Who's Who in Finance and Industry

Biographical Reference Works
Published by Marquis Who's Who

Who's Who in America

Who Was Who in America

   Historical Volume (1607-1896)

   Volume I (1897-1942)

   Volume II (1943-1950)

   Volume III (1951-1960)

   Volume IV (1961-1968)

   Volume V (1969-1973)

   Volume VI (1974-1976)

Who Was Who in American History—Arts and Letters

Who Was Who in American History—The Military

Who Was Who in American History—Science and Technology

Who's Who in the Midwest

Who's Who in the East

Who's Who in the South and Southwest

Who's Who in the West

Who's Who of American Women

Who's Who in Government

Who's Who in Finance and Industry

Who's Who in Religion

Who's Who in American Law

Who's Who in the World

Who's Who Biographical Record—Child Development Professionals

Who's Who Biographical Record—School District Officials

World Who's Who in Science

Directory of Medical Specialists

Marquis Who's Who Publications / Index to All Books

Travelers' Guide to U.S. Certified Doctors Abroad

Who's Who
in Finance and Industry ®

22nd edition
1981-1982

Marquis Who's Who, Inc.
200 East Ohio Street
Chicago, Illinois 60611 U.S.A.

Library of Congress Catalog Card Number 70-616550
International Standard Book Number 0-8379-0322-X
Product Code Number 030251

Distributed in the United Kingdom by
George Prior Associated Publishers
37-41 Bedford Row
London WC 1, England

Manufactured in the United States of America
1 2 3 4 5 6 7 8 9 10

Table of Contents

Preface vi

Standards of Admission vii

Key to Information in this Directory viii

Table of Abbreviations ix

Alphabetical Practices xiv

Biographies 1

Preface

The twenty-second edition of *Who's Who in Finance and Industry* represents the most recent efforts of the Marquis Who's Who editorial staff to reflect the steady growth and development of the business world.

Through continuing examination of the media and through frequent consultation with experts knowledgeable about business affairs, the editors have researched and compiled comprehensive biographical data on approximately 18,000 business executives. Included in this directory are executives and professionals in the fields of insurance; international banking; commercial and investment banking; factoring; mutual and pension fund management; commercial and consumer credit; international trade; real estate; investment services; manufacturing; retail trade; and other professions closely related to the business and financial worlds.

The biographical sketches in *Who's Who in Finance and Industry* are subject to constant revision. Each biographee must meet strict standards of selection, standards based specifically on business reference interest. Expert opinion and staff investigation confirm the publisher's experience that certain individuals who do not fall under the general reference interest standards governing admission to *Who's Who in America*, do meet the more specialized criteria of a special-interest reference directory such as this volume. These individuals qualify because of their professional standing in functional or "line-of-endeavor" career attainments. *Who's Who in Finance and Industry,* being a functional biographical directory, is intended to serve particular reference needs that *Who's Who in America* may not provide. Thus, in this edition of *Who's Who in Finance and Industry,* the publishers have attempted to focus to a greater degree upon identifying leaders of businesses that are not necessarily judged in terms of size or capitalization but are of high commercial "rating" or are prominent in an area of highly specialized yet far-reaching activity. The names of many businessmen and professionals listed in *Who's Who in Finance and Industry* may be unfamiliar in the communities in which they live, but are well known and highly regarded in their special fields of endeavor. The opposite may also hold true; that is, an executive listed in this volume may be quite well known in his home region, but may not be widely recognized in his or her area of expertise.

Each candidate for inclusion in *Who's Who in Finance and Industry* is invited to submit biographical data about his or her life and business career. This information is reviewed by the Marquis editorial staff before being written into sketch form. A prepublication proof of the sketch is sent to the biographee for his or her verification. The verified sketch, when returned and finally accepted by Marquis Who's Who is rechecked and put into final Who's Who format.

In the event that a reference-worthy individual fails to submit biographical data, the Marquis staff engages in careful investigation of that subject in order to prepare a sketch that is as accurate and up-to-date as possible. Such sketches in this volume are denoted by an asterisk.

Each sketch provides such information as name, position, vital statistics; education; family status; career and career-related activities; civic and political activities; non-professional directorships; military record, decorations and awards; lodges and clubs; writings; and address.

Marquis Who's Who editors exercise the utmost care in preparing each biographical sketch for publication. Occasionally, however, errors do appear, despite all precaution taken to minimize such occurrences. All users of this directory are requested to draw the attention of the publisher to any errors found so that corrections can be made in a subsequent edition.

The task of assembling this volume demands a keen knowledge of all aspects of business activity. As publishers of forty-one biennial editions of *Who's Who in America,* Marquis Who's Who is uniquely qualified to meet this task. It is our intention that this new twenty-second edition of *Who's Who in Finance and Industry* continue the tradition of excellence established with the publication in 1899 of the first edition of *Who's Who in America.*

Standards of Admission

In the process of compiling names for inclusion in *Who's Who in Finance and Industry*, the aim has been to select those qualified men and women in all lines of useful and reputable financial endeavor. The standards of admission provide for the selection of those individuals who because of prominence in a particular branch of business, have become subjects of interest, inquiry, or discussion in the business world. Others are chosen because of positions held in financial and industrial concerns of certain sizes or "rating" standings.

The first of these groups comprises persons who have accomplished some conspicuous achievement that distinguishes them from the majority of their business contemporaries. Frequently appearing are names of individuals who are prominent in some special field, but who are little known in their own communities. A man or woman whose commercial activities may be quite extensive may be scarcely known in the particular locality in which he or she lives. He or she is often a person whose business specialization is better known than he or she is. On the other hand, some of the biographees may be well known in their own communities, but are not widely recognized in their particular fields of endeavor. It is pertinent information concerning such individuals that the editors have attempted to gather and disseminate.

The second group embraces the following, without regard to notability or prominence in any other respect; principals of financial and industrial concerns capitalized at or above a certain figure; principals of business organizations of the type not readily judged on capitalization alone, but of high commercial "rating"; principals of leading firms engaged in international industry or finance; and principals of a select list of highly specialized concerns considered to be exposed to widespread interest because of exceptional characteristics of those businesses, regardless of their sizes in terms of capital, sales volumes, profits, or plant.

Key to Information in this Directory

❶ BURKE, GEORGE ALLEN, ❷ toy mfg. co. exec.; ❸ b. Highland Park, Ill., Mar. 23, 1926; ❹ s. Miles Benjamin and Thelma (Allen) B.; ❺ B.S., Northwestern U., 1949; ❻ m. Leota Gruber, Jan. 28, 1946; ❼ children—Evangeline Marie Burke Rossett, Joseph Paul, Harvey Edwin. ❽ With Millington Toy Mfg. Co., Peoria, Ill., 1950—, sales mgr., 1955-66, v.p., 1960-69, pres., 1969-76, chmn. bd., 1976—, also dir.; dir. Peoria Title and Trust Co., 1970—; lectr. Peoria Community Coll., 1967-68. ❾ Active Boy Scouts Am.; bd. govs. Lincolnwood Home for the Aged; sec. Ill. Gov.'s Commn. on Pub. Safety, 1972-76; mem. Peoria Heights Bd. Edn., 1956-58. ❿ Served with USNR, 1943-45; PTO. ⓫ Decorated Purple Heart; recipient Silver Beaver award Boy Scouts Am., 1967. ⓬ Mem. AIM, NAM, Beta Theta Pi. ⓭ Democrat. ⓮ Presbyterian. ⓯ Clubs: Masons, Shriners, Peoria Lake Country, Chgo. Athletic. ⓰ Contbr. articles to bus. publs. ⓱ Home: 903 Spring Dr Peoria Heights IL 61613 ⓲ Office: 1912 Main St Peoria IL 61606

Key:

❶ Name
❷ Occupation
❸ Vital Statistics
❹ Parents
❺ Education
❻ Marriage
❼ Children
❽ Career
❾ Civic and political activities
❿ Military record
⓫ Awards and certifications
⓬ Professional and association memberships
⓭ Political affiliation
⓮ Religion
⓯ Clubs (including lodges)
⓰ Writings and special achievements
⓱ Home address
⓲ Office address

The biographical listings in *Who's Who in Finance and Industry* are arranged in alphabetical order according to the first letter of the last name of the biographee. Each sketch is presented in a uniform order as in the sample sketch above. The abbreviations used in the sketches are explained in the Table of Abbreviations.

Table of Abbreviations

The following abbreviations and symbols are frequently used in this Directory

* (An asterisk) following a sketch indicates that it was researched by the Marquis Who's Who editorial staff and has not been verified by the biographee.

A.A. Associate in Arts
AAAL American Academy of Arts and Letters
AAAS American Association for the Advancement of Science
AAHPER Alliance for Health, Physical Education and Recreation
A. and M. Agricultural and Mechanical
AAU Amateur Athletic Union
AAUP American Association of University Professors
AAUW American Association of University Women
A.B. Arts, Bachelor of
AB Alberta
ABC American Broadcasting Company
AC Air Corps
acad. academy, academic
acct. accountant
acctg. accounting
ACDA Arms Control and Disarmament Agency
ACLU American Civil Liberties Union
A.C.P. American College of Physicians
A.C.S. American College of Surgeons
ADA American Dental Association
a.d.c. aide-de-camp
adj. adjunct, adjutant
adj. gen. adjutant general
adm. admiral
adminstr. administrator
adminstrn. administration
adminstrv. administrative
adv. advocate, advisory, adviser
advt. advertising
A.E. Agricultural Engineeer
A.E. and P., AEP Ambassador Extraordinary and Plenipotentiary
AEC Atomic Energy Commission
aero. aeronautical, aeronautic
aerodyn. aerodynamic
AFB Air Force Base
AFL-CIO American Federation of Labor and Congress of Industrial Organizations
AFTRA American Federation TV and Radio Artists
agr. agriculture
agrl. agricultural
agt. agent
AGVA American Guild of Variety Artists
agy. agency
A&I Agricultural and Industrial
AIA American Institute of Architects
AIAA American Institute of Aeronautics Astronautics
AID Agency for International Development
AIEE American Institute of Electrical Engineers
AIM American Institute of Management
AIME American Institute of Mining, Metallurgy, and Petroleum Engineers
AK Alaska
AL Alabama
ALA American Library Association
Ala. Alabama
alt. alternate
Alta. Alberta
A&M Agricultural and Mechanical
A.M. Arts, Master of
Am. American, America
AMA American Medical Association

A.M.E. African Methodist Episcopal
Amtrak National Railroad Passenger Corporation
AMVETS American Veterans of World War II, Korea, Vietnam
anat. anatomical
ann. annual
ANTA American National Theatre and Academy
anthrop. anthropological
AP Associated Press
APO Army Post Office
apptd. appointed
apt. apartment
AR Arkansas
ARC American Red Cross
archeol. archeological
archtl. architectural
Ariz. Arizona
Ark. Arkansas
Arts D. Arts, Doctor of
arty. artillery
ASCAP American Society of Composers, Authors and Publishers
ASCE American Society of Civil Engineers
ASHRAE American Society of Heating, Refrigeration, and Air Conditioning Engineers
ASME American Society of Mechanical Engineers
assn. association
asso. associate
asst. assistant
ASTM American Society for Testing and Materials
astron. astronomical
astrophys. astrophysical
ATSC Air Technical Service Command
AT&T American Telephone & Telegraph Company
atty. attorney
AUS Army of the United States
aux. auxiliary
Ave. Avenue
AVMA American Veterinary Medical Association
AZ Arizona

B. Bachelor
b. born
B.A. Bachelor of Arts
B. Agr. Bachelor of Agriculture
Balt. Baltimore
Bapt. Baptist
B.Arch. Bachelor of Architecture
B.A.S. Bachelor of Agricultural Science
B.B.A. Bachelor of Business Administration
BBC British Broadcasting Corporation
B.C.,BC British Columbia
B.C.E. Bachelor of Civil Engineering
B.Chir. Bachelor of Surgery
B.C.L. Bachelor of Civil Law
B.C.S. Bachelor of Commerical Science
B.D. Bachelor of Divinity
bd. board
B.E. Bachelor of Education
B.E.E. Bachelor of Electrical Engineering
B.F.A. Bachelor of Fine Arts
bibl. biblical
bibliog. bibliographical
biog. biographical
biol. biological
B.J. Bachelor of Journalism
Bklyn. Brooklyn
B.L. Bachelor of Letters
bldg. building
B.L.S. Bachelor of Library Science

Blvd. Boulevard
bn. battalion
B.&O.R.R. Baltimore & Ohio Railroad
bot. botanical
B.P.E. Bachelor of Physical Education
br. branch
B.R.E. Bachelor of Religious Education
brig. gen. brigadier general
Brit. British, Britannica
Bros. Brothers
B.S. Bachelor of Science
B.S.A. Bachelor of Agricultural Science
B.S.D. Bachelor of Didactic Science
B.S.T. Bachelor of Sacred Theology
B.Th. Bachelor of Theology
bull. bulletin
bur. bureau
bus. business
B.W.I. British West Indies

CA California
CAA Civil Aeronautics Administration
CAB Civil Aeronautics Board
Calif. California
C.Am. Central America
Can. Canada, Canadian
CAP Civil Air Patrol
capt. captain
CARE Cooperative American Relief Everywhere
Cath. Catholic
cav. cavalry
CBC Canadian Broadcasting Company
CBI China, Burma, India Theatre of Operations
CBS Columbia Broadcasting System
CCC Commodity Credit Corporation
CCNY City College of New York
CCU Cardiac Care Unit
CD Civil Defense
C.E. Corps of Engineers, Civil Engineer
CENTO Central Treaty Organization
CERN European Organization of Nuclear Research
cert. certificate, certification, certified
CETA Comprehensive Employment Training Act
CFL Canadian Football League
ch. church
Ch.D. Doctor of Chemistry
chem. chemical
Chem. E. Chemical Engineer
Chgo. Chicago
chirurg. chirurgical
chmn. chairman
chpt. chapter
CIA Central Intelligence Agency
CIC Counter Intelligence Corps
Cin. Cincinnati
Cleve. Cleveland
climatol. climatological
clin. clinical
clk. clerk
C.L.U. Chartered Life Underwriter
C.M. Master in Surgery
C.& N.W.Ry. Chicago & Northwestern Railway
CO Colorado
Co. Company
COF Catholic Order of Foresters
C. of C. Chamber of Commerce
col. colonel
coll. college
Colo. Colorado
com. committee
comd. commanded
comdg. commanding

comdr. commander
comdt. commandant
commd. commissioned
comml. commercial
commn. commission
commr. commissioner
condr. conductor
Conf. Conference
Congl. Congregational
Conglist. Congregationalist
Conn. Connecticut
cons. consultant, consulting
consol. consolidated
constl. constitutional
constn. constitution
constrn. construction
contbd. contributed
contbg. contributing
contbn. contribution
contbr. contributor
Conv. Convention
coop., co-op. cooperative
CORDS Civil Operations and Revolutionary
  Development Support
CORE Congress of Racial Equality
corp. corporation, corporate
corr. correspondent, corresponding,
  correspondence
C.&O.Ry. Chesapeake & Ohio Railway
C.P.A. Certified Public Accountant
C.P.C.U. Chartered property and casualty
  underwriter
C.P.H. Certificate of Public Health
cpl. corporal
CPR Cardiac Pulmonary Resuscitation
C.P.Ry. Canadian Pacific Railway
C.S. Christian Science
C.S.B. Bachelor of Christian Science
CSC Civil Service Commission
C.S.D. Doctor of Christian Science
CT Connecticut
ct. Court
CWS Chemical Warfare Service
C.Z. Canal Zone

d. daughter
D. Doctor
D.Agr. Doctor of Agriculture
DAR Daughters of the American Revolution
dau. daughter
DAV Disabled American Veterans
D.C., DC District of Columbia
D.C.L. Doctor of Civil Law
D.C.S. Doctor of Commercial Science
D.D. Doctor of Divinity
D.D.S. Doctor of Dental Surgery
DE Delaware
dec. deceased
def. defense
Del. Delaware
del. delegate, delegation
Dem. Democrat, Democratic
D.Eng. Doctor of Engineering
denom. denomination, denominational
dep. deputy
dept. department
dermatol. dermatological
desc. descendant
devel. development, developmental
D.F.A. Doctor of Fine Arts
D.F.C. Distinguished Flying Cross
D.H.L. Doctor of Hebrew Literature
dir. director
dist. district
distbg. distributing
distbn. distribution

distbr. distributor
disting. distinguished
div. division, divinity, divorce
D.Litt. Doctor of Literature
D.M.D. Doctor of Medical Dentistry
D.M.S. Doctor of Medical Science
D.O. Doctor of Osteopathy
D.P.H. Diploma in Public Health
D.R. Daughters of the Revolution
Dr. Drive
D.R.E. Doctor of Religious Education
Dr.P.H. Doctor of Public Health, Doctor
  of Public Hygiene
D.S.C. Distinguished Service Cross
D.Sc. Doctor of Science
D.S.M. Distinguished Service Medal
D.S.T. Doctor of Sacred Theology
D.T.M. Doctor of Tropical Medicine
D.V.M. Doctor of Veterinary Medicine
D.V.S. Doctor of Veterinary Surgery

E. East
E. and P. Extraordinary and Plenipotentiary
Eccles. Ecclesiastical
ecol. ecology, ecological
econ. economic
ECOSOC Economic and Social Council
  (of the UN)
E.D. Doctor of Engineering
ed. educated
Ed.B. Bachelor of Education
Ed.D. Doctor of Education
edit. edition
Ed.M. Master of Education
edn. education
ednl. educational
EDP electronic data processing
Ed.S. Specialist in Education
E.E. Electrical Engineer
E.E. and M.P. Envoy Extraordinary and
  Minister Plenipotentiary
EEC European Economic Community
EEG electroencephalogram
EEO Equal Employment Opportunity
EKG electrocardiogram
E.Ger. German Democratic Republic
elec. electrical
electrochem. electrochemical
electrophys. electrophysical
elem. elementary
E.M. Engineer of Mines
ency. encyclopedia
Eng. England
engr. engineer
engring. engineering
entomol. entomological
environ. environmental, environment
EPA Environmental Protection Agency
epidemiol. epidemiological
Episc. Episcopalian
ERA Equal Rights Amendment
ERDA Energy Research and Development
  Administration
ESEA Elementary and Secondary Education Act
ESSA Environmental Science Services
  Administration
ethnol. ethnological
ETO European Theatre of Operations
Evang. Evangelical
exam. examination, examining
exec. executive
exhbn. exhibition
expdn. expedition
expn. exposition
expt. experiment
exptl. experimental

F.A. Field Artillery
FAA Federal Aviation Administration
FAO Food and Agriculture Organization
  (of the UN)
FBI Federal Bureau of Investigation
FCA Farm Credit Administration
FCC Federal Communication Commission
FCDA Federal Civil Defense Administration
FDA Food and Drug Administration
FDIA Federal Deposit Insurance Administration
FDIC Federal Deposit Insurance Corporation
F.E. Forest Engineer
FEA Federal Energy Administration
fed. federal
fedn. federation
fgn. foreign
FHA Federal Housing Administration
fin. financial, finance
FL Florida
Fla. Florida
FMC Federal Maritime Commission
FOA Foreign Operations Administration
found. foundation
FPC Federal Power Commission
FPO Fleet Post Office
frat. fraternity
FRS Federal Reserve System
FSA Federal Security Agency
Ft. Fort
FTC Federal Trade Commission

G-1 (or other number) Division of General Staff
Ga., GA Georgia
GAO General Accounting Office
gastroent. gastroenterological
GATT General Agreement of Tariff and Trades
gen. general
geneal. genealogical
geod. geodetic
geog. geographic, geographical
geol. geological
geophys. geophysical
gerontol. gerontological
G.H.Q. General Headquarters
G.N.Ry. Great Northern Railway
gov. governor
govt. government
govtl. governmental
GPO Government Printing Office
grad. graduate, graduated
GSA General Services Administration
Gt. Great
GU Guam
gynecol. gynecological

hdqrs. headquarters
HEW Department of Health, Education and
  Welfare
H.H.D. Doctor of Humanities
HHFA Housing and Home Finance Agency
HI Hawaii
hist. historical, historic
H.M. Master of Humanics
homeo. homeopathic
hon. honorary, honorable
Ho. of Dels. House of Delegates
Ho. of Reps. House of Representatives
hort. horticultural
hosp. hospital
HUD Department of Housing and Urban Develop-
  ment
Hwy. Highway
hydrog. hydrographic

IA Iowa
IAEA International Atomic Energy Agency
IBM International Business Machines Corporation
IBRD International Bank for Reconstruction and Development
ICA International Cooperation Administration
ICC Interstate Commerce Commission
ICU Intensive Care Unit
ID Idaho
IEEE Institute of Electrical and Electronics Engineers
IFC International Finance Corporation
IGY International Geophysical Year
IL Illinois
Ill. Illinois
illus. illustrated
ILO International Labor Organization
IMF International Monetary Fund
IN Indiana
Inc. Incorporated
ind. independent
Ind. Indiana
Indpls. Indianapolis
indsl. industrial
Inf. infantry
info. information
ins. insurance
insp. inspector
insp. gen. inspector general
Inst. institute
Instl. institutional
instn. institution
instr. instructor
instrn. instruction
Internat. international
intro. introduction
IRE Institute of Radio Engineers
IRS Internal Revenue Service
ITT International Telephone & Telegraph Corporation

J.B. Jurum Baccolaureus
J.C.B. Juris Canonici Bachelor
J.C.L. Juris Canonici Lector
J.D. Juris Doctor
j.g. junior grade
jour. journal
jr. junior
J.S.D. Jurum Scientiae Doctor
J.U.D. Juris Utriusque Doctor
Judge Adv. Gen. Judge Advocate General

Kans. Kansas
K.C. Knights of Columbus
K.P. Knights of Pythias
KS Kansas
K.T. Knight Templar
Ky., KY Kentucky

La., LA Louisiana
lab. laboratory
lang. language
laryngol. laryngological
LB Labrador
lectr. lecturer
legis. legislation, legislative
L.H.D. Doctor of Humane Letters
L.I. Long Island
llc. licensed, license
L.I.R.R. Long Island Railroad
lit. literary, literature
Litt. B. Bachelor of Letters

Litt. D. Doctor of Letters
LL.B. Bachelor of Laws
LL.D. Doctor of Laws
LL.M. Master of Laws
Ln. Lane
L.&N.R.R. Louisville & Nashville Railroad
L.S. Library Science (in degree)
lt. lieutenant
Ltd. Limited
Luth. Lutheran
LWV League of Women Voters

m. married
M. Master
M.A. Master of Arts
MA Massachusetts
mag. magazine
M.Agr. Master of Agriculture
maj. major
Man. Manitoba
M.Arch. Master in Architecture
Mass. Massachusetts
math. mathematics, mathematical
MATS Military Air Transport Service
M.B. Bachelor of Medicine
MB Manitoba
M.B.A. Master of Business Administration
MBS Mutual Broadcasting System
M.C. Medical Corps
M.C.E. Master of Civil Engineering
mcht. merchant
mcpl. municipal
M.C.S. Master of Commercial Science
M.D. Doctor of Medicine
Md., MD Maryland
M.Dip. Master in Diplomacy
mdse. merchandise
M.D.V. Doctor of Veterinary Medicine
M.E. Mechanical Engineer
ME Maine
M.E. Ch. Methodist Episcopal Church
mech. mechanical
M.Ed. Master of Education
med. medical
M.E.E. Master of Electrical Engineering
mem. member
meml. memorial
merc. mercantile
met. metropolitan
metall. metallurgical
Met. E. Metallurgical Engineer
meteorol. meteorological
Meth. Methodist
Mex. Mexico
M.F. Master of Forestry
M.F.A. Master of Fine Arts
mfg. manufacturing
mfr. manufacturer
mgmt. management
mgr. manager
M.H.A. Master of Hospital Administration
M.I. Military Intelligence
MI Michigan
Mich. Michigan
micros. microscopic, microscopical
mil. military
Milw. Milwaukee
mineral. mineralogical
Minn. Minnesota
Miss. Mississippi
M.I.T. Massachusetts Institute of Technology
mktg. marketing
M.L. Master of Laws
MLA Modern Language Association
M.L.D. Magister Legnum Diplomatic

M.Litt. Master of Literature
M.L.S. Master of Library Science
M.M.E. Master of Mechanical Engineering
MN Minnesota
mng. managing
Mo., MO Missouri
moblzn. mobilization
Mont. Montana
M.P. Member of Parliament
M.P.E. Master of Physical Education
M.P.H. Master of Public Health
M.P.L. Master of Patent Law
Mpls. Minneapolis
M.R.E. Master of Religious Education
M.S. Master of Science
MS Mississippi
M.Sc. Master of Science
M.S.F. Master of Science of Forestry
M.S.T. Master of Sacred Theology
M.S.W. Master of Social Work
MT Montana
Mt. Mount
MTO Mediterranean Theatre of Operations
mus. museum, musical
Mus.B. Bachelor of Music
Mus.D. Doctor of Music
Mus.M. Master of Music
mut. mutual
mycol. mycological

N. North
NAACP National Association for the Advancement of Colored People
NACA National Advisory Committee for Aeronautics
NAD National Academy of Design
N.Am. North America
NAM National Association of Manufacturers
NAPA National Association of Performing Artists
NAREB National Association of Real Estate Boards
NARS National Archives and Record Service
NASA National Aeronautics and Space Administration
nat. national
NATO North Atlantic Treaty Organization
NATOUSA North African Theatre of Operations
nav. navigation
N.B., NB New Brunswick
NBC National Broadcasting Company
N.C., NC North Carolina
NCCJ National Conference of Christians and Jews
N.D., ND North Dakota
NDEA National Defense Education Act
NE Nebraska
N.E. Northeast
NEA National Education Association
Nebr. Nebraska
neurol. neurological
Nev. Nevada
NF Newfoundland
NFL National Football League
Nfld. Newfoundland
N.G. National Guard
N.H., NH New Hampshire
NHL National Hockey League
NIH National Institutes of Health
NIMH National Institute of Mental Health
N.J., NJ New Jersey
NLRB National Labor Relations Board
NM New Mexico
N.Mex. New Mexico
No. Northern

NOAA National Oceanographic and Atmospheric Administration
NORAD North American Air Defense
NOW National Organization for Women
N.P. Ry. Northern Pacific Railway
nr. near
NRC National Research Council
N.S., NS Nova Scotia
NSC National Security Council
NSF National Science Foundation
N.T. New Testament
NT Northwest Territories
numis. numismatic
NV Nevada
NW Northwest
N.W.T. Northwest Territories
N.Y., NY New York
N.Y.C. New York City
N.Z. New Zealand

OAS Organization of American States
Ob-Gyn obstetrics-gynecology
obs. observatory
O.D. Doctor of Optometry
OECD Organization of European Cooperation and Development
OEEC Organization of European Economic Cooperation
OEO Office of Economic Opportunity
ofcl. official
OH Ohio
OK Oklahoma
Okla. Oklahoma
ON Ontario
Ont. Ontario
ophthal. ophthalmological
ops. operations
OR Oregon
orch. orchestra
Oreg. Oregon
orgn. organization
ornithol. ornithological
OSRD Office of Scientific Research and Development
OSS Office of Strategic Services
osteo. osteopathic
otol. otological
otolaryn. otolaryngological

Pa., PA Pennsylvania
P.A. Professional Association
paleontol. paleontological
path. pathological
P.C. Professional Corporation
PE Prince Edward Island
P.E. Professional Engineer
P.E.I. Prince Edward Island
PEN Poets, Playwrights, Editors, Essayists and Novelists (international association)
penol. penological
P.E.O. women's organization (full name not disclosed)
pfc. private first class
PHA Public Housing Administration
pharm. Pharmaceutical
Pharm.D. Doctor of Pharmacy
Pharm.M. Master of Pharmacy
Ph.B. Bachelor of Philosophy
Ph.D. Doctor of Philosophy
Phila. Philadelphia
philharm. philharmonic
philol. philological
philos. philosophical
photog. photographic

phys. physical
physiol. physiological
Pitts. Pittsburgh
Pkwy. Parkway
Pl. Place
P.&L.E.R.R. Pittsburgh & Lake Erie Railroad
P.O. Post Office
PO Box Post Office Box
polit. political
poly. polytechnic, polytechnical
P.Q. Province of Quebec
P.R., PR Puerto Rico
prep. preparatory
pres. president
Presbyn. Presbyterian
presdl. presidential
prin. principal
proc. proceedings
prod. produced (play production)
prof. professor
profl. professional
prog. progressive
propr. proprietor
pros. atty. prosecuting attorney
pro tem pro tempore
PSRO Professional Services Review Organization
psychiat. psychiatric
psychol. psychological
PTA Parent-Teachers Association
PTO Pacific Theatre of Operations
pub. publisher, publishing, published
publ. publication
pvt. private

quar. quarterly
q.m. quartermaster
Q.M.C. Quartermaster Corps
Que. Quebec

radiol. radiological
RAF Royal Air Force
RCA Radio Corporation of America
RCAF Royal Canadian Air Force
R.D. Rural Delivery
Rd. Road
REA Rural Electrification Administration
rec. recording
ref. reformed
regt. regiment
regtl. regimental
rehab. rehabilitation
rep. representative
Rep. Republican
Res. Reserve
ret. retired
rev. review, revised
RFC Reconstruction Finance Corporation
R.F.D. Rural Free Delivery
rhinol. rhinological
R.I., RI Rhode Island
R.N. Registered Nurse
roentgenol. roentgenological
ROTC Reserve Officers Training Corps
R.R. Railroad
Ry. Railway

s. son
S. South
SAC Strategic Air Command
SALT Strategic Arms Limitation Talks
S.Am. South America
san sanitary
SAR Sons of the American Revolution

Sask. Saskatchewan
savs. savings
S.B. Bachelor of Science
SBA Small Business Administration
S.C., SC South Carolina
SCAP Supreme Command Allies Pacific
Sc.B. Bachelor of Science
S.C.D. Doctor of Commercial Science
Sc.D. Doctor of Science
sch. school
sci. science, scientific
SCLC Southern Christian Leadership Conference
SCV Sons of Confederate Veterans
S.D., SD South Dakota
SE Southeast
SEATO Southeast Asia Treaty Organization
sec. secretary
SEC Securities and Exchange Commission
sect. section
seismol. seismological
sem. seminary
sgt. sergeant
SHAEF Supreme Headquarters Allied Expeditionary Forces
SHAPE Supreme Headquarters Allied Powers in Europe
S.I. Staten Island
S.J. Society of Jesus (Jesuit)
S.J.D. Scientiae Juridicae Doctor
SK Saskatchewan
S.M. Master of Science
So. Southern
soc. society
sociol. sociological
S.P. Co. Southern Pacific Company
spl. special
splty. specialty
Sq. Square
sr. senior
S.R. Sons of the Revolution
S.S. Steamship
SSS Selective Service System
St. Saint
St. Street
sta. station
statis. statistical
stats. statistics
S.T.B. Bachelor of Sacred Theology
stblzn. stabilization
S.T.D. Doctor of Sacred Theology
subs. subsidiary
SUNY State University of New York
supr. supervisor
supt. superintendent
surg. surgical
SW Southwest

TAPPI Technical Association of Pulp and Paper Industry
Tb Tuberculosis
tchr. teacher
tech. technical, technology
technol. technological
Tel.&Tel. Telephone & Telegraph
temp. temporary
Tenn. Tennessee
Ter. Territory
Terr. Terrace
TESL Teaching English as a Second Language
Tex. Texas
Th.D. Doctor of Theology
theol. theological
Th.M. Master of Theology
TN Tennessee
tng. training

topog. topographical
trans. transaction, transferred
transl. translation, translated
transp. transportation
treas. treasurer
TV television
TVA Tennessee Valley Authority
twp. township
TX Texas
typog. typographical

U. University
UAW United Auto Workers
UCLA University of California at Los Angeles
UDC United Daughters of the Confederacy
U.K. United Kingdom
UN United Nations
UNESCO United Nations Educational, Scientific and Cultural Organization
UNICEF United Nations International Children's Emergency Fund
univ. university
UNRRA United Nations Relief and Rehabilitation Administration
UPI United Press International
U.P.R.R. Union Pacific Railroad
urol. urological
U.S. United States
U.S.A. United States of America
USAAF United States Army Air Force
USAF United States Air Force

USAFR United States Air Force Reserve
USAR United States Army Reserve
USCG United States Coast Guard
USCGR United States Coast Guard Reserve
USES United States Employment Service
USIA United States Information Agency
USIS United States Information Service
USMC United States Marine Corps
USMCR United States Marine Corps Reserve
USN United States Navy
USNG United States National Guard
USNR United States Naval Reserve
USO United Service Organizations
USPHS United States Public Health Service
U.S.S. United States Ship
USSR Union of the Soviet Socialist Republics
USV United States Volunteers
UT Utah

VA Veterans' Administration
Va., VA Virginia
vet. veteran, veterinary
VFW Veterans of Foreign Wars
V.I., VI Virgin Islands
vice pres. vice president
vis. visiting
VISTA Volunteers in Service to America
VITA Volunteers in Technical Service
vocat. vocational
vol. volunteer, volume

v.p. vice president
vs. versus
VT., VT Vermont

W. West
WA Washington
WAC Women's Army Corps
Wash. Washington
WAVES Women's Reserve, U.S. Naval Reserve
WCTU Women's Christian Temperance Union
W. Ger. Germany, Federal Republic of
WHO World Health Organization
WI Wisconsin
Wis. Wisconsin
WSB Wage Stabilization Board
WV West Virginia
W. VA. West Virginia
WY Wyoming
Wyo. Wyoming

YK Yukon
YMCA Young Men's Christian Association
YMHA Young Men's Hebrew Association
YM & YWHA Young Men's and Young Women's Hebrew Association
YWCA Young Women's Christian Association
yr. year

zool. zoological

Alphabetical Practices

Names are arranged alphabetically according to the surnames, and under identical surnames according to the first given name. If both surname and first given name are identical, names are arranged alphabetically according to the second given name. Where full names are identical, they are arranged in order of age—those of the elder being put first.

Surnames beginning with De, Des, Du, etc., however capitalized or spaced, are recorded with the prefix preceding the surname and arranged alphabetically, under the letter D.

Surnames beginning with Mac are arranged alphabetically under M. This likewise holds for names beginning with Mc; that is, all names beginning Mc will be found in alphabetical order after those beginning Mac.

Surnames beginning with Saint or St. all appear after names that would begin Sains, and such surnames are arranged according to the second part of the name, e.g., St. Clair would come before Saint Dennis.

Surnames beginning with prefix Van are arranged alphabetically under letter V.

Surnames containing the prefix Von or von are usually arranged alphabetically under letter V; any exceptions are noted by cross references (Von Kleinsmid, Rufus Bernhard; see Kleinsmid, Rufus Bernhard von).

Compound hyphenated surnames are arranged according to the first member of the compound.

Compound unhyphenated surnames common in Spanish are not rearranged but are treated as hyphenated names.

Since Chinese names have the family name first, they are so arranged, but without comma between family name and given name (as Lin Yutang).

Parentheses used in connection with a name indicate which part of the full name is usually deleted in common usage. Hence Abbott, W(illiam) Lewis indicates that the usual form of the given name is W. Lewis. In alphabetizing this type name, the parentheses are not considered. However if the name is recorded Abbott, (William) Lewis, signifying that the entire name William is not commonly used, the alphabetizing would be arranged as though the name were Abbott, Lewis.

Who's Who in Finance and Industry

AADAHL, JORG, airlines systems analyst; b. Trondheim, Norway, June 16, 1937; came to U.S., 1966; s. Ottar P. and Gurli (Lockra) A.; M.Sc.M.E., Tech. U. Norway, 1961; M.B.A., U. San Francisco, 1973; m. Inger R. Holst, July 13, 1973; children—Erik, Nina. Research fellow Tech. U. Norway, Trondheim, 1961-62; mgr. arc welding devel. NAG, Oslo, 1964-66; mfg. engr. Varian Assos., Palo Alto, Calif., 1966-67; bus. mgr. United Airlines, San Francisco, 1974-75, sr. systems analyst, 1977—; owner, gen. mgr. Internat. Contacts & Cons., San Mateo, Calif., 1976—. Recipient Certificate of Honor, San Francisco Bd. Suprs., 1973. Mem. Am. Inst. Indsl. Engrs. (Sr.), Leif Erikson League (pres. 1973), Assn. of M.B.A. Execs., Norwegian Soc. Profl. Engrs. Club: Young Scandinavians (v.p. 1971). Author: Strength Analysis, Welded Structures, 1967; contbr. articles in various fields to profl. jours.; editor, Nordic Highlights, 1972. Home: 1707 Monticello Rd San Mateo CA 94402 Office: United Airlines San Francisco Internat Airport San Francisco CA 94128

AADAL, MANOU CHARLES, automobile and leasing exec.: b. Persia, Dec. 26, 1926; came to U.S., 1954, naturalized, 1970; s. Reza and Touran (Kazimoff) A.; M.B.A., U. Teheran, 1949; postgrad. Bennett Coll., Sheffield, Eng., 1952, N.Y. U., 1960, Wharton Sch., U. Pa., 1978; m. Violet B. Bach, June 21, 1959; children—Mark, Lisa, Wayne, Scott. Pres., Monarch Trading Co., N.Y.C., 1954-60, Aqua Internat. Corp., N.Y.C., 1958—, Sunchris Realty, N.Y.C., 1960—, Mongaup Properties, Inc., N.Y.C., 1969—, Airports Rent-A-Car, Richmond Hills, N.Y., 1969—. Treas., World Mission Bd., Congregational Ch., Manhassett, N.Y.; committeeman Nassau chpt. Conservative Party. Recipient letter of commendation Transp. Mgmt. div. GSA. Mem. Am. Soc. Internat. Execs., Am. Car Rental Assn., Car and Truck Rental Assn. N.Y. (dir.), Am. Automotive Leasing Assn., U.S. Indsl. Council, Found. Christian Living. Clubs: Lake Success Golf, Sunrise Lakes Country. Home: 30 Jeffrey Ln Lake Success NY 11020 Office: 132 77 Metropolitan Ave Richmond Hills NY 11418

AAGRE, CURT, mdse. broker; b. Grimstad, Norway, Oct. 11, 1909; s. George and Tecla (Nilsen) A.; student Columbia, 1927-28, N.Y. U., 1929-30; grad. Pace Inst., 1933; postgrad. Harvard, 1948; m. Helen Winter, Oct. 19, 1946; children—Phyllis Kim, Carol Dee. Various positions to asst. div. sales mgr. Corn Products Refining Co., N.Y.C., 1926-40, fgn. rep., Mexico, 1947-48, Europe, 1949-52; asst. sales mgr. Hubinger Co., N.Y.C., 1953-59; sales mgr. Connell Rice & Sugar Co., Westfield, N.J., 1960-63; sales mgr. nat. accounts Olavarria & Co., N.Y.C., 1963; asst. v.p. Lamborn & Co., Inc., N.Y.C., 1964-69, v.p., mgr. diversification program, after 1969; now pres. Curt Aagre Co., Westfield, N.J. Trustee, Westfield Adult Sch. Served to maj. AUS, 1941-46. Decorated D.S.M. Mem. Harvard Assn., Am. Inst. Mgmt., Nat. Confectioners Salesmen Assn., N.Y. Sugar Club, N.Y. Preservers Assn., Sales Exec. Club, Candy Exec. Club, VFW. Presbyn. Club: Rotary (Westfield). Address: 858 Boulevard Westfield NJ 07090

AARON, HOWARD BERTON, mfg. co. exec.; b. Bklyn., Dec. 2, 1939: s. Max and Sara M. Aaron; B.Metall.Engring., Cornell U., 1962; M.S.Metall. Engring., U. Ill., 1963, Ph.D. (Sloan Found. fellow 1963-64), 1967; M.B.A. with distinction, U. Mich., 1973; m. Judith E. Kirsch, June 23, 1962; 1 dau., Nadine Wendy. Research asst. Cornell U., 1960-61; sr. technician Battelle Meml. Inst., Columbus, Ohio, summers 1961, 62; grad. research asst. U. Ill., 1962-63, 64-66, research asso., 1966-67; with Ford Motor Co., 1967-78, mgr. central lab. services, 1974-78; v.p., gen. mgr. transmission products div. D.A.B. Industries, Inc., Troy, Mich., 1978—; mem. faculty Henry Ford Community Coll., 1973, Wayne State U., 1976-77. Bd. dirs., mem. exec. com. Epilepsy Center Mich.: adv. bd. Protection and Advocacy Service, Lansing, Mich. Served to capt. U.S. Army, 1967-69. Mem. Am. Soc. Metals (div. chmn. materials testing and quality control 1980-81), Soc. Automotive Engrs., ASTM, Metall. Soc., Detroit C. of C., Mich. Assn. Children with Learning Disabilities. Jewish. Contbr. articles to profl. pubis. Home: 4677 Rolling Ridge Rd West Bloomfield MI 48033 Office: 466 Stephenson Hwy Box 2801 Troy MI 48084

AARON, JEAN-CLAUDE, builder; b. Marseilles, France, Aug. 2, 1916; s. Raoul and Jeanne (Reinach) A.; grad. in law, French Law Faculty; m. Marie-Louise Ripper, 1957; children—Sophie, Jean-Michel. Tech. adviser to Prime Minister, 1948-49; builder, land developer, initiator Rental Guarantee Programs, 1953-56; pres., dir. gen. Societe d'Etudes Financieres et de Realisations Immobilieres Internationales (SEFRI Internat.) Paris, 1956—; adminstr. Union Internationale Immobilière (U.I.I.), 1974—; adminstr., v.p. Consortium de Financement Immobilier a Long Terme; adminstr. Union Financiere de Participations, Compagnie Générale de Banque (SOFICAM), Groupe Drouot, Société Nouvelle de Participations, Barclays Bank S.A. France, Parisien Libere; mgr. Société Civile de Placement et d'Investissement; v.p. Consells de Gerance des S.C.I. de la Tour Maine-Montparnasse; former pres. Federation Nationals des Promoteurs Constructeurs; mem. econ. adv. com. C.N.P.F. Decorated Croix de Guerre, Rosette de la Resistance, comdr. Legion d'Honneur. Home: 54 Ave d'Iéna Paris VIeme France Office: Tour Maine-Montparnasse 33 Ave du Maine 75755 Paris Cedex 15 France

AARON, MERIK ROY, educator, fin. exec.; b. N.Y.C., May 22, 1947; s. Harry and Gertrude S. (Scherl) A.; B.A., L.I. U., 1969, M.A., 1971; profl. diploma Hofstra U., 1974. Dist. sci. coordinator Carle Place (N.Y.) Public Schs., 1969-80; dist. sci. supr. Lawrence (N.Y.) Public Schs., 1980—; pres. G.N.S. Investment Fund, N.Y.C., 1971—; v.p. Mervic Enterprises, Huntington, N.Y., 1978—; adj. prof. Nassau Community Coll., Syracuse (N.Y.) U. Mem. Environ. Planning Commn., Town of North Hempstead (N.Y.), 1980. Named Educator of Yr., Carle Place Public Schs., 1978. Mem. Nat. Assn. Investment Clubs, Nat. Sci. Tchrs. Assn., Nat. Sci. Suprs. Assn. (exec. bd.), N.Y. State Sci. Suprs. Assn. (exec. bd.). Republican. Clubs: Civic, Kiwanis, Masons. Home: 104 Ward St Westbury NY 11590

AARONSON, NORMAN, state agy. adminstr.; b. Bklyn., July 25, 1939; s. Emanuel and Florence (Lutzkey) A.; m. Lucy Zeldin, Jan. 19, 1959; children—Robert Michael, Andrew H., Elaine Cheryl. Asst. mgr. Family Fin. Corp., Bronx, N.Y., 1959-61; sr. tax collector N.Y. State Dept. Taxation and Fin., White Plains, 1963-68; head clk. personnel N.Y. State Dept. Social Services, Albany, 1968-70; adminstr. N.Y. State Social Devel. Planning Commn., Albany, 1970-71, N.Y. State Dept. Environ. Conservation, Region IV, Albany, 1971—. Mem. Am. Mgmt. Assn., Am. Soc. Public Adminstrn., Internat. Personnel Mgmt. Assn. Home: 41 Hunting Rd Albany NY 12205 Office: 50 Wolf Rd Albany NY 12233

AASEN, LAWRENCE OBERT, pub. relations exec.; b. Gardner, N.D., Dec. 5, 1922; s. Theodore and Clara Olina (Brenden) A.; M.S., Boston U., 1949; Ph.B., U. N.D., 1947; m. Martha Ann McMullan, Nov. 25, 1954; children—David Lawrence, Susan Clare. With McGraw Hill Pub. Co., N.Y.C., 1952-54; with N.Y. Life Ins. Co., N.Y.C., 1954-67, asst. v.p., to 1967; exec. sec. Better Vision Inst., N.Y.C., 1967—. Mem. Westport (Conn.) Democratic Town Com. Served with AUS, 1943-45. Mem. Pub. Relations Soc. Am., Am. Soc. Assn. Execs. Congregationalist. Home: 31 Ellery Ln Westport CT 06880 Office: 230 Park Ave New York City NY 10017

ABARR, CECIL DALE, real estate co. exec.; b. Blockton, Iowa, Jan. 25, 1929; s. Ardath Dale and Marietta Catherine (Bruner) A.; B.B.A., Simpson Coll., 1951; student Drake U., 1952-56; M.B.A., U. Chgo., 1976; m. Betty Lou Smith, July 7, 1979; children—Dennis, Sheila, Peggy. Treas., Frye Mfg. Co., Des Moines, 1951-65; v.p., gen. mgr. Massey Ferguson, Des Moines, 1965-69; v.p. fin. and adminstrn. Alodex Corp., Memphis, 1969-73; v.p., treas. Branitek, Inc., Savannah, Ga., 1973—. Served with AUS, 1946-47. Mem. Fin. Execs. Inst., Nat. Assn. Accts. Republican. Club: Marshwood Country. Home: 2 Windlass Ct Savannah GA 31411 Office: PO Box 14513 Savannah GA 31499

ABATE, MICHAEL F., indsl. ins. exec.; b. N.Y.C., Jan. 9, 1946; s. Alfred and Rose A.; B.A., Fordham Coll., 1967; M.S., U. Bridgeport, 1971. m. Roberta L. Schwartz, 1979. Indsl. ins. agt. Am. Mut. Ins. Co., Wakefield, Mass., 1970-78; pres. Libration Point Consultants, Ltd., Pension and Profit-Sharing Plans, New Canaan; pres., chief exec. officer Libration Point Ins. Services, Inc., Libration Point Internat. Risk Mgmt. Services, Ltd. Mem. Profl. Ins. Agts., Mensa. Clubs: K.C., Kiwanis (Stamford). Office: Box 14B East St New Canaan CT 06840

ABBICK, CHARLES ALOYSIUS, JR., oil co. exec.; b. Kansas City, Kans., Aug. 14, 1937; s. Charles Aloysius and Mary Helen A.; B.S. in Indsl. Relations, Rockhurst Coll., Kansas City, Mo., 1960; m. Rose Mary Franke, June 2, 1962; children—Annette, Christopher, Katherine, Nicholas. Electrician, Santa Fe R.R., Kansas City, 1958-61; with Travelers Ins. Co., various locations, 1961-69; mktg. mgr. St. Louis Ins. Brokerage, 1969-71; spl. group ins. mgr. Ins. Co. N. Am., St. Louis, 1971-74, regional mgr., Chgo., 1974-76; gen. ins. mgr. Gould Inc., Rolling Meadows, Ill., 1976-78; dir. corp. ins. dept. Clark Oil and Refining Corp., Milw., 1978—; pres., dir. Covey Ltd., Hamilton, Bermuda. Mem. Risk and Ins. Mgmt. Soc. Home: 1255 Church St Elm Grove WI 53122 Office: 8530 W National Ave PO Box 1994 West Allis WI 53201

ABBOTT, BENJAMIN EDWARD, JR., corp. exec.; b. Washington, Dec. 7, 1928; s. Benjamin Edward and Agnes (Campbell) A.; B. Indsl. Engring., U. Fla., 1953; m. Ellianna Gray, May 22, 1955; children—Celeni, Dawn, Mark, Scott. Indsl. engineer with E.I. DuPont de Nemours & Company, Martinsville, Va., 1951, Allis Chalmers, Milw., 1953, Pensacola (Fla.) Naval Air Sta., 1955-61; mem. exec. staff Dr. Wernher von Braun, Marshall Space Flight Center, NASA, Huntsville, Ala., 1961-68; v.p., dir. Investors Corp. of Am., Birmingham, 1968-75, Internat. Resorts, Inc., 1970-75; pres. Energy Systems Engrs., 1978—; dir. Pacific Am. Corp., San Francisco, 1969-74, Life Ins. Co. of Am., Birmingham, Ala., 1965-74. Served to lt. (j.g.) USNR, 1953-55. Registered profl. engr., Ala., Fla. Mem. Am. Inst. Indsl. Engrs. (sr.), Nat. Soc. Profl. Engrs., Ala. Soc. Profl. Engrs., ASHRAE, Assn. Energy Engrs., Pi Kappa Phi. Home: Route 2 Box 116-B Alpine AL 35014 Office: Energy Systems Engrs Inc 1055 24th St S Birmingham AL 35205

ABBOTT, CHARLES DENNIS, diesel mfg. co. exec.; b. Dayton, Ohio, Oct. 19, 1939; s. Wilbur Hollis and Bertha Elizabeth (Herbert) A.; B.S. in Bus. Adminstrn., Ohio State U., 1962; m. Anne Louise Maciorowski, Aug. 17, 1968; children—Elizabeth Anne, Steven Charles. With S.D. Leidesdorf & Co., N.Y.C., 1963-72, supervising sr. auditor, 1970-72; treas., sec. Comart Assos., Inc., N.Y.C., 1972-74; with Hawker Siddeley Inc., N.Y.C. (changed to Lister Diesels Inc., Olathe, Kans. 1976), 1974—, v.p. fin., sec., dir., 1974—; dir. H.S. Investments Inc. Bd. dirs., sec. Pinehurst Estates Homes Assn., 1977-78; chmn. bd. Cultural Arts Center, 1980—. Served with Army N.G., 1963. Mem. Am. Inst. C.P.A.'s, N.Y. State Soc. C.P.A.'s, Am. Mgmt. Assn. Roman Catholic. Clubs: Brookridge Country, Meadowbrook Racquetball. Office: Lister Diesels Inc 555 E 56th Hwy Olathe KS 66061

ABBOTT, DAVID HENRY, mfg. co. exec.; b. Milton, Ky., July 6, 1936; s. Carl and Rachel (Miles) A.; B.S., U. Ky., 1960, M.B.A., 1961; m. Joan Shefchik, Aug. 14, 1976; children—Kristine, Gina, Beth. With Ford Motor Co., Louisville, also Mpls., Dearborn, Mich., 1961-69; div. controller J.I. Case Co., Racine, Wis., 1970-73, gen. mgr. service parts supply, 1973-75, v.p., 1975—, v.p./gen. mgr. constrn. Equipment div., 1975-77, v.p., gen. mgr. Drott div., Wausau, Wis., 1977-79, exec. v.p. worldwide constrn. equipment, 1979—. Mem. Constrn. Industry Mfrs. Assn. (dir.), U.S. C. of C. (constrn. action council). Republican. Lutheran. Home: 3515 Corona Dr Racine WI 53406 Office: 700 State St Racine WI 53404

ABBOTT, DONALD FRANKLIN, mfg. co. exec.; b. Sidney, Ohio, Nov. 23, 1941; s. Carl J. and Grace (Davidson) A.; student U. Richmond, 1959-60, Edison State U., 1978; children—Gregg, Ric. With Sidney Oliver Store (IH Trucks), Sidney, 1960-62; machine tool rebuilder Sidney Machine Service, Inc., Sidney, 1962-76, pres., owner, 1977—. Mem. Sidney-Shelby County C. of C., Am. Motorcycle Assn. Republican. Baptist. Club: Moose. Home: 13000 CR 25A Anna OH 45302 Office: PO Box 198 Sidney OH 45365

ABBOTT, EDWARD LEROY, ins. co. exec.; b. Dayton, Ohio, Dec. 18, 1930; s. Roy Edward and Mildred Eileen (Filler) A.; A.B., Wittenberg U., 1952; postgrad. Ohio State U., 1952-53; m. Elizabeth Joan Grahame, June 8, 1957; children—Jay Edward, Julie Beth. Various positions Northwestern Mut. Life Ins. Co., Columbus, Ohio, 1956-64, asst. regional mgr., Dallas, 1964-68, mortgage loan regional mgr., Columbus, 1968-70, Washington, 1970-73; v.p. real estate Acacia Mut. Life Ins. Co., Washington, 1973-74, fin. v.p., 1974-78, exec. v.p., 1978—, treas., 1974—; dir. Acacia Fin. Corp., Acacia Equity Sales Corp., Ednl. Products Corp.; fin. v.p., treas., dir. Acacia Nat. Life Ins. Co. Served with U.S. Army, 1954-55. Mem. Washington Bd. Trade, Am., D.C. mortgage bankers assns., Am. Council Life Ins., Internat. Platform Assn., Friends of Kennedy Center, Alpha Tau Omega. Republican. Home: 6605 Goldsboro Rd Falls Church VA 22042 Office: 51 Louisiana Ave NW Washington DC 20001

ABBOTT, JOSEPH ALOYSIUS, communications co. exec.; b. Paterson, N.J., June 19, 1905; s. Henry Augustus and Mary (Roegiers) A.; B.S., Notre Dame U., 1930; m. Alice M. Hughes, Aug. 30, 1930; 1 son, Joseph A. With ITT, Nutley, N.J., 1942—, asst. personnel mgr., 1942-48, dir. personnel and labor relations, 1948-55, dir. pub. relations, 1955-66, dir. pub. relations ITT Def.-Space Group, 1966-75, dir. pub. relations ITT Aerospace, Electronics, Components and Energy Group, 1975-78; dir. pub. relations and advt. ITT Telecommunications and Electronics Group-N.Am., 1978—; dir. Fed. Electric Corp. Chmn. N.J. Little Hoover Commn., 1967-68; pres. Passaic Valley Water Commn., Clifton, N.J., 1964-66. Bd. dirs. St. Mary's Hosp., Passaic, N.J., 1961-68, Jr. Achievement, Passaic Clifton area, 1959-68. Recipient Boys' Club Medallion, Boys' Club Am., Clifton, 1963. Mem. Nat. Press Club, Air Force Assn., Pub. Relations Soc. Am., Clifton (N.J.) C. of C. (pres. 1956-68, 71-72); Navy League. Home: 25 E 40th St Paterson NJ 07514 Office: 500 Washington Ave Nutley NJ 07110

ABDEL-KHALIK, AHMED RASHAD, educator; b. Egypt, May 30, 1940; came to U.S., 1964, naturalized, 1975; s. Mohamed A. and Gamilah A. (El-Morsey) A.; B.Com. with honors in Acctg., Cairo (Egypt) U., 1961; M.B.A., Ind. U., 1965, M.A. in Econs., 1966; Ph.D. (Ernst and Ernst fellow), U. Ill., 1972; m. Maria E. Chaves, June 30, 1973; 1 dau., Jasmine C. Asst. to controller, main office Nat. Bank of Egypt, 1961; instr. Cairo U., 1961-64, U. N.C., Charlotte, 1967-69; teaching asst. U. Ill., 1969-72; asst. prof. Columbia U., N.Y.C., 1972-74, asso. prof., 1974-75; asso. prof. Duke U., Durham, N.C., 1975-77; Walter J. Matherly prof. acctg. U. Fla., Gainesville, 1977-80, grad. research prof. acctg., 1980—, dir. Acctg. Research Center, Sch. Acctg., 1977—. Mem. Am. Acctg. Assn., Am. Fin. Assn., Am. Econ. Assn., Inst. Mgmt. Scis., Am. Inst. Decision Scis., Fin. Execs. Inst., Beta Alpha Psi. Editor: (with Keller) The Impact of Accounting Research on Practice and Disclosure, 1978, Financial Information Requirements for Security Analysts, 1978; Government Regulation of Accounting and Information, 1980; contbr. articles to profl. jours. Home: 8409 SW 1st Pl Gainesville FL 32601 Office: Acctg Research Center U Fla Gainesville FL 32611

ABDUL, KATHERINE YOSHIE, realtor; b. Wailuku, Maui, Hawaii, Mar. 9, 1924; d. Yonosuke and Natsue (Ogawa) Kanada; student U. Hawaii, 1955-56; m. Daniel Lawrence Abdul, Mar. 14, 1945 (dec. Jan. 1963); children—Cassandra (Mrs. Larry Killion), Daniel Lawrence, Corinna Gay. Pres., Ka-ma-aina Realty, Inc., Honolulu, 1959-63; prin. broker Kay Abdul Realtor, Honolulu, 1964-71; pres. Kay Abdul Realtors, Inc., Honolulu, 1971—; sec.-treas. Kanab, Inc., 1969-76; partner Cassandra Co., 1967—, Waiehu Heights Assos., 1972—; developer Wailuku Indsl. Park Assos., 1977—, pres., dir. Wailuku Indsl. Park Owners Assn., 1977-80. Mem. Maui County Bd. Realtors, Nat. Assn. Home Builders, Internat. Platform Assn. Congregationalist. Home: 856 W Kaena Pl Wailuku Maui HI 96793 also 2552 Manoa Rd Honolulu HI 96822 Office: 1351 Lower Main St Wailuku Maui HI 96793

ABDUL-KAREEM, AMEEN, ins. agt.; b. Ridgeland, S.C., Nov. 29, 1938; s. Gilyard and Alma Norton; B.A. in Polit. Sci., Kean Coll., 1973; postgrad. in bus. adminstrn., Manhattan Coll. 1979—; m. Fareedah Nuri, July 31, 1977 (div.); 1 son, Dwayne. Pvt. investigator, Newark and N.Y.C., 1960-63; asst. loan mgr. Beneficial Fin. Co., Newark, 1964-69; loan mgr. Avco Fin. Services, East Orange, N.J., 1969-74; mgmt. trainee Bank of N.Y., White Plains, 1974-76; field underwriter Mut. of Omaha, Tarrytown, N.Y., 1976—; ins. broker. Served with U.S. Army, 1961-64. Muslim. Home: 9 New St Eastchester NY 10709

ABEDON, RICHARD LLOYD, ins. cons. co. exec.; b. Providence, Feb. 24, 1935; s. Bernard B. and Ann (Seidman) A.; grad. Colby Coll., 1959; LL.B., Boston Coll., 1969: m. Robin Gordon, June 16, 1957; children—Richard Lloyd, Todd, Tracy. Admitted to R.I. bar, 1959, Fla. bar, 1959; formerly asso. firm Abedon & Abedon, Providence; chmn. bd. Richard L. Abedon Co., Providence, 1977—; faculty N.Y. U. Law Sch. Inst. Taxation; judge of probate, Tiverton, R.I. Former pres. Tiverton Town Council; chmn. Tiverton Heart Fund; bd. dirs. Adaskin Found.; chmn. retirement com. R.I. League of Cities and Towns; chmn. citizens adv. bd. Newport County Mental Health Assn.; pres. Boys Club of Tiverton; chmn. R.I. Bottle Bill Coalition; mem. R.I. Council of Community Services, Settlements and Neighborhood Centers in Providence Study Com.; exec. bd. Moby Dick Council Boy Scouts Am.; vice chmn. State of R.I. Israel Bonds. Named to Nat. Assos. Hall of Fame, Mut. Benefit Life Ins. Co. Mem. Am. Bar Assn. (sect. on taxation, mem. com. employee benefits), R.I. Bar Assn. Democrat. Jewish. Lectr. to profl. groups; contbr. articles to pubis. Home: 150 North Ct Tiverton RI 02878 Office: 100 India St Providence RI 02903

ABEL, DEFOREST WILLIAMS, JR., ins. co. exec.; b. Providence, R.I., Apr. 14, 1929; s. DeForest Williams and Grace Isabel (Marshall) A.; student Nichols Coll., Dudley, Mass., 1948-49, U. Miami, 1949-51; children—DeForest Williams, Diane Christine, Wendy Lee, Richard Ellsworth, Virginia Caroline. With Amica Mutual Ins. Co., Providence, R.I., 1951—, dir., 1965—, pres., 1968—, chief exec. officer, 1971—; pres., dir. Amica Life Ins. Co.; chmn. bd. trustees Amica Pension Fund; pres., dir. Amica Services, Inc. Bd. dirs. R.I. Hosp. Trust Corp.; mem. corp. Women and Infants Hosp. R.I.; hon. trustee Bryant Coll., Smithfield, R.I., Nichols Coll., R.I. Sch. Design Mus.; mem. pres.' council Providence Coll. Served with USAF, 1951. Mem. Am. Inst. Property and Liability Underwriters (trustee), Ins. Inst. Am., Alliance Am. Insurers (dir.). Clubs: Squantum Assn., R.I. Country, University, Turks Head, British Empire, Agawan Hunt, Sea Island Golf, Boston Madison Square Garden. Office: 10 Weybosset St Providence RI 02940

ABEL, E. DONALD, accountant; b. Hawthorne, Nev., Feb. 8, 1931; s. Elmer and Josephine (Haeger) A.; student San Mateo Jr. Coll., 1949-51; A.A., Yuba Jr. Coll., 1952; B.A., Sacramento State Coll., 1957; m. Sept. 3, 1956. Accountant, J. George Harbinson, C.P.A.,

Sacramento, 1956-58; accountant C. S. Nicolas & Co., C.P.A.'s Placerville, Calif., 1958-61; partner Orville Stiff & Co., Modesto, Calif., 1961-77, Abel & Ellman, C.P.A.'s, Modesto, 1977—. Served with AUS 1952-54. C.P.A., Calif. Mem. Am. Inst. C.P.A.'s, Calif. Soc. C.P.A.'s, Aircraft Owners and Pilots Assn. Mason. Clubs: Del Rio Golf and Country (Modesto); Sportsmen of Stanislaus. Home: 904 Leveland Ln Modesto CA 95350 Office: 1104 12th St Modesto CA 95353

ABELES, TOM PETER, energy cons.; b. Louisville, Feb. 25, 1941; s. Gerd Hans and Ilse Rachael (Lowenstein) A.; B.S. cum laude, Wilmington Coll., 1963; postgrad. U. Mich., 1963-65; Ph.D., U. Louisville, 1968. Research asst./teaching asst. dept. chemistry U. Louisville, 1966-68; faculty dept. chemistry, Va. Poly. Inst. and State U., Blacksburg, 1968-71; asso. prof. Coll. Environ. Scis., U. Wis., Green Bay, 1971-76; cons. energy mgmt.; pres. I E Assos., Inc., Mpls., 1975—. Recipient Nat. Sci. Tchrs. Assn.-Gustav/Ohaus award in sci. teaching, 1974. Mem. Sigma Xi, Chi Beta Phi, Phi Lambda Upsilon, Phi Kappa Phi. Contbr. articles to profl. jours. Address: 3704 11th Ave Minneapolis MN 55407

ABELOV, STEPHEN LAWRENCE, uniform co. exec.; b. N.Y.C., Apr. 1, 1923; s. Saul S. and Ethel (Esterman) A.; B.S., N.Y.U., 1945, M.B.A., 1950; m. Phyllis S. Lichtenson, Nov. 18, 1945; children—Patricia C. (Mrs. Marvin Demoff), Gary M. Asst. div. mgr. Nat. Silver Co., N.Y., 1945; sales rep. Angelica Uniform Co., N.Y., 1945-50; asst. sales mgr., 1950-56, western regional mgr., Los Angeles, 1956-66, v.p. Angelica Uniform Co. of Calif., 1958-66, nat. v.p. sales, 1966-72, v.p. Angelica Corp. and Angelica Uniform, 1968—, group v.p. mktg., 1972—, exec. v.p., 1980—. Vis. lectr. marketing N.Y.U. Grad. Sch. Bus. Adminstrn. Vice comdr. Am. Legion; mem. vocational adv. bd. VA.; adv. bd. Woodcraft Rangers; bd. dirs. Univ. Temple. Mem. Am. Assn. Contamination Control (dir.), Am. Soc. for Advancement Mgmt. (chpt. pres.), Sales and Mktg. Execs. Assn., Am. Mktg. Assn., Health Industries Assn. Am. (dir.), various trade assns., St. Louis Council on World Affairs, Los Angeles C. of C. N.Y.U. Alumni Assn., Phi Epsilon Pi (treas.). Mem. B'nai B'rith (past pres.). Clubs: Men's (exec. v.p.); Town Hall, N.Y. U., Aqua Sierra Sportsmen. Contbr. articles to profl. jours. Home: 9821 Log Cabin Ct Ladue MO 63124 Office: 700 Rosedale Ave Saint Louis MO 63112

ABELSON, ALAN, editor, columnist; b. N.Y.C., Oct. 12, 1925; s. Harry Carl and Vivian A. (Finkelstein) A.; B.S. in Chemistry and English, CCNY, 1946; M.A. in Creative Writing, U. Iowa, 1947; m. Virginia Eloise Peterson, Sept. 1, 1951; children—Justin Adams, Reed Vivian. Reporter, N.Y. Jour.-Am., N.Y.C., 1949-56, columnist, 1952-56; feature writer Barron's Mag., N.Y.C., 1956—, mng. editor, 1965—, columnist Up and Down Wall Street, 1966—. Office: 22 Cortlandt St New York NY 10007

ABER, JOHN WILLIAM, educator; b. Canonsburg, Pa., Sept. 9, 1937; s. John William and Rose (Lauda) A.; S.B., Pa. State U., 1959; M.B.A. (McKinsey scholar), Columbia U., 1965; D.B.A. (Bus. Sch. leadership fellow, Div. of Research fellow), Harvard U., 1972; m. Cynthia Louise Sousa, Nov. 24, 1962; children—John, Valerie, Alexander. Cons., Univ. Affiliates, Inc., Boston, 1969-71; asst. prof. fin. Ga. State U., Atlanta, 1971-72; asst. prof. Boston U., 1972-78, asso. prof. fin., dir. mgmt. devel. program, 1978—; fin. cons. Served with USN, 1959-64. Mem. Am. Fin. Assn., Eastern Fin. Assn., Fin. Mgmt. Assn. Club: Harvard of Boston. Author: Beta Coefficients and Models of Security Return, 1973. Home: 51 Columbia St Brookline MA 02146 Office: 212 Bay State Rd Boston MA 02215

ABERCROMBIE, MARY LOUISE, plastic packaging co. exec.; b. Woodruff, S.C., Dec. 11, 1937; d. Paul Henry and Valma Mary (Perry) Fincher; student bus. Young Harris Jr. Coll., 1954-55; children—Kathryn Darlene, Robert Perry, Laura Lynn. Sec. patent dept. Cryovac div. W.R. Grace & Co., Duncan, S.C., 1962-65, sec. purchasing dept., 1968-73, purchasing asst., 1973-76, buyer, 1976—; sec. purchasing and physics dept. U. N.C., Chapel Hill, 1965-66. Mem. Purchasing Mgmt. Assn. Carolinas-Va. (2d vice chmn. Upper S.C. chpt. 1979-80). Home: 620 Edwards St Woodruff SC 29388 Office: Cryovac div WR Grace & Co PO Box 464 Duncan SC 29334

ABERNATHY, BOBBY FRANKLIN, oil co. exec.; b. Athens, Tex., June 25, 1933; s. George R. and Mary Lou (Jernigan) A.; B.S., U. Tex., Austin, 1955; m. Donna Jean Childers, Feb. 28, 1963; children—Julie Ann, Scott Franklin. With Amoco, 1955-72, chief engr., 1968-72; exec. v.p., dir. Quasar Petroleum Ltd., Calgary, Alta., Can., 1972-76; v.p. Am. Quasar Petroleum Co., Ft. Worth, 1973-76; sr. v.p. exploration and prodn., dir. Champlin Petroleum Co., Ft. Worth, 1976—; dir. Calnev Pipe Line Co. Del. to Tex. Republican Conv., 1964-68. Recipient Cedric K. Ferguson award, 1965. Mem. Ind. Petroleum Assn. Am. (exec. com.), West Tex. C. of C. (dir.), Am. Inst. Mining and Metall. Engrs., Soc. Petroleum Engrs. of AIME (Disting. lectr.), Am. Petroleum Inst., N.Mex. Oil and Gas Assn., Internat. Oil Scouts Assn., Ft. Worth Wildcatters (exec. com.), Phi Theta Kappa, Sigma Gamma Epsilon, Tau Beta Pi. Methodist. Clubs: Ft. Worth, Shady Oaks Country, Ft. Worth Petroleum. Home: 2005 Mt Royal Terr Fort Worth TX 76107 Office: PO Box 9365 Fort Worth TX 76107

ABERNATHY, K. BROOKS, mfg. co. exec.; b. Missoula, Mont., Aug. 30, 1918; s. Austin Irwin and Evelyn (Thompson) A.; B.A., Northwestern U., 1941; postgrad. Harvard Bus. Sch., 1967; m. Susan Koskinen, Mar. 7, 1942; children—Lynn (Mrs. Kenneth H. Stokoe), Gail (Mrs. Terrance Dickrell), Kenneth Brooks. With Gen. Electric Co., 1941-62; treas. Brunswick Corp., 1962-69, v.p., 1969-72, pres., chief operating officer, 1972—, now chmn., chief exec. officer, pres. internat. div., 1968-69, pres. Kiekhaefer Mercury div., 1969-72, also dir.; dir. Stone Container Corp., Nicor, Inc., Am. Nat. Bank & Trust, Walter E. Heller Internat. Corp. Mem. Am. Mgmt. Assn. Home: 52 Locust Rd Winnetka IL 60093 Office: Brunswick Corp One Brunswick Plaza Skokie IL 60077

ABIONA, DAVID AYOADE, computer programmer, educator; b. Nigeria, July 21, 1947; s. Benjamin K. and Florence A.; came to U.S., 1972, naturalized, 1976; B.Sc., Kean Coll., 1979, M.A., 1980; M.A., St. Peters Coll., 1981; m. Dec. 10, 1972. Computer operator Dun & Bradstreet, 1978-79; computer programmer Mayor's Office of Policy Devel., Newark, 1977-78; instr. computer programming Newark Skill Center, 1979-81; info. system designer Western Electric Co., Newark, 1981—; adj. prof. Essex County Coll., Newark, 1979—. Mem. Assn. Computing Machinery, Am. Mgmt. Assn. Office: Newark NJ

ABLAHAT, NEWTON ANDRE, business cons.; b. Chgo.; s. Haidow and Katie (Samuels) A.; B.S., Northwestern U., 1937; postgrad. U. Chgo., 1940, U. Colo., 1943, Johns Hopkins, 1953-55, Syracuse U., 1961, Am. U., 1965-67; m. Ella May Cason, June 14, 1947; 1 son, Roger Haydon. Mgr. mdse. research, mgr. credit research Spiegel, Inc., Chgo., 1938-41, mgr. market research, 1946-47, dir. policy, 1948-50; economist WPB, Washington, 1941-42; econ. intelligence officer, Yenan, China, 1943-45; exporter Trans World Assos., 1947; cons. Bur. Labor Statistics, Washington, 1950-53; analyst ORO, Johns Hopkins, 1953-56; head ops. research Gen. Electric Co., Phila., 1956-58; cons. Haskins & Sells, Chgo., 1958; cons. Gen. Electric Co., Syracuse, Europe and Washington, 1959-67; v.p. corp. planning dept. Investors Diversified Services, Inc., Mpls., 1967-80; pres. The Stratcon Group Inc., Mpls., 1980—; bus. cons. to fgn. firms; past cons. U.S. Dept. Transp. Bd. dirs. Twin Cities Citizens League, Suburban Community Services. Served with USNR, 1943; CBI. Mem. Am. Finance Assn., Nat. Assn. Bus. Economists, Ops. Research Soc., Inst. Mgmt. Scis., N.Am. Soc. Corp. Planners, Assn. for Corp. Growth. Home: 5200 Chantrey Rd Edina MN 55436 Office: 2240 Dain Tower Minneapolis MN 55402

ABLON, ARNOLD NORMAN, accountant; b. Ft. Worth, July 12, 1921; s. Esir R. and Hazel (Dreeben) A.; B.S., La. State U., 1941; M.B.A., Northwestern U., 1942; m. Carol Sarbin, July 25, 1962; children—Jan Ellen, Elizabeth Jane, William Neal, Robert Jack. Lectr. accounting So. Meth. U., 1946-47; auditor Levine's Dept. Stores, 1947-49; accountant Peat, Marwick, Mitchell & Co., 1946-47; sr. partner Arnold N. Ablon and Co., C.P.A.'s; partner W.T. Troth and Arnold Ablon, investments, Dallas; pres., dir. Ablon Enterprises, Inc.; dir. 1st Continental Enterprises, Inc., Wolf Textile Co., Hunsaker Truck Lease, Inc. Bd. dirs. Greenhill Sch., Spl. Care Sch., June Shelton Sch., Temple Emanuel. Served to capt. AUS, 1942-45. Mem. Am. Inst. C.P.A.'s, Tex. Soc. C.P.A.'s, Nat. Assn. Cost Accountants. Mason (Shriner). Clubs: Variety Internat., Columbian, Dallas, City (Dallas). Home: 9129 Clearlake Dallas TX 75225 Office: Republic Nat Bank Bldg Dallas TX 75201

ABLON, RALPH E., holding co. exec.; b. 1916; student Ohio State U., 1939. With Luria Bros. & Co., 1939-62, exec. v.p., 1948-55, pres., 1955-62, dir., 1962—; pres. Ogden Corp., N.Y.C., parent orgn., 1962-71, now chmn. bd., pres., dir. Served with USNR, World War II. Office: Ogden Corp 227 Park Ave New York NY 10027*

ABOUDARA, DEANE NORRIS, mfg. co. exec.; b. Los Angeles, Mar. 22, 1926; s. Jacques I. and Elizabeth V. (Vradenburg) A.; B.S.E.E., Calif. State Poly. U., 1950; m. Gwen M. Jost, July 8, 1950; 1 son, Bruce Scott. Test engr. Gen. Electric Co., 1950-52; jr. design engr. FMC Corp., 1952-53; transp. sales specialist, application engr. Gen. Electric Co., 1953-64; gen. supt. plant and equipment San Francisco Bay Area Rapid Transit Dist., 1964-69; mgr. transp. systems mktg. Philco-Ford Corp., 1969-70; project mgr. Gen. Electric Co., 1970; mktg. mgr. rapid transit div. Rohr Industries, 1970-73; exec. dir., dir. research-tech. services Transit Devel. Corp., Am. Public Transit Assn., 1973-79; mgr. tech. devel. transp. programs plastics bus. div. Gen. Electric Co., Washington, 1979—. Served with USNR, 1945-46. Registered profl. engr., Calif., Oreg., Va. Mem. IEEE, Nat. Soc. Profl. Engrs., Nat. Fire Protection Assn., Soc. Automotive Engrs., Soc. Plastics Engrs. Club: University. Contbr. articles to profl. jours. Home: 7308 Fox Pl Springfield VA 22151 Office: 777 14th St NW Washington DC 20005

ABRAHAM, RODNEY ELLIS, assn. exec.; b. Phila., Dec. 5, 1936; s. Walter and Rose Loretta (Mullin) A.; cert. in acctg. Temple U., also B.S. in Bus. Adminstrn.; cert. in agy. mgmt. Am. Coll., Bryn Mawr, Pa.; m. Lynn Reiner, June 30, 1957; children—Warren, Sharon, Brian, Lisa. Clk., Am. Coll., 1957-59; with Am. Soc. C.L.U., Bryn Mawr, 1959—, bus. mgr., 1960-72, asst. mng. dir., 1965-72, asst. mgr., dir. field and public relations, 1972-77, v.p. field and public relations, 1977-79, sr. v.p., 1979—; v.p., dir. Am.-Israeli Found. for Ins. Edn. C.L.U. Mem. Meeting Planners Internat. (charter, officer Delaware Valley chpt., gen. chmn. 1980 internat. conv.), Am. Soc. C.L.U., Ins. Conv. Planners, Life Assn. Communicators (chmn. 1977), Delaware Valley Soc. Assn. Execs. (officer). Republican. Jewish. Mem. editorial quality bd. Successful Meetings mag.; contbr. articles on assn. and conv. mgmt. to profl. publs. Home: 121 Merbrook Ln Merion Station PA 19066 Office: 270 Bryn Mawr Ave Bryn Mawr PA 19010

ABRAHAMSON, CAROL ANN, business exec.; b. Evanston, Ill., Aug. 19, 1950; d. Roland Axel and Lois Marie (Molinare) A.; B.A., Ohio Wesleyan U., 1971; M.B.A. in Fin., N.Y. U., 1976. Faculty, Logan Elm High Sch., Circleville, Ohio, 1971-72; portfolio mgr. Ohio Sch. Employees Retirement System, Columbus, 1972-73; security analyst Alliance Capital Mgmt. Corp., N.Y.C., 1973-74; asso. corp. fin. group Donaldson, Lufkin & Jenrette, Inc., N.Y.C., 1974-76; mgr. investor relations McGraw-Hill, Inc., N.Y.C., 1976-78; dir. pub. and fin. affairs PCA Internat., Matthews, N.C., 1978-79; v.p. investor relations Wendover Assos., Greensboro, N.C., 1979-80; dir. investor relations Foremost-McKesson, Inc., San Francisco, 1980—; faculty adviser N.Y. U. Grad. Bus. Sch.; dir. Natalie Kerr Designs, Inc.; cons. corps. and non-profit orgns. Mem. Fin. Women's Assn. (dir.), Pub. Relations Soc. Am., Nat. Investor Relations Inst., Home: 2323 Laguna San Francisco CA 94115 Office: One Post St San Francisco CA 94104

ABRAMS, ALBERT LEONARD, ins. co. exec.; b. Alpena Pass, Ark., Sept. 6, 1942; s. James Harold and Lois Lavern (Wheeler) A.; A.B., Ind. U., 1966; M.B.A., Chaminade U., 1978; m. Sandra Ray, Aug. 10, 1968; children—Robert Martin, Erika Marie, Lisa Michell. Underwriter, Fireman's Fund, 1969-71; gen. mgr. Bordallo Consol., 1971-74; v.p. Marianas Ins. Agy., Inc., 1974-76; account exec. Alexander & Alexander, Honolulu, 1976-77; sales rep. Wausau Ins. Cos., Indpls., 1978-80; chief operating officer Electronic Products, Inc., Indpls., 1980—; guest lectr. U. Guam, 1975, Chaminade, 1978; chmn. Guam Fire & Casualty & Marine Assn., 1973-74. Chmn., Guam Transit Authority, 1974-76. Served to lt. (j.g.) USNR, 1966-69. Mem. Inst. Mgmt. Acctg., Assn. M.B.A. Execs. Club: Elks. Office: 70 E 91st St Indianapolis IN 46206

ABRAMS, JULIUS, engr.; b. Butrimantzi, Lithuania, Oct. 27, 1902; s. Harry Isaac and Etta (Ginsberg) A.; brought to U.S., 1903; B.C.E., Northeastern U., 1925, D.Eng. (hon.), 1973; m. Eva Hodess, June 2, 1926; children—Fay Rosalind (Mrs. Louis Wilgoren), Benjamin Emanuel, Phillip. Civil and constrn. engr. Gleason Engring. Corp., Wellesley, Mass., 1932-36; chief engr. B.A. Gardett Corp., 1936-40; civil engr., supt. J. Slotnik Co., Boston, 1940-43; engr. Joseph Bennett Co., Boston, 1943-45; pres. Poley-Abrams Corp., Brookline, Mass., 1945—; pres. J. Abrams Constrn. Co. Inc., 1975—, chmn. bd., 1978—. Dir., past pres. Asso. Gen. Contractors of Mass. Past chmn. Greater Boston Hillel Com., mem., chmn. bd. of examiners Brookline Bldg. Dept.; mem. designer selection bd. Commonwealth of Mass., 1972-76, cons. to spl. commn. on state and county bldgs., 1979; chmn. adv. com. Northeastern U. Hillel; mem. corp. Northeastern U., Lesley Coll. Registered profl. engr., Mass. Fellow Am. Inst. Constructors; mem. Nat. Soc. Profl. Engrs., Am. Arbitration Assn., Am. Soc. Engring. Edn., Am. Council Constrn. Edn., Assn. Engrs. and Architects Israel (speaker 4th World Congress, Israel 1976), Alpha Epsilon Pi. Republican. Mason; mem. B'nai B'rith (past pres. Architects-Engrs. lodge). Home: 210 Nahanton St Newton MA 02159 Office: 45 Bartlett Crescent Brookline MA 02147

ABRAMS, PHILIP, constrn. co. exec.; b. Boston, Nov. 13, 1939; s. Julius and Eva (Hodess) A.; B.A., Williams Coll., 1961; m. Rosalyn Merle Heifetz, Aug. 23, 1970; children—Mark Solomon, Jonathan Samuel, Daniel Jason. Supt., project mgr. Poley-Abrams Corp., Brookline, Mass., 1961, 65-66; partner, treas. Abreen Corp., Needham Heights, Mass., 1966—. Mem. local bd. SSS, 1970-74; mem. Gov. Sargeant's Adv. Com. on Constrn. Industry, 1971-72; mem. Brookline Redevel. Authority, 1971-74. Served to lt. USNR, 1961-65. Mem. Asso. Gen. Contractors, Am. Inst. Constructors, Asso. Builders and Contractors (pres. 1975), Nat. Constrn. Industry Council (chmn. 1976-77), Nat. Def. Exec. Res. Republican. Jewish. Clubs: B'nai B'rith, Masons. Home: 32 Pickwick Rd West Newton MA 02165 Office: 140 Gould St Needham Heights MA 02194

ABRAMS, WILLIAM BERNARD, drug co. exec.; b. Atlantic City, July 15, 1922; s. Joseph Salzberg and Zelda (Coleman) A.; B.S., Rutgers U., 1944; M.D., Jefferson Med Coll., 1947; m. Berenda Weinberg, Mar. 4, 1945; children—James C., Andrew P., Joseph T., Julie A. Intern, Atlantic City Hosp., 1947-48; instr. bacteriology Jefferson Med Coll., 1948-49, adj. prof. medicine, 1977—; research fellow Children's Hosp., Phila., 1949-50; fellow in cardiology Phila. Gen. Hosp., 1950-51; fellow NIH, 1949-51; practice medicine specializing in internal medicine, Newark, 1955-58, Irvington, N.J., 1958-59; asso. in medicine Jefferson Med. Coll. Phila., 1959-64; research asso. prof. medicine Hahnemann Med. Coll. Phila., 1964-67, vis. prof., 1977—; clin. asso. prof. medicine N.J. Coll. Medicine, 1967-75; attending physician in medicine Newark City Hosp., 1964-75; dir. clin. pharmacology Newark Beth Israel Hosp., 1960-71; asso. medicine Newark Presbyn. Hosp., 1965-75; dir. dept. clin. pharmacology Hoffmann-LaRoche, Inc., Nutley, N.J., 1960-71; v.p. clin. research Ayerst Labs., N.Y.C., 1971-75; exec. dir. clin. research Merck, Sharp & Dohme, Inc., West Point, Pa., 1975—. Exec. com., trustee Essex County chpt. Am. Heart Assn., 1960—, sec., 1965—, pres., 1966, adv. bd. Council on High Blood Pressure Research, 1973—; trustee South Orange Community House; exec. sec. N.J. Scientists, Engrs. and Physicians for Johnson and Humphrey, 1964. Served to 1st lt., M.C., AUS, 1951-53. Fellow A.C.P., Am. Coll. Cardiology (gov. for N.J. 1970-73), Am. Soc. Clin. Pharmacology and Therapeutics (v.p. 1971-72, pres. 1975-76), Am. Coll. Chest Physicians, N.J. Acad. Medicine; mem. Am. Fedn. Clin. Research (past pres. N.J. chpt.), Am. Soc. Pharm. Exptl. Therapy (exec. com. clin. pharm. div.), Alpha Omega Alpha, Sigma Alpha Mu, Phi Delta Epsilon. Contbg. author: Coronary Heart Disease, 1962; Psychosomatic Medicine, 1962; The Theory and Practice Ausculation, 1963; Animal and Clinical Pharmacologic Techniques in Drug Evaluation, 1964; Cardiovascular Drug Therapy, 1965; Cardiovascular Diseases, 1968; Cardiovascular Therapy, 1971; Cardiac Arrhythmias, 1973; Hypertension Mechanisms and Management, 1973; Cardiovascular Disease, 1974; Principles and Techniques of Human Research and Therapeutics, vol. 1, 1974, vol. 2, 1976; New Antihypertensive Drugs, 1976; Pharmacology of Antihypertensive Drugs, 1980; asso. editor Davis Cyclopedia of Medicine, Surgery Spltys., 1965-71; editor Cardiovascular Drug Manual, 1972; editorial bd. Am. Heart Jour., 1980—; contbr. numerous articles to med. jours. Home: 220 Spruce Tree Rd Radnor PA 19087 Office: Merck Sharp & Dohme Inc West Point PA 19486

ABRAMSON, JOEL CHARLES, lighting products mfg. co. exec.; b. Malden, Mass., Oct. 26, 1946; s. Martin and Zelda (Silverman) A.; B.S., Boston U., 1969; m. Mary Pickering, June 26, 1977. Sales staff Chevron Oil Co., Perth Amboy, N.J., 1969-71; mgr. grocery sales GTE Sylvania, Danvers, Mass., 1971—; partner Cruise Enterprises, Lynn, Mass., 1979—; dir. Buddy Boy, Inc., Dennisport, Mass., 1979—; partner devel. investment properties, 1976—; dir. M.A.A.M. Inc. Hon. adm. Op Sail 80, also Sail On Boston. Mem. New Eng. Wholesale Food Assn., Greater Boston Conv. and Tourist Bur. Democrat. Jewish. Home: 47 Morton Rd Swampscott MA 01907 Office: GTE 60 Boston St Salem MA 01970

ABRAMSON, MICHELL NOBLE, JR., pub. relations exec.; b. San Francisco, Jan. 14, 1926; s. Michell N. and Edna (O'Brien) A.; A.B., U. Calif. at Berkeley, 1950; m. Mary Allerton Waldo, Feb. 4, 1965; children—Denise Louise, Karen Jaye; 1 stepdau., Colleen Anne. Reporter, Oakland (Calif.) Tribune, 1950-56; staff mem. Whitaker & Baxter-Campaigns, Inc., San Francisco, 1956-61, v.p., 1961—; v.p. Whitaker & Baxter Advt. Agy., San Francisco, 1961—; co-pub. Calif. Feature Service San Francisco, 1961—. Trustee Calif. Wildlife Found. Served with U.S. Mcht. Marine, 1943-46. Mem. Pub. Relations Soc. Am., Calif. Alumni Assn., Nat. Rifle Assn., Calif. Rifle and Pistol Assn., E Clampus Vitus, Sigma Delta Chi, Pi Kappa Alpha. Clubs: San Francisco Press, Commonwealth. Home: 99 Christopher Dr San Francisco CA 94131 Office: Flood Bldg San Francisco CA 94102

ABRASH, BRUCE MARVIN, numismatist; b. Bklyn., May 5, 1940; s. Louis and Rachel (Malofsky) A.; ed. SUNY, Buffalo, 1958-62; m. Catherine Faith Collings, May 27, 1973; children by previous marriage—Alex, Ross, Douglas, Lara. Pres., chmn. bd. Numis. Enterprises Corp., 1975—; pres. Numis. Funding Corp., also The Old Roman Nat. Coin Exchange, Melville, N.Y., 1964—; numis. authenticator U.S. Govt.; nominated to U.S. Assay Commn.; bd. govs. Inst. Numismatics and Philatelic Studies. Mem. Am. Numis. Assn. (life), Can. Numis. Assn. (life), Internat. Numis. Soc. (life), L.I. Businessmen's Assn. Republican. Jewish. Innovator direct mktg., advt. and sales techniques in numismatics. Office: 560 Broad Hollow Rd Melville NY 11747

ABS, HERMANN J., banker; b. Bonn, Germany, Oct. 15, 1901; Hon. pres. Deutsche Bank A.G., Frankfurt am Main, W. Ger.; chmn. mem., hon. chmn. supervisory bds. of major cos. Office: 5-11 Junghofstrasse Frankfurt am Main Federal Republic of Germany

ABT, CLARK CLAUS, social and econ. research and devel. co. exec.; b. Cologne, Germany, Aug. 31, 1929; came to U.S., 1937, naturalized, 1945; B.S., Mass. Inst. Tech., 1951, postgrad, 1961-65, Ph.D., 1965; M.A., John Hopkins, 1952; m. Wendy Peter, Nov. 3, 1972; children—Thomas, Emily. Research asst. social sci. Mass. Inst. Tech., 1950-51; instr. humanities Johns Hopkins, 1951-52; sr. staff engr. ops. analysis Raytheon Co., 1957-59, mgr. preliminary systems design Missile and Space div., 1960-61, mgr. Strategic Studies dept., 1962-63, mgr. advanced systems dept., 1964; pres., founder Abt Asso. Inc., Cambridge, Mass., 1965—; vis. lectr. Harvard U., 1969; vis. prof. State U. N.Y., 1976; mem. adv. bd. M.S. in Accounting program Bentley Coll., 1974; mem. vis. com. sociology dept Harvard U.; mem. vis. com. polit. sci. dept. M.I.T., 1979. Bd. dirs. League Sch. of Boston, Inc., 1969, Theatre Co. of Boston, 1972; incorporator Mt. Auburn Hosp., 1980. Served to capt. USAF, 1952-57. Recipient Grand prize Thoreau Landscape Architecture award, 1975, 79. Mem. Council for Applied Social Research (founder, pres. 1977). Author: Serious Games, 1970; The Social Audit for Management, 1977; Applied Research for Social Policy: The U.S. and Germany Compared, 1979; editor: The Evaluation of Social Programs, 1977; contbr. articles to profl. jours. Office: 55 Wheeler St Cambridge MA 02138

ACHOR, D. PERRY, educator; b. New Castle, Ind., May 1, 1936; s. Forest and Helen A.; B.S., Purdue U., 1958; M.A., Ball State U., 1964; m. Janet S. Rush, Aug. 17, 1958. Tchr., Crawfordsville (Ind.) Sr. High Sch., 1958-68; archtl. designer Nat. Homes Corp., Lafayette, Ind., 1968-76; prof. bldg. constrn. Purdue U., W. Lafayette, 1976—; cons. archtl. design. Mem. Lafayette Art Center. Recipient Pres.'s award Purdue U., 1976. Mem. Am. Inst. Constrn., Nat. Assn. Home Builders, Am. Soc. Interior Design (affiliate). Author: Estimating Laboratory Guide, 1971. Home: 511 Dodge St West Lafayette IN 47906 Office: Purdue U West Lafayette IN 47907

ACHTENTUCH, HERBERT, accountant; b. Vienna, Austria, Sept. 9, 1922; s. Herman and Paula (Kohn) A.; came to U.S., 1938, naturalized, 1944; B.B.A. magna cum laude, City Coll. N.Y., 1946; m. Marion Rosenbaum, Nov. 26, 1961; children—Jeanne Sharon, Harriet Rose. Owner Herbert Achtentuch, C.P.A., N.Y.C., 1949—. Cons. to pub. and pvt. cos. and founds. C.P.A., N.Y. Mem. N.Y. State Soc. C.P.A.'s, Am. Inst. C.P.A.'s, Inst. C.P.A.'s Israel (asso. internat. mem.), Beta Gamma Sigma. Home: 2 Middlemay Circle Forest Hills Gardens NY 11375 Office: 635 Madison Ave New York NY 10022

ACHZIGER, D'ARCY LEJEUNE, apparel mfg. exec.; b. Lackawanna, N.Y., May 22, 1950; d. Joseph P. and Gladys (LeJeune) Wilkinson; B.F.A., Carnegie Mellon U., 1972; divorced; 1 son, Josh. Sales staff Bergdorf Goodman, N.Y.C., 1976-77; asst. designer, sales rep. Drizzle, N.Y.C., 1977-78; sales mgr. Anne Klein Jeans, N.Y.C., 1978-80; v.p. designer lines Jerold Rayne Corp., N.Y.C., 1980-81; sales mgr. Jabé, N.Y.C., 1981—. Mem. N.Y. Fashion Council, Am. Mgmt. Assn., Council Profl. Women. Club: St. Bartholomew's. Home: 175 Riverside Dr New York NY 10024 Office: 575 Seventh Ave Ave New York NY 10018

ACKERBERG, NORMAN JAMES, contractor; b. Mpls., July 31, 1928; s. David and Eva (Fefereorn) A.; B.A., U. Minn., 1949; children—Lynn MMarie, Stuart Ira. Estimator, field clk. James Leck Co., Mpls., 1949-50; asst. v.p. Naugle-Leck Co., Mpls., 1950-64; pres. Norman Constrn. Co., Mpls., 1964—; owner NJA Ranch, sheep ranch, Wis. Pres. bd. dirs. Camp Tikvah, Mpls.; bd. dirs. Minn. Dance Theatre. Clubs: Decathalon Athletic, Oak Ridge Country, Inverrary Country, Le Club Internat., Jockey, Carleton, Masons, Shriners. Developer internat. village apt. concept. Home: 3700 Inverrary Dr Fort Lauderdale FL 33319 Office: 201 W 96th St Minneapolis MN 55420

ACKERMAN, GARY MARSHAL, mfg. co. exec.; b. Worcester, Mass., Jan. 31, 1950; s. Robert Elmer and Dorothy L. (Hulten) A.; A.A. in Econs., UCLA, 1973, A.A. in Music and Bus., Berkelee Coll. Music, 1974; postgrad. Worcester State Coll., 1975-76. Pres., chief exec. officer Auburn Indsl. Tool, Inc., Worcester, 1976—, AIT Corp., Worcester, 1978—, Advanced Indsl. Technologies, Worcester, 1979—; dir. Encryption Inc., Laser Graphics. Served with USN, 1968-70. Mem. Nat. Alliance Businessmen, Central Mass. Employers Assn. Club: Shrewsbury Racquet. Patentee digital indicator. Office: 95 Grand St Worcester MA 01610

ACKERMAN, LOIS VOLK, retail exec.; b. Sharon, Pa., Aug. 17, 1934; d. Louis and Sara Greenberger; B.B.A. magna cum laude, U. Pitts., 1955; m. Lawrence Volk, Dec. 25, 1955 (dec.); children—Valerie, David, Pamela; m. 2d, Sidney Ackerman, Sept. 3, 1978; stepchildren—Steven, Allan, Joel and Mitchell Ackerman, Eve Ackerman Rosenblatt. Instr., demonstrator Burroughs Corp., Pitts., 1956; owner, mgr., pres. Star Pharmacy, Inc., North Fort Myers, Fla., from 1971; pres. Star Gifts Inc., Fort Myers; sec.-treas. Star Gifts of Gainesville Inc., Star Gifts of Fla. Inc. Mem. Gift and Decorative Accessories Assn., S.E. Airport Mgrs. Assn., Jewelers Industry Council, Fla. League Arts, Beta Gamma Sigma. Democrat. Jewish. Club: Rotary Ann's. Home: 1715 Marina Terr North Fort Myers FL 33903 Office: 6611 Business 41-N North Fort Myers FL 33903

ACKERMAN, RICHARD PETER, mfg. co. exec.; b. Mineola, N.Y., Apr. 22, 1937; s. William DeWitt and Carmen Louise (Voss) A.; student Bklyn. Poly. Inst., 1954-55; B.A., Hofstra U., 1958; postgrad. Bklyn. Law Sch., 1963-64; m. Marian James, Aug. 27, 1960; children—Mary Lynn, Richard F. With Met. Life Ins. Co., Hempstead, N.Y., 1958-59; with Comml. Credit Corp., Hempstead, 1959-61, CIT Financial, Hempstead, 1961-63, Travelers Ins. Co., N.Y.C., 1963-67; asst. dir. ins. ITT Continental Baking Co., Rye, N.Y., 1967-69; dir. ins. and safety Sheraton Corp. Am., Boston, 1969-72; dir. ins. Westinghouse Electric Corp., Pitts., 1972-78; dir. asset and risk mgmt. R.J. Reynolds Industries, Winston-Salem, N.C., 1978—. Bd. dirs. Planned Parenthood, 1978. Mem. Am. Soc. Ins. Mgmt., Soc. Advancement of Mgmt., Am. Soc. Safety Engrs., Am. Mgmt. Assn. (mem. ins. council, dir. 1971—), Machinery and Allied Products Inst. (mem. ins. council 1972—), Nat. Assn. Corp. Real Estate Execs. Club: K.C. Contbr. articles to profl. jours. Home: 2825 Bartram Rd Winston-Salem NC 27106 Office: RJ Reynolds Industries Inc Winston-Salem NC 27102

ACKROYD, JOHN MARTIN, project engr.; b. Halifax, Eng., Mar. 10, 1934; s. Ernest Edgerton and Marion (Feavers) A.; came to U.S., 1967, naturalized, 1973; certificate Halifax Tech. Coll., 1955; A.A.S., Rochester Inst. Tech., 1976, B.S. in Mech. Engring., 1979; m. Barbara Corner, Sept. 13, 1958; children—Karen Ann, Robert Grahame. Mech. engr. Butler Machine Tool, Halifax, Eng., 1950-59, Asquith Machine Tools, Halifax, 1959-65, Churchill-Redman Machine Tools., Halifax, 1965-67; research technologist Eastman Kodak Co., Rochester, N.Y., 1967-76; project engr., machine tool engring. Farrel div. USM Corp., Rochester, 1976-79; project engr. Xerox Corp., Webster, N.Y., 1979—; mem. adj. faculty Rochester Inst. Tech., 1974—. Active Boy Scouts Am., Rochester, 1970-72; coach Greece Little Guy Soccer, Rochester, 1972-74. Served with RAF, 1955-57. Recipient Teaching award Rochester Inst. Tech., 1978. Mem. ASME. Home: 178 Quesada Dr Rochester NY 14616 Office: 800 Phillips Rd Webster NY 14580

ACORACE, JOSEPH JOHN, city fin. ofcl.; b. Lynn, Mass., Nov. 29, 1935; s. Dominic and Anna Eleanor (Calabro) A.; B.A. in Econs., U. N.H., 1960; M.B.A., Boston Coll., 1970; m. Carol M. Savoy, Feb. 16, 1957; children—Anthony Joseph, Elena Marie. Asst. gen. mgr. Jodi Shoe Co., Derry, N.H., 1960-69; city auditor City of Manchester, 1969-72, dir. fin., 1972—, treas. Manchester Retirement System, 1974—; chmn. bd. N.H. Retirement System, 1978-80. Mem. Manchester Bd. Mayor and Alderman, 1966-69; mem. exec. council State N.H., 1969-70; sec. bd. trustees Catholic Med. Center, Manchester, 1975-77, vice chmn., 1977-79, chmn., 1980—. Served with USNR, 1955-77. Named to Outstanding Young Men Am., U.S. Jaycees, 1967; lic. public acct., N.H. Mem. Mcpl. Fin. Officers Assn. Republican. Roman Catholic. Clubs: Joliet, Kiwanis. Office: 908 Elm St City Hall Manchester NH 03101

ACRIDGE, DOROTHY MARIE, Realtor; b. St. Louis, Aug. 8; d. William M. and Lillian (Matney) Herman; student Lindenwood Coll., 1948, U. Mo., 1950; m. Harvey Acridge, Dec. 13, 1968; 1 son, Dean Richard. Pres., Realty Execs. of Calif., San Diego, 1972—; pres. United Realty Assn., Inc., San Diego, 1978—. Republican. Office: 1277 Camino del Rio S San Diego CA 92108

ADACHI, JAMES SHOGO, lawyer; b. Wildwood, N.J., Apr. 8, 1920; s. Shogo and Fumi (Takashina) A.; A.B. cum laude, U. Wyo., 1942, J.D., 1942; m. Barbara Chase Curtis, June 1, 1949; children—Catherine Anthony, Daniel Curtis. Admitted to Wyo. bar, 1942, Tokyo, 1949; legal adviser Gen. Hdqrs. Supreme Comdr. for Allied Powers, Tokyo, 1946-50; practice law, Tokyo, 1950—; sr. partner firm Adachi, Henderson, Miyatake and Fujita, 1974—; individual practice, 1950-74; dir. various U.S.-Japan joint venture cos. Chmn., YMCA Fgn. Community Supporting Com., Tokyo, 1969, 76. Served with USAAF, 1943-46. Mem. Am.-Japan Soc. (council 1972—), Am. C. of C. in Japan (dir. 1963—, pres. 1971), Wyo. State Bar, First Tokyo Bar Assn. Episcopalian. Clubs: Tokyo Am. (dir.), Rotary, Tokyo Lawn Tennis (Tokyo); Hodogaya Golf, Karuizawa Golf, Fg. Corrs. Home: 19-3 Akasaka 6-Chome Minato-Ku Tokyo 107 Japan Office: 2-3-6 Otemachi Chiyoda-Ku Tokyo 100 Japan

ADAIR, JOHN DOUGLAS, mfg. co. exec.; b. Ardmore, Pa., May 24, 1920; s. Herbert J. and Margaret Lane (Douglas) A.; student Dartmouth Coll., 1938-39, George Washington U., 1940; m. Peggy Strickland Sawyer, Oct. 10, 1977; children—John Douglas, Richard Herbert. Chief estimator Kieckhefer Container Corp., 1939-41; insp. N.Y. Shipbldg. Corp., 1941; exec. asst. Kent-Moore Corp., Warren, Mich., 1946-47, pres., 1947—, also dir.; dir. Douglas & Lomason Co., City Bank & Trust Co., Jackson, Mich. Bd. dirs. Goodwill Industries Mich., 1951-64; trustee Village of Grosse Pointe Shores (Mich.), 1952-55; chmn. bd. dirs. Kidney Found. Mich., 1956—; v.p., bd. dirs. Mich. United Fund, 1964-73. Served to lt., U.S. Army, 1943-46. Clubs: Country, Detroit Athletic, Detroit, Economic, Hundred, (Detroit); Bloomfield Hills Country; Jupiter (Fla.) Hills; Seminole (Fla.) Golf; Pine Valley Golf. Home: 1201 Shore Club Dr Saint Clair Shores MI 48080 Office: 28635 Mound Rd Warren MI 48092

ADAM, RAY CHARLES, mfg. co. exec.; b. Aquilla, Tex., Jan. 12, 1920; s. Ernst and Margaret (Burt) A.; B.S., U. Ark., 1946; m. Dorothy Talley, May 2, 1948; children—Charles Randal, Laurie Wynn. With Mobil Oil Corp., 1946-72; div. pres. Mobil Chem. Co., N.Y.C., 1970-72, corp. v.p., 1970-72; exec. v.p., chief operating officer NL Industries, Inc., N.Y.C., 1972-74, pres., chmn. bd., chief exec. officer, 1974—, also dir.; dir. ABC, Bristol-Myers, Inc., Freeport Minerals Co., Met. Life Ins. Co., J.P. Morgan & Co., Morgan Guaranty Trust Co. Chmn., N.Y.C. Cerebral Palsy Fund Dr.; bd. dirs. United Cerebral Palsy Research and Edn. Assn. Served with AUS, 1942-46. Mem. Bus. Council. Clubs: Laurel Valley, Silver Spring; Blind Brook, Rolling Rock, Sky, Links. Home: Woods End Rd New Canaan CT 06840 Office: 1230 Ave of Americas New York NY 10020

ADAMS, ALLAN WILFRED, bus. cons., lawyer; b. Beloit, Wis., Aug. 23, 1910; s. Harry Wilfred and Prudence Mary (Bennett) A.; A.B., Harvard U., 1932; LL.B., U. Wis., 1935; m. Charlotte Amy Ray, Nov. 26, 1936; children—Allan Wilfred, Prudence B., Polly H., John B. Admitted to Wis. bar, 1935; partner firm Adams & Adams, Beloit, Wis., 1935-61; of counsel Hansen, Eggers, Berres & Kelley, Beloit, 1961—; pres. Adams Corp., Beloit, 1946-62; sec. Flakall Corp., Beloit, 1945-61; pres. Dell Foods, Beloit, 1957-61; pres. Adams Internat. div. Beatrice Foods Co., Beloit, 1962-75, cons., 1975-79; corp. sec. Regal-Beloit Corp., 1979—; dir. Heritage Bank Beloit, Nat. Mut. Benefit, Madison Wis., Wis. Power & Light Co., Madison, Regal Beloit Tool Corp. Pres., Beloit YMCA, 1955-64, dir., 1950-72; dir. Wis. Taxpayers Alliance, 1963—; bd. dirs. Beloit ARC, 1958-70; bd. dirs. United Givers, 1978—, Greater Beloit Steering Com., 1978—. With OPA-Rent Div., 1942-45. Paul Harris Rotary fellow, 1978. Fellow Am. Coll. Probate Counsel, Am., Wis. bar founds.; mem. Rock County Bar Assn. (pres. 1946), Am., Wis. bar assns. Republican. Congregationalist. Clubs: Rotary, Beloit Country, Madison, Elks, Wis. 49ers. Home: 1628 Emerson St Beloit WI 53511 Office: 419 Pleasant St Beloit WI 53511

ADAMS, BILLY JOE, bus. coll. dean; b. Forney, Tex., June 2, 1919; s. Garland John William and Bula Mae (Willmon) A.; B.S., Tex. A. and M. U., 1941, Ph.D., 1977; M.B.A., Tulane U., 1960; m. Martha Irelene Albright, July 19, 1942; children—Jack Lynn, Patricia Adams Manny. Chief accountant, asst. treas. Goldrus Drilling Co., Houston, 1946-47; chief accountant, office mgr. Gallery & Hurt, Houston, 1947-48; commd. 2d lt. U.S. Army, advanced through grades to col., 1963; bn. comdr., Korea, 1953-54; staff officer Pentagon, 1955-58; dir. computer simulation div. Army Logistics Mgmt. Center, Ft. Lee, Va., 1960-64, chief evaluation div., combat service support group, 1964-65; ret., 1965; asst. prof. Tex. Christian U., Fort Worth, 1965-66; asst. dir. exec. devel. programs Tex. A. and M. U., College Station, 1966-70, asst. dean Coll. Bus. Adminstrn., 1970—, dir. exec. devel. programs, 1970—, asst. prof. mgmt., 1967-79, asso. prof. mgmt., 1979—, dir. office continuing edn., 1978—. Served with AUS, 1941-46. Decorated Legion of Merit, Bronze Star with oak leaf. Mem. Data Processing Mgmt. Assn., Am. Soc. Tng. and Devel., Tex. Assn. Community Service and Continuing Edn., Beta Gamma Sigma, Sigma Iota Epsilon. Mem. Christian Ch. (Disciples of Christ). Editor Tex. Bus. Exec., 1975—. Home: 1207 Neal Pickett St College Station TX 77840 Office: Coll Business Adminstrn Tex A and M U College Station TX 77843

ADAMS, CHARLES ARTHUR, city ofcl.; b. Caldwell, Idaho, July 23, 1933; s. John Woodrow and Eileen (Vail) A.; B.A., Coll. Idaho, 1962; m. Susan Rae Donovan, Jan. 30, 1960; children—Michael C., Teresa M. Sales mgr. Hoppins Ins. Agy., Nampa, Idaho, 1961-63; auditor Indsl. Indemnity Ins. Co., Boise, Idaho, 1964-65, Argonaut Ins. Co., Portland, 1966-67; br. mgr. Am. Mut. Ins. Co., Portland, 1968-70; underwriting mgr. Alaska Pacific Assurance Co., Juneau, 1970-73; pres. A.I.M. Ins. Inc., Anchorage, 1973-78, pres. parent co. A.I.M. Corp., 1977-78, also sr. v.p. A.I.M. Internat., Tokyo, 1975-78; fin. officer City of Petersburg (Alaska), 1978, City of Homer (Alaska), 1979; fin. analyst Municipality of Anchorage, 1980—. Served with AUS, 1955-58; ETO. Mem. Resource Devel. Council Alaska, Homebuilders Alaska (dir. 1974-78), Homeowners Warranty Council Alaska (v.p. 1977), Porsche Club Am., Alaska Council Sports Car Clubs (dir. 1976-78), Alaska World Affairs Council, K.C. Clubs: Toastmasters (named Summit Club Speaker of Year 1969). Home: 2270 Lake George Dr Anchorage AK 99504 Office: Pouch 6-650 Anchorage AK 99502

ADAMS, CHARLES FRANCIS, advt. and real estate exec., assn. exec.; b. Detroit, Sept. 26, 1927; s. James R. and Bertha C. (DeChant) A.; B.A., U. Mich., 1948; postgrad. U. Calif., Berkeley, 1949; m. Helen R. Harrell, Nov. 12, 1949; children—Charles Francis, Amy Ann, James Randolph, Patricia Duncan. Pres., chief operating officer D'Arcy-MacManus & Masius, Inc., Bloomfield Hills, Mich., 1976-80; chmn., chief exec. officer Wajim Corp., Bloomfield Hills, 1979—; exec. v.p. and dir. Washington Office, Am. Assn. Advt. Agys., 1980—; former partner Hockey Club of Pitts.; owner Pitts. Penguins, Nat. Hockey League franchise; mem. steering com. Nat. Advt. Rev. Bd. Mem. exec. com. Oakland Univ., also chmn. steering com. Pres.'s Club. Mem. Am. Assn. Advt. Agys. (dir.), Advt. Fedn. Am. (past dir.), Nat. Outdoor Advt. Bur. (past chmn.), Theta Chi, Alpha Delta Sigma (hon.). Republican. Roman Catholic. Clubs: Bloomfield Hills Country, the Old, Nat. Golf Links Am., Muirfield Golf. Author: Common Sense In Advertising, 1965. Home: 3265 O St NW Washington DC 20007 also 1301 Clay St Nob Hill Pl San Francisco CA 94109 Office: Wajim Corp Bloomfield Hills MI 48013

ADAMS, D(ONALD) WAYNE, leasing co. exec.; b. Atlanta, July 8, 1947; s. John T. and Margaret E. Adams; student DeKalb Coll., Ga., 1965-69, Ga. State Coll., 1969-70; m. Patricia Ann Leptwich, July 15, 1967; children—Donald Austin, Dana Elizabeth. Br. mgr. Rollins Leasing Co., Conyers, Ga., 1971-73; part owner John Adams Food Co., Snellville, Ga., 1973-75; sales and br. mgr. lend lease Nat. Car Rental Co., Macon, Ga., 1979-80; regional lease devel. mgr. Saunders Leasing System, Atlanta, 1979—. Mem. staff Gov. Ga. Mem. N.G., 1975. Mem. Atlanta Traffic Club, Atlanta East Traffic Club (dir.), Am. Hist. Soc. Methodist. Clubs: Masons, All Traffic. Home: Route 1 Box 1 Oakwood GA 30566 Office: 4420 Chamblee Dunwood Rd Suite 275 Atlanta GA 30338

ADAMS, DAVID HOLMES, lawyer, constrn. co. exec.; b. Paintsville, Ky., Oct. 6, 1948; s. Stuart Holmes and Geneva L. (Honeycutt) A.; B.S., Pikeville Coll., 1970; J.D., U. Louisville, 1972; married; 1 son, Davin Holmes. Vice pres. Adams Constrn. Corp., Pikeville, Ky., 1970—; admitted to Ky. bar, 1972; asso. Hinton, Hall & Todd, 1972—; v.p. Adams Corps., WLSI Radio Sta. Mem. Ky. Bar Assn., Pike County Bar Assn., Phi Delta Tau, Delta Theta Phi. Clubs: Kiwanis, Shriners. Home and Office: PO Box 2853 Pikeville KY 41501

ADAMS, GEORGE JAMES, fin. co. exec.; b. Hobart, Okla., Jan. 14, 1934; s. William T. and Nina Mae (Barkley) A.; student Midwestern U., 1951, Pan Am. Coll., 1954, Southmost Coll., 1955; m. Virginia Caswell, Aug. 3, 1956; children—Robert Wayne, Debora Sara Adams Barnes. With First Mercantile Corp., Wichita Falls, Tex., 1958—, v.p., 1969-73, sr. v.p., sec., 1973—, also mem. exec. and credit coms., plan adminstr., trustee profit sharing trust. Served with USAF, 1954-58. Cert. consumer credit exec. Mem. Internat. Consumer Credit Assn. Republican. Methodist. Club: Sunrise Optimist (chmn. youth appreciation week, program com.).

ADAMS, JAMES CARLIE, II, mfg. co. exec.; b. Raleigh, N.C., Aug. 25, 1941; s. James Carlie and Julia Brown (Hobbs) A.; B.S., N.C. State U., 1963; m. Harriet Dana Heard, Aug. 19, 1968; children—James Carlie, Shannon Dana. Vice pres. Hobbs-Adams Engring. Co., Suffolk, Va., 1963—, J.C. Adams Inc., Willow Springs, N.C., 1970—; pres. Pioneer Processors Inc., Suffolk, 1970—, Two Adams Inc., Willow Springs, 1972—; dir. United Va. Bank. Served with U.S. Army, 1974. Mem. Nat. Bark Producers Assn. (pres.), Kappa Alpha. Club: Elks. Office: 1100 Holland Rd Suffolk VA 23434

ADAMS, JOHN OSCAR, lawyer, aircraft co. exec.; b. Chattanooga, Apr. 3, 1937; s. John M. and Queen M. (Smith) A.; B.S., Wayne State U., 1962; J.D., Loyola U., Los Angeles, 1970. Tchr., Detroit Pub. Schs., 1962-64; systems engr., instr., mgr. IBM Corp., Los Angeles, 1964-70; admitted to Calif. bar, 1971; atty. IBM, Armonk, N.Y. and San Jose, Calif., 1970-72; minority counsel Small Bus. com. U.S. Senate, Washington, 1972-75; dep. city atty. Los Angeles, 1975; individual practice law, Los Angeles, 1975—; asst. to pres. Wallace & Wallace Enterprises, Washington, N.Y.C. and Tuskegee, Ala., 1975-80; pres., chmn. bd. Adams Industries Inc. of Calif. Co-founder, bd. dirs. Green Power Found., Los Angeles; co-founder, past chmn. The Pendulum Inc. of Capitol Hill, Washington; past mem. advisory bd. Westchester (N.Y.) Urban League. Served with USN, 1958-62. Recipient Spl. contbns. award Los Angeles Urban League, 1968; Mgrs. award IBM, 1969. Mem. Am., Calif., Washington, N.Y., Fed., Nat. bar assns. Author: Notes of an Afro-Saxon, 1977. Home: 9000 Jefferson E Suite 1911 Detroit MI 48214 Office: 10001 Erwin St Detroit MI 48234

ADAMS, JOHN SMITH, II, warehouse exec.; b. Akron, Ohio, Aug. 26, 1930; s. John Smith and Eleanor (Cress) A.; student Fla. State U., 1950-53; children—John Smith III, Randy Cress, Lynn Fontaine, David Scott. Exec. trainee Allied Stores Corp., Tampa, Fla. and Kansas City, Mo., 1953-54, personnel dir. and selling cost controller, 1954-58; salaried personnel mgr. Black, Sivalls & Bryson, Kansas City, 1958-60; adminstrv. asst. to pres. Kansas City White Goods, 1960-62; personnel dir., selling cost controller Lamson's, Toledo, 1962-64; asst. personnel dir. Filenes, Boston, 1964-65; v.p., gen. mgr. D.H. Overmyer Co., Tampa and Orlando, Fla., 1965-69; v.p. Furniture Transport Co., Orlando, 1969-71; v.p., partner Bell & Norfleet Enterprises, Tampa, 1971-75; pres. Interstate Distbn. Services, Inc., Toledo, 1975—; dir. R.T. Systems, Inc. Trustee, Belle Grove, Inc., Nat. Trust for Historic Preservation; mem. Com. of 100, Tampa, Com. of 200, Orlando. Served with CIC, U.S. Army, 1954-56. Registered real estate broker, Fla. Republican. Episcopalian. Home: 2166 Blackthorn Dr Toledo OH 43614 Office: 302 S Byrne Rd Toledo OH 43615

ADAMS, JOHN WILLIAM, research co. exec.; b. Chgo., Feb. 23, 1923; s. Frank Alexander and Ruth Ella (Haas) A.; B.A., Pomona (Calif.) Coll., 1947; postgrad. Yale U., 1947-48; certificate Mgmt. Policy Inst., U. So. Calif., 1976; m. Suzanne Marie Joy, Dec. 27, 1942 (dec.); children—John Shepherd, Bradford Lee. Dir. pub. relations, producer/writer 20th Century-Fox Film Corp., Beverly Hills, Calif., 1948-53; mgr. Bur. Occupations, U. Calif. at Los Angeles, 1953-56; asst. to pres. for univ. relations Rand Corp., Santa Monica, Calif., 1956-61; dir. adminstrn., engring. div. Aerospace Corp., El Segundo, Calif., 1961-65; dir. pub. and fin. relations, asst. to chmn. and chief exec. officer Flow Gen. Inc., Santa Barbara, Calif., 1965—; chmn., chief exec. officer Adams Group, Inc., Carpinteria, Calif., 1979—. Commr., Boy Scouts Am., Los Angeles, 1957-58; vestryman St. Matthews Episcopal Ch., Pacific Palisades, Calif., 1957-62; bd. dirs. Santa Barbara council Girl Scouts, 1978—, Santa Barbara County Red Cross, 1979—. Served with USAAF, 1942-46; ETO. Decorated Air medal. Mem. Am. Electronics Assn. Nat. Alliance Businessmen, Western Coll. Placement Assn., Mchts. and Mfrs. Assn., Santa Barbara Personnel Assn. Republican. Club: Santa Barbara. Home: 1160 Estrella Dr Santa Barbara CA 93110 Office: 3375 Foothill Rd 324 Carpinteria CA 93013

ADAMS, LAURENCE JOSEPH, aerospace exec.; b. Madelia, Minn., Mar. 13, 1921; s. Nickolas H. and Mary (Keppers) A.; B. Aerospace Engring., U. Minn., 1948; m. Marguerite Helen Gaetz, June 7, 1951; children—Stephen, Teresa, Michael, Mary Louise, Susan. With Martin Marietta Corp., 1948—, successively tech. dir. Titan III, dir. engring. Denver div., v.p., gen. mgr. Denver div., now pres. Martin Marietta Aerospace, Bethesda, Md. Served with USNR, 1943-46. Recipient Outstanding Achievement award U. Minn. Regents: Outstanding Achievement award AF Systems Command: NASA Public Service award: Disting. Public Service medal. Fellow AIAA; mem. AF Communications and Electronics Assn. (nat. v.p.), Nat. Security Indsl. Assn. (exec. com.), Am. Def. Preparedness Assn., Air Force Assn., Assn. U.S. Army, Navy League U.S. (life). Republican. Roman Catholic. Office: 6801 Rockledge Dr Bethesda MD 20034

ADAMS, LAWRENCE (HIRAM) (LARRY), mgmt. cons.; b. Norwich, N.Y., Dec. 23, 1933; s. Nelson H. and Beulah M. (Pinney) A.; student Cornell U., 1952-54; M.B.A., Ariz. State U., 1977. Staff, Consumer Fin. Co., 1957-65; mgr. Seaboard Fin. Co., 1957-65; asst. mgr. comml. lending Valley Nat. Bank, 1965-71; adminstrv. mgr. Oxford Auto Lease, Phoenix, 1972-74; partner Advanced Mgmt. Services, Phoenix, 1974; owner Smada Inc., mgmt. cons.'s, Phoenix, 1976—; lectr. in field. Active United Fund; Mem. Christian Businessmen's Com. of Phoenix. Mem. Am. Mgmt. Assn., Nat. M.B.A. Assn., Assn. Mgmt. Consultants Inc. Republican. Mem. Christian Ch. Home and office: 2634 W Berridge Ln C-11 Phoenix AZ 85017

ADAMS, LOUIS NELSON, food co. exec.; b. Winthrop, Mass., Jan. 21, 1920; s. Edward Eldredge and Mary Elizabeth (Nelson) A.; B.A. cum laude, Calvin Coolidge Coll., 1941; m. Jean Ruth Scully, May 31, 1943. Asst. buyer Bigelow & Dowse Co., Needham, Mass., 1941, outside salesman, 1946-59; gen. sales mgr. Servend, Inc. (name now Seiler Corp.), Waltham, Mass., 1959-61, v.p. ops., 1961-71, sr. v.p. corporate devel., 1971—, sr. v.p., gen. mgr. Seiler's of New Eng., 1972-75, sr. v.p. adminstrv. services and corporate devel., 1975—, also sec., asst. treas., dir. Served with AUS, 1944-46. Mem. Mass. Automatic Merchandising Council (pres. 1968-70). Home: 57 Marlboro Rd Sudbury MA 01776 Office: 153 2d Ave Waltham MA 02154

ADAMS, MARION ROBERT, JR., feed and seed dealer; b. Springfield, Oreg., Oct. 2, 1923; s Marion Robert and Ida (Carson) A.; student U. Oreg., 1941; m. Bobbie Jean Taylor, Sept. 21, 1947; children—Marion Robert, Amy Carol, Sandra Lynn, Richard Arthur. Owner/mgr., Adams Feed & Seed, Springfield, Oreg., 1941—. Councilman, City of Springfield, 1974-76. Served with AUS, 1943-45. Mem. Am. Legion. Republican. Home: 1306 N St Springfield OR 97477 Office: 3545 Marcola Rd Springfield OR 97477

ADAMS, NON QUINCY, bank exec.; b. Mobile, Ala., June 1, 1925; s. Samuel Boyd and Dora W. A.; B.S., U. Ala., 1949, LL.B., 1950; m. Eran I. Jobe, Nov. 26, 1952; children—Laura Adams Ezell, Samuel Russell. With First Nat. Bank Mobile, 1951—, sr. exec. v.p., 1974-78, pres., 1978—; dir. T. R. Miller Mill Co., Turner Supply Co., M.W. Smith Lumber Co., Alco Land & Timber Co., Loyal Am. Life Ins. Co. Chmn., Allied Arts Dr., 1969; bd. dirs. Mobile C. of C., 1976—, Community Chest, Mobile, United Fund Mobile County; trustee Leukemia Soc.; mem. exec. bd. Mobile Area council Boy Scouts Am. Served to lt. j.g. USN, 1943-46. Mem. Ala. Bankers Assn. (pres. trust div. 1967), Associated Industries Ala. (v.p.). Baptist. Clubs: Country of Mobile, Lakewood Golf, Athelstan, Bienville, Kiwanis (dir. club). Office: PO Drawer 1467 Mobile AL 36621

ADAMS, RICHARD LEON, bank exec.; b. Scottsbluff, Nebr., July 19, 1921; s. Clyde Charles and Elizabeth (Sullvain) A.; student Okla. A. and M. Coll., 1940; diploma La. State U. Sch. Banking, 1963; m. Mildred Catherine Moody, Oct. 29, 1945; children—Janine Elaine, Richard Leon, Nancy Sue Adams Yawn), Charles C., Donna Jo. Clk., Scottsbluff Nat. Bank, 1937-41, teller, loan clk., 1945-47; with First Nat. Bank in Palm Beach (Fla.), 1947—, auditor, 1947-51, asst. cashier, 1953-57, asst. v.p., 1957-61, v.p., 1961-68, exec. v.p., 1968-79; pres., vice chmn. bd. Palm Beach Mall Bank, West Palm Beach, Fla., 1970—. Pres. Palm Beach County Heart Assn., 1974-75; adv. bd. Salvation Army, 1970—; bd. dirs. Palm Beach County Comprehensive Community Mental Health Center, Palm Beach Symphonette; bd. dirs. Fla. Bankers Assn. Ednl. Found., chmn., 1971-72. Served to maj. USAAF, 1941-46, USAF, 1951-53. Decorated D.F.C., Air medal with cluster. Mem. Am. (exec. com. real estate and housing div. 1972-75, governing council 1980—), Fla. (chmn. credit div. 1972-73, group chmn. 1971—, v.p. 1977-78, pres. 1979-80), Palm Beach County (pres. 1976) bankers assns., Soc. Real Estate Appraisers, Asso. Gen. Contractors, Home Builders Palm Beach County, Palm Beach Sales and Mktg. Assn., Palm Beach Islanders (treas., dir.), West Palm Beach (dir. 1973—, treas. 1979-80, pres. 1981—), Palm Beach (treas., dir. 19—), chambers commerce, Air Force Assn., Navy League, Quiet Birdmen, Flying Alligators. Methodist (mem. ch. bd., trustee 1960—). Clubs: Kiwanis (dir.), Sailfish (bd. govs. 1970—, pres. 1981—), Poinciana, Tuskawilua, Bankers. Home: 3101 Embassy Dr West Palm Beach FL 33401 Office: 151 Worth Ave Palm Beach FL 33480

ADAMS, ROBERT LYLE, real estate appraiser; b. Cape Girardeau, Mo., Feb. 20, 1947; s. Carroll Matthew and Mabel (Lee) A.; student S.E. Mo. U., Cape Girardeau; m. Laraine Rae Niswonger, Oct. 19, 1969; 1 dau., Merideth Allis. Real estate appraiser Colonial Fed. Savs. & Loan Assn., Cape Girardeau, 1974-79; ind. real estate appraiser, Jackson, Mo., 1979—. Mem. Jackson City Council, 1977. Served with USNR, 1968-69; Vietnam. Mem. Am. Inst. Real Estate Appraisers, Soc. Real Estate Appraisers, Nat. Assn. Rev. Appraisers, S.E. Mo. Real Estate Appraisers Assn., Cape Cirardeau County Bd. Realtors. Baptist. Club: Jackson Breakfast Optimist (dir. 1978). Home: 1414 Kimbeland Dr Jackson MO 63755 Office: 1404 Old Cape Rd Jackson MO 63755

ADAMS, WILLIAM BESLEY, JR., pension cons.; b. Portland, Oreg., Feb. 5, 1947; s. William Besley and Ruthe (Rolle) A.; B.S., U. Oreg., 1971; J.D., Northwestern U., 1974; m. Deborah R. Berg, Sept. 22, 1979. Asso. group legal dept. Standard Ins. Co., Portland, 1975-77; adminstrv. head employment agy. and farm labor div. State of Oreg., Portland, 1977-79; pension cons. Retirement Plans, Inc., Portland, 1979-80; producer, owner W.R. Reed & Co., Portland, 1980—; condr. pension plans for accts. Served with USMC, 1966-68. Mem. Nat. Assn. Pension Cons., Nat. Assn. Life Underwriters, Am. Mgmt. Assn. Republican. Episcopalian. Clubs: Mazama, Multnomah Athletic, Oreg. Rd. Runners, Ducks Unltd. Contbr. articles to profl. jours. Home: 4635 SE 44th Ave Portland OR 97206 Office: 4800 SW MacAdam Ave Portland OR 97201

ADAMSEN, JOHN RUSSELL, electronic equipment mfg. co. exec.; b. Seattle, June 18, 1939; s. Arthur Harry and Juanita Katherine (Day) A.; student Everett Jr. Coll., 1960-61, Edmonds Jr. Coll., 1970; m. Vickey Joy Averitt, Nov. 26, 1977. Assembly aid John Fluke Mfg. Co. Inc., Mountlake Terrace, Wash., 1962-63, electronic technician, 1963-66, supr. prodn., 1966-68, prodn. engr., 1968-69, tech. writer, 1969-70, tng. specialist, 1970-76, tng. mgr., 1976—. Served with U.S. Army, 1957-60. Mem. Am. Soc. Tng. and Devel. (chpt. treas. 1978). Lutheran. Home: 9011 202d Pl SW Edmonds WA 98020 Office: PO Box 43210 Mountlake Terrace WA 98043

ADAMSON, THOMAS JOHN, life ins. gen. agent; b. Brock, Nebr., Apr. 27, 1924; s. Thomas John and Alma Esther (Wilberger) A.; grad. Am. Coll. Life Underwriters, 1964; m. Eleanor Yates, July 21, 1945; children—Catherine Adamson Huwaldt, Nancy Adamson Leavitt, Susan Adamson Ballew. Farmer, owner Adamson farm store, Auburn, Nebr., 1941-54; agent Prudential Ins. Co., Auburn, 1954-57, div. mgr., Lincoln, Nebr., 1957-67, owner, operator Adamson Agency, Am. Mut. Life Ins. Co., Lincoln, 1967—; pres. Nebr. Assn. Life Underwriters, 1970-71; pres. Lincoln Chpt. Chartered Life Underwriters, 1973-74; instr. Life Underwriters Tng. Council, 1965-66. Recipient Distinguished Service award Auburn Jr. C. of C., 1955; named Man of Year, Auburn C. of C., 1955. Mem. Am. Soc. C.L.U.'s, Nat. Assn. Life Underwriters, Lincoln Estate Planning Council, Auburn Jr. C. of C. (pres. 1954), Nebr. Jr. C. of C. (sec. 1957). Republican. Presbyterian. Clubs: Lincoln Exec., Hillcrest Country, Masons, Shriners, Elks. Home: 6700 Everett Lincoln NE 68506 Office: FN Bldg Suite 300 100 N 56 St Lincoln NE 68504

ADDINGTON, WILLIAM HUBERT, rancher, granary exec.; b. Elkhart, Kans., Mar. 8, 1924; s. Emory Lee and Lucy (Latham) A.; A.B., U. Kans., 1948; m. Donna Lorene McCalla, Mar. 17, 1948; 1 son, Mark Wayne. Operator 6 grain elevators in Kans., 1948-66; operator ranches in N. Mex. and Wyo., 1956-67; pres. Haskell County Grain Co., Sublette, Kans., 1956-61, Am. Dairy Cow Co., Ft. Worth, 1977—; dir. East Side Bank. Commr., Kans. Hwy. Dept., 1955-57; mem. Kans. Ho. of Reps., 1958-61; Republican candidate for gov. Kans., 1960. Served from pvt. to lt. USAAF, 1943-48. Clubs: Masons, Shriners, Elks. Home: 3418 Henry Dr Fort Worth TX 76118

ADDIS, THOMAS HOMER, III, golf profl.; b. San Diego, Nov. 30, 1945; s. Thomas H. and Martha J. (Edwards) A.; student Foothill and Grossmont Jr. Coll., 1964-66; grad. Dale Carnegie course; m. Susan Tera Buckley, June 13, 1966; children—Thomas Homer IV, Bryan Michael. Profl. mgr. Sun Valley Golf Club, La Mesa, Calif., 1966-67; dir. golf ops., head golf profl. Singing Hills Country Club and Lodge, El Cajon, Calif., 1969—; staff instr. Nat. Golf Found. Seminars, 1978, 79, 80; pres. Calif. State Open. lectr. in field. Gen. chmn. Nat. Jr. Golf Championships, U.S. Golf Assn., 1973; area cons. Nat. Golf Found. Named So. Calif. Golf Profl. of Year, 1979. Mem. Profl. Golfers Assn. Am. (del. nat. 1978, 79, 80; mem. bd. control; A cert., pres. So. Calif. 1980-81, sec. So. Calif. 1978, 79; pres. San Diego chpt. 1978, 79, v.p. 1980, 81). Club: Rotary. Office: 3007 Dehesa Rd El Cajon CA 92021

ADDISON, MARK PENNINGTON, aerosol mktg. co. exec.; b. Chgo., Sept. 22, 1934; s. Earl H. and Margaret D. (Pennington) A.; B.A., U. Colo., 1960; m. Mary D. Kamps, Dec. 28, 1957; children—Douglas, Susan, Ann, Timothy, Sarah. With Design Products, Inc., Boulder, Colo., 1957-60, Binks Research & Devel. Corp., Boulder, 1960-61; with Colo. Dye & Chem. Co., Inc., Boulder, 1961—, pres., 1963—; propr. Art Matters, Boulder. Served with AUS, 1954-57. Recipient certificate appreciation N.Am. Ski Instrs. Congress, 1971; named III Internat. Schileherrfortbildungkurs, 1970. Mem. Am. Inst. Floral Designers (hon.), Soc. Am. Florists (wholesalers council; named Keyman 1971-73), Wholesale Florists and Florists Suppliers Am. (chmn. edn. com.), Profl. Ski Instrs. Am. (certificate appreciation 1974), Rocky Mountain Ski Instrs. Assn. (past pres.; exec. v.p., dir.; certificate appreciation 1969, 71), Phi Kappa Psi. Republican. Roman Catholic. Office: PO Box 1522 Boulder CO 80306

ADDISON, MICHAEL ROBERT, bus. exec.; b. Chgo., Dec. 9, 1941; s. Edward Alvin and Florence (Bauer) A.; M.S., Stanford, 1964; M.B.A., Harvard, 1974. Nuclear engr. Bechtel Corp., San Francisco, 1970-72; area mgr. Raychem Corp., Maple Shade, N.J., 1974-76, Bay Cities Auto Auction, 1976—. Served with USN, 1964-70. Mem. Am. Nuclear Soc., Tau Beta Pi. Jewish. Home: 16695 Shannon Rd Los Gatos CA 95030 Office: 48531 Warm Springs Blvd Fremont CA 94538

ADDLEMAN, JOHN CUSHING, banker; b. Chgo., Mar. 12, 1936; s. Arley Eugene and Margaret (Duncan) A.; B.S., U. Louisville, 1958; M.S., San Diego State U., 1963; m. Barbara Ann Dohm, May 5, 1975; children by previous marriage—Martin, Margaret Ann, John Cushing. Stockbroker, portfolio mgr. Shearson, Hammill, San Diego, 1964-71; v.p. new bus. devel., western asset mgmt. Western Bancorp., Los Angeles, 1971-75; v.p. bus. devel., comml. banking group Wells Fargo Bank, Los Angeles, 1976—. Advancement chmn. Boy Scouts Am.; commr., coach Am. Youth Soccer Orgn., 1972—; bd. dirs. Little League Baseball, 1972-80, coach, 1972-80, pres., 1978-80. Served with USNR, 1958-63. ROTC Scholar, 1954-58. Mem. Am. Mgmt. Assn. Republican. Episcopalian. Home: 27 Santa Bella Rd Rolling Hills Estates CA 90274 Office: Wells Fargo Bank 770 Wilshire Blvd Los Angeles CA 90017

ADDY, FREDERICK SEALE, oil co. exec.; b. Boston, Jan. 1, 1932; s. William R. and Edith (Seale) A.; B.A., Mich. State U., 1953, M.B.A., 1957; m. Joyce Marilyn Marshall, Mar. 26, 1954; children—Deborah, William, Brian. With Standard Oil Co. (Ind.) and its subsidiaries, 1957—, econ. analyst, 1957-61, econs. supr., 1962-67, acquisition mgr., 1968-71, treas. Am. Oil Co., Chgo., 1971-72, mgr. financial planning Standard Oil, 1972-73, gen. mgr. corp. planning and econs. 1975-77, treas., 1977—, v.p. adminstrn. Amoco Prodn. Co., 1973-75. Served with USAF, 1954-56. Mem. Soc. Petroleum Engrs. Home: 1230 Loch Ln Lake Forest IL 60045 Office: 200 E Randolph Dr Chicago IL 60601

ADELMAN, MARTIN HARRIS, instrument co. exec.; b. N.Y.C., Nov. 5, 1935; s. Sam G. and Pauline (Kletter) A.; B.S. Queens Coll., 1957; M.S., St. Josephs Coll., 1962; m. Glenda Sorsher, Sept. 6, 1958; children—Jill, Beth, Charles, Steven. Mktg. mgr. environ. sci. Technicon Corp., Tarrytown, N.Y., 1966-72; div. mgr. CEA Instruments, Stamford, Conn., 1972-77; pres., sales mgr., 1977—. Mgr., Little League; officer. N.J. Soc. Prevention Cruelty to Animals; trustee Temple Beth Sholom, also mem. sch. bd. Mem. Instrument Soc. Am. (sr.), ASTM, Air Pollution Control Assn., Mfrs. Agts. Nat. Assn., Am. Indsl. Hygiene Assn. Contbr. articles to profl. jours. Home: 58 Ralph Ave Hillsdale NJ 07642 Office: 15 Charles St Westwood NJ 07675

ADELMAN, MYLES HENRY, ins. agency exec.; b. Jersey City, Dec. 19, 1931; s. A. Harry and Beatrice S. A.; B.S. in Accounting, Lehigh U., 1953; M.S. in Fin., Columbia U., 1954; m. Elisabeth S., July 19, 1958; children—Mark, Rob, John. Exec. v.p. Middlesex Container Co. Inc., Milltown, N.J., 1956-63; pres. Basin & Basin Agency Inc. of N.J., Livingston, 1963-79; treas. Maj. Surplus Ltd., 1976-79; pres. Trans-Nat. Agy. Inc., 1980—. Served with U.S. Army, 1954-56. Mem. Ins. Premium Fin. Assn. N.J. (founder, dir.), Ins. Producers Council N.J. (exec. sec.), Essex County (N.J.) Ins. Agts. (v.p. 1978), Ins. Brokers Assn. N.J. (pres. 1974-76, Ins. Man of Year 1975), Ind. Ins. Agts. N.J., Profl. Ins. Agts., N.J. Surplus Lines Assn., Pi Lambda Phi, Alpha Kappa Psi.

ADELMAN, ROBERT JAMES, real estate exec.; b. Chgo., June 21, 1915; s. Samuel and Rose (Colitz) A.; A.B., U. Mich., 1936; m. Betty Friend, Feb. 4, 1941; children—Jean Ruth, Betty Sue. With Arthur Rubloff & Co., Chgo., 1936—, pres., 1952-70, chmn. bd., chief exec. officer, 1970-80, chmn bd., 1980—; dir. Chgo. Title & Trust Co., Avico, Ltd. Vice-pres., bd. dirs. Greater N. Michigan Ave. Assn.; mem. Chgo. Airport Study Commn., 1979; mem. Ill. Aeros. Bd., 1978—. Served to 1st lt. USAAF, World War II. Mem. Am. Soc. Real Estate Counselors, Northwestern U. Assos., Soc. Indsl. Realtors, Chgo. Assn. Commerce and Industry (aviation com.), Clubs: Standard, Tavern (Chgo.); Lake Shore Country (Glencoe, Ill.). Office: 69 Washington St Chicago IL 60602

ADENAUER, PETER CHRISTOPH, holding co. exec.; b. Neuss, Germany, Dec. 26, 1940; s. Hans C. and Gabriele M. (Werhahn) A.; came to U.S., 1965, naturalized, 1976; B.A. in Bus., Walsh Coll., 1967; M.S., Va. Commonwealth U., 1969; m. Sylvia Marie Ramirez, July 27, 1973; 1 dau., Carola Daniela. Asst. to mgr. mill div. Gebr. Boehler & Co., Duesseldorf, Germany, 1963-65; asst. to gen. mgr. E.W. Bliss-Henschel, Duesseldorf, 1965; asst. to controller Reynolds Internat., Inc., 1969-70; asst. to exec. v.p., asst. comptroller Bank of Va. Co., 1970-71; sr. analyst Wilh. Werhahn, OHG, Neuss, 1972-73; sr. acquisition analyst Ryder System, Inc., Miami, Fla., 1973-74; partner Wilh. Werhahn Neuss, Wilh. Werhan Can., Ltd., 1974—; sec.-treas. Restaurant Ventures, Inc., Miami, 1978-79, pres., 1979-80; cons. Mem. USCG Aux. Mem. Fla. Underwater Council. Roman Catholic. Clubs: Neusser Ruderverein e.v.; Coral Bay Yacht. Home: 13040 San Jose St Coral Gables FL 33156

ADKINS, GEORGE WOODROW, meat packing co. exec.; b. Salisbury, Md., Sept. 28, 1940; s. Woodrow Wilson and Blanche Elizabeth (Wilkins) A.; B.S., Coll. Agr., U. Md., 1962; m. Doris V. Smith, June 24, 1962; children—Elaine Marie, Grant Woodrow. With Swift & Co., Chgo., 1962-74, v.p. mktg. and sales Swift Processed Meats Co., 1970-74; v.p. Wis. Packing Co., Milw., 1974-77, pres., 1977—. Bd. dirs., v.p. Youth Ice Hockey Program, 1978-80; mem. bd. incorporation Milw. Boys Club, 1979-80. Danforth fellow, 1961—. Mem. Am. Meat Inst. (chmn. beef com. 1976-78), Am. Mktg. Assn., Young Presidents Orgn. (sec.), Classic Auto Club, Milwaukee County Zool. Soc. Republican. Clubs: Ozaukee Country, Innisbrook Country. Office: 4700 N 132d St Butler WI 53007

ADKINS, ROBERT DENNIS, elec. engr.; b. Kansas City, Mo., Aug. 14, 1952; s. Robert Worth, Jr. and Dorothy Lavon (Bundy) A.; B.S. in Elec. Engring., U. Mo., Rolla, 1974; M.B.A., U. Mo., Kansas City, 1979; m. Carolyn Sue Burchfield, Dec. 21, 1974. Power planning engr. Burns & McDonnell Engring. Co., Kansas City, Mo., 1974-79; corp. planning engr. Kansas City Power & Light Co., 1979—. Mem. IEEE, Nat., Mo. socs. profl. engrs., Assn. M.B.A. Execs., Planning Execs. Inst., Phi Kappa Phi, Beta Gamma Sigma. Presbyterian. Clubs: BMW of Kansas City; Mid Am. Rally. Home: 624 E 74th St Kansas City MO 64131 Office: PO Box 679 Kansas City MO 64141

ADKISON, DUANE TURNER, mortgage banker; b. Jacksonville, Fla., Nov. 19, 1937; s. Joe Turner and Louise (Fenner) A.; B.A., U. Fla., 1959, postgrad. Law Sch., 1963-64; m. Carol Dee Boykin, Aug. 12, 1962; children—Paul McEwen, Mark Carter. Vice pres. Wachovia Mortgage Co., Winston-Salem, N.C., 1965-74; pres., chief exec. officer So. Nat. Mortgage Co., Charlotte, N.C., 1974—, also dir.; dir. So. Nat. Bank N.C., Charlotte. Served with USN, 1959-63. Mem. Charlotte Mortgage Bankers Assn. (mortgage banker of yr. 1978-79; Mortgage Bankers Assn. Carolinas (dir.), Mortgage Bankers Assn. Am. Republican. Episcopalian. Clubs: Charlotte City, Myers Park Country. Home: 4617 Mullens Ford Rd Charlotte NC 28211 Office: PO Box 32246 Charlotte NC 28232

ADLER, ANTHONY WILLIAM, investment banker; b. Bronxville, N.Y., Sept. 4, 1939; s. William Frederick and Rita Evelyn (Hanzlik) A.; B.A., Columbia U., 1961; M.B.A., N.Y. U., 1966; m. Donna Andrea Olson, Sept. 10, 1960; children—Peter Christopher, Erik Erland. With trust dept. Chase Manhattan Bank, N.Y.C., 1963-66; with credit dept. Chem. Bank, N.Y.C., 1966-68; v.p. D.A. Campbell Co., N.Y.C., 1968-72; dir. research W.E. Burnet, N.Y.C., 1972-74; v.p., dir. Solar Services div. Muller & Co., N.Y.C., 1974—; cons. on solar energy, mem. photovoltaics adv. com. U.S. Dept. Energy; cons. on solar energy to various large corps. Mem. redesign com. Mamaroneck Union Free Sch. Dist., 1974; chmn. Emelin Theatre Com., 1974-76; trustee Mamaroneck Free Library, 1975—. Served with U.S. Army, 1961-63. Fellow Fin. Analysts Fedn.; mem. N.Y. Soc. Security Analysts, Solar Energy Industries Assn. (bd. govs., treas.), Am. Wind Energy Assn. (dir.), AAAS, Solar Energy Research and Edn. Found. (dir.). Presbyterian. Office: 25 Broad St New York NY 10004

ADLER, RITA TEITEL, bank exec.; b. Bklyn., Jan. 26, 1937; d. Bernard and Yetta Ada (Newman) Teitel; student U. Miami, 1954-56; certificate in Personnel and Mgmt., Yale Div. Coll., 1957; m. Harold J. Adler, June 14, 1973; children—Gary S. Ehrlich, Barbara Jo Ehrlich. Supr. dept. personnel Greist Mfg. Co., New Haven, 1956-58; asst. personnel mgr. Gray Mfg. Co., Hartford, Conn., 1958-59; office mgr. Shaw Employment Agy., Hartford, 1961-63; office mgr. M.A. Prescott, W. Hartford, Conn., 1963-68; sales woman Fenton & Muskat Realtors, Miami Beach, Fla., 1969-73; v.p. residential builder financing Washington Fed. Savs. and Loan Assn. of Miami Beach, from 1973, now v.p. savs. ops. Mem. Builders of S. Fla. Assn., NOW, Miami Beach Bd. Realtors, Nat. Assn. Realtors, Am. Mgmt. Assn., Nat. Forum for Exec. Women; Miami Beach C. of C. Jewish. Clubs: Calif., Top Draw, Carmel Tennis. Home: 20575 NE 6th Ct North Miami Beach FL 33179 Office: 1701 Meridian Ave Miami Beach FL 33139

ADLER, RONALD LESLIE, mgmt. cons.; b. Hartford, Conn., Dec. 6, 1946; s. Frank and Gloria Claire A.; B.S., U. Md., 1971; M.B.A., So. Ill. U., 1978; m. Lesli Ann Wolf, Aug. 24, 1969; children—Dana Claire, Lauren Evanne. Asst. store mgr. Singer Co., Bladensburg, Md., 1971-72; div. chief auditor Reed, Roberts Assos., Arlington, Va., 1973-75, asst. v.p., Phila., 1975-77, div. v.p., 1977-79, v.p. adminstrn., 1979—; cons., lectr. on unemployment ins. Vice chmn. bd. dirs. Chelsea Wood Condominium Assn., 1975-76. Served with USAF, 1964-68. Mem. Assn. M.B.A. Execs. (life), U. Md. Alumni Assn. Home: 3228 Byrd Pl Baldwin Harbor NY 11510 Office: 118 7th St Garden City NY 11530

ADRIAN, J. JACK, utility exec.; b. Beirut, Lebanon, Jan. 1, 1938; s. Simon and Araxie (Terzian) Lurchigian; came to U.S., 1956, naturalized, 1969; B.S. in Mech. Engring., Calif. State U., 1964; postgrad. U. Calif. (Los Angeles); m. Kathy Ofstad, Apr. 1, 1967; children—Jennifer Ani, Christine Shake. Engr., Bechtel Corp., Los Angeles, 1962-66; project engr. So. Calif. Edison Co., Los Angeles, 1966-69; v.p. engring. and constrn. Nat. Energy Systems Corp., Los Angeles, 1969-72; project mgr. high temperature gas cooled reactor and other projects So. Calif. Edison Co., Los Angeles, 1972-76, mgr. project engring. nuclear, fossil fuel, hydro, also other power generation projects, 1976—; cons. field of energy. Registered profl. mech. and nuclear engr., licensed gen. engring. A contractor, Calif. Mem. ASME, Am. Nuclear Soc., Atomic Indsl. Forum. Republican. Home: 18912 Canyon Circle Villa Park CA 92667

ADRIANI, FRANK NICHOLAS, road constrn. and services co. exec.; b. Bridgeport, Conn., Sept. 9, 1910; s. Nicola and Maria Lucia (Caseria) A.; student pub. schs., Bridgeport, m. Joan M. Schick, Feb. 8, 1941; 1 dau., Bonnie Lee. Painter, decorator, Bridgeport, 1928-43; with Silliman Co., Bridgeport, 1943—, pres., treas., 1955-70, chmn. bd., 1970—; pres. Woodbury Supply Co., 1960-67, Iron Ledge Co., 1960-67, Southbury Devel. Co., 1960-67; v.p. Better Bus. Bur.; mem. adv. bd. Conn. Nat. Bank. Bd. dirs. Archbishop Sheehan Center, Bridgeport, 1962—, chmn. bd., fin. sec., 1962-76; bd. dirs. Community Chest, Bridgeport, 1972—, Am. Cancer Soc., Bridgeport, 1963—, Jr. Achievement, Bridgeport, 1963—, St. Vincent's Med. Center, Bridgeport, 1964—; bd. dirs. U. Bridgeport, 1976—, hon. mem. bd. dirs., 1968—. Mem. Conn. Soc. Civil Engrs. (asso.). Roman Catholic. Clubs: Algonquin, Rotary, Elks. Home: 259 Victoria Lawn Stratford CT 06497

ADVANI, CHANDERBAN GHANSHAMDAS (G.A. CHANDRU), mcht.; b. Hyderabad, India, July 23, 1924; s. Ghanshamdas Gobindbux and Rukibai A.; B.A., Sind U., 1947; m. Devi K. Jagtiani, Nov. 30, 1958; children—Meera, Nalin. Mgr., V.H. Advani & Bros., Karachi, Pakistan, Narain Advani & Co., Karachi, French Drug Co., Karachi, Paragon Products Co., Karachi, 1941-48; pres. Nephew's Internat. Comml. Corp., Karachi, 1949-51; mgr. Indo French Traders, Pondichery, India, 1951-52; mgr. Ms. L. Mohnani, 1953-59; pres. G.A. Chandru Shokai, Yokahama, 1959—, Nephew's Internat. Inc., Yokohama, 1965—. Cons. in field. Recipient medal Mayor of Bombay; letter of appreciation Mayor of Yokohama. Mem. Indian Mchts. Assn. (hon. past pres.), Indian C. of C. Japan (hon. joint sec.). Propeller Club U.S.-Yokohama-Tokyo (past bd. govs.), Fgn. Corrs., Yokohama Fgn. Trade Inst., Yokohama-Bombay Sister-City Assn. (vice chmn.), Yokohama C. of C. and Industry. Mason (Shriner). Corr. editor Bharat Ratna, 1966—. Home: 502 NewPort

Bldg 25-6 Yamashita-cho Naka-ku Yokohama 231 Japan Office: Port PO Box 216 Yokohama 231-91 Japan

AELLEN, JOHN PAUL, JR., wine co. exec.; b. Bklyn., Dec. 25, 1927; s. John Paul and Elizabeth Margret (Cherouny) A.; B.S., Fordham U., 1948, M.S., 1950; M.B.A., Lehigh U., 1960; m. Lucille Greco, Jan. 20, 1951; children—John Paul III and Victor Thomas (twins), Lucia, Anthony, Elizabeth Ann, Eric. Methods engr. J.T. Baker Chem. Co., Phillipsburg, N.J., 1954-58; product devel. engr. Dixie Cup, Easton, Pa., 1960-64; with Sheridan Chem. Co., Bethlehem, Pa., 1956-69, pres., 1966-69; pres. Berrywine Plantations, Inc., Mt. Airy, Md., 1971—. Garden editor Dialogue With the Blind, 1969—. Served with USAF, 1951-53. Mem. Am. Chem. Soc., Am. Simmental Assn., Am. Soc. Enologists, Am. Wine Soc., Frederick C. of C. Home: 13601 Glisans Mill Rd Mt Airy MD 21771

AFFLECK, JAMES G., chem. co. exec.; b. 1923; B.A., Princeton, 1946; Ph.D., 1949; married. With Am. Cyanamid Co., 1947—, research chemist, tech. rep., mgr. new product devel. dept., 1949-57, mgr. rubber chem. dept., 1957-61, asst. gen. mgr. comml. devel. div., 1961-64, asst. gen. mgr. consumer products, 1964-65, asst. gen. mgr. internat. divs., 1965-67, gen. mgr. agrl. div., 1967-71, corporate v.p., dir., 1971, pres., 1972—, chmn., chief exec. officer, 1976—; dir. Potlatch Corp., Prudential Ins. Co. Am., N.J. Bell Telephone Co. Trustee, Found. Coll. Medicine and Dentistry N.J., 1974—; bd. dirs. Council for Fin. Aid to Edn., 1978—. Mem. Pharm. Mfrs. Am. (dir.), Chem. Mfrs. Assn. (dir. 1974—, exec. com. 1974—, chmn. exec. com. 1976-77, chmn. 1977—), U.S. C. of C. (dir. 1974-75), NAM (dir. 1978—), Conf. Bd. Clubs: Augusta (Ga.) Nat. Golf; Links (N.Y.C.); Blind Brook (N.Y.). Served to lt. USNR, 1943-46. Office: American Cyanamid Co Wayne NJ 07470

AGEE, WILLIAM MCREYNOLDS, mfg. co. exec.; b. Boise, Idaho, Jan. 5, 1938; s. Harold J. and Suzanne (McReynolds) A.; student Stanford U., 1956-57; A.A., Boise Jr. Coll., 1958; B.S. with high honors, U. Idaho, 1960; M.B.A. with distinction, Harvard U., 1963; D.Sc. in Indsl. Mgmt. (hon.), Lawrence Inst. Tech., 1977; D.Sc. (hon.), Nathaniel Hawthorne Coll., 1977; D.C.S., Eastern Mich. U., 1978, others. With Boise Cascade Corp., 1963-72, sr. v.p. and chief fin. officer, 1969-72; exec. v.p. and chief fin. officer The Bendix Corp., Southfield, Mich., 1972-76, pres., chief operating officer, 1976-77, chmn. bd., chief exec. officer, 1977—, dir., 1972—; dir. Equitable Life Assurance Soc. U.S., Dow Jones & Co., Inc., Gen. Foods Corp. Bd. dirs. Detroit Renaissance, Inc., Detroit Econ. Growth Corp., Nat. Council U.S.-China Trade, United Found., Assos. Harvard Bus. Sch.; trustee The Urban Inst., Citizens Research Council Mich., Cranbrook Ednl. Community; Investment Adv. Com., 1979; chmn. Pres.'s Indsl. Adv. Subcom. on Econ. and Trade Policy, 1978-79; mem. United Negro Coll. Fund, co-chmn. capital resource devel. campaign and bus. and industry com. Recipient Disting. Alumnus award Boise State U., 1972; Alumni Achievement award Harvard Bus. Sch., 1977; U. Idaho Alumni Hall of Fame, 1978. Mem. Conf. Bd., Council Fgn. Relations, Bus. Roundtable, Am. Inst. C.P.A.'s, Idaho Soc. C.P.A.'s, Mich. Assn. C.P.A.'s. Clubs: Econ. Detroit (dir.), Arid, Renaissance. Home: Bloomfield Hills MI Office: The Bendix Corp Bendix Center Southfield MI 48037

AGHIB, EDWARD GIULIO, internat. cons.; b. Milan, Italy, Apr. 16, 1922; s. Enrico C. and Olga (Romano) A.; certificate Brit. Inst., Cambridge, 1940; C.M.S., Sch. Engring., U. Lausanne (Switzerland), 1945; postgrad. N.Y. U., 1952; m. Joan H. Lewine, Nov. 11, 1951; children—Peter Romano, Lisa Gabriella. Came to U.S., 1948, naturalized, 1952. Indsl. engr. Olivetti Corp., Milan, 1945-46; systems engr. IBM, World Trade Corp., Oslo, 1946-48; various exec. positions to asst. to dir. product planning Univac div. Sperry Rand Corp., N.Y.C., 1948-58; dir. product planning Bus. Machines group Litton Industries, Orange, N.J., 1958-64; mgr. data systems planning ITT, N.Y.C., 1964-65; asst. group gen. mgr. ITT Data Systems Group, Paris, 1965-66, group gen. mgr. data services Europe, 1966-68, product line mgr. Data Systems Group, Brussels, 1968-73; v.p., product line mgr. data transmission and switching systems group ITT Europe Africa and Middle East, 1973-75; pres., chief exec. officer Comml. Trading Internat. subs. Control Data Corp., Brussels, Vienna, Frankfurt and Washington, 1975-79, v.p. Worldtech subs. CDC, 1978-79, also exec. cons.; pres., founder Aghib & Assos., Brussels, London, Washington, Paris, Verona and Tokyo, 1979—. Served Italian Underground, 1944-45. Mem. IEEE, Systems and Procedures Assn., Nat. Office Mgmt. Assn., Nat. Machine Accountants Assn., Assn. Computing Machinery, Brit. Antiquarian Horological Soc. Author: Work Simplification, 1950; Toll Roads and Accounting System, 1954; Belgian Clockmakers, 1973. Home: 16 Ave Jean Laudy Brussels B-1200 Belgium Office: 225 Ave Winston Churchill Bte 22 Brussels 1180 Belgium

AGNACIAN, GEORGE NUBAR, apparel mfg. co. exec.; b. Bucharest, Romania, Aug. 20, 1939; came to U.S., 1958, naturalized, 1970; s. Patric and Lucie (Muradian) A.; B.C.E., Rensselaer Poly. Inst., 1962, B.Mgmt. Engring., 1963; m. Joan Seibert, Sept. 14, 1968. Dept. mgr., internat. sales Foster Wheeler Corp., Livingston, N.J., 1963-71; sales dir. major projects Bank Bldg. Corp., St. Louis, 1971-73; founder McKinley Creations, Ltd., Chesterfield, Mo., 1974, pres., 1974—. Home: 229 Heather Crest Circle Chesterfield MO 63107 Office: 1307 Baur Blvd Saint Louis MO 63132

AGNEW, FRANKLIN ERNEST, III, food co. exec.; b. St. Louis, Apr. 13, 1934; s. Frank Ernest and Susanne (Kohlsaat) A.; A.B., Princeton U., 1956; M.B.A., Harvard U., 1958; m. Dorothy Powning, Feb. 17, 1962; children—Carolyn W., Timothy S., Jennifer S. Loan officer First Nat. Bank of Chgo., 1958-62; controller Rockwell Mfg. Co., Pitts., 1963-66, v.p. mfg. power tool div., 1966-68, v.p. mfg. valve div., 1968-69, v.p. fin., 1969-71; sr. v.p. fin. H.J. Heinz Co., Pitts., 1971-73, sr. v.p., 1973—. Trustee, Council of Ams., 1980, Princeton U., 1978—, Ellis Sch., 1980-81; bd. dirs. St. Margaret Meml. Hosp., 1980—. Mem. Fin. Execs. Inst., Conf. Bd. Clubs: Duquesne, Fox Chapel Golf. Office: PO Box 57 Pittsburgh PA 15230

AGNEW, JAMES KEMPER, advt. agy. exec.; b. Parkersburg, W.Va., May 10, 1939; s. James Pugh and Elinor Mary (Kemper) A.; B.B.A., U. Mich., 1961; M.B.A., U. Calif. at Berkeley, 1962; postgrad. spl. bus. studies U. Oslo (Norway); m. Ann Haughey, Sept. 15, 1962; children—Scott Kemper, Steven James, Derek John. With J. Walter Thompson, N.Y.C. and Paris, 1962-73, account exec., 1962-67, chmn. mgmt. com., Paris, 1967-70, v.p., mgmt. supr., N.Y.C., 1970-73; sr. v.p., group account dir. McCann-Erickson, Inc., N.Y.C., 1972-76, exec. v.p., gen. mgr., Los Angeles, from 1976, now pres. McCann-Erickson. Bd. dirs. Hastings Creative Arts Council. Mem. U. Mich. Alumnae Club N.Y., U. Calif. Berkeley Alumnae Club. Office: McCann-Erickson Inc 485 Lexington Ave New York NY 10017*

AGNEW, JOHN DANIEL, engring. exec.; b. Chgo., Dec. 7, 1929; s. Charles W. and Lillian (Martin) A.; student Purdue U., 1959-63; m. Anneliese Maier, May 7, 1974. With tool div. Ingersoll Milling Machine Co., Rockford, Ill., 1951-59; supr. tool engring. U.S. Steel Corp., Gary, Ind., 1959-68; mgr. product devel. Adamas Carbide Corp., Kenilworth, N.J., 1968—. Pres., Northwoods Assn., Liberty, Ind., 1966-68. Served with U.S. Army, 1950-51. Registered profl. engr., Calif. Mem. Soc. Profl. Engrs., Soc. Mfg. Engrs. (sr.), ASME, Soc. Carbide Engrs., Am. Nat. Standards Inst., Internat. Standards Orgn. Patentee machine tool. Home: PO Box 115 Waxhaw NC 28173 Office: 141 Market St Kenilworth NJ 07033

AGRATI, GUY JOHN, cons. co. exec.; b. N.Y.C., Feb. 9, 1941; s. Lorenzo Ernest and Elsie Elizabeth (von der Heyde) A.; A.B., Cornell U., 1963; M.B.A., Columbia U., 1969; m. Pamela Ann Patrone, Apr. 16, 1966; children—David Charles, Kristen Elizabeth. Investment analyst Blyth & Co., Inc., N.Y.C., 1969-70; v.p.-fin. and adminstrn. Chem. N.Y. Corp., subs. Realtime Systems, Inc., N.Y.C., 1971, mgr. control div. Chem. Bank, 1971-72; controller Russell Reynolds Assos., Inc., N.Y.C., 1972-75, v.p. and sec., 1975-78, sr. v.p.-fin. and adminstrn., 1978—. Mem. undergrad. secondary schs. com. Cornell U., 1973-77. Served to lt. USNR, 1963-68. Mem. Naval Res. Assn. (chpt. sec. 1974), Fin. Execs. Inst., Assn. Exec. Recruiting Cons.'s. Contbr. articles to profl. jours. Office: 245 Park Ave New York NY 10167

AGRAWAL, HARI MOHAN, constrn. equipment mfg. co. exec.; b. Allahabad, U.P., India, Jan. 3, 1935; came to U.S., 1963, naturalized, 1974; s. Brij Kishore and Suryamukhi Devi A.; B.S. in Agrl. Engring., U. Allahabad, 1954; M.S. in Agrl. Engring., U. Mass., 1965; M.S. in Mech. Engring., W.Va. U., 1967. Asst. prof., mech. engr. Govt. of Madhya Pradesh, India, 1954-63; research asst., design engr. U. Mass., Amherst, 1963-65; instr. indsl. engring. dept. W.Va. U., Morgantown, part-time, 1965-67; design engr. Allis Chalmers, Springfield, Ill., summer 1966; devel. engr. Barber Greene, Aurora, Ill., 1967-69, sr. design engr., 1969-73; project mgr. Stephens-Adamson, Inc., div. Allis-Chalmers, Aurora, 1973-78, contracts adminstrn., 1978—. Recipient engring. achievement award Barber Greene 1973; registered profl. engr., Ill. Hindu. Home: 565 High St Aurora IL 60505 Office: Stephens-Adamson Inc Div Allis-Chalmers Ridgeway Ave Aurora IL 60507

AGUSTIN, ALFREDO DE GUZMAN, Philippine govt. ofcl.; b. Markkina, Metro-Manila, Philippines, Aug. 24, 1949; s. Manuel (Luanzon) and Ester (de Guzman) A.; B.A. in Public Adminstrn., U. Philippines, 1970; cert. in bus. adminstrn. UCLA Extension, 1972; m. Adelia Motus, Oct. 30, 1971; 1 son, Mark Lester Motus. Asst. export mgr. Jemelee Shoes, Quezon City, Philippines, 1966-72; asst. export analyst Bd. Investments, Makati, Philippines, 1972-73, export analyst, 1973-74; chief Philippine House Coordinating Office, Makati, 1975-77; comml. attache Philippine consulate gen., N.Y.C., 1977—; mgr. Philippine Center, N.Y.C., 1977—. Bremen (Germany) Econ. Soc. grantee, 1976; World Trade Inst. grantee, 1979. Mem. Philippine Am. C. of C., Assn. Asian Comml. Attaches in N.Y. Club: Kiwanis. Home: 35 Stillwell St Huntington NY 11743 Office: 556 Fifth Ave New York NY 10036

AHLGREN, LLOYD CHALMERS, banker; b. Brockton, Mass., Aug. 6, 1920; s. Ivan Frederick and Esther Victoria (Johnson) A.; B.Sc. cum laude, Harvard, 1941, M.B.A. (Baker scholar), 1943; m. Dorothy Brede, June 18, 1949; children—Dana Lloyd, Tyler Grey, Ann. C.P.A., Price Waterhouse, Inc., N.Y.C., 1946-49; treas.-controller Perkin-Elmer Corp., Norwalk, Conn., 1949-56; v.p., partner Booz, Allen & Hamilton, Inc., Chgo., 1956-68; sr. v.p. devel. Warnaco Inc., Bridgeport, Conn., 1968-75; chmn. Kanebo-Warnaco Ltd., Osaka, Japan, 1974-75; v.p. Banco Lar Brasiliero, subs. Chase Manhattan Bank, Rio de Janeiro, Brazil, 1975—. Served with USNR, 1943-46. Decorated Purple Heart. Clubs: Harvard (N.Y.C.), Tokeneke (Darien, Conn.); Yacht of Rio de Janeiro. Home: 16 E Trail Tokeneke Darien CT 06820 also 898 Appleby Rd Boca Raton FL 33431

AHLSTROM, RICHARD MATHER, chem. co. exec.; b. Painesville, Ohio, Nov. 25, 1934; s. William McKinley and Janice M. (Mather) A.; A.B., Harvard U., 1956; postgrad. Amos Tuck exec. program Dartmouth Coll., 1974; m. Beverly J. Sowle, Apr. 6, 1957; children—Thomas R., Michael C. Budget analyst Diamond Shamrock Corp., 1960-63, corp. devel. analyst, 1963-64, chief fin. officer S.Am. subs., 1964-66, mgr. adminstrn. Specialty Chems. div., 1966-68, asst. treas., 1968-71, treas., 1971-76, v.p. fin., 1976—; dir. Stouffer's Inn on the Sq., Tex. Commerce Bank. Vice pres. exploring N.E. Ohio council Boy Scouts Am., 1977-79; trustee Fine Arts Assn. Lake County, Ohio, 1976-79; bd. dirs. Lake County chpt. Ohio Archaeology Soc., 1975-79, Tex. Assn. Taxpayers, Inc. Served with U.S. Army, 1957-59. Recipient Spoke award Jaycees, 1963, Boss of Year award Lake Erie chpt. Am. Businesswoman's Assn., 1970. Mem. Fin. Execs. Inst., Nat. Assn. Accountants, Greater Cleve. Growth Assn., NAM, Cleve. Treas. Club (past dir.). Clubs: Bent Tree Country, Cleve. Athletic. Author: Prehistoric Pipes of the Reeve Road Site, Lake County, Ohio 1979. Home: 5412 Bent Tree Dr Dallas TX 75248 Office: Diamond Shamrock Corp 717 N Harwood Dallas TX 75201

AHMANSON, WILLIAM HAYDEN, savs. and loan and ins. holding co. exec.; b. Omaha, Oct. 12, 1925; s. Hayden W. and Aimee (Talbod) A.; B.S., U. Cal. at Los Angeles, 1950; LL.D., Creighton U., 1972; m. Gloria June Gamble, July 10, 1964; children—Mary Jane, Patricia Ann, Amy Catherine, Dorothy, Joanne, Kimberly. With H. F. Ahmanson & Co., Los Angeles, 1950—, chief exec. officer, 1969—, chmn. bd., 1969—; pres. Nat. Am. Ins. Co., Omaha, 1966-75, chmn., 1975—; chmn. Home Savings & Loan Assn., 1969—, Stuyvesant Ins. Group, Allentown, Pa., 1974—, Nat. Am. Ins. Co. Calif., Nat. Am. Life Ins. Co. Calif., Nat. Am. Title Ins. Co. Mem. Founders of Music Center, Los Angeles. Bd. dirs. Hosp of Good Samaritan; trustee, v.p. Ahmanson Found., Los Angeles, 1952—; trustee Greater Los Angeles Zoo Assn., Los Angeles County Museum Art, Cal. Inst. Arts; visitor U. Cal. at Los Angeles. Served with USNR. Clubs: Wilshire Country, Chevalier Du Tastevin, Jonathan. Office: 3731 Wilshire Blvd Los Angeles CA 90010*

AHMED, AFTAB, real estate and med. equipment exec.; b. Lucknow, India, May 15, 1930; came to U.S., 1959, naturalized, 1962; s. Ahmad and Afaq Jehan (Begum) Hussain; student Prince of Wales R.I.M. Coll., Dehra Dun, India, 1940-45, Cambridge U., 1945-47; B.Sc. with honors, Air Force Coll., Pakistan, 1950; postgrad. Ariz. State U., 1959-61; m. Mary Louise Khan, May 16, 1958; children—Altaf Hussain, Arif Ben. Commd. officer Pakistani Air Force, 1950, advanced through grades to maj., 1957; squadron comdr. jet fighter squadron; ret., 1959; exec. owner Am. Bldg. Co., Phoenix, 1966—, Astro Comfort Stores, Phoenix, 1963—; dir. AKCO Mortgage Co., AA Oil & Gas, Hotel Mgmt. Co. Sec. Am.-Mex. Trade Assn., 1963-65. Lic. real estate broker, Ariz. Mem. Nat. Assn. Pilots, U.S.-Mex. Bus. Improvement Assn., Better Bus. Bur., Phi Beta Kappa. Democrat. Islam. Club: Elks.

AHRENS, ALLAN JAY, constrn. co. exec.; b. Cin., May 22, 1923; s. Edwin J. and Eleanor (Bernet) A.; student Miami U., Oxford, Ohio, 1943; B.S. in Applied Arts, U. Cin., 1948; m. Patricia Reeves Parker, Nov. 8, 1952; children—Alison Parker, Allan Jay. Mem. sales staff Crosley div. AVCO, Cin., 1948-49, Atlanta, 1949, Cleve., 1949-50; salesman C. Schmidt Co., Cin., 1951; v.p. Modern Distbg. Co., Cin., 1952-57; owner, mgr. Allan Jay Ahrens, Cin., 1958—; pres. Stonington Corp., Lebanon, Ohio, 1980—. Trustee, Home Builder Assn. Greater Cin. Pension Fund; deacon, trustee Presbyn. Ch. Served with USN, 1942-46; PTO. Mem. Home Builders Assn. Greater Cin. (pres. 1968), Omicron Delta Kappa, Phi Eta Kappa, Delta Phi Delta, Theta Alpha Phi, Phi Delta Theta. Republican. Clubs: Medi, Mason (Scottish Rite), Circus Fans Am. Home: 8392 Squirrelridge Dr Cincinnati OH 45243

AHRENS, FREDERICK PHILLIP, JR., lawyer, mfg. co. exec.; b. Kansas City, Mo., Oct. 6, 1937; s. Frederick Phillip and Adeline A. (Cutsford) A.; B.S. in Econs., Xavier U., Cin., 1959, M.B.A., 1962; J.D., Marquette U., 1962; m. Carolyn J. Thomas, Jan. 17, 1962 (div. Dec. 1977); children—Tracey Elizabeth, Sean Frederick. Admitted to Wis. bar, 1962, Mich. bar, 1963, Tex. bar, 1978; indsl. relations rep. steel div. Ford Motor Co., Dearborn, Mich., 1962-65; indsl. relations mgr. motor truck div. Internat. Harvester Corp., Springfield, Ohio, 1965-70; dir. indsl. relations Paper Mate div. Gillette Corp., Chgo., 1970-73; indsl. relations dir. microelectronics group Gen. Instruments Co., Hicksville, N.Y., 1973-74; v.p. indsl. relations Wylain Co., Inc., Dallas, 1974-80; v.p. human resources Friedrich Air Conditioning & Refrigeration Co., San Antonio, 1980—; instr. labor law Wittenburg U., 1966-67, Ohio U., 1968-70. Served with USAF Res., 1962. Mem. Am., Wis., Mich., Tex. bar assns. Roman Catholic. Clubs: Canyon Creek Country, Willowbend Polo. Office: PO Box 1540 4200 N Pan Am Expy San Antonio TX 78295

AHRENS, ROBERT MORTON, videotape and film producer/packager; b. Bklyn., Apr. 10, 1937; s. George Philip and Eleanor (Lipschutz) A.; B.S. in Communications, Syracuse U., 1958; m. Maxine Rosenzweig, Aug. 19, 1966; children—Daryl, Jody. Asso. producer Met. Probe, WNEW/TV, N.Y.C., 1959-60; coordinator Am. TV Commls. Festival, 1960-62; asst. producer, then producer Grey Advt., 1963-66; dir. TV prodn. Daniel & Charles Advt., 1967-68; advt. prodn. coordinator Block Drug Co., 1970-73; v.p. mktg./prodn. Video Software & Prodn. Center, Yonkers, N.Y., 1973-78; pres. Bob Ahrens Prodns., N.Y.C., 1978—. Pres., Richmond Estates Civic Assn., S.I., N.Y., 1972-73, 76-77, mem. exec. com., 1972-78. Recipient comml. award Am. TV Comml. Festival, 1968, Art Dirs. Club N.Y., 1968; Silver Screen award U.S. Indsl. Film/TV Festival, 1980; Silver award Internat. Film and TV Festival, 1980. Mem. Nat. Acad. TV Arts and Scis., Internat. Tape Assn. (sec. video adv. bd. 1977-78), Internat. TV Assn., Internat. Assn. Bus. Communicators. Office: Bob Ahrens Prodns 62 W 45th St New York NY 10036

AHRENSDORF, ROBERT EDGAR, publisher; b. Kearny, N.J., Jan. 26, 1916; s. Herrman Edgar and Elisabeth Murray (Winton) A.; A.B., Northwestern U., 1936; m. Sheila Jane Sanford, Mar. 16, 1976; children by previous marriage—Wendie Marie, Robert Edgar. Vice pres., gen. mgr. Rogers Pub. Co., Detroit, 1946-53; pres. Robert E. Ahrensdorf Co., Los Angeles, 1953-60; v.p. Hayden Pub. Co., N.Y.C., 1960-68; pres. Thomas Internat. Pub. Co., N.Y.C., 1968—; chmn. bd. Incom Co., Ltd., Tokyo, Incom Pub. Asia, Ltd., Hong Kong, Interasia Publs., Inc., Hong Kong, Internat. Communications, Ltd., Hong Kong, I.E.N.-Europe, N.V., Brussels; dir. Til Publicacoes Industrials, Ltda., Sao Paulo, Brazil; pres., dir. Western Hemisphere Mktg. Services Co., N.Y.C. Served with USAAF, 1942-45. Mem. Internat. Execs. Assn. Republican. Roman Catholic. Clubs: Met. (N.Y.C.) Apawamis (Rye, N.Y.). Home: 118 E 60th St New York NY 10022 Office: 1 Penn Plaza New York NY 10001

AHUJA, SUSHIL KUMAR, actuary; b. Muzafargarh, West Pakistan, May 1, 1941; s. Ladha R. and Jai D. (Pahwa) A.; B.S. with honors, U. Bombay, 1962; M.A., U. Delhi (India), 1968; m. Adarsh Narang, Oct. 10, 1970; children—Renuka, Raj, Rita. Came to U.S., 1970, naturalized, 1975. Actuarial student Ben Standard Life Ins. Co., Los Angeles, 1970-72; sr. acturial analyst Travelers Ins. Co., Hartford, Conn., 1973; actuarial mgr. Martin E. Segal Co., Washington, 1974-78; actuary U.S. Dept. Energy, Washington, 1978--. Served with Indian Armed Forces, 1964-70. Mem. Soc. Actuaries, Am. Acad. Actuaries. Home: 2234 Malraux Dr Vienna VA 22180 Office: PO Box 23049 Washington DC 20024

AIBEL, HOWARD JAMES, lawyer; b. N.Y.C., Mar. 24, 1929; s. David and Anne (Fishman) A.; A.B. magna cum laude, Harvard Coll., 1950, J.D. cum laude, 1951; m. Katherine Walter Webster, June 6, 1952; children—David Webster, Daniel Walter, Jonathan Brown. Admitted to N.Y. State bar, 1952, U.S. Supreme Ct. bar, 1957; asso. firm White and Case, 1952-57; litigation counsel Gen. Electric Co., 1957-64; with ITT, N.Y.C., 1964—, sr. v.p., gen. counsel, 1968—; dir. ITT World Communications, ITT Continental Baking Co., Internat. Standard Electric Co. Served to lt. comdr. USNR, ret. Office: 320 Park Ave New York NY 10022

AIDEKMAN, ALEX, food corp. exec.; b. 1915. Salesman, Good Deal Market Co., Irvington, N.J., until 1942, Uniondale Foods, Inc., 1946-55; founder, pres., dir. Wakefern Food Corp., 1955-67; chmn. bd. Supermarkets Operating Co. (merged into Supermarkets Gen. Corp. 1966), 1956-66, chmn. bd., dir., 1966—. Served with AUS, 1942-46. Office: Supermarkets General Corp 301 Blair Rd Woodbridge NJ 07095

AIDINOFF, M(ERTON) BERNARD, lawyer; b. Newport, R.I., Feb. 2, 1929; s. Simon and Esther (Miller) A.; B.A., U. Mich., 1950; LL.B., Harvard, 1953; m. Celia Spiro, May 30, 1956; children—Seth G., Gail M. Admitted to N.Y. bar, 1954; law clk. to Judge Learned Hand, U.S. Ct. of Appeals, N.Y.C., 1955-56; with firm Sullivan & Cromwell, N.Y.C., 1956—, partner, 1963—; dir. Gibbs & Cox, Inc., Goody Products, Inc. Trustee Spence Sch.; mem. adv. com. Gibbs Bros. Found.; mem. vis. com. Harvard U. Law Sch.; mem. adv. com. to Commr. IRS, 1979-80. Served as 1st lt. Judge Adv. Gen. Corps, AUS, 1953-55. Mem. Am. (vice chmn. taxation sect. 1974-77), N.Y. State bar assns., Assn. Bar City N.Y. (exec. com. 1974-78, chmn. exec. com. 1977-78, v.p. 1978-79, chmn. taxation com. 1979—), Am. Law Inst. (cons. subchpts. C and K income tax project), Council Fgn. Relations, Confrerie des Chevaliers du Tastevin, Commanderie de Bordeaux, India House, Phi Beta Kappa. Editor-in-chief: Tax Lawyer, 1974-77. Home: 1120 Fifth Ave New York NY 10028 Office: 125 Broad St New York NY 10004

AIGD, KENNETH WARREN, residential devel. co. exec.; b. 1943; B.S. in Mktg., U. So. Calif., 1966, M.S. in Systems Mgmt., 1969. Mgr. residential mktg. Irvine Co., Newport Beach, Calif., 1971-73, dir. residential mktg., 1973-76, v.p. sales and mktg., 1976-78; prin. Market Profiles, Inc., Irvine, Calif., 1978-79, sr. v.p. Mayer Group Inc., Downey, Calif.; guest lectr. U. So. Calif., U. Calif., Irvine, Calif. State U., Fullerton; speaker various orgns. Served to capt. USAF, 1967-71. Decorated Air Force Commendation medal. Mem. Bldg. Industry Assn. (Max C. Tipton award 1976), Sales and Mktg. Council (v.p. Orange County chpt., state v.p. 1976-78). Home: 29 Montpellier Newport Beach CA 92660 Office: 8121 E Florence Avenue Downey CA 90240

AIKEN, HUGH HOLCOMBE, JR., investor, real estate devel. co. exec.; b. New Orleans, Dec. 9, 1943; s. Hugh Holcombe and Patricia Hale (Parkhurst) A.; B.S.E. with high honors in Elec. Engring., Yale U., 1965; m. Robin Lynn McAllister, Mar. 18, 1978; 1 dau., Simone. Mktg. exec. IBM, Africa and Middle East, 1965-73; founder, dir. Marine Concrete Structures, New Orleans, 1973-76; chmn., chief exec. officer Gen. Computer Systems, Inc., Dallas, 1976-78; pres. Telex Computer Products, Inc., Tulsa, 1978-79; owner, mgr. Aiken

Real Estate Devel. Co., Tulsa, 1979—; now pres., chief exec. officer Braegen Corp., Cupertino, Calif. dir. Great S.W. Industries, Inc., Tulsa. Served to capt., inf. U.S. Army, 1966-67. Decorated Bronze Star with V. Republican. Episcopalian. Club: New Orleans Country. Home and office: 1029 E 21st St Tulsa OK 74114

AIKEN, KENNETH JAMES, designer; b. Bellows Falls, Vt., Jan. 6, 1952; s. Ralph Eugene and Marion Mable (Nies) A.; student U. Vt., 1970-72, Goddard Coll., Plainfield, Vt., 1976-78; m. Caresse Marlene Pecor, June 7, 1975. Designer products from ancient artifacts, sunken Spanish treasure galleons, 1977—; engaged in jewelry trade, 1972-76; instr. jewelry making Community Coll. Vt., Montpelier, 1977; pres. Designers Edit. Ltd., Plainfield, 1978—; cons. Internat. Coins & Currency, Inc., 1977-79, Seaquest Internat., Inc., 1979-80. Recipient Craftsman award Rock and Gem mag., 1977. Mem. Soc. N.Am. Goldsmiths, Vt. Jewelers Alliance, Am. Numis. Assn., Mfg. Jewelers and Silversmiths Am. Club: Masons. Author papers on anthropology. Inventor jewelers bench converter. Address: PO Box 218 Plainfield VT 05667

AIKMAN, ROBERT EDWIN, petroleum co. exec.; b. Oklahoma City, Feb. 7, 1932; s. Claud E. and Gladys Jesse Aikman; student U. Colo., 1950; B.B.A., U. Okla., 1952; m. Rachel Stockton, May 8, 1950; children—James S., Melanie, Lucia, Amy. Landman, Cities Service Oil Co., Jackson, Miss., 1952-54, dist. landman, Amarillo, Tex., 1955-56; pres. Aikman Bros. Corp., also v.p. Mana Oil Corp., Amarillo, 1957-59; pres., chmn. bd. Mana Resources Inc., Amarillo and Dallas, 1969-71, pres. Dorchester Exploration Inc., also Aikman Bros. Inc., Amarillo, 1971-77, Aikman Oil and Gas Co., 1977—; dir. Dorchester Gas Corp., Energy Resources Corp. Bd. dirs. Campfire Girls Council, Amarillo Area Found., Amarillo Coll. Found., West Tex. State U. Pres.'s Council. Mem. Ind., Tex. Mid-Continent (dir. 1977—) petroleum assns., Panhandle (dir. 1973—), Tex. ind. producers and royalty owners assns. Republican. Episcopalian. Clubs: Amarillo, Amarillo Country; Dallas Country, Dallas Petroleum. Home: 3201 Hawthorne Dr Amarillo TX 79109 Office: 300 Bank of SW Bldg Amarillo TX 79109

AILLONI-CHARAS, DAN, marketing services co. exec.; b. Ploiesti, May 22, 1930; s. Max and Felicia (Lupescu) C.; A.B. with honors, U. Calif. at Berkeley, 1952, M.A., 1953, Coro Found. fellow, 1953-54; Ph.D. (Univ. Honors scholar), N.Y. U. Grad. Sch. Bus., 1968; m. Miriam C. Taytelbaum, Oct. 8, 1957; children—Ethan Benjamin, Orrin, Adam. Project dir. Marplan div. Communications Affiliates, Inc., N.Y.C., 1958-60; supr. advt. studies NBC, N.Y.C., 1960-62; dir. consumer and communications research Forbes Research, Inc., N.Y.C., 1962; mgr. market research Chesebrough-Pond's, Inc., N.Y.C., 1963-64, new product mgr., 1964-68, mgr. internat. market services dept., 1968-69; pres. Stratmar Systems, Inc., N.Y.C., 1969—; asst. prof. mktg. Pace U. Grad. Sch. Bus. Adminstrn., from 1963, now prof.; bd. dirs. Young Men's Bd. of Trade, 1960-61, 62-63, Philharmonic Symphony of Westchester, 1977-80; trustee Inst. Advanced Mktg. Studies, 1965-66; program chmn. mktg. mgmt. track Internat. Mktg. Conf., 1978; bd. advisors AdExpo, 1978. Fellow Inst. of Dirs. (London); mem. Am. Mktg. Assn. (pres. N.Y. chpt. 1965-66, nat. v.p. 1970-71), N.Am. Soc. for Corp. Planning (dir. 1970-72), Promotion Mktg. Assn. Am. (dir. 1978—, chmn. edn. com. 1979—), AAUP, Delta Sigma Chi, Phi Sigma Alpha. Editor Mktg. Rev., 1960-63; Proc., 1st Ann. Conf. on Research Design, 1964; New directions in Research Design 2d Conf., 1965; Planning, 1968-71. Home: Woodland Dr Town of Rye NY 10573 Office: 385 Madison Ave New York NY 10017

AINLEY, ROBERT WALLACE, advt. exec.; b. Perry, Iowa, Aug. 18, 1922; s. Oscar Albert and Goldie (Beatty) A.; student Kemper Mil. Sch., 1940-41, State U. Iowa, 1941-43; A.B., Drake U., 1947; m. Ila June Inman, Apr. 15, 1949; children—Robert Kent, Leslie Ann. With sales dept. Maytag Co., Newton, Iowa, 1947-48; sales rep. Upson Co., Des Moines, 1948-54; advt. sales rep. Wallace Farmer, Des Moines, 1954-65; advt. mgr. Prairie Farmer Pub. Co., Chgo., 1965-75, supr. Midwest unit farm publs., Chgo., 1968-74, promotion mgr., 1974-76; mem. Chgo. plans bd. State Farm Mag. Bur., 1971-76, mgr. advt. sales, Indpls., 1976—. Past bd. dirs., pres. Churchill and Hawthorn Grade Sch PTA, Glen Ellyn, Ill.; trustee Prairie Farmer Pension Trust, 1970-73; pres. N.Am. Farm Show Council, 1975-76; mem. adminstrv. bd. Greenwood United Meth. Ch. Served with AUS, 1943-46, 50-51. Decorated Bronze Star medal. Mem. Nat. Agrl. Mktg. Assn. (dir. Mid-South), Memphis Federated Advt. Club, Ind. Agri-Bus. Club, Greenwood High Sch. Band Parents Assn., 69th Inf. Div. Assn., Am. Legion, V.F.W., Sigma Delta Chi. Republican. Elk. Home: 754 Colonial Way Greenwood IN 46142 Office: 2346 S Lynhurst Dr Indianapolis IN 46241

AINSWORTH, GRANVILLE LLOYD, mgmt. cons. co. exec.; b. Kingston, Jamaica, West Indies, Aug. 23, 1940; came to U.S., 1963, naturalized, 1980; s. Harold George and Rubena Esmie (Taylor) A.; B.A. in Econs., Howard U., 1970; M.B.A., Fordham U., 1972; m. Sonia May Pennicooke, Jan. 15, 1972; children—Alister, Alexis. Sr. acct., mgmt. cons. Peat, Marwick, Mitchell & Co., N.Y.C., 1970-76; sr. mgmt. analyst Capital Formation, Inc., N.Y.C., 1977-78, sr. fin. cons., 1978—; instr. Medgar Evers Coll., City U. N.Y.; corp. treas. Black Agenda, Inc. Chmn. fin. com. Owens Creative Arts Center, Jamaica, N.Y. Served with U.S. Army, 1965-67. Mem. U.S. Jaycees. Roman Catholic. Home: 90-09 Northern Blvd Jackson Heights NY 11372 Office: 1150 Carrol St Brooklyn NY 11225

AIRHEART, FRANKLIN BENJAMIN, brake mfg. co. exec.; b. San Francisco, Apr. 12, 1930; s. Ted S. and Dorothy (DeDici) A.; B.S., U. So. Calif., 1956; children—Eric Jeffery, Erin June. Asst. project engr. Lockheed Aircraft, Burbank, Calif., 1956-57; chief engr., v.p. engring. Airheart Products, Inc., Van Nuys, Calif., 1957-67; chief engr., v.p. engring. Hurst/Airheart, Chatsworth, Calif., 1967-72, exec. v.p., 1972-78; pres. Am. Dibranetics, Inc., Sylmar, Calif., 1978—. Served to 1st lt. AUS, 1952-54. Recipient Nat. Office Mgmt. award, 1956. Mem. Soc. Automotive Engrs. Republican. Patentee in field. Office: 15751 Sorbonne St Sylmar CA 91342

AITKEN, ROBERT PETERS, mktg. cons.; b. Mpls.; s. Robert A. and Rosa (Peters) A.; B.C.S., Drake U., 1934; M.S., Columbia, 1936; m. Marjorie Dorothea Jackson, Apr. 24, 1943; children—Robert G., Bruce E., Gerald T. Mem. pres. of sales corp. staff Johns-Manville Corp., N.Y.C., 1936-39, indsl. engr. forcasting and prodn. scheduling staff, 1939-41; analyst Supplee-Wills-Jones, Phila., 1941-51; dir. market research Eastern div. Sealtest Foods, Phila., 1951-54, nat. dir. market research, 1954-72; pres. RPA Mktg. and Consulting Services, Walden, N.Y., 1972—; adj. instr. Orange Community Coll., Rockland Community Coll.; mem. econs. of distbn. seminar Columbia U., N.Y.C., 1968-73. Auditor Warminster Twp., Bucks County, Pa., 1948—; mem. adv. com. U.S. Bur. of Census, 1972-73. Served as lt. USNR, 1943-45. Recipient certificate appreciation U.S. Dept. Commerce, 1975. Mem. Sales Execs. Club of N.Y., Am. Mktg. Assn. (v.p.), Grand Jurors Assn. Westchester County, Mil. Order World Wars. Home: 75 F Lake Osiris Rd Walden NY 12586 Office: PO Box 453 Walden NY 12586

AKCHURIN, OMAR ESMAIL, internat. trade co. exec.; b. Flushing, N.Y., Dec. 21, 1945; s. Esmail Ishak and Rukiye Omar (Starkow) A.; B.S., Temple U., 1967; B.Fgn.Trade, Am. Inst. Fgn. Trade, Phoenix, 1968; postgrad. Thunderbird Grad. Sch. Mgmt., Glendale, Ariz., 1969; M.S.L.S., L.I. U., 1980; m. Evelyn Diane Cowie; 1 son, Justin. Mgr., The Akchurin Corp., Hempstead, N.Y., 1972-74, treas., mgr. internat. ops., 1976—; asst. mgr. auto service equipment div. Drake Am. Corp., N.Y.C., 1974-76; cons. in field. Active local Little League, Boy Scouts Am. Served to capt. C.E., U.S. Army, 1969-72; maj. Res. Decorated Army Commendation medal. Mem. Am. Importers Assn., Islamic Cultural Center N.Y. (fin. com.). Republican. Office: PO Box 186 Hempstead NY 11551

AKERMAN, JOSEPH HARRY, JR., real estate co. exec.; b. Miami, Fla., Apr. 7, 1940; s. Joseph Harry and Anne (Durr) A.; B.S.E.E., Yale U., 1962; M.B.A., Stanford U., 1969; m. Terry Farrel Maull, Dec. 14, 1969. Weapon systems engr. Hughes Aircraft, 1962-67; v.p. Dean Witter Reynolds, San Francisco, 1969-74; with Dillon Read & Co., 1974-75; asst. treas. Fairchild Camera & Instruments, Mountain View, Calif., 1975-77; chmn. Compass Investment Group, Woodside, Calif., 1979-80; pres. J.H. Akerman Assos., 1977—. Mem. IEEE, Peninsula Mfrs. Assn. Club: New Ventures. Address: 240 La Questa Way Woodside CA 94062

AKERS, CAROLYN, investment co. exec.; b. Goshen, N.Y., Aug. 6, 1946; d. Leslie and Catherine (Tuthill) A.; A.S., Becker Jr. Coll., 1966. Cost analyst Pratt & Whitney Aircraft div. United Technologies Corp., East Hartford, Conn., 1966-68; sr. equities adminstr. Travelers Equities Sales Inc., Hartford, Conn., 1968-72; ops. mgr. CG Investment Mgmt. Co., Hartford, Conn., 1972-76, controller, 1976—; fin. mgr. common stock div. Conn. Gen. Life Ins. Co., Hartford, 1978—, controller Group of Mut. Funds, 1979—. Mem. adv. bd. Investment Co. Inst., Washington, 1976—; mem. zoning bd. appeals Town of Granby, Conn., 1974-80, mem. bd. fin., 1980—, Democratic Town Com., 1977—. Methodist. Home: 20 Pendleton Rd Granby CT 06035 Office: 950 Cottage Grove Rd Bloomfield CT 06002

AKERS, CHARLES DAVID, lawyer; b. Atlanta, Jan. 6, 1948; s. James Ires and Lillian M. (McDonald) A.; B.A., Vanderbilt U., 1970, J.D., 1973. Admitted to Tenn. bar, 1973; legis. atty. Tenn. Legis. Council, Nashville, 1974-76; staff atty. Tenn. Dept. Public Health Div. Water Quality Control, Nashville, 1976-79, Office of Gen. Counsel, Nashville, 1979-80, counsel for legis., 1979-80; gen. counsel Tenn. Commn. for Human Devel., Nashville, 1980—. Served with U.S. Army, 1973. Mem. Nashville Area Jr. C. of C., Am. Bar Assn., Tenn. Bar Assn., Tenn. Bot. Gardens and Fine Arts Center, Mensa, Nashville Striders, Descs. of Ft. Nashboro Pioneers. Unitarian. Office: 535 Church St Room 208 Nashville TN 37219

AKERT, BENJAMIN BRUCE, pub. co. exec.; b. McCook, Nebr., July 9, 1927; s. Paul and Cyla A. (Moseley) A.; A.B. Nebr. Wesleyan Coll., 1951; M.Ed., U. Nebr., 1954; m. Jacqueline R. Harrison, Aug. 10, 1952; children—Leonard Alan, Bruce Eugene. Tchr., Whittier Jr. High Sch., Lincoln, Nebr., 1951-53, prin., 1953-54; supt. schs., Elkhorn, Nebr., 1954-57; with Scott, Foresman & Co., Glenview, Ill., 1957—, Nebr. agt., Lincoln, 1957—. Mem. Nebr. Profl. Bookmen (pres. 1961-62), NEA (life), Pi Beta Alpha (pres. 1962-63, sec. 1968-69, nat. pres.-elect 1978-79, pres. 1979-80), Nebr. Wesleyan Alumni Assn. (v.p. 1979-80), Phi Delta Kappa. Served with AUS, 1945-46. Address: 1800 S 51st St Lincoln NE 68506

AKIN, THOMAS RUSSELL, III, mfg. co. exec.; b. Alton, Ill., June 22, 1940; s. Thomas Russell and Audra Berry (Curdie) A.; B.A. in Sociology, Tulane U., 1963; postgrad. U. Calif., Hastings, 1963-64; m. Mary Elizabeth Macfarlane, Feb. 14, 1976; children—Thomas R., Ronald C., Gabrielle E., John M. Casualty underwriting trainee Firemen's Fund Am. Ins. Cos., San Francisco, 1964-65, sr. casualty underwriter, 1965-67, spl. agent, 1967; sr. ins. rep. Kaiser Aluminum and Chem. Corp., Oakland, Calif., 1967-69; v.p. Huntington Corp. of Calif., San Francisco, 1969-70; asst. ins. mgr. E & J Gallo Winery, Modesto, Calif., 1970-75, benefits mgr., 1975—. Chmn. criminal complaints com. Stanislaus County (Calif.) Grand Jury; Cub Scout leader Yosemite council Boy Scouts Am., Modesto, 1972-73. Mem. Risk and Ins. Mgmt. Soc. Republican. Office: PO Box 1130 Modesto CA 95353

AKINS, GEORGE CHARLES, jewelry co. exec.; b. Willits, Calif., Feb. 22, 1917; s. Guy Brookins and Eugenie (Swan) A.; A.A., Sacramento City Coll., 1941; m. Jane Babcock, Mar. 27, 1945. Accountant, auditor Cal. Bd. Equalization, Dept. Finance, Sacramento, 1940-44; controller-treas. DeVons Jewelers, Sacramento, 1944-73, v.p., controller, 1973-80, v.p., chief fin. officer, 1980—; individual accounting and tax practice, Sacramento, 1944—; dir. De Vons Jewelers, Inc. Accountant, cons. Mercy Children's Hosp. Guild, Sacramento, 1957-77. Served with USAAF, 1942. Mem. Soc. Calif. Pioneers, Nat. Soc. Pub. Accountants, U.S. Navy League, Calif. Hist. Soc., English-Speaking Union, Drake Navigators Guild. Democrat. Roman Catholic. Clubs: Commonwealth of Calif., Comstock. Contbr. to Portfolio of Accounting Systems for Small and Medium-sized Businesses, 1968, 77. Home: 4417 Marion Ct Sacramento CA 95822 Office: 1009 9th St Sacramento CA 95814

AKINS, WILLIAM JOHN, security and investigation co. exec.; b. Rockford, Ill., Apr. 26, 1947; s. Donald Leroy and Marion Elizabeth (Drohan) A.; grad. Rock Valley Jr. Coll., Rockford, 1968; m. Lynn Ann Black, May 25, 1973; children—Erin Elizabeth, Kelly Jane. Asst. mgr. Karl Schoening & Sons, Rockford, 1968-70; controller Colonial Builders, Rockford, 1970-71, Fairview Builders, Rockford, 1971; spl. projects cons. Pinkerton's, Inc., Oak Park, Ill., 1971—; pres. Midwest Indsl. Emergency Planning Group; dir. Unit Systems, Addison, Ill. Served with USAR, 1966-72. Cert. protection profl. Mem. Am. Asso. Bar Assn., Am. Soc. Indsl. Security (editor newsletter 1979-80), Am. Fedn. Police. Republican. Roman Catholic. Home: 4012 Wagner St Schiller Park IL 60176 Office: 1010 Lake St Oak Park IL 60301

AKRAWI, SAMI TAWFIC, health care co. exec.; b. Iraq, Jan. 30, 1935; s. Tawfic and Mary (Fargo) A.; came to U.S., 1953, naturalized, 1968; B.A., Columbia Union, 1955; M.B.A., U. Md., 1956; postgrad. Golden Gate U.; children—Sherry, Ray, Randy. Instr., Sch. Bus. Adminstrn., U. Baghdad (Iraq), 1956-58; asst. mgr., dir. Union Trading Co., Kuwait, 1958-63; mgmt. cons., Los Angeles, 1963-66; adminstr., dist. mgr. Hy-Lond Enterprises, Sonoma, Calif., 1966-71, sr. v.p., corp. sec., 1971-77, pres., chief exec. officer, 1977—, also dir. Author: Business Methods, 1957; Human Relations in Management, 1970. Home: 6605 N Marty Ave Fresno CA 93711 Office: 1391 W Shaw Ave Fresno CA 93711

AKRIDGE, GREGORY ALLAN, oil and gas exploration co. exec.; b. Chgo., Sept. 13, 1949; s. Andrew Albert and Lois M.; B.S., U. Ill., 1971; m. Barbara Ann Bellamy, July 12, 1969; children—David Allan, Jonathan Andrew, Joel Aaron. Sr. programmer Zenith Radio Corp., Chgo., 1971-74; programmer analyst Fed. Res. Bank Chgo., 1974-80, team mgr. telecommunications, 1977-80; sr. network planner Ind. Petroleum Co., Dallas, 1980—; dir. Amway Distbrs. Assn. Recipient Pres.'s Award for Excellence, Fed. Res. Bank Chgo., 1979. Mem. GUIDE. Republican. Home: 3401 Greenbriar St Plano TX 75074 Office: 411 N Akard St IPB 5229 Dallas TX 75221

AKSELRAD, JOSEPH, detergent mfg. co. exec.; b. Poland, June 20, 1920; s. Nathan and Feiga (Dortort) A.; student Stanford U., 1943; B.A. in Econs., Bklyn. Coll., 1969; M.B.A. in Mgmt., Bernard M. Baruch Coll., 1972; postgrad. in bus. Univ. City N.Y., 1969-73; m. Blanche Markowitz, Sept. 6, 1942; children—Phyllis Ann, Nina Ruth. With Epic Chems. Inc., Bklyn., 1946—, v.p., 1973-77, pres., 1977—; condr. sanitation products seminars with distbrs., distbr. orgns. Treas. Loch Sheldrake (N.Y.) Home Owners Assn., 1952-54, v.p., 1954-58, pres., 1958-60; treas. Hebrew Congregation of Loch Sheldrake, 1967-78, pres., 1978. Served with U.S. Army, 1942-45; ETO. Recipient Presdl. citation for USAR service, 1949. Mem. Am. Mgmt. Assn., Bklyn. Coll. (Alumni in Fin. award 1969), Bernard W. Baruch Coll. alumni assns., Nat. Food Distbrs. Assn., N.Y. Food Dealers Assn. N.Y. State Sanitary Supply Assn., Hon. Order Ky. Cols., Alpha Sigma Lambda. Office: 89 Coffey St Brooklyn NY 11231

AKTURK, HANS, instrument mfg. co. exec.; b. Kars, Turkey, May 10, 1932; s. Huseyin Ragip and Meliha Akturk; came to U.S., 1957, naturalized, 1970; M.S., Turkish Naval Acad., 1956; B.S., U. Mich., 1961; M.S., U. Istanbul, 1962; m. Charlotte Ann Morton, June 15, 1967; 1 dau., Lisa. Project engr. Applied Dynamics, Inc., Ann Arbor, Mich., 1963-65, systems programmer, 1966-69; systems and programming cons., 1970-71; mgr. systems and programming Gelman Instrument Co., Ann Arbor, 1971—. Mem. Data Processing Mgmt. Assn. Home: 4785 Lake Ct Ann Arbor MI 48103 Office: 600 S Wagner St Ann Arbor MI 48103

ALALA, JOSEPH BASIL, JR., lawyer, public accountant; b. Aleppo, Syria, Apr. 29, 1933; s. Joseph Basil and Waheda A.; B.S., U. N.C., 1957, J.D. cum laude, 1959; m. Nell Powers, Dec. 19, 1954; children—Sheron, Tracy, Joseph Basil. Acct., Arthur Anderson & Co., Charlotte, N.C., 1959-62; admitted to N.C. bar, 1959, U.S. Tax Ct., 1962, U.S. Supreme Ct., 1978; asso. firm Garland & Eck, Gastonia, N.C., 1962-63; mng. partner Garland & Alala, attys., Gastonia, 1962—; dir. Independence Nat. Bank, Gastonia, Fiber Controls Corp., others. Bd. dirs. Salvation Army, Boys Club, Garrison Community Found., Belmont Abbey Coll.; past pres. YMCA. Served with AUS, 1954-55. C.P.A., N.C. Mem. Gastonia Jaycees (past pres.), Gastonia C. of C. (dir.), Am. Bar Assn., N.C. Bar Assn., Gaston County Bar Assn., Am. Assn. Attys.-C.P.A.'s, Am. Inst. C.P.A.'s, N.C. Assn. C.P.A.'s. Democrat. Roman Catholic. Clubs: Gaston Country (past pres.), Charlotte Athletic, Rotary, Grand Knights Malta. Editorial bd. N.C. law Rev., 1957-59; contbr. articles to profl. jours. Home: 1216 South St Gastonia NC 28052 Office: 192 South St Gastonia NC 28052

ALAR, JOHN, tobacco co. exec. Pres., Brown & Williamson Tobacco Corp., Louisville. Office: Brown & Williamson Tobacco Corp 1600 W Hill St Louisville KY 40232*

ALBAN, GEORGE CURTIS, advt. agy. exec.; b. Moscow, Idaho, Jan. 29, 1925; s. Arthur Henry and Emma Lillian (Kienholz) A.; student public schs., Chewelak, Wash.; m. Doris Mae Anderson, July 22, 1972; 1 son, Jack Iamar. Spl. agt. Firemans Fund Ins. Co., San Francisco and San Diego, 1946-67; partner Franklin Ins. Agy., San Diego, 1967-71, Family Life Seminars, San Diego, 1971-72; owner, mgr. The George Alban Co., San Jose, Calif., 1973—. Bd. dirs., mem. exec. com. Arthritis Found. Served with U.S. Mcht. Marine, 1942-45. Recipient cert. of merit Arthritis Found., 1978, 79. Republican. Home: 1076 Scaletta Ln San Jose CA 95120 Office: 186 E Gish Rd San Jose CA 95112

ALBAN, ROGER CHARLES, constrn. equipment distbn. co. exec.; b. Columbus, Ohio, Aug. 3, 1948; s. Charles Ellis and Alice Jacqueline (Hosfeld) A.; student public schs.; m. 2d, Rebecca Lynn Gallicchio, Aug. 12, 1978; 1 dau. by previous marriage, Allison Ann. With Alban Equipment Co., Columbus, 1963—, sales mgr., 1972-75, gen. mgr., 1975—, treas., 1978—. Mem. Grandview Heights Bd. Edn., Columbus, 1978—, pres., 1979, v.p., 1980, legis. liaison, 1978-79; mem. Met. Ednl. Council. Mem. Associated Equipment Distbrs. (lt. dir. region 6), Am. Rental Assn., Builders Exchange Central Ohio, Am. Mgmt. Assn., Nat. Right To Work Com., Nat. Fedn. Ind. Bus., Am. Mensa Ltd. (chpt. exec. com. 1979-80). Roman Catholic. Clubs: Sertoma, Downtown Columbus. Home: 1358 Wyandotte Rd Columbus OH 43212 Office: 1825 McKinley Ave Columbus OH 43222

ALBANESE, THOMAS, plumbing mfg. co. exec.; b. Passaic, N.J., June 27, 1930; s. Charles and Viola (Guerity) A.; student pub. schs., Garfield, N.J.; m. Theresa Mary Perez, Aug. 8, 1953; children—Thomas II, John, Theresa Lynne, Richard C., Michael Q. Pres., Thomas Albanese Inc., bathroom design and remodeling, 1958-60; research and devel. plumbing installations and systems, 1960-69; founder, pres. Albanese Products, Inc., Las Vegas, Nev., 1969—. Served with USAF, 1951-55. Mem. Am. Soc. San. Engrs. (pres. Nev. chpt. 1976), Am. Soc. Plumbing Engring., Air Force Assn., United Assn. Plumbers and Pipefitters. Patentee plumbing systems and products; creator MPB System. Home: 116 Norlen St Las Vegas NV 89107

ALBANESIUS, JANET GIBBS, grain co. exec.; b. Birmingham, Eng., Dec. 9, 1950; came to U.S., 1957, naturalized, 1963; d. Arthur Horton and Sheila Frances (Noake) Gibbs; B.A. in History and Lit., Am. U., 1972; m. Jon Howard Albanesius, Oct. 18, 1975; 1 dau., Chloe Gibbs. Research asso. Urban Inst., Washington, 1973; adminstrv. asst. U.S. Brewer's Assn., Washington, 1973-74; staff asst. Standard Brands Corp., N.Y.C., 1974-75; public relations coordinator Continental Grain Co., N.Y.C., 1975—. Mem. Am. Poetry Soc. Democrat. Episcopalian.

ALBAUGH, KENNETH CLOCKER, JR., mgmt. cons.; b. Balt., Dec. 17, 1922; s. Kenneth C. and Margaret (Griffin) A.; B.S. summa cum laude, U. Balt., 1951; certificate U. Mich. Grad. Sch. Bus., 1962; m. Lorraine Warner, Oct. 21, 1942 (div. Apr. 1966); children—Suzanne W. Lucas, Margaret V. Hanson; m. 2d, Hertha Sherwood, Nov. 30, 1969; 1 dau., Doreen S. Casuto. Registration and research officer VA, Balt., 1945-47; controller Empire Cleaners, Balt., 1951-55; mgr. corporate ins. and employees benefits The Glenn L. Martin Co., Balt., 1955-60; dir. ins. Columbia Gas Systems, Inc., N.Y.C., 1960-62, asst. to treas., 1962-63, dir. corporate taxes, 1963-66, asst. controller, 1966-67, operating group treas., 1967; sr. v.p. Phillips & Blackstone Ltd., mgmt. cons., N.Y.C., 1967-70; v.p., treas., cons. Adams Express Co., N.Y.C., 1970-78; v.p., treas., cons. Petroleum Corp. Am., N.Y.C., 1970-78; mgmt. cons., 1978—. Served with USAAF, 1941-45. Mem. Fin. Execs. Inst., Beta Alpha, Sigma Alpha Omicron. Home and Office: 6105 Caminito Baeza San Diego CA 92122

ALBERGER, WILLIAM RELPH, govt. ofcl.; b. Portland, Oreg., Oct. 11, 1945; s. Relph Griffin and Ferne (Ahlstrom) A.; B.A., Willamette U., 1967; M.B.A., U. Iowa, 1971; J.D., Georgetown U., 1973; m. Patricia Ann LaSalle, June 2, 1971; 1 son, Eric Griffin. Adminstrv. asst. to U.S. Rep. Al Ullman, Washington, 1975-77, House Ways and Means Com., 1977; mem. U.S. Internat. Trade Commn., Washington, 1977—, vice-chmn., 1978-80, chmn., 1980—; admitted to D.C. bar, 1974. Mem. Am. Bar Assn. (standing com.

customs law), D.C. Bar Assn. Democrat. Office: 701 E St NW Washington DC 20436

ALBERS, HARRY ROBERT, found. adminstr.; b. Jersey City, Mar. 6, 1938; s. Harry Robert and Lee (Vetreno) A.; B.S. in Physics, U. Pitts., 1960; M.S. in Physics, Cornell U., 1963; postgrad. Boston U., 1968-69; M.B.A., George Washington U., 1971; m. Jean Ellen Cherry, Jan. 26, 1963; children—Harry R., Robert S., Steaphan H. Mgr. satellite tracking program Smithsonian Astrophys. Obs., Cambridge, Mass., 1966-69; bus. mgr. Smithsonian Instn., Washington, 1970-72; dir. Smithsonian Research Found., Washington, 1967-72; dir. adminstrn. Kitt Peak Nat. Obs., Tucson, 1972-76; v.p. fin. and adminstrn. Barnard Coll.-Columbia U., 1976-78; dir. San Diego State U. Found., 1978—; cons. in field. Mem. Nat. Assn. Coll. and Univ. Bus. Ofcls., Am. Assn. Higher Edn., Soc. Research Adminstrs., Nat. Council Univ. Research Adminstrs. Home: 10019 Mozelle Ln La Mesa CA 92041 Office: San Diego State U Foundation San Diego CA 92182

ALBERT, ARTHUR JOSEPH, estate planning exec.; b. Scranton, Pa., Aug. 13, 1947; s. Eli Herman and Ruth (Alinkoff) A.; B.B.A., U. Miami (Fla.), 1969; postgrad. Purdue U., 1975; m. Sharon Justan, Aug. 31, 1974; 1 dau., Nicole Ruth. Adminstrv. asst. Congressman Claude Pepper, Washington, 1969-70; adminstrv. asst. Office Mayor of Miami (Fla.), 1972-73; exec. v.p. Eli H. Albert Agy., Scranton, 1974—. Bd. dirs. Health Systems Agy., Scranton Jewish Community Center; mem. White House Staff inaugural com., 1972. Served with AUS, 1970-72. Decorated Order St. Barbara. Mem. Scranton Assn. Life Underwriters (dir.), Nat. Assn. Ind. Public Adjusters, Delta Sigma Pi, Alpha Delta Sigma. Democrat. Jewish. Clubs: Glen Oak Country, Masons, B'nai B'rith. Home: 108 Belmont Ave Clarks Green PA 18411 Office: 701 Connell Bldg Scranton PA 18503

ALBERT, KARL DANIEL, data processing exec.; b. New Orleans, Sept. 16, 1950; s. Alonzo Joseph and Dora Cecilia A.; student Columbia Sch. Broadcasting, Harbor Coll. Data processing exec. Gen. Telephone & Electronics, Marina del Rey, Calif. Chief exec. officer Nat. Republican Congl. Com. Served with USAF. Licensed 3d class radiotelephone operator. Mem. Communications Workers of Am., Smithsonian Instn. Roman Catholic. Club: Playboy Internat. Home: 1303 Park Western Dr San Pedro CA 90733

ALBERT, P. C., mktg. exec.; b. Milw., Aug. 13, 1948; s. Theodore L. and Ann B. Albert; B.S., U. Wis., 1970; M.B.A., U. Chgo., 1980; m. Elizabeth Rowe, Aug. 15, 1970; children—Christopher, Lisa. Gen. mgr., v.p. Gen. Pet Supply of Ill., 1970-73; ops. mgr., pres., Gen. Pet Distbg. Co., 1973-78; sec.-treas. Pet's Pro Shop Ltd., 1977-79; pres. Genuine Pet Dealer Center, Inc., 1977—; dir. contingency div. Prusha/Wolfe, 1978-79; mktg. bus. credit services div. TRW, Inc., Niles, Ill., 1979-80; in mktg. Quaker Oats Co., Chgo., 1980—. Mem. Indian Princess council YMCA, La Grange, Ill.; chmn. West Suburban Boy Scouts Am. Served with U.S. Army, 1970-71. Mem. Am. Mgmt. Assn., Nat. Assn. Credit Mgrs., Pet Industry Distbrs. Assn., Am. Pet Products Mfrs. Assn., Am. Vet. Med. Assn., Am. Boarding Kennel Assn. Home: Box 282 Western Springs IL 60558 Office: Merchandise Mart Plaza Chicago IL 60654

ALBERT, ROBERT HARTMAN, mag. editor, businessman; b. Hershey, Pa., June 18, 1924; s. Thomas Warren and Hazel Noreen (Hartman) A.; B.A., Pa. State U., 1948; M.A., Stanford, 1950; postgrad. U. N.C., 1950-52. With New Yorker Mag., N.Y.C., 1956-58, Newsweek Mag., N.Y.C., 1959-61; Sunday editor N.Y. Herald Tribune, 1961-63; editorial dir. McCalls Corp., N.Y.C., 1963-64; editor, exec. v.p. Sales and Mktg. Mgmt. Mag., N.Y.C., 1964—; corporate v.p. Bill Communications, N.Y.C., 1971—; pres. Oley Furnace Vineyards, 1978—. Bd. dirs. Friends Theatre Music Collection, Mus. City N.Y. Served with USNR, 1943-46, 50-51. Mem. Advt. Research Found., Am. Mktg. Assn., Am. Soc. Bus. Press Editors, Am. Soc. Mag. Editors, ACLU, Pa. State U. Alumni Assn. Clubs: Sales Execs.; Wyomissing (Reading, Pa.); Overseas Press. Home: 10 Park Ave New York City NY 10016 Office: 633 3d Ave New York City NY 10017

ALBERT, SAMUEL OSCAR, computer mfg. co. exec.; b. Washington, Dec. 4, 1931; s. Jack and Lena (Levine) A.; B.A., Am. U., 1954; student Law Sch., N.Y. U., 1954, 56; m. Joyce Alpert, May 29, 1961; children—Corey-Jan, Gavin. Announcer, Sta. KELP, El Paso, Tex., 1956-58, tchr. Tennis Sch. of Air, Sta. KELP-TV, El Paso, Tex., 1956-58; tennis profl. Plantation Swim Club, Louisville, 1958, also tennis tchr. Sta. WAVE-TV, Louisville; salesman IBM, N.Y.C., 1959-61, instr., data processing div., N.Y.C., 1962-64, mgr. mktg. div., Forest Hills, N.Y., 1967-69 program adminstr. cons. data processing div., White Plains, N.Y., 1972—, mgr. consultants industry, 1972—; instr. Pace Coll., 1961-63; tennis sportscaster Sta. WFAS, White Plains. Cubmaster pack 4 Cub Scouts Am., Scarsdale, N.Y. Served with U.S. Army, 1956-58. Root Tilden scholar, 1954-57. Pres., E Club, booster orgn. Edgemont Sch. Dist., Scarsdale, 1979-80. Mem. Inst. Internal Auditors, U.S. Profl. Tennis Assn., EDP Auditors Assn., N.Am. Cons. Conf., So. Greenville Assn. (dir.), Nat. Assn. Accountants, Am. Mgmt. Assn., Omicron Delta Kappa. Home: 27 Kingwood Rd Scarsdale NY 10583 Office: 1133 Westchester Ave White Plains NY 10604

ALBERTI, KERRY BARTON, business exec.; b. Spokane, Wash., July 26, 1944; s. Robert Lynn and Kathleen (Steele) A.; B.B.A. in Econs., U. Iowa, 1967, M.A. in Bus. Mgmt., 1968; m. Linda Jean Nelson, Aug. 12, 1966; children—Thomas Scott, Tamara Sue. Mgr. computer ops., physics dept., U. Iowa, Iowa City, 1966-68; 2d v.p. Chase Manhattan Bank, N.A., N.Y.C., 1972-73, v.p., corp. planning group, 1973-77, v.p. deptl. planning, mgmt. info. and fin. controls exec. corp. banking dept., 1977-79; v.p. strategic mgmt. Avis, Inc., 1979—; bus. cons. N.Y. Philharmonic Orch. Treas., New Providence Presbyn. Ch., 1976-78. Served to capt. USAF, 1968-72. Decorated Air Force Commendation medal with oak leaf cluster. Republican. Home: 27 Glen Oaks Ave Summit NJ 07901 Office: 1114 Ave of Americas New York NY 10036

ALBERTS, JOHN HARRY, JR., ins. broker; b. Chgo., Apr. 21, 1950; s. John H. and Monette T. A.; B.A., Knox Coll., 1972; m. Judith C. Zabinski, Sept. 10, 1972. With Wm. H. Thompson & Co., Chgo., 1972—, sec., treas., 1976-78; regional v.p. Chgo. Bd. Underwriters, 1979—. Vice pres. Crestwood (Ill.) Pub. Library Dist., 1976—. Mem. Chgo. Bd. Underwriters (chmn. personnel lines com. 1977, dir., chmn. comml. lines com. 1978, 79), Independent Ins. Agents of Ill. (regional v.p. 1979—), Independent Ins. Agents Am., ACLU.

ALBERTSON, WILLIAM LEON, real estate broker; b. Wheeling, Mo., Aug. 26, 1906; s. William Robert and Blanche (Gillispie) A.; student University Place, Lincoln, Nebr., 1922; m. Frances A. Lee, Oct. 20, 1966. Real estate broker, Albertson Realty Co., San Bernardino, Calif., 1929—. Co-chmn. County March of Dimes, 1962; mem. atty. gen.'s adv. council State of Calif., 1972—. Res. Officer San Bernardino County Sheriff. Mem. Calif. Real Estate Assn., San Bernardino Realty Bd. Home: 841 Mountain View Ave San Bernardino CA 92401 Office: 459 4th St San Bernardino CA 92401

ALBERTSSON, STIG LENNART, recreation equipment mfg. co. exec.; b. Lindas, Sweden, Dec. 13, 1930; s. Albert Theodor and Karin Maria (Stenberg) A.; M.M.E., Katrineholms Tekniska Skola, 1952; m. Lilly Maria Karlsson, July 6, 1957; children—Susanne, Peter, Christine, Hans. Pres., Flyght Canada, Ltd., Montreal, Que., 1955-57, Flygt Corp., Norwalk, Conn., 1957-71; pres., treas. Bromley, Inc., Manchester Center, Vt., 1975—; introducer indsl. submersible pumps, Alpine Slide to N. Am. market; dir. Bromley Ski Ednl. Fund, Manchester Center, 1972—; corporator Putnum Meml. Hosp., Bennington, Vt., 1975—; bd. dirs. Friends of Hildene, Manchester, 1978—. Served with Swedish Army, 1953. Lutheran. Home: Box 297 Manchester VT 05254 Office: Box 626 Manchester VT 05254

ALBRECHT, ARTHUR JOHN, advt. agy. exec.; b. Woodhaven, N.Y., June 11, 1931; s. Charles Arthur and Anna (Klingner) A.; B.A. cum laude, Fla. State U., 1957; m. Sandi Edith Roberson, May 14, 1952; 1 dau., Sherylyn. Salesman, Vick Chem. Co., Louisville, St. Petersburg, Fla. and N.Y.C., 1958-60, sales promotion mgr., 1960-61, product mgr., 1961-63; group product mgr. Whitehall Labs., N.Y.C., 1963-65; v.p. mktg. J. B. Williams Co. Inc., N.Y.C., 1965-66; v.p. mktg. Mitchum Thayer Inc. div. Revlon, N.Y.C., 1966-68, sr. v.p. mktg., 1968-71; sr. v.p. William Esty Co., Inc., N.Y.C., 1971—; adj. asst. prof. Pace U., 1977—; lectr., cons. advt.; dir. Damon Therapeutics, N.Y.C. Pres., Villard Hill Assn., 1973-74. Served with USMCR, 1950-55. Recipient Alpha Delta Sigma Outstanding Service award, 1968. Mem. Proprietary Assn., Pharm. Advt. Club, Nat. Assn. Chain Drug Stores, Wholesale Drug Assn., Internat. Platform Assn., Fla. State U. Alumni Assn., Phi Beta Kappa, Phi Kappa Phi, Phi Eta Sigma, Alpha Delta Sigma (chpt. pres. 1956-57). Republican. Unitarian. Clubs: Century, Indian Springs Country. Author: Magic Town, U.S.A., 1977. Home: 144 Judson Ave Dobbs Ferry NY 10522 Office: 100 E 42d St New York NY 10017

ALBRECHT, EDWARD DANIEL, lab. apparatus mfg. co. exec.; b. Kewanee, Ill., Feb. 11, 1937; s. Edward Albert and Mary Jane (Horner) A.; B.S. in Metall. Engring., U. Ariz., 1959, M.S., 1961, Ph.D. (NDEA fellow 1959-62), 1964; profl. degree Metall. Engr. (hon.), 1973; m. Mignon Buehler, Jan. 1, 1973; 1 dau. by previous marriage, Deborah; stepchildren—Renata, Paul. Research asso. U. Calif. Los Alamos (N.Mex.) Sci. Lab., 1959, 60, 61; metallurgist, program mgr. U. Calif. Lawrence Livermore (Calif.) Lab., 1964-71; with Buehler Ltd. and Adolph I. Buehler Inc., Evanston, Ill., 1971—, v.p., gen. mgr., 1972-76, pres., chmn. bd., 1976—; founder, pres. Metall. Innovations Inc., Pleasanton, Calif., 1969-71; dir. Tech-Met Can. Ltd., Toronto, Ont., Banner Sci. Ltd., Coventry, Eng. Treas., bd. dirs. Danville (Calif.) Homeowners Inc., 1966-67; trustee, fellow Lake Forest (Ill.) Acad.-Ferry Hall. Fellow Am. Soc. Metals (metallographic com. 1975—, chmn. Tucson 1961); mem. Internat. Metallographic Soc. (pres. 1973-75, bd. dirs. 1971—, gen. chmn. tech. meetings San Francisco 1969, Chgo. 1972, Brighton, Eng., 1980), Sigma Gamma Epsilon. Clubs: Chicago; Onwentsia. Contbr. tech. papers to publs.; patentee in field. Office: 2120 Greenwood St Box 1459 Evanston IL 60201

ALDAG, CHARLES AUGUST, JR., chem. co. exec.; b. Indpls., May 17, 1932; s. Charles August and Mabel I (Robishaw) A.: B.S., Purdue U., 1954; M.B.A., Ind. U., 1955; m. Doris Lee Kelleher, Sept. 10, 1955; children—James C., Philip R., Charles A. With Sherex Chem. Co., Inc. and predecessor cos., various locations, 1955-72; v.p. chem. products div. Ashland Chem. Co., Dublin, Ohio, 1972-79; pres. Sherex Chem. Co. subs. Schering A.G. W. Ger., Dublin, 1979—. Mem. Planning Com. Upper Arlington (Ohio), 1971-74. Mem. Fatty Acid Producers Council div. Soap and Detergent Assn., Chem. Mfrs. Assn. Republican. Lutheran. Office: 5777 Frantz Rd Dublin OH 43017

ALDAN, DAVID RICHARD, bath fixtures mfg. co. ofcl.; b. New Castle, Pa., May 6, 1946; s. Traean Richard and Dorothy Jean (Thompson) A.; student Youngstown State Coll., 1965-68; m. Cynthia Luann Leicht, June 28, 1969; children—Erika Lyn, Brandon Todd. Laborer, D.D. Davis Constrn. Co., Youngstown, Ohio, 1968-71; moldmaker helper Universal-Rundle Corp., New Castle, Pa., 1972-75, research asst. fiberglass div., 1975-77, research asst. china div., 1977-78, safety dir. vitreous china plant, 1978—. Co-chmn. indsl. dr. Lawrence County chpt. Am. Heart Assn., 1978; active United Fund, Easter Seal Soc. Mem. Am. Mgmt. Assn., Indsl. Mgmt. Club. Republican. Clubs: Masons, Lions, Eagles. Home: 25 West Mill St Mount Jackson PA 16102 Office: E Cherry St Ext New Castle PA 16102

ALDEN, ANNA MARIE, whitewater outfitter; b. Pasadena, Calif., Dec. 12, 1945; d. Charles Donald and Maryene Florentine (Shramek) Alden; student UCLA, 1965-66; B.A., U. Calif., Hayward, 1972. Home office group rep. N.Y. Life Ins. Co., Sacramento, 1975-77; pres. Osprey River Trips, Inc., Wilderville, Oreg., 1977—; instr. Whitewater Guide Schs., 1978—. Mem. Outdoor Edn. Assn. (dir. 1978—), Inst. for Managerial and Profl. Women, Nat. Women's Polit. Caucus, NOW, Western River Guides Assn. Democrat. Metaphys. Ch. Address: 6109 Fish Hatchery Rd Grants Pass OR 97526

ALDEN, CAROLYN CARLTON, fin. cons.; b. Tulsa, Feb. 27, 1941; d. Henry Ellis and Estelle Mildred (Baker) Carlton; student Tulane U., 1959-62; B.S. magna cum laude, Okla. State U., 1966; m. Richard J. Alden, Aug. 29, 1964. Supr., Coopers & Lybrand, Dallas, 1967-72, project mgr., N.Y.C., 1972-76, nat. dir. profl. edn., 1976-79; mng. partner Alden & Assos., N.Y.C. and Newport Beach, Calif., 1979—; mem. U.S. Senatorial Bus. Adv. Bd. Pledge dr. sponsor Madison Ave. Presbyn. Ch., N.Y.C., 1975; sponsoring mem. Girls Club N.Y., 1975. C.P.A., N.Y. Mem. Am. Inst. C.P.A.'s, N.Y. Soc. C.P.A.'s, Am. Soc. Tng. and Devel., Tex. Soc. C.P.A.'s, Am. Women Soc. C.P.A.'s, Nat. Assn. Accts. Republican. Presbyterian. Club: Tex. Exec. Alumni of N.Y. Home: 203 Garnet St Newport Beach CA 92662 Office: 10 W 66th St Suite 8F New York NY 10023

ALDEN, RAYMOND MACDONALD, telecommunications co. exec.; b. Palo Alto, Cal., Nov. 17, 1921; s. Raymond Macdonald and Barbara (Hitt) A.; A.B. in Engring., Stanford, 1944; m. Sara Wills, Aug. 30, 1946; children—David Wills, Merritt Ann Alden Booster, John Lee. Engr., Western Union Telegraph Co., 1946-50; engr. Hawaiian Telephone Co., Honolulu, 1951-62, v.p., 1962-64; exec. v.p. United Telecommunications, Inc., Kansas City, Mo., 1964-73, pres., chief ops. officer, 1973-80, vice chmn., 1981—; dir. C.J. Patterson Co., United Mo. Bank Kansas City. Served with USNR, 1944-46. Registered profl. engr., Hawaii, Kan. Mem. IEEE (sr.), Nat. Soc. Profl. Engrs. Home: 4550 Warwick Blvd Kansas City MO 64111 Office: PO Box 11315 Kansas City MO 64112

ALDERMAN, MINNIS AMELIA, psychologist, bus. exec.; b. Douglas, Ga., Oct. 14, 1928; d. Louis Cleveland and Minnis (Wooten) A.; A.B., Ga. Coll. at Milledgeville, 1949; M.A., Murray State U., 1960; fellow U. Utah, summers 1974, 75. Camp counselor Camp Sloan, Conn., summer 1949; music dir. Umatilla (Fla.) Pub. Sch., 1949-50, Campbell High Sch., Fairburn, Ga., 1950-54; music and drama dir., tchr. English and speech Wells (Nev.) High Sch., 1954-59; tchr. English and history Sinking Fork Sch., Hopkinsville, Ky., 1960; counselor White Pine High Sch., Ely, Nev., 1960-68; instr. psychology, guidance and counseling Murray (Ky.) State U., summers 1961, 62; instr. guidance and counseling U. Nev. Extension, 1963-68, mem. home econs. adv. bd., 1977—; psychologist Ely Mental Health Center, 1969-75, Nev. Job Service, 1975—; owner Minisizer Exercising Salon, 1969-71, Minimimeo Mimeographing, 1969—, Knit Knook, 1969—, Gift Gamut, 1977—, City Service Sta.; sec.-treas. Great Basin Enterprises Corp., 1969-71; test supt. Coll. Entrance Exam. Bd. and Am. Coll. Testing, 1960-68. Pres. White Pine County Mental Health Assn., 1960-63, 78—; mem. Gov.'s Mental Health State Commn., 1963-65; bd. dirs. White Pine County Sch. Employees Fed. Credit Union, 1961-68, pres., 1963-68; 2d v.p. White Pine Community Concert Assn., 1965-67, pres., 1967, treas., 1975—; dir. Community Choir, 1975—; mem. Gov.'s Commn. on Status Women, 1968—; sec.-treas. White Pine Rehab. Tng. Center for Retarded Persons, 1973-75; mem. Gov.'s Commn. on Hwy. Safety, 1979—; dir. Ret. Sr. Vol. Program, 1973-74; vice chmn. Great Basin Health Council, 1973-75; sec.-treas. Great Basin chpt. Nev. Employees Assn.; vice chmn. White Pine Council on Alcoholism and Drug Abuse, 1975-76, chmn., 1976-77; grants author, originator Community Tng. Center for Retarded People, 1972, Ret. Sr. Vol. Program, 1974, Nutrition Program for Sr. Citizens, 1974, Sr. Citizens Center, 1974, Home Repairs for Sr. Citizens, 1974, Sr. Citizens Home Assistance Program, 1977, Creative Crafters Assos., 1976. Precinct reporter ABC News 1966. Mem. NEA (life), Nev. Edn. Assn., Counselors on Alcoholism, Addictions and Related Dependencies, AAUW (pres. 1964-65, state area rep. in edn. 1965-67; state implementation chmn. edn. 1967-69, state area adviser 1969-73), Bus. and Profl. Women's Club (1st v.p. 1965-66, pres. 1966-68, asst. dist. dir. 1967-68, state civic participation chmn. 1967-68, dist. dir. 1968-70, state 2d v.p. 1969-70, state rec. sec. 1968-69, state 1st v.p. 1970-71, state pres.-elect 1971-72, state pres. 1972-73), DAR, Internat. Platform Assn., Mensa (test adminstr. 1966—), Am. Personnel and Guidance Assn. (state memberships chmn. 1962-65), Am. Sch. Counselors Assn., Nat. Vocat. Counselors Assn., Nat. Fedn. Ind. Bus. (dist. chmn. 1971—), Nat. Assn. Women Deans and Counselors, Nat. Assn. Female Execs., NOW, Delta Kappa Gamma (2d v.p. 1964-66, state program chmn. 1965-69, 1st v.p. 1966-68, state 1st v.p. 1967-69, chpt. pres. 1968-72, state pres. 1969-71), Gen. Fedn. Women's Clubs (dist. pres. 1970-75), Beta Sigma Phi (chpt. sponsor 1970-72). Clubs: White Pine Knife and Fork (pres. 1970-71, sec.-treas. 1978—), Ely Woman's (pres. 1969-70). Methodist (lay speaker 1967—, lay leader to regional conf. 1977—, choir dir. 1960—). Author: Handbook for Counselors; Guidance Handbook for Teachers; Guidance Handbook for Administrators; Discipline Handbook, also articles. Home: 945 Ave H PO Box 457 East Ely NV 89315 Office: 1113 Ave F Murry St PO Box 457 East Ely NV 89301

ALDRICH, CLYDE FRANK, reins. co. exec.; b. Pulaski County, Ark., Aug. 28, 1925; s. Frank and Mary (Haynes) A.; J.D., St. Louis U., 1950; m. Gloria Lea Notwell, Dec. 30, 1972; children—Christopher F., Stephen L., Gary L., Laurie A., Robin L., Barry L. Admitted to Mo. bar, 1950, U.S. Patent Office bar, 1958; individual practice law, St. Louis, 1950-58; asst. gen. counsel Kemper Ins. Cos., Long Grove, Ill., 1958-69, pres. Kemper Reins. Co., 1969—, also dir.; atty. City of St. Ann, Mo., 1950-52. Served with U.S. Army, 1943-46. Mem. U.S. council Internat. C. of C. (trustee 1975—). Office Kemper Reinsurance Company Long Grove IL 60049

ALDRICH, FRANK NATHAN, banker; b. Jackson, Mich., June, 8, 1923; s. Frank Nathan and Marion (Butterfield) A.; student U. Md., summer 1943; A.B. in Govt., Dartmouth, 1948; postgrad. Harvard, summer 1948; m. Edna Dora DeJan, Nov. 21, 1956; children—Marion Dolores, Clinton Pershing. Sub-mgr. First Nat. Bank of Boston, Havana, Cuba, 1949-60, Rio de Janeiro, Brazil, 1961-62, sub-mgr., Sao Paulo, Brazil, 1963-64, mgr., 1965, exec. mgr., Rio de Janeiro, 1966, v.p. Brazilian brs., 1966-69, v.p. overseas operations, Boston, 1969-70, v.p. Latin Am.-Asia-Africa-Middle East div., Boston, 1970-73, sr. v.p. Latin Am. div., Boston, 1973—; exec. v.p., dir. Boston Overseas Financial Corp., Boston; chmn. bd. Bank of Boston Trust Co. (Bahamas) Ltd., Nassau; chmn. bd., pres. Caribbean Am. Service Investment & Finance Ltd., Cayman Islands; dir. Corporacion Financiera Boston, S.A., LaPaz, Bolivia, Corporacion Internacional de Boston S.A., San Jose, Costa Rica, Banco de Boston Dominicano S.A., Santo Domingo, Sociedad Anonima Servicios e Inversiones, Buenos Aires, Boston S.A. Administracao E Empreendimentos, Sao Paulo, Brazil, Arrendadora Industrial Venezolana C.A., Caracas, Venezuela, Boston Internat. Fin. Corp., Curacao, Netherlands Antilles, Bank of Boston Internat., N.Y.C., also Los Angeles, Miami, Fla. Served with USAAF, 1943-46. Decorated Air medal with 4 oak leaf clusters, D.F.C.; Medalha Marechal Candido Mariano da Silva Rondon (Brazil). Asso. fellow Brit. Interplanetary Soc.; mem. Air Force Assn., Res. Officers Assn., Inst. Navigation, Royal Astron. Soc. Canada, Md. Hist. Soc., Am. C. of C. Rio de Janeiro, Am. C. of C. Sao Paulo, Sphinx Soc., Beta Theta Pi. Mason (Shriner). Clubs: International (Washington); Dartmouth College, Yale (N.Y.C.); American (Miami, Fla.); Harvard (Boston). Home: Indian Spring Rd Dover MA 02030 Office: 100 Federal St Boston MA 02106

ALDRIDGE, DOUGLAS E., air conditioning co. exec.; b. Claude, Tex., Nov. 6, 1926; s. William George and Octa Ann (McCaugh) A.; student Chaffey Coll., 1949-50, Bakersfield Coll., 1950-51, Maricopa Tech. Inst., 1978-80; m. Oneta May Robinson, Sept. 19, 1950; children—Deborah Joy, Diana Elaine, Gayla Deane, Peggy Doreen, Douglas Dean. Sales mgr. Babcock Air Conditioning Co., Phoenix, 1966-73, Consol. Trades, Inc., Phoenix, 1974-78; salesman Wards, Phoenix, 1973-74; pres., sales mgr. Az-Nev, Inc., Phoenix, 1978—, also dir. Served with U.S. Army, 1944-49. Mem. Refrigeration Service Engrs. Soc., Electric League Ariz., Blue Flame Inst. Democrat. Methodist. Clubs: Elks, Moose. Home: 4400 W Missouri St Apt 135 Glendale AZ 85301 Office: 2418 W Indian School Rd Phoenix AZ 85015

ALESSANDRI, PETER, accountant; b. Springfield, Mass., Nov. 18, 1938; s. Pietro and Mondina Louise (Fornarciari) A.; B.S. in Bus. Adminstrn., Northeastern U., Boston, 1961, M.B.A., 1970; m. Eleanor J. Fales, Feb. 9, 1963; children—P. David, Paul G. With Haskins & Sells, C.P.A.'s, 1961-77, mgr., Boston, N.Y. and Providence, 1967-73, San Juan, P.R., 1974-77; v.p. fin., dir. April Industries, Inc., San Juan, 1977—; prof. Bryant Coll., Providence, 1967, Inter-Am. U., San Juan, 1974; dir., treas. Caribbean Consol. Schs., Inc., 1976-78. Clk. fiscal study com. Town of Walpole, Mass., 1970-71, chmn. fin. com., 1971-73. Served to capt. AUS, 1961-63. C.P.A., Mass., R.I., La., P.R. Mem. Am. Inst. C.P.A.'s, Nat. Assn. Accountants, Mass. Soc. C.P.A.'s. Clubs: Dorado Beach Golf and Tennis, Rotary, K.C. Home: Calle Hamilton C-16 Parkville Guaynabo PR 00657 Office: Luna St 155 San Juan PR 00901

ALEWINE, JAMES WILLIAM, financial exec.; b. Williamston, S.C., Apr. 26, 1930; s. David Andrew and Ruby Mae (Moore) A.; B.A., Carolina Sch. Commerce, 1961; m. Bobbie Sue Crawford, June 18, 1949; children—David, Susan. With Daniel Internat. Corp., 1947—, mgr. internal audit, Greenville, S.C., 1970-72, adminstrv. mgr. M & M div., 1972-73, fin. adminstr., Jenkinsville, S.C., 1973-77, mgr. accounting M-E-T Group, Greenville, 1977-78, asst. treas., 1978—. Served with USN, 1952-55. Cert. internal auditor, S.C. Mem. Inst. Internal Auditors (pres. Palmetto chpt. 1975-76). Baptist. Clubs: Masons (past grand high priest, knight York grand cross of honour),

Elks. Home: 2 Broad St Williamston SC 29697 Office: Daniel Bldg Greenville SC 29602

ALEX, RALPH PAUL, aircraft co. exec.; b. Brockton, Mass., Dec. 19, 1916; s. William J. and Christine C. A.; m. Louise A. Pesanelli, 1942; children—Paula A., Paul A. Aero. engr. Bell Aircraft Corp., Buffalo, 1937-39, Republic Aviation Corp., Farmingdale, N.Y., 1939-40, Wallace-Martin Aircraft Corp., Long Island City, N.Y., 1940-41; project engr., sr. product design engr., head product components design, asst. chief design and devel. Sikorsky Aircraft div. United Technologies, Stratford, Conn., 1941-77, chief mktg. research and devel.; pres. Ralph P. Alex & Assos., Inc., aero. consultants, 1977—; aero. cons. Investment Trust Co., N.Y.C., 1938; tech. adviser NRC, USAAF Volcano Expdn., Uruapan, Mexico, 1945; cons. FAA, 1954—; lectr. helicopter tech. Recipient certificate of merit aerospace vehicle com. Am. Inst. Aeros. and Astronautics, 1963; Pioneer award Helicopter Assn. Am., 1973; Yuri Gagarin award USSR Sporting Aviation Club, 1977. Mem. Am. Helicopter Soc. (pres. 1943-44, 59-60, certificate of merit 1947, chmn. bd. 1960, hon. fellow 1964, chmn. nat. heliport com. 1965-67, chmn. Helicopter Ops. Forum 1973, v.p. internat. affairs 1970—, Alexander Klemin award 1976), Soc. Automotive Engrs., Air Force Assn., Am. Def. Preparedness Assn. (chpt. pres. 1977, vice chmn. council), Nat. Aeros. Assn. (dir. 1959-62), Army Aviation Assn. Am., Fedn. Aeronautique Internat. (pres. internat. helicopter com. 1961—, chief juror 1st, 2d and 3d World Helicopter competitions), Internat. Order Characters, 1st Calvary Div. Assn. (life), Helicopter Club Am. (pres.). Club: Milford (Conn.) Yacht. Contbr. to Helicopter Section Science and Technology, 1968, Weapons Systems Acquisition Process, 1970; contbr. articles to tech. jours. and news media. Patentee in field. Home and office: 1037 Stratfield Rd Fairfield CT 06432

ALEXANDER, DANIEL CAREY, TV exec.; b. Geneva, N.Y., Jan. 13, 1953; s. Robert Louis and Sansa Rita (O'Connor) A.; B.A., U. Pacific, 1975; m. Gail Margaret Smith, Aug. 15, 1975. Engr., Sta. KUOP-FM, Stockton, Calif., 1971-77, also disc jockey, public service producer; comml. producer, disc jockey Sta. KSRT-FM, Stockton, 1977-78; v.p. Alexander & O'Connor, Inc., Sacramento, 1971—, M.F.C. Properties, Inc., 1971—; comml. producer, chief crew, head photography Big Valley Cablevision, Stockton, 1974-76; partner Media Services, Sacramento, 1979—; owner, pres. S.E.E. Teleprodns., Sacramento, 1978—. Originator, producer, antique film series, Sacramento County Library, 1978-79. Mem. Soc. Motion Picture and TV Engrs. Office: 5738 Marconi Ave #11 Carmichael CA 95608

ALEXANDER, DONALD CRICHTON, lawyer; b. Pine Bluff, Ark., May 22, 1921; s. William Crichton and Ella Temple (Fox) A.; B.A. with honors, Yale U., 1942; LL.B. magna cum laude, Harvard U., 1948; LL.D., St. Thomas Inst., 1975; m. Margaret Louise Savage, Oct. 9, 1946; children—Robert C., James M. Admitted to D.C. bar, 1949, Ohio bar, 1954, N.Y. bar, 1978; asso. firm Covington & Burling, Washington, 1948-54, Taft, Stettinius & Hollister, Cin., 1954-56, partner, 1956-66; partner firm Dinsmore, Shohl, Coates & Deupree, Cin., 1966-73; commr. of Internal Revenue, Washington, 1973-77; partner firm Olwine, Connelly, Chase, O'Donnell & Weyher, N.Y.C. and Washington, 1977-79, Morgan, Lewis & Bockius, Washington and N.Y.C., 1979—; cons. Treasury Dept., 1970-72; mem. Commn. on Fed. Paperwork, 1975-77. Served with AUS, 1942-45. Decorated Silver Star, Bronze Star. Mem. Am. Bar Assn., Am. Law Inst., U.S. C. of C. Clubs: Yale (N.Y.C.); Cin. Country; Chevy Chase (Md.); Met. (Washington); Nantucket Yacht (Mass.); Mill Reef (Antigua, B.W.I.). Home: 2801 New Mexico Ave NW Washington DC 20007 Office: 1800 M St NW Washington DC 20036

ALEXANDER, EVA ETHEL GALLMAN, bus. exec.; b. Spartanburg, S.C., Feb. 23, 1898; d. Joe and Etta Emily (Lancaster) Gallman; m. George F. Alexander, Apr. 24, 1923 (div. June 1930); children—Frank Harold, Wilbur Gallman, Mary Fay (Mrs. Jay Bodenheimer). With account dept. City of High Point, N.C., 1930-35; sec., bookkeeper Rhodes Press, 1935-56; owner, operator Arts by Alexander, High Point, 1956—; pres., treas. Alexander Press, Inc., High Point, 1960—. Chmn., High Point Crippled Children and Adults Soc., 1959; hon. mem. Boy's Home of Lake Waccamaw, N.C., 1963; treas. High Point Fine Arts Guild, 1969-70; mem. Democratic Com., 1964. Recipient Medallion award for oil Guildford County Fine Arts Exhbn., 1956; silver cup for oil Sears Traveling Exhibit, 1964; 1st prize in High Point Fine Art Juried Show, 1967; Beautification award High Point Garden Council. Mem. Am., N.C. iris socs., Carolina Club Printing House Craftsmen, Printing Industry High Point (sec.-treas. 1958—), High Point C. of C. (civic com. 1964-68), Nat. Home Fashions League. Baptist. Club: Pilot (pres. High Point 1962, chmn. extension com. 1964-66, dist. extension chmn. 1965-66, internat. extension com. mem. 1966-68, chmn. safety com.). Home: 708 Willoubar Terr High Point NC 27262 Office: 701 Greensboro Rd High Point NC 27260

ALEXANDER, JAMES ATWELL, poultryman; b. Stony Point, N.C., July 23, 1911; s. J. Will and Mary Emma (Alexander) A.; A.B., Davidson Coll., 1929, M.A., 1931; postgrad. Colo. Sch. Mines, 1930, U. N.C., 1932-34; m. Anna Pauline Hill, Dec. 23, 1938; children—Mary Anna, Eva Pauline. Seismologist, Shell Oil Co., Houston, 1937-40; owner, mgr. Alexander Poultry Farm, Stony Point, 1940—; mem. exec. com. Northwestern Bank, 1971; chmn. Alexander County Poultry Council, 1953-55, Alexander County Bd. Agr., 1955, Catawaba Soil Conservation Dist. Suprs., 1949-51; mem. Adv. Commn. on Poultry Test, 1958—. Mem. Bd. Commrs. Alexander County, 1950-54, Welfare Bd., 1952-54; mem. N.C. State Bd. Agr., 1955—, N.C. Gov.'s Com. on Nuclear Energy, 1957—, Gov.'s Com. on Mental Health, 1960—, Gov.'s Com. on Manpower Tng., 1963—; mem. Fair Commn., Dixie Classic Fair, Winston-Salem, N.C.; chmn. N.C. Gov.'s Adv. Com. on Agr., 1965—; adv. com. Sch. Agr., N.C. State U., 1960-63; exec. com. Gov.'s Council for Econ. Devel.; mem. exec. com. N.C. Agribus. Council, 1969, hon. dir., 1978—; vice chmn. bd. dirs. Alexander County Hosp.; chmn. bd. dirs., exec. com. N.C. Agrl. Found. Named Man of Year, Grange of Alexander County, 1957; recipient N.C. Outstanding Farm Mgr. award, 1965; Distinguished Citizenship award Northwest N.C. Devel. Assn., 1969, N.C. State County Agrl. Agts. award, 1971; named to N.C. Poultry Industry Hall of Fame, 1976. Mem. N.C. Acad. Sci., N.W. N.C. Devel. Assn. (pres., chmn. agrl. div.), C. of C. Alexander County (dir., named Man of Year 1967), N.C. Egg Mktg. Assn. (pres. 1961-63), N.C. Poultry Council (pres. 1963—), N.C. Vocat. Agrl. Tchrs. Assn. (hon.), Sigma Xi, Gamma Sigma Epsilon, Sigma Gamma Epsilon, Gamma Sigma Delta. Democrat. Club: Lions (past pres., zone chmn.). Office: Stony Point NC 28678

ALEXANDER, JAMES EDWIN, bus. exec.; b. Indianola, Iowa, Feb. 16, 1930; s. James Eugene and Lillian Esther (Gamble) A.; B.A., U. Pacific, 1959; S.T.B., Boston U., 1962; M.A., Claremont Grad. Sch., 1965; Ph.D., Vanderbilt U., 1972, postgrad. in Law, 1976; m. Joan Frances Harris, June 28, 1952 (div. 1981); children—James Michael, Michele Alene, Marsha Ann. Chief engr. Radio Sta. KJOY, Stockton, Calif., 1955-59; instr. broadcasting U. Pacific, 1956-59, lectr. Bible, 1963-65; owner, operator Stockton Teletronics, 1956-59; studio engr. Radio Sta. WHDH, Boston, 1960; teaching fellow Boston U., Coll. Bus. Adminstrn., 1960-62; ordained to ministry Methodist Ch., 1960; pastor Gleasondale (Mass.) Meth. Ch., 1960-62; asso. pastor Central Meth. Ch., Stockton, 1962-65, Claremont (Calif.) Meth. Ch., 1966-67; dir. printed resources Meth. Bd. Edn., United Meth. Ch., Nashville, 1967-70, asst. gen. sec., 1970-75, exec. dir. communications, 1976-78; exec. dir. The Other Sch. System, Inc., 1978—; pres. Music City Thirty, Inc., 1979—, TV 52 Broadcasting, 1980—; dir. Public Service Satellite Corp. Mem. Calif. Gov.'s Council on Aging, 1964-65, panel distinguished scholars New Media Bible, 1975—; mem. exec. bd. Christian Youth Publs., 1967-75; mem. adv. com. Nat. Orgns. Corp. for Public Broadcasting, 1974—; mem. Lake Placid Winter Olympics Com., 1977-80; mem. adv. com. Edn. Futures Internat. Served with USN, 1947-55. Decorated Letter of Commendation; recipient Walker awards for excellence in classical studies U. Pacific, 1956, 57, 58, citation Senate and Assembly State of Calif. for TV series, 1965; Jacob Sleeper fellow Boston U., 1965. Mem. Am. Acad. Religion, Am. Mgmt. Assn., Nat. Assn. Ednl. Broadcasters, Soc. Bibl. Lit., Religious Pub. Relations Council, Soc. for Antiquity and Christianity. Author: Abstracts from Federal Communications Law, 1958; Audiovisual Facilities for Churchmen, 1970; Ethical Factors in Management Decision, 1972; Mass Media Models of Education, 1975; Emerging Developments in Educational Television, 1976; Footprints in Space: Religious Applications of Communications Satellites, 1977; contbr. articles to religious publs. Exec. producer The Other School System, 1978. Home: PO Box 120311 Nashville TN 37212 Office: 2700 City Nat Bank Tower Oklahoma City OK 73102

ALEXANDER, JEANNE MERCHANT, mfg. co. exec.; b. Haskell, Tex., Dec. 2, 1942; d. Ralph W. Merchant and Helen Kindley Tanner; student Western Conn. State Coll., 1979-80; m. Charles H. Alexander, July 7, 1962; 1 son, Charles Bradley. Dental asst./office mgr. Dr. H. Gustavus, Abilene, Tex., 1961-63; credit interviewer Betterman's Furniture Co., St. Louis, 1965-66; accounts receivable specialist Kimball Wholesale Grocery, Abilene, 1963-65; asst. market group coordinator Ridgefield Group (Conn.), 1974-75; office mgr. Curken Scientific, Inc., Danbury, Conn., 1975—, treas., 1978—, v.p., 1980—; participant confs. Ch. sec. Broadview Bapt. Ch., Abilene, 1964; active PTA, Conn., 1973-74, chmn., 1973-74, co-chmn. sch. fair, 1973-74; fin. com. United Meth. Ch., Danbury, 1980—. Notary pub., Conn. Mem. LWV, Washington Women's Network, Nat. Thespian Soc. Democrat. Clubs: Newcomers, Rocking Roosters Sq. Dance (pres. 1977-78, treas. 1976-77). Home: East Hayestown Rd Danbury CT 06810 Office: PO Box 584 Danbury CT 06810

ALEXANDER, KLAREN KEITH, accountant; b. Preston, Minn., Sept. 26, 1943; s. Kenneth Noble and Rebecca Adah (Grabau) A.; B.S., Mankato State U., 1965; m. Helen Louise Anderson, Apr. 24, 1964; children—Krista, Chad, Craig. Staff acct. Peat, Marwick, Mitchell & Co., Mpls., 1965-66; staff acct. to partner Reese, Abdo, Gazzola & Co., Northfield, Minn., 1966-71; supr. to partner Fox & Co., Mpls., 1972-77, asst. partner-in-charge, 1977—; instr. St. Olaf Coll., Northfield, 1969-71. Scoutmaster, Boy Scouts Am., 1969-71; dist. chmn. United Fund, 1973. C.P.A., Minn. Mem. Am. Inst. C.P.A.'s, N.Y. State Soc. C.P.A.'s, Jaycees (chpt. treas. 1971, recipient key-man award 1971). Republican. Methodist. Home: 22 Manitou Rd Westport CT 06880 Office: 1211 Ave of Americas New York NY 10036

ALEXANDER, LEELAND NEILL, fin. exec.; b. Little Rock, Jan. 1, 1945; s. Emmit Calvin and Ellanore Isabell (McIntosh) A.; B.S., Okla. State U., 1968; m. Diana Lynn Stivers, June 3, 1967; children—Douglas Chad, Christopher Neill, Carey Lynn, Craig William. Staff acct. Okla. State U., Stillwater, 1966-68, acct., 1968-70; chief acct. Tulsa Jr. Coll., 1970-74; asst. dean for adminstrn., bus. mgr. U. Okla. Tulsa Med. Coll., 1974-80, asso. dir. adminstrn. and fin., 1980—; fin. cons. Tulsa Med. Edn. Found., Inc., 1974—, others. Chmn., Brotherhood of Deacons, So. Hills Bapt. Ch., 1979-80, chmn. com. on coms., 1979-80, chmn. staff com., 1980—, chmn. Lay Renewal Week, 1980—; mem. record book judging com. Tulsa County 4-H Club, 1975—. Nat. 4-H winner, 1963; Okla. 4-H winner, 1963; Okla. Key Club winner, 1962; Danforth award, 1962; named Outstanding Freshman Air Force Cadet, Okla. State U., 1964. Mem. Nat. Assn. Coll. and Univ. Bus. Officers, Central Assn. Coll. and Univ. Bus. Officers, Nat. Assn. Accts., Am. Assn. Univ. Adminstrs., Okla. Assn. Coll. and Univ. Bus. Officers, Delta Sigma Alpha (pres. 1964-65). Republican. Home: 3714 E 81st Pl S Tulsa OK 74136 Office: 2808 S Sheridan Rd Tulsa OK 74129

ALEXANDER, LOUIS G., banker; b. Houston, Feb. 14, 1910; s. Louis G. and Elizabeth (Burney) A.; student Bishop Coll., 1927-29; ed. elec. engring. Armour Inst. Tech., 1929-33; m. Irma O. Alexander, Mar. 31, 1941 (dec.); 1 son, Louis G. III. Pres. Practical Electronics Co., 1953-63; owner, operator Louis G. Alexander & Assos., cons., 1961—; v.p. marketing Amalgamated Trust & Savs. Bank, Chgo., 1967—; cons. govt. contracts adminstrn. Mem. Ill. Health Facilities Authority, 1973—; mem. Dept. Commerce Exec. Res. Bd. dirs. Better Boys Found., Chgo. chpt. NAACP, Ill. Humane Soc., Chgo. Boys Clubs; trustee Absalom Jones Theol. Sem., Atlanta. Served with AEF, 1942-45. Recipient Good Guy award Lawndale Scholarship program. Unitarian Universalist. Home: 5124 S Kenwood Ave Chicago IL 60615 Office: 100 S State St Chicago IL 60603

ALEXANDER, NORMAN E., chem. co. exec.; b. N.Y.C., 1914; A.B., Columbia, 1934, LL.B., 1936; m. Marjorie Wulf; four children. Chmn. bd., chief exec. officer Sun Chem. Corp., N.Y.C., 1957—, also dir.; chmn. bd. Chromalloy Am. Corp., 1980—; chmn. Ampacet Corp., Mt. Vernon, N.Y.; dir. Walter Kidde & Co., Asso. Madison Cos., Inc., Am. Distilling Co. Mem. The Conf. Bd. Office: 200 Park Ave New York NY 10017

ALEXANDER, ROBERT LEO, instrumentation co. exec.; b. N.Y.C., Dec. 13, 1930; s. Leo and Calistra (Luces) A.; student Howard U., 1950-52, N.Y. Community Coll., 1956-58; M.B.E., U. Pitts., 1976; m. Victorai Gomez, Dec. 29, 1966; 1 dau., Lisa Alexander. Chem. technician Barclay Corp., N.Y.C., 1958-60; coating chemist Tenax Corp., Newark, 1960-62; lab. technologist Mobil Oil Corp., Bklyn., 1962-66; tech. sales rep. Standard Sci. Corp., N.Y.C., 1966-68; area mgr., regional sales mgr. Technicon Corp., Tarrytown, N.Y., 1970-75, gen. mgr. Eastern Technicenter, 1975—. Served with AUS, 1953-55. Recipient Black Achievement award YMCA, N.Y.C., 1979. Mem. Am. Mgmt. Assn., Sales Exec. Club N.Y., Am. Soc. Clin. Lab. Mgrs. and Suprs., Omega Psi Phi. Republican. Roman Catholic. Home: 392 Central Park W New York NY 10025 Office: 511 Benedict Ave Tarrytown NY 10591

ALEXANDER, ROBERT WARREN, steel and wire mfg. co. exec.; b. Ann Arbor, Mich., Feb. 4, 1901; s. Clay William and Mary (Chalmers) A.; B.S. in Engring., U. Mich., 1923; m. Doris Gormley, June 28, 1939; 1 son, Jack Spencer. With Westinghouse Electric Co., East Pittsburgh, Pa., 1923-24, Allied Engrs., Jackson, Mich., 1924-31, Anaconda Wire and Cable Co., N.Y.C., 1931-41; pres. Hackensack (N.J.) Cable Corp., 1941-74, Carolina Steel and Wire Corp., Lexington, S.C., 1970—. Registered profl. engr., N.Y. State, N.J., S.C. Mem. IEEE. Republican. Presbyterian. Clubs: Summit, Forest Lake (Columbia, S.C.). Patentee in field. Home: 1718 Madison Rd Apt 301 Columbia SC 29204 Office: Carolina Steel and Wire Corp Box 829 Lexington SC 29072

ALEXANDER, SAMUEL ALLEN, JR., electronics co. exec.; b. Washington, Oct. 9, 1938; s. Samuel Allen and Mary Pearl (Last) A.; B.S. and B.A., Tufts U., 1962; postgrad. in biochemistry George Washington U., 1963; m. Susan Karinch, Aug. 25, 1973; children—Carolyn, Samuel Allen, Emily, Jonathan, David, Susan M. Investment banker, registered rep. Ferris & Co., Washington, 1966-69; pres. Command Fin., Washington, 1969-72, Potomac Fed. Corp., Washington, 1973-75; v.p. adminstrn. and ops. officer Potter Instrument Co., Gonic, N.H., 1975-78, pres., chief exec. officer, 1978—; participant investment banking seminar Wharton Sch. Bus., U. Pa., 1968-69. Mem. Delta Tau Delta. Roman Catholic. Clubs: Chevy Chase (Md.); Lake Sunapee Yacht (Sunapee, N.H.). Office: 10 Main St Gonic NH 03867

ALEXANDER, STEPHEN ALLAN, state ofcl.; b. Warren, Mich., Jan. 29, 1943; s. Peter Basil and Doris Helen (Carney) A.; B.S., U. Mich., 1965; M.B.A., U. Utah, 1978; m. Sept. 17, 1966; children—Kimberly, Kristen, Matthew, Joshua, Jacob. Actuary, Indsl. Indemnity Ins. Co., San Francisco, 1970-74, Foremost Ins. Co., Grand Rapids, Mich., 1974-76; ins. broker, Salt Lake City, 1976-79; risk mgr. State of Utah, Salt Lake City, 1980—. Served with USAF, 1966-70. Mem. Phi Kappa Phi, Beta Gamma Sigma. Home: 1192 E Edenbrook Dr Sandy UT 84070 Office: 147 State Capitol Bldg Salt Lake City UT 84114

ALEXANDER, THOMAS EATON, JR., mfg. co. exec.; b. New Orleans, July 28, 1912; s. Thomas Eaton and Dora A. (Hingle) A.; B.S., Tulane U., 1935; m. Jeanne Perrodin, July 28, 1951; children—Thomas Eaton, Sidney D., James H. Mech. engr. Equitable Equipment Co., New Orleans, 1936-39, sales engr., 1939-44; sales and service engr. Crane Packing Co., Baton Rouge and New Orleans, 1944-58; pres. KP Industries, Inc., mfr. check valves, Baton Rouge, 1967—; pres. Power Packing Co., Inc., mfr. mech. seals and packings, Baton Rouge, 1958—. Dir., 1st Meth. Ch., 1969—, Baton Rouge Assn. Retarded Citizens. Registered profl. engr., La. Mem. ASME (dir. Baton Rouge chpt. 1966-70), Baton Rouge Council Engrs. and Sci. Soc. (pres. 1961), La. Engrs. Soc. (pres. Baton Rouge 1960), Nat. Soc. Profl. Engrs. Clubs: Baton Rouge Country, Sherwood Forest Country, City (Baton Rouge). Home: 11308 Goodwood Blvd Baton Rouge LA 70815 Office: 2769 Mission St Baton Rouge LA 70805

ALEXANDER, UREY WOODSON, ednl. adminstr.; b. Owensboro, Ky., Sept. 10, 1915; s. Hamilton and Elizabeth Ford (Woodson) A.; B.S. in Engring., U.S. Mil. Acad., 1940; M.A. in Internat. Affairs, George Washington U., 1961; grad. U.S. Command and Gen. Staff Coll., Armed Forces Staff Coll., U.S. Army War Coll.; LL.D. (hon.), Dickinson Sch. Law, 1980; m. Ella Marie Cain, June 27, 1944; children—Urey Woodson, Buford C., Marie E. (dec.). Commd. 2d lt. U.S. Army, 1940, advanced through grades to col., 1954; comdr. 386 F.A. Bn., Europe, 1942-45; corps and arty. adv., Greece, 1949-50; sr. Army mem. Navy Spl. Devices Center, L.I., 1950-53; U.S. Mil. attache, Warsaw, Poland, 1955-57; mem. faculty U.S. Army War Coll., Carlisle (Pa.) Barracks, 1958-61, 67-70, dir. instrn., 1968-70; comdr. Heavy Arty. Group, Germany, 1961-63; force planner SHAPE, Paris, 1963-64; sr. army rep. Joint Targeting Staff, Omaha, 1964-67; ret., 1970; treas., bus. mgr. Dickinson Sch. Law, 1971—. Vice pres. Lake Meade Property Owners Assn., Adams County, Pa., 1971-78. Decorated Bronze Star, Legion of Merit. Mem. Nat. Assn. Coll. and Univ. Bus. Officers, Assn. U.S. Army Nat. Timberwolf Assn. Democrat. Baptist. Club: Rotary (pres. 1973-74, dist. gov. 1977-78) (Carlisle). Home: 624 Yorkshire Dr Carlisle PA 17013 Office: Dickinson Sch Law Carlisle PA 17013

ALF, JOHN JAMES, chem. co. exec.; b. Aurora, Ill., May 7, 1936; s. Frank Peter and Anne Mary (Urlaub) A.; B.S., St. Mary's Coll., Winona, Minn., 1958; M.B.A., U. Mich., Ann Arbor, 1966; m. Marianne E. Schmidt, Jan. 24, 1959; children—Christine, Julie, Elizabeth, Eric. Chemist, Chemetron Corp., Rockhill Labs., Newport, Tenn., 1960-63, sr. chemist N.W. Chem. div., Detroit, 1963-65; mgr. adminstrv. services Vulcan Labs., Inc., Pontiac, Mich., 1965-68; v.p. ops. water mgmt. div. Clow Corp., Pontiac, 1968—. Mem. Am. Chem. Soc., Mensa. Home: 35306 Lancashire Ct Livonia MI 48152 Office: 408 Auburn Ave Pontiac MI 48058

ALFIN, IRWIN, fragrance co. exec.; b. N.Y.C., Oct. 6, 1929; s. Louis and Bertha (Green) A.; B.Sc., Rutgers U., 1951; m. Betsy Eckerson, Dec. 23, 1951; children—David, Susan. Vice pres. Sacony Co., 1953-63, Revlon Co., 1963-69; pres. Chanel Inc., N.Y.C., 1969-73; pres. Max Factor Inc., Los Angeles, 1973-76; pres. Alfin Fragrances, Inc., N.Y.C., 1976—. Mem. adv. bd. St. Francis Hosp., Port Washington, N.Y.; mem. Cardinal's Com. for Inner-City Scholarships, N.Y.C. Served with inf. U.S. Army, 1951-53. Decorated Bronze Star medal with V; recipient medal City of Paris. Mem. Fragrance Found., Cosmetics Toiletries Fragrance Assn., Chevaliers de Tastevin. Club: North Hemstead Country. Office: 9 W 57th St New York NY 10019

ALFORD, DAVID ALLAN, banking cons.; b. Chgo., July 30, 1947; s. Morris Harold and Evelyn Delores (Andrews) A.; B.S. in Bus. Adminstrn., Ill. Wesleyan U., 1969; grad. Ill. Bankers Sch., Carbondale; m. Cheryl Anne Kmetty, Nov. 3, 1972; 1 dau., Jennifer Lynn. Comptroller of currency Dept. Treasury, Chgo., 1969-73; exec. v.p., cashier 1st Nat. Bank, Lincolnshire, Ill., 1973-74, pres., dir., chief exec. officer, 1974-79; v.p. Denver Equities Ltd., 1979—; exec. v.p. J. Turner Assos., Chgo., 1979—; dir. Half-Day Devel. Corp. Chmn., Vernon Twp. Boy Scouts Am., 1975, co-dir. Lake County fund, 1978; bd. dirs. Cardiac Charities of Lake County, 1977-79. Mem. Am., Ill. bankers assns., Assn. for Modern Banking in Ill., Lake County Bankers Assn., Half-Day Lincolnshire C. of C. (pres. 1973—, Business Person of Year 1975). Republican. Presbyterian. Home: 6630 E Heritage Pl S Englewood CO 80111 Office: 730 17th St Suite 850 Denver CO 80202

ALI, HUSSIEN, candy mfg. co. exec.; b. San Antonio, Nov. 22, 1948; s. Chester and Eleanor (Applewhite) Logan; B.S. in Bus. Adminstrn., Tex. So. U., 1970; m. Jacquelyn E. Wilson, June 6, 1974; children—Waseem, Musheer. Regional mgr. Midwest Co. Good Food Inc., Cleve., 1976; chief exec. officer Golden Keetle Candy Co., San Antonio, 1978-80; pres. H & A Distbg. Co., San Antonio, 1980—; chmn. bd. H & A Real Estate Rev., San Antonio, 1980—; fin. cons. Zegobea Candy Co., Apache Dist. Mem. Nat. Candy Wholesalers Assn., Nat. Confectioners Assn. (Candy Maker of Yr. award 1979-80), Internat. Consumer Credit Assn. Democrat. Islamic. Club: Wood Lake Country. Home: 6706 Stone Lake San Antonio TX 78244 Office: 212 E Houston St Suite 1023 San Antonio TX 78205

ALI, SHARON HAMMOND, bus. exec.; b. Long Branch, N.J., Feb. 23, 1948; d. Edward Leonard (stepfather) and Merrial (Kyler) Joshua; B.A. in Sociology, Brandeis U., 1970; certs. in mktg., advt., cash flow analysis, credit and collections, personnel policies and practices, bus. planning Del. Tech. and Community Coll.; m. Rudolph Ali, Aug. 26, 1975; children—Abdul-Rahman, Michelle, Abdul-Raheem, Naeemah, Aliyah, Latifa, Kareem, Hasan. Model, Copley Models, Boston, 1970; teller, securities clk. Bank of Del., Dover, 1971-72; adminstrv. asst. Assn. Greater Wilmington (Del.) Neighborhood Centers, 1973-74; adminstrv. asst., statistician Wilmington Bus. Opportunities and Devel. Corp., 1975; exec. sec. Ali Enterprises, Wilmington, 1977-78, corp. sec., 1978-79, v.p., 1980—; dir.

adminstrn. and fin. Ali Baking Co., Wilmington, 1978—. Active Baynard Blvd Neighborhood Assn., Wilmington, Haynes Park Civic Assn., Wilmington, Nat. Tax Limitation Com. Named Small Bus. Person of Yr. for State of Del., SBA, 1980. Mem. Am. Soc. Profl. and Exec. Women, Am. Muslim Mission, U.S. C. of C., Del. State C. of C., New Castle County C. of C. Democrat. Home: 2812 Baynard Blvd Wilmington DE 19802 Office: 3013 Lancaster Ave Wilmington DE 19805

ALIAS, FRED VINCENT, hotel and motel exec.; b. Clarksdale, Miss., Sept. 12, 1946; s. William Anthony and Aline (Faccini) A.; B.B.A. in Mktg. and Sales, U. Miss., Oxford, 1968; m. Rebecca Susan Hendee, Apr. 23, 1977; 1 son, Shaler. Public relations attache to gov. Miss., 1968-69; from sales rep., Los Angeles to asst. to sr. v.p. mktg. and advt. Holiday Inns, Inc., Memphis, 1969-73; v.p. mktg., then v.p. devel. W.B. Johnson Properties, owner, operator 11 Holiday inns and 6 Marriott hotels, Atlanta, 1973-78, exec. v.p., 1979-80, pres., 1980—; mem. nat. adv. com., advt. and mktg. com. Internat. Assn. Holiday Inns; speaker, cons. in field. Active local United Way, Campus Crusade for Christ. Served with Air N.G., 1969-75. Recipient numerous salesmanship awards. Mem. Hotel Sales Mgmt. Assn., Discover Am. Tour Orgn., Nat. Tour Brokers Assn., U. Miss. Alumni Assn. Roman Catholic. Clubs: Cherokee Town and Country, Commerce (Atlanta). Home: 3355 Chatham Dr Atlanta GA 30305 Office: 2175 Parklake Dr NE Suite 103 Atlanta GA 30345

ALIBRANDI, JOSEPH FRANCIS, diversified indsl. exec.; b. Boston, Nov. 9, 1928; s. Paul and Anna (Amendolia) A.; B.S. in Mech. Engring., M.I.T., 1952; m. Lambertha A. Araskiewicz, May 12, 1957; children—Paul, Ann-Marie, Carolyn. With Fairchild Engring. & Airplane Corp., 1951; mgr. indsl. engring. dept. Raytheon Co., Lexington, Mass., 1952-56, asst. plant mgr. Lowell, Mass., 1956-58, plant mgr., 1958-62, ops. mgr., 1962-65, v.p., gen. mgr., 1965-68, sr. v.p., gen. mgr., 1968-70; exec. v.p., dir. Whittaker Corp., Los Angeles, 1970, pres., 1970—, chief exec. officer, 1974—; dir. Fed. Res. Bank of San Francisco, 1973-76, chmn., 1977-79; dir. Daniel, Mann, Johnson & Mendenhall, Los Angeles, 1979—; mem. Western region adv. bd. Arkwright-Boston Ins., San Francisco, 1978—. Mem. corp. vis. com. Sloan Sch. of Mgmt., M.I.T., 1972—, corp. vis. com. dept. biology, 1979—, mem. corp. devel. com., 1973—, nat. bus. com., 1977—; chmn. bus. adv. council UCLA, 1976—, exec. com. bd. visitors Grad. Sch. Mgmt., 1979—; bd. councilors Sch. Bus. Adminstrn., U. So. Calif., 1977—; bd. dirs. Los Angeles World Affairs Council, 1980—. Served with U.S. Army, 1946-48. Mem. U.S. C. of C. (internat. policy com., 1978—). Office: 10880 Wilshire Blvd Los Angeles CA 90024

ALIG, FRANK DOUGLAS STALNAKER, constrn. co. exec.; b. Indpls., Oct. 10, 1921; s. Clarence Schirmer and Marjory (Stalnaker) A.; student U. Mich., 1939-41; B.S., Purdue U., 1948; m. Ann Bobbs, Oct. 22, 1949; children—Douglas, Helen, Barbara. Project engr. Ind. Hwy. Commn., Indpls., 1948-49; pres. Alig-Stark Constrn. Co., Inc., Indpls., 1949-57, Frank S. Alig, Inc., Indpls., 1957—; chmn. bd., pres. Concrete Structures Corp., Indpls., 1965—; pres. Home Stove Realty Co.; v.p. Bo-Wit Products Corp., Edinburg, Ind.; pres. Home Land Investment Co. Served with AUS, 1943-46. Registered profl. engr., Ind. Mem. U.S., Ind. socs. profl. engrs., Prestressed Concrete Inst., Ind. Assn. Credit Men, U.S., Ind., Indpls. chambers commerce. Republican. Presbyn. (deacon). Clubs: Woodstock, Dramatic, University, Lambs (Indpls.). Home: 8080 N Pennsylvania St Indianapolis IN 46240 Office: Concrete Structures Corp 4849 W 96th St Indianapolis IN 46268

ALIHAN, MILLA, indsl. psychologist, sociologist, mgmt. counsel; b. Vladikavkas, Russia; d. Alexander and Maria Sidamon (Tolpar) A.; M.A., Smith Coll.; Ph.D., Columbia; m. Bertram Cecil Eskell, July 16, 1938 (dec.). Lectr. sociology Smith Coll., Barnard Coll., Columbia; editorial adviser Can. Forum publ.; pub. relations exec. Transp., Housing and Welfare sects. N.Y. World's Fair; publicity dir. Beekman Downtown Hosp., Bldg. and Maintenance Fund; simultaneous interpreter Nuremberg trials, U.S. War Dept., 1946; pres. Milla Alihan Assos., 1945—; mgmt. counsel Kollsman Instrument Corp., Genesco, Inc., H.J. Heinz & Co., Inc., Walter Kidde & Co., Inc., Walter Kidde Constructors, Inc., Avien, Inc., Colvin Labs., McKinsey & Co., Inc., Eastern Airlines, Seaboard World Airlines, others; mem. faculty Internat. Grad. U. in Switzerland, Fla. Inst. Tech.-Internat. Grad. Sch. Behavioral Scis. Trustee Morton Prince Clinic for Hypnotherapy; bd. dirs. Inst. Research in Hypnosis; v.p. Russian Orthodox Theol. Fund. Fellow Am. Sociol. Assn.; mem. Am. Psychol. Assn., Am. Acad. Psychotherapists, Aviation Writers Assn., Am. Mgmt. Assn., Internat. Platform Assn., Caucasion Soc. Allaverdy, Mensa. Club: Smith Coll. Author synchronized Eng. film script, Wait for Me; author: Social Ecology, 1938, 64; Corporate Etiquette, 1970 (pub. in German 1970, Portuguese 1971, paperback Am. edit. 1974, German paperback, 1976). Editor: America; Illustrated America; contbr. articles, brochures in field. Home: 15 Litchfield Rd Port Washington NY 11050 Office: 25 E 83d St New York NY 10028

ALLAN, JAMES HENDRY, dairy exec.; b. Travancore, India, Sept. 7, 1930; immigrated to Can., 1967, naturalized, 1972; s. James Stanley and Margaret Black (Hendry) A.; ed. George Watson's Coll., Edinburgh, Scotland; married; children—Gordon, Bruce, Sarah. With Howden & Molleson, Chartered Accts., Edinburgh, 1953-60, Courtaulds, Ltd., Coventry and London (Eng.), 1960-62; chief acct., co. sec. Marglass Ltd., Dorset, Eng., 1962-65; sr. systems analyst, mgr. Westland Aircrafts Ltd., 1965-67; div. controller No. Electric Ltd. Can., Montreal, Que., 1967-76; v.p. fin. Puretest/Perrette Group of Cos., Laval, Que., 1976-81. Served with Royal Arty., 1950-52. Mem. Inst. Chartered Accts. of Scotland. Office: 999 St Martin Blvd Laval PQ H7S 1M6 Canada

ALLAN, WILLIAM NORMAN, investment co. exec.; b. Toronto, Ont., Can., May 30, 1925; s. Leslie Brown and Annie Lillian (Morrison) A.; B.A., U. Toronto, 1948, M.B.A., 1951; m. Jean Mary Pryzdial, May 22, 1965; Economist, asso. dir. Econ. Survey Ont., Ont. Treasury Dept., 1950-52; cons. bus., Toronto, 1952-57; exec. asst. to Minister of Fin. of Can., Ottawa, Ont., 1957-61; chmn. bd., pres. Gt. Lakes Comml. and Holding Corp. Ltd., Toronto, 1952—; chmn. bd., pres. Fiscal Investments Ltd., Toronto, 1961—; chmn. bd. and chief exec. officer Transprovincial Fin. Corp. Ltd., Econ. Realty Corp. Ltd., Fairstone Fin. Corp. Ltd.; founder Anglo-Permanent Corp. Holdings Ltd.; chmn., pres. Gt. North Uranium & Energy Resources Inc.; exec. v.p. Res. Acceptance Co. Ltd.; mem. Bd. Trade Met. Toronto. Bd. govs. Royal Humane Soc., London; chmn. bd. dirs. Fidelity Charitable Found., Toronto. Fellow Royal Econ. Soc. (life), Royal Commonwealth Soc. (life); mem. Nat. Trust for Scotland (life), Victoria Coll. Alumni Assn., Grad. Sch. Bus. Adminstrn. Alumni Assn. U. Toronto Alumni Assn., Kappa Sigma Frat. Alumni Assn. Toronto. Conservative. Clubs: Albany, Bd. Trade, Bus. Met. Toronto (Toronto); Univ. (Ottawa); Kensington Fishing (Gatineau, Que., Can.); Sommerville Recreation and Country (Haliburton, Ont.). Home: 157 Golfdale Rd Toronto ON M4N 2C1 Canada Office: 44 Eglinton Ave W Suite 410 Toronto ON M4R 1A1 Canada

ALLARDYCE, ROSS LEONARD, data processing co. exec.; b. Melbourne, Australia, Feb. 8, 1945; came to U.S., 1969; s. Leonard Charles and Jean Thelma A.; student Melbourne U., 1962, Caulfield Tech. Coll., 1963-65; m. Ruth Louise Lime, Sept. 15, 1979. Project leader, computer cons. and software Adaps Pty. Ltd., 1967-69; dir. mgr., tech. staff Firemans Fund Ins. Co., San Francisco, 1969-76; v.p. software devel. Advanced Software Techniques, San Francisco, 1976-79; pres. Advanced Micro Techniques, San Mateo, Calif., 1979—; cons. computer performance.

ALLDREDGE, ROBERT JUSTIN, forest products mfg. co. exec.; b. Port Huron, Mich., Sept. 6, 1942; s. William Herdis and Augusta (Blosfeld) A.; B.A. in Acctg., Mich. State U., 1964, M.B.A. in Fin., 1966; m. Victoria Elberts Doyer, Nov. 28, 1970; children—Michele Maryke, Marc Justin. Mgmt. cons. Touche-Ross & Co., San Francisco, 1966-69; treas., controller Young Am. Corp., St. Louis, 1970; sr. planner Boise (Idaho) Cascade Corp., 1971-74; corporate planner Weyerhauser Co., Tacoma, Wash., 1974-77; dir. corp. devel. Southwest Forest Industries, Phoenix, 1977—; dir. planning and analysis Syntex Ophthalmics, Phoenix, 1981—. Bd. dirs. Planned Parenthood, Boise. Cert. mgmt. accountant. Mem. Assn. Corp. Growth, Inst. Mgmt. Acctg. Republican. Congregationalist. Clubs: Ariz., West Side Tennis. Home: 314 W Northview St Phoenix AZ 85021 Office: PO Box 7548 Phoenix AZ 85011

ALLEN, ALICE, pub. relations exec.; b. N.Y.C., May 31, 1943; d. Claxton Edmonds and Helen (McCreery) Allen; student Conn. Coll. Women, 1961-63; 1 dau., Helen Pell. Publicity dir. Hawthorn Books, N.Y.C., 1964-67, Walker & Co., N.Y.C., 1967, J.B. Lippincott Co., N.Y.C., 1967-70; pres. Alice Allen, Inc., publicity and mktg., N.Y.C., 1970—; pres. a.a.d. advt., inc., N.Y.C.; cons. Assn. Am. Pubs. Mem. coms. Legal Aid Soc., 1971-78; co-chmn. pub. relations com. N.Y. Jr. League, 1973-74, communications v.p., 1977-78, mem. exec. com., 1978-79, bd. mgrs., 1977-79. Mem. Publishers Publicity Assn. (pres. 1969-70, v.p. 1968-69, dir. 1971), Brotherhood Book Travelers, Pub. Ad Club, Coordinating Orgn. Book Assns. (pres., co-founder 1978—), N.Y. Assn. Women Bus. Owners (dir. 1977-78), Women in Communications, Women's Nat. Book Assn. Episcopalian. Home: 930 Park Ave New York NY 10028 Office: 515 Madison Ave New York NY 10022

ALLEN, ARTHUR CLINTON, III, fin. cons.; b. Brockton, Mass., Feb. 6, 1944; s. Arthur Clinton and Lorraine Martha (Renaud) A.; B.A., Harvard U. 1967; m. Lawson Prince, July 17, 1971; children—Samantha, Walker, Lawson. Partner, Advest Co., Hartford, Conn., 1970-76; pres. Advest Fin. Communications, Boston, 1976—; dir. Hills Court Inc., Advest, Inc. Trustee Stonehill Coll. Mem. Nat. Investor Relations Inst., Aircraft Owners and Pilots Assn. Clubs: Union (Boston); Mid Ocean (Bermuda); Dedham Country and Polo; Harvard (N.Y.C.); Bankers (San Francisco and Miami); Dallas Petroleum; Union Boat; Houston; Board Room. Author: Aerial Photography, 1977; Flying Free, 1979. Home: 710 South St Needham MA 02192 Office: Advest Fin Communications 225 Franklin St Boston MA 02110

ALLEN, BILLY JAMES, constrn. and oilfield co. exec.; b. Soccoro, N.Mex., Apr. 6, 1937; s. Roger Monroe and Lola Grace (Lacy) A.; m. Doris June Mace, Jan. 14, 1957; children—Shannon Sue Allen Knowlton, Mark James, Tammy Todd Allen Kerrigan. Various supt. positions with engring. and constrn. cos., 1956-69; chmn. bd. VECO, Inc., Anchorage, 1969—; mng. dir., partner Allen & Leslie, Stavenger, Norway and Aberdeen, Scotland, 1973-76; chmn. bd. Norcon, Inc., 1974—, OFC of Alaska, 1975—, VECO Drilling Co., Grand Junction, Colo., 1978—, V.E. Systems, 1977—, VEMAR, Inc., 1979—; pres., chmn. bd. VECO Internat., Inc., 1979—; dir. PS Contractors A/S, Stavenger, 1977-79, VECO/NANA Drilling Co., Inc., 1980—. Mem. Nat. UN Day Com., 1978. Mem. Petroleum Club Anchorage. Republican. Club: Elks. Office: 5151 Fairbanks St Anchorage AK 99503

ALLEN, CHARLES MICHAEL, elec. engr.; b. New Castle, Pa., Sept. 1, 1942; s. Charles Moore and Betty Jane (Wise) A.; B.S.E.E., Carnegie Inst. Tech., 1964, M.S.E.E., 1965; Ph.D. in Systems Engring., State U. N.Y., Buffalo, 1968; m. Kathleen Riemer, Sept. 4, 1965; children—Charles Reed, James Michael. Instr., lectr. State U. N.Y., Buffalo, 1968, asst. prof., 1968-74; design engr. Lenlab, Inc., Lockport, N.Y., 1971-72, chief engr., 1972-73; pres., head design engring. CMA Assos., Inc., Charlotte, N.C., 1973—; asso. prof. U. N.C., Charlotte; engring. cons.; co-founder Internat. Symposium on Multiple-Valued Logic. Sec.-treas. Assumption Sch. Bd. Edn. NSF fellow, 1965-66; recipient 2 Office of Naval Research grants. Mem. IEEE (treas., dir. Charlotte sect.), Assn. Computing Machinery, Charlotte Computer Soc. Republican. Roman Catholic. Club: Queen City Optimists (treas.). Contbr. articles to profl. jours., chpt. in book. Home: 6541 Grove Park Blvd Charlotte NC 28215 Office: EAD Dept UNCC Station Charlotte NC 28223

ALLEN, CHARLES RICHARD, financial exec.; b. Cleve., Mar. 10, 1926; s. Charles Ross and Jennie (Harmon) A.; student Occidental Coll., 1943; B.S. in Bus. Adminstrn., U. Cal. at Los Angeles, 1945; m. Marion Elizabeth Taylor, Aug. 17, 1946; children—Kathleen Allen Templin, Jeanne Allen Duffy, Kenneth. Accountant, N.Am. Aviation, Inc., Los Angeles, 1946-55; div. controller TRW, Inc., Los Angeles, 1955-63, asst. controller, Cleve., 1964, controller, 1966-67, v.p., 1967-77, exec. v.p., 1977—, chief fin. officer, 1967—, also dir. Advisor New Court Partners, N.Y.C. Mem. Los Angeles Town Hall, 1961-64. Served with USNR, 1943-45. Mem. Greater Cleve. Growth Assn., Am. Mgmt. Assn., Financial Execs. Inst., Am. Finance Assn., Inst. of Dirs. (London). Clubs: Shaker Heights Country, Union, Pepper Pike (Cleve.); Wall Street (N.Y.C.). Home: 17503 Shelburne Rd Cleveland Heights OH 44118 Office: 23555 Euclid Ave Cleveland OH 44117

ALLEN, EUGENE, JR., mfg. co. exec.; b. Chgo., Nov. 7, 1937; s. Eugene and Pearl (Smith) A.; B.S., Ill. Inst. Tech., 1970; M.B.A., U. Chgo., 1976; m. Ledell Fields, Apr. 16, 1961; children—Sheryl, Karla, Nicole, Eugene M. Chemist, formulator, paint technologist Sherwin-Williams Co., 1963-67; materials engrs. Libby, McNeill & Libby, 1967-69; prodn. supr., div. sales mgr. Avon Products, Inc., 1969-74; exec. trainee, ops. mgr. Jewel Cos., Inc., Chgo., 1974-75; v.p., dir. mktg. and sales Valeer Industries, Inc., Mundelein, Ill., 1975-76; sr. v.p., dir. mktg. and sales Hub States Corp., Indpls., 1976-79; pres., chief operating officer Clinitemp, Inc., Indpls., 1979—. Bd. dirs. Youth for Christ, Indpls., 1979—, Ivy Hill Civic Assn., Arlington Heights, Ill., 1972-76; pres. Stony Island Heights Civic Assn., Chgo., 1968-70; adv. bd. Lawrence Twp. Sch. Dist., Indpls., 1978-79. Served with USAR, 1961-63. Recipient Paint Technologist award Nat. Paint Industry Edn. Com., 1966. Mem. Am. Mgmt. Assn., Dist. Export Council Ind., Indpls. C. of C. Home: 7527 N Cape Cod Ln Indianapolis IN 46250 Office: 8549 N Zionsville Rd Indianapolis IN 46250

ALLEN, FRED TIRRELL, bus. equipment mfg. co. exec.; b. Providence, Sept. 20, 1916; s. Lewis Leprelate and Fannie (Pike) A.; B.S., Brown U., 1938; m. Charlotte Ann MacIntyre, June 21, 1940; children—Fred Tirrell, William C., Richard M., Kathleen. With Pitney-Bowes, Inc., Stamford, Conn., 1938—, prodn. control mgr., 1948-55, v.p. mfg., 1955-63, exec. v.p. products, 1963-69, pres., chief operating officer, 1969-73, chmn. bd., pres., chief exec. officer, 1973—, also dir.; dir. Fidelity Trust Co., Caldor, Inc. Bd. dirs. United Way of Tri-State, Conn. Econ. Devel. Corp., 1980, Stamford Econ. Assistance Corp., 1980, U. Bridgeport, 1978; trustee Stamford Hosp., 1972—, treas., 1978. Mem. Stamford Area Commerce and Industry Assn. (dir. 1974—), Computer and Bus. Equipment Mgmt. Assn. (dir.). Office: Walter H Wheeler Jr Dr Stamford CT 06904

ALLEN, GEORGE FERGUSON, hosp. adminstr.; b. Lewiston, Maine, May 24, 1923; s. Shirley Burbank and Marion Evelyn (Ferguson) A.; B.A., Bates Coll., 1950; M.Ed., Boston U., 1953; M.A. in Hosp. Adminstrn., State U. Iowa, 1960; m. Judith Margaret Hawkins, Aug. 14, 1949; children—Douglas Ferguson, Carolyn Diane, David VanNuys, Donald Brown, Dorothy Elizabeth, Derek Fraser. Intelligence specialist USAAF, ETO, 1943-46, non-commd. officer USAF Med. Service, 1950-51; commd. 2d lt. U.S. Air Force, 1951, advanced through grades to maj., 1964; med. adminstrv. officer, psychologist, 1951-67, ret., 1967; exec. dir. Corning (N.Y.) Hosp., 1967-77; dir. hosp. and med. care div. Conn. Dept. Health, Hartford, 1977-81; health care mgmt. cons. Roncalli Inst., Cromwell, Conn. Instr. Macdill AFB campus Fla. So. Coll., 1953-54; lectr. psychology Ramey AFB (P.R.) campus Fla. State U., 1954-57; prof. hosp. mgmt. Ga. State Coll., Atlanta, 1964-65; active numerous local, area, regional and state orgns. devoted to health planning and delivery, mental health, environ. health, pub. info. and health orgn. relationship to state, fed. legis. reps. Mem. Air Force Assn., Am. Coll. Hosp. Adminstrn., N.Y. State Hosp. Assn. (mem. com. mgmt. engring. 1970—), Am. Hosp. Assn., Corning C. of C. (dir. 1968—). Presbyn. Mason. Home: 248 Maple Ave Higganum CT 06441

ALLEN, GEORGE WILLOUGHBY, veterinarian; b. Lethbridge, Alta., July 20, 1938; s. George Willoughby and Anne (Powell) A.; D.V.M., U. Toronto, 1962; M.Sc., Iowa State U., 1963; m. Marilyn Ruth Pearcey, May 28, 1960; children—Billy, Blair, Sally. Practive vet. medicine, Taber, Alta., 1963-76; Arabian horse breeder, Taber, 1976—; cons. Recipient High Gold award U. Toronto, 1962. Mem. Can. Vet. Assn., Am. Assn. Equine Practitioners, Internat. Arab Horse Assn., Can. Equestrian Fedn., Am. Horse Shows. Anglican. Contbr. articles to profl. jours. Address: PO Box 1690 Taber AB T0K 2G0 Canada

ALLEN, HENRY JOSEPH, tech. mktg./mgmt. cons. co. exec.; b. Passaic, N.J., Sept. 6, 1931; s. Edward J. and Mary B. A.; student Fairleigh Dickinson U., 1950-52, Am. Grad. U., 1975—; m. Clare B. Reardon, Jan. 21, 1956; children—Patricia Ann, Mark Terrence. Service engr. Curtiss-Wright Corp., Woodridge, N.J., 1952-56, customer service rep, 1956-60, mil. salesman, 1960-64, sr. sales engr., 1964-66, mgr. mktg., 1966-77, dir. mil.-govt. mktg., 1977-79; corp. dir. mktg. Advanced Technology, Inc., McLean, Va., 1979-81; pres. Challenger Assos., Elmwood Park, N.J., 1981—. Served with U.S. Army, 1952-55. Fellow Anglo-Am. Acad. Cambridge (hon.); mem. Tech. Mktg. Soc. Am., Am. Boat and Yacht Council, Assn. U.S. Army, Am. Mktg. Assn., Am. Def. Preparedness Assn. Republican. Roman Catholic. Home and Office: 21 Roosevelt Ave Elmwood Park NJ 07407

ALLEN, HERBERT, steel works exec.; b. Ratcliff, Tex., May 2, 1907; s. Jasper and Leona (Matthews) A.; B.S. in Mech. Engring., Rice Inst., 1929; m. Helen Daniels, Aug. 28, 1937; children—David Daniels (dec.), Anne (Mrs. Jonathan Taft Symonds), Michael Herbert. Engaged in miscellaneous research, 1929-31; chief engr. Abercrombie Pump Co., Houston, 1931-35; chief engr. Cameron Iron Works, Inc., 1935-41, v.p. engring. and mfg., 1942-50, v.p., gen. mgr., 1950-66, pres., 1966-73, chmn. bd., 1973-77, also dir.; dir. Big Three Industries, Inc., Tex. Commerce Bank. Bd. dirs. Houston Symphony Soc.; trustee emeritus William Marsh Rice U. Named Engr. of Year, San Jacinto chpt. Tex. Soc. Profl. Engrs.; Inventor of Yr., Houston Patent Atty. Assn., 1977; recipient Outstanding Engr. of Yr. award Rice U. Engring. Alumni, 1975, gold medal for distinguished service Assn. Rice U. Alumni, 1975; named to Nat. Acad. Engring., 1979. Registered profl. engr., Tex. Mem. ASME (hon. mem., award petroleum div. 1977), C. of C. (dir. 1952-54, 62, v.p. 1954-55), Am. Inst. Mining, Metall. and Petroleum Engrs., Am. Petroleum Inst., Houston Philos. Soc., Tex. Soc. Profl. Engrs., Houston Engring. and Sci. Soc., Newcomen Soc. N. Am., Tau Beta Pi. Episcopalian. Clubs: Ramada, River Oaks Country; Metropolitan (N.Y.C.); Petroleum, Houston, Bayou. Patentee in field. Home: 3207 Groveland Ln Houston TX 77019 Office: PO Box 1212 Houston TX 77001

ALLEN, HERBERT A., investment co. exec.; b. N.Y.C., 1908. Pres., chief exec. officer Allen & Co., N.Y.C., also dir. Address: Allen & Co 30 Broad St New York NY 10004*

ALLEN, HOWARD PFEIFFER, electric utility exec.; b. Upland, Calif., Oct. 7, 1925; s. Howard Clinton and Emma Maud (Pfeiffer) A.; B.A. cum laude, Pomona Coll., 1948; J.D., Stanford, 1951; m. Dixie Mae Illa, May 14, 1948; 1 dau., Alisa Cary. Admitted to Calif. bar, 1952; asst. dean, asst. prof. law Stanford Law Sch., 1951-54; with So. Calif. Edison Co., 1954—, v.p., 1962-71, sr. v.p., 1971-73, exec. v.p., 1973—; dir. Calif. Fed. Savs. & Loan Assn., PSA Inc., ICN Pharms., So. Calif. Edison, Republic Corp. Mem. Los Angeles County Election Commn. Bd. dirs. Los Angeles County Fair Assn., Calif. State U. and Colls. Found., Los Angeles Civic Light Opera, Friends of Claremont Colls., Pacific Coast Elec. Assn., bd. fellows Claremont U. Center; bd. visitors Stanford U. Law Sch.; trustee Pomona Coll., 1978—; vice-chmn. bd. dirs., mem. exec. com. Mayor's Spl. Com. on Olympics; mem. Los Angeles Olympic Organizing Com. Mem. Los Angeles C. of C. (dir., pres. 1978, chmn. 1979), Am., Los Angeles County bar assns., State Bar Calif., Bar Assn. San Francisco., Phi Beta Kappa, Phi Delta Phi. Mason (Shriner). Clubs: Jonathan, California, Los Angeles and Pacific-Union, Bohemian (San Francisco). Office: 2244 Walnut Grove Ave Rosemead CA 91770

ALLEN, IRA, communications cons.; b. N.Y.C., Dec. 26, 1946; s. Harley and Harriet (Kaiser) Bartfeld; student Bradley U., 1964-66; B.A., Queens Coll., CCNY, 1966-68; postgrad. Yale U., 1970, So. Conn. State Coll., 1971. Editorial trainee N.Y. Daily News, N.Y.C., 1966-67; researcher N.Y. Times, N.Y.C., 1968; cons. communications, New Haven, 1969-74; reporter Nat. Enquirer, New Haven, 1974-77; communications cons. Cook County Hosp., Chgo., 1977-79; cons., project mgr. Info. Mgmt. Services, Inc., Chgo., 1979—. Vol., trainer bd. dirs. Metro Help/Nat. Runaway Switchboard, Chgo. Contbr. articles to profl. jours. Home: 168 Menomenee Chicago IL 60614 Office: 188 W Randolph Chicago IL 60601

ALLEN, J. D., oil and gas exploration and drilling co. exec.; b. Ardmore, Okla., Mar. 26, 1947; s. Harry Dale and Blanche (Porter) A.; B.A., U. Okla., 1970, also M.Fin. Landman, Mobil Oil Co., Corpus Christi and Houston, 1970-72; pres. Helix Mineral & Oil Corp., Oklahoma City, 1973-74; pres. L-X Exploration, Oklahoma City, 1975-77; pres. Longhorn Gas Co., Inc., Oklahoma City, 1976—; chmn. bd. Longhorn Gas Internat. Ltd., 1979—; chmn. bd. J. D. Allen Industries, Inc., Oklahoma City, 1975—; founder Texoma Resources, Inc., Continental Resources, Inc.; part-owner High Plains Drilling Co., Denton Bros. Drilling Inc., Continental Drilling Co., Tex. Oilfield Supply, Diversified Oilfield Industries, Inc.; dir. Intrepid Drilling, Inc. Co-chmn. fin. com. Republican Nat. Com. Mem. Ind. Gas Producers Com., Ind. Petroleum Producers Assn., Ind. Assn. Drilling Contractors. Methodist. Office: 11th Floor Oil Center Bldg 2601 Northwest Expressway Oklahoma City OK 73112

ALLEN, JOE WILLIAM, variety store chain exec.; b. Covington, Ga., Mar. 28, 1943; s. Joseph O. and Mattie Lee (York) A.; B.A., Furman U., 1965; M.B.A., Ga. State U., 1973; m. Marilyn Jean Hames, Aug. 18, 1963; children—Joseph Kenton, Andrea Leigh. Supr., buyer Allen Bros. Co., Inc., Acworth, Ga., 1969-71, pres., 1972—; pres. Type 356 South, Kennesaw, Ga. Chmn. adminstrv. bd. Acworth United Methodist Ch. Served to capt. AUS, 1965-68. Recipient distinguished service award U.S. Jaycees, 1970. Mem. Ga. Retailers Assn. (dir.). Clubs: Optimists Internat., Sports Car of Am., Pinetree Country (Kennesaw). Home: 3796 Club Dr Kennesaw GA 30144 Office: 2960 Cobb Pkwy PO Box 149 Acworth GA 30101

ALLEN, JOHN ORLO, assn. exec.; b. Provo, Utah, Mar. 16, 1928; s. D. Orlo and Erma (Christenson) A.; B.S., Brigham Young U., 1952; Lent D. Upson fellow, Wayne State U., 1952-53; M.P.A., U. Pitts., 1965; m. Jean Conder, Dec. 14, 1949; children—David, Pamela, Steven, Cynthia, Phillip, Laurel. Research fellow Citizens Research Council, Detroit, 1952-53; exec. sec. Greene County br. Pa. Economy League, Waynesburg, 1953-55; research analyst Utah Found., Salt Lake City, 1955-56; sr. research analyst public affairs Research Council La., Baton Rouge, 1956-58; v.p., gen. mgr. ALCO, Inc., Orem, Utah, 1958-61; instr. public adminstrn. U. Pitts., 1961-64; dir. Office Tax Policy, Govtl. Research Inst., Cleve., 1965-67; exec. dir. Wyo. Taxpayers Assn., Cheyenne, 1967—; Wyo. legis. cons. Gen. Motors Corp.; dir. Rocky Mountain Fed. Savs. & Loan Assn.; pres. TAWS; mem. adv. bd. Advanced Monitoring Systems, Inc. Former pres. Cheyenne Community Council. Mem. Govt. Research Assn. (past trustee), Western States Taxpayers Conf., Nat. Taxpayers Conf. (chmn.), Greater Cheyenne C. of C. (past v.p. public affairs), Wyo. Assn. Trade Execs. (sec.), Phi Sigma Alpha. Republican. Mormon. Clubs: Young Men's Literary, Rotary. Office: 2515 Warren Ave Suite 300 Cheyenne WY 82001

ALLEN, LEE HARRISON, wholesale co. exec.; b. Cleve., Oct. 12, 1924; s. Horace Joseph and Eleanor Quayle (Malone) A.; B.Engring. Metallurgy, Yale U., 1948; m. Marieke Sellenraad, Sept. 18, 1954; children—Horace, Jan, Adrian, Carel, Eleanor. With Hickman, Williams & Co., supplier raw materials to iron and steel industry, Detroit, 1948—, metallurgist, 1951-70, div. mgr., 1970—, v.p., dir., 1971-76, pres., 1976—; owner L.H. Allen & Sons, wholesale tree nursery, Frankenmuth, Mich., 1969—. Trustee Grosse Pointe Bd. Edn., 1968-76. Mem. Am. Arbitration Assn., Am. Coal and Coke Chem. Inst., Am. Inst. of Mining and Metall. Engrs., Am. Iron and Steel Inst., Am. Foundrymen's Soc. Clubs: Yale of N.Y.C.; Country of Detroit, Economic of Detroit, Detroit Athletic. Home: 71 Moross Rd Grosse Pointe Farms MI 48236 Office: 100 Renaissance Center Suite 1875 Detroit MI 48243

ALLEN, NANCI JEAN, automobile parts co. exec.; b. Dundee, Ill., July 13, 1939; d. Walter Earl and Florence D. (Freeman) Anderson; m. Lowell Wesley Allen, Aug. 27, 1960; children—Beth Ann, Scott Jeffrey, Shawn Patrick. Lab. technician Sherman Hosp., Elgin, Ill., 1958-59; dept. mgr. Santa's Village, Dundee, Ill., 1959-61; pres. Lans Auto Parts, Inc., Sycamore, Ill., 1978—. Chmn., service chmn. local Parent Tchrs. League, 1969-76; mem. Immanuel Sch. bd., Dundee, 1974-79; cubmaster Cub Scouts troop, 1979—. Mem. Nat. Auto Parts Assn. Home: Route 2 Box 330 West Dundee IL 60118 Office: 550 Dekalb Ave Sycamore IL 60178

ALLEN, R. GARY, architect; b. N.Y.C., Sept. 13, 1928; s. Rembert Gary and Dorothy (Sigman) A.; student George Washington U., 1949; B.Arch., Pratt Inst., 1958; m. Nancy Creighton McAvoy, Aug. 23, 1974. Architect, Philip C. Johnson & Assos., N.Y.C., 1958-62, Carson Lundin & Shaw, N.Y.C., 1962-63, Tucker, Sadler & Bennett, San Diego, 1963-64; v.p., dir. design Frank L. Hope & Assos., San Diego, 1964-77; owner, prin. firm Gary Allen, architect, Del Mar, 1977—. Bd. dirs. La Jolla Chamber Music Soc. Served with AUS, 1953-55. Mem. AIA (Nat. Honor award 1969, award for sch. architecture 1973, award for top 10 mfg. facilities 1969, award for Naval Facilities Engring. Command 1976). Designer San Diego Stadium, Nat. Cash Register Computer Plant, San Diego, Creative Arts Center, City Coll., San Diego, Naval Underseas Center, San Diego, Western Med. Inst. Research, San Francisco, Mesa Coll. Sci. and Adminstrn. Facility, Hemet Valley Hosp. Addition, Sharp Hosp. Addition, Linkabit Corp. Hdqrs., La Jolla. Home: 750 Hoska Dr Del Mar CA 92014 Office: 1307 Stratford Ct Del Mar CA 92014

ALLEN, RALPH EDWARD, assn. exec.; b. Nelson County, Va., June 10, 1944; s. Walter Morris and Lena Nora (Rose) A.; student Benjamin Franklin U., 1964-66, George Washington U., 1974-76; m. Gerturde Rosetta Bailey, Mar. 7, 1966; children—Ralph Edward, Ross Jeffrey. With Am. Pulic Power Assn., Washington, 1965—, asst. treas., 1971-80, controller, 1980—. Democrat. Baptist. Office: 2600 Virginia Ave NW Washington DC 20037

ALLEN, RICHARD ALCOKE, concrete block mfg. co. exec.; b. White Plains, N.Y., Mar. 9, 1932; s. Kenneth D. and Helen (Kearney) A.; B.A. in Polit. Sci., Widener Coll., 1953; m. Judith G. Palmer, Apr. 24, 1954; children—Gregory, Patricia, Douglas, Susanne. Prodn. engr. Electric Regulator Corp., Norwalk, Conn., 1953-54; service adjuster Pontiac div. Gen. Motors Corp., Boston, 1957-58; sales mgr. Renault, Inc., N.Y.C., 1961-65, service and parts mgr., 1958-61; pres., gen. mgr. Star Steel Corp., Shrewsbury, Mass., 1965-71; gen. mgr., asst. to pres. Gen. Builders Supply Co., Norwood, Mass., 1972-74; pres., gen. mgr. Joral Constrn. Corp., Norwood, 1974-75; mgmt. cons., 1976; v.p., gen. mgr. masonry div. Plasticrete Corp., North Haven, Conn., 1976-78; pres. Plasticrete Block & Supply Corp., North Haven, 1978—. Vice pres. Lake Morey Protective Assn., Fairlee, Vt., 1975-77, pres., 1977-80. Served to capt. U.S. Army, 1954-57. Mem. Nat., New Eng. (sec. 1977-78) concrete Masonry assns., Am. Welding Soc., Am. Mgmt. Assn. President's Assn., Mensa. Roman Catholic. Home: 43 Currier Way Cheshire CT 06410 Office: 99 Stoddard Ave North Haven CT 06473

ALLEN, RICHARD CLEMENT, electronics and computer co. exec.; b. Neptune, N.J., Jan. 19, 1938; s. Clement L. and Florence Beatrice Allen; B.S. in Elec. Engring., Rutgers U., 1955-59, postgrad., 1959-61; m. Constance H. Rohr, June 26, 1959; children—Daniel Edward, Lara Jean. Engr., Electronic Assos. Inc., Long Branch, N.J., 1959-61; chief engr. Computer Products Inc., Farmingdale, N.J., 1961-64; v.p. engring. Simulation Systems Inc., Farmingdale, 1964-65; supr. computer system devel. Raytheon, Santa Ana, Calif., 1965-70; v.p. engring. Computer Products Inc., Santa Ana, 1970-71; v.p. engring. Varian Data Machines, Irvine, Calif., 1971-75, Memorex Corp., Santa Clara, Calif., 1976-77, v.p., gen. mgr., 1977-79; gen. mgr. micrographic systems div. NCR Corp., Mountain View, Calif., 1980—. Served with Signal Corps, U.S. Army, 1960. Mem. IEEE, Assn. Computing Machinery.

ALLEN, ROBERT COX, bank exec.; b. Phila., Mar. 16, 1924; s. Bertram Risley and Mary Catherine (Cox) A.; A.B. cum laude, Dartmouth Coll., 1947; M.B.A., U. Pa., 1949; m. Elizabeth J. Purvis, Sept. 9, 1950; children—Robert C., Deborah E., Meredith A. Asst. treas. Corn Exchange Nat. Bank, Phila., 1949-51; with Girard Bank, Phila., 1954-78, br. adminstr., sr. v.p., 1968-70, mktg. head, 1970-72, retail banking head, exec. v.p., 1972-78; pres. Farmers Bank of State of Del., Wilmington, 1979—. Bd. dirs. Jr. Achievement; chmn. exec. com. Med. Coll. Pa., 1974-76. Served with USNR, 1942-46. Mem. Del. Bankers Assn. Republican. Episcopalian. Clubs: Greenville Country; Univ., Whist (Wilmington). Author articles in field. Office: 107th & Market Sts Wilmington DE 19899

ALLEN, ROBERT FAY, air conditioning co. exec.; b. Syracuse, N.Y., Oct. 7, 1923; s. Fay O. and Ruth (Gorman) A.; B.S. in M.E., Princeton U., 1945; m. Vivian R. Rott, May 31, 1951; children—Kathleen, Joan, Barbara, Thomas, Robert. With Carrier Corp., 1945—, exec. v.p., 1978—; dir. Jenn-Air Co., Indpls., Elizando S.A., Monterrey, Mex., LeCompresseur Frigorifique, Montleul, France, Lincoln First Bank-Central, Syracuse. Mem. council Upstate Med. Center, SUNY, 1975—; mem. adv. bd. Syracuse U. Sch. Mgmt.; bd. dirs. Opera Theatre of Syracuse. Mem. Air Conditioning and Refrigeration Inst. (chmn. certification and policy com.). Clubs: Princeton (N.Y.C.), Century, Onondaga Golf and Country. Office: Carrier Corp div United Technologies PO Box 4808 Carrier Pkwy Syracuse NY 13221

ALLEN, ROBERT HAROLD, chem. co. exec.; b. Oklahoma City, 1928; grad. Tex. A&M U., 1950; married. With J.L. Block & Co., C.P.A.'s, 1953-57; with Gulf Resources & Chem. Corp., Houston, 1957—, pres., chief exec. officer, 1960-75, chmn. bd., chief exec. officer, 1975—, also dir.; dir. First City Nat. Bank, Fed. Express Corp., Dimark, Inc., Energex Minerals, Inc. Bd. dirs. Am. Mining Gongress; trustee Colo. Outward Bound Sch., Baylor Coll. Medicine. Office: Gulf Resources & Chems Corp 47th Floor 1100 Milam Bldg Houston TX 77002

ALLEN, ROBERT WAYNE, mfg. co. exec.; b. Indpls., Apr. 13, 1922; s. Stephen B. and Mary Amelia (Byerly) A.; student Purdue U., 1951, UCLA, 1956-58, U. Santa Clara, 1969; B.S. in M.E., Kensington U., 1976, M.B.A., 1978, postgrad., 1979—; m. Bernice Emily Meredith, 1940 (dec. 1972); 1 son, Robin Wayne; m. 2d, Francine Lile Wishner, July 3, 1976; stepchildren—Alan Jay Pollock, Meri Ellen Pollock. Machinist Allison div. Gen. Motors, Indpls., 1940-42, sr. tool designer, 1943-45; sr. tool and gage designer, mfg. planner Hoosier Enging. Co., 1946-47; chief tool designer Marmon Herrington Co., Inc., Indpls., 1947-48, asst. to plant supt., 1949-52, chief insp. 1953-54; supr. tool engring. Solar Aircraft Co., San Diego, Calif., 1954-55, chief prodn. engr., 1956-57, mgr. quality control and reliability, 1958-60; mgr. mfg. engring. Aerojet-Gen. Corp., Azusa and Sacramento, Calif., 1960-66, mgr. quality control and reliability, 1967-68, mgr. mfg. services, operations dir., 1969-70, corp. prodn. mgr., 1970-73; v.p. Graver Tank & Mfg. Co., El Monte, Calif., 1973-76; pres. Harcord Mfg. Co., Inc., Jersey City, 1976—, C.H. Leibfried Mfg. Corp., Bklyn., 1977—, Transfer Tech., Inc., Jersey City, 1977—; lectr. in field. Served with C.E., U.S. Army, 1945-46. Registered profl. engr., Calif. Mem. Am. Soc. Mfg. Engrs. (cert. mfg. engr.), Am. Soc. Quality Control. Mem. Ch. Religious Sci. Club: Masons (32 deg.). Copywrighter trigonometry computations. Home: 17 Berkshire Pl Englewood Cliffs NJ 07632 Office: 125 Monitor St Jersey City NJ 07304

ALLEN, TRUETT EVANS, banker; b. Sparta, Va., Apr. 16, 1933; s. Thomas Cheek and Ruth (Cutts) A.; A.B., U. Richmond, 1954; M.B.A., Harvard, 1962; m. Barbara Fagan, Dec. 18, 1966; children—Jefferson Madden, Riley Evans. Bank examiner, adminstrv. asst. Fed. Res. Bank Richmond, 1954-60; with Irving Trust Co., N.Y.C., 1962—, asst. sec., 1963-64, asst. v.p., 1964-67, v.p., 1967—, dist. head So. dist., nat. div., 1969-76, dept. mgr. So. dept. Fin. Instns. Banking div., 1976-80, dept. mgr. Securities Industry dept., 1980—. Served with AUS, 1956-58. Mem. Am. Arbitration Assn. (panel of arbitrators), Am. Textile Mfrs. Inst., Phi Gamma Delta. Clubs: Harvard (N.Y.C.); Timber Ridge (Windham, Vt.). Home: 135 E 71st St Apt 7-A New York NY 10021 Office: 1 Wall St New York NY 10015

ALLEN, VERNON EUGENE, mfg. co. exec.; b. Cleve., Dec. 24, 1919; s. Vernon LaFayette and Beatrice (Figgins) A.; grad. high sch.; m. Florence Wilma Stanard, Mar. 5, 1942; children—Vernon William, Carol Jean (Mrs. Charles Holmes), Gregory, Holly L. (Mrs. James May). Punch press operator Tinnerman Products Inc. (became div. Eaton Corp. 1969), Cleve., 1938-46, devel. engr., 1946-47, sales supr., 1947-70, sales mgr. Eaton Corp., 1970-72, div. mktg. mgr., 1972-80, dir. community liaison, 1980—. Capt., Ohio Hwy. Patrol Aux., 1968-70. Served with C.E., AUS, 1940-46; PTO, NATOUSA, ETO. Decorated Bronze Star. Mem. Sales Marketing Execs. Inc., Am. Legion (comdr. Ohio 1964-65), VFW, Soc. Automotive Engrs., Home Appliance Mfrs. Assn. Republican. Club: Wedgewood Country. Home: 14181 Cherokee Trail Middleburg Heights OH 44130 Office: Eaton Corp PO Box 6688 Cleveland OH 44101

ALLEN, VINCENT HENRY, JR., oil investment mgmt. co. exec.; b. Elmhurst, Ill., June 6, 1931; s. Vincent Henry and Elsie (Lesman) A.; B.A., Westminster Coll., 1953; m. Carole Ann Koch, Sept. 7, 1954; children—Vincent Henry III, Gordon Kelley, Jill E. With Investors Diversified Services, Oklahoma City, 1956-68; v.p. sales, midwestern region Financial Services Corp. Am., Oklahoma City, 1968-70; v.p. instl. and pvt. placement sales, Petro-Search, Inc., Denver, 1970-75; pres. Vince Allen & Assos. Inc., Denver, 1975—; cons. Anderson Petroleum Inc., Denver, 1975-76; v.p. Financial Service Corp. Am., Oklahoma City, Fundamental Service Corp. Am., Atlanta, 1968-70. Dir., coach Evergreen Am. Legion Baseball Team, 1974-75. Precinct leader Republican party, Oklahoma City, 1961-62, co-ward chmn., 1963-64. Served with AUS, 1954-56. Recipient Nat. Regional Mgrs. award Financial Service Corp., 1969. Clubs: Sales Executive, Village Methodist Men (pres.), President's (Oklahoma City). Home: 30421 Wingfoot Dr Evergreen CO 80439 Office: Suite 403 180 Cook St Denver CO 80206

ALLEN, WARREN WILLIAM, JR., brick co. exec.; b. St. Louis, Jan. 2, 1924; s. Warren William and Edith (Eilers) A.; student Purdue U., 1942-43; B.S. in Chem. Engring., Wash. U., 1948; m. Ruth Reddish, June 11, 1949; children—William Reddish, Margaret, John Warren. Sales engr. Presstite Engr. Co., 1948-51; with Hydraulic Press Brick Co., St. Louis, 1951—, sales engr., Cleve., 1951-52, sales mgr., Cleve., 1952-55, mgr. Haydite div., 1955-63, v.p., St. Louis, 1963-67, pres., Cleve., 1967—, also dir.; dir. St. Louis Steel Casting Inc. Dir. Expanded Shale Clay and Slate Inst. Served with AUS, 1943-46. Mem. Am. Ceramic Soc., Am. Concrete Inst., ASTM, Alpha Chi Sigma, Phi Delta Theta. Home: 1690 E Shore Dr Martinsville IN 46151 Office: PO Box 7 Brooklyn IN 46111

ALLEY, JAMES CULLEN, accountant; b. Mississippi County, Ark., July 17, 1929; s. Kenneth Carmie and Rethie Omillie (Whitby) A.; B.B.A., U. Tex., Austin, 1952; m. Ada Lee Langston, May 6, 1967; children—James W., Deborah L., Catherine A., E. Kenneth. With Aluminum Co. Am., 1953—, beginning as trainee, successively supply foreman, asst. supply mgr., constrn. supply mgr., ops. supply mgr., asst. acctg. mgr., constrn. acctg. mgr., constrn. adminstrv. mgr., mgr. fgn. constrn. acctg., mgr. constrn. acctg. Alcoa of Australia, Ltd., Melbourne, 1953-81; mgr. fin. services Compagnie des Bauxites de Guinée, Kamsar, Guinea, 1981—. Warden, mem. council, lay reader Episcopal Ch.; scoutmaster, dist. and council mem., dist. commr. Boy Scouts Am.; bd. dirs. Jr. Achievement, 1966. Served in USAF, 1946-49, to lt. AUS, 1952-53. Ky. col. Mem. Nat. Assn. Accts. Republican. Club: Rotary (sec., dir. 1963-67). Office: care Halco (Mining) Inc 900 Two Allegheny Center Pittsburg PA 15212

ALLISON, DON ALDEN, investment broker, furniture exec.; b. Las Animas, Colo., Sept. 11, 1907; s. Morgan Donaldson and Ada (Collins) A.; E.E., U. Calif. at Los Angeles, 1929; spl. courses U. So. Calif. Extension, 1932, 37-38; N. certificate U.S. Power Squadron, 1943; m. Mildred Evelyn Sallee, Jan. 1, 1940; children—Don Alden, Sallie Irene. Jr. partner Brown-Collins Co., 1929-30; v.p. House of Chesterfields, 1931; pres. Don Allison Co., Los Angeles, 1932—. Mem. Am. Power Boat Assn. (pres. western region 1942). U.S. Power Squadron (comdr. Los Angeles 1941). Inst. of Navigation, World Affairs Council, Bel Air Guild, Delta Sigma Phi. Clubs: Sertoma; Tuna (pres. 1953); Hollywood Yacht (commodore 1940). Mem. U.S. Sharp Cup Team. 1954, 55, 56; Am. Athletic Union del. Nat. Charity League. Home: 9398 Monte Leon Ln Beverly Hills CA 90210 Office: 8271 Beverly Blvd Los Angeles CA 90048

ALLISON, DONALD GEORGE, fin. exec.; b. Suffern, N.Y., Feb. 28, 1950; s. George Suffern IV and Jacquelin King (Badger) A.; B.S., U. Pa., 1972; M.B.A., Northwestern U., 1973; m. Janet Lodge Wright, May 22, 1976. Money market trader Chem. Bank, N.Y.C., 1973, asst. mgr., 1974, asst. sec., 1976; asst. sec. Irving Trust Co., N.Y.C., 1977, asst. v.p., 1978, v.p. 1979—, sr. mcpl. bond trader, 1979—. Mem. U. Pa. Gen. Alumni Exec. Bd., 1978—; v.p. bd. deacons Brick Presbyn. Ch., N.Y.C., 1979—. Mem. Theta Xi (nat. dir. 1974—, treas. 1980—). Republican. Clubs: Mask and Wig, St. Nicholas Soc., Princeton, U. Pa. of N.Y. (gov. 1974—). Home: 1192 Park Ave New York NY 10028 Office: 1 Wall St New York NY 10015

ALLISON, ROBERT JAMES, JR., oil co. exec.; b. Evanston, Ill., Jan. 29, 1939; s. Robert James and Mary Susan (Rohrer) A.; B.S., Kans. U., 1960; m. Carolyn Jean Grother, June 17, 1961; children—Amy, Ann, Jane. Petroleum engr., area engr. Amoco Prodn. Co., Okla., Kans., Miss., La., Tex., 1960-68, engr. Amoco Internat. Oil Co., Chgo., 1968-70, chief engr. Amoco Trinidad, Port-of-Spain, 1970-72; adviser Iran Pan Am. Oil Co., Tehran, 1972-73; v.p. ops. Anadarko Prodn. Co., Houston, 1973-75, pres., chief operating officer, dir., 1976-79, pres., chief exec. officer, 1979—. Mem. Soc. Petroleum Engrs. Am. Inst. Mining, Metall. and Petroleum Engrs., Ind. Petroleum Assn. Am., mid-Continent Oil and Gas Assn., Am. Petroleum Inst., Inst. Pertoleum Trinidad. Home: 5618 Green Springs St Houston TX 77066 Office: PO Box 1330 Houston TX 77001

ALLMAN, KATHERINE MIRIAM, coll. adminstr.; b. Berkeley, Calif., June 24, 1945; d. Ernest Daniel and Zelma Ann (Harding) A.; A.A., Laney Coll., 1968; B.S., U. Calif. at Berkeley, 1971, M.B.A., 1973. Mgmt. trainee Levi Strauss, San Francisco, 1972; accountant Price Waterhouse, Oakland, Calif., 1973-74; bus. mgr. Patten Bible Coll., Oakland, Calif., 1974—, instr. math. Patten Acad. Christian Edn., 1977-78, instr. math. Patten Bible Coll., 1977—. Treas. minority bus. assistance Student Devel. Found., 1971-75. Mem. Black Masters of Bus. Adminstrn. Student Assn. (co-chairperson 1971-72), Nat. Assn. Black Accountants, Western Assn. Coll. and Univ. Bus. Officers. Christian Evangel. Ch. Am. Home: 3701 Malcolm Ave Oakland CA 94605 Office: 2433 Coolidge Ave Oakland CA 94601

ALLMON, JOSEPH THURMAN, textile co. exec.; b. Mize, Miss., Mar. 20, 1921; s. William Richard and Susan Elizabeth (Huff) A.; student East Central Jr. Coll., 1938-40; B.A., Miss. Coll., 1942; Th.M., So. Bapt. Sem., 1945; postgrad. N.Y. U., 1948; m. Vauda Carolyn Burson, Sept. 25, 1945; 1 son, Warren Douglas. Personnel dir. Riegel Textile Corp., Conover, N.C., 1957-59, supr. mgmt. devel., N.Y.C., 1959-63, dir. indsl. relations, Ware Shoals, S.C., 1963-69, v.p. indsl. relations, 1969-73, v.p., Greenville, S.C., 1973—; adj. prof. mgmt. U. S.C., Columbia, 1974-75. Pres. Greenville Urban League, 1974-76; vice chmn. council affiliate press. Nat. Urban League, 1975-76; chmn., bd. trustees Ednl. Resources Found.; civil service commr., Greenville; chmn. Goodwill Industries Upper S.C. Served with USNR, 1945-46. Mem. Silver Bay Indsl. Mgmt. Conf. (past chmn.). Republican. Unitarian. Editor: How to Organize and Conduct a Management Development Group, 1950. Home: 101 E Lanneau Dr Greenville SC 29605 Office: Green Gate Park Greenville SC 29606

ALLSTROM, H. WILLARD, actuary, ins. co. exec.; b. Mpls., Aug. 2, 1918; s. Henry and Edith (Kleine) A.; B.A., U. Minn., 1940; B.S., Rutgers U., 1944; m. Lenore Boberg, June 28, 1952; children—Peter, Mark. Supr., Met. Life Ins. Co., N.Y.C., 1940-57; v.p., sr. actuary Union Labor Life Ins. Co., N.Y.C., 1957—; mem. Joint Bd. Enrollment of Actuaries. Served with AUS, 1942-45. Mem. Am. Acad. Actuaries, Soc. Actuaries, Conf. Actuaries in Public Practice, Am. Pension Conf. Office: 850 3d Ave New York NY 10022

ALLWARD, BRIAN ROSS, automotive co. exec.; b. Montreal, Que., Can., Mar. 19, 1944; s. Ross Murray and Dorothy Grace (Clendinneng) A.; Chartered Acct., McGill U., 1967; m. Maria J. Manzi, Aug. 13, 1966; children—Eric, Marc. Exec. v.p. Lansair Ltd. and subs., Montreal, 1968-78, also dir.; v.p. RK Elliott Group of Cos., Toronto, 1978—; cons. in field. Mem. Can. Inst. Chartered Accts. Home: 2 Cantrill Ct Brampton ON L6Z 1A3 Canada Office: 61 Rayette Rd Concord ON L4K 1B6 Canada

ALLY, CARL JOSEPH, advt. exec.; b. Detroit, Mar. 31, 1924; s. Carl and Mary (Miglio) A.; A.B., U. Mich., 1949, student Grad. Sch., 1953; certificate Georgetown U. Sch. Fgn. Service, 1952; m. Patricia M. Nusco, Jan. 15, 1952; children—Christopher Jonathan, Patricia Ann, Matthew Carl. Advt. exec. Gen. Electric Co., Schenectady, 1948-51; mgr. N.Y.C. office Campbell-Ewald Co., 1955-60; v.p. Papert, Koening, Lois, Inc., N.Y.C., 1960-62; founder, 1962, since chmn. bd., chief exec. officer Carl Ally Inc. (name now Ally and Gargano, Inc.), N.Y.C.; lectr. New Sch. Social Research, 1964—; Served to capt. USAAF and USAF, 1942-45, 50-52. Decorated D.F.C., Air medal with 3 oak leaf clusters. Mem. Sigma Nu. Clubs: Wings (N.Y.C.), Pequod Yacht. Author: History of Mary Washington College, 1973. Office: 437 Madison Ave New York NY 10022*

ALMOND, HAROLD COX, stove mfg. co. exec.; b. Tennga, Ga., Feb. 11, 1916; s. Claude Harle and Ethel Cox (Almond); student Draughon Bus. Coll., Knoxville, 1935-36; m. Ruthanna Stratton, June 5, 1937; children—Ann Almond Pope, Charles L. With Hardwick Stove Co., Cleveland, Tenn., 1937—, exec. v.p., 1961-74, pres., 1974—; dir. Am. Nat. Bank, Chattanooga; adv. dir. Liberty Mut. Ins. Co. Pres., bd. dirs. Jr. Achievement; bd. dirs. Boys Club Am., Tenn. Taxpayers Assn. Named to Bradley County Businessmen Hall of Fame, 1979. Mem. Cleveland Associated Industries, Tenn. Mfrs. Assn. Home: 3209 Ocoee St NW Cleveland TN 37311 Office: 240 Edwards St SE Cleveland TN 37311

ALOE, MARK ARTHUR, coal co. exec.; b. Pitts., July 21, 1947; s. William T. and Francis A.; B.S., Robert Morris Coll., 1970; m. Carol Fair, Dec. 2, 1972; children—Edith Francis, Carlin Fair. Asst. to pres. Aloe Coal Co. subsidiary Pullman, Inc., Imperial, Pa., 1967, gen. mgr. sanitary div., 1968-74, chmn. bd., pres. Aloe Coal Co., Midway Coal Co., Imperial Land Co., 1974—. Mem. Keystone Bituminous Coal Assn. (dir., exec. bd.), Western Pa. Bituminous Coal Operators (exec.

bd., dir.), Mining and Reclamation Council Am. (vice-chmn.). Clubs: Pittsburgh Athletic, Fellows. Office: Box 50 Imperial PA 15126

ALONZO, MARTIN VINCENT, mining co. exec.; b. N.Y.C., Apr. 8, 1931; s. Mariano and Mary (Traina) A.; B.B.A. cum laude in Acctg., Bernard M. Baruch Coll., CCNY, 1952, M.B.A. in Fin. and Investments, 1971; m. Sabina Gallucci, June 7, 1952; children—Martin Vincent, Marlene, Sabrina. With Eisner and Lubin, C.P.A.'s, N.Y.C., 1952-57; treas., controller Credit-Am. Corp., N.Y.C., 1957-60; asst. v.p. indsl. time sales financing and leasing A.J. Armstrong Co., Inc., N.Y.C., 1960-65; treas., sec. So. Nitrogen Co., Savannah, Ga., 1965-67; asst. to fin. v.p. AMAX, Inc. (name formerly Am. Metal Climax, Inc.), Greenwich, Conn., 1967-68, mgr. fin. planning, 1968-69, asst. controller, 1969, controller, 1970, v.p. and controller, sr. v.p. controls and adminstrn., 1978—; dir. Alumax Inc., San Mateo, Calif., 1970—; mem. various task forces Fin. Acctg. Standards Bd., 1975—. Bd. dirs. Greenwich Health Assn. C.P.A., N.Y. State. Mem. Am. Mining Congress (pension com., chmn. acctg. com. 1980—), Nat. Assn. Accts. (chmn. mgmt. acctg. practices com. 1976-79), Machinery and Allied Products Inst. (fin. council), Am. Inst. C.P.A.'s, N.Y. State Soc. C.P.A.'s, Fin. Execs. Inst., Extractive Industries Luncheon Group (chmn. 1978-79), AIME, Japan Soc., Beta Alpha Psi, Beta Gamma Sigma. Republican. Roman Catholic. Home: 31 Baldwin Farms N Greenwich CT 06830 Office: AMAX Center Greenwich CT 06830

ALPER, ALLEN MYRON, materials mfg. co. exec.; b. N.Y.C., Oct. 23, 1932; s. Joseph and Pauline (Frohlich) A.; B.S., Bklyn. Coll., 1954; Ph.D., Columbia (Univ. fellow, Dyckman Inst. Scholar, Univ. pres.'s scholar), 1957; m. Barbara Marshall, Dec. 20, 1959; children—Allen Myron, Andrew Marshall. Sr. mineralogist Corning Glass Works (N.Y.), 1957-59, research mineralogist, 1959-62, mgr. ceramic research, also sr. research asso., 1962-69; with GTE Sylvania Inc., Towanda, Pa., 1969—, chief engr., 1971-72, dir. research and engring., 1972-78, ops. mgr., 1978—, v.p. Syltron, P.R., 1979-80, pres. GTE Walmet, Royal Oak, Mich., 1980—. Mem. Pa. Gov.'s Adv. Panel on Materials, 1971—; mem. exec. bd. Gen. Sullivan council Boy Scouts Am.; chmn. adv. com. Materials Research Lab., Pa. State U. Recipient grant, fellowship N.Mex. Bur. Mines, 1954-57. Fellow Am. Ceramic Soc., Geol. Soc. Am., Am. Inst. Chemists; mem. Brit. Ceramic Soc., Am. Soc. Metals, Geophy. Union, Am. Chem. Soc., Explorers Club, Internat. Platform Assn., Internat. House, Sigma Xi. Presbyterian. Clubs: Towanda Country, Lake Wesauking Assn. Patentee in field. Contbr. to profl. jours. Editor: Phase Diagrams: Materials Science and Technology, 5 vols., 1970; High Temperature Oxides, 4 parts, 1970-71. Editorial bd. High Temperature Sci. jour., 1969—, High Temperature Chemistry, 1973—, Materials Handbook, 1974—; editor Materials Sci. and Tech. Series, Acad. Press, 1972—. Contbr. articles to profl. jours. Home: 880 Great Oaks Blvd Rochester MI 48063 Office: GTE Walmet Royal Oak MI 48068

ALPERIN, IRWIN EPHRAIM, clothing co. exec.; b. Scranton, Pa., Apr. 29, 1925; s. Louis I. and Bessie (Wickner) A.; B.S. in Indsl. Engring., Lehigh U., 1947; certificate mech. engring. Pa. State U., 1945; m. Francine Leah Friedman, Dec. 5, 1948; children—Barbara Joy, Jane Leslie. Mgmt. trainee Mayflower Mfg. Co., Scranton, Pa., 1947-49, sec., 1952-79, pres., 1980—; with Triple A Trouser Mfg. Co., Inc., Scranton, 1952, v.p., treas., 1958-79, pres., 1980—; with Gold Star Mfg. Co., Inc., Scranton, 1956, pres., 1956—; sec. Astro Warehousing, Inc., Scranton, 1962—; sec.-treas. Bondeal, Inc., Scranton, 1978—; v.p. Mortgage Inc., 1979—; dir. Sacquoit Industries Inc., Scranton. Bd. dirs. Econ. Devel. Council N.E. Pa., Avoca, Pa., 1974—, v.p., 1978—; bd. dirs. ARC, Scranton, 1968—, Jewish Home N.E. Pa., Scranton, 1970—, Jewish Community Center, Scranton, 1971—, Community Services Pa., Harrisburg, Pa., 1973-78, Scranton Mental Health-Mental Retardation Center, 1975—, Pa. Assn. for Retarded Children, 1979-80; pres. Planning Council Social Services Lackawanna County, 1972-74, now life mem.; pres. Jewish Fedn. Lackawanna County, 1967-70, now life bd mem.; v.p. United Way Lackawanna County, 1974-78; pres. Alperin Found., Scranton, 1962—; treas. Scranton-Lackawanna Jewish Council, 1973-75, bd. dirs., 1975—. Served with C.E., AUS, 1944-46. Named Man of Year Jewish Community Center, 1973. Mem. Am. Inst. Indsl. Engrs. (sr.). Jewish (temple pres. 1969-71). Mason (Shriner), Elk; mem. B'nai B'rith. Club: Glen Oak Country (Clarke Summit, Pa.). Home: 600 Colfax Ave Scranton PA 18510 Office: Meadow and Maple Sts PO Box 470 Scranton PA 18503

ALPERN, ANDREW, architect; b. N.Y.C., Nov. 1, 1938; s. Dwight K. and Grace M. (Michelman) A.; B.Arch., Columbia, 1964; Sc.D. (hon.), London (Eng.) Coll. Applied Sci., 1971. With Haines Lundberg Waehler, architects, N.Y.C., 1962-67; project dir. Saphier, Lerner, Schindler, Environetics, space planning and design, N.Y.C., 1968-72; v.p., dir. architecture Environ. Research & Devel., Inc., Space Planning and Design, N.Y.C., 1972-75; dir. research Corp. Planners & Coordinators, Inc., real estate, cons. and brokers, N.Y.C., 1973-75; project mgr. Hellmuth Obata & Kassabaum, architects, engrs. and planners, N.Y.C., 1977-78; mgr. real estate and facilities planning Coopers & Lybrand, N.Y.C., 1978—; pvt. practice as cons. architect, also research and analysis, feasibility studies, programming, archtl. problem solving, N.Y.C., 1964—. Cons. urban real estate and architecture, 1967—; lectr. City U. N.Y., Inst. Architecture and Urban Studies, Grolier Club. Mem. adv. bd. Inst. Applied Psychotherapy, 1969-72, therapist cons. state-funded program drug abuse prevention, 1970-72; mem. nat. panel arbitrators Am. Arbitration Assn., 1971—. Registered architect, N.Y. State, Pa., Calif., W.Va., Washington; certified Nat. Council Archtl. Registration Bds. Mem. AIA, Archtl. League N.Y., Soc. Archtl. Historians, N.Y. Hist. Soc., Nat. Trust Hist. Preservation, L.I. Hist. Soc., Bronx County Hist. Soc., Mcpl. Art Soc., N.Y. State Assn. Architects, Assn. Collegiate Schs. Architecture, Real Estate Bd. N.Y., Brownstone Revival Com., Friends of Cast-Iron Architecture, Met. Assn. Urban Designers and Environ. Planners. Author: Apartments for the Affluent: A Historical Survey of Buildings in New York, 1975; Garret Ellis Winants: 1813-1890, 1976; Alpern's Architectural Aphorisms, 1979; Handbook of Specialty Elements in Architecture, 1981; Holdouts, 1981. Editor-in-chief: Legal Briefs for Architects, Engineers and Contractors, 1978—. Address: 315 8th Ave New York NY 10001

ALPERT, WARREN, corp. exec.; b. Chelsea, Mass., Dec. 2, 1920; s. Goodman and Tena (Horowitz) A.; B.S., Boston U., 1942; M.B.A., Harvard, 1947. Mgmt. trainee Standard Oil Co. of Calif., 1947-48; financial specialist Calif. Oil Co., 1948-52; pres. Warren Petroleum Co., 1952-54; pres., chmn. bd. Warren Equities, Inc., 1954—; pres., chmn. Ritz Tower Hotel; dir. Mass. Gen. Life Ins. Co.; asst. sec. state Dept. State, 1962. Mem. U.S. Com. for UN, 1960; exec. com. SBA, 1958; mem. Nat. Bd. Field Advisers, 1957. Trustee, mem. exec. com. Boston U., Emerson Coll., Boston, Petroleum Marketing Edn. Found.; trustee Jerusalem Inst. Mgmt.; bd. dirs. Harvard Bus. Sch.; pres. Sutton Pl. Synagogue, N.Y.C. Served with Signal Intelligence, AUS, 1943-45. Mem. Young Presidents Orgn. (past dir.), Am. Petroleum Inst. (dir. mktg. com.), Harvard Bus. Sch. Assos. (dir.). Clubs: Harvard (Boston, N.Y.C.); 29. Home: 465 Park Ave New York NY 10022 Office: Warren Equities Inc 10 E 53d St New York NY 10022

ALSHUK, THOMAS JOHN, computer systems co. exec.; b. Waterbury, Conn., Aug. 4, 1949; s. Thomas and Zenobia Phyllis (Neminski) A.; B.S., Cornell U., 1973; M.S. in Engring. Sci., Rensselaer Poly. Inst., 1976; diploma in intermediate Russian, Vidil-Rock Sch. Modern Langs., 1976; m. Rebecca Kay Crossley Coyle, Mar. 26, 1977; 1 dau., Alexandra Tamara. Engr.-systems analyst Waterbury Farrel Co. div. Textron Inc., 1969-71; ind. cons. computer hardware, software, systems, 1971-73; mgr. control systems Fenn Mfg. Co. div. AMCA Inc., Newington, Conn., 1973-80; pres. The Anser Corp., Newington, 1980—. Mem. bd. advisers (Russian) Vidil-Rock Sch. Modern Langs., 1976—. Registered profl. engr., Conn; certified in data processing. Mem. Am. Nat. Standards Inst., Nat. Machine Tool Builders Assn., Conn. Soc. Profl. Engrs. (Young Engr. of Year award 1976, sec. state bd. dirs. 1978-79, chpt. v.p. profl. engrs. in industry sect. 1978-79, chpt. treas. 1979-80, chpt. pres. 1980-81), IEEE, Assn. for Computing Machinery. Democrat. Roman Catholic/Russian Orthodox. Patentee in field. Home: 7 Wilcox St Old Wethersfield CT 06109 Office: PO Box 11920 Newington CT 06111

ALTBAIER, CURTIS HENRY, marketing exec.; b. Vilshofen, Germany, Feb. 15, 1921; came to U.S., 1939, naturalized, 1944; s. Gustav H. and Frieda (Haag) A.; M.E., U. Cin., 1949; Ph.D. in Bus. Adminstrn., Colo. State Christian Coll., 1972; m. Lea Cronstein, Apr. 22, 1943; children—Robert, Sherry. With Cin. Milacron, 1939—, sales mgr. spl. machine div., 1958-63, asst. export mgr., 1963-65, export mgr., pres. Amertool Service, Inc., 1965-75, dir. multinat. project, 1975-77, dir. internat. mktg., 1977—, v.p., dir., 1963—; dir. Cin. Milacron Japan Ltd., Tokyo, Cin. Milacron S.E. Asia, Singapore. Mem. Pres. Export Adminstrn. Council, 1973-78; chmn. Numerical Control Tech. Adv. Com., Washington, 1973-75; mem. Regional Export Expansion Council, 1969-75; mem. fgn. credit ins. com. U.S. Export-Import Bank, 1969-75. Served with C.E., U.S. Army, 1944-46; CBI. Registered profl. engr., Ohio. Mem. Engring. Soc. Cin., Nat. Machine Tool Builders Assn. (internat. trade com.), Mu Pi Kappa, Sigma Delta Gamma. Clubs: No Name; Tennis, Indoor Tennis (pres.) (Cin.). Home: 3096 Clubcommons Rd Mason OH 45040 Office: 4701 Marburg Ave Cincinnati OH 45209

ALTENHOFF, NORMAN RICHARD, accountant; b. Chgo., May 30, 1934; s. Alexander and Beulah P. (Potts) A.; student Georgetown U., 1952-56; B.S. in Bus. Adminstrn., Roosevelt U., 1970, M.S., 1973; m. Janet Barbara Saad, June 12, 1960; children—Alexander, Allison. System engr. IBM, Chgo., 1964-67; div. comptroller First Nat. Bank of Chgo., 1967-73; mgmt. cons. Lester B. Knight & Asso., Inc., Chgo., 1973-76; v.p. Citizens Bancorp., Sheboygan, Wis., 1976-78; pres. Comml. Services Co., St. Petersburg, Fla., 1979—; instr. Grad. Sch. Bus., De Paul U., Chgo., 1975. Bd. dirs. St. Petersburg Opera Co. Served in USNR, 1956-58. Certified data processor Data Processing Mgmt. Assn. Mem. Nat. Assn. Accts., St. Petersburg C. of C. Clubs: River Forest Tennis, Happy Hollow Country. Home: 730 S Village Dr Saint Petersburg FL 33702 Office: 7901 4th St N Saint Petersburg FL 33702

ALTER, GERALD L., realty co. exec.; b. Rensselaer, Ind., Aug. 24, 1910; s. Leslie and Lettie (Willis) A.; student Bus. Coll., 1927-28; m. Margaret A. Davis, Sept. 15, 1939; children—Judith Ann (dec.), John Edward. Clk. and office mgr., 1929-35; bldg. contractor, 1936-45; real estate broker and ins. agt. Alter Realty Inc., Torrance, Calif., 1946—; pres. Alter Realty & Ins., Alter Devel. Co., Leads, Inc., Alter Ins. Agy., Inc., REMCO; sec. Developers & Builders. Mem. Torrance Planning Commn.; capt. Torrance Police Res., 1946-61. Past bd. dirs. Harbor Area United Way. Served with AUS, 1945-46. Mem. Torrance-Lomita-Carson Bd. Realtors (past dir., chmn. by-laws com., pres. 1978, v.p., multiple listing chmn. 1981), Calif. Real Estate Assn. (past dir., chmn. planning and zoning com.), Nat. Assn. Real Estate Bds., Calif. Assn. Realtors (dir. 1978—, 21st dist. legis. chmn. 1981), Torrance C. of C. (past dir.). Republican. Clubs: OX-5, Rotary (Torrance). Home: 709 Madrid Ave Torrance CA 90501 Office: 2305 Torrance Blvd Torrance CA 90501

ALTHOFF, JAMES CORNELIUS, retail liquor co. exec.; b. Lansing, Iowa, Dec. 8, 1922; s. Henry Theodore and Anna Christine (Teeling) A.; m. Agnes Stroik, Oct. 17, 1945; children—Patricia Ann, Michael James. Pres., Ernies Wine and Liquor Corp., South San Francisco, 1964-72; pres. Althoff Corp., Burlingame, Calif., 1977—; pres. Prestige Investments. Served with USAAF, 1942-45, USAF, 1951-53. Decorated D.F.C., air medal with 5 oak leaf clusters. Mem. Nat. Liquor Stores Assn. (pres. 1973-75), Calif. Retail Liquor Dealers Assn. (pres. 1969-71), Wine and Spirits Guild Am. Republican. Roman Catholic. Club: St. Francis Yacht (San Francisco). Home: 2 Mt Vernon Ln Atherton CA 94025 Office: 1300 Burlingame Ave Burlingame CA 94010

ALTHOFF, JAMES LEWIS, contracting co. exec.; b. McHenry, Ill., June 9, 1928; s. William H. and Eleanora M. Althoff; grad. high sch.; m. Joan Andreen, June 18, 1949; children—Timothy, Betsy, Tod, Katy, Patti, Jim, Karyn. Owner liquefied petroleum gas distbg. co., McHenry, 1952-60; founder, pres. J. Althoff & Assos., McHenry, 1960—, Althoff Industries, Inc., McHenry, 1960—. Pres., Fire Dist., 1966-78, Bd. Edn. Dist. 156, 1969-78; mem. Law Enforcement Commn. Lake and McHenry Counties, 1979—; bd. govs. Ill. Colls. and Univs., 1979—; trustee Plumbers Welfare Fund. Chgo., 1974—. Recipient Service award McHenry High Sch. Dist., 1979, Bradley U., 1976, McHenry Fire Dist., 1978. Mem. Chgo. Contractors Assn., Nat. Plumbing Contractors Assn. Home: 508 Green St McHenry IL 60050 Office: 809 Front St McHenry IL 60050

ALTIER, WILLIAM JOHN, mgmt. cons.; b. Drexel Hill, Pa., July 22, 1935; s. William John and Gertrude (Soule) A.; B.A., Lafayette Coll., 1958; M.B.A., Pa. State U., 1962; m. Mileen Rishel Bower, June 21, 1958; children—William Clark, Dwight Douglas. Asso., Kepner-Tregoe Inc., Princeton, N.J., 1964-68; gen. mgr. div. Princeton Research Press, 1970-75, sr. asso., 1975-76; asso. Applied Synergetics Center, Waltham, Mass., 1968-69; dir. mktg. Comstock & Wescott Inc., Cambridge, Mass., 1969-70; pres. Princeton Assos. Inc., Buckingham, Pa., 1976—; grad. asst. Dale Carnegie Courses; guest lectr. Grad. Sch. Mgmt., New Sch. for Social Research. Co-chmn. indsl. div. United Community Fund, Carlisle, Pa., 1963; ruling elder Doylestown Presbyterian Ch. Mem. Am. Chem. Soc., Am. Vacuum Soc., Armed Forces Communications and Electronics Assn., Am. Mgmt. Assn., Product Devel. and Mgmt. Assn., Indsl. Mgmt. Club, Kappa Sigma Alumni Corp. (chpt. pres.). Club: Exchange (bd. control 1960-64) (Carlisle). Research and devel. fundamental analytical thinking processes relative to change; patentee, author articles in field. Home: RD 4 Doylestown PA 18901 Office: PO Box 820 Buckingham PA 18912

ALTMAN, ALLAN, lawyer; b. Holyoke, Mass., Sept. 4, 1929; s. Leo and Elsie Eleanor (Siegel) A.; A.B., Bklyn. Coll., 1951; LL.B., Bklyn. Law Sch., 1956; m. Marcia Ann Edelman, Dec. 6, 1959; children—Steven Lawrence, Michael Jay. Asst. mng. clk. Messrs. Cravath, Swaine & Moore, N.Y.C., 1953-56; admitted to N.Y. bar, 1957, since practiced in N.Y.C.; asso. firm Henry F. Dressel, Esq., 1957-65; partner Dressel & Altman, 1965—. Trustee, Temple Beth Elohim. Served with USMC, 1951-53. Mem. Assn. Bar City N.Y., N.Y. County Lawyers Assn., Am., N.Y. bar assns. Home: 19 Faulkner Ln Dix Hills NY 11746 Office: 150 Broadway New York City NY 10038

ALTMAN, DON JOHN, accountant; b. Brookville, Pa., May 12, 1941; s. Arthur L. and Edith M. (Diegel) A.; B.S., Clarion State Coll., 1969; m. Isadora T. Shupack, Nov. 25, 1972; children—Dawn Jo, Dennis Shupack. Staff accountant Price Waterhouse Co., N.Y.C., 1969-72; div. controller Gulf & Western Industries, N.Y.C., 1972-73; corp. fin. mgr. Black Clawson Co., N.Y.C., 1973-76; pvt. practice accounting Don J. Altman, C.P.A., Brookville, 1976—; dir. H & H Hauling, Inc. Bd. dirs. Brookville Ambulance Service, 1976—; mem. Brookville Area High Sch. Bd. Served with U.S. Army, 1964-66. C.P.A., N.Y. State, Pa. Mem. Am., Pa. insts. C.P.A.'s, N.Y. Soc. C.P.A.'s. Clubs: Pinecrest Country (dir. 1976-80, sec.-treas. 1978—). Home: 54 Jenks St Brookville PA 15825 Office: 100 Franklin Ave Brookville PA 15825

ALTSCHUL, CRAIG ALAN, public relations and advt. co. exec.; b. Los Angeles, Apr. 22, 1941; s. John Lewis and Dorothy Gladys (Jacobsen) A.; A.A. in Journalism, Los Angeles Valley Coll., 1961; B.A. in Journalism, Calif. State U., Northridge, 1964; m. Peggy F. Simmons; 1 dau., Kimberly Ann. News editor Chronicle newspaper, Simi Valley, Calif., 1964-66; dir. pub. relations YMCA of Conejo Valley, Calif., 1966-67; asso. exec. dir. East Valley YMCA, Los Angeles, 1967-69; asst. dir. and dir. pub. relations YMCA of Met. Los Angeles, 1969-72; exec. dir. pub. relations Nat. Council YMCA's in U.S., N.Y.C., 1972-75; pres. Craig A. Altschul & Assos., New Haven, 1975—; writer syndicated column Ski Tips, 1968—. Mem. met. bd. dirs. YMCA Greater New Haven. Recipient award for communications excellence So. Calif. Indsl. Editors Assn., 1970, Thompson trophy Studio City Rotary Club, 1968, writing award Ski Industries Am., 1976. Mem. U.S. Ski Writers Assn., Assn. Profl. YMCA Dirs. U.S., Hotel Sales and Mktg. Assn., Sigma Delta Chi. Republican. Author: A Bunny's Guide to Skiing, 1971. Editor: Perspective jour. Contbr. articles to nat. mags. Office: 81-89 Church St New Haven CT 06510

ALTSCHULER, BRUCE CHARLES, investment co. exec.; b. Hackensack, N.J., May 6, 1946; s. Robert Alexander and Adelaide Stoutenburgh (Raynolds) A.; B.S. (Nat. Coll. Athletic Assn. scholar), U. Wyo., 1969; m. J. Angela Baines, June 4, 1977; stepchildren—Timothy B. Webb, Kelly A. Webb. Mgmt. trainee Comml. Trust Co. of N.J., Jersey City, 1969-70; municipal investment officer United Jersey Bank, Hackensack, 1970-76; v.p. John J. Ryan & Co., W. Orange, N.J., 1976—. Served with Army N.G., 1966. Mem. Bond Club N.J., Kappa Sigma. Presbyterian. Home: 268 Sollas Ct Ridgewood NJ 07450 Office: 80 Main St West Orange NJ 07052

ALTY, CHARLES MAYHEW, bus. exec.; b. Fall River, Mass., Jan. 23, 1940; s. Charles M. and Doris F. Alty; B.S., Southeastern Mass. U., 1961; M.B.A., St. John's U., 1965; Ph.D., Am. U., 1974; m. Antoinette Parent, Mar. 11, 1960; children—Charles Gregory, Jeffrey Scott, Jonathan Charles, Jenifer Ann. Mem. employee relations staff Babcock & Wilcox Co., N.Y.C., 1961-63; asso. Booz, Allen & Hamilton, N.Y.C., 1963-67; asso. prof. Lynchburg Coll., 1967-74; pres. Alty Assos./Corp. Performance Services; owner Venture Capital of Lynchburg, Inc., 1971—; exec. v.p., gen. mgr. Meredith/Burda, Lynchburg, 1979—. Episcopalian. Home: 2324 Indian Hill Rd Lynchburg VA 24503 Office: PO Box 11829 Lynchburg VA 24506

ALVES, MANUEL JOHN, mgmt. cons.; b. Lowell, Mass., Aug. 24, 1929; s. Manuel John and Mary C. (Freitas) A.; B.S., U. Dayton, 1955; M.B.A., Ind. U., 1956; m. Nancy E. Frueh, June 9, 1956; children—David, Julia. Corp. personnel mgr. Owens-Corning Fiberglas Corp., Toledo, 1956-69; mgr. Deliotte Haskins & Sells, Chgo., 1969-76; pres. Alves-Hill & Assos., Inc., Oak Brook, Ill., 1976—, dir., 1979—; dir. Romer Investments; partner HRA Partners; v.p., dir. Mgmt. Edn. Research Corp. Bd. dirs., alumni exec. council Ind. U. Sch. Bus., 1958—; adviser exec. devel. program Ind. U., 1979—. Served with USN, 1947-50. Named Outstanding Salesman, Mktg. and Sales Execs. Club, Toledo, 1966. Mem. Indsl. Relations Assn. Chgo., Chgo. Orgn. Devel. Assn., Ill. Mgmt. and Exec. Search Cons., Ind. Soc. Chgo., Ind. U. Alumni Assn., Chgo. Assn. Commerce and Industry, Sigma Iota Epsilon. Republican. Roman Catholic. Clubs: Union League, Naperville Country (v.p.), Toledo, Plaza. Home: 1511 Coral Berry Ln Downers Grove IL 60515 Office: Suite 1110 1301 W 22d St Oak Brook IL 60521

ALVINE, ROBERT, chem. rubber mfg. co. exec.; b. Newark, Aug. 25, 1938; s. James C. and Marie A.; B.S., Rutgers U., 1960; postgrad. Harvard Bus. Sch., 1972; m. Diane C. Marzulli, May 6, 1961; children—Robert James, Laurie Anne. With Celanese Corp., 1960-77, product mgr. Celanese Plastics Co., Newark, 1969-72, mktg. mgr. Celanese Piping Systems, Hilliard, Ohio, 1972-75, v.p. comml. Celanese Polymer Spltys. Co., Louisville, 1975-77; dir. strategy planning and bus. devel. Uniroyal, Naugatuck, Conn., 1977—, v.p. corp. planning and devel., Middlebury, Conn., 1978—; v.p., gen. mgr. Uniroyal Tire Co., 1979—; pres. Uniroyal Devel. Co., 1980—. Served with AUS, 1962-68. Mem. Am. Inst. Mgmt., Nat. Planning Execs. Inst., Soc. Plastics Industry, Soc. Plastics Engrs., Mfg. Chemists Assn., Rubber Mfrs. Assn., Comml. Devel. Assn., Nat. Paint and Coatings Assn., Hon. Order Ky. Cols. Mem. Ch. of Christ. Home: 55 N Racebrook Rd Woodbridge CT 06525 Office: Uniroyal Benson Rd Middlebury CT 06749

ALVORD, JOEL BARNES, banker; b. Manchester, Conn., Nov. 29, 1938; s. Martin Earl and Elizabeth (Barnes) A.; A.B., Dartmouth Coll., 1960, M.B.A., 1961; m. Anne Stilson, June 23, 1962; children—Sarah, Seth. With Hartford Nat. Bank & Trust Co. (Conn.), 1963—, v.p., 1968-71, sr. v.p.-investments, 1971-75, sr. v.p. and div. mgr.-investments, 1971-75, exec. v.p.-investments, 1976-78, pres., dir., 1978—, exec. v.p. Hartford Nat. Corp., 1976—; dir. Hartford Steam Boiler Inspection & Ins. Co., Bristol Press Pub. Co. Bd. dirs. Inst. of Living; trustee Loomis Chaffee Sch. Served with Ordnance Corps, U.S. Army, 1961-62. Mem. Res. City Bankers Assn. Congregationalist. Office: 777 Main St Hartford CT 06115

AMADOR, VICTOR JOHN, mfg. co. exec.; b. Bklyn., July 7, 1928; s. Victor John and Mary V. (Semerena) A.; B.S.E.E., Newark Coll. of Engring., 1955; m. Theresa Rackett, Sept. 23, 1950; children—Claudia (Mrs. Douglas Wright), Cindy, Peter. Gen. mgr. Plessey Inc., Bronx, N.Y., 1962-66; v.p., gen. mgr. McDonald div. BSR Ltd., Blauvelt, N.Y., 1966-72, pres. consumer group, 1974—; pres. Acoustic Research div. Teledyne Inc., mfr. high fidelity equipment, Norwood, Mass., 1972-74. Served with AUS, 1946-48, 50-51; ETO. Mem. Audio Engring. Soc., Inst. High Fidelity (dir.), Norwood C. of C., A.I.M. (pres.'s council). Democrat. Roman Catholic. Home: 10 Patriots Trail Totowa NJ 07512 Office: BSR (USA) Ltd Rt 303 Blauvelt NY 10913

AMBROSE, JAMES PAUL, fin. planner; b. Ft. Lauderdale, Fla., Jan. 23, 1938; s. Paul Crumbly and Effie Valerie (Cheek) A.; B.S., Fla. So. Coll., 1960; m. Judith Ann Shannon, Apr. 17, 1965; children—Sheryl Ann, James Paul. Account exec. Reynolds Securities Inc., Ft. Lauderdale, 1965-75, mgr. investment planning, 1975-76, v.p. sales, 1976-77, v.p. investments, 1978—; tchr. investments and fin. Broward County (Fla.) Sch. System, 1965—; fin.

columnist E. Broward Tribune, 1966—, Hi-Rise Mag., 1969—; panel mem. Ft. Lauderdale News & Sun Sentinel Investment Forum, 1971-72; mem. Investors Info. Com. Greater Ft. Lauderdale, 1971-73; gen. info. coordinator N.Y. Stock Exchange. Mem. adv. com. for securities and investing Broward County (Fla.) Sch. System, 1977—. Served with U.S. Army, 1961-63. Cert. tchr., Fla.; cert. fin. planner; registered mgr., N.Y. Stock Exchange. Mem. Assn. Investment Brokers, Internat. Assn. Fin. Planners, Inst. Cert. Fin. Planners, Greater Miami Stockbrokers Soc., Delta Sigma Pi, Tau Kappa Epsilon. Republican. Methodist. Clubs: Masons, Shriners. Contbr. articles to profl. jours. Home: 5241 NE 17th Ave Fort Lauderdale FL 33334 Office: 3535 Galt Ocean Dr Fort Lauderdale FL 33308

AMBROSE, JERE BRITTON, engr., inventor, automobile industry products mfg. co. exec.; b. Detroit, Mar. 6, 1939; s. Richard Wright and Mary (Van Allsburg) A.; B.S., Trinity U., 1961; m. Norma Jean Nicol, Sept. 8, 1961; children—Joe, Nicole, Richard. Sales engr. No. Fibre Products Co., Holland, Mich., 1961-64, sales mgr., Birmingham, Mich., 1964-66, v.p., 1966-73, exec. v.p., 1973-79, pres., 1979—; dir. 1st Mich. Bank, Zealand, 1980—. Served with U.S. Army, 1962. Recipient Ray S. Erlandson award. Republican. Presbyterian. Patentee in field. Home: 5645 Lakeshore Dr Holland MI 48423 Office: 50 W 3d St Holland MI 49423

AMBROSON, SARA LAURETTA HENRIETTA, banker; b. Charlson, N.D., Apr. 18, 1920; d. Halvor and Sara (Huglen) Ambroson; grad. high sch. Planimeter and calculator operator McKenzie County Agrl. Soil Conservation Service office, Watford City, N.D., 1939-41; clerk McKenzie County War Price and Rationing Bd., Watford City, 1942-43, chief clerk, 1944-45; bookkeeper, clerk-buyer Forest City (Iowa) Hardware, 1946-53; teller Forest City Bank & Trust Co., 1954-66, asst. cashier, 1967—; mayor Leland, Iowa, 1954-57. Mem. Young Peoples Luther League (tour mgr. 1955-57), Luth. Daus. of Reformation. Lutheran (sec., treas. congregation 1969—). Home: 505 S Clark St Forest City IA 50436 Office: PO Box 290 Forest City IA 50436

AMELANG, KARL JOHN, investment builder; b. Houston, Nov. 7, 1933; s. Karl Henry and Olga (Sweda) A.; B.S. in Mech. Engring. (Alpha Tau Omega scholar 1956-57), U. Tex., Austin, 1958; M.B.A. (Herbert Hoover fellow 1958-59), Stanford, 1960; m. Julia Montgomery, Sept. 4, 1957; children—Karl Andrew, Julia Robbins, Kathleen Adele. Asst. to pres. Scurlock Oil Co., Houston, 1960-64; project mgr. Gerald D. Hines Interests, Houston, 1965; partner Amelang/Gilchrist Investment Builders, Houston, 1966—. Vice pres. Houston Met. YMCA, chmn. internat. com.; v.p. Assn. for Community TV, Sta. KUHT. Served with U.S. Army, 1953-55. Methodist Clubs: Houstonian, Univ., Houston. Home: 35 Stillforest St Houston TX 77024 Office: 8868 Interchange Dr Houston TX 77054

AMELIA, THOMAS BAYARD, r.r. and leasing co. exec.; b. Balt., May 5, 1942; s. J. Donald and Elva N. Amelia; A.A., U. Balt., 1964, B.S., 1967; m. Elizabeth Jean Braden, June 6, 1964; children—Elizabeth Jean Kathleen Corrigan. Account mgr. IBM, Balt., 1967-75, product mgr., Washington, 1975-77; area dir. rail div. Itel Corp., Atlanta, 1977; v.p. Atlantic & Western Fin. Corp., Sanford, N.C., 1978—, Atlantic & Western Ry. Co., Sanford, 1978—. Mem. Data Processing Mgmt. Assn., Nat. Assn. Shippers Adv. Bds., Am. Short Line R.R. Assn., Assn. Am. R.R.'s, Car Officers Assn. Republican. Episcopalian. Clubs: Carolina Trace Country, Sherwood Forest, W. Lake Valley, Advocate of Balt. (dir. 1969-77). Home: 1626 Briarcliffe Dr Sanford NC 27330 Office: 317 Chatham St Sanford NC 27330

AMES, FRANCES JOHNSON, tax cons.; b. Bklyn., Apr. 14, 1923; d. Karl DeWitt and Gertrude Frances (Lehrfeld) Johnson; A.B., Bryn Mawr Coll., 1944, M.A., 1948; postgrad. in social work, Columbia U., 1963-64; 1 dau., Elizabeth Freeman. Fgn. econ. analyst Standard Oil Co. (N.J.), 1948-56; asst. mgr. H & R. Block, Montclair, N.J., 1975; partner Kirwin Assos., 1976-78; ind. tax cons., Roseland, N.J., 1978—. Chmn., Citizens Community Needs Study, Montclair, N.J., 1960-61; bd. dirs., sec. United Community Services of North Essex, 1961-68; trustee Montclair Kimberley Acad., 1975—. Mem. Nat. Assn. Enrolled Agts. Mem. United Ch. of Christ. Club: Montclair Golf. Home and Office: 28 Minnisink Dr Roseland NJ 07068

AMES, OAKES, glass co. exec.; b. Boston, Sept. 21, 1926; s. Oakes Ingalls and Harriet H. (Hatch) A.; A.B., Harvard U., 1947, M.B.A., 1949; m. Dorothy Cooper, Apr. 19, 1952; children—Oakes I., Anne, Pennel. Various positions Corning Glass Works (N.Y.), 1949-64, v.p., gen. mgr. TV products div., 1965-69, v.p., controller, 1969-77; chmn., mng. dir. Corning Ltd., Washington, Tyne and Wear, Eng., 1977—. Bd. dirs. Corning Hosp., 1966-77, pres. bd., 1972-75. Served with USAAF, 1945. Office: Corning Ltd Parsons Indsl Estates Washington Tyne and Wear England

AMIDON, PAUL CHARLES, pub. co. exec.; b. St. Paul, July 23, 1932; s. Paul Samuel and Eleanor Ruth (Sons) A; B.A., U. Minn., 1954; m. Patricia Jean Winjum, May 7, 1960; children—Karen, Michael, Susan. Bus. mgr. Paul S. Amidon & Assos., Inc., Mpls., 1956-66, pres., 1966—. Served with AUS, 1954-56. Home: 1582 Hillcrest Ave St Paul MN 55116 Office: 1966 Benson Ave St Paul MN 55116

AMISS, ROBERT THOMAS, transp. co. exec., bus. cons.; b. Malden, Mass., Sept. 27, 1927; s. Eugene Lorenzo and Margaret (Broderick) A.; student U. Hawaii, 1946; A.B., Tufts U., 1954; M.B.A., U. R.I., 1965; m. Catherine Elizabeth McDermott, Mar. 2, 1949; children—Catherine M. Amiss Bramley, Barbara J. Amiss Hagerty, Roberta A. Mgmt. trainee Mut. of N.Y., 1954-56; various positions Gibson Inc., Cin., 1956-67; pres., treas. Vinyl Packaging, Inc., Pawtucket, R.I., 1967-75, Plastic Devel. Inc., Providence, 1972-75; pres., chmn. bd., chief exec. officer B.J.T. Transport, Inc., Riverside, R.I., 1975—, also dir. Mem. U. R.I. Pres.'s Club; Served with Submarine Service, USN, 1944-48. Mem. Am. Trucking Assn., R.I. Truck Owners Assn., Submarine Vets. World War II, DAV. Clubs: U. R.I. Alumni, Pres.'s, Tufts of R.I. Roman Catholic. Contbr. articles to profl. jours. Home: 47 Timberland Dr Riverside RI 02915 Office: PO Box 4485 East Providence RI 02915

AMMERMAN, DAN SHERIDAN, electronic media tng. sch. exec.; b. Tyrone, Pa., June 10, 1932; s. Eugene Harry and Helen L. (Morrow) A.; m. Mary T. Graca, Jan. 10, 1953; children—Terri L., Mark Alan. Broadcast journalist Sta. WVAM, Altoona, Pa., 1950-59, Sta. KGNC-AM-TV, Amarillo, Tex., 1959-66, Sta. KTRH, Houston, 1966-67; contbg. corr. CBS Radio Network, 1967-68; anchorman KTRK-TV, Houston, 1968-72; with ABC Radio Network, 1972-73; founder, pres. Ammerman Enterprises Inc., Houston, 1973—. Served to 2d lt. U.S. Army, 1947-52; Korea. Named Big Bro. of Yr., Amarillo, 1965. Mem. Pub. Relations Soc. Am. (Tex. dir.), Radio and TV News Dirs. Assn. Republican. Roman Catholic. Clubs: Press, Sugar Creek Country (Houston). Home: 11715 Dorrance Ln Stafford TX 77477 Office: Ammerman Enterprises Inc 8323 SW Freeway Suite 920 Houston TX 77074

AMMIDON, HOYT, banker; b. Balt., June 30, 1909; s. Daniel Clark and Estelle H. (Hoyt) A.; B.A., Yale U., 1932; LL.D., Hofstra U., 1968; m. Elizabeth MacI. K. Callaway, May 19, 1933; children—Hoyt, Lee Ammidon Thorne. With Central Hanover Bank & Trust Co. (now Mfrs. Hanover Trust Co.), 1932-52, asst. sec., 1937-43, asst. v.p., 1943-50, v.p., 1950-52; chief exec. Office of Vincent Astor, 1953-57; chmn. bd. Public Sq. Inc., 1955-57; pres., dir., chmn. exec. com. U.S. Trust Co. of N.Y., 1958-61, chmn. bd., chief exec. officer, 1962-70, chmn. bd., 1970-74; dir., mem. fin. com. Am. Express Co., Am. Express Internat. Banking Corp.; vice chmn., dir. G.T. Investment Fund; chmn. bd. Westamerica Properties, S.A.; dir. Pacific Gen. Devel. Co., Fireman's Fund Am. Life Ins. Co., Fireman's Fund Ins. Co., Bullock Fund, Ltd., Carriers & Gen. Corp., Dividend Shares, Inc., High Income Shares, Inc., Monthly Income Shares, Inc., Nation-Wide Securities Co., Ltd., Howard Johnson Co.; dir., mem. exec. com. Gt. No. Nekossa Corp., Nypen Co., Inc.; trustee Greenwich Savs. Bank, also mem. securities com., exec. com.; hon. trustee U.S. Trust Co. N.Y.; mem. adv. council N.Y. chpt. Am. Inst. Banking, 1959-74; mem. clearing house com. N.Y. Clearing House Assn., 1971-74. Mem. nat. businessmen's com. A Better Chance, 1969-73; trustee, v.p. Vincent Astor Found., 1953-58; bd. dirs. N.Y. div. Am. Cancer Soc., 1969-73; bd. govs. N.Y. Coll. Osteo. Medicine; mem. Council Fgn. Relations Inc., 1961-79, Econ. Devel. Council N.Y.C., Inc.; chmn. Lincoln Center Fund; bd. dirs. Lincoln Center for the Performing Arts, Inc.; bd. dirs. Music Theater of Lincoln Center, Inc., 1963-71, chmn., 1963-68; mem. nat. emergency com. Nat. Council on Crime, 1967-70; mem. adv. council N.Y. Pub. Library, 1958-72; mem. Republican Nat. Finance Com., 1969-73; trustee emeritus Am. Acad. Rome; founding mem., trustee Bus. Com. for the Arts, Inc., treas., 1970-73; trustee emeritus Cooper Union for Advancement of Sci. and Art, 1964-72; trustee The Loomis Sch.; pres., bd. dirs. Am. Ditchley Adv. Council of The Ditchley Found., Whaling Museum Soc., Inc. Served as lt. USCGR, 1942-45. Decorated grand ofcl. Order of the Crown of Italy; Fundacion Internacional Eloy Alfaro (Panama); officer Am. Soc. Most Venerable Order of Hosp. of St. John Jerusalem, 1975; hon. comdr. Order Brit. Empire, 1976; recipient medal of Merit, St. Nicholas Soc. N.Y.C., 1969; Gold medal St. Paul's Cathedral, London; Distinguished Service award Loomis-Chaffee Sch., 1974. Fellow Pierpont Morgan Library, 1960-74; mem. Marine Hist. Assn. (adv. com.), Assn. Internat. Anciens Roseens, Cruising Club Am., France-Am. Soc., Grad. Club Assn., Nat. Golf Links Am., Pilgrims in U.S., Soc. Colonial Wars, Soc. Mayflower Descs., U.S. Sr. Golf Assn., Chi Psi. Clubs: Econ. N.Y., Yale Elihu (grad. pres. 1958-60), Links, Piping Rock, River; Royal and Ancient Golf Club of St. Andrews (Scotland); Jupiter Island; St. Nicholas Hockey. Home: 11 Chicken Valley Rd Old Brookville Glen Head NY 11545 Office: 45 Wall St New York NY 10005

AMMON-WEXLER, JILL DIANE, bus. writer, cons.; b. Highland Park, Mich., Dec. 19, 1939; d. Bernard Andrew and Dorothea Clarissa (Ammon) Wechsler; A.A., San Jose Jr. Coll., 1961; B.A., Calif. State U., 1966, M.A., 1969. Advt. prodn. coordinator Long Advt. Co., San Jose, Calif., 1960-62; research asso. Sylvania Electronic Def. Labs., Mountain View, Calif., 1962-64; pub./communications cons., San Francisco, 1964-73; founder, program dir. Human Dynamics Workshop, Boulder Creek, Calif., 1969-72; communications dept. mgr. GTE/Novar Corp., Mountain View, 1970-71; dir. new bus. Mgmt. Systems Assos., San Jose, 1973-74; pres. Mercury Communications Corp., Santa Cruz, Calif., 1974-79, chmn. bd., 1974-77; cons. to corps. Author: How to Create a Winning Proposal; Info-Sources Directory; Getting Your Share of the R & D Funds; Energy-Info Directory; contbr. articles to profl. jours. Home: PO Box 966 Felton CA 95018

AMODIO, JOSEPH JOHN, JR., info. systems analyst; b. Trenton, N.J., Sept. 1, 1947; s. Joseph John and Lillian Marie (Barricelli) A.; B.S., U. Nev., 1973. Asst. controller Ewell div. Gulstream Land & Devel. Co., Lakeland, Fla., 1973-75; internal auditor Jim Walter Corp., Tampa, 1975; accountant Harper, Van Scoik & Co. C.P.A.'s, Clearwater, Fla., 1975-77; partner Profl. Analytic Service, Clearwater, 1977-79; controller Dick Mills div. Airtron Inc., 1978-80; group controller Fla. Group, Airtron Inc. div. ARCO, 1980—; fin. and communication analyst Video Prodn. Assos. and Diagnostic Clinic, Trenton, N.J., 1971-73. Treas., Nye Hall Assos., 1972-73. Served with AUS, 1966-68. C.P.A., Fla. Mem. Am. Inst. C.P.A.'s, Fla. Inst. C.P.A.'s (com. on mems. industry and govt.), Internal Audit Assn., Nat. Assn. Accountants, Am. Mgmt. Assn. Republican. Roman Catholic. Home: 365-2 114th Ave N Saint Petersburg FL 33702 Office: PO Box 5286 Clearwater FL 33517

AMORUSO, VICTOR ANTHONY, banker; b. Bronx, N.Y., Apr. 27, 1945; s. Anthony Joseph and Marge (D'Esposito) A.; A.B.A., Suffolk Community Coll., 1974; B.B.A., Dowling Coll., 1976; m. Shawn E. McLaughlin, Feb. 19, 1966; children—Victor Anthony, Donna Marie, William Michael, Denise, Melissa. Investment asst. Bank of N.Y., N.Y.C., 1968-73; investment officer Chem. Bank, N.Y.C., 1973-76; asst. v.p. Australia and N.Z. Banking Group, Ltd., N.Y.C., 1976—. Mem. Selden (N.Y.) Vol. Fire Dept., 1969-75, treas., 1973-74; mem. exec. bd. Patchogue (N.Y.) Regional Cath. Sch., 1979—. Served with USN, 1963-65. Republican. Club: World Trade (N.Y.C.). Home: 71 Inwood Ave Selden NY 11784 Office: 63 Wall St New York NY 10005

AMOS, JOHN BEVERLY, ins. co. exec.; b. Enterprise, Ala., June 5, 1924; s. John Shelby and Mary Helen (Mullins) A.; B.A., U. Miami (Fla.), 1944; J.D., U. Fla., 1949; m. Elena Maria Diaz-Verson, Sept. 23, 1945; children—John Shelby, Maria Theresa. Admitted to Fla. bar, 1949; founder, editor Jay Tribune, weekly newspaper, Santa Rosa County, Fla., 1938-42; individual practice law, Ft. Walton Beach, Fla., 1949-55; owner, operator, founder Am. Family Life Assurance Co., Columbus, Ga., 1955—; chmn., chief exec. officer Am. Family Corp., 1972—. Trustee Morris Brown Coll.; mem. Ga. Properties Commn.; mem. nat. com. Nat. Museum Jewish History, Phila.; mem. exec. com. Hubert H. Humphrey Inst., Mpls.; mem. exec. com. Democratic Nat. Com. Mem. Nat. Assn. Life Cos. (v.p.), Fla. Bar Assn. Episcopalian. Clubs: Met. (N.Y.C.); Big Eddy and Harmony (Columbus). Home: 3952 Steam Mill Rd Columbus GA 31907 Office: 1932 Wynnton Rd Columbus GA 31999

AMSBAUGH, JEFFRY KENT, oil co. exec.; b. York, Pa., Aug. 31, 1941; s. Carroll Miller and Kathryn Louise (Wilhelm) A.; Asso. Sci., York Coll., 1962; B.S., Pa. State U., 1964, M.S., 1966. Mgr. computer ops. Sun Oil Co., Phila., 1964-70, mgr. resources and standards Sun Services Co., St. Davids, Pa., 1970-72, various fin. positions Sun Oil Co. (Pa.), Tulsa, 1972-74, sec., treas. Sun Oil Co. (Del.), Dallas, 1974-76, chief fin. officer Suntech. Inc., Valley Forge, Pa., 1976-80, v.p. Sun Ocean Ventures, 1980—, also dir., dir. ops. planning Sun Co., 1977—; pres. Ocean Mining Assos., 1981—, also dir.; dir. Sun Calvert Co., Calvert Geothermal Co., Aquaprawns; asst. prof. diagnostic radiology Hahnemann Med. Sch., 1972—. Mem. Assn. for Computing Machinery, Am. Mgmt. Assn., Soc. Petroleum Accountants. Author: Fortran as a Data Processing Language, 1966. Home: 205 Garden Pl Radnor PA 19087 Office: Gloucester Point VA 23002

AMUNDSON, DUANE MELVIN, gas co. exec.; b. Niagara, Wis., Apr. 3, 1925; s. Melvin Oscar and Thalia (McSweeny) A.; B.S. in Civil Engring., Purdue U., 1950; m. Marian Force, Nov. 21, 1948; children—Melvin, Robert, Jeffrey, Kimberly. With Ind. Gas Co., Inc., Indpls., 1950—, v.p. ops.-engring., 1963-74, sr. v.p. ops.-engring., 1974-77, exec. v.p., 1977-78, pres., chief exec. officer, 1980—, also dir.; pres., chief exec. officer, dir. Ohio River Gas Co., Ohio River Pipeline Corp. Served with USNR, 1943-46, 51-52. Mem. Nat., Ind. socs. profl. engrs., Am., Ind. gas assns. Mason, Lion, Elk. Home: 19720 Allisonville Ave Noblesville IN 46060 Office: 1630 N Meridian St Indianapolis IN 46202

ANDERS, HOWARD GARY, mfg. co. fin. exec.; b. N.Y.C., July 16, 1943; s. Morris and Dora (Krell) A.; B.A., Rutgers U., 1965; postgrad. Bernard Baruch Sch. Bus. and Public Adminstrn., 1966-68, Program Mgmt. Devel., Bus. Sch., Harvard U., 1979; m. Joan Florence Lewis, Apr. 9, 1967; children—David, James. Credit analyst Dun & Bradstreet, N.Y.C., 1965-67; asst. credit mgr. Lesney Prodn. Corp., N.Y.C., 1967-70; with Am. Can Co., Greenwich, Conn., 1970—, treas.'s dept., 1970-73, exec. dir. Am. Can Co. Found., 1973-77, mem. exec. com., bd. dirs. found., 1973—, dir. corp. program control, tech. and devel., 1977-79, dir. bus. resources Am. Can Internat., 1979—; guest lectr. Smithsonian Inst., Conn. Coll.; dir. ARLI (Antigua) Ltd. Mem. exec. bd. Heathcote PTA, Scarsdale, N.Y.; mem. Republican Nat. Com. Mem. Soc. Research Adminstrs., Assn. of Polit. Risk Analysts (treas. and sec.). Club: Beach Point. Home: 68 Fayette Rd Scarsdale NY 10583 Office: Am Can Co 75 Holly Hill Ln Greenwich CT 06830

ANDERSEN, DAVID WELDON, transp. co. exec.; b. Storm Lake, Iowa, Mar. 21, 1950; s. Weldon H. and Erma L. (Silver) A.; B.S. in Indsl. Adminstrn., Iowa State U., 1972; m. Jennifer L. Thompson, Aug. 28, 1971; children—Kristian D., Elyse M. Staff asst. Arthur Andersen & Co., Chgo., 1972-74, tax sr., Mpls., 1974-76; tax mgr. Gateway Transp. Co., Inc., La Crosse, Wis., 1976-78, controller, 1978-79; controller, chief fin. officer Renner's Express, Inc., Indpls., 1979—; lectr. acctg. U. Wis., La Crosse, 1977-79; instr. Ind. Central U., 1980. Advisor, Jr. Achievement, 1977-79. C.P.A., Ill. Mem. Am. Inst. C.P.A.'s, Nat. Assn. Accts. (dir., pres. LaCrosse-Winona chpt. 1979-80). Republican. Methodist. Home: 6760 Live Oak Ct Indianapolis IN 46224 Office: 1350 S West St Indianapolis IN 46225

ANDERSEN, GALEN EWOLDT, energy co. exec.; b. Caldwell, Idaho, Sept. 18, 1945; s. Ralph Vigaleous and Phyllis Norene (Ewoldt) A.; B.S., Washington and Lee U., 1967. Accountant, Tex. Gulf Sulpher Corp., N.Y.C., 1970-71; pres. Nokota Co., Bismarck, N.D., 1971—; pres., dir. Nokota Mining Co., Eagle Corp. Mem. exec. com. N.D. Lignite Council. Campaign dir. for candidates U.S. Congress, 1970, lt. gov., 1972. Served to capt. Ordnance Corps, AUS, 1967-69. Mem. AIME, Asian-U.S. Bus. Council, Mining Club N.Y. Office: PO Box 1633 316 N 5th St Bismarck ND 58501

ANDERSEN, HAROLD WAYNE, publishing co. exec.; b. Omaha, July 30, 1923; s. Andrew B. and Grace (Russell) A.; B.S. in Edn., U. Nebr., 1945; m. Marian L. Battey, Apr. 19, 1952; children—David, Nancy. Reporter, Lincoln (Nebr.) Star, 1945-46; with Omaha World-Herald, 1946—, pres., 1966—; dir. Salzburg Seminar in Am. Studies; past chmn. Fed. Res. Bank Kansas City; dir. Raleigh (N.C.) News & Observer Pub. Co., A.P.; chmn. World Press Freedom Com. Pres., Downtown Omaha, Inc.; trustee U. Nebr. Found.; bd. dirs. Newspaper Advt. Bur.; trustee Jr. Achievement Omaha, pres., 1964-65; trustee Freedom of Info. Found. Mem. Council on Fgn. Relations, Am. Newspaper Pubs. Assn. (past chmn.), Omaha C. of C. (v.p. 1964-65, bd. dirs. 1970—), Internat. Fedn. Newspaper Pubs. (past pres.), Phi Beta Kappa, Phi Gamma Delta. Republican. Presbyn. Home: 6545 Prairie Ave Omaha NE 68132 Office: Omaha World-Herald World-Herald Sq Omaha NE 68102

ANDERSEN, HARRY EDWARD, oil equipment co. exec.; b. Omaha, Apr. 25, 1906; s. John Anton and Caroline (Ebbensgaard) A.; student pub. schs. and spl. courses, including Ohio State U., 1957, U. Okla., 1959, Ga. Inst. Tech., 1960; Ph.D. in Bus. Adminstrn., Colo. State Christian Coll., 1972; m. Alma Theora Vawter, June 12, 1931; children—Jeanenne Dee (Mrs. Gaylord Fernstrom) and Maureen Lee (Mrs. Roger Podany) (twins), John Harry. Founder, N.W. Service Sta. Equipment Co., Mpls., 1934, chmn. bd., 1956—; owner Joint Operations Co., Mpls.; dir. Franklin Nat. Bank. Spl. dep. sheriff Hennepin (Minn.) County, 1951—; hon. fire chief Mpls., 1951—; pres. Washington Lake Improvement Assn., 1955. Mem. Shrine Dirs. Assn. (N.W. gov.), Nat. Assn. Oil Equipment Jobbers (pres. 1957-58, dir. 1954-56), C. of C., Upper Midwest Oil Man's Club. Lutheran. Mason (32 deg., K.T., Jester, Shriner). Clubs: Viking; Engineers; Toastmasters; Mpls. Athletic; Golden Valley Golf; Le Mirador Country (Lake Geneva, Switzerland). Home: 2766 W River Pkwy Minneapolis MN 55406 Office: 2520 Nicollet Ave Minneapolis MN 55404

ANDERSEN, KJELL JUNKER, diversified mfg. co. exec.; b. Oslo, Norway, s. Leif J. and Karen (Jurgensen) A.; came to Can., 1953, naturalized, 1962; came to U.S., 1970; Chem. Engr., U. Stockholm, 1951; grad. Toronto U., Can., 1966-68, York U., Can., 1968-69; M.S., Columbia U., 1973; postgrad. Kent State U., 1973-75; m. Elaine Pervin. Various engring. positions in chem. mfg. indsl. firms, Oslo, 1951-53, Toronto, Ont., Can., 1953-62; exec. v.p. Guy-Chart Tools, Ltd., Toronto, 1962-66; divisional controller Reeves Bros., Inc., Toronto, 1966-69, N.Y.C., 1970-72; asst. sec., controller Copperweld Splty. Steel Co., Warren, Ohio, 1972-74; controller Chgo. dist. Youngstown Sheet & Tube Co., East Chicago, Ind., 1974-78; dir. corp. fin. and operational analysis Am. Can Co., Greenwich, Conn., 1978—, asst. corp. controller, 1979—. Chmn., Met. Toronto Young Progressive Conservatives, 1959-61, sr. met. Toronto organizer Progressive Conservative Party, 1961-63; sec. Ont. Progressive Conservative Policy Com., 1962-63; chmn. League of Norsemen, Toronto, 1961-62; chmn. Christ Lutheran Ch., Toronto, 1961-63; sec. Toronto Interethnic Council, 1962-63; bd. dirs. East Ohio Blue Cross, 1972-76; chmn. World Humanist Day, Chgo., 1978; pres. S.W. Conn. UN Assn., 1980. Mem. Inst. Mgmt. Scis., Nat. Assn. Accountants, Fin. Execs. Inst., Soc. Long Range Planning, Planning Execs. Inst., Nat. Assn. Bus. Economists.

ANDERSON, ALAN T., business exec.; b. 1927. pres. Apgar Food Products Co., 1974-79; pres. Patrick Cudahy Inc.; pres., chief operating officer Bluebird Inc., 1979—. Office: Bluebird Inc 2000 Market St Philadelphia PA 19103*

ANDERSON, ALBERT DAVID "PETE", acct.; b. Casper, Wyo., Oct. 12, 1923; s. George and Cora Evelyn (Sheldon) A.; B.S. in Acctg., U. Wyo., 1960; m. Doris Rae Law, June 5, 1954; children—Lori Kay, Thomas David. Div. auditor Mountain States Power Co., Casper, 1949-51; div. office mgr., dist. acct. Seaboard Oil Co., Casper and Powell, Wyo., Billings, Mont., 1951-58; acct. Texaco Inc., Casper, 1958-60; owner, acct. A.D. "Pete" Anderson, Casper, 1960—; sec.-treas. Dix. Distbg. Corp., 1973-77, Bonanza Sirloin Pit, Billings, 1968-76. Served with USN, 1943-45; PTO. Mem. Casper C. of C., Wyo. Public Accts., Nat. Soc. Public Accts., Republican. Presbyterian. Clubs: VFW, Am. Legion, Elks; Paradise Valley

Country (sec.-treas. 1969-79). Home: 1914 Fremont Casper WY 82601 Office: 1634 S Poplar Casper WY 82601

ANDERSON, ARTHUR ROLAND, engring. co. exec.; b. Tacoma, Wash., Mar. 11, 1910; s. Eivind and Aslaug (Axness) A.; B.S., U. Wash., 1934; S.M., Mass. Inst. Tech., 1935, Sc.D., 1938; m. Barbara Hinman Beck, June 5, 1938; children—Martha Anderson Slocumb, Karl, Richard, Elisabeth, Deborah. Mem. staff Mass. Inst. Tech., 1936-38, 39-41; design engr. Klonne Steel Co., Dortmund, Germany, 1938-39; head tech. dept. Cramp Shipyard, U.S. Navy Bur. Ships, Phila., 1941-46; cons. engr., Stamford, Conn., 1946-51; co-founder Concrete Tech. Corp., Tacoma, Wash., 1951—, sr. v.p., 1957—; bd. chmn. ABAM Engrs., Inc., Tacoma, 1951, chmn. bd., 1977—; pres. Anderson Enterprises, Tacoma, 1957—; vis. lectr. U. Wash., 1954-55, now mem. vis. com.; trustee State Mut. Savs. Bank. Mem. public utility bd. City of Tacoma, 1954-69, chmn., 1968-69; mem. collegium Pacific Luth. U.; mem. Wash. Council for Post Secondary Edn. Recipient Lindau medal, 1971; Roger Corbetta award, 1973; Disting. Alumnus, U. Wash., 1980. Mem. ASCE (T.Y. Lin award 1971), ASTM, Soc. Exptl. Stress Analysis, Am. Concrete Inst. (hon., pres., Construction Practice award 1962, Whitney medal 1976, Turner medal 1978), Prestressed Concrete Inst. (hon., pres. 1970, Medal of Honor 1975), Japan Concrete Inst. (hon.), Nat. Acad. Engring., Fedn. Internationale de la Precontrainte, Royal Norwegian Sailing Assn., Sigma Xi, Tau Beta Pi, Chi Epsilon. Republican. Presbyterian. Clubs: Yacht, Kiwanis (pres. 1965), Engrs. (pres. 1963), Tacoma). Tested first prestressed concrete bridge in U.S. Contbr. articles to U.S. and fgn. profl. jours. Patentee in field. Home: 502 Tacoma Ave N Tacoma WA 98403 Office: 1123 Port of Tacoma Rd Tacoma WA 98421

ANDERSON, CAROLE LEWIS, investment banker; b. Stroudsburg, Pa., Oct. 7, 1944; d. William Ashley and Rosamond (Lewis) A.; B.A. in Polit. Sci., Pa. State U., 1966; M.B.A. in Fin., N.Y. U., 1976. Contracts coordinator Black Sivalls & Bryson Ltd., London, 1967-69; dir. franchise devel. Data Power Inc., Boston and N.Y.C., 1970-71; v.p. research Paine Webber Jackson & Curtis, Inc., N.Y.C., 1971-77; v.p. Blyth Eastman Paine Webber, Inc., N.Y.C., 1977—. Vol., Urban Cons. Group, In-Touch Network; bd. dirs. N.Y. U. Mgmt. Decision Stimulation program; polit. intern U.S. Ho. of Reps., 1965; bd. dirs. regional Young Democrats Pa., 1976-77; Dem. committeewoman Manhattan County, 1976—; mem. N.Y. Adv. Com., U.S. Commn. Civil Rights, 1980—. Mem. Fin. Women's Assn. N.Y. (past dir.), N.Y. Soc. Security Analysts, Investment Assn. N.Y., Forum for Women Dirs. (dir.). Club: 7th Regiment Tennis. Home: 679 Madison Ave New York NY 10021 Office: 1221 Ave of the Americas New York NY 10020

ANDERSON, DELFORD LEE, pipeline constrn. co. exec.; b. Barrie, Ont., Can., Apr. 26, 1944; s. Donald Delford and Emma Jean A.; B.B.S., Calif. Western U., 1979; m. Lois Margaret Shenton, Apr. 8, 1971; children—Phillip Delford, Marcus Eric, Charissa Lee. Journeyman lineman No. Can. Power Commn., 1964-65, line foreman, 1965; salesman Federated Life Ins. and Mut. Funds Co., 1967-69; asst. to gen. mgr. B.C. Equipment Co., 1969-71; asst. to woods mgr. Peace Woods Products Co., 1971-75; project adminstr. Leonard Pipeline contractors, Ltd., N. Am., Australia, Indonesia, 1975-78; adminstrv. mgr. Al-Qahtani-Shaw-Leonard, Ltd., Houston, 1978-79; field adminstr. PE Ben Pipelines Ltd., Edmonton, Alta., Can., 1979—; pres. Progene (Cattle) Internat. Ltd. Served with Royal Can. Signal Corps., 1961-64. Home: 9852 Athens Rd SE Calgary AB T2J 1B9 Canada

ANDERSON, DONALD SWAN CONSTANTINE, water co. exec.; b. Los Angeles, May 7, 1901; s. Swan S. and Ida C. (Constantine) A.; A.B. in Chemistry, U. Redlands, 1922; postgrad. chem. engring. Calif. Inst. Tech., 1923; postgrad. U. Calif., 1924, U. Hawaii, 1956; m. Gertrude M. McCunn, Apr. 12, 1930; children—Jean McC., Janet McC. Dep. agr. commr. San Bernardino County, Calif., 1923-26; sec., mgr. Paine Fumigating Co., Redlands, Calif., 1926-46; citrus rancher, cons. entomologist, Redlands, 1946-55; pres. San Bernardino Valley Water Conservation Dist., 1956-76, Bear Valley Mut. Water Co., Redlands, Calif., 1965—; dir. First Am. Title Co., Sunkist Inc. Chmn. county civil service chmmn., 1946-73; life trustee Lincoln Shrine, 1960-76; city councilman, mayor City of Redlands, 1952-56; elder Presbyn. Ch.; mem. county Republican central com., 1938-42; pres. U. Redlands Alumni Assn., 1927-29; pres. U. Redlands Fellows, 1960-62; mem. county Hist. Soc.; bd. dirs., treas. So. Calif. Presbyn. Homes, 1958-74; pres. Redlands Coop. Fruit Assn., 1956-76; bd. dirs., v.p. Redlands Highland Fruit Exchange, 1947-76. Mem. So. Calif. Entomol. Soc., Citrus Adv. Bd. State of Calif., Crafton-Mentone Protective Assn. (sec./mgr. 1928—). Clubs: Fortnightly, Rotary, Masons, Town Hall of Calif. Contbr. publs. local history. Home: 228 Grandview Dr Redlands CA 92373 Office: 101 E Olive Ave Redlands CA 92373

ANDERSON, GARY LEE, state ofcl.; b. Harlan, Iowa, Feb. 3, 1946; s. Lake Nels and Helen Margaret Anderson; A.B., Creighton U., Omaha, 1969; M.P.A., U. Nebr., 1975; m. Jeanne Kwapiszeski, Oct. 15, 1977. Supr., Panganerix, Omaha, 1969-71; asst. adminstr. Doctors' Hosp., Omaha, 1971-73; mem. research team Social Security Adminstrn., Omaha, 1974; dir. Nebr. Dept. Pub. Instns., Lincoln, 1975-80; systems analyst Mut. of Omaha, 1980—. Home: 6006 N 109 Plaza Omaha NE 68164 Office: 33d and Dodge Sts Omaha NE 68131

ANDERSON, GLENN ELWOOD, investment banker; b. Asheville, N.C., July 24, 1914; s. James Garrett and Lottie Lee (Alexander) A.; A.B., Duke U., 1934; m. Grace Elizabeth Curtis, Oct. 10, 1936; children—Glenn Elwood, Charlotte Anderson Straney. With Carolina Securities Corp. (name formerly Kirchofer & Arnold, Inc.), Raleigh, N.C., 1934—, sec., asst. to pres., exec. v.p., 1945-55, pres., 1955—, also dir.; dir. N.C. Natural Gas Corp., Fayetteville, Raleigh, Golden Corral Corp., Raleigh, Mid-South Holding Corp., Raleigh. Past v.p. United Fund Raleigh and Wake County; trustee Rex Hosp., Raleigh, Greensboro (N.C.) Coll.; former mem. ofcl. bd., trustee, chmn. fin. and stewardship commn. Hayes Barton United Meth. Ch., Raleigh. Mem. Nat. Assn. Securities Dealers (gov. 1958-60, chmn. bus. conduct com. 1959, chmn. bd. 1960), Securities Industry Assn. (chmn. Southeastern group 1962, gov. 1967-69), Sigma Phi Epsilon. Clubs: Raleigh-Durham Bond (past pres.), Sphinx (pres. 1965), Carolina Country, Capital City (gov.) (Raleigh). Home: 121 Pasquotank Dr Raleigh NC 27609 Office: PO Box 1071 Raleigh NC 27602

ANDERSON, HARLAN EUGENE, investment co. exec.; b. Freeport, Ill., Oct. 15, 1929; s. Arthur Hewitt and Lydia Amanda (Schroeder) A.; B.S. in Engring. and Physics, U. Ill., 1951, M.S. in Physics, 1952; postgrad. Exec. Devel. Program, Grad. Sch. Bus., Stanford U., summer 1966; m. Lois Jean Kahl, Sept. 16, 1950; children—Brian Arthur, Gregory Scott, Susan Elizabeth. Tech. staff Mass. Inst. Tech., Cambridge, 1952-57; founder, v.p., treas., dir. Digital Equipment Corp., Maynard, Mass., 1957-66; dir. tech. Time, Inc., N.Y.C., 1966-69; gen. partner Anderson Investment Co., New Canaan, Conn., 1969—; pres. New Canaan Inn Inc., 1977—; dir. Adage Inc., Computone Systems Inc., Summagraphics Corp., Pneumo Precision Inc., Termiflex Corp., Conn. Women's Bank, Videochart Corp., Infotecs Corp., Internat. Data Group Inc.; chmn. U.S. Com. for Internat. Computer Congress, Stockholm, 1974, vice chmn., Yugoslavia, 1971; chmn. U.S. Spring Joint Computer Conf., 1966. Mem. U. Ill. Found., 1973—, Pres.'s Club, 1972—, Northwestern U. John Evans Club, 1976—; trustee, treas. New Canaan Library, 1975—; trustee Harlan E. Anderson Found., 1969—, King Sch., 1971-74, A.B.C. Inc. of New Canaan, 1974-78, Norwalk Hosp., 1979—, Rensselaer Poly. Inst., 1980—; membership com. United Way of New Canaan, 1977; deacon Congregational Ch. New Canaan, 1971-74. Mem. Nat. Venture Capital Assn. Republican. Clubs: Woodway Country (Darien); Algonquin (Boston); Hemisphere (N.Y.C.); Landmark (Stamford). Home: 67 Dunning Rd New Canaan CT 06840 Office: 49 Locust Ave New Canaan CT 06840

ANDERSON, JACK GARNER, aerospace co. exec.; b. Memphis, Apr. 21, 1922; s. Wilfred John and Ruth (Garner) A.; B.S. in Chem. Engring., U. Louisville, 1943; B.Sc., USAF Inst. Tech., 1950; m. Patricia Menacher, Dec. 8, 1945; children—Judith, Jack, James, Jerold, Richard, William, Donald, Mark. Served as enlisted man U.S. Army Air Force, 1941-42, commd. lt., 1942, advanced through grades to maj., 1951, ret., 1954; v.p. mktg. Hoffman Electronics Corp., Los Angeles, 1954-60, Gen. Dynamics Electronics, Rochester, N.Y., 1960-61, Kollsman Instrument Corp., Elmhurst, N.Y., 1961-68; pres. Kaman Aerospace Corp., exec. v.p. Kaman Corp., Bloomfield, 1969-72; pres., chief exec. officer, ILC Industries, Inc., Bohemia, N.Y., 1972—, pres., chief exec. officer, chmn. bd. ILC Data Device Corp., Bohemia, 1976—. Fellow Radio Club Am.; mem. Am. Mgmt. Assn., Am. Rocket Soc., Am. Helicopter Soc., Am. Inst. Aeros., Astronautics. Electronics Industries Assn. (dir. govt. dir. 1977—, Nat. Security Indsl. Assn. (v.p. 1972-76), Nat. Aero. Assn. (trustee 1976—), Air Force Assn., Assn. U.S. Army, Armed Forces Communications Electronics Assn., Quarter Century Wireless Assn. (dir.), Nat. Aviation Club, Aviation Hall of Fame (bd. nominations 1967—). Club: Avon (Conn.) Country. Home: 28 Winged Foot Rd Dover DE 19901 Office: PO Box 266 Harrington Rd Frederica DE 19946

ANDERSON, JAMES BLAKELY, JR., mgmt. cons.; b. Jefferson, N.C., Mar. 3, 1942; s. James Blakely and Florence (Wade) A.; B.A., Furman U., 1964; Ph.D., Tulane U., 1969; m. Catherine Abbott, June 3, 1978; stepchildren—David Modrak, Keren Modrak, Raissa Modrak. Bus. mgr. Green River Prodns., Washington, 1971-72; prodn. asst. Surrender at Appomattox, CBS-TV, Hollywood, Calif., 1971; head prodn. Media-8 Prodns., Washington, 1972-73; sr. asso. Robert Ventre Assos., Inc., Bethesda, Md., 1973-77; creator, dir. Tae Kwon Do Is, TV comml., Washington, 1976; dir. communications World Blackbelt League, Washington, 1975-76; dir. internat. mktg. Jhoon Rhee Safety Equipment Co., Washington, 1975-76; dir. Anderson Communications (name changed to Anderson Mgmt. Group, Inc. 1979), Alexandria, Va., 1977-79, Vienna, Va., 1979—, pres., 1979—; founder, partner The Nexus Group, Washington, 1980—. Served from 1st lt. to capt. U.S. Army, 1969-71; Vietnam. Decorated Bronze Star. Mem. Am. Soc. Tng. and Devel., Am. Mgmt. Assn., Nat. Space Inst., AAAS, World Future Soc., Scabbard and Blade, Blue Key, Sigma Xi, Phi Mu Alpha Sinfonia. Composer: Slipping through the Cracks, 1971. Office: 413 Victoria Ct NW Vienna VA 22180

ANDERSON, JAMES KENNY, real estate co. exec.; b. San Rafael, Calif., Aug. 3, 1935; s. Ira John and Margaret (Kenny) A.; B.S. in Elec. Engring. and Math., San Jose State U., 1959; grad. Realtors Inst., U. Hawaii, 1974. Mem. profl. staff Northrop Corp., 1961-64, TRW Systems, 1964-67; mgr. facility Center Advanced Studies, Gen. Electric Co., Pearl Harbor, Hawaii, 1967-71; profl. staff Palisades Geophys Inst. div. Columbia U. Lamont Geol. Obs., 1971, Center Naval Analysis, U. Rochester, 1972-73; salesman/broker Grubb & Ellis Comml. Brokerage Co., Honolulu, 1973-76; prin. broker Cushman & Wakefield Hawaii, Inc., Honolulu, 1977; ind. broker, Honolulu, 1977-78; founder, chief operating officer, chmn. bd. Anderson Enterprises, Honolulu, 1978—; cons. to various fin. instns., developers. Mem. Republican Central Com. Hawaii, 1969-74; bd. dirs. Kaimuki-Waialae YMCA Indian Guide Program, Honolulu, 1975-77, chmn., 1976-77, founder, bd. dirs. Indian Princess Program, 1977-79. Served with U.S. Army, 1959-61. Named Salesman of Yr., Grubb & Ellis, 1975. Mem. Honolulu Bd. Realtors, Hawaii Assn. Realtors, Nat. Assn. Realtors (cert. comml. investment mem.), Realtors Nat. Mktg. Inst. Episcopalian. Clubs: Exchange (dir. 1976-77, Man of Yr. 1977), Honolulu, Outrigger Canoe (chmn. com. bldg. and grounds). Author: Voter Identification Program Manual, 1972; also numerous confidential publs. Office: 900 Fort St Mall Suite 1410 Honolulu HI 96813

ANDERSON, JAMES LEON, mfg. co. exec.; b. Sharon, Pa., June 14, 1933; s. Wilbert Seth and Beatrice Blackburn (Dotson) A.; B.S. in Bus. Adminstrn. cum laude, Youngstown State U., 1960; postgrad. Ohio State U., Kent State U.; M.B.A., Syracuse U.; m. Mary Elizabeth Passerrello, Aug. 31, 1957; children—Bradley J., Gregory L. Accountant, Fuller & Welkers, C.P.A.'s, Youngstown, Ohio, 1959-60; with B.F. Goodrich Co., Akron, Ohio, 1960-69, plant controller, 1966-68; controller Joy Mfg. Co., Claremont, N.H., 1969-72; div. controller Worldwide, Ingersoll Rand Co., Painted Post, N.Y., 1972-80, controller Gas Compressor Group, Houston, 1980—; instr. Pa. State U. Bd. dirs. council Boy Scouts Am., 1972-74; bd. dirs. United Way, 1970-72, campaign chmn., 1978-79. Served with USN, 1952-56. Mem. Corning C. of C., Nat. Assn. Accountants (dir.). Republican. Clubs: Kiwanis, Rotary, Hunting and Fishing. Home: 9523 Arcade Dr Spring TX 77373 Office: West Belt Houston TX 77024

ANDERSON, JAMES OLIVER, retail store exec.; b. Kokomo, Ind., Aug. 30, 1929; s. Oliver C. and Mary L. (Baker) A.; A.S., Vincennes U., 1950; B.S., Denver U., 1957; M.S., Butler U., 1961; postgrad. Ind. U., 1963; m. Charlotte R. Scott, Feb. 25, 1950. Internal auditor, office mgr. L.S. Ayres & Co., Indpls., 1957-61; asst. buyer, then buyer Stix, Baer & Fuller, St. Louis, 1961-62; asst. controller Allied Stores Corp., N.Y.C., 1962-67, corp. controller, 1967-69; v.p. control and fin. The May Co., Cleve., 1969-76; corp. v.p., chief fin. officer Gimbel Bros., Inc., N.Y.C., Pitts., 1976—. Served with USAF, 1951-55. Mem. Pa. Retailers Assn. (chmn., dir.), World Affairs Council Pitts., U.S. C. of C., Nat. Retail Mchts. Assn. Office: 339 6th Ave Pittsburgh PA 15222

ANDERSON, JERRY WILLIAM, JR., mfg. co. exec.; b. Stow, Mass., Jan. 14, 1926; s. Jerry William and Heda Charlotte (Petersen) A.; B.S. in Physics, U. Cin., 1949, Ph.D. in Econs., 1976; M.B.A., Xavier U., 1959; m. Joan Hukill Balyeat, Sept. 13, 1947; children—Katheleen, Diane. Research and test project engr. meteorol. equipment, Wright-Patterson AFB, Ohio, 1949-53; project engr., electronics div. AVCO Corp., Cin., 1953-70, program mgr., 1970-73; program mgr. Cin. Electronics Corp. (successor to electronics div. AVCO Corp.), 1973-78; pres. Anderson Industries Unltd., 1978—; chmn. dept. mgmt. Xavier U., 1980—; lectr. No. Ky. U., 1977-78; tech. adviser Cin. Tech. Coll., 1971—. Mem. Madeira (Ohio) City Planning Commn., 1962—; founder, pres. Grassroots, Inc., 1964; active United Appeal, Heart Fund, Multiple Sclerosis Fund; co-founder, tech. Presbyterian Ch., Cin., 1964. Served with USNR, 1943-46. Named Man of Year, City of Madeira, 1964. Mem. Soc. Non-Destructive Testing, Nat. Wood Carvers Assn., Assn. Energy Engrs. (charter), Am. Legion (past comdr.), Acad. Mgmt., Madeira Civic Assn. (past v.p.), Omicron Delta Epsilon. Republican. Contbr. articles on lasers, infrared detection equipment, air pollution to govt. publs. and profl. jours. Home and Office: 7208 Sycamorehill Ln Cincinnati OH 45243

ANDERSON, JOHN FREDRICK, agribus. exec.; b. Scottsbluff, Nebr., Apr. 12, 1924; s. John Fredrick and Larren (Tison) A.; grad. U. Mo., 1949; m. Phyllis Rose Dye, July 13, 1945; children—Marsha Jo Anderson Swainston, Jeffrey Bryan. Process engr. Consumer Coop. Assn. (co. name changed to Farmland Industries, Inc.), Coffeyville, Kans., 1949-58, supt. Coffeyville refinery, 1958-61, v.p. fertilizer mfg., Kansas City, Mo., 1971-74, exec. v.p. mfg. and prodn., 1974-78, pres., chief exec. officer, 1978—; chief engr. CRA subs. Farmland Industries, Inc., Kansas City, 1961-62, plant supt. Coop. Farm Chems. Assn. subs., Lawrence, Kans., 1962-68, v.p., 1968-71; dir. Commerce Bank, Kansas City. Mem. Clay County Devel. Com.; trustee U. Mo., Kansas City, Midwest Research Inst., Kansas City. Served with AC, U.S. Army, 1942-45. Mem. Am. Inst. Chem. Engrs., Nat. Petroleum Refiners Assn. Kansas City C. of C. (dir.). Office: Farmland Industries Inc 3315 N Oak Trafficway Kansas City MO 64118*

ANDERSON, JOHN NEVEL, mfg. co. exec.; b. Detroit, Aug. 13, 1942; s. Carl E. and Lois E. (Huffstutter) A.; B.S., Southeastern U., 1965; m. Judi R. Henrickson, June 15, 1974; children—Judith Lynn, Janna Renee. Sales rep. Moore Bus. Forms, 1965-66; med. center rep. Roche Labs., Charottesville, Va., 1966-72; with direct sales co., Salem, Va., 1972-75; dist. sales mgr. Soabar, Dallas, 1975-80, gen. sales mgr., Phila., 1980—. Mem. Sales and Mktg. Execs. Dallas (dir. 1979—). Lutheran. Home: 4005 Nicole Dr Hatboro PA 19040 Office: 7722 Dungan Rd Philadelphia PA 19111

ANDERSON, JOHN ROBERT, automobile co. exec.; b. Boston, June 26, 1936; s. Robert Elmer and Alma Evelyn (Webster) A.; A.B., U. S.C., 1958; M.B.A., Stanford, 1963; m. Carole Kilgore, Jan. 5, 1980; children by previous marriage—Robin Evelyn, Douglas Carl, Dana Katharine, Judith Carol. Mgr. facilities dept. Ford Motor Co., Dearborn, Mich., 1969-72, asst. controller, 1972-73, dir. diversified products analysis, 1973-74, asst. treas., 1974-77, dir. fin. ops. planning Office of Pres., 1977-78; pres. Ford Motor Land Devel. Corp., 1978—. Served to lt. USNR, 1961. Republican. Methodist. Clubs: Fairlane, Detroit Yacht. Home: 18171 Dunblaine Ave Birmingham MI 48009 Office: Ford Motor Land Devel Corp One Parklane Blvd Suite 1500E Dearborn MI 48126

ANDERSON, JOHN ROBERT, radio sta. exec.; b. Coopersville, Mich., May 1, 1927; s. Harold E. and Ruth E. (Soderman) A.; student Mich. State U., 1944-45; B.R., Radio Inst. Chgo., 1953; m. Anneliese R. Lorenz, May 23, 1948; 1 dau., Monica A. Announcer, program dir. Sta. WBAT, Marion, Ind., 1950-53; dir. sports and spl. events Sta. WWTV, Cadillac, Mich., 1953-54; sta. mgr. Sta. WPBN-TV, Traverse City, Mich., 1954-60; pres., gen. mgr. Sta. WCCW, Traverse City, 1960—; dir. Empire Nat. Bank. Bd. dirs., pres. Nat. Cherry Festival, 1968, mem. Grand Traverse Republican Com. Served with U.S. Army, 1944-48. Mem. Nat. Assn. Broadcasters (dir. 1974-78), Mich. Assn. Broadcasters (pres. 1973), Mich. C. of C. (dir. 1976—), Traverse City Area C. of C. (pres. 1973, Citizen of Yr. award 1978). Congregationalist. Club: Traverse City Rotary. Home: 7114 Cherrywood Ct Traverse City MI 49684 Office: 346 E State St Traverse City MI 49684

ANDERSON, KARL STEPHEN, newspaper exec.; b. Chgo., Nov. 10, 1933; s. Karl William and Eleanore (Grell) A.; B.S. in Editorial Journalism, U. Ill., 1955; m. Saralee Hegland, Nov. 5, 1977; children by previous marriage—Matthew, Douglas, Eric. Successively advt. mgr., asst. to pub., plant mgr. Pioneer Press, Oak Park and St. Charles, Ill., 1955-71; asst. to pub., then pub. Crescent Newspapers, Downers Grove, Ill., 1971-73; asso. pub. and editor Chronicle Pub. Co., St. Charles, 1973-80; asso. pub. Chgo. Daily Law Bull., 1981— Treas. St. Charles Softball Assn.; mem. St. Charles Econ. Devel. Commn.; mem. bd. Hotel Baker Sr. Living Center, Kane County Republican Central Com. Recipient C.V. Amenoff award dept. journalism No. Ill. U., 1976. Mem. Ill. Press Assn. (Will Loomis award 1977, 80), Nat. Nat. Newspaper Assn., No. Ill. Newspaper Assn., Soc. Profl. Journalists-Sigma Delta Chi, Chi Psi. Clubs: Palisades Park Country, Rotary. Home: 520 S 12th St Saint Charles IL 60174 Office: 415 N State St Chicago IL 60610

ANDERSON, KENNETH WARD, food processing co. exec.; b. Evanston, Ill., Dec. 14, 1931; s. Sydney Clemenson and Grey (Simpson) A.; B.S., Northwestern U., 1953; m. Jean Jensen, Mar. 21, 1953; children—Kenneth Ward, Richard S., Wendy Lynne. Asst. v.p. United Calif. Bank, Los Angeles, 1956-63; v.p. fin. T.I.M.E.-DC, Inc., Lubbock, Tex., 1963-70; sr. v.p. fin. Campbell Taggart, Inc., Dallas, 1970—, also dir.; dir. Offshore Logistics, Inc., Park Cities Bank. Chmn. bd. trustees Am. Bankers Assn. Retirement Plan, 1979-81. Served with AUS, 1953-56. Mem. Fin. Execs. Inst. (1st v.p. Dallas chpt. 1980-81). Club: Bent Tree Country. Home: 6120 Dilbeck St Dallas TX 75240 Office: Campbell Taggart Inc PO Box 222640 Dallas TX 75222

ANDERSON, MARSHALL LEE, exec. search co. exec.; b. Sherman, Tex., July 20, 1942; s. Marshall Elmer and Margaurite Lucille (Ivy) A.; B.B.A., U. Tex., Austin, 1966, M.B.A., 1968; m. Paula Jane Collier, Feb. 25, 1978; 1 son, James Marshall. Cons., Peat Marwick Mitchell & Co., Houston, 1967-70, sr. cons., 1970-71; partner Egan & Anderson, Houston, 1971-73; sr. asso. Korn-Ferry Internat., Houston, 1973-74; v.p. Paul R. Ray & Co., Inc., Ft. Worth, 1974-77; sr. v.p., 1977—. Republican. Baptist. Clubs: Prestonwood Country, City of Dallas, Chapparral. Home: 7631 Cliffbrook Dallas TX 75240 Office: 5383 First Internat Bldg Dallas TX 75270

ANDERSON, PETER SCOTT, data systems co. exec.; b. Cambridge, Mass., Oct. 22, 1942; s. Edwin Julius and Margaret (Doig) A.; student Coll. William and Mary, 1960-61; B.A. cum laude, Boston U., 1964; m. Mary Jeanne McKenna, Aug. 5, 1972; children—Mark Brian, Jonathan Scott. Mktg. rep. IBM Corp., Waltham, Mass., 1964-68, dist. staff, 1968-70; Eastern regional mgr. Raytheon Co., Norwood, Mass., 1970-71, mgr. product mktg., 1971-72; v.p. info. systems div. Bunker Ramo Corp., Trumbull, Conn., 1972-75; gen. mgr. comml. data systems div. Gen. Instrument Corp., N.Y.C., 1975-77, v.p., gen. mgr. bus. systems, 1978-78, v.p. mktg. devel., 1978-79; pres. N.Am. group Mohawk Data Scis. Corp., Parsippany, N.J., 1979—. Mem. Am. Mgmt. Assn. Republican. Episcopalian. Home: 7 Meyersville Rd Chatham Township NJ 07928 Office: 1599 Littleton Rd Parsippany NJ 07054

ANDERSON, PHILIP CARLTON, research co. exec.; b. Lincoln, Nebr., Dec. 12, 1918; s. Carl Louis and Harriet (Barnett) A.; student U. Nebr., 1936-38; m. Norma Gene France, Nov. 4, 1940; children—Mark, Kent, Dale, Sara, Jane, Paul. Pres., founder Feed Service Corp., Crete, Nebr., 1951, Tricarbon Corp., Crete, 1976—. Mem. N.Y. Acad. Sci., Nebr. Acad. Sci., Soc. Applied Spectroscopy, Internat. Platform Assn. Patentee chem. and mech. devices, animal feeding devices. Home: 1225 Jasmine Rd Crete NE 68333 Office: PO Box 242 Crete NE 68333

ANDERSON, PHYLLIS REINHOLD, mgmt. cons.; b. Denver, July 29, 1936; d. Floyd Reinhold and Minerva Eva (Needham) A.; Metall. Engr., Colo. Sch. Mines, 1962; M.B.A., U. Chgo., 1968; children—Kristin Elizabeth, Michele Ann. Mill metallurgist, supr. U.S. Steel Corp., 1962-66; research and devel. sr. metallurgist, supr., planner Continental Can Co., 1966-73; mgr. corp. planning B. F. Goodrich Co., 1973-76; regional asso. Strategic Planning Inst., Cambridge, Mass., 1975-76; project mgr. corp. planning, sales engring., then project mgr. corp. devel. Signode Corp., Glenview, Ill., 1976-80; mgmt. cons., 1974—; pres., prin. cons. Corp. Devel. Assos., Inc., Oak Brook, Ill., 1980—; initial exec. com., chmn. membership com. Strategic Planning Inst., 1975-76; dir. Quest Assos. Mgmt. and Quality Consultants; instr. bus. analysis methods. Active psychiat. support services, career counseling women's groups and individuals. Recipient leadership award Chgo. YWCA, 1977. Mem. Am. Soc. Metals, Soc. Women Engrs., Am. Mktg. Assn., N.Y. Acad. Scis., Women in Mgmt., AAAS, Nat. Assn. Woman Bus. Owners, Mensa. Home: 2201 S Highland Ave Lombard IL 60148 Office: PO Box 946 Oak Brook IL 60521

ANDERSON, RAYMOND QUINTUS, mfg. co. exec.; b. Jamestown, N.Y., Nov. 27, 1930; s. Paul Nathaniel and Cecille (Ogren) A.; B.S. in Engring., Princeton U., 1953; postgrad. Grad. Sch. Indsl. Mgmt., M.I.T., 1954; m. Sondra Rumsey, June 5, 1954; children—Heidi, Kristin, Gerrit, Mitchell, Tracy, Brooks. With Dahlstrom Corp., Jamestown, 1957-76, v.p., 1958-65, exec. v.p., 1965-68, pres., 1968-76; founder, pres. Aarque Steel Corp., 1976-78, Aarque Mgmt. Corp., Jamestown, 1978—; pres. Jamestown Industries, Inc.; chmn. Van Huffel Tube Corp., Kardex Systems, Inc., Jamestown, Furniture Mart, Inc., Lincoln First Bank, N.A. Chmn., Jamestown United Fund dr., 1964, 74. Served to lt. USNR, 1954-57. Mem. Mfrs. Assn. Jamestown Area (pres. 1967—), Empire State C. of C. (pres. 1974—), Tau Beta Pi. Republican. Episcopalian. Clubs: Moon Brook Country (Jamestown); Sportsmen's (Chautauqua, N.Y.); Met., Union League, Buffalo (N.Y.C.). Patentee in field. Home: 65 E Terrace Ave Lakewood NY 14750 Office: 111 W 2d St Jamestown NY 14701

ANDERSON, RICHARD, mining co. exec.; b. Phila., Aug. 24, 1937; s. James Earl and Ellen (Lawson) A.; student Lincoln Law Sch., Sacramento, 1976; A.A., Sacramento City Coll., 1977; student New Coll. Calif. Sch. Law, 1978; B.A., Calif. State U., Hayward, 1979, postgrad. in public adminstrn., 1980—; children by previous marriage—Ashley Benton, Fawhn Lynette. Partner, v.p. Baco Industries, Los Angeles, 1967-70; v.p. Arleo Mfg., Inc., Los Angeles, 1972-73; asst. dir. Los Angeles New Careers Orgn., 1972; pres. Amal. Enterprises, Inc., Beverly Hills, Calif., 1972—, Anderson Devel. Assn., Sacramento, 1970—; dir. Internat. Minority Bus. Seminar, Sacramento, 1972—; employment agt. Gen. Electric Co., Rockville, Md., 1973—; owner Profit Concepts & Systems Design Co., Sacramento, 1974—; exec. v.p. Fawhn Wholesale Distbg. Co., Sacramento, 1974—. Past chmn. exec. bd. small bus. adv. bd. Calif. Senate Select Com. on Small Bus. Enterprises; past cons. to Econ. Devel. Office, U.S. Dept. Justice. Served with USN, 1955-56. Mem. Nat. Lawyers Guild. Democrat. Baptist. Author: (plays) Twenty Fourth Day, 1966; A Thought of My People, 1977; The Strange Land, 1977; (books) Nostalgia, 1977; Sight and Fancy, 1977; Confluence, 1977; Colloquilism, 1977; Mind Poet, 1977; Themes, 1977. Home: 2516 Ivy Dr Oakland CA 94606 Office: PO Box 160213 Sacramento CA 95816

ANDERSON, RICHARD L., retail co. exec.; b. 1935; B.A., Amherst Coll., 1957; married. With F.W. Woolworth Co., N.Y.C., 1958—, asst. to gen. sales mgr. and field personnel dir., 1961-65, v.p. Kinney of Can., 1965-68, v.p. retail Kinney Corp., 1968-75, pres. Kinney Shoe Corp., 1978, v.p. F.W. Woolworth Co., 1979-80, sr. exec. v.p., 1980, pres., chief operating officer, 1980—, also dir. Office: FW Woolworth Co 233 Broadway New York NY 10007*

ANDERSON, RICHARD VONDERSMITH, mfrs.' rep.; b. Passaic, N.J., Sept. 3, 1913; s. Vondersmith and Mary Alice (Page) A.; B.S. in Indsl. Engring., Rensselaer Poly. Inst., 1937; m. Elaine Richert, June 3, 1944; children—Christine, Edward, Bonnie, Richard, James. Steel mill electric control specialist Clark Controller Co., Cleve., 1937-39; automotive engr. Arthur B. Sonneborn Co., Detroit, 1939-51; pres. Anderson & Hildebrand Co. (formerly Richard V. Anderson Co.), Royal Oak, Mich., 1951-79, chmn. bd., 1979—. Pres. Three Lakes Assn., Bellaire, Mich.; pres. Bloomfield Hills (Mich.) Parent Tchrs. Orgn. Mem. Am. Welding Soc. (chmn. 1974-75), Soc. Automotive Engrs., Indsl. Elec. Engring. Assn., Assn. Iron and Steel Engrs. Clubs: Torch Lake Yacht and Country (commodore 1962-63), Western Mich. Yachting Assn. (commodore 1968), Village, Shanty Creek Golf. Office: PO Box 868 Royal Oak MI 48068

ANDERSON, ROBERT, mfg. co. exec.; b. Columbus, Nebr., Nov. 2, 1920; s. Robert and Lillian (Devlin) A.; B.S. in Mech. Engring., Colo. State U., 1943, LL.D., 1966; M.S. in Automotive Engring., Chrysler Inst. Engring., 1948. With Chrysler Corp., 1946-68, v.p. corp., gen. mgr. Chrysler-Plymouth div., 1965-67; with Rockwell Internat. Corp., 1968—, pres. comml. products group, 1968-69, v.p. corp., 1968-69, exec. v.p., 1969-70, pres., chief operating officer, 1970-74, chief exec. officer, 1974—, chmn. bd., 1979—, dir., 1968—; dir. Security Pacific Nat. Bank and Security Pacific Corp. Los Angeles, Owens-Ill., Inc., Toledo, Celanese Corp., Hosp. Corp. Am.; dir. Nat. Council U.S.-China Trade. Trustee, Carnegie-Mellon U., Calif. Inst. Tech.; corp. mem., mem. exec. com. bus.-higher edn. forum Am. Council on Edn. Served to capt. F.A., AUS, 1943-46. Named Exec. of Yr., Nat. Mgmt. Assn., 1980. Mem. Soc. Automotive Engrs., U.S. C. of C. (dir.), Phi Kappa Phi, Tau Beta Phi, Sigma Nu. Clubs: Rolling Rock, Laurel Valley Golf (Ligonier, Pa.); Duquesne, Fox Chapel Golf (Pitts.); Los Angeles Country. Office: Rockwell Internat Corp 600 Grant St Pittsburgh PA 15219

ANDERSON, ROBERT EDWARD, III, distbg. co. exec.; b. Richmond, Va., Apr. 30, 1934; s. Richard Edward, Jr. and Vienna (Cobb) A.; B.S. in Commerce, U. Va., 1955; m. Pauline Stella Roberts, Dec. 10, 1955; children—Robert Edward, Radclyafe, Deirdre. Vice pres. Powers & Anderson Dental Co., Richmond, 1958-66, Powers & Anderson, Inc., surg. supply, Richmond, 1967-76, Owens Minor Bodeker, Inc., Wholesale drugs and surg. supply, Richmond, 1976—. Bd. dirs. Richmond chpt. ARC, 1975—, pres., 1978—; bd. dirs. Tng. Center Mentally Retarded, Richmond, 1975—, treas., 1978—. Served to 1st lt. AUS, 1955-57. Mem. Am. Surg. Trade Assn. (dir. 1972—, pres. 1978—), Nat. Assn. Wholesalers (trustee 1978—), Am. Surg. Trade Found. (trustee 1978—). Episcopalian. Clubs: Country of Va., Pinehurst Country. Home: 6 Greenway Ln Richmond VA 23226 Office: 2015 Staples Mill Rd Richmond VA 23230

ANDERSON, ROBERT FERDINAND, mining co. exec.; b. Hibbing, Minn., Apr. 26, 1921; s. A.G. and Anna (Tanquist) A.; B. Engring., Mich. Tech. U., 1946; m. Marjorie Mahon, Mar. 9, 1944; children—Judith A., Christopher R., Mark M. With Hanna Mining Co., 1947—, exec. v.p., from 1969, now pres., chief exec. officer, also dir. and mem. exec. policy com.; chmn., dir. Iron Ore Co. Can., Que. N. Shore and Labrador Ry. Co., 1974—; dir. Hollinger North Shore Exploration Co., Ltd., St. John d'el Rey Mining Co., Society Corp., Society Nat. Bank. Served with USAAF, 1943-46. Mem. Am. Inst. Mining, Metall. and Petroleum Engrs., Am. Iron and Steel Inst., Am. Iron Ore Assn. Clubs: Cleve. Athletic, Clevelander, Pepper Pike Union (Cleve.); Laurel Valley Golf (Ligonier, Pa.); Mount Royal (Montreal); Rolling Rock (Latrobe, Pa.); Duquesne (Pitts.). Home: 3585 Eldorado Dr Rocky River OH 44116 Office: 100 Erieview Plaza Cleveland OH 44114

ANDERSON, ROBERT LENNARTH, II, beverage co. exec.; b. Geneva, N.Y., Apr. 18, 1947; s. Robert Lennarth and Alicia Betty (Parker) A.; B.S. in Econs., U. Pa., 1969; m. Alice Louise Hicks, Jan. 4, 1979; children—Lisa Marie, Robert Lennarth III. With Rochester Coca-Cola Bottling Corp. (N.Y.), 1963—, beginning as cashier and bookkeeper, successively route salesman, acct., acct. and asst. corp. sec., 1963-77, corp. treas., 1977—; asst. corp. sec. ATA Service Corp. Served with AUS, 1970-71. Decorated Bronze Star. Mem. Nat. Assn. Accts., Inst. Internal Auditors. Presbyterian. Clubs: Masons, Shriners. Office: 123 Upper Falls Blvd Rochester NY 14605

ANDERSON, ROBERT MILTON, JR., chem. co. exec.; b. Phila., Sept. 27, 1931; s. Robert Milton and Margaret Elizabeth (Mitchell) A.; student Asbury Coll., 1950-52, U. Houston, 1959-63; m. Frances C. Carlock, July 4, 1954; children—Kathryn Elizabeth, Robert Milton. Design draftsman United Carbon, Houston, 1954-63; project engr. Ashland Chem., Houston, 1964-68, project mgr., Speyer, Germany, 1969-70, design engring. mgr., Columbus, Ohio, 1971-74, project mgr., Tampico, Mexico, 1975-77, project mgr., Valencia, Venezuela, 1977-78, mgr. project engring., Columbus, Ohio, 1979—. Served with AUS, 1952-54. Methodist. Club: Masons. Patentee in field. Home: 7080 Rieber St Worthington OH 43085 Office: PO Box 2219 Columbus OH 43216

ANDERSON, ROBERT ORVILLE, industrialist; b. Chgo., Apr. 13, 1917; s. Hugo A. and Hilda (Nelson) A.; B.A., U. Chgo., 1939; m. Barbara Phelps, Aug. 25, 1939; children—Katherine, Julia, Maria, Robert Bruce, Barbara Burton, William Phelps, Beverley. With Am. Mineral Spirits Co., Chgo., 1939-41; pres. Malco Refineries, Inc. (now Hondo Oil and Gas Co.), Roswell, N.Mex., 1941-63; chmn. bd., chief exec. officer Atlantic Richfield Co., Los Angeles; owner Diamond A Cattle Co., Roswell. Mem. Com. Econ. Devel., Nat. Petroleum Council, Washington. Chmn., Aspen Inst. for Humanistic Studies; chmn. Lovelace Found.; trustee Calif. Inst. Tech., U. Chgo. Mem. Am. Petroleum Inst. (dir.). Clubs: Century (N.Y.C.); California (Los Angeles); Metropolitan (Washington); Chicago; Pacific-Union (San Francisco). Home: PO Box 1000 Roswell NM 88201 Office: 515 S Flower St Los Angeles CA 90071

ANDERSON, ROGER E., banker; b. Chgo., July 29, 1921; s. E. L. and June (Delang) A.; B.S. in Commerce, Northwestern U., 1942; m. Marilyn Spence, Feb. 12, 1949; children—Blair, David. With Continental Ill. Nat. Bank and Trust Co. Chgo., 1946—, trainee, asst. cashier, v.p., 1957-65, sr. v.p., 1965-68, exec. v.p., 1968-72, vice chmn. bd., 1972-73, chmn., 1973—, also dir.; now chmn. Continental Ill. Corp. dir. Amsted Industries, Inc., Eastman Kodak Co., Internat. Harvester Co., S.C. Johnson & Son, Inc. Served as lt. USNR, 1942-46. Methodist. Home: 2423 Bennett Ave Evanston IL 60201 Office: Continental Ill Corp 231 S LaSalle St Chicago IL 60609*

ANDERSON, RONALD TRUMAN, writer, cons.; b. Utica, N.Y., Mar. 20, 1933; s. Stanley Truman and Corabelle (Livingston) A.; B.S.B.A., U. Fla., 1955, J.D., 1959; M.S., Fla. State U., 1961, Ph.D., 1966; 1 son, Charles Theodore. Admitted to Fla. bar, 1960; claims rep. State Farm Ins., Tallahassee, 1959-60; asst. dean Law Sch., Fla. State U., 1960-70; exec. v.p. Soc. C.P.C.U.'s, Malvern, Pa., 1970-75; cons., writer, lectr., Steamboat Springs, Colo., 1975—; books include: Insurance Agency Computer Power, 1978; Agent's Legal Responsibility, 1980; mem. Colo. Ins. Bd., 1977—. C.P.C.U.; C.L.U. Mem. Fla. Bar Assn., Am. Risk and Ins. Assn., Soc. C.L.U.'s, Soc. C.P.C.U.'s. Democrat. Home and Office: PO Box 2114 3005 Trails Edge Rd Steamboat Springs CO 80477

ANDERSON, ROY ARNOLD, aerospace co. exec.; b. Ripon, Calif., Dec. 15, 1920; s. Carl Gustav and Esther (Johnson) A.; A.B., Stanford, 1947, M.B.A., 1949; m. Betty Leona Boehme, June 10, 1948; children—Ross David, Karyn Dale, Debra Elayne, James Patrick. With Westinghouse Electric Corp., 1952-56; mgr. accounting and finance, then dir. mgmt. controls Lockheed Missiles & Space Co., 1956-65; dir. finance Lockheed-Ga. Co., 1965-68; asst. treas. Lockheed Corp., 1968-69, v.p., controller, 1969-71, sr. v.p. finance, 1971-75, vice chmn. bd., chief financial and adminstrv. officer, 1975-77, chmn. bd., chief exec. officer, 1977—; dir. Avantek, Santa Clara, Calif., Granite Rock Co., Watsonville, Calif., United Calif. Bank, Los Angeles, So. Calif. Edison Co. Served with USNR, 1942-46, 50-52, C.P.A., Calif. Mem. Phi Beta Kappa. Office: 2555 N Hollywood Way Burbank CA 91503

ANDERSON, SONYA LEE, glass mfg. co. exec.; b. Upland, Calif., Oct. 17, 1937; d. Ashley Long and Lillian Lee (Haswell) Woods; student Occidental Coll., 1955-56; B.S., Calif. State Poly. U., 1960; student Exec. Mgmt. Program, Claremont Grad. Sch., 1980—. Home economist So. Calif. Gas Co., Los Angeles, 1960-62; statistician T.H. Garner Co., Inc. (name changed to Garner Glass Co. 1979), Claremont, Calif., 1962-67, programmer analyst, 1967-69, data processing mgr., 1969—. Blood group chmn. ARC, 1976—. Mem. Data Processing Mgmt. Assn. (internat. sec.-treas. 1977-78, recipient Gold and Silver individual performance awards). Club: Toastmasters Internat. (awarded Competent Toastmaster designation). Home: PO Box 252 Claremont CA 91711 Office: 177 S Indian Hill Blvd Claremont CA 91711

ANDERSON, TERRY DALE, baby products co. exec.; b. Galesburg, Ill., Feb. 3, 1945; s. Richard Lloyd and Mary Clemmons (Simmons) A.; B.S., Bradley U., Peoria, Ill., 1968; m. Sandra Kay Smith, May 6, 1977; children—Donna Denise, David Donald. With Johnson & Johnson, Chgo., 1968-73, asst. engring. mgr., 1973-74; supt. maintenance, then engring. projects mgr. Johnson's Baby Products Co., Piscataway, N.J., 1974-76, nat. energy coordinator, after 1976, now adminstrv. asst. to dir. engring., mgr. packaging engring. Mem. Am. Mgmt. Assn., Nat. Assn. Energy Engrs., N.J. Assn. Energy Engrs., Pi Kappa Alpha. Baptist. Home: Hopewell/Lambertville Rd Box 235 Hopewell NJ 08525 Office: Grandview Rd Skillman NJ 08554

ANDERSON, THOMAS WILLIAM, civil engr., concrete mfg. co. exec.; b. Tacoma, Mar. 15, 1912; s. Eivind and Aslaug Emily (Axness) A.; B.S.C.E., U. Wash., 1936; S.M., M.I.T., 1937; L.H.D. (hon.), Pacific Luth. U., 1978; m. Kathryn Alice Madden, Mar. 25, 1938; children—Thomas R., James R., Stephen P. Pres., Concrete Technology Corp., Tacoma, 1951-78, chief exec. officer, chmn. bd., 1978—; treas. ABAM Engrs., Inc., Tacoma; dir. Pacific Nat. Bank Wash., Chem-Nuclear Systems, Inc., High Life Helicopters, Inc. Mem. Wash. Coordinating Council Occupational Edn., 1969-74; bd. dirs. Economic Devel. Council Puget Sound, v.p., 1979; chmn. bd. trustees St. Joseph Hosp.; chmn. regents Pacific Luth. U., 1973-76, now regent; mem. adv. com. Coll. Econs. and Bus., Wash. State U. Recipient Silver Beaver award Boy Scouts Am. Registered profl. engr., Wash. Fellow ASCE, Am. Concrete Inst.; mem. Safety Tng. and Research Assn. (dir.). Office: 1123 Port Tacoma Rd Tacoma WA 98421

ANDERSON, VERNON RUSSELL, mfg. co. exec.; b. San Francisco, July 3, 1931; s. Elmer O. and Ethel (Carlson) A.; B.S. in Mech. Engring., Stanford U., 1953, M.B.A., 1957; m. Lysbeth Warren, Dec. 27, 1953; children—Brenton, Lysanna, Dane. Engr., Trane Co., La Crosse, Wis., 1953-55; mgr. Sierra Electronic Corp., Menlo Park, Calif., 1957-59; pres., co-founder Vidar Corp., Mountain View, Calif., 1959-72; cons. United Telecommunications, Inc., Kansas City, Mo., 1975-77, L.M. Ericsson Telephone Co. (Sweden), 1976-77; dir. Telecommunications Tech. Inc., Continental Capital Corp.; instr. Stanford, 1968-72; guest lectr. Stanford Grad. Sch. Bus., 1964-71. Mem. adv. council Stanford Bus. Sch. 1971-77; mem. bus. adv. council Resource Center for Women. Mem. IEEE. Home: 25225 La Loma Dr Los Altos Hills CA 94022 Office: PO Box 85 Los Altos CA 94022

ANDERSON, WARREN M., multi-product co. exec.; b. Bklyn., Nov. 29, 1921; s. John M. and Ida M. (Peterson) A.; A.B., Colgate U., 1942; LL.B., Western Res. U., 1956; m. Lillian K. Christensen, Feb. 22, 1947. Chem. sales rep. Union Carbide Co., N.Y.C., 1945, v.p. sales and mktg. Olefins div., 1962, pres. Process Chems. div., 1967-69, v.p., 1969-73, exec. v.p., 1973—, dir., 1974—, pres., 1977—. Served with USNR, 1943-45. Mem. Am. Chem. Soc., Soc. Chem. Industry, Am. Bar Assn. Office: 270 Park Ave New York NY 10017

ANDERSON, WILLIAM CARL, cons. engr.; b. Vinton, Iowa, Sept. 24, 1943; s. Ivan Dale and Lois Bernice A.; B.S.C.E., Iowa State U., 1967; m. Elizabeth Ann Dingman, Nov. 12, 1966; children—William Carl III, Erica Dawn. Asst. pub. health engr. N.Y. State Health Dept., Utica, 1967; dir. environ. health Cayuga County (N.Y.) Health Dept., Auburn, 1968-73; mng. partner Pickard and Anderson, Auburn, 1973—. Health and safety commn. Cayuga County council Boy Scouts Am., 1969—. Served with USNR, 1967-68. Recipient Philip F. Morgan medal Water Pollution Control Fedn., 1973, Lewis Van Carpenter award N.Y. Water Pollution Control Assn., 1974; lic. profl. engr., N.Y., N.J., Iowa; lic. wastewater treatment plant operator, N.Y.; diplomate Am. Acad. Environ. Engrs. Mem. ASCE (environ. engring. div. exec. com. 1976-80, chmn. exec. com. 1980, com. on solid waste mgmt. 1970-75, chmn. 1973-75, profl. coordination com. 1977—, chmn. task force to prepare manual 1975, tech. cons. 1975—, feature speaker ann. conv. 1976), Am. Cons. Engrs. Council (environ. com. 1976—, chmn. task force on solid waste 1977-79), Chessman Hon. Soc. (Iowa State U.), Knights of St. Patrick Engring. Hon. Soc. (Iowa State U.), Chi Epsilon. Republican. Roman Catholic. Clubs: Owasco Country, Rotary, Iowa State U. Alumni Syracuse (pres. 1972-75). Expert witness in field U.S. Ho. of Reps., 1975, 76; rev. panel for procedures manual EPA, 1976; author, co-author articles in profl. publs. Home: 74 Adams Ave Auburn NY 13021 Office: 69 South St Auburn NY 13021

ANDOLSHEK, RICHARD ANDERS, retail stores exec.; b. Crosby, Minn., Mar. 13, 1952; s. Albin Henery and Alice Louise (Arvidson) A.; student U. Minn., 1970-73; m. Lonna Mae Schultz, Dec. 18, 1971; children—Kimberly, Albin. Owner, operator Crosslake IGA Grocery Store (Minn.), 1973—, Dick's Package Liquor Store, Crosslake, 1973—, Andy's Restaurant, Crosslake, 1973—; v.p. Country Printing Enterprises Inc., Pequot Lakes, Minn., 1977-80, LAR, Inc., night club and restaurant, Crosslake, 1977—; pres. Jonable Inc., chain restaurant, Crosslake, 1979—. Mem. Crosslake Planning and Zoning Commn., 1973-74, Region 5 Devel. Commn., 1975-77; mem. Ind. Sch. Dist. 186 Bd. Edn., Pequot Lakes, Minn., 1975—, chmn., 1977. Named Minn. Liquor Retailer of Yr., Midwest Beverage Jour., 1977. Mem. Minn. Food Retailers, Minn. Liquor Retailers (pres.), Crosslake C. of C., Nat. Fedn. Small Bus. Club: Elks. Home and office: Box 98 Crosslake MN 56442

ANDRE, JACQUES PIERRE, exec. search cons.; b. Warren, Ohio, Aug. 29, 1937; s. Armand Jules and Marion E. (Binder) A.; B.B.A., U. Miami, 1959; m. Kathleen Ann McCarthy, Sept. 19, 1959; children—Jacques P., Michelle M. Asst. personnel dir. Sealtest Foods, Balt., 1960-64; sr. employment specialist P. Ballentine & Sons, Newark, 1964-65; mgr. exec. search service Ernst & Ernst, N.Y.C., 1965-75; v.p. Paul R. Ray & Co., Inc., N.Y.C., 1975—. Served to capt. U.S. Army. Mem. Am. Soc. Personnel Adminstrn., N.Y. Personnel Mgmt. Assn., Am. Compensation Assn., Assn. Exec. Recruiting Cons., N.Y. Bd. Trade (mem. steering com. internat. sect. 1979—). Republican. Lutheran. Club: Toastmasters Internat. Home: 506 Lawrence Ave Westfield NJ 07090 Office: 277 Park Ave New York NY 10172

ANDREAS, DWAYNE O(RVILLE), corp. exec.; b. Worthington, Minn., Mar. 4, 1918; s. Reuben P. and Lydia (Stoltz) A.; student Wheaton (Ill.) Coll., 1935-36; m. Bertha Benedict, 1938 (div.); 1 dau., Sandra Ann McMurtrie; m. 2d, Dorothy Inez Snyder, Dec. 21, 1947; children—Terry Lynn Bevis, Michael D. Vice pres., dir. Honeymead Products Co., Cedar Rapids, Iowa, 1936-46; v.p. Cargill, Inc., Mpls., 1946-52; chmn. bd., chief exec. officer Honeymead Products Co. (now Nat. City Bancorp.), Mankato, Minn., 1952-72; exec. v.p. Farmers Union Grain Terminal Assn., St. Paul, 1960-66; chmn. bd., chief exec. officer Archer-Daniels-Midland Co., Decatur, Ill., 1970—; pres. Seaview Hotel Corp., 1958—; dir. Columbia Pictures, Inc., Lone Star Industries, Greenwich, Conn.; dir., exec. com. Archer-Daniels-Midland Co.; dir. Norwestern Nat. Life Ins. Co., Mpls., 1962-73. Mem. Pres.'s Gen. Adv. Com. Fgn. Assistance Programs, 1965-68, Pres.'s Adv. Council on Mgmt. Improvement, 1969-73; pres. Andreas Found.; mem. nat. bd. Boys Clubs Am.; trustee U.S. Naval Acad. Found. Mem. Fgn. Policy Assn. N.Y. (dir.). Clubs: Union League (Chgo.); Minneapolis, Minikahda (Mpls.); Indian Creek Country (Miami Beach, Fla.); Links (N.Y.C.); Blind Brook (Port Chester, N.Y.). Home: The Sea View 9909 Collins Ave Bal Harbour Miami Beach FL 33154 Office: Archer Daniels Midland Co Box 1470 Decatur IL 62525

ANDREASEN, CHARLES PETER, supply co. exec.; b. Bklyn., Mar. 18, 1930; s. Peter Kristian and Marie Paulene Andreasen; student Coll. Agr., Rutgers U., 1948-49; student statis. quality control Middlesex County Coll., 1970-71; m. Julia Kerekes, Nov. 27, 1952; 1 dau., Jane Mary. Quality control engr. Gorn Aircraft Controls Co., Stamford, Conn., 1962-63; quality control supr. Lily-Tulip Cup Corp., Holmdel, N.J., 1963-70; corp. quality control lab. supr. Purolator Products Co., Rahway, N.J., 1970-73; mgr. quality control Scovill Mfg. Co., Waterbury, Conn., 1973-78; quality assurance mgr. All-State Legal Supply Co., Mountainside, N.J., 1979—. Sgt.-at-arms Clara Barton Democratic Club, 1978-79; active Edison Dem. Assn. Mem. Am. Soc. for Quality Control (exec. bd.). Roman Catholic. Clubs: Danish Brotherhood in Am.; Elks (Metuchen, N.J.). Home: 24 Burchard St Edison NJ 08817 Office: 269 Sheffield St Mountainside NJ 07092

ANDRES, PAUL ANTHONY, ins. exec., investment adviser; b. Tulsa, Feb. 7, 1928; s. Paul Hall and Helen (Ardizzone) A.; student Georgetown U., 1946-47, U. Wis., 1947-50; B.A. in Journalism, U. Okla., 1950; postgrad. Washington U. 1951; B.A. in Geology, Oklahoma City U., 1957; m. Ann Simmons Alspaugh, July 24, 1954 (div. Jan. 1963); children—Holly Antoinette, Louis Howard, Paul Anthony; m. 2d, Deena Anderson, May 30, 1964; 1 son, Kevin

Michael. Information asst. pub. relations dept. Southwestern Bell Telephone Co., Oklahoma City, 1950-51, gen. information supr., gen. information dept., St. Louis, 1951-52; dir., editor, pres. Paul Andres Publs., Inc., 1953-62; pres., dir. Adcraft Mail of Okla., Inc., 1957-62; v.p. Cunningham, Andres & Co., Inc., Oklahoma City, 1958-62; gen. mgr. Paul Andres Realty to 1962; v.p. Sey-Co Products Co., Inc., Van Nuys, Calif., 1963-72; dir. Robert Bye Assos., Houston, 1972-80, ASK Realty, 1972—; partner Andres, Schildhauer, Kutner Cons., 1975—. Served from 2d lt. to capt. USAF, 1952-53. C.L.U. Mem. Nat. Assn. Securities Dealers, Nat., Houston assns. life underwriters, Tex. Real Estate Commn., New Eng. Life Leaders Assn. (life mem. Hall of Fame), Million Dollar Round Table. Club: Pine Forest Country. Home: 14630 Carolcrest Dr Houston TX 77079 Office: Suite 300 550 S Post Oak Houston TX 77027

ANDRES, WILLIAM A., dept. store exec.; b. Fayette, Iowa, 1926; B.A., Upper Iowa U., 1948; M.A., U. Pitts., 1949. With Dayton-Hudson Corp., 1958—, v.p., 1963-67, gen. operating mgr., 1966-67, sr. v.p. operations, 1967-68, sr. v.p., 1969-71, exec. v.p. retail operations, 1971-74, pres., 1974-77, chief operating officer, 1974-76, chief exec. officer, 1976, chmn., chief exec. officer, 1977—, also dir.; chmn. Dayton Co., 1968-69; dir. First Bank System, St. Paul Cos., Inc., Internat. Multifoods Corp. Office: Dayton-Hudson Corp 777 Nicollet Mall Minneapolis MN 55402

ANDRESEN, FINN OLE, liquid filtration and mining equipment co. exec.; b. Lillestrom, Norway, Nov. 7, 1932; s. Erik and Marie (Magnussen) A.; Examen Artium, Lillestrom Interkommunale Hogere Almenskole, 1952; student Molstad and Moen U., 1952-54; m. Kari von Krogh, July 14, 1957; children—Erik Johan, Elisabeth. Prodn. planning mgr. Aanonsen Fabrikker Co., Oslo, 1954-58, adminstrv. asst., 1958-60, sales adminstrn. mgr., 1960-68; v.p. mktg. IBM, Oslo, 1968-71; pres. Polyclon Co., Woburn, Mass., 1971—; founder, pres., owner Euro-Trade, Inc., export-import co., Weston, Mass., 1978—. Trustee, Waltham (Mass.) Hosp., 1979—. Served with Royal Guard, Norway, 1951-52. Mem. ASME, Filtration Soc. New Eng. (chpt. pres. 1972—). Clubs: Royal Norwegian Yacht, Royal Norwegian Automobil (Oslo). Home: 15 Pond Brook Circle Weston MA 02193 Office: 15 6th Rd Woburn MA 01801

ANDRESEN, FREDERICK RICHMOND, sportswear mfg. and importing co. exec.; b. El Paso, Tex., Mar. 1, 1932; s. Arthur Rinehart and Delka (Muller) A.; B.S. in Forestry, Colo. State U., 1954; B.Fgn. Trade, Am. Grad. Sch. Internat. Mgmt., Phoenix, 1958; m. Betty Romayne Palmer; children—Frederick Palmer, Joy Christiane, Lilli-Mari. Export service mgr. Monsanto Chem. Co., Springfield, Mass., 1958-60; cons. Geoffrey Ladhams Assos., N.Y.C., 1960-62; founder, pres. Scandia Trading Co., Inc., Winchester, Mass., 1962-73: founder, pres. Cevas, Inc., Quechee, Vt., 1977—. Trustee Camps Owatonna and Newfound, Harrison, Maine, 1977-79; bd. dirs. Hanover Chamber Orch. Soc., 1979-80. Served with U.S. Army, 1954-56. Mem. Ski Industries Am. (dir. 1966-76, pres. 1973-75), Am. Ski Fedn., U.S. Ski Found. (trustee 1974-76). Republican. Christian Scientist. Clubs; Woodstock Country, Masons. Home: Pomfret Rd Woodstock VT 05091 Office: Deweys Mills Rd Quechee VT 05059

ANDRETTA, EVELYN BOUINGTON, Realtor; b. Manatee, Fla.; d. Alex Jessie and Etna Mae (Fender) Bouington; student U. Tampa, 1950-51, Hillsborough Coll., 1972-74; m. Ralph Louis Andretta, Apr. 14, 1945; children—Denise Christine, Gregory Ralph, Richard Louis. With J.L. Hearin, Inc., Tampa, Fla., 1948—, v.p., 1969—. Mem. Tampa Citizens Zoning Sub-com., 1976-77, Hillsborough County Citizens Adv. Com. Horizon 2000, 1976—; bd. dirs. Suncoast council Girl Scouts U.S.A., 1965-74. Mem. Nat. Assn. Realtors, Soc. Indsl. Realtors (v.p. State chpt.), Nat. Mktg. Inst., Tampa C. of C. (dir., com. of 100), Fla. Indsl. Devel. Council. Democrat. Episcopalian. Clubs: Krewe of Venus, Palma Ceia Golf and Country, Tower, Tampa Woman's. Home: 3902 San Rafael St Tampa FL 33609 Office: 1st Fla Tower Suite 3030 111 Madison St Tampa FL 33602

ANDREW, J. R. BRUCE, mfg. co. exec.; b. Toronto, Ont., Can., Apr. 6, 1946; s. Robert and Irene A.; m. Lyn, Sept. 10, 1967; children—Lori Lynn, Tracy Leah. Internal auditor Toronto Transit Commn., 1965-68: comptroller Electronic Assos. Can., Ltd., Downsview, Ont., 1969-74; sec., treas., comptroller Sentrol Systems Ltd., Downsview, 1975—. Home: 1 Gosford Blvd Downsview ON Canada M3N 2G7 Office: 4401 Steeles Ave W Downsview ON Canada M3N 2G7

ANDREW, THEODORE STUART, mining co. exec.; b. Dundee, Scotland, Nov. 6, 1930; immigrated to Can., 1977; s. Theodore and Isabella Elizabeth (Simpson) A.; grad. Fettes Coll., Edinburgh, Scotland, 1949; m. Elizabeth C. Zimbler, June 4, 1955; children—Eric, Kathryn. Auditor, Price Waterhouse Peat & Co., Nicosia, Cyprus, 1962-64; chief acct. Cyprus Mines Corp., Skouriotissa, Cyprus, 1965-76; comptroller Cyprus Anvil Mining Corp., Vancouver, B.C., Can., 1977-79, v.p. comptroller, 1979—. Served to lt. Royal Arty., U.K., 1949-51. Fellow Assn. Cert. Accts. U.K. Office: Cyprus Anvil Mining Corp 330 355 Burrard St Vancouver BC V6C 2G8 Canada

ANDREWS, ARTHUR LAWRENCE, aerospace co. exec.; b. East Orange, N.J., Apr. 26, 1931; s. Bjorn Secker and Linnea Rongheld (Lindbloom) A.; M.E., Stevens Inst. Tech., 1953; M.S., U. So. Calif., 1974; m. Marilyn Bernice Wieboldt, Sept. 26, 1954; children—Deborah Lee, Ronald Andreassen. Test engr. Curtiss Wright, Woodridge, N.J., 1953-54; with McDonnell Douglas Astronautics Co., 1957—, chief logistics engr., Huntington Beach, Calif., 1970—; pres. Andreassen Enterprises, Rancho Palos Verdes, Calif., 1976—. Vice chmn. South Bay dist. exec. com. Boy Scouts Am., Los Angeles, 1973—; bd. dirs. Ascension Lutheran Ch., Rancho Palos Verdes, 1975-77, pres., 1977-78. Served with USAF, 1954-57. Recipient Silver Beaver award Boy Scouts Am., 1978. Mem. Am. Inst. Aeros. and Astronautics (chmn. nat. tech. com. on support systems 1976-78), Soc. Logistics Engrs., Nat. Assn. Watch and Clock Collectors. Club: Activi"8"ters Sq. Dance. Home: 27837 Longhill Dr Rancho Palos Verdes CA 90274 Office: 5301 Bolsa Ave Huntington Beach CA 92647

ANDREWS, DAVID VOLK, bank exec.; b. New Haven, May 13, 1923; s. Edward Deming and Faith E. (Young) A.; B.A., Yale U., 1949; m. Phyllis Camp, 1947; children—Edward, Garrett, Peter. Vice pres. Chase Manhattan Bank, N.Y.C., 1950-76; pres. Fidelity Trust Co., Stamford, Conn., 1976—. Served to lt., USAAF, 1942-45. Republican. Episcopalian. Clubs: Yale, St. Andrews, Woodway Country. Office: 129 Atlantic St Stamford CT 06902

ANDREWS, GERALD LEE, cash register co. exec.; b. Phila., June 8, 1945; s. Maurice Lee and Francis Jessie (Chambers) A.; student Kutztown State Coll., 1964-67; m. Robin Lee Geissler, June 21, 1969; 1 son, Micah Lee. Tech. service rep. Nat. Cash Register Co., Reading, Pa., 1968-72; mgt. tech. services Capital Bus. Equipment Co., Reading, 1972-76, H.C. Korner Co., 1976-77; sales mgr. Cash Register div. Clauser Office Equipment Co., Reading, 1977-78; pres. Capital Cash Register, Inc., Reading, 1978—. Dist. camping chmn. Hawk Mountain council Boy Scouts Am.; water safety instr. trainer ARC. Mem. Nat. Office Machine Dealers Assn. (dir.), Central Pa. Office Machine Dealers Assn. (pres. 1978-80, dir.), Ind. Cash Register Dealers Assn., Pa. Ind. Cash Register Dealers Assn. (dir.), Order of Arrow (chief 1965). Club: Reading Rotary (membership chmn.). Office: Capital Cash Register Inc Route 61 and Bellevue Ave Reading PA 19605

ANDREWS, HARVEY WELLINGTON, med. co. exec.; b. Stowe Twp., Pa., Sept. 9, 1928; s. Robert W. and Theresa R. (Reis) A.; B.B.A. cum laude, U. Pitts., 1952; M.B.A., Harvard, 1957; m. Jane Garland, Aug. 9, 1969; children—Marcia Lynne, Glynis Suzanne, Elizabeth Jane. With Gen. Electric Co., Syracuse, N.Y., 1952-55, Scovill Mfg. Co., Waterbury, Conn., 1957; comptroller Alcon Labs., Inc., Ft. Worth, 1958-61, comptroller, treas., 1961-65, v.p. finance, 1964-68; founder, pres. Medimation, Inc., Ft. Worth, 1968—, Tarrant Health Protection Plan, Inc., 1978—; dir. Med. Scis. Computor Corp., 1st Clin. Labs., Dalworth Med. Labs.; exec. dir. Tarrant Med. Ind. Practice Assn., 1978—. Bd. dirs., mem. exec. com. Fort Worth Opera Assn. Served with AUS, 1946-48. Mem. Am. Acad. Polit. and Social Scis., A.A.A.S., Ft. Worth C. of C., Soc. Advancement Mgmt. Order Artus, Scabbard and Blade, Golden Eagle Assn., Sigma Alpha Epsilon. Lutheran. Mason (32 deg.). Clubs: Rotary, Met. Knife and Fork, Tex. Christian U. Pres.'s Round Table Assn., Colonial Country, Century II. Home: PO Box 1786 Fort Worth TX 76101 Office: 1300 Summit Ave Fort Worth TX 76102

ANDREWS, JESSIE MAE, Realtor; b. Richfield, Idaho, Jan. 18, 1918; s. Clyde Osborn and Golda Pearl (Meyer) Ewing; student Santa Maria Jr. Coll., 1936-37; m. Forest Merl Andrews, Apr. 20, 1946. Sec., Kraft Foods, Aberdeen, Idaho, 1963-64; ins. sec. real estate salesman H.T. Breazeal Agy., Rupert, Idaho, 1964-69, real estate broker, 1969-73; asso. broker Bailey-Roberts Realty, Rupert, 1973-74; asso. broker sec.-treas., co-owner, mgr. Rupert office Big Wood Realty, Inc., 1974-75; broker, owner Trend Realty, Rupert, 1975—. Mem. Rupert Uniform Bldg. Codes Appeals Bd., 1974—. Mem. Burley-Rupert Bd. Realtors (sec.-treas. 1969-70, dir.), Nat. Inst. Farm and Land Brokers. Methodist (ass. treas. woman's soc. Christian service 1967-68). Home: 817 15th Dr Rupert ID 83350 Office: 638 Fremont Ave Rupert ID 83350

ANDREWS, STEELE, gage mfg. co. exec.; b. Bklyn., Dec. 9, 1927; s. Charles Edmund and Mabel Elizabeth (Steele) A.; B.Mgmt.Engring., Rensselaer Poly. Inst., 1951, certificate Exec. Devel. Program, 1965; certificate Mgmt. Devel. Program, New Haven Coll., 1960; m. Ingrid Elizabeth Heitman, June 10, 1950; children—Charles Erik, Dean Elise, Kristian Hartley, Dwight Nilsson, Dale Louise, Bradford Steele, Nils Emerson. Engring. trainee Torrington Co. (Conn.), 1951-52, project engr., 1952-53, chief insp., 1953-55, plant quality control mgr., 1955-71, quality control mgr. A. Bearing div., 1971-76, metrication mgr., 1975-76; exec. v.p. Standard Gage Co., Poughkeepsie, N.Y., 1976-79; adminstrv. mgr. Edmonds Mfg. Co., Farmington, Conn., 1979-80; mng. dir. The Torrington Co., Darlington, Eng., 1980—. Active Boy Scouts Am., 1951—, mem. troop com., 1952-72, dist. commr. Tunxis council, 1958-60; active YMCA, United Fund. Served with Signal Corps, U.S. Army, 1946-47. Mem. Am. Soc. for Quality Control (certified quality engr.; sec. Mid-Hudson chpt. 1977-78, vice chmn. 1978-79), Am. Prodn. and Inventory Control Soc., Torrington Aero Modelers (pres. 1954-55), Phi Kappa Tau. Republican. Mem. Reformed Ch. Home: RFD 3 Forest Dr Burlington CT 06013

ANDREWS, VERA JEAN, apparel mfg. co. exec.; b. Chester County, S.C., Jan. 1, 1941; d. Burt M. Andrews and Ersie S. Andrews Stewart; student Clemson U., 1962, Fashion Inst. Tech., 1964, U. S.C., 1967-69. With Skyline Mfg. Co. Inc., Camden, S.C., 1959—, dir. mfg., 1974-80, gen. mgr., 1980—. Mem. adv. bd. Kershaw County Vocat. Sch., 1979-81, co-author tng. manual. Recipient Disting. Service award City of Camden, 1963; Disting. Service cert. Kershaw County Vocat. Sch., 1978. Mem. Am. Mgmt. Assn., Am. Apparel Mfg. Assn. (edn. com.), Bus. and Profl. Women's Club (pres. local club 1969, chmn. state standing com. 1968), S.C. Needle Trade Assn. Home: 100 Chesnut St Camden SC 29020 Office: Dicey Creek Rd Camden SC 29020

ANDREWS, WILLIAM FREDERICK, mfg. corp. exec.; b. Easton, Pa., Oct. 7, 1931; s. William F. and Lydia Nielsen (Cross) A.; B.S. in Bus. Adminstrn., U. Md., 1953; student Georgetown Law Sch., 1956; M.B.A. in Mktg., Seton Hall U., 1962; m. Carol Beaman, Feb. 8, 1962; children—William Frederick, Whitney Leigh, Carter Beaman, Clayton Cross, Sloane Meadow. Mgmt. trainee W.R. Grace & Co., 1957; sales rep. Kaiser Aluminum, 1957-58; sales rep. Scovill Mfg. Co., Waterbury, Conn., 1958-59, br. sales mgr., 1959-62, dist. sales mgr., 1962-65, product mgr., 1965-68, v.p., gen. mgr. fluid power div., 1968-73, group v.p. automotive and fluid power group, 1973-78, pres., 1979—, chmn., 1981; dir. Scovill Inc., McM Corp., Raleigh, N.C., Colonial Bank, Waterbury. Trustee, Waterbury Hosp., Mattatuck Mus., Am. Indian Archaeol. Inst.; bd. dirs. Waterbury chpt. ARC, Easter Seals, Conn. Jr. Republic, St. Margaret's-McTernan Sch. Served to capt. USAF, 1953-56. Mem. Greater Waterbury C. of C. Office: 500 Chase Pkwy Waterbury CT 06720

ANDREWS, WILLIAM LEE, III, business exec.; b. Roanoke, Va., July 26, 1950; s. William Lee and Nancy Lee (Deacon) A.; B.A. in Econs., Washington and Lee U., 1972; M.B.A., Coll. William and Mary, 1974; m. Melynda Lea McNeil, July 26, 1975; children—Melynda McNeil, William Lee. Gen. mgr. Red Line, Inc., Roanoke, 1974-75, pres., treas., 1975—; chmn. Andrews Athletic Clubs, Inc., 1977—; chief exec. officer The Mansion, Inc., Roanoke, 1977—; chmn. Steer House, Inc., Roanoke, 1978—; gen. partner Swensen's of Ala., Roanoke, 1978—, Andrews Properties, Roanoke, 1976—, Andrews Leasing Co., Roanoke, 1978—; dir. Va. Nat. Bank, Roanoke. Mem. vestry St. John's Episcopal Ch., 1977-80. Mem. Washington and Lee Alumni (pres. 1977-79). Republican. Clubs: Shenandoah, Jefferson, Roanoke German, Roanoke Athletic, Roanoke Country. Office: 4504 Starkey Rd Roanoke VA 24014

ANDROULAKIS, COSTA EMMANUEL, hotel exec.; b. Heraklion, Crete, Greece, Mar. 2, 1936; s. Emmanuel George and Katherine Konstantine (Louloudakis) A.; B.S., Cornell U., 1969. With Hotel Zumstorhen, Zurich, Switzerland, 1961, Athens Hilton, 1963-66; exec. asst. mgr. Hilton Inn, Newport, R.I., gen. mgr. Hilton Inn, Logan Airport, Boston, 1970-74; gen. mgr. Carlton Hotel Corp., Boston, 1975-76; gen. mgr. Holiday Inn-Center City, Phila., 1976—, also legis. alert chmn. Bd. dirs. Phila. Opera Co. Served to 1st lt. Greek Army, 1958-60. Recipient Pride award Holiday Inns, Inc., 1976, Govt. Affairs award, 1977. Mem. Cornell Soc. Hotelmen, Greater Phila. Hotel Motor Inn Assn. (treas., pres.), Greater Phila. C. of C., Phila. Conv. and Visitors Bur., Am. Hellenic Ednl. Progressive Assn. Club: Skal. Office: 1800 Market St Philadelphia PA 19103

ANDROVIC, G. RICHARD, oil co. exec.; b. N.Y.C., Aug. 3, 1943; s. George and Stella (Gervat) A.; B.A., Kent State U., 1965; M.A., Am. Grad. Sch. Internat. Mgmt., 1968; m. Kathleen Fox, Oct. 11, 1970; children—Chris, Holly, Scott. With M.B.A. program in human resources, Port of N.Y. Authority, N.Y.C., 1968-70; asst. to v.p. Am. Express, N.Y.C., 1970-72; mgr. benefits planning and adminstrn. Hertz (RCA Corp.), N.Y.C., 1972-74; mgr. compensation and benefits ops. Internat. Paper Co., N.Y.C., 1974-80; corp. div. world wide compensation and benefits Conoco Inc., Stamford, Conn., 1980—; pres. Internat. Service Co., U.K. Mgmt. Com.; cons. ins. co.; lectr. in field of human resources. Served with U.S. Army, 1965-67. Mem. Oil Industry Compensation and Benefits Assn. (chmn.), Paper Compensation Assn. (chmn.), Council of Employee Benefits (chmn.), NAM, Internat. Personnel Assn. (compensations and benefits steering com.), N.Y. Personnel Assn., Am. Compensation Assn. Home: 31 Robinson Dr Bethpage NY 11714 Office: High Ridge Rd Stamford CT 06830

ANDRZEJEWSKI, EDWARD FRANCIS, ins. cos. exec.; b. Amsterdam, N.Y., Dec. 23, 1943; s. Stanislaus John and Sophie Mary (Wozniak) A.; B.B.A. in Acctg., Siena Coll., 1966; M.B.A. in Taxation, N.Y. U., 1975. Acctg. analyst Glens Falls Ins. Group (N.Y.), 1966-69, supr. acctg., 1969-71; tax acct. Continental Ins. Cos., N.Y.C., 1971-74, supr., 1974-76, asst. sec. Diners Club and other non-ins. affiliates, 1974-78, asst. sec. Continental Corp., Continental Ins. Cos., 1976-78; dir. taxes-compliance Am. Internat. Group, Inc., N.Y.C., 1978—. Mem. Soc. Ins. Accts., Tax Execs. Inst. Home: 201 E 87 St New York NY 10028

ANEROUSIS, JOHN PETER, chem. co. exec.; b. Riverside, N.J., Aug. 29, 1949; s. Peter G. and Georgia B. Anerousis; B.S. in Chem. Engring., U. Del., 1972, B.S. in Chem. Engring. Adminstrn., 1972; M.B.A., Drexel U., 1978. Staff engr./specialist Betz Labs., Inc., Trevose, Pa., 1972-75, resident project engr., Los Angeles, 1975-76, project supr., Trevose, 1976-78; dir. tech. mgmt. Betz Process Chems., Inc., The Woodlands, Tex., 1978—. Registered profl. engr., Calif., Tex. Mem. Am. Inst. Chem. Engrs., Nat. Assn. Corrosion Engrs., Am. Mgmt. Assn., U. Del. Alumni Assn., Sigma Phi Epsilon. Club: Rotary. Contbg. author: Beta Handbook of Industrial Water Conditioning, 7th edit., 1976; contbr. articles to profl. jours. Home: 3 Greenblade Ln The Woodlands TX 77380 Office: Betz Process Chems Inc The Woodlands TX 77380

ANFUSO, VICTOR L'EPISCOPO, JR., lawyer; b. Bklyn., Sept. 17, 1932; s. Victor L'Episcopo and Frances (Stallone) A.; A.B. magna cum laude, St. John's U., Jamaica, N.Y., 1954, J.D., 1959; m. Kathy Ann Shea, Apr. 8, 1967; children—Dina, Michelle, Victor Thomas, William Paul, Adrienne. Admitted to N.Y. bar, 1959, since practiced in N.Y.C.; partner firm Wildes, Weinberg & Anfuso, 1980—; founder Anfuso Consultants, Yuba City, Calif., 1981; pres. Excelsior Found., 1965-67. Bd. dirs. World Rehab. Fund, 1972-78; pres. N.Y. State Young Citizens for Johnson, 1964. Served to lt. USNR, 1955-57. Mem. Assn. Immigration and Nationality Lawyers, N.Y. State Bar Assn., Full Gospel Businessmen's Fellowship Internat. (pres. Manhasset chpt. 1979). Author articles in field. Office: 515 Madison Ave New York NY 10022

ANGELIDES, MICHAEL JOHN, design co. exec.; b. Lewiston, Maine, Nov. 24, 1951; s. Harry Emmanuel and Julia Caroline A.; A.B., (Demarest scholar) Rutgers U., 1970-74; student Harvard U., 1973; m. Lucy Lundie Guerard, Aug. 21, 1975. Asst. research analyst Cities Service Research & Devel. Co., Cranbury, N.J., 1972; founder Investment Alts., Princeton, 1973-75, chmn., 1975; pres. The Beverage Warehouse Group Ltd., Lewiston, 1975-77; spl. cons. Urban Systems Research & Engring. Co., Cambridge, Mass., 1977-78; v.p. fin. Turnbull & Co., Cambridge, 1978-79; pres., chief exec. officer, 1979—; outside cons. Arthur D. Little Inc., Cambridge, 1979-80; adv.-in-residence bus. and bus. careers South House, Harvard U., 1977. Trustee, Maine United Fund, 1976. Mem. Am. Mgmt. Assn.

ANGELINE, JOHN FREDERICK, food co. exec.; b. Somerville, Mass., Sept. 29, 1929; s. Jack L. and Edith (Ciavatti) A.; B.S., Northeastern U., 1952, M.B.A., 1963; m. Doris Helen L'Heureux, Nov. 9, 1957; children—Karen E., Rachel A., Andrea M. Research and mgmt. cons. Arthur D. Little, Inc., Cambridge, Mass., 1952-77; v.p. research and devel. Quaker Oats Co., Barrington, Ill., 1977-80. Served with U.S. Army, 1954-56. Mem. Inst. Food Technologists, Am. Chem. Soc., AAAS, N.Y. Acad. Sci., Phi Tau Sigma. Republican. Contbr. numerous articles to profl. jours.

ANGELL, RAYMOND COOK, steel co. exec.; b. Pitts., Jan. 1, 1935; s. William Raymond and Dot Ida (Jones) A.; B.S. in Metall. Engring., U. Pitts., 1959; m. Lois A. Riegler, June 9, 1957; children—Susan L., Tom R., With Babcock & Wilcox Co., Beaver Falls, Pa., 1959—, gen. sales mgr. tubular products group, 1976-78, v.p., gen. sales mgr., 1978—; mem. metallurgy faculty Geneva Coll., 1963-64. Bd. dirs. Beaver Falls Jaycees, 1964. Mem. Steel Service Center Inst., Am. Iron and Steel Inst., Am. Soc. Metals, Beaver Valley C. of C. Methodist. Clubs: Beaver Valley Country, Seven Oaks Country. Office: PO Box 401 Beaver Falls PA 15010

ANGEVINE, GEORGE BRAUD, steel co. exec.; b. Newark, June 26, 1918; s. Lewis James and Eugenia Marie (Braud) A.; B.A., Rutgers U., 1940; LL.B., U. Pitts., 1948; m. Margaret Muse Collin, Apr. 3, 1976; children by previous marriage—Paula (Mrs. David Douglas Craig), Sheryl, Katherine (Mrs. Clifton Leith), Barbara. Admitted to Pa. bar, 1948; mgr. labor relations West Penn Power Co., Pitts., 1948-56, partner firm Thorp, Reed & Armstrong, Pitts., 1956-63; v.p., gen. counsel, sec. Nat. Steel Corp., Pitts., 1963—. Bd. dirs. Allegheny Trails council Boy Scouts Am., Pitts., Health and Welfare Assn. Allegheny County, Pitts.; trustee Chatham Coll., Pitts. Served with USAAF, 1942-46. Decorated D.F.C., Air medal. Mem. Am. Iron and Steel Inst., Am., Pa., Mich., Allegheny County bar assns. Presbyn. (deacon). Clubs: Duquesne (Pitts.); Allegheny Country (Sewickley, Pa.); Edgeworth (Pa.); Rolling Rock (Ligonier, Pa.); Williams Country (Weirton, W.Va.). Home: 625 Pine Rd Sewickley PA 15143 Office: 2800 Grant Bldg Pittsburgh PA 15219

ANGIER, KEITH ALAN, business exec.; b. Morris, Minn., Mar. 29, 1934; s. Roland Sydney and Edythe Barbara (Landes) A.; B.A., Drake U., 1957; M.P.A., Ind. U., 1967; m. Joan Kay Foehlinger, Apr. 18, 1954; children—Kent Alan, Thomas Dean, Megan Jill. Intelligence officer CIA, Washington, 1957-69; dir. data processing State of Alaska, Juneau, 1969-71; dir. systems services for hosps. and dir. univ. adminstrv. data processing U. Wash., Seattle, 1971-73; dir. Wash. State Dept. Gen. Adminstrn., Olympia, 1973-77; v.p. adminstrn. Crowley Maritime Corp./N.W. and Alaska div., 1977-78; pres., chmn. bd. Applied Audio-Video Systems, Inc., Tacoma, 1978—; pres., chmn. bd. Pacific Commerce Co., Inc., Mercer Island, Wash., 1979—; mem. steering com., exptl. tech. incentives program Nat. Bur. Standards; dir. Pub. Procurement Research Found. NASPO, Inc., Lexington, Ky., 1975-76. Active Boys Scouts Am., Falls Church, Va., 1965-68; pres. Babe Ruth Baseball League, Juneau, 1970; chmn. site and accommodations com. White House Conf. on Handicapped Individuals, State of Wash., 1976; active Alaska Gubernatorial Campaign, 1970; Sunday sch. tchr. Immanuel United Methodist Ch., Annandale, Va., 1967-68, Mercer Island (Wash.) Presbyn. Ch., 1973-74. Recipient Career Edn. award, Nat. Inst. Pub. Affairs, 1966-67; Nat. Inst. Pub. Affairs fellow, 1967. Mem. Am. Soc. Pub. Adminstrn., Wash. State Hist. Adv. Council, Nat. Assn. State Purchasing Ofcls. Republican. Methodist. Club: Rotary. Home: 9248 SE 59th St Mercer Island WA 98040 Office: Maritime Business Park 5308 12th St E Tacoma WA 98424

ANGLIN, MAX MILLARD, foundry exec.; b. Leesburg, Ind., Sept. 24, 1935; s. H.B. and Mae G. (Stookey) A.; student Manchester Coll., 1953-56, Wabash Coll., 1973-75; m. Janice Reed, Aug. 7, 1954; children—Gary Wayne, Tammie Lynn, April Ann. With First Nat. Bank, Warsaw, Ind., 1955-56; asst. purchasing agt. Dalton Foundries, Warsaw, 1956-58, sales engr., 1958-65, sales mgr., 1965-71, v.p. sales, 1971—. Active Salvation Army, fund dr. Girl Scouts U.S.A., YMCA; chmn. County Republican Com., 1966-70, del. state conv., 1966-68, congl. campaign mgr., 1968; sch. bd. trustee, 1978-80, pres., 1981; pres. Bd. Aviation, 1980-81. Served with Ind. NG, 1953-61. Recipient Distinguished Service award United Fund, 1971. Mem. Gray Iron Foundry Soc. (mktg. chmn., Gredee award 1978), Am. Ordnance Assn. (sec. casting sect.), Am. Foundry Soc. Methodist. Clubs: Kiwanis, Masons (past master), Scottish Rite, Shriners, Optimist, Elks. Home: Rural Route 2 Warsaw IN 46580 Office: Lincoln and Jefferson Sts Warsaw IN 46580

ANGUS, MELVYN GRAHAM, corp. dir.; b. Stratford, Ont., Can., Jan. 19, 1911; s. William D. and Elizabeth (Graham) A.; B. Comm., U. Toronto (Ont.), 1932; m. Ada M. Hutchison, Sept. 30, 1936; children—William David, Elizabeth (Mrs. G.H. Eberts), Gillian (Mrs. Michel Cote). Staff Dominion Mortgage & Investments Assn., Toronto, 1932-35, asst. sec.-treas., 1935-36; asso. Angus & Co., mem. Toronto and Montreal Stock Exchanges, 1936-41; dir. Clark Ruse Aircraft Ltd., Dartmouth, N.S., 1941-45; pres. Lunham & Moore Ltd. and Asso. Cos., Montreal, 1945-80, Madeg Holdings Inc., Montreal, 1980—; dir. Nat. Trust Co. Ltd., Toronto, Comml. Union of Can. Holdings Ltd., Toronto. Chmn. Montreal Gen. Hosp. Found. Clubs: Mt. Royal, St. James's, Univ., Mt. Bruno (Montreal); Nat. (Toronto). Home: 2 Westmount Sq Montreal PQ H3Z 2S4 Canada Office: Suite 1410 One Westmount Sq Montreal PQ H3Z 2R5 Canada

ANGUS, ROBERT CARLYLE, JR., respiratory therapist; b. Grand Rapids, Mich., July 23, 1946; s. Robert Carlyle and Violet Ileen (Weidman-Deiters) A.; student Grand Rapids Community Coll., 1974; diploma respiratory therapy, St. Mary's Hosp., Grand Rapids Community Coll., 1974; diploma respiratory therapy, St. Mary's Hosp., Grand Rapids. Tech. dir. St. Mary's Hosp., 1970-73; staff therapist Grand Rapids Osteo. Hosp., 1973-74; head dept. respiratory therapy Hackley Hosp., Muskegon, Mich., 1974-76; dept. head cardiovascular lab. and pulmonary div. Am. Internat. Hosp., Zion, Ill., 1976-79; med. dir. and physician's asst. in medicine Mauer Clinic, Zion, Ill., 1978—; cons., lectr. in field; speaker numerous profl. confs. Active local Big Bros./Big Sisters, Boy Scouts Am. Served with USAF, 1964-67; Vietnam. Fellow Am. Coll. Respiratory Therapists; mem. Nat. Bd. Respiratory Therapy, Am. Assn. Respiratory Therapy, Nat. Soc. Cardiopulmonary Technologists, Am. Cardiology Technologists Assn., Mich., Ill. socs. respiratory therapy, Ill. Soc. Cardiopulmonary Technologists. Lutheran. Home: 1106 Oak Forest Dr Zion IL 60099 Office: Mauer Clinic 1819 27th St Zion IL 60099

ANKER, TIIA KARI, business exec.; b. Poltsamaa, Estonia, Apr. 11, 1937; came to U.S., 1949, naturalized, 1960; d. Handu and Vera (Masso) Kari; B.S., Washington U., 1958; M.B.A., Columbia U., 1975; children—Philip Allen, Kent Kari. Exec. trainee Bloomingdale's, N.Y.C., 1958-59; asso. buyer Frederich Atkins, N.Y.C., 1959-61; asst. fashion dir. Nat. Cotton Council, N.Y.C., 1961-64; ind. cons., N.Y.C., 1965-73; asst. to pres. Furnishings div. Sperry Hutchinson Co., N.Y.C., 1975-80; account supr. Peter Martin Assos., N.Y.C., 1980-81; chmn. and chief exec. officer Laurence Handprints N.J., Inc., N.Y.C., 1981—. Mem. Washington U. Alumni Council, 1960—, Columbia U. Alumni Adv. Council, 1975—; bd. dirs. YWCA, Darien, Conn., 1970-72; mem. drug abuse and prevention and art edn. com. Jr. League, 1970-73; active PTA, Darien, and N.Y.C., 1970—. Nat. Honor scholar, Washington U., 1954-58. Mem. Nat. Home Fashions League (treas. 1978-80, Am. Mktg. Assn., Mortar Board. Home: 531 Main St New York NY 10044 Office: 979 3d Ave New York NY 10022

ANSCHER, BERNARD, plastics mfg. co. exec.; b. Bklyn., June 9, 1922; s. Abraham and Esther (Draznin) A.; student Sch. Tech., CCNY, 1939-42; B.Mech. Engring., N.Y. U., 1948, M.B.A., 1953, postgrad., 1953-65; m. Marcia Daniel, Mar. 7, 1942; children—William, Marlene, Joseph. Chief, metall. and fabrication devel. reactor materials br. AEC, N.Y.C., 1946-50; devel., mgr., gen. sales mgr. domestic sales, asst. to v.p. Loewy-Hydropress, Inc., N.Y.C., 1950-55; cons., mfrs.' rep. Mercury Engring. Co., N.Y.C., 1955-65; founder, pres. Nat. Molding Corp., Farmingdale, N.Y., 1965—; pres. Custom Molds, Opa Locka, Fla., 1975—; founder, instr. mktg. program in community coll., N.Y.C., 1962-65; mem. industry adv. group Underwriters Labs. Queens County committeeman Republican Party, 1960-68. Served with AUS, 1943-46; PTO. Recipient Spl. award Manhattan Dist., 1946; registered profl. engr., Calif. Mem. N.Y. State Mktg. Educators (chmn. curriculum research com. 1964), Soc. Mfg. Engrs., Soc. Plastics Engrs., Am. Mgmt. Assn., Am. Mus. Natural History (asso.), N.Y. U. Alumni Assn., John Jay Assos. Columbia. Reviewing editor Die Design Handbook, 1954-55; patentee; contbr. publs. in field. Office: 5 Dubon Ct Farmingdale NY 11735

ANSPACH, HERBERT K., appliance mfg. co. exec.; b. Ada, Ohio, Sept. 3, 1926; s. Eldred and Della (Kephart) A.; B.S.M.E., U. Wis., 1947; J.D., U. Mich., 1952; m. Elizabeth McKenzie, June 5, 1952; 1 dau., Heather. Devel. engr. Goodyear Tire & Rubber Co., St. Mary's Ohio, 1947-49; labor relations rep. Kaiser Motors, Willow Run, Mich., 1953, supr. indsl. relations, Shadyside, Ohio, 1953-54; patent examiner U.S. Dept. Commerce, Washington, 1954-55; with Whirlpool Corp., Benton Harbor, Mich., 1955-75, v.p. personnel until 1975, pres., chief operating officer, 1977—; exec. v.p. Inglis Ltd., Toronto, Ont., Can., 1975, pres., chief operating officer, 1975-76, chmn. bd., 1976-77. Served with USN, 1944-46. Clubs: Met., Union League (Chgo.); Toronto; Point o' Woods (Benton Harbor, Mich.). Home: 2792 Sandra Terr Saint Joseph MI 49085 Office: 2000 US 33 N Benton Harbor MI 49022

ANTHONY, CLEON EARL, JR., investment and financial services co. exec.; b. San Luis Obispo, Calif., June 9, 1931; s. Cleon Earl and Olwyn Eudora (Hawbecker) A.; grad. Realtors Inst., 1974; m. Shirley Wardona, Oct. 31, 1953; children—Lorynn Donnell Anthony Tinder, Cleon Russell, Theresa Doreen, Donnell Amy. Mgr., Merc. Laurentide Fin. Co., Fresno, Calif., 1954-63; pres., realtor Anthony Investment Properties, Inc., Fresno, 1967—; pres. Anthony Investments and Fin. Services, Fresno, 1979—. Served with USN, 1950-54. Lic. real estate broker, life ins. agt., Calif. Mem. Fresno Assn. Realtors, Calif. Assn. Realtors, Nat. Assn. Realtors, Internat. Assn. Fin. Planners, Internat. Soc. Financiers, Am. Mortgage Brokers Assn., Nat. Mktg. Inst., Internat. Exchangors Assn. Republican. Mormon. Home: PO Box 207 Friant CA 93626 Office: PO Box 598 Pinedale Fresno CA 93650

ANTHONY, EDWARD LOVELL, II, editor, publisher; b. Boston, Sept. 24, 1921; s. DeForest and Dorothy Heath (Dodge) A.; A.B., Harvard, 1943, M.B.A., 1952; m. Constance Foss, Oct. 2, 1954; children—Edward L., Victoria N., Richard G. D. Asst. to pres. Daltry Opera Co., Middletown, Conn., 1938-40; asst. to head master, Manter Hall Sch., Cambrige, Mass., 1941; asso. editor Pub. Affairs Press, Washington, 1945-46; asst. chief photo intelligence tng. U.S. Navy, Washington, 1946-50; chief publs. div. SBA, Washington, 1952-62; editor Harvard Bus. Sch. Bull., Boston, 1962—, asso. Office Career Services and Off-Campus Learning; treas., dir. Lomel Corp. Trustee, Vermont Acad., Pine Manor Coll.; chmn. fin. com. Dr. Franklin Perkins Sch.; mem. publs. adv. com. Cambridge C. of C. Served in U.S. Army, 1942-45. Mem. Council for Advancement and Support of Edn., Nat. Freelance Photographers Assn., Internat. Council Small Bus., Order of Lafayette, English-Speaking Union, Nat. Assn. Retarded Citizens, Navy League U.S. Republican. Episcopalian. Clubs: Country (Brookline, Mass.); Harvard (Boston); The Hundred Club of Mass.; Harvard (N.Y.); Univ. (Washington); Friends of Boston Symphony Orch. Contbr. articles in field to profl. jours. Editor Exec. Letter, 1965-69. Home: 68 Woodcliff Rd Wellesley Hills MA 02181 Office: Harvard Bus Sch Boston MA 02163

ANTHONY, GUY MAULDIN, retail exec.; b. Cleveland, Okla., Apr. 26, 1915; s. Charles Ross and Lutie Lillian (Mauldin) A.; B.S., Wharton Sch., U. Pa., 1936; m. Christine Elizabeth Holland, Mar. 27, 1945; children—Charles Ross, Guy Mauldin, Robert Holland, Roy Jay, Jack Holland, Tom Albert. With C.R. Anthony Co., Oklahoma City, 1936—, v.p., dir. personnel, 1942-72, pres., chmn. exec. com., 1972—; dir. Liberty Nat. Bank, Community Nat. Bank (both Oklahoma City), Quaker Life Ins. Co., Tulsa. Bd. dirs. Northside YMCA, Oklahoma City, Cassady Sch., Last Frontier council Boy Scouts Am., United Fund Oklahoma City; chmn. for Okla., Nat. Com. Employer Support of Guard and Res., 1979—. Served with U.S. Army, World War II. Decorated Bronze Star with oak leaf cluster. Mem. Okla. C. of C., Oklahoma City C. of C., Sigma Nu. Democrat. Methodist. Clubs: Oklahoma City Golf and Country (dir.), Rotary, Economic, Men's Dinner. Office: PO Box 25725 Oklahoma City OK 73125

ANTHONY, PERRY, transp. co. exec.; b. Phila., July 8, 1940; s. Fredrick and Marjorie (Perry) A.; B.A., Grove City Coll., 1963; postgrad. Newark State U., 1964-65; m. Alyce Anderson, Aug. 17, 1963; children—Victoria Lynn, Theodore Perry. Mgr. mktg. communications Westinghouse Electric Corp., Pitts., 1968-69, mgr. nat. distbn., 1970-74; v.p. transp. Allied Van Lines, Inc., Omaha, 1976-80, v.p. household goods div., 1980—; rep. to energy com. Am. Trucking Assn. Mem. Nat. Traffic Club, Assn. Nat. Advertisers, Research Inst. Am. (exec. mem.), Omaha C. of C. Home: 1111 Ridgewood Ave Omaha NE 68124 Office: 10225 Allied Circle Omaha NE 68134

ANTHONY, RICK (LEE), bank exec.; b. Warrensburg, Mo., May 8, 1953; s. E.L. and Fern Anthony; B.S. in Econs., U. Mo., Columbia, 1975; M.B.A., Drury Coll., 1980; grad. Nat. Comml. Lending Sch.; cert. Am. Inst. Banking, 1978; m. Monica L. Blair, June 1, 1979. Br. mgr. Jefferson City Prodn. Credit Assn. (Mo.), 1975-77; v.p. 1st Nat. Bank & Trust Co., Joplin, Mo., 1977-78; v.p. First Nat. Bank, Mt. Vernon, Mo., 1978-80; exec. v.p., chief exec. officer Bank of Wheaton (Mo.), 1980—; dir. Farmer's Mut. Ins. Co.; guest prof. Drury Coll., Springfield, Mo. Pres. Indsl. Devel. Com., Wheaton. Mem. Am. Bankers Assn., Mo. Bankers Assn., Mt. Vernon C. of C., Am. Soc. Farm Mgrs. and Rural Appraisers. Roman Catholic. Clubs: Rotary, Lions, K.C. Home: 421 W Dallas Mount Vernon MO 65712 Office: PO Box 17 Wheaton MO 64874

ANTHONY, THOMAS NILE, ins. co. exec.; b. East Liverpool, Ohio, Oct. 25, 1935; s. Norman H. and Jane (Gessford) A.; student Ohio U., 1954-57; diagnostic X-ray degree U. Western Pa., 1958; children—Thomas N., Matthew D., Stephen G., Christopher T., Mark A. Sales rep. Warren Taad, Inc., Jamestown, N.Y., 1958-61; mgr. sales IBM, Jamestown, 1961-65; brokerage rep. Conn. Gen. Ins. Co., Miami, 1965-67; asst. to pres. Cockaigno, Inc., Jamestown, 1964-65; mgr. Md. Life Ins. Co., Miami, 1967-69; pres. Thomas Anthony Assos., Inc., Ft. Lauderdale, Fla., 1969—; pres. Hollywood Meml. Gardens; dir. Atlantic Telephone Equipment Co. Pres. Ft. Lauderdale Community Service Council, 1973-77; bd. dirs. Help on Wheels, 1973-77; bd. dirs., pres. Adv. Council Transp. for Sr. Citizens; bd. dirs. Emergency Family Housing Center; bd. dirs., v.p. Star of David Meml. Gardens; bd. dirs., mem. exec. com. Broward County Health Planning and Rehab. Council, pres., 1978—; mem. Broward County Drug Abuse Council; mem. Broward County Estate Planning Council; bd. dirs. Govt. Adv. Council Health Rehab. Services, Tenn. Adv. Council Manpower, Hospice of Broward, Inc., 1980; chmn. Coll. for Human Services, 1980; mem. ADOC, So. Fla. State Hosp. Broward County Assn. Life Underwriters. Republican. Lutheran. Clubs: Tower, Tennis, Le Club Internat., Touchdown, Marian Bay, Coral Ridge Country, Player's, Elks. Office: 5100 N Federal Hwy Fort Lauderdale FL 33308

ANTIL, FREDERICK HOLMAN, educator; b. Cortland, N.Y., Aug. 11, 1933; s. Michael Charles and Mary Margaret (Holman) A.; B.S., Cornell U., 1955; LL.B., Blackstone Sch. Law, 1963; M.S., George Washington U., 1968; children—Victoria Elizabeth, Frederick Holman, Michele Cathleen. Dir. tng. and mgmt. devel. Marriott Corp., Washington, 1959-67, Playboy Internat., Chgo., 1968-69; v.p. ednl. services Aims Edn., Inc., Lake Success, N.Y., 1969-71; v.p. edn. and tgn. div. Life Office Mgmt. Assn., N.Y.C., 1972-77; v.p. in-house devel. and tng. div. Am. Mgmt. Assn., N.Y.C., 1977—; text reviewer Addison Wesley, McGraw-Hill; lectr. Cornell U., Mich. State U., Pa. State U., Pratt Inst., U.S. Army Quartermaster Sch.; lectr. profl. orgns., corps. Republican precinct capt., Northbrook, Ill., 1968; mem. Cornell Alumni Secondary Sch. Com., 1972—; col. Manhasset United Givers Fund, 1974; adv. bd. N.Y. State Regents External Degree Program; mem. Manhasset Continuing Edn. Com.; mem. White House Career Opportunities for Youth Program, 1966-67. Served to 1st lt., USMC, 1956-59. Accredited personnel diplomate. Fellow Life Mgmt. Inst.; mem. Nat. Assn. Trade and Tech. Schs. (adv. bd.), Am. Soc. Tng. and Devel., Internat. Platform Assn., Hotel and Restaurant Assn. India (asso. editorial and mgmt. bd. 1974-75), Delta Upsilon. Republican. Roman Catholic. Clubs: Cornell of L.I. (v.p.), Toastmasters of Arlington (past pres.). Editorial bd. Tng. Mag., 1978-80; contbr. articles to profl. jours. Office: 135 W 50th St New York NY 10020

ANTOINE, ROY WILLIAM, mktg. devel. co. exec.; b. Lowell, Mass., June 9, 1957; s. Ramon Edwin and Eleanor Elizabeth (MacFarlane) A.; B.S., Purdue U., 1978; M.B.A., Harvard U., 1980. Regional sales, tng. supr. Chromalloy Am. Corp., St. Louis, 1979; fin. cons. AAMCO, Bridgeport, Pa., 1980; pres. Surcan Corp., Salem, N.H., 1980—. Apptd. mem. Salem Bd. Adjustment, 1979. Mem. Smithsonian Instn., Kappa Delta Rho. Republican. Congregationalist. Club: Northmeadow Tennis. Office: Surcan Corp 157 Bluff St Salem NH 03079

ANTON, ALBERT JOSEPH, JR., investment analyst; b. N.Y.C., Jan. 6, 1936; s. Albert Joseph and Helen (Cichoski) A.; A.B., Columbia, 1957; M.B.A., U. Pa., 1959; m. Sara Jane Lembcke, Sept. 6, 1958; children—Claire Elizabeth, Christopher Paul, Thomas Robert. Vice pres., div. exec. Chase Manhattan Bank, N.Y.C., 1959-69; partner Carl H. Pfozheimer & Co., N.Y.C., 1970—; mem. investment com. Petroleum and Trading Corp., N.Y.C., 1970—, dir., 1978—; dir. Burnwood Corp., N.Y.C. Vice chmn. South Orange-Maplewood YMCA, 1973-77, chmn., 1977-78; bd. dirs. YMCA of the Oranges, Maplewood and West Essex, N.J., 1975—, treas., 1977—; trustee Village of South Orange, 1971-73, also chmn. fin. com., 1971-73; mem. bd. sch. estimate South Orange-Maplewood, 1971-73; mem. bd. St. Benedict's Prep. Sch., Newark, 1978—. Served with USAF, 1961-62. Chartered fin. analyst. Mem. Inst. Chartered Fin. Analysts, N.Y. Soc. Security Analysts, Ind. Petroleum Assn. Am., Nat. Assn. Petroleum Investment Analysts (dir. 1976—, treas. 1976-78, sec. 1978-79, pres. 1979—), Oil Analysts Group N.Y., Internat. Assn. Energy Economists, Soc. Mining Engrs., Delta Upsilon. Roman Catholic. Club: City Mid-day. Home: 332 Beech Spring Rd South Orange NJ 07079 Office: 70 Pine St New York NY 10005

ANTON, HARVEY, textile co. exec.; b. N.Y.C., Nov. 10, 1923; s. Abraham J. and Byrdie (Casin) A.; student Western State Coll. Colo., 1941, Savage Sch. Edn., 1941-42; B.S., N.Y. U., 1949; m. Betty L. Weintraub, Dec. 18, 1949; children—Bruce Norman, Lynne Beth. Pres., Anton Yarn Corp. (merged 1959 with Robison Textile Co. to form Robison-Anton Textile Co.), N.Y.C., 1949-50, exec. v.p., 1959-73, pres., 1973—. Trustee, Emerson Jewish Center, 1958-59, Ezra Charitable Found.; pres. Anton Found. Served to 1st lt. AUS, 1943-46. Mason, K.P. Club: N.Y. U. Letter (N.Y.C.). Home: 41 Longview Dr Emerson NJ 07630 Office: Bergen Bldg Fairview NJ 07022

ANTON, MARK J., propane gas exec.; b. Newark, Feb. 12, 1926; s. Mark and Adele (Buecke) A.; B.A., Bowdoin Coll., Brunswick, Maine, 1951; m. Elizabeth Flower, Oct. 31, 1953. With Suburban Propane Gas Corp., Morristown, N.J., v.p. sales, 1958-61, exec. v.p., dir., 1961-63, pres., chief exec. officer, dir., 1963-79, pres., chief exec. officer, chmn. bd., 1979—; dir. The Pittston Co., Horizon Bancorp, Am. Nat. Bank & Trust Co. of N.J. Served with U.S. Navy, 1944-46. Mem. N.J. C. of C. (dir.), Nat. LP Gas Assn. (hon. dir.), Twenty-Five Year Club Petroleum Industry. Clubs: Baltusrol Golf (Springfield, N.J.); Beacon Hill (Summit, N.J.). Office: PO Box 2165R 334 Madison Ave Morristown NJ 07960

ANTONICELLO, ANTHONY NICHOLAS, investment co. exec.; b. Jersey City, Feb. 13, 1931; s. Giacomo and Angelina (Coniglio) A.; m. Apr. 25, 1965. Pres., Consol. Parker Inc., North Bergen, N.J., also RonLou Realty, L & R Meadowlands Corp., Coniglio & Towers Inc. Club: Moose. Office: Consol Parker Inc 1500 47th St North Bergen NJ 07047

ANTONINI, MARION HUGH, diversified mfg. co. exec.; b. Clinton, Ind., June 7, 1930; s. Valentine and Josephine (Dal Sasso) A.; B.S. in Mech. Engring., U. Toledo, 1952; m. Penelope Sue Fromong, Dec. 20, 1971; children—Caryn Marie, John Marius. Gen. foreman on spl. assignment to works mgr. Willys Motors Inc., Toledo, 1952-54; mgr. assembly and mfg. services Willys Overland Export Corp., Toledo, 1955-59; asst. mng. dir. Willys Overseas S.A., Zug, Switzerland, 1959-61; adminstrv. dir. Kaiser Jeep Internat. Corp., Toledo, 1961-64, v.p., mng. dir., Oakland, Calif., 1964-66; group v.p. Eltra Corp., pres. Prestolite Internat. Co., N.Y.C., 1967-75; pres. Eltra Internat. Co., N.Y.C., 1973-75; corp. v.p. Xerox Corp., 1975—, pres. Xerox Latin Am. Group, 1975-78, group v.p. for Can.-Latin Am. and Middle East, 1978-80, group v.p. and pres. internat. ops., 1980—. Mem. U.S. Export Expansion Council, 1960, Commn. U.S.-Brazil Relations, 1980; chmn. bd. Codel Nat. Council, 1974. Bd. dirs. Friends of Philippines Found.; bd. dirs., mem. exec. com. Council of Ams.; vice-chmn. United Way campaign, New Canaan, New Canaan YMCA dr. Named Toledo's Outstanding Young Man, 1957, One of Ohio's Five Outstanding Young Men, 1957, One of America's Outstanding Young Men, 1966. Mem. Soc. Automotive Engrs., Woodward Engring. Soc. (pres.), U. Toledo Alumni Assn. (pres.), Blue Key, Kappa Sigma Kappa (pres.). Home: 79 Ferris Hill Rd New Canaan CT 06840 Office: Xerox Corp Long Ridge Rd Stamford CT 06904

ANTOS, JOHN JEFFREY, mgmt. cons., real estate developer; b. Chgo., Jan. 13, 1949; s. Frank J. and Estelle (Petko) A.; B.S. in Bus. Adminstrn., U. Ill., 1971; M.B.A., U. Chgo., 1976; m. Lana Ethelyn Uryasz, Feb. 12, 1978. Asst. sales mgr. Southwestern Co., Nashville, 1968-73; pres. Antos & Assos., Chgo., 1973-75; fin. analyst Marsh & McLennan, Chgo., 1975-77; sr. cons. W.A. Golomski & Assos., Chgo., 1977-79; mgmt. cons., real estate developer, Chgo. and Riviera Beach, Fla., 1980—; tchr. grad. acctg. Roosevelt U., Chgo. Founder, pres. Young Execs. Club, Chgo., 1974-77; co-founder Republican Assos., Chgo., 1978. Mem. Nat. Assn. Accts., Am. Soc. Quality Control, Midwest Planning Assn. Home: 701 Deer Chase Rd Lake Zurich IL 60047 Office: 150 Bradley Pl Suite 614C Palm Beach FL 33480

AOYAMA, KENNETH MOTOHARU, agrl. and forestry engring. and mgmt. co. exec.; b. Newell, Calif., Jan. 1, 1945; s. Dan M. and Miyoke Aoyama; B.S. in Agrl. Engring. and Agronomy (Agrl. Edn. Found. fellow, 1975-76), Calif. State Poly. U., 1967; m. Katsue Miyahira, Feb. 14, 1970; 1 dau., Jennifer. Pres., owner Cal Delta Farm, Inc., Lodi, Calif., 1970-78, Ag West, Inc., Sacramento, 1973—; pres., co-owner Poly Ag Inc., Lodi, 1971-78; cons. agrl. engring. projects in Spain, Libya, Jordan, 1976—. Served to capt. USMC, 1967-70. Decorated Navy Commendation medal with combat V, Vietnamese Cross Gallantry. Mem. Am. Soc. Agrl. Engrs., Am. Soc. Farm Mgrs., Council Calif. Growers, Agrl. Leadership Assn., Geothermal Council, Calif. Jaycees (dist. v.p. 1971-72), Calif. State Poly. U. Alumni Assn. Alpha Zeta. Republican. Patentee aide for harvesting cannery tomatoes, mech. harvesting of cannery tomatoes apparatus, loading and transporting vehicle for module cotton, milti-till implement. Home: 803 Mace Blvd Davis CA 95616 Office: 1451 River Park Dr Suite 150 Sacramento CA 95815

APANA, ROGER GLENN, trucking co. exec.; b. Honolulu, Apr. 12, 1950; s. Carl Marmion and Joyce (Matsue) A.; B.B.A. in Acctg., U. Hawaii, 1974; m. Charmaine Je Niwa, Apr. 13, 1974; children—Michelle, Kristy, Raun. Labor and office clk. Maui (Hawaii) Scrap Metal Co., 1974-77; mgr. Maui Trucking, 1977—; mgr., dir. Maui Scrap Metal Co., Inc. Mem. Hawaii Transp. Assn. (dir.), Maui Contractors Assn. Home: 2762 Iolani St Pukalani HI 96788 Office: 1791 Waiinu Rd Wailuku Maui HI 96788

APONTE, JUAN B., banker; b. Gurabo, P.R., July 13, 1929; s. Bautista and Esperanza (Vasquez) A.; B.S., U. P.R., 1950; M.S. in Actuarial Math., U. Mich., 1955; Ph.D. in Applied Econs. and Ins., U. Pa., 1962; m. Milagros Mendez; children by previous marriage—Ines, Maribel, Marines. Asso. prof. ins. Wharton Sch. Fin. and Commerce, U. Pa., Phila., 1966-69; chmn. Govt. of P.R. Commn. on Universal Health Ins., San Juan, 1972-74; dean faculty bus. adminstrn. U. P.R., Pio Piedras, 1969-73; chmn. bd. Banco Metropolitano de Bayamon (P.R.), 1974-76; pres. First Fed. Savs. & Loan Assn. P.R., San Juan, 1975—; dir. Fed. Home Loan Bank N.Y.; cons. actuary various govt. agys., pvt. enterprises; prof. ins. Grad. Sch. Bus., U. P.R. Served to 1st lt. U.S. Army, 1950-52. Fellow Heubner Found. Ins. Edn. Mem. Am. Acad. Actuaries, Conf. Actuaries in Pub. Practice. Active in establishing ins. coops. in P.R., adoption of structure by Peru, Chile, Ecuador; author, co-author various reports for govt. of P.R.; contbr. numerous articles in field to profl. jours. Office: Box 9146 Santurce PR 00908

APOSTOLOU, ALEXANDER, pharmacologist-toxicologist; b. Athens, Greece, Mar. 3, 1926; came to U.S., 1965, naturalized, 1973; s. John and Angeliki A.; D.V.M., Ecole National Veterinaire de France, 1951; Ph.D. in Comparative Pharmacology and Toxicology, U. Calif., Davis, 1969; m. Lynn C. Davis, May 13, 1977. Head vet. drug div. ADELCO Pharm., Athens, 1960-64; sr. scientist Litton-Bionetics, 1970-72; chief pharmacology-toxicology Gulf South Research Inst., North Iberia, La., 1972; research fellow Merck Sharp & Dohme, West Point, Pa., 1972-76; dir. dept. pharmacology-toxicology Westwood Pharms. div. Bristol-Myers, Buffalo, 1977—. Served to maj., Vet. Corps, Greek Army, 1951-65. Diplomate Am. Bd. Toxicology. Mem. AVMA, Am. Soc. Toxicology, European Soc. Toxciology, Am. Coll. Toxicology, Am. Coll. Vet. Toxicology, Nat. Soc. Med. Research, N.Y. Acad. Scis., AAAS, Soc. Comparative Ophthalmology, Am. Soc. Photobiology, Pharm. Mfrs. Assn. Found., Inflammation Research Assn., Am. Acad. Dermatology. Home: 1350 Amherst Buffalo NY 14216 Office: 468 Dewitt Buffalo NY 14213

APPEL, ARTHUR, conv. mgmt. exec.; b. Bklyn., June 10, 1935; s. Benjamin and Sarah (Weiner) A.; student Hunter Coll., 1952-54, Coll. City N.Y., 1954-55; m. Jill Lynne Ginsberg, Apr. 28, 1977; children—Lori, Gary, Stacie. Bus. agt. Internat. Ladies' Garment Workers Union, Bridgeport, Conn., 1957-69; pres. Conv. and Group Travel Assos., Ltd., Bridgeport, 1969-74; dir. congress/convs. Thomas Cook, N.Y.C., 1974-76; v.p. meetings/convs. Unitours, Inc., N.Y.C., 1976-79; pres. Conv. Dimensions Inc., Orangeburg, N.Y., 1979—; conv. cons. Air France, Alitalia, El Al airlines. Mem. Am. Soc. Assn. Execs., Assn. Group Travel Execs., Meeting Planners Internat. Club: Lions. Author pamphlets in field. Office: Prel Plaza Orangeburg NY 10962

APPEL, BERNARD SIDNEY, electronic co. exec.; b. Boston, Jan. 10, 1932; s. Max and Sophie (Altshuler) A.; A.A. in Bus. Adminstrn., Boston U., 1959; m. Shirley Lane Blair, Mar. 8, 1980; children—Arlene R., Gerald I. Store mgr., buyer S & W Distbg. Co., Boston, 1949-59; buyer Radio Shack Co., Boston, 1959-66, mdse. mgr., Boston, 1967-70, v.p. merchandising, Fort Worth, 1970-78, sr. v.p. merchandising and advt., 1979-80, exec. v.p. mktg., 1980—. Vice pres. Holbrook (Mass.) Jewish Community Center, 1958-59; v.p., founder Temple Aliyah, Needham, Mass., 1969-70; pres. Congregation Ahavath Sholom, Fort Worth, 1979-80; bd. dirs. Jewish Fedn. Fort Worth, 1975—. Served with USCG, 1951-54. Mem. Electronic V.I.P. Club. Clubs: Masons, Shriners, Frog (Tex. Christian U.). Home: 3520 Arborlawn Dr N Fort Worth TX 76109 Office: 1600 One Tandy Center Fort Worth TX 76102

APPELBAUM, MURRAY, wholesale distbg. co. exec.; b. Poland, May 2, 1938; came to U.S., 1951, naturalized, 1956; s. Charles and Jennie A.; B.B.A., CCNY, 1960; m. Estelle Novick, Nov. 14, 1959; children—Eilene, Cheryl. Partner, Appelbaum Food Markets, Bronx, N.Y., 1959-69; pres. Selecto Products Co. Inc., Ardsley, N.Y., 1969—. Mem. Housewares Club N.Y. Club: B'nai B'rith. Office: Selecto Products Co Inc One Elm St Ardsley NY 10502

APPERSON, MARJORIE MAY, newspaper exec.; b. San Francisco, Apr. 22, 1929; d. John Philip and Jessie Lucille (Earl) Sampson; B.A., Stanford, 1950; children—Virginia, April, John. Co-owner, editor Mt. Shasta (Calif.) Herald, 1950—, Weed (Calif.) Press, 1970—; co-pub., editor So. Siskiyou Newspapers, Inc.; panelist Western Newspaper Found. Seminar, 1975. Mem. Mt. Shasta Planning Commn., 1966-70, chairperson, 1969; mem. Overall Econ. Devel. Planning Com. Siskiyou County (Calif.), 1970; mem. archtl. adv. com. Siskiyou County Planning Commn., 1974—. Mem. AAUW, Calif. Newspaper Pubs. Assn. (v.p. 1975, pres. Mid-Valley unit 1976; dir. 1977-78, 80-81; govtl. affairs com. 1977-80, membership chairperson 1980—). Home: 806 McCloud Ave Mount Shasta CA 96067 Office: PO Box 127 Mount Shasta CA 96067

APPLE, PETER GILBERT, rubber products, machinery and chems. co. exec.; b. Dayton, Ohio, Oct. 17, 1929; s. Donald W. and Vera V. (Gray) A.; ed. U. Dayton, State U. N.Y. at Buffalo; LL.B., LaSalle Extension U., 1969; m. Mary L. Wheeler, Aug. 23, 1947; children—Rebecca Sue, Steven Lynn. Dist. sales mgr. Precision Rubber Products Corp., Dayton, Ohio, 1950-70; pres., owner Apple Rubber Products, Inc., Lancaster, N.Y., 1970—. Republican. Clubs: Country of Buffalo, Rotary Internat. Home: 316 Brantwood Rd Snyder NY 14226 Office: 310 Erie St Lancaster NY 14086

APPLE, THOMAS LLOYD, bank exec.; b. Balt., Jan. 25, 1954; s. Charles Spicer and Dolores Jean (Wilburne) A.; B.A., Towson State U., 1975; M.B.A., Johns Hopkins U., 1979. Pres., Apple Prodns., Inc., Balt., 1974-75; v.p. Marshall Electronics, Joppa, Md., 1975-77; chief exec. Apple Industries, Inc., Balt., 1977—; cons. Creative Entertainment Services, 1976-79; with comptroller's acting services group Md. Nat. Bank, 1979—; dir. Sheffield Recordings, Ltd., 1977-79. Republican. Episcopalian. Home: PO Box 9 Phoenix MD 21131 Office: 10 Light St Baltimore MD 21203

APPLEBAUM, HERBERT AARON, constrn. co. exec.; b. Bklyn., Oct. 15, 1925; s. Herman and Rose A.; B.S. in Econs., Columbia U., 1950; M.A. in Sociology, Gannon Coll., 1971; M.A. in Anthropology, SUNY, Buffalo, 1975, Ph.D. in Urban Anthropology, 1979; m. Mika Nye, Aug. 12, 1979; children—Stephen, Michael, Amanda, Robert, Aleta, Eric, Alexia. Controller, Raymar Contracting Corp., Long Island City, N.Y., 1951-60; constrn. cons. Home Ins. Co., also Glens Falls Ins. Co., 1960-62; pres. Stevens Constrn. Co., N.Y.C., 1962-66; chief contract adminstr. Baldwin Bros., Erie, Pa., 1967-70; v.p. First Allegheny Constrn. Co., Erie, 1970-72; project mgr. Albert Elia Bldg. Co., Niagara Falls, N.Y., 1972—; tchr. econs., sociology and anthropology, adult edn. and evening classes, various community colls., 1965-78. Served with USN, 1943-46. Werner-Gren Found. fellow, 1978. Fellow Am. Anthrop. Assn., Soc. Applied Anthropology; mem. Am. Ethnology Assn., Northeastern Anthrop. Assn. Author: Royal Blue-The Culture of Construction Workers, 1980. Home and office: 509 Shunpike Rd Erie PA 16508

APPLEBY, WESLEY RAY, constrn. co. exec.; b. Grand Saline, Tex., May 23, 1929; s. Peter Wesley and Candace (Reid) A.; B.Arch., Tex. Technol. U., 1952; m. Betty Ann Norman, Aug. 2, 1952; children—Linda Denise, Wesley Ray. Mng. partner La Casa Builders, Odessa, Tex., 1954-61; pres. W.R. Appleby, Inc., Midland, Tex., 1961-70; gen. partner W.R. Appleby Constrn. Co., Ltd., Anchorage, 1970-74, Appleby Constrn. Co., Ltd., 1974—. Mem. Nat. Assn. Home Builders, Home Owners Warranty Council Alaska (pres. 1978-80). Address: 6701 Lunar Dr Anchorage AK 99504

APPLEGATE, ORAL LESTER, mfg. co. exec.; b. Maysville, Ky., Jan. 14, 1917; s. Earl and Marguerite (Macy) A.; m. Ruth D. Hensgen, Sept. 14, 1935; children—Ruth Ann, Oral L. Mem. bd. edn., City of Cin., 1938-42; chief plant engr. Standard Brands, Inc., 1942-45, staff engr., 1945-49, plant mgr., 1949-55, v.p. engring., 1955-58, v.p. mfg., 1958-67, sr. v.p., 1967-76, asst. to pres., 1976-78, exec. v.p., 1978, pres., 1978-80, vice-chmn., 1980—, also dir. Mason (Shriner). Office: Standard Brands Inc 625 Madison Ave New York NY 10022*

APPLEMAN, MARK JEROME, publisher, cons.; b. Columbus, Ohio, May 4, 1917; s. Phillip and Rose (Singer) A.; m. Marguerite Reinhold, Dec. 19, 1959. Group head J. Walter Thompson Co., 1956-61; gen. partner Francis I. duPont & Co., 1961-71; dir. mktg. Oppenheimer & Co., N.Y.C., 1971-73; prin. Mark. J. Appleman Co., mgmt. cons., N.Y.C., 1973—; pres., editor, pub. Corp. Shareholder, Inc., N.Y.C., 1973—. Served to capt., field arty., U.S. Army, 1941-45; PTO. Recipient Disting. Service award Investment Edn. Inst., 1979. Mem. Newsletter Assn. Am., Authors Guild, Authors League. Club: Overseas Press. Author: (film) Invitation to Happiness, 1940; The Liberation of Manhattan, 1949; (stage play) Stockade, 1954; The Winning Habit, 1970; Psychological Aspects of Investing, 1973; Organizing and Managing the Marketing Function, 1973; Conveying the Quality of Management, 1978; Building a Shareholder Constituency, 1979; The Annual Meeting Handbook, 1980. Home: 41 Park Ave New York NY 10016 Office: 271 Madison Ave New York NY 10016

APRUZZI, GENE, stock broker; b. Trani, Bari, Italy, Feb. 16, 1934; s. Francesco and Giulia (Tritto) A.; grad. Istituto Tecnico Commerciale, Bari, 1952; student Universita Di Bari Sch. Econs., 1952-56, N.Y. U., 1956-58; m. Ida G. Italiano, May 12, 1956; 1 dau., Claire J. Came to U.S., 1956, naturalized, 1959. Accountant, Am. Hull Ins. Syndicate, N.Y.C., 1956-58, F.I. duPont & Co., N.Y.C., 1958-59; asst. ops. mgr. Cyrus J. Lawrence & Sons, N.Y.C., 1959-61, ops. mgr., 1961-67, gen. partner charge ops. and adminstrn., mem. exec. com., 1968-73, exec. v.p., chief fin. and ops. officer, dir., mem. exec. com. Cyrus J. Lawrence Inc., 1973—; v.p., treas., dir. C.J. Lawrence & Co., Inc., 1973—; pres., dir. Cyrus J. Lawrence Realty Group, Inc.; dir. Tamcor, Inc., 1966-69, Tamlease Corp., 1967-69, Tamdata Corp., 1969-72. Dir. Brokers and Dealers Com. on Taxation, 1970-72; mem. Am. Stock Exchange, Boston Stock Exchange, Pacific Stock Exchange, Midwest Stock Exchange, Phila. Stock Exchange. Bd. govs. Strathmore Village Civic Assn., Manhasset, N.Y., 1970-73; chmn. bd. Cathedral Sch. of St. Mary, Garden City, N.Y., 1976—. Mem. Securities Industry Assn. Clubs: World Trade Center, Downtown Athletic (N.Y.C.); Plandome (N.Y.) Country. Home: 74 Dover Rd Manhasset NY 11030 Office: 115 Broadway New York NY 10006

APTON, RALPH JULIUS, investment adviser, business and fin. cons.; b. Cologne, Germany, Oct. 16, 1930; s. Adolph A. and Erna (Neu) A.; came to U.S., 1935, naturalized, 1940; B.A., U. Chgo., 1950, M.B.A., 1954; m. Renate Sickinger, Dec. 30, 1959; children—Kory Kim, Keith Jerrard. Fgn. trade and investment asst. AID, U.S. State Dept., Washington, 1954, asst. indsl. analyst, New Delhi, India, 1955-57, dep. regional tech. aids coordinator for Latin Am., Mexico City, 1957-59; dep. exec. sec. Pres. Task Force for Fgn. Econ. Assistance, Washington, 1960-61; chief mgmt. analysis br. Bur. for Latin Am. Affairs, Washington, 1962; devel. loan officer, Quito, Ecuador, 1963-65, AID del. to Ecuadorian Hwy. Transp. Com., 1963-65; chief pre-investment loans Inter-Am. Devel. Bank, Washington, 1966-76; real estate operator; pres. Apton Investment Adviser, Inc.; partner Apton-Cullen Corporate Fin.; cons. Dominion Sash & Door; chmn., treas. Tack N'Teake Ltd.; trustee Stonewall Farm; instr. U.S. Dept. Agr. Grad. Sch. Mem. Fairfax County Republican Com. Mem. Am. Fin. Assn., Am. Mktg. Assn., U.S. C. of C., Fairfax County C. of C., Psi Upsilon. Clubs: U. Chgo. of Washington, Internat. (Washington); River Bend Country (Va.); Quito Golf and Tennis. Home: 9610 Beach Mill Rd Great Falls VA 22066 Office: 6736 Old McLean Village Dr McLean VA 22101

AQUINO, FELIX RAMON, health adminstr.; b. Guaynabo, P.R., May 3, 1936; came to U.S., 1961; s. Antonio and Tomasa (Ridriguez) A.; B.A., U. P.R., 1966; m. Carmen I. Fontanez, Aug. 20, 1960; children—Iribeliz, Edwin Felix. Dir. purchasing Bronx (N.Y.) Lebanon Hosp., 1966-70; asso. exec. dir. Lincoln Med. and Mental Health Center, Bronx, 1970—; asso. clin. prof. Lehman Community Coll., Bronx. Served with AUS, 1955-57. Mem. Internat. Material Mgmt. Assn. (chpt. dir.), Hispanic Assn. Health Services Execs. Democrat. Roman Catholic. Clubs: Lions, Odd Fellows. Home: 1750 Garfield St Bronx NY 10460 Office: 234 E 149th St Bronx NY 10451

ARAFAT, MAHMOUD ZAKY, cons. engr., educator, city engr.; b. Cairo, Feb. 20, 1935; s. Zaky Ibrahim and Fahima Ahmed (Gad) A.; B.C.E., Ein-Shams U., Cairo, 1957; Ph.D., Sci. Research Inst. Concrete and Reinforced Concrete, Moscow, USSR, 1965; postgrad. U. Paris, 1970-71; m. Helen So-Ching; 1 son, Tarek. Came to U.S., 1971, naturalized, 1977. Mem. faculty Sch. Civil Engring., Ein-Shams U., Cairo, Egypt, 1966, asst. prof., to 1969; practice as cons. and research structural engr., with various corps. and govtl. agys. throughout world, 1960—; rep. of Egypt at 2d Internat. Conf. Structures, Budapest, Hungary, 1969, U.S. rep. VII Internat. Congress Prestressed Concrete, N.Y.C., 1974; supervising prin. engr. City of Jersey City; vis. asso. prof. engring. Pratt Inst., Bklyn.; mem. adv. bd. on ethnic heritage studies Jersey City State Coll. Registered profl. engr., N.Y. State, N.J., France, Egypt; profl. planner, N.J.; certified constrn. ofcl., N.J. Mem. ASCE, Am. Concrete Inst., Prestressed Concrete Inst. (chmn. com. precast prestressed concrete storage tanks), Post-Tensioning Inst., Assn. Egyptian-Am. Scholars. Contbr. tech. articles and reviews to profl. jours. Home: 10 Huron Ave Jersey City NJ 07306 Office: Dept Community Devel Div Bldgs 88 Clifton Pl Jersey City NJ 07304

ARAI, YONEO, banker; b. N.Y.C., Aug. 26, 1889; s. Rioichiro and Tazu (Ushiba) A.; A.B. cum laude, Harvard U., 1912, postgrad. Bus. Sch., 1912, 28-29; m. Mitsu Okabe, Oct. 1, 1917; 1 son, Ryozo. With Morimura Arai & Co., N.Y.C., 1913-23, partner, 1917-23; investment banking Harris Forbes & Co., 1929-30, Chase Harris Forbes Corp., N.Y.C., 1930-31; liaison officer Tokio Marine & Fire Ins. Co., N.Y., 1933-60; pres. Yamaichi Internat. (Am.) Inc. (formerly Yamaichi Securities Co. of N.Y., Inc.), N.Y.C., 1955-58, chmn. bd., 1958-76, hon. dir., 1976—; dir. Bank Tokio Trust Co., N.Y.C., 1956-74, hon. dir., 1974—. Mem. Harvard overseers com. for Far Eastern Studies, 1947-57; sec. Soc. Japanese Studies, N.Y.C., 1938-54; del. to Japan, Korea, Formosa and Hong Kong, N.Y. World's Fair, 1961; bd. dirs. Japan Soc. N.Y., 1942-70, v.p., 1955-70, hon. dir., 1970—. Decorated Order of Sacred Treasure for outstanding contbns. to furtherance of Japan-U.S. friendly relations through econ. and cultural activities Emperor Japan, 1968; recipient award Japanese-Am. Citizens League, 1969. Clubs: Riverside (Conn.) Yacht (hon.); Tokio Golf; Hodogaya Golf; Field (Greenwich, Conn.); Harvard (hon.) (N.Y.C.). Home: 309 Marks Rd Danville CA 94526 Office: Yamaichi Internat (America) Inc 1 World Trade Center New York NY 10048

ARANDA, LUIS, lawyer, educator; b. Nogales, Ariz., Mar. 3, 1936; s. Tomas N. and Maria G. (Covarrubias) A.; Mus.B., U. Ariz., 1964, M.Ed., 1965; J.D., Ariz. State U., 1973; children—Louis Anthony, Lydia Adrienne. Tchr., Clark County Sch. Dist., Las Vegas, Nev., 1965-70; trust officer and fin. planner Valley Nat. Bank, Phoenix, 1973-75; mem. faculty Coll. Bus. Adminstrn. Ariz. State U., Tempe, 1975—, asso. prof. adminstrv. services, 1980—, undergrad. program adv., 1975—, dir. Small Bus. Inst., 1976—; cons. research projects and tng. programs various legal and bus. firms, 1975—; mem. adv. bd. Sta. KIFN, Phoenix, 1979—, Nat. Econ. Devel. Adminstrn., Phoenix, 1975—; chmn. Nat. Assn. Hispanic Profs. of Bus. and Econs., 1980. Bd. dirs. Nat. Found. March of Dimes, Phoenix, 1976-77, Ariz. Bus. Resource Center, Phoenix, 1977-78. Served in USAF, 1955-59. Named Outstanding Educator of Year, Nat. Econ. Devel. Assn., 1976; recipient award of Commendation, SBA, 1977; Office of Minority Bus. Enterprise grantee, 1978. Mem. Am. Bus. Lawyers Assn., Am. Assembly Collegiate Schs. Bus., Internat. Council Small Bus., Mexican-Am. C. of C., Am. Inst. Decision Scis., Nat. Small Bus. Inst., Pacific Southwest Bus. Law Assn., NCCJ, League United Latin Am. Citizens (adv. to state dir. 1974-77), Order of Red Red Rose. Democrat. Roman Catholic. Contbr. articles on small bus. enterprise to profl. publs. Home: 1815 E Yale St Tempe AZ 85283 Office: Coll Bus Adminstrn Ariz State Univ Tempe AZ 85281

ARANYOS, ALEXANDER SANDOR, internat. ops. exec.; b. Zilina, Czechoslovakia; s. Ludwig and Ethel (Wilhelm) A.; Degree in Comml. Engring. cum laude, U. Prague (Czechoslovakia), 1931; m. Gertrude Reisman, Aug. 22, 1937; children—Alexander Paul, Vivian Jane. Adminstrv. asst. to pres. and export mgr. Coburg Mining & Foundry Co., Bratislava, Czechoslovakia, 1933-40; mgr. import div. Gen. Motors Distbrs., Panama, 1940-41; mgr. Latin Am. div. Van Raalte Co., N.Y.C., 1945-53; with Fruehauf Corp., Detroit, 1953—, v.p. internat. ops., 1956—, dir., 1973—; pres., dir. Fruehauf Internat. Ltd., 1957-76, chmn., dir., 1976—; mem. adminstrv. council Viaturas PNV-Fruehauf S.A., Sao Paulo, Brazil; dir. Fruehauf Trailers (Australasia) Pty. Ltd., Fruehauf Finance Corp. Pty., Ltd. (both Melbourne, Australia), Crane Fruehauf Ltd., Hayes, Middlesex, Eng., Fruehauf France S.A., Ris-Orangis, Fruehauf de Mexico, S.A., Coacalco, Nippon Fruehauf Co., Ltd., Tokyo, NETAM-Fruehauf B.V., N.V. Nederlandsche Tank Apparaten-en Machinefabriek, Rotterdam, Netherlands, Henred-Fruehauf Trailers (Pty.) Ltd., Johannesburg, S. Africa, Fruehauf, S.A., Madrid, Forss-Parator AB, Sweden, Industrias Colombo Andina Inca S.A., Bogota, Colombia; asso. dir. Clyde Industries, Ltd., Sydney, Australia. Mem. regional export expansion council U.S. Dept. Commerce, 1970-73. Mem. Detroit Bd. Commerce, Research Inst. Am., A.I.M., C. of C. U.S. (internat. com.), Am. Australian Assn. N.Y., Internat. Execs. Assn. Clubs: Rotary; World Trade of Detroit; Rockefeller Center Luncheon (N.Y.C.); Detroit Athletic. Home: 2 Bridle Ln Sands Point NY 11050 Office: 30 Rockefeller Plaza New York NY 10020 also 10900 Harper Ave Detroit MI 48232

ARASKOG, RAND VINCENT, bus. exec.; b. Fergus Falls, Minn., Oct. 30, 1931; s. Randolph Victor and Hilfred Mathilda A.; B.S.M.E., U.S. Mil. Acad., 1953, postgrad. Harvard U., 1953-54; m. Jessie Marie Gustafson, July 29, 1956. Spl. asst. to dir. Dept. Def., Washington, 1954-59; dir. mktg. aero. div. Honeywell, Inc., Mpls., 1960-66; v.p. ITT, group exec. ITT Aerospace, Electronics, Components and Energy Group, Nutley, N.J., 1971-76, pres., chief exec. ITT Corp., N.Y.C., 1979—, chmn. bd., chmn. exec. and policy coms., 1980—; dir. ITT Corp., Hartford Ins. Served with U.S. Army, 1954-56. Mem. Aerospace Industries Assn. (bd. govs.), Air Force Assn. (mem. exec. council). Episcopalian. Office: ITT World Hdqrs 320 Park Ave New York NY 10022*

ARAYA, PEDRO ALFONSO, cons.; b. Valparaiso, Chile, Jan. 19, 1922; s. Francisco Araya and Nella Proromant; B.S. in Mech. Engring., Chilean Naval Coll., 1943; B.A., U. Chile, 1945; M.S. in Indsl. and Mgmt. Engring., Columbia, 1963; m. Esther Emma Roussillion, Apr. 17, 1957; 1 dau., Carla Francesca. Came to U.S., 1955, naturalized, 1963. Various positions with rubber and plastics industry, 1949-59; gen. mgr. Coca-Cola Export Corp., Venezuela, 1959-61; indsl. mgmt. cons., Mexico and C. Am., 1961-63; asst. area mgr. Coca-Cola Export Corp., Middle East, North Africa and South West Asia, 1963-67, marketing mgr., S. Am., 1968-69; corporate cons. prodn. and operations Coca-Cola Co., Atlanta, 1970—; pres. Global Growth and Devel. Co., Wilmington, Del., 1973—. Served to lt. Chilean Navy, 1943-45. Fellow AAAS; mem. Am. Inst. Indsl. Engrs. (sr.) Inst. Environ. Scis., ASME, Soc. Naval Architects and Marine Engrs., Marine Tech. Soc., Am. Chem. Soc., Am. Soc. Quality Control, IEEE, Illuminating Engrs. Soc., Am. Inst. Plant Engrs., Soc. Advancement Mgmt., Assn. Iron and Steel Engrs., Ops. Research Soc. Am., Ops. Research Soc. Japan, Acad. Applied Sci., Nat. Soc. Corporate Planning, Am. Phys. Soc., Soc. Packaging and Handling Engrs., Nat. Council Phys. Distbn. Mgmt., Soc. Gen. Systems Research, Am. Marketing Assn., Am. Soc. Agrl. Engrs., Inst. Food Technologists, Am. Agrl. Econs. Assn., Internat. Cargo Handling and Coordination Assn. (Eng.), Colo. Sci. Soc., Ga. Engring. and Archtl. Soc., Assn. Computing Machinery, Am. Geophys. Union, Forage Grass Council (Australia). Clubs: American, Lawn (Buenos Aires); Union (Santiago, Chile). Contbr. articles to profl. jours. Home: Avenida del Libertader 2930 2d floor 1425 Buenos Aires Argentina Office: Suipacha 1111 17th Floor Piso Buenos Aires Argentina

ARBOLEYA, CARLOS JOSE, banker, civic worker; b. Havana, Cuba, Feb. 1, 1929; s. Fermin and Ana (Quiros) A.; student Havana U., 1947-58; D.(hon.), U. Internat. Moctezuma, Paris, 1972; D. Banking Sci. (hon.), U. Leonardo da Vinci, Italy, 1973; m. Marta Quintana, Aug. 29, 1954; 1 son, Carlos. Asst. mgr. Trust Co. of Cuba, Havana, 1957-59, chief auditor Banco Continental Cubano, Havana, 1959-60; clk. to office mgr. and comptroller Allure Shoe Corp., Miami, Fla., 1960-62; ops. officer and personnel dir. Boulevard Nat. Bank, Miami, 1962-64, v.p. and cashier, sec. to bd. dirs., 1964-66; exec. v.p. Fidelity Nat. Bank of South Miami (Fla.), 1966-67, pres., 1967-73, vice-chmn. bd., 1970-73; co-propr., pres., dir. The Flagler Bank, Miami, 1973-75; pres., dir. Barnett Bank at Westchester, Miami, 1975-76, Barnett Bank of Midway, Miami, 1975-76; chmn. bd. Barnett Bank BankAmericard Center, Miami, 1975—, chief exec. officer, 1977—; pres., chief operating officer and dir. Consol. Barnett Banks of Miami, 1977—; pres. Barnett Leasing Co., 1977—; instr. Am. Inst. Banking, Miami, 1967-72, Bank Adminstrn. Inst., Miami, 1969-72, U. Miami Sch. Bus. Adminstrn., 1972; lectr. various schs. and community orgns., 1964—; econ. adv. Latin C. of C., 1964—; mem. adv. bd. SBA, 1972-75; mem. Nat. Adv. Council on Econ. Opportunity, Washington, 1974-76. Mgr., Saints Peter and Paul Youth Center, Miami, 1962-65; asst. commr. S. Fla. council Boy Scouts Am., 1963-66, mem. exec. bd., 1962—; judge nat. vol. awards Nat. Center for Voluntary Action, Washington, 1974; adv. Jr. Achievement, Miami, 1965-70; mem. Children's Rehab. Center Com., Havana, 1957-60; mem. Citizens Adv. Planning Com., Miami, 1972-74; mem. numerous civic and community bds. including: ARC, Speak Up for America Program, Miami, YMCA Internat. Jose Marti, Miami, Nat. Softball Assn., Havana, Ballet Concerto of Miami, Internat. Center of Fla., Jr. Achievement Greater Miami; trustee numerous schs. and orgns. including: Barry Coll., Miami, Mus. of Sci. and Space Transit, Leukemia Soc. Am., Miami; bd. govs. Invest in America Nat. Council, Phila., 1974-78; mem. bd. advs. Duquesne U., Pitts., 1972-73. Recipient numerous awards including: Silver Beaver award Boy Scouts Am., 1973; George Washington Honor medal Freedoms Found. at Valley Forge, 1974, 75, 76, 77; Horatio Alger award Am. Schs. and Colls. Assn., 1976; keys to cities of Miami, Coral Gables, Jacksonville, Miami Beach and South Miami (all in Fla.), 1970; Saint George emblem Roman Catholic Ch., 1971; Lincoln Marti award Fed. Govt., 1971; Banker of Year award Nat. Econ. Devel. Assn., 1972; Carlos J. Arboleya park named in his honor, Miami, 1978; others; decorated knight Order St. John of Jerusalem, 1979; C.P.A. Mem. Bank Adminstrn. Inst. (pres. 1971-72), Am. Inst. Banking (v.p. 1970-71), Am. Arbitration Assn. (dir. 1969-73), Fla. Bankers Assn. (dir. 1969-72, Fla. Council Internat. Devel., Nat.

Alliance Businessmen (Miami adv. bd. 1971-72), InterAm. Assn. Businessmen (dir. 1970-71), Nat. Assn. Bank Audit Control (dir. 1968-73), Dade County Bankers Assn. (dir. 1970-71), Heart Assn. Greater Miami (dir. 1969-72), Delta Sigma Pi (hon.). Home: 1941 SW 23d St Miami FL 33145 Office: 1201 Brickell Ave Miami FL 33125

ARCHER, CARL MARION, oil and gas co. exec.; b. Spearman, Tex., Dec. 16, 1920; s. Robert Barton and Gertrude Lucille (Sheets) A.; student Tex. U. at Austin, 1937-39; m. Peggy Garrett, Aug. 22, 1939; children—Mary Frances, Carla Lee. Pres., Anchor Oil Co., Spearman, 1959—, Carl M. Archer Farms, Spearman, 1960—; gen. mgr. Speartex Grain Co., Spearman, 1967—, Speartex Oil & Gas Co., 1974—; dir. Panhandle Bank & Trust Co., Borger, Tex. Chmn. County Democratic Com., 1969—. Mem. Tex. Grain Dealers Assn., Ind. Royalty Owners and Producers Assn., Nat. Grain Dealers Assn., Am. Petroleum Landmen Assn., Nat., Tex. bankers assns. Mem. Ch. of Christ. Clubs: Perryton, Borger Country, Amarillo. Home: 304 S Endicott Spearman TX 79081 Office: 514 Collard St Spearman TX 79081

ARCHIBALD, RUSSELL DEAN, mfg. co. exec.; b. Independence, Mo., Jan. 10, 1924; s. David Myron and Henrietta McKinley (Roberts) A.; B.S., U. Mo., 1948; M.S. in Mech. Engring., U. Tex., 1956; m. Marion Alice Ebbets, May 25, 1946; children—Donna, Barbara, Robert, Mark. Mech. engr. Creole Petroleum Corp., Venezuela, 1948-51; sr. engr. Aerojet Gen. Corp., 1959-60; dept. mgr. Hughes Aircraft Co., Los Angeles, 1961-62, Hughes Dynamics, 1963-64; pres. CPM Systems, Inc., Los Angeles, 1964-65, v.p. CPM Systems, div. Informatics, Inc., Los Angeles, 1965-67; asso. Booz Allen & Hamilton, Los Angeles, 1967-69; v.p., gen. mgr. Symcon Marine Corp., Long Beach, Calif., 1969-70; asst. dir. Office of pres., IT&T, N.Y.C., 1970-75; dir., spl. projects Societe Anonyme DBA (Bendix), Paris, 1975-76; dir. bus. devel. Bendix Corp., Southfield, Mich., 1977—. Served with USAAF, 1943-46, USAF, 1951-58. Mem. Soc. Automotive Engrs., Engring. Soc. Detroit, Project Mgmt. Inst. (past v.p.), Internat. Mgmt. Systems Assn., Internat. Bus. Council. Episcopalian. Author: (with R.L. Villeria) Network Based Management Systems, 1967; Managing High Technology Programs and Projects, 1976. Office: Bendix Center Southfield MI 48037

ARCHIBALD, WILLIAM EDDIE, mfg. co. exec.; b. Gillette, Wyo., Apr. 6, 1940; s. U. Staley and Pearl Marguerite Archibald; student Tulane U., 1958-60; B.S. in Elec. Engring., U. Wyo., 1963, M.S., 1967; postgrad. U.S. Internat. U., 1968-70, U. Ariz., 1971-73; m. Carolyn Antoinette Brown, June 24, 1963; children—Patrick William, Cynthia Lee. Test equipment engr. Convair div. Gen. Dynamics, San Diego, 1967-70; test equipment engr., product engr., product design engr., pilot prodn. mgr., mfg. engring. mgr., systems mfg. mgr. Burr-Brown Research Corp., Tucson, 1971-79; ops. mgr. Granville-Phillips Co., Boulder, Colo., 1979—. Served to 1st lt. U.S. Army, 1963-65. Mem. IEEE, Instrument Soc. Am., Soc. Mfg. Engrs., Am. Prodn. and Inventory Control Soc. Republican. Office: Granville-Phillips Co 5675 E Arapahoe Ave Boulder CO 80303

ARCUNI, ANTHONY ORESTE, banker; b. N.Y.C., Feb. 20, 1939; s. Oreste and Teresa (De Luca) A.; B.S., Fordham Coll., 1960; J.D., Fordham U., 1963; m. Evelyn A. Leary, Aug. 6, 1965; children—Philip, Suzanne. With Citibank, N.Y.C., 1965-78, v.p., 1978; v.p. Bankers Trust Co., N.Y.C., 1978-79, sr. v.p., 1979—, group head, internat. investment mgmt. group, 1978—. Served to 1st lt. U.S. Army, 1963-65. Decorated Army Commendation medal. Mem. N.Y. State Bar Assn. Republican. Roman Catholic. Club: Seven Bridges Field (past pres.) (Chappaqua, N.Y.). Contbr. articles to profl. jours. Home: One Winthrop Rd Chappaqua NY 10514 Office: Bankers Trust Co 280 Park Ave New York NY 10017

ARDEN, JOHN RÉAL, lawyer; b. Louisville, Aug. 17, 1944; s. Sylvan Sherwin and Marie Theresa (LaLiberté-Daigneau) A.; A.S., Flint Community Jr. Coll., 1964; B.S., Mich. State U., 1967, postgrad., 1968-69; J.D., U. Notre Dame, 1972; m. Margot deNise Elkin, Aug. 9, 1969; children—Michael John-Réal, Stephen Patrick, Catherine Elizabeth. With Gen. Motors Corp., Flint, Mich., 1965-69; admitted to Mass. bar, 1973; asso. firm Donald P. Conway, West Springfield, Mass., 1972-73; research editor Ronald A. Anderson, Phila., 1973-74; tax atty. The Research Group, Inc., Charlottesville, Va., 1974; individual practice law, Northampton, Mass., 1974—; adj. prof. Western New Eng. Coll. Law Sch., Springfield, Mass., 1977, Greenfield (Mass.) Community Coll., 1978—; partner Arden Internat., Southampton, Mass., 1977—; cons. in field. Mem. fin. com. Town of Southampton, 1976-80, chmn., 1977-80; dir. Hampshire Community Action Commn., Northampton, 1978-80, chmn. exec. com., 1978-79. Mem. Am., Mass., Boston, Hampshire County bar assns., Tau Beta Pi, Eta Kappa Nu. Independent Democrat. Roman Catholic. Home: 23 Sandra Rd Easthampton MA 01027 Office: 181 Main St Suite 2 Northampton MA 01060

ARDITTI, FRED D., economist; b. N.Y.C., Jan. 30, 1939; s. David A. and Marie (Ben Nathan) A.; B.S. in Elec. Engring., M.I.T., 1960, M.S. in Indsl. Mgmt., 1962, Ph.D. in Econs., 1966; 1 dau., Elizabeth. Economist, Rand Corp., Santa Monica, Calif., 1965-67; lectr. U. Calif., Berkeley, 1967-68, asst. prof. finance, 1968-71; asso. prof. fin. and econs. U. Fla., Gainesville, 1971-73, Walter J. Matherly prof. fin. and econs., 1974-80, chmn. dept. econs., 1977-80; v.p. research Chgo. Mercantile Exchange, 1980—, chief economist, 1980—; vis. prof. fin. U. Toronto, Can., 1976-77, Hebrew U., Jerusalem, Israel, 1973; cons. to Fed. Energy Adminstrn., 1975-76, Dept. of Energy, 1978-79; mem. adv. com. on edn. Chgo. Bd. of Trade, 1977-79. NSF fellow, 1968-70, Dean Witter Found. research fellow, 1971; Ford Found. grantee, 1964. Mem. Am. Econs. Assn., Am. Fin. Assn. Jewish. Contbr. numerous articles to fin. and econs. jours. Office: Chicago Mercantile Exchange 444 W Jackson Blvd Chicago IL 60606

ARDIZZONE, JOSEPH, bus. consulting co. exec.; b. Bklyn., June 26, 1933; s. Thomas and Lillian A.; degree in bus. adminstrn. Suffolk Coll., 1970; m. Josephine Impoco, Sept. 8, 1956; children—Donna, Christopher, Glen. Traffic mgr. Helena Rubinstein Inc., 1961-65; prodn. control mgr. Amperex Electronics, 1965-71; owner, mgr. Carvel Ice Cream, Medford, N.Y., Dale's Ice Cream, Smithtown, N.Y., 1971-79; owner mgr. Binex Systems Co., East Northport, N.Y., 1977—; owner Philly Mignon Restaurant, Queens, N.Y., 1979—. Served with U.S. Army, 1951-52. Mem. Am. Mgmt. Assn., Ind. Cons. Am. Club: K.C. Home and Office: 2 Upland Dr East Northport NY 11731

AREEN, GORDON ERIC, fin. co. exec.; b. Chgo., Feb. 10, 1918; s. Eric G. and Tillie S. (Nyberg) A.; ed. Northwestern U., 1940; m. Pauline J. Payberg, June 28, 1942; children—Judith Carol, Patricia Ann, Richard Gordon. With Arthur Andersen & Co., Chgo., 1945-46, Allstate Ins. Co., Chgo., 1946-47; various positions to exec. v.p. Assos. Investment Co., South Bend, Ind., 1947-64; pres., dir. Chrysler Fin. Corp., Troy, Mich., 1964-80, chmn. bd., chief exec. officer, dir., 1980—; v.p. Chrysler Corp., 1974—; pres., dir. Chrysler Ins. Corp., 1964—. Pres. Jr. Achievement Southeastern Mich., 1978; vice chmn. bd. trustees Alma (Mich.) Coll., 1980. Served with AUS, 1940-46. C.P.A., Ill. Mem. Econ. Club Detroit, Am. Inst. C.P.A.'s Republican. Presbyterian. Clubs: Oakland Hills Country, Detroit Renaissance, Masons, Shriners. Home: 3932 Maple Hill E West Bloomfield MI 48033 Office: 900 Tower Dr Troy MI 48098

ARENA, ANGELO RICHARD, retail co. exec.; b. Lynn, Mass., May 29, 1928; s. Simon J. and Grace M. (Nicoletti) A.; B.S., M.I.T., 1949; M.S. in Bus., Columbia U., 1951; m. Alice Palazuelos, Mar. 24, 1968; children—Maria, Christine, Angela, Marisa, Alexa. Vice pres. Bullock's, Los Angeles, 1969-72; exec. v.p. merchandising and sales Weinstock's, Sacramento, 1972-73; pres. The Emporium, San Francisco, 1973-75; chmn. Neiman-Marcus, Dallas, 1975-77; pres., chief exec. officer Marshall Field & Co., Chgo., 1977—; dir. Harris Bankcorp, Inc. Chmn. exec. com. Lyric Opera, Chgo., 1978—; trustee Orch. Assn., 1978—, Rush-Presbyterian Med. Center, 1978—, Chgo. Mus. Sci. and Industry. Served with USAF, 1954-56. Roman Catholic. Clubs: Racquet, Econ., Chgo., Comml. (Chgo.); Onwentsia, Carlton, Balboa (Newport Beach, Calif.); Eastern Yacht (Marblehead, Mass.). Office: 25 E Washington St Chicago IL 60690

ARENS, WINDON GIBBS, fin. exec.; b. Los Angeles, May 1, 1924; s. Winfried Bernard and Treasure (Hartman) A.; student Whittier Coll., 1948-49, Pasadena City Coll., 1949-50; A.A., U. So. Calif., 1950-52; student in econs. UCLA, 1952-53; m. Jill Iris Medby, Aug. 19, 1977; 1 dau., Treasure Biro. Owner, pres. Windon G. Arens & Co., Los Angeles, 1948—; cons. Heil Constrn. Co., Monterey Park, Calif., 1953-55; partner D & A Land Devel., Simi, Calif., 1955-57; asst. v.p. in charge planning Calif. City Devel. Co., Los Angeles, 1957-58; v.p. in charge constrn./planning Best Investment Co., Los Angeles, 1958-59; pres. Nationwide Mortgage Corp., Los Angeles, 1960-62; pres. S & S Builders/Surety Constrn. Cons., Los Angeles, 1965-66; owner Lenders Property Mgmt. Co., Hollywood, Calif., 1966-67; owner, pres. Dolphin Fin., Inc., Coronado, Calif., 1978—. Served with U.S. Army, 1943-46. Decorated Bronze Star, Purple Heart; lic. real estate broker, Calif; lic. ins. broker, Calif.; lic. life disability agt., Calif. Republican. Episcopalian. Clubs: Hotel De Coronado Swim and Tennis, SAR, Vets. of Strategic Services. Office: PO Box 606 Corando CA 92118

ARENSTEIN, JUDY, telephone co. adminstr.; b. N.Y.C., Aug. 11, 1946; d. Seymour and Florence (Taback) Simonson; B.A. in Math., Wilkes Coll., Pa., 1968; M.B.A. with distinction, Pace U., 1976; m. Robert D. Arenstein, June 30, 1968. Programmer Long Lines AT&T, White Plains, N.Y., 1968-71, data processing supr., 1971-74, engr., EDP cons., 1974, labor negotiator, 1974-78, dist. ops. mgr., 1976-78, dist. accounting mgr., 1978—. Trustee Wilkes Coll.; drive capt. United Way, 1977, dept. coordinator, 1979; area coordinator U.S. Savs. Bonds, 1978—. Mem. Am. Mgmt. Assn., Delta Mu Delta, Wilkes Coll. Alumni Assn. (pres.). Club: Newcomers. Home: 15 Tanglewood Rd Scarsdale NY 10583 Office: 440 Hamilton Ave White Plains NY 10601

ARGABRIGHT, WILLIAM KEITH, accountant; b. Lakeview, Oreg., May 17, 1928; s. Estle O. and Genevieve D. Argabright; B.S., U. Nev., 1950; postgrad. U. Calif., 1953; m. Beverly Ann Gilbert, May 21, 1978; children—Dana Ann, James W., Sharon A., Catherine, Celia E. With Main Hurdman & Cranstoun and predecessors, 1954—, mng. partner San Francisco, 1967-69, regional mng. partner, 1969-79, Western regional mng. partner, mem. ops. com., mem. policy bd., 1979—. Served to 1st lt. USAF, 1951-53. C.P.A., Calif. Mem. Associated Acctg. Firms Internat. (treas. and mem. exec. com. 1968-78), Calif. Soc. C.P.A.'s (dir. San Francisco chpt. 1971-74), Am. Inst. C.P.A.'s, Nat. Assn. Accts., Am. Mgmt. Assn. Republican. Presbyterian. Club: Family (San Francisco). Home: 777 Camino Ricardo CA 94556 Office: 2 Embarcadero Center Suite 2500 San Francisco CA 94111

ARGYLL, MARION H.G., real estate broker; b. New Orleans, Jan. 29; d. Franklin Johns and Sarah (Henry) Gustine; attended pvt. schs.; widow; 1 son, James E. Med. records librarian Doctors Hosp., Washington, 1944-47; asst. to neurosurgeon VA, Washington, 1948-51; electroencephalographic tech. service NIH, 1952-55; tchr. real estate Washington Real Estate and Ins. Sch., 1958-60; real estate broker, Washington, 1958—, Va. 1958—, Md., 1959—, W.Va., 1960—. Recipient award in recognition of services to Nation, Pres. U.S., 1940, award for vol. work with United China Relief, 1942. Mem. So. Electroencephalography Soc. Club: Kenwood Golf and Country (Bethesda, Md.). Author: Moonlight Poems; also scenarios under pseudonym Julie de Quistine. Patentee san. disposable baby bottle, payroll safety box, adjustable automobile seat, protective garment, sludge transporter and converter, others; creator Argyll Mortgage Plan, one or 2 percent interest control plan. Home: 15 E Irving St Chevy Chase Village MD 20015 Office: 810 18th St Washington DC 20004

ARLEDGE, CHARLES STONE, mfg. co. exec.; b. Bonham, Tex., Oct. 20, 1935; s. John F. and Madeline (Jones) A.; B.S., Stanford, 1957, M.S. (Standard Oil Co. Calif. scholar), 1958, M.B.A., 1966; m. Barbara Jeanne Ruff, June 18, 1966; children—John Harrison, Mary Katherine. With Shell Oil Co., Los Angeles, 1958-64; v.p., dir. Signal Cos., Inc., Beverly Hills, Calif., 1966—; dir. UOP Inc., Des Plaines, Ill. Chmn. natural resources sect. Town Hall of Calif., Los Angeles, 1967-70; trustee Orme Sch. Clubs: Los Angeles Country, Calif. (Los Angeles). Home: 775 Chaucer Rd San Marino CA 91108 Office: 9665 Wilshire Blvd Beverly Hills CA 90212

ARLUKE, ALAN BRUCE, sports and entertainment mktg. exec.; b. Trenton, Dec. 13, 1944; s. Nat Rod and Alyce Gloria (Shapiro) A.; B.A. in Sociology, Temple U., 1967; m. Linda Lee Hertz, June 26, 1966; children—Lisa Beth, Seth Brian, Adam David. Account exec. Bache Halsey Stuart Shields Inc., Cherry Hill, N.J., 1971-74; nat. mktg. mgr. PML Securities Co (Provident Mut. Life Ins. Co.), Phila., 1974-77; dir. event sales Spectrum, Ltd., Phila., 1977—; pres. S. Jersey Automatic Machines; trustee Consumer Credit Corp. of S. Jersey. Served to capt. USAF, 1967-70. Recipient Achievement award Big Bros., 1979. Author: (photographs) Reflections, 1972, Week of Fire, 1973. Home: 217 Lamp Post Ln Cherry Hill NJ 08003 Office: Spectrum Ltd Broad and Pattison Sts Philadelphia PA 19148

ARMILLEI, JACOB BENJAMIN, audio visual supply co. exec.; b. Plains, Pa., May 31, 1931; s. Gene and Sophie (Chopka) A.; student Pa. State U., 1955-56; B.S. in Edn., Wilkes Coll., 1959; postgrad. Montclair Coll., Ind. U.; m. Mary Ann Wolczyk, Apr. 7, 1956; 1 son, David James. Dir. audio visual Bergenfield (N.J.) Sch. Dist., 1959-70; pres., owner Media Masters, Inc., East Stroudsburg, Pa., 1970—. Served with U.S. Navy, 1949-53. Mem. Nat. Audio Visual Assn. Roman Catholic. Club: Ham Radio. Office: RD 5 Box 327 East Stroudsburg PA 18301

ARMOUR, ALLAN A., film co. exec.; b. Bklyn., Apr. 25, 1933; s. Arthur Harris and Gertrude (Kornblue) A.; student New Inst. Film and Television, 1952, N.Y. U. Film Inst., 1956, Sch. Bus., 1956-60; m. Susan Lois Newman, June 25, 1967; children—Steven Douglas, David Newman. Asst. film editor Bray Studios, N.Y.C., 1951-53, asst. to film producer, 1955-57; TV film producer Milton Wynne Advt. Agy., Babylon, N.Y., 1957-59; owner, co-founder Cine Magnetics, Inc., N.Y.C., 1961—, also dir.; pres. Projection Systems, Internat., N.Y.C., 1964—. Trustee, Lenox Sch., N.Y.C. Served with Signal Corps, AUS, 1953-55. Mem. Nat. Audio Visual Assn. (cons.), Soc. Motion Picture Engrs. Contbr. numerous articles on audio visuals to various publs. Home: 501 E 79th St New York City NY 10021 Office: 730 3d Ave New York City NY 10017

ARMOUR, T. STANTON, fin. cons.; b. Chgo., Jan. 3, 1924; s. Lester and Mary Leola (Stanton) A.; grad. St. Mark's Sch., Southboro, Mass., 1942; B.A., Yale, 1949; m. Jean Ann Reddy, July 3, 1948; children—Audrey Lester, Thomas Stanton. With Marathon Corp., Menasha, Wis., 1949-56, regional sales mgr., 1955-56; with Mitchell, Hutchins, Inc., investments, Chgo., 1957—, pres., 1967-69, chmn. operating com., 1970-73, chmn. bd., 1973-77, sr. mng. dir., 1977-78, also dir.; sr. v.p., dir. Paine Webber, Jackson & Curtis Inc., 1977-78; sr. v.p., dir. Paine Webber Mitchell Hutchins, Inc., Chgo., 1979-80; dir. Paine Webber Inc., N.Y.C. Bd. dirs. Northwestern Meml. Hosp., Chgo.; trustee Shedd Aquarium, Chgo.; vice chmn. adv. bd. Chgo. Salvation Army. Served with USNR, 1943-46. Mem. Northwestern U. Assn., Comml. Club Chgo. Clubs: Attic (Chgo.); Onwentsia, Shore Acres, Winter (Lake Forest); Metropolitan (Chgo.). Office: 55 W Monroe St Suite 3800 Chicago IL 60603

ARMSTRONG, CHARLES N., life ins. co. exec.; b. Truro, N.S., Can., Aug. 5, 1936; s. Charles D. and Annie M. (Hayman) A.; B.S. in Econs., Acadia U., 1960; m. Patricia Anne Baiden, Aug. 20, 1960; children—Kimberly, Michael, Deanna. With Met. Life Ins. Co., 1960—, v.p. personal ins. ops. New Eng. head office, then v.p. in charge Atlantic head office, 1974-78, pres. Can. ops., Ottawa, 1978—. Bd. govs. U. Ottawa; bd. dirs. Canadian Opera Co.; co-vice chmn. devel. campaign com. Ottawa Civic Hosp.; co-chmn. achievement fund campaign com. U. Ottawa. Mem. Canadian Assn. Accident and Sickness Insurers, Canadian Life Ins. Assn., Bus. Council Nat. Issues. Club: Rideau. Office: Met Life Ins Co 99 Bank St Ottawa ON K1P 5A3 Canada

ARMSTRONG, CRAIG STEPHEN, energy public relations cons.; b. Columbus, Ohio, Jan. 18, 1947; s. Albert James and Margaret Ann (Dreschler) A.; B.S. in Edn., Ohio State U., 1972; m. Tamara Taggert, Nov. 26, 1966; children—Amber, Kirsten, Ann-Elise. Announcer, producer WOSU-TV, Columbus, Ohio, 1966-68, 70-72; newscaster WBNS-TV, Columbus, 1968-69; pub. relations counselor Pub. Service Co. of N.H., Manchester, 1969-70, 72-79; owner, chief exec. officer CS Armstrong Assos., energy communications cons.; chmn. Videotape Task Force, Executive Council New Eng.; cons. in field. Active Boy Scouts Am.; bd. dirs. Hancock Found., 1975—; mem. Contoocook Valley Regional Sch. Bd., Sharon, N.H., 1975-78. Served with USAR, 1966-77. Mem. Pub. Relations Soc. Am. (accredited), Internat. Assn. Bus. Communicators, Indsl. TV Assn., Sharon Taxpayers Assn. (pres.). Home: Rural Route 2 McCoy Rd Peterborough NH 03458 Office: 10 Elm St PO Box 526 Peterborough NH 03105

ARMSTRONG, DANIEL RAYBURN, constrn. co. exec.; b. Plainview, Tex., Oct. 20, 1946; s. Welcolm Mexas and Ruth Elaine (Kingery) A.; B.S.C.E., U. N.Mex., 1969; m. Glenda Ellison, Aug. 20, 1968; children—Krista, Daniel, Sarah. With Plant Constructors, Albuquerque, 1968-70, Bradbury & Stamm, Albuquerque, 1971-78; pres. Armstrong Bros. Inc., Albuquerque, 1978—. Mem. Constrn. Specifications Inst., ASCE, Asso. Gen. Contractors. Office: 2720 Broadbent Pkwy Albuquerque NM 87107

ARMSTRONG, DONALD WALLACE, JR., forest products mfg. co. exec.; b. Chgo., Oct. 24, 1936; s. Donald W. and Ethel I. (Hawkins) A.; B.S. in Indsl. Econs., Purdue U., 1959; m. Linda Frae Crockett, Feb. 16, 1962; children—David W., Carrie S. Part owner, officer, dir. Premier Porcelain, Inc., Indpls., 1959-62; planning mgr. Inland Container Corp., Phila., 1963-66, corp. personnel mgr., Indpls., 1966-75, asst. v.p. govt. affairs, 1975-78, asst. v.p. human resources, 1978—; guest lectr. DePauw U., 1978—. Treas., bd. dirs. Indpls. Clean City Com., 1979—; mem. Select Joint Com. on Orgn. Ind. State Govt., 1977-78; cons. project bus. div. Jr. Achievement, 1979—; pres. Greenbriar Assn., 1977. Mem. Indpls. C. of C. (vice chmn. govt. affairs council 1976—, trustee polit. action com. 1978—). Home: 8116 Hoover Ln Indianapolis IN 46260 Office: 151 N Delaware St Indianapolis IN 46206

ARMSTRONG, JAMES THOMAS, bldg. systems co. exec.; b. Los Angeles, Dec. 13, 1938; s. James Floyd and Mary Louise (Harris) A.; student Santa Rosa Jr. Coll., 1956-57, San Francisco City Coll., 1958-59, U. Calif., 1964-65; m. Virginia Carol Williams, Nov. 4, 1972; children—Alyson Louise, James Floyd, Dawn Lynn, Victoria Ruth. Research, devel. Speedspace Corp., Santa Rosa, Calif., 1966-68; engring. mgr. Trus-Joist Calif. Corp., Santa Rosa, 1968-69; owner, cons. Armstrong & Assos., Santa Rosa, 1969-71; ops. mgr. Pacific State Components, Sonoma, Calif., 1971-72; pres. Creative Bldg. Systems, Santa Rosa, Calif., 1972—. Active YMCA, 1969—, asst. chief Indian Guides, 1969-70. Served with C.E., AUS, 1957. Mem. Forest Products Research Soc., Beta Phi Beta. Developer FHA-approved criteria for manufactured wood building system. Office: 2841 Cleveland Ave Suite B Santa Rosa CA 95401 also PO Box 3432 Santa Rosa CA 45402

ARMSTRONG, JOHN ARCHIBALD, oil co. exec.; b. Dauphin, Man., Can., Mar. 24, 1917; s. Herbert H. and Louisa I. (McDonald) A.; B.Sc. in Geology, U. Man., 1937; B.Sc. in Chem. Engring., Queen's U., 1942. With Imperial Oil Ltd., 1940—, successively gen. mgr. producing dept. exec. v.p., dir., now chmn. bd., pres., chief exec. officer; asst. coordinator producing coordination dept. Standard Oil Co. (N.J.), 1959; dir. Alta. Gas Trunk Line Co. Ltd., 1958-59, Royal Bank Can. Mem. Brit.-N.Am. Commn., Can.-Am. Commn.; trustee Fraser Inst. Meml. Conf. Bd. Office: 111 St Clair Ave W Toronto 7 ON Canada*

ARMSTRONG, JOHN ARCHIBALD, petroleum co. exec.; b. Dauphin, Man., Can., 1917; B.Sc. in Geology, U. Man., 1937; B.Sc. in Chem. Engring., Queen's U., 1942. Formerly with Geol. Survey Can.; with Imperial Oil Ltd., 1940—, dir., 1961—, responsible for mktg. ops., 1963-65, exec. v.p., 1966-70, pres., 1970-79, chief exec. officer, 1973—, chmn. bd., 1974—; dir. Royal Bank Can. Vice chmn. bd. trustees Fraser Inst.; chmn. adv. com. Sch. Bus. Adminstrn., U. Western Ont. Mem. Brit.-N. Am. Com., Conf. Bd., Internat. C. of C. (exec. bd.). Address: Imperial Oil Ltd 111 St Clair Ave W Toronto ON M5W 1K3 Canada

ARMSTRONG, JOHN KENASTON, ins. and fin. services corp. exec.; b. Springfield, Mass., Sept. 2, 1929; s. Ralph A. and Avice E. (Bliss) A.; B.S. (Olin scholar), Wesleyan U., Middletown, Conn., 1950; M.B.A. (Baker scholar), Harvard U., 1956; m. Katharine Kipp, Dec. 17, 1955; children—Leigh K., Stephen Kipp. Budget mgr. W.R. Grace & Co., N.Y.C., 1956-58; asst. controller Ford Motor Co., Dearborn, Mich., 1958-63, mktg. dir., 1963-68; fin. v.p. Keene Corp., N.Y.C., 1968-77; exec. v.p., chief fin. officer INA Corp., Phila., 1977-80, exec. v.p., also pres. Investment Group, 1980—; dir. INA Capital Advisors, INA Internat. Corp., INA Life Ins. Co., INA Reinsurance Co., Ins. Co. N. Am., Life Ins. Co. N. Am., Hosp. Affiliates Internat., Inc., Paine Webber, Inc., Sealed Air Corp., Investors Life Ins. Co. N. Am., INA Comml. Fin., Inc., Phila. Investment Corp. Trustee Thomas Jefferson U., 1977—, Wesleyan U., 1979—; bd. dirs. Phila. Conv. and Visitors Bur. Served with Signal Corps, U.S. Army, 1951-53. Mem. Phi Beta Kappa. Republican. Clubs: Union League of Phila., Wesleyan of Phila., Phila. Country, Harvard Bus. Sch. of Phila. Office: 1600 Arch St Philadelphia PA 19101

ARMSTRONG, RICHARD QUINE, beverage co. exec.; b. Boston, July 27, 1935; s. Oren Arthur and Katherine Isobel (Quine) A.; B.A. cum laude, Bowdoin Coll., 1957; m. Pamela Barthelomew, Oct. 7, 1961; children—Matthew, Rod. Mgmt. positions, various advt. agys., N.Y.C., 1959-72; v.p. Dobbs-Life Savers Internat., N.Y.C., 1972-76; pres. Canada Dry Internat., N.Y.C., 1976-79, Canada Dry Corp., N.Y.C., 1979—, also dir. Mem. vestry Christ Ch., Greenwich, Conn., 1979-80. Served to 1st lt. U.S. Army, 1957-59. Mem. Bowdoin Alumni Assn. Clubs: Union League, Pinnacle (N.Y.C.); Milbrook (pres. bd. govs. 1972-76) (Greenwich, Conn.). Office: 100 Park Ave New York NY 10017

ARMSTRONG, SEBERT RAY, machinery mfg. co. exec.; b. Madison, W.Va., Nov. 26, 1935; s. Walter Walker and Stella Rhoda A.; B.S.M.E., U. Cin., 1958; postgrad. Fenn Coll., 1959; M.B.A., George Washington U., 1961; m. Patricia J.; children—Lynne Michelle, Roslyn Jane. Sales engr. Gen. Time Corp., San Marino, Calif., 1962-65; v.p. mktg. ESNA Ltd., Toronto, Ont., Can., 1965-70; pres. Armstrong Engring. Co., Old Lyme, Conn., 1970-77; pres. Carlyle Johnson Machine Co., Manchester, Conn., 1977—, also dir.; dir. Conn. Bank & Trust. Served with USAF, 1959-62. Home: 18 Pine Tree Ln Avon CT 06001 Office: 52 Main St Manchester CT 06040

ARMSTRONG, THEODORE MORELOCK, corporate exec.; b. St. Louis, July 22, 1939; s. Theodore Roosevelt and Vassar Fambrough (Morelock) A.; B.A., Yale U., 1961; LL.B., Duke U., 1964; m. Carol Mercer Robert, Sept. 7, 1963; children—Evelyn Anne, Robert Theodore. Admitted to Mo. bar, 1964; with Mo. Pacific Corp. and subs.'s, St. Louis, 1964—, corp. sec., 1971-75; corp. sec. River Cement Co., 1968-75; asst. v.p. Mississippi River Transmission Corp., 1974-75, v.p. gas supply, 1975-79, exec. v.p., 1979—. Mem. Am., Met. St. Louis bar assns., Mo. Bar, So. Gas Assn., Tenn. Soc. St. Louis (dir.), Phi Alpha Delta. Republican. Presbyn. (deacon). Clubs: Bellerive, Clayton, Yale (St. Louis); Yale (N.Y.C.). Home: 307 Woodside Dr Saint Louis MO 63122 Office: 9900 Clayton Rd Saint Louis MO 63124

ARMSTRONG, WALTER PRESTON, JR., lawyer; b. Memphis, Oct. 4, 1916; Walter Preston and Irma (Waddell) A.; A.B., Harvard, 1938, J.D., 1941; D.C.L. (hon.), Southwestern at Memphis, 1961; m. Alice K. McKee, Nov. 3, 1949; children—Alice Kavanaugh, Walter Preston III. Admitted to Tenn. bar, 1940; asso. Armstrong, Allen, Braden, Goodman, McBride & Prewitt, and predecessor firms, 1941-47, partner, 1948—; hon. consul for France, Mpls., 1978—; mem. Tenn. Commn. on Uniform State Laws, 1947-67. Pres., Memphis Bd. Edn., 1956-61; mem. Tenn. Comm. Higher Edn., 1967—, Tenn. Hist. Commn., 1969-80. Served pvt. to maj., AUS, 1941-46. Fellow Am. Bar Found. (sec. 1960-62), Am. Coll. Trial Lawyers; mem. Am. (ho. of dels. 1952-75), Tenn. (pres. 1972-73), Memphis and Shelby County, Inter-Am., Internat. bar assns., Am. Law Inst., Nat. Conf. Commrs. on Uniform State Laws (pres. 1961-63), Assn. Bar City N.Y., Harvard Law Sch. Assn., Am. Judicature Soc., Scribes (pres. 1960-61), Order of Coif, Phi Delta Phi, Omicron Delta Kappa. Contbr. articles to profl. jours. Home: 1530 Carr Ave Memphis TN 38104 Office: 1900 One Commerce Sq Memphis TN 38103

ARMSTRONG, WILLIAM, metal working co. exec.; b. Belfast, No. Ireland, Mar. 24, 1928; s. William and Martha (McClatchey) A.; Asso.Engr., Newark Coll. Engring., 1949; B.S., Rutgers U., 1953, M.B.A., 1957; m. Doris E. Schmider, Aug. 6, 1955; children—Allyson Dawn, Deborah Joy, Melody Faith. Came to U.S., 1935, naturalized, 1936. Model maker, research engr., asst. chief indsl. engring. Thomas A. Edison Industries, West Orange, N.J., 1945-59; mgr. indsl. engring. Curtiss Wright Corp., 1959-63; mgr. mfg. engring. Singer Corp., Elizabeth, N.J., 1963-66; asst. to pres., chief indls. engring. Hillyer Corp., Mountainside, N.J., 1966-68; gen. mgr. Cozzoli Machine Co., Plainfield, N.J. 1968-78; v.p., gen. mgr. Beckley Perforating Co., Garwood, N.J., 1978-81; dir. ops. Hoglund Triordinate Corp., Berkeley Heights, N.J., 1981—; mem. staff dept. mgmt. Rutgers U., 1966—; guest lectr. Fairleigh Dickinson U., 1975—. Mem. Republican County Com., 1967. Mem. Soc. Mfg. Engrs., Packaging Inst. (speaker seminars 1977). Editor: Ratio Delay and Work Sampling—Guide to Productivity Improvement (F.H. Lambrou), 1968. Home: 86 Bennett Ave Cedar Grove NJ 07009 Office: Hoglund Triordinate Corp Berkeley Heights NJ

ARNDT, MICHAEL PAUL, electronics co. exec.; b. Mt. Vernon, N.Y., Aug. 30, 1930; s. Stanley Morris and Helen (Wood) A.; student Occidental Coll., 1948-49; B.A., Pomona Coll., 1952; M.B.A., Harvard, 1954. Analyst investment dept. N.Y. Life Ins. Co., San Francisco, 1954-56; v.p. Fin. Control Electronics Group, TRW Inc., Los Angeles, 1956—. Mem. Fin. Analyst Soc. San Francisco, Fin. Execs. Inst., Phi Delta Alumni Assn. (sec-treas., dir. 1964). Club: Mar de Cortez (dir. 1963) (La Paz, Mexico). Home: 251 S Barrington Ave Los Angeles CA 90049 Office: 10880 Wilshire Blvd Los Angeles CA 90024

ARNDT, ROBERT EWINS SUMNER, chem. mfg. co. exec.; b. Phila., July 24, 1930; s. Robert Norton Downs and Alice (Sumner) A.; A.B. cum laude, Amherst Coll., 1952; M.B.A., Harvard U., 1957; m. Virginia Mae Robertson, June 26, 1954; children—John Ewins, Peter Grant, Stephen Channing, Robert Sumner. With Essex Research Corp., Needham, Mass., 1957-60; sales mgr. Williamson Corp., Concord, Mass., 1960-63; v.p., gen. mgr. Duralectra Inc., Natick, Mass., 1963-71; v.p. Coatings Engring. Corp., Sudbury, Mass., 1971-75; pres., chmn. bd. dirs. Wallace Clark Inc., N.Y.C., 1975—. Served to lt. (j.g.) USN, 1952-55. Mem. Soc. Mfg. Engrs., Master Metal Finishers N.E. (pres., dir.), Am. Soc. for Metals, Newcomen Soc. Club: Pequot Yacht. Home: 976 Pequot Rd Southport CT 06490

ARNETT, JAMES EDWARD, educator, ins. co. dir.; b. Gullett, Ky., Oct. 3, 1912; s. Haden and Josephine (Risner) A.; A.B., San Jose State Coll., 1947, M.A., 1955; Ed.S., Stanford, 1959; m. Helen Mae Vallish, Mar. 23, 1943. Tchr., prin. pub. schs., Salyersville, Ky., 1930-41; tchr., adminstr. pub. schs., Salinas, Calif., 1947-52; owner-mgr. Arnett Apts., Salinas, 1950-53; tchr., Innes High Sch., Akron, Ohio, 1953-73; owner-mgr. Arnett Apts., Akron, 1953-72; dir. Educator & Exec. Co., 1962-73, Educator and Exec. Insurers, 1957-76, Educator and Exec. Life Ins. Co., 1962-76, Great Am. of Dallas Fire and Casualty Co., 1974-76, Great Am. of Dallas Ins. Co., 1974-76, J.C. Penney Casualty Ins. Co., 1976; cons., 1976-77. Mem. county, state central coms. Democratic party, 1952. Served with AUS, 1942-45. Mem. Nat. (del. conv. 1957), Ohio, N.E. Ohio, Akron edn. assns., San Jose State Coll., Stanford alumni assns., Phi Delta Kappa. Home: 691 Payne Ave Akron OH 44302 Office: 800 Brooksedge Blvd Westerville OH 43081

ARNHOLD, RALPH CHARLES, engring. co. exec.; b. St. Louis, July 12, 1933; s. Charles Edward and Louise Emma (Brunner) A.; B.S. in Elec. Engring., U. Mo., 1958; postgrad. So. Meth. U., 1959-60. Owner, operator Arnhold and Assos., Hermann, Mo., 1951—. Served with U.S. Army, 1954-56. Mem. Soc. Coll. and Univ. Planning. Republican. Home: 1 Lone Tree Hill Hermann MO 65041 Office: Route 1 Box 4A Hermann MO 65041

ARNING, LEE DONCOURT, ins. co. exec.; b. Palenville, N.Y., Aug. 12, 1923; s. Herman G. and Grace Todd (Doncourt) A.; B.S. in Adminstrn., Rutgers U., 1951. With Dun & Bradstreet, Inc., 1947-55; with N.Y. Stock Exchange, 1955-72, sr. v.p., 1971-72; exec. v.p., treas. Tucker, Anthony & R.L. Day, Inc., 1972-76; pres., dir. USLIFE Corp., N.Y.C., 1976—; bd. dirs. Chgo. Bd. Options Exchange, 1973-75; trustee Montclair Savs. Bank (N.J.), 1972-76. Chmn., Montclair chpt. ARC, 1975-77; trustee Montclair Art Mus., 1978—; pres. Eagle Rock council Boy Scouts Am., 1956; warden, vestryman St. James Episcopal Ch., Montclair, 1963-74; mem. Montclair Bd. Edn., 1966-71, v.p., 1971. Served with AUS, 1942-46. Office: 125 Maiden Ln New York NY 10038

ARNOLD, CALVIN LINCOLN, carbide cutting tool exec.; b. Williamstown, N.Y., Feb. 11, 1923; s. Samuel G. and Florence Alice (Nicholson) A.; B.S. in Engring., U.S. Mil. Acad., West Point, N.Y., 1946; M.B.A., Harvard U., 1948; m. Marilyn Jean Wyard, Aug. 5, 1950; children—Calvin Lincoln, Cynthia W., Susan L. Commd. 2d. lt., U.S. Army, 1946, advanced through grades to capt., 1951; mem. Army Gen. Staff; ret., 1954; mgr. fin. planning, v.p. mfg. Honeywell, Inc., 1954-72; v.p. ops. Kennametal, Inc., 1972-76; v.p. ops., dir. Newcomer Products, Inc., Latrobe, Pa., 1977-79, pres., chief exec. officer, 1980—; dir. Peerless Saw Co., Columbus, Ohio. Bd. dirs. Pa. Economy League. Mem. Cemented Carbide Producers Assn., U.S. C. of C., NAM, Delta Kappa Epsilon. Republican. Congregationalist. Club: Rolling Rock (Ligonier). Home: RD 4 Box A Ligonier PA 15658 Office: PO Box 272 Latrobe PA 15650

ARNOLD, DAVID CLEMENT, electronics co. exec.; b. Farson, Iowa, Sept. 28, 1919; s. David Edwin and Hazel (Brown) A.; B.S., Iowa State U., 1942; m. Ann Robel, Mar. 20, 1941; children—Nancy, Susan, John David, Robert Edwin. Engr., Gen. Electric Co., 1942-45, Gilfallen Bros., Los Angeles, 1945-48; with Collins Radio Co., 1948-59, dir. research and devel., until 1959; v.p. Alpha Radio, Richardson, Tex., 1959-61; ops. mgr. RCA Corp., Burlington, Mass., 1961-65; v.p., gen. mgr. Hoffman Electronics Corp., El Monte, Calif., 1965, exec. v.p., dir., 1965-66, pres., 1966-70; pres. Conductron Corp., 1970-71; corp. v.p. McDonnell Douglas Corp., St. Charles, Mo., 1971—, pres. McDonnell Douglas Electronics Co., 1971—. Mem. Electronic Industries Assn. (v.p. govt. products div., bd. govs.). Office: Box 426 2600 N 3d St St Charles MO 63301

ARNOLD, DAVID LEE, ch. bldg. co. exec.; b. Bowie, Tex., Sept. 22, 1935; s. Floyd E. and Jackie L. Arnold; B.S., Abilene (Tex.) Christian U., 1955; m. Martha L. Scarborough, July 25, 1953; children—Wes, Mike. Ordained to ministry Ch. of Christ, 1955; pastor in Tex. and Okla., 1955-71; exec. Sir Speeky Instant Printing Centers, Tex., Miss., Tenn. and Ky., 1972-75; pres. Bus. Motivation Research, Inc., Dallas, 1975-78, Ch. Bldgs. & Interiors Inc., Oklahoma City, 1978—, also dir.; pres. Timbercon Builders, Inc., 1980—; dir. I.B.I. Inc. Pres., PTA, Ada, 1967. Mem. Real Estate Agts. Assn. Tex. Republican. Club: Lions. Author: Delinquent Moms and Dads, 1960; Above All Things, 1967; A Study of Final Events, 1958. Home: 8004 Irish Dr Fort Worth TX 76118 Office: PO Box 18925 Fort Worth TX 76118

ARNOLD, G. DEWEY, JR., accountant; b. Montgomery, Ala., Jan. 30, 1925; s. G. Dewey and Janie Esther (Terry) A.; B.A. in Econs., U. South, 1949; postgrad. accounting U. Tenn.; m. Dorothy Louise Wenger, Dec. 4, 1954; children—Susan O., G. Dewey III. With Aladdin Industries, Inc., Nashville, 1949-50; with Price Waterhouse & Co., C.P.A.'s, 1950—, partner, 1961—, partner charge Washington office, 1966-76, mem. policy com., 1975—, regional mng. partner, 1976—. Instr. accounting Robert Morris Sch. Accounting, 1952-53; lectr., course dir. mgmt. accounting Inst. Mexicano de Administracion de Negocias, A.C., 1958-64. Bd. dirs. Landon Sch., 1975—, chmn. bd.; bd. dirs. GWETA, 1972—, Wolf Trap Found., 1976—, Redskin Found., 1975—; sec., mem. exec. com. Fed. City Council, 1966—; vice chmn. Bicentennial Commn. D.C.; mem. Am. Arbitration Assn., Washington Bd. Trade. Served with USNR, 1943-45. C.P.A., Pa., D.C., Md., N.C., Mich., La. Mem. Am., D.C., Md. insts. C.P.A.'s. Episcopalian. Clubs: Burning Tree, Chevy Chase, Congressional Country, Metropolitan, (Washington). Home: 3 Chalfont Ct Washington DC 20016 Office: 1801 K St NW Washington DC 20006

ARNOLD, HENRIETTA DOWS, corporate exec.; b. Cedar Rapids, Iowa, Oct. 19, 1921; d. Sutherland C. and Frances Daisy (Mills) Dows; student The Masters Sch., Dobbs Ferry, N.Y., 1936-37, Greenwood Sch., Ruxton, Md., 1938-39, Coe Coll., 1939-41, Chgo. Art Inst., 1945-46; m. Duane Arnold, Apr. 27, 1946; children—Margaret, Helen, Duane, Elizabeth, Mary. Sec., Iowa Electric Light & Power, Cedar Rapids, 1942-43; with advt. dept. Sunkist Fruit Growers, Los Angeles, 1943-45; exec. v.p., corp. dir. Dows Real Estate Co., Cedar Rapids, 1969—; v.p., dir. Dows Farms, Inc., Cedar Rapids, 1969—; dir. Sutherland Sq., Cedar Rapids. Bd. dirs. YWCA, 1965-70, Cedar Rapids Art Assn. Pub. Health Nursing Assn., 1950-65; trustee, mem. exec. com., bldg. com. Coe Coll., 1953—; trustee, mem. fin. com. and research com. Menninger Found., Topeka, Mem. Jr. League. Republican. Presbyn. (mem. religious edn. com., instr., trustee). Home: 321 Crescent St Cedar Rapids IA 52403 Office: 212 Dows Bldg PO Box 409 Cedar Rapids IA 52406

ARNOLD, JAMES ROMER, mgmt. cons.; b. Chgo., May 8, 1933; s. William Joseph and Beatrice (Romer) A.; B.S., Denison U., 1955; M.B.A., Northwestern U., 1957; m. June Lenore Clissold, Aug. 18, 1956; children—Kathryn Anne, Douglas Joseph, Robert Clissold. Asst. to exec. v.p. McGraw-Edison Co., Elgin, Ill., 1960-66; officer No. Trust Co., Chgo., 1966-68; pres. exec. search div. A.T. Kearney, Inc., Chgo., 1968—. Active Dean's Bus. Adv. Council, Sch. Commerce and Acctg. U. Ill. Served to 1st. lt. U.S. Army, 1957-60. Mem. Assn. of Exec. Recruiting Consultants (exec. v.p., bd. dirs.). Republican. Office: 222 S Riverside Plaza Chicago IL 60606

ARNOLD, LARRY GENE, ins. sales exec.; b. McPherson, Kans., Mar. 25, 1944; s. Robert A. and Doris J. (Klassen) A.; student Kans. State U., 1962-65; B.A. in Bus., Tabor Coll., 1967; postgrad. U. Kans., 1967-68, Colo. U., 1968; m. Patricia Jean Arnold, June 17, 1967; children—Betsy Jeanne, Maggie Lee. Broker, Northwestern Mut. Life Ins. Co., 1970-77; pres. Larry G. Arnold C.L.U. and Assos., Inc., Colorado Springs, Colo., 1978—; Chmn. bd. Mountain Valley chpt. Nat. Found. of March of Dimes; mem. Pikes Peak Econ. Devel. Assn.; fund raiser United Fund, Heart Fund, YMCA, Boy Scouts Am., CROP. Served with AUS, 1967-69. Named Man of Yr., Gen. Agts. and Mgrs. Assn., 1976, Distinguished Life Underwriter, 1976. Mem. Million Dollar Round Table (life and qualifying mem.), Colorado Springs Assn. Life Underwriters, N.E. Bus. Builders. Democrat. Methodist. Clubs: Rampart Range Kiwanis (pres. 1974-75, dist. lt. gov. 1978), Masons. Contbr. articles to trade jours. Home: 3112 Whileaway Circle W Colorado Springs CO 80917 Office: 105 E Vermijo St Suite 235 Colorado Springs CO 80903

ARNOLD, LESTER EDWIN, JR., metals mfg. co. exec.; b. Relay, Md., Mar. 3, 1939; s. Lester Edwin and Evelyn (Weir) A.; B.S., Johns Hopkins U., 1968; M.B.A., State U. N.Y., 1971, LL.B., 1977; postgrad. Harvard U. Bus. Sch., 1972, Mass. Inst. Tech., 1973; m. Ingrid S. Andersen, Aug. 22, 1970; children—Elizabeth, Jennifer, Andrew, Daniel. Controller, Westinghouse Electric Corp., Balt., 1957-63; asst. to pres. Rubber Millers, Inc., Balt., 1963-65; gen. mgr. Hedwin Corp., Balt., 1965-68; mgr. engring. mgmt. Hooker Chem. Corp., Niagara Falls, N.Y., 1968-75; v.p. ops. U.S. Sugar Co., Buffalo, 1975-76; mgr. engring. mgmt. electro-mineral div. Carborundum Co., Niagara Falls, 1976-79; with Anaconda Industries, Buffalo, 1979—; admitted to N.Y. bar, 1977; instr. State U. N.Y.; dir. Prestegous Bank, 2 cos. Mem. Williamsville (N.Y.) Sch. Bd. Recipient Jr. Achievement award, 1976, Pres's. award U.S. Govt., 1970; registered profl. engr., N.Y., Md. Mem. Buffalo C. of C., Acad. Mgmt., Soc. Fin. Adminstrs., Am. Mgmt. Assn., Soc. Advanced Mgmt., Businessmen's Alliance, Am. Inst. Indsl. Engrs., Phi Beta Kappa, Tau Beta Pi. Democrat. Methodist. Clubs: Country Golf, Buffalo Athletic, Buffalo Yacht; Masons (Balt.). Author: Will Automation Make People Obsolete?, 1968; (with G. Bechberger) Production Cost Control, 1970; contbr. numerous articles to profl. jours.; patentee in field. Home: 36 Troy View Ln Williamsville NY 14221 Office: Anaconda Industries Inc Buffalo NY 14240

ARNOLD, WILLIAM PERRY, retail exec.; b. Omaha, Mar. 21, 1925; s. John Chapel and Hariett H. (Heiss) A.; B.S. in Bus. Adminstrn., U. Mo., 1947; m. Barbara L. Powell, Feb. 17, 1949; children—Stephen P., Alice Lee Arnold Drogoul. Vice pres. mdse., publicity dir. L.S. Ayres, Indpls., 1947-68; chmn., chief exec. officer J.W. Robinson, 1968-74; pres. Associated Dry Goods Corp., N.Y.C., 1974—, chief exec. officer, 1979—. Active, Urban League. Mem. Purple Mark. Club: Masons. Office: 417 Fifth Ave New York NY 10016

ARNOLDUS, CLINTON LEE, internat. banker; b. Salt Lake City, Mar. 3, 1947; s. Franklin Lee and La Preel (Sorenson) A.; B.A., Brigham Young U., 1971; M. Internat. Mgmt., Am. Grad. Sch. Internat. Mgmt., 1972; m. Lesley Ann Tuft, Aug. 29, 1970; children—Jennifer, Nicole, Ted, Christine. Supr. sales adminstrn. Koehring Co., Amsterdam, Milw., 1972-75; asst. cashier Bank of Am., Chgo., 1975-77; asst. v.p., v.p. Security Pacific Nat. Bank, Los Angeles, Chgo., 1977-79, v.p., mgr., San Francisco, 1980—, mem. No. Calif. exec. com., 1979—, chmn. adminstrv. com., 1979—. Mem. Western Com. on Internat. Banking, San Francisco C. of C., Oakland World Trade Assn., Brit.-Am. C. of C., Can.-Am. C. of C., German-Am. C. of C. Clubs: Union League (Chgo.); World Trade (San Francisco). Home: Palo Alto CA Office: One Embarcadero Center San Francisco CA 94111

ARNOT, ODEN BOWIE, real estate cons.; b. Balt., Dec. 29, 1947; s. Nathaniel DuBois and Alice Carter (Bowie) A.; student Lehigh U., 1967-68; B.S., Syracuse U., 1972; m. Rhea Duke Inglehart, Aug. 28, 1971; 1 dau., Alice Carter. Project dir. N.Y. Urban Devel. Corp., 1972-73; dir. mktg. Les Byron Assos., Inc., real estate devel. co., Ft. Lauderdale, Fla., 1973-74; v.p. EMC Properties, Inc., Miami, Fla., 1974-76; v.p. new project devel. Charles Center-Inner Harbor Mgmt., Inc., Balt., 1976-79; owner, mgr. O. Bowie Arnot, real estate cons., Balt., 1979—. Clubs: Center, Elkridge, Maryland. Home and Office: 309 Northfield Pl Baltimore MD 21210

ARNTZ, GARY PAUL, banker; b. Massillon, Ohio, May 4, 1946; s. Paul C. and Mary Ellen (Ray) A.; B.S. in Bus. Adminstrn., Kent State U., 1968; certificate Bank Adminstrn. Inst., Cin., 1976; m. Lorraine M. Lenkey, Jan. 16, 1970. Mktg. asst. Third Nat. Bank, Dayton, Ohio, 1973-75, mktg. officer, 1975-77; asst. v.p. mktg. Bank of Commonwealth, Detroit, 1977—. Served with USAF, 1969-73. Mem. Am. Mgmt. Assn., Am. Mktg. Assn., Bank Mktg. Assn. Democrat. Roman Catholic. Home: 3499 Berkshire Detroit MI 48224 Office: 719 Griswold St Detroit MI 48226

ARNTZEN, WAYNE LEROY, railroad exec.; b. Serena, Ill., Apr. 18, 1929; s. Archie Leroy and Helen Louise (Fatland) A.; student in transp. George Washington U., Northwestern U.; grad. Advanced mgmt. program Harvard U.; m. Geraldine Marie Batalia, June 26, 1954; children—Steven, Kurt, Kandee. With Chgo., Burlington & Quincy (name changed to Burlington No. Inc.), 1947—, div. supt., 1968-72, asst. v.p. ops., 1972-77, v.p. Denver region, 1977—; dir. Denver Union Terminal Ry. Co. Adv. bd. Denver area council Boy Scouts Am. Served with transp. bn. U.S. Army, 1951-53; Korea. Mem. Nat. Def. Transp. Assn. (life), Denver C. of C. Methodist. Clubs: Denver, Lakewood Country. Office: 1405 Curtis St Suite 2000 Denver CO 80202

ARONIN, RICHARD M., art and auction appraising co. exec.; b. Bklyn., Dec. 2, 1952; s. Herbert J. and Bertha E. A.; B.S., Bklyn. Coll., 1973; m. Toby D. Takce, Dec. 24, 1973; 1 dau., Rachel S. Buyer, Metpath, Inc., 1978-79; asst. v.p., dir. corp. purchasing Sotheby Parke Bernet, Inc., N.Y.C., 1979—. Mem. Nat. Assn. Purchasing Mgmt., Am. Mgmt. Assn. Office: Sotheby Parke Bernet Inc 980 Madison Ave New York NY 10021

ARONS, ISAIAH, real estate broker; b. N.Y.C., Aug. 29, 1917; s. Alexander and Fanny (Gillman) A.; B.S., Coll. William and Mary, 1938; m. Norma Janet Spier, Oct. 1, 1950; children—Alan L., Ronald E. Real estate mgr., N.Y.C., 1938-42; mgr. real property Garment Textile Bus. Service Corp., 1946-78: real estate broker, appraiser, cons. Arons Co., N.Y.C., 1978—. Mem. EPA com., mem. police adv. com., mem. consumer affairs com. Town of Rockville Centre. Served with USAAF, 1942-46; PTO. Club: Masons.

ARPE, JOHN EDWIN, mfg. co. exec.; b. Milw., June 10, 1916; d. Walter Christian and Amanda (Bruck) A.; student U. Wis., 1938-42, Marquete U., 1943-46; grad. Advanced Mgmt. Program, Harvard U., 1966; m. Germaine Margaret Brever, Aug. 10, 1940; children—James F., John E., Christine M., Janet E. With Heil Co., Milw., 1934—, exec. v.p., treas., 1968-77, pres., 1977—; dir. W.A. Krueger Co., Scottsdale, Ariz., Valuation Research Corp., Milw. Trustee Good Samaritan Med. Center, Milw. Club: University (Milw.). Home: 12520 Stephen Pl Elm Grove WI 53122 Office: 777 E Wisconsin Ave Suite 2800 Milwaukee WI 53202

ARRINGTON, WENDELL S., pharm. co. exec.; b. Bklyn., Oct. 3, 1936; s. Joseph Earl and Genevieve (Thornton) A.; B.S., Rensselaer Poly. Inst., 1958, Ph.D., (NSF fellow), 1964; M.B.A., Temple U., 1973; children—Judy Ann, Michael, Theresa, Patricia. Asst. prof. physics SUNY, Albany, 1965-66; head research computer applications Merck & Co., West Point, Pa., 1966-67; mgr. biostatistics Wyeth Labs., Phila., 1968-72, asso. dir. sci. computer applications, 1972-74, dir. sci. computer applications, 1974—. Active United Fund, Boy Scouts Am. Cert. mgmt. acct.; cert. data processor. Mem. Drug Info. Assn. (dir. public relations 1975—), Assn. for Computing Machinery, Sigma Xi. Home: 175 E Kenilworth St Newtown Square PA 19073 Office: PO Box 8299 Philadelphia PA 19101

ARSHT, ADRIENNE, lawyer; b. Wilmington, Del., Feb. 4, 1942; d. Samuel and Roxana (Cannon) A.; B.A., Mt. Holyoke Coll., 1963; J.D., Villanova (Pa.) U., 1966; m. Myer Feldman, Sept. 28, 1980. Admitted to Del. bar, 1966; asso. firm Morris, Nichols, Arsht & Tunnell, Wilmington, 1966-69; with Trans World Airlines, N.Y.C., 1969-79, dir. govt. relations, 1969-79; atty. firm Bregman, Abell, Solter & Kay, Washington, 1979—; pres. Land Title Corp.; dir. Nat. Savs. & Trust Bank, Washington. Mem. Del. Bar Assn. Home: 2801 New Mexico

Ave NW Washington DC 20007 Office: 1900 L St NW Washington DC 20036

ARSTARK, LESTER D., advt. exec.; b. Hoboken, N.J., Sept. 7, 1924; s. Maurice T. and Sophia L. (Solomon) A.; A.B., Brown U., 1948; postgrad. Columbia U. Grad. Sch. Bus. Adminstrn., 1950; m. Janice M. Corn, June 29, 1952; children—Kim A. (dec. 1968), Dru A. News editor Bristol (R.I.) Phoenix, 1948-49, New Bedford (Mass.) Standard-Times radio stas., 1949-51; account exec. Kenyon and Eckhardt, N.Y.C., 1951-53, promotion supr. food products, 1954-57; advt. and sales promotion mgr. Hudson Pulp & Paper Corp., 1957-59, dir. communications, 1959-60; pres. L.D. Arstark & Co., Inc., N.Y.C., 1961—; lectr. pub. relations C.W. Post Coll., 1960-61; lectr. mktg. Bernard Baruch Sch., City Coll. N.Y., 1959-61; dir., mem. exec. com. Programming and Systems, Inc. Bd. dirs. Nat. Parkinson Found., 1962-69, mem. exec. com., 1962-64. Served with USAAF, 1943-46. Clubs: Brown U. of L.I. (pres., dir.); Brown of N.Y.; Mill River (Upper Brookville, N.Y.). Home: 190 Main St Roslyn NY 11576 Office: 420 Lexington Ave Suite 556 New York NY 10017 also 20 Crossways Bldg Woodbury NY 11797

ARTEMIS, JOHNNIE (JOHNETTA) MAE, computer mktg. exec.; b. Mt. Carmel, Ill., May 31, 1945; d. John Franklin and Thelma Mae (Dustman) Gore; student Fla. State U., 1963-65; m. Nathan A. Teichholtz, Feb., 1980. Programmer/analyst Nat. Life and Accident Ins. Co., Inc., Nashville, 1969-71; systems analyst State of Tenn., Nashville, 1971-72; sr. programmer/analyst Stone & Webster Engring. Co., Boston, 1972-74, Genesco Inc., Nashville, 1974-75; sr. mktg. specialist Digital Equipment Corp., Merrimack, N.H., 1975-78; nat. account mgr. telecommunications industry Data Gen. Corp., Westboro, Mass., 1978-80; v.p. mktg. Turnkey Computer Systems, Inc., Hollis, N.H., 1980—; lectr. on women in mgmt. and bus., women's rights. Asst. state coordinator NOW, N.H., 1977, state coordinator, 1977-78; del. N.H. Democratic State Conv., 1978; chmn. for Amherst, N.H., Anderson for Pres., 1980. Certified data processor. Mem. NOW (Greater Nashua chpt. and N.H. orgn.), ACLU. Home: Pavillion Rd Amherst NH 03031 Office: 9 Ash St Hollis NH 03049

ARTHUR, PATRICIA LORAINE, mfg. co. ofcl.; b. Nacogdoches, Tex., Feb. 22, 1947; d. Travis Neal and Mary Audrey (Purcell) A.; B.S., U. Houston, 1970, postgrad., 1971. Tchr. high sch., Houston, 1970-73; with Mobil Oil Corp., N.Y.C., 1973—, mgr. corp. activites employee relations, 1979—; speaker in field. Mem. Am. Assn. Personnel Mgmt. Home: 420 E 64th St New York NY 10021 Office: 150 E 42d St New York NY 10017

ARTIS, D. RICHARD, govt. ofcl.; b. Warren, Ohio, Sept. 6, 1939; s. Foster Lionel and Alice Mae (Jones) A.; A.B., U. Calif., Berkeley, 1963; postgrad. Am. U., 1965-67; m. Virginia Gowder, Aug. 31, 1963; children—Christopher, Joshua. Engring. adminstr. Gen. Dynamics, Pomona, Calif., 1963-65; legis. asst., Washington, 1965-66; mgmt. cons., Washington, 1966-71; v.p. The Assistance Group, Washington, 1972-77; exec. dir. Office on Aging, Govt. D.C., 1977—; chief exec. Washington Center for Aging Services, 1980—; cons. to govt. ofcls.; adv. com. Family and Child Services D.C., 1977—; community adv. com. Washington Home, 1978—. Nat. Center Edn. in Politics fellow, 1961-63. Mem. Urban Elderly Coalition (dir.), Nat. Assn. State Units on Aging, Nat. Assn. Area Agys. on Aging. Methodist. Club Commonwealth. Home: 2958 Northampton St NW Washington DC 20015 Office: 1012 14th St NW Washington DC 20005

ARTIS, EDWARD ALLEN, mortgage co. exec., educator; b. Highland Park, Ill., July 9, 1945; s. Edgar and Lenore (Healy) A.; student U. Calif., Berkeley, 1966-68, Glendale Community Coll., 1974; LL.D. (hon.), U. Saigon, 1972; m. Regina Carol Shermer, Feb. 8, 1975. Dist. mgr. Jr. Achievement So. Calif., N. Hollywood, 1973-75; realtor asso. Stevenson, Dilbeck Inc. Realtors, Glendale, Calif., 1975—; asst. treas. Advance Mortgage Corp., Van Nuys, Calif., 1976-78; exec. v.p., prin. Classic Fin. Corp., Panorama City, Calif., 1978-81; chief exec. officer Ed Artis & Assos., 1981—; prof. real estate fin. Los Angeles City Coll., 1979—. Bd. dirs. Nat. Research Found. on Aging, 1975—. Served as Spl. Forces Green Beret, U.S. Army, 1963-73. Decorated Silver Star (2), DFC, Bronze Star (3), Purple Heart (3); recipient Distinguished Service award City of Concord, Calif., 1972; named an Outstanding Young Man, Calif. Jaycees, 1971, Calif. Humanitarian of Yr., 1973. Mem. Calif. Jaycees (spl. presdl. asst. on child abuse 1974-76, pres. internat. USA Mexico Border Fedn. 1974), Glendale C. of C., Calif. Assn. Realtors, Nat. Assn. Realtors, Calif. Mortgage Bankers Assn., Assn. Profl. Mortgage Women, Glendale Bd. Realtors, Glendale Days of Verdugos Assn. Republican. Home: 2633 E Glenoaks Blvd Glendale CA 91206 Office: 2777 Van Nuys Blvd Suite 201 Panorama City CA 91402

ARTLEY, JOHN WILLIAM, electronics co. exec.; b. Williamsport, Pa., June 7, 1938; s. A. Sterl and Dorothy M. (Hammond) A.; A.B., U. Mo., 1961, B.J. in Advt. and Mktg., 1962; m. Peggy L. Pederson, July 26, 1971; 1 dau., Meleah Rogers. With Young & Rubicam, Inc., N.Y.C., 1962-64, Glenn Advt., Dallas, 1964-67; account exec. Creative Agy. Assos., Inc., Dallas, 1967-70; exec. v.p. REFAC Tech. Devel. Corp., N.Y.C., 1970-71; asst. to pres. Object Recognition Systems, Inc., N.Y.C., 1971-72, pres., 1972—. Mem. Am. Mgmt. Assn., Pattern Recognition Soc., Robot Inst. Am., Soc. Mfg. Engrs., Presidents Assn. of Am. Mgmt. Assn. Republican. Presbyterian. Office: 521 Fifth Ave Suite 1713 New York NY 10017

ARTMAN, PHILIP BARRY, vinyl heat-sealing mfg. co. exec.; b. Bronx, N.Y., Dec. 3, 1953; s. George and Margaret (Simonowitz) A.; B.S., Fairleigh Dickinson U., 1975. Acct., Friedman & Strulowitz, Livingston, N.J., 1975-77, Goldman & Krinintz, N.Y.C., 1977; comptroller, v.p. Vinaseal Co., Inc., Newark, 1978—. C.P.A., N.J. Mem. N.J. Soc. C.P.A.'s. Democrat. Jewish. Home: 41 Hemlock Terr Springfield NJ 07081 Office: 25 Prospect St Newark NJ 07105

ARVAN, JACK HARITUNE, JR., transp. co. exec.; b. Memphis, Jan. 1, 1947; s. Jack H. and Virginia L. (King) A.; B.S. in Bus. Mgmt., U. Tenn., 1967; m. Wilma Wilson, Feb. 5, 1965; children—Kathy, Ken, Brenda, Misty. With PPG Industries, 1964-76; with Golden State Transit, Los Angeles, 1976—, v.p., gen. mgr., dir. fleet adminstrn., 1980—; dir. Glata Inc. Mem. Nat. Assn. Fleet Adminstrs., Western Council Pvt. Fleet Owners, Soc. Automotive Engrs., Calif. Autobody Assn. Home: 24357 La Glorita New Hall CA Office: 1408 W 3rd St Los Angeles CA 90017

ARWOOD, JOHN REYNOLDS, shipping co. exec.; b. Greenville, S.C., Dec. 14, 1931; s. Earl Homer and Emma (Lane) A.; student U.S. Naval Acad., 1952-53; B.S. in Indsl. Engring., N.C. State U., 1956; postgrad. CCNY, 1958-59; m. Lee Hoagland, Feb. 27, 1965; children—Melissa Lee, Susannah Lane. Engr., Union Carbide Corp., 1956-60; mgr. ops. Continental Grain Co., 1960-64; div. gen. mgr. SeaLand Service, Inc., 1965-68; sr. v.p. Seatrain Lines Inc., 1969-71; chmn., chief exec. officer Enterprise Distribution, Inc., Elizabeth, N.J., 1971-76; pres., chief exec. office Trans Freight Lines, Inc., Wayne, N.J., 1976—, dir., 1976—; dir. Alltrans Internat. Group, TNT, Ltd., Bulkships Ltd., Seafast UK, TNT Transport Internat. (Netherlands). Bd. dirs. Bonnie Brae Boys' Home, 1971-76, United Way, 1975; trustee Mountainside Hosp., Montclair, N.J. Served with USN, 1953. Mem. Nat. Def. Transp. Assn., Naval Acad. Assn., Am. Inst. Indsl. Engrs., Theta Tau, Alpha Pi Mu, Tau Beta Pi. Clubs: Montclair Golf, Bay Head Yacht, Seabrook Island, Moose (life). Home: 4 Valley View Pl North Caldwell NJ 07006 Office: Trans Freight Lines Inc 145 Route 46 Wayne NJ 07470

ASCHER, JAMES JOHN, pharm. co. exec.; b. Kansas City, Mo., Oct. 2, 1928; s. Bordner Fredrick and Helen (Barron) A.; student Bergen Jr. Coll., 1947-48, U. Kans., 1946-47, 49-51; m. Mary Ellen Robitsch, Feb. 27, 1954; children—Jill Denise, James John, Christopher Bordner. Rep., B.F. Ascher & Co., Inc., Memphis, 1954-55, asst. to pres., Kansas City, Mo., 1956-57, v.p., 1958-64, pres., 1965—. Bd. dirs. Children's Cardiac Center, 1964—, pres., 1968-70; bd. dirs. Jr. Achievement of Middle Am., Inc., 1970—, pres., 1973-76, chmn., 1979—; mem. central governing bd. Children's Mercy Hosp., 1968-80. Served to 1st lt. AUS, 1951-53. Decorated Bronze Star, Combat Infantryman's Badge. Mem. Pharm. Mfrs. Assn., Mo. C. of C., Drug, Chem. and Allied Trades Assn., C. of C. Greater Kansas City, Midwest Pharm. Advt. Club, Sales and Advt. Execs. Club, VFW, Young Pres.'s Orgn. (ex-officio dir., chmn. leadership activities com., edn. chmn. 6th Internat. Univ., Athens, Greece), World Bus. Council, Chief Execs. Forum, Delta Chi. Clubs: Kansas City; Indian Hills Country (Prairie Village, Kans.); N.Y. Athletic. Lotos. Home: 6706 Glenwood Shawnee Mission KS 66204 Office: 5100 E 59th St Kansas City MO 64130

ASH, FREDERICK MELVIN, chem. co. exec.; b. Columbus, Ohio, June 15, 1941; s. Melvin Edward and Ida Belle (Berry) A.; student U. Cin., 1959-61; B.S. in B.A., Ohio State U., 1963; m. Karen Persichetti, Apr. 7, 1979. Staff acct. chem. plastics div. Gen. Tire & Rubber Co., Akron, Ohio, 1963-65, office mgr., 1965-67, acctg. mgr., Lawrence, Mass., 1968, controller, Newcomerstown, Ohio, 1968-70, Lawrence, 1971-73, plant mgr., 1974-76, v.p. film, Jeannette, Pa., 1977; pres. Gen. Tire & Rubber Plastic Film Co., Jeannette, 1977-78; bus. dir. plastics Tenneco Chems., Inc., Piscataway, N.J., 1978—. Advisor, Jr. Achievement, Akron, 1965; mem. budget com. Merrimack Valley United Fund, Lawrence, 1973-74, budget com. chmn., 1975, campaign chmn., 1976, dir., 1975-76; bd. dirs. United Way of Westmoreland County, 1977-78. U.S. Rubber scholar, 1961-63; recipient Pace Setter award Ohio State U., 1963. Mem. Westmoreland County C. of C., Nat. Assn. Accts., Ohio State U. Alumni Assn., Sigma Chi. Republican. Presbyterian. Club: Masons. Home: Aspen 7 Village 2 New Hope PA 18939 Office: Turner Pl Piscataway NJ 08854

ASH, ROY LAWRENCE, office equipment mfg. co. exec.; b. Los Angeles, Oct. 20, 1918; s. Charles K. and Fay E. (Dickinson) A.; M.B.A., Harvard U., 1947; m. Lila M. Hornbek. Nov. 13, 1943; children—Loretta Ash Ackerson, James, Marilyn Ash Hodge, Robert, Charles. With Bank of Am., 1936-42, 47-49; chief fin. officer Hughes Aircraft Co., 1949-53; co-founder Litton Industries, Inc., Beverly Hills, Calif., 1953-72, dir., 1953-72, pres., 1961-72; dir. Bank of Am. Corp., 1968-72, 76—; dir. Bank of Am., 1968-72, 78—; dir. Trus Joist Corp., Global Marine, Inc., 1965-72, 75—, Pacific Mut. Life Ins. Co., 1965-72; asst. to Pres. U.S., dir. Office Mgmt. and Budget, Washington, 1973-75; chmn. bd., chief exec. officer AM Internat.; dir. Consol. Foods Corp.; chmn. Pres.'s Adv. Council on Exec. Orgn., 1969-71; co-chmn. Japan-Calif. Assn., 1965-72. Trustee Calif. Inst. Tech., 1967-72, Com. Econ. Devel., 1970-72, 75—, Urban Inst., 1971-72; bd. dirs. Los Angeles World Affairs Council, 1968-72, 78—, pres., 1970-72; chmn. adv. council on gen. govt. Rep. Nat. Com.; vice-chmn. Los Angeles Olympic Organizing Com. Mem. Conf. Bd., Bus. Roundtable, C. of C. U.S. (dir.). Clubs: Bel Air Country, Harvard (Los Angeles). Office: 1900 Ave of Stars Los Angeles CA 90067

ASH, THOMAS GRAY, bank exec.; b. Casper, Wyo., July 6, 1939; s. Kenneth John and Marion Gertrude (Gray) A.; B.A., Stanford U., 1962; M.B.A., U. S.C., 1975; m. Arlayne Marie Plutte, May 1, 1965; children—Christopher Joseph, Timothy Kenneth. Sr. systems analyst System Devel. Corp., Santa Monica, Calif., 1965-67; asst. div. mgr., market planning div. Wilbur Smith & Assos., Cola, S.C., 1967-70; v.p., data processing dir. First Nat. Bank of S.C., Columbia, from 1970, now sr. v.p.; adj. prof. U. S.C., 1977-78. Bd. dirs. Palmetto Home. Served with USAF, 1962-65. Decorated Air Force Commendation medal. Mem. adv. bd. Cardinal Newman High Sch., 1979—; v.p. East Columbia Dixie Youth Baseball Commn., 1978—. Mem. Am. Bankers Assn. (edn. com.), S.C. Bankers Assn. (chmn. ops. com.), Data Processing Mgmt. Assn., Assn. Systems Mgrs. Republican. Roman Catholic. Clubs: Wildewood Country, Hunting Creek Swim and Racquet (pres. 1976-77). Home: 108 Steeplechase N Columbia SC 29209 Office: First National Bank of South Carolina 1628 Browning Rd Columbia SC 29210

ASHBRIDGE, G. HARRY, engring. exec.; b. Chincoteague, Va., Dec. 22, 1929; s. G. Harry and Laura (Thornton) A.; student Lehigh U., 1948-49; B.S. in Elec. Engring., Ill. Inst. Tech., 1953; m. Donna D. Thornburg, Mar. 14, 1975; children—Stephen Dale, Susan Lynn, Brian Lee, J. Casey Franklin. Devel. engr. Burroughs Corp., Paoli, Pa., 1955-58; product planning mgr. Bryant Computer Products div. Ex-Cel-O Corp., 1958-62; product mgr. tape memories Ampex Computer Products Co., 1962-63, sect. mgr. product planning, 1963-67, mgr. long range planning, 1967-68; mgr. product planning Gen. Electric Co., 1968-69; v.p. mktg. and product planning Telex Computer Products Corp., 1969-72, v.p. business and marketing opportunities, 1972-73; v.p. planning Control Data Peripheral Products Co., Mpls., 1973-74, v.p. new bus. ventures, 1974—; sec. bd. dirs. Peripheral Products Co.; dir. Magnetic Peripherals, Inc., MPI-Portugal, MPI-Germany; founder, dir. United Peripherals Ltd. Audio cons. Hi-Fidelity Systems, Inc., Roslyn, Pa., 1955—. Treas., Christian Lit. Evangelism, Inc. Served with USNR, 1949-53; with AUS, 1953-55. Mem. Research Soc. Am., IEEE, Tulsa C. of C., Nat. Assn. Evangelicals. Club: Triangle. Democrat. Author and lectr. Patentee in field. Home: 8501 W 133 St Apple Valley MN 55124 Office: Control Data 8100 34th Ave South Bloomington MN 55420

ASHBY, JOHN EDMUND, JR., marketing exec.; b. Dallas, Mar. 5, 1936; s. John Edmund and Lillian Eloise (Cox) A.; B.B.A., U. Tex., 1957; m. Martha DeLarios; children—Vicki, Dana, Suzanne, Shelley, Elizabeth. Salesman, IBM, Corpus Christi, Tex., 1959-64, sales mgr., 1964-67; regional mgr. Recognition Equipment Inc., Dallas, 1967-69, v.p., 1969—. Served with USMC, 1957-59. Recipient Sales award Sales and Mktg. Execs. Assn., 1961, IBM, 1964. Mem. Sales and Mktg. Execs. Assn., Beta Theta Pi. Presbyterian. Home: 3429 Cornell Dallas TX 75205 Office: PO Box 22307 Dallas TX 75222

ASHBY, MICHAEL H., farm orgn. exec.; b. Mattoon, Ill., May 20, 1948; s. Harold M. and Willa M. (Rennels) A.; B.A. in Polit. Sci., Western Ill. U., 1970; m. S. Marlene Davis, Nov. 29, 1969; children—Chad M., Jennifer M. Mgmt. trainee Ill. Farm Bur., 1972-73, sec. dist. V, 1978—; gen. mgr. DuPage County Farm Bur., Wheaton, Ill., 1973—; sec.-treas. Northeastern Ill. Consumer Info. Com., 1979—, Food for Thought Com., 1979—. Mem. citizen's adv. council Carol Stream (Ill.) Park Dist., 1979—; mem. 20th anniversary com. Village of Carol Stream, 1979—. Served with U.S. Army, 1970-72; Vietnam. Decorated Bronze Star, Air medal. Mem. Ill. Agrl. Assn., Am. Simmental Assn., Carol Stream Jaycees (charter, dir. 1976, v.p. 1977, treas. 1978-79), VFW. Republican. Clubs: Masons, Shriners, Elks. Editor: DuPage Farmer, 1973—. Office: 245 S Gary Ave Carol Stream IL 60187

ASHCRAFT, STEVEN HENDERSON, retail drug store chain exec.; b. Marshville, N.C., 1916; degree So. Sch. Pharmacy, Atlanta; m. Sarah Bobo, 1939; 1 dau., Julie Ashcraft Merritt. With Atlanta Ice and Coal Co., 1936-46, asst. v.p., 1943-46; with Eckerd Drug Stores, Charlotte, N.C., 1935-36; founder, owner Craft's Drug Stores, 1947, 1947-79; co. merged with Fay's Drug Stores, 1979, pres. So. div., Spartanburg, N.C., 1979—, also dir. parent co.; past pres. So. Chain Stores; founder, past pres. Affiliated Drug Stores; dir. Spartanburg Bank and Trust Co. Mem. Spartanburg City Council, 1964-68, Spartanburg Planning and Devel. Bd., 1974—. Mem. Nat. Assn. Chain Drug Stores (chmn. bd. 1975, hon. life dir. 1979—), Am. Pharm. Assn., Nat. Assn. Retail Druggists, S.C. Pharm. Assn. Episcopalian. Clubs: Shriners, Rotary, Spartanburg Country, Piedmont. Address: Crafts Drug Stores Box 5808 Spartanburg SC 29304

ASHE, OLIVER RICHARD, govt. ofcl.; b. Washington, Nov. 25, 1933; s. Paul Joseph and Mary (Tomardy) A.; B.S., Georgetown U., 1955; M.B.A., Hofstra U., 1971; postgrad. Pace U., 1972—; m. Helen Marie Curtin, Feb. 15, 1958; children—Mary, Pauline, Margaret, Kathleen, Oliver, Cecilia, Caroline. Regional personnel rep. Marriott Corp., N.Y.C., 1965-68; personnel specialist Navy Resale System Office, N.Y.C., 1968-70, head, career mgmt., 1970-74, dep. dir., indsl. relations, 1974-76; dir. civilian personnel programs and spl. asst. to asst. sec. navy, manpower, res. affairs and logistics U.S. Dept. Def., Washington, 1976—. Served to capt. U.S. Army, 1955-65. Recipient Sustained Superior Accomplishment award U.S. Govt., 1976, 78, 79. Author book chpt. in field. Home: 10600 Vale Rd Oakton VA 22124

ASHEN, PHILIP, chemist, chem. co. exec.; b. Bklyn., Nov. 5, 1915; s. Joel and Fannie (Hirt) A.; B.A., Bklyn. Coll., 1936; M.B.A., N.Y. U., 1957, Ph.D., 1968. Chief chemist Alco Mfg. Corp., Bklyn., 1936-48; mgr. chem. div. M.W. Hardy & Co., Inc., N.Y.C., 1948-63, v.p., 1963-77, pres., 1977—. Lectr. internat. trade Grad. Sch. Bus. Adminstrn., N.Y. U., 1954-56; cons. internat. trade in chems., 1957—. Gas reconnaissance officer U.S. Citizens Def. Corps, also lectr. chem. warfare U.S. Citizens Service Corps, 1940-45. Recipient citation U.S. Treasury Dept., 1944, citation N.Y. Com. Nat. War Fund, 1945, citation Civilian Def. Vol. Office, 1945, citation U.S. Treasury Dept. War Finance Com., 1945, award A.R.C., 1945, Founders Day Award N.Y.U., 1969, Roosevelt medal Theodore Roosevelt Assn. Fellow Am. Inst. Chemists (profl. chemist accredited 1964, chmn. profl. accreditation com. 1964—, treas. 1970—), AAAS; mem. Am. Chem. Soc., Chem. and Econs. Group, Soc. Am. Chem. Industry, N.Y. Acad. Scis., Chemistry Alumni Soc. Bklyn. Coll. (pres. 1966—), Bklyn. Coll. Alumni Soc. (dir. 1969—), Chemists Club. Author: A Study of Foreign Chemical Companies Engaged in International Trade, 1957; The American Selling Price Method of Valuation in U.S. Chemical Imports, 1969. Home: 2315 Ave I Brooklyn NY 11210 Office: 111 Broadway New York City NY 10006

ASHFORD, ROBERT HAROLD ASKOUNES, lawyer; b. Chgo., Sept. 10, 1943; s. Theodore A. and Venette (Tomaras) A.; B.A. summa cum laude, U. South Fla., 1965; postgrad. (Woodrow Wilson fellow) Stanford U., 1965-66; J.D. cum laude, Harvard U., 1969. Admitted to Calif. bar, 1970, N.Y. bar, 1980; practiced in San Francisco, 1970—; asso. firm Morrison and Foerster, 1969-70; partner firm Stephens and Ashford, 1970-72; atty. firm Louis O. Kelso, Inc., 1973-75; of counsel firm Kelso, Hunt, Ashford and Ludwig, 1975-77; individual practice law, 1977—; chief operating officer and gen. counsel Kelso & Co., San Francisco, 1975-77; asso. prof. law Syracuse (N.Y.) U. Coll. Law, 1978—, research asso. Maxwell Sch. Citizenship and Public Affairs, 1978—; vis. scholar Boalt Hall Sch. Law, U. Calif., Berkeley, summer 1979, 80; cons. Ozarks Regional Commn., Econ. Devel. Adminstrn., Dept. Commerce, 1976, Nat. Center for Econ. Alternatives, 1978. Mem. Am. Bar Assn., State Bar Calif., D.C. Bar, N.Y. Bar, Bar Assn. San Francisco (del. State Bar Calif. conf. of dels. 1972-77, dir. 1978), Barristers Club San Francisco (pres. 1974), Bankers Club San Francisco., Sigma Pi Sigma, Phi Kappa Phi. Contbr. articles to legal and bus. jours. Office: 111 Sutter St Suite 1800 San Francisco CA 94104

ASHINGTON-PICKETT, MICHAEL DEREK, constrn. co. exec.; b. London, Oct. 11, 1931; came to U.S., 1965, naturalized, 1971; s. Edward Robert and Mary Dorothy (Trewhella) Ashington-Pickett; Civil and Structural Engring. degrees, London U., 1956; m. Sandra Helen Smart, Nov. 20, 1976; children—Mary Hillary, Michael Derek II. Constrn. mgr. various firms in Eng., 1956-63; pres. So. Precast Holdings, London, 1963-65, Ashington-Pickett Constrn. Co., Inc., Orlando, Fla., 1965—, Country Side Properties, Inc., Orlando, 1972—; chmn. Orlando Constrn. and Licensing Bd., 1974; lectr. for Brit. Council, 1963-65. Served as officer Brit. Army, 1950-52; Korea. Recipient Disting. Service award Orange County Bicentennial Commn., 1976. Mem. Home Builders Assn. Am. (past dir.) Home Builders Assn. Mid-Fla. (pres., dir.), Fla. Home Builders Assn. (dir.), Orlando Jaycees, Orlando Area C. of C. (dir.), Sommeller Guild. Mem. Ch. of Eng. Clubs: Kiwanis, Citrus. Home: 2056 Countryside Circle N Orlando FL 32804 Office: PO Box 20252 Orlando FL 32814

ASHLEY, GEORGE LOUIS, banker; b. Portsmouth, Ohio, Dec. 16, 1953; s. George and Ruth Ann (Wetta) A.; B.S. cum laude in Bus. Adminstrn., Xavier U., 1976; M.B.A., Boston Coll., 1978; m. Margaret Counts, Dec. 28, 1974; 1 dau., Sara. Credit analyst Mellon Bank N.A., Pitts., 1978-79, area mgr. credit dept., 1979, systems officer Money Mgmt. div., 1979—. Mem. Assn. M.B.A. Execs. Republican. Roman Catholic. Office: Mellon Bank Room 2110 Mellon Sq Pittsburgh PA 15230

ASHLEY, LEE JAMES, florist; b. Ordway, Colo., July 13, 1925; s. Jeptha J. and Welhelmina (Roemmich) A.; student U. Colo., 1958-59; m. Eleanor Lou Hicks, July 2, 1950; children—Auralie Jeanne, David Lee, Lenita Ann. With Studebaker-Packard Corp., Denver, 1947-56, Brakuman's Foliage & Decorating Co., Denver, 1956-63, Shop-Rite Floral Co., Denver, 1963-68, 70th Avenue Florists Shop, Denver, 1968-70, Country Fair Garden Center, Denver, 1970-74, Granny's Gardens, Denver, 1974-78; owner, mgr. Ashley's Petite Flower Shoppe, Denver, 1978—; instr. Community Coll. of Denver, 1968—, Aurora (Colo.) Tech. Center, 1978—, Denver Bot. Gardens, 1959—; curator Gladiolus Hall of Fame, 1979—; judge Nat. Council State Garden Clubs, 1960—. Deacon, First Bapt. Ch. Denver. Recipient award of honor City and County of Denver Commn. on Community Relations, 1976, cert. of appreciation Aurora Parks and Recreation Dept., 1979. Mem. Florists Transworld Delivery Assn., Soc. Am. Florists, N.Am. Gladiolus Soc., Colo. Federated Garden Clubs, Colo. Gladiolus Soc. (v.p. 1979-80, pres. 19—). Club: Kibitzers Garden (pres. 1979-80). Home: 310 S Glencoe St Denver CO 80222 Office: 1668 Marion St Denver CO 80218

ASHLIMAN, JOSEPH LYLE, JR., leasing co. exec.; b. Pitts., May 29, 1927; s. Joseph Lyle and Katherine L. (Voegler) A.; m. Audrey C. Baguet, July 28, 1948; children—Shirley Anne, Tracey Jo, Joseph Lyle III. Used car sales mgr. Mt. Lebanon Motors, Pitts., 1947-51; asst. to v.p. sales Lease Motor Vehicle Co., Pitts., 1951-60; exec. v.p. Foss Rental Co., Pitts., 1960—; profl. drummer, percussionist, 1948—. Mem. Bethel Park (Pa.) Sch. Bd., 1972-79, pres., 1977-78. Served with USN, 1945-47. Mem. Nat. Assn. Fleet Adminstrs., Am. Legion, VFW. Clubs: Elks, Kiwanis (past pres.) (Bethel Park). Home: 407

Broughton Rd Bethel Park PA 15102 Office: Route 22 E PO Box 31 Murrysville PA 15668

ASHTON, DAVID JOHN, ednl. adminstr.; b. Somerville, Mass., June 29, 1921; s. Albert Carter and E. Edna (Spry) A.; B.S., Tufts Coll., 1942; M.B.A., Boston U., 1950; M.A., Fletcher Sch. Law and Diplomacy, 1952, Ph.D., 1959; m. Grace Christine Higgins, June 21, 1943; children—Leslie Jean Ashton Koles, Jeffrey Carter, John Mark. Instr., asst. prof. Coll. Bus. Adminstrn., Boston U., 1947-59, asso. prof., 1959-61, prof., 1961—, editor Bus. Rev., 1958-59, chmn. Internat. Bus. Curriculum, 1958-64, chmn. dept., 1964-68, 74-79, internat. curriculum coordinator, 1968—, mng. dir. Boston U.-Brussels (Belgium), 1972-74, 77-78; dir. Boston Adminstrv. and Research Corp. Econ. cons. U.S. Naval War Coll., 1963-64; vis. lectr. 1964-65; econ. and fin. cons. U.S. Dept. Commerce, U.S. Dept. Treasury, Fed. Res. Bank Boston, Fund for Adult Edn., Ednl. Testing Service, Internat. Exec. Service Corps, New Eng. Econ. Research Found., New Eng. Regional Commn. Mem. Arlington (Mass.) Bd. Public Edn., 1955-58, chmn. bd., 1957-58; mem. Planning Bd. Arlington, 1955-62; mem. Tufts Alumni Council, 1959—, mem. exec. com., 1959-62; v.p., bd. dirs. Internat. Bus. Center of New Eng.; mem. exec. bd. Fletcher Sch. Alumni Assn., 1958—; mem. Mass. Gov's. Adv. Council on Internat. Trade, 1964. Mem. rep. town meeting, Winchester, Mass., 1964—, vice chmn. com. on town govt. reorgn., 1968-70. Bd. dirs. Found. for Advancement of Edn. in Internat. Bus., 1962—, Beneficient Soc. of New Eng. Conservatory of Music. Served to lt. USNR, 1942-45. Decorated chevalier Ordre Leopold II (Belgium); recipient George L. Plimpton Distinguished Alumni Service award Tilton Sch., 1976. Mem. Am. Econ. Assn., Nat. Planning Assn., Am. Acad. Polit. and Social Sci., Assn. Edn. Internat. Bus. (v.p.), Am. Arbitration Assn., Delta Tau Delta, Beta Gamma Sigma, Alpha Kappa Psi. Author: New England Manufacturers and European Investments, 1963; The International Component in the New England Economy, 1968; (with R.D. Robinson) New England's Exports of Manufactures, 1975; (with B.K. Sternal) Business Services and New England's Export Base, 1978; also numerous articles in field. Mem. editorial bd. Internat. Exec. Home: 22 Myrtle St Winchester MA 01890 Office: 212 Bay State Rd Boston MA 02215

ASHTON, HARRIS JOHN, business exec.; b. Elizabeth, N.J., June 21, 1932; s. Earle S. and Dorothy (Black) A.; B.A., Yale U., 1954; LL.B., Columbia, 1959; m. Angela Murphy, Oct. 20, 1962; children—Kelly Elizabeth, Victoria Catherine. Admitted to N.Y. bar, 1960; asso. atty. Breed, Abbott & Morgan, 1959-62, Lovejoy, Wasson, Lundgren & Huppuch, 1962-64; partner firm Lovejoy, Wasson, Lundgren & Ashton, 1964-75, of counsel, 1975—; pres., chief adminstrv. officer Gen. Host Corp., 1967-69, chmn., chief exec. officer, pres., 1970—; chmn. exec. com. Cudahy Co., 1973—; former dir., mem. exec. com. Armour and Co., Armour-Dial, Inc.; dir. Royal Bank & Trust Co., Franklin Custodian Funds Inc. Bd. dirs. Madison Sq. Boys Club; trustee Greenwich Acad. Served to lt. AUS, 1955-57. Mem. Am., N.Y. State bar assns., Assn. Bar N.Y.C., Assn. Yale Alumni (founding bd., bd. govs.), Delta Kappa Epsilon. Clubs: Yale, Sky, Twenty-Nine (N.Y.C.); Blind Brook; Stanwich Country (Greenwich, Conn.). Home: Clapboard Ridge Rd Greenwich CT 06830 Office: 22 Gate House Rd Stamford CT 06902

ASHWILL, TERRY MAX, trucking co. exec.; b. Long Beach, Calif., Dec. 9, 1944; s. James Harmon and Lois Adessa (Green) A.; B.S., U. Oreg., 1966; M.B.A., Oreg. State U., 1972; m. Louanne Kay Thiel, June 10, 1966; 1 dau., Shelly Christine. Fin. analyst Ford Motor Co., Dearborn, Mich., 1972-74; sr. fin. analyst Ryder System Inc., Miami, Fla., 1974, mgr. profit planning, 1974-75, dir. fin. planning Ryder Truck Rental, 1975-77; dir. corp. strategic planning and devel. Ryder System, 1977-79, v.p. fin. spl. transp. div., 1979—; dir. Hasco, Inc., Ryder Fed. Credit Union. Republican. Presbyterian. Home: 19520 W Oakmont Dr Miami Lakes FL 33015 Office: PO Box 520816 Miami FL 33152

ASHWORTH, DELL SHEPHERD, architect; b. Salt Lake City, July 20, 1923; s. Paul P. and Jane (Ferrin) A.; student Brigham Young U., 1940-42, 46; A.B., U. Calif. at Berkeley, 1949; m. Bette Brailsford, Dec. 21, 1946 (dec. 1977); children—Brent, Mark, Anne, Christopher; m. 2d, Faughn Montague, Dec. 10, 1977. Partner, Ashworth Architects, Provo, Utah, 1958-71; propr. TAG Architects and Engrs., 1971-76, Dell S. Ashworth and Asso., Architect, 1976—; pres. The Ashworth Group, Inc., developers, 1971—; propr. B. Ashworth Shop, Costa Mesa, Calif.; v.p. TAG Ashworth Real Estate and Investments, 1972-77. Active Provo Dist. com. Boy Scouts Am., 1956-60; chmn. Provo City Planning Commn., 1960-66. Served with USNR, 1942-46. Mem. AIA, Provo C. of C. (pres. 1969, dir.), SAR (v.p. Utah State chpt.). Mem. Ch. Jesus Christ of Latter Day Saints (bishop). Club: Kiwanis (past pres.). Works include Provo City Center, Orem City Center, Edgemont Plaza, Provo, Springville High Sch., Geneva Fed. Credit Union, Orem, Utah, Juab County Center, Nephi, Utah, Payson (Utah) City Center, Nephi (Utah) City Center, Prospector Hills Planned Unit Devel., Salt Lake County, Utah, Allens Market, Provo, Valley Guest Nursing Home, Provo, Petty Pavillion, Ferron, Utah. Home: 1965 N 1400 E Provo UT 84601 Office: 36 E 400 N PO Box 479 Provo UT 84601

ASKEW, REUBIN O'DONOVAN, govt. ofcl.; b. Muskogee, Okla., Sept. 11, 1928; s. Leo Goldberg and Alberta Nora (O'Donovan) A.; B.S. (ROTC honor grad.), Fla. State U., 1951; LL.B., U. Fla., 1956; postgrad. U. Denver; LL.D. (hon.), Fla. So. Coll., 1972, U. Notre Dame, 1973, U. Miami, 1975, U. W.Fla., 1978, Barry Coll., 1979; D.P.A. (hon.), Rollins Coll., 1972; L.H.D., Eckerd Coll., 1973, Stetson U., 1973, Bethune-Cookman Coll., 1975, St. Leo Coll., 1975; m. Donna Lou Harper, Aug. 11, 1956; children—Angela Adair, Keven O'Donovan. Admitted to Fla. bar; partner firm Levin, Askew, Warfield, Graff & Magie, 1958-70; gov. of Fla., 1971-79; partner firm Greenberg, Traurig, Askew, Hoffman, Lipoff, Quentel & Wolff, 1979; U.S. trade rep., Washington, 1979—; vis. fellow Harvard U., Asst. county solicitor Escambia County, Fla., 1956-58; mem. Fla. Ho. of Reps., 1958-62, Fla. Senate, 1962-70, pres. pro tem, 1969-70; chmn. Select Commn. on Immigration and Refugee Policy, 1979; chmn. presdl. adv. bd. on ambassadorial appointments, 1977-79; keynote speaker Dem. Nat. Conv., 1972; chmn. edn. commn. of the states; vice chmn., chmn. So. Gov's. Assn., chmn. Nat. Dem. Gov's. Conf., Nat. Gov's. Assn., So. Growth Policies Bd.; trustee Inst. of Art, Dade County; chmn. Dade County Public Safety Dir. Selection Com.; chmn. Mildred and Claude Pepper Library. Served with paratroopers U.S. Army, 1946; served to capt. USAF, 1951-53. Named top freshman mem. Ho. of Reps., Fla.; most valuable senator, Fla. Senate; outstanding govt. ofcl. of yr. S.Fla. Coordinating Council; U. Fla. Law Rev. Alumnus of Yr., recipient Profiles in Courage award John F. Kennedy chpt. B'nai B'rith of Washington; Nat. Wildlife Fedn. Spl. Conservation award; Salvation Army Gen. William Booth award; John F. Kennedy award Nat. Council Jewish Women; Jewish Theol. Sem. Am. Herbert H. Lehman ethics medal; Protector of Environment award Fla. Engring. Soc.; Leonard L. Abess Human Relations award Anti-Defamation League; Theodore Roosevelt award, Internat. Platform Assn.; Hubert Harley award Am. Judicature Soc.; humanitarian award, Fla. Commn. on Human Relations; Collier County Conservancy silver medal; F. Malcolm Cunningham achievement award Fla. chpt. Nat. Bar Assn.; leadership honor award Am. Inst. Planners; medal of honor Fla. Bar Found.; Champion of Higher Ind. Edn. in Fla. award; disting. community service award Brandies U.; elected to Order of Jurisprudence Cumberland Law Sch.; Chubb fellow, Yale U. Mem. Am. Bar Assn., Fla. Bar Assn., Dade County Bar Assn., Am. Assn. Museums, Am. Judicature Soc., Fla. Council of 100, Am. Legion, Delta Tau Delta. Presbyterian. Clubs: Rotary, Scottish Rite, York Rite Shrine, Knights of Red Cross of Constantine. Office: 1800 G St NW #712 Washington DC 20506

ASKEW, STEPHEN EDWARD, refrigeration and air conditioning co. exec.; b. Los Angeles, Jan. 24, 1937; s. Peter and Mary Clare (Morgan) A.; student Calif. State Poly. Coll., 1956; m. Diane Beverly Firlotte, Jan. 26, 1957; children—Mark Kevin, Stephanie Lyn, Kristen Edward. Mech. engr. Lockheed Aircraft Co., Burbank, Calif., 1956; dir. tech. sales Missimers, Inc., Los Angeles, 1956-60; pres. Thermal Products, Inc., Los Angeles, 1960—; partner, Askew Investment Partnership, Los Angeles; pres. Askew Mgmt. Inc., 1977; dir. Thermal Products, Inc., Los Angeles. Pres. Glendale Crescent Campfire Girls, 1969; mgr. Little League Baseball, 1958-70; chmn. area United Way, Glendale, Calif., 1967-68; chmn. fund drive YMCA, Glendale, 1968-70; pack chmn. Verdugo Hills Council Boy Scouts Am., 1965-66. Recipient Presdl. Recognition award Campfire Girls, 1969, Community Leadership award City of Glendale, 1967, Gov's. award Cal. Jr. C. of C., 1967. Mem. Air Conditioning and Refrigeration Wholesalers (dir. 1970, pres. 1975), Refrigeration Service Engrs. Soc. (ednl. chmn. 1965-66), Am. Soc. Heating, Refrigerating and Air Conditioning Engrs., Refrigeration Engrs. and Technicians Assn., San Fernando Valley Power Squadron, Glendale Jr. C. of C. (pres. 1966), Summit Homeowners Assn. Republican. Clubs: Verdugo (Glendale); Lahaina Yacht (Hawaii); Bahia Corinthian Yacht (Newport Beach, Calif.). Home: 1891 Derby Dr Lenton Heights CA 92705 Office: 16924 Marquardt St Cerritos CA 90701

ASKINS, ARTHUR JAMES, bus. services co. exec.; b. Phila., Dec. 2, 1944; s. William and Rita (O'Brien) A.; B.S., LaSalle Coll., 1967; M.Ed., Rider Coll., 1971; m. Nancy E. Paulsen, Apr. 28, 1979. Tchr. high sch., Phila., 1967-69; sr. staff acct. various public acctg. firms, Jenkintown, Pa., 1969-74; staff McGinnis Assos., fin. cons., Pitman, N.J. and Phila., 1967-80; asst. to controller Hankin Enterprises, Willow Grove, Pa., 1975-79; mgr. internal audit Resorts Internat., Inc., Atlantic City, 1979—; part-time acctg. practice. Polit. campaign coordinator various Republican candidates, 1965-79, state del. Young Rep. State Conv., 1965, 67, nat. del., 1966; adv. Jr. Achievement, 1978-79; vol. Community Accts., 1978—. C.P.A. Mem. Nat. Assn. Accts. (chpt. sec. 1978-79), Am. Inst. C.P.A.'s, Am. Acctg. Assn., Pa. Inst. C.P.A.'s, Mcpl. Fin. Officers Assn. Roman Catholic. Club: K.C. Home: 43B Maplewood Dr Mapleshade NJ 08052 Office: PO Box 124 Mapleshade NJ 08052

ASNANI, MOHAN DOULATRAM plastics products co. exec.; b. Khairpur Mirs, India, Feb. 2, 1944; s. Doulatram V. and Lakham D.; came to U.S., 1964, naturalized, 1971; M.S., SUNY, Stony Brook, 1966; M.B.A., Eastern Mich. U., 1975; m. Padma Khatwani, Mar. 27, 1968; children—Ravi, Priya. Project engr. Raven Industries, 1966-69, Bendix Corp., Ann Arbor, Mich., 1969-73; product design engr. Ford Motor Co., Dearborn, Mich., 1973-80; automotive programs mgr. Gen. Electric Co., Southfield, Mich., 1980—. NASA fellow, 1965-66. Mem. Phi Kappa Phi. Office: Gen Electric Co 25900 Telegraph Rd Southfield MI 48034

ASNES, MARVIN ARTHUR, mfg. co. exec.; b. New Brunswick, N.J., May 18, 1928; s. Louis and Esther (Mirsky) A.; B.S., M.I.T., 1949; M.B.A., Harvard U., 1951; m. Norma Ketay, Sept. 27, 1959; children—Anthony Ketay, Andrew Edwin, James Louis. Research asst. Harvard Bus. Sch., 1951-52; asst. to pres. Clay Adams, N.Y.C., 1954-57, v.p., 1957-59, exec. v.p., 1959-64; dir. Becton Dickinson & Co., Rutherford, N.J., 1964—, pres. LSE div., 1965-69, group v.p., 1968-72, exec. v.p. parent co., 1972-74, chief operating officer, 1974-80, pres., chief operating officer, 1980—; dir. Harper and Row, N.Y.C., Gen. Telephone & Electronic, Inc., Gen. Am. Investors Co., N.Y.C. Mem. vis. com. M.I.T. Sloan Sch. Mgmt., 1971-75, M.I.T. Vis. Commn. Sponsored Research, 1975—; bd. dirs. Stanley M. Issaacs Neighborhood Center Inc., N.Y.C., 1968—, N.Y.C. Ballet, 1980—; trustee Mt. Sinai Sch. Medicine, 1978—, Camp Madison-Felicia, N.Y.C., 1964-72; trustee, treas. Bank Street Coll. Edn. Served as 1st lt. USAF, 1952-54. Mem. Hosp. Industries Mfrs. Assn., Sci. Appartus Makers Assn., Instrument Soc. Am., Tau Beta Phi. Club: Harvard (N.Y.C.). Patentee centrifuge, other lab. equipment and supply items. Office: Becton Dickinson & Co Mack Centre Dr Paramus NJ 07652

ASTA, PATRICIA ELLEN, banker; b. Port Chester, N.Y., July 5, 1945; d. David Norbert and Rita Julia (West) A.; B.S. in Psychology magna cum laude (N.Y. State Regents scholar), C.W. Post Coll., 1967; M.S. (scholar), U. Bridgeport, 1969; M.A. in Counseling (scholar), U. So. Calif., 1972; postgrad. bus. mgmt. Pace U., 1973. Dir., Pirmasens (Ger.) Nursery Sch., 1969; ednl. adminstr. U.S. VA, Kaiserslautern, Germany, 1970-73; asso. dir. counseling Pace U., Pleasantville, N.Y., 1973-76; dir. counseling, tng. and edn. Wildcat Service Corp., N.Y.C., 1975-76; asso. dir. N.J. Job Corps, Edison, 1976-78; mktg. account exec. mgmt. devel. program AT&T Long Lines, Parsippany, N.J., 1978-80; asst. v.p. Nat. State Bank, Elizabeth, N.J., 1980—; instr. psychology, bus. and edn. depts. Pace U.; trainer staff devel. ITEL Corp.; internat. bus. cons. New Brunswick Sci. Corp., 1979-80. Cons., group leader YWCA, North Brunswick, N.J., 1977—; mem. town council Port Chester, N.Y., Pres.'s Commn. Employment of Handicapped; speaker bus. mgmt. classes, civic, and ch. groups; mem. Mid-Hudson Affirmative Action Task Force. Recipient cash award Planned Parenthood, 1967; cert. life skills educator, guidance counselor, therapist, vocat. rehab. counselor. Mem. Am. Personnel and Guidance Assn., Am. Psychol. Assn., Nat. Vocat. Guidance Assn., Assn. Measurement in Edn. and Guidance, Nat. Assn. Student Personnel Adminstrs., Am. Soc. Tng. and Devel., Met. Mental Health Assn. (exec. bd. 1975-78), Nat. Assn. Bank Women (ednl. coordinator N.J. chpt.), Public Offender Counselor Assn., Am. Assn. Higher Edn., AAUW, Nat. Assn. Women Deans and Counselors, Am. Assn. Group Workers, Assn. Humanistic Psychologists, Nat. Assn. Bus. and Profl. Women, N.J. Mental Health Assn., Mensa, Mu Alpha Theta, Psi Chi, Sigma Tau Delta, Pi Gamma Mu. Author: Test Your Vocational Aptitude, 1976; How to Score High on the PACE Exam, 1978; contbr. articles to profl. jours. Address: RD 1 Box 90 Hoffman Station Rd Englishtown NJ 07726

ASTROP, WILLIAM BOWEN, investment counseling exec.; b. Charleston, S.C., Sept. 22, 1929; s. Robert Collins and Arretha Robertson (Bowen) A.; B.A., U. Richmond, 1950, M.B.A. (J. Spencer Love fellow), Harvard, 1953; m. Jean Anne Trimmer, Sept. 18, 1963; children—William B., Douglas DuBois. Vice pres. Fla. Capital Corp., Palm Beach, 1960-63, Stone & Webster Securities, N.Y.C., 1963-68, UniCapital Corp., Atlanta, 1968-70; chmn. bd. Atlanta Capital Mgmt. Co., 1970—; gen. partner Pamco Partners; dir. Seamount Holdings, Bermuda, Founders Corp., Palm Beach, Cavalier Capital Corp., Cin. Instr. U. Richmond, evenings 1958-60. Mem. Com. of 100, Emory U., 1971—; pres. High Museum of Art, Atlanta. Bd. dirs. High Museum, Atlanta Arts Alliance; bd. visitors Emory U. Served to lt. comdr. USNR, 1953-56; Res. ret. Chartered fin. analyst. Mem. N.Y., Atlanta socs. security analysts. Clubs: Harvard (Atlanta, Palm Beach); Commerce, Piedmont Driving (Atlanta); Everglades (Palm Beach). Home: 2415 Hanover W Ln NW Atlanta GA 30327 also 139 Sunrise Ave Palm Beach FL 33480 Office: 230 Peachtree St Atlanta GA 30303

ATCHESON, JAMES EDWARD, architect; b. Terrell, Tex., Jan. 26, 1906; s. Frank and Bessie (Barton) A.; B.Arch., Tex. Tech. Coll., 1936; m. Armista Lucille Heggen, June 20, 1936; children—Michael Edward, Daniel Benn, Timothy Jon, Anne Louise. Draftsman, Eickenroht & Cocke, architects, San Antonio, also part-time instr. Tex. Technol. Coll., 1928-34; designer O. R. Walker, architect, Lubbock, Tex., 1935-40; asso. architect engr. C.E., U.S. Army, Albuquerque and Pyote, Tex., 1942-44; partner Walker & Atcheson, architects, Lubbock, 1941-45-46; prin. James Atcheson, architects, Lubbock, 1947-48; partner Atcheson & Atkinson architects, Lubbock, 1949-55, Atcheson & Cartwright & Assos. (and predecessor firms), architects and engrs., Lubbock, 1956—. Mem. AIA (pres. Panhandle chpt. 1945, Lubbock chpt. 1963), Tex. Soc. Architects (v.p. 1960), Constrn. Specifications Inst. (pres. Lubbock chpt. 1966), Phi Delta Theta. Lutheran (pres. 1966-67, elder 1968—). Kiwanian (pres. 1973). Club: Lubbock Country. Prin. works include Lubbock Country Club, 1960, Citizens Nat. Bank, 1963, First Christian Ch., 1964, Telephone Bldg. (merit award for archtl. excellence), 1967, Am. State Bank, 1968, Courthouse, Fed. office Bldg., 1970 (all Lubbock). Home: 3203 26th St Lubbock TX 79410 Office: 4010 Ave R Lubbock TX 79412

ATCHESON, MARION MACK, synthetic fuels cons.; b. Graham, Tex., July 28, 1920; s. Frank and Bess (Barton) A.; B.S. in Chem. Engring., Tex. Tech. Coll., 1942; m. Marianne McLane, Dec. 13, 1946; children—Thomas Gavin (dec.) James Barton (dec.). Engr., research devel. dept. Elliott Co., Jeannette, Pa., 1946-49; process engr. El Paso Natural Gas Co. (Tex.), 1949-53, chief design engr., 1953-55, chief engr., subs. El Paso Products Co., 1956-59, asst. operating mgr. El Paso Products Co., 1959-60, mgr. engring and petrochem. devel., 1961-64, exec. engr., 1964-65, v.p. engring. constrn. El Paso Products Co., Odessa, Tex., 1965-72, dir. El Paso Products Co., 1966-72, dir. engring. constrn. Synfuels Div., 1972-74, v.p., affiliate Fuel Conversion Co., 1972-76, asst. v.p. El Paso Natural Gas Co., 1974-80, exec. v.p. affiliates El Paso Coal Co., Fuel Conversion Co., Mesa Resource Co., 1976-80; pres. Atcheson & Assos., Inc., El Paso, 1980—. Served with C.E., U.S. Army, 1942-46. Named Distinguished Engr., Tex. Tech. U., 1975. Mem. Am. Inst. Chem. Engrs., Tau Beta Pi. Home: PO Box 13036 El Paso TX 79912 Office: 220 Thunderbird Dr El Paso TX 79912

ATHA, GEORGE CRAWFORD, petroleum geologist; b. Fairmont, W.Va., Nov. 25, 1902; s. William Hunter and Jessie Julia (Dougan) A.; student in geology Ohio State U., 1922, Muskingum Coll., 1927; m. Gladys R. Wray, Apr. 7, 1948. Civil engr., Sebring, Fla., 1927; salesman, mgr. real estate, Lorain, Ohio, 1927-28; staff Midwest Re '28 Co., Roswell, N.Mex., 1928-29; staff City of Palo Verde Estates (Calif.), 1929-30; pres. Hiawatha Exploration Co., San Marino, Calif., 1947—; pvt. practice petroleum geologist San Marino, 1947—. Mem. Internat. Oil Scouts. Club: Long Beach Petroleum, Elks (life), Los Angeles Athletic. Inventor geophys. equipment. Address: 2221 California Blvd San Marino CA 91108

ATHERTON, HOLT, machinery co. exec.; b. Stockton, Calif., Sept. 8, 1920; s. Warren Hendry and Ann (Holt) A.; B.A., U. Calif., Berkeley, 1941; m. Flora Cameron Kampmann, Sept. 28, 1970; children—Holt, Steve, Geary, Megan. Check pilot Pan Am. World Airways, San Francisco, 1946-52; with Holt Machinery Co., San Antonio, 1952—, pres., 1963-79; chmn. bd. Atherton Industries, 1979—, Holt Machinery Co., 1980—; dir. Frost Nat. Bank, San Antonio, Cullen-Frost, Bankers; Pres., San Antonio Safety Council, 1958; vice chmn. bd. dirs. San Antonio Econ. Devel. Found., 1975—; co-chmn. San Antonio Air Force Community Council, 1978, 79; bd. regents U. of Pacific, Stockton, 1980—; trustee Southwest Research Inst., San Antonio, 1960-66, bd. dirs., 1975—; bd. dirs. Met. Gen. Hosp., 1974—, Tex. Assn. Taxpayers, 1981—. Served as brig. gen. USAAF, 1941-46, res., 1946-64. Mem. San Antonio C. of C. (dir. 1961-67, chmn. bd. 1977), Daedalians. Clubs: Bohemian, Pacific Union (San Francisco); Outrigger Canoe, Waialae Country, Waikiki Yacht (Honolulu). Office: PO Box 658 San Antonio TX 78293

ATHERTON, NEIL PIERCE, automotive parts co. exec.; b. Toledo, Jan. 21, 1924; s. Noel Benjamin and Zena Lucy (Pierce) A.; B.S. in Civil Engring., Case Inst. Tech., 1948; m. Jean Ellen Conger, Jan. 31, 1948; children—Paula, Andrea. With Champion Spark Plug Co., Detroit, 1949—, v.p. ceramic div., 1975—. Served with USNR, 1942-46. Mem. ASME, Engring. Soc. Detroit, Phi Delta Theta. Republican. Methodist. Club: Torch (Detroit). Home: 32801 Outland Trail Birmingham MI 48010 Office: Champion Spark Plug Co 20000 Conner Ave Detroit MI 48234

ATHEY, RICHARD EDWARD, mfg. co. exec.; b. Wheeling, W.Va., Jan. 12, 1935; s. Clayton Arthur and Iva Murdhe (Webber) A.; B.S. in Mktg., Marshall U., 1957; m. Jacqueline R. Roush, Oct. 23, 1954; children—Richard Douglas, Donald Clayton, Daniel Lee. Sales mgr. Phillips Petroleum Co., Cin., 1963-72; nat. OEM sales mgr. FrigiKing div. Cummins Engine Co., Dallas, 1972-76; v.p. mktg. John E. Mitchell Co., Dallas, 1978-80; v.p. Energy Resources Corp., Dallas, 1980—. Chmn. Mfrs. Council, 1979-80. Mem. Internat. Mobil Air Conditioning Assn. (pres. 1980—, award 1980). Republican. Lutheran. Club: 2001 (Dallas). Home: 1329 Glen Cove Richardson TX 75080 Office: 3800 Commerce St Dallas TX 75226

ATHOS, ETHEL PAPAGEORGE, real estate agt.; b. Ipswich, Mass., Dec. 20, 1926; d. Charles Peter and Anne (Speris) Papageorge; B.S., Burdett Coll., 1942; student mgmt. George Washington U., 1967-68; student real estate Towson State Coll., 1977-78, Grad. Realtors Inst., 1977-78; m. James T. Athos, June 17, 1951 (dec.); children—Anne, Janet. Budget officer Bur. Intelligence and Research, Dept. State, Washington, 1955-74, ret., 1974; real estate sales rep. Town & Country Properties of Md., North Bethesda, 1974—; sec. Women's Council Realtors, 1978-80. Sec., Pilot Internat., Washington, 1965-66, v.p., 1967-68, pres., 1968-69; pres. Philoptohos Soc., Greek Orthodox Ch. of St. George, Bethesda, Md., 1968-70. Recipient Outstanding Service award Dept. of State, 1970, Meritorious Service award, 1973; Town & Country Pres's. Club award, 1977. Mem. Grad. Realtors Inst., Montgomery County (Md.) (Outstanding Sales award 1977, 79), Washington (Outstanding Sales award 1979) bds. realtors, Women's Council Realtors (sec.), Nat. Assn. Ret. Fed. Employees (treas. 1980), Salvation Army Aux., Seton Guild. Club: Potomac Bus. and Profl. Women's. Home: 9811 Belhaven Rd Bethesda MD 20034 Office: 6935 Wisconsin Ave Chevy Chase MD 20015

ATKINS, BURRELL DWAIN, ins. broker; b. Dallas, Nov. 20, 1939; s. Albert T. and Lela E. (Powers) A.; student Sch. Ins. Mktg., La. State U., 1973, U. Tex., 1960-61; m. Diane Rae, June 9, 1961; children—Kyle, Angela, Janis, Julie, Seth. Salesman, So. Provident Life Ins. Co., Dallas, 1964, Am. Gen. Life, Dallas, 1967-74, Union Mut., Dallas, 1974-77; free-lance ins. broker, Dallas, 1977—. Deacon, First Baptist Ch., Dallas. Named to Ins. Salesmen's Star Honor Roll, 1965, 70, 71, 72; recipient Salesmanship Oscar, Am. Salesmaster, 1978-80; Karate Black Belt; Univ. track scholar, 1960-61. Mem. Nat. Assn. Life Underwriters, Advanced Assn. Life Underwriters, Million Dollar Round Table, Top of the Table (Nat. Sales Achievement award

1969-80), Tex. Assn. Life Underwriters. Clubs: Safari, Karate. Office: 2001 Bryan Tower Suite 1060 Dallas TX 75201

ATKINS, ORIN ELLSWORTH, oil co. exec.; b. Pitts., June 6, 1924; s. Orin E. and Dorothy (Whittaker) A.; student Marshall Coll., 1942-43, 46-47, LL.D., 1970; student U. Pa., 1943-44; LL.B., U. Va., 1950; m. Kathryn Agee, Nov. 25, 1950; children—Randall, Charles. Admitted to W.Va. bar, 1950, Ky. bar, 1952; with Ashland Oil & Refining Co. (Ky.) (now Ashland Oil, Inc.), 1950—, exec. asst., 1956-59, adminstrv. v.p., 1959-65, pres., 1965-69, pres., chief exec. officer, 1969-70, chmn. bd., chief exec. officer, 1972—, also dir.; dir. Cin. br. Fed. Res. Bank of Cleve., 1968-71. Chmn. bd. advisers Marshall U., Huntington, W.Va.; mem. nat. council Salk Inst. Served with AUS, 1942-46. Mem. Am., W.Va., Ky. bar assns., Am. Petroleum Inst., Conf. Bd. Presbyterian. Club: Wall St. Office: 1409 Winchester Ave Ashland KY 41101

ATKINS, THOMAS JAY, lawyer; b. Detroit, Apr. 21, 1942; s. Robert Albert and Dorothy Irene A.; B.S. Engring., Wayne State U., 1965; M.S. in Mgmt., Rensselaer Poly. Inst., 1967; J.D., San Joaquin Coll. Law, 1978; m. Shirley Roberta Green, Dec. 21, 1968. Cons., Center for Advanced Studies, Gen. Electric Co., Santa Barbara, Calif., 1967-70; pres., chmn. bd. Central Valley Distbrs., Visalia, Calif., 1970-79; admitted to Calif. bar, 1979; individual practice law, Visalia and Santa Barbara, 1979—; bus. cons. Fund raiser local candidates for polit. office, bldg. fund St. John's Episcopal Ch., Royal Oak, Mich. Recipient Research Commendation, NASA, 1969. Mem. Am. Mgmt. Assn., Engring. Soc. Detroit. Republican. Clubs: Santa Barbara Yacht, Visalia Country. Office: PO Box 3744 Visalia CA 93277

ATKINS, VICTOR KENNICOTT, mfg. exec.; b. Denver, Apr. 23, 1921; s. James George and Jessie (Kennicott) A.; B.S., U.S. Naval Acad., 1942; M.S., Mass. Inst. Tech., 1947; m. Elizabeth Tanner, Mar. 17, 1944; children—Victor Kennicott, Abigail, William T. Engring. and mfg. exec. Pacific Car & Foundry Co., Renton, Wash., 1947-51; pres., dir. Doran Co., 1951—; dir. CSAA Inter-Ins. Bur., Ameron, Inc., Worldwide Spl. Fund, N.V. Trustee, Calif. Inst. Tech.; vice-chmn. bd. fellows Claremont (Calif.) Univ. Center. Served with Submarine Service, USN, 1942-45; PTO. Decorated Silver Star. Mem. Calif., Oakland chambers commerce, Soc. Naval Architects and Marine Engrs., Marine Exchange San Francisco, Calif. Automobile Assn. (dir.), Sigma Xi. Clubs: Rotary (Oakland); San Francisco Golf; Propeller of U.S., Bohemian, Pacific Union. Home: 2815 Vallejo St San Francisco CA 94123 Office: 1899 7th St Oakland CA 94607

ATKINSON, HAROLD WITHERSPOON, utilities cons.; b. Lake City, S.C., June 12, 1914; s. Leland G. and Kathleen (Dunlap) A.; B.S. in Elec. Engring., Duke, 1934; M.S. in Engring., Harvard, 1935; m. Pickett Rancke, Oct. 6, 1946; children—Henry Leland, Harold Witherspoon. Various positions in sales, engring. Cambridge Electric Light Co. (Mass.), 1935-39, 46-73, asst. mgr. power sales dept., 1946-49, gen. mgr., 1957-73, dir., 1959—, exec. v.p., 1972-73; mgr. Pee Dee Electric Membership Corp., Wadesboro, N.C., 1939-46; gen. mgr. Cambridge Steam Corp., 1951-73, v.p., 1959-73, dir. 1955—. Chmn., Cambridge Traffic Bd., 1962-73; pres. Cambridge Center Adult Edn., 1962-64; v.p. Cambridge Mental Health Assn.; chmn. allocations com. Greater Boston United Community Services, 1971-72; chmn. Cambridge Commn. Services, 1955-56; adv. bd. Cambridge Council Boy Scouts Am. Mem. corp., chmn. camping com. Cambridge YMCA, 1964-71; chmn. Cambridge chpt. ARC, 1969-71; trustee of trust funds Town of Harrisville, N.H. Served from pvt. to capt. AUS, 1942-45. Registered profl. engr., Mass. Mem. I.E.E.E. (sr.), Mass. Soc. Profl. Engrs., Elec. Inst. (pres. 1971), Harvard Engring. Soc., Cambridge C. of C. (pres. 1957-58). Newcomen Soc. N.Am., Phi Beta Kappa, Tau Beta Pi, Pi Mu Epsilon. Clubs: Cambridge Boat (treas. 1962-65), Cambridge (pres. 1972-73); Union of Boston; Civitan (pres. Wadesboro 1940-41); Keene Country, Rotary (Keene, N.H.). Home: PO Box 125 Harrisville NH 03450 Office: PO Box 535 Marlborough NH 03455

ATKINSON, ROBERT WILMER, trade assn. exec.; b. Norristown, Pa., Sept. 26, 1928; s. Paul Gregory and Pauline Mary (Beckman) A.; B.S., Rutgers U., 1950; M.B.A., Case Western Reserve U., 1959; m. Willea Lenora Cason, Sept. 18, 1955; children—Wendy Sue, Robert Alan, William Andrew, Richard Lee. Sales trainee Continental Can Co., Inc., Phila. and Balt., 1950-52, sales rep., Cleve., 1954-55; market analyst Brush Electronics Co., Cleve., 1956-58; mem. staff Forging Industry Assn., Cleve., 1958—, exec. sec., treas., 1964, exec. v.p., 1968—. Scoutmaster Greater Cleve. council Boy Scouts Am., 1965-74. Served with USAF, 1952-54; Korea. Recipient Order of Merit award Newton D. Baker dist. Boy Scouts Am., 1972. Mem. Inst. Orgn. Mgmt. (chmn. trustees 1975), Am. Soc. Assn. Execs. (chartered assn. exec., Key award 1979). Presbyterian. Office: 55 Public Square Cleveland OH 44113

ATKINSON, RUSSELL WELSH, diversified mfg. co. exec.; b. Somerville, N.J., Sept. 22, 1947; s. Russell Edward and Betty Ramsey (Welsh) A.; B.A., Baldwin-Wallace Coll., 1969; m. Elizabeth Camerden Austin, Oct. 3, 1970; children—Geoffrey Martin, Jamie Lynn. Mgr. sales promotion Affiliated Mfrs. Inc., Whitehouse, N.J., 1969-71, product mgr., 1971-73, sales mgr., North Branch, N.J., 1973-76, v.p. mktg., 1976—; v.p., dir. Serigraphico Inc., Wichita Falls, Tex., 1974—, AMI West, Inc., Sun Valley, Calif., 1975—, MTI Systems Corp., Juyland, Pa. Mem. Internat. Soc. Hybrid Micro-Electronics (vice-chmn. chpt. 1972-73). Patentee in field. Home: Box 188 Barley Sheaf Rd Flemington NJ 08822 Office: Affiliated Mfrs Inc Box 5049 North Branch NJ 08855

ATOR, GEORGE JACOB, research co. exec.; b. Hazleton, Pa., Sept. 10, 1935; s. John Daniel and Adelaide (Skoff) A.; B.S., Pa. State U., 1958; postgrad. Duquesne U., 1961—; m. Mary Ann Welkie, June 27, 1959; children—Brian, Mark. Tech. fieldman Equitable Gas Co., Pitts., 1958-60; glass sales forecaster Pitts. Plate Glass Industries, 1960-64; research asso., sales officer Western Pa. Nat. Bank, Pitts., 1964-68; v.p., dir. Feldman & Kahn, Inc., Pitts., 1968-75; pres. Group One Research, Inc., 1976—, Econ. & Market Research Co., 1976—; lectr. Grad. Sch. Savs. Banking, Brown U., 1970, 73; instr. marketing mgmt. U. Mo./SIMSA Mktg. Mgmt. Inst., U. Mo./Credit Union Execs. Soc. Mktg. Inst.; speaker various fin. instn. trade assns. including Conn., N.Y. savs. bank assns., U.S. Savs. & Loan League, Hawaii Credit Union League, others. Ann. mem. United Fund Allegheny County. Chmn. Young Republicans of Baldwin-Whitehall, Pitts., 1961. Bd. dirs. Central Blood Bank of Pitts. Served with USNR, 1952-60. Mem. Savs. Instns. Mktg. Soc., Am. Mktg. Assn. (past dir. Pitts. chpt.), Pitts. Econ. Club, Pitts. Jr. C. of C., Alpha Kappa Psi. Contbr. articles profl. jours.; author credit union facilities planning book. Home: 3218 Longwood Dr Pittsburgh PA 15227 Office: Granite Bldg 6th and Wood Sts Pittsburgh PA 15222

ATTEBERRY, WILLIAM LOUIS, mortgage co. exec.; b. Houston, Aug. 5, 1939; s. William Louis and Una Louise (Varney) A.; B.S., U. Md., 1962; J.D., U. Balt., 1965; m. Judith Lou Reiman, Jan. 30, 1965; children—Alexander, Julie, Hunter. Realty specialist GSA, Washington, 1962-66; admitted to Md. bar, 1966; sec., gen. counsel Carl M. Freeman Assos., Inc., builder-developer, Silver Spring, Md., 1966-68; with Kissell Co., mortgage banking, Springfield, Ohio, 1968-74, sr. v.p., 1972-74; pres., chief exec. officer Mortgage Investment Securities, Inc., Clearwater, Fla., 1974—, also dir.; pres. James T. Barnes Mortgage Co., Clearwater and James T. Barnes of D.C., Inc., 1977-80; pres., dir. Lincoln Fin. Corp., Clearwater, 1980—; instr. St. Petersburg (Fla.) Jr. Coll. Trustee Young Republicans Clark County, Ohio, 1970-73; mem. Clark County Rep. Finance Com., 1971-73; treas. Non Partisan Candidates for Charter, Washington, 1964. Mem. Mortgage Bankers Assn., Md. Bar Assn. Christian Scientist. Author: Modern Real Estate Finance, rev. edit., 1980; co-author: Real Estate Law, 1974, 2d edit., 1978. Home: 421 Belle Isle St Belleair Beach FL 33535 Office: 1090 Bank of Clearwater Bldg Clearwater FL

ATTEBURY, WILLIAM HUGH, elevator co. exec.; b. Amarillo, Tex., Jan. 8, 1929; s. Arnold Gentry and Lula Vivian (Dunn) A.; student Iowa State Coll., 1947-49; B.A., Okla. U., 1951; m. Joyce B. Kallin, June 7, 1951; children—Julie Anne, William Arnold, Nancy Ellen, Elizabeth Grace, Edward Anton. Vice pres. Attebury Elevators, Inc., Amarillo, 1954—; pres. Bison Devel. Co., 1960—, A & S Steel Bldgs Inc., Amarillo, 1961—, El Poso Oil Co., Amarillo, 1969—, Bison Chem. Co., Port Neches, Tex., 1969—; dir. 1st Nat. Bank Amarillo, Master Films Co. Mem. Amarillo Bd. City Devel., 1969-73; bd. dirs. Village of Hope, 1972-74; elder Westminster Presbyterian Ch., 1970—. Served with USNR, 1951-54; Korea. Mem. Panhandle Producers and Royalty Owners, Southwest Systems Builders Assn., Metal Bldg. Dealers Assn., Panhandle Grain Dealers Assn. Clubs: Amarillo, Amarillo Country. Home: 3202 Lipscomb St Amarillo TX 79109 Office: POB 7446 Amarillo TX 79109

ATWATER, HORACE BREWSTER, JR., food co. exec.; b. Mpls., Apr. 19, 1931; s. Horace Brewster and Eleanor (Cook) A.; A.B., Princeton, 1952; M.B.A., Stanford, 1954; m. Martha Joan Clark, May 8, 1955; children—Elizabeth C., Mary M., John C., Joan P. Divisional v.p., dir. mktg. Gen. Mills, Inc., 1958-65, mktg. v.p., 1965-70, exec. v.p., 1970-76, chief operating officer, 1976—, pres., 1977—, also dir.; dir. Northwestern Nat. Life Ins. Co., N.W. Bancorp. Trustee, MacAlester Coll., Walker Art Center. Served to lt. (j.g.) USNR, 1955-58. Club: Woodhill Country (Wayzata, Minn.). Office: 9200 Wayzata Blvd Minneapolis MN 55426*

ATWOOD, HOWARD WRIGHT, savs. and loan exec., bldg. contractor; b. Tallmadge, Ohio, Feb. 14, 1923; s. Earnest Sackett and Geneva Gertrude (Wright) A.; B.A. cum laude in Bus. Adminstrn., Kent State U., 1948; m. Isabelle Therese Parseghian, Dec. 27, 1953; children—Loraine, Michelle, Diane. Owner, operator Atwood Constrn. Co., Tallmadge, 1948—, Atwood Devel. Co., Tallmadge, 1960—; chmn. Falls Savs. & Loan Assn., Cuyahoga Falls, Ohio, 1973—, dir., 1963—. Trustee Akron Regional Devel. Bd., 1978-83. Served with USAAF, 1943-47. Mem. Nat. Assn. Home Builders (life dir.), Soc. Real Estate Appraisers (asso.), Tallmadge C. of C. Republican. Home: 255 Ernest Dr Tallmadge OH 44278 Office: Falls Savs and Loan Assn 2335 2d St Cuyahoga Falls OH 44222

ATZBERGER, FRANK JOHN, indsl. mfg. co. exec.; b. Cleve., Nov. 10, 1937; s. Frank Aloysious and Helen Catherine (Boufford) A.; B.S., U. Detroit, 1959; m. Maureen Frances McCarthy, Nov. 30, 1963; children—John, Mark, Craig, Kristin Elizabeth. Accountant, Pickands Mather & Co., Cleve., 1959-62; corporate planner Hanna Mining Co., Cleve., 1962-69; acquisitions cons. Peat Marwick Mitchell & Co., Cleve., 1969-70; controller Am. Koyo Corp., Cleve., 1972-73, treas., 1974, mgr. mktg., 1975—; pres. Corplan, Inc., 1976—, also dir.; controller Selected Meat Co., Ohio Eastern Express, Inc., The Waldock Co. Mem. Cuyahoga County Republican Finance Com., 1962-70. Mem. U. Detroit Alumni Assn., Blue Key, Delta Sigma Pi. Rotarian. Clubs: Lakewood Country; Exec. West (Rocky River, Ohio). Home: 4583 Angela Dr Fairview Park OH 44126

ATZESBERGER, JOHN JOSEF, acct.; b. Vienna, Austria, Dec. 12, 1929; came to Can., 1951, naturalized, 1964; s. Johan Nepomuk and Maria Theresa (Tomicek) A.; student Vienna Bus. Coll., 1950; degree in Econ. Sci., U. Alta., 1968; m. Ursula Edith Pfeiffer, Feb. 20, 1961; children—Giselle, Peter, Charles, Jason J. P. Acct., mgr. Argyll Auto Rep. Ltd., Edmonton, Alta., Can., 1965-70; controller, partner Gilwood Oilfield Services, Ltd., Edmonton, 1970-76; controller Skytop Rig Co., Houston and Edmonton, 1976-79; pres., gen. mgr. Edmonton Machine Tool (Can.) Ltd., 1979—, Vindobona Mgmt. and Cons. Co., Ltd., Edmonton, 1979—; cons. in field. Treas., Pleasantview Community League, Edmonton, 1975—. Mem. Progressive Conservative Assn. Can. Roman Catholic. Club: Derrick Golf and Winter. Home: 10915 54th Ave Edmonton AB T6H 0V2 Canada Office: 6571 103rd St Edmonton AB T6H2J1 Canada

AUERBACH, HERSCHEL, cemetery owner; b. N.Y.C., June 3, 1918; s. Ephraim and Anna (Nissenson) A.; B.A., N.Y. U., 1940; m. Ruth Vodnoy, Nov. 1, 1941; children—Mark, Leonard. Meml. counselor Sharon Meml. Park (Mass.), 1955-56; exec. v.p. Shalom Meml. Park, Palatine, Ill., 1956-79, pres., 1979—; pres. Sunset Meml. Gardens, Sunset Investment Corp., Rockford, Ill., 1976—; chmn. Cemetery Care Adv. Bd. State Ill., 1965-69. Pres., Zionist Orgn. Chgo., 1969-71; v.p. Zionist Orgn. Am., 1969—; chmn. Capital for Israel, State Israel Bonds, 1979—. Served to maj. U.S. Army, 1941-46. Named Man of Year, Zionist Orgn. Chgo., 1967; recipient State of Ill. Public Service award, 1968. Mem. Nat. Assn. Cemeteries (public service award 1977, pres. 1979-80), Ill. Cemetery Assn. (pres. 1963-64), Am. Israel C. of C. for Midwest (v.p. 1961-71). Republican. Jewish. Club: Meadows (Rolling Meadows, Ill.). Home: 600 W Rand Rd Arlington Heights IL 60004 Office: PO Box 549 Palatine IL 60067

AUGEN, BERNARD LEON, accountant; b. N.Y.C., Sept. 30, 1927; s. Benjamin and Frieda (Olinger) A.; B.S. in Accounting, 1949; m. Joan Wildfire, Mar. 23, 1952; children—Jeffrey, Michael. With Joseph Getz & Co., Simonoff, Peyser & Citrin, (merged with Clarence Rainess & Co. 1973), N.Y.C., 1957—, partner, 1968-78; partner Richard A. Eisner & Co., N.Y.C., 1978—. Served with AUS, 1946-47; PTO. Mem. N.Y. Soc. C.P.A.'s, Am. Inst. C.P.A.'s (chmn. bankruptcy insolvency com.). Contbr. articles, lectr. various profl. groups on accountancy on bankruptcy and insolvency matters. Office: Richard A Eisner & Co 380 Madison Ave New York NY 10017

AUGUSTINE, JEROME SAMUEL, investment adviser; b. Racine, Wis., May 7, 1928; s. Lester Samuel and Pearl (Hilker) A.; A.B. cum laude, Harvard, 1950, M.B.A., 1952; m. Camilla Sewell, Feb. 7, 1953; children—Theodore Samuel Purnell, Julia Sewell Augustine Marshall, Elizabeth Stroebel. Cons., Scudder, Stevens & Clark, Boston, 1952-56; founder, treas., dir. Vencap, Inc., Boston, 1956-58; treas., dir. Consumer Products, Inc., Boston, 1956-58; founder, treas., dir. Microsonics, Inc., Hingham, Mass., 1956-58; treas., dir. Capitol Mgmt. Corp., Boston, 1956-58; cons. Kidder, Peabody, & Co., Boston, 1958-64; pres. Cosmos Am. Corp., N.Y.C., 1964-67; founder, pres., dir. Cosmos (Bahamian) Ltd., Nassau, 1964-70, Cosmos Securities Corp., N.Y.C., 1965-70; pres. Augustine Fin. Co., 1970—; 1st v.p. Van Alstyne, Noel & Co., 1973-75; v.p. Wright Investors' Service, Bridgeport, Conn., 1974—. Mem. Boston Fin. Research Assos. (gov. 1960-64, v.p. 1963-64), New Eng. Amateur Rowing Assn. (past pres.). Episcopalian. Clubs: Union Boat (Boston); Harvard (N.Y.C.); Noroton (Conn.) Yacht; Ox Ridge Hunt (Darien). Home: 155 Long Neck Point Rd Darien CT 06820 Office: Park City Plaza Bridgeport CT 06604

AUSNIT, TONI HALPERN, fin. cons.; b. N.Y.C., July 23, 1941; d. Ray O. and Helen S. (Morris) Halpern; B.A., Wellesley Coll., 1963; M.B.A., Columbia U., 1980; m. Peter C. Ausnit, Nov. 7, 1963; children—Peter Charles, Christopher Michael. Exec. v.p. 525 Park Ave. Corp., N.Y.C., 1968—; co-founder, partner Ausnit/La Rouche, N.Y.C., 1976-78; real estate asso. Citibank, N.Y.C., 1979; dir. UDAG Program of N.Y.C., Econ. Capital Corp. of N.Y.C., 1980—. Bd. dirs. Friends Council, Whitney Mus. Am. Art, 1976-79; mem. women's bd. N.Y. div. Am. Cancer Soc., 1968-81. Clubs: Town Tennis, Wellesley (N.Y.C.); New Milford (Conn.) Racquet and Swim. Office: Econ Capital Corp of NYC 12th Floor 17 John St New York NY 10038

AUSTIN, CHARLES ROGERS, actuarial cons.; b. Somerville, Mass., Nov. 1, 1945; s. Arthur H. and Marjorie M. (Rogers) A.; B.A., Northeastern U., 1968, M.B.A., 1974; m. Heidi Ann Bookmiller, May 11, 1974. Mgr. quality control Coca-Cola Bottling Co., Lynn, Mass., 1966-67; mathematician's asst. Avco/MSD, Wilmington, Mass., 1967-68; actuarial cons. Wyatt Co. (formerly Warner-Watson Inc.), Wellesley, Mass., 1968—. Served with U.S. Army, 1968-70. Decorated Bronze Star. Mem. Am. Acad. Actuaries (enrolled actuary). Republican. Clubs: Masons (master 1980-81), De Molay (dist. dep. Mass. 1977-80). Home: 34 Spring St Stoneham MA 02180 Office: 65 William St Wellesley MA 02181

AUSTIN, LARRY, travel agy. exec.; b. Bklyn., Dec. 17, 1930; s. Sol and Ada (Spinner) A.; B.B.A., CCNY, 1957; m. Eileen Altzman, Mar. 14, 1954; children—Jeffrey, Jamie, Stewart. Pres., Austin Travel Corp., Hicksville, N.Y., 1955—, Escapades Enterprises, Inc., 1969—, A/C Advt. Assos., 1964—, L.I. Travel Commn., 1978—, L.I. Tourism Commn., 1978—. Chmn., L.I. Better Bus. Bur., 1976-78; trustee N.Y. Better Bus. Bur., 1976—, Nassau YMHA; v.p. L.I. Assn., 1975—; chmn. industry div. United Jewish Appeal, L.I., 1978-80. Served with USNR, 1947-54. Mem. Assn. Retail Travel Agts. (dir.), Hickory Group (pres. 1977-80), L.I. Travel Agts. Assn. (pres. 1973-76, chmn. 1976-77). Club: Cold Spring. Author: Memoirs of a Travel Agent, 1969. Office: 560 S Broadway Hicksville NY 11801

AUSTIN, LESLIE JAMES, constn. co. exec.; b. Worthington, Minn., Feb. 4, 1941; s. Leo Leslie and Rose Marie Austin; B.Arch. with high honors, U. Kans., 1970, M.A. in Planning, 1970; M.B.A., Harvard U., 1972; m. Lynda Sue Hammons, Feb. 6, 1965; children—Lyndsey, Leslie. Vice pres. Sea Pines Co., Hilton Head Island, S.C., 1972-74, Kimberly Scott Co., Wilmington, N.C., 1974-75; v.p., div. mgr. Ryan Homes, Inc., Columbus, Ohio, 1975-77; pres. Austin Constrn. & Devel. Co., Inc., Hilton Head Island, 1977—. Mem. Am. Inst. Planners, Urban Land Inst., Asso. Gen. Contractors, Nat. Assn. Home Builders, Hilton Head Island Home Builders Assn. (pres.). Baptist. Club: Rotary (Hilton Head Island). Home: 6 Isle of Pines Rd Hilton Head Island SC 29928 Office: 14 Pope Ave Hilton Head Island SC 29928

AUSTIN, MICHAEL HERSCHEL, lawyer; b. nr. Water Valley, Miss., Nov. 7, 1896; s. Michael Green and Willie C. (Roberson) A.; student U. Miss., 1915-18, LL.B., 1922; postgrad. Akron U., 1919; J.D., Ohio State U., 1923; m. Esther Catherine Seebach, Nov. 26, 1920 (dec.); m. 2d, Inez Harpst. Tchr. pub. elementary sch., Miss., 1914-15; admitted to Miss. bar, 1922, Ohio bar, 1924, since practiced in Columbus, Ohio; partner firm Pfeiffer and Austin, 1927-30; atty. FHA for Franklin County (Ohio), 1963-70; atty. VA Franklin County, 1965-68. Mem. chmn.'s council Franklin Democratic Com. Served with U.S. Army, World War I. Recipient Cross of Honor, U.D.C., 1944, Wisdom award of honor, 1970. Fellow Truman Library Assn.; mem. Am., Ohio, Columbus bar assns., Am. Judicature Soc., Columbus Real Estate Bd. (asso.), Ohio State U. Alumni Assn. (Golden certificate), Columbus Area C. of C., Am. Legion (post comdr. 1944-45, county comdr. 1953-54, dist. comdr. 1955-56, state treas. 1958-59, pres. Big Four Vets. Council 1956-57, pres. Past Comdrs. Club 1960-61, Dist. Outstanding Legionnaire of Year, Outstanding Services award 1969, judge adv. 12th dist. 1968—), Internat. Platform Assn., Exec. and Profl. Hall of Fame, Phi Alpha Delta. Mason. Clubs: Franklin County Democratic, Columbus Lawyers (past sec.). Home: 47 Richards Rd Columbus OH 43214 Office: 85 E Gay St Columbus OH 43215

AUSTIN, T.L., JR., utility exec.; b. 1919; B.S. in Mining Engring., U. Ala., 1942; married. With Indsl. Generating Co., 1953-59; with Tex. Power & Light Co., 1959—, pres., chief exec. officer, 1967-72, chmn., 1972, also dir.; pres. Tex. Utilities Co., 1972-74, chief exec. officer, 1973—, vice chmn., 1974, chmn. bd., chmn. exec. com., 1975—, also dir.; dir. Dallas Power & Light Co., Tex. Electric Service Co. Served with USNR, 1942-45. Address: 2001 Bryan Tower Dallas TX 75201*

AUSTIN, WILLIAM BENNETT, JR., banker; b. Upper Darby, Pa., Feb. 10, 1932; s. William Bennett and Inez Katheryn (Brock) A.; A.B. in Econs., Princeton U., 1954; postgrad. in Bus. Adminstrn., N.Y. U.; m. Donna Frederick, 1964; children—William Bennett III, Abigail, Amy. Vice pres. Bankers Trust Co., N.Y.C., 1954-74; sr. v.p. South Shore Bank, Quincy, Mass., 1975, exec. v.p., 1975-77; pres. Multibank Leasing, Inc., Quincy, 1976-78, chmn. bd., 1978—, dir., 1976—: dir. Multibank Internat., Quincy, 1978—; pres., chief operating officer, dir. South Shore Bank, Quincy, 1977—; chmn. credit com. Multibank Fin. Corp.; dir. Better Bus. Bur. Eastern Mass., Inc., Multibank Service Corp.; com. mem. Progress/Downtown Quincy, Inc., 1979—, Quincy Devel. and Fin. Corp., 1979—; South Regional Assn. campaign chmn. United Way of Mass. Bay, Inc., 1977-79, mem. So. Regional Campaign, 1979—, mem. nominating com., 1979—. Served to 1st lt. arty. AUS, 1954-56. Mem. Mass. Bankers Assn. (dir. 1980—), N.E. Bankcard Assn. (dir.), South Shore C. of C. (dir. 1976—). Clubs: Marshfield Country, Neighborhood of Quincy. Office: 1400 Hancock St Quincy MA 02169

AUTORINO, ARTHUR ALLEN, gas turbine co. ofcl.; b. Worcester, Mass., Feb. 7, 1946; s. Arthur Albert and Ann Marie (Mercadante) A.; B.S.A.E. (scholar), U. Va., 1969; M. Indsl. Adminstrn., Union Coll., 1976; m. Georgia June Wirth, July 5, 1969; 1 dau., Molly Meghann. With Mfg. Mgmt. Program, Gen. Elec. Co., 1969-72; supr. airfoils Gen. Elec. Gas Turbine Co., Schenectady, N.Y., 1972, planning specialist, 1972, specialist programming and adminstrn., 1972-73, mgr. airfoils mfg., 1973-76, mgr. advanced materials, 1976-79, mgr. mfg. systems, 1979-81, mgr. rotor mfg., 1981—. Mem. U. Va. Alumni Assn. (class agt.). Roman Catholic. Home: 3492 Rosendale Rd Niskayuna NY 12309 Office: General Electric Co Bldg 49-218 1 River Rd Schenectady NY 12345

AVANT, DAVID ALONZO, JR., realty co. exec., photographer; b. Tallahassee, Apr. 11, 1919; s. David Alonzo and Fenton Garnett (Davis) A.; B.A., U. Fla., 1940; M.A., Cornell U., 1941; postgrad. Sch. Modern Photography, N.Y.C., 1946, Winona (Ind.) Sch. Photography, 1951; B.A., Fla. State U., 1958; m. Anne Leigh Wilder, Nov. 22, 1961 (div. Mar. 4, 1976); children—David Alonzo III, Eugenia Tatum Davis. Instr. art Fla. State U., Tallahassee, 1946-47; partner, owner, color portrait photographer L'Avant Studios, Tallahassee, 1947—; partner Avant Offices & Apts., Tallahassee, 1953—, Avant Tree Farms, Tallahassee, 1964—; dir. Indian Hills

Estates, Tallahassee br. Fla. Fed. Savs. & Loan. Pres. Old St. Augustine (Fla.) Estates, 1968. Chmn. Armed Forces Day Tallahassee, 1958. Bd. dirs. Salvation Army. Served to lt. col., USAAF, 1941-68. Named Territorial Krewe Chief Springtime Tallahassee Festival, Tallahassee Sesquicentennial Com., 1974. Mem. U.S. Navy League (v.p. 1975-76), Tallahassee Jaycees (dir.), Profl. Photographers Assn. Am. (Master of Photographery cert. 1964), Am. Soc. Photographers, Fla. Photographers' Assn., Fla. Pub. Relations Assn. (dir., Gold award 1966), Tallahassee Art League (pres. 1954-54), Tallahassee Camellia Club (pres. 1953-54 68-69), Soc. Cincinnati of Md., Tallahassee SAR (pres. 1957-58, 76-77, 77-78), Order of First Families Va., Order Founders and Patriots Am., Soc. Colonial Wars, Order Loyalists and Patriots, Soc. Descs. Colonial Clergy, Jamestowne Soc., Soc. War of 1812, S.R., Flagon and Trencher, Mil. Order World Wars, Mil. Order Fgn. Wars, Order Stars and Bars, Sons Confederate Vets., Huguenot Soc. S.C., St. Andrew's Soc. Tallahassee. Democrat. Methodist (steward). Rotarian. Author: (with others) More Money Selling Portraits, 1956; Tallahassee Sesquicentennial Pageant, 1974; Florida Pioneers and Their Alabama, Georgia, Carolina, Maryland and Virginia Ancestors, 1974. Contbr. articles to profl. photog. jours. Pub. Like a Straight Pine Tree, 1971; Professional Raccoon Trapping, 1979; The Davis-Wood Family of Gadsden County, Florida, 1979. Home: 2312 Don Patricio Dr Tallahassee FL 32304 Office: Box 1711 207 W Park Ave Tallahassee FL 32302

AVASTHI, DAVID, multinational ins. co. exec.; b. New Delhi, June 22, 1952; s. Sada Shanker and Rama (Misra) A.; B.A. in Econs., Christ Church Coll., Kanpur, India, 1972; post-B.A. diploma Coll. Mass Communication, New Delhi, 1973; M.B.A., Bernard M. Baruch Grad. Sch. Bus., 1976. Came to U.S., 1973. Account exec. Alfred Allan Advt., Ltd., New Delhi and London, 1972-73; supr. Rand McNally & Co., N.Y.C., 1973-75; merger analyst Niederhoffer, Cross & Zeckhauser, Inc., N.Y.C., 1976-77; sr. underwriter sensitive risks div. Am. Internat. Group, Inc., N.Y.C., 1977-79; exec. v.p., dir. INAMIC, Ltd., subs. INA Corp., N.Y.C., 1979—. Recipient New York State Scholar Incentive award, 1976. Home: 42-65 Kissena Blvd New York NY 11355 Office: 127 John St New York NY 10038

AVEDISIAN, ARMEN GEORGE, corp. exec.; b. Chgo., Oct. 28, 1926; s. Karekin Der and Kardovil (Ignatius) A.; B.S., U. Ill., 1949; m. Dorothy D. Donian, Nov. 22, 1952; children—Guy A., Vann, Donna A. Civil engr. Standard Paving Co., Chgo., 1949; constrn. supt. Gallagher Asphalt Corp., Thornton, Ill., 1950-55; v.p., dir. Am. Asphalt Paving Co., Chgo., 1956-64; chmn. bd., pres. Lincoln Stone Quarry, Inc., Joliet, Ill., 1964—, Avedisian Industries, Inc., Hillside, Ill., 1964—; chmn. bd. Delta Constrn. Corp., Joliet, 1968—, Swenson, Inc., Joliet, 1970—, Midstate Stone Corp., Gillespie, Ill., 1970—; chmn. bd., chief exec. officer Hillside Stone Corp. (Ill.), 1969—, Avedisian Co., 1978—; chmn. bd., chief exec. officer Geneva Capital Corp.; dir. Citizens Nat. Bank, Lake Geneva, Wis. Mem. pres.'s com., guarantor Lyric Opera, Chgo., 1968—; governing life mem. Men's Council, Art Inst. Chgo., 1961—; mem. exec. bd. Boy Scouts Am.; trustee Glenwood (Ill.) Sch. for Boys, Max McGraw Wild Life Found., Avery Coonley Sch., Downers Grove, Ill., Chgo. Symphony Orch., 1978—. Served with AUS, 1944-45. Mem. Ill. Rd. Builders Assn. (dir., treas. 1963), Am., Western socs. civil engrs., Midwest Crushed Limestone Inst. (pres. 1966-67), Ill. Assn. Aggregate Producers (pres., dir. 1968), Nat. Limestone Inst. (chmn. bd. 1971—), Nat. Crushed Stone Inst. (bd. govs. 1972—), Sigma Nu. Clubs: Chicago Athletic, Chicago Yacht, Chicago Racquet; Butterfield Country (Hinsdale, Ill.); Dunham Woods Riding (Wayne, Ill.); Butler National; Lake Geneva (Wis.) Country. Office: 900 Jorie Blvd Suite 120 Oak Brook IL 60521

AVEDON, BRUCE, ins. and securities exec.; b. Atlantic City, Dec. 31, 1928; s. N. Jay and Rosalie Ann (Sholtz) A.; B.S., Yale U., 1950; m. Shirlee Florence Young, May 19, 1951; children—Linda Michele, Bruce Frederick. Vice pres. Sholtz Ins. Agy., Inc., Miami, Fla., 1950-51; various positions to dir. planning State Mut. Life Assurance Co. Am., Worcester, Mass., 1953-69, also sec. Am. Variable Annuity Life Assurance Co., Worcester, 1967-69; v.p. equity products Ohio Nat. Life Ins. Co., Cin., 1969—, also v.p., dir. O.N. Equity Sales Co., Cin, 1973—; pres., dir. O.N. Fund, Inc., O.N. Market Yield Fund, Inc. Served to lt. AUS, 1951-53; maj. Finance Corps Res. ret. Mem. Am. Council Life Ins. (com. SEC matter, chmn. subcom. state matter), cont Investment Co. Inst. (pension com.), Life Office Mgmt. Assn. (equity products and annuity com.), Nat. Assn. Securities Dealers (variable contracts com.), Res. Officers Assn., Mil. Order World Wars. Republican. Methodist. Clubs: Yale (Cin.), Masons, Order Eastern Star. Home: 6601 Hitching Post Ln Cincinnati OH 45230 Office: 237 William Howard Taft Rd Cincinnati OH 45219

AVERETT, ELLIOTT, banker; b. Chatham, N.J., Jan. 6, 1918; s. Elliott and Martha (Snead) A.; student Harvard Bus. Sch., 1958; m. Julia Bancroft Fletcher, Dec. 12, 1947; children—Elliott III, Thomas Hamlett, Julia Hall. With Bank of N.Y., 1940—, asst. treas., 1949-52, asst. v.p., 1952-56, v.p., 1956-63, head nat. dept., 1958-63, exec. v.p., 1963-66, chmn. credit com., 1963-66, sr. exec. v.p., 1966-68, chief comml. banking officer, 1966-67, chief adminstrv. officer, 1967-73, pres., 1968-74, chief exec. officer, 1973—, chmn. bd., 1974—, also dir.; chmn. bd., chief exec. officer, dir. Bank of N.Y. Co., Inc.; chmn., dir. Bank of N.Y. Internat. Corp.; dir. Ennia Reins. of Am., Centennial Ins. Co., La. Land & Exploration Co.; trustee Atlantic Mut. Ins. Co.; mem. N.Y. State Adv. Com. on Comml. Bank Supervision, 1965-67. Mem. Life Saving Benevolent Assn. N.Y., Council Fgn. Relations, Inc.; treas. Seeing Eye, Inc., Morristown, N.J., 1958-70, pres., chmn., 1970-81, trustee, 1981—; treas., v.p., bd. dirs. Greater N.Y. Fund, 1968—, chmn., 1977; bd. dirs. Downtown Lower Manhattan Assn., UN Assn. U.S.A.; trustee Josiah Macy, Jr. Found.; mem. trustees com. N.Y. Community Trust, 1969-74; bd. govs. Hundred Year Assn. N.Y., Inc. Served to capt. AUS, 1941-46; ETO. Decorated Purple Heart, Silver Star. Mem. Assn. Res. City Bankers, Robert Morris Assos., N.Y. Clearing House Assn., Econ. Club N.Y., Am. Inst. Banking (chmn. adv. council N.Y. chpt. 1976—), Am. Bur. Shipping, Internat. C. of C. (U.S. council). Clubs: Chicago; Down Town Assn., Amateur Ski, Anglers (N.Y.C.); Somerset Hills Country; Pilgrims U.S.; Union; Sky. Office: 48 Wall St New York NY 10015

AVERS, RICHARD DENNIS, elec. constrn. co. exec.; b. Goshen, Ind., Aug. 31, 1949; s. John Herman and Emma (Miller) A.; B.S., Ind. U., 1971; Pres., The Electric Co., Inc., Bloomington, Ind., 1977—, also dir. Mem. Nat. Fedn. Ind. Bus., Nat. Elec. Contractors Assn., Nat. Small Bus. Assn., Elec. Industry Evaluation Bd. Clubs: Bloomington Athletic, Bloomington Racquet. Home: 823 W 6th St Bloomington IN 47401 Office: PO Box 154 Bloomington IN 47402

AVERY, CYRUS STEVENS, II, real estate co. exec.; b. Tulsa, Oct. 19, 1932; s. Gordon Stevens and Phoebe Jane (Heffner) A.; B.S., U.S. Mil. Acad., West Point, 1954; M.B.A., Harvard U., 1962; m. Ella Jane Wolverton, June 10, 1955; children—Cyrus Stevens, Allyson Anne. Sales rep. Ferris & Co., Washington, 1962-66, br. mgr., 1966-69, partner, 1968-71, sr. v.p., dir., 1971-74; asst. to pres. Internat. Bank, Washington, 1974-77; pres. United Fin. Corp. Va., Washington, 1976—, also dir.; dir. Fin. Internat. Corp., 1978-80. Chmn. bd. dirs. D.C. Devel. Corp., 1976-79. Served with U.S. Army, 1954-60. Mem. D.C. Soc. Investment Analysts, Met. Washington Bd. Trade, Washington Bd. Realtors, West Point Soc. D.C., Harvard U. Bus. Sch. Club Washington. Republican. Episcopalian. Home: 8016 Georgetown Pike McLean VA 22102 Office: 1701 Pennsylvania Ave NW Washington DC 20006

AVERY, JAMES STEPHEN, pub. affairs exec.; b. Cranford, N.J., Mar. 24, 1923; s. John Henry and Martha Ann (Jones) A.; B.A., Columbia, 1948, M.A. in History, 1949; m. Joan Showers, Jan. 22, 1977; children by previous marriage—Sheryl Ann, James Stephen. Tchr. history Cranford High Sch., 1949-56, head dept. history, 1954-56; nat. coordinator community relations Exxon Co. U.S.A. (formerly Humble Oil & Refining Co.), 1963-68, pub. affairs mgr. northeastern region, Pelham, N.Y., 1968—. Co-chmn. com. on housing Plainfield (N.J.) Human Relations Commn., 1958; vice chmn. adv. com. Vice Pres.'s Task Force on Youth Motivation, 1966-69, chmn., 1969; chmn. Union County (N.J.) Coordinating Agy. for Higher Edn., 1968—; vice chmn. energy policy com. Asso. Industries N.Y.; past chmn. exec. com. N.Y. State Petroleum Council; vice chmn. United Negro Coll. Fund campaign, 1962-64; mem. Plainfield Assistance Bd., 1960-68, chmn., 1962-67; mem. Plainfield com. Union County Psychiat. Clinic, 1954-60; trustee N.Y. State Traffic Safety Council, N.Y. State Council on Econ. Edn. Served with U.S. Army, 1942-46. Mem. Nat. Assn. Market Developers (pres. 1964-66, chmn. bd. 1967), Am. Petroleum Inst. (vice chmn. offshore subcom. 1976—), Omega Psi Phi (grand basileus 1970-73). Home: 1940 Inverness Dr Scotch Plains NJ 07076 Office: Exxon Co 101 Merritt 7 Norwalk CT 06851

AVON, RANDY KALANI, fin. cons.; b. Honolulu, Sept. 25, 1940; s. Randolph Scott and Pualani (Mossman) A.; B.S. in Bus. Adminstrn., U. Fla., 1962; m. Joan Messmore, June 29, 1973; children—Eve, Emmy Lou, Jaimie, Bob, Randy. S.E. div. mgr. Rums of P.R., Miami, Fla., 1962-68; v.p. mktg. Continental Inns Am., Memphis, 1966-70; pres. Creative Public Relations and Mktg., Inc., Ft. Lauderdale, Fla., 1970—; pres., chief exec. officer Corp. & Fin. Cons.'s, Inc., Ft. Lauderdale, 1976—; pres. Security Investment Corp. Fla., 1967—. Pres., United Cerebral Palsy, 1965; chmn. Ft. Lauderdale Community Relations Bd., 1966; trustee Ft. Lauderdale U., 1973-76; mem. Fla. Legislature, 1972-76. Recipient Outstanding Am. award Viva, 1974; Disting. Service award VFW, 1975; Legislator of Yr. award Condominium Owners Assn., 1976; Humanitatian award Broward County Rabbinical Assn., 1975; numerous others. Mem. Fla. Public Relations Assn. (v.p. 1971-72), West Broward C. of C. (v.p. 1978-79). Republican. Episcopalian. Clubs: Elks, Kiwanis. Author: The Future of The Tax Exempt Industry in Florida, 1980. Office: 104 SE 6th St Fort Lauderdale FL 33301

AWADA, MICHAEL, lawyer; b. Montreal, Que., Can., Nov. 16, 1930; s. Solomon Moses and Alice (Hanna) A.; B.A., Sir George Williams Coll., 1955; B.C.L., McGill U., 1956; m. Cheryl Sandra Zakaib, Sept. 30, 1962; children—Glenn, Kim. With sales dept. Merck & Co., Ltd., 1949-51; indentured to firm Heward, Holden, Hutchinson, Cliff, McMaster & Meighen, 1956-57; called to Que. bar, 1957, since practiced in Montreal; jr. asso. firm John Jacob Spector, 1957-60; partner firm Awada & Bey, 1960-68, Awada & Gareau, 1968-70, Awada, Gareau & Feifer, 1970-72, Awada & Gareau, 1972-73, Awada, Gareau & Sumbulian, 1973-74, Awada & Sumbulian, 1974—; lectr. RCAF Officers Sch., Royal Mil. Coll., Kingston, Ont.; dir. Canadian Granite Industries Assn., Hanna Mfg. Co., Ltd., Distributeurs Maisonneuve Inc., Montreal, George Courey & Sons Ltd., Montreal. Hon. legal adviser St. George Orthodox Ch., Montreal. Served with RCAF, 1951-56. Mem. Internat. Platform Assn. Exec. editor McGill U. Law Jour., 1955-56. Contbr. articles to law jours. Home: 11230 Joseph Casavant Montreal PQ H3M 2B7 Canada Office: 1010 Sherbrooke St W Suite 1011 Montreal PQ H3A 2R7 Canada

AWAN, MALIK MUHAMMED MAHMUD, optical co. exec.; b. Bhera, Sargodha, Pakistan, Dec. 25, 1951; came to U.S., 1973, naturalized, 1978; s. Malik G. Ali and Fateh (Ali) A.; B.A. (merit scholar), Punjab U., 1970, M.A., 1972; Ph.D. (research fellow), Clark U., 1976; m. Roohi S. Yaqub, July 30, 1978. Chmn. dept. mgmt. Central New Eng. Coll., Worcester, Mass., 1975-77, also fin. planning cons. Sun Life of Can. and Prudential Ins. Co., Worcester, 1975-77; dir. Grad. Sch. Bus. Adminstrn., Nichols Coll., Dudley, Mass., 1977-79; internat. product mgr. Am. Optical div. Warner Lambert Co., Southbridge, Mass., 1979—; bus. cons. Pilgrim Mgmt. Corp., Boston, N.E.D. Corp., Worcester; advisor Ministry of Prodn., Govt. of Pakistan, 1978. Bd. dirs. Internat. Center of Worcester, Inc., 1974-76; pres. Assn. Pakistan and Indic-Islamic Studies, 1979—; chmn. New Eng. Chpt. Pakistan Council of Asia, Inc., 1980—; asso. prof. mgmt. Am. Internat. Coll., Springfield, Mass. Mem. Am. Acad. Mgmt., Am. Econ. Assn., Am. Mktg. Assn., Assn. Asian Studies, Inc. Club: Webster-Dudley Rotary. Author: Foreign Capital and Development Process, 1977; Role of Foreign Capital in Pakistan's Development, 1978; editor in chief Punjab U. Econ. Bull., 1971-72. Office: 14 Mechanic St Southbridge MA 01550

AWENDER, RICHARD CARL, mgmt. analysis officer; b. Lefor, N.D., Apr. 3, 1930; s. Anton and Mary (Haas) A.; B.A., Belleuve Coll., 1974; m. Rose Alice Brazda, Apr. 28, 1951; children—Christine Rose, Catherine Ann, Richard Carl, Anton Rudolph, Melanie Sue. Enlisted U.S. Air Force, 1948, advanced through grades to sr. master sgt., 1969; ret., 1969; plant indsl. engr. Falstaff Brewing Corp., Omaha, 1969-70; mgmt. analysis officer U.S. Army Engring. Dist., Omaha, 1971-73, mgmt. analyst Missouri River div., 1973-78, mgmt. analysis officer, Omaha, 1978-79, budget officer, Middle East, 1979-80, mgmt. analysis officer, Omaha, 1980—. Instr. hunter safety State Mont., 1960-63; exec. adviser Jr. Achievement, 1977-78. Mem. Am. Inst. Indsl. Engrs. (sr.), Nat. Rifle Assn., Air Force Aid Soc. (life). Republican. Roman Catholic. Clubs: K.C., Gymnastic Sokol Soc. Home: 207 Orchard Dr Bellevue NE 68005 Office: US Army Engr Dist 6014 US PO and Courthouse Omaha NE 68102

AWTRY, JOHN H., lawyer, ret. army officer, ins. exec.; b. Quitman, Tex., July 29, 1897; s. Emmett and Elizabeth (Williams) A.; J.D., U. Tex., 1921; m. Nell Catherine Jacoby; 1 dau., Nell Catherine Awtry Gilchrist (dec.). With Fed. Res. Bank of Dallas, 1917-19; with Govt. Savs. Div., Dept. Treasury, 1919-20; admitted to Tex. bar, 1921, U.S. Supreme Ct., Ct. Mil. Appeals bars; partner firm Taylor & Awtry, 1921-23; handled ins. on intra and interstate motor buses and trucks 17 years; pres. First Reins. Co. of Hartford (Conn.), 1936-41, John H. Awtry & Co., Inc., N.Y.C.; owner John H. Awtry & Co., Dallas; commd. officer AUS, 1942; active mil. service, 1942-53; assisted planning, participated in invasion of Europe 1944; on War Dept. Gen. Staff, 1946; chief fraud unit War Dept., Dept. Army, 1946-49; chief (lt. col.) contract and procurement br. Judge Adv. Div., European Command, 1949-50; mem. Army panel Armed Services Bd. Contract Appeals, Office Asst. Sec. Army, Washington; col. (promoted by direct order Pres. U.S.), U.S. Army and U.S. Army Res., ret. 1953. Decorated Bronze Star medal, Legion of Merit. Mem. N.Y. So. Soc., 12th Army Group Assn. (life), Judge Advs. Assn., N.Y. State C. of C., Fed., Am., N.Y., Tex. (life), Dallas bar assns., Mil. Order World Wars, Am. Legion (life), Washington Tex. Soc., Fed. Grand Jury Assn., U. Tex. Ex Assn. (life), DAV, Ret. Officers Assn. (life), Lambda Chi Alpha. Baptist. Clubs: Masons (32 deg.), Shriners, High Twelve, Nat. Sojourners, Nat. Exchange (ct. of honor; nat. pres.), Drug and Chem., Downtown Athletic, Bankers of Am. (N.Y.C.); Town (life) (Scarsdale, N.Y.); Scarsdale Golf (Hartsdale, N.Y.); Hartford Comm. Dallas Athletic, Dallas Exchange (life, 1st pres.); Nat. Exchange (ex-pres.); Army and Navy (Washington). Opinions as mem. Armed Services Bd. Contract Appeals in Commerce Clearing House legal publs. Home: 3337-2A Punta Alta Rossmoor Leisure World PO Box 2833 Laguna Hills CA 92653

AWTRY, NELL CATHERINE (MRS. JOHN HIX AWTRY), real estate exec.; b. Dallas, Sept. 29, 1900; d. Henry Hibbler and Laura Jane (Harris) Jacoby; B.A., So. Meth U., 1935; postgrad. Columbia, 1941-42; m. John Hix Awtry, Apr. 24, 1922; 1 dau., Nell Catherine (Mrs. William W. Gilchrist) (dec.). Real estate saleswoman Prince & Ripley, Scarsdale, N.Y., 1948, Midgeley Parks, Scarsdale, 1949, Cleveland E. Van Wert, Inc., Scarsdale, 1954-60, Julia B. Fee, Inc., Scarsdale, 1960-72. Mem. Zeta Tau Alpha. Republican. Baptist. Mem. Order Eastern Star (worthy matron 1961, 67). Clubs: Dallas Athletic; Scarsdale Golf. Author poems and lyrics. Home: 3337-2A Punta Alta Rossmoor Leisure World POB 2833 Laguna Hills CA 92653

AXELROD, ROBERT A(LAN), real estate developer; b. N.Y.C., Apr. 27, 1948; s. Bernard M. and Helene G.; A.B., Princeton U., 1969; M.B.A., Harvard U., 1972. Asst. v.p. Capital Mortgage Investments, Chevy Chase, Md., 1972-79; v.p. Investment Group Devel. Corp., Washington, 1979—. Office: 1100 17th St NW Washington DC 20036

AXELSON, KENNETH STRONG, corp. exec.; b. Chgo., July 31, 1922; s. Charles F. and Katherine (Strong) A.; A.B., U. Chgo. (John Crerar scholar), 1944; grad. student Va. Poly. Inst., 1943-44; m. Roberta Bearhope, Jan. 23, 1943; children—Kenneth Strong, Jerrold Frederic, Stephen, John. Acct., Arthur Andersen & Co., Seattle, 1946-48; controller Columbia Lumber Co. of Alaska, Juneau, 1948-50; mgmt. cons. McKinsey & Co., Chgo., 1950-52; mgr. mgmt. controls dept. Peat, Marwick, Mitchell & Co. 1952-53, partner, 1953-63; v.p. finance J.C. Penney Co., Inc., N.Y.C., 1963-67, v.p. fin. and adminstrn., 1967-74, sr. v.p. fin. and adminstrn., 1974-78, sr. v.p. fin. and pub. affairs, 1978—, dir., 1964—; on loan as dep. mayor for fin. City of N.Y., 1975-76; mem. Emergency Fin. Control Bd., N.Y.C., 1976-77, Fin. Acctg. Standards Adv. Council, 1979; dir. Protection Mut. Ins. Co., Discount Corp. N.Y., Grumman Corp., Bus. Mktg. Corp. for N.Y.C., 1978-80; trustee Dry Dock Savs. Bank; mem. adv. com. on implementation central market system SEC, 1974-75. Trustee, Fin. Execs. Research Found., 73-80, pres., 1978-80; bd. dirs. Lincoln Sq. Neighborhood Center, 1970-77; mem. exec. com. Assn. for a Better N.Y. 1977—; bd. dirs. Ave. of Americas Assn., 1978—; trustee Fin. Acctg. Found., 1980—. Served as warrant officer AUS, 1943-46. Recipient 1st ann. lit. award Jour. Accountancy, 1976. C.P.A., Ill., Wash., Iowa, N.Mex., N.Y., Va. Mem. Am. Inst. C.P.A.'s (accounting prins. bd. 1968-70), Financial Execs. Inst. (pres. N.Y.C. chpt. 1975-76, dir. 1978-80, exec. com. 1978-80), N.Y. Soc. C.P.A.'s, U. Chgo. Club N.Y. (pres. 1961-62), Nat. Assn. Accountants, Council Fin. Execs. (chmn. 1979-80), Regional Plan Assn. (dir. 1978—), Sch. Bus. Assn. U. Chgo. (pres. 1957-58), Nat. Retail Mchts. Assn. (chmn. fin. com., treas. 1975-77), Phi Delta Theta. Baptist. Author: Responsibility Reporting, 1961. Editor Mgmt. Controls bus. jour., 1958-63. Home: 425 E 58th St New York NY 10022 Office: 1301 Ave of Americas New York NY 10019

AXTELL, OLIVER, chem. co. exec.; b. York, Neb., Sept. 5, 1926; s. Oliver and Myrtle (Bonner) A.; B.S. in Chem. Engring., Rice U., 1944; S.M. in Chem. Engring., Mass. Inst. Tech., 1947; m. Patricia Ann Dill, Apr. 9, 1955; children—Bonnie Jean, Steven Brian. With Celanese Chem. Co., N.Y.C., 1951—, econ. evaluation engr., 1955-63, mgr. comml. info., 1963—. Mem. Bd. Adjustment, Fanwood, N.J., 1970-76; mem. Union County Republican Com., 1963-69. Fellow Am. Inst. Chem. Engrs.; mem. Am. Chem. Soc., Sigma Xi, Phi Lambda Upsilon. Republican. Methodist. Patentee in field. Home: 7722 Chattington Dallas TX 75248 Office: 1250 Mockingbird Ln Dallas TX 75247

AYA, HELEN RIDDLE (MRS. RODERICK HONEYMAN AYA), ret. communications co. exec.; b. Oroville, Calif., Sept. 6, 1912; d. William Robert and Odessa (Miller) Riddle; student Sacramento Jr. Coll., 1933-34; m. Roderick Honeyman Aya, June 16, 1945; children—Roderick Riddle, Deborah Germaina (Mrs. Richard W. Reynolds). Ronald Honeyman. Staff asst. The Pacific Tel. & Tel. Co., San Francisco, 1942-52, spl. asst., 1952-65; accounting office supr. N.Y. Telephone Co., N.Y.C., 1965-67, internal auditor, 1968-77. Mem. Sacramento Symphony Orch., 1931-34, Sacramento Civic Ballet, 1938-39, San Francisco Symphony Found., 1959—. Mem. Belvedere Sailing Soc., Telephone Pioneers Am. (social activities chmn. San Francisco council). Traffic Mgmt. Women (chmn. 1961). Republican. Roman Catholic. Mem. Order Eastern Star. Clubs: Sports Car Am. (dir. San Francisco 1955-56, social chmn. 1955-56, race ofcl. 1954-57); Corinithian Yacht Aux. Home: Maid of Barra care Postmaster Rowayton CT 06853

AYA, RODERICK HONEYMAN, ret. corp. tax. exec.; b. Portland, Oreg., Sept. 17, 1916; s. Alfred Anthony and Grace Myrtle (Honeyman) A.; student U. Oreg., 1935-36, Internat. Accts. Soc., 1937-39, LaSalle Extension U., 1940-42, Walton Sch. Commerce, 1942, U. Calif. Extension, 1945; m. Helen Marjorie Riddle, June 16, 1945; children—Roderick Riddle, Deborah Germaine Aya Reynolds, Ronald Honeyman. Chief statistician Hotel Employers Assn., San Francisco, 1939-42; accountant Pacific Tel. & Tel. Co., San Francisco, 1942-52, spl. accountant, 1952-63; tax accountant 1963-65; spl. accountant AT&T, N.Y.C., 1965-68, mgr. tax studies, 1968-73, mgr. tax research and planning, 1973—; public acct., San Francisco, 1940—; music tchr., 1959—; v.p., treas., dir. Snell Research Assos., Inc.; guest lectr. on taxes Westchester County Adult Edn. Program. Committeeman, Marin County Sheriffs' Reserve, 1963-65; law enforcement liaison com. on Juvenile Control; sec. Am. Nat. Standards Inst. Com. on Protective Headgear. Vice pres., treas., bd. dirs. Snell Meml. Found.; trustee Snell Meml. Found. (U.K.), Ltd.; dir., past pres. Stuart Highlanders Pipe Band of San Francisco. Recipient Wisdom award of honor Wisdom Soc., 1970. Mem. ASTM, Nat. Soc. Pub. Accountants, St. Andrews Soc., Soc. Ethnomusicology (contbr. to jour.), U.S. Naval Inst., Phi Chi, Sigma Nu. Clubs: Corinthian Yacht (Tiburon, Calif.); Sports Car Am. (San Francisco region treas. 1957-58, dir. 1957-59); U.S. Yacht Racing Union. Author: The Legacy of Pete Snell, 1965; Determination of Corporate Earnings and Profits for Federal Income Tax Purposes, 2 vols., 1966. Home: Maid of Barra PO Box 148 Rowayton CT 06853

AYERS, JOSEPH WILLIAMS, chem. co. exec.; b. Easton, Pa., Jan. 6, 1904; s. Charles Pierson and Emma Cottman (Williams) A.; B.Chemistry, Cornell U., 1927, postgrad., 1927-28; m. Caroline Brooke Stone, Oct. 6, 1934; children—Katherine Ayers Hovey, Phyllis Ayers Harmon. Research dir. C.K. Williams & Co., Easton, 1930-48, v.p., 1945-62; gen. mgr. minerals pigments and metals div. Pfizer, Inc., N.Y.C., 1962-68, pres., 1968-69; pres. Calcium Chem. Corp., Adams, Mass., 1937-48; pres. Agrashell, Inc., Los Angeles, 1939-76, chmn. bd., 1976—; pres. J.W. Ayers, & Co., Easton, 1955-61, The Ayers Co., Easton, 1971—; pres., treas. Joseph Ayers, Inc., Bethlehem, Pa., 1973—; dir. New Eng. Lime Co., Foote Mineral Co. Chmn., Pa. Hosp. and Health Council, 1971-74; v.p. Northampton County Citizens for Regional Progress, 1973—; trustee

Greater Valley Council Girl Scouts U.S., Bach choir of Bethlehem (Pa.). Fellow N.Y. Acad. Scis.; mem. Am. Inst. Chem. Engrs., Am. Inst. Chemists, Am. Chem. Soc., AAAS, Soc. Chem. Industries (Eng.), N.Y. Chemist Club, Zeta Psi. Republican. Presbyterian. Clubs: Cornell, Union League (N.Y.C.); Northhampton County Country; Pomfret (Easton); Oyster Harbors, Wianno, Wianno Yacht (Osterville, Mass.); Beach (Craigsville, Mass.), Los Angeles Athletic. Contbr. articles in field to profl. jours. Patentee in field. Home: 22 N 14th St Easton PA 18042 Office: RFD 2 Bethlehem PA 18017

AYERS, RICHARD WAYNE, elec. mfg. co. ofcl.; b. Atlanta, Aug. 23, 1945; s. Harold Richard and Martha Elizabeth (Vaughan) A.; B.B.A., Ga. State Coll., 1967; M.B.A., Ind. U., 1969; m. Nancy Katherine Martin, Aug. 9, 1969. Specialist mktg. communications research Gen. Electric Co., Schenectady, 1969-70, copywriter Lamp div., Cleve., 1970-73, supr., distbr. advt. and sales promotion, 1973-75, supr. comml. and indsl. promotional programs Gen. Electric Lighting Bus. Group, 1975-79, supr. comml. and indsl. market advt. and promotional programs, 1979—; lectr. in field. Recipient Best Indsl. Promotion award Advt. Age, 1974, Premium Showcase award Nat. Premium Sales Execs., 1975, 76, Gold Key award Nat. Premium Mfrs. Reps., 1976, 77, Golden Key Communicators award Factory mag., 1976. Dir.-at-large Ga. Young Reps., 1966-67. Mem. Blue Key, Delta Sigma Pi, Beta Gamma Sigma. Methodist. Home: 23951 Lake Shore Blvd Apt 1213B Euclid OH 44123 Office: Nela Park Bldg 308 Cleveland OH 44112

AYERS, THOMAS G., utility exec.; b. Detroit, Feb. 16, 1915; s. Jule C. and Camilla (Chalmers) A.; A.B., U. Mich., 1937; LL.D., Elmhurst Coll., 1966; m. Mary Andrew, Nov. 25, 1938; children—Catherine Mary Ayers Allen, Thomas G., William Charles, Richard James, John Steven. With Pub. Service Co. of No. Ill., 1938-52, mgr. indsl. relations, 1948-52; asst. v.p. Commonwealth Edison Co., Chgo., 1952, v.p., 1953-62, exec. v.p., 1962-64, pres., 1964-73, chmn., chief exec. officer, 1973-80, also dir.; dir. 1st Nat. Bank of Chgo., N.W. Industries, Inc., G.D. Searle & Co., Tribune Co., Zenith Radio Corp.; chmn. Breeder Reactor Corp. Chmn., 1969 Met. Crusade of Mercy; chmn. Leadership Council Met. Open Communities, Dearborn Park Corp.; chmn. bd. trustees Northwestern U., Chgo. Symphony Orch. Mem. Chgo. Assn. Commerce and Industry (past pres., dir.); chmn. Chgo. Econ. Devel. Commn. Clubs: Chgo., Econ., Comml., Tavern, Mid-Day (Chgo.); Glen Oak Country (Glen Ellyn, Ill.). Home: 199 Montclair Ave Glen Ellyn IL 60137 Office: POB 767 1 First Nat Plaza Chicago IL 60690

AYKAN, KAMRAN, chem. co. exec.; b. Istanbul, Turkey, May 19, 1930; s. Mehmet Emin and Fatma (Hikmet) A.; student U. Hamburg (Germany), 1951-53; M.S., U. Istanbul, 1954; m. Irmgard Kopp, Jan. 17, 1957. Chemist, Bergbau A.G., Koenig Ludwig, Germany, 1956-57; chemist William T. Burnett & Co., Inc., Balt., 1957-58; with E.I. DuPont de Nemours & Co., Inc., 1958-71, staff scientist, 1969-71; mgr. chem. research Engelhard Industries div. Engelhard Minerals and Chems. Corp., Edison, N.J., 1971-72, tech. dir. autoexhaust catalyst group, 1972-74, dir. research and devel., 1974-76, v.p. research and devel., 1976—. Bd. dirs. Research and Devel. Council N.J. Served with Turkish Army, 1954-56. Mem. Am. Crystallographic Assn., Am. Chem. Soc., Indsl. Research Inst., Am. Ceramic Soc., Catalysis Soc. N.Y. Contbr. articles to profl. jours. Patentee in field. Office: Engelhard Industries Div Menlo Park Edison NJ 08817

AYLSWORTH, JOSEPH LYNN, JR., health care services exec.; b. Phila., June 30, 1916; s. Joseph Lynn and Margaret Eleanor (Wanner) A.; student Peirce Jr. Coll., Phila., 1938; m. Marjorie Jane Biedert, June 20, 1942; children—Susan A. (Mrs. Thad R. Murwin), Joseph Lynn, John Stephen. With Butcher Sherrerd, Phila., 1946; pres. Mortgage Assos., Inc., Phila., 1946-68; exec. v.p., sec. Am. Med. Affiliates, Inc., Jenkintown, Pa., 1968—, also dir. Chmn. Montgomery County chpt. Am. Cancer Soc., 1971—. Bd. dirs. Met. Hosp., Phila., Erie (Pa.) Osteo. Hosp., Kirksville (Mo.) Coll. Osteo. Medicine. Served to 1st lt. USAAF, 1943-45. Decorated Air medal. Mem. Am. Nursing Home Assn., Phila. Mortgage Bankers Assn. (past pres.), Health Care Facilities Assn. Pa. Lutheran. Club: Union League (Phila.). Home: 1332 Wright Dr Huntingdon Valley PA 19006 Office: Foxcroft Sq Apts PO Box 608 Jenkintown PA 19046

AYMAR, CATHERINE BEATRICE (MRS. CLARENCE PHILLIP AYMAR), real estate broker; b. Ferndale, Wash., Nov. 28, 1922; d. Morley Victor and Jessie Edna (Fredenberg) Pomeroy; student Santa Rosa Jr. Coll., 1963, DeAnza Jr. Coll., 1967—, U. Calif. at Berkeley, 1967, U. San Francisco, 1972; m. Clarence Phillip Aymar, July 27, 1955; 1 son, Patrick Mercer. Real estate salesman Mairanoma Realty, Petaluma, Calif., 1963-66, Vivian Krodel, Sunnyvale, Calif., 1967-68; real estate salesman Rylander & House, Sunnyvale, 1968-69, real estate salesman, real estate broker, 1969-71; real estate broker, pres. Aymar Properties, Cupertino, Calif., 1971—. Mem. Ming Quong Children's Guild, Los Gatos, Calif., 1968-72; mem. Sunnyvale (Calif.) Bd. Edn. com.; vol. ARC Mobile Blood Bank, Mended Hearts; visitor to heart patients' Family groups; mktg. adviser Jr. Achievement, 1977—; mem. County Project Bus. Com., 1978; county bd. dirs. Jr. Achievement and Project Bus., 1978—. Mem. Nat. Assn. Realtors (pub. relations com. 1978), Grad. Realtors Inst., Assn. Profl. Mortgage Women, Nat. Notary Assn., Sunnyvale Bd. Realtors, Women's Council Realtors (corr. sec. San Jose chpt. 1974, v.p. Santa Clara Valley chpt. 1975, editor chpt. newsletter 1980, pres. 1976, Woman of Yr. 1977, chmn. pub. relations com. 1978; sec. Calif. chpt. 1977, v.p. 1978, pres. 1979), Am. Mgmt. Assn., San Jose Real Estate Bd. (mem. multiple listing com. 1972—, equal rights com. 1974, public relations com. 1978, polit. action com. 1980). Republican. Mem. United Ch. of Christ. Clubs: Santa Clara Toastmistress (pres. 1972), Quota (internat. dir.). Home: 917 Kennard Way Sunnyvale CA 94087 Office: 3600 Pruneridge Ave Santa Clara CA 95051

AYMOND, ALPHONSE HENRY, lawyer, former public utilities exec.; b. St. Louis, Sept. 27, 1914; s. Alphonse H. and Anne (Putz) A.; A.B., Northwestern U., 1936; J.D., U. Mich., 1939; LL.D. (hon.), Olivet Coll., 1970; D.Pub. Service (hon.), Western Mich. U., 1974; m. Elizabeth Shierson, Sept. 30, 1939; children—Charles H., Robert D., William G. Admitted to Ill. bar, 1939, Mich. bar, 1947; with Miller, Gorham, Wescott & Adams, Chgo., 1939-44, Commonwealth and So. Corp., N.Y.C., 1946-47; atty. Consumers Power Co., Jackson, Mich., 1947-51, gen. atty., 1951-55, v.p., gen. counsel, 1955-57, exec. v.p., 1957-60, chmn. bd., 1960-79, pres., 1972-75; dir. City Bank & Trust Co., Nat. Bank Detroit, Am. Seating Co., Kellogg Co., K Mart Corp.; trustee Northwestern Mut. Life Ins. Co., Northwestern Mut. Life Mortgage and Realty Investors. Past pres., mem. exec. bd. Land O' Lakes council, past mem. exec. bd., chmn. fin. com. East Central region Boy Scouts Am.; mem., past chmn. Mich. Colls. Found.; pres., trustee Jackson Found.; trustee W.K. Kellogg Found., Citizens Research Council. Served as lt. (j.g.), Supply Corps, USNR, 1944-46. Mem. Am. Bar Assn., Order of Coif, Assn. Edison Illuminating Cos. (past pres., exec. bd.), Edison Electric Inst. (past pres., mem. advisory bd.), Theta Xi, Phi Delta Phi. Episcopalian (past trustee diocese of Mich.). Clubs: Town, Country (Jackson); Detroit; Lost Tree (North Palm Beach, Fla.). Home: 1912 4th St Jackson MI 49203 Office: 180 W Michigan Ave Jackson MI 49201

AYRES, RICHARD WAYNE, credit union exec.; b. Kalamazoo, Sept. 21, 1932; s. Russell and Dora Evelyn A.; B.S., Wayne U., 1960; m. Dawn Ladell Williams, Mar. 21, 1973; children—Russell, Ladera, Douglas, Renee, Daniel, Carla, Matthew, Cynthia. Accounting supr. City of Garden City, Mich., 1961-63; field cons. Mich. Credit Union League, Detroit, 1963-69; mgr. Central Credit Union Mich., Detroit, 1969-74, 80—; gen. mgr. U.S. Central Credit Union, Madison, Wis., 1974-80; v.p. Internt. Credit Union Services Corp., 1974-80; treas. Credit Union Card Services Corp., 1977-80. Served with U.S. Army, 1952-54. Mem. Credit Union Execs. Soc. Libertarian. Episcopalian. Author: Loser's Handbook; contbr. articles to trade publs.; editor Central Coordinator, 1974-78. Home: 24608 Walden Rd W Southfield MI 48034

BAAMONDE, JOSEPH, JR., pharm. co. ofcl.; b. Tampa, Fla., Aug. 31, 1944; s. Joseph and Lupe (Randon) B.; B.A., Parsons Coll., 1972; m. Judith Frisk, June 9, 1973; 1 dau., Jennifer Judith. With Mallinckrodt, Inc., Brandon, Fla., 1973-80, regional sales mgr. S.E. region, 1978-80; dist. sales mgr. Wallace Labs., 1980—. Pres., Luth. Churchmen of Salem Luth. Ch., Peoria, Ill., 1977; pres. sch. bd. Immanuel Luth. Ch. Sch., Brandon, Fla., also mem. ch. council, chmn. Christian edn. Named Mgr. of Yr., Mallinckrodt, Inc., 1978. Mem. Am. Mgmt. Assn., Profl. Pharm. Mfrs. Reps. Assn. (v.p. Peoria 1976-77), Theta Chi. Republican. Address: 1306 Brandonwood Dr Brandon FL 33611

BAAR, JAMES A., public relations exec., author; b. N.Y.C., Feb. 9, 1929; s. A.W. and Marguerite R. B.; A.B., Union Coll., 1949; m. Beverly Hodge, Sept. 2, 1948; 1 son, Theodore Hall. Washington corr. U.P.I., various other wire services and newspaper assignments, 1949-59; sr. editor Missiles and Rockets mag., 1959-62; mgr. various News Bur. ops. Gen. Electric Co., 1962-66, mgr. European mktg. communications ops., 1966-70; pres. Internat. Mktg. Communications Cons.'s, Gen. Electric Co., 1970-72; sr. v.p., dir. public relations Lewis & Gilman, Inc., Phila., 1972-74; exec. v.p. Creamer Dickson Basford, Inc., 1974-78; pres. Creamer Dickson Basford-New Eng., 1978—. Mem. Nat. Investor Relations Inst., Public Relations Soc. Am. (exec. com. Counselors Acad.), Aviation/Space Writers Assn., Internat. Public Relations Assn., Chi Psi. Republican. Episcopalian (vestryman). Clubs: Nat. Press, Overseas Press, Agawam Hunt, Hope, Dunes, Mohawk (Schenectady). Author: Polaris, 1960; Combat Missileman, 1961; Spacecraft and Missiles of the World, 1962; The Great Free Enterprise Gambit, 1980; also numerous articles on bus., aerospace and polit. subject. Office: 40 Westminster St Providence RI 02903 also 1301 Ave of Americas New York NY 10019

BAAR, LILLIAN MARY (MRS. WILLIAM D. BAAR), business exec.; b. Chgo.; d. James and Frances (Stanek) Shuss; student evening sch. J. Sterling Morton Jr. Coll., 1934-36; m. William D. Baar, July 25, 1942; 1 dau., Judith Barbara Baar Topinka. Sec. to pres. Thordarson Mfg. Co., Chgo., 1935-37; sec. to ofcls. Sears, Roebuck & Co., Chgo., 1937-43; real estate sales, Berwyn, Ill., 1943-44; co-owner, realtor, ins. broker Baar Realty Co., Berwyn, 1944-69; real estate cons., 1969-74; owner, mgr. Lillian Baar Ins. Agy., Berwyn, 1969—; co-founder Baar and Baar Realtors, 1976—. Bd. dirs. Berwyn Community Chest (name now United Way of Berwyn), 1968—, v.p., 1968-70, chmn., 1971-72; mem. Berwyn-Cicero Gov.'s Council Employment Handicapped; active ARC, Am. Heart Fund; trustee Dialogue, 1969—, 1st v.p., 1971-72, pres., 1972-74; bd. dirs. Berwyn Heart Fund, 1968; mem. Ladies Aid of Bohemian Home for Aged; v.p. Ill. Real Estate Council of City of Hope, 1976, chmn. bd., 1977-79. Recipient Meritorious Service award Dialogue, 1971; plaque Million Dollar Club of City of Hope Med. Center, 1976, 77, 78; honored in Town of Cicero resolution for outstanding bus. and civic leadership, 1972; named Citizen of Yr., Berwyn Rotary, 1975-76. Mem. Cermak Road Bus. Assn. (pres. 1961-64, dir. 1965—), Nat. Inst. Real Estate Brokers, West Towns Bd. Realtors (pres. 1965), Nat. (women's council), Ill. assns. Realtor bds., Nat. Inst. Realtor Bds., Nat., Ill., Berwyn (pres. 1973-75) fedns. bus. and profl. women's clubs, Ill. C. of C., Berwyn C. of C. (treas. 1979-80), Riverside C. of C., Women for Dialogue. Club: Mothers of Alpha Gamma Delta. Home: Riverside IL 60546 Office: 6335 W Cermak Rd Berwyn IL 60402

BABAYANS, EMIL, internat. trade co. exec.; b. Tehran, Iran, Nov. 9, 1951; s. Hacob and Jenik (Khatchatourian) B.; came to U.S., 1969; B.S., U. So. Calif., 1974, M.S.E.E., 1976; m. Annie Ashjian. Pres., Babtech Internat. Inc., Encino, Calif., 1975—. Mem. IEEE, Nat., Calif. socs. profl. engrs., Nat. Pilots Assn., Los Angeles Area C. of C., U. So. Calif. Alumni Assn., Am. Soc. Internat. Execs. Armenian Orthodox. Office: 15910 Ventura Blvd Suite 633 Encino CA 91436

BABB, BERT GRAYDON, retail grocer; b. Salem, Oreg., Feb. 4, 1933; s. Bert Graydon and Carrie Gail (Boak) B.; student Oreg. State U., 1951-52: m. Shirley Ann Hamilton, Oct. 9, 1953; children—Kimberley Sue, Konni Renee, John Michael. With McKay Markets-Mayfair Markets, 1955-69, head buyer, merchandizer Oreg. and Wash., Mayfair Markets, 1967-69; owner-mgr. Harolds Market, Veneta, Oreg., 1969—. Served with AUS, 1953-55. Mem. Food Mktg. Inst., Oreg. Food Industries, Inc., Oreg. Ind. Grocers. Republican. Clubs: Lions, Elks, Kiwanis (pres. Eugene 1962), Oreg. State U. Beaver. Home: 543 Echo Ln Eugene OR 97404 Office: 25101 Hwy 126 Veneta OR 94787

BABCOCK, MICHAEL JANE ALLEN (MRS. JAMES D. BABCOCK), computer co. exec.; b. Wichita, Kans., Sept. 17, 1926; d. Harry R. and Alma (Garrison) Allen; B.A., Roosevelt U., 1948; postgrad. U. Tex., 1948-49, U. Calif. at Los Angeles, 1960-62; m. James D. Babcock, Aug. 27, 1949 (div. Apr. 1969); 1 dau. Carla Anne. Sec.-treas. Allen-Babcock Computing, Inc., Los Angeles, 1965-67, exec. v.p., 1967-69, pres., 1969-73, also dir.; pres. Mitro Computer Corp., Los Angeles, 1973—. Bd. dirs. Century City Civic Council. Bd. dirs., exec. v.p. Know Found. Mem. Delta Phi Upsilon. Home: 805 San Vicente St Santa Monica CA 90402 Office: Suite 1204 1888 Century Park East Los Angeles CA 90067

BABCOCK, ROBERT ALLEN, constrn. co. exec.; b. Indpls., May 4, 1935; s. William Harvey and Beatrice Opal (Durst) B.; student Butler U., 1953-54; m. Virginia Ann Richardson, Sept. 2, 1955; children—Patricia Ann, Debra Sue. With William H. Babcock & Son, Indpls., 1954-70; owner Robert A. Babcock, Gen. Contractor, Indpls., 1970-77; pres. Babcock Constrn., Inc., Indpls., 1977—. Pres., Wayne Twp. Screening Caucus, 1970, pres. Danville Band Parents, 1972; trustee Danville United Methodist Ch., 1980—. Mem. Better Bus. Bur. Republican. Methodist. Clubs: Masons (Shriner). Home: Rural Route 6 Box 174 Danville IN 46122 Office: 951 Western Dr Indianapolis IN 46241

BABIONE, RICHARD FRANCIS, real estate broker; b. Toledo, Dec. 31, 1941; s. Francis Augustus and Beatrice (Harms) B.; student engring. and physics, Pa. State U., 1960-63; m. Carolyn S. Bucklew, Apr. 18, 1964; children—R. Kevin, Michelle D., Melinda S. Product mgr. Sci. instruments Nuclide Corp., 1965-69; realtor asso. James H. Williams, Realtor, 1969-73, Univ. Realty, 1973-76; broker, owner Nittany Realty, State College, Pa., 1976—; tchr. real estate appraisal Pa. State U. Bd. dirs. Penn Central Conf., United Ch. of Christ, exec. dir., 1980—, chmn. personnel com., 1979-80, asst. moderator Penn Central Conf., 1980—, moderator, 1982-84. Mem. Nat. Assn. Realtors (cert. real estate specialist, Grad. Realtors Inst.), Pa. Assn. Realtors, Centre County Bd. Realtors (dir. 1978-80), State College C. of C. (dir.). Democrat. Office: 315 S Allen St Suite 123 State College PA 16801

BABIUK, ZENON, paper co. exec.; b. Overiany, Poland, May 13, 1932; s. Theodore and Nida (Tereschyn) B.; grad. Sch. Polit. Scis., Germany, 1954; m. Oksana Macyk, Aug. 26, 1952; children—George Roxolana, Andrew, Tamara. Came to U.S., 1956, naturalized, 1962. Vice pres., sec. Am. Paper Goods Co., Bklyn., 1961-64; exec. v.p. Champion Envelope Mfg. Co., Bklyn., 1964-72; exec. v.p. Champion Industries, Inc., 1972-79; v.p., gen. mgr. Transo Envelope Co., 1979—. Bd. dirs. Harvard U. Ukrainian Studies Fund, Inc., 1960-78. Mem. Envelope Mfrs. Assn. (dir. 1975—), N.Y. and Eastern Envelope Assn. (dir. 1972-79). Editor Horizons, 1961-62. Home: 29 Fairview Terr Maplewood NJ 07040 Office: 184 Kent Ave Brooklyn NY 11211

BABSON, IRVING KONRAD, publishing co. exec.; b. Tel Aviv, Israel, Apr. 15, 1936; s. Matthew and Miriam Babson (father Am. citizen); B.B.A., Coll. City N.Y., 1957; m. Laurie Babson, Jan., 1980; children—Stacey B., Mia Lauren, Christopher. Exec. v.p., owner B.M.Y. Publs., Inc., N.Y.C., 1963—, also dir.; dir. Intercontinental Consultants Corp. Served with U.S. Army, 1956-57. Club: Friars (N.Y.C.). Home: 10 East End Ave New York NY 10021 Office: 254 W 31st St New York NY 10001

BABUDRO, EGIDIO A., med. equipment co. exec.; b. Rijeka, Yugoslavia, Feb. 18, 1936; s. Angelo and Maria (Kisic) B.; B.A., U. Minn., 1963, B.Sc.Ed., 1968; m. Victoria S. Klos, July 11, 1959; children—Pernell T.A., Angelique M.P., Angelica M.P., Parnell T.A. Regional service mgr. Midwest Narco Med. Services, Mpls., 1970-72; coordinator biomedical technology Bown Inst., Mpls., 1972-74; program dir. biomedical equipment technology Sch. Dist. 287, Eden Prairie, Minn., 1974—; founder, pres. Electronic Systems Internat. design and mfg., Mpls., 1972—, Med. Design Instrumentation, sales and service, Mpls., 1974—. Mem. Med. Electronic and Data Soc., Assn. Advancement Med. Instrumentation, Am. Soc. Hosp. Engrs., IEEE (chmn. engring. medicine and biology). Contbr. articles to profl. jours. Home: 10684 Terrace Rd NE Minneapolis MN 55434 Office: 540 Greenhaven Rd Anoka MN 55303

BACA, ALEX S., mktg. co. exec.; b. Taos, N.Mex., July 3, 1919; s. Jose M. and Adelida (Valdez) B.; B.S. in Bus. Adminstrn., U. Okla., 1947; m. Anna M. Adams, Jan. 5, 1945; children—Mark Ira, Michael Bruce. With IRS, 1947-48; life underwriter Mut. Life of N.Y., 1948-50; dist. agt. Continental Assurance Co., also Continental Casualty Co., 1950-60; gen. agt. Pacific, Fidelity Life Ins. Co., 1960-63, Continental Assurance Co., 1963-69, loan corr., 1969-73; chmn. bd., pres. Central Investment & Leasing Corp., Sacramento, 1969-71; sec. Nat Gas Mfg. Inc., Oakland, Calif., 1971-72; sec.-treas. Trinity Minerals, Inc., Sacramento, 1970-73; gen. agt. Security Life of Denver, 1973-74; chmn. bd., pres. CENPAC Fin., Inc., Sacramento, 1974—; part-owner Old Sacramento Cocktail, Inc., cocktail mix mfrs. Pres. Bowling Green PTA, 1959, now hon. life mem.; active Cub Scouts, 1960; commentator, lector St. Charles Borromeo Roman Catholic Parish, 1972—, mem. parish council, 1976—. Served with USAAF, 1941-45. Recipient Quality award Life Underwriters Assn., 1959, 63. Mem. Am. Begonia Soc. Republican. Club: K.C. Home: 6936 Ruskut Way Sacramento CA 95823 Office: 1900 Point West Way Suite 148 Sacramento CA 95815

BACH, FRED IVAN, businessman; b. San Francisco, Feb. 13, 1915; s. James Carl and Mercedes Enriqueta (Araujo) B.; student Loyola U., 1938; m. Leonor Ruffo, Aug. 2, 1947; children—Frederick, Leonor. Sales mgr. Continental Steel Bldgs., Los Angeles, 1950-53; founder, dir. Farma, S.A., Mexico City, 1954-80; founder, pres. Representaciones Mex-Am., S.A., Mexico City, 1955—; cons. Sociedad Angiología de México, Colegio Internacional de Cirujanos. Served to capt. U.S. Army, 1943-47; PTO. Mem. Asociación Mexicana de Medicina Ortomolecular (founder, pres.). Home: 441 Risco Jardines del Pedregal México 20 DF México Office: 264 Diagonal 20 de Noviembre México 8 DF México

BACH, FRED W(ILHELM), mgmt. cons.; b. Mannheim, W. Ger., Mar. 24, 1930; s. Wilhelm and Else (Mueller) B.; came to U.S., 1972; M.B.A., U. Mannheim, 1954; postgrad. U. Hamburg, 1955-57; m. Helga Gudrun Rieg, Dec. 5, 1970. Cons., Quickborner Team, Hamburg, W. Ger., 1960-66, partner, 1967—; exec. v.p., treas. Quickborner Team, Inc., Millburn, N.J., 1973-75, pres., 1975—; lectr. profl. groups and orgns. Mem. Adminstrv. Mgmt. Soc., Office Landscape Users Group, German-Am. C. of C. Contbr. articles on office planning and mgmt. to various publs. Home: New York NY Office: 402 E 87th St New York NY 10028

BACH, STANLEY GOTTER, real estate developer; b. Burbank, Calif., Apr. 1, 1938; s. Stanley Fredrick and Betty Jane (McCarthy) Gotter; A.A., Cypress Coll., 1969; m. Judith Ann Price, Apr. 1, 1959; children—Laura Leigh, James Richard. With Fox Food Fair, Los Angeles, 1956-68; v.p., controller Tri Sonic Inc., Los Angeles, 1968-69; asst. supermarket mgr. Alpha Beta, La Habra, Calif., 1969-72; owner, real estate salesman Red Carpet, Garden Grove, Calif., 1972-75; owner, operator S. G. Bach Devel. Co., Temecula, Calif., 1975—, Temecula Real Estate Brokers, 1980—; founding v.p., past pres. Rancho-Temecula-Murrieta Bd. Realtors; polit. affairs chmn. 14th dist. Calif. Assn. Realtors. Mem. camping com. Temescal dist., asst. scout master Boy Scouts Am.; founder U.S. Freedom Library, Temecula. Mem. Nat. Assn. Realtors, Calif. Assn. Realtors (dir.), Rancho-Temecula-Murrieta Multiple Listing Service (founding v.p., past pres.). Republican. Roman Catholic. Club: Kiwanis (charter mem., founding dir. Rancho-Temecula). Home: 24405 Fuerte Rd Temecula CA 92390 Office: SG Bach Devel Co 27884 Del Rio Rd Temecula CA 92390

BACHER, JUDITH ST. GEORGE, exec. search cons.; b. New Rochelle, N.Y., July 14, 1946; d. Thomas A. and Rose-Marie (Martocci) Baiocchi; B.S., Georgetown U., 1968; M.L.S., Columbia U., 1971; m. Albert Bacher, Jan. 2, 1972; 1 son, Alexander Michael. Researcher, Time mag., N.Y.C., 1968-71; librarian Mus. Modern Art, N.Y.C., 1971-72; cons. Informaco Inc., N.Y.C., 1972-74, Booz-Allen & Hamilton, N.Y.C., 1974-79; research dir. MBA Resources/Keating Grimm & Leeper, N.Y.C., 1979—; mem. Adv. Com. on Personnel, Exec. Office of Pres., 1979—. Mem. Phi Beta Kappa. Home: 119 W 87th St New York NY 10024 Office: MBA Resources Inc 717 Fifth Ave New York NY 10022

BACHER, RONALD THOMAS, business exec.; b. Elyria, Ohio, Apr. 9, 1940; s. Carl Walter and Hilda G. (Gillis) B.; B.M.E., U. Detroit, 1964, M.B.A., 1972; m. Claudine A. Lendo, June 20, 1964 (div. Apr. 1980); children—Bradley Thomas, Joanna Lynn, Jason Ronald. Cons., computer applications, research and devel. div. Fruehauf Corp., Detroit, 1967-71, mgr. finance contracts Fruehauf Fin. Co., 1971-77; owner, operator Pickle Barrel Bar, 1978—. Treas., Voice for Mentally Handicapped, 1976-77, trustee, 1976-78. Mem. Nat. Assn. Accts. Club: Optimists (dir. 1979-81, v.p. 1981-82). Home: 412 Center Ave Bay City MI 48706

BACHTOLD, HAROLD ERNEST, investment co. exec.; b. Walla Walla, Wash., July 28, 1912; s. Ernest Frederick and Christine (Rtzer) B.; A.A., Sacramento Jr. Coll., 1933; student San Francisco Law Sch., 1935-36; m. Louise Marie Hollingsworth, May 16, 1939; children—Barbara, Patricia, Christine. With So. Pacific Co., San Francisco, 1935-43; public relations Whitaker & Baxter, San Francisco, 1944-45; pres. H.E. Bachtold Co., Inc. subs. Am. Internat. Comml. Corp., N.Y.C. and Calif., 1946-50; exec. sec. Calif. State Assembly Com. on Govt. Reorgn., 1950-53; asst. to speaker Calif. State Legislature, 1953-57; sr. account exec. Dean Witter Reynolds, Inc., Sacramento, 1958—. Bd. regents Calif. Luth. Coll., 1965-68. Mem. San Francisco Press Club. Republican. Lutheran. Club: El Macero (Calif.) Country. Home: 2941 Garden Ct El Macero CA 95618 Office: 455 Capitol Mall Sacramento CA 95814

BACHYNSKI, MORREL PAUL, electronics co. exec.; b. Bienfait, Sask., Can., July 19, 1930; s. Nicholas and Karolina B.; B.Engring., U. Sask., 1952, M.S., 1953; Ph.D., McGill U., 1955; m. Slava Krkovic, May 30, 1959; children—Caroline Dawn, Jane Diane. Lab. dir. RCA Ltd., Montreal, Que., Can., 1960-65, dir. research, 1965-75, v.p. research and devel., 1975-76; pres. MPB Technologies Inc., Ste. Anne de Bellevue, Que., 1977—; chmn. bd. Bytek Electronic Inc. Recipient David Sarnoff award, 1963; Prix Scientifique du Que., 1974; Queens Silver Jubilee medal, 1977; Can. Enterprize award, 1977. Fellow Can. Aeros. and Space Inst., Royal Soc. Can., Am. Phys. Soc., IEEE. Author: (with others) The Particle Kinetics of Plasmas, 1968; contbr. articles to profl. jours. Home: 78 Thurlow Rd Montreal PQ H3X 3G9 Canada Office: PO Box 160 Sainte Anne de Bellevue PQ H9X 3L5 Canada

BACKE, LOUIS MICHAEL, III, electronics co. exec.; b. Phila., Aug. 19, 1927; s. Louis Michael and Ann (Strecker) B.; B.S., LaSalle Coll., 1951; m. Jeanne Marie Doran, May 4, 1957; children—Lisa Ann, Mark Joseph, Carol Marie, Joanne Clare, Michael Louis. Account exec. RCA Tube Div., S.E., 1954-59; pres. E. Coast Electronics, Orlando, Fla., 1959-63; exec. v.p. Electronic Wholesalers, Orlando, 1963-70; pres. Electronic Wholesalers, Hollywood, Fla., 1970-71; sr. v.p. Cramer Electronics, Newton, Mass., 1971-77; v.p. Arrow Electronics, S.E. and S. Central Region, Norcross, Ga., 1977—. Served with USMC, 1945-47, 51-53. Mem. Nat. Electronic Distbr. Assn., USMC Res. Officers Assn. Republican. Roman Catholic. Club: Jockey. Home: 7975 Monticello Dr Dunwoody GA 30338 Office: 2979 Pacific Dr Norcross GA 30071

BACKERT, VANCE RICHARD, real estate broker; b. Glendale, Calif., June 29, 1954; s. Ernest Walter and Beverley June Backert; A.A., Coll. of Canyons, Valencia, Calif., 1976; m. Jackie A. Vaughan, Nov. 25, 1978. Engaged in real estate, 1972—; propr. V.R.B. Co., Newhall, Calif., 1975—. Mem. Nat. Assn. Realtors, Calif. Assn. Realtors (regional v.p. 1981), Santa Clarita Valley Bd. Realtors (pres. 1979, 80). Nat. Fedn. Ind. Bus. Address: PO Box 780 Newhall CA 91322

BACON, J. RAYMOND, mfg. exec.; b. Chgo., Aug. 11; s. Elmer Winfield and Alma C. (Romburg) B.; diploma in commerce Northwestern U., 1943; M.A., Western U., 1950; m. Florence I. Burdine, Nov. 5, 1927 (dec. Nov. 1960); 1 dau., Grace Florence (Mrs. John W. Bacher); m. 2d, Margaret Austin, Nov. 30, 1963. Asst. mgr. King Woodworking Co., Chgo., 1926-34; dept. head Montgomery Ward & Co., Chgo. and Albany, N.Y., 1935-40; v.p., gen. mgr. O.D. Jennings & Co., Chgo., 1940-48; exec. v.p. Rockola Mfg. Co., Chgo., 1948-54; pres. F.H. Noble & Co., 1954-67, F.H. Noble & Co. (Can.) Ltd., 1956-67; chief exec. officer F.H. Noble & Co. Ltd. (Ireland), 1962-67; pres. Draftette Co., 1967—. Mem. AIM, Hemet C. of C., Calif. Mfrs. Assn., Art Inst. Chgo., Am. Mgmt. Assn., Soc. Advancement Mgmt. (past v.p.). Presbyterian. Club: Kiwanis. Home: PO Box 895 Hemet CA 92343 Office: 26951 Cawston Ave Hemet CA 92343

BACON, WILLIAM THOMPSON, JR., investment co. exec.; b. Chgo., Feb. 6, 1923; s. William Thompson and Martha (Smith) B.; grad. Phillips Acad., 1941; B.A., Yale, 1945; m. Margaret Hoyt, Apr. 18, 1942; children—William Thompson III, Catherine (Mrs. Von Stroh), Hoyt Wells, J. Knight, Christopher S. Asst. cashier First Nat. Bank of Chgo., 1946-55; partner Bacon, Whipple & Co., Chgo., 1956—; dir. Walbro Corp., Safecard Services, Inc. Trustee Hadley Sch. for Blind, Winnetka, Ill., Fountain Valley Sch., Colorado Springs, Colo. Served with AUS, 1943-44. Mem. Elihu, Delta Kappa Epsilon. Republican. Episcopalian. Clubs: Yale (pres. 1962-63), Chicago, University (Chgo.); Onwentsia (Lake Forest, Ill.); Shoreacres (Lake Bluff, Ill.); Old Elm (Ft. Sheridan, Ill.); Indian Hill (Winnetka, Ill.); Yale (N.Y.C.); Gulfstream Golf (Delray Beach, Fla.). Home: 1300 N Waukegan Rd Lake Forest IL 60045 Office: 135 S LaSalle St Chicago IL 60603

BACOT, JOHN CARTER, banker; b. Utica, N.Y., Feb. 7, 1933; s. John Vacher and Edna (Gunn) B.; A.B., Hamilton Coll., Clinton, N.Y., 1955; LL.B., Cornell U., 1958; m. Shirley Schou, Nov. 26, 1960; children—Elizabeth, Susan. Admitted to N.Y. bar, 1959; with firm, Utica, 1959-60; with Bank of N.Y., N.Y.C., 1960—, pres., 1974—, also dir.; dir. Cirfico Holdings Corp., Home Life Ins. Co., Am. Internat. Group, Bank of N.Y. Internat. Corp., Bank of N.Y. Co., Inc. Chartered fin. analyst. Mem. Econ. Club N.Y., Pilgrims of U.S., Assn. Res. City Bankers, N.Y. Community Trust. Episcopalian. Club: Montclair Golf. Office: Bank of NY 48 Wall St New York NY 10015*

BACZKO, JOSEPH RICHARD, cosmetic mfg. co. exec.; b. Deggendorf, Germany, June 10, 1945; came to U.S., 1956, naturalized, 1967; s. Joseph and Elizabeth (Csanitz) B.; B.S. in Fgn. Service, Georgetown U., 1967; M.B.A. (W.T. Grant fellow), Harvard U., 1974; m. Kathleen Adams, June 7, 1967; children—Laura, Stephen, David. Fin. adv. William Rosenwald & Assos., N.Y.C., 1974-76; v.p. ops. Baker & Taylor Co. div. W.R. Grace & Co., N.Y.C., 1976-78, group v.p. ops. and devel. parent co., 1978-79; v.p. devel. Max Factor & Co., Hollywood, Calif., 1979-80, mng. dir., chief exec. officer Max Factor U.K. and European Group, London, 1980—. Served to capt. USMC, 1969-72. Decorated Navy Commendation medal. Home: 3 Duryea Rd Upper Montclair NJ 07043 also Greenways Danes Hill Hockering Woking England Office: 16 Old Bond St London England

BADNER, BARRY, indsl. engr.; b. Bklyn., Dec. 15, 1937; s. Hyman and Ray (Wachtelkoenig) B.; B. Indsl. Engring., N.Y. U., 1959, M.S. in Ops. Research, 1964; m. Heather Laurie, July 16, 1967; children—Ray Ann, Bruce Mitchell, David Alan. Engr., Burndy Corp., Norwalk, Conn., 1960-63, Estes Industries, Inc., N.Y.C., 1964-65, Drake, Sheahan/Stewart Dougall, N.Y.C., 1966-68; pres. Zelner and Badner, Inc., N.Y.C., 1969—; treas., dir. Medinvent, Inc. Trustee Moriah Sch. of Englewood (N.J.), Congregation Ahavath Torah, Englewood. Served with U.S. Army, 1959-60. Mem. Soc. Profl. Mgmt. Consultants (v.p.), Am. Assn. Hosp. Planning, Assn. Advancement Med. Instrumentation. Co-inventor component mounting. Home: 261 Robin Rd Englewood NJ 07631 Office: 501 Fifth Ave New York NY 10017

BADOYEN, ANDREW, ins. co. exec.; b. Lihue, Kauai, Hawaii, Aug. 24, 1945; s. Telesforo and Harriet (Gifford) Alica; A.A., Maui Community Coll., 1966; m. Norma Ann Ganialongo, June 20, 1968; children—Dean Andrew, Kristi Lynn Malia. With 1st Ins. Co. of Hawaii Ltd., 1966—, asst. mgr., Wailuku, 1973-75, resident v.p., gen. mgr., 1975—. Bd. dirs. Maui council Boy Scouts Am. Mem. Nat. Assn. Life Underwriters, Hawaii Ins. Assn., Nat. Fedn. Ind. Bus., Nat. Home Builders Assn. Democrat. Home: 1133 Mano Dr Kula Maui HI 96790 Office: 30 N Church St Wailuku Maui HI 96793

BAEHREL, PETER WILLIAM, mfg. co. exec.; b. Jamaica, N.Y., July 15, 1940; s. William Julius and Frances Elizabeth (Gingell) B.; student U. Fla., 1958-60; m. Judith Geuder, June 20, 1970; children—Michael Christian, Suzanne Michelle. Office mgr. Mehron Inc., N.Y.C., 1960-64; supr. facilities AMF Inc., White Plains, N.Y., 1965-73, mgr. facilities and equipment, purchasing agt., 1974-77, mgr. adminstrv. services and purchasing agt., 1978—. Served with Army N.G., 1961-68. Mem. Soc. Food Service Mgmt., Purchasing Assn. Seven Counties, Nat. Fire Protection Assn. Home: 8 Van Dyke Ave Suffern NY 10901 Office: 777 Westchester Ave White Plains NY 10604

BAER, WILLIAM HAROLD, business exec.; b. Eatontown, N.J., Dec. 6, 1947; s. Irving and Martha Ann (Ruddy) B.; B.S. in Bus. Adminstrn., Waynesburg Coll., 1971. Pres., Baldinos, Inc., Fayetteville, N.C., 1976—, Rondout Country Club, Ltd., Accord, N.Y., 1979—. Served to 1st lt. USMC, 1971-75. Recipient Navy Achievement medal. Office: PO Box 194 Accord NY 12404

BAERNS, ROBERT RUDOLPH, crating and packaging co., holding co. exec.; b. Melrose Park, Ill., Mar. 2, 1937; s. Rudolph and Doris Viola (Behnke) B.; A.A., Pasadena City Coll., 1957; B.S. in Bus. Adminstrn., Calif. State U., Los Angeles, 1959; m. Marleen Marilynne Morris, Dec. 30, 1961; children—Jeffrey James, Scott Stuart, Lori Lynne, Corey Craig. Sales rep., area sales mgr. Colgate Palmolive Co., Los Angeles, 1962-66, 68-74, Phoenix, 1966-67; sales mgr. Wood Space Industries, Buena Park, Calif., 1974, pres., 1974—; founder, pres. Baerns Enterprises, Inc., 1980—. Vol. umpire-in-chief Little League, Santa Ana, Calif., 1975-79, also mgr. coach various teams. Served with U.S. Army, 1959-62. Mem. Soc. Packaging and Handling Engrs. (sec.-treas. Orange County chpt. 1977—). Republican. Lutheran. Home: 1013 E 21st St Santa Ana CA 92706 Office: 6400 Roland St Buena Park CA 90621

BAGATELLE, WARREN DENIS, publishing co. exec.; b. Mt. Vernon, N.Y., Aug. 19, 1938; s. S. Jerry and Rose F. B.; B.A. in Econs., Union Coll., 1960; M.B.A., Rutgers U., 1961; m. Hedy S. Schwartz, Nov. 22, 1962; children—David, Tracy, Adrien. Mgr., Arthur Andersen & Co., N.Y.C. and Rochester, N.Y., 1962-69; v.p. adminstrn. and fin. Ilex Optical Co., Inc., Rochester, 1969-73; pres. Meson Electronics Co., Inc., Rochester, 1973-74; v.p. fin. Cross River Products Inc., Rochester, 1974-77; exec. v.p. Univ. Soc. Inc., Mahwah, N.J., 1977—. Served with 1961-62. C.P.A., N.Y. Mem. Am. Inst. C.P.A.'s, N.Y. State Soc. C.P.A.'s. Home: 75 Urban Club Rd Wayne NJ 07470 Office: Colonial Office Bldg Whitney Rd Mahwah NJ 07430

BAGBY, JOSEPH RIGSBY, investment banker, restaurant exec., real estate exec., author; b. Banner Elk, N.C., Aug. 23, 1935; s. Wesley Marvin, Jr. and Ila Paunee (Rigsby) B.; student Fla. State U., 1955; B.B.A. in Econs., U. Miami, 1959; m. Martha Lane Green, Jan. 1, 1966; 1 dau., Meredith Elaine. Supr., Miami Herald Pub. Co. (Fla.), 1953-63; with Oscar E. Dooly Assos., 1962-63; v.p. Jack Thomas Assos., 1963-66; real estate mgr., dir. real estate Burger King Corp., 1966-70; founder Property Resources Co., Inc., Miami, 1971, pres., 1971—, also dir.; pres. Joseph R. Bagby Assos., 1974—, Bagby, Alai & Co., Inc.; dir. Leisure Industries. Pres., U. Miami Young Democrats, 1958-59; dist. sec.-treas. Young Dems., 1959. Served with U.S. Army, 1959-61. Decorated 82d Airborne certificate of achievement; recipient Iron Arrow award U. Miami, 1958; Fla. Real Estate Golden Circle award, 1965; Recognition award Soc. Real Estate Appraisers, 1977. Mem. Internat. Real Estate Fedn., Fla. Mortgage Bankers Assn., Nat. Assn. Corp. Real Estate Execs. (founder, chmn. bd., pres. 1969-75, chmn. bd. trustees 1978—), Am. Mgmt. Assn., League of Econ. Devel. Orgns., Pres.'s Assn., Progress Club Miami (founder), Fla. State U., U. Miami alumni assns., Sigma Chi. Episcopalian. Club: Downtown Miami Optimist. Author: Real Estate Financing Desk Book, 1975. Co-editor: Hurricane campus newspaper, 1958-59. Contbr. articles to profl. jours. Office: 501 Spencer Dr West Palm Beach FL 33409

BAGBY, MARTHA L. GREEN (MRS. JOSEPH R. BAGBY), investment banker, mortgage banker, restaurant exec., author; b. West Palm Beach, Fla., June 17, 1937; d. Hampton and Louise (Lambert) Green; A.A., Palm Beach Jr. Coll., 1957; A.B., U. Miami, 1959; M.A., Pa. State U., 1964; m. Joseph R. Bagby, 1965. Tchr. English, journalism Palm Beach County, Fla., 1959-62; instr. journalism Pa. State U., 1962-63; city editor, writer Palm Beach News & Life, 1963-64; editor Alfred Hitchcock Mag., Riviera Beach, Fla., 1964; editor, supr. editorial services, pub. relations employee newspaper Nat. Airlines, Inc., Miami, Fla., 1965-73; corporate sec., chmn. bd. Property Resources Co., Coral Gables, Fla., 1971—; Ill. franchisee Burger King Corp.; lectr. journalism Dade and Palm Beach Counties; instr. Barry Coll., Miami. Mem. exec. bd. Childbirth and Parent Edn. Assn., Miami. Mem. Fla. Pub. Relations Assn., S. Fla. Indsl. Editors, Internat. Council Indsl. Editors, Airline Editors Conf., Air Transport Assn. Am. (chmn.), Women in Communications Inc. (pres. chpt.), Nat. Assn. Corporate Real Estate Execs. (trustee), Kappa Tau Alpha. Author: (novel) Stranglehold, 1977; co-author: The Complete Real Estate Book. Office: 471 Spencer Dr S Suite 3 West Palm Beach FL 33409

BAGLEY, RALPH COLT, grain co. exec.; b. Mpls., Apr. 13, 1915; s. Ralph Colt and Margaret Stanton (Noyes) B.; student Yale U., 1938; m. Mary Jim Foley, Sept. 13, 1960; children—Bridget, Florenel, R. Colt, George. With Bagley Grain Co., Mpls., 1929—, v.p., 1940-49, pres., 1949—. Councilman, Village of Orono (Minn.), 1952-66; warden St. Marins Ch., Minnetonka Beach, Minn., 1957-59; trustee St. James Sch., Faribault, Minn., 1954-79. Episcopalian. Clubs: Woodhill Country (trustee 1944-79) (Wayzata, Minn.); Mpls. Home: 905 Ferndale Rd W Wayzata MN 55391 Office: 654 Grain Exchange Bldg Minneapolis MN 55415

BAHL, JOHN CHARLES, banker; b. Nashville, July 19, 1943; s. Charles D. and Margaret J. (Hilberg) B.; B.S. in Fin., U. Ariz., 1965; postgrad. Stonier Coll., Rutgers U., 1973-76; m. Margaret D. White, Nov. 15, 1965; 1 son, Forrest John. Vice pres. corp. lending Provident Bank, Cin., 1967-77; pres., chief exec. officer Sun Bank St. Lucie County, Ft. Pierce, Fla., 1977—, also dir. Mem. Am. Bankers Assn., Fla. Bankers Assn. Club: Rioniar Bay Yacht. Home: 300 Harbour Dr Apt 102B Vero Beach FL 32960 Office: PO Box 8 Fort Pierce FL 33450

BAHR, WILLIAM AMEND, mfg. co. exec.; b. Kohler, Wis., June 30, 1928; s. Oscar H. and Wilhelmeta M. (Amend) B.; B.A., Valparaiso U., 1950; postgrad. Northwestern U., 1953-59; m. Carol J. Kiel, Dec. 1, 1951; children—Thomas, Jonathan, Pegge. With Am. Can Co., 1953-69, 73-77, 78—, mgr. ops., Chgo., 1966-69, plant mgr., Washington, N.J., 1973-75, dir. facilities evaluation, Greenwich, Conn., 1975-77, mng. dir. mfg. Am. Techs. div., Greenwich, 1978—; dir. prodn. Reads Ltd., Liverpool, Eng., 1969-73, also dir.; pres. Chempar Corp., Montgomeryville, Pa., 1978; v.p., dir. Hanover (Pa.) Indsl. Machinery Co. Trustee, Millneck Manor Found., Millneck Sch. for the Deaf. Served with Chem. Corps., U.S. Army, 1950-53. Mem. Chem. Soc., Am. Soc. Quality Control, Soc. Mfg. Engrs. Republican. Lutheran. Home: 33 Crescent Bend Allendale NJ 07401 Office: Am Can Co American Ln Greenwich CT 06380

BAICH, EDWARD V., pollution control co. exec.; b. Akron, Ohio, Jan. 11, 1936; s. Mary C. (Stitchko) B.; B.S. in Bus. Adminstrn., U. Akron, 1960; M.S. in Mgmt., Frostburg State Coll., 1971-73; children—Diane Lyn, Virginia Ann, Brenda Jean, Edward James. Sr. acct. Haskins & Sells, C.P.A.'s, N.Y.C., 1960-64; dir. acctg. Borden Foods Group Borden Co., N.Y.C., 1964-67; plant mgr., dir. finance Fairchild Industries, Hagerstown, Md., 1967-72; div. controller, Kama project mgr. Pangborn div. Carborundum Co., Hagerstown, Md., 1972-75; v.p., gen. mgr. pollution control div. Carborundum Co., Knoxville, Tenn., 1975-79; group v.p. environ. systems group Kennecott Devel. Co., Kennecott Corp., 1979—; past dir. Indsl. Gas Cleaning Inst., Inc. Bd. dirs. Jr. Achievement of Greater Knoxville, 1978-79. Served with AUS, 1954-56. Mem. Nat. Assn. Accts., Am. Mgmt. Assn., Indsl. Gas Cleaning Inst., Beta Delta Psi. Republican. Lutheran. Home: 222 Dublin Rd Knoxville TN 37919

BAILENSON, STEWART LEE, unemployment compensation cost control specialist; b. St. Louis, June 6, 1939; s. Albert and Ruth Bailenson; B.S. in Bus. Adminstrn., Washington U., St. Louis, 1961; m. Carol Sue Tennenbaum, Dec. 31, 1961; children—Mark, Kenneth, Melissa, Daniel, Alexander. Field service rep. R.E. Harrington Inc., Columbus, Ohio, 1965-68; asst. v.p. Reed, Roberts Assos. Inc., Garden City, N.Y., 1968-74; sr. v.p., regional mgr. James E. Frick Inc., St. Louis, 1974—; expert witness Mo. and Mich. legislatures, Nat. Commn. Unemployment Compensation. Mem. C. of C. of U.S. (labor com.), Mich. State C. of C. (labor com.), Ill. State C. of C. (unemployment compensation com.), Alpha Kappa Psi. Author: How to Control Unemployment Compensation Costs, 1976, 2d edit., Control Your Unemployment Compensation Costs, 1980; also articles. Home: 14818 South St Woodstock IL 60098 Office: 20 N Wacker Dr Chicago IL 60606

BAILEY, CARL FRANKLIN, telephone co. exec.; b. Birmingham, Ala., Sept. 17, 1930; s. Carl G. and Susan (Adair) B.; B.S. in Bus. Adminstrn., Auburn U., 1952; postgrad. Dartmouth Coll., 1967; m. Jean Jones Bailey, Dec. 15, 1956; children—Carl C., Jeffry F. With So. Bell Telephone Co., 1955-68, gen. mktg. mgr. Ala., Birmingham, 1964, asst. v.p. for Ala., 1965-68; exec. asst. AT&T, Washington, 1968-71; asst. to pres. S. Central Bell Telephone Co., co. hdqrs., Birmingham, 1971-72, gen. mgr. ops., 1972-75, v.p. customer and facility services, 1976, v.p. La., New Orleans, 1977—; dir. Rush Hampton Inc., Orlando, Fla. Trustee, YMCA; trustee, mem. exec. com. Public Affairs Research Council La., Inc.; trustee, chmn. gen. campaign United Way; bd. dirs. Internat. Trade Mart, Tidewater Devel. Assn., La. Assn. Bus. and Industry, Met. Crime Commn.; pres., bd. dirs. La. World Exposition, Inc.; bd. dirs., mem. exec. com. Econ. Devel. Council; sr. v.p., bd. dirs., mem. exec. com. Met. Area Com.; bd. dirs., mem. exec. com. New Orleans Philharm. Symphony, Council for a Better La.; mem. Bus. Task Force on Edn.; mem. pres.'s council Loyola U., New Orleans; mem. ann. fund council Dillard-Xavier. Served to 1st lt. AUS, 1952-55. Methodist. Office: 365 Canal St Suite 3000 New Orleans LA 70140

BAILEY, FREDERICK E., JR., chem. co. exec.; b. Bklyn., Oct. 8, 1927; s. Frederick E. and Florence (Berkeley) B.; A.B., Amherst Coll., 1948; M.S., Yale U., 1950, Ph.D., 1952; m. Mary Catherine Lowder, May 7, 1979. With Union Carbide Corp., South Charleston, W.Va., 1952—, research chemist, 1952-59, group leader in polymer chemistry, 1959-61, asst. dir. research and devel., 1962-69, tech. mgr. calendering, flooring and record products, 1964-65, technology mgr. vinyls, 1965-67, market study, 1968-69, mgr. market research chems. and plastics, 1969-71, sr. research scientist, 1971—, futures research specialist chem. industry, 1974-76; lectr. polymer chemistry U. Charleston, 1960-61, 65-66; lectr. phys. chemistry Kanawha Grad. Center, W.Va. U., 1959-60; adj. prof. chemistry Marshall U., 1975—; mem. council Gordon Research Conf. Fellow AAAS, Am. Inst. Chemists, N.Y. Acad. Scis.; mem. Am. Chem. Soc. (vice chmn. div. polymer chemistry 1975, chmn. div. 1976, councilor 1978—, sec. gen. macromolecular secretariat 1977, 78, sci. commr. 1978; vice chmn. div. officers caucus 1979-80, chmn. 1980—, div. activities com.), Am. Phys. Soc., Soc. Rheology, Gordon Research Conf. on Polymers (vice chmn. 1971, chmn. 1972), Phi Beta Kappa, Sigma Xi, Alpha Chi Sigma, Alpha Delta Phi. Contbr. articles to tech. jours. Patentee in field. Home: 848 Beaumont Rd Charleston WV 25314 Office: Technical Center PO Box 8361 South Charleston WV 25303

BAILEY, GLENN JOSEPH, ins. co. exec.; b. Dunbar, W.Va., Apr. 17, 1933; s. Roy Nathaniel and Odree (Bailey) G.; A.B., U. Pa., 1968; m. Barbara D. Behnke, Feb. 11, 1956; 1 dau., Patrice Lee. With Ins. Co. of N. Am., 1955-79, asst. v.p. INA Reins. Corp., Phila., 1977-79; sr. v.p. Burt and Scheld Corp., Ormond Beach, Fla., 1979—. Served with USAF, 1951-55. C.P.C.U. Home: 1 Fernwood Trail Ormond Beach FL 32074 Office: 140 S Atlantic Ave Ormond Beach FL 32074

BAILEY, JESSE EDWARD, Realtor; b. San Diego, Mar. 26, 1917; s. Jesse Wray and Huldah (Salquist) B.; B.A., San Diego State U., 1939; m. Marian Elizabeth Johnson, Jan. 20, 1945; children—Alan Edward, Karen E. Farley. With San Diego Ind. Newspaper Group, 1940-70, prodn. mgr., 1963-66, gen. mgr., publisher, 1966-70; sales exec. Land Cons. Am., San Diego, 1970-73; realtor Bailey & Assos., La Mesa, Calif., 1973—; prin. Bailey & Assos., publishers books on history of San Diego. Bd. dirs. Samarkand, Santa Barbara, Calif., Hearthstone Manor, Folsom, Calif., Homemakers for Children, San Diego; pres. Coop. Traders. Served as lt. USNR, World War II. Recipient newspaper circulation mgmt. service awards. Chmn. exec. bd. Mt. Miguel Covenant Village, Spring Valley, Calif., 1964—. Mem. Evang. Covenant Ch. Am. (nat. bd. benevolence, nat. social service commn.). Home: 8645 Butte St La Mesa CA 92041 Office: 8080 La Mesa Blvd Suite 106 La Mesa CA 92041

BAILEY, LEONARD LESLIE, JR., elec. engr.; b. Birmingham, Ala., Aug. 29, 1950; s. Leonard Leslie and Beverly June (Amerine) B.; B.S. in Elec. Engring., Auburn (Ala.) U., 1977; m. Mary Laraine McGowan, Feb. 18, 1978. Nuclear constrn. elec. engr. Electric Boat div. Gen. Dynamics Corp., Groton, Conn., 1977; nuclear ops. quality assurance engr. Ala. Power Co., Birmingham, 1978—. Served with Submarine Service, USN, 1971-75. Mem. Nat. Soc. Profl. Engrs., IEEE, Engring. Mgmt. Soc., Nuclear and Plasma Sci. Soc., Power Engring. Soc. Republican. Baptist. Home: 1 Town and Country Circle Birmingham AL 35215 Office: 600 N 18th St Room 732 Birmingham AL 35291

BAILEY, MICHAEL MAYNE, ins. co. exec.; b. Beloit, Wis., Aug. 3, 1936; s. Benjamin Franklin and Frances Jay B.; A.A., Jackson Jr. Coll., 1957; B.B.A., U. Mich., 1959, M.B.A., 1960; m. Pamela Jean Clark, Aug. 14, 1971; 1 dau., Nancy Ruth. Jr. accountant Arthur

Young & Co., Chgo., 1960-61; asst. treas. Interstate Fire & Casualty Co., Chgo., 1961-67; controller Foremost Life Ins. Co., Grand Rapids, Mich., 1967-78; life ins. accounting mgr. Pub. Service Life Ins. Co., Sioux City, Iowa, 1978—. Mem. Greenville (Mich.) Bd. Edn., 1971-78, v.p., 1972-75. Fellow Life Office Mgmt. Assn.; mem. Nat. Acctg. Assn. (v.p. membership Sioux City chpt. 1980-81), Inst. Internal Auditors (certified internal auditor), Sioux City Mus. Assn. (pres.). Clubs: Lions (past dist. sec./treas.) (Sioux City). Home: 4033 Sherwood Terr Sioux City IA 51106 Office: 814 Pierce St Sioux City IA 51101

BAILEY, ROBERT JACKSON, chemist; b. Sewickley, Pa., Dec. 23, 1941; s. Aaron Jackson and Madeline B.; student Bucknell U., 1960-63; B.S. in Chemistry, Am. U., 1968; Ph.D. in Organic Chemistry, Ohio State U., 1974; m. Sharon Kay Smith, Nov. 30, 1968. Chemist, W.R. Grace & Co., Columbia, Md., 1968-69; research asso. Ohio State U., Columbus, 1969-74; research chemist Mobay Chem. Corp., Pitts., 1974—, group leader elastomer application devel., 1979—, sect. mgr., 1980—. Mem. Am. Chem. Soc., Am. Contract Bridge League. Home: 323 Jenny Lynn Dr Coraopolis PA 15108 Office: Mobay Chem Corp Penn-Lincoln Pkwy W Pittsburgh PA 15205

BAILEY, RON KENNETH, builders assn. exec.; b. Lamar, W.Va., Mar. 7, 1941; s. Louis K. and Versie E. B.; A.A., No. Va. Community Coll., 1969; B.S., Strayer Coll., 1971; M.I.S., Am. U., 1975; postgrad. Western Colo. U., 1980—; m. Beverly J. Welsh, May 12, 1962; children—Ronnie Kyle, Ryon Kent. Computer programmer Bur. Customs, Washington, 1965; instr. Strayer Coll., Washington, 1977—; asst. comptroller, dir. data processing Nat. Assn. Home Builders, Washington, 1965—; dir. credit union, 1977—, treas. credit union, 1979-80. Treas., Loisdale Civic Assn., 1980. Served with U.S. Army, 1962-65. Electronic Data Processing Auditors Assn., Assn. Computer Programmers and Analysis (dir. 1980; Achievement award 1979), Data Processing Mgmt. Assn., Nat. UNIVAC Users Assn., Soc. Cert. Data Processors. Methodist. Contbr. articles to profl. jours. Home: 6801 Lois Dr Springfield VA 22150 Office: Nat Assn Home Builders 15th & M Sts NW Washington DC 20005

BAILEY, STANLEY ALLEN, mfg. corp. exec.; b. Stockton, Calif., July 20, 1944; s. Chester Issac and Ina Marie (Johnson) B.; B.A., San Jose State U., 1968; m. Fery Tavakolian; 1 dau., Saghi. Exec. dir. Mimax Corp., Teheran, Iran, 1973-74; pres. IDEACO, also cons. to govt. Iran, Teheran, 1974-76; sr. product mktg. mgr. Calcomp Corp., Anaheim, Calif., 1976-78; sales mgr. Info. Internat., Inc., Culver City, Calif., 1978—. Co-dir. Johnson for Pres. Campaign, Santa Clara, Calif., 1964. Mem. Am. Mktg. Assn., Internat. Mktg. Assn., Printing Industries Am., Nat. Micrographics Assn., Internat. Micrographics Congress. Democrat. Clubs: Imperial, Pars-Am. Office: 2102 Business Center Dr Suite 150 Irvine CA 92715

BAILEY, THOMAS R., holding co. exec.; b. Peoria, Ill., Dec. 5, 1932; s. Thomas L. and Grace D. (Rexroade) B.; B.B.A., U. Cin., 1959; postgrad. U. Chgo., 1960-61, U. Mich., 1962; m. Carol Bailey; children—Chris, Marty, Brian, Kyle, Linda K., Lori J. Mgmt. trainee, cost analyst U.S. Steel Corp., Gary, Ind., 1959-61; corp. fin. analyst Ford Motor Co., Dearborn, Mich., 1961-62; auditor Price Waterhouse, Peoria, Ill., 1962; acctg. mgr., controller Ingersoll Milling Machine Co., Rockford, Ill., 1963-68; sr. mgmt. cons. Coopers & Lybrand C.P.A.'s, Rockford, 1968-74; corp. v.p. fin., dir. Anderson Consol. Industries, Inc., Rockford, 1974—; chmn. bd. Anderson Packaging, Inc.; sec.-treas., dir. numerous subs. Served with U.S. Navy, 1952-56. Mem. Fin. Execs. Assn. Home: 8058 Hickory Trail Belvidere IL 61008 Office: 803 N Church St Rockford IL 61101

BAILEY, WILLIAM JAMES, mfg. exec.; b. Los Angeles, Aug. 29, 1914; s. William James and Helen (Davis) B.; student U. So. Calif.; m. Miriam Kelley, November, 4, 1944; children—Linda Ann Bailey Stevens, Robin Ann Bailey Barker, William James III. Assistant sales mgr. Day & Night Mfg. Company, 1939-42, asst. gen. mgr., 1942-44, pres., 1944-65; v.p., dir. Affiliated Gas Equipment, Inc., 1949-55; v.p. Carrier Corp., 1955-71, dir., 1968—, exec. v.p., 1971-72, pres., 1972-78, vice chmn. bd., 1978-79; pres. Carrier Air Conditioning Co., 1967-71; pres. Payne Company, 1949-65; chmn. bd. Spectrol Electronics Corp., 1954-65; dir. 1st Trust and Deposit Co., 1st Comml. Banks Inc., Crouse-Hinds Co. Chmn. bd. Community-Gen. Hosp. Mem. Air-Conditioning and Refrigeration Inst. (dir.), Mfrs. Assn. Syracuse (dir.), Greater Syracuse C. of C. (dir.). Clubs: California (Los Angeles); Century (Syracuse); Onondaga Golf and Country (Fayetteville, N.Y.). Office: Carrier Corp Carrier Tower PO Box 1000 Syracuse NY 13201*

BAILEY, WILLIAM O., ins. co. exec.; b. Syracuse, N.Y., July 1, 1926; s. William E. and Kate (Olliver) B.; A.B. in Econs., Dartmouth Coll., 1947; M.B.A. in Ins., Wharton Sch., U. Pa., 1949; m. Carole Watts; children—George, Janet, Thomas, Carolyn. Asst. sec. Nat. Bur. Casualty Underwriters, 1952-54; with Aetna Life & Casualty Co., Hartford, Conn., 1954—, sr. v.p. casualty and surety div., 1968-72, exec. v.p., dir., from 1972; dir. Insilco Corp., Terra Nova Ins. Co., Ltd. Corporator, mem. ins. com. Hartford Hosp.; bd. dirs. St. Francis Hosp., Coll. Ins., N.Y.C., U. Conn. Found., Inc.; trustee Hartford Easter Seal Rehab. Center, Inc., Loomis-Chaffee Sch., N.E. Utilities. Served with USNR, World War II. Mem. Property-Casualty Ins. Council (chmn.), Am. Ins. Assn. (vice chmn.), Soc. C.P.C.U.'s. Office: 151 Farmington Ave Hartford CT 06156

BAILLIE, MYRA ATKINS, pub. relations co. exec.; b. Phila., May 22, 1920; d. Robert and Lillian Atkins; student U. Miami (Fla.), 1940, Columbia Tchrs. Coll., 1939, Calif. Inst. Tech., 1942; m. Hugh Scott Baillie, Feb. 20, 1943; 1 son, Mark Mead. Tng. dir. Broadway Dept. Store, Pasadena, Calif., 1941-43; asst. buyer ready-to-wear, floor mgr. G.C. Willis Dept. Store, Champaign, Ill., 1944-45; personnel interviewer Helen Edwards Agency, Los Angeles, 1945; teen promotion dir., fashion coordinator Hale Bros. Stores Calif., San Francisco, 1946-48; buyer Bloomingdales, N.Y.C., 1949-51; resident dir. Field Coordinators, merchandising and mktg. service, N.Y.C., 1967; pres. Myra A. Baillie Cons.'s, pub. relations, mktg. and fund raising, San Francisco, 1968—; cons. in field. Mem. San Francisco Mayor's Com. Wine and Flower Festival, 1975-76, San Francisco Mayor's Litter Com., 1977-78; mem. central com. San Francisco Republican party, 1963—; mem. nat. com. Women's Crusade for Common Sense Economy, 1978-79; mem. San Francisco Conv. Bur., 1974—; bd. dirs. Bay Area Benefit Concerts, Light House for Blind Aux., Presbyterian Hosp. Aux., St. Luke's Hosp. Aux., Stanford Children's Hosp. Aux., The Annex, Mills Meml. Hosp. League, San Francisco Ambassadors, Am. Cancer Soc. Mem. English Speaking Union, Internat. Platform Assn., Pacific Musical Soc., Calif. Press Women, Escoffier Soc., Am. Soc. Interior Designers, Alta Bates Hosp. Found., Am. Conservatory Theatre Assn. Clubs: San Francisco Bay Area Publicity (dir. 1975—), Peninsula Press (chmn. 1977—), Commonwealth, San Francisco Garden (coordinator 1974-75), Alliance Francaise, St. Francis Ch. Episcopal Women's Guild (past pres.). Home: 100 Saint Elmo Way San Francisco CA 94127

BAINTON, DONALD J., diversified mfg. co. exec.; b. N.Y.C., May 3, 1931; s. William Lewis and Mildred J. (Dunne) B.; B.A., Columbia U., 1952; postgrad. Advanced Mgmt. Program, Rutgers U., 1960; m. Aileen M. Demoulins, July 10, 1954; children—Kathryn C., Stephen L., Elizabeth A., William D. With The Continental Group, Inc., 1954—, gen. mgr. prodn. planning, 1967-68, gen. mgr. mfg. Eastern div., 1968-73, gen. mgr. Pacific div., 1973-74, Eastern div., 1974-75, v.p., gen. mgr. ops. U.S. Metal, 1975-76, exec. v.p., gen. mgr. CCC-USA, 1976-78, corp. exec. v.p., pres. diversified ops., 1978-79, pres. Continental Can Co., 1979—, exec. v.p., operating officer parent co., 1979—, also dir. Continental Group; chmn. bd. Teepak, Inc.; dir. Continental Group Can., Ltd. Mem. adv. bd. Columbia U. Served with USN, 1952-54; Korea. Mem. Canadian-U.S. C. of C. (dir.), Can Mfrs. Inst. (dir.), Columbia U. Alumni Assn., Knights of Malta. Republican. Roman Catholic. Clubs: Milbrook Country (Greenwich, Conn.); Landmark (Stamford, Conn.); Pinnacle (N.Y.C.). Office: care Continental Group One Harbor Plaza Stamford CT 06902*

BAINUM, STEWART WILLIAM, hotel chain and nursing homes exec.; b. Detroit, June 10, 1919; s. Charles and Emma (Liesure) B.; student Columbia Union Coll., 1938-39; m. Jane L. Goyne, June 8, 1941; children—Barbara (Mrs. Arnold Renschler), Stewart Willaim, Roberta (Mrs. Fenton Froom), Bruce. Self-employed mech. contractor, developer apt. projects, office bldgs., 1943-57; owner several Quality Motels, 1957-63; chmn. bd., dir. Quality Inns Internat., Silver Spring, Md., 1972—; chmn. bd. dirs. Manor Care Inc., public co. with 23 nursing homes, 1 hosp., 2 alcohol rehab. projects, Silver Spring, 1972—, Realty Investment Co. Pres. Allied Civic Group, 1959-60, Burnt Mills Hills Citizens Assn., 1956-57. Named Lodging Industry Leader of Yr., Religious Heritage Am., 1972. Mem. Nat. Assn. Home Builders (lifetime dir.), Met. Washington Builders Assn. (pres. 1965), Aircraft Owners and Pilots Assn. Republican. Office: 10750 Columbia Pike Silver Spring MD 20901

BAIR, WARNER BRECKENRIDGE, II, banker, lawyer; b. Seattle, July 4, 1945; s. Warner Breckenridge and Elizabeth Ann (Beaumont) B.; B.S. in Public Adminstrn., U. Ariz., 1967, J.D., 1971; grad. Nat. Coll. Dist. Attys., 1972; m. Katherine Bartlo, Jan. 25, 1970; children—Warner Breckenridge, Tiffany Elizabeth. Admitted to Ariz. bar, 1971; dep. county atty. Maricopa County (Ariz.), Phoenix, 1971-73; chief criminal dep. Mohave County (Ariz.) Atty.'s Office, Kingman, 1973; individual practice law, Kingman, 1973-79; trust counsel, trust officer, atty. trust div. 1st Nat. Bank of Ariz., Phoenix, 1979—; mem. faculty Nat. Coll. Dist. Attys., 1973; former mem. res. faculty Mohave Community Coll. Served with AIS, 1968. Mem. Am. Bar Assn., Am. Trial Lawyers Assn., Ariz. Trial Lawyers Assn., Maricopa County Bar Assn., Central Ariz. Estate Planning Council, Valley Estate Planners, Western Pension Conf., Am. Film Inst., Ariz. Authors Assn., Am. Inst. Banking, Phi Alpha Delta. Club: Phoenix 100 Rotary. Home: 13847 N 41st Ave Phoenix AZ 85023 Office: PO Box 2669 100 W Washington St Phoenix AZ 85002

BAIRD, CHARLES FITZ, bus. exec.; b. Southampton, N.Y., Sept. 4, 1922; s. George White and Julia (Fitz) B.; A.B., Middlebury (Vt.) Coll., 1944; grad. Advanced Mgmt. Program, Harvard, 1960; m. Norma Adele White, Sept. 13, 1947; children—Susan Fitz, Stephen White, Charles Fitz, Nancy Williams. With Standard Oil Co. (N.J.) 1948-65, dep. European fin. rep., London, 1955-58, asst. treas., 1958-62; dir. Esso Standard SA Francaise, 1962-65; asst. sec. of navy (fin. mgmt.), 1965-67, undersec. of navy, 1967-69; v.p. finance Inco Ltd., 1969-72, sr. v.p., 1972-76, vice-chmn., 1976-77, pres., 1977-80, chmn., chief exec. officer, 1980—, also dir.; dir. Bank of Montreal, ICI Ams. Inc. Mem. President's Commn. Marine Sci., Engring. and Resources, 1967-69. Nat. Adv. Commns. on Ocean and Atmosphere, 1972-74. Trustee Bucknell U., 1969—; chmn. bd. trustees, 1976—; bd. advisers Naval War Coll., 1970-74. Served as capt. USMCR, 1943-46, 51-52. Mem. Council Fgn. Relations, Can. Inst. Mining and Metallurgy, Canadian-Am. Com., Chi Psi. Clubs: Chevy Chase (Md.); Metropolitan (Washington); India House, Economic (N.Y.C.); Short Hills (N.J.); Links; Union; Wequetonsing (Mich.) Golf; Toronto. Office: 1 New York Plaza New York NY 10004 also 1 First Canadian Place Toronto ON M5X 1C4 Canada*

BAIRD, G(EORGE) STEWART, JR., lease making co. exec.; b. N.Y.C., Aug. 3, 1929; s. George Stewart and Virginia (Robinson) B.; B.A., Brown U., 1951; m. Martha Jane Haskell, June 15, 1956; children—Laura Haskell, Randall Stewart. Salesman, Career Publs., N.Y.C., Detroit, 1953-54; regional mgr. New Eng., Control Engring. Mag., McGraw-Hill Pub. Co., Boston, 1954-61, Sci. Am. Mag., N.Y.C. and Needham, Mass., 1961-62; regional mgr. No. New Eng., Pepsico Leasing, Waltham, Mass., 1962-70; pres. Leasemakers and LVS Co. a div., Wellesley, Mass., 1970—; chmn. venture investment com. Bay Colony Ventures, Wellesley; author, speaker, panelist in field; co-developer proposed changes in lease accounting rules Fin. Accounting Standards Bd., N.Y.C., 1974, adopted, 1977; developer, chmn. panel meeting Lease or Sell, indsl. mktg. group, Am. Mktg. Assn., Boston, 1973. Producer, Movement Sound Light in Concert, Spingold Theatre, Brandeis U., 1974, Dover Ch. Choir, 1978—, deacon, 1981—, Reinterpretation Jazz Band, 1979—. Served with USNR, 1951-53; Mem. Am. Assn. Equipment Lessors, Keyman Network. Club: Maugus (Wellesley). Contbr. article to profl. jour. Office: 572 Washington St Wellesley MA 02181

BAIRD, JAMES DAVID, materials handling equipment mfg. co. exec.; b. Rochester, N.Y., Oct. 5, 1939; s. James and Margaret (MacFadyen) B.; B.B.A., Bryant Coll., 1961; m. Carol A. Pascale; children—Douglas James, Jeanne Elizabeth. With Castle div. Sybron Corp., Rochester, 1961-65, with contract sales, 1962-64, credit mgr., 1964-65; credit mgr. Am. Sterilizer Co., Erie, Pa., 1966-67, mgr. contract financing, 1967-68; treas. Lamson Div. Diebold Inc., Syracuse, N.Y., 1968-72, v.p. gen. mgmt., 1972—. Chmn. mfg. div. Onodaga County chpt. United Way, 1970-73; bd. dirs. Huntington Family Center, Syracuse. Mem. N.Y. Credit and Financial Mgmt. Assn., Nat. Assn. Controllers, Am. Mgmt. Assn., Am. Fin. Mgmt. Assn., Am. Subcontractors Assn., Mfrs. Assn. Syracuse, Syracuse C. of C. Clubs: Masons, University, Meadows Racquet, Lakeshore Yacht and Country (Syracuse). Home: 4177 Lucan Rd Liverpool NY 13088 Office: 1976 Lamson St Syracuse NY 13221

BAIRD, JOHN DAVID, ins. exec.; b. Evanston, Ill., Sept. 22, 1937; s. Guy C. and Mary L. (Ellerbush) B.; B.B.A., U. Tex., 1959, postgrad. in law, 1959-60; m. JoAn R. Novotny, June 10, 1960; children—Colleen, Karin, Brian. From sr. ins. clk. to ins. supr. Tenneco Inc., Houston, 1961-65; asst. corporate risk mgr. Anderson, Clayton & Co., Houston, 1965-68; mgr. corporate ins. G.W. Murphy Industries, Houston, 1968; corporate ins. mgr. Tracor, Inc., Austin, Tex., 1968-73, corporate mgr. financial services, 1973—; sec./treas., dir. Baird's Village Hobby Shop, 1977—. Guest speaker U. Tex. Grad. Sch. Bus.; corporate ins. cons. Bd. dirs. N.W. Austin Little League, 1973-76, pres., 1974-75; bd. dirs. N.W. Vikings Jr. Football, 1973-77, pres., 1975; bd. dirs. Brackenridge Hosp., 1976-78, N.W. Austin Pony-Colt League, 1977-79; mem. budget com. United Way, 1975—. Served to lt. AUS, 1960-61. Mem. Nat. Assn. Accountants (dir. Austin area chpt. 1972-76, v.p. 1975), Soc. Chartered Property and Casualty Underwriters (pres. Central Tex. chpt. 1973-74, treas. 1980-81), S. Tex. chpt. Risk and Ins. Mgmt. Soc., Inc., Austin C. of C., Austin Heritage Soc., Austin Citizens League, NW Austin Civic Assn., Delta Sigma Phi. Roman Catholic. Club: Austin Runners. Home: 4004 Greystone Dr Austin TX 78731 Office: 6500 Tracor Ln Austin TX 78721

BAIRD, JOSEPH EDWARD, petroleum co. exec.; b. Columbus, Ohio, Mar. 18, 1934; s. Edward Graham and Alice (Hoover) B.; B.A., Yale U.; m. Anne Marie Baird, 1958; 3 children. With Chase Manhattan Bank, 1959-66, Smith, Barney & Co. Inc., 1966-67; mng. dir., chief exec. officer Western Am. Bank (Europe) Ltd., London, 1968-73; pres., chief operating officer Occidental Petroleum Corp., 1973-79. Served with AUS, 1954-56. Address: 166 Groverton Pl Los Angeles CA 90024

BAIRD, OREN KENNETH, real estate exec.; b. Charlestown, Ind., Jan. 25, 1919; s. Orva J. and Mary C. (Crum) B.; grad. Central Normal Coll., 1939; B.S., Canterbury Coll., 1947; attended sales and bus. mgmt. course Internat. Harvester Central Sch., Chgo., 1953, Ind. Sch. Real Estate, Indpls., 1961, Dale Carnegie Sales Course, 1967; m. Phyllis Stoller, Aug. 22, 1947; children—Chrisa, David, Dwight, Beth, Mark, Bruce. Tchr., Charlestown, Ind., 1939-41; owner, mgr. Kenny's Restaurant, Charlestown, Ind., 1940-41; sales trainee Internat. Harvester Co., Indpls., 1947, retail truck salesman, Indpls., 1951-52; owner, mgr. O.K.'s City Restaurant, Danville, Ind., 1947-50; post info. and edn. officer Camp Atterbury, Ind., 1950-51; pres., mgr. in charge of sales Internat. Harvester Dealer Acton, Ind., 1952-60; tchr. Franklin (Ind.) Twp. Schs., 1960-64; ins. agent, 1960—; real estate sales, 1961—; real estate broker, pres. Baird Realty Co., Inc., Indpls., 1968—. Chmn. Hendricks County (Ind.) Crusade for Freedom, 1951-52; chmn. Danville (Ind.) Boy Scouts Fund, 1952, institutional rep. Boy Scouts Am., 1954-58. Pres. Acton (Ind.) Community Council, 1955; dir. of civilian defense, Hendricks County (Ind.), 1950; mem. Marion County (Ind.) Plan Commn., 1954-57; pres. Franklin Central High Sch. Bldg. Corp. 1958—. Trustee, Franklin Twp., 1967-79. Served to 1st lt. 83d Inf. Div., AUS, 1941-46. Decorated Purple Heart, Bronze Star medal; named Man of the Year, Suburban Multi-list Exchange (SMILE), 1972, Ind. Farm and Land Realtor of Yr., 1978. Mem. Indpls., Hancock County bds. of realtors, Nat. Inst. Farm and Land Brokers (pres. Ind. chpt. 1974-75), Nat. Inst. Real Estater Brokers, Nat. Assn. Home Bldrs. (asso. mem.), Suburban Multi-list Exchange (pres. 1972), Hot-Line Ltd. Inc. Realtors (E. rep. 1971—), Am. Legion, 40 and 8, DAV, Wanamaker Bus. Mens Assn., Canterbury Coll. Alumni Assn. (pres. 1950-51, Outstanding Achievement award 1974), Order Ky. Cols., Zeta Sigma Nu. Presbyn. (elder 1972—). Mason (Shriner). Home: 9960 Southeastern Ave Indianapolis IN 46239 Office: Baird Realty Co Inc 3416 S Post Rd Indianapolis IN 46239

BAIRD, SHEILA MAUREEN, stockbroker; b. Toronto, Ont., Can., May 13, 1937; d. Cyril and Nellie E. (Arnott) B.; B.Comm., U. Toronto, 1959. Partner, M. Kimelman & Co., 1966—; com. productivity and technol. devels., bus. research adv. council Bur. Labor Stats. Trustee, Hurricane Island, Outward Bound, St. Joseph's Coll. Mem. Market Technicians Assn., Fin. Women's Assn., N.Y. Soc. Security Analysts. Office: 100 Park Ave New York NY 10017

BAITINGER, HERBERT MILLER, JR., apparel mfg. co. exec.; b. Gary, Ind., Feb. 18, 1928; s. Herbert Miller and Virginia (Howells) B.; student Northwestern U., 1947; B.B.A., U. Miami, 1951; m. Jocelyn George, Nov. 28, 1951; children—Gail Ann, David George. Mgmt. staff J.C. Penney Co., Daytona Beach, Fla., 1953-56, Panama City, Fla., 1956-58, Jacksonville, Fla., 1958-62, Waycross, Ga., 1962-64, Daytona Beach, Fla., 1964-68; pres., owner ABC Sch. Uniforms, Inc., Hialeah, Fla., 1968—; sec.-treas. Cricket Casuals, Inc., Tampa, Fla., 1973-75; sec.-treas. Daisy Uniform Co., Miami, 1976-77. Served with AUS, 1951-53. Mem. U.S., Power Squadron, S.A.R., Sigma Alpha Epsilon, Alpha Kappa Psi, L'Apache. Presbyn. Kiwanian, Lion. Club: Country (fleet capt. 1974-75, fleet commodore 1977-78) (Coral Gables, Fla.). Home: 5501 Riviera Dr Coral Gables FL 33146 Office: 1085 E 31st St Hialeah FL 33013

BAITZ, ARTHUR GEORGE, controls co. exec.; b. Buffalo, Aug. 22, 1918; s. Arthur George and Clara (Pfeil) B.; student Tri State Coll., 1937, U. Buffalo, 1938; m. Ruth Elizabeth Finkle, Mar. 15, 1950; children—Lisa, Arthur George III. Sales engr. Landers Engring. Co., Buffalo, 1940-41; test engr., fgn. service rep. Sterling Engine Co., Buffalo, 1940-45; sales engr. D.W. Mason Co., Buffalo, 1945-51; sales engr. Robertshaw Controls Co., Richmond, Va., 1951-54, dist. sales mgr., 1954-59, dir. sales tng., 1959-60, dir. engring., planning, 1960, dir. marketing, 1961, asst. v.p., gen. mgr. Eastern Research Center, King of Prussia, Pa., 1961-68; v.p., gen. mgr. Phone-Alert subs., 1968-71, asst. v.p., dir. marketing Robertshaw Controls Co., Richmond, 1971-76, asst. v.p., dir. planning, 1976—. Mem. Soc. Automotive Engrs., Am. Relay League, Am. Mgmt. Assn., Richmond Power Squadron, Beta Chi Epsilon. Republican. Presbyn. Clubs: Sandy Beach Yacht; Anchorage Yacht; Mathews Yacht. Home: 919 St Anns Pl Richmond VA 23225 Office: 1701 Byrd Ave Richmond VA 23226

BAKA, JOHN GEORGE, mfg. co. exec.; b. Mt. Vernon, N.Y., May 26, 1933; s. George E. and Julia T. (Puzio) B.; B.A., U. Pa., 1955, M.G.A. (Samuel Fels fellow), 1957; B.S., L.I. U., 1959; M.B.A., N.Y. U., 1962; m. Dorothea A. Noonan, June 22, 1957; children—Julia, Lynne Ann, Christie. Vice pres. mgmt. U.S. Lines, N.Y.C., 1969-73; dir. fin. planning/EDP, Sea Train Lines, N.Y.C., 1973-75; controller N.Y. Times, N.Y.C., 1975-79; v.p., chief fin. officer Tech. Tape Co., N.Y.C., 1979—. Mem. twp. bds., Clinton, N.J., 1972-76. Served with USAF, 1957-60. Mem. Fin. Execs. Inst., Nat. Assn. Accts. Roman Catholic. Home: 131 Upper Kingtown Rd Pittstown NJ 08867 Office: Tech Tape Co 1 LeFevre Ln New Rochelle NY 10801

BAKER, BRUCE FREDERICK, savs. bank exec.; b. Seattle, Sept. 23, 1930; s. Frederick Edward and Edel (Peterson) B.; B.A., U. Wash., 1954; m. Joyce Marie Norwick, Jan. 24, 1951; children—Jeffry L., David A., Bryan E. Account rep. Anacortes (Wash.) Am. Newspaper, 1954; with Cappy Ricks & Assos., advt. agy., Seattle, 1954-56; v.p., dir. Frederick E. Baker Advt., Inc., Seattle, 1956-68, N.W. Ayer-F. E. Baker, Inc., Seattle, 1968-69; resident mgr. Boyden Assos., Inc., Seattle, 1969-71; v.p. marketing Pacific 1st Fed. Savs. & Loan Assn., Tacoma, 1971-74; sr. v.p. marketing Wash. Mut. Savs. Bank, Seattle, 1974—; v.p., dir. Exchange Systems, Inc., Seattle, 1974—; dir. Great Northern Insured Annuity Corp. Mem. exec. bd. Chief Seattle council Boy Scouts Am., 1958—, v.p., 1976-80, pres., 1981—; trustee Seattle Symphony Orch., 1978—, Corporate Council for Arts, 1978—; trustee Medina Childrens Service, 1958-64, pres., 1963; bd. dirs. United Way King County, 1978—. Served with USAF, 1951-52. Republican. Congregationalist., Clubs: Rotary (dir. 1977—, sec.-treas. 1980—), Washington Athletic (gov. 1976—), Rainier. Home: 2916 26th St W Seattle WA 98199 Office: Wash Mut Savs Bank 1101 2d Ave Seattle WA 98101

BAKER, CHARLES MANDERVILLE, III, economist, fin. cons.; b. New Orleans, Dec. 24, 1926; s. George Fisher and Cecile Olga (Bacarisse) B.; B.S. in Bus. Adminstrn., U.N.Y., 1949; student Union Coll., 1947-48; m. Alyse Maude Otvos, May 19, 1979. Mgr. sales dept. Gen. Instrument Corp., Elizabeth, N.J., 1950-55; br. office ops. mgr. Merrill Lynch, Pierce, Fenner & Smith, Inc., N.Y.C., 1955-59; partner Kelly, McCarter & D'Arcy, N.Y.C., 1959-60; mgr. firm relations div. N.Y. Stock Exchange, 1960-65; regional v.p. Putnam Funds, N.Y.C., 1965-71; v.p. Prudential Group, Inc., N.Y.C., 1973-75; exec. v.p., treas. Mineral Rights Corp., N.Y.C., 1976-77; pres., treas. Charlyse Corp., Pitts. 1980—; economist, fin. cons.

Energy Related Investments, Pitts., 1979—; merger, acquisitions cons. Corp. Finance Assos., Pitts., 1980—; lectr. on econs. and fin. Served with U.S. Army, 1945-46, USAR, 1946-49. Mem. Wall St. Tng. Dirs. Assn. (founding mem.). Protestant. Club: Elizabeth Town and Country (past v.p., dir.). Office: 515 Glen Arden Dr Pittsburgh PA 15208

BAKER, CLARENCE ALBERT, SR., structural steel constrn. co. exec.; b. Kansas City, Kans., July 2, 1919; s. Earl Retting and Nancy Jefferson (Price) B.; student Kans. U., 1939-40, Finley Engring. Coll., 1937-39, Ohio State U., 1967, 69; m. Marjorie Ellen Yoakum, Mar. 19, 1959; children—Clarence Albert, Jorgeann (Mrs. Harry L. Hiebert); stepchildren—Robert Beale, Barbara Anne Stegner (Mrs. Robert T. Kenney II). With Kansas City (Kans.) Structural Steel Co., 1937—, shop supt., 1959-68, v.p., plant mgr., 1968-73, v.p. plant operations, 1973-76, v.p. engring., 1976—, dir., 1969—. Curriculum adv. Kansas City (Mo.) Met. Jr. Coll., 1971-72, Kansas City Vocat. Tech. Sch., 1973—. Committeeman, Republican Party, 1970-72; chmn. City of Mission (Kans.) Rep. Party, 1970-72; councilman City of Merriam (Kans.), 1957-59; adv. bd. Wentworth Mil. Acad.; bd. dirs. Kansas City Jr. Achievement. Served with USNR, 1944-46. Mem. Am. Welding Soc. (pres. 1970-71, chmn. 1970, code com.; cert.), ASTM, Kans. Engring. Soc., Kansas City C. of C. Club: Masons. Home: 6635 Milhaven Dr Mission KS 66202 Office: 21st and Metropolitan Sts Kansas City KS 66106

BAKER, CLIFF, aero. research mfg. co. exec.; b. St. Louis, Oct. 26, 1899; s. Robert Benton and Sarah (Hinman) B.; student U. Calif. at Los Angeles, 1936; LL.D., Pepperdine U.; m. Ann Warga, Jan. 3, 1942; children (by previous marriage)—Girard C., Barbara Arlette. Pres., Vanguard Oil Co., Los Angeles and Bakersfield, Calif., 1933-41, Cliff Baker Industries (formerly Elcon Mfg. Co.), Los Angeles, 1942—; owner Cliff Baker Ranches, Riverside, Merced and Mariposa Counties, Calif., 1955—. Mem. Founding 400 Pepperdine U. Assos.; bd. dirs. Pepperdine U. Mem. SAR, U.S. Trotting Assn. Club: St. Francis Yacht (San Francisco). Patentee improved aircraft elec. connector. Home: Van Nuys CA 91401 also La Grand CA 95333 Office: 251 S Lake Ave Pasadena CA 91101 also 9993 E Mission Ave Le Grand CA 95333

BAKER, CLIFFORD HOWARD, instn. adminstr.; b. Paoli, Ind., Oct. 14, 1932; s. James A. and Alice (Limeberry) B.; B.S., U.S. Mil. Acad., 1956; M.S., Purdue U., 1965; Ph.D., N.C. State U., 1972; m. Joan B. Meyer, Feb. 4, 1958; children—Steven Conrad, Bradford Nelson, Paul Milton, Jeffrey Todd, Douglas Ross, Matthew Kent. Indsl. mktg. exec. Tex. Instruments, Dallas, 1959-61; market research exec. Gen. Motors Corp., Kokomo, Ind., 1961-65; supr. market analysis Corning Glass Works, Raleigh, N.C., 1965-70; pres. Market Research and Statistics Co., 1970-71, Indsl. Edn. Inst., Mailmax, Raleigh and Columbia, S.C., Village Printer, Raleigh; v.p. Su Casa Mexican Restaurants, Raleigh, Quinn Mfg., Chapel Hill, N.C. Served with AUS, 1956-59. Recipient Nat. Def. Service medal West Point, 1956. Mem. IEEE, Assn. Grads. West Point. Mem. Ch. of Christ. Republican. Home: 4816 Deerwood Dr Raleigh NC 27612 Office: 4505 Creedmoor Rd Raleigh NC 27612

BAKER, DAVID HODGE, JR., investment co. exec.; b. N.Y.C., July 4, 1933; s. David Hodge and Estaleah (Harmsen) B.; B.S. with first honors, U. Md., 1955; M.B.A., Harvard U., 1961. Research analyst Lehman Bros., N.Y.C., 1961-63; dir. research Rotan Mosle, Houston, 1963-66; sr. portfolio mgr. Goldman Sachs, N.Y.C., 1966-68; pres. Van Cleef Jordan & Wood, N.Y.C., 1968-69; pres. Forty Four Mgmt., Inc., Alexandria, Va., 1969—, Forty Four Mgmt., Ltd., Cayman Islands, B.W.I., 1978, Forty Four Sales, Inc., 1980—, 44 Wall St. Fund, Inc., 1969—, 44 Wall St. Equity Fund, Inc., 1980—, also dir. Served as lt. j.g. USNR, 1956-59. Mem. No Load Mut. Fund Assn., Investment Co. Inst., N.Y. Soc. Security Analysts, Chartered Fin. Analysts, Sigma Chi Alumni Assn., Delta Sigma Pi. Republican. Club: Harvard Bus. Sch. N.Y. Home: S Church George Town Cayman Islands BWI Office: 150 Broadway Suite 914 New York NY 10038

BAKER, DAVID PERRY, savings and loan exec.; b. Bridgeport, Conn., Dec. 26, 1933; s. Leon Frederick and Inez (Carey) B.; B.A., Kans. U., 1955; student Grad. Sch. Savings and Loan, Ind. U., 1967-68, Colo. Sch. Banking, U. Colo., 1971; m. Jane Underwood, Aug. 3, 1957; children—Mark David, Laura Ann. Asst. cashier First Nat. Bank, Topeka, Kans., 1955-60; pres., mgr. Topeka Morris Plan, 1960-64; v.p. First Fed. Savs., Hutchinson, Kans., 1964-68; exec. v.p., dir. Central State Bank, Hutchinson, 1968-72; pres., dir. S.W. Fed. Savs. and Loan, Wichita, Kans., 1972—. Pres. Greater Downtown Wichita, 1980; bd. dirs. United Way, 1980—. Recipient Young Man of Yr. award Jaycees, Topeka, 1962, Hutchinson, 67. Mem. U.S. League Savs. Assns., Wichita C. of C., Kans. C. of C., Kans. Savs. and Loan League, Wichita Bd. Realtors, Wichita Builders Assn., Rho Epsilon, Pi Kappa Alpha. Republican. Congregationalist. Clubs: Crestview Country, Wichita, Albert Pike Lodge, Scottish Rite, Shriners. Contbr. articles in field to profl. jours. Office: 130 N Market St Wichita KS 67202

BAKER, DEANNA, travel agy. exec.; b. Jamestown, Ky., Jan. 20, 1937; d. William and Edna Alice (Bunch) Bolin; A.A., Alan Hancock Coll., Calif., 1974; m. Marion K. Baker, May 27, 1956; children—Gregory Michael, Brenda Diane, Douglas Richard, Kimberly Ann. Travel agt. Bon Voyage Travel, Schaumburg, Ill., 1974; travel agt. Valley Travel, Goleta, Calif., 1975-76, asst. mgr., 1976-77, v.p., gen. mgr., 1977-80; partner, gen. mgr. Am. Travel Agy., Inc., Santa Barbara, Calif., 1980—. Recipient Mil. Wife of Yr. award USAF, 1972. Baptist. Home: 4342 Scorpio Rd Lompoc CA 93436 Office: 818 State St Santa Barbara CA 93102

BAKER, DEXTER FARRINGTON, air products corp. exec.; b. Worcester, Mass., Apr. 16, 1927; s. Leland Dyer and Edith (Quimby) B.; B.S., Lehigh U., 1950, M.B.A., 1957; m. Dorothy Ellen Hess, June 23, 1951; children—Ellen L., Susan A., Leslie A., Carolyn J. Sales engr. Air Products & Chemicals, Inc. Allentown, Pa., 1952-56, gen. sales mgr., 1956-57, pres., chief exec. officer, 1978—, dir., 1964—, mng. dir. Air Products Ltd., 1957-67, group v.p., 1967-78, exec. v.p., 1968-78. Trustee, chmn. vis. com. chem. engring. Lehigh U.; bd. assos. Muhlenberg Coll.; exec. bd. Minsi Trails Council Boy Scouts Am.; bd. Pennsylvanians for Effective Govt., Lehigh Valley Public Telecommunications Corp. Served with USN, 1945-46, with U.S. Army, 1950-52. Mem. Am. Inst. Chem. Engrs., Soc. Chem. Industry, Am. Mgmt. Assn., Nat. Assn. Mfrs. (bd. dirs.), Chem. Mfrs. Assn. (bd. dirs.). Republican. Presbyterian. Club: Asa Packer Soc. (Lehigh U.), Theta Chi. Office: Box 538 Allentown PA 18105

BAKER, DOUGLAS, bus. cons.; b. New Orleans, Feb. 22, 1930; m. Arturo Artemis Stephanos Lullius and Lola Fairchild; m. Mildred Mary Ann Breaux, Aug. 15, 1949; children—Deborah Ann, Bonnie Lou, Douglas Earl, Rodney Anthony. Owner, Jerry's Woodcraft Co., Westwego, La., 1953-78; prin., owner Mgmt. Cons. Concepts, New Orleans, 1978—. Served with U.S. Army, 1948-51. Mem. Am. Mgmt. Assn. Roman Catholic. Address: 3660 Rue Mignon New Orleans LA 70114

BAKER, FREDERICK LLOYD, III, computer co. exec.; b. Chgo., May 11, 1941; s. Frederick Lloyd and Suzanne Berkeley (Budge) B.; B.S., Washington and Lee U., 1963; M.B.A. (Roswell C. McCrea scholar), Columbia U., 1965; m. Mary York Reidy, June 8, 1968; children—Frederick Lloyd, IV, Marian York, Timothy Maurice Carr. Pricing analyst IBM World Trade Corp., N.Y.C., 1966-70, IBM World Trade Asia Corp., Tokyo, 1970-73; fin. analyst IBM World Trade AFE Corp., Westchester, N.Y., 1973-76, strategic planning mgr., 1976-78, mgr. functional planning, 1979-80, mgr. fin. ops.-Americas, 1980—. Rep., Greenwich (Conn.) Town Meeting, 1976—. Served with USNR, 1965-66. Republican. Presbyterian. Clubs: Riverside Yacht, S.R. Office: Town of Mt Pleasant Route 9 North Tarrytown NY 10591

BAKER, GEORGE DORSET, data processing forms corp. exec.; b. London, Feb. 8, 1926; s. William Alfred and Aileen (Dorset) B.; student London Poly. Inst., 1948-50; came to U.S., 1958, naturalized, 1969. Mgmt. trainee John Dickinson & Co., London, 1948-52, v.p. prodn., Hamilton, Ont., Can., 1952-58; gen. mgr. Data Forms, Inc., Rochester, N.Y., 1958-64; pres. Datagraphic, Inc., Rochester and Atlanta, 1964—; lectr. Distributive Edn. Clubs Am., 1971-74, Summer Inst. on Am. Economy, Invest-in-America Nat. Council. Mem. nat. adv. council Nat. Fedn. Ind. Bus., 1972—, N.Y. state chmn., 1972—. Served to capt. Brit. Army, 1942-48. Mem. Nat. Fedn. Ind. Bus. (state chmn. 1972—), Forms Mfrs. Credit Assn. (chmn. 1969-70). Contbr. articles to various publs. Home: Rt 2 Bailey Rd Woodstock GA 30188 Office: 8565 Dunwoody Pl Atlanta GA 30188

BAKER, HARRY LUTHER, ins. broker; b. Butte, Mont., Apr. 28, 1939; s. Harry Willard and Isabelle Lois (Storey) B.; B.S., Mont. State U., 1961; m. June Judy Langworthy, May 23, 1964; children—Gregory, Matthew, Jennifer. Underwriter, Safeco Ins. Co., Seattle, 1965-74; gen. mgr. spl. programs div. Providence-Wash. Ins. Co., 1974-78; pres. Profl. Ins. Consultants, Seattle, 1978—; cons. Active P.T.A., Little League. Mem. Comml. Market Masters Club (life), Ins. Inst. Am. Republican. Episcopalian. Contbr. articles ins. jours. Office: 211 6th Ave N Suite 2105 Seattle WA 98109

BAKER, JAMES ALLAN, banker; b. Dayton, Ohio, Mar. 4, 1942; s. Wilbur and Lucille (Heck) B.; B.S. in Bus. Adminstrn. (Wall St. Jour. Student Achievement award 1964), Bowling Green (Ohio) State U., 1964; M.B.A., Ind. U., 1966; m. B. Lyn Wallace, Aug. 25, 1962; children—J.J., S.W., J.D. With City Nat. Bank, Columbus, Ohio, 1966-75, banking officer, 1971-75; pres., chief exec. officer Bank One Mansfield (Ohio), 1975—. Chmn. Mansfield United Fund drive, 1976, chmn. allocation com., 1976—; trustee Mansfield Art Center, 1980—; bd. dirs., v.p. Richland County Growth Corp., 1975—; bd. dirs., treas. Area Indsl. Growth, 1975—, Mansfield Growth Corp., 1977—; pres. Mansfield United Community Service, 1978. Named Boss of Year, Mansfield Jaycees, 1977. Mem. Am. Banking Assn., Banking Adminstrn. Inst., Young Pres. Orgn., Ohio Bankers Assn., Ohio Citizens Council (v.p. 1980). Republican. Episcopalian. Clubs: Westbrook Country, Brookside Country, 51, University. Office: 28 Park Ave W Mansfield OH 44902

BAKER, JAMES EDWARD SPROUL, lawyer; b. Evanston, Ill., May 23, 1912; s. John Clark and Hester (Sproul) B.; A.B., Northwestern U., 1933, J.D., 1936; m. Eleanor Lee Dodgson, Oct. 2, 1937 (dec. 1972); children—John Lee, Edward Graham. Admitted to Ill. bar, 1936, U.S. Supreme Ct. bar, 1957; practice in Chgo., 1936—; asso. firms Cutting, Moore & Sidley, 1936, Sidley, McPherson, Austin and Burgess, 1937-41, 46-47, partner firms Sidley, Austin, Burgess & Harper, 1948-49, Sidley, Austin, Burgess & Smith, 1949-67, Sidley and Austin, 1967—; lectr. Northwestern U. Sch. Law, Chgo., 1951-52. Nat. chmn. Stanford Parents Com., 1969-75; bd. visitors Stanford Law Sch. Served to comdr. USNR, 1941-46. Fellow Am. Coll. Trial Lawyers (regent 1973-77, sec. 1977-79, pres. 1979-80); mem. Am., Ill., Chgo. bar assns., Bar Assn. 7th Fed. Circuit, Soc. Trial Lawyers Ill., Order of Coif, Phi Lambda Upsilon, Sigma Nu. Republican. Methodist. Clubs: Univ., Legal, Law, Mid-Day (Chgo.); Westmoreland Country (Wilmette, Ill.). Home: 1300 N Lake Shore Dr Chicago IL 60610 Office: 1 First National Plaza Chicago IL 60603

BAKER, JOHN LANGSTON, air-conditioning equipment co. exec.; b. Oklahoma City, Oct. 10, 1930; s. John Wesley and Bessie Lou (Crouch) B.; B.S.M.E., U. Okla., 1953; m. Beverly Jean Goudelock, May 31, 1953; children—Marsha Lynn Baker Roberts, John Scott. Field application engr. Carrier Air Conditioning Co., Dallas, 1953-58, sales engr., Oklahoma City, 1958-64, br. mgr., 1964-71, dist. mgr., Dallas, 1971—. Group chmn. United Way of Dallas, 1973, firm chmn., 1974-80; patron Richardson Symphony Orch. Served with USNR, 1954-55; ETO. Recipient Expert Rifle medal. Mem. ASHRAE, Nat. Soc. Profl. Engrs., Nat. Rifle Assn. (life), Dallas Mus. Fine Arts, Res. Officers Assn., Shakespeare Guild, U. Okla. Alumni Assn. (life), Pi Kappa Alpha. Republican. Mem. Disciples of Christ. Ch. (elder, chmn. gen. bd.). Clubs: Brookhaven Country, Rotary. Home: 5 Pebblebrook Circle Richardson TX 75080 Office: 1801 Gateway PO Box 2875 Richardson TX 75080

BAKER, LAWRENCE COLBY, JR., ins. co. exec.; b. Carleton, Mich., Oct. 6, 1935; s. Lawrence Colby and Margaret Ellen (Close) B.; B.A., U. Mich., 1957; m. Ida Wasil, June 26, 1960. Dist. mgr. Tavelers Ins. Co., Los Angeles, 1961-71; chief dep. commr. Calif. Dept. Ins., Los Angeles, 1971-75; pres. Argonaut Ins. Co., Menlo Park, Calif., 1975—, also dir.; dir. Argonaut-Midwest Ins. Co., Argonaut-NW Ins. Co., Argonaut-SW Ins. Co., Ga. Ins. Co. Served as lt. (j.g.) USN, 1957-60; v.p. Calif. Workers' Compensation Inst., 1979; trustee Ins. Forum San Francisco, 1978. Mem. Assn. Calif. Ins. Cos. (dir.), Calif. Ins. Guarantee Assn. (vice-chmn.), Nat. Assn. Ind. Insurers (dir., chmn. workers' compensation com.). Office: 250 Middlefield Rd Menlo Park CA 94025

BAKER, MARION, mfg. co. exec.; b. Carson City, Nev., Nov. 21, 1930; s. Dayton M. and Phoebe A. (Taylor) B.; student San Francisco State Coll., 1948-51. Asst. to sales mgr. Royal Typewriter Co., San Francisco, 1951-53, dir. dept. store typing schs. Western U.S. and Can., 1953-56, nat. dept. store specialist, N.Y.C., 1956-61, promotion specialist, 1961-69, sales mgr. nat. accounts, 1971-74; dir. premium and mass mdse. Olivetti Corp., Tarrytown, N.Y.; v.p. spl. markets Silver-Reed Am., Inc., Greenwich, Conn., 1980—. Mem. Nat. Assn. Catalogue Showrooms (chmn. asso. mems.), Sales Exec. Club N.Y. (dir.), N.Y. Premium Sales Exec. Club. Republican. Home: Box 155 Goldens Bridge NY 10526 Office: Silver-Reed Am Inc 2 Sountview Dr Suite 100 Greenwich CT 06830

BAKER, MARTIN CHARLES, transp. auditing and cons. exec.; b. Montreal, Que., Can., July 2, 1944; came to U.S., 1964; s. Walter J. and Mary E. (McDonald) B.; student U. Minn., 1963-64; B.S., La. Tech. U., 1969; postgrad. S. Tex. Coll. Law, 1973; m. Jean V. Robson, June 1, 1977; children—Robson McDonald, Danielle Jean. Sales exec. Sperry Univac, Houston, 1969-74; exec. v.p. SSA Cos., Houston, 1974-79; pres., chief exec. officer Kona Tech. Corp., Houston, 1979—, So. Shippers Assn., Inc., Houston, 1979—. Clubs: Houstonian; Galveston Country. Home: Route 1 Box 147 V 4 Galveston TX 77551 Office: 4000 Dover St Houston TX 77087

BAKER, MILTON BARETZ, stainless steel flatware co. exec.; b. New Haven, July 8, 1908; s. Max L. and Gertrude (Baretz) B.; Ph.B., Yale U., 1929; m. Clara Sverd, Dec. 17, 1953; children—Barbara, Stuart. Sec., Majestic Silver Co., New Haven, 1929-45, pres., treas., 1945—, dir., 1929—; pres., treas., dir. Regal Splty. Mfg. Co., New Haven, 1932—. Served to lt. comdr. USNR, 1942-45. Jewish. Club: Woodbridge Country. Home: 17 Pleasant Hill Rd Woodbridge CT 06525 Office: Majestic Silver Co 241 Wolcott St New Haven CT 06513

BAKER, PHILIP GORDON, financier; b. Framingham, Mass., May 4, 1933; s. Orrin Gordon and Fannie Alma (Davis) B.; B.S., Boston U., 1955; m. Carolyn Atwell, Dec. 26, 1955; children—John P., Stephen G. Pres., Baker-Inman Corp., Presque Isle, Maine, 1957-62, Exec. Leasing Service, Portsmouth, N.H., 1963-70, 1st Mgmt. and Mktg. Corp., Portsmouth, 1971—, Bus. Investment Adv. Corp., Portsmouth, 1979—, Hampshire Capital Corp., Portsmouth, 1979—; dir. State St. Securites Corp. Chmn., New Castle (N.H.) Republican Town Com., 1964—. Served to capt., USAF, 1955-57. Econ. Devel. Adminstrn. grantee, 1979. Mem. Nat. Assn. Small Bus. Investment Cos. Congregationalist. Home: Wild Rose Ln New Castle NH 03854 Office: 48 Congress St Portsmouth NH 03801

BAKER, RAYMOND EMERSON, forest products co. exec.; b. Salem, Ind., Feb. 27, 1913; s. James Blaine and Mabel May (Miller) B.; A.B., DePauw U., 1935; M.S., Inst. Paper Chemistry, 1937, Ph.D., 1940; m. Jane E. Lesselyong, June 8, 1940; children—James Edward, Bonita Ann, John Clinton, David Blaine. Research chemist Brown Co., Berlin, N.H., 1940-41; pulp mill supt. Munising Paper Co. (Mich.), 1941-45; tech. dir. BFD div. Diamond Match Co., Plattsburg, N.Y., 1945-47; with pulp and paperboard div. Weyerhaeuser Co., 1947-60, v.p. mfg., 1955-60; exec. v.p. Southwest Forest Industries, Phoenix, 1960-72, pres., chief exec. officer, 1973-75, chmn. bd., 1975—, chief exec. officer, 1975-78, also dir.; dir. Valley Nat. Bank. Mem. TAPPI, Sigma Nu. Club: Phoenix Country. Home: 5307 Questa Tierra Dr Phoenix AZ 85012 Office: PO Box 7548 Phoenix AZ 85011

BAKER, REX GAVIN, JR., lawyer, savs. and loan exec.; b. Beaumont, Tex., Apr. 22, 1920; s. Rex Gavin and Edna (Heflin) B.; B.A., U. Tex., 1941, J.D., 1947; m. Jeannette M. Russell, Sept. 6, 1947; children—Jeannette (Masraff), Bess (Sharman), Ann (Wise), Rex Gavin III. Admitted to Tex. bar, 1946; practice law, Houston, 1947—; partner Berry, Richards & Baker, 1947-57, Roberts, Baker, Richards, Elledge & Heard, 1957-62, Baker, Heard, & Elledge, Houston, 1962-70, Baker & Heard, 1970-75, Baker, Sharman, Wise & Stephens, 1975—; dir., chmn. exec. com. United Savs. Assn. Tex.; chmn. bd. Southwestern Group Financial Inc.; pres., dir. Blanca Devel. Co., Baker Properties, Inc.; dir. Kaneb Securities, Inc., Total Systems, Inc., United Guaranty Corp., Sugar Creek Nat. Bank; past dir. Fed. Home Loan Bank Bd., Little Rock. Mem. fin. commn. State of Tex., 1963-73; councilman, Bellaire, Tex., 1948-49; mem. Houston Juvenile Delinquency and Crime Commn., 1955-56; chmn. exec. com. Pres.'s Council, U. Tex.; mem. Tex. Hi-Y Council, 1957-61; bd. dirs. Holly Hall, Inst. Religion, Houston Housing Devel.; past chmn. devel. bd. U. Tex. Served to lt. USNR, 1942-46. Named Distinguished Alumni U. Tex., 1977. Mem. Inter-Am., Am., Tex., Houston bar assns., Nat. League Insured Savs. Assns. (past pres., mem. exec. com.), Tex. Partners of Alliance with Peru (past pres.), Inter-Am. Savs. and Loan Union (past pres.; dir., exec. com.), Internat. Union Bldg. Soc. (council), Kappa Sigma. Baptist (past bd. deacons). Clubs: Nat. Lawyers, Georgetown (Washington); Headliners (Austin); River Oaks Country, Sugar Creek Country, Ramada, Houston (Houston). Home: 2200 Willowick Houston TX 77027 Office: 333 Southwestern Blvd Sugarland TX 77478

BAKER, ROBERT MAURICE, uniform and linens rental co. exec.; b. Odessa, Mo., Feb. 11, 1928; s. William F. and Lillian B.; B.S., Central Mo. State Coll., 1951; m. Marilyn D. Strode, Feb. 2, 1979; children—Deborah E., James E., Richard M., Ross A., Michelle L. Audit mgr. Arthur Andersen & Co., St. Louis, 1951-63; treas. Angelica Corp., St. Louis, 1963—. Active Boy Scouts Am. Served with AUS, 1946-47. C.P.A., Mo. Methodist. Office: 10176 Corporate Square Dr Saint Louis MO 63132

BAKER, ROLAND CHARLES, ins. co. exec.; b. Chgo., Aug. 12, 1938; s. William T. and Ruth J. (Carrington) B.; B.S., U. Calif., 1961; M.B.A., U. So. Calif., 1962; m. Aug. 17, 1961; children—Scott, Stephen, Stefanie. Budget adminstr. N. Am. Rockwell Corp., Anaheim, Calif., 1962-64; analyst Ampex Corp., Culver City, Calif., 1964-65; staff asst., controller Beneficial Standard Life Ins. Co., Los Angeles, 1965-75, sr. v.p., 1975-77; sr. v.p., chief fin. officer Colonial Penn Ins. Co., Phila., 1977-79, exec. v.p., 1979—, also dir.; sr. v.p. Colonial Penn Group, Inc., Phila., 1979—; exec. v.p., dir. Colonial Penn Franklin, Colonial Penn Life Ins. Co.; speaker at univs., seminars. Bd. dirs. Fund for An Open Soc., Phila., Phila. Zool. Soc.; mem. central allocations com. United Way of Southeastern Pa. Served with USMCR, 1962-65. C.P.A., Calif. Fellow Life Ins. Office Mgmt. Inst.; mem. Am. Inst. C.P.A.'s, Fin. Execs. Inst., Calif. Soc. C.P.A.'s, Pa. Inst. C.P.A.'s, Am. Soc. C.L.U.'s. Clubs: Phila. Racquet, Los Angeles Athletic. Home: Villanova PA 19085 Office: 5 Penn Center Plaza 30th Floor Philadelphia PA 19181

BAKER, STANLEY DAVID, agrl. co. exec.; b. Dallas, Oreg., Nov. 3, 1951; s. Pat Nobel and Doris Lucille B.; ed. Portland (Oreg.) Community Coll.; m. Michele Marie Hearn, May 27, 1972; children—Adell, Carmen. Asst. gen. mgr. Montavilla Sheet Metal Co., Inc., Portland, 1971-75; gen. mgr. Oreg. ops. Berger & Plate Co., div. Pacific Molasses Co., Inc., 1975-77; gen. mgr. Green Valley Seeds, Inc., Monmouth, Oreg., 1977-78, Seedco Enterprises, Inc., Dallas, 1978-79; exec. v.p., gen. mgr. Barenbrug USA, Inc., Dallas, 1979—. Served with USAR, 1970-71; Vietnam. Decorated Combat Inf. badge, Army Commendation medal, Gallantry cross with palm. Mem. Am. Seed Trade Assn., Oreg. Seed Assn. Republican. Mem. Apostolic Faith Ch. Home: 1171 SE Shelton St Dallas OR 97338 Office: 289 E Ellendale Ave Dallas OR 97338

BAKER, STEPHEN LEON, mfg. co. exec.; b. Brockton, Mass., Sept. 9, 1947; s. Stanley Lane and Jean Grace (Remick) B.; B.S. in Bus. Adminstrn. Mgmt., Northeastern U., 1970; M.B.A., Boston Coll., 1975; m. Anne M. Lodie, Mar. 7, 1970; children—Mark C., Erin L. Prodn. scheduler Garland Corp., Brockton, Mass., 1970-71; adminstr. Raytheon Co., Brockton, 1971-74; mgr. cost acctg. ERT Inc., Lexington, Mass., 1974-76; mgr. fin. planning and analysis Analytic Scis. Corp., Reading, Mass., 1977-79; mgr. engring. adminstrn. Compugraphic Corp., Wilmington, Mass., 1979—; instr. mgmt. Boston U., evenings 1977—. Mem. Adminstrv. Mgmt. Soc. Office: 80 Industrial Way Wilmington MA 01887

BAKER, WILLIAM CHARLES, restaurant chain exec.; b. Port Arthur, Tex., May 14, 1933; s. Harry Winters and Martha Emily (Newby) B.; B.B.A., U. Tex., 1955, LL.B., 1957; m. Janice Yeteva Haskin, Jan. 14, 1965; children—William C., Cynthia Carol, Lisa Lanette, Stacy Allison, Catherine Suzanne. Admitted to N.Y. bar, 1957, Tex. bar, 1959, U.S. Supreme Ct. bar, 1959; trial atty. U.S. Dept. Justice, Washington, 1957-59; mem. firm Zock, Petrie, Sheneman & Reid, N.Y.C., 1959-62, Wynne, Jaffe & Tinsley, Dallas, 1962-64; gen. counsel Great S.W. Corp., Arlington, Tex., 1964-67, chmn., pres.,

1968-70; pres., dir. Macco Corp., Newport Beach, Calif., 1967-70; partner firm Baker & Caldwell, Newport Beach, 1970-71; pres., dir. Perimeter Corp., Newport Beach, 1971-73; prin. B.H. Miller Devel. Co.; partner Baker-Miller & Assos., Santa Ana. 1973-76; chmn. bd., dir. Del Taco, Inc., Costa Mesa, Calif., 1976—, Del Taco Corp., Atlanta, 1978—. Served to capt. U.S. Army. Licensed real estate broker, Calif. Mem. Urban Land Inst., Am. Mgmt. Assn. Clubs: Balboa Bay, Big Canyon Country (Newport Beach); Coto de Caza (Trabuco Canyon, Calif.); Capital City, Commerce, Cherokee Country (Atlanta); Dallas. Home: Rt 3 Box 300 Madison GA 30650 Office: 345 Baker St Costa Mesa CA 92626

BAKER, WILLIAM FRANKLIN, TV co. exec.; b. Cleve., Sept. 20, 1942; s. William Franklin and Rita Marie (Huebner) B.; B.A. in Communications, Case Western Res. U., 1965, M.A., 1968, Ph.D., 1972; m. Jeannemarie Gelin, June 22, 1968; children—Christiane, Angela. Exec. producer Sta. WEWS-TV, Clevel., 1971-74, asst. gen. mgr., 1975-78; v.p., gen. mgr. Sta. WJZ-TV, Balt., 1978-79; pres. Group W Prodns., Hollywood, Calif., 1979, Group W TV, N.Y.C., 1979—; lectr. John Carroll U., U. Ark. Nat. Assn. Broadcasters grantee, 1968. Mem. Nat. Assn. Radio-TV Program Execs., Nat. Acad. TV Arts and Sci. Roman Catholic. Author: Power & Decision Making in American Television, 1971. Office: 90 Park Ave New York NY 10016

BAKER, WILLIAM HERBERT, hosp. assn. exec.; b. Buffalo, Oct. 23, 1932; s. Guy Andrew and Ella Mae (Beeler) B.; B.S. in Econs., Purdue U., 1954; postgrad. Ball State U., 1956-58, Rider Coll., 1980; children—Scott Andrew, Karen Lynn. Prodn. supr., safety dir., labor relations supr. Gen. Motors Corp., Muncie, Ind., New Brunswick, N.J., Anderson, Ind., 1956-69; dir. personnel mgmt. N.J. Hosp. Assn., Princeton, 1969-75, v.p., 1975—; mem. faculty hosp. seminars. Mem., v.p. Montgomery Twp. Bd. Edn., pres., 1977—; former bd. dirs. Am. Heart Assn. N.J. affiliate; officer, former bd. dirs. Princeton Area United Fund. Served with CIC, AUS, 1954-56. Mem. Am. Mgmt. Assn., Soc. Advancement Mgmt. Lutheran. Home: 420 Stockton St Hightstown NJ 08520 Office: 760 Alexander Rd CN-1 Princeton NJ 08540

BAKER, WILLIAM OLIVER, research chemist; b. Chestertown Md., July 15, 1915; s. Harold May and Helen (Stokes) B.; B.S., Washington Coll., 1935, Sc.D., 1957; Ph.D., Princeton, 1938; Sc.D., Georgetown U., 1962, U. Pitts., 1963, Seton Hall U., 1965, U. Akron, 1968, U. Mich., 1970, St. Peter's Coll., 1972, Poly. Inst. N.Y., 1973, Trinity Coll., Dublin, Ireland, 1975, Northwestern U., 1976, U. Notre Dame, 1978; D.Eng., Stevens Inst. Tech., 1962, N.J. Inst. Tech., 1978; LL.D., U. Glasgow, 1965, U. Pa., 1974, Kean Coll. N.J., 1976, Lehigh U., 1980; L.H.D., Monmouth Coll., 1973, Clarkson Coll. Tech., 1974; m. Frances Burrill, Nov. 15, 1941; 1 son, Joseph Burrill. With Bell Telephone Labs., 1939—, in charge polymer research and devel., 1948-51, asst. dir. chem. and metall. research, 1951-54, dir. research, phys. scis., 1954-55, v.p. research, 1955-73, pres., 1973-79, chmn. bd., 1980—; dir. Ann. Revs., Inc., Summit and Elizabeth Trust Co., Sandia Corp., Babcock & Wilcox Co., 1962-78, Bell Telephone Labs., Inc., Am. Bell Internat., Inc., 1975-79, Western Electric Co., Inc., 1975-80, Western Electric Internat., Inc., 1978-80, Johnson & Johnson, 1980—; vis. lectr. Northwestern U., Princeton U., Duke; Schmitt lectr. U. Notre Dame, 1968; Harrelson lectr. N.C. State U., 1971; Herbert Spencer lectr. U. Pa., 1974; Charles M. Schwab Meml. lectr. Am. Iron and Steel Inst., 1976; NIH lectr., 1958; Metall. Soc. Am. Inst. Mining Engrs./Am. Soc. Metals distinguished lectr., 1976; Miles Conrad Meml. lectr. Nat. Fedn. Abstracting and Indexing Services, 1977; Wulff lectr. M.I.T., 1979; cons. Office Sci. and Tech., 1977—. Mem. Princeton Grad. Council, 1956-64; bd. visitors Tulane U., 1963—; mem. commn. sociotech. systems NRC, 1974-78, also chmn. adv. bd. on mil. personnel supplies, 1964-78; mem. com. on phys. chemistry of div. chemistry and chem. tech., 1963-70, also steering com. Pres.'s Food and Nutrition Study Commn. Internat. Relations Nat. Acad. Scis.-NRC, 1975; mem. panel on phys. chemistry Office Naval Research, 1948-51; past mem. Pres.'s Sci. Adv. Com., 1957-60, nat. sci. bd. NSF, 1960-66; past chmn. Nat. Sci. Info. Council, 1959-61; mem. sci. adv. bd. Nat. Security Agy., 1959-76, cons., 1976—; cons. Dept. Def., 1958-71, to spl. asst. for sci. and tech., 1963-73, to Panel of Ops. Evaluation Group, USN, 1960-62; mem. N.J. Bd. Higher Edn., 1967—, exec. com., 1970—, vice chmn., 1970-72; mem. liaison com. for sci. and tech. Library of Congress, 1963-73; mem. Pres.'s Fgn. Intelligence Adv. Bd., 1959-77; chmn. Pres.'s Adv. Group Anticipated Advances in Sci. and Tech., 1975-76; vice chmn. Pres.'s Com. Sci. and Tech., 1976-77; bd. regents Nat. Library Medicine, 1969-73; bd. visitors Air Force Systems Command, 1962-73; mem. mgmt. adv. council Oak Ridge Nat. Lab., 1970—; mem. Nat. Commn. on Libraries and Info. Scis., 1971-75, Commn. on Critical Choices for Ams., 1973-75, Nat. Cancer Adv. Bd., 1974—; mem. panel advisory Inst. Materials Research, Nat. Bur. Standards, 1966-69; mem. Council Trends and Perspective U.S. C. of C., 1966-74; chmn. tech. panels adv. to Nat. Bur. Standards, Nat. Acad. Scis.-NRC, 1969-78; mem. Nat. Council Ednl. Research, 1973-75; mem. energy research and devel. adv. council Energy Policy Office, 1973-75; mem. Project Independence adv. com. Fed. Energy Adminstrn., 1974-75; mem. Gov.'s Com. to Evaluate Capital Needs N.J., 1974-75; mem. governing bd. Nat. Enquiry into Scholarly Communication, 1975-79; advisory council N.J. Regional Med. Library, 1975—, Gas Research Inst. Advisory Bd., 1978—, Commn. o Humanities, 1978—; adv. bd. N.J. Sci./Tech. Center, 1980—. Mem. sci. advisory bd. Robert A. Welch Found., 1968—; vis. com. for chemistry Harvard, 1959-72; vis. com., div. chemistry and chem. engring. Calif. Inst. Tech., 1969-72; vis. com. on scis. and math. Drew U., 1969—; asso. in univ. seminar on tech. and social change Columbia, 1969—; vis. com., dept. materials sci. and engring. Mass. Inst. Tech., 1973-76; bd. overseers Coll. Engring. and Applied Sci. U. Pa., 1975—; bd. dirs. Council on Library Resources, 1970—, Clin. Scholar Program Robert Wood Johnson Found., 1973-76, Third Century Corp., 1973-76; trustee Urban Studies, Inc., 1960-78, Aerospace Corp., 1961-76, Carnegie-Mellon U., 1967—, Princeton, 1964—, Fund N.J., 1974—, Harry Frank Guggenheim Found., 1976—, Gen. Motors Cancer Research Found., 1978—, Charles Babbage Inst., 1978—, Newark Mus., 1979—; trustee Rockefeller U., 1960—, vice chmn., 1970-80, chmn., 1980—; trustee Andrew W. Mellon Found., 1965—, chmn., 1975—. Named 1 of 10 top scientists in U.S. industry, 1954; recipient Perkin medal, 1963; Honor scroll Am. Inst. Chemists, 1962; award to execs. ASTM, 1967; Edgar Marburg award, 1967; Indsl. Research Inst. medal, 1970; Frederik Philips award IEEE, 1972; Indsl. Research Man of Year award, 1973; Procter prize Sigma Xi, 1973; James Madison medal Princeton, 1975; Mellon Inst. award, 1975; Soc. Research Adminstrs. award for distinguished contbns., 1976; Fahrney medal Franklin Inst., 1977; von Hippel award Materials Research Soc., 1978; N.J. Sci./Tech. medal, 1980; Harvard fellow 1937-38, Procter fellow, 1938-39. Fellow Am. Phys. Soc., Am. Inst. Chemists (Gold medal 1975), Franklin Inst., Am. Acad. Arts and Scis.; mem. Dirs. of Indsl. Research, Am. Chem. Soc. (past mem. com. nat. def., cons., past mem. com. chemistry and pub. affairs, Priestley medal 1966, Parsons award 1976, Willard Gibbs award 1978, Madison Marshall award 1980), Am. Philos. Soc., Nat. Acad. Scis. (council 1969-72, com. sci. and pub. policy 1966-69), Nat. Acad. Engring., Inst. Medicine (council 1973-75), Indsl. Research Inst. (dir. 1960-63), Sigma Xi, Phi Lambda Upsilon, Omicron Delta Kappa. Clubs: Chemists of N.Y. (hon.), Cosmos, Princeton of Northwestern N.J. Contbr.: High Polymers, 1945, Symposium on Basic Research, AAAS, 1959, Rheology, Vol. III, 1960, Technology and Social Change, 1964, Science: The Achievement and the Promise, 1968, Ann. Rev. Materials Sci., 1976, various other books. Mem. editorial adv. bd. Jour. Applied Polymer Sci., Sci., Tech. and Human Values, 1979-80; adv. bd. Info. and Soc., 1979—; past mem. adv. editorial bd. Research Mgmt., Chem. and Engring. News; hon. editorial adv. bd. Carbon. Contbr. numerous articles to tech. jours. Holder 13 patents. Home: Spring Valley Rd Morristown NJ 07960 Office: 600 Mountain Ave Murray Hill NJ 07974

BAKER, WILLIAM WALLACE, newspaperman, educator; b. Kansas City, Mo., July 2, 1921; s. William Reaune and Grace (Wallace) B.; A.B., U. Mich., 1947; m. Virginia Elizabeth Graham, Dec. 21, 1941 (dec.); 1 son, William Wallace (dec.); m. 2d, Betty Krall Thomas, Nov. 16, 1979. U. Mich. corr. Detroit Times, 1940-41; with SSS, 1945; with Kansas City Star, 1947-77, editorial writer, 1954-63, asso. editor, 1963-67, editor, 1967-77, exec. v.p., 1971-75, pres., 1975-77, also dir.; asst. prof. William Allen White Sch. Journalism, U. Kans., Lawrence, 1978—. Served with AUS, World War II; PTO. Decorated Bronze Star. Mem. Am. Soc. Newspaper Editors, Am. Newspaper Pubs. Assn., Nat. Conf. Editorial Writers, Sphinx, Phi Beta Kappa, Phi Kappa Phi, Phi Eta Sigma, Sigma Delta Chi. Episcopalian. Club: Kansas City Press. Home: 2 W Terrace Trail Lake Quivira KS 66106 Office: Room 105 Flint Hall Univ Kansas Lawrence KS 66044

BAKEWELL, CHARLES ADAMS, energy econs. cons.; b. Hartford, Conn., Apr. 12, 1940; s. Henry Palmer and Hester Livingstone (Adams) B.; B.A., Yale, 1963; M.B.A., Columbia, 1966; m. Lucia Ruth Urban, June 22, 1963; children—Geoffrey Ward, Andrea Whitney, Christine Ashley. Various fin. positions Gen. Foods Corp., White Plains, N.Y., 1966-74, category fin. mgr., 1974-75; mgr. budget and profit analysis and gen. accounting Sperry Remington Consumer Products Div., Bridgeport, Conn., 1975-78; sr. fin. analyst Gruy Fed., Inc., Arlington, Va., 1978—. Treas., Westport (Conn.) chpt. Am. Field Service, 1970-71; vestryman Christ Holy Trinity Ch., Westport, 1974-77, canvass chmn., 1974, 75; treas. Westport Republican Town Com., 1978-79; del. Conn. Rep. Conv., 1978; participant Campaign Mgmt. Inst., 1977. Home: 7900 Old Falls Rd McLean VA 22102 Office: 2001 Jefferson Davis Hwy Suite 701 Arlington VA 22202

BAKKEN, GLENN P., mfg. co. exec.; b. Mpls., Jan. 12, 1919; s. Luther G. and Ida (Skappel) B.; B.S. in Mech. Engring., U. Minn., 1942; m. Helen E. Moorehouse; children—Laurie, Leslie, Richard. Plant mgr. Aluminum Co. Am., 1942-46, Reynolds Metals Co., 1946-54; exec. v.p., dir. Chase Brass & Copper Co. Inc. subs. Kennecott Copper Corp., 1955-57, pres. subs., 1957, corp. sr. v.p., sec., 1979, exec. v.p., pres. Kennecott Minerals Co., 1979-80, pres., chief operating officer Kennecott Copper Corp., 1980—; dir. Kennecott Corp. Office: Kennecott Corp Ten Stamford Forum Stamford CT 06904

BALACEK, THOMAS VINCENT, corp. exec., engr.; b. N.Y.C., Sept. 24, 1937; s. Theodore Vincent and Margaret Alice (Tuohy) B.; student Acad. Aeros., 1956-60; m. Joyce Eldeene Iden, Nov. 19, 1960 (dec. May 5, 1978); children—Thomas Vincent, Valerie Anne, William Theodore, Paul Frederick. Engr., Executone, Inc., N.Y.C., 1958-60, U.S. Testing Co., Inc., Hoboken, N.J., 1961; sales engr. Nuclear-Chgo. subsidiary G.D. Searle Des Plaines, Ill., 1961-65, regional mgr., 1966-67, sales mgr., 1968, advt. mgr., 1969; v.p. sales and mktg. Telemed Corp., Hoffman Estates, Ill., 1969-76; founder, pres., chief exec. officer Cardiassist Corp., Hoffman Estates, 1976—. Home: 506 N River Rd Fox River Grove IL 60021 Office: 2400 W Hassell Rd Hoffman Estates IL 60195

BALBOS, PAUL HOWARD, mfg. co. exec.; b. Balt., May 9, 1948; s. Leslie and Anne (Weitzman) B.; B.S., Drexel U., 1971. Mfg. engr. Westinghouse Electric Corp., Lester, Pa., 1971-74, planning supr., 1974-75, systems analyst, 1975-76; dir. ops. Carefree of Colo., Broomfield, 1976-79; broker, owner A-1 Realty Inc., 1979—; prodn. mgr. Gerico, Northglenn Co. Home: 24 Scott Dr N Broomfield CO 80020

BALCAR, GERALD P., glass mfg. co. exec.; b. Elizabeth, N.J., July 2, 1932; s. Frederick Rhinehart and Genevieve (Pierce) B.; A.B., Cornell U., 1954; m. Carol Mintern Edlund, June 17, 1955 (div.); children—Sherry Elizabeth, Peter Rhinehart, Joanne Wendell. Mem. staff Tradeways, Inc., marketing consultants, 1954-58; supr. mktg. research Collins Radio Co., Richardson, Tex., 1958-60; asst. to pres. Acoustica Assos., Inc., Los Angeles, 1960-62; asst. to pres. Atco Chem. Indsl. Products, Inc., Franklin, N.J., 1962-65; nat. sales mgr. Potters Bros., Inc., Carlstadt, N.J., 1965-71; v.p. mktg. Potters Industries, Inc., 1971—, also v.p. devel. Chmn. Pub. Affairs Com.; chmn. West Milford Bd. Edn., 1971-73. Mem. Soc. Aerospace Material and Process Engrs., Am. Ordnance Assn., Internat. Platform Assn. Club: Chemists (N.Y.). Home: 73 Timber Ln Newfoundland NJ 07435 Office: 377 Route 17 Hasbrouck Heights NJ 07604

BALCH, WILLIAM EMMETT, JR., ins. co. exec.; b. Carter Nine, Okla., Nov. 9, 1929; s. WIlliam E. and Mary E. (Davis) B.; B.S. in Edn., Eastern Ill. U., Charleston, 1952; M.S. in Edn. (Grad. Fellow), U. Ill., 1953; certs. Ins. Inst. Am., Life Ins. Agency Mgmt. Assn.; m. Patricia L. Field, Feb. 11, 1951; children—Kerry L., Denice O., Lynn Valentine, Kayla J. Asst. coach U. Ill., Champaign-Urbana, 1952-53; head coach Byron (Ill.) Comml. High Sch., 1953-55; with State Farm Ins. Co., 1955—, ins. agt., Effingham, Ill., 1955-60, agency sales mgr., Decatur, Ill., 1960-61, agency supr., 1961-62, dir. tng. and edn. Ill. and Iowa, 1962-64, agency dir. charge of mktg., recruiting, sales promotion, Bloomington, Ill., 1964—. Pres. Jr. C. of C., 1958-59; tchr., youth sponsor Eastview Christian Ch., bd. dirs., 1960-74. Served with USN, 1947-48. Cert. C.L.U. agency mgmt. Mem. Bloomington Assn. Commerce, Ill. Life Underwriters Assn. Clubs: Am. Legion, Masons. Contbr. items on sales mgmt., agency mgmt. to house publ. Home: 1015 E Grove St Bloomington IL 61701 Office: 2309 E Oakland St Bloomington IL 61701

BALCH, WILLIAM FRANKLIN, investment counseling co. exec.; b. Mpls., Dec. 15, 1934; s. Richard Carlisle and Virginia (Finley) B.; B.A., Dartmouth Coll., 1956, M.B.A., 1957; m. Sally J. Ciancimino, Sept. 19, 1970. Salesman, Minn. Mining & Mfg. Co., St. Paul, N.Y.C., 1957-59; registered rep. Dean Witter & Co. Inc., Berkeley, Calif., 1959-64, v.p., head computer research dept., 1964-73; co-founder, pres. Balch, Hardy, Inc. (merged with Peter W. Scheinman Co. 1977), N.Y.C., 1973-77; pres. Balch, Hardy & Scheinman Investment Counseling, N.Y.C., 1977—. Served with USAF, 1957. Chartered fin. analyst. Mem. Inst. Chartered Fin. Analysts, N.Y. Soc. Security Analysts, N.Y. Instnl. Options Soc., Investment Tech. Assn. Home: 4455 Douglas Ave Riverdale NY 10471

BALDERSTON, THOMAS WILLIAM, investment banker; b. Phila., Feb. 28, 1941; s. Hugh Eastburn and Pauline (Schaaf) B.; B.S., Pa. State U., 1963; M.B.A., U. So. Calif., 1973; m. Louise Talmage, June 5, 1971; 1 dau., Kristin Clark. Mktg. rep. Rohm & Haas Co., Phila., 1966-72; asst. v.p. Warburg Paribas Becker Inc., N.Y.C., 1973-77; sr. v.p. Blyth Eastman Paine Webber Health Care Funding Inc., N.Y.C., 1977—, also dir.; dir. Naked Zebra, Inc. Served to 1st lt. C.E., U.S. Army, 1963-65. Mem. Am. Hosp. Assn. Republican. Club: Round Hill (Greenwich, Conn.). Home: 34 Lake Dr S Riverside CT 06878 Office: 1221 Ave of Americas New York NY 10020

BALDRIGE, MALCOLM, mfg. co. exec.; b. Omaha, Oct. 4, 1922; s. Howard Malcolm and Regina (Connell) B.; B.A., Yale U., 1944; m. Margaret Trowbridge Murray, Mar. 31, 1951; children—Megan Brewster Baldrige Murray, Mary Trowbridge. With Eastern Co., 1947-62, v.p., 1957-60, pres., 1960-62; with Scovill Mfg. Co., Waterbury, Conn., 1962—, pres., from 1963, chmn., chief exec. officer, 1969—; dir. AMF, Inc., ASARCO, Inc., Bendix Corp., Conn. Mut. Life Ins. Co., Eastern Co., Uniroyal, Inc.; trustee Swiss Re-ins. Co. Chmn., Nat. Corp. Giving, Yale U., 1976-79; incorporator Easter Seal Soc.; chmn. Waterbury Mayor's Citizens' Adv. Com.; dir. Waterbury ARC; chmn. Central Valley Drug Help Drive; del. Republican Nat. Conv., 1964, 68, 72, 76; chmn. Conn. Rep. State Fin. Com., 1969; chmn. Conn. Bush for Pres. Com., 1979-80; mem. Conn. Citizens' Commn. on State Legislature; mem. Conn. Rep. State Central Com. on Labor. Served to capt. U.S. Army, 1943-46. Mem. Bus. Council, Council Fgn. Relations, Internat. C. of C., Greater Waterbury C. of C. (past chmn.). Office: Scovill Inc 500 Chase Pkwy Waterbury CT 06720

BALDWIN, ELLEN JANE (MRS. HAL WEST) real estate co. exec.; b. N.Y.C., d. Whitney and Edna Estelle (Bolles) Eckert; student N.Y. Sch. Design, 1956-58, New Sch. Coll. City N.Y., 1958-60; m. Hal West, Oct. 18, 1968; children (by previous marriage)—Richard A., Suzanne E. Real estate Salesman, 1963-71; owner Baldwin West and Assos., San Rafael, Calif., 1971—. Sec., Marin County (Calif.) Cerebral Palsy, 1962-64. Cert. residential specialist; grad. Realtors Inst. Mem. Santa Margarita Valley Homeowners Assn. (dir. 1972—, v.p. 1972-76, pres. 1976—), Nat. Assn. Realtors, Calif. Assn. Realtors, Realtors Nat. Mktg. Inst., Marin County Bd. Realtors (dir. 1979—), Million Dollar Club (life), Nat. Million Dollar Real Estate Club. Home: 16 Galleon Way San Rafael CA 94903 Office: 200 Northgate One San Rafael CA 94903

BALDWIN, ESTHER EBERSTADT (MRS. ROBERT HOWE BALDWIN), personnel and ins. co. exec.; b. East Orange, N.J.; d. Edward Frederick and Elenita Contreras (Lembcke) Eberstadt; B.A., Notre Dame Coll. Md., 1919, M.A. (hon.), 1941, LL.D., 1958; Mus.B., Am. Inst. Applied Music, 1921; m. Robert Howe Baldwin, June 7, 1933. Pres., Mrs. E.E. Brooke, Inc., Personnel Cons., N.Y.C., 1923—, Robert H. Baldwin, Inc., Ins. Brokers, N.Y.C., 1955—; v.p. Davis, Dorland & Co., N.Y.C., 1955—; lectr. to colls., bus. and profl. groups. Mem. nat. council U.S. Com. for Refugees, 1963-64; mem. White House Conf. For World Refugee, 1963; mem. nat. council Am. Friends of Middle East, 1956-63, Pakistan-Am. Students Assn., 1957-62; mem. Greater N.Y. council Boy Scouts Am., 1956-58; Greater N.Y. chpt. ANTA. Pres. Robert H. Baldwin Found., 1956—. Mem. bd., exec. Com. Women's Nat. Republican Club, 1956-60, now life member. Bd. dirs., chmn., pres. Am. Com. to Befriend Arab Refugees, 1958—; bd. dirs. Council on Islamic Affairs, 1957-65, vice-chmn., 1958-63; bd. dirs. Near East Found., Notre Dame Coll. Md., Camp Fire Girls, Inc., Internat. Ednl. Devel.; mem. nat. council Met. Opera, 1967—; mem. Pres.'s Council Columbia U.; co-founder Arab and Am. Friendship Assn. Decorated Order Chevalier Ct. by Shah of Iran; recipient Pres.'s Medal Coll. Notre Dame. Fellow Archeol. Inst. Am., Am. Geog. Soc.; founding mem. Jr. League of Oranges (Orange, N.J.); life mem. Acad. Polit. Sci., Am. Mus. Natural History, Assistance League So. Cal. Met. Mus. Art, N.Y. Zool. Soc.; mem. Nat. Inst. Social Scis., Pakistan-Am. C. of C., Soc. Women Geographers, AAUW, English Speaking Union, Columbia Assos., Soc. of Jesus (hon.), Delta Epsilon Sigma. Author: The Girl and Her Job, 1933; Career Clinic, 1940; The Right Job For You and How To Get It, 1944; Career Guide, 1943; Guide to Career Success, 1947; You and Your Personality, 1949. Contbr. articles to Cosmopolitan, Good Housekeeping, Mademoiselle, others. Home: 4 Pleasant St Woodstock VT 05091 Office: Davis Dorland & Co 2 World Trade Center New York NY 10007

BALDWIN, FREDERICK HENRY, JR., gen. contracting co. exec.; b. Medford, Mass., Aug. 13, 1946; s. Frederick Henry and Barbara Constance (Beal) B.; student Lowell Technol. Inst., 1964-72; m. Ellen F. Connolly, Aug. 6, 1971; children—Christopher P., Kathleen E. Founder, pres., treas. F.H. Baldwin, Jr., Inc., Tewksbury, Mass., 1964—; dir. Selecto-Therm, Inc., Motion Control Devices Co. Mem. Tewksbury Planning Bd., 1969-73, chmn., 1970; mem. No. Middlesex Area Planning Commn., 1970-74, Tewksbury Bd. Selectmen, 1970-74. Mem. Home Builders Assn., Homeowner Warranty Council (pres.). Democrat. Episcopalian. Clubs: Elks, 100 of Mass. Home: 29 Magna Vista Circle Tewksbury MA 01876 Office: 853 Main St Tewksbury MA 01876

BALDWIN, JESSE ANTHONY, filter mfg. co. exec., philanthropist; b. Knox, Ind., June 27, 1896; s. Monroe and Lulu (Hopkins) B.; degree in Mech. Engring., U. Mich., 1921; postgrad. Purdue U., 1922; m. Marie Alice Phalem, June 5, 1923 (dec. Mar. 1932); children—Colleen Marie Baldwin Eaton, Theodore Gregory; m. 2d, Fern A. Holte Farquhar, May 21, 1944. Test engr. Maxwell Motor Car Co., Detroit, summer 1921; testing engr. Packard Motor Car Co., Detroit, 1922-25; testing, developing carburetors Marvel Carburetor Co., Flint, Mich., 1926; testing, designing, developing carburetors Detroit Lubricator Co., 1927-29; experimenter, developer filters, Eau Claire, Wis., 1930-32; owner, gen. mgr. J.A. Baldwin Co., Eau Claire, 1932-42; asso. engr. WPB, Wis. dist., 1942-46; Wis. dist. mgr. Smaller War Plants Corp., 1945-46; pres., gen. mgr., charge engring. and designing J.A. Baldwin Mfg. Co., Kearney, Nebr., 1953—. Served with U.S. Army, 1917. Baldwin Bldg. at Mayo Clinic named for him. Mem. Soc. Automotive Engrs., N.A.M., Automotive Service Industry Assn., U.S., Kearney chambers commerce. Patentee numerous carburetors, filters for mech. constrn., chem. formulas. Designer renewable-type filter; designer, builder spl. machines for prodn. filters. Home: 16 Hillscrest Dr Kearney NE 68847 Office: PO Box 610 Kearney NE 68847

BALDWIN, JOHN LUCIAN, glass co. exec.; b. Fitchburg, Mass., Aug. 21, 1926; s. Roy Duane and Elsie (Fuller) B.; B.A., Yale U., 1949; grad. Advanced Mgmt. Program, Harvard U., 1969; m. Nancy Church McDowell, Apr. 21, 1951; children—John M., Sarah C. With PPG Industries, Inc., 1949-78, v.p. contract and supply, glass div., 1971-78; pres., chief exec. officer Pittsburgh Corning Corp., Pitts., 1978—. Served with USN, 1944-46. Episcopalian. Clubs: Duquesne (Pitts.); Edgeworth (Sewickley, Pa.). Office: Pitts Corning Corp 800 Presque Isle Dr Pittsburgh PA 15239

BALDWIN, LARELL HARDISON, ins. co. exec.; b. Hanford, Calif., May 12, 1940; s. Leo H. and Bernice (Gash) B.; student Pasadena Coll., 1958-61; grad. Alexander Hamilton Inst. Bus., 1967; m. Kathleen L. Hardison, June 23, 1979; children—Jennifer Lin, Leslie Kari, Richard Allen, Michael Maxwell. Vice-pres. mortgage lending div. Standard Life & Accident Ins. Co. of Okla., Phoenix, 1961-64; sales mgr. Peterson Baby Products Inc., Burbank, Calif., 1964-67; v.p. sales Rotorway Aircraft Corp., Tempe, Ariz., 1967-69; pres. Trans World Arts Inc., San Jose, Calif., 1969-75, Baldwin Assos. Devel. Corp., Santa Cruz, Calif., 1975-80; partner, nat. dir. mktg. Assurance Distbg. Co. Ltd., Santa Ana, Calif., 1979—; nat. cons. ins.

cos.; dir. Am. Acrylic Industries. Home: 8 Deer Trailway Scotts Valley CA 95066 Office: 1010 N Main St Suite 525 Santa Ana CA 92701

BALDWIN, MELVIN DANA, II, machinery mfg. co. exec.; b. Evanston, Ill., Sept. 8, 1941; s. Ralph Belknap and Lois Virginia (Johnston) B.; B.S. in Indsl. Engring., U. Mich., 1964; m. Mary Nell Wiese, Sept. 13, 1969; children—Peter Dana, John Belknap. With Oliver Machinery Co., Grand Rapids, Mich., 1964—, v.p., mktg. mgr., 1974-80, v.p., gen. mgr. machine tool div., 1980—. Bd. dirs. Grand Rapids YMCA, 1975-78, Grand Rapids Art Mus., 1977—. Mem. Woodworking Machinery Mfrs. Am. (treas. 1978-80, v.p. 1980—, dir. 1977—). Republican. Congregationalist. Clubs: Kent Country, Grand Rapids Yacht, University (pres. 1978-80) (Grand Rapids). Office: 445 6th St NW Grand Rapids MI 49504

BALDWIN, ROBERT HAYES BURNS, bus. exec.; b. East Orange, N.J., July 9, 1920; s. John Frank and Anna (Burns) B.; A.B., Princeton U., 1942; m. Geraldine Gay Williams, May 28, 1949; children—Janet Kimball, Deborah Gay Baldwin Fall, Robert Hayes Burns, Whitney Hayes, Elizabeth Brooks. With Morgan Stanley & Co., N.Y.C., 1946—, gen. partner, 1958-65, 67-75, ltd. partner, 1965-67; pres., mng. dir. Morgan Stanley & Co., Inc., N.Y.C., served as under sec. of navy, 1965-67; dir. Urban Nat., Inc. Trustee, Presbyn. Hosp. City N.Y., Morristown (N.J.) Meml. Hosp., Geraldine Rockefeller Dodge Found., Seeing Eye, Inc., Orgn. Resources Counselors, Inc. Served to lt. USNR, 1942-46. Mem. Securities Industry Assn. (governing council, vice chmn. bd. dirs.), Council Fgn. Relations, Phi Beta Kappa. Republican. Presbyn. Clubs: Links (N.Y.C.); Chevy Chase (Md.); Metropolitan (Washington); Morris County Golf (Convent, N.J.); Morristown (N.J.) Field; Bridgehampton (N.Y.); Chicago; Augusta (Ga.) Nat. Golf. Home: Village Rd New Vernon NJ 07976 Office: 1251 Ave of Americas New York NY 10020

BALGOCHIAN, PETER KACHADOUR, JR., mfg. co. exec.; b. Boston, Sept. 10, 1935; s. Peter K. and Mary (Moosesian) B.; A.A. in Elec. Engring., Northeastern U., 1963, B.S. in Indsl. Tech., 1965, M.B.A., 1968; m. S. JoAnne Bazarian, Apr. 8, 1956; children—Peter Kachadour, Mardi Kristen. Project engr. Sylvania, Boston, 1963-67, Avco Missile Systems Div., Wilmington, Mass., 1967, TRW, Boston, 1968; northeastern sales mgr. Litton Industries, Boston, 1969; engr.-in-charge Sylvania, Boston, 1970-73; mgr. product test Xerox Corp., El Segundo, Calif., 1973—; cons. SBA. Campaign mgr., Mass. State Senator candidate, 1972. Served with U.S. Army, 1957-59, 61. Mem. Am. Mgmt. Assn., Soc. for Advancement of Mgmt. (pres. Los Angeles chpt. 1979-80, area dir. 1980-81). Mem. Armenian Apostolic Ch. Club: Lions. Office: 555 S Aviation Blvd El Segundo CA 90245

BALKCOM, JAMES ROBBINS, JR., mfg. co. exec.; b. Atlanta, May 19, 1944; s. James Robbins R.; student Ga. Inst. Tech., 1962-63; B.S., U.S. Mil. Acad., 1967; M.B.A., Harvard U., 1973; m. Linda Purcell, June 30, 1967; children—Julie Ann, Mary Kathryn. Vice pres. Peachtree Bank & Trust Co., Atlanta, 1973-76; v.p. Techsonic Industries, Eufaula, Ala., 1976-77, pres., 1977—, also dir.; dir. Eufaula Bank & Trust Co. Vice chmn. Bass Research Found., Starkville, Miss., 1977—; chmn. Tourism and Conv. Commn., Eufaula, 1978-79; dir. United Way, Eufaula, 1979. Served with U.S. Army, 1967-71. Decorated Bronze Star with oak leaf cluster. Mem. Am. Fishing Tackle Mfrs. Assn., Boating Industry Assn., Harvard Bus. Sch. Club Atlanta, West Point Soc. Atlanta, Young Pres.'s Orgn. Methodist. Office: 1 Humminbird Ln Eufaula AL 36027

BALKIE, FRANCIS WILLIAM, pub. co. exec.; b. Phila., Aug. 2, 1932; s. William Francis and Alice (Spur) B.; R.N., Pa. Sch. Nursing, 1954; B.S., Temple U., 1960; M.B.A., Fordham U., 1975. Pvt. practice anesthesia nursing, San Francisco, 1960-67; cons. Calif. Nurses Assn., San Francisco, 1967-71; dir. ednl. services div. Am. Jours. Nursing Co., N.Y.C., 1971-73, dir. mags., 1973-76, dep. pub. dir., 1976—, sr. v.p., sec., 1977—. Served with AUS, 1954-56, to capt. USAF, 1960-64. Decorated Air Force Commendation medal. Mem. Mag. Pubs. Assn., Am. Nurses Assn., Am. Assn. Nurse Anesthetists, Temple U. Alumni Assn. Democrat. Roman Catholic. Club: N.Y. Athletic (N.Y.C.). Home: 187 Sandcastle Key Harmon Cove Secaucus NJ 07094 Office: 555 W 57 St New York NY 10019

BALKOVEC, PETER HENRY, steel co. exec.; b. Pitts., Nov. 5, 1944; s. Peter Henry and Mary Helen (Simonic) B.; B.S., U. Pitts., 1977, postgrad., 1977—. Draftsman PDM Steel Co., Pitts., 1963-66, 67-69, cost estimator, 1969-74, project mgr., 1975, contract adminstr., 1976-78, mgr. estimating, 1978—; draftsman Am. Optical Co., Pitts., 1966-67; lectr. in field. Rep. bd. visitors U. Pitts., 1977—. Univ. scholar U. Pitts., 1976-77, Tappe leadership awardee, 1977. Mem. Am. Assn. Cost Engrs. (asso.), U. Pitts. Alumni Assn., Delta Sigma Pi (life), Alpha Sigma Lambda. Roman Catholic. Home: 4912 Hatfield St Pittsburgh PA 15201 Office: PDM Steel Co Grand Ave Neville Island Pittsburgh PA 15225

BALL, GENE LOWTHER, petroleum co. exec.; b. Williamson, W.Va., June 11, 1929; s. Robert Edgar and Willa Eleanor (Lowther) B.; B.S., Marshall U., 1953; m. Linda Borchers, Aug. 31, 1974; children—Gene Lowther, Cynthia. Expeditor govt. contracts Polan Industries, Huntington, W.Va., 1955-56; spl. rep. Ashland Oil Inc. (Ky.), 1958-70, coordinator petroleum pitch, 1970-75, mgr. splty. products, 1975-77, mgr. petroleum pitch, 1977—. Vice pres. Belhaven (N.C.) Civic League, 1967-68; pres. Ashland Oil-Marshall Found., Ashland, Ky., 1970—. Served with AUS, 1952-54; Korea. Mem. Am. Inst. Mining and Metall. Engrs., Am. Soc. Lubrication Engrs., Tau Kappa Epsilon. Republican. Presbyn. Elk. Club: Bellefonte Country. Home: 1015 Radford Dr Russell KY 41169 Office: Ashland Oil Exec Hdqrs Russell KY 41169

BALL, GEORGE L., securities co. exec.; b. Evanston, Ill.; B.A., Brown U. Pres., E. F. Hutton Group Inc. and E. F. Hutton & Co., N.Y.C. Mem. Securities Industry Assn. Office: E F Hutton Group Inc 1 Battery Park Plaza New York NY 10004

BALL, JEAN GAIL LYONS (MRS. EDWIN LEE BALL), realtor; b. Elizabeth City, N.C., Jan. 17, 1927; d. George Cluster and Dorothy Louise (Tillett) Lyons; student Temple U., 1945; diploma Moore Inst. Design, 1945, Kesley Jenney Coll., 1959, Anthony Schs. Real Estate, 1970; m. Edwin Lee Ball, June 28, 1946; 1 dau., Dianna Lee. Profl. fashion model, singer with various agys. including Neufelt, Phila., Walters, Balt., Powers, San Diego, N.Y.C., Fashionality, San Diego, intermittently, 1942-58; owner, broker Ball Realty, El Cajon, Calif., 1970-80; pres. Gail Ball & Assos., Internat. Real Estate Investment Corp., El Cajon, 1980—; pres., gen. mgr. Gail Ball & Asociados S. A. de C.V., Baja California, Mex., 1980—; broker, gen. partner Internat. Fin. Co., 1980—; pres. Ball/McKinnon, Inc.; owner Dyana's Beauty Salons, El Cajon, 1973—. Exhibited art in shows at Tivoli Hotel Little Gallery, C.Z. various commns. Mem. Nat. League Am. Pen Women, Inc., El Cajon Valley Bd. Realtors, Calif. Real Estate Assn., Nat. Assn. Real Estate Bds. Home: 1787 Hillsdale Rd El Cajon CA 92020 Office: 772 E Washington Ave El Cajon CA 92020

BALL, JOHN FRANKLIN, bldg. materials co. exec.; b. Clay, Ky., Mar. 20, 1937; s. Herman Franklin and Agnes L. (Newman) B.; B.S., U. Ky., 1959; grad. in bus. mgmt. Stanford U., 1974; m. Patricia L. Bibbee, Aug. 25, 1979; children—Kathryn Leigh, John Franklin. Product mgr. Johns-Manville Sales Corp., Denver, 1964-69, product group mgr., 1969-71, asst. gen. sales mgrs., 1971-72, v.p., mdse. mgr., 1972-77; dir. mktg. Knauf Fiber Glass, Shelbyville, Ind., 1978—. Chmn., Old Tappan (N.J.) Planning Bd., 1969. Served with U.S. Army, 1959-60. Mem. Soc. Advancement Mgmt. (pres.), Mineral Insulation Mfrs. Assn. (pres.), Beta Gamma Sigma. Republican. Methodist. Club: Republican (pres. 1968). Home: 3547 Walnut Grove Ct Columbus IN 47201

BALL, LEWIS EDWIN, II, energy co. exec.; b. Huntsville, Tex., July 1, 1931; s. William Perry and Ethel (Osborne) B.; B.B.A., U. Tex., 1952; m. Marion Buchanan, June 5, 1954. With firm Ernst & Whinney, C.P.A.'s, Houston, 1952-71, mgr., 1962-71; v.p., treas. Stewart & Stevenson Services, Inc., Houston, 1971-80; v.p. fin. Intercontinental Consol. Cos., Inc., Houston, 1981—. Treas. Soc. Performing Arts, Houston, 1970-72, v.p., 1972-74, also bd. dirs., 1969—; treas. Houston Mus. Natural Sci., 1976—, also trustee, 1970—; bd. dirs. Retina Research Found., 1979—; treas. Children's Mental Health Services Houston, 1974-76, v.p., 1976-78, also bd. dirs., 1972-78; mem. adv. bd. Vol. Lawyers and Accountants for the Arts, 1981—; trustee com. Am. Assn. Museums, 1976—, mem. exec. com., 1978—; bd. dirs., treas. Park People, Inc., 1980—; mem. Cultural Arts Council Houston, 1977—, mem. allocations com., 1978—, chmn., 1980—. C.P.A., Tex. Mem. Financial Execs. Inst., Am. Inst. C.P.A.'s, Nat. Assn. Accountants. Methodist. Clubs: Ramada, Houston Country, Garden of the Gods, Riverhill, Houstonian. Home: 6122 Valley Forge St Houston TX 77057 Office: 600 Jefferson Suite 2000 Houston TX 77002

BALL, REX MARTIN, architect, urban designer; b. Oklahoma City, June 14, 1934; s. Ralph Martin and Sarah Mae (Kellner) B.; B. Arch., Okla. State U., 1956; M. Arch., M.I.T., 1958; m. Margie E. Crowley, Jan. 1, 1960; children—Julie Kay, Linda Carol, Sharon Louise, Renee Marie. Vice pres. Oklahoma City office HTB, Inc., 1958-62, v.p., dir. office, Tulsa, 1962-74, exec. v.p., Oklahoma City, 1974-75, pres., 1975—. Trustee, Frontier Sci. Found.; past chmn. Met. Tulsa Transit Authority; chmn. fed. procurement task force White House Conf. on Small Bus.; bd. dirs. Okla. Theatre Center. Served with C.E., U.S. Army, 1956-58. Fellow AIA (past pres. Okla. soc.); mem. Am. Inst. Cert. Planners, Am. Soc. Planning Ofcls., Soc. Am. Mil. Engrs. (sustaining mem.), Nat. Mcpl. League (governing council, regional v.p.), M.I.T. Alumni Assn. (past pres. Okla.), Oklahoma City C. of C. (chmn. edn. council, chmn. Tchr. of Year program), Nat. Housing Conf. (dir., legis. com.), Nat. Trust Hist. Preservation, Okla. Heritage Assn. Home: 2917 Charing Cross Rd Oklahoma City OK 73120 Office: 1411 Classen Blvd PO Box 1845 Oklahoma City OK 73101

BALLARD, EATON WALLING, dept. store exec.; b. Seattle, June 27, 1911; s. Roy Page and Olive (Murphy) B.; A.B., Stanford U., 1932; M.B.A., Harvard U., 1937; m. Beverly Holtenhouse, Dec. 28, 1933; children—Sarah Eaton Ballard Pileggi, Gretchen Walling Ballard Guard, Jonathan Roy. With Marshall Field & Co., Chgo., 1937-38, May Co., Los Angeles, 1939-46; with Carter Hawley Hale Stores, Inc., Los Angeles, 1947—, treas., 1956-63, v.p., 1959-67, exec. v.p., 1967-77, dir., 1956-77, cons., 1977—; chmn. bd. Whittaker Corp., Los Angeles; dir. Christiana Cos., Inc., Fundamental Investors, Inc., Airborne Freight Corp., Am. Mut. Fund, Inc., Anchor Growth Fund, Inc., Pacific Am. Income Shares; pres. Music Center Operating Co. Chmn. bd. trustees Pacific Oaks Coll.; trustee Calif. Inst. Arts, Children's Hosp. of Los Angeles. Served to lt. USNR, 1943-45. Clubs: Calif., Stock Exchange (Los Angeles). Office: 550 S Flower St Los Angeles CA 90071

BALLARD, GEORGE HENRY, III, urbanologist; b. Phila., Aug. 23, 1952; s. George Henry and Nancy (Medley) B.; B.S. in Econs. (Fed. Res. Bank. Pa. scholar), U. Pa., 1974; student Gen. Electric Fin. Mgmt. program, 1974-76; m. Doretha Ann Williams, Aug. 23, 1973; children—Sean J., George. Fin. analyst asst. Vertrol div. Boeing, 1969; research asst. in econs. Fed. Res. Bank of Phila., 1969-74; program acct. Gen. Electric Co., Phila., 1974-77; asst. treas. Am. Baptist Chs., U.S.A., Valley Forge, Pa., 1977-79; urbanologist, exec. dir. Citizens for Urbanism, Phila., 1979—; bd. dirs. Religious Conv. Mgrs. Assn., 1978-79. Mem. Nat. Council Chs. (audit com.), World Council Chs. (fin. resource group), Wharton Sch. Profl. Club. Democrat. Baptist. Office: Citizens for Urbanism Zion Broad St & Venango St Philadelphia PA 19140

BALLARD, JOHN WAYNE, gas co. exec.; b. Hosston, La., Aug. 26, 1914; s. John William and Nora (Wynn) B.; student Centenary Coll., Shreveport, La., 1941-45; m. Annie Lee Bickham, July 3, 1937; children—John R., Milton R. Admitted to La. bar, 1952, Lab. technician, Shoreline Oil Co. (La.), 1934-37, Talco Asphalt & Refinery, 1937-41, Stanolind Oil & Gas Co., Vivian, La., 1941-42; chief chemist Princeton Refining Co., Shreveport, La., 1942-45; asst. chief engr., asst. chief chemist Bayou State Oil Co., 1946-55, asst. supt., 1948-55; v.p., plant supr. Caddo Pine Island Corp., Shreveport, 1955-68, pres., gen. mgr., 1968—; pres. B&G Oil Co., 1970—; dir. Caddo Trust & Savs. Bank, Belcher, La. pvt. practice law, Oil City, La., 1952—. Mem. Am. Bar Assn., La. Bar Assn., Shreveport Bar Assn. Democrat. Baptist. Clubs: Rotary, Masons. Office: Rt 1 Box 60 Oil City LA 71061

BALLARD, JOSEPH GRANT, photographer, photog. co. exec.; b. Greenville, N.C., Nov. 29, 1928; s. Charlie Edgar and Mary Velma (Keel) B.; B.S., Calif. Western U., 1976, M.B.A., 1978; grad. Woodward Sch. Photography, 1949, Modern Sch. Photography, N.Y.C., 1950; Ph.D. (hon.), Pacific Coll., 1976; m. Sherry Rae Hall, May 2, 1961; children—Jeffrey Grant, Warren Scott, Vikki Kristine, Joseph Grant, Patricia, Michael, Ronnie, Don. Exec. v.p. Goldcraft Studios, Cin., 1951-61; pres. Photoland, Inc., Cleve., 1961-71, Nelson's Photography, Inc., Cleve., 1972—; cons. in mktg., promotions, budget controls and fund raising to various bus. firms and orgns., 1975—. Mem. Bicentennial Commn., Cleve., 1975; pres. Recreation Advisory Bd., North Olmsted, Ohio, 1977—; chmn. com. of Child Evangelism Fellowship of Cleve., 1977-79, 80-81; trustee Nat. Child Evangelism Fellowship, Warrenton, Md., 1980—. Served with USAAF, 1945-47. Recipient numerous awards for portrait photography, 1953—; Joseph G. Ballard Day proclaimed in honor by mayor of Cleve., April 4, 1975. Mem. Profl. Photographers of Am. Assn., Wedding Photographers of Am. Assn., Ohio Assn. Chiefs of Police, Fraternal Order of Police, Cleve. Ad Club, Ohio Profl. Photography Assn. Home: 5612 Allandale Dr North Olmsted OH 44070 Office: 41 Colonial Arcade Cleveland OH 44115

BALLENGEE, JAMES RICHARD, pulp and paper co. exec.; b. Covington, Va., Aug. 18, 1935; s. Otto Lee and Edna Lovern B.; B.S., Va. Tech. Inst., 1958; m. Betty May Rose, Aug. 31, 1957; children—James R., Robert S., Elizabeth, Jennifer. With Westvaco Corp., 1958—, nat. sales mgr. Kraft div., N.Y.C., 1971-76, gen. mgr. plant, Columbus, Ga., 1976—. Bd. dirs. United Way of Columbus; mem. Mayors Pvt. Industry Council, 1979—; bd. dirs. Columbus Symphony, 1979—. Served with U.S. Navy, 1953. Mem. Mfrs. Council Columbus, Columbus C. of C. (dir.). Presbyterian. Clubs: Rotary, Green Island Country, Big Eddy. Home: 7146 Leighton Rd Columbus GA 31904 Office: PO Box 6709 Columbus GA 31907

BALLES, JOHN JOSEPH, banker; b. Freeport, Ill., Jan. 7, 1921; s. Louis J. and Kathleen P. (O'Connor) B.; B.S., State U. Iowa, 1942, M.A., 1947; Ph.D., Ohio State U., 1951; m. Mira Jane Knupp, June 16, 1944; children—Nancy, Janet. Instr., then asst. prof. econs. and bus. adminstrn. Ohio State U., 1947-54; sr. economist, then v.p. Fed. Res. Bank Cleve., 1954-59; sr. v.p., chief economist Mellon Nat. Bank & Trust Co., Pitts., 1959-72; pres. Fed. Res. Bank San Francisco, 1972—; dir. N. Am. Rockwell Corp., 1966-72. Bd. dirs. Bay Area Council, San Francisco, 1974—. Served with AUS, 1943-46. Decorated Bronze Star with oak leaf cluster. Mem. Am. Finance Assn. (dir. 1962-63), Am. Bankers Assn. (govt. relations council 1970-72), Nat. Assn. Bus. Economists (council 1964-66), Pa. Bankers Assn. (pres. 1965-66), Am. Econ. Assn. Author (with Richard W. Lindholm and John M. Hunter): Principles of Money and Banking, 1954. Office: PO Box 7702 San Francisco CA 94120

BALLEW, HAROLD WAYNE, high tech. co. exec.; b. Abbott, Tex., Sept. 22, 1924; s. Wayne Garland and Ruby Kathlene (Hammer) B.; B.S., Tex. Tech U., Lubbock, 1948, M.S. (State of Tex. physics fellow) 1949; m. Maxine Broadaway, July 7, 1944; children—Elizabeth Ann Ballew O'Neil, Kathlene Marie. Research physicist Magnolia Petroleum Co., Dallas, 1949-51; sr. engr. Western Electric Co., Winston-Salem, N.C., 1953-55; sr. engr. to middle mgmt. Gen. Electric Co., Schenectady, N.Y. and Phila., 1955-65; pres. Applied Radiation Corp., Walnut Creek, Calif., 1965-69; mgmt. cons., Walnut Creek and San Francisco, 1969-72; pres., dir. Nuclepore Corp., Pleasanton, Calif., 1972-80; cons., investor, 1980—. Chmn. bd. regents John F. Kennedy U., Orinda, Calif. Served with AUS, 1942-45, to 1st lt. U.S. Army, 1951-53. Mem. IEEE, Pleasanton C. of C. (dir., mem. indsl. com.). Republican. Methodist. Clubs: Masons (Shriner); Lions. Contbr. articles to profl. jours. Patentee in field. Home: 1750 Orchard Way Pleasanton CA 94566 Office: 7035 Commerce Circle Pleasanton CA 94566

BALLHAGEN, LLOYD WILL, publs. and broadcasting cos. exec.; b. Peever, S.D., Aug. 21, 1931; s. Frank Clinton and Vesper Henrietta (Metz) B.; B.A., U. S.D., 1958; m. Eunice Elaine Arndt, June 15, 1957; children—Kurt Laine, Clint William. Reporter, Watertown (S.D.) Public Opinion, 1956-57; exec. intern Harris Group, 1958-61; asst. to pub. Hutchinson News, 1961-66; editor, pub. Daily Reporter, Spencer, Iowa, 1966-69, Hays (Kans.) Daily News, 1970-72; asst. gen. mgr. Harris Enterprises, Inc., Hutchinson, Kans., 1972-75, newspaper gen. mgr., 1975-78, pres., 1978—. Chmn., Kans. Public TV Services, 1977-79; bd. dirs. Kans. Sci. and Arts Found., ARC. Served with USMC, 1951-54. Mem. Inland Daily Press Assn. (dir. 1976-79), Am. Newspaper Pubs. Assn., Nat. Advt. Bur. Methodist. Home: 1602 Aurora Hutchinson KS 67501 Office: 616 1st National Center Hutchinson KS 67501

BALLIETT, JOHN WILLIAM, bus. cons., publisher; b. Rochester, N.Y., Sept. 10, 1947; s. Charles Garrison and Burnetta Elizabeth (Purtell) B.; B.S. in Physics, Grove City Coll., 1969; postgrad. U. Rochester, 1969-71; m. Betsy Jane Van Patten, Jan. 25, 1969; 1 dau., Noelle Elizabeth. Devel. engr. Eastman Kodak Co., 1969-70; scientist Tropel Inc., 1970, mgr. applied optics, 1971-72, mktg. mgr., 1972-73; exec. v.p., dir. Quality Measurement Systems Inc., Penfield, N.Y., 1973-77; pres. QMS Internat., Inc., Penfield, 1974-77, Balliett Assos., Sarasota, Fla., 1978—, Shore Lane Devel. Corp., 1981—; pres., pub. Suncoast TV Facts, Inc., Sarasota, 1979—. Mem. U.S. C. of C., Sarasota County C. of C. Patentee optical systems. Home: Shore Ln Boca Grande FL 33921 Office: Suite 703 Ellis Bank Bldg Sarasota FL 33577

BALLIETT, PIERRE BOUCHER, pub. co. exec.; b. Kansas City, Mo., June 11, 1934; s. Carl Arthur and Mary Echo (Dummit) B.; student Dartmouth Coll., 1952-54; A.B., U. Miami, 1956; postgrad., 1956-57; m. Shirley Ann Sudds, Sept. 12, 1955; children—Della-Lisa Balliett Kron, Elsa Lia. Instr., U. Miami, 1955-57; dir. Lang. Sch., Centro de Bellas Artes y Letras de Maracaibo (Venezuela), 1957-58; writer Prudential Ins. Co., Newark, 1958-59; research editor Holt, Rinehart & Winston, Inc., Bloomington, Ind., and N.Y.C., 1959-65; resident mgr. McGraw-Hill Book Co., Buenos Aires, Argentina, 1965-68; resident mgr. CBS Edn. Internat., Mexico, 1968-71; sales mgr. Nueva Editorial Interamericana, CBS, Mexico, 1971-73; asst. mgr. internat. dept. Houghton Mifflin Co., Boston, 1973-75, mgr., 1975-77, v.p., dir., 1977—; dir. Houghton Mifflin Can. Ltd., 1977—; dir., sec. Houghton Mifflin Pubs. Ltd., U.K., 1977—. Served with USNR, 1951-55. Study tour grantee German Fed. Republic, 1976. Mem. Assn. Am. Pubs. (mem. exec. council internat. div., del. to People's Republic of China 1979, del. to Interam. Pubs. Group, Internat. Pubs. Assn. 1980—), Friends of Marlborough (Mass.) Library. Office: 1 Beacon St Boston MA 02107

BALLINGER, RICHARD MOORE, pub. co. exec.; b. Merchantville, N.J., Feb. 26, 1915; s. Charles Perkins and Mable H. (Moore) B.; B.S. in Mech. Engring., Drexel U., 1938; postgrad. U. Pa., 1945; m. Nancy Annan, May 15, 1948; children—June Ridley, James Charles. Jr. account exec. media dept., research dept. Ward Wheelock Co., advt. agy., Phila., 1946-50; advt. salesman Woman's Home Companion mag., N.Y.C., 1950-55; regional mgr. House and Home div. Time Inc., N.Y.C., 1955-62; mktg. dir. housing Better Homes and Gardens mag., N.Y.C., 1962—; chmn. mktg. com. Nat. Home Improvement Council, 1968—, treas., 1974-75, exec. com., 1975—, trustee, 1979—, recipient Pub. Service award, 1973. Served to 1st lt. USAAF, 1942-45. Mem. Nat. Assn. Home Builders (former chmn. coms. Nat. Council Housing Industry, recipient Industry Service citation 1972, 75). Episcopalian. Club: Masons. Author: Illustrated Guide to the Houses of America, 1971; studies in Better Homes and Gardens. Home: 57 W Meadow Rd Wilton CT 06897 Office: 750 3d Ave New York NY 10017

BALLMAN, BENEDICT GEORGE, lawyer; b. N.Y.C., Feb. 7, 1931; s. Bernard George and Claire Ballman; B.; A.A., U. Md., 1950; B.S., Am. U., 1955, LL.B., 1958; LL.M., Georgetown U., 1963, LL.M. in Taxation, 1980; m. Frances Lucas Hurst, Jan. 3, 1959; children—Deborah Lee Watson, Lynda Hurst, Benedict George, Kimberly Sprague. Admitted to D.C. bar, 1957, Md. bar, 1958; practice in Kensington, Md. and Washington, 1960—; law clk. Dow, Lowhnes & Albertson, 1955-57; atty. FCC, 1957-58; atty. Staley & Prescott, 1958-60; sr. partner Ballman & McDonald, 1960-65; sr. partner law office B. George Ballman, 1965; now pres. Staley, Prescott & Ballman. Past pres. The Counsellors; committeeman Nat. Capitol Area council Boy Scouts Am., 1961-63; camp chmn. Camp Echo Lake, 1965-67, chmn. fund raising campaign, 1965, pres., 1969-71. Bd. dirs. Montgomery County Young Democrats, 1960-61, mem. exec. com., 1960. Treas., bd. dirs. Bethesda-Chevy Chase Rescue Squad. Recipient Distinguished Service award Bethesda Jr. C. of C., 1965. Mem. Montgomery Investors (pres.), Am., Md., Montgomery County (past pres., dir., com. chmn.) bar assns., Bethesda-Chevy Chase C. of C. (past dir.), Delta Theta Phi. Rotarian. Clubs: Bethesda Exchange (past pres.), Congressional Country. Book rev. editor Law Rev., 1956-57. Home: 12002 River Rd Potomac MD 20854 Office: Citizens Savs Bldg Kensington MD 20795

BALOCK, JOHN, JR., excavating co. exec.; b. Melstone, Mont., Oct. 24, 1927; s. John and Mary Agnes (Leonard) B.; student pub. schs., Melstone; m. Heather J. Thompson, July 3, 1958;

children—Rita, Debra, Edward. Railroad crane operator, Melstone, 1943-50; partner Balock-Mills Co., Melstone, 1950-55; owner J. Balock Jr. Co., Melstone, 1955-68; pres. Balock Excavating, Inc., Melstone, 1968—. Mem. Melstone Study Commn., 1973-75; bd. dirs. Roundup Hosp., 1978—. Served with USNR, 1944-45. Recipient Good Neighbor award Musselshell Valley C. of C., 1975. Roman Catholic. Clubs: Rotary, Moose.

BALOGUN, JACOB OLAKAYODE, educator, fin. exec.; b. Lagos, Nigeria, June 20, 1952; came to U.S., 1973; s. Talsim and Deborah (Abraham) B.; B.S., Youngstown State U., 1976, M.B.A., 1977; Ph.D., La. State U., 1980; m. Gwendolyn Randolph Feb. 2, 1976. Tchr., Lagos, 1968-70, 71-72; instr. Kent (Ohio) U., 1974-76; bus. devel. specialist, Warren, Ohio, 1977-78; grad. asst., bus. cons. La. State U., Baton Rouge, 1978-80; asst. prof. So. U., Baton Rouge, 1980—; asst. prof. Va. Commonwealth U., Richmond, 1981—; cons. Acct., sec. Gilead House Community Center, Youngstown, 1977-78; v.p. Sunshine Child Day Care Center, Youngstown, 1977-78. Recipient Instr.'s award Kent State U., 1974-75. Mem. Am. Fin. Assn., Inst. Internal Auditors, Ohio Registered Public Accts. Office: Va Commonwealth U Sch Bus 1015 Floyd Ave Richmond VA 23284

BALOTSKY, EDWARD ROBERT, hosp. mgmt. co. ofcl.; b. Phila., Sept. 26, 1950; s. Edward Robert and Stella Mary (Lash) B.; B.S. in Bus. Adminstrn., Phila. Coll. Textiles and Sci., 1977; M.B.A., Temple U., 1979. Adminstrv. resident Nazareth Hosp., Phila., 1978-79; asst. adminstr. Lake Community Hosp., Leesburg, Fla., 1979-81; asst. to v.p. Gateway Hosp. Mgmt. Corp., Clearwater, Fla., 1981—. Served with USAF, 1969-73. Mem. Am. Coll. Hosp. Adminstrs., Am. Acad. Med. Adminstrn., Am. Mktg. Assn. Club: Civitan (Leesburg). Home: 10081 12th Way N Saint Petersburg FL 33702 Office: 2500 E Bay Dr Clearwater FL

BALTAZZI, EVAN SERGE, consulting co. exec.; b. Izmir, Turkey, Apr. 11, 1921; s. Phocion George and Agnes Sylvia (Varda) B.; Dr. Sci. Physiques, Sorbonne U., Paris, 1949; Ph.D., Oxford U., 1954; m. Nellie D. Biolaro, July 17, 1945; children—Angie, James, Maria. In charge research French Nat. Research Center, Paris, 1947-59; group leader organic chemistry research NALCO, Chgo., 1959-61; mgr. organic chemistry sect. Research Inst., Ill. Inst. Tech., Chgo., 1961-63; dir. research lab Addressograph Multigraph Corp., Chgo. and Cleve., 1963-77; pres. Evanel Assocs., Northfield, Ohio, 1977—. Recipient Citizen of the Yr. award Citizenship Council Met. Chgo., 1964; Outstanding Achievement award in sci. Immigrants Service League, 1965, citation, 1965; Recognition award Gordon Research Confs., 1976; Outstanding Program award YMCA, 1967; fellow Nat. Research Council Can., 1955, British Council, 1952-54. Fellow Am. Inst. Chemists (vice-chmn. Chgo. chpt. 1970); mem. Am. Chem. Soc. (sr.), Soc. Photog. Scientists and Engrs. (pres. Cleve. chpt. 1979—). Clubs: Masons, Shriners. Author: Basic American Self-Protection, 1972; Kickboxing, 1976; Stick-Footfighting, 1979; Self-Protection at Close Quarters and Beyond, 1980; contbr. articles in field to profl. jours; patentee numerous items. Home and Office: 825 Greengate Oval Sagamore Hills OH 44067

BAMBAS, KARL JOHN, nuclear services co. exec.; b. Buffalo, Aug. 8, 1933; s. Julius John and Martha Rebecca (Ochsner) B.; B.S. in Chem. Engring., Syracuse U., 1955, M.S. in Chem. Engring., 1957; M.B.A., Harvard U., 1960; m. Kathleen Gorga, Mar. 18, 1978. Fin. analyst Union Carbide Corp., N.Y.C., 1960-69; fin. mgr. Allied Chem. Corp., Morristown, N.J., 1969-72, div. controller, 1972-75, asst. to div. pres., 1975-76; v.p. fin. and adminstrn. Allied-Gen. Nuclear Services Co., Barnwell, S.C., 1976—, v.p. safeguards, 1979—. Served to capt. USAF, 1957. Mem. Atomic Indsl. Forum (com. on domestic safeguards), Fin. Execs. Inst., Inst. Nuclear Materials Mgmt. Home: 219 Northwood Dr Aiken SC 29801 Office: Box 347 Barnwell SC 29812

BANACH, ART JOHN, graphic art exec.; b. Chgo., May 22, 1931; s. Vincent and Anna (Zajac) B.; grad. Art Inst. Chgo., 1955; pvt. painting studies Mrs. Melin, Chgo.; m. Loretta Anne Nolan, Oct. 15, 1966; children—Heather Anne, Lynnea Joan. Owner, dir. Art J. Banach Studios, 1949—, cartoon syndicate for newspapers, house organs and advt. functions, 1954—, owned and operated advt. agy., 1954-56, feature news and picture syndicate, distbn. U.S. and fgn. countries. Recipient 1st award Easter Seal contest Ill. Assn. Crippled, 1949, 3 scholarships Chgo. Public Sch. Art Soc., 1952. Mem. Artists Guild Chgo., Am. Mgmt. Assn., Am. Mktg. Assn., Advt. Execs. Club, Art Dirs. Club Chgo., Chgo. Federated Advt. Club, Internat. Platform Assn., Chgo. Soc. Communicating Arts. Clubs: Toastmasters, Columbia Yacht. Office: 1076 Leahy Circle E Des Plaines IL 60016

BANASZEWSKI, THOMAS WILLIAM, coll. bus. officer; b. Amsterdam, N.Y., Nov. 25, 1940; s. William Anthony and Anne Loretta (Lenahan) B.; B.A., Ricker Coll., 1963; m. Nancy Louise Sullivan, Aug. 24, 1963; children—Lynne, Lisa, Craig, Jill. Asst. treas. Hickey Freeman Co., Inc., Rochester, N.Y., 1963-73; treas. St. Bernard's Sem., Rochester, 1973—; treas. Rochester Center for Theol. Studies, 1977—; treas. Seminary Mgmt. Assn. Vice-chairperson Rochester-Monroe County Youth Bd.; pres. Cath. Youth Orgn., 1974, Holy Cross Parish Council, 1973, Holy Cross Bd. Edn., 1971-72; town leader Greece (N.Y.) Democratic Com.; bd. dirs. Jr. Achievement Rochester, 1975, United Community Chest Rochester. Mem. Nat. Assn. Coll. Univ. Bus. Officers, Nat. Assn. Accountants, Council Advancement Student Edn., Rochester Area C. of C. (trustee), Greece C. of C. (v.p.), Rochester (pres. 1974-75), U.S. (hon. life; ambassador) Jaycees. Home: 83 Wood Smoke Ln Rochester NY 14612 Office: 2260 Lake Ave Rochester NY 14612

BANCROFT, CHRISTOPHER MARLER, electronics cons.: b. Norwalk, Conn., Feb. 17, 1948; s. Charles and Jean (Coburn) B.; B.S. in E.E., U. Rochester, 1971, B.A. in Physics, 1971. Engring. technician "C", Hughes Aircraft, Culver City, Calif., 1967-70; engr. Raytheon Corp., Bedford, Mass., 1972-74; chief engr. Diano Corp., Woburn, Mass., 1974-76; with Taylor Instrument Corp., Rochester, N.Y., 1977; cons. electronics and physics, Wakefield, N.H., 1977—. Mem. Soc. Applied Spectroscopy (councilor 1974-80). New Eng. Computer Soc., IEEE. Republican. Inventor in field. Address: Route 153 Wakefield NH 03872

BANCROFT, JAMES RAMSEY, lawyer, bus. exec.; b. Ponca City, Okla., Nov. 13, 1919; s. Charles Ramsey and Maude (Viersen) B.; A.B., U. Calif., Berkeley, 1940, M.S. in Bus. Adminstrn. (Flood fellow 1940-41), 1941, J.D. Hastings Coll. Law, 1949; m. Jane Marguerite Oberfell, May 28, 1944; children—John Ramsey, Paul Marshall, Sara Jane. With McLaren, Goode, West & Co., C.P.A.'s, San Francisco, 1946-50; admitted to Calif. bar, 1950; partner firm Bancroft, Avery & McAlister, San Francisco, 1950—; pres. Madison Properties, Inc., San Francisco, 1967—, Adams Properties, Inc., 1969-79, Adams-Western, Inc., 1969-78; vice chmn., dir. Primark Corp., Reno, 1969-80; chmn. bd. dirs. United Nuclear Corp., Falls Church, Va., 1972—, UNC Resources, 1978—; dir. Recortec, Inc., Mountain View, Calif. Pres., trustee Harvey L. Sorensen Found.; trustee Dean Witter Found.; past dir. Suisun Resource Conservation Dist., Solano County, Calif. Served to lt. USNR, 1942-46. Mem. Am. Bar Assn., Calif. Bar Assn., Phi Beta Kappa. Clubs: Bohemian, Pacific Union, Olympic (San Francisco). Office: UNC Crescent Plaza 7700 Leesburg Pike Falls Church VA 22043 also 601 Montgomery St Suite 800 San Francisco CA 94111

BANCROFT, PAUL, III, investment co. exec.; b. N.Y.C., Feb. 27, 1930; s. Paul and Rita (Manning) B.; B.A., Yale, 1951; postgrad. Georgetown Fgn. Service Inst., 1952; m. Monica M. Devine, Jan. 2, 1977; children by previous marriage—Bradford, Kimberly, Stephen, Gregory. Account exec. Merrill Lynch Pierce Fenner & Smith, N.Y.C., 1956-57; asso. corporate finance dept. F. Eberstadt & Co., N.Y.C., 1957-62; partner Draper, Gaither & Anderson, Palo Alto, Calif., 1962-67; with Bessemer Securities Corp., 1967—; v.p. Venture Capital Investments, 1967-74, sr. v.p. securities investments, 1974-76, pres., chief exec. officer, dir., 1976—; dir. Am. Standard, Inc., Measurex Corp., Fotomat Corp., Intersil, Inc., Scudder Devel. Fund, Scudder Spl. Fund; founder, past chmn. Nat. Venture Capital Assn. Served from 2d lt. to 1st lt. USAF, 1952-56. Clubs: River, Yale (N.Y.C.); Pacific Union, Bohemian (San Francisco); Burlingame (Calif.). Home: 238 Newtown Turnpike Redding CT 06896 Office: 245 Park Ave New York NY 10017

BANDEEN, ROBERT ANGUS, ry. exec.; b. Rodney, Ont., Can., Oct. 29, 1930; s. John Robert and Jessie Marie (Thomson) B.; B.A., U. Western Ont., 1952, LL.D. (hon.), 1975; Ph.D., Duke, 1959; LL.D. (hon.), Dalhousie U., 1978; D.C.L. (hon.), Bishop's U., 1978; m. Mona Helen Blair, May 31, 1958; children—Ian Blair, Mark Everett, Robert Derek, Adam Drummond. Asst. economist Canadian Nat. Rys., Montreal, Que., 1955-56, research statistician, 1956-58, staff officer planning, 1958-60, chief costs and statistics, 1960, chief devel. planning, 1960-66, dir. corporate planning, 1966-68, v.p. corporate planning and fin., 1968-71, v.p. Great Lakes region, 1971-72, exec. v.p. finance and adminstrn., 1972-74; pres. and chief exec. officer Canadian Nat. Rys. System, 1974—; chmn. bd., dir. Grand Trunk Corp., Central Vt. Ry., Duluth Winnipeg & Pacific Ry., Grand Trunk Western R.R., Detroit Toledo & Ironton R.R., CN (France), CNCP Telecommunications; dir. Crown Life Ins. Co., Mortgage Ins. Co. Can., Sport Participation Can., Intercast S.A., Eurocan. Shipholdings Ltd. Chancellor, Bishop's U.; hon. v.p. Que. council Boy Scouts, hon. mem. Nat. council; mem. Home Inst. Policy Analysis Com., Can. Transp. Research Forum; senator Stratford Shakespearean Festival Found. Can. Decorated knight Order of St. John. Mem. Brit.-N.Am. Com., Can. Ry. Club, Toronto Ry. Club, Nat. Freight Traffic Assn. Clubs: Montreal AAU, Mount Royal, Saint James's (Montreal). Home: 3120 Daulac Rd Westmount PQ H3Y 2A2 Canada Office: 935 Lagauchetiere St W Montreal PQ H3C 3N4 Canada

BANDER, NORMAN ROBERT, communications and info. mgmt. cons.; A.B., Dartmouth Coll., 1954; postgrad. Harvard U., Columbia U., U. Pa., N.Y. U. Former sales research dir. Benton & Bowles, Inc., N.Y.C.; media program research dir. Lennen & Newell, Inc., N.Y.C.; dir. mktg. test analysis Gillette Co., Boston; dir. creative communication evaluation and advt. research J. Walter Thompson Co., N.Y.C.; now pres. Bander & Assos., Sarasota, Fla., 1968—. Served as clin. psychologist, M.C., AUS, 1954-56. Mem. Am. Mktg. Assn. Clubs: Dartmouth, Yale (N.Y.C.). Author studies on mktg. and advt. effectivness, consumer behavior and pub. opinion. Office: PO Box 190 Sarasota FL 33578

BANDER, ROBERT NELSON, broadcasting co. exec.; b. Washington, Jan. 15, 1944; s. Myrick Edward and Anne H. (Plevinsky) B.; B.A. in English and History, Tufts U., 1965; M.B.A. in Fin., Columbia U., 1966; m. Anne Lawson Grimsley, Feb. 18, 1979. Asso., Booz, Allen & Hamilton, Washington, 1970-75; dir. research Pres.'s Commn. on Olympic Sports, Washington, 1975-76; dir. Coopers & Lybrand, Washington, 1976-78; spl. cons. EPA, Washington, 1978-79; pres., gen. mgr. Moonshadow Broadcasting Co., Inc., Sta. WYNA, Raleigh, N.C., 1979—; asst. prof. hosp. adminstrn. Baylor U., 1967-68; adj. instr. mktg. St. Mary's U., San Antonio, 1968. Active Lakepark Citizens Assn. Served to capt. AUS, 1967-70. Decorated Army Commendation medal. Mem. Triangle Area Radio Broadcasters Assn. (sec.-treas. 1980-81), Triangle Advt. Fedn., N.C. Assn. Broadcasters, Nat. Assn. Broadcasters, Raleigh C. of C. Democrat. Jewish. Author govt. publs. Home: 6215 Lookout Loop Raleigh NC 27612 Office: PO Box 30099 Raleigh NC 27622

BANDLER, MICHAEL LOUIS, telephone co. exec.; b. N.Y.C., Mar. 1, 1938; s. Louis C. and Elaine W. Bandler; B.E.E., Cornell U., 1960; M.B.A., N.Y. U., 1968; m. Linda Ruth Goldberg, Nov. 11, 1961; children—David, Karen, Joanna. Div. engr. for network planning N.Y. Telephone Co., N.Y.C., 1971-73, div. network mgr., 1973-75, chief engr., 1975-76, asst. v.p. product mgmt., 1977—. Served as officer arty. U.S. Army, 1960-61. Mem. Cornell Soc. Engrs. (pres. 1973-75), Cornell U. Alumni Assn. N.Y.C. (dir.). Office: 1095 Ave of Americas New York NY 10036

BANDLER, RICHARD, advt. exec.; b. N.Y.C., July 12, 1917; s. Maurice and Edna (Lee) B.; m. Eleanor Slater Trenholm, Jan. 7, 1966; children—Judith Finch, Patricia Hornblower, Elise, Tatiana. Dir. purchasing B. T. Babbitt Co., N.Y.C., 1939-42; nat. sales mgr. Reuben H. Donnelley Corp., N.Y.C., 1946-49; founder, pres. Richard Bandler Co. Inc., directory advt., N.Y.C., 1949—. Served with U.S. Army, 1942-45. Decorated Purple Heart with three battle stars. Mem. Masters of Foxhounds Assn., Greenville County (S.C.) Hounds (founding master) Am. Roman Catholic. Clubs: Union League, Turf and Field. Home: RD 4 Succabone Rd Mount Kisco NY 10549 Office: 30 E 60th St New York NY 10022

BANDY, PHILIP ROBERT, communication exec.; b. St. Louis, Nov. 16, 1949; s. Robert Fred and Jane Rose (O'Malley) B.; B.A., So. Ill. U., 1971; M.A., Mich. State U., 1972; m. Roberta Kay Pilgrim, June 14, 1969; children—Robert William, Elisabeth Grace. Floor dir. KMOX-TV, St. Louis, cameraman WMSB-TV, East Lansing, Mich., 1971-72; instr. Lake Mich. Coll., Benton Harbor, Mich., 1972-73; continuity writer/producer WOTV, Time-Life Broadcast, Grand Rapids, Mich., 1973-75, promotion mgr., 1975-79, client services dir., 1979—; formulator TV-radio course of study for Lake Mich. Coll. Mem. citizen adv. com. Grand Rapids public schs. millage election, 1980; chmn. Citizen to Elect Dorothy Moser Com., 1978; mem. Grand Rapids City ad hoc com. on equal employment, 1975. Award winner, NBC-TV 1976 Promotion Mgrs. Competition; Award of Merit, 6th Dist. AM. Advt. Fedn., 1977, others. Mem. Broadcasters Promotion Assn. (dir. 1978-80), Kent County Assn. for Retarded Citizens. Lutheran. Club: Grand Rapids Advt. Office: 120 College St SE Grand Rapids MI 49503

BANE, BERNARD MAURICE, pub. co. exec.; b. Salem, Mass., Nov. 23, 1924; s. Julius and Rhoda (Trop) B.; student Northeastern U., 1946-48, Law Sch., 1948-49. Engaged in sales and merchandising, 1949-55; with The Ivy League Enterprise, Boston, 1955-65; with BMB Pub. Co., Boston, 1965—, pub., 1970—. Chmn. local Miss Am. Pageant, 1961. Mem. Am. Soc. Notaries. Author, pub.: The Bane in Kennedy's Existence, 1967; Is President John F. Kennedy Alive. . . and Well?, 1973, 11th edit., 1981. Home: 854 Massachusetts Ave Cambridge MA 02139 Office: PO Box 1622 Boston MA 02105

BANE, MARILYN ANNETTE, advt. exec.; b. Ft. Worth, Aug. 26, 1943; d. Forest Nelson and Wilma Grace (Orr) Bane; A.B., U. Tex., Austin, 1967. Copywriter, Ted Bates and Co., Inc., N.Y.C., 1967-69, Grey Advt., Inc., N.Y.C., 1969-70; v.p., copy supr., Gary F. Halby Assos., Inc., N.Y.C., 1970-73; v.p., account supr., Chester Gore Co. Inc., N.Y.C., 1973-78, sr. v.p., 1980—; v.p., account supr. Wells, Rich, Greene, Inc., N.Y.C., 1978-80; mktg. and advt. prof., Marymount Weekend Coll., Tarrytown, N.Y., mktg. advisory com. to bd. trustees; mktg. cons. to bd. dirs. Consumer Credit Counseling Service, N.Y. Pub. relations com. Al-anon Family Group Hdqrs., N.Y.C., 1973-76. Republican. Episcopalian. Office: 515 Madison Ave New York NY 10022

BANGEL, KENNETH ROY, merger and acquisition cons.; b. Bklyn., July 10, 1932; s. Maurice Bruce and Clair (Berger) B.; B.B.A., U. Pa., 1954; postgrad. Pace Coll., Hofstra U.; m. Ruth L. Ziman, Sept. 7, 1958; children—Cara Jill, Elyssa Anne. Strategic planning acquisition studies and profit improvement program Texaco Inc., 1960-66; group controller for univ. ops. Yale U., New Haven, 1966-73; mgr. fin. services Burns and Roe Inc., Oradell, N.J., 1973-76; gen. mgr. Edison Mgmt. Co., 1977; pres. Bus. Brokerage Group, Ramsey, N.J., 1978—; partner Mac Assos., Ramsey, 1978—; prin., cons. Kenroy Assos., Ramsey, 1978—; profit improvement McKinsey & Co., Ramsey, 1976—. Div. chmn. United Way; sr. adv. Jr. Achievement; mem. disbursements com. charities drive Yale U.; bd. dirs. Sr. Personnel Registry; troop leader Boy Scouts Am.; mem. Upper Saddle River Police Res. Served with U.S. Army, 1953-55; Korea. Cert. in real estate, mgmt., financing, cons. Mem. Am. Mgmt. Assn., Soc. for Advancement Mgmt., N.J. C. of C., Arnold Air Soc., VFW. Jewish. Clubs: Lago Mar, Yale Faculty, Saddle River Valley. Home: 60 Carlough Rd Upper Saddle River NJ 07458 Office: 79 N Franklin Turnpike Ramsey NJ 07446

BANGERT, HAROLD WALLACE, investment banker; b. Sheldon, N.D., Oct. 12, 1905; s. Charles George and Sarah Elizabeth (Wallace) B.; student, U.N.D., 1923-28; J.D., George Washington U., 1931; m. Mary K. Jeffries, Sept. 5, 1931; 1 son, Charles Jeffries. Admitted to N.D. bar, 1934, D.C. bar, 1931; atty. FTC, Chgo., 1931-33; mem. firm Bangert & Bangert, Fargo, N.D., 1937-76; atty., dist. dir., nat. dir. Price Control Bds. Office Price Adminstrn., Fargo, Chgo., also Washington, 1942-46; organizer, chmn. Statesman Group Inc., Des Moines, 1959-72; organizer, chmn. Bangert & Co. Investment Bankers, San Francisco, 1971-75; dir., chmn. emeritus Bangert, Dawes, Reade, Davis & Thom, San Francisco, 1975—; organizer, dir., chmn. emeritus Am. Life & Casualty Ins. Co., Fargo, N.D., 1949—. Mem. Am., N.D. bar assns., Phi Delta Phi, Delta Tau Delta. Republican. Episcopalian. Clubs: Mpls., Chgo., Merchants Exchange. Home: 839 Terra California Dr Walnut Creek CA 94595 Office: 650 California St San Francisco CA 94108

BANKER, DIPAK VINODKUMAR, fin. and bus. planning exec.; b. Hyderabad, Pakistan, Dec. 6, 1943; s. V. C. and J. V. Banker; B.S. in Mech. Engring., U. Baroda (India), 1965; M.S. in Indsl. Engring. with honors, Ill. Inst. Tech., 1967; M.B.A. with honors, Rochester Inst. Tech., 1974; m. Smita Parikh, Mar. 2, 1970; children—Sanjay, Samir. Indsl. engr., systems analyst Electronics div. Gen. Dynamics, Rochester, N.Y., 1967-69; bus. analyst, unit mgr. fin. planning and analysis Xerox Corp., Rochester, 1969-76; controller Am. Instrument div. Baxter Labs., Silver Spring, Md., 1976-78; bus. mgr. Norden div. United Technologies Corp., Norwalk, Conn., 1978-80; dir. planning and control Bristol Labs. div. Bristol-Myers Co., Syracuse, N.Y., 1980—. Mem. Assn. M.B.A. Execs., Am. Mgmt. Assn., Planning Execs. Inst., Phi Kappa Phi, Alpha Pi Mu. Home: 4885 Firethorn Circle Manlius NY 13104 Office: Bristol Labs Div Bristol-Myers Co Thompson Rd Syracuse NY 13201

BANKER, EDWARD KEITH, banker; b. Columbus, Ind., Nov. 27, 1925; s. John Keith and Mildred (Marr) B.; student Purdue U., 1943-44; A.B., DePauw U., 1948; M.B.A., Northwestern U., 1949; m. Thelma Barnes, Sept. 12, 1953; children—John Barnes, Judith Marr. With Harris Trust & Savs. Bank, Chgo., 1949—, v.p., 1965-69, div. adminstr., 1969-72, sr. v.p., group exec., U.S. group, 1972-75, group exec., internat. banking group, 1975-79, sr. v.p., group exec., fin. group, 1979—. Bd. dirs. Met. Housing and Planning Council, Chgo., 1976—, pres., 1978-79; pres., dir. Lakefront Gardens, Inc., 1979—; bd. dirs. Open Lands Project, 1978—. Served with USAAF, 1944-45. Recipient Alumni award Northwestern U., 1973. Mem. Bankers Assn. for Fgn. Trade (dir. 1979—), Chgo. Council Fgn. Relations. Republican. Episcopalian. Clubs: Univ., Econ. (Chgo.); Geneva (Ill.) Golf; Farmington Country (Charlottesville, Va.). Home: 311 S 1st St Geneva IL 60134 Office: Harris Trust and Savs Bank 111 W Monroe St Chicago IL 60603

BANKER, JOHN HOWARD, transp. exec.; b. Bayonne, N.J., Aug. 27, 1940; s. John Joseph and Alva Frances (Long-Tingle) B.; B.S. in Bus. and Fin., Parsons Coll., 1964; m. Mary Louise Borra, Dec. 23, 1978. Acct., Nat. Newark and Essex Bank, Newark, 1964-66; tax mgr. Roadway Express, Inc., Akron, Ohio, 1966-74; asst. sec. Coastal Industries, Inc. and Subsidiaries, Akron, 1974—; cons. state tax compliance and fual tax reporting systems for motor carrier industry. Mem. N.Am. Gasoline Tax Conf., Tax Execs. Inst. (Cleve. chpt.), Am. Assn. Motor Vehicle Adminstrs., Nat. Tax Assn., Tax Inst. Am., Am. Trucking Assn., Nat. Acctg. and Fin. Council, Ohio Acctg. Council. Contbr. article to jour. in field. Office: 250 N Cleveland-Massillon Rd Akron OH 44313

BANKIER, JACOB (JACK) DAVID, plastics co. exec.; b. Karabalta, Russia, May 24, 1945; s. Leon and Fela (Boberman) B.; came to U.S., 1951, naturalized, 1956; B.S., U. Ill., 1966; M.S., Roosevelt U., 1972; m. Marianne Dina Schonfeld, Apr. 18, 1970; children—Seth Joseph, Rachel S., Nanci Ruth. Mem. tech. staff Amoco Chems. Plastics div. Standard Oil Co. (Ind.) Research Center, Naperville, Ill., 1968-70; chemist Polymer Synthesis Research, Borg-Warner Corp., Roy C. Ingersol Research Center, Des Plaines, Ill., 1970-72; Midwest sales mgr. Adell Plastics, Inc., Balt., 1972-75; v.p. mktg. Plastron Corp., Bensenville, Ill., 1975-79; pres. Bankier & Co., Inc., 1979—. Dir. young leadership div. Jewish United Fund, 1976-80; mem. nat. young leadership cabinet United Jewish Appeal, 1979—; chmn. div. Chgo. fedn. Jewish United Fund, 1980-81; ex-officio bd. mem. Michael Reese Hosp., 1977-78. Recipient David Ben Gurion award for Plastics div. Man Yr. award, 1975. Mem. Soc. Plastics Engrs., Am. Chem. Soc. Club: B'nai B'rith. Home: 1724 Longvalley Dr Northbrook IL 60062 Office: 70 Rawls Rd Des Plaines IL 60018

BANKS, ARTHUR EDWARD, research and engring. co. exec.; b. Everett, Mass., Nov. 29, 1943; s. Arthur F. and Elizabeth (Cornell) B.; B.A., U. N.H., 1965; M.P.A. (research asst.), Pa. State U., 1969; m. Karen Nesbitt, Aug. 9, 1965; children—Mark Franklin, Mary Frances, Elizabeth Cornell. Indsl. relations recruiter Ford Motor Co., Ypsilanti, Mich., 1969-70; salary adminstrn. analyst Exxon Research and Engring. Co., Florham Park, N.J., 1970-72, employee relations group head., 1972-74, office services adminstr., 1974-77, labor relations exec., expatriate policies adminstr., 1977-79, mgr. benefits compensation and systems sect., N.Y. employee relations office Exxon Corp., N.Y.C., 1979—. Served to capt. U.S. Army, 1965-68. Home: 37 Harvard Dr Hartsdale NY 10530 Office: 1251 Ave of Americas New York NY 10020

BANKS, EUGENE WILSON, stock broker; b. Wailuku, Hawaii, Sept. 18, 1944; s. Jean Wilson and Ella Kuikuiehu (Keanini) B.; B.A., Brigham Young U., 1968; M.B.A., U. Wash., 1972; m. Evelyn Hubbard, Apr. 3, 1968; children—Tiffany Kamaile, Trent Wilson, Nicole Kauilani, Tyler Eugene, Troy Robert, Rochelle Kanani. Account exec. Merrill Lynch, Phoenix, 1972, sr. account exec., 1978, asso. mgr., Sun City, Ariz., 1978, mgr., asst. v.p., 1978-80, resident mgr., Honolulu, 1980—. Active Boy Scouts Am.; bishop Ch. of Jesus Christ of Latter Day Saints. Served with U.S. Army, 1969-71. Mem. U. Wash. M.B.A. Alumni Assn. Republican. Club: Rotary (pres.-elect, Paul Harris fellow). Home: 6732 Hahaione Pl Honolulu HI 96825 Office: Merrill Lynch 190 S King St Honolulu HI 96813

BANKS, PAUL IRVING, constrn. co. exec.; b. Dorris, Calif., Aug. 15, 1922; s. Roy R. and Maybelle (Otey) B.; student U. Minn., 1944-45; B.S., U. Kans., 1948; grad. Harvard Advanced Mgmt. Program, 1963, Stanford Exec. Program, 1976; m. Julie Anne Briant, June 11, 1944; children—Jana, Paul, Kirk, Sara, Kelly. Civil engr. Calif. Hwy. Dept., Los Angeles, 1948-50; constrn. supt. Philips Petroleum Co., Bartlesville, Okla., 1950-58; v.p., dir. E.E. Black Ltd., Honolulu, 1958-66; constrn. mgr. Hawaiian Dredging and Constrn. Co., Honolulu, 1966-69, v.p., 1969-75, pres., chief exec. officer, 1975—. Bd. trustees Hawaii Sch. for Girls. Served with U.S. Navy, 1940-45. Mem. Gen. Contractors Assn. Hawaii (past pres., dir.), Tau Beta Pi. Republican. Episcopalian. Club: Kaneohe Yacht. Home: 590 Kaimalino Kailua HI 96734 Office: 614 Kapahulu Ave Honolulu HI 96815

BANKS, REBECCA BETH, ins. broker; b. Bellaire, Ohio, Jan. 22, 1951; d. John A. and Mary L. (Troyanovich) Balek; cert. of completion Offshore Oil Sch., U. Tex., 1977; m. David W. Banks, Oct. 15, 1975. With Associated Gen. Contractors, Washington, 1970-71, Am. Internat. Underwriters, Tulsa, 1971-73, Marsh & McLennan, Inc., Tulsa, 1973-75; mktg. ofcl. So. Marine and Aviation Underwriters, 1975-76; asst. v.p., br. mgr. J.H. Blades, Inc., Tulsa, 1976—. Mem. Okla. Surplus Lines Assn., Internat. Assn. Drilling Contractors (hon.), Met. C. of C. Republican. Presbyterian. Home: 2233 E 22d Pl Tulsa OK 74114 Office: 5800 E Skelly Dr Tulsa OK 74135

BANKS, RICHARD ALLEN, apparel co. exec.; b. Circleville, Ohio, Apr. 10, 1939; s. Carl E. and Nana L. (Watson) B.; student Ohio Wesleyan U., 1957-59; B.A., Ind. U., 1962; m. Rebecca Ann Robles, Sept. 4, 1971; children—Terri M., Scott H., Matthew R., Benjamin T., Channing R. Ohio, F & R Lazarus, Columbus, Ohio, 1964-66; v.p. mktg. Bobbie Brooks, Cleve., 1969-73; pres. S.F. Gold Co., San Francisco, 1973-75, Harris & Stroh, Hayward, Calif., 1975-77, women's wear div. Levi Strauss, San Francisco, 1980—. Mem. Republican Senatorial Adv. Com. Recipient Outstanding Bus. Achievement award B.R.A.G., N.Y.C., 1980. Republican. Roman Catholic. Club: Bankers (San Francisco). Office: 2 Embarcadero San Francisco CA 94106

BANKS, RUSSELL, chem. corp. exec.; b. N.Y.C., Aug. 2, 1919; s. Thomas and Fay (Cowan) B.; B.B.A., Coll. City N.Y., 1936-40; LL.B., N.Y. Law Sch., 1960; m. Janice Reed, June 19, 1949; children—Gordon, L. Banks. Sr. accountant Selverne, Davis Co., N.Y.C., 1940-45; pvt. practice as C.P.A., N.Y.C., 1945-61; admitted to N.Y. bar, 1961, since practiced law, N.Y.C.; exec. v.p. Met. Tele-communications Corp., Plainview, N.Y., 1961-62; pres., chief exec. officer Grow Group, Inc., N.Y.C., 1962—, aiso dir.; dir. Bairnco Corp. C.P.A., N.Y. Mem. N.Y. County Lawyers Assn., Am. Mgmt. Assn. (gen. mgmt. planning council 1966—), Nat. Paint and Coatings Assn. (dir., mem. exec. com.), Phi Delta Phi. Club: Met. (N.Y.C.). Editor: Managing the Smaller Company for Growth. Home: Harmony Rd Pawling NY 12564 Office: 345 Park Ave New York NY 10022

BANKS, TALCOTT MINER, lawyer; b. Englewood, N.J., June 23, 1905; s. Talcott M. and Olive H. S. (Dawes) B.; ed. Hotchkiss Sch., Lakeville, Conn.; A.B., Williams Coll., 1928, LL.D., 1975; J.D., Harvard, 1931; LL.D., Northeastern U., 1971; m. Kathleen Macy Hall, July 23, 1935 (dec. May 1966); children—Ridgway Macy, Oliver T., Helen M. m. 2d, Ann S. Monks, June 23, 1967 (dec. Mar. 1970); m. 3d, Elisa C. Brooks, Aug. 8, 1973 (dec. Oct. 5, 1979). Pres. Nat. Intercoll. Lawn Tennis Assn., 1927-28; mem. editorial staff Time Mag., admitted to Mass. bar, 1931; asso. firm Palmer Dodge in practice of law, Boston, 1931-41; gen. counsel Bd. Investigation and Research, 1941-44; mem. Palmer & Dodge and predecessor firms, 1944-78, of Counsel, 1977—; dir Comstock & Wescott, Inc. Chmn. bd. emeritus Boston Symphony Orch.; trustee emeritus Williams Coll.; trustee N.E. Conservatory Music; hon. trustee Sterling and Francine Clark Art Inst.; hon. pres. Boston Opera Assn.; past dir. Williams Coll. Alumni Fund, People's Symphony Orch.; trustee emeritus Fessenden Sch. Mem. Am. (chmn. spl. com. on securities laws and regulations, 1940-42), Mass., Boston bar assns., Am. Law Inst., Kappa Alpha, Phi Beta Kappa. Unitarian. Clubs: Somerset, University (N.Y.); St. Botolph (pres. 1949-53), Cruising of Am., Am. Alpine; Dunes (Narragansett); Hope (Providence). Contbr. articles to legal periodicals, mags. Home: Bedford Rd Lincoln MA 01773 Office: One Beacon St Boston MA 02108

BANKS, WARREN EUGENE, educator, lawyer; b. Hot Springs, Ark., Feb. 1, 1929; s. Warren Eugene and Helen Frances (Shaw) B.; B.S., U. Ark., 1950, J.D., 1953, M.B.A., 1960, Ph.D., 1968; postgrad. Georgetown U. Law Center, 1957, U. Colo., summers 1962, 63; m. Carolyn Beth Duty, Dec. 27, 1952; children—Karen Marie, Keith Randolph. Admitted to Ark. bar, 1953; mem. firm C.T. Cotham, Atty., Hot Springs, 1953; investigator GAO, Washington, 1955-57; instr. U. Ark., Fayetteville, 1957-59, asst. prof., 1959-64, asso. prof., 1964-70, prof. finance, 1970—, chmn. dept. fin., 1978—, part-time faculty Sch. Law, 1957—. Served to 1st lt. USAF, 1953-55. Recipient Faculty Achievement award Ark. Alumni Assn., 1973. Mem. Am., Southwestern fin. assns., Fin. Mgmt. Assn., Am. Trial Lawyers Assn., Ark. Bar Assn., Omicron Delta Kappa, Beta Gamma Sigma, Beta Alpha Psi, Alpha Kappa Psi, Sigma Pi, Phi Alpha Delta. Episcopalian. Contbr. articles to profl. jours. Home: 1109 Sunset Dr Fayetteville AR 72701

BANKSTON, EDDIE WILSON, educator; b. Albany, La., Nov. 9, 1938; s. Woodrow Wilson and Mamie (Miller) B.; B.B.A., U. Southwestern La., 1963; M.B.A., La. State U., 1967, D.B.A., 1975; J.D., U. Ark., 1981; m. June Williams, Nov. 21, 1964; children—Shelly Lynn, Forrest Edward, Leah Christine. Personnel dir. Petroleum Helicopters, Inc., Lafayette, La., 1964-65; instr. mgmt and mktg. La. State U., New Orleans, 1967-68; asst. prof. mktg. U. Southwestern La., Lafayette, La., 1968-70; asso. prof. mgmt. U. N.D., Minot, 1972-73; asst. prof. mgmt. and pub. service adminstrn. U. Tenn., Nashville, 1973-74; asso. prof. mgmt. Middle Tenn. State U., Murfreesboro, 1974; chief adminstrn. services div. ARO, Inc., Tullahoma, Tenn., 1974-76; asso. prof. mgmt. U. Ark., Little Rock, 1976—; cons. in gen. mgmt., indsl. relations, and managerial devel. Served with USMC, 1957-59. La. State U. Grad. Sch. fellow, 1971. Mem. Acad. Mgmt., Indsl. Relations Research Assn., Am. Soc. Personnel Adminstrn., Beta Gamma Sigma. Democrat. Roman Catholic. Club: K.C. Home: Route 5 Box 493 GG Little Rock AR 72212 Office: 33d and University Sts U Ark Little Rock AR 72207

BANNARD, WILLIAM NEWELL, III, investment banker; b. Hazleton, Pa., June 12, 1918; s. William Newell, Jr. and Emily (Markle) B.; grad. Hill Sch., 1937; B.A., Yale, 1941; m. Marion H. Sutphen, Oct. 22, 1942; children—Marie S. (Mrs. William Cartier), David N., Barbara M. Haller. With Graham, Parsons & Co., N.Y.C., 1946-50; v.p., chmn. exec. com. Am. Securities Corp., 1950—, now pres., dir. Trustee, pres. Huntington Hosp. Served with USNR, 1942-46. Decorated Silver Star. Mem. Nat. Assn. Dealers (vice chmn. dist. bd.), N.Y. Soc. Security Analysts, Kappa Beta Phi (mem. council), Chi Psi. Clubs: Huntington Country (dir.); Bond (gov.) (N.Y.C.); Piping Rock; Mid-Ocean. Home: White Hill Rd Cold Spring Harbor NY 11724 Office: 25 Broad St New York NY 10004

BANNES, LORENZ THEODORE, constrn. co. exec.; b. St. Louis, Oct. 24, 1935; s. Lawrence Anthony and Louise Clair (Vollet) B.; B.S. in Civil Engring., St. Louis U., 1957; m. Janet Ann Bruening, Aug. 10, 1957; children—Stephen W., Michael F., Timothy L. From project engr. to exec. v.p. Gamble Constrn. Co. Inc., St. Louis, 1960-69, pres., 1969-72; founder, pres. Bannes-Shaughnessy Inc., 1972-78, chmn. bd., 1978—; tchr. civil engring. dept. St. Louis U., 1969—; tchr. contracting and basic constrn. skills Minority Contractors Devel. Corp., 1971—; tchr. concrete constrn. methods and contracting U. Mo. Extension Center, 1970—; tchr. constrn. mgmt. Grad. Engring. Center, U. Mo., St. Louis, 1968—, Washington U. Sch. Architecture, 1974—; tchr. Nat. Assn. Women in Constrn., 1973—, Florissant Valley Community Coll., 1974—. Mem. Human Rights Commn. Archdiocese of St. Louis, 1980—; mem. nat. bd. Living and Learning, Jesuit Program for Disadvantaged; bd. dirs. Little Sisters of Poor, Home for Aged; trustee Christian Bros. Coll. High Sch., St. Louis, 1980—. Served as officer USAF, 1957-60. Recipient Alumni Merit award St. Louis U., 1972. Mem. Nat. Soc. Profl. Engrs. (Mo. Young Engr. of Year 1971), Mo. Soc. Profl. Engrs. (Young Engr. of Year award St. Louis chpt. 1971), Nat. Assn. Women in Constrn. (hon.), Concrete Council St. Louis (pres. 1972-73, Outstanding Achievement award 1973), Asso. Gen. Contractors St. Louis (chmn. ednl. com. 1968—, Chmn. of Year 1973-74), ASCE, Young Pres.'s Orgn., Engrs. Club St. Louis, Asso. Gen. Contractors Am. (Nat. Build Am. award 1974), Circle Club Engrs., Xe Chi Epsilon. Home: 724 Paschal Dr Saint Louis MO 63125 Office: 6780 Southwest Ave Saint Louis MO 63143

BANNISTER, STEPHEN CHARLES, mgmt. cons.; b. Auburn, N.Y., Apr. 18, 1946; s. Russell Joseph and Mary Jane (Piccaro) B.; student M.I.T., 1963-64; B.S. in Econ. Theory, U. Ill., 1968; m. Judith E. Swagler, Nov. 26, 1980. With fin. dept. Ford Motor Co., 1968-71; staff cons. Kurt Salmon Assos., Princeton, N.J., 1971-79, Nashville, 1980—, prin., 1978—. Served with U.S. Army, 1968-70; Thailand. Decorated Joint Service Commendation medal. Mem. Beta Gamma Sigma. Club: Pine Beach Yacht (vice commodore). Office: Kurt Salmon Assos 4525 Harding Rd Nashville TN 37205

BANTON, JAMES FOWLER, mfg. co. exec.; b. Chgo., May 29, 1937; s. Fowler Boyton and Margaret Collin (Gilruth) B.; B.S. in Acctg., U. Ill., Champaign, 1959; M.S. in Engring., Ill. Inst. Tech., 1963; m. Susan Mary Abendroth, Sept. 1, 1966; children—James Andrew, Pembrook Collin and Bridget Gilruth (twins). Mgr. project control Automatic Elec. Co. subs. Gen. Telephone & Electronics, Northlake, Ill., 1961-64, program dir. ops. analysis, 1964-68; cons. mgr. Rexnord, Inc., Milw., 1968-79; v.p. operational devel. Agribusiness-Blount, Inc., Montgomery, Ala., 1979—; lectr. U. Wis., 1966-72; guest lectr. Harvard U., 1973-76. Mem. Brookfield (Wis.) Parks and Recreation Commn., 1975-79, chmn., 1977-79; alderman Fourth Dist., Brookfield, 1978-79. Served with Army N.G., 1955-63. Mem. Inst. Mgmt. Scis. (chmn. Milw. chpt. 1965-66; nat. v.p. meetings 1977), Ops. Research Soc. Am. (chmn. chpt. 1965-66, nat. publs. com. 1966-73, nat. meetings com. 1968-77, chmn. 1973-76, chmn. joint nat. meetings com. 1973-75, chmn. 43d nat. meeting). Clubs: Capital City, Rolling Hills Country (Montgomery). Contbr. articles to profl. jours. Home: 3202 Bankhead Ave Montgomery AL 36106 Office: 4520 Executive Park Dr Montgomery AL 36192

BANTON, JULIAN WATTS, internat. banker; b. Gladstone, Va., Aug. 8, 1940; s. John Dorman and Elizabeth (Watts) B.; B.S., Va. Commonwealth U., 1965; M.B.A., U. Richmond, 1968; grad. advanced mgmt. program Harvard U., 1977; m. Donna L. Brown, July 9, 1960; children—Courtney, Stephanie. With Bank of Va., Richmond, 1965-80, exec. v.p. until 1980; pres. Bank of Va. Internat., Richmond, 1980—; instr. Grad. Sch. Banking, U. Va.; lectr. Center Internat. Banking, U. Va.; mem. edn. policy and steering com. Grad. Sch. Banking U. Va., 1970—. Bd. dirs. Sci. Museum Va., Richmond, 1977—. Served with U.S. Army, 1958-61. Mem. Bank Assn. Fgn. Trade, Robert Morris Assos. Methodist. Clubs: Harvard (N.Y.C.); Westwood. Office: 11011 W Broad St Rd Richmond VA 23260

BANVILLE, ANNE, pub. relations co. exec.; b. Washington, Mar. 26, 1942; d. William Francis and Anne (Zuk) B.; B.A. with honors, U. Md., 1965; cert. U. Paris, 1963. Public relations asst. Sheraton-Park Hotel, Washington, 1965-66, Washington Hilton Hotel, Washington, 1966-67; research asst. Office Public Affairs, Am. Bar Assn., Washington, 1967-68; asso. John Hoving, Washington, 1968-72; owner, prin. Anne Banville, Washington, 1972—; dir. Washington office Carlson, Rockey & Assos., Inc. Am. Field Service Internat. scholar, 1959. Mem. Nat. Assn. Women Bus. Owners, Women's Legal Def. Fund (dir.), Public Relations Soc. Am., Capital Press Women, Am. Newspaper Women's Club, Nat. Press Club, Kappa Kappa Gamma. Home: 10009 Kensington Pkwy Kensington MD 20795 Office: 1000 Connecticut Ave NW Washington DC 20036

BANZER, JERRY LEE, aerospace co. exec.; b. Wichita, Kans., Aug. 23, 1938; s. Edward Victor and Inez (Baker) B.; B.S. in Mech. Engring., Kans. State U., 1961; M.B.A., Wichita State U., 1968; postgrad. (Sloan fellow) Stanford, 1975; m. Barbara Ann Junker, Sept. 3, 1961; children—Melody, Jacqueline. Reliability engr. Hercules Co., Salt Lake City, 1961-63, Gen. Dynamics Corp., Pomona, Calif., 1963-65; flight control engr. Boeing Co., Wichita, 1965-68, asst. mgr. structures and mechanics, Houston, 1968-69, strategy planning mgr., Wichita, 1970-74, div. planning mgr. 1975-79, dep. mgr. Oak Ridge ops., 1979—. Mem. Kans. Gov.'s Problem Identification Team, 1976, Gov.'s Steering Com. on Effective Mgmt. in State Govt., 1976-78; bd. dirs. Roane/Anderson County Econ. Devel. Council, Oak Ridge World Trade Com., E. Tenn. Big. Bros./Big Sisters, fund raising com. Children's Mus. Recipient Apollo Achievement Award, 1969. Mem. ASME, Ops. Research Soc. Am., Oak Ridge C. of C., Stanford Alumni Assn. Home: 1134 W Outer Dr Oak Ridge TN 37830 Office: 465 Laboratory Rd Oak Ridge TN 37830

BANZHAF, CLAYTON HARRIS, financial exec.; b. Buffalo, Dec. 24, 1917; s. Joseph Maximilian and Elizabeth (Harris) B.; M.B.A., U. Chgo., 1954; m. Dolores J. Gavins, Dec. 30, 1962; children by previous marriage—Barbara A. (Mrs. Thomas T. Grimmett), Debra R. (Mrs. Stephen T. York), William Clay. With Sears, Roebuck & Co., 1936—, trainee, Buffalo, retail auditor, Phila., 1939-41, retail controller, Washington, 1946-48, Pitts., 1949-50, wage and salary adminstr. nat. personnel dept., Chgo., 1951-57, corp. asst. treas., 1958-60, sr. asst. treas., Chgo., 1961-74, treas., 1975-76, v.p., treas., 1976—; pres., chief exec. officer, dir. Sears Roebuck Acceptance Corp., Wilmington, 1963-72, dir., 1972—; treas. Sears Internat. Finance Co., Sears Roebuck Overseas Inc., Sears Roebuck de Puerto Rico S.A., Seraco Enterprises Inc., Fleet Maintenance Inc., Lifetime Foam Products Inc., Terminal Freight Handling Co., Tower Ventures, Inc.; asst. treas. other Sears subsidiaries; dir. Homart Devel. Co., Banco de Credito Internacional S.A., Lake Shore Land Asso. Inc., Sears Overseas Finance N.V., Curacao, Western Forge Corp., Colorado Springs, Barclays Am. Corp., Charlotte, N.C. Mem. exec. bd. Chgo. Area council Boy Scouts Am., 1963-68, mem. adv. bd., 1969—; mem. bus. adv. council Coll. Bus. Adminstrn., U. Ill., Chgo. Circle; bd. dirs. Council for Community Services, Chgo., 1975-77, United Way Met. Chgo., 1977—; trustee Elmira (N.Y.) Coll., 1975—. Served to maj. AUS, 1941-45. Mem. Financial Execs. Inst. (pres. Chgo. chpt. 1972-73, nat. dir. 1975-78, mem. exec. com. 1976-77, v.p. Midwest area 1977-78), U. Chgo. Alumni Assn. (Exec. Program, Grad. Sch. Bus., dir. 1966-67, v.p. 1968, pres. 1969, mem. alumni council Grad. Sch. Bus. 1969, pres. 1972-75), C. of C. U.S. (com. on banking and monetary policy 1967-72, com. on banking, monetary and fiscal affairs 1972-74), AIM (pres. council, fellow), Am. Assembly Collegiate Schs. Bus. (accreditation mem.), AMA (com. allied health edn. and accreditation). Republican. Presbyterian. Mason. Clubs: Arts, Economic, Medinah Country, Metropolitan, Executives, Saddle and Cycle, Union League Chgo. (dir. 1969-72, chmn. house com. 1969-71, v.p., dir. 1977-78). Home: 1130 N Lake Shore Dr Chicago IL 60611 Office: Sears Tower Chicago IL 60684

BAPTISTA, ERNEST PETER, ins. broker; b. Providence, July 4, 1950; s. Ernest and Carmela B.; B.S., Boston U., 1973; m. Sharon Williams, May 11, 1980; 1 dau., Jennifer Ann. Pension and ins. broker Worrell, Passananti and Radoccia, Inc., Providence, 1973—. Active Jr. Achievement, United Way, R.I. Philharm., YMCA; mem. R.I. Gov.'s Small Bus. Forum. Mem. Nat. Life Underwriters, Small Bus. Assn. New Eng. (chmn. legis. sect.). Roman Catholic. Club: Kirkdrae Country. Home: 14 Stevens Rd Cranston RI 02910 Office: 144 Westminister St Providence RI 02903

BARAKET, EDMUND S., JR., gen. contractor, contracting cons.; b. N.Y.C., Oct. 10, 1947; s. Edmund S. and Agnes B.; student Pa. State U., 1967-68; A.A., Lehigh County Community Coll., 1971; m. Maryann; children—Christopher, Melissa, Joseph. Insp. metall. layout Bethlehem Steel Corp., 1967-69, mem. research and devel. staff, 1970-73; owner, mgr. Ed Baraket Gen. Contractors, Allentown, Pa., 1973—. Recipient award for restoration of early colonial family residences Keystone Publs., 1978. Mem. Gen. Contractors Assn. Lehigh Valley, Concrete Contractors Assn., Am. Soc. Concrete Constrn. Office: 1322 Tweed Ave Allentown PA 18103

BARAS, CAROL ROSE FORMOST (MRS. WILLIAM T. BARAS), pub. relations exec.; b. Chgo., Oct. 1, 1930; d. August and Celestina (Ristucce) Formost; student San Diego State Coll., 1947-49, U. Calif. at La Jolla, 1967, 70-71, U. London, 1971; m. William T. Baras; children—Gary Rose, Frank Rose, Linda Rose. Disc jockey Carol's Frolics, Radio Sta. KSDO, San Diego, 1947; record mgmt., receptionist, 1948-49; pub. relations Circus Foods, 1948-51; bookkeeper Sunset Engraving, 1948-49; copy writer program scheduling Radio Sta. KGB, 1950-51; exec. sec. programming, copywriting Radio Sta. KSDO, 1951-52; mgr. Formost Rental Agy., 1952-54; instr., mgr., cons. Roman Health Spa, 1967-68; partner, decorator Formost Furniture, 1973—; owner, dir. Hypnos Morpheus Center, San Diego, 1968—; condr. weekly self-hypnosis tng. programs VA Hosp., La Jolla, Calif., 1973—; partner, pub. relations exec. Formost Advt., San Diego, 1969—; treas., Universal Jet, Inc., San Diego, 1971-76; treas. Santa Clara (Calif.) Mobile Homes, 1974-78, Palm Springs (Calif.) Country Club Mobile Homes, 1974-76; partner SEB Enterprises, Escondido, Calif., 1973-76; v.p. Woots Corp., 1976—; co-owner Mom's Natural Foods from Mother Earth, 1977—; partner Jacumba Hot Springs Hotel & Spa., 1979—. Formerly active Salvation Army Assn., Zool. Soc. San Diego, San Diego County Assn. Retarded Children; bd. dirs. Big Sisters League Inc., 1979—; co-founder Baras Found., 1978—; originator 291-Kids, 1978. Mem. Am. Parapsychol. Research Found., Assn. to Advance Ethical Hypnosis, Calif. Profl. Hypnotists Assn. (chmn. hypnotists examing council 1975-77), Calif. Assn. Ethical Hypnosis, Calif. State Hypnosis Assn., San Diego C. of C., Advt. and Sales Club, Better Bus. Bur. (nat panel consumer arbitrators), Media Club, Internat. Platform Assn., Nat. Acad. TV Arts and Scis. (bd. govs.), Alpha Phi. Office: Suite 300 2255 Camino del Rio S San Diego CA 92108

BARBA, J. WILLIAM, lawyer; b. Arlington, N.J., May 22, 1923; s. John and Rose (Lettiere) B.; A.B., Princeton, 1947; LL.B., U. Pa., 1950; m. Susan Vartanian; children—Susan Elizabeth, Christina. Admitted to N.J. State bar, 1950, D.C. bar, 1969; practiced in Newark, 1950-53; asst. spl. counsel to Pres. U.S., 1954-57; partner law firm Shanley & Fisher, Newark, 1957—. Chmn. N.J. Republican Finance Com. Served as lt. (j.g.) USNR, 1943-46. Mem. Am., D.C., Essex County bar assns. Roman Catholic. Clubs: Metropolitan (Washington); Essex (Newark), Baltusrol Golf. Asso. editor U. Pa. Law Rev. Home: Long Hill Rd New Vernon NJ 07976 Office: 550 Broad St Newark NJ 07102

BARBER, ANDREW BOLLONS, banker; b. Joliet, Ill., Apr. 8, 1909; s. Charles and Pauline Inez (Bollons) B.; student U. Ill., 1929-31; B.S., Northwestern U., 1939; m. Bette Jo Johnson, May 1, 1963; children—Suzanne (Mrs. Terrence J. Ryan), Nancy, Mary Jane (Mrs. Robert Holt). With Union Nat. Bank, Joliet, Ill., 1940—, pres., 1972-73, chmn. bd., 1974—; dir. Citizens Nat. Bank, Waukegan, Ill., Nat. Bank North Chicago (Ill.), Streator (Ill.) Nat. Bank. Chmn. Will County Savings Bond Program, 1946-74; mem. Salem Village Bd. Trustees; chmn. Will County Land Clearance Commn., 1968-72; mem. Joliet (Ill.) Parking Commn., 1950-70; mem. Luth. Welfare Services Bd.; bd. dirs. Credit Bur. Will County, Midwest region Boys Club Am.; trustee Lewis U., Lockport, Ill. Mem. C. of C. Kiwanian. Clubs: Country (Joliet, Ill.); Three Rivers Yacht (Wilmington, Ill.); Chgo. Yacht. Home: 415 Western Ave Joliet IL 60435 Office: 50 W Jefferson St Joliet IL 60431

BARBER, CHARLES FINCH, metals co. exec., lawyer; b. Chgo., Feb. 26, 1917; s. Henri Newton and Lillian (Wanner) B.; B.S., Northwestern U., 1939; LL.B., Harvard, 1942; M.Phil., Oxford U., 1948; LL.D. (hon.), Mont. Tech., 1976; m. Lois Helen LaCroix, Aug. 30, 1947; children—Charles Bradford, Ann McDonald, Robin Goodhue, Elizabeth Louise. Admitted to D.C. bar, 1942; asso. Covington & Burling, Washington, 1948-54; asst. solicitor gen. U.S., 1954-56; gen. counsel Asarco Inc. (formerly Am. Smelting & Refining Co.), N.Y.C., 1956-63, v.p., 1959-63, exec. v.p., 1963-69, pres., 1969-71, chmn., 1971—, also dir.; dir. Chase Manhattan Bank, Continental Corp., So. Peru Copper Corp., Desarrollo Indsl. Minero, S.A. Bd. mgrs. Swarthmore Coll., 1966-74; trustee Conf. Bd., Council of Ams.; chmn. Nat. Legal Center for Public Interest; mem. council Woodrow Wilson Center for Scholars, Rockefeller U.; bd. dirs. UN Assn. U.S.A. Served to lt. comdr. USNR, 1941-46. Decorated Legion of Merit. Mem. Am. Bar Assn., AIME (asso.), Council Fgn. Relations, Am. Mining Congress (dir., chmn.), Phi Beta Kappa. Clubs: Wall St., Down Town Assn., Harvard, Mining (N.Y.C.); Metropolitan (Washington); Belle Haven (Greenwich). Office: 120 Broadway New York NY 10271

BARBER, GEORGE CULLEN, mfg. co. exec.; b. Paterson, N.J., May 22, 1917; s. George and Ruth (Shaw) B.; B.Mech. Engring., U. Va., 1942; M.B.A., Harvard U., 1948; m. Elaine Ardell Sprague, Feb. 11, 1945; children—Jeffrey, Bruce, Douglas. Mfg. engr. Otis Elevator Co., 1948-50; with Anchor Hocking Corp., 1950—, group v.p. packaging, 1974-76, pres., chief operating officer, Lancaster, Ohio, 1976-77, pres., chief exec. officer, 1977—, also dir. Served to lt. USNR, 1942-46. Mem. Glass Packaging Inst. (past dir.), Nat. Canners Assn. (past dir.). Republican. Clubs: Lancaster Country; Muirfield Village Golf (Columbus, Ohio). Home: 134 Crown Ct Lancaster OH 43130 Office: 109 N Broad St Lancaster OH 43130

BARBER, RICHARD ALLEN, bldg. contractor; b. Vanduser, Mo., July 17, 1940; s. James Arthur and Lucille (Moxley) B.; B.S., UCLA. Vice-pres., Pacific Funding Corp., Inglewood, Calif., 1967-71; v.p. 1st Los Angeles Corp., Los Angeles, 1971-73, Internat. Mortgage, Irvine, Calif., 1973-75; pres. Kaufman & Broad Homes, Detroit, 1976, Kaufman and Broad of So. Calif., Irvine, 1976-80, Anden of Fla., Longwood, 1980—. Served with USMC, 1961-64. Mem. Bldg. Industry Assn. Republican. Home: 181 Columbus Circle Longwood FL 32750

BARBIERI, ARTHUR ROBERT, chem. co. exec.; b. Paterson, N.J., June 10, 1926; s. Otto Arthur and Sadie (Maxwell) B.; student Rutgers U., 1957-58, Utah State U., 1962-69, Weber Coll., 1980—; m. Carole Jones, Dec. 26, 1979; children by previous marriage—Elaine, Debra, Donna. Asst. buyer Allen B. Dumont Labs., Clifton, N.Y., 1947-54; field supr. Housing Guild, Inc., Smithtown, N.Y., 1954-56; buyer Thiokol Co., Denville, N.J., 1956-60, sr. buyer, Brigham City, Utah, 1960-72, purchasing agt., 1972—. Bd. dirs. Brigham City Community Theatre, Thiokol Credit Union. Served with USN, 1944-46; PTO. Democrat. Clubs: Elks, Masons (past master), Shriners (asso. grand guardian 1978), Job's Daus. Home: 8615 S Hwy 89-91 Brigham City UT 84302 Office: 3350 Airport Rd Ogden UT 84403

BARBOUR, ALFRED RAYMOND, ingot mfg. co. exec.; b. Pitts., Dec. 6, 1917; s. Alfred Charles and Irene Marie (Schlegel) B.; B.A., Princeton U., 1940; m. Mary Louise Dunnington, Dec. 30, 1944; children—Melissa Ann, Mary Louise, Alfred. Salesman, Roessing Bronze Co., Mars, Pa., 1945-50, sec., treas., 1950-56, v.p., 1956-62, pres., 1962-79, chmn., 1979—. Served as capt. Pa. N.G., 1946-49; trustee Foundry Edn. Found., 1973-75. Served with U.S. Army, 1940-45. Mem. Assn. Brass and Bronze Ingot Makers (pres. 1965-67), Am. Copper Council (dir. 1974; treas. 1978—), Brass and Bronze Ingot Inst., Am. Foundrymen's Soc., ASTM. Republican. Presbyn. Clubs: Duquesne, Longue Vue, Masons (32 deg., Shriner). Patentee in field. Home: 1200 Bennington Ave Pittsburgh PA 15217 Office: PO Box 547 Mars PA 16046

BARBOUR, ROBERT FRANKLIN, acct., fin. exec.; b. Wirt, Okla., June 29, 1930; s. Frank Burney and Bonnie Caroline (Barton) B.; B.S., Okla. A. and M. Coll., 1955; m. Dolores Dawson, Nov. 23, 1950. Internal auditor Halliburton Oil Well Cementing Co., Duncan, Okla., 1955-58; comptroller Compania Halliburton de Cementacion Y Fomento, Maracaibo, Venezuala, S. Am., 1958-62; C.P.A., Harrison, Ark., 1962-73; fin. analyst Jobbers' Motor Supply Inc., Harrison, 1973-77; with Guaranty Savs. and Loan Assn., Harrison, 1977—, v.p., 1979—. Treas. John Paul Hammerschmidt Re-election Com. to U.S. Ho. Reps., 1970-77. Served with U.S. Army, 1948-50. Mem. Am. Inst. C.P.A.'s, Ark. Soc. C.P.A.'s, Am. Mgmt. Assn., Beta Alpha Psi. Democrat. Baptist. Lion. Home: Cottonwood Rd PO Box 35 Harrison AR 72601

BARCLAY, EDWARD STEARNS, advt. agy. exec.; b. Oak Park, Ill., Aug. 15, 1921; s. Arthur Jackson and Marion Elizabeth (Stearns) B.; B.S., U. Fla., 1943; certificate in Advt. Design, Pratt Inst., N.Y.C., 1953; postgrad. Art Students League, N.Y.C., 1951-53, Chgo. Art Inst., 1937; m. Mary Elizabeth Weaver, Nov. 11, 1944; 1 son, David Edward. Artist promotion dept. Allied Stores, N.Y.C., 1950-53; asst. mgr., sales promotion mgr. Davis Dept. Store, Winston-Salem, N.C., 1953-57; sr. promotion artist St. Petersburg (Fla.) Times, 1957-70; v.p., creative dir. Russell, Brantley & Peterson, Inc., St. Petersburg, 1970—. Merit badge counselor Boy Scouts Am., 1972-74. Served to capt. AUS, 1942-46; PTO. Mem. Fla. Outdoor Writers Assn., Nat. Rifle Assn. (life), Am. Fishing Assn. (life), Fla. League Anglers, Outdoor Writers Assn. Am., Bass Anglers Sportsmens Soc., Delta Sigma Phi. Episcopalian. Home: 14557 Tanglewood Dr Largo FL 33540 Office: 5013 Central Ave St Petersburg FL 33710

BARCLAY, JAMES CRAWFORD, textile co. exec.; b. New Rochelle, N.Y., Aug. 31, 1940; s. Hartley Wade and Marjorie Kathleen (Whitley) B.; student Gettysburg Coll., 1958-60; B.A., Hofstra U., 1962; m. Donalda Elizabeth Banks, Mar. 2, 1968; children—James Crawford, William Whitley. Mgmt. devel. program Allstate Ins. Co., White Plains, N.Y., 1963-68; exec. Jute Industries Ltd., White Plains, 1968—, corporate sec., 1969-72; corp. sec. Sidlaw Industries Ltd., White Plains, 1972-73; asst. v.p. Colox Corp., White Plains, 1973-75; v.p. Stevens Textile Supply Co. Inc., Dalton, Ga., 1975, pres., 1976—; treas., dir. Trueset Yarns, Inc., Dalton; chmn. bd. Waretex Industries, Inc., Dalton, Royce Industries Ltd., Dalton; dir. Richco Textile Sales, Inc., Dalton, Southeastern Textile Sales, Inc., Dalton. Founder Westchester Research Assos., White Plains, N.Y. Recipient Sales and Marketing Execs. award for excellence, 1964. Mem. Commerce and Industry Assn., Am. Importers Assn., Carpet and Rug Inst., Jute Carpet Backing Council N.Y., Phi Delta Theta. Republican. Episcopalian. Clubs: Dalton Golf and Country, Battlefield Golf and Country. Home: 604 Audubon Way Dalton GA 30720 also Who-Torok Estate King St Port Chester NY 10573 Office: 302 S Thornton Ave Dalton GA 30720

BARD, GERALD WILFORD, food processing co. exec.; b. Milw., Oct. 7, 1932; s. Alex and Jean (Lifschultz) B.; B.S., U. Wis., 1955; M.B.A., Iona Coll., 1970; m. Sandra Ann Laskin, July 28, 1956; children—Loryn, Nancy, Jeffrey, Corey, Betsy. Supr. organic lab. RexNord, Milw., 1955-60; asst. dir. research and devel. Duncan Foods Co. div. Coca Cola, 1960-62, corp. staff engr., 1962-64; group leader process engring. Beechnut Life Savers Inc., Port Chester, N.Y., 1964-68, mgr. engring. devel. dept., 1968-71; gen. mgr. Brookhill Frozen Meat Co., N.Y.C., 1972; gen. prodn. mgr. Frozen Foods div. Libby McNeill & Libby Co., Chgo., 1972-74, gen. mgr. Frozen Foods div., 1974-75, dir. indsl. devel., 1976-77; dir. engring. planning and devel. Kraft, Inc., Chgo., 1978-79, dir. process engring., grocery and oil products, 1979—; instr. bus. adminstrn. Coll. Lake County. Chmn., Deerfield Village Youth Council; scoutmaster Boy Scouts Am., 1977—. Served with AUS, 1955-57. Registered profl. engr. Wis., Tex. Mem. Nat. Soc. Profl. Engrs., Inst. Food Technologists, Am. Inst. Chem. Engrs., Phi Tau Sigma, Alpha Chi Sigma. Home: 1215 Arbor Vitae Rd Deerfield IL 60015 Office: 500 N Peshtigo Ct Chicago IL 60690

BARDT, NATHAN NORMAN, pub. accountant; b. Bklyn., Nov. 29, 1922; s. Andrew S. and Fannie (Tolkan) B.; B.B.A., Pace Coll., 1950; m. Patricia Faber, June 19, 1949; children—David R., Allison Sue, Leslie Ellen. Pvt. practice accounting, Rockville Centre, N.Y.; cons. on estate planning. Served with Signal Corps, AUS, 1941-44. Mem. Am. Inst. C.P.A.'s, N.Y. State Soc. C.P.A.'s, Nat. Soc. Pub. Accountants, Fla. Inst. C.P.A.'s, Empire State Assn. Pub. Accountants, Tax Inst. Clubs: Lions (treas. 1961-62), B'nai B'rith. Home: 6885 Bianchini Circle Boca Raton FL 33433 Office: 119 N Park Ave Rockville Centre NY 11570

BAREFOOT, BRIAN MILLER, fin. services co. exec.; b. Cin., Apr. 11, 1943; s. John Roy Jr. and Marjorie Isabel (Miller) B.; student Union Coll., 1961-63; B.S. in Bus. Adminstrn. Babson Coll., 1966; M.B.A., Pace Coll., 1969; m. Pamela Howell Porter, Sept. 7. 1968; children—John, Katharine. Trainee Merrill Lynch, Pierce, Fenner & Smith, N.Y.C., 1967-68, analyst, 1968-70, instl. salesman, Chgo., 1970-72, asst. br. mgr. Cleve., 1972-75, nat. instl. sales mgr., 1975-76, Western instl. sales dir., San Francisco, 1976—; guest lectr. Babson Coll., Baldwin Wallace Coll. Asst. chmn. United Fund Dr., Cleve.; dir. fund raising Jr. Davis Cup, Cleve. Served with USAR, 1967-73. Mem. Newcomen Soc. N.Am., Babson Coll. Alumni Assn. (dir.), Chi Psi, Delta Sigma Pi. Clubs: Beacon Hill (Summit, N.J.); Bond (Chgo., Cleve., San Francisco); Bankers, Mchts. Exchange (San Francisco); Orinda (Calif.) Country. Office: 300 California St San Francisco CA 94104

BARGFREDE, JAMES ALLEN, lawyer; b. Seguin, Tex., Sept. 10, 1928; s. Herman Fred and Elsie (Vorpahl) B.; B.S., Tex. A. and M. U., 1950; postgrad. Ohio State U., 1952-53; J.D., St. Mary's U., 1957; m. Virginia Felts, Nov. 27, 1970; 1 son, Charles Allen. Engr., Signal Corps, San Antonio, 1950-52; elec. engr. San Antonio Pub. Service Bd., 1953-58; admitted to Tex. bar, 1957; patent counsel Hubbard & Co., Chgo., 1958-59; practiced in Chgo., 1959-60, Houston, 1960—; mem. firm Butler, Binion, Rice, Cook & Knapp, 1960-68; individual practice, 1968-74, 75—; patent and legal counsel HydroTech Internat., Inc., 1977-81; mem. firm Bargfrede and Thompson, 1974-75. Served with USAF, 1952-53. Mem. Am., Houston (chmn. automated equipment com. 1971-75) bar assns., State Bar Tex., Am., Houston patent law assns., Assn. Former Students Tex. A. and M. U., Houston Livestock Show and Rodeo, Delta Theta Phi. Baptist. Club: Briarcroft Civic (pres.). Home: 5649 Piping Rock Ln Houston TX 77056

BARIBEAU, MICHAEL HENRY, real estate exec.; b. Brunswick, Maine, Feb. 4, 1953; s. Henry Michael and Elizabeth Helen (Crooker) B.; B.A., Beloit (Wis.) Coll., 1975. Appraiser, Baribeau Appraisal Assos., Brunswick, 1976-80; mgr., broker Baribeau Agy., Brunswick, 1977-78, dir. mgmt./investments, 1979—; owner, mgr. photography by Baribeau, Baribeau Print Shop, Brunswick, 1979—. Mem. Nat. Bd. Realtors, Merry Meeting Bd. Realtors (charter), Nat. Realtors Mktg. Inst., Brunswick C. of C. Office: 51 Pleasant St Brunswick ME 04011

BARICKMAN, JAMES HALL, advt. agy. exec.; b. Mpls., Oct. 5, 1924; s. John B. and Mary Jane (Hall) B.; B.B.A., U. Minn., 1947; m. Mary Mischler, Jan. 28, 1974; children—Nancy, James H.J., Julie K., Robert John, Daniel W. With trust dept. Northwestern Nat. Bank, Mpls., 1947-49; W. Coast advt. mgr. Pillsbury Co., Los Angeles, 1949-52; partner Brewer Advt., Kansas City, Mo., 1952-59; chmn., chief exec. officer Banrckman Advt., Kansas City, Mo., 1959—; dir. Columbia Union Nat. Bank. Pres., Jr. Achievement Kansas City, 1959-60. Served with C.E., U.S. Army, 1943-44. Recipient Am. Advt. Fedn. Silver Medal award, 1976. Mem. Am. Mktg. Assn., Assn. Advt. Agys., Internat. Am. Assn. Advt. Agys. Clubs: Kansas City, Univ., Indian Hills Country, Wolf Creek Country, Carriage, La Quinta Country, Hillcrest Country, Friars, Williams. Home: 6417 Verona Rd Shawnee Mission KS 66208 Office: 421 W 12th St Kansas City MO 64105

BARISH, JEAN ELLEN, newspaper exec.; b. N.Y.C., June 13, 1952; d. Norman N. and Esther (Braverman) B.; B.A. with honors, Wesleyan U., 1974; M.B.A., Harvard U., 1978. Cons., Data Resources, Inc., Lexington, Mass., 1974-76; analyst Inco Ltd.-Venture Capital Mgmt., N.Y.C., 1977; asst. to v.p. mfg. Washington Post Co., Washington, 1978-79, bus. mgr. TV Mag., 1980—. Trustee Wesleyan U., 1978—. Mem. Nat. Women's Edn. Fund. Clubs: Wesleyan U. Alumni, Harvard Bus. Sch. (Washington). Home: 1880 Columbia Rd NW Apt 202 Washington DC 20009 Office: Washington Post Co 1150 15th St NW Washington DC 20071

BARISH, MICHAEL SIGMUND, investment co. exec.; b. N.Y.C., Dec. 29, 1939; s. Albert and Irene (Diamond) B.; B.B.A., U. Mich., 1960; m. Joyce F. Day, June 11, 1963; children—Brian, Grant. Security analyst Fin. Programs Co., Denver, 1960-65, portfolio mgr., 1968-69; security analyst Moore & Schley, Inc., N.Y.C., 1965-68; portfolio mgr. Cambridge Mgmt. Corp., Denver, 1969-73, Cambiar Investors Inc., Denver, 1973—; dir. Guaranty Nat. Corp. Served with USCG, 1962-63. Chartered fin. analyst. Mem. Fin. Analysts Fedn., N.Y. Soc. Security Analysts. Republican. Jewish. Home: 5761 E Nassau Pl Englewood CO 80111 Office: 3600 S Yosemite St Suite 1000 Denver CO 80237

BARKDOLL, GERALD LEE, govt. ofcl.; b. Waynesboro, Pa., Feb. 14, 1934; s. Paul Brison and Myrtle Geneva (Patterson) B.; B.S., Drexel U., 1957, M.B.A., 1963; m. Linda Alice Suydam, Dec. 30, 1978. Sr. methods and standards engr. Firestone Tire & Rubber Co., Akron, Ohio, 1964-65; controller Englander Co., also sr. econ. analyst Union Carbide Corp., Chgo. and N.Y.C., 1965-70; Central regional mgr. on-line decisions FDA, Rockville, Md., 1970-71, dep. asso. commr. for planning and evaluation, 1971-72, asso. commr. for planning and evaluation, 1972—; Served with C.E., U.S. Army, 1957-59. Recipient FDA award of merit, 1974; HEW Hon. "A" Award, 1974; registered profl. engr., Md. Mem. Planning Exec. Inst., Am. Inst. Indsl. Engrs. Unitarian. Contbr. articles to profl. jours.; editorial rev. bd. Evaluation and the Health Professions, 1976—. Home: 7001 Oak Forest Ln Bethesda MD 20034 Office: 5600 Fishers Ln Rockville MD 20857

BARKER, A. CLIFFORD, electronics co. exec.; b. Phoenix, June 7, 1933; s. Alva Clifford and Gertrude Theresa (Gertzen) B.; B.S. in Engring. with highest honors, UCLA, 1959, M.S. in Engring., 1962; m. Shirley Ray Mueller, May 30, 1975; children—Alexandra Caton, Adrienne Caren. Sr. engr. Litton Industries, Woodland Hills, Calif., 1959-63; mgr. advanced nav. systems Teledyne, Inc., Los Angeles, 1963-67; exec. v.p. Internat. Engring. Co. div. ATO, Inc., Arlington, Va., 1967-70; v.p. Hastings-Raydist div. Teledyne, Inc., Hampton, Va., 1970-73; chmn. bd., pres. Navidyne Corp., Newport News, Va., 1973—. Bd. dirs. Va. Ballet, Inc., 1979—. Served with USMC, 1953-56. Recipient Most Outstanding Undergrad. Student award UCLA Coll. Engring., 1958. Mem. John Birch Soc. (nat. council 1968—), IEEE, Inst. of Nav., Internat. Omega Assn., Tau Beta Pi. Club: Rotary. Contbr. articles to profl. jours. Patentee in field. Office: 11824 Fishing Point Dr Newport News VA 23606

BARKER, COLIN EDWARD, real estate devel., constrn. corp. exec.; b. Birmingham, Eng., May 21, 1947; came to U.S., 1952, naturalized, 1958; s. Cyril Ernest and Joan Kathleen (Spurrier) B.; B.Indsl. Engring., Ga. Inst. Tech., 1971; m. Charlene Denise Campbell, Mar. 10, 1979. Project mgr. Project Mgmt. Consultants, Atlanta, 1970-72, Consol. Equities Corp., Atlanta, 1972-75; v.p. Glen Properties, Inc., Atlanta, 1975—; cons. Public Service Commn., Savannah, Ga., 1970-71. Served with AUS, 1967-69. Decorated Bronze Star. Mem. Nat. Assn. Homebuilders (Recognition award Research Found. 1980), Apt. Owners and Mgrs. Assn., Nat. Remodelers Assn. Clubs: Lake Lanier Sailing, Court South Racquet. Home: 3001 Saint Anne's Ln Atlanta GA 30327 Office: Glen Properties Inc Suite 224 5299 Roswell Rd Atlanta GA 30342

BARKER, DAVID ALLEN, ins. rep.; b. Columbus, Ohio, Oct. 29, 1940; s. Jesse Sebert and Eleanor Emma (Baber) B.; B.A., Morris Harvey Coll., 1971; postgrad. Marshall U., 1972; m. Brenda Gail Amick, Mar. 2, 1979; children—Pamela Dawn, Andrew David, Rebecca Lynn, Katherine Renae. Sales rep. Met. Life Ins. Co., Charleston, W.Va., 1973-76, sales mgr., Columbus, 1976—. Pres., Marmet (W.Va.) City Planning Commn., 1973-74, Marmet Civic Welfare Council, 1972-75. Served with USNR, 1958-61. Mem. Nat. Assn. Life Underwriters, Poca River Hunting and Fishing Club, V.F.W. (officer). Methodist. Club: Masons. Home: 3758 Palm St Columbus OH 43213 Office: 4150 E Main St Columbus OH 43213

BARKER, GERALD PATRICK, mgmt. cons.; b. Montreal, Que., Can., Oct. 26, 1942; s. Kenneth Paul and Lucille Elizabeth (Murphy) B.; B.A., Loyola Coll., 1963; m. Joan Skelly, Dec. 14, 1968; children—Kenneth, Joanne, Sharon. Jr. exec. officer Govt. of Can., External Aid Office, Ottawa, Ont., 1963-65; adminstr. wages and salaries RCA Victor Co., Ltd., Montreal, 1966-67; mgr. compensation and benefits Can., RCA Ltd., Montreal, 1968-70; mgr. indsl. relations RCA Records-Can., Smiths Falls, 1970-71; mgr. employee relations Toronto (Ont.) Star, 1972-74; dir. personnel Monenco Ltd., Montreal, 1974-79; pres., mng. dir. Katimavik Cons., Montreal, Toronto, London, Ont., 1979—. Dir., Verdun Young Liberal Assn., 1967; treas. Lachine Liberal Assn., 1978-79; campaign chmn. Fed. Election, 1979, Lachine Liberal Assn. Recipient Am. Compensation Assn. award for contbns. to mgmt., 1969. Fellow Royal Commonwealth Soc.; mem. Am. Compensation Assn. (chpt. v.p. 1970), Can. Cons. Engrs. Personnel Group (treas. 1977-80). Liberal. Roman Catholic. Author: Manual for Commonwealth Scholars in Can., 1964. Home: 915 Inverhouse Dr Mississauga ON Canada Office: 1300 Bay St Toronto ON M5R 3K8 Canada

BARKER, GREGSON LEARD, business forms printing co. exec.; b. Chgo., Jan. 19, 1918; s. Walter R. and Margaret (Gregson) B.; m. Mary Louise Nichols, Sept. 8, 1939; children—Margaret Louise (Mrs. George H. Thompson), John Leard, Eric Walter, William Jordan; m. 2d, Betty McPherson King, Apr. 27, 1968; m. 3d, D'Arcy Timmons, Aug. 19, 1978. With UARCO Inc., designers, printers bus. forms, Barrington, Ill., 1937—, v.p., 1949-51, exec. v.p., 1951-55, pres., 1955—; dir. LaSalle Nat. Bank, Chgo., 1st Nat. Bank & Trust Co., Barrington, Chgo. Profl. Basketball Corp., Hammond Corp., Carson Pirie Scott & Co. Mem. citizens bd. U. Chgo.; bd. dirs., v.p. Jr. Achievement, Chgo.; bd. dirs. Infant Welfare Soc. Chgo., Chgo. Hearing Soc. Mem. Ill. Mfrs. Assn. (pres., dir.), Chgo. Assn. Commerce and Industry (v.p., dir.), Ill. State C. of C. (dir.), Employers Assn. Chgo. (dir.), Chgo. Pres.'s Orgn., Northwestern U. Assos. Republican. Episcopalian. Clubs: Economic, Executives, Chicago Commonwealth, Chicago, Mid America, Commercial, Racquet (Chgo.); Metropolitan (N.Y.C.); Barrington Hills Country; Lyford Cay (New Providence, Bahamas); Meadow. Home: 81 Meadow Hill Rd Barrington IL 60010 Office: UARCO Inc W County Line Rd Barrington IL 60010

BARKER, JOHN MICHAEL, computer sci. cons.; b. Pitts., Oct. 13, 1953; s. William H. and Lora M. (Crumley) B.; B.S. in Computer Scis., Point Park Coll., Pitts., 1976; postgrad. in computer sci. Johns Hopkins U., 1978—; m. Martha Elizabeth Higgins, Sept. 1, 1979. Programmer, analyst Fortune Nat. Life Ins., Pitts., 1976-77, Computer Scis. Corp., Silver Spring, Md., 1977-79; cons. Booz, Allen & Hamilton, Bethesda, Md., 1979—. Mem. Assn. Computing Machinery, Phi Kappa Theta. Home: 8421 Church Ln Bowie MD 20715 Office: 4330 East West Hwy Bethesda MD 20014

BARKER, KEITH RENE, investment banker; b. Elkhart, Ind., July 28, 1928; s. Clifford C. and Edith (Hausman) B.; A.B., Wabash Coll., 1950; M.B.A., Ind. U., 1952; m. 2d, Elizabeth S. Arrington, Nov. 24, 1965; 1 dau., Jennifer S.; children (by previous marriage)—Bruce C., Lynn K. Sales rep. Fulton, Reid & Staples, Inc. (formerly Fulton, Reid & Co.), Ft. Wayne, Ind., 1951-55, office, 1955-59, asst. v.p., 1960, v.p., 1960, dir., 1961, asst. sales mgr., 1963, sales mgr., 1964—, sr. v.p., 1966-75, pres., chief exec. officer, 1975—, also dir.; dir. Nobility Homes, Inc.; mem. exec. com. Cascade Industries. Pres. Historic Fort Wayne; cons. to Mus. of Historic Ft. Wayne, Inc.; bd. dirs. Ft. Wayne YMCA, 1963-64. Served to lt. USNR, 1952-55. Recipient Achievement certificate Inst. Investment Banking, U. Pa., 1959. Mem. Ft. Wayne Hist. Soc. (v.p.), Alliance Francaise, V.F.W. (past comdr.), Smithsonian Assos., Co. Mil. Historians, Am. Soc. Arms Collectors, Phi Beta Kappa. Episcopalian. Mason. Club: Beaver Creek Hunt. Home: 351 Cranston Dr Berea OH 44017 Office: Bond Court Bldg Cleveland OH 44114

BARKER, NORMAN, JR., banker; b. San Diego, July 30, 1922; s. Norman and Grace (Bolger) B.; B.A., U. Chgo., 1947, M.B.A., 1953; m. Sue Keefe, June 27, 1947; children—Peter, Timothy, Michael, Beth. Asst. cashier Harris Trust & Savs. Bank, Chgo., 1947-55; credit mgr. Am. Can Co., 1955-57; with United Calif. Bank, Los Angeles, 1957—, chmn. bd., chief exec. officer, 1968—; dir. Western Bancorp., So. Calif. Edison Co., Carter Hawley Hale Stores, Inc.; dir. Carnation Co., Lear Siegler Inc. Trustee Occidental Coll., U. Chgo. Served to lt. USNR, 1944-46, 50-52. Mem. Delta Kappa Epsilon. Home: 111 N June St Los Angeles CA 90004 Office: 707 Wilshire Blvd Los Angeles CA 90017

BARKER, ROBERT RANKIN, bus. exec.; b. Brookline, Mass., July 12, 1915; s. James Madison and Margaret (Rankin) B.; A.B. magna cum laude, Harvard U., 1936; m. Elizabeth VanDyke Shelly, Mar. 7, 1942; children—James Robertson, Ann Shelly, William Benjamin, Margaret Welch. With investment and credit analysis, investment adv. depts. J.P. Morgan & Co., 1936-49; with William A.M. Burden & Co., N.Y.C., 1949-78, gen. partner, 1954-78; gen. partner Robert R. Barker & Co., 1973—; spl. asst. to asst. sec. commerce for air, 1942-43. Mem. vis. com. univ. resources Harvard U.; trustee Am. Mus. Natural History, Florence V. Burden Found., J.M.R. Barker Found., Hudson Inst.; former chmn. Adv. Com. on Endowment Mgmt., Ford Found. Served as officer USNR, 1943-46. Mem. Council Fgn. Relations, N.Y. Soc. Security Analysts, Phi Beta Kappa. Clubs: Century, Hemisphere, Univ., Harvard, Brook (N.Y.C.). Home: 809 Oenoke Ridge New Canaan CT 06840 Office: 630 Fifth Ave New York NY 10111

BARKER, VIRGIL DALE, ins. co. exec.; b. Owensboro, Ky., Aug. 31, 1946; s. George S. and Tina P. (Crowe) B.; B.S., Western Ky. U., 1969; grad. Life Underwriters Tng. Course, 1979; m. Sandra K. Lyons, June 1, 1968; children—Cassandra G., Virgil D. Mgr., W.T. Grant, Muncie, Ind., 1969-75; agt. Met. Ins. Co., Anderson, Ind., 1976-77; agt. Prudential Ins. Co., Owensboro, 1977—. Served with U.S. Army, 1970-72. Recipient Leader award Gen. Agts. and Mgrs. Assn., 1978. Mem. Nat. Assn. Life Underwriters (nat. quality award 1979, nat. sales achievement award 1979). Republican. Baptist. Home: 1221 Rosehill Dr Owensboro KY 42301 Office: PO Box 1216 Owensboro KY 42301

BARKER, WILLIAM MCKINLEY, textile co. exec.; b. Alva, Okla., May 25, 1931; s. Elisha McKinley and Ruby Louisa (Branch) B.; student accounting Palmer Bus. Coll., 1956-59; m. Ann Gloria Usry, Sept. 3, 1949; children—William Wayne, John McKinley, David Branch. Cost accountant John P. King Mfg. Co., Augusta, Ga., 1955-57; div. controller Riegel Textile Corp., Johnston, S.C., 1957-67, Ware Shoals, S.C., 1967-70, Trion, Ga., 1970-76, adminstrv. mgr., Fries, Va., from 1977, now exec. v.p. Riegel Sports Div., Dallas, N.C.; chmn. ops. research Com., tech. adv. Com. Inst. Textile Tech., Charlottesville, Va. Sec. treas. Trion (Ga.) Community Found., 1970-76; state exec. committeeman Edgefield County (S.C.) Republican Party, 1963-64; treas. Chattooga County (Ga.) Presbyn. Ministries, 1974-76. Mem. Data Processing Mgmt. Assn. (local pres. 1967), Galax-Carroll-Grayson C. of C. (pres. 1979). Club: Galax Rotary (pres. 1980). Home: 108 E Ridge St Kings Mountain NC 28086 Office: 205 E Robinson St Dallas NC 28034

BARKLEY, CAROLYN ESTHER, TV account exec.; b. Austin, Tex., Nov. 21, 1944; d. Edward M. and Hermine Winifred (Pearce) B.; B. in Journalism, U. Tex. at Austin, 1967. Public info. specialist Austin (Tex.) Parks and Recreation Dept., 1967-69; community info. coordinator Austin City Mgr.'s Office, 1969-70, Austin Public Info. Dept., 1970; dedication office staff mem. L.B. Johnson Library Dedication Office, U. Tex. at Austin, 1971; spl. asst. to campaign dirs. Dolph Briscoe for Gov. State Hdqrs., Austin, 1972; dir. public relations United Way Capital Area, Austin, 1973-76; account exec. Sta. KTVV-TV, 1976—. Del. Travis County Dem. Conv., 1968, 72, alt. del. Tex. State Conv., 1974; treas. Dist. 8, Tex. Fedn. Dem. Women; bd. dirs. Austin YWCA, 1978—; mem. public relations bd. ARC, 1976—. Named Miss Austin Aqua Beauty, Austin Aqua Festival, 1970. Mem. Austin Advt. Club (dir. 1978—, sec.-treas. 1979—). Home: 2501 E St Elmo Rd Austin TX 78744 also 1306 Darter Ln Austin TX 78746 Office: KTVV PO Box 490 Austin TX 78767

BARKSDALE, ARLEN O'NEIL, investment and devel. co. exec.; b. San Diego, Apr. 8, 1945; s. Earlie Nathaniel and Carmen Pauline (Wilson) B.; A.A., Weatherford Coll., 1967; B.S., U. Tex., Arlington, 1969; M.A., Rice U., 1971, Ph.D., 1972; m. Ruby Diane Haynes, June 3, 1966; children—Julie Elisabeth, Shane Arlen. Prodn. planner Aerospace div. LTV, Grand Prairie, Tex., 1967; lab. technician, materials research Bell Helicopter, Ft. Worth, 1968; ops. mgr. silicon mfg. Tex. Instruments, Sherman, 1973-77; chmn. bd., chief exec. officer Cory Enterprises, Inc., Arlington, Tex., 1977—; chmn. bd. Tex. & So. Quarter Horse Jour., 1979—; chmn. bd., chief exec. officer Lanier Machine Works, Inc., Petrocast, Inc., 1980—; owner Sealcrest Homes, 1977—, Barksdale Orchards, 1975—, Hytec Engring. Consultants, 1974—. Served with USAF, 1963-65. AEC spl. fellow, 1969-72; NDEA fellow, 1972-73; U. Tex. grantee, 1967-69. Mem. Am. Phys. Soc., C. of C., Tex. Quarter Horse Assn., Am. Forestry Assn., Smithsonian Instn., AAAS, Phi Beta Kappa, Sigma Xi. Clubs: Lions, DeMolay. Contbr. articles to profl. jours. Home: 4722 Anchorage Dr Arlington TX 76016 Office: 5026 Mansfield Rd Fort Worth TX 76119

BARLETT, ALVAN CURTIS, chem. engr.; b. Phila., May 10, 1939; s. Albert F. and Elenor (Fielder) B.; B.S. in Chem. Engring., Drexel U., 1962; m. Elizabeth A. Habecker, July 1, 1961; children—Scott, Melissa. Research and devel. engr. E.I. duPont de Nemours & Co., Inc., Wilmington, Del., 1962-65; project engr. Allied Chem. Corp., Phila., 1965-66, tech. supr., Peoria, Ill., 1966-67; plant supr. Celotex Corp., Carteret, N.J., 1967-69; with Standard Brands, Dover, Del., 1969-76; coatings application engr. Reichhold Chem., Dover, 1976—. Mem. Am. Inst. Chem. Engrs. Republican. Presbyterian. Address: PO Drawer K Dover DE 19901

BARLOW, CHARLES BUFORD, JR., petroleum engr., natural resource co. exec.; b. Bakersfield, Calif., Nov. 9, 1934; s. Charles Buford and Martha (Johnson) B.; B.A., Pomona Coll., 1956; B.S. in Engring., U. Okla., 1958; M.S. in Engring., U. So. Calif., 1961; postgrad. Harvard Bus. Sch.; m. Laura Geraldine Lush, June 12, 1959; children—Charles Buford and David Simpson (twins), Cheryl Lynn. Gen. mgr. United Testers Ltd., Calgary, Alta., Can., 1958-60; pres. Barlow Devel. Ltd. and Barlow Bros., Ltd., Calgary, 1961—, Dacker Resources Inc.; dir. Maloney Steelcrafts Ltd., Bugaboo Helicopter Skiing Ltd., Heli-Skiing Cariboo Ltd., Calgary Cable TV Ltd., Chinook Stables Ltd., Pigeon Mountain Recreations Ltd., Gascan Resources Ltd. Pres., Pastoral Inst., Calgary. Profl. engr., Alta. Mem. Engring. Inst. Can., Am. Petroleum Inst., Am. Inst. Mining, Metall. and Petroleum Engrs., Econ. Soc. Alta., Canadian Inst. Mining and Metall. Engrs., Phi Kappa Phi, Kappa Mu Epsilon, Sigma Gamma Epsilon. Home: 4403 Britannia Dr SW Calgary AB T2S 1J4 Canada Office: Room 614 816 7th Ave SW Calgary AB T2P 1A1 Canada

BARLOW, CHARLIE (CHUCK), duplicating equipment mfg. co. exec.; b. Jackson, Ga., Nov. 7, 1949; s. Eulus Paul and Helen Louise (Carr) B.; B.S., Morris Brown Coll., 1971; m. Shirley Ann McCou, Apr. 29, 1973; children—Algernon Nicole, Charlie F., Shayla C. Retail mgmt. trainee Abraham & Straus, N.Y.C., 1970; mgmt. trainee MONY Ins. Co., N.Y.C., 1971; sales rep. Xerox Corp., Atlanta, 1973-75, sales specialist, St. Petersburg, Fla., 1975-79, sales mgr. community involvement/public relations, 1979-80, br. mktg. mgr., Atlanta, 1980-81, regional sales support mgr., 1981—. Mem. policy bd. Pinellas Headstart; bd. dirs. Urban League, Big Brothers, OIC, Bethel Baptist Ch.; dir. social activities, jr. deacon Macedonia Bapt. Ch. Served with AUS, 1971-73. Mem. Alpha Phi Alpha. Clubs: Rotary (dir.), Toastmasters (area gov., pres.). Home: 1708 Delowe Dr SW Atlanta GA 30311 Office: 1801 Peachtree Rd NE Atlanta GA 30309

BARLOW, F(RANK) JOHN, mech. contracting co. exec.; b. Milw., July 12, 1914; s. Ernest A. and Alice E. (Norton) B.; B.S. in Mech. Engring., U. Wis., 1937; m. Dorothy M. Marx, Oct. 13, 1935; children—Joyce D., Bonnie M., Joan C., Grace M., Jacqueline S., Wendy J., Terri L., Alice M. Engr., Buffalo Forge Co., 1937-40, sales engr., Chgo., 1940-42; plant engr. A.O. Smith Corp., Milw., 1942-44; chief mech. engr. Western Condensing Co., Appleton, Wis., 1944-46, prodn. mgr., 1946-53; owner Azco, Inc., Appleton, 1953—, pres., 1959—; pres. Sanco, Inc., Appleton, 1959—, B & B Leasing Co., Appleton, 1965—, Tippy's Taco House, 1968—, Schlafer Inc., 1969—, Schlafer Supply Co., 1969—, Downey Co., 1970—; treas. Winagamie Corp., 1965—; v.p. Azco Fire Protection, Inc., 1953—; dir. First Nat. Bank Appleton. County chmn. March of Dimes, 1957—, state co-chmn., 1958, industry chmn. com. fund dr., 1968-69. Bd. dirs., exec. com. Air Wis.; chmn. bd., pres. AAD, Inc., 1977; trustee Azco Employees Profit Sharing Trust. Recipient Industry award Wis. Soc. Profl. Engrs., 1967. Mem. Mech. Contractors Assn. Am. (pres. 1974—, nat. dir.), Mech. Contractors Assn. Wis. (pres. 1969-70), Wis. Soc. Profl. Engrs. (chpt. pres. 1968-69, dir.), Am. Soc. Heating, Refrigeration and Air Conditioning Engrs., Appleton C. of C. (dir.), Am. Assn. C.E., Am. Welding Soc., Flying Engrs., Civil Air Patrol, Nat. Pilots Assn., Nat. Soc. Profl. Engrs., Am. Soc. Cost Engrs., TAPPI, Sigma Chi. Mason (32 deg., Shriner), Rotarian, Elk (past exalted ruler). Club: Butte des Morts Golf (pres. 1961-63, dir.). Home: 178 River Dr Appleton WI 54911 Office: PO Box 567 Appleton WI 54911

BARLOW, WILLIAM PUSEY, JR., accountant; b. Oakland, Calif., Feb. 11, 1934; s. William P. and Muriel (Block) B.; student Calif. Inst. Tech., 1952-54; A.B. in Econs., U. Calif. at Berkeley, 1956. Accountant, Barlow, Davis & Wood, San Francisco, 1960-72, partner, 1964-72; partner J. K. Lasser & Co., San Francisco, 1972-77; partner Touche Ross & Co., San Francisco, 1977-78; pvt. practice acctg., Oakland, 1978—. Treas., Friends of Bancroft Library, 1970-74, 80—, chmn. bd., 1974-79; pres. Gleeson Library Assos., 1970-74. C.P.A., Calif. Mem. Am. Water Ski Assn. (dir., regional chmn., 1959-63, pres. 1963-66, chmn. bd. 1966-69, 77-79), World Water Ski Union (mem. exec. bd. 1961-71, 74-78). Clubs: Grolier (N.Y.C.); Roxburghe (San Francisco), Book of Calif. (dir. 1963-76, pres. 1968-69, treas. 1970—). Home: 1474 Hampel St Oakland CA 94602 Office: 1330 Broadway Suite 1600 Oakland CA 94612

BARNABAS, BENTLEY, psychologist, mgmt. cons.; b. Albany, N.Y., May 2, 1908; s. Leander and Josephine (Califano) B.; B.S. in Bus. Adminstrn., U. Wichita, 1929; M.S. in Indsl. Psychology, Kans. State Coll., 1953; m. Pearl Richardson, Feb. 17, 1931; children—Clare Jane Templeton, George Richardson. Asst. v.p. Kans. Gas and Electric Co., 1933, advt. mgr., 1940; cons. The Coleman Co., Inc., Beech Aircraft Corp., Chevrolet div. Gen. Motors, Am. Machine Tool Distbrs. Assn., Saunders Truck Leasing System, Jam Handy Orgn., other concerns, 1944—; sales promotion mgr. S.A. Long Co., Inc., 1948-52; pres. Asso. Personnel Technicians, Inc., 1945-79, Associated Bus. Cons.'s, 1979—; instr. indsl. psychology Friends U., 1946, Kans. U. Extension Center, Wichita, 1947-48; spl. lectr. U. Wichita, 1951-52. Pub. info. chmn. Sedgwick County chpt. A.R.C., 1942-44, disaster chmn., 1944-45, 48-49, bd. dirs., 1943-44. Housing commr. Wichita Housing Authority, 1968; chmn. Mayor's Adv. Com. on Crime Control, 1970-71. Served with Civil Air Patrol, active duty anti-submarine task force Parksley, Va., 1942, 2d Air Force Courier Service, 1942-45, intelligence officer Kans. Wing, 1942-46, rank of maj. Mem. Am. Psychol. Assn., Nat., Kans. (pres. 1963-65) assns. for mental health, AIM (dir. 1955-63), Wichita State U. Alumni Assn. (pres. 1966-67), Sigma Xi, Pi Kappa Delta, Pi Alpha Pi, Wichita U. Honor Five. Republican. Episcopalian. Clubs: C. of C. Ambassadors (pres. 1960—); Wichita Country, Wichita. Author: Develop Your Power to Deal with People, 1971; also articles; lectr. sales tng., aptitude testing. Home: 14720 Lakeview Springdale Wichita KS 67230 Office: 1403 Douglas Bldg Wichita KS 67202

BARNARD, JOHN, JR., fin. services co. exec.; b. Cleve., Aug. 13, 1917; s. John and Mildred (Safford) B.; B.A., Harvard U., 1939, LL.B., 1947; m. Cornelia Bridge, Sept. 4, 1943; 1 son, Jeremy. Admitted to Mass. bar, 1947; asso. Gaston, Snow, Rice & Boyd, Boston, 1947-51; partner Gaston, Snow, Motley & Holt, Boston, 1951-63; gen. counsel Mass. Fin. Services, Inc., Boston, 1963-69, v.p., dir., 1969-77; chmn., mng. partner Mass. Fin. Services Co., Boston, 1977—; pres., dir. Mass. Investors Growth Stock Fund; trustee Suffolk Franklin Savs. Bank, Boston; underwriting mem. Lloyd's of London, 1970—. Trustee, mem. investment and audit coms. New Eng. Deaconess Hosp., 1975—. Served to capt. C.E., U.S. Army, 1942-46. Mem. Nat. Assn. Securities Dealers, Inc. (mem. investment cos. com., bd. govs.), Investment Co. Inst. (bd. govs.), Greater Boston C. of C. (v.p., dir.). Home: 70 Black Horse Ln Cohasset MA 02025 Office: 200 Berkeley St Boston MA 02116

BARNARD, ROLLIN DWIGHT, savs. and loan exec.; b. Denver, Apr. 14, 1922; s. George Cooper and Emma (Riggs) B.; B.A., Pomona Coll., 1943; m. Patricia Reynolds Bierkamp, Sept. 15, 1943; children—Michael Dana, Rebecca Susan (Mrs. Paul C. Wulfestieg), Laurie Beth (Mrs. Kenneth J. Kostelecky). Clk., Morey Merc. Co., Denver, 1937-40; partner George C. Barnard & Co., gen. real estate and ins., Denver, 1946-47; v.p. Foster & Barnard, Inc., 1947-53; instr. Denver U., 1949-53; dir. real estate U.S. Post Office Dept., Washington, 1953-55, dep. asst. postmaster gen., bur. facilities, 1955-59, asst. postmaster gen., 1959-61; exec. v.p. Midland Fed. Savs. & Loan Assn., Denver, 1961-62, pres., 1962—, also dir.; mem. nat. adv. council Urban Am., 1967-70; dir. Fed. Home Loan Bank Topeka, 1965-66. Bd. dirs. Downtown Denver Improvement Assn., 1962-71, pres., 1965; exec. bd. Denver Area council Boy Scouts Am., 1962—, pres., 1970-71; mem. nat. council Pomona Coll., 1963—; bd. dirs. Denver Area Fellowship Christian Athletes, 1963-76, Children's Hosp., 1979—, Bethesda Found., 1973—; bd. dirs., chmn. bd. Colo. Council on Econ. Edn., 1971-76; trustee Mile High Fund, 1969-72; trustee, v.p., treas. Morris Animal Found., 1969-74, pres., chmn., 1974-78; trustee Denver Symphony Assn., 1973-74; mem. Greenwood Village (Colo.) Planning and Zoning Commn., 1967-73, chmn., 1969-73; mem. Greenwood Village City Council, 1975-76. Served to capt. AUS, World War II. Nominated one of ten outstanding young men in Am., U.S. Jr. C. of C., 1955, 57; Distinguished Service award Postmaster Gen. U.S., 1960, Silver Beaver award Boy Scouts Am., 1969. Mem. Denver Bd. Realtors (v.p., dir. 1949-53), U.S. League Savs. Assns. (nat. legis. com. 1962—, dir. 1972-77, mem. exec. com. 1974-77, 79—, v.p. 1979-80, pres. 1980-81), Savs. League Colo. (dir. 1962-64, 69-72, pres. 1971-72), Denver C. of C. (dir. 1964-67, pres. 1966-67), Western Stock Show Assn. (dir. 1971—), Colo. Assn. Commerce and Industry (dir. 1971-76), Nu Alpha Phi. Republican. Presbyterian. Clubs: 26 (pres. 1970), Rotary (dir. 1979—, 2d v.p. 1980— (Denver); Mountain and Plains Appaloosa Horse (pres. 1970-71, dir. 1970-73), Roundup Riders of Rockies (dir. 1980—). Home: 101 Long Rd Littleton CO 80121 Office: 444 17th St Denver CO 80202

BARNED, ANTHONY ROGER, bank exec.; b. Louth, Lincolnshire, Eng., May 19, 1945; s. Walter and Joyce (Day) B.; student grammar schs., Louth, Eng.; m. Carol Raine, Dec. 6, 1969; 1 son, Alexander St. John. Clk., Lloyds Bank Ltd., Lincolnshire, Eng., 1963-66; with Barclays Bank Internat. Ltd, Maiduguri, Nigeria, 1966-67, Blawtyre/Mzuza, Malawi, 1967-74, credit analyst, London, 1974-77, 1st v.p., mgr. N.Y.C. br., 1977—. Mem. Inst. Bankers (asso.). Conservative. Mem. Ch. of Eng. Clubs: St. Georges Soc. (N.Y.C.); Royal Overseas League (London). Office: 100 Water St New York NY 10005

BARNES, ANDREW IMRI, computer exec.; b. Preston, Eng., Sept. 28, 1945; came to U.S., 1952, naturalized, 1971; s. Andrew Imri and Alice Ann (Woodacre) White; B.S. in Bus., U. Nev., 1968; M.Bus., U. Santa Clara, 1979; m. Valerie Ann Erickson, Feb. 26, 1972; 1 dau., Angela Lee. With Burroughs Corp., Las Vegas, 1968-72, Tektronix Inc., Santa Clara, Calif., 1972-78; sales mgr. computer supplies Inmac, Sunnyvale, Calif., 1978-79; sr. sales rep. Digital Equipment Corp., Santa Clara, 1980—; partner Cygnet Cellars Winery, 1979—; owner Haircrafters Styling Salon, 1979-80. Named to Burroughs Legion of Honor, 1970, 71; named Salesman of Yr., Tektronix, 1974, Master, 1976, 77. Mem. R.R. Passengers Assn., Data Processing Mgmt. Assn., U. Nev. Alumni Assn., Santa Clara U. Alumni Assn. Republican. Baptist. Home: 796 Amanda St San Jose CA 95136 Office: 2525 Augustine St Santa Clara CA 95051

BARNES, ARTHUR JAMES, auditor; b. Manila, Ala., July 21, 1952; s. Roosevelt and Pearlie Mae Dennis; B.A., Stillman Coll., 1974. With B.F. Goodrich Co., 1974—, auditor, Akron, Ohio, 1976—. Div. chmn. United Negro Coll. Fund; active Boy Scouts Am. Mem. Congress of Community Orgns., Am. Ethnic Sci. Soc., Alpha Phi Alpha. Baptist. Home: 315 Utah Ave Mobile AL 36610 Office: City of Mobile Mobile AL

BARNES, EARLE B., corp. exec.; b. 1917; m. B.S., Tex. Christian U., 1938; M.S., U. Nebr., 1940. With Dow Chem. Co., 1940—, gen. mgr. Tex. div., 1961-67, dir. corp. mfg., engring. and maintenance, 1967-68, corp. v.p., gen. mgr. U.S. area, 1968-71, mem. corp. exec. com., pres. Dow Chem. U.S.A., 1971-75, corp. exec. v.p., 1975-79, mem. exec. com., 1975—, chmn., 1979—; dir. Dow Corning Corp., Asahi Dow Chem. Co., Dow Banking Corp. Office: Dow Chem Co 2030 Dow Center Midland MI 48640

BARNES, FRANK EDWARD, III, investment banker; b. Mineola, N.Y., May 22, 1949; s. Frank Edward, Jr., and Margaret Eleanor (Smith) B.; B.A., U. N.C., 1971, M.B.A., 1973; m. Joan Alexandre Herrick, Apr. 29, 1978. With Bankers Trust Co., N.Y.C., 1973-74, ofcl. asst., 1974-75, asst. treas. So. div. U.S. banking dept., 1976, asst. v.p. Eastern Banking div., 1976-77, asst. v.p., tng. dir. comml. banking tng., 1977-78, v.p. Far West div. Los Angeles rep. office, 1978-79; with investment banking group Warburg Paribas Becker Inc., N.Y.C., 1979-80, pvt. investments-communications group, 1980—; dir. Brookside Assos. Inc., Smithfield, N.C. Pres., bd. dirs., treas. exec. com. Friends of Henry St. Settlement; mem. So. Calif. campaign com. United Negro Coll. Fund. Mem. N.C. Soc. N.Y., Alumni Assn. U. N.C., Alpha Tau Omega. Republican. Episcopalian. Clubs: Rockaway Hunting (Cedarhurst, N.Y.); Manursing Island (Rye, N.Y.); N.Y. Athletic, Racquet and Tennis (N.Y.C.); Ducks Unltd. (chpt. dir.) (Los Angeles and N.Y.C.). Home: 161 E 90th St New York NY 10028 Office: 55 Water St New York NY 10041

BARNES, GEOFFREY WICKHAM, computer software co. exec.; b. Toronto, Ont., Can., Oct. 25, 1949; s. John Wickham and Martha Janet (Roe) B.; came to U.S., 1974; B.A., U. Toronto, 1972; M.Mus., Yale U., 1974. Profl. bassoonist, Toronto, New Eng., 1970-75, New Haven Symphony, 1973-74; systems analyst Burndy Corp., Norwalk, Conn., 1974-75, mgr. fgn. subs. customer service, 1975-76; systems cons. Decision Strategy Corp., N.Y.C., 1976-77, dir. customer support, 1977-78, v.p. customer support and quality control, 1979—; prin. bassoonist New Amsterdam Symphony Orch., 1976—. Author: Computers: the Programmer's Reference Guide to the Terminal Application Processing System, 1978. Home: 131 Midland Terr Yonkers NY 10704 Office: 708 Third Ave New York NY 10017

BARNES, JOHN DAVID, banker; b. Oil City, Pa., Aug. 23, 1929; s. Alfred David and Rachael Marian (Kerr) B.; B.A., Allegheny Coll., Meadville, Pa., 1951; LL.B., Harvard, 1954; m. Suzanne Franklin Robbins, Nov. 26, 1960. With credit div. Mellon Nat. Bank & Trust Co., Pitts., 1956-58, asst. v.p., v.p. nat. dept., 1958-72; v.p., sr. v.p. Mellon Nat. Corp. and Mellon Bank, N.A., Pitts., 1972, now pres. Mellon Nat. Corp.; chmn. bd., chief exec. officer Freedom Fin. Services Corp.; chmn., chief exec. officer Local Loan Co., Chgo., 1976—; v.p., sec., dir. Penn's SW Assn.; dir. Diamond Shamrock Corp., Allomon Corp., Mellon Nat. Mortgage Co. of Colo., Mellon Nat. Mortgage Co. of Ohio, Carruth Mortgage Corp. Pres., chmn. bd. trustees Ellis Sch., Pitts. Assn. for Improvement of Poor. Served with AUS, 1954-56. Clubs: Duquesne; Harvard-Yale-Princeton; Fox Chapel Golf; Fox Chapel Racquet. Office: Mellon Nat Corp PO Box 15629 Pittsburgh PA 15244*

BARNES, JOHN JAMES INGALLS, utilities co. exec.: b. Detroit, July 4, 1936; s. Russell Curtis and Ruth Constance (Ingalls) B.; A.B. in Econs., Harvard U., 1958; 1 son, Andrew Harrison. Trainee, Ford div., Fort Motor Co., 1961-63; research analyst, copywriter J. Walter Thompson, Detroit, 1963-65; copywriter Gray & Kilgore Advt., 1965-67; sr. copywriter: creative supr. Young & Rubicam Advt., Atlanta and Detroit, 1967-70; creative dir. Detroit News, 1970-74; gen. adminstrv. asst., mgr. advt. and sales promotion Mich. Bell Yellow Pages, Detroit, 1974—; cons. AT&T, mem. nat. promotion com. Episcopalian. Home: 159 Marlborough Dr Bloomfield Hills MI 48013 Office: 882 Oakman Detroit MI 48238

BARNES, JUDITH ANNE, retail store exec.; b. Rochester, N.Y., Feb. 28, 1948; s. Robert William and Louise (Marriott) B.; B.A., Russell Sage Coll., 1970; M.S., Rensselaer Poly. Inst., 1971, Ph.D., 1981. Graphic designer, 1970—; instr. Russell Sage Coll., 1975-76; spl. cons. communication and design Inst. Man and Sci., 1975-78; advt. dir. The Mayfair Group Stores, Albany, N.Y., 1978—; cons. Co-founder, exec. v.p. bd. Music Hall Corp. Mem. Hudson-Mohawk Indsl. Gateway, Rensselaer County Hist. Soc., Hist. ALbany Found. Author: Understanding Freedom of Speech in America, 1976.

BARNES, KENDALL MONTAGUE, lawyer; b. Coldwater, Mich., Aug. 28, 1909; s. George Emerson and Myrtle Kendall (Montague) B.; B.A., Princeton U., 1931; LL.B., U. Pa., 1934; Certificat, U. Dijon, 1930; m. Greta Pauline Armel, Aug. 18, 1943; children—Kendall Montague, Gayle Barnes Blomme, Nancy Elizabeth. Admitted to Pa. bar, 1933, N.Y. bar, 1934; asso. firm Mitchell, Taylor, Capron & Marsh, N.Y.C., 1934-41; atty. War Prodn. Bd., Washington, 1942-44; atty. civil div. Dept. Justice, Washington, 1944-64; gen. counsel U.S. Army Materiel Command, Washington, 1964-74; individual practice law, Alexandria, Va., 1974—; instr. U.S. Army Logistics Center, 1965-74. Recipient Tom C. Clark award Dept. Justice, 1960. Mem. Phi Beta Kappa Assn. D.C. Democrat. Presbyterian. Club: Princeton Washington). Home and office: 8609 Waterford Rd Alexandria VA 22308

BARNES, MARGARET ANDERSON, math. statistician; b. N.C., Feb. 8, 1938; d. Rosa Lee (Cole) Anderson; B.S., N.C. Central U., 1958; M.A., U. Md., 1975; m. Benjamin Barnes; children—Obren V., Kimberly R. Chmn. math. dept. Tarboro (N.C.) Schs., 1959-60; supervisory math. statistician Bur. Census, Suitland, Md., 1962-67, mgr. research and methodology, 1969-70; math. statistician D.C. Govt., 1967-68; profl. cons. NIH, 1970-72; chief data standards and clearance and planner HEW, 1972-76; pres. MA Barnes Cons. Assos., Inc., Lanham, Md., 1978—; adv. bd. Prince George's State Bank, 1980—. Instr. Prince George's (Md.) Community Coll., 1978—. Commr., Md. Accident Fund, 1979—; chmn. Md. com. edn. and tng. minority businesspersons Office of Minority Affairs, 1980—; mem. Glenwood Park Civic Assn.; Mem. Nat. Assn. Women Bus. Owners, Am. Statis. Assn., Am. Mgmt. Assn., Am. Public Health Assn., Nat. Bus. League, Alpha Kappa Alpha. Episcopalian. Author papers, reports in field. Home: Lanham MD Office: 9332 Annapolis Rd Lanham MD 20801

BARNES, MICHAEL A., food service co. exec.; b. Detroit, Oct. 28, 1942; s. Albert Howard and Shirley Bernice (McShane) B.; corr. student U. Mich., 1961-62; student U. Alaska, 1962-64; children—Shannon, Brydie, Casey. Dist. mgr. Lake Central area Canteen Corp., Detroit, Chgo., Columbus and Dayton, Ohio, 1967-71; region v.p. Service Systems Corp., Detroit, Albany, N.Y. and Boston, 1971-76; v.p. ops. ARA Services, Inc., Phila., 1976-78; group v.p. Ogden Food Service Corp., East Boston, Mass., 1978—, also officer, dir. Dir. U.S. Jaycees, Livonia, Mich., 1967-73. Recipient Pres.'s award youth activities, 1966, award Town of Concord 200th Anniversary Am. Revolution, 1975. Mem. Nat. Restaurant Assn., Nat. Automatic Mdsg. Assn., Soc. Food Service Mgmt., Harness Tracks Am., Am. Greyhound Track Operators Assn., Thoroughbred

Racing Assn., Internat. Assn. Auditorium Mgrs. Roman Catholic. Office: 111 Waldemar Ave East Boston MA 02128

BARNES, PAUL HOWARD, banker; b. Hazlewood, Ind., Aug. 28, 1916; s. Conard Wilson and Emma (Turner) B.; grad. U. Wis. Banking Sch., 1958; m. Marilou Muir, Aug. 30, 1945; children—Sandra (Mrs. Robert L. Barber), Emilou (Mrs. Geoffrey Griswold), Paula. With Albuquerque Nat. Bank, 1935-73, asst. cashier, auditor, 1948-53, asst. v.p., auditor, 1953-56, v.p., auditor, 1956-63, v.p., controller, 1963-65, sr. v.p., controller, 1965-69, sr. v.p., cashier, 1970-73; pres. 1st N.Mex. Bankshare Corp., 1973—, also chief exec. officer, 1974—. Pres., N.Mex. Conf. Meth. Found. Past trustee McMurry Coll., Manzana Day Sch., Albuquerque Little Theater. Served with AUS, 1941-45; ETO, PTO. Mem. Eastern N.Mex. U. Alumni Assn. (hon. life). Methodist (trustee ch.). Clubs: Four Hills Country, Albuquerque Country, Albuquerque Petroleum. Home: 6918 Shoshone Rd NE Albuquerque NM 87110 Office: 303 Roma Ave NW Albuquerque NM 87101

BARNES, ROBERT GILBERT, JR., engring. exec.; b. Flushing, N.Y., Feb. 19, 1929; s. Robert Gilbert and Sophie Amelia (Blazej) B.; B.S., Stevens Inst. Tech., 1950; m. Joan Comolli, June 25, 1955; children—David, Nancy, Karen. Engr., Clark Bros. div. Dresser Industries, Olean, N.Y., 1953-55; with AMF Cuno div. AMF, Inc., Meriden, Conn., 1956—, div. v.p. engring., 1970-79, group v.p. engring. AMF Splty. Materials group, 1980—. Pres., Meriden Bd. Edn., 1978—; vice chmn. Meriden Planning Commn., 1972-76. Served with U.S. Army, 1951-53. Mem. Meriden C. of C. (v.p. 1979—), Tau Beta Pi. Republican. Unitarian. Home: 631 Brownstone Ridge Meriden CT 06450 Office: 400 Research Pkwy Meriden CT 06450

BARNES, SAMUEL LEE, ins. co. exec.; b. Shelby County, Ala., Aug. 2, 1941; s. Jesse Winsor and Mamie Jane (White) B.; B.S. in Math., Jacksonville (Ala.) State U., 1963; m. Charlotte Virginia McCain, Apr. 1, 1963; children—Kenneth Lee, Jeffery Dwayne. Actuarial trainee, asst. actuary Volunteer State Life Ins. Co., Chattanooga, 1963-69; asso. actuary, v.p. group underwriting Horace Mann Life Ins. Co., Springfield, Ill., 1969—. Sunday sch. tchr., deacon Williamsville Christian Ch.; coach summer baseball program, 1970-75; treas. Williamsville Jr. C. of C., 1970-72, Williamsville-Sherman Water Commn., 1972-73; bd. dirs. Aid to Retarded Citizens; trustee Village of Williamsville, 1979—. Mem. Group Underwriters Assn. Am., Nat. Assn. Health Underwriters. Republican. Club: Masons. Home: 408 E Jones St Williamsville IL 62693 Office: 1 Horace Mann Plaza Springfield IL 62715

BARNES, THOMAS WILLIAM, steamship agy. exec.; b. Montreal, Que., Can., Mar. 15, 1938; s. Howard William and Margaret Helen (Staniforth) B.; diploma in civil tech. Ryerson Inst. Tech., Toronto, Ont., 1961; m. Heather Arlene Freure, June 16, 1962; children—Leah Christine, Lorie Ellen, Lesley Heather. Mktg. mgr. Gilbarco Can. Ltd., Brockville, Ont., 1966-73; pres. Carrier Air Conditioning, Montreal, 1973-75, Seafast Internat. Ltd., Montreal, 1975—. Clubs: Montreal Transp. League, Montreal and Toronto Transp., Grunt. Office: 276 Quest Rue St Jacques Montreal PQ H2Y 1N3 Canada

BARNETT, BERNARD HARRY, lawyer; b. Helena, Ark., July 13, 1916; s. Harry and Rebecca (Grossman) B.; student U. Mich., 1934-36; J.D., Vanderbilt U., 1940; m. Marian Spiesberger, Apr. 9, 1949; 1 son, Charles Dawson. Admitted to Ky. bar, 1940; practiced in Louisville, 1940-42; asso. firm Woodward, Dawson, Hobson & Fulton, 1946-48; partner firm Bulitt, Dawson & Tarrant, 1948-52, firm Greenbaum, Barnett, Wood & Doll, 1952-70, firm Barnett & McConnell, 1972, firm Barnett, Greenebaum, Martin & McConnell, 1972-74, firm Barnett, Alagia, Greenebaum, Miller & Senn, 1974-75, Barnett & Alagia, 1975—; dir. Bank of Louisville, John B. Coleman Co., Cook United, Inc., Fuqua Industries, Inc., Hasbro Industries, Inc., Sealy Mattress Co. Oreg.; mem. adv. group Joint Com. on Internal Revenue Taxation, U.S. Congress, 1953-55, Com. on Ways and Means, U.S. Ho. of Reps., 1956-58. Chmn., Louisville Fund, 1952-53; mem. Louisville and Jefferson County Republican Exec. Com., 1954-60; chmn. Ky. Rep. Finance Com., 1955-60. Served as lt. USNR, 1942-45. Mem. Am., Ky., Louisville bar assns. Home: 331 Zorn Ave Louisville KY 40206 Office: Ky Home Life Bldg Louisville KY 40202

BARNETT, DON BLAIR, plumbing contractor; b. Mt. Vernon, Ohio, Oct. 21, 1921; s. Homer V. and Bessie (Skeels) B.; student public schs., LaRue, Ohio; m. Virginia V. Ireland, June 24, 1943; children—James, Faye. Maintenance and supervision positions Perfection Steel Body Co., Galion, Ohio, 1942-44; owner, operator Barnett Plumbing and Hearing, Galion, 1948—. Active, Jehovah's Witness Ch., supr. installation and maintenance, nat. and internat. convs., 1950—. Mem. Galion Plumbing Contractors Assn., Christian Labor Union Assn. Home and Office: 127 Wilson Ave Galion OH 44833

BARNETT, GILBERT LANE, soft drink co. exec.; b. Hammond, Ind., Aug. 20, 1945; s. Eldon G. and Imogene (Lane) B.; B.S. in Mktg., Ind. U., 1967; M.B.A., U. Mo., Kansas City, 1974; m. Cheryl D. Wilson, Dec. 17, 1966; children—Brent, Beth. Account mgr. Continental Can Co., 1971-76; dir. sales Continental Can Internat., 1976-78; v.p., gen. mgr. Mid-Continent Bottlers, div. Universal Foods Co., Des Moines, 1978—. Served to 1st lt. USMCR, 1969-71; Vietnam. Decorated D.S.M. Mem. Am. Mgmt. Assn., Des Moines C. of C., Des Moines Com. Fgn. Relations. Office: 1675 NE 51st St Ave Des Moines IA 50306

BARNETT, LOUIS HERBERT, plastic and chem. cons.; b. Malden, Mass., Nov. 22, 1918; s. Max and Molly G. B.; B.B.A. in Chem. Engring. and Indsl. Mgmt., Northeastern U., 1944, D. Engring. (hon), 1977; D.Sc., Tex. Christian U., 1974; m. Madlyn Brachman, May 3, 1945; children—Laurie Barnett Werner, Eliot B., Rhoda Barnett Bernstein. Founder, chmn. bd., chief operating officer Loma Industries, 1947-66; cons. plastics and chems., fabrication technologies, new products, creative mktg., oil and gas exploration, Ft. Worth, 1966—; chmn. bd. Petrochems. Co., Inc., Ft. Worth, Originala Petroleum Corp., Ft. Worth; dir. Robintech, Inc., Overton Park, Nat. Bank of Ft. Worth, Chattem, Inc., Chattanooga. Trustee Tex. Christian U., Ft. Worth Children's Hosp.; mem. com. Harris Hosp. Devel. Council, Ft. Worth. Served with inf., AUS, 1941. Recipient medal for outstanding accomplishment to Ft. Worth and Israel, Prime Minister of Israel, 1973. Mem. Soc. Plastics Engrs., Soc. Plastic Industry, Tex. Inventors Assn., Am. Chem. Soc., United Inventors and Scientists Am., Nat. Rifle Assn., Jewish Fedn. Ft. Worth (past pres.). Republican. Jewish. Clubs: Chevaliers du Tastevin, Ft. Worth Kennel, Am. Kennel (judge), Ft. Worth Dog Tng. (past pres.). Contbr. articles on plastics. tech. research and devel. to tech. publs.; pioneer in rotational modling and casting; designer 1st injection modling machine; patentee plastic houseware designs. Home: 3631 Encanto St Fort Worth TX 76109 Office: 404 Fort Worth Club Bldg Fort Worth TX 76102

BARNETT, MARILYN, advt. agy. exec.; b. Detroit, June 10, 1932; d. Henry and Kate (Boesky) Schiff; B.A., Wayne State U., 1953; children—Rhona, Ken. Supr. broadcast prodn. Northgate Advt. Agy., Detroit, 1968-73; founder, part-owner, exec. v.p. Mars Advt. Co., Southfield, Mich., 1973—. Mem. AFTRA (dir. 1959-67), Adcraft. Women's Adcraft. Office: 18470 W Ten Mile Rd Southfield MI 48075

BARNETT, NORMAN LAWRENCE, investment advisor; b. N.Y.C., Mar. 16, 1935; s. Herman Ben and Goldie Ann (Feiner) B.; B.S., N.Y. U., 1961; M.B.A., Harvard U., 1963, D.B.A., 1967; m. Rosalind Chait, Oct. 20, 1963; children—Jonathan David, Amy Elizabeth. Research fellow Harvard Bus. Sch., Boston, 1966-67; cons. Market Structure Studies, Inc., Cambridge, Mass., 1967-69, Venture Research & Capital Corp., Newton, Mass., 1969-71; v.p. White, Weld & Co., Boston, 1972-79; v.p., mgr. Cowen Investors Mgmt. Services, Boston, 1979-81; prin. Norman L. Barnett & Co., Boston, 1981—. Mem. com. on resources Harvard Med. Sch., Boston, 1978—; dir. Big Bros. of Boston, 1976-78. Served with U.S. Army, 1956-58. Recipient Founders Day award N.Y. U., 1961. Club: Harvard. Contbr. articles to profl. jours. Home: 21 Partridge Hill Rd Weston MA 02193

BARNETT, RICHARD EARL, lawyer, film distbg. co. exec.; b. Lake Charles, La., Aug. 1, 1927; s. George and Freida (Goldsmith) B.; student Princeton, 1944-45; B.A., Amherst Coll., 1950; LL.B., Columbia, 1953; m. Harriet Schottland, July 21, 1950; children—Pamela Jane, James Richardson, Thomas Schuyler. Admitted to N.Y. bar, 1953; practiced in N.Y.C., 1953-56; atty. with gen. counsel's office N.Y. Central R.R., 1956-58; v.p., dir. Modern Film Corp., N.Y.C., 1958-71, sec., 1961-71, pres., 1971—; pres., dir. Movies En Route, Inc., N.Y.C.; dir. Walport (Overseas) Ltd., London. Served to warrant officer U.S. Mcht. Marine, 1945-47. Mem. Am., N.Y.C. bar assns., Theta Xi, Phi Delta Phi. Home: 225 Clinton Ave Dobbs Ferry NY 10522 Office: 1540 Broadway New York NY 10036

BARNETT, TEDDY, bus. exec.; b. Freeport, N.Y., Mar. 12, 1948; s. William and Mary B.; B.S. in Bus. Adminstrn., Boston U., 1970; m. Carol Ann Grier, July 4, 1971; children—Carol Joell, Jason Theodore, Jordan Dai. Sr. acct. Price Waterhouse & Co., N.Y.C., 1973-75; dir. internal audit Bedford Stuyvesant Restoration Corp., Bklyn., 1976-78, dir. fin. and adminstrn., 1978-79, v.p. fin. and adminstrn., 1980—; Bd. dirs. Enock Star Restoration Housing Devel. Fund, Inc.; active Stearns Park Civic Assn. Recipient Black Achievers in Industry award, 1974. Mem. Nat. Assn. Accts., Nat. Assn. Black Accts. Methodist. Office: 1368 Fulton St Brooklyn NY 11216

BARNETTE, CURTIS HANDLEY, lawyer, steel mfg. co. exec.; b. St. Albans, W.Va., Jan. 9, 1935; s. Curtis Franklin and Garnett Drucella (Robinson) B.; A.B. with high honors, W.Va. U., 1956; diploma (Fulbright scholar) in Internat. Law, U. Manchester, Eng., 1957; J.D., Yale, 1962; postgrad. Harvard Bus. Sch., 1974-75; m. Loris Joan Harner, Dec. 28, 1957; children—Curtis Kevin, James David. Admitted to Conn. bar, 1962, Pa. bar, 1968; atty. Wiggin and Dana, New Haven, 1962-67; atty. Bethlehem Steel Corp. (Pa.), 1967-70, gen. atty., 1970-72, asst. sec., 1972-76, asst. gen. counsel, 1972-77, asst. to v.p., 1974-76, sec., 1976—, asst. v.p., 1976-77, v.p., gen. counsel, 1977—; law tutor Yale Law Sch., New Haven, 1962-67; lectr. U. Md., Frankfort, Ger., 1958-59. Bd. dirs. Yale Law Sch. Fund, Minsi Trails council Boy Scouts Am.; mem. legal adv. council Mid-Atlantic Legal Found., Sta. WLVT-TV, W.Va. U. Found.; chmn. nominating com. Pa. Trial Ct. Served with Intelligence Corps, U.S. Army, 1957-59; to maj. Res., 1959-68. Mem. Am., Pa., Fed., Northampton County, Conn. bar assns., Am. Iron and Steel Inst., Am. Judicature Soc., Am. Law Inst., Assn. Gen. Counsel, Am. Soc. Corporate Secs., Southwestern Legal Found., Pa. Soc., Phi Beta Kappa, Beta Theta Pi, Phi Alpha Theta, Phi Delta Phi. Clubs: Saucon Valley Country, Blooming Grove Hunting and Fishing, Bethlehem; New Haven Lawn; Yale (N.Y.C.); Nat. Lawyers (Washington). Home: 1112 Prospect Ave Bethlehem PA 18018 Office: Martin Tower Room 2018 Bethlehem PA 18016

BARNEY, LYNN BAGLEY, banker; b. Salt Lake City, Apr. 29, 1947; s. Ralph Shupe and Laura Fern (Bagley) B.; B.A., U. Utah, 1972, M.B.A., 1974; m. Linda Christine Locke, July 17, 1969; children—Jennifer, Joanna, Jared, John. Missionary for Mormon Ch., Italy, 1966-69; salesman Am. Western Life Ins., Salt Lake City, 1969-70; mgmt. trainee, ops. officer, comml. loan officer, br. mgr., asst. v.p. Zions 1st Nat. Bank, Salt Lake City, 1971-78; pres., chmn. bd. Cottonwood Security Bank, Salt Lake City, 1978—; cons. Stockdale Corp. Local and state del. Republican Conv., 1972. Served with AUS, 1965-66. Mem. Am. Inst. Banking, Robert Morris Assos., Assn. Exec. M.B.A.'s, Beta Gamma Sigma, Phi Kappa Phi. Office: 3826 S 2300 E Salt Lake City UT 84109

BARNEY, WALTER FLEMING, mgmt. cons.; b. Washington, Mar. 13, 1926; s. Walter Van and Ruby (Fleming) B.; B.M.E., Ga. Inst. Tech., 1949, M.S. in Indsl. Engring., 1950; S.M. in Mgmt. (Alfred P. Sloan fellow 1963-64), M.I.T., 1963; m. Carol Bomstad, Aug. 3, 1965; children—Glen Steven, Bruce Alan. Chief, mgmt. officer Anniston (Ala.) Ordnance Depot, 1950-56; chief mgmt. services br. Army Ballistic Missile Agy., Huntsville, Ala., 1956-60; chief program coordination and mgmt. office Kennedy Space Center, Fla., 1960-63, chief ADP div., 1964-72; chief info. systems div. U.S. Dept. Transp., Washington, 1972-76; chief ADP systems rev. and devel. U.S. Dept. Energy, Washington, 1976-79; sr. cons. Calculon Corp., Gaithersburg, Md., 1979—; lectr. dept. indsl. and systems engring. U. Fla., 1964-65. Served with USN, 1944-46. Mem. Am. Inst. Indsl. Engrs., ASME, Nat. Soc. Profl. Engrs., Tau Beta Pi, Pi Tau Sigma. Republican. Presbyterian. Home: 9409 Chatteroy Pl Gaithersburg MD 20760 Office: 656 Quince Orchard Rd Suite 404 Gaithersburg MD 20760

BARNHARD, IVAN HAROLD, educator, investment co. exec.; b. Bklyn., Jan. 2, 1934; s. Daniel S. and Sydelle (Lowenthal) B.; B.A., L.I. U., 1956; M.A., Auburn U., 1962, Ph.D., 1969; m. Vivian Blancato, June 20, 1957; children—David William, Linda Carol, Lisa Ann. Tchr., adminstr. pub. schs., Yonkers, N.Y., 1962—; pres. Profl. Investment Group, 1967—; chmn. Hudson Holding Assos., 1969—, Marine Investor Assos., 1969—, Pine Investment Assos., 1969—; exec. v.p. Ednl. Analysis Assos., 1971—; vice chmn. bd. Peoples Nat. Bank of Rockland County; dir. P.I.A. Inc., Packease-Servease Corp., Electro Motion Corp., Peoples Nat. Bank Rockland County. Recipient Jenkins Meml. award Yonkers P.T.A., 1970. Mem. Am. Ednl. Research Assn., Nat. Assn. Secondary Sch. Prins., N.Y. State Assn. Secondary Sch. Adminstrn., Ga. Acad. Sci., Mensa, Phi Delta Kappa, Tau Delta Phi, Phi Beta Mu. Author numerous articles on edn. and investments. Home: 29 Culver Dr New City NY 10956

BARNHARD, SHERWOOD ARTHUR, printing co. exec.; b. Newark, Mar. 14, 1921; s. Charles L. and Blanche (Tarnow) B.; B.S., Franklin and Marshall Coll., 1942; m. Esther Lasky, Feb. 21, 1946; children—Ronald Harris, Paul Ira. With Lasky Co., Millburn, N.J., 1946—, exec. v.p., 1956-61, pres., 1961—; pres. Web and Sheetfed Color Lithographers. Bd. dirs. Jewish News Essex County, 1962—; trustee Temple Israel, South Orange, N.J.; bd. govs. Pleasant Valley Home For Aged, West Orange, N.J. Mem. Printing Industries N.J. (pres.), Printing Industries Met. N.Y. (mem. bd.), Met. Lithographers Assn. (dir., mem. labor com.), Mktg. Communications Execs. Internat., Advt. Club N.Y. Zeta Beta Tau. Clubs: Village (South Orange); Crestmont Golf and Country (West Orange). Home: 408 Long Hill Dr Short Hills NJ 07078 Office: 67 E Willow St Millburn NJ 07041

BARNHARDT, WILLIAM HORACE, textile mfg. co. exec.; b. Harrisburg, N.C., Feb. 3, 1903; s. John Addison and Sarah E. (McClellan) B.; B.E., N.C. State Coll. Sch. Textiles, Raleigh, 1923; m. Margaret McLaughlin, Oct. 8, 1927; children—William M., Nancy Barnhardt Thomas, Charles F. (dec. 1975), John David. Pres., treas., dir. Barnhardt Bros. Co., Charlotte, N.C., 1938—, Barnhardt Elastic Corp., 1945—, Barnhardt Internat. Corp., 1945—, Am. Textile Corp., Charlotte, Tryon Processing Co. (N.C.), Am. Realty Corp., Charlotte, Novelty Yarns Corp., Charlotte; chmn., dir. So. Webbing Mills, Inc., Greensboro, N.C.; v.p., dir. Sharon Corp., Charlotte; treas., dir. Providence Acres, Inc., Riverview Acres Corp., Univ. Heights, Inc., Carolinas Corp., Providence Assos., Univ. Plantation (all Charlotte); dir. Standard Bonded Warehouse Co., Charlotte, N.C. Nat. Bank, Charlotte, Dan River Mills, Inc., Danville, Va. Pres., treas., dir. Barnhardt Found., Inc.; past pres., chmn. investment com. N.C. Textile Found.; former trustee Barber-Scotia Coll., Concord, N.C.; trustee, mem. exec. com., chmn. fin. com. Queen's Coll., Charlotte, 1946-75; former trustee, chmn. fin. com. Crossnore (N.C.) Sch., Johnson C. Smith U., Charlotte; trustee, nat. chmn. patrons fund Protestant Radio and TV Center, Atlanta; life trustee Charlotte Country Day Sch.; former trustee, treas. Greater Charlotte Found.; chmn. Found. U. N.C. at Charlotte, 1963-66; mem. regional com. Boy Scouts Am., mem. adv. council Mecklenburg council; past v.p., chmn. capital funds bd. United Community Services; past chmn. exec. and bldg. coms. Hist. Found., Montreat, N.C.; campaign chmn. Charlotte Citizens for Freedom Park; mem. bldg. com., past pres. Charlotte YMCA; mem. exec. com. Interstate YMCA; former deacon, elder, vice moderator Myers Park Presbyterian Ch. Recipient Silver Beaver award Boy Scouts Am., 1947, Silver Antelope, 1949; Algernon Sydney Sullivan award Queens Coll., 1953; Service Youth award Charlotte YMCA, 1954; NCCJ award, 1966; named Man of South, Dixie Bus. Publ. poll, 1973; various bldgs. named in his honor. Mem. N.C. Textile Mfrs. Assn. (past dir.), Royal Soc. Knights Carrousel (governing council, king 1955), Carolina Yarn Assn. (pres. 1946), Newcomen Soc. N. Am., Phi Kappa Phi, Pi Kappa Alpha. Presbyterian. Clubs: Charlotte Textile, Quail Hollow Country (pres. 1963, 64, 65), Executives (pres. 1956), Charlotte City (past v.p.), Charlotte Country (past v.p.); Met., N.Y. Athletic (N.Y.C.); Travelers Century. Home: 1512 Queens Rd W Charlotte NC 28207 Office: NC Nat Bank Bldg Charlotte NC 28202

BARNHART, EDWIN LOUIS, environ. engr.; b. N.Y.C., Nov. 22, 1936; s. Edwin Leroy and Rose Barnhart; B.C.E., Manhattan Coll., 1959, M.San. Engring., 1965; postgrad. N.Y. U., 1960-62; m. Joan F. Ryder, Feb. 2, 1958; children—Laura, Linda, Cheryl, Edwin, Fred. Research asso. Manhattan Coll., 1959-61; with Hydrosci. Inc. (subs. Dow Chem. Co. 1972), Westwood, N.J., 1962-80, pres., 1972-80, bus. mgr. parent co., 1976-80; founder, pres. ELBA Inc., Dallas, 1980—; adj. prof. So. Meth. U., 1980—. Bd. dirs. N.J. council Girl Scouts U.S.A., 1977-79. Diplomate Am. Assn. Environ. Engrs.; registered profl. engr., N.Y. State, N.J., Tex., Tenn., Pa.; lic. profl. planner, N.J. Mem. ASCE (nat. chmn. com. on environ. standards), Am. Inst. Chem. Engrs., Water Pollution Control Fedn., Oceans Soc., Bergin County C. of C. (chmn. environ. law com.). Republican. Contbr. numerous articles to profl. publs. Home: 601 Balboa Dr Irving TX 75062 Office: 1545 W Mockingbird Ln Dallas TX 75235

BARNHILL, GREGORY HURD, investment banker; b. Balt., Feb. 20, 1953; s. Robert Bell and Margaret Katherine (Hurd) B.; student Institut d'Etudes Européenes, Banque Nat. de Paris, 1974; B.A. in Econs., Brown U., 1975; postgrad. Inst. Fin., N.Y.C., 1975. Registered rep. Alex. Brown & Sons, Investment Bankers, Balt., 1975—; v.p., dir. BOACO, Inc. T.E.G. Devel. Corp.; partner Barnhill/Griffith; dir. CPU, Inc. Adv. bd. Institut d'Etudes Européenes; mem. Mayor's Ball Com.; affiliate Balt. Mus. Art; mem. Walters Art Gallery. Lic. N.Y. Stock Exchange/Nat. Assn. Securities Dealers. Mem. Bond Club Md., Nat., Md. assns. realtors, Greater Balt. Bd. Realtors, Md. Hist. Soc., Brown U. Club—Md. (pres. 1976—), McDonogh Sch. Alumni Assn. (dir. 1976—), Hist. Soc. Balt. (trustee 1978-81), Sigma Chi. Republican. Club: Md. Home: Bond Ct 628 Washington Blvd Baltimore MD 21230 Office: Alex Brown & Sons 135 E Baltimore St Baltimore MD 21202

BARNHILL, JOHN WILLIAMSON, JR., ice cream co. exec.; b. Brenham, Tex., Nov. 18, 1936; s. John Williamson and Cecilia Low (Morriss) B.; B.J., U. Tex., Austin, 1959; m. Katherine Jane Cook, Aug. 22, 1959; children—Jane Elizabeth, John Williamson III, Ted Cook. Asst. pres. sec. to Gov. Tex., 1958-59; editorial staff writer Houston Press, 1959-60; dir. sales promotion Blue Bell Creameries, 1961-64; gen. mgr. Houston br., 1964-72, gen. sales mgr., Brenham, Tex., 1972—, v.p. sales, 1977—, also dir. Trustee, Brenham Ind. Sch. Dist., 1974-75; bd. dirs. Vol. Services Council Brenham State Sch., 1976—, Bohne Meml. Hosp., Brenham, 1979—; ruling elder Brenham Presbyterian Ch., 1974—; chmn. Brenham Parks and Recreation Bd., 1979—; pres. Washington County chpt. Am. Heart Assn., 1979-80, Brenham Maifest Assn., 1979—. Served to 1st lt. U.S. Army, 1961-62. Mem. U. Tex. Ex-Students Assn. (life, pres. Washington County 1976-77), Washington County C. of C. (dir. 1974-76), Mktg. Communications Execs. Internat. (pres. Houston chpt. 1969-70), Dairy Products Inst. Tex. (dir. 1974-76), Tex., Houston retail grocers assns., Houston Livestock Show and Rodeo (life), Heritage Soc. Washington County (life), Kappa Alpha (pres. Houston chpt. alumni orgn. 1969-70). Clubs: Brenham Gun and Rod, Brenham Rotary (pres. 1975-76). Home: Old Chappell Hill Rd Rural Route 1 Box 540 Brenham TX 77833 Office: PO Box 1807 Loop 577 Brenham TX 77833

BARNHILL, KENNETH SMALTZ, JR., mining co. exec.; b. Mesilla, N.Mex., Aug. 2, 1928; s. Kenneth Smaltz and Rega (Ragan) B.; B.S. in Chem. Engring., N.Mex. A. and M. U., 1952; m. Patricia Jean Boney, Aug. 10, 1950; children—Jane, Martha. Engr., supr. TMCA, Henderson, Nev., 1952-60; engring. mgr. U.S. Borax, Carlsbad, N.Mex., 1960-64; constrn. mgr. U.S. Borax, Saskatoon, Sask., Can., 1964-68, engring., mining and refinery mgr., Boron, Calif., 1968-74; mgr. project field constrn. Gulf Mineral Resources Co., Grants, N.Mex., 1974-79, gen. mgr. N.Mex. uranium ops., 1979—; mining adv. bd. N.Mex. Inst. Tech., 1977. Bd. dirs. Camp Stoney Episcopal Ch., 1978—. Served with AUS, 1946-48. Named Man of Year, Henderson Jr. C. of C., 1955, 56. Mem. Grants C. of C. (dir. 1976-77), Am. Inst. Chem. Engrs., AIME, Can. Inst. Mining and Metallurgy, Am. Underground Assn., Colo., N.Mex. mining assns. Democrat. Club: Elks. Patentee in field. Home: 812 Mount Taylor Ave Grants NM 87020 Office: PO Box 1150 Grants NM 87020

BARON, JOEL RICHARD, lawyer; b. N.Y.C., Feb. 25, 1938; B.S. in Acctg., Bklyn. Coll., 1959; LL.B., Bklyn. Law Sch., 1963. Admitted to N.Y. State bar, 1964; acct. Simoniff Peyser & Citrin, N.Y.C., 1960-63; asso. dir. bus. affairs news div. CBS, N.Y.C., 1963-66; owner Scotties by Cromwell, Inc., N.Y.C., 1966-70; asst. to pres. Boyle Midway div. Am. Home Products Corp., N.Y.C., 1972-80, div. v.p. adminstrn., 1980—. Mem. Am. Bar Assn. Home: 860 Fifth Ave New York NY 10021 Office: 685 3d Ave New York NY 10017

BARON, SYDNEY STUART, pub. relations co. exec., mgmt. cons.; b. N.Y.C., May 30, 1920; s. Hyman C. and Anne (Stuart) B.; B.S., St. John's U., 1942; m. Sylvia Schreibman, Oct. 23, 1938; children—Barbara Baron Balsam, Eric, Richard, Daniel Henry.

Practice as publicist, 1940-50; chmn. bd. Sydney S. Baron and Co., Inc., N.Y.C., 1952—; dir. United Aircraft Products, Inc., Shopwell, Inc.; instr. polit. sci. N.Y. U., N.Y.C., 1954-58; public relations and mgmt. cons. Aluminum Co. Am., 1956—, Am. Can Co., 1966—, Taiwan Ministry Econ. Affairs, 1976—, Columbia U., 1967—, Atlantic Cement Co., Inc., 1965—, Commodity Exchange, 1976—, Nat. Alliance Businessmen, 1976—, Electronic Industries Assn. Japan, 1972—, Japan Bearing Indsl. Assn., 1978—, Am. Shipbldg. Co., 1976—, Pullman Inc., 1979—, Windham Properties Ltd., 1979—; dep. commr. N.Y.C. Dept. Marine and Aviation, 1950; dep. commr. dir. promotion N.Y.C. Dept. Commerce, 1951. Dir. N.Y.C. bd. dirs. Nat. Assn. Retarded Children, N.Y.C. Big Bros. Movement; chmn. bd. dirs. Beth Jacob Schs., N.Y.C., 1956—; trustee Maimonides Hosp., N.Y.C. Recipient Civic Merit award N.Y.C., 1951; certificate commendation Jewish War Vets. U.S.A., 1960. Mem. A.I.M. (pres.'s council), Pub. Relations Soc. Am., U.S. C. of C., Am. Mgmt. Assn., Soc. of Silurians. Democrat. Mason. Clubs: Board Room, Lone Star Boat, Friars (N.Y.C); Fenway Golf (White Plains, N.Y.); International, George Town (Washington). Author: One Whirl, 1942; Men without Humor, 1944; The Bells Ring Loudly, 1946. Contbr. numerous articles to popular mags. Producer other Broadway stage shows including Tambourines to Glory. Home: Scarsdale NY 10583 Office: 540 Madison Ave New York NY 10022

BARON, THEODORE, public relations co. exec.; b. Harbin, China, Aug. 20, 1928; s. Solomon and Bella (Gelesny) B.; came to U.S., 1946, naturalized, 1952; B.A. in Journalism, U. Calif., Berkeley, 1950; LL.B., N.Y. U., 1957; m. Irene Cunnington, Oct. 24, 1958; children—Susan, Michael. Reporter-editor Coalinga (Calif.) Record, 1950-51; editor AP, San Francisco, 1951-52; writer, account exec. Med. and Pharm. Info. Bur., N.Y.C., 1952-56, Ruder & Finn, N.Y.C., 1956-57, Lobsenz & Co., N.Y.C., 1957-58; admitted to N.Y. State bar, 1958; founder, pres. Ted Baron, Inc., N.Y.C., 1959—; founder, chmn. bd. Baron/O'Brien, Inc., N.Y.C., 1979—. Mem. Am. Bar Assn., Nat. Investor Relations Inst., Pub. Relations Soc. Am. (accredited; pres., dir. N.Y.C. chpt.). Clubs: Overseas Press, Princeton, Theodore Gordon Flyfishers (dir.). Contbr. numerous articles on pub. and investor relations to profl. jours. Office: 1440 Broadway New York NY 10018

BARONE, ANTHONY JOSEPH, sales exec.; b. Leroy, N.Y., July 25, 1917; s. Joseph Anthony and Jovana (Maloni) B.; student Ithaca Coll., 1936-40; m. Betty Lou Poe, May 20, 1966; children—John Barone, Marietta, Toni-Ann. Mgr. Western Auto Stores, Newark, also Passaic, Paterson, N.J., 1941-49; gen. agt. Gen. Am. Life Ins. Co., Miami, Fla., 1960-64; salesman franchises, Birmingham, Ala., 1965-70; pres. Organ Center, Inc., Sound Advt. Media, Inc., Huntsville, 1970—. Mem. Sales and Mktg. Execs. Assn., Internat. Platform Assn., C. of C., Phi Mu Alpha. Democrat. Roman Catholic. Clubs: Elks, Lions. Home: 404 Weatherly Rd Huntsville AL 35803 Office: 2801 S Memorial Pkwy Huntsville AL 35810

BAROODY, THOMAS ALOYSIUS, investment co. exec.; b. Buffalo, Oct. 25, 1933; s. Thomas Asa and Florence Rose (Welch) B.; B.S. in Econs., Villanova U., 1955; m. Mary Kathleen Maloney, Jan. 20, 1973; children—Thomas Aloysius, III, Timothy A., Terrence A., Tara A., Tracey A., Todd A., Kieran Charles, Sean. Sales mgr. Reynolds & Co. (name changed to Reynolds Securities Co.), Phila., 1955-62; v.p. CEM Securities Corp., Balt., 1962-64; sr. partner Baroody & Co., Ft. Lauderdale, Fla., 1964-73; exec. v.p., dir. Castlewood Internat. Corp. (name now Flanigan Enterprises), Miami, Fla., 1962-64, 73-74; pres. Baroody-Price Trading Corp., Ft. Lauderdale, 1973—, The Baroody Group, Inc., 1975—; dir. Hoffman Publs.; v.p. internat. Sales Harmsco Export, Inc., N. Palm Beach, Fla.; v.p. Saudi Arabia, Dravo Internat., Pitts., 1978—; mng. dir. Dravo Arabia Ltd., Pitts., 1978—; cons. Todd Industries. Chmn. Villanova U. Sports awards com., 1959-60; dir. finance div. Catholic Charities, Phila., 1960-61; chmn. Holy Cross Hosp. Charity Ball, Ft. Lauderdale; bd. dirs. Childrens Genetic Found. of Fla. Mem. N.Y., Am. (asso.) stock exchanges, Ft. Lauderdale C. of C. Clubs: Coral Ridge, Le Club International, The Tower, Gold Coast Internat. Yachting and Sailing (pres.) (Ft. Lauderdale); Racquet (Miami). Home: 601 Solar Dr Fort Lauderdale FL 33301 Office: 2455 E Sunrise Blvd Internat Bldg Fort Lauderdale FL 33304

BAROWSKY, ANDREW PHILLIP, bakery exec.; b. Holyoke, Mass., May 21, 1950; s. Mischa Daniel and Norma Josephine (Magidson) B.; B.A., U. Rochester, 1972; M.B.A., U. Mich., 1974. Tax specialist Arthur Andersen & Co., Boston, 1974-77; sr. v.p., treas., dir. F.R. Lepage Bakery Inc., Auburn, Maine, 1977—; reviewer, acctg. and bus. texts Harper & Row, Inc. Bd. dirs. LPL/APL Arts Council, 1977. C.P.A., Mass. Mem. Am. Inst. C.P.A.'s, Am. Bakers Assn. (bd. govs.). Home: 65 Garden Circle Auburn ME 04210 Office: 60 2d St Auburn ME 04210

BARR, DAVID ABEEL, info. services exec.; b. Tarrytown, N.Y., Apr. 8, 1939; s. Frederick Albert and Mary Byrd (Saunders) B.; B.S. in B.A. with distinction, N. Central Coll., 1962; m. Judith Gaden, Apr. 22, 1961; children—Dianne Lynn, Lynda Kaye. Br. sales mgr. Honeywell Info. Systems, Inc., Chgo., 1967-69; dir. customer ops., product devel. Exec. Computer Systems, Inc., Oak Brook, Ill., 1969-72; v.p. mktg. Tran Telecommunications Corp., Marina Del Rey, Calif., 1972-76; asst. v.p. mktg. Ill. Bell Telephone, Chgo., 1976-80; pres. SMS/COMPCOM div. Situation Mgmt. Systems, Inc., Oak Brook, 1980—; cons. in field. Fund raising chmn. Girl Scouts of DuPage County, 1972-75; class rep./alumni fund raising chmn. N. Central Coll., 1977—. Served with U.S. Army, 1957. Mem. Am. Mktg. Assn. Methodist. Home: 203 Westmoreland Ln Naperville IL 60540 Office: Oak Brook IL

BARR, JOHN WATSON, III, banker; b. Louisville, Mar. 22, 1921; s. John McFerran and Anita L. (Carrington) B.; B.A. in Econs. and Polit. Sci., Princeton U., 1943; m. Mary Louise Engelhard, Nov. 10, 1945; children—John McFerran II, Charles Carrington. With 1st Nat. Bank, Louisville, 1946—, chmn. bd., 1974—, also dir.; with 1st Ky. Trust Co. and affiliates, Louisville, 1946—, chmn. bd., 1974—, also dir.; chmn. bd. 1st Ky. Nat. Corp., holding co., Louisville, 1974—, also dir.; dir. Collins Co., Belknap, Inc., Louisville Gas & Electric Co., Louisville Cement Co., Capital Holding Corp., Churchill Downs, Inc., Dixie Warehouse & Cartage Co. Bd. dirs. and/or officer Salvation Army, Louisville Central Area, Louisville Devel. Corp., Louisville Fund for Arts, Cave Hill Cemetery Co., Am. Printing House for Blind, Ky. Higher Edn. Assistance Authority, Ky. Ind. Coll. Found., YMCA, U. Louisville Found.; bd. overseers U. Louisville. Served to capt. F.A., U.S. Army,1942-45; ETO. Decorated Air medal with 3 oak leaf clusters, Bronze Star with V device; recipient awards Jr. Achievement Kentuckiana, Old Ky. Home council Boy Scouts Am., Am. Inst. Banking, City of Hope, Spirit of Louisville Found. Mem. Am. Bankers Assn., Ky. Bankers Assn., Assn. Res. City Bankers, Assn. Bank Holding Cos., Bank Adminstrn. Inst. (award), Robert Morris Assos., Ducks Unltd., Princeton Alumni Assn. Presbyterian. Clubs: Rotary, Louisville Country, River Valley, (Louisville); Princeton, Univ. (N.Y.C.). Office: First Nat Tower 101 S 5th St Louisville KY 40202

BARR, JOSEPH WALKER, corp. dir.; b. Vincennes, Ind., Jan. 17, 1918; s. Oscar Lynn and Stella Florence (Walker) B.; A.B., DePauw U., 1939; M.A., Harvard, 1941; LL.D., Vincennes U., 1966, DePauw U., 1967; m. Beth Williston, Sept. 3, 1939; children—Bonnie (Mrs. Michael Gilliom), Cherry (Mrs. Donald N. Briggs), Joseph Williston, Elizabeth Eugenia (Mrs. Andrew Losasso), Lynn Hamilton. Mem. 86th Congress from 11th Ind. Dist.; asst. to sec. of treasury, 1961-64; chmn. FDIC, 1964-65; under sec. of treasury, 1965-68, sec. of treasury, 1968-69; pres. Am. Security & Trust Co., Washington, 1969-72, chmn. bd., 1973-74; chmn. Fed. Home Loan Bank, Atlanta, 1978—; dir. 3M Co., Comml. Credit Co., Control Data Corp., Burlington Industries, Inc., Washington Gas Light Co., Manor Care Inc., Conrail. Bd. dirs. Student Loan Marketing Assn.; bd. regents Georgetown U. Served to lt. comdr. USNR, 1942-45. Decorated Bronze Star. Mem. Phi Beta Kappa. Democrat. Home: Houyhnhnm Farm Hume VA 22639 Office: 734 15th St NW Washington DC 20005

BARR, KENNETH JOHN, petroleum and mining co. exec.; b. Birmingham, Ala., Aug. 25, 1926; s. Archie and Mable Leona (Griffith) B.; B.S. in Chem. Engring., Auburn U., 1947; postgrad. Inst. Mgmt. Northwestern U., 1964; m. Jeanne Bonner, Jan. 22, 1951; children—Marsha Jeanne, Kenneth John, Darren Clint. With Amoco Prodn. Co., 1948-1965, 70-73, 75-79, jr. petroleum engr., Hobbs, N.Mex., 1948-49, chief engr., 1962-65, v.p. and div. mgr., New Orleans, 1970-73, mgr. prodn. and v.p. prodn. Amoco Can. Petroleum Co., Calgary, Alta., Can., 1965-70; gen. mgr. supply and coordination dept. Standard Oil Co. Ind., Chgo., 1973-75; exec. v.p. Amoco Internat. Oil Co., Chgo., 1975; exec. v.p., dir. Amoco Prodn. Co., Chgo., 1975-79; pres., dir. Cyprus Mines Corp., Los Angeles, 1979—, Amoco Minerals Co., Denver, 1980—; dir. Cypress Anvil Mining Co. Served with USAAF, 1945. Mem. Am. Petroleum Inst., Soc. Petroleum Engrs. of AIME, Tex. Mid-Continent Oil and Gas Assn., Phi Lambda Upsilon. Clubs: Mid-Am. (Chgo.); Calif. (Los Angeles); North River Yacht. Office: 7000 S Yosemite Englewood CO 80112

BARR, ROY RASSMANN, lawyer; b. Chgo., Sept. 28, 1901; s. Alfred Eugene and Pauline (Rassmann) B.; student Northwestern U., 1918-20; Ph.B., U. Chgo., 1923; J.D., John Marshall Law Sch., 1924; m. Katharine Roberts, Sept. 9, 1924; children—Robert Roy (dec.), Barbara Ann (Mrs. Robert E. Newlin), Alfred Eugene, II. Admitted to Ill. bar, 1924; mem. firm Barr & Barr, 1924-26, later Barr, Barr & Corcoran; now individual practice. Trained with S.A.T.C. U.S. Army, 1918. Mem. Am., Ill., Chgo., W. Suburban bar assns., Am. Judicature Soc., Pierce Arrow Soc., Phi Sigma Soc. of Chgo. and Oak Park, Delta Sigma Phi. Conglist. Mason. Clubs: Antique Automobile Club of Am.; Horseless Carriage; Classic Car of Am.; Interfraternity (Chgo.). Home: 1116 Randolph St (2d) Oak Park IL 60302 Office: 10 S La Salle St Chicago IL 60603

BARR, SUSAN MCADOO, corp. exec., civic worker; b. Detroit, May 2, 1935; d. Joseph Stanly and Jessie E. (Colquhoun) McAdoo; B.S., La. State U., 1957; m. Gavin Chaundy Barr, June 21, 1958; children—Susan, Jessie Jo, Gavin Chaundy, Bryce C. Social welfare worker N.J. Bd. child Welfare, Camden, 1957-60; with G.C. Barr, M.D., P.C., Bethlehem, Pa., 1971—, v.p., 1972—. Bd. dirs. Young Reps. Lehigh County, 1963-66, Council Rep. Women, 1964-68, Lehigh County unit Am. Cancer Soc., 1966-78; trustee Lehigh Valley Child Care, Allentown Art Mus., 1972-75, 80—, Lehigh Valley chpt. ARC, 1980—, Sta. WLVT-TV, 1980—; trustee, v.p. Moravian Acad.; pres. Soc. of Arts of Allentown (Pa.) Art Museum, 1972-74; mem. community adv. bd. Jr. League; mem. St. Luke's Ball Com.; gen. chmn. Sta. WLVT-TV Great On-Air Auction, 1978. Kate Duncan Smith Sch. grantee, Ala., 1971;. Named Pa.'s outstanding jr. mem. D.A.R., 1971, nat. outstanding jr. mem., 1971. Mem. D.A.R. (chpt. vice regent 1968-74, nat. vice chmn. jr. membership in charge sales 1971-74, chpt. regent 1974-77, 78-80, nat. chmn. pub. relations 1974-77, state conf. chmn. 1978, Pa. chmn. schs. com. 1977-80, state corr. sec. 1980—), Woman's Aux. Northampton County Med. Assn. (pres. 1975), Lehigh County Aux. Med. Soc., Moravian Acad. Parents Assn. (pres. 1977), Internat. Platform Assn. Clubs: Altrusa, Alpha Omicron Pi Alumni, Saucon Valley Country (Bethlehem). Home: RD 5 Whiteacre Dr N Bethlehem PA 18015

BARRACK, THOMAS JOSEPH, JR., real estate corp. exec.; b. Los Angeles, Apr. 28, 1947; s. Thomas Joseph and Mamie Mary (Fadel) B.; A.B., U. So. Calif., 1969, J.D., 1972; m. Ann Christine Watson, June 11, 1971; children—Jodi Christine, Thomas Joseph. Admitted to Calif. bar, 1972; asso. firm Kalmbach, DeMarco, Knapp and Chillingsworth, Los Angeles, 1972-74; partner firm Barrack and Wilkinson, Newport Beach, Calif., 1974-75; pres., dir. Dunn Internat. Corp., Newport Beach, 1975—; dir. Newport Fin. Corp. Apptd. U.S. del. to 19th gen. conf. UNESCO, Nairobi, Kenya, 1976; mem. Calif. State Bldg. Standards Commn. Mem. State Bar Calif., Orange County, Los Angeles County bar assns. Clubs: Big Canyon Country (Newport Beach); Jonathan (Los Angeles). Office: 1600 Dove St Suite 210 Newport Beach CA 92660

BARRANCO, PASCAL CHARLES, retail exec.; b. New Orleans, Oct. 2, 1941; s. Pasquale C. and Edna K. (Byrnes) B.; student La. State U., 1975-76, Am. Inst. Banking, 1962, Loyola U., New Orleans, 1970-73; m. Flora Ann Perez, Apr. 29, 1962; children—Lisa Ann, Paul Charles, Amy. Bookkeeper, Hibernia Nat. Bank, New Orleans, 1961-62; paymaster Touro Infirmary, La. Hosp., New Orleans, 1962-64; sr. acct. Auto-Lec Stores, Inc., New Orleans, 1964-69; asst. controller Leon Godchaux Clothing Co., New Orleans, 1969-73; controller Porter-Stevens Clothing Store Co., New Orleans, 1973-78; pres., controller The Varsity Shops, Baton Rouge, La., 1978—. Treas., Inter-Lec Fed. Credit Union, 1964-69, The Leon Godchaux Credit Union, 1969-73, N. Bridgedale Civic Assn., 1976-77; bd. dirs. La. chpt. Nat. Hemophilia, treas., 1977-80. Mem. Nat. Assn. Accts. Clubs: Shriners, Eagles (treas. 1975-76), Last Minute Carnival (pres. 1977-78), Alisi. Home: 13517 Buckley St Baton Rouge LA 70816 Office: 340 Florida St Baton Rouge LA 70801

BARRETT, CHARLES MARION, physician, ins. co. exec.; b. Cin., Mar. 10, 1913; s. Charles Francis and May (Ryan) B.; A.B., Xavier U., 1934, LL.D. (hon.), 1974; M.D., U. Cin., 1938; m. May Belle Finn, Apr. 27, 1942; children—Angela (Mrs. Ernest Eynon), Charles, John, Michael, Marian, William. Asso. med dir. Western-So. Life Ins. Co., Cin., 1942, med. dir., 1951-73, exec. v.p., 1965-73, pres., 1973—, also dir.; prof. depts. surgery and radiology U. Cin. Coll. Medicine, after 1957, prof. emeritus, 1974—; dir. Eagle Savs. Assn., Procter & Gamble Co., Cin. Bell, Inc., Eagle-Picher Industries, Inc., So. Ohio Bank. Bd. dirs. Our Lady of Mercy Hosp., U. Cin., Bethesda Hosp. and Deaconess Assn. Recipient Taft medal U. Cin., 1973, Spl. award Ohio Radiol. Soc., 1974. Fellow Am. Coll. Radiology; mem. A.M.A., Life Ins. Assn. Am. Home: 2581 Grandin Rd Cincinnati OH 45208 Office: 400 Broadway Cincinnati OH 45202

BARRETT, JAMES EDWARD, JR., mgmt. cons.; b. Lowell, Mass., Dec. 9, 1929; s. James E. and Margaret A. (Holland) B.; A.B., Harvard U., 1951; postgrad. Washington U., 1952-53, Air Command and Staff Coll., 1952; m. Dorothy G. Walle; children—James Edward, Dorothy Anne, William H., Mark S. Asst. prof. Harvard U., 1955-58; systems analyst, mgr. Raytheon Co., 1958-62; mgmt. cons., 1963-68; mktg. mgr. Kepner-Tregor, Inc., Princeton, N.J., 1962-65; mgr., dir. K-T Europe, 1966-67, pres., 1967-68; pres. Cresheim Co., Inc., Phila., 1968—, chmn. Chresheim, Ltd. (U.K.), 1979—, Cresheim do Brasil, Sao Paulo, 1980—. Pres., Wyndmoor (Pa.) Community Assn., 1977-79. Served to capt. USAF, 1951-55. Mem. Am. Assn. Small Research Cos. (pres. Phila. chpt. 1977—), Inst. Mgmt. Cons.'s (v.p. chpt. 1977-), Instructional Systems Assn., Inst. Dirs. (U.K.). Clubs: Harvard (N.Y.C., Phila.); American (London). Contbr. numerous articles to profl. jours. Home: 8315 Flourtown Ave Wyndmoor PA 19118 Office: Cresheim Co Inc 1408 E Mermaid Ln Philadelphia PA 19118

BARRETT, JAMES EMMETT, ins. co. exec.; b. Omaha, May 30, 1923; s. John C. and Elizabeth M. (Wilson) B.; LL.B., Creighton U., 1948; m. Mary Ann Forsyth, Oct. 20, 1944; children—Mary Margaret Barrett Slye, Susan Elizabeth, Joanne Barrett Gates, James Emmett. Admitted to Nebr. bar, 1948; with Mut. of Omaha Ins. Co., 1948—, v.p., 1959-65, exec. v.p., 1965—; vice chmn. bd. dirs. Tele-Trip Co., Inc., Omaha, 1964—; dir. Companion Life Ins. Co., N.Y.C. Mem. Met. Washington Bd. Trade; pres.'s council Creighton U.; founding pres., dir. U.S. Phys. Edn. and Sport Devel. Found.; trustee Behrend Found., Washington; trustee Nat. Capital chpt. Nat. Multiple Sclerosis Soc., chmn., 1973-78, nat. conf. chmn., 1976; bd. dirs. The Heights Sch., Washington, 1974-78; world pres. USO, Inc., chmn. exec. com., 1977-78, v.p. Nat. Capital USO, dir. USO Met. N.Y. Served as officer, inf., AUS, World War II; ETO. Recipient Community Service award Sales and Mktg. Execs. Washington, 1978. Mem. Health Ins. Assn. Am. (dir. 1966-68; nat. health care programs com.; chmn. task force vets. affairs), Am., Fed., Nebr. bar assns., Nebr. Soc. Washington (pres. 1962), HEROES, Inc. (charter), C. of C. U.S. (health care com. 1974-79), Newcomen Soc., Washington Inst. Fgn. Affairs, Nat. Assembly of Nat. Voluntary Health and Social Welfare Orgns. Inc. (colleague), Delta Theta Phi, Alpha Sigma Nu. Clubs: Kenwood Golf and Country, F St., Capitol Hill (Washington). Home: 5017 Sentinel Dr Washington DC 20016 Office: 1700 Pennsylvania Ave NW Washington DC 20006

BARRETT, JAMES ROBERT, mgmt. cons.; b. Perth Amboy, N.J., June 8, 1941; s. Eugene Edward and Genevieve Rita (Poling) B.; A.B., Seton Hall U., South Orange, N.J., 1964; m. Patricia Elinor Blazo, Oct. 22, 1966; children—Kathleen E., Jennifer C., James R. Mktg. rep. Jersey Central Power & Light Co., Morristown, N.J., 1966-68; staff cons. Handley-Walker Co., Montvale, N.J., 1968-69; ops. mgr. Brooks Internat. Corp., Montvale, 1969-79; partner, dir. Mgmt. Tech. Corp., Secaucus, N.J., 1979—. Pres. Keyport (N.J.) Jaycees, 1965, Holmdel (N.J.) Jaycees, 1968; sec. bd. trustees Keyport Library, 1964-66; mem. Monmouth (N.J.) County Republican Com., 1965. Mem. Assn. Productivity Specialists. Roman Catholic. Home: 722 Holmdel Rd Holmdel NJ 07733 Office: 401 Whimbrel Ln Secaucus NJ 07094

BARRETT, JOHN FINN, banker; b. Cin., Mar. 16, 1949; B.B.A., U. Cin., 1971. With Bank of N.Y., 1971—, asst. v.p., 1976-78, v.p., team leader nat. div. Midwest region, N.Y.C., 1978—. Home: 125 E 82d St Apt 9 New York NY 10028 Office: 48 Wall St New York NY 10015

BARRETT, M(AXIE) EDGAR, educator, bus. cons.; b. Portland, Oreg., Oct. 21, 1941; s. Maxie E. and Naomi E. (Leaf) B.; B.S. with honors, Portland State U., 1967; M.B.A. (Alfred P. Sloan Found. fellow), Stanford U., 1969, Ph.D. (Arthur Andersen doctoral fellow, Am. Acctg. Assn. doctoral fellow), 1971; m. Patricia Ann Kinney, Mar. 23, 1969; children—Jennifer Lee, Stephanie Paige, Laura Louise. Asst. prof. Harvard U., 1971-74, asso. prof., 1974-77; ind. bus. cons., Dallas, 1968—; dir. Maguire Oil and Gas Inst., So. Meth. U., Dallas, 1978—, prof. bus., 1977—; cons. exec. edn. Served with USAR, 1963-64. Recipient Outstanding Acctg. Student award Portland State U., 1967. Mem. Am. Acctg. Assn., Fin. Mgmt. Assn. Republican. Methodist. Contbr. articles to Fin. Analysts Jour., Harvard Bus. Rev. Home: 8706 Middle Downs Dr Dallas TX 75243 Office: Cox School of Business Dallas TX 75275

BARRETT, ROBERT OWEN, carpet mfg. co. exec.; b. Gettsburg, Pa., June 2, 1944; s. Edward Earl and Elizabeth Louise (Plank) B.; B.A., Pacific U., 1966; postgrad. U. Oreg., 1969; m. Elisabeth Taylor Hayes, Mar. 25, 1972; 1 dau., Susan. Sales rep. Crown Zellerbach, Portland, Oreg., 1966, Eugene, Oreg., 1967; with Lees Carpets, various locations, 1970—, ter. mgr., Medford, Oreg., 1970, Seattle, 1971-72, comml. terr. mgr., Washington, 1973-74, comml. sales mgr., San Francisco, 1975-78, asst. nat. comml. sales mgr., King of Prussia, Pa., 1978-79, Eastern regional comml. sales mgr., 1979—. Mem. Nat. Republican Com. Mem. Soc. for Advancement of Mgmt., Am. Mgmt. Assn. Presbyn. Club: Wash. Athletic. Home: 519 Greenhill Ln Berwyn PA 19312 Office: Valley Forge Corp Center King of Prussia PA 19406

BARRETT, WILLIAM JOEL, investment banker; b. Darien, Conn., Aug. 26, 1939; s. William J. and Virginia Barrett; B.A., DePauw U., Greencastle, Ind., 1961; M.B.A., N.Y. U., 1963; m. Sara Schrock, Sept. 1, 1962; children—William, Brian, Christopher, Peter. Investment analyst Met. Life Ins. Co., 1961-66; v.p. Gregory & Sons, investment bankers, 1966-69, G.A. Saxton, investment bankers, 1969-74; sr. v.p., dir. Janney Montgomery Scott, Inc., N.Y.C., 1974—, also dir.; dir. Exploration Surveys, Inc., Patrick Industries, Plastics & Rubber Products Co., RMS Electronics, Inc. Republican. Episcopalian. Clubs: Navesink Country, Univ., Broad St., Shrewsbury Sailing and Yacht, Sea Bright Lawn Tennis. Office: 26 Broadway New York NY 10004

BARRIENTOS, EMMANUEL ALCIBIADES, mfg. co. exec.; b. Dominican Republic, Dec. 2, 1938; came to U.S., 1969; s. Julio and Elvida Mireya (Marcelino) B.; B.A. in Acctg., Universidad Autonoma Santo Domingo, 1964; postgrad. Sch. of Bus., Santo Domingo, 1965-67, Williams Paterson Coll., 1978-81; children—Ramon, Emmanuel, Rene, Fatima. Sr. auditor Sociedad Industrial Dominicana, 1959-65; auditor IRS Center of Dominican Republic, 1965-67, Publicitaria Dominicana C. por A., 1967-69; controller John H. Graham & Co. Inc., Oradell, N.J., 1969—. Mem. Nat. Assn. Accts., Oradell C. of C. Roman Catholic. Club: Lions. Home: 188 Oakdene Ave Teaneck NJ 07666 Office: John H Graham & Co Inc 617 Oradell Ave Oradell NJ 07649

BARRIGER, JOHN WALKER, IV, railroad exec.; b. St. Louis, Aug. 3, 1927; s. John Walker and Elizabeth Chambers (Thatcher) B.; B.S., M.I.T., 1949; C.T., Yale U., 1950; m. Evelyn Dobson, Dec. 29, 1955; children—John W., Catherine Brundige. With Santa Fe Ry., 1950-68, 70—, supt. transp., 1965-68, mgr. staff studies and planning, Chgo., 1970-77, asst. v.p. fin., 1977-79, asst. to pres., 1979—; mgr. transp. controls div. Sylvania Info. Systems, Waltham, Mass., 1968-70; mem. vis. com. dept. civil engring. M.I.T., 1972-75; chmn. M.I.T. Mgmt. Conf., Chgo., 1974. Trustee, Village of Kenilworth (Ill.), 1978—, chmn. sts., sanitation and public works. Served with USN, 1946. Recipient Bronze Beaver award M.I.T., 1975, Employee Campaign Chmn. of Yr. award United Way/Crusade of Mercy, 1979. Mem. Am. Assn. R.R. Supts. (dir. 1958-68), Am. Ry. Engring. Assn., Ry. Planning Officers Assn. (chmn. 1971-76), Transp. Research Bd., Transp. Research Forum, Western Ry. Club (pres. 1979-80), Newcomen Soc., M.I.T. Alumni Assn. (dir. 1968-72), Delta Kappa

Epsilon. Republican. Roman Catholic. Clubs: Econ. Chgo. Exec. Chgo., M.I.T. Chgo. (pres. 1972-73), Kenilworth, Mich. Shores, Union League Chgo. Home: 155 Melrose Ave Kenilworth IL 60043 Office: 80 E Jackson Blvd Chicago IL 60604

BARRIS, ROBERT LEE, indsl. drilling co. exec.; b. Cleve., Jan. 14, 1922; s. Floyd Clayton and Emma Elizabeth (McVeen) B.; student Cuyahoga Community Coll., 1968-69; m. Bernice M. Sebek, Feb. 22, 1941; children—Susan Lee, Robert James, Charles Britt. Sheet metal worker Swarthout Co., Cleve., 1940-42, carpenter, 1950-57; erection supt. Mills Metal Partition Co., 1945-60; owner Hupp Well & Pump subs. ABC Drilling, Cleve., 1957—; pres. Evergreen Builders, Cleve., 1976—; partner Barris & Difini, Cleve., 1968—. Committeeman, Boy Scouts Am., 1959-68; mem. council Highland Heights Consol. Health Fund, 1959—; mem. CAP, Coast Guard Aux.; mem. Highland Heights City Council, 1957-59, 65-78, mayor, 1959-63. Served with USAF, 1943-45. Decorated Purple Heart, Air medal with five clover leafs. Mem. Businessmen Assn., Aircraft Owners and Pilots Assn. Mem. Ch. of Christ. Clubs: Masons, Lions. Office: 4996 Campbell Rd Willoughby OH 44094

BARRON, ALEX E., investments co. exec.; b. Paris, Ont., Can., Aug. 4, 1918; s. Frederick and Ethel (Rutherford) B.; student schs., Paris, Ont.; m. Nina Marion Burrows, June 1, 1946 (dec., 1976); children—Paul, James; m. 2d Beverley Mollett, May 5, 1978. With Fry & Co. Ltd., 1938-59, pres., 1955-59; officer Canadian Gen. Investments Ltd., Toronto, Ont., 1959—, now pres., dir.; pres., dir. 3d Can. Gen. Investment Trust Ltd.; chmn., dir., exec. com. Domtar Inc.; chmn., dir. Can. Tire Corp. Ltd.; dir., exec. com. Can. Trust Co., Can. Trustco Mortgage Co.; v.p., dir. Spinrite Yarns & Dyers, Ltd. Listowel; dir. Haliburton Co., Dallas, Tex., Steel Co. Can. Ltd. Clubs: Toronto, Rosedale Golf, Granite of Toronto, Briars Golf and Country. Office: 110 Yonge St Suite 1702 Toronto ON M5C 1T4 Canada

BARRON, JAMES BRENDAN, banker; b. Boston, Jan. 4, 1931; s. Thomas J. and Mary M. (Murphy) B.; B.S. cum laude, Boston Coll.; postgrad. Boston U. Sch. Bus., Internat. Banking Sch., London Inst. Bankers Christ Ch. Coll. Oxford U.; m. Mary R. Naclerio, Aug. 1958; children—Kelly, James Brendan, Michael F., M. Rachel, Stephen R., Aimee L. Vice pres. New Eng. Mchts. Nat. Bank, Boston, 1955-70; pres. Middleborough Trust Co., Middleboro, Mass., 1970-76; pres. First Nat. Bank of New Bedford (Mass.), 1976—; pres., chmn. First Melville Bancorp., Inc., holding co. Served with U.S. Army, 1952-55. Mem. Mass., Am. (certified comml. lender) bankers assns., Am. Arbitration Assn. (arbitrator). Roman Catholic. Clubs: Wamsutta, Elks, Lions. Home: 132 Cedar St Braintree MA 02184 Office: PO Box C-906 New Bedford MA 02741

BARRON, JANE ELIZABETH, banker; b. Providence, Nov. 15, 1947; d. Irving R. and Joan (Kelsey) Lockwood; student So. Sem. Jr. Coll., Buena Vista, Va., 1965-66. Asst. buyer dress salon Gladdings Dept. Store, Providence, 1966-67; mgr. Village Lane, splty. shop, Warwick, R.I., 1967-69, The Waethervane, Warwick, 1969-71; from teller to ops. asst. Oldstone Bank, Providence, 1971-76; br. mgr. Am. Nat. Bank, Middlefield, Conn., 1977-79, comml. banking officer, mgr., 1979—. Mem. adv. bd. Middlesex Community Coll. Mem. Am. Inst. Banking, Middlesex C. of C. Episcopalian. Office: Am Nat Bank Middlefield CT 06455

BARROW, THOMAS DAVIES, mining co. exec.; b. San Antonio, Dec. 27, 1924; s. Leonidas Theodore and Laura Editha (Thomson) B.; B.S., U. Tex., 1945, M.A., 1948; Ph.D., Stanford, 1953; grad. Advanced Mgmt. Program, Harvard, 1963; m. Janice Meredith Hood, Sept. 16, 1950; children—Theodore Hood, Kenneth Thomson, Barbara Loyd, Elizabeth Ann. With Humble Oil & Refining Co., 1951-72, regional exploration mgr., New Orleans, 1962-64, dir., 1965-72, sr. v.p., 1967-70, pres., 1970-72; sr. v.p., dir. Exxon Corp., N.Y.C., 1972-78; exec. v.p., dir. Esso Exploration, Inc., 1964-65; chmn., chief exec. officer Kennecott Corp., Stamford, Conn., 1978—; mem. Commn. on Natural Resources, NRC; mem. marine petroleum and minerals adv. com. U.S. Dept. Commerce; mem. Woods Hole Oceanographic Instn., 20th Century Fund-Task Force on U.S. Energy Policy. Bd. dirs. N.Y. Philharmonic; trustee Am. Mus. Natural History. Served to ensign USNR, 1943-46. Recipient Disting. Achievement award Offshore Tech. Conf., 1973, Disting. Engring. Grad. award U. Tex., 1970; named Chief Exec. of Year in Mining Industry, 1979. Fellow N.Y. Acad. Scis.; mem. Nat. Acad. Engring., Am. Mining Congress, Copper Devel. Assn., Am. Assn. Petroleum Geologists, Geol. Soc. Am., Internat. Copper Research Assn., AAAS, Am. Soc. Oceanography (pres. 1970-71), Am. Geophys. Union, Am. Petroleum Inst., Am. Geog. Soc., Sigma Xi, Tau Beta Pi, Sigma Gamma Epsilon, Phi Eta Sigma, Alpha Tau Omega. Episcopalian. Clubs: Links, Sky (N.Y.C.); Landmark (Stamford); Clove Valley; Round Hill Country. Home: 589 North St Greenwich CT 06830 Office: Ten Stamford Forum Stamford CT 06904

BARRY, JAMES ALBERT, JR., investment adviser; b. Arlington, Mass., Sept. 27, 1935; s. James Albert and Irene Madlin (Flynn) B.; student Burdett Coll., 1960; m. Rosemarie Clasani, Dec. 5, 1953; children—Rosemarie, Irene, James. Sales mgr. Hartford Ins. Group, Boston, 1960-69; sr. v.p. Putnam Mgmt. Co., Boston, 1969-76, also with Putnam Fund Distbrs., Inc., Boca Raton, Fla.; pres., chmn. bd. Asset Mgmt. Corp., Boca Raton, 1976—. Past trustee Coll. Fin. Planning, Denver; found. mem. Fla. Atlantic U., Boca Raton. Served with AUS, 1953-56. Certified fin. planner. Mem. Nat. Assn. Security Dealers (prin.), Internat. Assn. Fin. Planners (pres. Gold Coast chpt. 1974-77), Jr. C. of C. (v.p. Cambridge, Mass. chpt. 1968). Club: Golden Harbour (Boca Raton). Home: 531 Silver Ln Boca Raton FL 33432 Office: 1499 W Palmetto Park Rd Suite 220 Boca Raton FL 33432

BARRY, JEFFREY ALAN, investment co. exec.; b. N.Y.C., June 9, 1950; s. Herbert G. and Ruth B.; B.B.A., Pace U., 1974. Partner, Blank & Barry, Washington, 1969-71, N.Y.C., 1971—; mem. staff Deloitte Haskins & Sells, N.Y.C., 1973-76; exec. v.p., dir. Savs. Devel. Corp., Los Angeles, 1976-77, mng. dir., Greenwich, Conn., 1977—; sr. v.p., dir. City Fin. Services Co., N.Y.C., 1979—; dir. Athabasca Capital Investments Ltd., Familliant, Gallieni & Cie., The Landmark Cos., Inc., Tunlaw Realty Holdings Ltd., Cortlandt Oil & Gas Corp., Metaconta Internat. Fin. N.V., Metalics Explorations & Mining Co. Ltd., Oasis Energy Resources, Inc., Houston. Mem. Regional Plan Assn. Clubs: Triborough, Univ.; Landmark (Stamford). Home: PO Box 87 Greenwich CT 06830 Office: 341 Madison Ave 3d Fl New York NY 10017

BARRY, ROBERT RAYMOND, bus. exec., former congressman; b. Omaha, May 15, 1915; s. Ralph and Ethel (Thomas) B.; student Hamilton Coll., 1933-36, Dartmouth Coll., 1936-37, Sch. Finance, N.Y. U., 1938, Law Sch., 1946-47; m. Anne Rogers Benjamin, July 19, 1945; children—Cynthia Herndon Bidwell, Henry Huttleston Rogers. Investment banker Kidder Peabody & Co., 1937-38; with Mfrs. Trust Co., 1938-40; mgr. exec. Bendix Aviation Corp., 1940-44; asst. to pres. Yale & Towne Mfg. Co., 1945-50; pres. Plumas Mining Co., 1945-50, Calicopia Corp., 1965—; dir. Vanderbilt Growth Fund, Vanderbilt Income Fund, Pegasus Income and Capital Fund; engaged in ranching, Coachella, Calif., in mining, Quincy, Calif.; mem. 86th-87th Congresses, 27th Dist. N.Y., mem. 88th Congress 25th Dist. N.Y., mem. coms. govt. ops., 1959-61, post office and civil service, 1959-65, fgn. affairs, 1961-65. Mem. Nat. council Boy Scouts Am.; active campaign Dewey for dist. atty., 1937, Willkie presdl. campaign; mem. N.Y. Republican County Com., 1945; statistician for Dewey, Rep. Nat. Conv., mem. Rep. Nat. Campaign Com., Washington, 1948; personal staff Eisenhower campaign tour, Denver, Chgo., 1952; chmn. finance com. N.Y. State Congl. Campaign Com., Citizens for Eisenhower, 1954; chmn. Yonkers Citizens Eisenhower Com., 1956; U.S. del. NATO Parliamentarian Conf., 1959, 60, UNESCO Conf., 1963; mem. Nixon-Agnew Nat. Staff; nat. vice chmn. Congressional Speaker Reform Com. Bd. dirs. Greater N.Y. bd. YMCA; active community, civic affairs. Mem. Acad. Polit. Sci., Internat. Seaman's Union, Sierra Club, Alpha Delta Phi. Presbyterian. Clubs: Eldorado Country, Thunderbird Country (Palm Springs, Calif.); St. Andrews Golf (Hastings, N.Y.); Econ., Blue Hill Troupe, Dartmouth Coll., Met. (N.Y.C.); Met., Capitol Hill (Washington). Home: 3001 Normanstone Dr NW Washington DC 20008 Office: 8500 Wilshire Blvd Beverly Hills CA 90211

BARSALONA, FRANK, theatrical agy. exec.; b. S.I., N.Y., Mar. 31, 1938; s. Peter and Mary (Rotunno) B.; student Wagner Coll., 1955-58, Herbert Berghof Sch., 1959-60; m. June Harris, Sept. 1, 1966. Singer, actor; agt. Gen. Artists Corp., N.Y.C., 1960-64; founder, pres. Premier Talent Agy., N.Y.C., 1964—; lectr. in field. Bd. govs. T.J. Martell Leukemia Found., 1975—; pres. Phila. Fury, 1978—. Named Talent Agt. of Yr., Billboard Pubs., 1976, 77. Office: 3 E 54th St New York NY 10022

BARSANTI, ROBERT RANDOLPH, ins. co. exec.; b. San Francisco, Mar. 25, 1932; s. John G. and Lilias E. (Harrison) B.; student Stanford U., 1950-52; m. Diane Diehl, Nov. 15, 1952; children—Candace D., Robert G., Valerie K. Loss control engr. Continental Ins. Cos., San Francisco and Los Angeles, 1952-59, spl. agt., Los Angeles and San Diego, 1959-65, br. prodn. mgr., 1965-68, comml. underwriting mgr., 1968-71, br. mgr., Phoenix, 1971-75, asst. sec., personal lines underwriting officer, San Francisco, 1975-78, sec., personal lines officer, Chgo., 1978-79, asst. v.p. Mid-Western underwriting and prodn., 1979-80, v.p. and regional mgr., Dallas, 1980—; mem. adv. com. Nat. Automobile Theft Bur., 1977-78; mem. governing bd. Western Auto Ins. Plans, 1975-78. Pres., Van Nuys (Calif.) Sch. Bd., 1969-71. Cert. Ins. Inst. Am. Office: 1810 Commerce St Dallas TX 75201

BARSHAY, STANLEY FREDERICK, pharm. and consumer products co. exec.; b. N.Y.C., Sept. 8, 1939; s. Julius and Sadie B.; B.S., Long Island U., 1960; student N.Y.U., 1962-65; m. Ilene Hally Juliber, June 9, 1963; children—Lawrence Neal, Scott Allan, Melissa Hope. Acct., Rosenblum, Zwicker C.P.A.'s, N.Y.C., 1960-64; adminstrv. asst. Boyle-Midway div. Am. Home Products Corp., N.Y.C., 1964-66, product mgr., 1966-67, asst. to pres., 1967-69, group product mgr., 1969-71, v.p. mktg., 1971-72, pres., from 1972; v.p. Am. Home Products Corp., from 1975, also mem. ops. com.; pres. Whitehall Labs. div. Am. Home Products Corp., from 1978. Served with USN. Meadowbrook Nat. Bank Scholar; recipient Outstanding Acctg. Student award. Mem. Proprietary Assn., Old Westbury Homeowners Assn., Residents Assn. of Old Westbury. Club: Yale. Office: 685 Third Ave New York NY 10017

BARTEK, VICTORIA JEAN (VEE JAY), engr.; b. Pitts., Aug. 14, 1945; d. Elmer and Victoria (Mroz) B.; student U. Pitts., nights 1974-77. With G.C. Murphy Co., Pitts., 1961-64; gen. clk. Bell Telephone, Pitts., 1964-67, staff aide, 1967-68, tech. asst., 1968-69, engring. technician, 1969-70, engring. asso., 1970-78, engr., Phila., 1978-79, Pitts., 1979—. Mem. Future Pioneers Am. Democrat. Roman Catholic. Office: 25 W Mall Plaza Carnegie PA 15106

BARTELSTONE, JAY LARRY, credit card co. exec.; b. Bridgeport, Conn., July 8, 1943; s. Maurice and Minerva (Peffer) B.; B.A. in Polit. Sci., U. Conn., 1964; M.B.A. in Mktg., Fordham U., 1970; m. Helen Einhorn, Aug. 20, 1965; children—Alyse, David. Asst. product mgr., br. sales mgr. data services div. ITT, N.Y.C., 1968-73; mktg. mgr. Docutel Corp., Dallas, 1973-74; mktg. dir. card products div. Citicorp, N.Y.C., 1974-76; v.p., ops. head, area dir. N.Y. banking div. Citibank, N.Y.C., 1976-78; v.p. internat. planning and devel., product planning and devel., Carte Blanche Corp., Los Angeles, 1978—. Served with USAR, 1960-61. Mem. N.Y. C. of C., Fifth Ave. Assn., U. Conn. Alumni Assn., Fordham Alumni Assn.

BARTH, CHRISTINE LEEMARIE, sales cons.; b. Detroit, Aug. 28, 1946; d. Stanley and Stella Mary (Koziara) Woloszyn; m. Duane D. Barth, Jan. 24, 1970; children—Michael, James, Jeffrey and John (triplets), Shawn, Nichall. Histology technician Meadville (Pa.) City Hosp., 1966-68; auditor Leamington Hotel, Mpls., 1968-69; v.p. Barth Devel. Corp., Burnsville, Minn., 1970-80; sales cons. Christian Builders, Inc., Rogers, Minn., 1980—. Mem. Minn. State Assn. Realtors, Dakota County Bd. Realtors. Club: Minnetonka Christian Women's. Home: 375 Lakeview Ave Tonka Bay MN 55331

BARTH, ERNEST, chem. co. exec.; b. Vienna, Austria, Feb. 17, 1926; s. Jacob and Regina (Hecht) B.; m. Rita Spiegel, Dec. 30, 1951; 1 dau., Karen Nina. Pres., Continental Fertilizer Corp., N.Y.C., also v.p. Continental Ore Corp., 1953-72; pres. Agrico Internat., Inc., Tulsa and N.Y.C., 1972-73; pres. Beker Internat. Corp., Greenwich, Conn., also sr. v.p. Beker Industries, 1973-75; v.p. Philipp Bros./Engelhard Minerals & Chem. Corp., N.Y.C., 1975—; sr. v.p. Beker Industries Corp., Greenwich, 1977—; pres., dir. Superfos Am., Inc., Greenwich, 1979—; dir. Mineral GMBH, Hamburg, Germany, Minex Corp. subs., Greenwich, 1978—; dir. affiliated cos. Mem. White House Food for Peace Council, 1962; co-chmn. U.S. Indsl. Mission to Korea, 1962. Home: 25 Lindsay Dr Greenwich CT 06830 Office: 35 Mason St Greenwich CT 06830

BARTH, NIKOLAUS STEPHEN, acct.; b. Switzerland, Sept. 21, 1943; came to U.S., 1955, naturalized, 1962; s. Stephan L. and Irene E.B.; B.A., St. Michael's Coll., 1966; m. Louise Bourgie, July 3, 1965; children—Nicholas, Natalie Andrew. Account exec. Burroughs Corp., 1968-70, Victor Bus. Products, 1977-78; comptroller Secant Constrn., Stowe, Vt., 1967-68, Fanny Allen Hosp., Winooski, Vt., 1965-67; pres. Delphi Systems, Inc., Orlando, Fla., 1978—. Republican. Roman Catholic. Club: Sertoma. Office: 831 N Mills Ave Orlando FL 32803

BARTH, RALPH THOMAS, indsl. control co. exec.; b. Pitts., Apr. 3, 1935; s. Ralph John and Leoba M. (Hoebler) B.; B.S., Duquesne U., 1957; M.S., Carnegie Mellon U., 1967; children—Gregory T., Rebecca Suzanne. Sr. research engr. Gulf Oil Co., Pitts., 1957-67; sr. staff engr. Westinghouse Electric Co., Pitts., 1967-68; cons. Control Data Corp., Pitts., 1969-70; v.p. mktg. Metromation Inc., Princeton, N.J., 1971-75, pres., 1975-79, chmn. bd., 1975-79, pres. Process Analyzers Inc. subs., 1975-79; pres. Hitec, San Jose, Calif., 1979—. Pres., O'Hara Civic Assn., 1968-69. Mem. Am. Inst. Chem. Engrs., Assn. Computing Machinery. Club: Almaden Golf and Country. Contbr. articles to profl. publs. Home: 6880 Hampton Dr San Jose CA 95120 Office: 1109 Silver Oak Ct San Jose CA 95120

BARTH, VERNON CHARLES, marine service co. exec.; b. St. Louis, Dec. 21, 1920; s. Charles A. and Ottilia M. (Ripplinger) B.; B.B.A., Washington U., 1948; student U. Mo., 1940-41; M.E., Okla. U., 1943; m. Virginia Viola Franz, July 10, 1944; children—Roger, Cheryl, Janice. Asst. to v.p. installment loan dept. Miss. Valley Trust, St. Louis, 1947-48; asst. to Lubricants mgr. Shell Oil Co., St. Louis, 1948-49, indsl. rep., 1950-55, lubrication engr., 1956-60, mgr. inland waterways, 1960-74; with Ory Bros. Marine Service of Am., Inc., Hartford, Ill., 1974—, v.p. sales/public relations/adminstrn., 1974-78, sr. v.p., 1979—. Trustee, Forest Haven Grantwood Village, 1958-62, bldg. commr., 1958-59, st. and sewer commr., 1960-62, mayor, 1962-64. Served with U.S. Army, 1942-46. Decorated Purple Heart, Bronze Star. Mem. Nat. River Acad., U.S. Mcht. Marine Acad. Alumni Assn. Republican. Clubs: St. Louis Propellor, E. Side Indsl. River Men's Assn. (dir. 1970-80 pres. 1976-77, chmn. bd. 1978-79). Office: Foot of Hawthorne St Hartford IL 62048

BARTHELMES, NED KELTON, stock broker; b. Circleville, Ohio, Oct. 22, 1927; s. Arthur and Mary Bernice (Riffel) B.; B.S. in Bus. Adminstrn., Ohio State U., 1950; m. Marjorie Jane Livezey, May 23, 1953; children—Brooke Ann, Richard Thomas. Stock broker Ohio Co., Columbus, 1953-58; pres. First Columbus Corp., stock brokers and investment bankers, 1958—; pres., dir. Ohio Financial Corp., Columbus, 1960—; trustee, chmn. Am. Guardian Financial, Republic Financial; dir. Nat. Foods, Midwest Capital Corp., Lancaster Colony Corp., United Capital Corp., Conditioned Power Corp., Liebert Corp., Mid-Continent Capital Corp., Medex, Inc., 1st Nat. Equity Corp., Union Nat. Corp., Franklin Nat. Corp., Midwest Nat. Corp., Gen. Nat. Corp., 1st Columbus Realty Corp., Court Realty Co. (all Columbus). Served with Adj. Gen.'s Dept., AUS, 1945-47. Former mem. Am., N.Y., Midwest stock exchanges; mem. Nat. Assn. Securities Dealers (past vice chmn. dist. bd. govs.), Investment Bankers Assn. (exec. com.), Investment Dealers Ohio (pres. 1973), Nat. Stock Traders Assn., Young Pres. Orgn. (pres. 1971), Nat. Investment Bankers (pres. 1972), Columbus Jr. (pres. 1956), Ohio Jr. (trustee 1957-58), Columbus Area (dir. 1956, named an outstanding young man of Columbus, 1962) chambers commerce, Newcomen Soc., Phi Delta Theta. Kiwanian. Clubs: Executives, Stock and Bond, Columbus, Scioto Country (Columbus); Crystal Downs Country (Frankfort, Mich.). Home: 1000 Urlin Ave Columbus OH 43212 Office: 1241 Dublin Rd Columbus OH 43215

BARTHOLDI, THEODORE GEORGE, cons. co. exec.; b. Duluth, Minn., Feb. 7, 1932; s. Theodore G. and D. B.; B.A. cum laude, U. Minn., 1955; m. Dorothy J. Jurmu, Dec. 21, 1951; children—Carol, Kathryn, Lizette, Theodore George. With IBM Corp., 1957-69; v.p., gen. mgr. DPF, Inc., N.Y.C., 1969-70; v.p. Photon, Inc., Wilmington, Mass., 1970-71; founder, 1971, since pres. Bartholdi & Co., mgmt. cons., Wellesley, Mass.; dir. GRI Computer Co. Served with USAF, 1950-51. Mem. Assn. Exec. Recruiting Cons., U.S., Boston chambers commerce. Club: Wellesley Country. Office: 65 William St Wellesley MA 02181

BARTHOLOMAY, WILLIAM CONRAD, ins. brokerage exec.; b. Evanston, Ill., Aug. 11, 1928; s. Henry and Virginia (Graves) B.; student Oberlin Coll., 1946-49, Northwestern U., 1949-50; B.A., Lake Forest Coll., 1955; children—Virginia T., William T., Jamie C., Elizabeth S., Sara C. Partner, Bartholomay Bros., Bartholomay & Clarkson, 1951-63; v.p. Bartholomay & Clarkson div. Alexander & Alexander, 1963-65; pres. Olson & Bartholomay, Chgo. and Atlanta, 1965-69; sr. v.p. Frank B. Hall & Co., Inc., N.Y.C. and Chgo., 1969-72, pres., 1973—, vice-chmn. bd., 1974—, chmn. exec. com., 1978—, dir., 1969—; dir. Turner Broadcasting Systems, Inc., Nat. Security Bank Chgo., Xcor Corp., Xcor Internat., N.W. Fin. Corp., Eastman & Beaudine, Inc.; chmn. bd. Atlanta Nat. Baseball Club, Inc. Commr., Chgo. Park Dist., 1980—. Served with USNR, 1951-54. Mem. Nat. Assn. Life Underwriters, Chief Execs. Forum, Million Dollar Round Table, Chgo. Assn. Life Underwriters. Clubs: Chicago, Racquet, Saddle & Cycle, Univ., Commonwealth, Econ., Casino, Met. Onwentsia, Shore Acres (Chgo.); Links, The Brook, Dougles, Deepdale, Regency Whist, Econ., Racquet and Tennis (N.Y.C.); Peachtree, Piedmont Driving, Commerce, Country (Atlanta). Home: 180 E Pearson St Chicago IL 60611 also Hotel Carlyle 35 E 76th St New York NY 10021 Office: 230 W Monroe St Chicago IL 60606 also 261 Madison Ave New York NY 10016

BARTHOLOMEW, ARTHUR PECK, JR., accountant; b. Rochester, N.Y., Nov. 20, 1918; s. Arthur Peck and Abbie West (Dawson) B.; A.B., U. Mich., 1939, M.B.A., 1940; m. Mary Elizabeth Meyer, Oct. 4, 1941; children—Susan Bartholomew Hall, Arthur Peck, James M., Virginia L. With Ernst & Whinney, 1940-79, successivley jr. acct., partner charge Eastern dist., Detroit, 1940-64, nat. office, Cleve., 1964-65, N.Y. office, 1965-79, also mem. mng. com.; dir. E.F. MacDonald Co.; instr. acctg. U. Mich., 1940, George Washington U., 1945-46; mem. Mich Gov.'s Task Force for Expenditure Mgmt., 1963-64, The Conf. Bd. Bd. dirs. Detroit League for Handicapped, 1952-64; treas. Grosse Pointe War Meml. Assn., 1961; mem. exec. bd. Greater N.Y. council Boy Scouts Am. Served from pvt. to capt., AUS, 1942-46. Mem. Nat. Assn. Accountants (pres. Detroit 1963-64, nat. v.p. 1968-69, pres. 1974-75), Mich., N.Y. socs. C.P.A.'s, Am. Inst. C.P.A.'s, Phi Beta Kappa, Phi Kappa Phi, Beta Gamma Sigma, Phi Eta Sigma, Beta Alpha Psi, Phi Kappa Sigma. Republican. Presbyn. Clubs: Country (Detroit); Greenwich Country (gov.); Wall St. (gov., pres. 1976-78), Indian Harbor Yacht, Home: 103 Doubling Rd Greenwich CT 06830 Office: Citicorp Center 153 E 53d St New York NY 10022

BARTHOLOMEW, TRACY, II, geol. economist; b. Pitts., June 17, 1952; s. George Anderson and Nancy Davis (Large) B.; B.A. in Econs., Ohio Wesleyan U., 1975; m. Rebecca Joan Phillips, Apr. 5, 1975. Geol. asst. Huntley & Huntley, Inc., Pitts., 1973-75, exec. asst. to pres., 1975-79, asst. sec., 1975—, v.p. ops., 1979—. Deacon, Third Presbyn. Ch., Pitts., 1976—, rec. sec., 1978—. Mem. Am. Mgmt. Assn., Soc. for Advancement of Mgmt., Soc. Petroleum Engrs., Am. Assn. Petroleum Geologists, Ind. Oil and Gas Assn. W.Va., Am. Assn. Petroleum Landmen, Pitts. Geol. Soc., Engrs. Soc. Western Pa., Pa. Oil, Gas and Minerals Assn., Ohio Oil and Gas Assn., Internat. Oil Scouts Assn. Republican (dist. chmn. 1972 presdl. election). Clubs: Univ., Longue Vue, Laurel River. Home: 505 Kerrwood Rd Pittsburgh PA 15215 Office: 1700 Benedum-Trees Bldg 221 4th Ave Pittsburgh PA 15222

BARTH-WEHRENALP, GERHARD, chem. co. exec.; b. Teplitz-Schoenau, Czechoslovakia, Oct. 19, 1920; s. Burghard and Kaethe (Bechert) von B. W.; came to U.S., 1951, naturalized, 1957; Ph.D. max. cum laude, U. Innsbruck (Austria), 1949; m. Waltraut von Weber, Apr. 8, 1952; children—Christian, Gerald, Markus. Chemist, Inst. Beverage Tech., Bad Homburg, Germany, 1943-44, Breganzia Food Corp., Bregenz, Austria, 1945-46; lectr., asst. U. Innsbruck, 1949-51; research asso. Temple U., 1951-52; asst. prof. LaSalle Coll., Phila., 1952-54; research chemist Pennwalt Corp., Phila., 1953-55, group leader, 1955-57, dir. inorganic research, 1957-63, mgr. research, 1963-70, asst. to chmn. bd., 1970-71, v.p., tech. dir., 1971-74, sr. v.p., tech. dir., 1974—; Austrian rep. to Younger Chemists Internat. Project, Tech. Assistance Program, 1951; chmn. phosphorus-nitrogen chemistry symposium Gordon Research Conf., 1960. Mem. council of pres.'s assos. LaSalle Coll., Phila.; bd. dirs. U.S.

Com. for WHO. Mem. Am. Chem. Soc., Soc. Chem. Industry, Am. Com. Econ. Edn., Am. Rocket Soc. (pres. Phila. sect. 1958). Editorial bd. Research Mgmt. Contbr. articles to profl. jours. Holder U.S., Canadian, Brit., German, French, Italian patents. Office: Pennwalt Tech Center 900 First Ave King of Prussia PA 19406

BARTINE, ALLEN RUSSELL, mfg. co. exec.; b. Marshalltown, Iowa, Apr. 2, 1945; s. Edwin Willard and Orpha L. (Froning) B.; B.S., Iowa State U., 1967; M.B.A., Ind. U., 1969; m. Margot Claire Friese, June 8, 1968; children—Todd Allen, Erin Marie. Sr. auditor, cons. Touche Ross & Co., Chgo., 1969-74; corp. controller Am. Tara Corp., Chgo., 1974-75, sec.-treas., 1975-77, v.p. fin., sec.-treas., pension plan adminstr., 1978—. Mem. Am. Inst. C.P.A.'s, Ill. Soc. C.P.A.'s, Internat. Bus. Forms Inst., Nat. Bus. Forms Assn., Printing Industry Am., Chgo. West Central Assn. (mem. urban redevel. com. 1978, v.p. and dir. 1981). Republican. Presbyterian. Clubs: Lake Bluff Bath and Tennis, Mid-Town Racquet. Office: 1311 W Lake St Chicago IL 60607

BARTLETT, BRUCE L., mfg. co. exec.; b. Denver, July 14, 1944; s. Edgar E. and Genevieve J. Bartlett; B.A., Adams State Coll., 1967; M.A., U. Colo., 1971; m. Joyce L. Klein, Mar. 13, 1976; children—Erin A., Christine M., Jason E. Founder, exec. dir. Community Group Homes, Denver, 1971-75; grant adminstr. Com. for Econ. Devel., City of Tucson, 1975-76; city mgr. City of Bethel (Alaska), 1976-77; dir. NW Econ. Devel. Center, Seattle, 1977-78; v.p. Roberge Sheet Metal Inc., Seattle, 1978-79, owner, pres., 1979—; mem. adj. faculty U. Puget Sound. Bd. dirs. King County (Wash.) Assn. for Retarded Citizens, Children's Home Soc. Wash. Mem. Soc. Mfg. Engrs., Internat. City Mgmt. Assn. Republican. Roman Catholic. Home: 16424 164th Ave Woodinville WA 98072 Office: 2922 Western Ave Seattle WA 98121

BARTLETT, HALL, motion picture producer, dir.; b. Kansas City, Mo., Nov. 27, 1925; s. Paul Dana and Alice (Hiestand) B.; grad. Yale, 1942; m. Lupita Ferrer, Apr. 30, 1977; children—Cathy, Laurie. Propr., Hall Bartlett Prodn., Inc., Los Angeles, 1952—; producer films Navajo, 1952, Crazylegs, 1953; producer-dir. Unchained, 1954, All The Young Men, 1960, Drango, 1956, Zero Hour, 1957, The Caretakers, 1964, Sol Madrid, 1968, Changes, 1969, The Sandpit Generals, 1972; producer, dir. Jonathan Livingston Seqgull, Cleo Laine Special, The Search of Zubin Mehta, The Children of Sanchez, Come Back to Me, 1981. Bd. dirs. Hollywood Greek Theatre. Patron Music Center. Served with USNR, 1942-46. Recipient 11 Acad. award nominations, Film Festival awards from Cannes, 1961, 63, Venice, 1959, 65, Edinburgh, 1952, San Sebastian, 1969, Grand prize Internat. Moscow Film Festival, 1971; Motion Picture of Year award Nat. Conf. Christians and Jews, 1955, Fgn. Press awards. Mem. Motion Picture Acad. Arts and Scis., Acad. Television Arts and Scis., Friends of Library, Cinema Circulus, Phi Beta Kappa. Presbyterian. Club: Bel-Air Country (Los Angeles). Home: 861 Stone Canyon Rd Los Angeles CA 90024 Office: 9200 Sunset Blvd Los Angeles CA 90069

BARTLETT, THOMAS EDWARD, research exec.; b. Tulsa, Sept. 3, 1920; s. Michael Leo and Elizabeth (Stadden) B.; B.A., U. Okla., 1942; M.S., Columbia U., 1947; postgrad. Purdue U., 1957-59, U. Fla., 1965, Ariz. State U., 1966. Engr., Montgomery Ward & Co., 1947-48; chief indsl. engr. Bank of Am., 1948-50; mem. tech. staff Hughes Research and Devel., 1950-54, Ramo-Wooldridge, 1954; prof. Purdue U., 1955-63; mem. teaching staff Calif. State Poly. Coll., 1964-65; ops. research cons., 1965-67; dir. ops. research Lester Gorsline Assos., 1967-68; pres., chmn. bd. dirs. Wyvern Research Assos., Inc., Mill Valley, Calif., 1968—; cons. Truck Ads, Inc. Served with CIC, U.S. Army, 1942-46. Registered profl. engr., Calif. Mem. Am. Inst. Indsl. Engrs., Inst. Mgmt. Scis., Ops. Research Soc. Am., Fedn. Am. Scientists, Am. Soc. Info. Scis., AAAS, Am. Soc. Personnel Adminstrn., Sigma Xi, Phi Kappa Phi, Phi Kappa Psi. Home: 1 Lincoln Dr Sausalito CA 94965 Office: 2670 Bridgeway Sausalito CA 94965

BARTLETT-GOODRICH, HELEN ELIZABETH (NESBIT), engrng. co. exec.; b. Lowry City, Mo., May 26, 1921; d. Charles Dwight and Beulah E. (Dawson) Nesbit; student Sch. Bus. Adminstrn., U. Mo., 1954-56; m. Harvey S. Bartlett, Aug. 24, 1958 (dec. July 1972); m. 2d, James Lynn Goodrich, PE, July 28, 1977. Real estate broker Bissman Real Estate & Ins. Co., Springfield, Mo., 1950-57; legal sec. firm Lincoln, Lincoln, Haseltine, Forehand & Springer, Springfield, Mo., 1957-58; exec. sec. Pullara, Bowen & Watson, architects-engrs., Tampa, Fla., 1958-59; pvt. sec. Seaborn Collins Real Estate & Ins. Co., Las Cruces, N.Mex., 1960-61; legal sec. Darden, Caffey & Mechem, attys., Las Cruces, 1961-66; legal sec. to atty., E. Forrest Sanders, Las Cruces, 1966-67; legal sec. firm Galvan, Lenko, Triviz, Las Cruces, 1968; chief fiscal officer Las Cruces Urban Renewal Agy., 1968-73; partner Goodrich-Bartlett & Assos., Las Cruces, 1973—. Mem. Am. Inst. Aeros. and Astronautics (sec. Inland Missile Range sect. 1973—, Nat. Spl. Event award 1975); Nat. Assn. Legal Secs. (pres. N.Mex. chpt. 1968-69); Nat. Assn. Ind. Ins. Agts., Am. Def. Preparedness Assn. (life). Presbyterian. Co-author: Energy Sufficiency, 1975; collaborated with cons. Engr. James L. Goodrich on conduct of major engrng.-econ. feasibility studies and preparation for reports on numerous projects, programs, plans, including: Progress Village, Inc., a Planned com., Manatee River Water Supply and Conservation Program, Manhattan Mutual Apt. Project, Palmetto Sanitary Sewerage System, (all in Fla. 1958-59); also design, organization, conduct and compilation of proceedings on SKYLAB-ERTS Conf., Albuquerque, 1973, Energy Consumers' Contribution to Problems of the Energy Crisis, N.Mex. State U. and U. Tex. at El Paso, 1973, assessments of U.S. Pres.'s Energy Messages to Congress, 1974, 77. Home: 1105 Gardner St Las Cruces NM 88001 Office: Goodrich Bartlett & Associates 1105 Gardner Las Cruces NM 88001

BARTLING, JUDD QUENTON, physicist, sci.-tech. and market research co. exec.; b. Muncie, Ind., July 24, 1936; s. Hubert George and Hildagarde (Good) B.; B.A., U. Calif., 1959, Ph.D., 1969; M.S., Purdue U., 1964; m. Madeline Levesque, June 9, 1973; stepchildren—Mary Johnson, Michael Johnson. Research asso. U. Calif., 1965-69; cons. solid state physics, Quantum electronics-electro-magnetics, Riverside, Calif., 1969—; pres. Azak Corp., Chatsworth, Calif., 1971—. NSF fellow Inst. in Quantum Chemistry and Biology, Gainsville, Fla., 1969. Mem. Am. Phys. Soc. Research in bus., solid state physics, radar, electro-magnetics and quantum physics. Office: 9738 Nevada St Chatsworth CA 91311

BARTOLOTTA, PETER LOUIS, telephone co. ofcl.; b. Bklyn., Apr. 11, 1947; s. Louis Peter and Ida Rita (Melito) B.; A.A., Nassau Coll., 1968; m. Deirdre Elizabeth Giglio, Feb. 13, 1971; children—Heather Louise, Derek Peter, Adam George. Sales rep. SCM, L.I., 1970-71; mfg. systems specialist Xerox Corp., L.I., 1971-74; nat. mktg. mgr. corr., electronic mail systems Bowne Time Sharing Co., N.Y.C., 1974-78; mktg. mgr. AT&T, Basking Ridge, N.J., 1978—. Scout master Nassau County council Boy Scouts Am. Mem. Soc. Consumer Affairs Profls. in Bus., Electronic Mail Users Assn. (charter mem.), Associated Data Processing Service Orgns., Am. Mgmt. Assn., Sales Exec. Club (N.Y.). Episcopalian. Home: 25 Williamson Ln Chester NJ 07930 Office: 295 N Maple Ave Basking Ridge NJ 07920

BARTON, BLAYNEY JONES, govt. ofcl.; b. Beaver City, Utah, Oct. 22, 1910; s. Ray Hunter and Emma Jay (Jones) B.; student U. Utah, 1929-30, 33; LL.B., George Washington U., 1938; m. Hazel Lavina Whitaker, July 31, 1937; 1 son, John Whitaker. Admitted to Utah bar, 1938, D.C. bar, 1938, U.S. Supreme Ct. bar, 1964; spl. agt. FBI, N.Y., Va., Nebr., Calif., Utah, 1940-44; dir. indsl. and pub. relations Bayer Aspirin, Winthrop-Stearns Pharm. Co., Sterling-Winthrop Research Inst., Rensselaer, N.Y., 1945-51; dir. employee relations M & M Woodworking Co., Portland, Oreg., 1952-53; dir. labor relations Am. Stores Co. (name changed to Acme Markets, Inc.), Phila., 1954-56, v.p. labor relations, 1957-68; acting dir. fed. labor-mgmt. relations Dept. Labor, Washington, 1968—. Nat. committeeman Boy Scouts Am., 1950-51, commr. Ft. Orange council, Albany, N.Y., 1948-51; asst. dir. Albany Community Chest. 1949-51; v.p. YMCA, 1950-51. Mem. panel Am. Arbitration Assn. Mem. Ch. of Jesus Christ Latterday Saints. Kiwanian, Rotarian. Club: Union League (Phila.). Home: PO Box 99 Berwyn PA 19312 Office: US Dept of Labor 14th St and Constitution Ave NW Washington DC 20210

BARTON, GEORGE ALAN, bank exec.; b. Chgo., Oct. 14, 1934; s. George K. and Kazimiera (Wypysynski) Cizinauskas; B.S. in Bus. Adminstrn. cum laude, U. N.H., 1964; postgrad. Tuck Sch. Bus., Dartmouth, 1965; m. Arlene Anne Buonanno, June 12, 1960; children—George David, Alan David. Methods analyst Douglas Aircraft Co., Long Beach, Calif., 1957; field engr. B-J Electronics, Santa Ana, Calif., 1957; sr. elec. engr. Raytheon Co., Oxnard, Calif. and Andover, Mass., 1958-60; trainee Worcester (Mass.) County Nat. Bank, 1965-67, asst. research and devel. officer, 1967-69, ops. officer, 1969-70, asst. v.p., 1970-72, v.p., 1972-73, sr. v.p., 1973-78; sr. v.p. ops. Royal Trust Bank Corp. subs. Royal Trust Co. Can., Miami, Fla., 1978—; mem. transfer/distbn. com. New Eng. Automated Clearing House; pres. Worcester Clearing House Assn., bd. dirs. Worcester County Postal Customers Council. Served with USAF, 1952-57. Recipient Whittemore Sch. Bus. Mktg. award. Mem. Worcester Users Group, Worcester Econ. Club, Bank Adminstrn. Inst., Mass. Bankers Assn. (bank automation/ops. com.), Am. Mgmt. Assn. (speaker). Democrat. Roman Catholic. Club: Kiwanis (v.p.). Home: 16823 SW 79th Place Miami FL 33157 Office: Royal Trust Bank Corp Royal Trust Tower 701 SW 27th Ave Miami FL 33135

BARUCH, RALPH MAX, communications co. exec.; b. Frankfurt, Ger., Aug. 5, 1923; came to U.S., 1940, naturalized, 1948; s. Bernard and Alice B.; ed. Sorbonne, Paris; m. Jean Ursell de Mountford, June 9, 1963; children by previous marriage—Eve, Renee, Alice, Michele. Account exec. SESAC, N.Y.C., 1947-50, Dumont TV Network, N.Y.C., 1950-54; account exec. CBS, N.Y.C., 1954-57, Eastern sales mgr. CBS Films, 1957-59, dir. internat. sales CBS, 1959-61, v.p. internat. sales, 1961-67, v.p., gen. mgr. CBS Enterprises, 1967-71, group pres. CBS, 1971; pres., chief exec. officer Viacom Internat., Inc., N.Y.C., 1971-78, chmn. bd., chief exec. officer, 1979—. Bd. dirs., mem. exec. com. Internat. Rescue Com., 1975—. Mem. Internat. Radio and TV Soc. (dir.), Nat. Cable TV Assn. (past dir., sec.; chmn. rewrite com.), Acad. TV Arts and Scis. (past pres. internat. council). Clubs: City Athletic (N.Y.C.); Poor Richards (Phila.). Office: Viacom Internat 1211 Ave of Americas New York NY 10036

BARUH, MORTON GOLDMAN, liquor exec.; b. San Francisco, Mar. 15, 1923; s. Harold F. and Doris (Goldman) B.; student Marin Jr. Coll., 1940-41, San Francisco Inst. Accountancy, 1941-42; m. Marilyn Felix, Aug. 10, 1944; children—Barry F., Terye E. (Mrs. Jacob Levy), Randie (dec.). Treas., merchandising mgr. Goldman's Store, Oakland, Calif., 1946-53; v.p. Baruh Liquors, Inc., San Jose, Calif., 1953-60, exec. v.p., 1960-69, pres., 1969-70; v.p. E. Martinoni Co., San Francisco, 1954-69, chmn. bd., chief exec. officer, 1969-79; v.p. Goldman's Walnut Creek, Inc., Walnut Creek, Goldman's Alameda, Inc., Alameda, 1958-79; pres. James A. Robertson of Wash., Seattle, 1969—; chmn. bd. Am. Constrn. Assos., Menlo Park, Calif., 1962-64; treas. Goldman's Hayward, Inc., Hayward, Calif., 1952-53. Bd. dirs. Randie Lynn Baruh Research Found. for Leukemia; trustee Leukemia Soc. Am., 1980—. Served from pvt. to flight officer USAAF, 1943-45. Decorated Air medal (Army). Mem. Nat. Alcoholic Beverage Control Assn., Calif. Distilled Spirits Rectifiers Assn. (pres.). Mason. Office: care E Martinoni Co 543 Forbes Blvd San Francisco CA 94080

BARZELAY, ROSS, food co. exec.; b. Malden, Mass., Sept. 28, 1922; s. Henry and Etta (Bell) B.; B.S. in Edn., Boston U., 1946; grad. Advanced Mgmt. Program, Harvard, 1965; student Aspen (Colo.) Inst., 1971; m. Jean Barzelay, Oct. 27, 1946; children—William D., Caren A., Michael A. Mktg. exec. Van Brode Milling Co., 1946-50; with Gen. Foods Corp., 1961—, v.p., 1969-72, gen. mgr. Jell-O div., 1969-72, exec. v.p., from 1972, now pres., dir.; dir. Uniroyal; trustee Consol. Edison Co. N.Y., Inc. Bd. dirs. Jr. Achievement; trustee Boston U., Com. for Econ. Devel. Served with AUS, 1943-46, 50-52. Decorated Purple Heart, Silver Star, Bronze Star with 3 oak leaf clusters, Combat Inf. badge; Mil. Cross (Eng.). Home: 25 W Branch Rd Westport CT 06880 Office: 250 North St White Plains NY 10625

BASCH, GEORGE F., mktg. exec.; b. Vienna, Austria, Mar. 9, 1937; came to U.S., 1938, naturalized, 1943; s. Felix P. and Anne Marie (Urban) B.; B.S. in M.E., M.I.T., 1959; M.B.A., Northwestern U., 1961; m. Carole Anne Shute, Apr. 28, 1962; children—Susan, Paul. Dir. product devel. Sawyer's Inc., Chgo. and Portland, Oreg., 1962-65, GAF Corp., N.Y.C., 1965-68; pres. Consol. Mktg. Services, Inc., Denver, 1968—. Trustee Colo. Acad., 1974—, treas., 1975-77, v.p., 1977-79. Mem. Nat. Assn. Home Builders, Internat. Council Shopping Centers, Am. Land Devel. Assn. Home: 1384 Lupine Way Golden CO 80401 Office: 1825 Lawrence St Suite 466 Denver CO 80202

BASH, JAMES FRANCIS, ins. exec.; b. Indpls., Aug. 10, 1925; s. S. Douglas and Pauline C. (Beattey) B.; A.B., Butler U., 1946; J.D., Ind. U., 1949; With Standard Life Ins. Co. Ind., 1949—, pres., 1967—, chmn., 1979—, also dir., mem. exec., investment coms.; admitted to Ind. bar, 1949; sec., treas. All Funds Mgmt. Corp., 1963-66, v.p., 1966-74, pres., 1974—, also dir. Bd. dirs. Central Ind. Better Bus. Bur., 1967-73. Mem. Am., Ind. bar assns., Nat. Assn. Life Underwriters, Am. Council Life Ins. (state v.p. 1979—), Ind. Assn. Life Ins. Cos. (pres. 1979—), Ind. U. Alumni Assn. (ins. com. 1972—, exec. council 1975-78, v.p. 1980—), Sigma Chi (treas. 1973-75, v.p. 1975-77, pres. 1977-79, exec. com. 1973—). Methodist (trustee, sec. bd. 1958-73, vice chmn. 1974, chmn. 1975—). Clubs: Masons (32 deg.); Indpls. Athletic, Columbia, Meridian Hills Country. Home: 8160 N Meridian St Indianapolis IN 46260 Office: 300 E Fall Creek Blvd Indianapolis IN 46205

BASHAW, PETER GIRARD, credit and collections ofcl.; b. Two Rivers, Wis., Aug. 23, 1954; s. Alvin Lyle and Genevieve Theresa (Herzog) B.; B.B.A. in Fin. (Hamilton Good Fellowship acad. scholar), U. Wis., Oshkosh, 1976. Collection clk. Lenox Candles, Inc., Oshkosh, 1976, asst. credit mgr., 1977, credit mgr., 1978-80; credit mgr. Eaton Corp./Cutler-Hammer Products, Milw., 1980—. Mem. Nat. Assn. Credit Mgrs., YMCA. Roman Catholic. Club: Rotary (hon.). Home: 6745 N 75th St Milwaukee WI 53223 Office: 4201 N 27th St Milwaukee WI 53216

BASKETT, JOHN LESLIE, constrn co. exec.; b. Mountain View, Mo., Apr. 5, 1922; s. Charles Monroe and Mable Marguerette (Hoover) B.; B.S. in Civil Engring., Mont., State U., 1952; m. Shirley Ann Cottle, June 18, 1950; children—John Leslie, Andrea Helene. Eastern dist. mgr. spl. projects Peter Kiewit Sons Co., Omaha, 1952-65; pres., dir. Freeport Constrn. Co., Ltd., (Bahamas) 1965-70; group v.p., Willamette-Western Corp., Portland, Oreg., 1970-73; exec. v.p., dir. Reid Burton Constrn. Co., Inc., Fort Collins, Colo., 1973—. Mem. Ft. Collins Urban Renewal Authority. Served with U.S. Army, 1942-47. Mem. Freeport, Bahamas C. of C. (dir., 1968), Crestview Water Assn. (dir.), Am. Inst. Constrn., Asso. Gen. Contractors, Am. Arbitration Assn. (comml. panel). Republican. Presbyterian. Clubs: Toastmasters, Masons, Shriners, Jesters, Rotary. Patentee in field. Home: 720 Cottonwood Fort Collins CO 80521 Office: 301 E Lincoln Fort Collins CO 80521

BASS, CORNELIUS GRAHAM, business exec.; b. Latta, S.C., May 28, 1918; s. Howard H. and Sarah (Carmichael) B.: B.S. in Bus. Adminstrn., U. S.C., 1940; m. Ann Blair, May 23, 1942 (div. Jan. 6, 1976); children—Ann Blair Bass Crowder, Cornelius Graham. With Latta Cotton Co., 1940-41; asst. mgr. Dilmar Oil Co., Latta, 1941-42; mgr. Santee Oil Co., 1945-47, sec.-treas., 1947-71, gen. mgr., 1947—, v.p., 1971—; partner, gen. mgr. S & P Tire Co., Kingstree, S.C., 1949—; sec.-treas., gen. mgr. Services, Inc., Kingstree, 1950-71; pres. Warsaw Mfg. Co., Kingstree, 1958-63; pres. Bass Farms, Inc., Latta, 1963—; pres., gen. mgr. Santee Broadcasting Co., Inc., 1963-69, sec.-treas., 1972-76; sec.-treas. King's Tree Inn, Inc., 1967-70; pres. Kingstree Indsl. Corp., 1958—, T.A.B. Enterprises, Inc., 1976—, Sunrise, Inc., 1976—, Sun Up, Inc., 1976—, Airport Beverage Corp., 1976—. Chmn., Williamsburg County Bd. Edn., 1957-62. Served with AUS, World War II. Decorated Bronze Star. Mem. Kingstree C. of C. (v.p. 1956-58), S.C. Oil Jobbers Assn. (pres. 1954, 55). Lion (past pres. Kingstree), Moose (past gov. Kingstree, treas.). Clubs: Kingstree Country (pres.), Kingstree Optimist (past pres.). Home: US Hwy 52 N PO Box 567 Kingstree SC 29556

BASS, FRANK GARDNER, ins. co. exec.; b. Griffin, Ga., Jan. 28, 1946; s. Pomroy Hamlin and Addie Ruth (Gardner) B.; B.B.A., Ga. State U., 1969; m. Mary Irene Collins, Apr. 30, 1966; children—Pamela Lynn, Paula Michelle. Vice pres. Ga. Internat. Life, Atlanta, 1968-77; v.p. United Am. Ins. Co., Dallas, 1977—. C.L.U. Mem. Am. Soc. C.L.U., S.W. Ins. Assn., Ga. Claims Assn., Internat. Claim Assn., So. Claim Conf. Methodist. Home: 1921 E Collins Blvd Richardson TX 75081 Office: 2909 N Buckner Blvd Dallas TX 75221

BASS, JOSEPH DANIEL, banker; b. Bklyn., July 9, 1950; s. Harry and Betty Bass; B.B.A. in Acctg., Hofstra U., 1975; m. Marion Elizabeth Lord, Aug. 7, 1977. Sr. accountant Deloitte Haskins & Sells, Woodbury, N.Y., 1975-79; mgr. Citibank, N.A., N.Y.C., 1979—. Bd. dirs. Smithtown (N.Y.) Landmark Soc., 1977—. C.P.A., N.Y. Mem. Am. Inst. C.P.A.'s, N.Y. State Soc. C.P.A.'s, Am. Mgmt. Assn. Club: K.P. Home: 90 S Park Ave Rockville Centre NY 11570 Office: 111 Wall St New York NY 10043

BASS, LEWIS, lawyer; b. Bklyn., Oct. 22, 1947; s. Alexander and Doris Bass; B.S. in Mech. Engring., City U. N.Y., 1964-69; M.S. in Engring., U. So. Calif., 1971; J.D. cum laude, U. Santa Clara (Calif.), 1976. Safety engr. Lockheed Missiles and Space Co., Sunnyvale, Calif., 1971-76; admitted to Calif. bar, 1976; atty. firm Caputo, Liccardo, Rossi and Sturges, San Jose, 1976-78; corp. counsel Rose Mfg. Co., Englewood, Calif., 1978; individual practice, Palo Alto, 1978—; dir. Hans W. Wynholds Co.; lectr. Inst. Safety and Systems Mgmt., U. So. Calif. Registered profl. engr., Calif. Mem. Am. Bar Assn., Assn. Trial Lawyers Am., Am. Soc. Quality Control, System Safety Soc., Calif. Trial Lawyers Assn., Santa Clara County Bar Assn. Address: 3179 Bryant St Palo Alto CA 94306

BASS, PAUL ERNEST, real estate broker; b. Sauk County, Wis., July 16, 1925; s. Ernest George and Mildred Vee (McGaw) B.; student Wis. schs.; m. Mary Elizabeth Warner, Sept. 14, 1946; children—Lawrence George, John William. Engaged in farming, 1946-50; car salesman, 1950-54; sales mgr. 7-Up Bottling Co., Janesville, Wis., 1954-69; real estate broker, Janesville, 1969—; propr. Bass Realty, 1969—; cons. in field, also builder and subdivider. Recipient various sales awards. Mem. Nat. Bd. Realtors, Wis. Bd. Realtors, Janesville Bd. Realtors. Roman Catholic. Clubs: Exchange, K.C., Elks, Eagles. Office: 7 N Academy St Janesville WI 53545

BASS, STEVEN PAUL, project planner; b. Springfield, Mo., Nov. 3, 1947; s. Floyd Harold and Mary Emma (Thomlinson) B.; B.S., Pitts. State U., 1969; m. Linda Kay Campbell, Aug. 29, 1969; children—Aimee Nichole, Jocelyn Rene. Project engr. Temperature Engring., Kansas City, Mo., 1970-71; engr., asst. mgr. Natkin Service Co., Kansas City, 1971-76; regional mgr./v.p. Natkin Energy Mgmt., Dallas, 1976-79; project planner Austin Co., Kansas City, 1979—. Mem. ASHRAE, Jr. C. of C. (v.p. 1975). Republican. Baptist. Home: 10426 Hauser St Lenexa KS 66215 Office: 3100 Broadway Kansas City MO 64111

BASSETT, CONSTANCE COLT, investment co. exec.; b. Buffalo, Feb. 1, 1915; d. Henry Van Schaick and Julia Kennett (Whitaker) Colt; student Chateau Brillamont, Lausanner, Switzerland, 1928-30, Ecole Vinet, Lausanne, 1930-32; m. William B.K. Bassett, Sept. 15, 1943; children—Carroll C., Nancy L., Constance K., Julia Bassett Aronson. Sec. Free French, Radio City, N.Y.C., 1941-42; coordinator info. and Office Strategic Services, 1942-45; treas. Sterling Security Corp. and Moorland Farms of S.C., Inc., from 1954, pres., 1975-80; vice chmn. Bassett Found., Inc., 1973—. Club: Springdale Hall (Camden, S.C.). Home: Box 43 Route 3 Camden SC 29020 Office: Box 302 Pottersville NJ 07979

BASSETT, HARRY HOOD, banker; b. Flint, Mich., May 6, 1917; s. Harry Hoxie and Jessie Marie (Hood) B.; B.S., Yale, 1940; children—Harry Hood, George Rodney, Patrick Glenn; m. 2d, Florence Schust Knoll, June 22, 1958. Asst. trust officer First Nat. Bank, Palm Beach, Fla., 1940-42, chmn. bd., 1965-71, also dir.; asst. v.p. First Nat. Bank, Miami, 1947-48, dir., 1947-48, v.p., 1948-56, asst. to pres., 1951—, chmn. exec. com., dir., 1959—, pres., 1962-66, chmn. bd., 1966-76; dir. Wometco Enterprises, Eastern Airlines, Inc.; chmn. bd. S.E. Banking Corp., Inc. Mem. Orange Bowl Com. Chmn. bd. trustees emeritus U. Miami. Served as pilot Civil Coastal Patrol (anti-submarine), 1941-42; 1st lt. USAAF, 1944-46. Decorated Air medal. Mem. Fla. Bankers Assn., Assn. Res. City Bankers (dir.), Assn. Bank Holding Cos. Episcopalian. Clubs: Bath (Miami Beach); Links, River (N.Y.C.); Lyford Cay (Nassau, Bahamas); Everglades (Palm Beach, Fla.); Biscayne Bay (Fla.) Yacht; Bohemian (San Francisco); Metropolitan (Washington). Home: Coconut Grove FL Office: 100 S Biscayne Blvd Miami FL 33131

BASSIN, GILBERT, electronics co. exec.; b. N.Y.C., 1932; s. Benjamin and Rose Bassin; B.M.E., N.Y. U., 1953; m. Doreen Rosen, Dec. 25, 1961; children—Pamela, Elisabeth, William. Engr., Cornel Dubilier Electric Co., Cambridge, Mass., 1953-56; chief engr. component div. Litton Industries, Mt. Vernon, N.Y., 1956-61; owner Bassin Tech. Sales Co., Mamaroneck, N.Y., 1961—; owner, pres. Logicomp Electronics Inc., Mamaroneck, 1967—. AirTrol Corp., Mamaroneck, 1976—. Registered profl. engr., N.Y. Mem. ASME,

Nat. Electronics Distbrs. Assn., Am. Crafts Council, Pi Tau Sigma. Contbr. articles to tech. jours. Home: 52 Fayette Rd Scarsdale NY 10583 Office: 895 Mamaroneck Ave Mamaroneck NJ 10543

BAST, JOHN ALLING, nuclear engr.; b. Balt., Apr. 19, 1936; s. Louis and Evelyn Francis (Alling) B.; B.Marine Engring., SUNY Maritime Coll., Bronx, 1958; M.S. in Nuclear Engring., M.I.T., 1960; m. Georgia Ellen Doolittle, Sept. 7, 1959; children—Kenneth, Kyle, Kristian, Katherine. With Gen. Electric Co., 1965-70, 72—, mgr. reactor equipment, Schenectady, 1974-76, mgr. battery energy systems, 1976—; devel. apparatus rep. AEC, New Haven, also mgmt. cons. naval reactors program, 1970-72. Pres. bd. trustees East Glenville Community Evang. Ch., Scotia, N.Y., 1968-70; chmn. local troop com. Boy Scouts Am., 1975-79. Registered profl. engr., N.Y. State. Home: 23 Pinewood Dr Clifton Park NY 12065 Office: Gen Electric Co 1 River Rd Schenectady NY 12345

BASTARDI, ANTHONY VINCENT, mktg. exec.; b. Newark, Aug. 30, 1944; s. Anthony V. and Josephine (Gerardo) B.; B.Engring. with honors, Stevens Inst. Tech., 1966; M.S. in Indsl. and Mgmt. Engring., Columbia, 1967; m. Marilyn P. Petrozzino, June 24, 1967; children—Noelle, Anthony V. III, Matthew, Christian. Pres., chmn. bd. Mgmt. Computer Systems Corp., Florham Park, N.J., 1968-73, Am. Recycling Corp., Cedar Knolls, N.J., 1973-77; adminstrv. v.p. SmokEnders, Inc., Phillipsburg, N.J., 1977-78; v.p. mktg. Evelyn Wood Reading Dynamics, Inc., N.Y.C., 1979-80; v.p. Celentano Bros. Inc., Verona, N.J., 1980—. Mem. Tau Beta Pi, Phi Sigma Kappa. Home: 40 Polhemus Terr Whippany NJ 07981 Office: 225 Bloomfield Ave Verona NJ 07044

BASTIAN, ROYAL RICHARD, banker; b. New Orleans, July 5, 1946; s. Royal Richard and Elizabeth (Morphy) B.; B.A., U. Pa., 1969; postgrad. Stonier Grad. Sch. Banking, Rutgers U., 1972-74; m. Georgeanne Call; children—Jonathan, Matthew. Vice pres. Bank of Okla., Tulsa, 1975-77; exec. v.p. Republic Bank & Trust Co., Tulsa, 1977, pres., chief exec. officer, 1977—. Trustee Tulsa Indsl. Authority; bd. dirs. Tulsa Arts and Humanities Council. Republican. Office: Republic Bank & Trust Co PO Box 1656 Tulsa OK 74101

BATCHELOR, ANDREW JACKSON, SR., glass co. exec.; b. Sharpsburg, N.C., Jan. 30, 1931; s. Octavious T. and Luncinda A. (Stallings) B.; B.S. in Elec. Engring., N.C. State Coll., 1953; B.S. in Mgmt., Rutgers U., 1957; M.B.A. summa cum laude, Fairleigh-Dickinson U., 1960; postgrad. N.Y. U., 1962-65, Northeastern U., 1970-71, Ohio U., 1972-80; m. Gladys Mary Purchess, June 8, 1957; children—Allison Jay, Andrew Jackson. Design engr. Westinghouse Meter div., Newark, 1953-54; mgr. bus. planning ITT, N.Y.C., 1956-61; dir. advance planning Gen. Precision, Inc., Little Falls, N.J., 1961-65; asst. to group v.p. Mohasco Industries, Inc., Amsterdam, N.Y., 1965-71; v.p. adminstrn. Anchor-Hocking Corp., Lancaster, Ohio, 1971-74, corporate v.p. strategic planning and acquisitions, 1974—; electronics instr. ITT Labs., Nutley, N.J., 1957-59. Active Boy Scouts Am. Served with Signal Corps, AUS, 1954-56. Mem. World Future Soc. (life, chpt.), Planning Execs. Inst., Real Estate Assn. Columbus (dir.), Ohio Hist. Soc., U.S. Chess Fedn. (life), Eta Kappa Nu, Phi Kappa Tau. Club: Lancaster Country. Author: Ionosphere Theory and Electronics, 1956. Home: 1260 Ridgewood Way NE Lancaster OH 43130 Office: 109 N Broad St Lancaster OH 43130

BATCHO, RONALD FRANK, shirt mfg. co. exec.; b. Hackensack, N.J., Mar. 31, 1947; s. Edward Stephen and Anna (Korley) B.; A.A.S., Fashion Inst. Tech., 1967; m. Mary Lou Ohleyer, Sept. 26, 1970; children—Ronald Frank, Rebecca Louise. Indsl. engr. Can. Garment Ltd., Winnipeg, Man., 1967-68; asst. product mgr. Eastern Isles, Inc., N.Y.C., 1968-73; product mgr. Windjammer Fashions, N.Y.C., 1973-77; pres. Crewco, Inc., Cornelius, N.C., 1977—; mem. Cornelius bd. Piedmont Bank and Trust Co., Davidson, N.C., 1980—. First lt. Maywood (N.J.) First Aid Squad, 1975-77; CPR instr. Am. Heart Assn., Englewood, N.J., 1975-77. Mem. Am. Mgmt. Assn., Central Piedmont Employers Assn. Democrat. Roman Catholic. Office: Crewco Inc Hwy 115 Cornelius NC 28031

BATEMAN, DOTTYE JANE SPENCER, Realtor; b. Athens, Tex.; d. Charles Augustus and Lillie (Freeman) Spencer; student Fed. Inst., 1941-42, So. Meth. U., Dallas Coll., 1956-58; m. George Truitt Bateman, 1947 (div. Apr. 1963); children—Kelly Spencer, Bethena; m. 2d, Joseph E. Lindsley, 1968. Sec. to state senator, Tyler, Tex., 1941-42; sec. to pres. Merc. Nat. Bank, Dallas, State Fair of Tex., Dallas, 1942-48; realtor, broker, Garland, Tex., 1956—; co-partner Play-Shade Co.; appraiser Asso. Soc. Real Estate Appraiser; auctioneer, 1963—; developer Stonewall Cave, 1964—. Pres., Central Elementary Sch. PTA, 1955-56, Bussey Jr. High PTA, 1956-57; den mother Cub Scouts Am., 1957-59; chmn. Decent Lit. Com., 1956-58; chmn. PTA's council, 1958; dir. Dallas Heart Assn., 1960, local chmn., 1955-57, county chmn., 1957-60; spl. dir. Henderson County Red Cross, 1945; local chmn. March of Dimes, 1961-63; mem. Dallas Civic Opera Com., 1963-64; mem. homemaker panel Dallas Times Herald, 1955-74. Named Outstanding Tex. Jaycee-Ette Pres., 1953, hon. Garland Jay-Cee-Ette, 1956, hon. Sheriff, Dallas County, 1963; headliner Press Club Awards dinner, 1963-68. Mem. Garland, Dallas (chmn. reception com., past dir., mem. comml.-investment div., mem. make Am. better com. 1973-78, mem. beautify Tex. council 1977-78, by-laws com. 1977-78) bds. realtors, Auctioneers Assn., Internat. Real Estate Fedn., Soc. Prevention Cruelty to Animals, Dallas Women's (project chmn.), Garland (chmn. spl. services com. 1955-56) chambers commerce, Consejo Internacional De Buena Vecindad, Delphian Study Club, Eruditis Study Club, D.A.R. (Daniel McMahan chpt.). Christian Scientist. Clubs: Garland (past v.p., pres.), Tex. (past treas., ofcl. hostess) Jaycee-Ettes, Garland Fedn. Women's (past pres.), Garland Garden, Trinity Dist. Fedn. Women's (past pres.), Pub. Affairs Luncheon, Dallas Press (dir. 1973-74), chmn. house com. 1973-74, chmn. hdqrs. com. 1973-74). Home: 6313 Lyons Rd Garland TX 75043 Office: 5518 Dyer St Dallas TX 75206

BATEMAN, EDWARD LEE, fin. exec.; b. Bklyn., May 23, 1945; s. William Lee and Dana Louise (Barber) B.; student Coll. of Charleston, 1963-66, 78—; m. Karen Michele Schnekser, Aug. 14, 1965; children—Michele, Sherri, Jeffrey. With GMAC, Charleston, S.C., 1966-68; loan officer Citizens & So. Nat. Bank of S.C., Charleston, 1968; asst. mgr. CAB Fed. Credit Union, Charleston, 1968-77, gen. mgr., 1977—. Active Charleston YMCA, 1979—. Named Boss of the Yr., Flowertown Bus. and Profl. Women's Club, 1979. Mem. S.C. Credit Union League (dir. 1976—, pres. 1979—), Charleston Area Chpt. Credit Unions (sec. 1975, treas. 1976, pres. 1977-79), Credit Union Exec. Soc. Republican. Roman Catholic. Clubs: Toastmasters (treas. 1975, ednl. v.p. 1976, pres. 1977), Charleston. Home: 678 Jane Circle Charleston SC 29412 Office: PO Box 409 Charleston AFB SC 29404

BATEMAN, RAYNARD MARA, constrn. co. exec.; b. Nashville, Dec. 3, 1925; s. Norman Silver and Veda Moncrieff (Maxwell) B.; B.A.Sc. with honors, U. Toronto, 1951; m. Daphne D. Erlendson, Mar. 29, 1969; children—Lynn Raynard, Raynard Larus. Field engr. C.A. Pitts Gen. Contractors, Toronto, Ont., Can., 1951-54; field engr. Stolte Inc., San Leandro, Calif., 1954-56; estimator, chief estimator (thermal power) Bechtel Corp., San Francisco, 1956-69; mgr. cost engring., mgr. div. tech. services Los Angeles power div. Bechtel Power Corp., Norwalk, Calif., 1969—. Served with U.S. Army, 1944-46. Mem. Am. Assn. Cost Engrs., Assn. Profl. Engrs. Ont. Republican. Methodist. Home: 16252 Typhoon Ln Huntington Beach CA 92649 Office: 12400 E Imperial Hwy Norwalk CA 90650

BATEMAN, TERRY SPENCER, systems engr.; b. Spokane, Wash., Sept. 6, 1935; s. Cecil Leonard and Lolita Blackford (Spencer) B.; B.S., Stanford U., 1958; M.B.A., Harvard U., 1960. Project engr. Space Tech. Labs., Inc., San Bernardino, Calif., 1963-64; with TRW, Inc., 1964—, sr. staff engr., then project mgr., 1966-70, asst. program mgr. energy systems group, Redondo Beach, Calif., 1977-79, project mgr., 1979—; gen. mgr. Oceans '77 Conf. Treas. S. Bay Concert Singers, 1966-68, chmn. exec. com., 1970-72. Served with USAF, 1960-63. Decorated Air Force Commendation medal. Mem. Stanford U. Alumni Assn., Harvard U. Bus. Sch. Alumni Assn., Tau Beta Pi. Republican. Club: A & E Flying (pres. 1967-71) (Los Angeles). Home: 7804 Flight Ave Los Angeles CA 90045 Office: 1 Space Park Redondo Beach CA 90278

BATES, BARBARA J. NEUNER (MRS. HERMAN MARTIN BATES, JR.), town ofcl.; b. Mt. Vernon, N.Y., Apr. 8, 1927; d. John Joseph William and Elsie May (Flint) Neuner; B.A., Barnard Coll., 1947; m. Herman Martin Bates, Jr., Mar. 25, 1950; children—Roberta Jean, Herman Martin III, Jon Nicholas. Confidential clk. to supr. town Ossining (N.Y.), 1960-63; pres. BNB Assos., Briarcliff Manor, N.Y., 1963—, Upper Nyack Realty Co., Inc., Briarcliff Manor, 1966-71; receiver of taxes Town of Ossining, 1971—. Vice pres. Ossining Young Republican Club, 1958; pres. Young Women's Rep. Club Westchester County (N.Y.), 1959-60; regional committeewoman Assn. N.Y. State Young Rep. Clubs, 1960-62; mem. Westchester County Rep. Com., 1963—. Mem. Jr. League Westchester-on-Hudson, D.A.R., Hackley Sch. Mothers Assn. (pres. 1966-68), Nat. Fedn. Bus. and Profl. Women's Clubs, N.Y. State Assn. Tax Receivers and Collectors, Westchester County Assn. Receivers of Taxes (legis. liaison), R.I. Hist. Soc., Am. Soc. Notaries, Ossining Bus. and Profl. Women's Club. Club: Ossining Emblem. Congregationalist. Home: 78 Holbrook Ln Briarcliff Manor NY 10510 also RFD 2 Chepachet RI 02814 Office: Town Hall Ossining NY 10562

BATES, CHARLES WALTER, personnel exec.; b. Detroit, June 28, 1953; s. E. Frederick and Virginia Marion (Nunneley) B.; B.A. cum laude, Mich. State U., 1975, M. Labor and Indsl. Relations, 1977; postgrad. DePaul U. Law Sch., Chgo., 1979—. VISTA vol., paralegal Legal Aid Assn. Ventura County, Calif., 1975-76; substitute tchr. social studies Lansing, Holt and Okemos (Mich.) sch. systems, 1976-77; job analyst Gen. Mills, Inc., Mpls., 1977-78, plant personnel asst., Chgo., 1978-80, asst. plant personnel mgr., 1980, personnel mgr. mktg. divs., 1980—. Asst. scoutmaster Boy Scouts Am., 1971—, Eagle Scout, 1969, Scouter's Tng. award, 1979; active Nat. Eagle Scout Assn. Mem. Indsl. Relations Research Assn., Am. Soc. Personnel Adminstrn., Am. Bar Assn., Minn. Bar Assn., Mich. State U. Alumni Assn., Sierra Club, Order of Arrow, Phi Alpha Delta. Libertarian. Unitarian-Universalist. Home: 3905 Lancaster Ln #325 Plymouth MN 55441 Office: Gen Mills Inc 3 SW 9200 Wayzata Blvd Golden Valley MN 55426

BATES, EDWARD BRILL, ins. co. exec.; b. Lexington, Mo., May 14, 1919; s. Worth and Faye (Brill) B.; A.A., Wentworth Mil. Acad., 1938; B.A. in Bus. Adminstrn., U. Chgo., 1940; m. Mary Louise Van Sickle, May 11, 1946; children—Lynn Louise (Mrs. Edward W. Russell, III), Stephen Worth. With Conn. Mut. Life Ins. Co., 1946—, agt., gen. agt., Kansas City, Mo., gen. agt., Los Angeles, 2d agy. v.p., 1960-61, v.p., 1961-62, exec. v.p., 1962-67, pres., 1967—, chmn., chief exec. officer, 1977—, dir., 1962—; trustee N.E. Utilities; dir. Conn. Bank and Trust Co., Heublein, Inc., Stanley Works. Bd. regents U. Hartford. C.L.U. Mem. Am. Coll. Life Underwriters (trustee). Clubs: Country of Fla. (Delray Beach); Hartford Golf (West Hartford, Conn.); Hartford (Conn.). Home: 46 Ironwood Rd West Hartford CT 06117 Office: 140 Garden St Hartford CT 06115

BATES, LEWIE LANHAM, JR., rehab. equipment co. exec.; b. Greenville, S.C., Feb. 22, 1930; s. Lewie Lanham and Annie Mae (Rogers) B.; B.S. in Elec. Engring., Clemson U., 1951; m. Helen Virginia Tollison, June 6, 1951; children—Lewie Lanham III, Elizabeth Ann. Staff engr. Gen. Electric Co., Syracuse, N.Y., 1951; mgr. Byrum & Bates, Greenville, 1953-54; pres. AARO Med. Service, Greenville, S.C., 1954—, treas., dir.; treas., dir. Med. Equipment Distbrs. Dir., treas. Cancer Soc. Greenville; dir. Sr. Action Council; med. equipment adv. Easter Seal Soc., Muscular Dystrophy Assn., Multiple Sclerosis Soc. Served to 1st. lt. Signal Corps U.S. Army, 1951-53. Named Man of Yr., Rental Service Assn., 1962; recipient service cert. Muscular Dystrophy Assn., 1973. Mem. Rehab. Engring. Soc. N.Am. (charter), Am. Congress Rehab. Medicine (asso.), Nat. Affiliation of Durable Med. Equipment Cos. (dir.). Republican. Methodist. Home: 1047 Parkins Mill Rd Greenville SC 29607 Office: 1010 Laurens Rd Greenville SC 29607

BATES, RONALD ESLEY, cons. co. exec.; b. Wauwatosa, Wis., Aug. 30, 1935; s. Edwin George and Avis Isabelle (Iaatsch) B.; B.S., U. Wis., 1959; m. Yvonne Williams, Aug. 31, 1957; children—Susan, Linda. Human resources mgr. Fibreboard Co., San Francisco, 1966; sr. cons. Touche Ross Co., Mpls., 1966-70; founder, pres. Integro, Mpls., 1973—, also offices throughout U.S. and 15 countries. Served to capt. U.S. Army, 1959-61. Mem. Am. Soc. for Tng. and Devel. Author numerous manuals on tng. and devel. Office: 650 E Grant St Minneapolis MN 55404

BATONGMALAQUE, RODIE LORENZANA, bank exec.; b. Davao City, Philippines, Oct. 12, 1947; s. Erasto R. and Herminia M. (Lorenzana) B.; came to U.S., 1969; B.S. in Mgmt., Woodbury Coll., 1973; postgrad. Golden Gate U., 1976—; m. Isabel V. Gandionco, Nov. 26, 1971; children—Michelle Lee, Mark Lewis. Farm mgr. L-B Ranches, Philippines, 1967-69; bus. mgr. J.L. Batongmalaque, Los Angeles, 1970-74; accounting clk. Joseph Goldinger Fabrics Inc., Los Angeles, 1972-73; comml. loan officer Bank of Calif., Los Angeles, 1974-77; asst. v.p. Calif. Overseas Bank, Los Angeles, 1977-80, v.p. brs. adminstrn., 1981—, mem. sr. loan com., 1978—; partner Wing Advt.; dir. Lejers Internat. Corp. Pres. Amoma Para Sa Sugbu, Los Angeles, 1976—. Mem. Credit Mgrs. Assn., Woodbury Alumni Assn., Far West Ski Assn., Nat. Rifle Assn., U.S. Jaycees. Phi Theta Pi. Clubs: Las Canchas Racquet (Rolling Hills, Calif.); Mountain Gate Country; Ambassador Tennis. Home: 2512 Date Circle Torrance CA 90505 Office: 3701 Wilshire Blvd Los Angeles CA 90010

BATSON, LEONORA L., retail exec.; b. Asbury Park, N.J., July 14, 1936; d. William and Elizabeth (Labagh) Little; student Ind. U., 1953-56; B.S. in Mus., Julliard Sch. Music, 1958; M.B.A. in Fin., N.Y. U., 1978; m. Robert G. Batson, Jan. 13, 1962; 1 son, James A. Mgmt. cons. Booz Allen & Hamilton, N.Y.C., 1972-76; personnel mgr. DHJ Industries, Inc., N.Y.C., 1976-77, dir. personnel and indsl. relations, 1977-79; dir. corp. human resources The Stop and Shop Cos., Boston, 1979—. Mem. adv. bd. middle mgmt. continuing edn. program Babson Coll., Wellesley, Mass., 1980. Mem. Am. Soc. Tng. and Devel., Am. Soc. Personnel Adminstrn., Am. Compensation Assn., Pi Kappa Lambda, Pi Lambda Theta. Episcopalian. Home: 8 Wilshire Dr Scituate MA 02066 Office: PO Box 369 Boston MA 02101

BATT, BERMAN, ins. co. exec.; b. St. Louis, Oct. 18, 1926; s. Joseph S. and Reva (Berman) B.; B.S. in Mech. Engring., Washington U., St. Louis, 1948; m. Jill Peltason, Apr. 1, 1961; children—Sarah Batt Winkler, Susy Batt Adams, Joseph, Walter. Vice pres. Southwestern Splty. Co., San Antonio, 1948-61; pres. S. Tex. Hotel Supply Co., San Antonio, 1961-65; owner 1890 Sweet Shop, San Antonio, 1963-68; owner, pres., chief exec. officer Batt & Assos., San Antonio, 1965—. Served with USNR, 1942-45. C.L.U. Mem. Nat. Assn. Life Underwriters, San Antonio Assn. Life Underwriters, San Antonio C. of C., Million Dollar Round Table. Clubs: Turtle Creek Country, Plaza. Home: 14442 Sir Barton St San Antonio TX 78248 Office: Batt & Assos Suite 200 7334 Blanco Rd San Antonio TX 78216

BATT, COLIN BRIAN, printing ink mfg. co. exec.; b. Gillingham, Kent, Eng., Feb. 14, 1939; came to Can., 1969, naturalized, 1975; s. Stanley Sylvester and Doris Phyllis (Dixon) B.; student Borough Poly., London, 1957-60, 62-64; final diploma City & Guilds (London), 1964; m. Jean Florence Kelly, Sept. 12, 1959; children—Phillip Graham, Karen Theresa. Lab. technician Johnson & Bloy Ltd., London, 1957-59, plant tech. mgr., 1961-69; research dir. Can. Printing Ink div. Reichhold Ltd., 1969—. Served alt. mil. duty U.K. Nat. Service, 1959-61. Mem. Oil and Color Chemists Assn., Flexographic Tech. Assn., Can. Owners and Pilots Assn. Patentee in radiation curable compositions. Home: Lot 3 Conc 7 Rural Route 2 Acton ON L7J 2L8 Canada Office: 111 Brockhouse Rd Toronto ON M8W 2W9 Canada

BATTEN, CARL ROGER, constrn. co. exec.; b. Biscoe, N.C., June 7, 1939; s. Carl Winford and Willie L. (Spikes) B.; student Coll. San Mateo (Calif.), 1968-72, Calif. State U., Hayward; C.L.U., Am. Coll. Life Underwriters, Bryn Mawr, Pa., 1972; m. Collette Gurthet; children—Debra, Rebecca, Bruce, Tim. Field underwriter Sacramento gen. office N.Y. Life Ins. Co., 1961-65, asst. mgr. Westlake (Calif.) gen. office, 1965-68, mgmt. asst., N.Y.C., 1968, gen. mgr. Redwood City (Calif.) gen. office, 1968-71, gen. mgr. Hayward gen. office, 1971-76; exec. v.p. Middle East Mgmt. and Constrn. Corp., 1976—; pres. World Trade Import Inc., 1977—. Dist. commr. Boy Scouts Am., 1964-67. Asso. mem. Calif. Republican Central Com., 1969-70; mem. Bay Area Rep. Alliance, 1969—. Served with USAF, 1956-60. Mem. Soc. Chartered Life Underwriters, So. Alameda County Life Underwriters (pres.), So. Alameda County Gen. Agts. and Mgrs. Assn. (pres.). Home: 425 Dartmouth Ave San Carlos CA 94070 Office: 166 Gerry St San Francisco CA 94108 also Thong Tock Bldg Suite 210 15 Scotts Rd Singapore 9 Singapore

BATTEN, WILLIAM MILFRED, stock exchange exec.; b. Reedy, W.Va., June 4, 1909; s. Lewis Allen and Gurry Frances (Goff) B.; B.S. Ohio State U., 1932, L.H.D., 1977; LL.D., Morris Harvey Coll., 1960, W.Va., U., 1966, Alderson-Broaddus Coll., 1971, W.Va. Wesleyan Coll., 1974; L.H.D., Marietta Coll., 1965, Hofstra U., 1978; m. Kathryn P. Clark, Aug. 10, 1935; children—David Clark, Jane Louise. Formerly sales promotion rep. Kellogg Co., Battle Creek, Mich.; with J. C. Penney Co., Inc., N.Y.C., 1935-74, asst. store mgr., 1937-40, tng. dir., 1940-46, zone personnel rep., 1946-51, asst. to pres., 1951-58, v.p., 1953-58, pres., chief exec. officer, 1958-64, chmn. bd., chief exec. officer, 1964-74; chmn. bd. dirs. N.Y. Stock Exchange, 1976—; dir. Boeing Co.; mem. bd. adv. council Tex. Instruments, Inc. Mem. Bus. Council, 1961—, chmn., 1971-72. Served to lt. col. AUS, 1942-45. Clubs: Links, Creek, Recess, Bond, Economic (pres. 1967-68) (N.Y.C.); North Hempstead Country. Home: Heather Ln Mill Neck NY 11765 Office: 11 Wall St New York NY 10005

BATTLE, MATTHEW ANTHONY, property mgr.; b. Nashville, July 28, 1943; s. Lonnie Eugene and Emma (Maxwell) B.; B.S., Tenn. State U., 1966, M.S., 1972; M.S., Vanderbilt U., 1975, Morgan State U., 1978; m. Lauranetta Brown, Apr. 8, 1977; children—Sherry, Joycelynette, Damon Lewis, Matthew Anthony. Tchr., Memphis Sch. System, 1966-68; mem. Met. Nashville Police Dept., 1968-71; store mgr. Goodyear Service Stores, Nashville, 1971-72; property mgr. Realty Mgmt. Assos., 1972-74; asst. regional mgr. N.C.H.P. Property Mgmt., Inc., Emeryville, Calif., 1974—. Mem. Mayor's Council Children and Youth; dir. membership Memphis youth div. NAACP, 1966. Mem. Greater Balt. Bd. Realtors, Inst. Real Estate Mgmt., Alpha Kappa Alpha. Democrat. Methodist. Home: 3226 Ursa Way Hayward CA 94541 Office: 5901 Christie Ave Emeryville CA 94608

BATTLES, ROBERT EUGENE, ins. exec.; b. Oakland, Calif., Jan. 31, 1912; s. Eugene and Tomasina (Abernathie) B.; A.B. in Economics, U. Calif. at Los Angeles, 1933; m. Dorothy McDonald, Mar. 4, 1939; 1 son, Brenton E. Planting overseer United Fruit Co., Panama, 1933-36; with R.A. Rowan & Co., Los Angeles, 1936—, exec. v.p., gen. mgr., dir., 1954—; pres. South Boston Co.; chmn. Rowan-Wilson Ins., The William Wilson Co.; dir. Mchts. Fireproof Bldg. Co. Mem. bd. electors Ins. Hall Fame, 1971-74. Trustee, Rep. Assos. Served as lt. col. AUS, asst. mil. attache U.S. Embassy, Mexico City, 1942-46. Decorated Order of Mil. Merit (Mexico); War Dept. Commendation medal (2) (U.S.). Mem. Ins. Assn. Los Angeles (past pres.), Calif. Assn. Ins. Agts. (past pres.; Ramsden award), Nat. Assn. Ins. Agts. (past pres.; Woodworth Meml. medal 1959). Los Angeles C. of C. (dir. 1961-63), Native Sons Golden West, Phi Gamma Delta. Clubs: Los Angeles Stock Exchange; Univ. (Pasadena, Calif.); Annandale Golf. Author: The Agency System in Relation to Insurance Economics, 1958. Contbr. articles to ins. mags. Home: 982 Linda Vista Ave Pasadena CA 91103 Office: 180 S Lake Ave Pasadena CA 91101

BATTS, WARREN LEIGHTON, diversified food co. exec.; b. Norfolk, Va., Sept. 4, 1932; s. John Leighton and Allie Belle (Johnson) B.; B.E.E., Ga. Inst. Tech., 1961; M.B.A., Harvard, 1963; m. Eloise Pitts, Dec. 24, 1957; 1 dau., Terri Allison. With Kendall Co., Charlotte, N.C., 1963-64; exec. v.p. Olga Co., Van Nuys, Calif., 1964-66; v.p. Douglas Williams Assos., N.Y.C., 1966-67; founder Triangle Corp., Orangeburg, S.C., 1967, pres., chief exec. officer, 1967-71; exec. v.p., gen. mgr. Mcht. group and Paper and Related group Mead Corp., Dayton, Ohio, 1971-73, pres. Mead Corp., 1973-80, chief exec. officer, 1978-80; pres., chief operating officer Dart Industries, subs. Dart & Kraft, Inc., Los Angeles, 1980—; dir. 1st Nat. Bank of Atlanta, 1974-80, B.C. Forest Products, 1974-80, Dart & Kraft, Inc., 1980—; adj. prof. U. S.C., 1970-71. Mem. alumni adv. bd. Ga. Inst. Tech.; mem. exec. council Harvard Bus. Sch. Alumni Assn., 1978—. Author: (with others) Creative Collective Bargaining, 1964. Home: 1120 Harman Ave Dayton OH 45419 Office: Dart Industries PO Box 3157 Terminal Annex Los Angeles CA 90051

BATTY, W. LAWSON, JR., plastic and chem. mfg. co. exec.; b. Lawrence, Mass., July 8, 1927; s. Wilfred Lawson and Inez P. (Chambers) B.; A.B., Dartmouth Coll., 1950; postgrad. in indsl. adminstrn. Yale U., 1959; m. Eleanor Trumpold, Apr. 14, 1951; children—Robert L., John C., Paul R. Salesman, Mallinckrodt Chem. Works, N.Y.C., 1950-52; from salesman to mktg. mgr. Chem. div. Gen. Electric Co., Waterford, N.Y., Schenectady, 1952-73; dir. mktg. E.D. Bullard Co., Sausalito, Calif., 1973-74; central devel. mgr. Gamlen div. Sybron Corp., San Francisco, 1974-76, v.p. mktg. Nalge Co. div., Rochester, N.Y., 1976—; instr., lectr. Rochester Inst. Tech., 1979—. Served with USN, 1945-47. Mem. Am. Chem. Soc., Sci. Apparatus Makers Assn., Rochester Sales and Mktg. Execs. Club (instr., lectr.). Republican. Club: Oak Hill Country (Rochester).

Home: 11 Cranston Rd Pittsford NY 14534 Office: 75 Panorama Creek Dr Box 365 Rochester NY 14602

BAUDOIN, MATTHEW DUPLAN, investment banker; b. Neuilly, France, Apr. 17, 1947; s. Denis Henri and Madeleine Rosine (Duplan) B.; B.S., Georgetown U., 1970; M.B.A., Cornell U., 1974; m. Susan Louise Yerkovich, June 24, 1972; children—Madeleine, Claudia. With Oppenheimer & Co., Inc., 1974-75; corp. fin. dept. Bache Halsey Stuart Shields & Co., Inc., N.Y.C., 1975-77; gen. partner Fahnestock & Co., N.Y.C., 1977—; dir. Perarma, S.A., Paris. Republican. Roman Catholic. Clubs: Winged Foot Golf (Mamaroneck, N.Y.); Racing de France (Paris). Home: 156 Taymil Rd New Rochelle NY 10804 also La Garenne Bonnelles Yvellines France. Office: 110 Wall St New York NY 10005

BAUER, BETTY ESTELLE, publisher; b. Lincoln, Nebr., Feb. 1, 1928; d. Walter Anthony and Lucille Bernice (Ludwig) B.; B.S. in Bus. Adminstrn., U. Mo., 1952. With nat. advt. dept. New Mexican, Santa Fe, 1953-55; with health and social services dept. State of N.Mex., Santa Fe, 1955-71, dir. system div., 1968-71; founder, pub., partner, gen. mgr. Santa Fean mag., Santa Fe, 1972—. Vice pres. bd. Santa Fe Festival of Arts; mem. Mayor's Promotion and Conv. Com. Mem. Los Comprades, Santa Fe C. of C. (dir. 1978—, pres. 1980-81), U. Mo. Alumni Assn. Republican. Club: Santa Fe Press (pres. 1976). Home and Office: 1701 Aqua Fria Santa Fe NM 87501

BAUER, CARL ALBERT, chem. co. exec.; b. Rome, Ga., Sept. 28, 1924; s. Carl Albert and Rita Christina (Mull) B.; B.S., N. Ga. Coll., 1949; m. Mary Elizabeth Burton, June 12, 1947; children—Franklin Page, Carl Albert III, Mary Beth. Lab. supr. Brunswick Chem. Co. (Ga.), 1949-53; prodn. mgr. Flag Sulphur & Chem. Co., Tampa, Fla., 1953-55; prodn. mgr. Valley Chem. Co., Greenville, Miss., 1955-56, v.p., 1957-58, pres., 1959—; dir. Planters Bank & Trust Co., Ruleville, Miss., Riverside Land Co., Greenville. Served with USNR, 1943-46. Decorated Air medal with 2 stars. Mem. Nat. Agrl. Chem. Assn. (dir.), Am. Legion. Methodist (chmn. ofcl. bd.). Clubs: Rotary (pres. Greenville 1968-69), Greenville Golf and Country. Home: 1134 Cloverdale Dr Greenville MS 38701 Office: Valley Chem Co PO Box 1317 Raceway Rd Greenville MS 38701

BAUER, EDMOND S., chem. and equipment co. exec.; b. Astoria, N.Y., May 12, 1918; s. Edmond S. and Alice Gertrude (Cavanaugh) B.; B.S. in Chem. Engring., Newark Coll. Engring., 1939; m. Jean L. Benney, May 22, 1943; children—Carl Thomas, Jay Scott. With Monsanto Co., St. Louis, 1942-79, gen. mgr., 1969-71, corp. v.p., 1971-74, group v.p., 1974-75, group v.p., mng. dir., 1975, exec. v.p., 1975-79, now dir.; chmn., pres., chief exec. officer Fisher Controls Corp. of Del., Fayton, Mo., 1979—. Mem. Soc. Chem. Industry, Groupement International des Associations Nationales de Fabricants de Pesticides (dir. 1973-75), Nat. Agrl. Chems. Assn. (dir. 1970-76, chmn. 1974-75, mem. exec. com. 1972-76). Clubs: Old Warson Country, St. Louis (St. Louis); Ponte Vedra (Fla.). Contbr. articles on resins and their uses to profl. jours. Office: Fisher Controls Corp of Del 7711 Bonhomme Ave Clayton MO 63105*

BAUER, EDWARD EWING, mfg. co. exec.; b. Moline, Ill., Dec. 18, 1917; s. Harry E. and Elma (Ewing) B.; B.S., U. Wis., 1939; M.S., U. Pa., 1945; LL.B., LaSalle U., 1954; m. Margaret Lamont McConnell, May 17, 1941; children—Annette Louise Bauer Tucker, Barbara Ann Bauer Erickson, Cheryl Ewing Bauer Rowder. Application engr. Gen. Electric Co., Pitts., 1939-45, gen. mgr., 1952-59; sales mgr. Food Machinery Corp., Chgo., 1945-50; sales mgr. Heyl & Patterson, Pitts., 1950-52; v.p., gen. mgr. Aerovox Co., New Bedford, Mass., 1959-63; became v.p. mfg. LeTourneau Westinghouse, Peoria, 1963, later v.p. mktg. Constrn. Equipment div. Westinghouse Air Brake Co.; v.p., dir. Wabco Distbg. Co.; group v.p. constrn. and mining equipment A-T-O Inc., Willoughby, Ohio; v.p., gen. mgr. hard rock mining div. Joy Mfg. Co., Denver. Registered profl. engr., S.C. Mem. Soc. Automotive Engrs., Am. Mgmt. Assn., Am. Inst. Mining Engrs. Presbyterian. Clubs: Columbine Country, Cactus, N.Y. Mining. Home: 4505 S Yosemite Stoney Brook Denver CO 80237 Office: PO Box J39 Denver CO 80239

BAUER, PAUL DAVID, retail food co. exec.; b. Buffalo, July 25, 1943; s. Norman Thomas and Rita Anne (Maloney) B.; B.S. in Bus. Adminstrn., Boston Coll., 1965; m. Donna Marie Szlosek, May 6, 1967; children—David, Lisa. With Peat, Marwick, Mitchell & Co., Buffalo, 1965-70; with Niagara Frontier Services, Inc., Buffalo, 1970—, v.p. fin. Treas., Studio Arena Theatre, 1969-76; sec. Amherst (N.Y.) Youth Hockey, 1977-79; mem. Council on Accountancy, Canisius Coll., Buffalo. Mem. Nat. Assn. Accts., Fin. Execs. Inst. Republican. Roman Catholic. Club: Park Country. Home: 49 Oakview Dr Williamsville NY 14221 Office: 60 Dingens St Buffalo NY 14206

BAUER, PETER ALEXANDER, mfg. co. exec., lawyer; b. Berlin, Germany, Aug. 11, 1923; s. Siegfried and Amelie (Gerstle) B.; B.A. magna cum laude, Marietta Coll., 1947; J.D., Harvard U., 1952; m. Elizabeth D. Bull, Oct. 29, 1960. Admitted to N.Y. bar, 1952, Ill. bar, 1958; atty. NLRB, 1953-57; with legal dept. Helene Curtis Industries, Inc., Chgo., 1957-61; v.p. Continental Materials Corp., Chgo., 1961-76, sec., 1976-79, dir., 1976—; partner firm Antonow & Fink, Chgo., 1970-79; asso. gen. counsel Interpace Corp., Parsippany, N.J., 1979—. Bd. dirs. Lincoln Park Conservation Assn., Chgo., 1965-72, pres., 1970; mem. Lincoln Park Conservation Community Council, 1969-79, chmn., 1976-79. Served with U.S. Army, 1943-46. Mem. Am., Ill., Chgo. bar assns., Nat. Assn. Housing and Redevel. Ofcls., Phi Beta Kappa. Club: Harvard (Chgo.). Home: 166 N Wyoming Ave South Orange NJ 07079 Office: 260 Cherry Hill Rd Parsippany NJ 07054

BAUER, RAYMOND GALE, mfrs. rep.; b. Merchantville, N.J., June 19, 1934; s. Robert Irwin and Florence Winifred (Guyer) B.; A.A., Monmouth Coll., West Long Branch, N.J., 1955; B.B.A., U. Miami, 1958; m. Jayne Whitehead, Feb. 15, 1955; 1 dau., Linda Joan. Div. mgr. R.J. Reynolds Tobacco Co., Winston-Salem, N.C., 1959-68; Middle Atlantic mgr. U.S. Envelope Co., Springfield, Mass., 1968-74; div. sales mgr. Eastern Tablet Corp., Albany, N.Y., 1974-75; owner Ray Bauer Assos., mfrs. reps., Haddonfield, N.J., 1975—. Served with USAF, 1959-64; officer Air Force Aux. Mem. Friends of Haddonfield (N.J.) Library, Haddonfield Civic Assn., Smithsonian Assos., Monmouth Coll., U. Miami alumni assns., Nat. Philatelic Soc., Am. Security Council, Air Force Assn., Am. Conservative Union, Am. Mgmt. Assn., Lambda Sigma Tau, Lambda Chi Alpha. Clubs: Republican, U.S. Senatorial, Arrowhead Racquet, Iron Rock Swim and Country. Home and office: 132 Maple Ave Haddonfield NJ 08033

BAUGH, COY FRANKLIN, accountant, food co. exec.; b. Mt. Vernon, Ark., Feb. 7, 1946; s. Oather Lee and Eula Faye (Barnett) B.; A.A., Glendale Coll., 1969; B.S. in Bus. Adminstrn., Calif. State U., Los Angeles, 1971; postgrad. exec. devel. program Cornell U., 1978; m. Cheryl Ann Linscott, June 22, 1968; 1 son, David Franklin. Staff accountant to sr. accountant Ernst & Ernst, Los Angeles, 1971-73, sr. tax accountant, Sacramento, 1973-74; auditor to audit supr. Amfac, Inc., San Francisco, 1974-76, controller to v.p. fin. Fisher Cheese div., Wapakoneta, Ohio, 1976—. Served with U.S. Army, 1964-67; Vietnam. Decorated Air Medal. Mem. Am. Inst. C.P.A.'s, Calif. Soc. C.P.A.'s. Clubs: Sertoma, Elks. Home: 801 Aster Dr Wapakoneta OH 45895 Office: PO Box 409 Wapakoneta OH 45895

BAUGH, L. DARRELL, fin. exec.; b. Prairie Grove, Ark., Oct. 7, 1930; s. Lacey D. and Mary Grace (Brown) B.; B.S. in B.A., U. Ark., 1954; M.S. in B.A., U. Colo., 1960; C.L.U., Am. Coll., 1967; m. Wileeta Claire Gray, June 15, 1958; children—Adrienne Leigh, John Grayson. With Penn Mut. Life Ins. Co., 1961-71, gen. agt., Sacramento, 1968-71; pres. Nat. Estate Planning Inst., Boulder, Colo., 1974—; lectr. in field; cons. U. Colo. Center for Confs. Mgmt./Tech. Programs, 1975-80; sponsor ednl. programs for profl. estate planners and estate owners. Served with U.S. Army, 1954-56. Mem. Boulder C. of C., Am. Soc. C.L.U.'s, Boulder County Estate Planning Council (pres. 1972-73), Sacramento Estate Planning Council. Contbr. articles to profl. jours. Home: 92 Caballo Ct Boulder CO 80303 Office: 75 Manhattan Dr Boulder CO 80303

BAUGHER, KENYON LOREN, dental co. exec., real estate developer; b. Hurdland, Mo., Aug. 3, 1913; s. Loren Victor and Leona (Cable) B.; B.S. in Mech. Engring., U. Colo., 1936; M.B.A., Stanford U., 1938; m. Joan Aiken, Jan. 25, 1975. Vice pres. Densco, Inc., Denver, 1949-62; with VanSchaack & Co. Real Estate, Denver, 1962-68; owner Denpro Co., Denver, 1968—; v.p. Planet Realty, Inc., Denver, 1975—. Mem. Denver Bd. Realtors, Am. Dental Trade Assn., Sigma Tau, Delta Tau Delta. Democrat. Unitarian Universalist. Club: Rotary. Home: 340 Oswego Ct Aurora CO 80010 Office: 1751 Franklin Denver CO 80218

BAUGHMAN, ERNEST THEODORE, former banker; b. Ackworth, Iowa, Dec. 27, 1915; s. Lawrence E. and Nellie (Booth) B.; B.S. in Econs., U. Minn., 1939, M.S., 1941; m. Esther M. Bajari, Aug. 28, 1940; children—Carol Mae Baughman Dudzik, Verna Lee, Francine Lou Baughman Davies. Instr., U. Minn., 1939-41; economist Council Farm Coops., 1942; with Fed. Res. Bank Chgo., 1946-74, 1st v.p., 1970-74; pres. Fed. Res. Bank Dallas, 1974-81; lectr. Sch. Banking, U. Wis., 1950-74; cons. White House, 1954-55. Bd. dirs. Farm Found.; adviser grad. programs in mgmt. and adminstrv. scis. U. Tex. at Dallas, center for banking edn. Tex. So. U. Served with USNR, 1943-45. Mem. Am. Farm Econ. Assn. (editorial bd. 1956-57), Am. Finance Assn. Editor Bus. Conditions, 1959-70. Home: 3714 Northview Ln Dallas TX 75229

BAUGHMAN, GEORGE WASHINGTON, III, univ ofcl., fin. cons.; b. Pitts., July 7, 1937; s. George W. and Cecile M. (Lytel) B.; B.S. in Psychology, Ohio State U., 1959, M.B.A., 1961, postgrad., 1961-63; 1 dau., Lynn. Pres., Advanced Research Assos., Worthington, Ohio, 1960—; asst. instr. fin. Ohio State U., Columbus, 1961-63, research asso., office of controller, 1964-66, dir. data processing, 1966-68, 70-72, dir. adminstrv. research, 1966-72, asso. to acad. v.p., 1968-70, exec. dir. univ. budget, 1970-72, dir. spl. projects, office of pres., 1972—; chmn. bd. Hosp. Audiences, Inc., 1974—; dir. Clear Creek Foods, Inc., 1978—, Cedar Hill Assos., Inc., 1979—. Founding bd. dirs. Coll. and U. Machine Records Conf., 1971-73; bd. dirs. Uniplan Environ. Groups, Inc., 1970-73, chmn., 1971-73; chmn. Franklin County (Ohio) Republican Demographics and Voter Analysis Com., 1975-79; mem. Ohio Dental Bd., 1980—. Am. Council on Edn. grantee, 1976-77; Reisman fellow, 1962; Nat. Assn. Coll. and Univ. Bus. Officers grantee, 1977-79; Ohio Bd. Regents grantee, 1978-79; NSF grantee, 1980—. Mem. Assn. Instl. Research, AAAS, Coll. and U. Systems Exchange, Internat. Trade Exchange, Phi Alpha Kappa, Delta Tau Delta. Republican. Presbyterian. Author: (with D.H. Baker) Writing to People, 1963; (with R.W. Brady) University Program Budgeting, 1968, Administrative Data Processing, 1975; University Price Index Calculation Systems, 1977; contbr. articles to profl. publs. Home: 833 Lakeshore Dr Worthington OH 43085 Office: 190 N Oval Mall Columbus OH 43210

BAUGHMAN, LEWIS EDWIN, banker; b. Warren, Ohio, Nov. 15, 1923; s. Milton Day and Katherine B. (Boone) B.; B.S.B.A., Ohio State U., 1947; grad. Stonier Sch. Banking, Rutgers U., 1955; m. Ann Hawkins Buker, July 7, 1946; children—Milton Day, James Lewis. With Second Nat. Bank Warren 1948—, v.p., 1959-62, pres., 1962—, chmn. bd., 1974—; dir. Sommer Electric Co., Gus Orwell, Inc. Trustee, treas. Trumbull Meml. Hosp., Warren; trustee Jr. Achievement, Warren; chmn. Downtown Devel. Com. Warren, Urban Renewal Design and Devel. Com. Warren. Served to sgt. Transp. Corps, U.S. Army, 1943-46; ETO. Named Young Man of Yr., Warren Jr. C. of C., 1954, Man of Yr., 1964; recipient Silver Beaver award Western Res. council Boy Scouts Am., 1970, Alumni Citizenship award Ohio State U., 1975. Presbyterian. Office: 108 Main Ave Warren OH 44481

BAUGHN, JOSEPH HAUSER, bus. exec.; b. Columbia City, Ind., Mar. 29, 1943; s. Winston Reece and Martha Fay (Hauser) B.; B.S. (journalism scholar 1963-64), Ball State U., 1966, postgrad., 1967; postgrad. Ind. Central U., 1971-72; m. Sandra Yvonne May, Oct. 18, 1969; children—Andrew Joseph, James Anthony. Tchr., C.A. Beard Meml. Sch. System, Knightstown, Ind., 1966-68; with loan dept. Citizens State Bank, New Castle, Ind., 1968-69; Midwest regional credit mgr. Bostitch Textron, Inc., Indpls., 1969-75, Midwest regional bus. mgr., 1975—. Past sec., v.p. council United Ch. of Christ. Recipient Honors award for distinguished service in journalism Ball State U., 1964. Mem. Ind. State Mus., Early Am. Soc. (founding). Club: Masons, Economic (Indpls.). Home: 3636 Holly Circle Indianapolis IN 46227 Office: 420 S Kitley Ave Indianapolis IN 46219

BAUKNIGHT, CLARENCE WILLIAM, III, utility co. exec.; b. Wilkes-Barre, Pa., Apr. 28, 1951; s. Clarence William and Bernice Mae (Griffin) B.; B.A. in Urban Adminstrn., Syracuse U., 1973; M.P.A., Rutgers U., 1978; m. Toni Renee Tilghman, Sept. 1, 1973; 1 dau., April Celeste. Asso. dir. Urban League Union County, Elizabeth, N.J., 1973-77; supr. employment and urban relations Elizabethtown Gas Co. and Elizabethtown Water Co., Elizabeth, 1977-79, mgr. urban affairs and employment, 1979—; mem. Union County Employment and Tng. Adv. Council, 1978—; mem. Union County Pvt. Indsl. Council, 1980—. Bd. dirs., treas. Urban League Union County, 1978—; v.p. Egenolf Day Nursery, Elizabeth, 1978—; pres. Indsl. Community Center, Elizabeth, 1979—; bd. dirs. United Way Eastern Union County, 1978—. Mem. N.J. Gas Assn., N.J. Utilities Assn., Am. Soc. Public Adminstrn., Eastern Union County C. of C. Home: 757 Sheridan Ave Roselle NJ 07203 Office: One Elizabethtown Plaza Elizabeth NJ 07207

BAUM, ARNOLD RHEINHOLD, real estate, ins. and investment co. exec.; b. Union Hill, N.J., May 27, 1924; s. Adam Rheinhold and Margaretha Catharine Susanna (Arnold) B.; student Cambridge (Eng.) U., 1946; B.S. in Bus. Adminstrn., Syracuse U., 1950; M.S. in Ednl. Adminstrn., U. So. Calif., 1970; postgrad. Ball State U., 1970, N.Y. U., 1971-73; m. Patricia Ann Caffrey, Aug. 27, 1951; children—Valerie Ann, Willow Ann. Ind. ins. field underwriter, 1948-50; enlisted man U.S. Army, 1943-46; commd. 2d lt. U.S. Air Force, 1950, advanced through grades to maj., 1963; ret., 1970; sr. mem. Baum Assos., Callicoon, N.Y., 1970—; exec. reservist in response and recovery Fed. Emergency Mgmt. Agy., 1979—; pres. bd. dirs. Dover (Del.) Fed. Credit Union, 1963-67. Mem., v.p., pres. Delaware Valley Central Sch. Dist. Bd. Edn., Callicoon, 1971-74; mem. task force on tenure N.Y. State Sch. Bds. Assn., 1973-74; bd. dirs. sec., treas. Hortonville Cemetery Assn. Corp., 1975—. Decorated Bronze Star, Air Force Commendation medal, Combat Inf. badge, others; recipient N.Y. State Conspicuous Service Cross, 1955; citation for meritorious service Nat. Credit Union, 1966; cert. of merit N.Y. State Sch. Bd., 1975; lic. ins. and real estate broker, N.Y. State; cert. tchr. and sch. dist. adminstr. and supr., N.Y. State; cert. tchr., Calif. Mem. Am Arbitration Assn., Air Force Assn., AAUP, Mil. Order World Wars, Res. Officers Assn. U.S., Am. Security Council (nat. adv. bd.), Ret. Officers Assn., VFW. Home: RD 1 Box 129-B Callicoon NY 12723

BAUM, GEORGE FREDERICK, JR., investment co. exec.; b. Corsicana, Tex., Dec. 17, 1932; s. George Frederick and Priscilla Camille (Hartzell) B.; grad. Phillips Exeter Acad., 1951; student Oxford U., Eng., 1953; A.B., Harvard, 1955; LL.B., So. Meth. U. 1963; m. Catherine Margaret McLemore, May 1, 1965; children—George Frederick III, Mary Katherine, Edward McLemore, Elizabeth Hartzell. Partner, Baum Properties, 1957—; admitted to Tex. bar, 1963; enforcement atty. SEC, Fort Worth, 1963-64; estate tax atty. U.S. Treasury Dept., Dallas, 1964-66; practice law, Dallas, 1966-69; sec., gen. counsel Capital S. W. Corp., Dallas, 1969-76; asst. gen. counsel Mich. Gen. Corp., 1976-79; sec., gen. counsel Mesbic Fin. Corp. Dallas, 1977-78; pres. 1st Bancorp Capital, Inc., Corsicana, Tex., 1979—. Served with USAF, 1955-57. Mem. Am. Dallas (sec.-treas. corp. counsel sect. 1975, vice chmn. 1976, chmn. 1977) bar assns., State Bar Tex. (sec.-treas. corp. counsel sect. 1976, vice chmn. 1977, chmn. 1978), Nat. Assn. Small Bus. Investment Cos. (mem. legal com. 1975), S.W. Legal Found., Am. Soc. Corp. Secs., Assn. for Corp. Growth (dir. Dallas-Ft. Worth chpt. 1978-79), U.S. (nat. dir. 1963), Tex. (v.p. 1963) jr. chambers commerce, Sons Republic Tex. (1st v.p. Dallas chpt. 1973, pres. 1974), Mil. Order World Wars. Mem. Christian Ch. Club: Harvard co-chmn. schs. com. 1966-68, (Dallas). Home: 4331 Lorraine St Dallas TX 75205 Office: 1st Nat Bank Bldg Corsicana TX 75110

BAUM, RICHARD THEODORE, engring. co. exec.; b. N.Y.C., Oct. 3, 1919; B.A., Columbia U., 1940. B.S., 1941, M.S., 1948. Engr., Electric Boat Co., Groton, Conn., 1941-43; with Jaros, Baum & Bolles, N.Y.C., 1946—, partner, 1958—. Mem. adv. council, faculty of engring. and applied sci. Columbia U., 1972—. Served to 1st lt. USAAF, 1943-46. Registered profl. engr., Nat. Bur. Engring. Registration, N.Y., D.C., 20 other states. Fellow Am. Cons. Engrs. Council, ASME, ASHRAE; mem. Nat. Soc. Profl. Engrs., Nat. Soc. Energy Engrs., Am. Arbitration Assn. (panel of arbitrators 1973—), Council on Tall Bldgs. and Urban Habitat (steering group, chmn. mech., elec. and vertical transp. coms.). Club: University (N.Y.C.). Office: 345 Park Ave New York NY 10154

BAUM, STANLEY ALLEN, advt. exec.; b. N.Y.C., Mar. 6, 1928; s. Louis and Olga (Pasternack) B.: B.A., N.Y. U., 1949. Advt. writer Dancer-Fitzgerald-Sample, Inc., N.Y.C., 1950-56, copy supr., 1956-60, v.p., 1960-70; pres. Stanley Baum Assos., N.Y.C., 1970—. Mem. N.Y. U. Alumni Assn., ASCAP, Am. Guild Authors and Composers, Copy Research Council, Sigma Delta Omicron. Clubs: N.Y. U., Players. Home: 235 Lincoln Pl Brooklyn NY 11217 Office: 330 E 49th St New York NY 10017

BAUM, ZELDA BRODY, assn. exec.; b. Newark, N.J., Dec. 20, 1927; d. Harry and Anne (Helfmann) Brody; B.A., N.Y. U., 1949; postgrad. Seton Hall U., 1957, Fairleigh Dickinson U., 1959; m. Ward Joseph Baum, July 7, 1946; children—Link Z., Craig Z., Duffy Z. Comml. interior designer, N.J., 1958-65; adminstrv. asst. Baum Assos., 1965-70; exec. asst., acting dir. Nat. Found. for Ileitis and Colitis, N.Y.C., 1970-75; exec. dir. Nat. Cooley's Anemia Found., N.Y.C., 1975-78; exec. dir. Mktg. Agts. for Food Service Industry, N.Y.C., 1978—. Bd. dirs. Am. Jewish Congress, 1958, Congregation Beth El, 1960-66; mem. Am. Council Jewish Women. Mem. N.Y. Soc. Assn. Execs. (chairperson membership com.), N.Y. Soc. Fund Raisers, Am. Soc. Assn. Execs. (membership com.), Am. Mgmt. Assn., Am. Mktg. Assn., Meeting Planners Internat. Democrat. Club: Hadassah (life). Home: 215 E 24th St New York NY 10010 Office: 15 E 26 St Suite 1914 New York NY 10010

BAUMAN, JOSEPH F., textile co. exec.; b. N.Y.C., July 23, 1924; s. Alexander and Rose B.; student Harvard Coll., 1943-44; B.S.M.E., Rensselaer Poly. Inst., 1950; M.A. in Physics, Trenton State Coll., 1971; m. Jeannie R. Bauman; children—Neil, Ward. Engr., Foster Wheeler Co., N.Y.C., 1948-49, Davidson Indsl. Contracting Co., N.Y.C., 1950-51; contracts adminstr. Maxson Electronics, N.Y.C., 1952-53; v.p. sales Emanuel Roth Co., Inc., Secaucus, N.J., 1954-60, v.p. fin., dir., 1971—; v.p. engring., corporate sec. Acme Hamilton Mfg. Co., Trenton, 1960-71. Served with U.S. Army, 1943-45. Decorated Purple Heart, Combat Infantryman's badge. Home: 860 Lower Ferry Rd West Trenton NJ 08628 Office: Emanuel Roth Co Inc 400 County Ave Secaucus NJ 07094

BAUMAN, LAWRENCE SCOTT, lawyer; b. Washington, Oct. 29, 1948; s. Philip and Esther Louise B.; B.A. summa cum laude, Oberlin Coll. 1970; J.D., Stanford U., 1973. Admitted to Ill. bar, 1973, Pa. bar, 1977; asso. firm Sonnenschein Carlin Nath & Rosenthal, Chgo., 1973-76, firm Blank Rome Comisky & McCauley, Phila., 1978—. Mem. Am. Bar Assn., Pa. Bar Assn., Phila. Bar Assn. Editor, Stanford Law Rev., 1972, note editor, 1973.

BAUMANN, FREDERICK WILLIAM, JR., paper co. exec.; b. Lexington, Ky., May 27, 1945; s. Frederick Wilhelm and Elizabeth Pauline (Goetz) B.; B.S. in Bus. Adminstrn., Western Ky. U., 1968; m. Mitchell Ann Ward, Jan. 25, 1974; 1 dau., Hilary Mitchell. With Baumann Paper Co., Inc., Lexington, 1968—, v.p., 1975-79, pres., 1980—. Served with inf. U.S. Army, 1969-70. Decorated Bronze Star, Army Commendation medal with oak leaf cluster. Mem. Sales-Mktg. Execs. Assn., Nat. Paper Trade Assn., Ky. Restaurant Assn. (dir.), Ky. Hotel-Motel Assn. (cert. of appreciation 1974). Democrat. Presbyterian. Club: Spring Lake Country. Office: PO Box 13022 Baumann Dr Lexington KY 40512

BAUMEISTER, HERBERT ALFONS, investment advisor, fund raiser, cons.; b. Bklyn., Aug. 25, 1943; s. Alfons Joseph Baumeister and Friederike Doretta (Harms) Baumeister Diedin; B.S. in Investment Banking, N.Y. U., 1966. Asst. to research dir., registered rep. Kahn, Peck & Co., Inc., N.Y.C., 1966-68; asst. to research dir., registered rep. and trader Diamond, Turk & Co., N.Y.C., 1968-71; registered rep. analyst and trader D.H. Blair & Co., N.Y.C., 1971; dir. research, registered rep. and trader J.R. Radin & Co., Inc., N.Y.C., 1971-72; account exec. fin. public relations Ron Como & Assos., Inc., N.Y.C., 1972-76; account exec. J.S. Alden Public Relations, Inc., N.Y.C., 1977-78; sr. security analyst, registered rep. Old Ct. Securities, Great Neck, N.Y., 1978; registered investment advisor Herbert Baumeister & Assos., Bklyn., 1978—. Mem. council Bethleham Lutheran Ch., Bklyn., 1974-80, fin. sec., 1974-78, mem. fin. commn.; mem. N.Y. State Legis. Adv. Com. Recipient cert. of commendation Nat. Republican Congressional Com. Mem. N.Y. Soc. Security Analysts, Fin. Analysts Fedn., N.Y. U. Alumni Assn., Ft. Hamilton High Sch. Alumni Assn., Nat. Trust Hist. Preservation, N.Y. Zool. Soc., Am. Assn. Account Execs. Club: N.Y. Univ. Home and Office: 152 77th St Brooklyn NY 11209

BAUMER, BEVERLY BELLE, journalist; b. Hays, Kans., Sept. 23, 1926; d. Charles Arthur and Mayme Mae (Lord) B.; B.S., William Allen White Sch. Journalism, U. Kans., 1948. Summer intern reporter Hutchinson (Kans.) News, 1946-47; continuity writer, women's program dir. Sta. KWBW, Hutchinson, 1948-49; dist. editor Salina (Kans.) Jours., 1950-57; commd. writer State of Kans. Centennial Year, 1961; contbg. author: Ford Times, Kansas City Star, Wichita (Kans.) Eagle, Ojibway Publs., Billboard, Modern Jeweler, Floor Covering Weekly, other bus. mags., 1962-69; owner and mgr. apts., Hutchinson, 1970—; info. officer, maj. Kans. Wing Hdqrs. CAP, 1969-72. Recipient Human Interest Photo award Nat. Press Women, 1956; News Photo award AP, 1952. Mem. Nat. Soc. Magna Charta Dames, Nat. Soc. Daus. Founders and Patriots Am., Nat. Soc. Daus. Am. Colonists, Kans. Soc. Daus. Am. Colonists (organizing regent Dr. Thomas Lord chpt.), Nat. Soc. Sons and Daus. Pilgrims (elder Kans. br.), D.A.R., Ben Franklin Soc. (nat. adv. bd.), Daus. Colonial Wars, Order Descs. Colonial Physicians and Chirurgiens, Colonial Daus. 17th Century, Plantagenet Soc., Internat. Platform Soc. Author book of poems, 1941. Home and Office: 204 Curtis St Hutchinson KS 67501

BAUMGART, STEPHEN WAYNE, trading co. exec.; b. St. Louis, Oct. 25, 1940; s. Sylvestor John and Cornelia (Bitz) B.; B.S., U.S. Naval Acad., 1963; m. Margaret Gayle Hosse, June 15, 1963; children—Michael Kenneth, Margaret Kay. Commd. ensign USN, 1963, advanced through grades to lt., 1969; naval adviser to Pres.'s Sci. Adv. Com., mem. staff Chief of Naval Ops., 1963-69; cons. to IBM Fed. Systems, Raybestos-Manhattan, Dept. Def., Owner B Assos., 1970-74; chmn., chief exec. officer Gateway Internat. Co., 1974—; dir. Chemimetal S.A., Brussels, ITCC, Sharjah, Simex-Gabon, Gabomer S.A., Gabon. Decorated Bronze Star with Combat V and Gold Star; commendation Sec. of Navy. Home: 11216 South Shore Rd Reston VA 22090 Office: PO Box 17253 Gateway One Bldg Dulles Airport Washington DC 20041

BAUMGARTNER, ALLAN RODNEY, computer co. exec.; b. N.Y.C., May 27, 1938; s. John Herbert and Claire Regina (Strobele) B.; B.S., Carnegie Inst. Tech., 1960; m. Dolores Zalewski, Dec. 4, 1976; children—Yvette Selena, Brendon Allan Hans. Product mgr. Westinghouse Electric Corp., Sunnyvale, Calif., 1966-67, data processing devel. mgr., 1967-71; data communications designer Pacific Telephone Co., San Francisco, 1971-74, internal cons., 1974-78; cons. to advanced communications system AT&T, Morristown, N.J., 1976-77; dir. tech. strategy Nat. Semicondr. Corp., San Diego, 1979-80, dir. software mktg. subs. Nat. Advanced Systems, Inc., Mountain View, Calif., 1980—; cons. mgmt. and data processing. Served to capt. C.E., U.S. Army, 1960-65. Mem. Data Processing Mgmt. Assn., IEEE, Assn. Data Processing Service Orgns. Republican. Home: 14820 Satanas St San Diego CA 92129 Office: 800 E Middlefield Rd Mountain View CA 94043

BAUMGARTNER, RICHARD MATHIAS, ins./investments co. exec.; b. Bird Island, Minn., Apr. 3, 1913; s. William and Theresa Baumgartner; B.A. in Bus. Adminstrn., Coll. of St. Thomas, St. Paul, 1937; m. Anne Jane Durkan, May 22, 1943; children—Marcia Sue Baumgartner Wilkowski, Shelley Anne Baumgartner Machacek, Mary Elizabeth Baumgartner Sawdey, Robyn Lynn. With Federated Muts. Co., Mpls., 1937-42; owner, mgr. R.M. Baumgartner Agy., Bemidji, Minn., 1946—; pres. Baumgartner, Inc., Bemidji, 1964—, IPS Inc., Bemidji, 1970—; pres. Valley View, Inc., St. Paul, 1962-67, chmn. bd., 1967—. Bd. dirs. Bemidji State U. Found., 1974-79, Bemidji Devel. Corp. Served with USN, 1942-46. Mem. Nat. Assn. Mut. Agts., Minn. Assn. Ins. Agts. (dir. 1963, cert. of merit 1965), Ind. Ins. Agts. Minn., Minn. Assn. Profl. Ins. Agts., Profl. Ins. Agts. Polit. Action Com., Am. Legion, VFW, Bemidji C. of C. (pres. 1971-72). Republican. Roman Catholic. Clubs: K.C. (grand knight 1951-52), Elks, Moose, Bemidji Blue Line, Presidents (Benidji State U. Found.), Bemidji Town and Country (pres. 1954-55), Leech Lake Yacht, Birchmont Tennis, Bemidji Gun, Bemidji Curling, Ducks Unlimited, Lions. Home: 3042 Birchmont Dr Bemidji MN 56601 Office: 210 Beltrami Ave PO Box 808 Bemidji MN 56601

BAUMHART, RAYMOND CHARLES, univ. pres.; b. Chgo., Dec. 22, 1923; s. Emil and Florence (Weidner) B.; B.S., Northwestern U., 1945; Ph.L., Loyola U., 1952, S.T.L., 1958; M.B.A., Harvard, 1953, D.B.A., 1963; LL.D. (hon.), Ill. Coll. Joined Jesuit Order, 1946; ordained priest Roman Catholic Ch., 1957; asst. prof. mgmt. Loyola U., Chgo., 1962-64, dean Sch. Bus. Adminstrn., 1964-66, exec. v.p., acting v.p. Med. Center, 1968-70, pres., 1970—; research fellow Cambridge Center for Social Studies, 1966-68; dir., Jewel Cos., Inc., Continental Ill. Corp. Trustee Boston Coll., 1968-71, St. Louis U., 1967-72; bd. dirs. Council Better Bus. Burs. Served to lt. (j.g.) USNR, 1944-46. Decorated Order of Cavalier (Italy); recipient Râle medallion Boston Coll.; John W. Hill fellow Harvard, 1961-62. Mem. Assn. Jesuit Colls. and Univs. (dir.), Fedn. Ind. Ill. Colls. and Univs. (dir.). Clubs: Commercial, Economic, Mid-America (Chgo.). Author: An Honest Profit, 1968; (with Thomas Garrett) Cases in Business Ethics, 1968; (with Thomas McMahon) The Brewer-Wholesaler Relationship, 1969. Corr. editor: America, 1965-70. Home: 6525 N Sheridan Rd Chicago IL 60626 Office: Loyola U Sch Bus Adminstrn 820 N Michigan Ave Chicago IL 60611

BAUR, STEPHEN, high-technology products co. exec.; b. N.Y.C., Sept. 29, 1922; s. Stephen A. and Elsie (Reckert) B.; B.Mech. Engring., N.Y. U., 1949; m. Gloria Patricia Scheib, May 11, 1954; children—Nancy Ann, Robert Charles. Design engr. Fairchild Camera & Instrument Corp., Jamaica, N.Y., 1941-43; asso. editor Iron Age mag., N.Y.C., 1949-50; dist. mgr. Harry W. Smith, Inc., Chgo., 1950-54; dir. pub. relations Harris D. McKinney, Inc., Phila., 1954-59, Erwin Wasey, Ruthrauff & Ryan, Inc., Phila., 1959-64; dir. corp. communications ESB, Inc. (formerly Electric Storage Battery Co.), Phila., 1964-76; v.p. corp. relations Ambac Industries, Inc., Carle Place, N.Y., 1976-78, Harris Corp., Melbourne, Fla., 1978—. Served with USAAF, 1943-46. Mem. Pub. Relations Soc. Am., Nat. Investor Relations Inst., Bus./Profl. Advt. Assn., ASME, NAM (chmn. public relations council 1972), Machinery and Allied Products Inst., Psi Upsilon. Home: 2600 S Patrick Dr Indialantic FL 32903 Office: Harris Corp Corporate Hdqrs Melbourne FL 32919

BAXENDALE, MICHAEL STANLEY, publisher; b. Brighouse, York, Eng., Sept. 27, 1937; s. Stanley and Dora Marie (Day) B.; ed. U. Toronto; m. Anna Ozvoldik, May 5, 1966; children—Dean, Bradley, Alison. Asst. to v.p. Kelvinator of Can., 1958-60; market analyst Montreal Standard Pub. Co., 1960-62, sales and mktg. mgr., 1962-67, asst. dir., 1968-71; dir. info. services div. Montreal Star, 1971-75; founder, pub. Optimum Pub. Co., Ltd., Montreal, 1975—, now chief operating officer; pub., chief operating officer Les Editions Optimum Limitée; lectr. in field. Bd. dirs. Montreal Internat. Book Fair. Served with Royal Canadian Regiment, 1955-58. Mem. Am. Mktg. Assn. (past v.p., dir.), Canadian Book Pubs. Council, Bd. of Trade. Anglican. Author: Role of Marketing in Corporate Growth; co-author books, numerous mag. articles. Home: 27 Place de Bretagne Candiac PQ J5R 3M9 Canada Office: 245 Saint Jacques St W Montreal PQ H2Y 1M6 Canada

BAXTER, GENE KENNETH, engring. mgmt. exec.; b. Emmett, Idaho, Sept. 4, 1939; s. Glen Wilton and Mable Velhelmina (Casper) B., Sr.; A.A. in Mech. Engring. (scholar), Boise Jr. Coll., 1959; B.S. in Mech. Engring., U. Idaho, 1961; M.S. in Aero. Engring. (NDEA fellow), Syracuse U., 1966, Ph.D. in Mech. Engring., 1971; m. Laraine Marie Mitchell, Jan. 20, 1968; children—Gretchen Lynn, Aaron Gregory. Engr. Pratt & Whitney Aircraft Co., East Hartford, Conn., 1961; teaching and research asst. Syracuse (N.Y.) U., 1962-67; engr. Galson & Galson Cons. Engrs., Syracuse, 1968; sr. mech. engr., staff engr. electronic systems div. Gen. Electric Co., Syracuse, 1968-77; advanced project mgr., space div., Daytona Beach, Fla., 1977, mgr. mech. design engring., 1977—; tchr. refresher course N.Y. State Profl. Engrs., Syracuse, 1975-76. Chmn. fin. and stewardship com. United Ch. of Christ, Liverpool, N.Y., 1974-77, chmn. bd. trustees, 1977; pres. Ormond Beach (Fla.) Presbyterian Ch., 1979-80, ruling elder, 1980—, chmn. stewardship com., 1979-80. Recipient design award Machinery Mag., 1961; Raymond J. Briggs award Idaho State Bd. Engring. Examiners, 1961; profl. licensed engr., N.Y. Mem. IEEE (sr.; treas. Daytona sect. 1978-79, chmn. 1979-80), ASME, Nat. Soc. Profl. Engrs., Sigma Xi, Phi Kappa Phi, Tau Beta Pi, Phi Theta Kappa. Club: Tomoka Oaks Country. Panelist, speaker numerous profl. conferences; contbr. over 30 research papers in field. Home: 10 Pebble Beach Dr Ormond Beach FL 32074 Office: Gen Electric Co PO Box 2500 Daytona Beach FL 32015

BAXTER, HARRY STEVENS, lawyer; b. Ashburn, Ga., Aug. 25, 1915; s. James Hubert and Anna (Stevens) B.; A.B. summa cum laude, U. Ga., 1936, LL.B. summa cum laude, 1939; postgrad. Yale, 1939-40; m. Edith Ann Teasley, Apr. 4, 1943; children—Anna Katherine (Mrs. Paul Worley) (dec.), Nancy Julia (Mrs. John Adams Sibley III). Admitted to Ga. bar, 1941; instr. U. Ga. Law Sch., Athens, 1941; asso. Smith Kilpatrick, Cody, Rogers & McClatchey, Atlanta, 1942-51; partner Kilpatrick & Cody, Atlanta, 1951—; mem. State Bd. Bar Examiners Ga., 1960-66, chmn., 1961-66; mem. Ga. Jud. Qualifications Commn., 1979—; dir. Latex Contrns. Co., Atlanta. Pres., Atlanta Community Chest, 1963; mem. bd. visitors U. Ga. Law Sch., 1965-68, chmn., 1965-66, chmn. alumni adv. com. on reorgn., 1962-64, chmn. alumni adv. com. on selection dean, 1972-73; chmn. chancellor's alumni adv. com. on selection of pres. U. Ga., 1966-67; gen. co-chmn. Joint Ga. Tech.-Ga. Devel. Fund, 1967-68. Trustee William E. Honey Found., St. Joseph's Infirmary, Atlanta; chmn. bd. trustees U. Ga. Found., 1973-76. Served with AUS, 1942-45. Recipient Distinguished Alumnus award U. Ga. Law Sch., 1967. Fellow Am. Bar Found.; mem. Am. Law Inst., Am., Ga., Atlanta bar assns., Atlanta C. of C. (dir. 1959-62), Atlanta Legal Aid Soc. (pres. 1956-57), Phi Beta Kappa, Phi Beta Kappa Assos., Phi Kappa Phi, Omicron Delta Kappa, Phi Delta Phi. Clubs: Capital City (pres. 1965-67), Lawyers (pres. 1958-59), Piedmont Driving, Commerce, Univ. Yacht (Atlanta). Home: 3197 Chatham Rd NW Atlanta GA 30305 Office: Equitable Bldg Atlanta GA 30043

BAYDALA, EDWARD THOMAS, coll. adminstr.; b. Munson, N.Y., Sept. 18, 1919; s. Andrew and Josephine (Zatorski) B.; B.S., U. Md., 1954; M.B.A., George Washington U., 1955; m. Eileen M. Bellion, July 31, 1943; children—Aileen, Thomas, Nancy, Robert, Susan, John. Statis. clk. N.Y. Stock Exchange, 1936-40; bond specialist Fed. Res. Bank, N.Y.C., 1940-42; commd. 2d lt. USAAF, 1942, advanced through grades to col., USAF, 1964; dir. budget Air Def. Command, Mitchel Field, N.Y., 1946-50; budget br. chief USAF, Washington, 1950-54; asst. controller European Command, Paris, 1955-58; resident auditor Richards-Gebaur AFB, Mo., 1958-59; chief internal audits So. Dist., Ft. Worth, 1959-62; data automation tech. br. chief USAF, Washington, 1963-65, data automation program br. chief, 1965-67; dir. profl. controller course Air U., Maxwell AFB, Ala., 1967-68; ret., 1968; dir. budget State U. Coll., Fredonia, N.Y., 1968-69, v.p. for adminstrn., 1969-79; bus. mgr. Fla. Inst. Tech., Melbourne, 1979—; instr. bus. adminstrn. U. Md., 1955-56, 63-67; instr. accounting No. Va. Community Coll., 1966-67. Treas. Fredonia Coll. Found., 1968—. Decorated Bronze Star medal, Air Force Commendation medal with 2 oak leaf clusters, Army Commendation medal. Mem. Air Force Assn., Ret. Officers Assn., Risk Mgmt. Soc., Fla.-Columbia Partners. Republican. Roman Catholic. Club: Suntree Country. Author: State of the Art - Optical Scanners, 1964; Development of Data Systems within the Air Force, 1966; The Impact of U.S. Military Forces Overseas on U.S. Balance of Payments, 1968; Operations of Residence Halls within State University, 1972. Home: 500 Inverness Ave Melbourne FL 32935

BAYNARD, MILDRED MOYER (MRS. ROBERT S. BAYNARD), business exec., club woman; b. Lincoln, Nebr., May 10, 1902; d. Charles Calvin and Flora (Harter) Moyer; student Sullins Coll., 1921, U. So. Calif., 1922; B.A., U. Nebr., 1925; m. Robert S. Baynard, May 24, 1927; 1 son, Lester B. Tchr. pub. schs., Lincoln, 1926-27, Crescent City, Fla., 1925-26; sec. Venice Land Co., Inc., 1949-69; sec. Fla. Bridge Co., 1960-68; partner Ind. Parking, 1965-72; v.p. Venice-Nokomis Bank, Venice, Fla., 1947-63, dir., 1947-63; pres. Venice Land Co., 1969-72. Mem. Fla. State Dist. Welfare Bd., 1948-52; pres. bd. dirs. YWCA, 1953-56; Fla. chmn. Nat. Soc. Prevention Blindness, 1957-60, bd. dirs., 1960-67, v.p., 1963-66; nat. v.p., pres. Fla. Soc. Prevention Blindness, 1958-64, v.p., 1967-68, also mem. Fla. exec. com., hon. life mem.; dir. Center for Blind, 1956; pres. Suncoast div. Arthritis Found. Inc., 1966-67; mem. nat. voter adv. bd. Nat. Security Council; pres. North Ward P.T.A., 1938; sec. St. Petersburg (Fla.) Woman's Club, 1945-46; corr. sec. St. Margaret's Guild, St. Thomas Episcopal Ch., St. Petersburg; Democratic precinct committeewoman, 1936. Recipient Outstanding Citizen's award Pinellas County Commn., 1964, Sarah Schwab Deutsch award, 1978. Mem. Internat. Platform Assn. (sec. So. region 1965), Stuart Soc., St. Petersburg Hist. Soc., Mus. Fine Arts, All Childrens Hosp. Guild, U. Neb. Alumni Assn., Museum of Fine Arts, Nat. Soc. for Lit. and Arts, Am. Council World Freedom, Nat. Taxpayers Union, D.A.R., Delta Gamma (province officer 1950-56, conv. chmn. 1964, Cable award 1964, Shield award 1973, house corp. 1969—, hon. fellow found. 1974—). Clubs: Sorosis; Rotary Ann. (pres. Venice 1962); Yacht of St. Petersburg, Panhellenic, Women's, Interlock (sec. 1942-44) (St. Petersburg, Fla.); Venice Nokomis Woman's (life). Mem. editorial adv. bd. Florida Lives. Home: 627 Brightwaters Blvd NE Saint Petersburg FL 33704

BAYNE, WILLIAM HENRY, JR., mgmt., pub. relations cons.; b. Kearny, N.J., Dec. 13, 1912; s. William H. and Margaret W. (Aitken) B.; student Rutgers U., 1932-35, Columbia, 1935-37; m. Adele Wehman, May 29, 1946; children—Edward J., William H. III. Reporter, N.Y. World, N.Y. Herald-Tribune, Newark Evening News, 1935-40; dir. pub. relations Brewster Aero. Corp., Long Island City, N.Y., 1940-43; chief instrn. and edn., dept. medicine and surgery VA, Washington, 1946-48; editor, pub. Handicap Pub. Co., Washington, 1948—, pub., 1976—; editor, pub. Washington Med. News Bur., 1950; pres. Bayne Assos., mgmt. and pub. relations cons., Washington, 1955—; exec. dir. Asso. Builders and Contractors Va., 1968-70; exec. v.p., gen. mgr. Paulen Industries, Inc., Paulen Chem. Co., Beltsville, Md., 1970-75; pres. Rehab. Services Advisors, 1973—; dir. Md. Maritime Assos., Hosp. Systems, Med. Systems Advisors, Surg. Research & Devel. Corp., Central Am. Liaison Corp. Mem. steering com. Pres. Truman's Nat. Health Assembly, 1948; mem. Pres.'s Com. on Employment of Physically Handicapped, 1948-76; mem. White House Conf. Handicapped Individuals, 1976-77; bd. dirs. Prince Georges Scholarship Fund, Greater Washington Sci. Fair Assn., Spina Bifida Assn. Am. Served with AUS, 1943-47. Mem. AAAS, Am. Chem. Soc., Am. Inst. Mcht. Shipping, Am. Mgmt. Assn., Nat. Rehab. Assn., Soc. Plastics Engrs., Am. Med. Writers Assn., Nat. Assn. Execs. Mason. Home and Office: 5709 38th Ave Hyattsville MD 20782

BAYS, KIRK VAN, ins. co. exec.; b. Springfield, Mo., June 22, 1951; s. Robert Newell and Gertha Bernice (Huddleston) B.; B.S. in Bus. Adminstrn. (scholar), Nicholls State U., 1973; postgrad. U. Tex., 1978-79; m. Cindy Fondren, June 9, 1973. Credit mgr. Terrebonne Bank & Trust Co., Houma, La., 1973-74; agt. Aetna Life & Casualty Co., New Orleans, 1974-75, agt., asst. supr., Tampa, Fla., 1975-76, estate and bus. analysis mgr., Dallas, 1976—; sales cons. to various orgns.; cons. Pres. Young Republicans, Thibodaux, La., 1972-73; mem. Nat. Rep. Com., 1976—. Recipient Nat. Sales Achievement award, 1974-77, 79, 80; Nat. Quality award, 1975-77, 79, 80; Man of Yr. award Aetna Life & Casualty, New Orleans, 1974, Tampa, 1975; named to Million Dollar Roundtable, 1975-76, 79, 80; recipient Sales Mgmt. award, 1976, 77, 78. Mem. Nat. Assn. Life Underwriters, Dallas Assn. Life Underwriters, Fellowship of Christian Athletes. Baptist. Home: 1704 Tulane Dr Richardson TX 75081 Office: 8350 N Central Expressway Suite M-2100 Dallas TX 75206

BAYTOS, LAWRENCE MICHAEL, food co. exec.; b. Youngstown, Ohio, May 15, 1937; s. John Stephen and Helen Marie B.; B.B.A., Youngstown U., 1959; M.B.A., Harvard U., 1961; m. Carol Ann Moore, June 23, 1962; children—Laura, Lisa. Mem. indsl. relations staff Procter & Gamble, 1961-64; cons. Hewitt Booz Allen, 1964-69; dir. personnel Fed. Signal Co., 1969-72; v.p. corp. personnel Quaker Oats Co., Chgo., 1972—. Bd. dirs. Chgo. Alliance for Bus., Edn. and Tng., 1979—. Served with AUS, 1961. Mem. Employers Assn. Greater Chgo. (dir. 1979—), Am. Soc. Personnel Adminstrn. (mem. pres.'s council). Roman Catholic. Clubs: Mid Am., Mdse. and Mfrs. Home: 109 W Farnham Wheaton IL 60187 Office: Merchandise Mart Plaza Chicago IL 60654

BAYUK, ANNE MARIE, investment adviser; b. Farrell, Pa., May 7, 1916; d. John and Helen (Baron) Kmetz; R.N., Allegheny Gen. Hosp., 1938; student U. Pitts., 1938-40; children—Dennis John, Bonita Anne, Darryl Anthony. Mgr., Bel-Park Anesthesia Assn., Youngstown, Ohio, 1968-78; sec.-treas., dir. Beachwood Investments, Inc. (Ohio), 1977—. Recipient awards for appreciation Coop. Office Edn., 1968—. Mem. Internat. Assn. Fin. Planners. Home: 1323 St Albans St Youngstown OH 44511 Office: 24300 Chagrin Blvd Beachwood OH 44122

BAYUK, DENNIS JOHN, investment broker and adviser, real estate developer; b. Youngstown, Ohio, Jan. 20, 1947; s. Anthony Joseph and Anne Marie (Kmetz) B.; B.S., U. Miami (Fla.), 1968; M.S., U. Akron (Ohio), 1974; m. Linda Elizabeth LaBelle, July 26, 1974. Options prin. Nat. Assn. Securities Dealers, Beachwood, Ohio, 1978—, fin. and ops. prin., 1977—, gen. securities prin., 1977—; registered investment adviser SEC, Lyndhurst, Ohio, 1977-78; pres., dir. Beachwood Investments, Inc., 1977—, La Belle Capital Corp., 1979—; instr. securities Wall St. Internat. Cert. fin. planner. Mem. Internat. Assn. Fin. Planners. Home: 5228 Lynd Ave Lyndhurst OH 44124 Office: 24300 Chagrin Blvd Beachwood OH 44122

BAYUS, BRIAN EDWARD, ins. co. exec.; b. Bridgeport, Conn., Mar. 17, 1945; s. Stephen Zachary and Rita Alice B.; B.A., U. Mich., 1971, J.D., 1973; m. Carol Anne Marr, May 14, 1966; children—Catherine, Christopher. Admitted to Mich. bar, 1974, Conn. bar, 1974, Ill. bar, 1976, D.C. bar, 1980; atty. Travelers Ins. Co., Hartford, Conn., 1973-76; asst. v.p., legal counsel Ill. Mut. Life & Casualty Co., Peoria, 1976-78; v.p., sec., gen. counsel Consumers United Ins. Co., Washington, 1978—; dir. Forest Hills, Inc. Served with U.S. Navy, 1966-68. Fellow Life Mgmt. Inst.; mem. Am. Bar Assn., Conn. Bar Assn., Mich. Bar Assn., Ill. Bar Assn., Am. Trial Lawyers Assn., Am. Judicature Soc., Am. Council Life Ins., Am. Coll. Life Underwriters. Roman Catholic. Clubs: Rox Mills Woods Tennis, Reston Country. Home: 2521 Heathcliff Ln Reston VA 22091 Office: 2100 M St NW Washington DC 20037

BAZIN, ALBERT JEIL, corp. exec.; b. Caracas, Venezuela, Sept. 20, 1904; s. Miguel Uzcategui and Rosa (Sarria) B.; B.C.S. cum laude, N.Y. U., 1929; m. Mildred Davidson, July 18, 1931 (dec. 1971); 1 son, James D.; m. 2d, Frances Sichel Lahey, Apr. 7, 1973. Came to U.S., 1910, naturalized, 1935. Asst. treas. Jaeger Watch Co., N.Y.C., 1929-35; sec.-treas. Albert B. Ashforth, Inc., N.Y.C., 1935-59, v.p., treas., 1959-71, sr. v.p., treas., 1971-75, sr. v.p., 1975—, dir., 1935—; sec.-treas. Albert B. Ashforth, Ltd., 1961-75, also dir.; gen. mgr. Venezuelan Supply Corp., N.Y.C., 1965—; sec.-treas., dir. Duff & Conger, Inc., Comml. Mgmt. Corp., 1946-75; dir. Western Hemisphere Export Co. Trustee Employees Profit Sharing Retirement Trust. Licensed real estate broker, N.Y. State, Conn. Mem. Real Estate Bd. of N.Y., Greenwich Bd. Realtors, Beta Gamma Sigma, Alpha Kappa Psi. Club: Wykagyl Country (past gov.). Home: 25 Old Orchard Rd Port Chester NY 10573 Office: 2 Greenwich Plaza Greenwich CT 06830

BEACH, KAREN OVERBAUGH, advt. agy. exec.; b. Schenectady, Jan. 13, 1950; d. Merrill V. and Arleyne D. (Knizek) Overbaugh; B.A., SUNY, 1972; M.B.A., U. Conn., 1979; m. Jeffrey W. Beach, Apr. 27, 1974. Market research project dir. The Stop & Shop Cos., Inc., Boston, 1975-77; tchr. German/French, Shaker Jr. High Sch., Latham, N.Y., 1972-75; v.p. research, dir. Creamer, Inc., Hartford, Conn., 1977-78, v.p., account supr., 1978—. Vice chmn. Neighborhood Alliance, Hartford, 1979-81. Mem. Am. Mktg. Assn. (chpt. dir. 1979—). Office: 100 Constitution Plaza Hartford CT 06103

BEACH, MARY ELINOR THOMPSON, lawyer; b. Washington, Jan. 28, 1935; d. Jesse Albert and Ethel Catherine (Lowrey) Thompson; B.S., Ohio State U., 1957; M.B.A., George Washington U., 1961, LL.B., 1965; m. Donald F. Beach, Apr. 22, 1963; children—Patrick Clarence, Catherine Maryon, Harry Thompson. Rep., Ferris & Co., 1957-58; fin. analyst div. corp. fin. SEC, 1958-66, br. chief div. corp. fin., 1966-72, chief Office of Disclosure Policy and proc., 1972-76, staff dir. SEC Adv. Com. on Corp. Disclosure, 1976-77, asso. dir. div. corp. fin., 1976—; lectr. Columbus Sch. Law, Cath. U. Am. Mem. Fed. Bar Assn. Office: 500 N Capitol St Washington DC 20549

BEACH, MORRISON H., ins. co. exec.; b. Winsted, Conn., Jan. 10, 1917; s. Howard Edmund and Edith (Morrison) B.; B.A., Williams Coll., 1939; postgrad. Mass. Inst. Tech., 1942; J.D., U. Conn., 1954; m. Evelyn R. Harris, Sept. 6, 1942; children—Howard, Linda, Deborah. With Travelers Corp., Hartford, Conn., 1939—, asst. actuary, 1950-54, asso. actuary, 1954-57, actuary, 1957-59, v.p., actuary, 1959-62, 2d v.p., 1962-64, v.p., 1964-65, sr. v.p., 1965-70, exec. v.p., 1970-71, pres., chief adminstrv. officer, 1971-73, chmn., chief exec. officer, 1973—, also dir.; dir. numerous Travelers subs.'s, Travcan Ltd., Greater Hartford Corp., Conn. Econ. Devel. Corp. Co-chmn. Conn.-Western Mass. region NCCJ; mem. White House Conf. on Aging, 1981, Greater Hartford Community Council; mem. nat. adv. com. Nat. Multiple Sclerosis Soc.; bd. dirs. Hartford Hosp., Greater Hartford chpt. ARC; trustee Hartford Grad. Center, Trinity Coll., Kingswood-Oxford Sch., Horace Bushnell Meml. Hall Corp.; corporator Hartford Sem. Found., Inst. of Living, Winsted Meml. Hosp. Served to maj. USAAF; ETO. Fellow Soc. Actuaries; mem.

Conn. Bar Assn., Am. Council Life Ins. (dir.), Internat. Ins. Seminars, Inc. (dir.), Ins. Assn. Conn. (dir.), Conf. Bd., Bus. Round Table, Greater Hartford C. of C. (dir.). Home: 100 Uplands Dr West Hartford CT 06107 Office: One Tower Sq Hartford CT 06115

BEACHAM, FRANK WILLIAM, printing co. exec.; b. Buffalo, Mar. 10, 1932; s. George Robert and Joan Constance B.; student (Acad. scholar) U.S. Coast Guard Acad., 1950-52; B.S.I.E., U. Buffalo, 1955; M.B.A., SUNY, Buffalo, 1970; m. lly Marie Milligan, May 21, 1955; children—Michael, Michele, Maureen, Mark. Cost estimator Esso Research & Engring. Co., Linden, N.J., 1955-57; project engr. J.W. Clement Co., Buffalo, 1957-58; chief engr. Clement Colortype Co., Chgo., 1958-64; mfg. services mgr. Arcata-Graphics Co., Buffalo, 1964-69, dir. mfg., 1969-71, mgr. engring. services, 1971-74; mgr. engring. Arcata Publs. Group, Los Angeles, 1974-76, Stamford, Conn., 1976—, v.p. tech. services, 1978—. Mem. Gravure Research Inst. (adv. bd.), Research and Engring. Council (exec. com.), Gravure Tech. Assn., Printing Assn. Am. Roman Catholic. Club: K.C. Patentee in field. Home: 890 Cedar Rd Southport CT 06490 Office: 2 Landmark Sq Stamford CT 06901

BEAGAN, CHARLES JOHN, investment co. exec.; b. N.Y.C., Dec. 4, 1941; s. Charles Hackett and Alice Ethel (O'Connor) B.; A.B. in History, Coll. of Holy Cross, 1963; M.A. in History (Maude E. Warwick scholar), N.Y. U., 1969. Vice pres., dir. Re-Con Systems Corp., N.Y.C., 1968-70, Ednl. Guidance Systems Corp., N.Y.C., 1970-71; salesman, adminstr. Teltronics Services Inc., N.Y.C., 1971-74; account exec. Merrill Lynch, Pierce, Fenner & Smith, N.Y.C., 1974-76; regional syndicate mgr. E.F. Hutton & Co. Inc., N.Y.C., 1976—. Mem. Investment Assn. N.Y., Securities Industry Assn. (vice chmn. com. govt. relations N.Y. dist.), Internat. Platform Assn., U.S. Strategic Inst., Friends of Musica Sacra. Democrat. Roman Catholic. Club: Holy Cross (N.Y.C.). Home: 444 E 58th St New York NY 10022 Office: 1 Battery Park Plaza New York NY 10004

BEAIRD, BYRON BRYANT GRADY, fin. exec.; b. Apr. 28; s. Grady Milford and Nancy Isabelle (Bryant) B.; ed. Northwestern U.; m. Evelyn Ruth Frost, Oct. 18; children—Richard Charles, John Michael. Owner, Beaird's Cafe, 1936-38; mgr. Rex Cafe, 1939-41; with E. I. DuPont de Nemours & Co., Inc., Wilmington, Del., 1942-43; cost acct. Douglas Aircraft Co., Santa Monica, Calif., 1944-45; maitre d'hotel Ladd's Supper Club, Santa Monica, 1946-49; dining car steward A.C.L., N.Y.C. and Union Pacific R.R., Denver, 1950, supr. dining car and hotel dept., 1964-71, supr. commissary, 1971—; pres., founder Ice Creations Unltd., Denver, 1970-75; now pres. M-M Investment Prodn. Co., Los Angeles. Mem. Griffith Park Hills Republican Assembly, Los Angeles County Rep. Assembly, Calif. Rep. Assembly. Mem. Soc. of Geneva, Rocky Mountain Restaurant Assn. Methodist. Clubs: Portland Press, Ranch Country, Internat. House, Beverly Hills Optimist, U.S. Navy League, Rosicrucian Order. Patentee in field. Home: 1841 Thayer Ave Los Angeles CA 90025 Office: Wilshire Tower Suite 406 5514 Wilshire Blvd Los Angeles CA 90036

BEAIRD, DAN LAGETTE, real estate co. exec.; b. Tyler, Tex., Nov. 21, 1937; s. Bryant LaGette and Abbie (Asbury) B.; B.B.A., U. Tex.; m. Martha Lou Hester, Mar. 6, 1965; children—Gayden, Benjamin. Life ins. salesman Dan Beaird & Assos., 1958-67; pres., chief exec. officer Dan Beaird Inc., Dallas, Okla. Exploration, 1967—, also dir.; dir. Murray Savs. Mem. exec. com. Highland Park Community League, 1978—. Served to 2d lt. AUS, 1959-63. Mem. Dallas Real Estate Bd., Comml. and Indsl. Real Estate Bd. Presbyterian (elder). Office: Dan Beaird Inc 2412 Homer St Dallas TX 75206

BEAL, GARY MICHAEL, banker; b. Hobbs, N.Mex., Mar. 22, 1947; s. Bingham and Betty G. (Beal) B.; B.B.A., U. N.Mex., 1969; postgrad. Southwestern Grad. Sch. Banking, So. Meth. U., 1978; m. Dianne Beal; 1 child. Staff accountant, auditor Moore & Nials, C.P.A.'s, Hobbs, N.Mex., 1965-68, Daniel M. Smith & Co., C.P.A., Albuquerque, 1968-69; mgmt. trainee, credit analyst, sales rep. United Calif. Bank, Los Angeles, 1969-71; with N.Mex. Bank & Trust, Hobbs, 1971-80, v.p., mgr., 1974-80; v.p., sr. loan officer 1st Nat. Bank, Springdale, Ark., 1981—; instr. N.Mex. Jr. Coll. Div. chmn. United Way, Hobbs, 1973-74; exec. dir. Miss N.Mex. Pageant, 1976-78. Bd. dirs. N.Mex. Assn. Retarded Citizens; bd. dirs., treas. Lea Sheltered Activity Center, Hobbs Assn. Retarded Children; chmn. city planning bd. City of Hobbs; mem. Gov.'s Council on Disabled, State of N.Mex.; mem. exec. com. U. N.Mex. Alumni Assn. Named Outstanding Jaycee of Year, Hobbs Jaycees, 1972, Outstanding Young Man Am., 1975, Outstanding Young Citizen of Hobbs, 1978. Mem. U.S. Jaycees (nat. dir. N.Mex. 1973-74), Hobbs Jaycees (pres. 1972-73), Hobbs C. of C. (dir.). Methodist. Home: 1638 Cartwright Circle Springdale AR 72764 Office: PO Box 249 Springdale AR 72764

BEAL, ROBERT LAWRENCE, real estate exec.; b. Boston, Sept. 10, 1941; s. Alexander Simpson and Leona M. (Rothstein) B.; B.A. cum laude, Harvard, 1963, M.B.A., 1965. Vice pres., partner Beacon Cos., Boston, 1965-76; gen. partner The Beal Cos.; exec. v.p., treas. Beal and Co., Inc., Boston, 1976—; trustee Provident Instn. Savs.; vice-chmn., dir. Mass. Indsl. Fin. Agy., 1976—; instr. real estate Northeastern U., 1969-75. Pres., dir. Boston Zool. Soc., 1972—; mem. vis. com. Sch. Mus. Fine Arts, Boston; overseer Boys Club Boston, 1975—; mem. corp. Belmont Hill Sch.; mem. bldg. com. Beth Israel Hosp.; dir. Harvard Coll. Fund Council, 1972-73; exec. bd. Boston chpt. Am. Jewish Com., 1979—; bd. dirs. Boston Municipal Research Bur., 1978—. Mem. Nat. Realty Com. (dir., treas. 1975—), Mass. Assn. Realtors (dir. 1979—), Greater Boston Real Estate Bd. (dir. 1970-72, 76—, pres. 1978-79), Bldg. Owners Mgrs. Assn. Boston (dir. 1970-72), Ripon Soc. (nat. treas. 1968-73, nat. governing bd. 1979—), Beacon Hill Civic Assn. (dir. 1975-78), Greater Boston C. of C. (execs. club). Republican. Jewish. Home: 21 Brimmer St Boston MA 02108 Office: Suite 800 15 Broad St Boston MA 02109

BEALL, CHARLES CLYDE, JR., banker; b. Oxford, Miss., Mar. 28, 1935; s. Charles Clyde and Jennie Dale (Buford) B.; B.B.A., U. Miss., 1957, M.B.A., 1961; grad. Southwestern Grad. Sch. Banking, So. Meth. U., 1966; m. Ines Anne Watts, July 21, 1961; children—Charles Clyde III, Craig Alan. Joined Tex. Commerce Bank, Houston, 1961, mem. credit dept., 1962-64, comml. loan dept., 1964-65, with Nat. div., 1966-68, Met. div., 1969-73, exec. v.p., mgr. banking dept., 1974-77, pres., 1978—. Served with USAF, 1957-60. Office: 712 Main St PO Box 2558 Houston TX 77001

BEALL, DONALD RAY, mfg. co. exec.; b. Beaumont, Calif., 1938; s. Ray C. and Margaret Irene (Murray) B.; B.S., San Jose State Coll., 1960; M.B.A., U. Pitts., 1961; postgrad. UCLA. Controller, Ford Motor Co., Palo Alto, Calif., 1967-68, mgr. corp. fin. planning and contracts, Phila., 1966-67, fin. mgmt. positions, Newport Beach, Calif., 1961-66; exec. dir. corp. fin. planning N. Am. Rockwell, El Segundo, Calif., 1968-69, exec. v.p. electronics group, 1969-71; exec. v.p. Collins Radio Co., Dallas, 1971-74; pres. Collins Radio Group, Rockwell Internat. Corp., 1974-76, pres. electronics ops. parent co., 1976-77, exec. v.p., 1977-79, pres., chief operating officer, 1979—, also dir.; dir. 1st Nat. Bank, Dallas. Past mem. bd. dirs. So. Methodist U. Found. Sci. and Engring., United Way Met. Dallas; gen. campaign chmn. W. Pa. affiliate Am. Diabetes Assn., 1979; trustee U. Pitts.; bd. dirs. United Way Allegheny County. Recipient award of distinction San Jose State U. Sch. Engring., 1980. Mem. Armed Forces Communications and Electronics Assn. (nat. dir.), Electronic Industries Assn., Aerospace Industries Assn. (bd. govs.), Soc. Automotive Engrs., Def. Preparedness Assn., Navy League U.S., Young Pres.'s Orgn. (Dir.'s Table), Beta Gamma Sigma, Sigma Alpha Epsilon. Clubs: Allegheny, Balboa Bay, Balboa Yacht, Cat Cay, Duquesne, Fox Chapel Golf, Rolling Rock. Office: Rockwell Internat Corp 600 Grant St Pittsburgh PA 15219

BEAM, THOMAS JOSEPH, fin. and mgmt. cons.; b. Phila., Jan. 1, 1946; s. Thomas J. and Jeannette H. (Templin) B.; B.S. in Acctg., Temple U., 1967; Ph.D. in Acctg. and Ops. Research (NDEA fellow), N.Y. U., 1976; children—Meredith S., Kimberly J. Mem. staff Arthur Andersen & Co., Newark, 1969-72; fin. mgr. Am. Hoechst Corp., Somerville, N.J., 1972-80; cons. AMIC Research Assos., Jersey City, 1980—; asso. prof. acctg. Fairleigh Dickinson U., Madison, N.J., 1980—. Mem. Nat. Assn. Accts. (dir. local chpt.), N. Am. Soc. Corp. Planning, Am. Inst. C.P.A.'s, Pa. Inst. C.P.A.'s, Am. Acctg. Assn., Am. Fin. Assn., Beta Alpha Psi, Beta Gamma Sigma. Office: AMIC Research Assos 1 Exchange Pl Jersey City NJ 07302

BEAMAN, BRUCE EDWARD, mfg. co. exec.; b. Greensboro, N.C., Oct. 24, 1924; s. William J. and Susie (Oliver) B.; B.M.E., N.C. State U., 1948; postgrad. in Elec. Engring., U. Pitts., 1949-50; m. Janet Simpkins, Oct. 11, 1960; children—Bruce, Lisa, Karleigh, Janet, Nancy. Engr., Westinghouse Corp., Pitts., 1950-51; pres. Beaman Corp., Greensboro, 1952—, Bardex Corp., Greensboro, 1970—; dir. Triangle Engring. Co., Central Engring. Co., Beaman Realty Co. Active YMCA, Boy Scouts Am. Served with inf. AUS, 1941-45. Decorated Bronze Star. Mem. ASME, Pi Tau Sigma, Pi Kappa Alpha. Republican. Christian Scientist. Clubs: Kiwanis, Greensboro Country, Greensboro Engrs. Home: 3103 Greenbrook Dr Greensboro NC 27408 Office: 800 W Smith St Greensboro NC 27420

BEARDEN, DONN ROBERT, banker; b. Berkeley, Calif., May 3, 1933; s. Prewitt Henry and Esther (Brickman) B.; B.S., U. Calif., Berkeley, 1955; grad. Bank Adminstrn. Inst. Sch. Banking, U. Wis., Madison, 1978; m. Eleanor Whitmore, Aug. 15, 1959; children—Paul Robert, Lisa. Cost acct. to div. analyst U.S. Steel Corp., Pittsburg, Calif., 1959-68; acctg. officer Exchange Bank, Santa Rosa, Calif., 1968-73, v.p., controller, 1973—. Active, YMCA; pres. Handicapped Vocat. Tng. Workshop, 1973. Served to lt. USNR, 1955-58. Mem. Nat. Assn. Accts., Bank Adminstrn. Inst. (pres. San Francisco chpt. 1977-78, nat. treas. 1979-80). Republican. Office: Exchange Bank PO Box 403 Santa Rosa CA 95402

BEARDEN, GARY EDWARD, oilfield equipment mfg. co. exec.; b. Beaumont, Tex., May 8, 1946; s. John Louis and Dorothea Alice (Carley) B.; B.B.A., Tex. A&M U., 1969; m. Dorothy Jean Stiebing, Aug. 3, 1969; children—Alise, Garrick, Melissa. Auditor, Touche Ross & Co., Houston, 1969-72; asst. to chmn. bd. Hycel, Inc., Houston, 1972-76; v.p. fin. B.S. & B Safety Systems Group, Tulsa, 1976-78; v.p. fin. F.H. Maloney Co., Houston, 1978—, dir., 1980—. C.P.A., Tex., Okla. Mem. Am. Prodn. and Inventory Control Soc., Okla. Soc. C.P.A.'s. Republican. Mormon. Author: (with Stolle) Auditing Computer Generated Accounts, 1971. Home: 11914 Normont St Houston TX 77070 Office: PO Box 287 Houston TX 77001

BEARE, DAVID C., commodities trading co. exec.; b. Urbana, Ill., July 10, 1941; s. Glen R. and Sarah Nell Beare; student Highland Park Coll., 1959-61, Alexander Hamilton Inst.; m. Nancy Joyce Birdsall, June 22, 1963; children—Christian, Dawn, Lance. Regional dir. Alexander Hamilton Life Ins. Co., Lansing, Mich., 1965-71; with Internat. Diversified Corp., 1970—, Internat. Montetary Exchange, Ltd., 1974—; with Internat. Trading Group, Ltd., San Francisco, 1975—, now chmn. bd., pres.; mem. N.Y. Merc. Exchange; mem. Commodity Futures Trading Commn., N.Y. Stock Exchange; dir. OMNI World Wide Ltd., also all subsidiaries, Parker, Weissenborn & Moynahan. Registered commodity trading adviser. Mem. Internat. Assn. Fin. Planners, Nat. Assn. Security Dealers, Internat. Assn. Commodity Traders, Futures Industry Assn., Mich. Life Leaders. Club: Alpine Hills Tennis. Editor-in-chief: Commodity Option Newsletter; contbg. editor: Homeowner's Moneyletter. Office: Internatl Trading Group Ltd 120 Montgomery St Suite 2375 San Francisco CA 94104

BEASLEY, JAMES GEORGE, civil engr., surveyor; b. Cin., Apr. 27, 1949; s. John Henry and Harriet Frances (Copas) B.; B.S. in Civil Engring., Ohio State U., 1972, M.S. in Engring., 1973; m. Alta Mae Farrell, Aug. 15, 1970. Research asso. Ohio State U., Columbus, 1973; staff engr. Ohio Dept. Natural Resources, Columbus, 1973-74, engr.-in-charge, flood plain sect., 1974-75; asst. county engr. Brown County, Georgetown, Ohio, 1975-79, county engr., 1981—. Owner, operator Beasley Engring. & Surveying, Georgetown, 1977—. Adv. 4-H Club, 1976-80. Served to 2d lt. U.S. Army, 1972, to capt. USAR. Registered profl. engr., lic. surveyor, Ohio. Mem. Profl. Land Surveyors Ohio (treas. SW chpt. 1978-80, v.p. 1981), Georgetown Am. Legion, Brown County Hist. Soc., Ohio Georgetown Jaycees, Nat. Assn. County Engrs., Ohio Valley Antique Machinery Assn., Brown County Ohio State U. Alumni Assn. (sec.-treas. 1979-80). Club: Brown County Sq. Dance (sec. 1979-80, v.p. 1980-81). Clubs: Russellville Kiwanis, Brown County Farmers Union.

BEASLEY, ROBERT L., farm supply co. exec.; b. Poplar Bluff, Mo., Mar. 6, 1929; B.A. in Journalism, U. Mo., 1952; m. Betty Beasley; 2 children. With various newspapers, Mo., Iowa, Wis.; with Farmland Industries, Inc., Kansas City, Mo., 1957—, v.p. info. and pub. relations dept., 1971—, mem. exec. council. Vice chmn. bd. govs. Greater Kansas City YMCA; past vice chmn. Kansas City Philharm. Assn.; bd. dirs. Public Broadcasting Channel 19, Kansas City United Way. Mem. Internat. Coop. Alliance, Coop. League U.S.A. (past chmn.), Kansas City C. of C. Office: Farmland Industries Inc PO Box 7305 Kansas City MO 64116

BEASLEY, WILLIAM HOWARD, III, chem. co. exec.; b. Dallas, Oct. 1, 1946; s. William Howard, Jr. and Doris Ann (Waddell) B.; A.B. with distinction (Scholar Athlete award 1966), Duke U., 1968; M.B.A., U. Tex., Austin, 1969, Ph.D., 1971; m. Jean Childers, June 10, 1972; 1 son, William Howard, IV. Interviewer, Nat. Ednl. TV, Austin, 1969; mem. fin. faculty U. Tex., Austin, 1968-71; spl. asst. to sec., also dep. sec. Treasury Dept., 1971-73; dir. minority staff com. banking, housing and urban affairs U.S. Senate, 1973-75; spl. asst. to pres. Northwest Industries, Inc., Chgo., 1975-78; vice chmn. bd. Velsicol Chem. Corp., Chgo., 1978-79, pres., chief exec. officer, 1979—; pres., chief exec. officer Beasley Enterprises, Dallas. Served with USAF, 1968-70. Mem. Am. Enterprise Inst. (asso.), Chgo. Council Fgn. Relations (exec. com., com. fgn. affairs). Republican. Presbyterian. Clubs: Union League, Execs. (Chgo.); Calyx (Dallas). 341 E Ohio St Chicago IL 60611

BEASON, DONALD RAY, fin. co. exec.; b. Mt. Airy, N.C., Oct. 10, 1938; s. Grover Ray and RIrene (Spencer) B.; m. Janet Thacker, Mar. 12, 1958; children—Mark Christopher, Natalie Joan. Bus. mgmt. cons., to 1974; dep. sec. commerce State of N.C., Raleigh, 1972-74, sec. commerce, 1974-77; pres., chief exec. officer N.C. Savs. Guaranty Corp., Raleigh, 1977—. Chmn., N.C. Rural Electrification Authority, N.C. Land Use Council, Capital Bldg. Authority, Legis. Tax Study Commn. Served in U.S. Army, 1958-60. Mem. Nat. Assn. Credit Union Regulators (dir.), Nat. Assn. Savs. and Loan Regulators (dir.). Baptist. Office: PO Box 2688 Raleigh NC 27602

BEATRICE, GEORGE, life ins. co. exec.; b. East Paterson, N.J., Oct. 18, 1937; s. Michael and Mary Jane (Penna) B.; student Fairleigh Dickinson U., 1955-57, Am. Coll. Life Underwriters, Bryn Mawr, Pa., 1974; m. Barbara Breen, Aug. 8, 1959; children—Gary, James, Geralyn, Teresa, Robert G. Agt., Met. Life Ins. Co., Pomton Lakes, N.J., 1959-67; with Am. Gen. Life Ins. Co., Cin., 1967—, brokerage mgr., East Orange, N.J., 1967-71, gen. mgr., 1971-73, dir. brokerage sales, 1973-75, regional dir. sales, Cin., 1975-78, regional v.p., 1978-79, Eastern divisional v.p., dir. agys., Ft. Mitchell, Ky., 1979—. Active Little League. Mem. Kenton County, Covington Latin, Crescent Springs, PTA's. Served with N.J. N.G., 1957-72. Cert. instr. mng. interpersonal relationships. Mem. St. Joe's Men's Soc., Met's. Pres. and Hon. Clubs (regional outstanding leadership award 1977), Nat., Cin. assns. life underwriters, Cin. Assn. C.L.U.'s. Republican. Roman Catholic. Clubs: Republican (mem. pistol team), Summit Hills Country, No. Ky. Racquet. Home: 26 Linden Hill Ct Crescent Springs KY 41017 Office: 211 Grandview Dr Suite 307 Fort Mitchell KY 41011

BEATTIE, TEODOZJA KUREK, typographic co. exec.; b. Poreba-Zawiercie, Poland, Mar. 27, 1922; d. Piotr and Marianna (Wronski-Makowka) Kurek; came to U.S., 1946, naturalized, 1950; student U. Hartford, 1957-60; children—Sylvia Teodozja, Christopher Andrew. Supr. internat. banking Hartford Nat. Bank & Trust Co., 1962-64; econ. research asst. Fed. Res. Bank Mpls., 1966-67; internat. Banking officer, internat. econ./polit. analyst Wachovia Bank & Trust Co., Winston-Salem, N.C., 1967-75; pres., founder T.K.B. Internat. Corp., Winston-Salem, 1976, pres. Hendricks Miller Typog. Co. div., Washington, 1977—, Global Trading Corp., Washington, 1977—. Mem. Printing Industries Am., Printing Industry Met. Washington (dir.), Internat. Typographers Assn., Small Bus. Assn. Home: 500 23d St NW B-1106 Washington DC 20037 also 2870 Robinhood Rd Winston-Salem NC 27106 Office: 2363 Champlain St NW Washington DC 20009

BEATTIE, WILLIAM JOHN, III, foundry exec.; b. St. Louis, Nov. 18, 1933; s. William John and Mary Ellen (Chipley) B.; student Washington U., St. Louis, 1951-54, Tex. Christian U., 1958-61; m. Rebecca Sue Czeschin, July 11, 1970; children—William, Ann, Todd, Chad, David. Engring. supr. Emerson Electric Co., St. Louis, 1966-69; asst. mktg. mgr. Meyer Labs. Inc., Maryland Heights, Mo., 1969-70; v.p., gen. mgr. Forecast, Inc., Kirkwood, Mo., 1970-74; pres. St. Charles Aluminum Casting Co. (Mo.), 1974-78; v.p. ops. Mfrs.'s Brass & Aluminum Foundry, Inc., Blue Island, Ill., 1979-80; v.p. ops. Balcar, Inc., Carrollton, Tex., 1980—. Planning and zoning commr. City of St. Charles, 1976-79; bd. dirs. Boys Club St. Charles. Served with USAF, 1954-56; Korea. Mem. Am. Foundrymen's Soc., Sigma Chi. Republican. Presbyterian. Home: 1922 Castille Dr Carrollton TX 75007 Office: 1745 Sandy Lake Rd Carrollton TX 75006

BEATTY, LESTER ROBERT, data processing exec.; b. Natrona Heights, Pa., Sept. 29, 1937; s. Lester R. and Virginia E. (Rumbaugh) B.; B.S., Carnegie Inst. Tech., 1960; M.B.A. magna cum laude, U. Bridgeport, 1970; m. Anita Ruth Ruben, July 27, 1963; children—Virginia, Sandra, Brian. Sci. programmer Carnegie Inst. Tech., Pitts., 1958-60; sci. programmer Allegheny Ludlum Steel, Natrona Heights, 1960-64; benefits programming project leader U.S. Steel, Pitts., 1964-66; software sr. analyst RCA, Palm Beach Gardens, Fla., 1966-68; applications project leader Bunker-Ramo, Trumbull, Conn., 1968-70; systems mgr. Champion Internat., Hamilton, Ohio, 1970-79; dir. mgmt. info. and computer systems Cin. Electronics, 1979—; data processing cons.; 1968—; guest lectr. U. Cin., 1979. County bus. chmn. United Way, Ohio, 1975; county chmn. Young Republicans, 1967-68; senate pres. Ohio Model Legislature, 1974; nat. honor guard Rep. Nat. Conv., 1968. Served as 1st lt. Signal Corps, U.S. Army, 1960-61. Named outstanding state chmn. in U.S., U.S. Jaycees, 1968; outstanding local pres. in Pa., Pa. Jaycees, 1964; cert. data processor. Mem. Assn. for Systems Mgmt., Paper Industry Mgmt. Assn. (nat. EDP com.), Am. Water Ski Assn., Mensa (local editor 1975-76), SAR. Presbyterian. Clubs: Kiwanis, Masons (32 deg.), Shriners. Home: 10224 Lochcrest Dr Cincinnati OH 45231 Office: 2630 Glendale-Milford Rd Cincinnati OH 45241

BEATTY, WILLIAM CHARLES, food service co. mgr.; b. Medford, Oreg., Oct. 22, 1950; s. Robert Charles and Mary Edgarda (Heine) B.; B.A.B.A., Linfield Coll., 1972. Food service mgr. Saga Corp. at Colo. Coll., 1972-73, food service dir., 1976-78, at Coll. Idaho, 1974-76, at 1st Nat. Bank of Oreg., Portland, 1979-80, dist. mgr., Santa Fe Springs, Calif., 1980—; mgmt. trainee U.S. Nat. Bank of Oreg., Portland, 1978; terr. mgr. Canteen Co. Oreg., Portland, 1978-79. Mem. Pi Sigma Epsilon. Republican. Episcopalian. Club: Kiwanis (Caldwell, Idaho). Home: 20822 Cortner Ave Lakewood CA 90715 Office: 12631 E Imperial Hwy Suite 100 F Santa Fe Springs CA 90670

BEATY, RAYMOND CARL, JR., public relations exec.; b. Chandlerville, Ill., June 11, 1941; s. Raymond C. and Marie (Updike) B.; B.A., Western Ill. U., 1964, M.A., 1965; Ph.D. in Communication, Ohio U., 1971; student George Washington U., 1959-60; postgrad. N.Y. U., 1977; m. Catherine Cain, June 10, 1967 (div. 1976). Dir. forensics Ohio U., Athens, 1968-76; dir. tng. Reddy Communications, Inc., Greenwich, Conn., 1976-78, v.p., 1978—; nat. seminar lectr. Public Relations Soc. Am., 1979—. Exec. sec. Nat. Forensic Assn., 1973-76; coach nat. championship forensic program Ohio U., 1972, 73, 74, State of Ohio, 1970-76. Named nat. forensics coach of yr. Nat. Forensics Assn., 1975. Mem. Am. Forensic Assn., Am. Mgmt. Assn., Speech Communication Assn., Internat. Assn. Bus. Communicators, Am. Soc. Tng. and Devel. Editor RCI Communicator, 1978—. Office: Reddy Communications Inc 537 Steamboat Rd Greenwich CT 06830

BEAUCHAMP, DOUGLAS ARTHUR, mfg. co. exec.: b. Peterborough, Ont., Can., Jan. 1, 1947; s. George Arthur and Irene Edith (Nattress) B.; registered indsl. acct., McMaster U., 1972; m. Erica Sue Anderson, Aug. 30, 1969; children—Erica Fleur, Melanie Sue. With Canadian Gen. Electric, Peterborough, 1965-72; with Borg Warner Chems., Cobourg, Ont., 1972—, acctg. mgr., 1972—; chmn. Canadian Plastics Credit Group. Dep. warden, chmn. adv. bd. St. Peter's Ch., Cobourg, 1978-79. Mem. Soc. Mgmt. Accts., Assn. Systems Mgmt. Anglican. Ch. Club: Cobourg Figure Skating (v.p. 1980-81). Home: 435 Westwood Dr Cobourg ON K9A 4M5 Canada Office: PO Box 10 Cobourg ON K9A 4K2 Canada

BEAUCHAMP, WILLIAM HUNT, utility co. exec.; b. Bklyn., Mar. 6, 1921; s. James Mercer and Elsie Patterson (Meuser) B.; Sc.B., Brown U., 1942; M.B.A., Pepperdine U., 1976; Ed.D., U. So. Calif., 1979; m. Jun-Ko (Diana) Nakamori, July 26, 1969; 1 son, Christopher Y. Served to capt., AUS, 1942-46; commd. capt. C.E., U.S. Army, 1951, advanced through grades to lt. col., 1967; staff/faculty Command and Gen. Staff Coll., 1951-52; constrn. planner U.S. Army/Alaska, 1952-55; dir. phaseout ops., Tokyo and Yokohama, Japan, 1957-59; constrn. def. sites, Calif. and Korea, 1961-64; dir. public works U.S. Civil Adminstrn., Ryukyus, 1965-67, chmn. bd.

Ryukyu Electric Power Co., Okinawa, 1965-67, ret., 1967; auditor, accountant Chase Manhattan Bank, Tientsin, China and Tokyo, 1947-49; dep. gen. mgr., mgmt. services Vietnam Power Co., Saigon, 1967-70; mgr. support services dept. Hawaiian Electric Co. Inc., Honolulu, 1973—; lectr. mgmt. U. Hawaii, 1980—. Mem. platform Republican party State Com., 1975-81; clk. of vestry Holy Nativity Episcopal Ch., Honolulu, 1976-79. Registered profl. engr., Wis.; lic. gen. engrng. contractor, Hawaii. Mem. Hawaii Soc. Corporate Planners (pres. 1978-79), Nat. Soc. Prof. Engrs., ASCE, Far East Soc. Architects and Engrs. (life). Club: American (Tokyo, life). Home: Apt 1117 1778 Ala Moana Blvd Honolulu HI 96815 also 3-37-2 Izumi Suginami-ku Tokyo Japan 168 Office: PO Box 2750 Honolulu HI 96840

BEAUDOIN, GREGORY DAVID, retailer; b. Cadillac, Mich., Feb. 14, 1947; s. William Francis and Flora Jeanette (Sawin) B.; student Northwestern Mich. Coll., 1965-66, No. Mich. U., 1966-67; B.S., Central Mich. U., 1967-69; m. Patricia Agnes Sivak, May 10, 1969 (dec. Feb. 9, 1981); children—Anne-Terese Renee, David Gregory, Daniel Stephen. Tchr. sci. Fowler (Mich.) Pub. Schs., 1969-70; mgr., v.p. Bill's Motor Sales, Cadillac, 1971—; owner, mgr. Vehicle Appraisal Assos., 1979—, Central Excavating, 1980—, Beaudoin Tree Co., 1980—. Chmn. Wexford County Republican Party, 1977-79; mem. Wexford County Rep. Exec. Com., 1976; dir. Wexford County Juvenile Ct. Vols., 1974-78; mem. Haring Twp. Bd. Appeals, 1976-79; chmn. Haring Twp. Bldg. Com., 1976-78; vol. United Way of Wexford County, 1975, 76; trustee Haring Twp. Bd. Suprs., 1976-79; bd. dirs. U.S. 131 Area Devel. Assn., 1974—. Served with U.S. Army, 1970-71. Mem. Mich. Christmas Tree Growers Assn., Am. Legion. Republican. Roman Catholic. Club: Moose. Home: 4665 E 32d Rd Cadillac MI 49601 Office: 1129 N Mitchell St Cadillac MI 49601

BEAUDRY, MARK JEROME, indsl. and comml. real estate broker; b. Stamford, Conn., Oct. 24, 1948; s. Paul E. and Margaret M. (Konisky) B.; student U. Dayton (Ohio), 1966-68, SUNY, Plattsburgh, 1971, U. Conn., 1972; B.S. cum laude in Bus. Adminstrn., Mercy Coll., White Plains, N.Y., 1979; m. Jill A. Czarnecki, Oct. 12, 1968; children—Mark J., Christopher S. Salesman, Beaudry Assos., Inc., Stamford, Conn., 1972-75, v.p., 1975-80, pres., 1980—, prin. owner, 1977—. Served with USAF, 1968-72. Mem. Nat., Conn., Stamford bds. realtors, Stamford Area Commerce and Industry Assn., Delta Mu Delta. Office: 222 Summer St Stamford CT 06901

BEAUPRE, EUGENE EDWARD, safety engr.; b. La Broquerie, Man., Can., May 27, 1927; s. Joseph Charles and Marie Louise (Morin) B.; m. Jeannine Andrea Bilodeau, Aug. 20, 1951; children—Regent, Gerald, Francois, Daniele, Andre. Served with Royal Can. Navy, 1948-53; commd. Royal Can. Army, 1953, advanced through grades to maj., 1974; ret., 1974; safety engr. Davie Shipbldg. Co., Lauzon, Que., 1975—; lectr. Red River Coll., U. Man., 1973, also various assns. and groups on safety subjects, 1975—. Mem. Am. Soc. Safety Engrs., Can. Soc. Safety Engrs., Indsl. Accident Prevention Assn. (adminstr., exec. council 1979-80), Nat. Safety Mgmt. Soc., Soc. des Consellers en Securite Industrille du Que., Royal Can. Legion, Can. Mil. Inst., Que., Maritime Group. Liberal. Roman Catholic. Home: 4795 Pl Nobel Charlesbourg PQ G1H 4E9 Canada Office: Davis Shipbldg & Repairs Lauzon PQ G6V 6N7 Canada

BEAVER, RALPH LESLIE, computer co. planner; b. Rochester, Pa., Mar. 29, 1942; s. Curtis Sidney and Elizabeth Sara (Kiedaisch) B.; B.A., W.Va. Wesleyan Coll., 1964; m. Beverly Ann Ryan, July 2, 1964; children—Dawn Marie, David Jay, Amy Michele. Mgr., J.C. Penney Co., 1964-65; claims adjuster Am. Mut. Ins. Co., 1965-66; salesman Pa. Life Ins. Co., 1966-67; systems engr. IBM Corp., Phila., 1967-72, product planner, Rochester, Minn., 1972—. Active flood recovery group Olmsted County, 1978-79; vice chmn. citizens adv. com. Olmsted County CD; v.p. Rochester Council Chs., 1979—; exec. com. Rochester Area Chs. Republican. Baptist. Home: 711 28th St NW Rochester MN 55901 Office: IBM Corp 37th St NW Rochester MN 55901

BEAVERS, VALDEAN RAY, banker; b. Davenport, Nebr., Mar. 5, 1933; s. Francis Loyal and Fay Louise (Ray) B.; student Hastings Coll., 1955, U. Nebr., Omaha, 1957-58; m. Lenore Alice, Oct. 10, 1958; 1 son, Gary. With Dial Finance Co., Hastings, Nebr. and Omaha, 1959-68; v.p. First Nat. Bank, Wahoo, Nebr., 1968-75; pres., chmn. bd. dirs. First Nat. Bank, Stanton, Nebr., 1975-76; pres., chmn. bd. dirs. First Nat. Bank of Tekamah (Nebr.), 1975—. Served with U.S. Army, 1953-55. Mem. Nebr. State Bankers Assn., Tekamah C. of C., VFW, Am. Legion, Burt County Feeders Assn., Nat. Cattlemen's Assn., Ak-Sar-Ben (ambassador). Democrat. Methodist. Office: 448 S 13th St Tekamah NE 68061

BECERRA, LAWRENCE, mfg. co. exec.; b. N.Y.C., Sept. 22, 1926; s. Rosendo and Adeline (Diaz) B.; B.S. in Aero. Engring., Acad. Aeros., 1948; postgrad. in Bus., U. Paris, 1952; LL.B., Atlanta Law Sch., 1959; exec. program U. Chgo., 1969, M.B.A., M.B.M., Sussex (Eng.) Coll. Tech., 1975; m. Virginia Warren, Aug. 12, 1975; children by previous marriage—Linda Ruberto, Laurie Demma, Larry, Carla Siegel, Dawn, Lisa, Maria. With Sperry Gyroscope Co., 1949-54, Bendix Corp., 1955-61, Sprague Electric Co., 1961-65, P.R. Mallory Co., 1965-67, Fansteel Corp., 1967-69; with Golconda Corp., Chgo., 1969-71; v.p. internat. ops. Rockwell Internat. Co., Detroit, 1971-74; v.p. internat. ops. Essex Group subs. United Tech. Corp., Detroit, 1974-78; cons. internat. bus., 1978-80; dir. internat. ops. Avco Corp., 1980—; dir. Gen. Technologies Corp. Served with AUS, 1943-44. Mem. Internat. Execs. Assn., Am. Soc. Internat. Execs., Licensing Execs. Soc., Classic Car Club, Rolls Royce Owners Club, Jaguar Club, Sigma Delta Kappa. Home: 2685 Amberly Rd Bloomfield Village Birmingham MI 48010

BECHTEL, STEPHEN DAVISON, JR., engr., exec.; b. Oakland, Cal., May 10, 1925; s. Stephen Davison and Laura (Peart) B.; student U. Colo., 1943-44; B.S., Purdue U., 1946, Dr. Engring. (hon.), 1972; M.B.A., Stanford, 1948; m. Elizabeth Mead Hogan, June 5, 1946; 5 children. Engring. and mgmt. positions Bechtel Corp., San Francisco, 1941-60, pres., 1960-73, chmn. cos. in Bechtel group, 1973—; dir. Hanna Mining Co., IBM Co., So. Pacific Co. Vice chmn., mem. Bus. Council; life councillor, past chmn. Conf. Bd.; mem. Presdl. Com. on Urban Housing, 1967-69; mem. Nat. Indsl. Pollution Control Council, 1970-73, Nat. Productivity Commn., 1971-74; mem. Cost of Living Council, 1973-74; mem. Nat. Commn. Indsl. Peace, 1973-74, Labor-Mgmt. Group, 1974—. Nat. Adv. Council on Minorities in Engring., 1974—. Trustee, Nat. Fund Minority Engring. Students, Calif. Inst. Tech.; bd. govs., mem. pres.'s council Purdue U. Served with USMC, 1943-46. Registered profl. engr., N.Y., Mich., Alaska, Calif., Md., Hawaii, Ohio, D.C., Va. Decorated officier Legion of Honor (France); recipient Disting. Alumnus award Purdue U., 1964, Stanford U., 1974. Fellow ASCE (Parcel-Sverdrup award 1979); mem. Nat. Acad. Engring. (fin. com. 1975-77), AIME, Calif. Acad. Scis. (hon. trustee), Chi Epsilon, Tau Beta Pi. Clubs: Pacific Union (San Francisco); Claremont Country (Oakland, Calif.); Cypress Point (Monterey Peninsula, Calif.); Thunderbird Country (Palm Springs, Calif.); Vancouver (B.C.); Ramada (Houston); Bohemian, San Francisco Golf (San Francisco); Links, Blind Brook (N.Y.C.); Augusta (Ga.) National Golf; York (Toronto); Mount Royal (Montreal). Office: 50 Beale St San Francisco CA 94105

BECHTLE, REID RONALD, mfg. co. exec.; b. Phila., Oct. 8, 1952; s. Charles Ronald and Jenny (Manchur) B.; B.B.A., U. Pa., 1978; m. Dorothy Marie Wise, June 1, 1974; children—Amy Marie, Lori Jean. Ops. mgr. Spiegel Inc., Phila., 1971-76; mfg. mgr. Braceland Bros., Phila., 1976-79; dir. mgr. The Drawing Board, Dallas, 1979—; condr. seminars in mfg., fin. ratio analysis, since 1975—. Com. leader Phila. Republican Com., 1978-79. Mem. Am. Mgmt. Assn., Printing Industries Am., Am. Assn. M.B.A. Execs., Wharton Alumni Assn. Home: 4409 Cleveland Dr Plano TX 75075 Office: 256 Regal Row Dallas TX 75222

BECHTOLD, EDWIN LOUIS, diversified co. exec.; b. Perry, Okla., Nov. 2, 1922; s. Edwin Flynn and Gladys Belle (Holt) B.; student U. Okla., 1940-41, 45; B.S. in Mech. Engring., Okla. A. and M. U., 1948; postgrad. in bus. U. Houston, 1950-51; m. Betty Jean Woolsey, Oct. 8, 1943; children—Suzanne (Mrs. Joaquin Estrada), Mary Jane (Mrs. William Fahey, Jr.). Sr. design engr. Hughes Tool Co., Houston, 1949-54; div. mgr. engring. and mfg. Dresser Industries Inc., Dallas, 1954-59; gen. mgr. Equipos Petroleros Nacionales, S.A., Mexico City, 1959-62; dir. mfg. domestic and fgn. Mission—TRW, Houston, 1962-68; gen. mgr. pumps and gen. products Norris div. Dover Corp., Tulsa, 1968-77, exec. v.p., 1977-78, pres., 1978—. Served to 1st lt. USAAF, 1942-45. Mem. Soc. Petroleum Engrs., Tex. Soc. Profl. Engrs., Houston Engring. and Sci. Soc., Pi Tau Sigma. Republican. Methodist. Clubs: University (Mexico City), Tulsa Country, Petroleum, Summit (Tulsa). Research on closed die engring. process. Home: 6214 S Indianapolis St Tulsa OK 74136 Office: 10 N Elwood St Tulsa OK 74101

BECK, BURTON, retail exec.; b. Newark, Nov. 8, 1930; s. Jerome Gibian and Blanche (Goldsmith) B.; student Rutgers U., Newark, 1948-50; B.A., Seton Hall U., South Orange, N.J., 1953; m. Elaine Marie Gettenberg, Mar. 20, 1954; children—Lynn Ellen, Carol Leslie. Asst. public relations dir. WATV, Channel 13, Newark, 1955-56; asst. public relations dir. Clairol, 1956; clk. to pres. Charles I. Beck & Son, South Orange, N.J., 1956—; chmn. adv. bd. Village Bank of N.J., 1977—. Treas. N.J. Housewares Club, 1970-75; pres. South Orange C. of C., 1976-78; com. mem. Econ. Devel. Com. South Orange. Served with U.S. Army, 1953-55. Recipient award for service Retail Hardware Assn., 1975, Mental Health Assn. Essex County, 1979. Mem. Pa.-Atlantic Seaboard Hardware Assn. Jewish. Club: B'nai B'rith. Home: 45 Ocean Ave Monmouth Beach NJ 07750 Office: 57 S Orange St South Orange NJ 07079

BECK, GARY GORDON, indsl. corp. ofcl.; b. Altoona, Pa., Nov. 8, 1943; s. Gordon Leroy and Evelyn Elaine (Huffman) B.; student Taylor U., 1962-65; A.B.A., Internat. Coll., 1967; children—Marla Jenee, Matthew Gordon. Data analyst Gen. Telephone of Ind., Ft. Wayne, 1967-68; program dir., sales mgr. Ft. Wayne Broadcasting Co., 1968-71; adminstrv. asst. to pres. Aldersgate Found., Kissimmee, Fla., 1971-72, Oxford Found., Leesburg, Fla., 1972-76; pvt. practice real estate, Leesburg, 1976-78; gen. mgr. C.L. Industries, Inc., Orlando, Fla., 1978—. Lic. real estate broker, mortgage broker, Fla. Mem. Nat. Assn. Realtors, Aircraft Owners and Pilots Assn. Republican. Author paper in field of real estate. Home: 394 Strawberry Fields Winter Park FL 32792 Office: 8360 S Orange Ave Orlando FL 32809

BECK, GEORGE RICHARD, real estate investment exec.; b. Hanford, Calif., Jan. 18, 1917; s. George Anthony and Mabel (Strunk) B.; B.S., U. Calif. at Berkeley, 1938; postgrad. Harvard, Mass. Inst. Tech.; m. Mary Elizabeth Russell, Aug. 17, 1940; children—Elizabeth Rae, Richard Russell. Surveyor Kings County, Calif., 1938-40; mineral rights appraiser Kings County, 1940-42; radio engr. Fed. Telephone and Radio Corp., Newark, 1946-50; product devel. engr. Hughes Aircraft Co., Culver City, Calif., 1950-53; program mgr. Bendix Pacific, North Hollywood, Calif., 1954-57; sr. staff radioplane div. Northrop Corp., Van Nuys, Calif., 1958; product engring. mgr. TRW Systems, Redondo Beach, Calif., 1959-70; v.p. adminstrn. Altrad Corp., Tarzana, Calif., 1970-71; investment mktg. Burreson Investment Co., Inc., North Hollywood, 1971-73; v.p. mktg. Mariel Realty, Inc., Canoga Park, Calif., 1973-76; owner George Beck & Assos., real estate investments, Woodland Hills, Calif., 1976—. Scoutmaster, Boy Scouts Am.; bd. dirs. Valley Youth Cathedral, Inc., Northridge, Calif. Served to lt. comdr. USNR, 1942-46. Mem. IEEE (sr.), Nat. Assn. Realtors, Los Angeles, San Fernando Valley bds. Realtors, Gideons Internat., Naval Res. Assn., Internat. Platform Assn. Baptist. Contbr. articles to sci. mags. Home: 24153 Gilmore St Canoga Park CA 91307 Office: 6355 Topanga Canyon Blvd Woodland Hills CA 91367

BECK, JOHN GUNGL, ins. co. exec.; b. Nagymányok, Hungary, Aug. 5, 1925; came to U.S., 1951, naturalized, 1957; s. Abraham and Theresia (Gungl) B.; diploma Teachers' Coll., Budapest, Hungary, 1944; m. Irmgard Helene Kernwein, Nov. 1, 1978; children—Stephen John, Michael Francis, Thomas Paul. Asso. actuary Irwin Solomon & Co., N.Y.C., 1956-61; v.p., actuary, Citadel Life of N.Y., 1962-66; sr. v.p. Cologne Life Reins. Co., Stamford, Conn., 1966-79; exec. v.p. Frankona Am. Life Reins. Co., Kansas City, Mo., 1979-80, pres., 1981—. Home: 10311 Howe Dr Leawood KS 66206 Office: 2440 Pershing Rd Kansas City MO 64108

BECK, JOHN ROLAND, biol. cons. co. exec.; b. Las Vegas, N.Mex., Feb. 26, 1929; s. Roland Lycurgus and Betty Lind (Shrock) B.; B.S., Okla. A. and M. Coll., 1950; postgrad. U. Tex., 1954; M.S., Okla. State U., 1957; postgrad. George Washington U., 1965; m. Doris Aliene Olson, Feb. 9, 1951; children—Elizabeth Joan, Thomas Roland, Patricia Lind, John William. Biologist, King Ranch, Tex., 1950-51; wildlife mgmt. fellow Okla. A. and M. Coll., 1951, asst. instr., 1952-53; instr. physiology U. Tenn., 1954-55; control agt. U.S. Fish and Wildlife Service, N.D., 1953-54, research biologist, Idaho, 1955-57, control biologist, Ohio, 1957-65, Va., 1967-69; dir. Job Corps Center, U.S. Dept. Interior, Okla., 1965-67; v.p. Bio-Serv Corp., Troy, Mich., 1969-78; prin. Biol. Environ. Cons. Services, Detroit, 1978—; lectr. preventive medicine Ohio Coll. Vet. Medicine, 19S7-65; lectr. econ. biology Bowling Green State U., 1958-76; grain sanitation cons. Ohio Grain and Feed Dealers Assn., 1958-65; mem. Interagy. Bd.-U.S. Civil Service Examiners, Dallas, 1965-67; mem. Ohio Gov.'s Com. on Pesticides, 1961-63; chmn. adv. bd. pesticide tech. Ferris State Coll., 1972-76, mem. adv. bd. Sch. Allied Health, 1977-79; mem. pesticide adv. com. Mich. Dept. Agr., 1977-79. Bd. dirs. Braes of Bloomfield, 1970-72, pres., 1971; bd. dirs. Birmingham YMCA, Detroit YMCA. Registered sanitarian, Ariz., Ohio; cert. wildlife biologist. Fellow Explorers Club, Royal Soc. Health (London); mem. Mich. Pest Control Operators Assn. (pres. 1970-72, dir. 1973-76), Nat. Pest Control Assn. (dir. 1972-75, award 1970, chmn. reorgn. com. 1976-78), ASTM (chmn. com. on vertebrate pesticides 1973-78, chmn. Symposium on vertebrate control test methods 1978, chmn. com. pesticides 1980—), Nat. Environ. Health Assn., Wildlife Soc., Entomol. Soc. Am., Pi Chi Omega (dir. 1972-78, pres. 1977). Republican. Baptist (deacon 1957-75). Clubs: Masons, Rotary (chmn. youth support com. Detroit 1972-73). Contbr. articles to profl. publs. Home: 3631 W Pasadena Phoenix AZ 85019

BECK, LELAND WHITCOMB, mfg. exec.; b. Fremont, Ohio, June 29, 1926; s. Leo Emil and Josephine Amanda (Whitcomb) B.: B.S.M.E., U. Mich., 1947; children—Charles, Thomas, Anne. Area mgr. Tool div. Ingersoll-Rand, Milan, Italy, 1963-65, mng. dir., Stockholm, 1965-70, v.p. Ingersoll-Rand Internat., Woodcliff Lake, N.J., 1970-76, v.p., gen. mgr. Power Tool div. Ingersoll-Rand, Liberty Corner, N.J., 1976—. Served with USNR, 1943-46. Mem. Compressed Air and Gas Inst., Material Handling Inst. Republican. Presbyterian. Clubs: Fiddlers Elbow Country, Mt. Kemble Lake Country, Keyport Yacht. Home: Pfizer Rd Bernardsville NJ 07924 Office: PO Box 1776 Liberty Corner NJ 07938

BECK, LEWIS ALFRED, mfrs. rep.; b. Denver, July 13, 1919; s. Alfred and Lillie May (Groesbeck) B.; B.S. in Elec. Engring., U. Colo., 1941; m. Priscilla M. Ryder, Dec. 29, 1941; children—Lewis Alfred, Georgina Lee. Engr., Gen. Electric Co., Schenectady, 1941-47; sales engr., then v.p. Peterson Co., Denver, 1947-67, pres. 1967—. Mem. Elec. Equipment Reps. Assn. (pres. 1971), Rocky Mountain Elec. League (pres. 1975). Clubs: Lakewood Country, Garden of Gods, Mt. Vernon Country. Home: 1851 Winfield Dr Lakewood CO 80215 Office: 4949 Colorado Blvd Denver CO 80216

BECK, LOUIS GEORGE, med. supply co. exec.; b. Bklyn., May 31, 1946; s. Louis and Carmen Mildren (De Rosa) B.; A.A., Temple U., 1969; B.S. in Med. Tech., Cleve. State U., 1971; m. Mary Catherine Manley, Aug. 10, 1974; children—Kelly Ann, Christopher Louis, Michael Joseph. Med. technician Episcopal Hosp., Phila., 1967-69; dir. purchasing Healthco-Schuemann-Jones Co., Cleve., 1969-72; mfrs. rep. Christiansen & Barber Assoc., Chgo., 1972-76; pres. Corpsman Med. Supply Co., Lodi, Ohio, 1976—. Served with USN, 1964-67; Vietnam. Decorated Air medal with 3 oak leaf clusters, Purple Heart with 2 oak leaf clusters, Bronze Star, Navy Cross, Silver Star, Navy Commendation medal, Vietnamese Cross of Gallantry, Vietnamese Army Service medal; certified med. lab. Technologist, blood bank technologist, notary public. Mem. Am. Legion, VFW, DAV. Republican. Roman Catholic. Club: Medina Kiwanis. Home: 8721 Chippewa Rd Chatham OH 44254 Office: PO Box 179 Lodi OH 44254

BECK, RICHARD PAUL, computer mfg. co. exec.; b. St. Johnsbury, Vt., May 12, 1933; s. Harold Conrad and Ruth (Taylor) B.; B.S., Babson Coll., 1957, M.B.A., 1960; m. Judith McCarthy Beek. Asst. controller Cool-Ray, Inc., Boston, 1960-63; v.p., treas. Controlled Environment, Inc., Whitman, Mass., 1963-68; pres., dir. Particle Tech., Inc., Sunnyvale, Calif., 1968-70; exec. v.p., dir. Apogee Chem. Co., Inc., Richmond, Calif., 1970-71; v.p., treas. MB Assos., San Ramon, Calif., 1971-72; partner San Francisco Cons., 1972-75; prin. Beck & Assos., 1975-76; sr. v.p., treas., dir. HealthGarde Corp., Salt Lake City, 1976-78; sr. v.p. fin., treas. Beehive Internat., Salt Lake City, 1978—. Mem. exec. bd. Utah Opera Co., 1980—. Served with USAF, 1950-54. Home: 1 Payday Dr Park City UT 84060

BECK, ROBERT A., ins. co. exec.; b. N.Y.C., Oct. 6, 1925; s. Arthur C. and Alma W. Beck; B.S. in Mgmt. and Ins. summa cum laude, Syracuse U., 1950; agy. mgmt. diploma Am. Coll., 1961; m. Frances Kenny, Aug. 7, 1948; children—Robert, Arthur, Kathleen, Stephen, Theresa. Fin. analyst Ford Motor Co., Detroit, 1950-51; with Prudential Ins. Co. Am., 1951—, agy. mgr., Cin., 1956-57, dir. agy., Jacksonville, Fla., 1957-63, exec. gen. mgr., Newark, 1963-65, v.p., 1965-66, sr. v.p., Chgo., 1966-67, Newark, 1967-70, exec. v.p. mktg., 1970-74, pres., 1974-78, chmn., chief exec. officer, 1978—, also dir.; dir. Xerox Corp., Campbell Soup Co. Trustee Syracuse U.; adv. council Columbia U. Grad. Sch. Bus.; bd. dirs., chmn. planning com. United Way Am.; mem. Bus. Com. for the Arts, Bus. Arts Found. Served to 1st lt. AUS, 1943-48. C.L.U. Mem. Am. Soc. C.L.U.'s, Nat. Assn. Life Underwriters, Am. Council Life Ins. (dir.), Life Ins. Mktg. Research Assn. (past chmn.), Conf. Bd., S.A.R., Greater Newark C. of C. (past chmn.), N.J. Hist. Soc. (past pres., dir.), Knights of Malta, Beta Gamma Sigma. Clubs: Navesink; Essex; Ocean Reef; Seabright, Boca Grande. Home: 8 Somerset Dr Rumson NJ 07760 Office: Prudential Plaza Newark NJ 07101

BECK, ROBERT RANDALL, investment mgmt. co. exec.; b. San Francisco, July 2, 1940; s. Lester L. and Eunice (Hague) B.; A.B. with certificate in pub. affairs, Woodrow Wilson Sch., Princeton, 1962; M.B.A., Harvard, 1967. Producer, dir., Les Films Numero Uno, Paris, France, 1963-65; with State St. Research & Mgmt. Co., Boston, 1967—, partner, 1973—; dir. Edn. for Mgmt., Inc., United Artists Theatres, Inc., Graphics Mktg. Group, Inc., Coline Distbn. S.A., Paris. Mem. corp. New Eng. Deaconess Hosp. Served with USN, 1962-64. Mem. Boston Soc. Security Analysts. Home: Forest Rd East Alstead NH 03602 Office: 222 Franklin St Boston MA 02110

BECK, ROGER THOMAS, resort mgr.; b. Seattle, Mar. 1, 1950; s. William Henry and Opal Lorraine (Moe) B.; B.A. (Hotel Sch. scholar 1972), Wash. State U., 1972; M.B.A. (Thorberg fellow 1977-79), Stanford U., 1979. Asst. mgr. hotel ops. Sun Valley (Idaho) Resort, 1973-74, dir. mktg., 1974-77; gen. mgr. Snowmass Resort Assn., Snowmass Resort, Colo., 1979—. Vice pres. Snowmass Transit Authority, 1979—; dir. Anderson Ranch Arts and Crafts Center, 1979—; co-chmn. Ski the Rockies, 1976. Mem. Aspen C. of C. (dir. 1979—), Idaho Ski Area Assn. (vice chmn. 1975-77). Club: Aspen Athletic. Home: PO Box 5714 Snowmass Village CO 81615 Office: PO Box 5566 Snowmass Village CO 81615

BECKER, HAROLD SAMUEL, mgmt. cons.; b. Chgo., June 24, 1929; s. Morris and Ruth B.; B.Aero. Engring., Ga. Inst. Tech., 1951; M.Engring., UCLA, 1959; m. Marilyn Hope Lerner, Feb. 15, 1953; children—Debra Ann, Donna Sue, Linda Joan. Mgr. spl. projects Aerospace Corp., dir. launch vehicles, advanced systems N.Am. Aviation, Downey, Calif., 1963-66; dir. advanced projects office and dep. dir. advanced systems NASA, Huntsville, Ala., 1966-69; treas., sr. fellow Inst. for Future, Middletown, Conn., 1969-71; exec. v.p., treas. Futures Group, Glastonbury, Conn., 1971—; tchr., lectr. policy analysis, tech. assessment, futures research, forecasting, mgmt. NSF grantee. Mem. Am. Acad. Sci., AIAA (dir.). Contbr. numerous articles to tech. jours. Office: 76 Eastern Blvd Glastonbury CT 06033

BECKER, IVAN ENDRE, plastics co. exec.; b. Budapest, Hungary, June 14, 1929; came to U.S., 1946, naturalized, 1953; s. Dezso and Kato (Irsay) B.; student N.Y. U., 1953-54, New Sch. for Social Research, 1953-54; m. Nancy Helen Greenglass, Feb. 11, 1962; children—David Michael, Kenneth Andrew. With mktg. and prodn. depts., asst. prodn. mgr. Exxon Film div. Exxon Co., N.Y.C. and Pottsville, Pa., 1955-67, tech. services mgr., 1958-64; founder, pres. Edison Plastics Co. div. Blessings Corp., mems. Am. Stock Exchange, South Plainfield, N.J., 1967—, dir. 1976-78, mem. adv. com. to bd. dirs., 1978—; pres. Blessings Internat. Inc., Piscataway, N.J., 1980—, also dir. Served with Signal Corps, U.S. Army, 1951-53. Mem. Soc. Plastics Industry, Soc. Plastics Engrs., Flexible Packaging Assn., Internat. Disposables Assn., TAPPI. Clubs: Econ., Chemists (N.Y.C.). Home: 306 Shady Brook Ln Princeton NJ 08540 Office: PO Box 297 South Plainfield NJ 07080

BECKER, LAFOLLETTE, communications, urban affairs, community relations cons.; b. N.Y.C., July 4, 1924; d. Frank and Friedy (Wegeli) B.; ed. N.Y. U., Columbia. Advt. exec. Ben Sackheim, Inc., 1951-53; indsl. pub. relations editor-writer, George Fischer Ltd., Schaffhausen, Switzerland, 1953-56; advt. exec. Hazard Advt. Co., Inc., 1957; pub. relations asso. Nat. Council Chs., 1958-61; ednl. pub.

relations-alumni devel. exec. Pratt Inst., Bklyn., 1961-62; dir. corporate pub. relations, consumer-trade advt. Incabloc Corp., N.Y.C., 1963; dir. financial pub. relations Franklin Soc. Fed. Savs. & Loan Assn., N.Y.C., 1965-68; cons. communications, mktg., advt. pub. relations programs for banks, business and govt., 1969-72; state housing ofcl. Empire Housing Found. N.Y. State Div. Housing and Community Renewal, 1972-75; cons. communications, urban affairs, community relations to banks, bus. and govt. agys., 1976—; mem. regional adv. council SBA, 1976; lectr. continuing edn. Columbia U., 1978-80. Mem. Manhattan Community Bd. 8, N.Y.C., 1975-77; Republican candidate for State Assembly, 1964; founder Community Action Council, 1970. Recipient Editorial award Am. Alumni Council, 1962; Mktg. awards Savs. Inst. Mktg. Soc. Am., 1968; Freedoms Found. award, 1968; Good Citizenship Silver medal Nat. Soc. SAR, 1977. Mem. Pub. Relations Soc. Am., East Mid-Manhattan C. of C. (dir. 1972, v.p. 1973, 1st woman pres. 1976, mem. exec. com. 1977—, Achievement awards for community relations programs 1973-77), N.Y. U. Alumni Fedn. Contbr. articles to financial and other publs. Home: 305 E 88th St New York NY 10028

BECKER, ROBERT DAVIS, mfg. co. exec.; b. Des Lacs, N.D., Dec. 23, 1920; s. Robert D. and Mary R. (Healy) B.; B.S. in Mech. Engring., U. Calif., Berkeley, 1942; m. Lorrayne Grassel, Aug. 4, 1944; children—Lynne E., Ward R., Reid C. Part owner, operator F.B. Becker Co., Des Lacs, 1942-55; v.p. Algas Industries, Industry, Calif., 1955-65; prodn. mgr. Pennwalt Corp., Monrovia, Calif., 1965-68; exec. v.p. Grover Mfg. Corp., Montebello, Calif., 1968—. Mem. Petroleum Equipment Inst., Automotive Service Industries Assn. Club: Elks. Home: 914 Kings Canyon Way Brea CA 92621 Office: 620 S Vail Ave Montebello CA 90640

BECKER, SHERBURN M., investment co. exec.; b. Milw., 1906; grad. Princeton U., 1928. Partner, Fahnestock & Co., N.Y.C.; pres. Phila. Fund, Inc. Home: 620 Park Ave New York NY 10021 Office: Fahnestock & Co 110 Wall St New York NY 10005*

BECKER, STEPHEN PHILIP, cons. co. exec.; b. Newton, Mass., Apr. 4, 1943; s. Frederick Leon and Julia Jean (Rattet) B.; B.S., Boston U., 1966, M.Ed., 1968, certificate advanced grad. study adult edn., 1971; m. Brenda Phyllis Marmer, May 28, 1967; children—Adam Jay, Marc Austin, Sheri Jill. Mgmt. tng. specialist Polaroid Corp., Cambridge, Mass., 1968-70; v.p. tng. St. Johnsbury Trucking Co., Cambridge, 1970-77; v.p. organizational devel. M/A-COM, Burlington, Mass., 1978-79; pres. Learncom Inc., Boston, 1979—. Mem. Adult Edn. Assn. Mass. (dir.), Am. Soc. Tng. and Devel., Nat. Soc. Performance and Instrn. (Outstanding Communication award 1978), Adult Edn. Assn. U.S.A., Nat. Orgn. Devel. Network, Mgmt. Devel. Forum, N.Y.C., Phi Delta Kappa. Contbr. articles Tng. mag. Home: 23 Swanson Rd Framingham MA 01701 Office: 113 Union Wharf E Boston MA

BECKER, WILLIAM ADOLPH, ins. assn. exec.; b. Kenosha, Wis., July 2, 1933; s. Adolph Gustav and Helen Marie (Rasmussen) B.; B.A., William and Mary Coll., 1957; diploma Cornell U., 1958; m. Mildred Lois Behr, Dec. 13, 1952; children—Verne W., Bradford S., Gregory T. Mgr., Commodore Maury Hotel, Norfolk, Va., 1957-59; field underwriter Home Life Ins. Co. of N.Y., Norfolk, 1959-61; asst. to gen. agt. Union Mutual Life Ins. Co., Richmond, Va., 1961-65; supr. Aetna Life & Casualty, Richmond, 1965-70, mktg. dept. field dir., 1970-71, gen. agt., Utica, N.Y., 1971-74, Syracuse, N.Y., 1974-77; v.p. Life Underwriter Tng. Council, Washington, 1977—; instr. C.L.U. diploma program, 1973-74, Life Underwriter Tng. Council, Richmond, 1964-68. Mem. Va. Health Ins. Council Hosp. Relations Com. Served with USN, 1950-54. Recipient Louis I. Dublin award for pub. service, 1976, 77. C.L.U. Mem. Am. Soc. C.L.U.'s (pres. Mohawk Valley chpt. 1973-74), Central N.Y. Personnel Mgrs. Assn., Utica Assn. Life Underwriters (pres. 1972-73), N.Y. Assn. Life Underwriters (regional v.p. 1977-78), Soc. Advancement Mgmt., Am. Soc. Personnel Adminstrs., Am. Mgmt. Assn., Gen. Agts. and Mgrs. Assn., Richmond Assn. Life Underwriters, Nat. Assn. Health Underwriters, Richmond Assn. Health Underwriters, Va. Assn. Health Underwriters. Republican. Club: University. Contbg. editor Med. Economics Co. Publs., 1978, LIMRA Mgrs. Mag. Office: 1922 F St NW Washington DC 20006

BECKER, WILLIAM ELLIOT, real estate mktg. cons.; b. Somerville, Mass., Jan. 25, 1927; s. Joseph and Dorothy (Spivak) B.; B.S., N.Y. U., 1950, M.B.A., 1952; m. Marilyn Berniker, Oct. 18, 1953; children—Donna, June, Gary. Sales promotion mgr. Ronson Corp., 1950-55; asst. advt. and promotion mgr. Evans Chemetics, N.Y.C., 1955-57; advt. and sales promotion mgr. Kenneth Draperies div. United Merchants and Mfrs., N.Y.C., 1957-60; v.p. mktg. Leisure Tech. Corp., Lakewood, N.J., 1960-64; pres., chmn. bd. William E. Becker Orgn., Teaneck, N.J., 1964—; adj. prof. mktg. Real Estate Inst. N.Y. U., 1966—; founding trustee, chmn. admissions com. Inst. Residential Mktg., 1976—. Served with USNR, 1945-46. Recipient Million Dollar Lifetime Circle award, 1966; Nat. Assn. Home Builders award, 1966; Multi-Housing Leadership award Gralla Publs., 1978; named Idea Man of Year, 1976. Mem. Nat. Assn. Home Builders, Urban Land Inst., Regional Plan Assn. Am. Mktg. Assn. Jewish. Club: Masons. Author: Marketing from the Ground Up, 1979. Home: 894 Barbara Dr Teaneck NJ 07666

BECKETT, JOHN R., business exec.; b. San Francisco, Feb. 26, 1918; s. Ernest J. and Hilda (Hansen) B.; A.B., Stanford, 1939, M.A., 1940; m. Dian Calkin, Nov. 27, 1947 (dec. June 1968); children—Brenda Jean, Belinda Dian; m. 2d, Marjorie Abenheim, July 1969. Valuator, Pacific Gas & Electric Co., 1941-42; utility financial analyst Duff & Phelps, 1942-43; utility financial expert SEC, 1943-44; asst. to pres. Seattle Gas Co., 1944-45; investment banker Blyth & Co., 1945-60, v.p., 1955-60; pres. Transamerica Corp., 1960-79, chmn. bd., chief exec. officer, 1968—, chmn. bd., 1981—, dir., 1960—, also dir. all subs. cos.; dir. Kaiser Aluminum & Chem. Co., Tex. Eastern Corp. Clubs: San Francisco Golf, Menlo Circus, Pacific Union, Bohemian (San Francisco); California (Los Angeles); Links (N.Y.C.); Cypress Point (Pebble Beach, Calif.). Home: PO Box 7928 San Francisco CA 94120 Office: 600 Montgomery St San Francisco CA 94111

BECKMAN, FREDERICK IRA, metals co. exec.; b. Bklyn., June 3, 1944; s. Michael L. and Rose D. Beckman; student U. Ga.; m. Merrill R. Sosis, May 27, 1979; children—Shannon L., Michael M. Salesman, asst. to comptroller I.G. Ely Co., Atlanta, 1962-64; salesman Carpetland, Rockville, Md., 1965-67; asst. Mid-Atlantic regional mgr., then Mid-Atlantic regional mgr. J.C. Best Carpet Co., Braintree, Mass., 1967-69; salesman, gen. mgr. carpet div. Legum Distbg. Co., Balt., 1969-78; dir. mktg. Superior Metal Moulding Co., Balt., 1978—. Democrat. Jewish. Office: 1120 Whistler Ave Baltimore MD 21224

BECKMAN, GLEN LEONARD, consumer and trade show exec.; b. Los Angeles, July 22, 1930; s. Glenn Leonard and Lillian Nell (Etie) B.; m. Karen Marie Nielsen, Aug. 18, 1956 (dec.); 1 dau., Tracy Lynn. Sales and adminstrn. Archtl. Arts, 1955-60; partner Continental Exchange Corp., Los Angeles, 1960-63; v.p. Fortune of Calif., apparel mfg., Los Angeles, 1963-65; exec. dir. Los Angeles chpt. Bldg. Contractors Assn. Calif., 1965-67; pres. Industry Prodns. Am., Los Angeles, 1967-70, Industry Prodns. of Calif., Los Angeles, 1976—; producer-dir. Beckman's Gift Show, Gifts and Decorative Accessories Show, Profl. Arts, Crafts and Indoor Plants Show, Western Invitational Advt. and Sales Promotion Show, Mobile Merchandising Tour Am., numerous others since 1967. Served with USN, 1951-54. Recipient commendations, mayor Los Angeles, bd. suprs. Los Angeles County, Los Angeles City Council. Mem. Advt. Club Los Angeles, Nat. Assn. Exposition Mgrs., Fgn. Trade Assn. So. Calif. Address: 10992 Ashton Ave Los Angeles CA 90024

BECKMAN, JOHN STEPHEN, life ins. co. exec.; b. Berwyn, Ill., Apr. 16, 1936; s. Lloyd John and Esther (Hubbard) B.; B.B.A. with spl. distinction, U. Okla., 1958; M.B.A. with distinction, Harvard U., 1963; m. Barbara J. Arado, Dec. 2, 1967; 1 son, John Stephen. Asso., McKinsey & Co., Inc., Chgo., 1963-70, partner, 1970-72; v.p. Continental Investment Corp., Boston, 1972-74; pres. United Investors Life Ins. Co., Kansas City, Mo., 1974—, also dir.; exec. v.p. Waddell & Reed, Inc., Kansas City, 1974—, also dir. Regent, Coll. for Fin. Planning, 1977—, chmn., 1980—. Served with USAF, 1958-61. Republican. Club: Carriage (Kansas City). Office: PO Box 1441 1 Crown Center Kansas City MO 64141

BECKMANN, NEAL WALTER, design and constrn. co. exec.; b. St. Louis, July 23, 1941; student Washington U., 1973-74, St. Louis U., 1974-77; m. Jacqueline R. Beckmann, Aug. 1, 1969; children—Michael W., Michelle L., Marcus W. With Am. Materiel Co. affiliate Bank Bldg. and Equipment Corp. Am., St. Louis, 1974—, pres. purchasing, 1978—; adj. prof. St. Louis U.; lectr. Meramec Community Coll., Washington U.; chmn. bd. Pro-Con Internat., Ltd., Beckmann Found.; cons. E.F. Hutton and Co., Inc., Gould, Ind., Gulf Oil Corp., Dealer's Choice Interiors; dir. Mark Twain Bancshares Inc. Alderman Village of Edmundson, Mo., 1975-76, also park commr., dir. youth activities, dir. sr. citizens activities; mem. exec. bd. Old Trails council Boy Scouts Am., St. Louis. Served with U.S. Army, 1967-69. Recipient Khoury League Sportsman award for community service, Khoury League Baseball, 1975. Mem. Purchasing Mgmt. Assn. St. Louis (chmn. purchasing techniques com. 1974-76, dir. 1976-78, sec. 1978—), World Trade Club, Internat. Fedn. of Purchasing and Materials Mgmt., Nat. Assn. Purchasing Mgmt. (certified), Minority Purchasing Council Met. St. Louis (chmn. 1974-75), Backstoppers Club, Mo-Kans. Dist. Export Council. Author: Negotiations: Understanding The Bargaining Process, 1977; (with Dr. G.R. Banville) Negotiations: Understanding The Bargaining Process - A Study Guide, 1977; feature writer St. Louis Purchaser Mag., 1974—. Home: 147 Rue Grand Lake Saint Louis MO 63367 Office: 1144 Hampton Ave Saint Louis MO 63139

BECKMEYER, HAROLD EDWARD, electronics co. exec.; b. Yorktown, Tex., Oct. 6, 1920; s. Edward L. and Ella (Schneider) B.; B.A., Tex. Tech. U., 1941; M.B.A., Stanford U., 1953; m. Nov. 26, 1948; 1 son, James E. With Continental Oil Co., Ft. Worth, 1941-42; commd. ensign, U.S. Navy, 1942, advanced through grades to capt., 1962, ret., 1965; with Watkins Johnson Co., Palo Alto, Calif., 1965—, treas., adminstrv. dir., 1976—. Mem. Palo Alto C. of C. (chmn. congressional action com. 1970-77, dir. 1973-74), Nat. Assn. Purchasing Mgmt., Ret. Officers Assn. Republican. Methodist. Club: Rotary. Home: 490 Pine Ln Los Altos CA 94022 Office: 3333 Hillview Ave Palo Alto CA 94304

BECKWITH, RODNEY FISK, mgmt. cons.; b. Passaic, N.J., Oct. 24, 1935; s. Raymond Fisk and Nancy Angel (Oberdorf) B.; B.M.E. with distinction, Cornell U., 1958; M.B.A. with distinction, Harvard U., 1963; m. Elizabeth Ann Wedemann, July 23, 1960; children—Allison Collins, Kimberly Hall. Plant engr. Western Electric Co., Kearny, N.J., 1960-61; sr. asso. Cresap, McCormick and Paget, Inc., N.Y.C., 1963-68, prin., N.Y.C., 1968-72, v.p., Melbourne, Australia, 1972-77, v.p., dir., exec. com., N.Y.C., 1977—; dir. Am. C. of C., Australia, 1975-77. Served with USN, 1958-60, to lt. USNR, 1960-65. Mem. Inst. Mgmt. Cons.'s (founding), Delta Upsilon. Presbyterian. Clubs: Harvard Club N.Y.C., Pinnacle (N.Y.C.); Australian Club (Melbourne); Wee Burn Country (Darien, Conn.). Home: 8 Nolen Ln Darien CT 06820 Office: 245 Park Ave New York NY 10017

BEDELL, CATHERINE DEAN, govt. ofcl.; b. Yakima, Wash., May 18, 1914; d. Charles Henry and Pauline (Van Loon) Barnes; B.A., U. Wash., 1936, M.Ed., 1937; m. Donald W. Bedell, Nov. 14, 1970; children by previous marriage—James C. May, Melinda May Sullivan. Tchr. public schs., Chehalis, Wash., 1937-40; radio writer and commentator Sta. KMO, Tacoma, 1940-41, Sta. KOMO, Seattle, 1941-42; head radio dept. Strang-Prosser Advt. Agy., Seattle, 1942-43; radio writer Sta. WEAF, N.Y.C., 1944-46; radio broadcaster Sta. KIT, Yakima, 1948-56; mem. Wash. Ho. of Reps., 1952-58; mem. 86th to 91st Congresses; mem., incorporator Nat. R.R. Passenger Corp., Washington, 1970-71; chmn. U.S. Tariff Commn., Washington, 1971-75; mem. U.S. Internat. Trade Commn., 1975—. Mem. Nat. Commn. on Food Mktg., 1964-66. Mem. Alpha Chi Omega. Republican. Office: 701 E St NW Washington DC 20436

BEDIER, MARILYN DEE, banker; b. Warrensburg, Mo., Aug. 19, 1939; d. William and Margaret Lee (Drinkwater) Draper; student Central Mo. State Coll., 1958; m. Bruce A. Bedier, July 30, 1978; children by previous marriage—William Allen, Larry Neil, John Byron, Donald James, Knox. With Security Nat. Bank, Kansas City, Kans., 1968—, v.p. ops., sr. ops. officer, 1980—. Mem. Nat. Assn. Bank Women, Women's C. of C., Am. Banking Assn., Assn. Systems Mgmt., Am. Inst. Banking, Bank Adminstrn. Inst., Women's C. of C. (treas. 1977). Democrat. Methodist. Office: Security Nat Bank One Security Plaza Kansas City KS 66117

BEDINGER, KENNETH LAWRENCE, real estate broker; b. Portales, N.Mex., June 3, 1943; s. Andrew Emitt and Lillie Lois (Oney) B.; B.B.A., Eastern N.Mex. U., 1970, M.B.A., 1971; m. Sandra Ann Hardisty, Nov. 4, 1967; children—Sonja Denise, Brett Aaron. Mgmt. trainee J.C. Penney Co., Lompoc, Calif., 1963-66, asst. mgr., Portales, N.Mex., 1966-71, sales mgr. Schumpert Real Estate, Portales, 1971-72; owner Master Realty, Portales, 1972—; real estate cons., guest lectr. Eastern N.Mex. U., 1971—. Pres. Roosevelt County Bd. Realtors, 1972-73. Chmn., bd. dirs. Portales United Fund, 1974-75. Mem. Nat. Assn. Realtors, Phi Beta Lambda, Rho Epsilon (pres. 1970). Kiwanian (pres. Sundowners 1974-75). Home: 1416 S Globe St Portales NM 88130 Office: 712 W 1st St Portales NM 88130

BEDOYA, IVAN M., internat. mgmt. cons.; b. Pereira, Colombia, June 27, 1939; came to U.S., naturalized, 1962; m. Lijardo and Trinidad (Moreno) B.; degree N.Y. U., 1967; grad. Mgmt. for Execs., L.I. U., 1980. Asst. to public relations mgr. El Espectador newspaper, Bogota, Colombia, 1961; computer programmer/operator N.Y. U., N.Y.C., 1963-69; sales rep. Lanica Airlines, N.Y.C., 1969-79, dist. sales and interline mgr., 1979-81; v.p. J.B.J., Inc., N.Y.C., 1981—. Vol. tchr. for Spanish-speaking adults Our Lady of Sorrows Sch., Corona, N.Y.; mem. Am. Mus. Natural History. Mem. Colombia Cultural Assn. N.Y.C. Office: 919 Third Ave Suite 1701 New York NY 10022

BEDROSSIAN, PETER STEPHEN, chem. co. exec.; b. Hoboken, N.J., Sept. 15, 1926; s. Nishan Bedrossian and Helen (Jamagotchian) B.; B.B.A., St. Johns U., 1949, J.D., 1954; m. Jean M. Reynolds, Jan. 1951 (div. Oct. 1962); children—Peter, Alice Marie; m. 2d, JoAnn H. Thompson, Nov. 15, 1962; children—Stephanie Ann, Jennifer Ann. Admitted to N.Y. bar, 1954, Calif. bar, 1973; chief accountant Stauffer Chem. Co., N.Y.C., 1948-58, dir. taxes, 1958—, asst. treas., 1961—; v.p., dir. Stauffer Chem. Internat., Geneva, 1959-62; dir. Kali-Chemie Stauffer, Hannover, Germany, Stauffer Chem. Co. Internat.; asso. firm Dobbs & Nielsen, San Francisco, 1975-77; chief fin. officer, v.p.-legal Nanon Electronics, Inc., Cupertino, Calif., 1978—; vice chmn. Nitron, Inc., 1978—; dir. Parrott Ranch Co., San Francisco. Served with AUS, 1944-46. Mem. Am., N.Y., Calif. bar assns., Tax Execs. Inst. (pres. N.Y. chpt.), Internat. Assn. Assessing Officers, Nat. Assn. Rev. Appraisers, Internat. Fiscal Assn., Am. Legion, Phi Delta Phi, Alpha Kappa Psi. Club: N.Y. Athletic. Home: 400 Kings Mountain Rd Woodside CA 94062 Office: 10420 Bubb Rd Cupertino CA 95015

BEEBE, WILLIAM THOMAS, airline exec.; b. Los Angeles, Jan. 26, 1915; s. Dewey Sheldon and Elsie (Thomas) B.; B.B.A., U. Minn., 1937; m. Nancy Lee Gragg, Feb. 3, 1951; children—Marshall J., Linda Lee, Deborah Susan. Coll. trainee Gen. Electric Co., 1938-40; personnel mgr. United Aircraft Corp., Hartford, Conn., 1940-46; v.p. Delta Air Lines, Inc., Atlanta, 1946-67, sr. v.p. adminstrn., 1967-70, pres., 1970-71, chmn. bd., 1971—, also dir.; dir. Provident Life & Accident Ins. Co., Citizens & So. Nat. Bank, Am. Bus. Products. Mem. nat. adv. council Nat. Multiple Sclerosis Soc. Mem. Air Transport Assn. Episcopalian. Office: Hartsfield Atlanta Internat Airport Atlanta GA 30320

BEEBER, ALLAN R(OBERT) A(NDREW), bus. exec.; b. Mar. 1, 1913; B.S., CCNY, 1936; M.S., Columbia U., 1941, Ph.D., 1945; 4 children. Tech. dir. Keuffel & Esser, Hoboken, N.J., 1939-57; v.p. research Arkwright-Interlaken Inc., Fiskeville, R.I., 1957-59; tech. cons. Altec, A.G., Zurich, Switzerland, 1959-73, Ozalid Ltd., London, 1960-73; chmn. bd., mng. dir. WIFO, AG, Zurich, 1972-77; dir. Ozalid Group Holdings Ltd., London, 1973-77; chmn. bd., mng. dir. Transworld Tech. Ltd., R.I., 1975-77; chmn. bd., chief exec. Arkwright Inc., 1974-77, Arkwright Internat. Inc., R.I., 1974-77, TWT Labs. Inc., R.I., 1973-77, Photonics Co., St. Louis, 1975-77; vice chmn., dir. group tech. Technographics World Trade Corp., Darien, Conn., 1977-79; chmn. bd., pres. Spectrum Communications Tech., Inc., Darien, 1978—; pres. Zuritec, AG, Zurich, 1979—. Mem. Inst. Dirs., Royal Photog. Sci., Soc. Photog. Engrs. and Scientists, Am. Chem. Soc., Am. Inst. Chemists, AAAS, N.Y. Acad. Sci., Assn. Research Dirs. Chemists Club, N.Y. Acad. Sci. Inventor, patentee in field, U.S., Eng., Switzerland. Address: 837 Hollow Tree Ridge Rd Darien CT 06820

BEEKMAN, JEFFREY SCOTT, packaging co. exec.; b. Rockville Centre, N.Y., Mar. 7, 1953; s. Cecil H. and Barbara K. Beekman; B.B.A. with honors, Hofstra U., 1975; M.B.A. with distinction, Cornell U., 1978; m. Janice Long, July 31, 1976. With Continental Group, Continental Can Corp., 1978-79, mgr. licensing and bus. devel. plastic beverage bottles div., 1979-80, New Eng. sales rep., Merrimack, N.H., 1980—. Recipient Student Achievement award in fin. Wall St. Jour., 1978. Mem. Am. Mgmt. Assn., Soc. Advancement Mgmt., Beta Gamma Sigma. Home: 9 Sarah Dr Merrimack NH 03054 Office: 14 Continental Blvd Merrimack NH 03054

BEEN, FREDDIE EDMOND, fin. exec.; b. Covington, Okla., Apr. 5, 1936; s. Dewey C. and Hanna M. (Westphal) B.; B.S., Okla. State U., 1957, postgrad., 1957-58; postgrad. Tulsa U., 1958-59; m. Charlcie Lee Appelgate, Aug. 27, 1955: children—Tamera Lou, Dana Lynn, Criston David. Staff acct. Deloitte, Haskins & Sells, C.P.A.'s, Tulsa, 1957-62; chief acct. Tyler-Dawson Supply Co., Tulsa, 1962-68, controller, 1968-76, sec.-treas., 1976-79, fin. v.p., 1979—; v.p. fin. T-D Oilfield Supply Co., Tulsa, 1979—. Adv. bd. acctg. Tulsa Jr. Coll., 1977—; trustee Sunset Bible Camp. C.P.A., Okla.; recipient Jaycees Spoke award, 1960. Mem. Okla. Soc. C.P.A.'s, Am. Mgmt. Assn. Republican. Mem. Christian Ch. Club: Meadowbrook Country. Home: 9645 S 193rd St E Ave Broken Arrow OK 74012 Office: 6310 E 13 St Tulsa OK 74112

BEER, CELSO, flavor and fragrance mfg. co. exec.; b. Rio de Janeiro, Feb. 7, 1941; came to U.S., 1978; s. Carlos Waldemar and Maria Eleanora (Kappaun) B.; student sci. and engring. Colegio Esdadual Washington Luiz, 1958-60; student adminstrn. Centro de Estudos Boletim Cambial, 1966-67; m. Cely Mussel, Sept. 20, 1961; children—Evandro Roni, Elaine Regina. Plant mgr. Internat. Flavors & Fragrances, Brazil, 1960-73, ops. mgr., Indonesia, 1974-75, tech. cons., 1975; ops. mgr. for Latin Am., Polak Frutal Works, Brazil, 1976-78, group v.p. for ops. and logistics, Middletown, N.Y., 1978—. Mem. Am. Mgmt. Assn. Roman Catholic. Office: 33 Sprague Ave Middletown NY 10940

BEER, GORDON ALBERT, mgmt. exec.; b. Summerland, B.C., Can., May 23, 1930; came to U.S., 1936, naturalized, 1942; s. Albert James and Mary (Lister) B.; student Santa Monica City Coll., 1949-51; B.S. with honors, UCLA, 1953; postgrad. exec. program in bus. adminstrn. Columbia U., 1973; m. Joyce Darlene Wolfe, Dec. 19, 1953; children—Teri Lynn, Jeffrey Allen, Kenneth Lister. Naval architect Mare Island Naval Shipyard, 1953-56, sect. head Nuclear Power div., 1956-60, br. head, 1960-62; dept. head Aerojet Gen. Corp., 1962-64, sr. project engr., 1964-67; quality assurance unit mgr. Liquid Metal Engring. Center, Santa Susana, Calif., 1967-70, operation mgr., 1970-71; dir. quality assurance Consol. Edison Co. N.Y., Inc., N.Y.C., 1971-79, dir. on exec. staff, 1979-80, mem. nuclear facilities safety com., 1976-80; v.p. Mgmt. Analysis Co., San Diego, 1980—; mem. practices and procedures com. nuclear tech. adv. bd. Am. Nat. Standard Inst., 1973-76. Registered profl. engr., Calif. Mem. ASME (vice chmn. nuclear quality assurance standards com., mem. gen. requirements subcom.), Am. Soc. Quality Control (sr.), Am. Nuclear Soc., Am. Mgmt. Assn., Tau Beta Pi. Home: 9982 Del Dios Hwy Escondido CA 92025 Office: 11095 Torreyana Rd San Diego CA 92121

BEER, JOHN WALTER, mgmt. cons.; b. N.Y.C., Feb. 11, 1932; s. Walter Eugene and Florence Fay B.; A.B., Harvard U., 1954, postgrad., 1956-57; m. Rosemary Tyson, Dec. 28, 1957; children—Thomas, Amy, Jeffery. Vice pres., dir. Drexel Harriman Ripley, Inc., N.Y.C. and Paris, 1963-69; pres., dir. Dean Witter Internat., London, 1969-71; pres. Atlantic Partners Inc., Litchfield, Conn., 1971—. Served to comdr. USMCR, 1954-56. Clubs: Down Town Assn., Harvard (N.Y.C.); Bucks (London); Travellers (Paris); Racket (Montreal). Home: East Chestnut Hill Litchfield CT 06759 Office: Box 553 Litchfield CT 06759

BEESLEY, JOSEPH L., ins. exec.; b. Alert, Ind., Aug. 24, 1904; s. John W. and Mary (Stephenson) B.; A.B., DePauw U., 1926; m. Alta M. Biddinger, June 27, 1924; children—Lester, John E. With Equitable Life Assurance Soc. U.S., 1926—, beginning as trainee, successively cashier, Denver, Phoenix, Syracuse, asst. cashier, N.Y.C., cashier, Chgo., agy. mgr., Syracuse, field v.p. charge N.Y. area agencies, 1953, sr. v.p. charge sales, 1955-61, sr. v.p., asst. to chmn., 1961-69, spl. rep., 1969—; mem. Equitable Group Millionaires, Equitable Nat. Leaders Corps, 1971-73, Equitable Order Excalibur, 1973, Equitable Pres.'s Cabinet, 1971, 73. Commr., treas. Nat. Commn. Community Health Services, 1962-66. Trustee Am. Fund for Dental Edn., 1961-69, DePauw U. C.L.U. Mem. Nat. Assn. Life

Underwriters (chmn. edn. com. Chgo.; dist. dir. Syracuse 1947-48), Life Agy. Mgrs. Assn., Syracuse Life Trust Council, Life Ins. Agy. Mgmt. Assn. (dir. 1961-63), Am. Coll. Life Underwriters (pub. relations com.), Am. Life Conv. (chmn. agy. sect. 1960), Agy. Officers Round Table (chmn. 1959-60), Phi Beta Kappa, Delta Chi. Methodist. Mason. Clubs: Rotary; Garden City Country, Union League. Home: 63 Osborne Rd Garden City NY 11530 Office: 3333 New Hyde Park Rd New Hyde Park NY 11042

BEETS, F. LEE, ins. co. exec.; b. Paola, Kans., Apr. 2, 1922; s. William Francis and Nellie (Bryan) B.; B.B.A., Tulane U., 1945; postgrad. Harvard U., 1945, evening sch. U. Kansas City, Rockhurst Coll.; m. Dorothy Loraine Shelton, June 20, 1945; children—Randall Lee, Pamela Lee. Sr. acct. Lunsford Barnes & Co., Kansas City, Mo., 1946-49; v.p., gen. mgr. Viking Refrigerators, 1949-53; v.p., sec.-treas. Equipment Finance Co., 1949-53; exec. v.p., treas., gen. mgr. T.H. Mastin & Co., Consol. Underwriters, Mo. Gen. Ins. Co., Plan-O-Pay, Inc., Mid-Am. Data Co., B O L Assos., Inc., 1953-69; now chmn. bd. chief exec. officer Fin. Guardian Group, Inc., Fin. Guardian, Inc., Fin. Compensation Cons., Inc., Worldsurance, Inc., F G Tech. Services, Inc., Fin. Guardian Internat. B.V. Served with USNR, 1942-45. C.P.A., Mo. Mem. Mo. Soc. C.P.A.'s, Am. Inst. C.P.A.'s, Soc. C.P.C.U.'s, Pi Kappa Alpha, Sigma Tau Gamma, Phi Mu Alpha Sinfonia. Club: Masons. Home: 7901 Bristol Ct Prairie Village KS 66208 Office: 3100 Broadway Kansas City MO 64111

BEHNKE, WALLACE BLANCHARD, JR., elec. utility co. exec.; b. Evanston, Ill., Feb. 5, 1926; s. Wallace Blanchard and Dorothea (Bull) B.; B.S., Northwestern U., 1945, B.E.E., 1947; m. Joan F. Murphy, Sept. 24, 1949; children—Susan F., Ann B., Thomas W. With Commonwealth Edison Co., Chgo., 1947—, dist. supt., Crystal Lake, Ill., 1956-58, div. engr., Joliet, Ill., 1958-60, area mgr., Mt. Prospect, Ill., 1960-62, div. v.p., Chgo., 1962-66, asst. to pres., 1966-69, v.p., 1969-72, exec. v.p., 1972-80, vice chmn., 1980—; chmn. bd. Project Mgmt. Corp.; dir. Lake View Trust & Savs. Bank, Commonwealth Edison Co., Standard of Am. Life Ins. Co. Bd. dirs., chmn. Robert Crown Center for Health Edn.; bd. dirs. United Way Met. Chgo.; trustee Ill. Inst. Tech., Protestant Found. Chgo., Northwestern Meml. Hosp., Chgo.; bd. dirs., vice chmn. Atomic Indsl. Forum. Served to lt. USNR, 1943-46, 50-52. Fellow IEEE; mem. Am. Nuclear Soc., Nat. Acad. of Engring. Western Soc. Engrs., Phi Delta Theta. Clubs: Econ., Chgo., Comml., Hinsdale (Ill.) Golf. Home: 311 S Oak St Hinsdale IL 60521 Office: 1 First Nat Plaza Chicago IL 60690

BEHR, RALPH STEVEN, food mfg. co. exec.; b. N.Y.C., June 19, 1951; s. Paul and Sylvia (Kurus) B.; B.A., SUNY, Albany, 1973; J.D., Hofstra U., 1976. Admitted to Oreg. bar, 1976, N.Y. bar, 1977; legis. asst. N.Y. State Legislature, 1971-73; individual practice law, Portland, Oreg., 1976-77; v.p., counsel Food Oils Corp., Carlstadt, N.J., 1978—; instr. Hofstra U., 1975-76; vol. atty. Family Ct. of N.Y.C. Mem. Oreg. Bar Assn., Am. Bar Assn., Bar Assn. City of N.Y., Pvt. Label Mfrs. Assn. (dir. 1980—). Contbr. in field; legal editor Pvt. Label mag. Office: 145 Grand St Carlstad NJ 07072

BEHRAKIS, GEORGE D., pharm. mfg. co. exec.; b. Lowell, Mass.; s. Dracoulis K. and Stella (Zaroulis) B.; B.S. in Pharm. Scis., Northeastern U.; m. Margo Pergakis, July 30, 1961; children—Drake, Stephanie, Joanna, Elena. Salesman, McNeil Labs., N.H. and Vt., 1959-62, hosp. salesman, Va. and N.C., 1962-64, regional supr. Northeastern U.S., 1964-67; founder, pres. Dooner Labs., Haverhill, Mass., 1967-77; owner Muro Pharm., Inc., Tewksbury, Mass. Pres., Holy Trinity Ch., Lowell; bd. dirs. Lowell Boys Club, Lowell Girls Club; founder, bd. dirs. New Eng. Allergy Found.; bd. dirs. Maliotis Cultural Center, Hellenic Coll.; bd. dirs. Bldg. Authority U. Lowell, mem. advisory bd. Sch. Mgmt. Served with U.S. Army, 1957-59. Mem. Northeastern U. Alumni Assn., Asso. Industries of Mass., Pharm. Advertisers Club N.Y., Am. Pharm. Assn., Am. Chem. Soc., Ahepa. Club: Vesper Country. Research on patterns of the solublization of theophylline in an aqueous solution without the use of alcohol. Office: Muro Pharmaceutical Inc 890 East St Tewksbury MA 01876

BEHRENFELD, WILLIAM HAROLD, lawyer, C.P.A.; b. Bklyn., Apr. 9, 1936; s. Herman Boyce and Belle (Wexler) B.; B.S. in Bus. Adminstrn., Boston U., 1957; J.D., Fordham U., 1963; LL.M., N.Y. U., 1967; m. Nancy Schep, Aug. 30, 1964; children—Craig, Randi, Jodi. Admitted to N.Y. bar, 1963, U.S. Tax Ct. bar, 1966, U.S. Supreme Ct. bar, 1967; tax mgr. Main Lafrentz & Co., N.Y.C., 1968-71; tax mgr. Richard Eisner & Co., N.Y.C., 1971-72; individual practice law, Nanuet, N.Y., 1972-77; partner firm Gurevitch and Behrenfeld, Pearl River, N.Y., 1977—; adj. asst. prof. Manhattanville Coll. Served to 1st lt. U.S. Army, 1957-59. Mem. Am. Bar Assn., Am. (pres.-elect), N.Y. (past pres.) assns. atty.-C.P.A.'s, Am. Inst. C.P.A.'s. Author: Estate Planning Desk Book, 4th edit., 1977. Home: 3 Gem Ct Spring Valley NY 10977 Office: 500 Bradley Hill Rd Blauvelt NY 10913

BEHRENS, RAYMOND WALTER, ins. co. exec.; b. N.J., July 19, 1933; s. Max Gustau and Jean B.; B.A., Rutgers U., 1955; m. Judith A. Harvey, Nov. 14, 1970; children—Elizabeth, John. Commd. officer USAF, 1956, resigned, 1963; brokerage cons. Conn. Gen. Life Ins. Co., Los Angeles, 1964-69, account mgr., 1970—; seminar speaker. Active in charitable fund raising, local community and polit. fund raising. Served with USAF, 1956-63. Recipient awards for profl. achievements Conn. Gen. Life Ins. Co. Republican. Originator exec. compensation design techniques. Home: 27925 Ridgebrook Ct Rancho Palos Verdes CA 90274

BEINECKE, FREDERICK WILLIAM, II, business exec.; b. Stamford, Conn., June 3, 1943; s. William and Elizabeth Barrett (Gillespie) B.; B.A., Yale U., 1966; J.D., U. Va., 1972; student Program Mgmt. Devel., Harvard Bus. Sch., 1977; m. Candace Krugman, Oct. 2, 1976; 1 son, Jacob Sperry. Admitted to N.Y. bar; asso. firm Hughes Hubbard & Reed, N.Y.C., 1972-73; gen. counsel, dep. mng. dir. South St. Seaport Mus., N.Y.C., 1973-75; mgr. real estate ops. Sperry & Hutchinson Co., N.Y.C., from 1975, corp. v.p., 1977-80, pres., 1980—, also dir.; pres. The Gunlocke Co. subs. Trustee, Phillips Acad., Andover, Mass., South St. Seaport Mus.; bd. dirs., treas. N.Y.C. Ballet; bd. dirs. N.Y. Urban League. Served to capt. USMC; Vietnam. Decorated Bronze Star with Combat V. Mem. Assn. Bar City N.Y., Am. Bar Asn. Clubs: River, Yale, Angler's, St. Hubert's, Ausable (N.Y.C.). Office: Sperry & Hutchinson Co 330 Madison Ave New York NY 10017

BEINECKE, WILLIAM S., ret. bus. exec.; b. N.Y.C., May 22, 1914; s. Frederick William and Carrie (Sperry) B.; B.A., Yale U., 1936, M.A. (hon.), 1971; LL.B., Columbia U., 1940; LL.D. (hon.), Southwestern U., 1967, Cath. U. Am., 1972; m. Elizabeth Barrett Gillespie, May 24, 1941; children—Frederick W. II, John B., Sarah S., Frances G. Former asso. law firm Chadbourne, Wallace, Parke & Whiteside; co-founder law firm Casey, Beinecke & Chase; became gen. counsel The Sperry and Hutchinson Co., N.Y.C., 1952, gen. counsel, v.p., 1954-60, dir., 1955—, pres., 1960-67, chmn. bd., chief exec. officer, 1967-80; trustee Consol. Edison Co., N.Y.C. Trustee, Am. Mus. Natural History, Yale U.; bd. mgrs. N.Y. Bot. Garden. Served to comdr. USNR, World War II. Recipient Alumni medal Alumni Fedn. Columbia U., 1971. Mem. Council Fgn. Relations. Clubs: Yale, Sky, The Links (N.Y.C.); Baltusrol Golf (Springfield, N.J.); Eastward Ho Country (Chatham, Mass.); Cotton Bay (Eleuthera); Country of Fla. (Delray). Home: 21 E 79 St New York NY 10021 Office: The Sperry and Hutchinson Bldg 330 Madison Ave New York NY 10017

BEINHOCKER, GILBERT DAVID, investment banker; b. Phila., July 7, 1932; s. Joseph A. and Florence (Shlifer) B.; B.A., Pa. State U., 1954; M.S., U. Pa., 1958; D.Eng., U. Detroit, 1968; m. Barbara Broadley, Dec. 17, 1960; children—Eric David, Elizabeth Broadley, Robert Marc. Engring. dir. Epsco, Inc., 1958-61; pres. Syber Corp., Natick, Mass., 1961-64; div. mgr. Tech. Measurement Corp., 1964-65; dir. advanced planning Am. Optical Co., 1965-66; chmn. bd. Microdyne Instruments, Inc., Waltham, Mass., 1967-69; pres., chief exec. officer, dir. Mgmt. Scis., Inc., Cambridge, Mass., 1968—; dir. Nat. Info. Services Inc., Cambridge; chief exec. officer, dir. Eurocom Inc., Cambridge, 1975—; dir. corp. finance Moors and Cabot, Boston, 1976—; dir. Stranway Corp., Elmendorf Board Corp., Green Cross Oxygen Inc., Valpey-Fisher Corp., Evergreen Energy Corp., Moors & Cabot Assos. Inc.; sr. lectr. U. Detroit, 1967-68. Recipient Nat. Fight for Sight citation Nat. Council to Combat Blindness, 1963. Mem. AAAS, IEEE, Assn. Computing Machinery, Internat. Fedn. Med. Electronics and Biol. Engring., Internat. Soc. Clin. Electroretinography, Assn. Research Ophthalmology, Am. Def. Preparedness Assn., Am. Mgmt. Assn., Instrument Soc. Am., Am. Assn. Med. Instrumentation, Pi Lambda Phi. Democrat. Author: Theory and Operation of Stardac Computers, 1960, also articles. Patentee in field. Home: 36 Beatrice Circle Belmont MA 02178 Office: Moors and Cabot Devonshire St Boston MA 02168

BEINHORN, JEFFERY MICHAEL, furniture retailer; b. Roanoke, Va., Oct. 21, 1940; s. Sam and Ruth Muriel (Schwartz) B.; ed. U. Miami. With B & L Maytag Co. Inc. of Va., Grundy, sec., v.p., 1978—; pub. Cy. Fair Catalog, 1973-78. Adv. Interact Club, 1964-78; bd. dirs. March of Dimes, 1969-70; fund raiser ARC, 1978-80. Served with USAR, 1964-70. Recipient Interact award, 1972. Mem. C. of C., So. Home Furnishings Assn. (dir. 1974-78). Jewish. Clubs: Islander, Rotary (pres. 1969-70), Moose. Home: PO Box Y Slate Creek Rd Grundy VA 24614 Office: PO Box Y E Main St Grundy VA 24614

BEISWINGER, GEORGE LAWRENCE, retail co. exec.; b. Salem, Mo., Mar. 15, 1924; s. Lawrence and Bessie (Pines) B.; B.S., Washington U., St. Louis, 1949, postgrad., 1953; postgrad. Harvard, 1949; M.J., Temple U., 1980; m. Virginia Marie Graves, Dec. 24, 1950; children—Gail Anne Beiswinger Rexon. George William. Personnel mgr. Continental Baking Co. (name now changed to ITT Continental Baking Co.), St. Louis, 1953-58; supr. tng. and communication Monsanto Co., Columbia, Tenn., 1958-63; communication coordinator Dodge Truck Plant, Chrysler Corp., Detroit, 1963-64; communication supr. research and styling Chrysler Engring., Detroit, 1964-66, group mgr. communication, car assembly group, 1966-67; corporate dir. communication Acme Markets, Inc., Phila., 1967-77, v.p. communication, 1977-79, v.p. public relations, 1979—. Served with USAAF, 1942-46. Recipient award Freedoms Found., 1963. Mem. Pub. Relations Soc. Am. (pres. Phila. chpt. 1976—). Republican. Episcopalian. Office: 124 N 15th St Philadelphia PA 19101

BEITEL, HERBERT MANSON, exec. recruiter, cons.; b. Kokomo, Ind., Apr. 1, 1925; s. Orville Charles and Vesta Ann (Oliver) B.; student Emory U., 1943-44; B.S. cum laude, U. S.C., 1946; J.D., U. Chgo., 1949. Admitted to Ind., Ill. bars, 1950; asst. chief title examiner Calumet Title Co., Crown Point, Ind., 1950-52; asst. to pres., atty. First Fed. Savs. & Loan Assn., Chgo., 1952-55; legis. counsel, eastern mgr., counsel Nat. Automatic Merchandising Assn., Chgo., 1955-60, 66-68, sec., dir. Cantop Machinery Corp., Bala Cynwyd, Pa., 1960-65; exec. dir. Pa. Automatic Merchandising Council, Phila., 1963-68; pub. editor Vend mag. Billboard Publs., Inc., N.Y.C., 1968-72; dir. adminstrv. systems Servomation Corp., N.Y.C., after 1972, dir. mktg. services and communications 1977-79; pres. The Wayne Hammond Group, N.Y.C., 1979—. Pres., Mid-Atlantic Center for Arts, 1981; nat. treas. Young Republicans, 1951-53, asst. gen. counsel, 1953-55. Served to lt. (j.g.) USNR, 1943-46. Recipient Jesse H. Neal award journalism. Mem. Am., Ill., Ind. bar assns., Newcomen Soc., Blue Key, Phi Beta Kappa. Club: Masons. Contbr. articles to profl. jours. Home: 283 8th St Jersey City NJ 07302 Office: New York NY

BEITZEL, GEORGE B., bus. machines co. exec.; b. Springfield, Pa., Apr. 25, 1928; s. George Breuninger and Mary Elizabeth (Bickley) B.; B.A., Amherst Coll., 1950; M.B.A., Harvard U., 1955; m. Mary Louise Elliott, July 26, 1952; children—George Elliott, Mary Elizabeth, David Nelson. With IBM Corp., 1955—, pres. IBM Data Processing div., 1966-68, v.p., 1968-72, gen. mgr. Data Processing Group, 1969-72, group exec. Gen. Bus. Group, 1972-79, sr. v.p., 1972—, dir., 1972—; dir. Bankers Trust Co., Flight Safety Internat., Inc., Phillips Petroleum Co. Bd. trustees Amherst Coll., No. Westchester Hosp. Office: IBM Corp Old Orchard Rd Armonk NY 10504

BEJARANO, JOSÉ RAFAEL, engring. exec.; b. Mexico City, Mex., Apr. 15, 1915; s. Jose Miguel and Trinela (Lillo) B., came to U.S., 1916, naturalized, 1948; B.S. in Elec. Engring., Columbia, 1937, M.S., 1938; m. Blossom Helen Smiley, July 2, 1948; children—Michele Helene, Barbara Alexandra Coleman, Gregory Andres. Mgr. spl. projects dept. Westinghouse Electric Internat., N.Y.C., 1942-44; gen. mgr. Industria Electrica de Mexico, Mexico City, 1945-47; mng. dir. Brasmotor S.A., Sao Paulo, Brazil, 1951-59; pres., sr. v.p., dir. RCA Internat. Ltd., Montreal, Que., Can., 1960-63; group v.p., pres. Latin Am. group Xerox Corp., Stamford, Conn., 1964-75, sr. v.p. Xerox Corp. and Xerox Consultants Inc., Stamford, 1975-76; dir. Parsons Brinckerhoff Inc., N.Y.C., Parsons Brinckerhoff Internat. Inc., Parsons Brinckerhoff Devel. Co., 1977—; internat. bus. cons. Mem. Uniao Cultural Brasil-EEUU, Tau Beta Pi, Epsilon Chi, Theta Tau. Club: Univ. (N.Y.C.); Landmark (Stamford). Home: 138 Pecksland Rd Greenwich CT 06830

BEKES, GREGORY EDWARD, food co. exec.; b. Phila., Feb. 15, 1950; s. Walter Thomas and Ethel Florence (Finger) B.; student Eastern Baptist Coll., 1968-70; B.A., Glassboro State Coll., 1971; M.B.A., So. Ill. U., 1978; m. Kathleen Moore, Feb. 12, 1972; children—Jason, Matthew. Shipping supr. Campbell Soup Co., 1971-78; quality control supr. Underwood Co., Hannibal, Mo., 1978-79; personnel mgr., asst. to gen. mgr. Hunt-Wesson Foods, Inc., Valparaiso, Ind., 1979—; lectr. bus. adminstrn. Ind. U. Mem. budget and allocations com. United Way Porter County. Mem. Am. Soc. Personnel Adminstrn., Valparaiso C. of C., Beta Gamma Sigma. Home: 35 S Sunset Hebron IN 46341 Office: PO Box 468 Valparaiso IN 46383

BEKKUM, OWEN D., gas co. exec.; b. Westby, Wis., Mar. 2, 1924; s. Alfred T. and Huldah (Storbakken) B.; B.B.A., U. Wis., 1950; postgrad. Northwestern U.; m. Dorothy A. Jobs, Aug. 26, 1950. With Arthur Andersen & Co., 1951-57, Hertz Corp., 1957-62; with No. Ill. Gas Co., 1963—, mgr. tech. acctg., 1964-66, asst. comptroller, 1966-68, comptroller, 1968-70, adminstrv. v.p., 1970-73, exec. v.p., 1973-76, pres., 1976—, also dir.; dir. all NICOR and NI-Gas subs.'s.; dir. Andrew Corp. Bd. dirs. Protestant Found. Greater Chgo., 1975—, Pace Inst., 1977—. Served with AUS, 1943-46. C.P.A., Wis., Ill. Mem. Am. Mgmt. Assn., Am. Inst. C.P.A.'s, Am. Gas Assn. (dir. 1978—), Inst. Gas Tech. (trustee 1978—). Clubs: Mid-Day, Economic (Chgo.). Home: 46 Royal Vale Dr Oak Brook IL 60521 Office: PO Box 190 Aurora IL 60507

BELAN, ROBERT DUANE, mfg. co. exec.; b. Smithfield, Pa., July 19, 1940; s. John L. and Katherine B.; B.S. in Bus. Mgmt., St. Vincent Coll., 1962; postgrad. exec. mgmt. program Pa. State U., 1977; m. Bonita L. Warner, Oct. 26, 1968; children—Robert, Jamie Lynn. Mgmt. trainee Rockwell Internat., Uniontown, Pa., 1966-68, prodn. control mgr., 1968-75, factory mgr., 1975-77, gen. plant mgr., 1977—. Bd. dirs. Fayette County Devel. Council, Fayette Heritage; bd. trustees Greater Uniontown Indsl. Fund; exec. bd. Fayette-Westmoreland council Boy Scouts Am.; bd. dirs., membership campaign com., new bldg. com. YMCA, Uniontown; adv. com. Fayette County Area Tech. Sch.; mem. Fayette County com. Pa. Economy League; corp. gifts chmn. Am. Heart Fund Assn. Served to lt. USN, 1962-66; Viet Nam. Mem. Am. Water Works Assn., Uniontown Area C. of C. (dir.). Roman Catholic. Club: Rotary. Office: PO Box 487 Uniontown PA 15401

BELCHER, DONALD WILLIAM, engring co. exec.; b. N.Y.C., July 13, 1922; s. Donald Ray and Mary Carver (Williams) B.; B.E. in Chem. Engring., Yale, 1943; m. Dariel Keith, March 23, 1946; children—Dariel Jean Belcher Sellers, Donald Richard, Susan Keith Belcher Penedos, David Todd, Jonathan Rockwood. Chem. supr. E. I. DuPont de Nemours & Co., Inc., muriatic acid dept., Grasselli, N.J., 1946; asst. dept. supt., silicate dept., 1946-48; project design engr. Bowen Engring. Inc., North Branch, N.J. (name now Stork Bowen Engring. Inc., Somerville, N.J.), 1948-51, mgr. functional design, 1951-57, v.p. and chief engr., 1957-72, v.p. and tech. dir., 1972-76, exec. v.p., dir., 1976-78, pres., dir., 1978-79, exec. v.p., dir., 1979—. Bd. dirs. YMCA, Westfield, N.J., 1959-64. Served in USNR, 1943-46. Registered profl. engr., N.J., La. Mem. Am. Inst. Chem. Engrs. Home: 550 Prospect St Westfield NJ 07090 Office: Box 898 Somerville NJ 08876

BELDOCK, DONALD TRAVIS, financial exec.; b. N.Y.C., May 29, 1934; s. George and Rosa (Tribus) B.; B.A., Yale, 1955; m. Lucy Geringer, Apr. 23, 1971; children—John Anthony, Gwen Ann, James Geringer Christopher. Mdse. exec. R.H. Macy & Co., N.Y.C., 1955-60; fin. cons. D.T. Beldock & Co., N.Y.C., 1961-66; chmn. fin. com. Basic Resources Corp. (formerly White Shield Corp., N.Y.C., 1966-69, pres., chmn. bd., chief exec. officer, 1970—; pres., dir. Beaver St. Research Corp., N.Y.C., 1966—, Fast Food Systems Corp., Westport, Conn.; dir. Automatic Toll Systems, Inc., N.Y.C., Solar Reliance Corp., Westport, Phila. Printing Properties, Inc., Fundamental Properties, N.Y.C., Dynaflair Ltd., Montreal, Que., Can. Trustee, treas. Strang Clinic-Preventive Medicine Inst.; bd. advisers Colo. Timberline Acad.; trustee Am. Symphony Orch. Clubs: Yale; Westchester Country, Lotos. Home: 784 Park Ave New York NY 10021 Office: 595 Madison Ave New York NY 10022

BELFER, NORMAN C., real estate developer; b. Wodzislaw, Poland, Sept. 27, 1922; s. Benjamin S. and Hinda Belfer; m. Elinor Renfield, Jan. 5, 1952; children—Andrew, James, Lauren, Carolyn. Corp. sec., gen. mgr. Belfer Corp., Bklyn., 1950-53; pres. Knickerbocker Feather Corp. and Belfer Bros. Co., 1954-63; chief officer, gen. partner Belfer Devel. Co., Belfer Realty Assos., Great Neck, N.Y. and Guttenberg, N.J., 1964—; chmn. bd. United Feather and Down, Inc., Bklyn. and Chgo., 1979—. Club: Palm Beach (Fla.) Country. Address: 100 Sunrise Ave Palm Beach FL 33480

BELHUMEUR, JEAN MARC R., JR., acct., business exec.; b. Woonsocket, R.I., Aug. 7, 1933; s. Jean Marc R. and Marie Therese (Major) B.; B.S. in Acctg. and Fin., Bryant Coll., 1954; m. Lea E. Dextraze, Oct. 10, 1956; children—Denise, Jeannie, Paulette, Michelle. Acct., mgmt. cons. Howell & Co., Washington, 1956-58; acctg. analyst Litton Industries, Washington, 1958-60; acctg. mgr. U.S. Industries, Washington, 1960-63; controller Curtis Bros., Washington, 1963-65, Leasco Systems, Washington, 1965-69; v.p., treas. PST Inc., Boston, 1969-70; v.p. Gould, Inc., Newton, Mass., 1970-73; sec.-treas. Scan-Optics, Inc., East Hartford, Conn., 1973-76, v.p., 1976-78, pres., 1978-79, chmn., pres., 1979—. Served with U.S. Army, 1954-56. C.P.A., D.C. Mem. Am. Inst. C.P.A.'s, Conn. Soc. C.P.A.'s, Nat. Assn. Accts., East Hartford C. of C. (dir.). Clubs: Rotary, French. Home: 156 Box Mountain Dr Vernon CT 06066 Office: Scan-Optics Inc 22 Prestige Park East Hartford CT 06108

BELISLE, JACQUELINE THERESE, bus. economist; b. Woonsocket, R.I., Sept. 16, 1933; d. J. Armand and Delia M. (Desilets) B.; B.S. in Bus. Adminstrn., Boston U., 1956; M.B.A., N.Y. U., 1960. Research asst., internat. dept. Mfrs. Hanover Trust Co., N.Y.C., 1956-60; research asso. dept. econs. and research Am. Bankers Assn., N.Y.C., 1960-67, asst. economist, 1967-69; sr. industry analyst, corp. devel. ITT, N.Y.C., 1969-72, economist, bus. econs., corporate devel., 1972—. Mem. Am. Econ. Assn., Nat. Assn. Bus. Economists. Home: 300 E 34th St New York City NY 10016 Office: 320 Park Ave New York City NY 10022

BELK, IRWIN, mcht.; b. Charlotte N.C., Apr. 4, 1922; s. William Henry and Mary Leonora (Irwin) B.; student Davidson Coll.; grad. U. N.C., Chapel Hill, 1946; LL.D. (hon.), Mo. Valley Coll.; m. Carol Grotnes, Sept. 11, 1948; children—William Irwin, Irene G. Belk Miltimore, Marilyn Belk Bryan, Carl G. Trained in mercantile field; pres. Belk Enterprises, Inc., Charlotte; chmn. bd. Monroe Hardware Co. (N.C.); exec. v.p. Belk Stores Services, Inc., Charlotte; pres. Belk Finance Co., Charlotte, Belk Stores Ins. Reciprocal, Charlotte; v.p., dir. PMC, Inc., Belk Group Stores; dir. Adams Millis Corp., First Union Nat. Bank, Lumbermen's Mut. Casualty Co., Cameron Financial Corp., Stonecutter Mills, Fidelity Bankers Life Ins. Co. Mem. Nat. Council on Crime and Delinquency; mem. N.C. Ho. of Reps., 1959-62; mem. N.C. Senate from Mecklenburg County, 1963-66; mem. N.C. Legis. Council, 1963-64; mem. Legislative Research Commn., 1965-66; mem. Dem. Nat. Com., 1969-72; del. Dem. Nat. Conv., 1956, 60, 64, 72. Chmn. bd. advisers Belk Found.; chmn. bd. N.C. div. Am. Cancer Soc.; bd. dirs., exec. com. N.C. Assn. for Blind; bd. dirs., past pres. N.C. chpt. Nat. Soc. for Prevention Blindness; bd. dirs. Med. Found. N.C., Carolina Carrousel, Charlotte Opera Assn., Sch. Design at N.C. State U., Charlotte and Mecklenburg div. Am. Heart Assn., Bus. Found. N.C., N.C. State Coll. Found.; chmn. U.S. Olympic Com. for N.C.; trustee Queens Coll., Charlotte; bd. advisers Chowan Coll.; bd. govs., former trustee U. N.C., Chapel Hill; adv. council Wingate (N.C.) Coll.; nat. ho. of dels. Am. Cancer Soc., 1972; bd. visitors Babcock Grad. Sch. Mgmt. Wake Forest U.; bd. advisers Meredith Coll., Raleigh, Erskine Coll., Due West, S.C.; elder Myers Park Presbyterian Ch.; former deacon, active synod N.C. Presbyn. Ch. Served with USAAF, World War II. Named one of 10 Outstanding Young Men of Charlotte, 1954-57. Mem. Charlotte C. of C. (dir., exec. com.), N.C. (past pres., state dir.), Charlotte mchts. assns., Kappa Alpha, Delta Sigma Phi. Democrat. Mason (Shriner), Lion (past dist. gov.). Clubs: Charlotte Country, Myers Park Country, Executives (dir.), City (Charlotte); Raleigh City (Raleigh, N.C.); Sky (N.Y.C.). Home: 2519 Richardson Dr Charlotte NC 28211 Office: 308 E 5th St Charlotte NC 28202

BELK, THOMAS MILBURN, corp. exec.; b. Charlotte, N.C., Feb. 6, 1925; s. William Henry and Mary Leonora (Irwin) B.; B.S. in Mktg., U. N.C., 1948; m. Katherine McKay, May 19, 1953; children—Katherine Belk Morris, Thomas Milburn, Hamilton McKay, John Robert. With Belk Stores Services, Inc., 1948—, pres., 1980—; dir. NCNB Corp., Mut. Savs. & Loan Assn., Bus. Devel. Corp. of N.C. Bd. dirs. Mecklenburg County council Boy Scouts Am., Presbyn. Home at Charlotte; bd. dirs. YMCA, pres., 1978, 79; gen. chmn. Shrine Bowl of Carolinas, 1963-64, United Appeal, 1959; past pres. United Community Service; trustee Charlotte Community Coll. System, 1958-65, Montreat-Anderson Coll., 1964-68, St. Andrews Presbyn. Coll., Laurinburg, N.C., 1967-71, Crossnore (N.C.) Sch., Inc., Davidson (N.C.) Coll., 1974—, U. N.C., Charlotte, 1975—, Endowment Fund, 1975-78, Presbyn. Hosp., Charlotte. Served to lt. (j.g.), USN, 1943-46. Named Young Man of Year, Jr. C. of C., 1960, Man of Year, Charlotte News, 1962, Tarheel of Week, Raleigh News & Observer, 1964, Man of Year, Delta Sigma Pi, 1962. Mem. Charlotte C. of C. (chmn. 1977), N.C. Citizens Assn. (past pres.), Central Charlotte Assn. (pres. 1965-66), Mountain Retreat Assn. (past chmn. bd. trustees). Democrat. Clubs: Rotary, Masons, Shriners, Charlotte Country, Quail Hollow Country, Country of N.C., Biltmore Forest. Home: 2441 Lemon Tree Ln Charlotte NC 28211 Office: 308 E 5th St Charlotte NC 28202

BELL, BRYAN, real estate, oil investment exec., educator; b. New Orleans, Dec. 15, 1918; s. Bryan and Sarah (Perry) B.; B.A., Woodrow Wilson Sch. Pub. and Internat. Affairs, Princeton, 1941; M.A., Tulane U., 1962; m. Rubie S. Crosby, July 15, 1950; children—Rubie Perry, Helen Elizabeth, Bryan, Beverly Saunders, Barbara Crosby. Pres., Tasso Plantation Foods, Inc., New Orleans, 1945-66; partner Bell Oil Cos., New Orleans, 1962—, also 12 apt. complexes; pres. Bell & Assos., Inc., New Orleans, 1970—; dir. Royal St. Louis, Inc., New Orleans, Prentiss Creosote & Forest Products, Inc., Gautier Oil Co., Inc., Marine Concrete Structures, Inc. Instr. econs. of real estate devel. Sch. Architecture, Tulane U., New Orleans, 1967—. Mem. Garden Dist. Assn., 1964—; bd. dirs. United Fund for Greater New Orleans Area, 1964-71, pres., 1968-69; chmn. Human Talent Bank Com., New Orleans, 1969—. Mem. City Planning Commn., New Orleans, 1956-58; mem. bd. Met. Area Com., 1968—, pres., 1971—; bd. dirs. Bur. Govtl. Research, 1966—, pres., 1971—; chmn. com. Met. Leadership Forum, 1969—; mem. bd. New Orleans Area Health Council, 1966-70; bd. dirs. Tulane-Lyceum, 1947-51, Family Service Soc., 1951-58, pres., 1956-58; bd. dirs. St. Martin's Protestant Episcopal Sch., 1964-68, Metairie Park Country Day Sch., 1967-71; bd. dirs. Trinity Episcopal Sch., chmn., 1958-68; chmn. Trinity Christian Community, 1975—; bd. dirs. Christ Spirit of 76 Com., Fedn. Chs., 1975—. Served to 1st lt. AUS, World War II. Mem. New Orleans C. of C., Princeton Alumni Assn. La. (pres. 1962-63), Fgn. Realtions Assn. Democrat. Episcopalian (vestry 1960—, jr. warden 1968-70, sr. warden 1970-72). Clubs: Internat. House, Boston, New Orleans Lawn Tennis, Wyvern, Lakeshore, Pickwick. Address: 1331 3d St New Orleans LA 70130

BELL, CHARLES SUMNER, gas co. exec.; b. New Orleans, June 14, 1922; s. Robert Edwin and Louise (Wingerter) B.; B.B.A., Tulane, 1943; postgrad. mgmt. program for execs. U. Pitts., 1964; m. Leslie Bartels, Dec. 18, 1944; children—Linda Elizabeth, Judi Alice, Robert Charles. Mem. fin. staff Esso Standard Oil Co., Baton Rouge and New Orleans, Pelham, N.Y. and N.Y.C., 1943-61, coordinator mktg. accounting, 1957-61; coordinator corp. analysis Humble Oil & Refining Co., Houston, 1961-64; controller Esso Chem. Co., N.Y.C., 1964-70; asst. to vice chmn., mgr. spl. projects Houston Natural Gas Corp., 1971—. A founder, chmn. bd. Forty Plus of Houston. Mem. Fin. Execs. Inst., Office Execs. Assn., Nat. Assn. Accountants (research coordinator Accounting Prins. Bd.), Beta Gamma Sigma, Beta Alpha Psi. Home: 402 Sancroft Ct Katy TX 77450 Office: 1200 Travis St Houston TX 77001

BELL, DAVID ARTHUR, advt. agency exec.; b. Mpls., May 29, 1943; s. Arthur E. and Frances (Tripp) B.; B.S., Macalester Coll., 1965; m. June 22, 1968; children—Jenney L., Jennifer L., Jeffrey D. With Leo Burnett Co., Chgo., 1965-67; with Knox Reeves Advt., Mpls., 1967-75, pres., 1974-75; exec. v.p., gen. mgr. Bozell & Jacobs Internat., Mpls., 1975—. Broadcast chmn. Mpls.-St. Paul United Way, 1974, chmn. gen. bus. downtown sect., 1975, chmn. pub. relations, 1976; coordinator United Way Am., 1977-78; chmn. sustaining membership YMCA, Mpls., 1977; bd. dirs. Mpls. Metro Girl Scouts. Served with Minn. Air N.G., recipient Airman of Yr. award, 1967. Recipient Charter Centennial medallion Macalester Coll., 1974. Presbyterian. Clubs: Minn. Press, Mpls. Athletic, Mpls. Golf, Omaha. Home: 3121 Chowen Ave S Minneapolis MN 55416 Office: 100 N 6th St Minneapolis MN

BELL, DENNIS LLOYD, dry cleaning exec.; b. Delaware, Ohio, Sept. 14, 1945; s. Earl L. and Dorothy R. (Kinnell) B.; B.S., Miami U., Oxford, Ohio, 1967. Asst. store mgr. K-Mart, Cleve., 1970-71; asst. br. mgr. Society Corp., Cleve., 1971—; adminstrv. officer br. banking Central Nat. Bank, Cleve., 1971-73; v.p. savs. and spl. services Central Savs., Columbus, Ohio, 1973-78; v.p. secondary market savs. mktg. R.R. Savs., Columbus, 1978-79; owner, operator Johnstown Cleaners, Sunbury (Ohio) Cleaners and Coin Laundries, 1979—; lectr. in field. Advisor, Jr. Achievement, 1971-72; mem. Sunbury Planning and Zoning Com., 1978-80, Sunbury City Council, 1979-80; mem. Lake County Central Com., 1971-73, exec. com., 1971-73. Mem. Ohio Dry Cleaners Assn., Nat. Fabricare Inst. Republican. Methodist. Clubs: Lions, Sertoma. Home: 613 Cheshire Rd Sunbury OH 43074 Office: 23 W Granville St Sunbury OH 43074

BELL, DONALD JOSEPH, elec. engr.; b. Tulsa, June 16, 1944; s. Doneal Jay and Larcita Vivian (Cato) B.; A.S.E.E., Allen Hancock Coll., Santa Maria, Calif., 1964; B.S.E.E., Calif. Poly., 1966; m. Virginia Watkins, Feb. 26, 1966; children—Sheila Diane, Kartaka Rai, Sandra Donnice, Lisa Meshun, Byron Gerald, Corey Elizabeth. Chief operating officer Beltrol, Inc., Dallas, 1967-74; digital design engr. Dahlgren Mfg., Dallas, 1974-76; chief exec. officer Daeco Bell Inc., Dallas, 1977—; pres. Daeco Inc., Dallas, 1977—; evaluator computer ops. at sea Sedco Inc., Dallas, 1977-78. Campaign dir., com. chmn. for Bill Clements, 1978. Recipient Tex. Assn. Developing Colls. award, 1970. Republican. Baptist. Club: Rep. Men's. Inventor in field. Home: 2208 Worthington St Dallas TX 75204

BELL, DRUMMOND CRILLEY, chem. co. exec.; b. Balt., Mar. 13, 1916; s. Crilley Drummond and Ella (Witten) B.; student Loyola Coll., Balt., 1934, Johns Hopkins, 1935-38, U. Balt., 1946; m. Ruth Ann McCarthy, Feb. 3, 1940; children—Drummond Crilley III, Richard James. With Montgomery Ward & Co., 1935-56, successively mail order house controller, asst. controller for corp., 1935-53, co. personnel mgr., 1953-56, v.p., personnel dir., 1955-56; asst. to pres. Bridgeport Brass Co., 1956-57, controller, 1957-58, v.p., controller, 1958-61, v.p. finance, 1961-62; v.p. Nat. Distillers & Chem. Corp., 1962-68, exec. v.p., 1968, pres., dir., 1968—, chief exec. officer, 1970—, chmn. bd., 1975—; dir. Continental Corp., Panhandle Eastern Pipe Line Co., Houston, Almaden Vineyards Inc., (Calif.), Surveyor Fund, Inc., N.Y.C. Trustee Presbyterian Hosp., N.Y.C. Clubs: Country of Fairfield (Conn.); Union League, Pinnacle (N.Y.C.); Biltmore Forest (N.C.) Country. Office: 99 Park Ave New York NY 10016

BELL, HENRY NEWTON, III, lawyer; b. Temple, Tex., Mar. 5, 1941; s. Henry Newton and Mildred (Smith) B.; B.B.A., U. Tex., 1965; J.D., Baylor U., 1968; m. Pamela Roberts, July 25, 1964; children—Regina Eleanor, Henry Newton. Admitted to Tex. bar, 1970; pvt. practice law, Austin, Tex., 1970—; sr. trial counsel Barnhart Supply, Inc., Austin, 1973—; owner Bell Ranches, Bastrop and Burleson Counties, Tex. Lobbyist various spl. interest groups; judge Internat. Moot Ct. Competition, U. Tex. Sch. Law, 1980; bd. dirs. First Meth. Ch., Bastrop, Tex., 1980. Served with QMC, U.S. Army, 1968-70. Decorated Bronze Star; recipient cert. of Honor, Tex. Dept. Agr., 1974. Mem. Internat. Bar Assn., Fed. Bar Assn., Am. Bar Assn., Tex. Bar Assn., Am. Judicature Soc., Assn. Am. Trial Lawyers, S.A.R. (sec. 1979), Sons Republic of Tex. (v.p. 1981), SCV, Phi Delta Phi. Democrat. Methodist. Home: PO Box H Bastrop TX 78602 Office: Suite 210 300 E Huntland St Austin TX 78752

BELL, HERBERT AUBREY FREDERICK, ins. co. exec.; b. Toronto, Ont., Can., Jan. 15, 1921; came to U.S., 1946, naturalized, 1954; s. Kenneth J. and Mabel (Clarke) B.; student Washington U., St. Louis, 1953; grad. Am. Coll. Advanced Mgmt. Inst., 1954; m. Gretta Nisbet, May 16, 1946; children—Cathryn Pat, T. Scott, Paul Conway. Asso., G.A. John Hancock Mut. Life, Syracuse, N.Y., 1947-53; asst. agy. dir. Jefferson Nat. Life, Indpls., 1953-56; v.p. Mich. Life Ins. Co., Royal Oak, 1956-65; exec. v.p. Phila. Life Ins. Co., 1965—. Lectr. ins. mgmt. Mich. State U., 1961. Recipient Leading Agt. award Gen. Agts. and Mgrs. Assn., Syracuse, 1947-48. C.L.U. Mem. Nat. Assn. Life Underwriters, Am. Soc. C.L.U.'s, Life Underwriters Assn. (past dir. public relations), Agy. Mgmt. Assn. Clubs: Toastmasters Internat., Diablo Country. Contbr. articles to profl. jours. Office: 1700 Montgomery St San Francisco CA 94111

BELL, HOWARD R., indsl. co. exec.; b. Chgo., Dec. 29, 1946; s. Herman E. and Ida S. (Schultz) B.; B.S. in Bus. Adminstrn., Roosevelt U., 1968; postgrad. Chgo.-Kent Coll. Law, 1968-69; m. Ruth Ellen Sang, July 15, 1976; children—Michael Kevin, Jonathan Eric, Harris Matthew, Rachel Lyn. Acct., H. Schoenbrod & Co., Chgo., 1966-69; mgr. spl. projects, v.p., gen. mgr. leasing subs. Allied Products Corp., Chgo., 1969-78; chief fin. officer, corp. sec. Florasynth, Inc., N.Y.C., 1978—; cons. indsl. revenue bond issues. Active Cancer Found., Leukemia Found., 1964-75; treas. Greenbrook Swim Team, 1975; mem. Young Men's Jewish Council, 1977; bd. dirs. young leadership div. Jewish Fedn. Met. Chgo., 1976-78, treas., 1978-79; mem. United Jewish Appeal, N.Y.C., 1978—. Mem. Inst. Internal Auditors. Jewish. Club: Standard (Chgo.). Author: Auditing Through the Computer, 1968. Home: 35 Sutton Pl New York NY 10022 Office: 410 E 62d St New York NY 10021

BELL, JAMES ALBERT, mech. engr.; b. Eudora, Ark., s. James Garfield and Willie Mae B.; B.S.M.E., Tenn. State U., 1966-71. Engring. trainee U.S. Steel Co., Gary, Ind., 1967-68; with Gen. Foods-Kool Aid div. Chgo. Engring. Corp., 1969-70; with Bethlehem Steel, Burns Harbor, 1970-71; engring. trainee Union Carbide Chem. Co., Texas City, Tex., 1974-77, mech. engr., 1974-77; pres. Bevco Inc., Houston, 1977—, La. Stainless Inc., New Orleans, 1979—. Mem. Nat. Assn. Black Mfrs., ASME, Am. Assn. Blacks in Energy, Nat. Minority Purchasing Council, Houston Regional Minority Purchasing Council, Houston Citizens C. of C., Kappa Alpha Psi. Baptist. Address: Bevco Inc Box 61003 Houston TX 77208

BELL, JAMES ALVIN, accountant; b. Jefferson, Tex., Oct. 22, 1932; s. James Alex and Daisy (Washington) B.; B.A., San Francisco State Coll., 1956; m. Shelley May Dixon, Oct. 18, 1954; children—Kenneth, Lisa, Marquerite. Accountant, So. Calif. Gas Co., Los Angeles, 1957-62; controller Safety Savs. & Loan, Los Angeles, 1962-64, v.p., gen. mgr. 1964-66; mgmt. cons. Westminster, Inc., Los Angeles, 1966-67; pres. Westminister Data Corp.; adminstrv. v.p. Sussex Records, Inc., Hollywood, Calif., 1970-74; mem. profl. staff York Smith & Co., C.P.A.'s, 1974-76; prin. James Bell, C.P.A., 1976—. Home: 900 S Longwood Ave Los Angeles CA 90019 Office: 4929 Wilshire Blvd Los Angeles CA 90010

BELL, JEFFREY GRAHAM, exec. recruiting cons.; b. Montclair, N.J., Aug. 28, 1945; s. Graham and Barbara (Burgess) B.; B.A., Wesleyan U., 1968; M.B.A., U. Pa., 1973; m. Tara Anne Whiteley, July 5, 1969; 1 dau., Whitney Page. Comml. banking officer Brown Bros. Harriman & Co., N.Y.C., 1973-75; corp. fin. asso. Blyth Eastman Dillon & Co., Inc., N.Y.C., 1975-76; v.p. Russell Reynolds Assos., Inc., N.Y.C., 1976—. Served to capt. USMC, 1969-71. Decorated Air Medal (3). Mem. Assn. Exec. Recruiting Cons., Wesleyan U. Alumni Council (trustee nominating com.). Clubs: Union (N.Y.C.); Beacon Hill (Summit, N.J.). Home: 31 Overhill Rd Summit NJ 07901 Office: 245 Park Ave New York NY 10167

BELL, LLOYD WILLIAM WEIDENER, JR., banker; b. Ellenville, N.Y., June 13, 1941; s. Lloyd William Weidener and Elsa Marjoria (Mihalko) B.; B.S., Cornell U., 1963; M.B.A., N.Y. U., 1967; m. Jane-ann P. Schiera, Sept. 9, 1962; children—Carolyn, Lloyd, Christopher. Vice pres. Mfrs. Hanover Trust Co., N.Y.C., 1964-72; sr. v.p. O'Hare Internat. Bank, N.A., Chgo., 1972-74; v.p. Union Commerce Bank, Cleve., 1974-79; sr. v.p. BancOhio Nat. Bank, Cleve., 1979—. Mem. Cleve. Treasurers Club. Clubs: Cleve. Athletic, Chagrin Valley Country. Home: 120 Greentree Rd Chagrin Falls OH 44022 Office: 1101 Euclid Ave Cleveland OH 44115

BELL, RICHARD BRYAN, Realtor; b. Bremen, Ga., Feb. 15, 1939; s. James Henry and Joyce Marion (Wester) B.; B.S. in Indsl. Mgmt., Ga. Inst. Tech., 1961; m. Gail Lucinda Howard, June 16, 1962; children—Richard Bryan, Ansley Howard. Salesman, Remington Office Machines, Inc., Atlanta, 1965-66; salesman Pope & Carter Co. (name now Carter & Assos., Inc.), Atlanta, 1966—, v.p., 1971-76; owner Richard Bell Co., 1977; partner Bell, Cowart & Jackson, Atlanta, 1978—. Mem. adminstrv. bd. Peachtree Rd. United Meth. Ch., 1975—; chmn. 5th Dist. Republican Com., 1975-77; mem. state exec. com. Ga. Rep. Party, 1975; chmn. legis. sect. 40th Senatorial Dist., 1975—; sec., trustee Wesley Found. at Ga. Inst. Tech.; trustee Leadership Atlanta Alumni Assn., 1976. Served to lt. (j.g.) USNR, 1962-65. Mem. Soc. Indsl. Relators (dir. 1979—; pres. Ga. chpt. 1977), Atlanta Bd. Realtors, Atlanta C. of C. (dir. 1972, chmn. membership campaign 1972), Ga. Inst. Tech. Nat. Alumni Assn. (trustee, chmn. 29th ann. fund drive 1975, pres. 1980-81). Club: Ansley Golf. Office: 1809 Gas Light Tower 235 Peachtree St NE Atlanta GA 30303

BELL, THOMAS DALE, automotive parts mfg. co. exec.; b. Tulsa, Apr. 6, 1938; s. Eugene and Jewel B.; B.S., U. Okla., 1960; grad. Advanced Mgmt. Program, Harvard Bus. Sch., 1977; m. Frances Lander, Mar. 30, 1959; children—Mark, David, Kathryn. With Wagner Electric Corp., Parsippany, N.J., 1960—, pres., chief exec. officer, 1979—. Mem. Am. Trucking Assn. Found., Soc. Automotive Engrs., Automotive Pres.'s Council, Truck Trailer Mfrs. Assn. Office: 100 Misty Ln Parsippany NJ 07054

BELLAMY, THOMAS NATHANIEL, army officer; b. Winnabow, N.C., Oct. 12, 1946; s. Oliver H. and Mary E. B.; B.S. in Bus. Adminstrn., N.C. A&T State U., 1969; M.B.A., U. Utah, 1973; m. Emma Vesta Ree Bell, Oct. 11, 1969. Commd. 2d lt. U.S. Army, 1969, advanced through grades to maj., 1979; budget analyst Walter Reed Army Med. Center, Washington, 1974-75; chief mgmt. assistance br. comptroller div., 1975-76; comptroller Walter Reed Army Inst. Research, Washington, 1976-79; dep. comptroller, chief force devel. br. Letterman Army Med. Center, San Francisco, 1980—. Decorated Army Commendation medal. Methodist. Club: Fort Mason Officers. Home: 1282A Lendrum Ct San Francisco CA 94129 Office: Presidio of San Francisco CA 94129

BELLANGER, SERGE RENÉ, banker; b. Vimoutiers, France, Apr. 30, 1933; s. René Albert and Raymonde Maria (Renard) B.; M.B.A., Paris Bus. Sch., 1957. With Citibank, 1966-73, Paris br., 1966-69, world corp. relations officer for Europe, N.Y.C., 1969-73, asst. v.p., 1969-71, v.p., 1972-73; sr. v.p., gen. mgr. N.Y. br. Crédit Industriel et Commercial and U.S. rep. of Crédit Industriel et Commercial Group, 1973-79, exec. v.p., gen. mgr., 1979—; prof. banking French Banking Inst., 1961-64; mem. cons. com. French House, Columbia U., 1976—. Served with French Air Force, 1958-60. Decorated Algeria Commemorative medal. Mem. French-Am. C. of C. (adv. 1973-76, exec. com. 1976-80, v.p. 1980—), French Overseas Assn. (adv. fgn. trade for France 1979—), Inst. Fgn. Bankers (trustee 1975-77, v.p. 1977-79, chmn. 1979—), N.Y. Futures Exchange (dir. 1980—). Clubs: Board Room, River (N.Y.C.); Automobile de France (Paris). Home: 860 UN Plaza Apt 23/24C New York NY 10017 Office: 280 Park Ave New York NY 10017

BELLET, ALAIN ALPHONSE, reins. co. exec.; b. Paris, France, Feb. 27, 1946; came to U.S., 1974; s. Alphonse Henri and Renee Marie-Louise (Cotte) B.; Master of Law, Faculty of Law, Paris, 1971; m. Cynthia Ann West, Nov. 21, 1977; children—Sabine, Christel. Multiple line insp. Assurances du Groupe de Paris, 1967-69; group life sales mgr AGF, Paris, 1969-70; U.S. dept. mgr. Société Commerciale de Reassurance Paris, 1970-74; exec. v.p. SCOR Reins., Dallas, 1974-78, pres., 1978—, also dir.; pres., dir. SCOR Re Life; chmn. BIND, Inc., Dallas, SCOR Risk Mgmt., Dallas, SIRCO, Dallas; counselor fgn. trade for France. Served with French Army, 1966-67. Mem. Pres.'s Assn., French-Am. C. of C. (pres. Dallas/Ft. Worth chpt. 1979—), Dallas C. of C. Home: 3520 Rock Creek Dallas TX 75204 Office: PO Box 220032 Dallas TX 75222

BELLINGER, JOHN DOOLEY, bank exec.; b. Honolulu, May 13, 1923; s. Eustace L. and Lei Camelia (Williams) B.; student U. Hawaii, 1941-42; m. Joan Louise Simms, Apr. 7, 1945; children—Dona, Jan, Neil. With First Hawaiian Bank and predecessor, Honolulu, 1942—, pres., chief exec. officer, 1969-79, chmn. bd., chief exec. officer, 1979—, also dir.; chmn. bd., pres., chief exec. officer First Hawaiian, Inc., also dir.; chmn., chief exec. officer Hawaii Thrift & Loan, Inc., also dir.; chmn. bd. dirs. Japan Hawaii Fin. Kabushiki Kaisha; dir. Alexander & Baldwin, Inc., Matson Navigation Co., Aloha Airlines, Inc., Hawaii Meat Co., Ltd., Hawaiian Telephone Co., Hawaii Seiyu, Ltd.; mem. adv. bd. Hawaii Pacific Metro; Hawaii chmn. Japan-Hawaii Econ. Council. Civilian aide to Sec. of Army for Hawaii; chmn. Civilian Adv. Group Steering Com., U.S. Army Western Command; trustee Francis Brown Found., Honolulu, Japan-Am. Inst. Mgmt. Sci., Honolulu, Punahou Sch., Honolulu. Served with fin. dept. U.S. Army, 1946-47. Recipient Service to Mankind award Sertoma Club, 1972, Citizenship award Honolulu Police Dept., 1975; named Hawaii's Salesman of Yr., Sales and Mktg. Execs. of Honolulu, 1973. Mem. Hawaii Bankers Assn., Honolulu C. of C., Navy League, U.S. Air Force Assn., Assn. U.S. Army, 200 Club (pres. 1975-76, treas. 1980—), Hawaiian Civic Club. Clubs: Waialae Country, Oahu Country, Outrigger Canoe. Office: 165 S King St Honolulu HI 96813

BELLINGER, THOMAS, bank exec.; b. Shreveport, La., July 17, 1921; s. John Ramsey and Norma Isabelle (Ayers) B.; B.S., La. State U., 1949; M.B.A., Columbia, 1951. With Chase Manhattan Bank, N.Y.C., 1951-74, sr. v.p., mktg. and planning, 1974; pres., chief exec. officer, Security Trust Co., Rochester, N.Y., dir. Security N.Y. State Corp., 1974; v.p. Financial Gen. Bankshares, Washington, 1975-79; sr. exec. v.p. Bank of New Orleans & Trust Co., 1979—; chmn. credit policy com. Am. Security Bank, N.A., Washington. Served with USAF, 1941-45. Republican. Roman Catholic. Clubs: Union League (N.Y.C.); University (Washington). Home: 3443 Esplanade Ave New Orleans LA 70119 Office: Bank of New Orleans 1010 Common St New Orleans LA

BELLMAN, MAURICE, drapery mfg. co. exec.; b. Montreal, Que., Can., June 22, 1938; B.Comm., Sir George Williams U., 1960; C.A., McGill U., 1963; M.B.A., Concordia U., 1972. Partner, Zittrer, Siblin, Stein, Levine & Co., Montreal, 1960-72; v.p. fin. and adminstrn., Magnasonic Can. Ltd., Montreal, 1972-76; v.p. fin. Consol. Textiles Ltd., Montreal, 1976-78; pres. Nat. Drapery Ltd., Toronto, 1978—; lectr. acctg. Concordia U., Montreal, 1972-78, York U., Toronto, 1978—. Mem. Inst. Chartered Accts. Office: 4100 Weston Rd Weston ON M9L 1W7 Canada

BELLMANN, GUENTER PETER, banker; b. Hof Saale, Germany, Oct. 3, 1941; s. Gottfried F. and Johanna K. (Spitzbart) B.; B.S., U. Calif., Berkeley, 1971, M.B.A., 1972. Program analyst Bechtel Corp., San Francisco, 1967-68; sr. lending officer Bank of Am. NT&SA, San Francisco, and Cologne, W. Ger., 1973—; cons., fgn. currency, multi-nat. corps. Mem. World Affairs Council, San Francisco C. of C., German-Am. C. of C., Calif. Council Internat. Trade, Phi Beta Kappa, Beta Gamma Sigma. Club: World Trade. Home: 15 Tappan Rd San Anselmo CA 94960 Office: 555 California St San Francisco CA 94104

BELLMORE, LAWRENCE ROBERT, JR., truck, automobile sales co. exec.; b. Flint, Mich., May 1, 1947; s. Lawrence R. and Vaneta O. (Wortz) B.; B.S. in Mech. Engring., Gen. Motors Inst., 1970; m. Patricia Antonopolos, Dec. 27, 1969; 1 son, Lawrence Robert III; m. 2d, Susan Marie Thompson, Aug. 1979; 1 stepdau., Stacy Marie Thompson. Engr. in tng. Gen. Motors Inst., Flint, Mich., 1969-70; dist. service and parts mgr. Detroit zone, Buick Motor Div., 1970-72; mgr. fleet maintenance N.Am. Van Lines, Ft. Wayne, Ind., 1972-74, Eazor Express, Pitts., 1974-75; br. mgr. Pullman Trailmobile, Inc., Lancaster, Pa., 1975-79, Jersey City, N.J., 1976-77, Balt., 1977-79; pres. Lyco Truck Sales & Service, Inc. and Lyco Leasing, Inc., Montoursville, Pa., 1979—. Bd. dirs. Black Hawk Home Owners Assn., 1972-74. Mem. Pa. Motor Truck Assn. (regional dir.), Md. Motor Truck Assn., D.C. Motor Truck Assn., Dela. Motor Truck Assn., Lancaster Traffic Club, Theta Tau. Republican. Clubs: Rotary, Sertoma. Home: 1600 James Rd Williamsport PA 17701 Office: 232 Howard St Montoursville PA 17754

BELLO, ANTHONY EMIL, broadcasting co. exec.; b. St. Louis, June 11, 1924; s. Dominic A. and Louisa M. B.; student Washington U., 1946-48; m. Dorothy Jane Schueddig, Jan. 28, 1956; children—David Anthony, Julie Ann. Radio announcer Sta. WJPF, Herrin, Ill., 1947-49; newscaster, mutual network announcer Sta. KWK, St. Louis, 1949-52; account exec., gen. sales mgr. Sta. KMOX, CBS Radio, St. Louis, 1953-60; account exec., nat. sales mgr., gen. sales mgr. Sta. KSD-TV, St. Louis, 1960-79; v.p. sales Pulitzer TV, Sta. KSDK, St. Louis, 1979—. Bd. dirs. St. Louis Heart Assn., 1977-80, Children's Home Soc. Mo., 1978—. Served with USAAF, 1943-46. Roman Catholic. Clubs: Advt., Media (St. Louis). Office: 1010 Market St Saint Louis MO 63101

BELLU, RENATO RENE, jewelry co. exec.; b. Rome, Italy, June 26, 1936; s. Salvatore and Concetta (Masala) B.; came to U.S., 1954, naturalized, 1965; B.A., Bklyn. Coll., 1961, B.S. in Accounting summa cum laude, with honors in Econs., 1963; M.B.A., Pace U., 1976; m. Elena Mennella Oct. 11, 1957; children—Paola, Flavia, Renato, Roberto. Comptroller, Belt Corp., N.Y.C., 1957-68; asst. gen. mgr. Pirelli, U.S.A., N.Y.C., 1968-73; pres. Aurea Jewelry Creations, Inc., N.Y.C., 1973—; v.p. ops., dir. J.M.S. Jewelry Mfg. Co., Inc., 1978—; instr. Henry George Sch., N.Y.C. Mem. Am. Mgmt. Assn., Am. Amateur Skiing Assn., Italy-Am. C. of C. (chmn. jewelry com.). Clubs: West Side Tennis (Forest Hills, N.Y.); Karat of N.Y.C. Home: 59 Continental Ave Forest Hills Gardens NY 11375 Office: 580 Fifth Ave New York NY 10036

BELLVILLE, RALPH EARL, banker; b. Lynn, Mass., June 15, 1925; s. Harold Eugene and Edith Floy (Simpson) B.; A.B., Harvard U., 1950; m. Crescentia Ranftl, Oct. 16, 1954. Asst. mgr. No. Trust Co., Chgo., 1955-60; v.p. United Calif. Bank, Los Angeles, 1960-69; exec. v.p. Security Pacific Nat. Bank, Los Angeles, 1969—; dir. Bank of Canton (Hong Kong), Security Pacific Bank (Panama) S.A.; chmn. bd. Security Pacific Internat. Bank, N.Y.C., Security Pacific Overseas Corp., Security Pacific Overseas Investment Corp. Served with inf. U.S. Army, 1943-46. Decorated Bronze Star with oak leaf cluster. Mem. Bankers Assn. Fgn. Trade (dir. 1975-77), Nat. Fgn. Trade Council. Clubs: Jonathan, Internat., Harvard of So. Calif. (Los Angeles). Office: 333 S Hope St Los Angeles CA 90071

BELSERE, ARTHURO ARTHUR, hotel exec.; b. Vienna, Austria, Oct. 7, 1922; s. Jaques A. and Frieda (Goldfarb) B.; came to U.S., 1952, naturalized, 1956; grad. Ecole International D'Hotel, Lausanne, Switzerland, 1939; B.A. in Bus. Adminstrn., N.Y. U., 1955. Chef de reception Shephard's, Cairo, 1940-41, Ritz Carlton, Paris, 1939-40; dir. food and beverage King David Hotel, Jerusalem, 1947-51; asst. chef de reception George V Hotel, Paris, 1945-47; v.p., gen. mgr. Tuscany Towers, Tuscany Hotel, Doral Park Ave. Hotel and Doral Inn, N.Y.C., 1968—; guest lectr. Culinary Inst., N.Y.C. Served to lt. col. Brit. Commandos; Middle East. Mem. N.Y. Hotel Assn. (dir., dir. pension fund), Sales Execs. Club. Office: Doral Park Ave Hotel 70 Park Ave New York NY 10016

BELSHO, EDWARD, bus. equipment mfg. co. exec.; b. Orange, Ohio, Sept. 27, 1925; s. Vincent and Margaret B.; B.S. in Journalism, Ohio U., 1950; m. Betty Virginia Coleman, Mar. 31, 1961. With Cleve. Press, 1943; free-lance publicist, news stringer, 1950-51; sports editor Athens (Ohio) Messenger, 1951; with Gen. Motors Co., Cleve., 1953-54; advt. mgr. data processing equipment Royal McBee Corp., N.Y.C., 1954-59, public relations dir., 1959-61, asst. to pres., 1961-65; gen. mgr. Automatic Typing div. Royal Typewriter Co., 1965-66, v.p., asst. to pres., 1966-68, dir. mfg. Imperial Typewriter Co., Leicester, England, 1973-76, also European ops. Royal Imperial div., 1973-76; pres. McBee Loose Leaf Binder Products, Springfield, Mo., 1976—; v.p. Office Communications Equipment Group, Litton Industries, Inc., N.Y.C., 1968-73. Served with USNR, 1943-46. Home: 1528 S Forrest Heights Ave Springfield MO 65804 Office: 424 N Cedarbrook St Springfield MO 65802

BELTZ, FRED WALLACE, JR., mfg. co. exec.; b. Honolulu, Dec. 29, 1922; s. Fred W. and Sara Bean (Keely) B.; B.S., U. Mich., 1944; m. Elizabeth Ann Pratt, July 26, 1947; children—Fred Wallace III, Stewart M., William K. With Transam. Delaval Inc., Trenton, N.J., 1949—, gen. mgr. Condenser and Filter div., 1970-77, v.p., gen. mgr. Turbine and Compresser div., 1978—. Served with U.S. Mcht. Marine, 1945-49. Registered profl. engr., N.J., Pa. Fellow Inst. Marine Engrs.; mem. ASME, Soc. Naval Architects and Marine Engrs. (past chmn. Phila. sect.), Heat Exchange Inst. (past pres.), U.S. Power Squadron, Theta Delta Chi. Clubs: Rotary, Toms River Yacht, Masons. Home: 2308 Stackhouse Dr Yardley PA 19067 Office: c/o Transam Delaval Inc PO Box 8788 Trenton NJ 08650

BEMBRY, MARSHA JEWEL, chem. co. ofcl.; b. Ft. Riley, Kans., Sept. 20, 1948; d. Thomas Jule and Minnie (Baker) Bembry, Jr.; B.A., Hampton Inst., 1970. Promotion dir. Sta. WKAT, Miami Beach, Fla., 1970-71; continuity dir., disc jockey Sta. WRBD, Ft. Lauderdale, Fla., 1971-72; plant tng. supr. Mobil Chem. Co., Covington, Ga., 1979-80, prodn. supr., 1980—. Served as officer Signal Corps, U.S. Army, 1972-79. Decorated Army Commendation medal, Meritorious Service medal. Mem. Alpha Kappa Alpha. Office: Mobil Chem Co Alcovy Rd Covington GA 30209

BEMIS, HAL LAWALL, engring. and bus. exec.; b. Palm Beach, Fla., Jan. 30, 1912; s. Henry E. and Elise (Lawall) B.; B.S., M.I.T., 1935; m. Isabel Mead, June 27, 1942; children—Elise, Carolyn, Claudia. With Campbell Soup Co., 1935-53, mgr., asst. to pres., v.p., dir. Campbell Soup Co., Ltd., 1946-53; organizer, pres. Mariner Corp., 1954—; v.p. Hosp. Food Mgmt., Inc., 1954-57; sec., treas. Bell Key Corp., 1955—; v.p. Coral Motel Corp., 1963—; pres. Jennings Machine Corp., 1957—; cons. Coopers & Lybrand, 1973—; dir., mem. exec. and audit coms. Publicker Industries; chmn., dir. Phila. Reins. Corp.; dir. Ott, Hertner, Ott & Assos., Colonial Savs. Bank. Past pres. Commn. Twp. Lower Merion, Pa.; bd. dirs., vice chmn. Spring Garden Coll.; exec. bd. Com. of 70; chmn. bd. Am. Cancer Soc.; bd. dirs. Delaware Valley area Nat. Council on Alcoholism; adv. bd. Salvation Army; past trustee Haverford Sch.; dir. Phila. Port Corp., West Phila. Corp., Phila. Indsl. Devel. Corp.; trustee United Fund, Young Men's Inst.; pres., trustee Greater Phila. Found.; bd. dirs. Am. Diabetes Assn., M.I.T. Devel. Found., Broad St. So. Com.; mem. corp. bd. Goodwill Industries, Garrett-Williamson Found. Served 1st lt. to lt. col. AUS, 1942-45. Decorated Legion of Merit with oak leaf cluster, Bronze Star medal; Croix de Guerre (France). Mem. Greater Phila. C. of C. (past chmn. bd., past pres.), SAR, S.R., Pa. Soc., Newcomen Soc., Mil. Order World Wars, Mil. Order Fgn. Wars, Am. Legion (past comdr.), Tau Beta Pi, Delta Psi. Clubs: Union League (pres.), St. Anthony, Racquet, Rittenhouse (Phila.); Pine Valley Golf (N.J.); St. Anthony (N.Y.C.), Merion Golf (Ardmore); Merion Cricket (dir.) (Haverford), Bachelor's Barge, IV Street; Pine Valley Golf, Sunday Breakfast, Right Angle, Penn, Toronto Golf, Royal Canadian Yacht, Brit. Officers. Home: 256 W Montgomery Ave Haverford PA 19041 Office: 355 Lancaster Ave Haverford PA 19041

BEMIS, RICHARD LEE, accountant; b. Kansas City, Mo., June 11, 1946; s. Duaine Clair and Helen Ann (Smith) B.; B.B.A. in Acctg., St. Cloud (Minn.) State U., 1971. Loan officer, SBA, Corpus Christi, Tex., Chambersburg, Pa., 1971-72; v.p. White, Bemis, Sluyter, Inc., Corpus Christi, 1972-78; owner, mgr. Richard L. Bemis, C.P.A.'s, Corpus Christi, 1978—; co-owner Cantina Santa Fe, Inc., 1980—. Served with U.S. Army, 1968-70. Decorated Bronze Star; C.P.A., Tex. Mem. Corpus Christi Bus. and Estate Planning Council, Am. Inst. C.P.A.'s, Tex. Soc. C.P.A.'s. Club: Conquistadors. Home: 3122 Nassau Corpus Christi TX 78418 Office: PO Box 1537 Corpus Christi TX 78403

BEMLEY, JESSE LEE, govt. ofcl.; b. Memphis, Apr. 17, 1944; s. Timothy D. and Paralee (Lewis) B.; B.S. with honors in Mathematics, Miss. Valley State U., 1963; M.S. in Tech. of Mgmt., Am. U., 1977; postgrad. Walden U., 1978—; m. Barbara Ann Grant, Apr. 1, 1973. Tchr. mathematics Moss Point (Miss.) Municipal Sch. System, 1966; mathematician U.S. Army Topographic Command, Dept. Computer Services, Washington, 1968-71; computer systems analyst D.C. Bd. Elections, Washington, 1971-74; instr. data processing Strayer Coll., Washington, 1978, asst. chmn. data processing dept., 1980—; computer specialist Drug Enforcement Adminstrn., Dept. Justice, Washington, 1974—; dir. Afro American Datanamics, Inc., 1975-76. Served with U.S. Army, 1966-68. Certified tchr., Miss. Mem. Assn. for Computer Programmers and Analysts (officer Capital chpt. 1978—), Am. Soc. Pub. Adminstrs., Soc. Mgmt. Info. Systems, Phi Delta Kappa. Democrat. Baptist. Home: 2316 Naylor Rd SE Washington DC 20020 Office: 1405 I St NW Washington DC 20537

BENCKENSTEIN, CHARLES HAIGHT, JR., temporary help service exec.; b. New Orleans, Mar. 18, 1918; s. Charles Haight and Margaret (Hortman) B.; student U. Tex., 1935-36, Rice U., 1936-39; m. Clara Helbing, Sept. 30, 1939; children—Stephen Couch, Leonard Fredrick, Margaret Alma, Stanley Peterson. Purchasing agt. Consol. Western Steel, Orange, Tex., 1940-46; asst. mgr. purchases Consol. Western Steel div. U.S. Steel, 1946-52; gen. mgr. Lutcher-Moore Lumber Co., Orange, 1952-58; pres. House and Home Inc., Beaumont, Tex., 1958-63; pres. Manpower Inc. of Beaumont-Port Arthur, Beaumont, 1963—; sec.-treas. Remex Inc. Pres., Orange County Nav. Dist. Tex., 1956-58; trustee, vice chmn. St. Stephen's Episcopal Sch., Austin, Tex., 1956-58. Mem. Nat. Assn. Purchasing Agts., Tex. Assn. Bus. Office: 1255 Broadway Beaumont TX 77701

BENDAT, JULIUS SAMUEL, cons., author; b. Chgo., Oct. 26, 1923; s. Benjamin M. and Frieda (Korn) B.; B.A. cum laude, U. Calif. at Berkeley, 1944; M.S., Calif. Inst. Tech., 1948; Ph.D. in Math., U. So. Calif., 1953; m. Mildred Rosen, July 27, 1947; children—James Russell, Lucinda Ann. Asst. prof. aero. engring. U. So. Calif., Santa Maria, 1948-49; research engr. Northrop Aircraft, Inc., Hawthorne, Calif., 1953-55; sr. staff mem. Thompson Ramo Wooldridge, Inc., Canoga Park, Calif., 1955-62; pres. Measurement Analysis Corp., Los Angeles, 1962-68; v.p. Digitek Corp., Los Angeles, 1968-70; owner J.S. Bendat Co., Los Angeles, 1970—. Served as ensign USNR, 1945-46. Mem. Am. Math. Soc., Math. Assn. Am., Soc. Indsl. and Applied Math., Phi Beta Kappa, Sigma Xi, Pi Mu Epsilon. Author: Principles and Applications of Random Noise Theory, 1958; Measurement and Analysis of Random Data, 1966; Random Data: Analysis and Measurement Procedures, 1971; Engineering Applications of Correlation and Spectral Analysis, 1980. Home: 1231 Casiano Rd Los Angeles CA 90049 Office: 833 Moraga Dr Los Angeles CA 90049

BENDER, JULIET ANN, govt. ofcl.; b. Lodi, Calif., Sept. 1, 1952; d. Calvin Arthur and Erna Emilie (Ebertz) B.; B.A. (Calif. State scholar), U. Calif., Davis, 1974; student Georg-August U., W.Ger., 1972-73; M.A. (fellow), Johns Hopkins U., 1977. Coder analyst Office Spl. Trade Rep., Washington, 1977; program staff asst. NASA Hdqrs., Washington, 1978; economist FCC, Washington, 1978-79; internat. trade specialist Dept. Commerce, Washington, 1979—. Mem. So. Econ. Assn., Johns Hopkins U. Alumni Assn., Calif. Aggie Alumni Assn., AAUW, Commerce Overseas Service Assn., Nat. Democratic Women's Orgn., Delta Phi Alpha. Club: Internat. Editor: Astronautics and Aeronautics: A Chronology, 1976. Home: 2100 Connecticut Ave NW Apt 409 Washington DC 20008 Office: Dept Commerce 14th and Constitution Ave Room 4012 Washington DC 20230

BENDER, MILES DENNIS, computer supply co. exec., mgmt. cons.; b. Buffalo, Feb. 26, 1937; s. Samuel Arthur and Adele Ida (Altman) B.; B.A., U. Buffalo, 1959, postgrad. Law Sch., 1959-60; postgrad. Harvard Bus. Sch., 1965; m. Sue Ellen Rolader, Apr. 12, 1975; children—Carolyn Gilbert, Melissa Joan, Jami Brett, Elizabeth Anne. Registered rep. Bache & Co., Buffalo, 1960-65; dir. public relations, asst. to pres. Internat. Life Ins. Co. of Buffalo, 1966-67; pres. Wunderest Industries, Inc., Buffalo, 1967-68; dir. mktg. Hard Co., Buffalo, 1968-70; pres., chmn. bd. Syncom Inc., Orchard Park, N.Y.; 1970—; pres. Miles Bender & Assos., Inc., 1980—; dir. Graphic Arts Supply, Inc., Rochester, N.Y. Mem. Erie County (N.Y.) Legislature, 1966-68; chmn. Erie County div. Am. Cancer Soc. corp. gifts div., 1975, 76, 77; mem. Pres.'s UN Day Com., 1977, 78; mem. exec. com. Eric County Republican Party, 1966-70; lobbyist for Erie County, N.Y. State Legislature, 1968-70. Club: Orchard Park Country. Home: 360 Balboa Ct Atlanta GA 30342 Office: 3355 Lenox Rd Suite 750 Atlanta GA 30326

BENDETSEN, KARL ROBIN, lawyer, forest products mfr.; b. Aberdeen, Wash., Oct. 11, 1907; s. Albert M. and Anna (Bentson) B.; A.B., Stanford, 1929, J.S.D., 1932; m. Billie McIntosh, Sept. 8, 1938; 1 son, Brookes McIntosh; m. 2d, Maxine Bosworth, Sept. 19, 1947; 1 dau., Anna Martha; m. 3d, Gladys Ponton de Arce Johnston, Aug. 19, 1972. Admitted to Calif., Oreg., Wash., Ohio, N.Y., D.C. bars, also U.S. Supreme Ct.; in law practice, Aberdeen, Wash., 1932-40; mgmt. counsel, 1946-47; spl. cons. to Sec. Def., 1948; asst. sec. Army, 1948-51, undersec. Army, 1952; chmn. bd. Panama Canal Co., 1950-54; dir. gen. U.S. Railroads, 1950-52; with Champion Internat., Inc. (formerly U.S. Plywood-Champion Papers Inc.), Stamford, Conn., 1952-54, Tex. div. mgr., 1954-55, v.p., gen. mgr. Tex. div. Pasadena, Tex., 1955-57, v.p., gen. mgr. pulp and paper mfg., 1958-59, exec. v.p. ops. group, 1959-60, pres., 1960-72, chmn. bd., chief exec., also chmn. exec. com., 1973-75, also dir.; dir. Westinghouse Electric Corp. Mem. Nat. Indsl. Conf. Bd.; mem. governing bd. N.Y. Stock Exchange; spl. U.S. rep. to W. Ger. and Philippines with rank ambassador, 1956; chmn. adv. com. on gen. mil. instrn. to sec. Def., 1962; vice chmn. Def. Manpower Commn., 1974-76. Mem. council U. Chgo. Grad. Sch. Bus.; bd. visitors Stanford U. Law Sch.; overseer Hoover Instn., Stamford; vestryman St. Thomas Parish, Episcopal Ch., N.Y.C., 1968-74. Served in active mil. service, 1940-46; as col. Gen. Staff Corps. U.S. Army, 1940-46. Decorated D.S.M. with oak leaf cluster, Silver Star, Legion of Merit with 2 oak leaf clusters, Bronze Star with 2 oak leaf clusters and V device, Medal of Freedom, Distinguished Civilian Service award (U.S.), Croix de Guerre with palm, officer Legion of Honor (France), Order Brit. Empire (Eng.); knight comdr. Order St. John Jerusalem, Knights Malta. Mem. Theta Delta Chi. Clubs: Pacific Union, Bohemian (San Francisco); Wash. Athletic (Seattle); Tejas, Bayou, Houston Country, Petroleum (Houston); Commonwealth (Cin.); Met., Brook, Links (N.Y.C.); F St., Georgetown (Washington); Everglades, Bath and Tennis (Palm Beach). Home: 2918 Garfield Terr NW Washington DC 20008

BENEDETTO, RICHARD MICHAEL, copper mfg. co. exec.; b. Elizabeth, N.J., Aug. 3, 1940; s. Carmine and Josephine (Gordon) B.; B.S. in Bus. Adminstrn., Rutgers U., 1971; M.B.A. in Mktg., Mercy Coll., L.I. U., 1978; m. Jeri Anne Kalk, Jan. 17, 1969; children—Sharyn Anne, Toube Lynn. Div. controller knitting machinery div. Singer Co., Ozone Park, N.Y., 1967-72; div. controller ITT-Grinnell, Elmira, N.Y., 1972-75; bus. mgr. Whittaker Corp. Life Scis. Group, Rockville, Md., 1975-76; v.p. fin. Phelps Dodge Cable & Wire Co., Yonkers, N.Y., 1976-78, v.p. mfg., 1978-80; sr. v.p. Phelps Dodge Copper Products Co., Yonkers, 1981—; adj. prof. Marymount Coll. Mem. Nat. Assn. Accts., Am. Mgmt. Assn. Office: Phelps Dodge Copper Products Co Box 391 Yonkers NY 10702

BENEDICT, CLIFFORD HORACE, fin. and advt. cons.; b. Laredo, Tex., June 23, 1940; s. Horace and Amparo Benedict; B.A. in Spanish, U. Tex., 1963; B.S. in Human Services, Thomas A. Edison Coll., Trenton, N.J., 1965; B.S. in Anthropology, Pacific Northwestern U., 1967; B.A. in Roman History, Collegii Romanii, Rome, 1970; B.S. in Bus. Adminstrn., B.J., Gulf So. U., New Orleans, 1970, M.S., 1976, M.J., 1977; m. Bertha Garcia Lizovska, Mar. 23, 1979. Exec. v.p. Latin Am., Knobel Internat. AG, Switzerland, 1967-70; public relations and advt. dir. S.E. Mex., Ralston-Purina Co., 1971-73; public relations and dist. sales dir. Mex. div. W.M. Jackson Co., pubs., 1973-74; program dir., comml. producer Televisa, Mex., 1974-76; owner Benedict & Benedict, bus., fin. and multi-media advt. cons., Laredo, 1976—; pub. Perceptions, photonovel mag., 1980—; ind. TV producer, 1979—. Served with USAF, 1962-67. Mem. Internat. Enterpreneurs Assn. Home: 703 Corpus Christi St Laredo TX 78040 Office: PO Box 1922 Laredo TX 78041

BENEDICT, ROBERT MITCHELL, JR., mining co. exec.; b. Little Rock, Sept. 26, 1943; s. Robert Mitchell and Louise Ellen Benedict; B.S., U. Oreg., 1966, M.B.A., 1972; M.A. in Econs., Case Western Res. U., 1975; m. Susan Clark Van Tuyl, Mar. 24, 1965; children—Tobey Lynn, Todd Lewis, Christian Robert. Adminstrv. asst. Hanna Mining Co., Cleve., 1972-76, asst. treas., 1976—; asst. treas. Iron Ore Co. Can., Cleve. Fundraiser Republican Fin. Com., 1975-79; trustee Hiram House, Cleve., 1979-80. Served to capt. U.S. Army, 1966-70. Decorated Bronze Star. Mem. Treasurers Club Cleve., Bus. Economists Club Cleve., N.E. Ohio Cash Mgrs. Assn. Home: 37159 Deer Run St Solon OH 44139 Office: 100 Erieview Plaza Cleveland OH 44114

BENEKE, DEAN RICHARD, banker; b. Plover, Iowa, Feb. 7, 1929; s. Herman O. and Ethyl K. (Wilson) B.; B.A., Wartburg Coll., 1950; B.A., Stonier Grad. Sch. Banking, Rutgers U., 1963-65; m. Bernice M. Johnson, June 13, 1952; children—Terry, Robert, Susan. Sr. examiner Dept. Banking, State of Iowa, 1953-61; cashier Midway Nat. Bank, Cedar Falls, Iowa, 1961-62; with First Nat. Bank, Cedar Falls, 1962—, exec. v.p., 1963-79, pres., 1979—, dir., 1963—. Chmn. bd. Sartori Meml. Hosp., Cedar Falls, 1967-75; pres. Cedarloo Hosp. Council, 1972-74; bd. dirs. Jr. Achievement, 1977—. Served with AUS, 1951-53. Mem. Iowa Bankers Assn., Cedar Falls C. of C. (pres. 1967). Lutheran. Lion (pres. 1971). Home: 3116 Dallas Dr Cedar Falls IA 50613 Office: 302 Main St Cedar Falls IA 50613

BENENSON, JAMES, JR., financier; b. Moultrie, Ga., Mar. 9, 1936; s. James and Mary Watkins (Camp) B.; B.S., Mass. Inst., Tech., 1958; postgrad. (Woodrow Wilson scholar), Yale U., 1960; m. Sharen Statler, Aug. 28, 1966. Investment banker F. Eberstadt & Co., N.Y.C., 1961-65; v.p., dir. Walker Hart & Co., Inc., N.Y.C., 1965-68; founder, chmn. bd., pres. James Benenson & Co., Inc., 1968—; chmn. bd., chief exec. officer Bowline Corp., 1974—; pres., chief exec. officer Vesper Corp., 1979—; chmn. bd. Capitol Pipe and Steel Products Co. U.S.A., Penco Products, Inc., Cleve. Gear Co., Dynacure Pre-Coated Steel Co., 1980—; dir. Capitol Pipe and Steel Products (Can.) Ltd. Mem. M.I.T. Ednl. Council. Served with AUS, 1960. Andover Teaching fellow, 1958-59. Mem. Audubon Soc., Sierra Club, N.Y. Bot. Garden, N.Y. Mus. Natural History, Scenic Hudson Preservation Conf., Mass. Inst. Tech. Alumni Assn., Sigma Nu. Clubs: Coffee House, Yale, Madison Square Garden (N.Y.C.); Sag Harbor Yacht; Racquet (Phila.). Home: 1 Lexington Ave New York NY 10010 Office: 301 City Line Ave Bala Cynwyd PA 19004

BENEVENTO, FRANCIS ANTHONY, II, investment banker; b. Washington, May 15, 1947; s. Anthony Andrew and Dolores (Connor) B.; B.S. summa cum laude, Georgetown U., 1970; J.D., U. Va., 1973; m. Judith Lynn Free, Aug. 30, 1969; children—Francis Anthony III, Alexander Blaine Lee. Admitted to D.C. bar, 1975, Md. bar, 1974, U.S. Tax Ct., 1974; individual practice law, 1973-74; fin. cons., 1975-77; asso. firm Pierson Semmes Crolius & Finley, Washington, 1975-77; asso. Lehman Bros. Kuhn Loeb, Inc., N.Y.C., 1977—. Served with USAR, 1969-75. Mem. Am. Bar Assn., Va. Hist. Soc., MENSA. Republican. Roman Catholic. Club: Farmington Country (Charlottesville, Va.); Chevy Chase (Md.); Bronxville (N.Y.) Field. Home: 10 Plateau Circle Bronxville NY 10708 Office: 55 Water St New York NY 10005

BENGTSSON, RALPH ANDREW, bus. exec.; b. Turlock, Calif., Nov. 21, 1930; s. Ragnar Anders and Bertha (Johnson) B.; engring. degree Saffle Tekniska Aftonskola, 1963; bus. econs. degree Karlstad Gymnasium, 1974; m. Kerstin Margareta Andersson, Oct. 6, 1951; 1 son, Thomas Anders. Materials mgr. Electrolux AB, Saffle, Sweden, 1965-69; materials mgr. C.J. Wennberg AB, Karlstad, Sweden, 1969-74, products mgr., 1974-78; v.p. C.J. Wennberg, Inc., Atlanta, 1978-80. Mem. AIME, Metall. Soc. Inventor continuous mech. fabrication of starting sheets for electrolytic refining. Home: 1415 Floribunda Ave Burlingame CA 94010

BENHAM, ROBERT MILES, JR., retail co. exec.; b. Cin., May 16, 1939; s. Robert Miles and Jean (Murphy) B.; B.S. in Edn., Monmouth (N.J.) Coll., 1966; student Vanderbilt U., 1961-64; m. Ardys Dee Johnson, Nov. 29, 1969; children—Michael Robert, Elizabeth Maren. Buyer menswear, Steinbach Co., Asbury Park, N.J., 1966-69; asst. to exec. v.p. Famous Barr div. May Co., St. Louis, 1970-71, mdse. mgr. May D & F div., Denver, 1971-75; mdse. mgr. I. Magnin div. Federated Dept. Stores, San Francisco, 1976-77; pres. Halls Crown Center div. Hallmark Co., Kansas City, Mo., 1978, pres. Hallmark retail div., Kansas City, 1979—. Active Boy Scouts Am. Served with U.S. Army, 1961-64. Mem. Nat. Retail Mchts. Assn., Kansas City Mchts. Assn., Mo. Retail Assn. (dir.), Crown Center Mchts. Assn. (dir.). Republican. Presbyterian. Office: 200 E 25th St Kansas City MO 64108

BENISCH, HENRY JOHN, monument and mausoleum co. exec.; b. Bklyn., Aug. 22, 1899; s. Charles John and Anna Margaret (Rope) B.; B.C.E., Cornell U., 1920; m. Catharine Elizabeth Barr, Oct. 17, 1924; children—Barbara, Margaret Ann Benisch Anderson. With U.S. Geol. Survey, New London, Conn., 1917, McClintock Marshall Co., Pitts., 1920-21; owner, mgr. Henry J. Benisch Co. (doing bus. as Benisch Bros.), Bklyn., 1921—. Bd. dirs. Indsl. Home for Blind, 1940—, Greater N.Y. YMCA, 1938-42; bd. dirs. Big Bros., Inc., N.Y.C., 1949—, chmn. bd., 1972—; mem. nat. bd. YMCA, 1938-43. Served with U.S. Army, 1918. Mem. Cornell soc. Civil Engrs., Eastern Lawn Tennis Assn. (pres. 1964). Congregationalist. Clubs: West Side Tennis (pres. 1966-67) (Forest Hills, N.Y.); Heights Casino (Bklyn); Masons (Stonington, Maine). Home: 60 Exeter St Forest Hills NY 11375 Office: 840 Jamaica Ave Brooklyn NY 11208

BENJAMEN, LYSLE IRVING, business exec.; b. Detroit, July 20, 1927; s. Lysle Christopher and Ruth (Boss) B.; B.S., U.S. Coast Guard Acad., 1950; M.S., Rensselaer Poly. Inst., 1955; Ph.D., Mich. State U., 1966. Prod. engr. Eaton Mfg. Co., Battle Creek, Mich., 1955-57; asst. prof., finance and mgmt. Ferris State Coll., Big Rapids, Mich., 1958-59; engr. mgr. Dearborn Marine Engines, Inc., Madison Heights, Mich., 1959-62; exec. v.p. Midwest Machine Co. of Ind., Inc., Marysville, Mich., 1962-70, now dir.; partner Benjamen and Maurer Co., Birmingham, Mich., 1970-75, Benjamen and Co., 1975—; dir. Media Tech. Corp., Louisville, Sylbin Investments Ltd., Bloomfield Hills, Mich., Sylbin Credit Co. Ltd., Birmingham, Birmingham Mfg. Corp., Cairo, Mich., Gowani Corp., Birmingham, Carl Lasswell Motor Sales Ltd., Pontiac, Mich., Econ. Tng. Systems Ltd., Birmingham. Lectr. indsl. mgmt. U. Detroit. Served to lt. USCGR, 1945-54. Certified mfg. engr.; registered profl. engr., Calif., Mich. Mem. Engring. Soc. Detroit, Am. Soc. Naval Engrs., Soc. Mfg.

Engrs., Am. Arbitration Assn., Detroit Crisis Club, Sigma Xi, Phi Sigma Epsilon, Beta Gamma Sigma. Republican. Episcopalian. Elk. Mason (Shriner). Patentee in field. Home: 3860 Northdale St Bloomfield Hills MI 48013 Office: 725 S Adams Rd Suite L-2 Birmingham MI 48011

BENMOSCHE, ROBERT H., bank exec.; b. Bklyn., May 29, 1944; B.A. in Math., Alfred U., 1966; children—Nehama, Ari. Cons., project mgr. personnel systems Info. Sci., Inc., Montvale, N.J., 1970-73; sr. cons. personnel mgmt. systems Arthur D. Little Co., Englewood Cliffs, N.J., 1973-75; v.p. data processing Chase Manhattan, N.Y.C., 1975-77, v.p. human resources info. center, 1977—. Home: 91 Lime Kiln Rd Suffern NY 10901 Office: Chase Manhattan Bank 80 Pine St New York NY 10005

BENNACK, FRANK ANTHONY, JR., publishing co. exec.; b. San Antonio, Feb. 12, 1933; s. Frank Anthony and Lula W. (Connally) B.; student U. Md., 1954-56, St. Mary's U., 1956-58; m. Luella M. Smith, Sept. 1, 1951; children—Shelley, Laura, Diane, Cynthia, Julie. Advt. account exec. San Antonio Light, 1950-53, 56-58, adv. mgr., 1961-65, asst. pub., 1965-67, pub., 1967-74; gen. mgr. newspapers Hearst Corp., N.Y.C., 1974-76, exec. v.p., chief operating officer, 1975-78, pres., chief exec. officer, 1978—; dir. Council, N.Y.C. Chmn. bd. San Antonio Symphony, 1973-74. Trustee Our Lady of Lake Coll.; hon. trustee Witte Meml. Mus.; bd. govs. N.Y. Hosp., N.Y.C. Served with AUS, 1954-56. Mem. Tex. Daily Newspaper Assn. (pres. 1973—), Am. Newspaper Pubs. Assn., Greater San Antonio C. of C. (pres. 1971—). Rotarian (pres. 1974-75). Office: Hearst Corp 959 8th Ave New York NY 10019*

BENNER, BRUCE, JR., bank exec.; b. Chgo., Apr. 26, 1927; s. Bruce and Florence (Granert) B.; B.A., Dartmouth Coll., 1949; grad. Stonier Grad. Sch. Banking, Rutgers U., 1963; m. Ann Wheat, Aug. 28, 1954; children—Douglas, Joan. With Gen. Electric Co., Schenectady and N.Y.C., 1949-51; v.p. Continental Ill. Nat. Bank & Trust Co., Chgo., 1951-69; pres., chief exec. officer Ann Arbor Bank & Trust Co., Ann Arbor, Mich., 1969—; v.p. First American Bank Corp., Kalamazoo. City councilman, Ann Arbor, Mich., 1972-74. Trustee, Nat. Sanitation Found. Served with USNR, 1945-46. Clubs: Rotary Internat., Barton Hills Country. Office: 101 S Main St Ann Arbor MI 48107

BENNER, GLENN LYLE, supermarkets cons.; b. Laurel, Mont., Oct. 7, 1942; s. Alolph and Bertha (Schield) B.; B.A., Eastern Mont. Coll., 1965; student Portland State U., 1968-70; m. Betty Ellen Nelson, Mar. 23, 1963; children—Candace Jeanne, Scott Douglas. Salesman, Proctor & Gamble, Cin., 1965-67; store mgr. Bazar, Inc., Portland, Oreg., 1967-70; cons. Super Valu Stores, Hopkins, Minn., 1970-77; owner, mgr. Benner & Assos., Tualatin, Oreg., 1977—. Served with USN, 1960-62. Mem. Internat. Council Shopping Centers, N.Y. U. Research Dept., Nat. Assn. Ind. Retailers. Republican. Developed gravity computer model for supermarket site locations research. Home: 20917 SW Winema Dr Tualatin OR 97062 Office: PO Box 335 Tualatin OR 97062

BENNETT, BARRY F., educator, retailer; b. Reading, Pa., Nov. 15, 1945; s. Francis Jay and Dorothy M. (Heltzinger) B.; B.A., LaSalle Coll., 1967; M.Ed., Temple U., 1971; m. Faye A. Robertson, Dec. 16, 1971; children—Krista L., Thomas R. Sales & mktg. mgr. BankAmericard div. Am. Bank & Trust Co. of Pa., Reading, 1968-71; tchr. social studies Keith Valley Middle Sch., Willow Grove, Pa., 1971-73, Exeter High Sch., Reiffton, Pa., 1973—; instr. sociology Alvernia Coll., Reading, 1974-78; owner, mgr. Creative Arts & Crafts, Laureldale, Pa., 1975—. Fulbright fellow, India, 1977. Bd. dirs. Cerebral-Palsy Found. of Berks County, 1974-78. Mem. Middle Atlantic Craft & Hobby Industry Assn., Nat. Art Materials Trade Assn., Nat. Council Social Studies, Pa. Council Social Studies, Berks County Council for Social Studies (co-founder). Republican. Roman Catholic. Club: Lions (service award 1976). Editor: Berks County Social Studies Jour., 1974-78; contbr. articles in field to profl. jours. Home: 3304 Kutztown Rd Laureldale PA 19605 Office: 3424 Kutztown Rd Laureldale PA 19605

BENNETT, BRIAN GREGORY, fin. exec.; b. Bklyn., July 4, 1948; s. John William and Constance Rosemary (Sanderson) B.; B.S. in Sociology, Huron Coll., 1971; m. Cheryl Ann Hofer, Dec. 4, 1971; 1 dau., Jennifer Lynn. With Audiovox Corp., Hauppauge, N.Y., 1972—, nat. credit mgr., 1977—. Mem. Nat. Assn. Credit Mgrs. Home: 39 Summercress Ln Coram NY 11727 Office: 150 Marcus Blvd Hauppauge NY 11787

BENNETT, CEDRIC EUGENE, elec. supply co. exec.; b. Mattoon, Ill., June 7, 1926; s. Kenneth Ross and Dorothy Mae (Wilson) B.; B.S., U.S. Naval Acad., 1949; m. Fleur Ardis Norton, June 10, 1949; children—Cedric Eugene, Mark N., Michael C., John D., Ruth, Rebecca. Served as enlisted man U.S. Navy, 1944-45, commd. ensign, 1949, advanced through grades to lt., 1954; engring. officer U.S.S. Valley Force, 1950-52; pilot, 1952-55, adminstrv. officer, communications officer, legal office VP-26 Squadron, Brunswick, Maine, 1955-56, ret., 1956; partner C.P. Norton Memls., 1956-57; salesman Indsl. Nucleonics Corp., Balt., Richmond, Va. and Mobile, Ala., 1956-72, account mgr., 1972-75; chmn. bd. Nix & Bennett Supply Co. and Baldwin Elec. Supply Co., Fairhope, Ala., 1975—. Pres., Eastern Shore Emergency Services Assn., 1977-78, Fairhope Girls Softball League, 1977-78; vice-chmn. Fairhope Planning and Zoning Bd., 1979—; pres. Mobile-Baldwin County chpt. Coalition for Decency, 1980. Mem. Am. Home Lighting Inst., TAPPI, Nat. Assn. Elec. Distbrs., Nat. Home Builders Assn., Nat. Fedn. Ind. Businessmen, Eastern Shore C. of C. (dir. 1975-78), Ret. Officers Assn., U.S. Naval Acad. Alumni Assn., Nat. C. of C. Episcopalian. Clubs: Internat. Trade, Le Club, Optimist (dir. Fairhope 1975-78), Woodmen of World. Home: 257 Blue Island St Fairhope AL 36532 Office: 856 Fairhope Ave Fairhope AL 36532

BENNETT, DOUGLAS PHILIP, lawyer; b. White Plains, N.Y., Feb. 24, 1942; s. Philip C. and Anne B.; B.S., U.S. Mil. Acad., 1964; M.B.A. cum laude, Am. U., 1971; J.D., George Washington U., 1974; m. Sandra Seton Benedikt, May 18, 1968; children—Heather Seton, Douglas Stratton, Robyn Kirsten, Rebecca Blythe, Alexandra Benedikt, Jon Christian. Legis. asst. Congressman Alexander Pirnie, 1969-72; dir. legis. affairs Firestone Tire & Rubber Co., 1972-74; admitted to D.C. bar, 1977; spl. asst. legis. affairs Office Sec. Treasury, 1974; spl. asst. to Pres. U.S. for Legis. affairs White House, 1975; dir. Presdl. Personnel Office, White House, 1975-77; individual practice law, Washington, 1977—; appointed mem. Pres.'s Commn. on Personnel Interchange, 1976-79, Disting. Fed. Civilian Service Awards Bd., 1976-77. Bd. visitors U.S. Mil. Acad., vice-chmn., 1977, chmn., 1978-79. Served with U.S. Army, 1964-69. Decorated Bronze Star, Purple Heart, Air medal. Mem. Am. Bar Assn., D.C. Bar Assn. Republican. Roman Catholic. Club: Met. (Washington). Home: 9107 N Branch Dr Bethesda MD 20034 Office: 3238 Prospect St NW Washington DC 20007

BENNETT, EDITH THOMAN (MRS. CHARLES DANA BENNETT), found. exec.; b. Covington, Ky., July 15, 1900; d. Bernard H. and Elizabeth (Trenkamp) Thoman; B.A., U. Cin., 1921; student Am. Acad. Dramatic Art, 1921-22, Columbia, 1922; pvt. tutors in langs., Brussels and Berlin; m. Charles Dana Bennett, Sept. 20, 1924. Asso., Charles Dana Bennett Assos., Washington, 1945—; trustee Farm Film Found., 1946—, exec. v.p., 1948-76; dir. Elk Run Farm, Inc., 1947-57, Visual Edn., Inc., 1969—. Mem. steering com. Nat. Farm-City Week, 1955, mem. bd. dirs., nat. com. for Farm-City Week, 1956-57, mem. finance com., 1957; chmn. film com. Nat. Farm-City Council, Inc., 1958—, dir., 1959—, mem. exec. com., 1959-69; mem. Washington Film Council, 1958—; adv. council Univ. Film Found., 1965-78. Film juror Ednl. Film Library Assn., 1965-69; trustee Council on Internat. Non-theatrical Events, 1971-73, hon. life mem., 1973—. Recipient citation Nat. 4-H Club, 1956, Gold Clover, 1973; citations Boy Scouts Am., 1958, 62; Distinguished Service award Future Farmers Am., 1969, Hon. Am. Farmer degree, 1975. Asso. mem. U. Film Assn., Am. Assn. Agrl. Coll. Editors. Roman Catholic. Home: RD 3 Box 426 Vergennes VT 05491 Office: 1616 H St NW Washington DC 20006

BENNETT, EDWARD BLAIR, JR., banker; b. Indiana, Pa., Mar. 5, 1936; s. Edward Blair and Nelle Virginia (McGregor) B.; B.A., Yale U., 1958, J.D., 1963; children—(by previous marriage) Edward Blair III, Tristam Barclay; m. 2d, Nancy Jo Rice, May 1, 1967; children—Adam Rice, McGregor Blair. Admitted to N.Y. State bar, 1964; legal asso. Cadwalader, Wickersham & Taft, N.Y.C., 1963-65; pres., dir. M. Bennett & Sons, Indiana, Pa., 1966-75; dir. Nat. Bank of Commonwealth, Indiana, 1963—, pres., 1969—; dir. Berkshire Securities Corp., Indiana, 1977—; partner, dir. Tobias Knoblauch Pvt. Bank, Reading, Pa.; mem. nat. adv. com. to Office Comptroller of the Currency; chmn., chief exec. officer, dir. N.Mex. Bancorp., Santa Fe, 1979—; dir. 1st Nat. Bank Santa Fe. Mem. exec. bd. William Penn council Boy Scouts Am., 1967-71; mem. alumni bd. Yale, 1968-72; mem. Indiana County Bd. Assistance, 1972; mem. bd. Indiana County Community Action Program, 1972-75; mem. bd. Indiana County Planning Commn., 1972—, vice-chmn., 1974-77, chmn., 1977; mem. Pa. Republican Com., 1972-74. Served to 1st lt. USMC, 1958-60. Mem. Phelps Assn., Delta Kappa Epsilon, Phi Delta Phi. Clubs: New Haven Lawn; Duquesne (Pitts.); Yale (N.Y.C.); Allied (Indiana); Santa Fe Country; Elks. Home: Sena Plaza #35 Santa Fe NM 87501 Office: PO Box 6107 Santa Fe NM 87502

BENNETT, EDWARD HENRY, reins. co. exec.; b. Glens Falls, N.Y., July 22, 1917; s. Harry and Elizabeth Chandler (Clark) B.; A.B., Princeton, 1940; m. Louise Faris, Aug. 3, 1946; children—Faris Elizabeth, Anne Louise. With Guy Carpenter & Co., Inc., N.Y.C., 1940—, v.p., 1954-63, pres., dir., 1963-76, vice chmn., chief adminstrv. officer, 1976—; dir. Balis & Co., Inc., Phila., Reaseguradora Delta, C.A., Venezuela. Served to maj. USAAF, 1942-46. Decorated Legion of Merit. Mem. SAR. Republican. Episcopalian. Clubs: Wall St., Drug and Chem., Princeton (N.Y.C.); Nassau, Adirondack Mountain. Home: RFD 1 West Circle Bedford NY 10506 Office: 110 William St New York NY 10038

BENNETT, ERNEST RAY, airline exec.; b. Gwinnett County, Ga., July 2, 1928; s. Sim and Omie Lee (Hutchins) B.; LL.B., John Marshall Law Sch., 1957; m. Helen Frances Stephens, June 24, 1961; children—Fran Dee, Jennie Ann. Admitted to Ga. bar, 1959; with Delta Air Lines, Inc., Atlanta, 1945—, supr. data processing ops., 1957-63, gen. mgr. computer services ops., 1973—. Deacon, Sunday sch. tchr. Corinth Bapt. Ch., Stone Mountain, Ga., 1965—. Served with USNR, 1951-53. Mem. Ga., Gwinnett County bar assns. Democrat. Clubs: Masons, Shriners. Home: 1247 Hickory Dr Lilburn GA 30247 Office: Delta Air Lines Inc 3550 Greenbriar Pkwy Atlanta GA 30320

BENNETT, HARRY D., govt. data processing exec.; b. N.J., June 13, 1929; s. Harry and Mary (Null) B.; B.S., Dartmouth Coll., 1953; M.S., Stanford U., 1954; m. Paige Petroff, Apr. 27, 1978; children—Kathleen, Patricia, Christopher. Spl. rep. IBM Corp., Washington, 1953-62, 64-68, Paris, 1962-63; v.p. VIP Systems, Washington, 1968-72; regional mgr. Deltak Inc., Washington, 1972-73; dir. data processing Nat. Library of Medicine, Bethesda, Md., 1973—. Served with U.S. Army, 1946-48. Mem. Assn. Computing Machinery, Phi Beta Kappa. Episcopalian. Home: 9565 Fern Hollow Way Gaithersburg MD 20760 Office: Nat Library Medicine 8600 Rockville Pike Bethesda MD 20014

BENNETT, JAMES LOUIS, radar technician; b. Elmira, N.Y., Jan. 31, 1938; s. Albert Jr. and Vera Lena (Wheat) B.; B.B.A., U. Alaska, Fairbanks, 1969; M.B.A., U. Alaska, Anchorage, 1973; m. Edith Mildred Wagnon, Oct. 12, 1974; children—James Louis, Christy Lou, Harry A., Vera L., Dorothy. Housing mgmt. officer FAA, Anchorage, 1969-75; asso. prof. bus. adminstrn. Chapman Coll., Cold Bay, Alaska, 1975-78, Eastern Wyo. Coll., Lusk, 1981—; self-employed mgmt. cons., Alaska and Md., 1973-80; chief sector field office FAA, Cold Bay, 1975-78, radar technician Balt.-Washington Internat. Airport, Md., 1978-80, chief sector field office, Lusk, Wyo., 1980—; dir. J&J Enterprises, Willard Fisheries Co. Served with USN, 1956-60. Recipient Spl. Achievement award FAA, 1971, Meritorious Service award, 1969, Outstanding Achievement award, 1979, 80. Mem. Am. Soc. Public Adminstrn., Internat. Conf. Sports Car Clubs (regional chmn. 1967-69), Fairbanks Sports Car Club (pres. 1966-68), Alaska Sports Car Club. Republican. Jewish. Club: Shriners. Author: History of Air Traffic Control Development in Alaska 1968. Home: 711 W 3d St Lusk WY 82225 Office: Lusk Sector Field Office FAA Lusk WY 82225

BENNETT, JEROME VINCENT, fin. info. systems cons., educator; b. Jacksonville, Fla., Feb. 3, 1930; s. Oscar Vinson and Eula (Taylor) B.; B. Textile Engring., Ga. Inst. Tech., 1951; M.B.A., U. N.C., 1955; Ph.D. in Accounting, U. S.C., 1976; m. Anne Jenkins; 1 dau. by previous marriage, Christelle. Indsl. engr. E.I. DuPont de Nemours & Co., Kinston, N.C., 1955-57; indsl. engr. Riegel Paper Corp., Milford, N.J., 1957-58, mgr. cost accounting, 1958-61, div. controller, paper div., 1961-65; mgr. spl. projects, 1965-66, dir. mgmt. info., 1966; controller fiber and textile div. Uniroyal, Inc., 1966-69; exec. v.p. Lewis-Bennett Inc., 1966-69; pres. Consultronics Inst. Inc., 1968-70; fin. v.p. Wm. Heller Inc., 1968; dir. div. tech. utilization S.C. Budget and Control Bd., 1970-72; controller Tamper Inc., 1973; cons. Midlands Computer Assos., 1974-75, Pres.'s Reorgn. Project Cash Mgmt. Study, Washington, 1978; prof., cons. Newberry Coll. and U. S.C., 1973-76; prof., chmn. dept. accounting, cons. U. Richmond (Va.), 1976—. Treas., Milford (N.J.) Library Commn., 1958-60; mem. Milford Bd. Ed., 1962-66; trustee Warren Hosp., 1965-66; bd. dirs. Stuart Circle Center, 1980—. Served as lt. (j.g.) USNR, 1951-54; ETO. Registered profl. engr., Pa., S.C.; certified in mgmt. accounting and data processing. Mem. Am. Inst. Indsl. Engrs., TAPPI, Soc. for Advancement Mgmt., Nat. Assn. State Info. Systems, Am. Mgmt. Assn., Ops. Research Soc. Am., Fin. Execs. Inst., Assn. Systems Mgmt., Data Processing Mgmt. Assn., Am. Accounting Assn., Am. Inst. Decision Scis., Nat. Assn. Accountants, Phi Kappa Tau. Delta Kappa Phi, Beta Alpha Psi, Beta Gamma Sigma. Clubs: Toastmasters, Bull and Bear. Author: Administration of the Company Accounting Functions. Home: 2500 Fox Harbor Ct Richmond VA 23235 Office: Robins Sch Bus U Richmond Richmond VA

BENNETT, JOHN PHILLIP, pharm. co. exec.; b. Portsmouth, Eng., June 12, 1931; came to U.S., 1967; s. Charles Risby and Doris Isabel (Peckham) B.; B.Sc. with honors (Portsmouth Higher Award fellow), London U., 1953, B.Sc. (spl.), 1954; Ph.D., Cambridge (Eng.) U., 1963; advanced mgmt. cert. Stanford U., 1974; m. Margaret Anne Kettel, Dec. 29, 1956; children—Julian Fraser, Simone Margaret. Head endocrinology research, dep. head biol. research Brit. Drug Houses Ltd., 1963-67; head dept. reproductive physiology Syntex Research Corp., Palo Alto, Calif., 1967-70, dir. research adminstrn., 1970-72; corp. dir. adminstrn. Syntex Corp., Palo Alto, 1972, v.p. adminstrv. services, 1972-74, v.p. Corp. Adminstrn. and Communications div., 1978—; v.p. Syntex (USA), 1974—; nat. del. for Gt. Brit. V World Congress Fertility and Sterility, Stockholm, 1966; doctorate examiner U. Sydney (Australia), 1974; lectr. in field. Bd. dirs. Liaison Bay Area Council, San Francisco, 1976-78. Served with Ednl. Corps, Royal Army, 1954-56. Recipient Queens award to industry, 1966. Mem. Am. Soc. for Reprodn., Am. Fertility Soc., Soc. for Study Fertility, Internat. Word Processing Assn., Nat. Micrographics Assn., N.Y. Acad. Sci. Mem. Ch. of England. Author: Chemical Contraception, 1974; contbr. numerous articles to profl. jours.; patentee in field. Office: Syntex Corp 3401 Hillview Ave Palo Alto CA 94304

BENNETT, JOSEPH PALMER, mfg. co. exec.; b. Pitts., Aug. 14, 1929; s. Keenan A. and Winifred (Palmer) B.; B.B.A., U. Wis., 1951; postgrad. Case Western Res. U., 1952; m. Jean N. Wall, May 8, 1953; children—Thomas J., Charles K. Salesman, Hankins Container Corp., Cleve., 1952-60; pres. Trio Products, Inc., Elyria, Ohio, 1960—; dir. Ameritrust, Nat. Solvents Corp., Contour Packaging Co., W. Park Packaging. Mem. Soc. Plastics Industry, Ohio Bankers Assn. Club: Cleve. Yacht. Address: PO Box K Elyria OH 44036

BENNETT, LAFELL DICKINSON, market research firm exec.; b. Keene, N.H., Apr. 17, 1954; s. Robert A. and Jane (Dickinson) B.; B.A. in Govt., Skidmore Coll., 1976; M.B.A. in Mktg., U. N.H., 1978; m. Joan Duffett, Aug. 28, 1976. Founder, pres. Blake & Dickinson, Inc., Manchester, N.H., 1977—. Nat. pollster Anderson for Pres. Com., 1980. Named Outstanding Young Man of Yr., 1979. Mem. Am. Mktg. Assn., N.H. Ad Club. Republican. Developer primary voter model. Home: 21 Whig Dr Manchester NH 03104 Office: 922 Elm St Rm 408 Manchester NH 03101

BENNETT, LAYTON ALDEN, flying service exec.; b. Woodland, Wash., Apr. 12, 1919; s. Frank Henry and Edith Alice; student pub. schs., Forest Grove, Oreg.; m. Agnes Lourene Wilder, Feb. 27, 1944; children—Eric L., Lynn Norris, Barton Rhett. Pres. Lab Flying Service, Haines, Ark., 1958—. Served with USAF, 1942-46. Republican. Methodist. Office: Lab Flying Service Haines AK 99827

BENNETT, LEON LEDON, JR., electronics co. exec.; b. Birmingham, Ala., Aug. 22, 1928; s. Leon LeDon and Mary Ophelia (Oswalt) B.; B.S., Ga. Inst. Tech., 1953; m. Susan Lee Paul, June 11, 1950; children—Donna Susan, Steven Paul, David Wayne. Salesman Sylvania Electric Products, Photolamp div., New Orleans, 1954, dist. sales mgr., 1957, So. regional sales mgr., Atlanta, 1960; So. regional sales mgr., consumer products GTE Sylvania, Atlanta, 1971, nat. sales mgr., Danvers, Mass., 1975—. Served with AUS, 1946-48, USAF, 1950-52. Mem. George and Christina Oswalt Assn. (pres. 1970—), Sales and Mktg. Execs. Democrat. Congregationalist. Home: 1 Olde Planters Rd Beverly MA 01915 Office: 100 Endicott St Danvers MA 01923

BENNETT, MICHAEL MIDDLETON, mus. instrument co. exec.; b. Jackson, Tenn., Aug. 27, 1943; s. Floyd Kenneth and Thelma (Middleton) B.; B.Mus., MacPhail Coll. Music, 1965; m. Janet Leck, Sept. 2, 1964; children—Jay, Peggy. Dist. sales mgr. Norlin Music, Musical Instrument div., 1970-73, regional sales mgr., 1973-75, dir. sales, 1975-77, nat. sales mgr. Band and Orch. Div., 1978; now nat. sales mgr. W.T. Armstrong Co., Elkhart, Ind. Bd. dirs., v.p. Elkhart County Symphony Assn. Named Salesman of Yr., Norlin Music, Musical Instrument div., 1971. Republican. Clubs: Elcona, Phi Mu Alpha. Office: 1000 Industrial Blvd Elkhart IN 46514

BENNETT, RICHARD EARLE, corp. exec.; b. N.Y.C., Oct. 6, 1919; s. David L. and Augusta (Levanthal) B.; B.Mech. Engring., Coll. City N.Y., 1941; grad. student Stevens Inst. Tech., 1947-49; m. Helen Pitsillidis, Nov. 22, 1961; 1 son, Gerald Richard; 1 dau. by previous marriage, Nancy (Mrs. Hervey Friss). Mfg. engr. Western Electric Co., 1945-50; owner, operator Fairmount Tool Co., Newark, 1950-51; gen. mgr. various divs. Daystrom, Inc., later Weston Instruments, Inc., 1952-64; with Internat. Tel. & Tel. Corp., 1964—, exec. v.p. office of chief exec., 1978-80, sr. exec. v.p., 1980—, also dir., 1968—; dir. various subsidiaries; chmn. bd. ITT Ind. Can., 1978—. Served with AUS, 1942-44. Mason. Patentee wire wrap tool used in electronic assembly. Home: 18 Laurie Dr Englewood Cliffs NJ 07632 Office: 320 Park Ave New York City NY 10022

BENNETT, RICHARD EDWIN, shopping center exec.; b. Oshkosh, Wis., July 29, 1943; s. Richard Howell, Jr. and Dorothy Coroline (Brain) B.; student U. Wis., 1961-63, 67-68; m. Priscilla Kowalski, Nov. 25, 1967; children—Richard Howell, Jean Ann, Carol Ann. Asst. mgr. Robert Hall Clothes, Janesville, Wis., 1968-69; v.p., gen. mgr. Bennett Industries, Inc., St. Petersburg, Fla., 1969-72, dir., 1969—; asst. mgr., then mgr. W.T. Grant Co., Mt. Dora, Fla., 1972-76; asst. gen. mgr. Rouse Co., Tampa (Fla.) Bay Center, 1976-78, v.p., gen. mgr. Charlottetown Mall, Charlotte, N.C., 1978—. Served with AUS, 1963-66. Mem. Greater Charlotte C. of C., Internat. Council Shopping Centers. Home: 5116 Chestnut Lake Dr Charlotte NC 28212 Office: 601 Charlottetown Mall Charlotte NC 28204

BENNETT, RICHARD JOSEPH, corp. exec.; b. Bklyn., Jan. 20, 1917; s. Richard and Gertrude (McGuire) B.; A.B., Fordham Coll., 1938, LL.B., 1942; m. Eileen P. O'Neill, May 4, 1946; children—Susan, Richard. Admitted to N.Y. bar, 1942; mem. firm Whedon & Bennett, N.Y.C., 1945-46; staff atty. Schering Corp., 1947-55, asst. sec., asst. gen. counsel, 1955-59, sec., gen. atty., 1959-70, v.p., sec., gen. counsel, 1970-72; v.p., sec., gen. counsel Schering-Plough Corp., 1971-73, sr. v.p. adminstrn., 1973-76, pres., 1976-80, chief operating officer, 1976—, chmn. bd., 1980—; dir. New Eng. Nuclear Corp.; exec. dir. Pharm. Mfrs. Assn. Chmn. bd. trustees Fordham U.; pres. bd. trustees Found. Coll. Medicine and Dentistry N.J. Served with USAAF, 1942-45. Mem. Am., N.Y. State bar assns., N.Y. County Lawyers Assn. Office: Schering-Plough Corp Kenilworth NJ 07033

BENNETT, RICHARD THOMAS, chem. co. exec.; b. Trenton, N.J., Jan. 7, 1930; s. George and Gladys (Burgess) B.; B.S. in Chemistry, Yale U., 1952; M.S. in Organic Chemistry, Rutgers U., 1954, Ph.D., 1956; m. Bertha B. Wilson, Jan. 24, 1958; children—Sandra Jean, Richard Burgess, Terri Lynn, David Wilson. From research chemist to tech. rep. duPont Co., 1956-62; tech. dir. Am. Bag & Paper Corp., Phila., 1962-64; with Allied Chem. Corp., 1964-76, mem. task force splty. chems., Morristown, N.J., 1975-76; pres., dir. Plaskon Products, Inc., Toledo, 1979—; trustee NW Ohio Blue Cross, 1980—. Pres. Wilmington (Del.) Jaycees, 1959-60, Del. Jaycees, 1960-61, Morris Plains (N.J.) PTA, 1967-68; chmn. fin. commn. St. Paul's Episcopal Ch., Morris Plains, 1969-71, jr. warden, 1971-72, sr. warden, 1972-73; chmn. sustaining membership program Morris Plains council Boy Scouts Am., 1972; bd. dirs. Community

Chest, Toledo, 1978-80; vestryman St. Michael's Episcopal Ch., Toledo, 1979-80, jr. warden, 1980—; v.p. Toledo United Way, 1980. Named Outstanding Local Pres., Del. Jaycees, 1960. Mem. Soc. Plastics Engrs., Ohio Chem. Council (vice chmn. 1977-80), Ohio Mfrs. Assn., Toledo C. of C. Home: 2155 Hawthorne Rd Toledo OH 43606 Office: 2829 Glendale Ave Toledo OH 43614

BENNETT, ROBERT EUGENE, JR., mfg. co. exec.; b. Camden, N.J., Oct. 20, 1939; s. Robert Eugene and Ida B. (Trout) B.; B.S., Ursinus Coll., 1962; M.S., Rochester Inst. Tech., 1976, M.B.A., 1978; m. Leanne M. Fowler, June 30, 1962; children—Robert L., Randolph K. Mgr. systems and programming Ednl. Testing Service, Princeton, N.J., 1965-72; EDP auditor, systems cons. Xerox Corp., Rochester, N.Y., 1972-78; audit mgr. Air Products & Chems. Co., Allentown, Pa., 1978—. Treas., Nat. R.R. Hist. Soc., Rochester, 1977-78. Served to 1st lt. USAF, 1962-65. Cert. data processor, EDP auditor. Mem. Inst. Internal Auditors, EDP Auditors Assn. Contbr. articles to profl. publs. Home: 157 Hillcrest Dr Macungie PA 18062 Office: PO Box 538 Allentown PA 18105

BENNETT, ROBERT JOHN, banker; b. Fitchburg, Mass., June 7, 1941; s. N. Raymond and Mabel Ruth (Stoddard) B.; B.S., Babson Coll., 1963; M.B.A., U. Mass., 1966; grad. Advanced Mgmt. Program, Harvard U., 1981; m. A. Kathleen Dessert, Apr. 10, 1971; children—Burke M., Kristin D., Kimberly A., Richard L. Mem. controller's staff Norton Co., Worcester, Mass., 1966-68, supr. systems devel., 1968-69, v.p. mktg. ops., Boston, N.Y.C., 1969-70; pres. Beren Assos., Boston, 1970-71; sr. mgmt. cons. Touche Ross & Co., N.Y.C., 1971-75; v.p. Boatmen's Nat. Bank of St. Louis, 1975-76; sr. v.p. Boatmen's Bancshares, Inc., St. Louis, 1976—; dir. Boatmen's Bank of Troy, Boatmen's Life Ins. Co. Mem. Fin. Execs. Inst., St. Louis Corp. Growth Assn., Club: Bellerive Country. Office: Boatmens Bancshares Inc Box 236 Saint Louis MO 63166

BENNETT, ROBERT LYNN, diversified co. exec.; b. Plymouth, Ind., Aug. 10, 1941; s. Robert Lee and Edith Marie (Lane) B.; B.S., U.S. Naval Acad., 1963; M.S. in Adminstrn., George Washington U., 1973; m. Delores Ann Sallee, June 6, 1963; children—Leah Lynn, Eliabeth Ann. With Sperry Univac, Washington, 1970—, br. sales mgr., Washington, 1978-79, br. mgr., 1979—. Served with USN, 1963-70; Vietnam. Home: 8177 Murphy Rd Fulton MD 20759 Office: 2121 Wisconsin Ave NW Washington DC 20007

BENNETT, ROY FREDERICK, automotive co. exec.; b. Winnipeg, Man., Can., Mar. 18, 1928; s. Charles William and Gladys Mabel (Matthews) B.; student North Toronto Collegiate Inst., 1942-47; C.A., Inst. Chartered Accountants, 1953. With Ford Motor Co. of Can., Oakville, Ont., 1956—, dir., 1966—, pres., 1970, pres., chief exec. officer, 1971—. Mem. Premier's Advisory Com. on Econ. Future, Ont.; policy com. Bus. Council on Nat. Issues; mem. Can.-Am. Com. C.D. Howe Research Inst.; bd. govs. York U., Niagara Inst. Fellow Inst. Chartered Accountants Ont.; mem. Motor Vehicle Mfs. Assn. (dir.). Clubs: Mississauga Golf and Country; Toronto. Office: Canadian Rd Oakville ON L6J 5E4 Canada

BENNETT, SCOTT WAYNE, real estate developer; b. Ogden, Utah, Dec. 28, 1943; s. George H., Jr. and Gladys Norma (Ellery) B.; B.S. in Agrl. Econs., Utah State U., 1969; m. Ruth Marie Clayton, Sept. 9, 1979; children—Blaine, Teresa, Brock, Britanny. County supr. Farmers Home Adminstrn., 1969-70; sales rep. McCulloch Oil Land Co., 1970-73, Sweetwater Park, Bear Lake, Utah, 1974-75; founder, 1976, since pres., sec.-treas. Swan Creek Village, Inc., Salt Lake City; pres. Thundermountain Ranch. Recipient various sales awards. Mem. Home Builders Assn., Am. Land Devel. Assn. Republican. Mormon. Home: 1613 E Park Pl N Salt Lake City UT 84101 Office: 345 Trolley Sq Salt Lake City UT 84102

BENNETT, SHELDON WELLS, mgmt. cons. co. exec.; b. Seattle, Feb. 25, 1942; s. Manson Otis and Lucile (Divine) B.; B.S., U. Wash., 1964; Ph.D. in Physics, Columbia U., 1970; m. Mary Katherine Mattfield, Jan. 19, 1974; children—Marta Hope, Erin Elizabeth, Gabrielle Marie. Asst. prof. physics Harvard U., Cambridge, Mass., 1968-71; project mgr. Wasserman Devel. Corp., Cambridge, 1972-75; sr. v.p. Kent Corp., constrn. mgmt. consultants, Boston, 1975—; mem. constrn. industry panel Am. Arbitration Assn., 1977—. Corporator, Children's Mus. Lic. builder, Boston. Mem. Project Mgmt. Inst. Contbr. articles on exptl. high energy physics, neutral K meson physics to profl. jours. Office: 45 Broad St Boston MA 02109

BENNETT, WALLACE L., pvt. investment co. exec.; b. Washington, Oct. 31, 1944; s. Luther Eric and Margaret Jeannette (Persons) B.; A.B., U. Va., 1965; D.M., Episcopal Theol. Sch., 1969; M.B.A., Washington U., St. Louis, 1972; m. Sharon Lynn Brewer, June 1, 1968; children—Charles Stuart, John Daniel. With Merrill Lynch White Weld Capital Markets Group, and predecessors, N.Y.C., 1972-78, v.p., 1975-78; gen. partner Old Port Co., Alexandria, Va., 1979—; dir., mem. exec. com. Pinehurst Airlines, Greenville, S.C., Alexandria Cablevision Co. Home: 6210 Foxcroft Rd Alexandria VA 22307 Office: 424 N Washington St Alexandria VA 22314

BENNITT, ELMER CLARKE, agrl. exec.; b. Jersey City, Jan. 11, 1906; s. Frederick Henry and Jessie (Marvin) B.; student pub. schs.; m. Margaret Y. Yoder, Oct. 2, 1943; children—Frederick Y., George S. Salesman, Whitney and Kemmerer Coal Co., N.Y.C., 1925-29; asst. supt. Gt. Atlantic & Pacific Tea Co., Newark, 1929-35; sales supr. P. Ballantine and Sons, 1935-41; plant mgr. Yoder Bros., Ashtabula, Ohio, 1946-50; chmn. bd. Butler County Mushroom Farm, Inc., West Winfield, Pa., 1950—; chmn. bd. Yoder Bros. Inc., Barberton, Ohio. mem. adv. bd. Mellon Nat. Bank and Trust Co., Butler. Served with USNR, 1941-46. Mem. Am. Mgmt. Assn., Pa. Economy League (chmn. 1959, dir. 1963-64), N.A.M., U.S. C. of C. Episcopalian. Elk, Rotarian (pres. 1961-62). Clubs: Butler Country (dir.); Univ. (Pitts.); Ponte Vedra (Ponte Vedra Beach, Fla.); John's Island (Vero Beach, Fla.). Home: 519 N McKean St Butler PA 16001 Office: Worthington PA 16262

BENOIT, RICHARD CHARLES, JR., electronic engr.; b. East Orange, N.J., May 16, 1917; s. Richard Charles and Mary F. (Tierney) B.; student RCA Insts., 1936-37; certificate Air U. Command and Staff Coll., 1958; grad. Syracuse U. Modern Engring. Program, 1969; D.Engring., Clayton U., 1976, D.Internat. Affairs (hon.), 1976; m. Josephine M. Rasulo, June 5, 1943 (dec. June 1971); children—Richard Joseph, Joseph Edward; m. 2d, Marilyn Heit Chazan, Apr. 28, 1973. Self employed in radio theatre sound servicing, Highland, N.J., 1934-40; electronic technician U.S. Army Signal Corps Labs., Ft. Monmouth, N.J., 1940-42; project engr. USAF Watson Labs., Red Bank, N.J., 1945-50; with USAF Rome Air Devel. Center, Griffis AFB, N.Y., 1950—, unit chief to sect. chief in areas of radio navigation and telecommunications, chief communications processing and distbn. sect., 1968—; tech. adviser Hdqrs. USAF Europe, 1953, 55; mem. U.S. del. to NATO Telecommunications Conf., 1959-67; USAF tech. adviser on telecommunications to Spanish Air Force; spl. communications cons. Albany (N.Y.) Med. Coll., Union U., 1959-64; U.S. project officer for telecommunications, tech. data exchange program between U.S. and NATO nations, also Republic of Korea, 1959—; gen. chmn. Ann. Mohawk Valley Mgmt. Seminars, 1960, 61; pub. relations dir. IEEE Nat. Communications Symposium, 1955-58, exec. vice chmn., 1959, gen. chmn., 1960, bd. govs., 1961-66. Chmn. non-partisan tech. adv. com. to Congressman Mitchell (N.Y.); mem. citizens adv. council Marcy (N.Y.) Psychiat. Center. Served as ensign USCGR, 1942-45. Recipient Key to City of Utica (N.Y.) from Utica C. of C., 1959, also from Mayor of Utica, 1960, four cash awards and certificates for invention contbns. Dept. Air Force, 1959-69, Superior Performance award Dept. Air Force, 1963, Air Force Systems Command certificate of merit, 1973. Fellow IEEE (internat. dir. 1974-75, dir. Region I, 1974-75, regional activities bd. 1974-75, U.S. activities bd. 1974-75, 77-78, chmn. Mohawk Valley sect. 1969-70, sec. 1967-68, mem. del. to USSR 1974), AAAS; mem. N.Y. Acad. Sci. Roman Catholic. Contbr. articles in field to profl. jours. Office: Rome Air Devel Center DCLT Griffiss Air Force Base Rome NY 13441

BENSIGNOR, SAMUEL, adminstr.; b. Phila., July 28, 1929; s. Jacob and Mazaltob (Levy) B.; student Columbia U., 1954-55. Clk., Brown Instrument div. Mpls.-Honeywell Corp., Phila., 1952-53; office mgr. Earl B. Lovell-S.P. Belcher, Inc., N.Y.C., 1953-70, asso., 1970—. Served with AUS, 1948-52. Asso. mem. N.Y. State Assn. Profl. Land Surveyors. Jewish. Home: 216 Garfield Pl Brooklyn NY 11215 Office: 53 Park Pl New York NY 10007

BENSON, LAWRENCE EDWARD, ins. co. exec.; b. Mpls., July 31, 1916; s. Linus Edward and Hilma Agnita (Olausson) B.; student Bethel Coll., 1936-37; B.S., U. Minn., 1939; m. Phyllis Elaine Newman, Aug. 23, 1941; children—Laurel, Natalie, Lois, Philip, Kjersti. Underwriter, Employers of Wausau, Mpls., 1940-48; underwriting mgr. Federated Mut. Ins. Co., Owatonna, Minn., 1948-50; underwriting mgr. Mut. Service Ins. Co., St. Paul, 1950-56, dir. underwriting, 1956-61, dir. casualty actuarial dept., 1961-72, v.p. personnel, 1972-76, v.p. casualty, 1976—; dir., chmn. Minn. Ins. Guaranty Fund, Minn. FAIR Plan. Bd. mgmt. YMCA, Mpls., 1955-72, chmn., 1964-66; bd. regents Bethel Coll. and Sem., St. Paul, 1959-64, treas., 1960-62, vice chmn., 1962-64, mem. bd. President's Assos., 1967—; mem. Minn. Central Republican Com., 1966-69; bd. dirs. United Way, St. Paul, 1973-80. Served with U.S. Army, 1942-46. Recipient service award YMCA, 1963, Bethel Coll. and Sem., 1965, Minn. Central Rep. Com., 1966, also various PTA's; cert. Life Office Mgmt. Assn. Mem. Soc. C.P.C.U.'s (cert.), Am. Acad. Actuaries (cert.), Am. Swedish Inst. Republican. Baptist. Club: Midland Hills Country. Contbr. to ins. publs.

BENSON, LAWRENCE KERN, lawyer; b. Lake Charles, La., Jan. 19, 1906; s. George William and Lotta Emma (Tannehill) B.; LL.B., Tulane U., 1927; m. Adele Foster, Aug. 24, 1933; children—Lawrence Kern, Robert George. Admitted to La. bar, 1927, Tex. bar, 1929, U.S. Supreme Ct. bar, 1964; pvt. practice, Hammond, La., 1927-29; asso. firm Baker, Botts, Parker & Garwood, Houston, 1929, asso. firm Milling, Benson, Woodward, Hillyer, Pierson & Miller, and predecessors, New Orleans, 1929-35, partner, 1936—; prof. law Tulane U., 1962-64. Past pres., sec.-treas. Atchafalaya Land Corp.; ret. dir. La. Land and Exploration Co. Mem. civil law sect., mem. adv. com. mineral law project La. Law Inst., 1963-74; vice chmn. adv. com. La. Coastal and Marine Resources, 1971-73; mem. La. Sea Grant Adv. Council, 1974-77, Pub. Affairs Research Council, Council for Better La., Met. Area Com. New Orleans; bd. visitors St. Martin's Protestant Episcopal Sch. Fellow Am. Bar Found.; mem. Am., La., New Orleans bar assns., Assn. Bar City N.Y., Am., La. (chmn. continuous revision com. of mineral code 1977—) law insts., Am. Judicature Soc., Ind. Petroleum Assn. Am., Mid-Continent Oil and Gas Assn., Order of Coif, Sigma Phi Epsilon, Phi Delta Phi. Democrat. Presbyn. (trustee, elder). Clubs: Boston, Plimsoll, New Orleans Country, Petroleum (New Orleans); City (Baton Rouge). Home: 5544 Jacquelyn Ct New Orleans LA 70124 Office: Whitney Bldg New Orleans LA 70130

BENSON, RAY, educator; b. N.Y.C., Nov. 25, 1911; s. Julius M. and Rae (Benison) B.; B.A., L.I. U., 1932; J.D., Fordham U., 1935; M.B.A., U. Calif., 1962, Ph.D., 1969; m. Marion B. Lichtenstein, May 16, 1944; children—Susan Benson Cowan, Patricia Harriet, Janet Rhone. Pianist, orch. leader, N.Y.C., 1935-47; agt., exec. producer Music Corp. Am., Beverly Hills, Calif., 1947-52; exec. producer Dumont TV Network, N.Y.C., 1952-53; TV exec. John Gibbs Agy., Inc., N.Y.C., 1953-56, Paul Small Artists, Ltd., Beverly Hills, 1956-60; prof. law and adminstrn., fin. and industry, head arts adminstrn. program Calif. State U., Fresno, 1964—. Mem. Am. Economic Assn., AAUP, Am. Risk and Ins. Assn., Fin. Mgmt. Assn., Am. Bus. Law Assn., Beta Gamma Sigma, Sigma Iota Epsilon. Author: The Broadway Theater—A Problem of Stasis. Home: 9955 Durant Dr Beverly Hills CA 90212

BENSON, RICHARD HAROLD, acctg. co. exec.; b. Kenosha, Wis., Apr. 24, 1938; s. Harold Milton and Dorothy Marie (Cox) B.; B.B.A., U. Mich., 1960, M.B.A., 1961; m. Susan Eda Reed, Aug. 14, 1965; 1 dau., Kristi Sue. With Arthur Andersen & Co., 1961—, staff acct., Detroit, 1961-66, mgr., 1966-72, partner, 1972—, asst. to vice chmn. internat. ops., Chgo., 1972-75, mng. partner Athens, Greece, 1975-77, mng. partner Toledo, 1977—. Pres. Toledo Symphony Orch.; treas. Kidney Found Northwestern Ohio, 1978—, Birmingham (Mich.) Bd. Edn., 1970-72. Mem. Am. Inst. C.P.A.'s, Ohio Soc. C.P.A.'s, Am. Acctg. Assn. Republican. Presbyterian. Clubs: Inverness, Toledo. Office: Arthur Andersen & Co 300 Madison Ave Toledo OH 43604

BENSON, ROBERT BRONAUGH, retail lumber exec.; b. Pleasant Hill, Mo., May 16, 1923; s. Herbert Lowell and Sarah Amelia (Bronaugh) B.; student Kansas City U., 1942; B.A., Mo. U., 1951; m. Dorothy Ann Durick, May 8, 1954. Co-owner Benson Lumber Co., Columbia, Mo., 1958—; pres., treas., dir. Benson Lumber & Supply Co., Columbia, 1958—; v.p., dir. Benson Bldg. Materials, Inc., Columbia, 1958—; partner Osage Bldg. Supply Co., 1958—, Benson Bros. Enterprises, Columbia, 1952. Active Boy Scouts Am.; bd. dirs. Mid-Mo. Devel. Council, 1960-64. Served with AUS, 1943-46. Mem. Mid-Am. (dir. 1974), Southwestern (dir. 1970-73) lumbermen's assns., Mo. Archaeol. Soc., Am. Forestry Assn., Forest History Soc., Mo. Statewide Forest Com. (del.), Nat. Trust Historic Preservation, Native Sons of Kansas City. Presbyterian. Clubs: Country Mo. (Columbia); Kansas City; Westerners. Home: 1706 Green Meadow Rd Columbia MO 65201 Office: 710 Business Loop 70 W Columbia MO 65201 Mailing address: PO Box 3 Columbia MO 65205

BENSON, ROBERT DALE, financial mgmt. cons.; b. Little River, Kans., June 4, 1912; s. Leslie Robert and Vernena (Sherer) B.; grad. Hutchinson Jr. Coll., 1932; student Northwestern U., 1939-40; grad. Army Indsl. Coll., 1944; m. Nelle Malick Payne, Dec. 23, 1933 (dec.); children—Robert Payne, Robin Sherwood; m. 2d, Gertrude Marie Trudeau, June 21, 1975. Chief acct. Asso. Dairies Wichita (Kans.), 1933-34; with Spurrier & Wood, C.P.A.'s, Wichita, 1935; chief accountant, comptroller Steffen Ice and Ice Cream Corp., Wichita, 1936; partner Spurrier, Wood & Benson, accountants and auditors, Hutchinson, Kans., 1941-43; with firm P.H. Willems, accountants and auditors, McPherson, Kans., 1937; partner Willems & Benson, accountants and auditors, McPherson, 1937-43; chief fixed price audits, spl. audits and termination audits brs. Hdqrs., U.S. Army Air Force, 1943-47; chief spl. audit br., asst. chief indsl. audits div. Hdqrs., U.S. Army Audits Agy., 1947-48; dep. auditor gen. U.S. Air Force, 1948-53, dep. for accounting and fin. mgmt. to asst. sec. air force, 1953-58, dep. asst. sec. air force for fin. mgmt., 1958-69, prin. dep. asst. sec. air force, 1969-71; chmn. bd. Internat. Finance and Mgmt. Corp., Washington, 1971-72; pres. Robert D. Benson & Assos., mgmt. cons., Washington, 1972—; guest lectr. George Washington U., 1953-56. Mem. bd. U.S. Civil Service Examiners, 1955-71. Recipient Air Force Decoration for Exceptional Civilian Service, 1953, 55, 69-71; named Outstanding Young Man Kans., 1942. Mem. U.S. Jr. (v.p. 1943-44, treas. 1944-45, dir. 1941-45), Kans. (dir. 1942-43), Kans. Jr. (pres. 1942-43) chambers commerce, Assn. Govt. Accountants, Kans. State Soc. Licensed Municipal Pub. Accountants, Am. Accounting Assn., Air Force Assn., Ordre Des Compagnons Du Bontemps-Medoc et Graves Bordeaux France (hon. comdr.), Internat. Wine and Food Soc., Les Amis du Vin. Clubs: Kenwood Golf and Country (Bethesda, Md.); Manor Country (Rockville, Md.); Nat. Aviation (Washington); Montgomery Village Golf (Gaithersburg, Md.). Asso. editor Future Magazine, 1944. Home: 3506 Manor Rd Chevy Chase MD 20015

BENT, DOROTHY FLORENCE (MRS. ALLEN EMERY BENT), Realtor; b. Whitingham, Vt., June 1, 1920; d. Harold Edgar and Florence Vernette (Hicks) Plumb; B.S. (Cotting Meml. scholar), U. Mass., 1942; M.A. in Teaching, U. Vt., 1968; m. Allen Emery Bent, Nov. 11, 1944; children—Kim Allen, David Emery, Douglas Gene, Robert Arnold, Cynthia Lee. County 4-H club agt. Chittenden County, Burlington, Vt., 1942-43, Orange County, Middletown, N.Y., 1943-44; acting county club agt. Orange County, Chelsea, Vt., 1954; tchr. Whitcomb High Sch., Bethel, Vt., 1960-67; county extension agt. Windsor County, Woodstock, Vt., 1967-72; realtor Pyramid Realty & Mortgage Corp., Winter Haven, Fla., 1974—. Cons., instr. handicapped homemakers. Adviser Windsor, Springfield family centers; mem. tech. adv. com. Health Care and Rehab. Services Southeastern Vt., Inc., 1970-72; Orange County rep. to Vt. 4-H Club Found., 1952-53; mem. Orange County Extension Adv. Bd., 1965-67; mem. sub-com. on edn. Gov.'s Com. on Children and Youth, 1971-72; den. mother Cub Scouts, 1957-58; pres. Randolph Unit PTA, 1961-63; mem. Vt. Inter-Agy. Council on Smoking and Health, 1971-72, Vt. Preschool Planning Com., 1971-72; del. White House Conf. on Children, 1970. Town auditor Town of Braintree (Vt.), 1950-55; mem. Orange County Republican Com., 1961-62, Polk County Rep. Exec. Com., Winter Haven Tourist Com. Trustee Downer 4-H Camp; bd. dirs. Central Vt. Community Action Council, First Chance Project of Pre-Sch. Edn. Centers, Windsor County and Vt. Community Coordinated Child Care Com.; named Mrs. Vt. of 1963, Mrs. America Homemakers Council. Founder-fellow Internat. Inst. Community Service; mem. Nat. Congress Parents and Tchrs. (life mem.; mem. health and welfare commn. 1969-72, mem. nat. bd. mgrs. 1969-72), Vt. PTA (pres. 1969-73), Nat., Vt. (v.p. 1969-71), New Eng. (sec. 1969-71) assns. extension home economists, Winter Haven Bd. Realtors (edn. and polit. action coms.), Nat., Fla. assns. realtors, Cert. Bus. Counselors Inst., Grad. Realtors Inst., Messiah Assn. of Winter Haven, Braintree Hist. Soc. (charter mem.), Vt. Hist. Soc., DAR, Orange County 4-H Leaders Assn. (pres. 1952-53), Vt. 4-H Hon. Soc., Mass. All-Stars 4-H Hon. Soc., Conglist. Office: 1478 6th St NW Winter Haven FL 33880

BENTEL, ROBERT BRIGGS, banker; b. San Diego, Sept. 20, 1938; s. Carr Eugene and Gladys (Briggs) B.; B.A., Dartmouth Coll., 1960; M.B.A., Stanford U., 1964; m. Alma Baltodano, Apr. 16, 1966; children—John Carr, Elizabeth Anne. With The Bank of Calif., 1964—, br. mgr., San Francisco, 1968-69, asst. v.p., mgr. central credit dept., 1969-70, v.p. met. div., 1970-72, v.p., dir. tng., 1972-73, v.p., London, 1973-75, v.p. comml. loan supervision, 1975-76, sr. v.p., div. head loan rev. div., 1976—. Bd. dirs. Vis. Nurse Assn. of San Francisco, Inc. Served with USNR, 1960-62. Mem. Robert Morris Assos. Clubs: Commonwealth of Calif.; Guardsmen. Home: 2900 Ocean Ave San Francisco CA 94132 Office: 400 California St San Francisco CA 94108

BENTELE, RAYMOND, corp. exec.; b. 1936; B.S., N.E. Mo. State Coll., 1960; married. Accountant, S.D. Leidesdorf & Co., 1960-65, treas., controller Germania Savs. and Loan Assn., 1965-67; with Mallinckrodt, Inc., St. Louis, 1967—, asst. controller, 1969-71, controller, 1971-74, v.p., 1974-76, v.p. fin. and adminstrn., 1976-77, v.p. internat. group, 1977-78, sr. v.p., group exec., 1978-79, pres. 1979—, chief exec. officer, 1980—, also dir. Office: Mallinckrodt Inc 675 Brown Rd St Louis MO 63134*

BENTLEY, FRED DOUGLAS, lawyer; b. Marietta, Ga., Oct. 15, 1926; s. Oscar Andrew and Ima (Prather) B.; A.B., Presbyn. Coll., 1945; LL.B., Emory U., 1948, J.D., 1961; student Wright Jr. Coll., 1946, U. Ga., 1950; m. Sara Tom Moss, Dec. 26, 1953; children—Fred D., Robert Randall. Admitted to Ga. bar, 1948; practiced in Marietta, 1949—; mem. firm F. D. Bentley, 1949-53, Bentley and Dew, 1953-55, Bentley, Awtrey and Bartlett, 1955-57, Edwards, Bentley, Awtrey and Bartlett, 1957-63, Edwards Bentley, Awtrey and Parker, 1963-72, Bentley & Bentley, 1980—; prin. Fred D. Bentley, Sr., 1972-80; pres. Bentley & Sons, Inc., 1976—, Pine Mountain Estates Inc., 1965—, Beneficial Investment Co., 1972—, Market Sq., Inc., Market Sq. of Cartersville, Inc., Community Investment, Inc., Happy Valley, Inc.; v.p. Newmarket Mall, Inc. Active in Ga. Mental Health Assn., Community Chest; pres. Kennestone Hosp. Guild, 1972; chmn. Ga. Gov.'s Fine Arts Com.; county atty.; mem. Ga. Ho. of Reps. 1951-57; mem. Ga. State Senate, 1959; mem. Ga. Democratic Exec. Com., 1964-65. Bd. dirs. League of Women Voters; adv. dir. YWCA. Served with USNR, 1945-46. Mem. Am., Ga., Cobb County, Nacca bar assns., Am. Trial Lawyers Assn., C. of C., Cummer Mus., High Mus., Nat. Hist. Soc., Nat. Trust Historic Preservation, Alpha Lambda Tau, Phi Alpha Delta, Gamma Beta Phi. Methodist. Clubs: Lawyers, Toastmasters (pres. 1957), Kiwanis, Rotary, Salmagundi, Governor's, President's. Home: Beaumont Kennesaw GA 30144 Office: 272 Washington Ave Marietta GA 30060

BENTON, ALLAN MORTON, investment banker; b. Pittsfield, Mass., June 20, 1937; s. Kenneth Hiram and Edna Alma (Morton) B.; B.A. in Chemistry, Williams Coll., 1959; M.S. in Chem. Engring., U. Minn., 1962; m. Ann Hall Freiberg, May 4, 1973; children—Amy Ann, Kenneth Hall. Project mgr. corp. devel. Dow Corning Corp., Midland, Mich., 1962-66; mgr. synthetic fuels Chem. Systems, Inc., N.Y.C., 1967, 70-71, London, 1968-69; chem. analyst, v.p. corp. fin. Blyth Eastman Dillon, N.Y.C., 1972-73; treas. Hooker Chem. Corp., Houston, 1974-75; with Salomon Bros., Dallas, 1976-77, N.Y.C., 1978—, now v.p. corp. fin., also mgr. chem. group. Mem. Am. Chem. Soc., Am. Inst. Chem. Engrs., Am. Petroleum Inst. Republican. Club: Petroleum (Oklahoma City). Author: (monograph) Selection of Projects and Production Processes for Basic and Intermediate Petrochemicals in Developing Countries, 1969. Office: 1 New York Plaza New York NY 10004

BENTON, DOUGLAS GEORGE, bldgs. mgr.; b. Denver, Feb. 4, 1946; s. Nicholas and Dorothy Revilla (Sloan) B.; B.A. in Journalism, Colo. State U., 1971, postgrad., 1978-80; Electronics technician Colo. Engring. Expt. Sta., Nunn, Stanley Aviation, Denver, 1972; bldg. mgmt. asst. Gen. Services Adminstrn., Denver, 1973-74, bldgs. mgr., Casper, Wyo., 1974-78, Colorado Springs, Colo., 1978-79, chief maintenance and utilities sect., 1979-80, area field supr., Denver, 1980—. Chmn., Casper Combined Fed. Campaign, 1976-78; bd. dirs.

Natrona County United Way. Served in USN, 1965-69. Decorated Navy Commendation medal with Combat V. Mem. Casper Fed. Execs, Council (v.p. 1975-76, pres. 1977). Methodist. Home: 3005 S Xeric Ct Denver CO 80231 Office: GSA Bldg 41 Denver CO 80225

BENTON, F. FOX, JR., oil and mineral co. exec. Pres., chief exec. officer, dir. Houlston Oil & Minerals Corp. Office: Houston Oil & Minerals Corp 1100 Louisiana St Houston TX 77002*

BENTON, FREDERICK RAYMOND, real estate broker; b. Westerville, Ohio, June 26, 1939; s. Frederick Raymond and Edith May B.; B.S. in Bus. Mgmt. and Orgn., Andrews U., 1970; m. Janet Arlene Roush, Apr. 26, 1958; children—Gary Michael, Jeffrey Lee Roy, William Raymond, Pamela Kay. Property mgr. Berrien Enterprises Inc., Berrien Springs, Mich., 1971-72; real estate and fin. supr. City of Benton Harbor, Mich., 1972-74; v.p., asso. real estate broker, Findling and Assos. Inc., St. Joseph, Mich., 1974-79; asso. real estate broker Tipton and Assos., Inc., Albuquerque, 1979—. Pres. PTA, 1967-68; scoutmaster Southwestern Mich. council Boy Scouts Am., 1967-71; mem. State of Mich. Advisory Council on Vocat. Rehab.; chmn. advisory council Vocat. Rehab., Benton Harbor, 1976-78. Served with USN, 1957-63. Mem. Southwestern Mich. Bd. Realtors (chmn. econ. devel. com.), Realtors Nat. Mktg. Inst., Mich. Assn. Realtors Exchange Div. (Exchangor of Yr., 1977), Albuquerque Bd. Realtors (Exchangor of Yr. 1979), Delta Mu Delta (pres. 1970-71). Mem. Disciples of Christ. Home: 4308 San Andres NE Albuquerque NM 87110 Office: 2301 San Pedro NE Albuquerque NM 87110

BENTON, NICHOLAS, pub. exec.; b. Boston, Oct. 18, 1926; s. Jay Rogers and Frances (Hill) B.; grad. Phillips Exeter Acad., 1945; A.B., Harvard, 1951; m. Kate Lenthal Bigelow, June 5, 1954; children—Frances Hill, Kate, Emily Weld, Louisa Barclay. Promotion writer Life mag., N.Y.C., 1951-55, Fortune mag., 1955-56; staff writer Time Mag., 1956-57; advt. promotion mgr. Archtl. Forum, 1957-64; gen. promotion mgr. Time-Life Books, N.Y.C., 1965-68, pub. relations dir., 1968—, v.p., 1977—. Mem. Nat. Book Awards Com., 1971, co-chmn., 1975-79; mem. Am. Book Awards Com., 1981. Pres., E. 69th St. Assn., 1963-64; 1st v.p. Soc. Meml. Sloan-Kettering Cancer Center, 1963-64, asst. treas., 1964-66, treas., 1967-68. Served with AUS, 1945-46. Mem. Pubs. Publicity Assn. (pres. 1970-71), New Eng. Historic Geneal. Soc. (trustee 1979—), N.Y. Geneal. and Biog. Soc., Assn. Am. Pubs. (Freedom to Read Com. 1974-78, pub. relations com. 1976-79, internat. freedom to publish com. 1979—). Clubs: Harvard (bd. mgrs. 1971-73) (N.Y.C.); Bourne Cove Yacht (Wareham, Mass.); Coffee House. Author: A Benton Heritage, 1964. Co-producer musical Salad Days, 1958. Home: 1007 Turkey Run Rd McLean VA 22101 Office: Time-Life Books Inc Alexandria VA 22314

BENTON, PETER, mgmt. cons.; b. Boston, July 4, 1925; s. Jay Rogers and Frances (Hill) B.; grad. Browne and Nichols Sch., 1944; Asso. degree, Boston U., 1950, B.S., 1956; m. Marilyn M. Moore, Sept. 11, 1948; children—Jeffrey Willard, Douglas Chamberlin, Andrew Jay, Sarah Warren. With John Hancock Mut. Life Ins. Co., Boston, 1950-73, dir. pub. relations Midwest region, Chgo., 1963-73; v.p., dir. mktg. First Vt. Bank, Brattleboro, 1973-80; pres. Salmon Stream Assos., mgmt. cons., Dummerston, Vt., 1980—; mem. evening faculty Northeastern U. Coll. Bus. Adminstrn., 1958-63, also Keene State Coll. Asst. chmn. Greater Boston United Fund Health and Fitness Fair, 1961; mem. Chgo.-Cook County Com. on Criminal Justice, 1970-73; bd. dirs. Greater North Michigan Ave. Assn., 1968-73, Chgo. Conv. and Tourist Bur., 1972-73, Vt. Pub. Radio, Vt. Green Up, Inc.; bd. dirs., pres. Brattleboro Mus. and Art Center; governing mem. Chgo. Symphony Orch., 1968-71; trustee Browne and Nichols Sch., 1960-68, Vt. Symphony; mem. nat. alumni council Boston U. Served with USMCR, 1943-46. Recipient Francis W. Hatch awards, GAMMA award. Mem. Public Relations Soc. Am. (dir. New Eng. chpt. 1958-63, pres. 1961, chmn. 15th nat. conf. 1962, award for profl. excellence). Clubs: Chgo. Athletic Assn., Marine Meml. (San Francisco). Author: Vermont Firsts Collection. Designer 1st Vermont Bowl. Home: Dummerston Center VT Office: RD 2 Dummerston VT 05346

BENTZINGER, HARLAN ALBERT, citrus grower; b. Donnellson, Iowa, May 1, 1923; s. Albert Henry and Ruth Victoria (Schmitt) B.; B.S.M.E., Iowa State U., 1944; M.B.A., Harvard U., 1948; m. Pauline Jameson, May 29, 1948; children—Dana, Julia, Lisa. Prodn. and engring. mgr. Precision Chem. Pump, Waltham, Mass., 1951-65; div. mgr. Chem. Products Corp., East Providence, R.I., 1965-75; pres. Lake Delta Citrus Assn., Weslaco, Tex., 1977-79, Bentzinger Farms, Inc., Edinburg, Tex., 1966—; dir. Tex. Citrus Exchange, 1977-79, chmn., 1979. Mem. Rehoboth (Mass.) Sch. Com., 1969-75, chmn., 1971. Served with C.E., U.S. Army, 1944-46, 50-52. Registered profl. engr., Mass. Republican. Protestant. Patentee (6). Home: 923 E Canton Edinburg TX 78539 Office: PO Box 1 Weslaco TX 78596

BENZ, HERBERT LOUIS, tech. services co. exec.; b. Buffalo, Oct. 25, 1941; s. Herbert Conrad and Edna Elinor (Dinsmore) B.; student Buffalo State Tchrs. Coll., 1959-60, Erie County Tech. Inst., 1962-64, Harvard U. Bus. Sch., 1976; m. Carla Mae Trautman, July 22, 1961. Draftsman, Linde div. Union Carbide Corp., Buffalo, 1961-65; piping designer Clark Bros. div. Dresser Industries, Buffalo, 1965-67; project mgr. A.E. Anderson Constrn. Corp., engring. div., Buffalo, 1967-73; gen. mgr. Anderson Engring. div. Andco, Inc., Buffalo, 1973-76; v.p. Andco Tech. Services, Inc., Buffalo, 1976-79, pres., 1979—; guest lectr. Niagara Community Coll.; cons. field fgn. and domestic blast furnace design. Mem. Iron and Steel Soc. of Am. Inst. Mech. Engrs., Eastern States Blast Furnace and Coke Oven Assn. Republican. Club: GPA Investment (v.p.). Author articles, patentee in field. Home: 24 Pine Terr Orchard Park NY 14127 Office: 2005 Walden Ave Buffalo NY 14225

BENZAK, LOUIS RICHARD, investment counselor; b. Allentown, Pa., Aug. 27, 1939; s. Louis Anton and Emma Ann (Yany) B.; B.S., Pa. State U., 1961; m. Virginia Ann Scully, Nov. 17, 1973; children—Christopher Louis, Jeffrey John, Caroline Ann. Second v.p. Chase Manhattan Bank, N.Y.C., 1962-68; sr. v.p. Loeb Rhoades & Co., N.Y.C., 1969-77; pres. Spears Benzak & Co., Inc., N.Y.C., 1978—. Dir., treas. Muscular Dystrophy Assn. Am., 1977—. Served with U.S. Army, 1962. Mem. N.Y. Soc. Security Analysts. Clubs: Knickerbocker, City Midday (N.Y.C.); Apawamis (Rye, N.Y.). Home: 1 Ralston St Rye NY 10580 Office: 730 Fifth Ave New York NY 10019

BERANEK, LEO LEROY, bus. and engring. cons.; b. Solon, Iowa, Sept. 15, 1914; s. Edward Fred and Beatrice (Stahle) B.; A.B., Cornell Coll., 1936, D.Sc. (hon.), 1946; M.S., Harvard, 1937, D.Sc., 1940; D.Engring. (hon.), Worcester Poly. Inst., 1971; D. Comml. Sci. (hon.), Suffolk U., 1979; m. Phyllis Knight, Sept. 6, 1941; children—James Knight, Thomas Haynes. Instr. physics Harvard, 1940-41, asst. prof. communication engring., 1941-43, dir. electro-acoustics and systems research labs., 1943-46; asso. prof. communication engring. Mass. Inst. Tech., 1947-58, lectr., 1958—; dir. Bolt, Beranek & Newman, Inc., research and devel., Cambridge, 1953—, partner, 1948-53, pres., chief exec. officer, 1953-69, chief scientist, 1969-71, cons., 1971—; chmn. bd. Mueller-BBM GmbH, Munich, Germany, 1962—; pres., chief exec. officer, dir. Boston Broadcasters, Inc., owners WCVB-TV, 1963-79, chmn. bd., 1980—; Thomas Hawksley lectr. Inst. Mech. Engrs., Eng., 1958. Trustee, Cornell Coll., 1955-71, Opera Co. Boston, 1961—, pres., 1961-63; trustee Emerson Coll., 1973-79; charter mem. bd. overseers Boston Symphony Orch., 1968—, chmn., 1977-80, trustee, 1977—; pres. World Affairs Council of Boston, 1975-78, vice chmn., 1980—; bd. dirs. Greater Boston Fund for Internat. Affairs, 1976—, chmn., 1978—; bd. dirs. Flaschner Jud. Inst., Mass., 1977—. John Simon Guggenheim fellow, 1946-47; recipient Presdl. certificate of merit, 1948; Cornell Coll. Alumni Citation, 1953; Abe Lincoln TV award Radio and TV Commn., 1975. Fellow Acoustical Soc. Am. (Biennial award 1944, Wallace Clement Sabine Archtl. Acoustics award, 1961; Gold Medal award 1975; v.p. 1949-50, pres. 1954-55), Am. Acad. Arts and Scis., Am. Phys. Soc., A.A.A.S., Nat. Acad. Engring. (com. pub. engring. policy 1966-71, council 1970-71, marine engr. bd. 1965-71, aero. and space engring. bd. 1966-69, 73-76), Groupement des Acousticiens de Langues Francais (1st Silver medal 1966), Inst. Noise Control Engring. (dir., charter pres. 1971-73), IEEE (chmn. profl. group on audio 1950-51), Audio Engring. Soc. (exec. v.p. 1966-67, pres. 1967-68, bd. govs. 1966-71, 1st Gold Medal award 1971); mem. Am. Nat. Standards Inst. (dir. 1963-66, mem. acoustical standards bd. 1955-70), Boston C. of C. (dir. 1972-79, v.p. 1976-79, Disting. Community Service award 1980), Boston 200 (dir. 1975-77), Mass. Broadcasters Assn. (dir. 1973—, treas. 1976-77, v.p. 1977-78, pres. 1978-79, Disting. Service award 1980), Phi Beta Kappa, Sigma Xi, Eta Kappa Nu. Episcopalian. Clubs: St. Botolph, Winchester Country, Harvard, M.I.T. Faculty. Author: Principles of Sound Control in Airplanes, 1944; Acoustic Measurements, 1949; Acoustics, 1954; Noise Reduction, 1960; Music, Acoustics and Architecture, 1962; Noise and Vibration Control, 1971. Contbr. numerous articles on acoustics and communications engring. to tech. publs. Home: 7 Ledgewood Rd Winchester MA 01890 Office: 5 TV Pl Needham MA 02192

BERBERIAN, H. NICHOLAS, lawyer; b. Phila., Dec. 27, 1952; s. Nicholas H. and Kay (Hamparian) B.; A.B., Kenyon Coll., 1974; M.B.A., U. Chgo., 1975, J.D., 1978; m. Nancy Ann Mikaelian. Asst. to dir. research Freehling & Co., Chgo., 1975; mgmt. cons. intern Ernst & Ernst, Chgo., 1975; admitted to Ill. bar, 1978; law clk. firm Friedman & Koven, Chgo., 1976, asso. atty., 1978—; instr. fin. and acctg. Northeastern U., Chgo., 1977—. Chmn. Chgo. admissions program Kenyon Coll. Mem. Am. Bar Assn., Ill. Bar Assn., Chgo. Bar Assn., Omicron Delta Epsilon. Home: 333 E Ontario St Apt 3110B Chicago IL 60611 Office: 208 S LaSalle St Chicago IL 60604

BERCHTOLD, KENNETH JOSEPH, fin. exec.; b. Mt. Angel, Oreg., Dec. 19, 1937; s. Joseph Jacob and Helen Marie (Saalfeld) B.; B.A. in Bus. Adminstrn., St. Martin's Coll., 1959; children—Michael, Joseph, Mary Heidi. Fin. mgr. Boeing Co., Seattle, 1959-70; controller comml. programs Northrop Corp., Hawthorne, Calif., 1970-73, pricing mgr., 1974-76, bus. mgr. Saudi Arabia ops., 1977-78, mgr. pricing and estimating, 1978-79, mgr. contracts and pricing, aircraft services div., 1979—; dir. fin. Iran Aircraft Industries, Tehran, 1973-74; mng. partner Bee Devel. Co., Hermosa Beach, Calif. Chmn. civil service commn., Mercer Island, Wash., 1968; councilman Mercer Island, 1969-70; chmn. 531 Esplanade Assn. Served with Air N.G., 1959-65. Mem. South Bay Bd. Realtors. Republican. Roman Catholic. Club: King Harbor Yacht. Home: 531 Esplanade #907 Redondo Beach CA 90277 Office: 3901 W Broadway Hawthorne CA 90250

BERDICK, LEONARD STANLEY, ins. broker; b. New Rochelle, N.Y., Aug. 13, 1938; s. Julius and Fay (Jaffe) B.; B.A., Colgate U., 1960; M.A., Columbia U., 1963; student U. N.C. Law Sch., 1960-61; m. Arlene Jean Kaufman, Oct. 31, 1968. Broker, dir., agt. Leonard S. Berdick Agy., S.I., N.Y., 1975—. Committeeman, Liberal Party, 1974—. Mem. Nat. Assn. Life Underwriters, N.Y. Ins. Brokers Assn., Life Suprs. Assn., Acad. Polit. Sci., Colgate U., Columbia U., U. N.C. alumni assns. Jewish. Home: 1302 Rockland Ave Staten Island NY 10314 Office: 355 Lexington Ave 20th Floor New York NY 10017

BERE, JAMES FREDERICK, mfg. exec.; b. Chgo., July 25, 1922; s. Lambert Sr. and Madeline (Van Tatenhove) B; student Calvin Coll., 1940-42; B.S., Northwestern U., 1946, M.B.A., 1946; m. Barbara Van Dellen, June 27, 1947; children—Robert Paul, James Frederick, David Lambert, Lynn Barbara, Becky Ann. With Clearing Machine Corp. div. U.S. Industries, Inc., 1946-53, gen. mgr. Clearing Machine Corp., 1953-56; gen. mgr. Axelson Mfg. Co. div., 1956, pres. 1957-61; pres., gen. mgr. Borg & Beck div., Borg-Warner Corp., Chgo., 1961-64, group v.p. parent co., 1964-66, exec. v.p. automotive div., 1966-68, pres. corp., from 1968, chief exec. officer from 1972, also chmn. bd.; dir. Continental Ill. Nat. Bank and Trust Co., Chgo., Abbott Labs. Trustee, Ill. Inst. Tech. Served as lt. AUS, 1943-45. Mem. Am. Mgmt. Assn., Soc. Automotive Engrs. Office: Borg-Warner Corp 200 S Michigan Ave Chicago IL 60604*

BEREND, ROBERT WILLIAM, lawyer; b. Miami Beach, Fla., Dec. 31, 1931; s. George Harry and Miriam (Wagner) B.; A.B., N.Y. U., 1952; LL.B., Yale, 1955. Admitted to N.Y. bar, 1955; practice law, N.Y.C., 1955—; asst. gen. atty. to trustee Hudson & Manhattan R.R. Co., N.Y.C., 1958-61; asso. Delson, Levin & Gordon, N.Y.C., 1961-65; partner firm Delson & Gordon, 1965-76; sec. Mgmt. Assistance Inc., 1970—, sr. v.p., gen. counsel, 1976—, also dir. Served with AUS, 1956-58. Mem. Am., N.Y. State bar assns., Assn. Bar City N.Y., Phi Beta Kappa. Jewish. Club: Yale (N.Y.C.). Home: 132 E 35th St New York NY 10016 Office: 300 E 44th St New York NY 10017

BERESFORD, JOHN P., advt. exec.; b. Short Hills, N.J., July 22, 1917; s. Percival and Ethel (Addenbrooke) B.; grad. Lawrenceville Sch., 1935; student Yale, 1936; m. Solita Arbib, Apr. 5, 1965; children—Sheila, Bridget, Stephen, Charles. Vice pres. Cecil & Dresbrey, Inc., N.Y.C., 1950-54; exec. v.p., dir. McCann-Erickson, Inc., N.Y.C., 1954-65; exec. v.p. Advt. Measurements, Inc., N.Y.C., 1965-67; pres. Data Base Corp., N.Y.C., 1967-69; chmn. exec. com., dir. Norman, Craig & Kummel, Inc. (now NCK Orgn. Ltd.), N.Y.C., 1969—. Served to capt. AUS, 1944-47; ETO. Home: 36 Sutton Pl S New York NY 10022 Office: 919 3d Ave New York NY 10022*

BERETTA, DAVID, rubber products co. exec.; b. Cranston, R.I., July 16, 1928; B.S. in Chem. Engring., U. R.I.; postgrad. R.I. Coll., U. Conn.; m. Serena Shuebruk, Nov. 1954; children— David, Norman, Martha. Research asst. Fram Corp., East Providence, R.I., 1949-51; engr. chem. div. Uniroyal, Inc., Middlebury, Conn., 1953-62, gen. foreman prodn. dept., Naugatuck, Conn., 1962-65, factory mgr., 1965-66, v.p. charge chem. ops. in Can., 1966-68, v.p. mktg. Uniroyal, Ltd., 1968-70, pres. Uniroyal Chem., 1970-72, group v.p. charge footwear, consumer, indsl., chem. and textile ops., 1972-74, operating officer, 1974, chmn., chief exec. officer, chmn. exec. com., dir. Uniroyal, Inc., Middlebury, 1975-80, pres., 1974-78, chmn., 1975—; mem. adv. bd. Colonial Bank & Trust Co., Waterbury, Conn.; dir. Rubicon Chems., Inc., Monochem, Inc., Geismar Industries, Inc. Mem. Conn. Pub. Expenditures Council. Chmn., Research Inst., U. Waterloo, Ont.; mem. adv. council Coll. Engring., Notre Dame U. Served with Chem. Corps, AUS, 1951-53. Mem. Am. Inst. Chem. Engrs., Am. Chem. Soc., Hwy. Users Fedn. (dir.), R.I. Soc. Profl. Engrs. Office: Uniroyal Inc World Hdqrs Middlebury CT 06749

BERETZ, PAUL BASIL, mfg. co. exec.; b. Washington, Oct. 15, 1938; s. O.P. and Marthe B.; B.B.A., U. Notre Dame, 1960, M.B.A., Golden Gate U., 1974; married; 5 children. Credit rep. Union Carbide Corp., N.Y.C., 1961-65, asst. credit mgr., Atlanta, 1966-67, San Francisco, 1967-69, mgr. Western credit region, 1970-79, mgr. central credit dept., N.Y.C., 1979—; instr. Nat. Assn. Credit Mgmt., San Francisco, 1976-78, Am. Mgmt. Assn., Los Angeles, 1976; mem. faculty St. Mary's Coll., Moraga, Calif. and Golden Gate U., San Francisco, 1979-80. Recipient Exec. award Stanford U., 1972. Mem. Nat. Assn. Credit Mgmt. (v.p., dir.), Nat. Chem. Credit Assn. (chmn. Pacific div. 1974-75), Nat. Inst. Credit (pres. San Francisco 1974). Republican. Roman Catholic. Club: Bay Area U. Notre Dame (past pres., dir.). Sponsor M-2 Calif. Prison Authority. Office: Union Carbide Corp 270 Park Ave New York NY 10017

BERG, ALAN SULZBERGER, oil co. exec.; b. Phila., June 7, 1930; s. Abram Sulzberger and Elsie (Friedman) B.; student Bergen Jr. Coll., 1948-49, Gen. Motors Inst. Tech., 1950-51. With Neatsfoot Oil Refiners Corp., Phila., 1952—, pres., 1968—; pres. Calber Chem., Inc., 1971-77, Glue Specialty Co., Inc., Phila., 1954—. Mem. Phila. Oil Trade Assn. (dir., golf chmn.), Am. Oils and Fats Assn. Club: Philmont Country. Home: 7911 Ronaece Dr Elkins Park PA 19117 Office: Neatsfoot Oil Refiners Corp E Ontario and Bath Sts Philadelphia PA 19134

BERG, EUGENE PAULSEN, mfg. co. exec.; b. Chgo., May 25, 1913; s. Christian Paulsen and Mae Olive (Mathews) B.; B.S. in Mech. Engring., Purdue U., 1937; M.B.A., U. Chgo., 1945; m. Margaret Louise Hughes, Jan. 21, 1939; children—Charles, Paula. With Link-Belt Co., Chgo., 1937-60, gen. mgr., 1950-60; exec. v.p. Bucyrus-Erie Co., South Milwaukee, Wis., 1960-62, pres., 1962-77, chmn. bd., 1963-77; pres., chmn. bd. Bucyrus-Erie Co. Can., Ltd., Toronto, Ont., 1963-77; chmn. bd. Ruston Bucyrus, Ltd., Lincoln, Eng., 1962-77; pres. Automatic Spring Coiling Co., Chgo., 1978—; dir. Interlake Inc., Chgo., Abex Corp., Cross & Trecker Corp., Research Cottrell, Rovac Corp., Gen. Am. Investors Co. Chmn., Pres.'s Council, Purdue U., 1973. Mem. ASME (chmn. Chgo. 1956), Delta Upsilon, Pi Tau Sigma. Clubs: Economic, Yacht (Chgo.); Westmoreland Country (Wilmette, Ill.); Bath and Tennis (Lake Forest); Onwentsia. Home: 24 Shawnee Ln Lake Forest IL 60045

BERG, GORDON HERCHER, investment banker; b. New Haven, May 14, 1937; s. John Edward and Dazma Charlotte (Hercher) B.; A.B., Ohio Wesleyan U., 1959; M.B.A., N.Y. U., 1962; postgrad Stonier Grad. Sch. Banking, 1968; m. Ruth Isabella Gardner, Aug. 26, 1961; children—Elizabeth Gardner, Deborah Brewster, Mary Chilton, Beatrice Gardner, Gordon Edward Gardner. Loan officer Irving Trust Co., N.Y.C., 1959-64; v.p. New Eng. Mchts. Bank, Boston, 1964-68; partner Sprague Co., Boston, 1968-71; pres. Berg & Co., Boston, 1971—; dir. various cos. Pres. bd. trustees Derby Acad.; v.p. Duxbury Hist. Soc.; past bd. dirs. Mass., Nat. assns. mental health. Mem. Mortgage Bankers Assn. Am., Mass. Mortgage Bankers Assn. (gov.), Hosp. Fin. Mgmt. Assn. Episcopalian. Clubs: Duxbury Yacht; Racquet (N.Y.C.); Masons. Contbr. articles to profl. jours. Home: Louisburg Sq Boston MA 02108 Office: 175 Federal St Boston MA 02110

BERG, LOUIS LESLIE, investment exec.; b. Vienna, Austria, Dec. 27, 1919; s. Gustav and Hedwig (Kohn) B.; came to U.S., 1938, naturalized, 1943; student U. Vienna, 1937-38, Coll. City N.Y., 1941-43; m. Minnette Whitman, Aug. 28, 1959; children—Sharon, Randee, Michel. Pres., Gt. Empire Corp., N.Y.C., 1946—, Bendalou Real Estate Corp., N.Y.C., 1950-60, Netherlands Securities Co., Inc., N.Y.C., 1959-62, Imported Automotive Parts, Ltd., Long Island City, N.Y., I.A.P. Inc., Lyndhurst, N.J.; dir. Internat. Aviation Corp., Cosmos Industries, Kane-Miller Corp., Knickerbocker Toy Co., Inc., Vernitron Corp., Jet Aero Corp., Fidelity Am. Finance Corp., S.W. Fla. Enterprises, Sulray Inc., U.S. Airlines, Commuter Airlines, Aviation Equipment. Mem. Am. Mgmt. Assn. Club: Wings. Home: 945 5th Ave New York NY 10021 also 50 Hagiva Savyon Israel Office: 220 Clay Ave Lyndhurst NJ 07071

BERG, SIEGFRIED KURT, electronics engr.; b. Gelsenkirchen, W. Ger., , May 4, 1922; s. Adolph Eduard and Ida Hedwig (Matz) B.; came to U.S., 1951, naturalized, 1958; grad. Behring-Sch., Hohenstein, Ger., 1939, Sch. Communications, Flensburg, Ger., 1941; m. Waltraud Rybak, May 13, 1952. Founder, owner Deutscher Rundfunk Chgo., German radio broadcasting, 1952—, interviewer, program dir., 1952-68; owner Orbit Printing and Advt. Service, Chgo., 1963-68; engring. constrn. technician GTE Automatic Electric, Northlake, Ill., 1968-73, process engr., 1973-77, test engr., 1977—; program dir. Deutscher Rundfunk Chgo., 19—. Cert. mfg. technologist Soc. Mfg. Engrs.; cert. profl. mcht. Bd. Trade and Industry and C. of C., Allenstein, Ger. Mem. IEEE. Lutheran. Clubs: Rheinischer Verein, Schlaraffia (Chgo.). Work included Blue Book Am. Photography, 1971-72. Home: 2124 W Giddings St Chicago IL 60625 Office: GTE Automatic Electric E-6 Northlake IL 60164

BERG, STEPHEN WARREN, govt. ofcl.; b. Washington, Jan. 21, 1948; s. Isidore and Dorothy (Faust) B.; B.A., Tulane U., 1970; M.S., Shippensburg State Coll., 1976; m. Linda Ann Burns, Nov. 7, 1975; children—Ashley Michelle, Marcus Alan. Program analyst Dept. of Army, New Cumberland, Pa., Ft. Monmouth, N.J., Chambersburg, Pa., 1972-75; program mgr. Army Office Environ. Program, Washington, 1975-76; chief, directorate support br. Army Corps of Engrs., Washington, 1976-78; chief coordination and support br. Public Bldgs. Service, Washington, 1978-79, chief mgmt. control and analysis br., 1979—. Mem. Am. Soc. Public Adminstrn. Home: 19201 Tilford Way Germantown MD 20767 Office: 18th and F Sts NW Washington DC 20405

BERG, WILLIAM MICHAEL, candy co. exec.; b. Grand Haven, Mich., Nov. 12, 1947; s. Lawrence William and Mary Helen (Nowacki) B.; B.B.A. (Regents Alumni Scholar 1966-70, Mich. Higher Edn. grantee 1966-70, Ednl. Opportunity grantee, 1966-67), U. Mich., 1970; M.B.A., DePaul U., 1980; m. Susan Marie Steffens, Aug. 28, 1976. Mgr. Seaway Party Store, Grand Haven, Mich., 1972-75; accounts payable mgr. Community Discount Centers, Chgo., 1975-76; accounts payable supr. G.D. Searle & Co., Skokie, Ill., 1976-77; cost analyst Sargent & Lundy, Chgo., 1977-78; acctg. supr. Curtiss Candy div. Standard Brands, Inc., Chgo., 1978—. Vol. worker 49th Ward Regular Democratic Orgn., Chgo. Roman Catholic. Club: U. Mich. (Chg.). Home: 1133 W Albion St Chicago IL 60626 Office: Curtiss Candy Div Standards Brands Inc 3638 N Broadway Chicago IL 60613

BERGE, OLE M., internat. trade union ofcl.; b. Swift Current, Sask., Can., July 22, 1921; came to U.S., 1948, naturalized, 1955; s. Thorstein and Thora (Bjorgum) B.; student Harvard U., 1963; m. Katherine Ann Anderson; children—Katherine Ann, Linda Maureen, Ola Loraine. Bridge and bldg. helper, carpenter, pipe-fitter Great No. Ry., Nelson, B.C., 1941; sec.-treas., chmn. grievance com., rec. sec., jour. agt. BMWE Lodge 1426, Seattle, 1948-66, mem. exec. bd. Great No. System div., 1953-66, staff asst., Chgo., 1966-73, Grand Lodge v.p., 1973-78, pres. Grand Lodge, Brotherhood of Maintenance-of-Way Employees, AFL-CIO & CLC, Detroit, 1978—.

Mem. Ry. Labor Execs. Assn. Lutheran. Office: 12050 Woodward Ave Detroit MI 48203

BERGE, PAUL MORTON, banker; b. Manitowoc, Wis., Nov. 11, 1937; s. Morton K. and Amanda E. (Peterson) B.; B.B.A., U. Wis., 1960; m. Mary Bernadine Roberta Kunz, Aug. 20, 1960; children—Robert, Maren. With Affiliated Bank of Madison (Wis.), 1959—, pres., 1976—; dir. Affiliated Bank Corp., Affiliated Banks of Hilldale, Middleton. Mem. Wis. Bankers Assn., Am. Mgmt. Assn., Bank Adminstrn. Inst., Greater Madison C. of C. (bd. dirs., past chmn. bd.). Lutheran. Clubs: Rotary, Shriners, Masons. Office: 1 W Main St Madison WI 53703

BERGEN, HOWARD SILAS, JR., chem. and plastics co. exec.; b. St. Louis, Apr. 4, 1921; s. Howard S. and Marion Leonie (Broyer) B.; B.S. in Chem. Engring., Washington U., St. Louis, 1942; m. Joan Town, Apr. 27, 1963; children—Lisa T., Laurie A.; children by previous marriage—Bruce H., Patricia A. Engaged in plasticizer devel. Monsanto Co., St. Louis, 1946-55, field sales specialist, 1955-57, product mgr. plasticizers, 1957-64, dir. sales, 1964-67, sales dir. functional fluids, 1967-68, bus. dir. functional fluids, 1968-70, bus. dir. specialty products, 1970-76; pres. Shintech, Inc., Houston, 1976-77; gen. mgr. resins Ga.-Pacific Corp., Atlanta, 1978-81, v.p., 1981—. Served to capt. USAF, 1942-46. Mem. Am. Chem. Soc., Soc. Plastics Industry, Paper Industry Mgmt. Assn., Pulp Chem. Assn., Sigma Xi, Alpha Chi Sigma. Methodist. Clubs: Forest Hills Country (Chesterfield, Mo.); Atlanta Athletic; Pine Forest Country (Houston). Contbr. articles in plastic field, market research to profl. lit. Home: 1792 Castle Way NE Atlanta GA 30345

BERGEON, JOSEPH STEPHEN, electronic component distributing co. exec.; b. N.Y.C., May 20, 1941; s. Joseph J. and Mary B. (Lappano) B.; B.E., CCNY, 1964; M.B.A., Ariz. State U., 1973; m. Annemari Brui, Feb. 25, 1968; children—William S., Yvonne M. Supr. engring. Philco Ford Corp., 1970-72; gen. mgr. Jensen Tools, Phoenix, 1973-77; pres. BK Sweeney Mfg. Co., Denver, 1977-80; v.p. Marshall Industries, Los Angeles, 1980—; lectr. in field. Served to capt. C.E., U.S. Army, 1964-66. Decorated Bronze Star. Mem. Am. Mgmt. Assn., ASCE. Home: 1912 E Alto Ln Fullerton CA 92631 Office: 9672 Telstar Ave El Monte CA 91731

BERGER, FRANK S., consumer products exec.; b. N.Y.C., Nov. 6, 1936; s. Ernest A. and Anna (Weiss) B.; B.A., Queens Coll., 1958; M.B.A., N.Y. U., 1960, postgrad. Law Sch., 1961; postgrad. IBM Exec. Edn. Center; m. Judith Kugel, Jan. 15, 1966; children—Evan, Stacey. Supr. mktg. and fin. analysis dept. Lever Bros., 1959-61; v.p. fin. and adminstrn. Pacific Enterprises, 1961-62; corp. mktg. staff Joseph E. Seagram & Sons, Inc., 1962-63; mktg. asst. to central div. mgr. Calvert Distillers, 1964, asst. state mgr., Fla., 1965, state mgr., N.J., 1966-67, asst. eastern div. mgr., 1967-68, so. div. mgr., 1969-70; v.p., gen. sales mgr. Frankfort Distillers, 1970-71, exec. v.p. mktg. and fin., 1972-73; pres. Gen. Wine & Spirits Co., N.Y.C., 1973-76; pres. Seagram Distillers Co., 1976-77, House of Seagram, 1978-79; chmn., pres. Quadrillon Investment Co.; chmn. bd. Hazel Bishop Industries, Inc. Chmn., N.Y. Lunch-o-Ree, Boy Scouts Am., United Jewish Appeal, Gaucho Basketball Assn., Cystic Fibrosis Soc.; exec. com. wine and spirits div. Anti-Defamation League; Pro-Am tennis sponsor Cerebral Palsy; bd. dirs. Bronfman Found. Served with AUS, 1958. Mem. Am. Mgmt. Assn., Am. Mktg. Assn., N.Y. C. of C., A.I.M., Young Pres.'s Orgn., Pres.'s Assn. Clubs: Advt. N.Y., N.Y. Sales Execs. Office: 185 Sumner Ave Kenilworth NJ 07033

BERGER, JOHN EDWARD, real estate exec.; b. Chgo., Feb. 18, 1929; s. Edward and Marie Dorothy (Mahoney) B.; B.S., Loyola U., 1952; m. Mary Rose Lennon, Nov. 17, 1956; children—John Edward, Michael G., William F., Mary Therese, Joan M., Nancy M. Owner, real estate broker John E. Berger & Co., Chgo., 1954-73 (merger McKey & Poague, Inc. 1973), v.p., 1973—; dir., 1974—, regional sales mgr., 1977, gen. sales mgr., 1978—, mem. exec. com., 1978—; pres. McKey & Poague Real Estate Sales Inc., 1980—, McKey & Poague Real Estate Services, 1980—. Vice pres. S.E. Community Orgn., Chgo., 1962-64. Served to lt. USMC, 1951-53. Mem. Chgo. Real Estate Bd. (v.p. 1970—, dir. 1968-70, gov. brokers div. 1967-68), South Side Real Estate Bd. (pres. 1973—, dir. 1968-70), Beverly Suburban Real Estate Bd. (sec. 1975, treas. 1976, dir. 1978), Chgo. Property Mgrs. Assn., Loyola U. Alumni Assn., Ill. Assn. Real Estate Bds. (dist. v.p. 1969-70), Chgo. Athletic Assn. Club: Flossmoor Country. Home: 1266 Berry Ln Flossmoor IL 60422 Office: care McKey & Poague Real Estate Sales Inc 10540 S Western Ave Chicago IL 60643

BERGER, JOHN HANUS, biol. and chem. co. exec.; b. Plzen, Czechoslovakia, May 5, 1919; s. Otto and Martha (Weigner) B.; came to U.S., 1960, naturalized, 1965; B.S. in Chem. Engring., Prague State Coll., Charles U., 1939; cert. in English, U. Cambridge (Eng.), 1944; mgmt. course UCLA, 1979; m. Magda Jakubovic, Jan. 18, 1953; 1 son, Joseph Abraham. Asst. plant maintenance engr. Consol. Refinerie Ltd., Brit. Petroleum, Haifa, Israel and London, 1949-57; prodn. mgr. Resimon-Montana, C.A., Caracas, Venezuela, 1957-60; resin house supr. Glidden Co., Chgo., 1960-63; plant mgr. Hooker Glass & Paint Mfg. Co., Chgo., 1963-68; dir. mfg. Enterprise Paint Mfg. Co., Chgo., 1968-71; cons. to major coating cos., 1971-76; mfg. mgr. bioproducts Beckman Instruments, Palo Alto, Calif., 1976—. Served with Brit. Army, 1940-45. Recipient award Nat. Safety Council, 1966. Mem. Soc. Coating Tech., Am. Chem. Soc., Nat. Safety Council, AAU. Developed fiberglass-polyester resin prodn. methods for boat and furniture industries; dispersion methods for sand mills; large-scale mfg. of peptides. Home: 707 Continental Circle Apt 621 Mountain View CA 94040 Office: 1117 California Ave Palo Alto CA 94304

BERGER, LOUIS WILLIAM, mfg. co. exec.; b. N.Y.C., Jan. 12, 1918; s. Abram and Gussie Berger; B.S., Fordham U., 1940; m. T. Deane Samuels, Sept. 7, 1941; children—Hope Amelia, Anthony Lincoln. Acct., Gen. Electric Co., Schenectady, 1940-43, 46; chief acct. Tach Airways, N.Y.C., 1946-48, Mohawk Airlines, Teterboro, N.J., 1948-51; v.p. fin., dir. Elkay Industries, Wilkes-Barre, Pa., 1952—. Served with U.S. Army, 1943. Mem. Nat. Assn. Accts., Fin. Execs. Inst. Republican. Jewish. Club: Westmoreland (Wilkes-Barre). Author: Direct Costing-Selected Papers, 1965. Home: RD 7 Box 44 Shavertown PA 18708 Office: 32 Forrest St Wilkes-Barre PA 18703

BERGER, MURRY PEARSON, food prodn. and distbg. co. exec.; b. McKeesport, Pa., Jan. 24, 1926; s. Charles and Fannie Berger; grad. Duquesne U., 1948; M.A., Hofstra U., 1952; m. Helen Walsh, Apr. 23, 1947; children—John Lee, Keith David. Sales mgr. Seapak Corp., St. Simon's Island, Ga., 1948-55; pres. and producer Carnations Seafoods, Oceans of the World, Inc., Gt. Neck, N.Y., 1955-69; pres., chief exec. officer Seabrook Internat. Foods (formerly Seabrook Foods, Inc.), Gt. Neck, 1969—; mem. outer continental shelf adv. bd. U.S. Dept. Interior, 1975-79; chmn. food import com. Nat. Council U.S.-China Trade, 1977-80. mem. internat. adv. bd. Columbia U. Grad. Sch. Bus., 1979-80; mem. N.J. Econ. Recovery Commn., 1974-77; bd. dirs. Duquesne U., 1978-80; trustee N.J. Pvt. Colls. Fund, 1970—, Frozen Foods Assn. Ins. Fund, 1965-80. Served with U.S. Army, 1943-46. Decorated Bronze Star; recipient Young Achiever award Golden Slipper Club of Phila., 1972. Mem. Nat. Assn. Corp. Dirs., Am. Seafood Distbrs. Assn. (pres. 1977-79), Nat. Fisheries Inst. (pres. 1976-77, chmn. bd. 1978), Am. Arbitration Assn., Eastern Frosted Food Assn. (Man of Year award 1974). Republican. Jewish. Contbr. numerous articles to profl. publs. Home: 343 Algonquin Rd Franklin Lakes NJ 07417 Office: 60 Cutter Mill Rd Great Neck NY 11021

BERGER, PAUL HAROLD, adminstrv. and loan co. exec.; b. Cleve., Oct. 14, 1924; s. Ted Ross and Helen (Hirsh) B.; student Tex. A. and M., 1942-43, So. Methodist U., 1946-47, U. Chgo., 1947-51; M.A. in Social Scis., U. Chgo., 1956; m. Phyllis Ottem, July 31, 1954; children—Jessica E., Avery Ross. Adminstrv. asst. to city alderman, Chgo., 1949-51; sales rep. Mich. Steel Supply, Chgo., 1951-53, Abbot Screw & Bolt, Chgo., 1953-54; campaign staff Merriam for Mayor Com., Chgo., 1945-55; ins. broker, Chgo., 1955-67; chmn. bd., pres. Hyde Park Fed. Savs. & Loan Assn., Chgo., 1961—. Treas., Mid South Side Health Planning Orgn., 1969-71; dist. chmn. Boy Scouts Am., 1968-69; bd. dirs. Mary McDowell Settlement, Chgo., 1957-64, v.p., 1960-61; bd. dirs. Southeast Chgo. Commn., 1964—, Hyde Park-Kenwood Community Conf., 1964-67; bd. dirs., treas. First Unitarian Soc. Chgo., 1963-64; treas. Gateway Houses Found., Inc., 1969-74; bd. dirs. Woodlawn Hosp., 1964-74; bd. dirs. Met. Fair and Expn. Authority, 1975-80, vice chmn., 1978-80; bd. dirs. Community Services and Research Corp., 1975-80; bd. dirs., pres. Hyde Park-Kenwood Devel. Corp., 1974—; bd. dirs. Chgo. Renewal Efforts Service Corp., 1973—, chmn., 1976—. Served to 1st sgt. AUS, 1943-46. Decorated Combat Infantryman's Badge with 2 battle stars. Mem. Million Dollar Round Table (life). Clubs: Econ. of Chgo., Quadrangle (Chgo.). Home: 5816 S Blackstone Ave Chicago IL 60637 Office: 5250 S Lake Park Ave Chicago IL 60615

BERGERAC, MICHEL C., cosmetic co. exec.; b. 1932; B.A., Sorbonne U., Paris, M.A. in Econs., 1953; M.B.A., U. Calif. at Los Angeles, 1955; married. Asst. factory mgr. U.S. Divers Corp., Los Angeles, 1956-57; sales rep., then mgr., v.p.-inter nat. Cannon Elec. Co., Los Angeles, 1957-66; chief exec. v.p., then pres. ITT Europe, Inc., 1966-74; pres., chief exec. officer, chmn. bd. Revlon, Inc., N.Y.C., 1974—, also dir.; dir. Mfrs. Hanover Trust Co., Mfrs. Hanover Corp. Bd. dirs. World Wildlife Fund-U.S. Office: Revlon Inc 767 Fifth Ave New York NY 10022*

BERGEVIN, YVON JOSEPH, constrn. materials exec.; b. Shoreham, Vt., Aug. 30, 1942; s. Louis and Jeanne (DeForge) B.; B.A., U. Vt., 1964; M.B.A., U. Chgo., 1977; m. Karen Gibson, June 13, 1970; children—Kristen, Christopher. Constrn. supt., mgr. F.A. Tucker, Inc., Rutland, Vt., 1966-68, v.p. ops., 1969-72; mem. corp. staff L.E. Myers Co., Chgo., 1973, v.p. Myers-Oak Communication Constrn. Inc., Chgo., 1974; with corp. estimating L.E. Myers Co., 1975-76, equipment mgr., 1977-79; v.p.-equipment Flintkote Stone Products' Co., Hunt Valley, Md., 1979—. Served to 1st lt. U.S. Army, 1964-66; Korea. Home: 14009 Greencroft Ln Cockeysville MD 21030 Office: Flintkote Stone Products Executive Plaza IV Hunt Valley MD 21031

BERGHORST, DAVID THEODORE, investment banker; b. Cadillac, Mich., Feb. 21, 1947; s. George Oren and Avis Louise (Thiebaut) B.; student Western Mich. U., 1965-67; B.B.A., U. Mich., 1969; M.B.A., Northwestern U., 1971; m. Deborah Burnham Hinckley, Sept. 14, 1975; 1 dau., Sarah Hinckley. Asst. v.p. 1st Nat. City Bank, N.Y.C., 1971-76; sr. v.p., group head Lawrence Systems, Inc. subs. INA Corp., San Francisco, 1976, Chgo., 1976-79; v.p. Kidder Peabody & Co. Inc., N.Y.C., 1979, Chgo., 1980—. Club: University (Chgo.). Home: 364 Jackson Ave Glencoe IL 60022 Office: 125 S Wacker Dr Chicago IL 60606

BERGLEITNER, GEORGE CHARLES, JR., investment banker; b. Bklyn., July 16, 1935; s. George C. and Marie (Preitz) B.; B.B.A., St. Francis Coll., 1959; M.B.A., Coll. City N.Y., 1961; m. Betty Van Buren, Oct. 29, 1966; children—George Charles III, Michael John, Stephen William. Dir. instl. sales A.T. Brod & Co., N.Y.C., 1965-66, Weis, Voisin & Cannon, Inc., N.Y.C., 1966-67; dir. sales C.B. Richard, Ellis & Co., N.Y.C., 1967-68; pres. M.J. Manchester & Co., Inc., N.Y.C., 1968—; chmn. Delhi Internat. Ltd.; dir. B.J.B. Graphics, Inc., First Coinvestors, Inc., Jay Co., Computer Holdings Corp., Anka Research Ltd., Microlab/ FXR, Devon Internat. Ltd., Computer Engring. Corp.; v.p., dir. Delhi Chems. Inc., Delhi Mfg., Delhi Industries. Chmn., Francisco Fathers Devel. Program; trustee Stamford Community Hosp.; mem. council regents St. Francis Coll.; bd. dirs., chmn. fund drive Stamford Community Hosp. Recipient Franciscan Spirit award, 1959; Honor Legion award N.Y.C. Police Dept., 1970; John F. Kennedy Meml. award, 1972; Internat. award for service to investment community, 1972. Mem. Assn. Investment Brokers, Cath. War Vets., Nat., Phila.-Balt.-Washington stock exchanges, N.Y. Merc. Exchange, Security Traders Assn. N.Y., Am. Inst. Mgmt., Alumni Assn. St. Francis Coll. (dir.), UN Assn. Republican. Clubs: K.C., Moose; Touchdown, Downtown Athletic, New York Athletic (N.Y.C.); Stamford Country, Rotary (pres.) (Stamford). Home: Hobart NY 13788 Office: Delhi Bldg Stamford NY 12167

BERGMAN, BARRY EDWARD, ins. exec.; b. Bronx, Aug. 13, 1945; s. Mortimer Aaron and Mary (Axelrod) B.; A.A., Queensborough Coll., 1965; B.A., Queens Coll., 1967; m. Iris Libow, Aug. 26, 1967; children—Jill Renee, Lauren Rae, Jeremy Scott, Jonathan Reid. Adminstrv. asst. to ops. partner Eastman Dillon & DuPont Glove Forgan Inc., N.Y.C., 1967-70; with Prudential Ins. Am., Bohemia, N.Y., 1970—, div. mgr., 1971-73, agy. mgr., 1973—. CLU. Mem. Nat. Assn. Life Underwriters, Gen. Agents and Mgrs. Conf., Am. Soc. CLU. Liberal. Club: Kiwanis. Home: 3 Tarleton Ct Fort Salonga NY 11768 Office: 40 Orville Dr Bohemia NY 11716

BERGMAN, PHILIP HARVEY, bus. educator; b. N.Y.C., Aug. 31, 1941; s. Abraham M. and Dorothy (Metsch) B.; B.B.A., U. Miami, 1962; M.S., Fla. Internat. U., 1975; m. Rochelle Carole Pachman, Nov. 22, 1962; children—Steven, David. Staff acct. Coopers & Lybrand, 1962-65; analyst, auditor James Talcott, Inc., Newark, 1965-67; controller Hotel America, Houston, 1967-69; supervising cons. Laventhol & Horwath, Miami, Fla., 1969-71; individual practice acctg., Miami, 1971-77; pres. Fin. and Adminstrv. Services, Inc., Miami, 1978-80; pres., chief exec. officer Disc Corp., Miami, 1980—; prof. commerce Fla. Internat. U., Miami, 1975—. Mem. Am. Inst. C.P.A.'s, Fla. Inst. C.P.A.'s. Clubs: Kiwanis, Masons. Office: 8101 Biscayne Blvd Suite 517 Miami FL 33138

BERGMAN, ROBERT SCRIBNER, toy mfr.; b. Aurora, Ill., Nov. 23, 1934; s. Ross Matthew and Mary (Ochsenschlager) B.; B.S. in Physics, Ill. Inst. Tech., 1956; postgrad. Stanford, 1956-58; m. Mary Patricia LeBaron, June 10, 1956; children—David Clinton, Lynne Mary, Joseph Ross. Engr., Hughes Aircraft Co., summer 1956, microwave labs. Gen. Electric Co., summer 1957; asso. engr. Varian Assos., 1957; engr. microwave products lab. Sylvania Electric Co., 1958-61; with Processed Plastic Co., Inc., Montgomery, Ill., 1961—, pres., 1969—; pres. Bergman Mfg. & Trading Co., Inc., 1962—, Processed Plastic (Can.) Ltd., Lachine, Que., 1974—; v.p. Moldrite Tool and Die Co., Moldrite Plastic and Engring. Co.; treas. Graphic Label Co., Intertoy; dir. David Lipman (Toys) Ltd., Leeds, Eng. Mem. Am. Mgmt. Assn. (pres.'s assn.), Alpha Sigma Phi, Sigma Pi Sigma. Conglist. Home: 1330 Monona Ave Aurora IL 60506 Office: 1001 Aucutt Rd Montgomery IL 60538

BERGMAN, YIGAL JACOB, apparel mfg. co. exec.; b. Petah Tikvah, Israel, Mar. 1, 1940; s. Joshua A. and Matilda (Gottlieb) B.; B.S., Phila. Coll. Textiles and Sci., 1965; M.B.A., Bernard M. Baruch Coll., 1974; m. Michelle Joyce Pines, June 27, 1967; children—Jed Isaac, Deborah Eve. Asst. to pres. Glenhaven Ltd., N.Y.C., 1965-67; merchandiser controller Mill Fabrics Co., N.Y.C., 1967-70; divisional merchandiser Contanc div. Miller Bros. Industries, N.Y.C., 1970—, now v.p. merchandising jeans and slacks divs. Bd. dirs. B'nai B'rith Hillel Found., Bklyn. Coll. Served with Israeli Army, 1958-60. Republican. Jewish. Office: 135 W 50th St New York NY 10020

BERGMANN, ROBERT LEWIS, data processing exec.; b. St. Louis, Jan. 21, 1926; s. William G. and Elvera O. (Baum) B.; B.S. in Commerce, St. Louis U., 1949; m. Dorothy E. Thoma, July 24, 1954; children—Laura A., Alice M., Thomas C., Karen S. Sr. auditor Arthur Andersen & Co., St. Louis, 1949-55; mgr. adminstrv. data processing McDonnell Aircraft Corp., St. Louis, 1955-64; v.p. data processing Merc. Trust Co. N.A., St. Louis, 1964-73, sr. v.p., 1973-80, exec. v.p., 1980—; chmn. bd. Payment and Adminstrv. Communications Corp./Payment and Telecommunications Services Corp., 1980—. Served with USAAF, 1944-45. C.P.A., Mo. Mem. Am. Inst. C.P.A.'s, Data Processing Mgmt. Assn., Assn. for Systems Mgmt. (past pres. St. Louis), Mo. Assn. for Systems Mgmt. (Merit award 1974). Clubs: K.C. (past pres. St. Louis), Mo. Athletic (St. Louis). Office: PO Box 524 St Louis MO 63166

BERGMOSER, J. PAUL, automobile mfg. co. exec.; b. 1916; student Wayne State U.; B.S., U. Detroit. With Ford Motor Co., 1946-79; exec. v.p. procurement and supply group Chrysler Corp., Detroit, 1979-80, pres., chief operating officer, dir., 1980—. Office: Chrysler Corp 12000 Lynn Townsend Dr Box 1919 Detroit MI 48231*

BERGQUIST, JAY CHISM, computer co. exec.; b. Logan, Utah, May 24, 1948; s. A. Lee and Mary C. Bergquist; student Idaho State U., Pocatello, 1966-68, U. Utah, 1968-70; m. Linda Crane, Jan. 15, 1970; children—Erika, Derek, Daks. Stock broker Kesko & Co., Salt Lake City, 1968-69; ops. mgr. Computer Mgmt. Corp., Salt Lake City, 1969-70; owner Computer Hub, Inc., Salt Lake City, 1970—, chmn. bd., 1974—; founder, 1976, since chmn. bd. Hubco Mgmt. Inc., also Hubco Properties Ltd.; founder Hubco Data Products Corp., 1976; dir. Paradox Resources Co. Club: Willow Creek Country (treas., dir. 1979-80). Office: 5899 S State St Salt Lake City UT 84107

BERGSCHNEIDER, MARC CHRISTIAN, investment banker; b. Fayetteville, Ark., June 22, 1951; s. Johnfried Georg and Francesca Ward (Birckhead) B.; B.A., Brown U., 1973; M.B.A. in Fin. and Acctg., U. Chgo., 1977; m. Theodora Ann Vender, June 17, 1978. Regional dir. mktg. S.E., Planned Equity Corp. subs. CNA Corp., 1973-75; asst. v.p. corp. fin. Kidder, Peabody & Co., N.Y.C., 1977—. Mem. Am. Fin. Assn. Republican. Greek Orthodox. Office: 10 Hanover Sq New York NY 10005

BERGSTEIN, ROBERT ALLEN, cons. co. exec.; b. Bklyn., Nov. 1, 1934; s. Bennett Lewis and Dorothy (Stavin) B.; B.S. in Econs., U. Pa., 1967; postgrad. in Econs., S.D. State U.; grad. Air Command and Staff Coll., 1969; M.B.A., Western New Eng. Coll., 1971; postgrad. Cath. U., 1974; m. Margaret Rose Macklin, Feb. 2, 1957; children—Lynn Ellen, Diane Alison, Bennett Edward. Mgmt. trainee Standard Toykraft, 1953; customer service technician State N.Y. Ins. Dept., 1954; commd. 2d lt. USAF, 1956, advanced through grades to lt. col., 1973; SAC combat crew mem., 1957-60, squadron comdr., 1960-64, dep. comdr. services, 1965-66, comdr. mgmt. engring. detachments, 1967-70; br. chief mgmt. engring. Hdqrs. SAC, 1970-72; Hdqrs. USAF staff manpower officer, 1973-75; pres., chmn. bd. Mgmt. & Profit Systems, Inc., Springfield, Mass., 1975—; dir. Better Bus. Bur. of Western Mass., Upper State St. Devel. Corp.; adj. prof. behavioral sci. Western New Eng. Coll., 1970, bus. adminstrn. Bellevue Coll., 1970-72; lectr. U. Mass. Inst. Govtl. Studies and SBA. Pres., PTA, Dow AFB, Maine, 1960, Anderson AFB, Guam, 1963; pres. Synagogue of the Hills, S.D., 1968. Mem. Am. Inst. Indsl. Engrs., Ret. Officers Assn., Springfield C. of C. (small bus. adv. com.), Tau Epsilon Phi. Office: 110 Maple St Springfield MA 01101

BERHALTER, WALTER ANTHONY, service co. exec.; b. Chgo., July 20, 1946; s. Howard Robert and Marilee A. (Miles) B.; B.A. in Communications, B.A. in Edn., Eastern Wash. State U., 1971, M.B.A., 1977; J.D. (scholar), Gonzaga U., 1978. Tchr., Wash., 1971-75; bus. mgr. M & M Corp., 1978; pres. Berhalter & Brown Bus. Services Inc., Grand Coulee, Wash., 1979—; chmn. bd. dirs. Acorn Services Inc., 1980—; gen. partner Acorn 1, 1980—; enrolled agt. IRS, 1979—; bus. cons. Bd. regents Gonzaga U.; res. police sgt. Grand Coulee Police Dept., 1978—. Mem. Grand Coulee C. of C., Wash. Bar Assn., Nat. Soc. Public Accts., Phi Alpha Delta, Phi Theta Kappa, Kappa Delta Pi, Pi Kappa Delta. Clubs: Elks, Eagles. Author: The Effects of Government Agency Regulation and Procedures on Business, 1977; The Three Little Flashlights, 1977. Home: PO Box 321 Grand Coulee WA 99133 Office: PO Box 777 Grand Coulee WA 99133

BERING, CONRAD, realtor; b. Houston, Dec. 20, 1895; s. August C. and Josephine (Pauska) B.; student U. Tex., 1914-17; m. Lorene Rogers, July 8, 1920 (dec. Nov. 1965); children—Conrad, Donald Rogers, Barbara (Mrs. Garrett S. Dundas). Owner, operator Conrad Bering Co., Houston, 1922—; chmn. bd. Longwoods Corp., Houston, 1952—; sec., treas. Bering Realty Corp., Houston, 1952—; sec.-treas. Rogers Investment, Inc., Austin, Tex. Life mem. bd. Methodist Hosp., Houston. Founder mem. Naval War Coll. Found., U.S. Naval Coll., Newport, R.I. Mem. Houston Bd. Realtors, Tex. Real Estate Assn., Navy League U.S. (hon. life pres. Houston council), Nat. Assn. Real Estate Bds., Houston C. of C. (mem. mil. affairs com.). Methodist (mem. bd.). Kiwanian. Clubs: Houston; Angleton Fishing and Hunting (mem. bd.). Home: 306 Fall River Ct Houston TX 77024 also Box 108 Route 5 Long Island Dr Lake Hamilton Hot Springs AR 71901 Office: Conrad Bering Co 2221 S Voss Rd Suite 121 Houston TX 77057

BERING, NORMAN JOSEPH, II, retail hardware store exec.; b. Houston, July 16, 1949; s. August Charles III and Lottie (Hutton) B.; B.Jour., U. Tex., 1973; m. Kelly Ann Mulligan, June 2, 1973; 1 dau., Blakely Edith. Vice-pres. Bering Home Center, Inc., Houston, 1973—; chmn. bd. Handy Hardware Wholesale, Inc., 1980—. Mem. Nat. Retail Hardware Assn., Nat. Home Center Inst. Republican. Presbyterian. Office: 6102 Westheimer Houston TX 77057

BERKELEY, NORBORNE, JR., banker; b. Bethlehem, Pa., June 5, 1922; s. Norborne and Dorothea (Randolph) B.; B.A., Yale, 1947; LL.B., U. Va., 1949; postgrad. Advanced Mgmt. Program, Harvard, 1966; m. Rowena B. Dewey, July 28, 1972; children by previous marriage—Sally, Anne, Norborne, III. Admitted to N.Y. bar, 1950; asso. firm Root, Ballantine, Harlan, Bushby & Palmer, N.Y.C., 1949-50; with Chem. Bank, N.Y.C., 1950—, exec. v.p., 1968-73, pres., 1973—, also dir.; pres., dir. Chem. N.Y. Corp., Chem. Bank; dir. Uniroyal, Inc., Middlebury, Conn., Wildcat Service Corp., Anglo Co. Ltd., N.Y.C., Freeport Minerals Co., N.Y.C. Mem. Pres.'s Adv. Com. on Trade Negotiations; bd. dirs. N.Y. Infirmary, Beekman Downtown

Hosp., N.Y.C., Vera Inst. Justice; trustee Whitney Mus. Am. Art, N.Y.C.; mng. dir. Met. Opera Assn., N.Y.C. Served with AUS, 1943-45. Mem. Assn. Res. City Bankers. Republican. Episcopalian. Clubs: Links, Yale, University (N.Y.C.); Bedens Brook (Princeton); Nat. Golf Links Am. (Southampton, N.Y.); Maidstone (East Hampton). Home: 41 Westcott Rd Princeton NJ 08540 Office: 20 Pine St New York NY 10005

BERKEY, DANIEL STEWART, small bus. cons.; b. New Brunswick, N.J., June 25, 1941; s. Richard Scott and Dorothy (Hayden) B.; B.A., Lehigh U., 1963; M.B.A., U. Pa., 1970; m. Ann Cabot Richardson, Feb. 22, 1975. Systems analyst Thomas J. Lipton, Inc., Englewood Cliffs, N.J., 1970-72; mgmt. cons. Dept. Interior, Washington, 1972-73; spl. asst. to asst. sec. Interior for energy and minerals, 1973-74; exec. asst. rates and regulatory affairs United Gas Pipe Line Co., Houston, 1975-76, mgr. research and devel., 1976-77; cons./owner Berkey & Assos. and Gen. Bus. Services, Oakland, Calif., 1977—; v.p., sec. Datatek Reprographics Inc. Bd. dirs. Kiwanis Club of Oakland Scholarship Found. Served to capt. U.S. Army, 1963-68; Vietnam. Decorated Bronze Star, Army Commendation medal. Mem. Nat. Small Bus. Assn. (Calif. legis. coordinator 1978—), Oakland C. of C. Republican. Episcopalian. Clubs: Kiwanis; Wharton (San Francisco). Home: 5100 Proctor Ave Oakland CA 94618 Office: 1845 A Berkeley Way Berkeley CA 94703

BERKEY, MAURICE EDWARD, JR., fin. exec.; b. Salem, Ind., Feb. 17, 1922; s. Maurice Edward and Ida Mae (Bush) B.; student Ind. Central Bus. Coll., 1940-41; 1 dau., Suzanne. Insp., Presto-lite Co., Inc., Speedway City, Ind., 1941, Union Carbide Co., Speedway City, 1941; with Internat. Harvester, San Antonio, 1946-59; with Roegelein Fed. Credit Union, San Antonio, 1960—, mgr., sec.-treas.; also acct. Roegelein Co., San Antonio. Served with inf. AUS., 1941-45. Mem. Smithsonian Inst., Audubon Soc., Hist. Preservation Soc., Nat. Hist. Soc. Mem. Christian Ch. Club: Masons (32 deg.).

BERKLEY, STEPHEN MARK, computer peripherols mfg. co. exec.; b. N.J., Apr. 19, 1944; s. Irving S. and Goldie A. (Karp) B.; student London Sch. Econs., 1964-65; B.A. in Econs., Colgate U., 1966; M.B.A., Harvard U., 1968; children—David, Michael. Mgmt. cons. Boston Cons. Group, 1968, 71-73; mgr. strategic planning Potlatch Corp., 1973-77; v.p. bus. devel. Qume Corp., IT&T, Hayward, Calif., 1977-80, v.p., gen. mgr. memory products div., 1980—; instr. bus. and econs. E. Carolina U., 1969-71. Served to lt. USNR, 1968-71. Mem. Corp. Planners Assn. (dir.), Harvard Bus. Sch. Club No. Calif. Office: Qume Corp IT&T 2323 Industrial Pkwy Hayward CA 94545

BERKMAN, JACK NEVILLE, lawyer, corp. exec.; b. London, Feb. 12, 1905; s. Hyman L. and Sarah (Hellman) B.; came to U.S., 1908, naturalized, 1922; A.B., U. Mich., 1926; J.D., Harvard U., 1929; m. Sybiel B. Altman, Aug. 27, 1933 (dec. May 1964); children—Myles P., Monroe E., Stephen L.; m. 2d, Lillian Duban Rojtman, Jan. 26, 1970. Admitted to Ohio bar, 1930; practice law, Steubenville, Ohio, 1930-68; chmn., pres., dir. Rust Craft Broadcasting Co., Steubenville, 1940-79, vice chmn., dir., 1979—; pres. Radio Buffalo, Inc.; chmn. exec. com., vice chmn., dir. Rust Craft Greeting Cards, Inc., N.Y.C. and Boston; pres., dir. Rust Craft Broadcasting N.Y., Inc., Rochester, Rust Craft Broadcasting Pa., Inc., Phila., also Pitts., Rust Craft Broadcasting Tenn., Chattanooga; dir. Rust Craft, Ltd., Toronto, Rust Craft Greeting Cards (U.K.) Ltd., Asso. Am. Artists, Inc., N.Y.C.; chmn., chief exec. officer, dir. Asso. Communications Corp., 1979—; past dir. Union Savs. Bank and Trust Co., Union BancShares, Sinclair Bldg. Co.; chmn. exam. com. S.E. dist. Eastern div. U.S. Dist. Ct. Ohio. Pres., trustee Sybiel B. Berkman Found.; pres. Temple Beth El; bd. dirs. emeritus Retina Found., Boston; past chmn. Tri-State Indsl. Com.; past pres. Tri-State Cerebral Palsy, Steubenville. Mem. Internat., Jefferson County (officer), Ohio (chmn. coms.), Am., FCC bar assns., Steubenville C. of C. (past officer and dir.), Radio and TV Execs. Soc., Am. Soc. for Technion (dir.), Am. Judicature Soc., Soc. of Friends Japan House N.Y. (founding mem.). Broadcasters (Washington); Steubenville Country; Culver Parents, Harvard-Yale-Princeton, Variety (Pitts.); Friars, Harmonie, Harvard (N.Y.C.). Author: (play) Playing God, 1931; also short stories, articles. Home: New York NY Office: 680 Fifth Ave New York NY 10019 also 320 Market St Steubenville OH 43952

BERKOER, MARILYN ARLENE, health care adminstr.; b. Bronx, N.Y., Feb. 8, 1944; d. William and Bernice (Goldstein) B.; student Bronx Community Coll., 1961-64, CCNY, 1965-67, West Community Coll., 1971-73, Mercy Coll., 1979—. Dir. food service New Rochelle (N.Y.) Nursing Home, 1971-73, Waring Nursing Home, also Riverside Nursing Home, Haverstraw, N.Y., 1973-78; dir. purchasing and central supply Kings Harbor Care Center, Bronx, 197S—. Mem. Hosp. Instl. Ednl. Food Service Soc. Home: 29 Hoke Dr Stony Point NY 10980 Office: 2000 E Gun Hill Rd Bronx NY 10469

BERKSON, ROBERT G., fin. cons.; b. Bklyn., Feb. 14, 1939; s. Martin and Jeanne (Wolin) B.; B.S. in Econs., Hofstra U., 1960; m. Deanna Feinberg, Mar. 26, 1972. Asst. to v.p. U.S. Trust Co., N.Y.C., 1959-61; sec./treas. Packer, Wilbur & Co., Inc., N.Y.C., 1961-70; pres. A.J. Carno Co., Inc., N.Y.C., 1971—; v.p. Berkson's Bldg. Corp., N.Y.C., 1961—, also dir.; pres. R.G. Berkson & Co., 1971—; v.p. First Jersey Securities Inc., N.Y.C., 1975—; v.p. Princeton Corporate Services 1972—, also dir.; pres. Qualitas Mgmt. Corp., N.Y.C., 1972—; dir. Rob-Len Amusement Corp. Mem. N.Y. Merc. Exchange. Home: 50 Georgian Ct East Hills NY 10577 Office: First Jersey Securities Inc 80 Broad St New York NY 10004

BERLIN, JEROME CLIFFORD, lawyer, real estate devel. co. exec.; b. N.Y.C., Aug. 23, 1942; s. Benjamin R. and Muriel (Weintraub) B.; B.S. Bus. Adminstrn., U. Fla., 1964, J.D., 1968; m. Gwen Tischler, July 30, 1977; children—Bret Jason, Sharon Nichole, Ashley Lauren. Accountant, Peat, Marwick, Mitchell & Co., Houston, 1968-69; mem. law firm Jerome C. Berlin, Miami, Fla., 1969-71; pres. Sterling Capital Investments, Inc., Miami, 1971-80; pres., chief operating officer Inprojet Corp., Miami, 1974-80; individual practice law, Miami, 1980—. Chmn., Dade County Zoning Appeals Bd., 1971-73; mem. exec. com. Anti-Defamation League, 1979—; mem. long range planning com. Variety Children's Hosp.; bd. dirs. Temple Beth-Em, Miami, Juvenile Diabetes Found. C.P.A., Fla., Tex. Mem. Am., Fla. insts. C.P.A.'s, Tex. Soc. C.P.A.'s, Fla. Bar Assn., Am. Assn. Attys. and C.P.A.'s. Jewish. Home: 5425 SW 92 St Miami FL 33156

BERLIN, RICHARD DAVID, stock broker; b. Bklyn., Aug. 11, 1933; s. Benjamin and Anna (Goldstein) B.; B.S., L.I. U., 1955; m. Norma H. Schader, Dec. 18, 1954; children—Gerri, Susan, Joyce. Prodn. mgr. Air King Luggage Co., Bklyn., 1955-63, Lifton Mfg. Co., Richmond Hill, N.J., 1963-65; sales mgr. Fedtro Inc., Rockville Centre, N.Y., 1965-69; v.p., resident mgr. Bache Halsey Stuart Shields, N.Y.C., 1969—; career cons. C.W. Post Coll., Adelphi U. Mem. Assn. Commerce and Industry L.I., Bay Shore C. of C. Club: K.P. Office: South Shore Mall 1701 Sunrise Hwy Bay Shore NY 11706

BERLINER, WILLIAM MICHAEL, mgmt. cons.; b. N.Y.C., Aug. 24, 1923; s. Samuel Louis and Anna S. (Josephine) B.; B.S., N.Y. U., 1949, M.B.A., 1953, Ph.D., 1956; m. Bertha A. Hagedorn, Apr. 27, 1946. Safety engr. Continental Casualty Co., 1941-42, 45-46; retail div. mgr. B.F. Goodrich Co., 1949-50; asst. purchasing agt. Cutler-Hammer, Inc., 1950-51; faculty mem. N.Y. U., 1951—, prof. mgmt., chmn. dept., 1965-74, prof. mgmt. and orgnl. behavior, 1974—; policy com. regents external degree program SUNY; cons. Kellogg Found.; bd. dirs., cons. OTI Services, Inc.; cons. Mfrs. Hanover Trust Co.; cons. exec. program Boys Clubs Am., 1961-67, Ford Found. Cons. Exec. Program, N.Y.C., 1961-67; cons. Am. Inst. Banking, Am. Bankers Assn., Bank Adminstrn. Inst.; faculty Stonier Grad. Sch. Banking, Rutgers U.; faculty Nat. Installment Credit Sch., Am. Bankers Assn. Served to 1st lt., USAAF, 1942-45. Decorated D.F.C., Air Medal with 6 oak leaf clusters, Purple Heart. Ford Found. grantee, 1970. Mem. Acad. Mgmt., Am. Mgmt. Assn., Am. Mktg. Assn., Beta Gamma Sigma, Alpha Kappa Psi. Republican. Club: N.Y. U. Author: (with F.A. DePhillips and J.J. Cribbin) Management of Training Programs, 1960; (with W.J. McLarney) Management Practice and Training, 1974; Managerial and Supervisory Practice, 1979. Home: 27 Perkins Rd Greenwich CT 06830 Office: 100 Trinity Pl New York NY 10006

BERMACK, CHARLES K(ALMON), pub. accountant, lawyer; b. Lutck, Russia, Mar. 17, 1902; s. Koss and Bessie (Wallach) B.; brought to U.S., 1912, naturalized, 1926; B.C.S., N.Y. U., 1924, J.D., 1928, LL.M. 1934; m. Lillian Freeman, Nov. 23, 1926; children—Eugene, Ruth (Mrs. Robert Rosenberg). Pvt. practice accounting, N.Y.C., 1927-39; sr. partner Charles K. Bermack & Co., C.P.A.'s, 1939—; admitted to N.Y. bar, 1934; now asso. Bermack & Bermack attys. Active Flatbush Jewish Comunity Council; past chmn., co-chmn. United Jewish Appeal, Roslyn area, L.I. Mem. orgn. com. Albert Einstein Med. Sch. C.P.A., N.Y. Mem. State Soc. C.P.A.'s, Jewish Chautauqua Soc., Zionist Orgn. Am., Am. Inst. C.P.A.'s, N.Y. Credit and Fin. Mgmt. Assn. Delta Mu Delta. Mason. Home: 45 Strawberry Ln Roslyn Heights NY 11577 Office: 175 Great Neck Rd Great Necks NY 11021

BERMAN, BARRY JOSEPH, stock broker, lawyer; b. N.Y.C., Apr. 8, 1942; s. Nathan Rubin and Hilda (Weiss) B.; B.B.A., Coll. Ins., N.Y.C., 1969; J.D., Fordham U., 1976. Mgr., Cosmopolitan Mut. Ins. Co., N.Y.C., 1966-69; instl. account exec. Merrill Lynch Co., Queens, N.Y., 1969-72, Oppenheimer & Co., Inc., N.Y.C., 1972-73; admitted to N.Y. bar, 1977, D.C. bar, 1979; v.p. Wertheim & Co., Inc., N.Y.C., 1973-77; v.p. B.W. Managed Accounts div. Dean Witter Reynolds Inc., N.Y.C., 1977-79; v.p., dir. fin. planning L. F. Rothschild, Unterberg Towbin, 1979—. Club: Jockey (Miami, Fla.). Home: 46 Deepdale Dr Great Neck Estates NY 11021

BERMAN, CARL MARTIN, med. supply co. exec.; b. Hartford, Conn., Mar. 22, 1945; s. Jack and Betty (Chervin) B.; B.A., U. Conn., 1968. Tchr., Lisbon (Conn.) Schs., 1969, 72; pres. Berman's Med. Service, Chgo., 1974-76, Lake Front Med. Services, Chgo., 1976—, Bio-Tech Systems, Chgo., 1977—; cons. A-K Home Med., DuPage Home Med-Care. Served with AUS, 1969-71. Decorated Bronze Star. Mem. Ill. Soc. Allergy and Clin. Immunology, Nat. Assn. Asthmatic Children, Chgo. Lung Assn., Ill. Tree House Animal Found. Club: Burnham Harbor Yacht. Office: PO Box 25417 Chicago IL 60625

BERMAN, DONALD FRANCIS, computer exporting co. exec.; b. Hartford, Conn., Jan. 30, 1941; s. Morris and Miriam (Karp) B.; B.A., U. Conn., 1962; M.A., Stanford U., 1963; m. Dorothy Ann Sherman, Apr. 11, 1970; children—Daniel, Miriam. With U.S. Dept. Labor, Washington, 1964-68; mgr. sales adminstrn., export mgr. Digital Equipment Corp., Maynard, Mass., 1968-71; pres., founder Techexport, Inc., Waltham, Mass., 1971—. Recipient U.S. Dept. Commerce Excellence in Exporting award, 1976. Mem. Assn. for Computing Machinery, Nat. Computer Graphics Assn. Jewish. Home: 17 Chatham Circle Brookline MA 02146 Office: 244 2d Ave Waltham MA 02154

BERMAN, GEORGE RICHARD, planning cons. co. exec.; b. N.Y.C., Aug. 11, 1935; s. Arthur Harold and Claire Cecile (Blumenthal) B.; B.Chem. Engring., Yale U., 1956, M.Eng., 1960; M.B.A., Columbia U., 1963; m. Rochel Udovitch, Sept. 10, 1961; children—Joshua Asher, Jonathan Eli. Mktg. tech. rep. Monsanto Chem. Co., Springfield, Mass., 1960-62; process/project engr. Shell Chem. Co., Woodbury, N.J., 1963-65; dir. bus. planning Philip Morris U.S.A., N.Y.C., 1965-77; pres. Devon Mgmt. Resources, Inc., Yonkers, N.Y., 1977—; lectr. stats. and ops. research Richmond (Va.) Coll., 1967, N.Y. U. Grad. Sch. Bus., 1969. Served to lt. USNR, 1956-59. Mem. Inst. Mgmt. Scis., N.Am. Soc. Corp. Planning, Am. Prodn. and Inventory Control Soc. Republican. Jewish. Clubs: Yale (N.Y.C.); Mory's. Contbr. articles to profl. jours. Office: 84 Franklin Ave Yonkers NY 10705

BERMAN, JACOB, banker; b. N.Y.C., June 17, 1948; s. Aaron and Tillie (Grumet) B.; B.A. cum laude, Queens Coll., 1970; M.B.A., U. Chgo., 1972; m. Helen E. Levine, Aug. 29, 1971; children—Michael Dov, Robin Lisa, Amy Lauren. With Citibank, N.Y.C., 1972-74, account officer, 1973-74; asst. v.p. Israel Discount Bank, N.Y.C., 1974-76, v.p., 1977-79, 1st v.p., mem. credit com., 1980—. Treas., bd. dirs. Yavneh Acad., Paterson, N.J., 1978—. Mem. Nat. Credit Conf., Robert Morris Assn. Club: B'nai B'rith. Home: 1655 Buckingham Rd Teaneck NJ 07666 Office: 511 Fifth Ave New York NY 10017

BERMAN, JESSE DAVID, lawyer; mfg. co. exec.; b. N.Y.C., Aug. 9, 1909; s. Benjamin and Ida (Salitsky) B.; A.B. (Blauvelt scholar), CCNY, 1930; LL.B., Columbia U., 1933, J.D., 1969; postgrad. in econs., fin. and accountancy Baruch Sch. Bus. and Civic Adminstrn., 1945-49; m. Ruth Hannah Redmond, July 24, 1937; children—Kenneth Richard, Stuart Alan. Admitted to N.Y. bar, 1934; asso. firm Samuel K. Beier, N.Y.C., 1934-35, Herman Methfessel, S.I., 1936-39, Michael H. Grae, S.I., 1940-45, Sulzberger & Sulzberger, N.Y.C., 1945-46; sect. chief tax dept. Darling Stores Corp., N.Y.C., 1946-48; controller Marjorie Lane Stores, N.Y.C., 1948-49; cost and price controller Weston Internat. Assos., N.Y.C., 1949-50; quality and material controller Republic Aviation Corp., Farmingdale, N.Y., 1951-64; bus. cons. material and manpower requirements, N.Y.C., 1964-66; manpower planner Grumman Aerospace Corp., Bethpage, N.Y., 1967-69; fin. adminstr. Target Rock Corp., East Farmingdale, N.Y., 1969—. Mem. Columbia Law Sch. Alumni Assn., Columbia U. Acad. Polit. Sci., Cousteau Soc., Nat. Audubon Soc., Linus Pauling Inst. Sci. and Medicine, Smithsonian Assos., Nat. Found. Cancer Research (founding), Nat. Wildlife Fedn., Am. Red Magen David for Israel. Jewish. Clubs: Smithtown Landing Country; K.P. (S.I.). Home: 20 Reeves St Smithtown NY 11787

BERMAN, LESLIE ROBERT, real estate and fin. exec.; b. Winnipeg, Man., Can., July 8, 1947: s. Arthur and Frances (Averbach) B.; student U. Winnipeg, 1967-70; m. Margo Silverman, Mar. 12, 1976. Pres., chief exec. officer Elbee Investments, Inc., Vancouver, B.C., Can., 1974—; v.p. Sonnenblick Goldman Corp. Calif., Los Angeles, 1980; pres. L.R. Berman & Assos., Ltd., Vancouver, Seattle, San Diego, 1980—; Mem. Adv. Planning Commn., Twp. of Richmond (B.C.), 1979-80. Home: 8780 Demorest Dr Richmond BC V7A 4M1 Canada Office: 8080 Granville Ave Richmond BC V6Y 1P3 Canada

BERMAN, MURIEL MALLIN (MRS. PHILIP I. BERMAN), civic worker; b. Pitts.; d. Samuel and Dora (Coopersman) Mallin; student U. Pitts., 1943, Carnegie Tech. U., 1944-45; B.S., Pa. State Coll. Optometry, 1948; postgrad. U. Pitts., 1950, Cedar Crest Coll., 1953, D.F.A., 1972; postgrad. Muhlenberg Coll., 1954; m. Philip I. Berman, Oct. 23, 1942; children—Nancy, Nina, Steven. Practice optometry, Pitts.; vice chmn., v.p., asst. sec., dir. Hess's, Inc., Allentown, Pa.; sec., dir. Fleetways, Inc., real estate; sec., treas., dir. Philip and Muriel Berman Found.; sec. D.F. Bast, Inc., Fleet-Power, Inc. Active in UNICEF, 1959—, ofcl. non-govtl. orgns., 1964, 74; founder, donor Carnegie-Berman Coll. Art Slide Library Exchange; mem. Aspen (Colo.) Inst. Humanistic Studies, 1965, Tokyo, Japan, 1966; chmn. exhibit Great Valley council, Girl Scouts U.S.A., 1966; adminstrv. head, chmn. various events Allentown Bicentennial, 1962; vice chmn. Women for Pa. Bicentennial 1976; co-chmn. Lehigh County Bi-Centennial Liberty Bell-Trek, 1976; patron Art in the Embassies Program, Washington, 1965—; chmn. Lehigh Valley Ednl. TV, 1966—, programs Fgn. Policy Assn., Lehigh County, 1965-67; treas. ann. symphony ball Allentown Symphony, 1955—; mem. Dieruff High Sch. Art Adv. Com., Allentown, 1966—; producer weekly College Speak-Out, TV Channel 39, 1967—, producer, moderator TV program Guest Spot; chmn. art com. Episcopal Diocese Centennial Celebration, 1971; mem. Pa. Council on Status of Women, 1968-73; chmn. numerous art shows; mem. YWCA, Art Collectors Club Am., Am. Fedn. Art, Friends Whitney Mus., Mus. Modern Art, Mus. Primitive Art, Jewish Mus. Met. Mus., Kemmerer Mus., Bethlehem, Pa., Univ. Mus., Phila., Skirball Mus., Los Angeles (all N.Y.C.), Archives of Am. Art, Detroit, Allentown Art Mus., Phila. Art Mus., Reading Art Mus., Met. Opera Guild, N.Y.C., Lincoln Center, N.Y.C. Mem. Electoral College, 1968; mem. Democratic Platform Com., 1972; de. Dem. Nat. Conv., 1972. Bd. dirs. Pa. Ballet, Allentown Symphony (treas. ann. ball), Lehigh Valley Ednl. TV (chmn. program com.), Hadassah (nat. dir.), Heart Assn. Pa., Allentown Art Mus. Aux. (art appreciation dir.), Phila. Chamber Symphony, Baum Art Sch., Lehigh County Cultural Center, Women's Club (v.p., arts chmn. 1960—), Fgn. Policy Assn.; trustee Kutztown State Coll., 1960-66, vice chmn. bd., 1965; trustee Lehigh Community Coll., also sec. bd.; trustee Pa. Council on Arts, Smithsonian Art Council, Bonds for Israel. Named Woman of Valor, Israel, 1965; recipient Centennial Year Hon. citation Wilson Coll., 1969; Henrietta Szold award Allentown chpt. Hadassah; Outstanding Woman award Allentown YWCA, 1973. Mem. League Women Voters, Hist. Soc. Lehigh County, Lehigh, Phila. art alliances, UN We Believe. Jewish religion (past v.p. Temple sisterhood). Club: Wellesley. Good will tours to Latin Am. for U.S. Dept. State, 1965. Catalogs, research curator Berman (art) collection. Address: 20 Hundred Nottingham Rd Allentown PA 18103

BERMAN, PAUL ARTHUR, real estate exec.; b. Bklyn., July 25, 1935; s. Abraham H. and Ethel (Lash) B.; B.S., N.Y. U., 1957; m. Shirley A. Segal, June 25, 1961; children—Jonathan Israel, Deborah Rachael, Sharon Esther. Salesman, Saul Kirshner Real Estate Co., Bklyn., 1953-57; salesman Joseph P. Day Inc., N.Y.C., 1957, sales mgr., 1957-59, v.p., 1959-67; prin. Berman Realty Assos., N.Y.C. and Hackensack, N.J., 1964-71; pres. Paul A. Berman Realties Inc., Hackensack & N.Y.C., 1971—; real estate cons. Ward Foods, 1960-64, Fairleigh Dickinson U., 1959—, Samuel & Lois Silberman Fund Inc., 1960—, Nat. Casket Co., 1961-63, Virgil M. Price Indsl. Park, Farmingdale, L.I., N.Y., 1961-64. Bd. dirs. Jewish Fedn. Family Services, 1972-74; trustee Bergen-Pasaic unit Assn. Retarded Citizens, 1980—. Served with U.S. Army Res., 1957-63. Recipient Outstanding Transaction award Joseph P. Day Inc., 1961-63; Certificate of Appreciation Jewish Community Relations Council Bergen County, 1975; named Outstanding Mem. Pascack Valley Lodge B'Nai B'Rith, 1973-74-75. Mem. Soc. Indsl. Realtors, N.J. Indsl. Real Estate Brokers Assn., Bergen County C. of C. (dir. 1976), C. of C. and Industry No. N.J. (dir.), Internat. Real Estate Fedn. Club: B'nai B'rith (pres. Pascack Valley lodge 1974-75, gov. Palisades council). Office: Two University Plaza Hackensack NJ 07601

BERMAN, RONALD HOWARD, crafts mfg. co. exec.; b. Portland, Oreg., Apr. 24, 1948; s. Edwin J. and Laverl D. Berman; B.A. in Mktg., U. Oreg., 1969; m. Jeannie T. Josephs, May 23, 1971; children—Jessica, Mandy. With Joseph's Inc. (now div. Ex-Call Home Fashion Co.), N.Y.C., 1972-77, gen. mgr., 1975-77; founder, pres. Rainbow Creations Inc., Portland, Cin., Toronto, Ont., Can., 1977—. Served with USNR, 1966-71; Vietnam. Recipient 2 nat. awards Hobby Craft Show Am., 1980. Mem. Portland C. of C. Republican. Jewish. Club: B'nai B'rith (pres. 1976-77). Office: 2535 NW Upshur Portland OR 97210

BERMONT, PETER L., investment banking co. exec.; b. Peoria, Ill., Jan. 7, 1945; s. William Allen and Tessa N. B.; B.B.A., Tex. Christian U., 1967; grad. N.Y. Inst. Fin., 1968; m. Ronni Joy Weksler, Sept. 1, 1968; children—Tracy Meredith, William Allen II. Stockbroker, H. Hentz & Co., Miami, Fla., 1968-72, Bache & Co., Miami, 1972-74; v.p., resident mgr. Drexel Burnham Lambert Inc., Miami, 1974-79, 1st v.p., Fla. regional mgr., Miami, 1979—; dir. Bank of Coral Gables (Fla.); pres. Miami Bond Club, 1978. Pres., Dade Monroe Dist. Mental Health Bd., Temple Israel Greater Miami, Mental Health Assn. Dade County; trustee Coral Gables Retirement System; mem. Jr. Orange Bowl Com.; bd. dirs. Health Systems Agy., Miami. Served with USAFR, 1967-73. Recipient Disting. Service award Coral Gables Jaycees, 1975. Clubs: Univ., Standard Miami, Bankers, Viscayans. Bond. Office: One SE Third Ave Suite 3100 Miami FL 33131

BERNALD, EUGENE, internat. corp. exec.; b. Rostov, Russia, Jan. 23, 1908; s. Edouard K. and Vera (Sviatoslav-Gurekoff) B.; came to U.S., 1913, naturalized, 1942; grad. Columbia U., 1929; m. Mary Blanche Dual, Dec. 15, 1940; children—Mary Ann, Eugene Robert, Edward Arthur, Barbara Elaine. Asso. with Mfrs. Trust Co., N.Y.C., 1929-30; jr. exec. trust dept. J. Schanzenbach & Co., N.Y.C., 1931-36; asst. to pres. PABCO, Inc., N.Y.C., 1936-47, v.p., 1947-65, pres., 1965—; dir. Pan Am. Broadcasting Co., Internat. Media Co., GMBH, Frankfurt, Germany, Radio Am. W.I., Inc., St. Croix, Radio Anchorage, Inc., South Eastern Alaska Broadcasters, Inc., Juneau, Drum Trading Corp. Ltd., Lagos, Nigeria. Adv. com. Operation Crossroads Africa, Inc., N.Y.C., 1960—. Adviser minority groups presdl. elections Republican Nat. Com., Washington, 1956-64. Chmn. radio industry com. Am. Korean Found., 1957—; bd. dirs. Asia Found., Internat. Broadcasting Soc. Mem. Internat. Advt. Assn., Lutheran Laymen's League. Club: Overseas Press (N.Y.C.). Author: Primer of International Broadcasting, 1938; Economics of Broadcasting, 1940; Broadcasting Overseas, 1948; Reaching Minority Groups, 1952; Communications for Underdeveloped Countries, 1960. Home: 83 Somerstown Rd Ossining NY 10562 Office: 275 Madison Ave New York NY 10016

BERNARD, BURTON, electronics co. exec.; b. July 30, 1932; s. Harry and Sarah (Fein) B.; student U. Ill., 1950-52, DeVry Tech. Inst., 1957-58, Wright Coll., 1958-60; m. Marjorie Lousie Tollas, Feb. 20, 1954 (div. 1974); children—Donald Steven, Mark Alan; m. 2d, Raquel Correa, Mar. 29, 1975; stepchildren—Cynthia Lucy, Laura Annette, Frank M. Applications engr. Radiation Electroncis Corp., Chgo., 1957-61; field sales mgr. Infrared Industries, Inc., Santa Barbara, Calif., 1961-63; product mgr. Huggins Labs., Sunnyvale, Calif., 1963-65; sales mgr. Electro Optical Industries, Santa Barbara,

1965-66; regional marketing mgr., vehicular traffic systems RCA, Santa Barbara, 1966-68; dept. mgr. GTE Sylvania, Mountain View, Calif., 1968-72; pres., gen. mgr. Gen. Photonics Corp., Santa Clara, 1972—, chmn. bd., 1972—. Bd. dirs. Theater Guild of San Francisco, 1979—. Served with USNR, 1952-56. Mem. Laser Inst. Am. (pres. 1973, dir. 1972—). Author: ABC's of Infrared, 1970. Contbr. articles to profl. jours. Patentee in field. Home: 282 Cresta Vista Way San Jose CA 95119 Office: 2255 Martin Ave Santa Clara CA 95051

BERNARD, GEORGE VINCENT, publ. co. exec.; b. Cleve., Sept. 3, 1924; s. George Alexander and Rose Ann (Kolda) B.; B.A., Lynchburg Coll., 1949; postgrad Am. U., 1956-57, George Washington U., 1952-53; m. Ann Wiley Faw, Aug. 11, 1951; children—Katherine, Susan. Prin., Pub. Schs., Fairfax County, Va., 1954-55; publishers rep. Scott, Foresman & Co., Staunton, Va., 1955-62, Washington rep., 1962-70, dir. fed. relations, 1970-74, Va. rep., 1974—; owner Bernard & Son Timber and cattle. Vestryman Trinity Episcopal Ch., Staunton, 1970-73, 75-78; trustee Woodrow Wilson Birthplace Found., Staunton, 1964-74. Served with USCG, 1943-45, 51, to lt. USCGR, 1949-74. Mem. Res. Officers Assn., Profl. Bookmans Assn. Clubs: Nat. Press (Washington). Forum, Rotary. Home: 29 Fallon St Staunton VA 24401 Office: Box 2336 Staunton VA 24401

BERNARD, J. THOMAS, real estate developer; b. Denver, June 26, 1943; s. C.A. and G.I. Bernard; Engr. Mines, Colo. Sch. Mines, 1966; M.B.A., Boston U., 1970; m. Jacqueline J. Ranthum, Feb. 1, 1969. With Bechtel Corp., 1966-67; with Cabot, Cabot & Forbes Co., 1970—, v.p., N.W. gen. mgr., Seattle, 1974—. Mem. Republican Exec. Forum, 1978—; bd. dirs. Bellevue Community Coll. Found., 1981—. Served as officer U.S. Army, 1967-69. Mem. Nat. Assn. Office and Indsl. Parks (pres. Seattle chpt. 1980), Bellevue Downtown Assn. (v.p., dir. 1980-81), Bellevue C. of C. (dir. 1980-81), Seattle C. of C. (com. chmn. 1979-80), Soc. Indsl. Realtors (asso.), Tukwila C. of C., Seattle Mcpl. League, Lambda Alpha. Club: Southcenter Rotary (dir. 1979-80) (Tukwila). Home: 1421 Shenandoah Dr E Seattle WA 98112 Office: 1003 Andover Park E Seattle WA 98188

BERNARD, JULES FRANK, food processing co. exec.; b. N.Y.C., June 12, 1920; s. Frank S. and Beatrice (Greenfogel) B.; grad. Strayer Bus. Coll., Washington, 1940; m. June Clark, Aug. 1, 1945; 1 son, Steven. Vice-pres., Milani Internat., Inc., Chgo., 1946-47; pres., chief exec. officer Bernard Food Industries, Inc., Chgo., 1947—; dir., chmn. bd. Stevens Packaging, Inc., Skokie, Ill., 1977. Served in inf. U.S. Army, 1942-46. Recipient Optimist of Yr. award, 1976. Mem. Chgo. Pres.'s Assn., Evanston C. of C. (dir. 1977-80), Inst. Food Techs., Calorie Control Council. Jewish. Clubs: Evanston Optimist, B'nai B'rith. Office: PO Box 1497 1125 Hartrey Ave Evanston IL 60204

BERNARD, THOMAS GILBERT, ins. co. exec.; b. Fitchburg, Mass., Mar. 25, 1947; s. Gilbert Authur and Blanche Mary (Burube) B.; B.S.A., Bentley Coll., 1968; M.B.A., Clark U., 1971; m. Margaret Katherine Gibson, Aug. 27, 1967; children—Lori Ann, Stacy Marie. Field auditor IRS, Worcester, Mass., 1968-69; acct., systems analyst State Mut. Life, Worcester, 1969-72; sr. acct., mgr. internal audit Hanover Ins. Co., Worcester, 1972-76; treas. Citizens Ins. Co. Am., Howell, Mich., 1976-78; v.p. fin., treas. Western Employers Ins. Co., Santa Ana, Calif., 1978—; dir. Heritage Ins. Services, Western Employer, Inc.; instr. Mount Wachusett Community Coll., 1976. Chmn., County of Howell United Fund drive, 1976, Jr. Achievement drive, 1977. Fellow Life Office Mgmt. Assn.; mem. Nat. Assn. Accts., Ins. Acctg. and Statis. Assn. Republican. Roman Catholic. Home: 26671 Cadenas Mission Viejo CA 92691 Office: 515 N Cabrillo Park Dr Santa Ana CA 92702

BERNARD, VINCENT EUGENE, food co. exec.; b. Waterloo, Iowa, Nov. 14, 1940; s. Vincent Leo and Evelyn Marie (Patava) B.; student public schs., Cedar Falls, Iowa; m. Nyleta Jean Nelson, Dec. 5, 1959; children—Christi (dec.), Kraig, Kristin, Brian (dec.), Perry. Tech. dir. Doerfer div. Container Corp. Am., 1969-74; v.p. engring. Jimmy Dean Cos., Dallas, 1974-76, v.p. ops., 1976-77, pres., chief exec. officer, 1977—, also dir. Served with USMC, 1958. Mem. Pres's Assn., Am. Meat Inst., Southwestern Meat Packers Assn., Nat. Oceanographic Soc. Club: K.C. Method and apparatus patentee in field. Office: 1341 W Mockingbird Ln Suite 1100E Dallas TX 75247

BERNE, ANDREW, accountant; b. N.Y.C., Oct. 8, 1920; s. David B. and Beatrice (Fish) B.; B.B.A., CCNY, 1942; student Hunter Coll., 1942, U.S. Dept. Agr. Grad. Sch., 1942-43; m. Shirley Feld Moses, Sept. 7, 1945 (dec. Jan. 1977); 1 son, Robert David; m. 2d, Danielle Beigel, June 6, 1979. Partner, office mgr. N.L. Fish & Co., N.Y.C., 1946-61; prin. Andrew Berne, C.P.A., 1961—; mgmt. cons. to pvt. investment group, 1961—. Served to 1st lt. USAAF, 1943-46. C.P.A., N.Y., N.J. Mem. Am. Inst. C.P.A.'s, N.Y. State Soc. C.P.A.'s, Accounting Research Assn., Friends of Earth, Sierra Club. Club: Upper Ridgewood Tennis. Home and Office: 255 Maple Ave Hillsdale NJ 07642

BERNFELD, LESTER, textile mfg. co. exec.; b. Chgo., Sept. 15, 1927; s. Benjamin and Dorothy B.; student public schs., Chgo.; m. Shirley Cagan, June 18, 1949; children—Lynn, Jay. Ind. sales rep., Chgo., 1948-50; dir. domestics Cham Tred Industries, Chgo., 1950-56; sales mgr. Purofied Down, Chgo., 1956-68; pres. Jerhart, Inc., Chgo., 1968—, also chmn. bd. Mem. exec. com. Nat. Jewish Hosp.; active Boy Scouts Am. Served with Air Corps, USN, 1944-48. Mem. Am. Arbitration Assn. (panel arbitrators). Home: 7922 Arcadia St Morton Grove IL 60053 Office: 2735 W Armitage Chicago IL 60647

BERNHARD, HENRY PAUL, advt. exec.; b. Washington, Nov. 12, 1927; s. Henry Albin and Lucie O. (Karge) B.; B.A., Union Coll., Schenectady, 1952; m. Helen Dorothea Albert, Aug. 9, 1952; children—Karen Irene, Eric Albert, Lisa Karge, David Paul. Exec. trainee McCann Erickson Advt., N.Y.C., 1952; mgr. mktg. services Life mag. Time Inc., N.Y.C., 1952-60; with Ogilvy & Mather Inc., N.Y.C., 1960—, chmn. continental European offices and mng. dir. Frankfurt, Germany, 1966-70, vice chmn., N.Y.C., 1971—, also dir.; dir. Ogilvy & Mather Internat., Mktg. Outlooks, Inc., Wasa Rye King Inc. Served with USNR, 1945-47. Club: Tuxedo Park. Office: Ogilvie & Mather Inc 2 E 48th St New York NY 10017*

BERNHARDT, ARTHUR DIETER, housing industry cons.; b. Dresden, Germany, Nov. 19, 1937; s. Rudolf and Charlotte B.; came to U.S., 1966; Dipl.Ing., Munich U. Tech., 1965; postgrad. U. So. Calif., 1966-67; M. City Planning, Mass. Inst. Tech., 1969. Various positions with bldg. projects, 1956-68; dir. Program in Industrialization of Housing Sector (PIIHS), Mass. Inst. Tech., Cambridge, 1969-76, pres. PIIHS, 1977—; internat. housing industry cons., Cambridge, 1973—; asst. prof. Mass. Inst. Tech., 1970-76. Fed. Republic Germany fellow, 1965, 66, 67, 68; Mass. Inst. Tech. fellow, 1968, 69; grantee Fed. Republic Germany, 1965, Mass. Inst. Tech., 1970, Alfred P. Sloan Found., 1970, Dept. Commerce, 1972, HUD, 1972, 74. Mem. exec. com. Mass. Gov.'s Advisory Com. on Mobile Homes, 1974-75; apptd. NRC del. 8th Gen. Assembly Internat. Council Bldg. Research, 1974. Mem. Internat. Council Bldg. Research, Am. Acad. Polit. and Social Sci., Am. Planning Assn., Deutscher Hochschulverband, Am. Judicature Soc. (asso.). Author book, articles in field. Home: Cambridge MA Office: PO Box 303 Cambridge MA 02141

BERNHARDT, DOUGLAS CARLOS, automobile sales co. exec.; b. Ann Arbor, Mich., Dec. 26, 1948; s. Douglas Alden and Silvia Elsa (Rodriguez) B.; student U. Houston, 1967-71; m. Margaret Joyce Hawkins, Oct. 26, 1974; children—Kimberly Anne, Annabel Kate. Dept. mgr. Deugro Transport U.K. Ltd., London, 1971-73; mng. dir. Transcar U.K. Ltd., London, 1973-79; founder, chief exec. officer Am. by Car Internat. Ltd., Hamilton, Bermuda, 1979—; dir. Transcar Projects Ltd., R.S.J. Aviation Ltd. Fellow Inst. Dirs. Lutheran. Clubs: Arts (London); Goodwood Flying, Gardens, Steering Wheel, Royal Automobile. Home: Audley House River West Sussex GU28 9AX England Office: 53 Upper Brook St London W1 England

BERNOSKY, HERMAN GEORGE, retail gasoline dealer; b. Minersville, Pa., Aug. 16, 1921; s. Peter and Mary Bernosky; student Rider Coll., Trenton, N.J., 1947-48. With Bernosky's Exxon Sta., Llewellyn, Pa., 1940-42, 46—, owner, operator, 1949—. Treas. Minersville Area Bicentennial, 1976. Served with AUS, 1942-46; ETO. Decorated Bronze Star (3). Mem. Am. Legion. Democrat. Roman Catholic. Club: Minersville Lions (past pres., dir. 1957—). Home: 622 Lytle St Minersville PA 17954 Office: PO Box 170 Llewellyn PA 17944

BERNS, THOMAS F., mgmt. cons.; b. Chgo., June 2, 1943; s. Christian H. and Marie A. (Corcoran) B.; B.S. in Math., No. Ill. U., 1966; postgrad. Ill. Inst. Tech., 1966-69; M.B.A., Loyola U., Chgo., 1969; m. Sharon Piccatto, Nov. 20, 1965. Indsl. engr. Western Electric Co., Cicero, Ill., 1966; tchr. math. Sch. Dist. 10Z, LaGrange, Ill., 1966-68, Sch. Dist. 86, Hinsdale, Ill., 1968-69; with Arthur Andersen & Co., 1969—, mgmt. cons., London, 1969—. Mem. IBM Guide Assn., EDP Auditors Assn., Computer Users Assn. U.K. Clubs: Oakbrook Racquet; Historic Wine (London); Battersea Tennis Assn. Home: 51 Drayton Gardens London SW 10 England United Kingdom Office: Arthur Andersen & Co 1 Surrey London WC2 England United Kingdom also Arthur Andersen & Co 69 W Washington St Chicago IL 60602*

BERNSTEIN, AARON, retail apparel exec.; b. Minsk, Russia, Oct. 30, 1904; came to U.S., 1908, naturalized, 1940; s. George and Anna B.; student public schs., N.Y.C.; m. Ida Lebowitz, June 3, 1928; children—Charlotte Strauss, Gloria Sir. Gen. mgr. Gordon Dept. Store, West Point, Miss., until 1940; pres. Ruth Shops, Inc., Columbus, Miss., 1940—. Jewish. Office: Ruth Shops Inc 101 104 109 S 5th Main St Columbus MS 39701

BERNSTEIN, HARRY EZEKIEL, lawyer; b. Newark, July 26, 1908; s. Benjamin Mayer and Jenny Lee (Deutsch) B.; A.B., Rutgers U., 1932, LL.B., 1934, J.D., 1970; m. Evelyn Del Stoler, June 10, 1937; children—Daniel Stoler, Janice Bernstein Simmons. Admitted to N.J. bar, 1934; mem. firm Sacher, Bernstein, Rothberg, Sikora and Mongello, and predecessors, Plainfield, N.J., 1934—, sr. partner, v.p., 1972—; dir., chmn. fin. com., mem. nominating com. Economics Labs., Inc., 1966—, Washington Distbrs., Inc., 1970-79; dir. Community Distbrs., Inc.; dir., v.p. Graybar Builders, Inc.; co-adj. faculty dept. govt. services, Rutgers U.-State U. N.J., 1978—; chmn. Gov's. Task Force on Housing, 1968-72; cons. on land use to 21 municipalities State of N.J.; atty. for Twp. Scotch Plains, N.J., 1940-66, for Piscataway Planning Bd., 1968-75, for Warren Bd. Adjustment, 1969—. Fin. com. Clifford E. Case senatorial campaign, 1970, Rep. candidates for state and county offices in N.J. various dates. Recipient award from Gov. Cahill, 1971, from Rutgers U., 1974, outstanding citizen award, Scotch Plains, 1969; Pres.'s Disting. Service award N.J. League Municipalities. Mem. Am., N.J., Union County, Plainfield bar assns., Peace Through Law Assn. Jewish. Clubs: Rotary, Masons, Shriners. Author: Legal Aspects of Planning and Zoning, 1971; contbr. articles on land use in N.J. to Planner, annually 1960—. Home: 1410 Cooper Rd Scotch Plains NJ 07076 Office: 700 Park Ave PO Box 1148 Plainfield NJ 07061

BERNSTEIN, JEFFREY, food industry exec.; b. Bklyn., Jan. 22, 1950; s. Gilbert E. and Shirley C. (Carpe) B.; B.A., Bklyn. Coll., 1972; m. Melody Baum, Feb. 18, 1979; 1 son, Jonathan Alan. Sales mgr. Harrison Food Brokerage Co., Inc., Roslyn Heights, N.Y., 1970-76, pres., 1977-79; v.p. food service Andorn, Bergida & Danks, Inc., 1973-79; v.p. sales Fruitcrest Corp., Garden City Park, N.Y., 1979—. Mem. Nat. Food Brokers Assn. Home: 30 Meadow Dr Manhasset Bay Estates NY 11050 Office: 250 Fulton Ave Garden City Park NY 11040

BERNSTEIN, LAWSON FREDERICK, lawyer; b. N.Y.C., Feb. 29, 1920; s. Benjamin and Ruth (Kleeblatt) B.; A.B., Columbia, 1940; student Yale, 1940-41; LL.B., N.Y. U., 1947; m. Charlotte Jane Baer, Dec. 20, 1955 (div. June 1969); children—Lawson Frederick, Richard Douglas; m. 2d, Mio Miriam Fredland, Nov. 22, 1969; 1 dau., Katherine Miriam Celia. Admitted to N.Y. State bar, 1947, U.S. Supreme Ct. bar, 1953; mem. Bernstein & Bernstein, N.Y.C., 1950-63; engaged in individual practice law, N.Y.C., 1963-66, 69-77; partner Pincus, Bernstein & Seeman, N.Y.C., 1966-69, Bernstein & Obstfeld, N.Y.C., 1977—; mem. exec. council Lionel Trilling seminars, Columbia U. Acting chmn. Nat. Enforcement Commn., 1952-53. Served from pvt. to capt. AUS, 1942-46. Mem. Am. Bar Assn., N.Y. County Lawyers Assn., Yale Law Sch. Assn., Assn. Bar City N.Y., N.Y. State Bar Assn. Mem. B'nai B'rith (pres. Midtown lodge 1959-61, dist. dep. 1961-63). Clubs: Yale (N.Y.C.); Wyantenuck Country (Gt. Barrington, Mass.). Home: 121 E 95th St New York NY 10028 Office: 1 Rockefeller Plaza New York NY 10020

BERNSTEIN, MOREY, corp. exec.; b. Pueblo, Colo., June 21, 1919; s. Samuel and Celia (Wagner) B.; B.S. in Econs. with distinction, U. Pa., 1941; postgrad. Columbia, 1953; m. Hazel Doris Higgins, Aug. 1, 1948. Partner, Bernstein Bros. Equipment Co., 1941—, Bernstein Bros. Investment Co., 1941—; chmn. bd. Double-B, Inc., 1970—, Wholesalers, Inc., 1970—; pres. Bernstein Bros. Machinery Corp., 1946-52; dir. Minnequa Bank, Pueblo, Colo., 1951-55. Chmn. Bernstein Bros. Parapsychology Found., 1969—. Mem. Am. Soc. Psychical Research, C. of C. Jewish. Author: The Search for Bridey Murphy, 1956. Patentee Instant Fence, Pronto Panels, Kwik-Lok portable corrals. Home: 1819 Elizabeth St Pueblo CO 81003 Office: 134 N Mechanic St Pueblo CO 81003

BERNSTEIN, PHILIP, JR., retail stock brokerage exec.; b. Chgo. Oct. 2, 1933; s. Philip and Mary Elizabeth (Frank) B.; B.S. in Econs., U. Pa., 1955; m. Rita M. Kruger, June 26, 1966; 1 dau., Lynn. Mgmt. trainee Werthan Industries, Nashville, 1955-58; with Freehling & Co., Chgo., 1959—, partner, 1967—. Vol., Michael Reese Hosp., Chgo. Asso. mem. N.Y. Stock Exchange. Clubs: Standard of Chgo., Old Willow Bath & Tennis, Rotary. Designed automated mailing system for brokerage industry. Home: 399 Fullerton Pkwy Chicago IL 60614 Office: 120 S LaSalle St Chicago IL 60603

BERNSTEIN, ROBERT LOUIS, book publisher; b. N.Y.C., Jan. 5, 1923; s. Alfred and Sylvia (Bloch) B.; B.S., Harvard U., 1944; m. Helen Walter, Nov. 23, 1950; children—Peter Walter, Tom Alfred, William Samuel. Gen. sales mgr. Simon & Schuster, Inc., N.Y.C., 1946-57; with Random House, Inc., 1957—, pres., 1966—, now also chmn. bd., chief exec. officer. Bd. dirs. Chamber Music Soc. Lincoln Center, Am. Book Pubs. Council, 1967-70, Dr. Seuss Found.; bd. dirs., v.p. Internat. League Human Rights; chmn. Fund for Free Expression; mem. nat. adv. com. Amnesty Internat.; chmn. Am. Helsinki Watch Com.; trustee Blythedale Children's Hosp. Served with USAAF, 1943-46. Mem. Assn. Am. Pubs. (chmn. 1972-73, chmn. com. Soviet-Am. pub. relations 1973), Council on Fgn. Relations. Clubs: Harvard, Century Assn., Univ. (N.Y.C.); Century Country (White Plains, N.Y.); Town (Scarsdale); International (Washington). Home: 20 Murray Hill Rd Scarsdale NY 10583 Office: 201 E 50th St New York NY 10022

BERNSTEIN, RONALD, steel co. exec.; b. Englewood, N.J., Feb. 2, 1942; s. Irving and Mae B.; B.S. in Fin., Rutgers U., 1972; m. Bonnie Wohl, Aug. 29, 1965; children—Michael, Stephen, Frances, Johanna. Tax cons. Mailman Bros., N.Y.C., 1970-77; tax specialist Empire Macinery Co., Mesa, Ariz., 1977-79; pres. Shelter Sales Co., Phoenix, 1979—. Home: 9521 N 52d Pl Paradise Valley AZ 85253 Office: 3100 S 7th St Phoenix AZ 85040

BERNSTEIN, SIDNEY, publishing co. exec., lawyer; b. Bronx, May 3, 1938; s. Meyer and Ethel (Sloop) B.; B.A., Columbia U., 1960; J.D., Cornell U., 1964; m. Joyce Elaine Blum, July 7, 1963 (div. 1980); children—Michael Louis, Sheryl Lyn. Admitted to N.Y. bar, 1965, U.S. Supreme Ct. bar, 1971; with Lawyers Co-op. Pub. Co., Rochester, N.Y., 1964-71, editor, 1965-68, asst. mng. editor, 1969-71; sr. mng. editor Matthew Bender & Co., Inc., N.Y.C., 1971-75, asst. to pres., 1976—; mem. faculty Coll. Advocacy, 1977-80; lectr. criminal constl. law. Mem. Am. Bar Assn. (gen. law editor Law Notes 1970-71), Assn. Trial Lawyers Am. (chmn. criminal law sect.), Scribes (pres. 1971), New City (N.Y.) Jewish Center. Club: Masons (N.Y.C.). Editor: Criminal Defense Techniques, 7 vols., 1971-76; author profl. reports; editor Case and Comment Mag., 1968-71; editorial bd. Am. Criminal Law Rev., 1972-74. Home: 15 Heritage Dr New City NY 10956 Office: 235 E 45th St New York NY 10017

BERNSTEIN, STANLEY JOSEPH, lawyer, mfg. co. exec.; b. Boston, May 9, 1943; s. David William and Irene (Eisenman) B.: A.B. in English and French Lit., Brown U., 1965; J.D., U. Pa., 1968; m. Lisbeth Tarlow, July 16, 1972; 1 son, Michael Aaron. Admitted to Mass. bar, 1968; mgmt. trainee Am. Biltrite Inc., Chelsea, Mass., 1968-69, plant mgr., Stoughton, Mass., 1969-71, v.p., gen. mgr. Consumer Products Div., Cambridge, Mass., 1972-77, v.p. corp. planning and devel. parent co., 1978—; dir. First Tuesday Assos. Mem. Am. Mgmt. Assn., N. Am. Soc. for Corp. Planning, Assn. for Corp. Growth. Club: Belmont (Mass.) Country. Office: 575 Technology Sq Cambridge MA 02139

BERNT, BENNO ANTHONY, battery mfg. co. exec.; b. Bielitz, Austria, Mar. 14, 1931; s. Victor and Grete (Meissner) B.; came to U.S., 1953, naturalized, 1961; B.S. in Engring. summa cum laude, Fed. Inst. Tech., Vienna, Austria, 1952; D.C.S. in Internat. Econs. summa cum laude, U. Commerce Vienna, 1953; M.B.A., Carnegie-Mellon U., Pitts., 1954; m. Constance Smigel, June 22, 1957; children—Karin, Eric, Steve. Financial and mfg. exec. Chrysler Corp., 1954-59; mfg. and bus. planning exec., subs. gen. mgr. Whirlpool Corp., 1959-68; Cissell Mfg. Co., pres. Louisville, 1968-70; gen. mgr. Simonds Abrasive Co., Phila., 1970-73; v.p. fin. ESB Ray-O-Vac Corp., Phila., 1973-76, exec. v.p., dir., 1977-78; pres. Ray-O-Vac Corp., Madison, Wis., 1979—. Mem. Regional Planning Commn., Marion, Ohio, 1962-65; pres. Marion Concert Assn., 1963-65; bd. dirs. Internat. House, Phila., Phila. Coll. Performing Arts. Recipient Distinguished Service award and named Outstanding Young Man of Yr., Ohio Jaycees, 1965. Mem. Fin. Execs. Inst., Young Pres.'s Orgn. Clubs: Maple Bluff Country, Union League (Phila.). Home: 1007 Hillside Ave Madison WI 53705 Office: Ray-O-Vac Corp 101 E Washington Ave Madison WI 53703

BERNTSON, STANLEY MARSHALL, banker; b. Chgo., Aug. 5, 1907; s. Bernard E. and Margurite (Nelson) B.; evening student Northwestern U., 1925-27; m. Lillian Adelaine Johnson, Oct. 14, 1933; children—Gail Lynda, Grant Morgan. Accountant, George Reinberg Co., Chgo., 1927-35, George May & Co., 1935-36; exec. sec. Derby Laundry, 1936-40; pres., chmn. bd. Fidelity Fed. Savs., Chgo., 1940—; v.p. Mars Realty Co., 1945—; exec. sec. Samuel Olson Mfg. Co., 1943-56. Bd. dirs. Elmhurst YMCA; chmn. bd. Home of Onesiphorus; trustee Trinity Sem.; bd. dirs. Lydia Children's Home. Mem. Nat. League Insured Assns. (legislation com.), Ill. Savs. and Loan League (legislation com.), Cook County Council Insured Savs. Assn. (pres.), C. of C. (dir.). Mem. Evang. Free Ch. Am. Kiwanian (dir.). Home: 211 Winthrop Ave Elmhurst IL 60126 Office: 5455 W Belmont Ave Chicago IL 60641

BERRA, ROBERT LOUIS, chem. co. exec.; b. St. Louis, June 24, 1924; s. Angelo J. and Clara (Stohl) B.; B.S. in Econs., St. Louis U., 1947; M.B.A., Harvard U., 1947; m. Nov. 22, 1944; children—Kathleen Patricia Berra Schrage, Patricia Susan Berra Babcock. Mem. faculty St. Louis U., 1947; various tng. and personnel positions Monsanto Co., St. Louis, 1951-70, v.p. personnel, 1974-80, sr. v.p. adminstrn., 1980—; v.p. personnel and pub. relations Foremost-McKesson Inc., San Francisco, 1970-74; dir. Fisher Controls Internat. Mem. adv. council St. John's Mercy Med. Center; mem. central services vis. com., chmn. subcom. on personnel Harvard Coll. Served to lt. USN, 1942-46. Recipient Alumni Merit award St. Louis U., 1977. Mem. Am. Soc. for Personnel Administrn. (past pres.), Indsl. Relations Assn., Am. Mgmt. Assn., Conf. Bd., Labor Policy Assn., Personnel Round Table. Roman Catholic. Club: Bellerive Country. Office: Monsanto Co 800 N Lindbergh Blvd Saint Louis MO 63166

BERRY, BUTCH, lab. adminstr.; b. Trinidad, Colo., July 5, 1949; s. Leslie William and Amelia (Fantin) B.; A.A.S., Trinidad State Jr. Coll., 1971; m. Margaret Baca, Jan. 31, 1970; children—Shana Lynn, Leslie Brian. Asst. mgr. EDP, Colo. Farm Bur. Mut. Ins. Co., Denver, 1972-75; mgr. systems devel. Cobe Labs. Inc., Lakewood, Colo., 1975—. Sec. Gateway Club Aurora (Colo.), 1976—. Served with USMCR, 1968-71. Decorated Vietnamese Cross Gallantry. Mem. Data Processing Mgmt. Assn., So. Calif., Rocky Mountain (pres. 1978—) datapoint user groups. Address: 8944 W 75th Way Arvada CO 80005

BERRY, CHARLES LEONARD, fin. exec.; b. Granite City, Ill., Sept. 21, 1940; s. P. Louis and Freida (Feltman) B.; B.S., St. Louis U., 1961, M.S., 1972; m. Lynn S. Moore, Oct. 28, 1967; children—Charles Leonard, Catherine, Christopher. With Eastman Kodak Stores, Inc., 1961-70, acct., St. Louis, 1961-63, credit mgr., 1963-66, office supr., San Diego, 1966-70; hosp. controller St. Louis U. Med. Center, 1970-75, adminstrv. controller, 1975-76; asso. controller Normandy Osteo. Hosps., St. Louis, 1977-79; asst. prof. Webster Coll., St. Louis, 1979-80; v.p. fin. McKendree Coll., Lebanon, Ill., 1980—; adj. faculty Maryville Coll., 1975—, Webster Coll., 1974—. Mem. Hosp. Fin. Mgmt. Assn., Alpha Kappa Psi. Home: 280 N Lindbergh Blvd Saint Louis MO 63141 Office: 701 College Rd Lebanon IL 62254

BERRY, CHARLES MIKE, banker; b. Benjamin, Tex., Dec. 18, 1919; s. John W. and Mary P. (Perry) B.; grad. Pacific Coast Sch. Banking, 1958, Advanced Mgmt. Program, Harvard U., 1973; m. Claire M. Schroeder, Mar. 31, 1944; children—Peggy, Robert, Patti, James. With Continental Nat. Bank, Ft. Worth, 1938-40, Lubbock Nat. Bank (Tex.), 1940-41, 44-47; with Seattle-First Nat. Bank, 1947—, asst. cashier, 1958-61, asst. v.p., 1961-62, v.p., 1962-65, v.p., mgr. mktg. planning, 1965-70, v.p., mgr. br. banking, 1970-73, exec. v.p., mgr. br. banking div., 1973-74, exec. v.p., mgr. Washington banking group, 1974-75, pres., mgr. Wash. banking group, 1975—; pres. SeaFirst Corp.; dir. Wash. Natural Gas Council. Bd. dirs. Wash. Internat. Trade Fair, Econ. Devel. Council, Wash. Council Econ. Edn.; adv. bd. Seattle Salvation Army; trustee U. Puget Sound. Served with USAAF, 1941-44. Mem. Seattle C. of C. (exec. com., trustee). Democrat. Clubs: Wash. Athletic (bd. govs.), Rainier, Harbor, Broadmoor Golf and Country, Tacoma, Long Acres Turf. Home: 2623 170th St SE Bellevue WA 98008 Office: 1001 4th Ave Seattle WA 98154*

BERRY, HARRY AUGUST, oil and gas co. exec.; b. Wilmington, Del., Mar. 24, 1934; s. Elmer and Sara Elizabeth (Missimer) B.; B.S. in Accounting, U. Del., 1961; M.B.A., U. Utah, 1977; m. Helen Amber Parks, Nov. 15, 1957; children—Harry, Sharon, Sandra, David. EDP mgr. Rohm and Haas, Bristol, Pa., 1968-71, sec./treas. Rohm Haas N.C. Inc., Fayetteville, N.C., 1973-78, also dir.; financial mgr. Sauquoit Fibers, Scranton, Pa., 1971-72; sec./treas. Carodel Corp., Fayetteville, N.C., 1974-78; v.p. fin. Canus Petroleum, Varez Exploration and Varez Petroleum, Denver, 1978—. Treas., Freedom Friendship Found., 1972-78. Served with AUS, 1955-57. Mem. Nat. Assn. Accountants (chpt. dir. 1974), Council of Petroleum Accountants Socs. Republican. Presbyterian. Home: 4041 S Magnolia Way Denver CO 80237 Office: 1700 Broadway Suite 1400 Denver CO 80290

BERRY, JAMES DOYLE, banker; b. Sapulpa, Okla., June 23, 1921; B.S., U. Okla., 1943; grad. Rutgers U. Sch. Banking, Advanced Mgmt. Program, Harvard U. Formerly with Am. Nat. Bank, Sapulpa; later with Republic Nat. Bank, Dallas; now chmn. bd., chief exec. officer, dir. Republic Tex. Corp., Dallas. Office: Republic Tex Corp Ervay & Pacific Dallas TX 75201

BERRY, LOREN MURPHY, bus. exec.; b. Wabash, Ind., July 24, 1888; s. Charles D. and Elizabeth (Murphy) B.; student Northwestern U., 1909-10; LL.D., Rio Grande (Ohio) Coll.; m. Lucile Kneipple, June 9, 1909 (dec.); children—Loren Murphy, Martha Sue Fraim, John William, Elizabeth Anne Gray; m. 2d, Helen Anderson Henry, Aug. 28, 1938 (dec.); 1 son, Leland; m. 3d, Ruth Heston, Apr. 21, 1976. Newspaper reporter, Wabash, Ind., Joliet, Ill. and Chgo.; sold telephone directory advt. in Marion, Ind., 1910, St. Louis, Louisville and Indpls., which developed into nat. sales orgn. of L.M. Berry & Co. (main office Dayton, Ohio), now vice chmn. bd.; dir. emeritus Third Nat. Bank, Dayton, United Telecommunications Inc., Kansas City, Mo.; dir. Super Food Services, Inc., Dayton. Bd. dirs. Jr. Achievement of Dayton; trustee Rio Grande Coll. Mem. U.S. Ind. Telephone Pioneers (pres. 1938-39), Bell Telephone Pioneers Assn. (v.p. N.C. Kingsbury chpt. 1939-40). Republican. Episcopalian. Clubs: Masons, Shriners, Kiwanis, Engrs., Dayton City, Dayton Country, Moraine Country, Bicycle (Dayton); Surf (bd. govs.), Com. of One Hundred, Bath, Indian Creek (Miami Beach, Fla.); Capitol Hill (Washington); Bohemian (San Francisco). Home: 1155 Ridgeway Rd Dayton OH 45419 Died Feb. 10, 1980.

BERRY, WILLIAM MARTIN, financial holding co. exec.; b. Chgo., June 21, 1920; s. William John and Mary Frances (Martin) B.; B.S. summa cum laude, St. Mary's Coll., Winona, Minn., 1941; M.A., DePaul U., 1949; m. Julia Vail, Dec. 1972; children—William E., Mary Patricia, Peter D. Div. controller Hughes Aircraft Co., 1951-55, TRW Co., 1955-58; mgr. mgmt. services Peat Marwick Mitchell & Co., C.P.A.'s, Los Angeles, 1958-61; v.p., also pres. Royal Typewriter Group, Litton Industries, Inc., 1961-74; chmn. bd. The NN Corp., 1974; dir. Marine Corp., Marine Nat. Exchange Bank, Astronautics, Inc. Bd. dirs. Milw. Boys' Club, Milw. Symphony, Med. Coll. Wis., Columbia Hosp. Served to 1st lt., C.E., AUS, 1941-45; ETO, PTO. Mem. Fin. Execs. Inst. Clubs: Union League (N.Y.C.); University (Chgo.); Milwaukee, Milw. Country. Home: 1003 W Shaker Circle Mequon WI 53092 Office: 731 N Jackson St Milwaukee WI 53202

BERRY, WILLIAM RANDALL, retail exec., Realtor; b. Leesville, La., Apr. 30, 1954; s. Theodore Lloyd and Elenore Denise (West) B.; student Northwestern State U. La.; m. Gayla Gibson. With West-Gibson, Inc., Leesville, La., 1974—, personnel mgr., asst. buyer, 1976-78, asst. gen. mgr., 1978—, also sec. treas.; sec. treas. Berry Realty Co. Treas. state rep. campaign Dist. 31, Republican Party, 1979, exec. committeeman, 1980-84. Lic. real estate agt., La. Mem. Leesville Jaycees (dir. 1978-79; external v.p., 1979, internal v.p. 1980; Outstanding project award 1977), La. Realtors Assn., Assn. U.S. Army, Leesville Vernon Parish C. of C. (retail mchts. com.), La. Lions League Crippled Children. Republican. Methodist. Club: Rotary (program chmn. 1979-80, sgt.-at-arms 1980-81, treas. 1981-82). Office: Hwy 171 N Leesville LA 71446

BERRY, WILLIAM WILLIS, pub. utility exec.; b. Norfolk, Va., May 18, 1932; s. Joel Halbert and Julia Lee (Godwin) B.; B.S. Elec. Engring., Va. Mil. Inst., 1954; M.C., U. Richmond, 1964; m. Elizabeth Wall Mangum, Aug. 23, 1958; children—Elizabeth Preston, William Godwin, John Willis. Engr., Gen. Electric Co., Schenectady and Pittsfield, N.Y., 1954-55; with Va. Electric & Power Co., Richmond, 1957—, mgr. electric ops., 1971-73, v.p.-div. ops., 1974-76, sr. v.p.-comml. ops., 1976-77, exec. v.p., 1978-80, pres., 1980—; dir. Va. Nat. Bankshares, Inc., Va. Nat. Bank, Richmond. Elder, 1st Presbyn. Ch., Richmond, 1976—. Served with AUS, 1955-57. Registered profl. engr., Va. Mem. IEEE, Va., Richmond chambers commerce. Republican. Clubs: Commonwealth, Country of Va., Kiwanis. Home: 6601 Three Chopt Rd Richmond VA 23226 Office: Vepco PO Box 26666 Richmond VA 23261

BERSCHE, JOSEPH EDWIN, constrn. co. exec.; b. Fairmont, W.Va., Oct. 17, 1931; s. G. Joseph and Jessie Naomi (Darling) B.; student Mich. State Normal Coll., 1949-50, Nyack Coll., 1950-51; m. Barbara Carol Stegmaler, June 9, 1956; children— Craig, Chris Kimberly-Jo, Curtis, Barbi-Jo. Pres. Bersche Constrn. Inc., Pontiac, Mich., 1956-67; exec. v.p. The Hannan Co., Cleve., 1967-77, also dir.; pres. Inland Constrn. Inc., Chgo., 1977—, also dir. Bd. mgrs. The Christian and Missionary Alliance, Nyack, N.Y.; trustee Nyack Coll., Alliance Theol. Seminary. Served with U.S. Navy, 1951-55. Mem. Builders Assn. Chgo., Asso. Gen. Contractors Am. Clubs: Chgo. Execs., Carlton, Hudson (Ohio) Country. Office: 845 N Michigan Ave Chicago IL 60611

BERST, JANET ROSE, data processing exec.; b. Hammond, Ind., June 25, 1937; d. John Albert and Mary Ruth (Barnes) B.; B.A. in Speech, Taylor U., Upland, Ind., 1959; diploma in programming Internat. Data Processing Inst., Cin., 1967. Lead programmer analyst Midland Mut. Life Ins. Co., Columbus, Ohio, 1969-72, Ohio Dept. Edn., Columbus, 1972-75; sr. programmer analyst Ohio Youth Commn., Columbus, 1975-77; sr. devel. analyst Lincoln Nat. Life Ins., Fort Wayne, Ind., 1977-79; tech. analyst Washington Nat. Ins., Evanston, Ill., 1979—. Active, Evanston Hist. Soc., Chgo. Architecture Found. Life Mgmt. Inst. fellow, 1979. Mem. Assn. Systems Mgmt., Assn. Computing Machinery (pres. Central Ohio chpt.), AAUW, Internat. Platform Assn. Methodist. Club: Photography. Author: Christianity and the Real World. Office: 1630 Chicago Ave Evanston IL 60201

BERTELSEN, THOMAS ELWOOD, JR., investment banker; b. Chgo., Feb. 13, 1940; s. Thomas Elwood and Virginia Marie (McKenna) B.; A.B., U. Kan., 1962; LL.B., Stanford, 1965; M.B.A., Columbia, 1966; m. Sandra Lee Morgan, May 9, 1970; children—Derek, Page. With Dean Witter Reynolds Inc., N.Y.C., 1966—, v.p., 1969—, mgr. corporate fin. dept., San Francisco, 1974, sr. v.p., 1975-80, mng. dir. investment banking, 1980—. Roman Catholic. Club: Bankers (San Francisco). Home: PO Box 397 Ross CA 94957 Office: 45 Montgomery St San Francisco CA 94106

BERTERMANN, EUGENE RUDOLPH, clergyman, broadcasting co. exec.; b. Bittern Lake, Alta., Can., Sept. 2, 1914; s. Ernest Henry and Anna Maria (Kaiser) B. (parents Am. citizens); student Concordia Coll., Milw., 1929-33; B.D., Concordia Sem., St. Louis, 1937; A.M., Washington U., St. Louis, 1938, Ph.D., 1940; LL.D., Concordia Tchrs. Coll., Seward, Nebr., 1968; Litt.D., Hanyang U., Seoul, Korea, 1976; m. Ruth Martha Hoffmann, Dec. 27, 1937; children—Delvin, David, Deborah. Ordained to ministry Lutheran Ch., 1940; dir. Lutheran Hour Luth. Laymens League, St. Louis, 1935-59, exec. dir. Luth. Laymens League, 1967-71; exec. dir. Luth. Found.; exec. sec. Luth. TV, Luth. Ch. Mo. Synod, St. Louis, 1959-67; exec. dir. Far East Broadcasting Co., 1971-79; asso. dir. Luth. Bible Translators, Orange, Calif., 1979—; dir. 1st Bank of Whittier. Bd. dirs. Luth. Braille Workers, Luth. Ch.-Mo. Synod, Pacific States U., Los Angeles. Mem. Nat. Religious Broadcasters (sec.), Internat. Christian Broadcasters (v.p.). Clubs: Ill. Athletic (Chgo.); Mo. Athletic (St. Louis). Author: Day by Day With Jesus Devotional Calendar, 1952—. Home: 2550 Shadow Ridge Ln Orange CA 92667 Office: PO Box 5566 Orange CA 92667

BERTHOLD, JOHN RICHARD, craft co. exec., educator; b. Huntington, W.Va., Mar. 17, 1937; s. John Grover, Jr. and Dorothy Ann (Waugh) B.; B.S., Wheeling Coll., 1959; M.B.A., Stanford U., 1965; m. Kathleen Anne Laband, Oct. 28, 1961; children—Jennifer Anne, Pamela Nelle, John Stephen. Asst. to pub. Lane Pub. Co., San Francisco, 1960-63; brand mgr. Procter and Gamble, Cin., 1965-68; v.p. mktg. The Leisure Group, Inc., Los Angeles, 1968-71; exec. v.p. GSC/Six Flags Inc., Los Angeles, 1971-73; pres. John Berthold & Co., Pasadena, Calif., 1973-75; exec. v.p. Saska Sports Industries, Brisbane, Calif., 1975-77; v.p. Sunset Designs, Inc., San Ramon, Calif., 1977—; lectr. bus. mgmt. Stanford Bus. Sch., 1979—. Sec., Jaycees, 1962; mem. Nat. Republican Com., 1971-72. Mem. Alpha Sigma Nu. Roman Catholic. Contbr. articles to publs. Office: 3401 Crow Canyon Rd San Ramon CA 94583

BERTRAND, RUSSELL EARL, retail grocery chain ofcl.; b. Houston, Aug. 4, 1948; s. Charles J. and Nancy M. (Hanks) B.; diploma Houston Fire Acad., 1967; B.S. in Edn., Howard Payne U., 1973; m. Katherine Ann Feuge, Aug. 15, 1970. With Kroger Co., Houston, 1976—, sr. personnel asst., 1977-78, personnel mgr., 1979-81, mgr. transp., 1981—. Served to 2d lt. USAF, 1973-76. Mem. Am. Soc. Tng. and Devel., Alpha Phi Omega. Republican. Baptist. Home: 803 Fawn Circle Rt 2 Box 2870 Porter TX 77365 Office: 701 Gelhorn PO Box 1309 Houston TX 77001

BERTSCHE, COPELAND GRAY, lawyer, telephone co. exec.; b. N.Y.C., Aug. 8, 1941; s. William I. and Louise C. B.; B.A., Colgate U., 1963; J.D., Seton Hall U., 1971; M.B.A., N.Y. U., 1976; m. Andree Gowen Wright; children—Alane W., Brijit M., Victoria G., Jessica H. Admitted to N.J. bar, 1971, U.S. Supreme Ct. bar, 1978; mgr. Lawyers' and Mchts. Transl. Bur., N.Y.C., 1966-71; also. firm John B. M. Frohling, Newark, 1971-74, firm Connell, Foley & Geiser, Newark, 1974-76; atty. N.J. Bell Telephone Co., Newark, 1976—, Montclair (N.J.) Bd. Edn., 1980—. Trustee, chmn. investment com. Assn. for Children of N.J., 1978—; trustee Essex County Heart Assn., 1974-78, Nat. Council on Alcoholism-No. Jersey, 1975—; trustee, 1st v.p. Child Service Assn., 1975-78. Served with U.S. Army, 1963-66. Mem. Am., N.J., Essex County bar assns., N.J. Assn. Corp. Counsel. Home: 147 S Mountain Ave Montclair NJ 07042 Office: 540 Broad St Newark NJ 07101

BERY, RAJENDRA NATH, engring. co. exec.; b. Cuttack, India, Dec. 4, 1930; s. Kashi R. and Bhagwati (Bhandari) B.; sr. sch. certificate U. Cambridge (Eng.), 1945; B.S. in Chem. Engring., U. Mo., 1951; M.S. in Chem. Engring., N.J. Inst. Tech., 1954, M.S. in Mgmt. Indsl. Engring., 1956; m. Marjorie Adele Bauernfeind, Apr. 14, 1956; children—Renuka, Rajan. Research engr. Agrico Chem. Co., Carteret, N.J., 1951-57; sr. tech. officer Imperial Chem. Industries Ltd., Calcutta, India, 1957-60; process mgr., proposal mgr., sales mgr. Foster Wheeler Corp., Livingston, N.J., 1960-78; chief exec. officer, dir. FW Mgmt. Ops. Ltd., Milan, Italy, 1979—; dir. Foster Wheeler Italiana (U.S.A.); cons. and tech. witness on synthetic gas energy, hydrogen mfg. Trustee Far Brook Sch., Short Hills, N.J., Am. Sch. of Milan. Mem. Am. Inst. Chem. Engrs., Am. Chem. Soc., Asia Soc. Contbr. articles to profl. jours. Research, devel., design on synthetic gas, hydrogen, fertilizers and metall. plants. Home: 42 Whittingham Terr Millburn NJ 07041 Office: FW Mgmt Ops Ltd Via Vittor Pisani 25 Milan 20124 Italy

BERZINS, ARNOLDS, constrn. co. exec., realtor; b. Riga, Latvia, Aug. 13, 1919; s. Jekabs and Katrine (Krumins) B.; student Manhattan Inst. Commerce, 1952-53, Hofstra U., 1956-59; m. Jolanta Treiverts, Sept. 20, 1950; children—Gints, Anita. Vice pres. Gen. Builders Corp., 1958-66, gen. mgr. Gen. Bldg. Supply Corp., 1954-66; owner, operator motel, restaurant, Saratoga Springs and Elka Park, N.Y., 1964-70; pres. Berzins Bldg. Corp., Nashua, N.H., 1970—, Berzins Realty Corp., Nashua, 1970—. Founder, DAV Recreation Center, 1962—; founder, trustee Latvian Meml. Park, Elka Park, N.Y. Served with Latvian Army, 1944-46. Mem. Nat. Assn. Home Builders, Nat. Assn. Real Estate Bds., Latvian Am. Disabled Vets. (trustee), Latvian Welfare Soc. Mass. (trustee), Latvian Heritage Found. Republican. Lutheran. Home: 3 Fairhaven Rd Nashua NH 03060 Office: 254 Daniel Webster Hwy S Nashua NH 03060

BESCHLOSS, MORRIS RICHARD, valve mfg. co. exec.; b. Berlin, Germany, Mar. 7, 1929; s. Ottokar and Manya (Levine) B.; B.A. in Commerce, U. Ill., 1952, B.S. in Journalism, 1952; m. Ruth Greenwald, Nov. 13, 1954; children—Michael, Steven. Asst. advt. mgr. Continental Casualty Ins. Co., Chgo., 1954-55; advt. mgr. Standard Screw Co., Bellwood, Ill., 1955-56; advt. mgr. Hammond Valve Corp., 1956-58, asst. sales mgr., 1958-61, field sales mgr., 1961-62, v.p. sales, 1962-63, pres., 1963-68, chmn. bd., 1968—, also chief exec. officer; pres. Conval Corp., Chgo., 1968—; v.p., dir. Condec Corp., Old Greenwich, Conn. Pres. Bd. Edn. Sch. Dist. 161, Flossmoor, Ill., 1968-73. Served to capt., Psychol. Warfare div. AUS, 1952-54. Recipient Free Enterprise Found. award, 1965; Distinguished Eagle award Boy Scouts Am., 1974. Mem. Valve Mfrs. Assn. N.Y. (pres. emeritus, dir.), Assn. Industry Mfrs. (charter pres.), Plumbing-Heating-Cooling Information Bur. Chgo. (chmn.), Young Pres.'s Orgn. Club: Econs. (Chgo.). Contbr. articles to profl. jours. Home: 180 E Pearson St Chicago IL 60611 Office: 875 N Michigan Ave Chicago IL 60611

BESHEARS, CHARLES DANIEL, ins. cons.; b. Vandalia, Mo., Sept. 6, 1917; s. Charles D. and Anabel (Baker) B.; grad. exec. program in bus. mgmt. UCLA, 1968; grad. Advanced Mgmt. Program, Harvard U., 1971; m. Mildred Domreis, Nov. 23, 1941; children—Jacqueline, Charles III, Scott, Melanie. With Farmers Ins. Group, Los Angeles, 1937-79; former v.p. Farmers Group, Inc.; former pres., dir. Farmers New World Life Ins. Co.; ins. cons., Santiago, Chile, 1979—. Served with AUS, 1942-45. Mem. C. of C., Assn. M.B.A. Execs., Am. Soc. C.L.U.'s, Internat. Platform Assn., VFW, DAV. Republican. Baptist. Club: Wash. Athletic. Office: Casilla 53 Miramonte L Condes Santiago Chile

BESSE, JANET ALICE, bus. exec.; b. Pitts., Dec. 1, 1948; d. Herbert J. and Ruth A. (Melhorn) Rigby; B.S. and B.A. in Math., Fla. State U., 1969; div. High sch. tchr. math. Fla. Sch. Bd., 1969-72; mktg. rep. Burroughs Corp., Anchorage, 1974-75; mktg. dir. Escom, Inc., Anchorage, 1975-78, gen. mgr., 1978-79; owner Phototech, Anchorage, 1976—, Floor Finishers, Anchorage, 1979—; ind. fin. cons., 1980—. Mem. steering com. Midtown Bus. Assn., 1980—. Mem. Am. Mgmt. Assn., Data Processing Mgmt. Assn. (dir. 1978), Nat. Fedn. Ind. Businessmen, Screen Printers Assn. Internat. Home: SRA Box 80A Anchorage AK 99502 Office: 2415 Spenard Rd Anchorage AK 99503

BESSETTE, EDGAR LEO, JR., corp. exec.; b. Providence, Feb. 28, 1941; s. Edgar Leo and Zelma Roberta (Whiteside) B.; B.S., U. R.I., 1967; m. Lois Judith Abranow, Aug. 22, 1970; children—Jeffrey Robert, Renee Suzzanne. Asst. plant acct. Allied Chem. Co., Pottsville, Pa., 1967-68, plant acct., Whippany, N.J., 1968-70; controller landscape div., Columbus (Miss.) div. C.H. Stuart Inc., Newark, N.Y., 1970-72, Nobility Prestige div., Gateway Home Decorators, 1973-75, adminstrv. mgr., Gateway Home Decorators, Printing div., 1975-78, div. controller Hanover Distbrs., Gateway Distbrs., Wolco div., Spl. Markets div., Quality Service div., 1978-80; dir. mfg. services Bastian Bros. Co., Rochester, N.Y., 1980—. Served with USMC, 1960-63. Mem. Nat. Assn. Accts. Jewish. Home: 59 Brentwood Ln Fairport NY 14450 Office: Bastian Bros Co 1600 N Clinton Rochester NY 14621

BESSON, MICHEL LOUIS, mfg. co. exec.; b. Nancy, France, Mar. 14, 1934; came to U.S., 1980; s. Marcel L. and Germaine (Savignac) B.; Ecole Centrale Des Arts et Manufactures, 1959; M. Chem. Engring., M.I.T., 1960; m. Marie Jose Ellie, May 19, 1967; children—Frederique, Pascal, Thomas. Supt. engr. Cellulose du Rin, Paris, 1962-68, resident mill mgr., 1968-72, v.p., 1972-74, exec. v.p., 1974-76, chmn. bd., chief exec. officer, 1977-80; vice chmn., pres., chief exec. officer Certain-Teed Corp., Valley Forge, Pa., 1980—. Mem. Alumni Assn. Ecole Centrale des Arts et Manufactures (v.p. 1978-80). Office: PO Box 860 Valley Forge PA 19482

BEST, RAYMOND MERLE, cons. engr.; b. Pottstown, Pa., Nov. 20, 1938; s. Raymond Earl and Mary Elizabeth (Altland) B.; student Pa. State U., 1956-59; m. Karen Joel Diener, Nov. 1, 1958; children—Raymond Karl, Lauren Elizabeth. Draftsman, Berger Assos., Harrisburg, Pa., 1957-58; from draftsman to resident engr. William E. Sees, Jr., cons. engr., Harrisburg, 1959-62; with Buchart-Horn, Inc., York, Pa., 1962—, asst. chief engr., 1969-73, v.p., 1972—, sec., 1976—, also dir. Chmn., Silver Spring (Pa.) Twp. Bd. Suprs., 1969—; del. W. Shore Council Govts., 1972—, pres., 1977-78. Registered profl. engr., Pa., Ga., Del., N.C., N.H., N.Y., Va., Ind. Mem. ASCE, Nat. Soc. Profl. Engrs., Pa. Soc. Profl. Engrs., Engring. Soc. Pa., Cons. Engrs. Council Pa., Am. Water Works Assn., Water Pollution Control Fedn., Water Works Operators Assn. Pa. (pres. 1979-80), Nat. Assn. Water Cos., Pa. Assn. Twp. Suprs. (past chpt. pres.). Republican. Lutheran. Home: 30 Timber Rd Mechanicsburg PA 17055 Office: 55 S Richland Ave PO Box M-55 York PA 17405

BEST, ROBERT M., ins. co. exec.; b. Newcomerstown, Ohio, May 9, 1922; s. Chester R. and Beatrice (Mulvane) B.; B.S., Ohio State U., 1947; m. Roselyn Welton, Aug. 12, 1944; children—Eric, Linda, Grant. Agt., Bus. Men's Assurance Co. Am., 1946-48; with Security Mut. Life Ins. Co., Binghamton, N.Y., 1948—, exec. v.p., 1966-69, pres., 1969—, pres., chief exec. officer, 1972—, chmn. exec. com., 1974-77, chmn. bd., 1977—; dir. Marine Midland Bank, Buckingham Mfg. Co., Binghamton and Utica Mut. Ins. Co. (N.Y.); mem. N.Y. State Adv. Bd. Life Ins. Examinations, N.Y. State Ins. Bd.; exec. com. Life Ins. Guaranty Corp. Dir., Broome County Community Charities, Inc., Craw Found., Valley Devel. Found.; chmn. Broome County Performing Arts Theatre Com.; mem. council SUNY, Binghamton; dir. Harpur Found., Harpur Forum, SUNY; trustee Am. Coll., Bus. Council N.Y. State; pres. Twintier Home Health Care; bd. govs. Internat. Ins. Seminars. Served to lt. USNR, 1942-46. Mem. Am. Council Life Ins. (past dir.), Life Ins. Council N.Y. (past dir.). Republican. Clubs: Binghamton, Econ. (N.Y.C.); Oteyokwa Lake (Hallstead, Pa.), Masons, Scottish Rite. Office: Court House Sq Binghamton NY 13902

BETHEA, BARRON, lawyer, elec. hardware mfr., former state legislator; b. Birmingham, Ala., May 20, 1929; s. Malcolm and Wilma (Edwards) B.; student U. of South, 1948-50; B.S., U. Ala., 1952, LL.B., 1953; m. Phyllis Parker, Sept. 8, 1967; children—Barron Augustus, Elizabeth Ann. Admitted to Ala. bar, 1953; practiced in Birmingham, 1953-54; founder Barron Bethea Co., Inc., elec. hardware mfrs., Birmingham, 1957, chmn., pres., sec., treas., 1957—. Mem. Ala. Democratic Exec. Com., 1958-62; mem. Ala. Ho. of Reps., 1962-66. Mem. mgmt. bd. Five Points YMCA, 1962. Served as 1st lt. USAF, 1954-56. Mem. Ala. State Bar, Birmingham Bar Assn., Asso. Industries Ala., Birmingham C. of C., Am. Judicature Soc., Scabbard and Blade, Phi Gamma Delta, Phi Alpha Delta. Methodist. Elk. Club: Downtown. Patentee in field. Home: 4963 Spring Rock Rd Birmingham AL 35223 Office: POB 2202 Birmingham AL 35201

BETLACHIN, VLADIMIR, state ofcl.; b. Teheran, Iran, June 28, 1946; came to U.S., 1965, naturalized, 1978; B.S. in E.E., W.Va. Inst. Tech., 1969. Mgr. data processing The Civil Servants Ins. Orgn., Teheran, 1972-73; mng. dir. Iran VJAT Co., Teheran, 1974-75; mgr. systems and data processing The Internat. Bank of Iran, 1975-78; dir. info. systems South Coast Air Quality Mgmt. Dist., State of Calif., El Monte, 1978—. Mem. IEEE. Office: 9150 E Flair Dr El Monte CA 91731

BETON, JOHN ALLEN, communications co. exec.; b. Chgo., Aug. 25, 1950; s. John Henry and Anne Marilyn (Joseph) B.; B.S., U. Ill., 1972; M.B.A., DePaul U., 1975. Market analyst ITT Telecommunications, Des Plaines, Ill., 1972-73, mgr. mktg. services, 1973-75, mgr. market planning, Hartford, Conn., 1975-77, area mgr., Detroit, 1977-80, mgr. mktg. ops., Des Plaines, Ill., 1980—. Mem. Am. Mktg. Assn., Am. Philatelic Soc., Pitcairn Islands Study Group, Phi Eta Sigma, Phi Kappa Phi, Beta Gamma Sigma. Presbyterian (deacon). Home: 2800 N Lake Shore Dr #1601 Chicago IL 60657 Office: 2000 S Wolf Rd Des Plaines IL 60018

BETSCH, PHILIP ANTHONY, pharm. co. exec.; b. N.Y.C., July 6, 1940; s. Robert A. and Josephine (Rizzo) B.; B.S. in Commerce, Rider Coll., 1963; m. Dianna T. Johnson, May 12, 1964; children—David Eric, Ceili Elizabeth. Asst. econ. attache Fgn. Service Office, Dept. State, Far East, 1964-68; acting mgr. profl. audit staff Price Waterhouse & Co., N.Y.C., 1968-71; corp. internat. controller Interpub. Group Cos. Inc., N.Y.C., 1971-73; controller, chief fin. officer Morton Norwich Products Inc. div. Norwich Internat., N.Y.C., 1973-76; v.p. fin. Far East region Sterling Asia Hdqrs., Makati, Philippines, 1976-79; v.p., treas. Sterling Products Internat. Inc., N.Y.C., 1979—; guest speaker internat. accounting topics and bus. affairs Pace U., Lions and Rotary clubs. Recipient Presdl. citation Outstanding Civilian Service, Vietnam, 1967; C.P.A. Republican. Methodist. Office: Sterling Drug Inc care Sterling Products Internat Inc 90 Park Ave New York NY 10016

BETTS, BARBARA LANG, lawyer, rancher; b. Anaheim, Calif., Apr. 28, 1926; d. W. Harold and Helen (Thompson) Lang; B.A., Stanford U., 1948; LL.B., Balboa U., 1951; m. Bert A. Betts, July 11, 1962; children—John Chauncey IV, Frederick Prescott, Roby Francis II, Bert Alan, Randy W., Sally Ellen, Bruce Harold. Admitted to Calif. bar, 1952, U.S. Ct. of Appeals, 1952, U.S. Supreme Ct. bar, 1978; pvt. practice law, Oceanside, Calif., 1952; partner law firm Roby F. Hayes & Barbara Lang Hayes, 1952-60; practiced in San Diego, 1960—; city atty. Carlsbad, 1959-63; partner ins. firm Fred Hayes & Sons, 1955-60; v.p. W.H. Lang Corp., 1964-70; sec. Internat. Prodn. Assos., 1967—, Margaret M. McCabe, M.D., Inc., 1976—. Chmn. Traveler's Aid, 1952-53; pres. Oceanside-Carlsbad Jr. Chambrettes, 1955-56; dir. No. San Diego County for Retarded Children, 1957-58; v.p. Oceanside Diamond Jubilee Com., 1958; vice chmn. Carlsbad Planning Commn., 1959; mem. San Diego County Planning Congress, 1959; mem. resolutions com. Dem. State Central Com., 1958-60, mem. exec. com., 1962—; co-chmn. 28th Congl. Dist., 1960—; del. Dem. Nat. Conv., 1960; candidate Calif. State Legislature, 77th Dist., 1954. Mem. Am., Calif., San Diego Co. bar assns., U.S. Supreme Ct. Hist. Soc., C. of C. (see Oceanside, 1956-57 v.p. 1957-58, dir. 3 terms, legislation chmn. 1954-60, edn. chmn. 1957-60), AAUW (Calif. status of women com. 1957-58, legislation chmn. 1954-59, Calif. legis. com. 1957-58, asst. Calif. legis. chmn. 1958-59, pres. Palomar br. 1959-61), D.A.R. (membership chmn. 1957-58, vice regent Oceanside chpt. 1958-60, regent 1960-61), Nat. Inst. Municipal Law Officers (com. city-state relations), Country Friends, San Diego Hist. Soc., Fullerton Jr. Assistance League, Calif. Scholarship Fedn. (life), No. San Diego County Asso. Chambers of Commerce (sec.-treas. 1960-61), Bus. and Profl. Women's Club (legislation chmn. So. dist. 1958-59), San Diego C. of C. (inter-Am. com.), Phi Beta Kappa. Presbyn. Clubs: Oceanside-Carlsbad Country Inc. (sec.), Soroptimist Internat. (pres. club 1958-59, sec. pub. affairs San Diego and Imperial counties, pres. council 1958-59), Barristers. Author: (with Bert A. Betts) A Citizen Answers, 1972. Home: Betts Ranch Elverta CA 95626 Office: 8701 E Levee Rd Elverta CA 95626 also 3119a Howard Ave San Diego CA 92104

BETTS, HUGH SUMNER, JR., ins. co. exec.; b. Winchendon, Mass., Aug. 4, 1925; s. Hugh Sumner and Luella Conkling (Sidney) B.; student Lawrence Acad., Groton, Mass., 1940-42, Dartmouth, 1943-44, U. N.H., 1945-48; m. Marguerite Eleanor Brophy, Aug. 17, 1946; children—Colleen A., Terri A. Agt., supr., gen. agt. Penn Mut. Ins. Co., 1948-56; asst. v.p. Continental Assurance Co., Chgo., 1956-65; v.p. div. Mayflower Life Ins. Co., Chgo., 1966; v.p. Continental Am. Ins. Co., Wilmington, Del., 1967-72; v.p. mktg. dir. N.Am. Co. for Life & Health, Chgo., 1972-74, exec. v.p., 1975; exec. v.p. mktg. Guarantee Res. Life Ins. Co., Hammond, Ind., from 1975; now pres. Hugh Betts & Assos., Inc., Chgo. dir. N.Am. Co. for Property and Casualty. Served with USMCR, 1943-45. Mem. Life Ins. Mktg. and Research Assn. Club: La Grange Country. Home: 705 S Brainard Ave LaGrange IL 60525 Office: 5901 N Cicero Ave Suite 401 Chicago IL 60646

BETTS, JAMES FRANKLIN, ins. holding co. exec.; b. Cleve., Apr. 6, 1932; s. John W. and Lois Ann B.; B.S.B.A., Washington U., St. Louis, 1957; m. Martha Goebel, Dec. 29, 1956; children—Nancy, Susan, Liza. With New Eng. Life Ins. Co., 1950-72, gen. agt., Richmond, Va., 1966-69, home office v.p., 1969-72, sr. v.p., 1972; pres. Life Ins. Co. Va., Richmond, 1973—, Continental Fin. Services Co., 1980—; chmn. bd. Life of Va., 1980—, Lawyers Title Co., 1980—; exec. v.p. Continental Group, Inc., 1980—; dir. Va. Electric and Power Co., Central Nat. Bank, Central Fidelity Banks. Bd. dirs. United Way, chmn. 1981 campaign United Way Greater Richmond; bd. dirs. Wolf Trap Found.; bd. sponsors Sch. Bus. Adminstrn., William and Mary Coll. Served with U.S. Army, 1954-56. Mem. Am. Soc. C.L.U.'s, Am. Council Life Ins. (com. field relations). Roman Catholic. Office: 6600 W Broad St Richmond VA 23230 also PO Box 27424 Richmond VA 23261

BETZ, FRANK THEODORE, investment sales exec.; b. Bklyn., Sept. 9, 1923; s. Frank T. and Elizabeth (Green) B.; student Manual Tng. High Sch., Bklyn., B.S., Rider Coll., 1946-49; m. Jean Hapanowicz, Apr. 18, 1949; children—Frank, Eleanor, Richard. Salesman, Knickerbocker Shares, Inc., 1948-52, sales mgr., 1952-53; sales mgr. Del. Distbr., Inc., Phila., 1953-54, v.p., dir. sales, 1955-58; pres. Robinson & Co., 1958-60; exec. v.p. H.A. Riecke & Co., Inc., 1960-63; dir., asso. Harry J. Woehr & Assos., 1963—; v.p., dir. sales Federated Plans, 1963-64; pres. Frank T. Betz & Co., 1964—, Equity Cons., Inc., 1971-72, Financial Internat., 1974—. Served as sgt. USMCR, 1942-45. Decorated Air medal. Clubs: Old York Road Country, Poor Richard, Penn Athletic (Phila.). Home: 1554 Hower Rd Abington PA 19001 Office: Phila Nat Bank Bldg Philadelphia PA 19107

BETZ, JEAN, investment securities co. exec.; b. Utica, N.Y., Mar. 1, 1927; d. Walter John and Anna (Pomichowska) Hapanowicz; student Utica Free Acad., 1941-45; B.S., Rider Coll., 1949; postgrad. Beaver Coll., 1964-65; m. Frank Theodore Betz, Apr. 18, 1949; children—Frank, Eleanor Jean, Richard Walter. Editorial writer Book Publishers Projects, Inc., N.Y.C., 1967-68; sec., dir. Frank T. Betz & Co., Inc., investment securities, Phila., 1966—. Editor: The First Book of Magic, 1968. Home: 1554 Hower Rd Abington PA 19001 Office: Philadelphia National Bank Bldg Philadelphia PA 19107

BETZ, JOHN FREDERICK, utility exec.; b. Phila., Oct. 19, 1914; s. Harry W. and Claire G. (Robar) B.; B.E.E., Rutgers U., 1937. Cadet engr. Pub. Service Electric and Gas Co., Newark, 1937-40, asst. engr., 1940-61, div. supt. Elizabeth (N.J.) area, 1961-67, gen. supt. distbn. gen. office, Newark, 1967-68, gen. mgr. engring., 1968-71, v.p. elec. ops., 1971-74, sr. v.p. engring. and prodn., 1974, pres., to 1980, now dir.; asso. Mgmt. Analysis Co., San Diego, 1980—. Exec. bd. Union (N.J.) council Boy Scouts Am., 1960-61; bd. dirs. YMCA Eastern Union County, 1960-61; trustee Union Coll. Registered profl. engr., N.J. Mem. IEEE, Edison Electric Inst. (exec. com. engring. and operating div. 1973—), Phi Beta Kappa, Tau Beta Pi. Republican. Episcopalian. Club: Plainfield Country (Edison, N.J.). Office: 80 Park Pl Newark NJ 07101

BETZ, NORMAN THOMAS, newspaper pub.; b. Boulder, Colo., July 17, 1949; s. Frederick McClean and Barbara Lee (Applebach) B.; certificate Lamar Community Coll., 1969; B.A. in Polit. Sci., U. Colo., 1978; m. Ava Marie Woolliscroft, July 24, 1971; children—Kathryn Melinda, Lucy Nicole. Press photographer Lamar (Colo.) Tri-State Daily News, 1966-69, co-pub., 1975—; pub. Holly (Colo.) Chieftain, 1975—, gen. mgr., 1978—; v.p. Betz Pub. Co., Lamar, 1976—, bus. mgr., 1978—. Trustee Town of Holly, 1976-78; mem. exec. bd. So. Colo. Econ. Devel. Dist., 1976—; bd. dirs. Prowers County Devel., Inc.; mem. So. Area Employment Council; chmn. Local Area Employment Advisory Council. Served with USN, 1969-73. Recipient photojournalism award Colo. Press Assn., 1968, 69, 74, best editorial award, 1975, 76, best story award, 1977. Mem. Colo. Press Assn., Nat. Newspaper Assn., Nat. Fedn. Ind. Bus., Alumni Assn. U. Colo., Am. Legion. Democrat. Methodist. Clubs: Lions, Comml., Odd Fellows (Holly). Home: 734 W Colorado Ave Holly CO 81047 Office: 310 S 5th St Lamar CO 81052

BEULKE, RICHARD ARMAND, r.r. exec.; b. St. Paul, Apr. 17, 1924; s. Herbert Fredrick and Lillian Bertha (Westphal) B.; student U. Okla., 1943-44, U. Minn., 1962-67, Advanced Mgmt. Program, Harvard U., 1969; m. Alice Ruth Kooistra, June 7, 1947; children—Diana Lou, Richard Jeffrey. Claim agt. Burlington No., Inc., Spokane, Wash., 1947-49, dist. claim agt., Glendive, Mont., 1949-50, dist. claim agt., St. Paul, 1950-51, Livingston, Mont., 1951-59, asst. corp. sec., 1959-66, corp. sec., 1966-67, dir. personnel, 1967-70, v.p. personnel 1970, v.p. Omaha region, 1970, v.p. Seattle-Portland region, 1973-80, v.p. Billings (Mont.) region, 1980—; pres., dir. Delta Alaska Terminal, Ltd.; trustee Oreg. Trunk Ry.; dir. Oreg. Elec. Ry. Co.; v.p., dir. Walla Walla Valley Ry. Co. Mem. Livingston City Council, pres., 1957-58, mayor, 1958-59; former chmn. Livingston City/County Planning Commn.; bd. dirs. Econ. Devel. Council Puget Sound; trustee Corp. Council for Arts; asso. gen. chmn. corp. divs. United Way of King County; bd. dirs. Green River Community Coll. Found.; metro chmn., mem. adv. bd. Nat. Alliance of Bus. Served with AUS, 1943-45. Mem. Seattle C. of C. (dir., exec. com.), Puget Sound Chambers of Commerce (chmn.), Ind. Colls. of Wash. (dir.), Nat. Def. Transp. Assn. (life). Republican. Lutheran. Clubs: Masons, Shriners. Office: 600 1st Northwestern Bank Center 175 N 27th St Billings MT 59101

BEVARD, RALPH EDWARD, eraser mfg. co. exec.; b. Newark, Ohio, Mar. 20, 1915; s. Leroy Herman and Elizabeth Sarah (Strear) B.; B.S. in Bus. Adminstrn., Syracuse U., 1962; m. Renate Monika Odorff, Sept. 15, 1967; children—Virginia, Ralph Edward, Peter, Marilyn Bevard Kegerreis, Karen Bevard Steenberg, Jon, James, Marcus. Prodn. mgr. Reliance Electric and Engring. Co., Cleve., 1935-47; pres. Am. Prodn. Co., Syracuse, N.Y., 1948—, Eraser Co., Inc., Syracuse, 1962—; dir. Eraser Internat. Ltd., Am. Prodn. and Grinding Co. Bd. dirs. Eraser Co. Pension Fund, Eraser Co. Profit Sharing Fund; pres. Community Council on Careers; mem. Citizens Found. Mem. Syracuse Jr. C. of C. (pres. 1949-50), U.S. Small Bus. Assn. (advisor 1952-64), Mfrs. Assn. Syracuse (dir.). Methodist (layleader-stewardship, chmn. adminstrv. bd., capital funds drive chmn.). Clubs: University, Syracuse Press. BeVard Theater in Civic Center named in his honor. Home: 108 Woodmancy Ln Fayetteville NY 13066 Office: 4961 Oliva Dr Syracuse NY 13221

BEVERETT, ANDREW JACKSON, real estate broker; b. Midland City, Ala., Feb. 21, 1917; s. Andrew J. and Ella Levonia (Adams) B.; B.S., Samford U., 1940; M.B.A., Harvard, 1942; m. Martha Sophia Landgrebe, May 26, 1951; children—Andrew Jackson III, James Edmund, Faye A. Various exec. positions in corporate planning and mgmt. United Air Lines, Chgo., 1946-66; dir. aviation econs., sr. marketing and econ. cons. Mgmt. and Econs. Research, Inc., Palo Alto, Calif., 1966-71; sr. economist Stanford Research Inst., Menlo Park, 1971-72; pres. Edy's on the Peninsula stores, Palo Alto, 1973-78; real estate broker and cons., Saratoga, Calif., 1979—. Served from ensign to lt. USNR, 1942-46. Mem. Am. Mktg. Assn., Nat. Assn. Realtors, Phi Kappa Phi, Pi Gamma Mu. Presbyterian. Club: Toastmasters. Home: 19597 Via Monte Dr Saratoga CA 95070 Office: Suite A 12175 Saratoga-Sunnyvale Rd Saratoga CA 95070

BEVERIDGE, JAMES RICHARD, mfg. co. exec.; b. Hilewood, Pa., May 19, 1932; s. James and Carrie Henry B.; student Indiana (Pa.) State Coll., 1956-61, Post Coll., Conn., 1976-77; m. Mary Ann Warholic, Oct. 24, 1953; children—James, David, Robert, Mark, John. Asst. quality mgr. Robertshaw Controls Co., Indiana, Pa., 1954-62; with Timex Corp., Waterbury, Conn., 1962—, mgr. corp. quality assurance, 1970-77, pres., gen. mgr. Timex Def. Products Corp., 1977—, also chmn., dir. Served with USMC, 1950-53; Korea. Mem. Am. Def. Preparedness Assn., Am. Soc. Quality Control, Conn. Bus. and Indsl. Assn., Smaller Mfrs. Assn. Waterbury, Watertown C. of C. Methodist. Home: 359 French St Watertown CT 06795 Office: PO Box 2126 Waterbury CT 06720

BEVINS, THOMAS PETER, II, pump mfr.; b. Seneca Falls, N.Y., June 26, 1936; s. Thomas Peter and Louise Bernadette (Stapleton) B.; student U. Notre Dame, 1957-59; B.A. in English and History, Hobart Coll., Geneva, N.Y., 1962; M.A. in Mgmt., Claremont (Calif.) Grad. Sch., 1975; m. Joyce Ann Bertino, Apr. 23, 1960; children—Thomas Peter, Kimberly Ann, Kelly Elizabeth, Martin Joseph, Julibeth Stapleton, Mary Kathleen. Trainee, Goulds Pumps, Inc., Seneca Falls, 1963-65, asst. supt. water systems plant, 1965-67, asst. supt. engring. plant, 1967-68, mgr. mfg. Vertical Pump div., Industry, Calif., 1970-73, v.p., gen. mgr., 1973-76, pres. Tex. div., Lubbock, 1967-77; plant mgr. U.S. Pumps, Lubbock, 1968-70; pres. Hydr-O-Matic Pumps div. Wylain, Inc., Ashland, Ohio, 1977-78; pres. W.L. Somner Co., Shreveport, La., 1978—, also dir.; dir. G & H Castings Corp., Slaton, Tex. Served with USNR, 1954-57; ETO. Licensed community coll. tchr. bus. and indsl. mgmt., Calif.; notary pub., Tex. Mem. Tex. Mfrs. Assn., Sump Pump Mfrs. Assn., Submersible Waste Water Assn., Lone Star Water Well Assn., Soc. Metal Prodn. of World, Lubbock C. of C., Am. Mgmt. Assn., Am. Nuclear Soc. Home: 4833 Camellia Ln Baird Rd #1221 Shreveport LA 71106 Office: PO Box 82 Shreveport LA 71161

BEXLEY, JAMES BYRON, bank exec.; b. Waco, Tex., Jan. 11, 1934; s. Joe Dan and Rubye Francis (Porter) B.; B.B.A., U. Tex. at El Paso; M.B.A., U. Houston; LL.B., Blackstone Sch. Law, Chgo.; m. Elsie Mae Murphy, Feb. 5, 1955; children—Byron Keith, Tammie Lynn. Petroleum landman El Paso Nat Natural Gas Co., 1957-64; staff landman Bank of the S.W., Houston, 1964-66, trust officer, 1966-68, v.p., 1968-71; sr. v.p., chief adminstrv. officer River Oaks Bank, Houston, 1971-73; pres. chief exec. officer Houston State Bank, 1973-75; pres., chief exec. officer First Bank of Houston, 1975-80; exec. v.p., chief operating officer 1st Nat. Bank, McAllen, Tex., 1980—; lectr. bank mgmt. Houston Community Coll., 1972—; mem. bd. dirs., lectr. Intermediate Banking Sch., So. Meth. U., 1978. Chmn. finance Western Div. Sam Houston Council Boy Scouts Am., 1973, dist. chmn. Karankawa Dist., 1971-73. Bd. govs. Houston Golf Assn. Served to lt., AUS, 1953-57. Recipient Outstanding Performance award Tex. Mid-Continent Oil & Gas Assn., 1964, Silver Beaver award Boy Scouts Am., 1973, outstanding teaching award Houston Community Coll., 1975, adult outstanding service award Sharpstown Sr. High Sch., 1975. Mem. Tex. Bankers Assn. (chmn. ops. com. 1970-72; electronic funds transfer com. 1977-78, legis. com. 1977), Bank Adminstrn. Inst. (mem. Nat. Trust Commn. 1968-72), Baptist (bd. Deacons, Finance Com.). Mason. Clubs: McAllen Country, Tower, McAllen Racquet, University, Sharpstown High Athletic Booster (pres. 1973-75). Author: Oil and Gas Forms for Petroleum Landmen, 1966; Banking Management, 1978; contbr. articles in field to profl. jours. Home: 1200 S Peking McAllen TX 78501 Office: PO Box 1000 McAllen TX 78501

BEYER, GERALD, lawyer; b. N.Y.C., Oct. 30, 1936; s. Jack and Betty (Gorman) B.; A.B., N.Y. U., 1959, LL.M., 1964; J.D., Bklyn. Law Sch., 1962; m. Marilyn Goldstein, Aug. 19, 1961; children—Lauren, Russell, Kimberly. Admitted to N.Y. bar, 1962, Fla. bar, 1970; with firm Riesner Jawitz & Holland, N.Y.C., 1964-67; sr. staff atty. U.S. SEC, 1967-69; with firm Stone Bittel Langer Blass & Corrigan, Miami, Fla., 1969-71; sr. partner firm Beyer Lerner & Puder-Harris, Ft. Lauderdale, Fla., 1971—; adj. prof. law Nova Law Sch., 1976, lectr. securities law, 1978—. Mem. Fla. Bar (co-chmn. securities com. 1972). Club: Woodlands Country. Office: 2691 E Oakland Park Blvd Fort Lauderdale FL 33306

BHARGAVA, BHARAT KUMAR, bank exec.; b. Jaipur, India, Apr. 19, 1937; s. Bhagwan Das and Sharda B.; came to U.S., 1965, naturalized, 1975; M.B.A., Harvard U., 1967; m. Yognidra Bhargava, Nov. 15, 1960; children—Jyotsna, Alok, Benu. Asst. area mgr. internat. ops. Rohm & Haas & Co., Phila., 1967-68, EDP systems project mgr., 1968-71; v.p. EMH, Inc., Phila., 1971-72; fin. planning officer Phila. Nat. Bank, 1972-75, dir. mgmt. info., 1975-76, v.p., 1976—; cons. in field. Pres. Narberth (Pa.) Civic Assn., 1972-73, PTA, 1974-76.; councilman Borough of Narberth, 1977—. Mem. Bank Adminstrn. Inst., Soc. Mgmt. Info. Systems, Phila. Jr. C. of C. (v.p. 1971-73). Democrat. Hindu. Home: 77 Wynnedale Rd Narberth PA 19072 Office: Broad & Chestnut Sts Philadelphia PA 19101

BHATIA, VIJAY, catering service exec.; b. New Delhi, India, Mar. 13, 1941; s. Vishvamitra and Taravati (Gupta) B.; came to U.S., 1974; student Hotel and Catering Inst. London, 1963-67; m. Suneeta Gupta, Aug. 30, 1970; children—Nikhil, Prateek. Mgr. various hotels, London, 1963-69; mgr. food and beverage service Hotel Imperial, New Delhi, 1970, mgr. flight kitchen and restaurant Chefair-Air India, New Delhi, 1970-74; mgr. Ashoka Restaurant, N.Y.C., 1975-76; gen. mgr. Vegetarian Catering Services, N.Y.C., 1976—; dir. Glamar Travel Service, Inc., Brindavan Restaurant, Inc.; mem. Adv. Panel on Restaurant Bus., N.Y.C., 1977. Recipient spl. certificate of merit Prime Minister of India, 1973. Mem. Hotel Catering and Instl. Mgmt. Assn., Am. Mgmt. Assn., Royal Soc. Health, Food & Cookery Assn. London. Club: Lions (Lion of Yr. award 1979). Author: Catering Digest, 1970. Home: 119 E 38th St Paterson NJ 07514 Office: 310 E 44th St New York NY 10017

BIAGGINI, BENJAMIN FRANKLIN, railroad exec.; b. New Orleans, Apr. 15, 1916; s. B.F. and Maggie (Switzer) B.; B.S., St. Mary's of Tex., 1936, LL.D. (hon.), 1965; grad. Advanced Mgmt. Program Harvard, 1955; m. Anne Payton, Sept. 9, 1937; children—Constance (Mrs. Jay Guittard), Marian Anne (Mrs. David M. Krattebol). With So. Pacific Co., 1936—, pres., 1964—, chief exec. officer, 1968—, chmn., 1976—, also dir.; chmn., dir. So. Pacific Transp. Co.; chmn., dir. St. Louis Southwestern Ry. Co.; dir. Tenneco Inc., Ticor; mem. Nat. Transp. Policy Study Commn., 1976—; mem. Bus. Council, Bus. Roundtable, The Conf. Bd. Trustee, Calif. Inst. Tech., Transp. Council Calif., Nat. Safety Council; chmn. Bay Area Council, Inc.; bd. dirs. SRI Internat. Mem. Assn. Am. Railroads (dir.), Calif. Roundtable (founder, vice-chmn.). Office: Southern Pacific Bldg One Market Plaza San Francisco CA 94105

BIALEK, DIETER HEINZ, machinery mfg. co. exec.; b. Dusseldorf, W. Ger., Mar. 4, 1951; came to U.S., 1973; s. Karl August and Adleheid Anna (Mushoff) B.; student Bus. Coll., Duesseldorf, 1968-71. Sales rep. Schloemann A.G., Duesseldorf, 1968-71; sales engr. Am. Artos Corp., Charlotte, N.C., 1974-76, mktg. mgr., 1976-78, product mgr., 1978-80, planning and project mgr., 1980—, mgr. wood div., 1981—. Served with German Air Force, 1971-73. Home: 5100 Cherrycrest Ln Charlotte NC 28210 Office: 3201 Interstate 85 N Charlotte NC 28213

BIANCHI, PHILIP WILCKES, stockbroker; b. N.Y.C., Apr. 12, 1931; s. Albert William and Helen Gladys (Wilckes) B.; grad. St. Paul's Sch., 1949; B.S. in Indsl. Mgmt., Mass. Inst. Tech., 1953; m. Marion Ayer Bigelow, Mar. 6, 1976; children by previous marriage—Felicia Anne, Elizabeth Alexandra. With USM Corp., Boston, 1957-77, mgr. balance payments, 1971-74, adminstr. policies, procedures, 1974-77; with Drexel Burnham Lambert Inc., Boston, 1977—; dir. The Hedix Corp. Served with USAF, 1953-55. Episcopalian. Clubs: Country (Brookline); Union Boat (Boston). Home: 62 Circuit Rd Chestnut Hill MA 02167 Office: One Federal St Boston MA 02110

BIASCO, SHARON CHRISTEL, musical instrument co. exec.; b. Chgo., Aug. 10, 1951; d. David Paul and Patricia Joyce (Christel) B.; A.B., St. Mary's Coll., 1973; M.B.A., St. Louis U., 1976. Mktg. asst., mem. advt. staff Biasco Musical Instrument Co., Chgo., summers 1965-74, sec., treas., 1978—; mem. staff stock transfer dept. Stein Roe & Farnham, Inc., Chgo., 1975; project dir. Elrick & Lavidge, Inc., Chgo., 1976-78. Mem. Am. Mktg. Assn. Club: Chgo. Execs. Office: 5535 W Belmont Ave Chicago IL 60641

BIBB, THOMAS FARRIS, mfg. co. exec.; b. Murfreesboro, Tenn., July 26, 1943; s. Charles McLean and Ann Larue (Farris) B.; B.S., La. State U. at New Orleans, 1964; m. Barbara Eliasen, Nov. 14, 1964; children—Patrick, Michael, John. Accountant, Ernst & Ernst, New Orleans, 1964-67, San Antonio, 1967-69: controller Conroy, Inc., San Antonio, 1969—, v.p., 1975-77, v.p.-fin., 1978-80, exec. v.p.-adminstrn., 1980—. C.P.A., Tex., La. Mem. Am. Inst. C.P.A.'s, Nat. Assn. Accountants, Fin. Execs. Inst. Roman Catholic. Home: 3743 Chartwell St San Antonio TX 78230 Office: 3355 Cherry Ridge Dr San Antonio TX 78230

BIBEAULT, DONALD BERTRAND, fin. exec.; b. Woonsocket, R.I., Nov. 14, 1941; s. George Bertrand and Rene (Hebert) B.; B.S. in Elec. Engring., U. R.I., 1963; M.B.A., Columbia U., 1965; Ph.D., Golden Gate U., 1979. Fin. analyst Gen. Electric Co., various locations, 1965-67; sr. fin. analyst Am. Airlines Co., N.Y.C., 1968-69; v.p. Calif. Windsor Co., San Francisco, 1970-74; v.p. fin. Pacific States Steel Corp., Union City, Calif., 1975-78; exec. v.p. PLM Inc., San Francisco, 1978—; dir. Harvest Industries, Inc., Monon Trailer Corp., Avalon Savs. & Loan Co.; mem. faculty Golden Gate U., 1970—. Served to lt. U.S. Army, 1965. Recipient award Danforth Found., 1959. Mem. Corp. Planners Assn., Fin. Execs. Inst., Bankers Club San Francisco. Roman Catholic. Club: Commonwealth. Contbr. articles to profl. jours. Home: 2240 Buchanan St San Francisco CA 94115

BICHKO, MICHAEL FRANCIS, JR., accountant; b. Colver, Pa., Nov. 19, 1947; s. Michael and Anna (Pavuk) B.; student U. Pitts., 1965-67; B.S. in Acctg., St. Francis Coll., Loretto, Pa., 1972. Bus. mgr. Blacklick Valley Sch. Dist., Nanty Glo, Pa., 1973—, also sec. Bd. Edn. Served with U.S. Army, 1968-70. Mem. Assn. Sch. Bus. Ofcls. U.S. and Can., Pa. Assn. Sch. Bus. Ofcls. Home: RD 4 Box 79 Ebensburg PA 15931 Office: 555 Birch St Nanty Glo PA 15943

BICKEL, FLOYD GILBERT, III, investment counselor; b. St. Louis, Jan. 10, 1944; s. Floyd Gilbert II and Mary Mildred (Welch) B.; B.S. in Bus. Adminstrn., Washington U., St. Louis, 1966; M.S. in Commerce, St. Louis U., 1968; m. Martha Wohler, June 11, 1966; children—Christine Carleton, Susan Marie, Katherine Anne, Andrew Barrett. With research dept. Yates, Woods & Co., St. Louis, 1966-67; asst. br. mgr. E.F. Hutton & Co., Inc., St. Louis, 1967-70; asst. v.p., resident mgr. Bache & Co., Inc., St. Louis, 1970-72; pres. Donelan-Phelps Investment Advisors, Inc., St. Louis, 1972-80; founder, dir. Brentwood Bancshares, Inc.; pres., dir. Biclan, Inc., Data Research Assos., Inc., Gilmar Realty, Inc.; asso. prof. finance Lindenwood Coll.; cons. various television prodns. Mem. City of Des Peres (Mo.) Planning and Zoning Commn., 1975-76; chmn. St. Louis County Bd. Equalization, 1976-79; pub. safety commr. City of Des Peres, 1977-80, mem. audit and fin. com., 1980—. Cert. employee benefits specialist. Mem. Internat. Found. Employee Benefit Plan, Am. Mgmt. Assn., St. Louis Soc. Fin. Analysts. Republican. Presbyterian. Clubs: Bellerive Country; St. Louis; Commanderie de Bordeaux. Contbr. bus. articles to mags. Home: 12120 Belle Meade Saint Louis MO 63131 Office: 1034 S Brentwood Blvd Saint Louis MO 63117

BICKEL, WILLIAM CROFT, ret. oil co. exec., performing arts hall exec.; b. Pitts., Feb. 20, 1918; s. William Forman and Florence Graham (Croft) B.; A.B., Princeton, 1939; m. Minnette Chapman Duffy, Jan. 3, 1947; children—Minnette Chapman, Susan B. Scioli. With Gulf Oil Corp., various locations, 1946-78, v.p. mktg., Tulsa, 1965-71, Atlanta, 1971-74; v.p. govtl. relations, Washington, 1974-75, mgr. community relations, Pitts., 1976-78; chmn. advisory bd., mng. dir. Heinz Hall for Performing Arts, 1979—. Bd. dirs. Pitts. Opera, Pitts. Symphony. Served as pilot USMC, 1941-46. Decorated D.F.C. with stars, Air medal with stars. Mem. Pa. (dir. 1975—), Pitts. chambers commerce. Presbyterian. Clubs: Harvard Yale Princeton, Pitts. Golf, Fox Chapel (Pitts.), Boston (New Orleans); Hyannisport (Mass.); Beach (Centreville, Mass.); Capitol Hill (Washington). Home: 816 St James St Pittsburgh PA 15232 Office: Heinz Hall for Performing Arts 600 Penn Ave Pittsburgh PA 15222

BICKFORD, EDWARD DAVIDSON, steel co. exec.; b. Toronto, Ont., Can., Jan. 18, 1909; s. Harold Childe and Mary (Davidson) B.; student Yale U.; m. Ann Watson, June 10, 1937; children—Mary Ann Bickford Patten, Patricia Bickford Greenough, Susan Bickford Thomas (dec.), Edward W., Peter W. With Bethlehem (Pa.) Steel Corp., 1929—, asst. v.p., 1963, v.p. sales, 1963-70, sr. v.p. comml., 1970-74, now dir.; dir. Ogden Corp., Thompson Steel Co. Asst. dir. charge prodn. and distbn., chmn. prodn. directive com. Iron and Steel div. Nat Prodn. Authority, 1951-52. Mem. Am. Iron and Steel Inst. Episcopalian. Clubs: Brook, Yale, Links (N.Y.C.); Saucon Valley Country, Bethelehem (Bethlehem); The Steel Division. Home: RD 4 Saucon Valley Rd Bethlehem PA 18015 Office: Bethlehem Steel Corp 1 Bethlehem Plaza Bethlehem PA 18018

BICKLING, JAMES ALLAN, hosp. exec.; b. Easton, Md., July 14, 1948; s. James Albert and Kathryn Marie (Voshell) B.; A.A. in Bus. Adminstrn., Chesapeake Coll., 1971; B.S., Salisbury State Coll., 1973; M.S. in Bus. Adminstrn., Johns Hopkins U., 1975; postgrad. Sch. Law, U. Balt., 1975-76; postgrad. in public adminstrn. Nova U.; cert. fin. mgmt. program Harvard U., 1979; m. Swan, Mar. 24, 1968; 1 dau., Enid Nicole. Asst. registrar, registrar Chesapeake Coll., Wye Mills, Md. until 1976, also instr. dept. bus. and econs.; asst. controller Meml. Hosp. at Easton 1976-78, dir. fin. services, 1978—, asst. adminstr., 1980—, also dir. Bd. dirs. Caroline Health Facilities Corp., 1978—, pres., 1979—; chmn. edn. St. Paul's Meth. Ch., 1973-74, mem. adminstrv. bd., 1974-75, chmn. fin. com., 1978—; chmn. Greensboro (Md.) Zoning Appeals Bd., 1974-75. Served with U.S. Army, 1966-69. Mem. Assn. Collegiate Registrars and Admission Officers, Middle States Assn. Collegiate Registrars and Officers of Admission, Assn. for Instnl. Research, Nat. Assn. Accts., Hosp. Fin. Mgmt. Assn., Student Bar Assn. Club: Lions. Home: PO Box 155 Greensboro MD 21639 Office: 219 S Washington St Easton MD 21601

BIDDLE, DONALD RAY, aerospace co. exec.; b. Alton, Mo., June 30, 1936; s. Ernest Everet and Dortha Marie (McGuire) B.; student El Dorado (Kans.) Jr. Coll., 1953-55, Pratt (Kans.) Jr. Coll., 1955-56; B.S. in Mech. Engring., Washington U., St. Louis, 1961; postgrad. computer sci. Pa. State U. Extension, 1963; certificate bus. mgmt. Alexander Hamilton Inst., 1958; m. Nancy Ann Dunham, Mar. 13, 1955; children—Jeanne Kay Biddle Dionne, Mitchell Lee, Charles Alan. Design group engr. Emerson Elec. Mfg., St. Louis, 1957-61; design specialist Boeing Vertol, Springfield, Pa., 1962; cons. engr. Ewing Tech. Design, Phila., 1962-66; chief engr. rotary wing Gates Learjet, Wichita, Kans., 1967-70; dir. engring. Parsons of Calif. div. HITCO, Stockton, Calif., 1971—. Cons. engr. Scoutmaster, counselor, instl. rep. Boy Scouts Am., St. Ann, Mo., 1958-61; mem. Springfield Sch. Bd., 1964. Mem. Am. Helicopter Soc. (sec.-treas. Wichita chpt. 1969), ASME, Am. Mgmt. Assn., ASTM, AIAA, Exptl. Pilots Assn. Republican. Methodist (trustee, chmn. 1974-76). Patentee landing gear designs, inflatable rescue system, glass retention systems, adjustable jack system, cold weather start fluorescent lamp, others. Home: 1140 Stanton Way Stockton CA 95207 Office: 3437 S Airport Way Stockton CA 95206

BIDDLE, NICHOLAS, JR., securities exec.; b. Boston, Nov. 15, 1940; s. Nicholas and Virginia (Morris) B.; A.B., Harvard U., 1963; postgrad. U. Va. Law Sch., 1963-64; m. Joan Alanson Moore, Dec. 10, 1966; children—Virginia M., Barbara M., Katharine M. Salesman, team leader Kidder, Peabody & Co., Inc., N.Y.C., 1964-70; salesman, v.p. Kuhn, Loeb & Co., N.Y.C., 1970-76; instl. salesman Paine, Webber, Jackson & Curtis, Inc., N.Y.C., 1976-77; v.p., stockholder Keefe, Bruyette & Woods, Inc., N.Y.C., 1977—. Bd. dirs. treas. Lloyd Harbor Hills Assn., Huntington, N.Y., 1973-75; victory fund sponsor Nat. Republican Congl. Com., 1972—; mem. Nat. Right to Work Com., 1976—; class agt. St. Paul's Sch., Concord, N.H., 1974-79, Harvard U., 1980—. Served with USMCR, 1964-65. Mem. Investment Assn. N.Y. Republican. Episcopalian. Clubs: C.S.H. Beach, Huntington Country. Home: 14 Harbor Hill Dr Lloyd Harbor Huntington NY 11743 Office: 1 Liberty Pl New York NY 10006

BIDDLE, W(ALTER) SCOTT, land devel. exec.; b. Ogden, Utah, Apr. 1927; s. Walter Stanley and Marjorie (Turner) B.; B.B.A., U. N.Mex., 1950; m. Nancy Ann Pellissier, Aug. 28, 1949 (div. 1962); children—John Gary, Gregory Scott; m. 2d, LaVonne Wickman, Apr. 11, 1964. Salesman, Pellissier Dairy Farms, Pico Rivera, Calif., 1950, dept. sales mgr., 1951, div. mgr. Yami Yogurt div., 1952-54; mgr. So. Calif. div. Milk Producers Assn. Central Calif., Modesto, 1954-56; gen. purchasing agt. Frank F. Pellissier & Sons, Inc., Pico Rivera, 1955-57, adminstrv. asst. to pres., dir., 1957-61; sec., gen. mgr. Molecular Engring., Inc., 1961-63; v.p., gen. mgr. Hercules Constrn. Co., Suburbia Homes, 1963-65; exec. v.p. Broadmoor Homes, Inc., 1965-72; pres. Biddle Kavanaugh Devel., Inc., Tustin, Calif., 1972-73; pres., chmn. Biddle Devel., Inc., Newport Beach, Calif., 1974-79; chmn. Biddle/Carter Devel. Corp., San Diego, 1976-79, The Biddle Group, Inc., 1979—; sec. Biddle/Semco Devel. Corp., 1978-79. Served with USNR, 1945-46. Mem. Aircraft Owners and Pilots Assn., Calif. State (v.p. 1957-59, pres. 1959-60), U.S. (nat. dir. 1958-59) jr. chambers commerce, Bldg. Industry Assn. (pres. 1977-78), Nat. Assn. Home Builders (dir. 1978—), Calif. State Bldg. Industry Assn. (dir. 1976—, v.p. 1978, treas. 1979, v.p. 1980-81), Kappa Sigma, Alpha Kappa Psi. Presbyterian. Clubs: Balboa Bay, Big Canyon Country. Home: 1907 Yacht Puritan Newport Beach CA 92660 also 72-420 Sommerset Dr Palm Desert CA 92260 Office: Biddle Bldg 17701 Mitchell N Irvine CA 92714

BIDERMAN, CHARLES, real estate investor; b. N.Y.C., Oct. 24, 1946; s. Jack and Pauline B.; B.A., Bklyn. Coll., 1967; M.B.A., Harvard U., 1971. Asso. editor Barron's Fin. Weekly, 1971-73; pres. Charles Biderman & Co., N.Y.C. and Nashville, 1973-77, Nashville Mgmt. Corp. (name changed to Market St. Devel. Corp.), 1976—; fin. editor Wall St. Final, N.Y.C. Bd. dirs. Tenn. Dance Theater, 1977—. Served with USAF, 1966-67. Home: 5329 Gen Forrest Ct Nashville TN 37215 Office: Wall St Final 66 Greene St New York NY 10012

BIEBER, ROBERT MORTON, county ofcl.; b. N.Y.C., Jan. 8, 1940; s. Louis and Dina (Blank) B.; B.B.A., Coll. of Ins., N.Y.C., 1969; Asso. in Risk Mgmt., Ins. Inst. Am., 1972; M.A., N.Y. U., 1972; m. Muriel Kaplan, Aug. 11, 1963; children—Jill Lauren, Lee Douglas. Workers compensation claims examiner Pub. Service Mut. Ins. Co., N.Y.C., 1962-63; life ins. agt. John Hancock Ins. Co., N.Y.C., 1963-69; asst. ins. mgr. Asso. Metals and Mineral Corp., N.Y.C., 1969-71; ins. and safety adminstr. City of Yonkers, N.Y., 1971-74; dir. risk mgmt. Westchester County, White Plains, N.Y., 1974—; instr. risk mgmt. Coll. Ins.; lectr. risk mgmt. and cons. to govts. Chmn. cardio-pulmonary resuscitation com. Westchester Heart Assn.; instr., trainer first aid ARC, Westchester and Rockland counties; 1st lt. Springhill Ambulance Corps, Spring Valley, N.Y. Served with U.S. Army, 1959-62. Recipient Merit citation Mayor N.Y.C., 1972, Excellence award N.Y. State Assn. Counties, 1977, Tech. Subject award Vets. of Safety, 1977, 2 Achievement awards Nat. Assn. Counties, 1977, 78. Mem. Risk and Ins. Mgmt. Soc., Public Risk and Ins. Mgmt. Assn. (pres.), Am. Soc. Safety Engrs., N.Y. State Assn. Emergency Med. Technician Instrs. Contbr. safety and risk mgmt. articles to profl. jours. Home: 26 Forshay Rd Monsey NY 10952 Office: County Office Bldg 148 Martine Ave White Plains NY 10601

BIELEY, PEGGY, cons. economist, banker; b. N.Y.C., June 5, 1934; d. Louis and Bella (Kenarik) Moses; B.S. magna cum laude, N.Y. U.; M.A., Stanford U.; student Columbia U., 1951-53; m. Alfred D. Bieley (div.); children—Harlan Clayton, Lily Beth. Research asst. Nat. Indsl. Conf. Bd., N.Y.C.; economist Jules Backman Assos., Nat. Manpower Council; chief economist, v.p. Langner Research Co., Miami, Fla.; pres., chief economist Bieley, Wagner & Assos., Econ. Data Bank, Inc., Miami; pres. Housing-Data Bank, Miami; economist-cons. Freedom Fed. Savs. & Loan Assn. Tampa, Fla.; v.p. Am. Savs. & Loan Assn. Fla., Miami Beach, 1977—; teaching fellow dept. econs. Stanford; instr. dept. econs. U. Miami. Mem. Am. Econ. Assn., Am. Statis. Assn. Contbr. articles to profl. jours. Home: 11601 SW 64th Ave Miami FL 33156

BIELLO, VINCENT, mgmt. and indsl. engring. cons. co. exec.; b. Casacalenda, Italy, Jan. 2, 1949; came to Can., 1956, naturalized, 1969; s. Giuseppe and Antonietta (Ruccolo) B.; B.Mech. Engring., McGill U., 1973; M.P.A., U. du Quebec, 1980. Indsl. engr. Canadian Nat. Railways, Montreal, Que., 1973-76, project officer, 1976-78, economic analysis and cost research officer, 1979; sr. cons. Intercan Logistical Services Ltd., Montreal, 1979—. Mem. Am. Mgmt. Assn., Young C. of C. of Montreal, Order of Engrs. Province Que., Am. Inst. Indsl. Engrs. (v.p. Montreal chpt.), Materials Handling Soc. Montreal (program dir. 1973-75). Home: 9119 Descartes Saint Leonard PQ H1R 3N2 Canada

BIERINGER, LEROY J., pub. relations counsel; b. Chgo., June 14, 1922; s. Benjamin S. and Sylvia (Sternheim) B.; student George Williams Coll., Chgo., 1943-45; m. Annette S. Orenstein, Aug. 12, 1945; children—Steven A., Garry J., Shelley J. Publicity dir. Chgo. council Boy Scouts Am., 1943-45; account exec. Pub. Relations Services, Chgo., 1945-48; owner Leroy J. Bieringer Assos., Chgo., 1948-49; vice-chmn. Harshe-Rotman & Druck, Inc., N.Y.C., 1950—; lectr. Am. Mgmt. Assn.; lectr. on role of pub. relations in marketing N.Y. U. Sch. Continuing Edn. Mem. nat. council Boy Scouts Am., 1967—; fund chmn. Hartsdale (N.Y.) chpt. ARC, 1962; mem. Hartsdale Bd. Edn., 1963-66, 69—, pres., 1963-66; bd. dirs. Am. Heart Assn., 1978-80, chmn. public info. working group, bd. dirs. N.Y. affiliate, chmn. public info. council, 1980. Served with USAAF, 1942-43. Mem. Public Relations Soc. Am. Home: 439 E 51 St New York NY 10022 Office: 300 E 44th St New York NY 10017

BIERWIRTH, GEORGE GRANGER, mgmt. cons. co. exec.; b. Chgo., June 28, 1918; s. Frederick W. and Ruth M. (Granger) B.; A.B. in Econs., Lafayette Coll., 1941; m. Helen Hosford, Nov. 27, 1941; children—Frederick, Bette Ann, Wendy, Charles, Robert. Personnel mgr. Johns-Manville Co.; dir. indsl. products Ingersoll Products div. Borg Warner Co., Chgo.; dir. employee relations, corp. mgr. labor relations GAF Corp., N.Y.C.; pres., dir., owner Straw and Wirth, Inc., Fairfield, N.J., 1972—; dir. Investors Syndicate Am. (IDS). Elder, West Milford (N.J.) Presbyn. Ch., 1978—. Served as pilot USAAF, 1941-45. Decorated Air medal with oak leaf clusters, Purple Heart. Mem. Delta Kappa Epsilon. Office: 387 Passaic Ave Fairfield NJ 07006

BIERWIRTH, JOHN COCKS, aerospace mfg. co. exec.; b. Lawrence, N.Y., Jan 21, 1924; s. John E. and Alice (Marguerite) B.; B.A., Yale, 1947; J.D., Columbia, 1950; m. Marion Moise, June 14, 1946. Admitted to N.Y. State bar, 1951; asso. firm White & Case, N.Y.C., 1950-53; asst. v.p. N.Y. Trust Co. (now Chem. Bank), 1953-57; asst. treas. Nat. Distillers & Chem. Corp., N.Y.C., 1957-58, v.p., 1958-69, head internat. div., 1963-69, exec. v.p., 1969-72; dir. Grumman Corp., Bethpage, N.Y., 1966-72, v.p. finance, 1971, pres., 1972, chief exec. officer, 1974, chmn. bd., 1976—; dir. Koppers Co., Inc., Gen. Reins. Corp.; trustee Atlantic Mut. Ins. Co. Trustee, L.I. U.; bd. dirs. Tri-State United Way, N.Y. Blood Center, Com. for Econ. Devel.; mem. pres.'s com. Smith Coll. Mem. UN Assn. for U.S.A. (trustee), Conf. Bd. Club: Yale (N.Y.C.). Office: Grumman Corp 1111 Stewart Ave Bethpage NY 11714

BIESER, CARL OTTO, cons. engring. exec.; b. Cin., May 28, 1928; s. Carl William and Adelaide Louise (Burger) B.; B.S.M.E., U. Mich., 1950; M.B.A., Northwestern U., 1951; m. Nancy Jane Taylor, Sept. 18, 1953; children—Richard Carl, Caroline Jane. Indsl. engr., quality control engr. Formica Corp., Cin., 1953-58, mgr. quality control, process control, 1958-67; mgr. corporate devel. Ortner Freight Car Co., Cin., 1967-69; dep. mgr., project mgr. indsl. planning Processes Research Inc. also Kintech Services Inc. affiliated cos. A.M. Kinney Inc., Cin., 1969-74, v.p. indsl. planning, 1974—; dir. Process Research; cons. in field. Dist. chmn. United Appeal, 1966. Served to 1st lt. USAF, 1951-53. Registered profl. engr., Ohio. Mem. Soc. Advancement Mgmt., Engring. Soc. Cin. Republican. Presbyterian. Clubs: Univ., Indian Hill, Masons. Patentee corn buttering devices. Home: 8350 Eustis Farm Ln Cincinnati OH 45243 Office: 2900 Vernon Pl Cincinnati OH 45219

BIGELOW, MARY D. (MRS. RUDY GRAY BURTON), elec. firm exec., tax cons.; b. Perry, N.Y.; d. Albert E. and Rebecca Ann (Miller) Davis; student Rochester Bus. Inst., Am. Inst. Banking, 1938, Woodbury Coll., 1944, U. Calif. at Los Angeles, 1945; m. Richard Harned Bates, Oct. 4, 1940 (div. Sept. 1947); m. 2d, Floyd Burget Bigelow, 1948 (div. May, 1952); 1 dau., Judith Lynne (Mrs. Bigelow McMullen); m. 3d, Rudy Gray Burton, Nov. 17, 1962. Various positions, 1931-36; banking, 1936-41, advt., oil bus., 1944-50; sec.-treas. Emerald Bay Community Assn., Laguna Beach, Calif., 1950-52, Tel-I-Clear Systems, Inc., Laguna Beach, 1952-54; owner, operator Bigelow Bus. Services, Laguna Beach, 1954—; co-owner, mgr. Burton Electric, Laguna Beach, 1963—. Asst., bd. dirs. Three Arch Bay Dist., South Laguna, 1957-73; com. mem. Opera League Laguna Beach, 1968—; mem. U. Calif. at Irvine Friends of Library, U. Calif. at Irvine Interfaith Found. Bd. dirs. Joe Thurston Found., 1957-64, First Nighters, Girls' Club Laguna Beach. Recipient various civic awards; named Leading Lady in Bus., Laguna News-Post, 1971. Mem. Nat. Soc. Pub. Accountants, Inland Assn. Tax Consultants, Soc. Calif. Accountants, Dana Point Power Squadron, Laguna Beach Hist. Soc. (dir.), World Affairs Council Los Angeles and Orange County, Laguna Beach C. of C. Mermaids (info. chmn. Festival of Arts 1966, 67, 68), Cousteau Soc. Clubs: Altrusa (treas., dir.) (Laguna Beach); West Coast Yacht; Riviera, Anchorettes. Address: 697 Catalina St Laguna Beach CA 92651

BIGG, GEORGE MALCOLM, banker; b. LaPorte, Ind., Dec. 10, 1946; s. George John and Helen Marie (Wainscott) B.; B.S., Ind. U., 1969; student Northwestern U., 1970, DePaul U., 1972; m. Judith Anne Massa, Mar. 4, 1972; children—Jason Wainscott, Ryan Julian. Comml. banking officer Continental Ill. Nat. Bank, Chgo., 1969-73; asst. v.p. Citizens Fidelity Bank & Trust Co., Louisville, 1973-74, v.p., 1974-76, sr. v.p., 1977—; pres. Citizens Fidelity Energy Co., Louisville, 1979—. Trustee, City of Crossgate (Ky.), 1978-79, Buckhorn (Ky.) Children's Center, 1978—. Served with USAR, 1970-76. Mem. Ky. Coal Assn. (dir.), Nat. Coal Assn., Robert Morris Assos., Lambda Chi Alpha. Republican. Presbyterian. Clubs: Jefferson, Louisville Athletic. Home: 1806 Warrington Way Louisville KY 40222 Office: Citizens Plaza Louisville KY 40296

BIGG, LESTER MICHAEL EDWARD, coll. fin. adminstr.; b. Franklin, N.J., Jan. 12, 1945; s. Lester Edward and Anne Veronica (Kisac) B.; B.A. in Human Relations, Salem Coll., 1973; M.S. in Student Personnel Services, Upsala Coll., 1978. Asso. dist. exec. Gt. Trails council Boy Scouts Am., Dalton, Mass., 1973-74; cons. Helpage Internat., London, 1974-75; acct. Picatinny Arsenal, U.S. Army, Dover, N.J., 1976-77; asst. dir. student fin. aid center Union Coll., Cranford, N.J., 1978—. Mem. community adv. bd. Edni. Opportunity Fund Program. Served with USN, 1963-72. Recipient Silver Beaver award Boy Scouts Am., 1970; Good Citizen award Am. Legion, 1961; Dr. F. Witcraft Leadership award Am. Humanics/Salem Coll., 1973. Mem. Am. Personnel and Guidance Assn., Am. Coll. Personnel Assn., Am. Public Health Assn., Eastern Assn. Student Fin. Aid Adminstrs., N.J. Assn. Student Fin. Aid Adminstrs., N.J. Assn. Community Coll., Student Fin. Aid Adminstrs., Alpha Phi Omega. Home: 111 Route 15 S Wharton NJ 07885 Office: Union Coll 1033 Springfield Ave Cranford NJ 07016

BIGGAR, EDWARD SAMUEL, lawyer; b. Kansas City, Mo., Nov. 19, 1917; s. Frank Wilson and Katharine (Rea) B.; A.B., U. Mich., 1938, J.D. with distinction, 1940; m. Susan Bagby, July 9, 1955; children—John Edward, Julie Anne, Nancy Rea, William Bagby, Martha Susan. Admitted to Mo. bar, 1940; asso. Stinson, Mag & Fizzell, 1948-50, partner, 1950—; dir. Ward Paper Box Co., Kansas City, Russell Stover Candies, Inc., Kansas City, Western Chem. Co., Kansas City, Cereal Food Processors, Inc., Kansas City, Johnson County Nat. Bank, Kansas City. Chmn. Transp. Planning Commn. Greater Kansas City, 1963-64; mem. Met. Planning Commn., Kansas City Region, 1967-70. Chmn. bd. govs. Citizens Assn. Kansas City, Mo., 1959-60; bd. dirs., pres. Met. YMCA, Kansas City, Mo., 1979—; pres. Kansas City unit Am. Cancer Soc., 1958-59. Trustee Sunset Hill Sch., Kansas City, Mo., 1971-77. Served to 1st lt., USAAF, 1942-45. Mem. Kansas City Lawyers Assn. (pres. 1966-67), Mo. Bar, Am., Kansas City bar assns., Am. Judicature Soc., Order of Coif, Phi Beta Kappa, Phi Delta Phi, Phi Delta Theta. Republican. Presbyn. Home: 1221 Stratford Rd Kansas City MO 64113 Office: 2100 Charter Bank Center Kansas City MO 64105

BIGGERS, JOHN ALVIN, automotive and indsl. exec.; b. Durham, Calif., Oct. 27, 1926; s. Alvin C. and Bessie I. (Green) B.; student pub. schs., Chico and Sacramento, Calif.; m. Esther L. Debler, Apr. 20, 1945; children—Curtis G., Merlene A. and Marlene J. (twins), Calvin B. With Globe Auto Supply Co., 1941-44; with Gerlinger Motor Parts Co., Sacramento, 1944—, v.p., 1959-68, pres., 1968—, gen. mgr., 1950—; partner Auto-Quip Leasing Co.; No. Calif. adv. Calif. Valley Bank. Chmn. automotive sect. United Crusade, Sacramento, 1959-61; dist. fin. com. Boy Scouts Am., Sacramento, 1960-61; active YMCA, mem. Gen. Assembly (internat.), Portland, 1964; del. Gen. Assembly (internat.) Kansas City, 1968, Miami Beach, Fla., 1972, Dallas, 1976, Kansas City, 1980; mem. Sacramento Safety Council; mem. adv. council mech. and elec. tech. Sacramento City Coll.; mem. adv. council automotive and heavy duty vocat. program, chmn. all industries area-wide bus. and career edn. Sacramento County Schs.; pres. Industry Edn. Council of Met. Sacramento, 1979—; mem. adv. council Preston Sch. Industries, Fairhaven Home for Unwed Mothers. Mem. Sacramento Parts Jobbers Assn. (chmn.), Sacramento Camelia Soc., Automotive Service Industries Assn., Calif. Automotive Wholesalers Assn., Young Execs. Forum, C. of C. Republican. Mem. Ch. of Nazarene (chmn. bd. stewards, sec. bd. dirs., chmn. fin. com., choir dir.; del. gen. assembly internat. 1972, 76, chmn. laymen's retreat bd. 1970-71, sec. dist. adv. bd. 1978-79). Home: 5372 Monalee Ave Sacramento CA 95819 Office: 2020 Kay St Sacramento CA 95814

BIGGS, BARTON MICHAEL, investment co. exec.; b. N.Y.C., Nov. 26, 1932; s. William Richardson and Georgene (Williams) B.; B.A., Yale U., 1955; M.B.A. with distinction, N.Y. U., 1963; m. Judith Anne Lund, June 12, 1959; children—Wende Hammond, Gretchen Greve, Barton William. Analyst, E.F. Hutton & Co., N.Y.C., 1961-65, partner, 1965; investment mgr., partner Fairfield Partners, Greenwich, Conn., 1965-73; partner, mng. dir. Morgan Stanley & Co., N.Y.C., 1973—, mgr. research, investment mgmt. depts., 1973-80; chmn. Morgan Stanley Asset Mgmt. Co., 1981—; dir. Rand McNally & Co. Trustee, Brookings Instn., 1975—, Lehrman Inst., 1980. Served to lt. USMCR, 1955-58. Clubs: Field (Greenwich); Chevy Chase (Washington); N.Y. Athletic (N.Y.C.). Contbr. articles to mags. Home: 390 Riversville Rd Greenwich CT 06830 Office: Morgan Stanley & Co 1251 Ave of Americas New York NY 10020

BIGGS, CHARLES LOUIS, mgmt. cons.; b. Akron, Ohio, Nov. 16, 1940; s. Alfred W. and Helen L. (Lambert) B.; B.S., Kent State U., 1963; m. Lynda Payne, Sept. 10, 1960; 1 dau., Mamie. Partner and dir. mgmt. cons. services Touche Ross & Co., Detroit, 1968—. Cert. mgmt. cons. Mem. Inst. Mgmt. Cons.'s, Assn. Computing Machinery. Clubs: Renaissance, Detroit Athletic; Union of Cleve.; Oakland Hills (Birmingham, Mich.). Author: Managing the Systems Development Process, 1980. Office: 200 Renaissance Center 16th Floor Detroit MI 48243

BIGGS, GLENN, banker; b. Eldorado, Tex., June 10, 1933; s. Bennie Austin and Clara Francis B.; B.A., Baylor U., 1956; m. Ann Carolyn, July 29, 1955; children—Barry, Brian. Asst. mgr. Abilene (Tex.) C. of

C., 1956-59; partner Millerman & Millerman, Abilene, 1959-65; exec. aide to speaker Tex. Ho. of Reps., 1965-68; pres. Nat. Western Life Ins. Co., Austin, Tex., 1968-70; pres., chmn. bd. First Nat. Bank, San Antonio, 1970—; dir. Continental Fidelity Ins. Co., San Antonio. Chmn. bd. dirs. City Public Service, San Antonio; pres. Met. Hosp., San Antonio. Mem. Tex. Bankers Assn. Baptist. Clubs: Oak Hills Country (San Antonio). Office: 6200 NW Hwy San Antonio TX 78213

BIGGS, ROBERT WILDER, JR., mfg. co. exec.; b. Lorain, Ohio, Jan. 21, 1934; s. Robert Wilder and Eleanor (Hughes) B.; B.S. in Bus. Adminstrn., Ind. U., 1958; m. Dolores Bonnadine Ward, July 9, 1955; children—Robert Wilder, Adrienne. In retail industry, 1958-60; asst. purchasing agt. Oglebay Norton Co., Cleve., 1960-64; mgmt. cons. Case & Co., Cleve., 1964-68; with Pickands Mather & Co., Cleve., 1968—, treas., 1974—; mem. adv. bd. Arkwright Boston, 1978—. Trustee, Cleve. Inst. Music, 1979—. Served with U.S. Army, 1954-56. Mem. Fin. Execs. Inst., Nat. Assn. Accts., Am. Iron and Steel Inst., U.S. Power Squadron, Cleve. Treas.'s Club (dir.). Clubs: Cleve. Athletic, Mid-Day, Sandusky Yacht. Office: 1100 Superior Ave Cleveland OH 44114

BIGLER, W(ILLIAM) PAUL, corp. exec.; b. nr. Franklin, Pa., Oct. 5, 1904; s. William and Carolin (Gilmore) B.; grad. Perkiomen Sch., 1923; m. Sarah Tate, Dec. 21, 1940; 1 dau., Nancy Ann (Mrs. James M. Kersey). Mgr. repair parts sales service Joy Mfg. Co., 1926-34, dir. purchases, 1934-37; indsl. purchasing agt. Semet Solvay Engring. Corp., 1937-38; div. mgr. editorial research McGraw-Hill Pub. Co., 1938-40; sales mgr. Mining Machine Parts, Inc., Cleve., 1940-43, gen. mgr., 1943-48, pres., chmn. bd., 1948-67; pres. L. W. Kelley Co., Inc., 1958-67, Compass Equipment Co., Wichita, Kans., 1957-67; pres. Bigler Investment Corp.; v.p. Circle Oil Co., Sage Drilling Co., 1957-67. Mem. Am. Inst. Mining, Metall. and Petroleum Engrs., Am. Mining Congress, Rocky Mountain, W.Va., Ill. mining insts. Clubs: Country; Cleveland Skating; Franklin; United Hunts; Metropolitan (N.Y.C.). Home: 828 Greengate Oval Greenwood Village Northfield OH 44067 also San Remo Club 22871 N Ocean Blvd Boca Raton FL 33431

BIGLEY, JAMES PHILIP, telephone co. exec.; b. Viroqua, Wis., July 28, 1912; s. Lawrence A. and Ellen (McCall) B.; m. Dorothy Bent, Aug. 28, 1948 (dec.); m. 2d, Betty Lou Simmons, Nov. 17, 1978. With State Bank of LaCrosse (Wis.), 1930-47; officer, dir. State Bank of Viroqua, 1947-55, dir., 1970—, chmn. bd., 1975—; dir. Viroqua Telephone Co., 1948—, sec., treas., mgr., 1954-63, pres., 1963—; pres., dir. Viroqua Bldg. Corp., 1965—; dir. Capital Indemnity Corp., Capital Trans Am. Corp. Chmn., commr. Viroqua Housing Authority; exec. sec. Wis. Republican Com., 1955-57. Served from pvt. to 1st lt. 32d Div., AUS, 1942-46. Mem. LaCrosse Jr. C. of C. (pres. 1939), 32d Div. Vets. Assn. (nat. pres. 1957-58), Am. Legion, VFW, Wis. State Telephone Assn. (pres. 1962-64), U.S. Ind. Telephone Assn. (dir. 1966—, v.p. 74-77, pres. 1977-78). Clubs: Elk, Eagle (pres. Wis. 1952-53, investment counselor 1953—, internat. pres. 1959-60, fin. adviser 1962-69). Home: 3 S Washington Heights Viroqua WI 54665 Office: 114 E Court St Viroqua WI 54665

BIGLEY, WILLIAM JOSEPH, JR., control engr.; b. Union City, N.J., May 8, 1924; s. William Joseph and Mary May (Quigley) B.; B.M.E., Rensselaer Polytech. Inst., 1950; M.S. in E.E., N.J. Inst. Tech., 1962, M.S. in Computer Sci., 1973; m. Hannelore Hicks, June 24, 1950; children—Laura C., William Joseph IV, Susan J. Project engr. Tube Reducing Corp., Wallington, N.J., 1953-58, Flight Support, Inc., Metuchen, N.J., 1958-59, Airborne Accessories, Inc., Hillside, N.J., 1959-61; sr. staff engr. in control engring. Lockheed Electronics Co. div. Lockheed Aircraft, Inc., Plainfield, N.J., 1961—. Prof. engring. electronics Newark Coll. Engring., 1961-62; prof. cons. engr. Automatic Control Systems, 1958—. Mem. council Boy Scouts of Am., Scotch Plains, N.J., 1960-63. Served with AUS, 1943-44; served with USNR, 1944-46. Named Engr.-Scientist of Yr., Lockheed Aircraft, Inc., 1980, recipient Robert E. Gross award for tech. excellence, 1980; registered profl. engr., N.Y., N.J., Calif. Mem. Nat. Soc. Profl. Engrs., IEEE, AAAS, ASME, Instrument Soc. Am., Am. Mgmt. Assn., Nat. Rifle Assn. Contbr. articles to profl. jours. Home: 1641 Terrill Rd Scotch Plains NJ 07076 Office: Lockheed Hiway 22 Plainfield NJ 07060

BIJUR, PETER I., petroleum co. exec.; b. N.Y.C., Oct. 14, 1942; s. Herbert I. and Marion Ellen (Halpert) B.; B.A., U. Pitts., 1964; postgrad. Columbia U. Grad. Sch. Bus., 1964-66; m. Anne Montgomery, Sept. 21, 1968; children—Kristin, Matthew, David. Various mktg. assignments Texaco Inc., 1966-70, dist. sales mgr., 1971-73, asst. to sr. v.p. public affairs, 1973-74, coordinator strategic planning, 1974-76, asst. to exec. v.p., 1977-80, mgr. refining/mktg. Rocky Mountains, Casper, Wyo., 1980—. Served with U.S. Army, 1967. Mem. United Ch. of Christ. Clubs: New Canaan (Conn.) Field; Casper Country. Home: 950 Waterford Casper WY 82601 Office: Texaco Inc PO Box 320 Casper WY 82602

BILES, DONALD M., hotel co. exec.; b. Phila., Nov. 2, 1922; s. Leslie G. and Margaret E. (Batty) B.; B.S., Cornell U., 1952; m. Eleanor Marie Milland, Sept. 13, 1947; children—Leslie Ann, Daniel Thomas, Robert Michael. Front office mgr. Skytop (Pa.) Lodge, 1952-53, asst. mgr., 1953-55, resident mgr., 1955-64, gen. mgr., 1964-74; pres., gen. mgr. Pocono Hotels Corp./Skytop Lodge, Inc., 1974—, also dir., mem. exec. com.; instr. resort mgmt. Cornell U., 1961-67. Trustee, Pocono Hosp., East Stroudsburg, Pa. Served with 82d Airborne div. U.S. Army, 1942-45. Decorated Bronze Star, Purple Heart, Combat Infantryman's badge, others. Mem. Am. Hotel and Motel Assn. (resort com.), Hotel Sales Mgmt. Assn., Pocono Vacationland Assn. (pres. 1954-56). Republican. Roman Catholic. Club: Skytop. Home: Box 203 Skytop PA 18357 Office: Skytop Lodge Skytop PA 18357

BILES, JAMES EDWARD, constrn. co. exec.; b. Borger, Tex., June 14, 1929; s. Howard and Anna Mae (Canfield) B.; B.S. in Mech. Engring., Tex. A. & M. U., 1951; m. Elizabeth Anne Cooper, Sept. 1, 1951; children—Deborah Kay, Elizabeth Susan, James Edward, David Howard. Asst. mech. engr. Tex. Power and Light Co., Trinidad, Tex., 1953-55; mech. engr., Frisco, Tex., 1955-57; maintenance engr. Southland Paper Mills, Inc., Lufkin, Tex., 1957-67, engring. asst., Houston, 1967-72, asst. supt. power and utilities, 1972-74; power staff engr. Ford, Bacon & Davis Constrn. Corp., Monroe, La., 1974-78, power sect. mgr., 1978—. Served with USAF, 1951-53. Registered profl. engr., Tex., La., Miss. Mem. ASME (past chmn. Monroe sub-sec.), TAPPI, Nat. Soc. Profl. Engrs., La. Engring. Soc. Baptist. Club: Masons. Home: 2107 Country Club Dr Monroe LA 71201 Office: Ford Bacon & Davis 3901 Jackson St Monroe LA 71201

BILES, RICHARD HAROLD, ins. benefits mktg. and adminstrn. co. exec.; b. Pasadena, Calif., July 21, 1919; s. Glenn Eugene and Elsie Fern (Williamson) B.; A.A., Pasadena Jr. Coll., 1938; m. Margaret W. Blumer, Dec. 30, 1944; children—Patricia, Beverly, Richard Kimberly. Franchiser, Troy Laundry, Pasadena, 1938-43; life ins. salesman, Los Angeles, 1946-48; regional group mgr. Cal/Western Life, Los Angeles, 1948-63; v.p. sales Plymouth Ins. Co., Los Angeles, 1964; exec. v.p. Biles-Killingsworth Co., Los Angeles, 1964-65; asst. v.p. Fed. Life & Casualty Co., Los Angeles, 1966-69; owner, pres. Biles & Cook Adminstrs., Inc., Los Angeles, 1969—; pres. Total Health Care Services Corp., Los Angeles, 1970—. Active Boy Scouts Am.; active Congregational Ch., San Marino, Calif., 1951—. Served with AC, U.S. Army, 1943-45. Mem. Employee Benefit Planning Assn., Soc. Profl. Benefit Adminstrs., Mass Mktg. Ins. Inst., Profl. Ins. Mass Mktg. Assn. Republican. Clubs: San Marino City, Los Angeles. Home: 6930 N Willard Ave San Gabriel CA 91775 Office: 2502 W 3d St Los Angeles CA 90057

BILLARD, GORDON YOUNGS, investment cons.; b. N.Y.C., Jan. 14, 1902; s. Harry Youngs and Alice (Hamfield) B.; B.S., M.I.T., 1924. Research partner J.R. Williston & Co., mems. N.Y. Stock Exchange, 1938-50; mng. partner Carreau & Co., mems. N.Y. Stock Exchange, 1950-67; limited partner Drysdale & Co., mems. N.Y. Stock Exchange, 1966-77; investment cons., N.Y. and Fla., 1977—. Trustee, Gordon Y. Billard Found. Served as engring. officer USNR, 1942-45. Fellow N.Y. Acad. Scis. (past dir., treas., chmn. fin. com.), Newcomen Soc., St. Nicholas Soc. Clubs: Met., Canadian, Lawyers, Downtown Athletic, M.I.T. (N.Y.C.); Rockway Hunt, Indian Creek Country, Navy League. Address: 860 UN Plaza New York NY 10017 also Fairfield Manor 9800 Collins Ave Bal Harbour FL 33154

BILLEN, THOMAS RAYMOND, brewery exec.; b. East St. Louis, Ill., Nov. 8, 1945; s. Harry Arnold and Stella Barbara B.; B.A. in Math., So. Ill. U., 1967; M.B.A., St. Louis U., 1971; m. Rose Marie Petraitis, Nov. 29, 1968. Computer programmer McDonnell Douglas Corp., St. Louis, 1967-69; with Anheuser Busch Cos., St. Louis, 1969—, dir. corp. planning, 1979—; dir. Anheuser-Busch Inc., Busch Entertainment Corp., Busch Properties, Inc. Roman Catholic. Office: Anheuser Busch Cos 721 Pestalozzi St Saint Louis MO 63118

BILLERA, FRANKLIN A., men's clothing mfg. co. exec.; b. Northampton, Pa., Feb. 21, 1936; s. Anthony and Anna (Licata) B.; grad. Pa. State U., 1956; m. Ann M. Eby, Jan. 26, 1957; children—Anthony, Charles. Mem. staff labor indsl. relations Cross Country Clothes, Northampton, 1956-65, asst. treas., asst. sec., 1965-70, v.p. mktg. and sales, N.Y.C., 1970-73, exec. v.p., 1974-75, pres., 1975—; partner B & C Motel Corp., 1960-70; sec.-treas. Holiday Bristol Motel Corp., 1967-72. Trustee, Cross Country Clothes Retirement Plan Fund; trustee Reuben Block Health Fund, exec. v.p., 1976-78; co-founder Lake Wallenpanpac Watershed Ecol. Assn., 1971. Named Clothing Mfr. of Year, Newark Designers Club, 1976. Mem. Sigma Chi (life). Club: N.Y. Athletic. Home: Litchfield Way Box 23 Alpine NJ 07620 Office: 1290 6th Ave New York NY 10019

BILLICK, L. LARKIN, bank holding co. exec.; b. Des Moines, Sept. 15, 1948; s. Lyle Larkin and Florence Carlson B.; B.S., U. Kans., Lawrence, 1970; grad. Inst. Bank Mktg., U. So. Calif., La. State U., 1978; m. Kathryn Rose Gildner, Aug. 14, 1971; children—Kelly Lynne, Brett Larkin. Group ins. trainee Bankers Life Co., Des Moines, 1970-71; nat. advt. rep. Stoner Broadcasting Co., Des Moines, 1971-74; advt. account supr. Mid-Am. Broadcasting, Des Moines, 1974-75; dir. public realtions and mktg. Iowa Bankers Assn., Des Moines, 1975-77; asst. v.p., advt. mgr. corp. staff Marine Banks, Milw., 1977-79, v.p. advt., 1979—. Bd. dirs. Grad. Inst. Bank Mktg., La. State U., 1978-79; chmn. communications Milwaukee County Performing Arts Center, 1978-79; advt., promotion cons. to polit. candidates; chmn. communications council United Performing Arts Fund Milw., 1978-79; dist. coordinator State Del. for Jimmy Carter, 1972-80; chmn. communications com. Milwaukee County council Boy Scouts Am., 1979-80. Mem. Bank Mktg. Assn. (chmn. advt. council 1980-81), Am. Bankers Assn. (mem. nat. mktg. conf. com. 1980), Am. Advt. Fedn. (public service com. 1980-81), Am. Mktg. Assn. Democrat. Roman Catholic. Home: 21400 Lower Cambridge Circle Brookfield WI 53005 Office: One Marine Plaza PO Box 481 Milwaukee WI 53201

BILLINGS, THOMAS NEAL, publishing and cons. co. exec.; b. Milw., Mar. 2, 1931; s. Neal and Gladys Victoria (Lockard) B.; A.B. with honors, Harvard U., 1952, M.B.A., 1954; m. Barta Hope Chipman, June 12, 1954 (div. 1967); children—Bridget Ann, Bruce Neal; m. 2d, Victoria Chipman, Nov. 5, 1968 (div. 1971); m. 3d, Nancy Kay Carstens, May 13, 1972; 1 stepdau., Alicia Laura. Vice pres. fin. and adminstrn. Copley Press, Inc., La Jolla, Calif., 1957-70; divisional pub. Harte-Hanks Newspapers, San Antonio, 1970-73; exec. v.p. United Media, Inc., Phoenix, 1973-75; asst. to pres. Ramada Inns, Inc., Phoenix, 1975-76; exec. dir. Nat. Rifle Assn., Washington, 1976-77; pres. Ideation Inc., Washington, 1977—; chmn. Bergen-Billings Inc., N.Y.C., 1977—; dir. The Assn. Service Corp.; guest lectr. in field. Bd. dirs. Nat. Allergy Found., 1973—, The Wilderness Fund, 1978—, San Diego Civic Light Opera Assn., 1965-69; v.p., gen. mgr. San Diego 200th Anniversary Exposition, 1969. Served with U.S. Army, 1955-57. Recipient Walter F. Carley Meml. award, 1966, 69. Mem. Am. Newspaper Pubs. Assn., Nat. Assn. Accountants, Inst. Internal Auditors, Inst. Newspaper Controllers, Am. Assn. V.P.'s (dir.), Sigma Delta Chi. Republican. Clubs: West Side Tennis, LaJolla Country, Washington Athletic, Elks. Author: Creative Controllership, 1978; editor The Vice Presidents' Letter, 1978—. Office: 230 Park Ave New York NY 10017

BILLS, CHARLES OLIVER, bookstore exec.; b. Hastings, Nebr., Nov. 2, 1944; s. Roscoe W. and Elna M. (Wightman) B.; B.A., Syracuse U., 1971; M.B.A., Rochester Inst. Tech., 1980; m. Elaine Christine Miller, Mar. 7, 1980; 1 son, Brian L. Sales clk. Nebr. Book Co., Lincoln, 1963-68; textbook dept. mgr. Syracuse (N.Y.) U. Bookstore, 1971-72; asst. mgr. Kans. U. Bookstore, Lawrence, 1972-74; mgr. Rochester (N.Y.) Inst. Tech. Bookstore, 1974-80; dir. Associated Students of U. Calif. Store, Berkeley, 1980—. Mem. Am. Mgmt. Assn., Berkeley C. of C. Address: ASUC Store U Calif Bancroft Way at Telegraph Ave Berkeley CA 94720

BILOTTI, CARLO FRANCO, fragrance and cosmetics co. exec.; b. Italy, Aug. 18, 1934; came to U.S., 1961, naturalized, 1966; s. Mario G. and Edvige and Miceli di Serradileo B.; law degree U. Naples (Italy), 1957; polit. and social scis. degree U. Palermo (Italy), 1959; m. Margaret E. Schultz, Sept. 1967; 1 dau., Lisa. Vice pres. internat. div. Shulton Inc., Clifton, N.J., 1966-72; pres. Parfums de Prestige Internat., Paris, 1972-75, Jacqueline Cochran Inc. div. Am. Cyanamid Co., N.Y.C., 1975—. Mem. Fragrance Found. N.Y. (dir.), Cosmetic, Toiletry, Fragrance Assn. N.Y., Accademia degli Incaminati Rome (hon.). Club: Univ. (N.Y.C.). Office: 630 Fifth Ave New York NY 10020

BILZERIAN, PAUL ALEC, real estate exec.; b. Miami, Fla., June 18, 1950; s. Oscar A. and Joan I. (Barrie) B.; B.A., Stanford U., 1975; M.B.A., Harvard U., 1977; m. Terri L. Steffen, Sept. 17, 1978. Asst. dir. World Data Analysis Center, Stanford, Calif., 1974-75; treasury asso. Crown Zellerbach Corp., San Francisco, 1977-78; chmn. bd. Internat. Broadcasters, Inc., Seminole, Fla., 1978-79; exec. v.p. Nat. Bus. Enterprises, Inc., Sacramento, 1979—; dir. So. Bus. Enterprises, Inc., St. Petersburg, Fla., The Fla. Cons. Group, Inc., St. Petersburg, SBE Mgmt. Co., Inc., St. Petersburg. Served to 1st lt. U.S. Army, 1968-71. Decorated Bronze Star. Club: Harvard Bus. Sch. Home: 1914 Carolina Ave NE Saint Petersburg FL 33703 Office: One Plaza Pl NE Suite 1010 Saint Petersburg FL 33701

BINDER, RICHARD FRANCIS, instrumentation co. exec.; b. Erie, Pa., Feb. 25, 1948; s. A. Francis and Nancy-lou (Knowlton) B.; B.S. in Mgmt., Canisius Coll., 1981. Lab. technician Niagara Blower Co., Buffalo, 1967-69; purchasing agt. Noremac Instrument Corp., Buffalo, 1969-72; purchasing agt., data processing mgr. PCB Piezotronics, Buffalo, 1972—. Served with U.S. Army, 1969. Mem. Purchasing Mgmt. Assn. Home: 214 Woodward Buffalo NY 14214 Office: PO Box 33 Buffalo NY 14225

BINDER, THEODORE RONALD, pub. co. exec.; b. Chgo., Mar. 13, 1935; s. Michael Cameron and Harriett Mary (Kouba) B.; B.S., Calif. State U., Long Beach, 1957; m. Sandra Lee Rogers, June 24, 1961; children—Kimberly Diane, Michael Kevin. Acct., Ira N. Frisbee & Co., C.P.A.'s, 1957-65; partner, founder Stotsenberg, Binder & Co., C.P.A.'s, 1966-69; pres. Bond, Parkhurst & Bond, Inc., Newport Beach, Calif., 1969-71; v.p., exec. pub. CBS Publs., Newport Beach, 1972-77; v.p. ABC Pub., 1978; pres. Nils Pub. Co. subs. ABC, Chatsworth, Calif., 1978-80; v.p., gen. mgr. T.L. Enterprises, Agoura, Calif., 1980—. Pres., Young Republicans, Orange County, Calif., 1964. Mem. Am. Inst. C.P.A.'s, Calif. C.P.A.'s. Office: 29901 Agoura Rd Agoura CA 91301

BINGAY, JAMES SCLATER, JR., banker; b. Seattle, Aug. 3, 1943; s. James S. and Margaret A. (Blackstock) B.; B.A. in Econs., Brown U., 1965; M.B.A. in Fin., U. Pa., 1967; m. Margaret Jean Meyer, June 14, 1969. Asso. corp. fin. dept. E.F. Hutton & Co., 1970-70; lending officer Citbank, 1970-76; v.p., gen. mgr. Citicorp, San Francisco, 1976-78; v.p., area mgr. Citicorp (U.S.A.), Inc., Cleve., 1978—. Fund raising capt. Musical Arts Assn., 1979-80. Served to lt., Supply Corps, USNR, 1967-69; Vietnam. Recipient Wall St. Jour. achievement award in econs., Brown U., 1965. Mem. Cleve. Growth Assn. Clubs: Olympic Golf, Univ. (San Francisco); Kirtland Country, Union (Cleve.). Office: Citicorp USA Inc 1300 E 9th St Bond Court Bldg Cleveland OH 44114

BINGHAM, JULES, ship broker; b. Amsterdam, Netherlands, Sept. 21, 1921; came to U.S., 1945, naturalized, 1951; s. David and Therese B.; student U. Amsterdam, 1940-42; B.A., Haverford Coll., 1947; M.A., Sch. of Advanced Internat. Studies, Johns Hopkins U., 1948; m. Helen Jarro, Sept. 27, 1956; 1 stepson, Laurence C.K. David. With W. Rountree, ship broker, N.Y.C., 1949-50, Shipping Enterprises Corp., N.Y.C., 1950-55, Ocean Freighting and Brokerage Corp., N.Y.C., 1955-60; pres. Bingham Bigotte Shipping Co., Inc. and affiliated cos., N.Y.C., 1960-76, sr. partner, 1976—. Mem. Assn. Shipbrokers and Agts. Club: Port Washington (N.Y.) Yacht. Home: 180 Sands Point Rd Sands Point NY 11050 Office: Bingham Bigotte and Co 90 Broad St New York NY 10004

BINGHAM, WARREN DAVID, printing and pub. co. exec.; b. Boston, Feb. 20, 1940; s. Warren Davis and Gertrude Agnes (White) B.; M.S. in Math., M.I.T., 1964; Ph.D. in Astronomy, Harvard U., 1969; postgrad. Wharton Sch. Bus., U. Pa., 1979; m. Janet Anne Ward, Oct. 18, 1960; children—Theresa, Michael, Leslie, Jill, Margaret. Sr. research asso. Harvard U., 1964-69; founder, pres. Harbor Press, Salem, Mass., 1969-74; v.p., gen. mgr. Dexter Colour (Can.) Ltd., 1974-78, dir., 1974—; pres. Dexter Press Inc., W. Nyack, N.Y., 1978—, Dexter Press (Can.) Ltd., 1978—, World Colour, Inc., 1978—. Mem. Am. Mgmt. Assn. (pres.'s assn.), Can. Mgmt. Centre, Nat. Assn. Printers and Lithographers, Printing Industries Am., Graphic Arts Tech. Found., Post Card Mfrs. Assn. Home: 208 New Hempstead Rd New City NY 10956 Office: Route 303 West Nyack NY 10994

BINKERD, EVAN FRANCIS, research exec.; b. Lynch, Nebr., Mar. 30, 1919; s. A. A. and Verna (Jones) B.; B.S., Iowa State U., 1942; m. Jerene M. Hallen, Oct. 10, 1942. Research chemist Armour and Co., Chgo., 1942-43, various research positions, 1946-67, dir. research Armour Foods, 1967-71, v.p. research and devel., 1971-78, v.p. Armour & Co., 1978—; participant White House Conf. Food, Nutrition and Health; mem. sci. com. Nat. Livestock and Meat Bd.; adviser U.S. Codex Alimentarius (FAO-WHO) Commn., advisor foot and mouth disease, Argentina. Mem. citizenship task force Ariz. Dept. Edn. Served from ensign to lt. USNR, 1943-46. Recipient Distinguished Achievement award Iowa State U., 1974; Alumni Merit award Iowa State U. Club, Chgo., 1975; Indsl. Achievement award Inst. Food Tech., 1979. Fellow Inst. Food Technologists (Hall of Fame 1978, Nicholas Appert medal 1980); mem. Am. Chem. Soc., AAAS, Am. Oil Chemists Soc., N.Y. Acad. Scis., Soc. Chem. Industry, The Westerners (sheriff Scottsdale Corral 1978), Am. Meat Inst. (chmn. sci. com. 1965-73, 77-78), Am. Meat Sci. Assn., Indsl. Research Inst., Calabash Soc., A.M.A. (chmn. food industry adv. com. 1976-77), Agrl. Research Inst., Inst. Food Technologists (exec. com. 1973-76), Phoenix Pvt. Industry Council, Western History Assn., Sigma Alpha Epsilon, Phi Tau Sigma. Republican. Methodist. Clubs: Arizona; Chicago Chemists. Patentee in field. Home: 3153 N 48th St Phoenix AZ 85018 Office: Armour Research Center 15101 N Scottsdale Rd Scottsdale AZ 85260

BINNING, GENE HEDGECOCK, air conditioning co. exec.; b. Casper, Wyo., Oct. 28, 1927; s. Lloyd Cecil and Vera (Rhodes) B.; B.S. in Mech. Engring., U. Wyo., 1949; postgrad. Oklahoma City U., Okla. State U.; m. Bette, May 4, 1952; children—Gene Barton, Barbara Jo, Bradford Jay. Sales engr. Trane Co., Denver, 1949-57; pres. Trane Co.-Gene H. Binning Co., Inc., Oklahoma City, 1957—, Comml. Devel. Co., 1968—, Binning Oil Devel. Co., 1970—. Served with AUS, 1946-47. Recipient Air Conditioning award Okla. State U., 1968. Registered profl. engr., Okla. Mem. Oklahoma City C. of C., Am. Soc. Heating, Refrigeration and Air Conditioning Engrs. (dir.), Sigma Nu. Presbyterian. Clubs: Kiwanis (v.p., dir.), Shriners, Quail Creek Golf and Country (past dir.). Author manuals. Address: 3800 Willow Springs Oklahoma City OK 73112

BINNING, JOHN HARLAN, ins. co. exec.; b. Dix, Nebr., Nov. 9, 1923; s. Gene and Myrtle (Andersen) B.; student U. Nebr., 1941-42, J.D., 1949; student Oberlin Coll., 1943; B.S., Northwestern U., 1944; m. Doris Frahm, Sept. 2, 1948; children—Robin, Brad C. Admitted to Nebr. bar, 1949, practiced in Lincoln, 1949-53; city prosecutor, Lincoln, 1955-56; asst. atty. gen. State of Nebr., 1956-57, dir. ins., 1957-59; mem. firm Crosby, Pansing, Guenzel & Binning, Lincoln, 1959-72; pres. 1st Greatwest Corp. subs. Pullman Inc., Lincoln, 1972—. Served with USMCR, 1943-46, 53-55. Mem. Lincoln C. of C., Nebr. Assn. Commerce and Industry, Phi Gamma Delta, Phi Alpha Delta. Clubs: Masons, Shriners, Univ., Lincoln Country. Home: 1512 Skyline Dr Lincoln NE 68506 Office: PO Box 81726 Lincoln NE 68501

BINNS, JAMES EDWARD, banker; b. Alameda, Calif., Oct. 5, 1931; s. Guy Vivian and Beatrice (Jury) B.; student U. Nev., 1950-51; grad. Sch. Bank Audit and Control, U. Wis., 1963, Am. Inst. Banking, 1964; m. Marjean Friesen, Feb. 21, 1951; children—Cheryl Jean Binns Smith, Jana Lee, Lori LeAnn. With Sierra Pacific Power Co., Reno, 1948-50; with First Nat. Bank of Nev., Reno, 1951—, asst. cashier, 1957-63, asst. to cashier, 1963-65, auditor, 1965—, asst. v.p., 1968-75, v.p., 1975—; instr. Am. Inst. Banking. Cert. internal auditor. Mem. Am. Inst. Banking (past pres. Sierra-Nev. chpt., past nat. asso. councilman), Bank Adminstrn. Inst. (charter pres. chpt., state dir.), Data Processing Mgmt. Assn. (charter mem. Sierra-Nevada chpt., past pres.), Inst. Internal Auditors (pres. chpt.; chartered bank auditor), Reno Jr. C. of C. (past treas.). Clubs: Masons, Shriners, Elks, Reno Toastmasters (past pres.). Home: 1720 Allen St Reno NV 89509 Office: PO Box 10026 Reno NV 89510

BINNS, JAMES HAZLETT, indsl. exec.; b. Salida, Colo., Dec. 23, 1912; s. Hazlett C. and May (Lacey) B.; A.B., U. Denver, 1934; m. Ruamie Hill, Dec. 29, 1936; 1 son, James Hazlett. Dir. placement and field work U. Denver, 1934-35; with Armstrong Cork Co. (name now Armstrong World Industries, Inc.), Lancaster, Pa., 1935—, successively sales trainee floor div., salesman floor div., Atlanta, acting dist. mgr., dist. mgr., asst. sales mgr., Lancaster, Pa., asst. gen. mgr. munitions div., asst. gen. sales mgr. floor div., gen. sales mgr., 1935-60, v.p., gen. mgr. floor and indsl. operations, 1961-62, sr. v.p., 1962-68, pres., 1968-78, chmn., 1978—, also dir.; dir. Campbell Soup Co., Woodstream Corp., Lititz, Pa. Bd. dirs. Bus.-Industry Polit. Action Com., Lancaster Gen. Hosp., Mid-Atlantic Legal Found., bd. dirs., mem. exec. com., vice chmn. Pennsylvanians for Effective Govt.; sr. mem. bd. Conf. Bd. Mem. Nat. Assn. Mfrs. (dir., vice chmn.), Bus. Round Table, Pa. Soc. N.Y., Newcomen Soc. N.Am., U.S. (dir.), Pa. (dir., vice chmn.), Lancaster (past dir.) chambers commerce, Omicron Delta Kappa, Kappa Sigma. Clubs: Pinehurst (N.C.) Country; Lancaster Country, Hamilton (Lancaster); Skytop (Pa.); DeAnza Desert County (Borrego Springs, (Calif.); Economic of N.Y. Office: Armstrong World Industries Inc Liberty and Charlotte Sts Lancaster PA 17604

BINNS, WALTER GORDON, JR., automobile mfg. co. exec.; b. Richmond, Va., June 8, 1929; s. Walter Gordon and Virginia Belle (Matheny) B.; A.B., Coll. William and Mary, 1949; M.A., Harvard U., 1951; M.B.A., N.Y. U., 1959; m. Alberta Louise Fry, Apr. 1, 1972; 1 dau., Amanda. Trainee, Chase Nat. Bank, N.Y.C., 1953-54; with Gen. Motors Corp., N.Y.C., 1954—, now asst. treas., sec. bonus and salary com. of bd., and coordinator pension fund investments. Served with U.S. Army, 1951-53. Mem. Fin. Execs. Inst. (chmn. com. on employee benefits 1977-80), Am. Pension Conf., Phi Beta Kappa, Beta Gamma Sigma. Clubs: Harvard (N.Y.C.); Recess (Detroit). Home: 8 Park Ave Bronxville NY 10708 Office: 767 5th Ave New York NY 10153

BIRCH, JOHN EDWARD, home builder, realtor; b. Chgo., Oct. 3, 1917; s. John Edward and Veronica (Motyka) B.; B.A. in Edn., B.S. in Banking and Fin., U. Ill., 1940; M.B.A., Northwestern U., 1942; Ph.D. (hon.), Colo. Christian Coll.; children—John Edward, Christopher J., Terrie J., Laurence P. Pres., John Birch & Co., Cherrywood Homes, Inc., Alert Carpentry Corp., Durable Masonry Corp., Oak Brook Terrace, Ill., 1955—, Country Club Hills, Oak Brook Terrace, 1956—, Terrie Birch & Co. Mem. Planning Commn. DuPage County (Ill.), Ill. Bldg. Authority; mem. adv. bd. Lyons Twp. (Ill.) Republican Party; sec. Mid-Am. Hearing Found., Wesley Meml. Hosp.; co-founder U. Ill. Sch. of Urban Econs.; founder Sch. Home Bldg., Central YMCA; trustee Mid-Am. Hearing Found. of Wesley Meml. Hosp., Chgo. Served with USAAF, 1942-46. Named Ky. col.; recipient Saturday Evening Post award distinguished home bldg. (2); Certificate of Appreciation Bus. and Profl. Hall of Fame, USN recognition award, Million Dollar Builders award, certificate of Appreciation, Oak Brook Terrace, Brand Name Found. citation. Mem. DuPage Bd. Realtors, Home Builder Assn. (life dir., gov.), Ill. (dir.), Chicagoland (dir.) home builders assns., Nat. Assn. Homebuilders (dir.), Ill. Assn. Real Estate Bds., Am. Legion, U.S. C. of C., Chgo. Assn. Commerce (urban affairs, aviation and world trade coms.), Art Inst. Chgo. Clubs: Rotary (Oakbrook, Ill.); Torch; Glen Oaks Country, Village (Oak Brook Terrace); Oak Brook Polo; Moose. Home: 17 W 421 Roosevelt Rd Oak Brook Terrace IL 60521 Office: PO Box 247 Lombard IL 60148

BIRCHER, EDGAR ALLEN, mfg. co. exec.; b. Springfield, Ohio, Apr. 28, 1934; s. John Clark and Ethel Ann (Speakman) B.; B.A., Ohio Wesleyan U., 1956; J.D., Ohio State U., 1961; m. Lavinia Brock, Sept. 30, 1978; children—Douglas, Stephen, Todd, Karen. Admitted to Ohio bar, 1962, Tex. bar, 1973; asso. mem. firm Fuller, Seney, Henry & Hodge, Toledo, 1962-64; with Cooper Industries, Inc., Houston, 1964—, v.p., 1977—, gen. counsel, 1977—. Served with USAF, 1956-59. Mem. Houston World Trade Assn. (v.p. 1974), Ohio Bar Assn., Tex. Bar Assn., Am. Bar Assn. Clubs: Houston, Sugar Creek Country, Bob Smith Yacht, Phi Delta Theta, Phi Delta Phi. Home: 635 Chevy Chase St Sugarland TX 77478 Office: Two Houston Center Suite 2700 Houston TX 77002

BIRD, HARRY LEWIS, mech. engr.; b. Indpls., Aug. 22, 1937; s. Harry Lewis and Evelyn (Pooler) B.; student U. Mich., 1955-59, M.I.T., 1964-66; B.S., SUNY, 1979; A.Arts and Scis., Dutchess Community Coll., 1976; postgrad. Marist Coll., 1979—; m. Barbara Couch, Dec. 27, 1958; children—Harry Lewis, Elizabeth Barrett, William Buss. Staff, M.I.T. Instrumentation Lab., 1963-66; with Metals & Controls, Attleboro, Mass., 1967; product design engr. Metal Bellows Corp., Sharon, Mass., 1967-68; staff engr. Stamp Inc., Rhinebeck, N.Y., 1968-70; owner Argos Gen. Constrn. Corp., Red Hook, N.Y., 1970-75; project engr. Virtis Co., Gardiner, N.Y., 1976-79; sr. design engr. Rotron Inc. div. EG&G, Inc., Shokan, N.Y., 1979—; notary public, N.Y. Bd. dirs. Red Hook Recreation Assn., 1978-79, Christ Ch. Tape Ministry, 1978—. Served with U.S. Army, 1960-63. A.M. Kitselman fellow, 1955; named Instr. of Yr., U.S. Army Security Agy. Sch., 1962; cert. mfg. engr. Mem. Soc. Mfg. Engrs. (chpt. sec. 1979—; sr.), Am. Soc. Metals, Refrigerating Engrs. and Technicians Assn., Mensa, Alpha Tau Omega. Republican. Episcopalian. Patentee in field. Home: 38 E Market St Red Hook NY 12571 Office: Rotron Inc DuBois Rd Shokan NY 12481

BIRD, JON ARTHUR, banker; b. Ypsilanti, Mich., Aug. 26, 1939; s. Harlan Robert and Alice Eva (Blauvelt) B.; A.B., U. Mich., 1961, M.B.A., 1966; m. Jan Brucker Eberly, June 24, 1961; 1 dau., Karen Alice. Credit analyst Bank of the Commonwealth, Detroit, 1966-68, asst. cashier, 1968-71, asst. v.p., 1971-75, v.p., nat. dept. mgr., 1975—. Served with USN, 1961-65. Mem. Robert Morris Assos., Nat. Consumer Fin. Assn., U. Mich. Alumni Assn., Res. Officers Assn., Naval Res. Assn., Chi Psi. Republican. Presbyterian. Club: Univ. (Detroit). Home: 1485 Yorkshire St Birmingham MI 48008 Office: 719 Griswold Detroit MI 48226

BIRD, L. RAYMOND, investor; b. Plainfield, N.J., Jan. 22, 1914; s. Lewis Raymond and Bessie (MacCallum) B.; student N.Y. U., 1946-47; m. May Ethel Siercks, June 5, 1949. With shipping dept. Horn & Hardart Co., 1936-46, control auditor, 1946-49, gen. supt. in commissary, 1949-51; asst. to treas. fin. and legal Lockheed Electronics Co. (formerly Stavid Engring., Inc.), 1951-55, treas., 1955-60; pres., dir. State Bank of Plainfield (N.J.), 1960-62; investor, 1962—. Plainfield area committeeman Young Life Campaign, Inc.; pres. Plainfield Camp of Gideons, 1956—; mem. exec. com., treas. Christian Bus. Men's Com. of Central Jersey, 1956—. Bd. dirs. Sudan Interior Mission; chmn. trustees, chmn. exec. com. Barrington Coll.; trustee Evangelistic Com. Newark and Vicinity. Served from pvt. to 1st lt. 6th Armored Div., AUS, 1941-45. Mem. Am. Mgmt. Assn., Plainfield Area C. of C. Baptist (deacon). Home and Office: 18 Maplewood Dr Whiting NJ 08759

BIRDWELL, JAMES EDWIN, JR., bank exec.; b. Chuckey, Tenn., Apr. 22, 1924; s. James Edwin and Mary Eleanor (Earnest) B.; A.B., Tusculum Coll., 1949, M.A., Vanderbilt U., 1951; m. Marilyn Gibson, Dec. 20, 1949; children—James Edwin, Amy Eleanor, Todd Gibson. Tchr., coach Doak High Sch., Greeneville, Tenn., 1948-50; field rep. Third Nat. Bank, Nashville, 1951-52; trainee Va. Nat. Bank, Norfolk, 1957-60, v.p., 1960-73; pres. Union Peoples Bank, Clinton, Tenn., 1973—, chmn. bd., 1977—; Bd. dirs. mem. exec. com. Roane-Anderson Econ. Council, 1978—; mem. exec. com. Melton Hill Regional Indsl. Assn., 1976—; chmn. Clinton Port Auth., 1978—; trustee Oak Ridge Hosp., 1977—; bd. dirs. Daniel Arthur Rehab. Center, 1974—. Served with USN, 1942-46, 52-57; PTO. Mem. Am. Bankers Assn., Tenn. Bankers Assn., Robert Morris Assos., Bank Adminstrn. Inst. Methodist. Clubs: Oak Ridge Country, Civitan, LeConte. Office: 245 N Main St Clinton TN 37716

BIREN, STEVEN ROBERT, lawyer; b. N.Y.C., Feb. 13, 1944; s. Irving H. and Helen S. (Buchbinder) B.; B.E.E., CCNY, 1965; M.S.E.E., N.Y. U., 1968, J.D., 1973; m. Phyllis L. Harrison, Aug. 24, 1969; children—Melissa, Rene. Electronic engr. Sperry Gyroscope Co., Great Neck, N.Y., 1965-67; sr. engr. Hazeltine Corp., Greenlawn, N.Y., 1967-70; asso. patent atty. Cooper, Dunham, Clark, Griffin & Moran, N.Y.C., 1973-76; patent counsel U.S. Philips Corp., Tarrytown, N.Y., 1976—; admitted to N.Y. bar, 1974, Patent bar, 1973. Bd. dirs. Marriage Encounter No. Westchester, 1977-79. Donald L. Brown fellow, 1971-73, Regents Coll. scholar, 1960-65. Mem. Am. Bar Assn. Club: Twin Oaks. Author: Computers in the Legal Profession, 1972; (with others) Patent Law, 1973; editor Moot Court Bd., 1972-73; patentee in field. Home: 40 Old Lyme Rd Chappaqua NY 10514 Office: 580 White Plains Rd Tarrytown NY 10591

BIRENBAUM, MARK, apparel mfg. co. exec.; b. St. Louis, Oct. 16, 1938; s. Harry and Sue Birenbaum; B.S.B.A. in Bus. Adminstrn. and Acctg., Washington U., St. Louis, 1965; postgrad. St. Louis U., 1967; m. Barbara J. Lapidus, Nov. 25, 1965; children—Richelle, Hylah. Buyer mgr. Stix Baer & Fuller, dept. store, St. Louis, 1964-65; mgr. inventory Angelica Corp., St. Louis, 1965-70; corp. mgr. materials mgmt. Superior Surg. Mfg. Co. Inc., Seminole, Fla., 1970—; cons. in field, 1972—. Co-chmn. sch. adv. bd., Pinellas, Fla., 1979-80. Served with U.S. Army, 1959-62. Mem. Am. Prodn. and Inventory Control Soc. (pres. L.I. chpt. 1974-75, nat. v.p. 1976-78). Author: Management and Control of Production and Inventory, 1980. Home: 1448 Rosetree Ct Clearwater FL 33516 Office: 10099 Seminole Blvd Seminole FL 33542

BIRGER, JORDAN, business exec.; b. Winthrop, Mass., Nov. 10, 1922; s. Louis John and Ruth (Berman) B.; B.S., Tufts U., 1943; m. Barbara Ann Featherman, Aug. 7, 1955; children—S. Chet Bradley, Jon Sanford. Founder, treas. Orkney Assos., Waltham, Mass., 1950-70; founder Bee Plastics, Inc., Waltham, 1960, pres., 1960-68; treas. 214 Assos., Inc., Waltham, 1966-68; partner Ridge Assos., Cambridge, Mass., 1968-69; mgr. consumer products div. Amoco Chem. Corp., Waltham, 1968—; founder, pres. Family Products, Inc., Tyngsborough, Mass., 1972—. Mem. alumni council Tufts U., 1974—. Served with AUS, 1944-46. Recipient Distinguished Service award Tufts U. Coll. Engring., 1973. Mem. Am. Chem. Soc., Soc. Plastic Engrs., Phi Epsilon Pi. Republican. Jewish. Mason. Home: 145 Sargent Rd Brookline MA 02124 Office: Family Products Inc Tyngsborough MA 01879

BIRK, ROGER EMIL, investment broker; b. St. Cloud, Minn., July 14, 1930; s. Emil S. and Barbara E. (Zimmer) B.; B.A., St. John's U., 1952; m. Mary Lou Schrank, June 25, 1955; children—Kathleen, Steven, Mary Beth, Barbara. Mgr., Merrill Lynch, Pierce, Fenner and Smith, Inc. (now Merrill Lynch & Co.), Fort Wayne, Ind., 1964-66, mgr., Kansas City, Mo., 1966-68, asst. div. dir., N.Y.C., 1968-70, div. dir., 1971-74, pres., N.Y.C., 1974-76, chmn., 1976—; pres. Merrill Lynch & Co., 1976—. Chmn., Saint John's U. Nat. Adv. Council, 1975-76. Served with AUS, 1952-54. Mem. Nat. Assn. Securities Dealers (mem. long-range planning com. 1975-78). Club: Navesink Country (Middletown N.J.). Home: 542 Navesink River Rd Red Bank NJ 07701 Office: Merrill Lynch & Co Inc One Liberty Plaza 165 Broadway New York NY 10006

BIRKENRUTH, HARRY HANS, mfg. co. exec.; b. Stiphausen, Germany, June 13, 1931; came to U.S., 1937, naturalized, 1944; s. Hermann and Erna (Vicktor) B.; B.A., CCNY, 1953; M.B.A., Harvard U., 1957; m. Honore A. Wilinski, Aug. 25, 1957; children—David, Todd. With treasurer's dept. Standard Oil Co. (N.J.), 1957-60; with Rogers Corp. (Conn.), 1960—, sec., dir., 1964—, treas., 1964-67, v.p. fin., 1967—; asso. dir. Conn. Bank & Trust Co., Danielson. Trustee, Windham (Conn.) Community Meml. Hosp. Served to 1st lt. U.S. Army, 1953-55. Mem. Fin. Execs. Inst., Am. Soc. Corp. Secs. Home: Rural Route 1 Ball Hill Rd Storrs CT 06268 Office: Rogers Corp Main St Rogers CT 06263

BIRLA, SUSHIL KUMAR, automotive mfg. co. exec.; b. Sirsa, Haryana State, India, Oct. 1, 1943; came to U.S., 1969, naturalized, 1978; s. Mahabir Prasad and Lalita Devi (Mohunta) B.; B.S.M.E., Birla Inst. Tech. and Sci., Pilani, India, 1965; M.S.E.E., Wayne State U., 1971; m. Pramila Kela, Dec. 14, 1972; children—Jyoti, Asheesh. Mng. partner Madhu Woodcraft Industries, Jaipur, India, 1965-66; supt. prodn. planning and control Hindustan Motors, Uttarpara, India, 1966-69; proposal, controls engr. Cross Co., Fraser, Mich., 1969-73; design engr. Excello Machine Tool Products, Detroit, 1973-76; sr. project engr. mfg. devel. Gen. Motors Co. Tech. Center, Warren, Mich., 1976—; mem. Machine Tool Task Force, USAF Materials Lab., 1978-80, recipient recognition for outstanding contbn. Vol. probation aide Macomb County, Mich., 1976-77; vol. probation counsellor Sterling Heights, Mich., 1979. Cert. mfg. engr. Mem. Soc. Mfg. Engrs. Home: 42380 Buckingham Dr Sterling Heights MI 48078 Office: Gen Motors Corp - Mfg Devel Gen Motors Tech Center Warren MI 48090

BIRMINGHAM, MATTHEW THOMAS, JR., publishing co. exec.; b. Boston, Apr. 30, 1920; s. Matthew Thomas and Beatrice (Strong) B.; B.A., Trinity Coll., 1942; m. Jane McCrady Gaillard, Nov. 8, 1947; children—Matthew T. III, Elizabeth (Mrs. Clark Cretti), Peter, James. Product dir. Street & Smith Pub. Co., N.Y.C., 1950-60; v.p., treas., dir., Ziff-Davis Pub. Co., N.Y.C., 1960-64; exec. v.p. Matthew Bender Co., N.Y.C., 1965-66, pres., 1966-74, chmn. bd., chief exec. officer, 1974—, dir., 1965—; group v.p. Times Mirror Co., Los Angeles, 1970—; chmn. bd., dir. Times Mirror Magazines, Inc., N.Y.C., Southwestern Co., Nashville, The Sporting News Co., St. Louis, Matthew Bender Co., N.Y.C., Select Mags., Inc., N.Y.C. Trustee Vt. Acad., Saxton's River, 1973—; patron Saratoga Performing Arts. Served to lt. USNR, 1942-46. Fellow Albany Art Inst. Clubs: Union League (N.Y.C.); Noroton Yacht (Darien, Conn.); Wee Burn Country (Darien, Conn.); Ft. Orange (Albany, N.Y.). Home: 521 Flax Hill Rd Norwalk CT 06854 also Cavendish VT Office: Times Mirror Co 235 E 45th St New York NY 10022

BIRNBAUM, ALLAN SANFORD, mfg., importing co. exec.; b. Bklyn., Nov. 6, 1937; s. Leo and Sylvia B.; B.S., Fairleigh Dickinson U., 1959; m. Ruth Stern, Mar. 10, 1962; children—Mark, David. With Bilt Well Umbrella Co., Inc., North Bergen, N.J., 1959—, pres., 1974—. Trustee, Congregation Beth Shalom, Teaneck, N.J., 1974—. Office: Bilt Well Umbrella Co Inc 1110 13th St North Bergen NJ 07047

BIRNBAUM, ROBERT BENJAMIN, mgmt. cons.; b. Wilkes-Barre, Pa., June 10, 1922; s. Louis and Elvira (Peters) B.; B.S., U. N.H., 1946; student U. Grenoble (France), 1945; postgrad. N.Y. U., 1946-47; m. Florence Harriet Green, Sept. 6, 1948; children—Marie Ann, William David. With various consumer and trade publs., 1947-52; sr. v.p. Breskin Publs., Inc., N.Y.C., 1952-65; exec. v.p. Franklin Sq. Agy., Teaneck, N.J., 1965-66; v.p. mktg. Billboard Publs., Inc., N.Y.C., 1966-70; v.p. pub. services Lebhar-Friedman, Inc., N.Y.C., 1970-76; pres. Bob Birnbaum Co., Mountainside, N.J., 1977—; dir. Breskin Publs., 1960-64; guest lectr. Fairleigh Dickinson U., 1976; chmn. Audit Bur. Circulations Businesspaper Industry Com., 1974-76; lectr. Folio mag. ann. seminars. Served with U.S. Army, 1943-46; ETO. Decorated Bronze Star. Mem. Mag. Pubs. Assn. (chmn. pub. mgmt. com. 1975-76), Am. Mktg. Assn., Advt. Club N.Y. Jewish. Contbr. articles in field to profl. jours. Office: 1173 Blazo Terr Mountainside NJ 07092

BIRNBAUM, ROBERT JACK, stock exchange exec.; b. N.Y.C., Sept. 3, 1927; s. Joseph M. and Beatrice (Herman) B.; B.S., N.Y. U., 1957; LL.B., Georgetown U., 1962; m. Joy E. Mumford, June 2, 1957; children—Gregg Gordon, Julie Beth. Admitted to D.C. bar, 1963; atty. SEC, Washington, 1961-66; with Am. Stock Exchange, N.Y.C., 1967—, pres., 1977—. Served with USCGR, 1945-46. Office: 86 Trinity Pl New York NY 10006

BIRNBERG, JACK, investment co. exec.; b. June 15, 1937; s. Max and Yetta (Halpern) B.; B.S., Fairleigh Dickinson U., 1959; m. Louise Rothstein, June 7, 1959; children—Michael, Steven, John, Jeffrey. Accountant firm Scholtz, Simon & Miller, 1960-61; controller, officer Scott, Harvey Co., Inc., 1962-63; pres., dir. M. A. Allan & Co., Inc., Clifton, N.J., 1963-71; dir. Williston Oil Corp., Kraftware Corp., N.Y.C., Edios, Inc., Joy Corp.; chmn. bd. Computerized Security Automation, Clifton, 1970—, Internat. Equities, Ltd., Clifton, 1970—; exec. v.p., dir. Tappen Zee Small Bus. Investment Corp., N.Y.C., Tappen Zee Capital Corp.; asso. dir. Home State Bank, Authenticolor Inc., Nat. Color Inc. Mem. Midwest Stock Exchange, 1968-76, Phila.-Balt.-Washington Stock Exchange, 1966-72. Pres., Passaic County Children's Shelter, 1967-74; bd. dirs. Boys Club, Paterson, N.J., 1970-77; chmn. met. div. United Jewish Appeal, 1970; bd. dirs. Barnert Hosp., Birnberg Found., Greater Paterson (N.J.) YW-YMHA, 1970-76; chmn. Expo 200, Barnert Temple, 1976—; chmn. bd. dirs. Employee Retirement Benefit Assn., 1975—; trustee Greater Clifton B'nai B'rith, 1962-64. Jewish. Home: 409 Carriage Ln Wyckoff NJ 07481 Office: 120 N Main St New City NY 10956

BIRNHOLZ, JACK, realtor; b. Newark, Jan. 16, 1931; s. Benjamin and Rebecca (Tullmon) B.; B.S., Rutgers U., 1957; postgrad. N.Y. U., 1958-61; also profl. and tech. courses; m. Shirley Sarasohn, Nov. 15, 1953; children—Harriet Ann, Robert Andrew, Richard Marc. Pres., Jack Birnholz & Co., Newark and North Miami Beach, Fla., 1958—; chmn. bd., pres. Appraisal Group, Inc., North Miami Beach, London and Munich, W. Ger., 1974—; pres. First Gen. Funding Corp., North Miami Beach, 1975—; adj. prof. real estate Rutgers U.; guest lectr. Am. Soc. Appraisers, Barry Coll., Fla., Am. Right of Way Assn. Conv. Bd. dirs. Jewish Chautaqua Soc.; mem. exec. bd. Nat. Fedn. Temple Brotherhoods, pres. So. Fla. council; mem. exec. com. Temple Sinai, North Miami Beach. Served with U.S. Army, 1951; Korea. Decorated Bronze Star, others; lic. real estate broker, Fla., N.J., N.Y., Pa. Mem. Nat. Assn. Rev. Appraisers, Am. Soc. Appraisers (1st v.p. Broward chpt.), Am. Acad. Cons.'s, Am. Indsl. Devel. Council, Nat. Assn. Realtors, Fla. Assn. Realtors, N.J. Assn. Realtors, Indsl. Real Estate Brokers Assn., Nat. Mktg. Inst., Am. Arbitration Assn., Farm and Land Brokers Inst., Internat. Real Estate Fedn., Real Estate Securities and Syndication Inst., Urban Land Inst., Am. Right of Way Assn., Newark Real Estate Bd., Miami Real Estate Bd., Soc. Real Estate Appraisers, Internat. Assn. Assessing Ofcls., Evaluators Inst., Nat. Assn. Corp. Real Estate Execs., Mortgage Brokers Assn. Fla., Nat. Soc. Fee Appraisers (past pres.), Nat. Assn. Rev. Appraisers. Office: 1558 NE 162d St North Miami Beach FL 33162

BIRO, STEVEN GEORGE MICHAEL, lawyer; b. Ankara, Turkey, Aug. 17, 1943; s. George G. and Lillian L. Biro; A.B. (Regents, Coll. scholar), Columbia Coll., 1965; M.A. in Polit. Sci., U. Wash., 1967; postgrad. N.Y. U., 1970-74; M.S. equivalent in Nuclear Engring., U.S. Navy Nuclear Power and Submarine Schs., 1967-68; J.D. (Law Sch. scholar), Fordham U., 1974; m. Sofiya Guzin Altiok. Adj. instr. polit. sci. N.Y. U., 1970-71; admitted to Conn. bar, 1974, N.Y. bar, 1975, U.S. Supreme Ct. bar, 1978, Fla. bar, 1979, also U.S. Tax Ct., U.S. Ct. Patent and Customs Appeals; law clk. to Justices Louis Shapiro and Joseph Longo, Supreme Ct. of Conn., 1974-75; law clk. Hon. T.J. Meskill, U.S. Ct. of Appeals for 2d Circuit, 1975; asso. firm Winthrop, Stimson, Putnam & Roberts, N.Y.C., Conn., Fla. and U.K., 1975-79; partner firm Hill & Spoliansky, Muscat, United Arab Emirates, 1979—. Mem. law com. Community Ch., 1976-79; co-chair rules com. Community Bd. 8, N.Y.C., 1978-79; pres. Democratic Club of Yorkville, 1977-79. Served to lt. USN, 1965-72. NIMH fellow, 1971-73, NIH fellow, 1973-74. Mem. Am., Fed., N.Y. State, Conn., Fla. bar assns., Assn. Bar City N.Y. (sec. com. on nuclear tech. and law), N.Y. County Lawyers Assn. (reporter com. on application of tech. to law), Phi Alpha Delta. Unitarian-Universalist. Club: Princeton. Contbr. articles to profl. jours. Home: 133 Arthur St Garden City NY Office: PO Box 190 Muscat Sultanate of Oman United Arab Emirates

BISCEGLIA, RAYMOND JAMES, banker; b. Middlesboro, Ky., Aug. 15, 1927; s. Anthony L. and Mary (Comparoni) B.; m. Patricia Hunt, Feb. 26, 1949; children—Judith Lynn, Theresa Ann, Anthony J., Joan Marie, William Thomas. Pres., chief exec. officer Nat. Bank, Middlesboro, Ky., 1974—. Served with USNR. Mem. Ky. Bankers Assn., Bank Adminstrn. Inst., Am. Banking Assn., Am. Legion. Roman Catholic. Club: Elks. Office: The National Bank PO Box 400 Middlesboro KY 40965

BISES, GEORGE RAYMOND, elec. products mfg. co. exec.; b. Rome, Aug. 7, 1920; came to U.S., 1939, naturalized, 1944; s. Arnold and Constance Bises; student U. Rome, 1937-39; B.S. in Mech. Engring., M.I.T., 1941; postgrad. Columbia U., 1946-47; m. Juliana Paola Nunes, Nov. 10, 1946; children—Laura, Ann, George. Mech. designer Stone & Webster, Boston, 1941-42; mech. engr. Ebasco Services, Inc., N.Y.C., 1942-43, 47-48; v.p. Sinex Projects, Inc., N.Y.C., 1948-50; asst. v.p., mgr. for Europe, Gibbs & Hill, Inc., N.Y.C., Milan, Italy and Madrid, Spain, 1950-63; area dir. power systems internat. Westinghouse Electric Corp., Milan and Geneva, 1963—; pres. Sopren S.p.A.; v.p. Westinghouse Electric S.p.A.; dir. Westinghouse Electric S.A.R.L., Geneva, Ercole Marelli S.p.A. Served as 1st lt. U.S. Army, 1943-46; ETO. Registered profl. engr., N.Y. State. Mem. ASME, Italian Atomic Forum, Am. C. of C. in Italy (dir.). Club: Golf (Milan). Home: 18 chemin Rieu Geneva 1208 Switzerland Office: 19 Place Longemalle Geneva 1204 Switzerland

BISHOP, GEORGE WILLIAMS, III, supply co. exec.; b. Williamson, W.Va., May 11, 1936; s. George W. and Dorothy Ann (Scott) B.; B.E.E., Va. Mil. Inst., 1958; postgrad. U. Va., 1959; m.

Nancy Lee Long, Dec. 4, 1976; 1 dau., Rebecca Lee; children by previous marriage—George Williams IV, Angela, Brett, Dale Scott. Mgr. elec. div. Buchanan Williamson Supply Co., Grundy, Va., 1962-64, exec. v.p., 1964-77, pres., chmn., 1977—, dir., 1964—; v.p., gen. mgr. Wingfield & Hundley, Inc., Richmond, Va., 1966-69, pres., 1969-72. Served to capt. USAF, 1959-62. Mem. Nat. Assn. Wholesalers, So. Indsl. Distbrs. Assn. Republican. Presbyterian. Clubs: Rotary, Brandermill Country, Jefferson. Home: 13600 Pebble Creek Ct Midlothian VA 23113 Office: BWS Co Grundy VA 24614

BISHOP, JACK LAWSON, JR., mfg. co. planner, economist; b. Rockville Centre, N.Y., Dec. 3, 1939; s. Jack Lawson and Elizabeth Janet (Blee) B.; B.S. in Chem. Engring., U. Colo., 1961; Ph.D. in Bus., U. Ill., 1972; m. Donna Norine Leavens, June 24, 1962; children—Elizabeth Anona, Jack Lawson, Kathleen Anne, Caroline Donna Van Alstine. Product devel. engr. Dow Corning Corp., Midland, Mich., 1961-72, mgmt. sci. specialist, 1968-72; instr. Central Mich. U., 1969-70; mgr. mgmt. sci. Ky. Fried Chicken, Louisville, 1972-73; mgr. econ. and gen. research May Dept. Stores, Inc., St. Louis, 1973-76; mgr. operational studies Brunswick Corp., Chgo., 1976—; cons. internat. econs., strategic planning. Exec. com. Midwest regional office Am. Friends Service Com., Chgo., 1979—; bd. dirs. Midwest Friends Housing Corp., 1980—; mem. Chgo. Council Fgn. Relations. Mem. Ops. Research Soc., Inst. Mgmt. Sci., Econometric Soc., Am. Econ. Assn., Am. Statis. Assn., Nat. Assn. Bus. Economists. Quaker. Author: Practical Emulsions, 1968; Insect Disease and Weed Control, 1972. Home: 916 Maple Evanston IL 60202 Office: 1 Brunswick Plaza Skokie IL 60077

BISHOP, JOHN FREDERICK, mfg. co. exec.; b. Yenangyaung, Burma, Jan. 3, 1924 (parents Am. citizens); s. Fay and Florence Louise (Larson) B.; B.S. in Mech. Engring., U. Calif., Berkeley, 1945; M.B.A., Harvard U., 1948; m. Ann Rix, Nov. 4, 1945; children—Caren Lee Bishop McDonald, John Bradford, Kimberly Ann Bishop Rothwell, Suzann Louise. With market research and distbn. dept. Owens-Corning Fiberglas Corp., Los Angeles, 1948-51; div. gen. mgr. Beckman Instruments, Inc., Fullerton, Calif., 1951-59; exec. v.p. Textron Electronics, Inc., Santa Ana, Calif., 1959-60; chmn. bd. EIP Microwave, Inc., Newport Beach, Calif., 1960—, Cushman Electronics, Inc., Newport Beach, 1960—; dir. ECCO, Inc., Baker Internat. Corp., Bentley Labs., Inc., San Francisco Real Estate Investors. Trustee, Webb Sch. Calif., 1970-73, Clarement Men's Coll., 1972-75; founding pres. UCI (U. Calif., Irvine) Found., 1968-69. Served as lt. (j.g.) USNR, 1943-47. Mem. ASME, IEEE, Instrument Soc. Am., Am. Electronics Assn., Young Presidents Orgn., World Bus. Council, Chief Execs. Forum, Mchts. and Mfrs. Assn. (dir. 1968-70). Republican. Episcopalian. Club: Calif. (Los Angeles); Balboa Bay, Big Canyon Country (Newport Beach). Home: 20 Linda Isle Newport Beach CA 92660 Office: 4500 Campus Dr Suite 235 Newport Beach CA 92660

BISHOP, LLOYD GEORGE ALFRED, real estate investment co. exec.; b. Kingston, Ont., Can., Apr. 13, 1942; s. Alfred Wesley and Claire Loyst (Ostrom) B.; B.Sc., Queen's U., 1965, M.Sc., 1973, M.B.A., 1973; m. Joan Elizabeth Haglund, May 22, 1971; 1 son, Douglas Craig. Asst. dept. head Northview Heights Secondary Sch., Toronto, Ont., 1966-69; leasing mgr. Met. Estates Property Corp., Can. Properties, Toronto, 1973-74; comptroller Allpak Ltd., London, Ont., 1979; v.p. Alcor Investments, London, 1979, pres., 1980—, also dir.; v.p., dir. City Centre (London) Ltd. Bd. dirs. London and Dist. Mental Retardation Assn. Mem. Liberal Party Can. Mem. United Ch. of Can. Home: 192 Bridport St London ON N6A 2A8 Canada Office: 233 Hyman St London ON N6A 1N6 Canada

BISHOP, WARNER BADER, fin. exec.; b. Lakewood, Ohio, Dec. 13, 1918; s. Warner Brown and Gladys (Bader) B.; A.B., Dartmouth Coll., 1941, M.B.A., 1942; A.M.P., Harvard U., 1955; m. Katherine Sue White, Dec. 15, 1944; children—Susan, Judith, Katherine, Jennifer; m. 2d, Barrie Osborn, Feb. 4, 1967; children—Wilder, Brooks. Successively sales rep., export mgr., sales mgr., div. gen. mgr., asst. v.p. Archer-Daniels-Midland Co., Cleve., 1946-56, v.p., 1956-59; pres. Fed. Foundry Supply Co., 1957-58, Wyodak Clay & Chem. Co., 1957-59, Basic, Inc., 1959-63, Union Fin. Corp., Cleve., 1963-74, Union Savs. Assn., 1963-74, chmn. bd., 1970—; pres., chmn. bd., chief exec. officer TransOhio Fin. Corp., Cleve., 1974—; dir. TransOhio Savs. Assn., Victoria and Grey Trust Co., Toronto, Med. Life Ins. Co.; trustee Nat. Mortgage Fund, Med. Mut. of Cleve. Sec., Foundry Ednl. Found., 1956-60; gen. campaign mgr. Cleve. Area Heart Assn., chmn. bd., 1960-61; bd. dirs. Fenn Coll., Ohio Heart Assn.; pres. Council High Blood Pressure, Am. Heart Assn., 1964-69. Recipient Disting. Service and Meritorious Service awards. Served to lt. USNR, 1942-45; ETO, PTO. Mem. Northeastern Ohio Savs. and Loan League, U.S. League Savs. Assns. Republican. Episcopalian. Clubs: Chagrin Valley Hunt; Union, Tavern (Cleve.); India House, Union (N.Y.C.); Meadow (Southampton, N.Y.). Contbr. articles to trade jours. Home: One Bratenahl Pl 409 Bratenahl OH 44108 Office: One Penton Plaza 1111 Chester Ave Cleveland OH 44114

BISSELL, BRENT JOHN, pub. co. exec.; b. Dearborn, Mich., July 10, 1950; s. Ernest Ross and Virginia Jane (Pete) B.; B.A., U. Toledo, 1971; m. Libby Schulak, Dec. 4, 1971; children—John, Sarah. Pres., chmn. bd. Bissell Advt. Inc., Toledo, 1976-79; v.p. Communications Concepts, Toledo, 1978-79; creative dir. Starkbro's Nurseries & Orchard Co., Louisiana, Mo., 1979-80; div. mgr. Consumer Pub. Co., Canton, Ohio, 1980—; pres. B. Urselv Communications. Nat. public relations dir. Nat. Assn. Congregational Christian Chs., 1979; active Torch Drive. Mem. Direct Mail Mktg. Assn. Club: Toledo. Home: 6153 Island Dr NW Canton OH 44718

BISSELL, EUGENE VAN NAME, III, cons. co. exec.; b. Mpls., July 9, 1953; s. Eugene Van Name and Janet Collier (Simpson) B.; B.A., Kalamazoo (Mich.) Coll., 1976; M.B.A., U. Pa., 1980. Investigator, lMich. Corp. & Securities Bur., Lansing, 1974; intern legis. action com. Ind. Businessman's Assn., Kalamazoo, 1975-76; petroleum allocation officer Mich. Energy Adminstrn., Lansing, 1976-77, dir. Office Fed. Relations, 1977-78; treas. XMCO, Inc., Springfield, Va., 1979—. Recipient Eugene P. Stermer award in public adminstrn., 1976. Mem. Am. Mgmt. Assn. Home: 2020 Peach Orchard Dr Falls Church VA 22043 Office: 6501 Loisdale Ct Springfield VA 22150

BISSELL, MARSHALL PHILIP, life ins. co. exec.; b. Bloomfield, N.J., June 20, 1914; s. Robert B. and Mary (Campbell) B.; B.S., U. Va., 1936; m. Claire Marie Flint; children—Beverley Anne (Mrs. Charles F. Wilson), Robert W., Marilyn B. (Mrs. Dennis W. Fread). With N.Y. Life Ins. Co., 1936—, beginning as mgr. bank relations successively asst. v.p., sec., 1936-58, v.p., asso. comptroller, 1958-60, v.p., comptroller, 1960-63, sr. v.p., 1963-69, exec. v.p., 1969-72, pres., 1972-80; dir. Mgmt. Assistance, Inc. Home: 13 Robert Dr Chatham NJ 07928 Office: 51 Madison Ave New York NY 10010

BISSELL, STEVEN LEWIS, TV prodn. co. exec.; b. Iowa City, Jan. 30, 1949; s. Lewis Austin and Berniece Margaret (Helmer) B.; student Kirkwood Community Coll., 1968, U. Iowa, 1968—. Founder, pres. Bissell Talent Agy., Iowa City, 1965—, New World Entertainment Agy. and New World TV Prodns., Iowa City, 1965—; founder, chmn., office mgr., advt. sales mgr. Student Producers Assn./Campus CableVision, U. Iowa, Iowa City, 1972-80; exec. asso. Collegiate Assns. Council, U. Iowa, 1977-79, 80, office mgr. student assns., 1979-80; cable programming dir., press agt. Iowa Public Interest Research Group, U. Iowa, 1980—; press agt. Congress Watch, U. Iowa chpt., 1980—. Served with USN, 1968. Recipient cert. of merit Charity Art Show, 1978. Mem. U.S. Jaycees (Presdl. citation 1978), Iowa City Jaycees (Presdl. award of honor 1978), Full Gospel Businessmen's Internat. Democrat. Roman Catholic. Home: 1030 E Washington Iowa City IA 52240 Office: Iowa Public Interest Research Group Activities Center Iowa Meml Union U Iowa Iowa City IA 52242

BISSEY, WILLIAM KARL, bank exec.; b. Columbus, Ind., Aug. 18, 1940; s. Harry Carl and Mary M. (Fleming) B.; B.S., Ind. U., 1962, M.B.A., 1964. Purchasing agt. Arvin Industries, Inc., Columbus, 1964-68; instr. Ohio No. U., Ada, 1968-73; credit analyst Mchts. Nat. Bank, Indpls., 1974-78; mgr. internat. econ. research Am. Fletcher Nat. Bank, 1978—. Served with U.S. Army, 1963-64. Ford fellow, 1960-63. Mem. Am. Philatelic Soc., Alpha Kappa Psi, Delta Sigma Phi, Beta Gamma Sigma, Omicron Delta Epsilon. Presbyn. Home: 8305 Sobax Dr Indianapolis IN 46268 Office: 111 Monument Circle Indianapolis IN 46226

BISSONNETTE, JAMES ARTHUR, electronics co. exec.; b. Nashua, N.H., Apr. 8, 1933; s. Arthur Joseph and Ann Jones (McAlpine) B.; B.A., St. Anselm's Coll., 1955; M.B.A., N.Y. U., 1961; postgrad. Boston Coll., 1959-60, Lowell U., 1973-75; m. Elizabeth Jane Murphy, Oct. 21, 1964; children—Ann, Jane, Carolyn, Noelle. Ins. rep. Travellers Ins. Co., Boston, 1957-59; ins. insp. Retail Credit Co., N.Y.C., 1959-61; supr. govts. contracts Raytheon Co., Andover, Mass., 1961-62, Sudbury, Mass., 1962-65, Bedford, Mass., 1965-69; mgr. procurement Ocean Systems div. Sanders Assos., Nashua, 1970-74, mgr. electronic warfare div. Ground Support Contracts, 1974-78, mgr. procurement Spl. Programs div., 1978—. Active Arts and Sci. Center, Nashua; pres. Nashua Symphony Assn., 1978-79, also bd. dirs. Served with U.S. Army, 1951-52. Mem. Nat. Contracts Mgmt. Assn. (certified profl. contracts mgr.), St. Anselm's Coll., N.Y. U. alumni assns., Assn. Old Crows. Roman Catholic. Club: Century. Home: 43 Farmington Rd Nashua NH 03060 Office: 95 Canal St Nashua NH 03061

BIVANS, ERNEST L., utility co. exec.; b. Ft. Lauderdale, Fla., May 3, 1919; s. William Weaver and Effa Beth (Brendla) B.; B.S. in Elec. Engring., U. Fla., 1942; exec. course Stanford U. Bus. Grad. Sch., 1974; m. Marjorie Alice Burns, Dec. 18, 1943; children—Barbara, Janet, William. With Fla. Power & Light Co., Miami, 1945—, asst. chief engr., 1960-70, chief engr., 1970-72, v.p. power supply, 1972-73, v.p. system planning, 1973—. Served with Signal Corps, U.S. Army, 1942-45; ETO. Decorated Bronze Star (5); registered profl. engr., Fla. Mem. Nat. Soc. Profl. Engrs., IEEE (sr.), Fla. Engring. Soc. (sr.), Phi Gamma Delta. Methodist. Clubs: Coral Gables Country, Dinner Key Cruising, Coral Bay Yacht, Univ. Yacht. Home: 12931 Deva St Coral Gables FL 33156

BIXBY, R. BURDELL, lawyer, former state ofcl.; b. Schenectady, Oct. 11, 1914; s. Raymond O. and Mabel A. (Rumsey) B.; A.B., Colgate U., 1936; LL.B., Albany Law Sch., 1940, J.D., 1968; m. Anne M. Hardwick, Oct. 25, 1941; 1 son, Robert Hardwick. Admitted to N.Y. bar, 1940; partner firm Dewey, Ballantine, Bushby, Palmer & Wood, N.Y.C., 1955—; asst. sec. gov. State N.Y., 1948-50, exec. asst., 1950-52, sec., 1952-54; sec.-treas. N.Y. State Thruway Authority, 1950-60, chmn., sec. treas., 1960-61, chmn., sec., 1961-74. Trustee Hudson (N.Y.) City Savs. Inst. Trustee Albany Law Sch. Served with USAAF, 1942-46. Mem. Am., N.Y. State, Columbia County bar assns., Am. Judicature Soc., Assn. Bar City N.Y., N.Y. County Lawyers Assn., Am. Legion. Mason. Club: City Midday (N.Y.C.). Home: 7 Joslen Pl Hudson NY 12534 Office: 140 Broadway New York City NY 10005

BIXBY, WILLIAM HERBERT, ret. elec. engr.; b. Indpls., Dec. 28, 1906; s. George Linder and Carrie (Tilton) B.; B.S.E., U. Mich., 1930, M.S., 1931, Ph.D., 1933; M.M.E., Chrysler Inst. Engring., 1935; m. Dorothy Bancroft, Jan. 17, 1963. Spl. problems engr. Chrysler Corp., Detroit, 1933-36; instr. to prof. elec. engring. Wayne U., 1936-56; cons. engr. Power Equipment Co., Detroit, 1937-56, v.p. for applied research Power Equipment div. North Electric Co., Galion, Ohio, 1956—. Fellow AAAS, IEEE; mem. Engring. Soc. Detroit, Sigma Xi. Home: 5274 Riverside Dr Columbus OH 43220

BIZZARO, WILLIAM, JR., indsl. designer; b. Bklyn., Nov. 4, 1938; s. William and Ethel Marie (Zobel) B.; B.S. in Indsl. Design, Pratt Inst., 1965; m. Louise Nancy Jaffe, May 1, 1964; children—Loree Wileen, Jeffrey William, Gregory Roy. Designer, Gen. Electric Co., Schenectady, 1965-67; sr. designer Atkins and Merrill Inc., Maynard, Mass., 1967-69; design dir. Dimensions Craft, Inc., Shrewsbury, Mass., 1969-70; owner, operator Expo Media William Bizzaro Assos., Framingham, Mass., 1970—. Served with USAR, 1957-63. Recipient Nat. Design award Playskool Research, 1964. Patentee in field. Home: 1667 Main St Concord MA 01742 Office: 1661 Worcester Rd Suite 401 Framingham MA 01701

BJERCKE, ALF RICHARD, bus. exec.; b. Oslo, May 30, 1921; s. Richard and Birgit (Brambani) B.; student Mass. Inst. Tech., 1939-41; m. Berit Blikstad, Mar. 15, 1946; children—Leif Richard Haakon Richard, Ingerid, Berit. With Alf Bjercke A/S, Oslo, 1945—, partner, 1950—, vice chmn., 1966-69, chmn., 1969—; dir. A/S. Jotungruppen, 1972—; with Addis Ababa, Nat. Chem. Ind. Ltd., 1966-75; chmn. Norwater (Norske Vannkilder A/S.), ABC Produkter A/S, Scanpump A/S, 1972-78; vice chmn., dir. Oplandske Dampskibsselskab; dir. Norwegian Shipping & Trade Jour.; chmn. Jotungruppen A/S, Kolding, Denmark; vice chmn. Akershus Broiler Co., Chilinvest A/S. Hon. consul gen. Tunisia in Norway; vice chmn. Norwegian Spring Water Assn.; chmn. council Kofoed Sch., 1962-80; mem. Norway's Olympic Com., 1971-74; mem. exec. com. Norwegian UNIDO Council, del. conf.; Norway del. Econ. Commn. for Africa; mem. Norwegian Arbitration Bd. for Competitive Questions; chmn. Soc. for Protection Ancient Towns, Soc. for Reconstrn. of Old Christiania, 1968-78; mem. council Norsk Sjofartsmuseum; chmn. bd. Norway's Bus. Mus., 1980—; Norwegian mem. adv. com. Sail Tng. Assn., London; past chmn. Norad Adv. Council for Industry; mem. Commn. 3 CIOR. Mem. campaign com. Norwegian Conservative party, 1974; bd. dirs. Artists Gallery of Oslo, 1957-69; vice chmn. East Norway Sailing Sch. Ship Assn., 1961-78; chmn. Norwegian-Ethiopian Soc., 1954-70; chmn. council Norway-Am. Assn.; chmn. fin. com. Norwegian World Wild Life Fund Bd. Reps.; Norwegian rep. Operation Sail 76; bd. dirs. A Smoke-free Generation, 1980. Served with Royal Norwegian Air Force, 1941-45; maj. Res. Mem. Norwegian Assn. Industries (past dir.), Color Council Norway (chmn. 1958-69, 72—), Norwegian Paint Mfrs. Assn. (past chmn.), Norway Athletic Assn. (chmn. 1968-72), Wine and Food Soc., World Wildlife Fund 1001 Club. Clubs: Rotary (dist. gov. 1980-81); Oslo Bus. Men's (dir. 1968-70). Contbr. articles in several fields to profl. jours.; columnist jour. Farmand. Home: 14 President Harbitzgate Oslo 2 Norway Office: Kongens gt 6 Oslo 1 Norway

BJORGAN, KENNETH HOWARD, ch. bus. adminstr.; b. Sioux Falls, S.D., Aug. 30, 1923; s. Oscar Melvin and Clara Elisa (Tiedeman) B.; B.A. in Econs. and Bus., U. Wash., 1949; m. Lyla Elizabeth Johnson, Sept. 4, 1943; children—Joy Lynn Bjorgan Carlisle, Laurie Kay. Office mgr. North Pacific Seafoods Co., Seattle, 1951-54; accountant Rainier Cos., Seattle, 1954-56; various mgmt. positions Western Farmers Assn., Seattle, 1956-71; ch. bus. adminstr. Phinney Ridge Lutheran Ch., Seattle, 1971—. Pres. View Ridge Community Club, Seattle, 1958-59; mem. Gov.'s Council for Reorgn. Wash. State Govt., 1966. Served with USN, 1942-45. Mem. Nat. Assn. Ch. Bus. Adminstrs. (pres. 1978-79), Greenwood C. of C. (pres.-elect 1980-81, rec. sec. 1975-78), U. Wash., Beta Alpha Psi alumni assns. Republican. Lutheran. Home: 7223 57th Ave NE Seattle WA 98115 Office: 7500 Greenwood Ave N Seattle WA 98103

BJORK, JOHN LAVERNE, distbn. services exec.; b. Rockford, Ill., June 13, 1927; s. Ivar A. and Lena (Johnson) B.; B.S.M.E., Ill. Inst. Tech., 1951; M.B.A., U. Chgo., 1957; m. Janice M. Ferm, June 17, 1950; children—Kimberly, Jon. Design engr. John S. Barnes Corp., Rockford, 1947-51; product sales mgr. Stewart-Warner Corp., Chgo., 1951-57, mgr. new products, 1957-59, group mktg. mgr., 1959-62; market analyst, long range planner Amsted Industries, Inc., Chgo., 1962-65; v.p., founding dir. Mgmt. Research & Planning, Inc., Evanston, Ill., 1965-66; dir. phys. distbn. Signode Corp., Chgo., 1966-70; v.p. distbn. services Libby, Nc Neill & Libby, Chgo., 1970-73; v.p. distbn. and devel. Keebler Co., Elmhurst, Ill., 1973-74; v.p., regional gen. mgr. Unijac div. IU Internat. Jacksonville, Fla., 1974-77; gen. mgr. ITT-Transp. Distbn. Services, Palm Coast, Fla., 1977—. Served with USAAC, 1944-46. Mem. Nat. Council Phys. Distbn. Mgmt. (pres. Chgo. chpt. 1968-69). Clubs: Skokie Country (Glencoe, Ill.); Ponte Vedra (Fla.), Masons. Office: ITT Transp Distbn Services Palm Coast FL 32051

BJORKSTEN, JOHAN, research chemist; b. Tammerfors, Finland, May 27, 1907; s. Walter and Gerda (Ramsay) B.; Ph.D., U. Helsinki (Finland), 1931; guest researcher U. Stockholm (Sweden), 1927-28, U. Minn., 1931-32; m. Christel E. Svedlin, Nov. 14, 1961; children—Sybil Joan (Mrs. Jurgen von Rennenkampff) (dec.), Oliver J. W., Dargar William, Nils Johan, Lennart Allen. Research chemist Felton Chem. Co., Bklyn., 1933-34, chief chemist, 1934-35; charge devel. Pepsodent Co., Clearing, Ill., 1935-36; chief chemist Ditto, Inc., Chgo., 1937-41; chem. dir. Quaker Chem. Products Corp., Conshohocken, Pa., 1941-44; founder, pres. Bjorksten Research Labs. Inc., Madison, Wis., 1944-76, chmn. bd., 1944—; pres. BEE Chem. Co., Lansing, Ill., 1945-48, chmn. bd., 1948-56; dir., co-founder Reef Industries, Inc., Houston, 1956—; co-founder, v.p., dir. A-B-C Packaging Machine Co., Tarpon Springs, Fla., 1940—. Pres., Bjorksten Research Found., 1952—. Mem. Am. Inst. Chemists (past pres.), AAAS, Am. Chem. Soc., Am. Assn. Cereal Chemists, Soc. Cosmetic Chemists, Am. Leather Chemists Assn., Am. Oil Chemists Soc., Am. Soc. Metals, Am. Soc. Testing and Materials, Am. Geog. Soc., Am. Geriatrics Soc., Chem. Arts Forum, Chgo. Soc. Paint Tech., Electrochem. Soc., N.Y. Acad. Scis., Gerontol. Soc., Soc. Plastics Industry, Soc. Plastics Engrs., TAPPI, Finnish Chem. Soc., Soc. pro Fauna et Flora Fennica, Alpha Chi Sigma, Gamma Alpha, Sigma Xi. Clubs: Cosmos (Washington), Chemists (N.Y.C.) (Chgo.); Rotary, Technical (Madison). Author: Polyesters and their Applications, 1956. Patentee in plastics, chem. processes, materials. Office: PO Box 9444 Madison WI 53715

BJORNSON, EDWARD LEE, confectionery mfg. co. exec.; b. Cleve., Oct. 19, 1931; s. Bjorn Adolf and Roberta Lida (Henniger) B.; B.A., Yale U., 1953; M.B.A., Harvard U., 1957; m. Frieda Garabedian, Oct. 16, 1954; children—Bjorn Gary, Eric Lee. Advt. mgr. Kordite Co. div. Nat. Distillers Co., Macedon, N.Y., 1957-60; sales promotion mgr. Nabisco Confections, Inc., Cambridge, Mass., 1960-65, asst. to pres., dir. mktg., 1965-75, v.p., gen. mgr. subs. Fred W. Amend Co., 1975-78, exec. v.p., 1978—. Served with U.S. Army, 1953-55. Mem. N. Andover Hist. Soc. (dir., v.p. 1974-78), New Eng. Mfg. Confectioners Assn., New Eng. Confectioners Club. Unitarian. Clubs: Harvard Musical Assn., Yale of Boston. Office: 810 Main St Cambridge MA 02139

BLABER, LEO BERNARD, JR., bank exec.; b. Bklyn., Aug. 18, 1928; s. Leo Bernard and Alice V. (Mullen) B.; B.S. in Bus. Adminstrn., U. Notre Dame, 1950; J.D., De Paul U.,'Chgo., 1957; m. Josephine R. Dooley, Sept. 6, 1952; children—Mary, Rowena, Mark, Peter, Christina, Vincent, David, Barbara, Ramona. With With Nat. Biscuit Co., Bklyn., 1950-51; asst. cashier Chgo. Nat. Bank, 1953-58; admitted to Ill. bar, 1957; v.p., gen. counsel 1st Fed. Savs. & Loan Assn., Chgo., 1958-68; exec. v.p. St. Paul Fed. Savs. & Loan Assn., Chgo., 1968-72, dir., 1969-80, pres., chief operating officer, 1972-80; pres. Fed. Home Loan Bank of Chgo., 1980—. Bd. dirs. Chgo. Area Renewal Effort Service Corp., Community Services Research Corp.; chmn. Oak Park (Ill.) Devel. Corp. Served with AUS, 1951-53. Mem. Am., Ill., Chgo. bar assns., Fed. Savs. and Loan Council (chmn. atty.'s com. Ill. chpt.), U.S. League Savs. and Loans (past chmn. atty.'s com.), Chgo. Area Council Savs. and Loan Assns. (past dir.). Roman Cath. Office: Fed Home Loan Bank 111 E Wacker Dr Chicago IL 60601*

BLACK, CHARLES HENRY, savs. and loan exec.; b. Atlanta, Sept. 12, 1926; s. Charles Henry and Elfrida (Peterson) B.; B.S., U. So. Calif., 1950; children—Charles Henry, Richard Swanton. Mgr. financial planning Lockheed Missiles & Space Co., Van Nuys, Calif., 1953-57; v.p. finance profl. group Litton Industries, Inc., Beverly Hills, Calif., 1957-70, treas., 1970—, corp. v.p., treas., 1976-80; exec. v.p. Gt. Western Fin. Corp., also Gt. Western Savs. & Loan Assn., Beverly Hills, Calif., 1980—; adv. bd. Investment Co. Am., 1972—; dir. Bond Fund Am., Nat. Health Enterprises; dir. Anchor Growth Fund, Fundamental Investors, Inc., Tax Exempt Fund Am.; trustee Cash Mgmt. Trust Am., 1976. Trustee, Brentwood Sch. Served with AC, USNR, 1944-46. Mem. Phi Kappa Psi. Clubs: Los Angeles Country; Bel Air Bay. Home: PO Box 5365 Beverly Hills CA 90210 Office: 8484 Wilshire Blvd Beverly Hills CA 90211

BLACK, CHARLES HOWARD, JR., hosp. ofcl.; b. Johnstown, Pa., June 30, 1938; s. Charles Howard and Mary Catherine (Porter) B.; Asso. Electronic Engring. Tech., DeVry Inst. Tech., 1965, B.Electronic Engring. Tech., 1969; m. Barbara Anne White, Feb. 15, 1960; children—Charles Warren, David Howard, Daniel James. Asso. engr. Western Electric Co., Chgo., 1965-67; sr. computer programmer Oliver Corp., Des Plaines, Ill., 1967-69; system engr. Scam Instrument Corp., Skokie, Ill., 1969-71, pres. Scam Instrument Corp. Credit Union, 1971; asst. dir. data processing Conemaugh Valley Meml. Hosp., Johnstown, 1978—, 1st v.p. Credit Union, 1978—. Served with USN, 1957-63. Mem. IEEE. Home: 117 Mabel St Johnstown PA 15905 Office: 1086 Franklin St Johnstown PA 15905

BLACK, CONRAD MOFFAT, corp. exec.; b. Montreal, Aug. 25, 1944; s. George Montegu and Jean Elizabeth (Riley) B.; B.A., Carleton U., 1965; LL.L., Laval U., 1970; M.A. in History, McGill U., 1973; LL.D., St. Francis Xavier U., 1979, McMaster U., 1979; Litt.D., U. Windsor, 1979; m. Shirley Gail Hishon. Chmn., co-owner Eastern Twps. Pub. Co., Ltd., La Societe de Publication de l'Avenir de Brome Missisquoi, Inc., Farnham, Que., Can., 1967; chmn. Sterling Newspapers Ltd., Vancouver, from 1971; chmn. Dominion Malting Ltd., 1976—; chmn. bd., chmn. exec. com. Argus Corp. Ltd., Toronto,

1979—; pres. Western Dominion Investment Co. Ltd., including Dominion Malting and Sterling Newspaper divs.; vice-chmn., chmn. exec. com. Hollinger Argus Ltd., 1979—, Norcen Energy Resources Ltd., 1980; chmn. Ravelston Corp. Ltd., Toronto adv. bd. Crown Trust Co.; mem. exec. com., dir. Can. Imperial Bank of Commerce, Dominion Stores Ltd., Standard Broadcasting Corp. Ltd.; dir. CFRB Ltd., Carling O'Keefe Ltd., Confedn. Life Ins. Co., Eaton's of Can. Ltd., T. Eaton Acceptance Co. Ltd., Iron Ore Co. Can., Labrador Mining and Exploration Co. Ltd., Clubs: Toronto, York, Toronto Golf; University (Montreal). Author: Duplessis, 1977. Office: 10 Toronto St Toronto ON M5C 27B Canada

BLACK, FREDERICK HARRISON, elec. mfg. co. exec.; b. Des Moines, Nov. 11, 1921; s. Frederick H. and Aurora (Brooks) B.; B.S. in Engring. Physics, Fisk U., 1949; M.B.A., Pepperdine U., 1972; D.Ed., U. Mass., 1975; m. Kay Browne; children—Joan, Lorna, Jai, Crystal. Field engring. mgr. Burroughs Co., 1955-59; sr. engr. Convair Astronautics, 1959-60; project engr. N.Am. Aviation, 1960-61, Gen. Electric Co., Phila., 1961-63, Aerospace Corp., 1963-66; mgr. minority relations Gen. Electric Co., Fairfield, Conn., 1966-73, mgr. equal opportunity, minority relations, safety and security, 1973-75, mgr. compliance spl. project, 1975—. Spl. asst. mayor Washington; exec. dir. Watts orgn.; bd. dirs. Interracial Council Bus. Opportunities and Nat. Minority Bus. Campaign. Served to 2d lt. AUS, 1941-44. Mem. AIAA, IEEE, Am. Soc. Personnel Adminstrn., AAUP. Home: 60 Prayer Spring Rd Stratford CT 06497 Office: 3135 Easton Turnpike Fairfield CT 06431

BLACK, JOHN GORDON, stationery engraving co. exec.; b. Mpls., Feb. 20, 1931; s. Samuel Oscar and Gladys Frances Gulliford) B.; Electronic Technician, Dunwoody Inst., 1955; student U. Minn., 1958; m. Nancy Lee Holsapple, June 16, 1956; children—David, Sandra, Karen. Engraver, pressman Standard Engraving Co., Mpls., 1955-58; v.p., gen. mgr. Perkins Engraving Co., Mpls., 1958-68, pres., 1965-68; pres. Excelsior div. Crane & Co., North Adams, Mass., 1968—; v.p., dir. Standard Engraving Co., San Leandro, Calif.; dir. Excelsior Printing Co.; cons. Crane of Venezuela, Caracas. Served with AUS, 1951-53. Mem. Engraved Stationery Mfrs. Assn. (dir.). Baptist (deacon). Club: Taconic Golf. Inventor variable speed envelope imprint machine. Home: 61 Gale Rd Williamstown MA 01267 Office: 50 Roberts Dr North Adams MA 01247

BLACK, JOHN JOSEPH, JR., fin. exec.; b. Mineola, N.Y., Jan. 11, 1947; s. John Joseph and Doris Irene (Favier) B.; B.S., U.S. Mil. Acad., 1969; postgrad. (Berol fellow 1974), Harvard U., 1974-75; M.B.A., Babson Coll. (grantee 1975), 1976; m. Elizabeth Anne Broere, Jan. 31, 1970; children—Candace Regan, Sean William, Ryan James. Fin. analyst Xerox Corp., Webster, N.Y., 1976-77, sr. fin. analyst, 1977-79, bus. analyst, 1979, mgr. fin. statements, 1979—; tax cons., 1977—; bus. fin. cons., 1978—; adj. asso. prof. acctg. Monroe Community Coll., 1981—. Chmn., SBA; active Corps of Execs., 1979; mem. Rochester Bus. Com. for the Arts, 1978-79, Small Bus. Council, 1980. Served with Signal Corps, U.S. Army, 1969-74. Decorated Army Commendation medal (2); recipient Xerox Mgmt. Assn. Outstanding Achievement award, 1978, 79. Mem. Rochester C. of C., Nat. Assn. Accts., Internat. Assn. Fin. Planners, Internat. Entrepreneurs Assn., Xerox Mgmt. Assn. (v.p. mgmt. devel. 1978-79, v.p. adminstrn. 1979-80 editor, pub. monthly publ. The Commentator 1979—). Roman Catholic. Home: 699 Finchingfield Ln Webster NY 14580 Office: Webster NY 14580

BLACK, JONATHAN TAYLOR, fin. cons.; b. N.Y.C., Sept. 10, 1947; s. William Adam and Zilita (Deshon) B.; B.S., U. Bridgeport, 1971; m. Kathleen Ann Fay, Aug. 29, 1970; children—Karen J., Jeffrey, Michael, Laurie. Ins. cons. Met. Life Ins. Co., Stamford, Conn., 1972-75; mgr. life dept. R.S. Weiss & Assos., Stamford, 1975-76; pvt. practice fin. cons., Bethel, Conn., 1976—. Mem. Nat. Assn. Life Underwriters, Western Conn. Estate Planning Council. Republican. Roman Catholic. Home: 29 Oak Ridge Rd Bethel CT 06801 Office: 53 Lake Ave Ext Danbury CT 06810

BLACK, KENNETH, JR., coll. dean; b. Norfolk, Va., Jan. 30, 1925; s. Kenneth and Margaret (Wolf) B.; B.A., U. N.C., 1948, M.A., 1951; Ph.D., U. Pa., 1953; m. Mabel Llewellyn Folger, Sept. 20, 1948; children—Kenneth III, Kathryn Anne. Partner, Colonial Ins. Agy., Chapel Hill, N.C., 1948-50; instr. U. Pa., 1952-53, Swiss Ins. Tng. Centre, Zurich, 1967; mem. faculty Ga. State U., Atlanta, 1953—, Regents prof. ins., 1959—, chmn. dept., 1953-69, dean Coll. Bus. Adminstrn., 1969—; exec. dir., trustee Ednl. Found., 1959—; pres., dir. gen., dir. Internat. Ins. Seminars, Inc.; dir. Swiss Reins. Co. U.S. subs. USLife Corp., Cousins Properties, Inc., Computone Systems, Inc., Haverty Furnitures Stores, Inc., Paul Manners Assos., Inc.; vice chmn. President's Commn. R.R. Retirement, 1971. Served with USNR, 1944-46. Recipient Outstanding Faculty award Ga. State U. Coll. Bus. Adminstrn., 1970; fellow S.S. Huebner Found., 1950-53. CLU; CPCU. Mem. Am. Soc. CLU's (editor jour.), CPCU's Soc., Am. Risk and Ins. Assn., So. Risk and Ins. Assn., So. Econs. Assn., Order Golden Fleece, Phi Beta Kappa, Alpha Kappa Psi, Beta Gamma Sigma, Omicron Delta Kappa, Phi Chi Theta, Phi Kappa Phi. Roman Catholic. Clubs: Capital City, Commerce, World Trade. Author, co-author or contbg. author books in ins. field. Office: University Plaza Atlanta GA 30303

BLACK, LEONARD J., retail store chain exec.; b. Bethlehem, Pa., Apr. 26, 1919; s. Morris and Reba I. (Perlman) B.; B.S., U. Pa., 1941; m. Betty Glosser, June 21, 1942; children—Susan Eiseman, Jodie Lichtenstein. With Glosser Bros., Inc., Johnstown, Pa., 1946—, merchandise mgr. ready to wear, 1954-59, exec. v.p. stores and supermarkets, 1959-69, pres., chief exec. officer, 1969— now chmn., chief exec. officer, dir.; v.p. Johnstown Savs. Bank; pres., dir. Globe Wholesale Co.; partner Morris Black & Sons. bd. dirs. Conemargh Valley Meml. Hosp.; Greater Johnstown Com., Cambria County War Meml., Johnstown Area Regional Industries, Johnstown chpt. ARC. Served to lt. comdr. USNR, 1940-46. Mem. Nat. Mass Retailing Inst. (dir.). Republican. Jewish. Clubs: Sunnehanne Country, Le Mirador Country (Switzerland). Home: 2207 Spear Ave Johnstown PA 15905 Office: Glosser Bros Inc Franklin and Locust Sts Johnstown PA 15901

BLACK, ROBERT PERRY, banker; b. Hickman, Ky., Dec. 21, 1927; s. Burwell Perry and Veola (Moore) B.; B.A., U. Va., 1950, M.A., 1951, Ph.D., 1955; m. Mary Rives Ogilvie, Oct. 27, 1951; children—Patty Rives, Robert Perry. Part-time instr. U. Va., 1953-54; research asso. Fed. Res. Bank, Richmond, Va., 1954-55, asso. economist, 1956-58, economist, 1958-60, asst. v.p., 1960-62, v.p., 1962-68, 1st v.p., 1968-73, pres., 1973—; asst. prof. U. Tenn., 1955-56; lectr. U. Va., 1956-57; mem. Gov.'s Adv. Bd. Revenue Estimates, 1980—. Mem. adv. bd. Central Richmond Assn.; trustee Collegiate Schs., also past chmn.; trustee Richmond Eye Hosp., Richmond Meml. Hosp.; past pres. United Way Greater Richmond; bd. dirs., mem. exec. com., chmn. fin. com. Downtown Devel. Unltd.; chmn. adv. com. Center for Banking Edn., Va. Union U., 1977—; bd. dirs., mem. exec. com. Central Va. Ednl. TV Corp., 1979—. Served with AUS, 1946-47. Recipient George Washington Honor Medal award Freedoms Found. Valley Forge, 1978. Mem. Am., So. econ. assns., Am. Fin. Assn., Richmond Soc. Financial Analysts, Am. Inst. Banking, Raven Soc., Assn. for Preservation Va. Antiquities, Phi Beta Kappa (past pres. Richmond chpt.), Beta Gamma Sigma, Alpha Kappa Psi, Kappa ALpha. Methodist. Club: Country of Virginia (Richmond). Contbr. articles to profl. jours. Home: 10 Dahlgren Rd Richmond VA 23233 Office: Fed Res Bank 701 E Byrd St Richmond VA 23219

BLACK, ROBERT STITT, public utility exec.; b. Newport News, Va., Oct. 31, 1951; s. William Holmes and Catherine Louise (Stitt) B.; B.A. cum laude in Econs., Kenyon Coll., 1973; M.B.A. in Fin., U. Mich., 1973-75; m. Christine Carr, Aug. 17, 1974; 1 son, Robert Stitt II. Regulatory affairs analyst El Paso Natural Gas Co. (Tex.), 1975-76; asst. to pres. Waterville Gas and Oil Co. (Ohio), 1976-77, pres., 1977—; spokesman for gas cos. at legis. and regulatory agy. hearings, 1978—. Mem. Ohio Gas Assn., Assn. M.B.A. Execs., Waterville C. of C. (dir. 1977-78). Republican. Episcopalian. Clubs: Toledo, Belmont Country, Rotary Internat., Mason. Home: 6204 River Rd Waterville OH 43566 Office: PO Box 40 Waterville OH 43566

BLACK, WILLIAM, philanthropist, restaurant exec.; b. Bklyn.; grad. Columbia, 1929, L.H.D., 1967; m. Jean Martin, 1951 (div. 1962); 1 dau., Melinda; m. 2d, Page Morton, Mar. 27, 1962. Checker, Washington Market; retail mcht. shelled nuts, N.Y.C.; organizer chain of stores Chock Full O'Nuts, N.Y.C., converted to restaurants, past pres., now chmn. bd., chief exec. officer; also owner coffee producing firm, Rheingold Breweries. Founder Parkinson's Disease Found., 1957; founder Page and William Black Post-Grad. Sch. Medicine at Mt. Sinai Hosp., William Black Hall Nursing at Lenox Hill Hosp., William Black Bldg. for Med. Research at Columbia U. Med. Center. Office: 425 Lexington Ave New York NY 10017

BLACK, WILLIAM FAULKNER, investment exec.; b. Oklahoma City, Nov. 19, 1933; s. William Harmon and Ruth (Faulkner) B.; B.A., Stanford, 1955; children—Kathleen Serena, Charles Randolph, Alexandra Sevier. Pres., La Jolla Properties (Calif.), 1958-61, 72—, also dir.; asst. cashier, asst. v.p., v.p., asst. to pres. Guaranty Bank, Phoenix, 1961-63; pres., dir. Bank of La Jolla, 1963-68; sr. v.p., mem. mgmt. com. So. Calif. First Nat. Bank, San Diego, 1968-70; dir. Landowners Oil Assos., Island Farms, Inc., Air Calif. Trustee, past chmn. Scripps Clinic and Research Found.; mem. Commn. of the Californias; trustee Ducks Unltd., Menlo Sch. and Coll., San Diego Aerospace Mus.; bd. dirs. Mexican-Am. Found. Served to 1st lt. USAF, 1956-58. Named one of five Outstanding Young Men, San Diego Jr. C. of C., 1964. Mem. Alpha Tau Omega. Episcopalian. Clubs: La Jolla Beach and Tennis, Cuyamaca, Univ. (San Diego); La Jolla Country; Calif. (Los Angeles); Venice Island (Stockton). Office: 7855 Ivanhoe Ave La Jolla CA 92037

BLACKBURN, JAMES H., ins. co. exec.; b. Columbus, Ohio, Sept. 6, 1943; s. Andrew Reif and Anne Elizabeth Blackburn; B.S. in Edn., Kent (Ohio) State U., 1965; postgrad. in mgmt. Harvard U., 1978; m. Susan Jay Pavell, Sept. 21, 1973; children—Reif Jonathon, Matthew Gregory. Secondary sch. tchr.-coach, 1965-69; engaged in ins. bus., 1969—; asst. dir. sales tng. Midland Mut. Ins. Co., Columbus, 1975-76, 2d v.p., dir. manpower devel., 1976-79, gen. agt., 1979—; instr. Life Underwriter Tng. Council; speaker in field; mem. Million Dollar Round Table, 1971-75. C.L.U. Mem. Nat. Assn. Life Underwriters, Am. Soc. C.L.U.'s, Gold Key Soc. Home: 1175 Autumn Creek Circle Westerville OH 43081 Office: 150 E Wilson Bridge Rd Worthington OH 43085

BLACKBURN, JAMES ROSS, JR., oil co. exec., airline pilot; b. Lakeland, Fla., Feb. 28, 1930; s. James Ross and Esther Louise (Flagle) B.; student Davidson Coll., 1948-49; B.B.A., U. Miami, 1953, postgrad., 1968-69; m. Joyce Gaynelle Green, Aug. 29, 1960; children—Linda Marie, Lisa Joyce. Pilot, Eastern Air Lines, 1957—, capt., 1969—; mktg. cons. Comrex Corp., 1967-72; pres. Surete Ltd., 1973; pres. J.R. Blackburn & Assos., 1974-76; pres. Blackburn Assos., Inc., (a Del. Corp.), Miami, Fla., 1977—. Mem. steering com. U.S. Senatorial Bus. Adv. Bd., Washington, 1980. Served with USAF, 1953-57. Mem. Air Line Pilots Assn., First Flight Soc., AMS/Oil Dealers Assn., Geneal. Soc. Greater Miami (past treas.), Am. Hall Aviation History (founding mem.) Quiet Birdmen, Soc. So. Families, Mil. Order Stars and Bars, Sigma Chi. Democrat. Baptist. Clubs: Masons, Country Club of Coral Gables. Home: 10745 S W 53d Ave Miami FL 33156 Office: PO Box 5 92032 AMF Miami FL 33159

BLACKBURN, JOHN HAILE, JR., oil co. exec.; b. Palo Alto, Calif., Aug. 29, 1934; s. John Haile and Winnefred (Denny) B.; B.S. in Chem. Engring., Stanford U., 1956, M.B.A. in Fin., 1962; postgrad. UCLA, 1964-66; children—Jennifer Jean, Annette Marie, Michelle Rene. Asst. v.p. investments Bank of Am., 1972; registered rep. John Nuveene Co., 1973; fixed income portfolio mgr. Citizens Savs., 1975; registered rep. Weeden & Co., 1976; registered rep., estate planner Equitec Fin. Group, 1977; chief exec. officer Apollo Oil Co., Mountain View, Calif., 1978—, Bargain Petroleum, 1978—, Apollo Oil Distbrs., 1979—; chief fin. officer Capacitor Tech., 1980—. Active Nat. Assn. Ski Patrollers; 1st aid instr., CPR. instr. ARC; ski proficiency instr., mountaineering instr., avalanche instr. Served to capt., USMC, 1956-60. Lic. real estate broker, stock and bond broker, life and health ins. agt. Mem. San Francisco Bond, Stockbrokers, South Bay Petroleum Club, Navy League. Republican. Episcopalian. Home: 2124 Rock St Apt 30 Mountain View CA 94043 Office: 1820 El Camino Real W Mountain View CA 94040

BLACKBURN, MARSH HANLY, food brokerage co. exec.; b. Ft. Thomas, Ky., Nov. 13, 1929; s. Hanly R. and Lois E. (Marsh) B.; student Wabash Coll., 1947-48; B.S. in Marketing, Ind. U., 1952; m. Mary Klimek; children—Steven, Kevin, Marsha. Retail sales mgr. Hoosier Brokerage Co., Indpls., 1953-58, pres., 1958-66; pres. Seavey & Flarsheim Brokerage Co., Oak Brook, Ill., 1966-73; pres. Sales Force Co., Inc., Schiller Park, Ill., 1973-79, chmn., chief exec. officer, 1979—; dir. Cen. Grain, Indpls., Franklin Nat. Life Ins. Co., Ft. Wayne, Ind., Tidewater Grain, Phila., Early & Daniel Co., Cin. Mem. exec. council Ind. U. Sch. Bus. Served to sgt. AUS, 1952-53; Korea. Decorated Bronze Star. Mem. Am. Marketing Assn. (gen. mgmt. council 1973—, nat. marketing council 1970-73, nat. planning council Pres.'s Assn. 1969-75), Nat. Food Brokers Assn., Food Distbn. Research Council (charter), World Bus. Council, Merchandising Execs. Club, Newcomen Soc. N.Am., Beta Theta Pi. Clubs: Chicago Yacht; I Men's (Ind. U.); Metropolitan; Ocean Reef. Office: Sales Force Cos Inc 4333 Transworld Rd Schiller Park IL 60176

BLACKHAM, ANN ROSEMARY (MRS. JAMES W. BLACKHAM, JR.), Realtor; b. N.Y.C., June 16, 1927; d. Frederick Alfred and Letitia L. (Stolfe) DeCain; A.B., Ohio Dominican Coll., 1949; M.A., Ohio State U., 1950; m. James W. Blackham, Jr., Aug. 18, 1951; children—Ann C., James W. III. Mgr. br. store Filene & Sons, Winchester, 1950-52; broker Porter Co. real estate, Winchester, 1961-66; sales mgr. James T. Trefrey, Inc., Winchester, 1966-68; pres., founder Ann Blackham & Co. Inc., Realtors, Winchester, Mass., 1969—. Mem. bd. econ. advisors to Gov., 1969-74; participant White House Conf. on Internat. Cooperation, 1965; mem. Presdl. Task Force on Women's Rights and Responsibilities, 1969; mem. exec. council Mass. Civil Def., 1965-69; chmn. Gov.'s Commn. on Status of Women, 1971-75; regional dir. Interstate Assn. Commn. on Status of Women, 1971-74; mem. Gov. Task Force on Mass. Economy, 1972; mem. Gov.'s Judicial Selection Com., 1972; mem. Mass. Emergency Finance Bd., 1974-75; corporator, trustee Charlestown Savs. Bank, 1974—; mem. regional selection panel White House Fellows, 1973, 74; mem. com. on women in service U.S. Dept. Def., 1977-80; 2d v.p. Doric Dames, 1971-74, bd. dirs., 1974—. Pres., Mass. Fedn. Republican Women, 1964-69; sec. Nat. Fedn. Rep. Women, 1967-71, 2d v.p., 1972-78; New Eng. regional dir., 1967-78; pres. Women's Rep. Club Winchester, 1960-62; dep. chmn. Mass. Rep. State Com., 1965-66; sec. Mass. Rep. State Conv., 1970, del., 1960, 62, 64, 66, 70, 72, 74, 78; state vice chmn. Mass. Rep. Finance Com., 1970; alt. del.-at-large Rep. Nat. Conv., 1968, 72; pres. Scholarship Found., 1976-78, Mass. Fedn. Women's Clubs. Recipient Pub. Service award Commonwealth of Mass., 1978, Merit award Rep. Party, 1969; named Civic Leader of Yr. Mass. Broadcasters, 1962; Pub. Affairs award Mass. Fedn. Women's Clubs, 1975. Mem. Greater Boston Real Estate Bd. (dir.), Mass. Assn. Real Estate Bds. (dir.), Nat. Assn. Real Estate Bd. (women's council). Brokers Inst., Winchester C. of C., Greater Boston C. of C., Nat. Assn. Women Bus. Owners. Republican. Clubs: Capitol Hill (Washington); Ponte Vedra, Winchester Boat, Winchester Country, Wychemere Harbor. Home: 40 Wedgemere Ave Winchester MA 01890 Office: 11 Thompson St Winchester MA 01890

BLACKMAN, DIANE DAILEY, accountant; b. Fort Meade, Md., Sept. 6, 1946; d. Howard Miller and Shirley Smith Dailey; B.A. in Govt., U. S.D., 1969; postgrad. U. Colo., 1973-74; m. Lawrence D. Blackman, Nov. 6, 1969. Staff accountant Stark, Hochstadt, Kark & Co., Denver, 1973-74; prin., Diane D. Blackman, C.P.A., Denver, 1974-77; pres. Diane D. Blackman, C.P.A., P.C., Denver, 1977—; sec., treas., dir. The Oxford Hotel Corp.; dir. Copas Electric Co., Inc., Narodno Ethnic Dance Ensemble. Mem. Am. Inst. C.P.A.'s, Am. Women's, Colo. socs. C.P.A.'s, Assn. Local Accounting Firms, AAUW. Clubs: The Forum, Altrusa Internat. Home: 2200 Dahlia St Denver CO 80207 Office: 1612 17th St Denver CO 80202

BLACKMAN, JAMES WAYNE, real estate and bus. developer; b. Peru, Ind., Feb. 20, 1944; s. Wayne S. and Lillian A. (Reuter) B.; B.S., Purdue U., 1966, M.S., 1968; m. Lynette M. Smith, Aug. 14, 1966; children—Jason Steele, Stacey Michelle. Tchr., Wainwright High Sch., Lafayette, Ind., 1966-70, Lafayette Jefferson High Sch., Lafayette, 1970-71; registered rep., dist. mgr. Equity Funding, Lafayette, 1970-72; partner franchise Perkins Pancake House, Mishawaka, Ind., 1972-77; pres. J. W. Blackman & Assos., Inc., Mishawaka, 1972-77; pres., chmn. bd. No. Ind. Devel. Co., Elkhart, 1973—, So. Mich. Devel. Co., Niles, 1973—, Mr. J's Family Restaurants of America, Inc. and predecessor, 1974—; pres., treas. BCJ Corp., Niles, 1974—, BJM Corp., Elkhart, 1974—; pres. The Parkmor "Hdqrs.", Inc., 1974-78, Asso. Leasing Co., Inc., 1975—; pres., chmn. bd. The Lobster Docks of Am., Inc., 1974—; owner Coffee Break Systems, 1975—; broker/agent Jackson Nat. Life Ins. Co. Mem. Am. Indsl. Arts Assn. (life), Nat. Assn. Securities Dealers, Elkhart C. of C., NEA, Iota Lambda Sigma. Club: Elks. Home: 3015 Greenleaf Blvd Elkhart IN 46514 Office: Parkmor Plaza Suite B 1130 W Bristol St Elkhart IN 46514

BLACKSTOCK, LEROY, lawyer; b. El Reno, Okla., Apr. 19, 1914; s. Herbert Austin and Ethel Mae (Gwin) B.; grad. Draughon's Bus. Inst., Tulsa, 1933; LL.B., U. Tulsa, 1938; m. Virginia Lee Lowman, Dec. 29, 1939; children—Craig, Priscilla, Birch, Lore, Trena. With Phillips Petroleum Co., Tulsa, 1933-41, asst. credit mgr., 1939-41; admitted to Okla. bar, 1938; practiced in Tulsa, 1941—; sr. partner firm Blackstock, Joyce, Pollard & Montgomery; dir., gen. counsel Tulsa Homebuilders Assn., 1959-68; pres. Skelly Stadium Corp., 1964—, Gt. Western Investment Trust; lectr. law office econs. and mgmt.; pres. Tulsa County Legal Aid Soc., 1961-62, bd. dirs., 1958-66; pres. Jud. Reform of Okla., 1966—; mem. Okla. Council Jud. Complaints, 1974—; chmn. Okla. Supreme Ct. Bar Orgn., 1966. Chmn. citizens adv. com. Tulsa County Bd. Commrs., 1963-66; pres. Tulsa Sci. Center, 1968-73, Tulsa Campfire Council, 1971-72; mem. Tulsa Mayor's Adv. Com. on Community Problems, 1957-58, Okla. Gov.'s Acad. for State Govt., 1966-68; chmn. Law Sch. com. Tulsa U., 1960-74; chmn. U. Tulsa Alumni Loyalty Fund, 1969-70; bd. dirs. Tulsa County Mental Health Assn., 1963-70, Tulsa Psychiat. Found., 1964-67, Tulsa Downtown YMCA; pres. Tulsa Baptist Laymen's Corp., 1962-66. Served with USNR, 1943-46. Recipient Distinguished Citizens award Okla. Psychol. Assn., 1963; Distinguished Alumni award U. Tulsa, 1969, Coll. Law, 1978; Boss of Yr. award Tulsa County Assn. Legal Secs., 1978. Fellow Am. Coll. Probate Counsel; mem. Am. (ho. of dels. 1965-67, com. on nat. coordination disciplinary enforcement 1969-72, standing com. profl. discipline 1973-77), Okla. (bd. govs. 1965-67, pres. 1966), Tulsa County (pres. 1962, Outstanding Atty. award 1961) bar assns., Tulsa County Bar Found. (pres., dir. 1962-66), World Assn. Lawyers (founding mem., judiciary com. 1976—), Practising Law Inst. (nat. adv. council), Tulsa County Hist. Soc. (founder), Photog. Soc. Am., Soc. Amateur Cinematographers, Phi Alpha Delta. Republican. Baptist (chmn. bd. deacons 1962, chmn. bldg. com. 1951-70). Club: Petroleum (Tulsa). Author: Paper Dolls; Lawyers' Fees. Home: 3740 Terwillegar St Tulsa OK 74105 Office: 300 Petroleum Club Bldg Tulsa OK 74119

BLACKWELL, CURTIS EDSON, fin. cons.; b. Sparland, Ill., Oct. 23, 1933; s. Vernon Suft and Leatha Mertle (Kimble) B.; B.S., No. Mich. U., 1956; M.B.A., So. Fla. U., 1972; m. Mary Yvonne Derrick, July 10, 1954; children—Denise, Derek, Daniel, Darren, Denette. Office mgr. Montgomery Ward, 1956-60; pres. Edson Foods and Edson Products Co., 1960-64; sr. staff acct. C.P.A. firm, 1964-68; pres. Blackwell Acctg., Marquette, Mich., 1968—; pres. Money Mgmt. Consultants, Inc., Fin. Resources & Consultants; owner Superior Letter Service; chmn. bd. Mus. Monetary Collectibles; financier. Served with U.S. Army, 1956-58; ETO. Mem. Mich. Accts. Assn., Nat. Fedn. Ind. Bus., Nat. Assn. Fin. Cons., Internat. Entrepreneurs Assn., Ind. Accts. Assn. Mich., Am. Legion. Methodist. Inventor portable foot and back rest. Office: 201 Rublein St Marquette MI 49855

BLACKWELL, JERRY EUGENE, business exec.; b. Walnut Springs, Tex., Apr. 17, 1937; s. Paul Willis and Ruth (Hill) B.; B.A., N.Y. U., 1954; postgrad. Pepperdine U.; 1 son, Forest. Editorial researcher Time mag., 1952-54; purchasing clk. Orientalia Inc., N.Y.C., 1954-55; exec. theater mgr. Loews Theatres, N.Y.C., 1956-60; theatre supr. M-G-M, 1960-64; chief exec. Pubs. Group, San Juan, P.R., 1964-67; exec. v.p., dir. Old Tucson Corp., 1973-79; officer, dir. Old West Corp., 1974-79, Fiesta Cabelvision Inc.; partner RFC Partners, Old Pueblo Cablevision; pres., dir. Sepia Pub. Corp. Bd. dirs. Community Orgn. for Drug Abuse, Awareness House; mem. Gov.'s Com. for Mex. Trade Relations, past pres.; mem. Ariz. Civic Theatre; past pres. Palo Verde Found.; mem. Planned Parenthood Assn., Cosanti Found. Arcosanti Festival, Nat. Assn. Pvt. Psychiat. Hosps., Hosp. Fin. Mgmt. Assn. Democrat. Clubs: Old Pueblo, Skyline Country. Home: 5800 W Gates Pass Rd Tucson AZ 85205

BLACKWELL, WILLIAM ALBERT, banker; b. San Antonio, June 12, 1935; s. William Albert and Aline Gertrude (Carley) B.; B.Sc. in Petroleum Engring., U. Tex., 1958; m. Martha Jean Vorheier, Aug. 25, 1956; children—William, John. Petroleum reservoir engr. Core Lab. Inc., Dallas-Maracaibo, 1956-68; sr. reservoir engr. Am. Overseas Petroleum Ltd., N.Y.C., 1968-69; v.p. Rockefeller Family and Assos., 1969-70, Morgan Guaranty Trust Co., N.Y.C., 1970-77; exec. dir. project fin. European Banking Co. Ltd., London, 1977—. Mem. Royal

Inst. Internat. Affairs, Soc. Petroleum Engrs., AIME, Nat. Soc. Profl. Engrs., Am. Assn. Petroleum Geologists. Democrat. Presbyterian. Club: Hurlingham (London). Office: 150 Leadenhall St London EC3V 4PP England

BLADES, JOSEPH HAMLET, ins. exec.; b. Houston, Aug. 8, 1925; s. William Hamlet and Agnes (Mills) B.; B.B.A., U. Tex., Austin, 1949; postgrad. in ins. U. Houston; m. Sarah Eloise Hand, July 11, 1953; children—Sarah Gaye Blades Cody, Robert H., Richard M., Barbara L. Founder, J.H. Blades & Co., Inc., Houston, 1952, J.H. Blades & Co. (Internat.) Ltd., St. John's Ins. Co. Ltd., Blades Mgmt. Co. (all Hamilton, Bermuda), 1971; chmn. Blades Group of Cos., 1973—; vice-chmn. Crum & Forster Mgrs. Corp.; underwriting mem. Lloyd's of London; lectr. profl. courses and meetings; dir. Tex. Commerce Bank-Greenway Plaza, N.A. Past pres. Greater Houston council Camp Fire Girls; bd. regents Tex. So. U., Houston; ofcl. bd. St. Luke's United Methodist Ch., Houston. Served with USMC, 1943-45. Recipient Ins. Mentor award U. Ala., 1974; Regent of Yr. award Tex. So. U., 1980. Mem. Houston C. of C. (internat. bus. com.), Nat. Assn. Profl. Surplus Lines Offices (v.p., dir.), Tex. Surplus Lines Assn. (past pres.), Am. Mgmt. Assns. (ins. and employee benefits council). Clubs: Houston, Univ., Houston Racquet, Rotary Univ. Area (Houston); City of London; Royal Hamilton Amateur Dinghy, Mid Ocean (Bermuda). Home: 6155 Doliver Dr Houston TX 77057 Office: 2640 Fountainview Dr Houston TX 77057 also PO Box 42808-BB Houston TX 77042

BLAGDON, W. RICHARD, mortgage banker; b. Cleve., June 28, 1927; s. Joseph Charles and Ann Blagdon.; B.A., Hiram Coll., 1950; m. Shirley Mills, Aug. 26, 1950; children—Joan, Paula, Douglas. With Howard S. Bissell, Inc., Cleve., 1954-74, pres., dir., 1969-74; pres., dir. CleveTrust Advisers, 1970-74; pres., trustee CleveTrust Realty Investors, 1970-74; pres. Blagdon Mortgage Corp., Cleve., 1974—. Mem. Solon Indsl. Devel. Commn., 1969-70; mem. Solon Planning and Zoning Commn., 1978—. Served with USNR, 1944-46. Mem. Mortgage Bankers Assn. Am., Nat. Assn. Review Appraisers, Soc. Real Estate Appraisers, Mortgage Bankers Assn. Met. Cleve. Club: Chagrin Valley Country. Home: 34040 Sherbrook Park Dr Solon OH 44139 Office: 23200 Chagrin Blvd Cleveland OH 44122

BLAIN, SPENCER HAYWARD, JR., savs. and loan assn. exec.; b. Beaumont, Tex., Apr. 3, 1936; s. Spencer Hayward and Clara (Marshall) B.; B.B.A., Lamar U., Beaumont, 1957; grad. U. Ind. Grad. Sch. Savs. and Loan, 1970; m. Bettye Joan Williams, Mar. 18, 1978; children—Clara M., Melissa A. Loan officer Beaumont Savs. & Loan Assn., 1958-61; exec. v.p., dir. Citizens Tex. Savs. & Loan Assn., Baytown, 1961-65; pres., dir. Orange Savs. & Loan Assn. (Tex.), 1965-72; exec. v.p. 1st Fed. Savs. and Loan Assn., Austin, Tex., 1972-78, pres., chief exec. officer, 1978—, dir., 1972—; dir. Fed. Home Loan Bank, Little Rock, 1979—; dist. dir. Savs. and Loan Polit. Action Com., 1978—; adv. com. Fed. Home Loan Mortgage Com., 1979—. Co-chmn. Bergstrom-Austin Community Council; mem. Bus. Com. for Arts; trustee Laguna Gloria Art Mus., Austin United Way; bd. advs., chmn. long range planning Seton Med. Center, Austin. Served with AUS, 1958. Mem. U.S. League Savs. Assns., Tex. Savs. and Loan League (dir. 1978—, chmn. legis. com. 1980—), Austin C. of C. (dir.), Alpha Tau Omega. Clubs: Admirals, Austin Country, Headliners, Westwood Country. Office: 200 E 10th St PO Box 1149 Austin TX 78767

BLAINE, DOROTHEA CONSTANCE RAGETTÉ, county ofcl.; b. N.Y.C., Sept. 23, 1930; d. Robert Raymond and Dorothea Ottilie Ragetté; B.A., Barnard Coll., 1952; M.A., Calif. State U., 1968; Ed.D., U. Calif., Los Angeles, 1978; J.D., Western State U., 1981. Mem. tech. staff Planning Research Corp., Los Angeles, 1964-67; asso. scientist Holy Cross Hosp., Mission Hills, Calif., 1967-70; career devel. officer and affirmative action officer County of Orange, Santa Ana, Calif., 1970-74, sr. adminstrv. analyst, budget and program coordination, 1975—. Bd. dirs. Deerfield Community Assn., 1975—, Orange YMCA, 1975-77. Mem. Nat. Women's Polit. Caucus, Fountain Valley Bus. and Profl. Women, NOW, Internat. Law Soc., Women Employees of Orange County, Orange County Trial Lawyers Assn., Am. Soc. Public Adminstrn., Am. Soc. Tng. and Devel., Human Factors Soc., Phi Delta Kappa. Office: 623 N Broadway Santa Ana CA 92701

BLAIR, CHARLES JACKSON, banker; b. Pitts., June 4, 1943; s. Charles Louis and LaVilla Janette (Orr) B.; B.A., Allegheny Coll., 1965; m. Pamela Beth Smithberger, June 15, 1968; children—C. Jackson, Mark J.H., Scott Buffington, Anne Pamela MacGregor. Dir. mgmt. devel. Mellon Bank N.A., Pitts., 1969-76; dir. human resources Morgan Stanley & Co., Inc., N.Y.C., 1976-78; sr. v.p., dep. chief adminstrv. officer Schroders Bank Trust Co., N.Y.C., 1978—. Mem. career planning bd. Grad. Sch. Bus., Duke U.; mem. alternative careers bd. Wharton Sch., U. Pa. Mem. Am. Bankers Assn., Assn. Internat. Students in Econs. and Commerce (dir.), Am. Soc. Personnel Adminstrn. Republican. Episcopalian. Clubs: Fairfield Country, Univ. (N.Y.C.); Univ. (Pitts.). Home: 75 Gray Rock Rd Southport CT 06490 Office: 1 State St Plaza New York NY 10015

BLAIR, CLAUDE MACLARY, banker; b. Columbia, Tenn., May 5, 1913; s. Anderson Maclary and Lucy (Howell) B.; LL.B., Atlanta Law Sch., 1949; m. Rose Bottagaro, June 9, 1945; children—Randy, Barbara, Julie. With AT&T, 1930-67, v.p. space communications program, 1961-63, pres. Ohio Bell Telephone Co., 1963-66, Pacific Northwest Bell Telephone Co.; now chmn., chief exec. officer Nat. City Corp.; dir. J. M. Smucker Co., Lamson-Sessions Co., Midland-Ross Co., Sifco; admitted to Ga. bar, 1949. Mem. adv. council Ohio Devel. Dept.; v.p., exec. bd. Greater Cleve. council Boy Scouts Am.; trustee, exec. com. Cleve. Devel. Found., Community Fund.; chmn. Greater Cleve. Growth Bd.; bd. dirs. NCCJ; trustee Mus. Arts Assn., Case-Western Res. U. Served to maj. Signal Corps., AUS, 1942-46, 51-52. Mem. Baldwin-Wallace Council Cleve. Bus. and Indsl. Leaders, Newcomen Soc., Bluecoats. Clubs: 50 of Cleve., The Country, Pepper Pike, Union, Clevelander, Tavern, Everglades, Rolling Rock. Office: 623 Euclid Ave Cleveland OH 44114

BLAIR, JAMES THOMAS, fin. mgmt. co. exec.; b. Circleville, Ohio, Aug. 22, 1939; s. Floyd M. and Hariett P. (Hanley) B.; B.A., U. Notre Dame, 1961; M.B.A., Am. U., 1968. Fin. analyst Irving Trust Co., N.Y.C., 1961-63; securities analyst SEC, Washington, 1967-69; dir. banking U.S. Postal Service, Washington, 1969-73; with Del. Investment Advisers, Phila., 1974—, sr. v.p. client services, 1978-79, sr. v.p. Del. Mgmt., 1979—. Served with USN, 1963-67. Republican. Roman Catholic. Clubs: Urban, Vesper. Home: 1420 Locust St Apt 37K Philadelphia PA 19102 Office: Del Investment Advisers 7 Penn Center Plaza Philadelphia PA 19102

BLAIR, LAWRENCE JOSEPH, fin. exec.; b. Vermillion, S.D., Aug. 1, 1940; s. Joseph P. and Kathryn B. (Mahan) B.; B.S. in B.A., U. S.D., 1963; children—Timothy Joseph, Tricia Ann. Loan officer Grinnan Mortgage, Dallas, 1976-77; asst. v.p. Lomas & Nettleton Co., Lubbock, Tex., 1977—. Active United Way, 1978-79; coordinator Heart Fund, 1979. Served with S.D. N.G., 1963-66. Mem. Mortgage Bankers Assn., S. Plains Mortgage Bankers, W. Tex. Builders Assn., Lubbock Bd. Realtors. Republican. Roman Catholic. Clubs: Lubbock, Hillcrest Country, Racquet, Elks. Home: 2116 48th St Lubbock TX 79413 Office: 8212 Ithaca St Lubbock TX 79423

BLAIR, RANDALL HOWELL, travel agency exec.; b. Oceanport, N.J., Apr. 30, 1946; s. Claude M. and Rose V. Blair; student London Sch. Econs., 1966-67; B.A., Dartmouth Coll., 1968; postgrad. Cleve.-Marshall Law Sch., 1973—; children—Michelle, Carolyn. Tchr. pub. schs., Cleve., 1968-70; pres. Konran Media, Cleve., 1970-73; pres. Travel Systems, Inc., Cleve., 1973—. Mem. Am. Soc. Travel Agts., Am. Soc. Assn. Execs., Greater Cleve. Growth Assn., Council of Smaller Enterprises. Club: Cleve. Athletic. Contbr. photog. illustrations to various textbook series. Home: 1801 E 12th St Cleveland OH 44114 Office: 609 Euclid Ninth Tower Cleveland OH 44115

BLAIR, ROBERT RUSH, oil co. exec.; b. Rawlins, Wyo., Sept. 22, 1928; s. James Scott and Ellen Scott (Rush) B.; B.S., Okla. State U., 1950; m. Carine Naveau de la Hault, Apr. 28, 1967; 1 dau., Tracy Catherine. With Sinclair Oil Corp., various locations, 1950-70, product coordinator Eastern Hemisphere, Brussels, 1964-67, gen. mgr., Algiers, 1967-70; v.p. Delhi Internat. Oil Corp., Dallas, 1970—; v.p., dir. Delhi Pacific Minerals Corp., Dallas, 1970—, exec. v.p. Delhi Internat. Oil Corp., Dallas, 1979—; chmn. bd., pres. CINCO Drilling Co., 1979—; dir. Natural Gas Pipeline Authority South Australia, Australian Mineral Found. Served with AUS, 1951-53; Korea. Registered profl. engr., Tex. Mem. Ind. Petroleum Assn. Am., Am. Petroleum Inst., Australian Petroleum Exploration Assn. (dir.), Soc. Petroleum Engrs., Am. Inst. Mgmt., Am. C. of C. in Australia, Australian Am. Assn. Methodist. Clubs: Dallas Petroleum, Northwood, Commerce South Australia, South Australian Cricket Assn. Home: 6749 Greenwich Ln Dallas TX 75230 Office: 3500 First Internat Bldg Dallas TX 75270

BLAIR, S. ROBERT, utility exec.; b. Aug. 13, 1929; s. Sidney Martin and Janet R. (Gentleman) B.; B.Sc., Queen's U., 1951; m. Lois Anne Wedderburn, June 13, 1951; children—Megan E., James S., Robert W., Martin B., Charlotte C. Engr. on pipeline and refinery constrn., Can. and U.S., 1951-58; engr. Alta. and So. Gas Co. Ltd. and Alta. Natural Gas Co., from 1958, v.p., mgr., 1961-66, pres., gen. mgr., 1966-70, also dir.; pres., chief exec. officer, dir. Alta. Gas Trunk Line Co., 1970—; chmn., dir. Algas Engring. Ltd., Alta. Gas Ethylene Co. Ltd.; pres., dir. Algas Resources Ltd., Algas Mineral Enterprises Ltd. Trustee Queen's U.; mem. Econ. Council Can. Mem. Assn. Profl. Engrs. Alta., Assn. Profl. Engrs. Ont., Can. Inst. Internat. Affairs. Presbyterian. Clubs: Edmonton Petroleum, Glencoe, Ranchmen's. Office: Alberta Gas Trunk Line Co Ltd 2800 Bow Valley Sq Calgary AB T2P 2N6 Canada*

BLAKE, NORMAN PERKINS, credit corp. exec.; b. N.Y.C., Nov. 8, 1941; s. Norman Perkins and Eleanor (Adams) B.; B.A., Purdue U., 1965, M.A., 1966; postgrad. Washington U., 1966-67, 71; m. Karen Cromwell, Sept. 12, 1965; children—Kellie, Kimberly, Adam. With Gen. Electric Co., 1967-74, 76—, mgr. strategic planning ops., plastics bus. div., Pittsfield, Mass., 1976-78, mgr. bus. devel. consumer products and services sector, 1978-79, staff exec., Fairfield, Conn., 1979; v.p., gen. mgr. comml. and indsl. fin. div. Gen. Electric Credit Corp., Stamford, Conn., 1979—; with Top, Inc., Troy, Mich., 1974-76, pres., 1976. Mem. Am. Mgmt. Assn. Office: 260 Long Ridge Rd Stamford CT 06904

BLAKE, VANCE GEORGE, collection agency exec.; b. St. Louis, Nov. 7, 1931; s. George H. and Marguerite D. (Olsen) B.; B.B.A., U. Mass., 1953; M.B.A., Northeastern U., 1962; m. Nancy Pike, June 27, 1953; children—Bruce W., Robert A., Carol Ann. Mgmt. trainee John Breck Co., West Springfield, Mass., 1953-54; credit exec. Dennison Mfg. Co., Framingham, Mass., 1956-59; with Worcester Dist. Med. Bur. of Economics, Worcester, Mass., 1959—, exec. dir., 1965-78, pres., 1978—. Served with USAF, 1954-56. Mem. Am., New Eng. collectors assns., Mass. Assn. Patient Account Mgrs., Hosp. Fin. Mgmt. Assn., New Eng. Assn. Patient Account Mgrs., Republican. Methodist. Home: 21 Oldham Rd Westboro MA 01581 Office: 340 Main St Worcester MA 10608

BLAKELY, JAMES RUSSELL, investment adv., fin. editor; b. Princeton, Ind., Mar. 21, 1935; s. Russell Harold and Mildred Mae (Newman) B.; B.A., U. Ill., 1957, postgrad. in law, 1957-58; m. Martha Marelen Mitchell, Aug. 31, 1968; children—Karen Holmes, Thomas Howard. Reporter, Champaign (Ill.) News-Gazette, 1964-65; feature writer Sunday mag. Chgo. American, 1965-67; consumer affairs editor Rochester (N.Y.) Democrat and Chronicle, 1967-72; asst. editor Consumer Reports Mag., Mt. Vernon, N.Y., 1972-74; mng. editor Gold & Silver Newsletter, New Rochelle, N.Y., 1974-76; editor/pub. Silver & Gold Report, Newtown, Conn., 1976-80; pres., treas., dir. Precious Metals Report, Inc., Gold Coin Jewelry Corp., Silver and Gold Money Mgmt. Corp., 1976-80; pres., treas., dir. James Blakely Investments, Inc., Sandy Hook, Conn., 1981—. Served with AUS, 1958-59. Mem. Soc. Profl. Journalists, Nat. Press Club, Phi Alpha Theta, Theta Delta Chi. Address: Old Green Rd Sandy Hook CT 06482

BLAKELY, WILLIAM HENDERSON, JR., minerals and chem. co. exec.; b. Warren, Ohio, Feb. 12, 1927; s. William Henderson and Romelia (Smith) B.; B.S. in Sociology and History with honors, N.C. A. & T. U., 1952; postgrad. Rutgers U.; m. Marcelle Wallace, May 23, 1954; children—Donna and Glenn (twins). Mem. staff Univ. Settlement, N.Y.C., 1952-62; eve. dir. Lillian Wald Recreation Rooms Settlement, N.Y.C., 1963-64; dir. Urban League Skills Bank, Newark, 1964-67; indsl. relations rep. Engelhard Industries, Newark, 1967-74; mgr. personnel relations Engelhard Minerals and Chems. Corp., Iselin, N.J., 1974—. Mem. N.J. corps. com. United Negro Coll. Fund; bd. dirs., past pres. Urban League Essex County; pres. bd. dirs. Leaguers, Inc.; commnr. juries Essex County, 1968-75; mem. chancellor's council N.C. A. and T. U.; exec. com. EDGES, Inc.; mem. Newark Community Affairs Group of Businessmen, Century club YMCA; trustee Kessler Inst. Rehab.; bd. dirs. Interracial Council for Bus. Opportunity, Better Bus. Bur., Project Pride. Recipient Achievement award Frontiersmen of Am., 1974; award Human and Civil Rights Assn. N.J., 1976; award Black Achievers in Industry, 1976, Project Pride, 1979, F.O.C.U.S. award, 1979, United Community Corp., Union County Urban League; named to N.C. A. & T. U. Hall of Fame, 1978. Mem. Nat. Urban League, Grand St. Boys Assn., C. of C. (regional urban affairs com.), N.C. A. and T. U. Alumni Assn., Sigma Rho Sigma, Omega Psi Phi. Home: 6 N Cobane Terr West Orange NJ 07052 Office: 70 Wood Ave S Iselin NJ 08830

BLANC, GÉRARD JOHN, civil engr.; b. St. Cloud, France, Oct. 15, 1924; s. Pierre Gabriel and Suzanne (Bouvier) B.; came to U.S., 1953, naturalized, 1957; M.S. in Civil and Indsl. Engring., Ecole Centrale des Arts et Manufactures, 1949; m. Carol Anderer, Dec. 30, 1978; children by previous marriage—Stephen, Laura. Constrn. engr. various cos., France and Can., 1942-53; with Harza Engring. Co., Chgo., 1953-67, asst. to pres., 1961-64; project mgr. Am. Electric Power Co., N.Y.C., 1967-72; internat. mgr. Chas. T. Main Internat., Inc., Boston, 1972—. Worked with French underground forces, 1943-44. Mem. ASCE, U.S. Com. on Large Dams. Episcopalian. Collector, authority field Oriental rugs, textiles. Office: CT Main Internat Inc Prudential Center Boston MA 02199

BLANCHARD, PATRICK G., banker; b. Appling, Ga., May 15, 1943; s. John Pierce and Mildred (Pollard) B.; B.B.A., Ga. So. Coll., 1965; m. Gwen Banks, Mar. 5, 1967; 1 dau., Mary Brannen. With Ga. R.R. Bank & Trust Co., Augusta, 1966-71, asst. v.p. mktg. 1970-71; asst. treas. State of Ga., Atlanta, 1971-72; fin. mgmt. officer Ga. Dept. Adminstrv. Services, Atlanta, 1972-74; pres., Ga. State Bank, Martinez, 1974—; also dir. bd. dirs. E. Ga. Lung Assn., Ga. Carolina council Boy Scouts Am., Columbia County unit Heart Assn., Columbia County Hist. Soc. Mem. Martinez Mchts. Assn., Ga. Bankers Assn., Bankers Adminstrn. Inst., Delta Sigma Pi, Alpha Tau Omega. Democrat. Baptist. Clubs: Rotary, Exchange, West Lake Country. Home: 8109 Sir Galahad Dr Evans GA 30809 Office: POB 4538 Martinez GA 30907

BLANCHARD, TOWNSEND EUGENE, diversified tech. services co. exec.; b. DuQuoin, Ill., Jan. 30, 1931; s. Townsend and Anna Belle (Jackson) B.; B.S., U. Ill., 1952; M.B.A., Harvard U., 1957; m. Norma Louise Barr, Dec. 18, 1960; children—John Barr, Susan Melody, Jayne Ann, Stephen Eugene. Cons., Ill. Sch. Cons. Service, Monticello, 1958-62; co-founder, treas., chief fin. officer Americana Nursing Centers, Monticello, 1962-75; v.p. finance, treas., chief fin. officer, chief staff Cenco Inc., Chgo., 1975-79; sr. v.p., chief fin. officer Dynalectron Corp., McLean, Va., 1979—. Served to lt. USNR, 1952-55. Decorated Spl. commendation. Mem. Fin. Execs. Inst., Am. Mgmt. Assn., Harvard Bus Sch. Club D.C., Delta Sigma Phi. Presbyn. (elder). Clubs: Econ. (Chgo.); U. Ill. Alumni (Washington). Home: 1222 Aldebaran Dr McLean VA 22101 Office: 1313 Dolley Madison Blvd McLean VA 22101

BLAND, E. A., moving van co. exec. Pres., chief operating officer Atlas Van Lines, Inc., Evansville, Ind. Office: Atlas Van Lines Inc 1212 St George Rd Evansville IN 47711

BLAND, THOMAS RAYMOND (T. RAY), ins. co. exec.; b. Greene County, Pa., June 13, 1937; s. Herbert Wesley and Margaret Anne (Wood) B.; B.S. in Bus., Miami U., Oxford, Ohio, 1959; postgrad. Golden State Law Sch., 1967; m. Joan Clair Coffman, Feb. 20, 1960; children—Julie Rae, Douglas Lynn, Laura Joan, Heather Robin, Michael Christopher. Adjuster, C.I.T. Fin., Sandusky, Ohio, 1959-60; agt., area dir. Coll. Life Ins. Co., Cin., 1960-69; tng. dir. Cal-Farm Ins. Co., Berkeley, Calif., 1969-73, regional dir., 1973-75, dir. mktg., 1975-79; v.p. mktg. Phila. Life Ins. Co., San Francisco, 1980-81; sr. v.p. mktg. West Coast Life Ins. Co., San Francisco, 1981—; lectr. U. Calif. Mem. Nat. Assn. Life Underwriters, Am. Coll. Life Underwriters, Oakland Assn. Chartered Life Underwriters, Phi Kappa Tau. Republican. Episcopalian. Home: 2079 Banbury Rd Walnut Creek CA 94598 Office: PO Box 3892 1275 Market St San Francisco CA 94119

BLANDER, MICHAEL LOUIS, food corp. exec.; b. Cin., Aug. 20, 1952; s. Ben and Doris B.; B.S., City U. N.Y., 1974, M.S., 1976. Prodn.-product engr. Food Service Dynamics, Inc., Bklyn., 1976-78; sec. AMB Catering Corp., Bklyn., 1978—; cons. engr. Madison Rich, Inc., Bklyn., 1978—, F.S.D. Industries, Lodi, N.J., 1977-80; indsl. engr. Germaine Monteil Cosmetiques Corp., Deer Park, N.Y., 1980—. Mem. Bklyn. Coll. Alumni Assn., Towne House Frat., Phi Beta Kappa. Home: 306 Ave M Brooklyn NY 11230 Office: 306 Ave M Brooklyn NY 11230

BLANKENSHIP, DOUGLAS PAUL, devel. co. exec.; b. Ky., Nov. 13, 1944; s. Herbert and Bertie Lee (Smith) B.; B.A. in History and Geography, Eastern Ky. U., 1964; M.A. in Adminstrn., U. Ky., 1966, M.A. in Transp., 1967; postgrad. UCLA, 1967-68; Ph.D., Ohio State U., 1969. Instr. high sch., dept. chmn. Pike County Sch. System, Pikeville, Ky., 1964-67; research asso. U. Ky., 1966; sr. transp. systems, planner Gen. Motors Corp., Los Angeles, 1967-72; project mgr. market research, asso. transp. planner Orange County Transit Dist., Santa Ana, Calif., 1972—; exec. v.p. transp. systems and mktg. Nat. Transp. Research Corp., Los Angeles, 1976, pres., chief exec. officer, 1976—; owner, pres. Pacific Coast Devel. Co.; guest lectr. U. So. Calif. Active System Task Force for Transit, Citizens Adv. Council, Modeling Task Force. Recipient Enoch Grehan Journalism award, 1964. Outstanding recognition in strategic and Guerrilla warfare gaming, 1968, Electronic Mus. award Los Angeles Mus. chpt., 1969. Creativity Recognition award Internat. Personnel Research, 1972; Ky. col. Mem. Am. So. Calif. mktg. assns., Am. Inst. Planning (asso.), Am. Soc. Planning Ofcls., Assn. Am. Georgraphers, Los Angeles Geog. Soc., Urban and Regional Info. Systems Assn., Transp. Research Bd., U. Ky. Alumni Assn. (pres. So. Calif.), Mensa, Kappa Iota Epsilon, Omicron Alpha Kappa. Democrat. Author: The Soviet Union-Expansion at Any Cost, 1969; Theories of World Power and Control, 1969; Multivariate Analysis of Power-A Ten Nation Study, 1969; A Tentative Theory of International Relations, 1969; A Model of International Message Flow, 1970; Cognition Related to Ten Branches of Philosophy, 1966; Human Freedom and Existentialism, 1966; Application of Raul Prebisch's ECLA Rationale to West Indies, 1968; The Nature of Some Geographical Theories, 1967; A Model of Guerrilla Engagements and Its Application, 1966; A Study of Directional Bias in International Lifelines, 1969; A Geographical Analysis of Entropy-Long Range Changes in Settlement Patterns Over Time, 1969. Contbr. articles on transp. system, modeling and quantitative market research to profl. jours. Home: 448 S Alexandria Ave Los Angeles CA 90020

BLANKENSHIP, VICTOR DALE, aerospace co. exec.; b. Topeka, Feb. 9, 1934; s. Robert Irvin and Maude (Kemble) B.; B.S., U. Kans., 1956; M.S., U. Notre Dame, 1959; Ph.D. (Rackham Grad. scholar NSF), U. Mich., 1963; m. Virginia Greco, Aug. 19, 1956; children—Mark Irvin, Scott Greco. Engr., Bendix Corp., South Bend, Ind., 1956-58, E.I. duPont Co., Orange, Tex., summer 1960; mem. tech. staff Aerospace Corp., San Bernardino, Calif., 1962-66, mgr. Advanced Ballistic Reentry Systems Program Definition Directorate, 1966-67, dir. Mark 18 Reentry System, 1967-68, dir. Mark 18 and reentry system concepts, 1968; lectr. U. Redlands, 1968, 75, 78, also fellow; mgr. reentry systems dept. TRW Def. and Space Systems Group, San Bernardino, 1968—; teaching fellow U. Mich., U. Notre Dame, 1958-61; lectr. grad courses U. So. Calif., 1963-66; chmn. testing panel advanced ballistic reentry materials workshop USAF, 1975; owner apt. complexes. Sci. adviser Explorer Post Boy Scouts Am., YMCA; trustee Valley Prep., 1970-71. Asso. fellow Am. Inst. Aeros. and Astronautics (chmn. council Arrowhead chpt. 1978, nat. com. fluid dynamics 1977-79, nat. com. public policy); mem. ASME (past chmn., sec.), N.Y. Acad. Sci., Sigma Xi, Sigma Tau, Pi Tau Sigma (past sec.), Sigma Nu. Methodist. Club: Optimists. Contbr. articles to profl. jours. Home: 1740 Canyon Rd Redlands CA 92373 Office: PO Box 1310 San Bernardino CA 92408

BLANKER, ALAN HARLOW, lawyer; b. Montague, Mass., Sept. 15, 1951; s. William C. and Ann H. B.; B.A., Colby Coll., Waterville, Maine, 1973; J.D., Georgetown U., 1976. Admitted to Mass. bar, 1977; mem. firm Levy, Winer, Hodos & Berson, P.C., Greenfield, Mass., 1976—; dir. Esleeck Mfg. Co., Inc., Turners Falls, Mass.; incorporator Franklin Savs. Instn., Greenfield. Incorporator, Camp Wiyaka Inc., Richmond, N.H., 1976—; mem. Greenfield Town Meeting, 1977—; chmn. Greenfield Sch. Bldg. Com., 1977—; bd. dirs. Big Bros./Big Sister Inc. of Franklin County, Mass., 1978-80; bd. dirs., clk. Greenfield Indsl. Devel. Area Corp., 1980—; incorporator

Greenfield Community Coll. Found., 1979—. Mem. Am. Bar Assn., Mass. Bar Assn., Franklin County Bar Assn. Republican. Congregationalist. Club: Kiwanis. Editor Georgetown Law Jour., 1975-76. Home: 56 Prospect St Greenfield MA 01301 Office: 277 Main St Greenfield MA 01301

BLANKFORT, LOWELL ARNOLD, newspaper publisher; b. N.Y.C., Apr. 29, 1926; s. Herbert and Gertrude (Butler) B.; B.A. in History and Polit. Sci., Rutgers U., 1946; m. April Pemberton; 1 son, Jonathan. Reporter, copy editor L.I. (N.Y.) Star-Jour., 1947-49; columnist London Daily Mail, Paris, 1949-50; copy editor The Stars & Stripes, Darmstadt, Germany, 1950-51, Wall St. Jour., N.Y.C., 1951; bus., labor editor Cowles Mags., N.Y.C., 1951-53; pub. Pacifica (Calif.) Tribune, 1954-59; free-lance writer, Europe, Asia, 1959-61; co-pub., editor Chula Vista (Calif.) Star-News, 1961-78; co-owner Paradise (Calif.) Post, 1977—, North Monterey County (Calif.) News, 1978—, Monte Vista (Colo.) Jour., 1978—, Center (Colo.) Post-Dispatch, 1978—, Del Norte (Colo.) Prospector, 1978—, Plainview (Minn.) News, 1980—, St. Charles (Minn.) Press, 1980—. Mem. Calif. Democratic Central Com., 1963. Named Outstanding Layman of Year, Sweetwater Edn. Assn., 1966, Citizen of Year, City of Chula Vista, 1976. Mem. ACLU (pres. San Diego chpt. 1970-71), Calif. Newspaper Pubs. Assn., Sigma Delta Chi. Contbr. articles on fgn. affairs to newspapers. Home: Old Orchard Ln Bonita CA 92002 Office: 835 3d Ave Chula Vista CA 92002

BLANTON, DAVID ANDERSON, III, investor relations cons.; b. St. Louis, Dec. 9, 1942; s. David Anderson and Bernard C. (Corrigan) B., Jr.; B.A., Georgetown U., 1964, M.A., 1968. Vice pres. G.H. Walker, Laird, Inc., St. Louis, 1970-74, A.G. Edwards & Sons, Inc., St. Louis, 1975-79; dir. Investor Relations div. Fleishman-Hillard, Inc., St. Louis, 1980—. State spl. events chmn. Am. Cancer Soc., 1978-79; bd. dirs. Theatre Project Co., 1976—; chmn. Stella Maris Day Care Center, 1976—. Mem. Nat. Investor Relations Inst., Public Relations Soc. Am., St. Louis Soc. Fin. Analysts. Home: 2 Lenox Pl Saint Louis MO 63108 Office: 1 Memorial Dr Saint Louis MO 63102

BLANTON, HOOVER CLARENCE, lawyer; b. Green Sea, S.C., Oct. 13, 1925; s. Clarence Leo and Margaret (Hoover) B.; J.D., U. S.C., 1953; m. Cecilia Lopez, July 31, 1949; children—Lawson Hoover, Michael Lopez. Admitted to S.C. bar, 1953; since practiced in Columbia; mem. firm Whaley & McCutchen, 1953-66, Whaley, McCutchen, Blanton & Richardson, 1967-72, Whaley, McCutchen, Blanton & Dent, 1973-74, Whaley, McCutchen & Blanton, 1974-80, Whaley, McCutchen, Blanton & Rhodes, 1980—; mem. Commn. Continuing Legal Edn. for Judiciary; dir. Legal Aid Service Agy., Columbia, chmn., 1972-74. Gen. counsel S.C. Republican Party, 1963-66; pres. Richland County Rep. Conv., 1962; del. Rep. State Convs., 1962, 64, 66, 68, 70, 74. Bd. dirs. Midlands Community Action Agy., vice chmn., 1972, 74; bd. dirs. Wildewood Sch., 1976-78. Served with USNR, 1942-46, 50-52. Mem. Am., Richland County (pres. 1980—) bar assns., S.C. State Bar (historian 1969-74), S.C. Bar (ho. of dels. 1975-76; chmn. exec. council fee disputes bd. 1978—), S.C. Def. Trial Attys. Assn., Assn. Ins. Attys. (state chmn. 1971-77, 80—, exec. council 1977-80), Def. Research Inst., Phi Delta Phi. Baptist. Clubs: Toastmasters (pres. 1959). Home: 3655 Deerfield Dr Columbia SC 29204 Office: 1414 Lady St Columbia SC 29201

BLANTON, WILLIAM SCOTT, cons./analyst; b. Los Angeles, Oct. 24, 1950; s. Robert Cronkite and Beverly Jean (Robertson) B.; student Liberty Baptist Coll., 1973-76, Upper Iowa U., 1978; corr. student Internat. Accountants Soc., Inc., 1969-71; m. Barbara Joanne Fahey, Dec. 24, 1968; children—Kerrie Rae, Scott Travis, Joel Kent, Noah Christian. Programmer/analyst Tri-Coll. Computer Center, Lynchburg, Va., 1974-76, Genesis Systems Inc., Lynchburg, 1976, Va. Bapt. Hosp., Lynchburg, 1976-77; sr. staff cons. Allen Services Inc., Dayton, Ohio, 1977-79; cons./analyst Convey, Inc., Dayton and partner DB Technology, Cedarville, Ohio, 1979—. Deacon, Emmanuel Baptist Ch.; asst. soccer coach Xenia Christian Day Sch.; referee Xenia Soccer Club. Served with USCG, 1968-71. Home: 277 Ledbetter Rd Xenia OH 45385 Office: 3400 S Dixie Dr Dayton OH 45439

BLANTON, WYNDHAM BOLLING, JR., physician, health care co. exec.; b. Richmond, Va., Dec. 21, 1918; s. Wyndham Bolling and Natalie Friend (McFaden) B.; B.A. in Econs., U. Richmond, 1943; M.D., Med. Coll. Va., 1950, M.S. in Physiology, 1959; m. Lucy Jane Bowman, July 3, 1940; children—Wyndham Bolling, Jane Bowman. Traffic mgr. C & P Telephone Co., Richmond, 1940-44, physician, 1952-70; intern Med. Coll. Va., 1950-51, resident, 1951-52; practice medicine specializing in internal medicine and allergy, Richmond, 1950—; mem. staff Stuart Circle Hosp., 1952—, chief of staff, 1969; v.p. med. affairs Charter Med. Corp., Macon, Ga., 1973—; asst. dean of medicine Med. Coll. Va., 1952-60, clin. prof., 1974—; owner, operator Cumva Farms, Farmville, Va., 1960—. Elder Presbyterian Ch.; bd. visitors Va. Commonwealth U., 1969—, rector bd. visitors, 1973—; exec. com. Atlantic Rural Expn. and Va. State Fair, Richmond, 1965—, v.p., 1970—; trustee Med. Coll. Va. Found., Richmond, 1973—, Richmond Profl. Inst. Found., Richmond, 1974—; mem. Nat. Profl. Standards Rev. Council, 1976—. Served to lt. (j.g.) USNR, 1945; PTO. Recipient award for greatest contbn. to dairy industry Va. Poly. Inst. Dairy Club, 1969. Mem. Va. (pres. 1976), Richmond, Am. socs. internal medicine, Richmond Acad. Medicine, AMA, So. Med. Assn., Am. Acad. Allergy, Va. Allergy Soc., Am. Coll. Chest Physicians, A.C.P., Am. Thoracic Soc., Med. Soc. Va., Med. Coll. Va. Alumni Assn. (trustee 1960-68), Royal Soc. Medicine, Am. (council on profl. services, council on patient services), Va. (dir.) hosp. assns., Fedn. Am. Hosps. (dir. 1975—), Assn. Am. Med. Colls., Am. Group Practice Assn., Va. Council Health and Med. Care (dir.), Va. Agribus. Council (dir.), Va. Assn. Professions, Va. Hist. Soc., Soc. Colonial Wars, Soc. of Cincinnati, S.R., Richmond, Va. State chambers commerce, Alpha Omega Alpha, Sigma Zeta, Alpha Sigma Chi, Alpha Mu Omicron, Delta Kappa Epsilon. Presbyterian. Clubs: Commonwealth, Bull & Bear, Country of Va., Farmington Country. Contbr. articles to profl. publs. Home: 1 Roslyn Rd Richmond VA 23226 Office: 1526 West Ave Richmond VA 23220

BLASCO, ALFRED JOSEPH, bus. and fin. cons., bank exec.; b. Kansas City, Mo., Oct. 9, 1904; s. Joseph and Mary (Bevacqua) B.; student Kansas City Sch. Accountancy, 1921-25, Am. Inst. Banking, 1926-30; Ph.D. (hon.), Avila Coll., 1969; m. Kathryn Oleno, June 28, 1926; children—Barbara (Mrs. Charles F. Mehrer III), Phyllis (Mrs. Michael R. O'Connor). From office boy to asst. controller Commerce Trust Co., Kansas City, Mo., 1921-35; controller Interstate Securities Co., Kansas City, 1935-45, v.p., 1945-53, pres., 1953—, chmn. bd., 1961-68; sr. v.p. ISC Fin. Corp., 1968-69, hon. chmn. bd., 1970-77, pres., 1979—; chmn. bd. Red Bridge Bank, 1966-72; chmn. bd. Mark Plaza State Bank, Overland Park, Kans., 1973-77; vice-chmn. bd. Anchor Savs. Assn.; spl. lectr. consumer credit Columbia, N.Y.C., 1956, U. Kans., Lawrence, 1963-64. Mem. Fair Pub. Accomodations Com., Kansas City, Mo., 1964-68; pres. Catholic Community Library, 1955-56; ward committeeman, Kansas City, Mo., 1972-76. Pres. hon. bd. dirs. Baptist Meml. Hosp., 1970-74; chmn. bd. dirs. St. Anthony's Home, 1965-69; chmn. bd. trustees Avila Coll., 1969—. Decorated papal knight Equestrian Order Holy Sepulchre of Jerusalem, 1957, knight comdr., 1964, knight grand cross, 1966, lt. No. Lieutenancy U.S., 1970-77, vice gov. gen., 1977—; named Bus. Man of Year, State of Mo., 1957; named Man of the Year, City of Hope, 1973; recipient Community Service award Rockne Club of Notre Dame, 1959, Brotherhood award NCCJ, 1979. Mem. Soc. St. Vincent de Paul (pres. 1959-67), Am. Indsl. Bankers Assn. (nat. pres. 1956-57), Am. Inst. Banking (pres. Kansas City chpt. 1932-33), Bank Auditors and Controllers Assn., Fin. Execs. Inst. Am. (pres. Kansas City chpt. 1928-29), Nat. Assn. Accountants, Kansas City C. of C. Rotarian. Clubs: Kansas City, Hillcrest Country, Serra (pres. 1959-60). Contbr. articles to profl. jours. Home: 11705 Central St Kansas City MO 64114 Office: 3100 Broadway St Kansas City MO 64141

BLASIUS, JACK MICHAEL, aluminum co. exec.; b. Atlanta, Feb. 29, 1932; s. Arthur George and Jessie Lee (Pate) B.; B.S. Indsl. Mgmt. and Accounting, U. Ala., 1954, M.B.A. in Mktg., 1957; m. Sybil Claire Watkins, Oct. 12, 1957; children—Michael Stribling, Kimberly Anne. Successively indsl. salesman, area sales mgr., nat. mgr. foundry ingot products Kaiser Aluminum Corp.; pres., gen. mgr. Batchelder-Blasius, Inc., Spartanburg, S.C., 1966—, also dir.; dir. Charles Batchelder Co., Botsford, Conn., Statewide Waste Oil & Chem. Corp., Spartanburg, 1st Nat. Bank, Spartanburg. Mem. Spartanburg City Council; exec. dir. Spartanburg YMCA; scholarship donor Clemson U.; trustee Spartanburg Day Sch.; bd. dirs. Spartanburg Girls' Home, Jr. Achievement, Spartanburg. Served with U.S. Army; ETO. Mem. Soc. Die Casting Engrs., Am. Foundryman Soc., Inst. Scrap Iron and Steel, Aluminum Recycling Assn. (dir.), Spartanburg Devel. Assn., Spartanburg C. of C. (dir.), U. Ala. Alumni Assn. Republican. Presbyterian. Clubs: Rotary (dir.), Spartanburg Country, Piedmont (Spartanburg); Atlanta Athletic, Ansley Golf (Atlanta); President's (Wofford Coll.); Founder's. Home: 1017 W O Ezell Blvd Spartanburg SC 29304 Office: Batchelder Blasius PO Box 5503 Spartanburg SC 29304

BLASS, WALTER PAUL, telephone co. exec.; b. Dinslaken, Germany, Mar. 31, 1930; came to U.S., 1941, naturalized, 1947; s. Richard B. and Malvi (Rosenblatt) B.; B.A., Swarthmore Coll., 1951; postgrad. Princeton U., 1951-52; M.A., Columbia U., 1953; m. Janice L. Minott, Apr. 2, 1954; children—Kathryn, Christopher, Gregory. Asst. Laos and Cambodia desk officer ICA, Washington, 1957-58; gen. mgr. R.B. Blass Co., Deal, N.J., 1958-61; economist AT&T, N.Y.C., 1961-66; country dir. Peace Corps, Afghanistan, 1966-68; asst. v.p. revenue requirement studies N.Y. Telephone Co., N.Y.C., 1968-70, dir. corp. planning, 1970—; cons., lectr. in field. Bd. dirs. N.Y. State Council on Econ. Edn.; trustee Guilford Coll., 1975—. Served to lt., j.g., USNR, 1953-56. Woodrow Wilson Found. sr. fellow, 1974—. Mem. N.Y. Acad. Scis., Soc. Values in Higher Edn., Am. Econ. Assn., Nat. Assn. Bus. Economists, N. Am. Soc. Corp. Planning (dir. 1972). Club: Princeton N.Y.C. Office: 1095 Ave Americas New York NY 10036

BLASZCZYK, JAMES SIGMOND, fiberglass co. exec.; b. Moses Lake, Wash., Sept. 9, 1955; s. Sigmond John and Helen Catherine (Cyzio) B.; B.S. in Econs., Wharton Sch., U. Pa., 1976; M.B.A. in Fin., Fairleigh Dickinson U., 1979. Sales rep. Owens Corning Fiberglas, Toledo, 1977-80, market devel. mgr., equipment mfrs. sect., 1980—. Mem. Omicron Delta Epsilon, Alpha Sigma Phi. Club: Wharton. Office: Owens Corning Fiberglas Fiberglas Tower Toledo OH 43659

BLATTE, NEIL HARVEY, bus. exec.; b. Bklyn., Apr. 10, 1942; s. Philip and Lydia B.; B.A., U. Mass., 1965; M.B.A., Coll. City N.Y., 1969; m. Ritchie Weinberg, Oct. 31, 1965; children—Eric, Pamela. Sr. product mgr. ITT Continental Baking Co., Rye, N.Y., 1971-74; market mgr. Cadbury Schweppes U.S.A. Inc., Stamford, Conn., 1974-77; dir. mktg. Schraft Candy Co. subs. Gulf & Western Industries Inc., Boston, 1977-79; pres. Bus. Service Centers, Inc., Wilton, Conn., 1979—. Mem. Am. Mgmt. Assn. Home: 530 Rock Ridge Rd Fairfield CT 06430 Office: One Danbury Rd Wilton CT 06897

BLATZ, DURAND BARRETT, mfg. co. exec.; b. Ventnor, N.J., July 27, 1918; s. John B. and Ethel (Barrett) B.; A.B., Cornell U., 1940; m. Joan Ipsen, Mar. 29, 1941; children—Durand Barrett, Ann Galen, Megan Eller, John Balthazar, Estelle Elizabeth. Treas., George C. Lewis Co., Phila., 1946-50; gen. controller Crosley and Bendix divs. Avco Mfg. Corp., Cin., 1951-57; controller Internat. Silver Co., Meriden, Conn., 1957-59, v.p., treas., 1959-65, pres., 1965-66; pres., chief exec. officer Insilco Corp., 1966-76, chmn. bd., chief exec. officer, 1976—, also dir.; dir. Aetna Life & Casualty of Hartford. Served to lt. col. F.A., AUS, 1940-46. Mem. Delta Upsilon. Republican. Episcopalian. Home: 39 Currier Pl Cheshire CT 06410 Office: 1000 Research Pkwy Meriden CT 06450

BLAUSTEIN, HOWARD YALE, ins. co. exec., painter; b. Hazelton, Pa., May 29, 1930; s. Alan Jacob and Ethel (Gauz) B.; student Syracuse U., 1951; m. Joyce Ellen Dean, Jan. 27, 1969; children from previous marriage—William, Jill Ellen, Joyce Nancy, Brian. Life ins. agt. Conn. Mut., Utica, N.Y., 1955-59; dist. mgr. Mass. Mut., Utica, 1959-65; gen. agt. Variable Life Ins. Co., Miami, Fla., 1965-67; v.p., also dir. of sales Variable Annuity Mktg. Co., Chgo., 1967-76; chmn. bd. Intangible Mktg., Inc., Unity Plan, Inc.; gen. partner Pub. Employees Adminstrn. and Computer Enterprises; sec., dir. Fin. Systems, Inc.; dir. Polo Stores; exhibited paintings in major Chgo. gallery; one-man shows, 1974, 75. Chmn., United Jewish Appeal, 1964; trustee Mus. Fin. Arts Research and Holographic Center. Served with U.S. Army, 1952-55. Recipient Mass. Mut. Man of the Year award, 1961-64, Variable Annuity Life Ins. Co. Glen Holden Mgmt. award, 1968. Mem. Million Dollar Round Table (life), Chgo. Life Underwriters Assn., Nat. Assn. Securities Dealers, Chgo. Assn. Commerce and Industry. Democrat. Jewish (dir. temple). Clubs: Masons, K.P., B'nai B'rith, Covenant; Whitehall; Ravinia Country; Lake Barrington Shores Golf; LaCosta Country. Home: 1100 N Lake Shore Dr Chicago IL Office: 180 N LaSalle St Chicago IL 60601

BLEDSOE, CHARLES WESLEY, indsl. supply co. exec.; b. Ellensburg, Wash., Feb. 26, 1912; s. Howard Franklin and Vera (De Weese) B.; B.A. in Econs. and Bus., U. Wash., Seattle, 1939; m. Marion McKenzie, Feb. 7, 1942; children—Charles Scott, James Barry. Mgr. men's dept. Roosevelt St. store Sears, Roebuck & Co., Seattle, 1945-46; chief ground instr. No. Aircraft Co., Seattle, 1946-49; sales rep. ITT Grinnel Co., Seattle, 1949-50; chmn. bd. Canal Indsl. Supply Co., Seattle, 1950—. Elder, United Presbyn. Ch., Seattle, 1952-79. Served as officer USAAF, World War II. Mem. Nat. Assn. Corrosion Engrs., Soc. Port Engrs., Assn. Gen. Contractors, ASHREA, Seattle C. of C., Common Cause, World Without War Council of Greater Seattle. Clubs: Swedish (Seattle); Ballard Kiwanis (pres. 1956). Home: 2626 25th St Seattle WA 98199 Office: 1516 NW 51st St Seattle WA 98107

BLEIBERG, LAWRENCE JAY, bus. exec.; b. Bklyn., Mar. 16, 1929; s. Edward M. and Frances (DuBroff) B.; B.S. in Econs., CCNY, 1949; M.S., Boston U., 1950; m. Judith Lieberman, June 14, 1952; children—Andrew Richard, Peter Mark, Steven David. Financial writer N.Y. Jour. Commerce, N.Y.C., 1950-55; security analyst Bache and Co., N.Y.C., 1955-58, asst. mgr. research dept., 1958-62, mgr., 1962-64, mgr. Bache Newswire, 1958-62; v.p. charge investment research Empire Trust Co., N.Y.C., 1964-66; dir. research Kohn Loeb & Co., 1966; mng. partner Boxwood Assos., 1967—; pres. Northfield Mgmt. Corp., 1969—. Served with AUS, 1951-53. Mem. N.Y. Fin. Writers Assn. (treas. 1955), N.Y. Soc. Security Analysts. Home: 16 Dewart Rd Greenwich CT 06830 also 770 S Palm Ave Sarasota FL 33577 Office: 175 Greenwich Ave Greenwich CT 06830

BLEICKEN, GERHARD DAVID, lawyer, ins. exec.; b. Newton, Mass., Aug. 29, 1913; s. Gerhard and Beatrice (Douglas) B.; student Gettysburg Coll., 1931-32; J.D. cum laude, Boston U., 1938; grad. Indsl. Coll. of Armed Forces, Nat. Air Tng. Sch.; student Aspen (Colo.) Inst. Humanistic Studies, 1957, Sch. Indsl. Mgmt., M.I.T., 1958; D.C.S. (hon.), Suffolk U., Boston, 1973; LL.D. (hon.), Boston Coll., 1977, Emmanuel Coll., Boston, 1978; L.H.D. (hon.), Northeastern U., 1977; m. Ellene T. Mailhot (div.); children—Kurt Douglas, Eric, Carl Weeman; m. 2d, Ann M. Meacham, children—David H., Neil G. Admitted to Mass. bar, 1938, U.S. Supreme Ct. bar, 1943; with John Hancock Mut. Life Ins. Co., Boston, 1939-79, chmn., chief exec. officer, 1970-79, dir., 1965—; dir. 1st Nat. Bank of Boston, 1st Nat. Boston Corp., Arthur D. Little, Inc., State St. Bank and Trust, Boston, 1966-70, Am. Research and Devel., Boston, 1970-72. Mem. adv. com. on C.D. to U.S. Dept. Def., 1954-69; mem. program adv. com. to Office Emergency Preparedness, 1958-73; trustee Boston U., Boston Urban Found.; bd. visitors U. Calif. at Los Angeles Grad. Sch. Mgmt., 1967-78; chmn. bd. trustees Boston U. Med. Center; bd. dirs. World Affairs Council; exec. com. Mass. com. Caths., Protestants and Jews; mem. Am. Battle Monuments Commn., 1969-78; trustee Tax Found., Inc., 1972-78; mem. Pres.'s Commn. on Personnel Interchange, 1974-77; bd. overseers Boston Mus. Fine Arts, Boston Symphony Orch. Served as lt. USNR, 1943-46; Recipient Distinguished Service award Pres. U.S., 1968; Distinguished Service citation Dept. Def., 1969; Distinguished Community Service award Brandeis U., 1973; Distinguished Citizen award Mass. Bay Federated councils Boy Scouts Am., 1977; Corp. Leadership award M.I.T., 1976; comdr.'s cross Order of Merit (W. Ger.), 1976; Christian Herter award Boston World Affairs Council, 1978; Andrew Cordier fellow Columbia U. Sch. Internat. Affairs; Benjamin Franklin fellow Royal Soc. Arts (London). Mem. Life Ins. Assn. Mass. (chmn. 1976-77), Conf. Bd., Am. Law Inst. (life), Bostonian Soc., UN Assn. U.S.A. (dir. 1963-80), Boston Mus. Sci. (trustee). Republican. Episcopalian. Clubs: St. Botolph, Wianno (Mass.) Yacht. Home: 18 Wood Rd Sherborn MA 01770 Office: 200 Berkeley St Room 800 Boston MA 02116

BLEMEL, MARLENE KAY, software co. exec.; b. Manistee, Mich., Jan. 27, 1937; d. Edward A. and Hazel (Downard) Kihnke; B.S., Edgecliff Coll., 1959; postgrad. U. Rochester, 1968-69, U. N.Mex., 1975-77; m. Kenneth G. Blemel, July 2, 1960; children—Kenneth, Maria, Peter, Edward, Michelle, Marlene. Treas., R/M Systems, Inc., Albuquerque, 1970-76; adminstrv. mgr. Hewitt and Assos. Inc., Mountaintek, Inc., Albuquerque, 1976-78; pres., treas. Mgmt. Scis. Inc., Albuquerque, 1978—. Home: 12412 Sierra Grande NE Albuquerque NM 87112 Office: 6022 Constitution St NE Albuquerque NM 87110

BLENDERMAN, RONALD JOHN, JR., mfg. co. exec.; b. Sioux City, Iowa, Dec. 28, 1927; s. Ronald John and Agnes (Smith) B.; B.S., U. Iowa, 1951; m. Shirley M. Dutreix, May 2, 1959; children—Deborah, Barbara, Wendy. With Amstar Corp., N.Y.C., 1953-78, v.p. and gen. mgr. grocery products div., asst. corp. v.p., 1970-75, v.p. planning, 1975-78; pres., chief operating officer Hardy Salt Co., St. Louis, 1978-79, also dir.; corp. v.p. ITC Corp., N.Y.C., 1979—, pres. spice & seasoning div., Totowa, N.J., 1979-81; pres., chief exec. officer, dir. B.F. Trappey's Sons, Inc., New Iberia, La., 1981—. Served with USCG, 1946-47, USAF, 1951-53. Mem. The Sugar Assn., The Salt Inst. Republican. Roman Catholic. Club: Mo. Athletic. Home: 410 Phillip Lane Watchung NJ 07060 Office: BF Trappey's Sons Inc New Iberia LA 70560

BLESCH, LARRY JOE, real estate exec.; b. Evansville, Ind., Nov. 3, 1944; s. Adolph Henry and Katherine Alma Jean (Weyer) B.; student pub. schs., Evansville; m. Kathy Suzann McBride, Aug. 17, 1974. With Ind. Bell Telephone Co., Evansville, 1964-70; owner Larry's Auto Sales, Evansville, 1970-73; carpenter, Evansville, 1971-73; mgr. Goff Realty, Evansville, 1974-78; pres. Blesch Realty, Inc., Evansville, 1978—. Pres., Hope of Evansville, Inc., 1977-78. Served with Army N.G., 1962. Mem. Nat. Assn. Ind. Fee Appraisers (v.p. 1979), Nat. Assn. Realtors, Ind. Assn. Realtors, Evansville Assn. Realtors, Farm and Land Inst., Womens Council Realtors, Nat. Auctioneers Assn., Ind. Auctioneers Assn., Nat. Assn. Review Appraisers. Republican. Baptist. Clubs: Osseo Haymakers Assn., Eagles, Civitan. Home: 3009 Oak Hill Rd Evansville IN 47711 Office: 3009 Oak Hill Rd Evansville IN 47711

BLESSEY, WALTER JEROME, IV, investment co. exec.; b. Biloxi, Miss., Apr. 17, 1939; s. Walter James and Geraldine Ann (Fountain) B.; B.B.A. in Accounting, U. Miss., 1961, J.D., 1964; m. Mary Alice Wingo, Dec. 18, 1960 (div. Aug. 1968); 1 son, Walter John V; m. 2d, Beverly Wartenbach Johnson, Sept. 29, 1968; stepchildren—Mitzi Lynn, Michael Louis. Instr. accounting U. Miss., 1962-64; admitted to Miss. bar, 1964; tax accountant Arthur Andersen & Co., Houston, 1966-69; ltd. partner, controller John E. Kilgore & Co., 1969—; v.p., dir. Indianola Co., Houston, 1971—; v.p., sec., treas., dir. Cambridge Royalty Co., Houston, 1970—; dir. Wicks 'n Sticks Inc., Houston. Served to 1st lt. AUS, 1964-66; Vietnam. Decorated Army Commendation medal. C.P.A., Tex. Mem. Am. Inst. C.P.A.'s, Am., Miss. bar assns., Tex. Soc. C.P.A.'s, Am. Legion, VFW, Delta Sigma Pi, Beta Alpha Psi, Phi Alpha Delta. Episcopalian (vestryman 1970-72, 76—). Clubs: University, Plaza, Woodlands Country. Home: 27222 Lana Ln Conroe TX 77302 Office: John E Kilgore & Co Suite 1200 San Jacinto Bldg Houston TX 77002

BLESSINGER, RICK, wood moldings mfg. co. exec.; b. Helena, Mont., Oct. 8, 1944; s. Philip Richard and Lois Elizabeth (DeBorde) B.; B.S. in Commerce, Mont. State U., 1968; student Dale Carnegie Sales Course, 1970; cert. Advanced Mgmt. Research Inst., 1978; m. Christine Lee Hahn, Mar. 1, 1975; 1 dau., Amanda Spring. Vice pres. Riklin Constrn. Co., Helena, 1968-74; asst. dir. contract adminstrn. Tri-County Transp. Dist. Oreg., Portland, 1975-78; pres. Constrn. Spltys., Inc., Helena, 1978—, chmn. bd. dirs., 1978—. Served with U.S. Army, 1964. Recipient cert. of appreciation Portland Traffic Safety Commn., 1977. Mem. Mont. Contractors Assn. (asso.), Mont. State U. Alumni Assn. Roman Catholic. Clubs: Helena Exchange, Carroll Coll. Century. Office: PO Box 4638 Helena MT 59601

BLEWITT, RICHARD FRANCIS, chem. co. exec.; b. Scranton, Pa., Mar. 26, 1947; s. Frank Joseph and Margaret (Kearney) B.; B.S. in Govt.-Politics, U. Md.; m. Laura Louise Sandone, Dec. 7, 1968; children—Mar Lynn and Carrie Ann (twins). Staff writer Scranton Times, 1966-68; asst. press relations Am. Trucking Assn., Washington, 1970-72; mgr. press relations Mfg. Chemists Assn., Washington, 1972-75; mgr. pub. relations FMC Corp. Chem. Group, Phila., 1975-78; v.p. corp. affairs Velsicol Chem. Corp., Chgo., 1978—; contbg. editor World Book Ency., 1973—. Served with USN, 1968-70. Mem. Pub. Relations Soc. Am., Profl. News Media Assn. N. Eastern Pa. (founder). Democrat. Roman Catholic. Club: Chgo. Press. Office: 341 E Ohio St Chicago IL 60611

BLICHFELDT, ROGER WENTWORTH, construction co. exec.; b. Chatauqua, N.Y., Apr. 18, 1918; s. Emil Harry and Eva Graham (Potter) B.; B.S. in Agronomy, Pa. State U., 1939, postgrad., 1940; m. Mary Elizabeth Ruppen, Aug. 20, 1947; children—Elizabeth, Roger, Mary, Louisa, Howard. With The Rust Engring. Co., Pitts., 1941—, mgr., 1965-71, v.p., 1971—, pres. Rust Chimney div., 1973-78, cons., 1978-79, gen. mgr., 1979—. Instl. rep. Allegheny council Boy Scouts Am., Pitts., 1958-65; v.p. parent tchr. guild St. Basil's Schs., Pitts., 1962-64. Served with USAAF, 1943-45. Decorated 2 Bronze Stars. Mem. Eastern States Blast Furnace and Coke Oven Assn., Am. Assn. Concrete Contractors, Nat. Wildlife Fedn., Am. Forestry Assn., Wilderness Soc., Am. Soc. Concrete Constrn., ASTM (task group cons.), Pa. State Alumni Assn. Republican. Methodist Episcopal. Club: University (Pitts.). Contbr. articles in field to profl. and trade jours. Home: 205 The Boulevard Pittsburgh PA 15210 Office: 600 Grant St Pittsburgh PA 15219

BLINCOE, CHARLES GONZA, machine tool distbg. co. exec.; b. Lebanon, Ky., Jan. 30, 1943; s. Charles Cambron and Mary Christine (Auberry) B.; B.S., U. Ky., 1965; M.B.A., U. Louisville, 1970; m. Bobbe Alexis De Spain, Nov. 30, 1968; children—Charles Cambron, David Ashley. Sales rep. Internat. Harvester Co., Bowling Green, Ky., 1965-67, Diehl Pump & Supply Co., Louisville, 1967-70; sales engr. Louisville Machinery Sales Co., 1970-74; v.p. Kentech Machinery Co., Louisville, 1974—. Mem. Beta Gamma Sigma. Democrat. Roman Catholic. Home: 3105 Yorkshire Dr Bardstown KY 40004 Office: 5611 Fern Valley Rd Louisville KY 40218

BLINDER, ABE LIONEL, publishing exec.; b. Osage, Iowa, Nov. 7, 1909; s. Heimer and Fanny (Goldstein) B.; Ph.B., U. Chgo., 1931; m. Henriette Levin, Oct. 19, 1947; children—Henry David, Jonathan. Circulation mgr. Apparel Arts, Chgo., 1932-33; circulation mgr. Esquire, Inc., Chgo., 1933-36, circulation dir. 1936-45, dir., 1945—, v.p., 1945-51, exec. v.p., 1952-61, pres., 1961-77, chmn. bd., 1977-79, vice-chmn. corp. devel. com., chmn. internat. ops., 1980—; dir. Ideal Toy Co. Mem. Phi Beta Kappa. Clubs: Harmonie (N.Y.C.); Metropolis Country. Office: Esquire Inc 488 Madison Ave New York NY 10022

BLINDER, MARTIN S., pub. co. exec.; b. Bklyn., Nov. 18, 1946; s. Meyer and Lillian (Stein) B.; B.B.A., Adelphi U., 1968; m. Donna Harman, Oct. 25, 1969. Account exec. Nordeman & Co., N.Y.C., 1968-69; v.p. Blinder, Robinson & Co., Westbury, N.Y., 1969-73; treas. BHB Prodns., Los Angeles, 1973-76; pub. Martin Lawrence Ltd. Edits., Van Nuys, Calif., 1976—, also dir.; dir. Corp. Art Inc., Gallery Hawaii; lectr. bus. symposia; TV and radio appearances. Patron, Guggenheim Mus., N.Y.C., Mus. Modern Art, N.Y.C., Los Angeles County s. Art, Hirschhorn Mus., Washington, Skirball Mus., Los Angeles. Contbr. articles to mags. and newspapers. Office: 7011 Hayvenhurst Ave Van Nuys CA 91406

BLISKO, LAWRENCE BERNARD, fin. cons.; b. Bronx, N.Y., Dec. 21, 1944; s. William and Pauline (Schmugler) B.; grad. Fairleigh Dickinson U., Rutherford, N.J., 1968; postgrad. Montclair (N.J.) State Coll.; m. Paula Sharon Lakind, Dec. 22, 1968; children—Marni Chandra, David Solomon. Tchr., Paterson (N.J.) Bd. Edn., 1968-70; chief reporter Spectator News Syndicate, Englewood, N.J., 1970-72; investigative reporter Union City (N.J.) Dispatch, 1972-74; v.p. Shena Pearl & Assos. Inc., Paterson, 1974-79; pres., chmn. bd. Econ. Devel. Assos., Inc., Paterson, 1979—; vice chmn. bd. Community Mgmt. Cons. Inc.; dir. SPA Research Co., W.G. DeWolfe Inc. Mem. Hudson County Overall Econ. Devel. Com., 1977-79, Hudson County Solid Waste Mgmt. Com., 1977-79, Hudson County Transp. Adv. Com., 1976-79, Hudson County Community Devel. Com., 1975-79, mayor's com. Hackensack Meadowlands Devel. Commn., 1976-79; active local Democratic Party. Mem. Am. Soc. Pub. Adminstrn., Am. Inst. Social and Polit. Sci., Acad. Polit. Scis., Pub. Relations Soc. Am., Am. Mgmt. Assn., N.J. Press Assn.

BLISS, CHARLES MELBOURNE, banker; b. Evanston, Ill., Oct. 9, 1921; s. Charles H. and Hazel (Whitmore) B.; A.B. magna cum laude, Harvard U., 1943; M.B.A. with distinction, Northwestern U., 1947; m. Margaret Soule, Jan. 1, 1943; children—Charles Melbourne, Marian (Mrs. William R. White), Emily (Mrs. Robert L. Crawford). With Harris Trust & Savs. Bank, Chgo., 1944—, pres., dir., 1976—, chief exec. officer, 1977—, chmn. bd., 1980—; dir. Kellogg Co., G.D. Searle & Co. Bd. dirs. Protestant Found. Greater Chgo., Children's Meml. Hosp., Chgo.; trustee Alonzo Mather Found., Chgo. Community Trust, Northwestern U.; treas. Chgo. Crusade of Mercy. Served with AUS, 1943. Mem. Assn. Res. City Bankers, Phi Beta Kappa, Beta Gamma Sigma. Episcopalian. Clubs: Casino, Chgo., Comml. (Chgo.); Glen View (Golf, Ill.); Met. (Washington). Office: 111 W Monroe St Chicago IL 60690

BLISS, H. PARRY, JR., ins. agy. exec.; b. Washington, Feb. 17, 1947; s. Henry P. and Joyce M. (Cancilla) B.; B.S. in Acctg., U. N.C., Charlotte, 1969. With Ernst & Whinney, Charlotte, 1969-75; treas., chief financial officer Johnson & Higgins Tex., Inc., Houston, 1975—. Served with USAR. Ernst & Whinney scholar; Alpha Kappa Psi scholar. Mem. Am. Mgmt. Assn., Am. Inst. C.P.A.'s, N.C. Assn. C.P.A.'s, Tex. Soc. C.P.A.'s, Nat. Assn. Accts., U. N.C. Alumni Assn. (past pres.), Alpha Kappa Psi. Episcopalian. Club: Houston. Home: 748 Augusta Dr Houston TX 77057 Office: Johnson & Higgins Tex Inc 1400 Capital Bank Plaza Houston TX 77002

BLISS, NANCY JEAN, retailer; b. Detroit, Nov. 13, 1947; d. Nolan Walter and Jeannette Evelyn Leach; Asso. with honors in Retailing, Oakland Community Coll., 1967; student bus. adminstrn. Wayne State U., 1968-71; m. James Edward Bliss, May 22, 1971; 1 dau., Jamie Lynne. Asst. store mgr. to store mgr. Winkelman Stores, Inc., 1968-72; customer rep. Savin Bus. Machines, 1973-74; founder, owner, mgr. Bliss Supplies Inc., Troy, Mich., 1974—. Active NOW. Mem. Nat. Office Products Dealers Assn. Office: 6496 Tutbury St Troy MI 48098

BLISS, THOMAS RICHARD. aviation mfg. co. exec.; b. Ames, Iowa, Oct. 2, 1954; s. Richard K. and Patricia Ann (Lounsbury) B.; B.S., Iowa State U., 1976; m. Michelle L. Wickersham, May 14, 1977. Mktg. programs specialist Cessna Aircraft Co., WiChita, Kans., 1976-77; mktg. advt. cons. Flood Assos., Tempe, Ariz., 1977-78; mktg. communications adminstr. Collins Gen. Aviation div. Rockwell Internat., Cedar Rapids, Iowa, 1978-80, mktg. communications specialist Sperry Flight Systems, Phoenix, 1980—. Served with USAFR, 1976. Mem. Gen. Aviation Mfrs. Assn., Aviation and Space Writers Assn. (asso.), Aircraft Owners and Pilots Assn. Republican. Office: Sperry Flight Systems 21111 N 19th Ave Phoenix AZ 85308

BLIWAS, PHILIP R., owner ins. agy.; b. Milw., June 28, 1920; s. Rubin and Caroline B.; student U. Wis., 1937-40; LL.B., Marquette U., 1947; postgrad. Columbia U., 1942, Ind. U. Law Sch., 1946-47; cert. farm estate planning U. Minn., 1977; cert. Keypact Inst. Advanced Studies, 1979; m. Joyce Shirley Strauss; children—James Charles, Janice M. Sec., Charles Strauss Shoes, Milw., 1947-51; pres., gen. mgr., chief exec. officer Korbe Shoe, Inc., Mpls., 1951-74; field underwriter N.Y. Life Ins. Co., 1975-79; gen. agt., owner Philip Bliwas Agy., Chaska, Minn., 1978—. Del. to county and state convs. Minn. Democratic Farm Labor Party, 1972, 76, 80; vol. work Carver County Family Services. Served to lt. USN, 1941-46; PTO. Recipient Life Ins. Nat. Sales Achievement award Nat. Assn. Life Underwriters, 1978, Nat. Quality award, 1977, 78. Mem. Nat. Assn. Life Underwriters, Million Dollar Round Table. Home: 110922 Von Hertzen Circle Chaska MN 55318 Office: Philip Bliwas Agy Chaska MN 55318

BLOCH, HENRY SIMON, economist; b. County Kehl (Baden), Germany, Apr. 6, 1915; s. Edward and Claire (Bloch) B.; M.B.A., U. Nancy (France), 1935, Dr. of Laws-Econs., 1937; fellow Acad. Internat. Law, The Hague, 1937; Dr. Econ., Polit. and Social Scis. (honoris causa), Univ. Libre de Bruxelles, Belgium, 1969; 1 dau., Miriam (Mrs. Henry Feuerstein). Came to U.S., 1937, naturalized, 1943. Research asst. then instr. econs., instr. Army and Navy officers program U. Chgo., 1938-45; cons. Fgn. Econ. Adminstrn., 1945; economist Treasury Dept., 1945-46, mem. Treasury del. tax treaty negotiations Western Europe, 1946; rising to dir. fiscal and fin. br., dir. bur. tech. assistance ops., dep. commr. tech. assistance UN, 1946-62; pres. Zinder Internat. Ltd., 1962-66; v.p., dir. E.M. Warburg Co., Inc., 1967-70; sr. v.p., dir. E.M. Warburg, Pincus & Co., Inc., 1970-75, exec. v.p., dir., 1976—, dir. affiliated cos.; adviser corps., banks, govt.; vis. prof. econs. Yale, 1955; lectr. law Columbia, 1955-63, adj. prof. law and internat. relations, 1963—; dir., chmn. UNITAR Seminar on Internat. Monetary Systems for 37 govts., 1972; spl. adviser UN Panel on Fgn. Investment, Amsterdam, 1969; adviser UN Consultative Com. for Asian Devel. Bank, Bangkok, Thailand, 1965. Decorated comdr. Order of Leopold II (Belgium), 1979; hon. asso. fellow Berkeley Coll., Yale U. Mem. Am. Econ. Assn., Soc. Royale d'Economie Politique de Belgique (hon.), Council Fgn. Relations. Clubs: Cosmos (Washington). Author: The Challenge of the World Trade Conference, 1965; Financial Strategy for Developing Nations, 1969; Export Financing Emerging as a Major Policy, 1976; Foreign Risk Judgment for Commercial Banks, 1977; co-author: Legal-Economic Problems of International Trade, 1961; The Global Partnership, 1968; Financial Integration in Western Europe, 1969. Office: 277 Park Ave New York NY 10017

BLOCH, IVAN SOL, realtor; b. Detroit, Nov. 16, 1940; s. Howard and Pauline Betty (Davis) B.; student U. Miami (Fla.), 1958-59, Oakland Community Coll., 1966-68; m. Linda Ehrlich, Oct. 14, 1963; children—Brian, Amy. Partner, Bloch Bros. Corp., Waterford, Mich., 1962-66; pres. Brian Realty, Brimingham, Mich., 1966—, Waterford Mortgage Co., Brimingham, 1968—, Uniprop/Mich. Mgmt. Co., Birmingham, 1969—; mem. adv. bd. Century Nat. Bank, Chevy Chase, Md. Co-chmn. finance Levin for Gov., 1970, 74, Kelly for State Senate, 1972; mem. central finance com. Mich. Democratic party, 1973—; mem. Dem. 500 Club. Hon. mem. Boys Town. Mem. Nat. Assn. Real Estate Brokers, Real Estate Security and Syndication Inst. Mem. B'nai B'rith (nat. humanitarian award com. 1971-72). Home: 1440 Old Salem Ct Birmingham MI 48009 Office: 480 Pierce St Birmingham MI 48011

BLOCH, RONALD BERNARD, investment co. exec.; b. Pitts., July 27, 1926; s. Alfred A. and Ruby (McCoy) B.; B.S., Edinboro State Coll., 1949; postgrad U. Pitts., 1951-52; m. Isabel J. Sorenson, July 14, 1951; children—Ronald Jeffrey, David Jon, Chris Sorenson. Art supr. pub. schs., Brentwood and Washington, Pa., 1949-59; v.p. Cleveland Crafts Co., Cleve., 1960-63; pres. Creative Hands Co., Pitts., 1964-73; partner Taunton Investment Co., Pitts., 1976—; v.p. Triarco Arts & Crafts Co., Addison, Ill., 1973—. Served with USNR, 1943-46. Mem. Pa. Assn. Sch. Bus. Ofcls., Nat. Art Edn. Assn., Art Edn. Exhbrs. Assn., Pa. Ednl. Salesmans Club, Pa. Parks and Recreation Assn., Nat. Art Material Trade Assn., Nat. Hobby Assn. Home: 137 Sunridge Dr Pittsburgh PA 15234 Office: 4146 Library Rd Pittsburgh PA 15234

BLOCK, KENNETH LEROY, mgmt. cons.; b. Newark, May 14, 1920; s. Herman J. and Flora E. (Wiehle) B.; B.B.A., U. Minn., 1942; B.S., M.I.T., 1946; M.B.A., U. Mich., 1948; m. Margaret Sally Sherratt, Aug. 22, 1947; children—Kenneth Lee, Timothy Douglas, Elizabeth Ann. With Honeywell, Inc., 1940, Ford Co., 1941, Chevrolet Aviation Engine Co., 1942; instr. bus. adminstrn. U. Mich., 1947-48; chmn. bd. A.T. Kearney, Inc., Chgo., 1948—, also dir.; dir. Lawter Chems., Inc., Tracor, Inc., Littelfuse, Inc., Safety-Kleen Corp., Capital Opportunities Fund, Inc., Stein Roe & Farnham. Bd. dirs. Community Fund of Chgo., Evanston Hosp., Chgo. Sunday Evening Club, Lyric Opera Chgo.; vice chmn. bd. dirs. Elmhurst Coll.; former chmn. bd. dirs. Bd. Benevolence, Evang. Covenant Ch. Am.; former pres. bd. dirs. Chgo. Crime Commn., Swedish Covenant Hosp.; bd. mgrs. YMCA Met. Chgo.; bd. overseers Stuart Sch. Mgmt. and Fin., Ill. Inst. Tech.; mem. vis. com. U. Chgo. Div. Sch. Recipient nat. award for excellence in mgmt. cons. Inst. Mgmt. Cons.-Assn. Cons. Mgmt. Engrs., 1980; registered profl. engr., N.H.; C.P.A.; cert. mgmt. cons. Mem. Conf. Bd. (dir.), Chgo. Assn. Commerce and Industry (dir.), Nat. Inst. Mgmt. Consultants (past pres.), Assn. Cons. Mgmt. Engrs. (dir. 1969-71), Assos. of Northwestern U., Iron Wedge, Beta Gamma Sigma, Delta Sigma Pi. Clubs: Union League of Chgo. (past pres., bd. dirs.), Chgo., Comml., Indian Hill Country, Union League of N.Y. Contbg. editor: Production Handbook, 1959. Office: 222 S Riverside Plaza Chicago IL 60606

BLODGETT, WILLIAM ARTHUR, SR., corp. exec.; b. Detroit, Feb. 19, 1937; s. Arthur Charles and Edwina McRoy B.; student U. Fla., 1959; children—William Arthur, Charles Clark, Matthew Scott, James David, Elyse Chantal. Columnist, sports editor Tampa (Fla.) Times, 1959-63; columnist Atlanta Constn., 1963-64; public relations mgr. Gen. Electric Co., Atlanta, 1964-65, Washington, 1965-67, N.Y.C., 1967-69, Schenectady, N.Y., 1969-70; dir. internat. public relations Cie Honeywell Bull, Paris, 1970-74; account exec. Carl Byoir & Assos., Boston, 1974-77, N.Y.C., 1977; v.p. corp. communications Gulf & Western Industries, Inc., N.Y.C., 1977—. Vice chmn. Nat. Kidney Found.; bd. dirs. Jr. Achievement. Served with U.S. Army, 1958-59. Mem. Public Relations Soc. Am. Democrat. Roman Catholic. Club: Overseas Press. Office: 1 Gulf & Western Plaza New York NY 10024

BLOEDE, VICTOR GUSTAV, advt. exec.; b. Balt., Jan. 31, 1920; s. Victor Gustav, Jr. and Helen (Yoe) B.; student St. John's Coll., Annapolis, Md., 1939, U. Md., 1941; m. Merle Huie, Mar. 11, 1945; children—Victor Gustav, Susan Lohn. Vice pres., copy chief French & Preston, N.Y.C., 1947-50; with Benton & Bowles, Inc., N.Y.C., 1950—, v.p., creative dir., 1957-61, sr. v.p., 1961-62, sr. v.p. charge creative services, 1962-63, exec. v.p., 1963-68, chmn. plans bd., 1963-67, pres., chief exec. officer, 1968-71, chmn. bd., 1971—, chief exec. officer, 1971-74. Dir. at large Am. Assn. Advt. Agys., vice chmn., 1972-73, chmn., 1973-74, chmn. adv. council, 1975—; dir. Am. Advt. Fedn., Nat. Outdoor Advt. Bur.; mem. Nat. Advt. Rev. Bd., 1975-78; adv. council PGA, 1980—. Bd. dirs. Am. Cancer Soc., 1976—, Travelers Aid Soc. N.Y.; bd. visitors and govs. St. John's Coll., 1972-78, 80—. Served to capt. USAAF, 1942-45. Decorated Air medal with 6 oak leaf clusters. Mem. Phi Sigma Kappa. Clubs: Sands Point (L.I.) Golf (gov. 1975-80); Coral Beach (Bermuda); Manhasset Bay Yacht, Cloud, Economic (N.Y.C.). Contbg. author: The Copy Writer's Guide, 1958. Home: 160 Bayview Rd Plandome Manor NY 11030 Office: 909 3d Ave New York NY 10022

BLOM, DANIEL CHARLES, lawyer, ins. co. exec.; b. Portland, Oreg., Dec. 13, 1919; s. Charles D. and Anna (Reiner) B.; B.A. magna cum laude, U. Wash., 1941, postgrad., 1941-42; LL.B., Harvard, 1948; postgrad. Faculte de Droit, Universite de Paris, 1954-55; m. Ellen Lavon Stewart, June 28, 1952; children—Daniel Stewart, Nicole Jan. Teaching fellow speech U. Wash., 1941-42; law clk. to judge Supreme Ct. Wash., 1948-49; admitted to Wash. bar, 1949, U.S. Supreme Ct. bar; practiced in Seattle, 1949—; asso. Graves, Kizer & Graves, 1949-51; gen. counsel Northwestern Life Ins. Co., 1952-54; partner Case & Blom, 1952-54; asso., partner Ryan, Swanson Hendel & Cleveland and predecessor firms, 1956—; v.p., gen. counsel Family Life Ins. Co., 1964-69, sr. v.p., 1969-77, exec. v.p., 1977—, gen. counsel, 1969—, also dir.; v.p., dir. Family Life Bldg. Co., 1970-76. Mem. industry adv. com. Nat. Assn. Ins. Commrs., 1966-68; mem. regulatory matters subcom. Am. Council Life Ins., 1980—; mem. Wash. Bd. Bar Examiners, 1954, 68-75, chmn., 1972-75; pres. Ins. Fund Found., 1971-73; chmn. jury Gov.'s Writers Day awards, 1976. Vice pres., trustee Bush Sch., Frye Mus., Friends of Freeway Park. Served to lt. AUS, 1942-45. Decorated Bronze Star medal. Mem. Am. (vice chmn. com. life ins. law 1971-76, chmn. 1976-78; council sect. tort and ins. practice), Wash., Seattle bar assns., Wash. Ins. Council (pres. 1971-73, trustee 1971—, gen. counsel 1975-78), Assn. Life Ins. Counsel, Harvard Law Sch. Assn., Am. Arbitration Assn., World Affairs Council (trustee 1971—), Estate Planning Council Seattle, Am. Judicature Soc., Phi Beta Kappa, Tau Kappa Alpha. Club: Harvard of Seattle and Western Washington (trustee 1976-77). Editor: Wash. State Bar Jour., 1951-52; author: Life Insurance Law of Washington, 1980. Home: 2424 Magnolia Blvd W Seattle WA 98199 Office: Park Pl Seattle WA 98101

BLOMFIELD, RICHARD BEST, mgmt. cons.; b. Kamuela, Hawaii, Mar. 24, 1919; s. John Harold Stewart and Eirene Alice (Best) B.; A.B. cum laude, U. Hawaii, 1945; postgrad. Harvard, 1945-46; M.A., Columbia, 1947; m. Laurel Currey, May 18, 1957; children—John Roe, Christiana Jane, Mary Rachel. Analyst Amfac Ltd., Honolulu, 1947-50; mgr. salary adminstrn. Union Carbide Corp., N.Y.C., 1950-59; dir. personnel adminstrn. Mack Trucks Inc., Plainfield, N.J., 1959-61; dir. personnel Am. Standard Inc., N.Y.C., 1961-63; v.p. Am. Mut. Ins. Cos., Wakefield, Mass., 1964-69; gen. partner Hornblower & Weeks-Hemphill, Noyes, N.Y.C., 1969-72; sr. v.p., sec., dir., mem. exec. com. Hornblower, Weeks, Noyes & Trask, Inc., N.Y.C., 1972—; pres. Blomfield Assos., Morristown, N.J., 1979—; dir. HWNT & Co., Inc., Henry Hornblower Fund, Inc.; allied mem. N.Y. Stock Exchange. Adv., Am. Cleft Palate Edn. Found.; mem. adv. bd. Ins. Inst., Boston U., 1967-69. Mem. town meeting, appropriations com., Lexington, Mass., 1966-69; mem. alumni adv. council Tchrs. Coll., Columbia U.; bd. dirs. Friends of Patriots Path. Served to lt. USNR, 1941-45. Mem. Am. Soc. Tng. and Devel., Securities Industry Assn., N.J., Morris County hist. socs., Nat. Geog. Soc., Internat. Oceanographic Found., Am. Hemerocallis Soc., Watnong Garden Club, Frelinghuysen Arboretum, Nat. Audubon Soc., Am. Mus. Natural History, Smithsonian Inst. Episcopalian. Clubs: Downtown Athletic (N.Y.C.); Randolph Hills Tennis. Contbr.: How to Prepare for Management Responsibilities, 1962; Leadership in the Office, 1963; A Guide to the Recruitment Process, 1965; A Guide to the Development Process, 1967. Contbr. articles to profl. jours. Home: 44 Rolling Hill Dr Morristown NJ 07960

BLOMQUIST, JOHN EMIL, metals co. exec.; b. Kansas City, Kans., Aug. 22, 1914; s. Arthur and Mary (Meeker) B.; A.B., U. Mo., Kansas City, 1938; m. Harriet Rohner, Sept. 25, 1943; 1 dau., Mary Blomquist Clary. Exec. v.p., dir., mem. exec. com. Reynolds Metals Co., Richmond, Va., chmn. bd., dir. Reynolds Aluminum Bldg. Products Co.; pres., dir. Indsl. Metals, Inc.; v.p., dir. Bushnell Plaza Devel. Corp., LoMer Devel. Corp., New Eastwick Corp., Presdl. Devel. Corp., Presdl. Manor Corp., Presdl. Plaza Corp., Reynolds Aluminum Deutschland, Inc., Reynolds Aluminum Export Corp., Reynolds Metals Devel. Corp., Reynolds Regency Corp., Weybosset Hill Devel. Corp.; dir. Alumina Transport Corp., Broad St. Road Corp., Caribbean Steamship Co., S.A., El Campo Aluminum Co., Ocean Trailer Transport Corp., Reynolds Alumina Stade, Inc., Reynolds Aluminio do Brasil, Ltda., Reynolds Aluminum Credit Corp., Reynolds Aluminum Sales Co. Del., Reynolds Energy Resources Corp., Reynolds Guyana Mines, Ltd., Reynolds Haitian Mines, Inc., Reynolds Jamaica Alumina, Ltd., Reynolds Jamaica Mines, Ltd., Reynolds Metals European Capital Corp., Reynolds Mineral Devel. Co., Reynolds Mining Corp., Reynolds Pipeline Co., Reynolds Research Corp., Reynolds Suriname Mines, Ltd., Tilo Co., Inc. Served with U.S. Nacy, 1942-46. Mem. Aluminum Assn. (chmn.). Office: Reynolds Metals Co 6601 Broad St Rd Richmond VA 23261*

BLOND, SUSAN JEANNE LARSON, retail exec.; b. Chgo., Feb. 2, 1950; d. Kenneth Rodney and Ruth Marie (Christensen) Larson; B.S., No. Ill. U., 1972, M.B.A., 1977. Adminstrv. asst. Keebler Co., Elmhurst, Ill., 1974; sales rep. 3M Co., Printing Products Div., Bedford Park, Ill., 1974-75; sales rep. Wallace Bus. Forms, Schiller Park, Ill., 1975-77, hosp. account specialist, Des Plaines, Ill., 1977-78, sr. account rep., Wichita, Kans., 1978; account rep. Maxwell House div. Gen. Foods Corp., Wichita, 1978-79; owner Dawn of Light book and gift store, also distbr. Neo-Life products, Wichita, 1979—. Clubs: Wallace Bus. Forms Outstanding Performance, Wallace Bus. Forms 100 Percent. Home: 201 S Green St Wichita KS 67211

BLOOM, EDWIN JOHN, JR., mgmt. cons., lectr.; b. Yonkers, N.Y., Nov. 12, 1931; s. Edwin John and Marion (Baude) B.; B.S., Cornell U., 1957, student Columbia U., 1950-51, 54; m. Mary C. Caciola, June 9, 1956; children—Mary Catherine, Edward Joseph, Theresa Ann, Donna Marie. Supr. employment and employee services GAF Corp., Binghamton, N.Y., 1957-65; mgr. indsl. relations Philco Ford Corp., Phila., 1965-70; dir. employee relations Rauland div. Zenith Radio Corp., Chgo., 1970-72; v.p. personnel Lechmere Sales subs. Dayton Hudson Corp., Cambridge, Mass., 1973-77; pres. Employee Relations Assos., Inc., Concord, Mass., 1977—; corporator Middlesex Instn. for Savs., 1980—; instr. Lasell Jr. Coll. and Bunker Hill Community Coll. Mem. Minuteman Assn. Retarded Citizens, Concord, 1973—, dir., 1974—, pres., 1977—, chmn. personnel com., 1975—; mem. bd. Concord area Mass. Dept. Mental Health, Region 3, 1975—, chmn. mental retardation sub-com., 1977, search com., 1976—; bd. dirs., pres. Eliot Community Mental Health Center, 1979—. Served with U.S. Army, 1951-54. Recipient certificate of merit United Way, 1974, Mass. Dept. Mental Health, 1978. Mem. Indsl. Relations Research Assn., Mass. Bus. Assn. Roman Catholic. Home: 265 Oak Hill Circle Concord MA 01742 Office: PO Box 1036 Concord MA 01742

BLOOM, HOWARD O., fin. cons.; b. Essex, Iowa, June 4, 1913; s. Chancie Paul and Lena Wilma (Hagedorn) B.; student public schs., Estherville, Iowa; m. Mardelle Fox, Mar. 24, 1936; children—Larry Howard, Dennis; m. 2d, Charlotte J. McDiarmid, Aug. 7, 1965; stepchildren—Janet Thompson, Robert McDiarmid. With Estherville Creamery, 1929-33, asst. butter maker, 1929-33; with Maytag Co., Newton, Iowa, 1933-36, dist. mgr., 1936; with Skelgas & Estate Stove Co., Mo. and Ind., 1936-40; dist. rep. George W. Helme Co., N.Y.C., 1940-45; owner, operator The Hob-Dee Ent., Des Moines, 1945-69, pres., 1974—; fin. cons., Des Moines. Mem. Direct Selling Legion, Upper Midwest Art and Gift Assn., Nat. Assn. Fin. Cons., New Inventions Research Assn., Assn. Retarded Children, Nat. Ret. Tchrs. Assn. Democrat. Methodist. Clubs: Country, Top Notchers. Home:

1146 39th St Des Moines IA 50311 Office: 3902 University Ave Des Moines IA 50311

BLOOM, PAUL, lawyer, photog. supply co. exec., trade show producer; b. Springfield, Mass., Jan. 1, 1916; s. Meyer and Anne (Hurwitz) B.; LL.B., Northeastern U., 1938; m. Charlotte Lannon, Dec. 5, 1937; children—Elliot Mayer Lewis, Ronni Susan. With Bloom's Photog. Supply Co., Springfield, 1934—, pres., 1948-80, chmn. bd., 1981—; admitted to Mass. bar, 1938; practiced in Springfield, 1938; founder, pres. Key Prodns., Inc., Hartford, Conn., 1972—, produces Conn. Indsl. Trade Expo., 1975—, also produces Am. Bus. Equipment and Communications Expo., N.E. Graphics Conf. and Trade Show; pres. Internat. Conv. Mgmt., Inc., Hartford; also numerous other bus. and real estate activities. Mem. Longmeadow (Mass.) Zoning Bd. Appeal, 1966—, vice chmn., 1976—; bd. dirs. Kodimoh Synagogue. Mem. Hampden County Bar Assn., Greater Hartford C. of C., Greater Hartford Conv. and Visitors Bur., Greater Hartford Passenger Traffic Assn., Council Photog. Suppliers (co-founder), Copier Dealers Assn., New Eng. Assn. Expn. Mgrs. (pres.), Nat. Assn. Expn. Mgrs. Republican. Clubs: Masons, Shriners. Author, producer: A Trap for the Fox, 1932. Office: 213 Worthington St Springfield MA 01103 also 410 Asylum St Hartford CT 06103

BLOOM, WILBUR (WIL) WAYNE, JR., real estate devel. co. exec.; b. Mpls., July 7, 1932; s. Wilbur Wilford and Hildegarde Amanda (Loman) B.; B.A., Ottawa (Kans.) U., 1954; postgrad. Eastern Baptist Theol. Sem., Phila., 1954-56; m. Dorothy Ann Burns, June 1, 1954; children—Carey Lynn, Jay Kristian, Jon Kirtley. Asst. minister Bala Cynwyd (Pa.) Methodist Ch., 1954-56; sales agt. Nat. Life Ins. Co. of Vt., Phila., 1956; br. mgr. Transam. Title Ins. Co., Phoenix, 1958-64, 67-69; v.p. Mfrs. Tire, Phoenix, 1964-65; account mgr. Allied Brands div. Uniroyal, Inc., 1965-67; dir. ann. fund Ottawa U., 1969-72; v.p. Cannon Devel. Corp., Scottsdale, Ariz., 1972—; adv. bd. Ottawa U. Coll. Without Campus, Phoenix, 1977—; career edn. adv. council Tempe (Ariz.) Area Schs., 1977-79. Served with U.S. Army, 1956-58. Cert. football ofcl., Ariz. Interscholastic Assn. Mem. Public Relations Assn. (v.p. 1971-72), Am. Bapt. Chs./Pacific SW (bd. mgrs. 1974—), Am. Bapt. Chs., U.S.A. (gen. bd. 1978—). Republican. Clubs: Tempe Racquet and Swim, Rotary, Tempe Diablos (exec. v.p. 1969, dir. 1973-78). Home: 3821 S Kenwood Ln Tempe AZ 85282 Office: 2130 E Brown Mesa AZ 85203

BLOOM, WILLIAM ROBERT, accountant; b. N.Y.C., July 31, 1946; s. William and Elizabeth (Carman) B.; A.A.S., SUNY, Farmingdale, 1971; B.B.A., Hofstra U., 1974; children—William Arvit, Erik Jon. Gen. acctg. supr. Potter Inst., Plainview, N.Y., 1969-73; chief acct. Ancorp Nat. Services, N.Y.C., 1973-74; controller George Malvese & Co., Hicksville, 1974-75; prin. William R. Bloom, C.P.A., Deer Park, N.Y., 1975—. Treas., L.I. Soccer Football League; coach Babylon United Soccer Club. C.P.A. Mem. Am. Inst. C.P.A.'s, N.Y. State Soc. Cert. Pub. Accts., Hofstra U. Bus. Alumni Assn., N.Y. State Pub. High Sch. Soccer Referees. Republican. Lutheran. Office: 2100 Deer Park Ave Deer Park NY 11729

BLOOMBERG, RICHARD SAMUEL, finance co. exec.; b. Mpls., June 30, 1929; s. John Nathaniel and Bertha Christine (Ehrenholm) B.; B.B.A., U. Minn., 1951; B. Fgn. Trade, Am. Inst. Fgn. Trade, 1958; m. Oliva Hernandez Betancourt, Feb. 20, 1960; children—Harriet, Gabriella, Erik. Mgr. for So. Caribbean, Pfizer Internat., 1961-64; gen. sales mgr. P.R., Pfizer Corp., 1964-66; product mgr. Syntex Internat., Mexico City, 1966-68; v.p., treas. Bloomberg Companies, Chanhassen, Minn., 1968—. Bd. dirs. Mpls. People to People, 1974—, Am. Dinner Theatre Inst., 1979—. Served to 1st lt. USAF, 1952-56. Mem. Nat. Assn. Accountants, Delta Upsilon. Presbyterian. Home: 1102 Hazeltine Blvd Chaska MN 55318 Office: 501 78th St W Chanhassen MN 55317

BLOOMFIELD, KEITH MARTIN, mgmt. cons.; b. Bronx, N.Y., Sept. 11, 1951; s. Monroe Louis and Shirley B. (Mason) B.; B.A., Windham Coll., 1973; M.S., Syracuse U., 1974; m. Adrienne Donna Young, Sept. 2, 1979. Personnel/cons. Automatic Data Processing Inc., Clifton, N.J., 1975-78; cons. European Am. Bank, N.Y.C., 1978-79; cons. Consol. Edison N.Y., 1979—; pres. Katbird Communications Inc., White Plains, N.Y., 1977—. Mem. Nat. Acad. TV Arts and Scis., Audio Engring. Soc., Syracuse U. Alumni. Contbr. short stories to various publs.; writer screen plays. Home: 25 Hillside Ave White Plains NY 10601

BLOSKAS, JOHN D., editor, pub. relations dir.; b. Waco, Tex., July 13, 1928; s. George and Alvina (Schrader) B.; B.A., Baylor U., 1953; m. Anna Louise Nelson, Feb. 7, 1955; children—Suzzanne (dec.), John D., Kenneth Douglas. Exec. sec. Waco Jr. C. of C., 1953-55; asso. editor Mexia (Tex.) Daily News, 1955-56; dir. publicity Valley C. of C., Weslaco, Tex., 1956-57; religion editor Houston Chronicle, 1957-58; v.p. pub. relations annuity bd. So. Bapt. Conv., Dallas, 1958—. Served with USNR, 1945-49, 50-51. Mem. So. Bapt. (past pres.), Tex. Bapt. (past pres.) pub. relations assns., Pub. Relations Soc. Am. (accredited), Religious Pub. Relations Council, Sales and Mktg. Execs., Fellowship of Christians in Arts, Media and Entertainment. Author: Staying in the Black Financially; Living Within Your Means. Editor: The Years Ahead. Home: 5816 Clendenin Dallas TX 75228 Office: 511 N Akard Bldg Dallas TX 75201

BLOUNT, JERRY CHARLES, cable TV co. exec.; b. Hamilton, Ohio, Jan. 9, 1949; s. James Reginald and Julia Blount; student in mgmt. Miami U., Oxford, Ohio, 1969-73; m. Dorothy Liford, June 29, 1968; children—Jeffrey, Jaime. Gen. mgr. Am. Cable TV, Napa, Calif., 1976-77; regional mktg. mgr. Telecommunications Inc., San Francisco, 1977-78; gen. mgr. Metro Home Theatre, Detroit, 1978-79; dir. ops. Am. Cable TV, Inc., Phoenix, 1979—. Mem. Nat. Cable TV Assn., Ariz. Cable TV Assn., Cable TV Adminstrn. and Mktg. Soc. Lutheran. Home: 5802 W Muriel Dr Glendale AZ 85308 Office: 2949 W Osborn Rd Phoenix AZ 85002

BLOUNT, TERRANCE GIRARD, fin. exec.; b. Washington, Sept. 5, 1946; s. Alvin V. and Geraldine (Exum) B.; B.S., Howard U., 1967; postgrad. N.C. Central U., 1967-68, Rutgers U., 1974-76; m. Patricia Hockaday, June 26, 1971; 1 son, Terrance G. Asst. treas. Bankers Trust Co., N.Y.C., 1971-76; v.p. Indsl. Bank of Washington, 1976-78; pres., chief exec. officer Equico Capital Corp., N.Y.C., 1979-80; asst. v.p. nat. corp. fin. dept. Equitable Life Assurance Soc. U.S., 1980—. Bd. dirs. Washington Urban League, 1976-78. Served with U.S. Army, 1968-71. Mem. D.C. Assn. Urban Bankers (pres. 1976-78), Nat. Assn. Urban Bankers (treas. 1978-79), Urban Bankers Coalition N.Y., One Hundred Black Men, Kappa Alpha Psi. Democrat. Roman Catholic. Club: Pigskin. Office: 1285 Ave of Americas New York NY 10019

BLOUNT, WILLIAM HOUSTON, bus. exec.; b. Union Springs, Ala., Jan. 3, 1922; s. William Madison and Clarabel (Chalker) B.; student U. Ala., 1940-42; m. Mary Frances Dean, Aug. 5, 1943; children—Barbara Dean Blount King, William Houston, Beverly Blount McNeil, David Dean, Frances Dean Blount Kansteiner. Partner, Blount Bros.; pres., dir. Southeastern Sand & Gravel; v.p. So. Cen-Vi-Ro Pipe, 1946-57; with Vulcan Materials Co., Birmingham, Ala., 1957—, pres. concrete pipe div., 1957-59, corp. v.p., mktg., dir., 1959-66, pres. SE div., dir., 1966-70, exec. v.p. constrn. materials group, dir., 1970-77, pres., chief operating officer, 1977-79, exec. com., 1970—, pres., chief exec. officer, also dir., 1979—; dir. Vulcan Life Ins. Co., Blount, Inc., Stateman Life Ins. Co., First Ala. Bank of Birmingham. Mem. exec. bd. Birmingham Area council Boy Scouts Am.; bd. dirs. Jr. Achievement of Jefferson County, Relay House, United Way; trustee Birmingham-So. Coll., YWCA, Camp Fire Youth Council; gen. chmn. United Way drive, 1975; chmn. Jr. Achievement drive, 1981. Served with AC, USN, 1942-46. Mem. Birmingham Area C. of C. (dir.). Republican. Methodist. Clubs: Mountain Brook (bd. govs.); The Club (dir.); Rotary, Chicago, River (N.Y.), Linville (N.C.) Golf. Office: PO Box 7497 1 Metroplex Dr Birmingham AL 35253

BLOWERS, JOHN GARRETT, broadcasting co. exec.; b. N.Y.C., Sept. 19, 1941; s. John Garrett and Joan D. (Lowery) B.; B.A., Mich. State U., 1963. Asst. to promotion mgr. Look Mag., Cowles Communications, N.Y.C., 1964-66; press rep., mgr. bus. info., dir. corporate info. ABC, N.Y.C., 1966-73; asso. dir., dir., v.p. investor relations CBS Inc., N.Y.C., 1973—. Mem. Nat. Investor Relations Inst. (v.p. programs N.Y. chpt. 1977-78, dir. N.Y. chpt. 1978-80), Nat. Acad. TV Arts and Scis., Pub. Relations Soc. Am., Internat. Radio and TV Soc. Club: Amateur Comedy (N.Y.C.). Home: 162 W 13th St New York NY 10011 also The Granary Barkers Island Rd Southampton NY 11968 Office: 51 W 52nd St New York NY 10019

BLUESTEIN, PAUL HAROLD, mgmt. engr.; b. Cin., June 14, 1923; s. Norman and Eunice D. (Schullman) B.; B.S., Carnegie Inst. Tech., 1946, B.S. in Mgmt. Engring. and B.Engring. in Mgmt. Engring., 1946; M.B.A., Xavier U., 1973; m. Joan Ruth Straus, May 17, 1943; children—Alice Sue Bluestein Greenbaum, Judith Ann. Time study engr. Lodge & Shipley Co., 1946-47; adminstrv. engr. Randall Co., 1947-52; partner Paul H. Bluestein & Co., mgmt. cons., 1952—; gen. mgr. Baker Refrigeration Co., 1953-56; pres., dir. Tabor Mfg. Co., 1953-54; pres., dir. Blujay Corp., 1954—, Blatt & Ludwig Corp., 1954-57, Jason Industries, Inc., 1954-57, Hamilton-York Corp., 1954-57, Earle Hardware Mfg. Co., 1955-57, Hermas Machine Co., 1956-58, Panel Machine Co., Ermet Products Corp., 1957—; gen. mgr. Hafleigh & Co., 1959-60; sr. v.p., gen. mgr., McCauley Ind. Corp., 1959-60; gen. mgr. Am. Art Works div. Rapid-Am. Corp., 1960-63; partner Companhia Engenheiros Industrial Bluestein do Brasil, 1971—; pub. Merger and Acquisition Digest, 1962—, Tyco Labs., Inc., 1968, All-Tech Industries, Inc., 1969; sec.-treas., dir. Liberty Baking Co., 1964-65; dir. Noramco, Inc.; pres. Duquesne Baking Co., Goddard Bakers, Inc., 1964-65; partner Seinsheimer-Bluestein Mgmt. Services, 1964—, Del. Tisco Corp., 1970-71; v.p. Famco Machine div. Worden-Allen Co., 1974-75; exec. v.p., gen. mgr. Peck, Stow & Wilcox Co., Inc., 1976-80; v.p. ops. Indsl. Plants Corp., 1979—. Served from pvt. to tech. sgt. AUS, 1943-46. Registered profl. engr., Ohio. Mem. ASME, Am. Inst. Indsl. Engrs., Joint Engring. Mgmt. Conf. Club: B'nai B'rith. Home: 3420 Section Rd Amberley Village Cincinnati OH 45237 Office: 3420 Section Rd Cincinnati OH 45237

BLUHDORN, CHARLES G., corp. exec.; b. Vienna, Austria, Sept. 20, 1926; came to U.S., 1942; student Coll. City N.Y., Columbia. Self-employed, 1946-56; dir. Mich. Plating & Stamping Co., Grand Rapids, 1956-57; chmn. bd., mem. exec. com., dir. Gulf & Western Industries, Inc., N.Y.C., 1958—; chmn. exec. com. Madison Sq. Garden Corp., N.Y.C.; dir. Paramount Pictures Corp., N.Y.C. Trustee, Trinity Sch., N.Y.C., Freedoms Found., Valley Forge; co-chmn. N.Y. chpt. Am. Cancer Soc. Served with USAAF, 1945-46. Recipient Disting. New Yorker award City Club N.Y. Office: Gulf & Western Bldg 1 Gulf & Western Plaza New York NY 10023*

BLUM, ALBERT ALEXANDER, ednl. adminstr.; b. N.Y.C., Apr. 5, 1924; s. Morris and Estelle (Kaplan) B.; B.S., CCNY, 1947; M.A., Columbia U., 1948, Ph.D., 1953; m. Roslyn Silver, Jan. 16, 1949; children—Steven Ephraim, David Joshua. Labor relations specialist Conf. Bd., N.Y.C., 1955-57; asst. prof. N.Y. U., 1958, Cornell U., 1958-59; asso. prof. indsl. relations Am. U., 1959-60; prof. Sch. Labor and Indsl. Relations, Mich. State U., East Lansing, 1960-74; prof. U. Tex., Austin, 1974-78; dean, prof. Stuart Sch. Mgmt. and Fin., Ill. Inst. Tech., Chgo., 1978—; labor arbitrator. Served with USAAF, 1943-45. Grantee Lyndon B. Johnson Found., 1976-77, Pacific Cultural Found., 1978-80. Mem. Am. History Assn., SW Labor Studies Conf. (exec. bd.), Indsl. Relations Research Assn. Author: A History of American Labor Movement, 1972; White Collar Workers, 1971; Teacher Unions and Associations: A Comparative Study, 1969; Drafted or Deferred: Practices Past and Present, 1967. Office: 10 W 31st St Chicago IL 60616

BLUM, KARL W., banker; b. N.Y.C., Oct. 13, 1932; s. Karl J. and Amalie C. B.; B.S., City U. N.Y., 1964; postgrad. N.Y. Law Sch., 1964-65, Stanford U., 1970-72; m. Elise Meehan, Aug. 23, 1958; children—Patrice C., Karl R., Elise A., Jean C., Kristine E. Asst. v.p. Citibank, N.A., Bklyn., 1969-74, N.Y.C., 1974-76; v.p. br. loan adminstrn. Am. Nat. Bank and Trust of N.J., Morristown, 1976-78, v.p., mgr. internat., 1978—. Mem. Roseland Bd. Adjustment, 1974-79. Served with U.S. Navy, 1953-55. Mem. Credit Research Found., N.J. Bankers Assn., Com. on Internat. Banking, Am. Mgmt. Assn., Morris County C. of C. Office: 225 South St Morristown NJ 07960

BLUMBERG, ARTHUR LESLIE, ins. co. exec.; b. Hartford, Conn., Apr. 7, 1937; s. Robert L. and Jean S. B.; B.Mktg., U. Vt., 1959; grad. life underwriter U. Conn., 1967; m. Ellen Meshken, June 30, 1963; children—Carolyn Beth, Matthew. Underwriter, A.S. Haller Ins., Hartford, 1959-61; life ins. specialist Underwriter Service Agy., 1961-63; founder, pres. Blumberg Assos., ins. brokerage, risk mgmt. co., Hartford, 1963—; pres. Programs Benefit Corp., 1978—, Warranty Records Service Center, Inc., USA, 1980—, Warranty Records Service Center, Ltd., Bermuda, 1980—; lectr. in field. Corporator Mt. Sinai Hosp., Hartford; 1974-79, Hartford Jewish Fedn.; bd. dirs. Bradley Air Field Mus., 1978-80. Recipient Pres's. award Banker's Nat. Life Ins., 1963; C.L.U. Mem. Million Dollar Round Table (life mem., HTFD group ins. award 1974-80, Nat. Quality award 1970-78, Gen. agts. award 1967), Mut. Agts. Assn., Life Agts. Assn. Gold Key, Hartford C. of C. Democrat. Designer spl. ins. program for ins. corp. Home: 30 Forest Hills Dr West Hartford CT 06117 Office: 100 Constitution Plaza Hartford CT 06103

BLUMBERG, BURTON STUART, hosp. cons.; b. Balt., Dec. 23, 1946; B.S., U. Md., 1968; M.B.A., George Washington U., 1970; m. Ana Delia Guerrero, Aug. 18, 1971; children—Johanna, Roland, Ricardo. Cons., Venezuelan Ministry Health, Caracas, 1971-73; adminstr. Coromoto Hosp., Maracaibo, Venezuela, 1973-74; dep. dir. planning Albert Einstein Coll. Medicine, Bronx, N.Y., 1974-76; pres. Joranna Assos., Balt. and Venezuela, 1976-77; hosp. cons. Friesen Internat.-AMI, Washington, 1977—. Recipient various service awards. Mem. Assn. Hosp. Planners. Home: 2806 Hogan Ct Falls Church VA 22043 Office: 1055 Thomas Jefferson St Washington DC 20007

BLUMBERG, DONALD FREED, mgmt. cons.; b. Phila., Jan. 30, 1935; s. Harry and Sara (Freed) B.; B.A., U. Pa., 1952, B.E.E., 1957, M.B.A., 1958, postgrad., 1963; m. Judith Toplin, June 16, 1960; children—Michael, Susan. Sr. planner IBM Corp., 1960-61; dir. planning and research services Pa. Research Assn., 1962-65; dir. ops. research and long range planning Philco Ford Corp., 1965-68; mgr. mgmt. sci. div. Sci. Mgmt. Corp., 1968; v.p. Computer Scis. Corp., 1969; pres., chief exec. officer Decision Scis. Corp., Jenkintown, Pa., 1969—; instr. U. Pa.; lectr. Am. Mgmt. Assn. Mem. Upper Dublin Twp. Govt. Study Commn., 1974-75; acting prin. dep. asst. sec. def. Dept. Def., 1975. Served to 1st lt., AUS, 1959-60. Memm. Inst. Mgmt. Scis., Ops. Research Soc. Am., IEEE. Democrat. Jewish. Contbr. articles in strategic planning, urban planning, long range planning and applications of mgmt. sci. techniques to profl. jours. Home: 1922 Audubon Dr Dresher PA 19025 Office: 528 Fox Pavillion Jenkintown PA 19046

BLUMBERG, PETER STEVEN, bus. exec.; b. Bklyn., Feb. 18, 1944; s. Howard G. and Lily (Goldberg) B.; B.S., U. Va., 1967; m. Judith E. Pauly, Apr. 22, 1967; children—Anne Pauly, Matthew Edward, Heather Rebecca. Salesman, The Coll. House, Inc., Mineola, N.Y., 1967-71, sales mgr., 1971-76, gen. mgr., 1977-78, pres., 1979—; pres. Blumberg Bros., Inc., Mineola, 1979—; treas., Sch. Tchrs. Supply Corp., Mineola, 1979—; dir. Sta. WUVA, Inc., Charlottesville, Va. Mem. Nat. Assn. Coll. Stores, Imprinted Sportswear Assn., Nat. Cath. Edn. Assn., Nat. Right-To-Work Legal Def. Found., Nat. Coalition to Ban Handguns, Handgun Control, Inc., Simon Wiesenthal Center for Holocaust Studies, Ams. Against Union Control of Govt. Jewish. Club: Les Amis du Vin. Home: 55 Hummingbird Dr East Hills NY 11576 Office: 96 Windsor Ave Mineola NY 11501

BLUME, FREDERICK ROSS, investment banker; b. Oakland, Calif., July 7, 1942; s. Frederick E. and Norma J. (Watson) B.; A.B., Stanford U., 1965, M.B.A., 1968; m. Margery Jean Friberg, Feb. 12, 1971. Asst. v.p. Bank of Am., 1968-72; v.p. corp. fin. Kidder Peabody & Co., 1972-77; v.p. corp. fin. Warburg Paribas Becker, 1977; now exec. v.p. Blyth Eastman Paine Webber Health Care Funding, Inc., Chgo., also dir. First aid instr. ARC, 1965-72. Club: Olympic (San Francisco). Contbr. articles in field to profl. jours. Office: 30 N LaSalle St Chicago IL 60602

BLUME, ROGER LEE, conglomerate co. exec.; b. Harvey, Ill., Aug. 1, 1943; s. Wilbur H. and Elda (Koehler) B.; B.A., Oberlin Coll., 1965; M.B.A. (fellow), U. Chgo., 1967; m. Camille Blume; 1 dau., Marie. Operations analyst Control Data Corp., Honolulu, 1967-69; mgr. systems devel. Control Data Corp., 1970-72; mgr. financial analysis Internat. Harvester, Chgo., 1972-74; asst. controller planning IU Internat., Phila., 1974-76, asst. treas., 1977-78, dir. strategic planning, 1979—. Mem. Fin. Execs. Inst., Phila. Treasurers Club, N.Am. Soc. Corp. Planning, Nat. Assn. Accountants. Club: Camac Health, Delaware Valley Tennis. Office: 1500 Walnut St Philadelphia PA 19102

BLUMENSON, PHILIP, lawyer; b. N.Y.C., Dec. 9, 1919; s. Alexander and May B.; A.B., Johns Hopkins U., 1939; J.D. cum laude, N.Y. U., 1948; m. Carolyn Greenfield, Sept. 2, 1945; children—Laura, Diane, Amy. Chmn. bd. dirs. Blumenson-Sussman Co., Inc., Great Neck, N.Y., 1945—; admitted to N.Y. bar, 1948; dir. Bronx Realty Adv. Bd., 1966—. Dep. mayor Village of Great Neck, 1961-62, trustee, 1958-61, mem. bd. zoning and appeals, 1955-58, mem. planning bd., 1953-55, village justice, 1965-75. Mem. N.Y. State, Nassau County bar assns. Jewish religion. Clubs: Lions, Elks. Office: 10 Cutter Mill Rd Great Neck NY 11021

BLUMENTHAL, GENE N., retail jeweler, public relations exec.; b. St. Paul, Oct. 31, 1946; s. Jerome E. and Tobie N. (Mintz) B.; B.A., Hartnell Coll., 1966; student Gemological Inst. Am., 1978—. Ventriloquist, comml. announcer, cameraman and pub. relations person, Sta.-KSBW-TV, Salinas, Calif., 1959-65; exec. v.p. BK &S Advt., Inc., Denver, 1969-72; in public relations ABC, Hollywood, Calif., 1972-74, C. of C. of U.S., Washington, 1974-77; owner Mr. B's Jewelers, Salinas, 1963—; owner, operator BK &S Advt., Salinas, free-lance producer TV commls. Active March of Dimes Nat. Found., 1960-77, including Monterey County T.A.P. chmn., 1961-65; producer stage shows for charity; mem. steering com. Jr. Achievement, Salinas; active local Republican polit. campaigns. Served with USAF, 1966-70. Recipient certificate of appreciation (7) March of Dimes, 1960-77, plaque (3), 1961, 62, 64, recognition numerous chambers commerce, including Palm Springs, Calif., 1976, North Hollywood, Calif., 1976, West Covina, Calif., 1976, Ventura, Calif., 1977. Mem. Salinas C. of C. (co-chmn. free enterprise com.), Salinas Jaycees (award 1977; dir.), Am. Legion. Club: Kiwanis. Author TV shows: The Newcomers, 1972-73, In Disguise, 1972-73. Office: 936 S Main St Salinas CA 93901 also 1 Midtown Ln Salinas CA 93901

BLUMENTHAL, SANFORD ELMORE, trade assn. exec.; b. San Francisco, May 24, 1921; s. Arthur and Rose (Hyman) B.; A.B., San Francisco State U., 1949; postgrad. Golden Gate Coll., 1951; m. Bessie Chernock, Dec. 21, 1941; children—Linda Susan, Phillip Allen. Auditor, State of Calif., San Francisco, 1949-52; internal auditor Montgomery Ward & Co., Oakland, Calif., 1953-55; mgmt. cons., exec. George S. May & Co., San Francisco, 1956-65; mgmt. cons. Nat. Elec. Contractors Assn., Washington, 1966-69, mgr. mgmt. services 1969—. Served with U.S. Army, 1942-46. Public acct., Calif. Mem. Am. Inst. Constructors, Am. Council for Constrn. Edn. (trustee), Associated Schs. of Constrn. Clubs: Masons, Shriners. Home: 5226 Farm Pond Ln Columbia MD 21045 Office: 7315 Wisconsin Ave Washington DC 20014

BLUMENTHAL, W. MICHAEL, sec. Treasury; b. Berlin, Germany, Jan. 3, 1926; s. Edward and Rose Valerie (Markt) B.; came to U.S., 1947, naturalized, 1952; B.S., U. Calif. at Berkeley, 1951; M.A., Princeton U., 1953, M.P.A., 1953, Ph.D., 1956; m. Margaret Eileen Polley, Sept. 8, 1951; children—Ann Margaret, Gillian, Jane Eileen. Research asso. Princeton U., 1954-57; labor arbitrator State of N.J., Trenton, 1955-57; v.p., dir. Crown Cork Internat. Corp., Jersey City, 1957-61; dep. asst. sec. state, Washington, 1961-63; ambassador, Pres.'s dep. spl. rep. for trade negotiations, Geneva, 1963-67; pres., chief operating officer Bendix Internat. (operating group of Bendix Corp.), N.Y.C., 1967-70; vice chmn. Bendix Corp., 1970, pres., chief operating officer, dir., 1971-72, chmn., pres., chief exec. officer, 1972-77, also dir. numerous fgn. affiliated cos.; sec. of Treasury, Washington, 1977-79; vice chmn. Burroughs Corp., Detroit, 1980—, also dir.; dir. Equitable Life Assurance Soc. U.S., Pillsbury Co., Chem. N.Y. Corp./Chem. Bank. Mem., trustee Rockefeller Found.; 1979—; bd. dirs. Council on Fgn. Relations, 1979—. Mem. Am. Econ. Assn., Phi Beta Kappa. Author profl. articles. Office: Burroughs Corp Exec Offices Burroughs Pl Detroit MI 48232

BLUMSTEIN, WILLIAM A., ins. brokerage and risk mgmt. co. exec.; b. N.Y.C., Mar. 21, 1948; s. Norman L. and Susan (Shapiro) B.; B.B.A., Pace U., 1970; postgrad. Coll. of Ins., 1977-79; m. Ellen Goldsmith, Sept. 12, 1970; children—Amy Beth, Sara Lynn. From trainee to casualty underwriter Hartford Ins. Group (Conn.), 1970-72; broker, agt. account exec. Barco Assos., Inc., N.Y.C., 1972-74; broker, agt. account exec. Blume & Blumberg Inc., N.Y.C., 1974-75, v.p., treas., 1975-80; pres. Blume & Blumstein, Inc., N.Y.C., 1980—. Trustee, Westchester Reform Temple, 1976—, pres. Men's Club, 1976-80, trustee Men's Club, 1980; trustee Jewish Home and Hosp for Aged, 1980—; mem. Greenacres Assn. Mem. Council Ins. Brokers

Greater N.Y., Sigma Zeta Chi Alumni Assn. (past pres., sec.). Clubs: Town (Scarsdale, N.Y.); Century Country; B'nai B'rith. Home: 20 Cambridge Rd Scarsdale NY 10583 Office: 501 Fifth Ave New York NY 10017

BLUNDELL, HARRY, elec. utility exec.; b. Salt Lake City, May 1, 1925; s. Henry James and Eliza Ellen (Terry) B.; B.S. in Philosophy and Math., U. Utah, 1949; postgrad. U. Mich.; m. Beverly Mae Martin, Aug. 26, 1944; children—Martin, James, John, Peter, Amy, Ann, Todd. With Utah Power & Light Co., Salt Lake City, 1949—, successively asst. treas., treas., v.p., sr. v.p., 1949-76, exec. v.p., 1976-79, pres., chief exec. officer, 1979—, dir., 1965—; dir. Walker Bank & Trust Co., Amalgamated Sugar Co., Ideal Basic Industries, Inc. Served with USNR, 1943-46. Mem. Salt Lake C. of C. (past v.p.), Phi Beta Kappa. Clubs: Rotary, Alta. Mormon. Office: 1407 W N Temple St PO Box 899 Salt Lake City UT 84110

BLUNSON, SAMUEL JAMES, ins. broker, fin. and export cons.; b. Houston, Dec. 8, 1931; s. Sam Thomas and Jessie Mae (Davis) B.; B.Th., Mt. Hope Bible Coll., 1972; B.A., Tex. So. U., 1977; m. Margaret Peterson, Feb. 12, 1968; children—Samuel James, Sebrena Joyce, Selina Jean, Stanford James, Sabenia Jos, Charlotte Jeanett, Chelah Jane. Dist. mgr. Am. Tchr. Mut. Ins. Co., 1964-65; investment and stock counselor Am. Capital Life Ins. Co., Houston, 1965-68; spl. agt. Bankers Life & Casualty Ins. Co., Houston, 1968-72; owner, broker Sunnyside Ins. Agy., Houston, 1972—; owner S. J. Blunson Fin. Services, 1980—; dir. Brotherhood Inc. Mem. Gov.'s Spl. Com. on Affairs, 1979—; mem. Nat. Com. on Human Resource Problems of Aging. Served with AUS, 1948-53. Mem. Internat. Assn. Fin. Planners, Nat. Soc. Cons.'s, Profl. Ins. Agts. Am., Nat. Small Bus. Assn., Nat. Assn. Evangelicals, World Relief Commn. Democrat. Baptist. Club: Shriners. Home: 4522 Keystone St Houston TX 77021 Office: 4703 1/2 Sauer St Houston TX 77004

BLUNT, FRANK CHRISTOPHER, III, investment banker; b. Eng.; came to U.S., 1966, naturalized, 1975; gen. cert. Cambridge U., 1957; student C.P.A. program McGill U. Sch. Commerce, 1959-62; m. Ann Wentworth Kerley, Dec. 1956; children—Gavin, Jason. Trainee, Touche Ross & Co., 1959-62; account exec. Merrill Lynch et al, 1962-65; v.p. Shearson Loeb Rhoades & Co., 1966-72; pres., dir. Blunt Internat. Ltd., Hamilton, Bermuda, 1973—; exec. v.p.-fin. Mid Ocean Mgmt., Inc., Wilmington, Del., 1973—; dir. Enertek Oil & Gas Corp., Houston, Clarendon Ins. Co. (Bermuda) Ltd., Hamilton. Served with RAF, 1956-59. Mem. Aircraft Owners and Pilots Assn., Asia Soc., Saint Georges Soc. of N.Y. Clubs: Met. (N.Y.C.); Mid Ocean (Bermuda). Home: 3410 Galt Ocean Dr Fort Lauderdale FL 33308

BLUNT, STANHOPE ECCLESTON, JR., advt. agy. exec.; b. LaJunta, Colo., Mar. 4, 1922; s. Stanhope Eccleston and Jane (Thompson) B.; B.B.A., U. Minn., 1946; m. Barbara Douglass, Apr. 2, 1949; children—Douglass. Brian, Melissa. Dist. sales mgr. Western Airlines, Mpls., 1948-57; account exec. Campbell-Mithun, Inc., Mpls., 1957-63, v.p., gen. mgr. Denver office, 1963-69, pres., Mpls., 1970-72, chmn. bd., 1972, chief exec. officer, 1975—. Mem. Minn. Advt. Rev. Bd. Sect. chmn. maj. firms div. United Way, 1973-74. Bd. dirs. Better Bus. Bur.; mem. adv. council U. Minn. Sch. Journalism. Served to 1st lt. USAAF, World War II; ETO. Mem. Advt. Club Minn., N.W. Advt. Golfers Assn. Clubs: Minneapolis; Tower (bd. govs.); Interlachen Country; Northwest Tennis. Home: 4 Merilane St Edina MN 55436 Office: Northstar Center Minneapolis MN 55402*

BLUTSTEIN, HARVEY M., ins. co. exec.; b. N.Y.C., June 17, 1927; s. Charles and Ethel (Zive) B.; B.S., N.Y. U., 1950; postgrad. Am. Coll., 1960; Exec. Devel. Program, Dartmouth Coll. Grad. Sch. Bus., 1979; m. Fanny Morgenstern, Nov. 26, 1956; children—Jeffrey Alan, Marcy Joy. Agt., Conn. Mut. Life, N.Y.C., 1954—, agy. supr., 1957-63, asst. gen. agt., 1963-68, gen. agt., 1968-80, agt. in pvt. practice, 1980—. Asst. dep. camp chief Boy Scouts Am., 1967-69. Served with U.S. Army, 1945-47; ETO. Recipient Nat. Mgmt. award, 1973-80; C.L.U. Mem. N.E. Mgmt. Forum (pres. 1978-79), Nat. Assn. Life Underwriters (dir. 1975-77), N.Y. Estate Planning Council, N.Y. Life Mgrs. Assn. (pres. 1975-76), Am. Soc. C.L.U.'s, Internat. Platform Assn. Jewish. Home: 66 Wykagyl Terr New Rochelle NY 10804 Office: 551 Fifth Ave New York NY 10176

BLYSTONE, FRANK LYNN, business exec.; b. La Habra, Calif., Aug. 28, 1935; s. Frank Edgar and Reta Lee (Taylor) B.; m. Patricia Louise Baker, Mar. 21, 1964; children—Jon Franklin, Ryan Taylor. Exec., YMCA of Kern County, Calif., 1963-70; owner Blystone Enterprises, Bakersfield, Calif., 1970-74; asst. to project mgr. Banister Pipelines, Alaska, Inc., 1974-76; mgr. spl. projects and corporate devel. Banister Pipelines Am., 1977-78, mgr. pub. and govt. relations, 1978-79; pres., chief exec. officer, dir. Petro Aviation Corp., Front Range Bldg. Systems, Inc.; pres. Bandera Land Co., Inc., Cherry Creek Venture Group, Denver; pres., chief exec. officer Merit Leasing Corp. of Colo.; dir. Tri Valley Oil & Gas Co., Aurora Internat., Inc. Served with U.S. Army, 1958-60, 61-62. Democrat. Club: Petroleum (Bakersfield). Home: 8320 E Hinsdale Ave Englewood CO 80112 Office: Suite 516 Colo Club Bldg 4155 E Jewell Ave Denver CO 80222

BOALT, JAMES ANTHONY, real estate co. exec.; b. Mpls., Mar. 2, 1928; s. Eben Lamberton and Bernice W. (Sweatt) B.; B.A., Yale U., 1950; M.B.A., Columbia U., 1962; m. Maria Antonia Rousseau, Mar. 16, 1974; children—Lisa L., Adam R., Amanda S., Christian A. Vice pres. Nichols Co., Inc., N.Y.C. and Detroit, 1962-68, Inverness Counsel, Inc., N.Y.C. and Palm Beach, Fla., 1970-77; pvt. investor, 1968-70; pres. Boalt Properties, Inc., Palm Beach, 1977—. Officer, bd. dirs. Palm Beach Civic Assn.; active Palm Beach chpt. Am. Cancer Soc.; charter mem. Republican Senatorial Inner Circle. Mem. Nat. Assn. Realtors, Fla. Assn. Realtors (dir. 1978-79), Palm Beach Bd. Realtors (dir. 1978-79), North Palm Beach Bd. Realtors, Palm Beach Brokers Assn. Clubs: Everglades (former gov.), Bath and Tennis, Seminole (gov.) (Palm Beach); Maidstone (former gov.) (East Hampton, N.Y.); Brook (gov.) (N.Y.C.); White's (London). Office: 400 Royal Palm Way Palm Beach FL 33480

BOAM, GARY CARL, mcpl. ofcl.; b. Scranton, Pa., Dec. 14, 1945; s. Carl and Dorothy Emily (Schild) B.; B.S. in Polit. Sci., Scranton U., 1967; m. Jean Marie Newton, June 14, 1969; children—Christopher Paul, Jeffrey Allan. Dir. residence young adult services YMCA, Scranton, 1967-68; dir. devel. Scranton Redevel. Authority, 1968-73; devel. adminstr., Wilkes-Barre (Pa.) Redevel. Authority, 1973-80; mgr. corp. real estate Jewelcor Corp., Inc., and Synfuel Energy Corp., 1980—; exec. dir. Downtown Wilkes-Barre Corp.; exec. dir. Wilkes-Barre II Corp.; lectr. King's Coll., U. Scranton. Chmn. Festival 500 Assn., 1975—. Served with USNR, 1962-68. Decorated Meritorious Service Medal. Mem. Nat. Assn. Rev. Appraisers (sr.), Dandy Lion Little League. Republican. Methodist. Home: 111 Terrace Dr RD 2 Moscow PA 18444 Office: 72 N Franklin St Wilkes-Barre PA 18773

BOAND, CHARLES W., lawyer; b. Bates County, Mo., Aug. 19, 1908; s. Albert and Edith Nadine (Pipes) B.; A.A., Jr. Coll. Kansas City; J.D. summa cum laude, U. Mo.-Kansas City; M.B.A., LL.B. cum laude, U. Chgo.; m. Phoebe Bard, Aug. 2, 1980; children—Bard, Barbara. Admitted to Mo. bar, 1931, D.C. bar, 1936, Ill. bar, 1937, U.S. Supreme Ct. bar, 1935, U.S. Circuit Ct. Appeals bars; asso. firm Moore & Fitch, St. Louis, 1933; atty. Gen. Counsel's Office, U.S. Treasury Dept., 1933-36; asso. Wilson & McIlvaine, 1937-42, partner, 1945—, chmn. exec. com., 1975—. Mem. council Grad. Sch. Bus., U. Chgo., 1961-68; mem. citizens bd. U. Chgo.; trustee Muskingum Coll., 1965-80. Served as officer USNR, 1942-45; lt. comdr. Res. (ret.). Mem. Am. (litigation Sect., nat. conf. lawyers and C.P.A.'s 1976—), Ill. (chmn. exec. com. corp. securities law sect. 1954-56), Chgo. (chmn. com. corp. law 1963-64), Fed., Seventh Circuit bar assns., U. Chgo. Alumni Assn. (pres. 1975-80, alumni cabinet 1964-70, 72-80, v.p. 1973-74), U. Chgo. Law Sch. Alumni Assn. (pres. 1968-70, dir. 1950-72), Order of Coif, Beta Gamma Sigma, Sigma Chi, Phi Alpha Delta. Presbyterian (stated clk. 1962-65). Clubs: Chgo., Mid-Am., Met., Law, Legal, Execs. (Chgo.); Barrington Hills (Ill.) Country (dir. 1947-55); Los Caballeros Golf (Ariz.); Nat. Lawyers (Washington). Editor: Case Notes, U. Chgo. Law Rev., 1932-33. Home: 250 W County Line Rd PO Box 567 Barrington Hills IL 60010 Office: 135 S LaSalle St Chicago IL 60603

BOARDMAN, ROBERT G., savings and loan co. exec.; b. Hereford, Tex., Apr. 9, 1934; s. Lester C. and Lorene M. (Talent) B.; student Inst. Financial Edn., U. New Mex., 1957-62; m. Mary L. Apr. 11, 1970. With First Nat. Bank of Albuquerque, 1949-53; with Bank of New Mex., Albuquerque, 1957-62, v.p. ops. and personnel, to 1962; field examiner Fed. Home Loan Bank of Little Rock, 1962-67; controller Mut. Bldg. and Loan Assn., Las Cruces, New Mex., 1967-69; pres. S.W. Savings & Loan Co., Santa Fe, New Mex., 1970-75; organizer Union Fidelity Savings & Loan Assn., El Dorado, Ark., 1975—, now pres., also dir. Bd. dirs. ARC, Las Cruces, 1968. Served with USAF, 1953-57. Mem. Inst. Financial Edn. (state dir. and instr. 1974-75), U.S., Ark. (ednl. com.) savs. and loan leagues, Nat. Assn. Rev. Appraisers, El Dorado C. of C. (dir. 1978—). Club: Civitan (sec.-treas. 1975). Home: 2215 W Oak St El Dorado AR 71730 Office: 125 W 5th St El Dorado AR 71730

BOBECZKO, MICHAEL STEVEN, mfg. co. exec.; b. Cleve., Aug. 6, 1946; s. Steve and Pauline Ellen (Kawalec) B.; B.S. in M.E., Purdue U., 1968; M.S., Carnegie-Mellon U., 1970; m. Ruth Ann Mugridge, Sept. 2, 1972; 1 dau., Lisa Ruth. Research engr. Westinghouse Electric Research & Devel., Pitts., 1968-70; sr. acoustical cons. Bolt Beranek & Newman, San Francisco, 1970-73; corp. noise control engr. Kaiser Aluminum & Chem. Corp., Oakland, Calif., 1973—; chmn. Aluminum Assn. Noise Control Com., Washington, 1977-79; engring. noise control cons. and expert witness to indsl. mfrs., equip. suppliers. Mem. Calif. Mfrs. Assn., Acoustical Soc. Am., ASME, Audio Engring. Soc., Inst. Noise Control Engrs. (dir. 1981—), Pi Tau Sigma, Tau Beta Pi, Pi Kappa Alpha. Contbr. articles to profl. jours.; patentee in field. Home: 2838 Jennifer Dr Castro Valley CA 94546 Office: 300 Lakeside Dr Oakland CA 94643

BOBERSKI, WILLIAM GEORGE, chemist; b. Hammond, Ind., Nov. 25, 1947; s. John and Arvilla Honnie (Guse) B.; B.S. in Chemistry, Purdue U., 1970; M.S., Northwestern U., 1971, Ph.D., 1974; m. Roberta Lavaughan West, Mar. 21, 1970. Sr. research chemist Coatings and Resins div. PPG Industries, Allison Park, Pa., 1974-78, research asso., 1978—. Mem. Am. Chem. Soc., N.Y. Acad. Scis., Sigma Xi, Phi Lambda Upsilon. Contbr. articles to chem. publs.; patentee in field. Office: PO Box 9 Allison Park PA 15101

BOBKER, HOWARD, bearings co. exec.; b. Newark, Feb. 14, 1925; s. Charles and Goldie (Harrison) B.; grad. high sch.; m. Edna Feldman, Jan. 19, 1946; children—Susan, Golda. With Bobker Bearings Co., Carlstadt, N.J., 1946—, partner, owner, pres., 1955—. Served with U.S. Army, 1943-45. Decorated Bronze Star. Mem. Bearing Specialist Assn. (past pres.), Power Transmission Distbr. Assn. Clubs: Crestmont Country, Millburn B'nai B'rith (past pres.). Home: 267 Dale Dr Short Hills NJ 07078 Office: 339 14th St Carlstadt NJ 07072

BOBO, DONALD ARTHUR, labor union ofcl.; b. Lawrence, Kans., Sept. 18, 1918; s. Drexel Morgan and Hazel Bobo; student public schs., Galveston, Tex.; m. Doris Johanna Evers, 1940; 1 son, Donald Arthur. With Order R.R. Telegraphers, 1952-62, gen. sec.-treas. 1959-60, gen. chmn. Santa Fe System, Div. 61, 1960-62; 1st v.p. Order R.R. Telegraphers, 1962-71; internat. v.p., asst. internat. sec.-treas. Brotherhood Ry. Airline Clks., Rockville, Md., 1972-75, pres. div. transp.-communications employees, 1972-75, internat. sec.-treas., 1975—. served to Sgt. U.S. Army, 1944-46. Named Boxing Middleweight Champion, Tex. Amateur Athletic Fedn., 1944, Army Middleweight Champion, U.S. Army, 1946. Mem. YMCA. Democrat. Club: Am. Legion. Office: 3 Research Pl Rockville MD 20850

BOBO, JACK EDWARD, ins. assn. exec.; b. Laurens, S.C., June 24, 1924; s. Floyd Lynn and Miriam Dorthea (Whyte) B.; m. Gladys Stromsholt, June 25, 1945; 1 son, Glen. Salesman, Stewart Warner Co., Phoenix, 1956; with N.Y. Life Ins. Co., Phoenix, 1956-78; partner Rasmussen/Bobo & Co., Phoenix; mem. Nat. Assn. Life Underwriters, past chmn. com. fed. law and legis., compensation com., public relations com., sec., 1975-76, pres. elect, 1976-77, pres., 1977-78, exec. v.p. 1979—, also trustee. Served as pilot AC, U.S. Army. Past pres. Phoenix Better Bus. Bur., Washington (Ariz.) Sch. Dist.; chmn. ins. div. Phoenix United Fund. Mem. Million Dollar Round Table. Home: 1101 S Arlington Ridge Rd Apt 416 Arlington VA 22202 Office: 1922 F St NW Washington DC 20006

BOCK, DONALD LEE, consumer electronics co. exec.; b. Davenport, Iowa, Aug. 13, 1942; s. Wilfred Edward and Louise Bock; B.A. in Acctg. and Econs., St. Ambrose Coll., Davenport, 1964; m. Berlyn Sue Miller, Apr. 1, 1967; children—David Edward, Rebecca Lyn. Public acct. Arthur Young & Co., Chgo., 1964-67; dir. fin. planning Allied Radio Corp., Chgo., 1967-70; asst. to fin. v.p. Tandy Corp., Ft. Worth, 1970-79, asst. treas., 1979—. Home: 3404 Acorn Run Fort Worth TX 76109 Office: 1800 One Tandy Center Fort Worth TX 76102

BOCK, LILLIAN LOUISE, plating co. exec.; b. Elkhart, Ind., Apr. 29; d. Charles Edward and Matie Ella (Ley) Rankin; student public schs.; m. George A. Bock, Jr., Nov. 28, 1935 (dec. May 1974). Various office and clerical positions, 1932; owner beauty shop, Elkart, 1930—; owner, pres. Ideal Plating Corp., Elkhart, 1964—. Lutheran. Clubs: Elkhart Zonta (dir.), Elks, Ladies Moose. Home: 1501 E Jackson Blvd Elkhart IN 46514 Office: 1913 S 14th St Elkhart IN 46515

BOCK, RICHARD FREDERICK, brokerage co. exec.; b. S.I., N.Y., Oct. 16, 1946; s. Edward Lawrence and Hilda Bertha (Herold) B.; B.A. in Polit. Sci., L.I. U., 1973; m. Kristin Heltne, May 24, 1980. Advt. exec. S.I. Advance, 1973-75; registered rep. Merrill Lynch, Piece, Fenner & Smith, N.Y.C., 1975-77, Bache, Halsey, Stuart, Shields, N.Y.C., 1977-78, Kidder, Peabody & Co., Inc., N.Y.C., 1978-79; v.p. West Coast, Bernard Herold & Co., N.Y.C., 1979—. Mem. Richmond County (N.Y.) Republican Exec. and County cons., 1975-77, N.Y. Rep. State Com., 1976-78; del. N.Y. Rep. Nominating Conv., 1978. Served with U.S. Army, 1967-70. Lutheran. Club: Grand Case Beach (St. Martin, F.W.I.) (dir.). Home: 1649 Appian Way Santa Monica CA 90401 Office: 450 Park Ave New York NY 10022

BOCKIAN, JAMES BERNARD, computer systems exec.; b. Jersey City, Sept. 16, 1936; s. Abraham and Evelyn (Skner) B.; B.A., Columbia, 1953; M.Pub. Adminstrn., U. Mich., 1955; M.A., Yale, 1957. Vice-consul, 3d. sec. Embassy, U.S. Dept. State, Washington and abroad, 1957-61; sr. systems analyst J.C. Penney Co., N.Y.C., 1961-67; mgr. systems services, head dept. systems projects adminstrn. McDonnell Douglas Automation Co., East Orange, N.J., 1967-76; prin. James B. Bockian & Assos., Morristown, N.J., 1976—; dir. info. systems Comml. Computer Systems, Inc., Norwalk, Conn., 1976-80; lectr. in field. Grad. fellow Yale, 1957. Mem. Internat. Assn. Cybernetics, Assn. Computing Machinery, Data Processing Mgmt. Assn., Am. Mgmt. Assn., Systems and Procedures Assn. Democrat. Jewish. Clubs: Yale (N.Y.); Royal Danish Yacht (Copenhagen). Author: Management Manual for Systems Development Projects; Project Management for Systems Development, 1979; AT&T User Guide to Information Systems Development, 1980. Contbr. treatises and articles to profl. publs. Home: 26 Farmhouse Ln Morristown NJ 07960 Office: Thomas Cook Ltd 380 Madison Ave New York NY 10017

BOCKSERMAN, ROBERT JULIAN, mfg. co. exec.; b. St. Louis, Dec. 20, 1929; s. Max Louis and Bertha Anna (Kremen) B.; B.S., U. Mo., 1952, M.S., 1955; m. Clarice Kreisman, June 9, 1958; children—Michael, Joyce, Carol. Chemist, Sealtest Corp., Peoria, Ill., 1955-56; prodn. mgr. Allan Drug Co., St. Louis, 1957-58; research chemist Monsanto Co., St. Louis, 1958-67, purchasing agt., East St. Louis, Ill., 1968; pres. Pharma-Tech Industries, Inc., Union, Mo., 1969—; v.p., dir. Sentinel Pharmacal Corp. Commr., Boy Scouts Am.; bd. dirs. Dielman Sch., Olivette, Mo., 1968-73; mem. adv. com. Sch. Engring. Mgmt., Coll. Engring., U. Mo., Rolla. Served with U.S. Army, 1952-54; Korea. Mem. Am. Chem. Soc., Packaging Inst., AAAS, Indsl. Pharmacists Assn. St. Louis, St. Louis Pharmacists Assn., Am. Technion Soc., Engrs. Club St. Louis, Soc. Cosmetic Chemists, Nat. Ethical Pharm. Assn., Inst. Food Technologists, Soc. Packaging Engrs., Regional Commerce and Growth Assn., Union (Mo.) C. of C., Sigma Xi, Sigma Alpha Mu, Phi Delta Chi. Club: Masons. Home: 54 Morwood Ln Creve Coeur MO 63141 Office: 521 Shilo Dr Union MO 63084

BOCZER, WILLIAM R., printer; b. Norwalk, Conn., Jan. 1, 1942; s. Paul and Olga B.; student Bullard Haven Tech. Sch., Bridgeport, Conn.; m. Patricia Ann Brown, Sept. 4, 1965; children—Karyn E., Amy C. With T.O. Toole & Son, then production mgr. Avery Hann & Co.; now owner, pres. Tech. Reproductions Inc., Norwalk. Served with USN, 1959-65; Cuba, Vietnam. Recipient 4 nat. awards Am. Show Car Assn. Mem. Norwalk C. of C. Club: South Norwalk Boat. Home: 9 Fireside Ct Norwalk CT 06850 Office: 326A Main Ave Norwalk CT 06851

BODEK, GORDON S., mfg. exec.; b. Phila., Dec. 23, 1920; s. Harry and Bessie (Miller) B.; B.A., U. Pa., 1942; m. Muriel Betty Pfaelzer, May 28, 1950; children—Marnie C., Hanley P., Janna M. Gen. sales mgr. Pfaelzer Bros., Chgo., 1953-57; v.p., dir. The Bobrick Corp., North Hollywood, Calif., 1957—; pres., dir. Bobrick Washroom Equipment, Inc., North Hollywood, 1969—; pres., dir. Bobrick Washroom Equipment of Can. Ltd.; v.p., dir. Franke-Bobrick AG, Switzerland; v.p., dir. Ednl. Inquiry, Inc.; dir. Theodor Mfg. Co. Bd. dirs., v.p. Natural History Mus. Alliance; trustee U. Pa. Served to lt. USNR, 1942-46. Decorated Air medal, Brit. citation. Mem. Internat. San. Supply Assn. (past pres., dir.). Clubs: U. Pa. (Los Angeles, past pres.); Univ. (Los Angeles); Riviera Tennis, Mask and Wig. Home: 148 S Bristol Ave Los Angeles CA 90049 Office: 11611 Hart St North Hollywood CA 91605

BODENHEIMER, VERNON BROADUS, chem. engr.; b. High Point, N.C., Dec. 20, 1922; s. David Carl and Roxie (Allen) B.; student U. N.C., 1939-41; B.S. in Chem. Engring., N.C. State Coll., 1948; m. Dorothy Sheffield, June 18, 1948; children—Vernon Broadus, Janice, David, Jill, Julie. Chem. engr. Champion Paper & Fibre Co., Canton, N.C., 1948-51; asst. pulp supt. Riegel Carolina Corp., Acme, N.C., 1951-52; So. mgr. Stebbins Engring. & Mfg. Co., Pensacola, Fla., 1952-56; pulp mill supt. Continental Can Co., Augusta, Ga., 1956-59, tech. dir., 1959-66; mgr. pulp and paper engring. Eastern Engring. Co., 1966-68; v.p. operation Prince Albert Pulp Co. Ltd. (Sask., Can.), 1968-72; v.p. Paper Industry Engrs., Inc., Atlanta, Ga., 1972-74; cons. to paper industry, 1974-78; sr. pulp engr. Ga. Pacific Corp., Atlanta, 1978—. Served to 1st lt. USAAF, 1942-45. Decorated Air medals; Distinguished Flying Cross (Eng.). Mem. T.A.P.P.I., Am. Inst. Chem. Engrs., Tau Beta Pi, Phi Kappa Phi. Baptist. Mason, Kiwanian. Clubs: Green Meadows Country, Prince Albert Curling and Golf. Home: 4929 Cambridge Dr Dunwoody GA 30338

BODIN, DAVID JOSEPH, mfg. co. exec.; b. Hamden, Conn., Aug. 7, 1933; s. Gustaf Henry and Jessie Martha (Butler) B.; B.S., Springfield Coll., 1955; postgrad. Clark U., 1957, Westfield State Coll., 1972-73, U. Mass., 1972; m. Jane Adeline Hudson, July 13, 1957; children—Kristi Ann, David Joseph, Richard Hudson. Instr., Norton Co., Worcester, Mass., 1959-63, field sale supr., 1963-65, head instr., 1965-68, editor pub. relations, 1968-70; asst. plant mgr. Fontaine Modular Structures, Northampton, Mass., 1970-73; field engr. Standard Mfg. Co., West Springfield, Mass., 1973-75, sales mgr., 1975-77, v.p., 1977—. Served with USNR, 1955-59. Mem. Photo Mktg. Assn., Assn. Photofinishing Labs. Contbr. to Ency. Brittanica; editor Grits & Grinds Mag., 1968-70. Home: 35 Maplewood Circle Amherst MA 01002 Office: 56 Doty Circle West Springfield MA 01089

BODINE, ALBERT GEORGE, physicist; b. Pitts., Mar. 17, 1914; s. Albert George and Anna (Minnick) B.; student U. Calif., 1937, Calif. Inst. Tech., 1934; m. Anna Thomsen, Apr. 30, 1939 (dec.); children—Linda Anne, Albert Jonathan. Research engr. Am. Liquid Gas Co., Los Angeles, 1938-39, chief engr., 1939-41; founder, owner, pres. Bodine Soundrive Co., 1942—; founder, dir. Soundrive Engine Co., 1946—, Soundrill Corp., 1949—, Soundrive Pump Co., 1950—, Soundrive Process Co., 1952—; tchr. extension div. U. Calif., 1937-40. Mem. patent adv. com. U.S. Patent Office. Bd. govs. Chapman Coll., Orange, Calif.; asso. Calif. Inst. Tech. Registered profl. mech., elec. engr., Calif. Fellow Acoustical Soc. Am. (mem. com. sonics and ultrasonics engring.); mem. Am. Soc. M.E., Soc. Automotive Engrs., Calif. Tech. Alumni Assn. Presbyn. Home: 13180 Mulholland Dr Beverly Hills CA 90210 Office: 7877 Woodley Ave Van Nuys CA 91406

BODINE, JAMES FORNEY, former state ofcl.; b. Villanova, Pa., June 16, 1921; s. William Warden and Angela (Forney) B.; grad. St. Paul's Sch., Concord, N.H., 1940; B.A., Yale, 1944; M.B.A., Harvard, 1948; m. Jean G. Guthrie, June 25, 1949; children—Jane G., Margaret F., Murray G., Tracy W. With First Pa. Bank (now First Pa. Corp.), Phila., 1948-78, v.p., 1958-63, sr. v.p., 1963-65, exec. v.p., 1965-68, sr. exec. v.p., dir., 1968-72, pres., 1972-78; sec. of commerce Commonwealth of Pa., 1979-80; mng. partner Greater Phila. Partnership, 1980—. Home: 401 Cypress St Philadelphia PA 19106 Office: 900 Western Savs Bldg Philadelphia PA 19107

BODINI, DANIELE DAMASO, real estate corp. exec.; b. Erba, Italy, Dec. 20, 1945; came to U.S., 1971; s. Franco and Cesarea (Martano) B.; M.Arch., U. Rome, 1970, M.Engring., 1968; M.B.A., Columbia U., 1972; m. Toni Allen Kramer, June 9, 1979. Asst. prof. Sch. Engring., U. Rome, 1968-70; trainee Blyth, Eastman Dillon, N.Y.C., 1973, v.p. realty, 1975-78; U.S.A. mgr. SGI, N.Y.C., 1974; exec. v.p., prin. Am. Continental Properties Inc., N.Y.C., 1978—. Served to lt. Italian Air Force, 1969-70. Lic. real estate broker, N.Y.; lic. architect, engr., Italy. Club: Racquet and Tennis (N.Y.C.). Home: 800 Fifth Ave New York NY 10021 Office: Am Continental Properties Inc 630 Fifth Ave New York NY 10111

BODNER, EMANUEL, indsl. scrap metals recycling co. exec.; b. Houston, July 25, 1947; s. Eugene and Eve (Pryzant) B.; B.B.A., U. Tex., Austin, 1969. Vice pres. Bodner Metal & Iron Corp., Houston, 1969—. Bd. dirs. Cy-Champ Utility Dist., 1978-79; mem. Tex. Legis. Council, Citizens Adv. Commn. Study of Vocat. Rehab., 1970-72; mem. removal of archtl. barriers com. Tex. Rehab. Assn., 1971; mem. handicapped access program task force Tex. Dept. Human Resources, 1978-79; mem. community relations agys. sub-budget com. Jewish Fedn. Greater Houston, 1978; mem. Israel Bond Dinner Com., Houston, 1978. Mem. Inst. Scrap Iron and Steel (nat. public relations com., nat. fgn. trade com.; dir. Gulf Coast chpt. 1977-80, chmn. chpt. public relations com. 1978-79, editor Gulf Coast Reporter 1978—), Ex-Students Assn. U. Tex., Alpha Epsilon Pi (life). Jewish. Clubs: Racquetball-Handball of Houston, Shriners, Masons (32 deg.). Office: 3660 Schalker Dr Houston TX 77026

BODONY, STEPHEN GERALD, mfg. co. exec.; b. Balt., Dec. 11, 1947; s. Stephen George and Martha Faye (Sharp) B.; B.S. in Bus. Adminstrn., Wright State U., 1970; m. Mary Margaret Bowman, Aug. 3, 1974; 1 son, Daniel Joseph. Office mgr. F.D. Borkholder & Co., Inc., Nappanee, Ind., 1970-73; cons. accountant Nappanee, 1972-74; controller Franklin Coach Co., Nappanee, 1973-74; controller, mem. mgmt. team, v.p. Newmar Industries, Inc., Nappanee, 1974-78; pres. MBC Corp., Nappanee, 1977-79; controller, asst. treas. Hanson Silo Co., Lake Lillian, Minn., 1980—; dir. Newmar Industries, Inc. Sec.-treas., bd. dirs. Kingdom Evang. Ch., New Paris, Ind., 1971-79; co. rep. Elkhart County United Fund Campaign, 1975—. Served with USMC, 1969. Home: 605 11th Ave SE Willmar MN 56201

BOE, ARCHIE R., ins. co. exec.; b. Estherville, Iowa, Feb. 27, 1921; s. Berge B. and Regina B. (Nelson) B.; B.C.S., Drake U., 1941, LL.B., 1976; M.B.A., U. Chgo., 1951; m. Elaine B. Jansson, May 11, 1973. With Allstate Ins. Co., 1941—, v.p., sec., 1960-66, pres., 1966-68, vice chmn., 1968-72; v.p., sec. Allstate Enterprises, Inc., 1960-66, pres., 1966-68, vice chmn., 1968-72, chmn., chief exec. officer Allstate Ins. and Allstate Enterprises, 1972—; dir. Sears, Roebuck & Co., Seraco Group, NICOR Inc., No. Ill. Gas. Co. Pres., Lyric Opera Chgo., 1980, Protestant Found. Greater Chgo., 1980. Served with USN, 1942-45. Mem. Property-Casualty Ins. Co., Health Ins. Assn. Am., Newcomen Soc. N.Am. Clubs: Chicago, Commercial, Executives, Economic, Mid-America (Chgo.); Metropolitan, Tavern, Sunset Ridge Country, Carlton. Home: Chicago IL Office: Allstate Plaza Northbrook IL 60062

BOECKMANN, MARLIN JAMES, mfg. exec.; b. St. Cloud, Minn., Apr. 13, 1945; s. Alfred Henry and Marvell Viola Boeckmann; B.S., St. John's U., 1969; M.A., U. Minn., 1974. Comml. auditor Arthur Andersen & Co., Mpls., 1968-74; cost containment mgr. Robert G. Engelhart & Co., Mpls., 1974-76; faculty St. John's U., Collegeville, Minn., 1976—, budget dir., 1977-79; pres. Ronby Co., Watkins, Minn., 1977—; ind. bus. cons. Served with U.S. Army, 1970-72. Mem. Minn. Soc. C.P.A.'s (mem. continuing edn. com. 1979-80). Home: 4065 82d Ave N Brooklyn Park MN 55443 Office: Econs and Business Adminstrn Dept St John's U Collegeville MN 56321

BOEHRINGER, LUDWIG CHARLES, JR., photog. mfg. co. exec.; b. Jersey City, Nov. 6, 1924; s. Ludwig Charles and Mabel Frances (Winans) B.; student (Naval scholar) Dartmouth Coll., 1943-44; B.S. in Mech. Engring., B.A. in Econs. (Naval scholar), U. Rochester, 1947. Indsl. engr. Indsl. Engring. div. Eastman Kodak Co., Rochester, N.Y., 1947-52, sr. indsl. engr., 1952-59, indsl. engring. asso., 1959-65, indsl. engring. supr., 1965-75, asst. dir. Indsl. Engring. div., 1975-76, asst. dir. Mgmt. Services div., 1976—. Served with USNR, 1943-46. Mem. Am. Inst. Indsl. Engrs., Rochester Engring. Soc., Rochester Indsl. Mgmt. Council, Kodak Mgmt. Club. Republican. Presbyterian. Club: Kodak Pioneers. Home: 58 Sunrise Crescent Rochester NY 14622 Office: Eastman Kodak Co Kodak Park Works 1669 Lake Ave Rochester NY 14650

BOEKENHEIDE, RUSSELL WILLIAM, paper co. exec.; b. St. Louis, Dec. 6, 1930; s. William George and Mildred (Hann) B.; B.A., Blackburn Coll., 1952; m. Barbro Martinson, June 18, 1966; children—Susan, Mark, Louise. Order and traffic mgr. Proctor and Gamble Distbn. Co., St. Louis, 1954-57; asst. personnel mgr. Knapp Monarch Co., St. Louis, 1957-59; plant personnel mgr. Vickers div. Sperry Rand Corp., Joplin, Mo., 1959-65; corporate dir. personnel Kendall Co., Boston, 1965-74; v.p. personnel Nestle Co., White Plains, N.Y., 1974-76; v.p. indsl. relations Union Camp Corp., Wayne, N.J., 1976—. Served with U.S. Army, 1952-54. Mem. Am. Soc. Personnel Adminstrs., Am. Paper Inst. (employee relations com.), U.S. C. of C. (labor relations com.). Congregationalist. Home: 352 Algonquin Rd Franklin Lakes NJ 07417 Office: Union Camp Corp 1600 Valley Rd Wayne NJ 07470

BOEMIO, VINCENT ANTHONY, oil co. exec.; b. Bklyn., May 29, 1948; s. Marco Louis and Rose (DeChiaro) B.; B.S. in Indsl. Distbn., Clarkson Coll. Tech., 1970; M.B.A. in Mktg., N.Y. U., 1972; m. Catherine Iannizzotto, Oct. 6, 1973; 1 son, David Vincent. Sr. mktg. rep. Exxon Internat., N.Y.C., 1972-75; asst. v.p. Philipp Bros. Minerals & Chems. Co., N.Y.C., 1976-77, v.p., 1977-78, group v.p., 1979; sr. v.p. Houston Oil & Refining Co., 1979-80, pres., 1980—. Active Head Start Program, Potsdam, N.Y., 1969-70; mem. U.S. Senatorial Adv. Bd., 1980—. Recipient AAUP award, 1970. Mem. Am. Petroleum Inst., Nat. Petroleum Refiners Assn., Oil Trades Assn. Roman Catholic. Clubs: Clarkson Alumni, Republican, Police Boys. Office: 11221 Katy Freeway Houston TX 77024

BOESAART, RONALD, controller; b. Amsterdam, Netherlands, Aug. 20, 1938; came to U.S., 1978; s. Nicolaas J.A. and Trijntje B.; M.B.A., S.P.D. in Acctg., U. Utrecht/Zwolle, 1973; m. Annette Braaksma, Mar. 13, 1967; children—Aletta, Marta. Adminstrv. mgr. automotive sect. Gulf Oil Nederland, Amsterdam, 1961-64; chief acct. Mecon, Teheran, Iran, 1964-71; mgr. budgets and planning Tyl, Zwolle, Netherlands, 1971-74; fin. adv., cons. H.V.A., Ghana and Tanzania, 1974-78; v.p., controller Euryza Foods, Inc., Orange, Tex., 1978—. Served with Dutch Army, 1957-61. Mem. Am. Mgmt. Assn., Photog. Soc. Am. Home: 2214 Lakeville Dr Kingwood TX 77339 Office: 1301 Childers Rd Orange TX 77630

BOESCHENSTEIN, WILLIAM WADE, glass products mfg. co. exec.; b. Chgo., Sept. 7, 1925; s. Harold and Elizabeth (Wade) B.; B.S., Yale, 1950; m. Josephine H. Moll, Nov. 28, 1953; children—William, Michael, Peter, Stephen. With Owens-Corning Fiberglas Corp., 1950—, br. mgr., Detroit, 1955-59, v.p. central region, 1959-61, v.p. sales br. ops., Toledo, 1961-63, v.p. mktg., 1963-67, exec. v.p., 1967-71, pres., 1971—, chief exec. officer, 1972—, also dir.; dir. Am. Electric Power Co., N.Y.C., FMC Corp., Chgo., Hanna Mining Co., Cleve. Trustee Phillips Acad., Andover, Mass. Clubs: Links, Econ., Univ. (N.Y.C.); Econ. (Detroit); Toledo, Inverness (Toledo); Belmont Country (Perrysburg, Ohio); Elec. Mfrs.; Country of Fla. (Delray Beach); Augusta (Ga.) Nat. Home: 3 Locust St Perrysburg OH 43551 Office: Fiberglas Tower Toledo OH 43659

BOESEL, JOHN PHILIP, JR., investment banker; b. Columbus, Ohio, May 14, 1932; s. John Philip and Marion (Andersen) B.; B.A., U. Wis., 1957; M.A., Mich. State U., 1961; m. Joan Mae Homme, June 11, 1955; children—John Philip III, Robert Mandt, Julie Ann. Various mgmt. positions to dir. materials Whirlpool Corp., St. Joseph, Mich., 1957-65; dir. materials Fisher Gov. Co., Marshalltown, Iowa, 1965-67; with R.G. Dickinson & Co., Des Moines, 1967—, pres., 1971—, also dir.; dir. Dealers Lumber Co. Adviser, Jr. Achievement, 1958-59; indsl. sect. capt. United Fund, 1963. Bd. dirs. Charles M. Boesel Found. Served with USAF, 1950-54. Mem. Securities Industry Assn. (mem. regional firms com., govt. relations com.), Nat. Assn. Securities Dealers (past chmn. dist. 8 com.), Young Pres.'s Orgn. (past chmn. Iowa chpt.). Republican. Mason. Home: 3008 Patricia Dr Des Moines IA 50322 Office: 910 Grand Ave Des Moines IA 50309

BOESEL, MILTON CHARLES, JR., business exec., lawyer; b. Toledo, July 12, 1928; s. Milton C. and Florence (Fitzgerald) B.; B.A., Yale, 1950; LL.B., Harvard, 1953; m. Lucy Laughlin Mather, Mar. 25, 1961; children—Elizabeth Parks, Charles Mather, Andrew Fitzgerald. Admitted to Ohio bar, 1953, Mich. bar, 1953; counsel Ritter Boesel, Robinson & Marsh (and predecessor firm), Toledo, 1956—; pres. Michabo, Inc., 1977—; dir. 1st Nat. Bank Toledo. Served to lt. USNR, 1953-56. Episcopalian. Mason. Clubs: Toledo, Toledo Country. Home: 2268 Innisbrook Rd Toledo OH 43606 Office: 240 Huron St Toledo OH 43604

BOESKY, IVAN FREDERICK, securities exec.; b. Detroit, Mar. 6, 1937; s. William H. and Helen (Silverberg) B.; J.D., Detroit Coll. Law, 1964; m. Seema Silberstein, Jan. 7, 1962; children—William Lehman, Marianne S., Theodore Emerson, Johnathan Brandeis. Admitted to Mich. bar, 1964; law clk. to judge U.S. Dist. Ct. for Eastern Mich., 1964-65; tax accountant Touce, Ross & Co., Detroit, 1965-66; security analyst L.F. Rothschild, N.Y.C., 1966-67; securities analyst First Manhattan Co., 1968-70; gen. partner Edwards & Hanly, N.Y.C., 1972—; mng. partner Ivan F. Boesky & Co., securities and arbitrage specialists, N.Y.C.; mem. N.Y., Am., Pacific, Phila. stock exchanges, CBOE; adj. prof. fin. Grad. Sch. Bus. Adminstrn., N.Y. U. Mem. Wall St. coms. Fedn. Jewish Philanthropies, United Jewish Appeal; trustee Albert Einstein Coll. Medicine, Trust for Cultural Resources of City N.Y., Hebrew Union Coll., Eagle Hill Sch., Greenwich, Conn., Temple Sholom, Greenwich; adv. mem. Jewish Theol. Sem.; pres. Jewish Theol. Sem. Library Corp. Fellow, Brandeis U. Mem. Am., Mich., Detroit bar assns., Delta Theta Phi. Democrat. Jewish. Clubs: Palm Beach (Fla.) Country; City Athletic (N.Y.C.); Burning Tree Country (Greenwich, Conn.). Office: 77 Water St New York NY 10005

BOETTCHER, ARMIN SCHLICK, banker; b. East Bernard, Tex., Apr. 12, 1941; s. Clem C. and Frances Helene (Schlick) B.; B.B.A., U. Tex., Austin, 1963, J.D., 1967; m. Virginia Nan Barkley, Apr. 13, 1963; children—Lynn Frances, Laura Anne. Various positions personal trust dept. Houston Nat. Bank, 1967-75, sr. v.p., trust officer, head trust dept., 1975—. Mem. Houston Bus. and Estate Planning Council, Houston Estate and Fin. Forum, Tex., Houston bar assns., Houston C. of C., Am. Inst. Banking, Houston Zool. Soc., Sigma Chi, U. Tex. Ex-Students Assn. (life). Methodist. Club: Houston Racquet. Office: 1010 Milam St Houston TX 77002

BOETTCHER, JAROLD WILLIAM, fertilizer co. exec.; b. Beloit, Kans., May 19, 1940; s. Harold J. and Zelma C. (Butcher) B.; B.S., Kans. State U., 1963; M.S. (Whitney scholar), M.I.T., 1966; m. Barbara E. Ball, Dec. 30, 1961; children—Christopher, Melinda, Andrew, Miranda. Security analyst Donaldson, Lufkin & Jenrette, N.Y.C., 1966-68; successively asst. v.p., v.p., dir. research, fund mgr., mgr. equity securities Waddell & Reed, Kansas City, Mo., 1968-79; pres. Boettcher Enterprises, Inc., Beloit, 1979—. Mem. Fin. Analysts Fedn. (cert. fin. analyst), Beloit C. of C. (dir.), Phi Kappa Phi. Clubs: Rotary, Elks, Masons. Home: 521 N Campbell Box 206 Beloit KS 67420 Office: 118 W Court St Beloit KS 67420

BOGAN, MARY FLAIR, stock broker, former actress; b. Providence, July 9, 1948; d. Ralph A.L. and Mary (Dyer) B.; B.A., Vassar Coll., 1969. Actress, Trinity Sq. Repertory Co., R.I., Gretna Playhouse, Pa., Skylight Comic Opera, Milw., Cin. Playhouse, Playmakers' Repertory, Va., also TV commls., 1970-77; account exec. E.F. Hutton & Co., Inc., Providence, 1977—. Soloist, St. Sebastian's Ch., 1979—. Mem. Providence Art Club. Club: Turks Head. Home: 15 Clarendon Ave Providence RI 02906 Office: 2414 Hospital Trust Tower Providence RI 02903

BOGAN, ROBERT FRANCIS, transp. equipment mfg. co. exec.; b. Newark, Dec. 15, 1925; s. James Francis and Kathleen Eleanor (Shannon) B.; B.S. in Civil Engring., Mich. State U., 1950; m. Joyce Quinn, June 9, 1951; children—Aletha, Patrick. With Pullman Standard Co., Chgo., 1951-65, asst. to pres., 1962-65; v.p. purchasing Trailmobile, Chgo., 1965-66, v.p. engring., 1966, v.p. ops., 1966-69; v.p. group Stanray Corp., Chgo., 1969-70; div. pres. Ecodyne Corp., Lenexa, Kan., 1970-74; pres. Am. Trailers, Oklahoma City, 1974-79; v.p., gen. mgr. Dorsey Trailers, Edgerton, Wis., 1979—. Chmn., Arlington Heights (Ill.) Caucus, 1954-55. Served with USAAF, 1944-45. Mem. Kans. Assn. Commerce and Industry (chmn. industry div. 1974), Truck Trailer Mfg. Assn. (chmn. 1977-78). Clubs: Janesville Country. Home: 2710 Dartmouth St Janesville WI 53545 Office: 405 E Fulton St Edgerton WI 53534

BOGAN, THOMAS ROCKWOOD, fin. mgmt. co. exec.; b. Chgo., July 7, 1941; s. Ralph A. L. and Alice (Rockwood) B.; B.S.M.E., M.I.T., 1963; M.B.A., U. Pa., 1965; m. Elizabeth S. Chapin, June 5, 1965; children—Nathaniel R., Andrew A. Cargo systems project engr. TWA, N.Y.C., 1967-69; securities analyst W. E. Hutton & Co., N.Y.C., 1969-73; v.p., securities analyst specializing in electronics and aerospace cos. Alliance Capital Mgmt. Corp., N.Y.C., 1973—. Served to lt. USN, 1965-67. Mem. N.Y. Soc. Securities Analysts, Aerospace Analysts Soc. N.Y. Congregationalist. Mem. panel on semi-condr. cos., panel on aerospace cos. Wall St. Transcript. Office: 140 Broadway New York NY 10005

BOGARDUS, PETER CHARLES, banker; b. Bradford, Pa., Oct. 14, 1937; s. Charles Thomas and Rowena Mary (Iverson) B.; B.S. in Bus. Adminstrn. cum laude, Kent State U., 1963; grad. Grad. Sch. Banking, U. Wis., 1972; m. Susan Mae Kelso, Aug. 17, 1963; children—David, Thomas, James. Examiner, Fed. Res. Bank, Cleve., 1963-65; with Peoples-Mchts. Trust Co., Canton, Ohio, 1965-78, v.p., 1973-78, mgr. comml. lending, 1976-78; fin. analyst H-P Products Inc., Louisville, Ohio, 1978-80; v.p. Pa. Bank & Trust Co., Warren, Pa., 1980—. Served with U.S. Army, 1955-58. Mem. Am. Bankers Assn. (certified comml. lender), Am. Registry Radiologic Technologists. Republican. Methodist. Clubs: Rotary, Masons, Robert Morris Assos. Home: 444 Conewango Ave Warren PA 16365 Office: Penn Bank Bldg Warren PA 16365

BOGARDUS, RAYMOND BRUCE, environ. cons. co. exec.; b. Oak Ridge, Tenn., May 26, 1946; s. Bruce Joseph and Muriel Viola (Palmer) B.; B.S. in Zoology, U. Tenn., 1968, postgrad., 1968-70; m. Diane Kathryn Messer, Aug. 23, 1973; children—Timothy Scott, Shawn Alan. Tech. asst. health physics div. Oak Ridge Nat. Lab., 1970; fisheries biologist WAPORA, Inc., Washington, 1971, mgr. field sta., Peoria, Ill., 1972, dir. midwest ecol. div., Charleston, Ill., 1973, v.p., 1974-79, sr. v.p., dir., 1979—; environ. cons. to electric utilities. Mem. N.Am. Benthological Soc., Am. Fisheries Soc., Am. Standard Testing Materials, Nat. Assn. Environ. Profls. (certified environ. profl.). Home: 11600 Shenorock St Gaithersburg MD 20760 Office: 6900 Wisconsin Ave NW Washington DC 20015

BOGARDUS, WILLIAM BROWER, govt. communications exec.; b. Torrington, Conn., Apr. 7, 1929; s. De Witt Brower and Henrietta Elizabeth (Burn) B.; student pub. schs., Torrington and El Monte, Calif.; m. Iva Irene Sims, Dec. 16, 1951; children—Karen L. Bogardus Thill, Linda L. Bogardus Waltz, Tracy Allyn, Mark W., Dorene E., Lynette A. Chief leased facilities Airways and Air Communications Service, Dept. Air Force, Andrews AFB, Md., Scott AFB, Ill., 1956-61; specialist comml. policy div. Def. Communications Agency, Dept. Def., Washington, 1961-66; dir. Comml. Communications Office, U.S. Army, Ft. Huachuca, Ariz., 1967—; Air Force contracting officer, 1957-61. Served with USAF, 1948-56. Decorated Meritorious Civilian Service medal Dept. Army, 1971. Mem. Armed Forces Communications and Electronics Assn. (1st v.p. Ariz. chpt. 1977-78), N.Y. Geneal. and Biog. Soc. Mormon. Home: 1381 Cholla Circle Sierra Vista AZ 85635 Office: US Army Comml Communications Office Fort Huachuca AZ 85613

BOGART, CREIGH ADAM, real estate exec.; b. Pitts., Feb. 19, 1948; s. Frank Larry and Patricia A. Bogart; student U. S.C., 1966; m. Roxanne Castleberry, July 20, 1980; children—Brent M., Kurt A. Salesman, Mattoon & Totty, Inc., Pitts., 1967-70, v.p., gen. mgr., 1970-77, sr. v.p., 1977—; pres. Com Vest Enterprises, Inc., 1979—; dir. Greater Pitts. Miltiple Listing Service. Mem. Greater Pitts. Bd. Realtors, Nat., Pa. assns. Realtors, Nat. Mktg. Inst., Inst. Real Estate Mgmt., Homebuilders Assn. Metro Pitts., Nat., Pa. assns. homebuilders. Republican. Club: South Hills Country. Home: Champion PA 15622 Office: 5019 S Park Rd Bethel Park PA 15102

BOGART, HOMER GORDON, paper and pulp co. exec.; b. New Rochelle, N.Y., July 28, 1922; s. Harold Garfield and Mildred Helen (Moses) B.; B.A. in History, Dartmouth Coll., 1945; m. Skaidrite Ozols, Feb. 22, 1962; children—Bonnie, Gary, David, Imants. Tchr., coach Vt. Acad., Saxtons River, 1945-48; owner, mgr. H.G. Bogart Distbg. Co., Kalamazoo, 1949-51; sales mgr. Food Processing Equipment Co., 1951-58; asst. sales engr. Sutherland Paper Co., Kalamazoo, 1958-61, sales mgr., Kalamazoo and N.Y.C., 1961-68; nat. sales mgr. Brown Co., N.Y.C., 1964-68; sales mgr. Perkins-Goodwin Co., Inc., Chgo., 1968-77, v.p. sales, 1975-77, pres., chief exec. officer, 1977—. Trustee, Paper Tech. Found., Inc., Western Mich. U., Kalamazoo. Served with U.S. Army, 1942-43. Mem. TAPPI. Republican. Episcopalian. Clubs: Sae, Marco Polo. Contbr. articles to profl. jours. Home: 3305 Robincrest Northbrook IL 60062 Office: 540 Frontage Northfield IL 60093

BOGDAN, ALBERT ALEXANDER, state econ. devel. exec.; b. N.Y.C., Feb. 28, 1936; s. Alexander Vincent and Blanche (Capp) B.; B.E.E., CCNY, 1958; M.B.A., U. Mass., 1972; m. Edwina H. Schachinger, June 6, 1959; children—Andrea E., Albert E., Stephen A., Alyssa B. Program mgr. Gen. Electric Co., Pittsfield, Mass., 1959-69; exec. dir. Pittsfield Urban Coalition, 1969-74; pres. Bridgeport (Conn.) Econ. Devel. Corp., 1974-76; mgr. tech. assistance Nat. Urban Coalition, Washington, 1976; exec. dir. Progress Com., Newport News, Va., 1976-78; Detroit regional dir. Mich. Office Econ. Devel., 1978—. Chmn., Berkshire Housing Fund, Pittsfield, 1971-74; chmn. Berkshire Manpower Planning Council, 1972-74; chmn. Pittsfield Mayor's Transp. Com., 1973-74; incorporator, bd. dirs. Downtown Cabaret Theatre, Bridgeport, 1975-76; bd. dirs. Peninsula Community Theatre, Newport News, 1977-78. Recipient Human Rights award Berkshire NAACP, 1971; Public Service award City Council Pittsfield and Nat. Urban Coalition, 1974. Mem. Nat. Assn. Housing and Redevel., Nat. Council Urban Econ. Devel. (ofcl.), Mich. Indsl. Devel. Assn., Internat. Downtown Exec. Assn., Urban Land Inst. Democrat. Unitarian. Home: 13342 Sherwood Huntington Woods MI 48070 Office: 1200 6th St Detroit MI 48226

BOGERT, JEREMIAH MILBANK, bus. corp. exec.; b. N.Y.C., Dec. 2, 1941; s. Henry Lawrence and Margaret (Milbank) B.; A.B., Yale U., 1963; M.B.A., U. Conn., 1973; m. Margot Beatrice Campbell, Nov. 2, 1963; children—Millicent Durant, Jeremiah Milbank. Editor, Random House, Inc., N.Y.C., 1963-68; asso. Mason B. Starring and Co., Stamford, Conn., 1968-73; pres. Bishop's Service, Inc., N.Y.C., 1973—; dir. Uniworld Group Inc., N.Y.C. Trustee, ICD Rehab. and Research Center, N.Y.C., 1976—, Bedford (N.Y.) Free Library, 1976—; treas. Bedford Republican Town Com., 1978. Episcopalian. Office: 41 E 42nd St New York NY 10017

BOGGS, MICHAEL DEAN, restaurant mgr.; b. Oak Hill, Ohio, Nov. 21, 1952; s. Vernon Edward and Melba Faye B.; B.B.A., Ohio U., 1974, M.B.A., 1975; m. Yvonne Fenice Smith, Aug. 3, 1974. Exec. mgr. Frisch's PiQua, Inc (Ohio), 1975-78; exec. mgr. Frisch's Norwood (Ohio) Tng. Center, 1978—; instr. Edison State Coll., 1977. Recipient award for outstanding cons. case study SBA, 1975. Club: Masons. Home: 88 E Maineville St Maineville OH 45039 Office: 4765 Montgomery Rd Norwood OH 45212

BOGOSIAN, JOHN SARKIS, photog. equipment co. exec.; b. Phila., July 17, 1927; s. Sarkis and Sirarpi (Savoulian) B.; student George Washington U., 1951; certificate of accounts and finances U. Pa., 1955; m. Marjorie Berberian, Nov. 6, 1955; children—John Paul, Joanne, Karen. With Camera Shop, Inc., Broomall, Pa., 1946—, v.p., 1955-60, pres., 1960—; pres. Visual Sound Co., 1967—; mem. retail adv. bd. Bell & Howell Co., Delaware County Community Coll.; mem. adv. bd. Argus and Singer; mem. Nat. Small Bus. Council. Pres., Armenian Students Assn. Am., 1954-56, trustee, 1956-71, chmn. bd. trustees, 1967-71; vice chmn. Armenian Bicentennial Com.; del. White House Conf. on Small Bus., 1980; mem. regional adv. bd. SBA, 1980—. Served with USNR, 1945-47, 50-52. Recipient B'nai B'rith award Delaware County, 1963; named Photog. Retailer of Year, 1975. Mem. Lawrence Park Mchts. Assn. (pres.), Delaware County C. of C. (dir., v.p., chmn. small bus. council), Master Photo Dealers and Finishers Assn., Nat. Audio Visual Assn., Photog. Research Orgn. (sec., dir.), Delaware Valley Photo Dealers Assn., Photo Mktg. Assn. (trustee-at-large 1974-80, chmn. legis. com. 1978-80), Knights of Vartan. Congregationalist. Club: Rotary (pres. 1973-74, gov.'s rep. dist. 1974-75). Home: 131 Charles Dr Havertown PA 19083 Office: 485 Parkway S Broomall PA 19008

BOGUE, BRUCE, ins. agt.; b. Los Angeles, Sept. 24, 1924; s. Charles Luther and Viola (Adam) B.; B.A., U. Calif. at Los Angeles, 1947; grad. Inf. Staff and Command Sch. U.S. Army, 1948; m. Tays Myrl Tarvin, Dec. 18, 1945; children—Tays Elizabeth, Charles Luther II.

Agt., Mut. Benefit Life Ins. Co., Los Angeles, 1948-55, prodn. mgr., 1955-62; gen. agt. Guardian Life Ins. Co., Los Angeles, 1962—; mem. adv. bd. Am. City Bank; tchr. ins. UCLA. Precinct capt., poll watcher, hdqrs. chmn., fund raising chmn., campaign chmn. for Rep. party. Served to capt., inf. AUS, 1942-46; ETO. Recipient Man of Affairs award Los Angeles Wilshire Press, Los Angeles Mirror News, 1958. Mem. Million Dollar Round Table (life), Am. Soc. C.L.U.s, Assn. Advanced Life Underwriters, Nat. Assn. Life Underwriters, Gen. Agts. and Mgrs. Assn., Los Angeles Life and Trust Council, U. Calif. at Los Angeles Alumni Assn. (life). Congregationalist. Clubs: Annandale Golf (Pasadena, Calif.); California (Los Angeles). Contbr. articles to profl. jours. Home: 2200 Homet Rd San Marino CA 91108 Office: 510 W 6th St Los Angeles CA 90014

BOHANNAN, RICHARD DOUGLAS, tool co. exec.; b. Wichita, Kans., Apr. 22, 1941; s. Joseph Henry and Marceil (Lemcke) B.; B.E., Lund Tech. U. (Sweden), 1965, M.E., 1967; m. Inger Helena Graman, Oct. 6, 1963; children—Brian Richard, Barbara Janet Michelle. Mktg. engr. HVDC systems Allmänna Svenska Elektriska Aktiebolag, Ludvika, Sweden, 1965-68, project engr. UHV systems devel., 1968-70: mng. dir. Bohannan & Schmidt Tool Co., Ludvika, 1970-80; exec. v.p. mktg. Seco Tools AB, Sweden, 1981—; chmn. bd. Snap-Tap (U.K.) Ltd., Seco Tools A/S Denmark, Seco Tools S.A., Brussels, Seco Snap-Tap, Inc.; dir. Snap-Tap Machine Accessories (India) Ltd., Seco Titan Australia, Seco Tools Japan, Seco Tools Austria, Seco Tools Italy, Seco Tools Taiwan, Seco Tools (U.K.) Ltd., Seco Tools do Brazil. Mem. Soc. Carbide and Tool Engrs., Soc. Mfrs. Engrs., Swedish Mekanforbund (mem. bd. mktg.). Jehovah's Witness. Clubs: Ludvika Flying, Hagge Golf. Patentee in field. Home: Box 4038 Eriksberg S-777 00 Smedjebacken Sweden Office: Fack 77301 Fagersta Sweden

BOHN, NELSON RANSON, former accountant; b. Frederick, Md., Oct. 27, 1920; s. Harry Howard and Mamie (May) B.; B.S., U. Md., 1951; m. Bettie Mae Stultz, Sept. 14, 1943; children—Phil D., William H., Robert T. Adminstrv. officer, comptroller U.S. Army, Ft. Terry, Plum Island, N.Y., 1951-54; pvt. practice C.P.A., Frederick, 1955-69; partner Stoy, Malone & Co., Bethesda, Md., 1969-78; pres. Catoctin Properties, Inc., Frederick, 1967—, B & N Enterprises, Inc., Frederick, 1968-78; dir. Moreland Farms, Inc. Pres. Frederick County Heart Assn., 1959-60. Served to 2d lt. USAAF, 1940-44. Mem. Md. Assn. C.P.A.'s (chpt. pres. 1969-70). Clubs: Lions (past pres.); Green Hills Yacht and Country, Wicomico (Salisbury, Md.). Home: 134 E Rustic Dr Salisbury MD 21801

BOHON, ELLIS G(RAY), accountant, mgmt. cons., tax cons.; b. LaBelle, Mo., Sept. 1, 1902; s. Frank W. and Lee (Ellis) B.; student Westminster Coll., Fulton, Mo., 1920-21; B.S. cum laude, Knox Coll., Galesburg, Ill., 1924; postgrad. Walton Sch. Commerce, 1927-29, Northwestern U., 1930-33, 1935, 1965-66, YMCA Community Coll., 1936-71, Chgo. Bd. Trade Grain Inst., 1955, 56 (all Chgo.); C.P.A., U. Ill., 1935; m. Joyce L. Finlayson, Apr. 15, 1939; children—Walter Duncan, Ellis Gray II (dec.). Staff accountant Ernst & Ernst, C.P.A.'s, Chgo., 1927-30; partner R. L. Pearce & Co., C.P.A.s', 1930-36; propr. E. G. Bohon & Co., C.P.A.'s, 1936—; former lectr. Am. Inst. Banking, Walton Sch. Commerce, Ill. Inst. Tech., Chgo., Lake Forest (Ill.) Coll. Former adviser, treas. Lakes chpt. Order DeMolay, bus. men's adv. council Jones Comml. High Sch. (Chgo.). Enrolled as atty. Tax Ct. U.S.A. C.P.A., Ill., Ky., Iowa, Mo., Ind. Mem. Am. Inst. C.P.A.'s, Am. Accounting Assn., Ill. (past chmn. tech. com.), Ia. socs. C.P.A.'s, Nat. Assn. Accountants, Am. Arbitration Assn. (panelist), Accounting Research Assn., ACE, Am. Inst. Laundering, Ky. Hist. Soc., Midwest Bus. Adminstrn. Assn., Phi Delta Theta. Presbyn. Clubs: Swedish Glee, Union League, Masons, Shriners. Author papers. Home: 523 E North Ave Lake Bluff IL 60044 Office: 19 S LaSalle St Chicago IL 60603

BOHON, MARLANE GELDART, wine importer; b. Haverhill, Mass., June 20, 1933; d. Clarence Benjamin and Jean Olivia (Kyle) Geldart; student Drexel U., 1951-52, Lebanon Valley Coll., 1952-53, Bucks County Community Coll., 1973-74, Villanova U., 1978—; children—Jeannie K., Kevin V. With Yale & Towne Mfg., Phila., 1954, Richarton Mints, Phila., 1955-56; with Wagner Wines & Spirits Co., Frazer, Pa., 1970—, v.p. adminstrn., 1976—; v.p., sec. Radnor Wines & Spirits Co., Frazer, 1977—. Bd. dirs. exec. sec. Western Assn. of Ladies for Relief and Employment of Poor, 1962—; bd. dirs. Southampton Free Library, 1968-70; pres. Friends Southampton Library, 1970-74. Mem. Am. Mgmt. Assn., Am. Bus. Women's Assn. Republican. Presbyterian. Club: Jr. Women's (pres. 1968-70). Home: 35 Chetwynd Rd Paoli PA 19301 Office: 53 Great Valley Pkwy Frazer PA 19355

BOHRER, THOMAS CARL, plastics and spltys. mfg. co. exec.; b. Bklyn., Nov. 8, 1939; s. Jack David and Henrietta (Pinas) B.; B.Chem. Engring., Rensselaer Poly. Inst., 1960; postgrad. in mgmt. N.J. Inst. Tech., 1962-64; postgrad. Wake Forest U., 1971; m. Janet Carol Jacobs, Jan. 23, 1966; children—Scott, Jeffrey. Jr. project engr. Organic Chems. div. Am. Cyanamid Co., 1960-62, project engr., 1962; chem. engr. Celanese Research Co., Summit, N.J., 1962-64, research engr., 1964-67, sr. research engr., 1967-69; group leader fibers research Celanese Fibers Co., Charlotte, N.C., 1969-71; mgr. tire cord and indsl. yarns devel. Celanese Fibers Mktg. Co., Charlotte, 1971-73, dir. spl. products devel., 1973-76; dir. planning Celanese Plastics Co., Chatham, N.J., 1976, v.p.-tech. and planning, 1976-78; dir. corp. planning Celanese Corp., N.Y.C., 1978-79; v.p.-tech. Celanese Plastics & Spltys. Co., Chatham, N.J., 1979—. Mem. Am. Chem. Soc., N.Am. Soc. Corp. Planning, Strategic Planning Inst., Soc. Chem. Industry. Patentee in field. Home: 22 Fielding Rd Short Hills NJ 07078 Office: 26 Main St Chatham NJ 07928

BOHROFEN, ELDON LAVERN, banker; b. Dallas Center, Iowa, July 14, 1941; s. Kenneth John and Lucille (Hawbaker) B.; B.S. (Nat. Merit scholar 1959-60), Drake U., Des Moines, 1963, J.D., 1966; diploma Nat. Grade Trust Sch., Northwestern U., 1972; m. Judith Beth Storey, Apr. 2, 1966; children—Heather Marie, Peter Charles. Admitted to Iowa bar, 1966, Wis. bar, 1974; mem. faculty U. Wis., Whitewater, 1966-68; trust officer First Nat. Bank, Sioux City, Iowa, 1968-69; v.p., trust officer Union Bank & Trust Co., Ottumwa, Iowa, 1969-74; v.p., sr. trust officer Citizens Bank Sheboygan (Wis.), 1974-79; pres. Citizens Trust Co., Sheboygan, 1979—; instr. comml. law Am. Inst. Banking, 1969. Bd. dirs., sec. Sheboygan Rotary Found.; mem. Bay Lake council Boy Scouts Am.; found. chmn. Sheboygan United Way; adv. com. endowment Lakeland Coll.; trustee endowment trust Sheboygan YMCA; mem. bd. edn. Trinity Lutheran Sch. Sheboygan. Mem. Sheboygan County Bar Assn., Sheboygan County Life Underwriters Assn., Phi Delta Theta. Clubs: Pine Hills Country; Rotary, YMCA Horizon (Sheboygan). Home: 423 Timberlake Rd Sheboygan WI 53081 Office: 636 Wisconsin Ave PO Box 171 Sheboygan WI 53081

BOILEAU, OLIVER CLARK, aerospace exec.; b. Camden, N.J., Mar. 31, 1927; s. Oliver Clark and Florence Mary Smith (Parker) B.; B.S.E.E., U. Pa., 1951, M.S.E.E., 1953; M.S. (Sloan fellow), Mass. Inst. Tech., 1964; m. Nan Eleze Hallen, Sept. 15, 1951; children—Clark Edward, Adrienne Lee, Nanette Erika, Jay Marshall. With Boeing Aerospace Co., Seattle, 1953-80, v.p., mgr., 1966-70, v.p., 1970-72, pres., 1972-80; pres. Gen. Dynamics Corp., St. Louis, 1980—, also dir.; dir. First Nat. Bank, St. Louis. Served with USN, 1944-46. Mem. AIAA, Navy League, Air Force Assn., Am. Defense Preparedness Assn., Assn. U.S. Army, Armed Forces Communications and Electronics Assn., Nat. Aeronautics Assn., Nat. Space Club, Naval War Coll. Found., Nat. Acad. Engring. Office: 7733 Forsyth Blvd Clayton MO 63105

BOISVERT, BARBARA SUE KIRKPATRICK, banker; b. Moultrie, Ga., June 6, 1943; d. Dale Croft and Edna Elizabeth (Gordon) Kirkpatrick; student La. State U., New Orleans, 1962-63, Memphis State U., 1969-70, Draughon Bus. Coll., 1970; m. William Francis Boisvert, May 19, 1972; 1 son by previous marriage, Russell Lloyd Patterson. Asst. municipal bond trader U.M.I.C., Memphis, 1968-70; asst. municipal bond underwriter Nat. Bank of Commerce, Memphis, 1970-72; household goods coordinator U.S. Naval Air Sta., Sigonella, Sicily, 1972-74; order coordinator Hewlett-Packard Co., New Orleans, 1974; exec. sec., trust dept. Bank of Am., Eureka, Calif., 1975-77, trust adminstr., trust dept., 1977—. Leader 4-H Club, 1976-77. Mem. Am. Bus. Women's Assn. Club: Quota. Home: 1819 I St Eureka CA 95501 Office: PO Box Q Eureka CA 95501

BOK, JOAN TOLAND, utility co. exec.; b. Grand Rapids, Mich., Dec. 31, 1929; d. Don Prentiss Weaver and Mary Emily (Anderson) Toland; A.B., Radcliffe Coll., 1951; J.D., Harvard U., 1955; m. John Fairfield Bok, July 15, 1955; children—Alexander Toland, Geoffrey Robbins. Admitted to Mass. bar, 1955; mem. firm Ropes & Gray, Boston, 1955-61; individual practice law, Boston, 1961-68; atty. New Eng. Electric System, Westborough, Mass., 1968-73, asst. to pres., 1973-77, v.p., sec., 1977-79, vice chmn., dir., 1979—; dir. New Eng. Merchants Nat. Bank, 1979—, Mass. Electric Co., 1977—, Narragansett Electric Co., 1977—, Conn. Yankee Atomic Power Co., 1977—, Maine Yankee Atomic Power Co., Vt. Yankee Nuclear Power Corp., Yankee Atomic Electric Co., 1977—, Norton Co., 1980—; vice chmn., dir. New Eng. Power Co., 1977—, New Eng. Power Service Co., 1977—, New Eng. Energy Inc., 1977—. Trustee Radcliffe Coll., 1980—; mem. bd. overseers Harvard U., 1980—. Mem. Boston Bar Assn., Electric Power Research Inst. (research adv. com.), Woods Hole Oceanographic Inst., Am. Antiquarian Soc., Phi Beta Kappa. Unitarian. Office: 24 Research Dr Westborough MA 01581

BOLAND, CHARLES MATTHEW, chem. co. exec.; b. Chgo., Sept. 15, 1943; s. Fred and Mary Ann (Clark) B.; student U. Ill., 1962-64; B.S., Ill. Inst. Tech., 1971; M.B.A., U. Chgo., 1974; m. Maureen Ann Sullivan, May 4, 1967; children—Laura Ann, Heather Lynn, Charles Matthew. Communications cons. Ill. Bell Telephone Co., 1964-66; internat. ops. auditor Dawe's Labs. Inc., Chicago Heights, Ill., 1966-74; materials mgr. Armour Pharms. Co., Kankakee, Ill., 1974-75; sales mgr. fine chems. div. Lonza Inc., Fair Lawn, N.J., 1975-78, div. mgr., 1980—; also dir. mktg. Hoffman-LaRoche, Nutley, N.J. Served with USMCR, 1965. Mem. Am. Feed Mfrs. Assn., Nat. Feed Ingredients Assn., Internat. Food Technologists, Am. Assn. Cereal Chemists. Home: 21 New England Dr Hiawatha NJ 07034 Office: 22-10 Route 208 Fair Lawn NJ 07410

BOLAND, GERALD LEE, financial exec.; b. Harrisburg, Pa., Apr. 2, 1946; s. Vincent Harry and Alice Jane (Geiste) B.; B.S., Lebanon Valley Coll., 1968; m. Elaine Frances Glenn, Oct. 25, 1980. Acctg. trainee Armstrong Cork Co., Millville, N.J., 1968; payroll supr., plant ops. accountant, 1969-70; sr. financial accountant Lancaster (Pa.) Gen. Hosp., 1970-71, mgr. gen. acctg., 1972; corp. acctg. mgr. HMW Industries, Inc., Lancaster, 1972; corp. controller Fleck-Marshall Co. subsidiary Gable Industries, Lancaster, 1973-74, sec.-treas., 1974-75; controller Dominion Psychiat. Treatment Center, Falls Church, Va., 1975-76; controller, dir. fin. Miller & Byrne, Inc., Rockville, Md., 1976-79; internal auditor Washington Hosp. Center, 1979—. Mem. Am. Acctg. Assn., Nat. Assn. Accountants, Hosp. Fin. Mgmt. Assn., Eastern Fin. Assn., Am. Hosp. Assn., Am. Mgmt. Assn., Fin. Mgmt. Assn., Inst. Internal Auditors. Methodist. Home: 2440 Hyannis Ln Crofton MD 21114

BOLAND, THOMAS EDWIN, banker; b. Columbus, Ga., July 8, 1934; s. Clifford and Helen Marjorie (Robinson) B.; student Emory U., 1952-54; B.B.A., Ga. State U., 1957; postgrad. Stonier Grad. Sch. Banking, Rutgers U., 1964-66; Advanced Mgmt. Program, Emory U., 1972; m. Beth Ann Campbell, May 23, 1959; children—Susan Ann, T. Edwin. With 1st Nat. Bank Atlanta, 1954—, v.p., 1968-71, group v.p., 1972-73, sr. v.p., 1974-78, exec. v.p., 1979—; corp. v.p. 1st Atlanta Corp., 1978—; v.p. 1st Atlanta Internat. Corp., 1979—; dir. alt. London Interstate Bank Ltd.; mem. investment com. Minbanc Capital Corp., Washington, 1978—. Trustee, Atlanta Bapt. Coll., 1970-72; trustee, treas. Ga. Bapt. Found., 1980—; bd. dirs. Ga. State U. Alumni Assn., 1979—; mem. pres.'s council Mercer U., Macon, Ga., 1980—. Served with AUS, 1957. Named Salesman of Yr., Atlanta Sales and Mktg. Execs. Club, 1968. Mem. Am. Bankers Assn. (cert. comml. lender, bank card com. 1964-66), Robert Morris Assos. (security dealers relations com. 1974-75, Atlanta Area chmn. 1979—, chmn., dir. Eastern group Southeastern chpt. 1981—). Club: Cherokee Town and Country (Atlanta). Office: PO Box 4148 Atlanta GA 30302

BOLCH, ADRIAN DAVIS, JR., oil co. exec.; b. Savannah, Ga., Feb. 14, 1931; s. Adrian Davis and Mildred Frances (Kight) B.; B.M.E., Ga. Inst. Tech., 1953; post baccalaureate in Chem. Engring. and Econs., U. Houston, 1968; m. Nancy Elizabeth Bowers, Aug. 18, 1956; children—Laurie W., Vaughan E. Mech. engr. Humble Oil & Refining Co., Baytown, Tex., 1956-60, sr. evaluation engr., Houston, 1960-63, head of forecasts and crude oil, Houston, 1963-65, sr. planning specialist, corporate planning, 1965-68; head of analysis, heavy fuel oil, Exxon Co. U.S.A., Houston, 1968-73, ops. coordinator, wholesale fuels, 1973-75; sr. v.p. Belcher Oil Co., Miami, 1975-76, exec. v.p., 1976—; dir., exec. v.p. Coastal Terminals, Inc.; corp. sec., dir. Belcher Oil Co., 1977—; exec. v.p., dir. Belcher Co., N.Y.C.; dir. Belcher New Eng., Inc. Bd. dirs. Jr. Achievement; precinct sec., del. to county and state convs. Democratic Party Tex., 1967-71. Served with U.S. Army, 1953-56. Registered profl. engr., Tex. Mem. Am. Mgmt. Assn., Am. Gas Assn., Fla. Bus. Roundtable, Fed. Energy Assn. (fuel oil adv. com.). Lutheran. Patentee petroleum leak detector. Home: 7405 SW 115th St Miami FL 33156 Office: PO Box 011751 Miami FL 33101

BOLDON, REGINALD DEWITT, savs. and loan exec.; b. Sparta, Wis., Nov. 2, 1934; s. Dean E. and Amalia (Schneider) B.; student U. Wis., 1952-53; m. Mary Anne Hanson, Nov. 7, 1953; children—Reginald Kim, Terry Lea, Bruce Alan, Bradford Charles. Owner, operator Boldon's Service Sta., 1953-55; field rep. Thorp Finance Corp., Rochester and Richfield, Minn., 1955, br. mgr., South St. Paul, Minn., 1957-62, br. mgr., LaCrosse, Wis., 1962-63; asst. sec.-treas., sec.-treas. Western Fed. Savs. & Loan Assn. (formerly Sparta Fed. Savs. & Loan Assn.), 1963-66, exec. v.p., 1966-72, pres., dir., 1972—; pres., dir. Western Service Corp. Chmn., Sparta Ins. Commn., 1971-72; capt. United Fund, Sparta, 1964-65; capt. fund-raising for St. Marys Hosp. and Methodist Edn. Bldg., 1963-64; past pres., bd. dirs. Sparta Indsl. Found.; past pres., bd. govs. St. Mary's Hosp., Sparta. Recipient Jaycee Spark Plug and Key Man awards, 1966-67. Mem. Wis. Savs. and Loan League (dir. Milw. 1972-74, past. pres. N.W. dist.), U.S. League Savs. Assns. (com. on FHLB system), Sparta C. of C., Sparta Jaycees (past treas. and v.p., Boss of Yr. award 1978). Republican. Methodist (past chmn. edn. com., past mem. ofcl. bd.). Clubs: Masons (past master), Shriners, Kiwanis (past pres., dir.). Home: 611 W Division St Sparta WI 54656 Office: 124 N Court St Sparta WI 54656

BOLIG, KENNETH LEROY, engr.; b. Lewisburg, Pa., Apr. 30, 1951; s. Earl Kenneth and Evelyn Mae B.; Asso. of Applied Sci., Williamsport Area Community Coll., 1973; B.Tech., Pa. State U., 1975; student Geometric Design of Hwys. workshop, Northwestern U., 1978; m. Susan Langham Walling, June 16, 1979. Constrn. insp. Pa. Testing Labs., Moosic, 1975-76; civil engr. Gerald E. Bickhart & Sons, Selinsgrove, Pa., 1976-78, Dept. Public Works Howard County, Ellicott City, Md., 1978—. Mem. ASCE, Howard County Employee Coalition. Lutheran. Project engr. 1st solar-heated animal facility for State of Md. Home: 8780 E Town & Country Blvd Ellicott City MD 21043 Office: 3430 Court House Dr Ellicott City MD 21043

BOLIN, ALPHA E., JR., elec. mfg. co. exec.; b. Madison, Ill., Mar. 4, 1927; s. Alpha E. and Cynthia B. (Putnam) B.; B.S. in Elec. Engring., Am. Inst. Engring. and Tech., Chgo., 1952; m. Shirley J. Wiseman, Jan. 7, 1956; children—Janis A., Nancy Jo, Donald A. Elec. engr. Wagner Electric Co., St. Louis, 1952-59; dir. research and devel. Precision Trans-Chgo., 1959-60; chief engr. Dowzer Electric Co., Mt. Vernon, Ill., 1960-63; founder VanTran Electric Corp., Waco, Tex., 1963, chmn. bd., pres., 1963—. Active Am. Cancer Soc., 1967-69; bd. dirs. Woodway Boys Club, 1975—, McLennan County Better Bus. Bur. Served with U.S. Army, 1945-47. Mem. N.A.M., Nat. Elec. Mfrs. Assn., Am. Hist. Soc., Waco Creative Art Center, Hist. Waco Soc., Nat. Trust for Hist. Preservation, Nat. Pilots Assn. Clubs: Woodland West Country (dir.); Vandalia (Ill.) Country; Waco Founders Lions. Home: 425 Whitehall Rd Waco TX 76710 Office: 7711 Imperial Dr PO Box 8355 Waco TX 76710

BOLIN, RUSSELL LEROY, constrn. co. exec.; b. Edgewood, Ill., Apr. 6, 1918; s. Fred Oscar and Lulu Margaret (Culley) B.; student Ill. Coll., 1936-38; B.S., Ind. State U., 1947; M.S., U. Ill., 1953; m. Anne May Mooney, Nov. 1, 1944; 1 dau., Diane Gege. Coach, Westville (Ill.) High Sch., 1947-51; with R.H. Bishop Co., Champaign, Ill., 1955—, sec., 1963—, v.p., 1970—. Served to maj. USAAF, 1941-46; as sr. pilot USAF, 1951-53. Decorated Air medal, D.F.C. Named Basketball Coach of Yr., Vermilion County (Ill.) Coaches, 1951; recipient YMCA award for service to youth, 1968. Mem. Plumbing, Heating and Cooling Assn. Central Ill. (pres. 1962-66, state dir. to Ill. Plumbing and Heating Assn. 1975-79), Am. Legion, V.F.W., Gamma Nu. Club: Moose. Home: Rural Route 1 Box 179 Fairmount IL 61841 Office: 3506 N Mattis Ave Champaign IL 61820

BOLINDER, SUE HOLLADAY, computer co. exec.; b. Tremonton, Utah, Sept. 6, 1938; d. James Eugene and Beatrice (Hawkins) Holladay; student public schs., Tooele, Utah; m. John Robert Bolinder, May 28, 1955; children—Eugene Jim, John Jay, Jack Karl, Susan Kay. Bookkeeping machine operator, fire ins. sec. Beneficial Life Ins. Co., Salt Lake City, 1960-61; sales sec. Hytronic Measurements Co., Salt Lake City, 1963-67; sales rep. J.F. Hurlbut Co., Salt Lake City, 1968-71; customer relations Applied Data Systems & Prudential Fed. Savs. Data Center, Salt Lake City, 1971-76; owner, mgr. Byte Shop Computers, Salt Lake City, 1977—. Mem. Elec. Reps. Assn. Mormon. Office: 3616 W 2100 S Salt Lake City UT 84120

BOLINGER, JOHN C., JR., mgmt. cons., gas co. exec.; b. Knoxville, Tenn., Feb. 12, 1922; s. John C. and Elsie M. (Burkhart) B.; B.S. in Fin., U. Tenn., 1943; M.B.A., Harvard, 1947; m. Helen McCallie, Jan. 26, 1944; children—Janet, Robert, John. Asst. sec. Lehigh Coal & Nav. Co., Phila., 1947-49, asst. to the pres., 1949-50, v.p., 1950-54; pres., dir. E. Tenn. Nat. Gas, Knoxville, 1957-61, Tenn. Bank & Trust Co., Houston, 1961-63; asst. to pres. Miss. River Corp., St. Louis, Mo., 1954-57, exec. v.p., 1963-67; pres. Mississippi River Transmission Corp., 1963-67; dir. Mo. Pacific R.R., 1963-67; pres., dir. Tenn. Natural Gas Lines, Nashville, 1970—; mgmt. cons., Knoxville, 1967—; pres., dir. Nashville Gas Co., 1973—; dir. Aladdin Industries, Inc., Home Fed. Savs. & Loan, Knoxville, Aladdin Ltd., London; dir. Nashville br. Fed. Res. Bank, 1975—; vis. lectr. Coll. Bus., U. Tenn., 1970—. Elder Presbyn. Ch., 1961—. Served to capt.; inf., U.S. Army, 1943-46; ETO. Decorated Purple Heart, Bronze Star; Croix de Guerre (France). Clubs: Cherokee Country, City (Knoxville); Belle Meade Country, Cumberland, Crocket Springs Golf and Country (Nashville); Lost Tree (North Palm Beach, Fla.). Home: 1400 Kenesaw Ave SW Knoxville TN 37919 also 1000 Lake House Dr S Lost Tree Village North Palm Beach FL 33408 Office: 2000 Parkway Towers Nashville TN 37219

BOLINGER, ROBERT STEVENS, banker; b. Mt. Union, Pa., July 22, 1936; s. Jesse Morrow and Nell Elizabeth (Stevens) B.; A.B. in Econs., Dartmouth Coll., 1958, M.B.A., 1962; m. Reba Mae Fleisher, June 17, 1962; children—Todd Wesley, Steven Morrow, Mark Andrew. Auditor, Irving Trust Co., N.Y.C., 1962, trainee, 1963, asst. sec. Wall St. div., 1964-66, asst. v.p. Met. div., 1966-70, with loan adminstrn. div., 1970-71, v.p., regional credit officer, 1971-72, v.p. McGraw Hill Office, 1972-75, v.p. Rockefeller Center Office, 1975; pres., chief exec. officer Farmers First Bank, Lititz, Pa., 1976—; dir. Farmers AgCredit Corp., Third Dist. Funds Transfer Assn. Bd. dirs. United Way Lancaster County. Served to lt. (j.g.) USN, 1958-61. Mem. Lancaster County Bankers Assn. (pres. 1980-81), Lancaster Assn. Commerce and Industry (dir.). Presbyterian. Club: Masons. Home: 1314 Stillwater Rd Lancaster PA 17601 Office: 9 E Main St Lititz PA 17543

BOLLMAN, DIANE ELIZABETH, county agy. adminstr.; b. Buffalo, Aug. 11, 1943; d. Earl Vincent and Annette Hattie (Bartz) Parsons; A.A.S., Erie County Community Coll., 1963; student Ouchita Bapt. Coll., 1965, Alfred U., 1977, Alfred State Coll., 1979-80; m., Sept. 14, 1963 (div. 1978); children—Beth Ann, Lori Jean. Dietitian, Charles E. Still Osteo. Hosp., Jefferson City, Mo., 1963-64, Ft. Worth Osteo. Hosp., 1964; asst. mgr. Holiday Inn, Camden, Ark., 1964-65; dietetic technician Mary's Nursing Home, Wellsville, N.Y., 1973-74; coordinator nutrition services Allegany County Office for the Aging, Belmont, N.Y., 1974-78, exec. dir., 1978—. Corp. bd. Allegany Transp. Systems, treas., 1978—; bd. dirs. Community Services; cons. Alfred U.; adv. bd. human services SUNY, Alfred; adv. com. on elderly affairs to Congressman Stanley Lundine, 1978—; profl. adv. bd. Public Health Dept., Belmont, 1978—; human resources com. W. Regional Planning Dept., State of N.Y., 1978—; mem. task force on health systems agys., Belmont, 1978—. Mem. N.Y. State Assn. Dirs. of Area Agys. on Aging, Nat. Assn. Dirs. of Area Agys. on Aging, Allegany County County Social Agys., Bolivar (N.Y.) Hist. Soc. Republican. Lutheran. Co-editor: The History of Bolivar, 1975. Home: 97 Wellsville St Bolivar NY 14715 Office: 17 Court St Belmont NY 14813

BOLNER, CLIFTON JOSEPH, mfg. co. exec.; b. San Antonio, Tex., July 30, 1928; s. Joe and Josephine (Grandjean) B.; B.S. (Disting. Mil. Grad.), Tex. A. and M. U., 1949; m. Rosalie Richter, Jan. 20, 1949; children—Tim, Mike, Deb, Cindy, Bev, Chris, Mary. Partner, Bolner's Grocery & Meat Market, San Antonio, 1949-55; pres. Bolner's Fiesta Products, Inc., San Antonio, 1955—, chief exec. officer, 1980—; a founder, dir. Exchange Nat. Bank, San Antonio,

1980—. Pres., Cath. Family and Children Services, San Antonio, 1968-69; chmn. fin. com. San Antonio Archdiocese, 1978-79; chmn. annual awards dinner NCCJ, 1974; bd. dirs. San Antonio Symphony Soc., 1973—, San Antonio Mus. Assn., 1973—, Opera Superman, 1975—, San Antonio Muscular Dystrophy Assn., 1975—; mem. devel. bd. Incarnate Word Coll., 1974—; San Antonio Cath. rep. NCCJ, 1978—. Served to 1st lt. USAF, 1950-52. Recipient Disting. Alumni award Central Cath. High Sch., 1979; Archbishop Furey Outstanding award medal, 1969. Mem. Produce Mktg. Assn. (dir. retail div. 1980—), Am. Spice Trade Assn. (membership com. 1977-79), Oblate Asso., Assn. of Holy Family Guilds. Roman Catholic. Clubs: K.C., San Antonio Serra Vocation, Italo Am. Young Men's, St. Paul's Men's, Soc. of Mary Assos. Home: 110 W Lynwood St San Antonio TX 78212 Office: 426 Menchaca St San Antonio TX 78207

BOLOGNA, GIACOMO JOSEPH, lawyer, cons. co. exec.; b. Detroit, Jan. 1, 1929; s. Salvatore and Cristina (Randazzo) B.; B.B.A. in Acctg., Detroit Inst. Tech., 1951; J.D., U. Detroit, 1957; D.Sc. (hon.) Ind. No. U., 1980; m. Jean A. Kolar, Feb. 16, 1957; children—James, Michael, Anne, Mary, Paul, Janine. With Nat. Bank of Detroit, 1950-52, Arthur Young & Co., 1953-54; with various U.S. govt. agys., 1955-68; v.p. Performance Systems, Inc., 1969-70, Intertel, Inc., Washington, 1971-73; pres. George Odiorne Assos., Inc., Plymouth, Mich., 1973—, Computer Protection Systems, Inc., Plymouth, 1980—; officer, dir. various profl. cons. groups, 1972—. Chmn. citizen's adv. council Plymouth Center for Human Devel.; mem. sch. bd. com. Our Lady of Good Counsel Ch. Mem. Am. Soc. Bus. and Mgmt. Consultants, Am. Mgmt. Assn., Data Processing Mgmt. Assn., N.Am. Soc. Corp. Planning, Nat. Assn. Accts. Contbr. articles to profl. jours.

BOLTE, CHARLES CLINTON, publishing exec.; b. Marshall, Mo., Jan. 8, 1945; s. Harry Ben and Laura Louise (Barnhill) B.; B.I.E., Ga. Inst. Tech., 1967; M.B.A., U. Va., 1972; m. Mary Elizabeth Tomaszewski, Sept. 2, 1973; children—Nicole Alison, Lauren Ann. Comml. mktg. rep. Letterflex, W. R. Grace & Co., Clarksville, Md., 1972-74; exec. dir. engring. William Byrd Press, Richmond, Va., 1974-76, exec. dir. market adminstrn., 1976-79, v.p. research and devel., 1979—; mem. research steering com. Graphic Arts Tech. Found. Served with U.S. Army, 1967-70. Mem. Am. Inst. Indsl. Engrs. (sr. mem.; graphic arts dir.). Episcopalian. Home: 4300 Croatan Rd Richmond VA 23235 Office: William Byrd Press Inc PO Box 27481 Richmond VA 23261

BOLTRES, HENRY WILLIAM, real estate investment cons.; b. Canton, Ohio, Apr. 7, 1936; s. Henry W. and Sarah A. Boltres; student Malone Coll., Ohio State U.; m. Doris Jean Kaufman, Aug. 9, 1958; children—Martin W., Christine A. With Addressograph-Multigraph Corp., Cleve., 1957-63, H.W. Boltres & Assos., Canton, 1963-65, Ohio Dept. Natural Resources, Columbus, 1965-75; pres. The Boltres Co., Newark, Ohio, 1975—; cons. U.S. investments. Mem. fin. com. Licking County Republican party, 1978-80. Served with USMC, 1953-54, U.S. Army, 1954-56. Mem. Nat. Bd. Realtors, Ohio Bd. Realtors, Licking County Bd. Realtors, Nat. Rifle Assn. Methodist. Clubs: Columbus Touchdown, Big Red Touchdown, Ducks Unltd. Home: 123 W Broadway Granville OH 43023 Office: 2112 Cherry Valley Rd Newark OH 43055

BOMZE, EDWARD LEMUEL, publisher; b. Belle Harbor, N.Y., Dec. 19, 1940; s. Henry Daniel and Anne (Herman) B.; student Duke U., 1958-62; B.A., Post Coll., 1964. Real estate salesman Charles Aug & Assos., N.Y.C., 1967-69; newspaper reporter Hudson Dispatch, North Bergen, N.J., 1970-73; asst. pub. Star Pub. Co., pubs. Racing Star, Am. Turf Monthly, N.Y.C., 1973-77, pub., 1979—. Served with U.S. Army, 1963. Republican. Jewish. Club: Midtown Health (dir.). Office: 505 8th Ave New York NY 10018

BONANNO, A. KENNETH, mfg. co. exec.; b. Lawrence, Mass., Apr. 17, 1949; s. Anthony Francis and Lucille Adella (Mignanelli) B.; B.S. in Accounting, Northeastern U., Boston, 1971; M.B.A. in Mgmt., N.H. Coll., Manchester, 1977; m. Julia Ann Chaykowsky, Apr. 29, 1972; children—A. Kenneth, Jason Thomas. Supr. gen. acoounting Shepard & Morse Co., Brookline, Mass., 1971-72; forecast accountant, supr. budgets and planning Sanders Assos., Nashua, N.H., 1972-74, sr. fin. analyst, 1974-76; adminstr. procurement planning Raytheon Co., W. Andover, Mass., 1976-78, sr. subcontract adminstr., 1978-79, asst. mgr. procurement planning, 1979-80, mgr. vendor performance, 1981—; mem. part-time faculty econs. and accounting Fitchburg (Mass.) State Coll, N.H. Coll. Adviser Greater Lawrence Jr. Achievement, named advisor of yr., 1978. Clara and Joseph Ford scholar, 1971. Mem. Nat. Assn. Accountants (chpt. pres. 1978, sec. regional council, mem. com. edn.), Assn. M.B.A. Execs., Raytheon-Andover Mgmt. Club, Delta Chi (alumni trustee). Democrat. Roman Catholic. Home: 314 Lowell St Methuen MA 01844 Office: 350 Lowell St West Andover MA 01810

BONAPARTE, TONY HILLARY, bus. educator; b. Grenada, W.I., June 13, 1938; s. Norman and Myra (McClean) B.; B.S., St. John's U., 1963, M.B.A., 1964; Ph.D., N.Y. U., 1967; m. Beverly Goodin, June 15, 1963; 1 dau., Yvette. Asst. prof. St. John's U., 1964-67, asso. prof., 1967-73; dir. Internat. Bus. Inst., Pace U., 1969-71, asso. dean Grad. Sch. Bus., 1971-74, dean, 1974—, prof. internat. bus., 1973—; research asso. Bus. Internat. Corp., 1968-70; dir. World Trade Inst., Schalkenbach Found.; sr. Fulbright prof. bus. adminstrn. Cuttington Coll., Liberia, 1973-74; vis. prof. U. Strathclyde (Scotland), 1977. Fellow AAAS; mem. Am. Econ. Assn., Acad. Mgmt., Acad. Internat. Bus., Fulbright Alumni Assn. Office: Pace Plaza New York NY 10038

BOND, CHARLES HERBERT, ednl. equipment mfg. co. exec.; b. Orange, N.J., Dec. 10, 1944; s. Charles Henry and Elizabeth Ann (McFall) B.; B.S. in Acctg., Rutgers U., 1972; J.D. cum laude, Seton Hall U., 1979; m. June W. Craft, July 17, 1977; children by previous marriage—Charles Herbert, Wendy Ann, Devon Edward. Various acctg. positions, 1964-70; mem. treas.'s staff Gulf and Western Industries, N.Y.C., 1970; sr. acct. Amerada Hess Corp., Woodbridge, N.J., 1970-74; with Tech. Engring. Co., Inc., Farmingdale, N.J., 1974—, controller, 1977-80, sec., 1980—, treas., 1980; admitted to N.J. bar, 1979; mem. adj. faculty Ocean County Coll. Bd. dirs. Shore Area YMCA, 1979-80. Mem. Am. Bar Assn., N.J. Bar Assn., Bricktown Jaycees (v.p. 1971-72). Roman Catholic. Home: 342 Dogwood Dr Bricktown NJ 08723 Office: PO Box 686 Farmingdale NJ 07727

BOND, NELSON LEIGHTON, JR., med. testing equipment co. exec.; b. Glen Ridge, N.J., Apr. 17, 1935; s. Nelson Leighton and Dorothy Louise (Hudson) B.; B.A., Lehigh U., 1957; M.B.A. (Foote Cone & Belding fellow), Harvard U., 1966; children—Sally L., Nelson Leighton, Trevor P., Elizabeth P., Susan J. Dist. mgr. McGraw-Hill, Inc., N.Y.C., 1957-58, 60-64; asso. McKinsey & Co., Inc., N.Y.C., 1966-68; fin. analyst Drexel Harriman Ripley, N.Y.C., 1968-69; instnl. salesman Faulkner, Dawkins & Sullivan, N.Y.C., also v.p. Alexander Brown & Sons, Balt., 1970-76; pres. Blood Pressure Testing, Inc., Reisterstown, Md., 1977—; pres., dir. Consumer Micrographics, Inc., Balt., 1980—. Pres., Parents Club St. Paul's Sch., 1978-79; chmn. Young Republicans, Verona, N.J., 1962-64. Served to 1st lt., intelligence, AUS, 1958-60. Clubs: Harvard Bus. Sch. of Md., Lehigh of Md. (pres.). Home: 13019 Old Hanover Rd Reisterstown MD 21136 Office: PO Box 354 Reisterstown MD 21136

BOND, PATERSON, stock broker; b. Bklyn., Apr. 1, 1909; s. Charles Grosvenor and Bertha Gildersleeve (Paterson) B.; B.A., Hamilton Coll., 1930; postgrad. N.Y. Inst. Finance, 1931-32; m. Gwen Stenehjem, May 26, 1945; children—Elinor Dorothy Martin, Geraldine Ann Laybourne, Deborah Gwen Bond-Upson, Charles Grosvenor III. With Orvis Bros., Plainfield, N.J., 1930-70, br. office mgr., 1938-62, 68-70, resident partner, 1962-67, mng. partner, 1967-68; resident v.p. Halle & Steiglitz Filor Bullard, Plainfield, 1970-73; v.p. Thomson McKinnon Securities, Inc., Plainfield, 1973—; trustee Savs. Bank Central Jersey. Bd. dirs. Somerset Valley Nursing Home, Bound Brook, N.J. Served with USNR, 1942-45. Mem. Plainfield Area C. of C. (past pres. 1971-72, dir.), Hamilton Coll. Alumni Assn. (council), Delta Kappa Epsilon. Club: Rotary. Home: 373 New Bedford Ln Rossmoor Jamesburg NJ 08831 Office: 145 Park Ave Plainfield NJ 07060

BOND, RUPERT WALDEMAR, acctg. exec.; b. Kansas City, Mo., Aug. 11, 1923; s. Charles V. and Minnie S. Bond; B.S., Wayne State U., 1955; postgrad. U. Md., Mercer U., U. Toledo; m. Dorothy A. Robinson, Feb. 22, 1966. Agt., IRS, Detroit, 1950-65; regional dir. H&R Block, Inc., Harrisburg, Pa., 1965-72; pres. Bond. Bookkeeping & Tax Co., Inc., Washington, 1972-75; controller United Black Fund, Inc., 1975—; dir. Bond Bookkeeping, Inc.; chief instr. H&R Block Tng. Schs.; instr. tng. div. IRS. Served with U.S. Army, 1943-46. Cert. tchr., Pa. Mem. Am. Mgmt. Assn., Am. Soc. Tax Cons., Washington Inst. Public Accts. Office: 1343 H St NW Washington DC 20005

BONDY, PETER JACOB, actuary; b. Guayaquil, Ecuador, Sept. 22, 1944; came to U.S., 1962, naturalized, 1977; s. Jorge and Ilse B.; B.S. in Math., Wake Forest U., 1967; m. Yvonne Schmitt, Mar. 13, 1971; children—Peter Jacob, Jennifer Marie, Julie Ann. Actuarial asst. Integon Life Ins. Co., Winston-Salem, N.C., 1966-68; actuarial asst. Pan-Am. Life Ins. Co., New Orleans, 1968-72, asst. actuary, 1972-73; v.p., mgr. Tillinghast, Nelson & Warren, Inc., New Orleans, 1973-79, v.p., prin., 1980—. Del., La. Gov.'s Conf. on Public Libraries. Fellow Soc. Actuaries, Conf. Actuaries in Public Practice; mem. Am. Acad. Actuaries, Southeastern Actuaries Club, Actuaries Club S.W., Internat. Actuarial Assn., Internat. Assn. Cons. Actuaries, Central Am. Actuarial Assn., New Orleans World Future Soc. Roman Catholic. Clubs: Metairie (La.) Rotary, Crescent City Stamp. Office: 3636 N Causeway Blvd Metairie LA 70002

BONEY, WILLIAM ANDREW, elec. equipment mfg. co. exec.; b. Forest Hills, Pa., June 2, 1933; s. William Gerard and Mary Ellen (Stewart) B.; B.M.E., Carnegie Mellon U., 1954; student U. Pitts., 1960; m. Margot M. Krautmacher, Nov. 1, 1958; children—Stephen William, Thomas Felix, John Robert. Various mktg., engring. positions, Phila., Pitts., Boston, 1954-73; gen. mgr. gas insulated products dept. ITE Imperial Corp., Greensburg, Pa., 1973-76; operation mgr. power breakers Gould Inc., Downey, Calif., 1976-78; v.p., gen. mgr. Brown Boveri Power Systems, Greensburg, 1978—; dir. ITE S.A., Mexico. Pres., High Acres Community Assn., 1972-73; bd. dirs. Westmoreland United Fund. Served with U.S. Army, 1956-58. Mem. Central Westmoreland C. of C. (dir.), IEEE. Methodist. Club: Latrobe Country. Office: Brown Boveri PO Box 98 Greensburg PA 15601

BONFIELD, GORDON BRADLEY, JR., paperboard co. exec.; b. Grand Rapids, Mich., May 23, 1926; s. Gordon Bradley and Helen Louise (Gutekunst) B.; B.A., Colgate U., 1950; student Advanced Mgmt. Program, Harvard, 1967; m. Ardella Mae Cowan, Aug. 27, 1949; children—Gordon Bradley III, Kenneth S. With Packaging Corp. Am. and predecessor cos., Evanston, Ill., 1941—, v.p. container div., 1966-73, sr. v.p. containerboard products div., 1973-74, pres., chief exec. officer, 1974—; chmn. bd. Tenn. River Pulp & Paper Co.; dir. State Nat. Bank, Evanston. Bd. dirs., mem. exec. com. Am. Paper Inst., Fourdrinier Kraft Board Group; trustee Inst. Paper Chemistry; pres. Am. Forest Inst., 1976-77. Served with U.S. Army, 1944-46. Mem. Am. Paper Inst., Paperboard Packaging Council. Clubs: Mid-Am. (Chgo.); Skokie (Ill.) Country. Office: 1603 Orrington Ave Evanston IL 60204

BONILLA-SOSA, SALVADOR, internat. investment advisor, former chem. co. exec.; b. Havana, Cuba, Dec. 23, 1913; A.B., Cin. U., 1935; M.D., Havana U., 1947; m. Vilma Mathe Sol, Sept. 20, 1953; children—Kristina, Victor, Ana Vilma, Salvador Vincente. Supr. Wm. S. Merrel & Co., Havana, 1940-47; med. dir., sales mgr. Lederle Labs., Havana, 1947-52; mgr. Pfizer Corp., Caribbean area, 1952-59; pres. Comercial Interamericana S.A., El Salvador, Guatemala, 1959-66; pres., chmn. bd. dirs. Corp. Bonima S.A. (Pharm.), El Salvador, 1963-66; pres., chmn. bd. Proquimia S.A. (Chem.), San Salvador, El Salvador, 1967-76; pres. Petroquimica Centroamericana S.A.. 1974-77, La Esmeralda S.A. (Coffee), 1974—; pres., chmn. bd. Corporacion Centroamericana de Inversiones S.A., Panama, 1969—; part-time prof. Havana U. Med. Sch., 1947-53. Pres. Instituto Salvadoreno de Cultura Hispanica; v.p. Pro-Arte El Salvador; pres. Comite Nacional de Ecologia, 1975—; pres. Consejo Superior Orquesta Filarmonica de la Habana, 1952-53; sec. Sociedad Bolivariana de El Salvador; mem. Circulo de Bellas Artes, Ateneo Habana, 1940-48; pres. Fedn. Salvadorena Yate y Remo; dir. Central Am. and Caribbean Yacht Racing Union; mem. Nat. Olympic Com. Mem. Decorated Order of Red Cross, Order of Comml. Merit, Order of Finlay, Order of Civil Merit of Spain, Order of S.S. and S. Brigida of Sweden. Assn. de Industriales, Pan Am. Cancer Citology Assn. (dir. 1967—, Pan Am. Med. Assn., (sec.) Clubs: Club de Ejecutivos, Rotary; Salvadoreno; Deportivo Internacional; American; Club Miami; Coral Gables (Fla.) Country. Office: Apartado 01-84 San Salvador El Salvador

BONIOL, EDDIE EUGENE, oil co. exec.; b. Port Arthur, Tex., Sept. 14, 1931; s. Willie Bernice and Leila Evelina (Chase) B.; diploma in acctg. Tyler Comml. Coll., 1949; student Baylor U., 1955-56, La. Coll., 1956; m. Margaret Faye Aguillard, Feb. 6, 1966; children—Joe Ed, Mark Eugene, Liesl Michelle. Various positions Comml. Credit Co., Bus. Services Group, Balt., 1959-73, area dir., 1970-73; freelance mgmt. cons. Dallas, 1973; v.p. Tex. Western Fin. Corp., Dallas, 1974-76; asst. v.p. Citicorp Bus. Credit Inc., Dallas, 1976-78; v.p. fin. and adminstrn., also chief fin. officer Superior Iron Works & Supply Co. Inc., Shreveport, La., 1978-80; sr. v.p. Latham Resources Corp., Shreveport, 1980—; cons. in field. Served with USN, 1950-53. Cert. credit analyst, credit and fin. analyst. Republican. Baptist. Clubs: Lions (pres. LeCompte, La., 1959-60), Rotary, East Ridge Country, Petroleum of Shreveport, Univ. Home: 8606 Rampart Pl Shreveport LA 71106 Office, Two American Tower Shreveport LA 71101

BONIS, LASZLO J., materials scientist, bus. exec.; b. Budapest, Hungary, May 31, 1931; s. Jozsef and Ilona (Hunvald) B.; came to U.S., 1957, naturalized, 1963; D.M. Ing., U. Tech. Sci., Budapest, 1953; postgrad. Mass. Inst. Tech., 1960; m. Eva Markovich, July 31, 1955 (div.); children—Andrea Christine, Peter Anthony Laszlo. Asst. dir. Material Research Labs., Inc., also asst. prof. U. Tech. Sci., Budapest, 1953-56; research asst. Mass. Inst. Tech., 1957-60; exec. v.p., tech. dir. Ilikon Corp., Natick, Mass., 1960-62, pres., treas., 1962-73, chmn. bd., tech. dir., 1973-77; chmn. bd., chief exec. officer Composite Container Corp. Am., Medford, Mass., 1977—. Pres., Boston Arts Council; pres., chief exec. officer Opera Co. Boston, 1966—. Named Outstanding Young Man of Greater Boston, 1966; recipient Golden Door award Internat. Inst. Boston, 1981. Registered profl. engr., Mass., Calif. Fellow Am. Inst. Chemists; mem. Am. Inst. Mining, Metall. and Petroleum Engrs., Am. Inst. Chemists, N.Y. Acad. Scis., Internat. Plansee Soc., Sigma Xi. Author: Fundamental Phenomena in the Material Sciences, 4 vols. Contbr. articles to profl. jours. Patentee in field. Home: 3 Sutton Pl Swampscott MA 01907 Office: 330 Middlesex Ave Medford MA 02155

BONNER, MARK HERBERT, JR., electric coop. exec.; b. Fort Necessity, La., Aug. 5, 1918; s. Mark Herbert and Emma Dee (Johnson) B.; La. Tech. U., 1938-41, La. State U. Law Sch., 1945-47; m. Janie Lee Coughran, Jan. 8, 1947; children—Janie Dee, Mark Herbert. Mng. editor Franklin Sun, Winnsboro, La., 1948-52; editor Rural La., dir. public relations and info. Assn. La. Electric Coops., 1952-62, exec. v.p., mgr., Baton Rouge, 1962—; free-lance feature writer-columnist, 1947—; dir. Cajun Electric Power Assn. Mem. La. Superport Com., 1972, La. Natural Resource Study Com., 1977—, La. Tax Study Com., 1976—. Served with USAAF, 1941-45. Decorated Bronze Star. Recipient numerous journalism awards including Best Editor of Yr. award La. Press Assn., 1951, Photo of Yr. award (2), 1953; La. State U. 4-H award, 1978; named Hon. State Farmer, Future Farmers Am., 1968; Conservationist of Yr., La. Forestry Assn., 1974. Mem. Nat. Rural Electric Mgrs. Assn. (pres.), Rural Electric Editors Assn. (pres.), Nat. Editors Assn., Am. Legion (post comdr.), VFW (comdr. 1946-48), La. Council of Farmer Coops, La. Priorities for the Future, La. Farm Bur., La. Press Assn., La. Broadcasters Assn., Baton Rouge C. of C., U.S. C. of C., Nat. Rifle Assn. Methodist. Clubs: Baton Rouge City, Optimist. Home: 1322 Casa Loma Dr Baton Rouge LA 70815 Office: Assn La Electric Coops 10725 Airline Hwy Baton Rouge LA 70816

BONNET, FRANKLYN RUDOLPH, investment adviser; b. N.Y.C., Dec. 28, 1915; s. Frank and Katharyne T. (Ronay) B.; B.B.A., Bernard Baruch Coll., N.Y.C., 1937; m. Alice Adelaide Botte, June 29, 1941; children—Alicia L., Franklyn Rudolph. Auditor, Hurdman & Cranstoun, C.P.A.'s, N.Y.C., 1946-49; fgn. accounting supr. Gen. Motors Corp., N.Y.C., 1949-53; fin. analyst Carborundum Corp., Niagara Falls, N.Y., 1953-55; internal auditor Gen. Time Corp., asst. treas., controller Westclox div., La Salle, Ill., 1956-63; dir. comml. services div. Fairbanks Morse Corp., N.Y.C., 1963-64; v.p. adminstrn. U.S. Berkel Corp., La Porte, Ind., 1964-70, dir., 1965-70; prin. Bonnet & Co., La Porte, 1970—; guest lectr. continuing edn. U. Notre Dame, N.Central campus Purdue U., Mich. State U., 1970—. Dir., chmn. finance com. La Porte United Fund, 1966-76; pres., bd. dirs. ARC, 1968—, Am. Field Service, 1968-71; treas., bd. dirs., mem. exec. and policy coms. La Porte County Comprehensive Mental Health Council, 1975—; bd. dirs. La Porte Community Hosp., 1967. Served to capt. U.S. Army, 1942-46; lt. col. Res. (ret.). Decorated Bronze Star medal, Army Commendation medal; C.P.A., N.Y., Ind. Mem. Fin. Execs. Inst., Am. Inst. C.P.A.'s, N.Y. State C.P.A. Soc., La Porte C. of C. (past dir., v.p.), La Porte Mfrs. Assn. (past pres.), South Bend Estate Planning Council. Roman Catholic. Clubs: Kiwanis (Disting. past pres., dir. Ind. Explorer div., adminstrv. chmn.); Elks (La Porte); Univ. (Chgo.). Home: PO Box 669 La Porte IN 46350 Office: 708 Jefferson Ave La Porte IN 46350

BONNET, FRED WILLIAM, mfg. co. exec.; b. N.Y.C., Oct. 23, 1936; s. William and Marie B.; B.S., CCNY, 1959; M.S. in Chem. Engring., SUNY, Buffalo, 1968; m. Dorothee H. Heym, June 23, 1961; children—Michael F., Thomas G. with Union Carbide, various locations, 1959—, mgr. environ. systems, Europe, 1971-76, mgr. catalyst bus. Linde div., Tarrytown, N.Y., 1976—. Mem. Am. Mgmt. Assn., Am. Inst. Chem. Engrs., Schlaraffia. Roman Catholic. Patentee rotary fluid contactor; contbr. articles to profl. jours. Home: 294 Canon Rd Wilton CT 06897 Office: 100 Clearbrook Tarrytown NY 10591

BONNIVIER, BERNARD WILLIAM, JR., mfg. co. exec.; b. Pittsfield, Mass., Dec. 6, 1942; s. Bernard William and Elsie Anna (Elfving) B.; B.S. in C.E., U. Mass., 1964; M.B.A., Purdue U., 1965; m. Marilynn Anderson, Mar. 23, 1963; children—Paige Leslie, Erika Leigh. Regional mgr. The Trane Co., LaCrosse, Wis., 1967-70, nat. sales mgr., 1970-71; dir. mktg. Nat. Homes Corp., Lafayette, Ind., 1971-73; CPD franchise holder The Trane Co., Indpls., 1973-78; v.p., gen. mgr. climate control div. Singer, Auburn, N.Y., 1978—. Co-chmn., United Way Cayuga County (N.Y.), 1979; mem. Republican Election Com. Upstate N.Y., 1980. Served with USAF ROTC, 1960-64. Mem. Auburn C. of C. (dir. 1979-80), ASHRAE, ASCE. Republican. Clubs: Skaneateles Country, Newcomers (dir. 1978-80), Elks. Contbg. editor The Effective Entrepreneur, 1972; contbr. articles to profl. jours. Office: 62 Columbus St Auburn NY 13021

BONNO, JAN HUFFCUT, banker; b. Peeksill, N.Y., Apr. 22, 1946; d. W. Harwood and Vernice Evelyn (Wood) Huffcut; B.A. in History, San Francisco, State U., 1969, B.A. in Polit. Sci., 1969; m. Gary Richard Clark, June 11, 1966 (dec. Dec. 1967); m. Charles Henri Bonno, Nov. 28, 1971. Supr. community services San Francisco Redevelopment Agy., 1969-73; with Bayview Fed. Savs. & Loan Assn., San Francisco, 1973—, asst. portfolio mgr., 1975, investment portfolio mgr., 1976-77, asst. v.p., 1977-79, v.p., 1979-80, chief fin. officer, 1980—. Adviser, Jr. Achievement, 1974; mem. exec. com. mayoral campaigns; mem. citizens budget rev. commn. City of Berkeley (Calif.), 1980—; pres.-elect Peninsula Ombudsmen; bd. dirs. Friends Outside, 1970-71. Mem. Financial Womens Club San Francisco, AAUW, League Women Voters, Calif. Savs. and Loan League (investment com. 1977-81), NOW. Democrat. Presbyn. Home: 5 Hillcrest Ct Berkeley CA 94705 Office: 2601 Mission St San Francisco CA 94110

BONO, PHILIP, aerospace engr.; b. Bklyn., Jan. 13, 1921; s. Julius and Marianna (Culcasi) B.; B.E., U. So. Calif., 1947, postgrad., 1948-49; m. Gertrude Camille King, Dec. 15, 1950; children—Richard Philip, Patricia Marianna, Kathryn Camille. Research and systems analyst N.Am. Aviation, Inglewood, Calif., 1947; engring. design specialist Douglas Aircraft Co., Long Beach, Calif., 1948-49; preliminary design engr. Boeing Airplane Co., Seattle, 1950-59; dep. program mgr. Douglas Aircraft Co., Santa Monica, Calif., 1960-62, tech. asst. to dir. advanced launch vehicles and space stas., Huntington Beach, Calif., 1963-65, sr. engr., scientist, Long Beach, 1973—; br. mgr. advanced studies, sr. staff engr. advanced systems tech. integration McDonnell Douglas Astronautics Co., Huntington Beach, 1966-72; pres. Cal-Pro Photo Accessories, 1974—; lectr. seminars, univs. and insts. including Soviet Acad. Scis., 1965; instr. engring. Wash., Calif. Served with USNR, 1943-46. Recipient Golden Eagle award Council Internat. Nontheatrical Events, 1964, A.T. Colwell merit award Soc. Automotive Engrs., 1968, N.M. Golovine award Brit. Interplanetary Soc., named engr. of distinction Engrs. Joint Council, 1971. Fellow AAAS, Royal Aero. Soc., Brit. Interplanetary Soc. (editorial adv. bd.), Am. Inst. Aeros. and Astronautics (asso.); sr. mem. Am. Astronautical Soc.; mem. N.Y. Acad. Scis., Internat. Acad. Astronautics, ASME, Soc. Automotive Engrs. (chmn. space vehicle com.). Author: Destination-Mars, 1961; (with K. Gatland) Frontiers of Space, 1969, translated into 6 fgn.

langs. Contbr. articles to profl. jours., chpts. to books. Inventor recoverable single-stage space shuttle for NASA. Home: 1951 Sanderling Circle Costa Mesa CA 92626 Office: 3855 Lakewood Blvd Long Beach CA 90801

BOOGAERTS, JOHN JOSEPH, JR., architect, urban planner, map pub.; b. Alexandria, La., Mar. 20, 1934; s. John Joseph and Eunice Loenie (Muse) B.; B.Arch., Tulane U., 1962; M.S. in Urban Planning, Columbia U., 1965; m. Florence May Macdonald, June 1, 1961; children—Charrette, Whitmore, Pieter, Wyngaert. Project planner Milan Engring., Ltd., Belize, Brit. Honduras, 1960-62; planner, mem. staff New Orleans City Planning Commn., 1962-63; planner John Graham & Co., N.Y.C., 1965-66; architect Skidmore Owings & Merrill, 1966-68; prin. urban designer N.Y.C. Housing and Devel. Adminstrn., N.Y.C., 1968-74; pres. Boogaerts & Assos., P.C., N.Y.C. and Riyadh, Saudi Arabia, 1975—; pres. Middle East Info. Co., Stamford, Conn. and Al Kohbar, Saudi Arabia, 1978—; cons. UN, 1975, 77, Central Planning Orgn., Yemen Arab Republic, 1975, Ministry of Mcpl. and Rural Affairs and Ministry of Info., Kingdom of Saudi Arabia, 1977-78; guest lectr. Columbia U., 1969, N.Y. U., 1975-76, Princeton (N.J.) U., 1975-76. Mem. Manhattan Community Bd. 8, 1968-75, chmn. E. 86th St. corridor com., 1968-75; Republican candidate Ho. of Reps. 18th Congl. Dist., 1974; mem. steering com. Carnegie Hill Neighbors, Inc., 1968-75, N.Y. Mcpl. Art Soc., 1968—; speakers bur. N.Y.C. Charter Revision Commn., 1975, Noroton Heights Assn., 1980—; pres. Columbia Archtl. and Planning Alumni, 1974-76. William Kinne Fellows travel grantee, 1964; registered architect Nat. Council Archtl. Registration Bds. Mem. A.I.A., Am. Inst. Planners. Republican. Roman Catholic. Club: Union (N.Y.C.). Producer, pub. series of guide maps cities of Saudi Arabia, annually. Home: 217 Hollow Tree Ridge Rd Darien CT 06820 Office: 1200 Bedford St Stamford CT 06905

BOOK, ANITA-BAKER (MRS. WILLIAM S. BOOK), mfr., designer; b. Essex, Ill.; d. John Benjamin and Dora (Greenwald) Baker; student Chgo. Bus. Coll., Columbia Conservatory, 1921-23, Am. Acad. Fine Arts; grad. Herzl Jr. Coll., 1936; student N.Y. U., 1936, U. Chgo., 1937-39, 40-41, U. Nebr., 1941; m. William Ship Book, Mar. 14, 1941. Tchr. dramatic art, Chgo., 1926-32; appeared various radio plays, Chgo., 1926-37; secretarial position, receptionist, Chgo., 1927-32; mgr. N.Y. import office, 1933-34; lectr. throughout U.S. with exhbn. wood carvings and handicrafts from Dutch East Indies, 1934-41; creator, designer Bells of Sarna, 1935; sec. Consairways, Fairfield, Calif., 1945; owner, exec. dir., designer Binita Fruit & Gift Wares, Skokie, Ill., 1945—, exhbns. maj. gift and trade shows throughout U.S.; past treas. Natural Hygiene Press. Commr., Village of Skokie Beautification and Improvement Commn., Skokie Bicentennial Commn. Bd. dirs., chmn. pub. relations Skokie League Women Voters; bd. dirs., chmn. Am. affairs Hadassah, Skokie; mem. Skokie Civic Theatre, Skokie Valley Symphony Orch. and Women's Guild; mem. nat. women's com. Brandeis U. Recipient award of merit U. Chgo. Alumni Fund. Hon. fellow Harry S. Truman Library Inst. Mem. Natural Hygiene Assn., Gift and Decorative Accessories Assn. (Quarter-century mem.), Natural Food Assn., Organic Growers No. Ill., UN Assn. U.S., Medic Alert, Skokie C. of C. (chmn. beautification com. 1968), U. Chgo. Alumni Assn., Art Inst. Chgo. (life), Nat. Fedn. Ind. Business Inc., Field Mus., Skokie Valley Bus. and Profl. Women's Club, Poets and Patrons, AAUW, Nat. Geog. Soc., Smithsonian Assos., North Shore Pub. Relations, M.M.S. Co-editor: Early Skokie, 1976. Home and office: 3811 Wright Terrace Skokie IL 60076

BOOK, EDWARD R., entertainment and hotel co. exec.; b. Harrisburg, Pa., May 9, 1931; s. Raymond John and Grace Elizabeth (Bergstresser) B.; B.S. in Hotel Adminstrn., Pa. State U., 1954; m. Inga M. Scheyer, Feb. 14, 1953; children—Sandra Book Liddick, Edward R., Frederick A. Restaurant mgr. Howard D. Johnson Co., Harrisburg, 1950-55; food and beverage mgr., asst. mgr. Hotel Harrisburger, Harrisburg, 1956-60; v.p., gen. mgr. Hotel Bethlehem (Pa.), 1960-68; gen. mgr. Hospitality Motor Inn, Cleve., 1968-69; gen. mgr. Hotel Hershey (Pa.), 1969; mng. dir. Hotel Hershey and Country Club, 1970; with HERCO, Inc. (now Hershey Entertainment & Resort Co.), Hershey, 1971—, chief exec. officer, chmn., 1974—; dir. Hershey Trust Co. Trustee, Harrisburg YMCA; campaign chmn. Tri-County United Way, Harrisburg; mem. exec. bd. Keystone council Boy Scouts Am., Hershey; bd. mgrs. Milton Hershey Sch. and M.S. Hershey Found.; trustee Pa. State U. Served to 1st lt. U.S. Army, 1954-56. Mem. Pa. State Alumni Assn. (past pres.), Pa. State Hotel and Restaurant Assn., Harrisburg Area C. of C. (past pres.), Travel Industry Assn. Am. (1st vice-chmn.), Ams. for Competitive Enterprise Systems, Inc., Am. Hotel and Motel Assn., Nat. Inst. Food Service Industry (trustee 1979). Presbyterian. Club: Skal. Home: 36 Brownstone Dr Hershey PA 17033 Office: 300 Park Blvd Hershey PA 17033

BOOKOUT, JOHN FRANK, JR., oil co. exec.; b. Shreveport, La., Dec. 31, 1922; s. John Frank and Lena (Hagen) B.; student Iowa Wesleyan Coll., 1943, Centenary Coll., 1946-47; B.Sc., U. Tex., 1949, M.A., 1950; D.Sc. (hon.), Tulane U., 1978; m. Mary Carolyn Cook, Dec. 21, 1946; children—Beverly Carolyn, Mary Adair and John Frank III (twins). Geologist, Shell Oil Co., Tulsa, 1950-59, div. exploration mgr., 1959-61, area exploration mgr., Denver, 1961-63, The Hague, Netherlands, 1963-64, exploration mgr., New Orleans, 1964, mgr. exploration and prodn. econs. dept., N.Y.C., 1965, v.p. Denver exploration and prodn. area, 1966, v.p. Southeastern exploration and prodn. region, New Orleans, 1967-70, pres., chief exec. officer, dir. Shell Can. Ltd., Toronto, Ont., 1970-74, exec. v.p., dir. Shell Oil Co., Houston, from 1974, now pres., chief exec. officer; dir. Irving Trust Co., Safeway Stores, Inc. Mem. So. regional adv. bd. Inst. Internat. Edn.; bd. dirs. Meth. Hosp., Houston; bd. visitors Tulane U. Served with USAAF, 1942-46. Decorated Air medal with 3 oak leaf clusters. Mem. Am. Petroleum Inst., Am. Assn. Petroleum Geologists (dir.), Nat. Petroleum Council, Conf. Bd., All-Am. Wildcatters Assn., 25 Yr. Club of Petroleum Industry (bd. govs. S.W. dist.), Internat. C. of C. (trustee U.S. council), Houston C. of C. (dir.), Bus. Roundtable, Found. for Bus., Politics and Econs. (trustee). Home: PO Box 13614 Houston TX 77019 Office: Shell Oil Co One Shell Plaza Houston TX 77001

BOOKSHESTER, DENNIS S., dept. store exec.; b. Chgo., Nov. 26, 1938; s. Jack and Dorothy (Goldblatt) B.; B.S., U. Ala., 1960; m. Karen V. Schwartz, July 11, 1967; children—Allison, Jacklyn. With Burdine's, Miami, Fla., 1960-77, sr. v.p. merchandising, 1974-77; pres. Sibley, Lindsay & Curr Co., Rochester, N.Y., 1977—, chief exec. officer, 1979—; dir. Security Trust Co., Rochester; v.p. Asso. Dry Goods Corp., N.Y.C. Bd. dirs. Rochester Bus. Com. for Arts, United Community Chest Rochester, Rochester Downtown Devel. Corp., Center for Govtl. Research; trustee Rochester Area Ednl. TV. Served with U.S. Army, 1960-61. Mem. Rochester Area C. of C. (trustee). Jewish. Clubs: Genesee Valley, Irondequoit Country (Rochester). Office: 228 Main St E Rochester NY 14604

BOONE, DANIEL C., JR., steel co. exec.; b. Mt. Sterling, Ky., Feb. 23, 1920; s. Daniel C. and Grace (Salyer) B.; certificate in accounting, Marquette U., 1947; m. Jayne Deardoff, July 28, 1970; 1 son, Terry. With Superior Lawrence Bag Co., 1937-41, Haskins & Sells, C.P.A.'s, Cin., 1947; with Armco Steel Corp., 1941-42, 47—, controller steel div., 1958-65, corp. controller, 1965-67, v.p. fin., 1967-69, sr. v.p. fin., 1969-73, exec. v.p., 1973-79, pres., chief operating officer, 1979—; dir. Armco Steel Corp., Winters Nat. Bank, Winters Nat. Corp., Duriron Co., Crystal Tissue Corp., Phillips Industries, Dayton Power & Light. Served with USAAF, 1942-45. Republican. Home: 2105 Tullis Dr Middletown OH 45042 Office: Armco Steel Corp Middletown OH 45042

BOONE, RALPH DAVIS, mfg. co. exec.; b. Turnersville, Tex., July 8, 1916; s. Tom and Birdie Chambers (Duckworth) B.; student public schs., Hamlin, Tex.; m. Velma Rea Leeth, July 27, 1938; children—Paula Boone Gough, Dan F. Pres., sales mgr. Three B Brush Mfg. Co., Inc., Lubbock, Tex. Mem. Am. Brush Mfrs. Assn. Office: 912 84th St Lubbock TX 79423

BOONE, TIMOTHY ALLEN, orgn. and mgmt. devel. cons.; b. Watsonville, Calif., June 14, 1945; s. Arthur Merle and Lillian Margaret (Rudolph) B.; B.A. magna cum laude in Psychology, Chapman Coll., Orange, Calif., 1975; M.A. in Human Resource Mgmt., Pepperdine U., Los Angeles, 1976; Ph.D. in Mgmt. and Orgn. Devel., U.S. Internat. U., San Diego, 1980; m. Linda Lee Snyder, Jan. 11, 1975; children—Jennifer Susan, Conor Patrick. Commd. 2d lt. U.S. Army, 1965, advanced through grades to capt., 1968; service in Thailand and Vietnam; resigned, 1976; gen. mgr. NTL/Learning Resources Corp., La Jolla, Calif., 1976-78; v.p. ops. Univ. Assos., Inc., La Jolla, 1978-79, v.p. profl. services, 1979-80; cons. Center for Leadership Studies, Escondido, Calif., 1980—; pres. T.A. Boone Assos., Inc., San Diego, 1980—; mem. faculty Calif. Am. U., Escondido, 1979—. Youth dir. Monterey Peninsula Jaycees, 1974; chmn. Los Penasquitos Sch. Goals Monitoring Com., 1977. Decorated Bronze Star (2), Meritorious Service medal, Air medal (3), Army Commendation medal (2), Purple Heart, Combat Inf. badge. Mem. Am. Soc. Tng. and Devel., Am. Acad. Mgmt., Orgn. Devel. Network. Author papers in field. Office: 14531 Yukon St San Diego CA 92129

BOORAS, NICKOLAS PERICLES, financier; b. Kalamata, Greece, June 23, 1944; s. Peter Pericles and Angelia (Demopolus) B.; came to U.S., 1919, naturalized, 1946; B.A., Mich. Lutheran Coll., 1968; m. Margaret Ferguson, Aug. 27, 1966; children—Heather, Amanda, Nickolas. With mktg. dept. Am. Can. Co., 1967-69, Texaco Inc., 1969-73; pres., chief exec. officer Thalasa Ltd., Birmingham, Mich., 1973—. Mem. Nat. Assn. Credit Mgmt., Builders Exchange, Birmingham, Troy chambers commerce. Greek Orthodox. Clubs: Rotary, Optimists (Troy). Home: 4621 Mill Pond Troy MI 48098 Office: 190 W Big Beaver Troy MI 48084

BOOSALIS, ELSIE, real estate mgmt. exec.; b. Cedar Rapids, Iowa, Dec. 1, 1913; adopted dau. of Peter and Rose (Halleck) B.; student Phoenix Bus. Coll., 1943-44, Northwestern U., 1952-53, U. Minn. Property mgr. Peter Boosalis Bldg. Trust, Mpls., 1953—, trustee, 1960—. Dir. Greater Lake St. Council; sustaining mem. council Girl Scouts; bus. mem. Powderhorn Devel. Corp.; active ARC. Mem. Mpls. Soc. Fine Arts, Minn., Hennepin County hist. socs., Mpls. C. of C., Minn. Orchestral Assn., English Speaking Union, Am. Swgdish Inst., Chgo.-Lake Assn. (dir.). Home: 4551 Dupont Ave S Minneapolis MN 55409 Office: 2951 Chicago Ave Minneapolis MN 55407

BOOTH, CHARLES DALE, mfg. co. exec.; b. Ft. Worth, July 18, 1953; s. Jesse Ray and Margaret Lucille Booth; student Tarrant County Jr. Coll., 1971-73; m. Vicki L. Miller, Apr. 6, 1974; 1 dau., Bridget Lyndale. Pres., All Am. Truck Sleeper Corp., Hurst, Tex., 1975—; lectr. on effective mfg. ideas, 1977—. Asst. 24th Congl. dist. leader One Nation under God Inc.; lectr. on abortion, def., polit. issues. Mem. Nat. Fedn. Ind. Bus., U.S. C. of C. Republican. Mem. Assembly of God Ch. Designer sleepers for tractor trucks. Office: 1501 Hurst Blvd Hurst TX 76053

BOOTH, WALLACE WRAY, distbn. mfg. co. exec.; b. Nashville, Sept. 30, 1922; s. Wallace W. and Josephine (England) B.; B.A., U. Chgo., 1948, M.B.A., 1948; m. Donna Cameron Voss, Mar. 22, 1947; children—Ann Conley, John England. mgr. Ford Motor Co., Dearborn, Mich., 1948-59; dir. finance, v.p. finance, treas. Ford Motor Co. Can., Ltd. Toronto 1959-63; mng. dir., chief exec. officer Ford Motor Co. Australia, Melbourne 1963-67; v.p. corporate staffs, indsl. products Philco-Ford Corp., Phila., 1967-68; sr. v.p. corporate staffs, mem. exec. com., dir. Rockwell Internat. Corp., El Segundo, Calif., 1968-75; pres., chief exec. officer, dir. United Brands Co., Boston, 1975-77; chmn., pres., chief exec. officer Ducommun Inc., Los Angeles, 1977—; dir. Litton Industries, Beverly Hills, Calif., United Calif. Bank, Los Angeles, Kaufman and Broad, Inc., Los Angeles. Pres., Los Angeles United Way. Served to 1st lt. USAAF, 1944-46. Club: Calif. (Los Angeles). Office: Ducommun Inc 612 S Flower St Los Angeles CA 90017

BOOTON, THOMAS MASON, auditor; b. Roslyn, N.Y., Nov. 10, 1949; s. Glenn S. and Franis (Igram) B.; B.A., St. John's U., 1973, M.B.A., 1978; m. Mary T. Dobsovits, May 15, 1973. Jr. auditor Irving Trust Co., N.Y.C., 1973-76; sr. and intermediate auditor European Am. Bank, N.Y.C., 1976-78; dep. auditor Bklyn. Savs. Bank, N.Y.C., 1978—. Cert. internal auditor; cert. data processing auditor. Mem. Inst. Internal Auditors, Am. Inst. Banking, Am. Mgmt. Assn., EDP Auditors Assn., Am. Inst. C.P.A.'s, Am. Legion, Republican. Roman Catholic. Home: 8557 106 St Richmond Hill NY 11418 Office: Brooklyn Savings Bank 211 Montague St Brooklyn NY 11202

BORCHERS, EDWARD LEO, mfg. co. exec.; b. Shelby County, Ohio, Jan. 8, 1939; s. Urban Frank and Elfrieda Elizabeth (Voisard) B.; A.A. in Higher Acctg., Miami Jacobs Coll., 1959; m. Merilyn G. Wagaman, July 14, 1962; children—Michele, Doug, David, Kim. Cost acct., bookkeeper, purchasing agt. Shelby Mfg. Co., Sidney, Ohio, 1959-66; part-owner, exec. v.p. Superior Aluminum Products Inc., Russia, Ohio, 1966—. Bd. dirs. Wilson Meml. Hosp., Sidney, 1979—; clk.-treas. Village of Russia, 1968-74, mayor, 1974—. Mem. Soc. for Advancement Mgmt., Cath. War Vets., Russia Civic Assn. Democrat. Roman Catholic. Club: K.C. (Public Service award 1979). Home: 111 Borchers St Russia OH 45363 Office: 211 W Main St Russia OH 45363

BORD, NANCY ARNONE, mgmt. cons.; b. West Hartford, Conn., Oct. 15, 1940; d. Frank Edward and Rita Marion (Moreau) Arnone; A.B. cum laude, Smith Coll., 1961; Ph.D., M.I.T., 1965. Economist, Center Urban Edn., N.Y.C., 1965-67; study dir. Inst. Ednl. Devel., N.Y.C., 1967-69; sr. asso. Cresap, McCormick & Paget, Inc., mgmt. cons., N.Y.C., 1969-75; mng. asso. Theodore Barry & Assos., Los Angeles, 1975-77; chief economist, mgr. planning Pacific Power & Light Co., Portland, Oreg., 1977-79; v.p. Planning and Anaylsis Group, N.Y.C., 1979—; mem. adj. faculty N.Y. U., City U. N.Y. Chmn. Gov. Oreg. Commn. Juvenile Services, 1978-79; chmn. planning com. N.W. Oreg. Health Systems, 1977-79; bd. dirs., v.p. Oreg. Vocal Arts Ensemble, 1977-79; adv. com. women in sci. NSF, 1973-75. Recipient Nat. Ednl. Press award, 1967. Mem. Nat. Assn. Bus. Economists, N.Am. Soc. Corp. Planning, Phi Beta Kappa. Clubs: Smith Coll., M.I.T. Alumni, Met. (N.Y.C.). Co-author: The Making of a Manager: A World View, 1975.

BORENSTEIN, MAX, comml. fin. exec.; b. July 2, 1920; s. Benjamin and Esther (Berches) B.; B.B.A., Coll. City N.Y., 1942; postgrad. Columbia U., 1945-46; m. Ruth Schreier, Oct. 19, 1946; children—Gary, Robert, Amy. Vice pres., treas. York Factors, N.Y.C., 1960-63; chmn. bd. IMFC Fin. Corp., N.Y.C., 1963-76; v.p. A.J. Armstrong Co. Inc., N.Y.C., 1976—. Served with Mil. Intelligence Service U.S. Army, 1942-45. Recipient Distinguished Citizen Service award Council for Distinguished Citizens, 1972; Silver Beaver award Boy Scouts Am., 1968. Mem. Nat. Comml. Fin. Conf., N.Y. Credit and Fin. Mgmt. Assn. Home: 270-060 Grand Central Pkwy Floral Park NY 11005 Office: 850 3d Ave New York NY 10022

BORENSTEIN, MILTON CONRAD, lawyer, cup co. exec.; b. Boston, Oct. 21, 1914; s. Isadore Sidney and Eva Beatrice B.; A.B. cum laude, Boston Coll., 1935; J.D., Harvard U., 1938; m. Anne Shapiro, June 20, 1937; children—Roberta, Jeffrey. Admitted to Mass. bar, 1938; practice law, Boston and Chelsea, Mass., 1938—; officer, dir. Md. Cup Corp., Owings Mills, 1960—, exec. v.p., treas., 1977—; officer, dir. Sweetheart Paper Products Co., Inc., Chelsea, 1944—, pres., 1961—; officer, dir. Sweetheart Plastics, Inc., Wilmington, Mass., 1958—, v.p., 1961—. Trustee, Boston Coll., 1979—, Combined Jewish Philanthropies, 1969—, N.E. Sinai Hosp., 1974—; pres.'s council Sarah Lawrence Coll., 1970-79, Brandeis U., 1980—; hon. pres. Congregation Kehillath Israel, Brookline, Mass.; bd. dirs. Am. Assos. Hebrew U., 1968—, Ben Gurion U., 1975—, Am. Jewish Congress, 1979—. Recipient Community Service award Jewish Theol. Sem. Am., 1970; bd. overseers Jewish Theol. Sem. Am., 1973—. Mem. Boston, Mass., Am. bar assns., Single Service Inst., Chelsea C. of C. (dir.). Clubs: Harvard (Boston); Harvard Faculty, 100, Masons. Home: 273 Eliot St Chestnut Hill MA 02167 Office: 191 Williams St Chelsea MA 02150

BORENSTINE, ALVIN JEROME, exec. search co. exec.; b. Kansas City, Mo., Dec. 14, 1933; s. Samuel and Ella (Berman) B.; B.A. in Econs., U. Kans., 1956; M.B.A. in Indsl. Mgmt. (Eddie Jacobson Found fellow, Systems and Procedures Assn. fellow), U. Pa., 1960; m. Roula Alakiotou, Dec. 31, 1976; children—Ella Marie and Sami (twins). Systems analyst Johnson & Johnson Co., New Brunswick, N.J., 1960-61; systems mgr. Levitt & Sons, Levittown, N.J., 1961-65; dir. systems and data processing Warren Bros. Co. div. Ashland Oil Co., Cambridge, Mass., 1965-71; corp. mgr. fin. and adminstrv. systems Esmark Inc., Chgo., 1971-72; pres. Synergistics Assos., Chgo., 1972—, chief exec. officer Ms. Exec. Search div., 1978—. Served with U.S. Army, 1956-58. Mem. Assn. Systems Mgmt. (pres. Boston chpt. 1968-69, chmn. internat. research com. 1966-68, Distinguished Service award 1970). Jewish. Clubs: Carlton, Whitehall (Chgo.); B'nai B'rith. Home: 6033 N Sheridan Rd Chicago IL 60660 Office: 875 N Michigan Ave Chicago IL 60611

BORER, EDWARD TURNER, investment banker; b. Phila., Nov. 30, 1938; s. Robert Chamberlin and Helen Elizabeth (Clawges) B.; B.S., U. Pa., 1960; m. Amy Hamilton Ryerson, Aug. 8, 1959; children—Edward Turner, Catherine Hamilton, Elizabeth Taft. Rep., Hopper Soliday & Co., Inc., Phila., 1960-67, v.p. research, 1967-73, sec., 1971—, sr. v.p., 1973—, also dir., dir. Manchester Gas Co. (N.H.), 1965—, pres., 1970, chmn. bd., chmn. exec. com., 1970—; founder, treas., sec., dir. Creative Information Systems, Inc., Chadds Ford, Pa., 1967-77; v.p. Sovereign Investors, 1980—. Chmn. West Met. Area-Wide Com., Regional Med. Program, 1969-70. Pres. Swarthmore Home and Sch. Assn., 1973; bd. dirs. Freedom Valley council Girl Scouts U.S.A., 1974-75, also chmn. finance com., chmn. investment com.; bd. dirs., mem. fin. com. Planned Parenthood Southeastern Pa., 1980—; treas., trustee George W. South Meml. Ch. of the Adv., Phila., 1978—. Served to 1st lt., Q.M.C., AUS, 1961-62. Chartered financial analyst. Mem. Financial Analysts Fedn., Phila. Securities Assn. (dir. 1979-80, v.p. 1980—), Fin. Analysts Phila. (treas. 1976-77), N.Y. Soc. Security Analysts, Delta Upsilon. Episcopalian (vestryman 1970-73, 74-77). Club: Union League (Phila.). Home: 125 Guernsey Rd Swarthmore PA 19081 Office: 1401 Walnut St Philadelphia PA 19102

BORGMANN, DMITRI ALFRED, research co. exec.; b. Berlin, Germany, Oct. 22, 1927; s. Hans and Lisa (Kalnitzkaya) B.; brought to U.S., 1936, naturalized, 1943; Ph.B., U. Chgo., 1946; D.D., Universal Life Ch., 1976; Ph.D. in Bus. Adminstrn., Sussex Coll. Tech., 1979; m. Iris Sandra Sterling, Oct. 27, 1962; 1 son, Keith Alan. Policy change supr. Central Standard Life Ins. Co., Chgo., 1946-61; actuarial asst. Harry S. Tressel & Assos., Chgo., 1961-65; ind. writer, columnist, researcher, Chgo., 1965-71; owner RC Research Co., also Jackpot Jubilee, Chgo., 1970-72, Dayton, Wash., 1972-75, Research Unltd., Dayton, 1975—, Intellex, Dayton, 1976—, Service Unltd., Dayton, 1976—; corporate identity cons., 1967—; ordained minister Universal Life Ch., Modesto, Calif., 1976; founder, pres. Divine Immortality Ch., Dayton, 1978—. Mem. Life Office Mgmt. Assn. Inst., Mensa, Word Guild, Nat. Puzzlers League. Author: Language on Vacation, 1965; Beyond Language, 1967; Curious Crosswords, 1970; columnist Games, 1979—. Home and Office: PO Box 300 Dayton WA 99328 Office: 227 E Park St Dayton WA 99328

BORLAND, VIRGINIA ANN, fashion specialist, fiber co. exec.; b. N.Y.C., Mar. 8, 1929; d. Charles Peter and Margaret Elise (Swane) Stockfish; B.A., Wells Coll., 1951; m. J. Nelson Borland, Nov. 13, 1969. Fashion publicist Grey Advt., N.Y.C., 1956-60; fashion dir. Cunningham & Walsh, advt., N.Y.C., 1960-61, Avtex Fibers, Inc. (formerly Am. Viscose Co.), N.Y.C., 1961—. Vol. pediatric ward Meml. Hosp., 1953—. Mem. Fashion Group (gov. 1975-77), Inner Circle, Am. Printed Fabrics Council (bd. dirs.), Color Assn. U.S.A. (chmn. women's apparel color selection com.), Round Table Fashion Execs., Fashion News Workshop, N.Y. Jr. League. Episcopalian. Home: 110 East End Ave New York NY 10028 Office: 1185 Ave of Americas New York NY 10036

BORMAN, FRANK, former astronaut, airlines exec.; b. Gary, Ind., Mar. 14, 1928; s. Edwin Borman; B.S., U.S. Mil. Acad., 1950; M.Aero. Engring., Cal. Inst. Tech., 1957; grad. USAF Aerospace Research Pilots Sch., 1960; grad. Advanced Mgmt. Program, Harvard Bus. Sch., 1970; m. Susan Bugbee; children—Fredrick, Edwin. Commd. 2d lt. USAF, advanced through grades to col., 1965, ret., 1970; assigned various fighter squadrons, U.S. and Philippines 1951-56; instr. thermodynamics and fluid mechanics U.S. Mil. Acad., 1957-60; instr. USAF Aerospace Research Pilots Sch., 1960-62; astronaut With Manned Spacecraft Center, NASA, until 1970; command pilot on 14 day orbital Gemini 7 flight, Dec. 1965, including rendezvous with Gemini 6; command pilot Apollo 8, 1st lunar orbital mission, Dec. 1968; sr. v.p. for ops. Eastern Air Lines, Inc., Miami, Fla., 1970-74, exec. v.p., gen. ops. mgr., 1974-75, pres., chief exec. officer, 1975—, bd. chmn., 1976—. Recipient Distinguished Service award NASA, 1965; Collier Trophy. Nat. Aeros. Assn., 1968. Address: Eastern Air Lines Inc Miami International Airport Miami FL 33148

BORMANN, DANIEL RAY, broadcast research and cons. co. exec.; b. Sioux Falls, S.D., Dec. 13, 1945; s. William John and Olga Florence (Hentschel) B.; B.S. in Bus. Adminstrn., U. S.D., 1971; certificate Gen. Electric Fin. Mgmt. Program, 1973; m. Ann Ruth Bonzer, Sept. 7, 1969; children—Adam Daniel, Nathan Paul. Fin. rep. Gen. Electric Co., Schenectady, 1971-74, corporate auditor, 1974-75; bus. mgr. KFSN-TV, WROW AM/FM, Fresno, Calif., 1975-77; controller

WCCO-TV, Mpls., 1977-78; v.p., chief adminstrv. officer Frank N. Magid Assos., Marion, Iowa, 1978—. Drive chmn. United Way, 1978-80. Served with U.S. Army, 1963-67. Mem. Broadcast Fin. Mgmt. Assn. (Contbg. Editor award 1979; personnel com.), Nat. Fedn. Ind. Bus., Beta Gamma Sigma. Democrat. Lutheran. Home: 7000 Parkdale Ln NE Cedar Rapids IA 52402 Office: 1 Research Center Marion IA 52302

BORMANN, EDWARD JOHN, chem. co. exec.; b. Bklyn., July 10, 1925; s. Julius E. and Bertha C. (Dreyer) B.; B.S., Coll. City N.Y., 1949, M.B.A., N.Y. U., 1958, postgrad., 1962-68; m. Gladys R. Bedigian, Oct. 23, 1949; children—Linda, Beverly, Emily. Chemist Magnus, Mabee & Reynard, N.Y.C., 1941-42; chief electronic insp. Sperry Gyroscope Co., Lake Success, L.I., 1943, 46; asst. operations mgr. Nat. Sugar Refining Co., Long Island City, 1949-54; sr. staff indsl. engr. S.B. Penick & Co., N.Y.C., 1954-64; sr. mgmt. cons., planning and evaluation, comml. devel. div. Am. Cyanamid Co., 1964-67; mgr. corp. evaluation and mgmt. planning Geigy Chem. Corp., 1967-70; planning and devel. coordinator CIBA-Geigy Corp., 1970-80, mgr. planning adminstrn., 1980—, cons. corp. acquisitions and new ventures, 1961-67. Served with USAAF, 1943-46. Mem. Am. Chem. Soc., Indsl. and Engring, Soc., Am. Inst. Chem. Engrs., Bergen County Hist. Soc., Am. Mgmt. Assn., N. Am. Soc. Corp. Planning. (treas. 1974-75, sec. 1975-77, dir. 1980—). Presbyn. (elder, trustee). Home: 693 Palmer Ave Maywood NJ 07607 Office: 444 Sawmill River Rd Ardsley NY 10502

BORMANN, RENNIE MAE, retail wallcovering co. exec.; b. Weslaco, Tex., Nov. 5, 1922; d. Harburd and Rennie May (Short) Tarpley; B.A. in Spanish, U. Tex., 1944; m. Edwin Murrie Bormann, June 16, 1946; children—Ronald Murrie, Rebecca Mae, Lois Ruth. Tchr. Spanish, Alamo Heights High Sch., San Antonio, 1944-46; bookkeeper Bormann's Paint & Supply Co., McAllen, Tex., 1950-72; mgr. Bormanns' Wallcoverings, Inc., McAllen, 1973-81, pres., 1981—. Mem. Nat. Decorating Products Assn., Nat. Assn. Ind. Bus., Rio Grande Valley Audubon Soc. Republican. Methodist. Office: 117 S McColl Rd McAllen TX 78501

BORMES, THOMAS G., dental co. exec.; b. St. Paul, Mar. 30, 1941; s. Louis A. and Ruth K. (Kinsella) B.; student St. John's U., 1959-62, Golden Gate U., 1970-72, U. Minn., 1962-63; m. Diann K. Marcus, June 8, 1968; children—Christopher Marc, Kimberly Jo. Founder, pres. MKB Tech., San Mateo, Calif., 1970-73; pres. APM-Sterngold, San Mateo, 1973-79, Mycone West, San Carlos, Calif., 1979—; founder, pres. PREAT, Inc., 1980—; dir. Time Track, Inc., Spectrolyte Inc. Bd. dirs. Boy Scouts Am., San Mateo, 1972-74. Republican. Roman Catholic. Clubs: Rotary, Ducks Unltd. Designer 5 precision attachments for dentistry. Home: 1596 Parkwood Dr San Mateo CA 94403 Office: 1661 Industrial Rd San Carlos CA 94070

BORNSTEIN, SUMNER, furniture mfg. co. exec.; b. Boston, Nov. 9, 1931; s. Jacob and Celia Doris Bornstein; B.S., U. R.I., 1954; m. Sarine Swartz, June 27, 1954; children—Barry Reid, Jack Alan, Scott Howard, Andrew Lee. Sales rep. Rowe Furniture Corp., Columbus, Ohio, 1960-65, asst. nat. sales mgr., 1966, v.p., nat. sales mgr., 1967-69; now dir.; pres. Kenwood Furniture Corp., Washington, 1970-74; exec. v.p. mktg. Jackson Furniture Cos., Bethesda, Md., 1975—; cons. Atlantic Furniture Corp., since 1971—. Pres., Md. Boys Club. Served to 1st lt. U.S. Army, 1955-57. Mem. So. Furniture Mfg. Assn. (mktg. com.), Ohio Wholesale Furniture Assn. (pres.). Republican. Jewish. Home: The Promenade 5225 Pooks Hill Rd Apt 1113N Bethesda MD 20014 Office: 7979 Old Georgetown Rd Suite 706 Bethesda MD 20014

BOROCHOFF, CHARLES ZACHARY, mfg. co. owner; b. Atlanta, Apr. 11, 1921; s. Isadore and Pauline (Reisman) B.; LL.B., Atlanta Law Sch., 1941; m. Ida Dorothy Sloan, Jan. 11, 1942; children—Lynn Borochoff Gould, Toby Ann Borochoff Bernstein, Jean Sue Borochoff Shapiro, Lance Mark. Exec v.p. So. Wire & Iron Works, Atlanta, 1936-63; pres. Borochoff Properties, Inc., real estate, Atlanta, 1954—, Designs Unlimited, Inc., Atlanta, 1964—, Scottdale Enterprises, Atlanta, 1972—; exec. v.p. Imperial SE; pres. CDR Mfg. Co. Mem. High Museum of Art, 1955—, Nat. Conf. Christians and Jews, 1967—, Planned Parenthood, 1970—. Trustee Atlanta Playhouse, 1971—; mem. program com. Nat. UN Day, 1977, 78. Mem. DeKalb C. of C. (econ. devel. com. 1975), Nat. Retail Wholesale Furniture Assn., Internat. Home and Furniture Reps. Assn., Nu Beta Epsilon. Jewish religion (trustee synagogue). Mason (Shriner, 32 deg.); mem. B'nai B'rith. Clubs: Atlanta Music, Progressive, Jockey. Home: 3450 Old Plantation Rd NW Atlanta GA 30327 Office: 3451 Church St Scottdale GA 30079

BOROWITZ, ALBERT IRA, lawyer: b. Chgo., June 27, 1930; s. David and Anne (Wolkenstein) B.; B.A. in Classics summa cum laude (Detur award 1948), Harvard U., 1951, M.A. in Chinese Regional Studies, 1953, J.D. magna cum laude (Sears prize), 1956; m. Helen Blanche Osterman, July 29, 1950; children—Peter Leonard, Joan, Andrew Seth. Admitted to Ohio bar, 1957; asso. firm Hahn, Loeser, Freedheim, Dean & Wellman, Cleve., 1956-62, partner, 1962—; dir. Bobbie Brooks, Inc. Mem. Am. Law Inst., Am. Bar Assn., Ohio State Bar Assn., Bar Assn. Greater Cleve. Clubs: Union, Rowfant, Ct. of Nisi Prius (Cleve.); Harvard N.Y.C. Author: Fiction in Communist China, 1955; Innocence and Arsenic: Studies in Crime and Literature, 1977; The Woman Who Murdered Black Satin: The Bermondsey Horror, 1981. Contbr. articles to profl. jours. Home: 2561 Coventry Rd Shaker Heights OH 44120 Office: 800 National City E 6th Bldg Cleveland OH 44114

BORRELLI, JOSEPH R., ins. co. exec.; b. Bronx, N.Y., July 17, 1939; s. Anthony J. and Santina M. (Miele) B.; m. Carol A. Burke, Feb. 10, 1961; children—Anthony, Theresa, Michael. Agt., John Hancock Ins. Co., 1966-67, staff mgr., 1967-77, regional dir. John Hancock Distbrs., 1978-79, dist. mgr. John Hancock Ins. Co., Brockton, Mass., 1979—. Mem. Nat. Assn. Life Underwriters (1st v.p.). Republican. Roman Catholic. Office: 1095 W Chestnut St Brockton MA 02401

BORST, ROBERT ORIN, mktg. exec.; b. Mpls., July 22, 1918; s. Robert E. and Judith (Sivertson) B.; M.E., U. Wis., 1941; postgrad. Calif. Inst. Tech., 1945-46; m. Miriam Fletcher, Aug. 29, 1947; children—Judith K., Barbra B. Cons. engr., 1954-57; mktg. mgr. Sierra Schroeder Controls, 1957-60; sales mgr. Aircraft div. Hughes Tool Co., 1960-61, applications engr. Nuclear div. Hughes Aircraft, 1961-62; mktg. and pres. Osborne-Borst Corp., 1964; mgmt. and engr. cons., 1962-64; mktg. mgr. Systems Mgmt. div. Western Gear Corp., 1964-66; mktg. mgr. spl. products Electronics div. Gen. Dynamics Corp., 1966-69; mgmt. cons., mktg. mgr. Marine Resources Inc., 1969-71; cons., dir. marketing and consumer affairs div. Bur. Domestic Commerce, U.S. Dept. Commerce, 1971-72; program mgr. terminal systems Cochran Western Corp., Salinas, Calif., 1972-75, cons., 1976-77; v.p. mktg. Vulcan Iron Works, West Palm Beach, Fla., 1977-78; mktg. Eastern region Carco Electronics, Menlo Park, Calif., 1978—. Mem. ASME (dir. Los Angeles aviation sect. 1955-57), Marine Tech. Soc., Nat. Soc. Profl. Engrs., Soc. Exploration Geophysics, Am. Arbitration Assn.

BORTLES, LARRY LYNEL, real estate investment co. exec.; b. Spokane, May 26, 1939; s. Ira and Evelyn (Wood) B.; B.A. in Econs., Cornell U., 1961; M.B.A. in Fin., Harvard, 1968; m. Leinani Keppeler, Oct. 12, 1963; children—Erin, Kristin, Gavin, Eden. Vice pres. Island Constrn. Co., Honolulu, 1963-66; asst. to sr. v.p. Fin. Sheraton Corp., Boston, 1967; mgr. mgmt. cons. div. Peat Marwick Mitchell & Co., Honolulu, 1968-69; pres. Hawaiiana Realty & Mgmt., Inc., Honolulu, 1969-72, Bortles & Assos., Inc., Honolulu, 1972—; dir. HI Econ. Devel. Corp., 1969-74, HI Internat. Mgmt. & Research Inst., 1969-74, Multi-Family Housing Council, 1970-72. Mem. Hawaii, Honolulu (dir. 1971-73) bds. realtors, Real Estate Securities Syndications Inst., Hawaii C. of C., Hawaii Visitors Bur., Home Builders Assn. Hawaii (dir. 1970-72), Wilder Regent Assn. Owners (dir. 1971-75), Waialae Iki Ridge Community Assn. (pres. 1972-75), Harvard Bus. Sch. Club Hawaii (pres. 1978—). Episcopalian. Home: 1437 Laamia St Honolulu HI 96821

BORUM, RODNEY LEE, printing corp. exec.; b. nr. High Point, N.C., Sept. 30, 1929; s. Carl Macy and Etta (Sullivan) B.; student U. N.C. 1947-49; B.S., U.S. Naval Acad., 1953; m. Helen Marie Rigby, June 27, 1953; children—Richard Harlan, Sarah Elizabeth. Design-devel. engr. Gen. Elec. Co., Syracuse, N.Y., Cape Kennedy, Fla., 1956-58, missile test condr. Cape Kennedy, 1958-60, mgr. ground equipment engrs., 1960-61, mgr. Eastern test range engring., 1961-65; adminstr. Bus. and Def. Services Adminstrn., Dept. Commerce, 1966-69; pres. Printing Industries Am., 1969—, mem. exec. com., 1969—, dir., 1969—; dir. Inter-Comprint Ltd., Strangers Cay, Ltd.; mem. governing bd. Comprint Internat. Mem. exec. council Cub Scouts Am., 1965; bd. dirs. Brevard County (Fla.) United Fund, 1964—, v.p., 1964-65; bd. dirs. Brevard Beaches Concert Assn., 1964; mem. edn. council, bd. dirs. Graphic Arts Tech. Found., 1970—; trustee, founder Graphic Arts Edn. and Research Trust Fund, 1978—. Republican candidate Fla. Ho. of Reps., 1960. Served to 1st lt. USAF, 1953-56. Named Boss of Yr., Ur. C. of C., 1965; recipient Bausch and Lomb sci. award, 1947, award Am. Legion, 1952. Mem. U.S. Naval Inst., U.S. Naval Acad. Alumni Assn., Graphic Arts Council N. Am. (dir. 1977—), Phi Eta Sigma. Methodist. Clubs: Columbia Country, City Tavern. Home: 4008 Glenrose St Kensington MD 20795 Office: 1730 N Lynn St Arlington VA 22209

BORUNDA, DAVID LEVINIO, lab. co. exec.; b. N.Mex., June 15, 1935; s. David Garcia and Jennie (Leyba) B.; student U. Md., 1957, U. N.Mex., 1958; certificate in traffic mgmt. Los Angeles Traffic Inst., 1969; m. Cheryl Kay Rein, Aug. 1, 1975; children by previous marriage—David Levinio, Dennis L., Donald L., Valerie Ann. Adminstrv. asst. to v.p. Par Industries, Los Angeles, 1962-63; supr. Appleton Electric Co., Los Angeles, 1963-65; plant traffic rep. Owens Ill. Glass Co., Los Angeles, 1965-69; mgr. distbn. Stuart Pharm. div. ICI Am., Pasadena, Calif., 1969-72, Cobe Labs., Inc., Lakewood, Colo., 1972—; instr. Community Coll. Denver, Opportunity Sch. Chmn. traffic and transp. adv. com. Community Coll. Denver, Emily Griffith Opportunity Sch. Served with USAF, 1954-58. Mem. Nat. Council Phys. Distbn. Mgmt., Traffic Club Denver (dir.), Internat. Trade Assn. Colo., Nat. Def. Transp. Assn., Rocky Mountain Air Cargo Assn. (pres., chmn. bd.), Delta Nu Alpha. Roman Catholic. Home: 12931 W Jewell Circle Lakewood CO 80228 Office: 1201 Oak St Lakewood CO 80215

BORUSZAK, JAMES MARTIN, ins. broker; b. Chgo., Dec. 9, 1930; s. Burton Victor and Priscilla Helena (Zohn) B.; B.S., U. Ill., 1953; C.L.U., 1962; m. Joan Kohlenbrener, June 14, 1953; children—Allan, Bruce, Beth. Asst. mgr. Met. Life Ins. Co., Chgo., 1956-62; asso. gen. agt. Pacific Mut. Life Ins. Co., Chgo., 1962-70; ins. broker, Northfield, Ill., 1970—. Pres., B'nai Torah Synagogue, Highland Park, Ill., 1969-71, Highland Park Depth Chargers, 1978; bd. dirs. Bonds for Israel, 1974; mem. pres.'s council U. Ill., 1980. Served with USAF, 1953-56. Recipient Earle S. Rappaport award Pacific Mut. Life Ins. Co., 1978, 79; C.L.U. Mem. Nat. Assn. Life Underwriters (dir. Chgo. chpt.), Am. Coll. C.L.U.'s, Million Dollar Round Table (knight), Golden Key Soc. Club: U. Ill. ALumni (treas. 1980) (Chgo.). Contbr. articles to ins. mags. Home: 1801 Winthrop Rd Highland Park IL 60035 Office: 540 Frontage Rd Suite 236 Northfield IL 60093

BORYS, EMIL, engr.; b. Chgo., Aug. 28, 1918; s. George and Della (Kielniarz) B.; student Wright Jr. Coll., Lawrence Inst. Tech.; m. Sophia E. Wojcicki, Feb. 5, 1944; children—Emil, George, Stanley. Tool engr. Aero. Products, Inc., 1940-44; chief engr. Walsh Press & Die Co., 1946-52; project engr. Bally Sales Corp., 1960-62; project engr. Automatic Canteen, Chgo., 1962-65; design engr. Sunbeam Corp., 1965-66; dir. engring. Wen Products, Chgo., 1966-69; engring., bus. cons., Lake Zurich, Ill., 1969—. Served with U.S. Army, 1944-46. Decorated Bronze Star. Mem. MENSA. Republican. Roman Catholic. Patentee in field. Address: 40 Pine Tree Row Lake Zurich IL 60047

BORYS, SVYATOSLAV, fin. cons.; b. Peremyshl, Western Ukraine, Nov. 21, 1931; s. Theodor Alexander and Theodora Maria (Leskiw) B.; came to U.S., 1949, naturalized, 1956; A.B. in Econs., St. Joseph's Coll., Ind., 1953; postgrad. in Accounting, Grad. Sch. Coll. City N.Y., 1957-60; m. Lorenza Natalie Bertolino, Sept. 5, 1953; children—Theodor J., Lisa Marie, James A., Peter M. Asst. dept. mgr. Kobacker's Inc., Buffalo, 1953-55; asst. buyer S. Klein-On-the-Square, N.Y.C., 1955-60; accountant, accounting mgr. Hertz Corp., N.Y. Hdqrs., 1960-63, controller for Germany and Austria, 1963-65, controller, asst. sec. for Can., 1965-67, controller ins. div. N.Y. Hdqrs., 1967-68; asst. fin. dir. (controller) Estee Lauder, Inc., Internat., N.Y.C., 1968-70; budget dir. internat. Coty Internat. Div. Pfizer Inc., N.Y.C., 1970-74; fin. mgr. internat. Digital Equipment Corp., Maynard, Mass., 1974-76; v.p. fin. Di-An Controls., Inc., Boston, 1976-77; partner Va. Bus. Cons.'s, Richmond, 1977—; exec. v.p. Video Tek, Inc., Mountain Lakes, N.J., 1979—. Greek Catholic. Home: 3504 Quail Hill Dr Midlothian VA 23113 Office: 8 Morris Ave Mountain Lakes NJ 07046

BOSAK, DONALD FRANCIS, residential alarm mfg. co. exec.; b. Stamford, Conn., Oct. 5, 1942; s. Chester Michael Bosak and Blanche Bosak Stevens; B.A., Boston Coll., 1964; m. Jane Bacon, Sept. 12, 1965; children—Noelle, Anne Elizabeth, William. Vice pres. Wendon Co. Inc., subcontracting mfg. co., Stamford, 1964-69; founder, pres. Transci. Co., Stamford, 1969—. Mem. exec. bd. Stamford Cath. Regional Sch. System, 1974-80. Mem. Security Equipment Industry Assn. (dir.), Nat. Burglar and Fire Alarm Assn. (industry rep. Dept. commerce study program on advanced residential reporting alarm system). Club: Woodway Country (Darien, Conn.). Office: 179 Ludlow St Stamford CT 06902

BOSCHMA, WILLIAM JOSEPH, retail co. exec.; b. Vincennes, Ind., Oct. 30, 1936; s. Riniji Dootsie and Dorothy Evelyn (Case) B.; B.A., Mich. State U., 1962; m. Betty Louise Dehart, Sept. 11, 1964; children—Bradley Christopher, Brett Andrew. Staff acct. Price Waterhouse & Co., Houston, 1962-65; controller Steve Kruchko Co., Drayton Plains, Mich., 1965-69, sr. acct. Price Waterhouse & Co., Houston, 1969-71, audit mgr., 1971-73; sr. v.p. Wicks 'N' Sticks, Inc., Houston, 1973—, also dir. C.P.A., Tex. Mem. Am. Inst. C.P.A.'s, Tex. Soc. C.P.A.'s, Nat. Assn. Accts., Assn. Corp. Growth. Roman Catholic. Clubs: Houstonian, Inwood Forest Country. Home: 13923 Britoak Ln Houston TX 77079 Office: PO Box 40307 Houston TX 77040

BOSS, BERDELL GLADSTONE, elec. motors mfg. co. exec.; b. Lake Geneva, Wis., Apr. 22, 1938; s. Robert Albert and Edna Victoria (Henderson) B.; A.A.S., Mohawk Valley Community Coll., 1959; B.S., Rochester Inst. Tech., 1962; m. Carolyn Chase, Aug. 8, 1959; children—Joel, Thad. Mfg. mgmt. program Gen. Electric Co., Schenectady, 1962-65, mfg. engr., 1965-67, mgr. prodn. control; 1967-69, mgr. quality control, product service, Scotia, N.Y., 1969-74; mgr. mfg. Rotron Inc., Woodstock, N.Y., 1974-78; mgr. mfg. Stow Mfg. Co., Binghamton, N.Y., 1978-80, v.p mfg., 1980—. Dist. chmn. Susquenango council Boy Scouts Am. Mem. Soc. Mfg. Engrs., Am. Product Inventory Control Soc., Soc. Die Casting Engrs. Republican. Unitarian-Universalist. Home: Box 640B Route 8 Old State Rd Binghamton NY 13904 Office: PO Box 490 Binghamton NY 13902

BOSSEN, WENDELL JOHN, ins. co. exec.; b. Vienna, S.D., Nov. 11, 1933; s. Hans Simonsen and Clara Patrina (Vorseth) B.; student S.D. Inst. Tech., 1952; grad. Am. Coll. Life Underwriters, 1972; m. Jan. 6, 1956; children—Mark, Monica. With Northwestern Nat. Life Ins. Co., 1957-76, br. mgr., Seattle, 1964-70, v.p., Mpls., 1970-76; exec. v.p. Inter Ocean Ins. Co., Cin., 1976—; speaker in field. Pres. ARC, Watertown, S.D., 1962-64; chmn. United Fund, Watertown, 1963-64; chmn. Codington County (S.D.) Republican Com., 1962-64; mem. S.D. State Rep. Exec. Com., 1963-64. Mem. Am. Coll. Life Underwriters, Nat. Assn. Life Underwriters, Gen. Agts., Mgr's. Assn. Lutheran. Clubs: Golden Valley Country, Lions, KG Tennis, Elks. Contbr. articles to trade publs. Home: 8184 Lakeridge Dr West Chester OH 45064 Office: 12195 Princeton Pike Cincinnati OH 45214

BOSSERT, JACQUES LOWELL, banker; b. Springfield, Ohio, May 31, 1928; s. George Julius and Florence Evelyn (Laird) B.; student Ohio State U., 1946; spl. courses Am. Inst. Banking, Case Western Res. U., Bankers Bus. Devel. Inst.; cert. in computer auditing Conf. State Bank Suprs., 1979; m. Violet Mae Shifley, Nov. 2, 1946; children—Jacques Lowell II, David A. Mgmt. positions Capital Fin. Services, Fremont, Ohio, 1950-57, Springfield Tool & Die, Inc., 1957-60, Winters Nat. Bank, Dayton, Ohio, 1960-69, Capital Nat. Bank, Cleve., 1969-70, No. Ohio Bank, Cleve., 1970-73; spl. projects loan specialist Greater Cleve. Growth Corp., 1973-74; exec. v.p., cashier 1st Bank Nat. Assn., Cleve., 1974—, also dir. Mem. Am., Nat., Ohio bankers assns., Bank Adminstrn. Inst., Am. Inst. Banking, Greater Cleve. Growth Assn. Republican. Lutheran. Clubs: City of Cleve., Masons. Home: 2382 Woodward Ave Lakewood OH 44107 Office: 232 Superior Ave NE Cleveland OH 44114

BOSSMAN, KENNETH LEROY, accountant; b. Harrisburg, S.D., Sept. 3, 1939; s. Harvey Joseph and Ethel Lorraine (Radloff) B.; student U. S.D., 1958-60, Nettleton Comml. Coll., 1960, 61, 63, Nat. Coll. Bus., Rapid City, S.D., 1967-69; m. Lois Lorraine Stabelfeldt, June 7, 1964; children—Edwin Raymond, Kyla Rachelle, Harlan Joseph, James Kenneth. Engring. aid S.D. Dept. Hwys., Pierre, S.D., 1964-67; accountant Ross Accounting, Mitchell, S.D., 1969-70, E.K. Williams Accounting, Sioux Falls, S.D., 1970-71, Ark. Enterprises for Blind, 1971-72; tax payer service rep. IRS, Aberdeen, S.D., 1972—. Mem. Nat. Treasury Employees Union (1st v.p. 1973-75), S.D. Assn. for Blind (treas. 1966-71, pres. 1972-74), Full Gospel Businessmen's Fellowship Internat. (sec.), Aberdeen Zool. Soc., Hub City Amateur Radio Club. Democrat. Mem. Assemblies of God. Clubs: Moose, Elks, Eagles, Masons, Lions (past pres.). Home: 1311 McGovern Ave SE Aberdeen SD 57401 Office: 115 4th Ave SE Aberdeen SD 57401

BOSTIAN, DAVID BOONE, JR., fin. co. exec.; b. Charlotte, N.C., Feb. 12, 1943; s. David Boone and Clara Edna (Kanoy) B.; A.B. (Distinguished Mil. grad.), Davidson Coll., 1964; M.B.A. (Bus. Found. scholar), U. N.C., 1965; m. Mary Rodgers Hunter, Sept. 11, 1965; 1 son, Robert Boone. Dir. market services Hayden, Stone Inc., N.Y.C., 1967-72; v.p. and dir. market research Loeb. Rhoades & Co., N.Y.C., 1972-76; pres. Bostian Research Assos., 1977—; lectr. N.Y. Inst. Fin., New Sch., Conf. Bd. Mem. bus. adv. council Nat. Rep. Congl. Com.; nat. policy com. Am. Tax Reduction Movement. Served to lt. U.S. Army, 1965-67. Named Outstanding Young Man U.S. Jaycees, 1978. Mem. Am. Fin. Assn., N.Y. Soc. Security Analysts (govt. relations com.), Inst. Chartered Fin. Analysts, Fin. Analysts Research Found., Nat., N.Y. assns. bus. economists, Nat. Bur. Econ. Research, Market Technicians Assn. N.Y., Nat. Platform Assn., Ballet Theatre Found., Alenda Soc. of Davidson Coll., Alpha Phi Omega. Republican. Methodist. Clubs: U.S. Senatorial, Economic of N.Y. Author: (with others) Methods and Techniques of Business Forecasting; (with others) Encyclopedia of Stock Market Techniques; A Question of National Economic Security, Market Analysis and Portfolio Strategy. Home: Suffolk Ln Tenafly NJ 07670 Office: 100 Park Ave New York NY 10017

BOSTIC, JAMES EDWARD, JR., textile co. exec.; b. Marlboro County, S.C., June 24, 1947; s. James Edward and Lula Mae (James) B.; B.S. with honors, Clemson (S.C.) U., 1979; Ph.D. (White House fellow), 1972; m. Edith A. Howard, July 12, 1975; 1 son, James Edward, III. Doctoral fellow, grad. residence counselor Clemson U., 1969; sr. research scientist Am. Enka Co., Enka, N.C., 1972; White House fellow, spl. asst. to sec. Dept. Agr., Washington, 1972-73, dep. asst. sec. agr., 1973-77; corp. regulatory dir. Riegel Textile Corp., Greenville, S.C., 1977—; dir. S.C. Nat. Bank, Greenville; mem. mgmt.-labor textile adv. com. U.S. Dept. Commerce. Trustee, Carver Research Found., Tuskegee Inst., 1978—; chmn., mem. S.C. Commn. Higher Edn., 1978—; bd. dirs. Greenville Urban League, 1977—, treas., 1978-79; mem. environ. preservation com. Am. Textile Mfrs. Inst., 1978-80. Served with U.S. Army Res., 1971-78. Ford Found. doctoral fellow for Black students, recipient 1969; Disting. Service award Greenville Jaycees, 1979. Mem. Am. Assn. Textile Chemists and Colorists, S.C. Textile Mfrs. Assn. Republican. Methodist. Home: 5 Swindon Ct Greenville SC 29615 Office: 25 Woods Lake Rd Suite 800 Greenville SC 29607

BOSTIC, STEVE A., optical co. exec.; b. St. Cloud, Minn., Feb. 11, 1949; s. Alva A. and May Ellen (Regan) B.; B.S., Black Hills State Coll., 1971; m. Sharon L. Stambaugh, Aug. 19, 1972; children—Stacy Jo, Melissa Jane. Dist. mgr. retail optical div. Dentsply Internat., 1974-76, gen. mgr., 1976-79; v.p. Optico Industries, div. Marion Labs., Tempe, Ariz., 1979-80; exec. v.p., sec., dir. Western States Optical, Tempe, 1980—. Mem. Nat. Assn. Mfg. Opticians (dir.), Wis. Assn. Optometrists and Opticians (past pres.). Republican. Methodist. Home: 2138 E Fountain Mesa AZ 85203 Office: 2204 W Southern Ave Tempe AZ 85282

BOSTON, WILLIAM GEOFFREY, mech. contracting co. exec.; b. Lackawanna, N.Y., Aug. 7, 1949; s. William Russell and Virginia Marie (Hulsmeier) B.; B.S. in Bus. Adminstrn., Xavier U., Cin., 1971; m. Maureen Ruth McNally, Oct. 2, 1971; children—Courtney Erin, Meaghan Kathleen, Patricia Molly. Asst. to pres. Roulston & Co., Inc., Cleve., 1971-73; corp. sec., project engr., mgr. C.L. Mahoney Co., Kalamazoo, 1973—. Mem. allocations and budget com. United Way, Kalamazoo. Lic. rep. all maj. stock exchanges; lic. mech. contractor. Mem. Mich. Plumbing and Mech. Contractors Assn.

Roman Catholic. Clubs: Rotary, Elks. Office: 438 Forest St Kalamazoo MI 49001

BOSTWICK, BURDETTE EDWARDS, mgmt. cons., author; b. Washington, Mar. 31, 1908; s. John Wilson and Harriet Caroline (Edwards) B.; J.D., Rutgers U., New Brunswick, N.J., 1935; m. Betty Bannister Brown, Sept. 19, 1936; children—Burdette E., Sherry B. Vice pres. J. Wiss & Sons Co., Inc., Newark, 1927-70; pres. B.E. Bostwick Co., Inc., N.Y.C., 1972—; author: Resume Writing: A Comprehensive How-To-Do-It Guide, 1976, rev. edit., 1980, How to Find the Job You've Always Wanted, 1977, rev. edit., 1980. Republican. Episcopalian. Clubs: Short Hills (N.J.). Home: 292 Short Hills Ave Springfield NJ 07081

BOSTWICK, WALLACE MANFORD, real estate appraiser; b. Spokane, Wash., Jan. 9, 1920; s. Wallace Manford and Dorothy Helen (Reinbolt) B.; B.S. in Land Econs., U. Idaho, 1948; m. Gertrude Utley, June 17, 1949; children—Lorne Patrick, Diane Denise, Moira Ann. With Fed. Housing Adminstrn., 1948-71, chief appraiser, Spokane, 1958-62, chief appraiser multifamily div. Western region, San Francisco, 1962-64, dir. Spokane insuring office, 1964-71; mortgage loan officer and chief appraiser for Eastern Wash., Fidelity Mut. Savs. Bank, Spokane, 1971—; tchr. U. Idaho, Spokane Community Coll., Wash. State U. Served in USAAF, 1942-45. Mem. Soc. Real Estate Appraisers (pres.), Spokane Bd. Realtors (dir. 1976-77, Service award 1971), Spokane Home Builders Assn. (dir. 1972—), Spokane Mortgage Men's Assn. (pres. 1974, award 1962), Am. Inst. Real Estate Appraisers (pres.). Congregationalist. Club: Rotary. Home: 4104 S Pittsburg St Spokane WA 99203 Office: W 524 Riverside St Spokane WA 99201

BOTELHO, RICHARD PAUL, mfg. co. exec.; b. Fall River, Mass., Oct. 31, 1949; s. William Couto and Alice Sylvia B.; A.S. in Acctg., Bristol Community Coll., Fall River, 1969; B.S. in Acctg., Johnson & Wales Coll., Providence, 1973; m. Diane Marie Luz, Sept. 27, 1969; children—Tracy Lynn, Julie Ann. Acct., Flint Bus. Service, Fall River, 1968-69; cost acct. Mt. Hope Machinery Co., Tauton, Mass., 1969-73; asst. comptroller Cliftex Corp., New Bedford, Mass., 1973; cost acctg. mgr. St. Regis Paper, Attleboro, Mass., 1974-77, materials mgr., 1977-78; comptroller Colonial Industries, Framingham, Mass., 1978—. Trustee, Darlington Congregational Ch., 1977-79; exec. v.p. Bristol County Young Republicans, 1968, 69. Mem. Bus. Adminstrn. Soc. (pres. 1969). Clubs: Eastern Star, Masons (master). Home: 168 Bishop St Attleboro MA 02703 Office: 2 Tripp St Framingham MA 01701

BOTHELL, LEE WILSON, mfg. co. exec.; b. San Francisco, Dec. 24, 1946; s. Lee W. and Estelle (Monahan) B.; B.A., St. Johns U., 1978; m. Janis A. Cruse, Jan. 20, 1968; children—Michael G., Bryan L. Office mgr. Household Fin. Corp., N.Y.C., 1970-71; credit man Walter E. Heller Corp., N.Y.C., 1971-74; asst. to corp. credit mgr. Leviton Mfg. Co., Little Neck, N.Y., 1974-78; credit mgr., computer mgr. Mitsui Machine Tool Sales subs. Mitsui and Co.-U.S.A., East Farmingdale, N.Y., 1979—. Scoutmaster, Cub Scout Pack 22, Boy Scouts Am., Island Park, N.Y., 1977—. Served with USMC, 1965-69. Republican. Methodist. Home: 7 Vause St Northport NY 11768 Office: 125 Sherwood Ave East Farmingdale NY 11735

BOTT, DUWAYNE THEODORE, banker; b. Lisbon, N.D., Apr. 29, 1933; s. Theodore Henry and Goldie Lillian (Olson) B.; B.S., Valley City State Tchrs. Coll., 1958; grad. Wis. Sch. Banking, 1972. Brakeman, Soo Line R.R., 1954-58; tchr., prin. Driscoll Sch., 1959, Sheyenne Sch., 1959-61, Adams (N.D.) Pub. Sch., 1962-66; v.p. Security State Bank, Adams, 1966-74; pres., cashier, dir. State Bank of Marion (N.D.), 1974—; pres. Dickey Marion Ins. Agy., Inc. Mem. Adams Town Bd., 1967-72, Adams Fire Dept., 1967-74; treas. 17th Dist. Republican Party, 1970-74; pres. Adams Ch. Council, 1973-74; mem. Marion Ch. Council, 1978. Served with U.S. N.G., 1952-62. Mem. Am., N.D., S.E bankers assns., Bank Adminstrn. Inst., Conf. State Bank Suprs., Am. Inst. Banking, AIM, Marion Improvement Assn., Greater N.D. Assn. Lutheran. Clubs: Eagles, Elks, Shriners. Home and office: Box 68 Marion ND 58466

BOTT, JOSEPH J., III, rubber co. exec.; b. Phila., July 25, 1930; s. Joseph C. and Dorothy Bott; student public schs.; m. Marie Violet O'Neill, Apr. 30, 1960; children—Denise, Joseph, Jeffrey. Sales rep. Republic Rubber Co., Phila., 1958-64; founder, 1964, thereafter pres. Colonial Rubber Co. Inc., Mt. Laurel, N.J.; dir. Fellowship Bank, Mt. Laurel. Mem. Mt. Laurel Twp. Com., 1970; chmn. Mt. Laurel Econ. Devel. Com., 1967-72; fin. chmn. Mt. Laurel Republican Party, 1968-69. Served with U.S. Army, 1951-54. Recipient various service awards. Mem. Fuel Mchts. Assn. S.Jersey, S.Jersey C. of C. Roman Catholic. Clubs: Propellor (Phila.); Mt. Laurel; Rotary (past pres.). Office: Elbo Ln and Texas Ave Mt Laurel NJ 08054

BOTT, RICHARD SCOTT, machinery mfg. co. exec.; b. Seattle, Apr. 7, 1949; s. Kenneth Leland and Nancy Isabel Bott; student Yakima Valley Coll., 1968-69, Belleville Area Coll., 1969-70; m. Patricia Jean Graves, Nov. 19, 1972; children—Ryan Phillip, Stacy Nicole. Mktg. rep. Cummins Mo. Diesel Corp., St. Louis, 1972-74; indsl. sales mgr. Cummins Northwest Diesel, Inc., Seattle, 1974-77; mgr. power div. Wallace Machinery Co., Oxnard, Calif., 1977-80; pres. Aladin Enterprises, Inc. and v.p. sales and engring. Aladin Engring. & Equipment Co. (both La Mirada, Calif.), 1980—. Instr., Jr. Achievement, 1976-77. Mem. Internat. Assn. Drilling Contractors, Associated Gen. Contractors, Elec. Generating Systems Mktg. Assn., Petroleum Club, Aircraft Owners and Pilots Assn., Nat. Pilots Assn., U.S. Coast Guard Aux. Republican. Episcopalian. Club: Elks. Home: 1093 Beechwood St Camarillo CA 93010 Office: 14400 E Firestone Blvd La Mirada CA 90638

BOTTORFF, THOMAS EDWARD, constrn. co. exec.; b. Oakland, Calif., July 16, 1953; s. Norman Eugene and Dorothy Eugene (Rodrigues) B.; B.S., U. Calif., Berkeley, 1975; M.S., Stanford U., 1976. Engr., economist U.S. Nuclear Regulatory Commn., Washington, 1976-78; mng. partner Clark Constrn. Co., Cobb, Calif., 1978—. Mem. exec. bd. Democratic party of Calif., 1979—. Mem. North Coast Builders Exchange, Tau Beta Pi, Eta Kappa Nu. Club: Commonwealth. Calif. collegiate boxing champion, 1974. Home: PO Box 512 Cobb CA 95426 Office: Clark Constrn Co 15285 Summit Blvd Cobb CA 95426

BOTTS, GUY WARREN, banker, lawyer; b. Milton, Fla., July 12, 1914; s. Alonzo O'Hara and Margaret (Land) B.; J.D., U. Fla., 1937; LL.B. (hon.), Jacksonville U., 1967; m. Edith M. Huddleston, Nov. 4, 1939; children—Edith, William. Admitted to Fla. bar, 1937; mem. firm Fleming, Hamilton, Diver & Jones, Jacksonville, 1937-39, 40-42; with law dept. Fla. br. Prudential Ins. Co. Am., Lakeland, Fla., 1939-40; mem. firm Fleming, Scott & Botts, and predecessor, 1942-55, sr. partner, 1955-57; sr. partner Botts, Mohoney, Chambers & Adams, and predecessor, Jacksonville, 1957-63; gen. counsel, dir. Barnett Nat. Bank of Jacksonville, 1955-63, pres., chief exec. officer, dir., 1963-70, vice chmn., 1970-73, chmn., 1973—; pres., chief exec. officer The Charter Co., 1960-63; chmn., dir. Charter Mortgage & Investment Co., 1960-63; pres. Barnett Banks Fla., Inc. (formerly Barnett Nat. Securities Corp.), 1963-72, chmn. bd., 1973—; chmn. bd. Nat. Bankamericard, Inc., 1973-75; dir. Gulf United Corp., Fla. Pub. Co. Past mem. Fla. Devel. Commn.; commr. Uniform State Laws Fla., 1955-59. Chmn. bd. trustees Jacksonville U., dir., past pres. Duval County Legal Aid Assn. Recipient Gold Key award U.S. Jr. C. of C., 1946; Ted Arnold award Jacksonville Jr. C. of C., 1963, 78. Mem. Am. Coll. Probate Counsel (past regent), Jr. (past pres.), U.S., Jacksonville Area (past pres.) chambers commerce, Am., Jacksonville (past pres.) bar assns., Fla. Bar (gov.), Am. Bankers Assn. (governing council), Fla. Bankers Assn., Assn. Bank Holding Cos. (past pres.), Phi Eta Sigma, Phi Alpha Delta, Alpha Kappa Psi, Delta Tau Delta. Clubs: River, Univ., Rotary, Fla. Yacht, Ponte Vedra, Timuquana Country. Compiled Brit. Statutes in Force in Florida, 1943. Editor Banks and banking statutes sect. Fla. Law Practice. Home: 3737 Ortega Blvd Jacksonville FL 32210 Office: 100 Laura St Jacksonville FL 32202

BOUCHARD, RENE JOSEPH, JR., advt. agy. exec.; b. Fall River, Mass., Aug. 16, 1931; s. Rene Joseph and Georgiana D. (Morin) B.; B.S., Bryant Coll., 1951; B.A., Brown U., 1958; M.A., M.A. in Edn., Bridgewater State Coll., 1961; m. Jean C. Cabral, Dec. 26, 1952; children—Betsy Jean, Rene Joseph, Amy Louise. Tchr., dept. head Holbrook (Mass.) High Sch., 1959-65; dir. Bur. Student Services, Commonwealth of Mass. Dept. Edn., Boston, 1965-73; founder, owner, pres. R.J. Bouchard & Co., Kingston, Mass., 1973—; producer/cons. LaBelle Industries, 1978—. Registrar, Town of Kingston, 1976—; chmn. Republican Town Com., Kingston, 1976—. Served with USAF, 1951-54. Mem. Smaller Bus. Assn. New Eng., Info. Film Producers of Am. Republican. Roman Catholic. Home: Indian Pond Rd Kingston MA 02364 Office: Bishop's Rd Kingston MA 02364

BOUDREAU, EDWARD JOSEPH, JR., ins. co. exec.; b. Cambridge, Mass., Oct. 16, 1944; s. Edward Joseph and Anella (Sakowich) B.; B.S., Boston U., 1966; postgrad. Am. U., 1966-67; M.B.A., Suffolk U., 1971; m. Janet Forsberg, May 26, 1968; children—Nancy, Mark. With John Hancock Mut. Life Ins. Co., Boston, 1967—, trainee, 1967-68, adminstrv. asst., 1968, treasury officer, 1968-70, treasury officer, asst. dir. banking relations, 1970-75, corp. banking service officer, 1975-78, gen. dir. banking and short-term investment, asst. treas., 1979, 2d v.p., 1980—; treas. John Hancock Subsidiaries, Inc., Boston; dir. John Hancock Fin. Services, Inc., Boston; treas./dir. Profesco Corp., N.Y.C.; adj. faculty Suffolk U. Served with USNG, 1967-73. Mem. Life Office Mgmt. Assn. (treasury ops. com.). Club: Winchester Country. Chmn. editorial bd. Life Treasurers' Roundtable; contbr. articles in field to publs. Office: John Hancock Pl PO Box 111 Boston MA 02117

BOUNDS, LAURENCE HAROLD, gas co. exec.; b. Newcastle, Wyo., Feb. 15, 1922; s. James Henry and Blanche Agnes (McKay) B.; B.S., Simpson Coll., 1943; postgrad. Columbia, 1943; m. Dorothy May Bostrom, Nov. 20, 1965. With comptroller dept. Kemper Ins., Chgo., 1947-51; sec.-treas. W&J Constrn. Co., 1951-64; auditor, Roosevelt Hotel, Jacksonville, Fla., 1964-66; v.p. Western Natural Gas Co., Jacksonville, 1966—, also sec., dir. Served to lt. USNR, 1942-46. Mem. Navy League, Jacksonville Symphony Assn., Alpha Tau Omega, Episcopalian. Clubs: Willow Lakes Golf and Country; Island (St. Simon's, Ga.); Tournament Players (Ponte Vedra, Fla.). Home: 6926 Bakersfield Dr Jacksonville FL 32210 Office: 2960 Strickland St Jacksonville FL 32205

BOUNDY, MARVIN DALE, investment co. exec.; b. Granite City, Ill., Jan. 22, 1949; s. Dale Dean and Dorelda Gene (Olson) B.; B.A., Coll. William and Mary, 1971; M.S., U. Va., 1977; m. Paula Ann Gwynn, July 28, 1979. Acct., Stanton, Minter and Bruner, C.P.A.'s, Alexandria, Va., 1971-76; acctg. supr. Minter, Morriston and Grant, C.P.A.'s, Alexandria, 1977-78; treas. Inverness Capital Corp., Alexandria, 1978—; treas. Old Port Co., Canal Way, Inc.; asst. treas. Inverness Resource Corp., Domino Internat., Inc. Mem. Am. Inst. C.P.A.'s, Methodist. Home: 6618 Elk Park Ct Alexandria VA 22310 Office: 424 N Washington St Alexandria VA 22314

BOURGOIN, BERT EDMOND, geologist; b. St. Leonard, N.B., Can., Feb. 3, 1934; s. Lorne and Corinne (Cyr) B.; B.Sc., St. Francis Xavier U., 1957; m. Suzanne Gauthier, May 27, 1961; children—Martin, Daniel. Project mgr. No. Exploration Ltd., Joutel, Que., 1962-67; exploration geologist Noranda (Que.) Exploration Co. Ltd., 1967-69; pvt. practice mining geol. cons., Rouyn, Que., 1969-74; mine mgr. Consol. Durham Mines & Resources Ltd., Prince William, N.B., 1974—, also dir. Mem. Prospectors and Developers Assn., Canadian Inst. Mining. Roman Catholic. Home: 139 Brookside Dr Fredericton NB E3A 1T9 Canada Office: Consol Durham Mines & Resources Ltd Prince William NB E0H 1S0 Canada

BOURNE, JOHN DAVID, city finance exec.; b. Barbados, West Indies, July 6, 1937; s. Daniel E. and Clarissa M. (Foster) B.; B.B.A., Baruch Coll., City U. N.Y., 1972; M.B.A., L.I. U., 1974. Mgr., Household Fin. Corp., N.Y.C., 1963-72, N.Y.C. Off-Track Betting Corp., 1972—; notary pub., 1964—. Served with USAF, 1959-63. Mem. Baruch Coll., L.I. U. alumni assns. Democrat. Home: 646 Rutland Rd Apt 3A Brooklyn NY 11203 Office: 1501 Broadway New York NY 10036

BOURNE, WILLIAM BURGELIN, mgmt. cons.; b. Trenton, N.J., May 27, 1927; s. William Cecil and Kathryn Harcourt (Newell) B.; student U. Buffalo, 1944-45, Temple U., 1948; m. Shirlie Ware Paul, June 23, 1951; children—Jeffrey Paul, Jennifer Ann. Quality control mgr. RCA, Moorestown, N.J., 1953-59; quality control mgr. Gen. Electric Co., Syracuse, N.Y., also Daytona Beach, Fla., 1959-65, mgr. mfg., 1965-69, mng. dir. fgn. subs., Singapore, 1969-71, ops. mgr. Utica (N.Y.) plant, 1971-72; v.p. ops. Smith Corona Group, SCM Corp., N.Y.C., 1972-79; pvt. practice mgmt. cons., Ormond Beach, Fla., 1979—. Chmn. fund dr. Am. Cancer Soc., Daytona Beach, 1967, chmn. edn. com., 1968. Served with USAAF, 1944-47. Mem. Daytona Beach Area C. of C. (chmn. pollution control com. 1968-69), Am. Inst. Indsl. Engrs. (sr.), Am. Soc. Quality Control (sr.). Republican. Episcopalian. Home and Office: 20 Sandalwood Ln Ormond Beach FL 32074

BOURNIVAL, JEAN MARC RAYMOND, mfg. co. exec.; b. Shawinigan, Que., Can., Oct. 26, 1943; s. Herve Maxime and Exaudina (Lampron) B.; B.Commerce, Montreal U., 1970, B.Com. in Acctg.; student in Mktg. Mgmt., Western U., London, Ont., 1980; m. Louise Kanemy, June 19, 1965; children—Eric, Julie, Patrick. Acct., Star Brush Ltd., Montreal, 1965-67, Que. Natural Gas Corp., Montreal, 1967-69; fin. analyst Sylvania Electric Ltd., Montreal, 1969—; sec.-treas. Eutectic & Castolin, Pointe Claire, Que. Mem. Montreal Bd. Trade, Pointe Claire C. of C., Montreal U. Grads. Assn. Clubs: Laurentide Camping, Masons. Home: 12560 27th Ave Riviere des Prairies Montreal PQ H1E 1Z9 Canada Office: 4200 Trans Canada Hwy Pointe Claire PQ H9R 1B6 Canada

BOUSQUET, DONAVON GAIL, motel exec.; b. Ponca, Nebr., May 21, 1942; s. Roger Joseph and Dorothy Marrie (Nelson) B.; student Wentworth Mil. Acad. Jr. Coll., 1964; m. Sandra Marie Bousquet, Jan. 25, 1972; 1 dau. Co-owner Sarasota Florida Travellodge, 1963—; owner Bousquet Inc., Sioux City, Iowa Imperial 400 Motel, 1964—; pres. Bousquet Investment Co., Sioux City, 1965—; owner-operator Donavons Reef Ships Lounge, Sioux City; owner Marshall (Minn.) Travelers Lodge, 1970-75; builder, owner Redwoodfalls (Minn.) Donavons Conf. Center, 1972-73; builder Donavons Best Western, Sioux Falls, S.D., 1975-76; regional coordinator for Friendship Inns of Am. Mem. Am. Hotel Mgmt. Assn. Republican. Lutheran. Home: 3060 Stone Park Blvd Sioux City IA 51104 Office: 110 Nebraska St Sioux City IA 51101

BOUSTANY, FREM FREM, JR., physician, wholesale bakery exec.; b. Lafayette, La., May 7, 1928; s. Frem Frem and Beatrice (Joseph) B.; B.S., Tulane U., 1948, M.D., 1950; m. Angell FaKouri, Jan. 6, 1957; children—Deborah, Jennifer, Stephanie. Intern, Charity Hosp., New Orleans, 1950-51, resident, 1951-54; practice medicine specializing in ob-gyn, Crowley, La., 1958-69; v.p. Huval Baking Co., Lafayette, 1950-70, pres., 1970-76, chief exec. officer, 1976—; dir. Flowers Industries, Inc., Thomasville, Ga., La. Bank & Trust Co., Crowley, City Savs. Bank & Trust Co., DeRidder, La. Bd. dirs. Lafayette Boys Club, 1972-75, Jr. Achievement, 1972-76; v.p. United Giver's Fund, Lafayette, 1974-78, bd. dirs., 1970-78. Served with M.C., USAF, 1954-56. Mem. AMA, La. Med. Soc., Am. Bakers Coop. (past chmn., pres.), Am. Bakers Assn., So. Bakers Assn. (gov.), Am. Inst. Baking. Democrat. Roman Catholic. Clubs: Bayou Bend Country, Crowley Town (Crowley); Lafayette Town, City, Krewe of Gabriel, Krewe of Zeus, Order of Troubadours (Lafayette); Camelot (Baton Rouge); K.C. Home: 244 W 17th St Crowley LA 70526 Office: Huval Baking Co Box 2339 Lafayette LA 70502

BOUSTEDT, ROBERT K., bus. systems cons.; b. N.Y.C., Dec. 6, 1942; s. Karl G. and Martha M. Boustedt; B.S. in Econs. and Bus., Hofstra U., 1964; m. Aileen Pierson, Dec. 3, 1978. Sr. analyst Aetna Life & Casualty, N.Y.C., 1967-70; v.p. mktg. and sales Datastream, Inc., N.Y.C., 1970-76; dir. devel. Datamatics Mgmt. Services, Inc., Englewood Cliffs, N.J., 1976-79, v.p. mktg. and sales, 1980—; pres. Resource Software Internat., Inc., Englewood Cliffs, 1978—. Vice pres., mem. exec. bd. Workshop in Bus. Opportunities. Served with C.E., U.S. Army, 1964-66. Home: 135 Hillside Ave Teaneck NJ 07666 Office: Englewood Cliffs NJ

BOUT, JAN, ret. ins. co. exec., editor; b. Rotterdam, The Netherlands, Apr. 7, 1915; s. Cornelius and Hendrika (Bosch) B.; ed. Rotterdam, Leiden and pub. schs., Pasadena, Calif.; m. Katherine D. Bassett, May 12, 1936; children—Jan II, Jacqueline. In trucking bus., C. Bout and Sons, 1934-36; tour mgr. Tanner Tours, Ltd., Grey Line, also ind. tours, 1936-40; with passenger traffic dept. A.T. & S.F. Ry., 1941-47; traffic and conv. mgr. Prudential Ins. Co. Am. 1947-56, mgr. travel and conf. div., 1956-66; dir. conf. arrangements Prudential Ins. Co., Newark, 1966-76, ret., 1976; contbg. editor Ins. Conf. Planner Mag., 1976—. Served to 1st lt. U.S. Army, 1943-46; ETO. Mem. No. N.J., Am. orchid socs., U.S. Inf. Assn. Contbr. articles to profl. jours. Home: 10349 NW 2d Ct Jacaranda Estates Plantation FL 33324

BOUTILLIER, ROBERT JOHN, accountant; b. Newark, Jan. 1, 1924; s. William and Millicent (Davies) B.; B.S., Rutgers, 1948; m. Marie C. Humphries, June 24, 1945; children—Robert Allan, Suzanne Marie. With Peat, Marwick, Mitchell & Co., 1943—, partner, 1955—, partner charge Newark office, 1960—, mem. exec. com. and Eastern area, partner, 1965—, partner charge U.S. ops., N.Y.C., 1970—, vice chmn., Eastern regional partner, dir., mem. operating com., 1977—; lectr. Rutgers U. Bd. dirs. Newark YM-YWCA; bd. overseers Rutgers U. Found. C.P.A., N.J. Mem. Am. Inst. C.P.A.'s, N.J. Soc. C.P.A.'s, Newark Jr. C. of C. (pres. 1956-57, outstanding young man of year award 1957), Newark C. of C., Delta Sigma Pi, Beta Gamma Sigma. Republican. Presbyterian. Clubs: Rotary of N.Y., Baltusrol Golf (pres., gov.). Home: 920 Minisink Way Westfield NJ 07090 Office: 345 Park Ave New York NY 10022

BOUTTE, ALVIN J., banker; b. Lake Charles, La., Oct. 10, 1929; B.S., Xavier U., 1951; married; 4 children. Pres., Ind. Drug Stores, 1956-64; pres. 79th St. Med. Corp.; co-founder, vice chmn. bd. Ind. Bank of Chgo., 1964-70, pres., 1970-80, chmn., chief exec. officer, 1980—; dir. Johnson Products Co. Bd. dirs. Better Bus. Bur. Served to capt. U.S. Army. Named Man of Yr., Chgo. Urban League, 1971. Office: 7936 S Cottage Grove Ave Chicago IL 60619

BOUVIER, HELEN SCHAEFER (MRS. JOHN A. BOUVIER, JR.), leasing co. exec.; b. McAlester, Okla., Sept. 11, 1910; d. William John and Anna (Perrin) Schaefer; student U. Fla., 1928-29, Northwestern U., 1929-30; m. John A. Bouvier, Jr., June 6, 1928; children—Helen Elizabeth (Mrs. William Spencer), John A. III, Thomas R. Sec., Sunset Rock & Sand Co., Miami, Fla., 1939-45, Coral Rock & Sand Co., 1945-48; pres., dir. Knight Manor, Inc., Miami; dir. West Kingsway, Inc., Miami, East Kingsway, Inc., Miami, South Kingsway, Inc., Miami, Fiftieth St. Heights, Inc., Miami, Karen Garden, Inc. Ft. Lauderdale, Fla.; pres. Miami Service Co., chief exec. officer, dir., 1972—, Knight Manor #1, Inc., Knight Manor #2, Inc., South Central Manor, Inc.; dir., pres. Nat. Leasing Corp., Miami, Fla. and N.Y.C., 1954—; chmn. bd. Nat. Leasing, Inc., 1967—; mgmt. cons., Miami, and N.Y.C., 1945—. Trustee Ella R. Bouvier Found. Presbyn. (pres. women's aux., pres. women's aux. synod). Clubs: Corinthian (Syracuse, N.Y.); Skaneateles (N.Y.) Country; Riviera Country (Coral Gables, Fla.); Beach Colony (Miami Beach, Fla.); Tower; Ponte Vedra. Home: 2756 NE 17th St Fort Lauderdale FL 33305

BOUVIER, JOHN ANDRE, JR., lawyer, investment counselor, corp. exec.; b. nr. Ocala, Fla., May 16, 1903; s. John Andre and Ella (Richardson) B.; student Davidson Coll., 1922-24; A.B., U. Fla., 1926, J.D., 1929; M.B.A., Northwestern U., 1930; D.H.L. (hon.), Windham Coll., 1977; m. Helen A. Schaefer, June 6, 1928; children—Helen Elizabeth (Mrs. William Spencer), John Andre III, Thomas Richardson. Admitted to Fla. bar, 1929, pvt. practice, Gainesville, 1929, Miami, 1930—, specialist corp., real estate, probate lawyer, cons.; gen. counsel Patterson & Maloney, Ft. Lauderdale; chmn. bd., pres. Pantex Mfg. Corp. (Delaware), 1958-60; pres. Pantex Mfg. Corp. (Can.), 1958-60; chmn. exec. com. Permutit Co.; chmn. bd. Prosperity Co. div., vice chmn. bd. Ward Industries Corp.; pres. Nat. Leasing Inc., Miami; pres. West Kingsway, Inc., 1952-73, East Kingsway, Inc., 1952-73, South Kingsway, Inc., 1952-73; chmn., dir. Knight Manor #1, Inc., Knight Manor #2, Inc., South Central Manor, Inc.; pres. Knaust Bros., Inc., West Coxsackie, N.Y., 1960-64, chmn., 1964-65; pres. K-B Products Corp., Hudson, N.Y., 1960-64, chmn., 1960-65; pres. Farm Industries, Inc., Iron Mtn. Atomic Storage Vaults, Inc.; v.p., sec. Miami Service Co., 1956-73, chmn., 1973—; sec. 50th St. Heights, Inc., Dade Constrn. Co., Miami, Karen Club Apt. Hotel, Ft. Lauderdale, 1951-67; dir. Ocean 1st Nat. Bank, Landmark Banking Corp. Commr. Dade County council Boy Scouts Am.; chmn. Malecon Com. Dade County; dir. Syracuse Govtl. Research Bur., Inc.; mem. Nat. Def. Exec. Res. Planning council Zoning Bd. Miami. Bd. trustees Parkinson Rehab., Diagnostic and Research Inst.; vice chmn. Nat. Parkinson Found.; pres. Ella R. Bouvier Fund; bd. dirs. Boys Club. Mem. Internat. Platform Assn., Am. Ordnance Assn., Am. Judicature Soc., Am., Fla., Dade County bar assns., N.A.M. (conservation of renewable natural resources com.), Mfrs. Assn. of Syracuse (dir.), Miami, Auburn civic music assns., Cayuga Mus. History and Art, Am. Acad. Polit. Sci., C. of C., Sigma Chi. Presbyn. (trustee, chmn., elder). Mason (Shriner), Elk, Rotarian. Clubs: Civitan (dir.), Miami Beach Rod and Reel, Surf, Riviera Country, Skaneateles Country; Tower; Ponte Vedra; Capitol Hill, Washington Lawyers. Author monographs, newspaper articles in field. Home: 2756 N E 17th St Fort Lauderdale FL 33305 Office: Box 14 Climax NY 12042

BOUWER, DENNIS RONALD, investment co. exec.; b. Republic of South Africa, Apr. 27, 1933; s. Jeremia J. and Catherine Elizabeth (De Beer) B.; B.Sc. in Chemistry, Rhodes U., South Africa, 1954; M.A. (Rhodes scholar), Oxford (Eng.) U., 1960; M.B.A. (Knox fellow), Harvard, 1963; m. Sara Margaret Holcroft, July 4, 1959; children—Consuelo Catherine, Richard J.A. Came to U.S., 1961, naturalized, 1966. Exec. trainee Bagshaw Gibaud & Co., Africa, 1951-54; math. master, asst. housemaster Kingswood Coll., South Africa, 1955; grad. chemist Am. Metal Climax, Zambia, 1955-57; marketing mgr. trainee Unilever Ltd., London, Eng., 1960-61; tng. mgr. Ford Motor Co., South Africa, 1961; econs. analyst Mobil Oil Corp., N.Y.C., 1962; with E.I. duPont de Nemours & Co., Inc., Geneva, Switzerland and Wilmington, Del., 1963-67; asst. to pres. chem. plastics div. Gen. Tire & Rubber Co., Akron, Ohio, 1967-68; asst. to chmn. Capital Research Co., Los Angeles, 1968—; v.p. Endowments, Inc., Bond Portfolio for Endowments, Inc.; v.p., asst. chmn. bd. Capital Strategic Services. Former adviser Coloured Peoples Advancement Assn., Africa. Served with RAF, 1957-61. Ford fellow, 1963. Chartered financial analyst; registered prin. Nat. Assn. Securities Dealers. Fellow Royal Commonwealth Soc. (life), Financial Analysts Fedn. (nat. dir., mem. nat. program com.); mem. Royal Air Force Assn. (life), Oxford Union (life), Africa Soc. (founder, pres.), Los Angeles Soc. Financial Analysts (gov., pres. program and nominating coms.; Most Disting. Mem. award), Exec. Council on Fgn. Diplomats (mem. advisory bd.), Harvard Bus. Sch. Club So. Calif. (gov.). Republican. Episcopalian. Clubs: Harvard (N.Y.C.); United Oxford and Cambridge Univs. (London); Los Angeles Athletic. Internat. rugby player. Home: 15937 Temecula St Pacific Palisades CA 90272 Office: 333 S Hope St Los Angeles CA 90071

BOUWER, JOHN D., recreation co. exec.; b. Missaukee County, Mich., Sept. 4, 1938; s. Benjamin and Minnie Bouwer; A.B., Calvin Coll., Grand Rapids, Mich., 1960; M.B.A., U. Mich., 1962; m. Marian F. DeVries, Aug. 24, 1961; children—Thomas John, Kathryn Frances, Gretchen Anne. Mktg. analyst Standard Oil Co. Ohio, 1962-64; mgr. mgmt. services. Touche, Ross & Co., C.P.A.'s, Detroit, 1964-72; dir. adminstrv. services Am. Seating Co., Grand Rapids, Mich., 1972-75; pres. Concordia Corp., Grand Rapids, 1975—. Bd. dirs. Jr. Achievement Grand Rapids, 1975-80, pres., 1979; pres. Jellema House, Grand Rapids, 1974-76. Served with USAR, 1962-64. Club: Peninsula. Home: 1540 Woodcliff St SE Grand Rapids MI 49506 Office: 201 Trust Bldg Grand Rapids MI 49503

BOVA, PAUL PETER, food co. exec.; b. Bronx, N.Y., July 26, 1941; s. Paul Peter and Rose Emily (Castellano) B.; B.S. in Econs., Fordham U., 1963; m. Diane Darry Pasquarelli, Sept. 14, 1963; children—Steven, Christopher, Paul. With Gen. Foods Corp., 1965-78, regional sales mgr. Maxwell House div., 1974-78; v.p. consumer sales ops. Am./Dixie Sales Co., div. Am. Can Co., Greenwich, Conn., 1978—. Served as officer U.S. Army, 1963-65. Mem. Grocery Mfrs. Am., Sales Execs. Club. Roman Catholic. Office: Am Can Co American Ln Greenwich CT 06830

BOVA, ROBERT JAMES, fin. planning co. exec.; b. Port Chester, N.Y., June 27, 1942; s. Angelo Nicholas and Harriet (Redding) B.; B.A., SUNY, Binghamton, 1967; M.B.A., U. Ky., 1981; m. Patricia Wellman, June 27, 1968; children—Christine Caryl, Jennifer, Ramsey. Account exec. Thomson McKinnon Securities, Inc., N.Y.C. and Lexington, Ky., 1968-70, asst. to exec. v.p., 1970-72, nat. sales coordinator, 1972-74, v.p., dir. fin. services dept., 1974-75, v.p., br. mgr., 1975-78; v.p. Kingsley Equipment Co., Lexington, 1978-80; pres., chief exec. officer Moneywatch Corp., Lexington, 1980—; sec.-treas. Group Services, Inc., Lexington, 1979-80, dir., 1979—. Sec., Friends of Lexington Public Library, 1978, pres., 1979—. Served to 1st lt. U.S. Army, 1961-64. Recipient Cert. of Merit, Ky. Epilepsy Found., 1977. Mem. Sales and Mktg. Execs. Assn. (pres. 1978-79). Republican. Roman Catholic. Club: Optimist. Office: 957 Turkey Foot Rd Lexington KY

BOVE, HENRY JOSEPH, chem. engr.; b. New London, Conn., Jan. 24, 1925; s. Loreto and Rose (Tolo) B.; B.S., Worcester Poly. Inst., 1947, M.S., 1948; m. Yolanda H. Ferrigno, Sept. 10, 1950; 1 son, Lawrence J. Design and mgmt. engr. Day & Zimmermann, Inc., Phila., 1948-68; project mgr., chem. div. United Engrs. & Constructors Inc., 1968—. Served with AUS, 1944-46. Registered profl. engr., Pa., N.Y., La., Ala., Ga., Ind., Del., Md. Mem. Am. Inst. Chem. Engrs., Am. Assn. Cost Engrs., Franklin Inst., Phila. Engrs. Club, Nat. Bur. Engr. Registration, Tau Beta Pi, Sigma Xi, Phi Kappa Theta. Republican. Roman Catholic. Home: 125 N Ormond Ave Havertown PA 19083 Office: 30 S 17th St Philadelphia PA 19101

BOVÉE, MICHAEL CHRISTOPHER, real estate broker; b. Los Angeles, July 15, 1943; s. John Lemuel Franklin and Margaret Keppler (Fowler) B.; A.A., Orange Coast Coll., 1965; B.S., U. East Fla., 1972; D. Comm. Sc., London Inst., 1973; m. Laura Mary Margaret Voegele, May 23, 1970; children—David Anthony, Jeffrey Michael. Owner, La Plage Enterprises, Newport Beach, Calif., 1964-71; dist. sales mgr. Valley Land Sales, Sherman Oaks, Calif., 1971; dir. property mgmt. Cal-Home Properties, Garden Grove, Calif., 1971-72; property mgr. Residential Leasing Corp., Garden Grove, Calif., 1972-73; dist. mgr. Grubb & Ellis Property Services, Inc., San Francisco, 1973-75; corporate broker, asst. sec., asst. dist. mgr. Property Mgmt. Systems, San Francisco, 1975-77; corporate broker, chmn. bd., pres. Pacific Property Services, Inc., Walnut Creek, Calif., 1977-78; v.p. property mgmt. div. Grubb & Ellis Property Services, Inc., Oakland, Calif., 1979—. Bd. dirs. Culverdale Community Assn., 1971-74, Rudgear Meadows Homeowners Assn., 1980—; cons. Homeowner Bd., Phase II, City of Irvine, 1972-73. Pres., Rudgear Meadows Community Assn., 1980—. Cert. property mgr. Mem. Inst. Real Estate Mgmt., Austin Apt. Assn., Mcht. Brokers Exchange, Internat. Real Estate Fedn., Native Sons Golden West, Ancien Roseens. Home: 2205 Kenton Ct Walnut Creek CA 94596 Office: 1333 Broadway Oakland CA 94612

BOVICH, EDWARD HUGH, cement co. exec.; b. N.Y.C., Sept. 20, 1924; s. Edward Francis and Beatrice Catherine (Gilmartin) B.; student Cathedral Coll., N.Y.C., 1942-44, U.S. Mcht. Marine Acad., Kings Point, N.Y., 1944-45; A.B., St. Basil's Coll. and Sem., Stamford, Conn., 1949; postgrad. Fordham U., 1950-51, DePaul U., 1954; m. Michele Maria Denaro, June 6, 1953; children—Mary Beatrice, Patricia Marie, Edward Philip, John Patrick. Instr., Fordham U., 1951; spl. agt. FBI, various locations, 1951-57; dist. dir. Nat. Safety Council, Pitts., 1957-59; exec. dir. Bd. Commerce, Wyandotte, Mich., 1959-62; dir. mktg. Wyandotte Chems. Corp., 1962-65, gen. mgr. cement div., 1966-70; pres. Wyandotte Cement, Inc., 1971-79, chmn. bd., 1974-79; pres. Ind. Cement Corp., Kingston, N.Y., 1977-79, now dir.; pres. Edward H. Bovich & Assos., Dearborn, Mich., 1980—; dir. Wyandotte Stone Co., Material Transfer Corp., Dearborn, Mich., N-Viro Energy Systems Ltd., Toledo; mem. adv. bd. Am. Mut. Ins. Co., 1973—. Spl. rep. Pa., Pres.'s Com. for Traffic Safety, 1958; pres. Sacred Heart Sch. Bd., Dearborn, 1967-68, Sacred Heart Council, 1969-70; chmn. Chem. Industry United Found., 1969-72; bd. mgmt. YMCA Detroit Met. Area, 1967-68; bd. dirs. Mt. Kelly Cemetery, Dearborn, 1974—, Nat. Found. for Philanthropy, Washington, 1980—. Served with USNR, 1945-46. Named Outstanding Young Man of Year, Wyandotte, 1961. Mem. Soc. Former FBI Agts. (past chmn. Mich. chpt.), Portland Cement Assn. Chgo. (dir.), Sales and Mktg. Execs. Detroit (past chmn. Speakers Bur.), Assn. Execs. Met. Detroit, Buffalo, Detroit, Rochester chambers commerce. Clubs: Buffalo; Dearborn Country; Ft. Orange (Albany, N.Y.); Renaissance (charter mem.) (Detroit); Fairlane (Dearborn). Author: CBS Radio Show, Your FBI, Chgo., 1957. Home: 752 Wagner Ct Dearborn MI 48124 Office: Box 420 Wyandotte MI 48192

BOWDEN, CURTIS DWIGHT, steel co. exec.; b. Bishop, Va., Aug. 19, 1943; s. Curtis Carl and Mildred Elaine (Perkins) B.; student mech. engring. W.Va. U., 1961-65; student bus. adminstrn. U. South Fla., 1979; m. Rebecca Sue Garten, Aug. 6, 1965; children—Timothy Wayne, Wyndalynn Dawn, Curtis Todd. Analyst Dun & Bradstreet, Charleston, W.Va., 1965-66; safety engr. Aetna Life & Casualty Co., Charleston, 1966-70; safety engr. Fla. Steel Corp., Tampa, 1970-72, mgr. safety, 1972—. Mem. Fla. Govs. Com. Safety Curriculum, 1972—; mem. com. Hillsborough Community Coll., 1972—. Served to 1st lt. Mil. Police, USAR, 1968-72. Mem. Nat. Fire Protection Assn., Nat. Safety Council, Am. Soc. Safety Engrs. (program chmn. 1973, sec. 1974, pres. 1975), Am. Iron and Steel Inst. (nat. safety com. 1972—), Concrete Reinforcing Steel Inst. (safety com. 1973—), Lambda Chi Alpha. Home: 902 Tomahawk Trail Riverview FL 33569 Office: Fla Steel Corp 1715 Cleveland St Tampa FL 33623

BOWDEN, DWIGHT RICHARD, realtor; b. Hope, Ark., Nov. 25, 1931; s. James Rister and Velma (Crews) B.; student Texarkana Coll., 1949-50, 52-53; m. Barbara Jean Orr, Dec. 9, 1953; children—Terry Michael, Scott Russell, Gary Raymond. With Wm. Cameron Co., Texarkana, Tex., 1952-53, Nat. Cash Register Co., Anchorage, 1954-59, Communications Engring., Inc., Anchorage, 1960-62; asst. v.p., br. mgr. First Fed. Savs. & Loan Assn., Anchorage, 1963-68; salesman Action Realty, Inc., Anchorage, 1969-70; owner, broker Bowden Co., realtors, Anchorage, 1971—; chmn. bd. Home Fed. Savs. & Loan Assn., Anchorage, 1974-76; pres. Superior Millwork, Inc., 1978—. Bd. dirs. Realtors Multiple Listing Service, Anchorage, 1971-72, 77-78. Served with USMCR, 1950-52. Mem. Anchorage Bd. Realtors (pres. 1971, dir. 1972), Nat. (dir. 1974), Alaska (pres. 1974) assns. realtors, Anchorage C. of C. Landlord and Property Mgrs. Assn. Alaska (dir. 1972—), Alaska Sports Car Club (pres. 1964). Methodist. Democrat. Elk. Home: 2101 Loussac Anchorage AK 99503 Office: 401 E Fireweed Ln Anchorage AK 99503

BOWDEN, LAWRENCE BERNARD, ins. co. exec.; b. Eccles, Lancashire, Eng., Dec. 25, 1927; came to Can., 1950, naturalized, 1976; s. Samuel Leslie and Elizabeth (Toole) B.; B.A. in English, De La Salle Coll., Pendleton, Eng., 1943; m. Sonja Florence Leporis, May 28, 1960; children—Mark Valent, Philip Andrew. Tchr. English, De La Salle Coll., Hopwood Hall, Lancashire, 1949-51; fire underwriter Phoenix of London Ins., Toronto, Ont., Can., 1951-54; fire supt. Continental Ins. Co., 1954-55, spl. agt., 1955-60; insp. Fireman's Fund, Toronto, 1960-62; insp. Great Am. Ins., Toronto, 1962-63, property mgr., 1963-64, underwriting mgr., 1964-67, asst. mgr. Can., 1967-71, gen. mgr. Can., 1971-76; sr. v.p. Canadian Gen. Ins. Co., Toronto, 1976—. Served with Royal Navy, 1946-49. Progressive Conservative. Roman Catholic. Clubs: Ont., Bd. Trade of Met. Toronto. Home: 21 Somerdale Sq West Hill ON M1E 1M9 Canada Office: 170 University Ave Toronto ON M5H 3B5 Canada

BOWDEN, OTIS HEARNE, II, mgmt. cons. firm exec.; b. Stuttgart, Ark., Jan. 2, 1928; s. Otis Hearne and Donna (Trice) B.; B.S. in Bus. Adminstrn., Washington U., 1950, M.B.A., 1953; m. Helen Carol Lamar, June 25, 1949. Financial analyst St. Louis Union Trust Co., St. Louis, 1950-53; dist. mgr. TRW, Inc., Cleve., 1953-63; dir. Mass Transit Center, B.F. Goodrich Co., Akron, Ohio, 1963-67; v.p. E.A. Butler Assos., Inc., Cleve., 1967-71; pres. Bowden & Co., Inc., Cleve., 1972—. Guest lectr. Akron U., 1972—. Nat. promotion dir. Laymen's Hour Radio Broadcast, 1959-63, trustee, 1975-79; chmn. commerce and industry div. United Fund of Greater Cleve., 1962; pres. Am. Baptist Men of Ohio, 1962-63. Trustee Alderson-Broaddus Coll., Philippi, W.Va., 1966-77, Eastern Coll., Phila., 1979—, Eastern Bapt. Theol. Sem., Phila., 1979—; alumni bd. govs., Washington U., St. Louis; mem. adv. bd. Salvation Army Greater Cleve., 1979—; bd. dirs. Am. Bapt. Fgn. Mission Soc., 1962-71; regional bd. dirs. Project Winsome Internationale. Served with USMCR, 1951. Paul Harris fellow Rotary, 1978. Mem. Am. Mgmt. Assn., Am. Mktg. Assn. Clubs: Union, Rotary (trustee Cleve. club 1975-77). Home: 1816 Brookshire Rd Akron OH 44313 Office: Liberty Plaza 5000 Rockside Rd Cleveland OH 44131

BOWDEN, RONALD JOSEPH, bus. exec.; b. Alturas, Calif., Dec. 26, 1951; s. Joseph Henry and Juanita Mae (Dunkin) B.; B.S., George Fox Coll., Newberg, Oreg., 1974; cert. Am. Inst. Banking, 1975, 76; m. Virginia Kathryn Martin, Oct. 12, 1974. Ops. officer I, U.S. Nat. Bank Oreg., Portland, 1975-76, br. banking officer II, Astoria, 1976-78; asso. dir. George Fox Coll. Found., 1978-79, exec. dir., 1979-80; sr. v.p. CL7 Devel., Inc., Portland, 1980—. Mem. Am. Bankers Assn., Am. Inst. Banking (past chpt. pres.), Am. Mgmt. Assn., Yamhill County Bd. Realtors. Republican. Quaker. Clubs: Sertoma (past club and dist. treas.), Kiwanis (past club treas., chmn. religious affairs com.). Home: 3101 SW McNary Pkwy Avocet 4 Lake Oswego OR 97034 Office: 711 SW Alder Suite 303 Portland OR 97205

BOWDEN, TOMMY H., computer co. exec.; b. Santa Anna, Tex., Feb. 12, 1938; s. Henry Floyd and Cora Myrtle (Norris) B.; B.M.E., So. Methodist U., 1963; m. Gayle Karen Kincaid, Aug. 20, 1971 (dec.); children—Jason, Thomas, Theresa. Div. mgr. Computer Complex, Houston, 1967-70; v.p. Tex. Sci. Corp., Houston, 1970-73; v.p. Western Union Teleprocessing, Inc., Mahwah, N.J., 1973-75; v.p. DMC Systems Inc., Santa Clara, Calif., 1975—; sr. partner Hand Bowden and Martell, 1974—; chmn. bd., dir. Sunrise Almaden Corp., 1976—. Mem. Sales and Mktg. Execs. Club, U.S. C. of C., Santa Clara C. of C. (dir.), Aviation Hall of Fame, Am. Mgmt. Assn. Republican. Club: Kenna. Home: 1133 Silver Oak Ct San Jose CA 95120 Office: 2300 Owen St Santa Clara CA 95051

BOWDIDGE, WILLIAM ALAN, constrn. co. exec.; b. San Francisco, Sept. 24, 1930; s. Herbert William and Anne Martha (Calahan) B.; B.S. in Bus. Adminstrn., U. Calif., 1952; m. Priscilla Furtado, Dec. 18, 1965; children—Robert, Anne. With Western Pacific R.R., 1953-66, sales rep. Oakland, Calif., 1962-64, asst. chief sales and service, San Francisco, 1964-66; traffic mgr. Guy F. Atkinson Co., South San Francisco, 1966—. Mem. Indsl. Traffic Club, Delta Nu Alpha. Democrat. Roman Catholic. Home: 2440 Lexington Way San Bruno CA 94066 Office: 10 W Orange St South San Francisco CA 94080

BOWE, RICHARD EUGENE, machine co. exec.; b. Van Wert, Ohio, Aug. 27, 1921; s. Hugh Horatio and Clara Magdeline (Heiby) B.; student U. Mich., 1939-40; B.S., U.S. Naval Acad., 1943; M.B.A., Harvard U., 1949; m. Virginia Welbourn Cooley, May 17, 1947; children—Richard Welbourn, Michael Ames, Peter Armistead. With Ellicott Machine Corp., Balt., 1954—, asst. sec., asst. treas., 1955-56, sec., treas., 1956-64, exec. v.p., 1964-65, pres., 1965—, chmn. bd., 1967—; chmn. bd. McConway & Torley Corp., 1963-78; dir. First Nat. Bank of Md.; adv. bd. Liberty Mut. Ins. Co., Arkwright-Boston Ins. Co. Trustee Balt. Mus. Art. Served to lt. comdr. Submarine Service, USN, 1940-47; PTO. Decorated Bronze Star, Gold Star, Silver Star. Home: 1135 Asquith Dr Arnold MD 21012 Office: 1611 Bush St Baltimore MD 21230

BOWEN, DENNIS PHILIP, ins. co. exec.; b. Williamsport, Pa., July 12, 1937; s. Raymond Charles and Claribel Bowen; B.S., Pa. State U., 1960; m. Barbara M. Roed, Aug. 12, 1962; children—Ingrid Leilani, Susan Marie. Sales rep. IBM Corp., 1963-70; dir. data processing Cogar Corp., 1970-71; v.p. electronic data processing Unity Mut. Life, Syracuse, N.Y., 1971—. Served with USN, 1960-63. Fellow Life Mgmt. Inst.; mem. Adminstrv. Mgmt. Soc. (pres. Syracuse chpt. 1977-78), Data Processing Mgmt. Assn. (dir. Syracuse chpt. 1979-80). Club: Skaneateles Sailing. Home: 16 Academy St Skaneateles NY 13152 Office: 1 Unity Plaza Syracuse NY 13215

BOWEN, HOWARD, research tech. exec.; b. Evanston, Ill., Apr. 29, 1932; s. Harvey N. and Sylvia E. (Turner) B.; student U. Chgo., 1949-50, Northwestern U., 1950-53; m. Carole E. MacDonald, May 19, 1956; children—Patricia Anne, Margaret Grace. Vice pres. Harwald Co., Evanston, Ill., 1961-69; sec., chmn. bd. dirs. Research Tech., Inc., Lincolnwood, Ill., 1970—; pres. Amms Co., Inc.; dir. IAV of Hong Kong. Served with U.S. Army, 1954-56. Mem. Nat. Audio-Visual Assn., Assn. Ednl. Data Systems, Assn. Ednl. Communications and Tech. Patentee fast moving films inspection. Home: 210 Catalpa Pl Wilmette IL 60091 Office: 4700 Chase Ave Lincolnwood IL 60091

BOWEN, JOHN SHEETS, advt. agy. exec.; b. Chelsea, Mass., Feb. 4, 1927; s. Charles Parnell and Helen Thomas (Sheets) B.; B.A., Yale U., 1949; m. Catherine Leigh Stander, June 28, 1952; children—Mark Stander, Charles Parnell, II, Holly Leigh. Unit mgr. Procter & Gamble, Inc., 1949-52; account exec. McCann Ericson, Inc., 1952-59; account supr., mgmt. supr., exec. v.p., pres., chief exec. officer Benton & Bowles, Inc., N.Y.C., 1959—. Served with inf., AUS, 1945-46. Mem. Am. Assn. Advt. Agys. (dir.-at-large), Econ. Club N.Y. Republican. Episcopalian. Clubs: Shenorock Shore, Manursing Island, Apiwamis. Home: 44 Grace Church St Rye NY 10580 Office: 909 3d Ave New York NY 10022

BOWEN, R. BRAYTON, JR., retail exec.; b. Coventry, R.I., June 12, 1940; s. Ralph Brayton and LillianDorothy (Phillips) B.; A.B., Brown U., 1962, A.M., 1965; student Am. Sch. Classical Studies, Athens, summer 1966; m. Judith Ann Briggs, Oct. 29, 1966; children—David N.G., Christopher P.T., Catherine A.C. Instr., Kent (Conn.) Sch., 1964-67, St. Paul's Sch., Concord, N.H., 1967-68; dir. employment-employee relations May Dept. Stores Co., G. Fox & Co., Hartford, Conn., 1968-72; v.p. ops. and personnel J. Homestock div. R.H. Macy & Co., Inc., Dedham, Mass., 1972-77; v.p. personnel Federated Dept. Stores, Rike-Kumler Co., Dayton, Ohio, 1977-79, sr. v.p. ops. and personnel, 1979—; speaker. Chmn., Medway (Mass.) Sch. Com., 1975-77, Democratic Town Com., 1976-77; bd. dirs. Goodwill Industries, 1980—; citizen founder, mem. steering com. Medway Citizen Adv. Group on Edn., 1974-75. R.I. Dept. Edn. scholar, 1960-62; Ford Found. intern, 1962. Mem. Am. Arbitration Assn., Am. Soc. Tng. and Devel., Conn. Personnel and Guidance Assn. (past pres. Hartford chpt.), Dayton C. of C. (labor relations com., legis. and govtl. affairs com.), Nat. Retail Mchts. Assn. (past chmn., dir., personnel bd. N.Y.). Home: 6619 Stamford Pl Dayton OH 45459 Office: Rike's Dept Stores 2d and Main Sts Dayton OH 45401

BOWEN, ROBERT CALLENDER, savs. and loan exec.; b. State College, Miss., Aug. 12, 1925; s. James Vance and Albye (Callender) B.; B.S., Auburn U., 1948; M.S., Pa. State U., 1952, postgrad., 1953; m. Doris Katherine Lee, Nov. 26, 1964. So. regional dir. Student Mktg. Inst., N.Y.C., 1953-56; asst. project dir. Crossley S-O Surveys, Inc., N.Y.C., 1956-57; mktg. and econ. research asso. N.Y. Stock Exchange, 1958-59; mktg. specialist Am. Bankers Assn., N.Y.C., 1959-62; met. div. mktg. officer Chem. Bank, N.Y.C., 1962-65; mktg. officer Franklin Nat. Bank, N.Y.C., 1965-66; pres. Lee/Bowen, Inc., N.Y.C., 1967, pres. Cleve., 1973-74; v.p., dir. mktg. research Cleve. Trust Co., 1968-72; v.p. mktg. First Fed. Savs. & Loan Assn. of Orlando, Fla. 1974—. Chmn. buyers'-sellers' guide com., chmn. research council Greater Cleve. Growth Assn., Cleve., 1970-74; trustee John Young Mus. and Planetarium, 1975-79, chmn. membership drive, 1976, treas., 1978; bd. dirs. Central Fla. Boys Club, 1976—, Council Arts and Scis. Central Fla., 1977—; chmn. nat. and local gifts campaign local Public Broadcasting Service, 1977; mem. United Arts Fund Steering Com., 1978—; mem. Orange County Cultural Adv. Bd., 1979—; mem. Indsl. Devel. Commn. of Mid-Fla., 1979—. Served with inf. AUS, 1943-46, 50-52. Mem. Am. Mktg. Assn. (chmn. finance sect. consumer div. 1964-66, publicity chmn. Cleve. chpt. 1968, chmn. attendance and hospitality Cleve. chpt. 1969, exec. v.p., pres. Cleve. chpt. 1970-72, pres.-elect Orlando chpt. 1979—), Bank Mtkg. and Pub. Relations Assn., Cleve. Advt. Club, Am. Mgmt. Assn. (chmn. modern practice in bank mktg. 1965-67), Am. Bankers Assn. (mem. edn. and tng. com. mktg./savs. div. 1969-70), Orlando Area Tourist Trade Assn. (dir. 1976—, pres. 1980—), Orlando Area C. of C. (chmn. promotion com. 1975, mem. steering com. 1975, viewpoint com. 1976, cultural affairs com. 1979—), Theta Chi, Phi Delta Kappa, Pi Gamma Mu. Clubs: Auburn U. Alumni (dir. 1977—, v.p. 1980—), Citrus; Winter Park (Fla.) Racquet, Univ. Author: Customer Analysis-A Profit Building Tool, 1961; Bank Holding Company Reporter, 1973; editorial bd. Fin. Mag., 1967, mktg. editor, 1968; contbr. articles to profl. jours. Home: 801 Pine Tree Rd Winter Park FL 32789 Office: PO Box 2073 Orlando FL 32802

BOWEN, WILLIAM JACKSON, gas co. exec.; b. Sweetwater, Tex., Mar. 31, 1922; s. Berry and Annah (Robey) B.; B.S., U.S. Mil. Acad., 1945; m. Annis K. Hilty, June 6, 1945; children—Shelley Ann, Barbara Kay, Berry Dunbar, William Jackson. Petroleum engr. Delhi Oil Corp., Dallas, 1949-57; v.p. Fla. Gas Co., Houston, 1957-60, pres., Winter Park, Fla., 1960-74; pres., chmn., chief exec. officer Transco Cos., Inc., Houston, 1974—; dir. S.W. Bancshares, Crown Zellerbach Corp., Gas Research Inst. Bd. dirs. YMCA, Houston, Houston Mus. Fine Arts. Served with AUS, 1945-49. Registered profl. engr., Tex. Mem. Am. Gas Assn. (dir.), Interstate Natural Gas Assn. Am. (adv. to bd. dirs.), Houston C. of C. (dir.), Delta Kappa Epsilon. Episcopalian. Home: 3702 Del Monte Dr Houston TX 77019 Office: PO Box 1396 S Post Oak at W Alabama Houston TX 77001

BOWER, DONALD L., oil co. exec.; b. Portland, Oreg., 1923; B.S., Oreg. State U., 1947; married. With Standard Oil Co. Calif., San Francisco, 1947—, corp. v.p., 1967-79, vice chmn., 1979—, also pres. Chevron U.S.A., 1977—; dir. Crocker Nat. Corp. Trustee Oreg. State U. Found. Office: Standard Oil Co Calif 225 Bush St San Francisco CA 94120*

BOWES, ARTHUR STUTZ, JR., bus. exec.; b. Chgo., Apr. 7, 1932; s. Arthur Stutz and Jane (Mattison) B.; student Purdue U., 1950-51; B.S., Northwestern U., 1958, M.B.A., 1959; m. Barbara Ann Hoops, Jan. 24, 1953; children—Linda Jane, Karen Ann. Investment analyst, research dir. H. M. Byllesby & Co., Chgo., 1960-64; v.p. and dir. Advance Ross Corp., Chgo., 1964-66; v.p. Utah Shale Land Corp.,

Chgo., 1964-66; pres. Lab Tronics, Inc., Chgo., 1965-66; pres. Wolf Ridge Minerals Corp., Denver, Colo., 1966-72; chmn. bd. Indsl. Resources, Inc., Chgo., 1972—, Advance Ross, Inc., 1976—; pres. Utah Shale Land & Minerals Corp., Chgo., 1980—, also dir.; dir. Holmes & Co., Columbia City, Ind. Served with AUS, 1952-55. Mem. Phi Gamma Delta, Beta Gamma Sigma. Republican. Clubs: Mid-Day, Tavern (Chgo.). Home: 1300 Lake Shore Dr Chicago IL 60610 Office: 111 W Monroe Chicago IL 60603

BOWIE, LOIS POWERS, real estate investment firm exec.; b. Grundy, Va., June 12, 1920; d. Thomas Benton and Amy (Stinson) Powers; Elementary Edn. Certificate, Hiwassee Coll., 1939; B.S. in Edn., Mary Washington Coll., 1942; postgrad. Mary Crest Coll., 1954-55; m. Roy Delp Bowie, Apr. 2, 1942; children—Elizabeth Anne (Mrs. Paul E. Brown, Jr.), Richard, Amy Lee (Mrs. Douglas Alan Williams), Nancy Carol (Mrs. Tom Carter). Elementary tchr., Harman, Va., 1940; real estate agt. firm Ruhl & Ruhl, Davenport, Iowa, 1952-54; receptionist Bowie Chiropractic Offices, Galax, Va., 1954-56; partner Bowie Swimming Pool Co., Bristol, Tenn., 1956—; owner, partner Bowie Investment Co., Bristol, 1960—; partner, owner Econo-Travel Motel, 1972—; co-owner, operator chain of Western Steer Family Steakhouses; partner Cedar Chalets of Bristol. Bd. dirs. YMCA, 1980—. Mem. Women's Soc. Christian Service, Delta Psi Omega. Methodist (mem. ofcl. bd. 1965-68, 74, evangelism commn. 1967-69, bd. dirs. child evangelism 1971—, mem. fin. com. 1969, tchr. Sunday sch. 1945—, adv. bd. Campus Crusade for Christ 1973-75). Club: Bristol Profl. Women's (fin. com.). Home: 1108 Glen St Bristol TN 37620 Office: 915 Anderson St Bristol TN 37620

BOWIE, WILLIAM JOSEPH, financial co. exec.; b. Oklahoma City, Mar. 23, 1936; s. Joe P. and Lou B.; m. Sue Botsford, Jan. 4, 1958; children—Joe, Patricia. Mgr., Askins, Inc., Oklahoma City, 1957-68; pres. CBS Fin. Services, Oklahoma City, 1968-79, chmn. bd., 1979—. Mem. World Bankers and Financiers Assn. (pres.), Internat. Mortgage Brokers, Internat. Bankers Assn. Democrat. Methodist. Clubs: Lions, Moose. Author: The Money Finders Directory. Office: 4540 NW 10th St Suite 202 Oklahoma City OK 73127

BOWLER, JOSEPH, JR., textile machinery sales and import co. exec.; b. New Bedford, Mass., Oct. 6, 1929; s. Joseph and Bertha E. (Mathews) B.; student New Bedford Textile Inst., 1948-50; U. N.C., 1960; m. Teresa M. Gillis, June 24, 1950; children—Joseph, Karen, Mary. Sales engr. Allen Co., New Bedford, 1950, dist. sales mgr., Greenville, S.C., 1950-52, Terrell Machine Co., Greenville, 1955-59, Am. Schlafhorst Co., Greenville, 1955-59, Lessona Corp., Greenville, 1959-61; v.p., gen. mgr. Dixon Corp., Monroe, N.C., 1961-62, also dir.; pres., treas. Bowler Industries, Inc., Greenville, 1962—; pres. Somet, Inc., Greenville, 1975-80, also dir. Served with U.S. Army, 1952-54. Recipient S.C. Bicentennial Service award, 1976. Mem. Am. Textile Mfrs., Inst., Am. Assn. Textile Tech., Am. Assn. Textile Chemists and Colorists, Ga. Textile Mfrs. Assn., Internat. Soc. Indsl. Yarn Mfrs., So. Textile Assn., Greenville C. of C. Republican. Episcopalian. Clubs: Greenville Country, Rotary, Greenville VIP. Contbr. articles to profl. jours. Home: 3 Darien Way Greenville SC 29615 Office: PO Box 1603 Greenville SC 29602

BOWLES, EDNA MATHILDA, govt. relations cons.; b. Callao, Peru, Mar. 7, 1928 (parents Am. citizens); s. James Martin and Eloise Matilde B.; B.S., Universidad Nacional de San Marcos, Lima, Peru, 1946; postgrad. Bryce Coll., 1947. Mem. staff, office of econ. counselors Argentine embassy, Washington, 1947-50; researcher, statistician Nat. Labor-Mgmt. Council on Fgn. Trade Policy, Washington, 1950-51; mgr. Washington office L.M. MacDonnell, 1951-53; asst. sec.-treas. Tech. Resources Corp., Washington, 1953-54; Washington editor, asst. to pub. Americas Daily/Diario Las Americas, Miami, Fla., 1954-66; govt. relations cons., 1966—; acting treas. Ten Eyck Assos., Washington, 1962-64; acting exec. dir. Inst. Socio-Econ. Studies, Ltd., Washington, 1973-74; asst. to pres. Lead-Zinc Producers Com., Washington, 1975; asso. govt. relations rep. Martin-Marietta Aluminum Co., Washington, 1975; dir. communications Am. Assn. Port Authorities, Washington, 1977. Dir. publicity D.C. Young Republicans, 1952-54; nat. dir. publicity Nat. Citizens Com. for Columbus Day, 1955-60; staff aide service D.C. chpt. ARC; vol. counselor Barney Neighborhood House, Washington. Mem. Soc. Internat. Devel., Nat. Planning Assn. Republican. Methodist. Office: Suite B-1105 3636 16th St NW Washington DC 20010

BOWLING, JOHN KNOX, JR., airline ofcl.; b. Duncan, Okla., Feb. 26, 1940; s. John Knox and Lula (Hatley) B.; B.A., U. Tex. at Austin, 1963, B.J., 1963; m. Diantha Lee King, July 13, 1967; 1 dau., Tanisha Lee. Advt. trainee Ted Bates & Co., Co., Inc., N.Y.C., 1963-64, comml. broadcast producer, 1964-66, broadcast supr., 1966-67; Western pub. relations mgr. Air France, Los Angeles, 1968-73, advt., merchandising and creative service mgr. for U.S.A., N.Y.C., 1973—. Recipient Grand Chevalier de lvOrdre de Vieux Moulin, France, 1963. Republican. Presbyterian. Clubs: Univ. N.Y., Blue Hill Troupe (N.Y.C.); Ardsley Country (Ardsley-on-Hudson, N.Y.). Home: Clifton Pl Irvington NY 10533 Office: 1350 Ave of Americas New York NY 10019

BOWMAN, ARNOLD PAUL, food co. exec.; b. Sikeston, Mo., Sept. 5, 1920; s. Arnold Paul and Margaret Dover B.; student S.E. Mo. U., 1938-41; B.S. in Chemistry, U. Wis., 1947-49; m. Jean Linville Welke, Mar. 7, 1941; children—Mary Linville, Melissa Hamilton. With Oscar Mayer & Co., Madison, Wis., ops. mgr., plant mgr., regional mgr., v.p., group v.p., also dir.; chmn., dir. Sci. Protein Labs., Quality Control Spice Co.; dir. Anchor Savs. & Loan Assn., Venezuelan Empoc Co., Claussens Pickles, Oscar Mayer S.A., Spain, Kantig Pak Machine Co., Iowa. Fin. chmn. Republican Party Dane County, 1962-63; trustee Baptist Ch., 1963; gen. chmn. United Givers Dane County, 1965, pres., 1968. Served to capt. USAAF, 1941-47. Mem. Am. Soc. for Quality Control, Am. Chem. Soc., Inst. Food Technologists, Wis. Alumni Assn., Inst. Mgmt. Sci., Madison C. of C. (pres. 1970). Club: Kiwanis (dir. 1963). Office: Oscar Mayer & Co PO Box 7188 Madison WI 53707

BOWMAN, DONALD EUGENE, investment counselor; b. Dayton, Ohio, July 9, 1930; s. John Peter Bowman and Delia Frances (Sink) Fry; B.A. in Finance, U. Wis., 1952; postgrad. Am. U., Johns Hopkins, U. Balt.; grad. Advanced Mgmt. Program, Harvard, 1973; m. Mary Louise Woodford, June 20, 1952; children—Clark W., Marylouise C. Theater mgr., Dayton, 1944-47; instr. econs., English composition U.S. Naval Acad., Annapolis, Md., 1954-56; investment counselor, economist T. Rowe Price, Balt., 1956-64, v.p., 1965-72, mem. exec. com., 1965-78, head counsel div., 1967-73, exec. v.p., 1973-74, pres., 1974-78, chief exec. officer, 1975-78, also dir.; pres., dir. Charles Center Properties, 1973-78; pres. Bowman Fin. Mgmt. Co., Balt., 1978—; past dir. T. Rowe Price Growth Stock Fund, Rowe Price New Era Fund, Rowe Price Prime Res. Fund, Rowe Price New Income Fund, Rowe Price Tax Free Fund; adj. prof. mgmt. and investments Loyola Grad. Sch. Bus. Trustee Roland Park Country Sch., Ind. Colls. Assn. Md., U. Wis. Found., U. Balt. Served with USN, 1952-56; capt. Res. Mem. Investment Counsel Assn. Am. (gov. 1972-78), Balt. Soc. Fin. Analysts, U. Wis. Bascom Hill Soc. (exec. com.). Presbyterian. Office: Bowman Fin Mgmt Co Suite 1106 2 Hopkins Plaza Baltimore MD 21201

BOWMAN, JAMES LEROY, glass co. exec.; b. Walterboro, S.C., May 3, 1945; s. Leroy A. and Mittie R. (Garrick) B.; B.S., S.C. State Coll., 1967; M.B.A., Fairleigh Dickinson U., 1979; m. Rosetta Jo Dalton, July 8, 1978. Commd. 2d lt. U.S. Army, 1967, advanced through grades to capt., 1975, discharged, 1975; sales rep. PPG Industries, Atlanta, 1975-76, sales rep., Pitts., 1976-77, account rep., N.Y.C., 1977-79, supr. customer service, organic chems., 1980, mgr. customer service, chem. div., 1980—. Instr., Jr. Achievement. Mem. Drug Chem. and Allied Trades Assn., Conn. Chem. Club. Home: 619 Deerwatch Rd Bridgeville PA 15017 Office: PPG Industries One Gateway Center Pittsburgh PA 15222

BOWMAN, L. ALLEN, slip ring mfg. co. exec.; b. Timberville, Va., Mar. 22, 1932; s. Vernon E. and Cora E. (Fansler) B.; student Berea Coll., 1949-50; B.S. in Bus. Adminstrn., Va. Poly. Inst. and State U., 1958; m. Marilyn Blankenship, Dec. 15, 1973; children—Steve A., Barry M. With Poly-Sci. div. Litton Industries, Blacksburg, Va., 1955—, pres., 1970—. Trustee, Montgomery County Hosp., 1978—. Served with USN, 1950-54. Mem. Am. Mgmt. Assn., U.S. C. of C., Blacksburg C. of C. (pres. 1974), Va. C. of C. (dir. 1976-79), Va. Mfrs. Assn. (dir. 1978—). Lutheran. Club: Blacksburg Country. Home: 1408 Palmer Dr Blacksburg VA 24060 Office: 1213 N Main St Blacksburg VA 24060

BOWMAN, R(OBERT) WALLACE, energy co. exec.; b. Gargrave, Yorkshire, Eng., July 30, 1921; came to U.S., 1950, naturalized, 1954; s. Sidney and Annie Isabel (Hoare) B.; B.Sc. (Econ. with honors, London Sch. Econs., 1949; M.S., Mont. State Coll., 1951; M.P.A. (Littauer fellow), Harvard U., 1953; m. Ruth Gurin, Nov. 2, 1967. Vice-pres., Studley Shupert, Boston, 1954-61; investment v.p. Delaware Mgmt. Co., Phila., 1962-65; investment mgr. Loews Corp., N.Y.C., 1966-73; sr. v.p. corp. devel. Tosco Corp., Los Angeles, 1973—. Served as pilot RAF, 1942-46. Decorated Brit. Air Force Cross, French Croix de Guerre. Mem. Fin. Analysts Fedn., Am. Econ. Assn. Home: 1008 Amalfi Dr Pacific Palisades CA 90272 Office: 10100 Santa Monica Blvd Los Angeles CA 90067

BOWMAN, VIRGINIA JUDITH, bank exec.; b. Chgo., June 18, 1940; d. Philip Gustav and Sara (Kinsey) B.; A.B., Smith Coll., 1962; M.B.A., Fordham U., 1978; Sorbonne U., 1964-65, U. Wroclaw (Poland), 1977. With State Dept., Washington, 1963-65; reporter Forbes Mag., N.Y.C., 1966-68; mng. editor East Europe Mag., N.Y.C., 1969; with Citicorp, N.Y.C., 1970—, v.p., 1979—. Trustee, Hollywood Arts Council. Home: 2024 Mayview Dr Los Angeles CA 90027 Office: Citicorp USA 515 S Flower St Los Angeles CA 90071

BOWYER, RICHARD CRAIG, engring. co. exec.; b. Yarmouth, N.S., Can., Nov. 22, 1944; s. James Laird and Margaret Jane (Moore) B.; P. Engring. in Mining, N.S. Tech. Coll. and Dalhousie U., 1968; m. Heather Ann Mattatall, Jan. 20, 1968; children—Bradley James, Nicole Alice, Michelle Margaret. Engr., Gulf Oil Can., Stettler, Alta., 1968-69, Calgary, Alta., 1969-71; sales engr. Camco Can., Calgary, 1971-75; pres. C.B. Engring. Ltd., Calgary, 1975—. Mem. Profl. Engrs. Alta., Canadian Inst. Mining & Metallurgy, Instrument Soc. Am. Anglican. Clubs: 400, Calgary Curling. Home: 413 Lake Simcoe Crescent SE Calgary AB T2J 5L3 Canada Office: #1 6320 11st SE Calgary AB T2H 2L7 Canada

BOX, WILLIAM THOMAS, mfg. co. exec.; b. Los Angeles, July 18, 1918; s. John Vincent and May (Youle) B.; B.S.M.E., U. Santa Clara (Calif.), 1940; m. Patricia Ryan Baxter, June 17, 1958; children—William T., John, Paul, Margaret, Anthony, Stephen, Robert, Jean. From test engr., sales engr. to v.p. ops. Byron Jackson, Inc. (now subs. Hughes Tool Co.), 1940-68; from asst. gen. mgr. to pres., chief exec. officer Trico Industries, Inc., Gardena, Calif., 1968—. Served in USMC, 1941-45. Mem. Soc. Petroleum Engrs., Petroleum Equipment Suppliers Assn. Republican. Roman Catholic. Club: Calif. Contbr. articles to mags. Office: 15707 S Main St Gardena CA 90248

BOYD, DONALD POYNTON, paper co. exec.; b. Phila., June 10, 1920; s. Roy Martin and Marguerite (Poynton) B.; B.S. in Econs. with distinction, U. Pa., 1942; m. Gertrude Stevenson, Oct. 11,1944; children—Mary Montgomery, Leslie Stevenson, Margaret Agnes, Christina Martin. With Curtis Pub. Co., Phila., 1946-68, mgr. purchasing, 1961, dir. purchasing, 1962-68; dir. purchasing Hammermill Paper Co., Erie, Pa., 1968-76, asst. v.p. materials and transp., 1976-80, v.p., 1980—; adj. faculty mem. Pa. State U. Vestryman, St. Stephan's Episc. Ch., Fairview, Pa. Served to maj. U.S. Army, 1942-46. Mem. Nat. Assn. Purchasing Mgmt. (asst. v.p.), Purchasing Mgmt. Assn. Erie (past pres.), St. Dunstan's Guild, Delta Upsilon. Republican. Clubs: Erie, Lake Shore Country. Office: Hammermill Paper Co E Lake Rd Erie PA 16533

BOYD, JOSEPH AUBREY, communications and info. handling equipment mfg. exec.; b. Oscar, Ky., Mar. 25, 1921; s. Joseph Ray and Relda Jane (Myatt) B.; B.S.E.E., U. Ky., 1946, M.S.E.E., 1949; Ph.D., U. Mich., 1954; m. Edith A. Atkins, May 13, 1942; children—Joseph Barry, Joel Edd. Prof. elec. engring., dir. Inst. Sci. and Tech., U. Mich., 1949-62; pres. Radiation Inc., 1962-67, merged with Harris Corp., 1967, exec. v.p., dir. Harris Corp., Melbourne, Fla., 1967-72, pres., 1972-78, chmn. bd., chief exec. officer, 1978—; dir. Quotron Systems, Inc. Fellow IEEE; mem. Machinery and Allied Products Inst. (dir., exec. com.), U.S. Armed Forces Communications and Electronics Assn. (dir., past pres.). Office: 1025 S Nasa Blvd Melbourne FL 32919

BOYD, RONALD ROADMAN, business exec.; b. Chelmsford, Mass., July 11, 1916; s. Richard T. and Jennie (Gates) B.; B.A., Harvard, 1938; m. Alyce Shirley Byron, Aug. 25, 1951; children—Bradford Marshall, Linda Maxwell, Ronald Roadman. With Textron, Inc., 1942-63, with parachute div., purchasing dept., Lowell, Mass., 1942-44, asst. to exec. v.p., N.Y.C., 1944-49, asst. to pres., 1949-51; v.p. Amerotron Co. div., N.Y.C., 1955-57, exec. v.p. of div., 1957-63; v.p. Deering Milliken, Inc., 1963-69, Indian Head, Inc., 1969-74; pres. R.R. Boyd, Mgmt. Cons., Greenwich, Conn., 1974—. Bd. dirs. Perkins Road Assn., Greenwich, Conn. Mem. Nat. Assn. Wool Mfrs. (dir., exec. com.), Woolens and Worsteds Am. (dir., steering com.), Am. Textile Mgrs. Inst. (chmn. man made fibers com.). New Eng. Soc. N.Y., Textile Salesman's Assn. Congregationalist. Club: Harvard (N.Y.C.). Home and office: 85 Perkins Rd Greenwich CT 06830

BOYD, VIRGIL EDWARD, former automobile mfg. co. exec.; b. Benton, Kans., July 8, 1912; s. Vitalis and Bertha (Klemm) B.; grad. Am. Bus. Coll., Omaha, 1931; L.H.D., Doane Coll., Crete, Neb., 1972; LL.D. (hon.), U. Neb., 1969; m. Berniece Nelson, Oct. 13, 1935; children—Sandra K. (Mrs. Robert M. Ireland), Richard N. Accountant, Gen. Motors Acceptance Corp., 1931-37; sales exec. Nash-Kelvinator Corp., 1937-47; owner, operator auto dealerships for Nash and Buick, 1947-54; with Am. Motors Corp., 1954-62; group v.p. sales Chrysler Corp., 1962-67, pres., 1967-70, vice chmn. bd., 1970-72, ret. Named Marketing Exec. of Year, Sales and Marketing Execs. Internat., 1963. Home: PO Box 893 Litchfield Park AZ 85340

BOYD, WILLIAM RICHARD, mfg. co. exec.; b. Stiefeltown, S.C., Oct. 27, 1946; s. Horace and Sara Louisa (Jones) B.; student Pepperdine Coll.; m. Ann Taylor, Dec. 27, 1970; 1 son, Robert Stephen. Motion time analyst John P. King, Augusta, Ga., 1962-67; sr. indsl. engr. M. Lowenstein & Sons, Lyman, S.C., 1967-70; asst. to v.p. mfg. Berkshire Internat. div. VF Corp., Reading, Pa., 1970-73; v.p. mfg. Shirey Co., Inc., Greenville, Tex., 1973—, dir., 1978—; sec., v.p. J & M Enterprises, Inc., 1977—. Mem. Tex. Vocat. Edn. Curriculum Bd., 1975-80; pres. Hunt County United Way, 1979; bd. dirs. YMCA, 1979-80; mem. adv. bd. Paris Jr. Coll., 1980—. Served with USMC, 1964-66. Mem. Tex. Assn. Bus. (life), Am. Inst. Indsl. Engrs., Am. Apparel Mfrs. Assn. Christian Ch. Clubs: Optimists (dir.), Lions (dir.), Gideons (dir.). Patentee in field; contbr. poetry to various newspapers, Christian poetry collections. Office: 1917 Stanford St Greenville TX 75401

BOYER, JAMES GAMBRELL, bank exec.; b. Ft. Benning, Ga., Dec. 22, 1928; s. Emile James and Mary Louise (Gambrell) B.; B.A., La. State U., 1950, J.D., 1951; m. Helen M. House, Nov. 9, 1963; children—William R., Catherine G. Admitted to La. bar, 1951, Tex. bar, 1954; partner firm Jones, Kimball, Harper, Tete & Wetherill, Lake Charles, La., 1951-70; city atty. City of Lake Charles, 1960-62; pres. Gulf Nat. Bank of Lake Charles, 1970—. Mem. State Central Democratic Com., 1963—; chmn. exec. com. Calcasieu Parish Dems., 1968—; pres. Calcasieu Parish bd. suprs. elections, 1976—. Served with USAF, 1951-53. Mem. La. Bankers Assn. (pres. 1978-79). Democrat. Episcopalian. Office: 825 Ryan Mall Lake Charles LA 70601

BOYKIN, JOHN CLAUDE, instruments mfg. co. exec.; b. Crandall, Tex., Jan. 24, 1935; s. Allie Carlton and Agnes (Henry) B.; student St. Benedict's Coll., 1953-54, Arlington State Coll., 1954-55; So. Meth. U., 1955-57, 62-68; m. Beverley Jo Stillings, Apr. 4, 1954; children—Shean Michael, Kevin Brady, Shannon Michele, Kathryn Colleen. Quality control technician Gen. Electric Co., Dallas, 1953-57; field service technician Space Corp., Dallas, 1957-59; mktg. mgr. Teledyne Geotech Co., Dallas, 1959-70; v.p. Electronic Flo-Meters, Inc., Dallas, 1970-78, pres., 1978—, also dir. Athletic dir. Diocese of Dallas, Catholic Youth Orgn., 1968-69; pres. Jesuit Coll. Preparatory Alumni Assn., 1974—. Mem. Am. Gas Assn. (asso.; spl. test adviser on turbine meter task group), Instrument Soc. Am., Am. Mgmt. Assn. Club: K.C. Home: 2420 El Cerito Dallas TX 75228 Office: 1621 Jupiter St Garland TX 75042

BOYLAN, GARY G., pharm. co. exec.; b. Newark, July 1, 1946; s. George P. and Florence E. (Grant) B.; A.A. in Bus., Union Coll., Crandford, N.J., 1972; B.S. in Mgmt. Sci., Kean Coll. of N.J., Union, 1976; m. Dolores C. Lacaskey, Apr. 27, 1968; children—Daniel, David. Mgr. prodn. planning and inventory control Bright Star Industries, Clifton, N.J., 1969-72; materials mgr. Ashland Chem., Newark, 1972-76; dir. materials mgmt. Westwood Pharms., Buffalo, 1976—. Pres., Country Pkwy. PTA, Williamsville, N.Y., 1979-80. Served with U.S. Army, 1965-67. Mem. Am. Prodn.-Inventory Control Soc., Am. Mgmt. Assn., Bristol-Myers Corp. Distbn. Council. Republican. Roman Catholic. Home: 368 Teakwood Terr Williamsville NY 14221 Office: 468 Dewitt St Buffalo NY 14213

BOYLE, CHARLES ALFRED, bus. exec.; b. Phila., July 6, 1916; s. John G. and Mae (Peterson) B.; student U. Pa., 1937-38, Brookings Instn., 1960, Ariz. State U., 1962-65, Indsl. Coll. of Armed Forces studies, 1955; m. Edith Christy, Sept., 1942. Manpower specialist Ariz. Govt. Service, Tucson, 1945-50, field supr. Ariz. Employment Service, 1951-54, chief, field operations, 1955-62, dep. adminstr., 1963, employment service adminstr., 1964-72; dir. unemployment ins., tech. assistance project, govt. edn. div. C & S Services Inc. div. Cordura Corp. (formerly Computing & Software, Inc.), Sacramento, 1972-75; now pres. Charles A. Boyle & Assos. Chmn. bd. Ariz. Bus.-Industry Edn. Council. Bd. dirs. Samuel Gompers Meml. Rehab. Center, Phoenix. Served with USAAF, 1940-45. Mem. Am. Acad. Polit. Sci., Internat. Platform Assn., Am. Legion, V.F.W., D.A.V., Urban League, Internat. Assn. Personnel in Employment Security, Ariz. Acad. Elk. Rotarian. Home and Office: 9747 Augusta Dr Sun City AZ 85351

BOYLE, J. ALLAN, banker; b. Orillia, Ont., Can., May 10, 1916; student Orillia Collegiate Inst.; grad. mgmt. tng. course U. Western Ont. With Toronto Dominion Bank, 1934—, gen. mgr. adminstrn., then dep. chief gen. mgr., 1968-72, exec. v.p., chief gen. mgr., 1972—, pres., 1978—; pres., dir. Torcred Devels. Ltd., Regtor Investments Ltd.; dir. Excelsior Life Ins. Co., Costain Ltd., Jannock Ltd., Aetna Casualty Co. of Can., Echo Bay Mines Ltd.; exec. v.p., dir. Toronto Dominion Centre Ltd., Toronto Dominion Centre West Ltd.; mem. Toronto Bd. Trade. Adv. com. Sch. Bus. Adminstrn. U. Western Ont.; chmn. Western Bus. Sch. Club Toronto; mem. Toronto Redevel. Advisory Council; bd. dirs., mem. exec. com. C.K. Clarke Psychiat. Research Found.; bd. govs. York U. Served with RCAF, 1940-45. Mem. Canadian Bankers' Assn. (past pres.). Clubs: Canadian (past pres. Toronto), Toronto, Granite, York, Thornhill Country; Sara Bay Country (Sarasota, Fla.). Address: Toronto Dominion Bank PO Box 1 Toronto Dominion Centre Toronto ON M5K 1A2 Canada

BOYLE, JOHN WILLIAM, retail co. exec.; b. Darlington, Wis., 1929; B.B.A., U. Wis., 1950; married. Partner, Arthur Andersen & Co., 1951-71; exec. v.p., controller May Dept. Stores Co., St. Louis, 1972-79, vice chmn., 1979-80, chmn. bd., chief fin. officer, 1980—, also dir.; dir. Boatmen's Nat. Bank St. Louis, Civic Center Redevel. Corp. Served with U.S. Army, 1951-53. C.P.A. Office: May Dept Stores Co 611 Olive St Saint Louis MO 63101

BOYLE, RICHARD JAMES, banker; b. Bklyn., Dec. 4, 1943; s. James Frances and Marie Eileen (Rodden) B.; A.B., Holy Cross Coll., 1965; M.B.A., N.Y. U., 1969; m. Denise Burke, Jan. 29, 1966; children—Anne Marie, Richard James. With Chase Manhattan Bank, N.Y.C., 1965—, v.p., 1971-74, sr. v.p., 1975—, dept. exec. in charge real estate fin., 1976—; chmn. Housing Investment Corp. Mem. adv. com., chmn. curriculum adv. com. Real Estate Inst. N.Y. U.; bd. dirs. Ave. of the Americas Assn., Inc. Served with USAR, 1969-75. Mem. Urban Land Inst., Real Estate Bd. N.Y. (gov.), Mortgage Bankers Assn. Am. Club: Baltusrol Golf. Office: Chase Manhattan Bank 1 Chase Manhattan Plaza New York NY 10081

BOYNTON, WILLIAM LEWIS, electronic mfg. co. ofcl.; b. Kalamazoo, May 31, 1928; s. James Woodbury and Cyretta (Gunther) B.; ed. pub. schs.; m. Kei Ouchi, Oct. 8, 1953. Asst. mgr. Speigel J & R, Kalamazoo, 1947-48; served with U.S. Army, 1948-74, ret., 1974; with Rockwell/Collins Divs., Newport Beach, Calif., 1974—, supr. materiel, 1978—; mem. faculty Western Mich. U., 1955-58. Decorated Bronze Star medal. Mem. Assn. U.S. Army, Air Force Assn., Assn. U.S. Army, Non-Commd. Officers Assn., Nat. Mgmt. Assn., Nat. Geog. Soc., Smithsonian Inst. (asso.). Republican. Roman Catholic. Home: 5314 Lucky Way Santa Ana CA 92704 Office: 4311 Jamboree Blvd Newport Beach CA 92663

BOYT, PATRICK ELMER, farmer, real estate exec.; b. Liberty, Tex., Sept. 22, 1940; s. Elmer Vernon and Kathleen (Nelson) B.; B.S. in C.E., U. Tex., 1963; m. Elizabeth Ruth Jefferson, June 16, 1962; children—Jefferson Elmer, Mark Cecil. Owner, mng. partner P.E.

Boyt Farms; sec. Boyt Realty Co.; v.p. Boyt Properties; dir. First State Bank, Liberty, 1978—, Beaumont State Bank, 1969-78. Bd. dirs. Beaumont Art Mus., 1973—, Devers Ind. Sch. Dist., 1974—, Am. Rice Growers, 1974—, Farm Air Service, 1976—; mem. Tex. Commn. for Arts, 1978—; bd. dirs. Kersting Meml. Hosp., 1976—; supr. Lower Trinity Soil and Water Conservation Dist., 1972—. Mem. Am. Brahman Breeders Assn., Tex. Rice Improvement Assn. (dir.), Coastal Cattlemen's Assn. (dir.), Tex. and Southwestern Cattleraisers Assn., Am. Quarter Horse Assn., Tex. Arts Alliance. Democrat. Presbyterian. Home and Office: Box 575 Devers TX 77538

BOZA, PHILIP STEVE, food co. exec.; b. Joliet, Ill., Oct. 30, 1945; s. Philip S. and Lillian Ann Boza; B.S., No. Ill. U., 1970; cert. Grad. Sch. Indsl. Adminstrn., Carnegie-Mellon U., 1976; m. Regina Saliga, Dec. 11, 1971; children—Joseph M., Walter W., Bradley S., Christine L. Bank examiner FDIC, 1970-74; sr. fin. analyst Interstate Brands Corp., Kansas City, Mo., 1974-78, asso. dir. corp. planning and devel., 1978, dir. corp. planning and devel., 1978—; asst. sec. DPF, Inc., 1978—; instr. Nat. Sch. for Bank Exam., 1974. Served with USMC, 1965-67. Recipient cert. of merit U.S. Jaycees, 1974. Republican. Roman Catholic. Home: 9818 W 101st Terr Overland Park KS 66212 Office: 12 E Armour Blvd Kansas City MO 64111

BRACEY, JAMES LEA, engring. adminstr.; b. Florence, S.C., Mar. 13, 1940; s. Cecil Perritt and Mary Louise (Lea) B.; B.B.A., Tex. Tech. Coll., 1963; M.B.A., Tex. Christian U., 1970; m. Ann Elizabeth Barger, June 13, 1964; 1 son, James McLeod. With Superior Decals, Inc., Dallas, 1956-62; adminstrv. asst. Gen. Dynamics, Fort Worth, 1963—. Active Tarrant County CD, Radio Amateur Civil Emergency Services, NOAA Skywarn. Mem. Nat. Mgmt. Assn., Am. Radio Relay League, SAR, Delta Sigma Pi. Home: 3955 Shannon Dr Fort Worth TX 76116 Office: PO Box 748 Fort Worth TX 76101

BRACKEN, RAY T., constrn. co. exec., banker; b. Harrisville, Miss., Aug. 8, 1926; s. Chester Parnell and Lela Rachel (Bounds) B.; student Copiah-Lincoln Jr. Coll., Wesson, Miss.; m. Sharron Navaille, July 22, 1972; children—Cindy, Holly, Michelle, Spencer. Payroll auditor U.S. Fidelity & Guaranty Ins. Co., 1953-63; now pres. Bracken Constrn. Co., Inc., Jackson, Brookwood Properties, Jackson; partner Central River Terminal, Vicksburg United Builders Supply, Inc., Jackson; chmn. bd. Bank of South, Crystal Springs. Served with USN, 1944-46. Mem. Am. Subcontractors Assn. Miss. (pres.), Asso. Gen. Contractors Miss., U.S. C. of C., Jackson C. of C., Am. Arbitration Assn. Methodist. Clubs: Shady Oaks Country, Brookwood Country, Moose, Masons, Shriners. Home: Route 1 Box 118-A Terry MS 39170 Office: PO Box 8399 Jackson MS 39204

BRACKEN, ROBERT JAMES, real estate sales co. exec.; b. Passaic, N.J., June 24, 1949; s. Harry Milton and Elsie B.; student pub. schs., Pompton Lakes, N.J. Pres., Bracken Printing Co., Pompton Lakes, 1968-72; sales mgr. Brooks, Ltd., Oak Ridge, N.J., 1972-74; pres. Bee Bee Constrn. Co., Hamburg, N.J., 1976—; gen. partner Valley Developers, Hamburg, 1977—, ELB Ltd., Hamburg, 1978—; pres. Telridge Assocs., Hamburg, 1974—. Treas. Hamburg 1st Aid Squad, 1978; chmn. Wanaque Indsl. Commn., 1973-76, Wanaque Planning Bd., 1974-75. Mem. Nat., N.J. assns. realtors, Sussex County Bd. Realtors (pres. 1979, M.L.S. chmn. 1980), N.J. Builders Assn., Nat. Home Builders Assn. Club: Rotary. Home: PO Box 265 Hamburg NJ 07419 Office: 100 Route 23 Hamburg NJ 07419

BRACKEN, THOMAS ROBERT JAMES, real estate developer; b. Spokane, Wash., Jan. 1, 1950; s. James Lucas and Frances (Cadzow) B.; B.A. with departmental honors, Yale U., 1971; M.B.A., Columbia U., 1972; m. Linda Diane Jacobson, Sept. 9, 1972; children—Karl Forrest, David Erskine. Sr. appraiser Prudential Ins. Co., N.Y.C. area, 1972-74, mgr. real estate investments, N.Y.C. and Newark, 1974-77; investment mgr. real estate investments, Seattle, 1977-78; v.p. First City Investments, Inc., Seattle, 1978-80; pres. Fenix, Inc., Kirkland, Wash., 1980—; guest lectr. U. Pa., N.Y. U. Mem. Nat. Assn. Indsl. and Office Parks, Internat. Conf. Shopping Centers. Presbyterian. Home: 4548 144th Ave SE Bellevue WA 98006 Office: Suite 206 12620 120th Ave NE Kirkland WA 98033

BRACY, JO AHNE C. PENNEY, publisher; b. Detroit, Sept. 25, 1947; d. George S. and Florence W. Penney; B.A. in Speech, Wayne State U., 1974, Cert. in Mortuary Sci., 1980; m. Lonnie Bracy, Oct. 3, 1965; children—Yvette M., Michael A. Jr. copywriter Celeste Advt. & Assos., Detroit, 1965-74; editor Community Bulletin Newspaper, Atlanta, 1975-76; pres. Express Yourself, Atlanta, 1975-76; news reporter Sta. WTVS-TV, Detroit, 1977—; social researcher Merrill Palmer Inst., Detroit, 1978—; editor, publisher Community Business Bulletin, Detroit, 1978—; exec. dir., founder When The Time Comes; cons. in field. Active Detroit Civic and Bus. League, Boy Scouts Am., Boys Club Am. Mem. AFTRA, Nat. Assn. Media Women, Am. Women in Communications, Toastmistress' Internat. Delta Sigma Theta, Sigma Delta Chi. Jewish. Club: Toastmistresses. Author: How To Pass Tests, 1976. Home: 12706 Pickford St Detroit MI 48235 Office: 3269 Webb St Detroit MI 48206

BRADEN, WILLIAM EDWARD, trading co. exec., cons.; b. Milw., Dec. 29, 1919; s. Armond Edward and Eve Ninette (Fuller) B.; A.B., Harvard U., 1941; m. Sonoyo Matsuda, Jan. 23, 1950 (dec.); children—Amy, Wythe Edward, Robert Fuller, William Samuel. Foreman, Procter & Gamble Mfg. Co., Quincy, Mass., 1941-42; civilian employee War Dept., Changchun, Manchuria, 1946-47; pres. Pacific Projects Ltd., Tokyo, 1948—; pres. Taihei Boeki Co., Ltd., Tokyo, 1955-80, chmn. bd., 1980—; dir. Ferro Far East Ltd., Hong Kong, Ferro Enamels (Japan) Ltd., Osaka, Nissan Ferro Organic Chem. Co., Ltd., Tokyo, Nichols Far East Ltd., Tokyo, Taiwan Neptune Co. Ltd., Taipei. Served with AF, USNR, 1943-45. Mem. Am. Japan Soc., Am. C. of C. in Japan, Japan Am. Soc. Honolulu. Clubs: Harvard (N.Y.C., Tokyo, Honolulu); Tokyo Am.; Fgn. Correspondents (Japan) (asso. mem.). Home: 211 Luika Pl Kailua HI 96734 Office: 10 1-Chome Muromachi Nihonbashi Chuo-ku Tokyo Japan 103

BRADFORD, HENRY ALEXANDER, III, research co. exec.; b. Detroit, May 26, 1939; s. Henry Alexander and Merle Louise (Scott) B.; B.A. with honors, U. Colo., 1961; M.S. in Biostatistics, U. Calif., Los Angeles, 1967; 1 dau., Lisbeth. Sr. biostatistician Abbott Labs., Chgo., 1967-69; asso. prof. biostatistics and epidemiology George Washington U., Washington, 1969-72; clin. prof. biostatistics Georgetown U., Washington, 1973—; pres. Biometric Research Inst., Inc., Washington, 1972—; Chmn. conf. on Naltrexone, Com. on Problems of Drug Dependence, Richmond, Va., 1976. Served with U.S. Army, 1962-65. USPHS fellow, 1966-67. Mem. Am. Statis. Assn. (mem. planning com. edn. sect. 1969-71), Biometric Soc., Food, Drug Law Inst., N.Y. Acad. Scis., Luther Rice Soc., U.S. Yacht Racing Union. Episcopalian. Office: Biometric Research Inst Inc 1010 Wisconsin Ave NW Washington DC 20007

BRADFORD, JAMES COWDON, investment banker; b. Nashville, Nov. 24, 1892; s. Alexander and Leonora (Bisland) B.; student Vanderbilt U., 1909-12; m. Eleanor Avent, May 11, 1926; children—Eleanor, James C. Partner Davis Bradford & Co., 1912-52; pres. Piggly Wiggly Stores Inc., 1923-25; partner J. C. Bradford & Co., Inc., now chmn.; pres., dir. Life Ins. Investors, Inc.; pres. Life Stock Research Corp. Served as 1st lt. F.A., U.S. Army, 1917-19. Episcopalian. Mason (32 deg., Shriner). Clubs: Belle Meade, Cumberland. Home: Belle Meade Blvd Nashville TN 37205 Office: 170 4th Ave N Nashville TN 37219

BRADFORD, ROBERT ERNEST, motion picture exec.; b. Berlin, Germany, May 25, 1927; s. Siegfried and Doris (Herzberg) B.; student Marie Curie Coll., Paris, France, 1937; A.B., U. Geneva (Switzerland), 1945; m. Barbara Taylor, Dec. 24, 1963. Came to U.S., 1946, naturalized, 1953. Prodn. cons. Distbn. Corp. Am., N.Y.C., 1946-53; exec. v.p. Jesse L. Lasky Prodns., Beverly Hills, Calif., 1953—; exec. v.p., dir. Samuel Bronston Prodns., N.Y.C., 1955—; head feature prodn. exec. producer Hal Roach Studios, Hollywood, Calif., 1959—; financial cons. Franco-London Film Corp., Paris, 1970, pres., 1970-73; chmn. Andes Internat. Film Corp.; pres., dir. Franco London Music Ltd. (Eng.), 1971—, Franco London Film S.A., Paris, 1971—; pres. Bradford Films Internat., Ltd.; dir. Franco London Film Internat., Ltd., Montreal, Que., Can., 1971—; dir. Financial Assistance Co. Del. Interatlantic Devel. and Investment Corp., Madrid, Interinvest, Madrid, Hy-Ford Prodns., Inc., Hy-Ford Europea, Rome, Italy, Jack London Prodns.; producer John Paul Jones, Warner Bros., 1958, The Scavengers, Hal Roach Studios, 1959, If You Remember Me, 1959-60, The Golden Touch, 1959-60, Simon Bolivar, 1965, The Conquest of Peru, 1965-66, To Die of Love, 1970, The Sweet Deception, 1971, Impossible Object, 1972. Fgn. Corr. Overseas News Agy., 1951—; lectr. internat. affairs, interracial problems, 1950—; press relations cons. Senator Herbert H. Lehman, 1952-53; cons., dir. Nat. Found. for Good Govt., 1952; cons. Internat. Study Tour Alliance, 1951—. Pub. relations dir. one world award com. Am. Nobel Anniversary Com. Served with French Intelligence, 1940-45. Recipient citation for outstanding work and civic achievements Greater N.Y. Citizens Forum, 1952. Mem. Internat. Inst. Arts and Letters (dir.), Internat. Jai Alai Assn. (chmn., dir.). Office: Empire State Bldg New York NY 10118

BRADLEY, A. VAL, mgmt. cons. co. exec.; b. Boston, May 9, 1922; s. John Edward and Ruth (Cheeseman) B.; B.A. summa cum laude, Bucknell U., 1952; student U. Mich. Law Sch., 1952-54; m. Catherine E. Kerstetter, Jan. 11, 1947; children—Carol, Bruce. Baseball player N.Y. Am. League baseball club, farm teams, 1941-43, 46-47; personnel dir. Chrysler Corp., Detroit, 1954-60; v.p. indsl. relations Overhead Door Corp., Hartford City, Md., 1960-62; sr. asso. L.B. Harris Assos. Inc., Chgo., 1962-64; pres. A. Val Bradley Assos. Inc., Mpls., N.Y.C. and Atlanta, 1964—; adj. prof. Pace U., 1977. Served with U.S. Army, 1943-45; ETO. U. Mich. Law Sch. fellow, 1952-54. Certified mgmt. cons., Inst. Mgmt. Cons.'s. Mem. Assn. Mgmt. Cons.'s (v.p. 1975—, rep. to Council Mgmt. Cons.'s. Orgn. 1976—), Phi Beta Kappa. Home: Office: A Val Bradley Assos Inc 757 Third Ave New York City NY 10017

BRADLEY, GILBERT FRANCIS, banker; b. Miami, Ariz., May 17, 1920; s. Ever and Martha (Piper) B.; grad. Pacific Coast Banking Sch., U. Wash., 1951-53, Advanced Mgmt. Program, Grad. Sch. Bus., Harvard U., 1968; m. Marion Bebb, June 21, 1941; children—L.P., Richard T., Steven E. With Valley Nat. Bank, Phoenix, 1937—, chmn. bd., chief exec. officer, 1976—. Trustee United for Ariz.; bd. dirs. Ariz. Tomorrow. Served to capt. USAF, 1942-45. Decorated D.F.C., Air medal with 3 bronze stars. Mem. Ariz. Bankers Assn. (pres., 1968-69), Fed. Res. System (pres. adv. council, 1978). Office: PO Box 71 Phoenix AZ 85001

BRADLEY, HERBERT LEE, communications exec.; b. Caldwell, Idaho, Oct. 2, 1941; s. Wendell Johnson and Irene Hazel (Huffman) B.; cert. Capitol Radio Engring. Inst., 1964; student U. Bridgeport, 1975-76, Calif. Western U., 1978—; m. Frauke H. Duwel, Apr. 5, 1969; children—Alexander Ernst, David Elliot. Technician, field project mgr. GTE Lenkurt Electric, San Carlos, Calif., 1964-70; regional mktg. mgr., tech. dir. GTE Internat., Middle E., 1970-73; mgr. liaison GTE Internat., Stamford, Conn., 1973-76; dep. gen. mgr. GTE Korea/Japan, dir. Samsung-GTE, Korea, 1976-78; div. dir. program devel. Comsat Gen., Washington, 1978—. Served with USAF, 1960-64. Lic. 1st class radio telephone operator. Lutheran. Office: 950 L'Enfant Plaza Washington DC 20024

BRADSHAW, MELVIN B., ins. co. exec.; b. Peoria, Ill., 1922; grad. Bradley U., 1949; postgrad. Harvard U., 1968. Pres., chief exec. officer Liberty Mut. Ins. Co., Boston, Liberty Mut. Fire Ins. Co.; pres. Liberty Life Ins. Co. Boston; chmn. Helmsman (Underwriting) Ltd., London, Liberty Mut. Ins. Co. (Mass.); dir. Nat. Shawmut Bank of Boston, Shawmut Corp. Office: Liberty Mutual Ins Co 175 Berkeley St Boston MA 02117*

BRADSHAW, THORNTON FREDERICK, oil co. exec.; b. Washington, Aug. 4, 1917; s. Frederick and Julia V. (See) B.; grad. Phillips Exeter Acad., 1936; A.B., Harvard, 1940, M.B.A., 1942, D.C.S., 1950; LL.D. (hon.), Pepperdine U., 1974; D.Social Sci. (hon.), Villanova U., 1975; m. Sally Davis, 1940 (div. 1974); children—Nancy M. (Mrs. Thomas Poor), Priscilla W. (Mrs. Richard Page, Jr.), Johathan G.; m. 2d, Patricia Salter West, May 11, 1974; children—Jeffrey D. West, Nicholas S. West, Andrew P. West, Eric R. West, Asso. prof. Grad. Sch. Bus. Adminstrn., Harvard, 1942-52; partner Cresap, McCormick & Paget, N.Y.C., 1952-56; v.p., dir. Atlantic Richfield Co. (formerly Atlantic Refining Co.), Los Angeles, 1956-62, exec. v.p., 1962-64, pres., 1964—, mem. exec. com., 1966—, also dir.; dir. RCA, Security Pacific Nat. Bank, Security Pacific Corp., NBC, Champion Internat. Bd. dirs., past pres. Los Angeles Philharmonic Assn.; bd. dirs. Conf. Bd., Aspen Inst. for Humanistic Studies, Am. Petroleum Inst., Los Angeles World Affairs Council; chmn. bd. fellows Claremont U. Center; trustee Conservation Found., Huntington Library and Art Gallery, Pasadena, Calif.; mem. vis. com. U. Calif. at Los Angeles Grad. Sch. Mgmt.; mem. bd. overseers Harvard U.; mem. bd. Center for Edn. in Internat. Mgmt.; mem.-at-large bd. govs. Performing Arts Council Los Angeles. Served to lt (j.g.) USN. Office: 515 S Flower St Los Angeles CA 90071

BRADSHAW, WILBERT CLINTON, asphalt and oil exec.; b. Wichita, Kans., Dec. 6, 1907; s. Wilbert Clinton and Nella May Herdic (Booher) B.; student Wichita U., 1927-28; M.E., U. Mich., 1929; student Internat. Corr. Schs., 1935-36; m. Clarice M. Buttner, Feb. 22, 1935; children—John Buttner, Wilbert Clinton III. With Gillespie Furniture Co., 1930-35; chief engr., mgr. Calif. Fresno Air Conditioning, 1936-41; owner W.C. Bradshaw Co., mech. contractors, engrs., 1942-52, W.C. Bradshaw, mgmt. cons., 1953—; v.p., mng. officer Calif. Fresno Asphalt Co., Fresno, 1952-72; sec., mng. officer Calif. Fresno Oil Co., Fresno, 1952-72; pres. Petroleum Chems., Inc., Fresno, 1952—; v.p. Calif. Fresno Investment Co., 1972—. Exec. v.p. United Cerebral Palsy Assns., Inc., N.Y., 1967-69, v.p., 1962-72; mem. adv. com. Calif. Dept. Spl. Edn., 1954-62; chmn. adv. council Calif. Dept. Rehab., 1960-67, mem., 1970—; chmn. Gov.'s Com. Employment of Handicapped, 1964—; pres. United Cerebral Palsy Assns. Calif., 1958-60; a founder Fresno City Sunshine Sch. for Cerebral Palsied, 1945; mem. Calif. Mental Retardation Bd., 1970-72, Calif. Developmental Disabilities Adv. Council, 1972—. Bd. dirs. Rehab. Enterprises, Inc., Fresno. Named Citizen of Year Phi Delta Kappa, Delta Xi, 1962; Roger S. Firestone award United Cerebral Palsy Assn. Mem. Am. Pub. Works Assn. Conglist. Kiwanian. Club: University-Sequoia Sunnyside. Co-inventor continuous flow asphalt slurry mixing and application machine. Home: 1465 N Harrison St Fresno CA 93728 Office: 2518 Railroad St PO Box 969 Fresno CA 93714

BRADSHAW, WILLIAM DANIEL, real estate co. exec.; b. Balt., May 24, 1933; s. William D. and Emily M. Bradshaw; B.A., Yale U., 1955; postgrad. Boston U.; divorced; children—Priscilla DeRosset, William Daniel. With R.M. Bradley & Co., Inc., comml. and indsl. real estate, Boston, 1955—, sr. v.p., 1970—, dir., 1980—. Chmn. real estate com. Mass. United Fund, 1971; treas. Wellesley chpt. Mass. Assn. Children with Learning Disabilities, 1969; mem. Wellesley Town Meeting, 1965-68. Mem. Nat. Assn. Indsl. and Office Parks (pres. New Eng. chpt. 1977-80), Greater Boston Real Estate Bd. (asso.), Greater Boston C. of C. Clubs: Harvard, Yale (Boston). Home: 780 Boylston St Apt 20J Boston MA 02199 Office: 250 Boylston St Boston MA 02116

BRADT, ACKEN GORDON, ret. banker, mgmt. cons.; b. Wichita, Kans., Sept. 22, 1896; s. Charles Edwin and Nellie (Acken) B.; A.B., Northwestern Univ., 1920, M.B.A., 1941; m. Aliff Bosier, June 18, 1918; children—Elizabeth Margaret (Mrs. Leonard S. Parsons), Virginia Helen (Mrs. W. Bruce Fullerton), Gordon Edwin. Asst. sec. Bd. Fgn. Missions Presbyn. Ch. U.S.A., 1920-28; with Continental Ill. Nat. Bank and Trust Co. Chgo., 1928-61, 2d v.p., 1943-49, v.p., 1959-61; now mgmt. cons. personnel adminstrn. and mgmt. devel. Lectr. mgmt., mem. faculty Northwestern U., 1944—; mem. faculty grad. sch. banking So. Methodist U., Dallas, 1958-63; sect. leader, lectr. Grad. Sch. Banking U. Wis., Pacific Coast Banking Sch., 1949-63, U. Wash., Sch. Pub. Relations Northwestern U., 1950-63; lectr. bank pub. relations sch. Princeton, Sch. Banking for South, La. State U., 1950-72. Past pres. United Community Services, Evanston; trustee Civic and Arts Found.; mem. adv. bd. Ill. Dept. Personnel; past chmn. bus. edn. adv. council Bd. Edn. Chgo. Pub. Schs.; vice chmn. Community Fund-Red Cross Joint Appeal Campaign, Chgo., 1958; vice chmn. budget com. Community Fund Chgo., Inc.; chmn. Mayor's New Generation Services Bd., Evanston; past pres. The Irving. Former sec., mem. exec. com., dir. McCormick Theol. Sem., Chgo.; past mem. exec. com. Evanston Council Chs.; past v.p., dir. Evanston YMCA; past trustee Evanston Pub. Library. Mem. Am. Inst. Banking (former chmn., regent), Financial Pub. Relations Assn. (treas.), Ill. Bankers Assn. (chmn. com. on edn.), Ill., Evanston (dir.) chambers of commerce, Chgo. Assn. Commerce and Industry, Evanston Hist. Soc. (life), Sigma Alpha Epsilon (life). Presbyn. (ruling elder). Kiwanian (dir.). Clubs: Union League (dir., 2d v.p.) (Chgo.); University (Evanston). Author: A Boy's Experiences Around the World; How To Triple Your Talents and Multiply Your Earning Power; The Secrets of Getting Results Through People; Five Keys to Productivity and Profits; also articles in mgmt. field. Home: 606 Michigan Ave Evanston IL 60202

BRADY, FRANK A., mktg. co. exec.; b. N.Y.C., July 10, 1946; s. Charles J. and Brenda V. (Madden) B.; B.A., Iona Coll., 1968; m. Lorraine C. Tretter, June 1, 1968; children—Jason, Kristen. Mktg. mgr. Sunbeam Corp., N.Y.C., 1965-68; dir. mktg. Seth Thomas Clock Co. div. Gen. Time Corp., Thomaston, Conn., 1968-76; pres. The Brady Mktg. Co., Concord, Calif., 1976—; free-lance cons. to major corps. in gourmet cookware field, 1976—. Recipient award Kiwanis Club, 1964. Mem. Pot and Kettle Club (San Francisco). Club: Round Hill Country. Patentee numerous designs. Office: 2190 Meridian Park Blvd Concord CA 94520

BRADY, RUPERT JOSEPH, lawyer; b. Washington, Jan. 24, 1932; s. John Bernard and Mary (Rupert) B.; B.E.E., Catholic U. Am., 1953; LL.B., J.D., Georgetown U., 1959; m. Maureen Mary MacIntosh, Apr. 20, 1954; children—Rupert Joseph, Laureen, Kevin, Warren, Jeannine, Jacqueline, Brian, Barton. Elec. engr. Sperry Gyroscope Co., L.I., N.Y., 1953-56; patent specification writer John B. Brady, patent atty., 1956-59; admitted to Ct. Customs and Patent Appeals, 1961, U.S. Supreme Ct. bar, 1969, Md. bar, D.C. bar; patent agt. B. P. Fishburne, Jr., patent atty., Washington, 1959-61; pvt. practice patent agt., Washington, 1961. patent atty., 1961—; sr. partner firm Brady, O'Boyle & Gates, Washington, 1963—. Mem. Am. Patent Law Assn., Am. Bar Assn., Senators Club Alumni. Patentee. Home: 7201 Pyle Rd Bethesda MD 20034 Office: 920 Chevy Chase Bldg 5530 Wisconsin Ave Washington DC 20015

BRADY, THOMAS PATRICK, pub. acctg. co. exec.; b. Des Moines, Dec. 28, 1945; s. Thomas P. and Helen (Howe) B.; M.B.A. in Fin. and Mktg., Northeastern U., Boston, 1977; B.B.S., U. Notre Dame, 1968; m. Patricia J. Keane, June 13, 1970. Staff and supervisory accountant Ernst & Whinney, Boston, 1968-71; asst. treas., dir. Ikor Inc., Burlington, Mass., 1971-76; divisional controller Omni Wave Electronics Corp. (Omni Wave/Ikor), Gloucester, Mass., 1976; prin. partner Rowe & Brady, C.P.A.'s, Winchester, Mass., 1977—; gen. partner BBH Assos.; lectr. acctg. Northeastern U. Mem. Boston Estate and Bus. Planning Council, Beta Gamma Sigma. Republican. Home: 40 Webb St Lexington MA 02173 Office: 661 Main St PO Box 312 Winchester MA 01890

BRADY, WINIFRED B., state ofcl.; b. Waterbury, Conn., Nov. 28, 1933; d. Percival T. and Ella (Jencks) Buskey; B.S., Rider Coll., 1954; M.B.A., Temple U., 1962; m. Richard E. Brady, July 9, 1963 (dec. 1978). With N.J. Dept. Labor and Industry, Trenton, N.J., 1963—, personnel and training dir., 1972-75, dir. job services, 1975—. Chmn. Burlington County (N.J.) Commn. on Women, 1976; mem. U.S.S. Trenton Commissioning com. City of Trenton, 1970-71. U.S. Civil Service Commn. fellow, 1970. Mem. Internat. Personnel Mgmt. Assn., Am. Soc. Personnel Adminstrs. (v.p. Region II 1978-80, dist. dir. Region II, 1975-77, nat. parliamentarian 1979-81, nat. sec. 1980-81), Nat. Fedn. Bus. and Profl. Women (state pres. 1976-77). Republican. Club: Soroptimist Internat. Home: 19 Spruce Ave Bordentown NJ 08505 Office: Room 1013 Labor and Industry Bldg Trenton NJ 08625

BRAFFORD, WILLIAM CHARLES, JR., lawyer; b. Pike County, Ky., Aug. 7, 1932; s. William C. and Minnie (Tackett) B.; LL.B., U. Ky., 1957; LL.M. (fellow), U. Ill., 1958; J.D., U. Ky., 1970; m. Katherine J. Prather, Nov. 13, 1954; children—William Charles III, David. Admitted to Ky. bar, 1957, Ga. bar, 1965, Ohio bar, 1966, Pa. bar, 1973, U.S. Sixth Circuit Court of Appeals, 1966, Tax Ct. U.S., 1965, Ct. of Claims, 1965, U.S. Supreme Ct., 1970; trial atty. NLRB, Washington, 1958-60; atty. Louisville & Nashville R.R. Co., Louisville, 1960-63, So. Bell Tel. & Tel. Co., Atlanta, 1963-65; asst. gen. counsel NCR Corp., Dayton, Ohio, 1965-72; v.p., sec., gen. counsel Betz Labs., Inc., Trevose, Pa., 1972—; dir. Betz Ltd., U.K., Betz S.A., France, Betz Ges, m.b., Austria, Betz Proprietory Ltd., Australia, Betz N.V. Belgium, Betz SUD S.p.A., Italy. Served to 1st lt., C.I.C., AUS, 1954-56. Editor Ky. Law Jour., 1953-54, 56. Home: 10 Fairfield Ln Doylestown PA 18901 Office: 4636 Somerton Rd Trevose PA 19047

BRAGDON, JOSEPH HENRY, investment counseling co. exec.; b. Boston, June 9, 1939; s. Joseph Henry and Marjorie (Saltonstall) B.; student Yale U., 1958-59; B.A., Am. U., 1963; M.A., Fletcher Sch. Law and Diplomacy, Harvard U., Tufts U., 1964; m. Brenda Whitmarsh Young, May 6, 1967; children—Caroline, Marjorie, Josiah. Meth. Bd. Edn. travel and study grantee, USSR, 1962;

economist U.S. Dept. Commerce, 1965-67; mgmt. trainee Ralston Purina Co., 1967-68; account exec., research analyst H.C. Wainwright & Co., Boston, 1968-73; gen. partner, founder Conservest Mgmt. Co., Boston, 1973—; dir. Input Output Computer Services; corporator Cambridge Savs. Bank; vis. scholar Brookings Instn., 1964. Trustee, 1st v.p. Mt. Auburn Hosp., 1975—; bd. dirs. Ossabaw Found., 1977—, Opera Co. Boston, 1972-76; bd. dirs., treas. Vision, Inc., 1971-79. Mem. Boston Com. Fgn. Relations. Clubs: Harvard (Boston); Cambridge (Mass.) Boat. Nat. rowing champion, 1967, 77, 78, 79. Home: 22 Fresh Pond Ln Cambridge MA 02138 Office: Conservest Mgmt Co 1 State St Boston MA 02109

BRAGG, BARRY ALLAN, banker; b. Charleston, W.Va., Oct. 13, 1946; s. Homer E. and Evelyn E. (Tincher) B.; B.A., W.Va. Wesleyan Coll., 1968; M.S., George Washington U., 1975. Mgmt. trainee Equitable Trust Co., Balt., 1968, br. mgr. Laurel Plaza and Laurel Shopping Center, 1969-73, area supr., 1973-79, supr. comml. lending, 1979—, 2d v.p., 1976—; lectr. in field. Mem. Laurel C. of C. (chmn. membership 1977). Republican. Methodist. Home: 9361 Our Time Ln Village Oakland Mills Columbia MD 21045 Office: 320 Main St Laurel MD 20810

BRAILSFORD, HARRISON DUDLEY, mfg. co. exec.; b. Louisville, July 7, 1898; s. James Harrison and Alice (Dudley). B; B.S. in Mech. Engring., U. Ky., 1923, E.E., 1938; postgrad. Mass. Inst. Tech., 1953; m. Juanita Messmore, July 19, 1929; 1 dau., Elizabeth Susan (Mrs. John Currier Gallagher III). Asso., Engr. Underwriters' Labs., Inc., N.Y.C., 1923-41; cons. engr., 1941—; pres. Brailsford & Co., Inc., Rye, N.Y., 1944—. Served with USN, 1917-19. Named to U. Ky. Hall of Distinguished Alumni. Registered profl. engr., N.Y. Fellow AAAS; mem. Am. Meteorol. Soc. (profl. mem.), Acoustical Soc. Am., Am. Inst. Physics, N.Y. Acad. Scis., Tau Beta Pi, Alpha Tau Omega. Republican. Episcopalian. Club: Larchmont Yacht. Patentee fields of instrumentation, radiosonde, telemetering, atmospheric measurement, brushless DC motors. Home: Fenimore Dr Harrison NY 10528 Office: Brailsford & Co Inc Rye NY 10580

BRAIN, DONALD CHESTER, ins. agt.; b. Beatrice, Nebr.; s. Clinton Chester and Bertha Susan (Jones) B.; B.B.S., U. Kans., 1940; m. Charleen McCann, Sept. 25, 1948; children—Donald Chester, David M. With Retail Credit Co., Kansas City, Mo., 1940-42; spl. agt. Hartford Accident and Indemnity Co., Los Angeles and Kansas City, 1946-48; asso. broker, then. gen. partner W.B. Johnson & Co., Kansas City, 1948-63; a founder, 1963, since pres. Brain & Fritson, Inc., Kansas City; trustee Harry J. Loman Found. Ins. Edn., 1964-68, chmn. bd., 1968; tchr. ins. courses U. Kansas City, 1952-56; trustee Am. Inst. for Property and Liability Underwriters, Inc., 1979—; elector Ins. Hall of Fame, 1970—; mem. public ins. com. city of Kansas City (Mo.), 1970-76, mem. sch. dist. ins. com., 1963-69; speaker in field, 1969—. Mem. Kansas City Crime Com., 1973—, Mayor Kansas City Prayer Breakfast Com., 1972—. Served with U.S. Army, 1942-45. Recipient citation 100th Ann. Mo. Ins. Dept., 1969; C.P.C.U., 1952. Mem. Soc. C.P.C.U.'s (past nat. pres.), Ind. Ins. Agts. Am. (pres. 1979), Mo. Assn. Ind. Ins. Agts. (past pres., Ins. Man of Yr. award 1976), Kansas City Assn. Ind. Ins. Agts. (past pres.), Kansas City Advt. and Sales Execs. Club, Kansas C. of C., Am. Legion (past post comdr.), 40 and 8, Serra Club (past pres. Kansas City, past dist. gov.). Clubs: Blue Hills Country, University. Address: 1100 United Missouri Bank Bldg Kansas City MO 64106

BRAKELEY, GEORGE ARCHIBALD, III, fundraising counsel; b. Princeton, N.J., Aug. 21, 1939; s. George Archibald and Mary Crozier Page (Brown) B.; B.A., Princeton U., 1961; M.B.A., U. Conn., 1976; m. Barbara Ann Nullmeyer, Aug. 28, 1965; children—William P., Kristin F. Salesman, Humble Oil & Refining Co., Wilmington, Del., 1965-69, sr. salesman, 1966-67, gen. sales supr., Salisbury, Md., 1967-69; with Brakeley, John Price Jones Inc., N.Y.C., 1969—, sr. v.p., 1978-79, exec. v.p., 1979—, also dir. Trustee, Congregational Ch. New Canaan (Conn.), 1980—, Princeton Prospect Found., 1979—; mem. exec. com. Princeton Alumni Council, 1971-77, treas., 1975-77. Served to capt. USMC, 1961-65. Republican. Clubs: Nassau (Princeton); Princeton of N.Y.; New Canaan Field. Home: 340 White Oak Shade Rd New Canaan CT 06840 Office: Brakeley John Price Jones Inc 6 E 43d St New York NY 10017

BRAKKE, JAMES GLENN, ins. exec.; b. Pomona, Calif., Apr. 16, 1942; s. Glenn Walden and Dessie Irene B.; A.A., San Jose City Coll., 1962; B.S., Colo. State U., 1964; Certified Ins. Cons., Orange Coast City Coll., 1975; m. Glenys E. Heaney, June 19, 1965; children—Tifani E., Xanne M., Richard S. Account exec. comml. ins. sales Sentry Ins., Whittier, Calif., 1966-69; v.p. sales Fenley & Assos., Inc., Orange, Calif., 1970-71; pres. Brakke-Schafnitz & Assos., Inc., Irvine, Calif., 1971—; v.p. Planned Community Mgmt., Newport Beach, Calif., 1976—; pres. Brakke-Schafnitz Investments, Inc., Newport Beach, 1979—; corp. sec., dir. Westwood Nat. Ins. Co.; dir. Pacific Nat. Bank, Irvine, Calif. Chmn. local dist. assembly race, 1977-78. Named Jaycee of Year, 1966; Profl. Adjuster of Year, Sentry Ins., 1967; Outstanding Salesman INA Life Ins., 1975-76, La. & So. Life, 1976, Pan Am. Life, 1978, Travelers Ins., 1975. Mem. Ins. Agts. Adv. Council (chmn.), Colo. State U. Alumni Assn., Gamma Iota Sigma (pres. 1973). Republican. Methodist. Clubs: Roosters of Chanteclair, Ritz Brothers. Home: 24871 Nellie Gail Rd Laguna Hills CA 92653 Office: 17911 Fitch Ave Irvine CA 92714

BRALOWER, EDWARD F., banker; b. Billings, Mont., Feb. 6, 1942; s. Frederick William and Martha Anne (Gray) B.; student U. Mont., 1960-62; B.A., Washington U., St. Louis, 1965; M.B.A., U. Chgo., 1967; m. Sara Jane Thirkell, June 21, 1970; children—Elizabeth Ann, Matthew Curtis, Emily Rebecca. Trainee, Harris Bank, Chgo., 1967-69, various positions in banking and trusts, 1969-76; asst. v.p. trusts First Nat. Bank of Chgo., 1976-80, v.p. trusts, 1980—, also dir. Bd. dirs. Francis Parker Sch., 1978—; active Little League. Mem. Am. Bankers Assn., Phi Beta Kappa. Club: Mid-America. Home: 713 W Barry Apt 1-N Chicago IL 60657

BRAMBLE, RONALD LEE, mgmt. cons.; b. Pauls Valley, Okla., Sept. 9, 1937; s. Homer Lee and Ethyle Juanita (Stephens) B.; A.A., San Antonio Coll., 1957; B.S., Trinity U., 1959, M.S., 1964; J.D., St. Mary's U. Sch. Law, 1975; D.B.A., Ind. No. U., 1973; m. Kathryn Louise Seiler, July 2, 1960; children—Julia Dawn, Kristin Lee. Mgr., buyer Fed-Mart, Inc., San Antonio, 1959-61; tchr. bus. San Antonio Ind. Sch. Dist., 1961-65, edn. coordinator, bus. tng. specialist, 1965-67; asso. prof., chmn. dept. mgmt. San Antonio Coll., 1967-73; prin. Ron Bramble Assos., San Antonio, 1967-77; pres. Adminstrv. Research Assos., Inc., 1977—. Lectr. bus., edn. and ch. groups, 1965—; cons. editor Prentice-Hall, Inc., Englewood Cliffs, N.J., 1969-71. Served with AUS, 1959. Recipient Wall Street Jour. award Trinity U., 1959, Distinguished Salesman award Sales and Marketing Execs., 1967, Merit award Adminstrv. Mgmt. Soc., 1968, U.S. Law Week award, 1975. Mem. San Antonio C. of C., Adminstrv. Mgmt. Soc. (pres. 1966-68), Bus. Edn. Tchrs. Assn. (pres. 1964), Sales and Marketing Execs. San Antonio (dir. 1967—), Internat. Platform Assn., Internat. Assn. Cons. to Bus., Nat. Assn. Bus. Economists, Acad. Mgmt., Phi Delta Phi. Republican. Methodist. Lion. Club: San Antonio Advertising. Contbr. articles profl. jours. Home: 127 Palo Duro San Antonio TX 78216

BRAMSON, FRANK HARRIS, stock brokerage co. exec.; b. Wausau, Wis., Aug. 27, 1946; s. Ronald Abert and Selma Jane (Greenwald) B.; B.A. in Fin., U. Ill., 1968. With Freehling & Co., Chgo., 1968—, account exec., 1969-78, partner, 1978—. Pres. jr. bd. dirs. Thresholds Mental Health Rehab. Center, Chgo., 1976-78; mem. fund-raising bd. Goodman Theatre. Mem. Chgo. Fgn. Relations Council, Bond Club Chgo. Republican. Home: 2736 Hampden Ct Chicago IL 60614 Office: 120 S La Salle St Chicago IL 60603

BRANAN, ROBERT NAPIER, systems analyst; b. Ft. Oglethorpe, Ga., Dec. 13, 1943; s. Fred Horton and Elizabeth Forbes (Ledbetter) B.; A.A., U. Md., 1974, certificate in mgmt., 1975. Student intern Inst. Def. Analysis, Arlington, Va., 1962-64; EDP trainee Honeywell Co., Arlington, 1964; computer operator Data Processing div. Md. Controller's Office, Annapolis, 1966-69, programmer, 1969-74, programmer-analyst, 1974, programmer/analyst specialist, 1974—. Bd. dirs. Youth Sanctuary Inc. Anne Arundel County (Md.), 1970-71. Cert. data processor Inst. Certification Computer Profls. Mem. Data Processing Mgmt. Assn. (certified), State Employers Mgmt. and Profl. Assn., Severn-Magothy Sq. Club. Democrat. Presbyterian. Club: Masons. Home: 2785 Hambleton Rd Riva MD 21044 Office: 60 West St Annapolis MD 21401

BRANDEIS, BARRY, jewelry mfg. co. exec.; b. Phila., May 3, 1946; s. Norman and Jennie (Yousin) B.; B.S. in Psychology, Pa. State U., 1968, M.B.A. in Mgmt., 1970; M.B.A. in Fin., Baruch Coll., City U. N.Y., 1974, A.B.D. Bus., 1975; m. Renee Riesenberg, Apr. 4, 1971; 1 son, Adam. Account exec. Meridian Securities Co., Bala Cynwyd, Pa., 1968-70; instr. Pace U. Grad. Sch., also Baruch Coll., 1968-75; asst. to chmn. Wasko Gold Products Corp., N.Y.C., 1975-77, v.p. fin., 1977-80, exec. v.p., 1980—; mem. U.S. Senate Bus. Adv. Bd.; adj. asst. prof. Pace U. Grad. Sch. Bus. Mem. AAUP, Internat. Precious Metals Inst. (charter), Assn. M.B.A. Execs., Internat. Platform Assn., Omicron Delta Kappa, Psi Chi. Home: 15 Cooper Dr Great Neck NY 11023 Office: 71 Fifth Ave New York NY 10003

BRANDEL, PAUL WILLIAM, lawyer, exec.; b. Chgo., Oct. 7, 1911; s. Carl P. and Christine (Johnson) B.; grad. North Park Acad., Chgo., 1928, North Park Coll. 1930, LL.D., 1973; J.D., Chgo. Kent Coll. Law 1933; LL.D., Trinity Coll., 1965; m. Vega G. Rundquist, July 2, 1938 (dec. Apr. 26, 1970); 1 dau., Carola Ruth; m. 2d, Bernice Peterson Stege, Jan. 3, 1976. Admitted to Ill. bar, 1933, since practiced in Chgo.; partner firm Brandel, Olson, Johnson & Erickson; chmn. bd. Stone-Brandel Center, Chgo.; pres., dir. Paul W. Brandel Enterprises, Inc.; chmn., dir. Schaumburg State Bank, Barrington State Bank, Edens Plaza State Bank, Countryside Bank, Woodfield Bank. Chmn. bd. benevolence Evang. Covenant Ch. Am.; mem. adv. com. on health, edn. and welfare to gov. of Ill.; mem. adv. bd. Salvation Army. Bd. dirs. Swedish Covenant Hosp.; bd. dirs. Chgo. Boys Clubs, Am. Found. Religion and Psychiatry, Nat. Health Assn.; trustee Ill. Inst. Tech., Goodwill Industries. Mem. Am., Ill., Chgo. bar assns., Law Inst., Gideons. Kiwanian. Clubs: Union League, Michigan Shores, Nordic Law, Chicago Athletic Assn., Swedish; N.Y. Athletic; Everglades (Palm Beach, Fla.); Lauderdale Yacht. Home: 2515 Mayapple Ct Northbrook IL 60062 Office: 500 Skokie Blvd Northbrook IL 60062

BRANDENBURG, JOE WILKIE, dietitian, army officer; b. Oneida, Ky., Nov. 15, 1948; s. Conley and Margie (Burns) B.; B.S., Berea (Ky.) Coll., 1971; M.S., U. So. Calif., 1978. Commd. 2d lt. U.S. Army, 1971, advanced through grades to capt.; dietitian Brooke Army Med. Center, Ft. Sam Houston, Tex., 1971-73; chief food production and service Wood Army Hosp., Ft. Leonard Wood, Mo., 1973-76; chief food service div. SHAPE Med. Center, Belgium, 1976-79, chief food service div. DeWitt Army Hosp., Ft. Belvoir, Va., 1980—. Decorated Army Commendation medal. Mem. Am. Dietetic Assn., Am. Hosp. Assn. Republican. Baptist. Home: 2830 Cambridge Dr Woodbridge VA 22060 Office: DeWitt Army Hosp Fort Belvoir VA 22060

BRANDER, REYNOLDS A., JR., lawyer; b. Grand Rapids, Mich., Nov. 22, 1937; s. Reynolds A. and Gertrude (Boot) B.; A.B., U. Mich., 1960; J.D., Wayne State U., 1966; m. Janice Ann Lusk, June 29, 1963; children—Gregory, Sara. Admitted to Mich. bar, 1966; mem. staff Kent County Prosecutor's Office, 1966-67; partner law firm Cholette, Perkins & Buchanan, Grand Rapids, Mich., 1967—. Served with USNR, 1960-63. Mem. Am., Mich. State bar assns., Internat. Assn. Ins. Counsel. Home: 634 Plymouth Rd Grand Rapids MI 49506 Office: 755 Old Kent Bank Grand Rapids MI 49503

BRANDES, THOMAS WESLEY, cons. engr.; b. Olean, N.Y., July 16, 1918; s. Wesley Charles and Gertrude Maude (Bell) B.; B.S., St. Bonaventure U., 1965; postgrad. Syracuse U., 1966-67; m. Agnes Ruth Roth, Mar. 1, 1945; 1 dau., Barbara Lynn. Research engr. Vander Horst Corp., Olean, N.Y., 1945-54, chmn. bd., 1950-53; mgr. research and devel. Viko div. Ethan Allen Co., Eldred, Pa., 1954-65; chem. process tech. engr. IBM Corp., Owego, N.Y., 1965-67; cons. chem. engr. Columbus McKinnon Co., Tonawanda, N.Y., 1967-77; cons. chem. engr., Olean, N.Y., 1977—. Dir. fund campaigns ARC, Am. Cancer Soc., 1945-55. Served with USAAC, 1941-45; ETO. Decorated Bronze Star (3), Air medal (5), Legion of Merit. Mem. Am. Chem. Soc., Patentee electrodeposition of chromium, iron, nickel, lead, copper, brass, organic chemistry and plastics. Address: 927 Delaware Ave Olean NY 14760

BRANDI, HENRY WILLIAM, resistor mfg. co. exec.; b. Naples, Italy, Mar. 3, 1924; s. Giovanni and Concetta (Davide) B.; came to U.S., 1948, naturalized, 1951; E.E., Livorno Naval Acad., 1943; m. Rose Desiderio, May 20, 1979; 1 son, John. Chief testing engr. Gen. Instrument, Newark, 1952-60; plant mgr. Weston Instrument, Newark, 1960-62; pres., gen. mgr., owner Vamistor Corp., Hanover Twp., N.J., 1962-73; pres., owner Res-Net Corp., Whippany, N.J., 1973—; dir. Marti Corp., Cedar Knolls, N.J. Served with Italian Navy, 1943-45. Mem. N.J. Mfrs. Assn., North Jersey Personnel Assn. Patentee in field. Office: 110 Route 10 Whippany NJ 07981

BRANDIN, ALF ELVIN, mining and shipping exec.; b. Newton, Kans., July 1, 1912; s. Oscar E. and Agnes (Larson) B.; A.B., Stanford, 1936; m. Marie Eck, June 15, 1936; children—Alf R., Jon, Erik, Mark. With Standard Group, Detroit, 1936-42; bus. mgr. and exec. officer charge land devel. Stanford, 1946-59, v.p. bus. affairs, 1959-70; sr. v.p., dir. Utah Internat., Inc., San Francisco, 1970—; dir. Saga Corp., Hershey Oil Corp. Gov. San Francisco Bay Area Council; dir. Am. Cancer Soc.; mem. VIII Olympic Winter Games Organizing Com. Vice pres. Reclamation Dist. 2087 Alameda, Calif.; mem. Stanford Athletic Bd.; bd. overseers Hoover Instn. on War, Revolution and Peace, Stanford U. Served as comdr., USNR, 1942-45. Mem. Zeta Psi. Elk. Clubs: Pauma Valley Country; Bohemian, Bankers, San Francisco Golf; Royal Lahaina (Honolulu). Home: 668 Salvatierra St Stanford CA 94305 Office: 550 California St San Francisco CA 94104

BRANDON, CRAIG STEVEN, mktg. and constrn. co. exec.; b. Columbus, Ohio, Aug. 17, 1947; s. Grant Godfrey and Gail Brandon; B.S. with honors in Bus. Adminstrn., Franklin U., 1970. Buyer, Florsheim Shoe Co., Chgo., 1970-74; corp. v.p. Consol. Internat. Co., Columbus, 1974-78; owner Midwest Mktg. Group, Casper, Wyo. (formerly Columbus), 1979—, Brandon Homes and Remodeling, Casper, 1979—; condr. fin. seminars; cons. in field. Mem. Nat. Home Builders Assn. Home: 324 Azalea Casper WY 82601 Office: PO Box 1857 Mills WY 82644

BRANDON, DALE EDWARD, oceanographer; b. Canonsburg, Pa., Sept. 22, 1938; s. George Edward and Mabel Elizabeth (Pugh) B.; B.S. in Geology, Wayne State U., 1965; M.S., Ph.C. in Oceanography, U. Mich., 1967, Ph.D. in Phys. Oceanography, 1970; postgrad. (Fulbright fellow) U. Sydney (Australia), 1967-69. Sr. research oceanographer Esso Production Research Co., Houston, 1970-73; environ. adminstr. Alyeska Pipeline Service Co., Anchorage, 1973-76; environ. coordinator Exxon Minerals Co., Houston, 1976-78; sr. program mgr. Environ. Research & Tech., Houston, 1978-80; dir. ocean sci. dept. Interstate Electronics Corp., Anaheim, Calif., 1980—. Served with USN, 1955-59. NSF fellow, 1965, 66, 67, 69, 70. Mem. AAAS, Am. Geophys. Union, Soc. Econ. Paleontologists and Mineralogists, Sigma Xi. Home: 201 19th St Huntington Beach CA 92648 Office: 1001 E Ball Rd Anaheim CA 92803

BRANDON, IRWIN, exec. recruiter; b. N.Y.C., Jan. 4, 1932; s. Joseph and Kitty (Quatel) B.; B.S., N.Y. U., 1956; m. Arlene Barnett, Oct. 11, 1961; children—Kyle, Mara, Avery. Owner, Brandon Ins., N.Y.C., 1960-67; exec. v.p. Hair Extension Center, Inc., N.Y.C., 1968-72, Hadley, Lockwood, Inc., N.Y.C., 1972—; bd. dirs. Hadley, Lockwood & Cutty Group, Inc. Served with U.S. Army, 1953-55. Clubs: N.Y. Road Runners, Princeton.

BRANDON, WILLIAM CLINT, mgmt. cons.; b. Chancellor, Ala., Oct. 9, 1918; s. John W. and Bess (Broxson) B.; B.S., U. Fla., 1942, M.A., 1948; m. Ethel I. Pool, Aug. 23, 1963; children—Deborah Jean, Eric, Michael, Wade Brandon. Territory mgr. Swift & Co., Miami, Fla., 1948-54, mgr. advt., merchandising, Chgo., 1954-58, Midwest sales mgr., Cleve., 1958-59, dir. tng. and devel., also personnel, Chgo., 1959-70; owner, pres. Agri-Bus. Tng. & Devel., Roswell, Ga., 1970—, Clint Brandon Assos., Roswell, 1977—. cons. Can. Feed Industry Assn. Served with U.S. Army, 1942-47. Danforth Found. fellow, 1942; Fla. Blue Key Leadership award, 1976. Mem. Am. Feed Mfg. Assn. (cons. personnel devel.), Nat. Agri-Mktg. Assn., Nat. Speakers Assn., Ga. Agri-Bus. Council, Res. Officers Assn. (life), Phi Gamma Delta, Alpha Zeta (chancellor). Baptist. Author: Motivation: Roots of Human Behavior, 1972, 80; Professional Clubs: U.S. Senatorial, Economic of N.Y. Selling in Agri-Business, 1972; Building and Developing Your Work Force, 1972; Closing Sales, 1979; Managerial Time Mgmt.: Work Orgn., 1979, others; contbr. articles to profl. jours.; editor-in-chief U. Fla. Mag., 1941-42. Home: 9370 Riviera Rd Roswell GA 30075 Office: 9370 Riviera Rd Roswell GA 30075

BRANDON, WILLIAM MILTON, fin. exec.; b. Shelbyville, Tenn., Nov. 6, 1943; s. William Moreland and Lucille (Blackburn) B.; B.A. U. Tenn., 1965. Dir. ops. Adler Communications, Balt., 1967-71; pres. Time & Space Advt., Balt., 1971-73; dir. mktg./advt. Merry Go Round Enterprises, Balt., 1973-75; exec. v.p. fin., chmn. bd. The Nurse Bank, Inc., Pikesville, Md., 1975—; cons. in field. Mem. U.S. Senatorial Bus. Adv. Bd. Mem. Am. Mgmt. Assn. Office: Unit 16 3701 Old Court Rd Pikesville MD 21208

BRANDSTROM, CHARLES HELMER, ry. products mfg. exec.; b. Union City, N.J., Apr. 19, 1932; s. Helmer and Gunhild Maria Brandstrom; M.E., Stevens Inst. Tech., 1955, M.S. in Indsl. Mgmt., 1963; m. Diane M. Hebert, July 27, 1976; 1 dau., Erica Lynn. Asst. gen. mgr. railroad sales dept. Union Carbide Corp., 1968-72; indsl. mktg. mgr. Pullman Standard, Pullman, Inc., 1972-77; gen. mktg. mgr. Airco Indsl. Gases, Airco, Inc., 1977-80; v.p. ry. products div. Gen. Industry Group, Allegheny Ludlum Industries, Inc., Chgo., 1980—. Served to 1st lt. USAF, 1955-57. Mem. Am. Mgmt. Assn., NW Maintenance of Way Assn., Chgo. Maintenance of Way Assn., St. Louis Maintenance of Way Assn., Chi Psi. Republican. Roman Catholic. Home: 6114 Shenandoah Dr Crystal Lake IL 60014 Office: 111 E Wacker Dr 15th Floor Chicago IL 60601

BRANDT, ELLEN B., fin. communications and media exec., educator; b. N.Y.C., Feb. 5, 1947; d. J. Michael and Martha Brandt; B.A., U. Pa., 1969, M.A., 1970, Ph.D., 1973. Tchr. researcher U. Pa., Phila., 1970-72; tchr. Pa. State U., King of Prussia, 1971-72; prof. U. S.C., Columbia, 1973-74; asst. to pres., dir. external affairs Azcon Corp., N.Y.C., 1974-75; dir. pub. affairs Certain-teed Corp., Valley Forge, Pa., 1975-76; pres. EB Corporate Fin. Communications, Sunnyvale, Calif., 1976—; chmn. Calif. Woman Media Syndications, Sunnyvale, 1979—; lectr. Sch. Bus. San Francisco State U., 1980—, Indian Valley Colls., Novato, Calif., 1980—. Mem. Nat. Investor Relations Inst., MLA, Women's Caucus Modern Langs., Nat. Women's Polit. Caucus, Popular Culture Assn., Am. Studies Assn., Women's Equity Action League, Bay Area Profl. Women's Network (bd. dirs.), World Affairs Council San Francisco, Kappa Kappa Gamma. Club: Commonwealth of Calif. Author: Susanna Haswell Rowson, America's First Best-Selling Novelist, 1975. Book reviewer Jour. Popular Culture, 1974—. Home and Office: 165 S Bernardo Ave Suite 35 Sunnyvale CA 94086

BRANDT, KEITH DELANO, welding electrode mfg. co. exec.; b. Lincoln, Nebr., May 22, 1934; s. John Henry and Martha Margaret (Mueller) B.; B.S., U. So. Calif., 1956, M.B.A., 1965; m. Mary Fay Mathes, Nov. 23, 1957; children—Stephen, Christopher, Patrick. Systems engr. IBM, 1959-62; mgr. electronic acctg. Specialty Engrs., 1963-65; dir. data processing Coca Cola Bottling Co., Los Angeles, 1965-70; mgr. mgmt. cons. services Coopers & Lybrand, Los Angeles, 1970-76; v.p. fin. sec. Stoody Co., Industry, Calif., 1976—; dir. Stoody Asean Sdn. (Malaysia) Berhad. C.P.A., Calif. Mem. Am. Inst. C.P.A.'s, Fin. Execs. Inst., Nat. Mgmt. Assn., Calif. Soc. C.P.A.'s, Commerce Assos. U. So. Calif., Navy League, Los Angeles World Affairs Council, Pasadena Men's Com. for Arts, Beta Gamma Sigma. Republican. Home: 2037 San Pasqual St Pasadena CA 91107 Office: 16425 Gale Ave Industry CA 91749

BRANDT, ROBERT BARRY, retail exec.; b. Lebanon, Pa., Nov. 13, 1948; s. Marlin Jay and Arlene Hilda (Bowman) B.; B.A., Lebanon Valley Coll., 1971; postgrad United Theol. Sem., 1971-73; m. Ruth Ann Peterson, June 6, 1970; 1 son, Matthew Scot. Licensed United Methodist Ch., 1968, Ordained to ministry, 1972; minister Enders Powells Valley, Pa., 1968-69; asst. minister Lebanon Covenant, Pa., 1969-71; asso. staff minister Christ Ch., Kettering, Ohio, 1971-73; computer operator Rike's Dept. Store of Federated Dept. Stores, Inc., Dayton, 1973-74, computer opns. mgr., 1974-77, computer systems analyst, 1977-78; asst. controller, dir. data processing Stewart div. Associated Dry Goods, Balt., 1978-80, implementation mgr. mdse. acctg. systems, N.Y.C., 1980—. Bd. dirs. Agape House, Dayton, 1977—. Democrat. Home: 189 Sheridan Ave Ho-Ho-Kus NJ 07423 Office: 417 5th Ave New York NY 10016

BRANDT, ROBERT KENNETH, mktg. exec.; b. Ft. Bragg, N.C., Oct. 2, 1947; s. Charles Kenneth and Doris (Hursey) B.; B.S. in Mktg., Pa. State U., 1970; m. Sandra Myra Smith, July 5, 1968. Market analyst Daily Express, Inc., Carlisle, Pa., 1971; bindery mgr. Maple Press Co., York, Pa., 1972-73, sales mgr., 1974-77; v.p. mktg. and sales Maple-Vail Book Group, York, 1978—. Served with Army N.G., 1970-76. Mem. Book Mfrs. Inst. (com. mem.). Republican. Home: 1221 Wiltshire Rd York PA 17403 Office: 210 E York St York PA 17403

BRANNAN, JOHN HAYES, mfg. co. exec.; b. Columbus, Ohio, Jan. 26, 1919; s. Thomas Hays and Kate (Warren) B.; student Ohio State U., 1936-39; B.S. in Civil Engring., Mass. Inst. Tech., 1941; m. Catherine Silbernagel, Mar. 31, 1941; children—Barbara Jane, Mary Lois, John Charles. With Union Carbide Corp., 1946—, dir. new bus. ventures Carbon Products div., N.Y.C., 1970-75, mng. dir. Union Carbide Iberica, SA, Madrid, Spain, 1977—, Union Carbide Navarra, SA, Pamplona, Spain, 1975-78, Brit. Acheson Electrodes Ltd., Sheffield, Eng., 1978—. Served with U.S. Army, 1941-46. Republican. Episcopalian. Club: Cleve. Yachting. Home: 18 Clarendon Rd Sheffield S10 England Office: British Acheson Electrodes Ltd Fountain Precinct Balm Green Sheffield S1 England

BRANNEN, JOEL THOMAS, broadcasting exec.; b. Waycross, Ga., May 25, 1942; s. Denver T. and Grace Wilma (Harper) B.; A.S. in electronics, So. Tech. Inst., Marietta, Ga., 1962; m. Freddie Carol Hubbard, Oct. 20, 1966; children—Gary, Amy. Engr., announcer, salesman Sta. WDLP, Panama City, Fla., 1962-67; engr., announcer Radio Sta. KCIL-FM, also engr., announcer, asst. mgr. Radio Sta. KJIN, Houma, La., 1967-69, gen. mgr. radio stas. KJIN and KCIL-FM, 1969-70, 75-77; pres., chmn. bd., gen. mgr. S. La. Broadcasters Inc., Houma, 1977—; owner, operator B & B Car Stereo Inc., Clearwater, Fla., 1970—, Brannen Real Estate Properties. Served with Army N.G., 1964-70. Mem. La. Assn. Broadcasters. Republican. Presbyterian. Home: 2307 Vanderbilt Dr Clearwater FL 33515 Office: 506 Virginia Ln Clearwater FL 33515

BRANNING, THOMAS EDWARD, ins. agt., motivation exec.; b. Bentonia, Miss., June 4, 1936; s. Henry Louis and Annie Mae (Partridge) B.; student U. Md., 1962-64, Troy State U., 1966-68; B.A. in History, U. Nebr., Omaha, 1971; children—Mark Henry, Stella Ann. Enlisted in U.S. Army, 1955, commd. 2d lt., 1961, advanced through grades to maj., 1968; signal officer, helicopter pilot; served in Vietnam; ret., 1975; fin. planner United Services Planning Assos., 1975-79; owner Branning Ins. Agy., Sierra Vista, Ariz., 1979—, Ariz. Leadership Dynamics, 1978—; guest speaker goal setting and motivation; condr. stress mgmt. seminars. Decorated Soldiers medal, Air medal. Home: 1000 Via Cabrillo Sierra Vista AZ 85635 Office: 25 El Camino Real Suite 3 Sierra Vista AZ 85635

BRANNON, TERENCE CARLIN, banker; b. Mobile, Ala., 1938; ed. Birmingham So. Coll. Pres., chief operating officer, dir. Central Bancshares of South, Inc., Birmingham, Ala.; dir. Central Bank of Mobile, Central Bank of Birmingham. Office: Central Bancshares South Inc 701 S 20th St Birmingham AL 35296*

BRANSON, ROBERT EMERY, chem. co. exec.; b. Amarillo, Tex., Feb. 5, 1934; s. William Leaton and Agnes Louise B.; B.B.A., U. Tex., 1956; m. Marilyn Elaine Hall, Aug. 10, 1963; children—Stephanie Ann, Suzanne Lynn. Area rep. West Coast Constrn. Materials div. Electrovert Inc., San Francisco, 1963-64, mgr. western sales, 1964-67; product specialist North Central heavy constrn. Constrn. Products Div. W.R. Grace & Co., Mpls., 1968-74, North Central sales mgr., 1974—; cons. in field. Served to lt., USNR, 1956-61. Named to Salesmaster's Council, Constrn. Products div. W.R. Grace & Co. Mem. Sales and Mktg. Execs. Mpls. (dir. programs 1979-80, 2d v.p. 1980—, Order of Bell award 1978, Chairperson of Yr. 1980), Producers Council, Constrn. Specification Inst., Mpls. Barbershop Chorus, Acacia Frat. Republican. Lutheran. Club: Masons. Home: 6620 Scandia Rd Edina MN 55435 Office: 4725 Olson Hwy Minneapolis MN 55422

BRASFIELD, CAROLYN A. (MRS. OTIS E. BRASFIELD), mfg. co. ofcl.; b. Spartanburg, S.C., Oct. 13, 1923; d. Edward Lucius and Alice Lucille (Bonner) Allen; grad. Harrison's Bus. Coll., Orlando, Fla., 1943; m. Otis E. Brasfield, Mar. 5, 1944; 1 son, Otis E., Jr. With Home Savings Assn., Odessa, Tex., 1962-78, asst. sec., 1967-70, sr. savings officer, asst. v.p., 1970-78; sec. Meister Industries, Odessa, 1978—. Active Boy Scouts Am., PTA, DeMolay Mothers Circle. Mem. DAR (regent 1975-77, vice regent 1979-81), Permian Basin Geneal. Soc., United Daus. of Confederacy (pres. 1961-62, 77-80), Magna Charta Dames. Republican. Baptist. Club: Order Eastern Star. Home: 3103 N Hancock Ave Odessa TX 79762 Office: 2301 W 42nd St PO Box 4693 Odessa TX 79763

BRASUELL, WILLIAM CHESTER, JR., telecommunications exec.; b. Buffalo, Jan. 5, 1936; s. William Chester and Ione Helen (Dresser) B.; B.Sc., Mass. Inst. Tech., 1957; M.B.A., San Jose State U., 1969; m. Carla Laree Atwell, Dec. 12, 1976; children by previous marriage—Allyson Lee, Christopher William. Devel. engr. Caterpillar Tractor Co., Peoria, Ill., 1957-61; sr. systems engr. Lockheed Missiles & Space Co., Sunnyvale, Calif., 1961-66; supr., adminstrv. systems Varian Assos., Palo Alto, Calif., 1966-74; mgr. worldwide telecommunications Fairchild Camera Instrument Corp., Mountainview, Calif., 1974-80; sr. cons. telecommunications DMW Group, Ann Arbor, Mich., 1980—; mem. faculty advisory bd. grad. program in telecommunications Golden Gate U. Mem. Assn. Data Communication Users (dir. No. Calif.). Address: 3235 Benton St Santa Clara CA 95051

BRASWELL, REX HARALSON, real estate exec.; b. Hattiesburg, Miss., Feb. 12, 1926; s. Rufus Haralson and Annie Elizabeth (Smith) B.; student Millsaps Coll., Jackson, Miss., 1945-46, U. So. Miss., 1958-61; m. Mary Alice Fancher, June 19, 1949; children—James Rex, John Haralson, Jerry Dumas. Owner, operator Rex's So. Cleaners, Hattiesburg, 1948-67; pres. Univ. Handbag Co., Inc., Hattiesburg, 1965-74; asso. Don Nace Realtor, Hattiesburg, 1975—. Pres. Hattiesburg Christian Bus. Men's Com., 1960-62, 78—; v.p. Hattiesburg Drug Edn. Council, 1972-74; trustee, chmn. fin. com. Clarke Coll., Newton, Miss. Served with USNR, 1944-47. Baptist (lay speaker, deacon). Home: 613 Cedarwood Dr Hattiesburg MS 39401 Office: 800 Westover Dr Hattiesburg MS 39401

BRATCHES, HOWARD, corp. exec.; b. Hammond, Ind., June 1, 1929; s. William Howard and Helen Lorraine B.; A.B., Washington and Lee U., 1951, LL.B., 1953; m. Patricia A. Kelly, June 21, 1951; children—Daryl, Janice, Beth, Kurt, Kyle. Personnel/labor relations exec. Shell Oil Co., Wood River, Ill., 1953-62; personnel and indsl. relations mgmt. Gen. Foods Corp., White Plains, N.Y., 1962-69; partner Thorndike Deland Assos., N.Y.C., 1969—. Bd. dirs. Rye United Fund, 1976; vestryman Christ's Episcopal Ch., 1976-78; pres. Rye High Sch. Dads' Club, 1974-76, Manursing Island Club, 1978-79. Mem. Am. Assn. Exec. Recruiting Cons.'s, Phi Alpha Delta. Republican. Club: Union League (N.Y.). Home: 51 Orchard Ln Rye NY 10580 Office: 1440 Broadway New York NY 10018

BRATMAN, CARROLL CHARLES, mus. instrument mfg. co. exec.; b. Balt., June 27, 1906; s. Lazar and Rebecca (Friedland) B.; grad. Balt. City Coll., 1926; postgrad. Peabody Inst., 1927-31, Curtis Inst., 1931-33; m. Beverly Kolman, Aug. 23, 1932; 1 son, Garry Samuel. Solo percussionist Nat. Symphony Orch., Washington, 1931-41, Stokowski All-Am. Youth Orch., U.S.A. transcontinental tour, 1941-42; staff percussionist NBC, CBS, N.Y.C., 1942-57; founder, pres., exec. dir. Carroll Mus. Instrument Service Corp., N.Y.C., 1945—; founder, pres. Electronics Lab., Paris, France, 1962—, Carroll Sound, Inc., N.Y.C., 1967—; pres. Ondotronics, Inc., N.Y.C., B.G.C. Mus. Instruments Distbg., Inc., N.Y.C.; mem. Philharmonic Symphony Orch. N.Y., N.Y.C., 1957-60; cons. condrs., composers, arrangers, schs., 1945—; producer Sound in Music in TV forum Nat. Acad. TV Arts and Scis., N.Y.C., 1967. Recipient citation Nat. Hosp. Denver, 1967; plaque Theatrical Sq. Club Greater N.Y., 1968. Mem. Am. Fedn. Musicians, ASCAP, Percussive Arts Soc. (dir.), Met. Mus. Art (life). Clubs: Montammy Golf (gov. Alpine, N.J.); Masons. Creator original percussion instruments and sound effects supplied to radio-TV networks, recs. and entire music industry, 1945—. Home: Apt 1-D 888 8th Ave New York NY 10019 Office: 351-53 W 41st St New York NY 10036

BRATT, PETER WALTER, fin. exec.; b. Palatine, Ill., Mar. 23, 1940; s. Theodore W. and Helen L. (Wolf) B.; B.S. in Acctg., Weber State Coll., 1971; C.P.A., Idaho, 1977; divorced; children—Julia, Karen. Acct., A.J. Canfield Co., Chgo., 1963-65; plant controller Morton Salt Co., Chgo., 1965-67; div. controller Stanray Corp., Los Angeles, 1967-70; controller LB Industries Inc., Boise, Idaho, 1970-76, v.p. fin., 1976—, also dir. Treas., Idaho Employee Rights Campaign, 1978; co-chmn. Idaho Freedom to Work Com., 1977. Served with USAF, 1957-62. Mem. Nat. Assn. Accts., Am. Mgmt. Assn., Am. Inst. C.P.A.'s, Idaho Soc. C.P.A.'s, Quarter Horse Breeders Assn., Weber State Coll. Alumni Assn. Republican. Address: LB Industries Inc Box 2797 Boise ID 83701

BRATTEN, ROSEMARY HATTIE, creamery exec.; b. Edwardsville, Ill., Sept. 30, 1930; d. John Lathon and Amelia Gertrude (Talleur) Jones; student pub. schs., Edwardsville; m. Maxwell W. Bratten, Aug. 18, 1948; 1 dau., Theresa Lynn. Inventory mgr. Montgomery Ward Co., Collinsville, Ill., 1948-52; head checker Hoover Bros. Grocery, Edwardsville, 1952-56; head bookkeeper Edwardsville Creamery Co., 1956-76, pres.'s asst., 1966-76, office mgr., 1976-78, mgr., 1978—; mem. Edwardsville Downtown Plan Commn.; mem. Edwardsville Econ. commn. Mem. Edwardsville, Land of Goshen (pres.), Metro East (pres.) chambers commerce, Edwardsville Bus. and Profl. Women, Ladies Aux. of United Transp. Union (pres. 1975-77), Royal Neighbors of Am. Democrat. Roman Catholic. Home: 662 Mill St Edwardsville IL 62025

BRAUN, JOHN GILBERT, business exec.; b. San Francisco, Jan. 16, 1913; s. Carl Franklin and Winifred Hughes (Gilbert) B.; student U. Calif., 1931-34; m. Ruth Richardson, Oct. 26, 1939; children—Beverly, Pamela. With C. F. Braun & Co., Alhambra, Calif., 1934—, pres., 1954-71, chmn. bd., chief exec. officer, 1971—; dir. Santa Fe Internat. Corp. Trustee Calif. Inst. Tech. Mem. ASME, Am. Chem. Soc. Republican. Clubs: California (Los Angeles); Annanadale Golf (Pasadena, Calif.). Home: 1750 Lombardy Rd Pasadena CA 91106 Office: CF Braun & Co 1000 S Fremont Ave Alhambra CA 91803*

BRAUN, WARREN L(LOYD), radio engr.; b. Postville, Iowa, Aug. 11, 1922; s. Karl William and Cornelia (Mueller) B.; student Valparaiso Tech. Inst., 1940-41, Capitol Engring. Inst., 1953, Alexander Hamilton Inst., 1953; m. Lillian Carol Stone, May 24, 1942; children—Warren L. (dec.), Dikki Carol. Chief engr. WKEY, 1941; chief engr. WSVA, 1941, later gen. mgr. WSVA-AM-FM-TV; v.p. EWSP Corp.; E.S.M.W.T.P. sect. head, 1942-45; charge installation stas. WSIR, WTON, WSVA-FM, WJMA, TV stas. WAAM-TV and WSVA-TV, Blue Ridge TV cable facilities, 1945-60; asst. gen. mgr., dir. engring. WSVA AM-FM-TV, 1959-63; owner Warren Braun Cons. Engrs., 1957—; v.p. Market Dimensions, Inc.; pres. ComSonics, Inc., 1972—, Shenandoah Valley Devel. Corp., 1972—. Panel 4 mem. TV Allocations Study Orgn.; chmn. Harrisonburg-Rockingham County Recreational Study Commn.; chmn. Upper Valley Regional Park Authority; mem. Va. Citizens Council for Recreation; mem. bd. Va. Air Pollution Control Bd., 1966-73; mem. Va. State Water Control Bd., 1974—, vice chmn., 1976-77, chmn., 1977-78; commr. Ohio River San. Commn., 1974—, chmn., 1978-80; v.p. Harrisonburg-Rockingham County Community Concert Assn.; mem. Va. Gov.'s Far East Trade Mission, 1972, 77; bd. dirs. Richmond Regional Export Council, Employee Stock Ownership Council Am., Va. Cultural Laureate Found. Recipient Jefferson Davis medal, 1961; A.S.E. Internat. award, 1969. Registered profl. engr., Va., S.C. Fellow Audio Engring. Soc., Internat. Consular Acad. (Reitzke Internat. award 1972); mem. Nat. Assn. Broadcasters (nat. chmn. tape standards com., engring. adv. com. 1966), IEEE, Va. Assn. Professions (v.p. 1972-73, pres. 1974-75), Va. Soc. Profl. Engrs. (dir., pres. Skyline chpt.; named Engr. of Year 1965, Distinguished Service award 1974), Acoustical Soc. Am., Soc. Motion Picture and Television Engrs., Am. Soc. Heating Refrigerating and Air Conditioning Engrs., Nat. Soc. Profl. Engrs. (mem. air pollution control task force), Electronics Industry Assn. (mem. broadband communications standards com.), Harrisonburg-Rock County C. of C. (Harrisonburg-Rockingham Man of Year 1965, pres 1965), Am. Soc. Testing and Materials, Va. Acad. Scis. (dir., exec. com.), Va. C. of C. (chmn. world trade com. 1969-71, dir. 1973-77, v.p. 1975-77). Clubs: Elks (Richmond). Home: 680 New York Ave Harrisonburg VA 22801 Office: Comsonics PO Box 1106 Harrisonburg VA 22801

BRAVERMAN, DOREEN, mfg. co. exec.; b. Vancouver, B.C., Can., Jan. 22, 1932; d. William James and Bernice Constance (Goulding) Montgomery; B.Ed., U. B.C., 1964, postgrad., 1980—; m. Jack Braverman, Aug. 20, 1965; children—William, Robert, Laura Jean, Susan Mary. Tchr., Vancouver Public Schs., 1962-65, 66-68; faculty asso. Simon Fraser U., Burnaby, B.C., 1965-66; gen. mgr., dir. J. Braverman Inc., Vancouver, 1974—; pres. Fleming Decal & Sign Ltd., Vancouver, Flag Shop, Inc., Calgary. Pres., West Point Grey Liberal Assn., 1971-72; treas. Liberal Party of B.C., 1972-73, pres., 1973-75, chmn. leaders com., 1975-77, co-chmn. nat. conv., 1975; fin. adv. B.C. Liberal Women's Commn., 1978—; bd. dirs. Royal Can. Mint, 1980—. Mem. Vancouver Bd. Trade, (dir. 1978—), Kitsilano C. of C., Kitsilano Bus. Assn., Screen Printers Assn. Can., N. Am. Vexillological Assn. Home: 3806 W 8th Ave Vancouver BC V6R 1Z4 Canada Office: 2081 W 4th Ave Vancouver BC V6J 1N3 Canada

BRAVERMAN, ROBERT JAY, multi-industry corp. exec.; b. Bklyn., Mar. 4, 1933; s. Arthur and Ruth Edith (Beck) B.; B.A. magna cum laude, Columbia U., 1954; postgrad. Harvard U. Law Sch., 1956-57, P.M.D., Bus. Sch., 1963; m. Alice Glantz; 1 son, John; m. 2d, Kate Hurney, Dec. 21, 1964; children—Sam, Amy. Partner, Harbridge House, Inc., mgmt. cons., Boston, 1957-66; with ITT, N.Y.C., 1966—, v.p., dir. mktg. and bus. strategy, 1970-79, v.p., group exec.-consumer services, publishing, home products, 1979—; coll. lectr., 1976-78. Served with U.S. Army, 1954-56. Mem. Phi Beta Kappa. Office: 320 Park Ave New York NY 10022

BRAVETTE, MICHAEL ANGELO, mfg. co. ofcl.; b. Newark, Sept. 19, 1926; s. Pasquale and Mamie (Bianco) B.; B.S. in Elec. Engring., N.J. Inst. Tech., 1949, M.S. in Mgmt. Engring., 1952; m. Florence Beltram, Nov. 17, 1951; children—Robin Ellen, Brian Patrick, Barry Alan. Sales engr. H.W. Stoddard & Sons, Nutley, N.J., 1948-54; dist. sales mgr. Indsl. Crane & Hoist div. Borg-Warner Corp., Bloomfield, N.J., 1955-58; proposal mgr. Kearfott Co., Little Falls, N.J., 1958-60; presentations mgr. Kearfott div. Singer Co., Little Falls, 1961—; speaker to engring. trainees 1965—. Lectr., N.J. Tercentenary Commn., 1964; mgr. Little League Baseball, 1970-74; mem. Democratic County Com., 1979—. Served with USN, 1945-46. Recipient Tercentenary Commemorative medal State of N.J., 1964. Democrat. Roman Catholic. Clubs: Toastmasters (pres. Kearfott chpt. 1962-63), Elks (exalted ruler 1973-74, trustee 1975—, state dist. public relations chmn. 1977-78). Editor tech. papers. Home: 23 Rockledge Pl Cedar Grove NJ 07009 Office: 1225 McBride Ave Little Falls NJ 07424

BRAVOCO, RALPH RICHARD, data processing exec.; b. Boston, Sept. 12, 1943; s. Ralph Angelo and Mary (Shepeluk) B.; A.B. in Math., Northeastern U., 1966, M.A. in Econs., 1969; Ph.D. in Bus., U. Mass., 1972; m. Vivian George, Aug. 28, 1966. Sci. programmer Mitre Corp., Bedford, Mass., 1962-67; dept. mgr. equipment div. Raytheon Co., Wayland, Mass., 1967-73; v.p., gen. mgr. internat. ops. SofTech, Inc., Waltham, Mass., 1973-78, v.p., gen. mgr. CADCAM div., 1977—; part time prof. Northeastern U. Mem. Walpole Town Meeting; active Heart Fund, United Fund, Jimmy Fund. Northeastern U. Trustee's scholar, 1961-62; Raytheon Co. fellow, 1969-71. Mem. Soc. Mfg. Engrs., Inst. Mgmt. Scis., Am. Mgmt. Assn., Smithsonian Assos., Nat. Geog. Soc., Soc. Natural History, Futurists, Assn. Computing Machinery. Author articles on computer aided mfg., computer solutions to bus. problems. Home: 7 Birchwood Ln Lincoln MA 01773 Office: 460 Totten Pond Rd Waltham MA 02154

BRAY, JOE PAUL, restaurant chain exec.; b. Tulsa, Sept. 4, 1951; s. Ralph Edward and Betty Jo (Walker) B.; student Okla. State U., 1970-74; m. JoAnne Maus, May 14, 1976; children—Ruth E., Emily, Kathrine C. Employee in food bus., 1967-69; fast food mgr., 1969-72; owner, operator restaurants, Stillwater, Okla., 1972-74; food service dir. Saga Foods, Tulsa, 1975-78; chief exec. officer Hungry Pelican Restaurants, Tulsa, 1979—; instr. Tulsa Jr. Coll. Mem. Nat. Restaurant Assn., Council of Hotel and Restaurant Trainers. Republican. Mormon. Office: Hungry Pelican Restaurants 852 S Harvard Ave Tulsa OK 74112

BRAY, PIERCE, telephone co. exec.; b. Chgo., Jan. 16, 1924; s. Harold A. and Margaret (Maclennan) B.; B.A., U. Chgo., 1948, M.B.A., 1949; m. Maud Dorothy Minto, May 14, 1955; children—Margaret Dorothy, William Harold, Andrew Pierce. Financial analyst Ford Motor Co., Dearborn, Mich., 1949-55; cons. Booz, Allen & Hamilton, Chgo., Manila, P.I., 1955-58; mgr. pricing Cummins Engine Co., Columbus, Ind., 1958-61, controller, 1961-66; v.p. finance Weatherhead Co., Cleve., 1966-67; v.p. treas. Mid-Continent Telephone Corp., Hudson, Ohio, 1967-70, v.p. finance, 1970—, dir., 1976—; dir. Cardinal Fund, 1969—; Instr. finance and econs. U. Detroit, 1952-54. Trustee, Beech Brook Children's Home, 1973—, v.p. fin., 1977-79, pres., 1979—. Served with AUS, 1943-46; PTO. Mem. Financial Execs. Inst., U.S. Ind. Telephone Assn. (chmn. investor relations com. 1974—), Inst. Public Utilities (exec. bd. of adv. com.), Cleve. Treasurers Club, Delta Upsilon. Presbyn. (elder). Clubs: Downtown Athletic (N.Y.C.); Union, Midday (Cleve.); Walloon Lake (Mich.) Yacht (chmn. bd. dirs.), Walloon Country. Home: 31173 Northwood Dr Pepper Pike OH 44124 Office: 100 Executive Pkwy Hudson OH 44236

BRAY, RANDALL CHARLES, savs. and loan exec.; b. Waterloo, Iowa, Jan. 22, 1944; s. Russell LaVerne and May Marie (Neipert) B.; B.A., U. No. Iowa, 1967; m. Margaret Jean Dexter, Aug. 12, 1967; children—Sara, Christopher. Youth dir. Waterloo YMCA, 1967-69; loan officer Bohemian Savs. & Loan, Cedar Rapids, Iowa, 1969-72, v.p., 1972-75, exec. v.p., 1975-76, pres., 1976—. Bd. dirs. Hawkeye Area council Boy Scouts Am., 1977-79; pres. bd. dirs. Central Cedar Rapids YMCA, 1979-80; bd. dirs. Mercy Hosp., Waterloo; exec. com. Greater Downtown Assn., 1980. Mem. Iowa Savs. and Loan League, U.S. League of Savs. Assns., Savs. Instns. Mktg. Soc. Am. Republican. Methodist. Clubs: Elmcrest Country, Rotary. Office: 320 3d St SE Cedar Rapids IA 52401

BRAY, WILLIAM EDWARD, software engr.; b. Pawtucket, R.I., Apr. 4, 1942; s. William C. and Ann Mary Bray; B.S., U. R.I., 1968. Jr. programmer RCA, Greenbelt, Md., 1968-74; analyst Computer Scis. and Technicolor Assos., Seabrook, Md., 1974-77; sr. software analyst Gen. Electric Co., Beltsville, Md., 1977-79, lead user support div. Landsat-D, Cheverly, Md., 1979—; pres. Unique Systems Approaches, cons., 1979—. Served with USNR, 1965-66. Roman Catholic. Clubs: Washington Bridge League, Bridge Club, Inc. Office: 4701 Forbes Blvd Lanham MD 20801

BRAYMAN, HAROLD, writer and public affairs cons.; b. Middleburgh, N.Y., Mar. 10, 1900; s. Channing and Minnie C. (Feeck) B.; A.B., Cornell U., 1920; LL.D., Gettysburg Coll., 1965; m. Martha Witherspoon Wood, Jan. 25, 1930; children—Harold Halliday, Walter Witherspoon. Tchr. Ft. Lee (N.J.) High Sch., 1920-22; reporter Albany (N.Y.) Evening Jour., 1922-24; asst. legislative corr. N.Y. Evening Post, 1924-26, legislative corr., 1926-28, Washington corr., 1928-33; Washington corr. Phila. Evening Ledger, 1934-40; Washington corr. Houston Chronicle and other newspapers, 1940-42; asst. dir. pub. relations dept. E. I. du Pont de Nemours & Co., 1942-44, dir., 1944-65; dir. Continental Am. Life Ins. Co. Chmn., bd. visitors Sch. Pub. Relations and Communications, Boston U., 1961-71; corp. exec. in residence Am. U., spring 1968; bd. dirs. Greater Wilmington Devel. Council; trustee Gettysburg Coll., Wilmington Med. Center. Chmn. 5th Nat. Conf. Bus. Pub. Relations Execs., 1948, chmn. sponsoring com. 1949 conf. Mem. Cornell U. Council, chmn., 1961-63, mem. adv. council grad. sch. bus. and pub. adminstrn., chmn., 1961-65, mem. Cornell Centennial Celebration Com.; trustee Found. Pub. Relations Research and Edn., 1956-62, v.p. 1960-62; v.p. Am. Acad. Achievement, 1967-73. Recipient citation for distinguished service Pub. Relations Soc. Am., 1963; Golden Plate award Am. Acad. Achievement, 1965; named Pub. Relations Prof. of Year, Pub. Relations News, 1963. Mem. U.S. C. of C. (pub. relations adv. com. 1952-54, com. on taxation 1954-60). Rotarian. Clubs: Gridiron (pres. 1941); Nat. Press (pres. 1938), Overseas Writers (Washington); Wilmington, Greenville Country, Wilmington Country (dir. 1952-64); University (N.Y.C.). Author: Corporate Management in a World of Politics, 1967; Developing a Philosophy for Business Action, 1969; (with A.O.H. Grier) Lincoln Club of Delaware: A History, 1970; The President Speaks Off-the-Record, 1976. Editor: Pub. Relations Jour., 1956. Home: Greenville DE 19807 Office: 1250 Montchanin Bldg Wilmington DE 19801

BRAZNELL, GEORGE THOMAS, packaging co. exec.; b. St. Louis, Mar. 20, 1936; s. G. Stuart and Bernice D. Braznell; student Monterey Coll., 1956-57; B.S. in Bus. Adminstrn., U. Mo., 1959; postgrad. Washington U., St. Louis, 1959-60, Lehigh U., 1960; m. Mary Ellen Lydon, Nov. 24, 1960; children—Mary E., Anne M., Ellen V., George T. Ops. dir. Braznell Co., St. Louis, 1959-64; pres. Spray-Chem. Corp., St. Louis, 1964-74; dir. sales, exec. v.p. Theochem Labs., Tampa, Fla., 1974-75; gen. mgr. Kare Kemical div. Interco, Miami, Fla., 1975-79; exec. v.p. Universal Packaging Co., Miami, 1979—. Served with U.S. Army, 1955-57. Mem. Phi Kappa Psi. Clubs: St. Louis, Elks. Home: 5990 SW 9th St Plantation FL 33317 Office: Universal Packaging Co 8200 NW 93d St Miami FL 33166

BREAKSTONE, ROBERT ALBERT, consumer products co. exec.; b. N.Y.C., Feb. 20, 1938; s. Morris E. and Minnie E. (Guon) B.; B.S., City Coll. N.Y., 1960; M.B.A., City U. N.Y., 1964; m. Eileen Fogel, Nov. 5, 1966; children—Warren, Ronald, David. Systems engr. IBM Corp., 1960-64; dir. fin. analysis and mgmt. systems Continental

Copper and Steel Industries, Inc., 1964-69; v.p., treas. Systems Audits, Inc., 1969-70; v.p., group exec. Chase Manhattan Bank, N.Y.C., 1970-74; corp. v.p. Chesebrough-Ponds, Inc., Greenwich, Conn., also pres. Health-Tex subs., 1974—; adj. asst. prof. Pace U., 1963-70; guest speaker and panelist profl. meetings, socs. and group sessions. Mem. Soc. Mgmt. Info. Systems, N.Am. Soc. Corporate Planning, Mu Gamma Tau (pres.). Home: CT 06903 Office: 33 Benedict Pl Greenwich CT 06830

BREALEY, JOHN, electronic exterminating co. exec.; b. Birmingham, Eng., Feb. 26, 1938; came to U.S., 1977; s. John Leslie and Phyllis Kathleen Brealey; student public schs., Eng. Mng. dir. Arden Plant Ltd., Poole, Dorset, Eng., 1959-61, Dorset Metals Ltd., Poole, 1962-68, G.B.A. Ltd., investment and holding co., Freeport, Bahamas, 1968-76; pres. Externa Pulse Internat. Inc., Panama, 1977—; pres. Electronic Exterminators Inc., West Palm Beach, Fla., 1978—. Developer electronic exterminating device. Office: 1442 10th Ct Lake Park FL 33403

BREDIN, J(OHN) BRUCE, real estate exec.; b. Wilmington, Del., June 1, 1914; s. Robert and Margaret (Starrett) B.; student Coll. William and Mary, 1930-32, U. Pa., 1938-40; m. Octavia M. duPont, Aug. 4, 1945; children—Stephanie S. du P. B. Speakman, Margaretta Starrett Bredin Brokaw, Jonathan Bruce, Alletta Bredin-Bell, Laura L. Bredin Cressman, Antonia duPont. Civilian employee U.S. Govt., 1934-38; with E.I. du Pont de Nemours & Co., 1939-45, 49-52; pres. Bredin Realty Co.; dir. Wilmington Trust Co. Participant in Smithsonian expdns. to Africa and West Indies; mem. spl. fine arts com. Dept. State; mem. adv. com. Longwood Found.; mem. devel. com. Woods Hole Oceanographic Inst.; pres. Bredin Found.; trustee Unidel Found., Inc., Wilmington Med. Center, Del. Inst. Med. Edn. and Research, St. Andrew's Sch., Henry Francis du Pont Winterthur Mus., Foxcroft Sch., U. Del.; bd. dirs. U. Del. Library Assos.; chmn. bd. dirs. Sweet Briar Coll.; bd. dirs. Greater Wilmington Devel. Council; bd. visitors Coll. William and Mary. Hon. fellow Smithsonian Instn.; mem. Del. Acad. Medicine (dir.), Hist. Soc. Del. (dir.), Am. Competitive Enterprise System, Confrerie des Chevaliers du Tastevin. Clubs: Vicmead Hunt, Greenville Country, Wilmington, Wilmington Country; Corinthian Yacht (Phila.); Gulf Stream Golf, Everglades, Gulf Stream Bath and Tennis (Palm Beach, Fla.); Nantucket Yacht, Sankaty Head Golf (Nantucket); Met. (Washington). Home: Greenville DE 19807 Office: PO Box 87 Wilmington Trust Bldg Wilmington DE 19899

BREECHER, CHARLES HERMAN, investment adv.; b. Vienna, Austria, July 26, 1916; came to U.S., 1938, naturalized, 1942; s. Siegfried and Elizabeth (Friedlander) B.; Absolutorium in Law, U. Vienna, 1938; LL.B., Lasalle U., 1957; M.B.A., Calif. Western U., 1978, D.B.A., 1979; m. Renee M. Sener, Nov. 7, 1946. Comptroller rys. U.S. Mil. Govt., Germany, 1946-49; transport and industry attache U.S. High Commn. and U.S. Embassy, Bonn, Germany, 1950-57; econ. counselor U.S. Mission to NATO, Paris, 1961-66; dir. devel. planning for Far East, Africa, Europe and Middle East, AID, State Dept., Washington, 1966-74; cons. investments, Washington, 1974—; Mem. adv. council on econ. affairs, mem. tax policy subcom. Republican Nat. Com. Served with inf. U.S. Army, 1942-45. Recipient Meritorious Service award AID/State Dept., 1960, Superior Honor award, 1970. Mem. Am. Soc. Internat. Law, Internat. Platform Assn., Am. Security Council. Roman Catholic. Clubs: Rep. Senatorial (charter), Rep. Congressional (charter). Author: Oil—The Big Rip-off, 1975; weekly fin. columnist Del. Coast Press, 1974—. Home: 113 Columbia Ave Rehoboth Beach DE 19971 Office: 1654 32d St Washington DC 20007

BREED, WILLIAM CONSTABLE, III, mgmt. co. exec.; b. N.Y.C., Feb. 18, 1935; s. William Constable and Ellen Harvey (Whitman) B.; B.A., Middlebury Coll., 1957; m. Rebecca Sherridan Sutter, Jan. 4, 1958; children—William C., Alan W., Michael S., Rebecca S. Asst. sec. Marine Midland Trust Co. of N.Y., N.Y.C., 1960-67; mgr. investment adv. dept. F. Eberstadt & Co., N.Y.C., 1967-69; pres. Cannell, Breed & Musser, N.Y.C., 1969-70; v.p. Channing Mgmt. Co., N.Y.C., 1970-74; pres. Edgewood Mgmt. Co., N.Y.C., 1974—. Bd. dirs. Manhattan Eye, Ear and Throat Hosp., 1967—; pres., dir. Stony Wold-Herbert Fund, N.Y.C., 1967—. Served with U.S. Army, 1958-60. Republican. Episcopalian. Clubs: Racquet and Tennis, Round Hill, Field of Greenwich. Home: 38 Calhoun Dr Greenwich CT 06830 Office: 201 E 42d St New York NY 10017

BREEDING, ROBERT EUGENE, SR., aerospace. co. exec.; b. Schuyler, Nebr., June 25, 1927; s. Clyde Elias and Grace Katheryn (Valish) B.; A.S. in Tool Engring., Hartford State Tech. Coll., 1955; B.S. cum laude, U. Hartford, 1955-59; grad., mgmt. devel. program Rensselaer Poly. Inst., 1968; m. Mary Ann Caramazza, June 26, 1947; children—Robert Eugene, Brian L., Mary Lou. Quality mgr. Bigelow-Sanford Textile Co., Enfield, Conn., 1948-50, Airline Mfg. Co., Warehouse Point, Conn., 1952-54; v.p. space systems Hamilton Standard div. United Aircraft Corp., Windsor Locks, Conn., 1954—. Served to 2d lt. 1st Cav. Div., AUS, 1945-48, 1st lt. 43d Inf. Div., 1950-52. Recipient Certificate of Appreciation, NASA, 1969, Pub. Service award, 1973; Distinguished Alumnus award U. Hartford, 1972; Victor Prather award Am. Astronautical Soc., 1973; Most Outstanding Alumnus award Hartford State Tech. Coll., 1978. Mem. Am. Inst. Aeros. and Astronautics, Am. Astronautical Soc., Internat. Astronautical Acad., Explorer's Club. Office: Hamilton Standard Div Bradley Field Windsor Locks CT 06096

BREEDLOVE, HOWELL ADAMS, JR., steel co. exec.; b. Monroe, Ga., June 25, 1935; s. Howell Adams and Annise Bell (Parker) B.; student Oglethorpe U., 1953-55; B.B.A., Emory U., 1957; grad. sr. exec. program M.I.T., 1976; m. Ann Forsyth Merkle, Sept. 3, 1955; children—Mark Howell, Alan Merkle, William Parker, Ann Marie, John Adams, Mary Helen. Trainee in fin. mgmt. Gen. Electric Co., Schenectady, 1957-59; various fin. positions Monsanto Co., Fla., N.Y. State, Conn., Mo., 1959-68, controller packaging div., St. Louis, 1968-71; controller Monsanto Comml. Products Co., St. Louis, 1971-73; controller Copperweld Corp., Pitts., 1973-74, v.p. and controller, 1974-75, dir., 1974, v.p. fin. and adminstrn., 1975, sr. v.p. fin. and adminstrn., 1975, exec. v.p., 1975—; dir. Equimark Corp./Equibank, Pitts., 1980—. Mem. fin. com. SW Pa. council Girl Scouts U.S.A., 1973-75; bd. dirs. YMCA, Pitts., 1979—. Mem. Am. Iron and Steel Inst., Steel Service Center Inst., Fin. Execs. Inst. Roman Catholic. Clubs: Duquesne, St. Clair Country, Oakmont Country, Rolling Rock. Home: 2015 Blairmont Dr Pittsburgh PA 15241 Office: Two Oliver Plaza Pittsburgh PA 15222

BREEDLOVE, JAMES GERALD, bus. exec.; b. Opp, Ala., Nov. 7, 1920; s. E. Marvin and Mary (Jeffcoat) B.; B. Ceramic Engring., Ga. Inst. Tech., 1950; m. Carolyn Elizabeth Archer, Nov. 27, 1947; children—Mary Carolyn Breedlove Peacock, Sally Elizabeth Breedlove Byrne, Donna Ellen. Ceramic engr. Tech. Ceramic Products div. 3M Co., Chattanooga, 1950-53, mgr. Titania div. lab., 1953-63, mgr. new product devel. lab., 1963-68, research supr., St. Paul, 1968—. Chief aux. police, Signal Mountain, Tenn., 1964-73. Served to sgt. AUS, 1941-45. Recipient Distinguished Community Service award Signal Mountain Lions Club, 1968. Mem. Am. Ceramic Soc., Inst. Ceramic Engrs. Democrat. Episcopalian. Patents and publs. in fields tech. ceramics, dielectrics, porcelain enamels. Inventor composite armor plate (ceramic-glass fiber). Home: 88 Walden St Burnsville MN 55337 Office: 3M Co Tech Ceramic Products Div Saint Paul MN 55101

BREEN, JOHN GERALD, mfg. co. exec.; b. Cleve., July 21, 1934; s. Hugh Gerald and Margaret Cecelia (Bonner) B.; B.S., John Carroll U., 1956; M.B.A., Case Western Res. U., 1962; m. Mary Jane Brubach, Apr. 12, 1958; children—Kathleen Anne, John Patrick, James Phillip, David Hugh, Anne Margaret. With Clevite Corp., Cleve., 1957-73, gen. mgr. foil div., 1969-73, gen. mgr. engine parts div., 1973-74; group v.p. indsl. group Gould Inc., Rolling Meadows, Ill., 1974-77; exec. v.p. Sherwin-Williams, Cleve., 1977-79, pres., chief exec. officer, 1979, chmn., pres., chief exec. officer, 1980—; dir. Parker-Hannifan Corp., Nat. City Bank, Clark Rubber & Plastics Co. Mem. vis. com. Case Western Res. U.; trustee John Carroll U.; bd. advisors Notre Dame Coll. Served with U.S. Army, 1956-57. Clubs: Pepper Pike, Union, Cleve. Skating (Cleve.). Home: 2727 Cranlyn Rd Shaker Heights OH 44122 Office: 101 Prospect Ave NW Cleveland OH 44115

BREEN, MARVIN GOLDEN, stock broker; b. New Orleans, Aug. 11, 1930; s. Nathaniel and Bluma (Teles) B.; B.S., La. State U., 1955; m. Carole Rambach, Dec. 23, 1956; children—Robin, Neff. Trainee Merrill Lynch Pierce Fenner & Smith, New Orleans, 1955, account exec., 1956-69, mgmt. staff, N.Y.C., 1969-70, partner, 1965, v.p., 1971—, br. mgr., Clayton, Mo., 1970-75; mem. Chgo. Bd. Options Exchange, 1975—; mem. Pacific Stock Exchange, 1976—, mem. governing com., 1977—. Served to capt. AUS, 1950-53. Home: 18 Noche Vista Ln Tiburon CA 94920 Office: Merrill Lynch Pierce Fenner & Smith 320 California St San Francisco CA 94104

BREHM, WILLIAM KEITH, consulting co. exec.; b. Dearborn, Mich., Mar. 29, 1929; s. Walter E. and Lucille (Hankinson) B.; B.S. with honors in Math., U. Mich., 1950, M.S. in Math., 1952; m. Delores Soderquist, June 28, 1952; children—Eric William, Lisa Karen. Asst. sec. Army, Dept. Army, Washington, 1968-70; v.p. corp. devel. Dart Industries, Los Angeles, 1970-73; asst. sec. def. Dept. Def., Washington, 1973-77; exec. v.p. Computer Network Corp., Washington, 1977-80; chmn. bd. Systems Research & Applications Corp., Arlington, Va., 1980—; cons. Dept. Def.; bd. visitors Nat. Def. U. Mem. parents' council Mary Washington Coll.; bd. dirs. Washington chpt. ARC. Recipient Disting. Civilian Service award Dept. Army; Disting. Public Service award Dept. Def. Mem. Ops. Research Soc. Am. Home: 4061 Ridgeview Circle Arlington VA 22207 Office: 2425 Wilson Blvd Arlington VA 22201

BREITBARTH, S. ROBERT, wire and cable cos. exec.; b. Newark, July 15, 1925; B.E.E., Cornell U., 1949; m. Laurel Patricia Stroh, Oct. 30, 1949; children—Meredith Jane, Jill Gretchen. Vice pres. Gen. Cable Corp., Greenwich, Conn., 1966-76, exec. v.p., dir., 1976-78; pres., dir. Gen. Cable Internat. Inc., 1979—; pres. Gen. Cable Export Corp., Greenwich, 1973-77, 79—; v.p. GK Techs., Inc., 1979—; dir. Cables Comunicaciones, S.A., Spain, Gen. Cable Ceat, S.A., Spain, Plasmica S.A., Spain, Saenger S.A., Spain; dir., v.p., Ceat Gen. de Colombia, Colombia; dir. pres. Electrofinance Ltd., Cayman Island; dir., v.p., Industria Venezolano de Cables Electricos, C.A., Venezuela; dir. Phillips Cables Ltd., Can. Mem. adv. bd. Council Americas; mem. conf. bd. Sr. Internat. Execs. Survey Panel. Sec., Stony Point Assn., Westport, Conn., 1973-75, treas., 1975-76, pres., 1976-77. Served with USAAF, 1944-46. Mem. Center Inter-Am. Relations, NAM (internat. investment subcom.), Wire Assn., U.S.-Spain C. of C. (dir., chmn. U.S. investment in Spain com.), IEEE, Cornell Soc. Engrs. Republican. Home: 2 Stony Point Westport CT 06880 Office: 500 W Putnam Ave Greenwich CT 06830

BREITEL, VIVIAN HOLLANDER, bank exec.; b. Albany, N.Y.; d. Charles David and Jeanne (Hollander) B.; B.A. with highest praise, U. Mich., 1966; M.A. in History, Harvard U., 1967. Teaching fellow in history Harvard U., 1968-69; lectr. in European history Boston Coll., 1971-74; mgmt. trainee Chem. Bank, N.Y.C., 1974-75, account officer, 1975-79, v.p., 1979—. Harvard traveling fellow, 1969-71. Mem. Phi Beta Kappa.

BREITENBECK, GREGORY ALLAN, aircraft co. exec.; b. Culver City, Calif., Sept. 9, 1946; s. John Woodrow and Elizabeth Marie (Quinsler) B.; A.A., Palm Beach Jr. Coll., 1966; B.A. in Polit. Sci., Fla. State U., 1968; M.A. in Internat. Relations, Boston U., 1974; M.B.A. in Internat. Mktg., Fla. Atlantic U., 1979; m. Elaine Joanne Windisch, July 14, 1975. Engring. aide Govt. Products div. Pratt & Whitney Aircraft, West Palm Beach, Fla., 1968-69, tech. reports engr., 1973-76, internat. market researcher, 1976-77, internat. mktg. mgr., 1977-79; regional dir. mktg. United Technologies (Europe), Brussels, 1979-81; internat. mktg. dir. govt. products div. Pratt & Whitney Aircraft, West Palm Beach, 1981—. Served with USAF, 1969-73. Recipient Harvard Book award, 1965; named Outstanding Freshman, Palm Beach Jr. Coll., 1965; Harold J. Ray Meml. award for mktg. Pratt & Whitney Aircraft, 1979. Mem. Assn. M.B.A. Execs., Phi Theta Kappa, Phi Kappa Phi, Beta Gamma Sigma. Clubs: La Coquille (Palm Beach); Cercle des Nations (Brussels). Home: 8041 Saint John W Boynton Beach FL 33437 Office: Govt Products Div Pratt & Whitney Aircraft PO Box 2691 West Palm Beach FL 33402

BREITLING, JULIUS, fin. cons. co. exec.; b. N.Y.C., Apr. 14, 1932; s. Carl and Minnie (Fleischman) B.; B.S. in Mech. Engring., CCNY, 1959; M.B.A. in Mgmt. Sci., Iona Coll., New Rochelle, N.Y., 1968; m. Ariane Henningson, Apr. 18, 1968. Sr. valuation engr. N.Y. Public Service Commn., 1959-67; sr. cons. Ebasco Services Inc., N.Y.C., 1967-69, prin. valuation cons., 1970-72; sr. engr. Jackson & Moreland div. United Engrs. & Constructors, Boston, 1969-70; exec. cons. Commonwealth Mgmt. Cons., N.Y.C., 1972-73; v.p. fin. mgmt. Ebasco Bus. Cons. Co., N.Y.C., 1973—. Served with U.S. Army 1952-54. Registered profl. engr., N.Y., Mass., Tex., Va. Sr. mem. Am. Soc. Appraisers; mem. Am. Gas Assn. (tech. assn. depreciation com.), Internat. Right of Way Assn., Nat. Soc. Profl. Engrs., N.Y. State Soc. Profl. Engrs. Author papers, reports in field; patentee talking photo album. Office: 2 World Trade Center New York NY 10048

BREMER, JOHN PAUL, mgmt. cons. co. exec.; b. St. Louis, Apr. 11, 1926; s. Jesse Currier and Eunice Sibylla (Schaus) B.; student U. Ill., 1946-47, U. Lausanne, 1947-48, U. Sorbonne, Paris, 1948; M.B.A., U. Chgo., 1955. Sales, tech. rep. IBM Corp., Washington, 1955-58; sr. data processing cons. Vaule & Co., Providence, 1958-63; co-founder, pres. Systemation, Inc., Boston, 1963-71; sr. cons., mgr. Mgmt. Cons. Group, Keane Assos., Wellesley, Mass., 1971-74; pres. Bremer Assos., Inc., Boston, 1974—. Served with AUS, 1944-46. Lutheran. Club: Charles River Yacht (vice-commodore). Home: 125 Newbury St Boston MA 02116 Office: 115 Newbury St Boston MA 02116

BREMERMANN, HERBERT JOHN, JR., ins. exec.; b. New Orleans, Dec. 9, 1922; s. Herbert John and Hilda Marie (Lemarie) B.; A.B., Tulane U., 1944, LL.B., 1949; m. Mary Gibson Parlour, Feb. 14, 1950; children—Eve P., Herbert John III. Spl. agt. FBI, 1949-53; with Black, Rogers & Co., New Orleans, 1953-56; with Md. Casualty Co., Balt., 1956—, beginning as resident v.p., successively v.p. casualty div., v.p. mktg. div., exec. v.p., 1956-76, pres., chief exec. officer, 1976—, chmn. bd., 1979—; sr. v.p., dir. Am. Gen. Corp., Houston; dir. Md. Nat. Bank, Md. Nat. Corp., Balt. Am. Ins. Assn., Ins. Services Office, Ins. Info. Inst., N.Y.C. Chmn. Pres.'s Council, Tulane U.; asso. gen. chmn. United Way of Central Md., 1979, now dir.; bd. dirs. Keswick Home for Incurables, Assn. Ind. Colls. in Md., Inc.; trustee Goucher Coll.; mem. Greater Balt. Com. Served to capt. USMC, 1943-46. Named Outstanding Alumnus, Tulane U. Sch. Law, 1977. Clubs: Balt. Country, Center, Maryland (Balt.). Office: 3910 Keswick Rd Baltimore MD 21211

BREMSER, GEORGE, JR., corporate exec.; b. Newark, May 26, 1928; s. George and Virginia (Christian) B.; B.A., Yale U., 1949; postgrad. U. Miami, 1959; M.B.A., N.Y. U., 1962; m. Marie Sundman, June 21, 1952 (div. July 1979); children—Christian Frederick, Priscilla Suzanne, Martha Anne, Sarah Elizabeth. Sales trainee Pitts. Plate Glass, South Bend, Ind., 1949-50; with McCann-Erickson, Inc., N.Y.C., 1952-61, asst. gen. mgr., Bogota, Colombia, 1955, gen. mgr., 1955-57, account supr., N.Y.C., 1958, v.p. mgr., Miami, Fla., 1959-61; asso. product mgr. Maxwell House div. Gen. Foods Corp., White Plains, N.Y., 1961-62, product mgr., 1962-63, advt. merchandising mgr., 1963-64, mktg. dir. Internat. div., 1964, area dir. Internat. div., 1965-66, asst. gen. mgr. Internat. div., 1966-67, v.p., gen. mgr. Gen. Foods Europe, 1967, pres. Gen. Foods Internat., 1967-71; v.p. Gen. Foods Corp., 1968-70, group v.p., 1970-71; pres., chief exec. officer, dir. Texstar Corp., Grand Prairie, Tex., 1971—, chmn. bd., 1972—; dir. C.I. Convertible Fund, 1972-74, Butler Internat., Inc. Vice pres. Citizens Com. for Conservation. New Canaan, Conn.; county committeeman 1st dist. Democratic Com., Ridgewood, N.J., 1962-63; town councilman, New Canaan, 1969-73; trustee Union Ch. Bogota (Colombia), 1956-57; bd. dirs. Soc. for Values in Higher Edn. Served to 2d lt. USMCR, 1950-52; capt. Res. Mem. New Canaan Audubon Soc. (dir.), Phi Beta Kappa, Beta Gamma Sigma, Beta Theta Pi. Congregationalist. Clubs: Brook, Met., Yale (N.Y.C.); New Canaan Field, New Canaan Winter, Country of New Canaan, Block Island; Great S.W. Golf (Dallas); Shady Oaks (Ft. Worth). Home: 705 Weed St New Canaan CT 06840 Office: 802 Ave J East Grand Prairie TX 75050

BRENNAN, DONALD P., paper co. exec.; b. N.Y.C., Dec. 31, 1940; s. Patrick James and Mary B.; B.S. in Marine Sci., SUNY, 1961; M.B.A., City U. N.Y., 1966, doctoral candidate in ops. research, 1967-70; married Sept. 22, 1962; children—Eileen, Donald, Maureen, Patrick, Jonahthan, Erin. Sr. planning analyst Corning (N.Y.) Glass Works, 1966-67; supr. mktg. planning Internat. Paper Co., N.Y.C., 1967-69, mgr. mktg. planning, 1969, dir. mktg. planning, 1969-71, v.p. container board div., 1971-72, Kraft Paper Bus. div., 1972-74, v.p. employee relations, 1974-76, exec. v.p. human resources and external affairs, 1976-77, exec. v.p. planning and adminstrn., 1977, exec. v.p. paper and packaging bus., 1977—, also dir.; chmn. bd. Bodcaw Co.; dir. Gen. Crude Oil. Trustee, Mary Baldwin Coll.; mem. Pres.'s Commn. on Exec. Exchange, 1977—. Served with USN, 1961-66; lt. comdr. Res. ret. Office: Internat Paper Co 220 E 42 St New York NY 10017

BRENNAN, EDWARD A., retail co. exec.; b. 1934; B.A., Marquette U., 1955; married. Buyer, Benson Rixon Co., 1955-56; with Sears, Roebuck & Co., 1956—, store mgr., Balt., 1967-69, asst. gen. mgr. N.Y. group, 1969-72, gen. mgr. Western N.Y. group, 1972-75, adminstrv. asst. to exec. v.p. East, 1975-76, gen. mgr. Boston group, 1976-78, exec. v.p. South, 1978-80, pres., 1980-81, chmn., chief exec. officer Sears Mdse. Group, 1981—, also dir.; dir. Allstate Ins. Co., Seraco Enterprises, Inc. Office: Sears Roebuck & Co Sears Tower Chicago IL 60684

BRENNAN, JAMES JOHN, coll. ofcl.; b. Bronx, N.Y., Nov. 29, 1948; s. Peter E. and Kathleen (Doroty) B.; A.A., St. John's U., 1969; B.S., Mercy Coll., 1978; M.B.A., L.I. U., 1980. Adminstr. drug and alcohol abuse program U.S. Army, Romulus, N.Y., 1971-73; coordinator of fed. funded program N.Y.C. Dept. of Parks, Bronx, 1973-77; coordinator adminstrv. services Mercy Coll., Bronx, 1977-80, dir. grants, 1980—; v.p. Brenbell Inc. Served with U.S. Army, 1971-73. Mem. Am. Mgmt. Assn., Am. Legion, Student Personnel Assn. N.Y. State. Democrat. Home: 676 Neried Ave Bronx NY 10470 Office: 2250 Williamsbridge Rd Bronx NY 10469

BRENNAN, JOSEPH CANTWELL, banker; b. Roslyn, N.Y. Sept. 26, 1910; s. Joseph P. and Evangeline (Walsh) B.; student LaSalle Mil. Acad., 1929; Ph.B., Georgetown U., 1933; m. Anne C. Patterson, Sept. 7, 1935; 1 dau, Constance C. With Mfrs. Trust Co., 1933-45, asst. sec., 1940-45; asst. treas. Bankers Trust Co., 1946-49, asst. v.p., 1949-51, v.p., 1951-52; v.p., asst. to pres. Emigrant Savs. Bank, N.Y.C., 1953-56, pres., 1957-67, chmn. bd., 1967-78, chmn. exec. com., 1979—, also trustee; dir. St. Joseph's Union, S.I., Savs. Patterson Fuel Oil Co., Floral Park, N.Y., Diamond Internat. Corp.; mem. Project Fin. Agy. of N.Y. State. Mem. Cardinals Com. of the Laity; dir. Cath. Youth Orgn., N.Y.C.; bd. dirs. United Hosp. Fund N.Y.; chmn. bd. N.Y.C. Community Preservation Corp. Served as lt. comdr. USNR, 1942-46. Decorated Bronze Star medal; recipient Nat. Brotherhood award NCCJ, 1969; Gold medal Cath. Youth Orgn., 1974; Good Scout award Boy Scouts Am., 1975; Knight of Malta. Mem. Friendly Sons of St. Patrick (treas.). Clubs: Union League; Westhampton Country. Home: 200 E 66th St New York NY 10021 Office: 5 E 42d St New York NY 10017

BRENNAN, PETER JOHN, pub. co. exec.; b. Dublin, Ireland, July 30, 1931; came to U.S., 1939, naturalized, 1957; s. Joseph Desmond and Ethna Mary (McDonald) B.; B.Chem.Engring., Cath. U. Am., 1953; m. Joan Tristram Hiller, May 15, 1954 (dec.); children—Phillip Alexander (dec.), Joan-Sarane Desmond, Peter Nicholas; m. 2d, Jilda F. Kicak, Oct. 27, 1973. Chem. engr. Union Bag & Paper Corp., Savannah, Ga., 1953-58; nuclear engr. Westinghouse Electric Co., Pitts., 1958-59; various editorial positions Chem. Engring. mag., N.Y.C., Houston, Phila., 1959-67; chief editor Engr. mag., N.Y.C., 1967-71; editor-pub. UN Indsl. Devel. Orgn., Vienna, Austria, 1971-73, sr. advisor to UNIDO, Overseas Pvt. Investment Corp., N.Y.C., 1978-79; chief editor Instruments & Control Systems mag., Radnor, Pa., 1973-75; founding editor Industria Quimica, Morristown, N.J., 1969, Internat. Instrumentation, Great Neck, N.Y., 1976; pres., pub. Worldtech Info. Services, N.Y.C., 1976—; cons. internat., tech. matters, 1970—. Recipient Am. Bus. Press Editorial Achievement award, 1976. Mem. N.Y. Bus. Press Editors (past dir., incorporator), World Trade Writers Assn. Democrat. Roman Catholic. Club: Overseas Press. Contbr. numerous articles on fin. and bus. to profl. jours. Office: PO Box 1345 Gracie Station New York NY 10028

BRENNAN, WILLIAM MARTIN, constrn. co. exec.; b. Wilkes Barre, Pa., June 15, 1950; s. William Martin and Lena Josephine B.; B.S.C.E., Pa. State U., 1972; postgrad. in bus. adminstrn. Pace U., N.Y.C., 1980. Field engr. Washington Dept. Hyws., 1971; asst. supt. Turner Constrn. Co., Fairfield, Conn., 1972-74; cost/scheduling engr. AT&T, Brominster, N.J., 1974-76; sr. project mgmt. control systems engr. N.Y. ter. Turner Constrn. Co., N.Y.C., 1976-79, corp. dir. project cost and control systems, dir. project. fin. reporting, 1979-80, project mgr., 1980—; cons. residential bdlg. constrn.; profl. ski instr., Hunter, N.Y. Active, Mus. Modern Art, Mus. Natural History. Mem. Pa. State Alumni Assn., ASCE (student chpt.), Eastern Profl. Ski Instr.'s Assn., Phi Kappa Phi, Tau Beta Pi, Sigma Tau (pres. Pa. State

U. chpt. 1972), Chi Epsilon (sec. Pa. State U. chpt. 1972), Phi Eta Sigma. Democrat. Roman Catholic. Clubs: Hackensack (N.J.) Golf, Hackensack Tennis, Riverview Racquet. Home: 321 Prospect Ave Hackensack NJ 07601 Office: 150 E 42d St New York NY 10017

BRENNEMAN, RALPH FRANCIS, mfg. co. exec.; b. Cedar Rapids, Iowa, Feb. 6, 1932; s. Ernest E. and Mary N. (Webster) Brenneman; m. Sandra Lee Matthews, Dec. 10, 1955; children—Brad, Lisa, Scott, Erin, R. David. Buyer, Collins Radio Co., 1954-59; asst. mgr. Deeco Inc., 1959-63; purchasing mgr. Collins Radio Co., 1963-73; founded Brenneman & Asso. Inc., 1973—. Mem. Chs. United, Cedar Rapids/Marion, Iowa; past pres. Lutheran Interparish Ministry, chmn. joint purchasing com.; chmn. task force for aux. funding Luth. Family Service; benevolence rep. Iowa Synod, Luth. Ch. in Am. Mem. Elks, Am. Assn. Small Businessmen, IEEE. Home: 1915 McGowan Blvd Marion IA 52302 Office: 201 35th St Marion IA 52302

BRENNEN, WILLIAM STUART, banker; b. Pitts., May 15, 1924; s. William M. and Irene (MacFarland) B.; B.S., U.S. Merchant Marine Acad., 1944; A.B., Columbia, 1947, LL.B., 1949; m. Justine Bright, Dec. 15, 1951; children—Stephen, Robert. Admitted to N.Y. bar, 1949; with firm Dow & Symmers, 1949-51, N.Y. State Banking Dept., 1951-53; 1st dept. supt. banks N.Y. State, 1959-63; with Greenwich Savs. Bank, N.Y.C., 1963—, pres., 1969—, chmn. bd., 1972—, also trustee; bd. memberships Found. Mortgage Co.; Mem. Ave. of Americas Assn., Real Estate Bd. N.Y., N.Y.C. Rent Guidelines Bd., Broadway Assn., Citizens Budget Commn., Assn. for Better N.Y., St. Vincent's Hosp.; chmn. bd. N.Y.C. Indsl. Devel. Agy.; pres. Greater N.Y. Safety Com. Republican. Episcopalian. Office: Greenwich Bank 1356 Broadway New York NY 10018*

BRENNER, JOSEPH DONALD, mfg. co. exec.; b. Carlisle, Pa., Mar. 1, 1917; s. Clyde E. and Pearl (Hastings) B.; Ph.B., Dickinson Coll., 1939; M.B.A., Harvard U., 1941; m. Jane B. Wimett, June 24, 1944; children—Margaret E. Brenner Bushey, Joseph Donald, Nancy E., Katherine H. Mfg. mgr. AMP Inc., Harrisburg, Pa., 1947, chief engr., asst. div. mgr., 1950-55, div. mgr. Automatic Machine div., 1955-58, ops. mgr., 1958-61, v.p. mfg. divs., 1961-67, corporate v.p. mfg., 1967-71, v.p. ops., 1971, pres., 1971—, chief exec. officer, 1972—; dir. Farmers Trust Co., Carlisle, United Telephone Co. of Pa., United Telecommunications Inc. Bd. dirs. Carlisle, Carlisle Hosp. Served to lt. USNR, 1944-46. Mem. Machinery Allied Products Inst. (exec. com.). Phi Kappa Sigma. Presbyterian. Home: 1051 Trindle Rd Carlisle PA 17013 Office: Eisenhower Blvd Box 3608 Harrisburg PA 17105

BRENNER, PAUL JAMES, steel co. ofcl.; b. Youngstown, Ohio, Jan. 6, 1943; s. Earl William and Margaret B.; B.S. in Math., A.B. in Edn., Youngstown State U., 1965; m. Barbara L. Schulz, Aug. 28, 1965; children—Deanne, Tracy, Wendy. Tchr. high sch. math., Struthers, Ohio, 1965-68; apprentice instr. Youngstown Sheet and Tube Co. (Ohio), 1968-71, conf. leader, 1971-74, mgmt. devel. specialist, 1974-76, mgr. supervisory tng., 1976-77; supr. tng. Rockwell Internat., Galesburg, Ill., 1977-78, Gt. Lakes Steel Co., Detroit, 1978—. First aid instr. ARC; CPR instr. Am. Heart Assn.; Hi-Y sponsor YMCA; umpire and coach softball and hardball. Mem. Struthers Ednl. Assn. (exec. com. 1966-67, chmn. contl. revision com. 1966-67, fin. chmn. 1966-68), N.E. Ohio Tchrs. Assn., Ohio Edn. Assn., Mahoning Valley Indsl. Mgmt. Assn., Nat. Mgmt. Assn. (mem. of yr. Youngstown Sheet and Tube chpt. 1975-76, pres., del. Keystone council, seminar chmn., bd. dirs.), Am. Soc. Tng. and Devel., Personnel Mgmt. Club. Republican. Roman Catholic. Clubs: Kiwanis Internat., Rotary (sponsor Interact Club). Editor local co. paper, 1978—. Home: 8187 Sandpiper Dr Canton MI 48187 Office: Great Lakes Steel Co Detroit MI 48229

BRENNER, RICHARD MICHAEL, bus. cons. exec.; b. Teaneck, N.J., June 12, 1948; s. Lawrence Martin and Dorothy Ruth (Botwen) B.; B.S., Fairleigh Dickinson U., 1972; m. Elizabeth Ann Ortz, Oct. 2, 1971. Controller, Autographic Bus. Forms, Inc., Mahwah, N.J., 1970-73; ops. center controller Nat. BankAmericard, Inc., San Mateo, Calif., 1973-74; dir. accounting container div. ITEL Corp., San Francisco, 1974-75, dir. accounting rail div., 1976-78, dir. fin. planning and adminstrn. rail div., 1978; owner, mgr. Brenner, Fassler & Co., Foster City, Calif., 1978—; v.p. U.S. Rail Services subs. U.S. Leasing Internat., Inc., 1979—. Clubs: Bayside Racquet, Island Sailing. Home: 1124 Halsey Blvd Foster City CA 94404 Office: 1124 Halsey Blvd Foster City CA 94404 also 633 Battery St San Francisco CA 94111

BRENTANO, LEWIS DOYLE, computer mfg. co. exec.; b. Santa Monica, Calif., May 22, 1949; s. August Doyle and Helen Lorraine (Hart) B.; B.S. in Aero. Engring., U. Notre Dame, 1971; M.S., Stanford U., 1973; postgrad. U. Calif., Berkeley, 1975—. Asst. engr. chem. systems div. United Technology Corp., Sunnyvale, Calif., 1972-75; mgr. data processing and software devel. URS/Blume Assos., San Francisco, 1975-77; mktg. mgr. Prime Computer, Wellesley, Mass., 1977—. Bd. dirs. Newton Country Players (Mass.), 1978-79. Mem. ASME, AIAA, Sierra Club. Home: 9 Maple Rd Wellesley MA 02181

BRENTON, WILLIAM HENRY, banker; b. Dallas Center, Iowa, June 30, 1924; s. Woodward Harold and Etta Spurgeon B.; B.S.C., U. Iowa, 1947; grad. Advanced Mgmt. Program, Harvard U., 1971; m. Natalie Graham, June 15, 1948; children—Woodward Graham, Natalie Gay, William Henry. Cashier, N.W. Brenton Nat. Bank, 1955, v.p., 1955-56, exec. v.p., 1956-58, pres., 1958-79; treas. Brenton Banks, Inc., 1955-64, pres., 1964-69, chmn. bd., 1969—; dir. Employers Mut. Cos. Bd. dirs. Iowa Methodist Hosp., trustee Drake U., Coffin Fine Arts Trust, Des Moines Art Center; v.p. Greater Des Moines Com.; pres. Iowa Nat. Heritage Found. Served with USAAF, 1943-45. Mem. Am. Bankers Assn., Assn. Registered Bank Holding Co., Iowa Bankers Assn., Beta Gamma Sigma. Clubs: Des Moines, Wakonda, Harvard, Univ., Chgo. Office: 2840 Ingersoll Des Moines IA 50312

BRES, PHILIP WAYNE, mgmt. services co. exec.; b. Beaumont, Tex., Mar. 6, 1950; s. DeFrance R. Bres and Edna Gene (Griffith) Rodemacher; B.B.A. with honors, Lamar U., 1972; M.B.A., Stephen F. Austin State U., 1973; m. Kathryn Anne Perkins, Sept. 8, 1973. Distbn. mgr., bus. mgmt. mgr. Mazda Motors Am., Houston, 1973-75; analyst cons. C.H. McCormack & Assos., Houston, 1975-76; asso. Frank Gillman Pontiac Co., Houston, 1976-79; sales rep. David Taylor Cadillac Co., Houston, 1979-80; pres. Braintrust Inc.; mgmt. services, Houston, 1980—. Mem. Am. Mktg. Assn., Am. Soc. Profl. Cons., Houston C. of C., Phi Kappa Phi, Phi Eta Sigma. Home and Office: 13032 Clarewood Dr Houston TX 77072

BRESCIANI, BESSIE MARTHA, banker; b. S.D., June 29, 1921; d. Anton John and Rose (Peterka) Vavra; student Chillicothe Bus. Coll., 1939-40, Modesto Jr. Coll., 1962-65, Pacific Coast Banking Sch., U. Wash., 1969-71; m. Louis L. Bresciani, Sept. 29, 1973; 1 dau., Helen Marie Williams. With Bank of Am., v.p., mgr. br., Modesto, Calif., 1978—. Mem. Modesto City Housing Rehab. Com.; bd. dirs. Girl Scouts U.S., 1978—, YMCA, 1980—. Mem. Nat. Assn. Bank Women, Am. Inst. Banking, Modesto C. of C. (past dir.). Republican. Roman Catholic. Clubs: Oakdale Golf and Country, Carousel Dance. Office: 1419 J St Modesto CA 95354

BRESLER, CHARLES SHELDON, real estate exec.; b. Phila., July 11, 1927; s. Samuel Harvey and Kathrine Louise Bresler; B.S. in Bus. Adminstrn., U. Md., 1949, M.A. in Urban Affairs, 1976; M.B.A., Southwestern U., 1974; m. Fleur Straus, Jan. 10, 1954; children—Sidney, Susan, Lynne, Edward, William, Carol. Chmn., chief exec. officer Bresler & Reiner Inc., Washington, 1955—; dir. Security Nat. Bank, Am. Med. Affiliates. Mem. Md. Legislature, 1962-65, Md. Senate, 1965-66; Md. nat. relations officer, spl. asst. to gov. State of Md., 1967-68. Served with Intelligence, U.S. Army, 1944-48. Clubs: Masons, Scottish Rite, Shriners. Home: 3217 Farmington Dr Chevy Chase MD 20015 Office: 401 M St SW Washington DC 20024

BRESSLER, RICHARD MAIN, r.r. exec.; b. Wayne, Nebr., Oct. 8, 1930; s. John T. and Helen (Main) B.; B.A., Darmouth Coll., 1952; m. Carol Gregory Leighton, Sept. 20, 1952; children—Kristin M., Alan L. With Gen. Electric Co., 1952-68; v.p., treas. Am. Airlines Inc., 1968-72, sr. v.p., 1972-73; v.p. finance Atlantic Richfield Co., Los Angeles, 1973-75, sr. v.p. fin., 1975-77; pres. Arco Chem. Co., 1977-78, exec. v.p., 1978-80; pres., chief exec. officer Burlington No., Inc., St. Paul, 1980—; dir. Gen. Mills, Inc., Scott Paper Co., Atlantic Richfield Co.; trustee Penn Mut. Life Ins. Co. Office: Burlington No Inc 176 E Fifth St Saint Paul MN 55101*

BRETT, ARTHUR CUSHMAN, JR., bank exec.; b. Bronxville, N.Y., Mar. 23, 1928; s. Arthur Cushman and Mary Kathryn (Clark) B.; B.S., Fordham U., 1953; M.B.A., N.Y. U., 1959; postgrad. Dartmouth Coll., 1962-63, Internat. Savs. Bank Summer Sch., Harpefoss, Norway, 1966; m. Mary Elizabeth Cunliffe, Aug. 21, 1954; children—Margaret, Catherine, John, Patricia, Matthew. Asst. v.p. Bowery Savs. Bank, N.Y.C., 1950-68; registered rep. Salomon Brothers, N.Y.C., 1968-71, 73-75, Blyth Eastman Dillon, Boston, 1971-72; v.p. Nat. Health & Welfare Mut. Life Ins. Assn., N.Y.C., 1975-78, East River Savs. Bank, N.Y.C., 1978-80; sr. v.p., treas. Harlem Savs. Bank, N.Y.C., 1980—. Mem. investors com. Social Sci. Research Council. Mem. N.Y. Soc. Security Analysts, Money Marketers. Republican. Roman Catholic. Office: 205 E 42 St New York NY 10017

BREWBAKER, WILLIAM STYNE, automobile agy. exec., farmer; b. Buchanan, Va., Oct. 24; s. Abram Joseph and Claudia (Styne) B.; student Roanoke Coll., 1925; m. Cassie Leta Garrett, June 22, 1929; 1 son, William Styne. Salesman, sales mgr. for various cos., 1925-40; chmn. bd., pres. Brebaker Motors, Inc., Montgomery, Ala., 1940—; pres., gen. mgr. W.S. Brewbaker, Inc., Montgomery, 1943—; owner, gen. mgr. Lingerwood Farms, Montgomery, 1947—; past dir. 1st Ala. Bancshares, Inc.; past adv. dir. 1st Ala. Bank Montgomery N.A. Chmn. women's div. United Appeal, Montgomery, 1957, campaign chmn., 1960-61, bd. dirs., 1958-61; past mem. Montgomery Indsl. Bd.; v.p. Montgomery Indsl. Park, Downtown Devel. Corp.; sec.-treas. Coosa-Alabama River Improvement Assn.; past mem. Community Council; trustee Huntingdon Coll., Montgomery; chmn. adv. bd. Montgomery Civic Center. Named Mr. Ala. Automobile Dealer, Automobile Dealers Assn. Ala., 1957, Boss of Year, Montgomery chpt. Nat. Secs. Assn., 1960. Mem. Ala. Automobile Dealers Assn. (pres. 1949), Montgomery Automobile and Truck Dealers Assn. (past pres.), So. Inst. Mgmt. (Founding), Montgomery (past dir.), U.S., Ala. chambers commerce, AIM (pres.'s council), English Speaking Union, Krewe of Phantom Host (dir., sec.), Downtown Unltd. (past pres.), Montgomery Mktg. and Sales Club (past pres.), Internat. Platform Assn., Blue and Gray Cols., Tau Kappa Alpha. Methodist (bd. stewards, trustee ch.). Clubs: Kiwanis (pres. Montgomery 1953); Men of Montgomery, Capital City, Montgomery Country, Beauvoir (Montgomery); Le Mirador Country (Mont Pelerin, Switzerland). Home: 435 E Fairview Ave Montgomery AL 36105 Office: Bibb & Molton St Montgomery AL 36104

BREWER, DAVID CLIFFORD, systems engr., bldg. contracting co. exec.; b. St. Paul, Aug. 4, 1919; s. Edward Vincent and Ida (Kueffner) B.; B.S., U. Minn., 1942; postgrad. U. So. Calif., 1942-43, U. Calif., 1944; m. Mary Louise Neilson; children—Stephanie, Dona Barbara, Diane, Anthony, Gabrielle, Heidi. Chief chemist Calif. Oil Refinery, Long Beach, 1946; sr. project engr., dir. Power Elements Hydraulic Lab., N.Am. Aviation Co., Downey, Calif., 1952-55; sr. systems engr. Convair div. Gen. Dynamics Co., San Diego, 1955-60, Fed. Cartridge Corp., New Brighton, Minn., 1968-72; owner, mgr. Brewer Constrn. Co., San Diego, 1960-68, Mindiego Corp., San Diego and St. Paul, 1972—. Served with USNR, 1944-45. Lic. bldg. contractor, Calif., Minn. Author textbook: Aircraft Fuels, Oils and Allied Systems; designer solar stills, biomass distillery; designer, supr. constrn. 1st computer-oriented automatic programmed checkout equipment, 1st lab. to check out high speed missile flight characteristics; research on ultra-high altitude fuel system; developer 1st electronic in-flight engine analyser (oscilloscope). Home: 4440 Del Monte Ave San Diego CA 92107 also 387 Pelham Blvd Saint Paul MN 55104

BREWER, GIVEN ANKENY, engring. co. exec.; b. Cleve., Dec. 8, 1913; s. Basil and Jean Armor (Given) B.; B.S., Mass. Inst. Tech., 1938; postgrad. Calif. Inst. Tech., U. So. Calif., 1944-46; m. Barbara Jenison, Oct. 19, 1940; children—Margaret Jean, Nicholas Given; m. 2d, Heidi Erika, Nov. 25, 1967; 1 child—Wiebke Given. Structures research engr. Lockheed Aircraft Corp., Burbank, Calif., 1938-42; asst. chief structures Bomber div. Ford Motor Co., Willow Run, Mich., 1942-44; structures project engr. Vultee Aircraft Corp., Downey, Calif., 1944-46, cons., 1946-50; founder, prin. Brewer Engring. Labs., Inc., Marion, Mass., 1950—; faculty exptl. stress analysis Mass. Inst. Tech., summers 1953—, mem. corp. vis. com. mech. engring., 1966. Served to capt. USMCR, 1948, Res. ret. Mem. Inst. Aero. Sci., Soc. for Exptl. Stress Analysis, Am. Soc. for Metals. Republican. Episcopalian. Patentee in field; contbr. to various profl. jours. Office: POB 288 513 Mill Marion MA 02738

BREWER, ROBERT JOSEPH, accountant; b. Washington, June 20, 1949; s. George Robert and Julia Ann (Salb) B.; B.A., U. Md., 1973; m. Adele Virginia Lee, Sept. 25, 1976; 1 dau., Jamie Lynn. Accountant, Wooden & Benson, Balt., 1974-75; mem. accounting staff Hugh Mitchell, C.P.A., White Plains, Md., 1975-77; pvt. practice pub. accounting, Indian Head, Md., 1977—. C.P.A., Md. Mem. Am. Inst. C.P.A.'s, Nat. Soc. Pub. Accountants, Md. Assn. C.P.A.'s, Indian Head Bryans Rd. Bus. Assn. Home: 205 Heather Dr Bryans Road MD 20616 Office: 1 Parran Bldg Indian Head MD 20640

BREWER, SUSAN CATHERINE, ins. sales rep.; b. Covington, Tenn., July 30, 1942; d. Daniel Fredrick and Mary (Lindsey) Jennings; student Memphis State U., 1960-61, 74—; m. Earl D. Brewer, Jan. 1981; 1 dau., Elizabeth Paige Watkins. Family lifestyles editor Covington Pub. Co., 1961-77; group sales rep. Equitable Life Assurance Soc., Memphis, 1977-78, mktg. rep. group ins. sales, 1978—; divisional sales leader, 1978—. Publicity dir. St. Jude Children's Research Hosp., 1976-77, Covington Little Theatre, 1970-77, Tipton County Bus. and Profl. Women's Club, 1974-77, Covington Jaycettes, 1970-72, Rev. Book Club, 1972-74. Recipient 1st and 2d press awards Tenn. Press Assn., annually 1969-77, 1st place award Tenn. Women's Press and Author Club, 1976-77, hon. mention U. Mo. Women's Editor contest, 1976; recipient 1st place art award in oils Tipton Art Assn., 1967. Mem. Sales and Mktg. Execs. Club, Nat. Career and Exec. Women's Club, Nat. Assn. Life Underwriters, DAR, Tipton County Art Assn., Women of 1812, Baptist. Club: Newcomer's (exec. bd. Memphis). Home: 3128 Court St Bartlett TN 38134 Office: 5100 Poplar Ave Suite 150A Memphis TN 38137

BREWSTER, DAVID, mfg. co. exec.; b. Ipswich, Eng., Jan. 18, 1933; came to U.S., 1966; s. Harold Seymour and Irene Hilda (Meyrick) B.; student public schs., Eng.; m. Myriam Marquess, Aug. 18, 1962; 1 dau., Sarah Louise. Regional mgr. Eutectic Welding Alloys, Gt. Brit. and U.S., 1962-69, Royfax, Div. Royal Typewriter Co., Cleve. and Atlanta, 1969-74, Nassau Corp., Highland Park, N.J., 1974-76; br. mgr. Royal Bus. Machines, Atlanta, 1976—. Served with Royal Corps of Mil. Police, 1951-53. Mem. Mktg. and Sales Mgmt. Assn., Inst. Mech. and Elec. Engrs., Brecksville C. of C. (hon.). Address: 2675 Johnson Rd Atlanta GA 30345

BREWSTER, GEORGE WHARTON, investment co. exec.; b. Washington, Aug. 7, 1932; B.S. in Bus. Adminstrn., Northwestern U., 1954; M.B.A., Harvard U., 1960; postgrad. U. Calif. at Los Angeles; m. Sheila; children—George Wharton, Douglas F., Sandra K. Pres., dir. Advisers Gen. Mgmt. Corp.; dir. Universal Heritage Investments Corp., Los Angeles; dir. Advisers Equity Corp.; exec. v.p., dir. Stonehedge Group, Inc. Mem. Torrance Youth Welfare Commn., 1963-64; mem. Intercity Hwy. Com., 1965-75; mem. Torrance Noise Pollution Control Com.; mem. steering com. Torrance Goals Program, 1968—; vice chmn. Torrance Planning Commn., 1964-70; councilman City of Torrance, 1970-78, vice mayor, 1975, 78; bd. mgrs. Torrance YMCA, 1968—, chmn. fund drive, 1970; bd. mgrs. Torrance-Lomita br. ARC., past chmn.; bd. dirs., v.p. So. Calif. Rapid Transit Dist., 1973-78. Served with USNR, 1954-58. Recipient Community Distinguished Service award U.S. Jaycees, 1963. Mem. Torrance Jaycees (life, pres. 1962-63, internat. senator), Aircraft Owners and Pilots Assn. Home: 443 Calle De Castellana Redondo Beach CA 90277 Office: 4040 Palos Verdes Dr N Rolling Hills Estates CA 90274

BREWSTER, ROBERT STEWART, mgmt. cons.; b. Bklyn., Jan. 7, 1940; s. Frederick Elbert and Gwendolyn Belle (Rock) B.; B.S.B.A. in Accounting, Babson Coll., 1963; m. Valerie Ellen Barber, Sept. 11, 1965; children—Michael Eric, Suzanne Elizabeth. With Arthur Young & Co., N.Y.C., 1963-68, sr. auditor, 1968-69, mgr. cons. dept., 1969-73, prin. cons. dept., 1973-78, dir. adminstrn., 1977—, dir. internat. fin. and adminstrn., 1978—, dir., organizer, author, cost accounting systems seminar, 1975-77. Mem. Planning and Zoning Bd. Twp. of Berkeley Heights (N.J.), 1972, chmn. citizens adv. com. master plan, 1974, chmn. citizens adv. com. zoning ordinances, 1975-77. Recipient Appreciation plaque Found. Accounting Edn., 1976. Mem. Am. Inst. C.P.A.'s, N.Y. Soc. C.P.A.'s (chmn. prodn. control com. 1973-76, chmn. fin. planning and control com. 1978-80). Presbyterian. Club: Beach Haven Park Yacht (vice commodore 1980—, chmn. fin. com. 1979—, dir. 1979—). Home: 60 Southview Dr Berkeley Heights NJ 07922 Office: 277 Park Ave New York NY 10017

BRIANTE, ROCCO ANTHONY, contractor; b. White Plains, N.Y., Jan. 14, 1932; s. Anthony Rocco and Lecia Ann (DeSepio) B.; student Westchester Community Coll., 1952; m. Rosita Tartaglia, Nov. 15, 1958; children—Rocco Anthony, Christopher, Laura Lee, Linda, Maria, Gregory, David. Mason foreman, White Plains, 1956-61; mason contractor R. Briante, White Plains, 1962-63; supt. Bilt-Rite Devel. Corp., White Plains, 1963-65, v.p. constrn., 1965—; pres. Rocco Briante & Sons, Inc., White Plains, 1967—, B.B.C. Realty Corp., 1975—. Bd. dirs. Kensico Little League, Valhalla, N.Y. Served with AUS, 1953-55. Named Man of the Year Kensico Little League, 1973. Mem. Westchester Bldg. Trade Employers Assn. (bd. govs. 1973—), Builders Inst. (dir. 1970-75), Builders Inst. Westchester. Roman Catholic (mem. parish sch. bd. 1973-75). Clubs: Rotary, K.C. Home: 15 Virginia Ln Thornwood NY 10594 Office: 720 Commerce St Thornwood NY 10594

BRICE, JAMES JOHN, accounting firm exec.; b. Chgo., Oct. 24, 1925; s. John Patrick and Margaret R. (Stookey) B.; student U. Ill., 1946-48; B.S., Northwestern U., 1950; m. Rosemary E. Freemuth, June 19, 1948; children—Susan, John, Kimberley, Pamela, Tracey. Accountant Standard Oil of Ind., 1950-51; staff accountant, mgr. Arthur Andersen & Co., C.P.A.'s, Chgo., 1951-60, partner, 1960-68, partner in charge, Los Angeles, 1968-72, vice chmn., 1972-74, co-chmn., mng. partner, Chgo., 1974—. Dir., pres. Mental Health Assn. Chgo., 1963-68; mem. Businessmen for Loyola U., 1963-67; dir. Arlington Heights (Ill.) United Fund, 1963-67; dir. United Way, Los Angeles, 1970-72; dir., chmn. Reading is Fundamental, Chgo., 1972—; dir., treas. United Charities, 1975—; trustee, v.p. Adler Planetarium, 1975—; prin. Chgo. United, 1973—; trustee, treas. Provident Hosp., 1975—; dir., v.p. Chgo. Crime Commn., 1974—; dir., chmn. Constl. Rights Found., Chgo. Project, 1974—; dir. nat. bd. Inroads, Inc., 1975—; mem. adv. bd. Urban Gateways, 1975—, pres., 1978; mem. Com. for Econ. Devel., Chgo., 1977—; exec. v.p. Lyric Opera Chgo., 1979. Served with USAF, 1944-46. Mem. Am. Inst. C.P.A.'s, Ill., Calif. socs. C.P.A.'s. Clubs: Chgo., Comml., Mid-Am. (Chgo.); Carlton, Mid-Day, Los Angeles; Barrington Hills Country, Butler Nat. Golf, Old Elm. Office: 69 W Washington St Chicago IL 60602

BRICK, STEVEN ROGERS, real estate broker, developer; b. Camden, N.J., Oct. 6, 1945; s. Justus Clark and Charlotte Martha (Carson) B.; B.A. with distinction, U. Va., 1968; M.B.A., Temple U., 1976; m. Lynne Dorothy Herbert, June 2, 1968; children—Scott Courtney, Adam Curtis. Pres., Brick Real Estate, Medford, N.J., 1972—. Bd. dirs. Cadbury, retirement community; treas. Delaware Valley Council of Homes for Living. Served with USAF, 1968-72. Mem. Nat. Assn. Realtors (cert. real estate brokerage mgr.), N.J. Assn. Realtors, Realtor Nat. Mktg. Inst., Burlington County Assn. Realtors. Republican. Quaker. Club: Island Heights Yacht. Home: 21 Maine Trail Medford NJ 08055 Office: Taunton Rd Medford NJ 08055

BRICKER, WILLIAM H., chem. co. exec.; b. Detroit, 1932; B.S., Mich. State U., 1953, M.S., 1954. Br. mgr. Ortho div. Calif. Chem. Co. 1954-57; gen. sales mgr. Chemagro, 1957-66; exec. v.p. Velsicol Corp, 1966-69; officer Diamond Shamrock Chem. Co., 1969-72, pres., 1972-74; v.p. Diamond Shamrock Corp., 1972-73, exec. v.p., 1973-75, chief operating officer, 1974-76, pres., 1975—, chief exec. officer, 1976—, chmn., 1980—, also dir.; dir. Soc. Nat. Bank, Soc. Corp., Lamson & Sessions & Samuel S. Moore & Co. Trustee John Carroll U., Univ. Hosp. Office: 2300 Southland Center Dallas TX 75201*

BRICKMAN, CHARLES ALFRED, investment Banker; b. Chgo., Apr. 3, 1932; s. Clarence J. and Caryl F.; B.A., Denison U., 1954; M.B.A., Northwestern U., 1959; m. Nancy Eshelman, Sept. 8, 1954; children—J. Bradley, Daniel J., Lizanne, C. Andrew. With Kidder, Peabody & Co. Inc., Chgo., 1960—, v.p., dir., 1970—; dir. MTS Systems Corp., Ill. Consol. Telephone Co. Trustee, George Williams Coll., 1973-78; trustee Denison U., 1974—, vice chmn. bd., 1977—. Served with USAF, 1954-57. Congregationalist. Club: Hinsdale (Ill.)

Golf (dir. 1972-75). Office: Kidder Peabody & Co Inc 125 S Wacker Dr Chicago IL 60606

BRIDGE, GARY L., securities analyst; b. Salt Lake City, Jan. 5, 1940; s. Gordon E. and Dorothy C. B.; B.S. in Fin., U. Utah, 1963; M.B.A. in Mgmt. with high honors, U. Miami, 1969; m. Lynda M. Spence, Apr. 22, 1967; children—Michael, Stefanie. Asst. divisional group mgr. group ins. Equitable Life Assurance Soc., 1963-68; asst. investment officer John Hancock Life Ins. Co., 1969-71; analyst, v.p. G.S. Grumman & Assos., 1971-76; v.p., analyst securities G.S. Grumman/Cowen, Boston, 1976—; tchr. Boston Security Analyst Soc. Named top photog. investment analyst in the country Instnl. Investor Mag., 1978, 79. Mem. Soc. Photog. Scientists and Engrs., Boston Security Analyst Soc. Club: Wellesley (Mass.) Country. Contbr. articles on photography and splty. chems. to profl. jours. Home: 25 Lincoln Rd Wellesley MA 02181 Office: 28 State St Boston MA 02109

BRIDGES, CHARLEY DAY, fin. and adminstrv. exec.; b. Wentworth, Mo., July 22, 1929; s. Walter Robert and Beula (Higgins) B.; A.S. in Engring. Sci., Mo. So. Coll., 1960, student in Math., 1961-62; student Kans. State Coll., Nat. Radio Inst. also data processing courses; m. Edith June McClinton, Aug. 20, 1948; children—Harold David, Lee Allen, Glen Wayne. Quality control analyst, test engr., sr. mathematician Rocketdyne div. N.Am. Rockwell Crop., Neosho, Mo., 1958-67, sr. computer programmer, analyst Tulsa div., 1967-68; mgr. systems and data processing Nat. Gypsum Co., Parsons, Kans., 1968-70; dir. finance and adminstrn., controller, adminstrv. services mgr. Day & Zimmermann, Inc., Parsons, 1970—; owner, mgr. Field Crop & Livestock Enterprise; chmn. bd., chief exec. officer Bridges Farms, Inc. Mem. Gen. Dist. 113 Bd. Edn., 1956-58; sec. Diamond Dist. R4 Bd. Edn., 1966-68; bd. dirs. Freedom Community Assn., 1960-65; leader Freedom 4-H Club, 1964-73; mem. Newton County Soil and Water Conservation Dist., 1972—; steward Diamond United Methodist Ch., 1960—. Recipient Day & Zimmermann Authors award. Mem. Nat. Mgmt. Assn. (past chmn., chmn. certification com., dir., mem. mgmt. devel. com., past pres. KAAP chpt., Silver Knight of Mgmt. award), Am. Def. Preparedness Assn., U.S. Army Assn. Republican. Club: Masons. Patentee tillage equipment. Home: Route 1 Sarcoxie MO 64862 Office: Kansas Army Ammunition Plant Parsons KS 67357

BRIDGES, JACKIE GARLEN, clergyman, bookstore exec.; b. Dodd City, Tex., Mar. 30, 1931; s. William G. and Laura T. Bridges; student Lee Coll., Cleveland, Tenn., 1950, Trinity U., San Antonio, 1952; m. Claudine Smith, Mar. 20, 1953; children—Gail, William, Anthony, John, Cynthia. Ordained to ministry Ch. of God, 1952; Fla. sec.-treas. Chs. of God, 1952-54, Tenn. sec.-treas., 1954-59; pastor Ch. of God, Knoxville, Tenn., 1959-65, Lawton, Okla., 1965-66, Mishawaka, Ind., 1966-69; mgr. Pathway Bookstore, Akron, Ohio, 1969—. Democrat. Club: Kiwanis (chmn. spiritual aims com.). Home: 1310 Carnegie Ave Akron OH 44314 Office: 75 S Broadway Akron OH 44308

BRIDGES, LEON GERALD, mortgage banker, builder, developer; b. Dublin, Ga., Jan. 28, 1943; s. Rowie Alexander and Lola Moye B.; B.B.A., U. Ga., 1968; student Woodrow Wilson Law Sch., 1970-72; m. Elizabeth Ellen Elrod, Dec. 27, 1969; children—Andrew Gerald, Denae M. Engr., Lockheed Ga. Co., Marietta, 1968-71; v.p., br. mgr. L.E.A. Mortgage Co., Marietta, 1972-74; pres., owner Mortgage Alliance Corp., Atlanta, 1974—; v.p. Alliance Ins. Corp.; sr. exec. v.p. Mortgage Title & Escrow Corp. Served with USAF, 1961-65. Mem. Am. Entrepreneurs' Assn., U.S. C. of C., Ga. Assn. Realtors, Cobb County Bd. Realtors, Atlanta Mortgage Bankers Assn. Republican. Baptist. Address: 3260 Powers Ferry Rd Suite A-215 Marietta GA 30067

BRIDGFORTH, ROBERT MOORE, JR., research specialist; b. Lexington, Miss., Oct. 21, 1918; s. Robert Moore and Theresa (Holder) B.; student Miss. State Coll., 1935-37; B.S., Iowa State U., 1940; M.S., Mass. Inst. Tech., 1948; postgrad. Harvard, 1949; m. Florence Jarnberg, Nov. 7, 1943; children—Robert Moore, Alice Theresa. Asst. engr. Standard Oil Co. of Ohio, 1940; teaching fellow Mass. Inst. Tech., 1940-41, instr. chemistry, 1941-43, research asst., 1943-44, mem. staff div. indsl. cooperation, 1944-47; asso. prof. physics and chemistry Emory and Henry Coll., 1949-51; research engr. Boeing Co., Seattle, 1951-54, research specialist, 1954-55, sr. group engr., 1955-58, chief propulsion systems sect. systems mgmt. office, 1958-59, chief propulsion research unit, 1959-60; chmn. bd. Rocket Research Corp., 1960-69, Explosives Corp. Am., 1966-69. Fellow Inst. Aero Scis. (asso.), Am. Inst. Chemists, Brit. Interplanetary Soc.; mem. Am. Astronautical Soc. (dir. 1959—), Am. Rocket Soc. (pres. Pacific N.W. sect. 1955), AAAS, N.Y. Acad. Scis., Am. Chem. Soc., Am. Inst. Physics, Am. Assn. Physics Tchrs., Tissue Culture Assn., Reticuloendothelial Soc., Combustion Inst., Sigma Xi. Home: 4325 87 Ave SE Mercer Island WA 98040

BRIDWELL, BOB S., energy equipment mfg. co. exec.; b. Oklahoma City, Dec. 28, 1940; s. Cecil Clinton and Gladys Izella (Tucker) B.; B.S., Calif. State U., 1966, M.B.A., 1968; m. Patricia Gayle Whitmer, June 19, 1964; 1 dau., Melissa Anne. Sect. chief Western Electric Co., Los Angeles, 1966-68; v.p. adminstrn., dir. Kanasi Schonnieson & Co., Los Angeles, 1968; v.p. corporate devel., dir. Am. Funding Corp., Beverly Hills, Calif., 1968-71; sr. v.p. fin., treas. CRS Design Assos. Inc., Houston, 1971-78; v.p. fin. Harte-Hanks Communications, Inc., San Antonio, 1979-80; pres., chief exec. officer Tescorp, Inc., 1980—. Mem. Fin. Execs. Inst., Newcomen Soc. N.Am. Clubs: Houston, Univ., Retama Plaza. Home: 3507 Marymont Dr San Antonio TX 78217 Office: 9 NE 410 Loop San Antonio TX 78219

BRIED, HENRY WILLIAM, elec. mfg. co. exec., mech. engr.; b. Teaneck, N.J., June 17, 1933; s. Henry F. and Rose M. Bried; M.E., Stevens Inst. Tech., 1955; M.B.A., Drexel U., 1965; married; children by previous marriage—Kathleen, James, Henry William, Stephen. Tech. planning engr. Gen. Electric Co., Phila., 1958-60, product design engr., Valley Forge, Pa., 1961-63, mgr. payload integration, 1963-65, mgr. mil. aerospace systems, Washington, 1965-68; mgr. WWMCCS Program, Honeywell Info. Systems, Phoenix, 1968-71, mgr. prodn. programs, 1968-74; mgr. info. systems Motorola, Inc., Phoenix, 1974-76, mgr. participative mgmt. program, 1976-80, corp. dir. program, 1980—. Pres., Kiva-Kaibab Little League, 1972-74, coach, 1969-76; coach Wheaton Boys Club, 1961-68; pres. Layhill Rd. Citizens Assn., 1965-68; bd. dirs. Ariz. Boys Community, 1976—; mem. Republican Nat. Com. Served to 1st lt., Ordnance Corps, U.S. Army, 1955-58. Mem. ASME, Air Force Assn., U.S. Navy League. Republican. Roman Catholic. Home: 8501 E Cholla St Scottsdale AZ 85260 Office: 8201 E McDowell Rd PO Box 1417 Scottsdale AZ 85252

BRIER, DANIEL LEWIS, mfg. exec.; b. Queens, N.Y., Dec. 29, 1932; s. Frederick and Teresa (Gluck) B.; B.S.T.E., Lowell Tech. Inst., 1954; B.B.A., U. Fla., 1956; postgrad. N.Y. U., 1958-60; m. Lynn E. Freeman, June 15, 1957; children—Frederick Nathan, Phillip David. Instr. engring. U. Fla., 1954-56; mktg. mgr. Tropical Delicacies, 1956-57; mktg. cons. Werner Mgmt. Cons.'s, 1958-59, dir. mktg. services, 1960-61; pres. Chemo Products, Inc. of Crompton Co., Inc., N.Y.C., 1961-63, dir. corp. market planning, 1964-65; asst. to pres. B.V.D. Co., Inc., N.Y.C., 1965, chief exec. officer The Alligator Co., 1966, dir. textile mfg. Knitwear group, 1967-69; pres. Corp. Planners, Inc., 1970, Brookdale Securities, Inc. and predecessor firm, N.Y.C., 1971-74; pres., dir. Rudin & Roth, Inc., Lincolnton, N.C., 1975—; former mem. N.Y., Pacific and Am. stock exchanges. Mem. Village of East Rockaway (N.Y.) Planning Commn., 1965-66. Served with USAR, 1956-64. Mem. UN Day Com., Am. Arbitration Assn., Alpha Kappa Psi, Pi Lambda Phi. Clubs: Catawba Country (Newton, N.C.); Ocean Reef (Key Largo, Fla.). Contbr. articles to profl. jours., chpts. in books. Office: PO Box 160 Lincolnton NC 28092

BRIGGS, EVERETT RIDLEY, banker; b. Paris, Tex., May 21, 1933; s. O.B. and Margaret (Billingsley) B.; B.S., Tex. A&M U., 1954, M.Ed., 1958; m. Shirley Ann Casey, Jan. 22, 1954; children—Cathy Ann, Carol Jean, David Ridley, Daniel Brian. Sr. v.p. First Bank & Trust Co., Bryan, Tex., 1963-71; pres. Elgin Bank of Tex., 1971-72, Paris Bank of Tex., 1973—. Pres. Paris and Lamar County United Fund, 1976. Served with USAF, 1954-57. Named Outstanding Young Man of Brezos County, Jaycees, 1964, Boss of Yr. of Paris, Jaycees, 1975. Mem. Am. Bankers Assn., Tex. Bankers Assn., Aircraft Owners and Pilots Assn., Paris and Lamar County C. of C. (pres. 1978-79). Baptist. Club: Lions. Home: 3015 Mahaffey St Paris TX 75460 Office: Paris Bank of Tex 1161 Clarksville St Paris TX 75460

BRIGGS, PAUL WELLINGTON, public utility exec.; b. Fairport, N.Y., Nov. 9, 1922; s. C. LeRoy and Erma B.; A. in Acctg. and Fin., Bentley Coll., Waltham, Mass., 1942; m. Beatrice Schroeder, Oct. 14, 1950; children—David, Peter, Thomas. Joined Rochester Gas & Elec. Corp. (N.Y.), 1945, asst. supt. gen. acctg. dept., 1955-57, asst. sec., 1957-60, sec., 1960-63, sec., asst. controller, 1963-65, sec., controller, 1965-69, v.p., controller, sec., 1969-71, sr. v.p. gen. services, 1971-73, sr. v.p. fin. and gen. services, 1973-74, pres., dir., 1974-80, chmn. bd., chief exec. officer, 1980—; dir. Security Trust Co., Security N.Y. State Corp. Vice chmn. bd. United Way Greater Rochester, 1980; vice chmn. Rochester Hosp. Service Corp.; v.p., bd. trustees Eastman Dental Center, 1980; bd. overseers Strong Meml. Hosp.; bd. dirs. Bus. Council of N.Y. State. Served to sgt., USAAF, 1943-45. Mem. Am. Gas Assn., Edison Electric Inst., Rochester Area C. of C. (trustee). Lutheran. Clubs: Univ. of Rochester, Country of Rochester, Genesee Valley. Office: 89 East Ave Rochester NY 14649

BRIGGS, PETER ALAN, envelope mfr.; b. Ann Arbor, Mich., Feb. 20, 1937; s. Robert Peter and Maxine (Corliss) B.; B.B.A., U. Mich., 1962, M.B.A., 1965; 1 dau., Rebecca Anne. Indsl. relations analyst Ford Motor Co., Dearborn, Mich., 1962-67; mgr. personnel and indsl. relations Western U.S., Packaging Co. Am., Denver and Evanston, Ill., 1967-74; dir. indsl. and employee relations Ball Corp. Metal Container Group, Lakewood, Colo., 1974-76; dir. personnel and indsl. relations Nekoosa Envelopes, Inc., Denver, 1976—, Butler Paper Co., 1981—; cons. in field. Vol. funds campaigner U. Denver, 1975. Served with AUS, 1956-57. Mem. Am. (accredited), Colo. socs. personnel adminstrn., U. Mich. Alumni Assn. (life). Republican. Episcopalian. Home: 565 Mohawk Dr Boulder CO 80303 Office: 23 Inverness Way E Englewood CO 80112

BRIGGS, REID RICHMOND, lawyer; b. Evanston, Ill., Aug. 25, 1911; s. Henry B. R. and Mary Florence (Dennis) B.; A.B., Stanford, 1932; J.D., George Washington U., 1938; m. Elizabeth Olwen Hughes, Aug. 23, 1935. Reporter, Los Angeles Record, 1932; clk. to U.S. Senator William Gibbs McAdoo, 1933-38; admitted to Calif. bar, 1938, D.C. bar, 1938, U.S. Supreme Ct. bar, 1945; with firm Lillick, McHose & Charles, Los Angeles, 1939-76, partner, 1950-76. Asso. founder Los Angeles Music Center; counsel Japanese Philharm. Orch., Los Angeles. Served from ens. to lt., USNR, 1942-46; lt. comdr. res., 1946-54. Recipient Gold Spike award Stanford U., 1976; Disting. Profl. Achievement award George Washington U. Law Assn., 1979. Mem. Los Angeles Bar Assn., Am. Judicature Soc., Stanford Assos. (bd. govs. 1961-69, v.p. 1964-65), Order of Coif. Unitarian/Methodist. Clubs: Univ. (pres. 1959-60) (Los Angeles); Chancery. Home: 3901 E California Blvd Pasadena CA 91107

BRIGHAM, JAMES BRIAN, retail chain exec.; b. Madison, Wis., Nov. 15, 1949; s. Donald Charles and Mary Etta B.; B.B.A., U. Wis., Eau Claire, 1975; m. Mary Elizabeth Clasen, Aug. 17, 1972; children—Sherry Marie, Brian Henry. Sr. auditor Ernst & Whinney, C.P.A.'s, Milw., 1975-78; nat. audit mgr. F. W. Woolworth Co., Milw., 1978-80, dir. auditing, 1980—. Bd. dirs. Milw. YMCA. Served with U.S. Army, 1968-71. C.P.A., Wis.; cert. internal auditor. Mem. Nat. Retail Mchts. Assn. (dir. internal audit group), Am. Inst. C.P.A.'s, Wis. Inst. C.P.A.'s, Inst. Internal Auditors, Am. Mgmt. Assn., Internat. Platform Assn., Phi Kappa Phi, Phi Eta Sigma. Home: 9220 N 70th St Milwaukee WI 53223

BRIGHT, GEORGE FRANK, mfg. co. exec.; b. Little Rock, Jan. 26, 1920; s. Nathan Henry and Sarah Alma (Carroll) B.; B.S. in M.E., U. Tenn., 1940; m. Gladys Marie Wright, June 6, 1947; children—Robert L., Don C. Gas engr. Black & Veatch, Cons. Engrs., Kansas City, Mo., 1940-42; faculty U. Tenn., Knoxville, 1946-47; mgr. mktg. Manning, Maxwell & Moore, Inc., Stratford, Conn., 1947-60; western sales mgr. Farris Engring. Corp., Palisades Park, N.J., 1960-62; with Anderson, Greenwood & Co., Houston, 1962—, v.p., 1971-79, v.p. internat. mktg., 1979—. Exec. v.p. Anderson-Greenwood Internat., Inc., Houston, 1972-80, pres., 1980—. Served to 1st lt. USAAF, 1942-45. Registered profl. engr., Tex. Mem. Am. Petroleum Inst. (sec. subcom. 1962—), So. Gas Assn. (asso. mems. com. 1976). Contbr. articles to various publs. Home: 10819 Atwell Dr Houston TX 77096 Office: Anderson Greenwood & Co PO Box 1097-TR Bellaire TX 77401

BRIGHT, LYN EDWARD, packaging machinery mfg. co. exec.; b. Sacramento, Apr. 7, 1947; s. Calvin Edward and Marjorie O. (Hensley) B.; B.S., Brigham Young U., 1969; M.B.A., U. So. Calif., 1971; m. Cheryl Ann Varone, Aug. 22, 1974; 1 son, Parker Hensley. Prodn. asst. Bright Foods, Inc., Turlock, Calif., part time 1963-69; project mgr. F.M. Stamper Co., Turlock, 1969-70; mgmt. trainee Wilson & Co., Buenos Aires, Argentina, 1968; asst. to pres., dir. A G I, Modesto, Calif., 1971-72; gen. mgr., cons. Woodside Properties, Turlock, 1972-75; gen. mgr., dir. B & H Mfg., Ceres, Calif., 1975—; dir. Valley Sales, Inc.; cons. CLS Investment. Republican. Mormon. Home: 3461 Rording Rd Ceres CA 95307 Office: 3461 Rording Ave Ceres CA 95307

BRIGHT, MADELINE ANN, bus. exec., investment counselor; b. Fresno, Calif., Jan. 5; d. Carl E. and Kathryn (Gilbert) McClurg; student Fresno State U., San Francisco State U.; divorced; children—Clinton Mart, Stephen Mart. Various positions in retail bus., 1951, 53-54; nurse Sequoia Hosp., Fresno, 1954-55; clk. Calif. Assigned Risk, San Francisco, 1959-60; owner, mgr. Madeline's Dog Salon and Boutique, Santa Clara, 1961—; co-founder United Dog Groomers Calif., Inc.; cons., tchr. in field. Co-founder Friends of Triton Mus., v.p., Santa Clara, 1975. Lic. realtor asso. Mem. United Dog Groomers (v.p. 1966-71). Democrat. Roman Catholic. Club: Santa Clara Soroptimist. Address: 1610 Pomeroy Ave Santa Clara CA 95051

BRIGHTBILL, L. O., III, bank holding co. exec.; b. Fairmont, W.Va., June 20, 1936; s. L.O. and Mary (Smith) B.; B.S. in Indsl. Mgmt., W.Va. U., 1960; grad. Advanced Mgmt. Program, Harvard U., 1975; grad. Southwestern Grad. Sch. Banking, 1971; m. Ruth Conley, Aug. 5, 1961; children—Mark, Amy, Ann, Cynthia. Vice pres. Ft. Worth Nat. Bank, 1972-73; v.p., exec. b.p. Tex. Am. Bancshares Inc., Ft. Worth, 1973-76, pres., 1980—; pres. Tex. Am. Bank, Dallas North, 1976-80; dir. Tex. Am. Bancshares. Trustee St. Paul Hosp. Found.; treas., dir. Circle Ten council Boy Scouts Am.; exec. com. Jesuit Coll. Prep. Sch.; campaign com. U. Dallas. Mem. Am. Inst. Banking. Roman Catholic. Clubs: Century II, Brookhollow Golf, Rotary (Ft. Worth). Office: 500 Throckmorton Fort Worth TX 76101

BRILL, ALAN RICHARD, fin. cons.; b. Evansville, Ind., July 5, 1942; s. Gregory and Bernice Lucille (Froman) B.; A.B., DePauw U., 1964; M.B.A., Harvard U., 1968; m. Bonnie Faye Phillips, May 26, 1973; children—Jennifer Leigh, Katherine Anne. Mgmt. cons. Peace Corps, Ecuador, 1964-66; sr. accountant, cons. Arthur Young & Co., N.Y.C., 1968-71; v.p. ops. Charter Med. Mgmt. Co., Inc. and v.p.-controller Hosp. Investors, Atlanta, 1972-73; v.p., treas., dir. Worrell Newspapers, Inc., and Worrell Broadcasting Inc., Charlottesville, Va., 1973-79; pres. Brill Assos., Charlottesville, 1979—. Mem. Am. Inst. C.P.A.'s, N.Y. State Soc. C.P.A.'s, Inst. Newspaper Controllers and Fin. Officers. Republican. Methodist. Clubs: Farmington Country (Charlottesville); Safari Internat. Home: Route 10 Box 1855 (Flordon) Charlottesville VA 22901 Office: PO Box 8147 Charlottesville VA 22906

BRILL, NICHOLAS STEVEN, health care services mgr.; b. Washington, Dec. 5, 1946; s. Daniel Herbert and Charlotte (Lobel) B.; B.A., Colgate U., 1969; M.B.A., Harvard U., 1974; m. Margaret Rose Warshaw, May 10, 1970. Urban affairs cons. Arthur D. Little, Inc., Cambridge, Mass., 1969-72; asst. commr. Mass. Pub. Health Dept., Boston, 1974-76; adminstr. Cambridge Center, 1976-80; dir. mgmt. services Harvard Community Health Plan, 1980—; v.p. bd. dirs. Health Planning Council Greater Boston, 1978-80. Chmn., Boston applicant relations com. Harvard Bus. Sch., 1976-78. Home: 12 Lincoln St Arlington MA 02174 Office: 1 Fenway Plaza Boston MA

BRILL, RALPH DAVID, architect, real estate developer; b. Cheltenham, Eng., Nov. 24, 1944; s. Walter and Irmgard (Levy) B.; came to U.S., 1949, naturalized, 1955; student U. Ill., 1962-66, in Urban Design, Kunstskolen, Copenhagen, 1967; m. Gail J. Koff, Oct. 8, 1978. Vice pres., founder Node 4 Assos., Inc., Bklyn., 1968-70; dir. devel. Townland Mktg. and Devel. Corp., Cherry Hill, N.J., 1970-72; pres. Ralph Brill Assos., Garrison, N.Y., 1973—; partner Brill Kawakami Wilbourne, Architects, Bklyn. and Cold Spring, N.Y., 1973—; pres. Finsky Group Inc., 1974—; founder Manitou Realty, Cold Spring, 1976—; archtl. critic Columbia U., 1969; adj. asst. prof. urban systems Farleigh Dickinson U., 1974-76. Bd. dirs. Garrison Art Center, 1976—; N.Y. State Hist. Preservation grantee, 1977. Registered architect, licensed real estate broker, N.Y. Mem. Soc. Indsl. Archeology, Center for Hudson River Valley. Jewish. Author: The Hudson River Catalogue, 1978. Home: PO Box 200 Garrison NY 10524 Office: 77 Main St Cold Spring NY 10516

BRILLHART, DAVID WINTHROP, banker; b. Bethlehem, Pa., Jan. 9, 1925; s. David H. and Elizabeth L. (Lehr) B.; B.S., U.S. Mil. Acad., 1946; M.B.A., N.Y. U., 1960; m. Joan Jeffris, Mar. 5, 1948; children—Jeff, Sally, Jon. Vice pres. Morgan Guaranty Trust Co., N.Y.C., 1954-72; exec. v.p. S.E. First Nat. Bank of Miami (Fla.), 1972-76; pres., chief exec. officer 1st Bancshares of Fla., Inc., Boca Raton, 1977-79; chmn. David Brillhart and Assos., Miami, 1979—; dir. Union Bank & Trust Co. Eastern Pa., Bethlehem. Served to capt. AUS, 1946-54. Mem. N.Y. Soc. Security Analysts, AIM, Am. Mgmt. Assn., Econ. Council Palm Beach County. Clubs: Standard, Miami (Miami); Royal Palm Yacht and Country (Boca Raton). Home: 5401 SW 98th Terr Miami FL 33156 Office: 1444 Biscayne Blvd Suite 212 Miami FL 33132

BRILLHART, MAXINE THORNTON, physician; b. Coffeyville, Kans., Nov. 11, 1915; d. Forest Clifton and Rena Harriet (Huffman) Thornton; M.D., U. Kans., 1950; m. Roy William Brillhart, Nov. 15, 1935; children—Robert Allen, Roy William. Intern, Providence Hosp., Kansas City, Kans.; gen. practice medicine, Kansas City, Kans., 1951—; mem. staff Bethany, Providence, St. Margaret's hosps.; owner, pres. Maxine T. Brillhart, P.A.; sec. Allied Investors Co., Med. Offices Lab.; preceptor med. students U. Mo. Kansas City Med. Sch., Kans. U. Sch. Medicine; preceptor Kansas City Coll. Med. and Dental Technicians. Past hon. trustee Kansas City Art Inst. Recipient Woman of Year in Medicine Matrix award Women in Journalism, 1969. Diplomate Am. Bd. Family Physicians. Mem. AMA, Kans. Med. Assn., Wyandotte County Med. Assn., Am., Kans., Dist. I acads. family physicians, SW Clin. Soc., World, Am., Greater Kansas City womens med. assns., World Med. Soc., Am. Med. Women's Assn., English Speaking Union, Univ. Assos., Fellows Nelson Gallery. Methodist. Clubs: Soroptimist (Woman of Year award 1962), Woman's City (Kansas City, Mo.). Home: 4540 County Line Rd Kansas City KS 66106 Office: 1610 Washington Blvd Kansas City KS 66102

BRILLIANDE, ROBERT, ins. exec.; b. Paris, France, Sept. 14, 1909; s. Isiah and Sophia (Gerine) B.; B.A., U. Hawaii, 1935; m. Irvine Tewksbury Baptiste, June 25, 1938; children—Robert Irving II, Gary Shawn, Timothy Wayne, Michael Bruce, Karen Joy. Editor, pub. Waikiki Pictorial News, 1935-37; engaged in ins. bus., 1937—; pres., treas. Brilliande Ins. Agy., Ltd., 1944-79, emeritus, 1979—; founder Financial Security Life Ins. Co., Ltd., Honolulu, 1950, pres., from 1950, chmn., from 1950, now emeritus chmn. and pres.; pres., treas. Reliable Investment Corp., Ltd., 1953—, Hawaii Underwriting Co., Ltd., 1953-79. Founder-patron Chamber Music Soc. Honolulu; patron Royal Circle of Honolulu Symphony Soc., Commedia, Inc., repertory theatre. Bd. dirs. Inst. Orch. and Ensemble Hawaii. Served with U.S. Army, 1930-36. Mem. Nat. Assn. Life Underwriters (life mem. Million Dollar Round Table), Ins. Accounting and Statis. Assn., Life Office Mgmt. Assn., Nat. Assn. Life Cos., Am. Mgmt. Assn., Gen. Agts. and Mgrs. Assn. Hawaii, Assn. Life Underwriters Hawaii, Hawaii Claims Assn., Am. Risk and Ins. Assn., Internat. Monetary and Fin. Soc. Hawaii (founder, 1st pres.), First Hawaii Shakespearean Soc. (pres. 1974), Nat. Skeet Shooting Assn., U.S. Tennis Assn. (past exec. com.), Hawaii Tennis Assn. (founder, 1st pres.) Lawn Tennis Assn., Amateur Athletic Union (bd. mgrs. for weightlifting, organizer, 1st pres. weightlifting assn. Hawaii), Honolulu Acad. Arts, U. Hawaii Theater Guild, Honolulu Community Theater (dir. 1979—), U. Hawaii Alumni Assn., Hist. Soc. Bishop Mus. Assn., N.Y. Shavians, African Soc. Denmark (hon. life), Game Conservation Internat., East African Profl. Hunters Assn. (hon. life), Internat. Platform Assn., Alliance Francaise, Phi Delta Phi. Clubs: Masons (K.T., 32d deg.), Safari Internat. (founder, 1st pres. Hawaii chpt., mem. internat. bd.), Aloha Skeet and Trap Hawaii (hon. life), Club de Regatas Corona Fishing (Tampico, Mexico), Hickam Rod and Gun (hon. life), Sailfish and Tarpon Mexico, Haura Marlin de Tahiti (founder), Hawaii, Kona Big Game Fishing, Honolulu Automobile, Honolulu Press (life). Home: 3671 Diamond Head Rd Honolulu HI 96816

BRIM, PHILLIP LAINE, banker; b. Richmond, Ind., Dec. 27, 1952; s. Joseph Clayton and Constance Fayetta (Palmer) B.; student Sinclair Community Coll., 1974-77, Ind. U. East, 1977, Earlham Coll. Inst. Exec. Growth, 1977. Clk., Richmond Automotive Supply Co., 1970-72; pipefitter Nat. Automatic Tool Co., Richmond, 1972-74; with Second Nat. Bank of Richmond, 1974—, teller mgr., 1976-77, depositor services officer, 1977-78, br. officer, 1978-80, tng. officer, 1980—; instr. bank teller procedures Ind. Vocat. Tech. Inst. Recipient Participation award United Way Wayne County (Ind.), 1975, 76, 77, 78. Mem. Richmond Personnel Assn., Richmond Jaycees (dir. 1974, 78, v.p. 1975, treas. 1976, presdl. asst. 1977), Ind. Jaycees (Region 6 Speaking award 1977, ambassador to W.I. 1977), U.S. Jaycees. Republican. Roman Catholic. Clubs: Toastmasters, Sertoma, Fraternal Order Police. Office: Second Nat Bank Promenade at Eighth St Richmond IN 47374

BRIMELOW, JOHN, investment banker; b. Warrington, Lancashire, Eng., Oct. 13, 1947; s. Frank S. and Bessie B.; B.A., U. Sussex (Eng.), 1970; M.B.A., Stanford U., 1972. With N.C. Nat. Bank, Charlotte, 1972-80; sr. v.p. John Muir & Co., N.Y.C., 1980—. Home: 250 Mercer St #D704 New York NY 10012

BRIMMEKAMP, CARL GERD, fgn. trade co. exec.; b. Hamburg, Germany, Aug. 7, 1928; s. Carl and Charlotte Eugenie (Steinwachs) B.; student U. Hamburg; B.A. in Econs., Bklyn. Coll., 1955; postgrad. N.Y. U., 1955-56; M.B.A., U. Calif., Berkeley, 1961; m. Ruth M. Lingg, Sept. 5, 1953; children—Thomas L., Susanne L., Kristina S. Sales engr. Ferrostaal Overseas Corp., N.Y.C., 1952-56; gen. mgr., sec.-treas. Ferrostaal Pacific Corp., San Francisco, 1957-62; pres. Carl G. Brimmekamp Co., San Francisco, N.Y.C., 1962-73; pres., chief exec. officer Krupp Internat., Inc., Harrison, N.Y., 1970-79, Carl G. Brimmekamp & Co., Inc., Stamford, Conn., 1979—; chmn. Brimmekamp & Horn Corp., Oakland, Calif., 1980—; dir. Automatik Maschinenbau U.S.A. Ltd., Stamford, Bruderhav Corp., Stamford. Co-founder, German-Am. Round Table, San Francisco, 1958; founder German-Am. Trade Adv. Bd., 1962-66. Served with U.S. Army, 1953-55. Mem. TAPPI, Wire Industry Assn., German-Am. C. of C. (dir. 1971-74, 76-79, exec. com. 1976-79). Republican. Presbyterian. Clubs: Landmark (Stamford); World Trade, Univ. (San Francisco); Greenwich (Conn.) Country; Met. Opera, Met. (N.Y.C.); Duquesne (Pitts.); Deutscher Verein. Office: 460 Summer St Stamford CT 06901

BRINCKO, JOHN PETER, mfg. co. dir., internat. mgmt. cons.; b. N.Y.C., Sept. 30, 1942; s. Peter and Justina (Strenk) B.; B.B.A., CCNY, 1965, postgrad., 1965-66; m. Jean A. Kraynak, Jan. 29, 1966; children—Justin, Danielle. Staff acct. Grey Advt., Inc., N.Y.C., 1961-65; comml. audit mgr. Peat, Marwick, Mitchell & Co., N.Y.C., 1965-70; v.p., treas. Eastern Pollution Control, Inc., N.Y.C., 1970-71; div. chief fin. officer Internat. Paper Co., N.Y.C., 1971-73; corp. controller Am. Home Products Corp., N.Y.C., 1973-76: sr. v.p., chief fin. officer Max Factor & Co., Hollywood, Calif., 1976-79; pres. J. P. Brincko Assos., Inc. and dir. Chateau St. Jean, Kenwood, Calif., 1979—; dir. Merzoian Enterprises, Elmco Vineyards, Inc., Poplar Grape Growers (all Porterville), St. Agnes Vineyards, Inc.; owner Technology AMS AG, Zurich, Switzerland. Mem. Am. Inst. C.P.A.'s, N.Y. Soc. C.P.A.'s, Fin. Execs. Inst. Republican. Roman Catholic. Club: Union League of N.Y. Home: 1349 Stone Canyon Rd Bel Air CA 90024 Office: 1801 Ave of Stars Los Angeles CA 90067

BRINER, JACK RICHARD, label brokerage co. exec.; b. Lancaster, Pa., Oct. 10, 1945; s. William McKelvey and Elsie May (Longenecker) B.; B.S. in Psychology, Pa. State U., 1967; m. Judith Ann Shronk, June 24, 1967; children—Jill Lynn, Jodie Linette, John William. Sales exec. IBM Corp., Phila., 1967-68; terr. mgr. Merck Sharp & Dohme, West Point, Pa., 1968-71; account exec. Reynolds Securities, Inc., Lancaster, 1971-72; pres. Conestoga Graphics, Inc., brokers and mfrs. reps., Lancaster, 1972—; dir. On Stage! mag. Pres. Neff Elem. Sch. Home and Sch. Assn., Lancaster, 1979-80; mem. adv. council to Mannheim Twp. (Pa.) Sch. Supt., 1978-80; steering com. Self-Study Com., Manheim Twp. Elem. Sch., 1978-80. Served with USAR, 1967-68. Mem. Mfrs. Agts. Nat. Assn., Direct Mail/Mktg. Assn. Republican. Presbyterian. Home: 2120 Landis Valley Rd Lancaster PA 17601 Office: PO Box 5130 Lancaster PA 17601

BRINGARDNER, THELMA LOIS, mfg. co. fin. exec.; b. Parkersburg, W.Va., Dec. 1, 1928; d. Everett Bernard and Leona May (Hendershott) Marshall; grad. Bur. Better Bus. Exec. Women's Workshop, 1975; m. Mar. 27, 1956 (div. Sept. 1977); children—Diana Jean, Linda Ruth, Candice Marie. Sec., bookkeeper Marcy Enterprises, Inc., Columbus, Ohio, 1972-75; rep. Wilma Boyd Airline & Travel Career Sch., Pitts., 1976; bookkeeper Aerospace Materials, Inc., Columbus, 1977; controller Formitex, Inc., Columbus, 1978-80; now liaison and bookkeeper Jones Electric Co. of Sanford (Fla.). Active PTA, Whitehall, Ohio, 1960-74: leader Ohio Trefoil council Girl Scouts U.S., 1959-62. Recipient award Norfolk (Va.) Naval Supply Center, 1952. Mem. Blennerhassett Dental Asst. Soc. (charter mem.; sec. 1947), Nat. Assn. Accountants, Am. Bus. Women Assn. Democrat. Mem. Assemblies of God Ch. Home: 136 Bedford Ct Carriage Cove Sanford FL 32771

BRINGHAM, WILLIAM TALBERT, assn. exec.; b. Normal, Ill., Dec. 16, 1924; s. Russell Wilson and Sarah E. (Talbert) B.; Ph.B., Ill. Wesleyan U., 1948; J.D., Vanderbilt U., 1951; m. Ruth Irene Jaeger, Jan. 10, 1947; 1 son, William Talbert. Spl. agt. FBI, 1951-52; exec. sec. Sigma Chi Frat., Evanston, Ill., 1954—, also exec. v.p. Sigma Chi Corp., also pub. Mag. of Sigma Chi; exec. dir. Sigma Chi Found., 1956—, also sec.; sec. bd. grand trustees Sigma Chi, sec. exec. com., and sec. Sigma Chi Corp. Former chmn. Wilmette (Ill.) Fire and Police Commn.; former trustee Village of Wilmette. Past v.p. Proviso Twp. (Ill.) Young Republicans; dep. committeeman Northfield Twp. Rep. Com.; presdl. elector from Ill., 1976. Served with USNR, 1942-46. Recipient Grand Consul's citation Sigma Chi; Order of Constantine; Certified Assn. Execs. award Am. Soc. Assn. Execs. Conv., 1967, Key award, 1973. Mem. Navy League, Travelers Protective Assn., Am. Legion, VFW, Frat. Execs. Assn. (past pres.), Am. Soc. Assn. Execs. (dir. nat. found.), Am. Assn. Higher Edn., Am. Personnel and Guidance Assn., Nat. Interfrat. Conf. (exec. com.), SAR (Ill. Soc.), Newcomen Soc., Kendall Coll. Corp., Phi Delta Phi. Methodist (ofcl. bd., trustee treas., past pres. Meth. Men). Mason (Shriner, K.T., 33 deg.). Kiwanian (past pres.). Clubs: University (dir., past pres.) (Evanston); Kickers; Westmoreland Country. Author booklet on alumni chpts. Sigma Chi. Chmn. com. which edited Visitation Manual for College Fraternities. Home: 4020 Bunker Ln Wilmette IL 60091 Office: Sigma Chi Corp 1714 Hinman Ave Box 469 Evanston IL 60204

BRINGHURST, NEALE CLARK, investment banker; b. Phila., Oct. 27, 1929; s. George Kendrick and Carrie Mildred (Scheu) B.; A.B., Harvard U., 1951, M.B.A., 1953; m. Carolyn Lee Carter, Apr. 29, 1967; children—Julia Lee, Amanda Carter. Trust investment officer 1st Pa. Bank, Phila., 1955-61; voting shareholder Drexel Harriman Ripley, Inc., Phila., 1961-68; v.p. 1st Pa. Bank, Phila., 1968-71; pres. Claneil Enterprises, Inc., Plymouth Meeting, Pa., 1971—; underwriting mem. Lloyd's (of London); vice-chmn. Mannin Trust Bank (Isle of Man); dir. Remington Rand Corp., Pa. Aviation, Inc., Penguin Industries Inc. mng. dir. Ballykisteen Ins. Corp. Ltd. (Bermuda). Bd. dirs. Claneil Found., World Trade Council, Union League of Phila. Served with U.S. Army, 1953-55. Republican. Episcopalian. Clubs: Met., India House (N.Y.C.); Phila. Aviation Country, Peale, Harvard (Phila.); Aronimink Golf; Harvard (Boston). Fin. editor Eastern Fin. Times. Office: Suite 511 1 Plymouth Meeting Plymouth Meeting PA 19462

BRINK, JOHN WILLIAM, transp. co. exec.; b. Chgo., July 14, 1945; s. M. W. and Alice L. (Nelson) B.; B.B.A., U. Wis., 1967; M.B.A., W. Tex. State U., 1970; m. Marcia Richards, June 17, 1967; children—Bethany, Peter. Comml. lending officer Huntington Nat. Bank Columbus (Ohio), 1970-72; asst. treas. Peabody Internat., Galion, Ohio, 1972-75; v.p., treas. Avis, Inc., N.Y.C., 1975—; prof. Evening Gen. Coll., Franklin U., Columbus, 1971-75. Served with AUS, 1968-70. Mem. Am. Mgmt. Assn. Clubs: Union League, Cherry Valley Country. Office: Avis Inc 1114 Ave of Americas New York NY 10036

BRINKER, THOMAS LYNN, ins. agy. exec.; b. Greensburg, Pa., June 27, 1946; s. Simon Kelley and Elizabeth Ann (Snyder) B.; student U. Pitts., 1964-68; m. Ann K. Sobota, Oct. 1, 1966; children—Melissa A., Jonathan T. Customer service mgr. Chamberlain Mfg. Corp., Derry, Pa., 1968-69; mgmt. trainee Modulus Corp., Mt. Pleasant, Pa., 1969-70; spl. agt. Prudential Ins. Co. Am., Greensburg, 1970-75, div. mgr., State College, Pa., 1975-78, agy. mgr., Allentown, Pa., 1978—. Asst. scoutmaster Boy scouts Am., 1962-63; mem. parish adv. council St. Joseph's Roman Cath. Ch. Served to 1st lt. U.S. Army, 1965-66. Mem. Lehigh Valley Assn. Life Underwriters, Lehigh Valley Gen. Agts. and Mgrs. Assn. (dir.), State College Life Underwriters Assn. (v.p. 1976-77). Home: 4115 Daisy Ct Orefield PA 18069 Office: 1201 Washington St Allentown PA 18102

BRINKERHOFF, PETER JOHN, indsl. products co. exec.; b. Hackensack, N.J., Aug. 1, 1945; s. James Walter and Janet Stoll (Mohair) B.; B.A. in Polit. Sci., Georgetown U., 1967; M.B.A. in Fin., Am. U., 1972; m. Jeannine T. Heneault, Aug. 2, 1969; children—Jodie, Peter John, Jill. Sr. trust investment mgr. Am. Security & Trust Co., Washington, 1969-71; mgr. corp. devel. ITT Co., N.Y.C., 1972-75; mgr. corp. market product devel. Chgo. Pneumatic Tool Co., N.Y.C., 1975-76, v.p. mktg. and sales, subs. Jacobs Mfg. Co., Bloomfield, Conn., 1976—. Served with USNR, 1967-69. Mem. Am. Supply and Mfrs. Assn., Am. Mktg. Assn., Western Hwy. Inst., Am. Machine Tool Distbrs. Assn. Club: Hartford. Home: 1 Ox Yoke Dr Simsbury CT 06070 Office: Jacobs Mfg Co Bloomfield CT 06002

BRINKLEY, CHARLES CLARENCE, bank exec.; b. Weatherford, Tex., June 27, 1926; s. Clarence Eston and Helen Miron (Wilson) B.; student Weatherford Jr. Coll., 1943-45, Tex. Christian U., 1945-48; m. Mary Pauline Cranford, Sept. 12, 1945; 1 son, Charles Michael. Bookkeeper, cashier M & F Bank, Weatherford, Tex., 1945-51; from asst. v.p. to 1st v.p., dir. First Nat. Bank, Weatherford, 1951-61; pres., chmn. N.E. Nat. Bank, Ft. Worth, 1961—; pres., chmn. N.E. United Bancorp of Tex., 1972—. Pres. adv. council S.W. Baptist Seminary, 1979-80; vice chmn. bd. devel. Hardin/Simmons U., Abilene, 1979-80. Recipient Outstanding Alumnus award Weatherford Coll., 1968, Outstanding Citizen award Haltom/Richland C. of C., 1964, 68; named Lion of Yr., 1979. Mem. Am. Bankers Assn., Tex. Bankers Assn., Nat. Assn. Economists. Republican. Baptist. Clubs: Lions, K.P. Office: PO Box 18000 Fort Worth TX 76118

BRINKMAN, MADELINE MARY, ins. agt., tax cons.; b. Dardanelle, Ark., Dec. 17, 1920; d. Robert Lee and Eula Ada (Robinson) Garner; student Lane Community Coll., 1971-72; m. Donald Emil Brinkman, Sept. 15, 1976; children—Richard Allan Howard, Donald LeRoy Howard. Tax preparer H&R Block, 1968-70; owner, mgr. Brinks Enterprises Ltd., Eugene, Oreg., 1970—; tax preparer Tax Corp. Am., Eugene, 1970—; ins. agt. Am. Bankers Ins. Co., Eugene, 1978—. Mem. Assn. Tax Consultants. Home: 2237 Wisconsin St Eugene OR 97402

BRINKMAN, RICHARD GENE, fuel co. exec.; b. LaPorte, Ind., Aug. 4, 1927; s. Wilbert C. and Ruth M. (Reeder) B.; student Valparaiso U., 1947; B.S. in Accounting, Ind. U., 1951, postgrad. 1951-53; postgrad. U. N.M., 1951; m. Audrey A. Benson, Aug. 13, 1955; 1 dau., Lisa B. With Texaco, Inc., N.Y.C., 1956—, asst. comptroller financial reporting, 1963-67, asst. comptroller internat., 1967-68, asst. controller adminstrn., 1968-69, staff coordinator strategic planning, 1969-71, treas., 1971-77, v.p.-fin. and econs., treas., 1977—; adv. bd. Mfrs. Hanover Trust Co. Bd. govs. White Plains (N.Y.) Hosp. Med. Center; past dir. parent council St. Mary's Coll., Notre Dame, Ind. Served with Signal Corps, AUS, 1945-47; as 1st lt. USAF, 1951-53. Mem. Am. Petroleum Inst. Club: Westchester Country. Office: Texaco Inc 2000 Westchester Ave White Plains NY 10650

BRINKS, JAMES THOMAS, exec. compensation cons.; b. Quincy, Ill., Feb. 22, 1938; s. Oscar Henry and Margaret Florence (Ott) B.; student Quincy Coll., 1957; B.A., St. Mary of Lake Sem., 1961, M.A., 1963, S.T.B., 1965; M.B.A., St. Louis U., 1971; m. Doris A. Krause, June 26, 1970; children—Rene Kendall, Bridget Claudine, Victoria Lynn. Ordained priest Roman Catholic Ch., 1965; personnel mgr. organic chems. div. Monsanto Co., St. Louis, 1969-70; v.p. mktg. and property mgmt. Levinson Co., Clayton, Mo., 1971-73; personnel mgr. corp. fin. Monsanto Co., St. Louis, 1973-74; mgr. compensation and manpower devel. Fisher Controls Co., Marshalltown, Iowa, 1974-78; mgr. human resources cons. Deloitte, Haskins & Sells, Chgo., 1978-80; prin. compensation cons. services Wyatt Co., Chgo., 1980-81, regional practice dir., Dallas, 1981—. Mem. Am. Soc. Personnel Adminstrs. (accredited), Am. Compensation Assn. (accredited), Am. Mgmt. Assn., Inst. Mgmt. Cons. Republican. Roman Catholic. Contbr. articles to profl. jours. Republican. Home: 305 Meadowcrest Dr Richardson TX 75080 Office: 1900 Republic Bank Tower Dallas TX 75201

BRINLING, JOHN CLYDE, computer mgmt. cons.; b. Pitts., June 8, 1936; s. William G. and Frances H. (Stasni) B.; B.S. in Pharmacy, Duquesne U., 1957; M.S. in Pharmacology, U. Ill., 1959; postgrad. U. Pitts., Ill. Inst. Tech., Columbia U.; m. Florence Stern, Jan. 11, 1975. Writer med. texts Basic Systems, Inc., 1964; tech. writer IBM, 1965-66; sr. cons. Advanced Computer Techniques, 1966-75; pres., sr. cons. Brinling Assos., Warren, Vt., 1977—. Mem. Assn. Computing Machinery, Mensa. Research in pharmacology. Home and Office: Prickly Mountain PO Box 75A Warren VT 05674

BRINSMADE, ROBERT TURGOT, lawyer; b. Puebla, Mex., July 24, 1913 (parents Am. citizens); s. Robert Bruce and Helen (Steenbock) B.; A.B. in Econs. summa cum laude, M.A. in Econs., U. Tex., 1934, LL.B., J.D., 1937; M.P.A. (Rockefeller fellow 1936-37), Nat. Inst. Public Affairs, Washington, 1936; D.C.L., U. Mex., U. Venezuela, 1943. Admitted to Tex. bar, 1937, Mex. bar, 1938, Venezuela bar, 1944; partner firm Basham, Ringe and Brinsmade, Mexico City, also dir., stockholder numerous Mexican firms, 1938-40; partner Venezuelan office firm Schuster, Feuille & Brinsmade, N.Y.C., 1940-45; sr. partner firm Brinsmade Calcaño and Vallenilla, N.Y.C., Mexico City, Caracas, Havana, Bogota, Rio de Janeiro and Buenos Aires, 1945-50; propr. firm Robert Turgot Brinsmade, N.Y.C. and Caracas, also dir., officer, prin. stockholder Am. and Venezuelan companies, 1940-58; pres. Industrias Unidas, 1948-58, Milprint de Venezuela, 1947-58, Clacraft, Tricontinental SA, 1948-58, Nat. Petroleum Co. Venezuela, 1947-58, La Calle Publns., 1952-58, Promotore Nacional de Industrias, 1942-58; propr. Robert Turgot Brinsmade and Assos., N.Y.C., Houston and Mexico City, 1958-76; prin. stockholder Mexican Shipping Co. Natumex, 1962-68; publisher, editor La Prensa, 1962-69; pres., prin. stockholder S.E. Asia Oil & Gas Co., Houston, 1965—; individual practice law, Washington, 1976—; legal cons. energy and related fields, 1935—; lectr. U. Tex., 1934-38, U. Mex., 1938-40, U. Venezuela, 1941-58. Founder, chmn. Energy Research and Devel. Found., 1978—; bd. dirs., gen. counsel Peace Found., 1979—. Mem. Sociol. Soc., Philos. Soc., Acad. Polit. Sci., Internat. Good Neighbor Council (pres. 1979), Internat. Council Religions (Tex. vice chmn.), Interam. Bar Assn., Am. Bar Assn., Sigma Alpha Epsilon. Roman Catholic. Clubs: Caracas Country, Valle Arriba Country, Mexico City Country, Dallas Country, Houston Petroleum. Contbr. articles to periodicals and news papers, U.S., Latin Am., Europe. Office: 600 New Hampshire Ave NW Suite 450 Washington DC 20037

BRINSON, RANDY EUGENE, cons.; b. Lafayette, Ind., Mar. 13, 1948; s. Charles William and Edna Mae (Denney) B.; student SUNY, 1966-71, 75, 77, De Vry Inst. Tech., Chgo., 1972-73. Field engr. Sorbus Inc., Albany, N.Y., 1973-74; purchasing mgr. Artcraft Concepts, Ballston Lake, N.Y., 1974-78; rep. Dow Hickam Pharms., Houston, 1979; owner Rebco, Clifton Park, N.Y., 1977—; co-organizer Am. Discovery, Inc., Buffalo, 1972. Co-chmn. Wayne Wagner for Congress Camp, 1974; mem. Volunteers in Tech. Assistance, Mt. Ranier, Md., 1975—; mem. Nat. Republican Com. Mem. Mensa. Mem. Reformed Ch. Am. Office: PO Box 357 Clifton Park NY 12065

BRINSON, RONALD DEAN, broadcasting exec.; b. Carbondale, Ill., July 26, 1944; s. Raymond J. and Etta M. Brinson; B.S., DePaul U., Chgo., 1972. Accounts receivable supr. Atlantic Richfield Co., Chgo., 1967-72; acctg. and office mgr. Edward Wax Casing Co., Chgo., 1973-74; mgr. acctg. Soil Enrichment Materials Corp., Chgo., 1973-75; dir. fin. WBBM-FM/CBS Radio, Chgo., 1975—. Mem. Broadcasters Credit Assn. Address: 6700 S Shore Dr Apt 16F Chicago IL 60649

BRISCOE, DANIEL DOUP, state ofcl.; b. Louisville, Apr. 10, 1943; s. Edward Doup and Jeanne C. (Cusick) B.; B.A., Centre Coll., 1965; J.D., U. Louisville, 1968. Admitted to Ky. bar, 1969—; spl. asst. to Mayor of Louisville, 1969-72; exec. asst., chief operating officer Mayor of Louisville, 1973-75; individual practice law, asso. firm Talbott, Mershon Sywers & Cunningham, 1975-80; commr. Ky. Dept. Ins., 1980—. Mem. Louisville and Jefferson County Planning Commn., 1977-78; bd. dirs. Ky. Youth Conf.; ex-officio mem. Ky. Derby Festival Commn.; mem. Ky. Democratic Central Exec. Com., 1972-76. Mem. Am. Bar Assn., Ky. Bar Assn., Louisville Bar Assn., Young Lawyers Ky. (v.p.), English Speaking Union. Roman Catholic. Office: Box 517 151 Elkhorn Ct Frankfort KY 40602

BRISCOE, JAMES AUSTIN, geol. exploration co. exec.; b. Tucson, July 30, 1941; s. James Watkins and Lura (Austin) B.; B.S., U. Ariz., 1964, M.S., 1967; children—Lura Kirsten, James Austin, Maribeth. Exploration geologist Am. Smelting and Refining Co., 1965-69; chief geologist Geodata, Inc., Orange, Calif., 1969-71; v.p., chief geologist Sierra Mineral Mgmt., Tucson, 1971-73; pres., founder Southwestern Exploration Assos., Inc., Tucson, 1973—. Registered profl. geologist, Ariz., Calif. Mem. Am. Inst. Mining and Metall. Engrs., AAAS, Ariz. Geol. Soc., N.Mex. Geol. Soc., Sigma Xi, Sigma Gamma Epsilon. Republican. Episcopalian. Office: 4500 E Speedway Suite 14 Tucson AZ 85712

BRISCOE, RALPH OWEN, corp. exec.; b. Trenton, Mich., Nov. 15, 1927; B.A., Kenyon Coll., 1950; M.B.A., Harvard U., 1952; m. Joan Trefry, Aug. 24, 1952; children—Ralph Jr., Donald, Stephen, Linda, Lisa. With fin. staff Ford Motor Co., 1953-56, Curtis-Wright Corp., 1956-57; asst. controller CBS, Inc., N.Y.C., 1958-73, controller, 1963-65, v.p. fin., 1965-69, group pres., 1969-73; chmn., pres., chief exec. officer Republic Corp., Century City, Calif., 1973—. Bd. dirs. Los Angeles chpt. NCCJ, 1975—. Mem. Los Angeles Area C. of C. (dir. 1978--). Office: 1900 Ave of Stars Suite 2700 Los Angeles CA 90067

BRITT, ROLLAND W., telephone co. exec.; b. Madison, Wis., 1922; B.A. in Accounting, U. Wis., 1943. With Arthur Andersen & Co., C.P.A.'s, 1943-49; v.p., dir. Gen. Telephone Co. Ill., 1949-67; pres., chief exec. officer Gen. Telephone Co. Pa., Erie, 1967-78, also dir.; pres., chief exec. officer, dir. Gen. Telephone Co. of S.W., San Angelo, Tex., 1978—; pres., dir. Bethel & Mt. Aetna Tel & Tel Co., 1967-78. Office: 2701 Johnson St San Angelo TX 76901

BRITTAIN, ALFRED, III, banker; b. Evanston, Ill., July 22, 1922; s. Alfred, Jr. and Sibyl (Collins) B.; grad. Phillips Exeter Acad., 1941; B.A., Yale, 1945; m. Beatrice Memhard, Dec. 18, 1948; children—Stephen M., Linda C. With Bankers Trust Co., N.Y.C., 1947—, mem. exec. com., 1966—, pres., dir., 1966-75, chmn., 1975—; dir. Collins & Aikman Corp., Philip Morris, Inc.; chmn., dir., mem. exec. com. Bankers Trust New York Corp.; mem. investment adv. com. Royal Globe Ins. Cos. dir. Bus. Mktg. Corp. Trustee, Com. Econ. Devel. Mem. Econ. Devel. Council N.Y.C. (dir.), N.Y. Chamber Commerce and Industry (dir.). Office: Bankers Trust Co 280 Park Ave New York NY 10017

BRITTAIN, JACK WILLIAM, electronics corp. exec.; b. Colorado Springs, Colo., Apr. 10, 1932; s. August Irvin and Elizabeth (Cole) B.; grad. tool and die maker VA apprenticeship program, 1958, Internat. Corr. Schs., 1960; student in bus. Santa Clara U., 1970; m. 2d, Ana Maria Ribiero de Paiva, Nov. 19, 1976; children—Jack William, Terri, Joni, Scott, Judith. Tool and die maker Colorado Springs Machine Corp., 1954-63; tool designer Qualitool Mfg. Co., Santa Clara, Calif., 1963-64; ops. mgr. Tempress Industries, Los Gatos, Calif., 1964-72, Kasper Instruments, Mountain View, Calif., 1972-73; sr. engr. Nat. Semiconductor, Santa Clara, 1973—, dir., gen. mgr. Nat. Semicondr. Electronics do Brasil, 1975-79; gen. mgr. Dismac Indsl. S/A, 1980—. Pres. Pikes Peak Fire Fighters, 1961-63; fire chief Stratton Meadows Fire Protection Dist., 1957-63; various offices Pikes Peak and Santa Clara County councils Boy Scouts Am., 1958—. Served with USN, 1950-54. Recipient various awards Boy Scouts Am. including Silver Beaver, 1974, various fire dept. awards; hon. life mem. Calif. PTA; cert. mfg. engr. Soc. Mfg. Engrs. Mem. Am. Soc. Metals, Am. Mgmt. Assn., Am. C. of C. for Brazil, Aprimesc-Abinee (Brazil). Office: Caixa Postal 837 Manaus Amazonas 69000 Brazil

BRITTENHAM, RAYMOND LEE, communications co. exec.; b. Moscow, Russia, Feb. 8, 1916 (parents U.S. citizens); s. Edward Arthur and Marietta (Wemple) B.; A.B., Principia Coll., Elsah, Ill., 1936; postgrad. Kaiser Wilhelm U., Berlin, Germany, 1937; LL.B., Harvard, 1940; m. Mary Ann Stanard, Nov. 3, 1956; children—Edward C., Carol. Admitted to Ill. bar, 1940, N.Y. State bar, 1946; asso. firm Pope & Ballard, Chgo., 1940-42, Mitchell Carroll, N.Y.C., 1947-56; with IT&T, 1957-80; sr. v.p. law, counsel, 1968-80, dir., 1965-80; with Lazard Freres, 1980—; pres. The Spanish Inst.; sec. U.S. sect. Internat. Fiscal Assn., 1950-57; bd. dirs. Nat. Fgn. Trade Council, 1961—. Served to maj. AUS, 1942-46. Decorated Bronze Star medal; Croix de Guerre (France and Belgium); chevalier Ordre de Leopold (Belgium). Mem. Am. Bar Assn., Council Fgn. Relations. Club: University (N.Y.C.). Home: 925 Park Ave New York NY 10028 Office: 1 Rockefeller Plaza New York NY 10020

BRITTON, DONALD ROBISON, opera co. exec.; b. Phila., Oct. 8, 1937; s. Frank Robison and Gladys Rebecca (Hoff) B.; student Haverford Coll., 1955, Chgo. City Coll., 1973; m. Susan Marchant, Mar. 3, 1964; children—Eve Marchant, Christopher Robison. Dist. mgr. Trans-Lux Theatres, N.Y.C., 1961-65; mng. dir. Meadow Brook Theatre, Detroit, 1966-70; founder, exec. dir. Upstage Detroit, Inc., 1971-72; bus. mgr. Lyric Opera of Chgo., 1972—; regional judge Am. Coll. Theatre Festival, 1971-72; co-founder, trustee Opera Sch. of Chgo., 1974—. Served with U.S. Army, 1960-61. Mem. Assn. Theatrical Press Agts. & Mgrs. Republican. Episcopalian. Clubs: Arts, Econ., Saddle & Cycle. Office: 20 N Wacker Dr Chicago IL 60606

BRIXEY, STEPHEN SIMMONS, JR., investment banker; b. Norman, Okla., Mar. 31, 1936; s. Stephen Simmons and Nondis L. (Zirkle) B.; B.S., U. Calif. at Los Angeles, 1959; Asso. Investment Bankers, U. Pa., 1967-70; m. JoAnne Wood, May 10, 1959; 1 son, Stephen. With Bateman Eichler, Hill Richards, Torrance, Calif., 1961-79, mgr., 1962-79, v.p., 1967-79, mng. dir. Century City office, Los Angeles, 1980—, dir., 1977—. Served to capt. AUS, 1959-62. Presbyterian (chmn. trustees ch. 1973-74). Club: Los Angeles Bond. Home: 1624 Via Arriba Palos Verdes Estates CA 90274 Office: 1900 Ave of Stars Los Angeles CA 90067

BROADBENT, ROBERT KENNETH, JR., sales exec.; b. Middleboro, Mass., Nov. 21, 1926; s. Robert and Alice (Laflamme) B.; student pub. schs.; m. Emily Pratt, Oct. 12, 1947; children—Linda, Joan, Karen, Cindy, Douglas, Kenny, Hazel. Salesman, Ralston Purina Co., St. Louis, 1965-70; sales mgr. Agway Inc., Syracuse, N.Y., 1971—, dist. mgr., 1971—. Mem. Cape Cod Mgrs. Assn. Republican. Baptist. Home and office: PO Box 627 Lakeside Ave Lakeville MA 02346

BROADBENT, ROBERT R., retail co. exec.; b. Lisbon, Ohio, May 25, 1921; s. Raymond and Ruth Edna (Schoonover) B.; B.S., U. Akron (Ohio), 1946; m. Mary; 1 son, William Stuart. Personal asst. to Cyrus S. Eaton, Cleve., 1946-49; various positions in retailing, 1949-58; exec. v.p., dir. Higbee Co., Cleve., 1958-73, pres., vice chmn. bd., 1979—, also dir.; chmn. bd., chief exec. officer Gimbel's, N.Y.C., 1973-76; pres., chief exec. officer Liberty House-Mainland, San Francisco, 1976-79; dir. Frederick Atkins, Inc., N.Y.C., 1976—; mem. Retail Mfrs. Adv. Bd., Williamsburg, Va., 1965-73. Bd. dirs. 34th St.-Midtown Assn., N.Y.C., 1973-76, Ave. Americas Assn., N.Y.C., 1973-76, Herald-Greeley Sq. Devel. Council, N.Y.C., 1973-76, San Francisco Spring Opera Theater, 1977—; v.p. Davis Cup and Wightman Cup com. Northeastern Ohio Tennis Assn., Cleve., 1959-73; v.p., trustee Cleve. Mental Health Assn., 1968-73, Cleve. Play House, 1969-73; trustee, exec. com. Glen Oak Girl's Sch., Cleve., 1971-73; pres. PEERS, suicide center, Cleve., 1972; vice chmn. region IV, Central Ski Assn., Cleve., 1968-73. Served with USAAF, 1943-45; ETO. Decorated D.F.C., Air medal with 4 oak leaf clusters. Clubs: Claremont Country (Oakland, Calif.); San Francisco Tennis; Cleve. Racquet, Cleve. Country, Union (Cleve.); Union League (N.Y.C.). Office: Higbee Co 100 Public Sq Cleveland OH 44113*

BROADHURST, NORMAN NEIL, foods co. exec.; b. Chico, Calif., Dec. 17, 1946; s. Frank Spencer and Dorothy Mae (Conrad) B.; B.S., Calif. State U., 1969; M.B.A., Golden Gate U., 1975; m. Victoria Rose Thomson, Aug. 7, 1976; 1 son, Scott Andrew. With Del Monte Corp., San Francisco, 1969-76, product mgr., 1973-76; product mgr. Riviana Foods, Inc., div. Colgate Palmolive, Houston, 1976-78; new products brand devel. mgr. foods div. Coca Cola Co., Houston, 1978-79, brand mgr., 1979—. Mem. Am. Mgmt. Assn., Am. Mktg. Assn. Clubs: Toastmasters Internat. (past chpt. pres.), Houston Met. Racquet. Home: 5714 Council Grove Houston TX 77088 Office: 7105 Old Katy Rd Houston TX 77005

BROADWOOD, THOMAS EDWARD, transp. exec.; b. Chatham, Ont., Can., Mar. 27, 1929; s. Thomas Walter and Lela Pearl (Morse) B.; student public schs., Ont.; m. Marguerite Schultz, Apr. 11, 1953; children—Kevin Randall, Kimberly. Traffic mgr. Lake Erie Coal & Nav., Blenheim, Ont., 1948-49; chief traffic control and rate clk. Internat. Harvester Co., Chatham, 1950-62; exec. v.p., partner Frederick Transport Ltd., Chatham, 1963—. Mem. Can. Indsl. Traffic League, Ont. Trucking Assn. (dir. 1979-80), Am. Trucking Assn., Mich. Trucking Assn., Chatham Transp. Club. Address: Rural Route 6 Chatham ON N7M 5J6 Canada

BROCK, JAMES DANIEL, airline exec.; b. Montgomery County, Ala., Feb. 19, 1916; s. Alexander Franklin and Rebecca Bookhart (Lamar) B.; student Tulane U., 1936-37; m. Alice Ferguson Jones, Jan. 8, 1948; children—James Daniel, Alice Timoxena, Franklin Laurens. Vice pres. TACA Internat. Airlines and TACA Corp., 1953-59, Frontier Airlines, 1959-62; v.p. traffic and sales Nat. Airlines, Inc., Miami Fla., 1962-73, v.p. mktg., 1973-77, v.p. internat., 1977-80, dir., 1974-80; v.p., asst. to pres. Pan Am. World Airways, Miami, 1980—; dir. Citizens Fed. Savs. & Loan, Miami; hon. consul Guatemala in Denver, 1960-62; trustee Met. Mus. and Art Center of Miami; bd. dirs. Lighthouse for Blind, Miami. Served to capt. USAAF, 1941-45. Mem. Caribbean Air Transp. Assn. (pres. 1956-59) Am. Soc. Travel Agts., Nat. Orgn. Travel Orgns. (dir.), Air Traffic Conf. Am. (pres. 1970), Discover Am. Travel Orgns. (dir.), Greater Miami C. of C. (gov.), Phi Delta Theta. Methodist. Clubs: Riviera Country; Biscayne Bay Yacht (Miami, Fla.). Home: 4107 Santa Maria Coral Gables FL 33146 Office: PO Box 592055 AMF Miami FL 33159

BROCK, JAMES MELMUTH, engring. co. exec.; b. Brockton, Mass., Jan. 12, 1944; s. James Melmuth and Ruth Eleanor (Copeland) B.; student U. Hawaii, 1964-65, Taiwan Normal U., 1969; m. Mary Soong, June 24, 1964; 1 dau., Cynthia. Survey apprentice Malcolm Shaw, Hanson, Mass., 1959-62; with Peace Corps, N. Borneo, 1962-64; engr. Austin, Smith & Assos., Honolulu, 1964-65, Trans-Asia Engrs., Vietnam, 1965-67; ops. mgr. Teledyne, Bangkok, Thailand, 1967-69; chief surveys Norman Saito Engrs. Hawaii, 1970-73; sr. prin. Brock and Assos., Maui, Hawaii, 1973—; dir. Pitt Engring. Inc., Brock Realty Ltd.; del. White House Conf. Small Bus., 1980. Registered land surveyor, Hawaii. Mem. Am. Congress Surveying and Mapping, Am. Water Works Assn., Profl. Services Mgmt. Assn., Hawaii Soc. Profl. Engrs. Democrat. Congregationalist. Home: 766 Kupulau Dr Kihei Maui HI 96752 Office: 48 Market St Wailuku Maui HI 96793

BROCK, KATHRYN JUSTER, Realtor; b. Wichita Falls, Tex., Feb. 22, 1922; d. Edward L. and Goldie (Mark) Juster; student Ohio State U., 1937-38; B.A., U. Minn., 1940, postgrad., 1940-41; m. Warren Richard Brock, Aug. 1, 1940; children—Rick, Jeffrey J., Bonnie Sy. Mgr., adressograph graphotype dept. Tucson Newspapers, Inc., 1947-48; office mgr. Perfect Block Co., Tucson, 1949-50; controller Larry Sakin Corp., Tucson, 1950-54; saleswoman Juster's Realty, Tucson, 1954-58, broker, 1958-69; broker New Age Realty, Tucson, 1969—; v.p., dir. Worldwide Travel, Tucson, 1967—. Pres., Democratic Women's Club, 1962; del. Dem. Nat. Conv., 1976. Mem. Pima County Bar Aux. (chmn. com. for jud. offices 1951-72), Nat., Tucson bds. realtors, Tucson Multiple Listing Service, AAUW, Sigma Delta Tau. Democrat. Jewish. Clubs: Tucson Women's, Ocotillo Women's. Home: 5242 Genematas Dr Tucson AZ 85704 Office: 244 W Drachman St Tucson AZ 85705

BROCK, WILLIAM GEORGE, fin. cons.; b. Dallas, Oreg., Dec. 6, 1928; s. Guy Glen and Sarah Jennie (Schriver) B.; student Linfield Coll., 1946-48; A.B., U. Wash., 1950, postgrad. Sch. Credit and Fin. Mgmt., 1961-63; postgrad. Mgmt., U. Calif., 1958-60; m. Carol June Sharp, Aug. 19, 1950; 2 sons, Geoffrey Stuart, Gregory Philip. With Nat. Bank of Commerce of Seattle, 1950-53; asst. trust officer, Alaska Nat. Bank, Fairbanks, 1953-56; credit analyst, Wells Fargo Bank, San Francisco, 1956-59, asst. cashier, 1959-62, asst. v.p., 1962-65, v.p. nat. div., 1965-67, v.p., mgr. corp. banking div., Los Angeles, 1967-73, sr. v.p., 1973-74; pres. Security Bank of Oreg., Portland, 1974; exec. v.p., B. M. Behrends Bank, Juneau, Alaska, 1974-76, pres., 1976-78; cons. corp. and project financing, Juneau, 1978—. Dir. Juneau C. of C., 1976-78, pres., 1977; mem. Juneau City and Borough Econ. Diversification Com., 1976-80, chmn., 1976-78; mem. Juneau City and Borough Housing Rehab. Com., 1979—, Juneau City and Borough Adjustment Commn., 1980—. Mem. Alaska Bankers Assn. (dir. 1975-78, pres. 1978), Med. Indemnity Corp. Alaska (bd. govs. 1976—, chmn. 1976-77). Republican. Clubs: Wash. Athletic, Juneau Yacht. Home: 1700 Angus Way Juneau AK 99801 Office: 326 4th St Suite 202 Juneau AK 99801

BROCKER, EDWARD EUGENE, fire protection and security co. exec.; b. Wausau, Wis., Apr. 20, 1951; s. Elroy Edward and Marilyn Mary (Tellock) B.; student Waukesha County Tech. Inst., Pewakee, Wis., 1975-78; m. Belinda C. LaRocque, Feb. 20, 1971. Asst. mgr. Falls Music Center, Memonomee Falls, Wis., 1966-72; with Harvey J. Winter & Co., Inc., fire protection, Milw., 1973—80, gen. mgr., 1979-80; pres., chief exec. officer Guardian Fire, Safety & Security, Inc., Menomonee Falls, 1980—; tchr. fire brigades, cons. to industry. Mem. Nat. Fire Protection Assn., Am. Mgmt. Assn., Nat. Assn. Credit Mgmt. Club: Kiwanis. Office: n88 w16675 Appleton Ave PO Box 266 Menomonee Falls WI 53051

BROCKMEYER, WILLIAM DONALD, ins. co. exec.; b. Balt., May 8, 1929; s. Richard Charles and Barbara (Rose) B.; B.S. in Edn., U. Md., 1951; B.S. in Meteorology, Pa. State U., 1952, M.S. in Meteorology, 1957; M.A. in Bus. Mgmt., U. Nebr., Lincoln, 1977; children—Lee A., Diane T., William D. II, Robert E. Commd. lt. U.S. Air Force, 1951, advanced through grades to col., 1977; ret., 1977; asst. prof. bus. mgmt. Dana Coll., 1977-78; tng. dir. Ins. Co. N. Am., San Jose, Calif., 1978—. Decorated Meritorious Service medal (2). Mem. Am. Mgmt. Assn., Am. Soc. Tng. and Devel., Omicron Delta Kappa. Roman Catholic. Office: PO Box 50055 San Jose CA 95150

BROD, HOWARD SEYMOUR, business exec.; b. N.Y.C., Feb. 15, 1919; s. Morris and Ann (Kauffman) B.; grad., Manlius Mil. Acad., 1935; B.A., Harvard, 1939, postgrad., 1939-41; m. Suzanne LaFrance, July 14, 1964; children by previous marriage—Della Ann, Howard Worrell. Sr. v.p. Wells/Jewelart Co., N.Y.C. Served with Am. Field Service, 1942-45; MTO, ETO. Home: 22 Arnold St Providence RI 02906 Office: 15 W 36th St New York NY 10018

BRODERICK, EDWARD MICHAEL, III, fin. and ins. exec.; b. Stamford, Conn., Nov. 4, 1947; s. Edward Michael and Lois Carolyn (Brown) B.; B.A., St. Anselm's Coll., Manchester, N.H., 1969; J.D., St. John's U., N.Y.C., 1973. Adminstrv. asst. legis. services Royal-Globe Ins. Cos., N.Y.C., 1969-74, atty., 1974-75; admitted to Conn. and N.Y. bars, 1974; corp. atty. Gen. Elec. Credit Corp. and Puritan Ins. Co., and predecessor, Stamford, 1975-79, asst. counsel, sec., 1976-79; sr. counsel ITT Fin. Corp., St. Louis, 1979—; asst. sec. and sr. counsel Lyndon Ins. Co., ITT Lyndon Life Ins. Co. and ITT Lyndon Property Ins. Co., St. Louis, 1979—. Mem. Am., N.Y. State, Conn. bar assns. Republican. Episcopalian. Home: 1968 Meadow Tree Ln Kirkwood MO 63122 Office: 700 Community Fed Center 12555 Manchester Rd Saint Louis MO 63131

BRODHEAD, JOHN, JR., ins. brokerage exec.; b. Springfield, Ill., Dec. 6, 1917; s. John and Dorothy (Farish) B.; A.B., Amherst Coll., 1940; postgrad. Washington U., St. Louis, 1949-50; m. Josephine Caree, Aug. 1, 1942; 1 dau., Josephine Brodhead Roberts. Partner, George D. Capen & Co., St. Louis, 1945-63; v.p., mgr. St. Louis office Marsh & McLennan, Inc., St. Louis, 1963-71, div. mgr., 1969-73, head nat. sales, 1973-75, head client/corp. devel., merger and acquisition, 1975-77, area mgr., 1977—, exec. v.p., 1969—, also dir. Bd. dirs. Easter Seal Soc., St. Louis, Mary Inst. Sch., St. Louis, St. Louis Country Day Sch., Child Guidance Clinic, St. Louis; active United Way of Greater St. Louis. Served with USNR, 1940-45. Decorated D.F.C., Air medal with gold star. Home: 4 Town & Country Dr Ladue MO 63124 Office: 515 Olive St Saint Louis MO 63101

BRODIE, DONALD GIBBS, investment co. exec.; b. N.Y.C., Oct. 24, 1938; s. Bruce James and Laurene Elizabeth (Rolf) B.; B.S., U. Pa., 1960; postgrad. U. Lausanne (Switzerland), 1962-63; M.B.A., N.Y. U., 1969; m. Gail Robison, Aug. 26, 1966; children—Lesley Thompson, Alexandra Paget, Ian Rolf. With Discount Corp. N.Y., N.Y.C., 1963—, v.p., asst. sec., 1970-72, v.p., sec., 1972-78, sr. v.p., sec., 1978—; sec. Discount Corp. N.Y. Advisers; sec., dir. Discount Corp. N.Y. Futures. Trustee, treas. Buckley Country Day Sch., Roslyn, N.Y. Served with USNR, 1960-62. Clubs: Univ., Downtown Assn. Office: 58 Pine St New York NY 10005

BRODIE, THEODORE HAMILTON, constrn. and distbn. co. exec.; b. Newton, Mass., Dec. 16, 1929; s. Theodore E. and Martha Washington (Hamilton) B.; B.A., Bowdoin Coll., 1952; m. Robin Fletcher Garland, May 20, 1978; children by previous marriage—Glenn A., Karen Lee, Beth Sprague. Salesman, Proctor & Gamble, 1952; sales engr. New Eng. Insulation Co., Canton, Mass., 1956-63, contract mgr., 1963-69, pres., 1969—, also gen. mgr.; pres., chief exec. officer Nat. Energy Inc., Canton; treas. A.F. Underhill Co. Inc., Somerville, Mass., Indsl. Insulation Co., Concordville, Pa.; chmn. bd. Insulation Supply Corp., Louisville, Ky.; gen. partner Hamilton Leasing Co., Duxbury, Mass.; owner Brodie Realty Trust, Portland, Maine. Moderator Pilgrim Congregational Ch., Duxbury, 1963-64; chmn. sch. com. Town of Duxbury, 1974-75; pres. Duxbury PTA; mem. Gov.'s Commn. on Rail Services, Mass., 1974—. Served with USNR, 1952-56. Mem. Young Pres. Orgn., World Bus. Council, Am. Arbitration Assn., Nat. Insulation Contractors Assn., World Insulation-Acoustic Congress Orgn. Republican. Clubs: Duxbury Yacht, Blue Water Sailing, N.Y. Yacht, U.S. Yacht Racing Union, Yacht Racing Union of Mass Bay, Masons, Rotary, Bowdoin of Boston, Execs. of Boston, Stadium.

BRODSKY, DAVID MICHAEL, lawyer; b. Providence, Oct. 16, 1943; s. Irving and Naomi Bernice (Richman) B.; A.B. cum laude, Brown U., 1964; LL.B., Harvard U., 1967; m. Barbara Banks, Aug. 22, 1965; children—Katherine, Peter Samuel. Admitted to N.Y. bar, 1968; law clk. to U.S. dist. judge So. Dist. N.Y., 1967-69, asst. U.S. atty. So. Dist. N.Y., 1969-73; asso. firm Guggenheimer & Untermyer, N.Y.C., 1973-75, partner, 1976-80; partner firm Schulte & McGoldrick, 1980—; dep. counsel to N.Y. State Moreland Act Commn. on Urban Devel. Corp., 1975-76; lectr. trial advocacy, chmn. broker-dealer liability Practising Law Inst., 1976—; chmn. legal com. Bklyn. Heights Assn., 1974-76, land use devel. com., 1976-78. Mem. Am. Bar Assn. (com. fed. regulation securities), Assn. Bar City N.Y., N.Y. County Lawyers Assn. (com. on securities and exchanges), Fed. Bar Council (2d circuit com.). Democrat. Jewish. Clubs: Brooklyn Heights Casino; Brown U. (N.Y.C.). Home: 24 Monroe Pl Brooklyn NY 11201 Office: 460 Park Ave New York NY 10022

BRODSKY, WILLIAM JAY, stock exchange exec.; b. N.Y.C., Jan. 29, 1944; s. Irwin A. and Helen (Kamen) B.; A.B., Syracuse U., 1965, J.D., 1968; m. Joan Breier, Dec. 17, 1966; children—Michael, Stephen, Jonathan. Asst. v.p. Model Roland & Co., Inc., N.Y.C., 1968-74; admitted to N.Y. bar, 1969; with American Stock Exchange, N.Y.C., 1974—, exec. v.p. ops., 1974—; dir. Options Clearing Corp.; lectr. N.Y. Inst. Finance, 1972—. Bd. visitors Syracuse U. Coll. Law, 1974—. Mem. Am. Bar Assn. Office: 86 Trinity Pl New York NY 10006

BROECKER, JOSEPH H., health care co. exec.; b. Indpls., Nov. 12, 1945; s. Cletus A. and Sarah H. (Yount) B.; B.B.A., U. Notre Dame, 1967; M.S., Purdue U., 1972; m. Dianna Crossland, Dec. 11, 1967; children—Joseph, Timothy. Supr. mgmt. cons. services Ernst & Ernst, Indpls., 1967-72, Chgo., 1972-73; dir. corp. planning Bio-Dynamics, Inc., Indpls., 1973-75, corp. v.p., 1975-77, pres. Environ. Systems div., 1977-78; pres. Bio-Dynamics Home Healthcare, Inc., Indpls., 1978—; dir. DePuy LatinoAmericano S.A., C & J Minerals Co., Design Systems, Inc. Bd. dirs., treas. Cathedral Prep. High Sch., Indpls., 1974-79; mem. Greater Indpls. Progress Com., 1975-78. C.P.A., Ind. Mem. Am. Inst. C.P.A.'s, Ind. Assn. C.P.A.'s, Am. Mgmt. Assn. (pres.'s assn.), Am. Public Health Assn., Healthcare Industry Mfrs. Assn., Nat. Wholesale Druggists Assn. Nat. Assn. Chain Drug Stores (asso.), Newcomen Soc. Roman Catholic. Clubs: Indpls. Athletic, Notre Dame (Indpls.); Hillcrest Country, K.C. Home: 6767 Springbrook Dr N Indianapolis IN 46219 Office: 6405 Castleway Ct Indianapolis IN 46250

BROFFMAN, MORTON HOWARD, mgmt. and media cons.; b. N.Y.C., Aug. 17, 1920; s. Samuel L. and Fannie B. (Mack) B.; B.A. cum laude, CCNY, 1940; M.A., N.Y. U., 1943; M.A. (teaching fellow 1949-50), Harvard U., 1950, M.P.A., 1951, Ph.D., 1953; m. Louise Hargrove, Dec. 24, 1969; children—Trudy, Jane, Michael. Vice pres., dir. mfg. and engring. Rayco Co., 1953-56, sr. v.p., dir. mktg. and retail stores, 1956-61; exec. v.p., gen. mgr. L.A. Darling Co., 1961-63; exec. v.p., chief operating officer United Brands Corp., N.Y.C., 1964-70; pres. Am. Biltrite, Inc., Boston, 1970-74; pres., chief exec. officer Combined Mgmt. Services Corp., N.Y.C., 1975-80, Public Media Inc., Wilmette, Ill., 1980—; dir. Sterndent Corp., Films, Inc., Public Media Corp., Bldg. Materials Distbrs. Co.; mem. faculty Northeastern U., Boston, 1950-51, Rutgers U., 1955-56. Bd. dirs. Save the Children Fedn., 1978—. Served with USN, 1944-46. Mem. Am. Mgmt. Assn., Conf. Bd., Am. Mktg. Assn., Inst. Indsl. Engrs. Clubs: Harvard (Boston and N.Y.C.); Manhattan, Drug and Chem., Internat., Whitehall, Touhy Tennis. Author, cons. editor profl. publs. Home: 1410 Sheridan Rd Wilmette IL 60091 Office: Public Media Inc 1144 Wilmette Ave Wilmette IL 60091

BROKAW, MARVIN JAY, JR., bank mktg. exec.; b. Kansas City, Mo., Nov. 14, 1938; s. Marvin J. and Eleanor Marie (Chitty) B.; B.A. in Market Research, Mich. State U., 1960; m. Charlotte Rosalie Carpenter, Jan. 20, 1968; 1 dau., Leslie Diane. Reporter, F.W. Dodge div. McGraw-Hill, Inc., Kalamazoo, 1960-61, dist. salesman, Mpls., 1964-69; sec.-treas. Compos-it, Inc., Montgomery, Ala., 1969-77; asst. mktg. officer 1st Ala. Bank, Montgomery, 1977-80, mktg. officer, 1980—; mem. Ala. Gov.'s Conf. on Library and Info. Services, 1979—, mem. exec. com., 1979—; mem. Citizens Adv. Com. on Public TV. Served with U.S. Army, 1961-64. Mem. Am. Inst. Banking, Advt. Club Montgomery (Silver Medal award 1978), Bank Mktg. Assn., Sales and Mktg. Execs. Club Montgomery. Club: Kiwanis. Home: 3010 Merrimac Dr Montgomery AL 36111 Office: PO Box 511 Montgomery AL 36134

BRONFMAN, EDGAR MILES, distillery co. exec.; b. Montreal, Que., Can., June 20, 1929; s. Samuel and Saidye (Rosner) B.; student Williams Coll., 1946-49; B.A., McGill U., 1951. Chmn. adminstrv. com. Joseph E. Seagram & Sons, Inc., 1955-57, pres., 1957-71; pres. Distillers Corp.-Seagrams Ltd., Montreal, 1971-75; chmn., chief exec. officer Seagram Co. Ltd., 1975—; chmn., dir. Clevepak Corp., Internat. Exec. Service Corps, Gulfstream Land and Devel. Corp.; hon. trustee Bank N.Y. Bd. dirs. Citizens Com. for N.Y.C., Interracial Council for Bus. Opportunity; Am. com. Weizmann Inst. Sci.; exec. bd. govs. N.Y. councils Boy Scouts Am.; trustee Park East Synagogue, Mt. Sinai Hosp., Sch. Medicine and Med. Center, Salk Inst. Biol. Studies; trustee, pres. Samuel Bronfman Found.; pres. World Jewish Congress. Mem. Center for Inter-Am. Relations, Council Fgn. Relations, Am. Technion Soc. (dir.), Hundred Year Assn. N.Y., United Jewish Appeal, Fedn. Jewish Philanthropies, Com. for Econ. Devel., Nat. Urban League, Fgn. Policy Assn., Bus. Com. for Arts, Inc. Office: Seagram Co Ltd 375 Park Ave New York NY 10052

BRONFMAN, EDWARD M., investment co. exec.; b. Montreal, Que., Can., Nov. 1, 1927; s. Allan and Lucy (Bilsky) B.; B.Sc. in Bus. Adminstrn., Babson Coll., 1950; children—Paul Arthur, David Eric, Brian Anthony. Chmn. bd., dir. Edper Investments Ltd., Toronto, Ont., Can.; dir. Ranger Oil (Can.) Ltd., Nat. Hees Enterprises Ltd., Trizec Corp. Ltd. Bd. govs. Montreal Gen. Hosp., Jewish Gen. Hosp., YMHA, Que. Student Inter-Exchange Program; bd. mgmt. YMCA; Eastern regional chmn. Can. Friends of Hebrew U. Jewish. Office: Edper Investments Ltd Royal Bank Plaza Suite 3601 PO Box 93 Toronto ON Canada*

BROODO, ARCHIE, cons. engr.; b. Wichita Falls, Tex., Feb. 3, 1925; s. Jack and Celia (Katz) B.; B.S. in Chem. Engring., Tex. A&M U., 1948, M.A. in Chemistry, 1950, Ph.D. in Phys.-Inogranic Chemistry, 1954; m. Dorothy Jean Marshall, Sept. 2, 1951; children—Marcia Rose, Charlene, Jack, Kenneth Chaim. Sr. materials engr. Convair div. Gen. Dynamics Corp., 1953-56; mem. tech. staff, research div. Tex. Instruments, Inc., 1956-59; mgr. engring., capacitor div. Gen. Electric Co., 1959-63; v.p. engring. capacitor div. Gen. Instruments Corp., 1963-66; div. mgr. hybrid microcircuits Varo Inc., 1966-68; pres. Technology Cons., Inc., 1968-71; pres., chmn. bd. AID Cons. Engrs., Inc., Dallas, 1917—. Mem. Dallas Explosive Appeals Bd. Served with U.S. Army, 1944-46. Mem. Am. Chem. Soc., Am. Soc. Metals, IEEE, Internat. Assn. Arson Investigators. Jewish. Co-author fire sci. series, audio-visual programs in fire investigation; patentee in field. Office: 2828 Merrell Dallas TX 75229

BROOKER, RICHARD HERBERT, pub. co. exec.; b. West Palm Beach, Fla., Mar. 7, 1930; s. Grant and Louise Catherine (Genthner) B.; student pub. schs. West Palm Beach, Fla.; m. Patricia Gibson, Dec. 28, 1963; children—Richard Herbert, Grant R., Kathleen A., James R., Scott G., Michael P. Southeastern sales mgr. Americana Corp. div. Grolier Inc., Washington, 1951-62; regional mgr. C.R.E.I. div. McGraw Hill Inc., Charleston, S.C., 1963-69, area mgr. electronic home study div., Norfolk, Va., 1969-78; area mgr. Mitre Sports, 1978—; sr. v.p. B&B Inc., Norfolk. Bd. dirs. Charity Fund of Lodge 1, Norfolk, Inc. Republican. Episcopalian. Club: Masons. Home: 7400 Spartan Ave Norfolk VA 23518 Office: PO Box 14395 Norfolk VA 23518

BROOKES, VALENTINE, lawyer; b. Red Bluff, Calif., May 30, 1913; s. Langley and Ethel (Valentine) B.; A.B., U. Calif., 1934, LL.B., 1937, J.D., 1967; m. Virginia Stovall Cunningham, Feb. 11, 1939;

children—Langley Brookes Brandt, Lawrence Valentine, Alan Cunningham. Admitted to Calif. bar, 1937; asst. tax counsel Calif. Francise Tax Commr., 1937-40; dep. atty. gen. State of Calif., 1940-42; spl. asst. to atty. gen. U.S., asst. to Solictor-Gen., 1942-44; partner firm Kent & Brookes, San Franciso, 1944-70, Alvord & Alvord, Washington, 1944-50, Lee, Toomey & Kent, Washington, 1950-79, Brookes and Brookes, San Francisco, 1971—; part time instr. Hastings Coll. Law, U. Calif., 1942-46; vis. lectr. U. Calif. Sch. Law, 1946-70. Regent St. Mary's Coll. (Calif.), pres. bd., 1970-72. Fellow Am. Bar Found.; mem. State Bar Calif. (com. on taxation 1946-52, chmn. 1950-52, 1960-61), San Francisco, Am. (council tax sect. 1960-63, chmn. com. on statute of limitations 1954-57) bar assns., Am. Law Inst., Soc. Calif. Pioneers (v.p.), Phi Kappa Sigma, Phi Delta Phi. Clubs: Pacific Union, Orinda Country, Bankers, World Trade (San Francisco). Author: The Continuity of Interest Test in Reorganization, 1946; The Partnership Under the Income Tax Laws, 1949; The Tax Consequences of Widows' Elections in Community Property States, 1951; Corporate Transactions Involving Its Own Stock, 1954; Litigation Expenses and the Income Tax, 1957. Home: 7 Sycamore Rd Orinda CA 94563 Office: Suite 1902 601 California St San Francisco CA 94111

BROOKFIELD, ARTHUR DUTTON, II, garment mfg. co. exec.; b. Kansas City, Mo., Oct. 4, 1946; s. Dutton and Betty Grace (Bell) B.; student Parsons Coll., 1966-67, U. Mo., 1969; m. Cynthia Cosgrove, Sept. 16, 1972; children—Arthur Dutton, John Tyler, Charles Cameron. With Unitog Co., Kansas City, Mo., 1970—, salesman, 1970-72, product mgr., 1973, nat. account mgr., 1974-75, regional sales mgr., 1976-77, v.p. materials mgt., 1978-79, sr. v.p. ops., 1979, pres., 1979—, dir., 1978—. Bd. dirs. Kansas City Mus., 1979, Heart of Am. Boy Scouts, 1979, Starlight Theatre, 1979; trustee Midwest Research Inst., 1980, Civic Council Greater Kansas City, 1980; bd. govs. Am. Royal Assn., 1977. Served with U.S. Army, 1967-69. Decorated Bronze Star. Mem. Young Pres.'s Orgn., NAM, Nat. Assn. Uniform Mfrs., Am. Apparel Mfrs. Assn. Republican. Presbyterian. Clubs: Kansas City Country; Kansas City; Rotary. Home: 42 Janssen Pl Kansas City MO 64109 Office: 101 W 11th St Kansas City MO 64105

BROOKMAN, ANTHONY RAYMOND, SR., lawyer; b. Chgo., Mar. 23, 1922; s. Raymond Charles and Marie (Alberg) B.; student Ripon Coll., 1940-41; B.S., Northwestern U., 1947; LL.B., J.D., Hastings Coll. Law, U. Calif., 1953; children—Meribeth Logan, Anthony Raymond, Lindsay Logan. Admitted to Calif. bar, 1953; law sec. Justice Jesse W. Carter, Calif. Supreme Ct. 1953-54; now partner firm Brookman & Hoffman Inc., specializing in trial of cases in state and fed. cts. Pres. Young Reps. of Calif., San Mateo County, 1953-54. Served with USAAF, 1943-46; PTO. Mem. Am., Alameda County bar assns., State Bar Calif. (lectr. continuing edn. of bar 1971), Oakland Mus. Assn., Thurston Soc., Am. Assn. Trial Lawyers, Calif. Trial Lawyers Assn., Beta Theta Pi, Phi Alpha Delta. Clubs: Elks, Athenian Nile, Athens Athletic; Lawyers of Alameda County. Home: 134 Rudgear Dr Walnut Creek CA 94596 Office: Walnut Creek Plaza Bldg Walnut Creek CA 94596 also Court Plaza Bldg Sacramento CA 95814

BROOKS, BERNARD EDWARD, mgmt. cons.; b. Camden, S.C., July 8, 1935; s. James and Bertha (Haile) B.; A.A.S. in Acctg., Bklyn. Coll., 1964; B.S. in Acctg., Fairleigh Dickinson U., 1973; M.S. in Mgmt., Pace U., 1978; m. Alice Lillian Morris, Sept. 22, 1956; children—Bernard E., Sharon, Karen, Susan, Theresa. Systems planning officer Chase Manhattan Bank, N.A., 1968-69; dir. data services adminstrn. Trans World Airlines, N.Y.C., 1969-70; prin. Arthur Young & Co., N.Y.C., 1970-74, dir., partner, 1978—; market mgr. AT&T, Morristown, N.J., 1974-78. Council, Twp. of Teaneck (N.J.), 1978—, dep. mayor, 1978-79; trustee Holy Name Hosp., Teaneck, 1979—. Served with USAF, 1952-56. Named Man of Yr., N. N.J. chpt. Negro Bus. and Profl. Women, 1979. Mem. Assn. Computing Machinery, Soc. Telecommunications Cons., Nat. Assn. Black Accts., Am. Mgmt. Assn., Alpha Phi Alpha. Roman Catholic. Club: Marco Polo (N.Y.C.). Home: 273 Glen Ct Teaneck NJ 07666 Office: Arthur Young & Co 277 Park Ave New York NY 10017

BROOKS, DANIEL TOWNLEY, lawyer; b. N.Y.C., Apr. 15, 1941; s. Robert Daniel and Mary (Lee) B.; B.S.E. cum laude, Princeton U., 1963; LL.B., Stanford U., 1967, M.S.E., 1968; m. Barbara Badertscher, June 16, 1973. Admitted to Calif. bar, 1968, N.Y. bar, 1969; gen. corp. atty. firm Cadwalader, Wickersham & Taft, N.Y.C., 1968-79; atty.-fellow office of market structure and trading practices, div. market regulation SEC, Washington, 1979—; chmn. commn. software issues in the 80's and PLI seminars on computer law, 1979, 80, 81. Mem. Computer Law Assn. (sec.), Am. Bar Assn., N.Y. Bar Assn., Calif. Bar Assn., Fed. Ct. Bar Council, Assn. Computing Machinery, IEEE. Clubs: Princeton (Washington); Blue Hill Troupe Ltd. Contbr. articles on computer law to profl. and trade jours. Office: Room 388 500 N Capitol St NW Washington DC 20549

BROOKS, EVANS BARTLETT, engraving co. exec., banker; b. New Albany, Ind., Jan. 28, 1900; s. William Wilson and Bertha (Evans) B.; student bus. adminstrn. Louisville YMCA Extension and Ind. U. Extension; m. Margaret Marby, Mar. 6, 1926; children—Marcia Jayne Brooks Browne, Sandra Lee Brooks Jordan. Vice pres. Delaware Engraving Co., Muncie, Ind., 1926-31, Ditzel-Brooks Co., Dayton, Ohio, 1931-32; v.p.-sec. Wayne Colorplate Co., Dayton, 1932-37, pres., treas., 1937—; v.p., treas. Brooks Investment Co., Dayton, 1956—, dir., 1966-72; chmn. bd. Third Nat. Bank & Trust Co., Dayton. Dir., past pres. Photo-Engravers Research Inst.; charter mem. Dayton Area Progress Council, 1961; founder mem., 1st pres. All-Dayton Com., 1945-47; trustee Dayton and Montgomery County Pub. Library (pres. 1961-64); pres. Dayton Art Inst., 1949-51; ex-chmn. Montgomery County chpt. ARC; past pres. Presbyn. bd. Home Missions (Ohio); past dir. Westminster Found., Dayton Community Chest, Dayton Council World Affairs; chmn. bldg. com. Air Force Mus., 1968—; chmn. Montgomery County Bldg. Com., 1968—; bd. dirs., past chmn. 169 Bd. Mentally Retarded; bd. dirs. Dayton Met. Housing Authority; past trustee U. Dayton. Mem. Am. Photoplatemakers Assn. (pres. 1959-62), Dayton Printing Industry Assn. (past pres.), Dayton C. of C. (pres. 1946-48), Council Graphic Arts (dir. research and engring.), Newcomen Soc. Presbyterian (elder). Clubs: Masons, Rotary (past pres.); Moraine Country, Engrs., Bicycle, Racquet, Dayton. Home: 4365 Delco Dell Rd Dayton OH 45429 Office: 40 E 1st St Dayton OH 45401

BROOKS, GARY, mgmt. cons.; b. Bklyn., Feb. 28, 1934; s. Nathan R. and Rose (Stern) B.; S.B., Mass. Inst. Tech., 1955; M.S., U. Rochester, 1959; m. Felice Ruth Dobbin, May 23, 1956; children—Andrew, Leslie Ellen. Project engr. Gen. Electric Co., Pittsfield, Mass., 1955-56; engr., new product supr. Eastman Kodak Co., Rochester, N.Y., 1956-64; v.p. ops. Peerless Photo Products, Inc., Shoreham, N.Y., 1964-68; cons., project mgr. Technomic Consultants, N.Y.C., 1969-71; v.p., div. gen. mgr. Scott Graphics, Inc., Holyoke, Mass., 1971-76; pres. Brooks & Assos., Inc., Longmeadow, Mass., 1976—; prin. Pace Cons. Group, Hartford, Conn., 1978—; adj. prof. U. Rochester, 1958-59, C.W. Post Coll., 1968-70, U. Mass., Amherst, 1978—. Pres. Temple Isaiah, Stony Brook, N.Y., 1970-71; trustee, v.p. Sinai Temple, Springfield, Mass., 1973—. Served with U.S. Army, 1956. Mem. Inst. Mgmt. Cons., Sales and Mktg. Execs. Internat., M.I.T. Alumni of Connecticut Valley (pres. 1979—), Sales and Mktg. Execs. Western Mass. (pres. 1980—). Republican. Clubs: Field of Longmeadow, Meadows Racquet. Office: 20 Hurlburt St West Hartford CT 06110

BROOKS, JERRY CLAUDE, food co. exec.; b. College Park, Ga., Apr. 23, 1936; s. John Bennett and Mattie Mae (Timms) B.; B.S., Ga. Inst. Tech., 1958; m. Peggy Sue Thornton, Feb. 26, 1961; children—Apryll Denise, Jerry Claude, Susan Vereen. Safety engr. Cotton Producers Assn., Atlanta, 1959-64, dir. safety and loss control, 1964-70; dir. corporate protection Gold Kist, Inc., Atlanta, 1970—. Instr., Ga. Safety Inst., Athens, Ga., 1971—. Bd. dirs. Greater Lithonia (Ga.) Homeowners Assn., Ga. Soc. Prevention of Blindness, Ga. Safety Council. Served with AUS, 1958-59. Mem. Am. Soc. Safety Engrs. (chpt. pres. 1968-69, regional v.p. 1974-76), Nat. Safety Council (gen. chmn. fertilizer sect. 1969-70), So. Safety Conf. (v.p. bus. and industry 1968-74, pres. 1974), Am. Soc. Indsl. Security, Ga. Bus. and Industry Assn. (dir.), Internat. Assn. Hazard Control Mgrs. (chpt. pres. 1979—). Clubs: Masons, Rosicrucians; Exchange (pres. 1969-70) (Lithonia). Home: 6411 Evans Mill Way Lithonia GA 30058 Office: 244 Perimeter Center Pkwy Atlanta GA 30338

BROOKS, JOHN WOOD, chem. mfr.; b. N.Y.C., Oct. 9, 1917; s. J. Arthur and Mary TenEyck (Oakley) B.; A.B., Harvard U., 1939; m. Patricia B. Bell, Dec. 20, 1941; children—Sylvia B., John W., Laurence O.; m. 2d, Margaret O. Maqoun, July 19, 1958; stepchildren—Anne MacKean Strong, Mary Ledyard Strong, Selina Clark Strong. Various sales, sales exec. positions in fibers industry, 1939-53; v.p., gen. sales mgr. Spring Mills, Inc., 1953-54; gen. mdse. mgr. textile div. Celanese Corp., N.Y.C., 1955, dir. mktg. fibers div., 1955-56, v.p., gen. mgr. fibers div., 1956-59; pres. Celanese Fibers Co., 1959-60; exec. v.p. domestic ops. Celanese Corp. 1960-61, exec. v.p. ops., 1961-65, dir., 1961—, pres., 1965—, chief exec. officer, 1968-77, chmn., 1971—; dir. ACF Industries, Bankers Trust Co., Dun & Bradstreet Inc. Co-chmn. bd. trustees Presbyn. Hosp. Clubs: Bedford (N.Y.) Golf and Tennis; Union, Univ., Links, Economic (N.Y.C.). Home: 363 Cantitoe Rd Bedford Hills NY 10507 Office: 1211 Ave of Americas New York NY 10036

BROOKS, PHILIP BARRON, ret. accountant banker; b. N.Y.C., Apr. 20, 1914; A.B. cum laude, Rider Coll., 1935; m. Betty R. Ralston; children—Richard L., Michael B., Philip J., Jeffrey R. Pvt. practice pub. accounting, Montclair, N.J., 1937-67; founder, chmn. bd., chief exec. officer Bank of Bloomfield (N.J.), 1972-74; past pres. Surf Club Apts., Inc., Surfside, Fla.; treas., dir. Computer Spltys. Corp., Palisades Park, N.J. Formerly lectr. tax subjects; panel mem. Am. Arbitration Assn. Former trustee, treas. Youth Employment Service Montclair, Montclair Urban Coalition, 1968-71; trustee Rider Coll.; former trustee Montclair Community Hosp. Recipient Distinguished Alumnus award Rider Coll., 1974. C.P.A., N.J., N.Y. Mem. AIM, Fla., N.J., N.Y., socs. C.P.A.'s. Am. Inst. C.P.A.'s, Rider Coll. Alumni Assn. (pres. 1965-67, past trustee), Grand Jury Assn. Essex County, N.J. Hosp. Assn., Eastern Srs. Golf Assn., Montclair C. of C. (dir., pres. 1966-69, past trustee), N.J. Hist. Soc., Zeta Beta Tau. Clubs: Spring Lake Bath and Tennis, Spring Lake Golf, Green Gables Croquet, New Racquet La Gorce Country, Grove Isle, Miami Legion of Honor, Com. of One Hundred (Miami, Fla.); Surf (sec., bd. govs.) (Surfside, Fla.); One Hundred (former trustee, treas.) (Montclair), Elks. Home: 20 Cherry Ct Spring Lake Heights NJ 07762 also (winter) Surf Club Apts Surfside FL 33154

BROOKS, ROGER KAY, ins. co. exec.; b. Clarion, Iowa, Apr. 30, 1937; s. Edgar Sherman and Hazel (Whipple) B.; B.A. magna cum laude, U. Iowa, 1959; m. Marcia Rae Ramsay, Nov. 19, 1955; children—Michael, Jeffrey, David. Joined Central Life Assurance Co., Des Moines, 1959, asst. to pres., 1966-67, asst. to pres. and asso. actuary, 1967-68, v.p., 1968-71, exec. v.p., 1971-72, pres., chief operating officer, 1972-75, pres., chief exec. officer, 1975—; dir. Iowa-Des Moines Nat. Bank. Fellow Soc. Actuaries; mem. Des Moines Actuaries Club (past pres.), Am. Acad. Actuaries, Des Moines C. of C. (dir.). Republican. Presbyterian. Clubs: Des Moines (dir.), Wakonda, Rotary. Office: 611 5th Ave Des Moines IA 50309

BROPHY, JOSEPH ALOYSIUS, JR., hotel exec.; b. Phila., May 29, 1950; s. Joseph Aloysius and Berenice Rose (Trainor) B.; B.S., Mt. St. Mary's Coll., Emmitsburg, Md., 1972; m. Barbara A. James, Dec. 6, 1975; 1 dau., Kelly Dawn. Asst. mgr. Whitebrier Hotel, Avalon, N.J., 1972-76, gen. mgr., 1977—, sec. corp., 1978—; mgr. Rustler Steak House, Pleasantville, N.J., 1976-77; tchr., br. mgr. Cape May County Vocat. Tech. Sch., 1977-81. Recipient Achievement award Cancer Soc., 1979. Mem. N.J. Restaurant Assn., N.J. Hotel Motel Assn., Cape May County C. of C. (dir. 1977—), Avalon C. of C. (dir. 1977—), Avalon Bowling League (dir. 1977—). Club: Stone Harbor Lions (dir. 1977—). Home: 7 Timothy Ln South Seaville NJ Office: Whitebrier Hotel 20th and Beach Sts Avalon NJ 08202

BROPHY, THEODORE F., telephone co. exec.; b. N.Y.C., Apr. 4, 1923; s. Frederick H. and Muriel W. (Osborne) B.; grad. Kent Sch., 1941; A.B., Yale, 1944; LL.B., Harvard, 1949; m. Sallie M. Showalter, Sept. 16, 1950; children—Stephen F., Anne R. Admitted to N.Y. bar; asso. with firm Root, Ballantine, Harlan, Bushby & Palmer, N.Y.C., 1949-55; gen. counsel Lummus Co., 1955-58; counsel Gen. Telephone Co., N.Y.C., 1958-59, v.p., gen. counsel Gen. Telephone & Electronics Corp., 1959-68, exec. v.p., gen. counsel, 1968-72, pres., from 1972, now chmn. bd., chief exec. officer, also dir. corp. and various subsidiaries; dir. Irving Bank Corp., Conoco, Inc. Mem. steering com. Nat. Urban Coalition; mem. adv. council Fairfield County council Boy Scouts Am.; Corp. mem. Greenwich Hosp. Assn.; mem. pres.'s com. Smith Coll.; mem. adv. com. Council for N.E. Econ. Action; bd. dirs. Boys' Clubs Am.; trustee Robert A. Taft Inst. Govt., Am. Shakespeare Theatre, Gen. Telephone & Electronics Found., Ind. Coll. Funds Am., Com. Econ. Devel., Tri-State United Way. Served to lt. (s.g.) USNR, 1944-46. Mem. Am., N.Y. State bar assns., Assn. Bar City N.Y., Fed. Communications Bar Assn., Bus. Council, Conf. Bd., Bus. Roundtable, Internat. C. of C. (trustee U.S. council), Conn. Com. Regional Plan Assn. Home: 9 Pecksland Rd Greenwich CT 06830 Office: One Stamford Forum Stamford CT 06904

BROSSEAU, LUCIEN, ins. co. exec.; b. Montreal, Que., Can., Jan. 28, 1920; s. Rosario and Zelia (Dufour) B.; Diploma Gen. Math., U. Laval (Can.), 1946; Actuarial Diploma, U. Edinburg (Scotland), 1951; m. Gilberte Brosseau, July 14, 1940; children—Michel (Mrs. Myren Puchuluteguy), Micheline (Mrs. James W. Gilbert), Lesley (Mrs. Andre Wery). Actuary, La Solidarite Ins. Co., Quebec City, Que., 1951-59; lectr. faculty of commerce U. Laval, Quebec, 1954-55; mng. dir. La Survivance Ins. Co., St. Hyacinthe, Que., 1959—, v.p., 1968-76, pres., 1976—, also dir.; pres. Hotel-Dieu de St-Hyacinthe, 1972—. Recipient Canadian Silver Jubilee medal. Mem. Corp. of Charted Adminstrs. Que. (pres. 1973-76), Can. C. of C. (pres. 1963-65), Montreal Inst. Investment Analysis, Am. Inst. Mgmt. (fellow pres.'s council), Actuarial Club Montreal. K.C. Home: 2580 St Pierre St W St Hyacinthe PQ J2T 4R9 Canada Office: 1555 Girouard W St Hyacinthe PQ J28 7C8 Canada

BROSSEAU, THOMAS EDWARD, real estate developer/broker; b. San Antonio, Nov. 2, 1951; s. Charles Martin and Elizabeth (Wiseman) B.; B.B.A., Tex. Tech. U., 1973; m. Karen Marie Jones, Dec. 1, 1979. Vice pres. Henry S. Miller Co., Dallas, 1973—. Active United Way Dallas, 1973—. Named Top Ten Producer, Henry S. Miller Co., 1977-79. Mem. Tex. Real Estate Assn., Greater Dallas Bd. Realtors. Republican. Methodist. Clubs: Dervish, Ghusto. Home: 4544 Belclaire St Dallas TX 75205 Office: 2001 Bryan Tower 30th Floor Dallas TX 75201

BROTMAN, PHYLLIS BLOCK (MRS. DON N. BROTMAN), advt. and public relations exec.; b. Balt., Mar. 22, 1934; d. Sol George and Delma (Herman) Block; ed. Balt. Jr. Coll., U. Va., Mary Washington Coll; m. Don N. Brotman, Aug. 16, 1953; children—Solomon G., Barbara Gay. Asso., Channel 13 TV, 1953-55; free lance pub. relations, 1960-66; coordinator pub. relations Md. Council Ednl. TV, 1965-66; pres. Image Dynamics, Inc., Balt., 1966—; lectr. Johns Hopkins, Baltimore County Pub. Schs., Inst. Politics, Duke, also in Jackson, Miss., Little Rock, New Orleans; cons. Bd. dirs. Hadassah, 1956-58, Nat. Jewish Fund, 1963-64, Asso. Jewish Charities, 1964—; internat. pres. B'nai B'rith Girls, 1952-53; bd. dirs. Nat. Council Jewish Women, 1964-66, Asso. Placement and Guidance Bur., 1964-65, Levindale Home and Infirmary Ladies Aux., 1963-64, Sinai Hosp. Aux., 1964-65; nat. commr. B'nai B'rith Youth Orgn., 1975—; dir. legis. info. program Md. Gen. Assembly. Recipient certificate of achievement Asso. Jewish Charities, 1965, award for outstanding community service Beta Omega Kappa, 1952, certificate for achievement in communications Md. Ho. of Dels., 1969—, certificate for outstanding achievement Md. Senate, 1970. Mem. Am. Assn. Advt. Agys., Pub. Relations Soc. Am. (certificate of achievement 1970, sec. Balt. chpt.), Advt. Club Washington, Advt. Assn. Balt. (dir.), McDonogh Field Assn. (pres. 1960—), S.W. Area Task Force, Md. Assn. Ednl. Broadcasters, C. of C. Met. Balt., Balt. Council Pub. Relations, Md.-Del.-D.C. Press Assn., Internat. Am. (div.) assns. polit. cons., Beta Omega Kappa. Democrat. Jewish religion (pres. P.T.A.; bd. congregation). Mem. B'nai B'rith Women. Instrumental in legislation to create state-wide ednl. TV network. Home: McDonogh Ln RFD 7 Box 554 Baltimore MD 21208 Office: Horizon House Calvert at Chase Sts Baltimore MD 21202

BROTT, JOSEPH W(ALTER), electronics sales co. exec.; b. N. Platte, Nebr., June 15, 1925; s. George W. and Faye O. (Barber) B.; student public schs.; m. June R. Davidson, June 30, 1946; children—Judy J., Jody J., Julie J. Machinist, U.P. R.R., 1947-56; staff asst. Nebr. Mil. Dept., 1956-68; salesman Motorola Co., 1968-78; owner Joe Brott & Assos., radio and electronics mfg. rep. and distbr., Omaha, 1978—. Served in AUS, 1943-46; lt. col. Res. (ret.). Republican. Baptist. Address: PO Box 10 Murray NE 68409

BROUGHTON, RAY MONROE, banker; b. Seattle, Mar. 2, 1922; s. Arthur Charles and Elizabeth C. (Young) B.; B.A., U. Wash., 1947, M.B.A., 1960; m. Margret Ellen Ryno, July 10, 1944 (div.); children—Linda Rae Broughton Hellenthal, Mary Catherine Broughton Boutin; m. 2d, Carole Jean Packer, 1980. Mgr. communications and managerial devel. Gen. Electric Co., Hanford Atomic Products Ops., Richland, Wash., 1948-59; mktg. mgr., asst. to pres. Smyth Enterprises, Seattle, 1960-62; dir. research Seattle Area Indsl. Council, 1962-65; v.p., economist (mgr. econ. research dept.) First Nat. Bank of Oreg., Portland, 1965—; mem. econ. adv. com. to Am. Bankers Assn., 1981—; mem. Gov.'s Econ. Adv. Council, 1981—; instr. bus. communications U. Wash., Richland, 1956-57. Treas., dir. Oreg. Heart Assn., 1972-78, chmn., dir., 1980—. Served to 1st lt. U.S. Army, 1943-46; ETO. Mem. Western Econ. Assn., Pacific N.W. Regional Econ. Conf. (dir. 1967—), Nat. Assn. Bus. Economists (co-founder chpt. 1971), Am. Mktg. Assn. (pres. chpt. 1971-72), Alpha Delta Sigma. Episcopalian. Author: Trends and Forces of Change in the Payments System and the Impact on Commercial Banking, 1972; contbg. editor Pacific Banker and Bus. mag., 1974-80. Office: 1300 SW 5th Ave PO Box 3131 Portland OR 97208

BROWER, PAUL GORDON, farmer coop. exec.; b. LaPorte, Ind., Oct. 10, 1938; s. Harold Herbert and Virginia Louise (Koch) B.; student Little Rock Jr. Coll., 1956-58, Little Rock U., 1960; B.B.A., Calif. Western U., 1976, M.B.A., 1979; m. Sandra Sue Wasson, Apr. 19, 1969; children—Kathryn Anne, Michael Paul. Reporter, Ark. Gazette, 1956-63; public relations dir. Ark. Savs. & Loan Assn., Little Rock, 1963-64; advt. mgr. Olin Corp., Little Rock, 1965-70, product advt. mgr. chems. group, Stamford, Conn., 1970-72; creative dir. Ward Archer Advt., Memphis, 1972-75; public relations mgr. Olin Corp., Little Rock, 1975-79; v.p. communications Gold Kist, Inc., Atlanta, 1979—. Mem. adv. bd. Future Farmers Am. Served with AUS, 1955-56, 61-62. Mem. Nat. Agri-Mktg. Assn., Nat. Assn. Farm Broadcasters, Agrl. Council Am., Am. Agrl. Editors Assn., Agrl. Relations Council. Episcopalian. Club: Rebel Bass. Home: 2442 Old Forge Ct NE Marietta GA 30062 Office: 244 Perimeter Center Pkwy NE Atlanta GA 30301

BROWN, ALLYN STEPHENS, newspaper publisher; b. New Castle, Ind., Feb. 7, 1916; s. Leroy Nicholas and Alice (Stephens) B.; A.B., Amherst Coll., 1938; m. Ellen Louise Kellogg, June 20, 1942; children—Allyn Stephens, Dianne Kellogg (Mrs. Daniel R. Cherry). With Evening Times, Sayre, Pa., 1939-50, co-pub. 1946-50; pres. Owego (N.Y.) Gazette, Inc., 1948-50; bus. mgr. Goldsboro (N.C.) News-Argus, 1950-52; with Graphic Equipment div. Fairchild Camera, Plainview, N.Y., 1953-56, 60-65; pres. pub. Brown-Thompson Newspapers, Inc., Union City, Pa., 1956—. Served with USAAF, 1943-46. Presbyn. Home: 22 1st Ave Union City PA 16438 Office: W High St Extension Union City PA 16438

BROWN, ARLON INMAN, Realtor, realty co. exec.; b. Bangor, Maine, Mar. 11, 1951; s. Eugene Ellis and Anne (Jacobs) B.; B.S.B.A., Boston U., 1973, M.B.A., 1974; M.B.A., Suffolk U., 1976; student Harvard U. Sch. Design Real Property Inst., 1977. Staff acct. Chester M. Kearney Co., C.P.A.'s, Bangor, 1976-77; pres., chief exec. officer Brown Realty Co., Bangor, 1977-78; mgr. comml. and indsl. div. J.F. Singleton Co., Bangor, 1978—; regent Indsl. Devel. Council Maine. Bd. dirs. Bangor Jaycees, 1978-80; ambassador Bangor C. of C., 1979-80. Served with ROTC, 1967. Mem. Nat. Assn. Realtors, Maine Assn. Realtors, Bangor Bd., Soc. Indsl. Realtors, Internat. Council Shopping Centers, Nat. Assn. Real Estate Bds. Clubs: Tarratine, Masons, Bangor/Brewer Mgmt. Home: 201 Husson Ave Bangor ME 04401 Office: 289 State St Bangor ME 04401

BROWN, BENNETT ALEXANDER, banker; b. Kingstree, S.C., June 1, 1929; B.S., Presbyterian Coll., Clinton, S.C., 1950; B.S., La. State U. Sch. Banking, 1960; grad. Advanced Mgmt. Program, Harvard Bus. Sch., 1965; m. Mary Alice Rustin, Nov. 30, 1957; children—Charlotte, Bennett, Leila, Katherine. With Chem. Bank, N.Y.C., 1950, Fed. Res. Bank Atlanta, 1953-55; with The Citizens & So. Nat. Bank, Atlanta, 1955—, chmn. and chief exec. officer, 1979—, also dir.; dir. Citizens & So. Holding Co., Piggly Wiggly So., Inc., Vidalia, Ga., Graniteville Co. (S.C.); mem. adv. bd. Ga. So. and Fla. R.R. Co. Served with U.S. Army, 1951-53. Mem. Atlanta C. of C. (dir.), Internat. Monetary Conf., Assn. Bank Holding Cos., Assn. Res. City Bankers. Presbyterian (elder). Clubs: Capital City, Commerce (dir.). Office: 35 Broad St Atlanta GA 30399

BROWN, CAMERON, ins. cons.; b. Chgo., Sept. 29, 1914; s. George Frederic and Irene (Larmon) B.; A.B., U. Ill., 1937; grad. Indsl. Coll. Armed Forces, 1941; m. Dorothea Fruechtenicht, May 10, 1947 (div. Feb. 1965); children—Reid L., Deborah Sue; m. 2d, Jean Mc Grew, Dec. 22, 1965; 1 dau., Sophia Lyn. Vice pres. R.B. Jones & Sons, Inc., 1938-41; dir. Geo. F. Brown & Sons, Inc., 1947-79, v.p., 1947-50, exec. v.p., 1950-53, pres., dir., 1953-64, chmn bd., dir. chief exec. officer, 1964-75; dir. Interstate Fire & Casualty Co., 1952-79, v.p., 1952-53, exec. v.p., 1953-56, pres., 1956-74, chmn., 1970-76; pres. Chgo. Ins. Co., 1957-74, dir., 1957-79, chmn., 1970-75; pres. Interstate Reins. Corp., 1961-74, dir., 1961-79, chmn., 1970-75; dir. Interstate Nat. Corp., 1968-79, pres., 1968-76, chmn., 1970-76; pres. Nat. Student Mktg. Corp., 1970-72, chmn., 1970-75, dir., 1970-79; pres. Cameron Brown, Ltd., Chgo., 1976—; underwriting mem. Lloyd's of London, 1971—. Bd. dirs., sec. Ill. Ins. Info. Service, 1961-76; bd. dirs. Chgo. area Planned Parenthood Assn., 1962-72, pres., 1969-72; bd. dirs. Planned Parenthood Fedn. Am., 1976-80, Exec. Service Corps, Chgo., 1978—, Nat. Multiple Sclerosis Soc. Chgo.; trustee U. Chgo. Cancer Research Found.; governing mem. Shedd Aquarium; mem. John Evans Club Northwestern U., pres.'s clubs U. Chgo., U. Ill.; mem. U. Ill. Found. Served from 2d lt. to lt. col. Gen. Staff Corps, U.S. Army, 1941-45. Decorated Bronze Star with oak leaf cluster. Mem. Assn. of Lloyd's Brokers (chmn. 1960), Surplus Line Brokers Assn. (chmn. 1954), Nat. Assn. Ind. Insurers (gov. 1961-77), La Confrerie des Chevaliers du Tastevin (officier-comdr.), Internat. Wine and Food Soc., Commanderie de Bordeaux (maitre), Psi Upsilon. Clubs: Executive (dir. 1968-73, 1st v.p. 1970-71), Economic, Casino, Onwentsia, Old Elm, Arts, Attic, Chicago, Shoreacres, Mid-Am. (Chgo.); Army-Navy Country (Washington); Pine Valley Golf (Clementon, N.J.); Birnam Wood Golf (Montecito, Calif.); Honourable Co. Edinburgh Golfers (Muirfield, Scotland); Royal and Ancient Golf St. Andrews (Scotland). Home: 600 S Ridge Rd Lake Forest IL 60045 Office: 222 E Wisconsin Ave Lake Forest IL 60045

BROWN, CARLTON AKIN, ins. co. exec.; b. Troy, N.Y., Jan. 24, 1922; s. Frederic M. and Ethel P. Brown; Asso. in Bus., Albany Bus. Coll., 1941; m. Dorothy Butler, Sept. 7, 1942; children—Richard I., Carol E. Brown Van Duzer. Bookkeeper, Addressograph Co., Albany, 1941-44, Constrn. Sales Corp., Albany, 1944-45; salesman Don Allen Chevrolet, Albany, 1945-54; ins. broker, pres., treas. Butler & Brown, Inc., Delmar, N.Y., 1954—. Mem. Profl. Ins. Agts. Assn., Albany County Agts. Assn. (dir.), Bethlehem C. of C., Republican. Club: Bethlehem Lions (pres. 1963). Home: 3 Herber Ave Delmar NY 12054 Office: 197 Delaware Ave Delmar NY 12054

BROWN, CAROL WILLIAMS, consulting co. exec.; b. Cleve., Apr. 8, 1941; d. Harter Whiting and Virginia Lambert (Templeman) Williams; B.A. in Econs., Wellesley Coll., 1962; cert. in systems and programming, N.Y. U., 1970; m. Cyrus Winthrop Brown II, Sept. 26, 1964; 1 dau., Laura Lambert Darby. Internal mgmt. cons. Met. Life Ins., N.Y.C., 1962-66; computer systems mgr. McKinsey & Co., Inc., N.Y.C., 1966-72; v.p. computer consulting Winthrop, Brown & Co., Inc., N.Y.C., 1972—. Licensed pvt. pilot. Mem. Canterbury Choral Soc. (sec.-treas. 1972), Computer Research Group, Assn. Computing Machinery (sec.-treas. bus. data processing group 1972—). Republican. Club: Jr. League (bd. mgrs. N.Y.C. 1974-76, community program v.p. 1979-80, exec. com. 1979-80). Contbg. author: Computer Handbook for Senior Management, 1978; author: The Minicomputer Simplified, 1980. Home: 266 West End Ave New York NY 10023 Office: 74 Trinity Pl New York NY 10006

BROWN, CARROLL F., dental co. exec.; b. Paulding, Ohio, Aug. 7, 1932; s. Floyd J. and Jessie J. (Meyers) B.; m. Norma Brown, Nov. 30, 1951; children—Gary, Dennis, Debi, Lisa. Mgr. water dept. City of Defiance (Ohio), 1955-61; mgr. equipment Litton Dental Co., Columbus, Ohio, 1961-75; mgr. Healthco Dental Co., Columbus, 1975—. Democrat. Presbyterian. Address: 1324 Dublin Rd Columbus OH 43215

BROWN, CHARLES EUGENE, mfg. co. exec.; b. Dubois County, Ind., Oct. 31, 1921; s. Lemoel C. and Bertha (McCormack) B.; B.S., Ind. U., 1948, M.B.A., 1950; grad Advanced Mgmt. Program, Harvard U., 1971;m. Elizabeth McAllister, Oct. 16, 1952; children—Deborah, Judith, Robert, Sarah. Indsl. relations mgr. Glidden Co., 1949-59; dir. indsl. relations Cleve. Pneumatic Tool Co., 1959-62; dir. indsl. relations Honeywell Inc., Mpls., from 1962, now v.p. employee relations. Bd. dirs., pres. Family and Childrens Service Mpls.; bd. dirs. Abbott Northwestern Hosp. Served with AUS, 1942-45. Decorated Purple Heart, Combat Inf. Badge. Mem. Aerospace Industries Assn., Personnel Round Table, Conf. Bd. Mgmt. and Personnel Adv. Council, Indsl. Relations Exec. Council Mpls. Clubs: Mpls., Edina Country. Mem. Minn. Advt. Council on Employment Services. Office: Honeywell Inc Honeywell Plaza Minneapolis MN 55408

BROWN, CHARLES IRVING, mining co. exec.; b. Bombay, India, Jan. 14, 1932; s. Charles Irving and Frances Belcher (Woods) B. (parents Am. citizens); B.A. in Geology, Williams Coll., 1954; M.B.A. with distinction, Harvard U., 1959; m. Kathleen Mae Shrum, July 2, 1960; children—Dana Scott, Tracy Ann, Kelly Mae. Asst. mgr. credit dept. First Nat. City Bank of N.Y., Rio de Janeiro, Brazil, 1954-57; v.p. fin. Western Nuclear Inc., Denver, 1959-73, also dir.; asst. treas. Indsl. Mineral Ventures, Inc., Golden, Colo., 1973-74; v.p. fin. and mktg. Energy Fuels Corp., Denver, 1974—, also dir.; dir. Citation Investment Co., Rawlins Nat. Bank (Wyo.), Western Utility Corp., Energy Fuels Nuclear Inc., Kerr Coal Co., Centurion Investment Co. Trustee Colo. Outward Bound, Colo. U. Research Found. Mem. Am. Inst. Mining Engrs., Fin. Execs. Inst. Clubs: Univ., Denver Athletic, Tower, Mt. Vernon Country. Home: 2691 Pinehurst Dr Evergreen CO 80439 Office: 1515 Arapaho St Suite 900 Denver CO 80202

BROWN, CHARLES LEE, JR., telephone co. exec.; b. Richmond, Va., Aug. 23, 1921; s. Charles Lee and Mary (McNamara) B.; B.S. in Elec. Engring., U. Va., 1943; m. Ann Lee Saunders, July 25, 1959; 1 son, Charles A. With AT&T and affiliates, 1946—, v.p., gen. mgr. Ill. Bell Telephone Co., 1963-65, v.p. ops., 1965-69, pres., 1969-74, dir., 1965-74, exec. v.p., chief fin. officer Am. Tel. & Tel. Co., N.Y.C., 1974-76, vice chmn. bd., chief fin. officer, 1976-77, pres., 1977-79, chmn. bd., 1979—, also dir.; dir. Chem. Bank & Chem. N.Y. Corp., E.I. DuPont de Nemours & Co., trustee Presbyn. Hosp., N.Y.C., 1977—. Served with USNR, 1943-46. Mem. Delta Upsilon, Theta Tau, Omicron Delta Kappa. Clubs: River, Links, Pine Valley Golf, Bedens Brook, Met., Augusta Nat. Golf. Office: 195 Broadway Room 2628 New York NY 10007

BROWN, CYRUS WINTHROP, II, investment co. exec.; b. Hartford, Conn., Mar. 11, 1938; s. Wallace Winthrop and Helen Elizabeth (van Dyck) B.; A.B., Harvard U., 1960; m. Carol Darby Williams, Sept. 26, 1964; 1 dau., Laura Lambert. Sr. credit analyst Mfrs. Hanover Trust, N.Y.C., 1960-66; corporate fin., venture capital officer F. S. Smithers & Co., Inc., N.Y.C., 1967-70; dir. corporate fin. Abraham & Co., Inc., N.Y.C., 1970-72; pres. Winthrop Ventures, N.Y.C., 1972—; lectr. on art of raising private capital, corporate role in venture capital at various univs. Mem. Canterbury Choral Soc., 1968—, pres., 1973-74; active Mayor's Action Center, 1975—, East Harlem Tutorial Program, 1975—. Served with SAC, USAF, 1960-63. Mem. AAAS, Aircraft Owners and Pilots Assn. Clubs: D.U., Hasty Pudding Inst. of 1770, Harvard (admissions com. 1979—, chmn. 1981—) (N.Y.C.). Author: Business Plan Guide, 1974. Home: 266 West End Ave New York NY 10023 Office: 74 Trinity Pl New York NY 10006

BROWN, DAVID, motion picture exec.; b. N.Y.C., July 28, 1916; s. Edward F. and Lillian (Baren) B.; A.B., Stanford U., 1936; M.S., Columbia U., 1937; m. Liberty LeGacy, Apr. 15, 1940 (div. 1951); 1 son, Bruce LeGacy; m. 2d, Wayne Clark, May 25, 1951 (div. 1957); m. 3d, Helen Gurley, Sept. 25, 1959. Apprentice, San Francisco News and Wall St. Jour., 1936; night editor, asst. drama critic Fairchild Publs., 1937-39; editorial dir. Milk Research Council, 1939-40; asso. editor Street and Smith Publs., 1940-43; asso. editor, exec. editor, editor-in-chief Liberty mag., 1943-49; editorial dir. Nat. Edn. Campaign, AMA, 1949; asso. editor, mng. editor Cosmopolitan mag., 1949-52; mng. editor, story editor, head scenario dept. 20th Century-Fox Film Corp. Studios, Beverly Hills, Calif., 1952-56, mem. studio exec. com., 1956-60, producer, 1960-62, also exec. story editor, head scenario dept.; editorial v.p. New Am. Library World Lit., Inc., 1963-64; exec. in charge story ops. 20th Century-Fox Film Corp., 1964-67, v.p., dir. story ops., 1967-69, exec. v.p. creative ops., 1969-70, also dir.; exec. v.p. creative ops., dir. Warner Bros., Inc., N.Y.C., 1971-72; exec. v.p., dir., producer Zanuck/Brown Co., 1972—, films include The Sting, Jaws, Jaws 2, MacArthur, The Sugarland Express, The Island. Final judge, best short story pub. in mags., ann. Benjamin Franklin Mag. awards, 1955-58. Mem. bd. trustees com. on film Mus. Modern Art, N.Y.C. Served as 1st lt., M.I., AUS, World War II. Mem. Acad. Motion Picture Scis., Producers Guild Am., Am. Film Inst. (trustee, mem. exec. com.). Clubs: Overseas Press, The Players (N.Y.C.); Nat. Press (Washington). Contbr. stories and articles to Am. Mag., Collier's, Harper's, Readers Digest, Am. Mercury, Sat. Eve. Post, Sat. Rev. Lit., Cosmopolitan, others. Contbr. to Journalists in Action, 1963. Editor: I Can Tell It Now, 1964; How I Got That Story, 1967. Home: 1 W 81st St New York NY 10024 Office: 40 W 57th St New York NY 10019

BROWN, DAVID GRAHAM, metals refining cons.; b. Charlottesville, Va., July 8, 1924; s. William Moseley and Gloria (Graham) B.; A.B., Colgate U., 1944; M.S., Newark Coll. Engring., 1955; m. Elizabeth Searles, Dec. 25, 1947; children—David Graham, Gregory H., Gary G., William L. Chemist, Foster D. Snell, Inc., N.Y.C., 1947; chemist, chem. engr. Air Reduction Co., Murray Hill, N.J., 1948-54; tech. dir. G.A.R. Precision Parts, Inc., Stamford, Conn., 1954-63; pres. Chem-Form, Inc., Danbury, Conn., 1963—; sr. v.p. Midland Processing, Inc., Pomona, N.Y., 1967-79; treas. Midland St. Jude Processing Corp., Mahanoy City, Pa., 1978-79. Served with USAAF, 1944-45. Mem. Am. Chem. Soc., Am. Inst. Chemists, Am. Inst. Chem. Engrs., Am. Soc. Metals, ASTM, Soc. Plastics Engrs., Phi Kappa Tau, Alpha Chi Sigma. Republican. Presbyn. Club: Chemists. Home: Rural Route 2 Robins Ct New Canaan CT 06840 Office: Wibling Rd Danbury CT 06810

BROWN, DONALD LAMONT, JR., mfg. co. exec.; b. N.Y.C., Apr. 25, 1921; s. Donald Lamont and Ethyl Davis (Broffe) B.; B.S., Yale U., 1943; m. Ann Wyper, Feb. 28, 1948; children—Christina Brown Ripple, Deborah, Kathryn Ann. With Pratt & Whitney Aircraft, East Hartford, Conn., 1946—, engr., 1951-54, asst. purchasing agt., 1954-55, purchasing agt., 1955-59, asst. purchasing mgr., 1959-68, purchasing mgr., 1968-76, v.p. purchasing, 1976-80, group v.p., 1980—. Served with USN, 1942-46. Address: 400 Main St East Hartford CT 06108

BROWN, DOUGLAS BARTON, musical booking agy. exec.; b. Sacramento, June 30, 1946; s. Wallace Barton and Virginia Ann (Keilholtz) B.; B.A. in Polit. Sci., U. Calif., Berkeley, 1968. Relocation aide San Francisco Redevel. Agy., 1969; speech writer, public relations dept. Wells Fargo Bank, San Francisco, 1970-72; founder, co-owner Good Music Agy., Inc., Mpls., 1973, pres., chief exec. officer, 1975—; asso. mem. adv. bd. Nat. Entertainment and Campus Activities. Mem. Nat. Assn. Orch. Leaders, Am. Fedn. Musicians, Internat. Theatrical Agys. Assn., C. of C., Am. Entrepreneurs Assn. Office: 100 N 7th St Suite 604 Minneapolis MN 55403

BROWN, DUANE HOLLIS, drafting cons.; b. Anthony, Kans., July 19, 1949; s. Hollis Edward and Inez Ethel (Cowell) B.; student Seible Sch. Drafting, 1970, Mesa Coll., 1968, Met. State Coll., Denver, 1967-68; m. Sallie Ruth Hovanyecz, June 22, 1974; children—Merrielle Andrea, Joanna Beth. Draftsman, Zeiler & Gray, Inc., Cons. Structural Engrs., Denver, 1970-75; chief structural draftsman KKBNA, Inc., Cons. Engrs., Denver, 1975-79; owner, prin. Duane H. Brown & Assos., Structural Drafting Services, Denver, 1979—. Mem. Inst. Cert. Engring. Technicians (cert.), Am. Inst. Design and Drafting. Baptist. Address: 9022 E Eastman Pl Denver CO 80231

BROWN, DUANE YALE, automotive exec.; b. Youngstown, Ohio, Apr. 29, 1938; s. Carl Leroy and May Lavern (Brubaker) B.; student Flint Jr. Coll., 1959-60, Gen. Motors Inst., 1956-60; B.B.A., Gen. Motors Inst., 1964; m. Mary Jean White, Nov. 24, 1962; children—Duana Jean, Craig Robert, Eric Lee. With Gen. Motors Corp., 1956—, service rep. Buick Motor div., Cin., 1960-62, Pitts., 1962-68, regional service coordinator central region, Birmingham, Mich., 1968-70, service devel. mgr., Detroit, 1971-73, dist. service mgr., Farmington, Mich., 1974-78, mgr. service ops. Chgo. zone, Oak Brook, Ill., 1978—; mem. Buick Parts and Service Field Activities Planning Council, Miami, Fla., 1965—. Pres. Fox Bay Civic Assn., Union Lake, Mich., 1974; chmn. Paul Bunyan Days Festival, 1972; pres. Douglass Houghton PTA, 1975-77; bd. dirs. Internat. Grad. Achievement, N.Y.C., 1957-58. Served with USCG, 1961-69. Recipient Grad. Key award Gen. Motors Inst., 1970; named Man of Year Buick Motor div., Pitts. zone, 1967; winner Buick Duffy's Dual, 1977, 78, 79, Buick All-Star Classic, 1978. Mem. Mich. (state v.p. 1973, mem. exec. com.), Union Lake (pres. 1972; award outstanding service 1974) Jaycees. Republican. Methodist. Home: 1043 Whirlaway Napeville IL 60540 Office: 2021 Spring Rd Oak Brook IL 60521

BROWN, EDWARD SHERMAN, mfg. co. exec.; b. Lansing, Mich., May 6, 1940; s. Raymond Edward and Jennie W. (Maki) B.; A.A., Compton (Calif.) Coll., 1970; A.A. in Bus. Adminstrn., Santa Ana Coll., 1975; B.A. in Mktg., Fullerton State U., 1976; 1 dau., Angela Renee. Sr. technician Rockwell Internat., Anaheim, Calif., 1962-69; sr. digital system technician Hughes Aircraft, Fullerton, Calif., 1969-70; engr. spl. systems Gen. Automation, Anaheim, 1970-76, engring. mgr., 1976-77, sales mgr., 1977-78, sales mgr. computer systems, Milw., 1978-80; sales engr. computer systems div. Perkin-Elmer, Brookfield, Wis., 1980—; cons. in field. Served with U.S. Army, 1959-62. Mem. Central Mich. Rocket Soc. (past v.p.), Pi Sigma Epsilon, Alpha Gamma Sigma. Club: Variety of Wis. (dir.). Home: 6933 W Kinnickinnic River Pkwy Milwaukee WI 53219 Office: Bishop's Woods W Suite 101 150 N Sunnyslope Brookfield WI 53005

BROWN, EDWIN LEWIS, JR., lawyer; b. Parker, S.D., Mar. 15, 1903; s. Edwin Lewis and Lucy Elizabeth (Lowenberg) B.; J.D., U. Nebr., 1926; m. Faye Hulbert, May 8, 1926; children—Betty Lou (Mrs. Philip Trainer), Lewis Charles. Admitted to Nebr. bar, 1926, Ill. bar, 1933, U.S. Supreme Ct. bar, 1960; practiced in Chgo., 1933—; partner firm Brown, Cook & Hanson, 1950—. Mem. wills and bequests com. Shriners Crippled Childrens Hosp., Chgo.; bd. dirs. Comml. Law Found. Recipient Time mag.-Narda Man of Year award, 1974. Mem. Am., Ill., Chgo. bar assns., Am. Judicature Soc., Comml. Law League Am., (pres. 1963-64), Phi Alpha Delta. Republican. Presbyn. Mason (32 deg., K.T., Shriner). Clubs: Monroe, Union League (Chgo.); Westmoreland Country (Wilmette, Ill.). Home: 2617 Hurd Ave Evanston IL 60201 Office: 135 S LaSalle St Chicago IL 60603 also 2114 Central St Evanston IL 60201

BROWN, ELIZABETH MYERS (MRS. KENT LOUIS BROWN), publishing co. exec.; b. Bklyn., Dec. 31, 1915; d. Garry Cleveland and Caroline (Clark) Myers; B.S., Cornell U., 1937; M.A., Case Western Res. U., 1960; m. Kent Louis Brown, June 26, 1940; children—Karen Elizabeth Brown Johnson, Kent Louis, David Stuart, Garry Myers. Tchr., Walden, N.Y., 1937-38, Auburn, N.Y., 1938-39, Cleveland Heights, Ohio, 1939-40; asst. Erie County (N.Y.) home demonstration agt. govt. extension service Cornell U., Ithaca, N.Y., 1940-42; editorial asst. Highlights for Children, Columbus, Ohio, 1962-64, asst. editor, 1964-66, asso. editor, 1966—, asst. sec., 1968—, dir., 1960—; dir. Zaner-Bloser Co., 1972—. Mem. Metro Writers Workshop, Cleve., 1970—; trustee New Day Press, Cleve., 1972-79; bd. dirs. Fedn. Cornell Women's Clubs, 1955-57, Fedn. Women's Clubs of Cleve., 1968-71; bd. dirs. Nutrition Assn. Greater Cleve., 1964-68. Mem. Women's Assn. Continuing Edn. (treas. 1959-61, pres. 1961-63), Women's Aux. Acad. Med. Cleve. (pres. 1969-70), Woman's Aux. Ohio Med. Assn. (chmn. mems.-at-large com. 1970-71, dir. 5th dist. 1975-77), Women's Nat. Book Assn. (dir. Cleve. chpt. 1978—). Home: 2861 Kersdale Rd Cleveland OH 44124 Office: 803 Church St Honesdale PA 18431

BROWN, FREDERICK HAROLD, ins. co. exec.; b. Troy, N.Y., Apr. 21, 1927; s. Harold Lamphere and Maida Adelaide (Wooden) B.; B.S. in Mech. Engring., Bucknell U., 1949; m. Mary Lee Lamar, Aug. 12, 1950; children—Deborah Elaine Wright, Frederick Harold. With INA Corp. and Subsidiaries, Phila., 1949-73, asst. v.p., 1970-71, v.p., 1971-73; founder, pres., chief exec. officer Jersey/Internat. Inc. affiliate W.R. Berkley Corp., N.Y.C., underwriting mgrs. for ins. cos. in splty., excess and surplus lines, Haddonfield, N.J., 1973—; pres. Admiral Ins. Co., Ensign Ins. Co., v.p. Queens Island Ins. Co. Mem. Phila. Fire Prevention Com., 1958-68; exec. treas. Camden County (N.J.) Republican Orgn., 1968-73; clk. bd. chosen freeholders of Camden County, 1969-73; active United Fund, Boy Scouts Am. Served with USNR, 1944-46. Named Citizen of Yr., INA, 1970. Registered profl. engr., Wis., Pa., Tenn. Mem. Soc. Fire Protection Engrs., Nat. Fire Protection Assn., Conf. Spl. Risk Underwriters, U.S. Jaycees (hon. life, Outstanding State V.P. 1961, Outstanding Nat. Dir. 1962). Episcopalian. Clubs: Tavistock (N.J.) Country; Crockford's (London); Kiwanis (Haddonfield); Union League (Phila.). Contbr. articles to profl. jours. Home: 165 Tavistock Ln Haddonfield NJ 08033 Office: 89 Haddon Ave Haddonfield NJ 08033

BROWN, FREDERICK WILLIAM, real estate exec.; b. N.Y.C., July 29, 1914; s. Frederick William and Rose Katherine (Hartel) B.; B.S., U.S. Naval Acad., 1948; J.D., George Washington U., 1954; m. Evelyn Magdelene Walther, July 11, 1940; children—Bruce Frederick, Bonnie Beth Brown Schuman, Laurie Anne. Commd. ensign U.S. Navy, 1938, advanced through grades to capt., aviator, 1958; service in Brazil, Panama, U.S.S. Enterprise; ret., 1963; social worker San Diego County Welfare Dept., 1965-73; exec. dir. several non-profit corps., 1973-75; realtor asso. J.D. Kelleher & Assos., San Diego, 1978—. Bd. dirs. San Diego County Assn. Mentally Retarded, 1968-70. Mem. San Diego County Bd. Realtors, Navy Inst., Am. Security Council, Coalition for Peace Through Strength, Am. Soc. Internat. Law, Am. Acad. Polit. and Social Sci., Heritage Found., Navy League, Ret. Officers Assn., Mil. Order World Wars, Naval Aviation Assn., Marine Meml. Assn., Friends of Handicapped. Home: 2640 Tokalon St San Diego CA 92110 Office: 828 Garnet Ave San Diego CA 92109

BROWN, G. HANK, feeding and processing co. exec., Congressman; b. Denver, Feb. 12, 1940; s. Harry W. and Anna Marie (Brown) B.; B.S., U. Colo., 1961, J.D., 1969; m. Nana B. Morrisson, Aug. 27, 1967; children—Harry, Christy, Lori. Tax accountant Arthur Anderson & Co., 1968-69; asst. to pres. Monfort of Colo., Greeley, 1969-70, corp. counsel, 1970-71, v.p. Monfort Food Distbg. Co., 1971-72, v.p. parent co. in charge corp. devel., 1973-76, v.p. charge internat. ops., 1976-79, v.p. lamb, 1979—; mem. Colo. Senate, 1972-76, asst. majority leader, 1975-76; mem. U.S. Ho. of Reps., 1981—. Served with USN, 1962-66. Decorated Air medal, Vietnam Service medal; recipient Jaycees Outstanding Young Man of Colo. award, 1973; Disting. Bus. Alumnus award U. Colo., 1978. Republican. Congregationalist. Clubs: Rotary, Elks. Home: 1741 35th Ave Ct Greeley CO 80631

BROWN, GEORGE PHILIP, bank exec.; b. N.Y.C., June 20, 1934; s. William Franklin and Marguerite Estelle (Martinez) B.; B.S. in M.E., U.S. Mcht. Marine Acad., 1956; postgrad. in Bus. and Fin., Hofstra U., 1960; m. Leona M. Lucas, Jan. 1, 1965; children—Kevin Charles, Gregory Scott, Barbara Lee. Project engr. Sperry Gyroscope Co., L.I., N.Y., 1956-59; v.p. IRE Investors Corp., L.I., 1959-61; pres. UNISEC Corp., L.I., 1961-62; mktg. mgr. Pharmaseal Labs., L.I., 1963-66; dir. mktg. NARCO Sci. Industries, Fort Washington, Pa., 1966-71; v.p. Nat. Fin. Mktg., Inc., Fort Washington, 1971-72; v.p. sales Phila. Saving Fund Soc., 1972—; instr. U. Wis., U. Mass.; cons. The Citation Group, Chalfont, Pa.; mem., cons. Pvt. Industry Council Phila. Served with USNR, 1953-56. Mem. Internat. Assn. Fin. Planners, Sales and Mktg. Execs. Phila. (pres. 1979-81), Fin. Sales Mgmt. Inst. (founder), Savings Instn. Mktg. Soc. Am., Nat. Assn. Mut. Savs. Banks. Clubs: Delaware Valley Aero, Lower Providence Rod and Gun. Home: 13 Langhorne Rd Chalfont PA 18914 Office: 1212 Market St Philadelphia PA 19107

BROWN, HARLAN JAMES, acquisition search and indsl. studies exec.; b. Altoona, Pa., Dec. 16, 1933; s. Lindsey A. and E. Grace (Ackerman) B.; M.Engr., Colo. Sch. Mines, 1957; M.B.A., George Washington U., 1967; 1 son, Harlan James II. Field engr. Beckman Instruments, Arlington, Va., 1957-59; partner Shaheen, Brown & Day, Denver, 1959-60; v.p. Nat. Engring. Service subs. NES, Inc., Washington, 1960-63; pres. NSC Internat., Washington, 1963-67; chmn. bd., chief exec. officer Harlan Brown & Co., Inc., McLean, Va., 1967—; seminar lectr. George Washington U., 1969, 70, 71, 75, U. Toronto, 1970, Fed. Res., 1975, Nat. Congress Community Devel., Washington, 1975, Allis Chalmers Co., Monsanto Co., 1980. Mem. IEEE, Am. Soc. Metall. Engrs., Am. Chem. Soc., Am. Mgmt. Assn., Blue Key, Theta Tau, Sigma Delta Psi, Alpha Tau Omega. Methodist. Clubs: Regency Racquet, Sporting, Nat. Jogging. Author: (with Mock and Shuckett) Financing for Growth, 1971. Produced first merger center experiment, Cherry Hill, N.J., 1969. Home: 1800 Old Meadow Rd McLean VA 22102 Office: 1307 Dolley Madison Blvd McLean VA 22101

BROWN, HAROLD MICHAEL, food industry exec.; b. Walkerville, Ont., Can., June 14, 1931; s. George M. and Germaine M. (La Rocque) B.; grad. Denby High Sch., Detroit; m. Jennie Marie Van De Water; children—Michael, Cheryl, Vicki, George, Harold,

Mark, David. Plant mgr. The Pillsbury Co., Gainesville, Ga., 1972-74, J-M Poultry Packing Co. Ltd., Gainesville, 1974-77; product mgr. Barker div. USI Agribus., 1977-78; gen. mgr. processing ops. Spring Valley Foods, 1978—. Mem. Inst. Food Technologists, SE Poultry and Egg Assn. (advisor). Lutheran. Clubs: Exchange (past dir.), Masons (past master). Home: 3808 Knollwood Dr Anniston AL 36201 Office: Spring Valley Foods Oxford AL 36203

BROWN, HARRY RONALD, stock broker; b. Chgo., Aug. 30, 1930; s. Arthur S. and Eleanor (Smith) B.; B.S., Purdue U., 1953; M.B.A., N.Y. U., 1957; m. Patricia Joan Miner, Aug. 2, 1952; children—Mitchell Ronald, Valerie Patricia. Security analyst E.W. Axe & Co., Tarrytown, N.Y., 1955-56, Stillman, Maynard, N.Y.C., 1956-61; instl. salesman Clark Dodge & Co., N.Y.C., 1961-67; gen. partner Buttonwood Assos., Jersey City, 1967-71; pres. Personal Investment Mgmt. Co., Mahwah, N.J., 1971-72; asst. v.p., account exec. E.F. Hutton N.Y.C., 1972-77; v.p. Dean Witter Reynolds, Inc., 1979—. Rockland County Republican committeeman, 1958-60. Served with U.S. Army, 1953-55. Mem. N.Y. Soc. Security Analysts, Inst. Chartered Fin. Analysts, Fin. Analysts Fedn., Kappa Sigma. Club: Scarsdale Golf. Contbr. articles to profl. jours. Home: 400 E 54th St New York NY 10022 Office: 130 Liberty St New York NY 10006

BROWN, HOWARD JORDAN, newspaper pub.; b. Chgo., July 31, 1923; s. Isidore and Gladys (Jordan) B.; B.A., Princeton U., 1946; M.S., Columbia U., 1948; m. Elizabeth Ahrend Kassel, Mar. 2, 1960; children—Lucille, Sarah, Amy. With Chgo. Sun-Times, overseas, 1948-49, Cleve. News-Plain Dealer, 1950-59, Ottaway Newspapers, 1959-62; pub. Kenosha (Wis.) News, 1962—; pres. United Communications Corp.; dir. 1st Nat. Bank of Kenosha. Served with AUS, 1943-45; ETO. Jewish. Office: 715 58th St Kenosha WI 53140

BROWN, JACK LEONDUS, sewer pipe co. exec.; b. Huntington, W.Va., Sept. 16, 1913; s. Wyatt Thornton and Lillian Vivian (Williams) B.; ed. pub. schs.; m. Lillian Louise Matchett, Jan. 5, 1935; children—Marjorie Bauman (Mrs. Linn Sheldon), Sally (Mrs. Alan C. Good), Jack Leondus III. With Am. Vitrified Products Co., 1935—, v.p., 1959-63, pres., 1963-68, also dir.; corporate gen. mgr. Superior Concrete Pipe Co., 1968—. Trustee Ohio Turnpike Commn. Mem. Clay Sewer Pipe Assn. (v.p.), Nat. Clay Pipe Inst. (dir.), Am. Concrete Pipe Assn. (past dir.), Ohio Contractors Assn. (dir.), Blue Coats. Baptist. Club: Acacia Country (Lyndhurst, Ohio). Home: 13514 Shaker Blvd Cleveland OH 44120 Office: 21200 Miles Ave Cleveland OH 44128

BROWN, JAMES, offset specialist; b. Scotland, Mar. 12, 1942; s. James Forbes and Eugenia (Trombik) B.; came to U.S., 1955, naturalized, 1960; B.A., U. Md., 1964; m. Gail Nobbs, Apr. 21, 1973; 1 dau., Carla Ann. With Pratt and Whitney Aircraft div. United Technologies Corp., E. Hartford, Conn., 1966-73, internat. procurement coordinator, 1970-73; mgr. internat. bus. devel. United Technologies Internat., Hartford, 1973-76, internat. benefits mgr. Pratt and Whitney Aircraft div., West Palm Beach, Fla., 1976—. Address: 8087 Coconut St Hobe Sound FL 33455

BROWN, JAMES EUGENE, apologetics co. exec.; b. Louisville, Aug. 4, 1929; s. Thurman Lewis and Virginia Della (Crosson) B.; student pub. schs., Cin.; m. Anne Louise Biddle, Sept. 8, 1972; children—Steve, Pamela Sue, Lori Ann, Carolyn Ruth. Pres., founder Creative Tape Systems, Inc., Cin., 1955-75, Nat. Label Systems, Inc., Cin., 1958-75, Internat. Machine Products, Cin., 1965-75, Graftek Systems Inc., Cin., 1965-75, Spectape Inc., Cin., 1967-75, Christian Communications Inc., Scottsdale, Ariz., 1975—; cons. to self-adhesive tape industry U.S.A. and Europe. Exec. asso. dir., trustee Christian Research Inst., 1978; pres. Christian Awareness Broadcasting Systems, 1978. Named mayor of Boys Week, Cin., 1948. Mem. Am. Mgmt. Assn., Sales Mgmt. Assn. Club: Toastmasters. Author: One Condition, 1978; contbr. articles to mags. Home: 8000 N Coconino Rd Scottsdale AZ 85253 Office: PO Box 80 Scottsdale AZ 85252

BROWN, JAMES LEHMON, chem. co. exec.; b. Detroit, Nov. 20, 1929; s. Abram Lehmon and Donnabelle (Chenoweth) B.; A.B., U. Mich., 1951, M.B.A., 1952; m. Judith Marsh Sinclair, June 28, 1952; children—Kirk, Scott, Kim, Carrie, Elizabeth. Propr. constrn. firm, Ann Arbor, Mich., 1955-58; sales mgr. Sinclair Mfg. Co., Toledo, 1958-64, pres., 1964-77, also chmn. bd.; chmn. Sinclair Mfg. Assos., Toledo, 1977—; dir. Monroe, Mich., Hunt Chem., Inc., St. Paul; dir. WGTE-TV, 1971-75, chmn. bd., 1980—. Mem. Toledo Citizens Com. for Effective Govt., 1971-72; pres. Toledo Area Govtl. Research Assn., 1974-75. Trustee Toledo Area council Boy Scouts Am., 1971—, exec. bd., 1970—, pres., 1975—; trustee U. Toledo Corp., 1975—. Served with AUS, 1952-55. Mem. Phi Eta Sigma, Theta Delta Chi, Sigma Delta Chi. Club: Toledo. Home: 30 Meadow Ln Toledo OH 43623 Office: 5644 Monroe St Sylvania OH 43560

BROWN, JANICE FOSTER, telephone co. ofcl.; b. Hyannis, Mass., Sept. 9, 1946; d. Philip Thayer and Irma Margarette (Ramsey) Foster; B.S. in Bus. Adminstrn., U. New Haven, 1976; m. John Andrew Brown, June 7, 1969. EDP keypuncher-computer operator High Standard Co., Hamden, Conn., 1967-70; computer operator Conn. Shoreline and Suburban Ednl. Computer Center, Hamden, 1970-73; mng. supr. student child care U. New Haven, West Haven, Conn., 1974-75; EDP programmer, software devel. programmer N.Y. Telephone Co., N.Y.C., 1976—; programmer Bell Labs., Holmdel, N.J., 1977-79; cons. Rocky Hill (Conn.) Town Planning Dept., 1975. Vol., N.Y.C. chpt. Nat. Heart Fund, 1979, N.Y.C. chpt. Leukemia Soc. Am., 1977, 79, New Haven Democratic Voter Registration Campaign, 1969; active Tri-State United Way. Recipient Outstanding Service award Leukemia Soc. Am., 1977, 79. Mem. Soc. for Advancement Mgmt., Am. Mgmt. Assn., Soc. Community and Profl. Employees, Nat. Assn. Negro Bus. and Profl. Women. Club: Generators Social (N.Y.C.). Home: 55 Austin Pl Staten Island NY 10304

BROWN, JAY DEAN, savs. and loan assn. exec.; b. Payson, Utah, Oct. 15, 1936; s. Darrel and Nadine Jane (Fowler) B.; B.S. in Accounting, Brigham Young U.; m. Avon Alleen Freudiger, Nov. 30, 1973; children—Steven Jay, Tamara, Linda Lee, Jay Darrel, Kelly Avon, Shauntelle Alleen, Brian Aaron. Semi-sr. auditor Haskins & Sells, C.P.A.'s, Los Angeles, 1962-65; asst. treas. Pacific Savs. and Loan Assn., Los Angeles, 1965-67; financial v.p. Investors Savs. and Loan Assn., Pasadena, Calif., 1967-68, Sterling Savs. and Loan Assn., Riverside, Calif., 1968-69; adminstrv. v.p. Mercury Savs. and Loan Assn., Huntington Beach, Calif., 1969-76; sr. v.p., treas. Great Northwest Fed. Savs. and Loan Assn., Bremerton, Wash., 1976-79; pres. Arrowhead Savs. & Loan Assn., 1979—. Rep. to Utah Boys State, 1954; account exec. United Crusade, 1972, 73; chmn. finance com. Pacifica dist. Boy Scouts Am., 1973; bd. dirs. Kitsap County chpt. ARC, 1977-79. Mormon (bishop 1966-71). Club: Lake Arrowhead Rotary (officer, dir. 1979—). Home: PO Box 997 Blue Jay CA 92317 Office: PO Box 277 Blue Jay CA 92317

BROWN, JEREMY EARLE, advt. exec.; b. Richmond, Va., Nov. 25, 1946; s. Earle Palmer and Barbara (McLaughlin) B.; B.A., Washington and Lee U., Lexington, Va., 1969; M.B.A., Harvard U., 1973; m. Sally McHugh, Feb. 2, 1980. Account exec. Leo Burnett Co., Chgo., 1973-74; pres. Earle Palmer Brown, Washington, 1974—. Mem. Nat. Fedn. Advt. Agencies (dir.), Washington Advt. Club (dir., Am. Mktg. Assn., Washington and Lee U. Alumni Assn. (class chmn. 1969), Phi Beta Kappa. Republican. Episcopalian. Club: Columbia Country. Home: 11397 Empire Ln Rockville MD 20852 Office: 4733 Bethesda Ave Bethesda MD 20014

BROWN, JERRY JOSEPH, tax specialist; b. Buffalo, Mar. 10, 1898; s. Jerry Patrick and Mary (Love) B.; student Niagara U., 1912-15; m. Emily F. Earle, May 27, 1921; children—Jerry E., Emily (Mrs. Bertram E. Himelstieb), Susan (Mrs. William E. Roschen, Jr.). Agt., Internal Revenue Service, 1923-45; partner Allen & Brown, N.Y.C., tax specialists, 1946—. Served with AS, U.S. Army, 1917-19. Mem. Nat. Soc. Pub. Accountants, Research Inst., Am. Legion. Club: N.Y. Athletic. Home: 11 Red Oak Dr Spring Lake NJ 07762 Office: 60 E 42d St New York NY 10017

BROWN, JOSEPH NATHANIEL, health care exec., educator; b. Durham, Maine, Apr. 12, 1924; s. Joseph Sandford and Charity Joyce B.; B.A., Bates Coll., 1950; M.A., U. R.I., 1968; m. Doris Fern Hastings, Apr. 11, 1944; children—Joseph, Sharon, David, Janice, Lloyd, Laurie, Paul, Debbie. Sales exec. Highland Meml. Park, Johnston, R.I., 1954-58; tchr. and sch. adminstr., R.I. and Mass., 1958-68; field coordinator-gerontology U. R.I., Kingston, 1968-71; founder, exec. dir. R.I. Meals on Wheels, Inc., Providence, 1969—; dir. Nursing Home Adminstrs.'s Inst., U. R.I. Extension, Providence, 1970—; pres. Bannister House, non-profit health care facility, Providence, 1978—. Served with U.S. Army, 1943-46. Mem. R.I. Adult Edn. Assn. (pres. 1971), Nat. Assn. Meal Programs (pres. 1976-78), Assn. Home Health Agencies R.I. (pres. 1978-80), R.I. Assn. Facilities for Aging (v.p. 1977-78), Nat. Council on Aging, U.S. Gerontol. Soc. Republican. Home: Box 521 RFD 1 North Scituate RI 02857 Office: 175 Mathewson St Providence RI 02903

BROWN, KENNETH RIDGEWAY, elec. equipment sales co. exec.; b. Newcastle, Eng., June 30, 1924; s. Reg R. and Ruby B.; came to U.S., 1963, naturalized, 1969; diploma in engring. U. London, 1944; grad. Royal Naval Engring. Coll., 1945; m. diane B. Litteljohn, Apr. 23, 1955; children—Christopher, Graeme, David. Grad. apprentice Met.-Vickers Elec. Co., Ltd., 1947-48, design engr., 1948-54, Western rep. Elec. Export div., Canada, 1954-58; Western mgr. Assos. Elec. Industries (Canada) Ltd., 1958-63; resident rep. U.S., Asso. Elec. Industries Internat., Ltd., 1963-66; v.p. A.E.I. Liason Services Ltd.-USA, 1967; pres. A.E.I. Turbine Generators, Inc., N.Y.C., 1968; v.p. A.E.I. Can. Ltd., Montreal, Que., 1969; sr. v.p., gen. mgr. Eastern Electric Co., Ltd., Montreal, 1970-73; pres., dir. English Electric Corp. USA, Elmsford, N.Y., 1973—; dir. Woods Fans Inc., Eugene Munsell Co., Marconi Electronics Inc., Ruston Gas Turbines Inc. Served with Brit. Navy, 1944-46. Mem. IEEE, Engring. Inst. Can., Instn. Mech. Engrs. Republican. Episcopalian. Office: English Electric Corp 500 Executive Blvd Elmsford NY 10523

BROWN, KENNETH STUART, electronics mfg. co. exec.; b. Bklyn., Aug. 15, 1931; s. Charles and Mimi Brown; B.A., Williams Coll., 1953; m. Carol Ann Brady, June 3, 1951; children—Michael, Peter, Debra, Christopher. Mgr. pubis. Sprague Electric Co., North Adams, Mass., 1955-58, mgr. indsl. relations, Visalia, Calif., 1958-61, Eastern area mgr. indsl. relations, 1961-68, adminstrv. asst. to sr. v.p. research and devel., 1968, corporate mgr. employee relations, 1968-69, corporate dir. materials, 1969-70, North Adams, 1961-70; dir. indsl. relations Optical Products div. Am. Optical Corp., Southbridge, Mass., 1970-73; staff v.p. corporate indsl. relations Bourns Inc., Riverside, Calif., 1973—. Pres. Williamstown (Mass.) Community Chest, 1968-69; bd. dirs. Inland Area Urban League, Calif., 1975—, v.p., 1977; bd. dirs. Riverside United Way, also v.p., chmn. campaign, 1978-79, pres., 1980. Served with USAF, 1953-55. Mem. Electronics Industries Assn. (exec. com. indsl. relations council 1977—), Am. Electronic Assn. Republican. Club: Victoria. Home: 2201 Archdale St Riverside CA 92506 Office: 1200 Columbia Ave Riverside CA 92507

BROWN, LELAND CLYDE, JR., mfg. co. exec.; b. Pitts., May 23, 1938; s. Leland Clyde and Virginia Jane (Montooth) B.; B.A., U. Pitts., 1961; m. Rachel Wofford Siviter, May 26, 1960; children—Leland Clyde, Rebecca Westmoreland. Salesman, mktg. and acquisition mgr. Airco, Inc., N.Y.C., 1964-68; exec. v.p. Weber, Inc., Pitts., 1968-69; pres. Brown & Co., Pitts., 1970—, U.S. Products Co., Pitts., 1972—, Home Services Unltd. Inc., Plantation, Fla.; dir. planning and devel. Ocean Divers, Ft. Lauderdale, Fla., 1979—, Viva Tanning Salons, Ft. Lauderdale, 1980—; mng. dir. Starts Engines, Inc., Ft. Lauderdale, 1979—; dir. devel. Mgmt. Services Inc., Pitts. Rep., Council Ind. Small Bus. Assns., Washington, 1977—; del. White House Conf. on Small Bus., 1980; scoutmaster, troop 152 Boy Scouts Am., Pitts., 1976-78; commr., coach Millvale Baseball Assn., Pitts., 1975-76. Served to capt. USAF, 1961-64. Master scuba diver. Mem. NAM, Smaller Mfrs. Council Pitts. (dir. 1977—, v.p. govt. relations), Nat. Small Bus. Assn., Council Ind. Small Bus. Assns. Nat. Fedn. Ind. Businesses, Abrasive Engring. Soc., S. Fla. Mfrs. Assn., Fla. Underwater Council, Am. Legion. Clubs: Amen Corner (Pitts.); Grove Isle (Miami, Fla.); Le Club Internat. (Ft. Lauderdale). Home: 2100 S Ocean Dr Fort Lauderdale FL 33316 Office: 1150 N Federal Hwy Fort Lauderdale FL 33304

BROWN, MARK LAWRENCE, SR., ins. broker; b. Washington, Sept. 21, 1950; s. Benjamin Franklin and Anna Mae (Brown) B.; B.S. in Acctg., U. Md., 1972; M.B.A. in Fin., Am. U., 1974; m. Suzanne Chase, Feb. 3, 1973; children—Franklin, Mark Lawrence, Grayson. Ins. agt., underwriter Benjamin F. Brown Ins. Agy., Inc., Bladensburg, Md., 1965-74; spl. agt. FBI, 1975; investment cons., ins. broker, Hyattsville, Md., 1976—. C.P.A., D.C.; C.L.U. Mem. Nat. Assn. Life Underwriters, Ind. Ins. Agts. Am., Nat. Assn. Accts., Am. Inst. C.P.A.'s, D.C. Inst. C.P.A.'s, Am. U. Alumni Assn., Nat. Rifle Assn. (life), Am. Security Council, Am. Def. Preparedness Assn., Ducks Unlimited, Friends of Geese. Democrat. Methodist. Clubs: Prince George Rod and Gun, Moose. Home: 13311 Forest Dr Mitchellville MD 21109 Office: 4312 Gallatin St Hyattsville MD 20781

BROWN, MELVIN FROMMEL, finance co. exec.; b. Carlinville, Ill., June 4, 1935; s. Ben and Selma (Frommel) B.; A.B., Washington U., St. Louis, 1957, J.D., 1961; m. Jacqueline S. Hirsch, Sept. 2, 1962; children—Andrew, Steven. Admitted to Mo. bar, 1961, Fed. bar, 1961; asst. to gen. counsel Union Electric Co., St. Louis, 1962-65; v.p., gen. counsel, sec. ITT Aetna Corp., Clayton, Mo., 1965-76, ITT Fin. Corp., Clayton, 1974-76; pres., chief exec. officer ITT Diversified Credit Corp., St. Louis, 1977—; dir. ITT Fin. Corp. Commr., St. Louis County Bd. Elections, 1968-70. Served with USAR, 1957-59. Mem. Bar Assn. Met. St. Louis, Mo. Bar Assn., Am. Bar Assn., Am. Jewish Com. Club: Univ. Office: 12555 Manchester St Saint Louis MO 63131

BROWN, MICHAEL GRIFFITH, automotive co. exec.; b. Nashville, Sept. 14, 1942; s. James Griffith and Ann Mae (Goodwin) B.; B.A., Evansville U., 1967; m. Donna Lee Wuerth, Nov. 20, 1962; 1 dau., Laura. Div. mgr. Sears Roebuck Co., Evansville, Ind., 1965; salesman Minn. Mining & Mfg. Co., Evansville, 1966-67, Gibson Co., Evansville, 1967-69; asst. dist. mgr. AWD Inc, Fort Wayne, Ind., 1968-69, dist. mgr., 1969-74; ops. mgr. Saunders & Neefus Inc., Cleve., 1975; pres., gen. mgr. Automotive Mfrs. Warehouse Inc., Pitts., 1976—; div. pres. Parts Warehouse, Inc., 1979—; mem. adv. council Standard Motor Products, Inc., 1980; mktg. adv. council Dayco Corp., 1980—; mem. mktg. council Monroe Automotive Equipment Warehouse Distbrs., 1978—. Mem. Automotive Warehouse Distbrs. Assn. Republican. Roman Catholic. Club: Masons. Home: 1050 Harvard Rd Monroeville PA 15146 Office: 211 Thomas St Pittsburgh PA 15122

BROWN, NEIL HARRY, advt. agy. exec.; b. Pitts., Oct. 3, 1938; s. Albert A. and Madeline B.; B.S., Carnegie Mellon U., 1960; m. Ruth Frances Bingham, Sept. 21, 1963; 1 son, William Bingham. With Ketchum, MacLeod & Grove, Inc., Pitts., 1957—, sr. v.p., 1978; chief exec. officer Vesely-Brown Co., Pitts., 1978—. Mem. Bus./Profl. Advt. Assn. (dir.). Republican. Clubs: Chartiers Country, Pitts. Athletic, Masons. Home: 4754 Wallingford Pittsburgh PA 15213 Office: 4 Gateway Center Pittsburgh PA 15222

BROWN, NIGEL RICHARDS, mortgage brokerage firm exec.; b. Hamilton, Bermuda, June 1, 1942; s. David Richards and Patricia (Seymour) B.; student City Coll. San Francisco, 1962-64; 1 son, Darin. Came to U.S., 1945, naturalized, 1957. Loan officer Advance Mortgage Co., San Francisco, 1971-74; mktg. dir. Citizens Savs. and Loan, San Francisco, 1974-76; mktg. dir. Ticor Mortgage Ins., Los Angeles, 1976-78; chmn. bd. Nat. Secondary Market (formerly Mortgage Center), Beverly Hills, Calif., 1978—; pres. The Mortgage Store, Beverly Hills, 1980—; cons. No. Calif. Savs. and Loan, Palo Alto, 1974. Served with USMC, 1963-65. Mem. U.S. Savs. and Loan League, Calif. Savs. and Loan League. Republican. Episcopalian. Home: 10037 W Wanda Dr Beverly Hills CA 90210 Office: 9441 Wilshire Blvd Beverly Hills CA 90212

BROWN, NORMAN M., lawyer, fin. cons., broker; b. Phila., Mar. 11, 1929; A.B., Temple U., 1950; LL.B., U. Pa., 1953; m. Renate Hennig, Feb. 23, 1967. Admitted to Pa. bar, 1956; practiced in Phila., 1956-66; v.p., gen. counsel, dir. Systems Capital Corp., Phila., 1966-68; pres. Nationwide Leasing Co., Chgo., 1969-70, 1st Securities Leasing Co., Chgo., 1971; mgr. leasing A.G. Becker & Co., Chgo., 1972-73; fin. cons., broker, Chgo., 1973—. Served to 1st lt. U.S. Army, 1953-55. Mem. Pa. Bar. Republican. Lutheran. Contbr. articles on leasing to profl. jours. Home and Office: 57 W Schiller St Chicago IL 60610

BROWN, O(WEN) BRUCE, wood stove co. exec.; b. Indpls., June 13, 1939; s. Irving Douglass and Eleanore Marie (Amos) B.; B.S., Fla. State U., 1961; Ed.D., Boston U., 1967; m. Marjorie Anne Pearce, June 8, 1958; children—Scott, Laurie, Gary, DeeDee. Asst. prof. Boston U., 1963-69, adminstr., 1969-71; pres. Abundant Life Woodstoves-Comforter Stove Works, Lochmere, N.H., 1973—. Elder, New Christian Fellowship Ch., Laconia, N.H.; pres. Full Gospel Businessmen's Fellowship, Laconia. Office: Abundant Life Woodstoves Box 188 Lochmere NH 03252

BROWN, P. ERWIN, mgmt. cons.; b. Cin., Jan. 13, 1944; s. Wallace Brown and Clara (Gibson) B.; B.A., Bernard M. Baruch Coll., 1970, M.B.A., 1972; postgrad. Fordham Law Sch., 1974-76. With Chem. Bank, N.Y.C., 1968-76, asst. v.p., 1968-76; dir. personnel and labor relations Western Psychiat. Univ. Health Center, U. Pitts., 1976-77; mgmt. cons. John Sheridan Assos., Des Plaines, Ill., 1977-80; pres. Brown Vessup & Assos., East Pitts., 1980—. Mem. Am. Soc. Personnel Adminstrn., Indsl. Relations Research Assn., Practising Law Inst., Pitts. Personnel Assn., Am. Mgmt. Assn., Pitts. Minority Purchasing Council, Pitts. Urban League, NAACP. Democrat. Home: 215 West St East Pittsburgh PA 15112 Office: PO Box 186 West St East Pittsburgh PA 15112

BROWN, PETER CAMPBELL, lawyer; b. Aug. 12, 1913; s. Peter P. and Ellen (Campbell) B.; A.B., Fordham Coll., 1935, LL.B., 1938; LL.D., St. Bonaventure (N.Y.) U., 1951; m. Joan Gallagher, June 8, 1943; children—Peter Campbell, Patricia Joan, Thomas, Michael, Robert Joseph. Admitted to N.Y. State bar, 1938; practiced in Bklyn., 1938-41; asst. U.S. atty. Eastern Dist. N.Y., Bklyn., 1946; 1st asst. criminal div. Dept. Justice, 1947-48; exec. asst. to atty. gen. U.S., 1948, spl. asst. to atty. gen., 1949-50; mem. subversive activities control bd. (under Internal Security Act of 1950), 1950-53, chmn., 1952-53; commr. investigation N.Y.C., 1954-55; corp. counsel N.Y.C., 1955-58; pvt. practice, mem. firm Manning, Hollinger & Shea, 1958-65, Brown Carlino & Emmanuel, 1965-72; counsel Winer Neuberger & Sive, 1972—; individual practice law, 1978—; dir. Thomas Pub. Co. Trustee St. Mary's Coll., Notre Dame, Ind. Served from pvt. to maj. AUS, 1942-45; ETO. Decorated 6 battle stars on European African Middle Eastern ribbon, Fourragère of Belgium for Battle of Ardennes (The Bulge). Fellow Am. Coll. Trial Lawyers; mem. Am., N.Y. State, Bklyn., City of N.Y. bar assns., VFW, Am. Legion, St. Patrick Soc. Bklyn. (past pres., dir.), Friendly Sons St. Patrick City N.Y., Fordham Coll. Alumni Assn. (past pres., dir.). Democrat. Roman Catholic (cardinal's com. laity). Clubs: K.C., Knight of Malta, Knight of Holy Sepulchre; Lawyers, Montauk (Bklyn.); N.Y. Athletic, Manhattan, Pinnacle (N.Y.C.); Army-Navy, Touchdown (Washington); Pelham Country; Westchester Country. Home: 275 N Ridge St Rye Town Port Chester NY 10573 Office: 90 Park Ave New York NY 10016

BROWN, PHILLIP STANLEY, mktg. co. exec.; b. Success, Ark., Mar. 10, 1940; s. Robert Hume and Katie Ozella (Shelton) B.; student public schs., Doniphan, Mo., 1954-58. Credit dir. GAC Fin. Corp., Paris, 1964-68; mktg. dir. Diversified Mktg. Internat., Frankfurt, W. Ger., 1968-69; mgr. Ramstein Audio Club W. Ger., 1969-70; pres. Brown Mktg. GmbH, Wiesbaden, W. Ger., 1970—; cons. Haden & Brown, Inc., Dallas; dir. Brown Sports GmbH, Munich, W. Ger. Served with U.S. Army, 1961-64. Home: 16 Adolfsalle Wiesbaden Federal Republic Germany D 6200 Office: 2 Egerstrasse Wiesbaden 32 Federal Republic Germany D 6200

BROWN, RALPH MANNING, JR., ins. exec.; b. Elizabeth, N.J., July 1, 1915; s. Ralph Manning and Anna Alethea (Rankin) B.; A.B., Princeton U., 1936; m. Margrette Burnham, Oct. 6, 1950; children—Anne Alethea Brown Hartnett, Ralph Manning. With Gen. Motors Acceptance Corp., 1936-51; asst. v.p. N.Y. Life Ins. Co., N.Y.C., 1951-53, v.p., 1953-62, exec. v.p., 1962-69, pres., 1969-72, chmn., chief exec. officer, 1972—; dir. La. Land and Exploration Co., J.P. Morgan & Co., Inc., Avon Products Inc., Union Carbide Corp., Union Camp Corp., Asso. Dry Goods Corp. Clubs: Links, Univ. (N.Y.C.); Pretty Brook Tennis (Princeton). Home: 50 Westcott Rd Princeton NJ 08540 Office: 51 Madison Ave New York NY 10010

BROWN, RAY LEE, business exec.; b. Columbus, Ohio, Nov. 25, 1930; s. John Lee and Audrey Louise (Cott) B.; B.S., Ohio State U., 1953, Ph.D., 1972; M.B.A., Harvard, 1963; m. June Edna Gibbs; children—Ellen, Sheryl, Linda, Victor, Gregory, Carol. Tax acct. Gen. Electric Co., Schenectady, 1953; commd. 2d lt. USAF, 1954, advanced through grades to col., 1974; assigned Office Comptroller USAF, also Office Sec. Def.; ret., 1975; asst. prof. acctg. U. Denver, 1975-80; v.p., chief fin. officer Congressional Info. Service, Inc., 1980—; cons., lectr. for several orgns. Decorated Legion of Merit; C.P.A.; cert. managerial accountant. Mem. Am. Acctg. Assn., Acad. Mgmt., Nat. Assn. Accts., Assn. Govt. Accts. (Research award 1978),

Beta Gamma Sigma, Beta Alpha Psi. Contbr. articles to profl. jours. including Harvard Bus. Rev. and Jour. of Accountancy. Address: 2420 S Queen St Arlington VA 22202

BROWN, RAYMOND DUTSON, assn. exec.; b. Phila., Feb. 3, 1933; s. Allen Webster and Helen Ruth (Belshaw) B.; B.A., Brown U., 1959; M.Div., Phila. Div. Sch., 1962; m. Joyce Marie Foor, Feb. 10, 1978; children by previous marriage—Raymond D., Timothy R., Katherine E., Lura A. Ordained to ministry Episcopal Ch., 1962; curate, Schenectady, 1962-63; vicar Whitefish (Mont.) Mission field, 1963-66; dean St. Peter's Cathedral, Helena, Mont., 1966-75; adminstr. Mont. Human Rights Div., Helena, 1975—; chaplain Mont. Ho. of Reps., 1967, 69. Mem. Helena Sch. Bd., 1973-76; pres. Lewis and Clark Search & Rescue, 1973-77; bd. dirs. St. Peter's Hosp., United Way; Served to s/sgt. USMC, 1951-54. Mem. Nat. Assn. Human Right Workers, Internat. Assn. Ofcl. Human Rights Agencies, Mont. Assn. Chs. (pres. 1973-74), Mont. Council Chs. (chmn. Indian task force 1968-70). Democrat. Home: 1748 Colorado Gulch Helena MT 59601 Office: Suite 300 Steamboat Block 616 Helena Ave Helena MT 59601

BROWN, RAYMOND LECLAIR, design and prodn. cons.; b. Framingham, Mass., Dec. 3, 1910; s. Cornelius Patrick and Josephine (LeClair) B.; B.S., M.I.T., 1933, M.S. in Elec. Engring., 1934; m. Josephine Partica, July 22, 1950; 1 son, Ronald. With Electrolux Corp., Old Greenwich, Conn., 1936-66, chief engr., mgr. product engring., 1959-66; mfg. cons. Singer Co., Elizabeth, N.J., 1966-75; cons. small motor design and prodn., Brewster, Mass., 1975—. Chmn., Brewster Econ. Devel. Commn., 1979—. Served with AUS, 1941-46. Decorated Bronze Star. Mem. IEEE (life). Republican. Patentee vacuum cleaner field. Home: 35 Tupelo Ln Brewster MA 02631 Office: PO Box 801 Brewster MA 02631

BROWN, RICHARD KING, ins. cons.; b. Buffalo, Nov. 5, 1942; s. Arnold A. and Ruth M. (King) B.; A.A., Wesley Coll., 1964; m. Janis Slayton, Sept. 7, 1970; children—Stacy Lynn, Jason Richard, Linsay Allison Pilar. Ins. salesman, 1967-73; pres. Corporate Ins. Cons. Ltd., Norristown, Pa., 1973—. Mem. Valley Forge C. of C. (past pres.), Norristown Jaycees, Nat. Assn. Life Underwriters, Health Assn. Underwriters. Contbr. chpt. to tech. text. Office: CIC Bldg 516 DeKalb St Norristown PA 19406

BROWN, RICHARD MYLES, lawyer; b. Chgo., Nov. 16, 1942; s. Leo and Esther (Balton) B.; B.A., UCLA, 1964, J.D., 1967; m. Sandra Barbara Spellman, July 28, 1971; children—Scott Matthew, Todd Andrew. Admitted to Calif. bar, 1968, U.S. Ct. Mil. Appeals bar, 1968; atty.-adv. FTC, Los Angeles, 1967-68, 71-72; atty. Xerox Corp., Los Angeles, 1972-73, Rochester, N.Y., 1973-74; div. counsel Bechtel Power Corp., Los Angeles, 1974-79; v.p., gen. counsel Avery Internat. Corp., San Marino, Calif., 1979—. Served as capt. JAGC, U.S. Army, 1968-71; Vietnam. Decorated Bronze Star, Army Commendation medal; named 1 of 20 Outstanding Graduating Srs., UCLA, 1964. Mem. State Bar Calif., Am. Bar Assn., Los Angeles County Bar Assn., Lawyers Club Los Angeles. Office: 415 Huntington Dr San Marino CA 91108

BROWN, ROBERT BRYCE, state ofcl.; b. Salisbury, Md., Sept. 28, 1942; s. Oscar E. and Laura (Wells) B.; A.A. and Gen. Bus. Adminstrn., Goldey Beacom Coll., 1961; m. Penny Elaine Hudson, Sept. 25, 1965; children—Ryan Bryce, Lori Lee. Auditor of accounts State of Del., Dover, 1962-76, state auditor III, 1976-80, chief adminstrv. auditor, 1980—. Served with Army NG, 1963-64. Mem. Intergovt. Audit Forum, Mcpl. Fin. Officers Assn., Del. Govt. Fin. Officers Assn. Democrat. Methodist. Clubs: Maple Dale Country, Del. Mobile Surf Fishermen. Home: RD 5 Box 246A Dover DE 19901 Office: Townsend Bldg PO Box 1401 Dover DE 19901

BROWN, ROBERT DANA, mgmt. cons.; b. Chgo., Aug. 19, 1920; s. J. Dana and Ethel (Crouch) B.; A.B., Dartmouth, 1946; postgrad. Northwestern U., 1946-47; m. Jane Tyne, Jan. 25, 1969; children by previous marriage—Robert Morse, Susan Beck. Labor relations exec. Richardson Co., 1946-51; sec., asst. treas. Fairbanks, Morse & Co., 1953-60; mgmt. cons. Stevenson, Jordan & Harrison, Chgo., 1961-62; asst. to pres. Fenestra, Inc., Chgo., 1963-65; v.p. Peabody Coal Co., St. Louis, 1966-68; v.p., gen. mgr. Jet Oil Co., Chgo., 1968-69; v.p. comml. banking Commerce Union Bank, Nashville, 1970-76; pres. R. Dana Brown & Assos., Nashville, 1976—; vice chmn. bd. Dobson & Johnson Ins. Co., Nashville. Served to maj. AUS, 1942-45. Decorated Legion of Merit, Bronze Star medal, Purple Heart (U.S.); Silver Cross of Merit with sword (Poland); Mil. Valor Cross (Italy). Clubs: Chicago, Racquet (Chgo.); Belle Meade Country, Cumberland (Nashville); Bath and Tennis (Palm Beach, Fla.). Home and Office: 5819 Hillsboro Rd Nashville IN 37215

BROWN, ROBERT HALL, JR., textile co. exec.; b. Boston, Nov. 12, 1931; s. Robert Hall and Laura (Aitken) B.; B.S.M.E., M.I.T., 1954; m. Joyce Hemenway, June 26, 1954; 1 dau., Elesse Throwbridge. With Belding Heminway Co., N.Y.C., 1954—, div. mgr., 1965-72, v.p., 1972-77, exec. v.p., 1977-79, pres., chief operating officer, 1979—, also dir. Trustee, Convent of the Sacred Heart, 1978—. Served with U.S. Army, 1954-56. Mem. The Thread Inst. (dir., 1973—), Sigma Xi, Tau Beta Pi, Pi Tau Sigma. Home: Upland Dr Greenwich CT 06830 Office: Belding Heminway Co 1430 Broadway New York NY 10018*

BROWN, SAMUEL JOSEPH, II, mech. engr.; b. New Orleans, May 6, 1941; s. Samuel Joseph and Camille Beatrice B.; B.S. in Mech. Engring., U. Southwestern La., 1966; M.S. in Mechanics (NDEA fellow), U. Fla., 1968; Ph.D., U. Akron, 1980; m. Josephine Monistere, Feb. 2, 1962; children—Troy Joseph, Tricia Maria, Kamryn Leigh. Engr., Middle South Utility, New Orleans, 1966; research asst., cons. U. Fla., 1969-70; analyst, design engr. Babcock & Wilcox, Barberton, Ohio, 1970-74, sr. engr. applied mechanics, 1974-78; mem. research and devel. staff J. Ray Mc Dermott, New Orleans, 1979-80; engr. O'Donnell & Assos., Pitts., 1980—; mem. faculty U. Akron. Registered profl. engr., Ohio, La. Mem. ASME, Soc. Exptl. Stress Analysis, Sigma Xi. Contbr. articles to profl. jours. Office: O'Donnell & Assos 241 Curry Hollow Rd Pittsburgh PA 15236

BROWN, SAMUEL THOMAS, railroad exec., bus. cons.; b. Patton, Pa., Apr. 18, 1896; s. Elmer Collins and Frances Betterton (Gregg) B.; M.E., Cornell U., 1917; m. Katherine Woodcock Kiefer, Feb. 9, 1921; children—Samuel Thomas, Mary Elizabeth, Elmer Collins. Pres., Glenside Coal Co., Bakerton Coal Co., Beaver Co., 1918-27; pres. Hughes-Brown-Moore Corp., real estate, Chgo., 1927—; partner firm Hughes Brown & Moore, investments, also exec. Wilson & Co., Inc., Chgo., 1936-38; v.p., dir. Climax Fire Brick Co. (Pa.), 1939; pres. Mechanics Laundry & Supply, Inc., Indpls., 1940; pres. Brown-Johnson Corp., 1942—; chmn., pres. Va. Iron Coal & Coke Co., Roanoke, 1945-60; dir. Monon R.R. (merged into L. & N. R.R. 1971), Chgo., 1956-71, pres., chmn. bd., chief exec. officer, 1967-71; chmn. bd. The Roanoke Corp. (Va.), 1960—; pres., chief exec. officer Chgo. & Western Ind. R.R. Co., 1972-76, chmn. bd., 1976—; cons. L. & N. R.R., 1972—. Served to ensign USN, 1917-21. Mem. Kappa Sigma. Republican. Presbyn. Mason (Shriner). Clubs: University (Chgo., N.Y.C.); Shenandoah, Country (Roanoke). Home: Private Huff Rd NW Roanoke VA 24012 Office: 418 W Campbell Ave Roanoke VA 24026

BROWN, SCOTT NEWTON, real estate, ins. exec., appraiser cons.; b. Chattanooga, May 3, 1909; s. C. Victor and Catherine (Colburn) B.; student Davidson Coll., 1926-28; B.S. in Commerce, U. Tenn., 1930; student Am. Inst. Banking, 1931; spl. courses Am. Inst. Real Estate Appraisers, 1947, 68; postgrad. Law Sch., LaSalle Extension U., 1966; m. Margaret Frierson Williamson, Dec. 2, 1939; children—Scott Newton, George W. Pres. Scott N. Brown Co.; exec. v.p. N.Am. Capital Corp. Mem. Tenn. Real Estate Commn., 1958-62; pres. Chattanooga Bd. Realtors, 1948, Insurors of Chattanooga, 1949-50; mem. Realtor's Washington Com., 1950-60, 62, chmn., 1951; chmn. Indsl. Com. of 100; trustee McCallie Sch., Inc., 1957-62; trustee, sec. McCallie Sch. Alumni Endowment Fund, Inc.; pres. Brown Found., Inc. Mem. Nat. Assn. Real Estate Appraisers, Nat. Apt. Assn., Am. Assn. Cert. Appraisers, Nat. Assn. Realtors, Tenn. Assn. Realtors, Nat. Assn. Ins. Agts., Tenn. Assn. Ins. Agts., Nat. Assn. Rev. Appraisers, Am. Coll. Real Estate Cons.'s, Am. Soc. Real Estate Profls., Chattanooga C. of C. (pres. 1958), Delta Sigma Pi, Pi Kappa Phi. Presbyn. (past elder). Clubs: Downtown Lions (past sec.; named Lion of Yr.), Walden. Home: 401 Crewdson Ave Chattanooga TN 37405 Office: 626 James Bldg Chattanooga TN 37402

BROWN, SUSAN O'CONNOR, bank exec.; b. Phila., Feb. 13, 1952; d. John Joseph and Suzanne Kelso (McLean) O'Connor; B.F.A., Rosemont Coll., 1974; postgrad. Temple U.; m. Michael J. Brown, May 16, 1975. Asst. mgr. women's boutique, 1972-74; with 1st Pa. Bank, Phila., 1974—, unit head consumer group planning area, 1977-78, div. head planning and fin. mgmt., 1978-79, nat. lending group, 1980—; cons. in field. Mgr. area campaign for state senatorial election 17th Pa. Dist., 1974. Mem. Am. Mgmt. Assn.

BROWN, THOMAS PAUL, oil co. exec.; b. Miles City, Mont., Aug. 5, 1927; s. Thomas Ambrose and Eleanor Ann (Boyce) B.; m. Virginia Sue Sayers, June 2, 1961; children—Dana, Tina, Nelson, Paul, Susan, Diane, David. With mktg. dept. Carter Oil Co., Billings, Mont., 1946-53; v.p. Modern Oil Co., Shelby, Mont., 1953-55, N.W. Oil & Refining, Billings, 1955-58, Berry Refining Co., Chgo., 1958-64, Pana Refining (Ill.), 1964-68; pres., chmn. bd. Synthetic Crude Devel. Co., Santa Barbara, Calif., 1980—; cons. Tosco Corp., Los Angeles, 1968-70, v.p., 1973-78, exec. v.p., 1978-80, also dir.; pres. Tosco Petro, 1970-73. Served with USAAC Res., 1944-45. Republican. Roman Catholic. Clubs: Los Angeles Petroleum, Calif., Jonathan, Los Angeles Athletic. Home: 4235 Cresta Ave Santa Barbara CA 93110 Office: 3892 State St Santa Barbara CA 93105

BROWN, THOMAS TOWNSEND, research co. exec.; b. Zanesville, Ohio, Mar. 18, 1905; s. Lewis K. and Mary (Townsend) B.; student Calif. Inst. Tech., 1922-23, Kenyon Coll., 1923-24, Denison U., 1924-25, Bowdoin Coll., 1941; m. Josephine Alberta Beale, Sept. 8, 1927; children—Joseph Townsend, Linda Ann. Lab. asst. electronics research dept. physics Denison U., Granville, Ohio, 1924-25; mem. staff astrophysics research lab. Swazey Obs., Granville, 1926-30; jr. physicist radiation and spectroscopy Naval Research Lab., Washington, 1930-33; state erosion engr. Fed. Emergency Relief Adminstrn., Columbus, Ohio, 1934; asst. adminstr. relief Ohio, dir. fed. student aid, dir. selection CCC, Ohio, 1934-35; research cosmic radiation observations Townsend Brown Found., Zanesville, Ohio, Laguna Beach, Calif., 1936-37; material and process engr. Glenn L. Martin Co., Balt., 1939-40; officer in charge magnetic and acoustic minesweeping research and devel. Bur. Ships, Navy Dept., Washington, 1940-41; radar cons. advanced design sect. Lockheed Aircraft Corp., Burbank, Calif., 1944-45; individual research biophysics, plant growth Island Kauai, Hawaii, 1948-52; cons. physicist Société Nationale Construction Aeronautique, Paris, France, 1955-56; chief cons. research and devel. Whitehall-Rand project Bahnson Co., Winston-Salem, N.C., 1957-58; pres. RAND Internat., Ltd., Nassau, Bahamas, 1958-74, Energy Resources Group, Ltd., Honolulu, 1974-80, Energy Internat., Inc., Chapel Hill, N.C., 1980—. Staff physicist Navy-Princeton Gravity Expdn., W.I., Navy Dept., 1932; physicist Johnson-Smithsonian deep sea expdn., Smithsonian 1933; cons. physicist Pearl Harbor Navy Yard, Honolulu, 1950; cons. Clevite-Brush Electronics Co., Cleve., 1954. Served to lt. comdr. USNR, 1933-43. Fellow AAAS; mem. Soc. Naval Engrs., Physics Soc., Geophys. Union. Address: PO Box 1565 Avalon CA 90704

BROWN, TRAVIS WALTER, oil drilling equipment co. exec., rancher, lawyer; b. Oklahoma City, June 18, 1934; s. H. Travis and Una Irene (Robison) B.; B.B.A., U. Okla., 1956; J.D., Oklahoma City U., 1962; m. Marilynn Davis, June 1, 1957; children—Deborah, Travis, Thomas, Darla. With Geolograph Co., Oklahoma City, 1948-79, pres., 1966-79, also dir.; pres., dir. Medearis Oilwell Supply Corp., Long Beach, Calif., 1973-79; sec., dir. Robinwood Farms, Ltd., Oklahoma County, Okla., 1968-79; v.p., dir. Geolograph Service Ltd., Edmonton, Alta., Can., 1960-79; chmn. bd. Geolograph Medearis Service (U.K.) Ltd., London, Aberdeen, Singapore, 1977-79; pres. Geolograph-Pioneer div. Geosource Inc., 1979—; chmn. bd. Robinwoods Poor Boy Feed Co., Edmond, Okla., 1980—; dir. Internat. pres. Cosmopolitan Internat. Civic Club, 1973-74, recipient Distinguished Service award, 1964, 67. Served with USNR, 1957-58. Recipient Wall St. Jour. award, 1952; named to Am. Cattle Breeders Hall of Fame, 1979. Mem. Okla., Oklahoma County (pres. 1974-75) cattlemen's assns., Am. Petroleum Inst., Internat. Assn. Oilwell Drilling Contractors, Ind. Petroleum Assn. Am., Soc. Petroleum Engrs., Canadian Inst. Mining and Metallurgy, Am. Mining Congress, Can. Diamond Drilling Assn., Am. Inst. Mining Engrs., Am., Okla. (Disting. Service award 1964), Oklahoma County bar assns., Okla. Zool. Soc., Palomino Horse Breeders Am. (nat. youth dir. 1973—, pres. elect 1980), Okla. Palomino Exhibitors Assn. (pres. 1978), Okla. (v.p. 1980—), Internat. Brangus breeders assns., Okla., Am. quarter horse assns., Nomads. Republican. Methodist. Contbg. author: Subsurface Geology, 1976; also papers on oilfield drilling and mining. Home: Route 1 Box 154 Oklahoma City OK 73131 Office: PO Box 25246 Oklahoma City OK 73125

BROWN, WALTER DANIEL, assn. exec.; b. Pitts., Nov. 25, 1917; s. David and Lillian Elizabeth (Waldschmidt) B.; B.S., U. Pitts., 1938, M.S., 1948; m. Elizabeth Logan Schmeck, July 29, 1944; children—David, Walter, Edward, Kenneth. Engr., Duquesne-Light Co., Pitts., 1939-50, asst. gen. supt. system ops., 1950-58; mgr. electric utility engring. Middle West Service Co., Chgo., 1958-64; system engring. editor Elec. World, McGraw-Hill, Inc., N.Y.C., 1964-70; adminstrv. mgr. Nat. Electric Reliability Council, Princeton, N.J., 1970-77, exec. v.p., 1977-80, pres., 1980—. Trustee Princeton United Meth. Ch., 1967-70. Served to lt. comdr. USNR, 1944-46. Registered profl. engr., Pa. Mem. IEEE, Scabbard and Blade, Sigma Tau, Eta Kappa Nu. Republican. Clubs: Nassau (Princeton); Army and Navy (Washington), Masons. Office: Terhune Rd Princeton NJ 08540

BROWN, WERNER CURT, chem. co. exec.; b. Berlin, Germany, Feb. 18, 1919; s. Robley Evans and Margaret (Hessler) B.; B.A. in Chemistry, Duke U., 1942; postgrad. Harvard Grad. Sch. Bus. Adminstrn., 1960; m. Maude S. Bulluck, Sept. 26, 1942; children—David B., Stephen R., Margaret B., Ernest M., Alice L., Richard E. With Hercules, Inc., Wilmington, Del., 1942—, v.p., mem. exec. com., 1966-80, mem. fin. com., 1969-80, pres., chief exec. officer, 1970-77, chmn. bd., 1977-80; dep. chmn. Fed. Res. Bank of Phila.; mem. Delmarva Power Bd., chmn. exec. com. Diamond State Telephone Co. Bd. dirs. YMCA of Wilmington, United Way of Del., Inc.; trustee Wilmington Med. Center, Duke U.; trustee, vice chmn., mem. exec. com., chmn. fin. com. U. Del. Mem. Am. Chem. Soc., Conf. Bd., Mfg. Chemists Assn. (past chmn.), Soc. Chem. Industry (past chmn. Am. sect., mem. exec. com.), Societe de Chimie Industrielle, Inc., Econ. Club N.Y. Clubs: Hercules Country; Wilmington, Wilmington Country; Links; Augusta Nat. Golf; Johns Island. Office: 910 Market St Wilmington DE 19899

BROWN, WILBUR FORMAN, JR., lab. exec.; b. Charleston, W.Va., Oct. 23, 1934; s. Wilbur Forman and Louise Chiles (Graves) B.; B.S., Colo. State U., 1956; m. Dorothy Ellen Jackson, July 20, 1955; children—Wilbur Clinton, Philip Pike, Kathryn Desha. Nuclear product specialist Picker X-Ray Corp., Arlington, Va., 1961-63; indsl. product specialist Picker Corp., Balt., 1963-68; treas. Reliance Testing Labs. Inc., Balt., 1968-73, pres., 1973—. Served with USN, 1957-61. Mem. Am. Soc. for Nondestructive Testing (chmn. Chesapeake Bay sect. 1969-70), ASTM, Nat. Rifle Assn. Am. Office: PO Box 85 2199 Greenspring Dr Timonium MD 21093

BROWN, WILLIAM L., banker; b. Hendersonville, N.C., Feb. 1, 1922; s. William W. and Sarah (Maxwell) B.; student Mars Hill Coll., Newberry Coll.; M.B.A., Harvard, 1947; m. Helen Presbrey, June 1947; children—Kathryn H., Richard P., Steven J., Melissa M. Pres., dir. First Nat. Boston Corp. and First Nat. Bank of Boston, dir. several subs. and affiliates; dir. Stone & Webster, Inc., N.Y.C., Standex Internat. Corp., Salem, N.H., Gen. Cinema Corp., Boston, Liberty Mut. Ins. Co., Boston and Liberty Mut. Fire Ins. Co., Boston. Trustee, Children's Hosp. Med. Center, Boston, Boston Coll., Mus. of Sci., Boston. Served to lt. USNR, World War II. Office: 100 Federal St Boston MA 02110

BROWN, WILLIAM MICHAEL, communications co. exec.; b. N.Y.C., Nov. 22, 1942; s. Herbert Joseph and Elizabeth Virginia (Allen) B.; B.S., Fordham U., 1963; m. Kathleen King, Mar. 7, 1964; children—William, Patrick, Michael, Carolyn, Michele, Daniel. Mem. audit staff Arthur Andersen & Co., 1963-67; asst. comptroller ITT World Communications, Inc., 1968-71; asst. comptroller O. M. Scott & Sons subs. ITT, 1972-73, v.p., comptroller, 1974-77; group comptroller, v.p. Communication Operating Group (U.S. Tel. & Tel.), ITT, N.Y.C., 1978-79, group v.p., exec. dir. Far East and European ops., 1979—. C.P.A., N.Y. State. Republican. Roman Catholic. Office: 67 Broad St New York NY 10004

BROWN, WILLIAM RICHARD, mfg. co. exec.; b. Poughkeepsie, N.Y., Aug. 1, 1929; s. Edmund and Grace (Lasher) B.; B.S., Rider Coll., Trenton, N.J., 1950; m. LaVerle Reynolds, Sept. 14, 1957; children—Craig, Peter, Christina. Dir. mktg. practices, mgr. budgets IBM Corp., White Plains, N.Y., 1954-69; v.p. Computer Tech./East, Inc., White Plains, N.Y., 1969-70; pricing and fin. analysis mgr. Xerox Corp., Stamford, Conn., 1970-71, dir. planning and bus. devel., 1971-72, pres., gen. mgr. spl. bus. div., El Segundo, Calif., 1972—; dir. Diablo Systems, Inc. and Versatec Inc. both subs. Xerox Corp. Dir. People's Coordinated Services of So. Calif., 1976—. Served with U.S. Army, 1951-53. Club: Palos Verdes Country. Home: 2700 Via Rivera Palos Verdes Estates CA 90274 Office: 701 S Aviation Blvd El Segundo CA 90245

BROWN, WILLIAM RUSSELL, lawyer; b. Holly Springs, Miss., July 5, 1914; s. Horace Brightberry and Aileen (Blackburn) B.; B.B.A., U. Tex., 1937, LL.B., 1937; m. Ruth Cunningham, Apr. 19, 1941; children—Betsy (Mrs. Thomas M. Smith III), Virginia, Russell. Admitted to Tex. bar, 1937, since practiced in Houston; partner firm Baker & Botts, and predecessors, 1948—; gen. counsel, dir. Houston Lighting & Power Co.; dir. Houston Industries Inc., Primary Fuels, Inc., Utility Fuels, Inc. Served to lt. USNR, 1943-45. Decorated Bronze Star. Fellow Tex. Bar Found.; mem. Am. (mem. council pub. utility law sect. 1974-77), Tex. (mem. council pub. utility law sect. 1976-77), Houston bar assns., Chancellors, Friar Soc., Newcomen Soc., Order of Coif, Delta Tau Delta, Beta Gamma Sigma. Democrat. Episcopalian. Clubs: Houston, Houston Country. Home: 5816 Bayou Glen Houston TX 77057 Office: 29th Floor One Shell Plaza Houston TX 77002

BROWN, WOODS ROBERT, mfg. co. exec.; b. Greenville, Pa., July 23, 1941; s. Woods R. and Naomi B.; B.S., Youngstown State U., 1965; M.B.A., Capital U., 1977; m. Jeanne McDermid, Aug. 28, 1965; children—Woods Robert II, Karyn W. Internal auditor Met. Life Ins. Co., N.Y.C., 1965-66; sr. acct. Xerox Corp., Rochester, N.Y., 1966-74; mgr. budgets and planning Borden, Inc., Columbus, Ohio, 1974-79; v.p. adminstrn. Kolux div. Gen. Indicator Corp., Kokomo, Ind., 1979-80; acting controller LaPointe Industries, Rockville, Conn., 1980; v.p., controller Integrated Electronics Corp., Dover, N.J., 1981—. Active Boy Scouts Am., 1974-77; cubmaster, 1974-75, Disting. Service award, 1976; bd. dirs. Howard County United Way, Kokomo, 1979-80; coach Westerville Jr. Baseball League, 1977-78; fin. cons. Big Walnut Sch. Dist., 1975-79; active Fairport-Perinton (N.Y.) Jaycees, 1968-70, named Outstanding Com. Mem. Republican. Methodist. Club: Sertoma. Home: 660 Dogwood Ct Noblesville IN 46060 Office: PO Box 213 Dover NJ 07801

BROWNE, ALAN KINGSTON, bank cons.; b. Alameda, Calif., Nov. 12, 1909; s. Ralph Stuart and Etta E. (Bouve) B.; student U. Calif., 1929; m. Elisabeth Leone Henrotte, Feb. 7, 1942. With Bank-Am. Co. (successor to securities div. Nat. Bankitaly Co.), 1929-41, successively clk., mgr. municipal bond dept., asst. v.p.; with Bank of Am. N.T. & S.A., 1941-71, successively asst. cashier, asst. v.p., mgr. municipal bond dept., v.p., 1952-64, head of investments, 1952-65, sr. v.p., 1965-71, cons., 1971-72; sr. v.p., dir. Drexel Firestone, Inc., N.Y.C., 1972-73; dir. Drexel Burnham & Co. Inc., 1973, cons., 1974. Past pres., dir. San Francisco Stadium, Inc. (Candlestick Park); past chmn. bd., pres. Friends San Francisco Pub. Library; chmn. adv. bd. on financing San Francisco Bay Area Rapid Transit Dist.; chmn. San Francisco Bay Area Rapid Transit Commn. Bd. dirs. Dist. Adminstrv. Bldg. Corp.; trustee U. Calif. Berkeley Found. Served from pvt. to maj., AUS, 1942-46. Recipient Distinguished Citizens award Nat. Municipal League, 1964. Mem. Securities Industry Assn. (past v.p., exec. com., gov.), Greater San Francisco C. of C. (past pres., chmn. sr. council), Air Force Assn., U. Calif. Alumni Assn. (alumni council), Assn. U.S. Army, Calif. Geneal. Soc., Calif. Hist. Soc., Mus. Soc., Mcpl. Forum N.Y., Mcpl. Fin. Forum Washington, S.A.R., Phi Kappa Sigma, others. Clubs: Pacific Union, San Francisco Bond (past pres.), San Francisco Stock Exchange, Olympic, Mcpl. Bond, Mchts. Exchange (San Francisco); Faculty (Berkeley). Home: 1113 Singing Wood Ct #6 Walnut Creek CA 94595

BROWNE, DAVID LEE, engring. co. exec.; b. Ancon, C.Z., Jan. 1, 1942; s. Carl Jacob and Ethel (Skinner) B.; B.A., Dartmouth Coll., 1963, B.E.E., 1964; M.B.A. candidate St. Mary's Coll., Moraga, Calif. Prin. engr. Kaiser Engrs., Oakland, Calif., 1969—; owner David Lee Browne Creations, 1975—. Served to lt. C.E., USN, 1964-69. Registered profl. engr., Calif., Fla. Mem. IEEE, Instrument, Soc. Am., Soc. Am. Mil. Engrs., IEEE Industry Applications Soc. (chmn. chpt.),

Dartmouth Soc. Engrs. Republican. Contbr. articles to profl. jours. Home: 1898 Queens Rd Concord CA 94519 Office: 300 Lakeside Dr PO Box 23210 Oakland CA 94623

BROWNE, FORREST REGINALD, JR., real estate and constrn. co. exec.; b. Bklyn., Apr. 23, 1939; s. Forrest Reginald and Rosita Marie (Anderson) B.; B.A. with honors, U. Mo., 1961; M.A. (Woodrow Wilson nat. fellow), U. Pa., 1962; m. Martha J. Schuetz, June 7, 1961 (div. May 1976); children—Lisa Lynn, Forrest Reginald III, Beneth Anderson; m. 2d, Mary Jo Alley, May 20, 1978; children—Jennifer Christen, Rebecca Josephine, Brooke Danae. Mem. fin. staff Chrysler Corp., Detroit, 1962-69; treas. Chrysler Realty Corp., Detroit, 1970-74, v.p., 1974-76; pres. Gt. Midwest Corp., Kansas City, Mo., 1976—, also dir. Bd. govs. Kansas City Philharm., 1976—, v.p., 1977-79, pres., 1979—, chmn. bd. trustees, 1979—. Mem. Young Presidents Orgn., Kansas City C. of C. Club: Kansas City. Home: Route 5 Box 361 Liberty MO 64068 Office: 8300 NE Underground Dr Kansas City MO 64161

BROWNE, HOUSTON LEE, investment exec.; b. Newport News, Va., Mar. 9, 1947; s. Houston LeRoss and Elizabeth Rose (Knapp) B.; B.A., Franklin and Marshall Coll., 1970; m. Jacquelyn Grace LaMalfa, July 16, 1977. Publisher, Colo. Property mag., Aspen, 1972-75; developed Colo. ranches, 1973-76; editor Sports Preview, newspaper syndication, 1975; partner, dir. Oxford Hill Ltd., Greenwich, Conn., 1976—; treas., dir. Environments for Human Services, Greenwich, 1976—; pres., dir. Greenwich Pharms. Inc., Greenwich, 1976—; dir. Bonanza Airlines, Aspen, Colo., 1976-78. Home: 465 Round Hill Rd Greenwich CT 06830 Office: 95 E Pitnam Ave Greenwich CT 06830

BROWNE, THEODORE DAVID, fin. cons. and research co. exec.; b. New Kensington, Pa., Dec. 2, 1932; s. Gordon Scott and Florence Llewllyn B.; B.S., Pa. State U., 1954; M.S. in Fin., U. Colo., 1957; m. Kathryn Vermillion, Nov. 28, 1959; children—Tamra D., Kristin A. Personnel specialist Martin Co., Denver, 1958-64; research economist U. Denver Research Inst., 1964-70; pres. Bickert, Browne, Coddington & Assos., Inc., Denver, 1970—; mng. partner Browne, Bortz & Coddington, Denver, 1979—; chmn., pres. Gunnison Indsl. Bank, Montrose Indsl. Bank; chmn. Delta Indsl. Bank. Served to lt. col. USMCR, 1954-56; ret. Res., 1977. Mem. Nat. Assn. Bus. Economists, Phi Gamma Delta. Republican. Club: Denver Execs. Home: 5525 Pemberton Dr Littleton CO 80121 Office: 155 S Madison St Denver CO 80209

BROWNING, CHARLES EDWARD, organ mfg. co. service mgr.; b. North Tonawanda, N.Y., Apr. 28, 1926; s. Frank Elmo and Martha Matilda (Meyers) B.; student pub. schs., Buffalo; m. Mary Ellen Woods, Jan. 4, 1954; 1 dau., Ellen Virginia. Clk., Fed. Res. Bank, Buffalo, N.Y., 1947-52; asst. service mgr. Wurlitzer Co., North Tonawanda, 1952-57; service mgr. Jordan Piano Co., Washington, 1957-64; dist. service mgr. Wurlitzer Co., DeKalb, Ill., 1964—; owner, operator Browning Organ Service, Washington, 1973—. Served with USN, 1943-45, U.S. Army, 1950-52. Home: 301 N Aspen Ave Sterling VA 22170

BROWNING, COLIN ARROTT, banker; b. Jersey City, June 24, 1935; s. Colin John Herbert and Ellenor May (Coughlin) B.; B.A., Cornell U., 1957; M.B.A., N.Y. U., 1964; m. Ellen Miriam McNeill, July 18, 1964; children—Colin Robertson, Paul William. With Chase Manhattan Bank, 1960-64; v.p. Midatlantic Nat. Banks N.J., 1964-70; with J. Henry Schroder Bank & Trust Co., N.Y.C., 1970—, sr. v.p., 1972-77, exec. v.p., mem. mgmt. com., 1977—; dir. Schroder Naess & Thomas. Trustee Upper N.J. chpt. Nat. Multiple Sclerosis, 1965-72, pres., 1969-70, 71-72. Served with U.S. Army, 1958-60. Mem. Corporate Fiduciaries Assn. Republican. Episcopalian.

BROWNING, DAVID STUART, lawyer; b. Amarillo, Tex., June 6, 1939; s. Stuart W. and Pauline (Rogers) B.; B.A., U. Tex., 1960, LL.B., 1962; M.A., Johns Hopkins U., 1964; m. Judith, July 31, 1957; 1 son, Mark. Admitted to D.C. bar, 1963; Tex. N.Y. bar, 1971; asso. firm Fulbright and Jaworski, Houston, 1964-70; asst. counsel Schlumberger Ltd., N.Y.C., 1970-76, sec., gen. counsel, 1976—. Mem. N.Y. Bar Assn., Tex. Bar Assn., Am. Soc. Internat. Law. Office: 277 Park Ave 41st Fl New York NY 10017

BROYHILL, ROY FRANKLIN, indsl. turf and agrl. equipment mfg. exec.; b. Sioux City, Iowa, June 20, 1919; s. George Franklin and Effie (Motes) B.; B.B.A., U. Nebr., 1940; m. Arline W. Stewart, Jan. 30, 1943; children—Lynn Diann (dec.), Craig G., Kent Bryan, Bryce Alan. Trainee mgr. Montgomery Ward Co., 1940; semi-sr. acct. L. H. Keightley, 1941-42; chief accountant Army Exchange Service, Sioux City, 1942-46; pres., chmn. Broyhill Co., 1946—; pres., dir. Star Printing & Pub. Co., South Sioux City, 1949—; pres., chmn. Broyhill Corp., 1953—; v.p. Broyhill Mfg. Co., 1978—; pres., chmn. bd. Broyhill Inc.; dir. 1st Nat. Bank, Sioux City. Mem. U.S.A. Exec. Res.; mem. Nebr. dist. adv. council Small Bus. Adminstrn., 1971—. Mayor of Dakota City, 1951-53; mem. Nebr. Republican Central Com., 1954-56. Past mem. local sch. bd. Trustee U. Nebr. Found. Served with AUS, 1940-41. Mem. Nitrogen Solutions Assn. (dir. 1956-60), Farm Equipment Mfrs. Assn. (dir., pres. 1971-72), Atokad Racing Assn. (dir., treas.), N.A.M., U.S., South Sioux City chambers commerce, Nebr. Assn. Commerce and Industry (dir. 1972-73), Alumni Assn. U. Nebr. (dir.), Beta Theta Pi, Alpha Kappa Psi. Presbyn. (elder). Mason (Shriner), Kiwanian. Home: 1610 Broadway Dakota City NE 68731 Office: Broyhill Co N Market Sq Dakota City NE 68731

BRU, JULIE MARTINEAU, ins. co. exec.; b. Annapolis, Md., Aug. 2, 1942; d. David Louis and Carole Elizabeth (Gregg) Martineau; B.A., George Washington U., 1963; m. Salvador Bru, July 12, 1969; 1 son, Alexander Nicolas. Teaching fellow econs. George Washington U., Washington, 1963-64; mgr. personal products div. Industrial Quimica Farmaceutica Iberica, Barcelona, Spain, 1964-69; mgr. planning and spl. projects Baskin-Robbins Ice Cream, Burbank, Calif., 1970-72; corporate analyst, dir. bus. planning Govt. Employees Ins. Co., Washington, 1972-79, asst. v.p. planning/research/analysis, 1979—. Mem. Phi Beta Kappa. Home: 4408 Garrison St NW Washington DC 20016

BRUBAKER, JAMES LINDLEY, data processing exec.; b. N.Y.C., Oct. 9, 1941; s. Carl Lindley and Marguerite Louise B.; B.A., Fla. Atlantic U., 1973; M.B.A., Nova U., 1977; m. Eleanor Carlee, Nov. 26, 1966; 1 son, Scott James. Sr. programmer, analyst Pompano Beach Bank (Fla.), 1968-71; programming mgr. Mangurian's, Inc., Fort Lauderdale, Fla., 1971-73; data processing mgr. Real Estate Computer Service, Pompano Beach, 1974-75; v.p. M.I.S., Fla. Bankshares, Inc., Hollywood, Fla., 1976—; adj. prof. Broward Community Coll. Served with U.S. Army, 1964-67. Mem. Assn. M.B.A. Execs., Data Processing Mgmt. Assn., Am. Inst. Banking. Republican. Methodist. Office: 2001 Hollywood Blvd Hollywood FL 33022

BRUCE, DAN ROBERT, career cons.; b. Detroit, Feb. 25, 1927; s. Jack and Edna (Togal) Berg; M.B.A., Stanford U., 1980; m. Carol E. Bodner, Feb. 11, 1956; children—Michele, Lori, Leslie. Vice pres. Nat. Album Co., Beverly Hills, Calif., 1967-69; nat. sales mgr., v.p. Pied Piper, Inc., Los Angeles, 1968; pres., chief exec. officer Bernard Haldane Assos., Los Angeles, 1969—; pres. West Coast Advt. Co., Los Angeles, 1978—; chmn. bd. Fin. Acceptance Corp. Served with U.S. Mcht. Marine, 1945-50. Recipient Outstanding Service Recognition award Am. Chem. Soc., 1978. Mem. Los Angeles C. of C. (dir.). Club: Civitan. Office: 3807 Wilshire Blvd Los Angeles CA 90010

BRUCE, ROBERT DOUGLAS, occupational health and environ. cons.; b. Livingston, Tex., Jan. 13, 1941; s. Vivian Eugene and Edna Lee (St. Clair) B.; B.S., Lamar U., 1963; M.S., Mass. Inst. Tech., 1966, E.E., 1966; m. Lydia Marcelyn Meynig, May 31, 1963; children—Robert Douglas, James Elliott. Asso. engr. Mobil Oil Co., Beaumont, Tex., 1963-64; teaching asst. Mass. Inst. Tech., 1965-66, asso. dir., summer 1972; cons. Bolt Beranek and Newman Inc., environ. and noise control techs., Cambridge, Mass., 1966-68, sr. cons., 1968-70, supervisory cons., 1970-73, mgr., 1970-74, asso. div. dir., 1974-75, dir. ops., 1975-77, dep. div. dir., 1977—; lectr. in field. Deacon West Acton (Mass.) Bapt. Ch. Fellow Acoustical Soc. Am. (past chmn. tech. com. on noise); mem. Inst. Noise Control Engring., Am. Indsl. Hygiene Assn., Air Pollution Control Assn., Am. Mgmt. Assn., Blue Key, Phi Kappa Phi, Eta Kappa Nu, Tau Beta Pi. Contbr. to publs. in field. Home: 26 Black Horse Dr Acton MA 01720 Office: Bolt Beranek Newman 50 Moulton St Cambridge MA 02238

BRUCKNER, WALTER SHERMAN, marketing exec.; b. Bronx, N.Y., June 5, 1935; s. Samuel Isaac and Marie (Blaustein) B.; B.A., L.I. U., 1956; M.B.A., U. Pa., 1958; m. Lenore Joan Miller, Nov. 20, 1971. Market research supr. RCA Record Div., N.Y.C., 1962-67; mgr. mktg. sales analysis ITT Continental Baking Co., Rye, N.Y., 1967-69; mgr. fin. planning Capitol Records, Hollywood, Calif., 1969-70; mgr. mktg. services Roberts Consol. Industries, Industry, Calif., 1970-74; dir. market planning and internat. mktg. Taylor Industries, Industry, Calif., 1974-76; pres. Walter S. Bruckner & Assos., Inc., Santa Monica, Calif., 1977-79; v.p., dir. mktg. Adhesive Industries Mfg. Co., Cerritos, Calif., 1979—. Served to 2d lt. AUS, 1958-60. Mem. Am. Mktg. Assn., Mfrs. Agts. Nat. Assn., Assn. M.B.A. Execs. Clubs: Toastmasters; Internat. Health (Los Angeles). Office: 5319 Vista Montana Yorba Linda CA 92686

BRUDER, ROBERT IRWIN, diversified co. exec.; b. Cleve., May 2, 1930; s. Leonard M. and Sarah (Doinwick) B.; student Ohio State U., 1948; m. Marcia Pullin, Mar. 18, 1973; children—Richard A., Ronald M., Stephen J., Scott P. Dir. mktg. Charles Corp., Cleve., 1955-58; founder, pres. Bruder & Co., Inc., Cleve., 1958-63; pres. Atherton-Bruder div. Litton Industries, Inc., Palo Alto, Calif., 1963-65; v.p., gen. mgr. Atherton div., Cleve., 1965-67, group v.p., 1968—; corp. v.p. Litton Industries, Inc., Beverly Hills, Calif., 1968; v.p. Stouffer Foods Corp. subs. Cleve., 1967-70; group v.p. Stouffer Restaurant & Inn, Stouffer Foods, Stouffer Food Systems divs; group v.p. Litton Food Services Group, Cleve., 1967-70; pres. Atherton div., 1970-73; pres. Litton Bus. Tel. Systems, 1973-74; group exec., pres. Litton Med. Products Group, Schiller Park, Ill., 1974-78; sr. v.p. corp. planning and devel. Gen. Telephone & Electronics Corp., Stamford, Conn., 1978—. Trustee, Mt. Sinai Hosp., Cleve. Mem. Bluecoats Fraternal Order Police. Jewish. Clubs: Brandeis U., Clevelander, Landmark, Stanwick Country. Patentee in microwave and electronic infra-red heating devices. Home: 35 W Brother Dr Greenwich CT 06830 Office: GT&E Corp One Stamford Forum Stamford CT 06904

BRUDNER, HARVEY JEROME, physicist, mfg. co. exec.; b. N.Y.C., May 29, 1931; s. Joseph and Anna (Fiddleman) B.; B.S. in Engring. and Physics, N.Y. U., 1952, M.S., 1954, Ph.D., 1959; m. Helen Gross, Dec. 18, 1963; children—Mae Ann, Terry Joseph, Jay Scott. Electronics engr. Bendix Corp., 1952; physicist Naval Ordnance Lab., 1953-54; prin. physicist Emerson Radio Corp., Washington and Jersey City, 1954-61; pres. Med. Devels. Inc., Jersey City, 1962; dean N.Y. Inst. Tech., N.Y.C., 1962-64; chief physicist Am. Can Co., Princeton, N.J., 1964-67; v.p. research and devel. Westinghouse Learning Corp., N.Y.C., 1967-71, chmn. and pres., 1971-76; pres. HBJ Enterprises, Highland Park, N.J., 1976—; guest scientist Rockefeller Inst., 1959-60; dir. Westinghouse Learning Corp., Ideal Sch. Supply, Ednl. Products Inc., Document Reading Services Ltd., Linguaphone Inst. Ltd., Info. Synergy, Inc., World Learning and Communications, Inc., Cambridge Learning Connection, Inc.; cons. Nat. Inst. Edn., M.I.T., Worcester Poly. Inst., Poly. Inst. N.Y., Rutgers U. Coll. Engring., U.S. Ho. of Reps. Com. on Sci. and Tech., Power Authority State N.Y. cons. steering com. project PROCEED NSF. Mem. planning com. Highland Park (N.J.) Bd. Edn., 1976; bd. advisers Middlesex County Coll., Ednl. Improvement Center of S. Jersey, 1967—. Fellow IEEE (photovoltaic systems com.); mem. AAAS, Am. Phys. Soc., Am. Math. Soc., Am. Inst. Physics, Soc. Motion Picture and TV Engrs., Am. Ednl. Research Assn., Am. Math. Soc., Am. Soc. Tng. and Devel., N.Y. Acad. Sci., Am. Judicature Soc., Council of Americas, Electronic Industries Assn., Nat. Security Indsl. Assn. Clubs: Chemists, N.Y. U. Patentee in field; author six math. and sci. textbooks, numerous articles in field. Home: 812 Abbott St Highland Park NJ 08904 Office: 333 Montgomery St Highland Park NJ 08904

BRUGGER, HUBERT ANTON, fin. holding co. exec.; b. Lindau, Germany, Feb. 26, 1933; came to U.S., 1961, naturalized, 1965; Betriebswirt, U. Munich, 1958; grad. internat. mktg. Northwestern U., 1961; m. Gisela Schruut, May 21, 1961; children—Joern-Eric Walter, Beatrice Caroline. Founder, pres. Autohaus Brugger, Inc., Redwood City, Calif., 1966—, Brugger Corp., fin. holding and investment co., Redwood City, 1968—, also chmn. bd.; chmn. bd. Brugger Natural Resources, Las Vegas. Mem. Internat. Economists Assn., Internat. Assn. Pvt. Investment Bankers. Home: 21 Haciendas Dr Woodside CA 94062 Office: 249 Main St Redwood City CA 94063

BRUMBACK-RICHARD, ALLEN, mgmt. cons.; b. Lorain, Ohio, Aug. 15, 1945; s. Harry Allen and Ester Mae (Cline) B.; B.S.I.E., Wayne State U., 1968; M.S. in Mgmt. Sci., Johns Hopkins U., 1972; m. Marion Sue Cowell, Aug. 8, 1969. Engr., Westinghouse Electric Corp., Balt., 1968-73; mgmt. cons., scientist JRB Assos., Inc., Sci. Applications, Inc., McLean, Va., 1973-77; mgmt. cons. Automated Scis. Group, Inc., Silver Spring, Md., 1977-78; v.p. ops. Wilson-Hill Assos., Inc., Washington, 1978—. Mem. Inst. Mgmt. Scis., Ops. Research Soc. Am. Home: 7441 Swan Point Way Columbia MD 21045 Office: Suite 900 1025 Vermont Ave NW Washington DC 20005

BRUMLEY, IRA JON, mfg. co. exec.; b. Pampa, Tex., 1939; B.B.A., U. Tex., 1961; M.B.A., U. Pa., 1963; married. Mgmt. cons. Towers, Perrin, Forster & Crosby, 1964-67; adminstrv. asst. Southland Royalty Co., Dallas, 1967-69, asst. to pres., 1969-70, v.p., 1970-71, exec. v.p., 1971-73, pres., 1973-74, pres., chief exec. officer, 1974—, also dir.; dir. Aztec Mfg. Co., Ft. Worth Nat. Bank, Millers Group. Served with U.S. Army. Office: Southland Corp 2828 N Haskell Ave Box 719 Dallas TX 75221*

BRUMMEL, CHARLES DWIGHT, bank exec.; b. Yates Center, Kans., Apr. 18, 1939; s. Gilbert Charles Clyde and Roberta Helena (Wade) B.; student U. Oreg., 1957-58, Pacific Coast Banking Sch., U. Wash., 1975-77, Nat. Comml. Lending Sch., U. Okla., 1973; m. Sandra Jean Thornburg, July 1, 1960; children—Pamela, Charles Dwight, Tina, Kevin. With Nationwide Fin. Co., 1960-70; with Security Bank of Coos County, Myrtle Point, Oreg., 1970—, asst. v.p., 1971-73, chief exec. officer, dir., 1974—; dir., chmn. bd. Computer Service Bur., 1979-80. Mem. Jr. Coll. Sch. Bd., 1979—, County Budget Com., 1979—, County Bd. Equalization, 1979—; chmn. City Myrtle Point Budget Com., 1977-80, Myrtle Point Career Edn. Adv. Com., 1977-78. Served with AUS, 1958-60. Recipient cert. appreciation Myrtle Point High Sch., 1977; named Outstanding Chmn., Richmond (Calif.) Jaycees, 1968. Mem. Oreg. Bankers Assn. (chmn. govt. affairs com. 1977-80), State Chartered Banks of Oreg., Western Ind. Bankers (dir. 1979-81), Am. Inst. Banks, Myrtle Point C. of C. Republican. Mem. Christian Ch. Clubs: Elks, Rotary (pres. Myrtle Point 1978), Lions, Kiwanis. Home: 1031 Spruce St Myrtle Point OR 97458 Office: Security Bank of Coos County 503 Spruce St Myrtle Point OR 97458

BRUMMER, ROBERT CRAIG, business exec.; b. Mar. 28, 1945; s. Emmett Anthony and Mary Ellen (Blue) B.; B.B.A., Eastern Mich. U., 1970; m. Jill Sutherland, Feb. 27, 1965; children—Anne Marie, Robert Craig. Ops. asst. mgr., shift leader, also dept. mgr. Interstate Stores, 1969-71, Midwest regional personnel mgr., 1971-72, Eastern regional personnel mgr., 1972-73, store mgr. in tng., 1973, asst. to dir. personnel and employee relations, 1973; dist. personnel mgr. Target Stores, Colo./Okla., 1973-74; regional personnel/ops. mgr. Tex./Okla., 1974-79; mgr. exec. placement and devel. Dayton Hudson Corp., Mpls., 1979—. Mem. Am. Soc. Tng. and Devel. Home: 7153 Willow Rd Maple Grove MN 55369 Office: Dayton Hudson Corp 777 Nicollet Mall Minneapolis MN 55402

BRUMMETT, CLAUDIA MAE, steel co. exec.; b. Amarillo, Tex., Feb. 28, 1927; d. Claude Jamieson and Mae (Kight) B.; student Amarillo Coll., 1944-46, U. Colo., 1946-48. Chief diversion and tracer clk. Santa Fe Ry. Co., 1948-68; partner JAL Co., JAL Ranch, Alvarado, Tex., 1968—; corp. sec. J & M Steel Co., Inc., Fort Worth, 1971—; v.p., sec. Western Tool & Mfg. Co., Alvarado; silversmith; one-man shows at Simpson Gallery, Amarillo, Tex., Square House Mus., Panhandle, Tex.; exhibited in group shows at Tex. Tech. Mus., Wichita Falls, Tex. Mus., Pan-Am. Mus., McAllen, Tex.; represented in permanent collection Carlin Gallery, Ft. Worth. Mem. State Democratic Exec. Com., 1962-70, mem. dist. exec. com., 1962-70; del. Dem. Nat. Conv., 1964, 68, 74, mem. rules com., 1964, mem. credentials com., 1968, 72; mem. del. selection commn. Dem. Nat. Com., 1973-74; co-chmn. Briscoe Campaign for Gov., 1972; dir. S. Central region Nat. Fedn. Dem. Women; nat. Dem. committeewoman, 1974-76; Republican precinct chmn., Johnson County, Tex. bd. dirs. Granbury Opera Assn.; pres. Johnson County Human Guidance Assn., 1977—. Mem. Tex. Designer Craftsman, Tex. Artists, Craftsman Guild. W. Tex. C. of C., Tex. Exec. Club, Tex. and Southwestern Cattle Raisers Assn., Tex. Fedn. Rep. Women, Nat. Fedn. Rep. Women. Baptist. Address: JAL Ranch Box 308 Alvarado TX 76009

BRUMMOND, ROBERT THOMAS, utility exec.; b. Belle Fourche, S.D., Dec. 29, 1950; s. Bruce and Mary Josephine (Waldron) B.; B.S. in Physics, St. Norbert Coll., DePere, Wis., 1973; M.S. in Civil Engring., U. Ill., Champaign-Urbana, 1974. Environ. engr. Lake County Public Works Dept., Waukegan, Ill., 1974-76, supr. ops., 1976—. Cert. wastewater operator, Ill. Mem. Am. Water Works Assn., Water Pollution Control Fedn., Ill. Soc. Water Pollution Control Operators (1st v.p.), Ill. Soc. Profl. Engrs. (asso.). Roman Catholic. Home: 73 Miller Rd Lake Zurich IL 60047 Office: 650 Winchester Rd Libertyville IL 60048

BRUNDAGE, JOHN DENTON, ins. co. exec.; b. Newark, Mar. 28, 1919; s. Edgar Ray and Salome (Denton) B.; A.B., Princeton U., 1941; m. Ann Lounsbury, Nov. 29, 1941; children—Elizabeth Ann, Susan, Patricia, John. Agy. asst. Bankers Nat. Life Ins. Co., Montclair, N.J., 1945-46, asst. to pres., 1953-54, adminstrv. v.p., 1955-57, exec. v.p., 1957-58, pres., dir., 1958-71; sales promotion mgr. Mut. Benefit Life Ins. Co., Newark, 1946-47, regional supt. agys., 1948-50, dir. agys., 1950-52, agy. mgr., N.Y.C., 1952-53; chmn., dir. Palisades Life Ins. Co., New City, N.Y., 1965-71; chmn., pres., dir. Ga. Internat. Life, Atlanta, 1972-74; pres., dir. Dominion Trust Life, Houston, 1972-74; chmn., chief exec. officer Globe Life Ins. Co., Chgo., 1974-77, 79—, pres., 1977-79. Chmn. Montclair Urban Coalition, 1969-70; chmn. bd. Am. Heart Assn., 1962-65; bd. govs. Chgo. Heart Assn., 1976—, chmn., 1980—; trustee Sch. of the Ozarks,1976—. Served from ensign to lt. comdr. USNR, 1940-45. Recipient Gold Heart award Am. Heart Assn., 1965; Citizens award for disting. community service N.J. Acad. Medicine, 1964; C.L.U. Fellow Life Office Mgmt. Assn.; mem. Nat. Assn. Life Underwriters, Am. Coll. Life Underwriters. Clubs: Princeton (N.Y.C.); Short Hills (N.J.); Indian Hill (Winnetka, Ill.); Chicago; Quadrangle (Princeton). Office: Globe Life Ins Co 222 N Dearborn St Chicago IL 60601

BRUNER, WILLIAM WALLACE, banker; b. Orangeburg, S.C., Nov. 6, 1920; s. Robert Raysor and Bessie (Livingston) R.; children—William W., Thomas W., James L. Accountant, J.W. Hunt & Co., C.P.A.'s, Columbia, S.C., 1945-48; with 1st Nat. Bank S.C., Columbia, 1948—, sr. v.p., 1961-64, pres., 1964—, chmn. bd., 1970—, also dir.; pres., dir. 1st Bankshares Corp. S.C., Columbia, 1969—; dir. Columbia Coca-Cola Bottling Co., Home Security Life Ins. Co., Durham, N.C., Spartan Mills, Spartanburg, S.C., Atlantic States Bankcard Assn., Raleigh, N.C. Treas., United Fund, Columbia, 1958-59, bd. dirs., 1956-58, chmn. large firms div., 1965; chpt. chmn. ARC, 1958-60, vice chmn. nat. fund, 1960-61; treas., chmn. bd. trustees Providence Hosp., Columbia; treas., trustee Bus. Partnership Found., U. S.C.; treas. S.C. Soc. Crippled Children and Adults, 1967-70, v.p., 1970-71, pres., 1971-72. Served to lt. comdr. USNR, 1941-45. C.P.A., S.C. Mem. Am. Inst. C.P.A.'s, S.C. Assn. C.P.A.'s, Am. (governing council 1972-74, dir. 1972-73), S.C. (pres. 1970-71) bankers assns., U.S. (banking, monetary and fiscal affairs com. 1977-80), Columbia (v.p. 1962) chambers commerce, Phi Beta Kappa, Beta Gamma Sigma, Sigma Nu. Methodist. Office: 1401 Main St PO Box 111 Columbia SC 29202

BRUNN, FREDERICK ALBERT, perfume co. exec.; b. Jersey City, July 19, 1936; s. Max Joseph and Elizabeth Maria (Mueller) B.; B.S. in Acctg., Seton Hall U., 1958; M.B.A. in Fin., Fordham U., 1972; m. Marguerite Kirchmann, Aug. 22, 1959; children—Mark, Laura, Matthew. Acct., Colgate Palmolive, N.Y.C., 1959-61; adminstrv. asst. Lanvin-Charles of the Ritz, N.Y.C., 1961-68; asst. treas. Faberge Inc., N.Y.C., 1968-72, treas., 1972—. Pres., Blauvelt (N.Y.) Free Library, 1974-79; bd. dirs. Cath. Charities N.Y. Archdiocese, St. Catharine's Ch., Blauvelt; trustee, pres. adv. com. Dominican Coll., Blauvelt. Served with U.S. N.G., 1958-64. Mem. Fin. Execs. Inst. (treas. N.Y.C. chpt.), Treas.'s Group N.Y.C. Club: K.C. Home: 707 Handwerg Dr River Vale NJ 07675 Office: 1345 Ave of Americas New York NY 10019

BRUNNER, GEORGE MATTHEW, mfg. co. exec.; b. Newark, Jan. 17, 1925; s. Mathais J. and Mary E. (Fuith) B.; A.B., Columbia U., 1949, M.A., 1950; m. Ruth E. Owens, Nov. 16, 1953. Devel. engr. J.T. Baker Chem. Co., Phillipsburg, N.J., 1950-53; plant mgr. Internat. Minerals and Chem. Corp., Niagara Falls, N.Y., Houston, 1953-62; mfg. and engring. mgr. Gen. Foods Corp., Hoboken, N.J., Houston, Lafayette, Ind., 1962-71; v.p. mfg. W.R. Grace & Co., St. Simon's

Island, Ga., 1971-73; pres., chief exec. officer, dir. S.A. Schonbrunn & Co., Inc., Palisades Park, N.J., 1973—. Served with U.S. Army, 1943-45. Decorated Purple Heart. Mem. Nat. Coffee Assn., Am. Chem. Soc., Am. Inst. Chem. Engrs., Electro-Chem. Soc., Fifth Armored Div. Assn., President's Assn. Home: 12 Roger Ct Woodcliff Lake NJ 07675 Office: 21 Grand Ave Palisades Park NJ 07650

BRUNNER, ROBERT RUSSELL, pharm. corp. exec.; b. Pana, Ill., July 3, 1953; s. Russell and Irene B.; B.S., Millikin U., 1975; m. Vonda Marie Williams, Dec. 31, 1979. Auditor, Arthur Andersen & Co., St. Louis, 1975-77; asst. controller Storz Instrument Co., St. Louis, 1977-78; treas., dir. Scherer Labs., Inc. Dallas, 1978—. C.P.A. Mem. Am. Inst. C.P.A.s. Club: Kiwanis. Home: 2644 Via La Paloma Carrollton TX 75006 Office: Scherer Labs Inc PO 400009 Dallas TX 75240

BRUNO, JIM NEIL, cons., former editor, pub.; b. N.Y.C., Sept. 5, 1946; s. Martin and Esther Alice (Youngwirth) B.; B.A., in Psychology, Coll. City N.Y., 1969; m. Gayle Thomas Whitaker, May 12, 1972; 1 son, D. Todd. Project dir. Lieberman Research, N.Y.C., 1969-70; editor Impact Info. Tech., also pub. Mgmt. World for Adminstrv. Mgmt. Soc., Willow Grove, Pa., 1972-79, mng. editor Adminstrv. Mgmt., 1979-80; partner Harvard (Mass.) Assos., 1979-80; dir. public relations Al Paullefton Co., 1980—; speaker mgmt. topics; cons. communications. Mem. Adminstrv. Mgmt. Soc., Public Relations Soc. Am., Del. Valley Assn. Communicators. Contbr. chpt. to Ency. of Profl. Mgmt., NBEA Yearbook, articles to bus. publs. including Adminstrv. Mgmt., Geyer's Dealer Topics, Office Equipment and Methods, Concepts, Mgmt. World, Generalist, Impact Info. Tech., Office Weekly. Home: 504 Penn St Newtown PA 18940 Office: Warren Ave Harvard MA 01451

BRUNO, NICHOLAS JOSEPH, mfg. co. exec.; b. New Canaan, Conn., Oct. 1, 1912; s. Dominick and Theresa (Cosentini) B.; grad. high sch.; b. Elizabeth Jane Schneider, July 10, 1939; children—Elizabeth, Theresa. Plant supt. Aerotec Corp., Greenwich, Conn., 1951-56; tech. procurement engr. Atomic div. Westinghouse Electric Co., Pitts., 1956-67; dir. purchases Target Rock Corp., East Farmingdale, N.Y., 1967—. Recipient Spl. Achievement award Westinghouse Electric Co., 1969. Republican. Roman Catholic. Club: K.C. Patentee dinner plate for handicapped. Home: 556 Rockland St Westbury NY 11590 Office: 1966 E Broadhollow Rd East Farmingdale NY 11735

BRUNSON, JOHN SOLES, lawyer; b. Houston, Jan. 8, 1934; s. Nathan Bryant and Jonnie E. (McMillan) B.; B.B.A., Baylor U., 1956, LL.B., 1958, J.D., 1965; m. Joan Erwin, Dec. 26, 1953: children—W. Mark, Dana Ruth. Admitted to Tex. bar, 1958, U.S. Supreme Ct. bar, 1961; asso. firm Dillingham, Schleider & Lewis, Houston, 1958-64; partner firm Brunson & Brill, Houston, 1964-70, Baker, Heard & Brunson, Houston, 1970-72, Brunson & Erwin, Houston, 1972—. Mem. Harris County (Tex.) Democratic Exec. Com., 1959-65; mem. Tex. Dem. Exec. Com., 1968-74. Mem. State Bar Tex., Houston Bar Assn., Am. Bar Assn. Baptist. Clubs: Houston, Houstonian. Home: 10314 Holly Springs Houston TX 77042 Office: 1700 Transco Tower Houston TX 77056

BRUSH, PETER NEWTON, electronic interconnections mfg. co. exec.; b. Manchester, N.H., May 2, 1937; s. Arthur Twitchell and Lois Elizabeth (Newton) B.; student Hofstra U., Hempstead, N.Y., 1957; m. Noelia Santana, Jan. 24, 1981; 1 dau. by previous marriage, Wendy. With photocircuits div. Kollmorgen Corp., 1965-78, v.p., 1977-78, pres. Multiwire div., Glen Cove, N.Y., 1978-80, dir. corp. planning Kollmorgen Corp., Stamford, Conn., 1980—, mem. mgmt. bd. Inland Motor Splty. Products div., Radford, Va., 1978—. Mem. Am. Electronics Assn., Inst. Interconnecting and Packaging Electronic Circuits. Office: 66 Gatehouse Rd Stamford CT

BRUSKE, GEORGE WILLIAM, farm supplies co. exec.; b. Pitts., May 22, 1927; s. Norbert and Marjorie (Glass) B.; B.A., U. Mich., 1951; m. Irene Ann Mooney, June 12, 1964; children—Regina Crosby, George Robert. With Standard Oil Co. Ind., various locations, 1951-67, marketing dir. Amoco Australia, Sydney, 1961-66; v.p. marketing Southwest Grease & Oil Co., Inc., Wichita, Kans., 1967-73; dir. sales promotion Farmland Industries, Kansas City, Mo., 1973—. Mem. advt. com. Universal Coop. Vice pres. marketing March of Dimes, Wichita, 1971-72; capt. Wesley Hosp. Fund Drive, Wichita, 1970; active United Fund, Wichita, 1971-72. Served with USAAF, 1945-46. Mem. Am. Petroleum Inst., Soc. Automotive Engrs., Am. Soc. Lubrication Engrs., Nat. Agri-Marketing Assn. (pres. Mo.-Kans. chpt., nat. membership chmn. 1980), Advt. and Sales Execs. Club, Theta Delta Chi, Sigma Delta Chi. Home: 6109 NW Webb Circle Kansas City MO 64151 Office: 3315 N Oak Trafficway Kansas City MO 64116

BRUSTKERN, MICHAEL FRANKLIN, steel corp. exec.; b. Elma, Wash., Sept. 24, 1940; s. LeRoy Eugene and Betty Jane (Zuvich) B.; A.B., U. Puget Sound, 1963; M.B.A., Gonzaga U., 1968; m. Patricia Dane Highsmith, Aug. 22, 1965; children—Von Franklin, Bo Daniel. Pres., ASC Industries, Inc., Spokane, Wash., 1975; v.p., gen. mgr. I&IP div. Gifford-Hill & Co., Inc., Spokane, 1976-77; pres. ASC Pacific, Inc., Tacoma, 1978—. Div. chmn. United Way of Spokane County, 1976-77; chmn. ann. giving U. Puget Sound, 1980-81. Mem. Presidents Assn., Am. Mgmt. Assn., Tacoma C. of C. Methodist. Clubs: Tacoma Country and Golf, Tacoma, Lakewood Racquet. Home: 7620 North SW Tacoma WA 90498 Office: ASC Pacific Inc 2141 Milwaukee Way Tacoma WA 98421

BRUXVOORT, KEITH EUGENE, mfg. co. exec.; b. Ft. Knox, Ky., June 14, 1953; s. Stanley Harold and Reuvena Marie (Dieleman) B.; B.A. in Bus. Adminstrn. (Coll. scholar), Calvin Coll., 1975; m. Beverly A. Scheeringa, Aug. 8, 1975. Tax intern Seidman & Seidman, Grand Rapids, Mich., 1975; daily ops. mgr. Bills Produce, Inc., Highland, Ind., 1975-76; credit mgr. films packaging Union Carbide Corp., Chgo., 1976-77; cost acct./asst. controller Land O Frost, Inc., Lansing, Ill., 1977-79, controller Ill. plant, 1979—; owner, operator acctg. firm, Highland, Ind. Comptroller First Christian Ref. Ch., Highland, 1977—, treas., 1978—. C.P.A., Ind. Mem. Nat. Assn. Accts., Am. Inst. C.P.A.'s, Ind. C.P.A. Soc. Office: 16850 Chicago Ave Lansing IL 60438

BRUYNES, CEES, mfg. co. exec.; b. Netherlands, Aug. 3, 1932; s. Arie and Petronella (Borst) B.; grad. Chr. Lyceum, Arnhem, Netherlands, 1951; m. Elly Nagel, Feb. 1, 1963; children—Irene W., Jan Paul. With N.V. Phillips' Gloeilampenfabrieken, Netherlands, 1953-71; pres., chief exec. officer Philips Can., 1971-74; exec. v.p. N. Am. Philips Corp., N.Y.C., 1975-78, pres., chief operating officer, 1978—. Served with Dutch Air Force, 1951-53. Clubs: Union League, Sky. Netherlands (N.Y.C.); Greenwich (Conn.) Country. Home: Khakum Wood Greenwich CT 06830 Office: 100 E 42d St New York NY 10017

BRYAN, ANTHONY JOHN ADRIAN, mfg. co. exec.; b. Mexico, Feb. 24, 1923; s. F.V.A. and Marjorie (Blackett) B.; student Ampleforth Coll., York, Eng.; M.B.A., Harvard, 1947; m. Pamela Zauderer, June 30, 1978; children—Caroline Bryan McCandless, Pamela, Jamie Robinson, George Robinson, Anthony John Adrian. With Monsanto Co., St. Louis, 1947-73, various positions in domestic mktg., 1947-67, bus. dir., 1968-69, gen. mgr. internat. div., 1968-73, corporate v.p., dir., 1969-73; pres., chief exec. officer, dir. Cameron Iron Works, Houston, 1973-77; chmn. bd., pres. Copperweld Corp., Pitts., 1977—; dir. Chrysler Corp., Hamilton Bros. Petroleum Corp.; dir. ITT, Fed. Express Corp., Imetal, Paris, Pitts. Nat. Corp. ITT. Bd. dirs. Am. Iron and Steel Inst.; bd. dirs., trustee numerous charitable and ednl. instns. Served with RCAF, 1940-45. Mem. Fgn. Policy Assn. (dir.). Home: 6530 Beacon St Pittsburgh PA 15217 Office: Copperweld Corp 2 Oliver Plaza Pittsburgh PA 15222

BRYAN, EUGENE LEE, cons. co. exec.; b. Apr. 18, 1934; s. Ray Kenneth and Ruth Orianna (Yinst) B.; B.S. in Forestry, U. Idaho, 1957; M.S. in Wood Tech., U. Calif., Berkeley, 1959, M.S. in Engring. Sci., 1961; Ph.D., U. Mich., 1963; children—Susan, Linda, Daniel. Project leader research staff U. Calif., Berkeley Forest Products Lab., 1957-62; research mgr. Black Clawson Co., Everett, Wash., 1963-65; asso. prof. forestry faculty Calif. State U., Humboldt, 1965-67; partner Bryan & Helm, Eureka, Calif., 1967-69; pres. Decision Dynamics, Inc., Portland, Oreg., 1969—; chmn. bd. Xytec Corp., Beaverton, Oreg., 1978—. Served with USNR, 1951-57. Recipient Wood award for Outstanding Research in Forest Products Field, 1963. Mem. Forest Products Research Soc. (chmn. mgmt. div. 1977-78), Soc. Am. Foresters, Ops. Research Soc. Am., Inst. Mgmt. Sci. Contbr. numerous articles in field to profl. jours. Home: 1901 Palisades Terr Lake Oswego OR 97034 Office: No 295 The Water Tower Portland OR 97201

BRYAN, JACOB FRANKLIN, III, ins. co. exec.; b. Jacksonville, Fla., Feb. 26, 1908; s. Jacob Franklin and Olive Julia (Gibson) B.; student Fla. Bus. U., 1927-28; LL.D. (hon.), Bethune-Cookman Coll.; m. Josephine Christian Hendley, May 25, 1935; children—Jacob Franklin, Carter Byrd, Kendall Gibson. With Ind. Life and Accident Ins. Co., Jacksonville, 1927—, successively agt., supt., mgr., 1927-48, v.p., dir., 1948-57, chmn. bd., pres., 1957-79, chmn. bd., chief exec. officer, 1979—; chmn. bd., pres. Herald Life Ins. Co., Jacksonville, 1960-79, chmn. bd., chief exec. officer, 1979—; dir., chmn. trust com. Fla. Nat. Bank; dir. Fla. Fed. Savs. and Loan Assn., 1955—, v.p., 1974; dir. Indsl. Am. Corp., Fla. Bus. Forum, Inc. Mem. U.S. Indsl. Council, 1967—, also mem. exec. com., v.p. for Fla., 1970—; com. mem. Bold New Jacksonville Program, 1968; bd. dirs. Community Planning Council Jacksonville Area, Inc., 1968—; mem. Fla. Pub. Sch. Bd., 1968-69; chmn. Citizens Com. Juvenile Ct.; mem. Fla. State Ins. Adv. Com.; mem. Fla. Council of 100, 1967—; chmn. Health Planning Council Jacksonville Area, Inc., 1964-70, mem. exec. com. and screening com.; mem. adv. council Jacksonville Hosps. Ednl. Program, 1966—; mem. state adv. group Fla. Regional Med. Programs, 1967—; mem. nat. adv. council SBA, 1970; mem. contact com. HUD, 1970—; chmn. Fla. Gov.'s Art Commn.; mem. Downtown Devel. Authority, 1968—; mem. Fla. Gov.'s St. Augustine Hist. Restoration and Preservation Commn., 1973, on Quality in Edn.; mem. Am. Bi-Centennial Commn. Jacksonville, 1973; mem. fin. com., 1973; exec. adviser N. Fla. council Boy Scouts Am., 1961—; vestryman Ch. of Good Shepherd Episcopal Ch., 1959-61, 63-65, 67-69, sr. warden, 1964-65, 67-68; mem. lay adv. bd. St. Vincent's Med. Center, 1972—; chmn. adv. com. Eartha White Nursing Home, Jacksonville; bd. dirs. Community First Corp., United Negro Coll. Fund, Jr. Achievement, Children's Mus., Children's Home Soc. Fla., March of Dimes, Child Guidance Clinic, Jacksonville Art Mus., 1968, United Way of Jacksonville; past bd. dirs. Greater Jacksonville Taxpayers Assn.; bd. dirs. Girls Club Jacksonville, 1972-74; bd. dirs. Fla. Heart Assn., 1968-70, hon. chmn. campaign, 1970, mem. community program com., 1968-69, mem. long-term planning and policy com., 1968-69, state chmn. fund drive, 1969-70; bd. dirs. N.E. Fla. Heart Assn., 1964-75, v.p., 1966-67, pres., 1968-69; nat. bd. dirs. Am. Cancer Soc., Life Underwriting Tng. Council, 1974—; bd. dirs. Fla. div. Am. Cancer Soc., v.p., mem. legacy and meml. com., also hon. life mem.; bd. dirs. Duval County unit Am. Cancer Soc., past pres., hon. life mem.; bd. dirs. Jacksonville Symphony Assn., pres., 1969-70; bd. dirs. Cathedral Found. Jacksonville, 1963-72, v.p., 1963-72, chmn. finance, 1969-72; trustee Bethune Cookman Coll.; trustee Jacksonville U., also mem. ops. com., devel. bd., past chmn. Coll. of Music com.; trustee Baptist Meml. Hosp., 1968—, mem. devel. council, 1967—; trustee, a founder, chmn. maj. gifts com., mem. corporate gifts com. Episc. High Sch., Jacksonville; bd. fellows U. Tampa, 1972—; trustee Life Underwriter Tng. Council, 1974—. Recipient Spl. award for outstanding service to cancer Fla. Cancer Soc.; Ted Arnold award for outstanding service and civic accomplishment Jacksonville Jaycees; Top Mgmt. award in commerce and industry Sales and Mktg. Execs. Club, 1968; Trail Blazers award Jacksonville Assn. Life Underwriters, 1969; C.H.I.E.F. award Ind. Colls. and Univs. Fla., 1971; named Boss of Year, Arlington Jaycees, 1960; Am. Bus. Women's Assn., 1965; named Man of Year, Fla. Assn. Life Underwriters, 1960; appointed chief Jacksonville Fire Div., 1976; others. Fellow Royal Hort. Soc. (Eng.); mem. Fla. C. of C. (dir.-at-large 1969—, mem. exec. com.), Jacksonville Area C. of C. (gov. 1962-64, 69-71, mem. downtown devel. com., com. of 100; past v.p.), Fla., Jacksonville hist. socs., Life Insurers Conf. (past bd. mem., mem. resolutions com. 1966—), Nat. Assn. Over the Counter Cos. (adv. council 1973—), Jacksonville Geneal. Soc., NAM (pub. affairs com., ednl. com.), Newcomen Soc., SAR (past pres. Jacksonville chpt.), SCV, Nat. Trust Hist. Preservation, Hist. St. Augustine Preservation Bd. (vice chmn. 1969-74), English-Speaking Union (past pres., dir.), Huxford Geneal. Soc., Inc., Univ. of South Vice-Chancellor's and Trustees' Soc., Internat. Platform Assn., 200 Club Jacksonville (charter), Order Stars and Bars, Alpha Kappa Psi (hon. life). Clubs: Seminole, Fla. Yacht, River, Timuquana Country, Ye Mystic Revellers. Home: 4255 Yacht Club Rd Jacksonville FL 32210 Office: 1 Independent Dr Jacksonville FL 32276

BRYAN, JOHN EDMUND, business exec.; b. Plymouth, Eng., Oct. 1, 1931; s. John Edmund and Marion Olive (Dowrick) B.; student Dunheved Coll., Cornwall, Eng., 1940-47, Somerset Agrl. Coll., 1949-50, Royal Bot. Garden, Edinburgh, 1952-55; came to U.S., 1961, naturalized, 1970; m. Willy Chichou, Jan. 25, 1958 (div. 1973); children—Daphne Desire, Jasmine Birgitta. Apprentice R.T. May Nurserymen, Elburton, Devon, Eng., 1947-49; student Bournemouth Parks Dept., (Eng.), 1950-52, Edinburgh (Scotland) Bot. Garden, 1952-55, Royal Hort. Soc. Gardens at Wisley, 1955-56, The Hague, Holland, 1956-57; landscape architect French Govt., 1957-58; mgr. herbaceous plant nursery Vilmorin, Paris, 1958-61; v.p., sales mgr. Oreg. Bulb Farms, Gresham, 1961-71; dir. Strybing Arboretum, San Francisco, 1971-79; pres. John E. Bryan Inc.; hort. cons. Govt. Malta, 1976. Chmn. Gresham (Oreg.) Park Commn., 1962-70; host PBS series Gardening from the Ground Up. Royal Hort. Soc. and Worshipful Co. Gardeners scholar, 1955-58. Fellow Royal Hort. Soc.; mem. Oreg. Assn. Nurserymen (state dir. 1966-68), Calif. Assn. Nurserymen, Internat. Dendrology Soc., Nat. Soc. Lit. and Arts, Royal Bot. Garden Guild, San Francisco Oakland Newspaper Guild, AFTRA. Clubs: Rotary, The Family, San Francisco. Author: (with Coralie Castle) Edible Ornamental Garden, 1973; Small World Vegetable Gardening, 1977. Contbr. articles to profl. jours. Garden columnist San Francisco Chronicle, 1976—. Home: 1326 Idylberry St San Rafael CA 94103 Office: 980 Magnolia Ave Suite 8 Larkspur CA 94139

BRYAN, JOHN H., JR., foods co. exec.; b. West Point, Miss., 1936; B.A. in Econs., Southwestern at Memphis, 1958; M.B.A., Miss. State U., 1960. With Bryan Packing Co., 1960-74, chmn. bd., pres., chief exec. officer to 1974; exec. v.p.-ops. Consol. Foods Corp., Chgo., 1974-75, pres., chief exec. officer, dir., 1975—. Office: Consol Foods Corp 135 S LaSalle St Chicago IL 60603

BRYAN, LESLIE AULLS, transp. economist; b. Bath, N.Y., Feb. 23, 1900; s. D(aniel) Beach and Anna (Aulls) B.; B.S., Syracuse U., 1923, M.S., 1924, J.D., 1929; Ph.D., Am. U., Washington, 1930; Sc.D. (hon.), Southwestern Coll., 1972; m. Gertrude Catherine Gelder, Aug. 22, 1931; children—Leslie A., George G. Prof. bus. adminstrn. Southwestern Coll., Winfield, Kans., 1924-25; asst. coach track Syracuse U., 1925-42, dir. athletics, 1934-37, also instr., 1925-28, asst. prof. transp., 1928-31, asso. prof. transp. and bus. law, 1931-39, prof., 1939-45, Franklin prof. transp., 1945-46; pres. Seneca Flying Sch., Syracuse, N.Y., 1943-46; dir. Inst. Aviation and prof. mgmt. U. Ill., 1946-68, emeritus, 1968—; aviation adv. bd. Norwich U., 1954-59; dir. aviation State of N.Y., 1945. mem. Pres. Kennedy's Task Force on Aviation Goals, 1961; U. Ill. faculty rep. Intercollegiate Conf. (Big Ten), 1959-68; dir. Univ. Fed. Savs. & Loan Assn., 1960-71. Bd. dirs. Nat. Found. Asthmatic Children, 1956-65. Served as lt., inf. U.S. Army, 1917-19; overseas, 1918-19; col. USAF Res. ret. Pres. Eastern Intercoll. Boxing Assn., 1936-38, N.Y. State Aviation Council, 1944-46, Traffic Club of Syracuse, 1942. Transp. cons. Nat. Resources Planning Bd., 1942-44; aviation cons. New Standard Ency., 1947—; mem. nat. aerospace ednl. adv. com. CAP, 1948-68; mem. bd. aero. advisers State of Ill., 1949-69; tech. assistance bd. Link Found., 1953-70, spl. cons., 1970—; adv. com. FCDA, 1957-60; chmn. Pres. Eisenhower's Gen. Aviation Facilities Planning Group, 1957-58; adv. com. Washington Internat. Airport, 1958-62; cons. FAA, 1959-62; mem. adv. bd. Air Tng. Command, 1964, cons., 1965-66. Pres. Arrowhead council Boy Scouts Am., 1954-60, mem. at large nat. council, 1960-70, regional exec. bd., 1959—. Awarded Sec. War Commdn., 1946; Arents medal, 1955; Brewer trophy, 1953; Sigma Delta Chi award, 1955; Air Power award, 1956; Silver Beaver award Boy Scouts Am., 1957, Silver Antelope, 1959; Tissandier diploma Fedn. Aeronautique Internat., 1958; disting. service award Am. Assn. Airport Execs., 1959; Continental Air Command cert. of recognition, 1960, Nat. Aero. Assn. cert. of recognition, 1966, FAA disting. pub. service award, 1965; Elder Statesman Aviation, 1966; Patriots medal S.A.R., 1968; Disting. Alumni award Am. U., 1969; Letterman of Distinction, Syracuse U., 1969; Minute Man award S.A.R., 1976, Gold Good Citizenship medal, 1976; Distinguished Service medal Nat. Huguenot Soc., 1976; Air Force Assn. citation, 1976. Fellow U. Aviation Assn. (pres., 1948-49; Wheatley award 1955); mem. Am. Soc. Traffic and Transp. (bd. examiners 1948-61), Nat. Aerospace Edn. Council (pres. 1952-53, 64-66, dir. 1953-54, 59-64, 66-67), Nat. Aero. Assn. (v.p. 1953-56, 60-61, 65-66, dir. 1950-52, 54-55, 57-59, 62-64), CAP (Disting. Service award 1954), Am. Assn. Airport Execs. (v.p. 1953-55; pres. 1955-56, dir. edn. 1952-68; hon. life mem.), AIAA, Acad. Mgmt., Assn. ICC Practitioners, Aerospace Writers Assn., Newcomen Soc. N.Am., Arnold Air Soc., Am. U. Alumni (chmn. 1970-71), Ill. State Geneal. Soc. (pres. 1972-74), Nat. Huguenot Soc. (pres. gen. 1977-79, hon. pres.-gen. 1979—), Ill. State Huguenot Soc. (pres. 1971-73), SAR (genealogist gen. 1973-75, pres. Ill. soc. 1974-77, trustee 1975-76, 78-79, 80—, v.p. gen. 1976-77), Soc. War 1812 (pres. Ill. soc. 1976—, asst. adj. gen. 1976—, v.p. gen. 1978—), Soc. of Cincinnati, Sigma Alpha Tau, Alpha Eta Rho, Phi Gamma Mu, Zeta Psi, Phi Delta Phi, Phi Kappa Alpha, Alpha Kappa Psi, Phi Kappa Phi, Alpha Phi Omega, Kappa Phi Kappa, Alpha Delta Sigma, Delta Nu Alpha, Tau Omega, Scabbard and Blade, Pershing Rifles, Beta Gamma Sigma. Author: Aerial Transportation, 1925; Industrial Traffic Management, 1929; Principles of Water Transmission, 1939; Aviation Study Manual (with others), 1949, Fundamentals of Aviation and Space Technology, 4th revision (with others), 1968; (with G.L. Wilson) Air Transportation, 1949; Traffic Management in Industry, 1953; Aulls Genealogy, 1974; Thomas Bryan and Some of His Descendents, 1979; also monographs and articles; adv. editor Nat. Air Rev., 1948-50; editorial adviser (aeros.) Holt, Rinehart & Winston, Inc., 1960-64; bd. editors Air Affairs, 1949-51; cons. Our Wonderful World, 1954-55; contbr. World Book Ency., 1952-68, Compton's Pictured Ency., 1959—, McGraw Hill Ency. of Sci. and Tech., 1959—; cons. editor Above and Beyond Ency., 1967-70. Home: 34 Fields E Champaign IL 61820

BRYAN, RICHARD RAY, real estate devel. exec.; b. Centerville, Iowa, Apr. 15, 1932; s. Ashley Chester and Celia Mildred (Wright) B.; B.S., Tex. A&M U., 1956; M.S., Stanford U., 1957; m. Shirley Erline Wilson, Dec. 17, 1955; children—Scott Douglas, Shari Kay. Project mgr. H.B. Zachry Co., San Antonio, 1957-63, 69-70, Zachry Internat., Lima, Peru, 1964-68; gen. mgr. Trans-Pecos Materials Co., Odessa, Tex., 1968-69; project mgr., v.p. Gerald D. Hines Interests, Houston, 1970-75, sr. v.p., 1979-80; dir., gen. mgr. Hines Overseas Ltd., Athens, Greece, 1976-78; sr. v.p. Cadillac Fairview, So. Region, Houston, 1981—. Mem. Adminstrv. bd. United Methodist Ch., Houston, 1971-73, 75-76, 78—. Served with USAF, 1950-52; Korea. Registered profl. engr., Tex. Mem. ASCE. Home: 12327 Overcup St Houston TX 77024

BRYAN, ROBERT EDWARD, JR., computer dealer and lessor; b. Peoria, Ill., June 11, 1929; s. Robert Edward and Jenny Alnore (Lawton) B.; B.A. in Gen. Sci., U. Iowa, 1951; M.S. in Mgmt. (Sloan fellow), M.I.T., 1969; m. Ann Shouvlin, June 6, 1959; children—Elizabeth, Amy, Molly. Asst. program contracts mgr., contracts mgr. The Glenn L. Martin Co., Balt., 1953-57, program sales mgr., 1958-59, European sales mgr., 1959-61; mgr., dir. contracts Martin Marietta Corp., Denver, 1961-68; exec. dir. Martin Marietta Data Systems, Denver, 1969-72, v.p., 1972-75; pres. Econ. Data Corp., Denver, 1975—. Served with USAF, 1951-53. Mem. Computer Dealers Assn., Nat. Contracts Mgmt. Assn. (dir. 1966-68). Club: University (Denver). Home: 4601 S Franklin St Englewood CO 80110 Office: 600 S Cherry St Suite 1011 Denver CO 80222

BRYAN, ROBERT FESSLER, investor; b. New Castle, Pa., Jan. 19, 1913; s. Harry A. and Nell (Fessler) B.; A.B. summa cum laude, Oberlin Coll., 1934; Ph.D. in Econs., Yale U., 1939; children—Diane Elaine, Barbara Norwood; m. 2d, Dorothy Darr Mackenzie, Aug. 11, 1961. Instr. econs. Yale, 1935-36, 37-39, Princeton, 1936-37; economist Lionel D. Edie & Co., Inc., N.Y.C., 1939-40, asst. v.p., 1943-45, v.p., 1946-48; price exec., rubber br. O.P.A., 1941-42; economist Goodyear Aircraft Corp., Akron, Ohio, 1943; asso. J.H. Whitney & Co., 1948—, partner, 1951-59; financial v.p., treas. Whitney Communications Corp., 1959-69, also dir.; dir. Merrill Lynch Capital Fund, Ready Assets Trust. Trustee Oberlin Coll., 1960-70. Mem Yale Grad. Sch. Assn. (exec. com.), Am. Econs. Assn., Phi Beta Kappa. Clubs: Blind Brook (Port Chester, N.Y.); Apawamis (Rye, N.Y.); Economic (N.Y.C.); Gulfstream Golf, Ocean (Delray Beach, Fla.). Home: 200 N Ocean Blvd Delray Beach FL 33444

BRYAN, ROBERT MELVIN, fin. exec.; b. Arlington, Va., Nov. 21, 1949; s. Robert Aubrey and Helen (Winn) B.; B.S. in acctg./econs. Shepherd Coll., 1972; m. Carole Teresa Scafone, Jan. 2, 1971; children—Michelle Marie, Robert Sean, Cheryl Lynn. Bus. mgr. New div. ABC, Washington, 1972-73, budget controller, 1973-77, mgr. fin. planning, N.Y.C., 1977; dir. adminstrn. Recreation Vehicle Industry Assn., Chantilly, Va., 1977-79, v.p. adminstrn., 1979—, treas. polit.

action com., 1978—. Active Boy Scouts Am., Mosby Woods Recreation Assn. Mem. Am. Soc. Assn. Execs., Delta Sigma Pi. Republican. Methodist. Home: 3204 Plantation Pkwy Fairfax VA 22030 Office: 14650 Lee Rd Chantilly VA 22021

BRYAN, WILHELMUS BOGART, III, mgmt. cons.; b. N.Y.C., Sept. 27, 1924; s. Wilhelmus Bogart, Jr., and Katharine Gilman (MacKenty) B.; A.B. in Psychology, Princeton, 1948; m. Charlotte Ann Leidy, Dec. 28, 1973; 1 son, Wilhelmus Bogart IV. Account mgmt. McCann-Erickson, N.Y.C., 1948-55, Benton & Bowles, N.Y.C., 1955-59, Foote, Cone & Belding, 1959-61; dir. mktg. and planning U.S. Borax & Chem. Corp., Los Angeles, 1961-67; group brand mgr. RJR Foods, N.Y.C., 1967-68; v.p., dir. Brennan Assos., N.Y.C., 1968-71; partner, sr. v.p., dir. William H. Clark Assos., N.Y.C., also v.p. Zehnder & Clark Internat., N.Y.C., 1971-76; mgmt. cons., exec. search, merger and acquisition search. Served with U.S. Mcht. Marine, 1943-45. Mem. Correctional Assn. N.Y. (vice chmn., dir.), Alumni Council Princeton U. Presbyterian. Clubs: Knickerbocker, Univ., Princeton, Quogue Field, Tower (Princeton), Nassau, Quogue Beach, Amateur Comedy of N.Y. Home: 215 E 72d St New York NY 10021 Office: 330 Madison Ave New York NY 10017

BRYANT, CECIL FARRIS, lawyer, ins. co. exec., former govt. ofcl.; b. Ocala, Fla., July 26, 1914; s. Charles Cecil and Lela Margaret (Farris) B.; student Emory U., 1931-32; B.S., U. Fla., 1935; LL.B., Harvard U., 1938; LL.D., Rollins Coll., Fla. Atlantic U., U. South Fla., Fla. So. Coll.; m. Julia Burnett, Sept. 18, 1940; children—Julie Lovett, Cecilia Ann, Allison Adair. Admitted to Fla. bar, 1939; partner firm Bryant, Miller and Olive, Jacksonville, Fla., 1970—; pres. Voyager Group, Inc., Jacksonville, 1965—, A.D.R. Warranty Corp.; chmn. bd. Voyager Life Ins. Co., Voyager Life Ins. Co. of S.C., Voyager Property and Casualty Ins. Co., Voyager Casualty Ins. Co., Voyager Warranty Corp.; chmn. bd., pres. First Protection Life Ins. Co.; dir. Fidelity Fed. Savs. and Loan Assn., Ocala, Fla., Air Fla. System, Inc. Trustee Jacksonville U., Fla. So. Coll., Met. YMCA, Jacksonville; mem. Fla. Ho. of Reps., 1942, 46-56, speaker of the Ho., 1953-54; gov. State of Fla., 1961-65; del. Democratic Nat. Conv., 1952, 60, 68; dir. Office of Emergency Planning, Exec. Office of the Pres., 1966-67; mem. Nat. Security Council, 1966-67; chmn. Adv. Commn. on Intergovernmental Relations, 1967-69; U.S. rep. NATO, 1966-67; vice chmn. Pres.' Cabinet Task Force on Travel, 1966-67. Mem. Fla. Bar Assn. Democrat. Methodist. Home: 3781 Ortega Blvd Jacksonville FL 32210 Office: PO Box 2918 Jacksonville FL 32203

BRYANT, DENNIS MICHAEL, bus. services co. exec.; b. Austin, Tex., June 30, 1947; s. L.D. and Mildred Virginia (Perkins) B.; B.S., Trinity U., San Antonio, 1970; m. Nancy Jane Louthan, Apr. 17, 1976; children—Dennis Michael, Sarah Elizabeth. Inside sales and rentals staff Hyco Equipment Co., Houston, 1973-74; sales rep. Briggs-Weaver Indsl. Truck div., Houston, 1974, mgr. San Antonio br., 1974—. Served to 1st lt. M.I., U.S. Army, 1971-73. Decorated Distinguished Service medal. Republican. Presbyterian. Club: Tex. Flying. Home: 14315 Ben Brush Dr San Antonio TX 78248 Office: 1014 Paulsun Dr San Antonio TX 78219

BRYANT, DONALD EUGENE, oil co. exec.; b. Shawnee, Okla., Mar. 26, 1933; s. Jacob Calvin and Ruby Jane (Smith) B.; B.B.A. with distinction, U. Okla., 1958, M.B.A. (Humble Oil and Refining Co. fellow), 1960; grad. (Harold Stonier fellow) Sch. Banking, U. Wis., 1973; m. Susan Epperson, Apr. 26, 1933; 1 son, Scott Dawson. Accountant, Peat, Marwick, Mitchell & Co., C.P.A.'s, Oklahoma City, 1959-60; asst. prof. econs. U. S.W. La., 1960-63; executor Estate of R.C. Smith, 1963-65; asso. prof. acctg. Bentley Coll., Boston, 1965-66; research asso. Harvard U. Bus. Sch., 1967-68, 71-73; asst. prof. adminstrn., asso. prof. acctg. Wichita (Kans.) State U., 1969-71, 73-75; asst. to pres. Alpha Exploration, Inc., Midland, Tex., 1975-76; v.p. Veritas Exploration, Inc., Midland, 1976—; controller RPM Energy, Inc., 1978—; sec. S. Gulf Oil Co., 1962-65; lectr. U. Tex., Permian Basin, 1975. C.P.A., Okla., Tex. Mem. Midland Real Estate Bd., Omicron Delta Kappa, Beta Gamma Sigma, Kappa Sigma (v.p. Wichita 1974). Republican. Episcopalian. Clubs: Harvard (Boston); Moose. Author papers in field. Home: 1 Linda Ct Midland TX 79701 Office: 228 Commercial Bank Towers Midland TX 79701

BRYANT, ROBERT LEE, mfg. co. exec.; b. Washington, Oct. 29, 1944; s. Howard Berkland and Alpha Geneve (Simmons) B.; student Prince George's (Md.) Coll.; m. Beverly A. Brodt, Dec. 17, 1977; 1 son, Robert Lee. Field engr. computer div. Gen. Electric Co., Washington, 1967-68; sales rep. data systems Xerox Corp., Washington, 1968-75; sales mgr. Digital Equipment Corp., Washington, 1975-80, mgr. European def. mktg., Reading, Eng., 1980—. Served with USN, 1962-67. Mem. Potomac River Power Squadron. Office: Fountain House The Butts Centre Reading RG1 7QN England

BRYANT, ROBERT PARKER, food co. exec.; b. S.I., N.Y., May 13, 1922; s. Thomas Vincent and Rosanna (McRoberts) B.; B.S., Cornell U., 1947; m. Barbara Carlson, Nov. 13, 1953; children—Elizabeth, Robert, Christine, Catherine, Martha. Food mgr. Pa. R.R. Dining Car System, 1952-56; cons. Booz Allen & Hamilton, N.Y.C., 1956-58; v.p. Frank G. Shattuck Co., N.Y.C., 1958-66; group v.p. Marriott Corp., Washington, 1966-74; v.p. Marc's Big Boy Corp. (Marriott franchise), Milw., 1974-75; group v.p. Burger King Corp., Miami, Fla., 1975-76; pres. Dobbs Houses, Inc. subs. Squibb Corp., 1976—; dir. Orgn. Renewal, Inc., Project Assos., Inc., Washington, West Electric Co., Toronto, Ont., Can.; dir., mem. exec. com. Commerce Union Bank. Bd. dirs. Jr. Achievement, Boy Scouts Am.; mem. curriculum council Memphis Bd. Edn.; mem. Ad Hoc D.C. Minimum Wage Bd. Served to 1st lt. AUS, 1942-46. Mem. Nat. Restaurant Assn., Phi Delta Theta. Clubs: N.Y. Athletic, Touchdown of N.Y.; Rotary, Univ. (Memphis). Home: 1217 Brookfield Rd Memphis TN 38117 Office: 5100 Poplar Ave Memphis TN 38137

BRYANT, TANYA MIFSUD (MRS. GLENDELL W. DOBBS), real estate exec.; b. Sliema, Island of Malta, May 15, 1920; d. Jose Louis and Vera (Jarmonkine) Mifsud; student pvt. schs.; m. Arthur J. W. Pitt, Nov. 17, 1937 (div. Feb. 1952); children—Natasha, Valerie Pitt Deeds, F. David, Micheline Pitt Magdaleno; m. 2d, William Cullen Bryant, Dec. 29, 1959 (div. June 1960); m. 3d, Jack F. Cutler, May 4, 1963 (div. Oct. 1968); m. 4th, Glendell W. Dobbs, Mar. 1969. Came to U.S., 1949, naturalized, 1957. Imported model Jacques Heim, Paris, France, 1949-50; Conover model all major fashion shows and TV shows U.S., 1950-52; sportswear buyer, exec. trainee Neiman Marcus, Dallas, 1952-54; mgr. ladies wear Broadway Dept. Store, Panorama City, Calif., 1954-56; owner, buyer Brides and Besides shops, Los Angeles, Bakersfield, Westwood, Calif., 1956-60; owner Tanya Bryant, Realtor, Stockton, Calif., 1957—. Originator, dir. Pamper House, Rockefeller Center, 1952. Staff asst. A.R.C., London, Eng., 1942-45; gray lady, Los Angeles, 1957-60. Bd. dirs. Better Bus. Bur., 1976—; mem. San Jose City Tenant/Landlord Com., 1975-79. Mem. Women's Council Nat. Assn. Real Estate Bds. (chpt. pres. 1966, 69), San Fernando Valley (dir. 1966), Stockton (chmn. investment div. Dist. 7) bds. Realtors, Calif. Real Estate Assn. (dir. 1966-72, chmn. pub. relations 1969, 70, polit. affairs com. 1972-74, legis. com. 1973), San Jose Real Estate Bd. (dir. 1970, sec. 1970), Internat. Platform Assn., C. of C. (dir. 1966), Internat. Traders Club. Contbr. articles to profl. jours. Home: 2621 W Hwy 12 Lodi CA 95240 Office: 41 W Yokuts Ave Stockton CA 95207

BRYANT, WALDO GERALD, chain mfg. co. exec.; b. Bridgeport, Conn., July 30, 1891; s. Waldo Calvin and Ida Gerold B.; Ph.B., Yale U., 1914; m. Ruth McCaskey, 1919 (dec. 1940); children—Ruth Ann, Waldo Dexter, Gerald Calvin; m. 2d, Sylvia Constance Jackson, Nov. 18, 1944. With Bead Chain Mfg. Co., Bridgeport, Conn., pres., treas., 1914-62, chmn. bd., 1962—. Episcopalian. Clubs: Yale (N.Y.C.); Fairfield County Hunt; Fairfield Country; Pequot Yacht; Mory's (New Haven); Masons, K.T., Shriners. Home: 330 Morehouse Ln Southport CT 06490 Office: Bead Chain Mfg Co 110 Mountain Grove St Bridgeport CT 06605

BRYERTON, ROBERT ALAN, paper converter co. exec.; b. Lock Haven, Pa., June 8, 1945; s. Jack Boyd and Nancy Elizabeth B.; B.A., Lycoming Coll., 1967; m. Bonnie Faye Karch, Feb. 3, 1973; children—Ashley Faye, Robert Alan. Chem. salesman Stein Hall & Co., N.Y.C., 1967-68, asst. to div. mgr. textiles, 1968-70; with C.A. Reed div. Westvaco Corp., Williamsport, Pa., 1970-80, customer service mgr., 1973-75, mgr. mktg. services, 1975-80. Republican. Methodist. Club: Masons. Office: PO Box 3128 Williamsport PA 17701 Died Oct. 8, 1980

BRZEZANSKI, JAY MARIAN, fin. exec.; b. Washington, Jan. 24, 1947; s. Henry Julian and Janina (Kamecki) B.; B.S., U. Md., 1968; M.S., U. Va., 1970; m. Rosemarie Raimo, Mar. 8, 1980. Internal auditor IBM, Armonk, N.Y., 1970-73; sr. staff acct. Gen. Cable Corp., Bayonne, N.J., 1973; sr. staff internal auditor K-Mart Corp., North Bergen, N.J., 1973-77; mgr. internal audit Robert Hall Clothes, N.Y.C., 1977, asst. controller, 1977; loss prevention mgr./dir. systems Abraham & Straus, Bklyn., 1977—. Commr., Boy Scouts Am., 1970-74, explorer advisor, 1971-75; mem. City Council Clifton, 1978, mem. Planning Bd., 1979; mem. Police Aux., CD, Clifton, 1975-78. Served with U.S. Army, 1966-69; capt. USAR, 1970—. Recipient D.A.R. Citizens award, 1970; CD award, 1974; others. Mem. Inst. Internal Audit, Systems Mgmt. Assn., Res Officers Assn. Democrat. Roman Catholic. Home: 16 Hover Dr Mount Arlington NJ 07856 Office: 500 Meadowland Parkway Secaucus NJ 07094

BUARON, ROBERTO, mgmt. cons.; b. Derna, Libya, May 14, 1946; s. Moreno and Rachele (Abravanel) B.; Ph.D. in Electronic Engring., Politecnico of Milan, 1968; M.B.A., European Inst. Bus. Adminstrn., Fontainebleau, France, 1970; M.B.A., Harvard U., 1974. Mgr. internat. mktg. Tex. Instruments, Houston, 1970-72, mgr. strategic planning, Houston, 1972-73; asso. McKinsey & Co., Inc., N.Y.C., 1974-80, principal, partner, 1981—. Mem. European Inst. Bus. Adminstrn. (INSEAD) Alumni Assn. U.S. (exec. com.). Clubs: Harvard, Harvard Bus. Sch. (N.Y.C.). Home: 400 E 56th St Apt 30K New York NY 10022 Office: 245 Park Ave New York NY 10017

BUCCINO, GERALD P., retail co. exec.; b. Belleville, N.J., Apr. 22, 1938; s. Charles and Jean (Fiscello) B.; student Fordham U., 1958-60; B.S. in Accounting, Seton Hall U., 1963; m. Lorraine Falivene, Aug. 20, 1960; children—Gerard, Lauren, Jennifer, Christopher. Sr. accountant Haskins & Sells, N.Y.C., 1963-66; accounting mgr. Becton Dickinson & Co., East Rutherford, N.J., 1966-70; asst. controller Stanray Corp., Chgo., 1970, controller, 1971-73, v.p. fin., 1973-76; sr. v.p., chief fin. officer Interstate United Corp., Chgo., 1976-79, chief adminstrv. officer, 1977-79; exec. v.p., dir. Goldblatt Bros. Inc., Chgo., 1979—, chmn. fin. com., mem. exec. com., 1979—. Bd. dirs., chmn. fin. com., chmn. audit com. Homan Services, Chgo., 1976-79; pres. Stanray Found., 1973-76; past pres. Tee and Green Homeowners Assn. Served with AUS, 1956-57. C.P.A., N.J., Ill. Mem. Am. Inst. C.P.A.'s., Fin. Execs. Inst., Planning Execs. Inst., Nat. Accounting Assn. Clubs: Union League (Chgo.); Glen Oak Country (Glen Ellyn, Ill.). Home: 1394 Shady Ln Wheaton IL 60187 Office: 333 S State St Chicago IL 60604

BUCHAN, DOUGLAS CHARLES, petroleum co. exec.; b. Bklyn., Aug. 4, 1936; s. Charles J. and Amelia P. (Petraca) B.; student U. Fla., 1954-56; m. Beverly Ann Wilcox, Mar. 7, 1970; 1 son, Paul Douglas. Pres., Buchan Gas Co., St. Petersburg, Fla., 1955—, Buchan Oil Co., St. Petersburg, 1966—, Clean Air Centers, St. Petersburg, 1975—. Pres., Pinellas County Republican Ivory Club; chmn. Pinellas campaign George Bush for Pres., also chmn. various polit. campaigns. Served to 1st lt. U.S. Army, 1958-65. Mem. Nat. Oil Jobbers Council, Nat. Liquified Petroleum Gas Assn., Fla. Petroleum Marketers Assn. (v.p.), Oil Fuel Inst. Fla. (pres., chmn. bd.). Episcopalian. Club: St. Petersburg Yacht. Home: 1067 42d Ave NE Saint Petersburg FL 33703 Office: Buchan Oil Co 4555 38th St N Saint Petersburg FL 33714

BUCHANAN, MARGARET ROSE, publishing co. exec.; b. Bryn Mawr, Pa., Feb. 23, 1948; d. William and Margaret (Murphy) B.; student Bryn Mawr Coll., 1965-67, Villanova U., 1965-66, St. Joseph's Coll., 1966-67; m. Thomas Francis McGuckin, July 22, 1967 (div. June 1979); 1 son, Patrick Thomas McGuckin. Cost analyst Gen. Electric Co., Valley Forge, Pa., 1968-70; contract and grant accountant U. Del., 1971-73; office mgr. Enterprise Pub. Co., Wilmington, Del., 1973-75, sec., treas., 1975—, v.p., 1977-79; exec. v.p. Enterprise Ventures, Inc., Enterprise Inst., 1979—; v.p. McGuckin Ins. Agy., 1975-77. Libertarian Party candidate lt. gov. Del., 1980; media chmn. Libertarian Party of Del., 1980—. Recipient Tribute to Women in Industry award Del. YWCA, 1980. Mem. Direct Mail Mktg. Assn., Am. Bus. Women's Assn., Am. Booksellers Assn. Home: 26 Cartier Rd Newark DE 19711 Office: 725 Market St Wilmington DE 19801

BUCHANAN, PETER T., investment banker; b. Orange, N.J., Sept. 12, 1934; s. Percy H. and Ruth C. (Townley) B.; A.B., Princeton U., 1956; m. Lane Eichhorn, Oct. 20, 1956; children—Richard, Linda. With The 1st Boston Corp., N.Y.C., 1956-57, 60—, v.p., 1967-73, mgr. equity securities dept., 1972-74, exec. v.p., dir. charge trading, sales, ops. and adminstrn., 1974-78, pres., 1978—, also dir. Served with USAF, 1957-60. Mem. Security Traders Assn. N.Y., Securities Industry Assn. (vice chmn.). Clubs: Bond, Princeton (N.Y.C.); Morris County Golf, Baltusrol Golf. Home: 32 Crescent Rd Madison NJ 07940 Office: First Boston Corp 20 Exchange Pl New York NY 10005

BUCHANAN, ROY LEVERN, railway co. exec.; b. Faulkner, Miss., Aug. 11, 1929; s. Acy Lamar and Bamma Francis (Jones) B.; B.S. in Bus. Adminstrn., Memphis State U., 1958; advanced mgmt. program Northwestern U., 1976, Columbia U., 1977; m. Mamie Lee Harrell, July 29, 1950; children—David Roy, Donald Levern, Karen Denise. With St. Louis San Francisco Ry. Co., Springfield, Mo., 1948—, terminal supt., 1968-72, div. supt., 1972-76, asst. v.p. labor relations, 1976-77, sr. asst. v.p. labor relations and personnel, 1977-78, v.p. labor relations and personnel, 1978—. Served with U.S. Army, 1952-53. Methodist. Clubs: Hickory Hills Country, Masons, Shriners, Order Eastern Star. Home: 2419 Berkeley St Springfield MO 65804 Office: 3253 E Trafficway St Springfield MO 65802

BUCHHEIT, LOUISE MARIE, fin. exec.; b. Oakland, Calif., May 16, 1942; d. David and Bertha Laverne (Des Longchamp) Meisinger; student Community Coll. Denver, 1970, U. Colo., 1972-73; m. Darvin Lee Buchheit, July 27, 1960. Office mgr., real estate closer Heide-Hulcy Realty, Aurora, Colo., 1972-73; with ICM Mortgage Corp., Aurora, Colo. and Casper, Wyo., 1973-79, office mgr., 1973-79; mgr., investment broker Biddle Creek Realty, Investment Properties Ltd., Casper, 1979—; underwriter Fed. Nat. Mortgage Assn., Los Angeles div., 1978-79. Mem. Nat. Bd. Realtors, Casper Bd. Realtors, Wyo. Bd. Realtors, Wyo. Arabian Horse Assn., Internat. Assn. Arabian Horses. Home: County Line Rd C 13756 Evansville Route Box 1 Evansville WY 82636 Office: 907 N Union Blvd Suite 240 Casper WY 82601

BUCHSBAUM, ROBERT GARY, devel. co. exec.; b. N.Y.C., June 12, 1950; s. Walter and Ann B.; B.A., U. Pa., 1971; M.A. in Biochemistry, UCLA, 1974, M.B.A. in Fin., 1976. Fin. analyst corp. devel. Tosco Corp., Los Angeles, 1976-77, sr. fin. analyst, coal div., 1977-78; sr. regulatory analyst Tosco Corp., 1979-80; mng. partner Silkie Enterprises, 1979-80; pres. Am. Century Real Estate, Inc., 1980—; fin. cons. WFI Corp.; instr. ops. research UCLA. Mem. Am. Fin. Assn., Assn. M.B.A. Execs., Nat. Assn. Accountants, Wilderness Soc. Club: U. Pa. Alumni (Los Angeles). Office: Am Century Real Estate Inc 2049 Century Park E Los Angeles CA 90067

BUCK, CHRISTIAN BREVOORT, former oil co. exec.; b. San Francisco, Oct. 18, 1914; s. Frank Henry and Zayda Justine (Zabriskie) B.; student U. Calif. at Berkeley, 1931-33; m. Natalie Leontine Smith, Sept. 12, 1948; children—Warren Zabriskie, Barbara Anne. Mem. engring. dept. U.S. Potash Co., Carlsbad, N.Mex., 1933-39; ind. oil operator, producer, Calif. and N.Mex., 1939—; former owner, operator farm, ranch, N.Mex., Calif. Served with RAF, 1942-45. Democrat. Episcopalian. Club: Riverside Country (Carlsbad). Home: 108 W Alicante Rd Santa Fe NM 87501 Office: PO Box 2183 Santa Fe NM 87501

BUCK, FRANK HENRY, JR., investor, former investment adviser, publisher; b. San Francisco, Jan. 15, 1912; s. Frank H. and Zayda (Zabriskie) B.; A.B., U. Calif., 1933; m. Corinne Hellier, Mar. 14, 1935; children—Walter H., Robert B. Investment adviser, Martinez, Calif., 1951—, Danville, Calif., 1951-68, Cedar Ridge, Calif., 1968-78; pub. The Buck Investment Letter, Served as civilian flight instr., CAA-WTS, Air Corps Res., World War II. Mem. Sigma Delta Chi, Theta Delta Chi. Presbyn. Home: 18564 Siesta Dr Penn Valley CA 95946 Office: Brunswick Rd at Colfax Ave PO Box 146 Cedar Ridge CA 95924

BUCK, LUCIUS A(DOLPHUS), lawyer; b. Abington, Va., July 3, 1905; s. E. C. and Mary (Lee) B.; student Emory and Henry Coll., Emory, Va., 1923-24; J.D., U. Va., 1929; m. Margaret Winters, Mar. 29, 1935; 1 son, David Mason V. Admitted to Va. bar, 1928, Fla., 1929, N.Y., 1940; practiced law, West Palm Beach, Fla., 1929-34; spl. asst. to U.S. Atty. Gen., 1934-38; sr. tax asso. Davis, Polk Wardwell Sunderland & Kiendl, N.Y.C., 1938-42, 45-48; pvt. practice, Jacksonville, Fla., 1948-51; sr. partner pvt. law firm, 1951—; chmn. com. fiscal policies of govt. Fla., 1955; chmn. Jacksonville Expressway Authority 1955-61. Trustee Episcopal High Sch., Jacksonville, Fla., 1966-74, also chmn. planning com. Served as officer AUS, 1942-45. Received Bronze Star, European-African-Middle East Theater Ribbon (with 9 bronze stars), Asiatic-Pacific Theater Ribbon, 2 War Dept. Gen. Staff Commendations, R.A.F. Field Commendation. Mem. Am., Jacksonville bar assns., Fla. Bar (chmn. tax sect. 1955-56), So. Acad. Letters, Arts and Scis. (dir. gen. 1971—), Order of Coif, Raven Soc., Phi Alpha Delta, Theta Chi. Episcopalian (sr. warden 1960-61, chmn. parish day sch. div. Diocese of Fla. 1959-62, chmn. bd. regents parish and diocesan schs. Diocese of Fla. 1962-67, vestryman 1973, chancellor Diocese of Fla. 1976-77). Club: River (Jacksonville). Home: 326 Ocean Blvd Atlantic Beach FL 32233 also (summer) Hot Ashes Dahlonega GA 30533 Office: 1120 Fla Title Bldg Jacksonville FL 32202

BUCK, MILTON, electronics sales co. exec.; b. Jersey City, Dec. 10, 1920; s. Israel and Gussie Buck; A.B. in Phys. Sci. and Math. magna cum laude, U. So. Calif., 1946; m. Ida Holanov, Jan. 17, 1943; children—Marcia Lynn, Clifford Russell. High sch. sci. tchr. Los Angeles County, 1947-51; asst. research and devel. engr. Calif. Metal Enameling Co., Los Angeles, 1951-53; tech. sales devel. dir. L.H. Butcher Co., Los Angeles, 1956-61; mgr. surfactants and plastics dept. E.S. Browning Co., Los Angeles, 1961-62; mgr. product devel., corp. mktg. Tretolite/Petrolite Co., Brea, Calif., 1962-63; aerospace product mgr. Kelite Corp., Los Angeles, 1964-66; product devel. mgr., then br. mgr. So. Calif. Chem. Co., Santa Fe Springs, 1966-70; founder, 1970, since pres. Buck Sales Co., Inc., Fremont, Calif. Served to 2d lt. AUS, World War II. Fellow Am. Inst. Chemists; charter mem. Calif. Inst. Chemists; mem. AAAS, Soc. Advancement Material and Process Engring., Am. Electroplaters Soc., Am. Chem. Soc., Calif. Circuits Assn., Phi Lambda Upsilon. Unitarian-Universalist. Home: 5246 Channel Dr Newark CA 94560 Office: 44700B Industrial Dr Fremont CA 94538

BUCKEL, HARRY JOHN, newspaper pub.; b. Indpls., Mar. 7, 1944; s. Harry J. and Delia (Spellman) B.; B.S.B.A. in Fin., Xavier U.; m. Helen McGrady, Dec. 16, 1966; children—Susan, Hailey, Sean Brandan. Group v.p. Panax Corp., Detroit, 1974-75, v.p., pub. Sun Reporter, Miami Beach, Fla., 1976-78; pres., pub. San Francisco Progress, Harte-Hanks Communications, Inc., 1978-79; pres. Ypsilanti (Mich.) Press, 1980; pres., pub. Gloucester County Times, Woodbury, N.J., 1981—. Served with U.S. Army, 1967-69. Mem. Am. Newspaper Pubs. Assn. Home: 190 Rugby Pl Woodbury NJ 08096 Office: 309 S Broad St Woodbury NJ 08096

BUCKEY, MALCOLM ADRIAN, JR., banker; b. Phila., July 15, 1936; s. Malcolm Adrian and Dorothy Elisabeth (Brickley) B.; grad. Wharton Sch. U. Pa., 1959; m. Susan Gurney, June 12, 1960; children—M. Robert, Nancy K., Elisabeth J., John E. With Mfrs. Hanover Trust Co., N.Y.C., 1959-63; instl. salesman Estabrook & Co., Phila. Nat. Bank Bldg., Phila., 1963-71; sales mgr. Hutchins, Mixter & Parkinson, Phila., 1971-72; sales mgr. F.S. Moseley & Co., Phila., 1972-73; v.p., mgr. instl. investment services Provident Nat. Bank, Phila., 1973-78, v.p., mgr. personal trust services sales dept., 1978—; dir. West Jersey Warehouse Co. Treas., mem. vestry Episcopal Ch. of the Messiah, Gwynedd, Pa.; bd. dirs. Lower Gwynedd Little League. Mem. Investment Assn. Phila. (pres. 1973), Phila. Securities Assn. (gov. 1974, 80). Republican. Clubs: Skytop (Pa.); Saw Grass, Ponte Vedra (Fla.); Vesper (Phila.). Home: Pheasant Run Gwynedd Valley PA 19437 Office: 1632 Chestnut St Philadelphia PA 19103

BUCKLES, ROBERT HOWARD, investment co. exec.; b. Champaign, Ill., June 30, 1932; s. Renick Hull and Ethel Maxine (Beach) B.; B.A., Stanford U., 1953; M.B.A., Harvard U., 1957; m. Linda Carol Porter, Dec. 27, 1958; children—Meredith Ann, Christopher John. Security analyst Lehman Corp., N.Y.C., 1957-65, v.p., 1965-69, exec. v.p., 1969-73, pres., 1973—, also dir.; pres. Gas Properties, Inc.; exec. v.p., dir. Lehman Mgmt. Co. Served with Security Agy., U.S. Army, 1954-56. Mem. N.Y. Soc. Securities Analysts. Contbr. to profl. publs. Home: 420 E 72d St New York NY 10021 Office: 55 Water St New York NY 10041

BUCKLEY, DAVID WEED, food industry exec.; b. Bryn Mawr, Pa., Apr. 10, 1931; s. James L. and Josephine (Weed) B.; A.B., Cornell U., 1952, M.B.A., 1953; m. Mary M. Smith, May 3, 1958;

children—Jeffrey, Matthew, Jonathan, Katherine, Sarah. Marketing trainee Lever Bros. Co., N.Y.C., 1955-56, sales supr., 1956-58, asst. product mgr., 1958-59, product mgr., 1960-65, mktg. dir., 1966-68, v.p., gen. mgr., 1969-71; pres. In-Store Publs., 1972-79; v.p. mktg. and sales Giorgio Foods, Temple, Pa., 1980—. Mem. Monmouth County Council Against Alcoholism, 1968-69. Mem. bd. edn. Rumson Sch.; pres. bd. edn. Holy Cross Sch.; class officer Cornell U. Served with AUS, 1953-55. Mem. Cornell Assn. Class Officers (dir.). Home: 6 Laurel Ln Box 278 Rumson NJ 07760 Office: Giorgio Foods Inc PO Box 96 Temple PA 19560

BUCKLEY, HERMAN G., merchandising exec.; b. Denver, Sept. 29, 1902; s. Joseph and Rose B.; student U. Colo., 1919-22; m. Gertrude Libowitz, Jan. 7, 1977; children—E. Michael, Joy Ann, J. Glen, H. Scot Buckley, Allan S., Dennis E., Luann J. Libowitz. With Goldblatt's Dept. Store, Chgo., 1923—, v.p. and dir. stores. 1955-63, v.p. and dir. merchandising, 1963-69, v.p., gen. mgr., 1969—; dir. merchandising div. Nat. Merchants Assn., 1968—. Served to 1st lt. AUS, 1943-45. Mem. Field Mus. Natural History. Mem. B'nai B'rith. Home: 1000 Lake Shore Plaza Chicago IL 60611 Office: 333 S State St Chicago IL 60604

BUCKLEY, JAMES OLUF, printing co. exec.; b. Hastings, Nebr., June 16, 1933; s. Leo Patrick and Helen Josephine (Gilbertson) B.; student Denver U., 1961; m. Phyllis Angela Hemberger, Nov. 19, 1953; children—James P., Susan M., Randall L., Kelly A. Inventory control clk. Eaton Metal Products Co., Denver, 1957-58; asst. office mgr. Rainbo Bread Co., Denver, 1958-61; office mgr. West Tape & Label Co., Denver, 1961-64; pres. Custom Tape & Label Co. Inc., Denver, 1965—. Mem. Flexographic Tech. Assn., Aurora (Colo.) C. of C. Roman Catholic. Clubs: Aurora Elks, Aurora K.C.; Denver Sertoma (charter). Home: 13295 E Ohio Ave Aurora CO 80012 Office: 4980 Monroe St Denver CO 80216

BUCKLEY, ROBERT JOSEPH, mfg. exec.; b. N.Y.C., Mar. 16, 1924; s. Thomas William and Catherine Alberta (Nolan) B.; B.A. with distinction, Wesleyan U., Middletown, Conn., 1950; J.D., Cornell U., 1953; m. Polly Dee, June 18, 1948; children—Robert Joseph, John Nolan, Peter Thomas, Clare Dee, Brian Burke, Mark Charles, Christopher Lawrence, Paul Gerard. Asst. plant engr. Nat. Cash Register Co., 1951-52; supr. N.Y. State Law Revision Commn., 1952-53, admitted to N.Y.bar, 1954; with Gen. Electric Co., 1953-61, mgr. union relations, Schenectady, 1959-61; with Baldwin-Lima-Hamilton Corp., 1961-68, gen. mgr. Standard Steel div., 1962-68, v.p. corp., 1962-68; exec. v.p. Ingersoll Milling Machine Co., Rockford, Ill., 1968-70, pres., 1970-71; pres. Allegheny Ludlum Industries, Pitts., 1971—, chief exec. officer, 1975—; dir. Mellon Bank, Wilkinson Match, Ltd., Tyco Labs, Inc., Bell Telephone of Pa. Pres., dir. Health Research Services Found. Pa.; bd. dirs. Pitts. Symphony Soc., Pitts. Ballet Theatre, Pitts. Opera, Duquesne U.; trustee Wesleyan U., Childrens Hosp. Pitts. Served with inf. AUS, 1942-46. Decorated Purple Heart. Mem. Am. Iron and Steel Inst. (dir.), N.Y. State Bar Assn., Pa. Mfrs. Assn., Am. Ordnance Assn., Transp. Assn. Am., Machinery and Allied Products Inst., Newcomen Soc. Knight of Malta, Knight of Holy Sepulchre. Clubs: Duquesne (dir.); (Pitts.); Edgeworth, Allegheny Country; 29, Metropolitan (N.Y.C.); Rolling Rock. Office: Allegheny Ludlum Inc 2700 Two Oliver Plaza Pittsburgh PA 15222*

BUCKLEY, ROBERT LAWRENCE, mfg. co. exec.; b. Quincy, Mass., Aug. 31, 1926; s. Charles F. and Anora M. Buckley; student Northeastern U.; m. Josephine A. Brennan, Apr. 5, 1954; children—Robert, Steven, Tom, Kevin, Susan, Kathy, Daniel. Salesman, advt. mgr. Westinghouse Electric Co., Boston, 1948-56; sales engr. air distbn. products Filters, Inc., Boston, 1956-66, Norman Assos., Needham (now Natick), Mass., 1966-70; pres., chief exec. officer Buckley Assos., Inc., Braintree, Mass., 1970—. Served with inf. U.S. Army, 1944-46. Mem. Nat. Fire Protection Assn., South Shore C. of C. Democrat. Roman Catholic. Clubs: K.C., Elks.

BUCKNAM, SUSAN, mail order co. exec.; b. Wakefield, Mass., Mar. 28, 1933; d. Charles Warren and Dorothy Alice (Jones) B.; A.A., Endicott Coll., 1952; B.A., U. N.H., 1954; M.B.A., Coll. St. Thomas, 1977. Coordinator giftstars program Carlson Cos., Mpls., 1964-65; adminstrv. asst. Gen. Mills, Inc., Mpls., 1965-69; v.p. fin. Northstar Industries, Mpls., 1969-76; pres. ARE, Inc., Greensboro, Vt., 1976—. Mem. alumnae council Endicott Coll., 1980—. Mem. Nat. Assn. Jewelers Retail. Home: RD 1 Box 86A East Hardwick VT 05836 Office: Box 8 Route 16 Greensboro Bend VT 05842

BUCKO, LEON HOMER, real estate broker and developer; b. Dearborn, Mich., Jan. 24, 1942; s. Leo W. and Evelyn Y. (Rousseau) B.; B.S. in Mktg., UCLA., 1964, M.B.A., 1965; m. Denise J. Barton, Mar. 2, 1969; children—Jennifer, Ryan. Research statistician McLatchy Newspapers, Sacramento, 1965-66; sales rep. nat. spot TV media sales and promotion Kelly Broadcasting, Sacramento, 1966-72; real estate sales rep. Coast Real Estate/Strout Real Estate, 1972-77; broker, owner Coast Real Estate, Inc., Florence, Oreg., 1977—; partner, owner Seafood Enterprise Assos.; staff instr. Lane Community Coll. Mem. Yachats Planning Commn., 1972; mem., chmn. Dunes City Planning Commn., 1973-77. Served wiht USCGR, 1965-71. Mem. Asso. Oreg. Industries, Cert. Bus. Counselors, Nat. Assn. Realtors, UCLA Alumni Assn., Florence Arts Council, Lane County Homebuilders Assn., Sigma Chi. Republican. Club: Triumph Vintage Registar. Home: 5400 Old County Rd 503 Dunes City OR 97439 Office: 100 Hwy 101 Florence OR 97439

BUCY, J. FRED, electronics co. exec.; b. Tahoka, Tex., July 29, 1928; s. J. Fred and Ethel (Montgomery) B.; B.Physics, Tex. Tech. U., 1951; M. Physics, U. Tex., Austin, 1953; m. Odetta Greer, Jan. 25, 1947; children—J. Fred, Roxanne, Diane. With Tex. Instruments Inc., Dallas, 1953—, corp. v.p., 1963-67, corp. group v.p. components, 1967-72, exec. v.p., 1972-75, exec. v.p., chief operating officer, 1975-76, pres., chief operating officer, 1976—, dir., 1974—; chmn. bd. Tex. Instruments Deutschland GmbH; rep. dir. TI Japan Ltd., gen. dir. several subs.'s. Mem. Technology Assessment of U.S. Congress, Comptroller Gen.'s Panel, Pres.'s Commn. for Nat. Agenda for 80's; chmn. bd. regents Tex. Tech. U. and Tex. Tech. U. Sch. Medicine. Recipient Disting. Engrs. award Tex. Tech. U., 1972. Fellow IEEE; mem. Nat. Acad. Engring., Soc. Exploration Geophysicists, Sigma Pi Sigma, Tau Beta Pi. Methodist. Clubs: Cosmos (Washington); Dallas Petroleum, Northwood (Dallas). Patentee in field (7). Office: PO Box 225474 M/S 236 Dallas TX 75265

BUCY, PAUL CRAIG, mktg. services corp. exec.; b. Chgo., Jan. 3, 1936; s. Paul Clancy and Evelyn Mary (Richards) B.; B.A., U. Iowa, 1957; M.B.A. with distinction, Northwestern U., 1959; m. Vivian Zajac, Jan. 28, 1980; children—Ann E., Sarah V., Emily E., Caroline C., Paul C. Brand mgr. mktg. dept. Procter & Gamble, Cin., 1959-64; pres. Chase div. Glendenning Cos., Westport, Conn., 1965-70; pres. First Mktg. Corp., Westport, 1970—; dir. Pix, Inc., 1973—, FIAI Ins. Co., 1978—; vis. lectr. Fairfield U., 1971—. Commr., Weston Little League, 1973-76. Mem. Beta Gamma Sigma. Republican. Methodist. Clubs: Aspetuck Valley Country; Univ. of Chgo. Author: A Wine Tour of France, 1972, NFL Playbook, 1973. Home: 35 High Noon Rd Weston CT 06883 Office: First Mktg Corp 32 Imperial Ave Westport CT 06880

BUDAYA, HARI, mfg. cons./exec.; b. Blitar, Java, Indonesia, Oct. 12, 1938; came to U.S., 1969, naturalized, 1977; s. Hernowo and Sutjiati (Tjiptoharsono) B.; B.Th., Bapt. Theol. Sem. Indonesia, 1962; B.A., U. Indonesia, 1966; A.A., Pasadena City Coll., 1979; M.B.A., Azusa Pacific Coll., 1977; m. May Ling, Feb. 26, 1965; children—Andrew, Angelique. Ordained to ministry Baptist Ch., 1962; minister Kebayoran Bapt. Ch., Jakarta, Indonesia, 1962-66; asst. editor/translator Bapt. Pub. House, Bandung, Indonesia, 1966-68; med. sales supr. Upjohn Internat., Hong Kong, 1968-70; asst. mgr. bookstore Calif. State U., Los Angeles, 1970; shareholder clk. So. Calif. Edison Co., Rosemead, 1972-78; staff exec. G. S. May Internat. Co., San Francisco; mgmt. cons./fin. analyst, mfg. analyst, Anaheim and Irvine, Calif., 1978—; project mg.nt. C.F. Braun Engring. & Constrn. Co., Alhambra, Calif. Nat. pres. Bapt. Youth Orgn., Indonesia, 1961; v.p. W. Java Bapt. Assn., Indonesia; pres. Indonesian Am. Soc., Los Angeles, 1978. Mem. Am. Mgmt. Assn., Nat. Mgmt. Assn., Profl. Bus. Cons.'s Assn. Home: 1625 Camden Pl Fullerton CA 92633

BUDD, EDWARD HEY, ins. co. exec.; b. Zanesville, Ohio, Apr. 30, 1933; s. Curtis Eugene and Mary (Hey) B.; B.S. in Physics, Tufts U., Medford, Mass., 1955. With Travelers Ins. Co., Hartford, Conn., 1955—, v.p., then sr. v.p., 1967-76, pres., 1976—, also dir.; pres., dir. Travelers Corp.; dir. Cushman Industries, Inc. Bd. dirs. United Way Greater Hartford, Greater Hartford Jr. Achievement; bd. visitors Sch. Bus. Adminstrn., U. Conn.; chmn. Greater Hartford Leadership Program; corporator, bd. dirs. Inst. of Living; corporator Hartford Hosp., St. Francis Hosp. Fellow Casualty Actuarial Soc.; mem. Am. Acad. Actuaries. Episcopalian. Clubs: Hartford, Hartford Golf; N.Y. Athletic. Office: 1 Tower Sq Hartford CT 06115

BUDGE, HAMER HAROLD, mut. fund co. exec.; b. Pocatello, Idaho, Nov. 21, 1910; student Coll. of Idaho, 1928-30; A.B., Stanford, 1933; LL.B., U. Idaho, 1936; m. Jeanne Keithly, Aug. 30, 1941; 1 dau., Kathleen. Admitted to Idaho bar, 1936; practiced in Boise, 1936-42, 46-51; dist. judge, Boise, 1961-64; commr. SEC, 1964-69, chmn., 1969-71; chmn. bd., dir. Investors Mut., Inc., Investors Stock Fund, Inc., Investors Selective Fund, Inc., Investors Variable Payment Fund, Inc., IDS New Dimensions Fund, Inc., IDS Progressive Fund, Inc., IDS Growth Fund, Inc., IDS Bond Fund, Inc., IDS Cash Met Fund Inc., Mpls., 1971—. Mem. Idaho Legislature, 1939, 41, 49, majority floor leader; mem. 82d-86th Congresses from 2d Dist. Idaho, mem. rules, appropriations and interior coms. Bd. dirs. Salvation Army. Served to lt. comdr. USNR, 1942-45. Mem. Am., Idaho bar assns., Sigma Alpha Epsilon. Republican. Mem. Ch. of Jesus Christ of Latter-day Saints. Clubs: Rotary; Mpls. (Mpls.); Mpls. (Washington); Burning Tree; Palm Desert; Thunderbird. Home: 46-790 Amir Dr Palm Desert CA 92260 Office: 1000 Roanoke Bldg Minneapolis MN 55402

BUDIKE, LOTHAR EDMUND STUART, mech. engr.; b. Paramaribo, Surinam, Dec. 30, 1931; s. David Gustaaf and Annie Antje (Budike) Polak; came to U.S., 1952, naturalized, 1956; B.S. in Marine Engring., U. Hague (Netherlands) Marine Acad., 1952; m. Alexandra Anderson, Nov. 27, 1954; children—Edward, Marianthe, Alexandra, Lothar Edmund Stuart. Engring. officer on bd. ship various cos., 1952-63; owner, pres. Avaley Engrs. Inc., Wallingford, Pa., 1964—; lectr. in field. Mem. Mech. Contractors Assn. Eastern Pa. Republican. Greek Orthodox. Club: Masons. Home and Office: 506 Georgetown Rd Wallingford PA 19086

BUDZINSKY, ARMIN ALEXANDER, investment banker; b. Steyr, Austria, Nov. 25, 1942; came to U.S., 1951, naturalized, 1957; s. Alexander Wladimir and Maria Gisella B.; A.B., John Carroll U., 1964; M.A. (NDEA fellow, Fulbright fellow), Rutgers U., 1969; M.B.A., U. Chgo., 1974; m. Pamela Plimmer, Oct. 29, 1978; 1 dau., Andrea. Instr. in English, Cleve. State U., 1969-72; corp. fin. cons. Citibank NA., N.Y.C., 1974-76; project fin. Dean Witter & Co., N.Y.C., 1976-77; v.p. oil and gas financing Merrill Lynch Pierce Fenner & Smith, N.Y.C., 1977—; mem. industry adv. com. N.Am. Assn. Security Adminstrs. Mem. Oil Investment Inst. Home: 4510 Shetland Ln Houston TX 77027 Office: First City Tower Suite 2466 1001 Fannin Ave Houston TX 77002

BUEGEL, HERMANN FREDERICK, JR., banker; b. Grand Forks, N.D., Aug. 4, 1927; s. Hermann Frederick and Lillian M. (Miller) B.; B.S. in Commerce, U. N.D., 1950; student Sch. Banking, U. Wis., 1964, Comml. Lending Sch., Norman, Okla., 1969; m. Judith E. Fiechtner, Nov. 14, 1973; children by previous marriage—John F., Donald S. With Red River Nat. Bank, Grand Forks, 1949-52; cashier 1st State Bank of Cando (N.D.), 1952-54; successively asst. cashier, asst. v.p., v.p., pres. Jamestown Nat. Bank (N.D.), 1954-66; pres., chmn. bd. successor bank 1st Bank of N.D. N.A., Jamestown, 1966—; dir. 1st Trust Co. of N.D.; pres. N.D. State Devel. Credit Corp. Former alderman City of Jamestown; mayor, 1970-74; trustee, treas. Jamestown Coll., 1967—; chmn. Jamestown Civic Center Commn., 1973—. Served with USNR, 1944-46. Recipient Disting. Service award Jaycees, 1964; named Outstanding Boss of Yr., Jamestown Jaycees, 1970. Mem. Am. Bankers Assn., N.D. Banking Assn., Jamestown C. of C. (pres. 1962), Am. Legion. Republican. Lutheran. Office: PO Box 1631 Jamestown ND 58401

BUEHLER, ALBERT CARL, JR., mfg. co. exec.; b. Chgo., July 27, 1923; s. Albert Carl and Goldie (Halquist) B.; B.A., Dartmouth Coll., 1945; m. Patricia Holmes; children—Albert Carl III, Karen Sue, John Holmes. With Victor Comptometer Corp., Chgo., 1943-77, v.p., 1954-63, exec. v.p., 1963-70, vice chmn., 1970-71, chmn., 1971-77. Clubs: Chicago; Skokie Country (Glencoe, Ill.). Home: 30 Bridlewood Rd Northbrook IL 60062 Office: 3900 N Rockwell St Chicago IL 60618

BUEHLER, SEYMOUR JACK, bowling exec.; b. Bklyn., Aug. 4, 1927; s. Gus and Bertha B.; student Mcht. Marine Acad., Kings Point, N.Y., 1945-47; B.S., Lehigh U., 1949; m. Joan Schwartz, Jan. 3, 1960; 1 son, Robert. Pres., N.Y. Bag Co., 1949-60, East Meadow (N.Y.) Bowl, 1960—; chmn. bd. Sycam Advanced Tech., 1979—. Mem. Bowling Proprs. Assn. Am. Republican. Jewish. Home: 1020 Park Ave New York NY 10028 Office: 1840 Front St East Meadow NY 11554

BUELL, EUGENE F(RANKLIN), lawyer; b. Elrama, Pa., Dec. 3, 1916; s. Frank Currey and Altina (Eckland) B.; B.S., St. Vincent's Coll., 1938; postgrad. Carnegie Inst. Tech., 1938-40, U. Pitts., 1941, John Hopkins, 1942; J.D., Duquesne U., 1944; m. Elizabeth Ellen Foster, December 28th, 1940; children—Erik Foster. Admitted to D.C. bar, 1949, to practice Canadian Patent Office, 1949; chemist U.S. Steel Corp., 1938-42, chief chemist Homestead works, 1942-45; with Stebbins, Blenko & Webb, lawyers, 1945-48; partner Blenko, Leonard & Buell, and predecessor firms, Pitts., 1949-73; pres. Blenko, Buell, Ziesenheim & Beck P.A.; pres. Tartan Industries, Inc.; sec. Porta-Drill, Inc.; dir. Metaltronics, Inc.; instr. patent law U. Pitts. Law Sch., 1954-59, adj. prof. law, 1959—. Past pres. Richland Com. for Better Govt. Mem. Am. Judicature Soc., Assn. Internationale pour la Protection Propriété Industrielle, Am., Inter-Am., Pa., Allegheny County bar assns., Assn. Bar City N.Y. (asso.), Engrs. Soc. Western Pa., Am. Patent Law Assn., Pitts. Patent Law Assn. (past pres.), Am. Arbitration Assn., Chartered Inst. Patent Agts., Licensing Exec. Soc., Order of Coif (hon.). Clubs: Masons, Pitts. Press, Duquesne, Allegheny, Amen Corner. Home: RFD 2 Box 418 Gibsonia PA 15044 Office: 301 5th Ave Pittsburgh PA 15222

BUENGER, CLEMENT L., banker; b. Cin., Apr. 27, 1926; s. Clement Lawrence and Estelle (Pelzer) B.; student U. Wis., 1943-44; B.S. in Bus. Adminstrn., Xavier U., 1950; m. Ann McCabe, Apr. 22, 1950. Acct., Kroger Co., Cin., 1950-51; exec. v.p. Selective Ins. Co., Cin., 1951-67, Life Ins. Co. of Ky., Louisville, 1967-69; pres. Fifth Third Bank, Cin., 1969—, also dir.; dir. Fifth Third Bancorp, Hooven & Allison Co. Trustee Thomas More Coll., Boys' Clubs Greater Cin., St. Xavier High Sch.; trustee, mem. pres.'s council Xavier U.; chmn. div. C, United Appeal, 1976; bd. dirs. ARC. Served with USNR, 1943-45. Mem. Assn. Res. City Bankers, Cin. Council on World Affairs. Republican. Roman Catholic. Clubs: Cin. Country, Bankers, Comml., Queen City. Home: 1029 Catawba Valley Dr Cin 45226 Office: 38 Fountain Sq Plaza Cincinnati OH 45202

BUERGER, JULIUS ALBERT, JR., real estate exec.; b. Denver, Dec. 26, 1932; s. Julius Albert and Roberta Carolyn (Cresup) B.; B.S. in Bus. Adminstrn., U. Denver, 1956; student U. Colo., 1954-55; m. Joanne Rae Ainsworth, Sept. 9, 1955 (div. July 1975); children—Julius II, Raymond, Holly, Matthew. Sec.-treas. Buerger Bros. Supply Co., Denver, 1956-63; real estate mgmt. Van Schaack & Co., Denver, 1964-69; sales and devel. Perry & Butler, Denver, 1970-73; v.p. Lincoln Co. real estate, 1973-75, Moore Realty, Denver, 1975-80, Property Brokers, Inc., Denver, 1980—. Tchr. piano and organ. Bd. mem. East Belleview Water and Sanitation Dist., 1967-74, treas., 1970-74; bd. dirs. Denver Mental Health Center, 1980-81; Republican precinct committeeman, 1968—, state and county del., 1968, 72, 74; bd. dirs. Denver br. Mental Health Assn. Colo., sec., 1977, 1st v.p., 1978-79. Certified property mgr.; lic. real estate broker, Colo. Mem. Timberline Toastmasters Internat. (pres. 1976, 79), Denver Round Table (dir.), Denver Musicians Assn., Beta Theta Pi. Home: 4351 W Ponds Circle Littleton CO 80123 Office: 2755 S Locust St Denver CO 80222

BUESCHER, ADOLPH ERNST, JR., aerospace exec.; b. St. Louis, Oct. 6, 1922; s. Adolph Ernst and Eugenie Katherine (Stroh) B.; B.S., U. Mo., 1946; M.S. (Standard Oil Co. Calif. fellow), Stanford U., 1950; postgrad. U. Calif., Los Angeles, 1951-52; m. Ruth Libbie Flemming, Aug. 21, 1948; children—Timothy, Philip. Engr., Eastman Kodak Co., Rochester, N.Y., 1946-49; flight test supr. Northrop Aircraft, Inc., Los Angeles, 1950-53; cons. engr., mgr. controls and instrumentation Sverdrop & Parcel, Inc., St. Louis, 1953-56; program mgr. Atlas System, Gen. Electric Co., Valley Forge, Pa., 1957-60, mgr. product planning, 1960-63, mgr. devel. plans, 1963-69, mgr. strategic planning aerospace group, 1969—; instr. U.S. Power Squadron, Phila., 1969—. Vice pres. Whitemarsh Citizens Council, 1961-66; mem. Whitemarsh Twp. Planning Commn., 1974—, chmn., 1975; mem. aviation com. Greater Phila. C. of C. Served with USAAF and AUS, 1942-46. Recipient Engr. of Year award Engrs. Club of Phila., 1960; registered profl. engr., N.Y., Calif., Mo. Asso. fellow Am. Inst. Aeros. and Astronautics; mem. Pi Tau Sigma, Tau Beta Pi. Republican. Lutheran. Clubs: Duffy Creek Yacht (Georgetown, Md.); Explorers (N.Y.C.). Patentee automatic celestial nav. systems. Home: 6044 Cannon Hill Rd Fort Washington PA 19034 Office: Box 8555 Philadelphia PA 19101

BUESSEM, NIELS C., publishing co. exec.; b. Berlin, Feb. 5, 1934; s. William R. and Gritta (Hennig) B.; B.A., Pa. State U., 1958; student Sorbonne U., Paris, 1956, U. Munich (Germany), 1955-56; m. Jan Evans, June 18, 1960; children—Christopher, William. Editorial dir. Charles Merrill Pub. Co., Columbus, Ohio, 1959-61; exec. editor Harcourt Brace Jovanovich Inc., N.Y.C., 1961-69; pres. Grune & Stratton, Inc., N.Y.C., 1969-73; v.p., gen. mgr. med. div. John Wiley & Sons, Inc., N.Y.C., 1973—; dir. Patient Care Publs., Inc. Served with USAF, 1958-59, 61-62. Mem. Am. Med. Publishers Assn. (past pres.), Assn. Ind. Clin. Publs. (dir.), Am. Inst. Ultrasound in Medicine, Am. Mgmt. Assn., Sci. Tech. and Med. Publishers Group. Home: 42 Lounsbury Rd Croton on Hudson NY 10520 Office: 605 3d Ave New York NY 10016

BUFFARDI, LOUIS JOSEPH, candy mfg. co. exec.; b. Chgo., Mar. 27, 1914; s. Salvatore J. and Carmella (Pagano) B.; student Northwestern U., 1932-35; LL.B., Kent Law Sch., 1938; m. Dorothy Ann Parrillo, Jan. 6, 1940; children—James S., Louis P., Carmellyn R., Donna T. Admitted to Ill. bar, 1938; practiced in Chgo., 1938-40; treas., atty. Ferrara Candy Co., Chgo., 1940-42, treas., atty., 1946—; electronic analyst Motorola, Inc., Chgo., 1942-44; bacteriological chemist Meadowmor Dairy, Chgo., 1944-46. Chgo. area candy industry sect. leader Community Fund, A.R.C., 1942-52. Bd. dirs. Villa Scalabrini, old peoples home. Recipient 10 year service award Red Feather, 1953. Mem. Ill. Bar Assn., Nat. Confectioner's Assn., N.A.M., Nat. Small Bus. Men's Assn., Catholic Lawyer's Guild, Chgo. Justinian Soc. Lawyers, Ill. C. of C., Chgo. Mus. Natural History, Lyric Opera Guild of Chgo., Northwestern U. Alumni Assn. Moose. Clubs: Chicago Candy Technology, Chicago Candy Production. Home: 121 Briarwood Loop Oak Brook IL 60521 Office: 7301 W Harrison St Forest Park IL 60131

BUFFINGTON, ARTHUR C., banker; b. Wesley, Iowa, June 13, 1928; s. Ross Phillip and Elna K. (Christensen) B.; ed. Iowa State U., spl. courses; m. Ardis J. Bosworth, June 17, 1951; children—Ann Margaret, Daniel Arthur, Ross Harmon, Thomas Allan. Asst. county supr. Farmers Home Adminstrn., Independence, Iowa, 1953-54; mgr. Fed. Land Bank Assn., Forest City, Iowa, 1954-58; asst. v.p. Fed. Land Bank of Omaha, 1958-68, v.p., 1968-74, pres., 1974—; mem. Farm Credit Fiscal Agy. Com. Trustee Wesleyan U. (Lincoln), Met. YMCA, Heritage Mus. (Omaha). Served with USAF. Recipient Alumni Achievement award Iowa State U. Mem. Am. Mgmt. Assn. (pres.'s assn.), Alpha Gamma Rho, Gamma Sigma Delta. Methodist. Clubs: Omaha, Toastmasters, Downtown Kiwanis (past pres.). Contbr. articles to agrl. and agrl. fin. jours. Office: 206 S 19th St Omaha NE 68102

BUFORD, CURTIS DONALD, transp. co. exec.; b. Sioux City, Iowa, July 6, 1920; s. Charles H. and Bess (Thomas) B.; B.S., Mass. Inst. Tech., 1942; m. Barbara Anderson, Apr. 29, 1947; children—Nancy Joanne, Jerome Donald, Roberta Jane, William Warwick, Ruth Elizabeth, John Anderson. With transp. and operating depts. N.Y. Central R.R., 1946-59; v.p. operations and maintenance Assn. Am. Railroads, Washington, 1959-64; exec. v.p. P. & L.E. R.R., Pitts., 1964, pres., dir., 1965-69; pres., dir. Trailer Train Co., Chgo., 1969—; dir. Allegheny Corp. Served to capt. AUS, 1942-46; PTO, ETO. Mem. Am. Soc. M.E., Newcomen Soc. in N.Am., Transp. Assn. Am. Clubs: Duquesne (Pitts.); Chicago; Glen View Country (Golf, Ill.); Metropolitan (Washington). Office: 101 N Wacker Dr Chicago IL 60606

BUFORD, WILLIAM HOLMES, JR., computer systems co. exec.; b. Ruston, La., June 15, 1934; s. William Holmes and Virginia (Holloway) B.; B.S. in Physics, La. State U., 1956; postgrad. U. So. Calif., 1958-61; m. Catherine de Montmeja, Mar. 17, 1979; children—William Holmes III, Deryl Louise, Elodie de Montmeja. Dir. advanced systems Marquardt Corp., Van Nuys, Calif., 1958-69; v.p. advanced studies Satellite Positioning Corp., Encino, Calif.,

1969-70; v.p. Seismark Internat.-System Engring., Reseda, Calif., 1970-71; pres. Codevintec Pacific, Inc., Woodland Hills, Calif., 1971-79, Electronic Frontiers Inc., Woodland Hills, 1979—; dir. Seismark Internat., Inc., Reseda. Served to 1st lt. USAF, 1956-58. Mem. Am. Nuclear Soc. Patentee nuclear tech., sonar navigation. Home: 19407 Shenango Dr Tarzana CA 91356 Office: 20121 Ventura Blvd Woodland Hills CA 91364

BUGBEE, LUTHER, pub. co. exec., cons.; b. Phila., Nov. 13, 1918; s. Luther (dec.) and Marguerite Louise (Jordon) B.; student Maria Ouspenskaya at Moscow Art Drama Sch., 1938-39, Coll. City N.Y., 1948-49; m. Elizabeth Sara Jennings, Dec. 25, 1941; children—Robin Alexander and Christopher Byron (twins), Bruce Gregory. Dist. sales mgr. circulation Macy Newspapers, Westchester County, N.Y., 1939-40; boy sales supr. MacFadden Publs., Inc., Mt. Vernon, N.Y., Poughkeepsie, N.Y., 1940-41; asst. dir. country div. Inter-Borough News Co., N.Y.C., 1945-49; nat. dir. newsstand circulation Popular Publs., Inc., N.Y.C., 1949-52; dir. newsstand sales Fawcett Pubs., Inc., Greenwich, Conn., 1953-68; sales dir. mag. div. Fawcett Publs., Inc., Greenwich and N.Y.C., 1968-69; v.p. circulation, mag. div., Greenwich, 1970-77; v.p., circulation dir. Womans group Consumer Pub. div. CBS, 1977—; pres. Luther Bugbee Assos., Inc., 1980—; guest lectr. N.Y. U. Sch. Continuing Edn., 1974. Bd. dirs. Bill Baldwin Day Fund, Inc., N.Y.C., 1973-76; hon. dir. 25 Year Club Ind. Distbn., Inc., N.Y.C., 1965-76, v.p., 1965-66. Served with AUS, 1941-46. Mem. Sales Exec. Club N.Y. (membership com.). Office: 1 Fawcett Pl Greenwich CT 06830

BUHAGIAR, MARION, editor; b. N.Y.C., Oct. 27, 1932; d. George and Mae (Pietrzak) B.; B.A. cum laude, Hunter Coll., 1953; 1 dau., Alexa Ragozin. Economist U.S. Dept. Commerce, Washington, 1954-57; bus. reporter Time Mag., N.Y.C., 1957-60; bus. reporter Fortune Mag., N.Y.C., 1960-63, asso. editor, dir. story devel., 1963-72; text editor Time-Life Books, N.Y.C., 1972-76; exec. editor, v.p. Boardroom Reports, N.Y.C., 1976—. Mem. Phi Beta Kappa. Office: 500 Fifth Ave New York NY 10110

BUHR, CARL EDWARD, banker; b. Bklyn., Dec. 27, 1941; s. Arthur H. and Agnes B.; A.B., Georgetown U., 1963; student N.Y. U., 1966-71. With U.S. Trust Co. N.Y., N.Y.C., 1966—, account exec., 1966—, asst. v.p., 1975-78, v.p., 1978—. Served to capt. U.S. Army, 1964-66, 68-69. Decorated Bronze Star. Mem. Fin. Analysts Fedn. Republican. Roman Catholic. Clubs: N.Y. Yacht, Port Washington Yacht, Yacht Racing Assn. L.I. Sound (treas.). Office: 45 Wall St New York NY 10005

BUINICKY, WILLIAM EDWARD, restaurant exec.; b. Claremont, N.H., Dec. 20, 1949; s. Henry Francis and Priscilla Ann (Langdon) B.; A.S., U. N.H., 1970. Chef, Sullivan County (N.H.) Nursing Hosp., 1970-72, Slope 'n Shore Inn, New London, N.H., 1972-73, Lakeview House, Sunapee, N.H., 1973-77; head chef, kitchen coordinator New London Inn, 1977-78; chef, mgr. Guideons Eating House, Plymouth, N.H., 1978—; with King B Caterers, 1979—; restaurant cons., 1980—; guest instr. Newport (N.H.) High Sch., 1973; mem. com. for advancement food service edn. U. N.H., 1976—. Democrat. Roman Catholic. Home: Thornton Terr Pasture Ln Campton NH 03223 Office: 1 Main St Plymouth NH 03264

BUIST, RICHARDSON, trust banker; b. Bklyn., Aug. 8, 1921; s. George Lamb and Adelaide (Richardson) B.; student Yale U.; m. Jean Mackerley, Oct. 2, 1948; children—Peter Richardson, Jean Morford, Mary Elizabeth Buist Taylor. Advt. copy writer Ecloss Co., Sparta, N.J., 1946-48; advt. mgr. Sussex County Ind., 1948-50, Dover Advance, 1950-53; bus. mgr. N.J. Herald, Newton, 1953-70; dir., v.p. The N.J. Herald, Inc., 1958-70, pub., 1967-70; asst. sec., asst. treas. Morford Co., 1965-72; trust officer Midlantic Nat. Bank/Sussex & Mchts., Newton, 1971—, Midlantic Nat. Bank, Newark, 1972—. Pres. Sussex County chpt. Am. Cancer Soc., 1956-58, Sussex County Music Found., 1959-61; mem. Morris-Sussex Area Health Facilities Planning Council, 1965-68; v.p. Sussex County Council Arts, 1971-73. Trustee Sussex County Music Found., 1955-75; v.p., chmn. fin. devel. com. Newton Meml. Hosp., 1966-68, pres. bd. govs., 1968-71, chmn., 1971-73; founding incorporator, trustee N.W. Jersey Health Care, 1971-76; trustee, mem. exec. com. regional health planning council Health Systems Agy., 1976—, v.p., 1978-79. Mem. N.J. Vet. Med. Soc. Aux. (del. 1979—), Am. Vet. Med. Soc. Aux. Club: Rotary (pres. 1967-68). Home: Rural Route 1 Box 668-A Hamburg NJ 07419 Office: 161 Madison Ave Morristown NJ 07960

BUKER, DAVID WILLIAM, mgmt. cons.; b. Portland, Maine, June 20, 1940; s. Myron William and Harriett Winifred (Bridge) B.; B.A. with honors in Econs., Wheaton Coll., 1966; M.B.A. in Fin., U. Chgo., 1975; m. Marilyn June Watkins, Aug. 4, 1963; children—Michelle Lynette, Bradley David. Material control mgr. Chgo. and Northwestern R.R., 1958-62; corp. materials cons. Hyster Co., 1966-69; dir. prodn. planning Barber-Greene Co., 1969-71; asst. to pres. Desa Industries, 1971-74; dir. materials Dresser Industries, Galion, Ohio, 1974-78; dir. mfg. indsl. edn. Arthur Andersen & Co., St. Charles, Ill., 1978-79; pres. David W. Buker, Inc., Antioch, Ill., 1979—, Fin. Services Co., Antioch, 1974—; chmn. bd. Vacation Island Properties, Sanibel Island, Fla., 1974—; dir., chmn. long-range planning com., chmn. fin. com. Sundial of Sanibel Island. Cert. practitioner in inventory mgmt. Mem. Am. Prodn. and Inventory Control Soc. (dir. cert. 1978), Internat. Materials Mgmt. Soc. (internat. v.p. 1972), Nat. Assn. Accts., Nat. Assn. Purchasing Mgrs. Republican. Mem. Evangelical Free Ch. Home: 24099 Bayview Rd Antioch IL 60002 Office: PO Box 475 Antioch IL 60002

BUKOWSKI, JOHN CHESTER, pharmacy exec.; b. Buffalo, July 9, 1936; s. Jesse J. and Irene (Firlik) B.; B.S., U. Buffalo, 1957; m. Barbara Pettis, Nov. 10, 1974; children—Mark, Kirk, Shari, Todd. Pres., Bukowski Pharmacy, Danville, N.Y., 1961—, Wayland, N.Y., 1966—, Perry, N.Y., 1977—; owner Bukowski Pharmacy, Livonia, N.Y., 1976—, Bukowski Avon Pharmacy (N.Y.), 1978—. Bd. dirs. Genesee Valley Home Care, 1973—; pres. United Fund, 1967. Served with USAF, 1957-59. Mem. C. of C. (dir. 1967-69), N.Y. State Pharm. Assn., Nat. Assn. Retail Druggists, Aircraft Owners and Pilots Assn., Nat. Assn. Flight Instrs., Dansville Pilots Assn. Club: Lions. Home: 7 Dugway St Danville NY 14437 Office: 168 Main St Dansville NY 14437

BULL, FRANK JAMES, architect; b. Chattanooga, June 25, 1922; s. Louis H. and Augusta (Clausius) B.; B.S., Ga. Inst. Tech., 1948, B.Arch., 1949; m. Betty Frances Graham, May 7, 1949; 1 son, Birney O'Brian. Pilot, Pan Am. World Airways, 1942-46; architect Aeck Assos., Atlanta, 1948-57; partner Bull & Kenney, Architects, Atlanta, 1957—; pres., dir. Atlanta Spring, Inc., 1967—. Bd. dirs. Galloway Schs., Inc., 1969-75, vice chmn., 1969-70, exec. com., 1971-75; trustee Holy Innocents Parish Day Sch., Atlanta, 1962-68, chmn., 1966; bd. dirs. Architects and Engrs. Inst., Atlanta, 1962-64. Recipient Rambusch prize Ecole de Beaux Arts, 1940; 1st recipient Producer's Council Service award Ga. chpt. AIA, 1957. Mem. AIA (corp. mem., treas. Atlanta chpt. 1976-78, chmn. com. systems sch. bldg. N.Ga. chpt. 1970-71, chmn. CEC joint com. 1975-76, dir. Ga. assn. 1971-74), Nat. Panel Constrn. Arbitrators, Am. Arbitration Assn., ANAK Honor Soc. Ga. Inst. Tech., Beta Theta Pi, Omicron Delta Kappa, Tau Beta Pi, Phi Eta Sigma, Phi Kappa Phi. Episcopalian. Club: Cherokee Town and Country (charter, governing bd. 1976-79, chmn. capital appropriations com., green chmn.). Contbr. articles to profl. jours. Major works include: sanctuary for Holy Innocents Episcopal Ch., Atlanta; speech sch. and clinic Atlanta Speech Sch.; Hummel Hall, Episcopal High Sch., Alexandria, Va.; Jekyll Island Golf Clubhouse, Jekyll Island (Ga.) State Park; McLarty Hall, Tull Hall, Turner Gymnasium at Westminster Schs., Atlanta. Home: 1795 Northridge Rd Dunwoody GA 30338 Office: 1261 Spring St NW Atlanta GA 30309

BULL, GERALD MILLER, data processing co. exec.; b. Camden, N.J., July 8, 1946; s. Walter Stephen and Mabelle (Miller) B.; B.S., Defiance Coll., 1969; M.S.A., George Washington U., 1975; m. Millie Louise Maxwell, Dec. 23, 1969; children—Robert Maxwell, Carolyn Mae, Melissa Michelle. Sr. software analyst Honeywell Info. Systems, Norfolk, Va., 1972-75; mgr. corp. computer services Peterson, Howell & Heather, Hunt Valley, Md., 1975-78; mgr. corp. data processing PHH Group, Hunt Valley, 1979—. Served from 2d lt. to capt., USAF, 1969-72. Cert. in data processing; cert. data educator. Mem. Assn. Computing Machinery (chmn. Balt. chpt. 1978-79), Honeywell Large Systems User Assn. (pres., dir.). Reviewer ACM Computing Revs., 1979-81. Office: PHH Group 11333 McCormick Rd Hunt Valley MD 21031

BULL, IVAN O., public accountant; b. Ottumwa, Iowa, Apr. 28, 1924; s. Rex Everett and Edna Farne (Epperly) B.; B.S.C., U. Iowa, 1947; m. Dorris Lucille O'Neal, Sept. 29, 1945; children—Dennis L., R. Warren, Peggy L., Tina M. With McGladrey Hendrickson & Co., Davenport, Iowa, 1947—, adminstrv. partner, 1960-66, mng. partner, 1966—; adv. bd. Paton Acctg. Center, U. Mich., 1975-77; profl. adv. bd. dept. accountancy U. Ill., 1976—; adv. council dept. acctg. U. Iowa, 1976—; trustee Fin. Acctg. Found., 1972-76; pres. Asso. Acctg. Firms Internat., 1968-70. Served with AUS, 1943-45. Decorated Bronze Star, Purple Heart. Recipient Disting. Alumni Achievement award U. Iowa, 1978; C.P.A., Iowa. Mem. Am. Inst. C.P.A.'s (chmn., 1975-76), Iowa Soc. C.P.A.'s, Ill. Soc. C.P.A.'s. Methodist. Clubs: Town (pres. Davenport 1968); Kiwanis (pres. 1960); Rock Island Arsenal Golf; N.Y. Athletic. Office: 908 Davenport Bank Bldg Davenport IA 52801

BULL, WALTER BERESFORD, JR., fin. services co. exec.; b. Rochester, N.Y., Jan. 30, 1933; s. Walter Beresford and Florence Blanche (Dash) B.; student Heidelberg Coll., 1951-52; B.S., U. Pa., 1955-58; postgrad. U. Rochester, 1958-60. Rep., Fahnestock & Co., Phila., 1969-73; v.p. Smith, Barney Harris Upham, Phila., 1973-76; v.p. Shearson Hayden Stone, Phila., 1976-77; pres. Allen, Rogers & Co., Inc., Phila., 1977—, Vigeant Motor Freight, 1975—, also Walmer, Inc., Market First Assos., Wyndon Group Ltd. Mem. Boston, Phila. stock exchanges. Clubs: Bond of Phila., Merion Golf, 4th St., Rochester Yacht, Union League, Rittenhouse. Home: 1010 Wyndon Ave Bryn Mawr PA 19010 Office: Suite 2822 1700 Market St Philadelphia PA 19103

BULLARD, CLAUDE EARL, newspaper and radio-TV co. exec.; b. Louisville, July 21, 1920; s. George Adolph and Clara Etta (House) B.; student U. Louisville, 1946-47; m. Mildred Gambert, July 24, 1943; 1 dau., Susan Earle. Owner, mgr. C. E. Bullard Printing Co., Louisville, 1938-43; journeyman printer Courier-Jour. & Louisville Times Co., 1946-65, supr. composing room, 1965-68, prodn. mgr., 1968-72; dir. ops., 1972-75; v.p. orgn. and planning for C.J. & T., WHAS Radio & TV, Standard Gravure Corp., 1975-81, sr. v.p. and dir., 1981—. Bd. dirs. Ky. Council on Alcoholism, Louisville, 1969-71, Plymouth Urban Center, Louisville, 1969-72, Little Saints Day Care Center, Louisville, 1973-76, Bridgehaven, 1978—, New Directions; mem. admittance com. Metro United Way. Served with U.S. Navy, 1943-45. Mem. Am. Newspaper Pubs. Assn., So. Newspaper Pubs. Assn. (mem. labor/personnel com. 1980-81), Am. Newspaper Personnel Assn., Am. Soc. Tng. Dirs., Louisville Personnel Assn., Rotogravure Labor Group, Soc. Am. Magicians. Clubs: Hon. Order Ky. Cols., 1st Tuesday Assn., Jefferson. Home: 3510 Hughes Rd Louisville KY 40207 Office: 525 W Broadway Louisville KY 40202

BULLARD, GILDA, state ofcl.; b. Chicago Heights, Ill., Dec. 12, 1927; d. Pietro Antonio and Philomena D'Antonoli; B.S., Calif. State U., Sacramento, 1967, M.B.A., 1973; 1 son, David L. Gard. With Pacific Telephone Co., 1945-61; with State of Calif., 1961—, fiscal specialist state welfare programs, 1966-74, adminstr. licensing div., 1974-76, hearing officer licensing regulations, 1976-78, mgr. audits and investigations div. Dept. Health Services, 1978—; part-time instr. community colls., 1974-78. Mem. Nat. Assn. Accountants (asst. treas., editor 1971—), AAUW, Calif. State Employees Assn. (past chpt. pres., editor, del.). Presbyterian. Home: 423 Alvarado Ave Davis CA 95616 Office: 714 P St Sacramento CA 95814

BULLARD, ROLAND KEITH, II, banker; b. Boston, Apr. 13, 1944; s. Richard Kendall and Nancy (Stone) B.; B.A., George Washington U., 1966, M.B.A., 1969; m. Nancy Denison, Jan. 30, 1964; children—Kurt William, Tracey Lee. Loan specialist Export Import Bank U.S., 1966-68; with Phila. Nat. Bank, 1968—, sr. v.p., mgr. internat. div., 1975-77, sr. v.p., mgr. multinat. div., 1977—; dir. Phila. Internat. Investment Corp., PNB Internat. Fin. Co., Sydney, Australia, Phila. Indsl. Devel. Corp. Mem. Internat. Bus. Forum Phila. (vice chmn.), Internat. C. of C. Home: 2186 Buttonwood Rd Berwyn PA 19312 Office: Phila Nat Bank Broad and Chestnut Sts Philadelphia PA 19101

BULLWINKLE, RICHARD, JR., mfg. co. exec.; b. Dallas, Nov. 5, 1937; s. Richard and Elizabeth Alden (Aller) B.; B.S. in Physics, Principia Coll., 1959; postgrad. Washington U., St. Louis, 1960; m. Mary Mosley, Mar. 31, 1972; children—Amy, Alden, Richard. Regional mgr. Kemp Engring. Co., Dallas, 1960-62; dir. contracts SCI Systems, Huntsville, Ala., 1962-66; v.p. mktg. Beta-Tek, Harriman, Tenn., 1966-68; pres. Option, Inc., cons. firm specializing in turn-around mgmt., Dallas, 1968-74; asso. pvt. investment group acquiring and rehabilitating distressed cos., 1974-76; pres., dir. Atlas Archtl. Metals, Inc., Dallas, 1977—. Club: Chandlers Landing Yacht. Home: 5322 Montrose Dr Dallas TX 75209 Office: 8230 Lovett St Dallas TX 75227

BULOW, RICHARD PAUL, coal co. exec.; b. Meadville, Pa., Jan. 23, 1938; s. Paul James and Mary Rita (Eager) B.; B.S., St. Francis Coll., 1959; m. Frances A. Diehl, May 12, 1962; children—Elizabeth, Kathryn, Matthew. Staff acct. Haskins & Sells, N.Y.C., 1959-61; staff acct. Maim, Lafrentz & Co., Johnstown, Pitts., 1962-64; partner Bulow, Hottle & Co., Somerset, Pa., 1965-75, Glessner Mines, Somerset, 1975—; v.p. Thought Products, Inc., Somerset, 1975—; mem. adv. bd. U.S. Nat. Bank, Johnstown. Bd. dirs. Somerset County YMCA, 1978. Served with U.S. Army, 1959. C.P.A., Pa. Mem. Am., Pa. (v.p. 1978-79) insts. C.P.A.'s, Somerset County C. of C. (dir. 1978-80). Clubs: Country (gov. 1978-79), Rotary (dir. 1975-80, pres. 1980-81) (Somerset). Mem. editorial bd. Pa. C.P.A. Spokesman mag., 1970-71. Home: 745 W Main St Somerset PA 15501 Office: RD 2 Somerset PA 15501

BUNCH, RICHARD LEE, fin. cons.; b. Pendleton, Oreg., Apr. 17, 1940; s. Laurence A. and Betty G. (Venable) B.; A.A., Boise State U., 1960; m. V. Anne Winters, Dec. 5, 1958; children—Richard, Lisa, Amy, Julie, Jennifer. Mem. mktg. staff Maxwell House Coffee div. Gen. Foods Corp., 1960-63; with mktg. and distbn. dept. Western Plastics Corp., Tacoma, 1963-66; incorporator, gen. mgr. Pacific Plastic Pipe Co., Portland, Oreg., 1966-70; pres. Financial Services Cons. of Oreg. Inc., Portland, 1970—, Artec N.W. Computer Word Processing, 1979—, Automated Word & Data Systems, 1981—; cons. to bus. Bd. dirs. Oreg. Christian Men's Group, 1972-73; chmn. bd. Aloha Community Baptist Ch., Hillsboro, Oreg., 1974-76; bd. dirs. local chpt. Full Gospel Businessmen's Fellowship Internat., 1975-79. Mem. Nat. Assn. Stock Dealers, Nat. Assn. Life Underwriters. Club: Masons. Home: Route 5 Box 293 Hillsboro OR 97123 Office: 433 Terminal Sales Bldg 1220 SW Morrison St Portland OR 97205

BUNDSCHUH, JOHN JOSEPH, JR., fin. cons.; b. New Rochelle, N.Y., Aug. 5, 1932; s. John J. and Quida N. (Louden) B.; B.S. in Fin., U. Notre Dame, 1954; postgrad. U. Pa., 1954-55; m. Dorothy E. Brown, Feb. 11, 1956; children—John G., Lauren E., D. Elizabeth, Geoffrey, Stphen R. Vice pres., dir. J.M. Louden, Inc., N.Y.C., 1957-68; pres., dir. The Marian Corp., New Haven, 1960-68; now pres. Bundschuh & Co., Fin. Cons., N.Y.C., First New Eng., Capital Corp., North Haven, Conn. Served with Fin. Corps, U.S. Army, 1955-57. Mem. N.Y. Soc. Security Analysts, Fin. Mgmt. Assn., Fin. Analysts Fedn. Roman Catholic. Club: Westchester Country. Home: 321 Betsy Brown Rd Port Chester NY 10573 and Millerton NY 12546 Office: 60 E 42nd St New York NY 10017

BUNDY, KENNETH ALVIN, newspaper editor, publisher; b. Alliance, Neb., Dec. 16, 1910; s. A. Floyd and Carolyn (Southard) B.; B.A. in Journalism, U. Colo., 1935; m. Virginia L. Carr, July 6, 1938; children—Stephen Allen, Paul Emerson. Editor, Estes Park Trail, 1935-36; advt. Fort Collins (Colo.) Express-Courier, 1936; reporter Boulder (Colo.) Daily Camera, 1936-37; reporter and photographer Denver Rocky Mountain News, 1937-42; owner, editor Gunnison (Colo.) Courier, 1945-55; mng. editor Cervi's Journal, 1955-56; pub., editor Aurora (Colo.) Star and Adams County News, 1956-70, pres. Star Publs., 1970—; dir. Aurora Nat. Bank, Montbello State Bank (Colo.). Editor plant newspaper, shell plant Kaiser Industries, Denver for War Manpower Bd., 1943-44. Mem. Colo. State Planning Commn., 1949-52; bd. regents U. Colo., 1950-56. Mem. Colo. Press Assn., Denver Press Club, Kappa Tau Alpha, Sigma Delta Chi. Democrat. Congregationalist. Club: Rotary. Home: 3435 S Ash St Denver CO 80222 Office: 1336 Glenarm Pl Denver CO 80204

BUNDY, THOMAS FREEBORN, JR., fin. exec.; b. N.Y.C., May 26, 1940; s. Thomas Freeborn and Mary (Regetz) B.; B.A., Trinity Coll., 1962; m. Judith Ann Cox, Dec. 18, 1965; children—Carter Alden, Graham Lewis. With U.S. Dept. Justice, Washington, N.Y.C. and Tampa, Fla., 1965-69; asst. sec., asst. v.p. nat. div. Chem. Bank, N.Y.C., 1969-73; asst. v.p. Bankers Trust, N.Y.C., 1973-74, v.p., group head Western dist. U.S. banking dept., 1974-78; v.p., mgr. corp. banking dept. Algemene Bank, Nederland, N.Y., 1979—. Served to 1st lt. USAF, 1962-65. Mem. Chinese Peoples Assn. for Friendship with Fgn. Countries. Episcopalian. Clubs: Onteora, Knickerbocker. Home: College Hill Rd Montrose NY 10548 Office: 84 William St New York NY 10038

BUNN, CHARLES NIXON, strategic bus. planning cons.; b. Springfield, Ill., Feb. 8, 1926; s. Joseph Forman and Helen Anna Frieda (Link) B.; student U. Ill., 1943-44; B.S. in Engring., U.S. Mil. Acad., 1949; M.B.A., Xavier U., Cin., 1958; m. Cecine Elizabeth Cole, Dec. 26, 1951; children—Siscine, Charles. Flight test engr. Gen. Electric Co., Cin., also Edwards AFB, Calif., 1953-59; sr. missile test engr., space systems div. Lockheed Aircraft Corp., USAF Satellite Test Center, Sunnyvale, Calif., 1959-60, 63-70, economist, advanced planning dept., 1961-63; economic and long-range planning cons., Los Altos, Calif., 1970-73; head systems planning, economist, strategic bus. planning, Western Regional hdqrs. U.S. Postal Service, San Bruno, Calif., 1973-78; strategic bus. planning cons., investment analysis cons., 1978-79; strategic bus. planning Advanced Reactor Systems dept. Gen. Electric Co., Sunnyvale, 1979—. Served with inf. paratroops U.S. Army, 1944-45, with inf. and rangers, 1949-53; Korea. Mem. Nat. Assn. Bus. Economists, World Future Soc., Sigma Nu. Episcopalian. Home: 172 Hamilton Ct Los Altos CA 94022 Office: 955 Arques St Sunnyvale CA 94086

BUNTING, JAMES WHITNEY, economist, coll. adminstr.; b. Phila., Nov. 23, 1913; s. George Miller Lewis and Helen Elizabeth (Whitney) B.; B.S., U. Pa., 1934; M.A., 1936, M.B.A., 1937, Ph.D., 1946; postgrad. U. Louisville, 1938-39; m. Mildred Eleanor Griscom, Oct. 14, 1939; 1 dau., Helen Whitney Bunting Pickett. Economist, Pa. State Planning Bd., Harrisburg, 1934-35; gen. freight agt. Preston Trucking Co., Md., 1935-36; instr. econs., mktg. and fin. Jr. Coll. Commerce, New Haven, 1937-39, coll. dean, 1949-50; asst. prof. bus. adminstrn. Hanover Coll., Ind., 1939-42; dir. pub. relations, prof. applied econs. Hobart Coll., Geneva, N.Y., 1945-49, asso., acting dean, 1946-48; prof. econs., chmn. dept. U. Ga., Atlanta, 1950-51; prof. econs. U. Athens (Ga.), 1951-52; exec. v.p. Oglethorpe U., 1952, pres., 1953-55; prof. fin. N.Y. U., 1957-62; dean Coll. Bus. Adminstrn. U. Ga., Athens, 1962-68; pres. Ga. Coll., Milledgeville, 1968—; dir. indsl. community program, 1947-48; asst. treas. Market Basket Corp., Geneva, N.Y., 1948-49; dir. Bur. Bus. Research U. Ga., Athens, 1951-52; cons. higher edn. and research Gen. Electric Co., 1955-62; cons. Exchange Bank of Milledgeville, Ga. Pub. Service Commn.; economist WPB, Washington, 1942; vice chmn. Atlanta Regional Export Expansion Council, 1971-74; chmn. com. on pub. affairs Am. Assn. State Colls. and Univs., 1970—; pres. Citizens Com. for Rye Pub. Schs.; mem. adv. bd. Concerned Educators Against Forced Unionism. Served as lt. Supply Corps, USNR, 1942-45. Recipient medal of Honor Freedom Found., Valley Forge, Pa., 1954; Am. Eagle award Invest-in-Am. Nat. Council, 1976. Fellow Internat. Inst. Arts and Letters (life); mem. Nat. Invest-in-Am. Com. (pres. nat. council, bd. govs. eastern regional chmn., exec. com.), Am. Econs. Assn., Am. Geog. Soc., Am. Mktg. Assn., Am. Acad. Polit. and Social Sci., Nat. Sales Execs., So. Economists Soc., Ga. Bus. and Industry Assn., Gamma Omicron Tau, Delta Sigma Pi, Delta Chi, Beta Gamma Sigma, Phi Kappa Phi, Pi Gamma Mu. Presbyterian. Clubs: Rotary. Author: Effective Retail Selling, 1953; Ethics for Modern Business Practice, 1953; Higher Education, A Twenty Year Look Ahead, 1957; Your Share in America's Prosperity, 1960; author, editor: Busines Leaders in People's Capitalism, 1959; editor Atlanta Econ. Rev., 1950-51, Ga. Bus., 1951-52; editor: Productivity-Some Thoughts for Business Leaders, 1977; contbr. econ. editor Elec. South, 1952-70; contbr. articles to profl. jours. Home: 120 S Clark St Milledgeville GA 31061 Office: Ga Coll PO Box 708 Milledgeville GA 31061

BUNTING, JOHN RICHARD, JR., banker; b. Phila., June 29, 1925; s. John Richard and Dorothy (McNair) B.; B.S., Temple U., 1950, M.A., 1952; m. Jane Anne Shuttleworth, June 29, 1946; children—Robin Anne, John Richard III. Economist, v.p. Fed. Res. Bank, Phila., 1950-64; economist, v.p., exec. v.p., pres., chmn., chief exec. officer First Pa. Corp., Phila., 1964-80; dir. Fidelity Mut. Life Ins. Co., City Stores, Inc. Chmn. WHYY, Inc.; co-chmn. Phila. Urban Coalition; pres. Pa. Soc. Served with AUS, 1944-46. Presbyn. Club: Seaview Country (Absecon, N.J.). Author: The Hidden Face of Free Enterprise, 1964. Office: Centre Square W 1500 Market St Philadelphia PA 19101

BUNZEL, FRED PAUL, title ins., trust co. exec.; b. Milw., Dec. 29, 1930; student U. Ala., 1953; B.S., Ariz. State U., 1960; children—Leslie Christine (Bunny), Fredrick Paul (Rick), Mary Melinda. Salesman real estate Phil Lind Realty, 1957-60; dep. sheriff Maricopa County (Ariz.), 1960-64; dep. marshall Town of Paradise Valley (Ariz.), 1964-68; pres. Blue Chip Realty, Phoenix, 1967-68; salesman Stewart Title & Trust Co., Phoenix, 1968-73; v.p. sales and mktg. Ariz. Title Ins. & Trust Co., Phoenix, 1973—. Active fund drs. Heart Fund, Salvation Army, United Way; v.p. Stat Employees Fed. Credit Union. Served with USAF, 1948-57; Korea. Mem. Ariz. Apt. Assn. (dir. 1971-72, pres. Central chpt. 1972-73), Phoenix Bd. Realtors, Farm and Land Inst., Nat. Mktg. Inst., Ariz. Assn. Realtors, Tri-City, Scottsdale bds. realtors, Nat. Assn. Indsl. Office Parks, Ariz. Assn. Indsl. Developers. Clubs: Civitan, Arizona Office: 111 W Monroe Suite 410 Phoenix AZ 85003

BURANDT, GARY EDWARD, advt. agy. exec.; b. Kansas City, Mo., Apr. 13, 1943; s. Herman Edward and Reka Lovice (Harrison) B.; B.J., U. Mo., 1966; m. Harriet Frances Krumrey, Aug. 12, 1966; children—Heather Lynn, Greta Anne. With Gen. Electric Co., Schenectady, 1966-68, advt. mgr., Pittsfield, Mass., 1971-74; account exec. Marsteller Inc., Chgo., 1974-79, account supr., 1979-80, mgmt. supr., v.p., 1979-80, group v.p., 1980-81, gen. mgr., v.p. Brussels office, 1981—; lectr. U. Wis., U. Mo., Northwestern U. Mem. Hinsdale (Ill.) Caucus, 1979-80. Served to lt. USN, 1968-71; Vietnam. Mem. Bus. Profl. Advt. Assn., Am. Assn. Advt. Agys., Chgo. Advt. Club, Newcomen Soc., Am. C. of C. in Brussels. Republican. Mem. United Ch. Christ. Clubs: Am., Chateau Ste. Anne (Brussels); Chgo. Athletic Assn. Office: 225 Ave Louise 1050 Brussels Belgium

BURBANK, RONALD E., business exec.; Pres., chief operating officer Consol. Freightways, Inc., San Francisco, 1980—. Office: Consolidated Freightways Inc International Bldg San Francisco CA 94108*

BURBIDGE, FREDERICK STEWART, transp. co. exec.; b. Winnipeg, Man., Can., Sept. 30, 1918; s. Frederick Maxwell and Susan Mary (Stewart) B.; B.A., U. Man., 1939, LL.B., 1946; m. Cynthia Adams Bennest, Apr. 27, 1942; children—John Bennest, George Frederick. With law dept. Canadian Pacific Ltd., Winnipeg, 1947-50, Montreal, 1950-60, asst. v.p. traffic, 1962-66, v.p. rail adminstrn., 1966-67, v.p., exec. asst., 1967-69, v.p. adminstrn., 1969, v.p. mktg. and sales CP Rail, 1969-71, sr. exec. officer CP Rail, also v.p. parent co., 1971-72, pres., dir., mem. exec. com. parent co., Montreal, Que., Can., 1972—; mem. adv. council to minister industry, trade and commerce; dir. Canadian Pacific Enterprises Ltd., Canadian Pacific Steamships Ltd., Canadian Pacific (Bermuda) Ltd., Canadian Pacific Transport Ltd., Canadian Pacific Air Lines Ltd., C-I-L Inc., Cominco Ltd., Marathon Realty Co., Ltd., Soo Line R.R. Co., Toronto, Hamilton & Buffalo Ry. Co.; dir., mem. exec. com. Bank of Montreal. Hon. v.p. Que. Provincial council Boy Scouts Am.; bd. dirs. Royal Victoria Hosp. Found.; mem. citizens adv. bd. Salvation Army; Mem. Gen. Council Industry, Montreal Bd. Trade, La Chambre de Commerce, Canadian Ry. Club, Traffic Club Montreal, Law Soc. Manitoba. Clubs: St. James's, Mt. Royal. Office: Canadian Pacific Ltd Windsor Sta Montreal PQ H3C 3E4 Canada

BURCKEL, CHRISTIAN EHRENFRIED, cons. publisher; b. Hamburg, Germany, Feb. 28, 1898; s. Christian O. and Clara E. (Husing) B.; brought to U.S. 1905; B.C.E., Ohio State U., 1922; M.A., Western Res. U., 1928; Ph.D., Tchrs. Coll. Columbia, U., 1941; m. Rutheda Fae Slemmons, Mar. 17, 1923. Asst. to san. engr. City of Cleve. 1922-23; tchr. Cleve. Pub. Schs., 1924-29, supt. sch., Xenia, Ohio, 1929; tchr. Lincoln Sch., Tchrs. Coll., Columbia U., 1930-36; pub. The Mount Vernon (N.Y.) News and The Pelham News, 1937-38, Coll. Blue Book, 1939-67; dir. guidance Stamford (Conn.) High Sch., 1939-40; cons. edn. and typography, 1940-42; spl. adviser to James L. Jackson, B.G. Tech. Data sect. USAAF, 1942-44; owner, dir. Christian E. Burckel and Assos., 1944-70; edn. editor Bell-McClure Syndicate, 1964-70; cons. mgmt. Pa. R.R., Gen. Electric, Internat. Harvester, Ward Leonard Electric Co., USAAF, Dept. Navy, C.E., Goodyear, 1944-70, Served with U.S. Army, 1918-19. Mem. N.E.A. (life), Am. Personnel and Guidance Assn. (life), Am. Mil. Engrs., Tech. Pubs. Assn. (pres.), Graphic Arts Industry Am. (research and engring. council), N.A.M., U.S. C. of C., Triangle, Am. Legion, Phi Delta Kappa. Mason (32 deg.). Clubs: Engineers, Nat. Republican, Lions; Mens Faculty (Columbia U.), President's of Ohio State University. Home: 13010 100th Dr Sun City AZ 85351

BURDICK, DANIEL HENRY, II, dept. store co. exec.; b. Utica, N.Y., Dec. 27, 1935; s. Harold Blake and Marion Thecla (Manske) B.; ed. Hamilton Coll., 1958; children—Victoria M.K., Vanessa M., Daniel Henry. Mgr., Kempf Properties, Utica, N.Y., 1961-66; asst. sec., U.S.A. and Can., S.S. Kresge Co. (name changed to K-Mart Corp. 1977), Troy, Mich., 1966-73, dir. property mgmt., 1973—. Served with U.S. Army, 1959-61. Republican. Roman Catholic. Club: Fort Schuyler (Utica). Home: 1011 N Woodward Ave Birmingham MI 48009 Office: 3100 W Big Beaver Rd Troy MI 48084

BURDICK, HERMAN HAROLD, assn. exec.; b. N.Y.C., Aug. 16, 1923; s. Jack and Anna (Kreitman) B.; B.S., CCNY, 1943; LL.B., Seton Hall U., 1955; m. Tina Pieroni, Aug. 31, 1946; children—Larry, Mark. Admitted to N.Y. bar, 1956; practiced law, N.Y.C., 1956-57; with European Exchange System, Nuremberg, Ger., 1957-61; gen. sec. Am. C. of C. in Italy, Milan, 1961—. Served as officer inf. U.S. Army, 1943-47, 51-53. Decorated Bronze Star. Mem. Assn. World Trade Chamber Execs. Pub. Italian Am. Bus., 1961. Home: 60 Via Plinio 20129 Milan Italy Office: Am C of C in Italy 12 Via Agnello 20121 Milan Italy

BURDON, WILLIAM FONTAINE, advt. agy. exec.; b. Ware, Mass., Dec. 21, 1926; s. Paul P. and Dorothy S. (Schaninger) B.; Asso. B.A., Curry Coll., Boston, 1951; m. Leonora Foronda, Sept. 10, 1954; children—Susan Lee, Linda Marie. With NBC, 1952-54; exec. v.p., creative dir. Marvin Hult & Assos., advt., Peoria, Ill., 1955-61; pres. Burdon Advt., Inc., Peoria, 1962—. Mem. adv. bd. YWCA; bd. dirs. Central Ill. Landmark Found. Served with AUS, 1945-47. Author published poetry. Home: 1827 W Sunnyview Dr Peoria IL 61614 Office: 200 Main St Bldg Peoria IL 61602

BURDORF, WALTER LOUIS, vinyl and rubber coated fabrics mfg. exec.; b. Miami, Fla., May 30, 1927; s. Walter Louis and Aleen Bruce (Schorr) B.; B.S. in Bus. Adminstrn., Ohio U., 1950; m. Judy Joan Von Thron, June 16, 1951; children—Walter Louis III, Joseph V., Edward S., Michael C. Salesman, Columbus Coated Fabrics Co. (Ohio), 1950-59, product mgr., 1959-62, dir. sales, 1962-65, v.p. mktg., 1965-70; gen. mgr. Mystik Tape Co., Northfield, Ill., 1970-72; asst. to pres. Crown Industries, Fremont, Ohio, 1972-74, v.p., gen. mgr., 1974-79; owner Sanford Rose Assos., Maumee, Ohio, 1980—. Served with USN, 1945-46. Mem. Beta Theta Pi. Home: 1967 N Carriage Ln Port Clinton OH 43452 Office: Huntington Bank Bldg 1446 Reynolds Rd Maumee OH 43537

BURDSALL, GERALD DALE, utility cons.; b. Tulsa, June 5, 1938; s. Glenn D. and Minnie I. Burdsall; B.S. in Elec. Engring., Wash. State U., 1960; widower; children—Randall D., Russell L., Richard A. With Gen. Electric Co., 1960-75, mgr. boiling water reactor contract services, nuclear energy div., San Jose, Calif., 1973-75; group v.p. Gen. Energy Resources, Inc., Beverly Hills, Calif., 1975-76; chmn., pres. BMK Services, Inc., San Jose, 1976—; chmn. bd. Asso. Project Services, Inc., San Jose, 1978—; mng. gen. partner BMK Investment Co., 1979—. Recipient Gen. Mgr.'s award Gen. Electric Co., 1971. Author papers in field. Home: 7171 Red Holly Ct San Jose CA 95120 Office: 2240 Lundy Ave San Jose CA 95131

BURG, GEORGE ROSCOE, journalist; b. New Lexington, Ohio, Apr. 1, 1916; s. Roscoe E. and Erie (Kreider) B.; B.S. in Journalism, Ohio State U., 1938, B.S. in Edn., 1939; m. Mary Vesta Ford, Oct. 31, 1941; children—George F., Mary Jane. Tchr., Pike Twp. High Sch., Madison County, Ohio, 1939-40; engaged in newspaper work, 1948—; mng. editor Kansas City (Mo.) Star, 1967-75, asso. editor, exec. asst. to pres., 1975—. Trustee U. Mo., Kansas City; bd. dirs. Kansas City Corp. for Indsl. Devel., Kansas City Indsl. Found. Served with AUS, 1940-48. Mem. Kansas City C. of C., A.P. Mng. Editors Assn., Mid-Am. Press Inst. (dir.), Mil. Order World Wars, Kansas City Area Safety Council (dir.), Tau Kappa Epsilon. Methodist. Elk. Club: Kansas City Press. Home: 4926 W 78th Terr Prairie Village KS 66208 Office: 1729 Grand Ave Kansas City MO 64108

BURG, LAWRENCE EDWARD, security analyst; b. LaPorte, Ind., Apr. 2, 1913; s. Clifford Ash and Hazel D. (Russell) B.; student bus. coll., spl. courses Northwestern U., 1946-47; m. Mary Ewing Glickauf, Jan. 10, 1942; children—Kenneth, Bruce, Louise, Mary. Salesman, Commonwealth Edison Co., Chgo., 1931-32, dist. rep., 1937-51; salesman Burg Typewriter Service, 1933, Williams & Meyer Co., 1934-35, Standard Oil Co. (Ind.), 1935-36; owner Minit-Fry Potato Co., 1951-54, pres. 1954-61; mgr. research dept., asst. sec. Wm. H. Tegtmeyer Co., 1961-65; registered rep., research cons., mut. funds specialist Woolard & Co., Chgo., 1965-79, Altorfer, Podesta, Woolard & Co., 1979—; owner Minit Calculator. Registered rep. Nat. Assn. Security Dealers. Served with AUS, 1941-45. Mem. Assn. Investment Brokers, Chgo. Contract Bridge Assn., Am. Legion, Am. Contract Bridge League, Internat. Platform Assn., Aerial Phenomena Research Orgn., Nat. Investigations Com. on Aerial Phenomena (asso.), Am. Security Council (nat. adv. bd.), Chgo. Chess Club, U.S. Chess Fedn., Toastmasters. Republican. Christian Scientist (1st reader 1959-62, asst. com. on publ. for Ill. 1962—). Home: 820 Elder Rd Homewood IL 60430 Office: 135 S LaSalle St Chicago IL 60603

BURGE, W. LEE, internat. bus. info. services co. exec.; b. Atlanta, June 27, 1918; s. William Frederick and Leona (Payne) B.; B.B.A., Ga. State U., 1942; LL.D., Mercer U., 1978; m. Willette Richey, Feb. 27, 1937; children—Roger, Judy Burge Cathcart. With Equifax, Inc., Atlanta, 1936—, v.p.-credit reporting affiliates, 1951-57, regional v.p., Pitts., 1957-59, chmn., pres., chief exec. officer, Atlanta, 1965—; dir. Nat. Service Industries, First Nat. Bank/First Atlanta Corp. Bd. dirs. United Way; trustee YMCA, Atlanta, 1960—; regional chmn. Nat. Alliance Businessmen, 1969. Served with U.S. Army, 1944-46. Recipient Disting. Community Service award Atlanta Urban League, 1979. Mem. Atlanta C. of C. (pres. 1966), So. Assn. Colls. and Schs. (accreditation com. 1976-80). Baptist (deacon). Club: Kiwanis (pres. 1965) (Atlanta). Office: Equifax Inc 1600 Peachtree St NW Atlanta GA 30309

BURGESS, ARTHUR HARRY, accountant; b. Sharon, S.C., Oct. 25, 1903; s. Arthur Calhoun and Mary (Love) B.; student Furman U., 1921-23; m. Sara Elizabeth Doll, Nov. 30, 1933; children—Sara Elizabeth Burgess Frazer, Arthur Harry. Pub. accountant, Hickory, N.C., 1928—; chmn. bd. Arthur H. Burgess & Co. Mem. adv. bd. trustees Queens Coll. Pres., Sharon Found. C.P.A., N.C. Mem. Am. Inst. C.P.A.'s, N.C. Assn. C.P.A.'s. Presbyn. (elder). Clubs: Rotary; Catawba (Newton, N.C.); Lake Hickory Country (Hickory); Charlotte City. Home: 322 3d Ave NE Hickory NC 28601 Office: 212 3d Ave NW Hickory NC 28601

BURGESS, DAVID, lawyer; b. Detroit, Nov. 30, 1948; s. Roger Edward and Claire Theresa (Sullivan) B.; B.S. in Fgn. Service, Georgetown U., 1970, M.S. in Fgn. Service, 1978, J.D., 1978. Research asso., adj. prof. Sch. Bus. Adminstrn., Georgetown U., Acad. in the Public Service, Washington, 1975-79; asst. editor Securities Regulation Law Report, Bur. Nat. Affairs, 1978-79; atty. Cadwalader, Wickersham & Taft, Washington, 1979—; speaker workshops Minority Legis. Edn. Program, Ind. Assn. Cities and Towns, Georgetown U. Continuing Edn. Program. Alumni rep. Internat. Sch. Bangkok, 1972-74. Served with USAF, 1970-74. Mem. Am. Bar Assn., D.C. Bar Assn., Am. Soc. Internat. Law, Am. Assn. Internat. Commn. Jurists, Amnesty Internat., Assn. Profls. in Internat. Affairs (founding), Am. Acad. Arts and Scis., Acad. Polit. Sci., U.S. Assn. Internat. Inst. Space Law, Washington Fgn. Law Soc., Inst. for Social Sci. Study of Space, Woodrow Wilson Assos., Princeton Space Studies Inst. Roman Catholic. Clubs: Eclectics, Georgetown U. Alumni Assn. (bd. govs. 1975—, class rep. 1971—). Author: Financing Local Government, 1977, 2d edit., 1978; Preparation of the Local Budget, 2 vols., 1976, 2d edit., 1978; Local Government Accounting Fundamentals, 2d edit., 1977; Improving Public Expenditure Decisions, 1979; Understanding Federal Assistance Programs, 2d edit., 1978; The POW/MIA Issue: Perspectives on the National League of Families, 1978; contbr. article to publ. Home: 3114 Pershing Dr Arlington VA 22201 Office: 1333 New Hampshire Ave NW Washington DC 20036

BURGESS, DONALD MYRON, constrn. co. exec.; b. Mt. Vernon, Ohio, Sept. 8, 1927; s. William Earl and Bessie Edith (Moore) B.; B.S. in Bus. Adminstrn., Bowling Green (Ohio) State U., 1950; m. Karen Evelyn Weaver, Aug. 17, 1968; children—Brett Martin, Scott Barton, Gregg Weaver. Mgr., partner G.R. Smith & Co., Mt. Vernon, 1950-62; systems analyst, acct. Cooper-Bessemer Corp., Mt. Vernon, 1962-70; treas. Kokosing Constrn. Co., Inc., Fredericktown, Ohio, 1970—, also dir. Republican. Baptist. Home: 1130 Gambier Rd Mount Vernon OH 43050 Office: Kokosing Constrn Co Waterford Rd Fredericktown OH 43019

BURGESS, RAYMOND RICHMOND, II, mfg. co. exec.; b. Forest City, N.C., May 3, 1947; s. Raymond Richmond and Alice Faye (McCall) B.; B.S., Ga. State U., 1971. Supr. data processing Montag Inc., Atlanta, 1965-68; coordinator data processing Nat. Services Ind., Atlanta, 1968-72; mgr. data processing, systems analyst Jacksonville (Fla.) Meml. Hosp., 1972-74; mgr. data processing Trailmobile div. Pullman Inc., Longview, Tex., 1974-75; mgr. Informatics, Columbus, Ohio, 1975-79; data processing mgr. Lancaster-Fairfield Hosp., Lancaster, Ohio, 1979—. Served with U.S. Army, 1966-68. Mem. Data Processing Mgmt. Assn., Am. Mgmt. Assn., Airline Passengers Assn., System Three Support Group. Democrat. Baptist. Clubs: Civitan, Mason. Home: 449 Shell Ct E Columbus OH 43213 Office: 401 N Ewing St Lancaster OH 43213

BURGESS, WAYNE THOMAS, computer systems analyst; b. Greensboro, N.C., Nov. 9, 1945; s. Clyde Smith and Edith Dow (Lynch) B.; B.A., East Carolina U., 1968; m. Joan Theresa Primavera, July 24, 1977; children—Wayne Thomas, James Andrew. Claims authorizer Social Security Adminstrn., HEW, Balt., 1968-72, computer specialist, 1972-80, supervisory computer systems analyst, 1980—; pres. Burgess Enterprises, Randallstown, Md., 1979—. Home: 4 Lanamer Ct Randallstown MD 21133 Office: 6401 Security Blvd 3-R-19 Operation Baltimore MD 21235

BURGIN, ROBERT AUGUSTUS, transp. co. exec.; b. Rolling Fork, Miss., July 20, 1924; s. Robert Augustus and Jane (Sullivan) B.; B.S., U. Tenn., 1949; m. Sara Porter Shofner, Dec. 4, 1948; children—Sally Burgin Margolis, Robert Augustus III, Christopher. Served with Oak Ridge Inst. Nuclear Studies, 1949-51; br. chief Dept. Def., Washington, and Albuquerque, 1951-56; cons. Stanford Research Inst., 1956-57; with TRW, 1956-78, v.p., asst. to chmn. bd. TRW Systems, 1965-67, v.p., gen. mgr. TRW Automotive Internat., 1967-71, v.p. planning and devel. Automotive Worldwide, 1972-73, v.p., gen. mgr. telecommunications, 1974-78, v.p. planning and devel. TRW Electronics, 1973-78; chmn., chief exec. officer Leaseway Transp. Corp., Cleve., 1978—; dir. Chagrin Valley Co., Ltd., Cleve., E.F. Johnson Co., Waseca, Minn., Storage Tech. Corp., Louisville, Colo., CFS Continental, Chgo., Provident Life & Accident Ins. Co., Chattanooga. Mem. exec. bd. Greater Cleve. Council Boy Scouts Am., 1979; mem. com. Hugh O'Brian Youth Found., 1977-79; bd. dirs. Greater Cleve. Growth Assn., 1979, trustee Fuller Theol. Sem., Pasadena, Calif., 1978, The ATA Found. Inc., Washington, 1979. Served to capt. USAAF, 1943-45, 51-52. Mem. Sigma Phi Epsilon. Clubs: Pepper Pike, Union. Office: 3700 Park East Dr Beachwood OH 44122

BURGIN, WILLIAM GRADY, JR., fin. planner; b. Waynesville, N.C., Apr. 26, 1943; s. William Grady and Lois (Lavender) B.; A.A., Brevard (N.C.) Jr. Coll., 1963; ed. N. Ga. Coll., Gainesville Jr. Coll., U. N.C., Ashville; m. Mary Lindley, Aug. 30, 1963; children—Kathy, Karen, William. Physicians asst., 1970-74; regional v.p. P.L. Styles & Assos., Asheville, 1974-78; owner Estate Ins. Agy., Asheville, 1978—. Chmn. fin. com. Owen High Sch. Band Boosters, 1979. Served as hosp. corpsman USNR, 1963-70; Vietnam. Club: Swannanog Valley Optimist (pres. elect 1980) (Black Mountain). Author articles in field. Home: 117 Beech Tree Dr Black Mountain NC 28711

BURGOON, DANIEL HUNTER, mfg. co. exec.; b. Norfolk, Va., Mar. 10, 1953; s. John R. and Margaret R. Burgoon; student public schs. Mgr., Solid State Music, Santa Clara, Calif., 1975-77; founder, pres. Hobby World Electronics, Northridge, Calif., 1977-79; owner, pres. Calif. Computer Systems Co., Sunnyvale, 1979—, Solid State Micro Tech., Santa Clara, 1978—. Served with USN, 1971-75. Office: 250 Caribbean Dr Sunnyvale CA 94086

BURGUN, J. ARMAND, architect; b. Rochester, Pa., Nov. 19, 1925; s. Paul John and Wilda (Whitehill) B.; B.Arch., Columbia, 1950; m. Muriel Ann DePowel, Dec. 30, 1944; children—Douglas Armand, Bruce Eric. Designer Ferrenz & Taylor, architects, N.Y.C., 1950-55; asst. dir. N.Y. State Joint Hosp. Planning Commn., Albany, 1955-60; asso. Rogers Burgun Shahine & Deschler, architects, N.Y.C., 1960-63, partner, 1963—. Archtl. cons. Hosp. Council of Greater N.Y., N.Y.C., 1957—, USPHS, VA; mem. Pres.'s Com. on Mental Retardation, Joint Commn. Accreditation Hosps. chmn. Dads Club, Pleasantville, 1962. Spl. lectr. Grad Sch. Med. Adminstrn., N.Y. Med. Coll. Served to lt. comdr. USCG, 1942-44. Decorated Purple Heart. Mem. A.I.A., N.Y. Soc. Architects, N.Y. State Assn. Architects, Am. Hosp. Assn., Nat. Fire Protection Assn. (dir., chmn. bd.), Internat. Hosp. Fedn., Am. Assn. for Hosp. Planning (pres.), N.Y. Bldg. Congress, Res. Officers Assn. Clubs: Winged Foot Country, Columbia University, Union League. Author: Handbook—Hospital Construction, 1958; Institutional Fires, 1977; also articles in field. Home: 235 Manville Rd Pleasantville NY 10570 Office: 521 Fifth Ave New York NY 10175

BURICK, MARY FRANCES, govt. ofcl.; b. Youngstown, Ohio, Dec. 22, 1952; d. Joseph and Carol Marie (Vlasic) B.; B.A. in Econs., Youngstown State U., 1975; M.A. in Econs., U. Okla., 1980. Fin. analyst examiner Ohio Div. Bank Supervision, Columbus, 1975; liquidator FDIC, Cleve., 1975—. Mem. Nat. Assn. Bus. Economists, Am. Mgmt. Assn., Am. Soc. Profl. and Exec. Women, Nat. Assn. Female Execs. Roman Catholic. Home: 931 Dravis Ave Girard OH 44420 Office: 550 17th St NW Washington DC 20429

BURK, JACK ANDREW, investment co. exec.; b. Springfield, Tenn., Mar. 19, 1935; s. Andrew Jackson and Elizabeth Ethelyne (Revels) B.; student Central Bible Inst., Springfield, Mo., 1953-54, So. Calif. Coll., Costa Mesa, 1955; student San Fernando Valley Coll., 1956; m. Alice Jean Jackson, Apr. 24, 1965; children—Teresa Lynn, Cheryl Ninette, Loren Dwayne. With Rocketdyne div. N.Am. Aviation Santa Susana Rocket Test sect., 1959-65; with Equity Funding Corp., 1965-73, area. v.p. So. Calif., Century City, 1970-71, v.p., resident mgr., Tarzana, Calif., 1972-73; founder, pres. Preferred Exec. Programs Inc., Woodland Hills, Calif., 1973-76; adv. com. Am. Pacific Life Ins. Co., San Rafael, Calif., 1973-76; mktg. officer Unimarc, Ltd., San Rafael, Calif., 1975-76; dir. fin. affairs Peoples Found., Fresno, Calif., 1977—. Mem. Nat. Assn. Securities Dealers, Nat. Assn. Life Underwriters, Nat. Assn. Charitable Estate Counselors, Internat. Assn. Fin. Planners. Republican. Home: 9391 E Ellery Fresno CA 93612

BURK, WILLIAM CHARLES, ry. co. exec.; b. Beaumont, Tex., Aug. 19, 1921; s. John Leonard and Dona Gertrude (Robinson) B.; student Central State Coll., Edmond, Okla., 1939-42, U. So. Calif., 1955, Cornell U., 1962; m. Mary Irene Meyer, Aug. 19, 1945; children—John Paul, Donald William, Mary Catherine. With Santa Fe Ry., 1946—, system photographer, Los Angeles, 1946-47, spl. pub. relations rep., Chgo., 1947-53, Topeka, 1953-61; mgr. pub. relations, Chgo., 1961-73, v.p. pub. relations, 1973—; past pres. Pub. Relations Clinic, Chgo., now mem. Trustee William Allen White Found. U. Kans. Served with USCGR, 1942-46. Recipient award Future Farmers Am., 1968. Mem. Pub. Relations Soc. Am., R.R. Pub. Relations Assn., Soc. Profl. Journalists, Am. Agrl. Editors Frat., Chgo. Headline Club, Chgo. Press Club, Kansas City Press Club, San Diego Press Club, Nat. Press Club, Alpha Tau Alpha. Republican. Episcopalian. Clubs: Masons, Shriners; Athletic Assn., Western Ry.; Michigan Shores. Home: 923 Cornell St Wilmette IL 60091 Office: 80 E Jackson St Chicago IL 60604

BURKE, ALEXANDER JAMES, JR., publishing co. exec.; b. N.Y.C., Apr. 24, 1931; s. Alexander James and Josephine Eleanor (McGrath) B.; B.A. cum laude, Holy Cross Coll., 1953; M.A., Fordham U., 1956; m. Suzanne Jeanne Gatti, June 25, 1955; children—James, Brian, Christopher, Nancy, Thomas, Matthew, Alexander John. Prof. English, Fordham U., 1953-56, 59-60; editor W. H. Sadlier Co., N.Y.C., 1959-60; mgr. Doubleday Bookstores, N.Y.C., 1952; with McGraw-Hill Book Co., N.Y.C., 1960—, gen. mgr., 1969-70, v.p., 1970-73, exec. v.p., 1973-74, pres., 1974—, now also chief exec. officer; dir. McGraw-Hill Ryerson, Ltd.; bd. dirs., exec. com. Book Industry Study Group, 1976-79; mem. adv. bd. Center for the Book, 1978-80. Bd. dirs. Adult Edn. Council St. Louis, 1965, Commn. on Radio and TV, Cath. Archdiocese St. Louis, 1968-72. Served with USAF, 1956-59. Mem. Assn. Am. Pubs. (dir., exec. com. 1978-81), Am. Soc. Curriculum Devel., Nat. Council Tchrs. English, Alpha Sigma Nu. Roman Catholic. Home: 455 Ryder Rd Manhasset NY 11030 Office: 1221 Ave of Americas New York City NY 10020

BURKE, JAMES EDWARD, bus. exec.; b. Rutland, Vt., Feb. 28, 1925; s. James Francis and Mary (Barnett) B.; B.S. in Econs., Holy Cross Coll., 1947; M.B.A., Harvard U., 1949; m. Alice Eubank, Apr. 27, 1957; children—Mary Clotilde, James Charles. Sales rep., then asst. brand mgr., brand mgr. Procter & Gamble, 1949-52; product dir. Johnson & Johnson, 1953-54, dir. new products, 1954-57, dir. advt. and merchandising, 1957-58, v.p. advt. and merchandising, 1958-62, gen. mgr. Baby Products Co. div., 1962-64, exec. v.p. mktg., 1964-65, gen. mgr. Johnson & Johnson Products Co. div., 1965-66, pres. 1966-70, chmn. bd., 1970-71, corporate dir., mem. exec. com., 1973-76, dir., mem. exec. com. parent co., 1965—, vice-chmn. exec. com., from 1971, chief exec. officer, chmn. bd. parent co., 1976—. Mem. vis. com. bd. overseers Harvard Coll. Med. Sch. and Sch. Dental Medicine; chmn. bd. United Negro Coll. Fund; trustee WNET/Channel 13; bd. govs., mem. exec. com. United Way Am.; mem. bus. com. Mus. Modern Art; trustee Council of Ams.; mem. Bus. Com. Arts. Served as ensign USN, World War II; PTO. Mem. Conf. Bd., Grocery Mfrs. Am. (dir.). Office: 501 George St New Brunswick NJ 08901

BURKE, JAMES LEO, paper mfg. co. exec.; b. Lewiston, Maine, Nov. 15, 1938; s. Francis John and Margaret Irene (Young) B.; B.S. in Chem. Engring., U. Maine, 1961; M.S. Inst. Paper Chemistry, Laurence U., 1963, Ph.D., 1966; postgrad. Harvard U. Bus. Sch., 1977; m. JoAnn Mary Joosten, May 15, 1965; children—Kelly Ann, Robert Kieth. With Mead Corp., 1966-78, mill mgr., Virginal, Belgium, 1973-74, v.p. mfg. forms div., Chillicothe, Ohio, 1975-78; v.p., gen. mgr. Garden State Paper Co., Pomona, Calif., 1978—, pres. subs. Great Western Fiber, Inc. Bd. dirs. Salvation Army, Chillcothe, 1977-78. Served with USCG, 1956-57. Mem. TAPPI, So. Calif. Mfg. Assn., Tau Beta Pi, Phi Kappa Phi. Republican. Roman Catholic. Home: 606 Delaware Dr Claremont CA 91711 Office: PO Box 2364 Pomona CA 91766

BURKE, JOHN MILES, mfg. co. exec.; b. Glendale, Calif., Nov. 5, 1938; s. Avery John and Dorice Katherine (Davidson) B.; B.A., Claremont Men's Coll., 1961; B.S., Stanford U., 1961; M.B.A., U. Calif. at Los Angeles, 1965, Ph.D., 1968; m. Barbara Dinsmore Gibbs, Feb. 23, 1963; 1 dau., Elena Katherine. Corporate planning staff Litton Industries, Beverly Hills, Calif., 1968-70, dir. bus. devel., machine tool group, Hartford, Conn., 1970-72; gen. mgr. Heim div. Rockwell Internat., Fairfield, Conn., 1972-74, gen. mgr. Admiral Audio div., Chgo., 1974-76; pres. MR Gasket div. W.R. Grace Co., Cleve., 1976-78, automotive group v.p., 1977-78; pres., chief exec. officer Woodhill Permatex group Loctite Corp., Cleve., 1978—. Ford doctoral fellow, 1965-68. Home: 172 Aurora St Hudson OH 44236 Office: 4450 Cranwood Ct Cleveland OH 44128

BURKE, PAUL STANLEY, JR., ins. co. exec.; b. St. Paul, Aug. 5, 1926; s. Paul Stanley and Loretta Josephine (Bertrang) B.; B.B.A., U. Minn., 1956; m. Irene Marie Wagner, Apr. 22, 1950; children—John, Steven, Nancy, Lawrence, Linda, James, Thomas. Regional mgr. Minn. Mutual Life Ins. Co., Los Angeles, 1950-61; pres. Paul Burke & Assos., Inc., ins. consultants and adminstrs., Mpls., 1961-73, Trust Life Ins. Co. Am., Scottsdale, Ariz., 1968-73, Purchase & Discount Buying Service Corp., 1977-79; chmn. bd. Larson & Burke, Inc., 1980—; dir. Lindbom & Assos., Inc., St. Paul. Pres., Boys Clubs of Mpls., 1974-76. Served with USAAF, 1944-47. Mem. Pilots Internat. Assn. (pres. 1966-73). Republican. Roman Catholic. Clubs: Mpls. Athletic, N. Am. Hunting (pres. 1978—), Interlachen Country, Olympic Hills Country. Home: 27 Circle W Edina MN 55436

BURKE, RICHARD WENDELL, fin. exec.; b. Phila., June 16, 1930; s. Wendell Lawrence and Sara Mary (McCullough) B.; pre-standard and standard certs. Am. Inst. Banking, 1954-61; NCO cert. Bankers Bus. Devel. Inst., 1970: m. Eleanor B. Aurand, Apr. 6, 1957; 1 son, Richard Wendell. Br. capt. Phila. Evening Bull., 1944-48, field auditor, 1948, br. mgr., 1948-49; clk. Nat. Bank of Germantown, 1949-54, proof operator, 1950-51, supr. proof dept., 1951-54; with Girard Bank, Phila., 1953-78, regional v.p. S.W. region, 1973, N.W. region, 1974, region I, 1976-78; regional adminstr. New Castle County, Farmers Bank of Del., Newark, 1978—. Dir., treas. Manoa Businessmen's Assn., 1963-66. Served with USMC, 1952-54. Recipient B'nai B'rith Citizenship citation, 1964. Mem. Am. Inst. Banking. Presbyterian. Clubs: Lions (treas., dir. 1970-72), Rotary (treas., dir. 1961-63). Home: 154 Plymouth Rd Springfield PA 19064 Office: 126 E Main St Newark DE 19711

BURKETT, HELEN LOUISE, med. service orgn. exec.; b. Vintondale, Pa., June 14, 1922; d. John Joseph and Helen (Balogh) Touris; B.A., Altoona (Pa.) Sch. Arts and Music, 1940; postgrad. George Washington U., 1953-56; m. Harding Theodore Burkett, Oct. 10, 1940; children—Helen Louise, Harding Theodore, Lynda S., Sallie L. Asst. supr. ARC, Washington, 1943-45; supr. ins. dept. George Washington U. Med. Center, Washington, 1953-55, billing office supr., 1955-58, asso. mgr. accounts, 1958-62, asso. mgr. credit dept., 1962-69, mgr. patient fin. admissions, 1969-75, exec. adminstrv. asst., 1975—, asst. dir. fin. ops., 1975—. Chmn. United Way, Washington, 1970; asst. Fairlington council Girl Scouts U.S.A., 1965-66. Mem. Credit Consumer Assn. (dir.), Am. Guild Patient Account Mgrs. (v.p. 1974-75), Soc. Certified Credit Consumer Execs., Nat. Found. Consumer Credit, Credit Women Internat., Am. Soc. Notaries. Club: Toastmasters Internat. (certified, pres. 1976-77, area gov. dist. 36 Region VII, Area XX, 1977-78, Able Toastmasters award 1977, Disting. Toastmistress award 1978). Home: 2931 Lawrence Dr Falls Church VA 22042 Office: 901 23d St NW Washington DC 20037

BURKEY, LEE MELVILLE, lawyer; b. Beach, N.D., Mar. 21, 1914; s. L. M. and Mina (Horner) B.; B.A., U. Ill., 1936, M.A., 1938; J.D. with honors, John Marshall Law Sch., 1943; m. Lorraine Burghardt, June 11, 1938; 1 son, Lee Melville. Tchr., Princeton, Ill., 1937-38, Harvey, Ill., 1938-43; admitted to Ill. bar, 1944; atty. Office of Solicitor, U.S. Dept. Labor, 1944-51; lectr. bus. law Roosevelt Coll., 1948-52; partner Asher, Gubbins and Segall, 1951-65, Asher, Greenfield, Gubbins & Segall, 1965-74, Asher, Greenfield, Goodstein, Pavalon & Segall, Ltd., 1974—; dir. LaGrange Fed. Savs. & Loan Assn. Trustee, Village of LaGrange (Ill.), 1962-68, mayor, 1968-73, village atty., 1973—; mem. Northeastern Ill. Planning Commn., 1969, pres., 1970-71; bd. dirs. Plymouth Pl., 1973—, Better Bus. Bur. Met. Chgo., 1975—; mem. corp. bd. homeland ministries United Ch. Christ, 1978—. Mem. Am., Ill., Chgo. bar assns., SAR, S.R., Order of John Marshall. Congregationalist. Clubs: LaGrange Country; Masons. Contbr. articles to profl. jours. Home: 926 S Catherine LaGrange IL 60525 Office: 228 N LaSalle St Chicago IL 60601

BURKLAND, SKOTT BARRE, exec. search cons. co. exec.; b. Phila., May 25, 1942; s. O. Jack and Virginia C. (Boston) B.; A.B. in Polit. Sci., Dickinson Coll., 1964; postgrad. in bus. Drexel U., 1964-68; children—Deborah, Julie, Laura. Fin. analyst E.I. Du Pont de Nemours & Co., Wilmington, Del., 1964-66; personnel rep. W.R. Grace & Co., N.Y.C., 1966-68; personnel officer 1st Nat. City Bank, N.Y.C., 1968-69; v.p. personnel Singer Co., N.Y.C., 1969-74; pres. Skott/Edwards Consultants, N.Y.C., 1974—. Vice chmn. Mountain Lakes (N.J.) Planning Bd. Served with arty. U.S. Army, 1965-71. Mem. Am. Mktg. Assn. Republican. Office: 250 Park Ave New York NY 10017

BURKS, WILLIAM FENTON, assn. exec.; b. Springfield, Mo., June 13, 1930; s. Theron T. and Ethyl (Frieze) B.; A.B. in Econs., U. Mo., 1952; m. Susanne Martin, Sept. 27, 1964; children—William Randolph, Julie Ann. Mgr. loan dept. Farm & Home Savs. Assn., Kansas City, Mo., 1954-61; v.p. People's Savs. Assn., Toledo, 1961-64; exec. v.p., mng. officer Home Savs. & Loan Assn., Albuquerque, 1964-67; pres., dir. Am. Savs. and Loan Assn., Albuquerque, 1967—; mem. adv. council Fed. Home Loan Bank; past pres. League Insured Savs. and Loan Assns. N.Mex., 1971-72; vice chmn. bd. dirs. Fed. Home Loan Bank of Little Rock 9th Dist., 1976-78, dir., 1973-78. Vice chmn. N.Mex. State Fair Commn., 1979—; treas., bd. dirs. Albuquerque Little Theatre, 1973-77. Served to col., USMCR, 1954—. Mem. U.S. League Savs. Assn., Albuquerque C. of C., Albuquerque Mortgage Bankers Assn., Am. Rose Soc., Bldg. Contractors Assn. N.Mex., Exec. Assn. Greater Albuquerque, Friend of Vista Sandia Hosp., Internat. Connoisseurs of Green and Red Chili, Marine Corps Res. Officers Assn., Navy League, Res. Officers Assn., Albuquerque Home Builders Assn. (asso.), Soc. Real Estate Appraisers (asso.), Albuquerque C. of C. (past dir.), Execs. Assn. Greater Albuquerque (former pres.). Clubs: Albuquerque Press, Masons, U. New Mex. Lobo (past v.p. past dir.). Office: 2400 Louisiana Blvd NE Albuquerque NM 87110

BURLEIGH, HUGH TAGGART, mfg. co. exec.; b. Franklin, N.H., Jan. 11, 1929; s. Joseph and Alice Josephine (Taggart) B.; cert. machine design, Wentworth Inst., Boston, 1948; B.A. in Econs., U. N.H., 1958; M.A. in Indsl. Mgmt. Programming candidate Yale U., 1960; m. Carol Louise Nickerson, June 29, 1957; children—Diane, Susan, Lawrence. With Singer Co., 1958-73, pres. Singer Industries France, Paris, 1969-73; v.p. mfg. Robert Bosch Corp., Charleston, S.C., 1973-78; pres. Hilti Industries, Inc., Tulsa, 1979—. Mem. Charleston Work Edn. Com., 1976-78, Charleston Devel. Bd., 1974-78, S.C. Govt. Indsl. Edn. Council, 1976-78; bd. dirs. S.C. C. of C., 1978. Served with AUS, 1951-53. Mem. Soc. Mfg. Engrs. Republican. Unitarian. Club: Tulsa Rotary. Home: 1336 E 26th Pl Tulsa OK 74114 Office: 5400 S 122 E Ave Tulsa OK 74145

BURLINSON, JOHN JOSEPH, JR., film equipment co. exec.; b. N.Y.C., Dec. 26, 1930; s. John Joseph and Alice Grace (Kenny) B.; B.S., Fordham U., 1953, M.A., 1959; m. Martha Marie Quigley, Dec. 29, 1954; children—Alice Gertrude, John Joseph, Monica Marie. Prodn. asst. Breyer Ice Cream Co., N.Y.C., 1954-57; salesman Henry Regnery Co., N.Y.C., Chgo., 1957-64; v.p. Quigley Pub. Co., N.Y.C., 1964-70; mgmt. exec. Nat. Screen Service Co., N.Y.C., 1970-75; gen. mgr. Nat. Theatre Supply, 1975—; v.p., gen. mgr. EPRAD, Inc., Toledo, 1977—, chief exec. officer, 1980—. Bd. dirs., sec. Found. Motion Picture Pioneers; mem. Cardinal's Com. Cath. Charities N.Y. Mem. Theatre Equipment and Supply Mfrs. Assn. (treas., dir. 1967—), Theatre Equipment Assn. (v.p. 1972—). Am. Soc. Assn. Execs., So. Soc. Motion Picture and TV Engrs., Brit. Kinematograph Soc. Clubs: Variety of N.Y.; Winged Foot Golf (Mamaroneck, N.Y.); Toledo Country, Rotary (Toledo). Contbr. articles to profl. jours. Home: 2617 Juniper Dr Toledo OH 43614 Office: 123 W Woodruff St Toledo OH 43620

BURMAN, ALDEN HAYWARD, nursing home exec.; b. Bellingham, Wash., Nov. 18, 1919; s. John A. and Winifred C. (Larson) B.; student health care adminstrn. U. Wash., 1967-68; m. Winifred L. Hartman, Mar. 16, 1951; children—Ronald Alden, Richard, James David, Shirley Ann. Pres., Marine View Nursing Home, Inc., Federal Way, Wash., 1951—; pres. Federal Way Convalescent Center, Inc., 1968—; pres., Parklane Convalescent Center, Inc., Aberdeen, Wash., 1969—; owner The Gallery gift and antique store, Ocean Shores, Wash., 1962—; v.p. Western Farms, Moses Lake, Wash.; owner Burmans Farm, Orting, Wash.; owner Afco Personnel Services, Buffalo and Seattle. Elder, Seventh Day Adventist Ch. Fellow Am. Coll. Nursing Home Adminstrs.; mem. Wash. State Health Facilities Assn. (state pres. 1962, bd. govs. 1961-65), Am. Nursing Home Assn. (bd. govs. 1962). Home: 424 N D St Tacoma WA 98403 Office: 29611 8th Ave SW Federal Way WA 98003

BURMAN, DAVID JAY, retail cons., educator; b. N.Y.C., June 11, 1938; s. Louis Robert and Frances B. (Cohen) B.; B.S., N.Y. U., 1961, M.S., 1962; M.P.A., Nova U., 1976; m. Luise L. Alterman, Aug. 23, 1964; children—Rona Susan, Michael Jonathan. Asst. gen. mdse. mgr. Gimbel's, N.Y.C. and Westchester, 1961-62; mgr. Ohrbach's, N.Y.C., 1962-63; pres. Merch-A-Matic, Bus. Cons., West Hartford, Conn., 1968—; asst. prof. bus. adminstrn. Central Conn. State Coll., New Britain, 1967—, also mem. Faculty Senate, dir. coop. edn.; adj. prof. bus. Tunxis Community Coll., Farmington, Conn., 1970—; adj. prof. Grad. Sch. Bus., U. Hartford; chmn. bd., dir. Vestamatic Enterprises, Inc., 1968-74. Pres., v.p. Beth-El Synagogue Asso. Mems., 1969-72; v.p. King Philip Sch. PTA, 1975—. Recipient Alexanders award for merchandising, 1962. Mem. Am. Mktg. Assn. (chpt. exec. v.p., named adv. of yr. coll. and univ. div.), Am. Soc. Pub. Adminstrn., Am. Collegiate Retailing Assn. (dir.), AAUP, Acad. Internat. Bus., Newcomen Soc. N.Am., Internat. Platform Assn., Am. Vocat. Assn., Am. Acad. Cons., U.S., West Hartford chambers commerce, Eta Mu Pi (nat. dir.), Pi Sigma Epsilon. Author: Downtown Cure Areas: Can They Survive?; monthly column Retail Thoughts; editor: Conn. Marketer. Home: 100 Mohawk Dr West Hartford CT 06117 Office: 1615 Stanley St New Britain CT 06050

BURNET, THORNTON WEST, mktg. exec.; b. Cin., Aug. 27, 1917; s. David and Agnes McClung (West) B.; B.S. in Commerce, U. Va., 1940; m. Mary Elizabeth Charlton, Aug. 14, 1948; 1 son, Thornton West. Asst. treas. Lincoln Service Corp., Washington, 1941-50, v.p., sec., 1950-59; v.p. mktg. Am. Finance Mgmt. Corp., Silver Spring, Md., 1959-76; v.p., treas., dir. Monet Constrn. Co., Fairfax, Va., 1962—; v.p. mktg. Am. Directory Service Agy., Silver Spring, 1976—; sec., dir. Worldwide Yellow Pages Service Co., Silver Spring, 1979—. Committeeman, Boy Scouts Am., 1945—. Pres. bd. trustees Fletcher Meml. Library, 1962. Served with AUS, 1940-43. Mem. Alpha Kappa Psi. Republican. Episcopalian (vestryman, past sr. warden). Home: 10800 Hunters Valley Rd Vienna VA 22180 Office: 35 Wisconsin Circle Chevy Chase MD 20015

BURNETT, CLAUDE HOWARD, railroad exec.; b. Maupin, Oreg., June 26, 1919; s. Melbourne L. and Daisy (Proost) B.; student U. Oreg., 1936-40; m. Evelyn J. Clarke, Aug. 18, 1943; children—Claudia B., Amanda L. With Union Pacific R.R., 1938—, asst. v.p. ops., Omaha, 1964-73, v.p. exec. dept., Portland, Oreg., 1973—; v.p. Oreg.-Wash. R.R. & Nav. Co.; dir. Fred Meyer, Inc., Portland Traction Co., Yakima Valley Transp. Co., DesChutes R.R. Ch., Mt. Hood R.R. Sr. v.p. Columbia Pacific council Boy Scouts Am., mem. nat. council; past pres. Tri County Community Council; bd. dirs., v.p. Portland Rose Festival Assn.; bd. dirs. Oreg. Hist. Soc., ARC, Portland-Sapporo (Japan) Sister City Com.; mem. adv. com. Portland Econ. Devel. Com.; chmn. adv. com. Portland Civic Auditorium. Mem. Nat. Alliance Businessmen (past chmn. Region X), Portland C. of C. (past chmn. bd.), World Affairs Council Oreg., Portland Com. on Fgn. Relations, Inst. Managerial and Profl. Women (dir.), Oreg. Ind. Coll. Found. (dir.), Assn. Portland Progress (dir.), NCCJ (dir.), Oreg. Symphony Soc., Portland Opera Assn. Republican. Episcopalian. Clubs: Waverley Country, Arlington, Portland City, Seattle Rainier, Rotary, Spokane. Home: 2221 SW 1st Ave Apt 2024 Portland OR 97201 Office: 921 SW Washington St Portland OR 97205

BURNETT, WILLIAM EARL, JR., ins. co. exec.; b. Louisville, Feb. 15, 1927; s. William E. and Bessie (Davis) B.; B.S., U. Louisville, 1949; m. Margaret Alberta Erny Crenshaw, Mar. 21, 1975; children by previous marriage—Bruce E., Suzanne L., John A. Treas., Louisville Fire & Marine Ins. Co., 1949-54; asst. sec.-treas. Ky. Ins. Agy., Lexington, 1955-59; sec.-treas. Ky. Central Life Ins. Co., Lexington, 1959-74, exec. v.p., 1975-76, pres., 1976—, mem. exec. and fin. coms., 1961—, dir., 1961—; pres. Ky. Central Life Ins. Co. and Property and Casualty Co. Subsidiaries, dir. Central Bank, Lexington, Peoples Comml. Bank, Winchester, Ky., Richmond (Ky.) Bank, First Nat. Bank, Georgetown, Ky., Ky. Fin. Co., Lexington; sec., dir. Triangle Found. Mem. Lexington Econ. Devel. Commn.; bd. dirs., treas. United Way of the Bluegrass; mem. Bluegrass council Boy Scouts Am.; mem. adv. council Coll. Bus. and Econs., U. Ky. Served with U.S. Army, 1945-47. Fellow U. Ky. Mem. Ins. Accts. and Statisticians Assn., Ky. C. of C., Lexington C. of C., Life Officers Mgmt. Assn., Am. Mgmt. Assn., Nat. Assn. Life Underwriters, Georgetown Coll. Assos. Presbyterian. Clubs: Lafayette, Shriners, Masons, Scottish Rite. Office: Kincaid Towers 300 W Vine St Lexington KY 40508

BURNETTE, JANIECE LEOLA, artist; b. Los Angeles, May 14, 1926; d. Walter William and Betty Olga (Lester) Burnette; B.S., U. So. Calif., 1950, M.S. in L.S., 1964, M.S. in Instructional Tech., 1970; student art Sorbonne, U. Munich (W. Ger.). Tchr., artist Los Angeles public schs., 1955—; pres. Ars Aristos, art design, Huntington Beach, Calif., 1972—, head designer stained glass mosaics, 1972—; prin. works include Angel and Saint, 1955, Fleeing Angel, 1967, Angel at the Organ, 1967, goblet with 2 lemons, 1978, Angels in Flight, 1980, Princess Balna, 1979, others. Mem. Gifts and Decorative Accessories Assn., Newport Harbor Art Mus. Republican. Address: 9571 Bay Meadow Dr Huntington Beach CA 92646

BURNISON, BOYD EDWARD, lawyer; b. Arnolds Park, Iowa, Dec. 12, 1934; s. Boyd William and Lucile (Harnden) B.; B.S., Iowa State U., 1957; J.D., U. Calif. at Berkeley, 1961; children—Erica LaFore, Alison Katherine. Admitted to Calif. bar, 1962, U.S. Supreme Ct. bar, 1971; dep. county counsel Yolo County (Calif.), 1962-65; counsel Davis and Woodland (Calif.) Unified Sch. Dists., 1962-65; asso. firm Steel & Arostegui, Marysville, Calif., 1965-66, St. Sure, Moore, Hoyt, Oakland, 1966-70; partner St. Sure, Moore, Hoyt & Sizoo, Oakland and San Francisco, 1970-75; v.p., dir. firm Crosby, Heafy, Roach & May, P.C., Oakland, 1975—; counsel Easter Seal Soc. Crippled Children and Adults, 1966-75, Easter Seal Found. Alameda County (Calif.), 1974-79. Adviser, Berkeley YMCA, 1971—, Yolo County YMCA, 1962-65; bd. dirs. Easter Seal Soc. Crippled Children and Adults of Alameda County, 1972-75, Yolo County YMCA, 1965, Moot Ct. Bd., U. Calif., 1960-61; trustee Easter Seal Found. Alameda County, 1975-79, hon. trustee, 1979—. Mem. Am. (equal employment opportunity law com. 1972—), Alameda County (dir. 1981—, mem. fee arbitration, memberships coms., mem. law office econs. com. 1972-78, chmn., 1975-77, mem. directory com., chmn. 1973-75, 80-81, mem. nominating com. 1974-79), Yolo County (sec. 1965), Yuba Sutter bar assns., State Bar Calif., Bar Assn. San Francisco, Boalt Hall Law Sch., U. Calif. at Berkeley, Iowa State U. alumni assns., Pi Kappa Alpha, Phi Delta Phi. Democrat. Clubs: Rotary, Oakland Athletic. Home: 3535 Old Mountain View Rd Lafayette CA 94549 Office: 900 Park Plaza Bldg 1939 Harrison St Oakland CA 94612

BURNLEY, WINSTON TOLBERT, graphic co. exec.; b. Atlanta, July 20, 1913; s. Richard Tolbert and Alzie Pearl (Grizzard) B.; student Emory U., 1929-33; m. Gladys Laurene Virgil, Dec. 15, 1973; children—Richard Norman, Linda Kaye Burnley Smith, Susan Rebecca, Candace Ann, Rita Jamieson. Staff mgr. real estate dept. Chgo. Herald & Examiner, Los Angeles Times, Georgian Am. and Atlanta Constitution, 1935-42; real estate salesman Gordon Bennett Real Estate Co., also Dimmitt-Rickhoff-Bayer Real Estate Co., 1944-55; sales mgr. Midwest Regions Assos., St. Louis, 1955-66; dir. sales Dynamic Graphics, Inc., Peoria, Ill., 1967-80. Lic. pvt. pilot. Mem. Phi Delta Theta. Republican. Methodist. Home: 2215 Cypress Gardens Blvd Winter Haven FL 33880

BURNS, ALEX ANDREW, life sci. co. exec.; b. Monroe, La., Sept. 15, 1940; s. Alex Andrew and Ollie M. (Hamilton) B.; B.S., So. U., 1962; postgrad. (NIH fellow) State U. N.Y., Buffalo, 1966-67. Asst. cancer research scientist Roswell Park Meml. Inst., Buffalo, 1964-69; mgr. cell culture prodn. Asso. Biomedic Systems, Buffalo, 1969-71, asst. to pres., 1971-73, v.p. corp. devel., 1973-74, exec. v.p., 1974-75, pres., 1975—, also dir.; chmn. bd., pres., dir. HTI Corp., Buffalo, 1975—; cons. Inst. for Sci. and Social Accountability, Washington, 1975—; mem. human subjects com. State U. N.Y., Buffalo, 1976—. Served with U.S. Army, 1962-64. Mem. Am. Soc. Microbiology, Tissue Culture Assn., Internat. Assn. Plant Tissue Culture, Buffalo Urban League, Alpha Phi Alpha. Home: 525 Humboldt Pkwy Buffalo NY 14208 Office: 872 Main St Buffalo NY 14202

BURNS, BARBARA M., editor; b. Evanston, Ill., July 4, 1929; d. Martin Hughes and Miriam Miller; B.A., Smith Coll., 1951; postgrad. U. London, 1974. Researcher Presdl. Appointments Office, White House, 1959; sec. to Senator Jacob Javits of N.Y., 1959-60; exec. asst. to asst. chmn. Republican Nat. Com., 1960-62, adminstrv. asst. to chmn., 1962-63; spl. asst. to chmn. John F. Kennedy Center, Washington, 1963-66; dir. Confs. for Corp. Execs., also editor SAIS Rev., Sch. Advanced Internat. Studies, Johns Hopkins U., 1966-69; dep. asst. sec. consumer services HEW, 1969-73; asst. to sec. interior and dir. internat. programs Dept. Interior, 1973-77; Washington editor Bus. and Society Rev., 1978—; mem. nominating com. for bd. govs. Am. Stock Exchange, 1972; mem. consumer council Am. Nat. Standards Inst., 1970-73, vice chmn., 1972-73; adv. com. Assn. Consumer Research, 1972, dir., 1972-73. Mem. Exec. Women in Govt. (a founder), Washington Jr. League (past dir.). Republican. Episcopalian. Clubs: 1925 F St., Sulgrave (Washington).

BURNS, DAN, mfg. co. exec.; b. Auburn, Calif., Sept. 10, 1925; s. William and Edith Lynn (Johnson) B.; 1 son, Dan. Dir. materials Menasco Mfg. Co., 1951-56; v.p., gen. mgr. Hufford Corp., 1956-58; pres. Hufford div. Siegler Corp., 1958-61; v.p. Siegler Corp., 1961-62, Lear Siegler, Inc., 1962-64; pres., dir. Electrada Corp., Culver City, Calif., 1964; now pres., chief exec. officer Sargent Industries and related cos.; chmn. chief exec. officer Arlington Industries, Inc. Served to capt. U.S. Army, 1941-47; aide-de-camp Gen. George C. Marshall. Clubs: Los Angeles Country (Los Angeles). Home: 10851 Chalon Rd Los Angeles CA 90024 Office: Sargent Industries 1901 Bldg Century City Los Angeles CA 90067

BURNS, GROVER PRESTON, physicist; b. nr. Hurricane, W.Va., Apr. 25, 1918; s. Joshua Alexander and Virgie (Meadows) B.; A.B., Marshall U., 1937; M.S., W.Va. U., 1941; student Duke U., 1939-40, U. Md., 1946; D.Sc. (hon.), Colo. State Christian Coll., 1973; m. Julia Belle Foster, Nov. 4, 1941; children—Julia Corinne Burns Jefferson, Grover Preston. Tchr. high sch., W.Va., 1937-40; fellow W.Va. U., 1940-41; instr. physics U. Conn., 1941-42; asst. prof. Miss. State Coll., 1942-44, acting head physics dept., 1944-45; asst. prof. physics Tex. Tech. Coll., 1946; asso. prof. math. Marshall U., 1946-47; research physicist Naval Research Lab., Washington, 1947-48; asst. prof., chmn. physics dept. Mary Washington Coll., 1948-68; asso. prof., chmn., 1968-69; supr. statis. analysis sect. Am. Viscose div. FMC Corp., 1950-67; pres. Burns Enterprises Inc., Fredericksburg, Va., 1958—; mathematician Naval Surface Weapons Center, 1967—. Served with AUS, 1945-46. Mem. Phys. Soc., AAUP, Am. Assn. Physics Tchrs., N.Y. Acad. Scis. Reviewer: Am. Jour. Physics; contbr. articles to profl. jours. Patentee in field of thermometers, conductivity testers, star finders. Home: 600 Virginia St Fredericksburg VA 22401

BURNS, JAMES WILLIAM, power corp. exec.; b. Winnipeg, Man., Can., Dec. 27, 1929; s. Charles William and Helen Gladys (Mackay) B.; B.Comm., U. Man., 1951; M.B.A., Harvard U., 1953; m. Barbara Mary Copeland, Aug. 12, 1953; children—James F.C., Martha J., Alan W. With Great-West Life Assurance Co., Winnipeg., Man., Can., 1953, with mktg. div., 1953-70, dir., pres., chief exec. officer, 1971-79, chmn., dir., 1979—; pres. Power Corp. of Can., Montreal, Que., 1979—; pres., dir. Trans-Canada Corp. Fund, Shawinigan Industries Ltd.; dir. Bathurst Paper Ltd., Consol.-Bathurst Inc., Genstar Ltd., IBM Canada Ltd., Investors Group, Montreal Trust Co., The CSL Group Inc. Trustee, Conf. Board, N.Y., Conf. Board in Europe, N. Am. Wildlife Found.; bd. dirs. Conf. Board in Can., Ottawa, Council for Bus. and the Arts in Can., Can. Council Christians and Jews. Hon. lt. col. Queen's Own Cameron Highlanders in Can. Clubs: St. Charles Country, Manitoba (Winnipeg); Albany (Toronto); Mount-Royal, Mount-Bruno Country (Montreal). Office: Power Corp of Canada 759 Victoria Sq Montreal PQ H2Y 2K4 Canada

BURNS, JOHN SPINNEY, bus. exec.; b. Evanston, Ill., June 30, 1943; s. John Lawrence and Beryl Mignon (Spinney) B.; A.B., Princeton U., 1966; postgrad. Harvard U., 1968; m. Dana Brown, July 15, 1972; 1 son, Geoffrey. Treas., Min-a-matic Inc., Absecon, N.J., 1968-69; exec. v.p. fin. Culligan Communications, Inc., N.Y.C., 1969-70; v.p. fin. Seaboard Am. Corp., N.Y.C., 1970-73; asst. v.p. Citibank, N.Y.C., 1973-75; pres., prin. Burns Aviation Inc., Newburgh, N.Y., 1975-77; pres. Interair, Inc., Greenwich, Conn., 1977—. Club: Round Hill (Greenwich). Home: Chateau Ridge Rd Greenwich CT 06830 Office: 32 Porchuk Rd Greenwich CT 06830

BURNS, LARRY DEMONT, controller; b. Greenville S.C., June 20, 1945; s. John Baylus Alston and Isabel Myrtle (Davis) B.; A.A., North Greenville Coll., 1965; B.A., William Carey Coll., 1967, B.S., 1970; student U. So. Miss., 1965, 69-70; postgrad. LaSalle Extension U., 1973-77; m. Norma Elaine Mills, Mar. 2, 1968; children—Rachelle DeLaine, Ashley DeMont. Tchr. Am. govt. and econs. Picayune (Miss.) Meml. High Sch., 1967-70; claims adjuster, claims adjuster trainer Nationwide Mut. Ins. Co., Greenville, 1970-72; accountant Lackey, Ferrell & Harris, C.P.A.'s, Greenville, 1972-73; div. controller Jim Pinnix Homes, S.C. div. Pinnix Corp., Greenville, 1973-75; internal auditor, fin. analyst Pinnix Corp., Greensboro, N.C., 1975-76, asst. to controller, corp. accountant, 1976-77, controller, asst. to pres., asst. treas., 1977-78; sec., treas. Addison Industries, Inc. (Ala.), 1977-78, B.C.H., Inc., Danville, Va., 1977-78; controller, sec., treas. High Point Sprinkler Co. (N.C.), 1978—; controller Hemisphere Homes Corp., Greensboro, 1976-78. Bd. dirs., treas. Battle Forest Village Townhouse Assn., 1976-79. Mem. Nat. Assn. Accts. (chpt. dir. 1980-81), Am. Accounting Assn., Am. Soc. Notaries, Alpha Psi Omega, Phi Beta Lambda. Republican. Methodist. Club: Wendover Hills Swim, Inc. (dir., asst. treas. 1980—). Home: 500 Hayworth Circle High Point NC 27262 Office: US Hwy 29-70S PO Box 2478 High Point NC 27261

BURNS, MICHAEL EDWARD, sales and mktg. exec.; b. Long Beach, Calif., July 11, 1943; s. Troy Alan and Vivian Frances (Clay) B.; B.A., Western State Coll., Colo., 1966; grad. Sales and Mktg. Exec. Program, U. Va., 1977; m. Jane Kathleen Slothower, Apr. 18, 1965; 1 dau., Heather Anne. Leader profl. ski patrol and mountain rescue Crested Butte (Colo.) Ski Area, 1968-70; pres. O Be Joyful, Inc., Charlottesville, Va., 1970—; v.p., co-founder The Plow and Hearth, Madison, Va., 1979—; chmn. bd. Blue Ridge Mountain Sports, Charlottesville, 1979. Judge, Town of Crested Butte, 1968-70; mem. chmn.'s com. U.S. Senatorial Bus. Adv. Bd. Mem. Eastern Outdoor Rep. Assn., Inc., Sigma Pi. Republican. Home and Office: 850 Emerson Dr Charlottesville VA 22901

BURNS, RANDY EUGENE, real estate exec.; b. Rockford, Ill., July 30, 1952; s. Robert Eugene and Evelyn Ruth B.; student N.W. Mo. State U., 1971-74; B.P.S. in Criminal Justice, SUNY, Utica, 1976; m. Dixie L. Jones, July 14, 1979. With Century 21, Michael Shinn & Assos., Denver, 1976—, dir. mktg. and investments, 1977—, instr. mktg. fin. and investment cons., 1977-0. Served with USAF, 1974-76. Mem. Nat. Assn. Realtors, Colo. Assn. Realtors, Denver Bd. Realtors (Disting. Sales award 1978), Sales and Mktg. Execs. Denver. Home: 292 S Salem Ct Aurora CO 80012 Office: Century 21 Michael Shinn & Assos 6630 E Hampden Ave Denver CO 80224

BURNS, RICHARD CARLTON, paper products exec.; b. Mexico City, Mar. 31, 1922; s. Robert Clyde and Lula Gertrude (Barkley) B.; student Tex. A. and M. Coll., 1938-40; B.A., George Washington U., 1942; m. Sara Eleanor Holmes, Nov. 14, 1942; children—Diane, Cynthia Barkley, Richard Carlton. Econ. investigator Am. embassy, Mexico, 1942-43; with Bethlehem Steel Export Corp., Mexico City office, 1943-44; gen. mgr. Dunlop y Cia., S.A., Mexico City (agts. Weirton Steel, Diamond Alkali, Kaiser Aluminum, Harshaw Chem., A.M. Byers cos.), 1947-60; v.p. Latin Am. ops. Spencer Stuart Internat., S.A. (affiliate Spencer Stuart & Assos., Inc., mgmt. cons., Chgo.), 1960-61; exec. v.p., dir. Sonoco de Mexico, S.A., Mexico City, 1961-62, pres., 1962—, also chmn. bd. Active Little League Baseball, Mexico City. Served with AUS, 1946-47. Mem. Am. C. of C. of Mexico (v.p., dir.), Omicron Delta Kappa, Delta Phi Epsilon, Acacia. Clubs: Univ. (dir.), Club de Golf Hacienda, de Industriales, Reforma Athletic (Mexico City). Home: Apartado Postal 10-734 Mexico 10 DF Mexico Office: care Sonoco de Mexico SA Apartado 92-Bis Mexico 1 DF Mexico

BURNS, VINCENT BROWN, banker; b. Boston, Feb. 22, 1935; s. Vincent Anthony and Mary Veronica (Corbett) B.; B.S. in Econs., Holy Cross Coll., Worcester, Mass., 1957; m. Vinita Murray, June 13, 1957; children—Paula, Vincent, Susan, Patrick, Margot. Sr. security analyst, asst. portfolio mgr. Govt. Employees Ins. Co., Washington, 1962-67; v.p., dir. research Wilmington Capital Mgmt. Co. (Del.), 1967-68; v.p., portolio mgr. Putnam Mgmt. Co., Boston, 1968-70; v.p., chmn. investment policy com., sr. investment officer Gardner & Preston Moss, Boston, 1970-74; v.p., portfolio mgr., mem. investment policy com., sr. mktg. officer Keystone Investment Mgmt. Co., Boston, 1974-75; 1st v.p. fin. mktg. John Hancock Life Ins. Co., Boston, 1975-80; v.p., sr. mktg. officer investment trusts Northeast Banks, Portland, Maine, 1980—; dir. Metal Images Boston, Gorman Comuter Systems, Washington. Chmn., Gov. Md. Blue Ribbon Govt. Study Com., 1964-65; bd. dirs. Prince Georges County (Md.) Mcpl. Improvement Co., 1965-66. Served to capt. USAF, 1959-62. Fellow Fin. Analysts Fedn.; mem. Am. Bankers Assn., Am. Mgmt. Assn., Boston Security Analysts Soc. Democrat. Roman Catholic. Home: Morrison Heights Wayne ME 04284 Office: 443 Congress St Portland ME 04101

BURNS, WARD, textile co. exec.; b. New Bedford, Mass., May 31, 1928; s. Frederick Lloyd and Pauline (Ward) B.; B.A., Amherst Coll., 1950; M.B.A., Harvard U., 1952; spl. student N.Y. U., 1955-57; m. Cynthia A. Butterworth, Dec. 19, 1964; children—Helen Abby, David Ward, Walton Lloyd. Mgr. Price Waterhouse & Co., C.P.A.'s, N.Y.C., 1954-62; asso. Laurence S. and David Rockefeller, Brussels, Belgium, 1962-65; with J.P. Stevens & Co., Inc., N.Y.C., 1965—, controller, 1969-78, group v.p., 1978-80, pres., 1980—; also dir., mem. exec. com.; dir. Foote & Davies, Inc., Atlanta, Ruralist Press, Inc., Elron, Tel Aviv; cons. ARS, Milan, Italy, HVL, Brussels, ARCO, Florence and Milan, 1963-65. Treas., dir. Internat. Sch. Brussels, 1963-65; pres. bd. dirs. Internat. Sch. Brussels Found., N.Y.C., 1965—; pres., bd. dirs. Friends New Cavell Hosp. Inc., N.Y.C., 1972-78. Served as capt. USAF, 1952-53. C.P.A., N.Y. Mem. Am. Inst. C.P.A.'s, N.Y. State Soc. C.P.A.'s, Financial Execs. Inst., St. Andrews Soc., Phi Alpha Psi, Phi Kappa Psi. Clubs: Univ., Econs. (N.Y.C.). Mem. editorial adv. bd. Jour. Accountancy, 1969-72. Office: JP Stevens 1185 Ave of Americas New York NY 10036*

BURNS, WILLIAM CHARLES, mfg. co. exec.; b. Phila., Aug. 5, 1927; s. William A. and Sadie M. (Deeney) B.; B.S. in Chem. Engring., Villanova U., 1950; J.D., Western States U. Coll. Law, 1978; m. Mary R. Holland, Aug. 27, 1955; children—Mary M., Joan, Kathleen, Barbara, Maureen, Theresa, William, Bernadette, Elaine, Colleen. Project mgr. Cochrane Crane Co., Phila., 1957-61; exec. v.p. Water Treatment Corp., City of Industry, Calif., 1961-71; pres. L & A Water Treatment div. Chromalloy, City of Industry, 1971—; dir., mem. exec. com. Water Treatment Corp., 1965—. Served with USN, 1945-46, 50-52. Mem. S.C. Contractors Assn., Soc. Petroleum Engrs., Indsl. Water Conditioning Inst. Republican. Roman Catholic. Club: 3 G's. Patentee in field; contbr. articles to profl. jours. Home: 1630 N Hollydale Dr Fullerton CA 92631 Office: 17400 E Chestnut St Industry CA 91749

BURNSIDE, WALDO HOWARD, dept. store exec.; b. Washington, Nov. 5, 1928; s. Waldo and Eleanor B.; B.S., U. Md., 1949; m. Jean Mae Culbert, June 24, 1950; children—Diane Louise, Leslie Ann, Arlene Kay, William Howard. With Woodward & Lothrop, Washington, 1949-80, divisional mdse. mgr., 1957-65, v.p., gen. mdse. mgr., 1965-74, exec. v.p., 1974-78, pres., 1978-80, also dir.; vice-chmn., chief operating officer Carter Hawley Hale Stores, Inc., Los Angeles, 1980—; dir. Asso. Mdse. Corp. Bd. dirs. Washington Blue Cross, 1974-77; bd. dirs. Washington Better Bus. Bur., 1973-77, pres., 1976-77. Episcopalian. Club: U. Md. Terrapin (pres. 1977-78). Office: Carter Hawley Hale Stores 550 S Flower St Los Angeles CA 90071*

BUROS, MELVIN SHELDON, inventor; b. Cleve., Dec. 9, 1920; s. Morris Jack and Minnie (Rose) B.; B.S. in Architecture, Western Res. U., 1943; m. Arline R. Bowytz, Oct. 11, 1943 (dec. 1971); m. 2d, Sylvia Okner, Jan. 10, 1976; children—William B., Barbara Anne. Engr., Boeing Aircraft, Seattle, 1943-44; gen. bldg. contractor, Phoenix, 1945-70, practice architecture, 1951—; pres. MICR-Shield Co., Phoenix, 1962—. Served with OSS, AUS, 1944-45. Recipient Distinguished Service award Ariz. State U., 1978. Life mem. pres.'s clubs Ariz. State U., U. Ariz. Mem. AIA, Internat. Carpenters Union. Clubs: Ariz., Phoenix Country, Masons, Shriners. Patentee bank computer-oriented inventions; designer, builder. Home: 1522 E Solano Dr Phoenix AZ 85014 Office: 4011 N Black Canyon Hwy Phoenix AZ 85015

BURR, KENNETH H(ERMAN), banker; b. Dayton, Ohio, May 11, 1942; s. Frederick K. and Violet E. (Noirot) B.; B.S., U. Dayton, 1964, M.B.A., 1968; m. Myra L. Coleman. Aug. 17, 1963; children—Kenneth, Keith, Kara, Kevin. With Winters Nat. Mortgage Corp., Dayton, 1965—, v.p., 1974—. Bd. dirs. Behavioral Scis. Center, Dartmouth U., 1973—. Mem. Nat. Assn. Rev. Appraisers, Home Builders Assn., Grad. Bus. Assn., St. Alberts Athletic Assn. (pres., dir.), Am. Inst. Banking, Greater Dayton Jaycees (Tower dir., treas. 1979). Republican. Roman Catholic. Office: Suite 404 Winters Bank Tower Dayton OH 45401

BURRELL, JOSEPH EARL, chem. mfg. co. exec.; b. Aurora, Ill., Sept. 7, 1919; s. Fred W. and Rosa (Greenman) B.; B.S., U. Mich., 1941; postgrad. Harvard, 1957; m. M. Margaret Macatee, Apr. 7, 1942; children—Robert, John, Marcia, Christopher, Jane, Susan. Chem. engr. research dept. and chem. div. ops. PPG Industries, Inc., Barberton, Ohio, 1952-56, asst. to v.p. ops., Pitts., 1956-58, ops. supt. Natrium, W.Va., 1956-58, v.p. ops., 1958-66, v.p., gen. mgr. chem. div., 1966-75, pres., 1976—, also dir.; dir. Pitts. Nat. Corp., Pitts. Corning, Duplate Can. Trustee, Marietta Coll., Nat. Safety Council; bd. visitors Sch. Bus., U. Pitts.; bd. dirs. Duquesne U. Mem. Mfg. Chemists Assn. (dir., exec. com.), Am. Inst. Chem. Engrs., Am. Chem. Soc., Profl. Engrs. Ohio. Office: PPG Industries 1 Gateway Center Pittsburgh PA 15222*

BURROWES, JOSEPH J., mfrs. rep.; b. Phila., Jan. 7, 1919; s. Joseph Thomas and Katie Lewis (McBlain) B.; B.A., Temple U., 1940, postgrad. Law Sch., 1940-42; m. Helen Leola Berkelbach, Nov. 10, 1942; children—Leola (Mrs. Robert Trainor Zintl, Jr.), Lisa Jo (Mrs. David A. Lough). Tech. sales rep. R.M. Hollingshead Corp., Camden, N.J., 1947-52; owner, Pakoil Co., Havertown, Pa., 1952—. Served as pilot, maj. AUS, 1942-46. Mem. Soc. Packaging and Handling Engrs. (nat. v.p. 1970-71, exec. v.p. 1972-73, pres. 1974-75, chmn. bd. 1976-77; Mem. of Year 1975, Fellow Mem. award 1978, hon. life), Am. Def. Preparedness Assn., Am. Ordnance Assn., Nat. Inst. Packaging and Handling and Logistics Engrs. Mason. Clubs: Lianerch County, Seaview Country. Home and office: 7 N Drexel Ave Havertown PA 19083

BURRUSS, MELVIN ALEXANDER, fin. exec.; b. New Haven, Feb. 13, 1946; s. Melvin Andrew and Anna (Webb) B.; B.S., U. Calif., Berkeley, 1973; M.B.A., Stanford U., 1975; m. Carla A. Cotton, Jan. 26, 1976; 1 child, Timnetra A. Mgmt. cons. Peat, Marwick, Mitchell, Washington, 1975-77; asst. to pres. and chief exec. officer Consol. Aluminum Corp., St. Louis, 1977-79; program fin. strategy cons. Xerox Corp., Rochester, N.Y., 1979—. Bd. dirs. Urban League, St. Louis, 1978, NAACP, St. Louis, 1978. Served with USN, 1965-69. Decorated Purple Heart; Ford Found. fellow, 1971-73; Peat, Marwick, Mitchell fellow, 1973-75. Mem. Am. Mgmt. Assn., Am. Mktg. Assn., Nat. Assn. Accts. (dir. 1977), Nat. Assn. Black Accts. (dir. 1976), Stanford U. Alumni Assn., U. Calif., Berkeley Alumni Assn., Rochester C. of C., Soc. Advancement of Mgmt. Clubs: Rotary, Masons. Home: PO Box 4025 Rochester NY 14604 Office: Xerox Sq 017 Rochester NY 14644

BURSON, HAROLD, pub. relations exec.; b. Memphis, Feb. 15, 1921; s. Maurice and Esther (Bach) B.; B.A., U. Miss., 1940; m. Bette Ann Foster, Oct. 30, 1947; children—Scott, Mark. Corr., reporter Memphis Comml. Appeal, 1938-40; dir. Ole Miss News Bur., Oxford, Miss., 1939-40; dir. pub. relations H.K. Ferguson Co., N.Y.C., 1941-43; chmn. Burson-Marsteller, N.Y.C., 1953—; dir., mem. exec. com. Marsteller, Inc., N.Y.C., Young & Rubicam, N.Y.C.; pres., dir. Burson-Marsteller (Can.), Ltd., Toronto, 1985—, Marsteller Internat. S.A., Geneva, 1961—; dir. Marsteller (Belgium) S.A., Brussels, Marsteller Internat. GmbH, Frankfurt, Germany, Burson-Marsteller Ltd., London, Burson-Marsteller (Asia) Ltd., Hong Kong, Burson-Marsteller (S.E.A.) Pte. Ltd., Singapore. Bd. dirs., mem. exec. com., chmn. pub. info. com. Joint Council on Econ. Edn.; former bd. dirs., exec. com., v.p. pub. info. Nat. Safety Council, 1968-76; bd. dirs. Kennedy Center Prodns., Washington, Catalyst Inc.; former trustee World Wildlife Fund, Found. for Public Relations Research and Edn.; mem. Commn. Fine Arts, Washington; adv. trustee Hackley Sch., Tarrytown, N.Y. Served with AUS, World War II. Named Pub. Relations Profl. of Year, Pub. Relations News, 1977; named to Alumni Hall of Fame, U. Miss., 1980. Mem. Am. (Gold Anvil award 1980), Internat. pub. relations assns., N.Y. Soc. Security Analysts, Am. Philatelic Soc., Blue Key, Omicron Delta Kappa. Clubs: Overseas Press, Marco Polo, Pinnacle (N.Y.C.); Mid-Am. (Chgo.); Internat. (Washington); Scarsdale (N.Y.) Golf. Home: 260 Beverly Rd Scarsdale NY 10583 Office: 866 3d Ave New York NY 10022

BURSON, THOMAS DANIEL, aerospace co. exec.; b. Hartselle, Ala., Jan. 7, 1936; s. Daniel Webster and Ardia (Starks) B.; B.M.E. with high honor, Auburn U., 1958; M.B.A., U. So. Calif., 1969; m. Mary Frances Wilson, June 7, 1958; children—Kelly Frances, Robyn Elizabeth, Thomas Scott. Asst. mgr. contract adminstrn. Hycon Co., Monrovia, Calif., 1961-63, mgr. customer contracts, 1963-66, asst. to pres., 1966-67, dir. mktg., 1967-71, v.p., 1969-71; dir. product and bus. planning Actron div. McDonnell Douglas Corp., Monrovia, 1971, dir. contracts and pricing, 1971-76, v.p. fiscal mgmt., 1976-78, v.p. indsl. control products McDonnell-Douglas Astronautics Co., 1978—. Served with USNR, 1958-61. Mem. ASME, Am. Inst. Aeros. and Astronautics, Nat. Contract Mgmt. Assn., Phi Kappa Phi, Tau Beta Pi, Pi Tau Sigma, Beta Gamma Sigma, Kappa Alpha. Democrat. Club: Glendora Country. Home: 1129 E Sierra Madre Ave Glendora CA 91740 Office: 700 Royal Oaks Dr Monrovia CA 91016

BURT, WALLACE JOSEPH, JR., ins. co. exec.; b. Burlington, Iowa, Apr. 1, 1924; s. Wallace Joseph and Lela (Catlow) B.; student Iowa State Coll., 1942, U. Wis., 1945; m. Alice Olmsted, June 22, 1946; children—Lockwood, David, Virginia. Vice pres., dir. 1st Ins. Fin. Co., Des Moines, 1946-50, Northeastern Ins. Co., Hartford, Conn., 1950-59; pres., owner Hail Reinsurance Mgmt., Inc., Ormond Beach, Fla., 1960—; chmn. Burt & Scheld, Inc., Ormond Beach, 1961—; chmn. U.S. br. Hamburg Internat. Reins. Co., 1976—; chmn. First N.Y. Syndicate Corp., 1979—, W.J. Burt Mgmt., Inc., N.Y.C., 1979—; pres. Ormond Reins. Co.; dir., v.p. Barnett Bank, Ormond Beach; underwriting mem. Lloyd's of London. Trustee, pres. Ormond Beach Meml. Hosp. Served to 1st lt. USAAF, World War II. Decorated D.F.C., Purple Heart, Air medal with 5 oak leaf clusters. Home: 222 Riverside Dr Ormond Beach FL 32074 Office: 146 S Atlantic St Ormond Beach FL 32074

BURTIS, THEODORE, chem. engr.; b. Jamaica, N.Y., May 17, 1922; s. Theodore Alfred and Florence Angela (Whalen) B.; B.Sc., Carnegie Inst. Tech., 1942; M.Sc., Tex. A. and M. Coll., 1946; D.Sc., Ursinus Coll., 1972; m. Billie Joyce King, June 2, 1945; children—Barbara, Theodore, Pamela. With Magnolia Petroleum Co., 1943-45, Owens-Corning Fiberglas Corp., 1946-47; with Houdry Process Corp., Phila., 1947—, pres., 1956-62, also chmn.; chmn. Catalytic Constrn. Co.; pres. Houdry Process & Chem. Co.; v.p., dir. Air Products & Chems. Inc., 1962-67; dir. comml. devel. Sun Oil Co., 1967-68, adminstrv. dir. research and engring., 1969-70, v.p. research and devel., 1970-72, v.p. mktg., 1972-74, pres. products group, 1974-75; exec. v.p., dir., from 1975, pres., 1976—, chief exec. officer, 1978—, chmn. bd., 1979—. Fellow Am. Inst. Chem. Engrs. (pres. 1967); mem. Am. Chem. Soc., Kappa Sigma, Tau Beta Pi. Clubs: Union League, Racquet (Phila); Aronimink (Newtown Square, Pa.). Office: 100 Matsonford Rd Radnor PA 19087*

BURTON, BERNARD HOWARD, financial exec.; b. Berlin, Germany, Apr. 7, 1924; s. Herman and Ray (Backer) B.; B.S. in Bus. Adminstrn., Rutgers U., 1951; M.B.A., N.Y. U., 1954; m. Helga Rosemarie Riemer, June 5, 1949; children—Vivian Jane, Monica Lynn, Michelle Annette. Came to U.S., 1945, naturalized, 1946. Sr. accountant Peat, Marwick, Mitchell & Co., N.Y.C., 1951-57; controller Internat. div. Olin Mathieson Chem. Corp., 1957-62; treas. Minerals and Chems. Philipp Corp., N.Y.C., 1962-67; v.p. Engelhard Minerals & Chems. Corp., N.Y.C., 1967-71; v.p. W.R. Grace & Co., N.Y.C., 1971-77; partner, v.p. fin. and adminstrn. THH Corp., N.Y.C., 1977-80; v.p. fin. and ops. Bucknell Press, Inc., Farmingdale, N.Y., 1980—. Mem. Financial Execs. Inst., Am. Inst. C.P.A.'s, N.Y. State Soc. C.P.A.'s, Home: 142 Monterey Dr Manhasset Hills NY 11040 Office: 240 Smith St Farmingdale NY 11735

BURTON, COURTNEY, mining and shipping co. exec.; b. Cleve., Oct. 29, 1912; s. Courtney and Sarita (Oglebay) B.; student Mich. Coll. Mining and Tech., 1933-34, B.S., 1956; m. Marguerite Rankin, Sept. 7, 1933 (dec. Apr. 17, 1976); children—Sarita Ann (Mrs. John Limbocker Jr.), Marguerite Rankin (Mrs. George M. Humphrey II); m. 2d, Margaret Butler Leitch, Dec. 20, 1978. Dir. E.W. Oglebay Co., Cleve., 1934-57, pres., 1947-57; v.p. Ferro Engring. Co., Cleve., 1950-57; pres. Fortuna Lake Mining Co., Cleve., 1950-57; treas., dir. Columbia Transp. Co., Cleve., 1950-57; v.p. Montreal Mining Co., Cleve., 1950-57; pres. N. Shore Land Co., Cleve., 1950-57; v.p., dir. Brule Smokeless Coal Co., Cleve., 1950-57; chmn. bd., chmn. exec. com. Oglebay Norton Co., Cleve., 1957—; dir. Cleve. Trust Co., 1950-76. Dir. Ohio Civilian Def. and Rationing, 1941-42; exec. asst. Office Coordinator Inter-Am. Affairs, 1942-44; mem. bd. commrs. Cleve. Met. Park Bd. Mayor, Village of Gates Mills, Ohio, 1948-61; chmn. Ohio Republican Finance Com., 1954-61, Rep. Nat. Finance Com., 1961-64. Trustee, Bethany Coll.; former trustee Nat. Park Found.; hon. trustee Univ. Hosp., Cleve., Oglebay Inst., Wheeling, W.Va.; pres. Am.'s Future Trees Found., Cleve. Zool. Soc., 1968-76. Served to lt. USNR, 1944-46. Mem. Am. Iron and Steel Inst., Nat. Coal Assn. Episcopalian. Clubs: Chagrin Valley Hunt (master of hounds 1946-54) (Gates Mills); Tavern, Union (Cleve.); Rolling Rock (Ligonier, Pa.); Fort Henry (Wheeling, W.Va.); Kirtland (Willoughby, Ohio). Office: 1100 Superior Ave Cleveland OH 44114

BURTON, EDWARD CLUFF, JR., utility co. exec.; b. Cambridge, Md., Feb. 11, 1928; s. Edward Carroll and Mildred Virginia (Cluff) B.; B.S., Salisbury State Coll.; m. Norma Lee Grupe, Mar. 17, 1950; children—Constance, Catherine, Karen. With Cambridge Gas Co., 1949—, pres., 1958—; with Chesapeake Utilities Corp., Salisbury, Md., 1958—, pres., 1972-80, chmn., 1980—, also dir.; chmn. and dir. subs. Eastern Shore Natural Gas Co., 1964—. Served with U.S. Army, 1945-47. Mem. Am. Gas Assn., Md.-D.C. Utilities Assn., South Eastern Gas Assn. Democrat. Episcopalian. Clubs: Masons, Elks. Office: 520 Commerce St Salisbury MD 21801

BURTON, JOHN CAMPBELL, accountant, educator; b. N.Y.C., Sept. 17, 1932; s. James Campbell and Barbara (French) B.; B.A., Haverford Coll., 1954; M.B.A., Columbia U., 1956, Ph.D., 1962; m. Jane J. Garnjost, Apr. 6, 1957; children—Eve Bradley, Bruce Campbell. Staff acct. Arthur Young & Co., 1956-60; prof. acctg. and fin. Columbia U., 1962-72, Arthur Young prof. acctg. and fin., 1978—; chief acct. SEC, 1972-76; dep. mayor for fin. City of N.Y., 1976-77; dir. Scholastic Inc., Commerce Clearing House. Pres. bd. trustees Millbrook Sch., 1977—; mem. Fin. Acctg. Standards Adv. Council, 1977—; cons. Comptroller Gen. of U.S., 1977—. Mem. Am. Inst. C.P.A.'s (mem. council), Fin. Analysts Research Found. (trustee), Am. Fin. Assn., Am. Econ. Assn., Am. Acctg. Assn. (v.p. 1980-81).

Author: (with W.T. Porter) Auditing, a Conceptual Approach, 1971; Accounting for Business Combinations, 1970; editor: Handbook of Accounting and Auditing, 1981, Corporate Financial Reporting, 1972. Home: 130 East End Ave New York NY 10028 Office: 625 Uris Hall Columbia University New York NY 10027

BURTON, ROY LUNN, fin. services cons.; b. Clarksburg, W.Va., Sept. 28, 1927; s. Roy Lunn and Helen Marguerite (Holland) B.; B.S., W.Va. U., 1951; m. Verna Louise Hall, Aug. 27, 1955; children—Amy, Ann, Christopher, Adam, William, Katherine, Polly. Advt. salesman Ironwood (Mich.) Daily Globe, 1951-55; advt. sales Barron's Bus. and Fin. Weekly, N.Y.C., 1955-56; advt. sales Marinette (Wis.) Eagle-Star, 1956-58; gen. mgr. Kettering-Oakwood (Ohio) Times, 1958-79; owner, mgr. Midwest Fin. Services, Kettering, Ohio, 1979—. Served with AUS, 1945-47. Mem. Kettering C. of C. (dir. 1968—), Dayton Area C. of C., Ohio Newspaper Assn. (dir. 1976-80), Buckeye Press Assn. (pres. 1966), Suburban Newspapers of Am. (dir. 1977-79), Nat. Newspaper Assn., Nat. Assn. Fin. Cons.'s. Club: Dayton Country. Home: 1313 Far Hills Ave Oakwood OH 45419 Office: 1424 Dorothy Ln Kettering OH 45409

BURWELL, THOMAS CARL, real estate exec.; b. Cleve., Mar. 3, 1943; s. Virgil and Marion Ann Burwell; B.B.A. in Acctg., St. Mary's U., San Antonio, 1969; m. Janet Farris, Aug. 15, 1965; children—Brian, Kevin. With Ernst & Whinney, San Antonio, 1969-71, Russ & Co., San Antonio, 1972; pres. Lakecroft Inc., San Antonio, 1972—. C.P.A., Tex. Mem. Nat. Assn. Accts., Tex. Soc. C.P.A.'s. Office: 8500 Village Dr San Antonio TX 78217

BUSCH, AUGUST ADOLPHUS, III, brewery exec.; b. St. Louis, June 16, 1937; s. August Adolphus, Jr. and Elizabeth (Overton) B.; student U. Ariz., 1957-59, Siebel Inst. Tech., 1960-61; m. Virginia L. Wiley, Dec. 28, 1974; children—August Adolphus, Susan Marie, Steven August, Virginia Marie. With Anheuser-Busch, Inc., St. Louis, 1957—, exec. v.p., gen. mgr., 1971-74, pres., 1974-75, pres., 1975—, chief exec. officer, 1975-77, chmn. bd., 1977—; chmn. bd., pres. Anheuser Busch Cos., Inc., 1979—; dir. Manu. Ry. Co., First Nat. Bank of St. Louis, Norfolk & Western Ry., Southwestern Bell Telephone Co., Laclede Gas Co., Gen. Am. Life Ins. Co. Active, Nat. Center for Resource Recovery, United Way Greater St. Louis, Boy Scouts Am., St. Louis Symphony Soc.; bd. dirs. Washington U., Wharton Sch. U. Pa., Sch. Bus. Adminstrn. Sponsors, Coll. William and Mary, St. John's Mercy Med. Center. Served with U.S. Army, 1956-57. Recipient Charles Coolidge Parlin award, 1973, St. Louis Argus award, 1975, Humanitarian award St. Louis Human Devel. Corp., 1975; named Packaging Man of Year, 1975, Chief Exec. Officer of Year, Financial World, 1976, 77. Mem. U.S. Brewers Assn. (chmn.). Clubs: St. Louis, St. Louis Country; Racquet; Log Cabin; Noonday; Stadium. Office: 721 Pestalozzi St Saint Louis MO 63118

BUSCH, MERRILL JOSEPH, public relations and publishing co. exec.; b. Jordan, Minn., July 25, 1936; s. Albert Meinrad and Hildegarde Sophia (Bauer) S.; student St. Thomas Coll., St. Paul, 1954-57; B.A. summa cum laude, U. Minn., 1958, postgrad., 1958-59; m. Mary D. Meteraud, Oct. 16, 1965; children—Christopher, Jennifer, Amy. Dir. publs., gen. mgr. Am. Assn. Cereal Chemists, St. Paul, 1965-72; editor Comml. West Mag., 1972-76; mng. editor, bus. and fin. editor Sun Newspapers, Inc., Mpls., 1972-78; editor, pub. Greater Mpls. mag., 1972—; pres. Busch & Partners, Mpls., 1980—; chmn. Prime, Inc., 1979—; dir. client relations Bozell & Jacobs, Inc., Mpls., 1978-80; dir. Cybx Corp. Bd. dirs. Butler Sch. Law, Groves Learning Center, Homeward Bound, Inc., Mpls. Film Commn., Minn. Motion Picture and TV Devel. Bd., De La Salle High Sch. Served with AUS, 1959-60. Mem. Info. Film Producers Assn., Mpls. C. of C., French Am. C. of C., Minn. Press Club, Phi Beta Kappa. Republican. Roman Catholic. Club: Mpls. Athletic. Writer, producer ednl. films and filmstrips. Home: 2120 Girard Ave S Minneapolis MN 55405 also 186 Shorewood Dr Saint Michael MN 55376 Office: 1111 W 22nd Street Suite 200 Minneapolis MN 55405

BUSH, JAMES DAVID, fin. corp. exec.; b. Dayton, Ohio, Apr. 28, 1951; s. D.J. and Vena B. (Pennington) B.; student Sinclair Coll., Wright State U.; m. Robin F. Cornell; children—Alyssa M., Nathan D., Amy E. Real estate sales Morgan Realty Co., Dayton, Ohio, 1972-74; asst. v.p., mgr. Advance Mortgage Corp., Van Nuys, Calif., 1974-78; pres. Classic Fin. Corp., Van Nuys, 1978—. Served with U.S. Army, 1970. Mem. Mortgage Bankers Assn. Am., Calif. Mortgage Bankers Assn., Jaycees. Home: 8378 Denise Ln Canoga Park CA 91304 Office: 8780 Van Nuys Blvd Suite 201 Panorama City CA 91402

BUSH, MARY KATE, banker; b. Birmingham, Ala., Apr. 9, 1948; d. Johnny and Augusta (Bennett) Bush: B.A. in Econs. and Polit. Sci., Fisk U., 1969; M.B.A., U. Chgo., 1971. Credit analyst Chase Manhattan Bank, N.Y.C., 1971-73; asst. treas. First Nat. City Bank, N.Y.C., 1974-76; asst. treas. Bankers Trust Co., N.Y.C., 1976-77, asst. v.p., 1977-79, v.p., team leader, 1979—. Mem. U. Chgo. Bus. Sch. Assn., U. Chgo. Alumni Assn., Phi Beta Kappa. Home: 788 Columbus Ave New York NY 10025 Office: 280 Park Ave New York NY 10017

BUSH, RALPH EVERETT, builder, developer; b. Lenoir, N.C., Aug. 26, 1903; s. Robert Burkhead and Siddie Anna (Underdown) B.; B.S., U. Va., 1925; m. Louise Cecelia Trice, Sept. 3, 1932; children—Mary Cuthbert (Mrs. John Joseph Digges), Nancy Louise (Mrs. Robert A. Lawson, Jr.). Bldg. contractor, Miami, Fla., 1925-27, Washington, 1927-28, Norfolk, Va., 1928-42; owner Bush Constrn. Co., Norfolk, Va., Washington and Balt., 1946—, also pres. subsidiary corps.; dir. emeritus Bd. dirs. Med. Center Hosps., Norfolk; mem. devel. com. Norfolk State Coll. Found. Served from capt. to maj. C.E., AUS, 1942-46. Mem. Soc. Am. Mil. Engrs., Nat. Assn. Homebuilders. Clubs: Norfolk Yacht and Country; Virginia; Harbor; University (Washington); Farmington Country (Charlottesville, Va.); Commonwealth (Richmond, Va.). Home: 601 Pembroke Ave Norfolk VA 23507 Office: 5532 Raby Rd Norfolk VA 23502

BUSHKIN, MERLE JEROME, banker; b. Dayton, Ohio, Mar. 21, 1935; s. Charles D. and Eva (Flagel) B.; A.B., Harvard U., 1956, M.B.A., 1960; m. Leone Edricks, Aug. 6, 1961; children—Elizabeth, Nancy. Mgmt. cons. Cresap, McCormick & Paget, N.Y.C., 1960-64; fin. and planning positions Mobil Oil Corp., N.Y.C., 1964-70; fin. v.p., treas., sec. Wollensak, Inc., Rochester, N.Y., 1970-71; v.p., mgr. merger and acquistion services CBWL-Hayden Stone, Inc., N.Y.C., 1971-72; pres. Bushkin Assos., Inc., N.Y.C., 1972—; lectr. in field. Bd. govs. chpt. Am. Jewish Com. Clubs: Harvard of N.Y.C., Harvard Bus. Sch. of N.Y., Harmonie. Home: 86 Caterson Terr Hartsdale NY 10530 Office: 555 Madison Ave New York NY 10022

BUSKIRK, RICHARD HOBART, educator; b. Bloomington, Ind., Jan. 24, 1927; s. Cyrus Hobart and Amiee Ruth (Borland) B.; B. in Bus. with distinction, Ind. U., 1948, M.B.A., 1949; Ph.D., U. Wash., 1955; m. Barbara Jean Lusk, June 14, 1947; children—Bruce David, Carol Ann. Instr. mktg. U. Kans., 1949-53, U. Wash., 1953-55; asst. prof. mktg. U. Okla., 1955-57; prof. mktg. U. Colo., Boulder, 1957-70, Calif. State U., Fullerton, 1970-73; prof. bus. adminstrn. U. So. Calif., Fullerton, 1973-74; Herman W. Lay chair mktg. So. Meth. U., Dallas, 1974-80; prof. mktg. and dir. entrepreneur program U. So. Calif., Los Angeles, 1980—; dir. Regiment Shops Colo., Boulder, 1963-70, A.R.F. Products, Inc., Raton, N.Mex., 1960-70, Health Wheels, Inc., 1970-74; cons. Delta Drilling Co., Tyler, Tex., 1978-79, Weyerhaeuser Co., Tacoma, 1962-64. Mem. Minority Bus. Opportunity Com. of Fed. Exec. Bd. Served with USN, 1944-46. Mem. Assn. Bus. Simulation and Exptl. Learning (past pres.), Am. Mktg. Assn. Methodist. Club: Northwood. Author: Cases in Marketing, 1970, 74; Concepts of Business, 1970; Business and Administrative Policy, 1970; Retail Selling, 1974; Machivelli and Modern Management, 1974; Your Career, 1975; Principles of Marketing, 4th edit., 1975; Handbook of Managerial Tactics, 1975; Retailing, 1979; Management of the Sales Force, 5th edit., 1979; Textbook of Salesmanship, 10th edit., 1979; How to Beat Men at Their Own Game, 1980. Home: 29206 Beachside Dr Rancho Palos Verdes CA 90274 Office: Sch Bus U So Calif Los Angeles CA 90007

BUSS, JERRY HATTEN, real estate co. exec., sports team owner; B.S. in Chemistry, U. Wyo., M.S., Ph.D. in Chemistry, U. So. Calif., 1957. Chemist, Bur. Mines; past mem. faculty dept. chemistry U. So. Calif.; mem. missile div. McDonnell Douglas, Los Angeles; partner Mariani-Buss Assos.; former owner Los Angeles Strings; chmn. bd., owner Los Angeles Lakers, Nat. Basketball Assn.; owner Los Angeles Kings, Nat. Hockey League. Office: care Los Angeles Lakers PO Box 10 The Forum Ingelwood CA 90306*

BUTCHER, HOWARD, IV, fin. co. exec.; b. Bryn Mawr, Pa., Nov. 27, 1936; s. Howard and Elizabeth C. (McBee) B.; student U. Pa., 1955-57, 58-59. Trainee, Dominick & Dominick, N.Y.C., 1959-61; with Butcher & Singer, Phila., 1961-71, 75-77, partner, 1965-71; territorial mktg. dir. Hornblower, Weeks, Hemphill & Hoyes, Phila., 1972-74; chmn. bd., pres. Butcher Internat., Phila., 1976—; v.p. Phila. Bourse, Inc.; dir. De Lancey, Pembroke & Co., Distribix, Phila. Bourse, Inc. Trustee Hill Sch., Voorhees U. Served with N.G., 1954-58. Republican. Episcopalian. Clubs: Racquet, Millreef, Union League. Home: 2018 Delancey Pl Philadelphia PA 19103 Office: 2018 Delancey Pl Philadelphia PA 19103

BUTCHER, WILLARD CARLISLE, banker; b. Bronxville, N.Y., Oct. 25, 1926; s. Willard F. and Helen (Calhoun) B.; student Middlebury Coll., 1945; B.A., Brown U., 1947; m. Sarah Catherine Payne, Oct. 8, 1949 (dec. Jan. 1955); children—Sarah Carlisle, Helen Catherine; m. 2d, Elizabeth Allen, Jan. 28, 1956 (dec. Aug. 1978); children—Barbara Downs, John Carlisle; m. 3d, Carole Elizabeth McMahon, Jan. 23, 1979; 1 son, Willard Carlisle, Jr. With Chase Nat. Bank (now Chase Manhattan Bank), N.Y.C., 1947—, asst. treas. Grand Central br., 1953-56, asst. v.p., 1956-58, v.p. 1958-61, sr. v.p., 1961-69, exec. v.p., 1969-72, vice chmn., 1972, pres., 1972—; dir. ASARCO, Inc., Firestone Tire & Rubber Co., Akron, Ohio. Trustee Brown U. Served with USNR, 1944-45. Mem. Phi Beta Kappa, Sigma Nu. Conglist. Clubs: Economic, Knickerbocker, Links (N.Y.C.); Silver Spring Country (Ridgefield, Conn.); Blind Brook (Port Chester, N.Y.); Norwalk (Conn.) Yacht. Home: Wilton CT Office: 1 Chase Manhattan Plaza New York NY 10081

BUTERA, REMO, lawyer; b. Norristown, Pa., Nov. 25, 1953; s. Joseph and Anne (Fabbri) B.; A.B., Brown U., 1975; J.D., Dickinson Sch. Law, 1978. Pres., Internat. Investment Services, Phila., 1976—; cons. Pa. Ho. of Reps., 1976-78; admitted to Pa. bar, 1978; corp. counsel Logan Sq. Inc., Norristown, Pa., 1978—; pres. Butera Devel. Co., 1979—; solicitor Montgomery County Office of Treasury, 1980—; asso. firm Cohen, Shapiro, Polisher, Shiekman & Cohen, Phila., 1981—. Coordinator field ops. Robert Butera for Gov. com., 1978; campaign cons. Lawrence Coughlin for Congress com., 1978; mem. Montgomery County Republican Com., 1978—; Montgomery County coordinator Bruce Kauffman for Supreme Ct. com., 1979. Mem. Internat. Council Shopping Centers, Pa. Bar Assn. Address: 22d Floor Phila Savs Fund Bldg 12 S 12th St Philadelphia PA 19107

BUTLER, BENJAMIN, lawyer; b. Farmington, Maine, Aug. 7, 1905; s. Frank W. and Alice (Smith) B.; A.B., Bowdoin Coll., 1928; LL.B., Boston U., 1932; m. Natalie C. Sturges, May 23, 1932; children—Diane Clare Butler Brinkman, Benjamin Sturges. Admitted to bar, 1932; pres., gen. mgr. Forster Mfg. Co., 1934-43; clk. Sugarloaf Mount Corp., 1955-74, dir., registrar, 1955-74; dir. Livermore Falls Trust Co., 1934-78; county atty., 1941-46; judge Franklin County Municipal Ct., 1961-65. State senator from Franklin County, 1953-58; trustee Franklin County Meml. Hosp., 1946-51; pres. Farmington Pub. Library, 1954—; assessor Farmington Village Corp., 1940-56, 60—; clk. Maine Citizens for Historic Preservation, 1972—, trustee, 1976—; treas. Farmington Hist. Soc., 1975—. Mem. Am., Maine, Franklin County bar assns., Newcomen Soc., Mayflower Soc. (gov., 1946-48, dep. gov.-gen. 1949-75), Chi Psi. Republican. Clubs: Masons, Shriners, K.T. Author: (with Natalie S. Butler) History Old South Church of Farmington from 1814 to 1965, 1966; also hist. booklets. Home: 93 Main St Farmington ME 04938 Office: 7 Broadway Farmington ME 14938

BUTLER, CHARLES HENRY, hosp. adminstr.; b. N.Y.C., Oct. 12, 1932; s. Charles Henry and Theresa Edith (Simmons) B.; A.A., N.Y. City Community Coll., 1960; B.S., L.I. U., 1962; M.P.A., N.Y. U., 1970; m. Lois Evelyn Belle, Jan. 14, 1956; children—Charles Henry, Craig Aron. Advt. claims adjuster N.Y. Times, N.Y.C., 1950-65; br. office mgr. Bklyn. Union Gas Co., 1965-67; corp. personnel specialist Endicott Johnson Corp., Endicott, N.Y., 1967-69; sr. indsl. relations rep. Kennecott Copper Corp., N.Y.C., 1969-70; dir. personnel N.Y.C. Health & Hosps. Corp., 1970—, Greenpoint Hosp., 1970-75, Queens Hosp. Center, 1975-78, Cumberland Hosp., Bklyn., 1978—; faculty Marymount Coll., Tarrytown, N.Y., 1975-76. Pres. PTA, N.Y.C., 1966-67; chmn. adv. com. Citizens Affirmative Action, N.Y.C., 1974-76. Served with USNR, 1953-55; maj. USAF Res. Recipient Certificate of Appreciation, N.Y.C. Bd. Edn., 1967; award N.Y. State Dept. Mental Hygiene, 1975. Mem. Am. Mgmt. Assn., Res. Officers Assn., NAACP, Soc. Advancement of Mgmt., N.Y. U. Alumni Assn., 100 Black Men, Council Concerned Black Execs., N.Y. Orgn. Devel. Network. Presbyterian. Contbr. articles in field to profl. jours. Home: 6 Foxcroft Dr Nanuet NY 10954 Office: 39 Auburn Pl Brooklyn NY 11205

BUTLER, ERNEST ALTON, mgmt. cons.; b. Greenville, N.C., Sept. 27, 1926; s. Walter Braxton and Mabel C. (Corrin) B.; student Columbia U., 1946. Sales exec. McCormick & Co., Balt., 1950; chmn. bd., chief exec. officer E. A. Butler Assos., mgmt. cons., Phila., N.Y.C., Los Angeles, Paris, Troy, Mich., Wellesley, Mass., Milw., Cleve., Montreal, Toronto, Dallas, Darien, Conn., 1953—; pres., chief exec. officer Heat Conservation Engring., Inc., Glens Falls, N.Y.; v.p. Panel-Ad, Inc.; chmn. The Little One; v.p., dir. Euromar, Paris, France; dir. Harlan Inc., Houston. Owner, Garnet Mountain Ski Area and Lodge. Mem. Soc. Profl. Mgmt. Cons. Methodist. Clubs: N.Y. Athletic (N.Y.C.); Campfire (Chappagua, N.Y.); Miami Yacht (Miami Beach, Fla.). Author: The Right Approach; How to Move In and Move Up, 1970; The Big Buck And The New Business Breed, 1972. Writer syndicated column On the Job, Chgo. Tribune. Home: 6 Ft Amherst Rd Glens Falls NY 12801 Office: PO Box 760 Glens Falls NY 12801

BUTLER, GEORGE ANDREWS, bank exec.; b. Westmount, N.J., Apr. 14, 1928; s. John T. and Kathryn B.; B.S. in Econs., U. Pa., 1950; m. Barbara Thomas, June 17, 1950; children—Lynn, William E., Thomas S., Pamela S. Asst. treas. First Pa. Bank, 1955-58, asst. v.p., 1958-68, exec. v.p., 1968-74, vice chmn., 1974-77, pres., chief operating officer, 1977-79, pres., chief exec. officer, 1979—; dir. Gen. Accident Group, Peirce Phelps. Bd. dirs. Presbyterian U. Pa. Med. Center. Served with U.S. Army, 1946-47. Mem. Robert Morris Assn., Assn. Res. City Bankers. Presbyterian. Clubs: Union League, Mfrs. Golf and Country. Office: 1500 Market St Philadelphia PA 19101

BUTLER, JOHN CHARLES, mfg. co. exec.; b. Pitts., Oct. 4, 1932; s. Francis Joseph and Mary Margret (Montgomery) B.; B.S., U. Pitts., 1958; m. Susan Clasier, Sept. 2, 1960; children—Cynthia, John F., Katherine. With Sperry Univac Co., 1970—, v.p., gen. mgr. internat. div., London, 1973-79, v.p., gen. mgr. Americas Nat. div., Blue Bell, Pa., 1979—; chmn. bd., pres. Sperry Rand Internat. Corp., Zurich; dir. SAAB Univac AB, Stockholm; dir., mem. supervisory bd. Sperry Rand Holland NV. Alumni trustee Kiskiminetas Springs Sch., Saltsbury, Pa. Served with AUS, 1954-58. Mem. Inst. Dirs., Am. C. of C. London. Republican. Presbyterian. Clubs: St. Davids Golf (Wayne, Pa.); Higate Golf, RAC, American (London). Author papers in field. Office: PO Box 500 Blue Bell PA 19422

BUTLER, JOHN MUSGRAVE, transp. co. exec.; b. Bklyn., Dec. 6, 1928; s. John Joseph and Sabina Catherine (Musgrave) B.; B.A., St. John's U., 1950; M.B.A., N.Y. U., 1951; m. Ann Elizabeth Kelly, July 9, 1955; children—Maureen, John, Ellen, Suzanne. Sr. accountant Lybrand, Ross Brothers & Montgomery, C.P.A.'s, N.Y.C., 1953-59; sr. auditor ITT, N.Y.C., 1959-62; asst. to controller Dictaphone Corp., Bridgeport, Conn., 1962-63, controller, Bridgeport, 1964-67, also Rye, N.Y., 1967-68; v.p. acctg. Chgo. and Northwestern Ry. Co., Chgo., 1968-69, v.p. fin. and acctg., Chgo. and Northwestern Ry. Co. and Chgo. and North Western Transp. Co., Chgo., 1969-79, also dir., sr. v.p. fin. and acctg. Chgo. and North Western Transp. Co., Chgo., 1979—. Served with USCGR, 1951-53. C.P.A., N.Y. Mem. Assn. Am. R.R.'s (mem. gen. com. acctg. div.), Am. Inst. C.P.A.'s, Fin. Execs. Inst. Roman Catholic. Office: 400 W Madison St Chicago IL 60606

BUTLER, OWEN BRADFORD, chem. co. exec.; b. Lynchburg, Va., Nov. 11, 1923; s. James Herbert and Ida Virginia (Garbee) B.; A.B., Dartmouth, 1947; m. Erna Bernice Dalton, Mar. 7, 1945; children—Nancy (Mrs. Wayne Archambault), James. With Procter & Gamble Co., Cin., 1945—, v.p. sales, 1968-70, v.p., group exec., 1970-73, exec. v.p., 1973-74, vice-chmn. bd., 1974-81, chmn. bd., 1981—, dir., 1972—; dir. Hosp. Corp. Am. Chmn. bd. trustees Good Samaritan Hosp.; bd. overseers Amos Tuck Sch. Bus. Adminstrn., Dartmouth Coll.; bd. dirs. Nat. Center for Resource Recovery. Com. Econ. Devel. (trustee), Phi Beta Kappa. Republican. Club: Queen City (Cin.). Office: PO Box 599 Cincinnati OH 45201

BUTLER, PARLEY NARVIN, mfg. co. exec.; b. Ogden, Utah, Dec. 22, 1928; s. Parley Arend and Louisa Ardelia (Thompson) B.; grad. Weber Coll., Ogden, 1950, grad. in Indsl. Engring., 1958; m. Wilma Johansen, Sept. 11, 1950; children—Susan, Curtis, Paul, Julie, Mary. Office mgr. Quaker Oats Co., Ogden, 1950-55, Joplin, Mo., 1955-59, Marion, Ohio, 1959-62, Chattanooga, Asheville, N.C. and Clarksville, Tenn., 1962-65, St. Joseph, Mo., 1965-73, controller subs. Magic Pan, Inc., San Francisco, 1973-74; asst. gen. mgr., controller Powder River Enterprises, Inc., Provo, Utah, 1974-75, asst. sec.-treas., 1975—, also controller; v.p., sec. Provo Aviation, 1978-80, Am. West Adv Inc., Provo, 1978—; sec.-treas. Powder River Motor Transport Corp., Provo, 1977—. Pres., Quaker Oats Employees Credit Union, St. Joseph, 1971-73; br. pres. Ch. Jesus Christ of Latter-Day Saints, Joplin, 1957-59, Marion, 1961-62, counselor to bishop, St. Joseph, 1968-71, stake high councilman, Independence, Mo., 1971-73. Served with JAGC, U.S. Army, 1946-48. Mem. Nat. Assn. Accts. (v.p. 1972-73), Adminstrv. Mgmt. Assn. Republican. Club: St. Joseph Lions (pres. 1971). Home: 625 E 60 N Circle Orem UT 84657 Office: 394 E 900 S Provo UT 84601

BUTLER, RICHARD COLBURN, banker, lawyer; b. Little Rock, Jan. 1, 1910; s. Richard Colburn and Edna (Clok) B.; student Little Rock Jr. Coll., 1929; A.B., U. Ark., 1931; m. Gertrude Remmel, Mar. 7, 1936; 1 son, Richard Colburn. Admitted to Ark. bar, 1933, U.S. Supreme Ct. bar; gen. practice law, Little Rock, 1933-63; partner firm House, Holmes, Butler & Jewell, 1941-63; pres., chmn. bd., sr. chmn. Comml. Nat. Bank Little Rock, 1963-80; chmn. bd. Livestock Bldg. Co., 1958—, Little Rock Abstract Co., 1970-80; chmn., dir. Peoples Savs. & Loan Assn. Little Rock; dir. First Ark. Devel. Finance Corp., Coca Cola Bottling Co. Ark., Kin-Ark Corp., Indsl. Devel. Co. of Little Rock. Pres. bd. trustees Little Rock U., 1961-63; bd. dirs. Little Rock Boys Club, pres., 1960; nat. asso. for Ark., Boys Clubs America, 1964-74; trustee, chmn. endowment com. Hendrix Coll., Conway, Ark.; pres. Pillars Club of United Way of Pulaski County. Served to maj. USAAF, 1942-46; CBI. Decorated Bronze Star. Mem. Am. Judicature Soc., Am., Ark. bar assns., Am. Iris Soc. (life, regional v.p. 1960-61), Am. Hemerocallis Soc., Bookfellows (pres. 1961), Little Rock C. of C. (pres. 1952). Methodist (chmn. bd. trustees). Clubs: Kiwanis, Little Rock Country, Little Rock, XV; Union League (Chgo.). Home: 36 River Ridge Rd Little Rock AR 72207 Office: 200 Main St Little Rock AR 72203

BUTKI, ARNOLD, steel co. exec., educator; b. Detroit, Apr. 25, 1935; s. Julius Joseph and Clara Tillie (Sadowski) B.; B.S., U. Mich., 1960; M.B.A., Claremont Grad. Sch., 1968; m. Joanne Ruth Schumacher, July 22, 1961; children—Jay Michael, Ellen Kay, Scott Andrew. With Kaiser Steel Corp., Fontana, Calif., 1960—, supr. indsl. engring., 1968-70, div. indsl. engr., 1970—, div. supr. operating practices, 1976—; asst. prof. mgmt. Calif. State U., Los Angeles, 1968—. Bd. dirs. YMCA Trail Blazers, 1976-80, dir., chief, 1968-71, 73-76; treas. Riverside Runners, 1981—. Served with U.S. Army, 1954-56. Registered profl. engr. Mem. Am. Iron and Steel Engrs., Am. Inst. Indsl. Engrs., Iron and Steel Soc. Am. Inst. Mining and Metall. Engrs., Nat. Soc. Profl. Engrs., Calif. Profl. Engrs., Claremont Grad. Sch. Alumni Assn. (fin. v.p. council 1969-73, pres. 1974-76). Republican. Roman Catholic. Contbr. articles to profl. jours. Home: 2180 Buckskin Pl Riverside CA 92506 Office: PO Box 217 Fontana CA 92336

BUTOROVICH, VERNON WILLIAM, mfg. co. exec.; b. Oakland, Calif., Nov. 24, 1939; s. Frank and Irene Diane B.; B.A., San Francisco State U., 1968; children—Colleen Marie, Theresa Lynn. Miner, construction Carrigan Mines, Inc., Sonora, Calif., 1957-61, also dir.; research asso. Sun Chem. Corp., San Leandro, Calif., 1965-66; physicist, design engr. Pacific Electric Motor Co., Oakland, Calif., 1968-74; pres. TechniTrek Corp., Union City, Calif. (formerly in San Leandro), 1974—, also dir. Served with U.S. Army, 1963-65. Mem. San Francisco State U. Alumni Assn. Republican. Designer accelerator beam optics electromagnets, magnetic separators for removal of contaminates from kaolin clay, coal and oil, heat exchanger systems for cooling elect. equipment, fusion research containment magnetic coils, fusion pulse transformers, solar energy collectors and solar systems, magnetic separators for food processing and wastewater purification, advanced flying insect control device. Home: 2108 Miramonte Ave San Leandro CA 94578 Office: 34701 7th St Bldg 1B Union City CA 94587

BUTSCH, WILLIAM MEREDITH, lawyer, acct.; b. Birmingham, Ala., Aug. 3, 1945; s. Leonard Milton and Felicia Ann (McLaughlin) B.; B.S., Auburn U., 1966; J.D., Woodrow Wilson Coll. Law, 1978. Admitted to Ga. bar, 1978; pvt. practice acctg., individual practice taxation law, Atlanta, 1980—. Served with USAF, 1967-68. Mem. Am. Bar Assn., Fed. Bar Assn., Ga. State Bar, Atlanta Bar Assn. Home: PO Box 8352 Atlanta GA 30306 Office: Suite 2301 1175 Peachtree St NE Atlanta GA 30361

BUTTERFIELD, BRUCE SCOTT, pub. co. exec.; b. N.Y.C., Feb. 4, 1949; s. Richard Julian and Mary (Hart) B.; B.A. cum laude, Amherst Coll., 1971; M.A., Harvard U., 1972; M.B.A., U. Conn., 1977. Adminstrv. asst. Golden Press div. Western Pub. Co., N.Y.C., 1972, editor, coordinator, 1973-74, sr. editor, 1975-76, mng. editor, adminstr., 1977, gen. mgr. Decisions Publs., 1978; pub. Scholastic, Inc., 1979—; cons. gen. bus.; cons. edn. Recipient Nat. Fedn. Music award, 1963; John F. Kennedy Meml. Brotherhood award, 1967; named Most Valuable Pitcher, Bergen Highlanders, 1969, All New Eng. Amateur Baseball Pitcher, 1971, All Am. Amateur Baseball Pitcher, 1971; recipient Wall St. Jour. Achievement Award, 1978. Mem. Am. Acad. Arts and Scis., Am. Acad. Polit. and Social Scis., Assn. Am. Publishers, Assn. M.B.A. Execs, Beta Gamma Sigma, Phi Delta Kappa, Phi Delta Sigma. Republican. Christian Scientist. Clubs: Forum, Harvard (N.Y.C.). Author: Fantasy and the Free School Thought: E.B. White and His Literature for Children, 1971; A Plea for Fantasy, 1972. Editor various books including: ABC's Wide World of Sports, 1975; Buccaneers, 1975; Book of the Mysterious, 1976; Chroma-Schema, 1977; Calculator Games, 1977; Children's Bible Stories, 1978; Oh Heavenly Dog, 1980. Home: 78 Heritage Hill Rd New Canaan CT 06840 Office: Scholastic Inc 50 W 44th St New York NY 10036

BUTTON, A. DWIGHT, banker; b. Wichita, Kans., Aug. 18, 1917; s. Albert D. and Helen Marie (Flynn) B.; m. Helen Margie Hawkins, Jan. 3, 1942; children—Gary D., Steven D., Thomas R. With 4th Nat. Bank & Trust Co., Wichita, Kans., 1937—, v.p., asst. to pres., pres., now chmn. bd.; chmn. bd. 4th Fin. Corp., Wichita; dir. Kaneb Services, Inc., Houston, Kans. Gas & Electric Co., Wichita, Ranger Nat. Life Ins. Co., Winnipeg, Can. Mem. Wichita Crime Commn.; bd. dirs. Wichita State U. Endowment Assn.; bd. advs. U. Kans. Sch. Bus. Served with U.S. Army, 1941-45. Decorated Bronze Star. Mem. Am. Bankers Assn., Kans. Bankers Assn., Wichita Area C. of C. (v.p., dir.), Kans. Assn. Commerce and Industry. Clubs: Wichita, Wichita Country. Office: PO Box 1090 Wichita KS 67201

BUTTON, BLAND BALLARD, investment banker; b. Louisville, June 25, 1915; s. Bland Ballard and Alleene Harwood (Wilson) B.; B.S., U. Chgo., 1938; m. Patricia Spooner, Sept. 20, 1969; children—Justine, Louise, Marcy, Kenneth. With Diversey Corp., Chgo., 1939-62, exec. v.p., 1959-62; v.p. Internat. Minerals & Chem. Corp., Libertyville, Ill., 1962-68; dir. spl. services Olin Corp., Stamford, Conn., 1969-72; investment banker F. Eberstadt & Co., N.Y.C., 1972-76; pres. Bland B. Button & Assos., Bronxville, N.Y., 1976—; chmn. bd., dir. Chemvet Labs., Inc., Kansas City, Kans.; dir. Bonewitz Chems. Inc., Burlington, Iowa. Mem. citizens bd. U. Chgo., 1958—. Republican. Episcopalian. Clubs: St. Andrews Golf, N.Y. Caledonian Curling, Indian Hill, University of Chicago. Home and office: 65 Durham Rd Bronxville NY 10708

BUTTON, JOHN WILLIAM, ins. co. exec.; b. Cromwell, Conn., Apr. 28, 1928; s. Milton Sherman and Ellen Louise (Johnson) B.; ed. U. Pa.; m. Jeanette Mae Erle, Nov. 25, 1954; children—Janice Lee, Joyce Ann, Judith Lynn. Payroll auditor Aetna Ins. Co., 1952-54; fieldman Employers Mut. Cos., 1954-64, underwriter, 1964-67, underwriting mgr., 1967-69, br. mgr., 1969-78; v.p., exec. asst. Employers Modern Life Co., Des Moines, 1978-79, chief operating officer, 1980-81, exec. v.p., 1981—; tchr. Phila. Ins. Soc., 1965-78. Fin. and ins. chairperson United Way, 1980; public relations officer USCG Aux. Served with USN, 1948-52. C.L.U., C.P.C.U. Mem. Soc. C.P.C.U.'s, Am. Soc. C.L.U.'s, Phila. Ins. Soc., Des Moines C. of C. Office: PO Box 712 717 Mulberry St Des Moines IA 50309

BUTTS, ARTHUR EDWARD, footwear mfg. co. exec.; b. Melrose, Mass., Mar. 6, 1947; s. Arthur E. and Anne (Wallace) B.; student Northeastern U., 1966-72; m. Nancy E. Dias, Sept. 9, 1967; children—Catherine A., Jeffrey A. Planning and control mgr. H.K. Porter Inc., Somerville, Mass., 1964-72: systems analyst J.F. McElwain Co. div. Melville Corp., Nashua, N.H., 1972-73, mgr. purchasing, 1973-78, dir. purchasing, 1978—. Trustee, Longmeadow Ch., 1978—; mem. Auburn Bd. Suprs., 1978—. Mem. Two-Ten Assos., Am. Mgmt. Assn. Republican. Home: 7 Rockwood Terr Auburn NH 03032 Office: 12 Murphy Dr Nashua NH 03061

BUTTS, JANE ESTHER DICKSON, comml. real estate broker; b. Washington, Apr. 3, 1920; d. Walter Stone and Helene Marguerite (Guerdrum) Dickson; student Lamar Coll. 1964; grad. Tex. A. and M. U., 1979; m. Jack Rockward Butts, Mar. 25, 1952; children—Victor Stone, Raymond Carl, Lawrence Lee, Loretta Ann. Operator pvt. dancing sch. Savannah, Ga., from 1936; traveling producer Empire Producers, Washington, 1937; singer, dancer various night clubs, Washington and Cleve. 1938; mem., dancer Roxyettes, Gay Foster Dancers, N.Y.C., Atlanta, Balt. 1939; instr. dancing, N.Y.C., 1940-41, Washington, 1941-43, Hawaii, 1946-47, Fla., 1947-54, Beaumont, Tex. 1954-63; real estate salesman, Beaumont, 1964-66; broker Butts Real Estate Co., Port Arthur, Tex. 1966—; cons. comml. real estate, specializing in shopping center leasing and mgmt. Mem. Greater Port Arthur C. of C., 1968-78; mem. Pride in Port Arthur, 1971-76, chmn., 1976. Recipient numerous letters of appreciation. Democrat. Christian Scientist and Methodist. Composer 57 songs. Home: 2312 Procter St Port Arthur TX 77640 Office: 4349 Procter St Port Arthur TX 77640

BUXTON, EDWARD F(ULTON), publisher, editor, author; b. Boston, May 8, 1917; s. Edward W. and Grace (Hurlurt) B.; B.A. in Journalism, U. Wis., Madison, 1940; postgrad. Northwestern U., 1940-41; m. Susan E. Abrams, Jan. 12, 1962; children by previous marriage—Gail, Leslie. With Wis. Press Bur., 1939-40, McCann Erickson, Chgo., 1940-42, Kenyon and Eckhardt Avt., N.Y.C., Compton Advt., N.Y.C. and J. Walter Thompson Advt., 1946-65; founder, pres., chief exec. officer Executive Communications, Inc., N.Y.C., 1965—; author: Promise Them Anything, 1973; Creative People at Work, 1977; contbr. articles to periodicals; lectr. coll. and bus. groups. Served with USNR, 1942-46. Recipient various creative advt. awards. Mem. Advt. Club N.Y., Copy Club N.Y., Alpha Delta Sigma. Democrat. Clubs: Wis. Alumni, Nat. W. Home: 185 E 85th St New York NY 10028 Office: 400 E 54th St New York NY 10022

BUYERS, JOHN WILLIAM AMERMAN, agribus. and splty. foods co. exec.; b. Coatesville, Pa., July 17, 1928; s. William Buchanan and Rebecca (Watson) B.; B.A. in History cum laude, Princeton U., 1952; M.S. in Indsl. Mgmt. (Sloan fellow), M.I.T., 1963; m. Elsie Palmer Parkhurst, Apr. 11, 1953; children—Elsie Buyers Viehman, Rebecca Watson, Jane Palmer. Div. ops. mgr. Bell Telephone Co. Pa., 1964-66; dir. ops. and personnel Gen. Waterworks Corp., Phila., 1966-68, pres., chief exec. officer, 1971-75; v.p. adminstrn. Internat. Utilities Corp., Phila., 1968-71; pres., chief exec. officer, dir. C. Brewer and Co., Ltd., Honolulu, 1975—; dir. First Hawaiian Bank, Calif. and Hawaiian Sugar Co.; mem. Gov.'s Adv. Council China Affairs, U.S. Army Civilian Adv. Group, Hawaii Joint Council Econ. Edn., Japan-Hawaii Econ. Council, Commn. on Jud. Discipline. Bd. dirs. Honolulu Symphony Soc.; trustee U. Hawaii Found. Served with USMC, 1946-48. Mem. Hawaiian Sugar Planners Assn. (chmn. bd. 1980-81, dir.), C. of C. Hawaii (vice chmn., dir.), Nat. Alliance Bus. (chmn. Hawaii Pacific Metro chpt. 1978), Newcomen Soc. N. Am., Donegal Soc., S.R. Presbyterian. Clubs: Cap and Gown (Princeton); Hilo Yacht, Oahu Country, Pacific, Plaza, Waiialae Country; Prouts Neck (Maine) Country; Racquet (Phila); Waynesborough Country (Paoli, Pa.). Home: 148 Poipu Dr Honolulu HI 96825 also Buckhaven Farm RD 3 Benton PA 17814 Office: 827 Fort St Mall Honolulu HI 96805

BUYS, CLIFFORD RICHARDS, assn. exec.; b. Wichita, Kans., Dec. 13, 1923; s. Ivan and Abbie Frances (Richards) B.; B.S. with honors in Banking and Fin., U. Ill., 1943; M.Bus. and Public Adminstrn., Southeastern U., 1978; m. Elva Catherine Quaglia, Nov. 20, 1945 (dec. 1969); 1 dau., Barbara Catherine Buys Fries; m. 2d, Jean Elizabeth Perryman Grande, Nov. 24, 1973. Acct., Am. President Lines, Yokohama, Japan, 1946-51; dir. case analysis Wage Stblzn. Bd., Richmond, Va., 1951-53; mgr. automation Allied Chem. Corp., N.Y.C., 1953-64; gen. mgr. Frantzreb & Pray Assos., N.Y.C., 1964-66; dir. mgmt. systems Am. Trucking Assn., Washington, 1966—; adj. instr. Fairleigh Dickinson U., Madison, N.J., 1964-66; bd. dirs. Transp. Data Coordinating Com., Inc., 1971—. Served with USMC, 1943-46. Cert. data educator. Mem. Ret. Officers Assn., Beta Gamma Sigma, Phi Kappa Phi. Republican. Methodist. Club: Army and Navy (Washington). Editor: Handbook of Data Processing in the Motor Carrier Industry, 1969. Home: 1709 Irvin St Vienna VA 22180 Office: 1616 P St Washington DC 20036

BUZBY, RUSSELL CONWELL, services mgmt. co. exec.; b. N.J., Feb. 13, 1934; s. Leland Stanford and Ethel Mae (McHenry) B.; B.A. with honors, Lafayette Coll.; m. Gloria Jean Landry, July 11, 1953; children—William James, Patricia Ann, Linda Sue, Mary Ellen. Personnel mgr. Armstrong Cork Co., Lancaster, Pa., 1959-64; personnel dir. Celanese Corp., N.Y.C., 1964-72; v.p. Ryder System, Miami, Fla., 1972-75; sr. v.p. ARA Services, Phila., 1975—. Bd. dirs. Phila. Drama Guild, Pa. Economy League, 1979—; chmn. Hospitality Employers' Council, 1979—. Served to capt. U.S. Army 1956-58. Mem. Labor Relations Council, Conf. Personnel Officers. Office: ARA Services Independence Square W Philadelphia PA 19106

BYE, RAYMOND SIGURD, ins. exec.; b. Mpls., May 30, 1919; s. Sigurd Hjalmer and Alice Marie (Johansen) B.; student Hamline U., 1940-42, U. Minn., 1944-46; m. Mary Clarissa Edwards, July 7, 1944; children—Monte R., Marianne, Joseph, Christine, Virginia. Packagine engr. 3M Co., Mpls. and St. Paul, 1945-49; regional dir. Saturday Evening Post, Curtis Pub. Co., Atlanta, Washington and Louisville, 1949-67; asst. to v.p., loan officer Monroe Mortgage Corp., Vienna, Va., 1968-72; with Comml. Security Bank, Salt Lake City, 1973-76; v.p. Travel Host of Utah, Salt Lake City, 1973-78; v.p. Mgmt. Corp. Unltd., Bountiful, Utah, 1973-78; nat. sales dir. Direct Line Communications Corp., 1978—; mktg. v.p. Travelhost Mag. of Utah, Salt Lake City, 1976—; mgmt. cons. Mayor, Town of South Arlington (Va.), 1962-63; mem. Atlanta Stake presidency Ch. of Jesus Christ of Latter-day Saints, 1955-60. Served with USAAF, 1939-43. Patentee packing list inserter; Scotchlite fabric. Home: 7596 Silver Fork Dr Salt Lake City UT 84121

BYER, MARSHALL, mech. engr.; b. Boston, Sept. 16, 1924; s. Selik J. and Flora (Goldsmith) B.; B.S., Mass. Inst. Tech., 1945, M.S., 1947; m. Dorothy Elaine VanVleet, June 13, 1949; children—Deborah E. Byer McLaren, Judith Y. Byer Freeman, Linda D. Test engr. high pressure boilers Foster Wheeler Corp., Dansville, N.Y., 1947-48; sr. engr. glass forming machinery, photosensitive glass devel. and mfr. Corning Glass Works (N.Y.), 1948-58; sr. engr., mgr. components product assurance, mgr. product environment tech. assignment IBM, Owego, N.Y., 1958-69, Endicott, N.Y., 1969—. Served with USNR, 1943-46, 51-53; lt. comdr. (ret.). Registered profl. engr., N.Y., Calif., Fla. Mem. ASME, Nat., N.Y. State socs. profl. engrs. Patentee composite glaceramic articles. Home: 921 Vestal Rd Vestal NY 13850 Office: IBM Corp PO Box 6 Endicott NY 13760

BYERS, BROOK HAMPTON, fin. mgmt. co. exec.; b. Belleville, Ill., Aug. 2, 1945; s. Kenneth Gunning, Sr., and Kathryn Worden (Hancock) B.; B.E.E., Ga. Inst. Tech., 1968; M.B.A. (Herbert Hoover fellow), Stanford U., 1970. Engr. FCC, Atlanta, 1963-67; div. gen. mgr. Behavioral Research Labs., Menlo Park, Calif., 1970-72; asso. Asset Mgmt. Co., Palo Alto, Calif., 1972-77, v.p., 1974-77; partner Kleiner & Perkins, San Francisco, 1977-78; gen. partner Kleiner, Perkins, Caufield & Byers, 1978—; chmn. Hybritech, Inc. Plexus Computers, Inc., Vitalink Communications Corp., Home Health Care Am., Inc. State youth chmn. U.S. Presdl. Campaign, 1968. Mem. Western (dir.), Nat. assns. venture capitalists. Clubs: San Francisco Bachelors, Baker St. Irregulars, Dolphin S. End Running, Stanford Bus. Sch. Nat. Alumni Assn. (dir.), Ga. Tech. Alumni No. Calif. (pres.). Contbg. author: Guide to Venture Capital, 1977. Office: Kleiner Perkins Caufield & Byers Two Embarcadero Center Suite 2900 San Francisco CA 94111

BYERS, EUGENE BENJAMIN, SR., computer co. exec., bus. cons.; b. Topeka, Nov. 24, 1943; s. Fletcher Dewitt and Laura Mae (Houston) B.; B.S., Morgan State Coll., 1965; M.B.A., Rutgers U., 1972; m. Barbara Jean Mulky, May 29, 1965; children—Derek, Eugene. With photo products div. E.I. Dupont de Nemours Co., Parlin, N.J., 1965-69; prodn. mgmt. staff Ethicon div. Johnson & Johnson, Somerville, N.J., 1969-71; mktg. rep., data processing div. IBM, West Orange, N.J., 1972—; pres./treas., bus. cons. EBB Enterprises, Inc., Hillside, N.J., 1969. Founder, bd. dirs. Edmund L. Houston Found., 1975-78; exec. bd. Elizabeth br. NAACP, 1977—; exec. dir. EBB Found.; chmn. bd. dirs. BHER Found.; bd. dirs. Newark/Essex chpt. Operation PUSH, 1977-78. Engelhard Minerals and Chems. grantee, 1972. Mem. Am. Mktg. Assn., Hillside Bus. and Profl. Assn., Union County Club of Nat. Assn. Negro Bus. and Profl. Women's Clubs, Inc., Am. Mgmt. Assn., Omega Psi Phi (named chpt. Man of Yr. 1980). Baptist. Club: Hillside High Sch. Afro-Am. Home: 56 Clark St Hillside NJ 07205 Office: 100 Executive Dr West Orange NJ 07102

BYRD, CHARLES DANIELL, mfg. co. exec.; b. Atlanta, May 3, 1925; s. Lloyd Porter and Gladys (Daniell) B.; B.Sc., Ohio State U., 1950; m. Suzanne Ballinger, May 18, 1952; children—Steven Daniel, Cynthia Suzanne. With Dresser Industries, 1952—; pres. oil tool div., Dallas, 1965-68, pres. petroleum equipment div., Salisbury, Md., 1968-71, pres. petroleum equipment group, Houston, 1971—; dir. AB Ljungmans Verkstader, Malmo, Sweden, Wayne, W. Africa, Lagos, Nigeria. Chmn. Greater Salisbury Com., 1973-75; trustee Peninsula Gen. Hosp., Salisbury, 1973-75; mem. com. for tomorrow Ohio State U., 1979-80; chmn. mfg. div. Combined Arts Corp. campaign, Houston, 1979-80. Served as officer USAAF, 1943-45. Mem. Am. Petroleum Inst., Am. Lift Inst., Gasoline and Pump Mfrs. Assn., Ohio State U. Assn. Republican. Methodist. Club: Houston Petroleum. Office: 2600 Dresser Tower 601 Jefferson St Houston TX 77002

BYRD, LUCID LINCOLN, engine parts mfg. exec.; b. Barberville, Fla.. Feb. 12, 1928; s. Kelly Bruce and Alice Edith (Crabtree) B.; B Indsl. Engring., Ga. Tech. U., 1952; children—Carol Jalane, Diana Margaret, Randolph Lucid. Foreman, mfg. engr., quality engr. Gen. Electric Co., Morrison, Ill., 1955-64; mgr. quality control ITT Controls & Instrument Div., Des Plaines, Ill., 1964-67; v.p. gen. mgr. Carter Precision Electric Co., Skokie, Ill., 1967-74; mgr. mfg., engine accessories operation Colt Industries, Beloit, Wis., 1974-79, mgr. ops. crucible compaction metals operation, Oakdale, Pa., 1979—. Presbyterian. Patentee elec. switch assemblies. Home: 1000 Westpointe Dr Pittsburgh PA 15205

BYRNE, MICHAEL JOSEPH, assn. exec.; b. Chgo., Apr. 3, 1928; s. Michael Joseph and Edith (Lueken) B.; B.Sc. in Mktg., Loyola U., Chgo., 1952; m. Eileen Kelly, June 27, 1953; children—Michael Joseph, Nancy, James, Thomas, Patrick, Terrence. Sales engr. Emery Industries, Inc., Cin., 1952-59; with Pennsalt Chem. Corp., Phila., 1959-60; pres. Oakton Cleaners, Inc., Skokie, Ill., 1960-70, Dataforms & Midwest Mktg. Assn., 1970—, Datatax Inc., 1974-75, Metro Tax Service, Inc., 1975—, Midwest Synthetic Lubrication Products, 1978—. Served with Ordnance Corps, AUS, 1946-48. Mem. AIM, VFW, Alpha Kappa Psi. Club: Toastmasters Internat. Home: 7350 Main St Niles IL 60648

BYRNE, RUSSELL FRANCIS, JR., mfg. co. exec.; b. St. Louis, July 8, 1943; s. Russell F. and Virginia M. B.; B.S. in Bus. and Public Adminstrn., U. Mo., 1967; m. Patsy J. Settles, Apr. 9, 1970; children—Jennifer, Russell, Kevin. Supr., Ernst & Ernst, St. Louis, 1970-77; dir. fin. and adminstrn. Worthington Service Corp., St. Louis, 1977-80; v.p., sec.-treas. Clayton Corp., St. Louis, 1980—. Served with U.S. Army, 1968-70. Mem. Fin. Execs. Inst., Am. Inst. C.P.A.'s, Mo. Soc. C.P.A.'s, Phi Kappa Theta. Home: 1798 Kimkirk Ct Kirkwood MO 63122 Office: 4205 Forest Park Blvd Saint Louis MO 63108

BYROM, FLETCHER LAUMAN, chem. mfr.; b. Cleve., July 13, 1918; s. Fletcher L. and Elizabeth C. Byrom; B.S. in Metallurgy, Pa. State U., 1940; m. Marie L. McIntyre, Feb. 17, 1945; children—Fletcher Lauman, Carol A. Byrom Conrad, Susan J. Byrom Evans. Sales engr. Am. Steel & Wire Co., Cleve., 1940-42; procurement and adminstrv. coordination Naval Ordnance Lab., also Bur. Ordnance and Research Planning Bd., Navy Dept., 1942-47; asst. to gen. mgr. tar products div. Koppers Co., Inc., Pitts., 1947-54, asst. v.p., also mgr. ops. in tar products div., 1954-55, v.p., asst. gen. mgr. tar products div., 1955-58, v.p., gen. mgr., 1958-60, pres., chief adminstrv. officer, 1960-67, chief exec. officer, 1968—, dir., 1960—, chmn., 1970—; chmn. Pitts. br. Fed. Res. Bank Cleve., 1966-68; adv. dir. Unilever; dir. N.Y. Stock Exchange, N.Am. Philips Corp., Mellon Nat. Corp., ASARCO, Mex. DeSarrollo Indsl. Minero S.A., Ralston Purina Co., Continental Group, Inc. Chmn. Conf. Bd., 1975-76; trustee, chmn. Com. for Econ. Devel.; mem. Bus. Council, Regional Indsl. Devel. Corp.; chmn. bd. trustees Presbyn.-Univ. Hosp., Kiski Sch. Recipient Distinguished Civilian Service award U.S. Navy Dept.; Distinguished Alumnus award Pa. State U., 1963. Mem. Am. Iron and Steel Inst., Am. Coke and Coal Chems. Inst., Am. Wood Preservers Assn., Eastern States Blast Furnace and Coke Assn., Engrs. Soc. Western Pa., Pa. State U. Alumni Assn. (pres. 1965-66), Phi Kappa Psi. Presbyterian (elder). Clubs: Duquesne, Fox Chapel Golf (Pitts.); Laurel Valley Golf, Rolling Rock (Ligonier, Pa.); Met. (Washington); Links (N.Y.C.); Little Egg Harbor Yacht (Beach Haven, N.J.); Desert Forest Golf (Ariz.). Home: Chatham Center Tower Pittsburgh PA 15219 Office: Koppers Bldg Pittsburgh PA 15219

CABOT, LOUIS WELLINGTON, chem. mfg. co. exec.; b. Boston, Aug. 3, 1921; s. Thomas Dudley and Virginia (Wellington) C.; A.B., Harvard, 1943, M.B.A., 1948; LL.D. (hon.), Norwich U., 1961; m. Mary Ellen Flynn de Pena Vera, Oct. 19, 1974; children by previous marriage—James Bass, Anne Louise Stewart, Godfrey Lowell II, Amanda Chilton Connolly, Helen. With Cabot Corp., 1948—, pres., 1960-69, chmn. bd., 1969—; mng. dir. Cabot Carbon, Ltd. (Eng.), 1949-51; v.p., treas. Godfrey L. Cabot, Inc. and subsidiaries, 1953-60; dir. Owens-Corning Fiberglas Corp., R.R. Donnelley & Sons Co., Chgo., New Eng. Tel. & Tel. Co., N.E. Mchts. Nat. Bank, 1953-69, Arthur D. Little, 1955-67; dir. Fed. Res. Bank Boston, 1970-78, chmn., 1975-78. U.S. rep. 15th Plenary Session UN Econ. Commn. for Europe, 1960; mem. bus. ethics adv. council Dept. Commerce, 1961-63; Boston chmn. Nat. Alliance Businessmen, 1968-69, dir., New Eng. chmn., 1970-72; chmn. Com. Corporate Support Pvt. Univs., Sloan Commn. Govt. and Higher Edn. Pres. Beverly Hosp., 1958-61; chmn. Harvard Coll. Fund Council, 1963-65; incorporator Boston Hosp. Women; mem. corp. M.I.T.; trustee Norwich U., 1952-77, Carnegie Corp. N.Y., 1966-78, Northeastern U., Boys Clubs Boston, Inc.; vice chmn. Brookings Instn.; v.p. Boston Mus. of Sci.; bd. overseers Harvard U., 1970-76. Served as lt. USNR, 1943-46. Recipient Bus. Statesman award Harvard Bus. Sch. Assn., Boston, 1966. Fellow Am. Acad. Arts and Scis.; mem. U.S. C. of C. (dir.), Internat. C. of C. (dir. U.S. council), Bus. Council, Conf. Bd., Bus. Com. for the Arts, Nat. Council U.S.-China Trade (dir.), Council Fgn. Relations, Phi Beta Kappa, Sigma Xi. Clubs: Harvard (Boston) (N.Y.C.); Somerset, Economic, Commercial (pres. 1970-72) (Boston); Metropolitan (Washington); Kandahar Ski; Wianno (Osterville). Office: 125 High St Boston MA 02110

CABOT, POWELL MASON, investment banker; b. Boston, Apr. 11, 1931: s. Powell M. and Virginia A. (Curtin) C.; A.B., Harvard U., 1953, M.B.A., 1959; m. Bernadette M. LeGuay, Apr. 29, 1961; children—Powell, Stephanie, Christopher. Vice pres., office mgr. Goldman Sachs & Co., 1959-70; dir. Oppenheimer & Co., Ltd., London, 1971-76, partner, 1973—; v.p. Oppenheimer Capital. Trustee, Mystic (Conn.) Seaport Mus. Served to lt. (j.g.) USNR, 1954-57; Korea. Republican. Clubs: Knickerbocker, Mashomack (N.Y.C.); Hurlingham, Lansdowne (London). Home: 16 Knollwood Dr Greenwich CT 06830 Office: 1 New York Plaza New York NY 10004

CABRAL, FRANCISCO ROBLEDO, bus. supply co. exec.; b. Ciudad Juarez, Chihuahua, Mexico, Aug. 8, 1946; came to U.S., 1960, naturalized, 1964; s. José Sanchez and Guadalupe (Robledo) C.; B.A., U. Tex., 1970; B.A., El Paso Community Coll., 1973-76; m. Elena Montes Roldan, Oct. 27, 1967; children—Claudia, Francisco, Yadira. Mgr. Abbott Labs., El Paso, Tex., 1970; mgr. WIGPO, El Paso, 1972-74; dir. fairs and expositions Nacional Juarez Mexico, Juarez, Mexico, 1975—. Served with U.S. Army, 1964-66. Decorated Viet-Nam medal, Airborne Wings. Mem. Nat. Assn. Fairs and Expositions, Nat. Assn. Adminstrn. Roman Catholic. Club: Lions. Home: 5029 Louis St El Paso TX 79904

CACCIA, PAUL ANTHONY, acct.; b. Forest Hills, N.Y., Nov. 13, 1947; s. Alexander L. and Gertrude L. (Yoell) C.; B.S., St. John's U., 1968, M.B.A., 1974. With Alpern & Bienes (now Avellino & Bienes), C.P.A.'s, N.Y.C., 1967-71, sr. acct., 1970-71; pvt. practice pub. acctg., N.Y.C., 1972-74; prin. Paul Caccia P.C., C.P.A., N.Y.C., 1974—; lectr. accounting various N.Y. colls. C.P.A., N.Y. Mem. Am. Inst. C.P.A.'s, N.Y. State Soc. C.P.A.'s, Accounting Research Assn. Home: 401 E 86th St New York NY 10028 Office: 30 E 42d St New York NY 10017

CADIEUX, EUGENE ROGERS, ins. co. exec.; b. Detroit, Feb. 14, 1923; s. Harold S. and Nadia (Rogers) C.; student U. Detroit Coll. Commerce and Finance, 1941-42, Sch. Law, 1952; m. Leontine Keane, May 10, 1975. With bond dept. Standard Accident Ins. Co.,

Detroit, 1951-54; bond mgr. Am. Ins. Co., Detroit, 1954-65, bond mgr. Fireman's Fund, Cin., 1965-66; bond mgr. Md. Casualty Co., Detroit, 1966-75, Zervos Agy., Detroit, 1976—; cons. to contractors, 1957—. Asst. dir. boys work Internat. Assn. Y's Mens Clubs, 1953; committeeman YMCA, Detroit. Trustee Joint Meml. Day Assn. Served with AUS, World War II. Mem. Surety Assn. Mich. (sec. 1958), Am. Assn. State and Local History, Mich., Detroit (trustee, sec. 1971—), Cin. (com. on library and acquisitions) hist. socs., S.A.R. (pres. Mich. soc. 1961-62, bd. mgrs., nat. Americanism com.), Friends of Pub. Library Cin., Grosse Pointe (hist. com.), Grosse Pointe Hist. Soc. (pres. 1980), Delta Sigma Pi, Gamma Eta Gamma. Clubs: Country of Detroit; Grosse Pointe Ski; Algonquin. Home: 208 Ridgemont Rd Grosse Pointe Farms MI 48236 Office: Zervos Agy 24724 Farmbrook Rd Southfield MI 48034

CADIGAN, PATRICK FINBAR, mfg. co. exec.; b. Stoneham, Mass., Mar. 1, 1935; s. Denis J. and Mary (Sullivan) C.; B.S., Boston Coll., 1957; M.B.A., Boston U., 1966; M.A., Claremont Grad. Sch., 1977, Ph.D., 1980; m. Barbara Ann Curran, June 13, 1959; children—Ann Kathleen, David Patrick, Maria Ann. Product mgr. Sylvania Electronic Systems, Waltham, Mass., 1961-67; gen. sales mgr. EECO Inc., Santa Ana, Calif., 1967-69, v.p., gen. mgr., 1969-73, pres., chief exec. officer, 1973—, also dir. Bd. dirs. U. Calif., Irvine Found. & Indsl. Assos.; bd. fellows Claremont U. Center. Served with U.S. Army, 1958-59. Mem. IEEE. Roman Catholic. Office: 1601 E Chestnut Ave Santa Ana CA 92701

CADILE, JOSEPH VINCENT, mech. engr.; b. Detroit, Feb. 19, 1944; s. Samual Joseph and Antionette Marie (Orlando) C.; student Ohio U., 1963; Grad. Salem Sch. Tech., 1965; m. Nancy Lee Grimm, Feb. 5, 1966; children—Michelle Sue, Paula Jo, Pamala Lynn. With Morgan Engring., Alliance, Ohio, 1965—, design engr. for standards, research and devel., 1965-75, supr. research and devel., 1975-79, system mgr., 1979—. Mem. ASME (main body com., chmn. exec. com. on cranes for nuclear power plants, mech. and structural subcoms.), Crane Mfrs. Assn. Am. (statis. com.), Assn. Iron and Steel Engrs. (main body com., mech. and structural working group for Standards #6, specification for electric overhead traveling cranes steel mill service, rep. coms. on cranes for nuclear power plants). Inventor earthquake stabilization device for cranes working above nuclear reactors used to generate elec. power; contbr. paper, standards for profl. orgns. Home: 14517 Beloit Snodes Rd Beloit OH 44609 Office: 947 E Broadway Alliance OH 44601

CADY, WILLIAM ROMYN, investment banker; b. St. Louis, July 2, 1926; s. William Romyn and Margaret Heiskell (Ball) C.; A.B., Princeton, 1948; m. Sara Ann Tarrant, July 7, 1948; children—Ann R. (Mrs. Hugh Scott III), Margaret B., Elise R. (Mrs. J. Tracey Leiweke). Reporter, St. Louis Star Times, 1948-51; account exec. T.W. Parry & Assos., 1951-52; account exec. Glee Stocker & Assos., 1952-58; pres. Kady, Inc., 1958-63; gen. partner Reinholdt & Gardner, St. Louis, 1963-74; v.p. Newhard, Cook & Co., Inc., 1974—; dir. Nat. Computer Service, Inc Vice pres., bd. dirs. Indsl. Devel. Corp. St. Charles County, Mo., Inc. Served with AUS, 1944-46. Recipient Distinguished Service award Jr. C. of C., 1961. Clubs: Bellerive Country (pres. 1976-77), Noonday, Univ. Home: 1240 Lay Rd Saint Louis MO 63124 Office: 300 N Broadway Saint Louis MO 63102

CAFFREY, RONALD JANSS, bldg. control and automation co. exec.; b. N.Y.C., Mar. 16, 1928; s. John Parker and Mildred Anna (Janss) C.; B.S. in Indsl. Engring. and Bus. Adminstrn., Yale, 1948; m. Suzanne Westermann, Apr. 2, 1949 (div. Jan. 1977); children—Carol Lyn, Karen Sue Caffrey Johnson; m. 2d, Kathleen Jakubiak; 1 son, Ronald Janss. With Johnson Controls, 1949—, sales engr., N.Y.C., 1949-64, br. mgr., 1964-69, regional mgr., Dallas, 1969-72, Chgo., 1972-74, v.p. mktg., Milw., 1974-76, v.p. mktg. and bldg. automation systems, Milw., 1976—. Bd. dirs. Port Washington (N.Y.) Estates Assn., 1960-63, United Fund, Dallas, 1969-70. Mem. Am. Soc. Heating, Refrigerating and Air Conditioning Engrs. (dir. 1974-77). Contbr. articles to profl. jours. Office: 507 E Michigan St Milwaukee WI 53202

CAFIERO, EUGENE ANTHONY, automobile co. exec.; b. N.Y.C., June 13, 1926; s. Anthony Eugene and Frances D. (Lauricella) C.; A.B., Dartmouth, 1946; postgrad. Rutgers U., 1947-48, Columbia, 1948-49, U. Mich., 1950-51; M.S. (Sloan fellow), M.I.T., 1959; D.Sc. (hon.), Wittenberg U.; m. Nancy Appleton Barnard, Jan. 23, 1960. With David Smith Steel Co., N.Y.C., 1947-49; with Ford Motor Co., Edgewater, N.J. and Dearborn, Mich., 1949-51; indsl. engr. Briggs Mfg. Co., Detroit, 1951-53; with Chrysler, Detroit, 1953—, v.p. Latin Am. ops., 1968-70, group v.p. U.S. and Can. automotive, 1970-72, group v.p. N.Am. ops., 1972, later sr. exec. v.p., dir, pres., chief operating officer, 1975-78, vice chmn., 1978-79; pres., chief exec. officer DeLorean Motor Co., N.Y.C., 1979—. Seved with USNR, 1946-47. Mem. Soc. Automotive Engrs., Nat. Mgmt. Assn., Soc. Sloan Fellows. Office: 280 Park Ave New York NY 10017

CAFIERO, FRANK ANTONY, acct./realtor; b. New Haven, May 29, 1953; s. Frank and Marie Theresa (Cagliotti) C.; B.S. in Acctg., U. Conn., 1975. Acct., Coopers & Lybrand, Hartford, Conn., 1975-77; with Mfrs. Life Ins., Hartford, 1977-78; adminstr. U. Conn., Storrs, 1978; with Personal Devel. & Research, N.Y.C., 1978-80; pres. Antony Enterprises, Tallahassee, 1980—. Bd. dirs. Countryside Condominium Assn., Newington, Conn., 1975-78, Assn. Student Commissaries, U. Conn., Storrs, 1975-78. Mem. Delta Sigma Pi. Home: 1852 Cottage Grove Rd Tallahassee FL 32303 Office: PO Box 4376 Tallahassee FL 32303

CAHALEN, GLENN MARTIN, assn. exec.; b. Loveland, Colo., Dec. 12, 1925; s. Herbert and Kathryn Elizabeth (Studeville) C.; student public schs., Iola, Kans.; m. Florence Elizabeth Gaskill, Nov. 9, 1945; children—Martha Jane Cahalen Proctor, Cheryl Ann, Glenn Michael, Daniel Mark. Fireman, Santa Fe Ry., Winslow and Seligman, Ariz., 1945-47; advt. mgr. Sears Roebuck & Co., Shawnee, Okla., 1948-49; salesman Gen. Foods, Tulsa, 1949-52; Pillsbury Mills, Tulsa, 1952-56, Cruden Martin Brokerage Co., Springfield, Mo., 1956-62; with U.S. C. of C., Tulsa, 1963-65; div. mgr. Nat. Fedn. Ind. Bus., Tulsa, 1965—. Baptist. Home and Office: 10319 E 21st Pl Tulsa OK 74129

CAHILL, ARNOLD JAMES, chem. co. exec.; b. Detroit, June 14, 1930; s. Joseph B. and Marie V. (Morris) C.; B.S. in Chemistry, U. Detroit, 1953, M.B.A., 1960; m. L. Jean Gidilewich, June 6, 1959; children—Patrick, James, Daniel, Robert, Suzanne, Mark. Sales corr. Union Carbide Chems. Co., 1953-55; with Wyandotte Chems. Co., 1957-65, product mgr., 1964-65; with Gulf Oil Chems. Co., 1966—, dist. sales mgr., 1968-72, product mgr., 1973-74, gen. mgr. mktg., petrochems. div., Houston, 1974—. Pres., Harris County Friends of Library, 1979; rep. Timberline Soccer Assn., 1977-80. Served with AUS, 1955-57. Mem. Am. Inst. Chem. Engrs. (Speakers award 1977), S.W. Chem. Assn., Drug, Chem. and Allied Trades Assn., Soap and Deteregent Assn., Am. Chem. Soc. Home: 1010 Klamath St Houston TX 77090 Office: PO Box 3766 Houston TX 77001

CAHILL, GERARD ALBIN, electronics co. exec.; b. N.Y.C., Dec. 21, 1936; s. Albin G. and Susan E. (Maschenic) C.; B.S. in Elec. Engring., Manhattan Coll., 1958; M.B.A., City Coll. N.Y., 1962; Ph.D., N.Y.U., 1973; m. Barbara Viator, July 5, 1969. With Western Electric Co. Inc., N.Y.C., 1959-67; div. controller Gen. Dynamics Corp., Orlando, Fla., 1967-68; corp. controller Library Equities orp., Washington, 1968-69; v.p. HETRA Co., Melbourne, Fla., 1969-71, CODI Corp., Fairlawn, N.J., 1971-73; v.p. finance, treas. Cablecom-Gen. Inc., Denver, 1973—; cons. in field. Ford Found. fellow, 1965. Registered profl. engr., N.Y. Mem. Inst. Mgmt. Sci., IEEE. Club: N.Y. Athletic. Home: 6568 S Niagara Ct Englewood CO 80111 Office: 8800 E Arapahoe Rd Englewood CO 80110

CAHILL, JOHN MICHAEL, fin. planner; b. San Francisco, May 28, 1944; s. Thomas Joseph and Margaret Mary (Smyth) C.; B.A., U. San Francisco, 1966; M.B.A., Golden Gate U., 1979; m. JoAnn de la Torre, Aug. 20, 1966. Zone mgr. Investors Diversified Service, Oakland, Calif., 1970-71; prin. Carroll/Cahill Assos., San Francisco, 1971—. Mem. mgmt. council U. San Francisco, 1977-78, fund raising com., 1972-78. Served to capt. Arty., U.S. Army, 1966-70: Vietnam. Decorated Bronze Star; C.L.U.; cert. fin. planner. Mem. Internat. Assn. Fin. Planners (internat. bd. dirs. 1978—), Inst. Cert. Fin. Planners, East Bay Assn. Fin. Planners (past pres.), Nat., San Francisco life underwriters assns., Nat. Assn. Security Dealers, Boston Stock Exchange, Alpha Sigma Nu. Home: 109 Roberta Ave Pleasant Hill CA 94523 Office: 680 Beach St San Francisco CA 94109

CAHN, JULIUS NORMAN, publishing co. exec.; b. N.Y.C., Oct. 26, 1922; s. Richard David and Frieda (Cohen) C.; B.S.S., City Coll. N.Y., 1942; M.A., Am. U., 1948; m. Ann Foote, Oct. 20, 1946; children—Gary Alan, Glenn Evan, Linda Jan, Carol Diane. Adminstrv. analyst U.S. Office for Emergency Mgmt., 1944; asst. to U.S. Senator Alexander Wiley, 1945-52; cons. fgn. relations com. U.S. Senate, Washington, 1952-58, staff dir. govt. ops. subcommittee, 1958-64; asst. to Vice Pres. Hubert Humphrey, Washington, 1965-69; publishing asso. Family Health Mag., N.Y.C., 1969-74; pres. Family Media Enterprises, Inc., N.Y.C., 1975—, also dir.; lectr. Am. U.; dir. The Washingtonian Mag. Dep. nat. chmn. Citizens for Humphrey-Muskie, 1968 presdl. campaign. Selected by Nat. Inst. Pub. Affairs and CSC for U.S. Govt. Internship Program for Exec. Tng. Mem. Sales Exec. Club N.Y. (dir. 1976), Soc. Fin. Counseling (past chmn.). Democrat. Jewish. Clubs: Washington Press, Nat. Press (Washington); Atrium (N.Y.C.). Contbr. articles in field to profl. jours. Home: 9211 Harrington Dr Potomac MD 20854 Office: 149 Fifth Ave New York City NY 10010

CAIN, ALBERT SPENCER, mfg. co. exec.; b. Poplar Bluff, Mo., Sept. 29, 1946; s. Albert P. and Elizabeth A. (Spencer) C.; B.S., St. Joseph's Coll., 1968; M.A., St. Louis U., 1972; m. Barbara Myers, Aug. 11, 1973. Market sales mgr. Motorola Inc., St. Louis, 1971-74; account rep. Graphic Scis. Inc., Danbury, Conn., 1974-75, sales tng. mgr., 1975-77; mgr. nat. accounts Rapicom Inc., Shaker Heights, Ohio, 1977-78, dist. sales mgr., Chgo., 1978—. Served with inf. AUS, 1969-71. Decorated Army Commendation medal. Mem. Am. Soc. Tng. and Devel., Am. Mgmt. Assn. Roman Catholic. Home: 1930 Ridgefield Ln Naperville IL Office: Rapicom Inc 4415 W Harrison St Hillside IL 61257

CAIN, GEORGE HARVEY, lawyer, business exec.; b. Washington, Aug. 3, 1920; s. J. Harvey and Madeleine (McGettigan) C.; B.S., Georgetown U., 1942; LL.B., Harvard, 1948; m. Patricia J. Campbell, Apr. 23, 1946; children—George Harvey, James C., John P., Paul J. Admitted to N.Y. bar, 1949, Ohio bar, 1972, Conn. bar, 1977; practiced in N.Y.C., 1949-71, Cleve., 1971-73, White Plains, N.Y., 1973-76, Stamford, Conn., 1976—; sec., gen. counsel Nat. Carloading Corp., 1949-54; mem. firm Spence & Hotchkiss, 1954-55; gen. atty., asst. sec. Cerro Corp., 1955-68, sec., gen. atty., 1968-71; sec. Cerro Sales Corp., 1956-71; sec., dir. Cerro Mining Co. of Can., Ltd., 1967-71; v.p., gen. counsel Pickands Mather & Co., Cleve., 1971-73; v.p., sec., gen. counsel The Flintkote Co., White Plains, 1973-80; spl. counsel firm Day, Berry & Howard, Stamford, 1980—; gen. counsel, dir. Atlantic Cement Co., Inc., 1962-71. Served to 1st lt. USAAF, 1942-46; to capt. USAF, 1951-52. Mem. Am., Ohio, Conn., N.Y. State, N.Y.C. bar assns., Am. Soc. Corporate Secs., Am. Arbitration Assn. (nat. panel arbitrators), Georgetown U. Alumni Assn. (mem. Alumni senate), Pi Gamma Mu. Clubs: Harvard (N.Y.C.); Milbrook (Greenwich, Conn.). Home: 12 Wildwood Dr Greenwich CT 06830 Office: 3 Landmark Sq Stamford CT 06901

CAINE, STEPHEN HOWARD, computer software co. exec.; b. Washington, Feb. 11, 1941; s. Walter E. and Jeanette (Wenborne) C.; student Calif. Inst. Tech., 1958-62. Sr. programmer Calif. Inst. Tech., Pasadena, 1962-65, mgr. systems programming, 1965-69, mgr. programming, 1969-70; pres. Caine, Farber & Gordon, Inc., Pasadena, 1970—; lectr. applied sci. Calif. Inst. Tech., Pasadena, 1965-71, vis. asso. elec. engring., 1976, vis. asso. computer sci., 1976—. Mem. Pasadena Tournament of Roses Assn., 1976—. Mem. Assn. Computing Machinery, Nat. Assn. Corrosion Engrs., AAAS, Am. Def. Preparedness Assn., Newcomen Soc. N.Am. Clubs: Athenaeum (Pasadena); Engrs. (N.Y.C.). Home: 77 Patrician Way Pasadena CA 91105 Office: 750 E Green St Pasadena CA 91101

CAIOLA, JAMES CLIFFORD, narrow fabric mfg. co. exec.; b. Bronx, N.Y., Nov. 2, 1933; s. Vincent James and Lola (DeFelice) C.; B.B.A., Iona Coll., 1955; children—Valerie, Vincent. With Arthur Young & Co., N.Y.C., 1955-59; asst. gen. mgr. Renault, Inc., N.Y.C., 1959-64; financial officer Baxter, Kelly & Faust, Inc., N.Y.C., 1964-69; with Murdock Webbing Co., Inc., Central Falls, R.I., 1969—, pres., dir., 1971—; pres., dir. subsidiaries U.S. Forge Craft Co., Inc., 1971—. Sec. planning bd., East Brunswick, N.J., 1966-67, chmn., 1968-69. Recipient Key Man award East Brunswick Jr. C. of C., 1965. C.P.A., N.J. Mem. Nat. Assn. Accountants, Am. Assn. Seat Belt Mfrs., Am. Inst. C.P.A.'s, R.I. Inst. C.P.A.'s, Textile Narrow Fabric Inst. Home: 100 Sunset Dr Seekonk MA 02771 Office: 27 Foundry St Central Falls RI 02863

CAIRNS, DONALD FREDRICK, engring. and mgmt. cons.; b. Coulterville, Ill., Sept. 9, 1924; s. Fred Barton and Elsie Loretta (Barbary) C.; B.S., U. Ill., 1950; M.B.A., St. Louis U., 1966, Ph.D., 1972; m. Marion Grace Huey, Sept. 4, 1950; 1 son, Douglas Scott. Asst. engr. Mo. Pacific R.R. Co., St. Louis, 1950-56; project engr., plant engr., asst. to pres., v.p. Granite City Steel Co. (Ill.), 1956-79; pres. Nat. Engrs. and Assos. unit Nat. Steel Corp., St. Louis, 1979—; pres., chmn. bd. Indsl. Waste Control Council; guest lectr. Washington U. Grad. Sch. Bus. Chmn. Webster Groves (Mo.) City Planning Commn., 1958; mem. St. Louis County Traffic Commn., 1960-61, Webster Groves Bus. Devel. Commn., 1962, St. Louis County Charter Commn., 1979; mem., chmn. St. Louis County Planning Commn., 1968-76; pres., dir. Edgewood Children's Center, 1963-72. Served with AUS, 1943-46. Decorated Bronze Star; recipient recognition for control of air pollution Pres.'s Johnson and Nixon, 1970; registered profl. engr., Mo., Ill. Mem. Nat. Soc. Profl. Engrs., Mo. Soc. Profl. Engrs., Am. Iron and Steel Inst., ASCE, Air Pollution Control Assn., Assn. Iron and Steel Engrs., Southwestern Ill. Indsl. Assn. (chmn. bd.). Club: Algonquin Golf. Home: 17 E Swon Ave Webster Groves MO 63119 Office: 7777 Bonhomme Ave Saint Louis MO 63105

CAIRNS, JOHN SHERWOOD, coal co. exec.; b. Oahu, Hawaii, Dec. 11, 1941; s. Edward F. and Gerry E. C.; B.A. in Edn. and Psychology, Biola Coll., 1966; m. Paula Weir, June 18, 1978. Personnel mgr. Container Corp. Am., Corona, Calif., 1969, 71-72, Los Angeles, 1970-72; tng. supr. FMC, Pocatello, Idaho, 1970; mgr. indsl. relations AMAX Co. Inc., Leadville, Colo., 1972-74, asst. dir. indsl./employee relations, Tucson, 1974-75, dir. indsl. employee relations, Indpls., 1975-79; mgr. indsl. relations Climax Moly Co., Leadville, 1972-74; asst. dir. indsl. relations Anamax Mining, Tucson, 1974-75; corp. dir. mgmt. and organizational devel. Amax Inc., Greenwich, Conn., 1979—. Republican. Baptist. Designer tng. program for systems approach to collective bargaining, 1973. Home: 114 Moody Ln Danbury CT 06810 Office: Amax Inc Greenwich CT 06830

CALAHAN, SCOTT CLAIR, ins. co. exec.; b. Balt., Dec. 25, 1943; s. Richard Clair and Jeanette C. (Gallagher) C.; B.S., Pa. State U., 1966; M.B.A. (fellow), U. Pitts., 1968; postgrad. Case Western Res. U., 1968-70; m. Linda Ballantyne, June 13, 1966; children—Douglas, Jill. With Gen. Tire & Rubber Co., Akron, Ohio, 1968-71, Assos. Corp. N. Am., South Bend, 1971-73; asst. v.p. corp. planning mgr. Integon Corp., Winston-Salem, N.C., 1973-78; v.p. Mortgage Fin. div. Investors Mortgage Ins. Co., 1978—. Mem. council Boston Symphony Orch., 1979—. Mem. Planning Execs. Inst., Ops. Research Soc. Am. Author: (with others) Direct Costing in Life Insurance Company Operations, 1978; asso. editor Jour. Ops. Research, 1972-74. Home: 133 Maynard Farm Rd Sudbury MA 01776 Office: 225 Franklin St Boston MA 02110

CALAME, BYRON EDWARD, newspaper exec.; b. Appleton City, Mo., Apr. 14, 1939; s. Harry Franklin and Gladys Verl (Neal) C.; B.J., U. Mo., 1961; M.A., U. Md., 1966; m. Kathryn Lee Boehm, June 9, 1962; children—Christine Lee, Jonathan David. Staff reporter Wall St. Jour., N.Y.C., 1965-67, Los Angeles, 1967-69, Washington, 1969-74, bur. mgr. Pitts., 1974-78, br. mgr., Los Angeles, 1978—. Served with USN, 1961-65. Office: 514 Shatto Pl Los Angeles CA 90020

CALANDRA, CARL ALDO, ins. co. exec.; b. Altoona, Pa., July 16, 1916; s. Cesare B. and Genevieve (DiCamillo) C.; ed. public schs., Altoona; m. Leanore Ferrari, Mar. 8, 1939; children—Anita, Carl W. Former owner, operator shoe making, repair and correctional shoe rebuilding service, later engaged in retail shoe bus.; gen. agt. Franklin Life Ins. Co., Lyndhurst, Ohio, 1952-65; regional mgr. Pioneer Am. Co., Lyndhurst, 1965-70, Am. Bankers Co., Euclid, Ohio, 1970-72; Ohio state mgr. Am. Fidelity Co., Northfield, 1972—. Mem. Million Dollar Club (nat. agy. expansion award 1959). Roman Catholic. Contbr. articles to profl. jours. Address: 1040 Canyon View Dr Sagamore Hills OH 44067

CALARCO, VINCENT ANTHONY, chem. co. exec.; b. N.Y.C., May 29, 1942; s. George Michael and Madeline C.; B.S., Poly. Inst. Bklyn., 1963; M.B.A., Harvard U., 1970; m. Linda Joyce Maniscalco, Apr. 10, 1971; children—David V., Christopher G. Chem. engr., Proctor & Gamble, St. Louis, 1963-66; engr. Johnson & Johnson, New Brunswick, N.J., 1968; with NL Industries, various locations, 1969-78, bus. mgr. splty. chems., Hightstown, N.J., 1974-76, bus. mgr. plastics and splty. chems., Hightstown, 1976-78; gen. mgr. chemicals Uniroyal Chem. Co. div. Uniroyal Inc., Naugatuck, Conn., 1978-79; gen. mgr. domestic ops. Uniroyal Chem. Co., 1979—, pres., 1979—; dir. Uniroyal S.p.A., Italy, Naugatuck S.p.A., Turin, Italy, Uniroyal Quimica, S.A., Buenos Aires, Uniroyal chem. Pty., Ltd., Edwardstown, Australia, Compania Quimica Ameyal, S.A., Mexico City, Rubicon Chem, Inc., Geismar, La., Synpol, Inc., Port Neches, Tex., Alpine Labs., Inc., Bay Minettee, Ala., Monochem, Inc., Giesmar, Premier Chem. Co. Ltd., Taiwan, Orchem. (Pty.) Ltd., Sasolburg, South africa, Sumitomo Naugatuck Co., Ltd., Osaka, Japan. Served with AUS, 1966-68. George F. Banker fellow, 1968-70. Mem. Soc. Plastics Industry, Internat. Inst. Synthetic Rubber Producers, Soc. Chem. Industry, Société de Chimie Industrielle, Chem. Mfrs. Assn., Nat. Agrl. Chem. Assn., Am. Inst. Chemists. Clubs: Chemists of N.Y., Harvard Bus. Sch. of N.Y. Office: Spencer St Naugatuck CT 06770

CALCATERRA, ANTHONY, ins. co. exec.; b. Bklyn., Feb. 15, 1945; s. Anthony J. and Catherine C.; student Manhattan Community Coll., 1969-71; cert. principles of individual health ins. Health Ins. Assn. Am., 1978; m. Linda Collins, Apr. 27, 1968; children—Cathy-Lynn, Anthony, Timothy. With Equitable Life Ins. Co., 1963—, asst. mgr. underwriting, adminstrn., mktg. and analysis, N.Y.C., 1978-79, div. mgr. individual med. expense claims, 1979, mgr. collection div., 1979—. Mem. Health Claim Assn., Accident and Health Club. Office: 1285 Ave of Americas New York NY 10019

CALCUT, GEORGE ALLEN, ins. co. exec.; b. Spokane, Wash., Jan. 13, 1938; s. John G. and Helen L. (Mayer) C.; student U. Md., 1959-60, Mont. Coll. of Mineral Sci. and Tech., 1960-61; C.L.U., Am. Coll. Life Underwriters, 1971; m. Geri L. Morck, July 9, 1961; children—Cindi L., Lori L., Kristin R., Nicole. Ins. agt., mgr. Western-So. Life, San Jose, Calif., 1961-67; ins. agt. Northwestern Mut. Life, San Jose, 1967-73; ins. broker George Calcut & Assos., Butte, Mont., 1973-78; pres. George A. Calcut & Assos., Inc., Butte, 1978—; instr. ins. courses Am. Coll. Life Underwriters, Butte, 1973-75; ins. cons. Gen. chmn. Butte Town Meeting, 1976; pres. Butte Anaconda Diabetes Assn., 1977—; bd. dirs. Mont. Diabetes Assn., 1978—. Served with U.S. Army, 1958-60. Mem. Butte C. of C. (exec. bd. 1975-77, 80), Southwestern Mont. Assn. Life Underwriters (pres. 1976-77), San Jose Life Underwriters Assn. (dir. 1966-67), Nat. Assn. Life Underwriters, Am. Soc. C.L.U.'s. Episcopalian. Club: Exchange. Home: 4 N Lake Dr Butte MT 59701 Office: Metals Bldg Suite 508 Butte MT 59701

CALDER, ALEXANDER, JR., bus. exec.; b. Bklyn., July 14, 1916; s. Alexander and Adelaide Fancher (Gunnison) C.; A.B., Dartmouth, 1938; M. B.A., Harvard, 1940; m. Rebecca Jane Holmes; children—Christie Holmes Calder Salomon, Alexander III. Sales trainee Union Bag-Camp Paper Corp. (now Union Camp Corp.), N.Y.C., 1940-41, asst. to dir. indsl. relations, 1941-46, asst. to v.p. charge sales, 1947-49, v.p., 1949-52, exec. v.p. and gen. mgr., 1952-56, now chmn. bd., chmn. exec. com., chief exec. officer, dir. Bank of N.Y. Co, Inc., Burlington Industries, Inc., Ingersoll-Rank Co., Bank of N.Y. Intelligence analyst Bd. Econ. Warfare, 1942-43. Served to lt. (j.g.) USNR, 1943-46, service overseas, 1944-45. Mem. Nat. Indsl. Conf. Bd., Am. Arbitration Assn. (dir.), Council Fgn. Relations, Phi Kappa Psi. Clubs: Montclair (N.J.) Golf; Pine Valley (N.J.) Golf; Mchts.; Madison (Conn.) Beach; Oglethorpe (Savannah, Ga.); University (N.Y.C.). Office: 1600 Valley Rd Wayne NJ 07470

CALDWELL, ALLAN BLAIR, health services co. exec.; b. Independence, Iowa, June 13, 1929; s. Thomas James and Lola (Ensminger) C.; B.A., Maryville Coll., 1952; B.S., N.Y.U., 1955; M.S., Columbia U., 1957; M.D., Stanford, 1964; m. Elizabeth Jane Steinmetz, June 13, 1955; 1 dau., Kim Allistair. Med. intern Henry Ford Hosp., Detroit, 1964-65; resident Jackson Meml. Hosp., Miami, Fla., 1956-57; admstr. Albert Schweitzer Hosp., Haiti, 1957-58; asst. admstr. Palo Alto-Stanford Hosp. Center, 1958-59; asso. dir. program in hosp. adminstrn. U. Calif. at Los Angeles, 1965-67; dir. bur. profl.

service Am. Hosp. Assn., Chgo., 1967-69; v.p. Beverly Enterprises, Pasadena, Calif., 1969-71; exec. v.p., med. dir. Nat. Med. Enterprises, Beverly Hills, Calif., 1971-73; pres., chmn. bd. Emergency Physicians Internat., 1973—, Allan B. Caldwell, M.D., Inc., 1973—; dir. indsl. medicine Greater El Monte Community Hosp., South El Monte, Calif., 1973—; pres. Am. Indsl. Med. Services, 1978—; chmn. bd. dirs. Technicraft Internat., Inc., San Mateo, Calif., 1970—; dir. Career Aids, Inc., Glendale, Calif., 1969-75; cons. TRW Corp., Redondo Beach, Calif., 1966-71; lectr. U. Calif. at Los Angeles, 1965—, Calif. Inst. Tech., 1971—, Calif. State U., Northridge, 1980—; examiner Civil Service Commn., Los Angeles, 1966; adviser Western Center for Continuing Edn. in Hosps. and Related Health Facilities, 1965—; cons. Los Angeles Hosp. and Nursing and Pub. Health Dept., 1965—; adv. council Calif. Hosp. Commn., 1972—; commr. Emergency Med. Services Commn. Bd. dirs. Comprehensive Health Planning Assn. Los Angeles County, 1972—; vice chmn. Emergency Med. Care Commn., Los Angeles County, 1977-78, chmn., 1978-79. Recipient Geri award Los Angeles Nursing Home Assn., 1966, Outstanding Achievement award Health Care Educators, 1978; USPHS scholar, 1961-63. Diplomate Am. Bd. Med. Examiners. Mem. Am., United (pres. 1971-72) hosp. assns., Am. Coll. Hosp. Adminstrs., Am., Calif. med. assns., Los Angeles County Med. Assn., Am. Coll. Emergency Physicians (v.p. 1975-77 dir. continuing med. edn. for Western U.S., Hawaii, Australia, N.Z., 1976—), Hosp. Fin. Mgmt. Assn. Home: 4405 Medley Pl Encino CA 91316

CALDWELL, HAROLD LEROY, petroleum engr.; b. Pawnee, Okla., Aug. 14, 1925; s. Harold Ralph and Eula P. (Buckner) C.; B.S. in Petroleum Engring., U. Tulsa, 1951; m. Patricia T. Poorman, Dec. 24, 1948; children—Michael Alan and Douglas Owen. Exploitation engr. Sunray Oil Co., 1951-55; chief engr. Keener Oil Co., Tulsa, 1955-59, gen. supt. prodn., 1959-63; engr. Fenix & Scisson, Inc., 1963-65; gen. supt. prodn. KWB Oil Property Mgmt., Inc., Tulsa, 1965-67; tech. asst. to chmn. bd. Resource Scis. Corp., Tulsa, 1967-74; v.p.-mgr. Perrault-Caldwell, Inc., Tulsa, 1974-76; engr. Keplinger & Assos., Tulsa, 1976-79; pres. Caldwell & Assos., Inc., cons. engrs., Tulsa, 1979—. Served with AUS, 1943-46. Registered profl. engr., Okla. Mem. Am. Inst. Mining Engrs., Am. Petroleum Inst., Okla. Soc. Profl. Engrs. Republican. Mem. Reorganized Ch. of Jesus Christ of Latter-day Saints. Home: 5129 S Richmond Tulsa OK 74135 Office: Suite 922 Mayo Bldg 420 S Main St Tulsa OK 74103

CALDWELL, JAMES ALLEN, lawyer, retail mcht.; b. New Castle, Pa., July 2, 1936; s. William James and Ruth Olive (McEwen) C.; A.B., Princeton U., 1958; J.D., U. Pitts., 1968: m. Margaret Jean Edmiston, Dec. 21, 1963; children—Russell James, Katherine Ruth. Admitted to Pa. bar, 1964; practiced law, New Castle, Pa., 1964—, Waynesburg, Pa., 1973—; asst. dist. atty. Lawrence County, Pa., 1970-72; spl. asst. dist. atty., Greene County, Pa., 1975-78; owner, operator Present Tense, West Alexander, Pa., 1979—. Served with USMCR, 1959-60. Mem. Am. Bar Assn., Pa. Bar Assn., Greene County Bar Assn., Lawrence County Bar Assn., Am. Guild Organists. Republican. Presbyterian. Clubs: Rotary, Masons (past master), Shriners, Elks. Home: RD 2 Waynesburg PA 15370 Office: PO Box 225 West Alexander PA 15376

CALDWELL, JAMES DAHL, pig farm exec.; b. Cardston, Alta., Can., June 25, 1928; came to U.S., 1953, naturalized, 1962; s. Edward Dahl and Una M. (Jensen) C.; B.S., Brigham Young U., Provo, Utah, 1957; M.S., U. Nebr., 1960; m. Dixie V. Flake, Dec. 20, 1954; children—Clay, Mark, Jill, Jackie, Bret, Janet, Julie, Ben, Tom. Fieldman, U. Nebr., 1957-60, Jackson & Krautman, Chillicothe, Mo., 1960-62; animal researcher U. Nev., Reno, 1962-64; pres., owner Snowflake Pig Farms, Inc. (Ariz.), 1964—; mem. Ariz. Livestock and San. Bd.; lectr. pig raising. Named Farm Family of Yr., for Ariz., Dept. Agr., 1973. Mem. Ariz. Pork Producers Assn. Republican. Mormon. Contbr. articles Jour. Vet. Med. Assn. Home and Office: PO Box AF Snowflake AZ 85937

CALDWELL, PHILIP, automobile mfg. co. exec.; b. Bourneville, Ohio, Jan. 27, 1920; s. Robert Clyde and Wilhelmina (Hemphill) C.; B.A. in Econs., Muskingum Coll., 1940, H.H.D. (hon.), 1974; M.B.A. in Indsl. Mgmt., Harvard U., 1942; m. Betsey Chinn Clark, Oct. 27, 1945; children—Lawrence Clark, Lucy Hemphill (Mrs. Thomas O. Stair), Désirée Branch. With Navy Dept., 1946-53, dep. dir. procurement policy div., 1948-53; with Ford Motor Co., 1953—, v.p., 1968-73, gen. mgr. truck ops., 1968-70, exec. v.p. internat. automotive ops., 1973-77, vice chmn. bd., 1977-80, chmn., chief exec. officer, 1980—, also dir.; dir. Philco-Ford Corp., Phila., 1970-71, v.p. mfg. group, 1971-72, chmn., chief exec. officer, dir. Ford of Europe, Inc., 1972-73; dir. Ford Latin Am., S.A. de C.V., Ford Mid-East and Africa, Inc., Ford Asia-Pacific, Inc., Ford Motor Credit Co. Mem. internat. council Conf. Bd.; mem. bus. advisory council Kent State U., 1968—; bd. dirs. World Affairs Council Phila, 1970-71, Detroit Symphony Orch.; trustee Muskingum Coll.; mem. Merrill-Palmer Inst. Served to lt. USNR, 1942-46. Recipient Meritorious Civilian Service award U.S. Navy, 1953; 1st William A. Jump Meml. award, 1950. Mem. Hwy. Users Fedn., Soc. Automotive Engrs., Engring. Soc. Detroit, Automobile Mfrs. Assn. (mem. motor truck mfrs. com. 1964-70), U.S. (transp. com. 1968-70), Internat. (exec. com. U.S. Council 1973—) chambers commerce. Clubs: Detroit Athletic, Bloomfield Hills Country, Renaissance. Office: Ford Motor Co American Rd Dearborn MI 48121*

CALDWELL, PHILIP MCINROY, transp. exec.; b. Beaver Falls, Pa., Apr. 16, 1921; s. Edward L. and Edna M. (McInroy) C.; B.S., U.S. Mcht. Marine Acad., 1944; B.M.E., Northwestern U., 1949; postgrad. Xavier U., 1958-61; m. Dorothy R. Enerson, Dec. 27, 1945; children—Philp McInroy, Arthur, Mary. Asst. plant engr. U.S. Gypsum Co., Gypsum, Ohio, 1949-52; mgr. facilities design and constrn. Gen. Electric Co., Cin., 1952-61, mgr. space environ. test facility, Valley Forge, Pa., 1961-65, mgr. tech. support, Bay St. Louis, Miss., 1965-70, mgr. tech. projects, 1970-72; mgr. facilities dept. Southeastern Pa. Transp. Authority, Phila., 1972-80, asst. gen. mgr. planning and constrn. div., 1980—. Treas., Trinity Episcopal Ch., Pass Christian, Miss., 1967-70. Served as lt. (j.g.) USNR, 1944-46. Registered profl. engr., Ohio, Miss., Pa. Mem. Am. R.R. Engring. Assn., Nat. Fire Protection Assn., Am. Mgmt. Assn., N.Y. Rwy. Club. Home: 1404 Wexford Circle West Chester PA 19380 Office: 200 W Wyoming Ave Philadelphia PA 19140

CALDWELL, WILLIAM MACKAY, III, business exec.; b. Los Angeles Apr. 6, 1922; s. William Mackay II and Edith Ann (Richards) C.; B.S., U. So. Calif., 1943; M.B.A., Harvard, 1948; m. Mary Louise Edwards, Jan. 16, 1946; children—William Mackay IV, Craig Edwards, Candace Louise. Sec.-treas., dir. Drewry Photocolor Corp., 1957-60, Adcolor Photo Corp., 1957-60; treas., dir. Drewry Bennetts Corp., 1959-60; sr. v.p., chief financial officer Am. Cement Corp., 1960-67, sr. v.p. corp., 1966-70, pres. cement and concrete group, 1967-70; pres., chmn. bd., chief exec. officer Van Vorst Industries, Los Angeles, 1970—; chmn. bd. Van Vorst Co., Seattle; pres. ELGEA I, 1970—, U.S. Bedding Co., 1979—, The Englander Co., 1979—, St. Croix Mfg. Co., 1979—; chmn. bd. So. Cross Industries, Atlanta, 1979—, Hawaiian Cement Corp.; v.p., dir. Am. Cement Internat. Corp., Am. Cement Properties; dir. Portland de Mailorca Internat. Concrete systems; cons. prof. U. So. Calif. Mem. men's com. Los Angeles Med. Center. Bd. dirs. Commerce Assos., U. So. Calif. Assos., bd. dirs. Pres.'s Circle; bd. dirs. Am. Cement Found. Served to lt. USNR, 1943-46. Mem. Newcomen Soc., Friends Huntington Library, Kappa Alpha (pres. U. So. Calif. 1943-44), Alpha Delta Sigma, Alpha Pi Omega. Presbyn. Toastmaster (pres. San Marino 1956-57). Clubs: Marrakesh Country, Eldorado Country (Palm Springs); Harvard Bus. Sch. of So. Calif. (dir. 1960-63); Los Angeles Met. Dinner, Los Angeles Country, Town Hall, Calif. (Los Angeles); Trojan; Annandale Golf; Big Canyon Country, Calif. Country. Home: 1880 Lombardy Rd San Marino CA 91108 Office: PO Box 927 Pasadena CA 91102

CALHOUN, JACK ROWLAND, electric utility exec.; b. Poplar, N.C., Oct. 21, 1919; s. Glenn David and Pearl Wanda (Willis) C.; B.E.E., Tenn. Tech. U., 1949; m. Jacqueline Capps, Sept. 23, 1944; children—Carol, Patrick, Janice, Susan. With TVA, 1954—, elec. maintenance supr. Johnsonville Steam plant, 1958-60, asst. supt. Shawnee steam plant, Paducah, Ky., 1960-64, asst. project mgr., gas-cooled reactor, Oak Ridge, 1964-68, asst. chief maintenance br., Chattanooga, 1968-71, supt. Brown Ferry nuclear plant, Decatur Ala., 1971-77, chief nuclear generation br., Chattanooga, 1977-79, dir. div. nuclear power, 1979-80; sr. v.p. (nuclear) Pa. Power and Light Co., Allentown, 1980—. Served in USN, 1938-45. Mem. Am. Nuclear Soc. (nat. chmn. reactor ops. div. 1977). Methodist. Home: 4010 Winchester Rd Allentown PA 18104 Office: Pa Power and Light Co Two N 9th St Allentown PA 18101

CALHOUN, LILLIAN SCOTT, public relations co. exec.; b. Savannah, Ga., June 25, 1925; d. Walter Sanford and Laura (McDowell) Scott; B.A., Ohio State U., 1944; m. Harold William Calhoun, Sept. 20, 1950; children—Laura, Harold, Walter, Karen. Columnist, feature editor Chgo. Defender, 1963-65; asso. editor Jet, Ebony, mags., 1961-63; reporter Chgo. Sun-Times, 1965-68; mng. editor Integrated Edn. mag., 1968-71; info. officer, acting info. dir. Dept. Labor, 1971-73; co-editor Chgo. Reporter, 1973-76; pres., founder Calmar Communications, Inc., Chgo., 1978—; columnist Crain's Chgo. Bus., 1978-80, Chgo. Journalism Rev., 1969-74. Vice-chairperson Ill. Commn. on Human Relations, 1973-75; mem. Gov.'s Commn. on Status of Women, 1965-67, Gov.'s Adv. Council on Manpower, 1973-75. Mem. Soc. Midland Authors, Alpha Gamma Pi. Episcopalian. Clubs: Chgo. Press, Publicity, Arts. Office: 500 N Dearborn St #1115 Chicago IL 60610

CALHOUN, THOMAS BARTLING, investment banker; b. Shanghai, China, Mar. 31, 1930 (parents Am. citizens); s. Alexander Dewey and Minna S. Calhoun; A.B., Harvard U., 1951, M.B.A., 1953; m. Charlotte Ford, Dec. 13, 1975. With Goldman, Sachs & Co., N.Y.C., 1957-66; 1st v.p. Smith, Barney & Co., San Francisco, 1966-77; v.p. E.F. Hutton & Co., San Francisco, 1977—; mem. adv. com. The Coldwell Banker Funds. Trustee, Ballet Theatre Found. (Am. Ballet Theatre). Served with USNR, 1953-57. Mem. Assn. Corporate Growth. Episcopalian. Clubs: Bohemian (San Francisco); Calif. (Los Angeles). Office: 505 Sansome St Suite 1700 San Francisco CA 94111

CALHOUN, WILLIAM BENJAMIN, III, health care corp. exec.; b. Tyler, Tex., Feb. 15, 1944; s. William Benjamin and Evelyn (Williams) C.; B.S., Southwestern U., 1966; M.A., U. Tex., 1969. Asst. editor Chem. Abstracts Service, Columbus, Ohio, 1969-72; sect. head tech. info. Philips Roxane Labs., Columbus, 1972-74; regulatory compliance coordinator Cordis Corp., Miami, Fla., 1974-75; mgr. tech. info. services Schering-Plough, Memphis, 1975-77; mgr. tech. info. systems Intermedics, Freeport, Tex., 1977—. Pres., Intermedics Employees Fed. Credit Union. NSF fellow, 1966-69. Mem. Am. Chem. Soc., Regulatory Affairs Profl. Soc. Episcopalian. Home: 60 Ranch House Loop Angleton TX 77515 Office: PO Box 617 Freeport TX 77541

CALIFF, ALVIN DAVID, banker; b. Memphis, Mar. 26, 1922; s. Mose and Alma (Dees) C.; student Sch. Banking South, La. State U., 1958-60, Grad. Sch. Bus. Adminstrn., Harvard, 1969; m. Mary Kay O'Connell, Sept. 16, 1944; children—Kathleen Ann, Michael David, Bernard Shawn, Mara Dees. Vice pres., cashier Coahoma Nat. Bank, Clarksdale, Miss., 1937-63; pres., chief exec. officer First Nat. Bank, Clarksdale, 1964—. Trustee Miss. Found. Ind. Colls., 1970, Carnegie Pub. Library, 1971. Served to lt. (j.g.) AC, USNR, 1942-46. Mem. Am. Legion, Am., Miss. (pres. jr. bankers sect. 1955) bankers assns., Clarksdale C. of C. (dir. 1959-66). Jewish. Clubs: Masons, Shriners, Lions. Home: 1120 Oakridge Rd Clarksdale MS 38614 Office: 402 E 2d St Clarksdale MS 38614

CALIGIURI, IRENE GLORIA, economist; b. Buenos Aires, Sept. 13, 1939; came to U.S., 1963, naturalized, 1969; d. Roque Nicolas and Angela (Andia) C.; student U. Law, Argentina, 1960; B.S. in Fin. and Acctg., N.Y. Inst. Tech., 1978, postgrad., 1979—; postgrad. Center for Profl. Advancement, 1980, NARUC Regulatory Studies Program, Mich. State U., 1980. Asst. sr. economist Zinder Cos., Washington, 1965-68; tech. asst. to Dr. F.J. Leerburger, econs. and engring. cons., N.Y.C., 1969-70; exec. asst. Allan J. Schultz, cons., N.Y.C., 1970-78; economist Power Authority State of N.Y., N.Y.C., 1978—. Mem. Delta Mu Delta. Home: 86-15 Broadway Elmhurst NY 11373

CALIRI, JOSEPH LOUIS, lawyer, corp. exec.; b. Rochester, N.Y., Mar. 16, 1916; s. Salvatore and Maria Teresa (Bottazzi) C.; A.B., U. Rochester, 1938; LL.B., Cornell, 1941; m. Dorothy Ann McGrath, Aug. 19, 1944; children—Robert Redmond, Barbara Jane. Admitted to N.Y. bar, 1941, Ill. bar, 1974; with law dept. Kraft, Inc., N.Y.C., 1941-51; asst. sec., 1951-52, sec., 1952—, v.p., 1971—; v.p. and sec. Dart & Kraft, Inc., 1980—. Former mem. West Islip Bd. Edn. Mem. Am. Judicature Soc., Am. Soc. Corporate Secs., Am., Ill., Chgo. bar assns., Cornell Law Assn., Phi Beta Kappa, Alpha Phi Delta. Republican. Clubs: Magoun Landing Yacht; Cornell of N.Y.; Execs., Union League (Chgo.); Michigan Shores, Westmoreland Country (Wilmette). Home: 1500 Sheridan Rd Wilmette IL 60091 Office: Kraft Ct Glenview IL 60025

CALKINS, FRANCIS JOSEPH, educator; b. Chgo., Oct. 15, 1910; s. Frank M. and Anna A. Calkins; A.B., Loyola U., Chgo., 1932, M.A., 1933; m. Rose Marie Schreiber, June 24, 1944; children—Edward J., Richard F., Anne R., Timothy J. Statistician, asst. supr WPA, Chgo., 1933-38; analyst Standard & Poor's Corp., N.Y.C., 1938-39; asst. prof. econs. and fin. U. Notre Dame (Ind.), 1939-45; prof. fin. Marquette (Mich.) U., 1945-65, Western Res. U., Cleve., 1965-67, Case Western Reserve U., Cleve., 1967-69, Cleve. State U., 1969-76, Emory U., Atlanta, 1976-78; vis. prof. fin. U. Nebr., Omaha, 1978-79, Wichita (Kans.) State U., 1979—. Mem. Am. Fin. Assn., Midwest Fin. Assn., Fin. Mgmt. Assn., Inst. Chartered Fin. Analysis, Fin. Analysts Fedn. Author: Cases and Problems in Investments, 1955; Investments, 1961. Home: 2121 Pine Forest Dr NE Atlanta GA 30345

CALKINS, GARY NATHAN, lawyer; b. N.Y.C., Mar. 1, 1911; s. Gary Nathan and Helen R. Williston C.; student Ecole Internationale, Geneva, 1926-27, Storm King Sch., 1927-29; A.B., Columbia, 1933; LL.B., Harvard, 1936; m. Constantia H. Hommann, June 22, 1940 (div. Dec. 1948; m. 2d, Susannah Eby, Nov. 19, 1949; children—Helen (dec.), Margaret, Sarah, Abigail. Admitted to N.Y. bar, 1936, D.C. bar, 1955, U.S. Supreme Ct. bar, 1965; asso. Beekman & Bogue, N.Y.C., 1936-41; staff CAB, 1941-56, chief internat. and rules div., 1947-56; mem. firm Galland, Kharasch, Calkins & Short, P.C., and predecessors, Washington, 1956—, N.Y.C., 1966-76, mng. partner, 1969-80, pres., 1980—; asst. sec. Philippine Airlines, 1974—. Mem. U.S. sect. Citeja, 1946-47; mem. U.S. del. legal com. Internat. Civil Aviation Orgn., 1947-55, del. chmn. 1st, 3d, 5th, 9th and 10th meetings; mem. drafting com. Mortgage Conv., Geneva, 1948, Rome Conv. on Surface Damage, 1952; chmn. U.S. del. Internat. Diplomatic Conf. for Revision of Warsaw Conv., The Hague, 1955; chmn. legal div. U.S. Air Coordinating Com., 1955-56. Served as lt. USNR, 1943-45. Mem. Am., D.C. bar assns., Am. Judicature Soc., Soc. Quiet Birdmen, Internat. Platform Assn. Clubs: George Town, Nat. Aviation (Washington). Asso. editor United States and Canadian Aviation Reports, 1956; asso. editor Jour. Air Law and Commerce, 1956-58, editor-in-chief, 1958-63. Author profl. papers. Home: 6504 Dearborn Dr Falls Church VA 22044 Office: Canal Sq 1054 31st St NW Washington DC 20007

CALKINS, SUSANNAH EBY, economist; b. Bucyrus, Ohio, Jan. 16, 1924; d. Samuel L. and Mae (McClure) Eby; A.B., Goucher Coll., 1945; M.S. in Econs. (Univ. scholar), U. Wis., 1947; m. Gary Nathan Calkins, Nov. 19, 1949; children—Helen E. (dec.), Margaret S., Sarah A., Abigail C. Fiscal analyst Bur. of Budget, Washington, 1945-50; economist U.S. Council Econ. Advisers, Washington, 1950-51, U.S. Office Price Stabilization, Washington, 1951-53, U.S. Bur. Budget, Washington, 1953-55; cons. U.S. Advisory Commn. on Intergovernmental Relations, Washington, 1972-73, 74-75, 77-79, sr. analyst, 1979—; cons. Brookings Instn., 1973-74. Mem. Am. Econ. Assn., Phi Beta Kappa. Presbyterian. Club: GeorgeTown. Author: (with R.P. Nathan, A.D. Manvel) Monitoring Revenue Sharing, 1975. Home: 6504 Dearborn Dr Falls Church VA 22044 Office: Advisory Commn on Intergovernmental Relations Washington DC 20575

CALLAGHAN, PETER, mfg. exec.; b. Sale, Cheshire, Eng., Oct. 13, 1934; came to U.S., 1978; s. John Tierney and May (Greenlees) C.; sch. cert. Joint Matriculation Bd., 1948, higher sch. cert., 1950; m. Pauline Dean, Dec. 26, 1953; children—Stephen Peter, Anthony Peter, Julia Pauline. Articled clerkship Cooper & Cooper, Chartered Accts., Manchester, Eng., 1950-55; sr. audit clk. Clarke, Eckersley, Prentice (Now Touche Ross), Manchester, 1956-57; co. sec. Furniture Distbrs. Ltd., Manchester, 1957-58; cost acct. Cunliffe Whittam Holdings Ltd., Manchester, 1958-63, co. sec., 1963-66, fin. dir., 1966-78, chmn. bd., 1978; pres. Pamarco, Inc., Roselle, N.J., 1978—. Chartered acct., Eng. and Wales. Fellow Inst. Chartered Accts. in Eng. and Wales. Roman Catholic. Office: 209 E 11th Ave Roselle NJ 07203

CALLAHAN, DANIEL JOSEPH, III, banker; b. Washington, May 7, 1932; s. Daniel Joseph and Anne Bailey (Scott) C.; B.A., Williams Coll., 1954; postgrad. Am. Inst. Banking, 1956-57, Internat. Banking Summer Sch., Oxford, Eng., 1964, George Washington U., 1956-57; m. Colleen Adrienne Mount, May 5, 1956; children—Daniel Joseph IV, Carey Scott, Caren Anne, Carolyn Patricia, Colleen Gerry. Trainee, Riggs Nat. Bank, Washington, 1956-58, exec. v.p., 1973-76, pres., dir., 1976—; v.p. Chase Manhattan Bank, N.Y.C., 1958-69; exec. v.p. Hambro Am. Bank & Trust Co., N.Y.C., 1969-72, also dir.; mng. dir. Merrill-Lynch-Brown Shipley Bank, Ltd., London, 1972-73; dir. Genway Corp., Chgo. Chmn. Mayor's Overall Econ. Devel. Adv. Com. D.C.; treas. Nat. 4-H Council; trustee Meridian House Internat., Capital Children's Mus.; bd. regents Georgetown U.; bd. dirs. D.C. Soc. Crippled Children. Served to capt. USAF, 1954-56. Mem. Assn. Res. City Bankers, D.C. Bankers Assn. (pres.), Am. Bankers Assn. (exec. com. comml. lending div.). Roman Catholic. Clubs: Metropolitan (dir.) (Washington) Chevy Chase (Md.); Knickerbocker (N.Y.C.); American, Buck's, Overseas Bankers (London); Sunningdale (Eng.) Golf; Burning Tree; Farmington Country, Alfalfa, Soc. Friendly Sons of St. Patrick. Office: 1503 Pennsylvania Ave NW Washington DC 20013

CALLAHAN, JAMES F., mfg. co. exec.; b. Rochester, N.Y., Sept. 15, 1919; s. Maurice James and Mary M. (Pigage) C.; student Rochester Bus. Inst., 1937-39, Niagara U., 1940, 41, N.Y. U., 1977; m. Berenice Norman, Mar. 12, 1945; 1 dau., Margaret Callahan Schofield. With Fasco Industries Inc., 1939—, v.p., 1972-80, exec. v.p., 1980, pres., chief exec. officer, vice chmn. bd., 1980—, dir., 1976—; pres. Rochester chpt. Nat. Assn. Cost Accts., 1956-57, nat. dir., 1957-58. Mem. Nat. Assn. Accts., Inst. Internal Auditors. Office: 601 N Federal Hwy Boca Raton FL 33432

CALLAHAN, JOHN MORGAN, coll. food service adminstr.; b. Ilion, N.Y., Aug. 22, 1930; s. John Lawrence and Helen Eileen (Rauscher) C.; B.S., Cornell U., 1959; m. Dolores Christine Izzo, Dec. 29, 1956; children—Sean Patrick, Mary Erin, Kerry Michael, Christopher Gabriel, Lawrence Joseph, James Brien. Asst. mgr. food service Clarkson Coll., Potsdam, N.Y., 1959-60; dir. food service Ithaca (N.Y.) Coll., 1960-62, mgr. Willard Straight Hall, 1962-66; dir. food service Harpur Coll., Binghampton, N.Y., 1966-67, U. Calif., Davis, 1967-69; ops. analyst New Eng. area ARA Inc., 1969-71, sales mgr. New Eng. area, 1971-73; owner, pres. Hospitality Cons., Inc., Newtonville, Mass., 1975—; dir. food service Boston Coll., Chestnut Hill, Mass., 1975—. Pres., PTA, Ithaca; leader Cub Scouts, Davis. Served with USN, 1951-54. Mem. Nat. Assn. Coll. and Univ. Food Services, Mass. Restaurant Assn., Cornell Soc. Hotelmen (pres. New Eng. chpt. 1979—). Democrat. Roman Catholic. Clubs: Nashawtuc Country (Concord, Mass.); Cornell (dir. 1980—). Home: 19 Brook St Hudson MA 01749 Office: Hospitality Consultants Inc 425 Newtonville Ave Newtonville MA 02160 also Boston Coll 74 Commonwealth Ave Chestnut Hill MA 02167

CALLAHAN, MICHAEL EDSON, instrument co. exec.; b. Tacoma, Wash., June 26, 1940; s. Edson Jess and Marjorie Mabel (Lee) C.; student Tacoma Vocat. Inst., U. Puget Sound; m. Lenita Marjean Hickok, Feb. 8, 1964; children—Kevin, Kelly. Instrumentation engr., research asst. Boeing Co., Seattle, 1960-68; sales rep. computer products Digital Equipment Corp., Seattle, 1968-70, mgr. Seattle office, 1970-77, mktg. mgr., Maynard, Mass., 1975-77; comml. group mgr. sales dept. Digitac Equipment Corp., Bellevue, Wash., 1977—. Bd. dirs. Eastside Amateur Hockey Assn., 1975-76. Mem. Am. Mgmt. Assn. Club: Elks. Author various articles in field. Home: 18916 197th Ave NE Woodinville WA 98072 Office: 11040 NE Main St Bellevue WA 98004

CALLAHAN, MONITA, business exec.; b. Grand Saline, Tex., Dec. 15, 1927; d. Cecil Stone and La Rue (Smith) Chaney; student So. Meth. U., 1945-48; m. Roy Haney Callahan, Dec. 27, 1952; children—Roy Haney, Michael Chaney, Monita. Vice pres., sec., dir. Round Hill Limousine Service, Inc., Greenwich, Conn., 1960-61; asst. sec., dir. Round Hill, Inc., 1960-61; asst. sec., dir. Wilder Transp. Co., 1960-61, pub. relations rep., 1962; sec., dir. Airport Service Corp., 1961, Mid-City Taxi Co., 1961—; exec. adminstr. N.Y. met. region Duracell Products. Co-chmn. Westport com. Mid-Fairfield County Child Guidance Council. Bd. dirs. Women's League of Mid-Fairfield County Youth Mus.; trustee Greenwich Country Day Sch., Whitley Sch. Mem. Greenwich C. of C. (edn. com. 1959-61), Round Hill Community Guild (chmn. children's fair 1959-60). Republican. Office: 1 Old Easton Turnpike Weston CT 06883

CALLAHAN, ROY HANEY, lawyer, bus. exec.; b. Marceline, Mo., July 7, 1904; s. William Paxton and Malvina (Haney) P.; A.B., U. Mich., 1926; J.D., 1929; LL.M., So. Meth. U.; m. Monita Chaney; children—Roy Haney, Michael C., Monita. Librarian, 1924-29; admitted to N.Y. State bar, 1931, Mich. bar, 1931, Tex. bar, 1949; practiced with White & Case, N.Y.C., 1931-40; mem. Callahan & Durant, Fort Worth, 1949-55, Kilgore & Kilgore, Dallas, 1955-56. Naval aviator, 1929-31, 40-46 as aircraft carrier exec. officer, task group ops. officer, task group chief of staff, asst. to dep. chief, Bur. Aeros, asst. to asst. sec. navy for air, also asst. to sec. navy; exec. dir. N.Y.C. Airport Authority, also asst. commr. Marine and Aviation for N.Y.C., 1946; v.p., gen. mgr. Airlines Terminal Corp., also Airlines Nat. Terminal Service Co., 1946-48; exec. dir. Greater Fort Worth Internat. Air Terminal Corp., 1950-51; lectr. U. Mich. Law Inst., 1940; pres. Simpson Grain Co., Inc., 1956—; pres. Swan Finch Oil Corp.; pres., dir. Keta Oil & Gas Co., Olean Industries, Inc., Doeskin Products, Inc. 1956-57; v.p. Epsco, Inc., 1959; pres., gen. mgr. Round Hill Limousine Service, Inc., 1960; exec. asst. to v.p. Eastern Air Lines, 1961-69; exec. v.p. Airlines Facilities Corp. Am., 1969—, AFCOA Inc., 1969—; dir. Bradley Facilities, Inc., Airlines Terminal Corp., Airlines Nat. Terminal Service Co. Mem. Navy Roper Bd., 1948, Bur. Aeros. Naval Res. Adv. Council, 1946—. Res. officer with U.S. Army, 1926-29, res. enlisted man or officer, 1929—, capt. USNR, 1945-55, rear adm., 1955—. Decorated Bronze Star, Air medal, Res. medal Pacific. Trustee Southwestern Inst. Alcohol Research; life mem. Southwestern Legal Found.; mem. Com. of 100 on behalf of U. Mich. Phoenix Project for Atomic Research. Mem. Am., City of N.Y., Tex., Fort Worth, Dallas bar assns. Clubs: Masons; Univ., N.Y. Athletic; Cipango (Dallas). Author: The Corporate Mortgage under Texas Law; Rescue and Salvage in the Everglades; A Neglected Air Market; The Robinson Patman Act; Impact of the Next Two Aircraft Generations on Airport Design; co-author: National Policy for Aviation, 1946; Airports for Future Aircraft—A Planning Guide. Home: 1 Old Easton Turnpike Weston CT 06883 Office: 318 Hillcrest Bank Bldg Dallas TX 75205

CALLAHAN, VINCENT FRANCIS, JR., publisher; b. Washington, Oct. 30, 1931; s. Vincent Francis and Anita (Hawkins) C.; B.S. in Fgn. Service, Georgetown U., 1957; m. Dorothy Helen Budge, Aug. 27, 1960; children—Vincent Francis, Elizabeth Lauren, Anita Marie, Cynthia Helene, Robert Bruce. Partner, Callahan Publs., 1957—; editor numerous publs., 1957—; past pres. Ind. Newsletters Assn., Washington; v.p., dir. McLean Savs. & Loan Assn. Republican candidate lt. gov. Va., 1965; chmn. Va. Rep. Finance Com., 1966; mem. Va. Ho. of Dels., 1968—; Rep. candidate for Congress, 1976; vice-chmn. No. Va. Community Found.; trustee McLean Citizens Found. Served with USMC, 1950-52. Mem. U.S. Naval Inst., Am. Def. Preparedness Assn., Ind. Newsletters Assn. (pres. 1964), Nat. Press Club. Republican. Roman Catholic. Clubs: Kiwanis (past pres.); Bull and Bear (Richmond, Va.). Author eight books including: Missile Contract Guide, 1958; Space Guide, 1959; Underwater Defense Handbook, 1963; Military Research Handbook, 1963. Home: 6220 Nelway Dr McLean VA 22101 Office: 6631 Old Dominion Dr McLean VA 22101

CALLAN, CHRISTOPHER BRADFORD, computer software devel. exec.; b. Bethesda, Md., July 5, 1946; s. William Bellinger and Norma Pauline (Hanson) C.; B.A., U. Richmond, 1969; m. Mary Eileen Lindsay, Aug. 21, 1971; 1 son, Malcolm Spencer. Mgr. energy/environ. data systems Applied Data Research Co., Vienna, Va., 1971-78; dir. Gulf Coast ops. Cexec, Inc., Houston, 1978—; cons. electric utility, coal and oil energy problems and regulatory matters. Mem. Nat. Energy Resources Orgn., Phi Beta Kappa. Clubs: Sudamericano de Rugby (a founder), Western Suburbs Rugby (a founder). Creator, editor monthly Fuel Price Analysis, 1976-78. Home: 6013 Burgoyne St Houston TX 77057 Office: 110/2411 Fountainview St Houston TX 77057

CALLARD, DAVID JACOBUS, bank exec.; b. Boston, July 14, 1938; s. Henry Hadden and Clarissa Cooley (Jacobus) C.; A.B., Princeton, 1959; postgrad. Union Theol. Sem., 1964-65; J.D., N.Y. U., 1969; children—Owen Winston, Francis Jacobus, Anne Lloyd, Elizabeth Hadden, Samuel Porter. With Morgan Guaranty Trust Co., N.Y.C., 1959-61, 65-72, asst. v.p., 1965-69, v.p., 1970-72; partner firm Alex Brown & Sons, Balt., 1972—; dep. exec. dir. Pres.'s Commn. on All Vol. Armed Force, 1969-70; chmn., dir. Alex Brown Realty, Inc.; dir., mem. exec. com. Waverly Press, Inc.; pres., dir. Hotel Investors Corp.; chmn., trustee Hotel Investors Trust. Trustee, treas. Peabody Inst.; trustee Kernan Hosp., Calvert Sch., Keswick Home. Served to lt. USMC, 1971-74. Boothe Ferris fellow, 1964-65. Republican. Episcopalian. Clubs: Union, Racquet and Tennis (N.Y.C.); Elkridge (Balt.). Home: 1025 Breezewick Rd Baltimore MD 21204 Office: 135 E Baltimore St Baltimore MD 21202

CALLAWAY, CHARLES FRANKLIN, greeting cards co. exec.; b. Bronson, Tex., Apr. 22, 1933; s. William Henry and Lesta Carmen (Taylor) C.; m. Margaret Jean Floyd, July 3, 1952 (div.); children—Don Charles, Robin Lynn, Michael Wayne, Virginia Lea; m. 2d Evelyn J. Jackson, June 20, 1978; children—Penny Lynn, Michelle Ann, Andrew Lawrence. With Am. Greetings Corp., Billings, Mont., 1960—, mgr. zone chain sales, Cleve., 1972-73, regional mgr., Cleve., 1973-76, mgr. nat. sales, supermarkets, Cleve., 1976—. Mem. Am. Mgmt. Assn. Home: 671 Pepperwood St Brunswick OH 44212

CALLAWAY, DAVID HENRY, investment banker; b. N.Y.C., July 3, 1912; s. David Henry and Mary (Sampson) C.; A.B., Dartmouth, 1934; m. Virginia A. Devoe, June 5, 1937; children—Nancy A. (Mrs. Martin L. Lyons), Patricia J. (Mrs. James R. McGrath). With Halsey, Stuart & Co., Inc., 1934-36; with First Mich. Corp., N.Y.C., 1936—, sr. v.p., 1956-62, pres., 1963-70, chmn. bd., chief exec. officer, 1970—, also dir. Pres., Municipal Forum N.Y., 1959-60. Mem. Municipal Bond Club, Am. Stock Exchange, Inc., N.Y. Stock Exchange. Clubs: Bond, Stock Exchange Luncheon (N.Y.C.); Detroit, Renaissance (Detroit); Wee Burn Country (Darien). Home: 17 Holly Ln Darien CT 06820 Office: 2 Wall St New York NY 10005 also 100 Renaissance Center Detroit MI 48243

CALLAWAY, WESLEY MONROE, investment co. exec.; b. Lampasas, Tex., Feb. 8, 1908; s. Oscar Monroe and Cara Ella (Graham) C.; B.A., So. Meth. U., 1961; m. Louree E. Galaway, May 3, 1931; children—Wesley Monroe, Kenneth G. Mgr., Gulf States Life Ins. Co., Taylor, Tex., 1931-35; v.p. South Coast Life Ins. Co., Beaumont, Tex., 1936-43, pres., 1943-53; pres., chmn. bd. South Coast Mortgage Co., Beaumont, 1953—; chmn. bd. Jefferson Investment Corp., Beaumont, 1955-78, Realty Mortgage Investment Corp., Austin, Tex., 1960-78; dir., chmn. planning com. Beaumont State Bank; dir. South Coast Mortgage Co. Dir. Tex. Life Conv., 1945-70. Mem. Tex. Mortgage Bankers Assn. (dir. 1953-73), Beaumont C. of C. Baptist (pres. men's Bible class; treas. Calder Ch. 1976-80, deacon 1976—). Clubs: Masons; Beaumont, Beaumont Country. Home: 1380 Audubon St Beaumont TX 77706 Office: 2050 N 11th St Beaumont TX 77704

CALLEN, JOHN HOLMES, JR., exec. search cons.; b. East Orange, N.J., June 19, 1932; s. John Holmes and Gloria (Batten) C.; student Princeton U., 1951-53; A.B. in History, Trinity Coll., Hartford, Conn., 1955; m. Carolyn Palmer Coleman, July 14, 1956; children—Paige Palmer, John Holmes, Lindsey Morrell, James Hunter. Sales rep. Peerless Woolen Mills div. Burlington Industries, 1958-61, Burlington Industries, 1958-77, exec. v.p. mktg. Burlington-Madison Yarn Co., 1960-73; pres. Galy & Lord div. Burlington Industries, 1973, Burlington Sportswear, 1973-77; partner, dir. Ward Howell Internat., N.Y.C., 1977—. Served as 1st lt., USMC, 1955-58. Republican. Clubs: Rumson Country (dir.), Sea Bright Lawn Tennis and Cricket, Princeton (N.Y.C.). Home: Black Point Horseshoe Rumson NJ 07760 Office: 99 Park Ave New York NY 10016

CALLENDER, ROBERT LEWIS, real estate co. exec.; b. Scranton, Pa., Aug. 31, 1930; s. Marion H. and Helen J. (Jones) C.; B.A., Dartmouth Coll., 1953, M.B.A., 1958; 1 son, William N. Nat. credit mgr. Gen. Foods Corp., White Plains, N.Y., 1961-64; v.p. Continental Ill. Bank, N.Y.C., 1964-67; pres. Computer Property Corp., N.Y.C., 1971—; vice chmn. bd. Fairfield Communities, Inc., Little Rock, 1971—. Served with USNR, 1954-57. Mem. Montessori Soc. Ark. (pres. 1976-78), Fin. Execs. Inst. Republican. Office: PO Box 3375 Little Rock AR 72203

CALLOWAY, JOHN CLYDE, fin. exec.; b. Birmingham, Ala., Jan. 29, 1921; s. John Clyde and Fannie (Lacey) C.; student U. Ala., 1941; m. Nettye Phillips, Apr. 2, 1950; children—Frances Amanda, Catherine Jayne. Founder, owner J.C. Calloway Merc Co., Bessemer, Ala., 1954-60; owner Skylite Corp., Tuscaloosa, Ala., 1944-54; partner BBC Investment Co., Birmingham, 1959-64; pres. Jolly Inns of Fla., Sarasota, 1964—, Intergulf Motels Inc., Jackson, Miss., 1964—, Intergulf Motels of Tex., Amarillo, 1973—; dir. Ala. Mchts. Assn., 1945-50. Bd. dirs. Master Hosts, 1960-65, Ala. Travel Council, 1957-65; bd. stewards Jones Meml. M.E. Ch., 1946-48; mem. ednl. bd. 1st Meth. Ch., Bessemer, 1949-51. Served to lt. comdr. USN, 1942-44. Mem. Ala. Motel-Hotel Assn. (pres. 1959-61, nat. dir. 1962-64), Jackson C. of C. Methodist. Clubs: Press, The Club. Home: 3800 Knollwood Dr Mount Brook Birmingham AL 35243 Office: 1 Flowood Blvd PO Box 5520 Jackson MS 39208

CALVERT, FRANCES LEON, bus. investments co. exec.; b. Sligo, Pa., Apr. 17, 1944; d. Francis Raymond and Alice Lucile (Myers) Miller; B.A., Sacks Sales U., 1970; m. John William Calvert, 1978; children by previous marriage—Tambra Dawn, Lonny Edward. Asst. purchasing agt. Monogram Industries, Los Angeles, 1968; buyer Barker Bros. Furniture, Los Angeles, 1969; bus. devel. officer Imperial Bank, Los Angeles, 1970-73, United Calif. Bank, Los Angeles, 1973-76; pres. Milliren Enterprises, Los Angeles, 1976-79; with Quail Place Properties, Newport Beach, Calif., 1978—. cons. in field; pilot. Recipient numerous sales certificates; named Bus. Devel. Officer of Yr., Imperial Bank, 1971, United Calif. Bank, 1976. Mem. Nat. Accountants Assn., Aircraft Owners and Pilots Assn., Calif. Real Estate Assn., Nat. Mgmt. Assn. Republican. Clubs: Skylark, Far West Ski Assn., Airguide. Developer real estate fin. packages, 1971—, software computer systems and usages, 1973-76. Office: 1400 Quail Place Newport Beach CA 92660

CALVIN, DONALD LEE, stock exchange exec.; b. Mt. Olive, Ill., Nov. 10, 1931; s. Mike H. and Mary Josephine C.; grad. U. Ill., 1955; m. Louise Peterson, Mar. 28, 1952; children—Jane Calvin Palasek, Sally Anne. Admitted to Ill. bar, 1956; individual practice law, Farmer City, Ill., 1956-57; atty. office of Sec. of State, Ill., 1957-58; Ill. securities commr., 1959-62; syndicate mgr. A.C. Allyn & Co., Chgo., 1962-63; atty. F. I. duPont & Co., Chgo., 1963-64; exec. asst. civic and govt. affairs N.Y. Stock Exchange, N.Y.C., 1964-65, v.p. civic and govt. affairs, 1966-77, sr. v.p., 1977-79, exec. v.p. market devel. and public affairs, 1979—; dir. Depository Trust Co., Nova Ancora Corp. Adv. bd. U. Calif. Securities Law Inst. Served with USMCR, 1951-56. Mem. Internat. Bar Assn., Am. Bar Assn., Ill. State Bar Assn., Chgo. Bar Assn. Clubs: Manhasset Bay Yacht (Port Washington, N.Y.), Met. of N.Y., N.Y. Stock Exchange Luncheon. Office: 11 Wall St New York NY 10005

CALVIN, LARRY THORTON, comml. fisherman; b. Huntington Beach, Calif., June 23, 1934; s. Frank Thornton and Gladys Evalyn (Henricksen) C.; B.A. in Bus. and Econs., Washington State Coll., 1958; m. Maryann Evalyn Henricksen, June 28, 1961; children—Kristopher, Eric, Leif, Karen. Mgr., Snow Pine Lodge, Alta, Utah, 1959-63; boat operator Alaskan Guide and Charter, Sitka, 1963-65; comml. diver Baranof Aquatic Co., Sitka, 1965-68; pres. Baranof Bldg. Supply, Inc., Sitka, 1968-80; owner Baranof Rentals; owner, capt. comml. fishing vessel Morning Mist. Mem., chmn. Alaska Fish and Game Adv. Com., Sitka, advisor del. Nat. Fisheries Plan. Mem. Alaskan, Sitka conservation socs. Republican. Office: Box 1170 Sitka AK 99835

CAMANGA, EUGENE ROY, JR., fin. and computer cons.; b. New Orleans, Sept. 13, 1951; s. Eugene Roy and Dolores (Matherne) C.; B.S. in Fin., U. New Orleans, 1973. Real estate salesman Latter & Blum, Inc., New Orleans, 1974; systems analyst, supr. Fed. Res. Bank, New Orleans, 1975-76; mgmt. cons. Alexander Grant & Co., C.P.A.'s, mgmt. cons., New Orleans, 1976-79; cons. Tymshare, Inc., New Orleans, 1979-80; sr. systems analyst Freeport Minerals, New Orleans, 1980—. Mem. U. New Orleans Alumni Assn., New Orleans Mus. Art. Home: 4629 Auron Blvd Metairie LA 70002

CAMBRIA, GUY, JR., banker; b. Middletown, Conn., Feb. 20, 1937; s. Guy and Frances Craft (Barnett) C.; B.A., Bard Coll., 1959; postgrad. Brown U., 1971; m. Barbara E. Lawton, Sept. 28, 1963; children—Suzanne Elizabeth, Stephen Barnett. Asst. treas. Mechanics Savs. Bank of Winsted, 1964-67; asst. v.p., sec. Union Savs. Bank of N.Y., 1967-70; v.p. mktg. Burritt Mut. Savs. Bank, New Britain, Conn., 1970-74; pres., chief exec. officer Tolland (Conn.) Bank, 1975—, also dir. Chmn. allocations com. Tri-Town United Way, 1977-80, v.p.; mem. allocations com. United Way of Capitol region, 1979—; v.p. Tolland High Sch. Scholarship Fund, 1975-78; chmn. Econ. Devel. Commn., Town of Tolland, 1977—; mem. adv. bd. Hockanum Valley Community Council, 1976-77; bd. dirs. Nathan Hale chpt. ARC, 1975-77; mem. adv. council Manchester Community Coll., 1975-77. Mem. Tri-Town C. of C. (dir.), Nat. Assn. Mut. Savs. Bank, Conn. Assn. Mut. Savs. Banks. Episcopalian. Clubs: Rotary, Shriners, Masons, Hartford. Home: 39 Hilltop Rd Tolland CT 06084 Office: 670 Tolland Stage Rd Tolland CT 06084

CAMBRON, JOHN RALPH, bus. assn. exec.; b. Asheville, N.C., Apr. 5, 1922; s. John Franklin and Carrie (Campbell) C.; A.B., U. N.C., Chapel Hill, 1951, J.D., 1953; M.A., U. N.C., Greensboro, 1978; m. Sylvia Anne Spivey, Mar. 2, 1962; children—Patricia Deborah, John Ralph, Andrew Bryan, Ellen Susan. Mem. legal dept. Pilot Life Ins. Co., Greensboro, 1953-63, v.p., 1963-72; pres. Better Bus. Bur. of Central N.C., Greensboro, 1972—; tchr. Guilford Tech. Inst. Pres. Greensboro Friends of Library, 1976—. Served with U.S. Army, 1942-45. Decorated Silver Star, Bronze Star, Purple Heart; recipient Silver medal Am. Advt. Fedn., 1980. Mem. Adminstrv. Mgmt. Soc. (pres. 1966), Personnel Assn. Greensboro (pres. 1970), Delta Theta Phi. Republican. Presbyterian. Clubs: Rotary (pres. 1972-73), Greensboro Writers. Book reviewer Greensboro Daily News, 1978-80. Office: 3608 W Friendly Ave Greensboro NC 27410

CAMERON, BRUCE DONALD, restaurant exec.; b. Detroit, Mar. 12, 1929; s. Duncan John and Elizabeth Helen (McPhillips) C.; B.S., U. Detroit, 1952, M.B.A., 1954. With Byron W. Trerice Co., Southfield, Mich., 1954-64; owner The Maple House Inc., Birmingham, Mich., 1964—; also 9 other restaurants, including Meating Place Inc., Orchard Lake, Mich., Midtown Cafe Inc., Birmingham. Served with U.S. Navy, 1949-50. Roman Catholic. Club: Oakland Hills Country. Home: 4695 Commerce Rd Orchard Lake MI 48033 Office: 3611 W Maple Rd Birmingham MI 48010

CAMERON, DONALD LEE, electronics mfg. co. exec.; b. Clonsilla, Okla., Feb. 9, 1936; s. Troy and Alice Marie (Harden) C.; B.S. in Elec. Engring., San Jose State U., 1959, M.S., 1964; m. Joyce Marie Gehrke, Sept. 20, 1974; children from previous marriage—Michael Lee, Laura Diane, Kelly Suzanne. Electronics design engr. Lawrence Radiation, Lab., Livermore, Calif., 1959-60; ordnance engr. Lockheed Missile Systems div., Sunnyvale, Calif., 1960-61; logic design engr. IBM, San Jose, Calif., 1961-63, systems design engr., San Jose, 1963-66, Hawaii, 1967-68, Palo Alto, Calif., 1968-71, mfg. industry application devel. mgr., Menlo Park, Calif., 1971-74, mgr. Industry Application Support Center, 1975—; partner Camtek, electronics devel. mfg. and distbn. firm, 1975—; pres. Camtronics, Inc., mfg. and distbn., 1979—. Pres., Mountain View Young Republicans, Palo Alto, 1973. Recipient Outstanding Contribution award IBM, 1973. Presbyterian. Home: 20315 Franklin Ave Saratoga CA 95070 Office: 2800 Sand Hill Rd Menlo Park CA 94025

CAMERON, DONALD ROYCE, real estate/fin. cons.; b. Jefferson City, Tenn., July 8, 1947; s. Simmie E. and Farris Joy (Thorpe) C.; B.S. in Agr., U. Tenn., 1975, M.B.A. in Real Estate and Fin., 1976; m. Sharon Lynn Blakley, June 15, 1974; 1 dau., Blakley D. Rep., Xerox Corp., Kingsport, Tenn., 1971-74; affiliate broker Zirkle-Rainwater Auction Co., Dandridge, Tenn., 1974-77; v.p. fin. Publix Oil Co., Inc., Morristown, Tenn., 1977-78; pres. Pegauss Corp., Knoxville, Tenn., 1978—; pres. Cameron, Downing & Co., Knoxville, 1979—; gen. partner various real estate syndications; appraisal cons. City of White Pine (Tenn.). Served with U.S. Army, 1966-69. Cert. real estate broker, Tenn. Mem. Am. Soc. Farm Mgrs. and Rural Appraisers (asso.), Tenn. Soc. Farm Mgrs. and Rural Appraisers, Knoxville Apt. Council, Tenn. Hotel/Motel Assn. Mem. Ch. of Brethren. Home: Route 2 Box 305 White Pine TN 37890 Office: 2510 United American Plaza Knoxville TN 37929

CAMERON, DONALD SEYMOUR, ins. co. exec.; b. Rochester, N.Y., Nov. 5, 1931; s. Thomas F. and Gertrude J. (Lash) C.; student Rochester Inst. Tech., 1949-50; m. Helen Marie Hynes, May 15, 1954; children—Anne, David, Susan. Head sales dept. Swift & Co., Rochester, 1952-57; agt. N.Y. Life Ins. Co., Rochester, 1957-63, 68-69, asst. mgr., 1963-68; gen. agt. Nat. Life of Vt., Rochester, N.Y., 1969—. Served with USMC, 1950-52. Recipient Rachel May Swain award, 1980; Pres.'s trophy Nat. Life of Vt., 1980. Mem. Rochester Life Underwriters (pres. 1968-69), N.Y. Assn. Life Underwriters, Gen. Agts. and Mgrs. Assn. (past pres.). Republican. Roman Catholic. Home: 104 Lake Lea Rd Rochester NY 14617 Office: 17 E Main St Rochester NY 14614

CAMERON, PAUL A., mfg. exec.; b. Wilmington, Del., Sept. 13, 1921; s. Willard and Mary (Fisher) C.; grad. U.S. Armed Forces Inst.; m. Carol Jean Mikkelson, Jan. 20, 1957; children by previous marriage—Victoria Nan Cameron Carlson, Kim Paul; children—Paul Carl, Michele Diane. Staff engr. TWA, 1946-52; mgr. Milw. div. Allstates Engring., 1952-55; pres., chief exec. officer Feedback Controls, Inc., 1955-63; product and market devel. mgr. Purolator, Inc., Piscataway, N.J., 1963-64, v.p. corp. devel., 1965-68, dir., 1967—, exec. v.p., chief operating officer, 1968-70, pres., chief exec. officer, 1970—; dir., chmn. examining com. Fidelity Union Trust Co.; dir. Mahle, Inc. Bd. dirs. Exec. Council on Fgn. Diplomates; chmn. bd. trustees Carrier Found.; pres. bd. trustees Animal Med.; adv. council Rockefeller U.; active Am. Diabetes Assn., Mus. Am. Indian. Served with USAAF, World War II. Named Chief Exec. Officer of Yr., Fin. World, 1979. Office: 255 Old New Brunswick Rd Piscataway NJ 08854

CAMERON, RANDOLPH WHITNEY, cosmetic co. exec.; b. Jersey City, Apr. 6, 1936; s. Hugh J. and Anneatta R. (Alleyne) C.; B.S., Del. State Coll., 1958; m. Martha R. Billingsley, Apr. 10, 1965; children—Randolph Whitney, Michele Renee. Mgr., D. Parke Gibson Assos., N.Y.C., 1962-64, v.p., 1966-71, dir., 1964-66; div. sales mgr. Avon Products, Inc., N.Y.C., 1972-73, mktg. dir., 1973-78, dir. gen. communications, 1978—. Served with U.S. Army, 1959-61. Mem. Nat. Assn. Market Developers, Am. Mktg. Assn., Del. State Coll. Alumni Assn. Home: 100 W 94th St New York City NY 10025 Office: Avon Products 9 W 57th St New York City NY 10019

CAMERON, STEELE CATHERWOOD, woodworking machinery mfr.; b. Poughkeepsie, N.Y., Aug. 9, 1923; s. Donald Palmer and Hazel (Catherwood) C.; student Princeton U., 1941-43; B.E., Yale U., 1944; M.B.A., Columbia U., 1949; m. Helen S. Runyon, Dec. 14, 1963; children—Elizabeth, Frances, Doris Ann. With James L. Taylor Mfg. Co., Poughkeepsie, 1949—, v.p., 1960-71, pres., dir., 1971—, chmn., 1974—; dir. Dutchess Bank & Trust Co.; dir. Internat. Woodworking Machinery and Supply Fair, 1980. Mem. Poughkeepsie Bd. Edn., 1960-64; pres. Dutchess Sr. Citizen Housing Corp., 1975-77; bd. dirs. Poughkeepsie YMCA, 1961-66, 68-73, pres., 1965-66, chmn. bldg. fund dr. 1967; trustee Am. Inst. Econ. Research. Served to ensign USNR, 1944-46, to lt., 1951-52. Mem. Woodworking Machinery Mfrs. Am. (dir. 1973—, v.p. 1976-77, pres. 1978-79), Yale Engring. Assn., Poughkeepsie Area C. of C. (dir. 1966-69, 76-79). Congregationalist. Home: 10 Jonathan Ln Poughkeepsie NY 12603 Office: 108-128 Parker Ave Poughkeepsie NY 12602

CAMICIA, NICHOLAS THOMAS, bus. exec.; b. Welch, W.Va., Apr. 23, 1916; s. Antonio and Antonia (Santini) C.; B.S., Va. Poly. Inst. and U., 1938; m. Virginia Brown, May 11, 1941; 1 dau., Caren Camicia Hollenbeck. Laborer to gen. mgr. ops. Island Creek Coal Co., 1938-57, v.p. ops., 1957-62, exec. v.p., dir., 1963-65; exec. v.p. Freeman Coal Mining Corp., Chgo., 1965-67, pres., 1967-69; pres. United Electric Coal Co., 1967-69; pres., chief exec. officer, dir. Pittston Co., N.Y.C., 1969—, chmn., 1977—; dir. Brink's, Inc., Ingersoll-Rand Co., Chessie Systems, Inc. Trustee, Fordham U. Served with AUS, 1941-45. Decorated Bronze Star, Order of Orange-Nassau (Netherlands); recipient Man of Conscience award Appeal of Conscience Found., 1975; Americanism award Anti-Defamation League, 1978; Erskine Ramsey medal AIME. Mem. Nat. Coal Assn. (past chmn.), Bituminous Coal Operators Assn. (past chmn.), Am. Mining Congress (chmn. bd. dirs.), Nat. Mine Rescue Assn. (past pres.), W.Va. Coal Mining Inst. (past pres.), Am. Inst. Mining, Metall. and Petroleum Engrs. Republican. Roman Catholic. Clubs: Blind Brook; Indian Harbor Yacht; Sky (gov. 1975); Greenwich Country. Contbr. articles to profl. jours. Home: 224 Round Hill Rd Greenwich CT 06830 Office: One Pickwick Plaza Greenwich CT 06830

CAMINKER, BERNIE, mfg. co. exec., design cons.; b. Los Angeles, Aug. 18, 1930; s. Elleck and Anna (Shevelenco) C.; student U. Calif., Berkeley, 1950-52; B.A., UCLA, 1956, postgrad., 1956-60; m. Irma

Judith Abramson, Aug. 22, 1954 (div.); children—Lisa Ellen, Evan Howard. Indsl. designer Henry Dreyfuss Indsl. Design, Pasadena, Calif., 1956-57; partner Powell-Caminker Indsl. Design, Los Angeles, 1957-63; mgr. indsl. design and project mgr. Packard Bell Computer, Los Angeles and Santa Ana, 1959-64; chief mech. engring. and devel. Eldorado Electronics, Walnut Creek, Calif., 1964-65; staff engr., head systems design group Hughes Aircraft Co., Fullerton, Calif., 1965-73; pres. Apex Diamond Tool Co., Santa Ana, Calif., 1974—; owner Camin Design Group, Santa Ana, 1978—; design, engring., graphics and archtl. cons. Served with Signal Corps, U.S. Army, 1952-54. Recipient Western Electronics show and conv. design awards of excellence, 1959, 60; Wescon Design award of merit, 1960. Contbr. articles to profl. jours.; patentee in field. Office: 1426 E Borchard Ave Santa Ana CA 92705

CAMMARATA, JACOB JOHN (JACK), med. devel. engr.; b. Milw., Oct. 29, 1938; s. Jacob and Anna C.; B.S. in Mech. Engring. and Bus. Adminstrn., Marquette U., 1963; m. Mary Alice Youngren, May 4, 1968; children—Tony Jacob, Nick William. Indsl. engr. Square D. Co., Milw., 1964-66, Louis Allis Co., Milw., 1966-67; mfg. engr. Donaldson Co., Mpls., 1967-70, Honeywell Co., Mpls., 1970-72; devel. engr. ADO Products, Mpls., 1972-74, Nortronics Co., Mpls., 1974, Medtronic Inc., Mpls., 1974—; cons. in personnel selection. Served with U.S. Army, 1962. Registered profl. engr., Minn. Mem. Am. Assn. Handwriting Analysts, Am. Handwriting Analysis Found. Lutheran. Patentee. Home: 5413 Fairview St N Minneapolis MN 55429

CAMMARATA, JOHN, bus. exec.; b. Bklyn., Oct. 6, 1922; s. Vincent and Mary (D'Oca) C.; B.E.E., Bklyn. Poly. Inst., 1943; M.B.A., Hofstra U., 1961; m. Nina Sicari, Feb. 14, 1954; children—Anna Marie, John. Test engr. Gen. Electric Co., Schenectady, 1943-46; engr. research devel. Arms div. Am. Bosch Arma Corp., Garden City, N.Y., 1946-50, sect. head, 1950-56, mgr. devel. services, 1957-59, asst. chief engr., 1960, mgr. product reliability, 1961-64, works mgr., 1964, dir. mfg. ops., 1965; exec. asst. Airborne Instrument Lab., Cutler Hammer Corp., Deer Park, N.Y., 1965-66; gen. mgr. Barden-Leemath div. Barden Corp., 1963-68; v.p. mfg. Trio Labs., Plainview, N.J., 1968—; mgr. indsl. engring. ITT, N.Y.C., 1968—; dir. Asia Pacific ops. devel. ITT Far East & Pacific Inc., Hong Kong, 1971—; mng. dir. ITT Niles Co., Ltd., Japan, 1973; gen. mgr. ITT Transelectronics (Malaysia) Sdn. Bhd., 1974; ops. exec. ITT, N.Y.C., 1975; v.p., dir. internat. ops. ITT Federal Electric Co., Paramus, N.J., 1976—; v.p., dir. ops. ITT Bus. Communications Div., 1980—. Served with AUS, 1943-45. Registered profl. engr., N.Y. Fellow Inst. Environ. Scis.; mem. Electronic Mfrs. Council (sec. dir.), IEEE, Nat. Soc. Profl. Engrs., Am. Mgmt. Assn., Tau Beta Pi, Eta Kappa Nu, Mu Gamma Tau, Alpha Phi Delta. Clubs: N.Y. Athletic; Huntington Crescent. Author: (with others) Handbook of Environmental Engineering, 1956. Home: 30 Lilac Dr Syosset NY 11791 Office: ITT Bus Communications Div 2000 S Wolf Rd Des Plaines IL 60018

CAMONIER, RENÉ DÉSIRÉ, indsl. engr.; b. Batavia, Dutch East Indies, May 26, 1929; came to U.S., 1962, naturalized, 1969; s. Wilhelm and Johanna (Bauwin) C.; M.S. in Maritime Engring., Royal Dutch Maritime Naval Acad., 1953; B.S. in M.E., U. Amsterdam, 1951; postgrad. Milw. Inst. Tech., 1964-66, Marquette U., 1966-67; 3 children. Founder, Transcript Ent. Internat. Corp., Pitts. and Rockford, Ill., 1973—; owner RDC Engring., 1971-75; cons. Project Metallurgic Import USSR/USA, Kamaz, USSR, 1971-73; staff prodn. engr. Colt Industries, Crucible, Inc., Midland, Pa., 1974-78; chief indsl. engr. Rockford Drop Forge Co. (Ill.), 1978—; chmn. bd., chief exec. officer Transcript Enterprises Internat. Corp. Served with Royal Dutch Air Force, 1955-57. Mem. Am. Inst. Indsl. Engrs., Data Processing Mgmt. Assn. Inventor air flow energy indicator, 1967. Home: 4471 Carthage Dr Apt 9 Rockford IL 61109

CAMP, EHNEY ADDISON, III, mortgage banker; b. Birmingham, Ala., June 28, 1942; s. Ehney Addison and Mildred Fletcher (Tillman) C.; B.A., Dartmouth Coll., 1964; m. Patricia Jane Hough, Sept. 17, 1966; children—Ehney Addison, Margaret Strader. Sr. v.p. Cobbs, Allen & Hall Mortgage Co., Inc., Birmingham, 1965-72; v.p., gen. mgr. The Rime Cos., Birmingham, 1972-75; pres. Camp & Co., Birmingham, 1975—. Bd. dirs. Community Chest/United Way Jefferson, Walker and Shelby Counties. Served with USAF, 1965, Ala. Air N.G., 1966. Mem. Am. (income property com.), Ala. mortgage bankers assns., Birmingham Real Estate Bd. Methodist. Clubs: Kiwanis (dir. 1977-78), Mountain Brook (bd. govs. 1976-77), Birmingham Country, The Club, Downtown, Ponte Vedra, Shoal Creek. Home: 3621 Rockhill Rd Birmingham AL 35223 Office: 3940 Montclair Rd Suite 502 Birmingham AL 35213

CAMPBELL, ALISTAIR MATHESON, ins. co. exec.; b. Argyllshire, Scotland, July 3, 1905; s. Peter and Catherine (MacRae) C.; student Inverness Royal Acad., 1917-23; M.A., U. Aberdeen, 1927; m. Barbara Hampson Alexander, Apr. 2, 1948; children—Michael Alexander, Catherine, Barbara, Jill. Joined Sun Life Assurance Co. of Can., Montreal, Que., 1928, asst. actuary, 1934-40, asso. actuary, 1940-46, actuary, 1946, asst. gen. mgr. and actuary, 1947, v.p., actuary, 1950, v.p. and chief actuary, 1954, exec. v.p., dir., 1956-62, pres., 1962-70, chmn., 1970-78, chmn. exec. com. of bd., 1978—; dir., chmn. Can. Enterprise Devel. Corp. Ltd., Canendev Investments Ltd.; dir., mem. exec. com. Royal Trustco, Ltd., Royal Trust Corp. Can.; dir. Royal Trust Co., Royal Trust Co. Mortgage Corp., Digital Equipment Can., Ltd.; provincial v.p. (Que.) Am. Life Conv., 1962-63, mem. exec. com., 1965. Bd. dirs. Can. Safety Council, 1968-73; past mem. bd. divisional trustees, v.p., 1950-53, hon. gov. Que. div. Can. Red Cross Soc., 1975. Served with Royal Can. Arty., 1940-45. Fellow Inst. Actuaries, Soc. Actuaries (past gov.); mem. Can. Assn. Actuaries (pres. 1947-48), Can. Life Ins. Assn. (pres. 1957-58), Life Ins. Assn. Am. (dir. 1968-71). Home: 4 Coltrin Pl Rockcliffe Ottawa ON K1M 0A5 Canada Office: Suite 604 255 Albert St Ottawa ON K1P 6A9 Canada

CAMPBELL, ANDREW GREGVER, health care exec.; b. Kansas City, Mo., Sept. 25, 1944; s. William Thaddeus and Ruth Logan (Coursault) C.; B.S., Cornell U., 1966; M.B.A., U. So. Calif., 1969; m. Martha Carolyn Roush, Oct. 18, 1972. Sr. auditor, cons. Harris, Kerr, Forster & Co., C.P.A.'s, Los Angeles, 1967-74; acctg. mgr. First Travel Corp., Encino, Calif., 1974-75; v.p. fin. Family Health Program, Fountain Valley, Calif., 1975—; dir. Health Maintenance Life Ins. Co., Providers & Consumers, Inc., Providers Protective Ins. Co.; mem. health maintenance orgn. adv. com. Calif. Corps. Commn.; bd. dirs., past pres. Health Services Polit. Action Com. Served with USAR, 1969-71. C.P.A., Calif. Mem. Am. Inst. C.P.A.'s, Group Health Assn. Am., Am. Mgmt. Assn., Calif. Soc. C.P.A.'s, Cornell U. Hotelmen's Soc., Internat. Food and Wine Soc., Les Amus Du Vin. Home: 425 Longfellow Ave Hermosa Beach CA 90254 Office: 9930 Talbert Ave Fountain Valley CA 92708

CAMPBELL, ARCHIBALD ROWLAND, JR., ins. co. exec.; b. Galveston, Tex., May 24, 1917; s. Archibald Rowland and Kate Wilson (Rountree) C.; student U. of South, Sewanee, 1935-37; B.A., U. Tex., 1940; m. Eugenia Davis Harris, Apr. 18, 1947; children—Eugenia, Archie, John, Douglas. With Am. Indemnity Co., Galveston, 1941—, v.p., 1969-80, now ret. Served to 1st lt. AUS, 1942-45. Club: Galveston Arty. Home: 4520 Caduceus Galveston TX 77550 Office: 2115 Winnie St Galveston TX 77553

CAMPBELL, BARBARA TOMON, bank exec.; b. Cleve.; d. Bert A. and Frances T. Tomon; B.A., Barat Coll., Lake Forest, Ill., 1967. Sales promotion mgr. Germaine Monteil Cosmetics, N.Y.C., 1967-74; dir. communications Lord & Taylor, N.Y.C., 1974-78; dir. mktg. Chem. Bank, N.Y.C., 1978—. Mktg. cons. Vol. Urban Cons. Group, 1979-80. Mem. Bank Mktg. Assns., Fin. Communications Soc. Clubs: Sandbar Sailing, Uptown Racquet, St. Bartholomew's Community. Contbr. articles to profl. jours. Home: 420 E 64th St New York NY 10021 Office: 1411 Broadway New York NY 10018

CAMPBELL, BARRIE CARVEL, research cons.; b. Salt Lake City, Mar. 15, 1946; s. Ezra Carvel and LaRue Jacobsen (Rawlings) C.; student (James T. Babb scholar) Yale U., 1964-66; B.S. in Physics, Brigham Young U., 1973, now postgrad.; m. Cathy Christensen, July 12, 1974; children—Amelia, Barrie Benoni, Bryan Roy. Engring. aid State of Idaho, Dept. of Water Adminstrn., Boise, 1969, 71; research physicist Billings Energy Corp., Provo, Utah, 1975-76, v.p. research, 1976-78, dir. electrochem. lab., 1978-79, dir., 1977-78; dir. Billings Computer Corp., 1976-78 pvt. cons.; research asst. Brigham Young U. Mem. Ch. of Jesus Christ of Latter-Day Saints. Club: Kiwanis. Contbr. articles in field to profl. jours. Home: 823 W 900 S Payson UT 84651 Office: Chemistry Dept Brigham Young U Provo UT 84602

CAMPBELL, BRIAN PHILLIP, mfg. co. exec.; b. Oak Park, Ill., Aug. 23, 1940; s. Andrew Frank and Elizabeth (Gabris) C.; B.S.C., DePaul U., 1963; M.B.A., Northwestern U., 1966; M.S. in Fed. Income Taxation, DePaul U., 1973; m. Mary Lucina Lincoln. With No. Trust Co., Chgo., 1963; asst. v.p. Walston & Co., Inc., Chgo., 1963-65; v.p. Glore Forgan Staats, Inc., Chgo., 1965-70; v.p. duPont Glore Forgan Inc., Chgo., 1970-73; v.p. Masco Corp., Taylor, Mich., 1974—, group v.p., 1980—; lectr. DePaul U., 1972-73. Bd. dirs. Chgo. Boys Clubs, 1972-73, Boys Clubs Met. Detroit, 1974—. Mem. Inst. Chartered Financial Analysts, Financial Execs. Inst., Planning Execs. Inst. Episcopalian. Clubs: Chgo., Univ. of Chgo., Economics (Chgo.); Barton Hills Country. Office: 21001 Van Born Rd Taylor MI 48180

CAMPBELL, BRUCE JACKSON, photog. co. retail exec.; b. Phila., Jan. 20, 1934; s. William Roland and Isabelle (Jackson) C.; B.A., Earlham Coll., 1956; m. Joyce Ann Olinger, June 16, 1956; children—Bruce Jackson, II Connie Sue, Douglas Paul, Andrew Marle. Successively buyer Rike Lumber Co., Dayton, Ohio; mgr. distbn. center E.F. MacDonald Stamp Co., mgr. distbn. analysis, Cleve.; regional distbn. mgr. GAF, Chgo.; dir. logistics Oxy Metal Industries, Detroit; v.p. distbn. and service Bell & Howell Co., Chgo., now v.p. ops., Bell & Howell-Mamiya Co., Chgo. Mem. Nat. Council Phys. Distbn. Mgmt. Office: 7100 N McCormick Rd Chicago IL 60645

CAMPBELL, CALVIN ARTHUR, JR., mining and tunneling equipment mfg. co. exec.; b. Detroit, Sept. 1, 1934; s. Calvin Arthur and Alta Christine (Koch) C.; B.A. in Econs., Williams Coll., 1956; B.S. in Chem. Engring., Mass. Inst. Tech., 1959; J.D., U. Mich., 1961; m. Rosemary Phoenix, June 6, 1959; 1 dau., Georgia Alta. With Exxon Co., N.Y.C., 1961-69; chmn. bd., treas. John B. Adt Co., York, Pa., N.Y.C., 1969-70; with Goodman Equipment Corp., Chgo., 1971—, pres., chief exec. officer, 1971—, chmn., 1980—, chmn. bd. subs. Improved Plastics Machinery Corp., 1979—; bd. govs. mfrs. div. Am. Mining Congress, Washington, 1972-80, bd. dirs., 1980—. Mem. Am., N.Y. bar assns., Am. Inst. Chem. Engrs., Ill. Mfrs. Assn. (dir. 1978), Newcomen Soc. N.Am., Young Pres.'s Orgn., Psi Upsilon, Phi Delta Phi. Clubs: Racquet (Chgo.); Glen View (Golf, Ill.); Skytop (Pa.). Home: 1320 N State Pkwy Chicago IL 60610 Office: 4834 S Halsted St Chicago IL 60609

CAMPBELL, CHARLES ALTON, furniture industry exec; b. Brunswick, Ga., Mar. 10, 1944; s. Rayford Monroe and Cecelia Elizabeth (Camilla) C.; B.Indsl. Engring., Ga. Inst. Tech., 1966; M.B.A., Harvard U., 1973; m. Mary Alla Traber, Aug. 15, 1970; children—Christine Beensen, Elizabeth Traber, Charles Traber. Mgr. ops. projects Camak Lumber Ops., ITT Rayonier, Thomson, Ga., 1974-75, mgr. ops. projects Wood Products Group, N.Y.C., 1975-77, dir. chems. devel. parent co., 1977-79, dir. operational planning and control, Seattle, 1979-80; pres. Fox Mfg. Co., Rome, Ga., 1980—. Served with C.E.C., USN, 1967-69. Mem. Planning Execs. Inst. Episcopalian. Club: Coosa Country. Home: Canterbury Pl Route 10 Rome GA 30161 Office: Drawer A Rome GA 30161

CAMPBELL, CHARLES BRYAN, constrn. co. exec.; b. Burley, Idaho, Mar. 9, 1922; s. James Rowe and Jane (Kelly) C.; B.S. in Bus., U. Idaho, 1949; m. JoAnne Voiten, Apr. 12, 1952; children—Bryan Joe, Douglas James. Accountant, Wells, Baxter & Miller, C.P.A.'s, Boise, Idaho, 1949-51; with Morrison-Knudson Co. Inc., Boise, 1951—, asst. controller, then controller, 1961-69, v.p. acctg., 1969—; employee trustee for Idaho, Am. Gen. Contractors-Teamsters Health and Welfare Fund, 1968—, Am. Gen. Contractors-Operating Engrs. Health, Welfare and Pension Funds, 1968—. Mem. Boise City Park Bd., 1966-71. Served with AUS, 1942-46. C.P.A., Idaho. Mem. Am. Inst. C.P.A.'s, Fin. Execs. Inst., Asso. Gen. Contractors Am. (sec.-treas. Idaho br. 1971-75), Idaho Soc. C.P.A.'s. Home: 6008 Lubkin St Boise ID 83704 Office: 400 Broadway Boise ID 83707

CAMPBELL, CHARLES GEORGE, banker; b. Andover, Eng., July 16, 1895; s. William T. and Grace (Calder) C.; brought to U.S., 1901, naturalized, 1919; grad. Ind. Bus. Coll., 1916; student U. Chgo., 1920-22; m. Helen I. Thompson, June 14, 1926; children—Claire E. (Mrs. David Locke, Jr.), Joyce C. (Mrs. Rodney Beals). Sec.-treas. Kamp Motor Co., Mt. Carmel, Ill., 1923-26, pres., 1926-59; v.p. Vigo Motor Co., Terre Haute, Ind., 1944-50; v.p. Security Bank and Trust Co., Mt. Carmel, 1937-59, pres., 1959-64, vice chmn. bd., until 1968, chmn. bd., 1968—, also dir.; pres. Am. Savs. & Loan Assn., Mt. Carmel, 1939-59, dir., 1937—; dir. Camray, Inc., Mt. Carmel, Mt. Carmel Area Devel. Corp. Mem. Mt. Carmel City Commn., 1963—; mayor Mt. Carmel, 1964-66. Served with U.S. Army, 1917-19; AEF in France. Mem. Mt. Carmel C. of C. (dir. 1959-62), Am. Legion (comdr. Wabash post 1937), 40 and 8, Wabash Valley Assn. Presbyterian. Clubs: Masons (Shriner), Elks, Moose, Eagles, Kiwanis (pres. Mt. Carmel 1935, dir. 1936). Home: 323 Cherry St Mount Carmel IL 62863 Office: 400 Main St Mount Carmel IL 62863

CAMPBELL, CHARLES INGALLS, JR., savs. and loan assn. exec.; b. Casper, Wyo., Jan. 9, 1923; s. Charles Ingalls and Ann Marie (Ryan) C.; student U. Mo., 1940-41, U.S. Naval Acad., 1941-43, Marine Corps Schs., 1943, Armed Forces Staff Coll., 1962; m. Kathryn Ryan, Feb. 7, 1953; children—Ann, Charles Ingalls III, Mary Kay, John. Commd. 2d lt. U.S. Marine Corps, 1943, advanced through grades to lt. col., 1970; ret., 1970; dir. personnel and purchasing Safety Fed. Savs. & Loan, Kansas City, Mo., 1971—. Hon. bd. dirs. Rockhurst Coll.; dep. election commr., Kansas City, Mo., 1972—. Decorated Air medal with three gold stars, Purple Heart, Navy commendation medal. Mem. Mo. Council Retired Officers Assn. (pres. 1975-76), Am. Soc. Personnel Adminstrn., Mil. Order World Wars, U. Mo. Alumni Assn., U.S. Naval Acad. Alumni Assn., Mo. Sheriffs Assn., DAV, Sigma Chi. Democrat. Roman Catholic. Clubs: Army-Navy Country (Washington); Brookridge Country (dir.) Homestead Country (Kansas City, Mo.). Home: 421 Westover Rd Kansas City MO 64113 Office: 910 Grand St Kansas City MO 64106

CAMPBELL, CHRISTOPHER JOHN, waste treatment mfg. co. exec.; b. London, Apr. 30, 1950; s. John Stephen and Marjorie Maude (Rapsey) C.; B.S. in Bus. Adminstrn., U. N.C. at Chapel Hill, 1973. Mktg. specialist Asia/Pacific Group, Corning-Glass Internat. Co., Corning, N.Y., 1973-74; product mgr. Air Power div. Ingersoll-Rand Corp., Painted Post, N.Y., 1974-75, water treatment div., 1975-77, IRAS div., Dayton, Ohio, 1977-78; sales engr. Thetford Corp., Ann Arbor, Mich., 1978—. Mem. So. Indsl. Devel. Council, Nat. Woodcarvers Assn. Episcopalian. Club: Toastmasters (charter) (area gov. 76-77, adminstrv. v.p. 1975-77). Home: 7601 Fernwood Ct Apt 4413 Richmond VA 23228 Office: PO Box 1285 Ann Arbor MI 48106

CAMPBELL, DAVID GWYNNE, petroleum exec., geologist; b. Oklahoma City, May 2, 1930; s. Lois Raymond Henager and La Vada (Ray) Henager Campbell; B.S., Tulsa U., 1953; M.S., U. Okla., 1957; m. Janet Gay Newland, Mar. 1, 1958; 1 son, Carl David. Geologist, Lone Star Producing Co., Oklahoma City, 1957-65; dist. geologist and geol. cons. Mid-Continent div. Tenneco Oil Co., Oklahoma City, 1965-77; exploration mgr. Leede Exploration, Oklahoma City, 1977-80; pres. Earth Hawk Exploration; Oklahoma City, 1980—. Active Last Frontier council Boys Scouts Am., 1960-73; Oklahoma County rep. to Cherokee Nation, 1976-78. Served with USNR, 1949-53, U.S. Army, 1953-55. Mem. Am. Petroleum Inst., Am. Assn. Petroleum Geologists (field trip chmn. 1978 conv., Ho. of Dels. 1980-83), Oklahoma City Geol. Soc. (public relations chmn. Speakers bur. 1963-64, chmn. stratigraphic code com. 1967-68, presdl. appointee 1969-70, advt. mgr. Shale Shaker 1969-71, rep. to AAPG Ho. of Dels. 1980-83), Okla. Ind. Petroleum Assn., Tulsa Geol. Soc., Am. Assn. Petroleum Landmen, Oklahoma City Geol. Discussion Group (pres. 1975-76), Oklahoma City Petroleum Club, Sigma Xi, Pi Kappa Alpha. Contbr. article to Jour. Cherokee Studies. Home: 6109 Woodbridge Rd Oklahoma City OK 73132 Office: 101 Park Ave Suite 1270 Oklahoma City OK 73102

CAMPBELL, DONALD MILLER, leasing co. exec.; b. Lincoln, Nebr., Oct. 18, 1939; s. John Miller and Doris Andrews C.; student Doane Coll., 1957-59; B.S. in Engring., U. Nebr., 1962; M.B.A., Stanford U., 1965; m. Virginia Schilling, Aug. 13, 1960; children—Jeffrey Erle, Brian Scott. Planning coordinator Boise Cascade Corp., Idaho, 1965-67; prodn. mgr. Finnigan Corp., Palo Alto, Calif., 1967-68; treas. Memorex Corp., Santa Clara, Calif., 1968-76; v.p. fin. ICD Leasing Group, Inc., Palo Alto, 1976-78; pres. Sequoia Capital Corp., Palo Alto, 1978-79, 80—; v.p., treas. Memorex Fin. Co., Sunnyvale, Calif., 1979-80. Mem. Fin. Execs. Inst., Am. Assn. Equipment Lessors. Home: 12870 Robleda Rd Los Altos Hills CA 94022 Office: 5 Palo Alto Sq Suite 1022 Palo Alto CA 94304

CAMPBELL, DOUGLAS A(RGYLE), investment banker; b. Toronto, Ont., Can., Jan. 13, 1929; s. Douglas Argyle and Dorothea (Turner) C.; came to U.S., 1960, naturalized, 1978; B.A., McGill U., 1951; M.B.A., Harvard U., 1953; Ph.D., Columbia U., 1972. Asst. to sr. partner Greenshields & Co., 1954-57; mem. research and sales staff Kidder, Peabody & Co., N.Y.C., 1957-60; propr. D.A. Campbell Co., Inc., Los Angeles and N.Y.C., 1960—; dir. Stanmil Corp. Bd. dirs. Dubnoff Center. Clubs: Racquet and Tennis, Knickerbocker (N.Y.C.); Marina City (Los Angeles); Mt. Bruno (Montreal). Author: The Third Market: A Catalyst for Change in the Securities Market; Environmental and Economic Implications of Enhanced Oil Recovery Processes-An Overview. Home: 1150 Brooklawn Dr Los Angeles CA 90024 Office: 1150 Brooklawn Dr Los Angeles CA 90024

CAMPBELL, DOUGLASS, fin. cons.; b. N.Y.C., Aug. 31, 1919; s. William Lyman and Helene (Underwood) C.; A.B., Yale U., 1941; m. Marion Danielson Strachan, Jan. 13, 1962. With N.Y. Central System, 1939-67, various positions including asst. to pres., supt., exec. rep., 1939-58, v.p. N.Y. Central R.R. and subs.'s, 1958-67, also in charge pub. relations and advt. dept., 1960-67, dir. affiliates and subs.'s.; chmn. bd., pres. Bowater Paper Co., Inc., N.Y.C. 1967-68; pres. Argyle Research Corp., N.Y.C. Served as maj. AUS, 1942-46. Episcopalian. Clubs: Down Town Assn., Yale, River, Econ. (N.Y.C.); Chagrin Valley Hunt (Cleve.); Chgo., Racquet (Chgo.); Saturn (Buffalo). Home: 3 E 71st St New York City NY 10021 Office: 800 3d Ave New York City NY 10022

CAMPBELL, FRANK, JR., cons. engr.; b. Adams, Ind., Nov. 9, 1931; s. Frank and Julia Elizabeth (Smith) C.; B.S., U. Wash., 1958; m. Marian Robison-Campbell, Oct. 31, 1953; children—Clifford Frank, Clare Lawrence. Sr. research engr. Bethlehem Steel Co. (Pa.), 1958-66; dir. tech. services Gen. Refractories Co., Phila., 1966-69; asst. gen. mgr. refractories div. Babcock & Wilcox, Augusta, Ga., 1969-75; pres. Leavesley-McCollum Corp., Houston, 1975-78; cons. engr., Houston, 1978—; dir. Leavesley-McCollum Corp. Pres., Jr. Achievement, Augusta, 1975. Served with USAF, 1950-54. Registered profl. engr., Tex. Mem. Nat. Soc. Profl. Engrs., Am. Ceramic Soc., Assn. Iron and Steel Engrs., Houston Engring. and Sci. Soc., Nat. Inst. Ceramic Engrs., Keramos. Republican. Methodist. Club: Exchange. Patentee in field. Home: 2274 Broadlawn St Houston TX 77058 Office: PO Box 58193 Houston TX 77058

CAMPBELL, GORDON W., banker; b. Waterloo, Iowa, Aug. 17, 1932; B.S. in Commerce, U. Iowa, 1954; M.B.A., Bradley U., 1961; m. Patricia Mayes; children—Mark, Melissa, Elizabeth, Andrea. With Comml. Nat. Bank, Peoria, Ill., then IBM Corp., Chgo.; later v.p., cashier, sr. v.p. banking State Nat. Bank, Evanston, Ill.; then exec. v.p., sec. Am. Nat. Bank & Trust Co., Chgo.; pres., chief exec. officer Exchange Bancorp., Tampa. Bd. dirs. Tampa Bay Art Center; mem. U. South Fla. Found. Fellow U. Tampa; mem. Am. Bankers Assn., Fla. C. of C. (dir.), St. Andrew's Soc. Clubs: Masons; University, Economics (Chgo.); University, Tower, Tampa Yacht, Palma Ceia County (Tampa). Home: 1106 Culbreath Isles Dr Tampa FL 33609 Office: Exchange Bank Bldg Tampa FL 33602

CAMPBELL, JAMES BOYD, sch. and office supply mfg. co. exec.; b. Jackson, Miss., May 11, 1931; s. James William and Evelyn (Flowers) C.; student Millsaps Coll., 1949-51; B.B.A., U. Miss., 1953; m. Martha Harris, June 12, 1953; children—James Boyd, Joe W., Alexander Boyd II, Martha H. Salesman, mgr. printing plant Office Supply Co., 1955-59; asst. to pres. Miss. Sch. Supply Co., 1959-60; pres. Gen. Equipment Mfg. Co., Crystal Springs, Miss., 1960-64, Miss. Sch. Supply Co., Jackson, 1964—; dir. 1st Capital Corp. 1st Nat. Bank, Unifirst Fed. Savs. & Loan, W.E. Walker Stores, Lamar Life Ins. Co. Pres., chmn. United Giver Fund, 1966-67; pres. Jackson Symphony Orch., 1970-71; chmn. trustees Millsaps Coll. Served with USAF, 1953-55. Mem. Jackson C. of C. (pres. 1975), Miss. Mfrs. Assn. (pres. 1971-72), Young Presidents Orgn., Nat. Office Product Assn., Nat. Sch. Supply and Equipment Assn. Methodist. Clubs: Jackson, Country of Jackson, Univ., Capital City Petroleum. Home: 4152 N Honeysuckle Ln Jackson MS 39211 Office: 4155 Industrial Dr Jackson MS 39205

CAMPBELL, JAMES DANIELS, III, chem. co. exec.; b. Phila., Dec. 3, 1925; s. James D. and Ruth L. (Koehler) C.; B.S. in Indsl. Engring., Pa. Mil. Coll., 1949; m. Evelyn M. Cressman, July 1, 1950; children—Susan, Douglas, James, Betsy. With E.I. duPont de

Nemours & Co., Inc. and subs., 1950—, product mgr., Bridgeport, Conn., 1968-70, mgr., Ilion, N.Y., 1970-73, sr. supr. engring. dept., Wilmington, Del., 1973-74, mfg. mgr. polymer products dept., 1974—. Chmn. troop com. DelMarVa council Boy Scouts Am., North Star, Del., 1964-66, Pomperaug council, Trumbull, Conn., 1968-70. Served with inf.-ordnance U.S. Army, 1944-46. Registered profl. engr., Del. Mem. ASME, Am. Mgmt. Assn., Nat. Soc. Profl. Engrs., Metal Powder Industries Fedn. (mem. safety policy bd. 1970-72). Patentee in field. Home: 231 North Star Rd Newark DE 19711 Office: E I duPont de Nemours & Co Inc Wilmington DE 19898

CAMPBELL, JAMES RAY, mfg. co. ofcl.; b. July 16, 1941; s. Ray E. and Anne Louise (Wooten) C.; B.S., U. Houston, 1965; postgrad. in behavioral sci. Case Western Res. U., 1967-68. Personnel asst. Standard Oil Co. (Ohio), Cleve., 1966-68; dir. equal opportunity programs Turner Constrn. Co., Cleve., 1968-73; employment project dir. Nat. Assn. on Drug Abuse Problems, N.Y.C., 1973-74; exec. dir. Cuyahoga Plan Ohio, Inc., Cleve., 1974-77; dir. equal employment opportunity compliance and community activities Continental Group, Inc., N.Y.C., 1978—; expert witness HUD, 1970, U.S. Ho. of Reps. subcom., 1972. Task force chmn., mem. steering com. Cleve. Fedn. for Community Planning's Manpower Planning and Devel. Commn., 1971-73; mem. Cleve. Press Community Adv. Bd., 1972; mem. Pres.'s Com. on Employment of Handicapped; mem. case selection and regulatory oversight com. Equal Employment Adv. Council, Washington. Served with USAF, 1958-62. Named 1 of 10 Outstanding Young Men of Yr., Cleve. Jr. C. of C., 1970, Outstanding Community Service award Urban League Cleve., 1972. Mem. Am. Soc. Personnel Adminstrn. (accredited personnel diplomate), Am. Mgmt. Assn., Am. Soc. Tng. and Devel., Human Resources Planning Soc., Nat. Alliance Bus. (corp. liaison program), World Future Soc., Omicron Delta Kappa (circle v.p. 1965, Gold Key 1965). Author profl. publs. Home: 130 W 67th St New York NY 10023 Office: One Harbor Plaza Stamford CT 06902

CAMPBELL, JERRY LEE, trade assn. exec.; b. Champaign, Ill., Dec. 4, 1934; s. Gerald William and Blanche Russeline (Florence) C.; B.S., Eastern Ill. U., 1960; m. Sandra De Etta Parrish, June 1, 1955; 1 son, Randal Lee. Auditor, safety engr. Hawkeye Security Ins. Co., Springfield, Ill., 1960-64; adminstrv. asst. Assn. Ill. Elec. Coops., Springfield, 1964-68; exec. v.p. Home Builders Assn. Ill., Springfield, 1968-77; exec. dir. Tenn. Valley Public Power Assn., Chattanooga, 1977—. Named Boss of Year, Springfield chpt. Nat. Women in Constrn., 1972. Mem. Ill. Soc. Assn. Execs. (pres. 1974), Am. Soc. Assn. Execs., Nat. Assn. Home Builders (exec. officers council, v.p. 1973-77). Clubs: Signal Mountain Golf and Country, Cosmopolitan of Springfield (pres. 1972). Pub. Ill. Home Builder Mag., 1975-77, TVPPA News, 1977—; contbr. articles to trade publs. Office: 831 Chestnut St Chattanooga TN 37402

CAMPBELL, LLOYD BEATON, plastic co. exec.; b. Lawrence, Kans., Mar. 21, 1922; s. John Howard and Mary Ethel (Ault) C.; B.S., U. Calif. at Berkeley, 1948; M.S., Air Force Engring. Sch., 1950; m. Betty Jo Fullerton, Dec. 31, 1969; children—Gary John, Corey Allan. Mgr. engring. div., aircraft div. Hughes Tool Co., Culver City, Calif., 1954-58; founder, v.p. Pyrodyne, Inc., Los Angeles, 1958-62; founder, pres. Camwil, Inc., precision plastics products, Honolulu, 1962—; founder, chmn. Camwil Communications, Ltd., Godalming, Surrey, Eng., 1979—. Served with USAAF, 1943-45, USAF, 1950-54; maj. Res. (ret.). Decorated Silver Star, D.F.C. (2), Air medal (7). Registered profl. engr., Calif. Mem. Nat. Fedn. Ind. Bus. (adv. bd. 1973—), Calif. Soc. Profl. Engrs. Clubs: Outrigger Canoe, Waikiki Yacht, Hawaii Yacht (dir. 1973) (Honolulu). Patentee in field. Home: 1744 Laukahi St Honolulu HI 96821 Office: 875 Waimanu St Honolulu HI 96813

CAMPBELL, LOUIS EUGENE, mfg. co. exec.; b. California, Mo., Feb. 12, 1941; s. Charles Louis and Flossie Mae (Sanders) C.; B.B.A. magna cum laude with dept. honors, Washburn U., 1974; M.B.A., So. Ill. U., 1976; m. Carol Susan Wall, July 15, 1960; children—Shelli Ann, Todd Alan, Marc Aaron. Joined U.S. Air Force, 1959, commd. 2d lt., 1962, advanced through grades to lt. col., 1979; exec. officer and pilot, Thailand, 1972-73, Dover AFB, Del., 1974-78; ops. insp. Mil. Air Lift Command Insp. Gen. Office, Scott AFB, Ill., 1978-81; ret., 1981; account rep. Burroughs Corp., St. Louis, 1981—. Decorated D.F.C. with oak leaf cluster, Air medal, Meritorious Service medal. Mem. Air Force Assn., Phi Kappa Phi, Beta Gamma Sigma, Nat. Eagle Scout Assn., Am. Numismatic Assn. Club: Order Daedalians (life). Home: 22 Lakeview Dr Freeburg IL 62243 Office: Burroughs Corp 11975 Westline Indsl Dr Saint Louis MO 63141

CAMPBELL, MICHAEL DUFF, communications co. exec.; b. Short Hills, N.J., Apr. 13, 1943; s. Donald L. and Elizabeth (Duff) C.; B.A., Lafayette Coll., 1964; J.D., Georgetown U., 1967; m. Pamela A. Moore, June 30, 1968; children—Sally Brennan, Michael Scott, Kathleen Moore. Asso., Steptoe & Johnson, Washington, 1969-74; admitted to D.C. bar, 1968, N.Y. bar, 1969; asst. gen. counsel Fairchild Industries, Germantown, Md., 1974-76; sec., gen. counsel Am. Satellite Corp., Germantown, 1976-78, v.p. law, 1978, v.p. ops. and law, 1979, sr. v.p. ops., 1980—. Served with U.S. Army, 1967-69. Decorated Bronze Star. Republican. Roman Catholic. Club: Kenwood Country. Home: 5705 Overlea Rd Bethesda MD 20016 Office: 20301 Century Blvd Germantown MD 20767

CAMPBELL, MYERS DALLAS, III, bank exec.; b. Kansas City, Mo., June 14, 1929; s. Myers Dallas C.; B.B.A., Northeast Mo. State U., 1954. With American National Bank, Midwest City, Okla., 1963-75, chmn., chief exec. officer, 1977—. Bd. dirs. Tinker br. YMCA, Met. YMCA. Served with USAF, 1951-53. Mem. Midwest City C. of C. (dir., v.p. 1969-73), Air Force Assn., Petroleum Club. Presbyterian (elder). Clubs: Okla. Skeet Shooters Assn., Nat. Skeet Shooters Assn., Oklahoma City Gun, Tinker AFB Gun. Office: 3013 N Glenoaks Midwest City OK 73110

CAMPBELL, NORMAN W., advt. exec.; b. Dallas, Dec. 29, 1933; student Arlington State Jr. Coll., 1951-53; B.J., U. Tex. at Austin, 1955; m. Barbara Ann Tidwell, Sept. 11, 1959. Advt. sales Dallas Morning News, 1955, Progressive Farmer Mag., 1956; account exec. Batten, Barton, Durstine & Osborn, 1956-63; mktg. services mgr. Pepsi-Cola Met. Bottling Co., N.Y.C., 1964-65, mktg. dir., 1964-65; dir., exec. v.p., mgr. Denver office Tracy Locke Co., Inc.; pres. Tracy-Locke Advt. & Public Relations, Inc., Dallas, dir., 1965—; dir. Tracy-Locke Co. Mktg. and Research Counselors Inc. Pres. adv. council U. Tex. Sch. Communication, 1977—; trustee Nat. Hemophilia Found.; bd. dirs. Shakespeare Festival; active United Way. Mem. Dallas C. of C., Dallas Advt. League, Salesmanship Club Dallas, Alpha Delta Sigma. Clubs: Northwood Country, Lancers, City. Office: 1407 Main St PO Box 50129 Dallas TX 75250*

CAMPBELL, RANDALL LEHNN, TV exec.; b. Covington County, Ala., Sept. 13, 1950; s. Fritz Fredrick (stepfather) and Lois Mae (Ballard) Duensing; grad. Career Acad. Sch. Broadcasting, Atlanta, 1968, Nat. Inst. Communication, 1975. Sta. mgr. CATV-Channel 13, Multivision N.W. Cablevision, Dalton, Ga., 1968-70; staff producer AFTV, Berlin, 1972-73; account exec. Buyers Guide, Santa Maria, Calif., 1974; owner, mgr. Randall Campbell Enterprises, Hollywood, Calif., 1975-77; gen. mgr. KECC-TV, El Centro, Calif., 1977—; guest lectr. Imperial Valley Coll., U. So. Calif. Bd. dirs. United Way of Imperial County, 1979-80. Served with AUS, 1970-73. Lic. 1st class radio operator FCC. Mem. Calif. Assn. Broadcasters. Club: El Centro Kiwanis. Office: 778 State St El Centro CA 92243

CAMPBELL, ROBERT KENNETH, utility exec.; b. Chgo., June 20, 1930; s. Donald E. and Jeanette A. Campbell; B.S. in Indsl. and Mech. Engring., Ill. Inst. Tech., 1952; M.S. in Mech. Engring., U. Ill., 1956; M.B.A., U. Chgo., 1958; J.D., Loyola U., Chgo., 1962; m. Alvina Oblinger; children—John E., Thomas L., Joseph A. With Western Electric Co., 1957-77, gen. mgr. Allentown (Pa.) works, 1972-76, gen. mgr. adminstrn., mfg. div., N.Y.C., 1976-77; pres., dir. Pa. Power & Light Co., Allentown, 1977—. Bd. dirs. Sacred Heart Hosp., Allentown, 1977—, United Way Lehigh County, 1978—; adv. bd. Big Bros. Am., Blue Cross; bd. assos. Muhlenberg Coll., Allentown, 1978—; trustee Cedar Crest Coll., Allentown, 1978—. Mem. Pa. Electric Assn. (dir. 1977—). Clubs: Lehigh Country, Saucon Valley Country. Home: 326 Lilac Rd Allentown PA 18103 Office: 2 N 9th St Allentown PA 18101

CAMPBELL, WALLACE ARNOLD, banker, financial exec.; b. Bayonne, N.J., June 2; s. Alexander and Louise (Hollenbach) C.; student Bowdoin Coll.; B.S., Columbia U.; M.B.A., N.Y. U.; m. Catherine F. Gray, July 22; 1 dau., Catherine Frances. Vice pres., fin. mgr., asst. treas. Citicorp., N.Y.C., v.p., treas. Citicorp Leasing Internat., Inc., Citicorp Leasing, Inc.; pres. Citicorp Funding, Inc., dir. Netherlands Antilles; mng. dir. Citicorp Overseas Fin. Corp. B.V.T.; dir., v.p., treas. Citilease, Inc., formerly v.p., treas. Carte Blanche Corp.; v.p. Citibank, N.Y.; pres. Citicorp Can., Ltd.; dir., exec. v.p., Am. Internat. Life Ins. Co.; pres. Nationwide Charge System; comptroller Am. Express Co.; dir., sec., treas. Omniswitch Corp.; lectr. Am. Mgmt. Assn., Bank Adminstrn. Inst. Served as 1st lt. Adj. Gen's. Dept., U.S. Army, 1942-49. Mem. Fin. Execs. Inst., Assn. Corporate Growth, Nat. Accounting Assn. Contbr. articles on orgn., fin., mgmt. and leasing to profl. publs. Home: 56 Rockwood Ln Greenwich CT 06830 Office: 399 Park Ave New York NY 10022

CAMPBELL, WILLIAM DONALD, ins. broker; b. Toronto, Ont., Can., Oct. 16, 1928; s. Elwood Kennedy and Lenamae Ruth C.; came to U.S., 1955; B.A., U. Toronto, 1951; grad. advanced mgmt. program Harvard U., 1976-77; m. Beverly B. Brown, Oct. 5, 1974; children—Brian, Karen, Martha; stepchildren—James, Thomas, Robina, Amy. With Aetna Life Ins. Co., Boston, 1951-69; dir. Boit, Dalton & Church, Boston, 1969-72; exec. v.p., dir. Frank B. Hall & Co. of Mass., Inc., Boston, 1972-78, pres., 1978—; dir. Colonial Penn Ins. Co. (Phila.). Anglican. Clubs: Brae Burn Country, Algonquin, Bald Peak Colony, Downtown, Boston-Madison Sq. Garden. Home: 543 Boston Post Rd Weston MA 02193 Office: 89 Broad St Boston MA 02110

CAMPBELL, WILLIAM HENRY, geologist; b. Kansas City, Mo., Sept. 20, 1923; s. Myers Dallas and Wilma (Morris) C.; student U. Kansas City, 1940-43; B.S., M.S. in Geology, Mo. State U., 1950; postgrad. Kans. U., 1946-47; Ph.D. in Archaeology, Biarritz U., 1965; m. Virginia Hargus, Oct. 8, 1955; children—Constance Lyn, William Arthur. Geologist, Phillips Petroleum Co., Venezuela, summer 1949; cons. geologist, oil field operator, 1950-55; pres. Campbell Mines, Inc., 1955-57; geologist, v.p. and dir. A.R. Jones Oil and Operating Co., Kansas City, Mo., 1957-58; geologist, v.p. Lotus and Trojan Oil Co., Kansas City, Mo., 1957-58; pres. Jones and Campbell, Inc., Prairie Village, Kans., 1958—; chmn. bd. Geol. Cons., Prairie Village, 1979--; dir. Ha Ha Tonka Park, Inc., 1968-73. Mem. Kans. Energy Adv. Council, 1976-78; bd. dirs. Gillis Home for Children. Served to capt. AUS, 1943-46. Decorated Purple Heart, Air medal, Silver Star, Bronze Star, and others; lic. pilot. Mem. Am. Assn. Petroleum Geologists, Soc. Mining Engrs., Assn. Profl. Geol. Scientists, Aircraft Owners and Pilots Assn., Phi Sigma Epsilon, Sigma Chi. Episcopalian. Clubs: Exchange, Kans. Bounders, University (Kansas City). Office: 4121 W 83d St Prairie Village KS 66208

CAMPBELL, WILLIAM ROBERT, mfg. co. exec.; b. Scranton, Pa., Nov. 6, 1929; s. Robert and Wilma (Grimes) C.; B.S., Clarkson Coll. Tech., 1953; M.S., Rensselaer Poly. Inst., 1959; m. Janice Lucille Williams, Dec. 26, 1949; children—William Robert, Dan Michael, David. Research chemist Am. Viscose Corp., Chester, Pa., 1954-55; mem. research and devel. staff Pratt & Whitney Aircraft Co., East Hartford, Conn., 1955-60; supr. tech. services Solvay Process Co. div. Allied Chem. Corp., Syracuse, N.Y., 1960-66; direct distbn. Amway Corp., Ada, Mich., 1965—; dir. Amway Distbrs. Assn. U.S. Served with U.S. Army, 1946-48. Mem. Buffalo C. of C. Republican. Roman Catholic. Club: Sea Pines Plantation.

CAMPER-TITSINGH, MARY ELISABETH, found. ofcl.; b. Monhein, Germany, Oct. 11, 1924; came to U.S., 1940, naturalized, 1952; d. Abraham Adrian Aurelius Gerard and Evelyn Julia (Gore) Camper-Titsingh; B.A., Lake Forest Coll., 1969; M.S., Columbia U., 1971; m. George W. Druliner, Jan. 15, 1945 (div. 1972); children—William, Bruce, Clifford. Mem. program staff Choate Found., Phoenix, 1964-65; investment research librarian Ford Found., N.Y.C., 1971-73, govt. research coordinator investment dept., 1973-76, social responsibility analyst investment dept., 1976—; cons. Investor Responsibility Research Center, 1976—, Center for Public Resources, Inc., 1979—. Founder, sec. Ariz. Democratic Council, 1960; sec. Ariz.-Maricopa County Dem. Central Com., 1964; bd. mgrs. Chgo. Child Care Soc., 1966; founder, sec. N.Y. Coalition on Hunger, 1974-77; bd. dirs. Forum for Corp. Responsibility, 1980—. Mem. Am. Polit. Sci. Assn., Spl. Libraries Assn., AAUW, ACLU, LWV, Planned Parenthood, Victorian Soc., Sierra Club, Amnesty Internat., Forum for Corp. Responsibility, Women's Econ. Round Table, Ams. for Dem. Action (nat. dir. 1966-77, mem. exec. com. 1970, N.Y. State sec. 1974-76), World Federalists U.S.A. (organizer, sec. Conn. chpt. 1970, sec. N.Y. Met. chpt. 1973-75). NOW (fund raising com. 1972). Contbr.: Business Roles in Economic Development, 1979; Forum for Corp. Responsibility Rev., 1980. Home: 35 E 35th St New York NY 10016 Office: 320 E 43d St New York NY 10017

CAMPION, RUSSELL RICHMOND, food service equipment mfg. co. exec.; b. Milw., Oct. 9, 1930; s. Russell Henry and Anna (Winne) C.; student U. Wis., 1948-49; m. Marguerite Schubert, Sept. 15, 1951; children—Jill Mary, Thomas Richmond, Jon Winne. Sales mgr. F.W. Boelter Co., Milw., 1952-62; sales mgr. Bastian Blessing Co., Chgo., 1962-67, mktg. mgr., Grand Haven, Mich., 1967-76, pres., 1976—, also dir.; dir. Service Action Corp. Mem. Nat. Assn. Food Service Equipment Mfrs. (dir. 1967—, pres. 1974, sec. 1980), West Mich. Mfg. Assn. (dir. 1976—, sec.), Tri-City C. of C. Roman Catholic. Clubs: Century (Muskegon, Mich.); Rotary (Spring Lake, Mich.). Home: 18183 Fruitport Rd Spring Lake MI 49456 Office: 422 N Griffin St Grand Haven MI 49417

CAMPMAN, ERIC PIERCE, aerospace parts mfg. co. exec.; b. Hollywood, Calif., May 1, 1953; s. Allen Earl and Dorothy Irene C.; student Merced Coll., 1971-73. Mgr. stores Gensler-Lee, Inc., jewelry chain, Stockton and Merced, Calif., 1973-76; exec. v.p. Classic Tool & Die Co., Inc., Paramount, Calif., 1976—; del. White House Conf. on Small Bus. Affairs, 1980. Mem. Nat. Tool, Die and Precision, Machining Assn., Nat. Fedn. Ind. Bus., Paramount C. of C. (dir. 1980—), Phi Beta Lambda (v.p. central sect. 1973). Republican. Office: 8112 E Rosecrans Ave Paramount CA 90723

CAMPOLUNGO, NEIL JAMES, legal services co. exec.; b. Albany, N.Y., Nov. 24, 1941; s. Neil V. and Anna F. (Lombardo) C.; student Cornell U., 1971, Sch. Indsl. Relations, 1975; m. Bernadette N. Lafond, Apr. 6, 1960; children—Barbara G., Natalie L. With Williams Press, Inc., Albany, 1963-76, dir. finishing ops., 1973-75; with Infosearch, Inc., Albany, N.Y., 1975—, v.p., gen. mgr., 1976—, also dir.; dir. Corp. Filing Service, Inc. Albany, Profl. Research Service, Inc., Doylestown, Pa. Mem. adv. council Albany Assn. Blind, active YMCA. Served with USAF, 1959-63; ETO. Recipient Cert. of Appreciation, Albany Assn. Blind, 1978. Mem. Internat. Assn. Printing House Craftsmen (award of Merit), Am. Mgmt. Assn., Public Records Research Assn., Cath. War Vets., Credit Mgmt. Assn. Eastern N.Y., Albany County C. of C. Republican. Roman Catholic. Home: 107 Wilkins Ave Albany NY 12205 Office: 170 Washington Ave Albany NY 12210

CANALE, WILLIAM JOHN, elec. contracting co. exec.; b. Bronx, N.Y., Sept. 11, 1947; s. Henry Joseph and Helen (Gregg) C.; m. Janet Ann Cavallo, May 25, 1969; children—Donna Marie, Jeneane Alyse. Elec. apprentice various cos., 1965-71; elec. mechanic Simpson Elec. Co., N.Y.C., 1971-79; exec. pres. P.E.S. Electric Services Inc., Bronx, 1979—. Mem. Internat. Brotherhood Elec. Workers, Sons of Italy. Roman Catholic. Office: 983 E 233d St Bronx NY 10466

CANALIZO, ALBERT EUGENE, fin. corp. exec.; b. St. Augustine, Fla., Dec. 26, 1943; s. Albert Eugene and Aline (McElroy) C.; B.S. in Bus., La. State U., 1964; Advanced Mgmt. Program, Harvard U., 1979; m. Marilyn Suzanne Belanger, Sept. 19, 1964; 1 dau., Donna Lynn. Mgr., All-State Credit Plan, Inc. div. U.S. Industries, New Orleans, 1964-78, v.p., dir. bus., 1979—. Co-founder, treas. Lakeshore Hebrew Day Sch., 1970—; mem. Jewish Burial Soc., 1970—, Agudath Israel, 1970—, Jewish Welfare Fund, 1971—; Boy Scouts master, 1968-70; notary public, 1970—; col. Mil. Dept. La., 1971—; a.d.c. Gov. La., 1970-72. Lemann-Stern fellow, 1975-76. Named Businessman of Year, Better Bus. Bur., 1973; Salesman of Year, All-State Credit Plan, 1976; Leader of Year, C. of C., 1972. Mem. Am. Mgmt. Assn., Nat. Consumer Fin. Assn., La. Consumer Fin. Assn., Audubon Soc. Republican. Clubs: B'nai B'rith, Lions (pres. 1967-68), Elks (pres. 1966). Pub. Jewish religious guides, 1974—, Notes of Credit, 1979—. Home: 6578 Louis XIV St New Orleans LA 70124 Office: All-State Credit Plan Inc 1201 Saint Charles Ave New Orleans LA 70124

CANAS, JOSE ANTONIO, metals co. exec.; b. Montpelier, Vt., Nov. 3, 1932; s. Manuel and Josephine (Diaz) C.; A.S., Vt. Coll., 1952; B.S., St. Michael's Coll., 1954; M.B.A., U. Conn., 1959, student Coll. Law, 1960-61; div.; children—Lisa, Lorrie, Leslie, Joseph. Fin. analyst, mgr. Nuclear Naval Reactors div. Corp. Combustion Engring., Windsor, Conn. and N.Y.C., 1956-61; asst. controller, prodn. mgr. Chapman Valve div. Crane Co., Indian Orchard, Mass., 1961-63; v.p. ops. and fin. The Heminway Corp., Waterbury, Conn., 1963-71; treas., controller Mossberg & Sons, Inc., New Haven and N.Y.C., 1972-76; sr. fin. cons. Alexander Proudfoot Co., Chgo., 1976-77; sr. v.p. Monarch Brass & Copper Corp., Waterbury, Conn. and New Rochelle, N.Y., 1977—; instr. mgmt. U. New Haven Grad. Sch. and Quinnipiac Coll., 1966-72. Bd. dirs. Jr. Achievement of Greater Waterbury; mem. Cheshire Bd. Edn., 1968-72. Served with USAF, 1953-54, U.S. Army, 1954-56. C.P.A., Conn. Mem. Conn. Soc. C.P.A.'s, Nat. Assn. Accts., VFW. Democrat. Roman Catholic. Home: 59 Melba St Milford CT 06460 Office: 75 Beechwood Ave New Rochelle NY 10801 also 240 E Aurora St Waterbury CT 06720

CANDLER, JOHN SLAUGHTER, II, lawyer; b. Atlanta, Nov. 30, 1908; s. Asa Warren and Harriet Lee (West) C.; A.B. magna cum laude, U. Ga., 1929; J.D., Emory U., 1931; m. Dorothy Bruce Warthen, June 13, 1933; children—Dorothy Warthen (Mrs. Joseph W. Hamilton, Jr.), John Slaughter. Admitted to Ga. bar, 1931; partner Candler, Cox, Andrews & Hanson and other law firms, 1931—; dep. asst. atty. gen. Ga., 1951-68; gen. counsel, sec., dir. The D.M. Weatherly Co., Weatherly Corp.; dir. Propane Gas Service, Inc., Sungas, Inc., Leon Propane, Inc., Equipment Sales Co., Inc., Ga. Motor Club, Inc., others. Pres., Atlanta Estate Planning Council, 1963-64; mem. Greater Atlanta council U.S.O., 1969—, exec. com., 1970—, pres., 1974-75; trustee Ga. Student Ednl. Fund; trustee Kappa Alpha Scholarship Fund, pres., 1970-72. Served from capt. to col. AUS, 1941-46. Decorated Commendation Ribbon. Fellow Am. Coll. Probate Counsel (bd. regents 1968-74), Internat. Acad. Law and Sci.; mem. State Bar Ga. (chmn. sect. fiduciary law 1964-65), Am., Atlanta bar assns., Lawyers Club Atlanta, Am. Legion (post comdr. 1949-50), Reserve Officers Assn. (state pres. 1946, nat. exec. com. 1947), Am. Judicature Soc., Nat. Tax Assn.-Tax Inst. Am. (adv. council 1969-72 Tax Inst. Am.), Internat. Platform Assn., Newcomen Soc., Mil. Order World Wars, English Speaking Union, U.S. Power Squadrons, Phi Beta Kappa, Phi Kappa Phi, Phi Delta Phi, Kappa Alpha Order, Sigma Delta Chi. Episcopalian (vestryman 1953-56, cathedral trustee 1957-67, lay reader 1971—, sr. warden 1955). Mason, Kiwanian (trustee Northside Atlanta Found. 1959—, chmn. 1962-79). Clubs: Piedmont Driving, Capital City, Commerce, Oglethorpe, Army-Navy, Peachtree Racket, Atlanta Touchdown, Ft. McPherson Officers. Home: 413 Manor Ridge Dr NW Atlanta GA 30305 Office: 2400 Gas Light Tower Atlanta GA 30043

CANDLER, JOHN STAPLES, paper co. exec.; b. Roanoke, Va., Feb. 17, 1941; s. Harry Louis and Katharine (Johnson) C.; B.A., Va. Mil. Inst., 1962; m. Linda Hill Stansbury, Aug. 25, 1962; children—Elizabeth Hamilton, Katharine Johnson. With Olin Corp., Pisgah Forest, N.C., 1962—, personnel mgr. alumnium div., 1968-70, Winchester div., 1971-73, mgr. orgnl. devel. and placement, 1973-75, dir. employee and community relations chems. group, 1975-78, v.p. mfg. Ecusta Paper & Film group, 1978—; dir. 1st Citizens Bank. Bd. dirs. Transylvania County United Fund, 1975-80, Jr. Achievement, 1976-80; chmn. bd. trustees Transylvania Community Hosp., 1979-80; mem. bd. Sch. Engring., N.C. State U., 1977-80, mem. pulp and paper tech. bd., 1980; bd. dirs. Transylvania Vocat. Services Found., 1980—. Served with U.S. Army, 1962-64. Mem. Brevard C. of C. Episcopalian. Clubs: Rotary, Glen Cannon Country, Elks. Address: PO Box 200 Pisgah Forest NC 28768

CANFIELD, GRANT WELLINGTON, JR., ednl. exec., mgmt. cons.; b. Los Angeles, Nov. 28, 1923; s. Grant Wellington and Phyllis Marie (Westland) C.; B.S., U. So. Calif., 1949, M.B.A., 1958; m. Virginia Louise Bellinger, June 17, 1945; 1 dau., Julie Marie. Personnel and indsl. relations exec., Los Angeles area, 1949-55; employee relations cons., regional mgr. Mchts. and Mfrs. Assn. Los Angeles, 1955-60; v.p., orgnl. devel. cons. Hawaii Employers Council, Honolulu, 1960-75; pres., dir. Hawaiian Ednl. Council, 1969—; exec. v.p. Hawaii Garment Mfrs. Assn., 1965-75, Assn. Hawaii Restaurant Employers, 1966-75; exec. dir. Hawaii League Savs. Assns., 1971-78; with Goodwill Vocat. Tng. Centers Hawaii, 1973-79; lectr. orgn. devel. and human resources mgmt. Bd. dirs. Hawaii Restaurant Assn., 1974-76, bd. dirs. Hawaii chpt. Nat. Assn. Accountants, 1963-67, nat. dir., 1965-66; bd. dirs. Vol. Service Bur. Honolulu, 1965-66, pres., 1966-68; bd. dirs. Vol. Info. and Referral Service Honolulu, 1972-75, Girl Scout council Pacific, 1961-65, 71-72; bd. dirs. Hawaii Com.

Alcoholism, 1962-71, co-chmn., 1964-68; pres., dir. Friends of Punahou Sch., 1972-75; mem. community adv. bd. Jr. League Hawaii, 1968-70; exec. bd. Aloha council Boys Scouts Am., 1962-65. Served to 1st lt., inf. AUS, 1943-46. Decorated Purple Heart, Combat Inf. badge. Mem. Am. Soc. Assn. Execs. (cert. assn. exec.), Am. Soc. Tng. and Devel., Internat. Assn. Agrl. Economists, Am. Agrl. Econs. Assn., Indsl. Relations Research Assn., Am. Soc. Personnel Adminstrn. Rotarian, Mason. Clubs: Pacific, Plaza (Honolulu); Kaneohe Yacht; Co-author: Resource Manual for Public Collective Bargaining, 1973. Home: 1605 Mokulua Dr Kailua HI 96734 Office: 1164 Bishop St Honolulu HI 96813

CANFIELD, JAMES A., III, public relations exec.; b. Queens, N.Y., Sept. 1, 1943; s. James A., Jr. and Muriel C. (Lyons) C.; B.A., St. John's U., Jamaica, N.Y., 1965; children—James, Kathleen, Christine. Vice pres., dir. advt. and public relations Security Nat. Bank, L.I., N.Y., 1969-75; asst. v.p., dep. dir. public relations Chem. Bank, N.Y.C., 1975-76; dir. corp. public relations Babcock & Wilcox Co., N.Y.C., 1976; sr. v.p., gen. mgr. Bozell & Jacobs, Inc., public relations, N.Y.C., 1976-79, pres., 1979—, also dir. Trustee Stony Brook (N.Y.) Fire Dept. Benevolent Assn., 1978-79; capt. Stony Brook Fire Dept. Rescue Co., 1974-79; bd. dirs. jobs program Nat. Alliance Businessmen, L.I. chpt., 1969. Mem. Public Relations Soc. Am., Nat. Acad. TV Arts and Scis., Fin. Communications Soc. Office: 220 E 42d St New York NY 10017

CANGEMI, JOSEPH, television repair co. exec.; b. Queens, N.Y., June 6, 1937; s. Guiseppi and V. (Pizzunno) C.; grad. high sch.; m. Michelina Odierno, Sept. 11, 1960; children—Vicki Ann, Nanci Ann, Gina Marie, Joseph. Pres., Accurate TV Co., Ltd., Hicksville, N.Y., 1960—; arbitrator Better Bus. Bur. L.I. and N.Y., 1970—; mem. nat. adv. council Nat. Fedn. Ind. Bus., 1960—. Asso. mem. Mus. Natural History; mem. Am. Com. on Italian Migration; active civic affairs. Served in M.C., U.S. Army, Kora. Mem. Nat. Rifle Assn. (life), L.I. Assn. Commerce and Industry, Sons of Italy (founder Ozone Park, N.Y. lodge, past venerable Columbus lodge). Clubs: Eagle Gun of L.I. (founder, past pres.). Address: 23 Blvd Dr Hicksville NY 11801

CANN, EUGENE WILLIAM, pub. co. exec.; b. Queens, N.Y., Nov. 1, 1941; s. Eugene W. and Mary (Horton) C.; B.B.A., St. Francis Coll., 1964; M.B.A., Adelphi U., 1974; m. Joan A. Volkomer, Sept. 26, 1970; children—Anne-Marie, Brian. Staff accountant Harris, Kerr, Forster & Co., C.P.A.'s, N.Y.C., 1964-67, Haskins & Sells, C.P.A.'s, 1967-70; asst. to controller, Doubleday & Co., Inc., Garden City, N.Y., 1971-72, mgr. corp. accounting, 1972-77; controller Dell Pub. Co., Inc., N.Y.C., 1977—; adj. asst. prof. accounting N.Y. Inst. Tech., Old Westbury and Commack, N.Y. Served with U.S. Army, 1964-65. Mem. Nat. Assn. Accts. (pres. L.I.-Nassau chpt.), Am. Accounting Assn. Home: 25 Maplelawn Dr Commack NY 11725 Office: Dell Publishing Co 1 Dag Hammarskjold Plaza New York NY 10017

CANN, HOWARD WHEELER, III, fin. services co. exec.; b. Monroe, La., Nov. 8, 1943; s. Howard Wheeler and Eleanor A. Cann, Jr.; B.S., U. Fla., 1965; M.B.A., U. Pa., 1970; m. Kristin Gail Blacken, June 5, 1965; children—Michael, Peter, Patrick. Vice pres., sect. head utilities Bank of Am., N.T. & S.A., San Francisco, 1970-78; mgr. fin. and mgmt. services Keith, Feibusch & Co., San Francisco, 1978-79, v.p., gen. mgr., 1979—. Pres., Homestead Valley Community Assn.; founder, bd. dirs. Homestead Valley Land Trust; chmn. County Service Area 14. Served to capt. U.S. Army, 1976-78; Vietnam. Mem. Am. Gas Assn., N.E. Electric Light and Power Assn., Pacific Coast Elec. Assn. (dir.). Republican. Episcopalian. Clubs: Bankers (San Francisco); Mill Valley (Calif.) Tennis. Home: 309 La Verne Ave Mill Valley CA 94941 Office: 220 Montgomery St San Francisco CA 94104

CANNALIATO, VINCENT, JR., investment banker, mathematician; b. Bklyn., July 12, 1941; s. Vincent and Margaret (Mancuso) C.; B.S. in Math., Fordham U., 1963; M.A. in Math., City U. N.Y., 1964; grad. certificate in system design U. Pa. Sch. Bus., 1970; m. June A Marino, Apr. 8, 1967; children—Amy June, Kimberly Dawn, Douglas Vincent. Systems analyst N.Y. Telephone Co., N.Y.C., 1969-70; account exec. CIT Leasing Corp., N.Y.C., 1970-72; v.p. Kidder Peabody & Co., Inc., N.Y.C., 1972-80, head leasing and project financing group corp. fin. dept., 1977-80; 1st v.p. Smith Barney, Harris Upham & Co., Inc., dept. head leasing and project fin., corp. fin., 1980—; vis. instr. Southwestern Grad. Sch. Banking, 1976-77; lectr. in field; adv. bd. U.S. Mcht. Marine Acad., 1974—, chmn., 1977—; instr. math. U. Md., 1966-69. Exec. bd., curriculum chmn. Gifted Child Soc., 1975—; nation chief Pampo Indian Guides and Princesses, Western Hills YMCA, 1980—. Served to capt. AUS, 1963-69. Decorated Bronze Star. Mem. Am. Assn. Equipment Lessors (fed. legis. com. 1975—, chmn. keyman com. 1978—), Acad. Magical Arts, Inc. Roman Catholic. Club: India House (N.Y.C.). Contbg. author: U.S. Taxation of International Operations, 1975, 77; Oil and Gas Taxes/Natural Resources Service, 1979; World Leasing Yearbook, 1980, 81. Home: 49 Cully Ln Wyckoff NJ 07481 Office: 1345 Ave of Americas New York NY 10019

CANNING, JESSIE MARIE, public relations cons. co. exec.; b. N.Y.C.; d. Robert James and Jessie Murray (Melville) C.; B.A., Marymount Coll, 1947; D.H.L. (hon.), Beth Jacob Tchrs. Coll., 1969. Exec. asst. to gen. counsel Met. Life Ins. Co., 1948-52; dir. govt. and bus. liaison Dept. Commerce, City of N.Y., 1952-53, asst. city adminstr., 1953-55; pres. Sydney S. Baron & Co., Inc., N.Y.C., 1955-80; chmn. bd. Baren/Canning and Co., Inc., N.Y.C., 1980—; instr. mgmt. sci. St. Frances Coll., N.Y.C., 1958-61; dir. Sr. Med. Consultants, Inc. Asso. dir. public relations N.Y.C. Democratic Com., 1952-60. Recipient Merit award City of N.Y., 1954. Mem. U.S. C. of C., Am. Mgmt. Assn., Pres.'s Assn. Roman Catholic. Clubs: Westchester Country (Rye, N.Y.); I.C. 100 (Montclair, N.J.); Georgetown (Washington). Author: Women in American Business, 1967. Office: 540 Madison Ave New York NY 10022

CANNON, ALEXANDER PIERRE, real estate exec.; b. Phila., Dec. 20, 1923; s. Alexander and Anita DeBost (Muller) C.; student Columbia U., 1946-49; m. Anne Bishop, Mar. 13, 1948. Real estate broker, bldg. mgmt., 1946-56; div. real estate mgr. Grand Union Co., Fairlawn, N.J., 1956-59; Eastern regional real estate mgr. Montgomery Ward & Co., N.Y.C., 1959-60; sr. asst. mgr. real estate dept. Equitable Life Assurance Soc. U.S., N.Y.C., 1960-68; asst. v.p. Citibank, N.Y.C., 1968—; on leave N.Y.C. Mayor's Office of Ops., 1979. Mem. N.Y. County Grand Jury, 1930. Served in U.S. Army, 1943-45. Decorated Purple Heart, Bronze Star. Mem. SCW (gov. N.Y. 1977—), St. Nicholas Soc. N.Y. (1st v.p. 1977—), SAR (N.Y. real estate and mus. coms.). Clubs: Madistone, Masons (past master). Home: 300 E 74th St New York NY 10021 Office: 399 Park Ave New York NY 10022

CANNON, CHARLES NIBLEY, engring. and constrn. co. exec.; b. Salt Lake City, May 7, 1922; s. George Mousley and Edna (Nibley) C.; student U. Utah, 1939-41; B.S. in Chem. Enging., U. Mich., 1947; m. Margie Moore, Mar. 2, 1945; children—Carolyn, Martha. Process engr. Fluor Corp., Los Angeles, 1947-51, in various sales and engring. positions, N.Y.C., 1961-66, Houston, 1966-68; v.p. FS West Co., Cons. Engrs., Whittier, Calif., 1951-60; mng. dir. Fluor Nederland N.V., Haarlem, Holland, 1968-71; pres. Fluor Engrs. & Constructors, Irvine, Calif., 1971—. Served to 1st lt. Ordnance Corps, U.S. Army, 1943-46. Mem. Am. Inst. Chem. Engrs., Am. Petroleum Inst., Nat. Petroleum Refiners Assn., Orange County Republican Assn. Clubs: Big Canyon Country, Balboa Bay, Eldorado Country. Office: Fluor Engrs Inc 333 Michelson Irvine CA 92730*

CANNON, JAMES HUGHES, recreation co. exec.; b. Los Angeles, Jan. 1, 1927; s. James Hughes and Lillian (Neyland) C.; B.M.E., Stanford U., 1951; m. Alison Duff, Mar. 17, 1969; children—Peter, Jane, Cathy; stepchildren—Donn, Jeffrey, Stuart, Shelley Randall. With Cannon Electric Co., Los Angeles, 1950-63; pres. Cannon Guild Inc., Cambridge, Mass., 1963-67; real estate investment trust trustee Cambridgeport Trust, Cambridge, 1967—; pres. Squash Club, Inc., Allston, Mass., 1976—; pres. Cannon Energy Co., Edgartown, Mass., 1967—; dir. U.S. Solar Harpsichord Co. Founding officer Pride's Beach Assn., 1967-72; founding officer Solar Harpsichord Research Found., 1978—. Served with USAAF, 1944-47. Mem. IEEE, Galpin Soc., Western Electronics Mfrs. Assn. (mem. govt. affairs com. chmn. 1960-63). Republican. Episcopalian. Clubs: Country, Edgartown Yacht, Tennis and Racquet of Boston, U.S. Ct. Tennis Assn., Racquet and Tennis Assn., Engl., World Atomic Squash Ball Devel. Corp. (pres. 1978-79). Address: 15 Gorham St Allston MA 02134

CANNON, JOHN, investment adviser; b. Phila., Jan. 17, 1930; s. John F. and Anne (Carlin) C.; B.S., U. Pa., 1954; M.B.A., Drexel Inst. Tech., 1956; m. Edythe Marple Grebe, Aug. 16, 1952; children—John, Lynne, Anne. Fin. analyst Bishop & Hedberg, Inc., Phila., 1956-58; rep. Stone & Webster Securities Corp., Phila., 1958-62; nat. sales mgr. municipal bond dept. Hallowell & Sulzberger, Phila., 1962-64; pres. Cannon & Co., Inc., Flourtown, Pa., 1964-71, chmn. bd., treas., 1971—; pres. PRO Fund, Inc., Flourtown, 1967-71, 75—, Pro Income Fund, Inc., Flourtown, 1975—, Med. Tech. Fund, Inc., Flourtown, 1979—; treas. Pro Services Inc., Flourtown, 1975—; gov. No-Load Mut. Fund Assn., Valley Forge, Pa., 1979—. Served with USMCR, 1950-51. Mem. Fin. Analysts Am. Republican. Episcopalian. Clubs: Masons; Mfr.'s Golf and Country (Oreland, Pa.). Home: 531 Willow Ave Ambler PA 19002 Office: 1107 Bethlehem Pike Flourtown PA 19031

CANNON, NATHANIEL LERENZO CARL, bus. exec.; b. Leesburg, Fla., Sept. 7, 1944; s. Leroy and Jessie M. Cannon; B.A. with honors, Bethune-Cookman Coll., Fla., 1971; J.D., George Washington U., 1974. With EEOC, 1973-76, atty.-adv., 1975-76; asso. firm Bergson, Borklan, Margolis & Adler, Washington, 1976; investigator Dept. Energy, 1976-77; dir. Office EEO/Affirmative Action, George Mason U., Fairfax, Va., 1977-79; dir. Office Civil Rights, Washington Met. Area Transit Authority, 1979-80; pres. The Heritage Corp., 1980—; lectr. No. Va. Community Coll. Recipient Meritorious Service award Nat. Law Center, 1972, Disting. Service award, 1973. Mem. Am. Public Transit Assn., Am. Assn. Affirmative Action (1st v.p. 1978-80), Coll. and Univ. Personnel Assn., Va. Social Sci. Assn., ACLU, Omega Psi Phi, Alpha Phi Omega. Methodist. Club: Masons.

CANNON, PETER JOHN, mktg. cons.; b. Chgo., Aug. 24, 1934; s. Peter J. and Veronica F. (Lyman) C.; B.S. in Engring., Notre Dame U., 1956, M.S., 1958; M.B.A., Case-Western Res. U., 1963; children—Kathleen, Daniel, Mary, Margaret, Edward. Evaluation engr. Honeywell, Inc., Mpls., summer 1956-57; applications engr., research engr. Rosemount Engring. Co., Mpls., 1958-60; mfrs. rep. Crossley Assos., St. Paul, 1960-61; tech. utilization officer NASA, Lewis Research Center, Cleve., 1961-64; mgr. bus. planning Booz-Allen & Hamilton, Inc., Bethesda, Md., 1964-67; Wash. rep. IIT Research Inst., Washington, 1967-73; cons. Cannon Assos., Reston, Va., 1973—; dir. Potomac Savs. and Loan Assn., KRS Assos. Inc.; instr. U. Notre Dame, 1956-58. Served to capt. USAF, 1961-64. Mem. Am. Mgmt. Assn., Instrument Soc. Am., Inst. Mgmt. Scis., Am. Mktg. Assn. Roman Catholic. Clubs: Reston Golf and Country; Univ. of D.C. Home: 1708 Red Oak Circle Reston VA 22090 Office: 11484 Washington Plaza Reston VA 22090

CANNON, SUSAN RHEA, banker; b. Independence, Mo., Dec. 7, 1946; s. Warren Martin and Alice Marie (Laxson) C.; B.A., Goucher Coll., 1968; M.B.A. with honors, Boston U., 1975. Asst. alumnae dir. Rosemary Hall, Greenwich, Conn., 1968-69; editor, materials coordinator, psychol. test scorer McBer & Co., also other behavioral sci. cons. cos., Boston, Cambridge, Mass., 1969-75; asst. v.p. mktg. and br. mgmt. Citibank, N.A., N.Y.C., 1975—. Co-chmn. Coalition for Better Amsterdam Avenue, 1980; mem. adv. bd. Oxford project Phoenix House, 1980. Office: 575 Lexington Ave New York NY 10022

CANNONE, JOHN DANIEL, mcpl. ofcl.; b. Cleve., May 3, 1922; s. John and Rose C.; student U. Akron, 1941-47; m. Marian Delores Comeriato, July 31, 1943; children—Daniel J., John F. With Bur. Public Utilities, City of Akron (Ohio), 1947-62, Dept. Fin., 1962; city treas. City of Akron, 1963—; active panelist mcpl. industry workshop programs. Chmn. city employees United Way, 1974, co-chmn., 1977. Cert. mcpl. fin. adminstr. Mem. Ohio Mcpl. Fin. Officers Assn., Mcpl. Fin. Officers Assn., Mcpl. Treas.'s Assn. (pres. Ohio chpt. 1975, trustee 1976, pres.'s award 1976), Mcpl. Treas.'s Assn. U.S. and Can. (pres.). Office: 166 S High St Room 102 Akron OH 44308

CANNY, J. FRANCIS, psychologist, bus. exec.; b. Norwich, N.Y., Feb. 20, 1913; s. Anthony Joseph and Bridgit (Redden) C.; B.A. in Psychology, U. Rochester, 1935; postgrad. Wharton Sch. U. Pa., 1935-36; M.A. in Personnel Adminstrn., Columbia U., 1946; m. Helen Jane Stofer, Apr. 20, 1940; 1 son, Christopher Richard. Sect. mgr. R.H. Macy & Co., Inc., N.Y.C., 1936-38, asst. to v.p. personnel, 1948-52; salesman Eastman Kodak Stores, Inc., N.Y.C., 1938-41; instr., vocat. counselor Bklyn. Poly Inst., 1946-48; dir. personnel adminstrn. McKinsey & Co., N.Y.C. 1952-54; pres. Canny, Bowen, Inc., N.Y.C., 1954-70, chmn. bd., 1970-77; sr. v.p. Golightly & Co. Internat., Inc., N.Y.C., 1978—; dir. Elmendorf Bd. Corp., Stranway Corp. Bd. dirs. Westchester United Fund, 1962-64, Council Social Agys., Westchester County, N.Y., 1954-64, Graham-Windham Child Care, 1968—, Parish Counseling Centers, Inc., 1971-73. Served to lt. comdr. USNR, 1941-45. Mem. Am., N.Y. State psychol. assns. Episcopalian (vestry 1965-73). Clubs: Cloud (dir. 1964-71); Columbia (gov. 1956-60); Wharton Grad. Bus. Sch. N.Y. (dir. 1971-73). Home: 45 Sutton Pl S New York NY 10022 Office: 1 Rockefeller Plaza New York NY 10020

CANONIE, ANTHONY CHARLES, constrn. co. exec.; b. South Haven, Mich., Oct. 10, 1946; s. Anthony and Marialyce (Welsh) C.; student U. Wis., 1965-68; 1 dau., Lindsey. With Canonie Constrn. Co., South Haven, Mich., 1969—, ops. mgr. Engine & Leasing Co. (later Canonie Constrn.), 1975, v.p. ops., 1976, pres., chief exec. officer, 1977—, also dir.; pres., chief exec. officer Canonie Cos., Inc., 1980—; pres. Lindsey Industries, Ltd.; pres., chief exec. officer Lindsey Leasing, Inc.; mng. partner Lindsey Group; dir. Bultema Dock & Dredge Co., LaCrosse Dredging Co., Bultema Marine Transp. Co. Vice chmn. fund raising program Chgo. area Boy Scouts Am., 1977. Mem. Young Presidents Orgn., Gen. Contractors of Am., Asso. Underground Contractors Mich. Republican. Roman Catholic. Clubs: Point O'Woods Country (Benton Harbor, Mich.); Mich. State U., Victors; South Haven Yacht; U. Wis. W; Chgo. Athletic. Home: Route 3 Box 184 Coloma MI 49038 Office: PO Box 509 South Haven MI 49090

CANTILLON, WILLIAM HOUCK, transp. co. exec.; b. Cleve., Sept. 17, 1943; s. Daniel James and Genevieve (Houck) C.; B.S., Case Inst. Tech., 1965; M.B.A., Butler U., 1968; divorced; children—Denice Renee, William Houck. Co-ordinator planning, parts div. Gen. Motors Corp., Flint, Mich., 1969-72; gen. mgr. Nat. Distbn. Service, Inc., Atlanta, 1972-75, Carson, Calif., 1976; gen. mgr. Yowell Transp. Service, Los Angeles, 1976, now div. mgr.-electronics. Mem. Am. Mktg. Assn., Nat. Council Phys. Distbn. Mgmt. Home: 18681 San Marcos St Fountain Valley CA 92708 Office: 1840 Cardington Rd Dayton OH 45409

CANTO, FERNANDO JOSE, garment mfg. co. exec.; b. Santiago, Cuba, Aug. 6, 1943; s. Fernando Juan and Dolores Maria (Marti) C.; came to U.S., 1962, naturalized, 1968; B.S.B.A. (Univ. Bd. Regents scholar), Creighton U., 1966; m. Ana Maria Repetti, Dec. 23, 1968; children—Fernando E., Roberto J., Eduardo I., Juan C., Ana M. Sr. auditor Haskins & Sells, San Juan, P.R., 1966-69; exec. v.p., sec., treas. Caribbean Leisurewear Inc., Rio Piedras, P.R., 1969—; pres., chmn. bd. FC Industries Inc., Carolina, P.R. Served with U.S. Army, 1963. Mem. Am., P.R. insts. C.P.A.'s, Nat. Assn. Accountants, Am. Security Council, Beta Gamma Sigma, Beta Alpha Psi. Club: AAA Gun. Home: B-9 Pontevedra Vistamar Marina Carolina PR 00630 Office: Box 30358 65th Inf Station Rio Piedras PR 00929

CANTON, JOHN RICHARD, advt. agy. exec.; b. Kansas City, Kans., Oct. 4, 1941; s. Richard Millard and Sedalia Elizabeth (Corwin) Canton; student Central Mo. State U., 1959-61; children—Jonna Renee, Heather Libra. Air personality Lexington Broadcasting Co., Sta. KLEX-AM (Mo.), 1958-59; program dir., news dir., air personality Ware Broadcasting Co., Sta. KZIX-AM, Ft. Collins, Colo., Sta. KOKO-AM, Warrensburg, Mo., 1959-61; program dir., music dir., air personality Rust Broadcasting Co., Sta. WHAM-AM-FM, Rochester N.Y., Sta. WRAW-AM, Reading, Pa., Sta. WNOW-AM-FM, York, Pa., 1961-63, 64-65; program dir., air personality Tele-Broadcasters, Inc., Sta. KUDL-AM, Kansas City, Mo., 1963-64; program dir., prodn. dir., music dir., air personality Westchester Corp., Stas. WIXY-AM, also WDOK-FM, Cleve., 1965-66, Storz Broadcasting Co., Sta. WDGY-AM, Twin Cities, Minn., 1966-77; host Bowling for Dollars, Hubbard Broadcasting Co., Sta. KSTP-TV, Twin Cities, 1977-78; exec. v.p. Masters & Assos., Inc., advt. agy., Mpls., 1977-78; air personality Midwest Radio & TV, Inc., Sta. WCCO-FM, Twin Cities, 1977—; pres. Canton Communications, Inc., advt. Agy., Mpls., 1978—; actor, model, narrator films, M.C. night clubs, 1960—. Mem. AFTRA, Advt. Fedn. Club. Club: Braemar Men's (Edina, Minn.). Home: 1126 Trailwood N Minneapolis MN 55343 Office: 6950 France Ave S Suite 10 Edina MN 55435

CANTOR, ALAN BRUCE, mgmt. cons.; b. Mt. Vernon, N.Y., Apr. 30, 1948; s. Howard and Muriel Anita (Feingold) C.; B.S. in Social Scis., Cornell U., 1970; M.B.A., U. Pa., 1973. Mgmt. cons. M & M Risk Mgmt. Services, N.Y.C., 1974-78, nat. services officer, spl. projects div. Marsh & McLennan, Inc., 1978-80, asst. v.p., 1979—, mgr. Marsh & McLennan Risk Mgmt. Services, Los Angeles, 1980—; co-mgr. Air Travel Research Group, N.Y.C., 1977-79; instr. Am. Mgmt. Assn. risk mgmt. program. Cons., Vol. Urban Cons. Group, N.Y.C. Mem. Cornell Alumni Assn. N.Y.C. (bd. govs., program chmn.), Cornell Alumni Assn. So. Calif. Clubs: Wharton Bus. Sch. (N.Y.C.); Los Angeles, Wharton (v.p.) (Los Angeles). Copyright airline industry model, 1975. Home: 428 N Palm Dr Beverly Hills CA 90210 Office: 3303 Wilshire Blvd Los Angeles CA 90010

CANTOR, DANIEL J., mgmt. cons.; b. Phila., Dec. 22, 1914; s. Michael H. and Sallie (Griver) C.; B.A. in Econs., U. Pa., 1935, postgrad. Wharton Sch.; postgrad. Sch. Law, Temple U.; m. Harriet Tannenholz; 1 dau., Joan Ellen. Exec. positions industry and govt., 1935-55; pres. Daniel J. Cantor & Co., Inc., Phila., 1955—; mem. faculty Temple U., 1952-57; lectr. Am. Law Inst., Practising Law Inst., 1959-70. Served as capt., Ord., World War II; PTO. Fellow Internat. Soc. Advancement of Mgmt.; mem. Conf. Am. Legal Execs. (founder), Soc. Advancement Mgmt. (pres. Phila. 1958), Inst. Mgmt. Cons. (founding), Presidents Assn., Am. Mgmt. Assn., Am. Judicature Soc., Am. Law Inst.-Am. Bar Assn. (advisory mem. peer rev. com.), Princeton Club N.Y. Club: Peale. Founding editor, Law Office Econs. and Mgmt., 1960-68. Author: Management for Tomorrow, 1958; Managing the Law Office, 1964. Contbr. mgmt. and econ. articles to legal jours. Home: Wynnewood PA Office: Philadelphia PA

CANTOR, ELI, typographic co. exec., writer; b. N.Y.C., Sept. 9, 1913; s. Sol M. and Bertha (Seidler) C.; B.S., N.Y. U., 1934, M.A. (Ogden Butler fellow in Philosophy), 1935; J.D., Harvard U., 1938; m. Beatrice Mink, Oct. 4, 1942; children—Ann, Fred. Of counsel CBS, N.Y.C., 1939; mem. editorial staff Esquire, Coronet mags., Chgo., 1940-41; editor-in-chief Research Inst. Report, Research Inst. Am., Inc., N.Y.C., 1951-61, chmn. prodn. com., 1951-59; pres. The Photo-Composing Room, Inc., N.Y.C., 1961-65; chmn. bd. The Composing Room, Inc., 1965-71, chmn. emeritus Composing Room, 1971—; cons. mgmt. graphic arts; chmn. bd. Printing Industries Met. N.Y., 1971—, Printing Industries Am., 1973-74; mem. printing industries adv. commn. Bd. Edn., N.Y.C., 1972—; journalism commn., 1976—; chmn. exec. com. Advt. Typography Assn., N.Y., 1967-70; chmn. research-tech. com. Graphic Arts Tech. Found., 1971—; industry rep. before Congress; adviser fed. graphics, panelist Nat. Endowment for Arts. Pres. Columbia Hook & Ladder Co., Croton Fire Dept., 1951; trustee Croton Free Library; fellow Menninger Found. Mem. Authors Guild, P.E.N., Poets and Writers. Club: Harvard of N.Y. Author numerous short stories, articles, poems for popular publs., TV plays NBC; author: (play) Candy Store, 1948; The Golden Goblet, 1959; (novels) Enemy in the Mirror, 1977; Love Letters, 1979; (as Gregory A Douglas) The Rite, 1979, The Nest, 1980. Lectr. and educator in fields of econs., bus., lit., graphic arts. Home and Office: 15 W 81st St New York NY 10024

CANTOR, MARTIN ROBERT, accountant; b. Bklyn., Sept. 7, 1947; s. Abraham and Zeena (Glass) C.; B.S. in Acctg., City U. N.Y., 1970; m. Debra L. Lowenthal, Dec. 2, 1972; 1 son, Bradley Ross. Auditor, Arthur Young & Co., N.Y.C.; internal auditor Allied Stores Corp., N.Y.C.; acctg. mgr. Transammonia, N.Y.C.; treas. Tahlg, Inc., N.Y.C.; controller, chief fin. officer Apex Tech. Sch., N.Y.C.; adj. lectr. dept. econs. Bklyn. Coll., City U. N.Y. Democratic committeeman Nassau County, N.Y.; mem. exec. bd. tax reduction action com., Nassau County; tax and bus. co-chmn. Assemblyman's Adv. Com.; founder Wantagh Park Dr. Assn., Nassau County. Served with U.S. Army. C.P.A., N.Y. Mem. Am. Inst. C.P.A.'s, N.Y. State Soc. C.P.A.'s (com. interim fin. statements). Democrat. Home: 2164 Wantagh Park Dr Wantagh NY 11793

CANTOR, ROBERT LEONARD, leasing co. exec.; b. N.Y.C., Apr. 30, 1928; s. Saul and Blanche (Bursutsky) C.; B.S., N.Y. U., 1952, M.A., 1953; m. Myra Werner, Dec. 8, 1966; children—Scott Howard, Nina Gail. In investment banking, 1955-60; exec. v.p., dir. C.F. Kirk Labs., N.Y.C., 1960-62; exec. v.p. Dragor Shipping Corp., N.Y.C., 1964-67; v.p. Am. Export Industries, N.Y.C., 1967-68; sr. v.p. Nat.

Equipment Rental, Ltd., N.Y.C., 1965-68, pres., chmn. 1968-69; chmn. exec. com., dir. Detroit Steel Corp., N.Y.C., 1969-71; financial cons., 1971-73; pres., dir. Barnett Leasing Co., subsidiary Barnett Banks of Fla. Inc., 1973—; dir. Barnett Bank of Port Everglades, Ft. Lauderdale, Fla., Barnett Bank of Broward County, Ft. Lauderdale. Served with USNR, 1946-48. Mem. AIM (mem. pres.'s council). Clubs: Tower (Ft. Lauderdale). Home: 2009 St Andrews Rd Hollywood FL 33021 Office: 1 Financial Plaza Fort Lauderdale FL 33302

CANTU, RODOLFO, food services cons.; b. Corpus Christi, Tex., Aug. 26, 1946; s. Melchor and Angelita (Hernandez) C.; A.A. in Archtl. Tech., Del Mar Tech., 1972; student Del Mar Coll., 1972-73, A & I U. Bus. Mgmt.; m. Anna Maria Abrego Pena, Sept. 17, 1977; 1 son, Lawrence Anthony; children by previous marriage—Melinda, Cindy, Chris. Draftsman, Central Kitchen Equipment Inc., Corpus Christi, Tex., 1969-71; asst. cons. Comml. Kitchens, Houston, Tex., 1971-72; head designer Central Kitchen Equipment Inc., Corpus Christi, Tex., 1972-78, gen. mgr., 1979—; propr., food service designer A & R Enterprises, Brownsville, Tex., 1978—; mem. Camden County Businessmen Adv. Council. Served with USMC, 1966-68; Vietnam. Mem. Tex. Restaurant Assn., Mr. Amigo Assn., Harlingen C. of C. Republican. Roman Catholic. Home: 1900 E Elizabeth Brownsville TX 78520 Office: PO Box 2216 Brownsville TX 78520

CANTUS, HOLLISTER, energy systems exec.; b. N.Y.C., Nov. 16, 1937; s. Howard J. and Eleanor E. (Hollister) C.; B.A., Williams Coll., 1959; postgrad. George Washington U., M.I.T., U. Hawaii, Columbia U., Pa. State U.,; m. Barbara Jane Park, Feb. 7, 1961; children—Charles H., Jane Scott. Mem. staff House Armed Services Com., 1970-74; dep. asst. sec. def., 1974; dir. congressional relations ERDA, 1975-77; mgr. energy programs Power Systems Div., United Technologies Corp., Washington, 1977—; pvt. cons. def. and energy. Served to lt. comdr. USNR, 1960-69. Decorated Joint Services Commendation; recipient Disting. Service award ERDA, 1978. Mem. Nat. Energy Resources Orgn. (v.p.), Nat. Security Industries Assn., NAM. Republican. Episcopalian. Clubs: Georgetown, Internat. of Washington, Capitol Hill. Home: 1173 Huntover Ct McLean VA 22102 Office: 1125 15th St NW Washington DC 20005

CAPELLO, THOMAS STONER, banker; b. Harrisburg, Pa., Dec. 17, 1943; s. Arthur Grant and Wilmina (Stoner) C.; B.S. in Econs., Pa. State U., 1965; m. Rita C. Capello, Oct. 19, 1968. Reporter, Dun & Bradstreet, Harrisburg, Pa., 1966; v.p. Pa. Devel. Credit Corp., Harrisburg, 1967-74; v.p. Commonwealth Nat. Bank, York, Pa., 1974—. Mem. Ball Com. March of Dimes, 1977-78, bank and fin. Com. Cancer Fund, small bus. com. Heart Fund. Served with USN, 1966. Mem. C. of C. (econs. com.), Robert Morris Assos. Club: Sertoma. Home: Route 1 Dover PA 17315 Office: Commonwealth Nat Bank Continental Square York PA 17405

CAPEWELL, JOHN, mgmt. cons., real estate appraising co. exec.; b. Trenton, June 25, 1931; s. John and Ellen Evelyn (Smith) C.; B.S. in Elec. Engring., Naval Postgrad. Sch., 1972; M.B.A., Golden Gate U., 1981; m. Ursula H. Felde, Feb. 14, 1980; children by previous marriage—JoAnn, John W. Commd. airman apprentice U.S. Navy, 1950, advanced through grades to lt. comdr.; 1975; ret., 1975; gen. partner Seyforth-Capewell, Pacific Grove, Calif., 1975-77; pres. Capewell & Capewell, Pacific Grove, 1977—; real estate appraiser, cons., 1975—; instr. real estate courses Monterey Peninsula Coll., 1976-78, Hartnell Coll., 1977-80. Active, Boy Scouts Am., 1943-68. Decorated D.F.C. with oak leaf cluster, numerous others; recipient award for scouting work Chief Naval Aviation Tng. Command, 1961. Mem. Am. Mgmt. Assn., Am. Soc. Appraisers (pres. San Jose chpt.), Internat. Council Shopping Centers (asso.), Nat. Assn. Rev. Appraisers (sr.). Republican. Club: Masons. Office: PO Box 478 Pacific Grove CA 93950

CAPLIN, HAROLD SHELDON, investment banker, bus. exec.; b. N.Y.C., Feb. 28, 1924; s. William and Rose (Eiss) C.; student N.Y.U., 1941-42, Kansas City U., 1944-45; children—Barbara, Diane, Laura, William, Mark. Vice pres., dir. Seamprufe, Inc., N.Y.C., 1942-59; owner Harold S. Caplin Enterprises, 1960; dir. corp. finance Sutro Bros. & Co., 1960-63; sr. partner H.S. Caplin & Co., investment bankers, 1963-64; chmn., pres. Tudor Industries Corp., 1964-71; pres., dir. Magic Marker Corp., 1966-69, chmn., chief exec. officer, 1969-70; chmn. White Card Corp., 1968-70, Writeworld Co., Inc., 1968-70, Spar Ribbon & Carbon, Inc., 1968-70, Custom Alloy Corp., 1968-69, Leafsaver Corp., 1968-70; chmn., pres. Sports-land Corp., 1968-74; sr. v.p. corp. fin. Roberts, Scott & Co. Inc., 1972-74, also dir.; sr. v.p. corporate finance Morgan Olmstead, Kennedy & Gardner, Inc., Los Angeles, 1974—; dir. Marker Corp. Japan, 1968-70, Magic Marker U.K., 1966-68, Standard Brands Paint Corp., 1961-63, Hawaii Land Corp., 1974-77, Am. Clipper Corp., 1977—. Chmn. bd. Am.-Israel Pavilion World's Fair Corp., 1963-65. Served with AUS, 1943-45. Club: University (N.Y.C.). Home: 1131 Alta Loma Rd Los Angeles CA 90069 Office: 606 S Olive St Suite 314 Los Angeles CA 90014

CAPORASO, JOHN JOSEPH PAUL, plastics co. exec.; b. S. Maria C.V., Naples, Italy, Jan. 1, 1924; s. Gaetano and Dosolina (De March) C.; B.A., Coll. Nazionale Arpino (Italy), 1942; M.S., Universita Pegli Studi Di Napoli, 1948; postgrad. Ill. Inst. Tech., 1955-56; m. Marsha J. Wohl, Aug. 25, 1979; 1 son, Marco G. H.; children by previous marriage—Andre, Anthony, David, Daniel, Laura, Silvia, Sandra. Came to U.S., 1955, naturalized, 1960. Chem. cons. 8 German leather and plastics factories, 1948-50; gen. mgr., owner S.A.L.P., Naples, 1950-52; sales mgr. Adesco, Caracas, Venezuela, 1952-55; prodn. supt. Chicago Rawhide, Chgo., 1955-56; chief chemist Koppers Co., Chgo., 1957; research mgr. Pipeline Service Co., Franklin Park, Elgin, Ill., 1958-60; pres. Abacus Polymer, Inc., Skokie, Ill., 1960-67; pres. Abatron Inc., Gilberts, Ill., 1963—; staff tech. cons. Dow Corning Corp., Midland, Mich., 1974—; founder, prin. writer Point Omega, Elgin, 1970-73; mem. mgmt. adv. panel Chem. Week mag. Chmn. Democratic Program Com., Elgin, 1971-75; precinct committeeman, Elgin, 1971-75; chmn. Human Unity Found., Elgin, 1970-73. Mem. Am. Heart Assn., Soc. Plastics Engrs., Am. Chem. Soc., Chgo. Council Fgn. Relations, Elgin C. of C. Home: 1852 Winmoor Ct Sleepy Hollow IL 60118 Office: 141 Center Dr Gilberts IL 60136

CAPPELLINI, BRUNO JOHN, lawyer, county ofcl.; b. N.Y.C., Oct. 4, 1934; s. Louis and Mary (Caramatti) C.; B.S. in Econs., Fordham U., 1956; J.D., St. John's U., 1960; M.B.A., N.Y. U., 1961. Admitted to N.Y. bar, 1961, U.S. Supreme Ct. bar, 1964; mem. firm Snyder and Zully, N.Y.C., 1961-62; legal cons. to Neighborhood Conservation Bur., N.Y.C., 1964, N.Y.C. Housing and Redevel. Bd., 1962-65; law sec. to judge of Civil Ct., N.Y.C., 1965-68; law sec. to Justice Manuel A. Gomez, Supreme Ct. State of N.Y., 1969-71; law sec. to Surrogate M.L. Midonick, N.Y. County, 1972-76; pub. adminstr. of N.Y. County, 1977—; guest lectr. Pace U., N.Y.C., 1974. Democratic candidate for N.Y. State Assembly, 1964; mem. Dem. County Com.; trustee Our Lady of Peace Roman Catholic Ch., N.Y.C., 1974—. Mem. Am. Judicature Soc., Am., N.Y. State bar assns., N.Y. County Lawyers Assn. (mem. surrogates ct. com. 1977—), Assn. of the Bar City of N.Y. (mem. com. on trusts, estates and surrogates cts. 1976-79), Nat. Assn. of Housing and Redevel. Ofcls., UN Assn. of N.Y., Yorkville Civic Council, Citizens Housing and Planning Council of N.Y., Citizens Union. Home: 340 E 62nd St New York NY 10021 Office: 31 Chambers St New York NY 10007

CAPPLEMAN, WILLIAM FRANKLIN, JR., ins. co. exec.; b. Winter Garden, Fla., Oct. 24, 1918; s. William Franklin and Ethel (McLean) C.; B.S. in B.A., U. Fla., 1940; m. Mary Virginia Brown, Jan. 21, 1945; children—Mary, Helen, William, John Mark. Auditor, Fla. Auditing Dept., Tallahassee, 1941; pres. Cappleman Agy., Inc., Winter Garden, Fla., 1946—; founding pres. Orange Fed. Savs. & Loan, 1958-76, chmn. bd., 1976—. Mem. Orange County Budget Commn., 1953-59; trustee W. Orange Meml. Hosp., 1955-62; founding pres. W. Orange Scholarship Found., 1958-72, dir., 1958—; mem. Orange County Hosp. Facilities Authority, 1977-80. Served to col. USMC, 1941-46. Named W. Orange County Man of Yr., 1960. Mem. W. Orange C. of C. (dir. 1976-80), Orlando-Winter Park Bd. Realtors, Fla. Assn. Ins. Agts., Nat. Assn. Ins. Agts., Profl. Ins. Assn. Democrat. Methodist. Clubs: W. Orange Country, Rotary, Masons, Shriners. Home: 1001 W Plant St Winter Garden FL 32787 Office: PO Box 189 60 W Plant St Winter Garden FL 32787

CAPPS, ANTHONY THOMAS (CAPOZZOLO), internat. pub. relations exec.; b. Pueblo, Colo.; s. Nicolo and Anna (Solomone) Capozzolo; student Los Angeles Bus. Coll., Pueblo (Colo.) Bus. Coll., 1929-33; ed. pvt. tutor, arts and music; m. Theresa Cecelia Harmon, Nov. 12, 1945. Dance dir., choreographer, producer motion pictures, TV and radio, featured profl. dance team Biltmore Bowl, Cocoanut Grove, Los Angeles, St. Catherine Hotel, Catalina, 1939-42; dance dir., producer NBC, ABC, KCOP-TV, Columbia Pictures, 20th Century Fox and Calif. Studios, 1940-60; numerous TV interviews on religion and politics, history of ballet and opera of last 500 yrs.; exec. dir. Lockheed and Vega Aircraft Co. activities, various locations, 1942-44; columnist Desert Sun Newspapers, 1959—; internat. pub. relations dir. Howard Manor, Palm Springs Key Club, 1960—, Country Club Hotel, Palm Springs Ranch Club, 1970-71, Kedes Radio, Cameron Center, 1971-73, Cameron Enterprises, Murietta Hot Springs Hotel, Health and Beauty Spa, 1972-73; founder, pres., dir. Tony Capps Enterprises, Palm Springs, Calif., 1959—, chmn., exec. dir. golf and tennis tournaments, benefit dinners, govt. ofcls., various fund-raising events; founder, pres. Capps-Capozzolo Art Gallery, City of Hope, Duarte, Calif. Chmn., exec. dir. Alan Cranston for Senator Dinner, 1963; Edmund G. (Pat) Brown Testimonial Dinner, 1964; Progressive Jet Set Party - Nat. Cystic Fibrosis Research Found. fund raising, 1968; United Fund Gala Premier Camelot Theatre Opening, 1967; United Fund Desert Circus Big Top Ball, 1971; founder, co-chmn. Nat. Football Found. Hall of Fame Golf Classic, Palm Springs, 1979. Mem. Assistance League Palm Springs Desert Area, Coachella Valley Colleagues, Desert Hosp., Palm Springs Desert Mus., Desert Art Center of Coachella Valley, Mary and Joseph League, Eisenhower Med. Center (charter), Women's Aux. Internat. Found., City of Hope Duarte (founder, pres.), Nat. Artists and Art Patrons Soc., Nat. Cystic Fibrosis Assn., AFTRA, Am. Security Council, Pathfinders, Palm Nat. Football Found. and Hall of Fame in Calif. (founder, pres. Tri-County chpt.), Palm Springs Friends of Los Angeles Philharmonic, Internat. Platform Assn., Nat. Hist. Soc. Gettysburg, Nat. Trust for Hist. Preservation, Smithsonian Instn., Jacque Costeau Soc., Palm Springs Pathfinders (life). Clubs: Balboa Bay, Newport Beach, Internationale Philanthropique Societe de Gourmet (founder). Home: 2715 Junipero Ave Palm Springs CA 92262 Office: 426-B N Maple Dr Beverly Hills CA

CAPPS, JACK ELIAS, engr.; b. Conway, S.C., Sept. 3, 1931; s. Jesse Jasper and Blanche Gertrude (Harward) C.; B.S. in Indsl. Engring., N.C. State U., 1958; m. Jessie Williams, July 19, 1959; children—Carmen Yvonne. Project engr. Western Electric Co., Burlington, N.C., 1958-63; rocket propulsion engr. NASA, 1963-80; systems engr. space shuttle program for NASA, Rockwell Internat. Co., Downey, Calif., 1974—; tech. cons. space engine valves. Served with USAF, 1950-53. Recipient Superior Performance award NASA, 1969, 76, 77, 79. Registered profl. engr., N.C. Democrat. Home: 17302 De Groot Pl Cerritos CA 90701 Office: 12214 Lakewood Blvd Downey CA 90241

CAPPS, ROBERT DAVID, ins. co. exec.; b. Gillette, Wyo., June 21, 1942; s. Walter LeRoy and Evelyn Grace (Stuart) C.; A.A., Casper Coll., 1962; C.L.U., Am. Coll. Life Underwriters, 1976; m. Jeannette Alice Douglas, Oct. 7, 1962; children—David, Roberta Jo; m. 2d, Leslie Ellen Hautala, June 2, 1977. Mgr. Wilsons Dry Goods, Gillette, 1962-71; floor mgr. Lou Taubert Ranch Outfitters, Casper, Wyo., 1971-72; dist. mgr. The Equitable Life Assurance Soc., Casper, 1972—, trustee Equitable C.L.U. Assn., 1978-80, sr. trustee, 1980-81. Dist. commr. Boy Scouts Am., Casper, 1971-75; speaker for blood bank Blue Envelope Health Fund, Casper, 1974; mem. Gillette City Council, 1970-71; mem. Central Wyo. Estate Planners Council, 1976—; fund-raising chmn. Neighborhood Housing Service. Recipient Nat. Citation award Dist. Mgr., Equitable Life Assurance Soc., 1975, 76, 77, 78, 79, also Nat. Sales Achievement award, 1974-75, 79, Nat. Quality award, 1977-78, 79. Mem. Nat. Assn. Life Underwriters, Central Wyo. Assn. Life Underwriters (pres. 1974-75), W. Central Wyo. Assn. Life Underwriters (pres. 1980—), Casper Area C. of C. Presbyterian (ruling elder 1974-77). Clubs: Sunrise Lions (chpt. sec. 1977-78, v.p. 1979-80), Maverick Sq. Dance, Riverton Hoedowners, Glenrock Yellowrockers, Casper Polka. Home: 150 Dahlia St Casper WY 82601 Office: PO Box 3294 Casper WY 82602

CAPURRO, DARYL EUGENE, trade assn. exec.; b. Reno, May 27, 1943; s. John Peter and Evelyn Hazel (Gault) C.; B.S. in Bus. Adminstrn., U. Nev., 1966; m. Gail Ann Gallagher, Feb. 14, 1978. Mng. dir. Nev. Motor Transport Assn., Inc., Reno, 1976—; exec. dir. Nev. Franchised Auto Dealers Assn., Inc., 1976—; mem. Nev. Gov's. Traffic Safety Adv. Com., 1975-77. Mem. parks recreation commn. City of Sparks (Nev.), 1970—. Served to capt. U.S. Army, 1966-68. Decorated Bronze Star with oak leaf clusters, Air medal; recipient Freedoms Found. award Valley Forge, 1967. Home: 3311 Montecito Dr Sparks NV 89431 Office: PO Box 7320 255 Glendale Ave Suite 6 Sparks NV 89510

CAPUTO, LUCIO, Italian govt. ofcl.; b. Monreale, Italy, May 22, 1935; s. Giuseppe and Gioacchina (Spinnato) C.; came to U.S., 1967; Law Degree, Palermo U., 1957, Journalism Degree, 1958, Degree in Polit. Sci., 1960, postgrad. economics, 1961; m. Maria Luisa Mayr, Oct. 5, 1967; 1 son, Giorgio. Journalist, Italy, 1950-65; admitted to Italian bar, 1961; asso. firm Studio Legale Caputo-Orlando, Palermo, Sicily, 1960-62; ofcl. Italian Fgn. Trade Inst., 1962—, mkt. researcher, Libya, Cyprus, 1963, dep., London, 1964-67, dir. study mission SE Asia, 1967, Italian trade commr., Phila., 1967-71, N.Y.C., 1972—; founder Italian Wine Promotion Center, N.Y.C., 1975—. Italian Trade Center, N.Y.C., 1981—; organizer annual Italian Week on 5th Ave., N.Y.C.; exec. sec., exec. com. Gruppo Esponenti Italiani, 1974—; advisory bd. Italy-Am. C. of C., 1972—; mem. bd. World Trade Center of Italy, 1978. Served to lt. Italian Air Force, 1959-61. Named Cavaliere Ufficiale all' Ordine del Merito della Repubblica Italiana, 1972, Commendatore, 1981. Mem. Italian Bar Assn., Italian Journalist Assn., Fgn. Consular Assn. Phila., Soc. Fgn. Consuls N.Y. Roman Catholic. Club: World Trade Center. Signer agreement between Italy and Peoples' Republic of China, 1967; editor trade mags.: Italy Presents, Quality (English, French, Spanish, German), 1962-64; contbr. articles to Italian mags. and newspapers. Office: 499 Park Ave New York NY 10022

CARABILLO, ERNEST ANTHONY, JR., med. products co. exec.; b. N.Y.C., July 29, 1938; s. Ernest Mario and Elvira (Genovesi) C.; B.S. in Pharmacy, St. John's U., 1960, J.D., 1964; m. Dolores C. Banculli, Sept. 7, 1964; children—Ernest Anthony III, Therese Lee. Owner, mgr. retail pharmacy, 1959-62; chief pharmacist Midwood Hosp., Bklyn., 1962-64; dir. med. legal research firm Garbarini, Decicco & Scher, N.Y.C., 1964-67; village atty., East Rockaway, N.Y., 1967-68; individual practice law, East Rockaway, 1964-68; spl. asst. to dep. dir. Bur. Narcotic and Dangerous Drugs, Dept. Justice, 1968-69, asst. to asst. dir. sci. support, 1969-72, chief drug control div., 1972-73; chief spl. programs div. Drug Enforcement Adminstrn., Dept. Justice, 1973-76, chief regulatory support div., 1976-77; asso. dir. regulatory affairs Office of Drug Abuse Policy, White House, 1977; dir. quality assurance and regulatory affairs Med. Products div. Union Carbide, Rye, N.Y., 1977—; vis. prof. Howard U. Mem. Parish Council, chmn. edn. com. St. Peter's Ch., Olney, Md., 1965-67. Served with U.S. N.G., 1956-64. Recipient Am. Jurisprudence prize for excellence in criminal law, 1960; hon. diplomate Am. Bd. Diplomates in Pharmacy; recipient citation of excellence, East Rockaway, 1968, excellence of performance award Bur. Narcotics and Dangerous Drugs, 1974, Superior Service award Drug Enforcement Adminstrn., 1976, award for excellence of performance, 1977. Mem. N.Y. State Bar Assn., Am. Soc. Quality Control. Roman Catholic. Office: 401 Theodore Fremd Ave Rye NY 10580

CARACCIOLI, KATHERINE FRANCES, mktg. research co. exec.; b. N.Y.C.; d. Louis N. and Catherine J. (Gargan) C.; B.A., N.Y. U., 1951, M.A., 1956. Mktg. analyst E.R. Squibb Internat., 1960-67; sr. market analyst Sudler & Hennessey Inc., N.Y.C., 1967-69; v.p. Deltakos div. J. Walter Thompson Co., N.Y.C., 1969-74; pres. KC Research Assos., N.Y.C., 1974—. Mem. Advt. Women N.Y., Am. Mktg. Assn., Mktg. Research Assn., Health Care Businesswomen's Assn., Pharm. Advt. Council, Biomed. Mktg. Research Group. Roman Catholic. Home: 205 E 66th St New York NY 10021 Office: 420 Lexington Ave New York NY 10017

CARAS, STANLEY ALAN, accountant; b. Malden, Mass., Apr. 5, 1945; s. Ernest Joseph and Vivian (Goodman) C.; B.S.A., Bentley Coll., 1966; m. Sharon Jane Feingold, May 27, 1967; children—Jill Heather, Joshua Brett. Sr. staff acct. Hertz, Herson & Co., 1966-71; pvt. practice acctg., 1971-72; partner Caras & Shulman, P.C., C.P.A.'s, Burlington, Mass., 1972—; lectr. actg. and mgmt. Bunker Hill Community Coll., Charleston, Mass.; adv. bd. Essex Bank. Chmn. Saugus Bus. and Indsl. Devel. Commn., 1977-80; v.p. Bentley Coll. Alumni Assn., 1971-73; mem. Lexington PTO Assn. Served with USAR, 1966-72. C.P.A., Mass. Mem. Am. Inst. C.P.A.'s, Mass. Soc. C.P.A.'s. Clubs: Saugus Rotary (dir. 1977-79), Masons (charter), 128 Roundtable Bus. Office: 121 Middlesex Turnpike Burlington MA 01803

CARAVASIOS, GEORGE NICHOLAS, lawyer; b. Wheeling, W.Va., Mar. 12, 1928; s. Nicholas G. and Katherine (Lias) C.: student Linsly Mil. Inst., 1941-45; A.B., Harvard, 1949, J.D., 1952. Admitted to W.Va. bar, 1952; gen. practice law, Wheeling, 1955—. Served with AUS, 1953-54. Mem. Am., W.Va., Ohio County bar assns., Am. Legion, Assn. Trial Lawyers Am., Am. Judicature Soc., Harvard Law Sch. Assn. W.Va., Order of Ahepa. Mem. Greek Orthodox Ch. Elk. Home: 813 Main St Wheeling WV 26003 Office: 77 12th St Wheeling WV 26003

CARAVETTA, PETER FRANK, jewelry mfg. co. exec.; b. Sheffield, Pa., Apr. 22, 1943; s. Frank Joseph and Maria Rose (Scarpelli) C.; B.S. in Mech. Engring., Stevens Inst. Tech., 1966; M.B.A., Rutgers U., 1970; m. Rosetta Preziosi, Mar. 22, 1975. Mfg. engr. Am. Can Co., Hillside, N.J., 1966-68; engring. mgr. Cert. Metals Co., Nutley, N.J., 1968-70; pres., co-owner Energex Lighting Industries, West Orange, N.J., 1970-77; pres., co-owner Metals Tech. Inc., Orange, N.J., 1977—. Mem. Mensa. Roman Catholic. Office: Metals Tech Inc 440 Washington St Orange NJ 07050

CARBONE, STEVEN JOHN, indsl. sales exec.; b. Newark, Sept. 4, 1951; s. Frank Albert and Sarina Renee (De Simone) C.; A.A. in Life Scis., Union Coll., Cranford, N.J., 1971; B.S. in Biology, Seton Hall U., 1973; m. Nancy A. Segear, Nov. 23, 1974. Retail salesman Federated Purchaser, Inc., Springfield, N.J., 1969-73, indsl. salesman, 1973-76, indsl. sales mgr., 1976—; tech. cons. on customer service. Roman Catholic. Office: 155 US Route 22 Springfield NJ 07081

CARBONELL, MARS AVENA, ins. agt.; b. Manila, July 15, 1935; s. Luis Tabor and Magdalena Velasquez (Avena) C.; B.S. in Bus. Adminstrn. (scholar), Far Eastern U., Manila, 1961; m. Flordeliza de Borja, Oct. 12, 1936; children—Christine, Mars Anthony, Christopher. Agt., Philippine-Am. Life Ins. Co., 1961-62, supr., 1962, asso. mgr., 1964-71; agt. John Hancock Mut. Life Ins. Co., 1971, agt., N.J., 1972-73, agt., N.Y., 1972-73, sales mgr., N.Y.C., 1974-80, gen. agt., Rego Park, N.Y., 1980—. Vice pres. Kapatirang Filipino, 1976-78. Recipient Nat. Quality award, 1975-77, 80; named Agy. Mgr. of Yr., 1974-80. Mem. Nat. Assn. Life Underwriters, Million Dollar Round Table, Philippines Life Underwriters Assn. Am. (dir.). Clubs: Philippine Bowling, K.C. Home: 40-47 Gleane St Elmhurst NY 11373 Office: 95-25 Queens Blvd Rego Park NY 11374

CARBRAY, SAM EDWARD, real estate investment exec.; b. Paris, Ark., July 23, 1935; s. John and Helen (Wells) C.; B.S. in Bus. Adminstrn., George Pepperdine Coll., 1957; m. Elizabeth Jean Forte, Mar. 9, 1963; children—Michael Gary, Teri Lynn, Kristin Elizabeth. Sales dir. Chism-Moody Realty Co., Los Angeles, 1961-65; partner Chism-Carbray Realty, San Mateo, Calif., 1966; pres. Carbray & Co., Real Estate Investments, San Mateo, 1967—; pres. Shelter Mortgage Inc., Shelter Devels. Inc. Served with USMCR, 1957-61. Mem. Sigma Tau Sigma. Baptist. Home: 360 Roblar Ave Hillsborough CA 94010 Office: 66 Bovet Rd San Mateo CA 94402

CARDIN, RICHARD W(ILFORD), accountant; b. Tellico Plains, Tenn., July 13, 1935; s. William C. and Mayola (Atkins) C.; B.S., East Tenn. State U., 1956, postgrad., 1957-58; m. Nancy Sue Cox, Sept. 1, 1956; children—Michael, Donna. With Arthur Andersen & Co., Nashville, 1958—, partner, 1968—, mng. partner, 1969—. Pres. Greater Chattanooga C. of C., 1976; mem. exec. com. United Way Chattanooga; bd. dirs. Chattanooga Chamber Found., Chattanooga Jr. Achievement; mem. adv. com. to dean Coll. Bus. U. Tenn., Knoxville, also East Tenn. State U. Named Outstanding Alumnus East Tenn. State U., 1978. Mem. Tenn. Soc. C.P.A.'s, Nat. Assn. Accts., Clubs: Rotary, Chattanooga Golf and Country (Chattanooga). Office: 300 Union St Nashville TN 37238

CARDINALE, LORETTA ANN (MRS. FRANK CARDINALE), Realtor; b. Beloit, Kans., Oct. 24, 1913; d. Charles Edward and Frances (Spannan) Rasher; grad. Am. Inst. Banking, 1941; student San Bernardino Valley Coll., 1965; m. Glen Clinton Lowry, Feb. 20, 1946 (dec. Feb. 1973); children—Nancy Ann (Mrs. Ronald Thomas Newcome), Elizabeth Jane (Mrs. Thomas King Krupka); m. 2d, Frank Cardinale; stepchildren—Frank, Dominic, Raymond. Asst. cashier First Nat. Bank, Beloit, 1943-46; co-owner, partner Lowry Real

Estate & Ins., Beloit, 1946-62; co-owner Lowry Real Estate, Calimesa, Calif., 1962—. Riverside County registrar voters, 1965-70; mem. Citizens Com. for New Gen. Plan for Riverside County, Residential and Comml., 1970-73; troop leader Girl Scouts U.S.A., Beloit, 1951-60. Mem. Nat. Assn. Real Estate Bds., Am. Assn. Ret. Persons, Am. Field Service Assn., V.F.W. Aux., Cath. Daus. Am., Bus. and Profl. Women's Club, Calif. Real Estate Assn., Sons and Daus. Soddies, Yucapia Balley Bd. Realtors (treas. 1966), Calimesa C. of C. (dir. 1965-71), Calif. Assn. Ind. Businessmen, Redlands Yucaipa Hort. Soc. Republican. Clubs: Soroptomist (charter), Yucaipa Women's. Home: PO Box 117 Calimesa CA 92320 Office: 543 W County Line Rd Calimesa CA 92320

CARDINELL, ROBERT HORACE, electric boat co. exec.; b. Columbia, Mo., June 14, 1922; s. Horace Albert and Norma (Waddell) C.; B.S., Mich. State U., 1947; M.B.A., Syracuse U., 1954; m. Francoise R. Mermod, Sept. 20, 1953; children—Robin Reneé, Laurie Anne. Commd. 2d lt. U.S. Army, 1944, advanced through grades to lt. col., 1962; served as infantry officer and as comptroller specialist, ret., 1967; cost analyst research and devel. firms including Am. Research Corp., Data Dynamics & Kaman Scis., 1967-71; founder, owner Vantage Boats, Falls Church, Va., 1970—, Advantage Electric Cars, 1975—; part time cons. bus. devel., 1971-74; dir. Found Services Inc., Tangerine Water Co. Decorated Bronze Star with oak leaf cluster, Legion of Merit. Mem. Assn. Syracuse Army Comptrollers, Ret. Officers Assn. Home and Office: Route 1 Box 309 6 Palm Ln Mount Dora FL 32757

CARDON, LOUIS CASIMIR, banker; b. Jouy-en-Josas (Yvelines), France, Dec. 20, 1904; s. Casimir J. and Louise (Ragoix) C.; diploma Hautes Etudes Commerciales, 1926; LL.D., Paris U., 1932; m. Helen Luise Barber, Apr. 18, 1939; step-children—Edgar B. Clark, Peter J. Clark. Dir., dir., hon. gen. mgr. Société Centrale De Banque, Paris, 1968—; hon. chmn. Société Financiere, Commerciale, Fluviale et Maritime, Paris, 1971, Credit Naval Paris, 1973; dir. charterhouse S.A., Paris, 1973. Conseiller Commerce Exterieur de la France, 1951, Conseiller honoraire, 1968. Served as 1st lt. G.H.Q. staff, 1940. Decorated officer Legion d'Honneur; comdr., officer fgn. orders. Mem. Commitee Assn. des Anciens Eleves des Hautes Etudes Commerciales (hon. chmn.). Contbr. articles to profl. jours. Home: 6 rue Adolphe Yvon Paris 16eme France Office: 47 rue Cambon Paris 1st France

CARDWELL, JOHN JAMES, food co. exec.; b. N.Y.C., Jan. 3, 1931; s. John Edward and Anne (Boyle) C.; B.S., U.S. Naval Acad., 1953; M.B.A., Harvard U., 1960; m. Mary Jean Carey, June 16, 1956; children—Mary Louise, Michael, Susan, Catherine, Anne, Joseph. With McKinsey & Co., Chgo., 1960-76, dir., mng. dir.; pres. Consol. Foods Corp., Chgo., 1976—; dir. FMC Corp. Bd. dirs. Northwestern U., Evanston Hosp. Served with USN, 1953-58. Clubs: Chgo., Glen View, Links. Home: 955 Hill Rd Winnetka IL 60093 Office: 135 S LaSalle St Chicago IL 60603

CAREY, DAVID J, bank exec.; b. Jackson Hole, Wyo., July 7, 1941; s. Burton Matthew and Dorothy Mae (Jenkins) C.; B.A. in Psychology, U. Rochester, 1963; M.B.A., Stanford U., 1971. Investment analyst Prudential Ins. Co. Am., Los Angeles, 1971-74; asst. v.p. corp. banking First Nat. Bank of Chgo., 1974-75; v.p. corp. banking Rainier Nat. Bank, Seattle, 1975-76, sr. v.p., mgr. corp. and corr. banking, 1976-80, sr. v.p., mgr. asset and liability mgmt. and planning div., 1980—; speaker groups including Assn. Wash. Bus. Chmn. bd. Shelter, Inc., 1977-78; mem. panel Family and Youth Services, United Way of King County. Served to lt. USN, 1964-69. Mem. Wash. Bankers Assn. Clubs: Rainier, Corinthian Yacht, Bellevue Athletic. Office: PO Box 3966 Seattle WA 98124

CAREY, MICHAEL CHARLES, hardgoods mfg. exec.; b. Kokomo, Ind., Sept. 6, 1949; s. Cornelius Joseph and Mary Jane Carey; B.A., Notre Dame U., 1971, M.B.A., 1974; m. Mary Gail Carey. Mktg. analyst SCM Corp., N.Y.C., 1974, field salesman, Dallas, 1974-75, mgr. sales planning, N.Y.C., 1975-76, product mgr. cartridges, New Canaan, Conn., 1976-78, dir. spl. products, 1978—; dir. Exec. Line, 1980. Mem. Am. Mktg. Assn., Nat. Office Products Assn., Wholesale Stationers Assn. Club: Notre Dame N.Y.C. Home: 447 S Broadway Upper Grandview NY 10960 Office: 65 Locust Ave New Canaan CT 06840

CAREY, THOMAS FRANCIS, cryogenics co. exec.; b. Hartford, Conn., Oct. 14, 1948; s. Thomas Anthony and Geraldine Elizabeth (French) C.; B.S. in Bus. Adminstrn., Am. Internat. Coll., 1970, Masters degree in Bus. Adminstrn., 1973; m. Jane Ellen Hollis, Oct. 2, 1976; children—Andrea Alison, Sarah Maria. Dist. rep. Gen. Motors Acceptance Corp., Springfield, Mass., 1971-73; quality assurance engr. San Onofre Nuclear div. Bechtel Corp., Norwalk, Calif., 1974-78; mgr. quality assurance Airco Cryogenics Co., Irvine, Calif., 1978—. Served with USMCR, 1969. Mem. Am. Mgmt. Assn., Am. Soc. for Quality Control, Assn. M.B.A. Execs., ASTM, Am. Soc. Non-Destructive Testing. Republican. Roman Catholic. Office: Airco Cryogenics Co 1900 Main St Irvine CA 92714

CAREY, WILLIAM JOSEPH, banking exec.; b. N.Y.C., May 15, 1922; s. Cornelius M. and Ellen (Gannon) C.; m. Barbara L. Garrison, Aug. 24, 1946; children—Kathleen, Eileen, Christine, Robert. Mgr., Ernst & Ernst, N.Y.C., 1949-59; controller Reynolds & Co., N.Y.C., 1959-61; exec. v.p. Bache & Co., Inc., N.Y.C., 1961-69; exec. partner Goodbody & Co., N.Y.C., 1970-71; v.p. Paine, Webber, Jackson & Curtis, N.Y.C., 1971-73; controller, treas., sr. v.p. J. Henry Schroder Bank and Trust Co., N.Y.C., 1973—; corporate v.p. fin. Schroders Inc., 1973—. Served with U.S. Navy, 1941-45. Decorated Purple Heart. Mem. N.Y. State Soc. C.P.A.'s, Am. Inst. C.P.A.'s, Fin. Execs. Inst., Nat. Assn. Security Dealers. Home: 861 Huron Rd Franklin Lakes NJ 07417 Office: 1 State St New York NY 10015

CARHART, KATHERINE MARY, Realtor; b. Newburgh, N.Y., Oct. 31, 1908; d. George Abdullah and Anna (Shayth) Mashnouk; grad. Spencerian Bus. Sch., 1927, Dinkin Sch. Real Estate, 1957; m. Eldred Perry Carhart, June 13, 1931 (dec. May 15, 1978); childreAnn Leanetta Carhart Stuart, Eldred Perry Jr. Stenographer, N.Y. Tel. Co., Newburgh, 1927-28; pvt. sec., dept. chemistry and electricity U.S. Mil. Acad., West Point, N.Y., 1929-37; salesman, Callahan Realty, Newburgh, 1956-57; founder, broker Carhart Agy., Inc., Newburgh, 1957—. Pres., P.T.A., 1946-47; treas. St. Agnes Whitney Meml. Ch., 1950-60; rec. sec., bd. dirs. McQuade Found. Mem. Newburgh Multiple Listing Service (pres. 1963), Newburgh Bd. Realtors (pres. 1966-67), Orange County Bd. Realtors (realtor of year 1970, dir. Multiple Listing Service 1975-76), Nat. Assn. Real Estate Bds., N.Y. State Assn. Real Estate Bds. (chmn. women's program com. 1966). Republican. Presbyn. Home: 70 Balmville Rd Newburgh NY 12550 Office: 111 S Plank Rd PO Box 7097 Newburgh NY 12550

CARL, ROBERT E., mktg. co. exec.; b. Independence, Mo., Sept. 1, 1927; s. Elmer T. Carl and Marion R. (Pack) C.; B.S., U. Kans., 1950; cert. in real estate So. Meth. U., 1965; certificate in investment analysis N.Y. Inst. Fin., 1967; m. Linda Arlene Sutton, Aug. 30, 1967; children—Melanie Ruth, Robert Brady. Vice pres. sales promotion Riverside Press, Inc., Dallas, 1951-54; pres., chief operating officer Jones-Carl, Inc., Dallas, 1954-62; v.p. mktg. communications Modern Am. Corp., Dallas, 1962-70; v.p. sales Dunn Properties of Tex., Inc., Dallas, 1970-71; sr. v.p. mktg. services Vantage Cos., Dallas, 1971—. Recipient legion of honor degree Internat. Supreme Council of Order of De Molay, 1957; Silver Anvil award Pub. Relations Soc. Am., 1958. Mem. Sales and Mktg. Execs. Dallas (pres. 1976-77, Distinguished Salesman's award 1954), S.W. Found. Free Enterprise (pres. 1975-76), Tex., So. indstl. devel. councils, Nat. Assn. Rev. Appraisers, Nat. Assn. Corp. Real Estate Execs., Sales and Mktg. Execs. Internat. (sr. v.p.). Republican. Methodist. Clubs: Big D. Toastmaster (pres. 1966), Press, Dallas, Masons, Shriners. Contbr. articles to profl. jours. Home: 4209 Gloster Rd Dallas TX 75220 Office: 2525 Stemmons Freeway Dallas TX 75207

CARLEN, RAYMOND NILS, steel co. exec.; b. Rockford, Ill., May 3, 1919; s. Charles and Hannah (Nystrom) C.; B.S. in Metall. Engring., U. Ill., 1942; M.S. in Bus. Adminstrn., U. Chgo., 1950; m. Jean Lovejoy, June 15, 1946; children—Cynthia Jean, Susan Joy. With Joseph T. Ryerson & Son, Inc., Chgo., 1946—, v.p. Eastern region, 1963-64, exec. v.p., 1964-68, pres., 1968—, chmn. bd., 1976—, also dir.; sr. v.p. Inland Steel Co., Chgo., 1976-78, vice chmn., 1978—, also dir., also chmn. bd. Inland Steel Container div., Alsip, Ill., 1976—; chmn. bd. Inryco, Inc., Chgo.; chmn., dir. Instud subsidiary Inland Steel Co., Inland-Ryerson Constrn. Products, Inc.; dir. Am. Nat. Bank and Trust of Chgo., Heller Internat., Pecker Plada Corp., Ltd., Tel Aviv, Israel, Hinsdale Fed. Savs. & Loan Assn. (Ill.), Lindberg Corp. Mem. Ill. Emergency Resources Planning Com., 1964—. Chmn. Hinsdale (Ill.) Community Caucus, 1963-64; pres. Chgo. area council Boy Scouts Am., 1970-74; active fund raising U. Chgo., Loyola U., Chgo., Passavant Meml. Hosp., Chgo., Met. Crusade of Mercy. Bd. dirs. Hinsdale Community House, 1957-60, Hinsdale PTA, 1957-60; mem. adv. council U. Chgo., 1960—, adv. council Coll. Engring., U. Ill., 1952—. Served to maj. C.E., AUS 1942-45; ETO. Mem. Chgo. Assn. Commerce and Industry, Ill. C. of C. Nat. (Leadership award 1961), Ill. mfrs. assns., Exec. Program Club Chgo. Clubs: Chicago Golf (pres. 1965, 66, dir. 1960-67) (Wheaton, Ill.); Hinsdale (Ill.) Golf; Chicago, Commercial, Economic (Chgo.). Home: 6 Oak Brook Club Dr Residence J305 Oak Brook IL 60521 Office: 30 W Monroe St Chicago IL 60603

CARLETON, BUKK G., III, real estate exec.; A.B. cum laude (Nat. Merit scholar), Harvard, 1961; M.B.A. (Stanford fellow), Stanford, 1964; m. Mary Oliver Lee, July 8, 1967; children—Samantha Lee, Heather Tucker. Investment analyst First Nat. City Bank, N.Y.C., 1961-62, Capital Research and Mgmt. Co., Los Angeles, 1963; fin. project mgr. Am. Friends Service Com., Phila., 1964-66; cons., 1966-68; partner Investment Assos., Washington, 1965—; founder, v.p. Landtect Corp., Phila., 1966-74, pres., 1974—, also dir.; pres. Landtect New Eng., 1976—, Burlington Tennis Co., Inc., 1977—, Waterville Valley Gateway, Inc., 1978—, Northeast Comml., 1979—; treas., dir. Benefit Systems, Inc., Balt., 1970—; cons. Stanford Research Inst., 1968-69. Mem. Soc. Indsl. Realtors, Am. Mgmt. Assn., Delta Upsilon. Clubs: Harvard, Racquet, Merion Cricket (Phila.); Harvard (N.Y.C.); Hasty Pudding Inst. (Cambridge). Home: Bragg Hill Rd Norwich VT 05055 Office: Suite 30 3 Lebanon St Hanover NH 03755

CARLETON, BUKK GRIFFITH, investment counsel; b. N.Y.C., May 30, 1909; s. Bukk G. and Clarice (Griffith) C.; A.B. magna cum laude, Harvard U., 1931, LL.B., 1934; m. Mary Elizabeth Tucker, June 16, 1934; children—Elizabeth Holland, Bukk Griffith. Admitted to N.Y. bar, 1935; asso. Larkin, Rathbone & Perry, N.Y.C., 1934-36; asst. counsel, asst. sec. Gen. Chem. Co., 1936-41; v.p., sec., dir. Perma-Bilt Homes, Inc., 1941-42; counsel RFC, 1942-44; head N.Y. law office Montgomery Ward & Co. 1944-46; mem. legal dept. Sinclair Refining Co., 1946-56; owner, investment counsel Griffith Carleton, 1946—. Trustee Hicks-Stearns Mus. Mem. Am., N.Y. bar assns., New Eng. Soc., Phi Beta Kappa. Quaker (com. nat. legis. 1957-58). Clubs: Met., Sleepy Hollow, Harvard (N.Y.C.); Woodway Country (Conn.); Quinnatisset Country (Conn.); R.I. Country; New Canaan Country, Harvard (New Canaan). Home: Parade Hill Ln New Canaan CT 06840 Office: Bukkskin East Killingly CT 06243

CARLIN, GABRIEL S., corp. exec.; b. N.Y.C., Mar. 19, 1921; s. Samuel and Lena (Franco) C.; B.S., N.Y. U., 1951, M.B.A., 1954; m. Rosalind Goldberg, Apr. 17, 1943; children—Donald B., Beverly J. Army-Navy purchasing coordinator U.S. Dept. Def., 1947-49; gen. sales mgr. Old Town Corp., Bklyn., 1949-60; div. gen. mgr., mem. world planning group Xerox Corp., Rochester, N.Y., 1960-64; exec. v.p. Savin Corp., Valhalla, N.Y., 1964—, dir., dir., 1965—. Served to 1st lt. AUS, 1942-46. Author: The Power of Enthusiastic Selling, 1962; How to Persuade and Motivate People, 1964. Home: 1807 Long Ridge Rd Stamford CT 06903 Office: Savin Corp Valhalla NY 10595

CARLIN, ROY HARRIS, lawyer; b. N.Y.C., May 30, 1939; s. Samuel H. and Shirley E. C.; B.A., Williams Coll., 1961; J.D., N.Y. U., 1964; m. Patricia L. Ladin, Jan. 26, 1964; children—Jennifer, John. Admitted to N.Y. bar, 1964, U.S. Supreme Ct. bar, 1975; law asst. appellate div. Supreme Ct., First Jud. Dept., 1965-66; asso. Krause Hirsch & Gross (merger Stroock & Stroock & Lavan), N.Y.C., 1968-72, partner, 1972—; chmn. programs Practicing Law Inst., Uniform Comml. Code. Mem. Am. Arbitration Assn. (panel of arbitrators), Am. Bar Assn. (subcom. uniform comml. code), N.Y. State Bar Assn., (com. on banking 1975—), Assn. Bar City N.Y. (subcom. uniform comml. code 1973—). Clubs: Princeton, Mid Hudson Patterns. Contbr. articles to legal jours. Home: 505 E 79th St New York NY 10021 Office: 61 Broadway New York NY 10006

CARLISLE, JOHN THOMAS, research co. exec.; b. Marion, Ohio, Jan. 13, 1941; s. Robert Moore and Corrinne (Claypool) C.; B.A. in English, U. Calif., Santa Barbara, 1963; m. Liberty Love Lealy, June 28, 1962; children—Robert Scott, John David, James Michael. With Santa Barbara Research Center subs. Hughes Aircraft Co., Goleta, Calif., 1967—, subcontract adminstr., 1970-72, supr. subcontracts, 1972-76, supr. procurement analysis, 1976-78, head procurement, 1978—, procurement mgr., 1979—; instr. purchasing mgmt. U. Calif., Santa Barbara, 1977—. Mem. Santa Barbara Research Center Mgmt. Club (founder, v.p. 1978). Office: 75 Coromar Dr Goleta CA 93017

CARLL, ELMER SAMUEL, title ins. co. exec.; b. Collingswood, N.J., Dec. 27, 1898; s. Samuel and Anna B. (Davis) C.; LL.B., Temple U., 1920; LL.D., Phila. Coll. Osteo. Medicine; m. Dorothy E. Brown, Feb. 12, 1955. With W. Jersey Title Guarantee Co. of Camden, N.J., 1916-18, Real Estate Title Ins. & Trust Co., Phila., 1918-22; title officer Frankford Trust Co. (Pa.), 1922-52, v.p., 1929-52, also dir.; pres. Indsl. Trust Co., Phila., 1952-61, chmn. bd., 1960-61; vice chmn. bd. Indsl. Valley Bank and Trust Co., Phila., 1961-63; exec. v.p. Indsl. Valley Title Ins. Co., Phila., 1964-70, vice chmn. bd., 1970—; dir. Germantown Ins. Co., Germantown Life Ins. Co., Indsl. Valley Title Ins. Co., Dist. Realty Title Ins. Corp. Recipient Disting. Service award Temple U. Alumni; 4th Ann. award Kensington Hosp., 1955; service award Boys Clubs Am., 1967. Mem. Mortgage Bankers Assn. (past pres. Phila. chpt.), Pa. Land Title Assn. (past pres.), Am. Bankers Assn., N.E. Phila. C. of C. (past dir.). Episcopalian. Clubs: Torresdale Frankford Country (past treas.); Union League (Phila.); Skytop; Masons (Haddonfield, N.J.); Shriners; Exchange (past pres., hon. nat. mem.) (Frankford). Home: 2073 Kent Rd Huntingdon Valley PA 19006 Office: Indsl Valley Title Ins Co 1700 Market St Philadelphia PA 19103

CARLSBERG, RICHARD PRESTEN, real estate corp. exec.; b. Stockton, Calif., Mar. 2, 1937; s. Arthur Walter and Lillian Marie (Presten) C.; student City Coll. of San Francisco, 1954-56; A.A., U. San Francisco, 1955; B.A. in Geology, UCLA, 1959; m. Barbara Ann Hearn, June 28, 1959; children—David Arthur, Rebecca Jane, Dawn Marie. Officer and/or dir. real estate, fin., devel., research, petroleum and acquisition corps.; pres. Carlsberg Corp., Santa Monica, Calif. Bd. dirs. UCLA Found., Calif. Pines Youth Found.; mem. Soc. of Blue Shield; elder Bel Air Presbyn. Ch. Served with N.G., 1959-65. Recipient award, resolution Calif. Legislature, 1965, 71, award of merit Los Angeles County, 1965, commendation County of Los Angeles, 1971, from U.S. Dept. Interior, 1971. Mem. Young Presidents Orgn. (Golden West chpt.). Clubs: So. Calif. Safari, Safari Internat., Game Coin, various conservation groups including Ducks Unltd. Office: 2800 28th St Santa Monica CA 90405

CARLSON, ARTHUR KENNETH GORDON, banker; b. N.Y.C., Jan. 8, 1922; s. John A. and Astrid (Sivertsen) C.; B.S., Fordham U., 1943; M.S., Columbia U., 1949, postgrad., 1949-50; diploma in Comml. Banking, Rutgers U., 1962; m. Georgene Clair Johnson, Feb. 6, 1954; children—Pamela Jean, Gail Lynn, Jill Susan. Commodity trader Merrill Lynch, Pierce, Fenner & Beane, Chgo., 1946-48; investment analyst N.Y. Life Ins. Co., N.Y.C., 1949-56; investment analyst Irving Trust Co., N.Y.C., 1956-59, asst. v.p. comml., 1959-67, v.p., dir. investment research, 1967-72; v.p. investment research First Nat. City Bank, N.Y.C., 1972-77; v.p., mgr. trust investments Valley Nat. Bank, Phoenix, 1977—; instr. econs. Fordham U., 1949-51. Pres. bd. dirs. Richmond Meml. Hosp., 1975-77; adv. bd. St. Joseph's Hosp. and Med. Center, 1980—. Served to lt. USNR, 1943-46. Mem. Am. Bankers Assn. (mem. trust investment com., trust div. 1980—), N.Y. Soc. Security Analysts (dir., pres. 1974-75), Steel Analysts Group N.Y. (exec. mem.), Non-Ferrous Metals Analysts (exec. mem.), Am. Inst. Mining and Metall. Engrs., Fin. Analysts Fedn. (dir. 1974-77). Clubs: Richmond County Yacht (N.Y.C.); Ariz. (Phoenix). Office: PO Box 71 Valley Nat Bank A-806 Phoenix AZ 85001

CARLSON, BARRY MARCUS, electronics co. exec.; b. Cin., May 23, 1947; came to Canada, 1953; s. Herbert Clifford and Ivy Winnifred (Field) C.; student Simon Fraser U., 1967-68; m. Taog Van Gyte, Nov. 26, 1966; children—Jesse Marcus, Zoe Martha. Prodn. mgr. Smith Barregar Ltd., Vancouver, B.C., Can., 1969-75; gen. mgr. Circuit Graphics Ltd., Burnaby, B.C., 1975-77, pres., chief exec. officer, 1977—. Mem. Sales and Mktg. Execs. of Vancouver. Libertarian. Home: 14128 114th Ave Surrey BC V3R 2M6 Canada Office: 8030 Winston St Burnaby BC V5A 2H5 Canada

CARLSON, CARL ALLEN, advt. exec.; b. Kenedy, Tex., Sept. 17, 1952; s. Carl Theodore and Mary Pearl (Allen) C.; B.A. in Communications, Tex. Lutheran Coll., 1974. Adminstrv. asst. Com. on House Adminstrn., Tex. Ho. of Reps., Austin, 1975-76; account exec. Neal Spelce Assos. Advt. and Public Relations, Austin, 1976-77, Gurasich, Spence, Darilek & McClure Advt., San Antonio, 1977—. Bd. dirs. Am. Heart Assn., Austin, 1975-76; bd. dirs., bd. regents Tex. Luth. Coll., 1976-78, bd. dirs. Devel. Bd., 1978—; vol. Bob Krueger for U.S. Senate, 1978. Mem. Tex. Assn. Bus. (dir. 1979-80), San Antonio Builders Assn., San Antonio C. of C., San Antonio Advt. Fedn., Tex. Luth. Coll. Alumni Assn. Democrat. Lutheran. Office: 1100 NE Loop 410 #655 San Antonio TX 78209

CARLSON, CURTIS LEROY, diversified internat. corp. exec.; b. Mpls., July 9, 1914; s. Charles A. and Leatha (Peterson) C.; B.A., U. Minn., 1937; D.Bus. Adminstrn. (hon.), Nathaniel Hawthorn Coll., 1976; m. Arleen Martin, June 30, 1938; children—Marilyn Carlson Nelson, Barbara Carlson Gage. Salesman, Procter & Gamble, Mpls., 1937-38; founder, pres., chmn. bd. Gold Bond Stamp Co., Mpls., 1938-72; pres., chmn. bd. Carlson Cos., Inc., Mpls., 1972—; chmn. bd., and/or com. mem., dir. Radisson Hotel Corp., Carlson Mktg. Group, Inc., PIC-Travel, Inc., TGI Friday's, Inc., Carlson Properties, Inc., Ardan, Inc., Commonwealth Premium Ltd. (Can.), Capital Hospitality Corp., A. Weisman Co., Prize Incentives Ltd., Carlson Leasing, Inc., Commonwealth Premium Sales Ltd. (Can.), CSA, Inc., ETAT, Inc., N. Am. Fin. Corp., Resort Hotels of Ariz., Inc., Superior Fiber Products, Inc., Tonkawa Ins. Co., WaSko Gold Products Corp., Radisson Atlanta Corp., Radisson Dallas Corp., Radisson Denver Corp., Radisson Grenelefe Corp., Radisson Mo. Corp., Radisson Raleigh Corp., Charles Shaffer, Inc., Schimmel Hotels Corp., Radisson Mpls. Corp., MIP Agy., Inc., CHC, Inc., Curtis Homes Employer, Inc., Frontier Savings Stamps, Inc. of Lubbock (Tex.), Gold Bond Stamp Co. of Okla., Premiums Internat. Ltd., Gold Bond Japan Ltd., Duraflex/Omega, Inc., Tozai Corp., Commerce Pl. Hotel Corp., Nat. Hotel Corp., Radisson Wilmington Corp., Reed Food Sales, Inc., Prandhur Corp., Naegele, Inc., Maj. Media, Inc., Maj. Media Mgmt. Corp., Maj. Media of S.E. Ltd., Maj. Media of Midwest Ltd., Naegele Outdoor Advt. Co. of Charlotte, Inc. (N.C.), Naegele Outdoor Advt. Co. of Calif., Inc., Bank Shares, Inc., MEI Corp., Marquette Nat. Bank, Mpls., Windhorst Outdoor Advt., Louisville. Bd. dirs. Fairview Community Hosps., Boys Club Mpls. (founder), Minn. Orch. Assn., Nat. Vinland Center, U. Minn. Research Found., Downtown Council Mpls.; mem. nat. bd. trustees Sigma Phi Epsilon Ednl. Found.; mem. adv. com. Minn. Exec. Program, Hubert H. Humphrey Inst. Public Affairs; trustee Mpls. Soc. Fine Arts, Am. Scandinavian Found.; bd. overseers U. Minn. Coll. Bus. Adminstrn. Recipient numerous awards including Minnesotan of Yr., Minn. Broadcasters Assn., 1976, Nat. Disting. Merit citation NCCJ, 1977, Capital City award St. Paul Area C. of C., 1977, Gt. Am. award Internat. B'nai B'rith Found., 1978, Horatio Alger award, 1979, U. Minn. Regents' award, 1979; named comdr. Royal Order of N. Star, King of Sweden, 1976. Mem. Mpls. C. of C. (exec. com.), U. Minn. Alumni Assn. (honors. com.), Detroit Swedish Council, Swedish Pioneer Hist. Soc. (Chgo.), Swedish Council Am. (exec. com.), Minn. Bus. Partnership, Sigma Phi Epsilon. Methodist. Clubs: Shrine Horsemen, Jesters, Masons; Northland Country (Duluth); Mpls., Mpls. Athletic; Minikahda; Ocean Reef Yacht (Miami, Fla.). Office: Carlson Cos Inc 12755 State Hwy 55 Minneapolis MN 55441

CARLSON, EDWARD ELMER, business exec.; b. Tacoma, June 4, 1911; s. Elmer E. and Lula (Powers) C.; student U. Wash., 1928-32; m. Nell Hinckley Cox, June 26, 1936; children—Edward Eugene, Jane Leslie. Mgr., President Hotel, Mt. Vernon, Wash., 1936-37, Rainier Club, Seattle, 1937-42; with Western Internat. Hotels, Inc., Seattle, 1946—, exec. v.p., 1953-61, pres., 1961-69, chmn. bd., 1969-71; pres., chief exec. officer United Air Lines, Inc., Chgo., 1971-74, now dir.; chmn. bd., dir. UAL, Inc., 1975—, pres., chief exec. officer, 1975-79; dir. Seafirst Corp., Seattle, Seattle First Nat. Bank, Western Internat. Hotels Co., GAB Bus. Services, Inc., Deere & Co., Dart & Kraft, Inc., Univar Corp.; internat. adv. council Wells Fargo Bank, 1st Nat. Bank of Chgo. Pres., Century 21 Expn., Inc., Seattle, 1957-59, chmn. bd., 1959-61, chmn. Wash. World's Fair Commn., 1955-63, Wash. Oceanographic Study Commn.; mem. Pres. Johnson's Industry-Govt. Task Force, 1968; mem. undersec. navy's adv. commn. to Navy Ships Store Office; mem. adv. bd. Grad. Sch. Bus., U. Wash. Hon. chmn. Pacific Sci. Center Found., Wash.; bd. dirs. Virginia Mason Med. Found.; trustee Henry J. Kaiser Family Found. Named 1st Citizen of Seattle, 1966, Outstanding Citizen, Municipal

League, 1970; recipient Alumnus Summa Laude Dignatus Award U. Wash., 1970. Mem. Order of St. John of Jerusalem. Clubs: Rainier, Seattle Golf, Bohemian, Comml. Office: PO Box 66919 Chicago IL 60666

CARLSON, EVERETT ARTHUR, cons. firm exec.; b. Norwood, Mass., Aug. 23, 1953; s. Oscar Theodore and Annie Elizabeth (Rozuck) C.; B.S. in Bus. Adminstrn., Northeastern U., Boston, 1976. Mgmt., ops. staff asst. St. Johnsbury Co., Cambridge, Mass., 1972-76; v.p., dir. Foundation Group, Ltd., Boston, 1976—. Mem. Greater Boston C. of C. Developer: Sourcebook Directory/Lexicon, 1976. Home: 51 Abbottsford Rd Brookline MA 02146 Office: 59 Temple Pl Boston MA 02111

CARLSON, JOHN FREDERICK, financial exec.; b. Stamford, Conn., Feb. 28, 1939; s. Frederick Reinhold and Gladys Elizabeth (Cahill) C.; B.A., Hofstra U., 1960; m. Judith Crockard, Dec. 3, 1961; children—Wendy Leigh, John Todd. Mgmt. cons., auditor Price Waterhouse & Co., N.Y.C., 1961-69; internat. controller Mennen Co., Morristown, N.J., 1969-73; controller consumer products Am. Cyanamid Co., Wayne, N.J., 1973-77; v.p. planning Shulton, Inc. subs. Am. Cyanamid Co., Wayne, 1978-79; fin. v.p. Viacom Internat. Inc., diversified entertainment and communications, N.Y.C., 1979—. Served with U.S. Army, 1960-61. C.P.A., N.Y. Mem. Financial Execs. Inst., Am. Inst. C.P.A.'s, N.Y., N.J. socs. C.P.A.'s. Club: Morris Country Golf. Home: High Ridge Rd RD 3 Dover NJ 07801 Office: Viacom Internat Inc New York NY 10036

CARLSON, RICHARD LAWRENCE, aerospace co. exec.; b. Providence, Apr. 12, 1937; s. Hans Lawrence and Bertha May (Strom) C.; B.S. in Mgmt. Engring., Rensselaer Poly. Inst., 1964; M.B.A., U. Conn., 1973; m. Johanna Mary Cornell, Aug. 27, 1960; children—Richard Lawrence, Suellen Marie. Indsl. engr. Johnson & Johnson, Watervliet, N.Y., 1961-64; quality control engr. Corning Glass Works (N.Y.), 1964; indsl. engr. United Technologies, East Hartford, Conn., 1965-66, supv. indsl. engring., 1966-68, gen. supv. material movement planning, 1968-76, materials engine program mgr., 1977—. Mem. exec. bd. Long River council Boy Scouts Am., Hartford, 1975—; bd. dirs. Woodland Summit Water Assn., 1965-67. Recipient Wheel award Modern Mfg. mag., 1968; registered profl. engr. Mass., Calif.; certified mfg. engr., material mgmt., material handling; Irving Subway Corp. grantee, 1962-63. Mem. Am. Mgmt. Assn., Soc. Advancement Mgmt., Am. Inst. Indsl. Engrs. (dir. 1965, treas. 1966-67, seminar chmn. 1967-68), Nat. Conn. soc. profl. engrs., Internat. Material Mgmt. Soc., Mensa., 1st Co. Gov.'s Horse Guards Conn., Rockville Fish and Game Club, British Balloon and Airship Club, Nat. Rifle Assn., Lighter Than Air Soc., Balloon Fedn., Am., Buckskin Shirts, Phi Kappa Phi, Beta Gamma Sigma, Alpha Phi Omega. Democrat. Lutheran. Home: 28 Willie Circle Tolland CT 06084 Office: 400 Main St East Hartford CT 06108

CARLSON, ROBERT L., bookbinding co. exec.; b. Rochester, N.Y., Feb. 12, 1921; s. Clarence Karl and Helen Estelle (Bartelson) C.; A.B., U. Mich., 1942; m. Jeanne Demaris Goudy, Sept. 22, 1942; children—Demaris Jeanne, Robert L., Donald K. With William F. Zahrndt & Son, Inc., Rochester, 1945—, pres., owner, 1968—. Chmn., Webster (N.Y.) Republican Com., 1958-64; mem. Monroe County Rep. Com., 1955-64. Served with inf. AUS, 1942-45. Decorated Purple Heart with 4 oak leaf clusters. Mem. Printing Industry of Am. (nat. dir., named Printing Man of Year 1979), U. Mich. Alumni Assn. (dir.). Republican. Club: Rochester Canoe. Home: 690 Lake Rd Webster NY 14580 Office: 1500 N Clinton Ave Rochester NY 14621

CARLSTON, RICHARD CHARLES, aerospace engr.; b. San Francisco, May 17, 1929; s. Charles Oliver and Gertrude Madeline (Green) C.; B.S., U. San Francisco, 1951; M.S., U. Mo., Columbia, 1954; Ph.D. in Chemistry, U. Kans., Lawrence, 1957; m. Margaret Elizabeth Schoenborn, July 19, 1956; children—Donald, Elizabeth, Stuart. Sr. chemist Sperry Gyroscope Co., Gt. Neck, N.Y., 1957-60; research engr. Grumman Aircraft Co., Bethpage, N.Y., 1960-62; head solid state physics dept. Aerojet Gen. Corp., Azusa, Calif., 1962-64; physicist Office Naval Research, Washington, 1964-68; asso. prof. metall. engring. Calif. Poly. State U., San Luis Obispo, 1968-72; research group leader EG&G Co., Santa Barbara, Calif., 1972-76; mgr. corrosion program for ICBM systems TRW Def. and Space Systems Group, Redondo Beach, Calif., 1976—. Co-founder, Plainedge (N.Y.) Public Library, 1961; active local Boy Scouts Am. Registered profl. engr., Calif. Fellow Washington Acad. Scis., Am. Inst. Chemists; mem. Nat. Assn. Corrosion Engrs., Air Pollution Control Assn., Am. Assn. Crystal Growth, Am. Crystallographic Assn., Electrochem. Soc., N.Y. Acad. Sci., Soc. Research Adminstrn., Sigma Xi. Republican. Roman Catholic. Club: K.C. Mem. editorial bd. Electrochem. Soc., 1967-72, chem. abstractor, 1960-65. Home: 3201 Flora St San Luis Obispo CA 93401 Office: Bldg 88/2012 TRW Redondo Beach CA 90278

CARLSTONE, EDWARD CHARLES, video prodn. services co. exec.; b. Chgo., Nov. 8, 1943; s. Paul Arthur and Helen Louise (Culberg) C.; B.S. in Elec. Engring., Northwestern U., 1966; M.B.A., U. Santa Clara, 1978; m. Nita Kay Flowers, Aug. 15, 1974; 1 son, Erik Davidson. Instr. electronics Hewlett-Packard Co., 1966-67, sales tng. mgr., 1967-70; co-founder TV Assos., Inc., Mountain View, Calif., 1970, pres., 1970—, gen. mgr., 1970—; instr. dept. theatre arts U. Santa Clara, 1971, guest lectr. Sch. Bus., 1974-77. Named Small Bus. Person of Yr., No. Calif. SBA, 1980. Mem. Beta Gamma Sigma. Home: 12071 Tiptoe Ln Los Altos CA 94022 Office: 2410 Charleston Rd Mountain View CA 94043

CARLTON, JOHN ROBERT, JR., financing, engring. and warehousing co. exec.; b. Roanoke, Va., Nov. 5, 1923; s. John Robert and Pauline (Strickler) C.; B.S. in Archtl. Engring., Va. Poly. Inst., 1949; m. Janet E. Keller McBride, Jan. 14, 1973; children—John Robert, William P.S.; stepchildren—Andrew, Jeffrey McBride. Archtl. draftsman, Lynchburg, Va., 1951-52; chief mech. engr. archtl. firm, Norfolk, Va., 1952-54; owner, pres., chief exec. officer Carlton Internat., Inc., Richmond, Va., 1954—; pres. Gateway Distbn., Atlanta; exec. v.p. Gateway Distbn. Center, Evansville, Ind. and Olathe, Kans. Bd. dirs. Blue Ridge Sch., Charlottesville, Va. Served with USAAF, 1943-46. Presbyterian (former deacon). Home: 201 Virginia Ave Richmond VA 23226 Office: 2107 N Hamilton St Richmond VA 23230

CARMEL, ALAN STUART, lawyer, diversified co. exec.; b. Balt., July 24, 1944; s. Isaac and Sylvia (Sirulnik) C.; A.A. magna cum laude, U. Balt., 1963, J.D., 1966; m. Ellen Freda Hobman, June 29, 1969; children—Shana Miriam, Jason Mark, Jarre Paige. Admitted to Md. bar, 1966; sec., asst. counsel 1st Federated Life Ins. Co., Balt., 1966-69; dir. equity mktg., U.S. counsel Mfrs. Life Ins. Co., Toronto, Ont., Can., 1970-75; v.p., dir. ManEquity, Inc., Denver, 1970-75; pres., dir. ManuLife Holding Corp., 1970-75; v.p., gen. counsel, sec., dir. Atlantic Internat. Corp., Balt., 1975-80, Atlantic Internat. Mktg. Corp., Balt., 1975-80, Atlantic Mfg. Corp., Balt., 1975-80; mng. dir. Atlantic Mobile GmbH, Frankfurt, W.Ger., 1976-80; gen. counsel AI Services, A.G., Zug, Switzerland, 1976-80; exec. mgr. Atliran P.J.S.C., Tehran, Iran, 1976-80; gen. counsel Brooks Shoe Mfg. Co., Inc., Hanover, Pa., 1980—. Fellow Life Mgmt. Inst.; mem. Internat., Am., Md. bar assns., Am. Soc. Internat. Law, Mensa, Am. Arbitration Assn. (panel arbitrators), Vintage Soc. Home: 2425 Diana Rd Baltimore MD 21209 Office: 131 Factory St Hanover PA 17331

CARMICHAEL, PAUL LOUIS, ophthalmic surgeon; b. Phila., July 8, 1927; s. Louis and Christina Ciamaichela; B.S. in Biology, Villanova U., 1945; M.D., St. Louis U., 1949; M.S. in Medicine, U. Pa., 1954; m. Pauline Cecilia Lipsmire, Oct. 28, 1950; children—Paul Louis, Mary Catherine, John Michael, Kevin Anthony, Joseph William, Patricia Ann, Robert, Christopher. Rotating intern St. Joseph's Hosp., Phila., 1949-50; resident in ophthalmology Phila. Gen. Hosp., 1952-54; certified isotape methodology Hahnemann Med. Coll., Phila., 1960, asst. prof. ophthalmology, 1960-66, clin. asso. prof. nuclear medicine, 1974—; radioactive isotope dept. Wills Eye Hosp., Phila., 1956-61, sr. asst. surgeon, 1961-65, asso. surgeon, 1966-72, asso. surgeon retinal service, 1972—; attending ophthalmologist Holy Redeemer Hosp., Meadowbrook, Pa., 1963-65; asso. ophthalmologist Grand View Hosp., Sellersville, Pa., 1958-75; instr. ophthalmology Grad. Sch. Medicine, U. Pa., Phila., 1956-63; clin. asso. prof. ophthalmology Temple U., Phila., 1967-72; clin. asso. prof. ophthalmology Thomas Jefferson U. Sch. Medicine, Phila., 1971—; chief ophthalmology N. Pa. Hosp., Lansdale, 1959—, pres. staff, 1959; pres. Ophthalmic Assos., Lansdale, 1969—, Carcon Leasing Co., Lansdale, 1975—. Pres. bd. dirs. N. Pa. Symphony, 1976-78. Served to capt., M.C., U.S. Army, 1950-51. Named Outstanding Young Man of Year, Lansdale Jaycees, 1959, Outstanding Young Man State of Pa. Jaycees, 1960. Diplomate Am. Bd. Ophthalmology. Fellow A.C.S., Internat. Coll. Surgeons, Coll. Physicians Phila.; mem. AMA, Montgomery County, Pa. State med. socs., Am., Pa. acads. Ophthalmology, Assn. Research in Ophthalmology, Inter-County Ophthalmol. Soc. (pres. 1975-78), Ophthalmic Club Phila. (pres. 1964). Roman Catholic. Co-author: Nuclear Ophthalmology, 1976; contbr. chpts. to books, papers to profl. confs., articles to publs. in field. Home: Box 395 Montgomeryville PA 18936 Office: 1000 N Broad St Lansdale PA 19446

CARMICHAEL, VIRGIL WESLY, coal co. exec.; b. Pickering, Mo., Apr. 26, 1919; s. Ava Abraham and Rosevelt (Murphy) C.; B.S., U. Idaho, 1951, M.S., 1956; Ph.D., Columbia Pacific U., 1980; m. Colleen Fern Wadsworth, Oct. 29, 1951; children—Bonnie Rae, Peggy Ellen, Jacki Ann. Asst. geologist Day Mines, Wallace, Idaho, 1950; mining engr. De Anza Engring. Co., 1950-52; hwy. engring. asst. N.Mex. Hwy. Dept., Santa Fe, 1952-53; asst. engr. U. Idaho, also minerals analyst Idaho Bur. Mines, 1953-56; mining engr. No. Pacific Ry. Co., St. Paul, 1956-67; geologist N. Am. Coal Corp., Cleve., 1967-69, asst. v.p. engring., 1969-74, v.p., head exploration dept., 1974—. Asst. chief distbn. Civil Def. Emergency Mgmt. Fuel Resources for N.D., 1968—. Served with USNR, 1944-46. Recipient award 'A' for Sci. writing Sigma Gamma Epsilon. Registered geol., mining, civil engr., geologist, land surveyor. Mem. Am. Inst. Profl. Geologists (past pres. local chpt.), Rocky Mountain Coal Mining Inst. (v.p. 1978-80), N.D. Geol. Soc., Am. Inst. Mining Engrs., Soc. Mining Engrs. (chmn. N.D. sect. 1979-80), Am. Mining Congress (bd. govs. Western div. 1973—), Sigma Xi. Republican. Clubs: Kiwanis, Masons, Elks. Home: 1013 N Anderson St Bismarck ND 58501 Office: Kirkwood Office Tower Bismarck ND 58501

CARNER, WILLIAM JOHN, banker; b. Springfield, Mo., Aug. 9, 1948; s. John Wilson and Willie Marie (Moore) C.; A.B., Drury Coll., 1970; M.B.A., U. Mo., 1972; m. Dorothy Jean Edwards, June 12, 1976. Mktg. rep. 1st Nat. Bank Memphis, 1972-73; asst. br. mgr. Bank of Am., Los Angeles, 1973-74; dir. mktg. Commerce Bank, Springfield, Mo., 1974-76; affiliate mktg. mgr. 1st Union Bancorp., St. Louis, 1976-78; pres. Carner & Assos., Springfield, Mo., 1977—; instr. Drury Coll., 1975. Publicity chmn. Am. Cancer Soc., Greene County, Mo., 1974-78; treas. Jackson Day Com.; bd. dirs. Springfield (Mo.) Muscular Dystrophy Assn., 1975-76, Greater Ozarks council Camp Fire Girls. Mem. Bank Mktg. Assn., Assn. M.B.A. Execs., Savs. Industry Mktg. Soc. Am. (research com.). Democrat. Mem. Disciples of Christ Ch. Clubs: Hickory Hills Country, Kiwanis, Mason, Shrine. Home: 3605 S Parkhill Springfield MO 65807 Office: PO Box 1482 SSS Springfield MO 65807

CARNES, CHARLES ROY, JR., video engr.; b. Harrisburg, Pa., Dec. 1, 1930; s. Charles Roy and Catherine Margaret C.; grad. DeVry Tech. Inst., Chgo., 1955; m. Eleanor Jean Kauffman, Feb. 25, 1951; children—Carol Elaine, Ronald Alan. Engr., WKBO Radio, Harrisburg, Pa., 1955-57; asst. studio supr. WTPA-TV, Harrisburg, 1957-68; sr. video engr. WITF-TV, Hershey, Pa., 1968—; dir. Ida W. Browning Audio-Visual Trust, Harrisburg, 1977—. Served with USAR, 1950-59. Mem. Soc. Broadcast Engrs. (cert. sr. broadcast engr.). Democrat. Lutheran. Club: Execs. of Central Pa. Home: 14 Fox Chase Dr RD 1 Harrisburg PA 17111 Office: PO Box Z Hershey PA 17033

CARNEY, DENNIS JOSEPH, steel co. exec.; b. Charleroi, Pa., Mar. 19, 1921; s. Walter Augustus and Ann (Nandor) C.; B.S. in Metallurgy, Pa. State U., 1942; Sc.D., Mass. Inst. Tech., 1949; m. Virginia M. Horvath, June 12, 1943; children—Colleen A., Dennis Joseph, Glenn P., Lynn C., Dianne V. With U.S. Steel Corp., Pitts., 1942-74, gen. supt., 1963-65, v.p. long range planning, 1965-68, v.p. applied research, 1968-72, v.p. research, 1972-74; v.p. operations Wheeling-Pitts. Steel Corp., 1974-75, exec. v.p., dir., 1975-76, pres., 1976—, chief operating officer, 1976-77, chief exec. officer, 1977—, chmn. bd., 1978—. Bd. dirs. Wheeling (W.Va.) Coll. Served to lt. (j.g.) USNR, 1943-46. Fellow Am. Soc. Metals (Grossmann award Pitts. chpt. 1959, trustee 1972—); mem. Am., Brit., Internat. iron and steel insts., Am. Inst. Mining, Metall. and Petroleum Engrs. (McKune award 1951, Benjamin F. Fairless award 1978), Am. Iron and Steel Engrs., Sigma Xi, Tau Beta Pi, Sigma Nu. Clubs: South Hills Country, Duquesne (dir.) (Pitts.); Laurel Valley Country, Fox Chapel Country. Author: (with others) Gases in Metals, 1956. Home: 4536 Brownsville Rd Pittsburgh PA 15236 Office: 4 Gateway Center Pittsburgh PA 15230

CARNEY, ROBERT ARTHUR, restaurant exec.; b. Camden, N.J., Aug. 20, 1937; s. George Albert and Margret (Hollworth) C.; B.A., Ursinus Coll., 1963; 1 dau., Lynn Ann. Procurement agt. Campbell Soup Co., Paris, Tex., 1963-69, mgr. procurement, Salisbury, Md., 1969-72, dir. procurement, Camden, N.J., 1972-78; v.p. procurement Burger King Corp., Miami, Fla., 1978—. Served to capt. U.S. Army, 1958-60. Mem. Nat. Restaurant Assn. Republican. Roman Catholic. Office: 7360 N Kendall Dr Miami FL 33152

CARNEY, ROBERT JOSEPH, airline exec.; b. Worcester, Mass., July 22, 1940; s. Joseph F. and Helen A. (MacVicar) C.; A.B., Brown U., 1961; M.B.A., Harvard U., 1963; m. Nancy L. Doerr, May 19, 1973. Asso., Dillon, Read & Co., Inc., N.Y.C., 1964-65, S.G. Warburg & Co., Inc., N.Y.C., 1965-66; partner Lorenzo, Carney & Co., Inc., N.Y.C., 1966—; pres., dir. Jet Capital Corp., N.Y.C., 1970—; exec. v.p., dir. Tex. Internat. Airlines, Houston, 1972—. Trustee, Contemporary Arts Mus., Houston, 1975-78, Mus. Fine Arts, Houston, 1978—; mem. corp. devel. com. Brown U., 1979—, chmn., 1981—. Served with U.S. Army, 1963. Mem. Phi Beta Kappa. Clubs: Harvard (N.Y.); Harvard Bus. Sch. (dir.) (Houston). Home: 559 Westminster Houston TX 77024 Office: Tex Internat Airlines 2 Allen Center Houston TX 77002

CARNICK, CRAIG EVANS, fin. services exec.; b. Detroit, June 20, 1946; s. Albert Lee and Geraldine (Bremen) C.; B.A., Wayne State U., 1966. Gen. mgr. Top of the Tower Restaurant, Toledo, 1970-72; mgr. Leelanau Homestead Hotel, Glen Arbor, Mich., 1972-74; pres. Food ServCo., Inc., Glen Arbor, 1974-78; dir. services No. Mich., Asso. Fin. Planning, Empire, 1978—. Bd. dirs. Oakland County chpt. Big Brothers Am. Mem. Profl. Photographers Am., Am. Hotel-Motel Assn., North-Am. Assn. Hospitality Execs. (pres. 1976-77), Glen Lake C. of C. (pres.). Office: Asso Financial Planning Empire MI 49630

CAROLAN, THOMAS ROBERT, equipment rental co. exec.; b. Indpls., Sept. 7, 1939; s. Francis James and Eva Lou (Hicks) C.; B.S., Purdue U., 1961; M.B.A., U. So. Calif., 1974; m. Rita Ann Argenta, Aug. 26, 1961; children—Jeffrey Thomas, Steven Robert. Controller, treas. Kaufman & Broad Home Systems, Los Angeles, 1973-74; group controller Republic Corp., Los Angeles, 1974-77, treas., 1977-78; pres. Cal-U-Rent, Thousand Oaks, Calif., 1978—; dir. Interco Underwriters. Served to lt., Supply Corps, U.S. Navy, 1961-65. Mem. Calif. Rental Assn., Am. Rental Assn. Republican. Presbyterian. Club: Las Posas Country (treas. 1978-80). Home: 1080 Valley Vista Dr Camarillo CA 93010 Office: 661 E Thousand Oaks Blvd Thousand Oaks CA 91360

CARON, ARTHUR EUGENE, mfg. co. exec.; b. Pawtucket, R.I., Jan. 1, 1937; s. Arthur Octave and Louisiane (Tetu) C.; B.S. in Bus. Adminstrn. summa cum laude, Bryant Coll., Providence, 1962; M.B.A., Northeastern U., Boston, 1967; m. Diana Theresa Studley, July 20, 1963; children—William, Arthur, Robert. Mgr. mfg. engring., asst. to gen. mgr. Chapman div. Crane Co., Indian Orchard, Mass., 1968-69; mgr. mfg. Springfield (Mass.) Cast Products div. Koehring Co., 1969-72, pres., gen. mgr., 1972-75; gen. mgr. Uniloy Springfield div. Hoover Ball & Bearing Co., 1975-78; pres., chief exec. officer Anchor/Darling Valve Co., Bala Cynwyd, Pa., 1978—; mem. bus. faculty, vis. lectr. M.B.A. program Am. Internat. Coll., Springfield, 1969-78. Served with USAF, 1954-58. Mem. Am. Prodn. and Inventory Control Soc. (past chpt. dir.). Home: 30 Williams Rd Haverford PA 19041 Office: 1 Belmont Ave Bala Cynwyd PA 19004

CAROTHERS, CRAIG HORN, mgmt. cons.; b. Platte City, Mo., Dec. 2, 1946; s. Victor L. and Margaret Helen (Horn) C.; B.A., William Jewell Coll., 1968; M.A., Sangamon State U., 1978; m. Linda S. Horvath, Feb. 6, 1971; children—Brian, Kevin. Programmer, analyst Nat. Car Rental Co., Bloomington, Minn., 1972-75; systems analyst Ill. Dept. Pub. Aid, Springfield, 1975-76, mgr. systems and program devel. Ill. Dept. Children and Family Services, 1976-78; cons. Resource Mgmt. Assos., Springfield, 1978-80; pres. Diversified Systems Services, 1980—. Served to capt. U.S. Army, 1968-72. Mem. Am. Pub. Welfare Assn. Home: 907 Belpre Dr O'Fallon IL 62269

CAROUSO, NICHOLAS HARRY, mining exec.; b. Oakland, Calif., Mar. 25, 1920; s. Victor Harry and Nina (Mitchell) C.: student St. Mary's Coll., 1946-47; B.A., U. Calif., 1950, M.S., 1959; postgrad. U. Nev., 1956-57, U. Ariz., 1968—; m. Barbara Elizabeth Stephenson, Feb. 2, 1952; children—Mark Nicholas, Joan Patricia, Valerie Elizabeth. Sr. research engr. Berkeley Research Co. (Calif.), 1957-59; geophys. engr. Phelps Dodge Corp., Douglas, Ariz., 1959; plant prodn. engr. Eitel-McCullough, Inc., San Bruno, Calif., 1959-61; concentrator metall. engr. Kennecott Copper Corp., Hayden, Ariz., 1961-65; mgmt. supr., cons. Bonanza-MJV, Superior, Ariz., 1969-70; pres., dir. Copper Mountain Mines, Inc., Payson, Ariz., 1966—, Geo-Processing, Inc., Miami, Ariz., 1971—; mining cons. Ibex Keystone Mine, Nev.; mineral exploration cons. Capt. Kearny Vol. Fire Dept., 1964-65. Served with USNR, World War II. Mem. Am. Inst. Mining, Metall. and Petroleum Engrs., Ariz. Geol. Soc., Am. Radio Relay League. Republican. Episcopalian. Inventor distance calculator, 1955. Home: 800 Ellendale Dr #19 Medford OR 97501

CARPENTER, BETTE MARIE (MRS. HERBERT LARSON CARPENTER), Realtor; b. Hemet, Calif., Mar. 8, 1927; d. Scott William and Eugenia LeProhon (de Beaufort) Carl; student Oceanside Jr. Coll., 1943-45, U. Calif. at Los Angeles, 1946-47; m. Herbert Larson Carpenter, May 6, 1944; 1 dau., Carolyn Lee Carpenter Dabbs. Propr., Bette M. Carpenter, Realtors, Carlsbad and Riverside, Calif., 1954-60; pres. Interstate Equities Corp., Carlsbad, 1960—; v.p., sec. LanInCo Corp. Nev., Las Vegas, 1964-75; v.p. mktg. Parkside Devel. Co., Santa Ana, Calif.; sec.-treas. Baylor Enterprises, Inc., Rancho, Calif., 1976—. Mem. Carlsbad Bd. Realtors (charter mem.), Calif. Real Estate Assn., Nat. Assn. Real Estate Bds., Nat. Inst. Real Estate Brokers, Urban Land Inst., Women Council Realtors, Carlsbad C. of C. Republican. Home: PO Box 254 Carlsbad CA 92008 Office: 4871 El Camino Real Carlsbad CA 92008

CARPENTER, LYLE DEAN, mortgage banker; b. Yuma, Colo., Aug. 3, 1941; s. Clifford Henry and Alice Emily C.; B.A., Colo. State U., 1964; m. Carole June Hauge, June 16, 1963; children—Randle Dean, Carrie Leigh. Broker, Mortgage Finance, Inc., Denver, 1964-65, loan officer, 1965-66, pres., dir., 1966—; pres., dir. Farm Appraisal Ranch Mgmt., Inc., Denver, 1971—. Nat. pres. Future Farmers Am., 1960-61. Mem. Nat. Assn. Rev. Appraisers (cert.; regional v.p. 1980), Denver Agrl. Livestock Club (pres. 1975), Omicron Delta Kappa, Alpha Gamma Rho. Republican. Methodist. Home: 5285 E 6th Ave Pkwy Denver CO 80220 Office: 1600 Broadway Denver CO 80202

CARPENTER, PENELOPE DAWN, hotel exec.; b. Portland, July 23, 1947; d. Donald Elmore and Magdalena Margaret (Lomnicki) C.; B.S., U. Oreg., 1969, postgrad. (fellow), 1979. Asst. dir. central recreation center City of San Mateo (Calif.), 1969-70; mgmt. trainee Sheraton-Palace Hotel, San Francisco, 1972-73; catering mgr. Valley River Inn, Eugene, Oreg., 1973-80, Hyatt Del Monte, Monterey, 1980—; guest lectr. Lane Community Coll., U. Oreg., Eugene Bus. Sch. Mem. Eugene Mayor's Commn. on Women; bd. dirs. Planned Parenthood, Eugene; precinct committeewoman Republican Party, Eugene. Mem. Am. Hotel Motel Assn., NW Hotel Motel Sales Assn., Emerald Empire Conv. Assn. (dir.), Mid-Oreg. Advt. Club, C. of C. (tourism and recreation commn.), AAUW (dir.; fellow to Women in Corp. World, Washington), Alpha Chi Omega, Patrons of Phi Beta Frat. Roman Catholic. Clubs: DAR, Jr. League of Monterey, Navy League U.S. Home: 500 Glenwood Circle #222 Monterey CA 93940 Office: One Old Golf Course Rd Monterey CA 93940

CARPENTER, RICHARD JOHN, JR., mgmt. cons.; b. Portland, Maine, May 3, 1940; s. Richard John and Eleanor Elizabeth (Marino) C.; student U. Maine, 1960-61; B. Psychology-Sociology, Western State Coll., Gunnison, Colo., 1963; M.B.A., U. Utah, 1969; M.S. in Edn., Wilkes Coll., 1975; postgrad. Law Sch., Gonzaga U., 1978—; m. Lois Virginia Stoker, Aug. 16, 1967; children—Ken Steven, Kristi Linda. Commd. 2d. lt. U.S. Air Force, 1964, advanced through grades to capt., 1979; logistical plans mgr., 1968-70; exec. to dir. material mgmt., 1970-72; adminstrv./ednl. liaison, 1972-75; ops. mgr., 1975-77; engring. comptroller, 1977-78, discharged, 1979; pres. Carpenter Cons. Assos., Spokane, 1976—. Founder, pres. Greater Spokane Racquetball League, 1976—; treas., elder Whitworth Community Presbyterian Ch.; past v.p. Farwell Elem. Sch. Parent Tchrs. Orgn. Decorated Commendation medal with 3 oak leaf clusters; award Freedoms Found. at Valley Forge, 1970; U. Mont.

fellow, 1964. Mem. Am. Purchase Mgmt. Assn., Christian Legal Soc., U.S. Racquetball Assn., Internat. Racquetball Assn., VFW (life). Republican. Clubs: Kiwanis, Toastmasters, North Park Racquet, Masons, Eagles. Home and Office: 15123 Little Spokane Dr Spokane WA 99208

CARPENTER, STANLEY WATERMAN, paper co. exec.; b. Lowell, Mass., June 25, 1921; s. Daniel Albert and Edith May (Redfern) C.; student Lowell Textile Inst., 1939-42; m. Marie Kurth, May 12, 1957; children—Cheryl J., Mark S. With Thorp & Martin Co., Boston, 1947-49; self employed distbr. Ditto, Inc., 1949-51; marketing mgr. U.S. Envelope Co., Springfield, Mass., 1951-65; with N.Y. Envelope Corp., L.I., N.Y., 1965—, v.p. sales, 1969-80, group v.p. mktg., 1980—. Asst. dir. CD, Bedford, Mass., 1946-49. Served with AUS, 1942-46. Decorated Army Commendation medal. Mem. Am. Mktg. Assn., So. Paper Trade, Midwest Paper Trade Assn. Clubs: Saugatuck Harbor Yacht (Westport, Conn.); Connecticut Gun Guild (Hartford). Home: 14 Owenoke Park Westport CT 06880 Office: 29-10 Hunters Point Ave Long Island City NY 11101

CARPENTER, VIVIAN LAVERNE, Mich. state ofcl.; b. Detroit, Nov. 3, 1952; d. Doyal W. and Jennie P. Thomas; B.S., U. Mich., 1973, M.B.A., 1975; m. Alden J. Carpenter, June 22, 1975. Research engr. Ford Motor Co., Dearborn, Mich., summers 1972, 73; sr. cons. Arthur Andersen & Co., Detroit, 1975-77; instr. U. Mich., 1977-78; dep. state treas. Mich. Dept. Treasury, Lansing, 1978—, disclosure chmn. Nat. State Auditors Coordinating Com., 1979-80, mem. User's Com., Nat. Council on Govtl. Acctg., 1980. Regional dir. Nat. Council on Alcoholism, 1980. Ford Found. grantee, 1978; C.P.A., Mich. Mem. Am. Inst. C.P.A.'s, Mich. Assn. C.P.A.'s, Nat. Assn. Black Accts., Mcpl. Fin. Officers Assn., Alpha Kappa Alpha. Office: Mich Dept Treasury Treasury Bldg Lansing MI 48922

CARPENTIER, POSEY (MRS. CHARLES NELSON CARPENTIER), real estate exec.; b. Hillsboro, Tex., Apr. 2, 1919; d. Homer H. and Itylene (Moore) Posey; A.A., Hillsboro Jr. Coll., 1939; B.A., U. Calif. at Los Angeles, 1975, M.A. in English; m. Charles Nelson Carpentier, Nov. 14, 1953 (dec. Oct. 23, 1978); children—Carla, Nelson. Dept. head Air Assos., Dallas, 1940-43, Los Angeles, 1943-45; personnel mgr. N.Am. Aviation Co., Los Angeles, 1947-50; dir. clerical personnel dept. Hughes Aircraft Co., Culver City, Calif., 1951-57; pres. Posey Carpentier Realty, Inc., Malibu, 1968—, Car-Nel Properties Investment Co., 1976—, Carpentier Mgmt. Co., 1978—; mgr., leasing agt. Pointe Dume Shopping Center, Malibu; dir., chmn. loan com. 1st Women's Bank of Calif., Los Angeles; mem. faculty Santa Monica (Calif.) Coll., 1975—; lectr. on property mgmt. and real estate. Pres. PTA, Webster Sch., Malibu, 1968-69, Malibu Park Jr. High Sch., 1971-72; historian Santa Monica PTA Council, 1972-73; bd. dirs. South Bay area Drug Abuse Council, 1971-73, Malibu Drug Action Bd., chmn., 1971-73; founder Los Angeles Music Center. Certified property mgr. Grad. Realtors Inst. Mem. Internat. Assn. Realtors, Nat. Assn. Realtors (dir. UCLA chpt.), Calif. Assn. Realtors (dir. 1973-77, vice chmn. property mgmt. div. 1977-78, regional v.p. 1978, mem. faculty, seminar speaker, editor Property Mgmt. mag. 1976-78), Malibu Bd. Realtors (dir. 1971-75, pres. 1972-73), Women in Bus., Nat. Women's Polit. Caucus, Women for Los Angeles County Mus. Contbr. articles to profl. publs. Democrat. Home: 3868 Rambla Orienta Malibu CA 90265 Office: 21361 Pacific Coast Hwy Box 116S Malibu CA 90265

CARR, ARTHUR, data communications mfg. co. exec.; b. Newark, July 9, 1931; s. Michael Thomas and Gertrude A. (Levy) C.; grad. pub. schs.; m. Virginia Lea Merry, July 11, 1953; children—Karen, Vickie, William. Field tech. specialist Remington Rand Univac, Boston, 1955-61; dir. mktg. Computer Control div. Honeywell, Framingham, Mass., 1961-68; v.p. mktg. Codex Corp., Mansfield, Mass., 1968-70, pres., chief exec., 1970—, also dir.; v.p. Motorola Inc., 1979—; dir. Prime Computer Inc. Mem. Recreation Com., Ashland, Mass., 1969. Served with USN, 1951-55. Mem. Ind. Data Communications Mfrs. Assn. (v.p., dir. 1971—). Mem. Federated Ch. (dir. 1964-69, 74-77). Home: 44 Donnelly Dr Dover MA 02030 Office: 20 Cabot Blvd Mansfield MA 02030

CARR, HAROLD NOFLET, airline exec.; b. Kansas City, Kans., Mar. 14, 1921; s. Noflet B. and Mildred (Addison) C.; B.S., Tex. A. and M. U., 1943; postgrad. Am. U., 1944-46; m. Mary Elizabeth Smith, Aug. 5, 1944; children—Steven Addison, Hal Douglas, James Taylor, Scott Noflet. Asst. dir. route devel. Trans World Airlines, Inc., 1943-47; exec. v.p. Wis. Central Airlines, Inc., 1947-52; mem. firm McKinsey & Co., 1952-54; pres. North Central Airlines, Inc., 1954-69, chmn., 1965-79; chmn. Republic Airlines, Inc., 1979—, also dir.; dir. Dahlberg Electronics, Inc., Ross Industries, Inc., Stange Co., Republic Energy, Inc., Governor's Sound, Inc., Cayman Water Co., Westland Capital Corp.; professorial lectr. mgmt. engring. Am. U., 1952-62. Bd. dirs. Minn. Safety Council; trustee Tex. A. & M. Research Found.; bd. nominations Nat. Aviation Hall of Fame; mem. adv. com. Tex. Transp. Inst., Tex. A. & M. U. System, devel. council Coll. of Bus., Tex. A & M U. Mem. World Bus. Council, Am. Mgmt. Assn., Air Transport Assn., Assn. Local Transport Airlines, Nat. Def. Transp. Assn., Am. Econ. Assn., Minn. Execs. Orgn., Greater Mpls., St. Paul Area chambers commerce, Am. Assn. Airport Execs., Nat. Aero Assn., Smithsonian Assos., Nat. Trust for Historic Preservation, Tex. A. & M. Former Students Assn. Clubs: Aero, Nat. Aviation (Washington); Stearman Alumnus (Wichita, Kans.); Mpls.; Aggie (dir.); Tex. A. & M. Century (College Station); Briarcrest Country (Bryan, Tex.); Racquet (Miami, Fla.); Wings (N.Y.C.); Gull Lake Yacht (Brainerd, Minn.). Address: PO Box H Bryan TX 77801

CARR, KENNETH WILLIAM, cosmetic mfg. co. exec.; b. Chgo., Jan. 27, 1940; s. William Wesley and Anita Leonie (Dickey) C.; A.S., St. Clair County Community Coll., 1960; student Mich. State U., 1960-63; m. Nancy Ellen Lowrie, Aug. 22, 1965; 1 son, Todd William. Key account sales rep. for Ohio, Mich. and Ind., Chesebrough-Pond's, N.Y.C., 1964-67; account mgr. for Ohio and Ill., Revlon, Inc., N.Y.C., 1967-72, Midwest regional mgr. Dept. Store div., 1972-74; Midwest regional sales dir. Orlane div. Norton-Simon Co., N.Y.C., 1974—. Mem. aesthetics com. Schaumburg. Mem. Am. Mgmt. Assn., Mercedes Benz Club N.Am. Home: 202 N Dewey Rd Inverness IL 60067 Office: 499 Park Ave New York NY 10022

CARR, RICHARD THOMAS, banker; b. Chgo., Dec. 22, 1936; s. Thomas W. and Shirley M. (Perrin) C.; student St. Mary's U., 1957-58, San Antonio Coll., 1957-58, Palm Beach Jr. Coll., 1958-60; Am. Inst. Banking, 1959-65; grad. Stonier Grad. Sch. Banking, Rutgers U., 1969, Inst. Fin. Mgmt., Harvard Grad. Sch. Bus., 1972; m. Doreen Susan Van Valkenburg, Mar. 3, 1962; children—Michael Orren, Thomas Perrin. Auditing, First Nat. Bank, Delray Beach, Fla., 1954-61; asst. nat. bank examiner Office Comptroller of the Currency, Atlanta, 1961-63, adminstrv. asst., Washington, 1963-64, dir. personnel planning and devel., 1964-66, nat. bank examiner 5th nat. bank region, Richmond, Va., 1966; cashier Calhoun (Ga.) Nat. Bank (name changed to Calhoun First Nat. Bank 1970), 1970-73, pres., 1973; chief exec. officer N.W. Ga. Bank, Ringgold, 1973-78, also mem. exec. com., dir.; asst. to pres. Jorges Carpet Mills, Ft. Oglethorpe-Rossville, Ga., 1978—; instr. in bus. devel. Ga. Bankers Sch., U. Ga., 1971-73. Pres. Gordon County (Ga.) Community Chest United Fund, 1967-68; chmn. advancement com. Gordon County unit Boy Scouts Am., 1967-69; pres. Am. Cancer Soc., Gordon County, 1968-69; chmn. City of Calhoun Bd. Edn., 1969-73; treas. Calhoun Presbyterian Ch., 1966-68; bd. dirs. ARC, Calhoun, 1966-67, State of Ga. YMCA, 1969-76; bd. dirs. Cherokee Boys Estate, chmn., 1971-76; bd. dirs. Jr. Achievement, Calhoun, counseling adviser, 1970-72. Served with USAF, 1955-58. Mem. Bank Mktg. Assn. (state chmn. 1969-73, ednl. adv. com. 1971-72), Small Bus. Assn., Ga. C. of C., Ga. Bankers Assn., Am. Inst. Banking (instr. 1969-71), Bank Adminstrn. Inst. Clubs: Kiwanis (pres. 1968-69), Rotary (dir. 1973-76, pres. 1977-78), Elks, Ringgold Athletic Booster. Home: PO Box 567 Ringgold GA 30786 Office: PO Box J Ringgold GA 30736

CARRABBA, MICHAEL PAUL, aircraft components mfg. co. exec.; b. Dayton, Ohio, Jan. 31, 1945; s. Paul G. and Margie (Nichols) C.; student Miami Dade Jr. Coll., 1962—; m. Carol Frances Young, Nov. 1, 1968. Gen. mgr. D.C. Airparts Corp., Hialeah, Fla., 1969-70, pres., owner, 1970—, also chmn. bd.; pres. D.C. Airparts Battery Co., Inc., 1974—, D.C. Airparts Battery of Europe, GmbH, D.C. Battery Co. (Exide). Served with USMCR, 1962-66. Mem. Nat. Pilots Assn., Helicopter Assn. Am., Nat. Bus. Aircraft Assn., Aviation Maintenance Found., Am. Helicopter Soc., Profl. Aviation Maintenance Assn., Nat. Air Transp. Conf. Home: 10175 SW 53 St Cooper City FL 33328 Office: 485 W 27th St Hialeah FL 33010

CARRAGHER, FRANK ANTHONY, chem. co. exec.; b. Belleville, N.J., Feb. 4, 1932; s. Frank A. and Margaret R. (Mallack) C.; B.S., Rutgers U., 1953; postgrad. Newark Coll. Engring., 1955; m. Eunice M. Burns, Oct. 2, 1955; children—Tracey, Phil, Judy, Matt, Susan, Frank, Marybeth. Dist. mgr. Ariz. Chem. Co., 1956-58; regional mgr. Humko div. Nat. Dairy Products, 1958-66; sr. v.p. mktg., research and devel. Glyco Chems., Inc., Greenwich, Conn., 1966-76, also dir.; exec. v.p. Petrochems. Co., Inc. subs. Chattem Drug & Chem. Co., Fort Worth, 1976-77; v.p., gen. mgr. Quad Chem. Corp., Long Beach, Calif., 1977-79; group v.p. chems. Ferro Corp., Cleve., 1979—; asso. dir. MCA. Mem. Wilton (Conn.) Sch. Bd. Served with USMC, 1953-55. Mem. Am. Oil Chemists Assn., Plastic Engrs. Soc., Soap and Detergent Assn., Am. Textile Assn., Comml. Devel. Assn. Roman Catholic. Clubs: Chemists, Cleve. Athletic, Univ. Home: 1080 Sheerbrook Dr Chagrin Falls OH Office: Ferro Corp One Erieview Plaza Cleveland OH 44114

CARRELL, TERRY EUGENE, controls co. exec.: b. Monmouth, Ill., July 1, 1938; s. Roy Edwin and Caroline Hilma (Fillman) C.; A.B., Monmouth Coll., 1961; M.B.A., Calif. State U., Los Angeles, 1967; D.B.A., U. So. Calif., 1970; m. Bonnie Lee Clements, July 11, 1964; children—Philip Edwin, Andrew David. Prin. engr. reconnaissance and communications N.Am. Aviation, 1963-67; mgr. avionics analysis and techs. B-1 div. Rockwell Internat., 1967-73, dir. engring. Morse Controls div., 1973-74; gen. mgr. Morse Controls div. Incom Internat. Inc., 1974-78, pres. indsl. div. Morse Controls, 1978-80, pres. Morse Controls, 1980—; cons.; lectr. U. So. Calif., 1967-70. Mem. Hudson (Ohio) Econ. Devel. Com., 1979—; dist. council commr. Boy Scouts Am., 1980—; mem. service rev. panel United Way of Summit County, 1980. NDEA fellow, 1961-63. Mem. Hudson C. of C. (trustee 1976-78), Boating Industry Assn. (chmn. steering task force 1974—), Am. Boat and Yacht Council (dir. 1980—). Contbr. articles to profl. jours. Patentee in field. Home: 7712 Valley View Hudson OH 44236 Office: 21 Clinton St Hudson OH 44236

CARRERE, CHARLES SCOTT, judge; b. Dublin, Ga., Sept. 26, 1937; B.A., U. Ga., 1959; LL.B., Stetson U., 1961. Admitted to Fla. bar, 1961, Ga. bar, 1960; law clk. to U.S. dist. judge, Orlando, Fla., 1962-63; asst. U.S. atty. Middle Dist. Fla., 1963-66, chief trial atty., 1965-66, spl. asst. to U.S. atty., 1966-67; partner firm Harrison, Greene, Mann, Rowe & Stanton, St. Petersburg, 1970-80; county judge Pinellas County (Fla.), 1980—. Served with inf. AUS. Mem. Am., Fla., St. Petersburg bar assns., Stetson Lawyers Assn. (dir. 1968), Phi Beta Kappa, Phi Delta Phi. Office: 115 17th Ave NE Saint Petersburg FL 33704

CARRET, PHILIP L., business exec.; b. Lynn, Mass., Nov. 29, 1896; s. James R. and Hannah (Todd) C.; A.B., Harvard, 1917, student Grad. Sch. Bus. Adminstrn., 1916-17; m. Elisabeth Osgood, Sept. 4, 1922; children—Gerard O., Donald, Diane E. Mem. staff Barron's Weekly, 1922-26; economist Blyth & Co., N.Y.C., 1927-32; partner various firms, 1932—; chmn. bd. Pioneer Fund, Inc.; pres. Carret & Co., Inc.; dir. various corps. Trustee Scarsdale Bd. Edn., 1941-46. Served to 1st lt. aviation sect. Signal Corps (later Air Corps), U.S. Army, 1917-19. Mem. Am. Legion. Republican. Conglist. Clubs: Harvard, Explorers (N.Y.C.); Scarsdale Golf. Author: The Art of Speculation, 1926. Contbr. mag. articles to Barron's and other publs. Home: 50 Popham Rd Scarsdale NY 10583 Office: 200 Park Ave New York NY 10017

CARRICO, JAMES EARL, govt. ofcl.; b. Beloit, Kans., Sept. 29, 1938; s. Elbert Charles and Winifred Marcella (Sheahon) C.; B.S., Kans. State U., 1961; m. Darby K. Costello, Nov. 6, 1971. Tng. adminstr. Naval Sea Systems Command, Washington, 1967-74; energy conservation specialist Fed. Energy Adminstrn., Washington, 1974-76; dir. field ops. Del. Carter-Mondale campaign, 1976; staff asst. to Sec. Navy, Washington, 1977; dir. tng., adminstrv. officer Chief of Naval Ops., Washington, 1977—; cons. engr., tech. writer Vector Research Corp., Gaithersburg, Md., 1976-77. Active Big Bros. Washington. Served to lt. USN, 1961-67. Decorated Vietnam Service & Campaign medal, Navy Expeditionary medal (Cuba). Mem. Res. Officers Assn. (pres. D.C. chpt.), Naval Res. Assn. (gen. chmn. congressional reception; D.C. chpt. pres.; dist. v.p.). Democrat. Roman Catholic. Club: Touchdown of Washington. Contbr. research articles to profl. publs. Home: 2555 Pennsylvania Ave NW Washington DC 20037

CARRIER, VIRGIL ELMER, lawyer, engr., corp. exec.; b. Winfield, Kans., Oct. 30, 1930; s. Virgil C. and Mary N. (Reeves) C.; student Wichita State U., 1948-50; B.S. in Mech. Engring., Kans. State U., 1955; J.D., U. Denver, 1968; m. Rita D. Ramos, Feb. 22, 1974; children—Chris Alan, Sheri Su, Clay Edward, William Jude, Andrew David. Cons. engr. E.E. Hysom & Assos., Wichita, Kans., 1955-56; dist. mgr. Trane Co., Denver, 1956-68; owner VEC Service Co., Denver, 1960-68; admitted to Colo. bar, 1968, also Fed. Dist. bar, 10th Circuit Ct. Appeals bar; asso. law Nagel & Clark, Denver, 1968-73; pres. VEC Corp., Denver, 1970-73; gen. counsel Beckett-Harmon Assos., Inc., Denver, 1973-76; pres. Energy Mgmt. Cons., Inc., Denver, 1973—, also dir.; v.p., sec., gen. counsel, dir. Beckett, Harmon, Carrier & Day Inc., Denver, 1976—; v.p., sec., dir. INDEVCO II, Inc., Denver, 1975—; dir. Mountain Internat. Corp., Marshall and Scott, Inc., Mobile Home Specialists Am., Inc., Denver; vis. lectr. Environ. Design Coll., U. Colo., 1974. Treas., Franklin Assn. for Childhood Edn., Franklin Sch., 1969; mem. budget com. Arapahoe County (Colo.) Pub. Schs., 1969; deacon S. Suburban Christian Ch.; bd. dirs. Christian Youth of Denver, 1970-72; mem. Greenbelt com. City of Greenwood Village (Colo.), 1977. Served with USAF, 1950-52. Recipient Commendation for outstanding performance of duty, Weather Service. Registered profl. engr., certified cons. engr., Colo., Kans., Okla. Mem. Am., Colo., Arapahoe County, Denver bar assns., ASHRAE, Assn. Energy Engrs., Cons. Engrs. Council, Internat. Trade Assn. Colo., Nat., Colo. socs. profl. engrs., Profl. Engrs. Colo., Colo. Soc. Engrs., Sigma Tau, Pi Tau Sigma. Republican. Club: Denver Athletic. Home: 1789 Green Oaks Dr Littleton (Greenwood Village) CO 80121 Office: 7200 W Alameda Suite 500 Denver CO 80226

CARRIKER, RUSSELL LLOYD, bus. and tech. tng. sch. adminstr.; b. Ord, Nebr., Dec. 29, 1932; s. Lloyd Franklin and Loye Goldie (Weber) C.; grad. in accounting Nat. Bus. Coll., Lincoln, Nebr., 1959; m. Jayne Elinor Wunderlich, Apr. 27, 1957; 1 son, Thomas Andrew. Engring. aide Nebr. Dept. Roads, Lincoln, 1951-57; dir. data processing Nat. Bus. Coll., Lincoln, 1959-61; co-founder, sch. dir. Automation Inst., Kansas City, Mo., 1961-69; sch. dir. Control Data Corp., Chgo., 1970-71, Manpower Bus. Tng. Inst., Manpower, Inc., St. Louis, 1971-73; with ITT Ednl. Services, Inc., 1973—; sch. dir. Hammel-Actual Coll., Akron, Ohio, 1973-74, ITT Tech. Inst., Boston, 1974-75, Taylor Bus. Inst., L.I., N.Y., 1976-79, ITT Tech. Inst., Chelsea, Mass., 1980—; past pres. Systems & Procedures Assn., Kansas City, Mo. Home: 26 Pine Ridge Rd North Reading MA 01864

CARROLL, CHARLES FRANCIS, public relations exec.; b. Cedar Rapids, Iowa, May 23, 1927; s. Frank Timothy and Florence Helen (Schulze) C.; B.A. in Journalism, U. Iowa, 1949, M.A., 1950; m. Yvonne Burkett, Oct. 1, 1954; children—Charles, Paul, Timothy, Anne, Martha, Amy, Kathryn, Jennifer. Desk editor Des Moines (Iowa) Register, 1950-54, Wall St. Jour., N.Y.C., 1954-55; editor, fin. writer N.Y. Herald Tribune, 1955-59; with Westinghouse Electric Corp., Pitts., 1959—, dir. corp. public relations, 1976—; lectr. journalism Drake U., 1953-54. Served with USN, 1945-46, 51-52. Mem. Nat. Investor Relations Inst., N.Y. Fin. Writers. Roman Catholic. Clubs: Pitts. Press. Home: 255 Inglewood Dr Pittsburgh PA 15228 Office: Westinghouse Bldg Gateway Center Pittsburgh PA 15222

CARROLL, DANIEL THUERING, mfg. co. exec.; b. Burlington, Vt., Mar. 21, 1926; s. Daniel B. and Viola T. (Thuering) C.; A.B., Dartmouth, 1947; M.A., U. Minn., 1948; postgrad. U. Chgo.; m. Julie Anne Virgo, Aug. 20, 1977; children—Laura L., Lisa D., Daniel K., Grant T. Asst. to mgmt. engring. Navy Dept., Washington, 1950-54; with Booz, Allen & Hamilton, Inc., 1954-72; pres., dir. Gould Inc., Chgo., 1972-80; pres., chief exec. officer, dir. Hoover Universal, Inc., 1980—; dir. Van Straaten Chem. Co., Conrac Corp., Nat. Bank & Trust Co. Ann Arbor, Diebold, Inc., Combined Internat. Corp., Wolverine WorldWide, Inc. Bd. dirs. Chgo. Urban League; trustee Case Western Res. U.; trustee, chmn. Colgate Rochester Div. Sch., Bexley Hall. Served with USNR, 1944-46. Home: 5183 Christine Dr Ann Arbor MI 48103 Office: PO Box 1003 Ann Arbor MI 48106

CARROLL, DONALD CARY, coll. adminstr.; b. Durham, N.C., Nov. 5, 1930; s. Dudley Dewitt and Eleanore Dixon (Elliott) C.; B.S. in Math., U. N.C., 1954; S.M., M.I.T., 1958, Ph.D. in Indsl. Mgmt., 1965; M.A., (hon.), U. Pa., 1972; children—Curtis James, Leah Anne. Staff asst. PPG Industries, Pitts., 1958-59; cons. Westinghouse Electric, Pitts., 1959-60; teaching intern M.I.T., 1960-61, asst. prof., 1961-65, asso. prof., 1965-68, prof., 1968-71; pres. TMI Systems Corp., Lexington, Mass., 1969-72, chmn., 1969—; Reliance prof. pvt. enterprise The Wharton Sch. U. Pa., 1972—, dean, 1972—; dir. Arlen Realty Inc., Monsanto Co., Morse Shoe Inc., SEI Corp., Nat. Railway Utilization Corp., Vestaur Securities Inc., MacAndrews and Forbes, Inc. Visitor Harvard U., 1974—, Tufts U., 1978—; trustee Bryn Mawr Coll., 1978—. Served with USMC, 1948-49, 54-56. Sloan fellow, 1960-61, Ford fellow, 1963-64. Mem. Inst. Mgmt. Scis., Phi Beta Kappa, Tau Beta Pi, Beta Gamma Sigma. Office: The Wharton School University of Pennsylvania Philadelphia PA 19104

CARROLL, GEORGE DEEKS, ins. co. exec.; b. Mpls., Mar. 27, 1916; s. Joseph Douglas and Dorothy Elizabeth (Deeks) C.; B.S. in Commerce, Northwestern U., 1937; m. Marguerite Ray, Nov. 19, 1938; children—George Deeks, Judith Ray Carroll Smith. With Spl. Agts. Sch., Employers Liability Assurance Corp., Boston and Chgo., 1938-42; with Marsh & McLennan Inc., Chgo., 1942—, asst. v.p., 1956-58, v.p., 1958—; past pres., dir. Ridge Investors Trust. Founder with White Sox, 1st Chgo. Little League, 1952; past pres., bd. dirs. Laguna Woods Home Owners Assn.; mem. exec. bd. Chgo. council Boy Scouts Am., 1962-76. Republican. Congregationalist. Clubs: Union League (Chgo.); Midlothian Country (dir.). Home: PO Box 461 Palos Park IL 60464 also Route 3 Box 26A Woodruff WI 54568 Office: 222 S Riverside Dr Chicago IL 60606

CARROLL, HARRY MATTERN, food co. exec.; b. Philipsburg, Pa., May 22, 1932; s. James Michael and Doris Elizabeth (Mattern) C.; B.A., Pa. State U., 1954, M.A., 1957; J.D., Duquesne U., 1968; m. Gloria Faye Mau, June 21, 1958. News dir., WCAE Radio, 1957-60; public relations asst. Blue Cross of Western Pa., 1960-65; public relations dir. Western Pa. Conservancy, 1965-67; U.S. public relations mgr. Heinz U.S.A., 1967-69; 1969-71. gen. mgr. communications, 1971—; public relations dir. Howard Johnson Co., Adv. bd. Bidwell Cultural and Tng. Center, 1973—; bd. dirs. Center for Assessment and Treatment Youth, Sickle Cell Anemia Soc. S.W. Pa., Pitts. Visitors and Convention Bur. Served with AUS, 1954-56. Mem. Public Relations Soc. Am., Am. Bar Assn., Soc. Consumer Affairs Profls., Pitts. Press Club. Office: Box 57 Pittsburgh PA 15230

CARROLL, JOHN, fin. cons.; b. Emmetsburg, Iowa, Nov. 14, 1926; s. Oliver Phillip and Marie Naoma (Ross) C.; B.S. in Bus. Adminstrn., Drake U., 1952; m. Joyce Irene Bradley, Dec. 11, 1947; children—John B., Victoria, Linda. Jr. auditor Haskins & Sells, Dallas, 1952-54; fin. analyst, prodn. acct. Caracas & Lagunillas, Venezuela, 1954-57; mgr. Deloitte, Plender, Haskins & Sells, Caracas, 1957-58; adminstr. Wyeth Labs., Caracas, 1958-60; v.p. Petare Textil, Caracas, 1961-63; mgr. internat. acquisitions Celanese Corp. Am., N.Y.C., 1963-65; controller Beauknit Textile, N.Y.C., 1965-66; sr. fin. cons. Middle West Service Co., Chgo., Saudi Arabia, S. Am., Africa, and SE Asia, 1966-74, prin. cons., Dallas, 1979-80; public utility industry specialist Deloitte, Haskins & Sells, Dallas, 1980—; sr. cons. Can. Internat. Power, S. Am. and Can., 1974-77, Charles T. Main Internat., Saudi Arabia and Boston, 1977-79. Served with U.S. Army and USAAF, 1944-49. C.P.A., Tex. Mem. Am. Inst. C.P.A.'s. Republican. Presbyterian. Home: 423 Cambridge Dr Richardson TX 75080 Office: One Main Pl Dallas TX 75250

CARROLL, JOHN FRANKLIN, JR., chem. co. exec.; b. Utica, N.Y., Apr. 25, 1932; s. John Franklin and Mabel Lisette (Berg) C.; B.Chem. Engring., Rensselaer Poly. Inst., 1953; m. Alice Florence Bruemmer, Dec. 20, 1958; children—John F. III, William Peter. With Hercules Inc., 1953—, corporate licensing mgr., Wilmington, Del., 1977—; pres. dir. Herdata, Inc.; speaker in field. Served with USMC, 1953-55. Mem. Am. Inst. Chem. Engrs., Nat. Def. Preparedness Assn., Licensing Execs. Soc. Office: 910 Market St Wilmington DE 19899

CARROLL, LAWRENCE WILLIAM, lawyer, super market exec.; b. Chgo., Mar. 7, 1923; s. Lawrence William and Lucille Bertha (Blackwell) C.; A.A., Herzl Jr. Coll., 1942; student U. Ill., 1942-44; J.D., Loyola U., 1950; m. Annie Lee Goode, June 28, 1947; 1 son, Lawrence William. Admitted to Ill. bar, 1950; with Chgo. Title & Trust Co., 1951—, sr. title examiner, title officer, 1964-73, asst. chief title officer, 1973-80, office counsel, 1975—; pres., chmn. bd. T.W.O./Hillman's Inc.; mem. Bd. Inquiry of Attys. Registration and

Disciplinary Commn. Deacon, Lincoln Meml. Ch.; former exec. v.p., counsel for housing Woodlawn Orgn.; former adviser to registrants Selective Service System, Local Bd. 18; sec., adviser to pres. Community Mental Bd. of Chgo.; former mem. lay-profl. adv. council Dr. Murray Brown, health commr. Bd. Health, Chgo.; bd. dirs. Woodlawn Community Devel. Corp., Mental Health Commn. Ill., Chgo. Coll. Osteo. Medicine. Served to 2d lt. as pilot USAAF, 1944-46. Mem. Nat. (bd. govs.), Cook County (dir.) bar assns. Democrat. Congregationalist. Home: 9651 S Michigan Ave Chicago IL 60628 Office: 111 W Washington St Chicago IL 60602

CARROLL, MICHAEL EUGENE, architect; b. Dover, Ohio, July 21, 1952; s. Max Eugene and Margaret Eloise (Belknap) C.; B.Arch., U. Cin., 1976; m. Kimberly Ann Carrigan, Aug. 19, 1978; 1 dau., Katherine Lee. Architect Bender, Grindle, Raike, Ashland, Ohio, 1976-77; asst. mgr. archtl. div. Raike Assos., Ashland, 1977-79; partner Brandstetter/Carroll & Assos., Lexington, Ky., 1979—. Mem. Nat. Council Archtl. Registration Bds., Nat. Park and Recreation Soc., AIA, Ky. Soc. Architects, Ky. Recreation and Parks Soc. Methodist. Home: 3504 Willowood Rd Lexington KY 40502 Office: 2040 Regency Rd Lexington KY 40503

CARROLL, MIRIAM GWYNN, real estate investor; b. Detroit, Sept. 21, 1938; d. Howard Robert and Ercel Greta (Oliver) C.; student public schs., Mt. Clemens, Mich.; children—David, Julie, Tamara. Real estate salesperson Petitpren Realtors, Mt. Clemens, Mich., 1968-71; real estate broker Banker's Realty, Mt. Clemens, 1971-73; owner Chateau Realtor, Mt. Clemens, 1973-76; pres., sole stockholder Briarwood Investment, Inc., 1973—; investor, sole owner Carroll Realtor, Mt. Clemens, 1978—. Mem. Macomb County Taxpayers Assn., 1980—. Licensed residential builder. Mem. Macomb County C. of C., Macomb County Bd. Realtors, Macomb Multiple Listing Service. Republican. Home: 219 Cass Ave Mount Clemens MI 48043 Office: 9 S Gratiot Ave Mount Clemens MI 48043

CARROLL, THOMAS EDMUND, publishing co. exec.: b. Columbus, Ohio, Apr. 21, 1928; s. Thomas Joseph and Dorothy (Danaher) C.; B.A., Yale U., 1950; J.D., U. Mich., 1952; M.B.A., Columbia U., 1959; divorced; children—Christopher Joseph, Andrew Keating. Admitted to Ohio bar, 1952, D.C. bar, 1973; with Time, Inc., 1953-67; exec. v.p. Evans Broadcasting Corp., N.Y.C., 1967-70; asst. adminstr. EPA, 1970-73; pres. Carroll Publishing Co., Washington, 1974—. Office: 1058 Thomas Jefferson St NW Washington DC 20007

CARROLL, THOMAS SYLVESTER, business exec.; b. N.Y.C., Oct. 1, 1919; s. Thomas Jeremiah and Johanna (Mulvihill) C.; A.B. cum laude, Catawba Coll., 1941; postgrad. Mass. Inst. Tech., 1941-42; M.B.A. with distinction, Harvard U., 1947; m. Sidney Burke, Sept. 27, 1947 (div.); children—Jeffrey Burke, Thomas Jeremiah (dec.), James Francis, Matthew, Charles Laurence. Brand mgr. Procter & Gamble Co., 1947-53; product dir. Gen. Foods Corp., 1953-55; mktg. mgr. Colgate Palmolive Co., 1955-57; v.p. George Fry & Assos., 1957-58; gen. mgr. mktg. services Lever Bros. Co., 1958-59, mktg. v.p., 1959-63, merchandising v.p., 1963-64, dir., 1963—, exec. v.p., 1964-67, pres., chief exec. officer, 1967-80; dir. Interpace Corp., Am. Airlines, Inc., Internat. Exec. Service Corps, C.I.T. Fin. Corp., Asso. Dry Goods Corp. Bd. dirs. Assos. of Harvard Bus. Sch., 1975—, Bus. Mktg. Corp. for N.Y.C., 1977—; trustee Catawba Coll., Mus. Modern Art; vis. com. Harvard Bus. Sch. Served from cadet to lt. col. USAAF, 1941-46. Mem. Grocery Mfrs. Am. (dir. 1968—, treas. 1971— vice chmn. 1976-78, chmn. 1978-80), Harvard Bus. Sch. Assn. (pres. 1973-74), Com. Econ. Devel. (trustee), Conf. Bd. Clubs: Country of New Canaan (Conn.); Racquet and Tennis, Econ. (N.Y.C.); Internat. (Washington); Pilgrims. Home: 67 Benedict Hill Rd New Canaan CT 06840 Office: 390 Park Ave New York NY 10022

CARROLL, WAYNE DOUGLAS, glass mfg. co. exec.; b. Richmond, Va., Apr. 30, 1938; s. Marion D. and Virginia M. (Horner) C.; B.S. in Mech. Engring., Duke U., 1961; M.B.A., Syracuse U., 1971; m. Barbara A. James, May 7, 1960; children—Diane M., Robin L. Forming specialist Owens-Ill. Glass Co., Clarion, Pa., 1961-62, glass container project engr., Toledo, Ohio, 1962-64; dept. foreman Corning Glass Works, Bradford, Pa., 1964-68, supr. process engring., Corning, N.Y., 1968-71; zirconia fibers prodn. supr. Union Carbide Corp., Tuxedo, N.Y., 1971-72, linde indsl. gases applications analyst, Tarrytown, N.Y., 1973-74, diagnostic reagents prodn. mgr., Tuxedo, 1974-76, membrane systems mfg. mgr., Tuxedo, 1976-77; mgr. prodn. Pitts. Corning Co., Port Allegany, Pa., 1978-79, plant mgr. Sedalia, Mo., 1979—. Mem. Citizens Adv. Bd. for Sch. Dist. Budget, 1975-76; mem. Mayor's Adv. Com. Public Transp., 1979. Club: Sedalia Country. Home: 906 S Barrett Sedalia MO 65301 Office: PO Box 716 Sedalia MO 65301

CARRUTHERS, CHARLES LEON, oil co. exec.; b. Prescott, Ark., Sept. 29, 1933; s. William Leon and Roxie Elizabeth (Faulkner) C.; B.S.E., Henderson State U., 1955; m. June Chambless, Jan. 3, 1958; 1 son, Brent Leon. Marketer, Lion Oil Co., Monroe, La., 1957-58, asst. tng. mgr., El Dorado, Ark., 1958-59, dist. mgr., Evansville, Ind., 1959-63; div. mgr. Merit Oil Corp., Phila., 1963-71, Cambridge, Mass., 1971—. Trustee North Shore C. of Christ, 1978—; active orgns. for children with learning disabilities. Served with U.S. Army, 1955-57. Democrat. Office: 299 Prospect St Cambridge MA 02139

CARRUTHERS, KAREEN MARIA, mortgage broker, personnel cons.; b. The Hague, Netherlands, Sept. 26, 1948; came to Can., 1956, naturalized, 1964; d. Emile Jacob and Klasina Agnes (Chaillet) Von Pohlreich; student U. Calgary (Alta., Can.), 1967-68. Acctg. clk. Nat. Tank, Calgary, 1967-69; with Martin Black Wire Ropes of Can. Ltd., Calgary, 1969-72; sec. to exec. officer Housing and Urban Devel. Assn. of Calgary, 1972-78; v.p. Palace Mortgage Ltd., Calgary, 1980—; pres. K.M. Carruthers Projects Ltd., Calgary, 1978—. Vol., Calgary Exhbn. and Stampede Bd. Com. Mem. Free Market Econ. Assn. of Can., Am. Soc. Assn. Execs., Nat. Assn. Expn. Mgrs., Housing and Urban Devel. Assn. Calgary. Home and Office: 4905 23d Ave NW Calgary AB T3B 5A8 Canada

CARSON, CLAUDE MATTESON (KIT), investment counselor; b. Farley, Mo., Sept. 26, 1907; s. Robert Walter and Mirtle Virginia Carson; student Advanced Mgmt. Program, Harvard, 1962; m. Helen Long, May 16, 1931. Pres. Hoerner Boxes, Inc., until 1966; sr. v.p. adminstrn., dir. Hoerner Waldorf Corp. (merger Hoerner Boxes, Inc. and Waldorf Paper Products Co.), St. Paul, 1966-73, 76—, also chmn. audit co., mem. exec. com.; chmn. audit com., dir. Puritan-Bennett Corp., Kansas City, Mo. Mem. Bus. Climate Task Force Com., State of Minn., 1971-73; active Boy Scouts Am. Bd. mgrs. Parker B. Francis Found.; bd. govs. Interlachen. Served with AUS. Fellow Am. Inst. Mgmt. (pres.'s council); mem. Fibre Box Assn. (chmn. bd., past pres.), TAPPI, Fourdrinier Kraft Board Inst., Internat. Corrugated Case Assn. (dir.). Rotarian. Clubs: Union League, Mid-Am. (Chgo.); Interlachen, Question, Minneapolis, St. Paul Pool and Yacht, Harvard Alumni. Home: 5209 Schaefer Rd Edina MN 55436 Office: Northwestern Financial Center 7900 Xerxes Ave S Suite 106 Minneapolis MN 55431

CARSON, JOSEPH GREGORY, economist; b. Youngstown, Ohio, Mar. 19, 1952; s. Louis Joseph and Hermina B. Carson; B.A., Youngstown State U., 1975, M.A., 1976; postgrad. George Washington U., 1977-79. Instr. in econs. Youngstown State U., 1977; staff economist Office of Chief Economist, Dept. Commerce, Washington, 1977-79; sr. economist mktg. staff Gen. Motors Corp., Detroit, 1979—. Mem. Am. Econ. Assn., Soc. Govt. Economists, Omicron Delta Epsilon. Roman Catholic. Contbr. articles to Bus. Am. Office: 3044 W Grand Blvd Room 9-247 GM Bldg Detroit MI 48202

CARSON, NORMAN RICHARD, cons. engr.; b. Rockford, Ill., Feb. 15, 1916; s. Clinton Kenneth and Fern (Hitchcock) C.; B.S. in Elec. Engring., U. Ill., 1937; m. Marjorie Alvina LaValle, Sept. 16, 1938; 1 dau., Barbara Kathryn. Elec. engr. Commonwealth Edison Co., Chgo., 1937-47; v.p., chief engr. T. Maseng and Assos., Inc., Chgo., 1947-49; chief elec. engr. Erik Floor and Assos., Inc., Chgo., 1950-55; partnership chmn., exec. partner R.W. Beck and Assos., Seattle, 1955—; chmn., dir. Precision Data Services, Inc., 1979-81; v.p., dir. Met. Office Corp., 1961-77. Pres., dir. Island Lake (Ill.) Property Owners Assn., Inc. 1950-55. Served to maj. AUS, 1942-46. Assn.; speaker in field. Mem. Nat. Democratic Club. Wash., Oreg., Alaska, Colo. Mem. Cons. Engrs. Council Wash. (pres., dir. 1961-63), IEEE, Soc. Am. Mil. Engrs., Eta Kappa Nu. Clubs: Wash. Athletic, Rainier (Seattle). Home: Capitol Hill. Blvd W Seattle WA 98199 Office: Tower Bldg Seattle WA 98101

CARSTENS, WILLIAM WRAITH, lawyer, real estate co. exec.; b. Denver, Mar. 12, 1931; s. Carl Eberhard and Erma Mabel (Wraith) C.; B.A. Occidental Coll., 1952; LL.B., U. So. Calif., 1955; m. Marylyn Triesch, June 21, 1953; children—Cheryl Lynn, Debra Lee, Connie Ann; m. 2d, Rosemary Simmons, Oct. 21, 1977. Admitted to Calif. bar, 1956; asso. firm White, Froehlich and Peterson, San Diego, 1959-61; partner firm Carstens and Shue, and predecessor, 1961-76; pres., owner Black Mountain Corp.; partner Black Mountain Venture; real estate developer Black Mountain Investments, 1976—, Rancho Bernardo Food and Convenience Center, 1975—, One Oaks North, 1975—, Miramar Devel. Co., San Diego, 1973—; instr. bus. law San Diego State Coll., 1961—; city atty. National City (Calif.), 1962-66. Bd. mgrs. San Diego YMCA. Served with USMCR, 1956-59. Mem. Am., San Diego County bar assns., State Bar Calif., Order of Coif, Apt. and Rental Owners Assn. (dir.). Home: 6254 Caminito Buena Suerte San Diego CA 92120 Office: 9393 Activity Rd Suite I San Diego CA 92126

CARSWELL, ROBERT, govt. ofcl.; b. Bklyn., Nov. 25, 1928; s. William Brown and Charlotte Edna (Riegger) C.; A.B. magna cum laude, Harvard U., 1949, LL.B. cum laude, 1952; m. Mary Killeen Wilde, Dec. 28, 1957; children—Kate, William. Admitted to N.Y. State bar, 1952, Calif. bar, 1954; with firm Shearman & Sterling, N.Y.C., 1955-62, partner, 1965-77; spl. asst. to sec. treasury, 1962-65, dep. sec. treasury, 1977—. Served to lt. j.g. USNR, 1952-55. Mem. Am. Bar Assn., Bar Assn. City N.Y., St. Andrews Soc. N.Y., Phi Beta Kappa. Clubs: Harvard (N.Y.C.). Home: 3700 33rd Pl NW Washington DC 20008 Office: Main Treasury Bldg Washington DC 20220

CARTER, CHARLES MCLEAN, mfg. co. exec.; b. Clyde, Ohio, Jan. 17, 1936; s. Howard Ellsworth and Dorothy Louise (McLean) C.; B.E.E., Rensselaer Poly. Inst., 1957; postgrad. Georgetown U., 1959-60; J.D., DePaul U., 1963; m. Linda Marie Parr, Apr. 24, 1965; children—Suzanne Marie, Debra Jean, Daniel William. Sales engr. Trane Co., LaCrosse, Wis., Pitts., 1957-59; patent asso. Western Electric Co., Washington, Chgo., 1959-62; admitted to Ill. bar, 1963; mem. firm Wolfe, Hubbard, Voit & Osaan, Chgo., 1962-64, Pendleton, Neuman, Seibold & Williams, Chgo., 1964-66; dir. corporate planning and legal, asst. sec. Warwick Electronics, Inc., Chgo., 1966-70; with Skil Corp., Chgo., 1970-80, gen. counsel, sec., 1971-80, v.p., 1975-80, corp. v.p., 1977-80; pres. Skil Internat., Inc., 1973-80; sr. v.p., treas., chief legal and fin. officer Stewart-Warner Corp., Chgo., 1980—, also dir. Mem. Chgo. Crime Commn. Mem. Am., Ill., Chgo., 7th Circuit bar assns., Am., Chgo. patent law assns., Licensing Execs. Soc., Tau Beta Pi, Eta Kappa Nu. Lutheran (deacon 1968-70, trustee 1973-76, pres. 1977-81). Club: Chgo. Execs. Home: 3491 Whirlaway Dr Northbrook IL 60062 Office: 1826 Diversey Pkwy Chicago IL 60614

CARTER, CURTIS REX, JR., investment co. exec.; b. Carthage, Mo., July 31, 1935; s. Curtis Rex and Ruth E. (Key) C.; B.S.M.E., U. Mo., 1957. Project engr. space flight vehicles LTV, 1962-68; v.p., tech. dir. Topaz Electronics, 1968-71; chmn. bd. Mission Bay Investments, Inc., Mission Data Systems, Regulus Corp., Organ Exchange, Inc., Consumark Electronics, San Diego, 1971—; lectr. bus. schs. So. Calif. Active in fin. Jimmy Carter campaign, 1976; active Zoo, Art Mus. Mem. Young Pres.'s Orgn., IEEE. Club: San Diego Yacht. Office: 3636 Camino Del Rio N San Diego CA 92108

CARTER, EDWARD WILLIAM, retail exec.; A.B., U. Calif. at Los Angeles, 1932; M.B.A., Harvard U., 1937; LL.D., Occidental Coll., 1962. Chmn., dir. Carter Hawley Hale Stores, Inc., Los Angeles; dir. AT&T, Del Monte Corp., Lockheed Corp., Pacific Mut. Life Ins. Co., So. Calif. Edison Co., Western Bancorp and subs. United Calif. Bank. Clubs: Pacific Union, Bohemian, Los Angeles Country, Calif., Burlingame Country, Cypress Point. Home: 626 Siena Way Los Angeles CA 90024 Office: 550 S Flower St Los Angeles CA 90071

CARTER, JAMES CALL, sugar co. exec.; b. Greensboro, N.C., Sept. 3, 1932; s. James Bain and Dorothy Rhoades (Call) C.; A.B., Harvard U., 1955; m. Sandra Faye Dickerson, Mar. 31, 1972; 1 son, James Call. Sales mgr. Am. Sugar Co., various locations, 1958-68, regional sales mgr., N.Y.C., 1968-72, gen. sales mgr. Amstar Corp., N.Y.C., 1972-75, v.p. grocery products, Am. Sugar div., 1975—. Clk. vestry St. Luke's Episcopal Ch., Montclair, N.J., 1977-79. Served with U.S. Navy, 1955-57. Mem. Sales Exec. Club N.Y.C. Republican. Clubs: Montclair Golf, Harvard of N.Y.C. Home: 67 Clinton Ave Montclair NJ 07042 Office: 1251 Ave of Americas New York NY 10020

CARTER, JOHN, JR., electronics exec.; b. Montclair, N.J., Oct. 30, 1945; s. John and Jane (Dill) C.; B.S., U. S.C., 1968; m. Alana Hartley, June 3, 1967; children—John III, Lee Hartley. With audit dept. Nat. Bank N.Am., 1968; prodn. mgr. Carter Semicondr., Ltd., 1969-70, v.p. mktg., 1970-75; pres., dir. Dumont Oscilloscope Labs., Inc., West Caldwell, N.J., 1975—, dir. Deforest Electronics, Inc. Officer, Mendham Soccer Club. Mem. Pres.'s Profl. Assn., Assn. Old Crows. Home: Valley View Dr Mendham NJ 07945 Office: 40 Fairfield Pl West Caldwell NJ 07006

CARTER, JOHN ALLEN, JR., real estate co. exec.; b. Plainfield, N.J., Dec. 30, 1934; s. John A. and Martha Apel (Conover) C.; B.A., Williams Coll., 1956; M.B.A., Rutgers U., 1969; m. Marian V. Taylor, Dec. 19, 1959; children—Mary Paige, Myles P. Pres. Stone & Webster Bldg., Inc., 1964—, Summer St. Realty Corp., 1974—, Stone & Webster Land Corp., 1978—, Sabal Corp., 1978—; v.p. Stone & Webster, Inc., N.Y.C., 1974—. Pres., Westfield Hosp. Assn.; treas. Westfield Bicentennial Corp. Served to lt., USNR, 1956-59, 61-62. Mem. Nat. Assn. Office and Indsl. Parks, Bldg. Owners and Mgrs. Assn., Nat. Assn. Real Estate Execs. Republican. Episcopalian. Home: 1592 Deer Path St Mountainside NJ 07092 Office: 90 Broad St New York NY 10004

CARTER, JOHN J., econ. cons.; b. Morgantown, Ind., Nov. 29, 1920; s. Julian G. and Marguerite W. C.; B.S., Ind. U., 1942; postgrad. (fellow) Am. Inst. Econ. Research, 1946; m. Margaret Jean Dunn, Jan. 1, 1943; children—Marcia Jean, Mary Susan, John Joseph. Dir. research, dean fellows Am. Inst. Econ. Research, 1948-51; economist Kingan & Co., 1951-53, Armour & Co., 1953; with Ind. Nat. Bank, Indpls., 1954—, v.p., economist, 1964-80, econ. cons., 1980—; pres., mng. dir. Research Assos., Inc., Indpls., 1970—; with Ball State U., 1978—, lectr., 1980—; dir. Ferdinand Furniture Co., Styline Co., Keller Mfg. Co.; chmn. Ind. Gov.'s Econ. Forecast Com. Served with USAF, 1943-46. Chartered fin. analyst. Mem. Inst. Chartered Fin. Analysts, Indpls. Soc. Fin. Analysts, Nat. Assn. Bus. Economists, Ind. Econs. Forum. Methodist. Club: Indpls. Athletic. Author: Economic Tides and Trends, 1948; Where Will Tomorrow's Opportunities Be, 1950; Business Trends, 1979; contbg. econs. editor: Bankers Monthly, 1968-80, CFA Digest, 1980—. Home: 795 W Main St Danville IN 46122 Office: PO Box 44640 Indianapolis IN 46244

CARTER, JOSEPH EDWIN, ret. nickel co. exec.; b. Jackson, Ga., Apr. 3, 1915; s. Charles Luther and Marilu (Holiman) C.; B.S., Ga. Inst. Tech., 1937; m. Virginia Meredith Crickmer, Apr. 8, 1939; children—Joseph Charles, Virginia Ann (Mrs. James Allan Colburn). Metallurgist, Internat. Nickel Co., Huntington, W.Va., 1937-40, various positions, 1940-52, mgmt. asst., 1952-57, works indsl. relations mgr., 1957-58, gen. supt., 1958-60, asst. v.p., mfg. mgr. Huntington Alloy Products div., 1960-62, v.p. mfg., mgr., 1962-67, exec. v.p., 1967-71, pres., 1971; v.p. Inco, Ltd., N.Y.C., 1971, exec. v.p., 1972-74, pres., 1974-77, chmn., chief exec. officer, 1977-80, also dir.; ret., 1980. Served to maj. AUS, 1942-45. Decorated Bronze Star. Mem. W.Va. Mfrs. Assn. (pres. 1970-71, dir.), Am. Chem. Soc., Phi Kappa Phi, Tau Beta Phi. Presbyterian (deacon). Clubs: Toronto, Granite, Canadian (Toronto); Univ., Recess, Econ. (N.Y.C.); Baltrusol Golf (N.J.); Guyan Country (W.Va.). Patentee in field. Office: One New York Plaza New York NY 10004 also Inco Ltd 1 First Canadian Pl Toronto ON M5X 1C4 Canada

CARTER, LEWIS HENRY, JR., distbr., contractor; b. Ruston, La., Mar. 5, 1926; s. Lewis H. and Minnie Lea (Davis) C.; B.S., U. Okla., 1948; m. Joan Patrica Beals, Sept. 10, 1965; children—Lewis Henry, Mary Kathleen, Susan Marie. Engr., Dykes Co., Shreveport, La., 1948-49; sales engr. C. Robert Ingram Inc., Oklahoma City, 1949-53; pres. Comfort Inc., Oklahoma City, 1953—, Comfort Distbrs. Inc., 1978—; sec.-treas. Air Mart Inc., Kansas City, Mo., 1974—; partner, C & D Investment Co., Oklahoma City, 1960—. Served to lt. (j.g.) USN, World War II. Named Outstanding Airtemp Distbr. in U.S., 1979; registered profl. engr., Okla.; cert. Nat. Environ. Balancing Bur. Mem. Sheet Metal Contractors Okla. (pres. 1957, 1971), Am. Soc. Heating, Refrigeration and Air Conditioning Engrs., Distbrs. Council Airtemp Corp. (chmn. 3 yrs.), Okla. Engring. and Tech. Guidance Council, Constrn. Specifications Inst., N. Am. Heating and Air Conditioning Wholesalers. Republican. Episcopalian. Home: 3308 Robin Ridge Rd Oklahoma City OK 73120 Office: 100 NE 34th St Oklahoma City OK 73105

CARTER, RICHARD DUANE, mgmt. cons. co. exec., educator; b. Canton, Ohio, Feb. 27, 1929; s. Herbert Duane and Edith Irene (Richardson) C.; A.B., Coll. William and Mary, 1951; M.B.A., Columbia U., 1960; Ph.D., U. Calif. at Los Angeles, 1968; m. Nancy Jean Cannell, Sept. 3, 1955; 1 son, Erich Richardson. Sales mgr. Republic Steel Corp., Birmingham, Ala., 1954-59; mgmt. cons. Arthur D. Little, Cambridge, Mass., 1960-62; chief exec. officer Human Resources Inst., prof. La. State U., Baton Rouge, 1968-70; dir. UN Indsl. Mgmt. and Cons. Services, Vienna, 1970-75; dean Sch. Bus., chmn. Center for Mgmt. Edn., Quinnipiac Coll., Hamden, Conn., 1977-80; chmn. research and publs. Columbia U. Orgn. and Mgmt. Seminar, 1976—; founder, mng. dir. Internat. Mgmt. Consortium, 1975—; chmn. bd. TCG Industries, Inc., N.Y.C., 1980—; sr. adviser, dir., pres.'s council Am. Mgmt. Assn., 1976-77. U.S. rep. UN Indsl. Devel. Program, Internat. Inst. Systems Analysis. Served with USMC, 1951-53. Fellow Internat. Acad. Mgmt.; mem. Acad. Mgmt., Am. Mgmt. Assn., Beta Gamma Sigma. Clubs: Univ. (Cleve.) (Boston); N.Y. Athletic. Author: Management: In Perspective and Practice, 1974; New Perspectives in Management Development, 1974—. Contbr. articles to profl. jours. Home: 46 Kings Hwy S Westport CT 06880

CARTER, STEPHEN ALLEN, urban designer; b. Augusta, Ga., Sept. 12, 1942; s. James Allen and Myrtle Elise (Parkman) C.; B. Arch., Clemson U., 1965; M. Urban Design, Archtl. Assn. (London), 1970; postgrad. London Sch. Econs., 1968, Imperial Coll., 1969; m. Susan Canders, July 1, 1972; children—Jeffrey Parkman, Timothy Stephen, Jeremy Brissette. Designer LBC & W Architects, Columbia, S.C., 1965-67; urban planner Greater London Council, 1968-70; v.p. Wilbur Smith & Assos., Washington, Miami, and Columbia, 1970-74; founder, mng. partner Stephen Carter & Assos., Columbia, 1974—; pres. Carter-Goble Assos., Inc., 1978—; adj. profl. Coll. Architecture, Clemson U.; adj. prof. econs. Bus. Coll., U. S.C.; dir. Geiger, McElveen and Kennedy, Inc., 1975—; mem. S.C. Legis. Com. on Pub. Transp.; mem. rev. com. Harbison New Town Design Devel.; mem. Econ. Devel. Commn. Columbia; mem. adv. com. for architecture and environ. arts S.C. Arts Commn. Recipient Alpha Rho Chi medal for architecture. Mem. Nat. Acad. Scis. (transp. research bd.), Am. Planning Assos., Met. Assn. Urban Designers and Environ. Planners, Nat. Council for Transp. Disadvantaged, Am. Soc. Psychoprophalaxis in Obstetrics. Author of U.S. position paper at UN Econ. Commn. of Europe, 1976, position paper transport policy and urban devel., Sao Paulo, Brazil, 1978. Office: 1501 Richland St PO Box 11287 Columbia SC 29211

CARTER, THOMAS SMITH, JR., railway exec.; b. Dallas, June 6, 1921; s. Thomas Smith and Mattie (Dowell) C.; B.S.C.E., So. Meth. U., 1944; m. Janet Ruth Hostetter, July 3, 1946; children—Janet Diane, Susan Jean, Charles T., Carol Ruth. Chief engr. Mo. Kans. Tex. R.R. Co., Dallas, 1954-61, v.p. ops., 1961-66; v.p. Kansas City (Mo.) So. Ry. Co., 1966, pres., dir., 1973—; chief exec. officer, 1981—; pres., dir. La. & Ark. Ry. Co., 1974, chmn. bd., 1981—; dir. Kansas City So. Industries. Served with USN, 1944-46. Mem. Assn. Am. R.R.'s (dir.), La. State Fair Assn., Nat. Soc. Profl. Engrs., ASCE, Am. Ry. Engring. Assn. Home: 9319 W 92d Terr Overland Park KS 66212 Office: 114 W 11th St Kansas City MO 64105

CARTER, WILLIAM CARL, JR., banker; b. Bedford, Pa., Nov. 24, 1943; s. William Carl and Ethel Emma (Lohr) C.; student Campbell Coll., 1962-64; B.A. in Polit. Sci., High Point Coll., 1967; grad. Sch. Banking of South, La. State U., 1979: m. Mary Christina Bolton, Jan. 23, 1966; children—William Neil, Kimberly Noel, Mary Allison, John Christopher. Tchr., John Gorrie Jr. High Sch., Jacksonville, Fla., 1967-69; cashier Barnett Banks of Fla., Jacksonville, 1969-72; cashier Northwestern Bank, Winston-Salem, 1972-78, city exec. Northwestern Bank, Clemmons, N.C., 1978-80; v.p., br. adminstr. Central Bank of Mobile (Ala.), 1980—. Mem. Northwest N.C. Econ. Devel. Commn., 1973-76; chmn. NW Jr. Steer Show, 1974-79; vice chmn. fund drive Winston-Salem Arts Council, 1977; co-chmn. Northwestern Bank Art Competition, 1976-76; bd. dirs. Lighthouse Rescue Mission, 1976; deacon Reynolds Presbyterian Ch., 1979—. Mem. Am. Inst. Bankers (dir. Forsyth County), Bank Mktg. Assn., N.C. Bankers Assn., Bank Adminstrs. Inst., Winston-Salem Personnel

Assn., Winston-Salem C. of C., Clemmons West Assn. Democrat. Club: Clemmons Civic. Office: PO Drawer 1288 Mobile AL 36606

CARTER, WILLIAM JOHN, banker; b. Ames, Iowa, Oct. 19, 1925; s. Sam. T. and Lorena M. C.; B.S., Iowa State U., 1949; student Morningside Coll., 1943; m. D. Vivian Smith, May 14, 1949; children—Christine, David, Deborah, Joseph. Tchr. public schs., Woodbury, Iowa, 1949-56; dist. mgr. livestock feed sales Allied Mills Inc., 1956-66; officer tng. Nat. Bank & Trust Co., Chariton, Iowa, 1966-67, asst. v.p. & farm rep., 1967-69, v.p., 1969-71, exec. v.p., 1971-73, pres., 1973—; dir. Iowa Bankers Mktg. Corp., Iowa Automated Clearing House. Served with U.S. Army, 1944-45, USAF. Decorated Air medal with 5 clusters. Mem. Iowa Bankers Assn. (agrl. com. chmn. 1974), C. of C. (pres.). Methodist. Club: Rotary. 1025 Braden Chariton IA 50049

CARTLIDGE, LINDA H(ESTER), expn. mgmt. co. exec.; b. San Francisco, Nov. 6, 1940; d. Edwin Lloyd and Hester Clara (Brown) Biggs; student San Jose City Coll., 1958-60, San Jose State U., 1960-61; 1 son, Cord. Computer mktg. Fairchild Semicondr. Co., Mountain View, Calif., 1966-68; v.p., nat. show dir. GGE, Inc., semicondr. shows, Santa Clara, Calif., 1972-75; pres. Cartlidge & Assos., Inc., Sunnyvale, Calif., 1975—; chmn. bd., producer Advanced Semicondr. Equipment Expn., Inc., S.W. Semicondr. Expn., Word Processing and Office Equipment Trade Show and Conf., Internat. Semicondr. Expo. Mem. Nat. Fedn. Ind. Bus., Peninsula Mktg. Assn., Nat. Assn. Expo Mgrs., San Jose C. of C., Santa Clara C. of C., Sunnyvale C. of C., San Jose Advt. Club. Home: 6074 Calle De Amor San Jose CA 95124 Office: 491 Macara Ave #1014 Sunnyvale CA 94086

CARTMELL, PETER, bank exec.; b. Clydebank, Scotland, Apr. 30, 1921; s. George Jack and Kate Banks (Griffin) C.; B.S., Rutgers U., 1943; grad. Sch. Credit and Fin. Mgmt., Dartmouth Coll., 1959; m. Constance Wingerter, May 26, 1945; children—Virginia Cartmell Cole, Peter B., Jennifer B., Elizabeth B., George D. With Fidelity Union Trust Co., Newark, 1946—, exec. v.p., 1964-69, pres., 1969-77, chief exec. officer, 1977—; pres. Fidelity Union Bancorp., Newark, 1970, chmn., chief exec. officer, 1980—; dir. Foster Wheeler Corp., Thomas & Betts Corp., United Steel & Aluminum Corp., Bamberger's. Bd. dirs. Greater Newark C. of C.; gov., trustee N.J. Hist. Soc. Served to capt. inf. U.S. Army, 1943-46. Mem. N.J. Bankers Assn. (hon. v.p.). Clubs: Down Town, Essex, Pine Valley Golf, Rumson Country, Sea Bright Beach, Econ. of N.Y. Office: 765 Broad St Newark NJ 07101

CARTO, DAVID LAWRENCE, resort exec.; b. Ft. Wayne, Ind., Aug. 5, 1930; s. Willis F. and Louise (Allison) C.; B.A., Ohio Wesleyan U., 1952; postgrad. U. Minn., 1954-55; m. Frances Eleanor Draffan, Sept. 18, 1954; children—David Draffan, Thomas James, Amy Louise, Steven Terrence. Asst. sales promotion mgr. Westinghouse Corp., Mansfield, Ohio and St. Louis, 1952-54; exec. asst. Ohio Brass Co., Mansfield, 1956-63; v.p. Didactics Corp., Mansfield, 1963-66; pres., treas., gen. mgr. Ohio Ski Slopes, Inc., Mansfield, 1961—; dir. Bank One of Mansfield. Trustee Rehab. Service N. Central Ohio, Mansfield, 1956—, pres., 1963-66: bd. dirs., past pres. Mansfield Area Tourist and Travel Bur. Served with U.S. Army, 1954-56. Mem. Nat. Ski Areas Assn. (dir.), Central Ski Areas Assn., Ohio Conf. Ski Area Operators (sec.-treas.). Republican. Congregationalist. Clubs: Kiwanis (past pres.) (Mansfield). Office: Ohio Ski Slopes Inc PO Box 163 Mansfield OH 44901

CARTWRIGHT, JAMES GLENN, ret. utility exec.; b. Hinton, Okla., Oct. 26, 1915; s. Oscar Glenn and Ella (Shawler) C.; B.S., Okla. State U., 1937; postgrad. Ga. Inst. Tech., 1964; m. Thelma Rosa Smith, Dec. 4, 1938; children—Clifford Glenn, Randall Joe. With Okla. Gas & Electric Co., Oklahoma City, 1937-81, asst. treas., 1962-65, asst. treas., asst. controller, 1965-69, controller, 1969-72, v.p. acctg., controller, 1972-78, v.p. acct., 1978, sr. v.p. acctg., 1978-81. Served to ensign USNR, 1942-45. Cert. internal auditor. Mem. Nat. Assn. Accts. (chpt. pres. 1969-70), Fin. Execs. Inst., Edison Electric Inst., Missouri Valley Electric Assn., Kappa Tau Pi, Pi Gamma Mu, Phi Kappa Phi, Beta Alpha Psi. Baptist.

CARTWRIGHT, WILLIAM HENRY, watch mfg. co. exec.; b. Chgo., Apr. 12, 1936; s. William Henry and Rose Helen (Kish) C.; B.S., St. Procopius Coll., 1959; postgrad. Ill. Inst. Tech., 1965; m. Barbara J. Knaack, Jan. 26, 1974; children—Robert S., William H. Corporate planner various cos., 1961-68, CNA Fin. Co., Chgo., 1968-70; mgr. corporate devel. Esmark Corp., Chgo., 1970-74; dir. planning and devel. Timex Corp., Waterbury, Conn., 1974—; asso. prof. bus. adminstrn. Ill. Inst. Tech. Bd. dirs. United Way, Waterbury; pres. Community Chest, Chgo. Served with U.S. Army, 1959-61. Mem. Assn. for Corporate Growth, Planning Execs. Inst., Corporate Planning Council. Home: 23 Hillside Rd Woodbury CT 06798 Office: Timex Corp Waterbury CT 06720

CARTY, JAMES PATRICK, nat. assn. exec.; b. Waltham, Mass., Mar. 13, 1938; s. James Edward and Mary Ellen (Carr) Carty; A.B., Providence U., 1961; LL.B., Boston U., 1964; LL.M., George Washington U., 1973; m. Gisela Leuschen, Aug. 13, 1966; children—Sean, Kristina. Admitted to Mass. bar, 1965, Va. bar, 1975; sr. trial atty. Fed. Trade Commn., Washington, 1969-73; counsel to Sen. Wm. L. Scott U.S. Senate, 1973-75; now v.p., mgr. Nat. Assn. Mfrs., Washington; lectr. Fed. Seminar Center, Oak Ridge, Tenn. Bd. dirs. Pinewood Lake Homeowners Assn., Fairfax, Va., 1970-75, pres. 1973-74. Served to maj., JAGC, U.S. Army, 1964-69. Decorated Distinguished Service medal. Mem. Mass., Va., Am. bar assns. Roman Catholic. Clubs: Internat. of Washington, Springfield (Va.) Golf, Providence U. Alumni of Washington (pres. 1979—). Contbr. articles to profl. jours.; editor: Regulatory Failure (3 parts), 1976, 77, 78, 80. Office: 1776 F St NW Washington DC 20006

CARUS, MILTON BLOUKE, chem. co. exec., publisher; b. Chgo., June 15, 1927; s. Edward H. and Dorothy (Blouke) C.; B.S.E.E., Calif. Inst. Tech., 1949; postgrad. Mexico City Coll., summer 1949, U. Freiburg (Germany), 1949-51, Sorbonne, Paris, 1951; m. Marianne Sondermann, Mar. 3, 1951; children—Andre, Christine, Inga. Devel. engr. Carus Chem. Co., Inc., LaSalle, Ill., 1951-55, asst. gen. mgr., 1955-61, exec. v.p., 1961-64, pres., 1964—; pres. Carus Corp., LaSalle, 1967—; editor Open Court Pub. Co., LaSalle, 1962-67, pub., pres., 1967—. Chmn. Ill. Valley Community Coll. Com., 1965-67; pres. chmn. bd. Internat. Baccalaureate, N. Am., 1977; co-trustee Hegeler Inst., 1968; mem. IBO Council, Geneva, 1977—. Served with USNR, 1945-46. Mem. Illinois Valley Indsl. Assn. (pres. 1970—), Chem. Mfrs. Assn. (dir. 1980—), Ill. Mfrs. Assn. (dir. 1972-77), Ill. C. of C. (edn. com. 1973), Phila. Soc., LaSalle County Hist. Soc. (dir. 1979). Home: 2222 Chartres St Peru IL 61354 Office: 1500 8th St LaSalle IL 61301

CARUSO, JOSEPH, banker; b. S.I., N.Y., Oct. 16, 1951; s. Michael and Martha Ann Caruso; B.S., Fla. Inst. Tech., 1973; M.B.A., Monmouth Coll., 1975; grad. Nat. Sch. Real Estate Fin., Ohio State U., 1978. With Citizens State Bank, Forked River, N.J., 1975—, v.p., 1978—, sr. loan officer, 1980—. Mem. Ind. Fees Appraisers N.J., Mortgage Bankers Assn. N.J., N.J. Bankers Assn. (mortgage com.), Ocean County Bankers Assn., N.J. Shore Builders Assn. (trustee), Pi Kappa Alpha. Contbr. articles on econs. to bldg. trade mags. Office: 106 N Main St Forked River NJ 08731

CARVEL, ELBERT NOSTRAND, banker; b. Shelter Island Heights, N.Y., Feb. 9, 1910; s. Arnold Wrightson and Elizabeth (Nostrand) C.; student Balt. Poly. Inst., 1924-28; J.D., U. Balt., 1931; LL.D. (hon.), Del. State Coll., 1964; m. Ann H. Valliant, Dec. 17, 1932; children—Elizabeth Carvel Palmer, Edwin V., Ann H., Barbara Carvel Krahn. Sales engr. Balt. G & E Co., 1931-36; treas., gen. mgr. Valliant Fertilizer Co., Laurel, Del., 1936-45, pres., 1945-68, chmn. bd., 1968—; dir. Sussex Trust Co., 1941-49, chmn. exec. com., 1947-49; dir. Peoples Bank & Trust Co., Laurel, 1957—, chmn. bd., 1975—; dir. Beneficial Corp., 1975—, Laurel Grain Co., 1965-75, Central Shore Commodities, 1976—. Co-chmn. Delawareans for Orderly Devel.; bd. dirs. Del. Wild Lands; chmn. Del. State Democratic Com., 1946, 54, 56; lt. gov. State of Del., 1945-49, gov., 1949-53, 61-65; hon. co-chmn. Del. Humanities Council, 1978—, Why Not Del. Com., 1978—; mem. Del. Electoral Coll., 1976—, chmn., 1977—; mem. Del. Jud. Nominating Commn., 1977—, Del. Com. on Judiciary, 1979—. Recipient Ann. award Del. chpt. NCCJ, 1949; Silver Beaver award Boy Scouts Am., 1967; Vrooman award, 1965; Alumnus of Year, Balt. Poly. Inst. decorated Order of Orange-Nassau, Queen of Netherlands, 1951. Mem. Del. Safety Council (v.p.), Del. Auto Club (v.p.). Episcopalian. Clubs: Laurel Lions, Queen Anne's Golf, Shriners, Masons (33 deg.). Home: 107 Clayton Ave Laurel DE 19956 Office: 1300 Market St Wilmington DE 19899

CARVER, DELBERT FRANKLIN, mgmt. cons.; b. Park Rapids, Minn., Apr. 14, 1951; s. Lawrence William and Nora Melissa (Peterson) C.; B.A., Concordia Coll., 1973; M.Internat. Mgmt., Am. Grad. Sch. Internat. Mgmt., 1974; m. Cynthia Renee Peterson, July 12, 1975. Market analyst Caterpillar Tractor Co., Peoria, Ill., 1975; parts merchandising mgr. Steiger Tractor Co., Fargo, N.D., 1975-78, service parts mgr., 1978-79; mgmt. cons. Trane Co., La Crosse, Wis., 1979—; instr. econs. Concordia Coll., Moorhead, Minn. Mem. Am. Mktg. Assn., Pi Kappa Delta. Lutheran. Club: Toastmasters. Home: 1214 Meadow Ln Onalaska WI 54650 Office: Trane Co La Crosse WI 54601

CARVER, JUANITA, plastic co. exec.; b. Indpls., Apr. 8, 1929; d. Willard H. and Golda M. Ashe; student Ariz. State U.; children—Daniel Charles, Robin Lewis, Scott Alan. Asst. librarian, sec., dir. CAMSCO, 1962-68; pres. Carver Corp., Phoenix, 1977—. Bd. dirs. Scottsdale Meml. Hosp. Aux., 1964-65, now asso.; active P.T.A.; den mother Cub Scouts; fund raiser Heart and Cancer campaigns. Republican. Methodist. Patentee latch hook rug yarn organizer. Home: 6255 E Avalon St Scottsdale AZ 85251 Office: 1810 S 19th Ave Phoenix AZ 85005

CARVER, KENDALL LYNN, ins. co. exec.; b. Spencer, Iowa, Nov. 4, 1936; s. Marion Wesley and Letha (Gaye) C.; B.S., U. Iowa, 1958; m. Carol, July 1, 1961; children—Merrian, Kendra, Lee, Christine. With Washington Nat. Ins. Co., 1958-77, mgr., Phoenix, 1968-74, regional dir., Evanston, Ill., 1974-77; pres., chief exec. officer Washington Nat. Life Ins. Co. N.Y., N.Y.C., 1977—; state health chmn. Health Ins. Council, Ariz., 1973-74. Fellow Life Mgmt. Inst.; mem. Am. Coll. Life Underwriters (C.L.U.), Nat. Assn. Life Underwriters, Life Ins. Council N.Y. (dir.). Republican. Home: 5 Tanglewood Trail Darien CT 06830 Office: 500 Fifth Ave New York NY 10036

CARVER, LUCILLE AVIS YOUNG (MRS. ROY JAMES CARVER, SR.), rubber mfg. co. exec.; b. Muscatine, Iowa, July 27, 1919; d. Merle Archie and Marie Anna (Kollman) Young; student U. Iowa; m. Roy James Carver Sr., Aug. 22, 1942; children—Roy James, John Alexander, Clayton Charles, Martin Gregory. With Carver Pump Co., Muscatine, sec., treas., dir., 1938—; treas., dir. Bandag, Inc., Muscatine, 1957—; with Carver Foundry Products, Inc., Muscatine, sec., treas., dir., 1954—; sec. Carver Tropical Products, Inc., Muscatine, 1968—. Bd. dirs. President's Club, U. Iowa. Recipient Distinguished Service award U. Iowa, 1972. Mem. Laura Musser Mus. Elk. Clubs: Ocean Reef (Key Largo, Fla.); Jockey, Internat. (Miami, Fla.); Geneva Golf and Country (Muscatine). Home: 2236 Mulberry Ave Muscatine IA 52761 Office: 1056 Hershey Ave Muscatine IA 52761

CARVER, RALPH DANIEL, JR., auto parts co. exec.; b. Denver, Oct. 7, 1932; s. Ralph Daniel and Beulah M. (Hill) C.; ed. high sch.; m. Lucinda Alice Carhart, Nov. 10, 1950; children—Delphine, Robert, James, Steven; m. 2d, Myrlis Jean Johnson, Mar. 4, 1978. Farmer, Dove Creek, Colo., 1950-56; diesel mechanic, asst. foreman I. Sanders Trucking Co., Naturita, Colo., 1957-60; owner, operator, pres., chmn. C & C Auto Parts Co., Naturita, 1960—, Montrose, Colo., 1963—, Delta, Colo., 1977—; chmn. bd. Ralph Carver Jr. Inc., Montrose, 1966—; land developer, Montrose, 1972—, dir. 1st Nat. Bank, Montrose. Chmn. bd. dirs. Colo. Western Coll., Montrose, 1969-72. Mem. Rocky Mountain Automotive Wholesalers Assn. (dir. Denver 1976—), Airplane Owners and Pilots Assn. Methodist. Clubs: Masons, Shriners, Elks. Home: 63524 Spring Creek PO Box 549 Montrose CO 81401 Office: 530 N Townsend St Montrose CO 81401

CARY, FRANK TAYLOR, bus. machines co. exec.; b. Gooding, Idaho, Dec. 14, 1920; s. Frank Taylor and Ida C.; B.S., UCLA, 1943; M.B.A., Stanford, 1948; m. Anne Curtis, 1943; children—Marshall, Bryan, Steven, Laura. With IBM, Armonk, N.Y., 1948—, pres. data processing div., 1964, v.p., group exec., 1966, sr. v.p., 1967, pres., 1971, chmn. bd., chief exec. officer, 1973—, also dir., chmn. exec. com.; dir. J.P. Morgan & Co., Morgan Guaranty Trust Co. N.Y., ABC, Inc., Merck & Co., Inc. Trustee Conf. Bd., Brookings Instn., Am. Mus. Natural History, Mus. Modern Art, Rockefeller U.; mem. corp. M.I.T., Bus. Council. Served with AUS, 1944-46. Office: IBM Old Orchard Rd Armonk NY 10504

CARY, TRACY GLEN, ins. co. exec.; b. Pampa, Tex., Apr. 29, 1929; s. J. Tracy and Leta Irene (Gillham) C.; student LaSalle Extension U. Sch. Law, 1948-52; B.B.A., Tex. Tech U., 1956; postgrad. So. Methodist U., 1960; grad. Am. Coll. Life Underwriters, 1977; m. Shirley Ann Hamlett, Aug. 24, 1957; children—Lance Hamleft, Shelley Ann. Mgmt. trainee Citizens Nat. Bank, Lubbock, Tex., 1956-57, new bus. devel. officer, 1957; agt. Gt. So. Life Ins. Co., 1957-58; v.p., dir. agys., exec. v.p., chmn. exec. com. Preferred Risk Life Assurance Co., 1958-62; pres. Glen Cary & Assos., 1966-67; asst. dir. agys., dir. agys., chief agy. officer Union Life Ins. Co., 1962-66; field v.p., v.p. and dir. gen. agys., v.p., dir. agys. and spl. markets, v.p. agys. Gt. Am. Res. Ins. Co., Dallas, 1967-79; exec. v.p., vice-chmn. exec. com., dir. First Pyramid Life Ins. Co., 1979—; chmn. bd. First Pyramid Mfg. Co., Inc., 1979—; dir. Computronics, Eden Isle Enterprises, Inc. Football coach YMCA, 1969-71; trustee Tex. Tech U. Loyalty Fund; fin. adv. council Tex. Tech. U.; mem. adv. com. Cotton Bowl, 1960-62. Served with AUS, 1948-52. Decorated Silver Star, Bronze Star, Army Commendation medal with pendant, Purple Heart, Combat Inf. badge, Legion of Merit; C.L.U. Mem. Nat. Assn. Life Underwriters, Sales and Mktg. Execs. Internat. (chmn. distinguished sales award com. 1961, dir. 1962), Ins. Club Dallas (dir.), Am. Coll. Life Underwriters, Internat. Platform Assn., Tex. Tech U. Ex-Students Assn. (nat. pres. 1976, nat. chmn. Old Red Club 1975), Phi Delta Theta (internat. bd. govs., internat. pres. 1978—), Delta Sigma Pi, Pi Sigma Epsilon. Clubs: Pleasant Valley Country; Brookhaven Country. Home: 17 Inverness Circle Little Rock AR 72212 Office: PO Box 2941 Little Rock AR 72203

CASAMO, WILLIAM ERNST, union ofcl.; b. N.Y.C., Nov. 29, 1916; s. Anthony R. and Hilda Marie (Johanson) C.; student Workers Sch., U. Wis., 1963, Inst. Mgmt. and Labor, Rutgers U., 1968; m. Eileen T. Moore, 1965; children—Cathryn, Vicki Lynn, William Anthony, Michael Jon, Jeffrey, Kevin. Pres. local 107, Packighouse Workers Orgn. Com., 1939-42; dist. dir. United Furniture Workers Am., 1943-53; rep. dir. dist. council 37, Am. Fedn. State, County and Mcpl. Employees Union, 1954-63; research asso., indsl. engr. Internat. Rep. Brotherhood Pulp, Sulphite and Paper Mill Workers, 1963; exec. asst. to pres. United Paperworkers Internat. Union, Flushing, N.Y., 1972—; mem. Labor Research Adv. Council, 1968-80, Manpower Area Planning Council, 1980; mem. coms. multilateral trade negitiations and fgn. labor and trade Dept. Labor, 1980. Bd. dirs. Day Care Council Westchester County; chmn. Cameron County (Pa.) Democratic Party; pres. Talcott Woods Assn.; town chmn. Queensbury (N.Y.). Served with USMCR, 1964. Mem. Indsl. Relations Research Assn., ACLU, Queens C. of C. Congregationalist. Club: Town of Scarsdale (N.Y.). Author tng. manuals. Home: 37 Talcott Rd Rye NY 10573 Office: 163-03 Horace Harding Expy Flushing NY 11365

CASE, ALBERT FOUNTAIN, JR., mgmt. systems cons.; b. Tampa, Fla., Mar. 2, 1955; s. Albert F. and Frances Elaine (Smith) C.; B.S. in Mgmt., SUNY, Buffalo, 1978; m. Deborah Ann Eigenman, Aug. 21, 1976; 1 dau., Kimberly Marie. Partner, Statewide Publs. Co., Niagara Falls, N.Y., 1972-74; asst. to dir. mgmt. info. systems Andco, Inc., Buffalo, 1974-76; analyst Service Systems Corp., Clarence, N.Y., 1976-77; bus. systems analyst M & T Bank, Buffalo, 1977—; exec. v.p. Maximus Systems, Inc., Williamsville, N.Y., 1977-79; pres. Case Info. Systems, Buffalo, 1979—; former dir. PJS Fed. Credit Union. Mem. Assn. Systems Mgmt., Assn. Computing Machinery. Democrat. Roman Catholic. Home: 6872 E High St Lockport NY 14094 Office: 1 Marine Midland Center 2SW Buffalo NY 14240

CASE, DEXTER KIMBALL, nursing home exec.; b. Hartford, Conn., May 8, 1946; s. Nathan Dexter and Ena Scott (Crockett) C.; B.S. in Bus. Adminstrn., Western New Eng. Coll., 1968; m. Rose Marie E. Connelly, Jan. 25, 1972; children—Brian, James, Scott, Laure. With Geri-Care Nursing Center Am., Manchester, Conn., 1969-72; owner, operator Ridgewood Ct. Nursing Home, Attleboro, Mass., 1972—, Camphill (Pa.) Nursing and Convalescent Center, Inc., 1976—, Hassler Home, Reading, Pa., 1978—; Oakmont (Pa.) Residence, 1978—. Mem. Pa. Health Care Assn. Republican. Address: 70 Mt View Rd Shillington PA 19607

CASE, MANNING EUGENE, JR., corp. exec.; b. Sioux City, Iowa, Mar. 1916; s. Manning Eugene and Loretta (Seims) C.; A.B., Western Res. U., 1938, J.D., 1941; m. Ernestine Bryan, July 26, 1941; children—Douglas Manning, Randall Bryan. Admitted to Ohio bar, 1941; asst. counsel B. F. Goodrich Co., Akron, 1941-52; sec., treas., gen. counsel, dir. Perfection Industries, 1952-55; sec. Hupp Corp., 1955-57; v.p. service and finance M & M's Candies div. Mars, Inc., 1957-60; asst. treas. Standard Brands, Inc., 1961-62, treas. 1962-77, v.p., 1968-78, v.p., chief fin. officer, 1977-78, sr. v.p., chief fin. officer, 1978-80, sr. v.p. personnel and investor relations, 1980—; dir. Excelsior Income Shares, Inc. Active, Boy Scouts Am. Served to col. JAGC, U.S. Army, 1942-46. Mem. Am. Soc. Corp. Secs., Am. Bar Assn., Phi Beta Kappa, Delta Sigma Rho, Omicron Delta Kappa, Beta Theta Pi, Phi Delta Phi. Clubs: Met. (bd. govs.), N.Y. Athletic; Morris County Golf, Conn. Golf. Home: 25 Lake End Pl Mountain Lakes NJ 07046 Office: 625 Madison Ave New York NY 10022

CASE, ROBERT ORMOND, electronics co. exec.; b. Portland, Oreg., Feb. 3, 1926; s. Robert Ormond and Evelyn (Smith) C.: B.Engring., Yale, 1949, M.Engring., 1950; m. Cynthia Tribou, June 28, 1947; children—Jennifer, Patricia Leigh, Victoria Jane, Robert Ormond. Devel. engr. Oak Ridge Nat. Lab., 1950-51; research engr. N.Am. Aviation, Inc., Downey, Calif., 1951-54, engring. supr., 1954-57, chief preliminary engring. sect., Anaheim, Calif., 1957-61; dir. research Tamar Electronics, Inc., Anaheim, 1962-63, v.p. engring. and marketing 1963-65, also dir.; with Ford Aerospace and Communications Corp., 1965—, dir. radar and intelligence operation, aeronutronic div., 1966-67, dir. air def. systems operation, 1967-72, dir. missile systems operation, 1972-80, asst. gen. mgr. Western devel. labs. div., Palo Alto, Calif., 1980—. Served with USNR, 1943-46. Mem. AAAS, Yale Sci. Assn., Assn. U.S. Army, Am. Def. Preparedness Assn., Air Force Assn., Sigma Xi, Tau Beta Pi. Republican. Methodist. Patentee in electronics field. Home: Saratoga CA Office: 3939 Fabian Way Palo Alto CA 94303

CASELL, R(OBERT) JAY, fin. exec.; b. Miami, Fla., June 14, 1939; s. Harold and Miriam (Berkowitz) C.; B.A., Franklin and Marshall Coll., 1960; grad. Am. Grad. Sch. Internat. Mgmt., 1962; m. Susan Clair, Feb. 14, 1971; children—Robert Jay, Jason Harold. Export mgr. Internat. Harvester, Kearny, N.J., 1962; asst. regional mgr. R.J. Reynolds Tobacco Co., P.R., 1962-63; dir. internat. devel. Inland Industries, N.Y.C., 1963; sales exec. Spanish Internat. Network, San Antonio, 1964; exec. v.p. P.S.A., San Antonio, Tex., 1964-67; mng. partner Bojay Ltd., Tex., Calif., 1966-76, Tex. Investment Council, 1967-69, Tex. Enterprises, 1967-69, Tex. Big Ten Prodns., 1967-69; regional sales exec. Communico, Houston, 1970-71, joint venture partner, 1971; pres. Alamo Group, San Antonio, 1971—. Chmn. bd. Alamo Plaza Assn., 1977-79; chmn. adv. bd. Tex. Tech. Sch. Mass Communication, 1979—; bd. dirs. Discover Tex. Assn., 1977—; nat. com. Discover Am. Travel Orgn., 1977-79. Served with USAF, 1960-61. Mem. Hotel Sales Mgmt. Assn. (dir. 1978-79), Paseo Del Rio Assn., Discover Am. Travel Orgn., Nat. Council Travel Attractions, Tex. Soc. Assn. Execs., Nat. Tour Brokers Assn., Greater San Antonio C. of C., San Antonio Conservation Soc., Tex. Travel Research Assn. Jewish. Clubs: Skal, B'nai B'rith. Home: 102 Chattington St San Antonio TX 78213 Office: 315 Alamo Plaza San Antonio TX 78205

CASEY, ALBERT VINCENT, airline exec.; b. Boston, Feb. 28, 1920; s. John Joseph and Norine (Doyle) C.; A.B., Harvard, 1943, M.B.A., 1948; m. Eleanor Anne Welch, Aug. 25, 1945; children—Peter Andrew, Judith Anne. With S.P. Ry., 1948-61, asst. v.p., asst. treas., San Francisco, 1953-61; v.p., treas. Ry. Express Agy., N.Y.C., 1961-63; v.p. finance Times-Mirror Co., Los Angeles, 1963-64, exec. v.p., dir., 1964-66, pres., mem. exec. com., 1966-74; chmn. bd., pres., chief exec. officer Am. Airlines, 1974-80, chmn., chief exec. officer, 1980—, also dir.; dir. Times Mirror Co., Colgate-Palmolive Co., Republic of Tex. Corp. Mem. council Stanford Research Inst.; bd. govs. Corp. Fund for Performing Arts, Kennedy Center, Washington; mem. bus. com. Mus. Modern Art, N.Y.C.; bd. dirs. Boys Clubs Am.; bd. overseers, chmn. fin. policy com. Harvard Coll.; bd. govs. Dallas Symphony Assn.; trustee Dallas Mus. Fine Arts. Bus. Served to 1st lt. AUS, 1942-46. Mem. Air Transp. Assn. (dir.). Clubs: Dallas, Dallas Country, Dallas Petroleum; Eldorado Country (Indian Wells, Calif.). Office: PO Box 61616 Dallas/Ft Worth Airport TX 75261

CASEY, ARTHUR FRANCIS, JR., mgmt. co. exec.; b. Boston, Apr. 20, 1951; s. Arthur Francis and Leona Elizabeth (George) C.; B.S., Boston Coll., 1973; m. Cheryl Lynn Volpe, Aug. 15, 1976. Exec. sec. to Mayor of Quincy (Mass.), 1976-78; comptroller O'Connell Mgmt. Co., Inc., Quincy, 1978—. Campaign mgr. city councillor, 1979. Served with USMC, 1973-74. Recipient commendation Fed. Energy Adminstrn. Developed and instituted 1st summer job lottery State of Mass., 1978. Home: 57 Woodcliff Rd Quincy MA 02169 Office: One Heritage Dr Quincy MA 02171

CASEY, EDWARD PAUL, mfg. co. exec.; b. Boston, Feb. 23, 1930; s. Edward J. and Virginia Pizzini (Paul) C.; A.B., Yale U., 1952; M.B.A., Harvard U., 1955; m. Patricia Pinkham, June 23, 1950; children—Patricia Estes Casey Shepherd, Lucile Tyler Casey Arnote, Jennifer Paul Casey Schwab, Sheila Pinkham, Virginia Louise. With Davidson Rubber Co. Inc., Dover, N.H., 1950-65, exec. v.p., 1955-65, pres., 1965; pres. McCord Corp., Detroit, 1965-78, Ex-Cell-O Corp., Troy, Mich., 1978—. Trustee Henry Ford Hosp., 1973—; bd. dirs. Detroit Symphony Orch., 1974—. Mem. Soc. Automotive Engrs., Engring. Soc. Detroit, Chief Execs. Forum. Clubs: Harvard Bus. Sch., Detroit, Detroit Athletic, Yondotega (Detroit); Grosse Pointe, Country of Detroit (Grosse Pointe); Eastern Yacht (Marblehead, Mass.), Union League (N.Y.C.); Bath and Tennis (Palm Beach, Fla.); Wig and Pen (London). Home: 4 Rathbone Pl Grosse Pointe MI 48230 Office: 2855 Coolidge Troy MI 48084

CASEY, JACK HESTWOOD, diamond investment counselor; b. Lexington, Va., Dec. 1, 1948; s. John H. and June B. (Bruyles) C.; B.A., Bradley U., Peoria, Ill.; m. Angela Suzanne Vasey, Mar. 1, 1979. Owner-operator Nat. Hearing Aid Center, Mattoon, Ill., 1975-76; pres. House of Hearing Aids, Inc., Mattoon, 1978-80; diamond investment counselor Internat. Diamond Corp., Mattoon, 1978—, also dir. tng., Great Lakes Region. Served with USMCR, 1968-71; Vietnam. Decorated Purple Heart. Mem. Nat. Fedn. Ind. Bus., Internat. Assn. Fin. Planners, Marine Corps League (past trustee Ill.; cert. of merit 1977), Ill. Notary Assn., Am. Legion, VFW. Republican. Methodist. Club: Shriners. Home: 1536 Crimson Ln Palatine IL 60067 Office: 1014 E Algonquin Rd Schaumburg IL 60194

CASEY, JOHN ROBERT, wood products co. exec.; b. Mason City, Iowa, May 9, 1928; s. Charles J. and Helen A. (O'Brien) C.; B.S. in Bus., U. Iowa, 1952; m. Polly A. Carnes, June 17, 1949; children—Stephen, Michael, Charles. Salesman advt. Charles J. Casey, Inc., Mason City, Iowa, 1952-54; sales engr. Rilco Laminated Products, Storm Lake, Iowa, 1954-57; Genesbo, Ill., 1957-62, Morton, Ill., 1962-65; archtl. engr. Weyerhaeuser Co., Naperville, Ill., 1965-67, area mgr., Peoria, Ill., 1967-70, adminstrv. asst., Palatine, Ill., 1970-73, adminstrv. and pricing mgr., St. Paul, 1973—. Mem. Variance Bd., Bloomington, Minn., 1977-78. Served with U.S. Army, 1946-48. Republican. Roman Catholic. Home: 10312 Stanley Circle Bloomington MN 55437 Office: Weyerhaeuser Co 7901 Xerxes Ave S Suite 316 Bloomington MN 55431

CASEY, LIONEL JAMES, cons. co. exec.; b. Lowland, N.C., May 4, 1930; s. Lionel James and Emma (Brothers) C.; student Coll. William and Mary, 1951-52; B.S., Tulane U., 1954; M.A., Emory U., 1955; m. Garnett Eighme Seifert, Oct. 12, 1958; children—Amy Lynn, Judith Anne, Mary Catherine, Lionel James III. Pilot, Pan Am. World Airways, N.Y.C., 1955-57; pres. Colonial Chem. Co., Inc., Washington, N.C., 1958-62, dir., 1958—; pres., dir. Constrn. Consultants, Inc., Norfolk, Va., 1962—; chmn. bd. Timberlane Farms, Inc., Apollo Farms, Inc. Served with AUS, 1947-51. Mason. Address: PO Box B132 Chesapeake VA 23321

CASEY, SAMUEL BROWN, JR., mfg. co. exec.; b. Pitts., Oct. 14, 1927; s. Samuel Brown and Constance (Connelly) C.; B.A., Pa. State U., 1950; m. Margaret Fox, Sept. 9, 1950 (div. 1978); children—Samuel Brown III, Ann, Meg; m. 2d, A.M. Dobbins, Nov. 8, 1980. Product mgr. Swindell-Dressler Co., 1950-60; pres. John F. Casey Co., 1960-69, chmn. bd., 1969—; pres., chief exec. officer Pullman, Inc., Chgo., 1970—, chmn., 1978-79; dir. Joseph Dixon Crucible Co., John F. Casey Co., Mellon Nat. Corp., Esmark, Inc., Mellon Bank N.A., Universal-Rundle. Pres., Pitts. Hosp., 1963-70; vice chmn. bd. Pitts. Stadium Authority, 1964; hon. trustee Carnegie Inst.; v.p., bd. dirs. John Crerar Library, Chgo.; bd. dirs. Mus. Sci. and Industry, Chgo. Served with USAF, 1945-46. Office: 1550 N State St Chicago IL 60610

CASEY, WILLIAM ROSSITER, customs broker, internat. freight forwarder; b. Los Angeles, June 15, 1922; s. William Rossiter and Clare (Gordon) C.; student Amherst Coll., 1940-42; B.S., U.S. Naval Acad., 1945; m. Carlyn Marie Temple, June 7, 1945; 1 son, Richard T. Successively treas., exec. v.p., pres. The Myers Group, Inc., Rouses Point, N.Y. and N.Y.C., 1953-76, chmn. bd., chief exec. officer, 1976—. Bd. dirs. Champlain Valley Physicians Hosp., Plattsburgh, N.Y., 1966-71; trustee SUNY, Plattsburgh, 1970-72; mem. Thousand Island Park Commn., Alexandria Bay, N.Y., 1971-77. Served with USN, 1942-53. Mem. Nat. Customs Brokers and Forwarders Assn. Am. (pres. 1979—), Customs Brokers Assn. No. U.S. Border (past pres.), Assn. Internat. Border Agys. (past dir.). Republican. Clubs: Downtown Athletic (N.Y.C.); Los Angeles Athletic. Contbr. articles to trade publs. Home: 310 Lake Rouses Point NY 12979 Office: Myers Bldg Rouses Point NY 12979 also One World Trade Center New York NY 10048

CASH, CLAYBOURNE ALLISON, ret. corp. exec.; b. McLean, Tex., Oct. 31, 1914; s. Claybourne Jeremiah and Lavada (Phillips) C.; student Tex. Technol. Coll., 1933-35; m. Juanita Ball, Sept. 13, 1936; 1 dau., Elaine (Mrs. C.D. Culver). With Shamrock Oil & Gas Corp., Amarillo, Tex., 1935-67, beginning as clk., successively chief clk., treating foreman, refinery, chief engr., asst. to v.p. charge ops., v.p., asst. to pres., 1955-57, exec. v.p., dir., 1957-60, pres., 1960-67; exec. v.p., dir. Diamond Shamrock Corp., 1967, pres. Diamond-Shamrock Oil & Gas Co. unit, 1967-69, chmn., 1969-71, vice chmn. Diamond Shamrock Corp., 1971, pres., chief operating officer, 1971-75, chmn. bd., 1975-80; dir. First Nat. Bank Amarillo. Mem. Am. Petroleum Inst. (dir.), Mid-Continent Oil and Gas Assn. (dir.), Nat. Gas Processors Assn., Newcomen Soc., Am. Chem. Soc., Panhandle Producers and Royalty Owners Assn. (dir.). Methodist. Mason. Clubs: Amarillo (pres. 1961), Amarillo Country; Dallas Petroleum; Petroleum (Houston). Home: 3000 S Lipscomb St Amarillo TX 79109 Office: Box 631 Amarillo TX 79173 also 1100 Superior Ave Cleveland OH 44114

CASH, TERRY LYNN, nursing home adminstr.; b. Spartanburg, S.C., Mar. 25, 1947; s. Arthur M. and Virginia H. (Henderson) C.; B.S. in Pharmacy, U. S.C., 1970; m. Janis Lewis, June 27, 1969; 1 son, Todd Lynn. Pharmacist, Boiling Springs Pharmacy, Spartanburg, 1970-72; pres. Health Resources Corp., Spartanburg, S.C., 1972-76; dir. ops. Oak Manor, Inc., Kinston, N.C., 1976-78; v.p. mgmt. and ops., dir. OMG Corp., Kinston, 1979—; v.p., dir. Med-Way, Inc., Kinston, 1979—. Mem. Am. Soc. Cons. Pharmacists, Am. Health Care Assn., N.C. Health Care Facilities Assn. (v.p. intermediate care), Am. Coll. Nursing Home Adminstrs. Methodist. Club: Rotary. Home: 2601 Brookhaven Dr Kinston NC 28501 Office: OMG Corp PO Box 969 Kinston NC 28501

CASHEN, JOSEPH LAWRENCE, real estate broker; b. Kansas City, Mo., May 10, 1931; s. John Lawrence and Anna May (Sutcliffe) C.; student real estate U. Calif. at Los Angeles, 1965-66; m. Michele Ann Hayes, June 15, 1960; children—Michael, Patricia, Kelly. Sales cons. chems. Economics Lab., Los Angeles, 1954-64; broker Forest E. Olsen Realtors, Canonga Park, Calif., 1964-67; pres. Property World, Inc., Woodland Hills, Calif., 1967-71; pres. Century 21 Real Estate #1, Inc., Woodland Hills, 1971—. Pres. Police Activity League, Woodland Hills, 1976; dir., mem. adv. council Pierce Coll. Rotoract, 1974-75. Served with USMC, 1950-54. Mem. San Fernando Valley Bd. Realtors, Calif. Assn. Realtors, Nat. Assn. Realtors, Nat. Inst. Farm and Land Brokers, Nat. Assn. Home Builders, Aircraft Owners and Pilots Assn., Woodland Hills C. of C. (pres. 1976). Clubs: K.C., Rotary (pres. 1974-75). Inventor in field. Office: 21021 Ventura Blvd Woodland Hills CA 91364

CASHION, WILLIAM RICHARD, data processor; b. Nashville, July 9, 1945; s. Eugene Hilton and Alice Catherine (Parks) C.; B.S., Tenn. Tech. U., Cookeville, 1972; m. Wilma Jean Hughes, Apr. 4, 1969; 1 dau., Alice Michelle. Data processing ops. mgr. Tenn. Tech. U., 1972-78, asst. dir. data processing, 1978—; partner Almica Co., Cookeville, 1978—. Served with USAF, 1967-69. Mem. Data Processing Mgmt. Assn. (chpt. pres. 1980). Home: 711 West Oak Dr Cookeville TN 38501 Office: Box 5071 Cookeville TN 38501

CASHMAN, JAMES CHESTER, bldg. contractor; b. Hartley, Iowa, Jan. 21, 1927; s. Chester Floyd and Kathryn (Fuller) C.; B.S. in Civil Engring., Iowa State U., 1949; m. Ethel Frances Goode, Sept. 4, 1949; children—Susan, James, Mary Elizabeth, David, Kevin. Asst. city engr. Sioux City (Iowa), 1950-52; city engr. South Sioux City (Nebr.), 1952-53; owner Cashman Engring. Co., Sioux City, 1953-57; mgr. Jennings Engring. Co., Los Angeles, 1957-58; supr. subdiv. constrn. H & H Constrn. Co., Los Angeles, 1958-62; pres. J & E Constrn. Co., Cashman Constrn. Co., Los Angeles, 1962-70; pres. Cashman & Sons, Inc., 1964-70; contracts mgr. Corona Land Co. 1970-72, pres., 1972-77; pres. The Homestead Co., Inc. Committeeman El Segundo council Boy Scouts Am.; mem. structural inspection adv. com. Riverside City Coll., 1974—. Bd. dirs. Centinella Valley YMCA, Inglewood, Calif., 1960—, also pres.; bd. dirs. Community Settlement House, Riverside, 1977—. Served with AUS, World War II. Mem. Bldg. Industry Assn. Calif. (pres. Riverside-San Bernardino chpt. 1976-77, 78), Nat. Assn. Home Builders (land use and devel. com. 1970—, pres. So. Calif. 1979-80, Builder of Year 1975-76), Exec. Secs., Inc., Phi Kappa Tau (pres. Ames, Iowa 1948-49). Mem. Trinity Christian Center (elder). Home and office: 2323 Mary St Riverside CA 92506

CASHMAN, RAY DUDLEY, printing co. exec.; b. Houston, Aug. 1, 1945; s. John Edgar and Mary Margaret (Dudley) C.; B.A., So. Meth. U., 1968; m. Susan Dean Odom, Jan. 2, 1970; 1 son, Ray Dudley. Pres., Times Jour. Pub. Co., Oklahoma City, 1968, asst. to pres., dir., 1970-72; salesman Gulf Printing Co., Houston, 1969-70, dir., 1974—, asst. v.p., 1974-75, v.p., 1975-77, pres., 1977—, also dir.; dir. Times Jour. Pub. Co., Gulf Pub. Co., Oklahoma City. Bd. dirs. Houston Youth Symphony and Allegro Ballet, 1978—. Office: 2210 W Dallas St Houston TX 77019

CASPER, JACK M., constrn. co. exec.; b. Phila. Sept. 10, 1945; s. John J. and Frances (Spinelli) C.; B.S., Drexel U., 1968; M.B.A., Okla. State U., 1970; m. July 18, 1970; children—Dana, John. Audit staff Deere & Co., 1970-71; fin. dir. John Deere Ltd., Australia, 1971-72; with Deere & Co., Moline, Ill., 1973, asst. controller, Kansas City, Mo., 1973-76; v.p. fin. Graney Cos., Inc., Kansas City, Mo., 1976—, also dir.; dir. Mo. Rental Machinery, Grain Valley Farms, Garney Cattle Co. Mem. Planning Execs. Inst., Am. Mgmt. Assn., Tax Execs. Inst., Fin. Execs. Inst., Pi Kappa Phi. Roman Catholic. Club: Kansas City Athletic. Home: 9206 W 112th Terr Overland Park KS 66210 Office: 1331 NW Vivion Rd Kansas City MO 64118

CASPERSEN, FINN MICHAEL WESTBY, finance co. exec.; b. N.Y.C., Oct. 27, 1941; s. Olaus Westby and Freda C.; B.A. in Econs. with honors, Brown U., 1963; LL.B. cum laude, Harvard, 1966; m. Barbara Morris, June 17. 1967. Admitted to Fla. bar, 1966, N.Y. State bar, 1967; asso. firm Dewey, Ballantine, Bushby, Palmer & Wood, N.Y.C., 1969-72; asso. counsel Beneficial Mgmt. Corp., Morristown, N.J., 1972-75, v.p., dir., mem. exec. com. Beneficial Corp., 1975, vice chmn., mem. exec. and fin. coms., 1975, chmn. bd., chief exec. officer, chmn. exec. com., 1976—; dir. Beneficial Ins. Group Cos.; gen. counsel Central Nat. Life Ins. Co. Omaha, Morristown, 1974-76, now dir.; pres. Westby Corp., Tri-Farms, Inc.; chmn. bd. Clark Hill Sugary; dir., mem. exec. com. Peoples Bank & Trust Co., Wilmington, Del., Spiegel Inc., Chgo., Western Auto Supply Co., Kansas City, Mo.; dir. Consol. Marine Ins., London, Nippon Beneficial Fin. Co. Japan. 1st Tex. Savs. Assn., Dallas, Cedix Holding Co., N.Z., Beneficial Fin. Co. Ireland Ltd. Trustee, N.J. Bd. Higher Edn., 1978-80; chmn. bd. trustees, chmn. exec. com. Peddie Sch., Hightstown, N.J.; trustee Brown U., Com. Econ. Devel., Camp Nejeda Found., O.W. Caspersen Found.; mem. nominating com. and retirement bd. Morristown Meml. Hosp.; bd. dirs. Exec. Council Fgn. Diplomats. Served from ensign to lt., USCG, 1966-69. Mem. Am., N.Y. State, Fla. bar assns., N.J. C. of C. (dir.), Del. Round Table; Nat. Consumer Fin. Assn. (dir., mem. exec. com.), Joint Econ. Com. (co-chmn. inflation seminar 1980). Clubs: Harvard, Knickerbocker (N.Y.C.); Faculty (Brown U.), Univ. (Sarasota, Fla.); Panther Valley Country (N.J.); Carlton (Chgo.); Univ. (Tampa, Fla.). Home: PO Drawer W Andover NJ 07821 Office: 200 South St Morristown NJ 07960

CASS, LEE HOGAN, retail co. exec.; b. Little Rock; d. William Frederick and Ora Lee (Baldridge) Meyer; student Little Rock U., 1938-39, So. Meth. U., 1941-42; m. Alonzo Beecher Cass, June 27, 1952 (dec. 1969); 1 dau., Julie Christopher; stepchildren—Timothy, Linda, Nicholas, Julie, Liza. Writer, producer, TV emcee NBC, Hollywood, Calif., 1946-54; fashion dir., sales promotion dir. Bullock's, Los Angeles, 1954-60; fashion dir., advt. dir. Catalina, Los Angeles, 1960-63; v.p. The Broadway, Los Angeles, 1966—. Mem. Los Angeles County Econ. Devel. Council, 1978—. Recipient Outstanding Communicator award Los Angeles Advt. Women, 1979. Mem. Hollywood Women's Press Club, Fashion Group Inc., Los Angeles County Mus. Art, Los Angeles County Mus. Art Costume Council, Los Angeles C. of C. (women's council). Baptist. Club: Balboa Yacht. Office: 3880 N Mission Rd Los Angeles CA 90031

CASS, ROBERT MICHAEL, lawyer, reins. co. exec.; b. Carlisle, Pa., July 5, 1945; s. Robert Lau and Norma Jean (McCaleb) C.; B.A., Pa. State U., 1967; J.D., Temple U., 1971; m. Patricia Ann Garber, Aug. 12, 1967; children—Charles McCaleb, David Lau. Benefit examiner Social Security Adminstrn., Phila., 1967-68; mktg. rep. Employers Comml. Union Ins. Co., Phila., 1968-70; asst. sec. Nat. Reins. Corp., N.Y.C., 1970-77; admitted to N.Y. bar, 1974; asst. v.p. Skandia Am. Reins. Corp., N.Y.C., 1977-80; mgr. Allstate Reins. Co., Northbrook, Ill., 1980—. Mem. Am. Bar Assn., N.Y. State Bar Assn., Soc. C.P.C.U.'s, Conf. Spl. Risk Underwriters, Excess/Surplus Lines Claims Assn. Home: 325 Old Mill Rd Barrington IL 60010 Office: 80 Allstate Plaza S Northbrook IL 60062

CASS, THOMAS RICHARDSON, lab. exec.; b. Peabody, Mass., Nov. 2, 1930; s. Thomas Edward and Alice Kimball (Richardson) C.; B.S., Merrimack Coll., Andover, Mass., 1952; m. Marjorie Ann Perry, June 30, 1962; children—Meredith, Thomas E. Sales engr., Hercules Powder Co., 1956-58; prodn. supr. Nat. Sugar Refining Co., 1958-59; plant mgr. Friend Bros. Inc., 1959-64; process engr. Bostik div. USM Corp., Middleton, Mass., 1964-67; mfg. mgr. Commodore Foods Inc., Lowell and Westford, Mass., 1967-70; pres. Aqua Labs. Inc., Amesbury, Mass., 1970—. Mem. Masconomet (Mass.) Regional High Sch. Bd., 1964-65. Served to lt. (j.g.), USNR, 1952-56. Mem. Nat. Assn. Corrosion Engrs., Small Bus. Assn. New Eng., Water Pollution Control Fedn., Sales and Mktg. Execs. Internat. Republican. Roman Catholic. Rotarian (dir. Amesbury 1976—). Home: 8 Taylor River Rd Hampton Falls NH 03844 Office: 36 High St Amesbury MA 01913

CASSAI, MILDRED ANN, accountant; b. Denver, Jan. 15, 1928; d. Pasquale and Josephine (James) Serravo; student Denver Opportunity Sch., 1964, 75—, Community Coll., 1974; m. Elmer Cassai, Oct. 31, 1948; children—Shirley (Mrs. Michael Demery), Gary, Michael, Pamela, Larry. With Denver & Rio Grande Western R.R., Denver, 1945-50; accountant Central Bookkeeping & Tax Service, 1964-73, partner, 1971-73; pvt. practice accounting, Denver, 1975—; legal sec. Justin D. Hannen, Atty., 1975—. Mem. Assn. Enrolled Agts. (dir., chmn. ethics com., pres. Colo. chpt.), Nat., Colo. socs. pub. accountants, Colo., Denver legal secs. assns., Epsilon Sigma Alpha. Republican. Roman Catholic. Club: Ports of Call Travel. Home: 1823 W 39th Ave Denver CO 80211 Office: Symes Bldg Denver CO 80202

CASSAR, JEAN-PAUL EDOUARD, systems analyst; b. Tunis, Tunisia, Feb. 29, 1948; immigrated to Can., 1975, naturalized, 1979; s. Paul L. and Marie D. (Gambin) C.; B.A. in Philosophy, U. Tunis, 1966; M.A. in Law and Adminstrn., Faculty of Law and Econ. Scis., Aix en Provence, France, 1972; m. Christiane Albrand, July 30, 1970; children—Yann-Philippe, Nicolas. Mgmt. cons. G. Prieur, Marseille, France, 1972-75; systems analyst Provincial Bank, Montreal, Que., Can., 1975-77; mgmt. cons. Police Dept., Montreal, 1977-79; systems mgr. Radio-Quebec, Montreal, 1979—. Mem. Que. Assn. Systems Mgmt. (pres. 1980-81), Fedn. de L'informatique de Quebec. Home: 906 Oak St Saint Lambert PQ J4P 1Z7 Canada Office: 1000 Fullum Montreal PQ H2K 3L7 Canada

CASSEL, JOHN ELDEN, accountant; b. Verden, Okla., Apr. 24, 1934; s. Elbert Emery and Erma Ruth (McDowell) C.; m. Mary Lou Malcom, June 3, 1953; children—John Elden, James Edward, Jerald Eugene. Plant mgr., also asst. gen. mgr. Baker and Taylor Co., Oklahoma City, 1966-71; paymaster, office mgr. Robberson Steel Co., Oklahoma City, 1971-76; pvt. investor, 1976—. Democrat. Methodist. Home: 2332 NW 118th St Oklahoma City OK 73120

CASSIDY, DWANE ROY, insulation contracting co. exec.; b. Bedford, Ind., Oct. 20, 1915; s. Leo Clayton and Lilly Fay (Robbins) C.; student Roscoe Turner's Sch. Aviation, 1944; m. Mary Catherine Shrout, Aug. 28, 1937; children—Gail (Mrs. Gordon Everling), Cheryl, Duane, Nina (Mrs. Robert McAnulty). With L. C. Cassidy & Son, Inc., Indpls., 1934—, now v.p.; v.p. L.C. Cassidy & Sons, Inc. of Fla., 1963—. Served with USN, 1944-45; PTO. Mem. Gideons Internat. Methodist. (dir.). Club: Optimist (Indpls.). Home: 644 Lawndale St Plainfield IN 46168 Office: 1918 S High School Rd Indianapolis IN 46241

CASSIDY, GERALD S. J., govt.-relations cons.; b. Flushing, N.Y., Apr. 14, 1941; s. John Joseph and Beatrice Veronica (Millott) C.; B.S. in Polit. Sci., Villanova U., 1963; J.D., Cornell U., 1967; m. Loretta Palladino, Mar. 7, 1964. Admitted to Fla. bar, 1967, D.C. bar, 1969; trial atty. S. Fla. Migrant Legal Services Program, Ft. Myers, 1967-69; profl. staff mem. U.S. Senate Select Com. on Nutrition and Human Needs, 1969, gen. counsel, 1970-73, 74-75; exec. dir., gen. counsel Democratic Nat. Com. Reform Commn., Washington, 1973; sec.-treas. Schlossberg-Cassidy and Assos., Inc., Washington, 1975—; mem. exec. legis. adminstrv. law sect. Am. Bar Assn.; speaker in field. Mem. Nat. Democratic Club. Recipient Speaker award Soc. Advancement Food Service Research, 1971, Food Service Mfrs. Assn., 1971. Mem. Am., Fla., D.C. bar assns., Am. Judicature Soc. Roman Catholic. Club: Capitol Hill. Home: 7733 Dower Ln McLean VA 22101 Office: 955 L'Enfant Plaza SW Washington DC 20024

CASSIDY, JAMES J(OSEPH), pub. relations counsel; b. Norwood, Ohio, Dec. 31, 1916; s. Martin D. and Helen (Johnston) C.; student U. Cin., 1934-38; m. Rita Hackett, Oct. 18, 1941; children—Claudia, James. Dir. spl. events, internat. broadcasts Crosley Broadcasting Corp., 1939-44, war corr., 1944-45, dir. pub. relations, 1946-50; war corr. NBC, 1944-45; account exec. Hill & Knowlton, Inc., N.Y.C., 1950-53, v.p., 1953-61, sr. v.p., 1961-66, exec. v.p., dir., 1966-71, pres., chief operating officer, 1971-74, vice chmn., 1974-75; vice chmn. Burson-Marsteller, Washington, 1975—. Recipient Variety award, 1944, citation for reporting in combat areas from Sec. War, 1945. Mem. Pub. Relations Soc. Am. (past pres. N.Y. chpt.), Profit Sharing Council Am. (past chmn.). Clubs: Overseas Press Am., Aviation Writers, Nat. Press, Sky, George Town, Internat., 1925 F St. Home: 2801 New Mexico Ave NW Washington DC 20007 Office: 1800 M St NW Washington DC 20036

CASSIDY, JAMES MARK, constrn. co. exec.; b. Evanston, Ill., June 22, 1942; s. James Michael and Mary Ellen (Munroe) C.; B.A., St. Mary's Coll., 1963; m. Bonnie Marie Bercker, Aug. 1, 1964; children—Micaela Marie, Elizabeth Ann, Daniel James. Estimator, Cassidy Bros., Inc., Rosemont, Ill., 1963-65, project mgr., 1965-67, v.p., 1967-71, exec. v.p., 1971-77, pres., 1978—; trustee Plasterer's Health & Welfare Trust, 1971—. Area fund leader constrn. industry salute to Boy Scouts Am., 1975; mem. pres.'s council St. Mary's Coll. Served with U.S. Army, 1963-64, USNG, 1964-69. Mem. Chgo. Plastering Inst., Builder Uppers Club (pres. 1973-74), Employing Plasterers Assn. Chgo. (pres. 1976-79), Great Lakes Council, Internat. Assn. Wall and Ceiling Contractors (chmn. 1977), Bldg. Constrn. Employers Assn. Chgo. (dir. 1976—), Assn. Wall and Ceiling Industries (dir. 1978—). Roman Catholic. Clubs: Abbey Springs Country (Fontana, Wis.); Courthouse. Office: PO Box 596 Rosemont IL 60018

CASSIDY, MICHAEL JAMES, fin. exec.; b. Schenectady, July 23, 1950; s. Donald Patrick and Helen Marcella (Hockford) C.; B.S., Rider Coll., 1972; M.B.A., Babson Coll., 1973. Sales rep. Prentice-Hall, Inc., Conn., 1973-75, I.D.S., New Haven, 1975-76; brokerage cons. Conn. Gen. Ins. Co., Boston, 1976-77; mktg. specialist Forum Corp., Boston, 1977-78; pres. Cassidy Assos., Woburn, Mass., 1978—; cons. in field. Address: 18 Mill St Woburn MA 01801

CASSILLY, WILLIAM SUTTER, realty co. exec.; b. St. Louis, Feb. 10, 1920; s. Edward John and Harriet Maude (Sutter) C.; B.S.B.A., Washington U., St. Louis, 1942; m. Anita Louise Crozat, Sept. 7, 1947; children—Louise, William Sutter, Anne, Mary, Joan, Ellen. Pres., Cassilly Realty Co., Ballwin, Mo., 1946—; dir. Mark Twain Bank. Bd. dirs. St. Joseph's Acad., St. Louis, camp dir. St. Louis council Boy Scouts Am., 1965-70. Served to capt. Transp. Corps, U.S. Army, 1942-46. Recipient Silver Beaver award Boy Scouts Am., 1966. Mem. Nat. Assn. Realtors, Am. Assn. Arbitrators (arbitrator), Nat.

Assn. Homebuilders (nat. dir. 1955-60, pres. St. Louis chpt. 1960-61), Beta Theta Pi. Republican. Roman Catholic. Home: 10 Kings Pond Rd Glendale MO 63122 Office: 753 Clubhouse Dr Ballwin MO 63011

CASSIMATIS, EMMANUEL JOHN, pharm. mfg. co. exec.; b. N.Y.C., Mar. 13, 1930; s. John Emmanuel and Angeliki (Fatseas) C.; B.S., N.Y. U., 1956, M.B.A., 1962; m. Patricia Ann Livingston, June 1, 1969; children—John Emmanuel, Andriana. Methods analyst Merrill Lynch, Pierce Fenner and Smith, N.Y.C., 1957-58; instr. acctg. N.Y.C. Community Coll., 1958-59; supr. cost dept. John W. McGrath Corp., N.Y.C., 1960-64; asst. to treas. AVCO Corp., Greenwich, Conn., 1964-69; asst. treas. Squibb Corp., N.Y.C., 1969—, Squibb Investments S.A., Luxembourg, 1974—, Squibb Internat. Fin. N.V., Netherlands Antilles, 1972—; treas. SQB Leasing Corp., N.Y.C., 1974—; mem. N.Y. adv. bd. Banco Popular, 1979—. Served with U.S. Army, 1951-53. Mem. Fin. Execs. Inst., Nat. Assn. Accountants, P.R. C. of C. in U.S. (dir. 1977-80), Beta Gamma Sigma, Beta Alpha Psi. Greek Orthodox. Club: Hellenic Univ. Home: 200 Winston Dr Cliffside Park NJ 07010 Office: 40 W 57th St New York NY 10019

CASSIN, WILLIAM BOURKE, natural gas co. exec.; b. Mexico City, Mexico, Sept. 11, 1931 (parents Am. citizens); s. William Michael and Elouise (Hall) C.; student Tex. Mil. Inst., 1947-49; A.B., Princeton, 1953; J.D. cum laude, U. Tex., 1959; m. Kristi Shipnes, July 15, 1961; children—Clay Brian, Michael Bourke, Macy Armstrong. Admitted to Tex. bar, 1959; clk. to judge 5th Circuit U.S., 1959-60; atty. Baker & Botts, Houston, 1960-70; v.p., gen. atty. United Gas Pipe Line Co., Houston, 1970-73, sr. v.p., gen. atty., 1973-74, exec. v.p., gen. counsel, exec. com., dir., 1974—; exec. v.p., gen. counsel, mem. exec. com., dir. United Energy Resources, Inc., 1976—. Gen. counsel Harris County Republican Party, 1963-64, 67-68. Bd. dirs. Houston Grand Opera Assn., gen. counsel, 1961-70; bd. dirs. Houston Ballet Found., Red Cross Youth; vestryman Christ Ch. Cathedral, Houston, 1971-73, 80—; trustee Armand Bayou Nature Center, Inc. Served to lt. AUS, 1953-57. Mem. Am., Houston, Fed. Power, Fed. bar assns., Tex. Bar, Order of Coif, Phi Delta Phi. Republican. Episcopalian. Clubs: Princeton Terrace, Houston Country, Bayou Ramada, Army and Navy, Houston Athletic; Princeton (N.Y.C.). Home: 1 S Wynden Dr Houston TX 77056 Office: 700 Milam Houston TX 77001

CASTELL, GEORGE COVENTRY, communications co. exec.; b. N.Y.C., 1936; s. George Oliver and Jane (Coventry) C.; student Columbia U., 1958; m. Marian Simmons Miller, 1964; children—William C., Gregory S. With Chase Manhattan Bank, N.Y.C., 1958-61; with CBS, Inc., N.Y.C., 1961-69, asst. treas., 1966-69; treas. Viacom Internat., Inc., N.Y.C., 1970-75, v.p. planning and devel., chmn. strategic planning com., 1976—; ltd. partner Lafer Amster & Co., N.Y.C., 1980—. Mem. exec. com. Nat. March of Dimes, 1975—; trustee Collegiate Sch., 1969—. Served with U.S. Army N.G., 1960. Mem. Assn. for Corporate Growth. Presbyterian. Clubs: Union League, Wee Burn Country. Office: 1211 Ave of Americas New York NY 10036

CASTERLIN, GEORGE GEYER, JR., health care adminstr.; b. Kingston, Pa., Apr. 20, 1935; s. George Geyer and Ruth (Davis) C.; B.S. in Econs., U. Pa., 1957; M.B.A., Rutgers U., 1962; m. Geraldine Hornyak, Dec. 20, 1973; 1 dau., Geraldine Ruth; children by previous marriage—Keith Stewart, Gail Arlene; stepchildren—Eileen Hornyak, Richard Hornyak. Mem. comptroller's staff N.J. Bell Telephone Co., Trenton and Newark, 1957-68; dean adminstrv. services, asst. prof. bus. Mercer County Community Coll., Trenton, 1969-74; pres., dir. United Presbyterian Home at Syosset, Woodbury, N.Y., Inc., 1974—; preceptor adj. faculty Ithaca Coll. Served with USAFR, 1957-63. Lic. nursing home adminstr., N.Y. Fellow Am. Coll. Nursing Home Adminstrs.; mem. Nat. Assn. Accts., Am., N.Y. (dir.) assns. homes for aging, Assn. Presbyn. Homes, Friars Sr. Soc., Internat. Narcotic Enforcement Officers Assn., Am. Mgmt. Assns., Pres.'s Assn., N.Y. Assn. Long-Term Care Adminstrs., Kite and Key Soc., Delta Tau Delta. Presbyterian (elder). Home: 4 Mill River Rd Setauket NY 11733 Office: 378 Syosset-Woodbury Rd Woodbury NY 11797

CASTLE, FRANK ELLES, mktg. co. exec.; b. Chgo., Nov. 12, 1932; s. Albert James and Edna Elizabeth (Turner) Castiglia; B.S. in Indsl. Engring., U. Ill., 1957; m. Pauline Richards, June 31, 1954; children—Nancy E., Janet E. Dist. and regional mgr. C.B.S. Electronics Co., Houston, 1958-61; regional mgr. tube div. Westinghouse Electric Co., Atlanta, 1961-65; regional and area mgr. Motorola Semicondrs. Co., Dallas, 1965-68, mgr. bus. planning, 1968-69; distbr. mktg. mgr. Tex. Instruments Co., Dallas, 1969-71; v.p. mktg. Sterling Indsl. Mktg. Co., Houston, 1971-74, pres., 1974—. Mem. Com. To Reelect John Tower, 1978; mem. Jersey Village (Tex.) Zoning and Planning Commn., 1977-79. Mem. Am. Mgmt. Assn. Republican. Presbyterian. Office: 4201 Southwest Freeway Houston TX 77027

CASTLE, VERNON CHARLES, recording co. exec.; b. Whitewater, Wis., May 17, 1931; s. Erwin Ellesworth and Anne Bertha (Nelson) C.; B.Ed., U. Wis., Whitewater, 1951; m. Jeanette C. Travis, Aug. 4, 1950. Profl. entertainer, musician, 1956-65; pres. Castle Prodns., Inc., Lake Geneva, Wis., 1966-79, Castle Rec., 1972-78, Recreational Recs., Ltd., 1972-77; broadcast advt. cons., 1979—. Served with Adj. Gen. Corps, U.S. Army, 1952-55. Home: 642 Birches Dr Lake Geneva WI 53147 Office: PO Box 628 Lake Geneva WI 53147

CASTLEMAN, BREAUX BALLARD, mgmt. cons.; b. Louisville, Aug. 19, 1940; s. John Pryor and Mary Jane Fish (Ballard) C.; B.A. in Econs., Yale U., 1962; postgrad. N.Y.U. Grad. Sch. Bus. Adminstrn., 1963; m. Sue Ann Foreman, Feb. 25, 1967; children—Matthew Breckinridge, Shea Breaux. With comml. credit dept. Bankers Trust Co., N.Y.C., 1962-65; founder, owner Castleman & Co., Houston, 1965-71; dir. program planning and regional economist HUD, Ft. Worth, 1971-73; v.p. Booz, Allen & Hamilton, Inc., mgmt. cons., Houston, 1973—. Trustee Houston Ballet Found., 1970-71. Recipient Disting. Service award HUD, 1973. Mem. N. Am. Soc. Corp. Planning, Assn. Corp. Growth, Am. Econ. Assn., Internat. Assn. Energy Economists. Club: Forest (Houston). Office: 1300 Main St Houston TX 77002

CASTLEMAN, RICHARD LAVERNE, corp. exec.; b. Taylorville, Ill., Aug. 10, 1934; s. Roy David and Evelyn (Mason) C.; B.S., Millikin U., 1956; 1 dau., Kelly Gale. Clk., Office Ill. Sec. of State, Springfield, 1953-55; sr. accountant firm Gauger & Diehl C.P.A.'s, Decatur, Ill., 1956-65; individual practice as C.P.A., Decatur, 1965—; comptroller Millikin U., Decatur, 1965-66; controller Progress Industries, Inc., Arthur, Ill., 1966-67, v.p. fin., sec., 1967-72; exec. v.p., gen. mgr., dir. Promanco Acceptance Corp., Arthur, 1967-72; asst. sec. Capital City Casket Co., Little Rock, 1967-70; sec., treas., dir. R.A.S., Inc., Decatur, 1968-76; pres., dir. Contemporary Leasing Co., Inc., Decatur, 1969—, Contemporary Enterprises, Inc., Decatur, 1970-77, Fincastle Enterprises, Inc., Decatur, 1978—; owner Contemporary Vending & Amusements, Decatur, 1977—; administrv. asst. logistics plans and tng. Signal Research and Devel. Labs., U.S. Army, Ft. Monmouth, N.J., 1957-59. Bd. dirs. Smith-Dickerson Found., Delta Sigma Phi Bldg. Corp. (both Decatur). C.P.A., Ill. Mem. Am. Inst. C.P.A.'s, Ill. C.P.A. Soc., Amusement and Music Operators Assn., Nat. Automatic Merchandising Assn., Ill. Mfrs. Assn. (legis. com. 1967-72), Order DeMolay (chpt. adviser 1959-65, Legion of Honor award 1960), Delta Sigma Phi. Republican. Clubs: Masons, Elks. Office: PO Box 1708 1325 N 22d St Decatur IL 62525

CASTNER, HARRY EDWARD, JR., mfg. co. exec.; b. Chgo., Dec. 12, 1931; s. Harry Edward and Betty Mabel (Farmer) C.; B.S. in Bus., Elmhurst Coll., 1957; M.B.A., Rutgers U., 1969; m. Claire June Van Reed, June 13, 1957; children—Ann, Vanessa, Arthur. Accountant, div. controller Liquid Carbonic div. Gen. Dynamics Corp., Chgo., 1957-63; controller Rutenberg Constrn. Co., Clearwater, Fla., 1963-65; plant controller, mgr. systems and budgets Celanese Corp., Newark, 1965-68; div. comptroller ITT, Clark, N.J., 1968-71; v.p. fin. Van Vlaanderen Machine Co., Paterson, N.J., 1971-75, exec. v.p., 1975; dir. adminstrn. Finley, Kumble, Wagner, Heine & Underberg, N.Y.C., 1976-77; pres. Allied Bus. Brokers, 1978—. Mgr., Little League, Nutley, N.J., 1972—; treas. Holy Trinity Luth. Ch., 1973, v.p., 1977; clk. of session Southminster Presbyn. Ch., 1978—. pres. Third Half Club of Nutley, 1976. Served with USN, 1951-55. Mem. Am. Mgmt. Assn., Nat. Assn. Accountants. Republican. Clubs: S. Halifax Kiwanis (v.p. 1979-80, pres.-elect 1980); S. Daytona Lions (1st v.p. 1980). Home: 1203 Golfview Dr Daytona Beach FL 32019 Office: 125 N Ridgewood Ave Daytona Beach FL 32014

CASTOR, MALCOLM OTIS, environ. scientist; b. Tampa, Fla., Dec. 23, 1946; s. Floyd Allan and Marcella Agnes (Webster) C.; B.S. in Chemistry, Newberry Coll., 1968; m. Patricia Grace Gray, Nov. 12, 1977; 1 dau., Elizabeth Katharine. Chemist, U.S. Air Force, various locations, 1968-72; environ. chemist EPA, Pa., Md., Va., Del. and W.Va., 1972-74, environ. scientist, Denver, 1974-78; regional tech. mgr. Ecology & Environment, Inc., Denver, 1978—. Recipient Profl. Merit award EPA, 1972, Sustained Superior Performance award for Outstanding Service, 1974. Republican. Lutheran. Home: 460 Ursula St Aurora CO 80011 Office: Suite 200 243 E 19th Ave Denver CO 80203

CASTOR, RICHARD GILBERT, corp. exec.; b. Woodbury, N.J., Dec. 26, 1927; s. George F. and E. Dorothy (Supplee) C.; B.A., Adelphi Coll., 1956; m. Constance R. Flink, Sept. 2, 1957; children—Kimberly Susan, Lisa Beth, Holly Jennifer, Jill Catherine. Pres., Interstate Risk Mgmt. Corp. and Interstate Coverage Corp., Redford, N.Y., 1951—. Chmn. bd. Scripture Union-U.S.A., Phila., trustee, 1959—; vice chmn. Union Biblica en Las Americas Consejo Regional, Lima, Peru; bd. mgrs. Am. Bible Soc., 1968—, exec. com., 1970-79, vice chmn., 1974; mem. corp. Inter-Varsity Christian Fellowship, 1955—, trustee, 1957-77. Served with USMC, 1945-46. C.L.U.; C.P.C.U. Mem. Profl. Ins. Agts. Assn. N.Y. (state bd. 1967-73, v.p. 1971-73), Soc. C.P.C.U.'s, Nat. Safety Council, Campus Safety Assn. Home: RFD 2 Box 72 Bedford Village NY 10506 Office: Hunting Ridge Mall Bedford NY 10506

CASWELL, W. CAMERON, mfg. corp. exec.; b. Boston, Aug. 14, 1916; s. Walter E. and Anne (Cameron) C.; A.B., Yale U., 1939; m. Ada-Chase Holcombe, Sept. 27, 1947; children—W. Cameron, John Marshall Holcombe, George Calvin II, Geoffrey Chase. Buyer, Allied Stores, N.Y.C., 1939-40; with Wesvaco Chem. Inc., N.Y.C., 1940-47, Eastern sales mgr., 1944-47; prin. McKinsey & Co., N.Y.C., 1947-67; v.p. Dover Corp., N.Y.C., 1967—; dir. C. Tennant & Sons Co., N.Y.C., Ronningen-Petter Co., Kalamazoo, Tranter Inc., Lensing, Mich., Dieterich-Standard Inc., Boulder, Colo. Chmn., Darien (Conn.) Bd. Fin., 1946-67. Served with cav. AUS, 1940-41. Mem. Am. Mgmt. Assn., Chem. Industry Assn., Am. Mktg. Assn. Clubs: Yale, Metropolitan (N.Y.C.); Tokeneke, Wee Burn Country (Darien). Contbr. articles to profl. jours. Home: Bumpalong Rd Darien CT 06820 Office: Dover Corp 277 Park Ave New York NY 10017

CATANIA, JOSEPH VINCENT, govt. auditor; b. N.Y.C., Sept. 2, 1917; s. Philip Joseph and Anne (Gianni) C.; B.S., St. Johns U., 1941; M.B.A., N.Y. U., 1950; m. Catherine Rosary Munna, Oct. 15, 1950; 1 dau., Anne Elizabeth (Mrs. William Armstrong Dixon). Cost accountant Bendix Aviation Corp., N.Y.C., 1942-43; accountant H.S. Pollack & Co., C.P.A.'s, N.Y.C., 1946-56; staff asst. for audits AEC (now Nuclear Regulatory Commn.), Washington, 1956—. Served with USAAF, 1943-46. Decorated Bronze Star. Mem. Assn. Govt. Accountants, Am. Accounting Assn., Inst. Nuclear Materials Mgmt., Financial Mgmt. Assn., Am. Mgmt. Assn. Roman Catholic. K.C. Home: 3613 Tarkington Ln Silver Spring MD 20906 Office: US Nuclear Regulatory Commn Washington DC 20555

CATHCART, CHARLES DEPASS, economist; b. N.Y.C., Mar. 27, 1940; s. James Armstrong and Mary Freeda (DePass) C., Jr.; B.A., U. Denver, 1965; M.A., U. Calif., 1966; Ph.D., U. Va., 1973; m. Evelyn Godshall, June 24, 1964; children—Scott D., Elizabeth S. Asst. prof. econs. Pa. State U., 1971-77; economist Chase Manhattan Bank, N.Y.C., 1977-79; v.p. bus. econs. group W.R. Grace & Co., N.Y.C., 1979-81; v.p. Citibank, N.Y.C., 1981—. Treas., trustee Tuxgdo Park (N.Y.) Sch.; vestryman St. Mary's Episcopal Ch., Tuxedo Park. Served with USAF, 1960-62. Named Outstanding Faculty Adv., Coll. Liberal Arts, Pa. State U., 1977. Mem. Nat. Assn. Bus. Economists, N.Y. Assn. Bus. Economists (v.p.), Am. Econ. Assn., Am. Fin. Assn., Atlantic Econ. Assn. Republican. Club: Tuxedo. Home: Tower Hill Rd Tuxedo Park NY 10987 Office: 1114 Ave of Americas New York NY 10036

CAUNTER, HARRY ALLEN, electronics co. exec.; b. Cleve., Dec. 21, 1935; s. Harry Albert and Ruth Olive C.; B.B.A., Case Western Res. U., 1961; children—Keith A., Christine A. With Gould, Inc., 1957—, pres., gen. mgr. engine parts div., 1976—, v.p. indsl. group, 1978—. Office: 10 Gould Center Rolling Meadows IL 60008

CAVANAGH, RICHARD EDWARD, mgmt. cons.; b. Buffalo, June 15, 1946; s. Joseph John and Mary Celeste (Stack) C.; A.B., Wesleyan U., Conn., 1968; M.B.A., Harvard U., 1970. Cons., McKinsey & Co., Inc., Washington, 1970-77, sr. cons., 1979—, prin., 1980—; exec. dir. fed. cash mgmt. Office Mgmt. and Budget, Washington, 1977-79; domestic reorgn. coordinator President's Reorgn. Project, White House, Washington, 1978-79; guest lectr. George Washington U., 1975-76, Brookings Instn., 1978-79; adv. N.Y.C. Partnership, 1979—. Staff mem., adv. Carter-Mondale Policy Planning Staff, 1976; cons. Carter-Mondale Presdl. Transition Team, 1976-77. Served with U.S. Army, 1968. Recipient Presdl. commendations, 1979, 80. Mem. Am. Soc. Public Adminstrn., Acad. Polit. Sci., Raimond Duy Baird Assn., Wesleyan U. Alumni Assn., Beta Theta Pi. Democrat. Roman Catholic. Club: Harvard (N.Y.C.). Home: 644 Massachusetts Ave NE Apt 101 Washington DC 20002 Office: 1700 Pennsylvania Ave NW Washington DC 20006

CAVANAGH, ROBERT T., electronics co. exec.; b. Winnipeg, Man., Can., May 31, 1922; s. Edgar L. and Margaret (Gillies) C.; B.A.Sc.E.E., U. Toronto (Can.), 1945; m. Ethel A. Ball, June 28, 1948; children—Thomas, Richard, Joanne. Came to U.S., 1947, naturalized 1957. Project engr. Cyclograph Services, Ltd., Toronto, Ont., Can., 1945-47; successively asst. to dir. research, chief engr. TV receiver div., dir. circuit research lab., gen. mgr. mil. operations Allen B. DuMont Labs., Clifton, N.J., 1947-60; with N.Am. Philips Corp., N.Y.C., 1960—, past gen. mgr. Philips Electronic Instruments, v.p. N.Am. Philips Co., Inc., PEPI, Inc., Philips Broadcast Equipment Corp., group v.p., v.p. corporate devel. and engring., now sr. v.p. Mem. IEEE, AAAS, Am. Inst. Aeros. and Astronautics, Electron Microscopy Soc. Am.; Ont. Soc. Profl. Engrs. Clubs: Sleepy Hollow Country; Union League (N.Y.C.). Home: 5 Birch Close Sleepy Hollow Manor North Tarrytown NY 10591 Office: 100 E 42d St New York NY 10017

CAVANAUGH, DENISE ELIZABETH, orgn. devel. firm exec.; b. Evergreen Park, Ill., Sept. 3, 1942; d. Vincent Paul and Nora Elizabeth (Sullivan) C.; B.A., St. Mary's Coll., Notre Dame, Ind., 1964; postgrad. U. Pitts. Sch. Public and Internat. Affairs, 1969-70. With Peace Corps, Peru, 1964-66, Headstart Program, Chgo., 1966-67; program officer VISTA, W.Va., 1967-69; trainer Leadership Inst. for Community Devel., Washington, 1970-73; owner Cook/Cavanaugh Assos., Washington, 1974—; adv. council First Women's Bank of Md., Rockville, 1978—. Mem. Nat. Assn. Women Bus. Owners (founder, pres. 1979-80), Am. Soc. Tng. and Devel. (chmn. conf. design com. 1979), Orgn. Devel. Network, Internat. Consultants Found., Washington Women's Network. Democrat. Roman Catholic. Office: Cook/Cavanaugh Assos 1725 K St NW Washington DC 20006

CAVENEY, WILLIAM JOHN, pharm. co. exec., lawyer; b. Wheeling, W.Va., Aug. 5, 1944; s. James Joseph and Esther Virginia (Ackermann) C.; A.B. cum laude, W.Va. U., 1966; J.D., Vanderbilt U., 1969; LL.M. in Taxation, N.Y. U., 1977, Advanced Profl. Cert., Grad. Sch. Bus. Adminstrn., 1979; m. Margaret Carol Serota, Sept. 18, 1971; children—Ryan Benjamin, Christine Joanna. Admitted to N.Y. bar, 1972, U.S. Supreme Ct. bar, 1976; tax mgr. Arthur Anderson & Co., N.Y.C., 1969-73; tax atty. Texaco, Inc., N.Y.C., 1973-76; mgr. tax planning Norton Simon, Inc., N.Y.C., 1976-78; dir. tax planning Warner-Lambert Co., Morris Plains, N.J., 1978-79, tax counsel, mem. fgn. exchange com., 1979—; lectr. Taxation and internat. fin. Mem. N.Y. State Bar Assn. (mem. exec. com. tax sect.), Am. Bar Assn., Am. Inst. C.P.A.'s, N.Y. State Soc. C.P.A.'s, Canadian Tax Found., Tax Execs. Inst., (mem. internat. tax steering com.), World Trade Inst. Contbr. articles to profl. jours. Home: 25 Meadowbrook Rd Short Hills NJ 07078 Office: 201 Tabor Rd Morris Plains NJ 07950

CAVIN, DANIEL CULVER, chem. engr.; b. Phoenix, Mar. 29, 1950; s. George Edmund and Norma Joanna (Priest) C.; B.S. in Chemistry, Iowa State U., 1972, B.S. in Chem. Engring., 1972, M.S., 1973; m. Barbara Sue Petersen, Aug. 25, 1973. Research chem. engr. Shell Devel. Co., Houston, 1973-77; sr. chem. engr. Esso Prodn. Malaysia, Kuala Lumpur, 1977-79; sr. gas engr. Exxon U.S.A., Houston, 1980—. Football coach Internat. Sch. Kuala Lumpur. Exxon Cos. Found. fellow, 1972-73; registered profl. engr., Tex. Mem. Tex. Soc. Profl. Engrs., Nat. Soc. Profl. Engrs., Am. Inst. Chem. Engrs., Am. Chem. Soc., Soc. Petroleum Engrs. Club: Malaysian SubAqua. Office: East Tex div Exxon Co USA PO Box 2180 4550 Dacoma St Houston TX 77001

CAVIN, F. G. (MOE), bank exec.; b. McKenzie, Tenn., Sept. 28, 1930; B.S. in Agr., U. Tenn., Martin; m. Sally Thornton; children—Virginia, Sarah, John, Carol. Exec. v.p. Farmers Exchange Bank, Union City, Tenn., 1968-71, pres., 1971-74; exec. v.p. First Amtenn Corp., Nashville, 1974-79, pres., 1979—, exec. v.p. First Am. Nat. Bank, 1979-80, vice-chmn. bd., 1980—. Chmn., Tenn. Indsl. Devel. Authority, 1972-78; chmn. fin. com. Brentwood United Methodist Ch. Clubs: Masons, Shriners. Office: First American Corp First American Center Nashville TN 37237

CAVINESS, GREGORY DON, ins. exec.; b. Oklahoma City, Mar. 14, 1946; s. Don Malcolm and Jo (Willey) C.; B.B.A. in Mktg., U. Tex., El Paso, 1972; m. Lori D. Childress, Oct. 11, 1968; 1 son, Eric Dawson. Br. mgr. Southland Life Ins. Co., Austin, Tex., 1972-74; v.p., gen. mgr. Mulder Corp., Austin, 1974-75; gen. agt. Am. Nat. Ins. Co., Denver, 1975-79; regional agy. mgr. Life Ins. Co. Va.; pres. Caviness Co., El Paso, 1979—; founder, mng. gen. partner Project Child Indemnity; pres. Adobe Prodn. Co.; v.p. 4 Bar C Land & Cattle Co., 1980—. Pres. Pheasant Run Home Owners Assn., 1977; co-chmn. ball com. Children's Diabetes Found. at Denver, 1978; chmn. Sun Bowl Press Host Com., 1979; chmn. devel. com., bd. dirs. El Paso Heart Assn. Served to 1st lt. U.S. Army, 1966-70. Decorated Army Commendation medal. Mem. Nat. Assn. Life Underwriters, Gen. Agts. and Mgrs. Assn. (bd. dirs.), C.L.U. Soc. Republican. Baptist. Clubs: El Paso Country, Miners Camp, Nugget, Sons of Sun, Kiwanis (El Paso). Home: 7001 Gineno St El Paso TX 79912 Office: 1170 Westmoreland St Suite 306 El Paso TX 79925

CAYLOR, RICHARD EUGENE, banker; b. Columbus, Ohio, Dec. 20, 1934; s. H. Russell and Lola L. (Huls) C.; B.Sc. in Psychology, Ohio State U., 1955; M.B.A. in Mktg., Mich. State U., 1964; m. Patricia Jo Kline, Jan. 30, 1960; children—Richard E., Michelle L. Mgr. employee relations Hammond Organ Co., Chgo., 1968-72; personnel mgr. Topco Assos., Inc., Skokie, Ill., 1972-74; dir. indsl. relations Anchor Coupling Co., Inc., Libertyville, Ill., 1974-76; v.p., dir. personnel Sears Bank and Trust Co., Chgo., 1978—. Chmn. policy com. Winnetka Caucus, 1975-76. Served to lt. USN, 1956-61. Mem. Am. Mgmt. Assn., Bank Personnel Assn. Chgo., Am. Soc. Personnel Adminstrs. Republican. Presbyterian. Home: 857 Ash Winnetka IL 60093 Office: 233 S Wacker Chicago IL 60606

CAYWOOD, JAMES ALEXANDER, civil engr.; b. Kona, Ky., Jan. 28, 1923; s. James A. and Mary V. (Crawford) C.; B.S., U. Ky., 1944; m. Carol Ann Fries, Mar. 20, 1959; children—Beverly Jo, James A., Daniel T., Malinda Ann and Elizabeth Carol (twins). Sr. instrumentman L. & N. R.R. Co., Latonia, Ky., 1946-47; asst. on corps B. & O. R.R. Co., Cin., 1947-50, asst. div. engr., 1950-52, div. engr., 1953-57, engr. maintenance of way, 1957-60, asst. chief engr., 1960-61, chief engr., 1961-64; gen. mgr. engring. planning for C.& O. - B.& O. R.R.'s, 1963-64; pres., dir. Royce Kershaw Co., Inc., 1964-65; pres. DeLeuw, Cather & Co., Cons. Engrs., Washington, 1965—, also dir. Served to lt. (j.g.), USNR, 1944-46; PTO. Registered profl. engr. in all 50 states, D.C., Canal Zone. Fellow ASCE; mem. Nat. Soc. Profl. Engrs., Am. Ry. Engring. Assn., Am. Ry. Bridge and Bldg. Assn., Soc. Am. Mil. Engrs., Roadmasters and Maintenance of Way Assn. Clubs: Univ.; Chgo. Athletic; Lakewood Country. Home: 24001 Whites Ferry Rd Dickerson MD 20753 Office: 1211 Connecticut Ave NW Washington DC 20036

CAZAN, SYLVIA MARIE BUDAY (MRS. MATTHEW JOHN CAZAN), realtor; b. Youngstown, Ohio, Nov. 17, 1915; d. John J. and Sylvia (Grama) Buday; student U. Bucharest, (Rumania), 1933-35, Youngstown Coll., 1936-38, Georgetown U. Inst. Langs. and Linguistics, 1950; m. Matthew John Cazan, July 14, 1935; 1 son, Matthew John G. Adminstrv. asst. statistics U.S. Dept. Def., 1941-52; spl. employee Dept. Justice, 1956-58; mgr. James L. Dixon & Co. Realtors, Falls Church, Va., 1959-70; mgr. Lewis & Silverman Inc., Chevy Chase, Md., 1970—. Mem. bd. Examiners Georgetown U., 1950. Bd. dirs. Magnolia Internat. Debutante Ball. Recipient Commendation and Meritorious award Dept. Justice, 1958. Mem. Gen. Fedn. Women's Clubs (pres. 1955-56), Interscholastic Debating Soc., Md. Bd. Realtors, Washington, No. Va. real estate bds. Mem. Rumanian Orthodox Ch. Home: 6369 Lakeview Dr Lake Barcroft

Estates Falls Church VA 22041 Office: 8401 Connecticut Ave Chevy Chase MD 20015

CAZEL, HUGH ALLEN, indsl. engr., educator; b. Asheville, N.C., Aug. 6, 1923; s. Fred Augustus and Agnes (Petrie) C.; B.S. in Indsl. Engring., N.C. State U., 1948, M. Indsl. Engring., 1972; m. Edna Faye Hawkins, Sept. 2, 1944; children—Audre Elizabeth, Hugh Petrie, Susan Margaret, Steven Sidney. Service mgr. Cazel Auto Service Co., Asheville, 1948-51; sales rep. Snap-On Tools Corp., Kenosha, Wis., 1951; estimator, cost accountant Standard Designers, Inc., Asheville, N.C., 1951-52; designer Robotyper Corp., Hendersonville, N.C., 1952-53; engr. Western Electric Co., Burlington, N.C., 1953-74; mgr. engring. So. Bell Telephone Co., Atlanta, 1974-79, ret., 1979; instr. math. Elon Coll., 1946-59; instr. engring. graphics and design Ga. Inst. Tech., 1977—. Mem. Dekalb County (Ga.) Adv. Com., 1979—. Served with AUS, 1943-46. Registered profl. engr., N.C., Ga. Mem. Am. Inst. Indsl. Engrs., Nat. Soc. Profl. Engrs., Profl. Engrs. N.C., Ga. Profl. Engrs. in Industry (chmn. 1976), AAAS, Ga. Soc. Profl. Engrs. (Ga. Engr. of Year in Industry 1976; energy com. 1979—). Republican. Methodist. Club: Odd Fellows. Home: 218-K Forkner Dr Decatur GA 30030 Office: Ga Inst Tech Atlanta GA 30332

CAZIER, JAMES HENRY, mining engr.; b. Wells, Nev., Nov. 23, 1912; s. Henry Hallowell and Neva (Dewar) C.; B.S. in Mining Engring., U. Nev., 1935; m. Dorothy Lynton, Oct. 5, 1940; children—Barry J., Stanley W. Engr. various locations Anaconda Co., Salt Lake City, 1935-41; asst. gen. supt. Lexington Mining Co., Neihart, Mont.; gen. supt. Callahan Consol. Mines, Inc., Wallace, Idaho, 1941-43; supervising engr. mine loan sect. RFC, Phoenix, also Salt Lake City, 1943-48; gen. supt. Goodwin Mining Co., Bagdad, Ariz., 1948-49, Bagdad Copper Corp., 1949-52; ind. mine operator, Bagdad, 1952-56; mining mgr. Anschutz Drilling Co., Inc., Denver, 1956-60; pres., dir. Webb Resources, Inc., 1961-68, mgr. mining div., 1976-79; mining cons., Denver, 1969-75, 79—. Served to lt. USNR, 1944-46. Registered profl. engr. Nev., Ariz., Colo. Mem. Am. Inst. Mining, Metall. and Petroleum Engrs., Am. Inst. Profl. Geologists, Colo. Mining Assn., Ariz. Nev. Mining Assn. Democrat. Clubs: Petroleum, Paradise Valley Country (Denver). Home: 2817 S Lansing Way Aurora CO 80014 Office: 1645 Court Pl Suite 300 Denver CO 80202

CECIL, DONALD, investment mgr.; b. N.Y.C., Jan. 3, 1927; s. Leopold and Viola (Osterweil) C.; student Williams Coll., 1944-45; B.S., Yale, 1947; m. Jane Grossman, Mar. 5, 1953; children—Leslie and Alec (twins). With Cecil Mfg. Co., Inc., N.Y.C., 1947-58, exec. v.p., 1953-58; research analyst Ira Haupt, N.Y.C., 1958-63; sr. instl. research analyst Eastman Dillon Union Securities, N.Y.C., 1963-64; dir. instl. research Shearson, Hammill & Co., Inc., N.Y.C., 1964, 1st v.p. in charge instl. sales and research, 1965-70; pres., dir. Shearson Hammill Mgmt. Co. Inc., 1967-70; v.p., dir. Contrails Growth Fund, 1968-70; v.p. Shearson Capital Fund, Inc., 1968-70; pres., dir. Shearson Appreciation Fund, 1969-70; gen. partner Cumberland Assos., N.Y.C., 1970—; dir. Grey Advt. Inc., Merrill Lynch Basic Value Fund, Merrill Lynch Equibond Fund, Fund Am., Merrill Lynch Ready Asset Fund. Former allied mem. N.Y. Stock Exchange. Bd. dirs., vice-chmn. Westchester County Bd. Transp.; v.p. Cage Teen Center. Served with USNR, 1944-45. Mem. N.Y. Soc. Security Analysis, Inst. Chartered Financial Analysts. Home: 20 Paxford Ln Scarsdale NY 10583 Office: 522 Fifth Ave New York NY 10026

CEDERLIND, JOHN ROGER, co. exec.; b. Portland, Oreg., Aug. 30, 1947; s. Irvin Murnane and Dorothy Jane (Eldridge) C.; B.S., Lewis & Clark Coll., 1969, M.A., 1970; B.S. cum laude, Portland State U., 1976, postgrad., 1976—; m. Karen Leah Young, Feb. 19, 1979. Registered rep. Aetna Life & Casualty, Portland, Oreg., 1970-73; crew mgr. Washington Inventory Service, Portland, 1973-75; staff coordinator material United Telephone Co. of NW, Hood River, Oreg., 1977-78, mgr. materiel, 1978-80; plant mgr. Maple Plain Co., Lake Oswego, Oreg., 1980—. Mem. Internat. Material Mgmt. Soc., Nat. C. of C., Lake Oswego C. of C., Lewis & Clark Coll. Alumni Assn. (dir.). Republican. Episcopalian. Clubs: Bellingham Yacht, Coll. of Seattle, Elks. Home: 6882 SW Montauk Circle Lake Oswego OR 97034 Office: 6024 SW Jean Rd Lake Oswego OR 97034

CEDERQUIST, STANLEY GUSTAF, food broker; b. Chgo., May 13, 1917; s. G. E. and Esther (Uron) C.; student U. Ill., 1936-40; m. Eleanor Nicholas, May 10, 1942; children—Eric S., Robert A. Chmn., Nicholas Co., Inc., Indpls., 1946—. Vice chmn. Dept. of Transp. Bd., City of Indpls., 1972-76; mem. Indpls. Pub. Transp. Corp. Bd., 1973—. Served with USAAF, 1941-46; to capt. USAF, 1950-52. Mem. Nat. (past nat. chmn.), Indpls. (past pres.) food brokers assns., Indpls. Assn. Mfrs. Reps., Contemporary Art Soc., Art Assn. Indpls., Ind., Indpls. chambers commerce, Mil. Order World Wars, Phi Kappa Tau. Episcopalian. Clubs: Columbia, Meridian Hills Country, Kiwanis, Sertoma (past pres.). Home: 8502 Bent Tree Ct Indianapolis IN 46260 Office: 2500 E 46th St Indianapolis IN 46205

CELAYA, AUGUSTINE, JR., indsl. co. exec.; b. Brownsville, Tex., Oct. 22, 1926; s. Augustine and Carmen (Barreda) C.; B.S., Tex. A. and M. U., 1948; m. Virginia Hillman, Sept. 10, 1962; children—Michael, Laura, Francisca. Rancher, farmer, Brownsville, 1948-55; asst. to mng. dir. N.Y. Potash Export Assn., Inc., N.Y.C., 1956-60; sales mgr. indsl. products Union Carbide Inter Am. Inc., Panama, asst. to v.p. Latin Am., N.Y.C., 1964-66, gen. mgr. consumer products div. Union Carbide Mexicana, S.Am., Mexico City, 1966-68, pres. Colombia, Ecuador, Bogotá, 1968-70, pres. Argentina sales, Buenos Aires, 1971-73, chmn. bd., pres. Union Carbide P.R., San Juan, 1973-76, v.p. engring. and mfg. agrl. chem. div. Union Carbide Corp., N.Y.C., 1976-78, v.p. internat. agrl. chem. div., 1978—; v.p. internat. ops. Houbigant, Inc. Served to 1st lt. USAF, 1945-46, 50-51. Recipient awards for conservation, commerce, sports. Roman Catholic. Clubs: N.Y. Yacht; Jockey (Buenos Aires). Home: 1208 Smith Ridge Rd New Canaan CT 06840 Office: 1135 Pleasantview Terr Ridgefield NJ 07657

CELLIERS, PETER JOUBERT, internat. pub. relations specialist; b. Vogelfontein, Union S. Africa; s. Bartilimy and Elsie Blanche (Goldberg) C.; ed. Eng., Continent; m. Helen Rassaby, Sept. 10, 1949; children—Gordon A.J., Jennefer A.J. Editor, to 1959; cons. to fgn. govts., internat. corps. Peter J. Celliers Co., N.Y.C., 1958-68; chief fgn. press services Olympic Organizing Com., Mexico, 1968; dir. for N.Am., Mexican Nat. Tourist Council, 1962-72; owner Ellis Assos., N.Y.C., 1969—; tech. adviser internat. market devel. to UN, hotels, carriers, govts. Mem. Public Relations Soc. Am. (Counsellors' Acad.), Soc. Am. Travel Writers (past pres.), N.Y. Assn. Travel Writers, Assn. Internat. Practical Tng. (nat. com.), Am. Soc. Journalists and Authors. Clubs: Nat. Press (Washington); Overseas Press, Dutch Treat (N.Y.C.). Home: 131 Fenimore Rd New Rochelle NY 10804 Office: 304 E 42d St New York NY 10017

CENSITS, RICHARD JOHN, food co. exec.; b. Allentown, Pa., May 20, 1937; s. Stephen A. and Theresa M. C.; B.S. in Econs., U. Pa., 1958; M.B.A., Lehigh U., 1964; m. Linda A. Malin, June 21, 1958; children—Debra, Mark, David. Sr. auditor Arthur Andersen & Co., C.P.A.'s, 1958-62; mgr. accounting Air Products & Chems., 1962-64; controller Hamilton Watch Co., Lancaster, Pa., 1964-69; v.p., controller IU Internat., Phila., 1969-75; v.p. finance Campbell Soup Co., Camden, N.J., 1975—. Trustee W. Jersey Hosp. Systems; class agt. U. Pa. Alumni. Mem. Fin. Execs. Inst., Nat. Food Processors Assn., Am. Inst. C.P.A.'s, Pa. Inst. C.P.A.'s, N.J. Soc. C.P.A.'s. Club: Union League. Home: 120 Partree Rd Cherry Hill NJ 08003 Office: Campbell Soup Co Campbell Pl Camden NJ 08101

CENTNER, RONALD MAURICE, mfg. co. exec.; b. Chgo., Sept. 19, 1934; s. Harry and Margaret (Gartner) C.; B.S., Ill. Inst. Tech., 1955; M.S., Mass. Inst. Tech., 1957; M.B.A., U. Mich., 1977; m. Sandra Marilyn Miller, Sept. 4, 1955; children—Steven Howard, Deborah Lynn. Research asst. Mass. Inst. Tech., 1955-57; with Bendix Corp. Research Labs., Southfield, Mich., 1959—, successively electronic engr., sr. engr., project engr., supervisory engr., 1959-68, mgr. control and data-handling systems dept., 1968-70, product dir., recognition systems program Bendix Advanced Products div., 1970-74, corp. dir. engring. planning, 1974-75, v.p., gen. mgr. Bendix Indsl. Controls div., 1975-78; v.p., gen. mgr. Bendix Instruments and Life Support div., Davenport, Iowa, 1978-80, v.p., gen. mgr. Air Transport Avionics div., Ft. Lauderdale, Fla., 1980—. Mem. Adminstrv. Civil Service Commn.. Southfield, 1967-75. Served to 1st lt. USAF, 1957-59. Mem. IEEE, Numerical Control Soc., Sigma Xi, Eta Kappa Nu, Tau Beta Pi, Alpha Epsilon Pi. Contbr. articles to profl. jours. Patentee in field. Home: 10894 NW 19th St Coral Springs FL 33065 Office: 2100 NW 62d St Fort Lauderdale FL

CERDAN, RICHARD, mgmt. cons.; b. N.Y.C., June 12, 1943; s. Aurelio and Henriette (Sorries) C.; B.S., Georgetown U., Washington, 1966; postgrad. in bus. adminstrn. Instituto de Estudios Superiores de la Empresa, Barcelona, Spain, 1966-67, law and econs. U. Geneva, 1968; children—Frederic, Isabelle. Personnel mgr. UN, Geneva and N.Y.C., 1969-73; asso. cons. Kepner-Tregoe, Princeton, N.J. and Wiesbaden, W. Ger., 1973-74; personnel mgr. Gen. Telephone and Electronics, Geneva, 1974-75; mng. dir. Charles Barker, Frankfurt, W. Ger., 1975-78; sr. asso. Heidrick & Struggles Internat., Frankfurt, 1979-80; v.p., Zurich, Switzerland, 1980—. Mem. Georgetown U., Alumni Assn. (pres.). Clubs: Rotary; Union Internat. (Frankfurt/Main) (dir.). Home: Alte Landstrasse 26 8702 Zollikon Switzerland Office: Gartenstrasse 14 8002 Zürich Switzerland

CERNIK, ARNOLD ALLEN, insurance broker; b. Oak Park, Ill., Nov. 25, 1937; s. Laddie J. and Gertrude C.; B.S., Utah State U., 1959; m. Sheridan Lee McCann, Sept. 7, 1976; children—Jacqueline J., Karyn A., Arnold Allen. Gen. mgr. Am. Mut. Ins. Co., White Plains, N.Y., 1960-74; project mgr. Deere & Co., Moline, Ill., 1974-75; prodn. coordinator Marsh & McLennan, Chgo., 1975-76; sr. v.p., mgr. Reed Stenhouse Inc., St. Louis, 1976—. Served with AUS, 1959-65. Mem. Am. Mgmt. Assn., Sales Execs. Club N.Y., Exec. Club Chgo. Clubs: Bridlespurt Hunt, Strathalbyn Farms, Clayton, Monroe. Home: Box 164 Manchester Rd Grover MO 63040 Office: 1010 Collingwood Dr Saint Louis MO 63132

CESARE, ANTHONY GIORGI, JR., writer; b. Chgo., July 31, 1943; s. Anthony Giorgi and Genevieve Stephanie (Lucas) C.; grad. St. John's Mil. Acad., Delafield, Wis., 1961; B.A. in English, Parsons Coll., 1965. Tech. writer T.M. Pubs., Chgo., 1965-67; copywriter Hilltop Advt., Battle Creek, Mich., 1967-68; mktg. and pub. relations coordinator Ad Art and Design, Kalamazoo, 1968-69; owner Cesare & Assos., Boulder, Colo., 1969-71; freelance writer, 1973-77; tech. editor Chemetron Fire Systems, Monee, Ill., 1971—; sr. tech. writer Allis-Chalmers Corp., 1979-80. Mem. Internat. Platform Assn., Am. Advt. Fedn., Writers Guild. Author: The Feathers Technique, 1980. Editor: Chemetron Fire Systems Halon 1301 Design Manual, 1978; inventor card game Snaffle, 1978. Home: Route 2 Box 30 Beecher IL 60401

CETRON, MARVIN JEROME, cons. co. exec.; b. Bklyn., July 5, 1930; s. Jack Student and Gertrude Leah C.; B.S. in Indsl. Engring., Pa. State U., 1952; M.S. in Bus. Adminstrn., Columbia U., 1959; Ph.D. in Research and Devel. Mgmt., Am. U., 1970; m. Gloria Rita Wasserman, June 29, 1955; children—Edward Jack, Adam Bruce. Civilian with USN, 1956-71; founder, 1971, since pres. Forecasting Internat., Ltd., Arlington, Va.; adj. prof. Am. U., M.I.T., Ga. Inst. Tech. Mem. research and devel. adv. com. USCG, 1974—. Served with USCGR, 1954-56. Mem. Ops. Research Soc. Am., IEEE, Tech. and Indsl. Mgmt. Soc., World Future Soc. Author: Technological Forecasting: A Practical Approach, 1969; Resource Management: Quantitative Methods, 1970; The Science of Managing Organized Technology, 4 vols., 1971; Industrial Applications of Technological Forecasting: Its Use in Research and Development Management, 1971; The Navy Technological Forecast, 3d edit., 1970; Technology Assessment in a Dynamic Environment, 1972; The Methodology of Technology Assessment, 1972; Quantitative Decision-aiding Techniques for Research and Development Management, 1972; Procs. NATO Advanced Study Inst. on Technology Transfer, 1974; Industrial Technology Transfer, 1977; editor-in-chief Tech. Assessment Jour., 1971-78. Office: 1001 N Highland St Arlington VA 22201

CHABRIS, PETER DANIEL, mgmt. and outplacement cons., corp. exec.; b. N.Y.C., Aug. 11, 1917; s. Louis and Esther Chabris; B.S., Columbia, 1939; m. Rosemary Melody Richardson; children—Margaret, Paul, John, Peter. Vice pres. Xerox Corp., Rochester, N.Y., 1962-65; sr. v.p., dir. Interpub. Group Cos., N.Y.C., 1965-68; corp. dir. planning Travelers Corp., Hartford, Conn., 1968-70; chmn. bd. Chabris & Assos., N.Y.C. and Essex Fells, N.J., 1970-76; v.p. Performance Dynamics Internat., Parsippany, N.J., 1976-80, sr. v.p., exec. v.p., 1980—. Commr. Rochester Human Relations Commn., 1962-65; bd. dirs. Memphis Symphony Orch., 1955-56, Sch. for Deaf, Rochester, 1962-65, Rochester Rehab. Center, 1963-65, Inst. Mktg. Communications, 1965-68; mem. orgn. planning council The Conf. Bd., 1962-67; mem. Assn. Corprate Growth, 1968-71. Served with U.S. Army, 1941-46. Republican. Episcopalian. Clubs: Univ. (N.Y.C.); Montclair Golf. Home: 27 Holton Ln Essex Fells NJ 07021 Office: 400 Lanidex Plaza Parsippany NJ 07054

CHACKO, GEORGE KUTTICKAL, educator, cons.; b. Trivandrum, India, July 1, 1930; s. Geevarghese Kuttickal and Thankamma (Mathew) C.; came to U.S., 1953, naturalized, 1967; M.A. in Econs. and Polit. Philosophy, Madras U., 1950; B.Commerce (Merit scholar 1950-52), Calcutta U., 1952; Ph.D. in Econometrics, New Sch. Social Research, 1959; m. Yo Yee, Aug. 10, 1957; children—Rajah Yee, Ashia Yo. Asst. editor Indian Fin., Calcutta, 1951-53; comml. corr. Times of India, 1953; research asst. in econs. Princeton U., 1953-54; asso. in math. test devel. Ednl. Testing Service, Princeton, 1955-57; dir. mktg. and mgmt. research Royal Metal Mfg. Co., N.Y.C., 1958-60; mgr. ops. research dept. semicondr. div. Hughes Aircraft Co., Newport Beach, Calif., 1960-61; asst. prof. bus. adminstrn. UCLA, 1961-62; ops. research cons. Union Carbide Corp., N.Y.C., 1962-63; mem. tech. staff Research Analysis Corp., McLean, Va., 1963-65, MITRE Corp., Arlington, Va., 1965-67; sr. staff scientist TRW Systems Group, Washington, 1967-70; vis. prof. U. So. Calif., 1970-71, prof. systems mgmt., 1971—; lectr. U.S. Dept. Agr. Grad. Sch., 1965-67; asst. professorial lectr. George Washington U., 1965-68; professorial lectr. Am. U., 1967-70, adj. prof., 1970; vis. prof. Def. Systems Mgmt. Coll., Ft. Belvoir, Va., 1972-73; def. systems cons. U.S. Dept. Def., Rand Corp., others; computer, space, technol. systems cons. Arthur Young & Co., Aries Corp., So. Ry. System, others; internat. devel. systems cons. York U., Toronto, UN, others; chmn. tech. evaluation panel NSF, 1976; speaker in field. Fellow AAAS (council 1968-73), Am. Astron. Soc. (v.p. 1969-71); mem. Ops. Research Soc. Am., Washington Ops. Research Council (trustee 1967-69), Inst. Mgmt. Scis., World Future Soc., AAUP. Democrat. Presbyterian. Club: Kiwanis. Author books, papers in field. Address: 6809 Barr Rd Washington DC 20016

CHADDICK, HARRY FRANCIS, real estate developer; b. Chgo., Aug. 27, 1905; s. William Baldwin and Maud M. (LeBlanc) C.; student public schs., Chgo.; m. Elaine M. Torbik, Apr. 27, 1955; 1 dau., Camille Hatzenbuehler. From truck driver to owner, chief exec. officer Am. Transp. Co.-Standard Freight Lines, Chgo., 1931-47; pres., founder Chgo. Indsl. Dist., Inc., 1961-75; developer Ford City complex, 1961-81; pres., chief exec. officer 1st Am. Realty Co., Chgo., 1964—, parent co. Near South Co., Inc., 1959-67, Harry F. Chaddick Assos., Inc., 1954—, Carnegie Constrn. & Devel., 1961—, Harry F. Chaddick Realty, Inc., 1966—, South Pulaski Corp., 1966—, Forest Park Mall, Inc., 1978—, Palm Springs Country Club and Fair Condominiums (Calif.), 1969—, Andreas Hills, 1972—, Spring Crest Water & Power Co., 1977—, Tennis Club and Hotel, 1961-80 (all Palm Springs); adviser, cons. ton transp. affairs re North African invasion to U.S. Govt., 1943; dep. dir. Chgo. CD Corps, 1948. Chmn., Chgo. Zoning Bd. Appeals, 1967-72; Chgo. Mayor's Com. on Rent Control, 1976-78; co-chmn. Chgo.'s Econ. Devel. Commn., 1976—. Recipient City of Hope award, 1967, Horatio Alger award, 1970, Golden Plate award, 1971; named Chgo.'s Outstanding Real Estate Developer, Little Flower Soc., 1965. Mem. Am. Trucking Assn. (past chmn. bd. gov.), Central Motor Freight Assn. (past pres.), Chgo. Assn. Commerce and Industry, Nat. Assn. Rev. Appraisers, Civic Fedn., Chgo. Real Estate Bd., Better Bus. Bur. Met. Chgo., Ill. C. of C., Chgo. Conv. and Tourism Bur., Am. Truck Hist. Soc., Lambda Alpha. Clubs: City, Hundred of Cook County, Mid-Am., Tower, Traffic, Executive (all Chgo.); Whitehall; Ridgemoor Country; O'Donnell Golf; Tennis; Palm Springs Country. Office: 123 W Madison St Chicago IL 60602

CHADSEY, WILLIAM LLOYD, III, research and devel. co. exec.; b. Miami, Okla., Sept. 25, 1942; s. William Lloyd and Vivian Evelyn (Hervig) C.; B.A. in Engring. and Applied Physics, Harvard U., 1965; M.S. in Physics, U. Pa., 1968; m. Mary Elizabeth Henschel, Feb. 2, 1980; children—Geoffrey, Gillian, Ian. Research and devel. engr. Gen. Electric Co., Phila., 1966-72; with Sci. Applications, Inc., McLean, Va., 1972—, v.p. electromagnetic tech. operation, 1977—. Mem. IEEE. Contbr. articles to profl. jours. Home: 4516 S 8th St Arlington VA 22204 Office: 1710 Goodridge Dr McLean VA 22102

CHAFIN, DON CARLYLE, elec. co. exec.; b. Logan, W.Va., Aug. 25, 1939; s. Marion R. and Virginia W. (Donevant) C.; B.S.E. with honors, W.Va. U., 1966; M.M.E., Rutgers U., 1968; grad. U.S. Army Engr. Sch., 1972; postgrad. in mech. engring. Ohio State U., 1974—; m. Nancy A. Helton, Dec. 22, 1978; children—Sherrie, Keith, Dawn, Victoria. Mem. tech. staff Bell Telephone Labs., Holmdel, N.J. and Denver, 1966-72; prin. engr. research and devel. center North Electric Co., Delaware, Ohio, 1972-75, mgr., asst. dir., 1975-78; asst. dir. N. Tech. Center ITT N.Electric Co., Delaware, 1978—; sr. engr., group leader GTE Automatic Electric Labs., Northlake Ill., 1975. Served with U.S. Army, 1961-64. Registered profl. engr., Colo. Mem. ASME (asso.), Soc. Am. Mil. Engrs., Nat. Mgmt. Assn., Res. Officers Assn., Pi Tau Sigma, Sigma Nu. Methodist. Clubs: Worthington Hills Country, Continental, Windsong. Home: 256 E Granville Rd Worthington OH 43085 Office: PO Box 20345 Columbus OH 43220

CHAIRNOFF, HUGH, banker; b. Phila., Apr. 4, 1939; s. Samuel and Vivian C.; B.S., Drexel U., 1961; M.B.A., Fla. State U., 1962; Ph.D., Mich. State U., 1966; m. Hedda Sandra Cohen, Aug. 19, 1962; children—Jeffrey, Deborah, Alicia. Research officer, economist Fed. Res. Bank of Phila., 1965-70, asst. v.p. credit, 1970-73, v.p. credit, bank services and regulation, 1973-78; v.p. fin. and planning N.J. Nat. Bank, Trenton, 1978—. Mem. vis. com. Coll. Bus. and Adminstrn., Drexel U. Mem. Robert Morris Assos. Club: Phila. Money Market. Office: NJ Nat Bank 1 W State St Trenton NJ 08603

CHAKRABARTI, PINAKI RANJAN, civil engr.; b. Calcutta, India, May 6, 1939; s. Bhola Nath and Uma Rani (Chatterjee) C.; came to U.S., 1964; B.C.E. (Govt. scholar), U. Calcutta, 1961; M.S. in Structural Engring. (John Cowles fellow), U. Minn., 1965; Ph.D. in Civil Engring., Rutgers U., 1976; m. Manjulika Chakraborty, Feb. 3, 1969; children—Indro, Indira. Trainee designer B.T.M. Co., Calcutta, 1961; project mgr. Shalimar Tar Products, Calcutta, 1961-64; design engr. Peter F. Loftus & Corp., Pitts., 1965-66; chief structural engr. T.Y. Lin Assos., N.Y.C., 1966-76; sr. engr. Burns & Roe, Oradell, N.J., 1976-78; prin. engr. A.G. Martin Assos., Los Angeles, 1978-79, Ralph M. Parsons, Pasadena, Calif., 1980—. Mem. Am. Concrete Inst., ASCE, Prestressed Concrete Inst., Tagore Soc. N.Y., Bengali Assn. Los Angeles, Chi Epsilon. Contbr. articles to profl. jours. Home: 1614 Naco Pl Hacienda Heights CA 91745 Office: 100 Walnut St Pasadena CA

CHAKRABORTY, SAMIR, telecommunications co. exec.; b. Ramgarh, India, Nov. 27, 1948; immigrated to Can., 1973, naturalized, 1977; s. Amalendu Nath and Sati (Bannerji) C.; B.E.E. with distinction (Govt. India Nat. Merit scholar), U. Kashmir, 1971; M.S. in Computer Systems (fellow), SUNY, Binghamton, 1973, M.S. in Gen. Systems, 1974; Centre for Advanced Engring. Study fellow, M.I.T., 1975; m. Rita Thappa, May 5, 1973; 1 child, Anjali. Systems engr. IBM, Endicott, N.Y., 1973; systems cons. Govt. Can., 1972-74; with N.B. Telephone Co., St. John, N.B., Can., 1974—, staff engr., 1974, tech. specialist, 1975, engring. mgr., 1976, project mgr. bus. info. systems, 1978, mgr. corp. planning, 1978—. Adv., Sch. Computer Sci., U. Windsor; loaned exec. United Way, 1980—. Registered profl. engr., N.B. Mem. Internat. Soc. Gen. Systems Research, IEEE, Assn. Computing Machinery, Austrian Cybernetics Soc., Assn. Profl. Engrs. N.B., Indo Can. Soc. (dir. 1980—), Sigma Xi. Contbr. articles to profl. publs. Home: 59 Park Dr Saint John NB E2H 1A5 Canada Office: Box 1430 1 Brunswick Sq Saint John NB E2L 4K2 Canada

CHALAKANI, JOHN Y., med. products mfg. co. exec.; b. Cairo, Egypt, Apr. 6, 1921; s. Hussein A. and Naomi (Hmeda) El Chalakani Bey; B.B.A., Ecole de Commerce, Paris, 1944; postgrad. U. Ill., 1955; m. Sherie Hart, Mar. 22, 1952; children—Paula Nadia (Mrs. Baier), Paul Scott, Michele Aida, Eric John, Jeffrey Hart, Joan Bernadette. Came to U.S., 1946, naturalized, 1949. With Austenal Med. Dental div. Howmet Corp., N.Y., 1948-66, v.p. internat. sales, 1965-66; v.p. marketing, corp. planning and fgn. subsidiaries Am. Cyctoscope Makers, Inc., Stamford, Conn., 1966-74, sr. v.p., 1975-76, pres., 1977—. Vol. Girl Scouts U.S.A., Hastings-on-Hudson, 1963-73. Recipient Pub. Service certificate State N.Y., 1958. Mem. U.S. Med.-Surg. Mfrs. Assn. (chmn. internat. affairs 1971-73). Home: 305 Crescent Pkwy Sea Girt NJ 08750 also 50 Glenbrook Rd Stamford CT 06902 Office: 300 Stillwater Ave Stamford CT 06902

CHALECKI, RON CHARLES, ins. agy. exec.; b. Chgo., July 29, 1931; s. Bruno Joseph and Helen Christine (Babiarz) C.; B.A., DePaul U., 1952, M.A., 1953; m. Carolyn J. Gledhill, Sept. 28, 1968; children—Robert C., Anthony J., Amy C. Sales mgr. Security Mut.

Casualty Co., Chgo., 1955-68; sales mgr. Blue Cross So. Calif., Los Angeles, 1968-71; agy. mgr. Mutual N.Y., Beverly Hills, Calif., 1971—; instr. Am. Coll., 1971-76. Active United Fund, 1971, Boy Scouts Am., 1968-72. Served with U.S. Army, 1953-55. Mem. Woodland Hills C. of C., San Fernando Valley, W. Los Angeles assn. life underwriters, Alpha Chi. Roman Catholic. Club: K.C. Home: 2733 Carlmont Pl Simi Valley CA 93065 Office: 9665 Wilshire Blvd # 500 Beverly Hills CA 90212

CHALFANT, JOSEPH SHAW, mgmt. cons.; b. Richmond, Ind., Apr. 12, 1936; s. Ray King and Margaret (Shaw) C.; B.S., Ind. U., 1958; postgrad. U. Louisville Sch. Law, 1959-62; m. Harriet Vaughan Strange, June 6, 1959; children—Martin Joseph, Matthew Christopher, Peggy. Sales, Colgate-Palmolive Co., 1958, merchandising rep., 1959-61; sales mgr. Mid-Continent Carton Corp., Louisville, 1961-72, pres., 1972—; pres. Shaw Internat., New Albany, Ind., 1972—; dir. various corp. and charity bds. Served with AUS, 1958-59. Cert. mgmt. cons. Mem. Sigma Alpha Epsilon, Alpha Delta Sigma. Republican. Methodist. Club: Ad. Home: Trimingham Rd New Albany IN 47150 Office: PO Box 375 New Albany IN 47150

CHALFANT, KENNETH PAUL, electronics co. exec.; b. Colorado Springs, Colo., July 31, 1953; s. Harry Ellis and Maxine Eleanor (Blunt) C.; student pub. schs., Colorado Springs; m. Rosemary Belle Chalfant. Technician, Maytronics Co., Colorado Springs, 1971, Western Sci. Co., Colorado Springs, 1972, cons. engr. Electric Co., Colorado Springs, 1971—; founder, owner, mgr. Chalfant Research & Devel. Co., Colorado Springs, 1974—; cons. in field. Hewlett Packard grantee, 1967-69; Tektronix Co. grantee, 1972; Bell Telephone Co. grantee, 1970; U. Colo. grantee, 1968. Mem. Florence Pioneer Mus. Hist. Soc.

CHALKER, ROBERT PHELPS, assn. exec.; b. Linden, Ala., Mar. 16, 1914; s. Isaac Watts and Harriet Marshall (Phelps) C.; student Birmingham (Ala.) So. Coll., 1929-31; A.B., Duke U., 1933, M.A., 1935; grad. student Heidelberg U. (Germany), 1936, U. Chgo., 1937, U. Paris, 1938, Fgn. Service Inst., Columbia U., 1950-51; m. Edna Violet Wood, Nov. 8, 1946; children—Janet, Jeffrey. Instr. pub. schs., Marianna and Panama City, Fla., 1934-35, Pensacola, Fla., 1935-38; instr. extension service U. Ala., 1939; vice consul, Berlin, 1939-42, sec. embassy, 1941-42, interned, Bad Nauheim, Germany, 1941-42; vice consul, Lisbon, Portugal, 1942, Birmingham, Eng., 1942-44; consul, sec. embassy, London, 1944-48; consul, Madras, India, 1948-49, Bremen, Germany, 1949-50, Duesseldorf, Germany, 1951-54; personnel ops. officer Office of Personnel, Dept. State, 1954-56; consul gen., Amsterdam, 1956-59; with U.S. Naval War Coll., 1959-60; Am. consul gen., Kobe-Osaka, Japan, 1960-64; counsellor Am. embassy, Dublin, Ireland, 1964-68; now exec. dir. U.S. C. of C. in Ireland, Dublin. Mem. Alpha Tau Omega. Clubs: Rotary (past pres.), Stephen's Green, Milltown Golf, Woodbrook Golf (Dublin). Office: 20 College Green Dublin 2 Ireland

CHALLANCIN, PAUL JOHN, constrn. mgmt. co. exec.; b. Hancock, Mich., Jan. 12, 1945; s. Paul V. and Elvira Selma (Nelson) C.; B.S., Mich. State U., 1969; m. Kathy R. Thomson, June 9, 1973; children—Tony, Susie. Western project mgr. N. Am. Constrn. Corp., Palm Beach, Fla., 1970-75; sec.-treas. Challancin-Weeks Corp., Snohomish, Wash., 1975—, pres., 1976—, dir., 1975—; v.p. Dejan Realty, Snohomish, 1980—, dir., 1979—. Mem. Master Builders Assn. Republican. Roman Catholic. Home: 23803 150th SE Monroe WA 98272 Office: 120 Ave A Snohomish WA 98290

CHAMBERLAIN, CARL EUGENE, farm coop. exec.; b. Everett, Pa., Sept. 22, 1925; s. John Thomas and Naomi Ruth (Edwards) C.; student Wittenberg Coll., 1943-44; m. Doris Suzanne Rearick, July 16, 1945; children—Steven Craig, Betsy Ann, Sally Leigh. Br. store mgr. Bedford Farm Bur. Co-op Assn., Everett, 1946-47, asst. assn. mgr., Bedford, Pa., 1947-48; store mgr. Pa. Farm Bur. Co-op. Assn., Indiana, Pa., 1949-51, dist. mgr., Lewistown, 1953-58, petroleum div. mgr., Harrisburg, 1959-61, retail services mgr., 1961-62, dir. distbn., 1962-65; regional mgr. petroleum div. Agway, Inc., Harrisburg, 1965, Ithaca, N.Y., 1966, asst. to dir. distbn., Syracuse, N.Y., 1966-71, ops. mgr. So. retail div., Harrisburg, 1971-73, dir. retail Eastern retail div., West Springfield, Mass., 1973—; pres. Pa. Assn. Farmer Coops., 1961-64; dir. N.Y. Council Retail Mchts., 1969-71. Sec. council St. John's Lutheran Ch., Lewistown, 1955-58; council St. John's Luth. Ch., Hoernerstown, Pa., 1961-64, Liverpool, N.Y., 1968-71; trustee Luth. Student Found., Syracuse U. Served with USAAF, 1943-46, USAF, 1951-53. Mem. West Springfield C. of C. (dir. 1976-79). Republican. Club: Masons. Home: 58 Beacon Hill Rd West Springfield MA 01089 Office: 95 Elm St West Springfield MA 01089

CHAMBERLAIN, FRANK MONROE, paint co. exec.; b. Alton, Ill., Mar. 9, 1931; s. Alexander S. and Dorothy M. (Monroe) C.; B.S., Yale U., 1953; M.B.A., Harvard U., 1959; m. Dixie Gwen Forgey, Jan. 25, 1958; children—Wendy, Pamela, Jennifer. Vice pres., gen. mgr. Arkwright Interlaken Co., Providence, 1967-68; pres. Cavrok Corp., Vernon, Conn., 1968-75; pres., dir. Porter Paint Co., Louisville, 1976—; dir. Maker's Mark Distillery; mem. bus. adv. council U. Louisville, 1978—. Vice pres. Historic Homes Found., Louisville, 1979-80; div. leader Met. United Way Louisville, 1980. Served with AUS, 1954-56. Mem. Young Pres. Orgn., Am. Mktg. Assn., Ky. Council Econ. Edn. Republican. Episcopalian. Clubs: River Valley, Harmony Landing Country. Home: 3365 Greenhill Ln Louisville KY 40207 Office: 400 S 13th St Louisville KY 40201

CHAMBERLIN, EDNA MAE, bank exec.; b. Dowagiac, Mich., Nov. 16, 1929; d. Michael J. and Mary T. (Luska) Sarabyn; A.A., South Bend Coll. Commerce, 1948; B.S. in Mgmt., Simmons Coll., 1979; postgrad. Grad. Trust. Sch., Northwestern U.; m. Donald P. Chamberlin, Sept. 13, 1952. Accountant dept. redevelopment City of Mishawaka (Ind.), 1963-68; cons. City Planning Assos., Mishawaka, 1968-73; trust officer Nat. Bank & Trust Co. of South Bend (Ind.), 1973—. Com. chmn. United Way, 1975-77. Mem. Nat. Assn. Bank Women, South Bend Estate Planning Council, Pilot Club of South Bend, Veronica's Profl. Women's Club. Republican. Roman Catholic. Clubs: Ladies of Elks. Home: 924 W Battell St Mishawaka IN 46544 Office: 112 W Jefferson Blvd South Bend IN 46601

CHAMBERLIN, JOHN STEPHEN, co. exec.; b. Boston, July 29, 1928; s. Stephen Henry and Olive Helen (McGrath) C.; A.B. cum laude, Harvard U., 1950, M.B.A., 1953; m. Mary Katherine Leahy, Oct. 9, 1954; children—Mary Katherine, Patricia Ann, Carol Lynn, John Stephen, Liane Helen, Mark Joseph. Lamp salesman Gen. Elec. Co., N.Y.C., 1954-57; mgmt. cons., 1957-60; mgr. product planning TV receiver dept., Syracuse, N.Y., 1960-63, mgr. mktg., gen. mgr. radio receiver dept., Utica, N.Y., 1963-70, v.p., gen. mgr. Housewares div., Bridgeport, Conn., 1971-74, v.p., gen. mgr. Housewares and Audio div., 1974-76; exec. v.p., dir. Lenox, Inc., Trenton, 1970-71, pres., chief exec. officer, dir., 1976—; dir. N.J. Nat. Corp.; Gulton Industries Inc. Bd. overseers Parsons Sch. Design. Clubs: Harvard, Union League (N.Y.C.); Bedens Brook (Princeton, N.J.); Sea View Country (Atlantic City). Home: 182 Fairway Dr Princeton NJ 08540 Office: Old Princeton Pike Lawrenceville NJ 08648

CHAMBERLIN, RONALD EUGENE, mfg. co. exec.; b. Chambersburg, Pa., May 21, 1947; s. Clifford Eugene and Betty Marie (Davidson) C.; B.A. magna cum laude, Gettysburg Coll., 1969; postgrad. Pa. State U., 1970-72; m. Frances Ann Petrosky, Mar. 22, 1969; children—Scott Charles, Megan Marie. Mgmt. intern Dept. Army, Washington, 1969-70; instr. polit. sci. Pa. State U., University Park, 1970-72; personnel mgr. Beistle Co., Shippensburg, Pa., 1973-76, v.p. for mfg., 1977—. Pres., Cumberland Valley chpt. Internat. Mgmt. Council, 1979-80, recipient Weaver prize, 1969. Mem. Am. Prodn. and Inventory Control Soc., Am. Polit. Sci. Assn., Phi Beta Kappa, Pi Lambda Sigma. Presbyterian. Home: 15055 West Creek Rd Shippensburg PA 17257 Office: 14-18 E Orange St Shippensburg PA 17257

CHAMBERS, DAVID EDSON, exec. search cons.; b. Mason City, Iowa, Mar. 6, 1938; s. Robert Edson and Louis Alice (Lennan) C.; B.S.B.A., U. Ariz., 1961; m. Traudl Steiger, Apr. 27, 1968; children—Scott David, Todd Robert, Andrea Suzanne. Employment rep. Pan Am. World Airways, Cape Canaveral, Fla., 1961-64; employment mgr. fin. Xerox Corp., Rochester, N.Y., 1965-66; pres. David Chambers Co., Chgo., 1966-68; employment dir. Allied Chem. Corp., N.Y.C., 1968-69; partner Antell, Wright & Nagel, Inc., N.Y.C., 1969-73; pres. exec. search div. Fry Consultants, Inc., N.Y.C., 1973-74; pres. David Chambers & Assos. Inc. (purchased Fry Consultants exec. search div.), N.Y.C., 1974—. Served with U.S. Army, 1961-63. Republican. Clubs: Union League (N.Y.C.); Winged Foot Golf (Mamaroneck, N.Y.). Office: 6 E 43d St New York NY 10017

CHAMBERS, JOHN EDWARD, ins. co. exec.; b. Boonville, Mo., Aug. 25, 1910; s. George E. and Margaret (Zollinger) C.; B.A., Stanford, 1932; m. Meta Ann Pearce, Feb. 17, 1940; children—Carol Ann (Mrs. Edward C. Mooney), John Edward. With Motors Ins. Corp., Albuquerque, 1934-47; v.p. Marathon Ins. Co., 1947-60, pres., dir., 1960-64; pres., dir. Spartan Ins. Co., also v.p., dir. Pacific Fidelity Life Ins. Co., 1960-64; v.p., dir. Olympic Ins. Co., 1951-64; pres., dir. Stuyvesant Ins. Co., Allentown, Pa., 1964-75, Mohawk Ins. Co., Allentown, 1972-75, Trans-Oceanic Ins. Co. San Juan, P.R., 1965-75, Stuyvesant Life Ins. Co., Allentown, 1964-75, Trans-Oceanic Life Ins. Co. San Juan, 1964-74, Health Maintenance Life Ins. Co., Long Beach, Calif., 1979—. Served to lt., USNR, 1942-45; PTO. Club: Stoneridge Country (Poway, Calif.). Home: 13423 St Andrews Pl Poway CA 92064

CHAMBERS, RAYMOND GEORGE, investment banker; b. Newark, Aug. 7, 1942; s. Herbert Blaine, II and Claire F. (Biebel) C.; B.S., Rutgers U., 1964; M.B.A. in Internat. Bus., Seton Hall U., 1970; m. Patricia A. Griffin, Oct. 17, 1965; children—Christine, Michael, Jennifer. Accountant, Price Waterhouse & Co., C.P.A.'s, 1965-68; pres., chief exec. officer Metrocare Inc., 1968-75; pres. Hampshire Capital Inc., Morristown, N.J., 1975—; dir. Windsor Life Ins. Co. Am. Office: 330 South St Morristown NJ 07960

CHAMBERS, ROBERT LEROY, mfg. co. exec.; b. Salt Lake City, Sept. 9, 1918; s. George B. and Vilate C. (Schofield) C.; B.A., U. Utah, 1939; M.A., Fletcher Sch. Internat. Law and Diplomacy, 1940; M.B.A., Harvard U., 1942; m. June Musser, 1940; children—Pamela Chambers Champe, Penelope Chambers Percy, James Henry. Founder, pres. Magna Power Tool Corp., Menlo Park, Calif., 1947-58; pres. BSP Corp., San Francisco, 1959-67; chief exec. officer, chmn. Envirotech Corp., Menlo Park, 1969-78, chmn., 1978—, also dir.; dir. The Herrick Corp., Memorex Corp., Consol. Freightways, Inc., Varian Assos. Mem. Young Pres. Orgn. (pres. 1957-58). Clubs: Bohemian (San Francisco); Menlo Country (Woodside, Calif.); Palo Alto (Calif.); Alta (Salt Lake City). Office: 3000 Sand Hill Rd Menlo Park CA 94025

CHAMPION, ELVERTON ROOSEVELT, ret. constrn. co. exec.; b. Edmonton, Alta., Can., Sept. 30, 1911; s. Ernest Charles and Sarah (Craig) C.; B.S., Pacific Coast U., 1936; grad. Advanced Mgmt. Program, Harvard, 1960; m. Gladys Ivy Lambert, Mar. 6, 1943 (dec. Aug. 1977); m. 2d, Glenna Marie Buscher, Feb. 16, 1980. Supt. Contractors Pacific Naval Air Bases, 1940-43; supt., acting dist. mgr. Raymond Concrete Pile Co., 1943-46; with Hawaiian Dredging & Constrn. Co. Ltd., Honolulu, 1946-59, v.p., 1959; v.p. Dillingham Corp., Honolulu, 1959-76, ret., 1976. Regional council mem. Boy Scouts Am.; pres. Friends of East West Center; pres. Flora Pacifica; mem. Oahu Pvt. Industry Council; bd. dirs. St. Francis Hosp., Maunalani Hosp.; founding trustee Hawaii Army Mus. Soc.; bd. dirs., pres. Hawaiian Humane Soc., Hawaiian Found. Am. Freedoms, Hawaii Visitors Bur.; trustee Leahi Hosp., Honolulu. Mem. Nat. Alliance Businessmen (chmn. Hawaii-Pacific), Pub. Relations Soc. Am., Soc. Am. Mil. Engrs., Engring. Soc. Hawaii, Pacific and Asian Affairs Council (dir.), Assn. U.S. Army (Hawaii pres.), Nat. Council on Crime and Delinquency (Hawaii chmn.), English-Speaking Union (pres.), Hawaii World Trade Assn. (pres.). Republican. Episcopalian. Clubs: Masons, Shriners, Jesters, Hawaiian Kennel (pres.), Pacific, Waia lae Country (Honolulu); Royal Melbourne (Australia); American (Sydney, Australia). Home: 525 Hakaka Pl Honolulu HI 96816

CHAN, FREDERICK MAN-HIN, architect, developer; b. Hong Kong, June 17, 1947; s. William Chak-Yan and Nancy Sui-Yin (Tse) C.; B.Arch., U. Calif., Berkeley, 1969; M.Arch., Harvard U., 1974. Architect, N.Y. State Urban Devel. Corp., N.Y.C., 1973-74; devel. mgr. community land devel. Ministry of Housing, Toronto, Ont., Can., 1974-78; pres. Nu West R.E.I. Corp., Los Angeles, 1978—, Kingsley Properties, Inc., Los Angeles, 1978—; treas. Pearl City Investments Corp., Los Angeles, 1978—. Mem. Am. Planning Assn., Ont. Assn. Architects, Urban Devel. Inst., Chinese C. of C. Los Angeles (dir.). Clubs: Marina City, Los Angeles Racquet, Internat. Home: 4314 Marina City Dr Marina Del Rey CA 90291 Office: 350 S Figueroa St Suite 555 Los Angeles CA 90071

CHAN, WALLACE LANE, physician, med. adminstr.; b. San Francisco, Dec. 30, 1923; s. Allan Lam and Rose Elsie (Sue) C.; student U. Calif., 1939-42; A.B., Stanford U., 1947, M.D., 1952; m. Emelda E., Oct. 14, 1948; children—Carolyn, Wallace, Jean, Elaine, Allan. Intern, Tripler Gen. Hosp., Honolulu, 1950-52; research dir. CIA, Washington, 1953-57; asst. research prof. physiology George Washington U. Sch. Medicine, Washington, 1956-57; exec. dir. Med. Scis. Research Found., Stanford, Calif., 1957-65, Bio-Research, Inc., San Mateo, Calif., 1957-59; med. dir., v.p. Resources Research, Inc., Washington, 1959-61; asst. clin. prof. medicine Stanford U. Sch. Medicine, 1957-61, asso. in medicine, Stanford, 1961-63; pres. Asian Exports, Inc. San Francisco, 1958-61; spl. asst. to dep. surgeon gen. and surgeon gen., dir. investigations USPHS, Washington, 1961-62; spl. asst. to chancellor U. Calif., Davis, 1962-63; incorporator Neuroscis. Research Found., M.I.T., Boston, 1962-66; med. dir. Alderson Convalescent Hosp., Woodland, Calif., 1966-67, Sunnydale Convalescent Hosp., Fremont, Calif., 1969-70, Mt. Oliver Convalescent Hosp., Carmichael, Calif., 1968-69, Norwood Hosp., Foxboro (Mass.) Area Health Center, 1977—; mng. dir. Marion Internat., Inc., Kansas City, Mo.; med. dir. Boston Chinese Community Health Services, Inc., Boston, 1974-76; dir. health services Mass. Dept. Corrections, 1974-77; chief exec. officer Norfolk (Mass.) Hosp.; practice family medicine, Pasadena, Calif., 1953, Washington, 1956-57, San Carlos, Calif., 1957-61, Sacramento, 1964-67, Oakland, Calif., 1967-71, Boston, 1974—; staff mem. Lemuel Shattuck Hosp., Norwood Hosp.; asst. clin. prof. Tufts Med. Sch., 1975—; asso. clin. prof. dept. community medicine U. Mass. Med. Sch., Boston, 1975—; dir. Intercommerce of Am., Banmerical, Inc., Western Industries, Inc., W. Ger., Bank of Commerce and Credit, San Jose, Costa Rica; pres. Allan Chan Improvement Corp., The Lane Corp., Foxboro Chinese Restaurant, Inc.; chmn. bd. Internat. Resource Mgmt., Inc., Wellesley Farms, Mass., 1973-74; cons. in field. Mem. Mass. Health Policy and Planning Council; mem. pub. health com. Sacramento County C. of C.; adviser Chinese Students Orgn. Served with U.S. Army, 1943-46, 51-53. Charles Murphy scholar U. Calif., 1940; named Man of Achievement, San Francisco C. of C., 1961. Mem. AMA, Pan-Am., Calif., Alameda-Contra Costa County med. assns., Am., Calif. acads. gen. practice, AAAS, Assn. Mil. Surgeons, N.Y. Acad. Sci., Am. Cancer Soc. (dir.). Clubs: Lions Internat. (past pres.), Internat. World Trade. Office: Norwood Hosp 800 Washington St Norwood MA 02062

CHANDLER, ALBERT GALLATIN, oil tool co. exec.; b. McKinney, Tex., Sept. 21, 1913; s. James T. and Eva G. (Hartin) C.; m. Oletha Althea Hollingsworth, Oct. 23, 1950; children—James Albert, John Emmet. Service engr. John Deere Tractor Co., Houston, 1934-36; service engr., dist. sales mgr., div. mgr. Reed Roller Bit Co., Houston, 1936-56; Eastern hemisphere mgr. Security Engring. Corp., Dallas, 1956-57, pres. Petroleum and Mining Equipment, Geneva, 1957—; owner, pres. Chandler Ranch and Petroleum Services Inc., Bastrop, Tex. Mem. Am. Petroleum Inst., Am. Inst. Mining, Metall. and Petroleum Engrs., Nomads. Home: Route 1 Box 62A Bastrop TX 78602 Office: 1249 Soral Geneva Switzerland

CHANDLER, COLBY H., photog. co. exec.; B.S., U. Maine, 1950; student M.I.T. Quality control engr. color control div., devel. engr. print and processing dept. color technol. div. Eastman Kodak Co., Rochester, N.Y. 1950-55, supr. Kodacolor quality control sect. and color technol. div., 1955-59, staff asst. tech. services, 1959-60, staff supr., 1960-63, asst. to gen. mgr. Kodak Park works, 1960-63, asst. to gen. mgr. color print and processing, 1963-64, asst. mgr., 1964-71, mgr., 1971, dir. photog. program devel. U.S. and Can. photog. div., 1971-73, div. dir. spl. projects, then gen. mgr., 1973-77, mem. sales estimating council, then corp. asst. v.p., exec. v.p., 1972-77, pres., 1977—, also dir.; exec. dir. Lincoln 1st Bank Rochester, Indsl. Mgmt. Council Rochester. Exec. dir. Rochester Civic Music Assn. Office: Eastman Kodak Co 343 State St Rochester NY 14650*

CHANDLER, OTIS, newspaper exec.; b. Los Angeles, Nov. 23, 1927; s. Norman and Dorothy (Buffum) C.; grad. Andover Acad., 1946; B.A., Stanford, 1950; children—Norman Brant, Harry Brant, Cathleen, Michael Otis, Carolyn. Various positions mech., editorial, circulation, advt. depts. Los Angeles Times, 1953-57; asst. to pres. Times Mirror Co., 1957-58, dir., 1962—, vice chmn. bd., 1968—, editor-in-chief. marketing mgr. Los Angeles Times, 1958-60, pub., 1960-80, chmn. bd., editor-in-chief Times Mirror, 1981—. Served to 1st lt. USAAF, 1951-53. Mem. Am. Newspaper Pubs. Assn., Am. Soc. Newspaper Editors. Club: California. Holder shot put record Pacific Coast Conf., 1950. Office: Times Mirror Sq Los Angeles CA 90053

CHANDLER, SCOTT STONER, business exec.; b. Kansas City, Mo., Dec. 6, 1932; s. Edwin and Sarah (Stoner) C.; B.S. with honors, Kans. State U., 1954, M.S., 1957; grad. A.M.P., Columbia U., 1978; m. Marjorie Kay Pinther, Sept. 22, 1962; children—Scott Stoner, Holly Ann. Tech. sales Armour Indsl. Chem. Co., Chgo., 1960-62, market devel., 1962-63, industry mgr., 1963-65; sr. mktg. analyst Internat. Minerals & Chem. Corp., Northbrook, Ill., 1965-67, mgr. sales analysis, 1967-68, product mgr., 1968-70, dir. supply and devel., 1970-74, dir. comml. devel., 1974-75; v.p., gen. mgr. Veterinary Products div. IMC Chem. Group, Inc. Mem. exec. bd. N.E. Ill. council Boy Scouts Am., 1974-75; bd. dirs. Animal Health Inst., 1977-80; bd. dirs. Kans. State U. Livestock and Meat Industry Council. 1979—. Served to 1st lt. USAF, 1954-56. Fellow Am. Inst. Chemists; mem. Midwest Chem. Mktg. Assn. (chmn. 1968-69, dir. 1969-70), Am. Chem. Soc., Midwest Planning Assn., Nat. Am. Indian Cattlemen's Assn. (agri-bus. advisory bd. 1977-78), Nat. Cattlemen's Assn. (co-chmn. nat. agri-bus. com., exec. com. polit. action com. 1980—), Beta Theta Pi, Gamma Sigma Delta, Alpha Zeta, Alpha Phi Omega. Republican. Mem. Evang. Convenant Ch. Am. Patentee in field.

CHANDLER, WINSTON GRIGGS, transp. corp. exec.; b. Clinton, Ark., Oct. 9, 1919; s. Lester W. and Mattie (Griggs) C.; student Coll. Ozarks, 1940; J.D., Ark. Law Sch., 1951; m. Ouida G. Hunnicutt, Sept. 16, 1942; children—Winston Griggs, Michael Lee, Jeffrey Scott. Owner Chandler 5 and 10, Clinton, Ark., 1946-48; safety insp. Ark. Pub. Service Commn., Little Rock, 1949-53; pres. Chandler Trailer Convoy, Inc., Little Rock, 1953—, chmn. bd., 1971—, also dir.; pres., dir. Chandler Agy., Little Rock, 1963—; pres. C & K Investment Corp.; dir. Safety Boom, Inc. Mem. Ark. Athletic Commn., 1954-56, Tenn. Walking Horse Breeding-Showing; chmn. Sch. Bd., Pulaski County, 1959-70; mem., chmn. Ark. History Commn., 1957-69; mem. exec. com. finance council, So. chmn. Democratic Fin. Council; mem. pres.'s devel. council Harding Coll., Searcy, Ark. Served to maj. USAAF, 1941-45. Mem. Am. Legion, Hon. Order Ky. Cols. Democrat. Mem. Ch. of Christ (elder). Lion. Home: 4 Arrowhead Ct Little Rock AR 72207 Office: 8828 N Benton Hwy Little Rock AR 72209

CHANDRA, GIRISH, steel co. exec.; b. Balia, Uttar Pradesh, India, July 1, 1941; came to U.S., 1970; s. Vindhyachal Prasad; B.Sc., Banaras Hindu U., India, 1959; M.B.A., Case Western Res. U., Cleve., 1972; m. Chander Kiran Sood, July 8, 1973; children—Ankur, Pravir, Nupur. Prodn. supr. New Central Jute Mills Co., Calcutta, 1964-68; office supr., 1968-69; purchase officer Jaipur Metals and Electricals, Ltd. (India), 1969-70; inventory control analyst Alcan Aluminum Corp., Warren, Ohio, 1972-77; inventory mgr. Wheatland Tube Co. (Pa.), 1978—. Mem. Am. Prodn. and Inventory Control Soc. Hindu. Home: 9061 Altura Dr Warren OH 44484 Office: 1 Council Ave Wheatland PA 16161

CHANDRA, SUNIL, electronics mfg. co. exec.; b. Dhanaura, India, Oct. 15, 1941; s. Sagar Mal Garg and Shakuntla Devi Singh; came to U.S., 1960; B.S., New Haven Coll., 1963; M.S., U. Conn., 1965; m. Cynthia Edith Wrisley, July 31, 1965; children—Candace, Stuart. Project mgr. Tex. Instruments Inc., Dallas, 1967-71, product mgr., Nice, France, 1971-73, mgr. mktg. application engring. and strategy, Rieti, Italy, 1974-75, mgr. European program, Paris, 1976-77, mgr. mktg., profl. calculators, 1977-78, time products div., 1979-80; mgr. strategic planning and devel. operation Gen. Electric Co., Lynchburg, Va., 1980—. Adviser, Jr. Achievement, 1967-68. Mem. Dallas Jr. C. of C. (dir. 1969-70). Unitarian. Home: 111 Deer Creek Dr Lynchburg VA 24502 Office: PO Box 4096 Lynchburg VA 24502

CHANEY, DENNIS WILLIAM, electronics co. exec.; b. Van Nuys, Calif., Nov. 6, 1947; s. William Leroy and Evelyn May (Kennedy) C.; B.S. with distinction, Ariz. State U., 1969; m. Sandra L. Emmons, Feb. 8, 1969; children—Robert Dennis, Deborah Ann. Elec. engr. Westinghouse Corp., 1969-70; engr.-supr. Mountain Bell Telephone Co., 1970-75; pres. Chaney Electronics Inc., Englewood, Colo.,

1975—. Mem. IEEE. Presbyterian. Office: Chaney Electronics Inc 2010 W Dartmouth St Englewood CO 80110

CHANEY, LARRY RANDALL, cleaning co. exec.; b. St. Louis, May 13, 1935; s. Elza Earl and Rossa Helen (Faries) C.; B.S. in Psychology, St. Louis U., 1963; m. Marcella Elizabeth Bokel, Sept. 1, 1962; children—Kim Marie, Julia Rose, Jeffrey Michael, James Earl, Christy Ann. Asst. pricing mgr., St. Louis div. Phillips Petroleum Co., 1962-64; asst. fleet mgr. St. Louis dist. Ford div. Ford Motor Co., 1964-66; exec. v.p. Power Magic Cleaning Co., 1966-70; exec. v.p. Multistate Service Co., St. Louis, 1970-73, also dir.; dist. mgr. Metal Finishing div. Stauffer Chem. Co., St. Louis, 1973-77; pres. Contecknix, Inc., Hazelwood, Mo., 1969—, also dir.; pres. Transi-Clean Co., 1975—; pres., dir. Transi-Chem. Supply Co., 1975—, Metal-Chem. Corp., 1979—; dir. Power Magic Cleaning Co., 1966-70, Specialty Leasing Co., 1968-70. Served with USAF, 1955-59. Decorated Commendation certificate. Mem. Am. Electroplating Soc., Psi Chi. Club: Oak (Oakland, Calif.). Patentee in field. Home: 1125 Woodcrest Ln Hazelwood MO 63042 Office: 5100 Bulwer Ave Saint Louis MO 63147

CHANEY, WILLIAM R., cosmetic co. exec.; b. Satanta, Kans., July 31, 1932; s. Alva Ross and Irene (Reeves) C.; B.A. in Bus. Adminstrn., U. Kans., 1953; m. Babette Carole Cooper, June 8, 1956; children—Carole Babette, Diana. With Avon Products, Inc., N.Y.C., 1955—, dir. personnel adminstrn., N.Y.C., 1966-67, v.p. personnel, 1967-68, group v.p. field ops., 1968-69, sr. v.p. ops., 1969-72, exec. v.p., 1972-77, pres., 1977—, also dir. Served to 1st lt. AUS, 1953-55. Mem. Advt. and Sales Execs. Club, Lambda Chi Alpha. Office: Avon Products Inc 9 W 57th St New York NY 10019*

CHANG, CHARLES KAM CHEW, lawyer; b. Honolulu, Dec. 3, 1924; s. William C. and Kam Bin (Lum) C.; B.A., U. Hawaii, 1953; J.D., Boston U., 1956; LL.M., N.Y. U., 1957; m. Winona P.J. Lee, May 29, 1951. Admitted to Mass. bar, 1956, Hawaii bar, 1957; asso. Carlsmith, Carlsmith, Wichman & Case, Hilo, Hawaii, 1957-59; partner Nevels & Chang, Honolulu, 1959-72; lectr. taxation; dist. magistrate, Hilo, 1959-62. Served with AUS, 1945-47. Mem. Am., Mass., Hawaii bar assns. Clubs: Elks, Masons, Shriners, Rotary. Office: Room 1020 1441 Kapiolani Blvd Honolulu HI 96814

CHANG, CHING MING, chem. co. exec.; b. Nanking, China, Oct. 13, 1935; s. Wen Pei and Su Hin (Pi) C.; came to U.S., 1968, naturalized, 1976; diploma in engring. Tech. U. Aachen (W. Ger.), 1962, Ph.D., 1967; m. Birdie Shiao-Ching Ku, Dec. 18, 1964; children—Andrew Liang-Ping, Nelson Liang-An. Research asst. Inst. Mechanics, Tech. U. Aachen, 1962-64, instr., 1964-67, research asso., 1967; vis. asst. prof. engring. mechanics N.C. State U., 1968-70, asst. prof., 1970-73; sr. engr. Linde div. Union Carbide Corp., Tonawanda, N.Y., 1973-75, cons., 1975, supr., 1975-78, engring. asso., 1978—; adj. asso. prof. engring. sci., aerospace engring. and nuclear engring. State U. N.Y. at Buffalo, 1975-79, adj. prof., 1979—. Registered profl. engr., Va., N.Y. Mem. AAAS, Am. Phys. Soc., Nat. Soc. Profl. Engrs. (dir. Erie-Niagara chpt. 1975-78, 2d v.p. 1978-79, 1st v.p. 1979-80, pres. 1980—), ASME, Air Pollution Control Assn., Sigma Xi, Phi Kappa Phi. Contbr. articles on fluid dynamics, heat transfer, two-phase flows, air pollution control, high-temperature gasdynamics, kinetic theory of gases to profl. jours.; asst. editor Plasma Physics, 1971-72; patentee electrostatic presipitation of particulates. Home: 171 The Paddock Williamsville NY 14221 Office: Linde Div Union Carbide Corp PO Box 44 Tonawanda NY 14150

CHANG, GARETH CHUN-CHUNG, aerospace co. exec.; b. Chengtu, China, Mar. 6, 1943; s. Peter Jen-Yiu and Joy Gan-Long (Ju) C.; A.A. in Engring., Fullerton Jr. Coll., 1963; B.A. in Math., Calif. State U. at Fullerton, 1965; postgrad. in Elec. Engring., U. So. Calif., 1965-71; M.B.A., Pepperdine U., 1978; m. Nancy Lee, Mar. 2, 1974; children—Michael Wai-Zsun, Michelle Wai-Li. Systems analyst, computer center Calif. State U., Fullerton, 1963-65; lectr. math. Calif. State U., Long Beach, 1965-67; lead engr. Minuteman guidance and control Autonetics div. N.Am. Rockwell, Anaheim, Calif., 1966-68; project engr. Honeywell, W.Covina, Calif., 1968-69; mgr., co-founder Systems and Computer Info. Inc., Inglewood, Calif., 1969-71; mgr. Xerox Data Systems, El Segundo, Calif., 1971-73; v.p.-engring. Actron div. McDonnell Douglas Corp., Monrovia, Calif., 1973-79; v.p. McDonnell Douglas China, Inc., Long Beach, 1980—; dir. Linkabit Corp., LaJolla, Calif. Co-chmn. Model UN, West Coast, 1965. Mem. IEEE, Am. Inst. Aeros. and Astronautics, Chinese Scientists and Engrs. Assn. So. Calif., Chinese Martial Arts Assn. Club: Old Ranch Tennis. Home: 3762 Seascape Dr Huntington Beach CA 92649 Office: 3855 Lakewood Blvd Long Beach CA 90846

CHANG, JOSEPH JUIFU, elec. engr., hotel exec.; b. Chungking, China, Dec. 1, 1928; s. Hsin-Yuan and Ching-Chien (Chia) C.; came to U.S., 1956, naturalized, 1963; B.S., Taiwan Coll. Engring., 1953; M.S., Purdue U., 1957, Ph.D., 1961; m. Mary Hsueh-Mei Yang, Jan. 1, 1954; children—Judy Pingo, Howard Feng-Hau, Mona Pinghua. Mem. tech. staff Bell Telephone Labs., Murray Hill, N.J., 1961-64; physics and electronics expert UN, 1964-65; project engr. Bendix Research Co., Southfield, Mich., 1965-66; with IBM, N.Y. and Vt., 1966—, microelectronics research mgr., 1967—; owner, gen. mgr. Holiday Inn, Springfield, Mass., 1978—; owner Ramada Inn, Chicopee, Mass., 1980—; chmn. bd. Trade Internat., Inc., Berkeley Heights, N.J., 1962-65, Chang Motels Corp., Poughkeepsie, N.Y., 1973—, Chang Hotel Corp., Springfield, 1978—; vis. prof. Chia-Tung U., Hsinchu, Taiwan, 1964-65. Mem. IEEE (sr.), Am. Phys. Soc., AAAS, Sigma Xi. Club: Rotary. Contbr. articles to profl. publs. Patentee in field. Inventor dielectric isolation and arsenic-emitter transistor. Home: 711 Dwight St Springfield MA 01100 Office: Holiday Inn Springfield MA 01100

CHANG, MARY HSUEH-MEI, hotel exec.; b. Tainan, Taiwan, Mar. 23, 1935; d. Ti and Yulan (Hsieh) Yang; m. Joseph Juifu Chang, Jan. 1, 1954; children—Judy, Howard, Mona. Pres., Trade Internat. Inc., Berkeley Heights, N.J., 1961-65; owner, gen. mgr. Dorchester Motor Lodge, Poughkeepsie, N.Y., 1973-78, owner, gen. mgr. Holiday Inn, Springfield, Mass., 1978-80, Ramada Inn, Chicopee, Mass., 1980—; pres. Yangti Hotel Corp., 1980—. Home: 711 Dwight St Springfield MA 01100 Office: Holiday Inn Springfield MA 01100

CHANNER, FREDERICK WYNDHAM, investment banker; b. Chgo., Nov. 23, 1909; s. George Stanton and Laura (Parsons) C.; Ph.B., U. Chgo., 1932; m. Georganne Gibson Dunshee, Oct. 12, 1944; children—Penelope, Christopher, Kendall. Engaged in investment bus., Chgo., 1933—; with Channer Securities Co., 1936-59, pres., 1957-59; pres. Channer Newman Securities Co., Chgo., 1959-72, chmn., chief exec. officer, 1972—. Served from pvt. to capt. Combat Intelligence, USAAF, 1942-45. Republican. Presbyterian. Clubs: Mid-Day, Bond, Municipal Bond (Chgo.); Inverness Golf (Palatine, Ill.). Home: 1894 W Stuart Ln Inverness IL 60067 Office: 39 S La Salle St Chicago IL 60603

CHANNER, STEPHEN DYER, trade assn. exec.; b. Chgo., Nov. 1, 1933; s. George Stanton and Maxine (Dyer) C.; B.A., Colo. Coll., 1956; m. Antoinette Persons, June 29, 1957; children—Stephen Persons, Wyndham Harvey. With American Seating Co., Grand Rapids, Mich., 1958-77; exec. dir. Business and Institutional Furniture Mfrs. Assn., Grand Rapids, 1977—. Served to 1st lt. U.S. Army, 1956-58. Mem. Am. Soc. Assn. Execs., Club: Grand Rapids Racquet. Contbr. articles to trade mags., jours. Office: 2335 Burton St SE Grand Rapids MI 49506

CHANT, DAVIS RYAN, real estate broker; b. Port Jervis, N.Y., Dec. 15, 1938; s. B. Ryall and Miriam C. (Cathy) C.; B.A., Belmont Abbey Coll., 1960; children—Tamara, Holley. Constrn. materials salesman, architect service U.S. Gypsum Co., Chgo., 1960-62; pres. Davis R. Chant, Inc., realtors, Milford, Pa., 1962—, Davis R. Chant Assos., Inc., realtors, Lords Valley, Pa., Davis R. Chant Inc., Realtors of N.Y. Chmn., Econ. Devel. Council NE Pa.; mem. Pres.' com. on Leisure Housing. Bd. dirs. Pike County Conservation Dist.; trustee Milford Reservation, Inc. Recipient nat. award for advt. Nat. Assn. Real Estate Brokers, 1971. Mem. Am. Right of Way Assn., Nat., N.Y. assns. real estate bds., Nat. Inst. Real Estate Brokers, Pa. Vacation Land Developers Assn., Pa., N.Y. assns. realtors, Internat. Real Estate Fedn., Sullivan County, Delaware County bds. realtors, Pike County (past dir.), Wayne County, Port Jervis, N.Y. chambers commerce, NE Soc. Farm Mgrs. and Rural Appraisers, Pike-Wayne County Bd. Realtors (past pres.), Monroe-Pike Builders Assn., Urban Land Inst., Nat. Inst. Farm and Land Brokers, Nat. Assn. Home Builders, Pocomo Mountain Vacation Bur., Community Assn. Inst. Am. (charter, dir.). Mason (32 deg.), Lion. Home: Twin Lakes Milford PA 18337 Office: 106 E Harford St Milford PA 18337

CHAO, BILL KEH-LUNG, mfg. co. exec.; b. China, Apr. 23, 1940; s. C.F. and Ti (Hsuing) C.; B.A., Tunghai U., China, 1962; M.A., U. Wash., 1966; M.B.A., Northwestern U., 1979; m. Shirley C. Chiu, Dec. 14, 1968; children—Jennifer, Kathleen. Data base adminstr. Deere & Co., 1969-72, sr. economist, 1972-74; mgr. bus. econs. dept., chief economist J.I. Case Co., Racine, Wis., 1975-79, dir. corp. planning, 1979—. Pres., Racine Chinese Assn., 1978. Mem. Nat. Assn. Bus. Economists, Am. Econ. Assn. Home: 6 Cherrywood Ct Racine WI 53402 Office: 700 State St Racine WI 53404

CHAO, GEORGE YAO TUNG, semicondr. mfg. co. exec.: b. Shanghai, China, July 4, 1946; came to U.S., 1950, naturalized, 1965; s. Di Wha and Polly Chao; B.S., Rensselaer Poly. Inst., 1970; M.B.A., SUNY, Albany, 1972. Asst. v.p. Bank of Canton of Calif., San Francisco, 1972-77; dir. microprocessor mktg. Nat. Semicondr. Corp., Santa Clara, Calif., 1977-80; v.p. mktg. and sales Cermetek Microelectronics, Sunnyvale, Calif., 1980—. Contbr. articles to profl. jours. Office: 2900 Semiconductor Dr Santa Clara CA 95051

CHAO, PEI-CHUNG, restaurant exec.; b. Shanghai, China, Apr. 24, 1922; came to U.S., 1946, naturalized, 1956; s. Chung Yin and Wen (Lee Ying) C.; M.Textile Engring., Lowell Inst. Tech., 1951; m. Rosana Hsu, Dec. 25, 1955; children—Rosalind, Raymond. Supr., Catalina Co., Los Angeles, 1955-59; propr. Chao's Chinese Restaurant, Garden Grove, Calif., 1959-64; pres. Chao Inc., Anaheim, Calif., 1963—. Mem. Chinese Culture Com. Assn., Los Angeles County Mus. Buddhist. Club: So. Calif. Opera. Office: 1560 S Harbor St Anaheim CA 92802

CHAPEL, JOHN WILLIAM, machine tool distbr.; b. Ashland, Ky., Feb. 28, 1935; s. William Albert and Margaret Jane (Youtsey) C.; student U. Cin. Evening Coll., 1953-60; m. Nancy Anne Lee, July 25, 1953; children—John William, Nancy Jane. Apprentice Gen. Elec. Co., Cin., 1953-57, mfg. planning and balancing specialist, 1957-60; sales engr. Cosa Corp. of Ohio, Cleve., 1960; owner, operator Chapel Machine & Tool Co., Cleve., 1961-68, inc., 1968, pres., 1968—. Sec., Euclid (Ohio) Jaycees, 1965, Outstanding Young Man of Yr., 1967; cubmaster Boy Scouts Am., 1964, dist. chmn., 1967-70; bd. dirs. Euclid YMCA, 1970-73; mem. Euclid Gen. Hosp. Assn., Euclid Devel. Corp. Mem. Euclid C. of C., Council Smaller Enterprises, Greater Cleve. Growth Assn. Republican. Baptist. Club: Euclid Rotary (pres. 1977-78). Home: 22651 Edgecliff Dr Euclid OH 44123 Office: 25901 Tungsten Rd Cleveland OH 44132

CHAPIN, CAROL LYNNE, oil co. exec.; b. Tulsa, Aug. 1, 1946; d. Robert Riley and Margaret Adelle C.; student Okla. State U., 1964-65, Tulsa U., 1970—. With Cities Service Co., Tulsa, 1966—, sec. to purchasing agt., 1966-68, sec. to mgr. purchasing, 1968-73, staff asst., 1973-77, office supplies buyer, 1977-79, material handling equipment buyer, 1979—. Mem. Purchasing Mgmt. Assn. Tulsa. Democrat. Home: 17596 N Peoria Skiatook OK 74070 Office: 110 W 7th St Tulsa OK 74145

CHAPIN, EDWARD YOUNG, IV, tourist attraction exec.; b. Chattanooga, Aug. 20, 1946; s. Edward Young III and Mildred (Toner) C.; B.S.E.E., Princeton U., 1967; postgrad. in bus. adminstrn. Emory U., 1980—; m. Linda Dale Standefer, July 22, 1967; children—Elizabeth Standefer, Edward Young V., John Charles. Gen. mgr., v.p. Sta.-WLOM, Chattanooga, 1967-70; asst. to pres. Rock City Gardens, Inc., Lookout Mountain, Tenn., 1970-74, pres., 1974—; 1st v.p., bd. dirs. Chattanooga Area Conv. and Vis.'s Bur. Bd. dirs. Chattanooga Area Regional Transp. Authority, 1973—, ARC, Chattanooga, 1976—, Am. Heart Assn., Chattanooga, 1979—. Recipient Disting. Service award, named Outstanding Young Man, Chattanooga Jaycees, 1976; named 1 of 3 Tenn.'s Outstanding Young Men. Tenn. Jaycees, 1977. Mem. Chattanooga C. of C., Ga. C. of C. (vice chmn. travel council), Ga. Hospitality and Travel Assn. (pres. travel div., named Outstanding Man in Travel Industry 1980), So. Highlands Attractions (pres.). Presbyterian. Home: 1301 Patten Rd Lookout Mountain TN 37350 Office: Rock City Gardens Patten Rd Lookout Mountain TN 37350

CHAPIN, ROY DIKEMAN, JR., automotive co. exec.; b. Detroit, Sept. 21, 1915; s. Roy Dikeman and Inez (Tiedeman) C.; A.B., Yale, 1937; m. Ruth Mary Ruxton, Oct. 29, 1937 (div.); children—Roy D., Christopher King, William Ruxton, Cicely Penny; m. 2d, Loise Baldwin Wickser, July 17, 1965; children—Alexandra, Robert L., Loise B., Hope B. With Hudson Motor Car Co. and Hudson Sales Corp., Detroit, 1938-54, dir. 1946-54; asst. treas., dir. Am. Motors Corp., 1954-55, treas., 1955, v.p., treas., 1956, exec. v.p., 1956-67, chmn. bd. 1967-78, chief exec. officer, 1967-77, now cons., dir., mem. corp. nominating com.; dir. Whirlpool Corp., Gould, Inc., Am. Natural Resources Co. Mem. exec. council Boy Scouts Am.; adv. bd. Leader Dogs for Blind; trustee Ducks Unltd. Found. Mem. Trout Unltd. (dir.), Ruffed Grouse Soc. (pres.). Clubs: Elihu Soc. (New Haven); Detroit Country, Grosse Pointe, Detroit Fontinalis (Detroit); Links (N.Y.C.); Pacific Union (San Francisco); Sankaty Golf (Nantucket). Office: American Motors Corp 27777 Franklin Rd Southfield MI 48034

CHAPMAN, ALGER BALDWIN, JR., bus. exec.; b. Portland, Maine, Sept. 28, 1931; s. Alger Balwin and Elizabeth (Ives) C.; A.B., Williams Coll., 1953; LL.B., Columbia, 1957; children—Alger Baldwin III, Samuel, Andrew, Henry. Admitted to N.Y. bar, 1957; atty. SEC, 1957-58, legal asst. to commr., 1958-59; mem. staff N.Y. Stock Exchange, 1959-67, v.p. civic and govtl. affairs, 1963-65, v.p. legal, civic and govtl. affairs, 1965-67; v.p. Shearson, Hammill & Co., 1967-68, exec. v.p., 1968-70, pres., chief adminstrv. officer, 1970-74, also dir.; co-chmn. bd. Shearson Loeb Rhoades Inc., 1974—; dir. Chgo. Bd. Options Exchange. Dir. Police Athletic League, N.Y.C. Mem. Am., N.Y. State bar assns., Securities Industry Assn. (mem. bd., mem. exec. com.), Sigma Phi, Phi Delta Phi. Home: 100 Central Park S New York NY 10019 Office: 2 World Trade Center New York NY 10048

CHAPMAN, ALVAH HERMAN, JR., newspaper exec.; b. Columbus, Ga., Mar. 21, 1921; s. Alvah Hermann and Wyline (Page) C.; B.S., The Citadel, 1942; m. Betty Bateman, Mar. 22, 1943; children—Dale Page (Mrs. Dennis Webb), Chris Ann (Mrs. Robert Hilton). Bus. mgr. Columbus Ledger, 1945-53; v.p., gen. mgr. St. Petersburg (Fla.) Times, 1955-57; pres., pub. Morning News and Evening Press, Savannah, Ga., 1957-60; pres. Savannah News-Press, Inc., 1957-60; exec. Knight-Ridder Newspapers, Inc., Miami, Fla., 1960—, exec. com., 1960—, exec. v.p., 1967-73, pres., 1973—, chief exec. officer, 1976—; v.p., gen. mgr. Miami Herald, 1962-70, pres., 1970—; lectr. Am. Press Insts., Columbia. Served from 2d lt. to maj. USAAF, World War II. Decorated D.F.C. with 2 oak leaf clusters, Air medal with 5 clusters (U.S.); Croix de Guerre; named one of five outstanding young men in Ga., 1951, Outstanding Young Man, Columbus Jr. C. of C., 1952, Dade County's Outstanding Citizen of 1968-69. Mem. Am., So. newspapers pubs. assn. Methodist. Home: 4255 Lake Rd Miami FL 33137 Office: Miami Herald 1 Herald Plaza Miami FL 33101

CHAPMAN, BRUCE, broadcasting co. exec.; b. N.Y.C., Aug. 12, 1905; s. William Brewster and Rose (Woodallen) C.; Ph.B., Brown U., 1926; m. Edna Coleman, June 10, 1932; 1 son, William Brewster. Cameraman, editor, Selznick Pictures, 1920-22; salesman, then N.Y. sales mgr. Bridgeport Chain Co., 1926-28; program mgr. Nat. Radio Homemakers, 1928-31; pres. Bruce Chapman Co., N.Y.C. and Grafton, Vt., 1931—. Cons. Assn. Electric Light & Power Cos., Edison Found., 1936-38, U.S. Econ. Coop. Adminstrn., 1949-52, U.S. Mut. Security Adminstrn. 1952-54, Fed. Republic Germany, 1953-54, USIA, 1953-55. Cons. N.Y. State Democratic Com., 1934-42, Nat. Republican Com., 1935-40. Trustee, Albert Payson Terhune Found., Grafton Assn. Mem. Broadcast Pioneers, Acad. TV Arts and Scis., Zeta Psi. Episcopalian. Author: Here's The Answer, 1946; Why Do We Say Such Things, 1947. Author (under pen name, Pete Howe) syndicated newspaper column, Here's Howe, 1945—. Office: Grafton VT 05146

CHAPMAN, ERSKINE CLIFFORD, constrn. equipment co. exec.; b. Huntington, W.Va., Apr. 4, 1920; s. Charles Corbett and Hazel Mae (Weekly) C.; degree in civil engring. U. Cin., 1942; m. Helen Frances Naisen, Nov. 27, 1948; children—Richard, David, Janet. With Caterpillar Tractor Co., Peoria, Ill., 1945—, v.p., 1965-78, exec. v.p., 1978—; pres. Caterpillar Overseas SA, Geneva, Switzerland, 1963-65; dir. Prospect Nat. Bank, Peoria. Served with C.E., U.S. Army, 1942-45. Decorated Bronze Star, Purple Heart. Home: 4421 Grandview Dr Peoria IL 61614 Office: Caterpillar Tractor Co 100 NE Adams St Peoria IL 61629

CHAPMAN, HOWARD DUDLEY, constrn. co. exec.; b. Norfolk, Va., July 30, 1938; s. James Dudley and Mary Elizabeth (Morrissette) C.; B.C.E. equivalent, Va. Polytech. Inst., 1960; m. Janice Marie Hauger, Dec. 29, 1959; children—Hunter Morrissette, Christopher Dudley. Civil engr. Constrn. Aggregates Corp., Chgo., 1960-71, constrn. mgr., 1971—, asst. v.p., 1974-77, v.p., 1977—; v.p. Bayview Urban Renewal Corp., 1975—, also dir.; v.p. Desconsa-Honduras C.A., 1979-80, pres., 1980—, also dir.; mgmt. trustee Gt. Lakes Tug and Dredge Pension Plan, 1975—. Mem. World Dredging Assn., Maritime Assn. Port N.Y., Internat. Found. Employee Benefit Plans, Western Soc. Engrs. Home: 450 Sussex Ct Buffalo Grove IL 60090 Office: 120 S LaSalle St Chicago IL 60603

CHAPMAN, JO(SEPHINE) LAWTON, corp. exec.; b. N.Y.C., Apr. 9, 1918; d. Wolcott Pitkin and Etta (Lawton) C.; student Breadloaf Writers' Conf., Middlebury Coll., 1948, 59, Pratt Inst. Evening Sch., 1955, U. Conn. Public Service Inst., 1979. Mem. suburban staff gen. news reporter Bridgeport Time-Star, 1934-40; asso. editor Westporter-Herald, 1940-43; town hall-polit. writer Greenwich Time, 1943-44; staff writer Port Chester Daily Item, 1944-46, Stamford Adv., 1946-52; corr. N.Y. Times, 1942-52, Asso. Press, 1944-52; own pub. relations bus. 1952—; aide Housing Authority of Town of Greenwich, Conn., 1962-65; owner Community & Pub. Relations Assos., Greenwich, 1966—; sec., dir. Pix Films Service, Inc., Greenwich, 1965-67; owner, editor pub. Greenwich Mail, 1965-80; with acctg. dept. Transact Internat. Inc., Stamford, Conn., 1980—; owner Chanticleer Publs., 1968—. Former distributive edn. instr. Conn. Dept. Vocational Edn. Past instr. first aid A.R.C., Fairfield and Greenwich Conn., past dir. Greenwich; pres. Greenwich Stamp and Coin Club, 1954-55, 69-70, life mem., 1977—; com. chmn. Greenwich Citizens Sch. Study, 1949. Nonpartisan mem. Rep. Town Meeting, Greenwich, 1945-57, 60-61, 68—, sec. 8th Dist. del., 1968-73, vice chmn., 1974-78, chmn., 1978—, mem. Community Devel. Action Program liaison com., 1968-71; mem. Selectmen's Civic Center Adv. Com., 1966-71; mem. Town Claims Com. 1973—; mem. Town Bicentennial Commn., 1975-77; mem. Town Rep. Com., 1974-80. Recipient Service award YMCA, Greenwich, 1957, citation for achievement, 1978. Mem. D.A.R. (dir. chpt. 1948-52, 68-71, chmn. pub. relations 1972-74), Crispus Attuck Assn. (past dir., treas.). Club: Soroptimist (pres. Greenwich 1956-58, 65-66, 73-74, com. chmn. N.E. region 1952-54, 60-62, 66-68, 74-78, chmn. Am. fedn. civic service objectives com. 1954-56, mem. Fedn. nominating com. 1964, chmn. resolution com. 1968-70). Home: 28 Decatur St Cos Cob CT 06807

CHAPMAN, JOHN SUTHERLAND, food mfg. co. exec., mgmt. cons.; b. Chgo., Dec. 24, 1925; s. Charles Williamson and Flora Naomi (Findlay) C.; student U. Wis., 1946-48; B.S. in Psychology, Ill. Inst. Tech., 1952, postgrad., 1952-54; postgrad. John Marshall Law Sch., 1964-66; m. Catherine M. Bobber, June 26, 1948; children—John Charles, Carl William, Mary Eileen. Asst. personnel mgr. Nabisco Inc., Chgo., 1948-53, personnel mgr., Atlanta, 1954-60, personnel mgr. Chgo. Mfg. Complex, 1961-71, regional personnel relations mgr., Naperville, Ill., 1971-74, regional personnel mgmt. cons., state govt. relations coordinator, 1975—; ind. cons. on indsl. relations and mgmt. devel., also equal employment opportunity; program chmn., conf. leader Am. Mgmt. Assn., 1968—. Mem. Ill. Gov.'s Adv. Com., 1969-71. Served with USNR, 1944-46. Mem. Am. Soc. Safety Engrs., Am. Soc. Personnel Adminstrn. (accredited exec. in personnel), Personnel Mgmt. Assn. (v.p. Chgo. 1971-72, pres. 1972-73), Ill. Mfg. Assn., Ill. C. of C. (labor relations com. 1977—), Chgo. Area Public Affairs Group, Psi Chi. Office: 1555 W Ogden Ave Naperville IL 60540

CHAPMAN, RICHARD PALMER, JR., savs. and loan assn. exec.; b. Cambridge, Mass., Feb. 7, 1935; s. Richard Palmer and M. Elizabeth (Smith) C.; B.A., Harvard U., 1957; postgrad. Columbia U. Grad. Sch. Bus. Adminstrn., 1957-58; m. Cynthia S. Miltimore, Sept. 13, 1958; children—Alison Chichester, Virginia Sebring, Richard Palmer, Elizabeth Marshall. With R.I. Hosp. Trust Co., Providence, 1958-67; security analyst, investment officer, investment counselor Standish, Ayer and Wood, Boston, 1967-72; pres. Brookline Savs. Bank (Mass.), 1973—; dir. John Hancock Bond Fund, John Hancock Investors, Inc., John Hancock Income Securities Corp., John Hancock Growth Fund, John Hancock Balanced Fund, Lumber Mut. Ins. Co., Savs. Banks Investment Fund; trustee John Hancock Tax Exempt

Trust; chmn., dir. Fambrook, Inc. Trustee New Eng. Aquarium, 1970—; v.p., trustee Boys and Girls Camps, Inc.; corporator Northeastern U., 1978—; mem. fin. mgmt. com., Brookline, Mass. Mem. Savs. Banks Retirement Assn. Mass. (vice chmn., trustee), Boston Soc. Security Analysts, Boston Econ. Club, Brookline C. of C. (v.p., chmn. exec. com.). Clubs: Union, Country. Home: 107 Upland Rd Brookline MA 02146 Office: 160 Washington St Brookline MA 02147

CHAPMAN, ROBERT BERRIEN, chem. co. exec.; b. Game, Ky., June 12, 1918; s. Theodore Robert and Alma Voris (Jordan) C.; B.A., Eastern Mich. U., 1940; M.Ed., Wayne State U., 1949; cert. in advt. mgmt. Ohio State U., 1961; m. Thelma Isabelle Light, June 14, 1941; children—Robert Bruce, Richard Keith, Ronald Edward. Tchr. schs., Farmington, Mich., 1940-44, YMCA, Detroit, 1944-47; mem. faculty bus. staff Eastern Mich. U., Ypsilanti, 1947-52; gen. office mgr. Chemstrand Corp., Decatur, Ala., 1952-55; treasury rep., Pensacola, 1955-58, ins. mgr., N.Y.C., 1958-61; ins. mgr. Monsanto Co., St. Louis, 1961-75, dir. risk mgmt., 1975-80, chmn. ins. subsidiaries, 1980—. Mem. Chem. Mfrs. Assn., Risk and Ins. Mgmt. Soc. (past pres. St. Louis chpt.), Phi Delta Kappa, Pi Kappa Delta. Home: 11 Ridge Crest Ct Chesterfield MO 63017 Office: 800 N Lindbergh Blvd Saint Louis MO 63166

CHAPMAN, WILLIAM PAUL, control mfg. co. exec.; b. Oakland, Calif., Oct. 19, 1919; s. William Porteus and Lucy A. (McCarthy) C.; B.S., U. Calif. at Berkeley, 1943; M.S., Purdue U., 1947; m. Beth Hartley, June 26, 1943; children—Bruce H., Craig S., Brian A., Dean O. Research engr. U.S. Steel Co., Pitts., 1947-50, field engr., 1950-56; adminstrv. dir. research Johnson Controls (formerly Johnson Service Co.), Milw., 1956-58, dir. research and devel., 1958-64, v.p. ops., 1964—; dir. Johnson Brass & Machine Foundry. Bd. dirs. St. Joseph-St. Michael's Hosp., Milw., 1979—; mem. adv. bd. St. Michael's Hosp., Milw., 1972—, pres., 1979-80; mem. steering com. Milw. Mayor's Council Sci. and Tech. Utilization; bd. dirs. Milw. Urban League, U. Wis.-Milw. Found. Served to capt. AUS, 1943-45; ETO. Decorated Purple Heart with cluster, Silver Star; named Milw. Engr. of Year, Engrs. and Scientists Milw., 1977; registered profl. engr., Wis., Pa. Fellow ASHRAE (dir. 1969-77, pres. 1976-77, Distinguished Service award 1969); mem. Nat. Soc. Profl. Engrs., Mgmt. Resources Adminstrs. Assn. Milw. (adminstrv. bd. 1972-78), Sigma Xi. Clubs: Town of Milw., Univ. Contbr. articles to profl. jours. Patentee in field. Home: 8260 N Gray Log Ln Milwaukee WI 53217 Office: PO Box 423 Milwaukee WI 53201

CHAPPELL, EUGENE WATSON, JR., mgmt. cons.; b. Newport News, Va., Jan. 1, 1945; s. Eugene Watson and Virginia Lee (Cathell) C.; B.E.E. (Navy scholar), U. Va., 1967. Asst. to gen. mgr. Northrop Services Inc., Arlington, Va., 1972-74; project dir. Sci., Engring. & Analysis, Inc., Arlington, 1974-77; pres. Fiscal Assos. Inc., Alexandria, Va., 1977-80, chmn. bd., 1977—; dir. Omnetics Inc., TOVFS, Inc.; sr. partner CAMS Enterprises, 1977—, The Company, 1976—. Served with USN, 1967-72. Mem. IEEE, Am. Mgmt. Assn., Data Processing Mgmt. Assn., Sigma Pi. Baptist. Clubs: Army Navy Country (Arlington); Shirley Racquet (Fairfax, Va.). Home: 6101 Edsall Rd W Apt 1107 Alexandria VA 22304 Office: 5911 Edsall Rd W Suite 1213 Alexandria VA 22304

CHARBONNEAU, JOSEPH JOHN, bus. exec.; b. Superior, Wis., July 8, 1940; s. Emery Earl and Marion Nell (Milroy) C.; m. Dawn Elaine Allen, Mar. 10, 1973; children—Joseph John, Charles Allen. Owner, Charbonneau Ins. Agy., Superior, Wis., 1961-69; pres. Personal and Profl. Devel. Inst., Mpls., 1969-76; v.p. Learning Dynamics, Inc., Boston, 1976-77; pres. Performance Group, Inc., Dallas, 1977—, Kangaroo Press, 1979—; chief exec. officer Info Systems, 1979—. Chmn. March of Dimes Nat. Found., 1965-66. Served with USNR, 1958-61. Mem. Am. Mgmt. Assn., Nat. Speakers Assn., Internat. Platform Assn., Dallas C. of C. Clubs: Masons, Shriners. Home: 6403 Genstar Ln Dallas TX 75252 Office: 13507 Branch View Ln Dallas TX 75234

CHAREST, GUY, educator; b. Acton-Vale, Que., Can., Aug. 28, 1937; s. Lucien and Germaine (Deslandes) C.; student Royal Mil. Coll. Can., 1956-61; M.A.S. in Chem. Engring., U. Montreal, 1963; M.S., London Sch. of Econs., 1967; Ph.D. in Bus. Adminstrn., U. Chgo., 1971; m. Helene Dargis, July 17, 1965; children—Pascale, Martin, Marie-Helene, Anne-Sylvie. Asst. prof. fin. Laval U., Quebec City, Que., Can., 1971-77, asso. prof. fin., 1977—, head fin. sect. Bus. Sch., 1977-78; dir. Fin. Research Found. of Can. M.P. candidate for Fed. Progressive Conservative Party, 1980. Served to lt. Royal Can. Engrs. Corps, 1961-66. Mem. Am. Fin. Assn., European Fin. Assn. Roman Catholic. Contbr. articles to profl. jours. Home: 1037 La Loire Ste-Foy PQ G1V 2Z6 Canada Office: Faculte d'Administration Universite Laval Ste-Foy PQ G1K 7P4 Canada

CHARITY, NEIL MITCHELL, mgmt. counsel, educator; b. Canandaigua, N.Y., Jan. 16, 1915; s. James Henry and Blanche Cordelia (Mitchell) C.; B.Chem. Engring., Cornell U., 1936; M.B.A., Harvard U., 1940; m. Lillian Santacreu, Oct. 1964; children—Mitchell, Andrew. Asst. plant mgr. Seagram Distillers Corp., N.Y.C., 1941-42, purchasing agt., 1946-49, asst. plant mgr. ops., 1950-52; asst. to pres. Coty, Inc., N.Y.C., 1953-64; internal cons. Pfizer, Inc., N.Y.C., 1965, div. controller 1966-67, long range planner, 1968-72; mgmt. counsel Econ. Devel. Council, N.Y.C., 1973-74, N.Y. State Court System, N.Y.C., 1975—; adj. asst. prof. N.Y. U., 1975—; Mes., dir. Orgn. Devel. Council, N.Y.C., 1978—. Served with USNR, 1942-46. Mem. Met. N.Y. Assn. Applied Psychology, Internat. Personnel Mgrs. Assn., Soc. Public Adminstrn. AAAS. Episcopalian. Clubs: Harvard (N.Y.C.); Harvard Business School New York. Home: 315 E 56th St New York NY 10022

CHARLES, JACOB EDWARD, ins. co. exec.; b. Marietta, Pa., Sept. 21, 1913; s. Jacob Mease and Minnie (Hoffman) C.; grad. U.S. Army Sch. Bus. Adminstrn., 1935; m. Edith Mae McKain, June 7, 1939; children—Patricia Anne, Jill Eilene. With Donegal Mut. Ins. Co., Marietta, 1938—, pres., treas., chief exec. officer, 1938—; pres., dir., treas. United Mut. Underwriters, Marietta; sec.-treas. Marietta Gravity Water Co.; dir. Miller's Mut. Ins. Co., Harrisburg, Pa., Heartland Group, Inc./N.Y. Ins. Exchange, Am. Bank & Trust Co., Reading, Pa. Bd. dirs. St. Anne's Home for Aged, Columbia, Pa.; past pres., past bd. dirs. Donegal Sch. Dist., Vo-Tech Schs., Lancaster County, Pa., Columbia Hosp. Served with U.S. Army, 1933-36. Mem. Ins. Fedn. Pa. (dir.), Internat. Platform Assn., Profl. Ins. Agts. Republican. Clubs: Masons (32 deg.), Shriners, Elks, Odd Fellows. Editor, Donegal News. Home: 676 W Market St Marietta PA 17547 Office: Route 441 Bypass Marietta PA 17547

CHARLTON, MARGARET ELLEN JONSSON, civic worker; b. Dallas, Aug. 7, 1938; d. John Erik and Margaret Elizabeth (Fonde) Jonsson; ed. Skidmore Coll., 1956-57, So. Methodist U., 1957-60; m. George V. Charlton, 1960; children—Laura, Emily, Erik. Civic worker, Dallas; dir. KRLD radio, Dallas, 1970-74; dir. 1st Nat. Bank, Dallas, 1976—, vice-chmn. dirs. trust com.; trustee Meth. Hosps., 1972—, mem. exec. com., 1977—; dir., chmn. exec. com. Lamplighter Sch., 1967—; mem. vis. com. dept. psychology M.I.T.; bd. dirs. Winston Sch., 1973—; bd. dirs., mem. exec. com. Episcopal Sch., 1976—; bd. dirs. Callier Center Communication Disorders, 1967—, v.p., 1974—; chmn. Crystal Charity Ball; bd. dirs. Children's Med. Center, Hope Cottage Childrens' Bur., Baylor Dental Sch., Dallas Health and Sci. Mus., Dallas YWCA, Day Nursery Assn. Margaret Jonsson Charlton Hosp. of Dallas named in her honor, 1973. Republican. Club: Dallas Women's.

CHARNLEY, SUSAN, consulting co. exec.; b. Kent, Ohio, Aug. 23, 1953; B.S. with distinction (grantee), U. Minn., 1976, M.A., 1978; student Travistock Inst. Human Relations, Leicester, Eng., 1975, Japan-Am. Inst. Mgmt. Scis. (grantee), 1978—. Admissions asst. U. Minn., 1972-74, asst. to mems. of faculty, 1974-76; tchr. Coll. St. Catherine, St. Paul, 1977; pres., con. Charnley Cons. Co., Mpls., 1977—; teaching asst. dept. speech U. Minn., 1977; pres. U. Student Telecommunications Corp., 1975-77; project asst. Bur. Econ. Research, N.Y.C., 1977. Dist. dir. United Fund, 1974; vol. coordinator alderman campaign Democratic Farm Labor Party, 1974, legis. researcher on child abuse and sr. citizens, 1975-77, reader city atty. race, 1977. Mem. Am. Acad. Polit. Sci., Speech Assn. Minn., Soc. Profl. Journalists, Am. Mgmt. Assn., Women In Communication, Sigma Delta Chi. Home: 215 Warwick St SE Minneapolis MN 55414

CHASE, ALLEN, investment banker; b. Los Angeles, Sept. 11, 1911; s. Edward Tilden and Lenna (Prather) C.; B.S., U. Calif. at Los Angeles, 1933; postgrad. London Sch. Econs., U. London (Eng.), 1934; m. Loriene Eck, Mar. 4, 1960 (div.); children by previous marriage—Charlene (Mrs. Alan Kreiger), Diane (Mrs. Jerome Randolph). Salesman, Chase Securities Co., Los Angeles, 1934-39; pres. Standardized Aircraft Co., Los Angeles, 1939—; chmn. bd. Esperence Plains Pty. Ltd., Australia, 1956—, Agra Paraguay, 1967—; pres. Allen Chase & Co., 1964—; dir. Allied Pastoral Co. Pty. Ltd., Australia. Conceived establishment of over one million virgin acres to agr. in single area by pvt. enterprise. Address: 4337 Marina City Dr Marina Del Rey CA 90291

CHASE, C(HARLES) WARD, ind. petroleum landman; b. Hartford, Conn., Feb. 28, 1908; s. Warren D. and Elizabeth S. (Ward) C.; B.A., Princeton, 1928; m. Olga Memi, Feb. 12, 1966. Drama critic, asst. dramatic editor Billboard mag., 1930-31; ins. editor Real Estate Record and Guide, N.Y., 1940-43; v.p. Butler and Baldwin, Inc., 1931-41; account exec. Johnson & Higgins, 1942, dept. mgr., 1950, v.p., 1953-69, dir., 1956-69; pres., dir. Johnson & Higgins (Can.), Ltd., 1955-63; chmn. bd. Johnson & Higgins Calif., 1964-65; pres. Chase Resources Co., 1970—. Served with USNR, 1943-46. Mem. Soc. Mayflower Descs. Clubs: St. James (Montreal); Players, Princeton (N.Y.C.); Eldorado, Indian Wells (Calif.). Home: 45-830 Pima Rd Indian Wells CA 92260 Office: PO Box 1704 Palm Desert CA 92261

CHASE, CHARLES VERNON, mktg. co. exec.; b. Berne, Switzerland, Nov. 17, 1945; s. Warren Montgomery and Simone Micheline (Steigelmann) C.; came to U.S., 1950, naturalized, 1964; student Cath. U. Am., 1962-64, Yale U., 1969, U. Chgo., 1969-70. With Advance Schs., Inc., Chgo., 1971-78, v.p. mktg., 1976-78; v.p. ops. U.S. Fin. Services, Inc., Mpls., 1978—. Mem. U.S. Olympic Com., 1972-76. Served with USAF, 1964-69. Decorated Bronze Star. Mem. Nat. Vocat. Guidance Assn., Chgo. Assn. Commerce and Industry, Am. Personnel and Guidance Assn., Am. Vocat. Assn. Roman Catholic. Home: 15610 Holdridge Rd E Wayzata MN 55391 Office: 300 Clifton Ave Minneapolis MN 55403

CHASE, DONALD CORNELIUS, lawyer; b. Plainfield, N.J., Oct. 16, 1939; s. Adam Benedict and Cora C.; B.A., Rutgers U., 1961, J.D., 1964; m. Dorothy Conover, Aug. 13, 1960; children—Jeffrey C., Bryan D., Gary B. Admitted to N.J. bar, 1964; partner Chase & Chase, Manville, N.J., 1964-72, Chase & Rzemieniewski, Manville, 1972-77, sr. partner, 1977—; chmn. bd. Jebryga Inc., Manville, 1978—; dir. Esahc Inc., Manville Savs. & Loan Assn.; sr. aide to Assemblyman Patero, 17th Dist. N.J., 1972—. Mem. Am., N.J. bar assns., Am. Judicature Soc., N.J. Municipal Attys. Assn., N.J. Sch. Bds. Assn., U.S. Tax Ct. Assn., Italian-Am. Assn., Ocean Heights Assn., U.S. Navy League, Tau Kappa Epsilon. Roman Catholic. Club: Elks. Home: 35 Woods Rd Somerville NJ 08876 Office: 220 S Main St Manville NJ 08835

CHASE, HELEN LOUISE, banker; b. Waukegan, Ill., Sept. 29, 1943; d. David William and Ruth V. (Sawyer) Chase; B.A., U. Ill., 1965; postgrad. in bus. Adminstrn., U. Chgo., 1975-76. With internat. dept. Continental Ill. Nat. Bank, Chgo., 1966—, internat. banking officer, 1973-76, 2d v.p., 1976-77, asst. rep., Brazil, 1977-80; group head Asia/Pacific sect. Continental Bank Internat., N.Y.C., 1980—. Mem. Kappa Alpha Theta. Presbyterian. Office: Continental Bank Internat One Liberty Plaza 48th Floor New York NY 10006

CHASE, MORRIS, internat. mgmt. cons.; b. N.Y.C., May 19, 1918; s. Samuel and Bessie (Rabinowitz) Cherkasky; B.B.A., CCNY, 1939; student econ. sci., U. Paris, 1959; m. Claire Pernitz, Mar. 14, 1942; children—Sylvia, Viviane. Mem. staff several C.P.A. firms, 1939-42; asst. to dir. fin. and acctg. Am. Joint Distbn. Com., 1946-48; dep. controller Marshall Plan mission to France, 1949; controller, fin. officer U.S. spl. econ. mission to Cambodia, Laos and Vietnam, 1950; controller U.S. spl. econ. mission to Yugoslavia, 1951; economist Office U.S. Rep. in Europe, Paris, 1952-53; chmn. Internat. Bd. Auditors for Infrastructure, NATO. Paris, 1954-60, dir. infrastructure program, 1961-68, chmn. def. installations com., 1966-68, chmn. payments and progress com; cons. NATO Air Def. Ground Environment Consortium, 1968—. Served to capt., USAAF, 1942-46; maj. Res. C.P.A., N.Y. State. Mem. Am. Inst. C.P.A.'s, N.Y. State Soc. C.P.A.'s, Fed. Accountants Assn. (pres. Paris 1961-62), Fed. Govt. Accountants Assn. Paris (pres. 1964-65), Beta Gamma Sigma. Home: Flaminia C Crans-sur-Sierre Valais Switzerland also 163 Ave Winston Churchill Brussels 1180 Belgium

CHASE, NORMAN BRADFORD, lumber co. exec.; b. Worcester, Mass., Jan. 25, 1924; s. Samuel Harold and Bessie Elizabeth (Bradford) C.; student Worcester Jr. Coll., 1946-47; m. Norma M. Liebmann, June 5, 1949; children—Susan P., Jonathan D., Lawrence A. Pres., owner Chase Industries, Ellington, Conn., 1950—, Brattleboro, Vt., 1970—. Trustee, Brooks Meml. Library, pres., 1974—; corporator Brattleboro Meml. Hosp., 1975—; trustee, mem. exec. com. Windham Coll., Putney, Vt., 1977—; mem. Vt. Ho. of Reps., 1975—, Vt. Human Services Bd., 1979—. Served with AUS, 1943-46. Mem. Am. Legion, Auto Club Vt. (v.p., trustee). Clubs: Mason, Shriner, Rotary. Home: Brookside Brattleboro VT 05301 Office: Corner Main St at High Brattleboro VT 05301

CHASES, MARK STEFAN, mfg. co. exec.; b. Allentown, Pa., Mar. 20, 1938; s. Morris and Jeannette (Binder) C.; B.S., Pa. State U., 1960, postgrad. 1962; children—Andrea, Elizabeth. Sr. analyst Gen. Motors Corp., Detroit, 1960-69; corporate controller Cole Nat. Corp., Cleve., 1969-71; pres. Swedlow Inc., Garden Grove, Calif., 1971—, chief operating officer, treas., dir., 1974—. Bd. dirs. Resources Council, 1978—; dir., adv. com. Calif. State U., Dominguez Hills, 1978—; exec. council Hoag Meml. Hosp., 1980—. Mem. Newport Harbor Mus., 1980—. Served with U.S. Army, 1956-62. Mem. Garden Grove C. of C., Alpha Kappa Psi. Home: 461 Promotory Dr E Newport Beach CA 92650 Office: 12122 Western Ave Garden Grove CA 92645

CHASTEEN, JOSEPH WILEY, JR., bus. exec.; b. Huntsville, Ala., Dec. 9, 1921; s. Joseph Wiley and Ola Lee (Brown) C.; A.B., William Jewell Coll., 1950; postgrad. U. Pa., 1952-55, Drexel Inst. Tech., 1956; M.B.A., Rollins Coll., 1962; m. Mae Lyndal Miller, Oct. 31, 1941; children—Joseph Wiley III, David A. Tchr., Central Tech. Inst., Kansas City, Mo., 1946-50; engr. RCA, Camden, N.J., 1951-56; group engr. Martin Co., Balt., 1956-57; asst. mng. engring. Martin Marietta Corp., Orlando, Fla., 1957-63, engring. mgr., 1963-67, tech. mgr., 1967-69; advance projects mgr., program mgr. space and electronics div. Emerson Electric Co., St. Louis, 1969-70; chmn. bd. dirs. PWC Assos., Inc., Orlando, 1970-73; mem. project office staff Honeywell, Inc., St. Petersburg, Fla., 1973-75; pres. Joseph W. Chasteen Real Estate Agy., Orlando, 1973-76; staff communications engr., design mgr., engring. coordinator, dep. dir. Dallah Avco Trans Arabia Corp., Jeddah, Saudi Arabia, 1976—; Chmn., Pine Hills Area Round Table, 1963-64; pres. Robinswood Civic Assn. 1963-65; commr. Pine Hills Fire Dist., 1964—, Orange County (Fla.) Local Govt. Study Group; treas. Pine Hill Community Council; bd. dirs. Robinswood Recreation Park, Orlando. Served with USNR, 1944-46, 50-51. Asso. fellow Am. Inst. Aeros. and Astronautics; mem. IEEE (sr.), Sigma Pi Sigma, Kappa Mu Epsilon. Contbr. articles to profl. jours. Home: 1824 Hastings Terr Orlando FL 32808 Office: PO Box 430 Jeddah Saudi Arabia

CHATMAN, ROXANNE LAW SHEFFIELD, packaging co. exec.; b. Pitts., Dec. 8, 1952; d. Waulnoth and Elizabeth Sheffield; B.A. with honors in Journalism, Mich. State U., 1974; m. Robert L. Chatman, Jr., Sept. 8, 1973. Packaging research specialist Mich. State U. Sch. Packaging, East Lansing, 1974-77; packaging specialist Rock Island Packaging Corp., Milan, Ill., 1977-78, ARCO Polymers, Inc., Phila., 1978—; bd. dirs. Packaging Edn. Found., 1979—. Mem. Packaging Inst. USA (edn. com.), Soc. Packaging and Handling Engrs. (nat. treas.), NAACP, Pi Kappa Gamma. Contbr. articles to profl. publs. Office: 1500 Market St Philadelphia PA 19101

CHATY, NORMA BOLOTIN, researcher, writer; b. Brockton, Mass., Feb. 13, 1931; d. Morris and Esta (June) Bolotin; B.A., U. Chgo., 1952; postgrad. Columbia, 1960; 1 dau., Gayle Anne. Tech. editor H.K. Ferguson Co., Cleve., 1956-58; pub. relations mgr. Jacob Ruppert Brewery, N.Y.C., 1958-60; tech. communicator Lummus Co., N.J., 1960—64; dir. creative services Avery Hand & Assos., Conn., 1964-67; editor Bus. Mgmt. mag., Greenwich, Conn., 1968-70; dir. market communications Emico ESP div. Envirotech Corp., Belmont, Calif., 1971-76; dir. corporate planning, info. services Cooper Labs., Inc., Palo Alto, Calif., 1976-77; partner The Wordsmith, Brisbane, Calif., 1977—. Recipient Silver Gavel award for legal research and writing Am. Bar Assn., 1980. Mem. Soc. Women Engrs., Environ. Writers Assn., Women Organized for Employment, Soc. Tech. Communicators, Mensa, Nat. Assn. Female Execs. Office: PO Box 357 Brisbane CA 94005

CHAU, ALFRED SHUN-YUEN, chemist, artist; b. Hong Kong, Nov. 20, 1941; came to Can., 1958, naturalized, 1963; s. Yat-Lun and Sue-Chong (Chan) C.; B.Sc., U. B.C., 1961; M.Sc., Carleton U., 1966; profl. diploma Sch. Modern Photography, 1970; m. Linda May Lim, Oct. 21, 1966; 1 son, Andrew T. M. Chemist, Dept. Agr., Ottawa, Ont., Can., 1965-70; head organic labs. Dept. Fisheries and Environ., Ottawa and Burlington, Ont., 1970-73; head spl. services sect. Dept. Environment, Burlington, 1973-80, head quality assurance and methods sect., 1980—; one-man show Beckett Gallery, Hamilton, Ont., 1977, 80; group shows: Beckett Gallery, 1976—, Manuge Galleries Ltd., Halifax, N.S., 1978, 79, 80, Agghazy Gallery, Calgary, Alta., 1979, 80, Gallery Danielli, Toronto, Ont., 1978, Que.-Ont. Cultural Exchange, 1978-79, LeFebvre Galleries Ltd., Edmonton, Alta., 1980—, Burlington (Ont.) Cultural Centre, 1979, Rodman Hall Public Art Gallery, St. Catherine, Ont., 1977, 78; represented in permanent collections: Beckett Gallery, Dominion Foundries and Steel Co.; coordinator Fed. Interdeptl. Com. on Pesticides, 1975—; asso. referee Assn. Ofcl. Analytical Chemists, 1977—. Recipient Caledon award, 1980; Dolfasco Can. Art Collection purchase award, 1980. Mem. Am. Men and Women of Sci., Am. Soc. Standards and Materials (chmn. task group), Chem. Inst. Can., Assn. Ofcl. Analytical Chemists, Hamilton-Wenworth Art Council, Can. and Chinese Art Soc. Contbr. articles, revs. to profl. jours.; author: Analysis of Chlorinated Hydrocarbon Pesticides, 1972; editor: (with others) Water Pollution: Chemical Analysis, 3 vols.; co-editor: Hydrocarbons and Halogenated Hydrocarbons in the Aquatic Environment, 1980. Office: 867 Lakeshore Rd Burlington ON L7R 4A6 Canada

CHAVEZ, FEDERICO, Mexican trade ofcl.; b. Mexico City, June 3, 1945; came to U.S., 1978; s. Jorge and Celia (Barajas) C.; Indsl. Engr. Degree, Engring. Faculty U. Mexico, Mexico City, 1969; Diplome d'Economie (Govt. France scholar), Ecole Coopératif Universitée de Paris, 1971; m. Jana Hornakova, July 3, 1971; children—Andrei, Jana. Sales and design engr. Procter & Gamble, Mexico City, 1968-69, Foxboro Co., Mexico City, 1969-70; asst. trade commr. of Mexico to Spain, 1973-75; to Can., Toronto, Ont., 1975-78, to Western U.S., Los Angeles, 1978—; plant adminstrn. prof. Faculty Engring. U. Mexico, 1968-69. Recipient commendation for public service Lt. Gov. Calif., 1979; Tunisian Govt. research grantee, 1970; Israeli Govt. research grantee, 1971. Mem. Mexico-Can. Cultural Assn. (founder, dir.). Author: Industrial Development in Third World Countries, 1970; Industrial Cooperatives in Developing Countries, 1972. Office: 8484 Wilshire Blvd Suite 808 Los Angeles CA 90010

CHAWLA, SHRI CHAND, electronic components co. exec.; b. Shikarpur, Pakistan, Nov. 25, 1947; came to U.S., 1978, naturalized, 1980; s. Chetandas and Atur (Bai) C.; B.E. in Elec. Engring., Jabalpur U., 1968, M.B.A., 1969; m. Sumitra, Mar. 4, 1972; children—Vijay Laxmi, Sony. Founder, pres. Micro Components Internat., engring. supplies, New Delhi, 1970-73, distbr. electronic components, 1973-79, Santa Clara, Calif., 1979—; cons. purchasing and mktg. Mem. U.S. C. of C., Santa Clara C. of C. Home: 698 Spruce Dr Sunnyvale CA 94086 Office: 3020 Scott Blvd Santa Clara CA 95050

CHAZEN, STEPHEN MARK, metals co. exec.; b. Harlan, Ky., Mar. 19, 1940; s. Julius L. and Ruth (Ettin) C.; student U. Okla., 1957-58; U. Chattanooga, 1958-60; m. Nanci E. Floyd, Mar. 12, 1976; 1 son, Jack. With So. Foundry Supply, Inc. a subsidiary SMC Corp., Chattanooga, 1960—, exec. v.p., 1965—. Served with Tenn. Air N.G., 1963-69. Mem. Am. Copper Council, Nat. Assn. Recycling Industries, Inst. Scrap Iron and Steel, Wire Assns., Bur. Internat. Recuperacion. Clubs: Chattanooga Tennis, Walden (Chattanooga); Fairyland (Lookout Mountain, Tenn.). Home: 1507 Chickamauga Trail Lookout Mountain TN 37350 Office: 540 McCallie Ave Chattanooga TN 37401

CHECCHI, ARTHUR ALFRED, cons. co. exec.; b. Calais, Maine, Aug. 13, 1922; s. Attilio R. and Dina A. (Pisani) C.; B.A., U. Maine, 1944; postgrad. Harvard U., 1944-45; m. Josephine Anne Soldati, Nov. 30, 1946; children—Alfred A., Anne Marie, Lisa A., Joanne M. Various positions (Boston, Kansas City, Denver), then staff mem. Office of Commr., FDA, Washington, 1945-59; v.p. Checchi & Co., Washington, 1960-75; pres., chmn. bd. Arthur A. Checchi, Inc., Washington, 1975—. Mem. Assn. Food and Drug Ofcls., Inst. Food Technologists. Roman Catholic. Home: 1303 Midwood Pl Silver

Spring MD 20910 Office: 1730 Rhode Island Ave NW Washington DC 20036

CHEEK, LOGAN MCKEE, III, venture capital co. exec., cons.; b. Glasgow, Ky., Sept. 21, 1938; s. Logan McKee II and Kathleen Lowndes (Jarrett) C.; A.B., Cornell U., 1960; postgrad. Mass. Inst. Tech., 1960-61, Cornell U., 1961-63; m. Pamela Louise Wilcox, Apr. 10, 1965; 1 dau., Christen Ashby. Supr., Charles Pfizer & Co., N.Y.C., 1968; asso. McKinsey & Co., Inc., N.Y.C., Dusseldorf, Germany, 1969-71; mgr. group plans control and analysis Xerox Corp., Rochester, N.Y., 1971-74, group program mgr., 1974, gen. mgr. Xemmco div., 1975, mgr. multinat. programs, 1976-78; mng. prin. The Pittsford Group (N.Y.), 1978—; pres., dir. Centex Mgmt., N.Y.C.; mgmt. cons.; dir. Pittsford Ventures, McDowell Coke Co., First Caribbean Bank & Trust; dir., chmn. fin. com. So. Region Energy Devel. Corp. N.Y. State finance chmn. Jimmy Carter Presdl. Campaign Com., 1976; nat. co-chmn. Bus. Execs. for Carter, 1976. Served to capt., Intelligence Corps, AUS, 1964-68. Decorated Silver Star, Bronze Star, Army Commendation medal; Ford scholar, 1956-60, Woodrow Wilson fellow, 1960-61. Mem. Pi Kappa Alpha. Club: Links of Martha's Vineyard. Author: Zero Base Budgeting Comes of Age, 1977; Zero-Base Budgeting: A Manual of Decision Packages, 1979. Home and Office: 8 Lodge Pole Rd Pittsford NY 14534 also 3 Farm Neck Way Oak Bluffs MA 02557

CHEEK, MICHAEL VERDON, wine co. exec.; b. Grantham, Eng., Nov. 21, 1944; came to U.S., 1946, naturalized, 1976; s. Verdon and Florence May (Ummel) C.; B.B.A., U. Ga., 1966; m. Runell Patricia Short, Nov. 14, 1964; children—Kelly, Andrea. With Carnation Co., 1966-75, gen. sales mgr. Southeastern U.S., 1975; sales mgr. Central and So. U.S., E&J Gallo Winery, 1975-79; v.p., dir. sales Wine Spectrum div. Coca-Cola Co., Atlanta, 1979—. Mem. Knights of Wine, Atlanta Commerce Club. Club: Atlanta Country. Address: 160 Marsh Glenn Point Atlanta GA 30328

CHEESEMAN, HENRY RICHARD, lawyer; b. Sault Ste. Marie, Mich., Aug. 16, 1946; s. Henry Benjamin and Florence Lorraine (Gaspar) C.; B.B.A., Marquette U., 1968; M.B.A., M. Tax, U. So. Calif., 1973; J.D., U. Calif., Los Angeles, 1973; postgrad. U. Chgo., 1976—; m. Kathleen Ney, June 15, 1968. Economist, Home Savs. & Loan Assn., Los Angeles, 1971-73; with Xerox Corp. Los Angeles, 1973-74; admitted to Calif. bar, 1973, Mich. bar, 1973; atty. firm Van Petten & Holen, Los Angeles, 1974-76; individual practice law, Los Angeles, 1976—; asst. prof. U. So. Calif., Los Angeles; dir. Mountain State Savs. & Loan Assn., Sun Valley, Idaho. Served with U.S. Army, 1968-70. Mem. Am., Calif., Mich. bar assns., Supreme Ct. Hist. Soc., U. So. Calif. Commerce Assos., U. Calif. at Los Angeles Law Alumni Assn., Beta Gamma Sigma. Republican. Contbr. articles in field to profl. jours. Address: 845 Lorraine Blvd Los Angeles CA 90005

CHELF, ROY L., business exec. Chmn. bd. Farmland Industries, Inc., Kansas City, Mo. Office: Farmland Industries Inc 3315 North Oak Trafficway Kansas City MO 64116*

CHEN, H. H., engring. and investment co. exec., educator; b. Taiwan, Apr. 11, 1933; s. Shui-Cheng and Mei (Lin) C.; student Ken-Tai Sch., 1952; m. Yehyeng-Lihua, Mar. 10, 1959; children—Benjamin Kuen-Tsai, Joe Chao-Kuang, Chao-Yu, Charmine Tsuey-Ling, Dolly Hsiao-Ying, Edith Yi-Wen, Yi-Fang. Owner, Tai Chang Indsl. Supplies Co., Ltd., 1967—; chmn. bd. Pirouette AG, Switzerland, 1974—; pres. Pan Pacific Indsl. Supplies, Inc., Toronto, Ont., Can., 1975—, H & B Internat. Investment Corp., Washington, 1981—; prof. First Econ. U., Japan. Mem Can.-Asia Commerce Assn. (dir.), Central Am. Econ. Deevl. Planning Council (advisor). Buddhist. Club: Internat. (Washington). Author: 500 Creative Designs for Future Business, 1961. Office: 1627 K St NW 9th Floor Washington DC 20006

CHEN, JOHN CHUNG-LIE, plastics co. exec.; b. Chengdoo, Szechuan, China, Feb. 17, 1940; came to U.S., 1962, naturalized, 1974; s. Yen-Kwong and Wah-Kwan C.; B.S., Cheng Kong U., 1961; M.Chem. Engring., U. Louisville, 1963; Ph.D., Princeton U., 1969; m. Julie Sy-Duan Yang, Apr. 4, 1964; children—Andrew, Vincent. Devel. engr. Union Carbide Co., 1964-65; research chemist Celanese Research Co., Summit, N.J., 1970-73, sr. research chemist, 1974-76, research supr., 1977-80; tech. supr. Celanese Plastics & Specialties Co., Summit, 1980—. Mem. N.Y. Acad. Sci., Sigma Xi. Office: Celanese Summit Tech Center 86 Morris Ave Summit NJ 07901

CHEN, MING YI, trade co. exec.; b. Chungking, China, June 6, 1939; s. Chao Hsung and Chuan Hui (Tang) C.; came to U.S., 1965, naturalized, 1981; Ph.D. in Chemistry, U. Chgo., 1970; m. Ching Yeh Chu, Dec. 15, 1977; children—San San (Carolyn), Yun Kai (Gene), Michelle. Research asso. Dept. Physics, U. Wis., Madison, 1970-71; pres. Chinese Native Products Ltd., N.Y.C., 1971—, Pearl River Chinese Products Emporium, Inc., N.Y.C., 1978—. Mem. Sino-Am. C. of C. (v.p. bd. dirs. 1979—), U.S.-China People's Friendship Assn. (steering com. 1971-74), Nat. Council U.S.-China Trade. Office: 393 W Broadway New York NY 10012

CHEN, SIMON KOSIANG, tech. cons., co. exec.; b. Shanghai, China, Oct. 13, 1925; s. Hoshien and Lin Sie (Chao) Tchen; B.M.E., Nat. Chiao-Tung U., 1947; M.M.E., U. Mich., 1949; Ph.D., U. Wis., 1952; M.B.A., U. Chgo., 1964; came to U.S., 1948, naturalized, 1955; m. Rosemary Yuhsia Ho, Jan. 17, 1952; children—Margaret, Lillian, Vivian, Victor. Div. chief engr., engine research and devel. Internat. Harvester Co., Melrose Park, Ill., 1952-69; v.p., gen. mgr. large engine operation, then v.p. engring. and application Fairbanks Morse Power Systems div. Colt Industries, Beloit, Wis., 1969-73; pres. Beloit Power Systems div. Tang Industries, 1973-79, Power & Energy Internat., Beloit, 1979—; chmn. mech. engrs. adv. com. Indsl. Tech. and Research Inst. Mem. Greater Beloit Com., 1976-77. Recipient Arch T. Colwell award Soc. Auto. Engrs., 1966, Distinguished Service award U. Wis. Alumni, 1973, Achievement award Chinese Inst. Engrs., 1976. Mem. Soc. Auto. Engrs., Soc. Naval Architects and Marine Engrs., ASME, Elec. Generating Systems Mktg. Assn. Contbr. articles to profl. jours. Home: 325 Racine St Delavan WI 53115 Office: 555 Lawton Ave Beloit WI 53511

CHENAULT, JAMES LEONARD, automatic garage door co. exec.; b. Flint, Mich., Feb. 23, 1929; s. Elmer Robert and Elva Marie (Slaubaugh) C.; student public schs., Flint. Painter, decorater, Flint, 1945-46; pattern-maker State of Mich., Iona, 1949-59; installer Cliff's Garage Doors, Flint, 1959, mgr., 1965; owner, pres. Automatic Garage Door Co., Burton, Mich., 1965—. Served with USN, 1946-48. Mem. Flint Home Builders Assn. (dir. 1979—), Nat. Home Builders Assn., Door and Operator Dealers of Am., Downtown Businessmen of Burton, Downtown Devel. Assn. Burton. Clubs: Masons, Moose. Office: G 4470 S Saginaw St Burton MI 48529

CHENEY, OAKLEY WILLIAM, JR., banker; b. Long Beach, Calif., June 27, 1936; s. Oakley William and Thelma Marie (Christenson) C.; B.S. in Commerce, U. Va., 1959; children—Oakley William III, George Spencer Wright, Elizabeth Tarlton. With 1st Nat. Bank Dallas, 1962—, asst. cashier, 1965-67, asst. v.p., 1967-68, v.p., 1968-71, sr. v.p., 1971-76, exec. v.p., 1977—. Mem. Bankers Assn. Fgn. Trade (dir. 1976-79, sec., treas. 1978-79), Robert Morris Assos., Internat. Lending Council, Am. Bankers Assn. (internat. banking div.). Republican. Episcopalian. Office: 1401 Elm St Dallas TX 75283

CHENG, DAVID GEE, Realtor, real estate developer; b. Shanghai, China, Sept. 1, 1915; s. Tsi Fei and Wai Wen (Liang) C.; came to U.S., 1966, naturalized, 1972; B.S. in Civil Engring., St. John's U., Shanghai, 1939; postgrad. Grad. Sch. of Design, Harvard U., 1966-67; children—David, Vida, Anthony. Pres., Nat. Housing Devel. Corp., Jakarta, Indonesia, 1956-66; minister of city planning and constrn. Republic of Indonesia, 1964-66; devel. dir. Hawaii Council of Housing Action, Honolulu, 1968-70; pres. DGC Devel. Corp., Honolulu, 1971—; asso. DRG Fin. Corp., Washington. Mem. transp. com. Oahu Devel. Conf., 1975—. Recipient Devel. Achievement medal Republic of Indonesia, 1964. Mem. Nat. Assn. Realtors, Honolulu Bd. Realtors. Roman Catholic. Club: Plaza (charter mem.). Office: 700 Bishop St Suite 1907 Honolulu HI 96813

CHENG, PAUL HUNG-CHIAO, engr., material handling and steel storage products co. exec.; b. AnHwei Province, China, Dec. 1, 1930; s. Yen-Teh and Shu-Ying (Tsou) C.; came to U.S., 1958; naturalized, 1973; B.S. in Civil Engring., Nat. Taiwan U., 1951; M.S. in Civil Engring., U. Va., 1961; m. Lucial Jen Cheng, Aug. 1, 1964; children—Maria, Elizabeth, Deborah, Samuel. Structural engr., Swift & Co., Chgo., 1963-67; sr. structural designer P & W.Engring., Chgo., 1967; sr. structural engr. A. Epstein & Son, Inc., Chgo., 1967-68, staff engr. Interlake, Inc., Chgo., 1968-71, supervising engr., 1971-73, chief structural engr., 1973-80, mgr. spl. structures, 1980, mgr. product engring., 1980—; cons. in field. Registered structural engr., Ill.; registered profl. civil engr., Calif. Mem. ASCE, Am. Concrete Inst. Home: 1620 Lawrence Crescent Flossmoor IL 60422 Office: 135th St and Perry Ave Chicago IL 60627

CHEQUER, JOHN HAMILTON, fin. exec., oil refiner; b. Piseco, N.Y., May 19, 1935; s. L. Hamilton and Frances (Dunham) C.; B.Engring., Yale U., 1957; M.B.A., Harvard U., 1963; m. Nan Guthrie Budde, May 30, 1963; children—Elizabeth, Anne, Laura. Vice-pres., First Nat. Bank of Boston, 1963-76; exec. v.p. Tosco Corp., Los Angeles, 1976—. Served to lt. (j.g.) USNR, 1958-61. Office: Tosco Corp 10100 Santa Monica Blvd Los Angeles CA 90067

CHERIS, SAMUEL DAVID, lawyer; b. Bklyn., Nov. 14, 1945; s. Hyman and Gertrude (Perlman) C.; B.S. cum laude, Bklyn. Coll., 1967; J.D., Stanford U., 1971, M.B.A. in Fin., 1971; m. Elaine Gayle Ingram, June 8, 1980; 1 son by previous marriage—Aaron Joseph. Admitted to Calif. bar, 1972, U.S. Ct. of Claims bar, 1972, Colo. bar, 1973, U.S. Tax Ct. bar, 1974; law clk. U.S. Ct. of Claims, Washington, 1971-72; asso. firm. Yegge, Hall & Evans, Denver, 1972-75; partner firm. Hall & Evans, Denver, 1976—; adj. prof. U. Denver; dir. Am. Stratigraphic Co. Vice pres. Stanford Law Sch. Fund, 1970-75; bd. dirs. Jewish Community Center of Denver, 1980—. Registered investment adv. Mem. Am. Bar Assn., Calif. Bar Assn., Colo. Bar Assn., Denver Bar Assn., Council of Petroleum Accts., Cheyenne Fencing Soc. Jewish. Home: 5730 Montview Blvd Denver CO 80207 Office: 2900 Energy Center Denver CO 80202

CHERNISS, NORMAN ARNOLD, newspaper editor; b. Council Bluffs, Iowa, July 16, 1926; s. David P. and Esther (Arenson) C.; B.A., State U. Iowa, 1950; postgrad. (Nieman fellow) Harvard, 1958-59, (Haynes fellow) U. Calif. at Los Angeles, 1960-61. Reporter, Council Bluffs Nonpareil, 1942-44; newswriter Sta. KOIL, Omaha, 1946; corr. Internat. News Service, Iowa City, 1948-49; editorial writer Des Moines Register and Tribune, 1949; Evansville (Ind.) Courier, 1951-53; editor editorial pages Riverside (Calif.) Press and Enterprise, 1953-68, asso. editor, 1968-71, exec. editor Press-Enterprise Co., 1971—; vis. lectr. U. Calif. at Los Angeles, 1965-66, U. So. Calif., 1968-69, 1970-71, 79; vis. prof. Columbia U., 1969-70. Served with USNR, 1944-46. Mem Am. Soc. Newspaper Editors, Nat. Conf. Editorial Writers, Soc. Nieman Fellows, Kappa Tau Alpha. Home: 2218 El Capitan Dr Riverside CA 92506 Office: Press-Enterprise Co Box 792 Riverside CA 92502

CHERNOFF, DANIEL PAREGOL, patent lawyer; b. Washington, Jan. 24, 1935; s. Bernard M. and Goldie S. (Paregol) C.; B.E.E. with distinction, Cornell U., 1957, LL.B., 1959; m. Nancy M. Kuehner, June 17, 1965; children—Scott, Graham. Instr., Cornell U., 1957-59, Oreg. Bd. Higher Edn., Portland, 1970-72; admitted to N.Y. bar, 1959, D.C. bar, 1959, Oreg. bar, 1968; practiced in N.Y.C., 1959-67, Portland, Oreg., 1967—; patent counsel Polarad Electronics Corp., Long Island City, N.Y., 1959-61; asso. firm Fish, Richardson & Neave, N.Y.C., 1961-67, Davies, Biggs, Strayer, Stoel & Boley, Portland, 1967-70; partner Chernoff & Vilhauer, P.C., Portland, 1970—. Mem. council Cornell U., 1975—; bd. dirs. Learning Resource Center, Inc., chmn., 1975-79; bd. dirs. Cardio-Pulmonary Research Inst., Seattle and Portland, 1974—. Mem. Oreg., N.Y., D.C. bar assns., Am., N.Y. (chmn. com. govt. relations to patents 1966), Oreg. (pres. 1973-74) patent law assns., Order of Coif, Tau Beta Pi, Eta Kappa Nu. Club: Multnomah Athletic. Home: 710 NW Winchester Terr Portland OR 97210 Office: 200 Wilcox Bldg Portland OR 97204

CHERRY, JAMES WASHINGTON, wholesale corp. exec.; b. Murfreesboro, Tenn., Nov. 10, 1926; s. Wheeler Morgan and Florence (Bybee) C.; student Milligan Coll., 1944-45, U. Louisville, 1945-46; B.S., Middle Tenn. State Coll., 1949; postgrad. Vanderbilt U., 1950; m. Susan Beazley, Oct. 30, 1952; children—James Gatewood, Susan Ann. Salesman, L.M. Berry Co., Dayton, Ohio, 1949-50; zone mgr. New Holland Machine Co. (Pa.), 1951-56; pres. Cherokee Sales Corp., Stanford, Ky., 1956—. Mem. Blue Grass Indsl. Council, Lexington, Ky., 1974; mem. service com. 4-H Club, Stanford, 1973-74; mem. Stanford Zoning Bd., 1976—. Served with USNR, 1944-47. Recipient award Future Farmers Am., 1973. Mem. C. of C. (pres. 1973). Clubs: Rotary (v.p. 1974), Masons (32 deg., Shriner). Home: 911 Lancaster St Stanford KY 40484 Office: Hwy 27N Stanford KY 40484

CHESTER, FRANCIS, lawyer, sheep farmer; b. Bklyn., Jan. 25, 1936; s. Frank and Mary (De Francesco) C.; B.A., Iona Coll., 1957; J.D., St. John's U., 1960; m. Diane G. Charlson, Oct. 29, 1966; children—Francis Scott, Angelique, Jennifer, Sabrina. Admitted to U.S. Dist. Ct. bar, 1962, U.S. Supreme Ct. bar, 1964, U.S. Ct. of Claims bar, 1964, Va. bar, 1969; individual practice law, Gordonsville, Va., 1969-80, Raphine, Va., 1980—; founder, owner Chester Farms, wool and sheep farm, wholesale distbrs. yarn, Gordonsville, 1968-80, Raphine, 1980—; guest lectr. community colls.; livestock orgns., 1978—. Mem. Va. Bar Assn., Louisa County Bar Assn., Nat. Columbia Sheep Breeders Assn., Eastern Columbia Sheep Breeders Assn. Republican. Roman Catholic. Home and Office: Route 1 Box 275 Raphine VA 24472

CHESTERFIELD, JAMES STUART, archtl. aluminum mfg. co. exec.; b. Indpls., June 4, 1952; s. John Morris and Erma Jeanne C.; A.B. in Econs., Ind. U., 1974; M.B.A. in Fin. and Mktg., U. Chgo., 1976; m. Gwen Kay Nevins, May 21, 1976. Mktg. rep. The Service Bur. Co. div. Control Data Corp., Chgo., 1976-78; treas., asst. corp. sec., asst. to pres. J-C Products Corp., Indpls., 1978—; v.p. CD Enterprises, Ltd., Chgo., also dir. Vice pres. bd. dirs. The Park of River Oaks Condominium Assn., Calumet City, Ill., 1978; active Monroe County Assn. Retarded Citizens. Mem. Am. Prodn. and Inventory Control Soc., Lambda Chi Alpha. Club: Econs. of Indpls. Office: J-C Products Corp 624 S Belmont Ave Indianapolis IN 46221

CHESTERFIELD, RHYDONIA RUTH EPPERSON, exec. financier; b. Dallas, Apr. 23, 1919; d. Leonard Lee and Sally Evelyn (Stevenson) Griswold; B.S., Southwestern U., 1952; B.S., N. Tex. U., 1954, M.E., 1956; Ph.D., Bernadean U., 1974; Ph.D., Calif. Christian U., 1974, LL.D. (hon.), 1974. Radio and evangelistic work with brother and sister as Griswold Trio, to 1958; tchr., psychologist, 1958-74; pres. Griswold-Epperson Fin. Enterprise, Los Angeles, 1974—. Fellow Internat. Naturopathic Assn.; mem. Los Angeles Inst. Fine Arts, Assn. Women in Edn. (hon.), Internat. Bus. and Profl. Women, Kappa Delta Pi (hon.), Pi Lambda Theta (hon.). Author several books, tchrs. guides for Little Citizens' Series; contbr. articles to various publs. Evangelistic worker in U.S. and Can. Office: 10790 Wilshire Blvd 202 Los Angeles CA 90024

CHESTERFIELD, ROBERT BRUCE, JR., mortgage banker; b. Seattle, Aug. 30, 1946; s. Robert Bruce and Marilyn (Sharpe) C.; B.A. with honors, Seattle U., 1969; M.Div., Harvard U., 1974. With Pacific Coast Investment Co., Seattle, 1974—, v.p., 1977—. Mem. King County Criminal Justice Planning Com., King County Health and Human Services Com. Mem. Mortgage Bankers Assn. Am., Realtors Nat. Mktg. Inst., Seattle-King County Bd. Realtors, Seattle C. of C., Mcpl. League Seattle. Republican. Roman Catholic. Clubs: Rainier. Harvard (Seattle). Home: 351 Lee St Seattle WA 98109 Office: 315 Norton Blvd Seattle WA 98104

CHESWICK, SUSAN REID, banker; b. Summit, N.J., Jan. 28, 1955; d. Richard R. and Ruth (Roberts) Cheswick; B.A., Wellesley Coll., 1977. Mgmt. trainee Citibank, N.Y.C., 1977-78, ops. officer, 1978-79, br. mgr., 1980—. Republican. Clubs: N.Y. Wellesley (fin. chmn. 1980—) (N.Y.C.); Wee Burn Country (Darien, Conn.). Home: 104 E 85th St New York NY 10028 Office: 1301 Ave of Americas New York NY 10019

CHEW, ERNEST BYRON, JR., coal mine exec.; b. Phila., Sept. 10, 1944; s. Ernest Byron and Myra Howard (Kreile) C.; B.S. in Chem. Engring., Carnegie-Mellon U., 1966; Ph.D. in Bus. Adminstrn., U. Ala., 1971; m. Stanlee Kley Chandler, June 2, 1967; children—Jennifer Chandler, Adrienne Chandler. Grad. teaching asst. U. Ala., 1969-71, adminstrv. asst. for continuing edn., 1970; asst. prof. bus. Delta State U., Cleveland, Miss., 1971-72; sr. research analyst Miss. Research and Devel. Center, Jackson, 1972-74; v.p. fin. affairs Birmingham-So. Coll., 1977-79, treas., bus. mgr., 1975-77, dir. Edward L. Norton Center, 1974-77; pres. Brownies Creek Collieries Harbert Constrn. Corp., Birmingham, 1979—. Pres. pro tem City Council of Vestavia Hills (Ala.), 1976—, chmn. adv. council on vocat. edn., 1978—; bd. dirs., v.p. Ala. Council on Epilepsy, 1978—; chmn. cities sect. United Way, Jefferson County, Ala., 1978. Served with USMC, 1966-68; NDEA fellow, 1968-71. Mem. Beta Gamma Sigma, Chi Alpha Phi, Kappa Phi Kappa, Omicron Delta Epsilon, Pi Tau Chi. Methodist. Office: 1 Riverchase Pkwy S Birmingham AL 35244

CHHEDA, PRAMILA MANILAL, fin. exec.; b. Bombay, India, Jan. 7, 1950; came to U.S., 1971, naturalized, 1980; d. Hansraj Deveshi and Tejbal Hansraj (Chheda) Shah; B.Com. with honors, Bombay U., 1970; M.B.A., U. Scranton, 1972; m. Manilal M. Chheda, Apr. 10, 1971; 1 child, Neha. Fin. analyst Silver Burdett Co., Morristown, N.J., 1973-75; with Taylor Bus. Inst., Inc., Ednl. Devel. Group, Livingston, N.J., 1975—, treas., 1980—. Home: 8 School Ave Chatham Township NJ 07928 Office: 600 S Livingston Ave Livingston NJ 07039

CHI, CHIA-DANN, banker; b. Nanking, China, Mar. 3, 1936; s. Lien and Far-Sen (Liu) C.; came to U.S., 1961, naturalized, 1973; B.S. in Agrl. Econs., Nat. Taiwan U., 1958; M.S. in Econs., U. Wis., 1964; m. Catarina Chen, Apr. 29, 1967; 1 son, Victor J. Economist, Thor Eckert & Co. Inc., N.Y.C., 1964; asst. treas. Asso. Maritime Industries Inc., N.Y.C., 1964-67; registered rep. Cohen, Simonson & Rea, Inc., N.Y.C., 1968-70; v.p., dir. research N.J. Bank N.A., Paterson, 1970-80, v.p., sr. investment officer, head investment div., trust dept., 1980—. Pres. Chinese Opera Club Am., 1972-75, 80, bd. dirs., 1970—. Fellow Fin. Analysts Fedn.; mem. N.Y. Soc. Security Analysts, Inst. Chartered Fin. Analysts. Address: 10 Laurel Ct Verona NJ 07044

CHIANG, JOSEPH SHING, mfg. co. exec.; b. Shanghai, China, Mar. 2, 1944; came to U.S., 1967, naturalized, 1980; s. Shin Ya and Kuei Tsen (Ma) C.; M. in Chem. Engring., U. Mo., 1970; m. Aug. 30, 1968; children—Joseph, Josephin. Dept. chmn. Chinese Overseas Student U., Taipei, Taiwan, 1966-67; sect. leader Borden Chem., Northfield, Ill., 1969-76; mng. dir. Mats Internat., Anaheim, Calif., 1975-76; pres. TA Industries, Inc., Anaheim, 1976—; dir. Taiwan Kawaski Wire & Cable, TA Devel. Served with Chinese Armed Forces, 1965-66. Roman Catholic. Office: 1875 S Lewis St Anaheim CA 92805

CHIAPPINELLI, JOSEPH, utility co. engr.; b. Newark, Jan. 1, 1950; s. Stanley and Ann (Mancino) C.; B.S.E.E., N.J. Inst. Tech., 1972; m. Beverly Ann Buonocore, May 12, 1979. Mgmt. trainee PSE&G of N.J., Newark, 1972, asst. engr., 1972-73, maintenance supr., 1973-75, sr. performance supr., 1975, sr. maintenance supr., 1975-77, sr. planning supr., 1977-78, sr. staff engr., 1978-80, sta. operating supr., 1980, sta. performance engr., 1980—. Lic. stationary engr., public sewage treatment plant supt. Clubs: Porsche of Am., 356 Registry. Home: 287 N Mountain Ave Upper Montclair NJ 07043 Office: Linden Generating Station Grasselli Area off Wood Ave S Linden NJ 07036

CHIAPPISI, ALPHONSE PHILIP, constrn. co. exec.; b. Roslindale, Mass., June 19, 1920; s. Philip and Mary Susie (Frasca) C.; student Needham (Mass.) pub. schs.; m. Mavis Louise Erath, Sept. 13, 1947. Apprentice plasterer Chiappisi Bros., Needham, 1938-41, estimator, 1947-51, partner, 1951—, treas., dir., 1967—; helper shipfitter U.S. Naval Shipyard, Charlestown, Mass., 1942, shipfitter, 1943, mold loftsman, 1944-45; salesman John Hancock Mut. Life Ins. Co., Newton, Mass., 1946; trustee Chiappisi Realty Trust; partner Chiappisi & Conte; treas. Paramount Water Purification Systems, Inc.; pres. Chiappisi Bros. Industries, Inc., 1980—. Mgmt. chmn., trustee Local 10 Boston Health and Welfare and Supplementary Unemployment Benefit Fund; mgmt. chmn., trustee Local 32 Newton Health and Welfare and Pension Fund. Recipient award of appreciation Contracting Plasterers' Lathers' Internat. Assn., 1964, 68, 71. Mem. Internat. Assn. Wall and Ceiling Contractors (dir. 1965-71, chmn. New Eng. conf. 1965-66, Mexico City award 1972), Asso. Subcontractors of Mass., Master Plasterers Assn. Boston and Vicinity, Vicinity Employers Assn. Roman Catholic. Clubs: Point Independence Yacht (Onset, Mass.), Great Blue Hill Power Squadron. Chmn. com. executing first written labor agreement between an internat. labor union and an internat. contractors assn., 1964. Home: 324 Country Way Needham MA 02192 Office: 199 Hillside Ave Needham Heights MA 02194

CHIARKAS, NICHOLAS LOUIS, JR., lawyer, educator; b. N.Y.C., Apr. 1, 1943; s. Nicholas Louis and Marie (Tedesco) C.; student N.Y.U., 1971; B.S., John Jay Coll., 1970, M.A., 1971; J.D.,

Temple U., 1978; M.Ed., Ed.D., Columbia U., 1979; m. Elizabeth L. Apple, Aug. 31, 1974; children—Erica Lynn, Nicky, Christopher, Adrienne. Officer, Police Dept., N.Y.C., 1965-71; prof. criminology dept. criminal justice Trenton State Coll., 1971-79; admitted to Pa. bar, 1978; practice law, Newtown, Pa., 1978-79; prof. law Cumberland Sch., Samford U., Birmingham, Ala., 1979—; bd. dirs. Newtown Crossing, 1976-79. Active, First Presbyn. Ch., Mountain Brook; Ala. Served with U.S. Army, 1962-65. Mem. Nat. Council Juvenile Ct. Judges, Pa. Bar Assn., Bucks County Bar Assn., Am. Bar Assn., Phila. Bar Assn., Fed. Bar Assn., Law and Soc. Assn., Internat. Assn. Chiefs of Police, Nat. Assn. Criminology, Internat. Crimonol. Soc., Acad. Criminal Justice Scis., Lambda Alpha Epsilon. Republican. Presbyterian. Home: 3772 River Ridge Circle Birmingham AL 35223 Office: Cumberland School of Law Samford U Birmingham AL 35209

CHICKERING, HOWARD ALLEN, lawyer; b. San Francisco, Mar. 21, 1942; s. Allen Lawrence and Caroline Cranford (Rogers) C.; B.S. Econs., U. Pa., 1966; J.D., Stanford U., 1971; m. Elizabeth D. Dalton, June 29, 1968; children—Philip Dalton, Caroline Howe. Admitted to Calif. bar, 1972; asso. firm Chickering & Gregory, San Francisco, 1971-76; sr. counsel ITEL Corp., San Francisco, 1976-79; v.p., gen. counsel, dir. Clarendon Ins. Co., 1979—. Co-author, acting campaign chmn. San Francisco Proposition C (Open Space), June 1974; campaign sec. Proposition J (Open Space and Park Renovation), Nov. 1974; chmn. city finances com., bd. dirs. Pacific Heights Assn., 1974-77. Served to lt. (j.g.) USN, 1966-68; lt. comdr. Judge Adv. Gen. Corps, USNR. Decorated Vietnam medals. Mem. Am. Bar Assn., Bar Assn. San Francisco, U.S. Naval Inst. Mechanics Inst., San Francisco Planning and Urban Renewal Assn., Calif. Hist. Soc. Republican. Episcopalian. Clubs: Belle Haven, Univ. (San Francisco), Commonwealth. Home: 80 Otter Rock Dr Greenwich CT 06830 Office: 655 Madison Ave 15th Floor New York NY 10021

CHICKLIS, BARBARA KAREN BURAK, computer cons.; b. Woonsocket, R.I., July 1, 1942; d. Steven and Stella Burak; B.S. in Math., Suffolk U., 1964; M.S.E.E. in Computer Sci., Northeastern U., 1974; children—Karen Barbara, Paul Steven. Systems programmer Raytheon Corp., Lexington, Mass., 1965-68, ITEK Corp., Lexington, 1968-71; project and staff leader Computation Center, Northeastern U., Boston, 1971-74; staff cons. Control Data Corp., Waltham, Mass., 1974—. Recipient award Internat. Profl. Services Analyst Symposium, 1977. Mem. Assn. Computing Machinery. Republican. Office: 60 Hickory Dr Waltham MA 02154

CHIDSEY, CHARLES WELLINGTON, JR., newspaper exec.; b. Springfield, Mass., June 12, 1923; s. Charles Wellington and Ruby Isabell (Sleith) C.; B.S., Northwestern U., 1947; postgrad in Bus., U. Calif. at Los Angeles, 1971-73, Columbia U., 1973; m. Mary Jacqueline Randell, June 26, 1948; children—Charles Wellington III, Carol Anne, Chidsey Tucker. Account exec. advt. dept. Chgo. Tribune, 1948-64; account exec. Cresmer, Woodward, O'Mara & Ormsbee, Inc., Chgo., 1965-67; Midwestern sales mgr. Los Angeles Times, 1968-70, asst. dir. mktg. research, 1971-73, dir. mktg. research, 1974—; dir. IAM Corp., Malibu, Calif., Sky Harbor Lithopress, Inglewood, Calif.; guest lectr. mktg. U. Calif. at Los Angeles, 1972-80, Calif. State U., Los Angeles, 1973-80. Republican precinct capt., Winnetka, Ill, 1954-71. Served with AUS, 1943-46; capt. USAR, 1947-55. Mem. Am. Mktg. Assn., So. Calif. Research Council, Internat. Newspaper Advt. Execs., Newspaper Research Council, Travel Research Assn. (dir. 1972-76), Los Angeles C. of C. Republican. Episcopalian (vestryman 1951-60, jr. warden 1960-63, sr. warden, 1963-66, treas. Chgo. diocese, 1960-63, mem. diocesian council 1954-63). Clubs: Chgo. Athletic; Palos Verdes Yacht. Home: 2200 Paseo del Mar Palos Verdes Estates CA 90274 Office: Los Angeles Times Times Mirror Sq Los Angeles CA 90053

CHIEN, TA-MU, engr.; b. Jiangin, China, Mar. 12, 1937; s. Chun-Pai and Yuan-Chuan C.; B.S., Nat. Taiwan U., 1959; M.S., U. Kans., 1962; Ph.D., Poly. Inst. N.Y., 1968; m. Blanche G. C. Shen, June 27, 1964; children—Lawrence, William, Catherine. Equipment and devel. engr. Western Electric Co., 1962-66; research fellow Poly. Inst. N.Y., Bklyn., 1966-68; mem. tech. staff Bell Telephone Labs., Holmdel, N.J., 1968—; dir. Hsintu Pub. Co., Inc., N.Y.C., Chinese English Lang. Service, Inc., Freehold, N.J.; chmn. China-Am. Mktg. Service, Inc., N.Y.C. Founder, Chinese-Am. Culture and Welfare Found., Freehold, N.J., 1976, pres., 1976-78, sec., dir., 1978—. Mem. IEEE. Democrat. Home: 15 Buckingham Way Freehold NJ 07728 Office: Bell Labs Holmdel NJ 07733

CHIHOREK, JOHN PAUL, electronics co. exec.; b. Wilkes-Barre, Pa., June 22, 1943; s. Stanley Joseph and Caroline Mary Chihorek; B.S.E.E., Pa. State U., 1965: postgrad. Calif. State U., San Diego, 1970-71; M.B.A., Calif. State U., Sacramento, 1972; m. Christina Maria Marroquin, Dec. 28, 1968; children—Jonathan, David, Crista. Program officer Hdqrs. Air Force Logistics Command, Dayton, Ohio, 1972-75; sr. engr. Hdqrs. Air Force Space Div., Los Angeles, 1975-78; mgr. software systems dept. Logicon Inc., San Pedro, Calif., 1978—; owner investment adv. firm. Mem. Congl. Adv. Bd., 1980; active PTA. Served with USN, 1965-70; Vietnam. Decorated Bronze Star. Mem. IEEE, Air Force Assn. Roman Catholic. Clubs: Lions, IOF. Office: 255 5th St San Pedro CA 90731

CHILCOTE, SAMUEL DAY, JR., trade assn. exec.; b. Casper, Wyo., Aug. 24, 1937; s. Sam D. and Juanita (Cornelison) C.; B.B.A., Idaho State U., 1959; m. Ellen Sheridan Spear, Nov. 11, 1966. Adminstrn. asst. Continental Oil Co., Glenrock, Wyo., 1960-63; asst. supt. pub. instruction Wyo. Dept. Edn., dir. Wyo. Surplus Property Agency and state sch. lunch program, Cheyenne, 1963-67; regional supr. Distilled Spirits Inst., Denver, 1967-71, dir. field div., Washington, 1971-73; exec. v.p. Distilled Spirits Council U.S., Inc., Washington, 1973-77, pres., 1978—; publicity dir. Wyo. Gov.'s Com. on Edn., 1963-64; mem. Joint Com. of States; mem. bd. dirs. Nat. Council on Alcoholism. Dep. state boxing commr., co-chmn. Wyo. Golden Gloves Tournament, 1962; pres. Sky Ranch Found. for Boys, 1975—. Served to capt. U.S. Army, 1959-60. Mem. Nat. Press Club, State Dirs. Sch. Food Service Assn. (v.p. 1964, pres. 1965), U.S. C. of C. (mem. taxation com.), Phi Kappa Tau. Clubs: George Town, Congressional Country (bd. govs.), Shriners, Elks, Masons. Office: Distilled Spirits Council 1300 Pa Bldg Washington DC 20004

CHILD ARTHUR JAMES EDWARD, food co. exec.; b. Guildford, Eng., May 19, 1910; s. William Arthur and Helena (Wilson) C.; B.Commerce, Queen's U., 1931; grad. Harvard Advanced Mgmt. Program, 1956; M.A., U. Toronto, 1960; m. Mary Gordon, Dec. 10, 1955. Chief auditor Can. Packers Ltd., 1938-52, v.p., 1952-60; pres. Canadian Dressed Meats Ltd., Jamar, Inc., Intercontinental Packers Ltd., 1960-66, Ajex Investments, Ltd.; pres., chief exec. officer Burns Foods Ltd., Calgary, Alta., Can., 1966—; chmn., dir. Palm Dairies Ltd., Scott Nat. Co., Ltd., Canbra Foods Ltd., Food Services Ltd., Stafford Foods Ltd.; dir. Allendale Mut. Ins. Co., Can. Life Assurance Co., LaVerendrye Mgmt. Corp. Ltd., Alta. Gas Chems. Ltd., Canoe Cove Mfg. Ltd., Grove Valve and Regulator Inc., Newsco Investments Ltd., Energy Equipment Systems Inc., Imperial Trust Co., WAGI Internat. Corp., Ronalds-Federated Ltd., Hydroblaster Inc., Nova. asso. prof. U. Sask., 1964-65 chmn., Can. West Found. Fellow Chartered Inst. Secs.; mem. Meat Packers Council Can. (past pres.), Inst. Internal Auditors (past pres.), Am. Mgmt. Assn., Inst. for Strategic Studies. Author: Economics and Politics in United States Banking, 1965; (with B. Cadmus) Internal Control, 1953. Home: 1320 Baldwin Crescent SW Calgary AB T2V 2B8 Canada Office: PO Box 2520 Calgary AB T2P 2M7 Canada

CHILDE, JAMES HENRY, econ. devel. co. exec.; b. Omaha, Oct. 7, 1943; s. James Gavin and Henry Dell (Ratcliff) C.; B.A., U. Nebr., 1965, J.D., 1968; grad. Indstl. Devel. Inst., 1975; m. Sharon Ann O'Hare, July 2, 1971; children—Kerry Lynn, Nancy Lea. Admitted to Nebr. bar, 1968; spl. programs coordinator Nebr. Dept. Econ. Devel., Lincoln, 1968-71; local coordinator Vision-17 Inc., Seward, Nebr., 1971-72; mgr. Kans. Center Midwest Research Inst., Topeka, 1972-75; exec. v.p. Bus. Devel. Corp. Nebr., Lincoln, 1975—. Certified indsl. developer. Mem. Nat. Assn. Bus. Devel. Corps. (v.p.), Am. Indsl. Devel. Council, Nebr. Indsl. Developers Assn. (past pres.), Am., Nebr. bar assns., Am. Judicature Soc., Phi Gamma Delta, Lincoln Alumni Assn. (sec. 1971). Clubs: Lincoln (dir. 1976-79, treas. 1980), Kaw Valley (pres. 1975) dog obedience, Jaycees. Participated in econ. devel. seminars, 1973-74. Home: 4741 S 57th St Lincoln NE 68516 Office: 1044 Stuart Bldg Lincoln NE 68508

CHILDERS, YILDIZ GUNDUZ, mfg. co. exec.; b. Gevas, Turkey, Nov. 28, 1939; d. Yosuf Ziva and Saduye (Buzkaya) Gunduz; came to U.S., 1960, naturalized, 1967; B.A., Istanbul Kiz Lisesi; m. William L. Childers, 1967 (dec. 1972). Pres. Childers Mfg. Co. Inc., mfrs. mobile and stationary heater tanks for indsl. liquids, Albuquerque, 1967—. Mem. Nat. Pavement Assn., Assn. Equipment Distbrs., Ladies Aux. of Nat. Asphalt Pavement Assn., Can. Assn. Equipment Distbrs., Asphalt Recycling and Reclaiming Assn., Asso. Gen. Contractors Am. Republican. Moslem. Clubs: Four Hills Country, Elks. Home: 1004 Cuatro Cerros SE Albuquerque NM 87123 Office: 2010 6th St NW Albuquerque NM 87197

CHILDS, CLINTON LANGWITH, real estate broker and developer; b. Honolulu, Sept. 14, 1922; s. Clinton Stibbs and Eleanor (Langwith) C.; B.B.A., U. Oreg., 1947; m. Frances A. Johnston, Jan. 6, 1944; children—Candis L., Patrick J., Christy S. With Bishop Nat. Bank, 1946-51; asst. to v.p. Lihue Plantation Co., 1951-65; Kauai mgr. comml. land devel. Amfac, Inc., 1965-68; pres. Kauai Helicopters, Inc., 1966—, Clint Childs, Inc., Realtors, Honolulu, 1974—, Alii Travel, Inc., 1977—; pres., mng. dir. Strategic Resources, Inc., 1980—. Served to capt. U.S. Army, 1944-46. Mem. Hawaii State C. of C. (pres. 1965), Kauai Bd. Realtors (pres. 1970-73), Kauai Mus. Assn., Acad. of Arts, Punahou Alumni Assn. (dir.), Sigma Alpha Epsilon. Republican. Episcopalian. Clubs: Kauai Golf and Yacht; Pacific, Plaza (Honolulu). Office: 4444 Rice Lihue HI 96766

CHILDS, JOHN DAVID, computer hardware and services co. exec.; b. Washington, Apr. 26, 1939; s. Edwin Carlton and Catherine Dorothea (Angerman) C.; student Principia Coll., 1957-58, 59-60; B.A., Am. U., 1963; m. Margaret Rae Olsen, Mar. 4, 1966; 1 son, John-David. Jr. adminstr. Page Communications, Washington, 1962-65; account rep. Friden Inc., Washington, 1965-67; Western sales dir. Data Inc., Arlington, Va., 1967-70; v.p. mktg. Rayda, Inc., Los Angeles, 1970-73, pres., 1973-76, chmn. bd., 1976—; sr. asso. World Trade Assos., Inc., 1976—. Pres. Coll. Youth for Nixon-Lodge, 1959-60, dir. state fedn.; mem. OHSHA policy formulation com. Labor Dept., 1967. Served with USAFR, 1960-66. Mem. Assn. Data Center Owners and Mgrs. (chmn. privacy com., 1975, sec. 1972-74, v.p. 1974). Democrat. Christian Scientist. Office: 15326 Sherman Way Suite 120 Van Nuys CA 91406

CHIN, CAROLYN SUE, telephone co. exec.; b. Washington, Nov. 28, 1947; d. Tin Wah and Oi Tuck (Ho) C.; B.S. in Mgmt. Engring., Rensselaer Poly. Inst., 1969; M.B.A., Harvard U., 1971; m. Gerald Bingham Sweeney, Sept. 18, 1976. Buyer, R.H. Macy's, Inc., N.Y.C., 1972-74, divisional mdse. adminstr. home accessories, 1974-75; mktg. mgr. design line, group product mgr. AT&T, Morristown, N.J., 1976, mktg. mgr. distbn. programs Bell System products, 1976-77, mdse. mgr. AT&T, Morristown, 1977-78, mgr. strategic planning, N.Y.C., 1980—; White House fellow, spl. asst. to sec. HUD, Washington, 1978-79; asst. to sec. HEW, Washington, 1979-80. Cons. N.Y. Emergency Fin. Control Bd.; mem. South Orange Econ. Devel. Com., 1977-78; bd. dirs. Albert Einstein Peace Prize Found., 1979—, Ind. Sector, 1980—. Named one of 10 Outstanding Young Working Women, Glamour mag., 1977, Outstanding Young Woman of N.J., 1977; elected to YWCA Acad. of Women Achievers. Home: Llewellyn Park West Orange NJ 07052 Office: AT&T 195 Broadway New York NY

CHIN, ROY, banker; b. N.Y.C., June 1950; s. Hong Chong and Jean C.; B.S., Rensselaer Poly. Inst., 1972; M.B.A., N.Y. U., 1980; m. Nancy Eng, Sept. 1972; 1 dau., Dana Alison. Asst. to pres. Am. Pioneer Corp., N.Y.C., 1972-73; credit analyst Chase Manhattan Bank, N.Y.C., 1974—, asst. treas., 1975, 2d v.p., 1976-79, v.p., 1979—. Home: 80 Lafayette St Chatham NJ 07928 Office: One Chase Plaza New York NY 10081

CHING, LARRY FONG CHOW, constrn. co. exec.; b. Honolulu, Mar. 15, 1912; s. Dung Sen and Dai (Chong) C.; B.C.E., U. Hawaii, 1935; postgrad. U. Utah Sch. Mining Engring., 1938-39; m. Beatrice Jook Yee Fong, Aug. 6, 1944; children—Randall Ming-Yu, Thalia Ping-Hsia. Instr. math. and engring. U. Yunan, Kunming, China, 1935-37; engr. Moses Akiona, Contractor, 1939-42, 45; supr. roads and airport constrn. U.S. Corps Engrs., 1942-44; mgr. Universal Contracting Co., 1945-47; constrn. supt. Associated Builders, 1948-49; pres., gen. mgr. Hwy. Constrn. Co., Ltd., Honolulu, 1949—; dir. Hawaii Franchise No-Joint Concrete Pipe, Hawaii Contractor's License Bd., 1960-63; pres., dir. Constrn. Industry Legis. Orgn., 1977-78; sub-chmn. design constrn. and maintenance Hawaii Hwy. Safety Council. Pres., Larry and Beatrice Ching Found., Hawaii Chinese History Center, 1971. Registered profl. engr., Hawaii. Mem. Asso. Gen. Contractors Am. (dir.), Gen. Contractors Assn. Hawaii (pres. 1968, dir.), Soc. Am. Mil. Engrs., Honolulu, Chinese (dir., pres. 1971-72), Hawaii (dir.) chambers commerce, Honolulu Better Bus. Bur., Friends of East-West Center, United Chinese Soc. (pres. 1980—), Tu Chiang Sheh (pres.). Home: 18 Kimo Dr Honolulu HI 96817 Office: 720 Umi St Honolulu HI 96819

CHINICH, ARNOLD, constrn. co. exec.; b. Newark, June 23, 1915; s. Barnet and Nettie Chinich; certificate in architecture Newark Sch. of Fine Arts, 1937; student Profl. Sch. of Bus., Union, N.J., certificate in pub. adjusting Sch. Bus. Adminstrn. Fairleigh Dickinson U., 1971. Engr., Newark Housing Authority, 1938-40, Jaehing & Peoples, Inc., Newark, 1940-42; archtl. engr. Dept. of Army, Newark, 1942-44; pres. Harvard Constrn. Co., Newark, 1944-69, Vassar Realty Corp., Newark, 1953—, Pitts Realty Corp., Newark, 1953—; self-employed cons., inst. agt., broker, adjuster, Newark, 1969—. Mem. Am. Assn. for Automotive Medicine, Internat. Platform Assn., Internat. Assn. for Accident and Traffic Medicine. Mason. Address: 815 S 11th St Newark NJ 07108

CHINICH, BESSIE (BESSIE CHINICH FEDERBUSH), lawyer; b. Newark; d. Barnet and Nettie (Chinich) Chinich; LL.B., Rutgers U., 1930, J.D., 1970; m. Harry Federbush, May 28, 1933; children—Paul Gerard, Roberta Dianne. Admitted to N.J. bar, 1930; practiced law, Newark, 1931-44, 48-51; conferee salary stblzn. unit U.S. Treasury Dept. N.Y.C., 1944-46; investigator Civilian Prodn. Authority, N.Y.C., 1946-47; claims examiner War Assets Adminstrn., N.Y.C., 1947-48; sr. investigator Nat. Prodn. Authority, U.S. Dept. Commerce, Newark, 1951-53; contract specialist U.S. Ordnance Dist., N.Y., 1953-65; admnstrv. contracting officer Def. Supply Agy., Springfield, N.J., 1965—. Atty., Newark Commn. Neighborhood Conservation and Rehab., 1962. Active local orphanages, home for aged, prevention of juvenile delinquency. Recipient awards N.Y. Ordnance Dist., 1953, 65. Mem. Nat. Council Juvenile Ct. Judges, Essex County Bar Assn., Rutgers Alumni Assn., Internat. Platform Assn., Am. Judicature Soc., Nat. Assn. Woman Lawyers. Address: 815 S 11th St Newark NJ 07108

CHINNERY, WILLIAM THOMAS, fin. planner; b. Kansas City, Kans., July 4, 1935; s. George Willian and Ardyce (Hardy) C.; B.A., Yale U., 1958; m. Wanda M. Shelp, Dec. 22, 1959; 1 dau., Melissa Christine. Gen. agent Bankers Life Nebr. Ins. Co., Kansas City, Mo., 1965-74; area mgr. Physicians Planning Service Corp., Western Mo. and Kans., 1970-77; independent fin. planner, ins. and investments fields, Shawnee Mission, Kans., 1977—; area sales mgr. Firemen's Fund Am. Life Ins. Co., Shawnee Mission, 1978-80. Bd. dirs. St. Paul's Episcopal Day Sch., Kansas City, Mo., 1970-71, Marillac Home for Children, Kansas City, Mo., 1977-78; v.p. Nat. Council on Alcoholism, Kansas City area, 1977-78. Mem. Internat. Assn. Fin. Planners. Episcopalian. Club: Yale of Kansas City (pres. 1967-68). Author: Tax Tangles, 1977; Tax Graffiti by Tax Graffiti, 1979. Home: 2020 W 61st Terr Mission Hills KS 66208 Office: 7721 State Line S-137 Kansas City MO 64114

CHINNOCK, RONALD JOHN, realtor; b. Grand Rapids, Mich., Oct. 5, 1903; s. Frederick C. and Margaret (Sullivan) C.; student Grand Rapids Jr. Coll., 1923-24, Northwestern U., 1925-26; m. Barbara Farr, Oct. 12, 1929 (dec.); children—John, Margot; m. 2d, Mary Swain, Dec. 29, 1948 (dec.); children—Christine, Michael, Peter, Mary Martha; m. 3d, Elizabeth Dickhoff, May 20, 1978. Partner, chmn. bd. Farr & Co., Chgo., 1929-52, Farr, Chinnock & Sampson, Inc., Chgo., 1952-69; chmn. bd. Chinnock & Doughty, Inc., 1969-73; sr. v.p. Chinnock & Doughty, Inc. subs. Strobeck, Reiss & Co., Chgo., 1973—; advisory dir. 1st Fed. Chgo.; dir. NW Trust and Savings Bank, Bank and Trust Co., Arlington Heights, Chgo. Short Line Ry. Pres. USO Chgo. Inc., 1966-68. Served as apprentice seaman World War I; capt. USN, World War II. Decorated Legion of Merit. Mem. Nat. (pres. 1954), Ill. (pres. 1947) assns. of realtors, Chgo. Real Estate Bd. (pres. 1942), Am. Soc. Real Estate Counselors, Soc. Indsl. Realtors, Am. Right of Way Assn. Republican. Clubs: Army-Navy, Univ., Mid-Day, Realty, Realtors Forty. Home: 1020 Grove St Evanston IL 60201 Office: 801 Davis St Evanston IL 60201

CHIOGIOJI, MELVIN HIROAKI, govt. ofcl.; b. Hiroshima, Japan, Aug. 21, 1939; s. Yutaka and Harumi (Yamasaki) C.; came to U.S., 1939; B.S., Purdue U., 1961; M.B.A., U. Hawaii, 1968; D.B.A., George Washington U., 1972; m. Eleanor Nobuko Oura, June 4, 1960; children—Wendy A., Alan K. Head, weapons gen. component div. Quality Evaluation Lab., Oahu, Hawaii, 1965-69; dir. weapons evaluation and engring. div. Naval Ordnance Systems Command, Washington, 1969-73; dir. Office Indsl. Analysis, Fed. Energy Adminstrn., Washington, 1973-75; asst. dir. div. bldgs. and community systems Dept. Energy, Washington, 1975-79, dir. div. fed. programs, 1979-80, dep. asst. sec., 1980—; prof. mgmt. sci. George Washington U., Washington, 1972—. Pres. Japanese Am. Citizens League, Washington, 1975; mem. Md. State Adv. Com. on Civil Rights, 1975-78; bd. dirs., treas. Seabee Meml. Scholarship Assn., 1980—. Served with USN, 1961-65. Registered profl. engr., Hawaii. Mem. Nat. Soc. Profl. Engrs., IEEE, Acad. Mgmt., Naval Res. Assn., Soc. Am. Mil. Engrs., Assn. Sci., Tech. and Innovation (pres. 1979—), Purdue Alumni Assn., Assn. C.E. Corps Officers, Armed Forces Mgmt. Assn., Hawaii Soc. Profl. Engrs. Episcopalian (vestryman 1977—). Author: Industrial Energy Conservation, 1979. Contbr. articles to profl. jours. Home: 15113 Middlegate Rd Silver Spring MD 20904 Office: 1000 Independence Ave NW Washington DC 20585

CHIOKE, CHRISTOPHER EKEMEZIE, mktg. co. exec.; b. Enugu, Nigeria, Dec. 25, 1941; s. Michael Zeigbo and Monica (Nwakaku) C.; came to U.S., 1968, naturalized, 1975; B.Sc. in Econs., U. London, 1965; M.A. in History, Yeshiva U., N.Y.C., 1971; Ph.D., Southeastern U., Greenville, S.C., 1975; postgrad. Harvard Bus. Sch., 1979. Dept. mgr. Lloyds & Scottish Bankers, London, 1964-67; ins. underwriter London & Overseas Ins. Co., 1967-68; sr. cost accountant Automatic Data Processing Co., Clifton, N.J., 1968-69; fin. and credit officer Fgn. Credit Ins. Assn., N.Y.C., 1969-71; pres., chief exec. officer Chioke Internat. Corp., N.Y.C., 1971—; dir. Elmwood Tool & Machine Co. Inc., Hartford, Conn. Bd. dirs. Deux Youth Found., N.Y.C., 1978—; mem. pres.'s council Democratic Nat. Com. Recipient certificate of recognition Black Enterprise mag., 1974, 75, 76, 77, 78, 79, 80; citation for bus. and community service Pres. Carter, 1978. Mem. Internat. Platform Assn., St. Georges Soc. N.Y.C., Brit.-Am. C. of C., UN Assn. Democrat. Roman Catholic. Home: 3001 Henry Hudson Pkwy Riverdale NY 10463 Office: 200 Park Ave New York NY 10017

CHIRURG, JAMES THOMAS, JR., investment co. exec.; b. Wellesley, Mass., May 21, 1944; s. James Thomas and Virginia Burtt (Low) C.; A.B., Cornell, 1964; M.B.A., Harvard, 1969; B.Litt. (Knox fellow), Oxford U., 1972; postgrad. U. Calif. at Berkeley. Asst. mktg. mgr. Gen. Mills Co., Tokyo, 1968; with corp. fin. dept. First Boston Corp., N.Y.C., 1969-70; gen. mgr. Protasis Trust, Ltd., London, 1971-72, lead partner, Berkeley, Calif., 1973—; dir. Protasis Holdings (S.A.R.L.), Luxembourg; lectr. U. Calif.; investment adv. AID Mission to Tanzania, 1980; cons. Bechtel Corp. Bd. dirs. World Affairs Council No. Calif., 1973-75; vice chmn. coastal zone com. Marine Tech. Soc., 1977—. mem. com. maritime preservation Nat. Trust. Historic Preservation, 1979—. Served to lt. (j.g.) USNR, 1964-67. Decorated Bronze Star with combat V; fellow Salzburg Seminar. Fellow Royal Asiatic Soc. (Eng.); mem. Acad. Internat. Bus., Internat. Assn. Advancement of Appropriate Tech. for Developing Countries, Soc. Internat. Devel., Am. Econ. Assn., Asia Soc., Chinese Culture Found., Soc. Asian Art, Navy League U.S., Brit. Inst. Mgmt., Royal Econ. Soc., Overseas Devel. Council, Naval Order U.S., Fraternal Order UDT/SEAL, Internat. Wine and Food Soc., Am. Mensa Ltd., Alpha Delta Phi. Clubs: Union League (N.Y.C.); Commonwealth (San Francisco); Harvard (Boston); United Oxford and Cambridge, Royal Naval (London); Internat. House Japan (Tokyo). Home: 2001 Broadway San Francisco CA 94115 Office: PO Box 4000 Berkeley CA 94704

CHISHOLM, TOMMY, utilities exec.; b. Baldwyn, Miss., Apr. 14, 1941; s. Thomas Vaniver and Ruby (Duncan) C.; B.S. in Civil Engring., Tenn. Tech. U., 1963; J.D., Samford U., 1969; m. Janice McClanahan, June 20, 1964; children—Mark Alan (dec.), Andrea, Stephen Thomas, Patrick Ervin. Civil engr. TVA, Knoxville, Tenn., 1963-64; with So. Services, Inc., 1963-73, coordinator spl. projects, Atlanta, 1971-73; admitted to Ala. bar, 1969; asst. to pres. So. Co., Atlanta, 1973-75, sec., asst. treas., 1977—; sec., house counsel So. Co. Services, Inc., 1977—; mgr. adminstrv. services dept. Gulf Power Co., Pensacola, Fla., 1975—. Active local United Appeal fund drives, 1967, 68, 72, 75, 78, 79. Registered profl. engr., Ala., Fla., Ga., Miss.

Mem. Am. Bar Assn., Ala. State Bar, ASCE, Phi Alpha Delta. Club: Rotary (officer, dir.). Home: 1611 Bryn Mawr Circle Marietta GA 30067 Office: The Southern Co PO Box 720071 Atlanta GA 30346

CHISM, JAMES ARTHUR, pharm. industry exec.; b. Oak Park, Ill., Mar. 6, 1933; s. William Thompson and Arema Eloise (Chadwick) C.; A.B., DePauw U., 1957; M.B.A. (Univ. fellow), Ind. U., 1959. Mgmt. engr. Uniroyal Co., Mishawaka, Ind., 1959-61, sr. mgmt. engr., 1961-63; with Miles Labs., Elkhart, Ind., 1963—, mgr. consumer products div. systems and programming, 1976-79, dir. adminstrn. and staff services—mgmt. info. services, 1979—; dir. adminstrn. and staff services—mgmt. info. services Cutter Labs., Emeryville, Calif., 1979—; asso. instr. Ind. U., South Bend, 1964-66; lectr. Am. Mgmt. Assn., 1969-74; mem. curriculum planning com. Southwestern Mich. Coll., 1974—. Bd. dirs. United Way Elkhart County, 1974-75. Served with U.S. Army, 1954-56. Mem. Assn. Systems Mgmt. (chpt. pres. 1969-70, div. council chmn. 1974-75, Merit award 1975, Achievement award 1977), Assn. Cons. Mgmt. Engrs., Assn. Internal Mgmt. Cons., Internat. Communications Assn., Am. Mgmt. Assn. Republican. Episcopalian. Clubs: Morris Park Country, Summit (South Bend). Editor: Am. Prodn. Inventory Control Soc. Glossary, 1980. Home: 504 Cedar Crest Ln Mishawaka IN 46544 Office: Miles Labs Inc PO Box 40 1127 Myrtle St Elkhart IN 46515

CHISMARK, KURT MICHAEL, camera co. exec.; b. Boston, June 7, 1945; s. Albert Henry and Janet Elizabeth (Hanley) C.; B.S., Cornell U., 1967; M.B.A., Ga. State U., 1975; m. Elizabeth Crane Yoder, Feb. 28, 1970; children—Kristin Ann and Karin Scott (twins). Asst. buyer Dey Bros. & Co., Syracuse, N.Y., 1967-68; sales mgmt. trainee Carnation Co., Atlanta, 1972-73, New Eng. sales supr., Boston, 1973-75, asst. dist. mgr., Chgo., 1975-77; Midwest area mdse. mgr. Polaroid Corp., Chgo., 1977-78, Midwest spl. accounts mgr., 1978, N.W. dist. sales mgr. San Francisco, 1978—. Active YMCA Indian Princess Program, Glen Ellyn, Ill., 1976-77 Served to capt. Spl. Forces, U.S. Army 1968-72; Vietnam. Decorated Bronze Star medal, Bronze Star with 2 oak leaf clusters, Air medal, Army Commendation medal. Mem. Phi Gamma Delta Alumni. Republican. Roman Catholic. Home: 4673 Gatetree Circle Pleasanton CA 94566 Office: 875 Stanton Rd Burlingame CA 94010

CHISOLM, CHARLES SMITH, foundry exec.; b. Selma, Ala., Sept. 10, 1916; s. James Satterfield and Ernestine (Smith) C.; B.S. in Chem. Engring., Auburn (Ala.) U., 1938, M.S., 1939; postgrad. Birmingham So. Coll., 1940; m. Martha Elizabeth Gilbert, Nov. 6, 1942; children—Betsy Chisolm Silberman, John Grier, Catherine. Instr. chemistry Auburn U., 1939; with metall. dept. U.S. Steel Corp., 1939-41; supt. metallurgy and quality control Wheland Foundry div. N. Am. Royalties, Chattanooga, 1946-56, gen. mgr., 1956—; pres. Valley Farms, Selma, 1950—, Chisolm Corp., Selma, 1969—, Satterfield Co., Selma, 1970—, Peter Pan Industries, Lookout Mountain, Tenn., 1954—. Vice chmn. Lookout Mountain Planning Bd., 1968—. Served to lt. col. AUS, 1941-45. Registered profl. engr., Tenn.; registered asso. real estate broker, Tenn. Mem. Am. Soc. Metals, Am. Foundrymen's Soc. (nat. dir. 1973-77), ASTM, Omicrom Delta Kappa, Spades, Kappa Alpha. Presbyterian (ruling elder). Clubs: Mountain City (Chattanooga); Fairyland (Lookout Mountain) (dir.). Home: 1213 Peter Pan Rd Lookout Mountain TN 37350 Office: 1800 S Broad St Chattanooga TN 37401

CHISOLM, WILLIAM ANDERTON, investment banking co. exec.; b. N.Y.C., Dec. 6, 1924; s. William G. and Ruth Chisolm; A.B., Princeton U., 1945; m. Frances, May 25, 1961; children—Richard, Allison, Page, Elizabeth. Mag. dir. First Boston Corp., N.Y.C., 1947-80; v.p. A.G. Becker Inc., N.Y.C., 1980—. Home: 47 E 88th St New York NY 10028 Office: A G Becker Inc 55 Water St New York NY 10041

CHITWOOD, ROBERT HODSON, oil co. exec.; b. Pratt, Kans., Oct. 2, 1930; s. Joe Vern and Blanche Katherine (Hodson) C.; B.S. in Bus. Adminstrn., Okla. State U., 1952; grad. exec. devel. program Cornell U., 1970; m. Barbara Ann Johnson, Mar. 10, 1952; children—Catherine Chitwood Hurst, Thomas Randall, Nancy Chitwood Ryan, Amalie Ann. With Cities Service Co., Tulsa, 1952—, v.p. supply and transp., 1970-74, pres., dir. Cities Services Gas Co., 1974-76, exec. v.p. parent co., pres., petroleum products group, 1976—; pres. Cities Service Mid-East, Inc., Cities Service Mid-East Trading Co., Cities Service S&T Europe-Africa Co., Cities Service Trading Co., Grand Bassa Tankers Inc.; v.p., dir. Cities Service Internat., Inc.; dir. Cities Service Gas Co., CSG Exploration Co., First Nat. Bank and Trust Co., Oklahoma City. Bd. dirs. Industries for Tulsa, Inc.; trustee Philbrook Art Center, Holland Hall Sch. Served with AUS, 1952-53. Mem. Okla., Tulas chambers commerce, Nat. Petroleum Refiners Assn. (chmn. bd.), Am. Petroleum Inst., Mid-Continent Oil and Gas Assn., Okla. Petroleum Council. Republican. Episcopalian. Clubs: Internat. (Washington); Tulsa, So. Hills Country, Petroleum, Utica 21 (Tulsa); Beacon (Oklahoma City). Home: 2108 E 29th St Tulsa OK 74114 Office: PO Box 300 Tulsa OK 74102

CHIUSANO, CHARLES, mfg. and services co. exec.; b. Bklyn., Oct. 21, 1917; s. John and Margargt (Di Santi) C.; B.C.S., N.Y. U., 1938; m. Ethel Mary Sandin, Nov. 15, 1939; children—John, Charles, Christine, Thomas, Frank, James, Laura, Mark. Dir. indsl. relations Childs Co., 1939-50, v.p. personnel and indsl. relations, 1952-55; dir. personnel Hilton Hotels Corp., 1950-52, v.p. personnel and indsl. relations, 1963-70; v.p. ops. Holly Corp., 1955-63; v.p., gen. mgr. Sherman House, 1970-72; pres. Aldeco Corp., N.Y.C., 1972—, also dir.; pres. Janine Corp., N.Y.C., 1972—, Airline Delivery Services Corp., N.Y.C., 1972—; dir. Roll-A-Grill Corp.; cons. on hotel manpower requirements for Tunisia, U.S. Govt., 1965. Republican. Roman Catholic. Club: Pelham (N.Y.) Country. Home: 334 Corlies Ave Pelham NY 10803 Office: 60 E 42d St New York NY 10017

CHLUSKI, JOHN J., bus. exec.; b. Warsaw, Poland, Aug. 12, 1923; ed. in France and Eng., degrees in mercantile law, commerce and econs.; m. 1948; 1 son, John. From dir. planning and procurement U.K. ops. and gen. mgr. French ops. to pres. Massey Ferguson Industries, Ltd., and Massey Ferguson Inc., Massey Ferguson Ltd., Toronto, Ont., Can., 1947-67; group v.p. internat. ops., group v.p. Tractomotive group Allis Chalmers Corp., Milw., 1968-71; with ITT, 1972—, exec. asst. and pres. ITT Europe and group gen. mgr. automotive products Europe, 1972-73, v.p. ITT, 1977, sr. v.p. ITT and group exec. engineered products Europe, 1979—. Served with Brit. and U.S. paratroop forces, 1943-45. Office: ITT 320 Park Ave New York NY 10022*

CHMELIK, JAMES JOSEPH, retail exec.; b. Oak Park, Ill., June 28, 1930; s. Arthur Francis and Belle (Svejda) C.; B.S., U.S. Naval Acad., 1955; M.B.A., U. Chgo., 1963; M. Pub. Adminstrn., Am. U., 1968; m. Patricia Ann Kinsella, Oct. 18, 1958; children—William, James, Joseph, Thomas, Edward, Rosemarie, Anthony. Commd. 2d lt. U.S. Marine Corps, 1955, advanced through grades to maj., 1966, inf. officer, 1955-68; data processing officer, 1969-75, ret., 1975; controller Smithsonian Museum Shops, Washington, 1975-76, dir., 1976—. Bd. dirs. Urbana Civic Assn., 1978-80. Decorated Navy Commendation medal; recipient outstanding service award Am. Soc. Mil. Comptrollers, 1975. Mem. Nat. Retail Mchts. Assn., Met. D.C. Bd. Trade, Marine Corps Assn., Smithsonian Resident Assn., VFW. Roman Catholic. Clubs: Eaglehead Country (chmn. bd. 1979-80), K.C. Home: 2941 Green Valley Rd Ijamsville MD 21754 Office: NHB Room C222 10th and Constitution Ave NW Washington DC 20560

CHMIELEWICZ, JOSEPH STANLEY, banker; b. Webster, Mass., Nov. 30, 1915; s. John Alexander and Stepania Mary (Skrzypek) C.; student pub. schs., Webster. With J.P. Ivascyn Ins. Co., 1936-42; sports editor Webster Times, 1940-55; mem. Webster Bd. Assessors, 1944-56, treas., 1957—; trustee Webster Five Cents Savs. Bank, 1968—. Bd. dirs. ARC, Webster-Dudley Boys' Club. Mem. Mass. Assessors Assn., New Eng. Fin. Officers Assn., Treas.'s Assn. U.S. and Can., Polish Am. Youth Fedn. (pres. 1960), Polish Nat. Alliance. Democrat. Roman Catholic. Clubs: Polish Am. Citizens (Man of Year 1962), Elks, Eagles, K.C. (4 deg.), Exchange. Home: 31 Morris St Webster MA 01570 Office: Town Hall Main St Webster MA 01570

CHMIELINSKI, EDWARD ALEXANDER, electronics co. exec.; b. Waterbury, Conn., Mar. 25, 1925; s. Stanley and Helen C.; B.S., Tulane U., 1950; postgrad. Colo. U., 1965; m. Elizabeth Carew, May 30, 1946; children—Nancy, Elizabeth, Susan Jean. Vice pres., gen. mgr. Clifton Products, Litton Industries, Colorado Springs, Colo., 1965-67; pres. Memory Products div. Litton Industries, Beverly Hills, Calif., 1967-69, Bowmar Instruments, Can., Ottawa, Ont., 1969-73; gen. mgr. Leigh Instruments, Carleton Pl., Ont., 1973-75; pres., dir. Lewis Engring. Co., Naugatuck, Conn., 1975—; pres., dir. Liquidometer Corp., Tampa, Fla., 1975—. Pres., Acad. Water Bd., 1963-65; bd. dirs. United Way, Colorado Springs, 1965-67. Served with USN, 1943-46. Mem. Am. Soc. Mining, Metall. and Petroleum Engrs., Am. Mgmt. Assn., C. of C., Pres.'s Council, Pres.'s Assn., Am. Mfrs. Assn., IEEE.

CHO, KAZUNOBU, mfg. co. exec.; b. Tokyo, Japan, Mar. 2, 1930; s. Keijiro and Take (Takase) C.; student Miyakojima Tech. Coll., 1945-48; m. Yoshiko Sakuraba, Nov. 8, 1958; children—Kaori, Michiru. Spl. interpreter SCAP Civil Info. Center, Osaka, 1948-52; info. adviser USIA, Osaka, 1952-60, labor adviser, 1960-66; spl. asst. to mng. dir. Japan Tupperware Co., Ltd., Tokyo, 1966, exec. v.p., rep. dir., 1967-74, pres., rep. dir., 1974—; pres. North Pacific ops. Tupperware Internat., 1976—; dir. Dart Industries Hong Kong, Ltd., 1972. Home: 2-3 Oyama-cho Shibuya-ku Tokyo Japan Office: 3-23 Kioi-cho Chiyoda-ku Tokyo Japan also care Pegasus Trading Co 904 Chiao Shang Bldg 92-104 Queen's Rd Central Hong Kong

CHOI, JOHN T., financial exec.; b. Chong-Ju, Korea, Dec. 22, 1935; s. Dong Sun and Young Soon (Park) C.; B.A. in Law, Chong-Ju U., Korea, 1959; B.S. in Accounting, Temple U., 1965; M.B.A., U. Del., 1970; m. Judy Kee Won; children—David, Jonathan. Accountant, Triangle Publs., Inc., Phila., 1960-64, operation mgr., 1964-66; sr. budget analyst Glen Alden Corp., Dover, Del., 1966-69; sr. auditor RCA Corp., N.Y.C., 1969, audit supr., 1969-71, audit adminstr., 1971-74, audit mgr., 1974-75; controller factory owned distributorships Fedders Corp., Edison, N.J., 1975-76, group controller, air conditioning group, 1976-77, dir. ops. analysis, 1977-78; audit mgr. Becton Dickinson & Co., Paramus, N.J., 1978—; chmn. seminar Auditing and the Computer - How, 1972. Bd. govs. Phila. chpt. Inst. Internal Auditors, 1971-73; treas. pack 73 Boy Scouts Am., 1977—; deacon Princeton Korean Ch., 1978—. Co-editor: Audit Scope, 1968. Office: Mack Centre Dr Paramus NJ 07652

CHOMICZ, JOHN JOSEPH, JR., plastics mktg. co. exec.; b. New Haven, May 17, 1933; s. John Joseph and Anna (Zaniewski) C.; A.S., Quinnipiac Coll., 1954, B.S., 1956; postgrad. Mich. State U., 1966; m. Margaret D. MacDonald, July 13, 1974; children—Steven Mark, Mark John, Lynne Marie. Nat. sales mgr. vinyl products B.F. Goodrich Co., Akron, Ohio, 1958-67; gen. sales mgr. Joclin-Quantum, Inc., Wallingford, Conn., 1967-68; mktg. mgr. Harvey Hubbell, Inc., Newtown, Conn., 1969-74; pres. Custom Plastic Products, Madison, Conn., 1974—. Mem. Soc. Plastics Industry, Soc. Plastics Engrs. Home: 52 Forest Hills Dr Madison CT 06443

CHOMITZ, MORRIS A., engring. and constrn. co. exec.; b. Phila., Dec. 5, 1925; s. Mendel and Sarah C.; Sc.B. in Chem. Engring., MIT, 1946; M.S. in Chem. Engring., Drexel U., 1954; m. Nancy Ruth Goodbread, Mar. 26, 1950 (dec.); children—Kenneth, Martha, Jonathan. Research and devel. engr. Allied Chem. Co., Bridesburg, Pa., 1946-49; project engr. Kuljian Corp., Phila., 1949-59; plant mgr. Baldwin-Ehret-Hill, Valley Forge, Pa., 1959-65; with Day & Zimmermann Inc., engring. and constrn., Phila., 1965—, mgr. project engring., 1972—, v.p. engring., 1977-79, sr. v.p. engring., 1979—. Served to lt. (j.g.) USNR, 1943-46. Registered profl. engr., Pa., N.J., N.C., N.Y. Mem. Project Mgmt. Inst. Office: Day & Zimmermann Inc 1818 Market St Philadelphia PA 19103

CHONG, LUIS A., engring. co. exec.; b. Paita, Peru, S.A., May 14, 1930; s. Isaac and Maria Victoria (Leon) C.; came to U.S., 1948, naturalized, 1960; B.S. in Mech. Engring., U. Ill., 1952; postgrad. U. Mich.; grad. A.M.P., Harvard Bus. Sch., 1979; m. Vivian A. Juco, May 23, 1953; children—Ana, Louis, Michael, Mary, Catherine, Paul. Various engring. positions Cummins Engine Co., Columbus, Ind., 1959-65; with Curtiss Wright Corp., Woodridge and Caldwell, N.J., 1966-71; with Otis Elevator Co., N.Y.C., 1972—, v.p. engring., 1974—; corporate dir. tech. planning United Techs. Corp. Republican. Roman Catholic. Clubs: Farmington Woods Country, Darlington Racquet. Home: 10 Chestnut Dr Avon CT 06001 Office: United Techs Bldg Hartford CT 06101

CHOPPA, EUGENE DANIEL, JR., architect; b. Glens Falls, N.Y., Sept. 9, 1936; s. Eugene Daniel and Martha Electa (Phelps) G.; B.Arch., U. Fla., 1961; m. Nancy Woodcock, Sept. 10, 1960; children—Richard, Robert, John, Margaret Electa. With Kirkpatrick & Pierson, Gainesville, Fla., 1956-58; draftsman, designer Arthur Lee Campbell, Architect, Gainesville, 1959-60; designer Baker & Henry, Architect & Engr., Glens Falls, 1960; designer, job capt. Milton Lee Crandall, Architect, Glens Falls, 1961-66; designer, project architect, asso. Crandell Assos., Architects, Glens Falls, 1966-70, also individual practice as Eugene D. Choppa, Jr., Architect, 1965-70; partner Cushing, Choppa & Collara, Architects, Glens Falls, 1970-72, Cushing, Choppa Assos., Architects, Glens Falls, 1972-76; staff architect, constrn. mgr Kamyr Installations, Inc., Glens Falls, 1976—. Mem. bldg. com. YMCA; dir. Young Republican Club; pres. Bulldog Boosters; bd. dirs. local chpt. ARC, Friends of Crandall Library; mem. adv. com. Warren-Washington Counties Indsl. Devel. Commn.; v.p. Salmon Pond Club; chmn. com., asst. scoutmaster Boy Scouts Am.; bd. dirs., mgr. Gansevoort, Wilton & Moreau Little League. Cert. gen. contractor, Fla. Mem. AIA, N.Y. State Assn. Architects, TAPPI. Clubs: Rotary (v.p./treas.), Jaycees (dir.), Glens Falls Country (tournament dir.). Address: Kamyr Installations Inc Glens Falls NY 12801

CHOU, CHIN-YUAN, internat. trade co. exec.; b. Tsing Tao, China, Feb. 25, 1946; s. Zen-Tee and Shu-Fan (Shu) C.; came to U.S., 1971, naturalized, 1975; M.S., W. Coast U., 1974; m. Si-Ling Tsao, Sept. 28, 1974. Sales engr. Hwa Sheng Electronic Co., Inc., Taiwan, 1970-71; owner Roady's Restaurant, San Dimas, Calif., 1974—; pres., owner E & C Trading Co., West Covina, Calif., 1975—; owner, v.p. Technologies Unlimited Inc., West Covina, 1976—. Mem. Am. Mgmt. Assn. Club: Civitan. Office: 160 W Bonita Ave San Dimas CA 91773

CHOU, MARK, importer; b. Peking, China, Apr. 1, 1910; came to U.S., 1949; M. European History, San Francisco U., 1950; postgrad. U. Calif., Berkeley; m. Florence Fong Ling Siu, Sept. 10, 1955; children—Raymond, Samuel, Theodore, Jadine. Pres., Mark Chou Gallery, Inc., Skokie, Ill., 1950—; tchr. Chinese antiques, investment in Oriental antiques. Author: A Discourse on Hung Hsien Porcelain; Dictionary of Jade Nomenclature; contbr. articles on Chinese antiques to periodicals. Home: 9024 Tripp Ave Skokie IL 60076 Office: PO Box 425 Skokie IL 60076

CHOYKE, PHYLLIS MAY FORD, ceiling co. exec., editor; b. Buffalo, Oct. 25, 1921; d. Thomas Cecil and Vera (Buchanan) Ford; B.S. summa cum laude (Bonbright scholar), Northwestern U., 1942; m. Arthur Davis Choyke, Jr., Aug. 18, 1945; children—Christopher Ford, Tyler Van. Reporter, City News Bur., Chgo., 1942-43; reporter met. sect. Chgo. Tribune, 1943-44; feature writer OWI, N.Y.C., 1944-45; sec. Artcrest Products Co. Inc., Chgo., 1951-63; v.p. 1963—; founder, dir. Harper Sq. Press, Chgo., 1967—. Mem. Phi Beta Kappa. Clubs: Arts (chgo.). Editor: Gallery Series One/Poets, 1967; Gallery Series Two/Poets—Poems of the Inner World, 1968; Gallery Series Three/Poets (Levitations and Observations), 1970—; Gallery Series Four/Poets— I Am Talking about Revolution, 1973; Gallery Series Five/Poets-To an Aging Nation (with occult overtones), 1977; (with others) Apertures to Anywhere (poems), 1979. Home: 29 E Division St Chicago IL 60610 Office: 401 W Ontario St Chicago IL 60610

CHRIS, HARRY JOSEPH, archtl. co. exec.; b. Beaumont, Tex., Sept. 13, 1938; s. Harry Adam and Lucille Helen (Junca) C.; B.Arch., Tulane U., 1961; M.B.A., Memphis State U., 1969; m. Jimmie Lea Bowen, Sept. 21, 1966; children—James, William, Mary Elizabeth, Mark, Lisa. Architect, Tex. State Bldg. Commn., Austin, 1966-68, Holiday Inn Am., Memphis, 1968-69; v.p. Club Corp. Am., Dallas, 1969-74, dir., 1972-74; pres. Architectural Designers, Inc., Dallas, 1969-74, RYA Architects, Inc., Dallas, 1974-78, H.J. Chris Architects Inc., Dallas, 1978—, Exec. Clubs of Am., Dallas, 1978—. Served to lt. comdr. USNR, 1961-66. Registered architect, Colo., Fla., Ky., La., Mo., N.J., N.Y., Ohio, Tex. Mem. Irving C. of C., AIA. Roman Catholic. Clubs: Lancers, Trophy Club Country (Dallas); K.C. Home: 417 San Jose St Irving TX 75062 Office: 8300 Douglas Suite 731 Dallas TX 75225

CHRISTENSEN, DAVID ALLEN, corp. exec.; b. Brookings, S.D., Mar. 25, 1935; s. Swend A. and Florence E. C.; B.S. in Indsl. Engring., S.D. State U., 1957; m. Mary Jo Peterson, Mar. 27, 1972; children—Dan W., Karen J., Scott A., Kristi L., Kathy L., Kathy A. Indsl. engr. John Morrell & Co., Sioux Falls, S.D., 1960-62; successively indsl. engr., prodn. mgr., v.p., exec. v.p., pres. and chief exec. officer and dir. Raven Industries, Inc., Sioux Falls, 1962—; dir. Northwestern Nat. Bank of Sioux Falls, N.W. Bancorp., No. States Power Co., Webb Co., Falcon Plastics, Inc., Sioux Falls Community Hotel Co. Campaign chmn. Sioux Falls United Way, 1979; bd. dirs. Sioux Falls Arena Bd., Sioux Falls Downtown Devel. Corp. Served with C.E., AUS, 1958-60. Named Sportsman of Yr., B'nai B'rith, 1977. Mem. NAM (dir.), Sioux Falls C. of C. Republican. Lutheran. Club: Minnehaha Country. Office: 205 E 6th St Sioux Falls SD 57117

CHRISTENSEN, DON ALAN, venture capital investment co. exec.; b. Denver, June 4, 1930; s. Herbert U. and Anne M. Christensen; B.S. in Chem. Engring., M.I T., 1952; M.B.A., Harvard U., 1958; m. Doris M. Judson, July 18, 1952; children—David, Susan, Tracy, Kim. Founder, pres. Greater Washington Investors, Inc., Washington, 1960—; dir. Airtronics, Inc., Capex Corp., Designpak, Inc., AUDYXX Corp., Nat. Demographics, Ltd. Served with U.S. Army, 1952. Mem. Am. Chem. Soc., Am. Inst. Chem. Engrs. Home: 9609 Weathered Oak Ct Bethesda MD 20034 Office: 1015 18th St NW Washington DC 20036

CHRISTENSEN, DONN WAYNE, ins. exec.; b. Atlantic City, N.J., Apr. 9, 1941; s. Donald Frazier and Dorothy (Ewing) C.; B.S., U. Santa Clara, 1964; children—Donn Wayne, Lisa Shawn. West Coast div. mgr. Ford Motor Co., 1964-65; agt. Conn. Mutual Life Ins. Co., 1965-68; pres. Christensen & Jones, Mgmt. and Ins. Services, Inc., Los Angeles, 1968—; v.p. Research Devel. Systems Inc. Pres., Duarte Community Drug Abuse Council, 1972-75, Woodlyn Property Owners Assn., 1972-73. Recipient Man of year award Los Angeles Gen. Agts. and Mgrs. Assn., 1969, 72, 73, 74, 75, 76, 77, 79. Mem. Nat. Life Underwriters Assn., Calif. State Life Underwriters Assn., Soc. Pension Actuaries, Foothill Community Concert Assn. (pres. 1970-73). Office: 1015 Wilshire Blvd Los Angeles CA 90017

CHRISTENSEN, ERNEST MARTIN, mortgage cons.; b. Marblehead, Mass., Aug. 14, 1933; s. Harry Martin and Amy Viola (Snow) C.; A.A., Boston U., 1958, B.S. in Pub. Relations, 1960; M.A. in Coll. Union Adminstrn., N.Y. U., 1963; m. Gail Sandra Bruno, May 17, 1961; children—Hans Martin, Kirsten Amy. Adminstrv. asst. YMCA, Marblehead, 1949-51; asst. dir. student activities Boston U., 1960-62, counselor, 1961-62; adminstrv. asst. Loeb Student Center, N.Y. U., 1962, dir. Religious Center, 1962-63; dir. Coll. Union, Ithaca (N.Y.) Coll., 1963-65, dean of men, 1964-65; asso. prof. U. Man. (Can.) at Winnipeg, 1966-71, dir. students union, 1969-71; dir. Stony Brook Union, Faculty Student Assn., State U. N.Y. at Stony Brook, 1971-73; v.p., treas. Over the Bridge, Inc., 1974-78; dir. exec. com. Annunity Account A Great West Life Assurance Co. (Can.), 1967-70; owner Over the Bridge Real Estate, 1976-80; mortgage cons. Mortgage Assistances, 1980—; edn. cons. Brandon U. (Can.), 1967-68, Mt. Royal Jr. Coll. (Can.), 1968—, U. Man., 1966-71, U. Winnipeg, 1969—, Del. State Coll. (U.S.A.), 1969-70, Normandale State Jr. Coll. (U.S.A.), 1969—. Founding mem. Friends of the Kennedy Center; bd. dirs. Tompkins County (N.Y.) chpt. ARC; v.p. Belfast Improvement Group, 1977, pres., 1978; adv. mgr. Belfast Broiler Festival; treas. Walt. County YMCA, 1978-79. Served in USAF, 1952-56. Recipient Judson Rea Butler award Boston U., 1958. Mem. Am. Personnel and Guidance Assn. (abstractor Jour. Am. Coll. Student Personnel 1966-74), Assn. Coll. Unions (nat. v.p., nat. exec. com. 1969-71; chmn. finance, devel. com. 1973-74), Assn. Coll. Concert Mgrs., Am. Assn. Higher Edn., Nat. Assn. Realtors, Mid-Coast Bd. Realtors, Nat. Campers and Hikers Assn., D.A.V., Scarlet Key, Tau Mu Epsilon. Methodist. Clubs: Rotary, Masons (32 deg). Author: (with Keith G. Briscoe) Directory of College Unions, 1963; College Unions at Work, 1967; contbr. articles to profl. jours. Home: 12417 Hadley St Whittier CA 90601

CHRISTENSEN, HAROLD, ins. co. exec.; b. North Bergen, N.J., Jan. 7, 1919; s. Frederick John and Olivia C.; B.S., N.Y. U., 1941; postgrad. St. Lawrence U. Sch. Law; m. Mildred Timm, Sept. 25, 1948; children—Linda L., Gail O. With Nat. City Bank, N.Y.C., 1935-37; treas. Am. Surety Co. of N.Y., 1937-58; treas. Am. Life Ins. Co. of N.Y., 1958-64; v.p. AFIA Worldwide Ins., Wayne, N.J., 1964-73, exec. v.p., 1973-75, sr. exec. v.p., 1975-76, pres., 1976—; dir. Paribas N. Am. Corp. Dir., Nat. Fgn. Trade Council; trustee The Coll. of Ins., N.Y.C.; dir. Greater Paterson Gen. Hosp., Wayne, N.J. Served to maj., AUS, 1941-45. Fellow Decorated Purple Heart, Bronze Star.

Fellow Fin. Analysts Found.; mem. N.Y. Soc. Security Analysts. Club: Union League (N.Y.C.). Office: 1700 Valley Rd Wayne NJ 07470

CHRISTENSEN, HARVEY FRANCIS, ins. co. exec.; b. San Francisco, Jan. 15, 1926; s. Willard Henry and Love Imelda (Derivan) C.; engring. student U. Wash., 1943; LL.B., La Salle U., 1951; m. Pamela Gay Christensen; children—Joseph Willard, Lawrence Harvey, Nancy Marie, Patricia Anne. Various positions radio, stage show bus., San Francisco, 1932-43; purchasing agt. U.S. Naval Purchasing Office, 1947-50; mfrs. rep. H.F. Christensen Co., San Francisco, 1950-52; sales engr. Benjamin Electric Mfg. Co., San Francisco, 1952-65; various positions Mut. Benefit Life Ins. Co., also Guarantee Mut. Life Ins. Co., Orange County, Calif., 1965-70; pres. Assurance & Fin. Cons. Corp., Anaheim, Calif., 1970—; v.p.-sec. Continental Gen. Ins. Brokers Inc., Anaheim, 1976-79; sales mgr. Ins. Benefits Inc., Tustin, 1979—. Mem. Orange County Grand Jury, 1972, City of Fullerton (Calif.) Traffic Commn., 1973-76; pres. Holy Family Adoption Agy., Santa Ana, Calif., 1974-76. Served with USMCR, 1943-46. Decorated Purple Heart. Mem. Fullerton C. fo C. (dir. 1972-74), Ind. Ins. Agts. Assn., Western Assn. Ins. Brokers, Marines Meml. Assn. San Francsico (charter). Republican. Roman Catholic. Office: 150 S Prospect Ave Tustin CA 92680

CHRISTENSEN, PHILLIP REX, tax cons.; b. San Antonio, Feb. 29, 1944; s. LaVerne Edward and Blanche Kathryn (Bennett) C.; student public schs. Phoenix; m. Lorelei Ellen, Sept. 2, 1972; children—Glen, Rory, Lorelei L., Peter, Chrisann. Commissary foreman Dept. Army, Anchorage, 1967-71; mil. account rep., sales rep. Kraft Foods Co., Anchorage, 1971-72; adminstrv. pay technician Alaska Army Nat. Guard, Kodiak, 1972-76; pres. Christensen Enterprises, Inc., Anchorage, 1976—. Served with USAF, 1962-66. Mem. Nat. Soc. Public Accts., Alaska Soc. Ind. Accts. (chmn. tax research div., pres.). Club: Moose. Research in tax refund errors Alaska Dept. Revenue. Home: 4300 Arctic Blvd #49 Anchorage AK 99503 Office: 4660 Stuart Way Suite A Anchorage AK 99503

CHRISTENSEN, RICHARD JON, bus. cons.; b. St. Paul, Sept. 17, 1937; s. Walter Albert and Mary (Lyttle) C.; B.A., U. Minn., 1959; m. Virginia Lee Mundale, Mar. 14, 1970 (dec. 1980); children—Dana Lee, Robert Lyttle. With Kaiser Aluminum & Chem. Co., Mpls., 1959-63, Minn. World's Fair Pavilion, Mpls., N.Y.C., 1963-64, Gould, Inc., St. Paul, 1964-66, Knox Reeves Advt., Mpls., 1967, Padilla & Speer, Inc., N.Y.C., 1967-68, Keating/Christensen & Assos., Inc., N.Y.C., 1968-73; v.p., partner Holiday Inn Pky., New Haven, Conn., 1970—; pres. Woodmont Assos., Inc., 1980—, Community Assos. of Vt., 1978—; dir. New Haven Motor Inc., 1970—, Iron Horse Restaurant, Inc., Bristol, Conn., 1971—, P & R Plastics, 1979—. Mem. Woodridge (Conn.) Town Com. Recipient Distinguished Service award, Publicity Club of N.Y., 1968. Mem. Chimney Hill Owners Assn. (pres. 1975-77), Wilmington C. of C. (sec.), Alpha Tau Omega (pres. 1966). Clubs: Publicity (bd. dirs. 1969-71) (N.Y.C.); University (St. Paul). Home: Castle Hill Rd Wilmington VT 05363 Office: PO Box 415 Wilmington VT 05363

CHRISTESEN, JOHN DENIS, bus. scientist; b. N.Y.C., July 16, 1936; s. Charles Nicholas and Mary (Koza) C.; B.A., Lehman Coll., 1970; M.B.A., Pace U., 1975; postgrad. Columbia U., 1976—; m. Barbara Jeanne Suchy, Nov. 21, 1964. Credit mgr. Butler Lumber Co., 1961-62; fiscal, sales staff Lever Bros., 1962-67; controller Sales Cycle Circus, 1967-70; v.p. Putnam Bicycle Importers Co., 1970-74; curriculum chmn. bus. adminstrn., asst. prof. Westchester Community Coll., Valhalla, N.Y., 1975—, dir. Mgmt. Inst., 1978—; dir. Investment Properties Corp., Computweather Corp. Chmn. urban devel. corp. Town of Lewisboro (N.Y.) Housing Com., 1973-75; adv. bd. Univ. Indsl. Mgmt., 1980—. Mem. Am. Mgmt. Assn., Nat. Econs. Club, Nat. Assn. Bus. Economists, Acad. Mgmt., Am. Inst. Higher Edn., Am. Acad. Polit. and Social Scis., Assn. M.B.A. Execs., Alpha Beta Gamma (nat. chmn. 1978-79, nat. devel. chmn. 1980-81), N.Y. State Assn. Two-Year Colls. (exec. bd. 1980-82), Sigma Lambda, Delta Mu Delta, others. Republican. Roman Catholic. Author: (with R. Wunsch) The Complete Resume Handbook, 1967; Management Miscellany, 1978; Introduction to Business (film series), 1980. Home: Waccabuc Rd Goldens Bridge NY 10526 Office: Westchester Community Coll 75 Grasslands Rd Valhalla NY 10545

CHRISTIAN, EDWARD KIEREN, radio sta. exec.; b. Detroit, June 26, 1944; s. William Edward and Dorothy Miriam (Kieren) C.; student Mich. State U., 1962-64; B.A., Wayne State U., 1966; M.A., Central Mich. U., 1980; m. Judith Dallaire, Nov. 21, 1966; children—Eric, Dana. Mgr., John C. Butler Co., Detroit, 1968-69; nat. sales mgr. WCAR Radio, Detroit, WSUN Radio, St. Petersburg Fla., 1969-70; v.p., gen. mgr. WCER Radio, Charlotte, Mich., 1970-74; exec. v.p. and dir. broadcasting WNIC AM-FM, Detroit, and WNOR AM-FM, Norfolk, Va., 1974—; chmn. Arbitron Radio Adv. Council; vice chmn. Mut. Affiliates Adv. Council. Bd. dirs. Greater Dearborn Safety Council, 1976-80, Broadcast Rating Council, 1978-80; pres. Charlotte United Fund, 1973: del. Republican State Conv., 1974. Mem. Broadcast Fin. Mgmt. Assn., Dearborn C. of C. (dir.), Alpha Epsilon Rho (nat. adv. council). Home: 795 Lakeland St Grosse Pointe MI 48230 Office: 15001 Michigan Ave Dearborn MI 48126

CHRISTIAN, MACK ALLEN, JR., petroleum co. exec.; b. Waco, Tex., Jan. 15, 1925; s. Mack Allen and Lura M. (Stanford) C.; student Centenary Coll., 1942-43, Ga. Sch. Tech., 1943-44; B.B.A., U. Houston, 1948; m. Ellen Ann Phillips, Nov. 26, 1948; children—Michael, Catherine, Paul. Computer scientist Texaco, Inc., Houston, 1948-63; gen. mgr. computer sci. and services Ashland Oil, Inc. (Ky.), 1963—. Pres., Ashland Community Concert Assn. Served to 1st lt. AUS, 1943-46, 51-52; ETO. Mem. Data Processing Mgmt. Assn., Assn. Computing Machinery, Am. Petroleum Inst., Inst. Mgmt. Sci., Ashland Area C. of C. Mason (Shriner), Rotarian. Home: 1621 Beverly Blvd Ashland KY 41101 Office: 1409 Winchester Ave Ashland KY 41101

CHRISTIAN, MARVIN MARTIN, sheet metal mfg. co. exec.; b. Mayville, Wis., Mar. 7, 1929; s. Martin Herman and Leona Esther (Baertschy) C.; student public schs., Mayville; m. Betty Jane Bilgrien, Sept. 2, 1950; children—Sharon Ann, Mary Luise, Jeri Lynn, Tracy Lee. With Maysteel Products Co., Mayville, 1945-50; Mayville Welding Industries, 1950; with Mayville Metal Products div. Ogden Metal Co., 1950—, v.p. mfg., 1968-75, exec. v.p., 1975—. Elder, congregation chmn. St. Johns Lutheran Ch., 1977-80. Mem. Am. Mgmt. Assn. Republican. Club: Mayville Golf (dir. 1968—, pres. 1976-77). Home: 619 River Dr Mayville WI 53050 Office: 1st and Highland Ave Mayville WI 53050

CHRISTIAN, RICHARD CARLTON, advt. exec.; b. Dayton, Ohio, Nov. 29, 1924; s. Raymond A. and Louise (Gamber) C.; B.S. in Bus. Adminstrn., Miami U., Oxford, Ohio, 1948; M.B.A., Northwestern U., 1949; student Denison U., The Citadel, Biarritz Am. U.; m. Audrey Bongartz, Sept. 10, 1949; children—Ann Christian Carra, Richard Carlton. Mktg. analyst Nat. Cash Register Co., Dayton, 1948, Rockwell Mfg. Co., Pitts., 1949-50; exec. v.p. Marsteller Inc., Chgo., 1951-60, pres., after 1960, now chmn. bd.; dir., chmn. Bus. Publs. Audit of Circulation, Inc., 1969-75; dir. Wilmette Bank; dir., council Better Bus. Bur., Chgo.; speaker, author mktg., sales mgmt., mktg. research and advt. Past trustee Northwestern U.; trustee Nat. Coll. Edn.; chmn. exec. com. James Webb Young Fund Edn., U. Ill., 1962-75; adv. bd. Sch. Journalism U. Ga.; adv. council J. L. Kellogg Grad. Sch. Mgmt., Northwestern U. Served with inf., AUS, 1942-46; ETO. Decorated Bronze Star, Purple Heart; recipient Gov.'s award State of Ohio. Mem. Am. Mktg. Assn. (dir. 1953-54), Indsl. Mktg. Assn. (founder, chmn. 1951), Bus. Publs. Advt. Assn. (life mem. Chgo.; pres. Chgo. 1954-55, nat. v.p. 1955-58, chmn., dir. 1969-75, G.D. Crain, Jr. award 1977), Northwestern U. Bus. Sch. Alumni Assn. (founder, pres.), Am. Mgmt. Assn., Am. Acad. Advt. (1st disting. service award 1979), Am. Assn. Advt. Agys. (dir., chmn. 1976-77), Nat. Advt. Rev. Council (pres. 1976-77), Northwestern U. Alumni Assn. (nat. pres. 1968-70), Chgo. Assn. Commerce and Industry, Council on Fgn. Relations, Alpha Delta Sigma, Beta Gamma Sigma, Delta Sigma Pi. Phi Gamma Delta. Baptist (trustee). Clubs: Sky (N.Y.C.); Chicago, Mid-America, Executives, Economic (Chgo.); Kenilworth; Westmoreland Country (Wilmette, Ill.); Pine Valley Golf (Clementon, N.J.). Home: 132 Oxford Rd Kenilworth IL 60043 Office: Marsteller Inc 1 E Wacker Dr Chicago IL 60601

CHRISTIANSEN, CLARENCE HERBERT, lawyer; b. Inwood, Iowa, July 2, 1923; s. Andrew and Ruth (Renshaw) C.; student State U. Iowa, 1941-43, 46-48, B.A., 1947, J.D., 1948; student Purdue U., 1943; m. Donna Mae Geertz, Mar. 20, 1943; children—Joan Lee, Dana Andrew, Scott Charles. Admitted to Iowa bar, 1948, U.S. Supreme Ct. bar, 1960; practiced in Davenport, Iowa, 1948—; partner firm Christiansen & Lowry, 1948; asso. firm Lambach, Kopf, and Berger, 1949-53, partner, 1953-54; sr. partner Kopf & Christiansen, 1954-63, Christiansen, Goebel, & Zogg, 1963-64, Lambach, Christiansen, Stevenson & Goebel, 1964-70; pres., treas., dir. Kopf & Assos., Ltd., 1961-72, Davenport Builders Land Devel. Corp., 1962-69; sec., dir. Profl. Arts Bldg. Ltd., 1961-70, Steel Valley, Inc., 1965-66; pres., dir. Franchise Mgmt., Inc., 1965-72; asst. sec.-treas. Guardian Securities Ltd., 1965-66; gen. counsel, sec.-treas., dir. Life Securities Iowa, Inc. (name changed to Fin. Security Life Corp. 1978), 1964-72, gen. counsel, 1964—, v.p. 1977—; v.p., gen. counsel Regency Life Ins. Co., 1967-70; sec., treas., dir. Kolar Corp., 1960-79; sec., dir. Main at Locust Pharmacy, Inc., 1965-79, Main Prescription Shop, Inc., 1965-72; exec. v.p., treas., gen. counsel Regency Nat., Ltd. (name changed to Regency Fin. Group, Inc. 1978), 1969-72, gen. counsel, 1972—, v.p., 1977—; exec. v.p., treas., gen. counsel, dir. Fin. Holding Corp., 1968-78; dir. Am. Security Life Ins. Co., 1967-70, pres., gen. counsel, 1968-70; sec., gen. counsel, dir. BEC Products, Inc., 1971-79, BEC Pressure Controls Corp., 1962-80, Electro Plasma, Inc., 1973—, BEC Industries, Ltd., 1975—; gen. counsel Fin. Security Life Ins. Co., 1969—, v.p., 1977—. Legal officer, law mem. Phys. Evaluation Bd. and trial counsel, Camp Pendleton, Calif., 1950-51. Mem. Am. (vice chmn. automobile com. ins. sect. 1965-66, life ins. com. 1970—), Fed. (securities com. 1977—), Iowa, Scott County bar assns., Fedn. Ins. Counsel (life ins. com. 1976, vice chmn. 1979—), Am. Legion, Delta Tau Delta, Gamma Eta Gamma. Clubs: Optimist (pres. Davenport 1950-51, Moline 1974-75), Elks, Nat. Lawyers, Davenport, Univ. Athletic, Masons (32 deg.), Shriners. Lutheran. Home: Carriage Club #4 3215 E Locust St Davenport IA 52803 Office: 103 Profl Arts Bldg Davenport IA 52803

CHRISTIE, DAVID GEORGE, ins. co. exec.; b. Glen Ridge, N.J., June 25, 1930; s. Francis Johnston and Catherine Fisher (Somes) C.; student Rutgers U., 1950-52; m. Diane Grace Wettyen, Mar. 23, 1950; children—Lindsey Diane, Mark Wettyen, Meredith Leigh. Asst. U.S. mgr. Union Re-ins. Co., Zurich, Switzerland, U.S. Br., 1956-64; v.p. Am. Re-Ins. Co., N.Y.C., 1964-71; v.p. Towers, Perrin Forster & Crosby Inc., N.Y.C., 1971-78; pres. Rochdale Ins. Co., exec. v.p. United Americas Ins. Co., sr. v.p., dir. Duncanson & Holt Inc., N.Y.C., 1979—; dir. Rochdale Ins. Co. Served with U.S. Army, 1953-54. Republican. Presbyterian. Club: Wall St. Home: 43 Rosedale Ln Princeton NJ 08540 Office: 99 John St New York NY 10038

CHRISTIE, GEORGE NICHOLAS, economist; b. Wilmington, N.C., Nov. 2, 1924; s. Nicholas and Helen (Lymberis) C.; B.B.A., U. Miami, 1948; M.B.A., N.Y. U., 1956, Ph.D., 1963; m. Mary Danatos, July 22, 1951; children—Sultana Helen, Stephanie Hope, Susan Adrianne, Sandra Alicia, Gregory Nicholas. With Dun and Bradstreet, Inc., N.Y.C., 1949-61, staff bus. writer, 1959-61; asso. dir. Credit Research Found., asst. dir. edn. Nat. Assn. Credit Mgmt., N.Y.C., 1961-63; asst. sec. credit policy com., small bus. credit com. Am. Bankers Assn., N.Y.C., 1963-64, sec., 1964-67; v.p., dir. research Credit Research Found., 1967-80, sr. v.p., 1980—; asso. dir. Grad. Sch. Credit and Financial Mgmt., dir. Nat. Inst. of Credit, 1967—. Instr. N.Y. Inst. Credit; lectr. Dartmouth, Stanford U.; asso. prof. L.I. U.; adminstr. 2d year banking course Stonier Grad. Sch. Banking, Rutgers U. Served with AUS, 1943-46. Mem. Am. Econ. Assn., Am. Fin. Assn., Fin. Mgmt. Assn. Contbr. articles to profl. publs. Home: 65 Nassau Rd Great Neck NY 11021 Office: 3000 Marcus Ave Lake Success NY 11042

CHRISTIE, JAMES CLAYTON, banker; b. Maryville, Mo., June 19, 1939; s. Virgil Glen and Harriet Winifred (Todd) C.; B.S., Kan. State U., 1962. M.B.A., U. So. Calif., 1971; m. Janice Lee Edwards, June 22, 1963; children—Jeffrey Charles, Christopher James. With Bank of Am. NT & SA, N.Y.C., 1962—, br. ops. mgr., Los Angeles, 1966-71, equipment leasing ops., acctg. and mktg. exec., So. and No. Calif., 1971-77, mgr. leasing mktg. for Calif., San Francisco, 1971-77, Asia Div. ship fin. officer, Tokyo, 1977-78, dep. head N. Am. ship fin. sect., N.Y.C., 1978-80, v.p., sect. head agribus. sect., Chgo., 1980—; cons. in field. Served with USNG, 1956-66. Mem. Am. Bankers Assn., Calif. Bankers Assn. Home: 123 W North St Hinsdale IL 60521 Office: 233 S Wacker Dr Chicago IL 60606

CHRISTIE, PETER GRAHAM, architect, planner; b. Balt., Nov. 8, 1920; s. Alexander Graham and Flora Ida (Brown) C.; student engring. Johns Hopkins U., 1939-40; student in architecture M.I.T., 1941; B.S. in Architecture, U. Va., 1943; M.Arch., Harvard U., 1949; children—Alison Graham Tucker, Jean Alden Farquhar, Gillian Turner Sears. Designer, Lucius R. White, architect, 1946-47; designer, architect Alex S. Cochran, architect, 1947-48, 49-50; partner Wilson & Christie, asso. architects, 1950-63; Christie, Niles and Andrews, 1963-67; partner The Archtl. Affiliation, Towson, Md., 1969-74; pres. TAA Inc (The Archtl. Affiliation), Towson, 1974—. Bd. dirs. Towson Devel. Corp., 1979—. Served with USAAF, 1943-46. Recipient archtl. awards Balt. C. of C., 1957, 58; registered architect, Pa., Del., D.C., Md. Mem. Am. Arbitration Assn., Am. Inst. Archaeology, Am. Inst. Planners, Constrn. Specifications Inst. (asso.), Citizens Planning and Housing Assn., Asso. Home Builders Assn. Md., Baltimore County C. of C., Internat. Hosp. Fedn., Nat. Fire Protection Assn. (sectional com. on residential occupancies), Engrs. Soc. Balt., Urban Land Inst., Balt. Mus. Art, Soc. Fire Protection Engrs., Royal Inst. Brit. Architects, Soc. Coll. and Univ. Planners, Alpha Delta Phi. Republican. Episcopalian. Club: L'Hirendalle. Prin. works include: Fire and Police Hdqrs., Baltimore County, 1954, 60, Greater Balt. Med. Center, 1966, Towson Plan, 1968, Merc. Bldg., Towson, 1970, Decker Coll. Center, Western Md. Coll., 1977. Home: 1905 Indian Head Rd Ruxton MD 21204 Office: TAA Inc 102 W Pennsylvania Ave Towson MD 21204

CHRISTIN, VIOLET MARGUERITE, banking cons.; b. Chgo., Oct. 4, 1903; d. Charles A. and Eva M. (Bosse) C.; student Northwestern U., 1936-37, Am. Inst. Banking, 1955. With Nat. Bank Austin, Chgo., 1922-76, asst. sec., 1953-57, sec., 1957-65, sec. mktg. com., 1977-79, sec., asst. v.p., 1965-76, cons., 1976—. Mem. Am. Inst. Banking, Ill. Bankers Assn. (50 Yr. Club), Assn. Chgo. Bank Women, Nat. Assn. Bank Women, Chgo. Fin. Advertisers (dir., treas.; Eagle award 1977). Clubs: Chgo. Press, Chgo. Advt., Execs. (Chgo.). Home: 805 N Grove Ave Oak Park IL 60302

CHRISTMAN, LARRY ALAN, hosp. fin. officer; b. Galion, Ohio, Sept. 24, 1949; s. Lewis T. and Evelyn M. (Holderness) C.; B.A. in Econs. and Bus. Adminstrn. cum laude (Hartke scholar), Capital U., 1971; m. Mary Beth Slattery, Aug. 23, 1975; 1 dau., Jennifer Ann. Staff auditor, sr. auditor, supr. Medicare audits Blue Cross of Central Ohio, Columbus, 1971-75; dir. cost and reimbursement, dir. fiscal services Ohio State U. Hosps., Columbus, 1975-79; chief fin. officer Lancaster (Ohio)-Fairfield County Hosp., 1979—. C.P.A., Ohio. Mem. Am. Inst. C.P.A.'s, Ohio Soc. C.P.A.'s, Central Ohio Hosp. Fin. Mgmt. Assn. (past pres., dir.), Nat. Assn. Accts., Columbus Hosp. Fin. Officers (chmn.), Tau Pi Phi. Lutheran. Club: Masons. Home: 1350 Coonpath Rd NE Lancaster OH 43130 Office: 401 N Ewing St Lancaster OH 43130

CHRISTOPH, HERMAN ATANASSOW, bus. exec.; b. Plovdiv, Bulgaria, Oct. 30, 1938; came to U.S., 1978; M. Electronic and Precision Mechanics, U. Sofia, 1962; 1 son, Frank A. Gen. mgr. systems services Olympia Office Machines, Italy, 1968-69; product mgr. Teleprint, Europe and West Germany, 1969-71; sales mgr. ITEL Corp., West Germany, 1971-72; pres. and gen. mgr. Central Europe, DATA 100 Corp., 1972-78; chmn. bd., pres. BELLCOM Corp., Los Angeles, 1979—. Mem. Fgn. Trade Assn. So. Calif., Century City C. of C. Contbr. articles on current computer bus. to trade and internat. jours. Home: 9670 High Ridge Dr Beverly Hills CA 90210 Office: 2049 Century Park E Los Angeles CA 90067

CHRISTOPHER, ANTHONY DOMENIC, mfg. co. exec.; b. Revere, Mass., June 10, 1918; s. John Anthony and Lena Evelyn (Church) C.; student Northeastern U., 1939-41, Northwestern U., 1968-69; m. Floy Gene Mangold, Apr. 13, 1957; children—Kathleen (Mrs. Louis P. Lalli), John A., Anthony Domenic. Commd. ensign USN, 1941, advanced through grades to capt., 1961; ret., 1963; exec. v.p. Murphy Leasing Co., Long Beach, Calif., 1963-68; v.p. Cruttenden & Co., Inc., Newport Beach, Calif., 1968-70; asst. to pres. Raypak, Inc., Westlake, Calif., 1970-71; v.p. Cruttenden, Gust & Merhab, Inc., Newport Beach, 1972-76; partner Computerized Alarm Systems Co., Newport Beach, 1976—; v.p. A & J Mfg. Co. Trustee, Mens Council, Our Lady Queen of Angels Ch. Decorated D.F.C., Air medal. Mem. Sales and Mktg. Execs. Internat. (v.p. 1964-67), Navy League (pres. council 1966-68). Republican. Roman Catholic. Rotarian. Home: 1233 Outrigger Dr Corona Del Mar CA 92625 Office: 14131 Franklin Ave Tustin CA 92680

CHRISTOPHER, GEORGE ALEXANDER, real estate exec.; b. Hamilton, Ont., Can., Aug. 15, 1917; s. Alexander George and Ethel Fern (McMaster) C.; came to U.S., 1935, naturalized, 1975; B.A.E., Syracuse U., 1941; B.Sc.M.E., Royal Mil. Coll., Kingston, Ont., 1943; m. Lillian Susan Terriah, Oct. 24, 1942 (dec.); children—Alexis Elizabeth, Martha Ann, Robert George. With G.A. Christopher Assos.—Architects & Engrs., St. Catharines, Ont., 1950-60; pres. Century Utilities Inc., W. Palm Beach, Fla., 1968—; sr. v.p. Cenrill Communities Inc., W. Palm Beach, 1968—; cons. engr. builder adv. bd. Gen. Electric. Corp. Served with Royal Canadian Engrs., 1942-46. Named Builder of Year, Sertoma, 1951, recipient Distinguished Service award, 1960; Developer award Fortune, 1972. Mem. Nat. Assn. Home Builders, Ont. Assn. Profl. Engrs. Republican. Episcopalian. Address: Cenvill Communities Inc North Haverhill Rd West Palm Beach FL 33406

CHRISTOPHERSON, WESTON, retail chain co. exec.; b. Walum, N.D., May 5, 1925; s. Carl and Ermie Marion (Larsen) C.; B.S., U. N.D., 1949, J.D., 1951; m. Myrna Louise Christensen, June 8, 1951; children—Mia Karen, Mary Louisa, Kari Marie. Admitted to N.D. bar, 1951, Ill. bar, 1952; with Jewel Cos., Inc., Chgo., 1951—, v.p., 1963-70, pres., 1970—, chief exec. officer, 1979—, also dir.; dir. Ill. Bell Telephone, GAJX Corp., Ill. Tool Works, Borg-Warner, Aurrera, S.A., Mexico City. Bd. dirs. Food Mktg. Inst., Children's Meml. Hosp., Lake Forest Hosp.; trustee U. Chgo. Presbyterian. Clubs: Economic, Chicago, Onwentsia, Old Elm, Commercial, Commonwealth. Home: 1696 S Oak Knoll Dr Lake Forest IL 60045 Office: 5725 NE River Rd Chicago IL 60631

CHRONLEY, JAMES ANDREW, fast food co. exec.; b. Springfield, Mass., July 31, 1930; s. Robert Emmett and Eleanor Agnes (Sullivan) C.; A.B., Brown U., 1952; student U. R.I., 1963; m. Monique Delpech, July 29, 1955; children—Mary E., James M., Jean L., Patricia, Joseph P., John P., Robert E. Dir. real estate Atlantic Richfield Co., Los Angeles, 1954-74; v.p. real estate restaurant group Marriott Corp., Washington, 1974-78; v.p. real estate Burger Chef Systems, Inc., Indpls., 1978-80, exec. v.p., 1980—. Pres., NACORE Restaurant Group, 1978, Md. chpt., 1978, Ind. chpt., 1979. Served with U.S. Army, 1952-54. Decorated Am. Spirit Honor medal, 1953; lic. real estate broker, sr. rev. appraiser. Mem. Nat. Assn. Corp. Real Estate Execs., Am. Right of Way Assn., Internat. Council Shopping Centers, Nat. Assn. Rev. Appraisers. Roman Catholic. Club: K.C. Office: 3500 DePauw Blvd Indianapolis IN 46268

CHRUSZ, PHILIP MITCHELL, retail chain exec.; b. Malden, Mass., Aug. 23, 1942; s. Joseph Miller and Eileen Jarrett (Reardon) C.; B.S. in Bus. Adminstrn., Northeastern U., 1969; m. Dianne Elaine DiStefano, June 24, 1967; children—Victoria, Joseph, Erica. Sr. auditor Coopers and Lybrand, Boston, 1969-71; v.p. mdse. controller, asst. to sr. v.p. fin., asst. controller, mgr. accounts payable, asst. to corp. controller, fin. control mgr. Zayre Corp., Framingham, Mass., 1971-78; v.p., controller Grossman's, Braintree, Mass., 1978—. Mem. Westford Indsl. Devel. Financing Authority, 1975-79; founder, pres. Westford Pop Warner Football Assn., 1973-79; pres. Wachusett Pop Warner Football Assn., 1975-77. Served with USMC, 1961-64. Mem. Nat. Assn. Accts. (dir. Mass. Route 128 chpt. 1974-76, Most Valuable Mem.-Spl. Achievement award 1975), Northeastern U. Alumni Assn. (pres. 1977-78, treas. 1974-77, chmn. steering com. on athletics 1977—). Roman Catholic. Club: Varsity (pres. 1974-76) (Northeastern U.). Home: 201 Bolas Rd Duxbury MA 02332 Office: 200 Union St Braintree MA 02184

CHU, ERNEST DAVID, high tech. and biomed. instrument co. exec.; b. N.Y.C., Sept. 15, 1946; s. Philip Mei Bao and Esther M. (Tang) C.; student U. Delhi (India), 1966-67; B.A. cum laude, Amherst Coll., 1968; postgrad. Columbia U., 1968-69; m. Rosalind M. Hale, Feb. 13, 1972 (div.); children—Christopher James, Jonathan Peter. Staff writer Wall St. Jour., Dow Jones News Service, N.Y.C., 1968-69; account exec. Carter, Berlind & Weill, N.Y.C., 1969-71; spl. asst. to exec. com. Walters, Yeckes & Gallant Co., 1971-72, v.p., 1972-73; allied mem. N.Y. Stock Exchange, 1972-73; sr. v.p., dir. Danes Cooke & Keleher, Inc., N.Y.C., 1973-76; v.p., mem. exec. com. Roussel Capital Corp., N.Y.C., 1976-77; chmn. bd., pres. Ernest Chu Assos., 1976—; v.p. fin., treas. Haber Inc., Towaco, N.J.; v.p., dir.

Sepradyne Corp., Towaso, N.J., 1979—; dir. various cos.; cons. in field. Active United Cerebral Palsy, 1974-76; bd. dirs. Nat. Com. Am. Fgn. Policy, 1979—; mem. alumni scholarship com. Amherst Coll.; bd. dirs. Orgn. Chinese Ams., Inc., 1976-79, v.p., 1977-79. Recipient Peace prize Lions Internat., 1966. Mem. Am. Profl. Platform Tennis Assn. (pro adv. bd. 1977-79), Asia Soc., Asian Mgmt. Bus. Assn. (chmn., chief exec. officer 1979-80), Amherst Alumni Assn. (dir. 1975—). Congregationalist. Clubs: Masons, Shriners. Contbg. author: Guide to Venture Capital Sources, 4th edit.; author: (with others) Winning Platform Tennis, Contemporary Platform Tennis; also articles; co-editor Valley Review of Books, 1968. Office: 470 Route 202 Towaco NJ

CHU, JEFFREY CHUAN, electronic data processing cons.; b. Tientsin, China, July 14, 1919; s. Yao and Ven-yl (Tang) C.; student U. Shanghai (China), 1938-40, Ill. Inst. Tech., 1950, Northwestern U., 1952; B.S., U. Minn., 1942; M.S., U. Pa., 1945; children—Lynnet (Mrs. Franz Helbig), Bambi (Mrs. Michael Ree), Deirdre. Came to U.S., 1940, naturalized, 1948. Engr. Philco Corp., Phila., 1942-43, engr. Reeves Instrument Co., N.Y.C., 1947-49; research asso. U. Pa., Phila., 1943-47; sr. scientist Argonne Nat. Lab., Chgo., 1949-56; dir. engring. Univac div. Sperry Rand Corp., Blue Bell, Pa., 1956-62; v.p. Electronic Data Processing div. Honeywell, Inc., Wellesley Hills, Mass., 1962-69, v.p. planning and devel. Honeywell Computer & Communication Group, Waltham, Mass., 1969-70, v.p. strategical planning Honeywell Information Systems, Inc., Waltham, 1970-71, v.p. license operations, 1971-73; sr. v.p. N.Am. marketing operations Wang Labs., Inc., Tewksbury, Mass., 1973-75; pres., chief exec. officer Sanders Tech. Systems, Inc., Amherst, N.H., 1980—; adv. Nat. Computer and Tech. Commn., Peoples' Republic of China. Bd. dirs. Tiao Tung U., Shanghai, China; trustee Moore Sch., U. Pa. Fellow IEEE; hon. mem. Chinese Acad. Social Scis. Home: 10 Baldwin Circle Weston MA 02193 Office: PO Box 1226 Nashua NH 03061

CHUCK, WALTER G(OONSUN), lawyer; b. Wailuku, Maui, T.H., Sept. 10, 1920; s. Hong Yee and Aoe (Ting) C.; Ed.B., U. Hawaii, 1941; J.D., Harvard, 1948; m. Marian Chun, Sept. 11, 1943; children—Jamie Allison, Walter Gregory, Meredith Jayne. Navy auditor, Pearl Harbor, 1941; field agt. Social Security Bd., 1942; labor law insp. Terr. Dept. Labor, 1943; admitted to Hawaii bar, 1949; law clk. Ropes, Gray, Best, Coolidge & Rugg, 1948; asst. pub. prosecutor City and County of Honolulu, 1949; with Fong, Miho & Choy, 1950-53; mem. Fong, Miho, Choy & Chuck, 1953-58; practicing individually, Honolulu, 1958-65; partner firm Chuck & Fujiyama, 1965-74, Chuck, Wong & Tonaki, 1974-76, Chuck & Pai, 1976-79, Walter G. Chuck & Assos., 1976—; dir. Pacific Guardian Life Ins. Co., Ltd.; treas. M. & W, Inc.; gen. partner Tripler Warehousing Co., Kapalama Investment Co.; dir. Pacific Resources, Inc., Gasco, Inc., Ala Moana Volkswagen, Inc., Princess Pauahi Coffee Shop, Inc., Hawaiian Ind. Refinery, Inc., Tongg Pub. Co. Ltd. Dist. magistrate Dist. Ct. Honolulu, 1956-63; Hawaii Employment Relations Bd., 1955-59; dir. Nat. Assn. State Labor Relations Bd., 1957-61; chief clk. Ho. of Reps., 1951, 53; govt. appeal agt. SSS, 1953-72; clk. of senate State of Hawaii, 1959-61; mem. Jud. Council, State of Hawaii, Dir. YMCA, Honolulu Theatre for Youth. Served as captain inf. Hawaii Territorial Guard. Fellow (dir.) Internat. Acad. Trial Lawyers; mem. Bar Assn. Hawaii (pres.). Am. (ho. of dels.), Hawaii bar assns. (mem. exec. com., jud. appointment com.), Asso. Students U. Hawaii, Chinese C. of C., Internat. Soc. Barristers, Newcomen Soc. N.Am., Law-Sci. Inst. Republican. Clubs: Waialae Country (pres., dir.); Pacific; Oahu Country. 2691 Aaliamanu Pl Honolulu HI 96813 Office: Suite 200 1022 Bethel St Honolulu HI 96813

CHUD, HARRY STEPHEN, acct.; b. Cambridge, Mass., Dec. 29, 1942; s. J. Morris and Minnie Chud; B.S. in Acctg., Pa. State U., 1964; cert. fin. planner Coll. for Fin. Planning, 1977; m. Faye Lynn Schwartz, July 30, 1972; children—Melissa Anne, Heather Stephanie. With Arthur Anderson & Co., Phila., 1967, Arthur Young & Co., Ft. Worth, 1970-71; pvt. practice acctg. as Harry Stephen Chud, C.P.A., Ft. Worth, 1971—. Served from lt. to capt. U.S. Army, 1964-66, 68-70. C.P.A., Tex. Mem. Am. Inst. C.P.A.'s, Tex. Soc. C.P.A.'s, Inst. Cert. Fin. Planners, Tex. Inst. Cert. Fin. Planners, Internat. Assn. Fin. Planners, Ft. Worth Execs. Assn., Arts Orgn. Jewish. Home: 4821 Overton St Fort Worth TX 76133 Office: 4210 W Vickery St Fort Worth TX 76107

CHUKS-ORJI, CHARLES EJIMOFOR, mfg. co. exec.; b. Enugu, Nigeria, Nov. 21, 1940; s. Orji and Maria (Nneze) (Nwachukwu); B.A., U. San Francisco, 1964, M.B.A., 1968; Ph.D., Calif. Christian U., Los Angeles, 1978. Came to U.S., 1960, naturalized, 1968. Ins. staff Golden State Mut. Ins. Co., Los Angeles, 1968-69, staff mgr., 1969-71; owner, operator franchise McDonald's, Oakland, Calif., 1971—; founder, owner Milanco Export Corp., Oakland, 1976—; dir. McDonald's Operators of Oakland, Unux Exco Co.; pres. Chuks-Orji Consol. Services, Oakland, 1977—; dir. Chuks-Orji Fin. and Ins. Co., Oakland, 1979—; chmn. exec. com. Macon's Group of Cos. Ltd., 1979—; group dir. Macon's Group (U.K.) Ltd., 1979—. Mem. Am.-Nigerian C. of C. Republican. Roman Catholic. Rotarian. Home: 919 45th St PO Box 3001 Oakland CA 94609 Office: McDonald's 4514 Telegraph Ave Oakland CA 94609

CHURCHILL, WILLIAM LEONARD KEY, constrn. equipment rental and service co. exec.; b. Roanoke, Va., Feb. 26, 1948; s. Robert Carr and Barbara Ann (Key) C.; B.A. in Bus. Mgmt., Coll. of William and Mary, 1970; m. Cheryl Gwin, Dec. 12, 1965; children—Gwin Ann, William. With Nat. Park Service, Williamsburg, Va., 1968-70; regional mgr. 3M Co., Roanoke, 1970-71; v.p. Churchill's Inc., Roanoke, 1972-79, pres., 1980—; dir., officer Designers II, Inc. Active Little League Athletics, Roanoke; vestryman St. John's Episcopal Ch., Roanoke. Mem. Soc. Advancement of Mgmt., Nat. Home Builders Assn., Associated Gen. Contractors, Portable Sanitation Assn. Internat. (past pres.). Republican. Episcopalian. Clubs: Roanoke Country, Squires. Home: 2905 Wycliffe Ave Roanoke VA 24014 Office: 1015 Rorer Ave Roanoke VA 24016

CHURCHMAN, JOSEPH BRUCE, corp. exec.; b. Dover, Del., Aug. 8, 1936; s. Joseph Emanuel and Mary Theresa (Roth) C.; B.S. in Accounting, Goldey Beacom Bus. Coll., Wilmington, Del., 1962; B.S. in Bus. Adminstrn., Ind. U., 1969; m. Madeline Jane Pugh, Feb. 16, 1956; children—Michele Lynne, Laura Carol, J. Bruce. Auditor, State of Del., 1958-59; plant accountant Tyler Refrigeration div. Clark Equipment Co., Smyrna, Del., 1959-64, asst. controller Tyler div., Niles, Mich., 1964-68, controller div., 1968-72; v.p., dir. Ardco, Inc., Chgo., 1972-75; mgr. corp. accounting Alco Standard Corp., Valley Forge, Pa., 1975-76, mgr. Alco Data Services, King of Prussia, Pa., 1976-79; exec. v.p. Alco Health Services Group, Inc., Devon, Pa., 1979—. Bd. dirs. Niles Day Care Center, 1968-72. Served with AUS, 1955-57. Recipient Spoke award Del. Jaycees, 1960. Mem. Fin. Execs. Inst., Nat. Assn. Accountants, Soc. Mgmt. Info. Systems. Club: Executives (Chgo.). Office: PO Box 959 Valley Forge PA 19482

CHUTORANSKY, PETER, JR., research chem. engr.; b. Framingham, Mass., May 18, 1941; s. Peter and Mary Frances (Gudzinowicz) C.; B.S., Worcester Poly. Inst., 1963, Ph.D. (Exxon Research Grantee 1963-67), 1968; m. Jacquelyn Ann McPartlen, Sept. 7, 1963; children—Elizabeth Mary, Peter III, Alexandra Rachel. Engr., Pratt and Whitney Aircraft, East Hartford, Conn., 1963; research chem. engr. Mobil Research and Devel. Corp., Paulsboro Lab. (N.J.), 1967-77; asso. engr. Mobil Chem. Corp., Edison Labs. (N.J.), 1977-80; venture mgr. Mobil Adminstrv. Service Co., Northeast Computer Center, Princeton, N.J., 1980—; adj. asst. prof. Rutgers U., 1978—. Pres. PTA, 1973-75, ch. council, 1973-75. Served to capt. U.S. Army, 1967-69. Mem. Am. Inst. Chem. Engrs. (chmn. So. Jersey Sect. 1974), Digital Equipment Corp. Users Soc., Sigma Xi, Alpha Tau Omega Alumni Assn. (treas. 1963-67). Roman Catholic. Contbr. articles on catalysis, kinetics, computers to profl. publs. Home: 12 Warner Dr Somerville NJ 08876 Office: PO Box 1025 Princeton NJ 08540

CHYLA, DAVID RAYMOND, exec. search co. exec.; b. Chgo., July 28, 1944; s. Raymond Walter and Helen Marie (Gradek) C.; B.S. in Chemistry, Purdue U., 1966; postgrad. Law Sch., U. Notre Dame, 1966-68; M.B.A., Ind. U., 1969; profl. acctg. cert. Northwestern U., 1970; m. JoAnne Marie Jalovecky, June 11, 1966; children—Kimberly Anne, Stacy Lynn. Sr. acct. Arthur Young & Co., Chgo., 1969-72; analyst Gould, Inc., Chgo., 1972-73; mgr. Peat, Marwick, Mitchell & Co., Chgo., 1973-76; v.p. William H. Clark Assos., Inc., Chgo., 1976—; asso. prof. Keller Grad. Sch. mt., Chgo., 1975—. C.P.A., Ill. Mem. Am. Inst. C.P.A.'s, Assn. Assn. Exec. Recruiting Consultants, Ill. Assn. Exec. Recruiting Consultants, Ill. Soc. C.P.A.'s, Hazel Crest Jaycees (charter, treas. 1974-75). Clubs: Young Execs., University (Chgo.). Office: 200 E Randolph Dr Suite 7912 Chicago IL 60601

CHYTROWSKI, ALLAN M., investment banker; b. Pszow, Poland, June 4, 1931; came to U.S., 1965, naturalized, 1972; s. Albert and Wanda (Trzoska) C.; B.A. in Econs., U. Cracow (Poland), 1953, M.B.A., 1955; Ph.D. in Polit. Econs. with great distinction, U. Vienna, 1965; m. Julie A.R. Dubach, June 27, 1959; 1 dau., Nancy Mary Paula. Asst. dept. head Coal Mine Constrn. Co., 1953-56; with turnkey projects Polimex, Warsaw, 1956-59, Krebs & Cie., Brussels, 1959-60, ITT Europe-Bell Telephone Mfg. Co., Brussels and Antwerp, Belgium, 1960-63; cons. to chief exec. officer Confinidus, Brussels, 1964-65; mgr. mktg. services Chem. Constrn. Co., N.Y.C., 1965-68; v.p. instl. sales Paine Webber, Jackson & Curtis, 1968-77, G. S. Grumman/Cowen, 1977-79; pres. Allan M. Chytrowski, Inc. and Allan Drilling Co., Belle Mead, N.J., 1979—. Author: The Role of a Concern-Bank in the Financial Policy of Concerns, 1965. Polish rep. in bobsledding and luge Olympic Games and world championships, 1948-59; Belgian rep. bobsledding, active U.S. luge Olympic Games and world championships, 1959-65. Home and Office: 52 Surrey Dr Belle Mead NJ 08502

CHYUNG, CHI HAN, mgmt. cons.; b. Seoul, Korea, Jan. 27, 1933; s. Do Soon and Boksoon (Kim) C.; came to U.S., 1954, naturalized, 1963, B.S., Kans. Wesleyan U., 1958; M.B.A., Mich. State U., 1960; postgrad. Mass. Inst. Tech.; m. Alice Yvonne Whorley, Dec. 23, 1961; children—Eric, Diana. Ops. analyst Chevrolet div. Gen. Motors Corp., Detroit and Flint, Mich., 1959-61; economist Internat. Harvester Co., Chgo., 1961-63; sr. analyst market div. Internat. Minerals & Chem. Corp., Skokie, Ill., 1963-66; mgr. market info. and planning Gulf & Western Industries, N.Y.C., 1966-68; dir. market planning and devel. Am. Standard, Inc., N.Y.C., 1968-71; pres. Oxytech Corp.; mgmt. cons., internat. market devel., Darien, Conn., 1971—; dir. Korea Hapsum Co.; cons. Govt. of Korea, Taisei Constrn. Co., Tokyo. Served with Korean Army, 1951-53. Mem. Inst. Mgmt. Scis., Am. Mktg. Assn., Ops. Research Soc., Am. Chem., N.Am. Corp. Planning Soc., Beta Gamma Sigma. Contbr. papers to profl. lit. Home: 5 Skytop Dr East Norwalk CT 06855 Office: 433 Post Rd Darien CT 06820

CIAMPA, DAN, mgmt. cons.; b. Cambridge, Mass., Dec. 14, 1946; s. Dante C. and Virginia (Dindio) C.; B.S., Boston Coll., 1969; M.Ed., Boston U., 1971; m. Elaine Nelson, June 28, 1970; 1 dau., Devon Laine. Asso., McBer & Co., 1969-70; mgmt. cons., 1970-72; sr. cons. Rath & Strong, Inc., Lexington, Mass., 1972-74, prin., 1974-76, div. dir., 1976—, v.p., 1976, dir. orgn. and mgmt. services, 1976—, group v.p., 1978—, also dir; vis. guest lectr. Harvard U., Boston Coll. Mem. Inst. Mgmt. Cons., Brit. Inst. Mgmt., Internat. Assn. Applied Social Scientists, Internat. Cons. Found. Office: Rath and Strong Inc 21 Worthen Rd Lexington MA 02173

CIANI, ROBERT MICHAEL, mortgage banker; b. N.Y.C., Jan. 5, 1935; s. R.P. and C. Virginia C.; B.A., Iona Coll., 1956; LL.B., St. Johns U., 1959, J.S.D., 1960; m. Georgette Luning, June 15, 1956; children—Lynn A., Robert P. Admitted to N.Y. bar, 1960; dir. First Fidelity Corp., Los Angeles, 1969-70; fin. v.p. ITT-Levitt Corp., Los Angeles, 1970-74; exec. v.p. Sonnenblick-Goldman Corp. of Calif., Los Angeles, 1974-75; founder, pres., chief exec. officer, dir. S-G Mortgage Corp., Panorama City, Calif., 1965—; lectr. instr. UCLA, 1960-80. Bd. dirs. Hidden Hills Homeowners Assn., 1973-75. Served with USMC, 1956-60. Mem. Mortgage Bankers Assn. Am., Calif. Mortgage Bankers Assn., So. Calif. Mortgage Bankers Assn. Republican. Roman Catholic. Club: Calabasas Tennis. Home: 5484 Jed Smith Rd Hiddgn Hills CA 91302 Office: S-G Mortgage Corp 8121 Van Nuys Blvd Panorama City CA 91402

CIANO, JOHN A., electronics exec.; b. Malden, Mass., Apr. 26, 1924; s. Pascal and Clorinda (Lecesse) C.; B.S. in Chem. Engring., Franklin Tech. Inst., Boston, 1950; B.S., Suffolk U., 1953; Ph.D., U. Beverly Hills, 1980; m. M. Patricia Riley, Sept. 19, 1970; children—Nancy Linda Concion, Kathryn Marie Ciano. Tech. foreman, jr. engr. Sylvania Electronics Div., 1950-55, Clevite Electronics, 1955-56; sr. engr. Raytheon Semiconductor Div., 1956-59; process engring. mgr. Fairchild Semiconductor, 1959-63; pres., chmn. bd. Inteconsal Assos., Inc., Palo Alto, Calif., 1963—; mktg. cons. Served with USNR, 1942-46; PTO. Registered profl. engr., Mass. Mem. IEEE, Internat. Soc. Hybrid Mfg., Electronic Reps. Assn., Mfrs. Agts. Nat. Assn., Electronics Assn. Calif., Mercedes Benz Owners Club. Republican. Episcopalian. Clubs: Palo Alto Hills Country, Univ. (Palo Alto), Masons, Shriners. Home: 1244 Sharon Park Dr Menlo Park CA 94025 Office: Interconsal Assos & Interconsal Asia Inc 991 Commercial St Palo Alto CA 94025

CIASULLO, JOSEPH JOHN, computer co. exec.; b. Phila., Dec. 24, 1936; s. Michael Joseph and Madeline Marie (Scarpiello) C.; B.S. in Acctg., LaSalle Coll., Phila., 1961; m. Lorraine Scappa, June 21, 1958; children—Michael, Joseph, Maria. Acctg. clk. CBS, Phila., 1955-56; with Sperry Univac Co., 1956—, v.p., controller, Phila., 1973-79, v.p., gen. mgr. internat. div., London, 1979—. Service with USAR, 1961-63. Mem. Soc. Advancement Mgmt., Fin. Execs. Inst., Inst. Dirs. Office: Sperry Univac Centre London NW10 8LS England UK

CIBELLA, ROSS CASIMIR, mgmt. cons.; b. Rochester, N.Y., Sept. 20, 1911; s. John S. and Grace (Castiglione) C.; B.S., Alfred U., 1934; student Western Res. U., 1934-35, Fenn Coll., 1935-36, U. Pitts., 1951-52; m. Marjorie Alice Sharp, Jan. 15, 1938; children—Richard S., James H., Robert Gordon. Tech. librarian titanium pigment div. Nat. Lead Co., Sayreville, N.J., 1936-37; librarian Calgon Corp. (formerly Hagan Chems. & Controls, Inc.), Pitts., 1937-50, personnel mgr., dir. library, 1950-69, asst. to pres., 1969-72, also dir. employee relations; mgmt. cons., 1972-73; dir. coop. edn. Allegheny Community Coll., Pitts., 1973-74; tng. dir. engring. works div. Dravo Corp., 1974-78, 80—; mgmt. cons., Bethel Park, Pa., 1978—. Mgr. support services Nat. Alliance Businessmen, 1970 (on loan); pres., dir. Central Blood Bank Pitts., Inc.; part time instr. Pa. State U. Extension, Robert Morris Coll.; pres. Downtown Br. YMCA, Pitts., 1943-44, Pennhills Br., 1953-54; chmn. indsl. council Sta. WQEX-TV, edn. TV; bd. dirs. Southwestern Pa. Jr. Achievement, Inc., 1960—; southeastern sect. chmn. United Fund Allegheny County, 1962. Mem. Pitts. Personnel Assn. (dir.), Chartiers Valley Personnel Assn. (dir.), Chartiers Valley Personnel Group, Spl. Libraries Assn. (pres. Pitts. chpt. 1940-42), Am. Chem. Soc., Pitts. Jr. (pres. 1947-48), Pitts. chambers commerce, Am. Soc. Tng. and Devel. (pres. 1972-73, chmn. bd. 1973-78). Methodist (bd.). Club: Masons. Author: Directory of Micro-film Sources, 1941; Trade Names Index, 1941. Editor: Calgon News; 1950-61. Home and Office: 1412 Stoltz Rd Bethel Park PA 15102

CICCHINO, DOMENIC ANTONIO, systems engr.; b. Isernia, Italy, June 27, 1949; s. Salvatore and Nicolina (Forte) C.; came to U.S., 1951, naturalized, 1962; B.S.E.E., Newark Coll. Engring., 1972, postgrad. studies, 1976—; m. Bonita S. Deerfield, May 24, 1980. Asst. to production engr. Regina Co., Rahway, N.J., 1973-74; indsl. engr. Johns Manville Corp., Denver, 1974-76, divisional engr., 1976-77, sr. divisional systems analyst, 1977-78; systems engr. Pantasote Inc., Passaic, N.J., 1978-80; mem. adminstrv. group Bell Labs., Piscataway, N.J., 1980—; dir. T.A.C.T. Inc., Lincroft, N.J., 1978—. Served with U.S. Army, 1972-73. Mem. Alumni Assn. N.J. Inst. Tech. Home: 2063 Nicholl Ave Scotch Plains NJ 07076 Office: Bell Telephone Labs 6 Corporate Pl Piscataway NJ 08540

CIERNIAK, REYNOLD EUGENE, chem. mfg. corp. exec.; b. Chgo., Jan. 11, 1940; s. Eugene Stanley and Jeanne Anne (Konopka) C.; B.A., St. Mary's Coll., Winona, Minn., 1961; M.S., Ariz. State U., 1966; M.B.A., U. Calif., Los Angeles, 1968; m. Rosemarie Dlouhy, Aug. 10, 1963; children—Eugene, John, Krysia, Reynold. Materials engr. rocketdyne div. North Am. Rockwell, Canoga Park, Calif., 1964-68; tech. sales rep. ICI Am., Los Angeles, 1968-69, central region sales mgr. ICI U.S., Chgo., 1969-75, production planning mgr., Wilmington, Del., 1975-80; pres. Recycling Research Inc., Morton, Pa., 1980—. Mem. Am. Chem. Soc., Soc. Plastics Industry. Republican. Roman Catholic. Club: Polish Roman Catholic Union. Home: 110 Fraser Pl Newark DE 19711 Office: ICI United States Inc Wilmington DE 19897

CIMILLUCA, MICHAEL ANGELO, fin. exec.; b. N.Y.C., July 1, 1939; s. Emanuel R. and Gertrude (Flores) C.; B.S., Fordham U., 1965; m. Audrey A. Stefani, June 18, 1966; children—Michael Steven, Gregory Scott. Supervising sr. Arthur Young & Co., C.P.A.'s, N.Y.C., 1965-71; asst. to corp. controller Am. lMaize Products Co., N.Y.C., 1971-73; v.p., controller S.A. Schonbrunn & Co., Inc., Palisades Park, N.J., 1973-75, v.p. fin., 1975—, v.p. adminstrn., 1979—. Mem. Piscataway (N.J.) Environ. Control Commn, 1973-74. Served with USAF, 1957-61. Mem. Am. Inst. C.P.A.'s N.Y. State Soc. C.P.A.'s, Nat. Assn. Accountants, Am. Accounting Assn., Assn. Corporate Controllers, Am. Mgmt. Assn. Roman Catholic. Home: 9 Beech Pl Denville NJ 07834 Office: Grand and Ruby Ave Palisades Park NJ 07650

CIMILUCA, ARTHUR EDWARD, chemist; b. East Rutherford, N.J., June 8, 1938; s. Philip M. and Katherine Christina (Gunther) C.; student Newark Coll. Engring., 1956-58; B.S., Fairleigh Dickinson U., 1961; postgrad. (grad. teaching asst.) Purdue U., 1961-62, Rutgers U., 1962-65; m. Maria Frances Bjelis, Jan. 25, 1964; children—Arthur Edward, Cheryl Ann, Kristen. Asst. chemist A.L. Wilson Chem. Co., Kearny, N.J., 1961; pilot lab. chemist Morning Star Paisley Corp., Hawthorne, N.J., 1962; research chemist Interchem. Corp., Carlstadt, N.J., 1963-65; dir. research, corp. v.p. A.L. Wilson Chem. Co., Kearny, 1965—, also now dir. research Novel Tech. Labs. div. Mem. Am. Mgmt. Assn., Chem. Engring. Product Research Panel, Am. Chem. Soc., N.Y. Acad. Scis., Nat. Rifle Assn. Mem. adv. panel Chem. Week, Modern Plastics, 1977; patentee in field. Home: 15 Old Wood Rd Bernardsville NJ 07924 Office: 1050 Harrison Ave Kearny NJ 07032

CINAMON, A. HARVEY, mail advt. and mail order co. exec.; b. Cambridge, Mass., Mar. 7, 1926; s. Max and Pearl Cinamon; student pub. schs., Brookline, Mass.; m. Marcia Shifrin, June 13, 1970; children by previous marriage—James S., Nancy A., David M.; stepchildren—Debra, Mitchell. With William M. Hirshberg Co., Boston, 1946-50; with Hub Mail Advt. Service, Inc., Boston, 1950-70, v.p. mktg. 1965-70; pres. Cinamon Assos., Inc., Brookline, 1971—; lectr., seminar participant and leader, 1960—. Served with USNR, 1943-46; PTO; CBI. Named Advt. Man of Year, Jr. Advt. Club Boston, 1961, Direct Mktg. Man of Year, Mail Advt. Club N.E., 1973. Mem. Direct Mail/Mktg. Assn., Mail Advt. Service Assn., Advt. Club Greater Boston (pres. 1964-65), Mail Advt. Club New Eng. (pres. 1968-69), Jr. Advt. Club Boston (pres. 1950-51). Home: 3 Addington Rd Brookline MA 02146 Office: 29 Harvard St Brookline MA 02146

CINELLI, MICHAEL ANTHONY, banker; b. Bound Brook, N.J., Dec. 10, 1934; s. Frederick and Mildred (Consalvo) C.; B.S., St. Peter's Coll., 1960; M.B.A., N.Y. U., 1962; m. Felicia Sena, Sept. 23, 1960; 1 son, Michael Frederick. Sr. credit analyst Chase Manhattan Bank and Empire Trust Co., N.Y.C., 1960-65; asst. cashier First Charter Nat. Bank, East Brunswick, N.J., 1965-67; v.p. Hermann Services, Inc., South Brunswick, N.J., 1967-73; pres. Hillsborough Nat. Bank, Belle Mead, N.J., 1973—. Pres. Hillsborough Twp. (N.J.) Bd. Edn., 1965-70; dep. mayor Hillsborough Twp. Com., 1970-73; mem. Hillsborough Twp. Indsl. Commn., Somerset County Coll. Adv. Council Community Relations; chmn. bd., trustee Somerset County (N.J.) Heart Assn. Recipient Outstanding Citizen award Hillsborough Twp. Jr. C. of C., 1970. Mem. N.J. Bankers Assn. (dir. mgmt. com.). Home: 16 Craig Dr Somerville NJ 08876 Office: Hillsborough Nat Bank Amwell Rd Belle Mead NJ 08502

CINNATER, ELMER FREDERICK, credit union exec.; b. St. Louis, May 11, 1908; s. William and Cecelia (Braun) C.; student public schs., St. Louis; m. Polly Ockunzzi, June 26, 1970; 1 son from previous marriage, Richard W. Clk., Shumate Cutlery Co., St. Louis, 1923-24; bookeeper Champion Shoe Machinery, St. Louis, 1925-28; acct. Mo. Pacific R.R., St. Louis, 1929-54, N. Am. Airlines, Burbank, Calif., 1955-58; mgr., asst. treas. Union Oil Center Fed. Credit Union, Los Angeles, 1958—. Mem. So. Calif. Council Credit Union Execs. (pres.), Calif. Credit Union League (dir.), So. Calif. Mgrs. Assn., Founders Club Credit Union Nat. Assn. Clubs: Elks, Dynasty, Table Tennis Hall of Fame. Home: 1828 Skyline Dr Fullerton CA 92631 Office: 461 S Boylston St Los Angeles CA 90017

CINOSI, NICOLA, economist; b. Villalfonsina, Chieti, Italy, May 18, 1942; s. Amelio and Angelina (Ventresca) C.; Ph.D., Fordham U., 1974. Instr. econs. Fordham U., 1970-71; economist Bur. Labor Statistics, Dept. Labor U.S., N.Y.C., 1971-73; internat. economist Bank Am. N.Y., N.Y.C., 1973-76, European Am. Bank, N.Y.C., 1976-80; v.p. Chem. Bank, N.Y.C., 1980—; adj. prof. internat. finance Fordham U., Tarrytown (N.Y.) campus, 1977, Pace U., 1980; asst. rep. Banca Popolare di Novara, N.Y.C. Earhart Found. fellow, 1968-69. Mem. Am. Econ. Assn. Author: Luigi Einaudi's

Contribution to Public Finance, 1974. Home: 27 Merlin Ave North Tarrytown NY 10591 Office: Chem Bank 20 Pine St York NY 10078

CIOCCA, ARTHUR A., wine industry exec.; b. Tarrytown, N.Y., Dec. 5, 1937; s. Angelo Arthur and Helen Theresa Ciocca; B.S., Coll. Holy Cross, 1959; M.B.A., Roosevelt U., 1963. Group product mgr. Gallo Winery, Modesto, Calif., 1968-73; gen. mgr. grocery products div. Oroweat, San Francisco, 1973-74; v.p. mktg. Franzia Winery, Ripon, Calif., 1974-75, pres., chief exec. officer, 1975-79; chmn., chief exec. officer Wine Group, Coca Cola Bottling, Ripon, 1979—. Served with USNR, 1962. Mem. Calif. Wine Inst. (dir., mem. exec. com.), Young Pres. Orgn., Pres.' Council Holy Cross Coll. Office: 177 Post St San Francisco CA

CIPRIANI, FRANK ANTHONY, coll. pres.; b. N.Y.C., Sept. 28, 1933; s. Domenico and Maria (DiGiesi) C.; B.A. in Polit. Sci., Queens Coll., 1955; M.A. in Edn., N.Y. U., 1961, Ph.D., 1969; m. Judith Pellathay; children—Mária, Frank, Michael, Dominique. Safety engr. Zurich-Am. Inst. Co., 1958-61; mem. adminstrv. staff State U. N.Y. Coll., Farmingdale, 1961—, v.p. adminstrn., 1969-78, pres., 1978—. Chmn. bd. Guide Dog Found. Blind, 1979—; chmn. Suffolk Energy Task Force. Served as capt. USAF, 1955-57. Mem. Middle States Assn. Colls. and Secondary Sch., L.I. Regional Advisory Council Higher Edn. (chmn.), Urban League L.I. Roman Catholic. Club: Half Hollow Hills Rotary. Address: State Univ Coll Melville Rd Farmingdale NY 11735

CIRIGNANO, JOHN JOSEPH, computer services exec.; b. Boston, June 9, 1940; s. Vito P. and Eleanor V. (Fiumedoro) C.; B.S. in Physics and Math., Tufts U., 1963; postgrad. in computer scis. Northeastern U., 1966, M.S. in Physics, 1965; M.B.A. with honors, Boston U., 1972; m. Florence Ruth Nicosia. Aug. 9, 1964; children—Paul David, Pamela Ruth, Mark Vito, Diane Florence. Teaching asst. in physics, Northeastern U., Boston, 1965; staff engr. Mass. Inst. Tech. Instrumentation Lab., Cambridge, 1963-68; project leader, design automation engring. Honeywell Electronic Data Processing Co., Waltham, Mass., 1968-69; asst. mgr. of program offices info. systems, Raytheon Co., Bedford, Mass., 1969-71; project mgr. ELectronic Data Systems Fed. Corp., Dallas, Tex., 1971-72; computer center mgr. Pratt & Whitney Aircraft, East Hartford, Conn., 1972-74; mgr. Xerox Computer Center ops., 1974-75, project mgr. computer bus. ops. planning Info. Services, Div., Xerox Corp., Rochester, N.Y., 1975—; dir. advanced systems planning div. Blue Cross Blue Shield of Del., Wilmington, 1976-77; sr. mgmt. cons. Coopers & Lybrand, Boston, 1977-78; mgr. computer devel. div. Environ. Research & Tech., Inc., Concord, Mass., 1978-79; gen. mgr. Computer Enterprise Inc. Scoutmaster, Boy Scouts Am., Winchester, Mass. Recipient cert. of commendation for contbn. to Apollo Primary Guidance, Navigation and Control System MIT, 1969. Mem. Soc. for Advancement of Mgmt., Am. Mgmt. Assn., Beta Gamma Sigma. Home: 7 Myrtle St Winchester MA 01890 Office: 85 Providence Hwy Westwood MA 02090

CISLAK, PETER JOHN, chem. co. exec.; b. Indpls., June 26, 1931; s. Francis Edward and Jeannette Grace (Huling) C.; student Swarthmore Coll., 1952; B.S., Purdue U., 1958, M.S., 1958; m. Margaret Frances Noble, June 6, 1953; children—Gregory Noble, Carol Margaret, David John, Susan Marie. Instr., Purdue U., 1958-62; statistician Reilly Tar & Chem. Corp., Indpls., 1962-64, data processing mgr., 1964-69, prodn. mgr. chem. div., 1969-77, sr. mgr. chems., 1977—; dir. Reilly Chems., Reilly Chem. S.A., Belgium; lectr. Ind. U.-Purdue U., Indpls., 1970. Asst. dist. commr. Boy Scouts Am., 1963—. Served with AUS, 1953-57. Mem. Am. Mgmt. Assn. (chmn. seminar), Am. Statis. Assn., Assn. Computing Machinery, Operations Research Soc. Am., Soc. Chem. Industry, Am. Inst. Chem. Engrs. (chmn. Indpls. sect. 1978), Ind. Soc. Mayflower Descs. (dep. gov. 1974-79). K.C. (4 deg.). Home: 8065 Morningside Dr Indianapolis IN 46240 Office: 151 N Delaware Indianapolis IN 46204

CISLER, WALKER LEE, consultant; b. Marietta, Ohio, Oct. 8, 1897; s. Louis H. and Sara S. (Walker) C.; M.E., Cornell U., 1922; Eng.D., U. Mich., Stevens Inst. Tech., S.D. Sch. Mines and Tech.; LL.D., U. Detroit, Wayne State U., Marietta Coll., U. Akron, No. Mich. U., Mich. State U., Detroit Coll. Law; D.Sc., U. Toledo, Ind. Tech. Coll., Mich. Technol. U.; L.H.D., Shaw Coll., Detroit; D.Econs., Tan Kook U. (Korea); D.Pub. Service, Detroit Inst. Tech.; m. Gertrude Demuth Rippe, July 28, 1939 (dec. 1975); adopted children—Richard Rippe, Jane Rippe Cisler Eckhardt. Various engring. positions Pub. Service Electric & Gas Co., Newark, 1922-41; with WPB, Washington, 1941-43; chief public utility sect. SHAEF, 1944; chief engr. power plants Detroit Edison Co., 1945-47, exec. v.p., 1948-51, pres., 1951-64, chmn. bd., 1964-75, also dir.; chmn. exec. com. of bd. Freuhauf Corp.; pres. Overseas Adv. Assos., Inc. Mem. Bus. Council; chmn. Thomas Alva Edison Found.; hon. chmn. internat. exec. council World Energy Conf.; mem. Nat. Acad. Scis.-Nat. Acad. Engring.; trustee emeritus Cornell U., Cranbrook Inst. Sci., Marietta Coll.; hon. trustee Atomic Indsl. Forum. Served to col. AUS, 1943-45. Decorated by several fgn. govts., U.S.; recipient Henry Lawrence Gantt Gold medal ASME, AMA, 1955; Washington award W. Soc. Engrs., 1957; Hoover medal Engring. Founders Soc., 1962, John Fritz medal, 1967; William Metcalf award Engring. Soc. Western Pa., 1963. Fellow IEEE (Edison medal 1965), ASME (pres. 1960, hon. mem., George Westinghouse Gold medal 1954), Am. Inst. Mgmt., Engring. Soc. Detroit, Am. Ordnance Assn., Soc. Am. Mil. Engrs. (pres. 1961, George W. Goethals award 1958), Edison Electric Inst. (pres. 1964), Engrs. Joint Council (pres. 1964), Newcomen Soc. N.Am. (hon. chmn. Mich. chpt.). Clubs: Detroit, Detroit Econ. (chmn. 1954-74), Country, Athletic (Detroit); Met. (Washington); Engrs., Univ., Cornell, Brook (N.Y.C.). Home: 1071 Devonshire Rd Grosse Pointe Park MI 48230 Office: 1300 Washington Blvd Bldg Detroit MI 48226

CISSEL, NORMAN RALPH, ret. accountant; b. Washington, Dec. 9, 1911; s. William and Emma (Pearson) C.; B.C.S., Benjamin Franklin U., 1935; m. Dorothy E. Fleming, Sept. 14, 1940 (div.); 1 son, William F. With V.I. Corp. (formerly V.I. Co.), Christiansted, 1936-51, comptroller, 1940-51; territorial accounting exec. OPS, Charlotte Amalie, V.I., 1952-53; supervisory auditor, asst. comptroller Govt. Comptroller of V.I., Charlotte Amalie, 1957-61; pvt. practice as C.P.A., St. Croix, V.I. 1952-66; sr. partner Cissel & Ellis, C.P.A.'s, 1966-71 (merged with Seidman & Seidman, C.P.A.'s, 1971); cons. partner Seidman & Seidman, C.P.A.'s, 1971-74. Mem. Food Commn. Municipality of St. Croix, 1946-49; mem. Banking Bd. of V.I., 1949-72, 77-79, chmn., 1949-54; mem. Tax Exemption Bd. Municipality of St. Croix, 1951-55; pres. V.I. Bd. Pub. Accountancy, 1957-72; mem. investment bd. V.I. Unemployment Compensation, 1963—; mem. V.I. Bd. Tax Rev., 1977—. C.P.A., V.I. Mem. Nat. Assn. State Bds. of Accountancy, Am. Inst. C.P.A.'s (council 1960-67), V.I. Soc. C.P.A.'s (pres. 1952-72), Inst. Internal Auditors, Nat. Assn. Accountants, Am. Accounting Assn., Municipal Finance Officers Assn. Home: Estate La Reine Box C Kingshill PO St Croix VI 00850

CITRON, RICHARD STEFAN (RUSTY), talent promotion cons.; b. N.Y.C., Jan. 20, 1953; s. Irving and Frieda Lea (Gordon) C.; B.A. with honors in Fine Arts and Journalism, U. Nebr., 1973; m. Jill Susan Henschel Greenberg, Sept. 9, 1978. Asso., David Frost, 1969-72; exec. Columbia Pictures TV, Lawrence Einhorn Prodns., Group W Prodns., Inc., ABC-TV, Easter Seals, booker maj. celebrities for TV and other public events, 1977—; pres. Citron Talent Services, Inc., North Hollywood, Calif., 1974-76; telethon producer Muscular Dystrophy, Arthritis, Fight for Sight, 1975-77; guest lectr. Internat. Council of Shopping Centers, Acad. TV Arts and Scis. Cons., Mt. Zion Hosp., San Francisco, Nat. Easter Seals, Chgo.; exec. com. for Man of Yr. Award, City of Hope, 1979. Mem. Nat. Acad. TV Arts and Scis., Alpha Epsilon Rho. Contbr. numerous articles on Hollywood bookings and celebrity market to in-house publs. Office: 10701 Riverside Dr Suite 14 North Hollywood CA 91602

CIUBA, STANLEY JOHN, research scientist; b. Polomia, Poland, June 24, 1940; s. John Stanley and Salomea (Pyra) C.; came to U.S., 1947; naturalized, 1958; B.S. in Chem. Engring., Newark Coll. Engring., 1968; M.S. in Environ. Engring., N.J. Inst. Tech., 1976; m. Frances A. Kuchar, Sept. 7, 1963; children—Stanley, Stephen, Susanne. Tech. service rep. Magnus Chem. Co., Garwood, N.J., 1960-67; project engr. Graver Water div. Ecodyne Corp., Union, N.J., 1967-68; water resources engr. Delaware River Basin Commn., Trenton, N.J., 1968-74; research scientist Betz Labs., Inc., Trevose, Pa., 1974-79, Econs. Lab., Inc., St. Paul, 1979—. Active Boy Scouts Am., Yardley, Pa., 1973-77; Democratic candidate for Borough Council, Yardley, 1977. Registered profl. engr., N.J. Mem. Am. Inst. Chem. Engrs., ASME, Air Pollution Control Assn. Roman Catholic. Patentee in field. Home: 12420 Allen Dr Burnsville MN 55337 Office: Econs Lab Inc St Paul MN 55118

CLABAUGH, ELMER EUGENE, JR., lawyer; b. Anaheim, Calif., Sept. 18, 1927; s. Elmer Eugene and Eleanor (Heitschusen) C.; B.B.A. cum laude, Woodbury Coll., 1951; B.A. summa cum laude, Claremont Men's Coll., 1958; J.D., Stanford U., 1961; m. Elizabeth Ellen Chapman, Dec. 25, 1954 (div. July 1966); children—Christopher Chapman, Matthew Martinson, Rindy M., Devra R.; m. 2d, Donna M. Organ, Dec. 1968. Fgn. service staff U.S. Dept. State, Jerusalem and Tel Aviv, 1951-53; field staff Pub. Adminstrn. Service, El Salvador, Ethiopia, U.S., 1953-57; admitted to Calif. bar, 1961; dep. dist. atty. Ventura County (Calif.), 1961-62; practiced in Ventura, Calif., 1962—; mem. firm Hathaway, Clabaugh, Perrett and Webster (and predecessor), 1962-79, Clabaugh & Perloff, Ventura, 1979—; state inheritance tax referee, 1968-78. Bd. dirs. San Antonio Water Conservation Dist., Ventura Community Meml. Hosp., 1964-80; trustee Ojai Unified Sch. Dist., 1974-79; mem. pres.'s adv. council Claremont Men's Coll. Served USCGR, 1944-46, USMCR, 1946-48. Mem. Calif. Bar Assn., Am. Arbitration Assn., Phi Alpha Delta. Clubs: Masons, Shriners, Lions. Home: 3510 Santa Paula-Ojai Rd Ojai CA 93023 Office: Citizens Savings Bldg 1090 Victoria Rd Ventura CA 93003

CLACK, DICK SCOTT, import-export co. exec.; b. Celina, Tex., Nov. 13, 1927; s. Clyde William and Tink (Blakemore) C.; B.S. in Wildlife Conservation, Okla. State U., 1952; postgrad. Hokkaido U., Sapporo, Japan, 1953-54, U. Hawaii, 1979; m. Yoshiko Eguchi, Oct. 1, 1955; children—Michael Bruce, Meiling Jade. Served as enlisted man U.S. Army, 1945-48, commd. 2 lt., 1952, advanced through grades to lt. col., 1967, stationed Japan, 1953-55; with mil. intelligence, 1957-60; stationed Ft. Polk, La., 1961-63; community relations officer PTO, 1967-70, ret., 1970; asst. v.p. Makaha Surfside Devel. Co., Honolulu, 1970-72; pres. D. Clack Inc., public relations cons., Honolulu, 1972-74; v.p. PCO Inc., Honolulu, 1974-76; exec. trustee Hawaii Army Museum Soc., Honolulu, 1976-78, trustee, 1976-80; v.p., dir. mktg. Traders Pacifica Ltd., Honolulu, 1979—; chmn. bd. dirs. Makaha Surfside Assos.; dir. Gt. Pacific Mortgage Co., 2211 Ala Wai Assos. Decorated Legion of Merit, Army Commendation medal with 3 oak leaf clusters; named hon. mem. City Council Kumagaya (Japan), 1954; recipient cert. of commendation Gumma Prefectural Govt. Japan, 1955, Saitama Prefecture Govt. Japan, 1955; named Okla. Col., 1957, Ark. Traveler, 1962, La. Col., 1963, Hon. Citizen New Orleans, 1964. Mem. Assn. U.S. Army (exec. com. Hawaii chpt. 1967-80), Mil. Order World Wars, Hawaii Mus. Assn., Pacific Regional Conservation Center, Assn. State and Local History Socs., War Mus. Can. Democrat. Clubs: Rotary (dir. public relations Dist. 500, 1974, 79, dir. internat. relations Dist. 500, 1980), Honolulu Press, VFW (chief of staff Hawaii 1973). Office: 821 A Cooke Honolulu HI 96813

CLAFFEY, GEORGE MICHAEL, accountant; b. Rochester, N.Y., Jan. 31, 1921; s. Michael Thomas and Kathryn Frances (Wimble) C.; student Shriveham Am. U., 1945, U. Rochester, 1946-48; m. Nancy Grace Ketterer, Sept. 23, 1950; children—Michael Thomas, Patricia Ruth, Barbara Anne, Victoria Grace, George Earl, Christopher Ketterer, Jonathan Phillip. Asst. to pres., v.p. Howe Plan Fund., Inc., Rochester, 1947-49; controller, v.p. fin. vets. Broadcasting Co., Rochester, 1949-65; controller Rust Craft Broadcasting of N.Y., Rochester, 1965-75, dir. fin., 1969-73; bus. mgr., controller Spartan Radiocasting Co., Spartanburg, S.C., 1976—. Mem. Inst. Broadcast Fin. Mgmt., Nat. Assn. Credit Mgmt. (dir. 1968-71). Republican. Roman Catholic. Club: Kiwanis. Home: 291 Harrell Dr Spartanburg SC 29302 Office: PO Box 1717 Intersection I-85 and I-26 Spartanburg SC 29304

CLAIR, JOHN MAURICE, investment co. exec.; b. Concord, Mass., May 24, 1943; s. Maurice and Ruth Gertrude (Bradley) C.; B.A. magna cum laude, Tufts Coll., 1965; LL.B., U. Pa., 1969; m. Andrea Henig, Dec. 4, 1970. Asso., First Boston Corp., N.Y.C., 1967-68; sr. asso. corporate fin. Salomon Bros., N.Y.C., 1969-76, v.p. corporate fin., 1976—. Vice chmn. bus. com. Met. Mus. Art. Mem. Fin. Analysts Fedn., N.Y. Soc. Security Analysts, Transp. Research Forum, Assn. Am. R.R.'s. Clubs: Down Town Assn., Univ. (N.Y.C.). Home: 1185 Park Ave New York NY 10028 Office: One New York Plaza New York NY 10004

CLAIRMONT, WILLIAM EDWARD, contractor, banker, rancher; b. Walhalla, N.D., Jan. 2, 1926; s. Emil O. and Mae E. (Bisenius) C.; student N.D. State U., 1948-49; m. Patricia Ann Filben, Oct. 7, 1950; children—Stephen, Julie, Cynthia, Nancy. Founder, William Clairmont, Inc., Bismarck, N.D., 1949, owner, 1949—; chmn. bd. Mandan Security Bank (N.D.), 1975—; land developer, Bismarck; owner farming and cattle ops., Costa Rica and N.D. Mem. City Council, Walhalla, 1955-56; chmn. bd. regents Mary Coll., Bismarck; trustee YMCA, Bismarck. Served with USMCR, 1944-46. Mem. N.D. Asso. Gen. Contractors (dir. 1964-67, pres. 1971). Club: Apple Creek Country. Home: 1938 Santa Gertrudis Dr Bismarck ND 58501 Office: 1720 Burnt Boat Rd Bismarck ND 58501

CLAMAN, JEFFREY ALAN, businessman; b. N.Y.C., Feb. 28, 1941; s. Jules L. and Shirley W. C.; B.S., N.Y. U., 1963, M.B.A., 1968; m. Susan E. Barrish, Dec. 22, 1963; children—Lawrence N., Jonathan L. Fin. analyst Mfrs. Hanover Trust Co., N.Y.C., 1963-65; sr. fin. analyst CBS, N.Y.C., 1965-68; v.p. Covington Funding Co. and Barrington Industries, Inc., N.Y.C., 1968-72; pres. Internat. Health Co., Pine Brook, N.J., 1972-80; mng. partner Terrill Manor Assos., 1977—, Med. Resources Internat., 1979—; pres. Am. Eagle Airways, Bayonne, N.J., 1977—; owner J.A.C. Enterprises Ltd., Bayonne, N.J., 1980—; gen. mgr. Bayonne Tomography, 1980—; mng. partner Mayfair Assos., 1980—. Mem. Am. Mgmt. Assn., Am., N.J. hosp assns. Office: JAC Enterprises Ltd 685 Broadway Bayonne NJ 07002

CLARK, ANDREW LAWRENCE, service co. exec.; b. Newark, Jan. 5, 1926; s. William Francis and Katherine Ann (Farrell) C.; A.B., Seton Hall U., 1949; J.D., Harvard U., 1954; m. Elizabeth Anne Brady, Apr. 11, 1959; children—Anne, Jacqueline, Peter. Admitted to N.Y. State bar, 1955; asso. firm Royall, Koegel & Rogers, and predecessors, N.Y.C., 1954-66; v.p., asst. to chmn. L.W. Frohlich & Co. and IMS Internat. Inc., N.Y.C., 1966-72; sr. v.p., sec. IMS Internat. Inc., N.Y.C., 1972—, also dir., dir. subs. Served with U.S. Army, 1945-47, 51-53. Mem. Am., N.Y. State, N.Y.C. bar assns. Republican. Roman Catholic. Home: 420 Colony Ct Wyckoff NJ 07481 Office: 800 3d Ave New York NY 10022

CLARK, BERNE HORTON, investment banker and advisor; b. Port Arthur, Tex., Feb. 26, 1935; s. Bernhard Franklin and Blanche (Keating) C.; B.B.A., Tex. A. and M. U., 1957; m. Elizabeth Estelle Price, May 4, 1973; 1 son, Andrew Keating. Account exec. Merrill Lynch Pierce Fenner & Smith, N.Y.C., 1966-67; v.p., nat. sales mgr. Arnold Bernhard & Co., N.Y.C., 1967-70; investment advisor, N.Y.C., 1970—; pub. Tax Shelter Monitor, N.Y.C., 1972—; cons. in field; pres. Gramercy Exploration Corp., N.Y.C., 1977—, Gramercy Securities Inc., Lancaster Securities Corp.; dir. Clark & Blum Pubs., Ltd., N.Y.C. Served to capt. USAF, 1958-65. Mem. Nat. Assn. Securities Dealers, Ohio Oil and Gas Assn., Am. Hereford Assn. Republican. Episcopalian. Clubs: Met., Bankers, Yale. Contbr. articles in field to profl. jours. Office: 331 Madison Ave Suite 1000 New York NY 10017

CLARK, CHARLES DANIEL, automobile dealer; b. Peoria, Ill., May 28, 1917; s. Richard Fardon and Melba Iona (Kirkpatrick) C.; B.A., U. Mich., 1939; m. Dorothy Elizabeth Van Gelder, Jan. 3, 1942; children—Kirk Allen, Robin Anne. Apprentice purser S.S. Santa Lucia, Grace Lines, N.Y.C., 1939-40; sales mgr. Carpenter Chevrolet Co., McAllen, Tex., 1940-41, v.p., 1945-50; pres. Charles Clark Chevrolet Co., McAllen, 1951—; dir. McAllen State Bank. City commr. City of McAllen, 1950-52; public mem. dist. 12-B grievance com. State Bar Tex. Served to maj., USAAF, 1941-45. Decorated D.F.C., Air medal with oak leaf clusters. Nat. com. Univ. Art Mus., U. Calif. at Berkeley, 1969-70; Council of Friends U. Mich. Mus. Art, 1972-78; mem. Coll. Fine Arts Found. adv. council U. Tex. at Austin, 1972—; mem. mus. adv. panel Tex. Commn. Arts and Humanities, 1972-74. Mem. McAllen C. of C. (pres. 1957, outstanding citizen 1958). Tex. Automobile Dealer Assn. (award personnel relations 1963, v.p. 1965-66), Delta Upsilon. Episcopalian. Home: 404 Lindberg Ave McAllen TX 78501 Office: PO Box 938 McAllen TX 78501

CLARK, CHARLES EDWARD, arbitrator; b. Cleve., Feb. 27, 1921; s. Douglas John and Mae (Egermayer) C.; student Berea Coll., 1939-41, King Coll., 1942; LL.B., U. Tex., 1948; m. Nancy Jane Hilt, Mar. 11, 1942; children—Annette S. Clark Gernhardt, Charles Edward, John A., Paul R., Nancy P., David G. Turret lathe operator Thompson Aircraft Products, Cleve., Euclid, Ohio, 1941-43; admitted to Tex. bar, 1948, Mass. bar, 1956, U.S. Supreme Ct. bar, 1959; practiced in San Antonio, 1948-55; prof. law, asst. dean St. Mary's U. Sch. Law, San Antonio, 1948-55; asst. editor-in-chief NACCA Law Jour., Boston, 1955-58; chief voting sect., legal asst. to vice-chmn. U.S. Commn. on Civil Rights, 1958-61; sr. compliance officer, asst. spl. counsel Office Fed. Contract Compliance, Washington, 1961-66; regional dir. EEO Commn., region VII, Kansas City, Mo., 1966-79; arbitrator, Kansas City, Mo., 1979—. Vice-chmn. D.C. chpt. Am. GI Forum, 1962-63; pres. sch. chpt. P.T.A., 1963-65; active Boy Scouts Am. Served with AUS, 1943-44; ETO. Recipient Wright Matthews Prize, Tex. Law Rev., 1948. Mem. Internat. Platform Assn., Indsl. Relations Research Assn. (treas. 1979—), Am. Arbitration Assn., State Bar of Tex., Phi Delta Phi. Author: Personnel Management: Policies and Practices Service, 1980; contbr. articles in field to profl. jours. Home and Office: 6418 Washington St Kansas City MO 64113

CLARK, DONALD CAMERON, financial exec.; b. Bklyn., Aug. 9, 1931; s. Alexander and Sarah (Cameron) C.; B.B.A., Clarkson Coll., 1953; M.B.A., Northwestern U., 1961; m. Jean Ann Williams, Feb. 6, 1954; children—Donald, Barbara, Thomas. With Household Finance Corp., Chgo., 1955—, treas., 1972-74, sr. v.p., 1974, dir., 1974—, exec. v.p., chief financial officer, 1976-77, pres., 1977—. Served to lt. U.S. Army, 1953-55. Mem. Nat. Consumer Finance Assn., Chgo. Com., Chgo. Council on Fgn. Relations. Presbyterian (elder). Clubs: Westmoreland Country; Mid-Am., Economic (Chgo.). Home: 2828 Blackhawk Rd Wilmette IL 60091 Office: 2700 Sanders Rd Prospect Heights IL 60070

CLARK, DONALD MALIN, assn. exec.; b. Buffalo, Feb. 11, 1929; s. Jack Malin and Louis Mary (Caccard) C.; B.S., Canisius Coll., 1950, M.A., 1952; Ed.D., SUNY, Buffalo, 1961, M.B.A., 1968; m. Joan Marie Coyle, Dec. 27, 1958; children—Kevin Malin, Michael John, Elizabeth Anne. Adminstrv. asst. Travelers Ins. Co., Buffalo, 1950-57; tchr. econs. Orchard Park (N.Y.) Sr. High Sch., 1957-66; dir. Center for Econ. Edn., State U. Coll., Buffalo, 1966-70; exec. dir. Niagara Falls (N.Y.) Industry-Edn. Council, 1970-79; pres. Nat. Assn. for Industry-Education Coop., Buffalo, Inc.; news commentator radio programs Economic Viewpoint and Reading Between the Lines, Sta. WADV, WBEN, Buffalo, 1961-78. Served to col. USAR. Recipient Kazanjian Found. award for Excellence in Teaching Coll. Econs., 1968; Freedom Found. award, 1965; U.S. Office of Edn. grantee, 1976-78. Mem. AAUP, Internat. Adminstrv. Mgmt. Soc., Am. Soc. Tng. and Devel., U.S. Army War Coll. Alumni Assn., Res. Officers Assn. U.S., Nat. Mil. Intelligence Assn., Phi Delta Kappa. Republican. Roman Catholic. Clubs: Sport and Fitness Center, Buffalo Tennis. Bi-monthly columnist Nat. Assn. for Industry-Edn. Coop. Newsletter, 1977—. Author: Handbook on Industry-Education Councils, 1973; Career Education Advisory Councils, 1978. Office: 235 Hendricks Blvd Buffalo NY 14226

CLARK, EARL, ins. co. exec.; b. Enid, Okla., Mar. 22, 1917; s. Owen Earl and Imogene (Timmons) C.; B.S., Kans. State Coll., 1939; m. Albertine Bernice Putnam, June 24, 1941; children—Kathleen Ann Clark Yankovich, Robert Hamilton, Cynthia Susan. With Occidental Life Ins. Co. Calif., 1940-44, 45—, v.p. agys., Los Angeles, 1959-63, pres., 1963-72, chmn. bd., 1972—, chief exec. officer, 1965—, dir., 1963—; chmn. bd., chief exec. officer Occidental Internat. Enterprises Inc.; chmn. bd. Arbor Life Ins. Co., Transamerica Income Shares Inc.; vice chmn., dir. Transamerica Corp.; dir. Am. Life N.Y., Can. Surety Co., Transam Investment Mgmt. Co., Trans Internat. Airlines. Served with USNR, 1944-45. C.L.U. Mem. Am. Coll. Life Underwriters (trustee 1964—), Am. Soc. C.L.U.'s, Pasadena Tournament of Roses Assn., Acacia Frat. Clubs: Big Canyon Country; Calif. (Los Angeles); San Francisco Golf. Office: 1150 S Olive St Los Angeles CA 90015*

CLARK, EARNEST HUBERT, JR., tool co. exec.; b. Birmingham, Ala., Sept. 8, 1926; s. Earnest Hubert and Grace May (Smith) C.; B.S. in Mech. Engring., Calif. Inst. Tech., 1946, M.S., 1947; m. Patricia Margaret Hamilton, June 22, 1947; children—Stephen D., Kenneth A., Timothy R., Daniel S., Scott H., Rebecca G. With Baker Oil Tools, Inc. (now Baker Internat.), Los Angeles, 1947—, v.p., asst. gen. mgr., 1958-62, pres., chief exec. officer, 1962-69, pres., chmn. bd., 1969—; div. v.p., dir. Kobe, Inc., Tech. Oil Tool Corp., Galigher Co.; dir. Bank of Calif., Beckman Instruments, Ban Calif. Tri-State Corp, Gold State Foods Corp. Bd. dirs. Downey (Calif.) YMCA, YMCA for Met. Los

Angeles; mem. nat. council YMCA; trustee Harvey Mudd Coll. Served with USNR, 1944-46, 51-52. Mem. ASME, Am. Petroleum Inst. (dir.), Petroleum Equipment Suppliers Assn. (dir.), Am. Mgmt. Assn., Mchts. and Mfrs. Assn. (dir.) Calif. C. of C. (dir.), Tau Beta Pi. Office: Baker Internat 500 City Parkway W Orange CA 92668*

CLARK, EDGAR SANDERFORD, ins. broker, cons.; b. N.Y.C., Nov. 17, 1933; s. Edgar Edmund, Jr., and Katharine Lee (Jarman) C.; student U. Pa., 1952-54; B.S., Georgetown U., 1956, J.D., 1958; postgrad. INSEAD, Fountainbleau, France, 1969, Golden Gate Coll., 1973, U. Calif., Berkeley, 1974; m. Nancy E. Hill, Sept. 13, 1975; 1 son, Schuyler; children by previous marriage—Alexandra, Pamela. Staff asst. U.S. Senate select com. to investigate improper activities in labor and mgmt., Washington, 1958-59; underwriter Ocean Marine Dept., Fireman's Fund Ins. Co., San Francisco, 1959-62; mgr. Am. Fgn. Ins. Assn., San Francisco, 1962-66; with Marsh & McLennan, 1966-72, mgr. for Europe, resident dir. Brussels, Belgium, 1966-70, asst. v.p., mgr. captive and internat. div., San Francisco, 1970-72; v.p., dir. Risk Planning Group, Inc., San Francisco, 1972-75; v.p. internat. div. Alexander & Alexander Inc., San Francisco, 1975—; lectr. profl. orgns.; guest lectr. U. Calif., Berkeley, 1973, Am. Grad. Sch. Internat. Mgmt., 1981. Served with USAF, 1956-58. Mem. Am. Mgmt. Assn., Am. Risk and Ins. Assn., Chartered Ins. Inst., Am. Soc. Internat. Law. Episcopalian. Editorial adv. bd. Risk Mgmt. Reports, 1973-76. Home: 72 Millay Pl Mill Valley CA 94941 Office: 1 Market Plaza San Francisco CA 94105

CLARK, ELMER BAILY, investment banker; b. Seattle, Feb. 2, 1918; s. Elmer Baily and Adah Mary (Spencer) C.; student Reed Coll., 1938, U. Ariz., 1940; A.B., U. Wash., 1942; m. Mary Jane Jacobs, Oct. 7, 1970. With Boeing Airplane Co., Seattle, 1942-46; v.p. Midland Coal & Lumber Co., 1944-62; v.p. Chemi-Serve, Inc., 1947-54, pres., 1954-57; pres. Natural Gas Transmission Co., 1961-62; with Hinton, Jones & co., 1964-68, sr. v.p. until 1968; ind. investment counselor, 1963—; dir. Math. Scis. N.W., Inc. Treas., Seattle Hospitality Com., 1953-64. Mem. Municipal League, Seattle Hist. Soc., Arboretum Soc. (trustee), Seattle Soc. Fin. Analysts, Zeta Psi. Republican. Episcopalian. Clubs: Seattle Tennis, The Highlands. Home: The Highlands Seattle WA 98177 Office: 601 Skinner Bldg Seattle WA 98101

CLARK, ERNEST LYNN, govt. ofcl.; b. St. Louis, May 12, 1947; s. John Clifton and Ella Mae (Baker) Morgan; A.A., St. Louis Jr. Coll. Dist., 1973; B.S. in Bus. Adminstrn., B.S. in Law Enforcement and Corrections, N.E. Mo. State U., 1975. Dep. clk., then asst. chief clk. Ct. Criminal Causes, St. Louis, 1969-70; cons. Ct. Adminstrs. Office, St. Louis, 1971-72; computer operator Gen. Bancshares Service Corp., St. Louis, 1971-75, N.E. Mo. State U., 1973-74; fed. funding specialist Mo. Ho. Reps., 1975, research analyst, 1975-76, 76-77; statewide campaign coordinator candidate for lt. gov. Mo., 1976; personnel specialist Bi-State Devel. Agy., St. Louis, 1977—; cons. fed. funding and mgmt.; sec. credit com. Real Estate Investor's Credit Union. Co-organizer 1st Nat. Alliance Businessmen's Job Fair for Vets., St. Louis, 1971; mem. rev. policy manual com. St. Louis Jr. Coll. Dist., 1971; founder Collegiate Vets. Mo., 1971; co-founder St. Louis Area Council Collegiate Vets., 1970. Served with USCG, 1965-69. Recipient various commendations, certs. recognition. Mem. Am. Criminal Justice Assn., Am. Mgmt. Assn., Acad. Polit. Sci., Mo. Sheriff's Assn., Mo. Apt. Owners Assn. (charter), St. Louis Real Estate Assn. Home: 2929 Magnolia St Saint Louis MO 63118 Office: 3869 Park Ave Saint Louis MO 63110

CLARK, FRED, legal writer, editor; b. Limon, Costa Rica, Dec. 12, 1930; came to U.S., 1968; s. Thomas C. and Irene (Penney) C.; student Central Am. Acad., 1944-49; B.Litt., U. Costa Rica, 1951; postgrad. Stafford Coll., 1956-57; barrister-at-law, Inner Temple, London, 1960; m. Dorothy Hyacinth James, Aug. 4, 1956; 1 son, Paul. Admitted to bar, Eng., 1960, Jamaica, 1960; master of langs. Merl Grove Sch., 1951-55; trust officer Govt. of Jamaica, 1960-61; individual practice law, Kingston, Jamaica, 1961-67; legal editor Corp. Trust Co., N.Y.C., 1968-69; sr. legal editor Prentice-Hall, Inc., Englewood Cliffs, N.J., 1969—; cons. commonwealth law. Trustee, United Ch. of Christ, 1970-78. Cert. in law Council Legal Edn. Mem. Internat. Commn. Jurists, Am. Mus. Natural History, Nat. Geog. Soc., Am. Ballet Theatre, Met. Opera Guild. Club: Rosicrucian Order. Editor, The Corp. Jour., 1968-69. Home: 39 W 4th St Freeport NY 11520 Office: Prentice-Hall Inc Sylvan Ave Englewood Cliffs NJ 07632

CLARK, GEORGE LEWIS, banker; b. Sidney, Mont., July 6, 1928; s. John Harry and Jean Elizabeth (Sherman) C.; B.A. in Liberal Arts, San Jose State Coll., 1958; m. Dixie C. Stiteler, May 10, 1973; children—Lisa, Patti. Examiner, FDIC, San Francisco, 1958-62; asst. v.p. Golden Gate Nat. Bank, San Francisco, 1962-64; v.p. San Diego Trust & Savs. Bank, 1964-68; exec. v.p. Security Nat. Bank, Roswell, N.Mex., 1968-73; asst. to chmn. First N.Mex. Bankshare Corp., Albuquerque, 1973-74; pres. First Nat. Bank, Albuquerque, 1974-78, Bank of Albuquerque, 1980—. Bd. dirs. Greater Albuquerque C. of C., 1975-78, United Way, Albuquerque, 1975-78. Served with USN, 1950-54. Decorated Air medal. Mem. N.Mex. Bankers Assn. (chmn. legis. com. 1977-78). Republican. Roman Catholic. Clubs: Elks, Albuquerque Country. Office: PO Box 947 Albuquerque NM 87103

CLARK, HENRY BENJAMIN, JR., food co. exec.; b. Chevy Chase, Md., Oct. 8, 1915; s. Henry Benjamin and Lena Hollida (Sefton) C.; B.S., Northwestern U., 1937; M.B.A., Harvard U., 1940; m. Geraldine Putman, July 24, 1942; children—Putman D., Sefton R. With Castle & Cooke, Inc., Honolulu, 1946—, treas., 1958-72, v.p., 1962-70, exec. v.p., 1970—, vice chmn. bd., 1980—, also dir. various affiliated cos.; dir. Bunker Hill Income Securities, Inc., Hawaiian Airlines, Hawaiian Ind. Refinery, Hawaiian Tel. Co., Honolulu Gas, Pacific Resources. Pres., Hawaii Prep. Acad.; bd. dirs. Honolulu Symphony, Goodwill Vocat. Centers of Honolulu, Honolulu Acad. Arts; Honolulu YMCA, Rehab. Hosp. of Pacific, Palolo Chinese Home, McInerny Found., Aloha United Way, Hawaii Loa Coll., Bishop Mus., Pacific and Asian Affairs Council. Served with USNR, 1940-45. Clubs: Pacific, Outrigger Canoe, Pacific-Union. Office: 130 Merchant St Honolulu HI 96813

CLARK, HERBERT TRYON, JR., banker; b. Glastonbury, Conn., Jan. 7, 1913; s. Herbert Tryon and Alice (House) C.; B.S., U. Conn., 1934; m. Barbara Richmond, Aug. 1, 1936 (dec. June 10, 1980); children—Herbert Tryon, LeRoy Richmond, Marjorie Ann. Asst. foreman assembly Royal-McBee Typewriter Co., Hartford, Conn., 1934-41; asst. plant mgr. Buffalo Arms Corp., 1941-44; procurement mgr. Gen. Ry. Signal Co., Rochester, 1945; purchasing agt. Frontier Industries div., Houdaille, Ind., 1946-49; pres. Geo. C. Field Co., Madison, Conn., 1949-78, Tuxis Lumber, 1957-68; pres. First Fed. Savs. & Loan Assn., Madison, Conn., 1957-64, chmn. bd., 1964-75; pres. Wildwood Properties Inc., 1965-78; arbitrator Am. Arbitration Assn., 1976—; dir. Coginchaug Devel. Corp. (now Lyman Farms, Inc.), 1967-78. Mem. Bd. Finance Madison, 1959-65, sec., 1962-65. Active Boy Scouts Am.; mem. Municipal Bldg. Study Com., 1967-69. Mem. Theta Sigma Chi. Conglist. Mason (32 deg.). Club: Exchange. Home: 23 Maplewood Ln PO Box 489 Madison CT 06443 Office: 107 Bradley Rd Madison CT 06443

CLARK, HOWARD LONGSTRETH, JR., fin. exec.; b. N.Y.C., Feb. 1, 1944; s. Howard Longstreth and Elsie (Dancaster) C.; B.S.B.A., Boston U., 1967; M.B.A., Columbia U., 1968; m. Sandra Little, Aug. 27, 1966; 1 son, Howard Longstreth III. Exec. v.p., chief investment officer Am. Express Co., N.Y.C., 1981—; dir. Palm Beach Co., Coca-Cola Bottling Co. of Miami, Inc., Magic Chef, Inc. Episcopalian. Clubs: River, Racquet and Tennis, Round Hill, Blind Brook, Links. Home: 1112 Park Ave New York NY 10028 Office: American Express Plaza New York NY 10004

CLARK, HUGH SCOTT, printing ink co. exec.; b. Detroit, Feb. 28, 1922; s. Frank Scott and Mary (Neff) C.; student U. Mich., 1938-40; B.A., Wayne State U., 1942; m. Florence Madden, Jan. 10, 1945; children—Michael, Hugh Scott, David, Jean, Mark, Suzanne. With Kohl & Madden Printing Ink Corp., Chgo., 1945—, pres., chief exec. officer, 1969—, chmn., 1978—, also dir.; dir. Rycoline Corp., 1420 Sheridan Road Bldg. Served as aviator USN, 1942-45. Mem. Graphic Arts Found. (Man of Yr. award 1978). Roman Catholic. Clubs: Tavern, North Shore Country, Bob O'Link Country. Home: 1420 Sheridan Rd Wilmette IL 60091 Office: 1132 S Jefferson St Chicago IL 60607

CLARK, JAMES GORDON, cons. engr., author; b. Kansas City, Mo., Dec. 23, 1913; s. John Arthur and Stella (Wright) C.; A.S., Kansas City Jr. Coll., 1933; B.S. with honors, U. Ill., 1935, M.S., 1939; m. Jeannette Hazel McKinstry, May 8, 1937; children—Nannette, Diana; m. 2d, Janice Elizabeth Winters, Nov. 28, 1952; children—Mary, Jane, James. Instr. civil engring. Ore. State Coll., 1935; jr. engr. U.S. Bur. Reclamation, Denver, 1936; from instr. to prof. civil engring. U. Ill., 1936-56; asso. Harry Blake Engrs.; owner James G. Clark, cons. engr.; partner Clark, Dietz, & Assos., Clark, Altay & Assos.; pres. Clark, Dietz, & Assos.-Engrs., Inc., until 1975, cons. to firm, until 1981; sr. v.p. ESCA Cons., Inc., 1981—; interim profl. work in structural engring. Am. Bridge Co., Bethlehem Steel Co., Howard, Needles, Tammen & Bergendoff, Curtiss Wright Corp., Consol. Vultee Aircraft Corp.; partner Balke & Clark; asso. Harry Balke Engrs. Chmn., James F. Lincoln Arc Welding Found. Award Programs. Mem. profl. engrs. examining com. for Ill. Trustee Ill. Bapt. Student Found., 1954—. Mem. Nat., Ill. socs. profl. engrs., ASCE (past pres. Central Ill. sect.), Am. Soc. Engring. Edn., Am. Ry. Engring. Assn., Am. Ry. Bridge and Building Assn., Am. Welding Soc., ASTM, Hwy. Research Bd., Am. Road Builders Assn., Assn. Commerce, Urbana (dir.), Sigma Xi, Tau Beta Pi, Chi Epsilon. Author; Elementary Theory and Design of Flexural Members, 1950; Welded Deck Highway Bridges, 1950; Welded Highway Bridge Design, 1952; Comparative Bridge Designs, 1954; Welded Interstate Highway Bridges, 1960. Home: 716 W Florida Ave Urbana IL 61801 Office: 302 W Elm St Urbana IL 61801

CLARK, JAMES LEROY, ret. plastic products mfg. co. exec.; b. Ottawa, Kans., Sept. 26, 1913; s. William Everett and Charlotte Daisy (Horn) C.; student Carnegie Inst. Tech., 1931-35; m. Harriet Elizabeth Janda, Nov. 24, 1937; children—Mary Elizabeth Clark Parsons, Virginia Lee. Sales mgr. Wis. Cuneo Press, Milw., 1937-41; divisional sales mgr. Milprint, Inc., Milw., 1941-43; pres. Clarvan Corp., Milw., 1943-53, Mark-Clark, Inc., Milw., 1953-62, Plastronics, Inc., Milw., 1962-79; dir. Mgmt. Resources Assos., Inc., 1977—. Vice pres., dir. Milw. Civic Alliance, 1976—; bd. dirs. Milw. Hearing Soc., De Paul Rehab. Hosp., Milw., 1976—; chmn. Bicentennial com. Greater Milw. Service Clubs, 1976—. Mem. Soc. Plastics Industry, Am. Mgmt. Assn., Wis. Mfrs. Assn., Health Industry Mfrs. Assn. (chmn. engring. com.), Friends of Museum, Milw. Art Center, Riveredge Found., Milw. Soc. Club: Sertoma. Patentee health care and other plastic products. Home: 4700 N Lake Dr Whitefish Bay WI 53211

CLARK, JAMES WHITLEY, food co. exec.; b. Springfield, Mo., Nov. 23, 1930; s. Henry B. and Dorothy (Demuth) C.; B.J., U. Mo., 1952; Program Mgmt. Devel., Harvard Bus. Sch., 1970; m. Frances Ann Seibert, July 5, 1952; children—Anne Louise, Janet Susan, John Demuth. Mgr. advt. Fleming Cos., Inc., Oklahoma City, 1959-60, store devel. rep., 1961-62, sales mgr., 1963-64, dir. advt., 1965-71, dir. communications, 1972-75, corp. sec., dir. communications, 1975-80, v.p., sec., 1980—. Served with USAF, 1952-53. Mem. Am. Soc. Corp. Secs. Methodist. Home: 1912 Westridge Dr Edmond OK 73034 Office: 6601 N Broadway Box 26647 Oklahoma City OK 73126

CLARK, JOHN FARRELL, banker, leasing co. exec.; b. N.Y.C., Jan. 19, 1927; s. John Ward and Katherine (Coyne) C.; student Am. Inst. Banking, 1947-51, Columbia U., 1952-54, N.Y. U., 1955; postgrad. Grad. Sch. Bus., N.Y. U., 1965-67. With Mfrs. Trust Co., N.Y.C., 1946-50, Bankers Trust Co., N.Y.C., 1951-56, Comml. Credit Corp., N.Y.C., 1956-59, European-Am. Banking Corp., N.Y.C., 1959-67; with N.J. Bank N.A., Passaic, 1967—, v.p., 1967-78; pres. Middle States Leasing Corp., Passaic, 1972-78; sr. v.p. Bank of Tokyo, N.Y.C., 1978—. Trustee, Garden State Credit Bur. Served with USNR, 1945-46, 51-52. Mem. Passaic County Bankers Assn. (past pres.), Dist. I Bankers Assn. (past v.p.), Robert Morris Assos., Bank Credit Assos., N.Y. Credit and Fin. Mgmt. Assn., N.J. Credit Execs. Republican. Roman Catholic. K.C. Home: 555 Gorge Rd Cliffside Park NJ 07010 Office: 100 Broadway New York NY 10005

CLARK, JOHN HOWARD, banker; b. Savannah, Ga., Aug. 15, 1937; s. John Stafford and Ellene Cora (Wallace) C.; B.S. in Bus. Adminstrn., The Citadel, Charleston, S.C., 1959; M.B.A., U. S.C., 1960; m. Judith Jane Weathersbee, Apr. 22, 1961; children—John C., Kelly E. Asst. cashier Fulton Nat. Bank of Atlanta, 1960-66, sr. v.p., 1974-78; v.p. First Ala. Bank, Birmingham, 1966-74; pres. Moultrie (Ga.) Nat. Bank, 1978—. Bd. dirs. Moultrie Housing Authority; ex officio dir. Moultrie Conquitt County Devel. Authority; bd. dirs. Moultrie YMCA; chmn. United Way of Colquitt County, Ga., 1980—. Served to maj. USAR. Mem. Am. Bankers Assn., Robert Morris Assos., Ga. State C. of C. (indsl. devel. council), Ga. Bankers Assn., Ind. Bankers Assn. Am., Assn. Citadel Men, Res. Officers Assn. Methodist. Clubs: Kiwanis, Elks. Office: PO Box 849 Moultrie GA 31768

CLARK, JOHN PAUL, banker; b. Bklyn., May 5, 1940; s. John Ambrose and Julia Catherine (Horgan) C.; B.A., Fordham U., 1961, J.D., 1965; m. Gloria Rice, 1967. Admitted to N.Y. State bar; securities analyst Erdman & Co., mems. N.Y. Stock Exchange, 1966-67; sr. securities analyst Coggeshall & Hicks, mems. N.Y. Stock Exchange, 1967-69; fin. v.p. Datron Systems, Inc., 1969-70; v.p. European banking group Citibank, N.A., N.Y.C., 1970—; dir. Bernuth Corp., Advanced Materials Systems, Inc. Vice chmn., treas. Interstate Sanitation Commn., 1975—; mem. Democratic Nat. Fin. Council, 1980—. Roman Catholic. Office: 399 Park Ave New York NY 10043

CLARK, JOHN WINTHROP, metals co. exec.; b. Sunderland, Mass., Sept. 14, 1928; s. Chester Augustus and Hazel Ruth (Keyes) C.; B.A., Gettysburg Coll., 1952; m. Geraldine Louise Snavely, May 31, 1952; children—Robert C., Thomas C. with Aluminum Co. of Am., 1954-68, mgr. distbn. and field sales Alcoa of Australia Ltd., 1964-68; pres., owner Clark Metals, Inc., Gardena, Calif., 1969—. Served with USAF, 1952-54. Mem. Nat. Assn. Alumnium Distbrs. (dir., chmn. producer relations com., chmn. Alcoa adv. council 1976). Clubs: Rolling Hills (Calif.) Country, Virginia (Calif.) Country. Office: 14605 S Main St Gardena CA 90248

CLARK, LYMAN HATHAWAY, fin. cons., resort property exec.; b. Berwyn, Ill., Dec. 29, 1944; s. Charles Dougherty and Agnes Theresa (Ogden) C.; A.B., Harvard U., 1968; M.B.A. (Bache & Co. scholar), Stanford U., 1971. Chief economic impact analysis br. Office of Planning and Evaluation, EPA, Washington, 1971-73; mortgage broker Sonnenblick-Goldman of Washington, Inc., 1973-74; econs., corporate fin. cons., Washington, 1974—; pres. Resort Properties Internat., Inc., Washington, 1980—. Tchr., transcendental meditation program Internat. Meditation Soc. Home: 1320 21st St NW 406 Washington DC 20036 Office: 1710 Connecticut Ave Washington DC 20009

CLARK, MELVIN EUGENE, chem. co. exec.; b. Ord, Nebr., Oct. 2, 1916; s. Ansel B. and Ruth J. (Bullock) C.; B.S. in Chem. Engring., U. Colo., 1937; postgrad. Columbia, 1952; Advanced Mgmt. Program, Harvard, 1961; m. Virginia M. Hiller, Sept. 16, 1938; children—John Robert, Walter Clayton, Dale Eugene, Merry Sue. Asst. editor McGraw-Hill Pub. Co., N.Y.C., 1937-41; chief program br. Chem. Bur., WPB, Washington, 1941-44 mgr. alkali sales Wyandotte Chem Co. (Mich.), 1944-53; v.p. marketing Frontier Chem. Co., Wichita, Kans., 1953-65; v.p., asst gen. mgr. chem. div. Vulcan Materials Co., Wichita, 1965-69, exec. v.p. Chems. div., 1969—. Recipient U. Colo. Alumni award, 1962; Chem. Market Research Assn. Meml. award, 1963. Mem. Am. Chem. Soc., Chem. Market Research Assn., Am. Inst. Chem. Engrs., Sales and Mktg. Execs. Wichita (pres. 1965-66), Chlorine Inst. (pres. 1978-80). Contbr. articles to trade mags. Home: 3200 Kiltie Ln Birmingham AL 35243 Office: Vulcan Materials Co PO Box 7689 Birmingham AL 35253

CLARK, R(UFUS) BRADBURY, lawyer, bus. exec.; b. Des Moines, May 11, 1924; s. Rufus Bradbury and Gertrude Martha (Burns) C.; A.B., Harvard, 1946, J.D., 1951; diploma in law (Fulbright fellow) Oxford (Eng.) U., 1952; m. Polly Ann King, Sept. 6, 1949; children—Cynthia Ann Clark Maxwell, Rufus Bradbury, John Atherton. Admitted to Calif. bar, 1952; asso. firm O'Melveny & Myers, Los Angeles, 1952-62, partner, 1962—; dir. 1st Charter Fin. Corp., Brown Internat. Corp., Automatic Machinery & Electronics, Inc., So. Calif. Water Co., Econ. Resources Corp. Chancellor, Episcopal Diocese Los Angeles. Served with U.S. Army, 1943-46. Decorated Bronze Star with oak leaf cluster, Purple Heart with oak leaf cluster. Mem. Am., Calif. (chmn. com. on corps. 1976-77), Los Angeles bar assns. Clubs: Calif., Alamitos Bay Yacht; Chancery (Los Angeles). Editor: California Corporation Laws (Ballantine & Sterling), rev. 4th edit., 1976. Home: 615 Alta Vista Circle S Pasadena CA 91030 Office: 611 W 6th St Los Angeles CA 90017

CLARK, ROBERT HENRY, JR., holding co. exec.; b. Manchester, N.H., Mar. 4, 1941; s. Robert Henry and Elva C. (Stearns) C.; B.S. in Bus. Adminstrn., Boston U., 1964; m. Rosalie Foster Case, Dec. 21, 1963; children—Robert Henry III, Hilary Eagan, Hadley Case. Municipal bond underwriter Merrill Lynch, Pierce, Fenner & Smith, N.Y.C., 1964-70; v.p. Case, Pomeroy & Co., Inc., N.Y.C., 1971-75, exec. v.p., 1975—, also dir.; v.p. finance Felmont Oil Corp., 1972-79, exec. v.p., 1979—; dir. Applied Optics Center Corp., Langdon P. Cook & Co., Inc., Case-Pomeroy Oil Corp., Essex Offshore, Inc., MFE Corp., Hazeltine Corp. Mem. Sigma Alpha Epsilon. Clubs: Downtown Assn., University (N.Y.C.); Leash; Bald Peak Colony (Melvin Village, N.H.); Round Hill. Home: Dogwood Ln Greenwich CT 06830 Office: 6 E 43d St New York NY 10017

CLARK, ROBERT OTTIS, fin. cons.; b. St. Paul, Nov. 20, 1930; s. Robert Dean and Elizabeth (Ottis) C.; A.B., Princeton U., 1952; M.B.A., Stanford U., 1957; m. Ruth Sargent, Nov. 28, 1959 (div. 1979); children—Hilary Cutler, Rebecca Dean, Daphne Kellogg. Sales engr. Kaiser Aluminum, Milw., 1957-60; cons. Booz Allen & Hamilton, N.Y.C. and Chgo., 1960-64; v.p. Laird Inc., N.Y.C., 1964-69; mng. dir. New Court & Partners subs. N.M. Rothschild & Sons Ltd., London, 1969-70, Fairmont Securities Inc., London, 1971—. Served with U.S. Army, 1952-54; Korea. Club: Princeton. Home: 11 Berkeley Gardens London W8 4AP England Office: 104 Park St London W1Y 3RJ England

CLARK, RUSSELL WARD, constrn. co. exec.; b. Shelby, Ohio, May 6, 1942; s. George William and Pauline Ruth (Bell) C.; B.S., Miami (Ohio) U., 1965; M.B.A., U. Dayton, 1977; m. M. Diane Hardin, June 20, 1970; 1 son, Mark Kerr. Staff acct. Arthur C. Jahn & Co., Columbus, Ohio, 1966-70, Arthur Young & Co., Columbus, 1970; controller Columbia Properties, Inc., Columbus, 1970-75; treas. Wallick Constrn. Co., Columbus, 1976—. Served with USAF, 1968-69. C.P.A., Ohio. Mem. Am. Inst. C.P.A.'s, Am. Mgmt. Assn., Nat. Assn. Accountants, Inst. Mgmt. Acctg., Ohio Soc. C.P.A.'s. Home: 2000 Riverhill Rd Columbus OH 43221 Office: 150 E Mound St Columbus OH 43215

CLARK, STUART ELWYN, restaurant mktg. co. exec.; b. Bridgeport, Conn., July 28, 1943; s. Albert J. and Dorothy Mae (Stuart) Nutile; student Hope Coll., 1962-64; B.S. in Bus. Adminstrn., Ferris State U., 1969; m. Mary Ellen Montei, Aug. 7, 1971; children—Sarah Marice, Jennifer Ellen, Stuart Charles Alden. Gen. mgr. R.C. Andresen, Inc., Big Rapids, Mich., 1969-70, Mt. Pleasant Community Hotel Corp. (Mich.), 1970-72, Precision Pettifoggery, Inc., Holland, Mich., 1973-80; pres. Crazy Horse Saloons, Holland, 1973-80, Clark Agency, Inc., Macatawa, Mich., 1978—; owner, regional franchiser Tidy Car, Inc.; owner, operator Quaker State, rustproofing franchise, Ugly Duckling, auto rentals franchise. Served with U.S. Army, 1967-69. Decorated Bronze Star, Air medal. Mem. Nat., W. Mich. restaurant assns., W. Mich. Tourist Assn., C. of C. Republican. Mem. Reformed Ch. Clubs: Elks, Optimists (v.p. Holland 1977-78). Home: 1926 96th St Zeeland MI 49464

CLARK, TIMOTHY GENEREUX, mgmt. cons.; b. Pasadena, Calif., May 24, 1939; s. Benjamin C. and Margaret G. (Genereux) C.; A.B., U. So. Calif., 1961; M.B.A., Harvard U., 1965; m. Diana Martell, Oct. 27, 1962; 1 dau., Pamela G. Sales supr., product mgr. Gen. Foods Corp., 1965-68; cons. Booz, Allen & Hamilton, Inc., 1968-72, v.p., Los Angeles, 1974—; v.p. mktg. Arrowhead div. Coca-Cola Bottling Co. of Los Angeles, 1972-74. Trustee, Center for Non-Profit Mgmt. Mem. Harvard Bus. Sch. Assn. So. Calif. (v.p.). Republican. Clubs: Annandale Golf (Pasadena, Calif.); Milbrook (Greenwich, Conn.); Harvard (N.Y.C.), Rotary, Jonathan (Los Angeles). Office: Booz Allen & Hamilton Inc 523 W 6th St Suite 550 Los Angeles CA 90014

CLARK, WILLIAM JAMES, ins. co. exec.; b. Kansas City, Mo., Oct. 1, 1923; s. William LeRoy and Margaret (Theobald) C.; student Kansas City Jr. Coll., 1941-42; B.S., U. Mo., 1947; m. Irene S. Dubreuil, July 15, 1974; children by previous marriage—Holly, Jane Clark Huegi, Nancy, Patty; stepchildren—Lynn Dubreuil Pugh, Lisa Dubreuil Wrisley. With Mass. Mut. Life Ins. Co., Springfield, 1947—, v.p. sales, 1967-70, sr. v.p., 1971-74, pres., 1974—, mem. exec. council, 1971—, also dir.; trustee 1st Nat. Bank Boston. Chmn., United Way Fund Pioneer Valley, 1973—. Bd. dirs. Springfield Coll.; v.p. Springfield chpt. United Fund. Served to 1st lt. USAAF, 1943-45. Mem. Life Ins. Mktg. and Research Assn. (dir.), Am. Council Life Ins. (mem. com. on field relations), Am. Soc. C.L.U.'s. Club: Longmeadow

(Mass.) Country; Colony (Springfield). Office: 1295 State St Springfield MA 01111

CLARKE, BERNARD JOSEPH, gas co. exec.; b. Phila., Sept. 26, 1920; s. Bernard and Bridget (Leonard) C.; B.S., Villanova U., 1942; M.S., U. Mich., 1948, postgrad., 1948-52; m. Agnes L. Flanigan, Sept. 4, 1948; children—Barbara, Mary, Louise, Richard, Bernard, Margaret, James, Joan. Research asst. U. Mich., Ann Arbor, 1950-52; engr. Columbia Gas System Service Corp., subsidiary Columbia Gas System Inc., Columbus, Ohio, 1952-53, sr. engr., 1953-54, sr. engr., N.Y.C., 1954-55, supervisory engr., 1955-57, chief supervisory engr., 1957-58, v.p. from 1958, chmn. bd., also dir.; pres. Columbia Gas System, Inc., 1970-75, chmn. bd., pres., 1975, now chmn. bd., also dir.; dir. Columbia Hydrocarbon Corp., N.Y.C.; sr. v.p., dir. Columbia Gas of Ohio, Inc., 1963-67, chmn. bd., 1967; sr. v.p., dir. Ohio Fuel Gas Co., 1963-67, chmn. bd., 1967—; sr. v.p., dir. Ohio Valley Gas Co., 1963-67, chmn. bd., 1967— (all Columbus). Served to lt. USNR, 1942-46. Office: 20 Montchanin Rd Wilmington DE 19807*

CLARKE, CHARLES PATRICK, electronics co. exec.; b. Chgo., Oct. 3, 1929; s. James Patrick and Elizabeth (McLaughlin) C.; student U. Ill., 1948-50; B.S., DePaul U., 1953. Auditor, Baumann Finney & Co., C.P.A.'s, Chgo., 1953-55; with Cuneo Press, Inc., Chgo., 1955-66, successively asst. gen. accounting supr., asst. chief corp. accountant, gen. auditor, 1955-61, systems, procedures and audit mgr., 1961-64, asst. to treas., 1964-66; comptroller Internat. Couriers Corp. (formerly Bankers Utilities Corp.), Chgo., 1966-69, treas., 1969-72, financial v.p., 1972-75; pres. C.P. Clarke & Assos., 1975-76; treas., corp. controller DC Electronics, Inc., Aurora, Ill., 1976—. C.P.A., Ill. Mem. Am. Inst. C.P.A.'s, Financial Execs. Inst., Ill. Soc. C.P.A.'s, Nat. Assn. Accts. Democrat. Roman Catholic. Home: 36 Parliament Dr W Palos Heights IL 60463 Office: 544 N Highland Ave Aurora IL 60506

CLARKE, CLIFFORD MONTREVILLE, assn. exec.; b. Ludowici, Ga., July 20, 1925; s. Clifford Montreville and Lella Bertrue (Hightower) C.; A.B. in Polit. Sci., Emory U., 1951. Radio engr., announcer Sta. WSAV, Savannah, Ga., 1941-43; pub. relations dir. Dept. Ga., Am. Legion, 1945-47; instr. Armstrong Coll., Savannah, 1947-48; asst. supt. Savannah Park and Tree Commn., 1951; instr., then supr. tng. dept. Lockheed Aircraft Corp., Marietta, Ga., 1951-52, mgr. employee services dept., 1952-53; exec. v.p. Asso. Industries Ga., 1953-66; pres. Ga. Bus. and Industry Assn., 1966-73; exec. dir. Bicentennial Council Thirteen Original States, 1973-74; pres. Arthritis Found., Atlanta, 1975—; mem. Am. Soc. Assn. Execs., 1955—, bd. dirs., 1958-67, mem. exec. com., 1960-67, treas., 1962-64, sr. v.p., 1964-65, pres., 1965-66; pres. Ga. Soc. Assn. Execs., 1958-60; v.p., chmn. state group Nat. Indsl. Council, 1966-68; mem. Ga. Urban and Tech. Assistance Adv. Council, 1965-68, Ga. Intergovtl. Relations Commn., 1966; mem. Ga. Ednl. Improvement Council, 1964-69, chmn., 1967-69; mem. Forward Ga. Commn., 1969-72, Ga. Commn. for Nat. Bicentennial Celebration, 1969-73, chmn., 1973-74; chmn. Chartered Assn. Exec. Chartering Bd., 1969-73; exec. com. Conf. State Mfrs. Assns., 1969-73. Bd. dirs. Atlanta Conv. Bur., 1968-72; mem. policy com. Grad. Sch. Bus., U. Ga., 1968-72; adv. bd. Ga. Vocat. Rehab., 1962-68; bd. dirs. Arthritis Found. Ga., 1965-71, Atlanta Community Services to Blind, 1965-72, Coop. Services for Blind, 1962-70, Atlanta Sch. Art. Served with inf. AUS, World War II. Decorated Purple Heart with 2 oak leaf clusters. Home: 2 Lullwater Pl NE Atlanta GA 30307 Office: Suite 1101 3400 Peachtree Rd Atlanta GA 30326

CLARKE, CORDELLA KAY KNIGHT MAZUY, ins. firm exec.; b. Springfield, Mo., Nov. 22, 1938; d. William Horace and Charline (Bentley) Knight; A.B. with honors in English, U. N.C., 1960; M.S. in Statistics, N.C. State U., 1962; m. M. Logan Clarke, Jr., July 22, 1978; children by previous marriage—Katharine Michelle Mazuy, Christopher Knight Mazuy. Statistician, Research Triangle Inst., Durham, N.C., 1960-63; statis. cons. Arthur D. Little, Inc., Cambridge, Mass., 1963-67; mktg. research project mgr. Polaroid Corp., Cambridge, 1967, dir. mktg. research, 1968-69, mgr. mktg. planning and analysis, 1969-70; dir. mktg. and bus. planning Transaction Tech., Inc., Cambridge, 1970-72; pres. Mazuy Assos., Boston, 1972-73; v.p. Nat. Shawmut Bank, Boston, 1973-74; sr. v.p., dir. mktg. Shawmut Corp., 1974-78; sr. v.p., dir. retail banking Shawmut Bank, 1976-78; v.p. corp. devel. Arthur D. Little, Inc., 1978-79; v.p. Conn. Gen. Life Ins. Co., 1979—; faculty Williams Sch. Banking; adv. com. Bur. of Census, 1978—; corp. adv. bd. Hartford Nat. Bank & Trust Co., 1980—; dir. McGraw Hill, Data Terminal Systems; tchr. Amos Tuck Grad. Sch. Bus., Dartmouth Coll., 1964-65, exec.-in-residence, 1978, 80, now bd. overseers; exec.-in-residence Wheaton Coll., 1978; vis. prof. Simmons Grad. Sch. Mgmt., 1978; mem. schs. adv. council Bank Mktg. Assn., 1976-78. Mem. Mass. Gov.'s Commn. on Status of Women, 1977-79; bd. corporators Babson Coll., 1977-80; adv. bd. Boston Mayor's Office Cultural Affairs, 1977-79; bd. dirs. Greater Hartford Arts Council, 1979—; trustee Children's Mus. Hartford, 1980—. Mem. Am. Statis. Assn., Am. Mktg. Assn., Phi Beta Kappa, Phi Kappa Phi, Kappa Alpha Theta. Columnist Am. Banker, 1976-78. Home: 31 Main St Farmington CT 06032 Office: Conn Gen Life Ins Co Hartford CT 06152

CLARKE, EDWIN V., JR., elec. mfg. co. exec.; b. 1925; B.S.I.E., U. Pitts., 1948; married. With Saginaw Bay Inc., 1951-54; with Westinghouse Electric Corp., 1950-51, 54—, v.p. mktg. industry and def., 1971-74, exec. v.p. components and materials, 1974-76, exec. v.p. transmission and distbn., 1976-78, pres. Industry Products Co., 1978—. Served to 2d lt. USAF, 1943-46. Office: Westinghouse Electric Corp Gateway Center Westinghouse Bldg Pittsburgh PA 15222*

CLARKE, GARY BATES, truck co. exec.; b. Jacksonville, Fla., May 19, 1946; s. Edgar Thomas and Ann Louise (Van Ormer) C.; B.S., Fla. State U., 1968, M.B.A. cum laude, 1969; m. Sherry Elayne Marrell, Aug. 5, 1966; 1 son, Todd. Sr. accountant, Arthur Andersen & Co., Miami, Fla., 1969-71; dir. finance Bati Services of Fla., Delray Beach, 1971-72; controller Devcon Internat. Corp., Pompano Beach, Fla., 1972-74, v.p., 1974-76; v.p., controller South Fla. Mack Trucks, Inc., Ft. Lauderdale, 1977—. Gulf Life Ins. Co. scholar, 1967-68; Fla. State U. fellow, 1968-69. C.P.A., Fla. Am., Fla. insts. C.P.A.'s, Nat. Assn. Accountants Fin. Execs. Inst., Beta Gamma Sigma. Republican. Presbyn. Recipient Sells award, 1969; Fla. C.P.A. Gold medal award, 1969. Home: 2920 NW 107th Ave Coral Springs FL 33065 Office: PO Box 21186 Fort Lauderdale FL 33335

CLARKE, GEORGE F. S., ins. co. exec.; b. Govan, Sask., Can., Feb. 1, 1921; s. Joseph Orville and Edra Francene Clarke; B.Commerce with honors, U. Man., 1950; m. Sheila Margaret Stewart, Sept. 18, 1945 (dec.); 1 dau., Georgia Margaret; m. 2d, Elsa Marian McLeod Eakins, May 7, 1977. With Mfrs. Life Ins. Co., 1950-67; actuary Sun Life Assurance Co. Can., Toronto, Ont., 1967-68, vp., chief actuary, 1968-70, sr. v.p., 1970-72, exec. v.p., 1972-78, pres., 1978—, dir., 1978—; chmn., dir. Sun Life Can. Investment Mgmt. Ltd., Sun Life Can. Benefit Mgmt. Ltd., Suncan Equity Services Co.; dep. chmn., dir. Sun Life Assurance Co. Can. (U.K.) Ltd.; pres., dir. Sun Life Assurance Co. Can. (U.S.), Suncan Benefit Services Co., Sun Growth Fund, Inc.; bd. dirs. Can. Cancer Soc. Served to lt. RCAF, 1942-46. Fellow Soc. Actuaries, Can. Inst. Actuaries; mem. Life Office Mgmt. Assn. (dir.), Internat. Congress Actuaries. Clubs: Royal Montreal Curling (past pres.), Royal Montreal Golf, Mount Royal, Granite, Toronto, Masons. Home: 45 Dunvegan Rd Toronto ON M4V 2P5 Canada Office: 20 King St W PO Box 4150 Station A Toronto ON M5W 2C9 Canada

CLARKE, GERALD SIMS, printing co. exec.; b. Monticello, Ark., July 27, 1945; s. Donald A. and Martha (Sims) C.; B.S. in Mech. Engring., U. Ark., 1968; m. Susan Kay Dennehy, June 14, 1969; children—Cable Shane, Casey Dawn. From foreman to sect. foreman engring. and prodn. mgmt. Corning Glass Works, Muskogee, Okla., 1972-76; quality control engring. supr., then quality control mgr. Teledyne Water Pik Co., Ft. Collins, Colo., 1976-78; v.p., dir. ops., corp. dir. Metric Machining Co., Monrovia, Calif., 1978-80; gen. mgr. ops. Richmark Printers Inc., Aurora, Colo., 1980—; co-founder, 1979, since dir. Pentad Corp. Served to capt. USAF, 1968-72; Vietnam. Decorated D.F.C., Air medal with 4 oak leaf clusters; Vietnamese Cross Gallantry. Mem. Am. Mgmt. Assn., Am. Soc. Quality Control (past regional vice chmn.), Mensa. Roman Catholic. Club: S. Suburban Met. Athletic (Denver). Home: 2638 E Fremont Pl Littleton CO 80122 Office: 3370 Peoria St Suite 205 Aurora CO 80010

CLARKE, JACK WELLS, corp. exec.; b. Abingdon, Va., June 26, 1914; s. James Sydnor and Ottie B. (Wells) C.; A.B., Williams Coll., 1935; postgrad. N.Y. U., 1935-37; m. Dorothy Irelan, Mar. 24, 1938. Bond analyst, statistician, N.Y.C., 1935-37; asst., later mgr. budget and statis. dept. Lion Oil Co., 1938-41, asst. to pres., asst. to chmn. bd., 1947-51; dir. pub. relations Tex. Eastern Transmission Corp., 1951-55; exec. v.p. Freestate Indsl. Devel. Co., 1955-56, pres., dir., 1956-68; pres., dir. North Shreveport Devel. Co., 1956-68; now ind. investor developer. Bd. dirs. Shreveport Econ. Devel. Found., Holiday in Dixie; past chmn. Caddo Parish Dem. Assn. Served from ensign to lt. USNR, 1942-45. Fellow Am. Indsl. Devel. Council (certified indsl. developer); mem. Shreveport C. of C., Am. Ordnance Assn., Urban Land Inst., Pub. Affairs Research Council La., Navy League, Shreveport-Bossier Bd. Realtors (v.p.), Shreveport Com. of 100, Internat. Council Shopping Centers, Ret. Officers Assn., Phi Delta Theta. Episcopalian. Clubs: Shreveport; Eldorado Country (Palm Desert, Calif.). Home: 708 Azalea Dr Shreveport LA 71106 Office: PO Box 6 Shreveport LA 71161

CLARKE, JOSEPH BRIAN, mfg. co. exec.; b. Toronto, Ont., Can., Dec. 2, 1938; s. Kirkwood Johnson and Ethel May (Thomas) C.; student Ryerson Inst. Tech., 1957-61; m. Odette Hamel, July 24, 1972; children—Johanna, Krystina. Sales supr. Moore Bus. Forms, Toronto, 1961-65; v.p. mktg. Deluxe Reading Corp., Toronto, 1966; exec. v.p. Coleco (Can.) Ltd., Montreal, 1967-78, pres., 1978—; v.p. mktg. Coleco Industries, Inc., Hartford, Conn., 1970—. Mem. Can. Export Assn., Can. Toy Mfrs. Assn., Econ. Initiative and Devel. Commn. Montreal. Office: 4000 St Ambroise St Montreal PQ H4C 2C8 Canada

CLARKE, NEIL J(ACKSON), SR., lawyer; b. Ava, Mo., Oct. 16, 1905; s. Joshua S. and Lucinda (Hayes) C.; student State Coll., Springfield, Mo., 1924-28, U. Mo., 1929-31; m. Gertrude McCollom, May 10, 1961; children—Neil Jackson, Elizabeth Hall. Prin., grade sch., Ava, 1926-27; admitted to Mo. bar, 1931; city atty., 1931-35; gen. practice Ava, 1931-40, Pasadena, Los Angeles, 1949—; referee Mo. Compensation Com., 1940-43; mem. Blackinton, Reid & Clarke, 1943-48; adjuster Asso. Indemnity, 1946-49; atty. Ink Makers Inc., Technol. Services Inc., Harold E. Simpson Landscape Constrn. Co. Inc., Welsh Printing Co., Inc., Tulleners Enterprises, Inc., Tie-Man, Inc., C.C.D.M. Inc., Product Diversification, Inc., Equine Services, Inc., Ahead With Houses Inc., Tulleners Constrn. Corp. Mem. Am., Mo., Calif., Pasadena bar assns., Los Angeles Lawyers Club, Delta Theta Phi. Republican. Presbyn. Club: Sierra. Home: 300 Monte Vista Rd Arcadia CA 91106 Office: 3814 E Colorado St Pasadena CA 91107

CLARKE, REGINALD LLOYD, fin. exec.; b. Edmonton, Alta., Can., Feb. 11, 1942; came to U.S., 1960, naturalized, 1960; s. Harold Wallace Vincent and Norma May (Steeves) C.; B.A., U. Alta., 1961; M.A., Am. Inst. Fin., 1964; m. Ghyslaine Fournier, Mar. 10, 1973. Pres., United Guaranty Group, Inc., Washington, 1965-67, First United Mortgage & Escrow, Inc., Washington, 1965-68; Far East sales mgr. Investors Overseas Services Co., Geneva, 1969-72; owner St. Petersburg (Fla.) Yacht Sales Co. 1974; mng. dir. Econ. Devel. Corp. Americas, 1978—; pres. I.R.E.X. Premium Acceptance Corp., 1978—, Internat. Res. Exchange Ins. Co. Ltd., 1979—; v.p. corp. acquisition N. Am. Biols. Inc., 1979-80; v.p. Capital Premium Fin. Corp., 1980—; exec. v.p. Grands Prix Assos., Inc. 1979—, Interkem Mix Master Chems., 1980—; cons. fin. mgmt. S. Am. Export Assn. Mem. Am. Mgmt. Assn., Am. Bankers Assn. (dir. 1967-71), Commodity Futures Trading Assn., Internat. Platform Assn., Internat. C. of C. (dir. 1976, 78). Democrat. Club: Bankers. Contbr. articles to profl. jours. Home: 8800 SW 68th Ct Miami FL 33156 Office: PO Box 524185 Miami FL 33152

CLARKE, ROBERT BRADSTREET, publishing co. exec.; b. Mountainside, N.J., Oct. 31, 1928; s. Bert and Antoinette L. (Bartlett Baker) C.; student U. Miami, 1947; m. Roberta Powell, Aug. 26, 1950; children—William, Cynthia. With Grolier Enterprises, Inc., Danbury, Conn., 1949—, pres., chief exec. officer, 1978—, also chmn.; dir. adv. bd. Union Trust Co., Stamford, Conn. Trustee Danbury Hosp.; dir. Western Conn. Corporate Coll. Council, 1978—. Mem. Assn. Am. Publishers, Direct Mail/Mktg. Assn., Direct Selling Assn. Club: Saugatuck Harbor Yacht (chmn., commodore 1972-73). Office: Sherman Turnpike Danbury CT 06816

CLARKE, SHEILA RISE, advt. sales and promotion co. ofcl.; b. Buffalo, Feb. 14, 1942; d. Harry L. and May (Idels) Niesen; student Los Angeles Valley Coll., 1958-59, Choinard Art Inst., 1959. Mng. editor Interface mag. So. Calif. Computer Soc., Los Angeles, 1975-76; owner, mgr. Cybergrafix Advt. Design, Canoga Park, Calif., 1975-80; dir. advt. InfoWorld, Palo Alto, Calif., 1980—. Mem. Microcomputer Industry Trade Assn., Peninsula Women in Advt. Office: 530 Lytton Ave Suite 311 Palo Alto CA 94301

CLARKSON, CHARLES ANDREW, real estate investment co. exec.; b. Grove City, Pa., Sept. 1, 1945; s. Harold William and Jean Henrietta (Jaxtheimer) C.; A.B., Princeton U., 1967; J.D., George Washington U., 1972; m. Patricia Holt, June 14, 1969; children—Thomas Byerly, Blair Elizabeth. Real estate negotiator Safeway Stores, Washington, 1968-69; mortgage banker J.W. Rouse Co., Washington, 1970-73; pres. Alex Brown Realty, Balt., 1973-76; founder, pres. Charles A. Clarkson, Inc., Balt., 1976-78, Jacksonville, Fla., 1978—. Home: 9688 Deer Run Dr Ponte Vedra Beach FL 32082 Office: 3205 Independence Sq 1 Independent Dr Jacksonville FL 32202

CLARKSON, DAVID MICHAEL, software products co. exec.; b. San Angelo, Tex., Jan. 21, 1948; s. William George and Ruth Garvene (Carlin) C.; B.B.A. (Rotary scholar, U. Tex. Chancellor's scholar), U. Tex., Austin, 1970, postgrad., 1970-77; m. Martha Jane Bradley, Nov. 9, 1968; 1 son, Robert Michael. Computer systems devel. Tracor, Inc., Austin, 1969-71, MRI Systems corp., Austin, 1971-72; exec. v.p. Data Base Mgmt. Systems, Inc., Miami, Fla., 1972-76; v.p., dir. data base mgmt. systems research and devel., 2d v.p. Calif. Software Products, Inc., Santa Ana, 1976—; instr. data base mgmt. U. Calif., Santa Cruz. Mem. Assn. Computing Machinery, Internat. Brotherhood Magicians. Mormon. Club: Photography. Reviewer tech. papers, books. Home: 24361 Borrego Ct Laguna Niguel CA 92677 Office: Suite 300 525 N Cabrillo Park Dr Santa Ana CA 92701

CLARKSON, GRAHAM ALBERT, electronics co. exec.; b. London, Oct. 26, 1918; came to U.S., 1961; s. Albert Thomas and Emily (Paine-Parker) C.; B.S. in Elec. Engring. equivalent, London U., 1948; m. Evelyn May Corbin, June 27, 1940; children—Valerie Annette, Richard David, Anthony Graham, Julie Marsha. Lectr. radio/radar Air Ministry, London, 1948-51; sr. design engr. Can. Marconi, 1952-57; mgr. EF&I Lenkurt of Can., 1957-61; spl. products engr. RCA, 1961-63; sales mgr. RFL Industries, Boonton, N.J., 1963-70; chief elec. engr. Sippican Corp., Marion, Mass., 1971-73; dir. research and devel., fiber-optics div. TII Industries, Copiague, N.Y., 1973—. Served with RAF, 1934-41. Mem. IEEE, Quantum Electronics and Applications Soc., Optical Soc. Am., Inst. Transp. Engrs. (affiliate). Home: 108A La Bonne Vie Dr E Patchogue NY 11772 Office: TII Industries 100 N Strong Ave Lindehurst NY 11757

CLARY, RONALD GORDON, ins. agy. exec.; b. Moultrie, Ga., May 2, 1940; s. Ronald Ward and Hazel Collins C.; student Young Harris Coll., 1958-60; B.B.A. in Ins., U. Ga., 1962; LL.B., Woodrow Wilson Coll. Law, 1966. Field rep. Comml. Union Ins. Cos., 1962-67; ind. ins. agt., 1967—; ins. agt., sec. of agy. Day, Reynolds & Parks, Gainesville, Ga., 1971—. Mem. Ga. Assn. Ind. Ins. Agts., Gainesville Assn. Ind. Ins. Agts. (past pres.), Am. Legion. Republican. Baptist. Club: Elks. Home: 1184 Cumberland Valley Rd NE Gainesville GA 30501 Office: Day Reynolds & Parks 631 Spring St Gainesville GA 30501

CLAUSEN, ALDEN WINSHIP, banker; b. Hamilton, Ill., Feb. 17, 1923; s. Morton and Elsie (Kroll) C.; B.A., Carthage Coll., 1944, LL.D., 1970; LL.B., U. Minn., 1949; student Advanced Mgmt. Program, Harvard, 1966; LL.D., Lewis and Clark Coll., 1978, Gonzaga U., 1978; m. Mary Margaret Crassweller, Feb. 11, 1950; children—Eric David, Mark Winship. Admitted to Minn. bar, 1949, Calif. bar, 1950; with Bank of Am., N.T. & S.A., 1949—, v.p., 1961-65, sr. v.p., 1965-68, exec. v.p., 1968-69, vice chmn. bd. dirs., 1969, pres., chief exec. officer, 1970—. Past chmn. Bay Area Council; mem. San Francisco Clearing House Assn., Bus. Council; past pres. Internat. Monetary Conf.; bd. govs. United Way of Am.; bd. dirs. San Francisco Opera, SRI Internat., Harvard Bus. Sch. Assos.; trustee Brookings Instn.; adv. council Stanford Grad. Sch. Bus.; mem. The Bus. Roundtable. Mem. Calif. Bar Assn., Res. City Bankers Assn., Conf. Bd., Am. Bankers Assn., Japan-Calif. Assn. (co-chmn.), Calif. C. of C. (dir.), Japan-U.S. Econ. Relations Group, Nat. Council for Minority Bus. (dir.). Clubs: Commonwealth, Bankers (San Francisco); Pacific Union, Bohemian. Burlingame Country; Links (N.Y.C.); Metropolitan (Washington). Office: Bank of America PO Box 37000 San Francisco CA 94137

CLAWSON, HARRY QUINTARD MOORE, bus. cons.; b. N.Y.C., Aug. 8, 1924; s. Harry Marshall and Marguerite H. (Burgoyne) C.; grad. Staunton Mil. Acad., 1943; student N.Y. U., 1951-52, New Sch. for Social Research, 1953; m. (div. June 1964); m. 2d, Annemarie Korntner Thinnes, Dec. 1967. Supr. transp. responsible adminstrn. and liaison with U.S. Army for ARC overseas, 1945-46; asst. to dir. personnel UNESCO, Paris, 1947; resident rep. Texas Co., Douala, French Cameroun, West Africa, 1948-50; asst. dir. overseas bus. service McGraw-Hill Pub. Co., 1951-58; dir. client service Internat. Research Assos., N.Y.C., 1958-61; v.p., sec., dir. Frasch Whiton Boats, Inc., gen. mgr. sailboat tng. facility, 1961-64; pres. Harry Q.M. Clawson & Co., Inc., 1961-76; dir. planning and adminstrn. splty. chems. div. Essex Chem. Corp., Sayreville, N.J., 1976-78; pres. Harry Q. M. Clawson & Co., Inc., Charleston, S.C., 1978—. Pres. Centre Island Assn., 1974-76; vice chmn. planning bd., then chmn. Village of Centre Island, also environ. commr., 1976-77. Served with inf., AUS, 1943-45, ETO. Decorated Bronze Star. Mem. Ex-Mems. Assn. Squadron A. Club: N.Y. Yacht (N.Y.C.). Contbr. articles to profl. jours. Home: 1 King St Charleston SC 29401 Office: 18 Broad St Charleston SC 29401

CLAWSON, RAYMOND WALDEN, ind. oil producer; b. San Jose, Calif., Nov. 15, 1906; s. Benjamin B. and Mae Belle (Names) C.; LL.B., Am. U., 1936; m. Barbara M. Robbins, 1965; children by previous marriages—Russell Miller, Raymond Walden. Vice pres. C.C. Warren & Co., Oakland, Calif., 1924-27, ind. operator, exploration and devel. oil properties, N.Mex., 1936—; pub. Los Angeles Mirror, 1945-47; pres. Ariz. Securities, Phoenix, 1947-50, Transcontinental Oil Co., Los Angeles, 1947-49; geophys. cons. in offshore drilling ops. Gulf of Mexico, 1963—, North Sea, 1970—; chmn., chief exec. officer Clawco Petroleum Corp., 1979—. Clubs: Balboa Bay, Acapulco Yacht. Home: Newport Beach CA 92663 Office: PO Box 2102 Newport Beach CA 92663

CLAXTON, ALLEN ENES, univ. adminstr.; b. Providence, July 24, 1937; s. Allen Enes and Lucy May (Denton) C.; A.B. cum laude, Princeton U., 1959; M.P.A., Syracuse U., 1960; m. Harriet Louise Ladlee, July 18, 1959; children—Catherine Anne, Allen Enes, Philip Andrew. Budget examiner U.S. Bur. of Budget, Washington, 1960-65; chief, program budget unit AID, Washington, 1965-68, dep. mission dir. to Uruguay, 1968-70; asst. budget dir. City of N.Y. Budget Bur., 1970-74; budget dir. CUNY, 1974-75; v.p. fin. N.Y. U., N.Y.C., 1976—. Treas., Broadway Temple Corp., 1978—; mem. internat. com. YMCA, N.Y.C., 1980. Recipient Profl. Achievement award Bur. of Budget, 1963, Meritorious award AID, 1969. Congregationalist. Club: Deer Lake. Office: 70 Washington Sq S New York NY 10012

CLAY, MICHAEL TRAVIS, air force officer; b. Middletown, Ohio, June 10, 1944; s. Jack Henry and Christine (Spears) C.; B.S. in Math., Otterbein Coll., Westerville, Ohio, 1966; M.S. in Systems Mgmt., U. So. Calif., 1974; disting. grad. USAF Air Command and Staff Coll., 1978; m. Marlie Ann Elliott, July 27, 1974. Commd. 2d lt. U.S. Air Force, 1966, advanced through grades to maj., 1977; pilot trainee, Del Rio, Tex., 1966-67; pilot, McGuire AFB, N.J., 1967-68; forward air controller, Rep. South Vietnam, 1968-69; flight examiner, Pope AFB, N.C., 1969-72; tactical air liaison officer Schofield Barracks, Hawaii, 1972-75; program evaluation group leader Wright Patterson AFB, Ohio, 1975-77; chief nav./communication br., directorate operational requirements Scott AFB, Ill., 1978—. Coach, Mil. Youth League Football, 1972-75. Decorated DFC, Air medal with 13 oak leaf clusters, Medal of Honor (Vietnam), Air Force Commendation medal with oak leaf cluster, Cross of Gallantry (Vietnam). Mem. Air Force Assn. Co-author: Air Force ROTC Field Training - A New Model, 1978. Home: 340 Lincolnshire Blvd Belleville IL 62221 Office: MAC/XPQ Scott AFB IL 62225

CLAY, RACHEL LOUISE, govt. ofcl.; b. Evington, Va., Oct. 18, 1942; d. Arthur and Mary Everene (Cooper) C.; A.A. with high honors, Prince George's Community Coll., 1974; B.S. (Md. State scholar 1975-76), U. Md., 1976; M.A., Central Mich. U., 1978; 1 dau., Tonya Everene. With Dept. Public Welfare, Washington, 1964-69, D.C. Personnel, Washington, 1969-72; adminstrv. asst. D.C. City

Council, 1972-75, legis. services specialist, 1975—. Democrat. Roman Catholic. Office: 14th and Pennsylvania Ave NW Washington DC 20004

CLAY, WILLIAM CALDWELL, JR., lawyer, corp. exec.; b. Mt. Sterling, Ky., Dec. 28, 1915; s. William Caldwell and Kathryn (Greene) C.; A.B., Dartmouth Coll., 1937; LL.B., Yale U., 1940; LL.D., Transylvania U., 1973; m. Esther Briggs, Apr. 13, 1946; children—Jeannette Dobbs, Sally Sue, Kathryn Caldwell. Admitted to Ky. bar, 1939, since practiced in Mt. Sterling and Lexington; with antitrust div. Dept. Justice, 1938-40; counsel, pub. relations Burley Auction Warehouse Assn., Mt. Sterling, 1946-56; v.p., dir. Exchange Bank Ky., 1954-69, chmn. bd., 1969—; sec., dir. Hwy. Drainage Pipe, Inc., 1949—; v.p., dir. Mt. Sterling Broadcasting Co., 1957—; pres., dir. The Cola Corp., 1960—; sec., dir. Cowden Enterprises, Inc., Top Yield Industries, Inc., 1979—; pres., dir. Ky. Pub. Co.; dir. Lee Basal, Inc., Morehead Co. Bd. curators, exec. com. Transylvania U. Mem. Am., Ky. bar assns., C. of C., Sigma Alpha Epsilon. Mem. Christian Ch. Clubs: Odd Fellows, Masons, Rotary. Author: Farmers Tax Manual, 1943; Farmers Tax Manual Account Book, 1943; How to Read and Understand the Bible, 1974; Dow Jones-Irwin Guide to Estate Planning, 1980; Estate Planning and Administration, 1977; How to Win Maximum Awards for Lost Earnings, 1980; Creative Estate Planning and Administration, 1980. Office: 50 Broadway Mount Sterling KY 40353

CLAYTON, JOHN MARK, drugs and cosmetics mfg. exec.; b. Kevil, Ky., Aug. 6, 1945; s. Hubert F. and Mary L. (Brooks) C.; B.S., Tenn. Tech. U., 1968; Ph.D., U. Tenn., 1971; m. Doris Jeffers, Aug. 14, 1970; children—Mark, Stephanie, Beth. Insts. Health predoctoral fellow, grad. research asst. U. Tenn. Med. Units, 1969-71; postdoctoral research asso. Pomona Coll., Claremont, Calif., 1971-72; research biologist FDA, Jefferson, Ark., 1972-73; asst. prof. drug design div. U. Tenn. Center Health Scis., 1974; clin. research asso. med. dept. Plough, Inc., Memphis, 1974-75, dir. clin. and regulatory services, 1975-78, v.p. quality control and clin. and regulatory services, consumer ops. Schering-Plough Corp., 1978—; asst. prof. U. Ark. Med. Sch., 1972-74. Mem. Acad. Pharm. Scis., Am. Chem. Soc., AAAS, N.Y. Acad. Scis., Regulatory Affairs Profls. Soc., Am. Soc. Quality Control, Rho Chi. Methodist. Author: (with W.P. Purcell and G.E. Bass) Strategy of Drug Design: A Molecular Guide to Biological Activity, 1973; contbr. articles profl. jours. Office: 3030 Jackson Ave Memphis TN 38151

CLAYTON, ROBERT THAYER, ins. exec.; b. Milw., Mar. 3, 1926; s. Thayer Zachariah and Helen Parker (Tozer) C.; student U. Wis., 1943-48, B.S. in Mech. Engring., 1948; m. Ann Clare Peterson, Dec. 17, 1972; children—Robert Thayer, Nency Leigh Clayton Stein. Instr. Coll. Engring., U. Wis., Madison, 1948; sec. George H. Russell Co., Milw., 1948-55; v.p., sec. Norris, Fitzgerald & Russell Co., Inc., Milw., 1955-62; pres., treas. Fitzgerald, Clayton, Noyes & Kasten, Inc., lMilw., 1962—. Treas., West Suburban YMCA, Wauwatosa, Wis., 1968; mem. archtl. rev. bd. Village of Oconomowoc Lake (Wis.), 1978—. Served with U.S. Army, 1945-46. Mem. Soc. C.P.C.U.'s, Ind. Ins. Agts. Am. (pres. 1976-77, presdl. citations 1976, 78), Ind. Ins. Agts. Wis. (pres. 1965-66, outstanding service award 1962), Ind. Ins. Agts. Milw. (pres. 1960-61, spl. award 1978), Am. Legion. Republican. Congregationalist. Clubs: Oconomowoc Lake (commodore), Wis., La Belle Yacht, Lake Country Racquet. Office: 757 N Broadway Milwaukee WI 53202

CLEAR, ALBERT FRANCIS, hardward mfg. co. exec.; b. N.Y.C., June 9, 1920; s. Albert Francis and Edna M. (Coyle) C.; B.S., M.I.T., 1942; M.B.A., Harvard U., 1948; m. Jeanne Posselt, Aug. 7, 1947; children—Geoffrey Posselt, Gregory Stuart. Vice pres., mgr. Mallory Div. John B. Stetson Co., Danbury, Conn., 1948-57; mng. asso. Booz-Allen & Hamilton, N.Y.C., 1957-65; v.p., gen. mgr. hardward div. Stanley Works, New Britain, Conn., 1965-69, v.p. consumer group., chmn. European ops., 1967-69, exec. v.p. The Stanley Works, 1969-76, pres., chief ops. officer, dir., 1976—; dir. Barden Corp., Danbury; Curtiscorp, Inc., Sandy Hook, Conn.; New Britain Bank and Trust; Stanley Home Products, Westfield, Mass.; First Bank, New Haven. Trustee, Hartford Grad. Center, Hartford Coll. for Women; bd. visitors U. Conn. Grad. Sch. Bus.; bd. dirs. Constructive Workshop, Inc., Housatonic Valley Assn; mem. Mcpl. Action Council, New Britain. Served to capt. U.S. Army, 1942-46. Office: Stanley Works 195 Lake St New Britain CT 06117

CLEARY, TIMOTHY FINBAR, govt. ofcl.; b. Cork, Ireland, Sept. 30, 1925; s. John Francis and Nora (Riordan) C.; B.S., Fordham U., 1955, J.D., 1959; m. Patricia Agnes Hanley, July 21, 1947; children—Timothy F. X., Maureen P., Therese A., Richard S., Gail P., Eileen P. Admitted to N.Y. bar, 1959; atty. N.Y.C. Police Dept., 1959-67; asst. counsel Fair Labor Standards div. U.S. Dept. Labor, Washington, 1967-71, chief counsel, 1971-73, commr., 1973-77; chmn. U.S. Occupational Safety and Health Rev. Commn., Washington, 1977—; lectr. labor law Practicing Law Inst., U. Wis., Washington and Lee U., Cumberland Sch. U., Ohio No. U., Brookings Instn., numerous others; Served with USN, 1943-45. Mem. Soc. for Occupational and Environ. Health, Am. Public Health Assn. Contbr. articles to legal jours. Home: 5709 Cheshire Dr Bethesda MD 20014 Office: Occupational Safety and Health Review Commission 1825 K St NW Washington DC 20006

CLEGG, CHARLES STEPHEN, investment co. exec.; b. Geneva, Ill., Aug. 16, 1950; s. William E. and Marie Jane C.; B.S., U.S. Air Force Acad., 1972; M.B.A., U. Chgo., 1975; m. Deborah Lynn Frakes, Mar. 18, 1978; 1 son, Casey Frakes. Vice pres. All-Brite Anodizing, Chgo., 1972-73; sr. analyst W.R. Grace & Co., N.Y.C., 1975-77; dir. internat. fin. Avis Inc., N.Y.C., 1977-79; asso. AEA Investors Inc., N.Y.C., 1979; dir. Midtown D.C. Inc. Served with USAF, 1968-72. Home: 801 W End Ave New York NY 10025 Office: 640 5th Ave New York NY 10019

CLEGG, LEE MILTON, JR., packaging machinery mfg. co. exec.; b. Cleve., Jan. 18, 1932; s. Lee Milton and Albertine (Ahrens) C.; B.S. in Indsl. Engring., Lehigh U., 1959; M.B.A., Harvard U., 1961; m. Elizabeth Pentland, July 1, 1973; children—Campbell Ahrens, Jasperdean Whitney, Kimberley. Application engr. FMC Corp., San Jose, Calif., Phila., 1961-67; gen. sales mgr. Control Print Corp., 1968-70; pres. Lee M. Clegg Assos. Inc., Morristown, N.J., 1970-72; v.p. mktg. Solbern Corp., Fairfield, N.J., 1973-78, Weldotron Corp., Piscataway, N.J., 1978-79; exec. v.p. Femia Food Processing Equipment Inc., subs. Femia S.A., Fairfield, 1979—; guest lectr. Packaging Inst. U.S.A., 1974. Served with USAF, 1952-56. Republican. Presbyterian. Club: Smoke Rise Rod and Gun. Home: 7 Esti Ct Madison NJ 07940 Office: 277 Fairfield Rd Fairfield NJ 07006

CLEMENKO, MICHAEL JAMES, restaurant chain exec.; b. Linden, N.J., Jan. 9, 1936; s. Michael P. and Rose (Zavada) C.; B.S. in Elec. Engring., Newark Coll. Engring., 1964; m. Judith E. Parrish, Apr. 12, 1969; children—Michael James, Andrew Charles. Auditor, A.C. Nielson Co., Chgo., 1964-67; cons. Alexander Proudfoot Co., Chgo., 1967-69; project mgr. Naus & Newlyn Inc., Paoli, Pa., 1969-71; project dir. Control Interval Scheduling, Inc., Rolling Hills, Calif., 1971-73; dir. mgmt. engring. Marriott Corp., Washington, 1973—; guest lectr. Pa. State U., 1980. Served with USAF, 1956-60. Mem. Am. Inst. Indsl. Engrs. Club: Toastmasters. Home: 17728 Queen Elizabeth Dr Olney MD 20832 Office: 1 Marriott Dr Washington DC 20058

CLEMENS, LEON JOHN, law enforcement cons.; b. Des Moines, Feb. 3, 1917; s. James L. and Nettie C. (Uhr) C.; grad. Des Moines Bus. U., 1936; student Drake U., 1941-43; grad. Delehanty Police Sch., N.Y.C., 1950; grad. in criminal law Blackstone Law Inst., 1951; grad. Am. Service Investigative Sch., Chgo., 1952, FBI Nat. Police Acad., Washington, 1953; m. Mary M. Palm, Feb. 5, 1938 (dec. July 2, 1980); 1 dau., Kay Clemens Edwards. Adminstrv. asst. to chief Des Moines Police Dept., 1940-64; chief investigator, asst. atty. gen. State of Iowa, 1945-53; personal aide and driver, presdl. campaign Harry S. Truman, 1947; clhief investigator Iowa Atty. Gen.'s Office, 1948-53; coordinator U.S. presdl. security, 1954-60; investigator U.S. Senate sub-com. on rackets in labor and mgmt., 1957-58; instr. FBI Acad., Washington, 1955-58; owner, operator Ford Gum M and M Candy Co., Tucson, 1963-72; with security and maintenance dept. Rocky Mountain Nat. Park, 1973-79; prin. Col. L. Clemens & Assos., crime prevention and security cons., Sun Lakes, Ariz., 1973—; prin. Exec. Escort Service. Mem. nat. adv. council Americans for Effective Law Enforcement; adv., investigator U.S. internat. affairs Am. Security Council, 1963—; dist. chmn. Democratic Party of Ariz., 1963-73; vol. adv. Am. and Ariz. consumer councils, 1963—; bd. dirs. Nat. Council on Crime and Delinquency, 1949—, Ariz. Boys' Ranch, 1963—, Alumni Assn. of Civilian Conservation Corps., 1972—; mem. police scholarship bd. U. Ariz., 1964-72; coordinator police course Pima Community Coll., 1968-72; govtl. appointee chief adv. consumer affairs for ret. and sr. citizens State of Ariz. Served with U.S. Army, World War II. Elected to Police Hall of Fame, 1953; recipient Korean Service Vets. medal, 1978; named Ambassador of Peace, Korea, 1978. Mem. Am. Law Enforcement Officers Assn. (nat. v.p. 1973—, dir. crime prevention and consumer affairs 1976—), Nat. Ret. Policeman's Assn. (nat. dir. crime prevention 1948—), Nat. Police and Fire Fighters Assn. (charter, dir. heroism awards), Iowa Assn. Chiefs of Police and Peace Officers (life), Am. Legion. Clubs: Home Lodge of Des Moines, Masons, Shriners. Home: Sun Lakes 9229 SE Cactus Sun Lakes AZ 85224

CLEMENT, RICHARD FRANCIS, business exec.; b. Chgo., Nov. 29, 1906; s. Robert Fawne and Jennie (Halvorson) C.; B.S., U. Wis., 1928; m. Margaret Buchanan, Aug. 11, 1934; children—Richard Bradley, Jane Elizabeth Clement Wilemon, Charles Frederic. Men's furnishings merchandiser Wilson Bros., Chgo., 1935-39; sportswear merchandiser Ely & Walker div. Burlington Industries, St. Louis, 1939-47, v.p., 1949-65, dir. sales, 1954-62, dir. marketing and planning, 1963-65; part owner, chmn. Clement and Benner Dept. Store, Los Alamos, 1959-79; partner Yates, Woods & Co. (now Rowland & Co.), St. Louis, 1965-69; v.p. Newhard, Cook & Co., St. Louis, 1969—; owner, operator Rippling River Ranch, Steelville, Mo., 1969—; pres. Champion Springs Ranch Co., Annapolis, Mo., 1977—; chmn. Precious Metals, Inc., St. Louis, 1979—, C & B Investment Assos., 1979—. Mem. Alpha Tau Omega. Congregationalist. Club: Algonquin Golf. Home: 55 S Gore Ave Webster Groves MO 63119 Office: 300 N Broadway Saint Louis MO 63102

CLEMENTS, B. GILL, business exec.; b. 1941; B.B.A., So. Meth. U., 1963; married. Loan officer First Nat. Bank Dallas, 1963-68; treas. Sedco Inc., Dallas, 1968-73, pres., 1973—, chief exec. officer, 1977—, also dir. Office: Sedco Inc 1901 N Akard St Dallas TX 75201*

CLEMENTS, GEORGE F., JR., ind. oil and gas producer; b. Waltham, Mass., Sept. 24, 1925; s. George F. and Florence (Pinkerton) C.; student Rensselaer Poly. Inst., 1943; B.S., Mass. Inst. Tech., 1949; m. Betty McDowell, May 23, 1964; children—Lisa M., George F., Sallie E. With Empire Trust Co., N.Y.C., 1949-61, v.p., 1959-61; v.p., dir. Empire Resources Corp., N.Y.C., 1954-61; pres., dir. Whitestone Petroleum Corp., N.Y.C., 1961-72; pres., dir. Whitestone Corp., Greenwich, Houston; dir. Whitestone Internat., Inc., Dallas, Barber Oil Corp., N.Y.C. Trustee nat. schs. com. for econ. edn. Greenwich (Conn.) Acad. Served to 2d lt. USAAF, 1943-46; 1st lt. USAF, 1950-51. Decorated Air medal. Mem. Am. Inst. Mining, Metall. and Petroleum Engrs. Clubs: N.Y. Yacht, Leash, India House, Sky, Storm Trysail, Cruising Am. (N.Y.C.); Royal Ocean Racing (London); Eastward Ho, Stage Harbor Yacht (Chatham, Mass.); Indian Harbor Yacht, Round Hill (Greenwich, Conn.); Ramada (Houston). Office: 283 Greenwich Ave Greenwich CT 06830

CLEMENTS, HARRY MICHAEL, physician; b. McKees Rocks, Pa., Apr. 14, 1942; s. Harry H. and Genevieve R. Clements; A.B., Dartmouth Coll., 1963; M.D., Jefferson Med. Coll., 1967; m. Chris Ann Bower, Feb. 14, 1972; Intern USPHS Hosp., New Orleans, 1967-68; physician U.S. Coast Guard, 1968-70; med. dir. ITE-Imperial Corp., Phila., 1970-72; indsl. physician Weirton (W.Va.) Steel div. Nat. Steel Corp., 1972—. Served with USPHS, 1967-70. Diplomate Nat. Bd. Med. Examiners. Mem. Am. Occupational Med. Assn., AMA, Am. Coll. Emergency Physicians, Am. Arbitration Assn. Home: 3951 Palisades Dr Weirton WV 26062 Office: Med Dept Weirton Steel Co Weirton WV 26062

CLEMONS, J. KING, ins. co. exec.; b. Columbus, Ohio, Jan. 21, 1936; s. Frank M. and Ethel K. Clemons; B.S. in Physics, Colorado Coll., 1958; M.S. in Statistics, U. Iowa, 1966; m. Ann Douglass, June 2, 1959; children—Mike, Steve, Karl. Research physicist White Sands Missile Range, N.Mex., 1958; actuarial asst. A.S. Hansen, Inc., Lake Bluff, Ill., 1966-67, cons. in tng., Lake Bluff, 1967-69, subject cons., Milw., 1969-70, subject cons., Los Angeles, 1970-72; pres. Western Res. Life Ins. Co., Grand Junction, Colo., 1972—; propr., broker Top Realty Co., 1972—. Pres., Grand Junction Eagles Baseball, 1976-78; active YMCA Fund Drive, Milw., 1969. Served to capt., Ordnance Corps, U.S. Army, 1958-64. Recipient Distinguished Service award YMCA, 1969. Mem. Western Colo. Estate Planning Council, North Ave. Trade Assn. (dir. 1978-79), Grand Junction C. of C. (v.p. 1977-79). Republican. Club: Lions. Home: 2561 I Rd Grand Junction CO 81501 Office: 2755 North Ave Grand Junction CO 81501

CLENDENEN, SHIRLEY HAMILTON, real estate broker; b. Detroit; d. Albert Joseph and Gertrude May (Mawby) Hamilton; grad. Realtors Inst., 1971; m. Roger B. Clendenen, Dec. 3, 1945; children—Deborah, Denise Clendenen Brasher, Rebecca Clendenen Maxwell, Kelly, Erin, Allison. Founder, Hobbs Welcome Service (N.Mex.), 1958-75; real estate saleswoman, 1958-61; owner, operator Clendenen Realty, Hobbs, 1961—; chmn. Realtors Polit. Action Com. N.Mex., 1978—. Active United Fund. Lic. real estate broker, N.Mex. Mem. Nat. Inst. Real Estate Brokers, Nat. Assn. Realtors, Realtors Assn. N.Mex. (dir. 1974-75, 79—, regional v.p. 1975-76), Hobbs Bd. Realtors (pres. 1974-75, Realtor of Year 1975), Women's Council of Realtors (charter mem., 1st pres. Lea County chpt.), Hobbs C. of C. (chmn. ambassadors, dir. 1978-80). Democrat. Roman Catholic. Home: 4000 N Grimes St Hobbs NM 88240 Office: 1919 N Turner Hobbs NM 88240

CLENDENIN, ROBERT JAMES, lawyer, banker; b. Monmouth, Ill., Oct. 12, 1904; s. J.W. and Louvisa (Stevenson) C.; A.B., Stanford U., 1926; J.D., U. Mich., 1930; L.H.D., Coll. of Ozarks, 1971; m. Louise Velde, Dec. 6, 1941; children—Robert J., John V., William H., Thomas. Admitted to Ill. bar, 1931; mem. firm Clendenin Burkhard and Butler, 1934—, asst. U.S. dist. atty. So. Dist. Ill., 1933-39; referee bankruptcy, master in chancery, 1939-53; spl. legal counsel Culver (Ind.) Mil. Acad., 1963-64; chmn. bd., dir. Monmouth Trust & Savs. Bank; dir. Monarch Engring. & Mfg. Co., Martha Brown Ltd., Monmouth. Pres., Edward Arthur Mellinger Ednl. Found.; trustee U.S. Naval Acad. Found., Monmouth Coll., 1961-63, 72—, Coll. of Ozarks Found., Clarksville, Ark. Served as lt. USNR, 1943-45, capt. Res. ret. Mem. Nat. Assn. Referees Bankruptcy, Am., Ill., Fed., Chgo., Peoria, Warren County bar assns., Soc. Barristers (U. Mich.), Am. Judicature Soc., Am. Legion, Tau Kappa Alpha, Alpha Sigma Phi. Democrat. Presbyn. Clubs: Masons (32 deg.), Shriners, Elks; Univ. (Chgo.); Creve Coeur (Peoria); Army and Navy (Washington). Home: 1111 E Euclid Ave PO Box 278 Monmouth IL 61462 Office: 1025 E Broadway Monmouth IL 61462

CLERK, NORMAN JEFFREY, advt. agy. exec.; b. Oakland, Calif., Mar. 3, 1923; s. Ira and Winifred (Mastick) C.; student Modesto Jr. Coll., 1942-43, Armstrong Coll., 1948-49, U. Calif. at Berkeley, 1949; m. Anne Linderman, Apr. 28, 1951; children—Norman G., Bradford L., Amyann M. Owner, N.J. Clerk & Asso., San Francisco, 1954-64; account exec. Kennedy, Hannaford & Dolman, Inc., Oakland, 1964-65, v.p., 1966-69; owner, pres. N.J. Clerk & Assos., Oakland, 1969—; instr. advt. Laney Jr. Coll., 1966-67. Chmn., Jr. Achievement Com., Oakland, 1967. Clubs: Elks, Aeolian Yacht, Encinal Yatch (Alameda, Calif.); Oakland Rotary. Contbr. articles to profl. jours. Home: 1809 San Jose Ave Alameda CA 94501 Office: 414 Pendleton Way Oakland CA 94621

CLEVELAND, CHARLES AMES, investment mgr.; b. New Rochelle, N.Y., Aug. 5, 1923; s. John Luther and Elizabeth Allen (Ames) C.; A.B., Dartmouth Coll., 1945; m. Thirza Helen Jones, July 1, 1954; children—Charles A., Helen T., Dwight M. Asst. cashier 1st Nat. Bank of N.Y., 1947-54; asst. v.p. to v.p. Morgan Guaranty Trust Co., N.Y.C., 1954-68; v.p. Bankers Trust Co., N.Y.C., 1968-72; mng. partner Squam Lakes Assos., Mpls., 1972—; dir. Overseas Oil & Gas Co. Trustee, Minn. Opera Co., 1975—. Served to lt. Mil. Intelligence, U.S. Army, 1943-46. Mem. Ind. Petroleum Assn. Am. Republican. Presbyterian. Clubs: Anglers, Shenorock, Blind Brook, Camp Fire (N.Y.C.); Minikahda, Minneapolis, Chevaliers du Tastevin (Mpls.). Office: 4508 IDS Center Minneapolis MN 55402

CLEVELAND, ROBERT RAHLYN, communications mfr.; b. Searcy, Ark., Nov. 22, 1948; s. Thomas Chester and Jennie Marie (Griffin) C.; student Tallulah (La.) public schs., spl. engring. courses; m. Beatriz Santiago, Nov. 25, 1968; children—Robert Michael, Shiela Michelle, Kenneth Eric. Broadcast engr. Am. Forces Radio and TV Service, Taiwan and Philippines, 1967-73; v.p. contracting and systems div., dir. Alexander Electronics, Inc., St. Louis and Kansas City, Mo., 1973-76; pres., chmn. bd. Video Masters, Inc., Kansas City, Mo., 1976—; pres. VMI Corp., Kansas City; dir. Video Systems Research, Inc. Sec., Home Owners Assn. Kansas City North, 1977-78; life mem. Republican Nat. Com. Served with USAF, 1967-73. Decorated Meritorious Service medal; registered profl. engr., Mo.; cert. elec. supr. City of Kansas City. Mem. Nat. Assn. Broadcasters, Soc. Broadcast Engrs., Am. Assn. R.R.'s, Ry. System Suppliers, Inc., Better Bus. Bur. Kansas City, Mo. City C. of C., Smithsonian Instn., Elec. Assn. Kansas City. Contbr. articles to Progressive Railroading, Ry. Age. Patentee rail car identification system using TV. Office: 1616 Broadway Kansas City MO 64108

CLEVELAND, TAMMY EARLENE, fin. and constrn. mgmt. co. exec.; b. Kings Mountain, N.C., Apr. 10, 1946; d. Ephraim Watkins and Nettie Viola (Hunt) C.; B.S., Iowa State U., 1969; postgrad. Roosevelt U., 1978—; m. Eban Anthony Cleveland. Corp. acct. Balt. News Am., 1973-74; asst. adminstr. child abuse program Sinai Hosp., Balt., 1974-75; corp. sec., adminstr. Druid Elec. Contractors, Balt., 1975-77; paralegal and office adminstr. Denis A. Kleinfeld & Assos., Ltd., Chgo., 1977-80; owner, mgr. Cleveland Enterprises, Chgo., 1977—. Mem. adv. bd. Conestoga council Girl Scouts U.S.A., Waterloo, Iowa. Mem. Ill. Paralegal Assn., Nat. Assn. Notary Publics, Nat. Assn. Women in Constrn. (dir. 1979-80), Nat. Assn. Female Execs., Nat. Assn. Bus. Women, Internat. Platform Assn. Democrat. Methodist. Club: Eastern Star. Home and Office: 2101 S Michigan Ave Chicago IL 60616

CLEVEN, DONALD LE ROY, constrn. co. exec.; b. Kendall, Wis., Mar. 11, 1931; s. Morris Edward and Anne Marie (Preuss) C.; Master of Accounts, Madison (Wis.) Bus. Coll., 1950; postgrad. Madison Area Tech. Coll., 1968-73, U. Wis., Madison, 1973-77; m. Maxine Eileen Schuchmann, May 18, 1958; children—Gina, Paul, Ruth. Acct. trainee, distbr. sales acct. Borden Co., Madison, Wis., 1950-57, internal auditor, Chgo., 1958; acct. Vogel Bros. Bldg. Co., Madison, 1958-69, treas., 1969—; dir., Vogel Bros. Bldg. Co., Madison, R. J. Lederer Co., Milw., Profl. Contractors, Inc., Lakeland, Fla. C.P.A. Mem. Nat. Assn. Accts., Am. Inst. C.P.A.'s, Wis. Inst. C.P.A.'s. Lutheran. Home: 1706 Wendy Ln Madison WI 53716 Office: 2701 Packers Ave PO Box 7696 Madison WI 53707

CLIFF, BARRY LEE, fin. planner; b. Reading, Pa., Mar. 31, 1943; s. James Denton and Virginia Mae (Kelly) C.; A.A.S., Capitol Inst. Tech., 1964; certificate in fin. planning Coll. Fin. Planning, Denver, 1977; postgrad. in Engring. Econs., Iowa State U., 1967-68. Dist. mgr. Equity Funding Securities Corp., Washington, 1969-73; br. mgr. Investors Fin. Services, Rockville, Md., 1973-74; co-founder, chief exec. officer, pres. Am. Fin. Cons., Silver Spring, Md., 1974—; mem. adj. faculty Coll. Fin. Planning, named to Hall of Fame, 1978. Served with USN, 1961-63. Mem. Internat. Assn. Fin. Planners. Home: 10112 Kensington Pkwy Kensington MD 20795 Office: 8555 16th St Suite 701 Silver Spring MD 20910

CLIFFORD, ARTHUR, former investment co. exec., civic worker; b. Bridgeport, Conn., Feb. 11, 1896; s. Charles and Mary Maud (Matts) C.; student pub. schs., Bridgeport, also spl. courses; H.H.D., Bridgeport Engring. Inst., 1976; m. Mabel Eva Brough, Apr. 14, 1921 (dec. May 1960); children—Arthur Charles, Elizabeth Mabel Clifford Clark. With efficiency dept. U.S. Steel Corp. coke plant, Gary, Ind., 1913-15, Youngstown Sheet & Tube Co., Struthers, Ohio, 1916; foreman LaBelle Ironworks, Steubenville, Ohio, 1917; gen. foreman Donner Union Coke Corp., Buffalo, 1919-22; with A.W. Burritt Co., Bridgeport, 1922-63, pres., 1955-63, chmn. bd., 1957-63, dir., 1938-63; asst. to pres. Burritt Lumber Sales Co., 1934-56, v.p., 1951-56, pres., 1956-58, chmn. bd., 1957-58, dir., 1944-58; v.p. Investors Capital Corp., Bridgeport, 1962-67, v.p., 1967-68, pres., dir., 1962-68. Bd. dirs. Lakeview Cemetery Assn., 1942—, v.p., 1967—; bd. dirs. and charter mem. steering com. Bridgeport region Urban Coalition, 1968; adviser, bd. assos. Bridgeport Engring. Inst., 1966—; chmn. bd. Bridgeport chpt. ARC, 1960; pres., dir. YMCA of Greater Bridgeport, 1960-62, trustee, 1964-70; bd. dirs., fin. adviser Bridgeport Police Athletic League, 1950—; bd. dirs. Bridgeport Family Welfare Service, 1960-63, Bridgeport Safety Council, 1946-57, Toys for Hosp. Tots, Inc., 1971—, Easter Seal Rehab. Center, 1972-75; chmn. individual gifts com. United Way, Bridgeport, 1974-75; chmn. Mayor's Action Com. for Better Bridgeport, 1966-71; chmn. Redevel. Agy. City Bridgeport, 1958-66; mem. organizing com., mem. community forum Fairfield U., 1966-73; life mem. bd. assos. U. Bridgeport, 1966—, adviser Coll. Bus. Adminstrn., 1960—; mem. adv. com., contest judge Brand Names Found., 1953-54, 58-59;

trustee Park City Hosp., Bridgeport, 1964-76, life mem., 1977—; dir. Liturgical Musical Festival, 1976—. Served as sgt. maj. USMC, 1917-19. Recipient Distinguished Citizens award Bridgeport C. of C., 1961; Sr. Civic Indsl. Bus. Leader, 1970; Outstanding Citizen of Bridgeport award Bridgeport Civitan Club, 1967; statuette for distinguished service 2d Div. Assn. U.S. Army, 1967-69, plaque, 1970, 72; distinguished citizen award Bridgeport Vol. Bur., 1969; Service to Youth plaque Bridgeport YMCA, 1970; Wisdom award of Honor, 1970; plaque Bridgeport Police Athletic League, 1971; outstanding service certificate of appreciation USMC, 1973; Algonquin Sachem of Year award, 1975; named Ky. Col. Mem. Nat. Retail Lumber Dealers Assn. (dir. and mem. edn. com. 1953-56), Northeastern Retail Lumbermens Assn. (hon. life mem.; pres. 1955, exec. com. 1951-57, dir. 1945-57), Lumber Dealers Assn. Conn. (pres. 1945-47, dir. 1940-48), C. of C. U.S. (policy com. 1956-60), New Eng. (hon.), Conn. (hon.) assns. police chiefs, Nat. Police Hall Fame, Greater Bridgeport C. of C. (pres. 1954; dir. 1945-56), VFW, Marine Corps League, Am. Legion. Episcopalian (organist, choir dir. 1942-47, mem. fin. com. 1965-72). Clubs: Masons, Rotary (dir. 1953-59, 68-71; pres. Bridgeport 1957-58); Rotarian of Century award 1971, internat. Paul Harris fellow 1974); Algonquin. Home: 45 Hickory St Bridgeport CT 06610

CLIFFORD, H. CURTIS, mktg. exec.; b. Lincoln Park, Mich., July 22, 1935; s. Harry Benjamin and Terressa Belle (Huff) C.; student in mech. engring. Ohio State U., 1953-57; B.S., SUNY; m. Sandra Jean Lamberson, Mar. 30, 1968; children—Daniel, Mark, James. Asst. chief draftsman Seagrave Fire Apparatus (div. FWD 1962), Columbus, Ohio, 1954-63, chief engr., Clintonville, Wis., 1963-66; chief engr. Ward LaFrance Truck Corp., Elmira, N.Y., 1966-68, sales mgr., 1968-71, sales mgr. Am. LaFrance, 1971-78, dir. customer services, 1978-80, v.p. mktg., 1980—. Mem. N.Y. State Assn. Retarded Children. Served with C.E., U.S. Army, 1955. Mem. Adminstrv. Mgmt. Soc., Nat. Fire Protection Assn., Nat. Assn. Service Mgrs. Methodist. Home: 1572 Belaire Dr Horseheads NY 14845 Office: 100 E LaFrance St Elmira NY 14902

CLIFFORD, STEWART BURNETT, banker; b. Boston, Feb. 17, 1929; s. Stewart Hilton and Ellinor (Burnett) C.; A.B., Harvard U., 1951, M.B.A., 1956; m. Cornelia Park Woolley, Apr. 26, 1952; children—Cornelia Lee Clifford Wareham, Rebecca Lyn, Jennifer Leggett, Stewart. With Citibank, N.A., N.Y.C., 1956—, asst. cashier, 1958-60, asst. v.p., 1960-63; exec. v.p., gen. mgr. Merc. Bank Can., Montreal, Que., 1963-67, v.p. adminstrn. comml. banking group, 1968-72, v.p., head World Corp. dept., London, 1973-75, head energy systems dept., 1975-78, sr. v.p. in charge domestic energy, 1978—; dir. Monumental Corp., Balt., Monumental Life Ins. Co. Trustee Spence Sch., N.Y.C.; pres. Woolley-Clifford Found.; trustee, elder Brick Presbyterian Ch. Served to lt. AUS, 1951-54. Clubs: Union, Univ. (N.Y.C.); Duxbury (Mass.) Yacht. Home: 120 East End Ave New York NY 10028 Office: 399 Park Ave New York NY 10043

CLIFTON, RUSSELL B., mortgage lending co. exec.; b. Maroa, Ill., Jan. 16, 1930; s. Russell Thomas and Clara Leoda (Luckenbill) C.; B.A. in Acctg. and Fin., Mich. State U., 1957; m. Mary Joyce Hartline, Oct. 10, 1948; 1 son, Steven Shawn. Acct., Arthur Andersen & Co., Detroit, 1957-59; v.p. mortgages Mich. Nat. Bank, Lansing, 1959-65; sr. v.p. Asso. Mortgage Cos., Kansas City, Mo., 1965-69; v.p. mortgages Fed. Nat. Mortgage Assn., Washington, 1969—; mem. adv. com. Home Owner's Warranty Corp., 1978—. Served in U.S. Army, 1952-54. Disting. fellow Nat. Assn. Cert. Mortgage Bankers; mem. Mortgage Bankers Assn. Am., Nat. Savs. and Loan League, U.S. League Savs. Assns., Nat. Assn. Mut. Savs. Banks, Nat. Assn. Home Builders, Nat. Assn. Realtors, Am. Bankers Assn., Community Assns. Inst., Nat. Acad. Conciliators (dir. 1979—), Phi Kappa Phi, Tau Sigma, Beta Gamma Sigma, Beta Alpha Psi. Methodist. Office: 3900 Wisconsin Ave NW Washington DC 20016

CLINE, RICHARD GORDON, retail distbn. co. exec.; b. Chgo., Feb. 17, 1935; s. William R. and Katherine A. (Bothwell) C.; B.S., U. Ill., 1957; m. Carole J. Costello, Dec. 28, 1957; children—Patricia, Linda, Richard, Jeffrey. With Jewel Cos., Inc., Chgo., 1963—, pres. Osco Drug, Inc. subs., 1970-79, sr. exec. v.p., 1979, vice chmn., 1979-80, pres., 1980—, also dir.; dir. NICOR, Inc., No. Ill. Gas Co., Aurrera, S. A., Mexico City. Bd. dirs. United Way Met. Chgo., Inc.; trustee Rush-Presbyterian-St. Luke's Med. Center; gov. and former chmn. bd. Central DuPage Hosp.; mem. adv. council Coll. Commerce and Bus. Adminstrn., U. Ill. Clubs: Econ., Chgo., Comml., Commonwealth, Chgo. Golf. Office: Jewel Cos Inc 5725 East River Rd Chicago IL 60631

CLINE, ROBERT ALEXANDER, JR., banker; b. Cin., June 8, 1935; s. Robert Alexander and Martha Louise (Kunkel) C.; B.A., Williams Coll., 1957; M.B.A., Xavier U., 1965; m. Rosalen Ehemann, Sept. 30, 1978; 1 son, John Emery. With advt. dept. Proctor & Gamble Co., Cin., 1960-63; fin. data processor IBM, Cin., 1963-65; with Fifth Third Bank, Cin., 1966—, div. mgr. consumer banking, 1974—, sr. v.p., 1975—; bd. dirs. Credit Bur. Cin., 1976—. Trustee exec. com. Children's Hosp. Med. Center, Cin.; pres., trustee Cath. Social Services of Southwestern Ohio. Served with USAF, 1957-58. Clubs: Cin. Country, Queen City (Cin.); Commonwealth. Office: Fifth Third Center Cincinnati OH 45202

CLINE, WILLIAM RUSSELL, JR., nat. football league team exec.; b. Ft. Walton, Fla., Oct. 15, 1943; s. William Russell and Virginia Frances (Kirkland) C.; B.S., William Jewell Coll., 1972; children—Lisa Lee, Lori Lynn. Edn., youth and counseling dir. Swope Park Bapt. Ch., Kansas City, Mo., 1966-75; dir. promotions and game prodn. Kansas City Chiefs, 1975—; lectr. in field; cons. in field. Area chmn. program/meetings United Way, 1979-80; bd. dirs. Big Bros., 1979—. Served with USAF, 1962-66. Recipient award for outstanding service, United Way, 1979; Excellence in Mktg. award, Am. Mktg. Assn., 1979. Mem. Advt. and Mktg. Execs. Assn. Democrat. Baptist. Home: 9308 Bales St Kansas City MO 64132 Office: 1 Arrowhead Dr Kansas City MO 64129

CLINEFELTER, JAMES WALTER, corp. exec.; b. Akron, Ohio, Oct. 3, 1927; s. James Claude and Gladys Madora (Fraze) C.; B.A., U. Akron, 1950, M.A., 1951; m. Barbara Joan Baugh, Apr. 13, 1957; children—James Christopher, Joan Lucinda, Laura Mélètine, Barbara Claudia. With J. C. Clinefelter Co., rubber and plastics extrusion insulation machinery sales, Akron, 1950—, sales rep., 1950-56, owner, 1956-65, pres., chmn bd., 1965—; pres. Wayne Equipment Corp., Akron, 1963—, chmn. bd. 1963—; Midwestern sales agt. John Royle & Sons, 1956-71, regional sales mgr., 1971-76, Ont. and Gt. Lakes regional sales mgr., 1976—; partner CZ Equipment Co., 1967—; pres. Empathy Internat., Akron, 1972—, chmn. bd., 1975—; partner Burke & Hare, 1976—; asst. instr. U. Akron, 1948-49, grad. asst. instr., 1949-50; dep. registrar motor vehicles State of Ohio, 1959-62. Mem. Summit County Democratic Exec. Com, 1953-68, treas., 1964-66; del. to state convs. 1956-64. Mem. Wire Assn., Nat. Rifle Assn. (life), Akron Rubber and Plastics Group, Monarchist League (life), Wire Machinery Builders Assn., Pi Sigma Alpha, Phi Alpha Theta. Episcopalian. Mason (Shriner). Clubs: Banyan Soc. (Toronto); Cascade (life) (Akron); Whatley Hall (Banbury, Oxford). Author: Ohio Congressional Districts 1803-1951; patentee. Home: 618 Ridgecrest Rd Akron OH 44303 Office: 1067 W Exchange St Akron OH 44302 also Adelans (Lure) Hte Saône 70200 France

CLINGAN, MELVIN HALL, lumber exec., publisher; b. Atchison, Kans., July 12, 1929; s. Frank E. and Hazel Ellen (Hall) C.; B.S. in Bus. (Summerfield scholar), U. Kans., 1951; m. Athelia Roberta Sweet, Apr. 7, 1956; children—Sandra, Scott, Kimberly, Marcia. Pres., Holiday Homes, Inc. and Clingan Land Co., Shawnee Mission, Kans., 1956—; pres. Johnson County Pubs., Inc., pub. Gardner News, De Soto News and Spring Hill New Era, 1965—; dir. R.L. Sweet Lumber Co. and subs.'s, Kansas City, Kans., 1959—, exec. v.p., 1973—. Vice pres. Westwood View Sch. Bd., 1965-68; Republican congl. dist. chmn., mem. state exec. com., 1966-72; bd. dirs. Johnson County Community Coll. Found., 1973—. Served with USAF, 1951-55. Mem. Home Builders Assn. Greater Kansas City (past pres.), Home Builders Assn. Kans. (past pres.), Nat. Assn. Home Builders (nat. life dir.), Mission C. of C. (pres. 1971), Sigma Nu (grand officer 1961-68), Omicron Delta Kappa, Beta Gamma Sigma, Sigma Delta Chi. Republican. Mem. Disciples of Christ Ch. Club: Mission Hills Country. Home: 5345 Mission Woods Rd Shawnee Mission KS 66205 Office: 4500 Roe Blvd Kansas City KS 66103

CLINGERMAN, EDGAR ALLEN, mfg. co. exec.; b. Wolf Lake, Ind., Dec. 27, 1934; s. Virgil Wilson and Jessie Pauline Clingerman; B.S. in Bus. Adminstrn., Ball State U., 1960; postgrad. Advanced Mgmt. Program, Harvard U., 1974; m. Betty Gean White, Dec. 9, 1966; children—Tamera, Sarah, Johnny, Edgar Allen. Mgr. cons. Cooper Lybrand and Co., Ft. Wayne, Ind., 1960-63; controller Monteith Bros., Inc., Elkhart, Ind., 1963-66; plant controller Joy Mfg. Co., Michigan City, Ind., 1966-68; v.p. Milton Roy Co., St. Petersburg, Fla., 1968—; dir. E-C Apparatus Corp. Bd. dirs. Arrowhead council Boy Scouts Am., 1972-78; deacon, bd. dirs. 1st Christian Ch., Largo, Fla. Served with USN, 1952-55. Mem. Contact Lens Mfg. Assn. (dir. 1976-80), Nat. Assn. Accts., Fin. Execs. Inst., Machinery Allied Products Inst. (exec. council III). Clubs: Masons, Rotary (dir. 1960-74). Home: 2534 Heron Ln N Clearwater FL 33520 Office: One Plaza Pl Saint Petersburg FL 33701

CLIPP, JAMES C., water purification co. exec.; b. Salem, Ind., Apr. 4, 1933; s. Wendell Vance and Blanche Merle (Elrod) C.; B.A., in Chemistry cum laude, David Lipscomb Coll., Nashville, 1955; m. Patsy Ann Humphrey, Dec. 14, 1957; 1 dau., Susan Elizabeth. Owner, mgr. Clipp Chem. Co., El Cajon, Calif., 1963-67; chief research chemist Havens Internat., San Diego, 1967-70; product mgr. ecol. systems div. Raypak Westlake Village, Calif., 1970-73; mgr. watermark systems KMS Industries, Irvine, Calif., 1973-75; founder, pres. Water Purification Systems, Inc., Los Angeles, 1975—. Served to lt. USNR, 1955-58. Mem. Nat. Water Supply Improvement Assn., Internat. Desalination and Environ. Assn., Credit Mgrs. Assn. of So. Calif., Conejo Valley Wine Soc., Smithsonian Assos. Republican. Club: Sunset Hills Country. Office: 3451 E 26th St Los Angeles CA 90023

CLONES, JULIA PANOURGIA, economist; b. Athens, Greece, Dec. 10, 1930; came to U.S., 1960, naturalized, 1968; d. Eustace and Ismini (Pallinginis) Panourgias; diploma Center for Stats., Athens, 1952; B.A., Athens Sch. Econs., 1951; M.Sc. (Greek State scholar), London Sch. Econs., 1956; postgrad. New Sch. Social Research, 1963; children—Daphne, Yannis. With econ. research dept. Bank of Greece, Athens, 1957-60; with Nat. Bur. Econ. Research, N.Y.C. and Washington, 1960-66, Brookings Instn., Washington, 1968-73; mem. Cost-of-Living Council, Exec. Office of Pres., Washington, 1973-74; mem. Consumer Product Safety Commn., Washington, 1974—. Recipient Chairman's award Consumer Product Safety Commn., 1978. Mem. Am. Econ. Assn., Atlantic Econ. Assn., Am. Acad. Polit. and Social Sci., Soc. Govt. Economists (pres. 1979-80), Nat. Economists Club. Club: Atheaneum Univ. (pres. 1977-78). Home: 6005 32d St NW Washington DC 20015 Office: 5401 Westbard Ave Bethesda MD 20207

CLONEY, JAMES MAURICE, chem. co. exec.; b. Kalamazoo, Mar. 5, 1919; s. Maurice Joseph and Edith (Caster) C.; B.A., Kalamazoo Coll., 1941; m. Margaret Reiser, Jan. 24, 1946; children—Sheila, James, Robert. With GAF Corp. (formerly Gen. Aniline & Film Corp.), N.Y.C., 1946—, v.p. internat. div., 1966-71, group v.p. office systems, 1971—, sr. v.p. govt. relations, 1974—. Served with AUS, 1942-46. Mem. Am. Mgmt. Assn., Washington Export Council, Navy League. Club: Tantallon. Home: 706 Carnoustie Ln Tantallon MD 20022 Office: 1101 15th St NW Washington DC 20005

CLONINGER, AVERY MITCHELL, paper co. exec.; b. Portland, Oreg., May 31, 1919; s. Mitchell Andrew and Lela (Yocum) C.; B.B.A., U. Oreg., 1940; M.B.A. (univ. fellow), U. Wash., 1941; m. Geneva Mary Stafford, Oct. 7, 1940; children—Mitchell Lloyd, Michael Avery. Gen. traffic mgr., dir. raw material procurement Longview Fibre Co. (Wash.), 1941-63; dir. transp. Great Northern Paper Co., N.Y.C., 1964-68, Central Nat.-Gottesman Corp., N.Y.C., 1969-70; cons. Nat. Com. on Internat. Trade Documentation, N.Y.C., 1970; mgr. transp. Dennison Mfg. Co., Framingham, Mass., 1971—; mgr. cons. firm A.M. Cloninger Assos., N.Y.C., 1968-75. Pres., United Fund, Longview, 1948-49; chmn. County Com. Republican Party, 1950-51. Recipient Fgn. Trade award U.S. Dept. Commerce-U. Oreg., 1941. Mem. Progressive Shippers Coop. Assn. (dir. Worcester 1973—, pres. 1976—), Nat. Indsl. Traffic League (dir. 1948-76), Nat. Assn. Shippers Adv. Bds. (pres. 1964-65), Sigma Alpha Epsilon. Republican. Episcopalian. Clubs: Traffic (N.Y.C.); Boston Traffic Assn.; Longview Transp. (Wash.). Contbr. articles to trade publs. Inventor AMCLO Zip Route. Home: 14 Temple St Apt 8F Framingham Centre MA 01701 Office: 300 Howard St Framingham MA 01701

CLOSE, DONALD PEMBROKE, mgmt. cons.; b. Orange, N.J., July 11, 1920; s. Charles Mollison and Simah C.; B.S. in Economics, Wharton Sch. U. Pa., 1942; m. L. Carolyn Reck, Apr. 22, 1950; children—Geoffrey Stuart, Cynthia Leigh, Sara Carolyn. Sales rep. IBM, Newark, 1946-47; asst. budget dir. L. Bamberger & Co., Newark, 1947-53; staff exec. Am. Express, N.Y.C., 1953; controller, sec. Ciba Co., Inc., N.Y.C., 1953-59; dir. fin. and control Avon Products Inc., N.Y.C., 1960-72; pres. Corp. Fin. Assos., Inc., N.Y.C., 1973-76; v.p. Nelson Walker Assos., N.Y.C., 1973-76, Internat. Mgmt. Advisers, Inc., N.Y.C., 1976—. Trustee, Morristown (N.J.) Beard Sch., 1974-77; pres. Jr. Essex Troop Cavalry, 1964-68. Served with AUS, 1942-46. Decorated Bronze Star, Letter of Commendation. Mem. Fin. Execs. Inst., Am. Soc. Corp. Secs., Systems and Procedures Assn., Nat. Assn. Accts., Human Resources Planning Soc., Phi Sigma Kappa (past sec.). Republican. Episcopalian. Clubs: University (N.Y.C.); Montclair Golf; Wharton. Home: 7 S Mountain Terr Montclair NJ 07042 Office: 485 Lexington Ave New York NY 10017

CLOSE, HUGH WILLIAM, textile mfg. exec.; b. Phila., Nov. 18, 1919; s. Hugh William and Marian Lucy (Crandall) C.; B.S., U. Pa., 1942; grad. Exec. Program. U. N.C., 1959; LL.D. (hon.), U. S.C., 1967; m. Anne Kingsley Springs, Nov. 23, 1946; children—Lillian Crandall Close Bowles, Frances Allison Close Hart, Leroy Springs, Patricia Close Hastings, Elliott Springs, Hugh William, Derick Springsteen, Katherine Anne. With Springs Mill, Inc., N.Y.C., 1946—, mem. sales staff, Fort Mill, S.C., successively apprentice Springs Cotton Mills, asst. supt., asst. mgr. Fort Mill plant, gen. supt. card and spinning, asst. gen. mgr., asst. to pres., v.p., 1946-59, pres., chief exec. officer, dir. Springs Mill, Inc., N.Y.C., Springs Mills, Inc., Fort Mill, S.C., 1959-69, chmn. bd., 1969—; chmn., dir. Central Carolina Bank, Carolina Loan & Realty, Inc., Kanawha Ins. Co., Lancaster & Chester Ry., Leroy Springs & Co., The Springs Co., L & C Devel. Corp., Springland, Inc.; dir. Norfolk & So. R.R. Co. Commr. 5th Congl. dist. for S.C. Dept. Parks Recreation and Tourism, 1967-78. Dir., chmn. Elliott White Springs Found., Inc., Frances Ley Springs Found., Inc.; bd. dirs. J.E. Sirrine Textile Found.; trustee S.C. Coll. Council. Served as pvt. AUS, 1942, to lt. USNR, 1942-46. Named Textile Man of Year, N.Y. Bd. Trade, 1963. Mem. Am. Textile Mfrs. Inst. (ex-officio dir., pres. 1972-73), S.C. Textile Mfrs. Assn. (v.p. 1977-78, ex-officio mem. bd.), Newcomen Soc. Am., Phi Gamma Delta, Beta Gamma Sigma. Episcopalian. Club: Lions. Home: Fort Mill SC 29715 Office: Springs Mills Inc Fort Mill SC 29715

CLOUGH, WENDELL SNOW, businessman; b. Barre, Vt., Sept. 6, 1914; s. Lester Pratt and Eunice Elizabeth (Snow) C.; B.F.A. in Architecture, Yale U., 1937; m. Frances Jean Robinson, June 1, 1940; children—Wendell S., Alison B. Asst. to pres. Libby-Owens-Ford Glass, Toledo, Ohio, 1938-43; asst. to pres. Bell & Gossett, Chgo., 1948-53; mgr. styling adminstrn. Ford Motor Co., Detroit, 1953-57; mng. dir. Chrysler Ltd., London, 1958-62; devel. mgr. ITT, London, 1963-68; v.p. Boyden Internat., London, 1968-74; sr. v.p. Paul R. Ray, Internat., London, 1974-79; pres. Clough Assos., Inc., Denver and London, 1979—. Trustee, Am. Sch. London, 1964—. Served to lt. USNR, 1943-46. Mem. Am. C. of C. (pres. 1969-71, dir.), Brit. Inst. Mgmt., Inst. Dirs., Soc. Long Range Planning. Clubs: Royal and Ancient Golf (St. Andrews, Scotland); Sunningdale Golf, Bucks (London); Am. (dir., pres.). Home: 36 Sloane Ct W London SW3 4TB England also Parasol Route D'Antibes Valbonne France Office: 87 Regent St Suite 73 London W1 England

CLOUGH, WILLIAM ALLEN, oil co. exec.; b. Ocean City, N.J., Aug. 7, 1921; s. Roy Graham and Anne Marion (Carson) C.; B.A., U. Va., 1947, M.S., 1949; m. Jean Morse Howell, Jan. 12, 1946; children—Gwen, Virginia, Elisabeth. Geologist, The Tex. Co., 1949-52; sr. geologist Anderson Prichard, 1952-55; v.p. exploration Anschutz Drilling Co., 1955-59; regional exploration mgr. Union Tex. Petroleum, Denver, 1959-68; v.p. Stuarco Resources Corp., Denver, 1968—. Served with USNR, 1942-45. Mem. Am. Assn. Petroleum Geologists, Rocky Mountain Assn. Geologists, Am. Inst. Profl. Geologists, Denver Petroleum Club, Sigma Xi. Republican. Presbyterian. Clubs: Valley Country, Garden of the Gods. Author: Geology of the Danforth Hills Anticline, Moffat County, Colorado, 1954. Home: 4021 S Cherry St Englewood CO 80110 Office: Suite 2117 1st National Bank Bldg Denver CO 80202

CLOW, JOHN W., fin. cons.; b. Denver, Oct. 14, 1930; s. John Bailey and Louise (Warner) C.; A.B., Dartmouth, 1952; M.B.A., U. Calif. at Berkeley, 1954; m. Martha H. de Mey, Apr. 10, 1956; children—Eric de Mey, Gregory Vincent, Amelia Bayley, Guy Rowan, Louise Crankshaw. Dept. mgr. J.C. Penney Co., San Francisco, 1954-58; mem. staff Webb & Webb, C.P.A.'s, San Francisco, 1958-62, partner, 1962-71; pres. Clow Accountancy Corp., San Francisco, 1972-76; partner Main Lafrentz & Co., San Francisco, 1976-79, corp. fin. cons., 1979—. Treas., Calif. Young Republicans, 1962, nat. committeeman, 1963. Served with USAF, 1952-54. C.P.A., Calif. Mem. Am. Inst. C.P.A.'s (council 1977-80), Calif. (dir., treas. 1974-77, trustee found. 1979—), San Francisco (pres. 1972-73) socs. C.P.A.'s, Dartmouth Alumni Assn. (pres. No. Calif., Nev. 1962-63). Club: Univ. San Francisco. Home: PO Box 1448 Ross CA 94957

CLOWE, KELLEY ABINGTON, banker; b. Tulsa, Sept. 27, 1942; s. Kendall Dean and Clare Curry (Abington) C.; B.A., Central Methodist Coll., Fayette, Mo., 1964; M.B.A., U. Pa., 1966; m. Virginia Sue Carroll, Mar. 21, 1964; children—Sean, Douglas, Malinda. Research asst. Gen. Foods Corp., White Plains, N.Y., 1966-67; mktg. research analyst Anheuser-Busch, Inc., St. Louis, 1967-69; mktg. research mgr. Ralston Purina Co., St. Louis, 1969-72; pres. Clowe-Mather Research Assos., Inc., Lakewood, Colo., 1972-74; asst. v.p. mktg. First Nat. Bank of Denver, 1974-80; sr. v.p., cashier Dominion Bank of Denver, 1980—; instr. Inst. Mktg. Research, Bank Mktg. Assn., 1975-81, Sch. Bank Mktg., 1975-76. Mem. Am. Mktg. Assn. (pres. Colo. chpt. 1976-77), Bank Mktg. Assn. (chmn. research and planning council 1977-78, chmn. mktg. planning conf. 1979). Author: (with Anthony N. Diina) The Basics of Bank Marketing Research, 1978. Home: 4414 Apple Way Boulder CO 80301 Office: 3251 Syracuse Denver CO 80207

CLOWER, WILLIAM DEWEY, assn. exec.; b. Salem, Va., Oct. 9, 1935; s. Alton Oliver and Addie Vane (Young) C.; B.S., U. Va., 1958; M.S., 1958; m. Shirley Carol Tuttle, Sept. 1, 1956; children—Candice Denise, Michael DeWayne, Catherine Dione. Applications engr. ITT, Nutley, N.J., 1958-60; regional mktg. mgr. Litton Industries, Washington, 1960-61; propr. W. D. Clower Co., Great Falls, Va., 1961-70; spl. asst. to Pres. U.S., White House, Washington, 1970-75; exec. v.p. CISPI, Washington, 1975-76; pres. Food Processing Machinery and Supplies Assn., Washington, 1976—; dir. Food Processors Inst., 1977-80. Mem. com. on campaign services steering com. Republican Nat. Com., 1977-80. Served with USAF, 1959-60. VA Gen. Assembly scholar U. Va., 1954-58. Mem. Am., Washington socs. assn. execs., Aircraft Owners and Pilots Assn., The Food Group, Gamma Delta Epsilon. Republican. Presbyterian. Clubs: Sertoma (pres. 1963-64), Capitol Hill, River Bend Golf and Country. Home: 1098 Fairbank St Great Falls VA 22066 Office: 1828 L St NW Washington DC 20036

CLOWNEY, WILLIAM D., ins. co. exec.; b. Atlantic City, Nov. 18, 1923; s. Frank Sherman and Mabel Erskine (Eastlake) C.; A.B., Princeton U., 1948; m. Mary Seaman, Dec. 11, 1954; children—Lester, Elizabeth, William, Michael, Janet. Exec. dir. Group Sales and Service Prudential Ins. Co. Am., 1967-73, v.p. group ins., 1973-75, v.p., 1975-78, pres. Eastern ops., South Plainfield, N.J., 1978—. Vice chmn. bd. trustees Morristown Meml. Hosp.; adv. bd. Center Alcohol Studies, Rutgers U. Served to capt. U.S. Army, 1942-46, 50-51. C.L.U. Mem. Nat. Assn. Life Underwriters. Republican. Episcopalian. Clubs: Morris County Golf, Morristown Field, Princeton (N.Y.C.), Essex (Newark). Office: 1111 Durham Ave South Plainfield NJ 07080

CLUETT, MAXWELL LEWIS, chem. co. exec.; b. Lunenburg, N.S., Can., Jan. 6, 1929; came to U.S., 1953, naturalized, 1961; s. William Pike and Dorothy (Selig) C.; B.Sc., Dalhousie U., 1949; M.A., U. Toronto, 1951; Ph.D. (Pratt fellow), U. Va., 1956; m. Lucy Catherine Gerhardt, Aug. 8, 1951; children—Jayne Candice, Marita Kathryn, Lisa Anne. Chemist, N. Am. Cyanamid Co., Welland, Ont., Can., 1951-53; research chemist E.I. du Pont de Nemours & Co., Inc., Wilmington, Del., 1956-60; sr. research chemist, 1960-63, research asso., 1963-66, supr. sales technical, 1966-68, sales rep., 1968-72, sales mgr., chems. and pigments dept., N.Y.C., 1975—; sales mgr. DuPont of Can., 1972-75. Mem. Am. Chem. Soc., Sigma Xi. Republican. Episcopalian. Contbr. articles to chem. jours. Home: 184 Beechwood Rd Ridgewood NJ 07450 Office: E I du Pont de Nemours and Co 350 Fifth Ave Room 1129 New York NY 10118

COANE, JAMES EDWIN, bldg. products co. exec.; b. N.Y.C., July 21, 1940; s. James Edwin and Mary Elizabeth (Brown) C.; B.A., Duke U., 1963; m. JoAnn Sabasteanski, May 23, 1968; children—James Edwin IV, Mary Ashley. Sales mgr. Am. Flagpole Equipment Co., Inc., N.Y.C., 1963-65, asst. v.p., 1965-68; div. mktg. mgr. Kearney Nat., Inc., East Setauket, N.Y., 1968-70, v.p., gen. mgr., 1968-78, v.p. ops., 1979—; pres. Am. Flagpole Co., 1978-79. Mem. devel. com. Stony Brook Sch., 1977-78; active Assn. Retarded Children, Inc. Served with U.S. Army, 1963-64. Recipient Appreciation award Police Athletic League, 1976, Certificate of Appreciation, Boy Scouts Am., 1975. Mem. Constrn. Specification Inst., Nat. Assn. Archtl. Metal Mfrs. (dir.), Stony Brook Sch. Alumni Assn. Contbr. articles to profl. jours. Home: 3 Constance Ct East Setauket NY 11733

COATES, JOHN DOUGLASS, transp. equipment leasing corp. exec.; b. Abington, Pa., Sept. 27, 1942; s. Charles Fearon and Cynthia (Douglass) C.; B.S. in Indsl. Engring. (Trask Ashton scholar), Pa. State U., 1964; M.B.A., U. Pa., 1966; m. Judianne E. Eynon, June 11, 1966. Indsl. engr. U.S. Steel Corp., Phila., 1964-65; asso. A.T. Kearney and Co., Chgo., 1968-72; dir. engring., v.p. ops., SSI Container Corp. div. Itel Corp., San Francisco, 1972-78, pres. Itel specialized container div., San Francisco, 1978—; del. Container Lessor's Trade Assn. Active ACLU; sponsor pub. Sta. KQED-TV. Served to lt. comdr. USN, 1966-68. Mem. Transp. Research Forum., Wharton Alumni Club. Clubs: Commonwealth of Calif., Bay (San Francisco); Lotus (N.Y.C.). Co-author: Guide to Equipment Inspection, 1975. Home: 45 Crecienta Dr Sausalito CA 94965 Office: 2 Embarcadero Center San Francisco CA 94111

COATS, HUBERT S., JR., bank exec.; b. Julesberg, Colo., Feb. 26, 1927; s. Hubert S. and Ruth (Lang) C.; pre-standard cert. Am. Inst. Banking, 1951, standard cert., 1955; grad. Pacific Coast Bankers Sch., 1970; m. Edna Mae, July 13, 1946; children—Larry Dale, Matthew Daniel. With First Security Bank, Jerome, Idaho, 1946-55, 57-59, asst. mgr. timeway credit, 1953-55, asst. mgr., 1957-59; asst. mgr. Hailey (Idaho) First Security Bank, 1955-57; v.p., cashier First Security Bank Twin Falls (Idaho), 1959-67; mgr. First Security Bank, Rupert, Idaho, 1967-69; v.p. ops. eastern div. First Security Bank, Pocatello, Idaho, 1967-72, v.p., asst. mgr., 1972-73, mgr., 1977; mgr., v.p. First Security Bank, Coeur d'Alene, Idaho, 1973-77; v.p., area mgr. Idaho Bank & Trust Co., Boise, 1977-78, sr. v.p., 1978—. Pres. PTA, Hailey, Idaho, 1955-56; treas. Pocatello Jr. Achievement, 1970-71, pres., 1969-70; chmn. Idaho Housing Agy.; chmn. bd. trustees First Methodist Ch., Coeur d'Alene; treas. Kootenai County (Idaho) YMCA, 1972-75, dir., 1972—; bd. dirs., chmn. gen. div. United Way, Boise. Served with USN, 1944-46. Named Businessman of Yr., Twin Falls Credit Women's Club, 1954, Man of Yr., Kootenai Family YMCA, 1975; recipient Distinguished Service award Coeur d'Alene C. of C., campaign award Kootenai County United Way, 1976. Mem. Boise C. of C. Clubs: Hillcrest Country, Arid (Boise). Home: 817 Argyll Dr Boise ID 83702 Office: PO Box 2800 Boise ID 83701

COBB, DONALD LEE, elec. engr.; b. Newport News, Va., May 10, 1949; s. Willie Herman and Rebecca Odelia (Harrelson) C.; B.S.E.E., N.C. Agrl. and Tech. State U., 1972; M.B.A., Pepperdine U., 1980; cert. in noise abatement, U. Wis., 1972; cert. in bus. mgmt., Cortez Peters Bus. Coll., 1973. Sr. project engr. Gen. Foods Corp., Chgo., 1972-74; engring./maintenance Supr. Container Corp. Am., Santa Clara, Calif., 1974-77; gen. supr. Hughes Aircraft Co., El Segundo, Calif., 1977-80; mgr. plant engring. Raytheon ESD, Goleta, Calif., 1980—. Bd. dirs. Chgo. Jaycees, recipient Key Man award U.S. Jaycees. Cert. environ. health engr., Ill., energy conservation engr., Calif. Mem. IEEE, Midwest Noise Council, Assn. Energy Engrs. Democrat. Presbyterian. Club: All Seasons Ski.

COBB, WILLIAM CHARLES, mgmt. cons.; b. St. Louis, Apr. 5, 1943; s. James R. and Eileen (Provost) C.; B.S. in Aero. Engring., U. Tex., Austin, 1966; M.B.A., Ohio State U., 1970; m. Nancy Hale, June 25, 1966; children—Marlo Jane, Haley Tribble. Mgmt. cons. Touche Ross & Co., Houston, 1970-73; exec. dir. law firm Bracewell & Patterson, Houston, 1973-77; pvt. practice mgmt. cons., Houston, 1978—; mem. faculty Practising Law Inst., N.Y.C., Inst. Continuing Legal Edn.; speaker Internat. Bar Confs., Am. Bar Assn. confs. Served as officer USAF, 1966-70. Mem. Am. Inst. C.P.A.'s, Tex. Soc. C.P.A.'s, Am. Inst. Aeros. and Astronautics, Am. Mgmt. Assn., Am. Mgmt. Assn. Pres.'s Assn., Houston C. of C. Club: Houstonian. Author: Am. Bar Assn. Planning Workbook for Law Firm Management. Office: 1100 Milam Bldg Suite 4720 Houston TX 77002

COBB, WILLIAM REEVES, chem. co. exec.; b. Astoria, N.Y., Dec. 30, 1944; s. Edward Ellis and Helen (Rohan) C.; student Dun & Bradstreet Bus. Schs., 1972-74; A.A.S., State U. N.Y., 1974; B.S., Elmhurst Coll., 1978; m. Maureen, Sept. 19, 1970; children—Kelly Ann, Kimberly Catherine. Asst. mgr. Household Fin. Co., Bayshore, N.Y., 1967-68; claims mgr. Tuition Plan Inc., N.Y.C., 1968-71; complex credit mgr. U.S. Plywood Co., Farmingdale, N.Y., 1971-74; dist. credit mgr., accounts receivable mgr. Westinghouse Electric Supply Co., Elmhurst, Ill., 1974-79; domestic credit mgr. Chems. group Olin Corp., 1979—. Served with U.S. Army, 1965-67; Vietnam. Fellow Nat. Inst. Credit; mem. Nat. Chem. Credit Assn. Nat. Assn. Credit and Fin. Mgmt., Southwestern Conn. Credit and Fin. Mgmt. Assn. Republican. Roman Catholic. Home: 3 Shortridge Dr Mineola NY 11501 Office: 120 Longridge Rd Stamford CT 06904

COBBS, CLARENCE EVERETTE, shoe co. exec.; b. Springfield, Tenn., Apr. 27, 1921; s. Clarence Everette and Lewise McDonald C.; B.S., Tenn. Tech. U., 1942; m. Jane Marcelle Gilman, May 5, 1945; children—Susan E., Robert L., Richard G., James C. With Genesco, Inc., Nashville, 1946-67, div. mgr., European coordinator, Brussels, 1966-67; sr. v.p. Acme Boot Co., Clarksville, Tenn., 1967-79; pres. John A. Frye Shoe Co., Inc., Marlboro, Mass., 1979—. Served with USNR, 1943-45. Mem. Clarksville-Montgomery County C. of C. (exec. com.). Republican. Methodist. Home: 17 Olde Coach Rd Westboro MA 01581 Office: 84 Chestnut St Marlboro MA 01752

COBLE, THOMAS CULVER, public warehousing exec., lawyer; b. Anderson, Ind., Aug. 9, 1938; s. Reid Donald and Gladys Ilene (Foley) C.; B.S., Ind. U., 1960, J.D., 1966; m. Barbara Merritt Evans, June 2, 1962; children—Katherine Anne, Robert Culver, Michael Reid. Asst. to pres. AAA Warehouse Corp., Indpls., 1965-70, v.p., gen. mgr., 1970—; admitted to Ind. bar, 1966, U.S. Supreme Ct. bar, 1966; partner Larman & Larman, Indpls., 1972—, Larman, Coble & Larman, Indpls., 1972—; pres. St. Clair Warehouse Corp., Indpls., 1978—; a founder, sec.-treas. Kostoff McKee Overhead Door Corp., Indpls., 1978—. Served to 1st lt. Signal Corp, U.S. Army, 1960-62. Mem. Am. Warehouseman's Assn., Indpls. Traffic Club, Ind. Warehouse Assn., Ind. Bar Assn. Republican. Roman Catholic. Office: 221 S Franklin Rd Indianapolis IN 46219

COBURN, FRANKLIN DELANO, savings and loan assn. exec.; b. Ridgeway, Pa., Dec. 9, 1933; s. George Clifford C.; B.Comml.Sci., Benjamin Franklin U., 1960, M.Comml. Sci., 1962; diploma Inst. Fin. Edn., 1964; children—David, Cathleen. With Northwestern Fed. Savs. & Loan Assn., Washington, 1956—, pres., 1973—; dir. Inst. Fin. Edn., 1970—, Met. Washington Savs. & Loan League, 1971-79. Served with USAF, 1952-56. Recipient Contbn. to Chpt. award Inst. Fin. Edn., 1979. Mem. U.S. League for Savs. Assns., Washington Bd. Realtors. Republican. Club: Kiwanis. Office: 1900 M St Washington DC 20036

COBURN, ROBERT BOWNE, stock broker; b. Manchester, Conn., May 19, 1906; s. Edward Hewitt and Lena (Carter) C.; B.S., Yale U., 1928; m. Elizabeth Mohun, June 15, 1929; children—Edward H., Elenor Coburn Smith, Barry M. Pres. Glastonbury Knitting Co., 1930-33; spl. partner Easland & Co., stock broker, 1932-34; partner Coburn & Middlebrook, 1934-48; treas., chmn. bd. Coburn & Meredith, Inc., Hartford, Conn., 1948—; pres., dir. Coburn Securities Corp., 1947—; pres., dir. Westminster Leasing Ltd., Kensington Leasing Ltd., Burnham Leasing Ltd.; dir. Plimpton & Hills Corp., Hartford; mem. Midwest Stock Exchange. Trustee Nettie Bowne Estate; bd. dirs. Conn. Prison Assn.; incorporator Mt. Sinai Hosp., Bloomfield, Conn. Mem. Miramichi Salmon Assn. (past dir.), Nat. Platform Assn. Congregationalist. Clubs: Harbor View, Yale (N.Y.C.); Hartford, Hartford Golf; Coventry Fish and Game. Home: 43 Juniper Rd Bloomfield CT 06002 Office: 17 Lewis St Hartford CT 06003

COCCIA, SILVIO D., pharm. co. exec.; b. Chester, Pa., Aug. 25, 1932; s. Saverio and Chiara (Marchetti) C.; B.S. in Pharmacy, Temple U., 1954; B.S. in Bus. Adminstrn., Widener Coll., 1962; m. Virginia Pasqualini, Apr. 26, 1958; children—Silvio, Mario, Marco, Bernard, Anthony. Pharmacist, Lloyd Pharmacy, Chester, Pa., 1954-57; with Geigy Pharm. div. Ciba Geigy Corp., Ardsley, N.Y., 1957—, salesman, 1957-62, sales tng. instr., 1962-66, sales promotion mgr., 1966-68, product promotion mgr., 1968-70, group product promotion mgr., 1970-72, copy supr., 1972-75, group sales promotion mgr., 1975-77, dir. sales promotion, 1977-80, dir. promotion planning and adminstrn., 1980—. Served with U.S. Army, 1954-56. Mem. Am. Pharm. Assn., Pa. Pharm. Assn., N.J. Pharm. Assn., Am. Inst. History of Pharmacy, Phi Delta Chi. Roman Catholic. Home: 20 Lawrence Dr Berkeley Heights NJ 07922 Office: 556 Morris Ave Summit NJ 07901

COCHRAN, JOHN FRAZER, petroleum engring. exec.; b. Los Angeles, June 23, 1908; s. Samuel Findley and Frances Eugenia (Frazer) C.; B.S., Ga. Inst. Tech., 1931; m. Maxine Cecilia Whiffin, Sept. 28, 1940; 1 dau., Barbara Frances Cochran Smith. Engr., Westinghouse Elec. & Mfg. Co., Pitts. and N.Y.C., 1931-38, Kaelin Elec. Co., Los Angeles, 1939, Hunter Engring. Co., Riverside, Calif., 1940-41, Consol. Western Steel Corp., Maywood, Calif., 1941-45, Eastman Oil Well Survey Co., Long Beach, Calif., 1946-50; with Driltrol, Inc., Long Beach, 1950—, pres., chmn. bd., 1954—; pres. Dynaquip, Inc., Signal Hill, Calif., 1961-68; chmn. bd. Montrose Lighting, 1964-69. Registered mech. and elec. engr., Calif. Mem. Am. Def. Preparedness Assn. (life), Am. Welding Soc., Petroleum Prodn. Pioneers, Christian Anti-Communism Crusade (life), Petroleum Equipment Suppliers Assn. (dir. 1974-76), Nat. Oilfield Mfrs. and Dels. Soc. (pres. 1965, nat. regent 1966-68). Democrat. Presbyterian. Clubs: Sertoma (pres. 1961-62), Old Ranch Country, Seal Beach. Patentee well-drilling tools. Home: 2825 E 2d St Long Beach CA 90803 Office: 1361 E Hill St Signal Hill CA 90806

COCHRAN, KERRY THOMAS, furniture mfg. co. exec.; b. Drayton, N.D., Sept. 19, 1940; s. Everard James and Kathleen Alta (Ferguson) C.; student Minot State Coll., 1958-61; m. Joan Florence Upham, May 1, 1971; children—Kari Lynn, Dawn Heather, Jennifer Lynn. Dept. mgr. Sears, Roebuck & Co., Minot, N.D., 1961-65, mdse. mgr., Kenosha, Wis., 1965-67, Waterloo, Iowa, 1967-70; adminstrv. asst. for nat. accounts Flexsteel Industries, Inc., Dubuque, Iowa, 1970-71, account exec., 1971-72, product mgr., 1972-73, nat. accounts sales mgr., 1973-77, regional sales mgr., Waxahacie, Tex., 1977—. Office: 1401 W Marvin St Waxahachie TX 75165

COCHRAN, RICHARD TIMOTHY, investment banker; b. Newark, Ohio, Mar. 12, 1939; s. Jacque P. and Lena H. (DeVito) C.; B.A., Ohio U., Athens, 1966; m. Annetta Marie Giesy, Oct. 31, 1972; children—Sean P. (dec.), Richard Sean, Scott Ellwood. Salesman, Wheeling Steel Co. (W.Va.), 1966-67, Anchor Hocking Glass Co., Lancaster, Ohio, 1967; with Merrill Lynch, Pierce, Fenner & Smith Inc., Columbus, Ohio, 1968—, sr. account exec., then asst. v.p., 1973-77, v.p., 1977—; leader option seminars. Mem. fin. com. Broad St. United Methodist Ch., Columbus, 1979-80. Mid-Am. Conf. athlete, 1965. Mem. Columbus Stock and Bond Club, Phi Beta Kappa. Republican. Clubs: Brookside Country, Columbus Athletic. Office: 180 E Broad St Columbus OH 43215

COCHRAN, VENITA RAE, exec. search co. exec.; b. Hawk Springs, Wyo., Dec. 18, 1936; d. Earl R. and Isis B. Hubbs; B.S. in Acctg., U. Wyo., 1960. Sr. budget analyst Thiokol Chem. Corp., Brigham City, Utah, 1961-62; payroll supr. U. Calif., La Jolla, 1963; sr. auditor Vicenti, Lloyd & Stuzman, C.P.A.'s, LaVerne, Calif., 1964-67; v.p., controller Cable Commuter Airlines, Ontario, Calif., 1967-69; sr. auditor Stegall & Easley, C.P.A.'s, San Bernardino, Calif., 1969-71; tax specialist S.D. Leisdesdorf & Co., C.P.A.'s, Los Angeles, 1971-72; tax. mgr., then dir. internal audit Collins Foods, Internat., Inc., Los Angeles, 1972-78; pres. Cochran Exec. Search, Ltd., Los Angeles, 1978—. C.P.A., Calif. Republican. Office: 10642 Santa Monica Blvd Los Angeles CA 90025

COCHRAN, WILLIAM HAROLD, traffic control systems co. exec.; b. Six Mile, S.C., Dec. 17, 1929; s. James Leon and Della Marie (Howard) C.; B.S., Clemson U., 1958; m. Jo Ann Dillard, Aug. 14, 1954; children—Hal, Cara. Indsl. engr. Deering Milliken, Clemson, S.C., 1958; salesman Exxon Corp., Greenville, S.C., 1958-63; owner, pres. Traffic Control Systems, Greenville, 1965—. Served with U.S. Army, 1951-53. Republican. Baptist. Office: PO Box 8171 Greenville SC 29604

COCHRANE, WILLIAM HENRY, mgmt. cons.; b. Norfolk, Va., Apr. 3, 1912; s. William F. and Gretchen (Schneider) C.; student Princeton U., 1931-32; m. Elizabeth J. Ballantine, Aug. 3, 1935 (dec. July 1979); children—William Henry, Elizabeth J. Cochrane Davis, Susan B. Cochrane Aspinwall, Peter B.; m. 2d, Deborah E. Collyer, June 14, 1978. With U.S. Indsl. Chems. Co., 1932-52, chemist, salesman, dist. mgr. market and sales analysis, mgr. detergent project; gen. mgr. indsl. div. Lever Brothers Co., 1952-57; exec. v.p. Neptune Internat. Corp., 1957-58, pres., 1958-69, chmn. bd., 1966-72, now dir.; v.p. Mountain Lake Corp., 1975-78, pres., dir., 1978—; dir. Los Angeles Soap Co., Harrower Enterprises, Inc. Trustee Lake Wales Hosp.; mem. Vero Beach (Fla.) City Council, 1980—; bd. dirs. Vero Beach Civic Assn. Served from lt. (j.g.) to lt., USNR, 1944-46. Mem. Soc. Chem. Industry, Fla. Colombia Alliance, UN Assn., Am. Water Works Assn., Newcomen Soc. N.Am. Clubs: Nassau, Econ., Princeton (N.Y.C.); Mountain Lake (Fla.); Riomar Bay Yacht, Riomar Bay Country. Home: 2320 Club Dr Vero Beach FL 32960 Office: City Hall Vero Beach FL 32960

COCKRELL, CLAUDE O'FLYNN, JR., container co. exec.; b. Memphis, May 10, 1937; s. Claude O'Flynn and Audrey (Roberts) C.; student Memphis State U., 1955, U. Miami, 1955-57; div.; children—Cana Lynn, Claude O'Flynn III. Pres., Shelby Paper Box Co., Memphis, 1952-56; pres.-owner Memphis Corrugated Container Co., 1956-61; adminstr., owner Cockrell Container Co., Memphis, 1961—; owner West Corp., Memphis, 1971—, Diamond Bar Ranch, Memphis, 1972—; pres. Tenn. Aviation, 1970—, Great Am. Container Corp., 1975—, Nashville Corrugated Box Inc., 1975—; pres., owner Am. Divers, 1972—, West Prodns., 1977—, Photo Finish, Inc., 1978—, TVC Internat., Inc., 1979—, Cockrell Communication Corp.; dir. So. Corrugated Box, Inc. State marshall Freedom Trail Found. Tenn., 1973—. Head campaign George Wallace for Pres., Memphis and Tri-state area, 1968. Mem. Tenn. Breeders and Racing Assn. (chmn. 1978), Pi Kappa Alpha. Presbyn. Moose. Home and Office: PO Box 90387 Nashville TN 37209

COCKRUM, WILLIAM MONROE, III, investment banker; b. Indpls., July 18, 1937; s. William M. and Katherine (Jaqua) Moore; A.B., DePauw U., 1959; M.B.A., Harvard U., 1961; m. Carol Anne Woodburn, June 10, 1961 (div.); children—Catherine Anne, William Monroe IV; m. 2d, Andrea Lee Deering, Mar. 8, 1975. With A.G. Becker Inc., Chgo., N.Y.C., Los Angeles, 1961—, v.p., N.Y.C., 1965—, mgr. corp. finance div. nationwide, 1969-71, mgr. pvt. investments, 1971-74, sr. v.p., 1974-78, vice chmn., 1978—, also dir. Mem. Bankers Club N.Y.C. Clubs: University (Chgo.); Delta Kappa Epsilon (N.Y.C.). Home: 666 Sarbonne Rd Los Angeles CA 90024 Office: One Century Plaza Los Angeles CA 90067 also 55 Water St New York NY 10004

COCKSHUTT, MALCOLM WILLIAM, elec. contracting co. exec.; b. Manchester, Eng., Sept. 9, 1940; came to U.S., 1967, naturalized, 1981; s. James Farnworth and Hilda Maude (Jackson) C.; student Cleve. Inst. Electronics, 1971-72, Jacksonville U., 1974; m. Enid Cockshutt, Mar. 14, 1960; children—Janice, Mandy. Gen. mgr. Continental Electric Corp., 1967-69, 76-78, also dir.; service and projects mgr. White Elec. Constrn., Atlanta, 1970-74; projects mgr. Miller Electric, Jacksonville, 1974-76; pres. Internat. Elec. Corp., Sterling, Va., 1978—. Served with Brit. Navy, 1962-66. Hon. lt. col. Ala., 1974. Registered elec. contractor, Va., Md., D.C. Mem. No. Va. Elec. Contractors Assn. (pres. 1979-81), Nat. Elec. Contractors Assn. (v.p. Fla. 1975). Clubs: U.S. Yacht Racing Union, West River Sailing, Chesapeake Bay Yacht Racing Assn., Pirates Cove Race. Home: 317 Hanford Ct Sterling VA 22170

COCRON, RONALD ROBERT, food distbn. co. exec.; b. Phila., Oct. 31, 1937; s. Nick Peter and Naomi Ruth (Hagy) C.; student U. Del., 1968; m. Gloria Jean MacLennan, Feb. 8, 1964; children—Lisa Ann, Cheryl Ann. Clk., Penn Fruit Co., Phila., 1955-60; salesman Samuel Zukerman & Co., Pennsuaken, N.J., 1963-65; supermarket mgr. Supermarkets Gen. Corp., Woodbridge, N.J., 1965-69; v.p. sales Progressive Brokerage Co., King of Prussia, Pa., 1975-78; sr. v.p. Samuel Zukerman & Co., Bensalem, Pa., 1969—. Served with AUS, 1960-63. Presbyterian. Home: Ridgeview Dr RD 2 Doylestown PA 18901 Office: I-95 Industrial Park Bensalem PA 19020

COE, HENRY SUTCLIFFE, rancher, mgmt. cons.; b. Oakland, Calif., May 30, 1906; s. Henry Huntington Willard and Rhoda Dawson (Sutcliffe) C.; student U. of Pacific, 1924-26; A.B., Stanford, 1929, postgrad., 1931-32; LL.B., Blackstone Coll. Law, 1941, J.D., 1942; m. Pearle Winnifred Hersey, Oct. 9, 1928; children—Nancy Patricia, Winnifred Hannah Verbica. Pub. accountant, San Jose, Calif., 1928-29; bookkeeper U.S. Steel Corp., San Francisco, 1929; salesman James A. Clayton Co., Real Estate, 1929; bookkeeper Del Monte Corp., 1930; cattle rancher, San Jose, 1932—; property mgmt. cons., San Jose, 1943—, Bangor, Maine, 1943—. Life bd. dirs., trustee, patron San Jose YMCA. Mem. Am. Def. Preparedness Assn. (life), Nat. (charter), Calif., Santa Clara County cattlemen's assns., Am. Forestry Assn. (life), Maine Forest Products Council, Calif. Hist. Soc. (patron), San Jose C. of C., Arabian Horse Registry, Arabian Horse Club No. Calif. Republican. Episcopalian. Clubs: Masons (32 deg.), Shriners, Camel Herders; Commonwealth of Calif. (San Francisco); San Jose Country. Home: 8610 San Felipe Rd San Felipe Valley San Jose CA 95135 Office: PO Box 877 San Saint James Park Sta Jose CA 95106 also PO Box 676 Rangor ME 04401

COE, WILLIAM CLITUS, JR., accountant; b. Swifton, Ark., Sept. 18, 1941; s. William Clitus and Mary Inez (McCall) C.; B.S. in Bus. Adminstrn., U. Ark., 1963; M.B.A., U. Pa., 1965; m. Yvonne Marie Ross, Nov. 16, 1968; children—Mary, Rebeecka. Office mgr. Frank Whitbeck for Gov., Little Rock, 1968; partner Ernst & Whinney, C.P.A.'s, New Orleans, 1968—. Adviser Jr. Achievement, New Orleans, 1971-72; mem. Spring Fiesta Assn., Mus. Art, Friends of Cablido; bd. dirs. Jefferson Place Civic Assn., New Orleans, 1971-76, pres., 1972-73, v.p., 1973-74; v.p., bd. dirs. New Orleans Floral Trail, 1973—; bd. dirs., treas. Community Service Center, 1976-79; bd. dirs. McGehee's Sch. for Girls, 1979-80, Internat. Trade Mart, 1979-80. Served to 1st lt. Fin. Corp. AUS, 1966-68. C.P.A., La., Ark. Mem. Goals to Grow Found., Am. Inst. C.P.A.'s, New Orleans, La. socs. C.P.A.'s, Fin. Analysts Soc., New Orleans Jr. C. of C. (dir. 1972-73, state dir. 1972-73), Phi Eta Sigma, Alpha Kappa Psi, Phi Delta Theta, Omicron Delta Kappa. Republican. Methodist. Clubs: Variety dir. 1973-75, 79-80), Young Men's Bus. (dir. 1971-73, 75-77, treas.; 1st v.p. 1978, pres. 1979) (New Orleans). Editor: Action, 1972-73, 74-75, 75-76. Home: 3708 Post Oak Ave New Orleans LA 70114 Office: One Shell Sq New Orleans LA 70139

COELHO, HORACE ALEXANDER, bus. systems and equipment mfg. co. exec.; b. Karachi, India, Feb. 26, 1943; came to Can., 1972, naturalized, 1978; s. Patrick Hubert and Martha Charlotte (D'Cunha) C.; B.A. with honours, U. Bombay, 1962, LL.B., 1964; m. Rita Maria Fonseca, May 4, 1974; children—Chantal Valerie, Craig André. Called to Indian bar, 1964; sales mgmt. trainee Colgate-Palmolive Co., India, 1965-70; divisional sales mgr. Havero Industries, India, 1971; with Pitney Bowes of Can., 1972—, br. mgr., Sudbury, Ont., 1979—; fellow English dept. St. Xavier's Coll., Bombay, India, 1962-63. Past pres. parish council St. Mary's Ch., Montreal. Mem. Canorient Assn. Montreal and Toronto (past dir.). Roman Catholic. Home: 2188 Robin St Sudbury ON P3A 4V3 Canada Office: Pitney Bowes of Can 1899 Lasalle St Sudbury ON P3A 2A3 Canada

COERPER, MILO GEORGE, lawyer; b. Milw., May 8, 1925; s. Milo Wilson and Rose (Schubert) C.; B.S., U.S. Naval Acad., 1946; LL.B., U. Mich., 1954; M.A., Georgetown U., 1957, Ph.D., 1960; m. Lois Hicks, Apr. 11, 1953; children—Milo Wilson, Allison Lee, Lois Paddock. Admitted to D.C. bar, 1954, since practiced in Washington; asso. firm Wilmer & Broun, 1954-60; asso. firm Coudert Brothers, 1961-63, partner, 1964—. Trustee, Sheridan Sch., chmn. bd., pres., 1974-76; ordained deacon Episcopal Ch., 1978, priest, 1979; priest St. Andrew's Ch., Clear Spring, Md., 1979—. Served to ensign USN, 1946-49, to lt., 1951-53. Mem. Bar Assn. D.C., Assn. Bar City N.Y., Am. Bar Assn., Md. State Bar Assn., Am. Law Inst., Am. Soc. Internat. Law, Internat. Law Assn. Clubs: Army and Navy, Met., Chevy Chase; Union League (N.Y.C.). Contbr. articles to profl. jours. Home: 7315 Brookville Rd Chevy Chase MD 20015 also Box 24 Clear Spring MD 21722 Office: 1 Farragut Sq S Washington DC 20006

COFFEY, GEORGE HAROLD, utilities co. exec.; b. New Haven, Apr. 27, 1943; s. Robert John and Marian L. (Taylor) C.; student Eli Whitney Tech., 1962-63, Bullard Havens Tech., 1963-64, U. Bridgeport, 1964-70; m. Diane Lee Eastman, Oct. 30, 1976 (div. Jan. 1980); 1 son, Robert (by previous marriage). Electrician, Avco Lycoming, Stratford, Conn., 1962-66, computer technologist, 1966-69; tech. asst. to mgr. sales Data Products, Stamford, Conn., 1969, quality assurance design engr., 1969-71; pres., owner G. H. Coffey Co., Inc., Internat., Gaysville, Vt., 1972—, dir., 1975—; pres., dir. C & D Realty & Devel. Co., Gaysville, 1976—; founder, pres., treas. N. Country Elec. Co., Rochester, Vt., 1976-78; v.p., dir. Bridgewater Constrn. Co., Randolph, Vt., 1977—; tech. advisor Assoc. Gen. Contractors Vt., 1977—. Mem. Am. Soc. Quality Control, Assoc. Builders and Contractors Assn., Assoc. Gen. Contractors Vt. Republican. Roman Catholic. Home: Lilliesvill Rd Bethel VT 05032 Office: PO Box 92 Route 107 Gaysville VT 05746

COFFEY, JAMES BAGSHAW, JR., govt. ofcl.; b. Lowell, Mass., Sept. 30, 1941; s. James B. and Dorothy (Webster) C.; B.A., U. Mass.,

Amherst, 1963; M.A., U. Maine, Orono, 1974; m. Pamela Washburn, Sept. 4, 1965; children—Bradford, Cara. Exec. dir. Presque Isle (Maine) Indsl. Council, 1964-68; dir. Eastern Maine Devel. Dist., Inc., Bangor, 1968-76. Chmn. Penobscot County Manpower Assn. 1971-73; mem. Maine Gov.'s Manpower Council, 1973-76; mem. Action Com. of 50, 1974-78; bd. dirs. Bangor YMCA, 1977-80, pres., 1980; bd. dirs. New Eng. Assn. Hosp. Devel., 1977—; dir. devel. Eastern Maine Med. Center, 1976—; trustee Husson Coll., 1981—. Served with U.S. Army, 1963-64. Fellow Am. Indsl. Devel. Council (dir. 1972-77); mem. Nat. Assn. Devel. Orgns. (dir. 1971-76), Indsl. Devel. Council Maine (pres. 1970). Club: Rotary. Home: 177 Silk St Brewer ME Office: 489 State St Bangor ME 04401

COFFEY, MICHAEL LEYMON, indsl. hygienist; b. Tulsa, Apr. 22, 1943; s. Ardie Walker and Margie Arlette (Miller) Tucker; B.S., UCLA, 1971, M.P.H. (HEW fellow), 1972; cert. health insp., OSHA Inst., Rosemont, Ill., 1975; student Lincoln U., Jefferson City, Mo., 1961-62, Azusa (Calif.) Pacific Coll., 1966-68. Indsl. hygienist Colo. Dept. Health, Denver, 1974-76; occupational safety and health evaluator Bristol Myers Co., East Syracuse, N.Y., 1977-80; sr. environ. health and safety engr. Hughes Aircraft Co., Fullerton, Calif., 1980—. Served with USAF, 1962-66. Mem. Am. Indsl. Hygiene Assn., Am. Public Health Assn. Club: World Future Soc. Home: 400 N Acacia A-14 Fullerton CA 92631 Office: PO Box 3310 Bldg TC11 H-106 Fullerton CA 92634

COFFIN, JERRY DEAN, broadcasting exec.; b. Spokane, Wash., Dec. 21, 1944; s. Joseph Herschel and Ella Audine (Meyer) C.; student Calif. Poly. U., 1962-65; m. Lynne Ann Shatzkin, Feb. 24, 1974; children—Julietta Dora, Jessica Daniele. Program exec. Quaker Action Group, Phila., 1967-69, War Resisters League, N.Y.C., 1967-72; gen. mgr. Sta. WBAI-FM, N.Y.C., 1972-73; account exec. London Wavelength, Inc., N.Y.C., 1974; pres. Am. Internt. Media Services, N.Y.C., 1974-75; sta. relations exec. NBC, N.Y.C., 1975-77; gen. mgr. BGI, N.Y.C., 1977-79; pres. Maggie Prodns., N.Y.C., 1979—; dir. WIN Mag., N.Y.C. Bd. dirs. War Resisters League, N.Y.C.; pres. A.J. Muste Inst., N.Y.C. Author: Organizing for the P.P.C., SCLC, 1968; A Manual for Direct Action, WRL, 1971; Start Your N.I.S. Station Right, NBC, 1976; also articles and monographs. Home: 23 Pierrepont St Brooklyn NY 11201 Office: Maggie Prodns 345 Lafayette St New York NY 10012

COFFIN, WILLIAM SARGENT, bus. cons.; b. Pittsfield, Maine, Dec. 16, 1914; s. Carl Sargent and Grace (Summerbell) C.; A.B., Bates Coll., 1937; grad. Am. Inst. Banking; m. Amelia Amanda Moore, Sept. 7, 1945; children—Thomas Carl, William Sargent. Clk., First Nat. Bank, Pittsfield, Maine, 1939-41; credit mgr. Sears Roebuck Co., Augusta, Maine, 1947-53; clk. Electric Boat div. Gen. Dynamics Corp., Groton, Conn., 1953-55; examiner Dept. Banks and Banking, Augusta, Maine, 1955-58; exec. dir. Devel. Credit Corp. Maine, Augusta, 1958-75; owner, gen. mgr. W.S. Coffin & Asso. Manchester, Maine, 1975—. Served to capt. AUS, 1941-46. Mem. Nat. Assn. Bus. Devel. Corps. (exec. v.p. 1973—), Indsl. Devel. Council Maine, Maine Bankers Assn., Maine Mchts. Assn. Republican. Clubs: Masons. Order Eastern Star. Home: Williamson Rd Manchester ME 04351

COFFMAN, FREDERIC SIMON, JR., consumer products co. exec.; b. Princeton, N.J., Oct. 12, 1931; s. Frederic S. and Lorlynne (Taylor) C.; student Princeton U., 1949-51; B.S., Babson Coll., 1953; m. Gail Frances Judge, Feb. 10, 1962; children—Peter Daniel, Margaret Jean. Vice-pres. A. G. Becker & Co., N.Y.C., 1964-71, Baker, Weeks & Co., N.Y.C., 1971-76; 1st v.p. White Weld & Co., N.Y.C., 1976-78; staff v.p. corp. planning Kimberly-Clark Corp., Neenah, Wis., 1978—. Mem. N.Y. Paper Analysts Group (pres. 1963-65), N.Y. Soc. Security Analysts. Republican. Presbyterian. Club: North Shore Golf. Office: Kimberly-Clark Corp N Lake St Neenah WI 54956

COFFMAN, HERBERT MCKINLEY, ch. exec.: b. Fruitland, Idaho, Mar. 1, 1933; s. McKinley and Elizabeth (Fahrney) C.; B.A., Manchester (Ind.) Coll., 1959; m. Janet Eller, Nov. 22, 1956; children—Amy, Lavonne, Kurt, Rhonda, Michael. Asso. European dir. Brethren Service Program, Kassel, W. Ger., 1960-62; dir. Centers and Disaster Service, New Windsor, Md., 1963-77; dir. service ministries Ch. of Brethren, New Windsor, 1977—; mem. unit com., disaster service com. Ch. World Service, 1977—, chmn. immigration and resettlement com., 1977—, spl. liaison rep. refugees, Indochina, Malaysia, Thailand and Cambodia, 1979; exec. com. Nat. Vol. Orgns. Active in Disaster, 1977—; dep. dir. Cuban Haitian Task Force, Ft. Chaffee, Ark., 1980—; vice chmn. Heifer Project Internat., Little Rock, 1977—; mem. spl. del. to Vietnam, Ch. World Service/World Council Chs., 1979; 2d alt. ofcl. U.S. Del. Refugees, Geneva, 1979; dir. New Windsor State Bank, 1977—. Recipient various service citations. Address: 1300 Wakefield Valley Rd New Windsor MD 21776

COFFMAN, LEROY CARL, savs. and loan assn. exec.; b. Chgo., May 1, 1929; s. Carl E. and Dorothy (Hill) C.; B.S. in Accounting and Econs. (Wall St. Jour. scholar), Aurora Coll., 1951; m. Marilyn K. Weiland, Aug. 23, 1952; children—Linda Lee, Kelly Jean. Mgr. br. Ward Lumber Co., Aurora, Ill., 1950-57; sec.-treas. Columbia Lumber Co. Alaska, Juneau, 1957-60; asst. cashier B.M. Behrends Bank, Juneau, 1960-63; pres., mng. officer Alaska Fed. Savs. and Loan Assn., Juneau, 1963—; pres. Alaska State Devel. Corp., 1971—; chmn. bd. Alaska Indsl. Devel. Authority, 1980—; dir. Fed. Home Loan Bank of Seattle. Mem. City Council Douglas, 1958-64; mem. Alaska New Capital Site Planning Commn.; bd. dirs. Juneau Receiving Home for Children, 1965—, pres., 1968-69, treas., 1965—. Served with AUS, 1953-55. Mem. Nat. (gov. 1966-70, dir. 1978), Alaska (pres. 1967-70, 73, exec. v.p. 1980—) leagues insured savs. and loan assns., Greater Juneau C. of C. (dir. 1970-72), U.S. Savs. and Loan League (dir. 1970), USCG Aux. Clubs: Rotary, Elks, Juneau Yacht (past commodore). Home: 108 Troy St Juneau AK 99801 Office: 301 N Franklin St Juneau AK 99801

COFFMAN, ROY WALTER, III, publishing co. exec.; b. Detroit, May 27, 1943; s. Roy Walter, Jr. and Adele Ruth Coffman; student U. Okla., part-time 1967-70; m. Brenda Lynn Spies, June 27, 1964; children—Christa Ruth, Eric Ross. Sales mgr. Christian Sci. Monitor, Boston, 1968-75; v.p. Logos Internat. Fellowship, Plainfield, N.J., 1975-77: promotion mgr. Aspen Systems Corp., Germantown, Md., 1977-78; v.p. Christianity Today, Carol Stream, Ill., 1978—; condr. seminars, cons. in field. Served with USAF, 1960-68. Home: 129 S Lancaster St Bolingbrook IL 60439 Office: 465 Gundersen Dr Carol Stream IL 60187

COGAN, DOLORIS CAROLYN COULTER, drug co. exec.; b. Potter, Nebr., July 28, 1924; d. George A. and Margaret Ann (Jensen) Coulter; B.A., Nebr. Wesleyan U., 1945; M.S., Columbia U. Grad. Sch. Journalism, 1946; m. Thomas J. Cogan, Oct. 6, 1950 (div. July 1967); children—Thomas J., Richard B., Douglas G. Editor, Inst. Ethnic Affairs, Washington, 1946-49; research dir. Nat. Indian Inst., Dept. Interior, Washington, 1949-50; adminstrv. asst. Pacific affairs Office of Territories, Dept. Interior, 1950-55; free-lance writer, 1955-65; asst. pub. relations mgr. Pepperidge Farm, Inc., Norwalk, Conn., 1965-67, mgr. pub. relations, 1967-72; dir. pub. relations Miles Labs., Inc., Elkhart, Ind., 1972—; mem. U.S. del. to 2nd Inter-Am. Indian Congress, Cuzco, Peru, 1949. Sec., Norwalk Charter Revision Commn., 1959; sec. Fact-Finding Com. on Sch. Bldg. Requirements, Norwalk, 1962; v.p. League Women Voters, Norwalk, 1959-61; publicity chmn. Am. Field Service, Norwalk, 1963-64; dir. pub. info. United Way of Elkhart County, 1973-75; mem. adv. council Career Center of Elkhart Area, 1976—, pres., 1980-81; bd. dirs. Elkhart YWCA, 1977—, Elkhart Urban League, 1977—; trustee Nebr. Wesleyan U., 1973—. Recipient citation First Guam Congress, 1950, Meritorious Service award Dept. Interior, 1955, Alumni Achievement award Nebr. Wesleyan U., 1976, Bus. Leadership award Elkhart YWCA, 1977. Mem. Pharm. Mfrs. Assn. Washington, Am. Women in Radio and TV (pres. Hoosier chpt. 1977), Soc. for Nutrition Edn., LWV, South Bend Press Club. Democrat. Unitarian. Clubs: Elcona Country (Elkhart); Altrusa. Home: 1616 N Bay Dr Elkhart IN 46514 Office: 1127 Myrtle St Elkhart IN 46514

COGGINS, THOMAS WAYNE, SR., tng. co. exec.; b. Henderson, N.C., Feb. 11, 1941; s. George Grady and Reba Alline (Garrett) C.; student U.S. Navy Enlisted Tech. and Mgmt. Schs., 1960-78; children—Debra Diane, Thomas Wayne, Mari Ellen. Enlisted in U.S. Navy, 1958, advanced through grades to chief petty officer, 1975, ret., 1978; chmn. bd. curriculum Devel. & Cons., Inc., San Diego, 1977—, cons., pres., 1979—; dir. Nav Tech Services Inc., San Diego, S.K. Tourney & Assos., San Diego. Decorated Silver Star, Purple Heart, Air medal. Mem. Nat. Soc. Performance and Instrn. Republican. Baptist. Club: Vikings of Scandia. Contbr. articles to profl. jours. Home: 9171 Ellingham St San Diego CA 92129 Office: 7525 Mission Gorge Rd Suite F San Diego CA 92120

COHEN, ALAN, investment banker; b. N.Y.C., Jan. 1, 1945; s. Harold and Edith (Schneider) C.; B.A. in Econs., Bklyn. Coll., 1967; postgrad. N.Y. U.; m. Carolyn Zacks, Jan. 3, 1970; children—Davi Melissa, Michael Jarrett. Commodity broker Reynolds Securities Inc., N.Y.C., 1977-78; v.p., regional commodity mgr. Loeb Rhoades Hornblower, N.Y.C., 1978-79; v.p., regional commodity dir. E.F. Hutton Co., N.Y.C., 1979-80; v.p., nat. commodities sales mgr. Bear, Stearns & Co.; N.Y.C., 1980—. Home: 7 Hemlock Ln Marlboro NJ 07746 Office: 55 Water St New York NY 10004

COHEN, ALAN LOUIS, communications co. exec.; b. Phila., June 8, 1956; s. Morton F. and Suzanne Cohen; B.S. summa cum laude, Boston U., 1978. Founder, pres. Alco Co., Phila., 1970-74; account exec. Yellow Book of Pa., 1976; nat. sales mgr., then asso. pub./bus. mgr. Commonwealth Monthly, Boston, 1975-77; pub., founder Stage Entertainment div. York Publs., Boston, 1977-78; mktg. analyst, coordinator market planning consumer pub. div. CBS, Inc., N.Y.C., 1978-80, mgr. market planning and analysis, 1980—. Mem. Communications Mktg. Assn. Home: 2 Soldiers Field Park Apt 108 Boston MA 02163

COHEN, ARTHUR CHARLES, real estate appraiser; b. N.Y.C., Jan. 26, 1940; s. Isidor Michael and Mary Frances (Eskew) C.; B.S., U. Wis., 1961; M.B.A., Columbia U., 1971; m. Eve L. Imberman, Mar. 19, 1966; children—Daniel, Alexander. Property mgr. Gerald Becker Inc., N.Y.C., 1962-65; area coordinator HUD, N.Y.C., 1965-69; prin. Arthur Charles Cohen, Inc., real estate cons. and appraiser, N.Y.C., 1970—. Vice pres. 110-118 Riverside Tenants Corp., 1975-77, Council West Side Coops., 1976-78. Served with Field Arty., U.S. Army, 1964. Mem. Am. Soc. Appraisers (v.p. N.Y. chpt., co-chmn. internat. bd. of examiners-real property, cert. of commendation 1979), Nat. Assn. Ind. Fee Appraisers (v.p. N.Y. chpt.), Am. Inst. Real Estate Appraisers. Home: 110 Riverside Dr New York NY 10024 Office: Arthur Charles Cohen Inc 200 W 57th St New York NY 10019

COHEN, BURTON JEROME, fin. exec.; b. Phila., Dec. 8, 1933; s. Alexander David and Esther (Mirrow) C.; B.S. in Accounting, Temple U., 1955; student exec. program Harvard U.; m. Jane McDowell, Mar. 16, 1968; children—Paul, Joshua, Douglas, Glen. Ops. v.p. Cakemasters, Inc., Phila., 1957-61; mgr. IBM, Phila., White Plains, N.Y., N.Y.C., 1961-70; partner Touche & Ross & Co., N.Y.C., 1970-77; nat. dir. fin. and adminstrn. Coopers & Lybrand, N.Y.C., 1977—; lectr. Am. Mgmt. Assn. seminars; adj. prof. Columbia U. Grad. Sch. Bus. Mem. advisory bd. Borough Manhattan Community Coll. Served with Finance Corps, AUS, 1955-57. Mem. Fin. Execs. Inst. Mason. Author: Cost Effective Informations Systems, 1971; Strategy Formulation in Information Systems; Setting Objectives, 1975. Home: 63 Adams Ln New Canaan CT 06840 Office: 1251 Ave of Americas New York NY 10020

COHEN, CARALI RAMEY, marketing exec.; b. N.Y.C., Mar. 11, 1939; d. Benjamin and Dutch (Young) Nezin; student creative art Hofstra Coll., 1957-58; m. M. David Cohen, Dec. 31, 1977; children—Stephen, Deborah. Display designer Am. Design Assos., N.Y.C., 1958-59; instr. graphic design Western Design Tech., Los Angeles, 1959-70; pres. sailing and nav. sch. Pacific Sailing Assn., Marina del Rey, Calif., 1970-75; v.p. marketing Soumaf Corp., Marina Del Rey, 1975—; chmn. bd. Universal Showcase Associates, Marina del Rey, 1976—, Calif. Med. Registries, Marina Del Rey, 1980—; pres. Carali Galleries, Los Angeles, 1978—. Mem. Am. Mgmt. Assn., Nat. Volleyball Assn., Western Tournament Chess Assn. (pres. 1976-77). Clubs: Marina City; Marina Yacht. Patentee in field. Home: 4240 Promenade Way Marina Del Rey CA 90291

COHEN, ED, business exec.; b. Bklyn., Jan. 7, 1943; s. Harry and Zella (Goldman) C.; B.F.A., N.Y. Inst. Tech., 1965; M.B.A., L.I. U., 1971; m. Eileen Dworkin, Aug. 29, 1965; children—Beth Robin, Stephen Foster. Salesman, William S. Merrell div. Richardson-Merrell, Inc., Cin., 1967-71; sales and mktg. exec. Pfizer Diagnostics div. Pfizer, Inc., N.Y.C., 1971-73; product mgr. Hyland div. Baxter-Travernol, Inc., Costa Mesa, Calif., 1973-75; bus. unit mgr. clin. div. Union Carbide Corp., Rye, N.Y., 1975—; dir. mktg. Technicon Instruments Corp., Tarrytown, N.Y., 1976—; dir. Technia Diagnostics, Ltd., London. Mem. Clin. Lab. Mgmt. Assn., Clin. Radioassay Soc., Am. Assn. Clin. Chemistry, Assn. M.B.A.'s. Home: 15 Ole Musket Ln Danbury CT 06810 Office: 511 Benedict Ave Tarrytown NY 10591

COHEN, EDWARD, cons. engr.; b. Glastonbury, Conn., Jan. 6, 1921; s. Samuel and Ida (Tanewitz) C.; B.S. in Engring., Columbia, 1946, M.S. in Civil Engring., 1954; m. Elizabeth Belle Cohen, Dec. 19, 1948 (dec.); children—Samuel, Libby, James; m. 2d, Carol Suzanne Kalb, Jan. 11, 1981. Asst. engr. Conn. Dept. Pub. Works, East Hartford, 1942-44; structural engr. Hardesty & Hanover, N.Y.C., 1945-47, Sanderson & Porter, N.Y.C., 1947-49; lectr. architecture Columbia, 1948-51; with Ammann & Whitney, cons. engrs., N.Y.C., 1949—, partner, 1963-77, sr. partner, 1974-77, mng. partner, 1977—; exec. v.p. in charge bldg., transp., communications, mil. and planning projects Ammann & Whitney Inc., 1963-78, chmn., chief exec. officer, 1978—; exec. v.p. Ammann & Whitney Internat. Ltd., 1963-73; pres. Safeguard Constrn. Mgmt. Corp., 1973—; cons. RAND Corp., Santa Monica, 1958-72, Dept. Def., 1962-63, Hudson Inst., Croton-on-Hudson, N.Y., 1967-71; Stanton Walker lectr. U. Md., 1973. Bd. dirs. Cejwin Youth Camps, 1972—; pres. N.Y.C. Concrete Industry Bd., 1978-79; deptl. adv. com. urban and civil engring. U. Pa., 1974—; trustee N.Y.C. Hall of Sci., 1976—. Recipient Illig medal applied sci. Columbia U., 1946; Patriotic Civilian Service award Dept. Army, 1973. Registered profl. engr., N.Y., Conn., Fla., Ga., Md., Del., N.J., D.C., Okla., Pa., Va., Wis. Fellow ASCE (Ridgeway award 1946, state-of-art civil engring. award 1974, Raymond Reese award 1976), Am. Cons. Engrs. Council; mem. Structures Research Council, chmn. com. on long term observations 1972-76, v.p. met. sect. 1978-79, pres.-elect 1979, pres. 1980), N.Y. Acad. Scis. (hon. life; chmn. engring. div. 1978, 79, Laskowitz Aerospace Research medal 1970), Am. Concrete Inst. (hon.; dir. 1966-74, v.p. 1970-72, pres. 1972-73; Wason medal 1956, Delmar Bloem award 1973; chmn. com. on bldg. code requirements for reinforced concrete 1963-71), Internat. Bridge and Turnpike Assn., Am. Soc. Planning Ofcls., Am. Welding Soc., Am. Nat. Standards Inst. (chmn. com. bldg. code requirements for design loads 1968—), N.Y.C. Concrete Constrn. Inst. (pres. Tall Bldgs. Council 1975—), Nat. Acad. Engring., Engring. Council Columbia U., Reinforced Concrete Research Council (chmn.), European Concrete Com., N.Y. Assn. Cons. Engrs. (bldg. code advisory com.), Nat. Council Engring. Examiners, Engrs. Club N.Y. (dir. 1974-76), Sigma Xi, Chi Epsilon (hon.), Tau Beta Pi. Jewish. Mem. B'nai B'rith. Contbr. to manuals profl. assns., articles to profl. jours. Home: 56 Chestnut Hill Roslyn NY 11576 Office: Ammann & Whitney Two World Trade Center New York NY 10048

COHEN, FLORENCE EMERY, ins. co. exec.; b. Paterson, N.J., Mar. 6, 1944; s. Claude John and Esther Ruth Emery; B.A., Temple U., 1965; M.A., U. Chgo., 1970; m. Harvey H. Cohen, Sept. 5, 1965; children—John Aaron, Jason Matthew. Quality control analyst credit ops. Standard Oil of Ind., Chgo., 1970; officer, product planning mgr. Penn Mut. Life, Phila., 1970-78; dir. market analysis Prudential Life Ins. Co., Newark, 1980—; speaker industry meetings, TV and radio appearances. Mem. F.L.M.I. Soc. of Greater N.Y. (dir.). Club: Soroptimists Internat. Contbr. articles to profl. jours. Home: 3 Stonelea Dr Princeton Junction NJ 08550 Office: Corp Office Prudential Life Ins Co Plaza Bldg Newark NJ 07101

COHEN, IRA, paper co. exec.; b. Boston, July 7, 1923; s. Joseph H. and Rose (Stone) C.; B.A., Amherst Coll., 1945; m. Alden Duer, Sept. 1, 1950; children—Jonathan, Matthew Leland, Douglas Duer, Priscilla Alden. Asst. buyer Abraham and Straus, Bklyn., 1950-53; with Schlosser Paper Corp., N.Y.C., 1953-61; with Lindenmeyr Paper Corp., Long Island City, N.Y., 1961—; v.p. Process Materials Corp., 1972—. Trustee, Village Temple, 1960-80; bd. dirs. Washington Sq. Music Assn., Washington Sq. Assn. Served as lt. (j.g.) USN, 1942-45. Mem. Am. Inst. Graphic Arts, Typophiles, Amherst Alumni Assn. N.Y. (v.p. 1977-80). Democrat. Jewish. Home: 182 Sullivan St New York NY 10012 Office: 53d Ave at 11th St Long Island City NY 11101

COHEN, IRVING ELIAS, real estate cons.; b. Bklyn., Nov. 7, 1946; s. Daniel Arthur and Shirley B. (Kanner) C.; B.A. in Psychology, City Coll. N.Y., 1968; M.B.A. in Fin., N.Y. U., 1973; m. Adriane Pinsker, Aug. 22, 1976. Mut. fund cashier Investors Funding Corp., Inc., 1968-69; syndication cashier Eastman Dillon, Union Securities, Inc., 1969-70; registered rep. Steiner, Rouse & Co., Inc., N.Y.C., 1970-72; instnl. rep. Shearson Hayden Stone, Inc., N.Y.C., 1972-74; exec. v.p. Howard P. Hoffman Assos., Inc. subs. Lehman Bros. Kuhn Loeb, Inc., N.Y.C., 1974—. Mem. Nat. Assn. Bus. Economists, Nat. Assn. Office and Indsl. Parks, Soc. Indsl. Archeology, Nat. Trust for Hist. Preservation, Preservation League of N.Y. State. Jewish. Contbr. articles to profl. publs. Home: 90-13 68th Ave Forest Hills NY 11375 Office: 100 Park Ave New York NY 10017

COHEN, IRWIN, financial economist; b. Bronx, N.Y., Feb. 29, 1936; s. Samuel and Gertrude (Levy) C.; B.S. in Accounting, N.Y. U., 1956, M.B.A. in Finance, 1964, M.A. in Econs., 1969; B.S. in Math., Coll. City N.Y., 1970. Financial analyst U.S. SEC, N.Y.C., 1965-67, Fed. Res. Bank N.Y., N.Y.C., 1967-72, Prudential Ins. Co. Am., 1973-74, SEC, N.Y.C., 1974—. Fellow Internat. Biog. Assn. (life), Am. Biog. Inst.; mem. Internat. Platform Assn (life), World-Wide Acad. Scholars (life), Math. Assn. Am., Am. Finance Assn., Econ. History Assn. Home: 372 Central Park Ave Apt 2K Scarsdale NY 10583

COHEN, JEFFERY MARLIN, corp. exec.; b. Harrisburg, Pa., June 12, 1943; s. Bernard L. and Lillian L. (Lax) C.; B.S.I.E. (Foundry Ednl. Found. scholar), Pa. State U., 1965; M.S. in Fin., George Washington U., 1969; m. Meryl Margolin, July 4, 1968; children—Nessa, Bradley. Budget mgr., fin. mgr. Aerospace div. and Urban Systems Devel. Corp. subs., Westinghouse Elec. Corp., 1967-72; sr. cons. Ernst & Whinney, Washington, 1972-74; v.p. Capitol Venture Group, Inc., Washington, 1974-78; v.p., sec. Washington Franchise, Inc., 1976-78; pres. Key Bridge Corp., Washington, also Baltic Corp., Silver Spring, Md., 1978—; cons. SBA. Advisor Jr. Achievement, 1973; mem. adv. bd. Automobile Owners Action Council. Mem. Nat. Assn. Accts., Alpha Pi Mu. Jewish. Club: B'nai B'rith. Home: 14120 Woodwell Terr Silver Spring MD 20906

COHEN, JEROME, office machines corp. exec.; b. Kansas City, Mo., Oct. 9, 1913; s. Rueben and Helen (Silverstein) C.; student Kansas City Jr. Coll., 1931, Huffs Bus. Coll., 1932, Central Bus. Coll., 1932-33, correspondence course U. Pa., 1933-34; m. Jeannett Baier, Nov. 25, 1934; children—Rosalyn Jacobson, Elaine Rubin. Asst. mgr. Edison Bros. Burt Shoe Store, 1931-34; chief clk. Old Age Assistance Div., State of Mo., 1935; mgr. Jackson County Welfare Dept., 1936-38; founder, pres. Tempo Co., Kansas City, Mo., 1938—, Kansas City Electronic Bus. Equipment, 1957—, Jefferson City (Mo.) Electronic Bus. Equipment, Inc., 1960—, St. Joseph (Mo.) Electronic Bus. Equipment, Inc., 1961—; adv. council Minn. Mining and Mfg.; past pres. Bus. Products Council, Internat. Microfilm Congress. Commr. Kansas City Park Bd., 1955-62; pres. commrs. sect. Am. Inst. Park Execs., 1962, conv. chmn., 1962; pres. Richards-Gebaur Base Community Council, 1961-62, Friends of the Zoo, 1973-74; exec. bd. Citizens Assn., 1940—, Camp Fire Girls, 1960-65, Kansas City Recreation Commn., 1955-65, Sr. Citizens Corp. Kansas City, 1955-80, Childs World; exec. com. Starlight Theatre, 1950-80, v.p., 1979-80; chmn. Mayor's Christmas Tree Assn., 1960-80, Kansas City Jewish Chatauqua Drive, 1962, Kansas City Soap Box Derby, 1947-60; life mem., v.p. Am. Humanics Found.; v.p. Mid-Town Assn.; gov. Am. Royal Assn., 1940-80; mem. Kansas City Bus. and Indsl. Commn.; pres. Temple B'nai Jehuda Brotherhood, 1965-66, Temple B'nai Jehudah, 1980-81; sec., adv. Mother chpt. DeMolay Temple Assn.; exec. com. Kansas City Safety Council, McCoy House, People to People; pres. Bus. Dist. League, 1960-62; bd. dirs. U. Kans. Sch. of Religion; adv. bd. Met. Jr. Coll.; Mo. mem. Nat. Com. for Support of Public Schs.; active Jewish Home for Aged, Japan Am. Soc., Hebrew Acad. Kansas City, Conservation Fedn. Mo., Am. Assn. Zoos and Aquariums, Mo. U. Assos., Kansas City Lyric Theatre Guild, Mayors Corps of Progress, City of Fountains Assn., Am. Jewish Com., Mayor's Prayer Breakfast Com., Jackson County Hist. Soc., Jewish Geriatric Convalescent Center, Jewish Vocat. Service, Friends of Art, U.S.-China Friendship Assn., Kansas City Crime Commn., Reform Jewish Appeal, NCCJ, Garden Center (life), YMCA. Served with USAR, 1940-45. Named to Legion of Honor, Order of DeMolay; Israel Bond honoree, 1971; hon. fellow Harry S. Truman Library Inst.; named Kansas City Mktg. Exec. of Yr., 1981; hon. trustee Boy Scouts Am.; hon. dir. Rockhurst Coll., Bapt. Meml. Hosp. Mem. Bus. Products Council Assn. (pres.), Kansas City (Mo.) C. of C., Kansas City (Kans.) C. of C., Mo. State C. of C. Clubs: Masons (33rd degree), Scottish Rite (master Council of Kadosh, 1959, venerable master Lodge of Perfection, 1972, membership chmn. Kansas City Consistory, 1961-69), Shrine (organizer, rajah Ararat Shrine Oriental Band, 1948-60), Rotary (dir. Club 13), B'nai B'rith, Meadowbrook Country, Kansas City Athletic, Elmers Fishing (pres. 1965-66), Bouroughs Nature, Navy League. Home: 6616 Ward Pkwy Kansas City MO 64113 Office: 1500 Grand Ave Kansas City MO 64108

COHEN, LESLIE JAY, personnel agys. exec.; b. Chgo., June 19, 1931; s. Jack and Sylvia Thelma (Sanders) C.; B.S. in Commerce, Roosevelt U., 1952. Asst. to pres. Jay Mills Co., Chgo., 1954-60; founder, pres. EDP Personnel, Inc., Chgo., 1960-64, Secretaries, Inc., Chgo., 1964—. Mem. industry liaison com. Better Bus. Bur. Served with AUS, 1952-54. Decorated Bronze Star. Mem. Nat. (past dir., past treas.; recipient Pres.'s award 1973), Ill. (past dir., past treas.; recipient Lincoln Meml. award 1976) employment assns., Nat., Chicagoland assns. temporary services, Temporaries Independents Profl. Soc. (treas. 1977-78, pres. 1978-79). Jewish. Home: 20 E Cedar St Chicago IL 60611 Office: Secretaries Inc Prudential Plaza Chicago IL 60601

COHEN, MARVIN SANFORD, lawyer; b. Akron, Ohio, Oct. 16, 1931; s. Norman J. and Faye (Abramovitz) C.; B.A., U. Ariz., 1953, LL.B., 1957; m. Frances E. Smith, June 19, 1953; children—Samuel David, Jeffrey Lee, Rachel Ann. Admitted to Ariz. bar, 1957, since practiced in Tucson; chief civil dep. Pima County atty., 1958-60; 1st asst. Tucson city atty., 1961; spl. asst. to solicitor Dept. Interior, Washington, 1961-63; mem. firm Bilby, Thompson, Shoenhair & Warnock, and successors, 1963-78; instr. U. Ariz. Coll. Law, 1965; mem., chmn. CAB, 1978—. Mem. Tucson Fgn. Relations Com., from 1968; chmn. Ariz. Anti-Defamation League, 1970. Pres. Young Democratic Clubs Ariz., 1960; pres. Democrats for Better Govt., 1964; del. Dem. Nat. Conv., 1964; chmn. Pima County Dem. Central Com., 1960; parliamentarian Dem. Party Ariz., 1970; chmn. Ariz. Dem. Telethon Com., 1974. Pres. Tucson Jewish Community Center, Ariz. Civic Theater, 1972-73, 75-76. Bd. dirs. United Community Campaign, Tucson Urban League Com., Ariz. Commn. on Arts and Humanities, 1975-77. Served to 1st lt. USAF, 1953-55. Named Young Man of Year, Tucson Jewish Community, 1966. Mem. Ariz. Civil Liberties Union, State Bar Ariz., Am. Bd. Trial Advs. Jewish (bd. dirs. temple). Office: CAB 1825 Connecticut Ave NW Washington DC 20428

COHEN, MICHAEL DAVID, accountant; b. Pitts., Aug. 18, 1942; s. Nathan David and Jacqueline Blanche (Radner) C.; B.A. in Bus. Adminstrn., Calif. State U., Fullerton, 1973; m. Renate Herkommer, May 1, 1965; children—Kira Danielle, Sabrina Mylene. Staff accountant Marriott & Held, C.P.A.'s, Alhambra, Calif., 1970-72; propr. Cohen & Assos. Bookkeeping & Tax Service, Brea, Calif., 1972-74; pres. Michael D. Cohen Accountancy Corp., Brea, 1974—. Recreation and parks commr. City of Brea. Served with U.S. Army, 1960-63. Recipient Distinguished Alumnus award, accounting dept. Sch. Bus. Adminstrn. and Econs., Calif. State U., Fullerton, 1978. C.P.A., Calif. Mem. Am. Inst. C.P.A.'s, Calif. Soc. C.P.A.'s, Brea C. of C. (dir.), Beta Alpha Psi. Democrat. Jewish. Clubs: Rotary (pres. 1980-81), Masons (Brea). Home: 560 Bonita Canyon Way Brea CA 92621 Office: 203 N Brea Blvd Suite 218 Brea CA 92621

COHEN, MITCHELL NORMAN, sales promotion co. exec.; b. Washington, Oct. 11, 1945; s. Daniel and Rebecca (Goldstein) C.; student Bowling Green U., 1963-65; B.S. in Econs., U. Md., 1967; M.B.A., N.Y. U., 1971; m. Rosemary Dale Luhrs, Sept. 1, 1968; children—Rebecca Anya, Arielle Joy. Account exec. Mktg. Showcase, N.Y.C., 1972-73; account exec., account supr. Park Ave. Group, N.Y.C., 1974; account supr., v.p.-sales John Blair Mktg., N.Y.C., 1975—; cons. Mem. Assn. M.B.A. Execs. Home: 26 Knightsbridge Rd Great Neck NY 11021 Office: 717 Fifth Ave New York NY 10022

COHEN, PHILIP HERMAN, accountant; b. Bklyn., Dec. 4, 1936; s. David J. and Toby (Jaeger) C.; B.S., N.Y. U., 1957; m. Susan Rudd; 1 dau., Davi Ellen. Accountant Touche Ross & Co., N.Y.C., 1957-64, supr., 1965, mgr., 1966-69, partner, 1969—; lectr. in field. Bd. dirs. Alpha Epsilon Pi Found. Inc., Nat. Interfrat. Conf., Jewish Bd. Family and Children Service; bd. dirs. joint purchasing com. Fedn. Jewish Philanthropies; del. Nat. Interfrat. Conf., 1975—. C.P.A., N.Y., La., N.C. Mem. Found. Accounting Edn., Am. Inst. C.P.A.'s, N.Y. State Soc. C.P.A.'s (admissions com. 1968-69, chmn. fin. and leasing com. 1972-74, com. on relations with the bar 1974-76, com. on real estate acctg. 1976-79, com. ins. 1980—), Am. Acctg. Assn., Nat. Assn. Accts., Ins. Accts. Statis. Assn., Soc. Ins. Accts., Alpha Epsilon Pi (supreme gov. 1966-73, nat. pres. 1974-76, mem. fiscal control bd. 1977—), Beta Alpha Psi, Areopagus. Jewish (bd. govs. synagogue 1964—). Clubs: Masons, N.Y. Alumni of Alpha Epsilon Pi. Home: 44 W 62d St New York NY 10023 Office: 1633 Broadway New York NY 10019

COHEN, PHILLIP, wholesale and retail co. exec.; b. Milw., Apr. 5, 1919; s. Jacob E. and Anna (Kurman) C.; B.A., U. Wis., 1941; m. Mildred Kaminsky, Aug. 5, 1945; children—Phyllis, Jay. Chmn. bd. Wis. Toy & Novelty Co., Milw., 1945—, Union Prescription Centers, Inc., 1960—; v.p., dir., exec. com. Unicare Services, Inc., Milw., 1969—; chmn. bd. Lou Spero Co., Inc., Boston, 1976—, Job Lot Trading Inc., N.Y.C., 1978—; pres. P.C. Sales Inc., Fort Lauderdale, Fla., 1978—. Served as capt. USAAF, 1941-45. Mem. Toy Mfrs. U.S. Jewish. Clubs: Bonaventure Country (Ft. Lauderdale); Brynwood Country (Milw.); World Trade Center (N.Y.C.), Masons. Address: 16541 Royal Poinciana Dr Fort Lauderdale FL 33326

COHEN, RALPH GORDON, stock broker, fin. cons.; b. Portsmouth, Va., Oct. 9, 1918; s. Nathan Joseph and Kate (Jacobson) C.; B.S. in Bus. Adminstrn., Va. Poly. Inst., 1940; m. Margot M. Roberts, July 20, 1970; children—Lauren Beth, Debrah Lynn. Partner, So. Candy Co., Portsmouth, 1946-54; pres. Fidelity Comml. Co., Norfolk, Va., 1954-76, Security Equity Corp., Norfolk, 1966-69; sec.-treas. Property Buyers Inc., Norfolk, 1963-68; gen. partner Exec. Investors, Norfolk, 1968-74; pvt. practice fin. cons., stock broker, Palm Beach, Fla., 1976—; dir. Fidelity Am. Bankshares, Am. Nat. Bank. Served to lt. USN, 1942-46; ETO; PTO. Mem. Am. Legion, Jewish War Vets. Democrat. Jewish. Club: Elks (Portsmouth). Home: 3575 S Ocean Blvd Palm Beach FL 33480

COHEN, ROBERT SHERMAN, elec. mfg. co. exec.; b. Boston, Nov. 20, 1933; s. Saul Josephmand Ruth (Aronstien) C.; B.S.E.E., U. Mass., 1955, M.S.E.E., 1963; m. Iris Carole Sidman, Nov. 27, 1958; children—Jeffrey, Andrew, Ruth. Test engr. Gen. Electric Co., Schenectady, N.Y., 1955, mgr. devel. programs, Pittsfield, Mass., 1974—; lectr. in field. Mem. Pittsfield Water Commn., 1965-76; mem. Pittsfield Solid Waste Commn., 1977—. Served with USAF, 1955-57. Recipient Borch award Gen. Electric Co., 1973. Mem. IEEE, Navy League Am., Elfun Soc., Nat. Soc. Profl. Engrs. Democrat. Jewish. Clubs: Berkshire Hills Country, Pittsfield Country, Rotary. Home: 38 Brunswick St Pittsfield MA 01201

COHEN, ROGER LEE, real estate exec.; b. St. Joseph, Mo., Oct. 4, 1935; s. Joseph A. and Esther L. (Wienstock) C.; B.S. in Bus. Adminstrn., U. Mo., 1957; m. Marjorie Critten, May 2, 1974; children—Robin, Cynthia, Bradley. Exec. trainee Sears, Roebuck & Co., Chgo., 1957; partner Karbank & Co., Realtors, Kansas City, 1959-68; pres. Roger L. Cohen & Co., Realtors, Kansas City, Mo., 1969—; chmn. bd. Cohen Asset Mgmt. Co.; dir. Barclay Evergreen Advt., Mark Twain Empire Bank, Electronic Realty Assos. Bd. dirs. Kansas City (Mo.) Real Estate Bd. Chmn. Jackson County (Mo.) Indsl. Commn., 1969; chmn. March of Dimes, Jackson County, 1965-66. Mem. bd. govs. Menorah Med. Center, Jewish Fedn., Kansas City, Mo.; bd. dirs. Performing Arts Found.; bd. assos. Trinity Luth. Hosp. Served with F.A., AUS, 1957-59. Mem. Soc. Indsl. Realtors (pres. Western Mo.-Kans. chpt. 1974-76, nat. dist. v.p. 1976—), Young Pres.'s Orgn., Am. Royal Assn. (bd. govs.). Jewish (v.p. bd. trustees temple). Clubs: Oakwood Country, Homestead Country, Kansas City. Home: 3700 W 64th Mission Hills KS 66208 Office: 1100 Main St City Center Sq Suite 850 Kansas City MO 64105

COHEN, SAUL, publishing co. exec.; b. N.Y.C., Dec. 11, 1918; s. Morris and Golde C.; B.S. in B.A., N.Y. U., 1954; m. Sylvia Kessler, Mar. 8, 1947; children—Barbara, Karen, Richard. Mgr., Neisner Bros., Rochester, N.Y., 1941-42; sales mgr. Raynard Optical Co., Bklyn., 1946-54; sr. v.p., dir. Childcraft Edn. Corp., Edison, N.J., 1954—. Bd. dirs., trustee Inst. and Mus. Fantasy and Play, Princeton, N.J., 1977—. Served to 1st lt., AUS, 1942-46; PTO. Decorated Army Commendation Medal. Mem. Direct Mail and Mktg. Assn., Nat. Sch. and Supply Equipment Assn., Nat. Retail Mchts. Assn. Democrat. Jewish. Club: Cornell (N.Y.C.). Home: 2 Grayson Ln Englishtown NJ 07726 Office: 20 Kilmer Rd Edison NJ 08817

COHEN, STANLEY J., fin. planning co. exec.; B.A., Cornell U., 1946; M.A., Columbia U., 1953, also postgrad. in Am. history and econs.; m. Fimi Zolas; children—Steven, Nora, Thomas. Mgr. Import-Export div. Hygrade Food Products Corp., 1959-66; with Eastman Dillon-Union Securities, later Butcher & Singer, from 1966; v.p. Moseley, Hallgarten, Estabrook & Weeden, Inc., N.Y.C.; cons. editor for econs. and fin. Gen. Books div. Reader's Digest; cons. on investments and fin. planning to law and acctg. firms, N.Y., N.J. Cert. fin. planner. Mem. Internat. Assn. Fin. Planners, Inst. Cert. Fin. Planners (dir., chmn. publs. com., founder Jour. Cert. Fin. Planners), N.Y. Investment Round Table (pres.), N.Y. Stockbrokers Forum. Clubs: N.Y. Stock Brokers, Amex. Home: 50 Riverside Dr New York NY 10024 Office: Moseley Hallgarten Estabrook & Weeden Inc One New York Plaza New York NY 10004

COHEN, WALLACE M., lawyer; b. Norton, Va., July 11, 1908; s. Jacob Edward and Annie (Hyman) C.; S.B., Harvard U., 1929, student Law Sch.; LL.B., Cornell U., 1932; m. Sylvia J. Stone, Sept. 7, 1932; children—Anne E. Cohen Winkelman, Edward S., David W. Admitted to Mass. bar, 1932, Md. bar, 1952, D.C. bar, 1946, also U.S. Supreme Ct. bar; practiced in Boston, 1932-38; staff NLRB, Dept. Labor, Shipbldg. Stblzn. Commn.; adv. commn. Council Nat. Def., OPA, Lend Lease Adminstrn., Fgn. Econ. Adminstrn., 1938-45; dep. administrv. asst. to Pres., 1944-45; mem. firm Landis Cohen Singman & Rauh, Washington, 1951—; v.p., gen. counsel, dir. Zinder Cos., Inc.; gen. counsel, officer, dir. Zinder-Neris, Inc., Zinder Can., Zinder Mgmt. Services, Inc.; gen. counsel, officer Zinder Engring., Inc., FRS, Inc., Zinder Realty, Inc., Zinder Oil & Gas Mgmt., Inc. Fellow Brandeis U.; mem. D.C. bd. Am. Jewish Com.; bd. dirs. Montserrat Bldg. Soc. Served with USCGR, 1943-45. Mem. Am., Fed., Fed. Communications, D.C., Mass., Md. bar assns., Fed. Lawyers Club. Clubs: Harvard (Boston and Washington); Woodmont Country (Rockville, Md.); Lonesome Pine Country (Norton); Federal City, Internat., Nat. Press, Harvard (dir.) (Washington). Home: 2444 Massachusetts Ave NW Washington DC 20008 Office: 1019 19th St NW Washington DC 20036

COHEN, WILLIAM ROY, mgmt. co. exec.; b. Newark, June 3, 1931; s. H. Edward and Ada (Goldbaum) C.; B.B.A., U. Miami, 1953; postgrad. Mich. State U., 1958, Harvard, 1973, 75, 76, Am. U., 1962; m. Lisetta Barr, Nov. 22, 1953; children—Lori, Michael, Ted, Gail. With Standard Overall Service Co., Irvington, N.J., 1953-54, gen. mgr. Standard Uniform Service, Mamaroneck, N.Y., 1954-56; gen. mgr. Standard Overall Service, Bklyn., 1956-61; pres. Renta Uniform Supply, Passaic, N.J., 1967-69; pres. Edisons Mgmt. Co., Hillside, N.J., 1970—; pres. Star Uniform Rental Co., N.Y.; pres. Moru Candy Co., Roselle, N.J., 1980—; cons. pvt. corps. Active Little League Baseball, Football, Children's Asthma Research Inst., Fight for Sight, United Jewish Appeal; trustee, panel arbitrators YM-YWHA Met. N.J. Mem. Inst. Indsl. Launderers, Linen Supply Assn., Young Pres.'s Orgn. Jewish. Clubs: Green Brook Country, Berkeley Tennis, Orange Lawn Tennis. Office: 35 Hillside Ave Hillside NJ 07205

COHN, BERTRAM JOSIAH, corp. exec.; b. Newark, Sept. 12, 1925; s. Julius Henry and Bessie Ruth (Einson) C.; A.B., Harvard Coll., 1949; M.B.A., N.Y. U., 1951; m. Barbara Ann Biard, June 20, 1956; children—Daniel, Susan, Diana. Vice pres. Decatur Iron & Steel Co., 1950-68; chmn. bd. Schuylkill Lead Corp., Baton Rouge, La., 1968-70, DPF Inc., Hartsdale, N.Y., 1971—; dir. Arrow Electronics, Bowne & Co., Orion Capital Corp. Served with U.S. Army, 1943-46. Jewish. Office: 414 Central Ave S Hartsdale NY 10530

COHN, DAVID D., investment holding co. exec.; b. Chgo., Dec. 30, 1937; s. Albert H. and Helen F. (Baker) C.; student (research honors) Am. U., 1958; B.A., Pomona Coll., 1959; M.A. in Social Service Adminstrn., U. Chgo., 1977; m. Elizabeth Ann Curtis, Dec. 29, 1960; children—David Curtis, Robert Curtis. Salesman, Universal Battery Co., Chgo., 1959-62, v.p., 1962-66, pres., 1966-69, pres. Universal Battery div. Whittaker Corp., Chgo., 1969-70; pres., dir. Universal Res. Corp., Chgo., 1966—; cons., lectr. employee assistance programs, orgns. and industry. Vice pres. Francis W. Parker Sch. Alumni Assn., 1969-71; bd. dirs. Albert H. Cohn Found., Tucson Symphony, 1979—; trustee Green Fields Country Day Sch., 1979—, exec. com., 1980—; mem. adv. bd. Ariz.-Sonora Desert Mus., 1981—. Mem. Nat. Assn. Social Workers, Council Social Work Edn. Unitarian. Clubs: Standard (Chgo.); Tucson Country, Skyline Country (Tucson). Research in field; speaker profl. confs. Home: 5455 E Camino Bosque Tucson AZ 85718 Office: 6801-A E Camino Principal Tucson AZ 85715

COHN, MICHAEL, publishing co. exec.; b. N.Y.C., Nov. 14, 1932; s. William and Pauline (Haber) C.; B.S., U. Pa., 1954; L.L.B., Harvard, 1957; m. Susan Cotton, Aug. 26, 1956; 1 son, Thomas; m. 2d, Suzanne Hazen, June 21, 1970; 1 son, Peter. Admitted to N.Y. State bar, 1957, U.S. Dist Ct. bar, 1958; individual practice law, N.Y.C., 1957-62; corp. sec., resident counsel New Am. Library, Inc., N.Y.C., 1962-68; v.p. adminstrn. World Publishing Co., N.Y.C., 1968-70; v.p., dir. book div. Playboy Enterprises, Inc., N.Y.C., 1970—; lectr. in field. Mem. Bar Assn. N.Y. State and So., Eastern Dists. of N.Y. Contbr. articles in field to profl. jours. Home: 1725 York Ave New York City NY 10028 Office: 747 Third Ave New York City NY 10017

COHN, NORMAN UNGER, bus. exec.; b. Waterloo, Iowa, Jan. 2, 1933; s. Maurice W. and Bess (Unger) C.; B.A., State Coll. Iowa, 1957; m. Suzanne Dubiecki, Feb. 14, 1965; five children. Chmn. bd. Nat. Bus. Services, Phila., 1949—, also dir.; dir. Comml. Bank Holding Co., Comml. Travel Agy., Santa Claus Industries, Twilight Oil Refiners, Am. Glass Decorators, Santa Claus Farms, Studio One, Creative Splty. Mfrs., Waterloo, Waverly and Cedar Falls, Iowa, Gifts Unlimited, Clayton, Mo., Internat. Mdse. Corp., Chgo., Nat. Bus. Services, Inc., Advt. Splty. Inst., Creative Advt. Service, Trevose, Pa., others. Active in Waterloo devel. activities; Pa. rep. and chmn. Council of the 13 Original States; chmn. Acapulco YPO U., 1974; bd. dirs. Congress of World Unity, Ct. Am. Achievements Program; chmn. bd. Cohn Family Trust; steering com. Phila. Art Mus. Served with AUS, 1957-62, Air N.G. Mem. Young Pres.'s Orgn. (dir.), Soc. Nat. Assn. Pubs., Info. Industry Assn., World Affairs Council (dir.), Confrerie de la Chaine des Rotisseurs (vice chancelor, treas., dir.). Home: 200 Pine Tree Rd Radnor PA 19087 Office: Studio One Bldg 425 Andrews Rd Trevose PA 19047

COHO, JAMES PRESTON, lawyer; b. Lancaster, Pa., July 6, 1919; s. Ralph W. and Lillie (Eby) C.; A.B., Franklin and Marshall Coll., 1941; LL.B., Dickinson Sch. Law, 1944, J.D., 1968; m. Helen E. Boetzel, Aug. 18, 1945; children—Linda, Jeffrey P. Admitted to Pa. bar, 1945; asso. firm G. T. Hambright, Esquire, 1945-48; partner firm Hamaker & Coho, 1949-51; pvt. practice, 1952—. Dir. Way Oil Co. Mem. adv. bd. St. Joseph Hosp., pres., 1977; trustee Dickinson Sch. Law, 1968-71. Mem. Am., Pa., Lancaster bar assns., Pa., Lancaster chambers commerce, Nat. Assn. Accountants, Am. Arbitration Assn., ICC Practitioners Assn., Lancaster Cemetery Assn. (pres. 1977—, dir.), Pa. Soc. N.Y., Pa., Lancaster hist. socs., Soc. Pa. Archaeology, Am. Judicature Soc., Internat. Platform Assn., Lancaster Traffic Club, Chi Phi. Republican. Mem. Evang. Ref. Ch. Mason (Shriner), Rotarian, Elk. Clubs: University (past pres.), Hamilton, Lancaster Country, Lancaster (Pa.) Pirates. Home: 23 Glen Moore Circle Lancaster PA 17601 Office: 53 N Duke St Lancaster PA 17602

COKE, ALDEN L., design, mktg. and sales co. exec.; b. Pasadena, Calif., Aug. 7, 1930; s. Wilbur S. and Lila Frances C.; B.A., Fresno State Coll., 1956; m. Constance Mangano, Mar. 11, 1977; children—Michelle, Peter, Christina. Right of way agt. Calif. Hwy. Div., 1957-58; owner Baby Butler Enterprises, Balt., 1958-61; sales, sales mgmt. Bankers Life & Casualty Co., Balt., 1961-75; owner Cokebury Estates, York, Pa., 1975-77; pres. Design and Funding, Inc., Balt., Willow Grove, Pa. and Washington, 1977—. Served with AUS, 1952-55. Mem. Mktg. Research Assn., Electronic Reps. Assn., Mfrs. and Agts., Nat. Assn., Am. Mktg. Assn. Club: Moose. Patentee, inventor: Super-Tenna, Grade Checker, Strip—O-Magic, Hair Topper, Power Steering Pump Bracket Tool, Spark Plug Wire Boot Puller, Pullmaster. Office: 8767 Satyr Hill Rd Baltimore MD 21234

COKE, C(HAUNCEY) EUGENE, cons. co. exec., educator; b. Toronto, Ont., Can.; s. Chauncey Eugene and Edith May (Redman) C.; B.Sc. with honors in Chemistry, U. Man., M.Sc. magna cum laude; M.A., U. Toronto; Ph.D., U. Leeds (Eng.), 1938; m. Sally B. Tolmie, June 12, 1941. Dir. research Courtaulds (Can.) Ltd., Cornwall, Ont., 1939-42, various exec. positions, Montreal, 1948-59; dir. research and devel. Guaranty Dyeing & Finishing Co., 1946-48; dir. research and devel., mem. exec. com. Hart-Fibres Co., 1959-62; tech. dir. textile chems. Drew Chem. Corp., 1962-63; dir. new products fibers div. Am. Cyanamid Co., 1963-68, dir. application devel., 1968-70; pres. Coke & Assos., Cons., Ormond Beach, Fla., 1970-80, now chmn.; vis. research prof. Stetson U., Fla., 1980—. Served from 2d lt. to maj. RCAF, 1942-46. Recipient Bronze medal Canadian Assn. Textile Colourists and Chemists, 1963. Fellow Royal Soc. Chemistry (life) (Gt. Britain), Textile Inst. (Gt. Britain), Soc. Dyers and Colourists (Gt. Britain), Inst. Textile Sci. (co-founder, 3d pres.), Chem. Inst. Can., AAAS, N.J. Acad. Sci.; mem. Am. Assn. Textile Technology (life, past pres., recipient Bronze medal 1971), Canadian Assn. Textile Colourists and Chemists (hon. life, past pres.; Bronze medal 1963), N.Y. Acad. Scis., Fla. Acad. Scis. Club: The Chemist's (life). Contbr. articles in field to profl. jours. Home: 26 Aqua Vista Dr Ormond Beach FL 32074 Office: Ormond by the Sea FL 32074

COLBERT, ROBERT REED, banker; b. Wellsville, N.Y., Dec. 13, 1924; s. J. Reed and Lillian J. (Fortner) C.; B.S., Cornell U., 1948; m. Barbara J. Schaefer, Sept. 1, 1948; children—Robert Reed, Colleen S., Thomas B., Constance A., Timothy J., Michele M., Jacqueline B., Kristin S. Real estate developer and investor; investment counselor to fin. instns.; exec. v.p., chief adminstrv. officer Savs. Bank of Tompkins County, Ithaca, N.Y., 1969—; pres. Tompkins Realty Inc. of Mich.; pres. INSTL Equities, Inc., Instl. & Investors Real Estate; lectr. Cornell U., Brown U.; faculty Sch. Spl. Studies Nat. Assn. Mut. Savs. Banks, also mem. com. on mortgage investments, N.Y. State, 1970-73. Bd. dirs. N.Y. State Bd. Realtors, Montessori Sch. mem. Ithaca Bd. Pub. Works, 1968-69, Charter Revision Com., 1968, Mayor's Adv. Com., 1963-64; pres. Friends of Ithaca Coll. Republican. Clubs: Ithaca College Faculty, Ithaca Yacht, Cornell (Ithaca). Home: 104 Homestead Rd Ithaca NY 14850 Office: 301 E State St Ithaca NY 14850 also 121 E Seneca St Ithaca NY 14850

COLBERT, ROBERT REED, JR., real estate developer; b. Ithaca, N.Y., June 13, 1949; s. Robert Reed and Barbara Jane (Schaefer) C.; B.S., Cornell U., Ithaca, 1971; m. Mary Elizabeth Murrin, Oct. 4, 1980. Dir. property mgmt. Pyramid Cos., DeWitt, N.Y., 1971-73; pres. Concept Property Mgmt. Group, Ithaca, 1973—; lectr. Architecture Coll., Cornell U., 1977-78. Roman Catholic. Clubs: Ithaca Yacht, Cornell, Quadrangle. Home: 602 Warren Rd Ithaca NY 14850 Office: 121 E Seneca St Ithaca NY 14850

COLBERT, VIRGIS WILLIAM, brewing co. exec.; b. Jackson, Miss., Oct. 13, 1939; s. Quillie and Eddie C.; student Earlham Coll., 1973-74; B.S., U. Toledo, 1974. With Toledo Machining Plant, Chrysler Corp., 1966-79, foreman, 1968-70, gen. foreman, 1970-73, mfg. supt., 1973-77, gen. mfg. supt., 1977-79; asst. to plant mgr. Miller Brewing Co., Reidsville, N.C., 1979-80, prodn. mgr., Ft. Worth, Tex., 1980—. Active Youth program Nat. Alliance Businessmen, NAACP. Mem. Am. Mgmt. Assn., Omega Psi Phi. Clubs: Moose, Shriners. Home: 1506 San Francisco Ct 219 Arlington TX 76012 Office: Ft Worth Container Plant Miller Brewing Co 6600 Will Rogers Blvd Fort Worth TX 76140

COLDEWAY, WILLIAM GUS, JR., businessman; b. Floresville, Tex., Nov. 20, 1920; s. William Gus and Emily (Stoltze) C.; m. Dorothy Strozier, Dec. 20, 1941 (dec.); children—Dian Beverly, Paula Mae, Mary Kay. Rt. mgr., asst. gen. mgr. Nat. Linen Service, Houston, 1946-53, gen. mgr., Lubbock, Tex., 1953-55, San Antonio, 1955-68, Houston, 1968-71; v.p., gen. mgr. Guess Towel and Uniform Supply, San Antonio, 1971—; dir. Mission Fed. Savs. and Loan Assn. Served with AUS, 1942-46. Mem. San Antonio Mfg. Assn. (bd. dirs.), S.W. Linen and Indsl. Assn. (past v.p., dir.). Republican. Presbyterian. Clubs: Lions (past pres., past dep. dist. gov.), Masons, Shriners. Office: 541 Roosevelt San Antonio TX 78210

COLE, BRUCE HERMAN, advt. exec.; b. Chgo., July 22, 1928; s. Leo L. and Kate (Mandelkern) C.; student U. So. Calif., 1948-50; A.B., Grinnell Coll., 1953; m. Jane Renwick Bagby, June 7, 1953; children—Rosemary, Dorothy, Robert Bagby, Frances. Advt. mgr. Gen. Electric Co., Schenectady, 1953-59; account exec. Reincke Meyer & Finn, Inc., Chgo., 1959-60; v.p., gen. mgr. Marsteller, Inc., Chgo., 1960-74, exec. v.p., 1974-78, dir., 1975-78; sr. v.p., gen. mgr. Bozell & Jacobs, Inc., Phoenix, 1978-80; exec. v.p. Cramer-Krasselt Co., Milw., 1980—; pres. Cramer-Krasselt-Southwest, 1980—; lectr. U. Wis. Mgmt. Center; instr. advt. Northwestern U. Extension. Bd. dirs. Marsteller Found., Milw. Sch. Engring., Phoenix Symphony Orch.; adv. bd. Salvation Army; vice chmn. Sun Country Council. Served with USN, 1946-48. Mem. Am. Mgmt. Assn. (lectr.), Am. Assn. Advt. Agys. (chmn. Chgo. council), Grinnell Coll. Alumni Assn., Chgo. (chmn. bd.), Chgo Advt. Club (dir.), Sigma Delta Chi. Clubs: Arizona; Univ. (Milw.); Oak Brook (Ill.) Polo; Univ. (Phoenix); Mid-Am., Econ. (Chgo.); Phoenix Country. Home: 4701 Sparkling Ln Paradise Valley AZ 85253 Office: Cramer-Krasselt Co 733 N Van Buren St Milwaukee WI 53202

COLE, CATHERINE ANNE, shipping co. exec.; b. Elysburg, Pa., Aug. 21, 1950; d. Joseph M. and Margaret R. C.; Ph.D. (hon.), London Center Research, 1972. Mgr. equipment control Crossocean Shipping Co., N.Y.C., 1974-76; mgr. container dept. Norton Lilly & Co., N.Y.C., 1976-78; cons. ops. Baltic Shipping Co., N.Y.C., 1978—. Vol. worker Met. Mus. Art, N.Y.C., Am. Cancer Soc. Mem. French

Am. C. of C. Republican. Home: 1600 Center Ave Apt 7-D Fort Lee NJ 07024 Office: 750 3d Ave Suite 1348 New York NY 10017

COLE, CHARLES SEYMOUR, franchise devel. analyst; b. Glendale, Calif., Oct. 20, 1951; s. Charles Seymour and Jane (Phillips) C.; B.A., Calif. State Coll., 1973; postgrad. Western Baptist Sem., Portland, Oreg., 1974-76. Minister stewardship 1st Bapt. Ch., Modesto, Calif., 1972-74; minister adminstrn. 1st Bapt. Ch., Visalia, Calif., 1974; investment real estate salesman Lou Beres & Assos., Portland, 1975-76; real estate developer, mgr. Dean Russel Real Estate, Modesto, 1977-78; real estate developer, loan broker Land Group Fin. Services, Modesto, 1978-80; franchise devel. analyst Expansion Systems, Inc., Hayward, Calif., 1980—; cons. HUD, 1976—. Mem. Mayor's Youth Prayer Breakfast Com., 1973; youth chmn. Greater Modesto Billy Graham Evangelistic Crusade, 1974. Mem. Nat., Calif., Modesto apt. assns., Modesto Bd. Realtors, Nat. Assn. Ch. Bus. Adminstrs. Republican. Home: 66 Cleary Ct Suite 210 San Francisco CA 94109 Office: 1201 San Luis Obispo Ave Hayward CA 94544

COLE, CHARLES STEVEN, bank exec.; b. Poplar Bluff, Mo., July 29, 1947; s. Harry Newell and Wanda Jean C.; B.S. in Acctg., S.W. Mo. State U., 1969; student U. Mo., Kansas City, 1977-78; m. Faith Adele Brown, July 14, 1967; children—Kelli Renée, Karen Lehann, Leah Elizabeth. Staff acct. Arthur Andersen & Co., Kansas City, Mo., 1970-71; asst. comptroller United Missouri Bancshares, Inc. Kansas City, 1971-75, asst. auditor, 1975-76; asst. cashier United Mo. Bank of Kansas City, N.A., 1977-78; pres. United Mo. Bank of Hickman Hills, Kansas City, 1978—; guest lectr. S.W. Mo. State U., Springfield, Rockhurst Coll., Kansas City, 1978-79. Coach, Little League Baseball, 1970; scoutmaster, Boy Scouts Am., 1975-78, vice chmn. Arrowhead dist., 1979—, mem. leadership devel. com., 1979—; adv. council St. Joseph's Hosp., Kansas City, 1979—; mem. base council Richards-Gebaur Air Force Base, 1979—. Recipient Woodbadge cert. Boy Scouts Am., 1975. Mem. Am. Inst. Banking (chmn. bank audit report seminar 1975-76), Bank Adminstrn. Inst., Mo. Bankers Assn., Am. Bankers Assn., Kansas City Retail Credit Assn. Republican. Mem. Assemblies of God Ch. Office: 11702 Hickman Mills Dr Kansas City MO 64134

COLE, DONALD JOSEPH, electronics co. exec.; b. Teaneck, N.J., Mar. 20, 1941; s. Eugene Frank and Irene Kathrine (Barr) C.; B.S., Cornell U., 1964, postgrad. Law Sch., 1964-65; postgrad. U. So. Calif. Sch. Bus., 1973-74; m. Ruth Kathleen Foster, June 19, 1965. Engr., Avion Electronics Co., Paramus, N.J., 1965-67; mgr. advanced systems Hoffman Electronics Co., El Monte, Calif., 1967-77; dir. engring. E-Systems Co., Salt Lake City, 1977-78; v.p. Audio Pulse Electronics Co., El Monte, 1978—, sec., dir., 1978—. Mem. IEEE, Nat. Mgmt. Assn. Republican. Congregationalist. Club: San Fernando Valley Computer. Home: 2640 Country Club Dr Glendora CA 91740 Office: Audio Pulse Electronics Co 4501 N Arden Dr El Monte CA 91731

COLE FRANKLIN ALAN, bank holding co. exec.; b. Park Falls, Wis., May 20, 1926; s. David A. and Elizabeth (Schwid) C.; B.A., U. Ill., 1947; J.D., Northwestern U., 1950; m. Joan Lauter; 6 children. Admitted to Ill. bar, 1950; practice in Chgo., 1950-63; asso. Lederer, Livingston, Kahn & Adsit, 1950-55; partner Cole, Wishner, Epstein & Manilow, 1955-63; exec. Walter E. Heller Internat. Corp., Chgo., 1963—, chmn. chief exec. officer, 1971—; chmn., chief exec. officer dir. Walter E. Heller & Co.; chmn., chief exec. officer Walter E. Heller Internat. Corp.; dir. Am. Nat. Bank & Trust Co. Chgo., Peoples Energy Corp., Chgo., Diebel Mfg. Co., Chgo., Oak Industries Inc., Rancho Bernardo, Calif. Trustee, Northwestern U. Home: 110 Acorn Ln Highland Park IL 60035 Office: 105 W Adams St Chicago IL 60690

COLE, GARY CHARLES, ins. co. exec.; b. Dallas, Aug. 12, 1943; s. Monroe C. and Ada K. Baechtel C.; B.B.A., Tex. Christian U., 1965; m. Betty Sue Foote, Aug. 16, 1963; children—Pamela, Michael, Carrie. With Southwestern Gen. Life Ins. Co., Dallas, 1965—, now sr. v.p. adminstrv. ops. Fellow Life Office Mgmt. Inst. Baptist. Author: Across the Frontier. Home: 1733 Tobin Trail Garland TX 75043 Office: PO Box 779 Dallas TX 75221

COLE, GEORGE WENDELL, stockbroker; b. McClure, Okla., Jan. 18, 1926; s. Alva A. and Mary Ethel (Masten) C.; student U. Okla., 1946-50; m. Marjorie Jane Bouws, Nov. 10, 1962; children—Paul W., Margaret Ann, George B. Stock salesman, 1962-66; with Shoemaker & Co., Oklahoma City, 1966-72, co-owner, 1969-72; owner, mgr., dir. George Cole & Co., Inc., Oklahoma City, 1972—; pres., dir. Dunlap Sporting Goods, Inc., Cole Exploration, Inc., Oklahoma City, Waveland Devel. Co. (Miss.). Served with USN, 1944-46. Democrat. Home: 3832 NW 67th St Oklahoma City OK 73116 Office: 1211 NW 23d St Oklahoma City OK 73106

COLE, JAMES EARL, mgmt. cons.; b. Sumter, S.C., July 18, 1950; s. Arthur Roy and Mildred Eva (Kuliner) C.; B.S. magna cum laude, Yale U., 1972; M.B.A., U. Chgo., 1975; m. Susan Tomilson Hill, Feb. 18, 1978. Systems engr. IBM Corp., Chgo., 1973-75; mgmt. cons. R.H. Hayes & Assos., Chgo., 1975-76, Touche Ross & Co., N.Y.C., 1976—. Clubs: Yale of N.Y., Knickerbocker Republican. Home: 230 E 50th St New York City NY 10022 Office: 666 5th Ave New York City NY 10019

COLE, JOHN HIBBERT, grain co. exec.; b. Toronto, Ont., Can., Oct. 25, 1946; came to U.S., 1950; s. Walter John and Margaret Storey (Hibbert) C.; B.S. in Microbiology, Colo. State U., 1969, B.S. in Bus. Adminstrn., 1970, M.S. in Bus. Adminstrn. (Grad. Sch. Bus. scholar, Am. Prodn. and Inventory Control Soc. scholar), 1971: student Jones Real Estate Sch., 1975; m. Shirley Ann Sawtelle, June 14, 1970; children—Shawn Davin, Dustin Michael, Kyle Christopher. Cons., Western Concentrates, Inc., Monte Vista, Colo., 1976-78; gen. mgr. Top of the World Farms of Public Service Land Co., Questa, N.Mex., 1978-79; mng. partner Am. Farms, Mosca, Colo., 1975—; pres. Intermountain Grain Co., Alamosa, Colo., 1978—; v.p. Williams Grain Co., Keenesburg, Colo., 1980—. Mem. Nat. Farmers Orgn., Alamosa Farm Bur., Nat. Rifle Assn., Assn. M.B.A. Execs., Colo. Grain and Feed Assn., Ariz. Grain and Feed Assn., Alamosa Jaycees, Alpha Gamma Rho. Methodist. Clubs: Elks, San Luis Valley Ducks Unltd. (pres. 1973). Home: 5 Mile Ln Mosca CO 81146 Office: Ln 106 N Mosca CO 81146

COLE, JOHN YOUNGLOVE, lawyer, mining co. exec.; b. San Francisco, Aug. 5, 1900; s. John Younglove and Viola (Odom) C.; S.B., Harvard, 1925, J.D., 1930; postgrad. Fordham U. Law Sch., 1941; m. Cicily Ainsworth, March 15, 1933; 1 son, John Younglove. Admitted to N.Y. State bar, 1942, U.S. Supreme Ct. bar, 1946, Calif. bar, 1960; practiced in N.Y.C., 1942-60, Palo Alto, Calif., 1960—; developer mining properties Can., U.S., 1925—; pres. Cole Gold Mines, Ltd., Red Lake, Ont., Can., 1932—. Mem. Am., Calif. bar assns., Assn. Bar City N.Y., Harvard Law Assn. Home: 2930 Ramona St Palo Alto CA 94306 Office: Red Lake ON Canada also Palo Alto CA

COLE, RICHARD, lawyer; b. Spokane, Wash., Aug. 28, 1936; s. Homer Jackson and Katharine Louise (Jolly) C.; B.A., Wash. State U., 1960; J.D., U. Wash., 1963; m. Mary K. Weber, Nov. 28, 1964; 1 son, Thomas Alan. Admitted to Wash. State bar, 1963; chief civil dep. pros. atty. Snohomish County (Wash.), 1964-66; judge Edmonds (Wash.) Dist. Ct., 1967-71; individual practice law, Edmonds, 1967—; gen. counsel Port of Edmonds, 1968—; gen. counsel, dir. Lynwood Savs. and Loan, 1979—; chmn. bd., gen. counsel Radio Northwest Broadcasting Co., Edmonds, 1979—. Pres. bd. trustees Sno-Isle Regional Library Bd., 1969-72, 79—; mem. Edmonds Parks and Recreation Adv. Bd., 1973-79, pres. bd., 1978-79; v.p. bd. trustees Snoline YMCA, 1976-78. Mem. Am. Bar Assn., Wash. State Bar Assn., Wash. Savs. League (atty.'s com. 1980—), Snohomish County Bar Assn. Club: Rotary (pres. 1975-76) (Edmonds). Home: 7313 Soundview Dr Edmonds WA 98020 Office: Suite 230 Harbor Bldg 100 2d Ave S Edmonds WA 98020

COLE, STEVEN ROBERT, real estate appraiser, developer; b. Morristown, N.J., Aug. 23, 1949; s. Wilton Donald and Gloria Cole; B.A. with high honors, U. Calif., Santa Barbara, 1971; M.B.A., UCLA, 1973. Asst. to pres. Washington Ednl. Research Assos., Culver City, Calif., 1971-73, now dir.; real estate appraiser, cons. Solot & Assos., Tucson, 1975—; developer Catalina del Sol, Tucson, 1978—; instr. econs. Pima Coll., 1975-76. Mem. Tucson Bd. Realtors, Nat. Assn. Realtors, Am. Inst. Real Estate Appraisers, Internat. Soc. Real Estate Appraisers (sr. real property appraiser). Home: 410 N Schrader Tucson AZ 85710 Office: PO Box 12339 Tucson AZ 85732

COLE, TODD G., financial co. exec.; b. Coushatta, La., Mar. 5, 1921; s. Ira and Lucie (Tricke) C.; student La. State U., 1935-37; LL.B., Woodrow Wilson Coll., 1947; m. Inez Hamilton, Feb. 9, 1953 (div. 1974); children—Michael H., Diane Janusz; m. 2d, Josephine Giovanetti, Oct. 1974; children—Paola Smith, Leda Sanford. With Delta Airlines, 1940-63, exec. v.p. adminstrn., dir., 1959-63; sr. v.p. fin. and adminstrn., dir. Eastern Airlines, 1963-67, vice chmn., chmn. fin. com., dir., 1967-69; v.p., asst. to pres. C.I.T. Fin. Corp., N.Y.C., 1969, v.p. fin., 1969-71, exec. v.p., 1971-73, pres., chief adminstrv. officer, 1973-80, pres., chief operating officer, 1980—, also dir., mem. exec. com.; dir. Emery Air Freight. C.P.A. Mem. Ga. Bar Assn. Home: Charter Oak Ln Greenwich CT 06830 Office: 650 Madison Ave New York NY 10022

COLE, WILLIAM HOWARD, mfg. co. exec.; b. Long Beach, Calif., Oct. 3, 1943; s. Dan Moody and Margaret Elizabeth (Kalm) C.; student U. N.Mex., 1962-63; m. Alma Ann Stark, Dec. 3, 1960; children—Shawn Vincent, Lyle Patrick. Vice-pres. Neon Products, Albuquerque, 1964, pres., 1964-66; zone sales mgr., account exec. Motorola C and E, Albuquerque, Dallas, 1967-71; mktg. mgr. Secode Electronics, Dallas, 1971-77; dir. nat. mktg. R.F. Communications div. Harris Corp., Rochester, N.Y., 1977—; dir. Worldwide Communications Cons., Dallas. Mem. IEEE, Amateur Radio Relay League, Petroleum Industry Elec. Assn., Armed Forces Communications Electronics Assn., Sales Mktg. Execs., Nat. Assn. Radiotelephone Services Mfrs. (co-dir. 1975-76), Radio Club Am., Ind. Telephone Pioneers. Republican. Methodist. Home: 52 Bent Oak Trail Fairport NY 14450

COLEGROVE, WILLIAM DANA, bank exec.; b. Remus, Mich., Jan. 19, 1912; s. William Dana and Carrie M. (Hoyt) C.; B.S., Mich. State Coll., 1931; m. Sena Verhage, Oct. 12, 1935; children—Marilyn, William. With Dow Chem. Co., Midland, Mich. and Freeport, Tex., 1935-77, exec. asst., 1950-70, mgr. community relations, 1970-77; mktg. dir. Angleton Bank of Commerce (Tex.), 1977—; chmn. bd. Brazosport Savs. & Loan Assn. (Tex.), 1960-62. Mayor, City of Lake Jackson, Tex., 1948-54. Named Brazosport Citizen of Year, C. of C., 1953. Democrat. Methodist. Club: Riverside Country (Lake Jackson). Columnist, Brazosport Facts, 1977—. Home: 52 Plantation Ct Lake Jackson TX 77566 Office: Angleton Bank of Commerce 201 E Mulberry St Angleton TX 77515

COLEMAN, JAMES JULIAN, lawyer, bus. exec.; b. New Orleans, May 5, 1915; s. William Ballin and Millie (Davis) C.; B.A., Tulane U., 1934, LL.B., 1937; m. Dorothy Louise Jurisich, July 30, 1940; children—James Julian, Thomas Blaise, Peter Dee, Dian Judith. Admitted to La. bar, 1937; sr. partner Coleman, Dutrey & Thomson; chmn. bd. Internat. Tank Terminals, Ltd., Internat. Tank Terminals, Ltd., Karachi, W. Pakistan, Chittagong, Bangladesh and Ulsan, South Korea, Daisy Oil Co., Loving Enterprises, Civic Center Site Devel. Co., Inc.; pres., gen. counsel Internat. Trade Mart. Former treas. Cordell Hull Found.; former pres. Adult Edn. Center, Inc.; past mem. exec. com. Internat. Relations Com., Mississippi Valley World Trade Council; mem. bd., past pres. Jr. Achievement New Orleans; pres. New Orleans Philharm. Symphony Soc.; trustee Loving Found., Bradley Family Found. Principia Coll.; past chmn. council Tulane U. Bus. Sch. Hon. consul gen. Republic Korea. Mem. Internat., Am., La., New Orleans bar assns., Am. Judicature Soc. (past dir.), Greater New Orleans Area (past pres.), U.S. (dir. 1964-68) chambers commerce. Christian Scientist. Home: 10 Audubon Pl New Orleans LA 70118 Office: 321 Charles Ave New Orleans LA 70130

COLEMAN, LESTER E., chem. co. exec.; b. Akron, Ohio, Nov. 6, 1930; B.Sc. in Chemistry, U. Akron, 1952; M.S. in Chemistry, U. Ill., 1953, Ph.D. in Chemistry, 1955; m. Jean Goudie Moir, Aug. 31, 1951; children—Robert Scott, Kenneth John. With The Lubrizol Corp., Wickliffe, Ohio, 1955—, asst. to pres., 1972-73, v.p. internat. ops., 1973-74, exec. v.p., 1974-76, pres., 1976—, chief exec. officer, 1978—, also dir.; dir. Norfolk & Western R.R., Society Nat. Bank, Society Corp., Ferro Corp., Cleve. Served with USAF, 1955-57. Mem. exec. bd. Northeast Ohio council Boy Scouts Am., Painesville, Ohio. Mem. Am. Chem. Soc. (past chmn. Northeastern Ohio sect.). Office: 29400 Lakeland Blvd Wickliffe OH 44092

COLEMAN, MARION LESLIE, ins. co. exec.; b. Mobile, Ala., Mar. 20, 1925; s. Luther Woodward and Carrie (Lockler) C.; student pub. schs.; m. Joyce Kelley, Aug. 29, 1944; children—Connie, Woodward L. and Franklin M. (twins). Agt., Life Ins. Co. Ga., Mobile, 1946-55, dist. mgr., El Dorado, Ark., 1955-56, Hattiesburg, Miss., 1957-60, Meridian, Miss., 1960-64; v.p., agy. dir. Nat. Preferred Life Ins. Co., Atlanta, 1964-65; v.p. tng. Found. Life Ins. Co., Atlanta, 1965—; v.p. Kelley-Blakely Land Corp., Mobile; pres. Yamaha Sports World, Meridian, Melco Ltd. Custom Tailors, Meridian, Meridian Motors, Buddy Coleman Enterprises, Meridian, Triple C Corp.; div. mgr. Jefferson Standard Life Ins. Co., Meridian; v.p. Merchandizers Inc. (Gibson Discount Center), Meridian; dir. Gulf Cascade Investment Properties, Inc., Long Beach, Miss. Served with USNR, 1943-46. Mem. Life Underwriters Assn., Sales and Mktg. Execs. Club. Home: 2100 23d Ave Meridian MS 39301 Office: 514 Citizen National Bank Bldg Meridian MS 39301

COLEMAN, WILLIAM ELIAH, psychologist; b. Utica, N.Y., May 30, 1921; s. Michael and Mildred (Hoffman) C.; B.A., Ohio State U., 1942, M.A., 1946, Ph.D., 1949; m. June Charna Juster, Oct. 3, 1943; children—Nancy, Lawrence, Karen. Asst. prof., then dir. testing and guidance U. Tenn., 1947-56; human factors scientist RAND Corp., 1956-60; dir. psychol. services Ward J. Jensen Co., 1960-61; pres. Coleman & Assos., mgmt. psychologists, Santa Monica, Calif., 1961—; instr. UCLA; lectr. Calif. Inst. Tech. Bd. dirs. Santa Monica Area NCCJ, 1970-73. Served with U.S. Army, 1942-46. Decorated Bronze Star, Purple Heart. Fellow Am. Psychol. Assn.; life mem. Am. Personnel and Guidance Assn. Democrat. Author: Pictorial Intelligence Test, 1960, Life Goals Inventory, 1966. Home: 349 Euclid St Santa Monica CA 90402 Office: 1640 5th St Santa Monica CA 90401

COLEN, ALLYN R., energy and air conditioning cons.; b. Cleve., Jan. 19, 1920; s. Morry M. and Ann (Minsky) C.; B.S., Ohio State U., 1949; B.A., Ariz. State U., 1967, M.A., 1970; m. Joy Rosalind Friedman, Mar. 20, 1949; children—Russell B., Laurel H. Engr., Modern Heating Co., Oklahoma City, 1950-54, Carnahan & Thompson, Oklahoma City, 1954-55; mgr. Ace Sheet Metal Co., Oklahoma, City, 1955-59; engr., Goettl Bros. Metal Products, Phoenix, 1959-70, 71-76; engr., Honeywell Infor. Systems, Phoenix, 1970-71; pvt. cons. to architects and contractors, Phoenix, 1970-78; engr. Enercom, Inc., Tempe, Ariz., 1978—; instr. Glendale Community Coll., 1971-72; adviser Maricopa Tech. Coll., 1972—. Served with AUS, 1941-45. Registered profl. engr., Ariz., Okla., Wash., Nev. Mem. Am. Soc. Certified Engring. Technicians (hon.), Am. Soc. Heating, Refrigerating and Air Conditioning Engrs., Am. Soc. Profl. Engrs., Assn. Energy Engrs., Kappa Delta Pi. Home: 3420 N 42d St Phoenix AZ 85018 Office: 2323 S Hardy Dr Tempe AZ 85282

COLER, MARK DAVID, lawyer; b. N.Y.C., Jan. 5, 1944; s. Myron Abraham and Viola Ethel (Buchbinder) C.; B.A. cum laude in Econs., Harvard U., 1966; J.D., U. Pa., 1969. Admitted to N.Y. bar, 1970, D.C. bar, 1973; VISTA atty. U.S. Office Econ. Opportunity, Albuquerque, 1969-70; individual practice law, N.Y.C., 1970-71, chief Wage Appeals br. Cost of Living Council, Washington, 1972-73; spl. asst. to dir. Bur. of East-West Trade, Dept. Commerce, Washington, 1973-74; dir. office Raw Materials and Oceans Policy Dept. Treasury, Washington, 1974-76, deputy to asst. sec. for N.Y. Finance, Dept. Treasury, 1976-77; chmn. Monetary Group, Ltd., N.Y.C.; dir. Coler Engring., N.Y., Southwark Housing Devel. Corp., Phila. Mem. Am., Washington bar assns., Washington Bd. Realtors, Urban Land Inst., Realtors Nat. Mktg. Inst. Clubs: Harvard (N.Y.C.); Sharswood Law (Phila.); Hasty Pudding Inst. (Cambridge, Mass.); Nat. Cathedral Tennis (Washington); Mamaroneck (N.Y.) Yacht. Office: Pan Am Bldg 200 Park Ave Suite 303 E New York NY 10017

COLES, CHARLES FURMAN, broker; b. Atlanta, Mar. 31, 1921; s. Marion and Katherine (Furman) C.; B.S. in Naval Architecture, Mass. Inst. Tech., 1943; grad. Advanced Mgmt. Program, Harvard, 1962; postgrad. Boston U., Northeastern U.; m. Cornelia Ford, Apr. 21, 1962; children—Lindsay Schnabel, John, Charles Furman. Dir. bus. planning USM Machinery Co., Boston, 1946-62; asst. to pres. U.S. Smelting & Refining Co., Boston, 1963-64; asst. to pres. The Reece Corp., Waltham, Mass., 1964-68; v.p. Pyrotector Inc., Hingham, Mass., 1969-71; resident mgr. Apache Programs Inc., Boston, 1968—; pres. Hydroflight Corp., Wenham, Mass., 1968—; pres. Romahoff Pen Corp., Wenham, 1971—. Mem. adv. bd. U.S. Dept. Commerce, 1960—. Corporater Beverly (Mass.) Hosp. Served as lt. USNR, 1944-46. Mem. Harvard Bus. Sch. Assn. (past gov.), Am. Marketing Assn. (past pres.), St. Anthony Club (past pres.), Schussverein Ski Club (past dir.). Clubs: Myopia Hunt, Manchester Yacht. Patentee boat designs. Home: 24 Main St Wenham MA 01984 Office: Box 484 Wenham MA 01984 also Apache Programs 20 Railroad Ave S Hamilton MA 01982

COLES, JAMES A., business exec.; b. San Jose, Calif., 1932; B.S., U. Santa Clara, 1953; married. v.p. U.S. Trust Co., 1970; dir. Office Bank Mgmt., Fed. Home Loan Bank Bd., Washington, 1970-72; pres. Fed. Home Loan Bank of Little Rock, 1972-78; pres. PMI Mortgage Co., 1978-79; pres., chief operating officer Imperial Corp. Am., San Diego, 1979—. Office: Imperial Corp Am 8787 Complex Dr San Diego CA 92123*

COLES, JOHN EDMUND, JR., bus., estate planning co. exec.; b. Balt., Aug. 20, 1948; s. John Edmund C.; B.A., Calif. State Coll., San Bernardino, 1970; m. Carol Ann Larsen, May 15, 1968; children—John Edmund III, Christopher, Heidi, Joseph, Adam, Natalie, Kimberly, Paul. Pres., John E. Coles Jr. and Assos. Inc., Riverside, Calif., 1975—; agency mgr. Beneficial Life Ins. Co., Riverside, 1975—; pres., chmn. bd. United Calif. Bus. and Estate Planning Inc., Riverside, 1976—; pres. United Bus. and Estate Planning (Utah) Inc., Riverside, 1978—, Am. Ins. Exchange, Inc., Unite Investment Res., Inc., Diamond Importers. Exec. sec. Riverside stake Ch. Jesus Christ Latter-Day Saints, 1978—. Recipient various nat. sales and mgmt. awards; qualifying mem. Million Dollar Round Table, 1972-77, 79. Mem. Riverside County Life Underwriters Assn. (pres.), Internat. Assn. Financial Planners, Gen. Agts. and Mgrs. Conf. Republican. Home: 141 E Manfield St Riverside CA 92507 Office: 1160 University Ave Riverside CA 92507

COLETTI, ALBERT F., fin. planning corp. exec.; b. Paterson, N.J., Apr. 15, 1943; s. Albert and Maria (Santilli) C.; A.A.S. in Bus., Suffolk County Coll., 1964; student Hofstra U., 1964-66; m. Victoria López, Apr. 2, 1967. Real estate investor, bus. cons.; asso. New Eng. Mut. Life Ins. Co., Melville, N.Y., 1968-73; pres. Designed Pension Plans, Inc. and Designed Exec. Compensation, Inc., Melville, 1973-75; founder, pres., chmn. bd. Design Capital Planning Group, Inc., Hauppauge, N.Y., 1975—; faculty instr. Dale Carnegie mgmt. seminars. Mem. Suffolk County Chpt. C.L.U.'s (pres. continuing edn. chmn.), Suffolk County Estate Planning Council (dir.), Assn. Commerce and Industry (chmn. V.I.P. com.), L.I. Assn. (ambassador's com.). Republican. Roman Catholic. Contbr. Insight, regular article in bus. publs.; contbg. author Inst. for Bus. Planning, 1979; speaker profl. confs. Office: 300 Vanderbilt Motor Pkwy Hauppauge NY 11787

COLEY, JOEL EDGAR, constrn. and real estate co. exec.; b. Indiahoma, Okla., Aug. 11, 1917; s. J.E. and Amanda Dottie (McCoy) C.; student Oklahoma City U., Oklahoma City Coll., U. Okla., Western Hills Bus. Coll., Okla. South Coll.; children—Carolyn Joan Coley Hume, Mickey Clinton. Pres., Joel Coley Constrn. Co., Oklahoma City, 1939—, Coley Lumber Co., 1949—, Coley Realty Co., 1950—, Home Owners Ins. Corp., 1955; real estate appraiser, 1944—; commr. Oklahoma City Housing Authority, 1971-74. Pres., Cerebral Palsy Oklahoma City, 1979, 80. Mem. Am. Soc. Appraisers (regional gov.), Oklahoma City Home Builders Assn. (life dir.), Oklahoma City Bd. Realtors. Democrat. Clubs: W. Side Lions (pres. 1975-76), Masons. Office: 3501 NW 36th St Oklahoma City OK 73112

COLL, EDWARD GIRARD, JR., univ. adminstr.; b. Pitts., Aug. 9, 1934; s. Edward G. and Alice V. (Ebeling) C.; B.A., Duquesne U., 1960; m. Carole Hulse, Feb. 3, 1958; children—Thomas, Jean, Peter, Karen, Kelly. Div. dir. United Fund of Allegheny County (Pa.), 1959-61, campaign dir. Dade County (Fla.), 1961-63; asst. to pres. U. Miami, Coral Gables, Fla., 1963-67, dir. devel., 1967-72, corporate sec., 1972-73, v.p. devel., 1973—; lectr. acad. adminstrn. Chmn. zoning appeals bd. Dade County, 1973—; bd. dirs. Dade County ARC, 1975—. Served with U.S. Army, 1953-56. Mem. Council for Advancement and Support of Edn., Am. Council on Edn. Democrat. Roman Catholic. Clubs: Miami, Standard, Kings Bay Yacht and

Country. Contbr. articles to profl. publs. Home: 15505 SW 77th Ct Miami FL 33157 Office: PO Box 248073 U Miami Coral Gables FL 33124

COLLAR, WILLIAM ARCHER, diversified service co. exec.; b. Warren, Pa., Sept. 25, 1929; s. John S. and Lucile (Proud) C.; A.A., U. Fla., 1953, B.Indsl. Engring., 1954; m. Mary Alice Casey, Sept. 6, 1953; children—Sammy G., John Lee, Sandra Lynne. Adminstr. cost estimating RCA, Camden, N.J., 1954-57; mfg. research engr. Martin Co., Orlando, Fla., 1957-59; mgr. advanced research Radiation, Inc., Melbourne, Fla., 1959-62; prin. engr. Honeywell, Inc., St. Petersburg, Fla., 1962-67; mfg. engring. supr. McDonnell-Douglas, St. Charles, Mo., 1967-68; dir. engring. Advanced Circuitry div. Litton Corp., Springfield, Mo., 1968-75; quality control and engring. mgr. TRW/Cinch-Graphik, Industry, Calif., 1975-77; pres. CDA Corp., Fullerton, Calif., 1977—, chmn. bd., 1978—; mfg. cons. Mem. Redevel. Commn. City of Fullerton. Served with USN, 1947-51. Registered profl. engr., Calif. Republican. Episcopalian. Clubs: Elks, Masons, Shriners. Office: 679-I S State College Blvd Fullerton CA 92631

COLLETT, WALLACE TIBBALS, ret. food service exec.; b. Wilmington, Ohio, Nov. 14, 1914; s. Howard and Mary S. (Tibbals) C.; A.B., Wilmington Coll., 1936, B.S. in Edn., 1936; M.A., Haverford Coll., 1937, LL.D., 1975; m. Carrie E. Hudson, 1937; children—Jonathan H., Jane Collett Moeller, Stephen W. Tchr., Hanover High Sch., Butler County, Ohio, 1937-40; allotment clk. drug products dept. Procter & Gamble Co., Cin., 1943-45; asst. mgr. Tibbals Co., Cin., 1940-45, mgr., 1945-51, owner, 1951-60; a founder Servomation Corp., N.Y.C., 1960, div. mgr., 1961-75, v.p., 1961-76, sr. v.p., 1976-78, dir., 1960-80, chmn. exec. com., 1972-80. Vice chmn. Cin. Mayor's Friendly Relations Com., 1956-62; mem. Cin. City Planning Commn., 1948-53, Hamilton County Planning Commn., 1949-53; bd. dirs. Am. Friends Service Com., Phila., 1964-70, treas. bd., 1970-71, chmn. bd., 1971-79, asso. exec. sec. fin., 1980; bd. mgrs. Haverford Coll., 1978—; trustee Wilmington Coll., 1960-74, chmn. bd., 1966-74; bd. dirs. Camp Joy, Cin., 1964—, pres. bd., 1964-69; chmn. Mayor's Com. for Urban Greenery, 1976—; bd. dirs. Cin. Hist. Soc., 1979—. Mem. Soc. Friends. Club: Queen City (Cin.). Home: 1181 Edwards Rd Cincinnati OH 45208

COLLIE, JOHN, JR., insurance agt.; b. Gary, Ind., Apr. 23, 1934; s. John and Christina Dempster (Wardrop) C.; student Purdue U., 1953; A.B. in Econs., Ind. U., 1957; m. Jessie Fearn Shaw, Aug. 1, 1964; children—Cynthia Elizabeth, Douglas Allan Hamilton, Jennifer Fearn. Operator, Collie Optical Lab., Gary, 1957-62; owner, operator Collie Ins. Agy., Merrillville, Ind., 1962—. Served as lt. col. U.S. Army Res., 1957—; instr. Command and Gen. Staff Coll., 1973-77. Mem. Profl. Ins. Agts. Assn. Ind. (dir.), Res. Officers Assn. (sec., v.p. army State of Ind.), Mil. Order World Wars, Internat. Platform Assn., Phi Kappa Psi. Republican. Presbyterian. Clubs: Masons (32 deg.), Shriners, Elks. Home: 717 W 66th Pl Merrillville IN 46410 Office: 5600 Broadway PO Box 8049 Merrillville IN 46410

COLLIER, ABRAM THURLOW, ins. co. exec.; b. Billerica, Mass., Oct. 26, 1913; s. Forrest Foster and Lucy Bryant (Foster) C.; A.B. cum laude, Harvard, 1934, LL.B., 1937; L.H.D., Northeastern U.; Litt.D., Babson Coll.; D.B.A., Boston Coll.; LL.D., Nasson Coll.; m. Eleanor Whitney, Dec. 11, 1937; children—Linda Collier Kenerson, Debora Collier Zug, Joyce Collier Fearnside, Charles. Admitted to Mass. bar, 1937; practiced in Boston, 1937-39; with John Hancock Mut. Life Ins. Co., 1939-66, vice chmn. bd., 1965-66; pres. New Eng. Mut. Life Ins. Co., Boston, 1966-74, chmn. bd., 1974-78, also dir.; dir. Houghton Mifflin Co., dir. New Eng. Mchts. Nat. Bank, Gen. Cinema Corp.; trustee William Underwood Co. Trustee Boston Symphony Orch., Wheaton Coll.; mem. corp. Northeastern U., Babson Coll., Boston Mus. Sci. Recipient McKinsey award Harvard Bus. Rev., 1960. Mem. Boston Bar Assn., Assn. Life Ins. Counsel (pres. 1962-63), Greater Boston C. of C. (pres. 1965-66, dir.). Unitarian. Clubs: Appalachian Mountain; Harvard, Comml. (pres. 1972-74) (Boston); Country (Brookline). Author: Management, Men, and Values, 1962. Office: 501 Boylston St Boston MA 02117*

COLLIER, JAMES DEWEY, assn. exec.; b. Birmingham, Ala., Oct. 18, 1926; s. Earl S. and Annie (Williams) C.; B.S., U. Ala., 1949; M.B.A. with distinction, N.Y. U., 1967. Asst. to controller cost control Freeport Sulphur Co., New Orleans, 1954-64; mgr. chpt. ednl. services Nat. Assn. Accountants, N.Y.C., 1964-68, dir. mem. services, 1968-72, dir. publs., 1972—, editor publisher Mgmt. Accounting, 1972—; cons. to industry. Treas., St. Tropez Condominium, N.Y.C., 1966-70. Served with C.E., AUS, 1944-46. Mem. Nat. Assn. Accts., Am. Soc. Assn. Execs., UN Assn., Met. Opera Guild, Am. Acctg. Assn., Beta Alpha Psi Forum. Contbr. articles to profl. jours. Home: 77 W 55th St New York NY 10019 Office: 919 3d Ave New York NY 10022

COLLIER, MICHAEL THOMAS, news agy. exec.; b. N.Y.C., Oct. 17, 1950; s. Patrick and Eileen (Casey) C.; B.A., Hunter Coll., 1975. Dir., Riverdale Protection Group, N.Y.C., 1975-77; supr. central services B'nai Jeshurun Community Center, N.Y.C., 1975-76; pres., treas. M.T.C.'s News Agy., Phila., 1976—; research cons. M.T.C., 1977—. Active Nationalities Service Center, ednl. services, Phila., 1979. Mem. AAAS, N.Y. Acad. Sci., Am. Enterprise Inst., Am. Acad. Arts and Sci. Address: 322 S 10 St Philadelphia PA 19107

COLLINGS, CHARLES LEROY, retail food and drug chain co. exec.; b. Wewoka, Okla., July 11, 1925; s. Robert Roy and Dessie Louise Collings; student So. Meth. U., 1943-44; U. Tex., 1944-45; m. Frances Jane Flake, June 28, 1947; children—Sandra Jane, Dianna Lynn. Sec., dir. Noble Meat Co., Madera, Calif., 1947-55; head acctg. dept. Montgomery Ward & Co., Oakland, Calif., 1956-57; office mgr. Raley's Sacramento, 1957-59, controller, 1960-62, sec., 1963-68, pres., 1969—, also dir.; dir. United Grocers Ltd., Data Factors, Inc. Bd. dirs. Youth for Christ, Pro Athletes Outreach. Served with USN, 1943-46. Mem. Calif. Grocers Assn. (dir.), No. Calif. Growers Assn. (dir.). Republican. Baptist. Home: 7465 French Rd # 31 Sacramento CA 95828 Office: 1515 20th St Sacramento CA 95813

COLLINS, CLAUDE CHARLES, fin. services co. exec.; b. West Palm Beach, Fla., Sept. 14, 1946; s. Claude Charles and Winifred (Farr) C.; student U. Fla., 1964-67; children—Christian, Cara. Ins. mktg. rep. State of Fla., 1967-68; fin. and mktg. cons. to several ins. cos., 1969-71; pvt. cons. investments, ins. and tax strategies; v.p. IMC Am., Tampa, Fla., 1973-75; propr. MDA Fin., DeLand, Fla., 1976-79; founder, pres. Seos Found., Inc., DeLand, 1977—, Sterling-Forbes Holdings, Inc., DeLand, 1979—; agt. and exclusive U.S. rep. Finlay Trust Group; internat. fin. cons. Served with U.S. Army, 1968. Mem. Nat. Assn. Fin. Cons., Real Estate Securities and Syndication Inst., Internat. Soc. Financiers, Mcht. Brokers Exchange. Republican. Club: Internat. Order Flangers. Home: Beresford Rd DeLand FL 32720 Office: PO Box 622 DeLand FL 32720

COLLINS, DAVID ALBERT, mfg. co. ofcl.; b. Dunmore, Pa., June 29, 1950; m. Donald Edward and Olive Blanche Collins; B.A., Rutgers U., 1974, M.B.A., 1981; m. Beverly Lee Harrison, Nov. 25, 1972; children—Jennifer Lee, Kristi Lee, Melissa Lee. Lab. technician, jr. chemist R.M. Hollingshead Corp., Camden, N.J., 1970-74; environ. chemist and engr. Westinghouse Electric Co., Phila., 1974-76; quality assurance mgr. Magic Marker Corp., Cherry Hill, N.J., 1976—. Mem. Am. Soc. for Quality Control (cert. quality engr., exec. com.), Am. Mgmt. Assn. Researcher and developer quality control and writing instrument systems. Home: 257 Champion Way Sewell NJ 08080 Office: 1 Magic Marker Ln Cherry Hill NJ 08003

COLLINS, EVA MAE LOMERSON, ins. co. exec.; b. Lake Orion, Mich., July 10, 1930; d. J.M. and Thelma Marie (Kimmery) Lomerson; ed. U. Mich., Wayne State U.; m. John Armstrong Collins, Feb. 24, 1968. Dept. mgr. Sears Roebuck & Co., 1951-69; personal lines mgr. Bingham & Bingham, Inc., ins., 1970-73, comml. accounts mgr., resident ins. agt., 1973-75, v.p., office mgr., 1975-77; underwriting mgr., v.p. InterCEDE Group, 1977—. Mem. Nat. Assn. Ins. Women, Ins. Women Met. Detroit (adv. chmn. 1976-77, rec. sec. 1977-78, corr. sec. 1978-79, treas. 1979-80, 2d v.p. 1980-81), DAR (chpt. chmn. good citizens program, jr. mems., regent, vice regent, state chmn. pages and jr. mems. 1967-70, state outstanding jr. mem. 1966), Am. Bus. Women's Assn. (pres. Land-O-Oak chpt. 1964-65, woman of year 1965), Nat. Hist. Soc., Hist. Soc. Mich., Detroit Soc. Geneal. Research, U. Mich. Alumni Assn. (life), Nat. Wildlife Assn., Nat. Trust Hist. Preservation, Nat. Assn. Female Execs., Am. Soc. Profl. and Exec. Women, Nat. Audubon Soc., Friends Detroit Public Library, Founders Soc. Detroit Inst. Arts, Daus. Colonial Wars. Clubs: Great Oaks Country; Club on Hill Women's; Women's Econ., Econ. (Detroit). Home: 1122 Mill Valley Rd PO Box 734 Rochester MI 48063 Office: 30700 Telegraph Rd S-4535 Birmingham MI 48010 Birmingham MI 48010

COLLINS, EVAN REVERE, JR., investment banking/brokerage co. exec.; b. Boston, Nov. 6, 1937; s. Evan Revere and Virginia (Lillard) C.; B.A., Dartmouth Coll., 1959, M.B.A., 1961; m. Daisy MacDonald Drews, Sept. 6, 1969; children—Evan Revere, Elizabeth Anne, Randell Revere, Lindsay McDonald. With Kidder, Peabody & Co., Inc., N.Y.C., 1961—, asst. v.p., 1969-71, v.p., 1971—, resident officer, 1978—; dir. Collins Racing Corp. Bd. dirs. Up With People, Tucson, 1972-75; bd. dirs. United Way of No. Westchester, Mt. Kisco, N.Y., 1976—, pres., 1977—; bd. dirs. United Way Westchester, White Plains, N.Y., 1978—. Mem. Investment Assn. Republican. Episcopalian. Clubs: N.Y. Yacht, African Safari. Home: October Farm Old Roaring Brook Rd Mount Kisco NY 10549 Office: 522 Fifth Ave New York City NY 10036

COLLINS, GALEN FRANKLIN, hosp. supply co. exec.; b. Winona Lake, Ind., Dec. 29, 1927; s. Harry Franklin and Elsie (Bahney) C.; B.S., Purdue U., 1949, M.S., 1952. Ph.D., 1954; m. Ann Elizabeth Averitt, Sept. 30, 1956; children—Galen Robert, Amelia, Scott. Grad. asst. Purdue, U., 1949-52, research fellow, 1952-53; pharm. chemist Miles Labs., Inc., Elkart, Ind., 1953-58, asst. to dir. Miles-Ames Pharm. Research Lab., 1958-59, sr. research scientist, sect. head Ames Products, 1959-60; sect. chief Norwich Products Devel., Norwich Pharmacal Co. (N.Y.), 1960-63; mgr. research div. S. E. Massengill Co., 1963-67, dir. research, 1967-71; v.p. research and devel. Dade div. Am. Hosp. Supply Corp., Miami, Fla., 1971-74, v.p., sci. dir., 1974—. Bd. dirs. Bristol unit Am. Heart Assn., pres., 1969-71. Fellow A.A.A.S., Am. Inst. Chemists; mem. Am. Assn. Clin. Chemists, Assn. Clin. Scientists, Acad. Pharm. Scis., Am. Chem. Soc., Am. Pharm. Assn., Rho Chi, Phi Lambda Upsilon, Sigma Xi. Congregationalist. Elk. Patentee in field. Home: 10800 SW 69th Ave Miami FL 33156 Office: POB 672 Miami FL 33152

COLLINS, GARELD JEFFERSON, automotive supply co. exec.; b. Sask., Can., July 4, 1913; s. Andrew Jackson and Amelia (Hartsook) C.; came to U.S., 1922, naturalized, 1968; student pub. schs.; m. June Blevins, July 1, 1940; children—Michael Lee, Lael Gareld. With Civilian Conservation Corps, Pistol River, Oreg., 1933-34; mechanic Del Rogue Garage, Grants Pass, Oreg., 1935-36; shipping clk. Western Auto, Grants Pass, 1927-39; sales rep. George Lawrence Co., Portland, Oreg., 1939-40; shipping clk. Littrell Parts, Yreka, Calif., 1940-41, sales rep., 1942-45, sales mgr., 1945-64, v.p., 1952-64, pres., 1965—; pres. Collins Enterprises, Inc., Yreka, 1970—, Littrell Welding Supply, Inc., Medford, Oreg., 1970—, Littrell Welding Supply, Redding, Calif., 1971—; dir. Timberline Community Bank, Automotive Parts Assn. Fed. Credit Union. Sec., Siskiyou County (Calif.) Sheriff's Posse, 1967, 73. Bd. dirs. Am. Buckskin Registry Assn., 1966-73, pres., 1972. Mem. Calif. Automotive Wholesalers Assn. (dir. 1974—). Mason (Shriner), Rotarian (dir. 1980—). Home: Route 1 Box 504 Yreka CA 96097 Office: 404 S Main St Yreka CA 96097

COLLINS, HARKER, fin. and investment mgmt. co. exec., publisher; b. Denver, Nov. 24, 1924; s. Clem Wetzel and Marie (Harker) C.; B.S., U.S. Naval Acad., 1945; m. Emily Harvey, Aug. 23, 1957; children—Catherine Emily, Cynthia Lee, Constance Marie. Asst. buyer Montgomery Ward & Co., N.Y.C., 1947-51; prodn. mgr. Diamond Hosiery Mills, High Point, N.C., 1953-55; v.p. Vanette Hosiery Mills, Dallas, 1955-59; v.p., dir. Grote Mfg. Co., Madison, Ind., 1959-71; group v.p., gen. mgr. Bendix Corp., South Bend, Ind., 1971-73; pres., dir. Bandag, Inc., Muscatine, Iowa, 1973-78, chief exec. officer, 1974-78; pres., chief exec. officer, dir. Harker Collins & Co., Inc., Brownsville, Tex., 1978—; pub. The Economy and You, Update, 1978—; instr. U. Denver, 1948. Bd. dirs. Hwy. Users Fedn., 1970—; chmn. automotive industry liaison com. with Dept. Transp., 1968—, automotive industry excise tax com., 1964-70, automotive industry tariff com., 1964-70, joint operating com. for automotive trade shows, 1969-77; mem. Pres.'s Com. Hwy. Safety, 1966-68. Bd. fellows Northwood Inst., 1974—. Served to ensign USN, 1945-47; to lt. USNR, 1951-53. Recipient Automotive Industry Leadership award, 1965, 74, Fin. World Top Chief Exec. Officer award, 1975, 77. Mem. Automotive Service Industry Assn. (v.p. 1966-67, pres. 1968-69, dir. heavy duty exec. com. 1969-71, chmn. safety and environ. protection com. 1962-67, 70—), Automotive Sales Council (dir. 1966-67, sec. 1971-72, v.p. 1972-73, pres. 1973-74), Am. Nat. Standards Inst. (chmn. task force on used vehicle standards 1966-74, mem. tech. bd. 1966-74), Home Products Safety Council (pres. 1960-63), Medicine Cabinet Mfg. Council (pres. 1960-63, dir. 1960-68), Truck Safety Equipment Inst. (pres. 1960-63, dir. 1960-68), Internat. Platform Assn. Clubs: 33 (treas. 1977-78), Rotary. Office: PO Box 3918 Brownsville TX 78520

COLLINS, HOWARD ELISHA, health care cons.; b. Medina, N.Y., Jan. 5, 1915; s. John F. and Nina G. (Blount) C.; accounting diploma Bryant & Stratton Bus. Coll., 1935; continuation edn. basic hosp. adminstrn. Columbia, 1964-65; m. Florence J. Phillips, June 30, 1937; children—Sharon Beth Collins Corriero, Beverly Faye Collins Galloway, John Howard. Gen. mgr. Collins Upholstery Mfg. Co., Silver Creek, N.Y., 1936-54; gen. mgr. Silver Creek Motors, 1954-58; pvt. practice accounting, Silver Creek, 1958-61; bus. mgr., adminstr. Lake Shore Intercommunity Hosp., Irving, N.Y., 1961-66; adminstr. Mohawk Valley Gen. Hosp. and Nursing Home, Ilion, N.Y., 1966-77; pres. Chart, Inc., Albany, N.Y., 1977—; com. mem. Mid-State Comprehensive Health Planning Com. for Oneida and Hekimer Counties, 1971-73; chmn. bd. trustees C.H.A.R.T., Inc., hosp. shared computer orgn., Albany, 1968-77. Fellow Am. Coll. Hosp. Adminstrs.; mem. Hosp. Fin. Mgmt. Assn. (advanced mem.), Am. Coll. Nursing Home Adminstrs., Hosp. Mgmt. Systems Soc., Am. Assn. Hosp. Planners, Am. Hosp. Assn., Hosp. Assn. N.Y. State (trustee, com. chmn.), Central N.Y. Hosp. Assn. (chmn. bd. dirs. 1975-76), Assn. Hosp. Adminstrs. Columbia U. Program Continuing Edn., Am. Mgmt. Assn. Republican. Presbyterian. Clubs: Masons, Moose. Home: 8 Summit Park Ballston Lake NY 12019 Office: Profl Bldg Northway 10 Executive Park Ballston Lake NY 12019

COLLINS, MICHAEL, museum ofcl.; b. Rome, Oct. 31, 1930; s. James L. and Virginia (Stewart) C.; parents Am. citizens; B.S., U.S. Mil. Acad., 1952; student Advanced Mgmt. Program, Harvard, 1974; D.Sc., Northeastern U., 1970, Stonehill Coll., 1970; LL.D., St. Michael's Coll., 1970, Southeastern U., 1975; m. Patricia M. Finnegan, Apr. 28, 1957; children—Kathleen, Ann Stewart, Michael Lawton. Commd. officer U.S. Air Force, advanced through grades to col., 1970; fighter pilot, flight comdr., U.S., Europe; exptl. flight test officer, Edwards AFB, Calif.; named astronaut NASA, 1963, pilot Gemini 10, 1966, space walker, comdr., Command Module pilot Apollo 11, 1963-69; apptd. asst. sec. state for pub. affairs, Washington, 1970-71; dir. Nat. Air and Space Mus., Smithsonian Instn., Washington, 1971-78, undersec. of Instn., 1978—. Bd. dirs. Air Force Hist. Found. Decorated D.S.M., D.F.C.; recipient Presdl. Mgdal of Freedom, NASA Disting. Service and Exceptional Service medals, Hubbard medal, Collier trophy, Goddard Meml. trophy, Harmon trophy, Gen. Thomas D. White USAF Space trophy, gold space medal Fedn. Aeronautique Internat. Fellow AIAA, Am. Astronautical Soc.; mem. Washington Inst. Fgn. Affairs, Soc. Exptl. Test Pilots, Order of Daedalians, Washington Nat. Monument Soc. Clubs: Cosmos, Alfalfa, Alibi. Author: Carrying the Fire, 1974; Flying to the Moon and Other Strange Places, 1976. Office: Smithsonian Instn Washington DC 20560

COLLINS, MICHAEL DEMAR, landscaping co. exec.; b. Southampton, N.Y., Oct. 26, 1944; s. Thomas Louden and Anna Elizabeth (Miller) C.; A.A.S., SUNY, 1964; B.S., Okla. State U., 1968; m. Janice M. Sanders, Nov. 24, 1967; 1 son, Brendan deMar. Mgr., Whitmore, Worsley, Inc., Amagansett, N.Y., 1969-72; gen. mgr. The Bayberry Inc., Amagansett, 1972-79, Marder's Landscaping, Inc., East Hampton, N.Y., 1979—. Mem. Springs Citizens Planning com., 1978-79; mem. Springs Fire Dept., 1965—. Mem. Nature Conservancy (chmn. 1979). Presbyterian. Office: 745 A Fire Place Rd East Hampton NY 11937

COLLINS, MICHAEL JAMES, ins. co. exec.; b. Orange, N.J., July 30, 1944; s. James Mitchell and Dorothy Colville (Dann) C.; B.A., Stanford U., 1967; grad. key man program Am. Inst. Fgn. Trade, 1968; M.B.A., Harvard U., 1970; 1 dau., Catherine Elise. Pres., Intracontinental Prodns., 1966-69; v.p. acquisition and new product devel. APC Industries, Inc., Austin, Tex., 1969-70; asst. to pres. Fidelity Union Life Ins. Co., Dallas, 1970-71, v.p. spl. ops., 1971-72, chmn. bd. dirs., pres., chief exec. officer, chief operating officer, 1972—, also dir.; pres., dir. Allianz Investment Corp., 1980—; partner Bucaroon Bay Assos., Vent-a Hood Co.; mem. exec. com. of bd. dirs. Allianz Am. Inc., 1979—; dir. First Nat. Bank Dallas, APC Industries, Inc. Subcom. chmn. Dallas Planning Commn.; bd. dirs., v.p. Carr P. Collins Found., Dallas; bd. dirs. Friends of Dallas Public Library, Goals for Dallas, Women for Change Center, Dallas; mem. Greater Dallas Planning Council; bd. dirs., trustee, co-chmn. fin. com., host Sta. KERA-TV, Public Broadcasting Service, Dallas; asso. mem. bd. dirs., mem. found. bd. So. Meth. U. Sch. Bus.; mem. devel. bd. Thanks-Giving Sq., Dallas; founder, trustee U.S.A. Film Festival, Dallas. Recipient Douglas MacArthur Freedom medal; Public Service commendation USCG; named 1 of 5 Outstanding Young Leaders of Dallas, Nation's Bus. mag.; named an Outstanding Young Man Am., U.S. Jaycees, 1978. Mem. Am. Council on Germany, Central Bus. Dist. Assn. (exec. com.), Dallas C. of C., Dallas Assembly, Dallas Citizens Council, Dallas Council World Affairs, Tex. Life Ins. Assn. (gov.), Young Pres.'s Orgn., Aardvark Soc., Common Cause, Five Hundred, Inc., Museum Modern Art N.Y., Cousteau Soc., Clubs: Bent Tree Country, City, Harvard, Petroleum, Preston Trail Golf, Idlewild, Stanford, Terpsichorean, Willow Bend Polo and Hunt. Office: 1511 Bryan St PO Box 500 Dallas TX 75221

COLLINS, RICHARD ANTHONY, data processing exec.; b. Lake Forest, Ill., Sept. 19, 1931; s. Anthony D. and Alice A. (Luedke) Czaikowski; B.A. magna cum laude, Augustana Coll., 1956; M.B.A., U. Wis., 1957, postgrad., 1966-70; m. Joan V. Krapfel, Apr. 17, 1965; children—Craig R., Clark A. Econ. statistician Eastman Kodak, Rochester, N.Y., 1957-59; mgr. mktg. research Ritter Co., mfr. dental and med. equipment, Rochester, N.Y., 1959-63; mktg. research supr. Oscar Mayer & Co., meat packing, Madison, Wis., 1964-66; mktg. program coordinator U. Wis. Extension, Madison, 1966-68; prof. U. Wis., Whitewater, 1968-72; mktg. exec. Anchor Savs. & Loan Assn., Madison, 1972-73; EFTS project dir. Fed. Home Loan Bank Bd., 1973-74; dir. EFT projects Credit Union Nat. Assn., Madison, 1974-76, v.p. fin. systems, 1976-78; exec. v.p. Cunadata Corp., Madison, 1978-80; v.p. mktg. Services Clark Sutton Assos., Inc., fin. cons., Madison, 1980—; ad hoc prof. mktg. programs for small bus. U. Wis. Extension, 1970-73; instr. Savings and Loan Inst. courses, 1965-72; Served with AUS, 1949-53. Mem. Am. Mktg. Assn. (chpt. seminar chmn. 1972-73). Author: (with George L. Herpel) Specialty Advertising in Marketing, 1972. Home: 2812 Waunona Way Madison WI 53713 Office: 802 W Broadway Suite L8-A Madison WI 53713

COLLINS, RICHARD ARTHUR, JR., newspaper exec.; b. Augusta, Ga., May 27, 1927; s. Richard Arthur and Margaret Lucille (Slater) C.; A.B., DePaul U., 1951; postgrad. Medill Sch. Journalism, Northwestern U., 1952-56, U. Chgo., 1959; m. Nancy Virginia Quinn, Oct. 6, 1951; children—Nanette V., Adrienne V., Marietta T., Mark R., Promotion asst. Chgo. Daily News, 1952-59; mgr. public services Chgo. Sun-Times, Chgo. Daily News, 1959-64; spl. events mgr. Halle Bros. Co., Cleve., 1964-65; circulation sales promotion mgr. Cleve. Press, 1965-69; asst. promotion mgr. Boston Globe, 1969-75, promotion dir., 1975—. Mem. Marblehead (Mass.) Hist. Commn., 1972—, chmn., 1975—. Served with U.S. Army, 1944-46. Mem. Internat. Newspaper Promotion Assn. (dir. Eastern region, sec.-treas. 1976-77, v.p. 1977-79, pres., 1979-80), internat. dir. 1980—), Acad. TV Arts and Scis. Roman Catholic. Club: Boston Yacht. Home: 269 W Shore Dr Marblehead MA 01945 Office: Boston Globe Boston MA 02107

COLLINS, ROGER WAYNE, mfg. co. exec.; b. Moline, Ill., Mar. 12, 1943; s. William Fredrick and Norma Theresa (Aguglia) C.; B.S., U. Ill., 1966; M. Ops. Research, Tulane U., 1972; m. Ellen Anne Evans, Aug. 8, 1964; children—Alice Norma, Maureen Barbara. Commd. 2 lt. U.S. Army, 1969, advanced through grades to major., 1975; ret., 1976; with Gen. Electric Co., 1976—, program mgr. for personnel systems research, Washington, 1978—. Decorated Bronze Star. Mem. Ops. Research Soc. Am., Data Processing Mgmt. Assn. Home: 5708 Heming Ave Springfield VA 22151 Office: 777 14th St NW Washington DC 20005

COLLINS, RUSSELL MAUL, JR., ins. co. exec.; b. St. Paul, June 15, 1933; s. Russell M. and Mary Collins; B.S. in Math., M.I.T., 1955; postgrad. U. Munster (Ger.), 1955, U. Tubingen (Ger.), 1956, U. Minn., 1956-57; m. Karla, Dec. 21, 1956; children—Russell, Richard, Renate. Actuary asst. Minn. Mutual Life Ins. Co., 1957-60, asst. actuary, 1960-64, asso. actuary, 1964, actuary, 1964-70, sec., v.p., 1966-68, v.p., 1968-70; actuary v.p. head actuary dept. Western Life

Ins. Co., St. Paul, 1970-73, sr. v.p. ins. ops., 1973-74; sr. v.p. ins. ops. St. Paul Life Ins. Co., 1973-74; v.p. J.C. Penney Fin. Services, N.Y.C., 1974—; dir. J.C. Penney Life Ins. Co., Great Am. Res. Ins. Co., J.C. Penney Casualty Ins. Co., J.C. Penney Reins. Co. Bd. dirs. St. Paul Human Resources Planning Council, 1969-74, sec., 1973; bd. dirs. Goodwill Industries, St. Paul, 1970-74. Danforth fellow, 1955-57; Fulbright scholar, 1955-56. Fellow Soc. Actuaries; mem. Am. Acad. Actuaries, Internat. Actuarial Assn., Nat. Assn. Securities Dealers. Lutheran. Clubs: St. Paul Athletic, North Oaks Golf, Minn., Greenwich Country. Office: 1301 Ave of Americas New York NY 10019

COLLINS, WILLIAM FINN, metals co. exec.; b. Edgar, Wis., May 5, 1919; s. Francis E. and Mary (Finn) C.; B.A., U. Wis., 1942, LL.B., 1942; m. Jacqueline Knee, Jan. 14, 1944; children—Michael, Katherine, Alexis, Benjamin, Sarah. Admitted to Wis. bar, 1945, N.Y. bar, 1947; asso. firm Cravath, Swaine & Moore, N.Y.C., 1945-52; asst. gen. counsel Revere Copper & Brass, Inc., Rome, N.Y., 1952-55, gen. counsel, N.Y.C., 1955-60, sec., 1960-71, dir., 1965—, v.p., 1965-67, exec. v.p. legal and fin., 1967-71, pres., mem. exec. com., 1971—, chief exec. officer, 1975—; v.p., dir. Ormet Corp.; dir. Servomation Corp., Copper Devel. Assn. Served to lt. USNR, 1942-45. Decorated Commendation medal. Mem. Am., N.Y. State bar assns., Order of Coif. Home: 136 E Hunting Ridge Rd Stamford CT 06903 Office: 605 3d Ave New York NY 10016

COLLINSWORTH, EVEN THOMAS, JR., corp. exec.; b. Knoxville, Tenn., Oct. 11, 1921; s. E.T. and Lillian (Smith) C.; B.S., U. Tenn., 1943; M.B.A., Harvard, 1950; m. Edith Merory, June 5, 1949; children—Even III, Eden, Sean. Sales mgr. Worthington Corp., Harrison, N.J., 1943-48; dir. bus. research Monsanto Chem. Co., St. Louis, 1950-52; pres., dir. Velsicol Chem. Corp., Chgo., 1953-59; chmn. bd. Velsicol Internat. Corp., 1955-59; pres., dir. Fansteel Metall. Corp., North Chicago, 1960-61; v.p. Armour & Co., Chgo., 1963-66, group v.p. indsl. products and agrl. chem. internat., 1966-68, group v.p. indsl. products and grocery products, 1968-69, exec. v.p., dir., 1969-72; pres., chief exec. officer Bliss & Laughlin Industries, Inc., Oak Brook, Ill., 1972—; dir. Bliss & Laughlin Corp., Sundstrand Corp., Bucyrus-Erie Co., Nicor Inc. Bd. dirs. Am. Grad. Sch. Internat. Mgmt.; trustee Glenwood Sch. for Boys. Registered profl. engr., N.J. Mem. Chgo. Council on Fgn. Relations (dir.); Chgo. Assn. Commerce and Industry (dir.), Conf. Bd. (dir.), Alpha Chi Sigma, Phi Gamma Delta. Clubs: Mid-Am., Chgo. (Chgo.); Waukegan (Ill.) Yacht. Home: 33 Briarwood S Oak Brook IL 60521 Office: 122 W 22d St Oak Brook IL 60521

COLLMER, RUSSELL CRAVENER, data processing exec.; b. Guatemala, Jan. 2, 1924; s. G. Russell and Constance (Cravener) C.; B.S., U. N.M., 1951; postgrad. Calif. Inst. Tech., 1943-44; M.S., State U. Iowa, 1955; m. Ruth Hannah Adams, Mar. 4, 1950; 1 son, Reed Alan. Staff mem. Mass. Inst. Tech., Lincoln Lab., Lexington, 1955-57; mgr. systems modeling, computer dept. Gen. Electric, Phoenix, 1957-59; mgr. ARCAS Thompson Ramo Wooldridge, Inc., Canoga Park, Cal., 1959-62; asso. mgr. tech. dir. CCIS-70 Bunker-Ramo Corp., 1962-64; sr. asso. Planning Research Corp., Los Angeles, 1964-65; pres. R. Collmer Assos., Benson, Ariz., 1965—; pres. Benson Econ. Enterprises Corp., 1968-69. Lectr. computer scis. Pima Community Coll., Tucson, 1970—. Served with USAAC, 1942-46, to capt. USAF, 1951-53. Mem. IEEE, Am. Meteorol. Soc., Assn. for Computing Machinery, Phi Delta Theta, Kappa Mu Epsilon. Republican. Baptist. Home: 191 E 8th St Benson AZ 85602 Office: PO Box 864 Benson AZ 85602

COLMAN, EUGENE WENDELL (PETE), mktg. co. exec.; b. Pasadena, Calif., Oct. 14, 1916; s. Fred O. and Ruth (Myers) C.; m. Maralyn Lee Brunk, Mar. 19, 1962; children—Sally Anne Colman Smolinski, Jean Susanne Colman Grodzen, Richard Michael, Cendra Lee, Christine Diane, James G.W., Debra Lynn. Profl. motorcycle racer, 1933-48; machinist Vard Engring., Pasadena, 1937-38; expt. insp. Wright Aero. Co., Patterson, N.J., 1938-39; asst. chief insp. Kinner Motors, Glendale, Calif., 1939-40; contact engr. Lockheed Aircraft Co., Burbank, Calif., 1940-42; v.p., dir. Johnson Motors, Inc., Pasadena, 1948-69, BSA Motorcycle Corp., Duarte, Calif., 1965-74, Triumph Motorcycle Corp., Duarte and Balt., 1969-74, Birmingham Small Arms Co., Inc., 1969-74; v.p. engring. Top Gear Access, Inc., Duarte and Balt., 1969-74; pres. Motorcycle Industry Services, Newport Beach, Calif., 1974-77, Sachs Motors Corp. USA, Cleve., 1977-78, Coleman & Assos., Newport Beach, 1978—; mem. Motorcycle Industry Council, Washington, 1964—, pres., 1970-72. Bd. dirs. Motorcycle Safety Found., 1973-74. Served as cadet A.C., 1942-43, to 1st lt. USAAC, 1943-45. Mem. Am. Motorcycle Assn. (trustee 1964-69), Soc. Automotive Engrs. (motorcycle com. 1969—). Home: 114 Coral Ave PO Box 10 Balboa Island CA 92662 Office: PO Box 10 Balboa Island CA 92662

COLMAN, MARALYN LEE BRUNK, cons. co. exec.; b. Ponca City, Okla., Nov. 13, 1939; d. Arthur and Twyla Marguerite (Kennedy) Brunk; student U. Calif. at Irvine; m. E.W. Pete Coman, Mar. 19, 1962; children—Richard Michael, Cendra Lee Colman Stewart, Christine Diane, James G.W., Debra Lynn. Account exec. Merceds Messenger News, Los Angeles Herald Examiner, Swiston Silver Co., 1958-61; research dir. Top Gear, Inc., Duarte, Calif. and Montclair, N.J., 1968-69; personnel and systems mgr. Colman Co., Claremont, Calif., 1970-72; pres., owner Industry Services, Ltd., Newport Beach, Calif., 1972-78, M.C.C., Inc., Newport Beach, 1978-80; specialized agt. N.Y. Life, Fullerton, Calif., 1980—; dir. Community Investments Corp.; cons. U.S. Dept. Commerce. Mem. Nat. Assn. Female Execs. (dir.), Women Enterpreneuers Assn., Internat. Orgn. Women Enterpreneurs, Motorcycle Industry Council, Internat. Trade League, Nat. Assn. Women Bus. Owners, Nat. Assn. Life Underwriters, Women's Research Inst. Bus. columnist. Home: 1227 S 10th St Arcadia CA 91006 Office: 8383 Wilshire Blvd Beverly Hills CA also 1440 N Harbor Blvd Fullerton CA 92635

COLMAN, MARTIN H., economist, fin. co. exec.; b. Tucson, Aug. 28, 1951; s. Martin and Alpha Victoria (Beede) C.; m. Mirka Nadraszky, Dec. 15, 1972. Partner, Colman & Assos., Los Angeles, 1970-74; pres. Indsl. Funding Corp., Beverly Hills, Calif., 1974; chmn. bd. Calif. Leisure Industries Inc., Beverly Hills, 1976—. Dir. task force Citizens Mgmt. Rev. Com., Los Angeles Unified Sch. Dist., 1976; chmn. subcom., budget and fin. com. Calif. Dem. party, 1977—. Mem. Beverly Hills C. of C., Los Angeles World Affairs Council. Author: Comecon—Is It Economically Viable?, 1977; Social Concern and Fiscal Responsibility, 1976; The U.S. and the Third World, 1976. Home: 211 Vance St Pacific Palisades CA 90272 Office: 9542 Santa Monica Blvd Beverly Hills CA 90210

COLMAN, SAGER TILDEN, export mgmt. co. exec.; b. Rio de Janeiro, Brazil, Sept. 15, 1923 (parents Am. citizens); s. George Tilden and Harriett Louise (Sager) C.; B.S. in Elec. Engring., Purdue U., 1948; m. Lucy Evelyn Gorham, July 14, 1951; children—Evelyn Louise, Paul Tilden. Export mgr. Sq. D Co., Secaucus, N.J., 1948-64; mgr. Internat. div. Fischer & Porter Co., Warminster, Pa., 1964-65, corp. sec., 1965-66; pres. Internat. Controls Co., Inc., Warrington, Pa., 1966—; cons. on internat. mktg., 1968-72; chmn. internat. com. 1978 Internat. Expn., Phila. Served with U.S. Army, 1941-45. Decorated Bronze Star. Mem. Instrument Soc. Am., Internat. Trade Devel. Assn. of Bucks County (founder, 1st pres.), Internat. Indsl. Mktg. Club (pres. N.Y.C. 1964-66). Democrat. Presbyterian. Clubs: Doylestown Country; Secaucus Rotary (v.p. 1960-64). Office: 2099 Maple Ave Warrington PA 18976

COLMENARES, EDUARDO, banker; b. Colombia, Apr. 6, 1937; s. Nicolas and Rosa (Abrajim) C.; came to U.S., 1964; B.Sc., U. Calif., Berkeley, 1959, cert. Exec. Program, 1978; divorced; 1 son, Eddie. Sec. of fin. City of Cucuta (Colombia), 1961-63; dir. econ. planning State of North Santander (Colombia), 1964; with Bank of Am., 1964—, v.p. heavy equipment group, Chgo. and San Francisco, 1974-76, v.p., group head, sr. office for Latin Am., Chgo., 1976—; hon. founding prof. econs. U. Francisco Paula Santander, 1963-64; mem. Govt. Task Force on Econ. Integration, Colombia-Venezula. Trustee Mcpl. High Sch., State U. Santander, 1962-64. Mem. World Trade Assn., Am. Mgmt. Assn. Roman Catholic. Clubs: Hunters, Tennis; Commerce (Colombia); Internat. Bus. (Chgo.). Office: care Bank of Am—Sears Tower 233 S Wacker St Chicago IL 60606

COLMENERO, CHARLES, agrl. machinery co. exec.; b. N.Y.C., Dec. 30, 1931; s. Aurelio and Consuelo María (Fernández) C.; B.S., N.Y.U., 1957; student U. Miami, 1957-58, Fairleigh Dickinson U., 1962-63; m. Sabra Ann Pryor, Feb. 20, 1954; children—Laura, Elena, Charles, Elisa, Mercedes, Anita, Aurelio. Indsl. engr. Pan-American, Miami, Fla., 1957-58; mgr. systems and procedures Radiation, Inc., Palm Bay, Fla., 1958-62; gen. analyst Continental Can Co., N.Y.C., 1962-64; mgr. logistics and ops. Xerox Corp. (Latin-Am.), Rochester, N.Y., 1964-68; dir. ops. Xerox De Mexico, S.A., Mexico City, 1968-71; exec. vice-pres., chief exec. officer Koehn Mfg. Inc., Watertown, S.D., 1971—; chmn. Mattson's Inc., Grafton, N.D., Repsel Assos. Inc., Watertown; dir. Daktronics, Inc., Brookings, S.D. Served with USAF, 1951-55. Mem. S.D. Mfrs. Assn. (charter dir., chmn. articles and by-laws com., chmn. membership com.), Watertown Mgmt. Council, Farm Equipment Mfrs. Assn., Nat. Assn. Mfrs., Am. Legion, Alpha Kappa Psi. Republican. Presbyterian. Club: Elks. Author: Technology - Its Impact on Enterprise, 1959. Office: 202 NW 1st Ave Watertown SD 57201

COLONEY, WAYNE HERNDON, civil engr.; b. Bradenton, Fla., Mar. 15, 1925; s. Herndon Percival and Mary Adore (Cramer) C.; B.C.E. summa cum laude, Ga. Inst. Tech., 1950; m. Anne Elizabeth Benedict, June 21, 1950; 1 dau., Mary Adore. Project engr. Fla. Rd. Dept., Tallahassee, 1950-55; hwy. engr. Gibbs & Hill, Inc., Guatemala, 1955-57, project engr., Tampa, Fla., 1957-59; project engr. J.E. Greiner Co., Tampa, 1959-62, asso., 1962-63; partner Barrett, Daffin, Bishop & Coloney, Tallahassee, 1963-66, Barrett Daffin & Coloney, Tallahassee, 1966-70; pres., gen. mgr. Wayne H. Coloney Co., Inc., Tallahassee 1970-77, chmn., chief exec. officer, 1977—; chmn., chief exec. officer The Coloney Co., cons. engrs., 1978—; pres. Tesseract Corp., 1975—; dir. Internat. Enterprises, Inc., 1967-73, pres., 1965-68. Pres., Fla. Heritage Found., 1967; chmn. Area Vocat. Adv. Com., 1965-79; pres. Leon County United Fund, 1971-72; bd. dirs. Springtime Tallahassee, 1970-72; bd. dirs. Lemoyne Art Found., 1973-75, v.p., 1974-75. Served with AUS, 1943-46; ETO. Registered profl. engr., Fla., Ga., Ala., N.C., Nat. Council Engr. Examiners. Fellow ASCE; mem. Nat. Soc. Profl. Engrs., Fla. Engring. Soc. (sr.), Koseme Soc., Anak, Phi Kappa Phi Omicron Delta Kappa, Sigma Alpha Epsilon, Tau Beta Pi. Episcopalian (vestry). Contbr. articles on san. sewage disposal to tech. jours. Patentee in field. Home: Argyle House 2540 Marston Rd Tallahassee FL 32312 Office: PO Box 5258 Tallahassee FL 32301

COLUSSY, DAN ALFRED, airline co. exec.; b. Pitts., June 3, 1931; s. Dan and Viola E. (Andreis) C.; B.S., U.S. Coast Guard Acad., 1953; M.B.A., Harvard, 1965; m. Helene Graham, June 3, 1953; children—Deborah, Jennifer. Applications engr. Jet Propulsion div. Gen. Electric Co., 1956-63; dir. ops. Am. Airlines, N.Y.C., 1965-66; v.p. mktg. N.E. Airlines, Boston, 1966-69; v.p., group head Wells, Rich, Green Advt. Agy., N.Y.C., 1969-70; v.p. mktg. devel. Pan Am. World Airways, N.Y.C., 1970-72, v.p. passenger mktg., 1972-74, sr. v.p. passenger mktg., 1974, sr. v.p. field ops., 1974-75, sr. v.p. mktg. and services, 1975-76, exec. v.p. mktg. and services, 1976-78, pres., chief operating officer, 1978—, also dir. Bd. dirs. N.Y. Conv. and Visitors Bur., USCGA Found.; trustee St. Francis Coll.; dir. N.Y. com. U.S. Ski Team; mem. N.Y.C. Mayor's Adv. Council; mem. travel and tourism industry adv. council of Senate Subcom. on Mcht. Marine and Tourism. Served to lt. USCG, 1953-56. Recipient Travelsphere award, 1976. Clubs: Sky, Larchmond Yacht, Harvard, Wings. Office: Pan Am Airways 200 Park Ave New York NY 10017*

COLVIN, JAMES MICHAEL, constrn. co. exec.; b. Shreveport, La., Mar. 21, 1952; s. James Henry and L'Marie (Bayles) C.; B.S. in Bldg. Constrn., N.E. La. U., 1974; m. Judy Kay Coon, Aug. 10, 1974. Cost analyst Ford, Bacon, Davis Constrn. Corp., Monroe, La., 1974-75, chief cost analyst, 1975-78, asst. to mgr. project mgmt., 1978-79, proposals mgr., 1979—. West Monroe rep. N.E. La. Indsl. Devel. Bd. Mem. Am. Assn. Cost Engrs., Project Mgmt. Inst., Am. Inst. Constructors, N.L.U. Bldg. Constrn. Alumni Found., Sigma Lamda Chi. Republican. So. Baptist. Clubs: Jaycees, Masons. Contbr. articles to profl. jours. Home: 207 DuPont Dr West Monroe LA 71291 Office: 3901 Jackson St PO Box 1762 Monroe LA 71201

COLWELL, BUNDY, mortgage banker; b. Ely, Nev., Aug. 24, 1912; s. Alfred Bundy and Pearl (O'Brien) C.; B.S. in Bus. Adminstrn., U. So. Calif., 1934; J.D., 1936; m. Anne Foster Jackson, Aug. 28, 1940; children—Stephen B., Penelope Anne. Admitted to Cal. bar, 1936; individual practice law, Los Angeles, 1936—; formerly v.p., dir. Cal. Fed.Svs. and Loa Assn., Los Angeles; chmn. The Colwell Co., mortgage bankers, Los Angeles. Served with USAAF, 1943-44. Mem. Am., Los Angeles bar assns., Nat. Assn. Real Estate Bds., Nat. Home Builders Inst., Nat. Inst. Real Estate Brokers, Mortgage Bankers Assn. Am. (gov., regional v.p.), Calif., So. Calif. mortgage bankers assns., U.S., Calif. Los Angeles chambers commerce, Alpha Kappa Psi, Phi Kappa Tau, Lambda Alpha, Phi Alpha Delta. Congregationalist (past moderator, trustee). Mason (Shriner). Clubs: Jonathan (Los Angeles); Trojan. Home: 4612 Vineta St La Canada CA 91011 Office: 3223 W 6th St Los Angeles CA 90020

COLYER, GILMORE CLIFTON, constrn. co. exec.; b. Jacksonville, Fla., Apr. 4, 1920; s. Robert Patten and Loula Parker (Smith) C.; student Auburn U., 1940-42; B.S., U. Fla., 1947; m. Elizabeth Schell, Dec. 27, 1941; children—Gilmore Clifton, Wilkie Schell, Robin Patten. Pres. G.C. Colyer & Co., Inc., Anniston, Ala., 1950—; dir. First Nat. Bank of Anniston. Trustee Internat. House, Jacksonville State U., 1968-71. Served with USMCR, 1942-45. Mem. Asso. Gen. Contractors of Am. (dir. Ala. 1970—), Anniston C. of C. (dir. 1958-73), Phi Delta Theta. Episcopalian (vestryman 1952-71). Club: Anniston Country (pres. 1971-73). Home: 535 Hillyer High Rd Anniston AL 36201 Office: 413 Quintard Ave Anniston AL 36201

COLYER, RALPH JOSEPH, telephone directory co. exec.; b. Newark, June 2, 1935; s. Ralph Mitchell and Violet May (Kreideweis) C.; B.S., Rutgers U., 1964; m. Grace Margaret Smith, Dec. 21, 1957; children—Donna Marie, Ralph Joseph, Lisa Rose. Accounting supr. N.J. Bell Telephone Co., Newark, 1953-64; staff accountant Ernst & Ernst, Newark, 1964-66, sr. accountant, 1966-68, supr., 1968-70; comptroller Nat. Telephone Directory Corp., Union, N.J., 1970-72, treas., 1972—, v.p., 1979—. Served with U.S. Army, 1954-56; ETO. C.P.A., N.J. Mem. N.J. Soc. C.P.A.'s, Am. Inst. C.P.A.'s, Nat. Assn. Accountants. Episcopalian. Home: 18 Baldwin Rd Edison NJ 08817 Office: Nat Telephone Directory Corp 1050 Galloping Hill Rd Union NJ 07083

COMBES, JAMES HOMER, financial exec.; b. Oak Park, Ill., Sept. 17, 1938; s. Homer McNeil and Virginia Elizabeth C.; B.S. in Indsl. Engring., Ill. Inst. Tech., 1960; M.B.A., Harvard U., 1962; m. Dorothy Anne Dziak, Aug. 29, 1959; children—Candace, Cheryl, Kevin, Stacey. Treas., Nat. Cash Register Co., Dayton, Ohio, 1962-75; exec. v.p. fin. Hertz Corp., N.Y.C., 1975-77; sr. v.p. fin. and adminstrn. AM Internat., Inc., Los Angeles, 1977—; mem. emerging problems com. Fin. Acctg. Standards Bd. Mem. Am. Mgmt. Assn., Fin. Execs. Inst. (nat. dir.), Machinery and Allied Products Inst. (mem. fin. council). Home: 2906 Elvido Dr Los Angeles CA 90049 Office: AM Internat Inc 1900 Ave of Stars Los Angeles CA 90067

COMBS, AUSTIN OLIN, real estate and ins. broker; b. Harr, Tenn., Aug. 5, 1917; s. Clyde Harmon and Bess (Widner) C.; student Stetson Bus. Coll.; m. Marjorie Thayer Mason, Dec. 28, 1947; 1 dau. by previous marriage, Hope; 1 dau., Carolyn; adopted children—Dianne, Marjorie, Dunnan Dowling III. Vice pres. Kipp & Combs, Inc., 1952-54; partner Combs-Sibley, 1954; pres. Austin O. Combs, Inc., Daytona Beach, Fla., 1954—; airplane pilot. Mem. Air Def. Command, Air Res. Adv. Bd., 1946-47. Trustee Volusia County Heart Assn., 1955-56, pres., 1965; trustee, chmn. bd. visitors Embry-Riddle Aero. U.; bd. dirs. YMCA; bd. dirs., pres. Fla. Internat. Festival Com. Served with USAAF, 1944-46. Mem. Flying Realtors, Fla. Aero Club, Aircraft Owners and Pilots Assn., Daytona Beach C. of C., Tomoka Gems and Minerals Soc. (past pres.), Internat. Platform Assn., Quiet Birdmen, UN Assn. U.S. Clubs: Masons, Shriners, Jesters, Elks, Moose, Rotary (past pres.); Elinor Village Country (past pres., dir.), Daytona Beach Yacht, (Daytona Beach); Miami Springs Executive, Oceanside Country. Home: 3756 Cardinal Blvd Daytona Beach FL 32019 Office: 2008 S Atlantic Ave Daytona Beach FL 32018

COMBS, DOUGLAS LEE, magazine pub. exec.; b. Cin., Dec. 16, 1946; s. Francis G. and Nellie Marie (Lauterwasser) C.; B.S. with honors in Advt., U. Fla., 1972; M.B.A., U. Ala., Birmingham, 1979; m. Sonya Rea Horowitz, July 17, 1969. Dir., Combs & Assocs., Gainesville, Fla., 1971; communications dir. Gainesville C. of C., 1972; dir. pub. relations Blount Bros. Corp., Montgomery, Ala., 1973-77; dir. promotions Southern Living, Decorating & Craft Ideas, Progressive Farmer mags., Birmingham, 1977—. Bd. dirs. United Appeal, 1975—. Served with Intelligence Corps, U.S. Army, 1964-68; Vietnam. Mem. Public Relations Soc. Am., Direct Mail Mktg. Assn., Soc. Profl. Journalists, Am. Soc. Personnel Adminstrs., Assn. M.B.A. Execs., Alpha Delta Sigma. Republican. Clubs: Econchati Toastmasters (pres.); Sertoma (Birmingham). Home: 3101 Lorna Rd Suite 1224 Birmingham AL 35216 Office: 820 Shades Creek Pkwy Birmingham AL 35209

COMBS, PAUL HOWARD, bus. exec.; b. New Brunswick, N.J., Oct. 23, 1925; s. Howard Leon and Lillian Marie (Knudson) C.; B.A. in Bus. Adminstrn., Rutgers U., 1950; m. Shirley Bertenshaw, July 21, 1962; children—Sharon (Mrs. Louis Martinez), Paul Clifford, Amy B., Debra A.; step-children, Norman Wiseman, Russell Wiseman. Purchasing exec. M.W. Kellogg Co., Houston, 1955-62; exec. v.p. Youngstown Steel Tank Co. (Ohio), 1963-64; mem. corporate staff ITT, N.Y.C., 1965-71; v.p., sec., dir. Chautauqua Hardware Corp., Jamestown, N.Y., 1971-78; pres., dir. Arbor Industries, Inc., Jamestown Lounge Co., 1978—; v.p., sec., dir. CHC Industries, Inc., N.Y.C., Period Brass, Inc., Falconer, N.Y. Decorative Hardware, Inc., Lincolnwood, Ill., 1971-78. Chmn. adv. bd. Jamestown Gen. Hosp.; bd. dirs. United Way Jamestown, Jamestown Labor/Mgmt. Com. Served with USAAF, 1943-46. Decorated Air medal with oak leaf cluster: featured in 1973 Newsweek Mag. article for devel. employee compensation. Mem. Mfrs. Assn. Jamestown Area (chmn. utilities com., dir.). Methodist. Mason. Author: Handbook of International Purchasing, 1971, 2d edit., 1976. Home: W Oak Hill Rd Jamestown NY 14701 Office: 40 Winsor St Jamestown NY 14701

COMEAU, CARL VICTOR, ins. co. exec.; b. Digby, N.S., Can., July 10, 1943; came to U.S., 1963, naturalized, 1968; s. Victor G. and Helen B. (Melanson) C.; B.S., St. Patrick's Coll., 1962; m. Helen M. Ratafia, Mar. 30, 1971; children—Lynn, Donna. Sr. ins. cons. Nat. Health and Welfare Retirement Assn., N.Y.C., 1962-70; partner Furman McDonagh & Comeau, N.Y.C., 1970-75; mgr. Comeau Assos., Provident Mut. Life Ins. Co., Waterville, Maine, 1975—; pres. Actuarial Cons. of Maine. Dir. profl. div. Mid-Maine United Way, 1979—; bd. dirs. Am. Cancer Soc., 1980—; chmn. bd. dirs. Greater Waterville Salvation Army, 1980—. Mem. Nat. Assn. Life Underwriters, Gen. Agts.-Mgrs. Assn. Democrat. Roman Catholic. Club: Waterville Country. Home: Great Pond Belgrade ME 04903 Office: 15 College Ave Waterville ME 04901

COMER, DONALD, III, textile co. exec.; b. N.Y.C., June 23, 1938; s. Donald and Isabel (Anderson) C.; B.S., U. Ala., 1962; m. Jane Stephens, May 4, 1962; children—Jason Legare, Luke McDonald, Carrie St. George. With Cowikee Mills, Eufaula, Ala., 1962-75, v.p., 1966-68, pres., treas., dir., 1968-75; pres., treas., chief exec. officer, dir. Avondale Mills, Sylacauga, Ala., 1975—; dir. Techsonic Industries, Eufaula, Ala.; dir. 1st Nat. Bank of Birmingham (Ala.); adv. bd. Am. Mutual Ins. Co., Boston. Trustee Avondale Ednl. and Charitable Found., Inc.; bd. dirs. Ala. Symphony Orch., Ala. Safety Council, Choccolocco council Boy Scouts Am.; past chmn. Ala. Ethics Commn. Served with USAF, 1961-64. Mem. Ga. Textile Mfrs. Assn. (dir.), Ala. Textile Mfrs. Assn. (pres., dir. 1967-73), Am. Yarn Spinners Assn. (past sec., dir.), Am. Textile Mfrs. Inst. (dir.), Inst. Textile Tech. (trustee). Clubs: Coosa Valley Country (Sylacauga, Ala.); Mountain Brook Country (Birmingham). Home: 1500 Stone Hill Rd Sylacauga AL 35150 Office: Avondale Mills Avondale Ave Sylacauga AL 35150

COMER, EVAN PHILIP, chem. and metall. co. exec.; b. Cumberland Gap, Tenn., May 29, 1927; s. Evan M. and Margaret Nola (Estep) C.; B.A. in Psychology, Carson-Newman Coll., 1948; M.A., Columbia U., 1949; m. Mary Blanc, Aug. 28, 1948; children—Vivian Kresslein, Jane. Asst. prof. psychology Furman U., Greenville, S.C., 1949-52, dir. student personnel and placement, 1949-52; supervisory conf. leader Union Carbide Nuclear Co., Oak Ridge, Tenn., 1953-55; instr. U. Tenn., Knoxville, 1955-56; plant personnel mgr. Foote Mineral Co., Sunbright, Va. plant, 1956-58, company mgr. safety and tng. Exton, Pa., 1958-59, dir. indsl. relations, 1959-63, v.p. indsl. relations, 1963-67, v.p. adminstrn., 1969-70, dir., 1970—, v.p., gen. mgr. chems. and minerals div., 1970-80, pres. and chief exec. officer, 1980—; pres. Southeastern Community Coll., Whiteville, N.C., 1967-69; vice chmn. bd. Met. Assos. of Phila., 1960-67; dir. Phila. Mfg. Mut. Ins. Co., 1981—; adv. bd. Liberty Mut. Ins. Co. Mem. bd. deacons Second Baptist Ch. of Germantown (Pa.), 1960-65; bd. dirs. ARC of Columbus County (N.C.), 1967-69, Family Service of Chester County (Pa.), 1964-67; adv. bd. Carson-Newman Coll. Served with USN, 1945-46. Mem. Am. Inst. Mining and Metall. Engrs., Phila. Indsl. Relations Assn. (dir. 1959-67), Mfg. Chemists Assn. (dir. 1969-71), Chester County Indsl. Relations Assn. (pres. 1964-67). Republican. Baptist. Clubs: Mining of N.Y.C.; Wilmington

(N.C.) Execs. Contbr. articles to various bus. and indsl. publs. Office: Foote Mineral Co Route 100 Exton PA 19341

COMERFORD, PHILIP MICHAEL, banker; b. Toledo, Apr. 20, 1931; s. L.C. and Regina M. (Heiler) C.; Asso. Sci., Jackson Jr. Coll., 1950; B.B.A., U. Mich., 1952, M.B.A., 1953; m. Diana Lange, Feb. 7, 1953; children—Philip Michael, Cynthia, David, Andrew. Audit mgr. Price Waterhouse & Co., 1957-65; asst. to treas. Standard Pressed Steel Co., Jenkintown, Pa., 1965-68; pres., dir. Eastern Bancorp., Phila., 1969—; pres., dir. State Nat. Bank of Md. Fin. chmn. Christ the King Regional Sch. Bd., 1972-75; mem. Haddonfield (N.J.) Bd. Edn., 1977-78. Served with USCGR, 1953-56; now comdr. Res. C.P.A., D.C., Pa. Mem. Am. Inst. C.P.A.'s, Pa. Inst. C.P.A.'s, Md. Bankers Assn. (govt. relations com.), Phila. Jaycees (pres. 1965-66, chmn. bd. 1966-67), Pa. Jaycees (state v.p. 1966-67), U. Mich. Alumni Assn. (sec.-treas. 2d dist. 1976-77, dist. dir. 1977-80), Bethesda-Chevy Chase C. of C. (legis. com.). Clubs: U. Mich. Alumni of Phila. (pres. 1973-75, dist. rep. 1975-77), U. Mich. Alumni of Washington (gov.), Union League (Phila.); Rotary; Vesper; Bethesda Country; Tavistock Country. Home: 7715 Savannah Dr Bethesda MD 20034 Office: 11616 Rockville Pike Rockville MD 20852

COMM, EDWARD DANIEL, engring. exec.; b. Fargo, N.D., Jan. 10, 1912; s. Otto Ben and Emily (Riebhoff) C.; B.S., N.D. State U., 1933; grad. U.S. Army War Coll., 1953. Practice civil engring., N.D., 1933-40; commd. 1st lt. C.E., U.S. Army, 1940, advanced through grades to col., 1944, ret. phys. disability, 1967; served N. Africa, Italy, France, Germany, 1942-45; exec. asst. to Q.M. Gen. and dir. logistics, Washington, 1946-52; asst. chief of staff logistics, France, 1953-56; engr. U. S. Army Engr. Dist., Louisville, 1956-58; mem. Joint Chiefs Staff, Washington, 1958-60; comdg. officer Advanced Individual Tng. Regiment, Ft. Leonard Wood, Mo., 1960-62; spl. asst. to dep. chief staff for logistics Dept. Army, Washington, 1962-67; cons. to Dept. Def., Washington, 1967-69; now dir. Washington ops. Howard, Needles, Tammen & Bergendoff, cons. engrs.; mem. directorate Presdl. Task Force on Structure SSS, 1967. Decorated D.S.M., Legion of Merit with two oak leaf clusters, Bronze Star; officer Order Brit. Empire; Legion of Honor, Croix de Guerre (France); comdr. Crown of Italy; Medahla de Guerra (Brazil). Registered profl. engr. Fellow ASCE; mem. Soc. Am. Mil. Engrs., Amateur Trapshooting Assn., Phi Kappa Phi, Tau Beta Pi. Clubs: Army and Navy (Washington); Army-Navy Country (Arlington, Va.). Home: 1111 Army Navy Dr Arlington VA 22202 Office: PO Box 11259 Alexandria VA 22312

COMMON, FRANK BREADON, JR., lawyer; b. Montreal, Que., Can., Apr. 16, 1920; s. Frank Breadon and Ruth Louise (Lang) C.; Diploma in Engring., Royal Mil. Coll., 1940; B.C.L., McGill U., 1948; m. Katharine Ruth Laws, Sept. 7, 1946; children—Katharine Ruth, Anne Elizabeth, Frank Breadon (dec.), Diana Melanie, Ruth E., Jane, James Lang. Admitted to Canadian bar, 1948; mem. firm Montgomery, McMichael, Common, Howard, Forsyth and Kerr, and successor firms; now sr. partner firm Ogilvy, Renault; vice chmn. bd., dir. PHH Can. Services Inc., Canadian Corps., Ltd.; pres. Brown Boveri Realty Corp.; dir., dep. chmn., dir. Cadbury Schweppes Powell Ltd.; dir. PHH Leasing Ltd. (U.K.), PHH Services Ltd. (U.K.), Sun Alliance Ins. Co., N. Am. Car Can., Royal Bank Can., Selco Mining Corp. Ltd., CIBA-GEIGY Can., Beneficial Finance Co. of Can., PHH Group, Inc. (U.S.), Internat. Paper Sales Co., Inc.; sec., dir. Ralston Purina Can. Lectr. in law McGill U., 1953-59. Past pres., bd. dirs. Que. div. Canadian Red Cross. Alderman, commr. finance and public works City Of Westmount, 1959-62, acting mayor, 1961-62. Bd. govs. Montreal Gen. Hosp., Montreal Symphony Orch.; past chmn. and gov. Douglas Hosp.; founder, 1st pres., gov. Canadian Found. Ednl. Devel. Officer Royal Canadian Engrs., 1940-45. Mentioned-in-dispatches. Mem. Canadian Bar Assn. (council 1956-58), Canadian Tax Found., Mil. Engrs. Assn. Can. (past pres. Montreal br.), Grad. Soc. of McGill U. (dir.), McGill Alma Mater (faculty chmn.). Mem. United Ch. Can. (com. stewards). Clubs: Mount Royal, Mount Bruno Country; Brook (N.Y.C.), others. Home: Gleneagles Apt B-101 3940 Cote des Neiges Rd Montreal PQ H3H 1W2 Canada Office: 700 Place Ville Marie Montreal PQ H3B 1Z7 Canada

COMMONS, DORMAN L., shipping co. exec.; b. Denair, Calif., 1918; student Stanford U. Staff acct. John F. Forbes & Co., 1943-47; sr. v.p., dir. Douglas Oil Co., 1947-64; sr. v.p. fin., dir. Occidental Petroleum Co., 1964-72; pvt. practice fin. cons., 1972-73; pres., chief exec. officer, dir. Natomas Co., 1974—; chmn. bd., chief exec. officer dir. Am. Pres. Lines subs Natomas Co., 1977—. Office: 601 California St San Francisco CA 94108

COMPTON, SAMUEL BENTON, advt. exec.; b. Meyersdale, Pa., Apr. 12, 1929; s. Ward Samuel and Eva (Miller) C.; student pub. schs.; m. Christina Petrillo, Oct. 14, 1961; children—Jennifer, Melissa. Operator, W.S. Compton Brick Co., Salisbury, Pa., 1953-61; advt. cons., Salisbury, 1961-63; advt. and sales promotion mgr. Trion, Inc., McKees Rocks, Pa., 1963-66; advt. mgr. Continental div. Fisher Controls Co., Coraopolis, Pa., 1966-69; product mgr. promotional lines CPS Industries div. Papercraft Corp., Pitts., 1969; supr. advt. services PPG Industries, Pitts., 1969-70; dir. mktg. services Seasonall Industries, Indiana, Pa., 1970-71; mgr. advt. and sales promotion ITT Reznor, Mercer, Pa., 1971-77; dir. communications, municipal and utility div. Rockwell Internat., Pitts., 1977-79; mgr. mktg. communications Jerrold div. Gen. Instrument Corp., 1979—. Served with M.C., AUS, 1951-53. Mem. Water and Wastewater Equipment Mfrs. Assn. (pub. relations com.), Soc. Tech. Writers and Pubs. (sr.), Assn. Nat. Advertisers. Democrat. Mem. United Ch. of Christ. Home: 1139 Carroll Ln Sharon PA 16146 Office: Rockwell Internat 400 N Lexington Ave Pittsburgh PA 15208

COMPTON, WALTER A(MES), health care industry exec.; b. Elkhart, Ind., Apr. 22, 1911; s. Herman A. and Grace (Cooper) C.; A.B., Princeton, 1933; M.D., Harvard, 1937; m. Phoebe Emerson, June 22, 1935; children—Cynthia, Joan, Phoebe, Walter Ames, Gordon. Intern, Billings Hosp., 1938; med. and research dir. Miles Labs., Inc., Elkhart, 1939-42, v.p. in charge of med. and research div., 1946-62, exec. v.p., 1962-64, pres., chief exec. officer, 1964-73, chmn., chief exec. officer, 1973—, also dir.; dir. Alimentos Proteicos Ltda., Neige des Cevennes, Quimexa, S.A., Laboratorios Miles de Mexico, Miles Devel. S.A., Miles Labs. Pan Am., Inc., Quimica Mexama S.A., Aramiles, S.A. de C.V., Miles Internat. Inc., Miles-Kyowa Co. Ltd., Miles-Sankyo Co. Ltd., Miles Mauri Pty. Ltd., Miles S.A., First Nat. Bank of Elkhart. Mem. adv. council South Bend Center for Med. Edn.; former mem. nat. adv. food and drug com. FDA; mem. adv. council Goshen Coll.; mem. adv. council Sch. Sci. of Notre Dame U.; mem. council biol. scis. U. Chgo. and Pritzker Sch. Med.; corp. vis. com. Sch. Med., Tufts U.; bd. govs. Weizmann Inst. Sci.; chmn. Elkhart Conf. Bd. dirs. Oaklawn Found. for Mental Health; trustee Royal Soc. Medicine Found. Served in M.C., AUS, 1942-46. Mem. AMA, Ind. Med. Assn., Elkhart County Med. Soc., Royal Soc. Medicine (Eng.), Royal Soc. Health (Eng.), AAAS, N.Y. Acad. Scis., Japan Soc. Presbyn. Office: Miles Lab Inc 1127 Myrtle St Elkhart IN 46515*

COMSTOCK, PETER HARWOOD, piano mfg. co. exec.; b. Essex, Conn., Aug. 29, 1915; s. Elliot M. and L. Marcia (Harwood) C.; student public and pvt. schs.; m. Charlotte Toppin, Nov. 30, 1940; children—Marcia Anne Littel, Barbara Johnstone, Constance, Patricia. With Pratt, Read & Co. (name changed to Pratt-Read Corp.), Ivoryton, Conn., 1936—, v.p., 1942-54, pres., 1954-70, chmn. bd., 1970—, chief exec. officer, also dir.; dir. Colonial Bank, Waterbury, Conn., Brit. Piano Actions, Ltd., Wales, Hitchcock Chair Co., Riverton, Conn., Springfield Wire Co. (Mass.), Tech-Art Plastics, Morristown, N.J.; adv. bd. Liberty Mut. Ins. Co., North Haven, Conn. Bd. govs. U. New Haven; trustee Conn. Public Expenditure Council. Mem. Nat. Piano Mfrs. Assn., Nat. Piano Found., Am. Music Conf. (dir.). Clubs: N. Am. Yacht Racing Union, Cruising of Am. (past commodore), Off Soundings, Royal Bermuda Yacht, Royal Ocean Racing, Storm Trysail, Essex Yacht, N.Y. Yacht. Office: Pratt-Read Corp Main St Ivoryton CT 06442

COMULADA, FERNANDO ANTONIO, banker; b. Ponce, P.R., July 31, 1943; s. Juan A. and Elba Comulada (Ortiz) C.; B.B.A., Cath. U. P.R., 1965; postgrad. Sch. Banking, Williams Coll., 1980—; m. Aida Berrios, May 19, 1966; children—Mia, Pierrette. Acct., Norden's div United Techs. Corp., Norwalk, Conn., 1970-71; sr. acct. Comptroller's Office, City of Norwalk, 1971-76; credit analyst Conn. Bank & Trust Co., Hartford, 1976-78, asst. v.p. Hartford comml. region, 1978—. Founder, pres. Com. for Puerto Rican Handicapped Children, 1973-80; bd. dirs. Long River council Boy Scouts Am., 1979-80; mem. Greater Hartford Leadership, 1980; participant White House Forum on Inflation, 1979. Served with U.S. Army, 1966-69; Vietnam. Decorated Bronze Star with oak leaf cluster, Army Commendation medal. Recipient awards P.R. chpt. Nat. Soc. for Easter Seals, 1978, 79, Bridgeport Spanish Mchts., 1976, Bridgeport Econ. Devel. Corp., 1976, Conn. chpt. P.R. Handicapped Com., 1979. Mem. Greater Hartford C. of C., Hartford Spanish Mcht. Assn. (asso.) Democrat. Home: 114 Westwood Rd New Haven CT 06515 Office: One Constitution Plaza Hartford CT 06106

COMYNS, KENNETH CHARLES, real estate co. exec.; b. Dublin, Ireland, Nov. 29, 1932; immigrated to Can., 1955, naturalized, 1961; came to U.S., 1980; s. Charles B. and Mary E. Comyns; B.A.I., in Civil Engring., Trinity Coll., Dublin, 1955, M.A. in Arts, 1961; m. Dorothy Marie Kathe, Aug. 17, 1979; children—Peter, Jennifer. Civil engr. Irish Electricity Supply Bd., 1955, Collen Bros., 1955; Ont. Hydro Co., 1955-58; civil engr. cons. Marshall, Macklin, Monaghan Ltd., Toronto, Ont., Can., 1958-59; twp. engr. Twp. of Chinguacousy (Ont., Can.), 1959-69; v.p. Markborough Property Ltd., Toronto, 1969-76; v.p. land Nu-West Devel. Corp., Calgary, Alta., Can., 1976-79; pres. Nu-West, Inc., Aurora, Colo., 1979—; dir. Nu-West Group Ltd., Carma Developers Ltd., Nu-West of Ariz. Mem. Assn. Profl. Engrs., Geologists and Geophysicists of Alta., Assn. Profl. Engrs. of Ont., Urban Land Inst. (large scale communities com.). Office: 3033 S Parker Rd Suite 500 Aurora CO 80014

CONANT, KENNETH JOHN, III, commodity-industry analyst; b. Cambridge, Mass., Dec. 2, 1952; s. Kenneth John and Margaret Mary (Wait) C.; B.S., U. Notre Dame, 1974; M.S. in Bus. Adminstrn., Boston U., 1978. Exec. officer 243d Ordnance Co., Owings Mills, Md., 1979-80, comdr., 1980—; commodity-industry analyst U.S. Internat. Trade Commn., Washington, 1980—. Served with U.S. Army, 1974-79. Mem. Am. Chem. Soc., Am. Def. Preparedness Assn., Res. Officers Assn., Coalition for Peace through Strength. Roman Catholic.

CONBOY, CHARLES EDWARD, real estate broker; b. Swampscott, Mass., Dec. 29, 1909; B.A., U. Hawaii, 1963; m. Muriel Veronica Abbey, Mar. 1, 1937; children—Alan Joseph, Charles Edward. Enlisted USN, 1928, advanced through grades to comdr., 1952, ret., 1958; salesman Windward Oahu Realty, Kailua, Hawaii, 1964-66; salesman, real estate broker Tropic Shores Realty, Honolulu, 1967-68; staff appraiser Hambleton & Asso., Inc., Honolulu, 1968-69, prin. broker, 1968-70; ind. fee appraiser, Honolulu, 1969—; ind. real estate broker, Honolulu, 1970—. Bd. dirs. Community Council Kailua, 1971-76; past pres. Community Assn., Hawaii. Treas., 25th rep. dist. Republican party Hawaii, 1967-78. Mem. Am. Right of Way Assn., Honolulu Bd. Realtors, Nat., Hawaii assns. real estate bds. Roman Catholic. Home: 1423 Mokolea Dr Kailua HI 96734 Office: 733 Bishop St Suite 1616 Honolulu HI 96813

CONDICT, EDGAR RHODES, med. instrument mfg. exec., med. health care exec., inventor; b. Boston, Apr. 27, 1940; s. Clinton Adams and Elizabeth May (Lane) C.; B.S., Bucknell U., 1962; m. Judith Pond, June 9, 1962; children—Edgar Rhodes, Robert Adams, Carolyn Helen. Chmn. bd., pres. Bio-Tronics Research, Inc., 1962—, Kearsarge Healthcare, Inc., 1978—, Kearsarge Rehab. Hosp., Inc.; pres. Medel Corp., patent devel. investment, 1965—; cons. U. Tex. Med. Sch., 1968-70; cons. in med. electronics, electronics, biophysics, telecommunications, environ. health and welfare. Chmn., Mantowa dist., exec. bd. Daniel Webster council Boy Scouts Am.; chmn. bd., pres., founder Kearsarge Rehab. Med. Center; chmn., pres. Kearsarge Rehab. Hosp. Recipient various grants in neuro-brain scis.; numerous med. awards from fgn. countries. Mem. Sigma Chi. Baptist. Author: A Theory of Anesthesia; Feedback Anesthesia; Electronic Pain-Killing Devices; others. Patentee in fields med. electronics, telecommunications. Address: Main St New London NH 03257

CONDON, JOSEPH FRANCIS, engring. and constrn. co. exec.; b. Bklyn., Jan. 22, 1925; s. Joseph F. and Helen M. (Carboy) C.; A.B., Brown U., 1950; cert. London Sch. Economics, 1951; m. Ann Merwin Foote, Jan. 16, 1954; children—Alicia Merwin, Joseph Francis, Susan Olney, Sarah Avery. Vice pres. internat. Parsons & Whittemore, Inc., N.Y.C., 1959-65; v.p. finance Parsons & Whittemore, Inc., N.Y.C., 1965-72; sr. v.p. internat. Wheelabrator Frye, N.Y.C., 1972-76; v.p. internat. finance The Lummus Co., Bloomfield, N.J., 1976—; v.p. internat. Combustion Engring., Inc., Stamford, Conn., 1978—; dir. D.P.F., Inc., Interstate Brands Corp., Kansas City, Mo., Viacom Internat., Inc., N.Y.C., CSA, Madrid, CE-rrey, S.A., Mexico City, EVT, Stuttgart, Ger., Stein Industrie, S.A., Velizy Villacoublay, Ateinsa, Madrid. Served with USN, 1943-46; PTO. Fulbright scholar, 1950-51. Mem. Am. Mgmt. Assn., Inst. Internat. Edn., Council on Fgn. Relations, N.Y. Export Council. Clubs: Metropolitan, Union League. Contbr. articles to profl. jours. Home: 25 Eton Rd Scarsdale NY 10583 Office: 900 Long Ridge Rd Stamford CT 06902

CONDRY, CARSON EMMITT, mech. engr.; b. Liberal, Kans., July 12, 1923; s. Sterling H. and Gladys B. (Carson) C.; B.S., Kans. State U., 1948; m. Martha Elizabeth Baker, July 9, 1944. Prodn. draftsman, design engr., asst. chief engr. J.B. Ehrsam & Son Mfg. Co., Enterprise, Kans., 1948-50; chief engr. Hamilton Constrn. Tex., Salina, Kans., 1950-51; with A.J. Boynton & Co. of Tex., Dallas, 1951-66, draftsman, design engr., project engr., asst. chief engr., 1951-61, chief engr., 1961-66; v.p., dir. Zetterlund-Boynton-Condry & Assos., Engrs., Tech. Counselors, Dallas, 1966-67; chmn. bd., pres. Condry Cayton Burford & Assos., Cons. Engrs. and Indsl. Specialists, Dallas, 1966—. Mem. Greater Dallas Planning Council. Served to 1st lt. A.C., AUS, 1941-45; ETO. Decorated Air medal; registered profl. engr., Tex., Okla., Kans. Mem. ASME, Tex., Nat. socs. profl. engrs., Joint Engrs. Council, Profl. Engrs. in Pvt. Practice, Cons. Engrs. Soc., Nat. Wildlife Fedn., Alumni Assn. Kans. State U., Nat. Geog. Soc., Dallas C. of C. Democrat. Methodist. Club: Forest Hollow. Home: 2216 Longwood Ln Dallas TX 75228 Office: 10901 Garland Rd Dallas TX 75218

CONFER, KERBY EUGENE, radio broadcasting co. exec.; b. Woodbury, N.J., Jan. 24, 1941; s. Clarence Eugene and Lela Myrtle (Maltby) C.; student Lycoming Coll., 1959-60; m. Beverly J. Dawson, Aug. 22, 1959; children—Kerby Scott, Rand Allen, Kristin Elizabeth. On air radio personality Sta. WMPT, Williamsport, Pa., Sta. WFEC, Harrisburg, Pa., Sta. WARM, Scranton-Wilkes-Barre, Pa., Sta. WCAO, Balt., 1957-65; on camera TV personality Sts. WDCA-TV, Washington, 1966-67, Sta. WBAL-TV, Balt., 1967-71; v.p., gen. mgr. Sta. WYRE, Annapolis, Md., 1969-75; pres. Pa. Radio Inc., Stas. WLYC-WILQ, Williamsport, 1975—, Berks Broadcasting Co., Sta. WHUM, Reading, Pa., 1977—, Crown Broadcasting Inc., Stas. WKRT-WNOZ, Cortland-Ithaca, N.Y., 1978—, 1st Com Corp., Sta. KSSN, Little Rock, 1979—, Keymarket Broadcasting, Sta. WGXL, Greenville, S.C., 1981—. Scoutmaster troop 758, Boy Scouts Am., Crofton, Md., 1970-75. Mem. Nat. Assn. Broadcasters (conv. speaker), Arbitron Radio Adv. Council, Nat. Radio Broadcasters Assn. (conv. speaker). Baptist. Office: Sta KSSN One Financial Centre 650 Shackleford Rd Little Rock AR 72212

CONFORTI, EMILE RALPH, plastic co. exec.; b. Torrington, Conn., Oct. 22, 1928; s. Emile Domenic and Catherine (LaStoria) C.; B.A. in Edn., Providence Coll., 1950; postgrad. Calif. State Coll. at Long Beach, 1957-58; m. Kathleen Ann Zullo, Dec. 27, 1953; children—Diane, Donna, David. Vice-pres., gen. mgr. Ryko Products, Inc. (acquired by Monsanto Co. 1963), Los Angeles, 1958-63, marketing mgr. Monsanto Co., Anaheim, Cal., 1963-68; pres., chief exec. officer Hollywood Plastics, Inc. (subsidiary Shell Chem. Co.), Los Angeles, 1968-74, also dir.; pres., chief exec. officer Ampro Corp., Anaheim, Calif., 1974—; dir. Placentia Linda Savs. & Loan. Served with AUS, 1951-53. Mem. Soc. Plastic Engrs., Soc. Plastic Industry, ASTM. Clubs: Yorba Linda (Calif.) Country; Ostomy Assos. of Orange County (pres.). Office: Ampro Corp 1340 N Jefferson Blvd Anaheim CA 92807

CONFOY, RICHARD HENRY, trust fund adminstr.; b. Mineola, N.Y., May 30, 1934; s. Harry Joseph and Ethlyn Muriel (Desnoes) C.; B.S., Villanova U., 1955; M.B.A., N.Y. Inst. Tech., 1976; m. Margaret Ann Lobdell, Nov. 22, 1958; children—Kerrie, Brian, Robert, Richard, Christy, Jennifer. Pres., Convoy Oil Co., Baldwin, N.Y., 1959-63; exec. v.p. L.J. Bennett Inc., Garden City, N.Y., 1963-69; registered rep. Conn. Gen. Co., Garden City, 1969-71; mgr. Phoenix Mut. Life Ins. Co., Garden City, 1971-73; mgr. Fidelity Mut. Life Ins. Co., Hauppauge, N.Y., 1973-75; dir. Suffolk County CESA Benefit Fund, Holtsville, N.Y., 1975—; dir. Raleigh Athletic Co., New Rochelle, N.Y., Ridon Industries, Setauket, N.Y. Bd. dirs., sec. West Meadow Beach Assn., Stony Brook, N.Y., 1976—. Served as lt. (j.g.) USN, 1955-57. C.L.U. Republican. Roman Catholic. Club: Stony Brook Yacht. Home: 65 W Meadow Rd Old Field NY 11733 Office: Suffolk County CESA Benefit Fund 755 Waverly Ave Holtsville NY 11742

CONGDON, ROBERT CLARENDON, II, constrn. co. exec.; b. Sumnter, S.C., June 7, 1945; s. Robert Clarendon and Wilma Elizabeth (Lindabury) C.; B.S. in Civil Engring., U. Tenn., 1968; m. Elizabeth Straubmueller, Oct. 24, 1977. Salesman, Congdon Assos., Whitehouse Station, N.J., 1968-69, pres., 1974-76; pres. The Clarendon Co., Clarendon Constrn. Co., Whitehouse Station, 1976—. Served as officer U.S. Army, 1969-74. Mem. Nat. Assn. Home Builders, Nat. Assn. Realtors, Internat. Entrepreneurs Assn., Hunterdon County Bd. Realtors. Republican. Methodist. Home: Box 185 7 Main St Whitehouse Station NJ 08889 Office: Box 185 Somerset St Whitehouse Station NJ 08889

CONGER, SUE ANN, mgmt. cons.; b. Akron, Ohio, Nov. 6, 1947; d. Scott Stanley and NormaMarie (Bauknecht) Summerville; B.S., Ohio State U., 1970; M.B.A., Rutgers U., 1976; postgrad. N.Y. U.; m. David Boyd Conger, July 3, 1971. Sr. programmer-analyst U.S. Dept. Agr., Washington, 1970-73; programming analyst Ednl. Testing Service, Princeton, N.J., 1973; 2d v.p. Chase Manhattan Bank, N.Y.C., 1974-77; tech. dir. Lambda Tech., Inc., N.Y.C., 1977-80; mgmt. cons. Mobil Oil Corp., N.Y.C., 1980—; cons. Mem. Morris Plains Bd. Edn., 1978—. Recipient U.S. Dept. Agr. Cert. of Merit, 1972. Office: 150 42d St New York NY 10017

CONGRO, PATRICK GERARD, mktg. exec.; b. N.Y.C., Oct. 14, 1938; s. Basil Anthony and Mary (Ferranti) C.; B.S. in Mktg., Nassau Coll., 1967; m. Diane Pepe, Aug. 22, 1965; children—Patricia Ann, Michael, David, Stephen. Div. mktg. rep. Texaco, Inc., N.Y.C., 1969-72; mktg. supr. Texaco, Inc., N.Y.C., 1973-76; v.p. mktg. Cray Energy, Inc., North Walpole, N.H., 1978—. Planning council mem. Little League, Walpole, 1976-80. Served with USMC, 1958-62. Mem. Nat. Oil Jobbers Council, Ind. Oil Men's Assn. New Eng., Nat. Assn. Texaco Wholesalers, N.H. Better Heat Council, New Eng. Fuel Inst., Vt. Petroleum Assn. Club: Lions (dir. 1978-80). Home: Wentworth Rd Walpole NH 03608 Office: 173 Main St North Walpole NH 05101

CONKEL, LEO SHERMAN, design engring. exec.; b. Minford, Ohio, July 5, 1925; Arthur Harrison and Emma P. (Warren) C.; student U. Ark., 1943-44; B.Engring., Ohio State U., 1950; m. Dolores A. Beduhn, July 5, 1967; children—Michele, Leo Sherman II. Sales mgr. Denison Engring. div., pres. Racine-Chgo. Engring. Corp., Addison, Ill., 1959-60, chmn. bd., 1960—; chmn. bd. Fluid-Scope, Inc., Dynamic Power Systems. Mem. Nat. UN Day Com.; mem. com. for tomorrow Coll. Engring. Ohio State U. Mem. Chgo. Assn. Commerce and Industry. Clubs: River Forest (Ill.) Golf (dir.), Ohio State U. Pres.'s, Elks, Masons, Moose. Office: 840 Fiene Dr Addison IL 60101

CONLAN, THOMAS LAWRENCE, lawyer; b. Detroit, July 24, 1912; s. Thomas L. and Margretta (Cook) C.; J.D., U. Detroit, 1936; m. Mary Helen Rabaut, Oct. 2, 1936; children—Thomas L., John Edwin, Gretta Marie Conlan Barclay, Maureen Catherine Conlan Hehman, Mary Carol Conlan Melton, Virginia Ann, Christine Helen. Admitted to Mich. bar, 1936, Ohio bar, 1942; gen. practice in Detroit, 1936-42; chief enforcement atty. Cin. OPA, 1942-45; instr. U. Detroit Coll. Law, 1937-42; spl. asst. U.S. dist. atty. for So. Dist. Ohio, 1942-46; mem. firm Kyte Conlan Wulsin & Vogeler, Cin., 1946-78; dir. So. Ohio Bank, Silco, Inc., H.A. Seinsheimer Co. Mem. Hamilton County Hosp. Commn.; mem. U.S. Pres.'s Commn. Mental Health, 1977-78; mem. Ohio Bd. Regents, 1973-75. Home: 3645 Traskwood Circle Cincinnati OH 45208 Office: Provident Tower Cincinnati OH 45202

CONLEE, JAMES KENT, corp. exec.; b. White Hall, Ill., Jan. 2, 1934; s. Thomas Harrison and Gussie (DeHart) C.; B.S., Western Ill. U., 1956; postgrad. in organic chemistry Washington U., St. Louis, 1956-57; m. Joan Cardwell, June 28, 1953; children—Teresa, Mark, Michael, Andrew, John. Research chemist Alton Box Board Co. (Ill.), 1956-58, Universal Match Corp., Ferguson, Mo., 1958-61; process engr. and project mgr. Union Starch & Refining Co., Granite City, Ill., 1961-66; chief engr. milling div. Cargill, Inc. and Corn Starch & Syrup Co., Cedar Rapids, Iowa and Dayton, Ohio, 1966-73; pres., dir. Modern Process Design, Inc., Dayton, 1973—; v.p., dir. NEMCO, S.A. (Mexico City), African N. Am. Process Industries, Inc.; officer, dir. Midwest Mfg., Inc. Registered profl. engr., Ohio. Mem. Nat., Ohio socs. profl. engrs., Order of Engrs., Am. Assn. Oil Chemists, Dayton Engrs., Full Gospel Businessmen's Fellowship Internat. (dir.).

Mem. Ch. of God. Developed new methods of producing corn syrups and starches. Home: 6437 Westford Rd Dayton OH 45426 Office: 4977 Northcutt Pl PO Box 1400E Dayton OH 45414

CONLEY, FREDERICK WEBESTER, health care exec.; b. Portland, Maine, Jan. 27, 1947; s. Fred Ellsworth and Sharlene Marie (Preston) C.; B.S. in Acctg., Husson Coll., Bangor, Maine, 1970; m. Linde J. Armstrong, Aug. 14, 1971; children—Candace Megan, Ryan Frederick. With Stone & Webster Engring. Co., Wiscasset, Maine, 1970, Nat. Grange Mut. Ins. Co., Keene, N.H., 1970-76; accountant, bus. mgr. Cooper, Stewarts, Gilmore & Horner, P.A., Bar Harbor, Maine, 1976—. Mem. Am. Mgmt. Assn. Baptist. Home: RFD 4 Box 443 Ellsworth ME 04605 Office: 37 Hancock St Bar Harbor ME 04609

CONLEY, ROBERT WILLIAM, health products mfg. co. exec., plant engr.; b. Portland, Maine, Nov. 18, 1944; s. William Martin and Barbara (Jordan) C.; B.S. in Agrl. Engring., U. Maine, 1967; postgrad. in bus. adminstrn. Fairleigh Dickinson U., 1980—; m. Maureen Catherine Mc Afee, Feb. 18, 1978. Prodn. supr. Charmin Paper Products Co., Mehoopany, Pa., 1967-68; with Johnson & Johnson Inc., 1968—, plant engr., New Brunswick, N.J., 1968-77, plant engr. subs. Ethicon, Inc., Somerville, N.J., 1977—, chief plant engr., 1980—. Bd. dirs. Big Bros./Big Sisters of Somerset County (N.J.), 1977—, pres., 1979-80; mem. Hillsborough Twp. (N.J.) Indsl. Commn., 1978—. Served with Army N.G., 1967-73. Mem. Am. Inst. Plant Engrs. Home: 502 Brookside Ln Somerville NJ 08876 Office: Ethicon Inc US Route 22 Somerville NJ 08876

CONLIN, FLOYD BRONSON, JR., financing co. exec.; b. Cambridge, Mass., Feb. 18, 1940; s. F. Bronson and Ruth Janet (Young) C.; B.A. in Psychology, U. Conn., 1968; m. Mary Elizabeth Empey, Sept. 21, 1975; children by previous marriage—Janice Diana, Floyd Bronson III. Mktg. rep. IBM, N.Y.C., 1968-72; part owner Murphy-Conlin, Inc., Darien, Conn., 1972-76; v.p. Handy Assos., N.Y.C., 1976-77; asso. Itel Corp., N.Y.C., 1977-79, J.M. Randolph & Assos., Inc., Greenwich, Conn., 1979—. Troop leader Boy Scouts Am., Rowayton, Conn., 1977-79. Served with USAF, 1961-65. Mem. U. Conn. Alumni Assn. (pres. Fairfield alumni chpt. 1968-70). Republican. Congregationalist. Clubs: Darien Lions (pres., dir.), Shore and Country. Home: Westview Ln Norwalk CT 06854 Office: J M Randolph & Associates Inc 537 Steamboat Rd Greenwich CT 06830

CONLIN, JAMES CLYDE, realty co. exec.; b. Ft. Dodge, Iowa, Aug. 12, 1940; s. Clyde Elwin and Evelyn C. (Olson) C.; student Wentworth Mil. Acad., 1959-61; m. Roxanne Elizabeth Barton, Mar. 21, 1964; children—Jacalyn Rae Alice, James Barton, Debra Ann, Douglas Klein. Sales mgr. Cooper Realty Inc., Des Moines, 1966-68; salesman Stanbrough Realty Co., Des Moines, 1968-72; gen. sales mgr. Iowa Realty Co., So. Offices, Des Moines, 1972-79; v.p. Iowa Realty Co. Brokers, 1979—; pres. Mid Iowa Mgmt., Southbrook Green, Indianola Village Ltd.; partner Alpha Partners. Bd. dirs. Des Moines Tax Payers Assn. Mem. Greater Des Moines Bd. Realtors, Real Estate Securities and Syndication Inst., Nat. Mktg. Inst., Grad. Realtors Inst. Iowa. Home: 6116 SW 48th Ave Des Moines IA 50321 Office: 2423 Ingersoll St Des Moines IA 50312

CONLIN, JOSEPH COSMAS, publisher; b. Bklyn., Nov. 23, 1952; s. Walter Francis and Joan A. (Dolan) C.; A.B. in English, Fairfield U., 1974; m. Linda A. Bernert, Aug. 10, 1974; 1 son, Paul J. Exec. v.p., editor, asso. pub., dir. Modern Indsl. Energy and IG Energy Newsletter, Pub. Dynamics, Inc., Stamford, Conn. Public relations cons. Conn. Visual Health Clinic. Mem. Assn. Energy Engrs. (charter), Bibl. Archaeol. Soc. (hon.). Editor: Modern Indsl. Energy mag. Home: 84 Garden Dr Fairfield CT 06430 Office: Two Selleck St Stamford CT 06902

CONN, ROBERT HENRY, accounting co. exec.; b. Boonton, N.J., June 8, 1925; s. Henry Hammond and Violet (Doremus) C.; B.B.A., U. Miss., 1955; M.S., Rochester U., 1962; D.B.A., Ind. U., 1965; m. Virginia Inness-Brown, July 6, 1946; children—Portia, Judith, Robert, Catherine, Patricia. Commd. ensign, U.S. Navy, 1946, advanced through grades to capt., 1967; asst. dir. budgets and reports Office of Naval Comptroller, Washington, 1969-72; ret., 1972; mgr. fed. liaison div. Arthur Andersen & Co., Washington, 1972—; asst. prof. naval sci. Rochester U., 1959-62; lectr. Armed Forces Indsl. Coll., U.S. Naval War Coll., Nat. War Coll. Bd. dirs. Navy Mut. Aid Soc. Decorated Legion of Merit. Mem. Am. Soc. Mil. Comptrollers, Assn. Govt. Accountants, Navy League, Sigma Iota Epsilon. Episcopalian. Clubs: N.Y. Yacht, Army and Navy, Capitol Hill. Author: Financial Management Systems for Political Campaigns, 1972. Home: 1621 Crescent Ln McLean VA 22101 Office: Arthur Andersen & Co 1666 K St NW Washington DC 20006

CONNAUGHTON, DAVID MICHAEL, mgmt. cons.; b. Youngstown, Ohio, Feb. 19, 1943; s. James Michael and Dorothy Edith (Roberts) C.; B.S. in Math., U.S. Air Force Acad., 1965; M.B.A., Harvard U., 1973; m. Marilyn J. Goscewski, Dec. 31, 1966; children—Erin, James. Commd. 2d lt. U.S. Air Force, 1965, advanced through grades to capt., 1968; resigned, 1971; asst. to chief operating officer Burton Duenke Constrn. Co., St. Louis, 1973-74; v.p. fin. Energystics, Inc., Toledo, 1974; sr. cons. Cambridge Communications Group (Mass.), 1975-77; v.p., dir. Plastic Forming Co., Woodbridge, Conn., 1977-79; prin. cons. David M. Connaughton & Assos., Kingston, N.Y., 1980—. Exec. summer intern Office of Sec. Air Force, 1972. Decorated Air medal (11). Home and Office: 70 Norma Ct Kingston NY 12401

CONNEEN, JAMES THOMAS, lawyer, mgmt. cons.; b. Orange, N.J., June 1, 1939; s. Thomas J. and Mary Elizabeth (Doyle) C.; B.S. (scholar), St. Peter's Coll., 1961; J.D. (scholar), N.Y. U., 1964; m. Maureen C. Rielly, Aug. 24, 1963; children—Elizabeth, Sheila, Martin. Admitted to Pa. bar, 1964, N.Y. bar, 1967; law clk. to chief justice Pa., Phila., 1964-65; asso. firm Breed, Abbott & Morgan, N.Y.C., 1967-69; v.p., gen. counsel, dir. Posi-Seal Internat., Inc., North Stonington, Conn., 1969-70; asso. counsel Union Camp Corp., Wayne, N.J., 1970-72; v.p. Syncronamics, Inc., Englewood Cliffs, N.J., 1972-75; chmn. bd. A. T. Hudson & Co., Inc., Paramus, N.J., 1975—, also dir. Served to capt., M.I., U.S. Army, 1965-67. Decorated Army Commendation medal. Mem. Am. Bar Assn., N.Y. Bar Assn., Pa. Bar Assn. Republican. Roman Catholic. Club: Ridgewood (N.J.) Country. Home: 299 Highland Ave Ridgewood NJ 07450 Office: A T Hudson & Co Inc 299 Forest Ave Paramus NJ 07652

CONNELL, CHARLES ALEXANDER, JR., securities co. exec.; b. Orange, N.J., Sept. 14, 1941; s. Charles Alexander and Elizabeth Dixon (Ralli) C.; A.B., Brown U., 1963; m. Susan Meredith Margetts, Aug. 5, 1967; children—Cynthia R., Katherine E., Amy M. Asst. v.p. Merrill Lynch, Pierce, Fenner & Smith Inc., N.Y.C., 1964-74; sr. govt. trader, v.p. Blyth Eastman Dillon Capital Markets, Inc., N.Y.C., 1974-79; sr. govt. trader Kidder, Peabody & Co., Inc., N.Y.C., 1979—. Mem. Harding (N.J.) Twp. Com., 1975—; pres. Harding Twp. Republican Club, 1973; bd. dirs. Harding Twp. Civic Assn., 1971-74; mem. New Vernon (N.J.) Vol. Fire Dept., 1971—; treas. New Vernon First Aid Squad, 1974-76. Presbyterian. Clubs: Morris County Golf; Morristown; Point O'Woods; Windermere Island (Eleuthere, Bahamas). Home: Shalebrook Dr New Vernon NJ 07976 Office: 10 Hanover Sq New York NY 10005

CONNELL, JOSEPH EDWARD, ins. co. exec.; b. Niagara Falls, N.Y., Oct. 8, 1930; s. George Kerr and Katharine Elsa (Vodra) C.; B.A., Antioch Coll., 1954; postgrad. George Washington U., 1956-58; m. Patricia Jane Parsons, Aug. 22, 1953; children—Douglas Edward, Marjorie Elsa. With Coopers & Lybrand, Detroit, Mpls. and Des Moines, 1958-74, partner, SEC specialist, 1973-74; exec. v.p., controller, treas. Rep. Nat. Life Ins. Co., Dallas, 1974—. Served to lt. USNR, 1955-58. C.P.A., Mich. Fellow Life Mgmt. Inst., Life Office Mgmt. Assn.; mem. Am. Council Life Ins., Tex. Life Ins. Assn., Am. Inst. C.P.A.'s, Tex. Soc. C.P.A.'s, Iowa Soc. C.P.A.'s, Minn. Soc. C.P.A.'s, Mich. Soc. C.P.A.'s, Nat. Assn. Accts., Fin. Execs. Inst. Unitarian. Clubs: Canyon Creek Country, Marathoner, White Rock. Office: Box 226210 Dallas TX 75266

CONNELL, WILLIAM FRANCIS, diversified co. exec.; b. Lynn, Mass., May 12, 1938; s. William J. and Theresa (Keaney) C.; B.S. magna cum laude, Boston Coll., 1959; M.B.A., Harvard, 1963; m. Margot C. Gensler, May 29, 1965; children—Monica Cameron, Lisa Terese, Courtenay Erin, William Christopher, Terence Alexander. Controller, Olga Co., Inc., Van Nuys, Calif., 1963-65; asst. treas. Litton Industries, Inc., also pres. div. Marine Tech., Inc., 1965-68; treas. Ogden Corp., N.Y.C., 1968-71, v.p., 1969-71, sr. v.p., 1971-80, exec. v.p., 1980—, also dir.; pres., chief exec. officer Ogden Leisure, Inc., 1972—; chmn., chief exec. officer Ogden Food Service Corp., Ogden Recreation, Inc., Ogden Security, Inc., Ogden Services, Inc. Active fund raising, trustee Boston Coll.; trustee St. Elizabeth's Hosp., Boston. Served to 1st lt. AUS, 1959-61. Mem. Greater Boston C. of C. (dir.), Beta Gamma Sigma, Alpha Sigma Nu, Alpha Kappa Psi. Roman Catholic. Clubs: Algonquin, University (Boston); Tedesco County Home: 111 Ocean Ave Swampscott MA 01907 Office: 111 Waldemar Ave East Boston MA 02128

CONNELLEY, EARL JOHN, JR., water and waste treatment co. exec.; b. Covington, Ky.; s. Earl John and Grace (Muzzio) C.; B.S., U. Cin., 1947, M.S., 1948; m. Eileen L. O'Connor, Feb. 20, 1965; children—Ann Lloyd, Carol Jeanne, Cynthia Jane. Research engr. Eckey Research Labs., Cin.; process engr. Permutit Co. subs. Zurn Corp., N.Y.C., sales engr., East Orange, N.J., Chgo., dist. engr., Cin., regional mgr., Chgo., sales mgr., Paramus, N.J., 1966-78; dir. Havens & Emerson Cons. Environ. Engrs., Saddle Brook, N.J., 1978—; instr. U. Cin., 1947-48; mem. industry com. Ann. Am. Power Conf. Registered profl. engr., Ohio, Ill., N.J., Ind., N.Y., Pa., Mass., Mich., Mo., Wis., Ky., Iowa, Tex., Minn. Mem. Am. Water Works Assn., Waste Pollution Control Fedn., Sales Execs. Club, Alpha Chi Sigma, Phi Kappa Theta, Scabbard and Blade. Roman Catholic. Club: Univ. (Cin.). Contbr. articles to profl. jours. Home: 8 Split Rock Rd Upper Saddle River NJ 07458 Office: 299 Market St Saddle Brook NJ 07662

CONNELLY, AUBREY BYRON, computer systems analyst; b. Hopewell, Va., Dec. 14, 1939; s. Aubrey Byron, Jr. and Elizabeth (Hudson) C.; B.S., Va. Commonwealth U., 1969; M.A., U. No. Colo., 1978; m. Arlene Viola Cassety, Aug. 3, 1963; children—Dawn Marie, Hope Lynn, Cheri Michele. Programmer trainee Allied Chem. Co., Hopewell, Va., 1965; programmer Mobil Chem. Co., Richmond, Va., 1966; programmer analyst Va. Commonwealth U., Richmond, 1966-68; computer specialist U.S. Army Computer Systems Command, Ft. Eustis, Va., 1968-70; sr. computer specialist U.S. Army Communications Command, W. Ger., Washington, Ft. Huachuca, Ariz., 1970—; instr., ADP credentials com. Cochise Coll.; cons., realtor asso. Exec. Realty and Investment Co. Candidate Sierra Vista City Council, 1977; mem. spl. com. Sierra Vista Pub. Schs., 1976; sec. So. Ariz. (Sierra Vista) Jewish Community, 1977-80; mem. com. to free Soviet Jewish Dissidents, 1978; pres. Huachuca Pony-Colt Baseball League, 1977; coach Sierra Vista Basketball and Ponytail Softball Leagues; coach U.S. Dependent Youth Assn. in Basketball and Girls Softball, Augsburg, W. Ger., 1973-75; mem. com. to improve German-Am. relations through sports and civic activities, 1973-75; bd. dirs. Kol Hamid bar, 1979—. Served with Army N.G., 1963-66. Named Coach of Year, U.S. Dependent Youth Assn. in Basketball, W. Ger., 1974; recipient letters of appreciation Va. Commonwealth U., 1968, U.S. Army, 1970, 75, Sierra Vista Pub. Schs., 1976, Sierra Vista Ponytail Softball League and Huachuca Pony-Colt Baseball League, 1977. Mem. Ariz. Assn. Realtors, Cochise County Multiple Listing Service, Assn. Laissez-faire. Republican. Jewish. Clubs: Optimist (v.p. Sierra Vista 1976), Kiwanis (dir. 1973-74), Elks (House chmn. 1980-81), Masons, Order Eastern Star, Scottish Rite, Shriners (ambassador Aahmes Shrine, permanent contbg. mem. to Crippled Children's Hosp., Sabbar Shrine). Author (with Dr. Stan Dunn): Establishment of Thruput Analysis Standards for Army Telecommunications, 1977. Home: 1968 Chateau Ln Sierra Vista AZ 85635 Office: Headquarters USACC Attn DSCOPS-PR Fort Huachuca AZ 85613

CONNELLY, DAVID ANTHONY, bank exec.; b. Bartlesville, Okla., Oct. 1, 1937; s. Donald L. and Martha H. C.; B.A., U. Tex., 1959, M.B.A., 1961; children—Donald, Jennifer, Laurence, Eileen. Asst. trust officer 1st City Nat. Bank, Houston, 1961-66; mktg. fin. analyst Exxon U.S.A., 1966-68; v.p. Tex. Commerce Bank, Houston, 1969-73; pres. Am. Bank, Odessa, Tex., 1973; v.p. Bank S.W., Houston, 1973-76; pres. Westbury Nat. Bank, Houston, 1976—. Mem. Robert Morris Assos. Republican. Roman Catholic. Club: Houston Country. Office: PO Box 35555 Houston TX 77035

CONNELLY, JOHN FRANCIS, industrialist; b. Phila., Mar. 4, 1905; LL.D. (hon.), LaSalle Coll., Villanova U., 1958; m. Josephine O'Neill, Apr. 1938; children—Josephine, Emily, John, Thomas, Judith, Christine. Dir. Crown Cork & Seal Co., Phila., 1956—, pres., 1957-76, chmn. bd., 1957—, chief exec. officer, 1979—; chmn. bd. Connelly Containers, Inc. Chmn. Archbishop's laity com. Office: Crown Cork & Seal Co 9300 Ashton Rd Philadelphia PA 19136*

CONNELLY, THEODORE SAMPLE, communications co. exec.; b. Middletown, Conn., Oct. 15, 1925; s. Herbert Lee and Mabel Gertrude (Wells) C.; B.A., Wesleyan U., 1948, postgrad., 1951; postgrad. U. Paris, 1950. Sec., Nat. Com. on Edn., Am. Trucking Assn., Inc., Washington, 1952-54; dir. pub. affairs Nat. Automobile Club, San Francisco, 1955-62; pres., chmn. The Connelly Corp., San Francisco, 1963—; treas. Ednl. Access Cable TV Corp.; dir. Mission Neighborhood Centers, Inc., Neighborhood Devel. Corp.; mem. adv. com. on Calif. motor vehicle legislation, 1955-62, Calif. State C. of C. com. on hwys., 1958-62. Trustee Lincoln U.; sec. Lincoln U. Found; bd. dirs. San Francisco Program for Aging; founder Communications Library, 1963, Communications Inst., 1978; founding mem. Calif. Council for UN Univ., 1976; organizer Internat. Child Art Collection; co-founder African Research Commn., 1970. Served with USNR, 1943-46. Recipient cert. of merit San Francisco Jr. C. of C., 1959; award of Merit USPHS Hosp., 1980. Mem. AAAS, AAUP, Pub. Relations Round Table of San Francisco, Atlanta Hist. Soc., Asian Mass Communication and Info. Centre (Singapore), NAACP, SAR, Press Club San Francisco, UN Assn. U.S.A., Nat. Sci. Tchrs. Assn. (bus.-industry sect.). Club: Dolphin Swimming and Boating (San Francisco). Author/compiler: BCTV Bibliography on Cabletelevision, 1975—; CINCOM: Courses in Communications-USA, 1978. Contbr. articles in field to profl. jours.; producer, writer, dir. numerous TV programs. Office: Communications Inst 1550 Bryant St San Francisco CA 94103

CONNER, GEORGE WILMARTH, telephone co. exec.; b. Mpls., Mar. 10, 1933; s. George Frederick and Marion (Wilmarth) G.; B.S., U.S. Naval Acad., 1955, M.B.A., Harvard U., 1962; m. Charlotte Kuhl, Oct. 23, 1965; children—Jennifer, Scott, Edward. Contract adminstr. McDonnell Aircraft, St. Louis, 1962-64; partner McKinsey & Co., Inc., N.Y.C., 1964-77; v.p. bus. and residence sector GTE Corp., Stamford, Conn., 1977—. Bd. dirs. Fairfield County chpt. Am. Cancer Soc., 1980. Served with USAF, 1955-60. Republican. Presbyterian. Clubs: Harvard (N.Y.C.); Rumson (N.J.) Country. Office: 1 Stamford Forum Stamford CT 06904

CONNER, HARRY LOUIS, fin. planner; b. Los Angeles, Dec. 2, 1920; s. Harry William and Mabel Frances (Rubly) C.; B.S., U. Md., 1958; M. Bus. Edn., San Diego State Coll., 1970; cert. in Fin. Planning, Coll. Fin. Planning, Denver, 1974; m. Muriel Rita McCune, Sept. 21, 1946; children—William S., Michael J., Mary K., Ann E., Mark L. Served as enlisted man U.S. Navy, 1942-45; commd. ensign, 1945, advanced through grades to lt. comdr., 1958, ret., 1965; div. mgr. Am. Gen. Capital Planning, Inc., San Diego, 1967—; enrolled agt. IRS. Past pres., bd. dirs. San Diego Navy Fed. Credit Union, 1965—. Mem. Internat. Assn. Fin. Planners (past pres. San Diego chpt.), Optimist Club of Coronado. Roman Catholic. Club: K. of C. (past grand knight). Home: 705 D Ave Coronado CA 92118 Office: 4111 Randolph St San Diego CA 92103

CONNINGTON, RICHARD DEWEY, corp. exec.; b. Hillside, N.J., May 9, 1931; s. Herbert James and Mildred (Dewey) C.; A.B., Columbia U., 1953; student Seton Hall U., 1957; m. Florence Kerber, June 24, 1954 (div. May 1978); children—Hilary F., Harry C., Onita C., Richard; m. 2d, Grace Evans, Aug. 19, 1978. Asst. sec. Hanover Bank (N.Y.), 1956-61, Mfrs. Hanover Trust, 1961-62; asst. v.p. Citizens Savs. Bank, Providence, 1962-64, Citizens Trust Co., 1962-64; v.p. Harbor Nat. Bank, Boston, 1964-65, sr. v.p., mem. exec. com., 1965-67, also dir.; exec. v.p. Central State Bank, N.Y.C., 1967-68; dir. orgn. and planning Computer Applications, Inc., N.Y.C., 1968-70, v.p., 1969-70; dir. Providence & Worcester R.R. Co., 1964-68, v.p., 1965-66, chmn. finance com., 1965-68, chmn. exec. com., 1966-68; chmn. exec. com., dir. Island Pond (Vt.) Nat. Bank, 1967-70; pres., dir. Dewey, Irwin & Co., Inc., N.Y.C., 1970—, chmn., 1971—; sec.-treas., dir. Pelham Mgmt. Systems, Inc., N.Y.C., 1970—; treas., dir. Venture Mgmt. Corp., Middletown, N.J., 1971—; chmn. finance com., dir. Acron Corp., Lakewood, N.J., 1971-77, pres., 1974-76, chmn., 1976-77; dir., chmn. finance com. Artium Inc., Roselle, N.J., 1973-77; chmn. Norca Corp., 1976-77; chmn., pres., dir. TELESAVE Corp., N.Y.C., 1976—; mng. partner Telesecurity Cons., 1977—; exec. v.p. and dir. Charter Group Internat., Inc., N.Y.C. and London, 1978—; dir. Enerco Inc., Atlanta, 1980—. Chmn., Montclair (N.J.) Young Republicans, 1959-61; pres. Montclair Rep. Club, 1961-62; vice chmn. Essex County Rep. Com., 1962; nat. chmn. Rockefeller Vols., 1973-76. Served with AUS, 1954-56. Clubs: Newcomen; Univ., Turks Head (Providence). Author: Information Management Through Data Processing, 1980. Home: PO Box 507 Woodstock NY 12498 Office: 601 6th St Brooklyn NY 11215

CONNOLLY, JOHN DOLAN, investment banker; b. N.Y.C., Oct. 28, 1943; s. Thomas Michael and Ann Dorothy (Dolan) C.; A.B. in Economics, Holy Cross Coll., 1965; M.B.A., Stanford, 1967; m. Elizabeth Pell Frazier, Jan. 18, 1975; 1 son, Thomas Pell. Securities analyst First Natl. City Bank, N.Y.C., 1967-69; Nat. Securities & Research Corp., 1969-71; v.p. Faulkner, Dawkins & Sullivan, 1971-77, sr. v.p., 1977; 1st v.p. White, Weld & Co., 1977-78; v.p. E. F. Hutton, 1978-79; sr. v.p. Shearson Loeb Rhoades, N.Y.C., 1979—. Mem. Bd. Trustees Village of Saltaire. Chartered fin. analyst, N.Y. Mem. Fin. Analysts Fedn., N.Y. Soc. Security Analysts, Stanford Alumni Assn. Clubs: Saltaire Yacht (past bd. govs.); Downtown Athletic. Contbr. articles to profl. jour. Home: 240 E 76th New York NY 10021 Office: Shearson Loeb Rhoades 14 Wall St New York NY 10005

CONNOLLY, SID, broadcasting co. exec.; b. Portland, Maine, Oct. 2, 1926; s. Michael Thomas and Mary Ann (Madden) C.; A.B., Bowdoin Coll., 1950; 1 dau., Hilary. Account exec. Cowles Pubs., N.Y.C., 1950-55, Chgo., 1955-60; account exec. Calif. Broadcasting Co., San Jose, 1960-66; sales mgr. Davis Broadcasting Co., San Jose, 1966-68; pres. gen. mgr. Sta. KGSC-TV, San Jose, 1968—, also dir.; dir. Continental Urban TV Corp., Washington. Served with USNR, 1944-46. Mem. Nat. Assn. Broadcasters, Calif. Broadcasters Assn., Nat. Acad. Arts and Scis., LWV, Psi Upsilon, Advt. Club San Jose, Advt. Club San Francisco. Clubs: Bowdoin No. Calif., Hawthorn (San Francisco); Sharon Heights Country; Cardinal of Stanford U.; Cheverus 300; Prouts Neck (Maine) Country. Home: 1850 Willow Rd Palo Alto CA 94304 Office: 1536 Kerley Dr San Jose CA 95112

CONNOR, JOHN HENRY, publisher; b. Phila., June 20, 1922; s. James Francis and Anna Marie Connor; B.A., Calif. State Coll., 1952; M.B.A., Calif. Western U., 1980; m. Helen L. Hatfield, June 6, 1956; children—Petrycia Louise, Jolene Petryce. Enlisted in USAAF, 1941, advanced through grades to col., 1967; service in PTO, Korea and Vietnam; insp. gen. AFCS, 1970-72; ret., 1973; from asst. dist. mgr. to area dir. Moore Bus. Service Inc., 1973-78, mng. editor, Lakeland, Fla., 1978—; leader seminars, lectr. in field. Decorated Legion of Merit (3), D.F.C. (2), Air medal (9), Bronze Star, Meritorious Service medal (2). Mem. Air Force Assn., Ret. Officers Assn., Caterpiller Club. Republican. Episcopalian. Author manuals on real estate, taxes, instrn. techniques. Home: 1430 Lake Mirror Dr NW Winter Haven FL 33880 Office: 404 N Ingraham Ave Lakeland FL 33801

CONNOR, JOHN MICHAEL, JR., fastener mfg. co. exec.; b. Hazelton, Pa., Mar. 30, 1946; s. John Michael and Mildred Jean (Dorneman) C.; B.A., Parsons Coll., 1968; postgrad. Babcock Sch. Mgmt., Wake Forest U., 1979—. Sales/service rep. Rau Fastener div. U.S. Industries Inc., Columbus, Ohio, 1968-69, Chgo., 1969-72, asst. mgr., 1973-75, dist. sales mgr., 1976-78, regional sales mgr., Greensboro, N.C., 1979—. Mem. Sigma Phi Epsilon. Democrat. Roman Catholic. Clubs: Amoco Rugby Football, U.S.A. Owls Rugby Football, Greensboro Rugby Football. Office: 3003 Pacific Ave Greensboro NC 27406

CONNOR, JOHN ROBERT, engring. exec.; b. Phila., Nov. 27, 1916; s. James A. and Juana (Guerrero) C.; B.S. in Civil Engring., U. Pa., 1939; m. Marion Leslie Horter, Dec. 17, 1943; children—Robert Brian, Cynthia Joan (Mrs. Boyd G. Hood), Marguerite Ann (Mrs. Denis Grillet), John Gregory, James Anthony. Engr. Panama Canal, C.Z., 1939-41; project mgr. Gahagan Constrn. Co., N.Y.C., 1945-48; project mgr. Frederick Snare Corp., N.Y.C., 1948-59, internat. mgr., 1959-62; with Kaiser Engrs., Oakland, Calif., 1962—, v.p. internat. operations; v.p. Latin Am., worldwide heavy constrn., 1962-64; asst. gen. mgr., v.p. Kaiser Industries, 1964—; gen. mgr. Consorcio Guri-Venezuela, 1967—; pres. Frederick Snare Overseas Corp., 1971; v.p., dir. Constructora Precom-Snare C.A., 1972; pres. Connor & Assos., Inc., St. Petersburg, Fla., 1980—. Served with USNR, 1941-45. Fellow Am. Soc. C.E.; mem. Internat. Commn. Large Dams, Soc. Profl. Engrs. Republic of Colombia, Pan Am. Union, Coll. Engrs. Republic of Venezuela Pan Am. Soc. Clubs: Internat. (Washington);

Caracas Country, Caraballeda Golf and Yacht; Princeton, Univ. (N.Y.C.). Home: 386 Briarwood Villas Sea Pines Plantation Hilton Head Island SC 29928

CONNOR, JOHN THOMAS, bank chmn.; b. Syracuse, N.Y., Nov. 3, 1914; s. Michael J. and Mary V. (Sullivan) C.; A.B. magna cum laude, Syracuse U., 1936; J.D., Harvard, 1939; m. Mary O'Boyle, June 22, 1940; children—John Thomas, Geoffrey Michael, Lisa Forrestal. Admitted to N.Y. State bar, 1939; asso. with Cravath, deGersdorff, Swaine & Wood, N.Y. City, 1939-42; gen. counsel Office Sci. Research and Devel., Washington, 1942-44; gen. atty. Merck and Co. Inc., Rahway, N.J., 1947, sec. and counsel, 1947-53, v.p., 1950-55, pres., chief exec., dir. 1955-65; U.S. sec. of commerce, 1965-67; pres. Allied Chem. Corp., N.Y.C., 1967-68, dir., 1967-80, chief exec. officer, 1968-79, chmn. bd., 1969-79; chmn. bd. Schroders, Inc., N.Y.C., 1980—; incorporator Communications Satelite Corp.; dir. Gen. Motors Corp., Warner-Lambert Co., ABC, Inc., ANECO Re-ins. Co. Ltd., Schroders Ltd., London, J. Henry Schroder Bank & Trust Co., N.Y.C. Trustee, Smith Coll., Syracuse U. Served from 2d lt. to capt. USMC, 1944-45, counsel Office Naval Research, spl. asst. to Sec. Navy, 1945-47. Mem. Bus. Council, Council on Fgn. Relations, Phi Beta Kappa, Phi Kappa Psi, Phi Kappa Phi, Phi Kappa Alpha. Roman Catholic. Clubs: Links, Harvard; Baltusrol; Metropolitan (Washington); Chevy Chase, Seminole. Office: Schroders Inc One State St New York NY 10004

CONNOR, JOHN THOMAS, JR., lawyer; b. N.Y.C., June 16, 1941; s. John Thomas and Mary (O'Boyle) C.; B.A. cum laude, Williams Coll., 1963; J.D., Harvard U., 1967; m. Susan Scholle Connor, Dec. 18, 1965; children—Seanna, Marin, John. Admitted to N.Y. State bar, 1968, D.C. bar, 1980; asso. firm Cravath, Swaine & Moore, N.Y.C., 1967-71; dep. dir. Office Econ. Policy and Case Analysis, Pay Bd., Washington, 1971-72; dep. dir. Bur. E.-W. Trade, U.S. Dept. Commerce, Washington, 1972-73; sr. v.p. U.S.-USSR Trade and Econ. Council, Moscow, 1973-76; asso. firm Milbank, Tweed, Hadley & McCloy, N.Y.C., 1976-79; partner firm Curtis, Mallet-Prevost, Colt and Mosle, Washington, 1980—. Exec. dir. Democratic party N.J., 1969-70; trustee Council for Religion in Independent Schs. Fulbright tutor Ferguson Coll., Poona, India, 1963-64. Mem. Internat., Am. (agy. adjudication com. of adminstrv. law sect.), N.Y. State, N.Y.C. (internat. law com.) bar assns., Council on Fgn. Relations, Phi Beta Kappa. Clubs: Met. (Washington); Union (N.Y.C.). Home: 2915 Woodland Dr NW Washington DC 20008 Office: 1735 Eye St NW Washington DC 20006

CONNORS, JAMES EDWARD, ins. co. exec.; b. Pitts., Apr. 28, 1933; s. Charles Joseph and Ruth Matilda (Costlow) C.; student U. Pitts., 1955-56, Harvard U., 1973; data processing certificate; postgrad. U. S.C. Mgmt. Center, 1975; m. Grace A. Moran, Feb. 9, 1957; children—James, Martin, Linda, Susan, Robert, Ann. Mgr. new systems RCA Corp., Cherry Hill, N.J., 1961-65; mgr. EDP systems Celanese Corp., Charlotte, N.C., 1965-67; dir. internat. market support Honeywell, Inc., London, Eng. and Wellesley, Mass., 1967-71; exec. v.p. Blue Cross & Blue Shield of S.C., Columbia, 1971—; exec. v.p., dir. Companion Life Ins. Co., Columbia, 1973—. Fund raising speaker United Fund. Served with USN, 1951-55. Mem. Am. Mgmt. Assn., Blue Shield-Blue Cross Assn., Am. Pub. Health Assn., Gamma Iota Sigma. Roman Catholic. Club: Summit. Home: 2617 Chatsworth Rd Columbia SC 29206 Office: Blue Cross and Blue Shield Columbia SC 29219

CONOLE, RICHARD CLEMENT, mgmt. exec.; b. Binghamton, N.Y., Dec. 7, 1936; s. Clement V. and Marjorie E. (Anable) C.; student U. Pa., 1955, 1960, Clarkson Coll., 1956-57; children—Margaret Ann, Linda Elizabeth; m. Sharyn Stafford, Apr. 18, 1969; 1 dau., Samantha Erin. Data processing dept. Campbell Soup Co., Inc., Camden, N.J., 1954; draftsman Gannett, Fleming, Corddry & Carpenter, Inc., Ardmore, Pa., 1955-56; plant mgr., office mgr. Tabulating Card Co., Inc., Princeton, N.J., 1957-59, asst. to pres., asst. sec.-treas., sec. 1959; pres., dir. Data Processing Supplies Co., Inc., Princeton, 1959; sec., dir. Whiting Paper Co., Inc., Princeton, 1959, pres. 1961-62; pres., dir. Mercer-Princeton Realty Co., Inc., Princeton, 1959-61; pres. Am. Bus. Investment Co., Inc., Princeton, 1960; pres., dir. Business Supplies Corp. Am., Skytop, Pa., 1962-65, Gen. Bus. Supplies Corp., Ardmore, 1965-71; chmn. bd. Nat. Productive Machines, Inc., Elkridge, Md., 1965-71; v.p., chmn. finance com., dir. Pocono Internat. Raceway Inc., 1964-74; pres. Gen. Automotive Supplies Co., 1971-72; pres., dir. Autoberfest, Inc., 1973—, Promotional Printing Ltd., 1973; pres. The World Series of Auto Racing Corp., 1973-78, Tex. World Speedway Inc., 1976—, Speedway Mgmt. Corp., 1978—; sales cons. Hess & Barker, 1972-76; mem. competition com. U.S. Auto Club, 1976—. Clubs: Skytop (Skytop, Pa.); Phila. Country, Merion Cricket (Haverford, Pa.); Manor (Pocono Manor, Pa.). Home: Box 9191 College Station TX 77840 Office: Box AJ College Station TX 77840

CONRAD, DAVID M., govt. ofcl.; b. Lawrence, Mass., Dec. 28, 1946; s. Michael Joseph and Genevieve (Gamble) C.; B.S. in Bus. Mgmt., Rensselaer Poly. Inst., 1968; M.B.A., Suffolk U., 1974; m. Rachel R. LeBlond, Aug. 29, 1971; children—Joseph Adam, Sarah Elizabeth. Contract adminstr., adminstrv. contracting officer, Def. Logistics Agy., Boston, Binghamton, N.Y., Needham, Mass., Lynn, Mass., Nashua, N.H., 1972-80; adminstrv. contracting officer GSA, Boston, 1980—; pres. Greenlands Assos.; asst. prof. evening sch. N.H. Vocat. Tech. Coll. Mem. Lawrence High Sch. Bldg. Com., 1976-77. Served with USN, 1968-71, USNR, 1972—. Mem. Nat. Contract Mgmt. Assn. (Boston chpt., cert. profl. contracts mgr.), VFW, Naval Res. Assn., Soc. of Old Crows, Patriots Roost. Roman Catholic. Office: GSA IFCA McCormick PO Courthouse Boston MA 02109

CONRAD, THERON DARLINGTON, investment banker; b. Sunbury, Pa., Sept. 10, 1902; s. Walter Ziegler and Maude (Neidig) C.; diploma LaSalle Extension U., 1932; m. Mabel Anna Yoxtheimer, Oct. 12, 1920; children—Theron Walter, James Henry, Patricia Ann (Mrs. John E. Hoover), Barry Lee. Agt., asst. supt., ordinary agt. Prudential Ins. Co. Am., Newark, 1925-40 pres. Theron D. Conrad & Co., Inc., investment banker and broker, Sunbury, 1945—. Charter mem., v.p. United Fund, Sunbury, 1961; bd. dirs. Salvation Army, Sunbury, also past pres.; bd. dirs. John R. Kauffman Jr. Pub. Library; trustee YMCA, Sunbury; past pres., trustee Sunbury Community Hosp. Mem. Phila. Stock Exchange, Nat. Assn. Securities Dealers, Central Susquehanna Valley C. of C. (past dir.), S.A.R. (state pres. 1980-81), pres. McClay chpt. 1973-74), Lambda Chi Alpha. Republican. Lutheran. Elk, Kiwanian (charter mem. Danville, Pa.). Home: 316 9th St Sunbury PA 17801 Office: 416 Market St Sunbury PA 17801

CONROY, DAVID JEROME, lawyer; b. New Orleans, Dec. 27, 1929; s. George E. and Lilyon (Bowling) C.; B.A., Tulane U., 1950, J.D., 1952; m. Ann Kathryn Gunderson, May 15, 1954; children—Kathryn Ann, David Michael, Elizabeth Helen, Mary Daire, Peter George Edward, Patrick Frank. Admitted to La. bar, 1952; partner firm Milling, Benson, Woodward, Hillyer, Pierson & Miller, New Orleans, 1956—, mng. partner, 1974—; sec. Jahncke Service Inc., New Orleans, 1961-69, Pub. Grain Elevator New Orleans, 1964—; sec., dir. C.B. Fox Co., New Orleans, 1965—. Mem. planning com. Tulane Tax Inst., 1975-79; del. La. Constl. Conv., 1973; bd. dirs. New Orleans Speech and Hearing Center, 1968-74, pres., 1970-72; bd. dirs. Louise S. McGehee Sch., 1970-77, pres., 1975-77; trustee Pub. Affairs Research Council La., 1974—; bd. dirs. Family Service Soc., 1972-77, United Way Greater New Orleans, 1974-80; bd. dirs., exec. com. Council for A Better La. Served with AUS, 1952-54. Mem. Am., La. (chmn. sect. corp. law 1968-69, chmn. com. on law reform 1977-78), New Orleans bar assns., Internat. House (dir. 1978—), St. Thomas More Cath. Lawyers Assn. (bd. govs. 1969-72, 78—, 1st v.p. 1971-72). Roman Catholic. Clubs: Pickwick, New Orleans Country, Plimsoll, Essex. Home: 437 Dorrington Dr Metairie LA 70005 Office: Whitney Bldg New Orleans LA 70130

CONSIDINE, FRANK WILLIAM, container corp. exec.; b. Chgo., Aug. 15, 1921; s. Frank Joseph and Minnie (Regan) C.; Ph.B., Loyola U., Chgo., 1943; m. Nancy Scott, Apr. 3, 1948. Partner, F. J. Hogan Agy., Chgo., 1946-47; asst. to pres. Graham Glass Co., Chgo., 1947-51; owner F.W. Considine Co., Chgo., 1951-55; v.p. Metro Glass div. Nat. Dairy Products Corp., Chgo., 1955-60; v.p., dir. Nat. Can Corp., Chgo., 1961-67, exec. v.p., 1967-69, pres., 1969—, chief exec. officer, 1973—, also mem. fin. com., chmn. exec. com., mem. corp. devel. com.; dir. Central Telephone & Utilities Corp., 1st Chgo. Corp., 1st Nat. Bank Chgo., Maytag Co., Internat. Minerals & Chem. Corp. Mem. governing bd. Ill. Council Econ. Edn.; chmn. U.S.-Egypt Bus. Council; trustee Mus. Sci. and Industry, Loyola U., Chgo.; bd. dirs. Can Mfrs. Inst., Evanston Hosp., Easter Seal Soc. Chgo., Lyric Opera of Chgo., Jr. Achievement Chgo., Econ. Devel. Com. Chgo.; mem. Chgo. Econ. Devel. Commn., Ill. Indsl. Devel. Authority. Served to lt. USNR, 1943-46. Mem. U.S. Brewers Assn. (asso. dir.), Am. Inst. Food Distbrn. (bd. trustees, chmn.), Chgo. Assn. Commerce and Industry (past pres.). Clubs: Econ., Comml., Mid Am. (Chgo.); Glenview. Office: 8101 Higgins Rd Chicago IL 60631

CONSIDINE, PATRICK JOHN, leather co. exec.; realtor; b. N.Y.C., Dec. 8, 1918; s. John Patrick and Alice Ann (Sizer) C.; m. Elizabeth Ceglio, Sept. 8, 1940; 1 son, Robert Patrick. Pres., P.J. Considine Co., Scarsdale, N.Y., 1950—; v.p., Hanson Realty Co., Scarsdale, 1965—. Served with USNR, 1942-43. Home: 199 Hanson Ln New Rochelle NY 10804 Office: 118 Brook St Scarsdale NY 10583

CONSIDINE, RICHARD, log house mfg. co. exec.; b. N.Y.C., Sept. 12, 1933; s. Thomas Joseph and Josephine (Chuzas) C.; student U. Va., 1970; m. Mary Zappulo, Jan. 6, 1956; children—Susan, Barbara, Cathy Ann. Pres., Lincoln Logs Ltd., Chestertown, N.Y., 1975—. Served with USN, 1951-54. Mem. Nat. Assn. Home Builders. Roman Catholic. Clubs: K.C., Rotary, (pres. 1974-75). Home: Spring St Chestertown NY 12817 Office: Riverside Dr Chestertown NY 12817

CONSIGLI, JOSEPH ANTHONY, real estate exec.; b. N.Y.C., Nov. 19, 1926; s. Joseph and Arduina (Malossi) C.; B.S. in Acctg., L.I. U., 1951; m. Rita Balcar, June 30, 1951; children—Robert, Michele. With Johns-Manville Sales Corp., Denver, 1951—, beginning as acct., successively auditor, mgr. sales services, dir. adminstrn. services, v.p. and gen. mgr. facilities planning, 1951-76, v.p., sr. dir. real estate, 1976—; vice chmn. bd. Johns-Manville Properties Corp.; works include Johns-Manville World Hdqrs. (AIA award), Elkhorn at Sun Valley, Idaho (AIA award), Ken-Caryl Ranch Planned Unit Devel. (Indsl. Research Council Environ. award). Dir. Youth Athletic League; scoutmaster Boy Scouts Am.; coach in baseball, football and hockey. Served with USMC, 1945-46. Mem. Nat. Assn. Real Estate Execs., Nat. Assn. Rev. Appraisers, Lakewood (Colo.) C. of C. Republican. Roman Catholic. Club: Columbine Country. Home: 1364 E Easter Circle Littleton CO 80122 Office: Ken Caryl Ranch Denver CO 80217

CONSTANT, CLINTON, chem. engr.; b. Nelson, B.C., Can., Mar. 20, 1912; s. Vasile and Annie (Hunt) C.; B.Sc. with honors, U. Alta., 1935, postgrad., 1935-36; Ph.D., Western Res. U., 1939; m. Margie Robbel, Dec. 5, 1965. Came to U.S., 1936, naturalized, 1942. Devel. engr. Harshaw Chem. Co., Cleve., 1936-38, mfg. foreman, 1938-43, sr. engr. semi-works dept., 1948-50; supt. hydrofluoric acid dept. Nyotex Chems., Inc., Houston, 1943-47, chief devel. engr., 1947-48; mgr. engring. Ferro Chem. Co., Bedford, Ohio, 1950-52; tech. asst. mfg. dept. Armour Agrl. Chem. Co. (formerly Armour Fertilizer Works), Bartow, Fla., 1952-61, mgr. research and devel. div., 1961-63, mgr. spl. projects (name now USS Agri-Chems.), Atlanta, 1963-65, project mgr., 1965-70; chem. adviser Robert & Co. Assos., Atlanta, 1970-79; chief engr. Almon & Assos., Atlanta, 1979—, Engring. Service Assos., Inc., Atlanta, 1980—. Registered profl. engr., Wis., Calif.; cert. profl. chemist and chem. engr. Fellow AAAS, Am. Inst. Chemists, Am. Inst. Chem. Engrs., AIAA (asso.); mem. Am. Chem. Soc., Am. Astron. Soc., Astron. Soc. Pacific, Royal Astron. Soc. Can., Am. Water Works Assn., N.Y. Acad. Scis., Soc. Mfg. Engrs. (cert. mfg. engr.), Ga., Ala. water and pollution control assns. Writer tech. reports, sci. fiction. Home: PO Box 1221 Atlanta GA 30301 Office: 1800 Water Pl Suite 200 Atlanta GA 30339

CONTAS, ARTHUR PETER, mgmt. cons.; b. Boston, Apr. 8, 1931; s. Peter Gouvalaris and Jennie (Badavas) C.; student Phillips Acad., Andover, 1948, Eastbourne Coll., Sussex, Eng., 1949; A.B. magna cum laude, Harvard U., 1952, M.B.A. with distinction, 1954; children—Jennifer Thompson, Alysia Nichols. Pres., J.S. Contas Bros., Inc., Boston, 1958-63, Kane Fin. Corp., Boston, 1969-73; v.p., dir. Boston Cons. Group, 1963-69, 73—; pres., dir. Mass. Capital Corp., 1969-72; vice chmn. Queches Lakes Corp., Vt., 1969-72; trustee Security Trust Assos., 1967—. Class sec. Harvard Bus. Sch., 1965—; mem. corp. Inst. Contemporary Art, Boston, 1965-72; bd. dirs. Playhouse, Boston, 1967-71; trustee Hellenic Coll., 1973-74; bd. overseers Boston Symphony Orch., 1975—; corp. mem. Winsor Sch., 1980—. Served to lt. USNR, 1954-57. Mem. Phi Beta Kappa. Greek Orthodox. Clubs: Harvard (Boston); Bay. Home: 85 East India Row 24B Boston MA 02110 Office: 1 Boston Pl Boston MA 02106

CONTI, JAMES JOSEPH, mortgage banker; b. Burlington, N.J., Dec. 19, 1926; s. Anthony F. and Alice (Conrey) C.; B.S., Rider Coll., 1949; certificate Sch. Mortgage Banking Northwestern U., 1958; m. Elizabeth Eileen Schoch, Aug. 23, 1947; 1 dau., Kimberly Sue. Loan mgr., Comml. Credit Corp., Camden, N.J., Harrisburg, Pa., 1949-52; asst. mgr. W.A. Clarke Mortgage Co., Harrisburg, 1952-62; v.p. mortgage opns. Cumberland County Nat. Bank, New Cumberland, Pa., 1962-69; regional dir. Central Pa., Mortgage Guaranty Corp., Milw., 1969—. Treas., Humane Soc. West Shore; bd. dirs., mem. fin. com. United Ch. of Christ Homes for Aged. Served with USN, 1944-46. Decorated Purple Heart. Mem. Inst. Real Estate Mgmt., Am. Legion, West Shore Area C. of C. (past pres.), Rider Coll. Alumni Club. Mem. United Ch. of Christ. Club: Lion, Moose. Home and office: 308 Allendale Way Camp Hill PA 17011

CONTRERAS, FERMIN M., banker; b. Santurce, P.R., Jan. 20, 1944; s. Benigno and Argelia (Bordallo) C.; B.B.A. cum laude, U. P.R., 1965; M.B.A., Inter-Am. U., 1971; m. Gisela Gómez, Sept. 3, 1965; children—Fermin, Omar, Gisela, Mariana. Trainee, Chase Manhattan Bank, San Juan, 1965-66, credit analyst, credit officer, 1966-67; asst. mgr. Banco Central Economias, San German, P.R., 1967-68, asst. v.p. in charge of ops. and personnel, 1968-69, v.p. in charge of S.W. credit ops., 1969-72, sr. v.p., 1972—, dir., 1977—. Mem. Am. Banking Assn. (certified comml. lender), Robert Morris Assn. Club: Mayaguez (P.R.) Hilton Tennis and Swimming. Home: Rd 108 K3-5 Mayaguez PR 00708 Office: Box 146 San German PR 00753

CONWAY, EDWARD JOHN, mgmt. cons. co. exec.; b. Ridgefield Park, N.J., Sept. 8, 1931; s. Thomas Anthony and Norma Jean (Scott) C.; B.S. in Acctg., U. So. Calif., 1957; student Fordham U., 1949-50; 1 son, Robert F. Asst. controller Continental Can Co., Los Angeles, 1954-61, Universal Pictures, Los Angeles, 1962-65, controller Universal City Tours, Los Angeles, 1965-68; asst. controller MCA Inc., Los Angeles, 1969-71, ABC Records, Los Angeles, 1972-76; v.p. fin. Casablanca Record & Filmworks, Los Angeles, 1976-78; pres. Sunstorm Mgmt. Cons., Los Angeles, 1978—. Served with U.S. Army, 1950-54. Decorated Bronze Star. Mem. Assn. Mgmt. Cons., Assn. Fin. Planners. Republican. Roman Catholic. Home: 938 3d St Santa Monica CA 90403 Office: 8230 Beverly Blvd Suite 27 Los Angeles CA 90048

CONWAY, EDWARD ROBERT, real estate broker; b. Concord, N.H., Aug. 27, 1925; s. Edward James and Frances (O'Brien) C.; B.S., U. N.H., 1950; postgrad. San Diego State U., 1970-72; advanced certificate in real estate U. Calif. at San Diego, 1974; grad. Realtors Inst. Calif.; m. Susan Jane Barto, Nov. 3, 1961; children—Craig William, Margaret Kathleen. Commd. 2d lt. U.S. Army, 1950, advanced through grades to lt. col., 1967, ret. 1969; real estate investment and exchange broker Conway Investment Realty, Rancho Sante Fe, Calif., 1972—. Served with AUS, 1942-46. Decorated Legion of Merit, Army Commendation medal (4). Mem. San Diequito Bd. Realtors, Calif. Assn. Realtors, Real Estate Forum San Diego (chmn. 1975—), Real Estate Cert. Inst., U. N.H. Alumni Assn., Ret. Officers Assn., Kappa Sigma. Republican. Address: Box 1777 Rancho Santa Fe CA 92067

CONWAY, FRANKLIN DANIEL, real estate investor; b. Denver, June 13, 1921; s. Franklin Daniel and Clara Belle (Phelps) C.; student San Francisco State Coll., 1947, San Mateo Jr. Coll., 1948, 52; m. Carol F. Upchurch, Nov. 21, 1972; children by previous marriage—Claire Conway Spence, Ivka, Marian; 1 stepdau., Jane Russell Parris. Diesel engr. Delta Lines, 1947; sr. technician, tng. supr. Pacific Tel. & Tel. Co., 1979; engaged in real estate investing, 1959—. Served as capt. CAP, 1950-59. Served with USNR, 1941-45. Mem. Telephone Pioneers Assn., Airplane Owners and Pilots Assn., Air Force Assn. Aux., Am. Legion (post vice comdr. 1958, chmn. nat. def. com. 1956-57). Republican. Roman Catholic. Clubs: Elks, Commonwealth Calif. Address: 12160 Mellowood Dr Saratoga CA 95070

CONWAY, JOHN EDWIN, cement mfg. co. exec.; b. N.Y.C., May 21, 1934; s. Edwin John and Mary (Condren) C.; B.S. in Chemistry, Holy Cross Coll., 1955; postgrad. U. So. Calif., 1965-67; m. Mary Ann Carpenter, Jan. 10, 1959; children—Mark, Susan. Asst. to v.p. ops. Riverside (Calif.) Cement Co., 1965-68, supr. quality, Oro Grande, Calif., 1968-70; v.p. mfg. Phoenix Cement Co., Clarkdale, Ariz., 1970—; vice chmn., dir. 1st State Bank of Sedona (Ariz.). Pres., trustee Mingus Union High Sch.; bd. dirs. Marcus J. Lawrence Meml. Hosp., Sedona Healthcare Corp. Served to capt. USAF, 1956-64. Mem. ASTM, Ariz. Sch. Ed. Assn., Am. Hosp. Trustees Assn. Republican. Roman Catholic. Clubs: Sedona Racquet, Jerome Elks. Home: PO Box 1032 Sedona AZ 86336 Office: PO Box 428 Clarkdale AZ 86324

CONZELMAN, BRUCE THOMAS, cons., developer; b. St. Louis, May 9, 1935; s. Fred H. and Lily Margarite (Kern) C.; B.E.E., U.S. Naval Acad., 1958; postgrad. U. Calif. at La Jolla, 1972. Founder, pres. Beach & Towne Realty, San Diego, 1965-72; exec. v.p., dir. mktg., sales tng. Grubb & Ellis Co., San Diego, 1974—, v.p. new home sales div., 1976—; founder, pres. Mktg. Advisors, San Diego, 1974—. Served to lt. USN, 1958-62. Mem. Am. Mktg. Assn., San Diego Bldg. Contractors Assn., San Diego C. of C., U.S. Naval Acad. Alumni Assn. Home: PO Box 733 Solana Beach CA 92075 Office: 1200 Third Ave Suite 1100 San Diego CA 92101

CONZEN, WILLIBALD HERMANN, pharm. co. exec.; b. Dortmund, Germany, Aug. 3, 1913; s. Friedrich Wilhelm and Elizabeth (Mathies) C.; abitur degree, Kaiserin Augusta Gymnasium, Koblenz, W. Germany, 1931; children—Elizabeth, Suzanne; came to U.S., 1952, naturalized, 1959. With Schering A.G., Berlin, Germany, 1931-38; with Scherag (Pty.) Ltd., Johannesburg, S. Africa, 1938-52, gen. mgr., 1941-52; with Schering Corp., U.S.A., Bloomfield, N.J., 1952—, v.p., 1959-65, sr. v.p., 1965-66, pres., chief exec. officer, 1966-72, chmn. bd., 1972-75; pres., chief exec. officer Schering-Plough Corp., 1971-76, chmn. bd., chief exec. officer, 1976-78, chmn., 1976-80, chmn. exec. com. of bd., 1980—; dir. Midlantic Nat. Bank, Midlantic Banks, Inc., Faber-Castell Corp., BDM Internat., Inc. Bd. dirs. People-to-People Health Found. Mem. Pharm. Mfrs. Assn., Internat. Fedn. Pharm. Mfrs. Assn. Clubs: Montclair Golf (N.J.); Union League, Sky, Economic (N.Y.C.). Office: Galloping Hill Rd Kenilworth NJ 07033

COOK, CLYDE CHILES, bus. cons.; b. Cortland, N.Y., Mar. 28, 1937; s. Clyde J. and Gracy C.; student Auburn Community Coll., 1969-70; m. Jacqueline Belknap, Aug. 22, 1959; children—Kurt, Cheryl, Daniel, Susan. Vice pres. David Harum Paint Co., Homer, N.Y., 1960-65; v.p., treas. Taurus Chem. Corp., Auburn, N.Y., 1965-69; pvt. practice bus. cons., Homer, 1969—. Served with U.S. Army, 1957-59. Mem. Nat. Assn. Accountants (v.p., dir.), Nat. Soc. Public Accountants, N.Y. Soc. Ind. Accountants, Nat. Fedn. Ind. Bus., United Comml. Travelers. Republican. Methodist. Club: Nat. Grange. Home: RD 1 Health Camp Rd Homer NY 13077 Office: 17 S Main St Homer NY 13077

COOK, DAVID FRETZ, banker; b. Easton, Pa., Apr. 5, 1939; s. Alan Riegel and Isabel Jane (Fretz) C.; B.S. in Bus. Adminstrn., Lehigh U., 1960; m. Cynthia Hawkins, Oct. 18, 1963 (div.); 1 son, Michael. With Girard Bank, Phila., 1966-79, v.p. in charge mortgage and comml. real estate loans and adminstrn., to 1979; exec. v.p. No. Nat. Corp., multi-bank and fin. holding co., Moorestown, 1980—. Mem. Riegelsville (Pa.) Zoning Bd., 1966-68; deacon, elder United Ch. of Christ, 1966-70. Served to lt. USNR, 1962-65. Mem. Phila., Bucks County bds. realtors, Phila. Mortgage Bankers Assn. Office: Northern Nat Corp 312 W Route 38 at East Gate Dr Moorestown NJ 08057

COOK, EARLE THEODORE, corp. exec.; b. Kingman, Ariz., Sept. 23, 1930; s. Earle Wayne and Sadie Louise (Rucker) C.; A.A., Highland Community Jr. Coll., Kans., 1970; student Harvard U., 1960, 62, 65, U. Kans., 1968-70; B.A., Williams Coll., Berkeley, Calif., 1972, M.A., 1974, D.B.A., 1975; D.D., Internat. Deliverance Chs., Dallas, 1979; m. Marlene A. Winters, Dec. 23, 1977; children—Earle W., Steve W. With Coca Cola Co., Kingman, Atlanta Jackson, Miss., Little Rock, Amarillo, Tex., Houston, 1953-68; ordained to ministry Internat. Deliverance Chs., 1978; pres., owner PMA Corp., mattress mfrs., Oakland, Calif., 1978—; capt. Vols. of Am., 1979; dir. Vols. of Am. Thrift Stores, Oakland and San Francisco, 1979—; speaker; TV appearances. Served to lt. U.S. Army, 1951-57; Korea. Cert. comml. pilot, lic. for single and multi-engine aircraft, instrument landing. Address: 989 40th St Oakland CA 94608

COOK, EDWARD WILLINGHAM, diversified industry exec.; b. Memphis, June 19, 1922; s. Everett Richard and Phoebe (Willingham) C.; A.B., Yale U., 1944; m. Patricia Long, Mar. 17, 1973; children—Edward Willingham, Everett Richard II, Barbera Moore Cook Brooks, Patricia Kendall. Chmn. bd., chief exec. officer Cook Industries, Inc., Memphis; dir. First Tenn. Nat. Corp., Tenn. Taxpayers Assn. Squire, Shelby County (Tenn.) Ct., 1948-66; mem. Cotton Adv. Commn., 1964-68; chmn. Memphis-Shelby County Airport Authority, 1968—; mem. exec. com. Nat. Council U.S. China Trade, 1973-78; mem. Pres.'s Export Council, 1973-79; dir. Chgo. Bd. Trade, 1974-76. Served to maj. USAAF, 1943-45; MTO. Decorated D.F.C., Bronze Star, Air medal with six oak leaf clusters. Mem. Am. Cotton Shippers Assn. (pres. 1966-67), So. Cotton Assn. (past pres.), Cotton Council Am. (dir. 1962-65), Cotton Council Internat. (dir. 1964-65), Memphis Area C. of C. (dir.). Democrat. Episcopalian. Clubs: Memphis Country, Memphis Hunt and Polo; Links (N.Y.C.); Island (Hobe Sound, Fla.); Old Baldy (Saratoga, Wyo.); Everglades (Palm Beach, Fla.). Home: Memphis TN Office: 855 Ridge Lake Blvd Memphis TN 38138

COOK, FORREST RUSSELL, JR., bank exec.; b. Salem, Mass., Jan. 25, 1933; s. Forrest Russell and Priscilla Cook; A.B., Bowdoin Coll., 1955; student Mass. Bankers Sch., Williams Coll., Stonier Grad. Sch. Banking, Rutgers U., Advanced Mgmt. Program, Grad. Sch. Bus. Adminstrn., Harvard U., 1973; m. June; children—Laurel, Russell. With pharm. sales Upjohn Co., 1956-58; with Rockland-Atlas Bank, Boston, 1958-61; successively corr. banking dept. head, credit card dept. head, retail div. head, sr. v.p., State St. Bank, Boston, 1961-74; pres. Bank of N.H., N.A., Manchester, 1974—; dir. United Life & Accident Ins. Co., Amoskeag Industries. Mem. AAA Adv. Bd.; trustee Elliot Hosp., 1977—; chmn. fund raising, bd. dirs. Fed. Arts of Manchester, 1979-80; chmn. corp. gifts Easter Seal Telethon, 1980. Served to capt. U.S. Army. Club: Manchester Rotary. Office: 300 Franklin St PO Box 600 Manchester NH 03105

COOK, GENE WALTON, food co. exec.; b. Dothan, Ala., Oct. 24, 1931; s. Frank Walton and Lottie Jeanette (White) C.; student U. N.C., 1949, U. Pa., 1950, William and Mary Coll., 1954-56; postgrad. Mich. State U., 1959-60; m. Irene Iris Roach, Dec. 2, 1952; children—Michael, Patricia J. With Gen. Foods Corp., 1954—, nat. sales mgr. for beverages, breakfast and pet foods divs., White Plains, N.Y., 1980—. Served with USAF, 1949-52. Mem. Am. Mgmt. Assn., Mich. State Alumni Assn., N.Y. Sales Execs. Club. Republican. Methodist. Home: 56 Cedar Dr Allendale NJ 07401 Office: 250 North St White Plains NY 10625

COOK, GEORGE LONGSHORE, savs. and loan assn. exec.; b. Sacramento, Dec. 30, 1924; s. Carroll Adams and Margaret (Irys) C.; student U. Santa Clara, 1942; Jane O'Dea, Jan. 25, 1945; children—Jane, Susan, Margaret, George, Catherine, John, Michael, Stephen, Mark, James, David. With Artz and Cook, Real Estate Brokers, Sacramento, 1945-52; with Sacramento Savs. & Loan Assn., 1952-60, pres., chmn. bd. dirs., 1956-60; pres., chmn. bd. dirs., chief exec. officer El Dorado Savs. & Loan Assn., Placerville, Calif., 1960—; dir. A. Teichert & Son; Fruitridge Vista Water Co. Served with USAAF, 1943-45. Mem. Calif. Savs. and Loan League (dir.), Sacramento Bd. Realtors (pres. 1961). Republican. Roman Catholic. Club: Cameron Park Country. Office: PO Box 1208 Placerville CA 95667

COOK, GRANVILLE POTTER, equipment mfg. co. exec.; b. Bono, Ark., Sept. 6, 1937; s. James C. and Letha (Lakey) C.; student Ark. State U., 1954-55; m. Ruth M. Lands, Apr. 29, 1966. Ins. agt. Lincoln Income Life, Jonesboro, Ark., 1957-59; material handler J.I. Case Co., Memphis, 1959-62, machinery biller, 1964-66, asst. mgr. equipment distbn., 1966-79, distbn. specialist, 1979—. Served with U.S. Army, 1962-64. Methodist. Home: 1265 Heathcliff Dr Memphis TN 38134 Office: 6363 Poplar Ave Memphis TN 38117

COOK, HERBERT, food co. exec.; b. Phila., 1932. With Bluebird, Inc., Phila., 1948—, now chmn. bd., chief exec. officer. Office: 2000 Market St Suite 1400 Philadelphia PA 19103

COOK, JAMES BALFOUR, fin. exec.; b. Kirkcaldy, Scotland, Dec. 5, 1948; came to U.S., 1963, naturalized, 1970; s. James B. and Kathleen (Sands) C.; B.A., Oakland U., 1973; m. Marilyn Renaldi, May 14, 1971; children—Justin, Jillian. Asst. mgr. Am. Fin. Corp., Detroit, 1972-73; sales mgr. Mich. Credit Union League, Southfield, 1973-74; collection mgr. Detroit Tchrs. Credit Union, 1974-77; mng. dir. Saguaro Credit Union, Tucson, 1978—, dir., 1980—. Served with U.S. Army, 1968-70. Mem. Credit Union Exec. Soc., Am. Mgmt. Assn. Democrat. Roman Catholic. Office: 1060 N Campbell Ave Tucson AZ 85719

COOK, JAMES SAMUEL, jewelry mfg. co. exec.; b. Needham, Mass., Sept. 12, 1928; s. William A. and Frances (Cohoon) C.; B.A., Brown U., 1950; m. Phyllis Towne, Sept. 12, 1953; children—Allison, James, Deborah, Jonathan, Susan. Personnel asst., fgn. mktg. analyst 1st Nat. Bank of Boston, 1952-56; with W.R. Grace & Co., Mass., S.C. and Pa., 1956-74, v.p. Jet Containers div., until 1974; pres., chief exec. officer L. G. Balfour Co., Attleboro, Mass., 1974—, chmn. bd., dir.; trustee, bd. investments Attleborough Savs. Bank. Trustee Sturdy Meml. Hosp. Served to capt. USMCR. Mem. NAM (dir.), Asso. Industries Mass. (dir.), Am. Mgmt. Assn. (pres.'s assn.), Mfg. Jewelers and Silversmiths Am. (dir.), Conf. Bd. (N.E. regional council), Attleboro C. of C.

COOK, LORA ELIZABETH, ednl. co. exec.; b. Sarepta, Miss., June 10, 1924; d. William Franklin and Ella (Lewis) C.; student Jackson (Miss.) Comml. Coll., 1942, Miss. State Coll., 1950, 51, 52, U. Miss., 1959, 60. Sec., Herschel Smith Co., Jackson, 1942-58; adminstrv. asst. Ednl. Projections Corp., Jackson, 1958-72, dir. instructional materials, Glenview, Ill., 1972-79; pres. Ednl. Projections Corp., Jacksonvlle Beach, Fla., 1979—; mktg. specialist Standard Projector and Equipment Co., Glenview, 1945—. Recipient Merit award Nat. 16mm Victory Film Com., 1945. Mem. Miss. Audio Visual Club (sec. 1969), Nat. Audio Visual Assn., Assn. Ednl. Tech. and Communication, DAR, Colonial Dames VII Century, Beta Sigma Phi. Democrat. Baptist. Home: 901 Ocean Blvd Apt 98 Atlantic Beach FL 32233 Office: 224 N 1st St Jacksonville Beach FL 32250

COOK, NOEL ROBERT, mfg. co. exec.; b. Houston, Mar. 19, 1937; s. Horace Berwick and Leda Estelle (Houghton) C.; student Iowa State U., 1955-57; B.S. in Indsl. Engring., U. Mich., 1960; m. Patricia Jane Henny, Aug. 17, 1962 (div. 1980); children—Laurel Jane, David Robert. Engr. in tng. Eaton Mfg., Saginaw, Mich., 1960-61; mgr. mfg. and contracting J. N. Fauver Co., Madison Heights, Mich., 1961-65; pres. Newton Mfg., Royal Oak, Mich., 1965—; sec. Indsl. Piping Contractors, Birmingham, Mich., 1969-75; pres. RNR Metal Fabricators, Inc., Royal Oak, Mich., 1974-78; chmn. bd. Kim Internat. Sales Co., 1978—; pres. Newton Sales Co., Royal Oak, 1978—. Served with U.S. Army, 1960-61. Mem. Fluid Power Soc., Nat. Fluid Power Assn., Birmingham Jr. C. of C. (past bd. dirs.). Patentee in field. Office: 4249 Delemere Blvd Royal Oak MI 48073

COOK, ROBERT EDGAR, computer services corp. exec.; b. Altoona, Pa., June 19, 1941; s. William R. and Dorothy M. (Baird) C.; B.S., Indiana U. of Pa., 1964; M.S., George Washington U., 1970; m. Georgia Ann Greene, Dec. 26, 1964; children—Camberly, Chadwick. Sales mgr. Boeing Computer Services, Inc., McLean, Va., 1971-74; product line mgr. - time sales, 1974-76; v.p. planning STSC, Inc., Bethesda, Md., 1978-79, sr. v.p. market devel., 1979—; chmn., dir. MTSC, Inc., Bethesda, 1980—. Served with U.S. Army, 1964-70. Decorated Bronze Star. Mem. Data Processing Mgmt. Assn., Assn. Data Processing Service Orgns. (dir. remote processing services sect. 1980—). Home: 10107 Nadine Dr Vienna VA 22180 Office: STSC Inc 7316 Wisconsin Ave Bethesda MD 20014

COOK, ROBERT EDWARD, real estate broker, developer; b. Alexander City, Ala., Oct. 19, 1946; s. Luther W. and Annie Lou (Moore) C.; B.B.A., U. Ga., 1968; M.S., S.D. State U., 1969; m. Kay Angela Eades, Oct. 9, 1948; children—Emily Lynn, Corbin Lee. With Jim Royer Realty, Atlanta, 1966; asso. broker Evans & Mitchell Industries, Inc., Athens, Ga., 1966-69; owner, broker Amprop-Am. Property Services, Inc., Rapid City, S.D., 1969-72; v.p. Bales Properties, Inc., Atlanta, 1973-76; pres. Southland Real Estate & Investment Corp., East Point, Ga., 1976—, also Southland Heritage Homes, Inc., Fayetteville, Ga. Served to capt. USAF, 1968-72. Mem. Nat. Assn. Realtors, Realtors Nat. Mktg. Inst., Mortgage Bankers Assn., Rho Epsilon. Republican. Club: Ansley Golf (Atlanta). Home: 3819 Brandy Station Ct NW Atlanta GA 30339 Office: 646 Morrow Ind Blvd Jonesboro GA also 2692 Harris St East Point GA 30344 also 1741 Hwy 138 Riverdale GA

COOK, STANTON R., newspaper pub.; b. Chgo., July 3, 1925; s. Rufus Merrill and Thelma Marie (Bogerson) C.; B.S. in Mech. Engring., Northwestern U., 1949; m. Barbara Wilson. Dist. sales rep. Shell Oil Co., 1949-51; prodn. engr. Chgo. Tribune, 1951-60, asst. production mgr., 1960-65, production mgr., 1965-67, production dir., 1967-70, dir. ops., 1970, gen. mgr., 1970-73, pub., 1973—; v.p. Chgo. Tribune Co., 1967-70, exec. v.p., 1970-73, pres., 1973-74, chief officer, 1974-76, chmn., 1974—; v.p., dir. Tribune Co., Chgo., 1973-74, pres., chief officer, from 1974; dir. Newspaper Advt. Bur., Inc.; 2d vice chmn., dir. AP; dep. chmn., dir. Fed. Res. Bank of Chgo. Mem. exec. com. Am. Newspaper Pubs. Assn. Research Inst.; bd. dirs. Chgo. Boys Clubs, Jr. Achievement Chgo.; trustee U. Chgo., Mus. Sci. and Industry, Field Mus. Nat. History (both Chgo.), Am. Newspaper Pubs. Assn. Found., Robert R. McCormick Trusts and Founds.; prin., mem. exec. com. Chgo. United. Mem. Chgo. Council on Fgn. Relations (dir.), Am. Newspaper Pubs. Assn. (dir., former pres.). Office: 435 N Michigan Ave Chicago IL 60611

COOK, SUSAN PAULA, retail exec.; b. Rochester, N.H., Feb. 16, 1947; d. Israel Jack and Molly (Landes) C.; A.B. cum laude (scholar), N.Y. U., 1968; scholar U. Madrid, 1967. Dept. mgr. Bloomingdale's, 1968, personnel mgr., 1969-70, corp. tng. dir., 1971-72; asst. personnel dir. I Magnin Co., San Francisco, 1971; personnel mgr. Macy's Calif., Palo Alto, 1973-74, staff tng. mgr., 1974-75, adminstr. tng., 1975-77, v.p. personnel devel., 1977-80, v.p. exec. personnel and devel., 1980—. Mem. United Way mgmt. assistance program United Jewish Appeal. Recipient Priscilla Lieber Kaufman Swimming medal. Mem. Am. Soc. Tng. and Devel. (exec. com.), Internat. Assn. Bus. Communicators, Nat. Soc. Performance Improvement, Nat. Retail Mchts. Assn., Profl. Women's Alliance. Democrat. Jewish. Editor: Israel's Numismatic Mag., 1970; editor, developer Faces, Bloomingdale's internal mag., 1971-72. Home: 21100 Gary Dr Apt 309 Hayward CA 94546 Office: PO Box 7888 San Francisco CA 94120

COOK, WILLIAM SUTTON, bus. exec.; b. Duluth, Minn., Sept. 6, 1922; s. Ellis Ray and Marjorie Sutton Cook; B.B.A., U. Minn., 1948. Various fin. positions Gen. Electric Co., 1948-62; comptroller, then v.p., comptroller Pa. R.R./Pa. Central Co., 1962-68; v.p., comptroller Ebasco Industries, Inc., 1968-69; v.p. fin., then exec. v.p. Union Pacific Corp., N.Y.C., 1969-77, pres., since 1977, also dir.; dir. U.P. R.R., Champlin Petroleum Co., Upland Industries Corp., Stauffer Chem. Co., Boise Cascade Corp., Royal Group, Inc. Served to capt. U.S. Army, 1943-46. Mem. Financial Execs. Inst. Clubs: Links, Brook, Econ., Board Room (N.Y.C.); Sleepy Hollow Country (pres. 1976-78), (Scarborough). Office: 345 Park Ave New York NY 10022

COOKSON, ALBERT ERNEST, tel. and tel. co. exec.; b. Needham, Mass., Oct. 30, 1921; s. Willard B. and Sarah Jane (Jack) C.; B.E.E., Northeastern U., 1943; M.E.E., Mass. Inst. Tech., 1951; Sc.D., Gordon Coll., 1974; m. Constance J. Buckley, Sept. 10, 1949; children—Constance J., William B. Group leader Research Lab. Electronics, Mass. Inst. Tech., 1947-51; lab. dir. ITT Fed. Labs., Nutley, N.J., 1951-59, v.p., dir. operations Internat. Elec. Corp. div., Paramus, N.J., 1959-62, pres. ITT Intelcom, Falls Church, Va., 1962-65; dep. gen. tech. dir. Internat. Tel. and Tel. Corp., N.Y.C., 1965-66, v.p., tech. dir., 1966-68, sr. v.p., gen. tech. dir., 1968—; chmn. bd. ITT Interplan; dir. Internat. Standard Electric, ITT Industries. Mem. Def. Communications Satellite Panel; adviser research and engring. on def. communications satellite systems Dept. Def.; mem. indsl. panel sci. and tech. NSF. Mem. Fairfax County Econ. and Indsl. Devel. Com., 1962-65; mem. nat. council Northeastern U.; mem. pride com. U. Hartford, 1973-76; elec. engring./computer adv. bd. Mass. Inst. Tech., 1977—. Served with USNR, 1943-46. Fellow IEEE; mem. Armed Forces Communications and Electronics Assn., Am. Mgmt. Assn., Am. Inst. Aeros. and Astronautics, Electronic Industries Assn., Sigma Xi, Tau Beta Pi. Patentee frequency search and track system. Home: 2 Baywater Dr Darien CT 06820 Office: 320 Park Ave New York NY 10022

COOLEY, BERNARD HENRY, hotel devel. and cons. exec.; b. N.Y.C.; s. Anthony Bernard and Annie Catherine (Smith) C.; ed. in U.S., Cuba and Eng.; m. Doris Joan Liebfried, Aug. 18, 1948; children—Carol E., Brenda J. Fgn. trade counsellor, N.Y.C., 1926-34; comml. attache Govt. Cuba, 1934-42; gen. mgr., asst. to pres. Brighton Hotel, Atlantic City, 1947-49; gen. mgr., pres. Colony Hotel, Palm Beach, Fla., 1949-59; cons. supr. El Colony, Isle of Pines, Cuba, 1958; v.p., operational and mgmt. cons. Old Port Village, Palm Beach, 1959-63; v.p., gen. mgr. Lost Tree Country Club, Palm Beach, 1959-63; v.p., dir. Westport Utilitie Corp. (Fla.), 1959-63; pres., dir. Hotel Consultants & Developers, Inc., Palm Beach, 1960—, Salco, Inc., Palm Beach, 1957-63; exec. dir. Kings Bay Yacht and Country Club, Miami, Fla., 1964-69; gen. mgr. Everglades Club, Palm Beach, 1969-70, Thunderbird Motor Hotel, Jacksonville, Fla., 1971—; asst. to pres. FPA Corp., Pompano Beach, Fla., 1970—; mem. adv. bd. Bank Palm Beach & Trust Co., 1969—; pres. Sapphire Valley Devel. Corp. (N.C.), 1974—. Commr. for 6th Congl. dist. Fla. Adv. Commn., 1954. Bd. suprs. St. Francis Coll., Loretto, Pa., 1958—. Served to maj. AUS, 1942-46; ETO. Mem. Fla. State (dir. 1953-58), Palm Beach County (pres. 1950-60) hotel assns., Fraternal Order Police Assos. (founder, trustee, pres. 1957-58). Clubs: Palm Beach, Everglades of Palm Beach, The Beach, Palm Beach; River of Jacksonville (Fla.). Home: 400 S Ocean Blvd Palm Beach FL 33480

COOLEY, RICHARD PIERCE, banker; b. Dallas, Nov. 25, 1923; s. Victor E. and Helen (Pierce) C.; B.S., Yale, 1944. With Wells Fargo Bank, N.A., San Francisco, 1949—, exec. v.p., 1965-66, pres., 1966-78, dir., chief exec. officer, 1966—, chmn., 1978—, pres., chief exec. officer, dir., Wells Fargo Bank Internat., 1967—, Wells Fargo & Co., 1968—; dir. United Airlines, Inc., Pacific Gas Electric Co., UAL, Inc., Howmet Turbine Components Corp., Pechiney Ugine Kuhlmann Corp.; trustee Rand Corp. Trustee, Calif. Inst. Tech., Pasadena, Children's Hosp., San Francisco; bd. dirs. San Francisco Opera Assn., Los Angeles Philharm. Assn. Served to 1st lt. USAAF, 1943-46. Decorated Air medal. Mem. Assn. Res. City Bankers, Smithsonian Instn. (dir.). Office: Wells Fargo Bank Nat Assn 770 Wilshire Blvd Los Angeles CA 90017

COOLIDGE, NICHOLAS JEFFERSON, investment banking exec., lawyer; b. Brookline, Mass., Feb. 12, 1932; s. Harold J. and Helen Carpenter (Isaacs) C.; grad. Groton Sch., 1950; A.B., Harvard, 1954, LL.B., J.D., 1959; m. Eliska Hasek, June, 1977; 1 dau., Alexandra Randolph; children from previous marriage—Nicole Rousmaniere, Peter Jefferson. Admitted to N.Y. bar, 1959; practiced in N.Y.C. until 1965; asso. firm Sullivan & Cromwell; with Kidder, Peabody & Co., Inc., N.Y.C., 1965-78, dir., v.p. corporate fin. dept., head leasing and project financing, Canadian and real estate groups; pres. Nicholas Coolidge Inc., Investment Banking Services, N.Y.C., 1978—. Served to 1st lt. USMRC, 1954-56. Mem. Council on Fgn. Relations. Home: 3200 Scott Pl Washington DC 20007 Office: 800 Fifth Ave Suite 20D New York NY 10021

COOLIDGE, ROBERT CANODE, computer co. exec.; b. Bloomington, Ill., Feb. 11, 1933; s. Clifford Newell and Margaret Jane (Canode) C.; student DePauw U., Greencastle, Ind., 1951-53, San Francisco State U., 1966-67; grad. Advanced Mgmt. Program, Stanford U., 1976; m. Marie Ann Handley, Apr. 6, 1974; children—Kimberly, John Case, Robert Todd, Christopher Lawrence. Western area mgr. Minn. Mining & Mfg. Co., St. Paul, 1959-67; regional mgr. Stromberg Data Graphics, Inc., San Diego, 1967-69; v.p. mktg. Distbn. Scis., Inc., Oakbrook, Ill., 1969-71, also dir.; sr. v.p. Boole & Babbage, Inc., Sunnyvale, Calif., 1972-79, also dir.; founder, pres. Internat. Data Processing Services, San Francisco, 1980—; dir. Computer Program Products, Ltd., London, European Software Co., The Hague, Netherlands. Served with U.S. Army, 1953-55. Mem. Users Automated Data Processing Equipment (past dir.), Western Electronics Mfrs. Assn., Assn. Data Processing Service Orgns. Republican. Address: 354 Pine Hill Rd Mill Valley CA 94941

COOLIDGE, WINTHROP KNOWLTON, investment co. exec.; b. Chgo., Nov. 14, 1901; s. Winthrop and Marie (Knowlton) C.; S.B., Mass. Inst. Tech., 1923; m. Laetitia B. Kelly, July 20, 1935 (div. Jan. 1961); children—Laetitia (Mrs. Robert G. Allen Jr.), Deborah Jean (dec.), Olga Elizabeth, Dexter Knowlton, Carol Marie (Mrs. Alexander Breckinridge); m. 2d, Catharyn June Cook, Dec. 30, 1968. With sales dept. Standard Oil Co. (Ind.), 1923-26; with Chgo. Copper & Chem. Co., 1927—, pres., 1949—. Bd. dirs. Tucson Symphony Orch., to 1980. Mem. English Speaking Union. S.A.R., Delta Kappa Epsilon. Clubs: Saddle and Cycle (Chgo.); White Lake (Mich.) Golf, White Lake Yacht; Tucson Country. Address: 2640 N Camino Valle Verde Tucson AZ 85715 also Michillinda Beach Assn Whitehall MI 49461

COOLING, WILMER COLEBROOK, mfg. exec.; b. Wilmington, Del., Apr. 16, 1921; s. Wilmer J. and Pauline (Kolck) C.; B.S. in Indsl. Engring., Pa. Mil. Coll., 1942, B.S. in Mil. Sci. (hon), 1946; M.B.A. in Indsl. Mgmt., Temple U., 1949; m. Louise Andrew Dalton, May 4, 1946; children—Andrew C., Janet L., Mary Louise. Indsl. engr. U.S. Rubber Co., Passaic, N.J., 1946, L. H. Gilmer div., Tacony, Pa., 1946-48; indsl. engr. Atlantic Refining Co., Phila., 1948-50; mgr. methods and standards Internat. Resistance Co., Phila., 1950-56; corp. chief indsl. engr. Engelhard Industries, Inc., Newark, 1956-62; dir. indsl. engring. Airtron div. Litton Industries, Morris Plains, N.J., 1962-63; corporate staff indsl. engr. Am. Radiator & Standard San. Supply Co., N.Y.C., 1963-66; dept. v.p., mgr. electro-mech. aerospace and marine systems Engelhard Minerals & Chems. Corp., East Newark, N.J., 1966-71, v.p. personnel and indsl. relations Engelhard div., 1971-73, dir. indsl. relations, 1973—; instr. Rutgers U., 1954, Temple U., 1955-56; shop adviser Wharton Sch., U. Pa., 1955-56; cons. to asst. sec. of def. for properties and installations, 1954-56; lectr. Mgmt. Center, Cambridge, 1968—. Served to capt. AUS, 1942-46. Decorated Bronze Star with cluster. Fellow Soc. for Advancement Mgmt. (past chpt. dir., profl. mgr.'s citation, Advancement of Mgmt. award Phil Carroll award 1972), Royal Soc. Arts; mem. Am. Inst. Indsl. Engrs., Indsl. Mgmt. Soc., English-Speaking Union. Mem. Ch. of Holy Communion (vestry). Clubs: Yacht of Sea Isle City (N.J.) (past treas.), Rock Spring. Author: Front Line Cost Administration, 1955; Low Cost Maintenance Control; Play Arbitration, Box Seat at a Labor Management Dispute. Contbr. chpts. to books, articles to tech. mags. Home: 368 Hillside Pl South Orange NJ 07079 Office: 80 Wood Ave S Iselin NJ 08830

COOLS-LARTIGUE, ANTHONY RONALD, tourist assn. exec.; b. Roseau Dominica, West Indies, June 7, 1931; s. Alexander Raphael and Sybil Alexandra Cools-Lartigue; student pvt. and parochial schs., W.I.; m. Ethel Yvonne Wilson, Nov. 27, 1952: children—Roger, Beverly-Ann, Stewart, Suzanne, Angela, Michael. Clk., Jonas Browne & Hubbard, Grenada, W.I., 1948-49; salesman Gerald S.W. Smith & Co., Grenada, 1949-50; airlines clk. Hazells Ltd., St. Vincent, W.I., 1951-56, mgr. airlines dept., 1957-73, dir., 1973-74; dir. N. Am., Eastern Caribbean Tourist Assn., N.Y.C., 1974—. Pres., St. Vincent Music Council, 1968-73; dep. chmn. St. Vincent Tourist Bd., 1971-73. Mem. Am. Soc. Travel Agts. (asso.), Caribbean Tourism Assn., Assn. of Nat. Tourist Orgns. Roman Catholic. Club: Lions. Home: 88 Fenimore St Brooklyn NY 10017 Office: Eastern Caribbean Tourist Assn 220 E 42d St Room 411 New York NY 10017

COOMBES, MARIEL, constrn. co. exec.; b. Pasadena, Calif., Aug. 5, 1938; d. Oscar Branche Jackson and Mary Lincoln (Hicks) Jackson Turner; adopted d. William Nathan Turner; m. Donald Ernest Coombes, June 12, 1957 (div. 1972); children—Scott Craig Goodwin, William Cullen, Anna Maria, Joel Howard. Sec., co-incorporator Mineral Harvesters Inc. (name changed to Ariz. Custom Mfg. Inc. 1971), Phoenix, 1966-72, pres., bus. mgr., 1976—; pres., bus. mgr. Ariz. Custom Steel, 1976—; former co-owner WCS Constrn. Inc., from 1976; pres., bus. mgr. Eagle Erectors, 1979—. Dist. coordinator Republican Party, Oreg., 1964. Mem. Ariz. Steel Fabricators Assn. (pres. 1978—), Tolsun Farms Homeowners Assn., Nat. Assn. Women Bus. Owners, Nat. Assn. Female Execs., Ariz. Network Profl. Women, Women Emerging, Internat. Platform Assn., Intertel, Mensa. Mem. Ch. Jesus Christ of Reorganized Latter Day Saints. Home: PO Box 641 Tolleson AZ 85353 Office: PO Box 626 Tolleson AZ 85353

COON, FRANK GARLAND, ret. hotel co. exec.; b. Chgo., June 19, 1908; s. John Garland and Marjorie Wills (Weeks) C.; student U. Tenn., U. Mich., Harvard; m. Jean Frillman, Aug. 29, 1958; 1 dau., Sandra Jean. Civilian employee Chinese govt., combat pilot Sino-Chinese war; various positions Morrison Hotel, Sherman Hotel, Drake Hotel, Chgo., 1932-41; owner, operator restaurant, St. Louis, 1946-52; v.p., gen. mgr. Congress Motel, St. Louis, 1952-55; chief investigator criminal investigator firm Butler & Coon, hotel attys., Chgo., 1955-60; gen. mgr. Hunter's Inn, Santa Maria, Cal., 1960-61; dir. sales Vandenberg Inn, Santa Maria, 1962, gen. mgr., 1963, dir. Santa Maria Visitor and Conv. Bur., 1963-65; gen. mgr. Mecca Motel, Anaheim, Cal., 1964-65; gen. mgr. Tropics, Palm Springs, Cal.,

1965-66; mgr. Nite-Kap Motel, Santa Maria, 1967-68, gen. mgr. Howard Johnson's Motor Lodge, Santa Maria, 1969-76; ret., 1976. Cons. hospitality industry; mem. Service Corps Ret. Execs., SBA; reservist Fed. Emergency Mgmt. Agy. Bd. dirs. Campfire Girls Am., Santa Maria. Served with AUS, 1942-46; ETO. Decorated Air medal with 13 oak leaf clusters, Purple Heart with 1 oak leaf cluster, D.F.C. with 1 oak leaf cluster, Bronze Star medal; Croix de Guerre (France). Mem. Santa Maria Valley C. of C. (dir. 1963), Santa Maria Hotel and Motel Assn. (pres. 1973—), Assn. Former Intelligence Officers, Calif. Hotel Motel Assn. (founding mem.). Elk, Rotarian (pres. club 1973—). Home: 920 Woodmere Rd Santa Maria CA 93454

COONEY, JOHN THOMAS, bus. co. exec.; b. Mpls., Apr. 17, 1921; s. John Thomas and Helen (Bork) C.; B.B.A., U. Minn., 1943; grad. advanced mgmt. program Harvard U., 1971; m. Margaret Frances Bonner, Oct. 30, 1948; children—Mary, John Thomas, Patricia Bell, David, Stephen, Michael, Thomas. Pub. relations M & O Paper Co., Mpls., 1946-49; ter. mgr. Univis, Inc., Ft. Lauderdale, Fla., 1949-52, regional sales mgr., 1952-57, product mgr., 1957-59, gen. sales mgr., 1959-61, v.p. mktg., 1961-68, group v.p. mktg. and distbn., 1968-71, exec. v.p., 1971-72; v.p. mktg. and distbn. Itek Vision Optical div. Itek Corp., Boston, 1972-74, pres. div., 1974-75; pres. Jack Cooney & Assos., Ft. Lauderdale, 1975— chmn. bd. The Griffith Co.; dir. Alexander Hamilton Nat. Bank. Chmn. bd. dirs. Boys' Clubs Broward County; chmn. bd. dirs. Inverrary Found.; bd. dirs. Broward Life Center. Served to maj. U.S. Army, 1943-46. Decorated Silver Star, Bronze Star, Legion of Honor, Crown of Leopold. Mem. Sales and Mktg. Execs. Ft. Lauderdale (past pres., dir.), Am. Mgmt. Assn. (pres.'s council), Broward County C. of C. (dir.), Beta Theta Pi. Roman Catholic. Club: Coral Ridge Country. Home: 48 Cayuga Rd Fort Lauderdale FL 33308 Office: 2601 E Oakland Park Blvd Fort Lauderdale FL 33306

COONROD, RICHARD ALLEN, food co. exec.; b. Mahaska, Kans., Mar. 30, 1931; B.S., Kans. State U., 1953; m. Phyllis Clark, Jan. 7, 1960; children—Amy, Wade, Paul. With Pillsbury Co., Mpls., 1956—, v.p., gen. mgr. commodity mdsg., 1975-77, v.p., gen. mgr. agri-products div., 1977-78, group v.p., gen. mgr. agri-products, 1978-79, exec. v.p., 1979—; dir. Northwestern Nat. Bank. Campaign chmn. Minn. United Negro Coll. Fund, 1979-80; bd. dirs. Mpls. Jr. Achievement, 1979-80, Urban Coalition, Art Inst. Mpls. Served to capt. USAF, 1954-56. Mem. Millers Nat. Fedn. (exec. com.), St. Louis Grain Exchange, Chgo. Bd. of Trade. Clubs: Mpls., Interlachen Country. Office: 608 2d Ave S Minneapolis MN 55402

COONS, ELDO JESS, JR., recreational vehicle mfg. co. exec.; b. Corsicana, Tex., July 5, 1924; s. Eldo Jess and Ruby (Allison) C.; student U. Calif., Los Angeles; m. Betty June Muntz, June 1, 1954; children—Cheryl Ann, Roberta Annette, Valerie Lucille. Owner, mgr. C & C Constrn. Co., Pomona, Calif., 1946-48; sgt. Pomona Police Dept., 1948-54; nat. field dir. Nat. Hot Rod Assn., Los Angeles, 1954-57; pres. Coons Custom Mfg. Inc., Oswego, Kans., 1957-68; chmn. bd. Borg Warner Corp., 1968-71; pres. Coons Mfg. Inc., Oswego, 1971—. Mem. adv. com. for State Architects Assn. Elected to Recreational Vehicle/Mobile Homes Hall of Fame, 1975; recipient Paul Abel award Recreation Vehicle Assn., 1978. Mem. Young Pres. Orgn., Am. Inst. Mgmt. (fellow pres.'s council). Home: 1315 North St Oswego KS 67356 Office: 2300 W 4th St Oswego KS 67356

COOPER, ALCIE LEE, JR., ins. co. exec.: b. Gadsden, Ala., Aug. 3, 1939; s. Alcie Lee and Jettie Merle (Farrabee) C.; A.B., Asbury Coll., 1961; B.D., St. Paul Sch. Theology, 1966; postgrad. Coll. Workers Compensation, 1979; m. Audrey May MacAuslan, Sept. 3, 1976. Claims adjuster Sentry Ins. A Mut. Co., St. Louis, 1967-69, claim supr., Kansas City, Kans., 1969-72, regional claims supr., Dallas, 1972-77; home office workers compensation cons. Houston Gen. Ins. Co., Ft. Worth, 1977-79, asst. claims mgr., 1979—; partner Al Cooper & Assos., distbrs. Amway products, Ft. Worth, 1977—; instr. Workers Compensation Sch. Mem. Free Enterprise Assos., Amway Distbrs. Assn., Citizens Choice. Republican. Club: U.S. Senatorial. Home: 4125 Alicante Ave Fort Worth TX 76133 Office: 4100 Equitable Dr Fort Worth TX 76113

COOPER, CHARLES EDWARD, mgmt. cons.; b. North Wildwood, N.J., Jan. 31, 1933; s. Bernard and Esther (Worobe) C.; B.S., Temple U., 1958; postgrad. in law Universidad de Santa María, Caracas, Venezuela, 1961; m. Judith Glijansky, Aug. 11, 1956; children—Ann, Robert, Bernard. Cons., Corp. Venezolana de Fomento, Caracas, 1958-60; gen. mgr. El Avila, Barquisimeto, Venezuela, 1960-62; cons. Distbr. Venezolana de Azucares, S.R.L., Caracas, 1961; owner, pres. Procesamiento Eléctrico de Datos, C.A., Caracas, 1962-65; rep. IBM World Trade, Caracas, 1965-66; dir. Texfin C.A., Caracas, 1966-68; v.p., dir. Computer Systems Tech., Inc., Jenkintown, Pa., 1968-70; v.p. Nat. Computer Analysts, Inc., Princeton, N.J., 1970-74; prin. Coopers & Lybrand, Phila., 1974—; dir. Princeton Transport. Bd. dirs. Children's Aid Soc. Pa. Served with USN, 1951-53. Recipient cert., Pres. Carter, 1978. Mem. Nat. Assn. Accts., Inst. Mgmt. Consultants, Bank Adminstrn. Inst. Clubs: Philmont Country, Union League (Phila.). Office: First Internat Plaza 1100 Louisiana Suite 4100 Houston TX 77002

COOPER, CHARLES G., toiletries and cosmetics co. exec.; b. Chgo., Apr. 4, 1928; s. Benjamin and Gertrude C.; B.S. in Journalism, U. Ill., 1949; m. Miriam Meyer, Feb. 11, 1951; children—Deborah, Ruth, Janet, Benjamin. Sales promotion mgr. Maidenform Co., N.Y.C., 1949-51; asst. circulation promotion mgr. Esquire Mag., Chgo., 1951-52; with Helene Curtis Industries Inc., Chgo, 1953—, pres. salon div., 1971-75, pres. consumer products div., 1975—. Served with U.S. Army, 1952-53. Mem. Nat. Wholesale Druggists' Assn., Nat. Assn. Chain Drug Stores. Jewish. Club: Mid-Am. (Chgo.). Office: 4401 W North Ave Chicago IL 60639

COOPER, CHARLES MALCOLM, diversified packaging co. exec.; b. Benton Harbor, Mich., Mar. 6, 1928; s. Charles E. and Louella Olive (Butzbach) C.; B.A. in Mktg., Mich. State U., 1954; m. Martha Jean Riley, Dec. 25, 1951; children—Kathleen, Scott, Tom, Patricia. Salesman, Owens-Ill., Inc., Toledo, 1954-66, div. v.p., dir. sales and mktg. Plastics div., 1966-71, corporate v.p., gen. mgr. div., 1971-78, gen. mgr. exec. and spl. ops. internat., 1976-78; pres., chief operating officer Kerr Glass Mfg. Corp., Los Angeles, 1978—, chief exec. officer, 1980—. Served with U.S. Army, 1946-47, 51-53. Mem. Newcomen Soc. N.Am., Theta Chi. Republican. Roman Catholic. Clubs: Mountain Gate Country (Brentwood, Calif.); California (Los Angeles); Sales Execs. (N.Y.). Home: 2161 Ridge Dr Los Angeles CA 90049 Office: 700 S Flower St Suite 2200 Los Angeles CA 90017

COOPER, DENYS GEOFFREY TYNDALE, research adminstr.; b. Nairobi, Kenya, Apr. 1, 1939; arrived Can., 1965, naturalized, 1972; s. Roger T. and M.J. (Tregoning) C.; B.Sc., U. Exeter (Eng.), 1962; Ph.D., U. Liverpool (Eng.), 1965; m. Jennifer A. Simpson, June 30, 1973; children—Bruce, Jillian. Research staff Plastics div. Imperial Chem. Industries, Welwyn Garden City, Eng., 1957-59; postdoctoral fellow in chemistry Nat. Research Council, Ottawa, Ont., 1965-67, project officer for indsl. research grants in chems., paper, and pharms., 1973—; exec. asst. Consol. Bathurst Ltd., Montreal, Que., Can., 1967-73. Mem. Can. Inst. Chemistry, Can. Pulp and Paper Assn., Innovation Mgmt. Inst. of Can., Canadian Field Hockey Assn. (v.p. 1972-74), Canadian Field Hockey Umpires Assn. (pres. 1976-79, sec. 1971-75), Hockey Fedn. Internat. (internat. umpire). Club: Outaouais Field Hockey (Ottawa). Home: 7 Madawaska Dr Ottawa ON K1S 3G5 Canada Office: Montreal Rd Ottawa ON K1A 0R6 Canada

COOPER, DOUGLAS JAMES, jewelry co. exec.; b. Bryn Athyn, Pa., Sept. 19, 1931; s. Fred J. and Aurora (Synnestvedt) C.; A.B.A., U. Pa., 1962; m. Diene Pitcairn, Jan. 9, 1960; children—Heather Diene, Lochlin Douglas, Christopher Ian. Pres., chief exec. officer F.J. Cooper, Inc., Phila., 1958—; pres. F. J. Cooper Internat. Co., Phila., Jamaica, 1964—. Chmn. ann. giving campaign U. Pa. Evening Sch., 1963-66; past pres. Singing City of Phila.; bd. dirs. Phila. Opera Co.; trustee, chmn. Oriental art com. Phila. Mus. Art; chmn. bd. Pa. Ballet, 1975-79, now bd. dirs.; bd. dirs. Settlement Mus. Sch., Beneficia Found., Elwyn Inst. Mem. Beta Nu, Delta Sigma Pi, Sigma Kappa Phi. Republican. Swedenborgian religion. Clubs: Racquet, Locust, Union League (Phila.); Montego Bay Yacht. Home: 5500 Wissahick on Ave Philadelphia PA 19144 also El Cerro Tamarind Hill Montego Bay Jamaica West Indies Office: 1406 Chestnut St Philadelphia PA 19110 also PO Box 306 2 Orange St Montego Bay Jamaica West Indies

COOPER, HAROLD HOMER, JR., lawyer; b. Tulsa, Aug. 3, 1940; s. Harold Homer and Marjorie (Burkett) C.; B.A., U. Tulsa, 1962, J.D., 1966; postgrad. So. Methodist U., 1958-60; div.; 1 son, Christopher Lee. Admitted to Tex. bar, 1968; corp. sec., gen. counsel Linbeck Constrn. Corp., Houston, 1967-72; asso. gen. counsel Mitchell Energy & Devel. Corp., Houston, 1972-74; v.p., gen. counsel, corp. sec. 1st Constrn. Group, Inc., Houston, 1974-77; v.p. and gen. counsel Houston div. Vantage Cos., 1978—. Bd. dirs. Houston Grand Opera Assn. Mem. Am., Okla. bar assns., State Bar Tex., Kappa Alpha, Phi Alpha Delta. Home: Houston TX Office: 4635 Southwest Freeway Suite 700 Houston TX 77027

COOPER, HOWARD KENNETH, electronics mfg. co. exec.; b. Chgo., Jan. 26, 1934; s. Milton B. and Julia (Peller) C.; B.S.E.E., Chgo. Tech. Coll., 1955; M.S.E.E., Pacific States U., 1965; m. Iris S. Speyer, June 26, 1955; children—Scott, Stacey, Stefanie. With Nucleonic Products, subsidiary Thompson SSF, 1964-73, pres., 1970-73; group v.p., pres. Gallil Corp. subs. Mica Corp., 1973-76; with electronic instrumentation div. Eaton Corp., City of Industry, Calif., 1976—, chief exec. officer, gen. mgr., 1976—. Mem. adv. bd. Calif. State U. Sch. Computer Sci. and Engring., Pacific States U.; v.p. chpt. City of Hope, 1969-72. Served to capt. USMC, 1955-57. Mem. IEEE, Soc. Exptl. Stress Analysis, Assn. Advancement Med. Instrumentation. Home: Woodland Hills CA 91367 Office: 19535 E Walnut Dr City of Industry CA 91748

COOPER, JEROME MAURICE, architect; b. Memphis, Jan. 24, 1930; s. Samuel and Bessie (Phillips) C.; B.S., Ga. Inst. Tech., 1952, B.Arch., 1955; postgrad. U. Rome (Italy), 1956-57; m. Jean Kanter, Dec. 29, 1957; children—David Franklin, Samuel Randolph, Beth Lauren. Draftsman, Willner & Millkey, Atlanta, 1955-56; Fulbright fellow, Rome, 1956-57; designer Abreu & Robeson, Atlanta, 1957-59, Heery & Heery, Atlanta 1959-60; pres. Cooper, Carry & Assos., Inc., 1960—. Served to lt. (j.g.) USNR, 1952-54. Fellow AIA (pres. chpt., nat. dir.). Prin. works include Classroom Arts Bldg. of W. Ga. Coll., Sheraton-Emory Inn, Chateau Fleur de Lis Restaurant, Briarcliff Village Shopping Center, Macon Youth Devel. Center, Gen. Motors Office Bldg., Northwest Med. Center, Landmark Exec. Center, Piedmont Plaza. Home: 1070 Judith Way NE Atlanta GA 30324 Office: 1819 Peachtree Rd NE Suite 500 Atlanta GA 30309

COOPER, NAOMI JUNNE, market research and shopping exec.; b. Oklahoma City, May 22, 1925; d. George Alexander and Sarah Ann (Williams) Manous; grad. pub. schs.; student Knapp Coll. of Bus., Tacoma; m. Nollie Cooper, Nov. 20, 1961; children—Francine Carter Campbell, Linda Carter Kendrick. Owner, mgr. Northwest Proficiency, market research and analysis services, Tacoma, Wash., 1973—. Mem. Am. Soc. Bus. and Mgmt. Consultants, Am. Inst. Profl. Consultants, Am. Mgmt. Assn. Tacoma Area Better Bus. Bur., Tacoma C. of C. Mem. Pentecostal Holiness, Ch. Club: Toastmistress Internat. Home: 3745 N 30th St Tacoma WA 98407 Office: 915 1/2 Pacific Ave Suite 401-G Tacoma WA 98402

COOPER, ROGER HARVEY, mfrs. rep.; b. Hackensack, N.J., Feb. 14, 1941; s. George Manning and Hazel (Rainey) C.; B.A. in Bus., Econs. and Sociology, Drury Coll., 1963; m. Vicki Lynn Vantrease, Feb. 12, 1961; children—Douglas, Deborah, Denise, Davis. With Standard Oil Co., 1957-63; mgr. Queen Anne Apts., 1962-63; self-employed salesman, 1963-72; founder Ozark Ry. Supplies, Inc., Nixa, Mo., 1973—; pres. Ozark Properties of Nixa, Inc., 1979—; tchr. seminars, 1977-79. Bd. deacons, lay ch. worker Parkcrest Baptist Ch. Mem. Roadmasters Assn., Am. Ry. Bridge and Bldg. Assn., Ill. Ry. Club, St. Louis Ry. Club. Club: Rotary. Designer Ozark Spike Re-Cla-Mer. Office: 80 Bellerive Dr Nixa MO 65714

COOPER, STEPHEN FORBES, financial cons.; b. Gary, Ind., Oct. 23, 1946; s. Leo Kenneth and Arlene (Davis) C.; B.A., Occidental Coll., 1968; M.B.A., U. Pa., 1970. Staff auditor Touche Ross & Co., N.Y.C., 1970, sr. auditor, 1971, asso. cons., 1972, sr. cons., 1973-76, mgr., 1976—, partner, 1979—. C.P.A.; cert. mgmt. cons.; cert. mgmt. acct. Trustee, treas. Nat. Sudden Infant Death Syndrome Found. Mem. Am. Inst. C.P.A.'s, N.Y. State Soc. C.P.A.'s, Inst. Mgmt. Acctg., Inst. Mgmt. Cons., Phi Gamma Delta, Wharton Grads. Club. Roman Catholic. Home: Anderson Rd Kent CT 06757 Office: 1633 Broadway New York NY 10019

COOPER, THEODORE WILBUR, scientist, author; b. Hillman, Mich., Apr. 27, 1923; s. Clayton T. and Vila M. (Spencer) C.; B.S., Mich. Tech. U., 1952, M.S. (R.R. Seeber research scholar 1952-53), 1953; m. Calla M. Franisco, Aug 8, 1942 (div.); children—Jeannie, Gary A.; m. 2d, Gwendolyn Anne Gleeson, May 16, 1970. Project engr. transistor devel. sect. Hughes Semicondr., 1953-56, head, transistor engr. dept., 1956-60; ops. mgr. Micro Systems, Inc., 1960-61, head microelectronic engring. Electro Optical System, 1961-63; mgr. prod. devel. dept. Centralab div. Globe Union, Inc., 1963-66; pres. Technicon Assos., Inc. of Wis., 1966-69; chmn., chief exec. officer Gen. Technicon Co., San Anselmo, Calif., 1969—. Mem. nat. adv. bd. Am. Security Council. Served with AUS, 1942-45. Mem. IEEE, AAAS, Acad. Polit. Sci., Mich. Engring. Soc., Mich. Tech. Alumni Assn., Internat. Platform Assn., Tau Beta Pi. Author: By Popular Choice, 1970; By Popular Choice, Why Not Vocalize the Silent Majority?, 1975; Functionality: A Revelation for Science, 1978. Patentee in field of semicondr. devices and processing, method and system for open cycle operation internal combusion engine. Home: 1269 Parkwood Dr Novato CA 94947 Office: PO Box 1413 Novato CA 94960

COORS, WILLIAM K., brewery exec.; b. Golden, Colo., 1916; grad. Princeton U., 1938. Former pres., now chmn., dir., chief exec. officer Adolph Coors Co., Golden. Office: Adolph Coors Co Golden CO 80401

COPELAND, MARGOT JAMES, bank exec.; b. Richmond, Va., Dec. 4, 1951; d. William Lloyd and Thelma (Taylor) James; B.S. in Physics, Hampton Inst., 1973; M.A. in Research and Stats., Ohio State U., 1974; m. Terence E. Copeland, Apr. 7, 1979; 1 dau., Kimberley. Legis. research cons. Ohio Ho. of Reps., Columbus, 1975-76; mktg. rep. Xerox Corp., Cleve., 1976-77; consumer service asso. Polaroid Corp., Cleve., 1977-78, regional ops. adminstr., 1978—, Midwest tng. coordinator, from 1978; now employee relations specialist Ameritrust Corp., Cleve. Mem. telethon planning com. United Negro Coll. Fund. Mem. Am. Soc. for Personnel Adminstrn., Nat. Assn. Female Execs., Blacks in Mgmt., Nat. Council Negro Women, NAACP, Ohio State U., Hampton Inst. alumni assns., Phi Delta Kappa, Delta Sigma Theta. Democrat. Baptist. Clubs: Women's Aux. Cleve. Bar Assn., 13th Ward Dem., Barristers' Wives, Women's City. Home: 16703 Talford Ave Cleveland OH 44120 Office: Ameritrust Corp 900 Euclid Ave Cleveland OH 44101

COPITHORNE, DONALD GORDON, real estate broker; b. Calgary, Alta., Can., Mar. 30, 1947; s. Clarence and Lillian Irene (Robertson) C.; student Olds (Alta.) Agrl. Coll., 1966-67, U. Calgary, 1969-71; m. Wynne Louise Anderson, Nov. 26, 1977. Owner, operator ranch, Cochrane, Alta., 1973; pres., gen. mgr. Courier Mgmt. Co., Calgary, 1974-76; salesman Block Bros. Realty Ltd., Calgary, 1976-80, S.W. Calgary Real Estate Ltd.-Realty World, 1980—. Bd. dirs. Calgary Jaycees, 1978-79, Calgary Buffalo, 1979-80; asso. Calgary Exposition and Stampede, 1979—. Recipient various awards, including Spoke award Calgary Jaycees, 1978, Outstanding Membership Recruitment award Internat. Jaycees, 1978, 79; winner Wild Horse Race, Calgary Stampede, 1971, 72, 74, mem. winning team Wild Horse Race, 1975, 77, 78, 79, 80. Office: Realty World Britannia Shopping Centre 822 49th Ave SW Calgary AB T2S 1G9 Canada

COPLEY, HELEN KINNEY, newspaper publisher; b. Cedar Rapids, Iowa, Nov. 28, 1922; d. Fred Everett and Margaret (Casey) Kinney; attended Hunter Coll., N.Y.C., 1945; m. James S. Copley, Aug. 16, 1965 (dec.); 1 son, David Casey. Asso., The Copley Press, Inc., 1952—, chmn. corp., dir., chmn. exec. com., 1973—, chief exec. officer, sr. mgmt. bd., 1974—; chmn. bd. Copley News Service, San Diego 1973—, chmn. editorial bd., 1976—; chmn. bd., dir., mem. exec. com. Union-Tribune Pub. Co., 1973—; pub. San Diego Union and Evening Tribune, 1973—. Mem. Friends of Internat. Center, La Jolla, La Jolla Mus. Contemporary Art, La Jolla Town Council, Inc.; life patroness Makua Aux.; charter mem. San Diego Womens Council, Navy League U.S.; life mem. San Diego Hall of Sci.; mem. San Diego Soc. Natural History; mem. womens com. San Diego Symphony Assn., Scripps Meml. Hosp. Aux., Social Service League of La Jolla; life mem. Star of India Aux., Zool. Soc. San Diego; mem. YWCA. Chmn. bd., trustee James S. Copley Found., 1973—; hon. chmn., bd. dirs. Washington Crossing Found.; bd. dirs. San Diego Mus. Art, Putnam Found.; trustee, bd. dirs. Freedoms Found. at Valley Forge; trustee, trustee devel. com. Scripps Clinic and Research Found.; trustee U. San Diego. Mem. Inter Am. Press Assn. (dir.), Calif. Press Assn., Newspaper Advt. Bur. (dir.), Am. Soc. Newspaper Editors, Am. Press Inst., Am. Newspaper Pubs. Assn. (dir.), Greater Los Angeles, Nat., San Diego, San Francisco press clubs, Nat. Newspaper Assn., Pres.'s Assn., Sigma Delta Chi. Republican. Roman Catholic. Clubs: Aurora (Ill.) Country; Cuyamaca, San Diego Yacht, Univ., U. San Diego Presidents (San Diego); De Anza Country (Borrego Springs, Calif.); La Costa Country (Carlsbad, Calif.); La Jolla Beach and Tennis, La Jolla Country. Office: PO Box 1530 La Jolla CA 92038*

COPPAGE, JAMES EDWIN, bus. exec.; b. Petroleum, Ohio, Jan. 19, 1928; s. John Robert and Helen Mae (Pearce) C.; student Youngstown Coll., 1946-54; M.B.A., U. New Haven, 1978; m. D. Marcella Zitnyar, Jan. 22, 1949; 1 dau., D. Lynn Coppage McGowan. Tech. specialist Westinghouse Electric, 1948-54; advt. mgr. Cramer div. Conrac Corp., Old Saybrook, Conn., 1954-61; promotion and public relations mgr. Burndy Corp., Norwalk, Conn., 1961-63; mktg. mgr. Consol. Controls Corp., Bethel, Conn., 1966-69; pres. Rapidprint, Inc., Middletown, Conn., 1969—. Served with USCG, 1945-46. Home: 682 Green Hill Rd Madison CT 06443 Office: 2055 S Main St Middletown CT 06457

COPPIETERS, EMMANUEL (COPPIETERS DE TER ZAELE, CHEVALIER EMMANUEL), economist, educator, lawyer; b. Bruges, Belgium, Jan. 1, 1925; s. Georges and Jeanne (de Halieux) C. de ter Z.; D.Juris, Louvain U., 1947 D.Econ. Scis., 1955; M.Scis. in Econs., London U., 1952; children—Arnold, Bruno, Beatrice, Johan. Barrister, 1947-57; prof. internat. econ. orgn., faculty econs. Nat. U., Antwerp, Belgium, 1954—; dir.-gen. Institut Royal des Relations Internationales, Brussels, 1954—; ofcl. auditor banks, 1962—; bank auditor Societe Francaise de Banque et de Depot, Am. Express Internat. Banking Co., Bank van Mariaburg, 1962—; prof. Royal Mil. Acad., Brussels, Belgium, 1963-66; consul gen. for Honduras in Belgium, 1961—; minister chargé d'affaires a.i. of Honduras to European Communities, 1973—. Mem. Belgium nat. commn. UNESCO, 1955—; gov. Assn. pour l'Etude des problemes of Europe, Paris, 1959—, European Cultural Found., 1973—; adviser on fgn. trade to Fgn. Ministry, 1960—. Served with Belgium and Brit. Armed Forces, 1944-45; now lt. col. Res. Decorated Resistance medals, War Vol. medal, officer Order of Leopola; comdr. Order Orange Nassau (Netherlands); Order Merit Luxemburg; Order Morazan (Honduras); Order Merit (Senegal); Order Holy Sepulchre (Vatican); knight Order Malta; Order Leopard (Zaire); officer Nat. Order Rwanda, Polonia Restitute; comdr. Order Romania. Mem. Royal Acad. Scis., Belgian Nat. Council Statistics, Mexican Acad. Internat. Law. Editor, Chronique de Politique Etrangere, 1954—; co-editor Internationale Spectator, Tijaschrift voor Internationale Politiek, 1961—. Author: English Bank Note Circulation 1694-1954, 1955; L'Accord Monetaire European et les Progres de la Convertibilite des Monnaies, 1959; Internationale Organizaties en Belgische Economie, 1960; La integracion monetaria y fiscal europea, culminacion de la integracion politica, 1963; contbr. articles in English, Dutch, French and Spanish to various publs. Home: 88 avenue de la Couronne 1050 Brussels Belgium also Vijverskasteel Loppem bij Brugge Belgium

COPULSKY, WILLIAM, chem. co. exec.; b. Zhitomir, Russia, Apr. 4, 1922; s. Boris and Betty (Bruman) C.; came to U.S., 1923, naturalized, 1929; B.A., N.Y. U., 1942, Ph.D., 1957; m. Ruth B. Brody, Dec. 26, 1948; children—Stephen, Jonathan, Lewis. Chemist, Ammeco Chem. Co., Rochester, N.Y., 1942; asst. research dir. J.J. Berliner Co., N.Y.C., 1946-48; research dir. R. S. Aries and Assos., N.Y.C., 1948-51; comml. dir. W.R. Grace and Co., N.Y.C., 1951-74, v.p. operations services group, 1974—. Served with AUS, 1942-46. Mem. Am. Chem. Soc., Chemists Club, Beta Gamma Sigma. Author: Marketing Chemical Products, 1948; Forecasting Chemical Commodity Demand, 1962; Practical Sales Forecasting, 1970; Entrepreneurship and the Corporation, 1974. Home: 23-35 Bell Blvd Bayside NY 11360 Office: 1114 Ave of Americas New York NY 10036

COQUIA, REYNALDO MANINGDING, ins. agt.; b. Calasiao, Pangasinan, Philippines, July 9, 1945; s. Feliciano Liwanag and Felisa (Maningding) C.; came to U.S., 1970, naturalized, 1976; B.S., Adamson U., Manila, Philippines, 1966; m. Helen Atienza Magtibay, Apr. 18, 1969; children—Jon, James. With Prudential Ins. Co., 1970-72; agt. Lincoln Nat. Life Ins., Oakland, Calif., 1973-74, asst. v.p., 1974-76, v.p., 1976-77; partner, agt. Coquia & Mejia Ins. Assos., Walnut Creek, Calif., 1977—. Mem. Nat., Calif. assns. life underwriters, Million Dollar Round Table (nat. sales achievement award). Roman Catholic. Home: 1954 Woodbury Ct Walnut Creek CA 94596 Office: 1776 Ygnacio Valley Rd Suite 103 Walnut Creek CA 94598

CORASANTI, EUGENE RUSSELL, med. equipment mfg. co. exec.; b. Utica, N.Y., Sept. 9, 1930; s. Joseph and Rose (Pastore) C.; B.B.A. in Acctg., Niagara U., 1952; m. Connie Nole, Aug. 11, 1962; children—Joseph J., David G. Pvt. practice public acctg., Utica, 1954-72; pres. Consol. Med. Equipment, Inc., Utica, 1973—; dir. Mohawk Hosp. Equipment, Inc. Profl. adv. com. div. bus. and public mgmt. SUNY Coll. Tech.; past mem. budget com. United Fund. Served with U.S. Army, 1952-54. Democrat. Roman Catholic. Clubs: Ft. Schyuyler, Yahnundasis Golf. Patentee in area of monitoring electrodes. Home: 9 Carmen Ln Utica NY 13501 Office: 10 Hopper St Utica NY 13501

CORBETT, GWEN ANN, tel. answering service co. exec.; b. Chgo., Aug. 24, 1938; d. Wesley Francis and Marie Ruth (Johnson) Evans; m. George Raymond Corbett, June 25, 1960; children—June Ellen, Lori Louise. Pres., Answer-All Secretarial Service Inc., Westminster, Colo., 1964—, Print-All Services, 1976—. Mem. vocat. adv. com. Adams County Sch. Dist. 50. Mem. Adams County C. of C., Asso. Tel. Answering Assn. (nat. dir. 1977—, sec.-treas. 1979-80, v.p. 1980—), Tel. Answering Services Mountain States (pres. 1975-76, exec. sec.), Bus. and Profl. Womens Club. Democrat. Mem. Reorganized Ch. Jesus Christ Latter-day Saints. Home: 10914 Pearl Ct Northglenn CO 80233 Office: 7145 Lowell Blvd Westminster CO 80030

CORBETT, WILLIAM BERTON, constrn. co. exec.; b. Green Forest, Ark., Apr. 1, 1923; s. Edwin Francis and Mary Evelyn (Patton) C.; student public schs., Raton, N.Mex., 1929-41; m. Karen Franko, Apr. 2, 1945; children—Bobette, Jeffrey (dec.). Surveyor, U.S. C.E., Costa Rica, 1942-43, Sietz-Perkins, Poughkeepsie, N.Y., 1946-49; surveyor Utah Constrn. Co., Denver, 1950-52, field engr., Ariz., Mo., Wyo., Calif, 1953-58; project mgr. Paul Hardemar Co., Lompoc, Calif., San Diego, Cheyenne, Wyo., 1959-66; project mgr. Morrison-Knudsen Co., Inc., Vietnam and Peru, 1966-70; v.p. ops. Morrison-Knudsen Engenharia, 1970-79; pres. Morrison-Knudsen Engrs., Rio de Janeiro, 1979; pres. Morrison-Kundsen Engenharia S.A., Rio de Janeiro, Brazil, subs. Morrison-Knudsen Co. Inc.; adminstrv. council dir. Internacional Engenharia S.A. Served with U.S. Army, 1943-46. Mem. Am. Soc. Rio de Janeiro. Republican. Clubs: Gavea Golf (Rio de Janeiro). Office: Morrison-Knudsen Engenharia SA 112 Rua Assuncao Rio de Janeiro RJ Brazil

CORBIN, HERBERT LEONARD, public relations co. exec.; b. Bklyn., Mar. 30, 1940; s. H. Dan and Lillian C.; B.A., Rutgers U., 1961; m. Carol Heller, June 2, 1963; children—Jeffrey, Leslie Faith. Staff corr. Newark News, 1961-63; asst. dir. dept. public relations News Service of Rutgers U., New Brunswick, N.J., 1963-65; account exec. A.A. Schecter Assos., N.Y.C., 1965-66, Barkis & Shalit Inc., N.Y.C., 1965-66; sr. account exec. Daniel J. Edelman, Inc., N.Y.C., 1967-69; founder, pres. Kanan, Corbin, Schupak & Aronow, Inc., N.Y.C., 1969—. Mem. Public Relations Soc. Am., Public Relations Soc. N.Y., Sigma Delta Chi. Clubs: Williams Coll., Old Oaks Country. Home: 31 Hathaway Ln White Plains NY 10605 Office: 99 Park Ave S New York NY 10016

CORBIN, ROBERT ELLIOT, real estate co. exec.; b. N.Y.C., Mar. 18, 1931; s. Richard Beverley and Lucy (Elliot) C.; A.B., Harvard U., 1953; postgrad. N.Y. Inst. Fin., 1966-67; m. Janet G. Gigliotti Hicks, Oct. 7, 1976. Trainee, Lambert & Feasley, N.Y.C., 1953-54; buyer Lorimex Corp., N.Y.C., 1955-56; research cons. Sullivan Stauffer Calwell & Bayles, N.Y.C., 1956-58, account exec., mgr., 1958-64; investment counselor Brundage, Story & Rose, N.Y.C., 1966-69; owner, mgr. Venture Capital, N.Y.C., Newport, R.I., 1969-78; real estate broker Carey, Richmond & Viking, Newport, 1978-80; partner, mng. dir., pres. Pvt. Properties, Inc., Newport, 1980—; pres. The Corbin Co., Newport, 1980—, The Vaucluse Co., Newport, 1980—, Vaucluse Realty Corp., Newport, 1980—; dir. VRI Corp. Bd. dirs. Seaman's Ch. Inst., N.Y.C., Holland Lodge Found., N.Y.C., Child and Family Services Newport County, Newport. Served with USAR, 1950-54. Mem. Newport County Bd. Realtors, R.I. Realtors Assn., Nat. Realtors Assn. Episcopalian. Clubs: Brook, Union (N.Y.C.); Newport Reading Room (gov.), Clambake of Newport (gov.), Spouting Rock Beach Assn., Masons. Office: 37 Bellevue Ave Newport RI 02840

CORBLEY, JOHN JAMES, ins. exec.; b. N.Y.C., Nov. 20, 1926; s. John Patrick and Rose Josephine (Gagan) C.; A.B., Iona Coll., 1950; J.D., N.Y. Law Sch., 1962; m. Renee M. Buck, Aug. 22, 1953 (dec.); m. 2d, June Audrey Ferris, July 24, 1971; children—John Roger, James Brian, Jeanne Marie. Admitted to N.Y. State bar, 1963, Md. bar, 1974; claim supr. Kemper Ins., N.Y.C., 1950-62; sec., mgr. Motor Vehicle Accident Indemnification Corp., N.Y.C., 1963-72; exec. dir. Md. Automobile Ins. Fund, Annapolis, 1973-76, chmn. bd. trustees, 1976—; guest lectr. bar assns.; apptd. sec. Md. Dept. Licensing and Regulation, Balt. Served with USN, 1944-46; Recipient Outstanding Achievement award in gov. Iona Coll., 1973. Mem. Def. Research Inst., Am., N.Y. State, Md. State, Anne Arundel County, Bronx County (3d v.p.) bar assns., N.Y. Claim Assn. (2d v.p.), Am. Arbitration Assn., N.Y. Law Sch. Alumni Assn. Home: 475 Fair Oak Dr Severna Park MD 21146 Office: One S Calvert St Baltimore MD 21202

CORCORAN, RICHARD LEE, ins. exec., cons.; b. Wheeling, W.Va., June 18, 1941; s. Charles Vincent and Evelyn Lee (Chambers) C.; student Richmond (Va.) Profl. Inst., 1962-64, Estate Planning and Bus. Sch., Purdue U., 1971; m. Regina Hudert, June 18, 1966; children—Richard Lee, Charles Vincent II, Sean Patrick, Anthony Cameron. Salesman to sales mgr. Herald Sales Co., Richmond, Va., 1962-66; freelance ins. agt., registered rep., investment adviser, Midlothian and Richmond, Va., 1966-79; owner RLC & Co., gen. agts., brokers, and ins. cons., Midlothian, 1979—. R.H.U. (registered health underwriter). Served with USN, 1958-62. Mem. Nat. (8 Nat. Quality awards, 3 Nat. Sales Achievement awards), Va. assns. life underwriters, Nat. Assn. Health Underwriters, Nat. Assn. Security Dealers, Million Dollar Round Table. Roman Catholic. Clubs: Millionaires (fin. sec. Midlothian chpt.), Shooters (dir.), Loyal Order Moose, K.C. Office: 11001 Midlothian Turnpike PO Box 311 Midlothian VA 23113

CORCORAN, ROBERT LEE, JR., bank exec.; b. Rochester, N.Y., Apr. 12, 1944; s. Robert Lee and Evelyn Gertrude (Askey) C.; B.B.A., U. Notre Dame, 1966; M.B.A., U. Pa., 1968; m. Sharon Radford Dorminey; 1 son, Alexander Macdonald. With Chem. Bank and subs., N.Y.C., 1968—, lending and credit officer corporate bank, 1969-73, v.p. for Europe, Middle East, and Africa Chemco Leasing, London, 1973-78; v.p., sr. internat. planning officer Chem. Bank, N.Y.C., 1978-79; exec. v.p., chief exec. officer, dir. Bank of Liberia affiliate Chem. Bank, N.Y.C., 1979-80; pres. Chem. Internat. Fin. Ltd., 1980—. Roman Catholic. Clubs: Univ. (N.Y.C.); Rockaway Hunting, Wharton Bus. Sch. Office: Chem Bank 20 Pine St New York NY 10005

CORCORAN, THOMAS ARMSTRONG, ski resort and real estate exec.; b. Yokohama, Japan, Nov. 16, 1931; s. David Merle and Harriet Huntington (Armstrong) C.; B.A., Dartmouth Coll., 1954; M.B.A., Harvard U., 1959; m. Daphne King Andresen, May 28, 1977; children—Linda, Daphne, Michael, Christine, Kathleen, Kerry. Fin. analyst Capital Enterprise Co., San Francisco, 1960-61; asst. to partner J. Barth & Co., Los Angeles, 1961-63; asst. to pres. Aspen Skiing Corp. (Colo.), 1963-65; pres., chief exec. officer Waterville Co., Inc., Waterville Valley, N.H., 1965—; dir. Carroll Reed Ski Shops, Inc., Mountain Media, Inc. Selectman, Town of Waterville Valley, 1966—; trustee U.S. Ski Ednl. Found., 1976—. Served with USNR, 1954-56. Mem. Nat. Ski Areas Assn. (2d v.p., dir.), Am. Land Devel. Assn. (dir.), Am. Ski Fedn. (dir., chmn.), U.S. Ski Assn. (dir. competition div.), U.S. Olympic Skiing Com. Democrat. Clubs: Boothbay Harbor Yacht, Waterville Valley Ski. Racing editor Ski mag., 1963-72. Home: Greeley Hill Rd Waterville Valley NH 03223 Office: Waterville Co Inc Waterville Valley NH 03223

CORD, MICHAEL JONAS, diversified co. exec.; b. Owyhee, Nev., Feb. 28, 1949; s. John Joseph and Rosa Elizabeth (Campbell) Gallagher; student Links Bus. Coll., Boise, Idaho, 1967-68; m. Susan Hester Brunelle, Nov. 11, 1977; children—Sean Michael, Justin Bley and Melissa Rose (twins). Computer operator Paine Webber, Los Angeles, 1969-70; owner Hippodrome Boutiques, Los Angeles, 1970-72; owner Cord Artist Mgmt. & Public Relations, Beverly Hills, Calif., 1971-74, Cordco-Mail Order, Los Angeles, 1972-76; dist. mgr. Luzier Cosmetics, Los Angeles, 1975-76; broker Hollywood Properties, Los Angeles, 1979-80; owner Famous Designers Forum, Beverly Hills, 1976-80, Graffiti Guard Specialty Coatings, Van Nuys, Calif., 1979—. Mem. Beverly Hills C. of C., Hollywood C. of C., Jaycees, Small Businessmen's Assn. Los Angeles, San Fernando Valley Bd. Realtors, Beverly Hills Bd. Realtors. Democrat. Mem. Ch. of Religious Sci. Home: 15715 Marlin Pl Van Nuys CA 91406 Office: PO Box 6411 Beverly Hills CA 90211

CORDEIRO, IVO AMORIM, Portuguese diplomat; b. Lisbon, June 6, 1933; s. Carlos Moraes Sarmento and Marina (Mello) C.; Bachelor's degree Portuguese Overseas Sch. Public Adminstrn.; m. Dorothy Harol, Jan. 25, 1964. Newspaper reporter, then asst. editor Noticies de Meçeu, Macau, 1958-61; trade del. in South Africa, Portuguese colonies Mozambique and Angola, 1962-71; dir. Portuguese Govt. Trade Office, Los Angeles, 1972—. Recipient cert. of achievement World Trade Inst., N.Y.C., 1972. Mem. Center Social Democracy. Roman Catholic. Clubs: North Ranch Country, Westshore Tennis (Westlake Village); Rotary (sec. Macau 1958-61). Author articles in field. Home: 1484 Eastkind Circle Westlake Village CA 91361 Office: Central Plaza 3440 Wilshire Blvd Suite 616 Los Angeles CA 90010

CORDELL, DOUGLAS HAMILTON, truck broker; b. Asheville, N.C., June 8, 1928; s. Luther Hamilton and Georgia Mary (Pearce) C.; student Stanford U., 1950-51; children—Constance Diane, Reginald David. Cargo pilot United Air Lines, San Francisco, 1951-53; br. mgr. Standard Brands, Inc., Miami, Fla., 1953-64; dist. mgr. C.I.T. Engring. Corp., Asheville, N.C., 1965-70; fleet sales mgr. Carolina Truck and Body Co., Inc., Asheville, N.C., 1970—. Served to comdr. USN, 1939-45. Mem. Nat. Pilots Assn., Aircraft Owners and Pilots Assn., Profl. Golfers Assn. Republican. Baptist. Club: Rotary. Office: 1895 Old Haywood Rd Asheville NC 28806

CORDELL, JOE B., acctg. corp. exec.; b. Daytona Beach, Fla., Aug. 4, 1927; s. Joe Wynne and Ada Ruth (Wood) C.; student Yale U., 1945-46, Fla. So. Coll., 1946-47; B.S. in Bus. Adminstrn., U. Fla., 1949; m. Joyce Hinton, June 16, 1951; children—Joe B., Coleman Wynn, Lauren. Intern, Price Waterhouse Corp., N.Y.C., 1948-49, staff acct., 1949-50, audit mgr., Atlanta, 1950-58; v.p. Jim Walter Corp., Tampa, Fla., 1958-70, sr. v.p., treas., 1970-74, pres., chief operating officer, dir., 1974—; dir. Royal Trust Bank of Tampa, Fla. Steel Corp., Gen. Instrument Corp. of N.Y. Past pres. U. Fla. Found.; trustee bus. adv. council U. Fla. Served with USNR, 1945-46. C.P.A. Mem. Am. Inst. C.P.A.'s, Ga. Inst. C.P.A.'s, Fla. Inst. C.P.A.'s, Greater Tampa C. of C., Com. of 100, Alpha Kappa Psi, Alpha Tau Omega. Methodist. Clubs: Tower of Tampa, Tampa Yacht and Country, Palma Ceia Golf and Country, University of Tampa, Ye Mystic Krewe of Gasparilla. Office: Jim Walter Corp 1500 N Dale Mabry Hwy Tampa FL 33607

CORDER, HENRY ROBERT, real estate exec.; b. Grand Junction, Colo., Mar. 13, 1920; s. Clarence Myron and Harriett Catherine (Jones) C.; B.A. cum laude with honors, Williams Coll., 1941; postgrad. Wesleyan Coll., 1941-42; m. Mary Allen Jackson, Apr. 3, 1943; children—Henry Robert, John Ellett. Exec. v.p. Continental Trading Corp., New Orleans, 1947-50; exec. v.p., sales mgr. C. Horton Smith Co., New Orleans, 1950-54; sales mgr. S.W. Regional packaging div. Mead Corp., New Orleans, 1954-69; real estate broker Latter & Blum, Inc., New Orleans, 1969-73, realtor, v.p., sales mgr., 1973—. Served with USN, 1942-45. Mem. Soc. Indsl. Realtors, Nat. Assn. Realtors, Nat. Inst. Real Estate Brokers, New Orleans Bd. Realtors, Navy League U.S. (New Orleans Council pres. 1955-57, La. State pres. 1957-59, nat. dir. 1955-60). Presbyterian. Clubs: Picwick, New Orleans Country. Home: 307 Betz Pl Metairie LA 70005 Office: Latter and Blum Inc 919 Gravier St New Orleans LA 70112

COREY, VIRGIL EDWIN, farmer, co-op. exec., state legislator; b. Morning Sun, Iowa, Sept. 23, 1916; s. John Leroy and Maxie Gwendolyn (Martin) C.; student Cornell Coll., Iowa, 1937-39; B.S., Iowa State U., 1942; LL.B., LaSalle Extension U., 1953; m. Elsie Lucille Gaide, May 2, 1941; children—Leroy Dale, Virgil Edwin, Carolyn Mae, John Edward. Vocat. agr. instr., Manilla, Iowa, 1942-44, Coggon, Iowa, 1944-50, Lone Tree, Iowa, 1965-69; farmer, Morning Sun, 1950—; mem. Iowa Ho. of Reps., 1979—; dir. Eastern Iowa Light & Power Coop., Wilton, 1959-78, pres., 1974—. Dist. commr. Soil Conservation Service, 1973-78, mem. area office programming and planning, 1974-78; local committeeman Republican Party, 1968-75; mem. Iowa Ho. of Reps., 1979—. Mem. Louisa County Farm Bur. (pres. 1956-57), Iowa Soybean Growers Assn. Methodist. Clubs: Masons, Order Eastern Star. Home: Morning Sun IA 52640 Office: Eastern Iowa Light & Power Coop 600 E 5th St Wilton IA 52778

CORMIE, DONALD MERCER, investment co. exec.; b. Edmonton, Alta., Can., July 22, 1922; s. George Mills and Mildred (Mercer) C.; B.A., U. Alta., 1944, LL.B., 1945; LL.M., Harvard, 1946; m. Eivor Elisabeth Ekstrom, June 8, 1946; children—John Mills, Donald Robert, Allison Barbara, James Mercer, Neil Brian, Bruce George, Eivor Emilie, Robert Ekstrom. Admitted to bar, 1947; Queens counsel, 1964; sessional instr. faculty law U. Alberta, 1947-53; sr. partner Cormie, Kennedy, Fitch & Patrick, Edmonton, 1954—; instr. real estate law Dept. of Extension, U. Alta., 1958-64; pres., dir. Prin. Group Ltd., Prin. Life Ins. Co. Can., Collective Securities, Ltd., Collective Mut. Fund Ltd., Cormie Ranch, Ltd., Prin. Certificate Series, Inc., Prin. Investors Corp. Served with Canadian Mcht. Marine, 1943-44. Recipient Judge Green Silver medal in Law. Mem. Law Soc. Alta., World Bus. Council, Chief Execs. Forum, Canadian Bar Assn. (mem. council 1961—, chmn. adminstrv. law com. 1963-66, v.p. Alta. 1968-69, chmn. taxation sect. 1970—). Home: 12436 Grandview Dr Edmonton AB T6H 4K4 Canada Office: 1600 Cambridge Bldg Edmonton AB T5J 1S3 Canada

CORN, IRA GEORGE, JR., business exec.; b. Little Rock, Aug. 22, 1921; s. Ira George and Martha (Vickers) C.; student Little Rock Jr. Coll., 1941; A.B., U. Chgo., 1947, M.B.A., 1948; m. Louise Touchstone, Feb. 8, 1947 (div. Mar., 1961); children—Jay, John, Laura. Trainee marketing Gen. Electric Co., N.Y.C., 1947-48; asst. prof. So. Meth. U., 1948-54; corporate, financial cons. in Dallas, 1954-66; pres. Community Water Service, Dallas, 1960—, Lakeshore Apts., Indpls., 1964—; co-founder Tyler Corp., 1966, dir., 1966—, chmn. C & H Transp. Co., 1966—, co-founder Mich. Gen. Corp., 1968, chmn. bd., chief exec. officer, 1968— (all Dallas); chmn. bd. Aces Internat., Inc., Dallas, Pinnacle Books, Inc., Los Angeles; TV economist Channel 33, Dallas; mem. exec. com. Com. of Publicly-Owned Cos., N.Y.C., 1978—. Speaker profl. orgns., Dallas, N.Y.C., Washington; trustee Aberrant Behavior Center, Dallas, Dallas Acad.; mem. council Grad. Sch. Bus., U. Chgo. Served from pvt. to sgt. U.S. Army, 1942-46. Mem. Am. Mgmt. Assn., Nat. Assn. Bus. Economists, Nat. Economists Club, U. Chgo. Alumni Assn. (chmn. Dallas chpt. 1955—, nat. com. corporate support 1969—), Am. Contract Bridge League (dir., pres. 1979-80), SAR, Sigma Chi. Presbyn. Author: Play Bridge with The Aces, 1972; The Story of the Declaration of Independence, 1977 (Significant Sig award 1979); Businessman Answers Questions of College Students, 1980; author syndicated column Aces on Bridge; founder Aces, world champion bridge team, capt., 1970, 71, 77. Home: 4829 Forest Ln Dallas TX 75234 Office: 8333 Douglas Ave Suite 1100 Dallas TX 75225

CORNARO, VITTORIO ANTONIO, banker; b. Bergamo, Italy, Aug. 14, 1905 (Swiss citizen); s. Giovanni and Antonietta (Scotti) C.; Dr. in Econ. and Comml. Sci., Comml. U. Luigi Bocconi, Milan, Italy, 1928; m. Teresa Costa, Oct. 31, 1935 (dec. 1970); children—Fabia (Mrs. L. Dell 'Acqua), Giovanna (Mrs. A. Folonari), Paolo. Mgr. head office Banco di Roma, Rome, Italy, 1942-45; gen. mgr. Banco di Roma per la Svizzera, Lugano, Switzerland, 1945-51; mng. dir. Corner Bank, Ltd., Lugano, 1952-79, vice chmn., 1963-79, chmn., 1979—; mng. dir. Navimar S.A., Lugano 1954—, chmn., 1969—; dir. Financial Securities, Ltd., Lugano, 1952—. Pres., Dr. Vittorio and Dr. Teresa Cornaro Found. for Acad. Scholarships. Decorated grand officer Order St. Gregory the Gt. (Vatican). Mem. Swiss Bankers Assn. Author: (with Mario Alberti) Banks of Issue, Currency and Monetary Policy in Italy from 1849 to 1929, 1931; also other publs. on econs. Home: 16 via Sole Suvigliana/6977 Ruvigliana Lugano Switzerland Office: 16 Via Canova Lugano Ticino Switzerland

CORNELIUS, IRA EARL, mfg. co. exec.; b. Pella, Iowa, Feb. 29, 1916; s. Jacob Earl and Kitty Mae (Bickford) C.; B.A., Central U. Iowa, Pella, 1947; Ph.D., St. Andrews Episcopal U., 1967; m. Lois Margaret Geronime, 1945; children—Sue, Ronnie, Gail, Earl, Margaret, Irene, Allison. With Montgomery Ward Co., 1947-53; budget group supr. indirect methods analysis Northrop Aircraft, 1953-54; engring. specialist group leader N.Am. Aviation Co., 1954-57; various mgmt. positions Hughes Aircraft Co., 1957-60; sr. corp. planner Lockheed Aircraft Co., 1960-61; with Rockwell Internat., various locations, 1961—, sr. exec. resource analysis, 1965-70, sr. exec. advisor advanced space programs, Downey, Calif., 1970—; instr. West Coast U., Los Angeles, 1974-75. Served with U.S. Army, 1943-45. Registered profl. engr., Calif. Mem. Am. Inst. Indsl. Engrs. (sr.), Tau Epsilon Pi, Sigma Tau Delta. Republican. Home: 1334 W Orangethorpe Ave Fullerton CA 92633 Office: 12214 Lakewood Blvd Downey CA 90240

CORNELIUS, LAWRENCE BERNHARD, constrn. co. exec.; b. Corpus Christi, Tex., Apr. 30, 1929; s. Bernhard G. and Lenora Engleking C.; student public schs., Tex.; m. Barbara Bowen, Oct. 7, 1948; children—Coiece Cornelius Pyle, Susan Dale, Lisa Lynn. With B.G. Cornelius Constrn. Co., Alice, Tex., 1948—, now pres., gen. mgr.; mem. builder adv. bd., dir. Alice Nat. Bank. Bd. dirs. Camp Fire, 1969-80, Luth. Found. of S.W., 1980; mem. Community Edn. Bd., 1972-77, Alice Airport Bd., 1979-80; mem. devel. bd. Tex. Luth. Coll., 1975-80, Luth. Social Services, 1980—; mem. U.S. Senatorial Bus. Adv. Bd., 1980-81; mem. Indsl. Found. Alice; chmn. Immanuel Luth. Ch. Bd. Served with U.S. Army, 1952-54. Mem. Alice C. of C. Republican. Lutheran. Club: Rotary (dir.). Home: 2020 Hwy 281 N Alice TX 78332 Office: PO Drawer 650 Alice TX 78332

CORNELL, ALLAN ROGERS, sales exec.; b. Carbondale, Pa., June 18, 1950; s. Rogers H. and Evalyne M. (Sampson) C.; A.B.A. with distinction, Pa. State U., 1975; m. Patricia M. Willis, Nov. 23, 1974; 1 son, Clinton Allan. Adjuster, North Eastern Bank of Pa., 1973-75; retail sales mgr., v.p. Gertrude Hawk Candies, Dunmore, Pa., 1975—, also dir. Served with USN, 1969-73. Mem. Pa. State Alumni Assn. Republican. Presbyterian. Mason. Home: 106 Templeton Dr Dickson City PA 18519 Office: 1325 E Drinker St Dunmore PA 18512

CORNELSEN, FRANZ ROBERT, publisher; b. Minden-Westphalia, Germany, July 22, 1908; s. Franz and Emely (Gaedecke) C.; M.A.; m. Hildegard Friedrichs, July 22, 1938; 1 son, Dirk. With overseas dept. Siemens and Halske, Berlin, Germany, 1933-45; pres. Found. Franz Cornelsen Verlag, 1946—, also Cornelsen-Velhagen & Klasing, Berlin, Cornelsen & Oxford U. Press. Mem. Assn. Textbook Pubs. Fed. Republic of Germany (pres. 1956-60, 74, 76), Assn. Cartographic Pubs. and Insts. (pres. 1957-65), Assn. for Promotion Ednl. Aid in Developing Countries (pres. 1963-65). Home: 29 Binger Strasse 1000 Berlin 33 Germany Office: 30 Lutzowstr 105 Berlin 30 Germany

CORNELSEN, PAUL FREDERICK, food co. exec.; b. Wellington, Kans., Dec. 23, 1923; s. John S. and Theresa Albertine (von Klatt) C.; student U. Wichita, 1939-41, 45-46; B.S. in Mech. Engring., U. Denver, 1949; m. Floy Lila Brown, Dec. 11, 1943; 1 son, John Floyd. With Boeing Airplane Co., 1940-41; with Ralston Purina Co., 1946—, v.p. internat. div., 1961-63, adminstrv. v.p., gen. mgr. internat. div., 1963-64, v.p., 1964-68, exec. v.p., 1968-78, vice-chmn. bd., chief operating officer, 1978—, dir., 1964—, pres. Ralston Purina Internat., 1964-77; dir. Boatmans Nat. Bank, St. Louis, Boatmen's Bancshares, Inc., St. Louis, Petrolite Corp., St. Louis; founding mem. Latin Am. Agribus. Devel. Corp., Miami. Adv. com. Nat. 4-H Council; trustee Ill. Coll., Jacksonville. Served to 1st lt. U.S. Army, World War II, also Korean War. Decorated Silver Star. Home: Home: 506 Fox Ridge Rd Saint Louis MO 63131 Office: Checkerboard Sq Plaza Saint Louis MO 63188

CORNETT, CHARLES ERNEST, transport refrigeration sales and service co. exec.; b. Va., Dec. 19, 1940; s. Ernest Reed and Louise Elizabeth (Williams) C.; student public schs.; m. Myra Earlene Tilson, Sept. 22, 1960; children—V. Elizabeth, Charles Ernest. Gen. mgr. Lakewood Truckers Paradise, Halifax, N.C., 1968-71, Frederick I-70 Truck City (Md.), 1971-72, P&M Plaza, Harrisburg, Pa., 1973-74; pres. BPC Service Corp., Billings, Mont., 1974—; dir. Billings Trophy Mfg. Co. Inc. Bd. dirs. Billings Sheltered Workshop. Served with USAF, 1959-65. Mem. Nat. Assn. Truck Stop Operators, N.C. Truck Stop Operators Assn. (charter), Husky Car/Truck Stop/Husky House Internat. Seminar. Republican. Presbyterian. Office: 5400 Laurel Rd Billings MT 59101

CORNETT, ROBERT BOYD, kitchen designer; b. Detroit, Apr. 12, 1929; s. Boyd and Samantha (Creech) C.; B.S. in accounting, U. Ky., 1957, postgrad., 1957-58; m. Lena Grace Nicholion, July 11, 1953;

children—Robert Dwaine, James Craig, Donna Jean, Ronald Lee. With Kitchen Planning Center, Inc., Lexington, Ky., 1958—, kitchen designer, 1972—, asst. sec.-treas., 1968—, comptroller, 1970—, sales coordinator, 1974—. Served with arty. U.S. Army, 1951-53. Certified kitchen designer. Mem. Am. Inst. Kitchen Dealers, Home Builders Assn. Lexington. Republican. Baptist. Clubs: Lexington Sportsman, Masons. Home: 982 Lakeland Dr Lexington KY 40502 Office: 101 W Loudon Ave Lexington KY 40508

CORNING, BLY ARGIE, mfg. co. exec.; b. Wexford County, Mich., Feb. 22, 1917; s. Clark E. and Nina B. (Milliman) C.; student Eastern Mich. U., 1937-40; m. Audry Tuttle, Sept. 27, 1940; 1 dau., Jenifer Blye. With AC Spark Plug div. Gen. Motors Corp., Flint, Mich., 1940-45; owner, pres. Corning Mfg. Co., Flint, 1949—. Bd. govs. William L. Clements Library Assos., U. Mich. at Ann Arbor. Served with U.S. Army, 1936-37. Mem. Kappa Phi Alpha. Club: Masons. Home: 1902 Hampden Rd Flint MI 48503

CORNWALL, ROBERT MAYNARD, plastic co. exec.; b. Chgo., Sept. 27, 1921; s. Paul Brooks and Gladys May (Maynard) C.; student Marquette U., 1939-40, Miami U., Oxford, Ohio, 1942-43; m. Janet J. Jones, Feb. 10, 1943; children—Thomas, Scot, Steven, Jeffry. With dept. purchasing Carnation Co., Oconomowoc, Wis., 1939-42, 45-47; with dept. purchasing Speed Queen div. McGraw Edison Co., Ripon, Wis., 1947-53, mgr. purchases, 1953-60, asst. to pres., 1960-68, pres., 1968-75; owner Nat. Exec. Search, Houston, 1975-78; pres., chief exec. officer Rotocast Plastic Products, Inc., Miami, Fla., 1978—. Served with USN, 1942-45. Home: 7440 SW 114th St Miami FL 33156 Office: 3645 NW 67th St Miami FL 33147

CORNWELL, JERALD MOYER, mining equipment mfg. co. exec.; b. Wilkes Barre, Pa., Jan. 14, 1928; s. Thomas H. and Margaret L. (Lehman) C.; B.S. in Bus. Adminstrn., U. Pitts., 1951; postgrad. Harvard U.; m. Barbara Kates, Apr. 12, 1952; children—Thomas L., Steven W., Kathryn Cornwell Wolbers. With Westinghouse Air Brake & Union Switch & Signal Corp., Swissvale, Pa., 1951-52; buyer Lycoming div. Avco Corp., Williamsport, Pa., 1952-56, purchasing agt. advanced Devel. div., Stratford, Conn., 1956-57, purchasing mgr. research and advanced devel. div., Lawrence, Mass., 1957-59, Missile Systems div., Wilmington, Mass., 1959-65, dir. materials, 1965-72; dir. purchasing Marion (Ohio) Power Shovel Co., 1972-73, v.p. purchasing, 1973-76; v.p. materials Marion Power Shovel div. Dresser Industries, Inc., 1976—; instr. indsl. mgmt. Boston U. Vice pres. Am. Field Service, Andover, Mass., 1966-67; dir. Little League Baseball, 1966-67; chmn. Marion County fund raising Am. Cancer Soc., 1975, bd. dirs., 1975—; mem. Marion Econ. Council, 1977—; chmn. advance gifts div. United Way of Marion County, 1978-79; mem. Republican Fin. Com., 1978—. Mem. C. of C., Nat. Assn. Purchasing Mgmt., Purchasing Mgmt. Assn. Columbus Area (pres. 1977). Lutheran. Clubs: Marion Country, Marion Power Shovel Mgmt., Golden Panther of U. Pitts. Alumni Assn. Contbr. articles to profl. jours. Home: 1035 Yorkshire Dr Marion OH 43302 Office: 617 W Center St Marion OH 43302

CORNYN, JOHN EUGENE, accountant; b. San Francisco, Apr. 30, 1906; s. John Eugene and Sara (Larkin) C.; B.S., St. Mary's Coll., 1935; M.B.A., U. Chgo., 1936; postgrad. N.Y. U. Law Sch., 1936-37; m. Virginia R. Shannahan, Sept. 10, 1938 (dec. May 1964); children—Virginia, Kathleen, John III, Madeleine, Carolyn; m. 2d, Marian C. Fairfield, Aug. 21, 1965. Sr. partner John E. Cornyn & Co., C.P.A.'s, Winnetka, Ill., 1952-73, pres. John E. Cornyn & Co., Ltd., 1973—; pres. Seven Seas, Inc.; treas. All Seas, Inc.; lectr. U. Chgo., 1947-54. Exec. sec. North Shore Property Owners Assn. Mem. Am. Inst. C.P.A.'s, Ill. Soc. C.P.A.'s, Fellowship Catholic Scholars (asso.). Roman Catholic. Office: 126 Bertling Ln Winnetka IL 60093

CORONEOS, TAS, ins. co. exec.; b. Balt., Aug. 19, 1920; s. Andrew and Mary (Gavriles) C.; grad. U. Pa., 1947; postgrad. Catholic U. Law Sch., 1966; m. Theodora Lambros, Nov. 28, 1948; children—Tas S. G., Anna Maria. With Met. Life Ins. Co., 1948—, agt., Washington, 1948-49, sales mgr., 1949-51, field trainer, 1951-52, territorial supr., N.Y.C., 1952-53, dist. mgr., Newport News, Va., 1953-55, Washington, 1955—; instr., lectr., cons. in field. Served with U.S. Army, 1943-47. Recipient Tower Trophy Met. Life Ins. Co., 1973. Mem. Nat. (chartered life underwriter), Newport News (dir.), Washington (fin. com.) assns. chartered life underwriters, Gen. Agents and Mgrs. Assn. Republican. Greek Orthodox.Clubs: Kenwood Golf and Country, Men's Garden (Bethesda, Md.); Rotary (Newport News). Home: 5801 Highland Dr Chevy Chase MD 20015 Office: 8701 Georgia Ave Silver Spring MD 20910

CORRAD, PAUL KENTON, glass co. exec.; b. Saginaw, Mich., Jan. 2, 1946; s. Thomas J. and Vietta Ruth (Wagner) C.; student Delta Jr. Coll., 1964-66; B.S. in Bus. Adminstrn., Central Mich. U., 1969; postgrad. East. Tex. State Coll., 1975; m. Celia Ella Thornton, Aug. 12, 1980; 1 son, Brent Thomas. Dist. rep. Libbey Owens Ford Co., Los Angeles, 1971-74, dist. rep., Dallas, 1974, sr. dist. rep., Dallas, 1975-76, asst. nat. market mgr., Toledo, 1977-78, sr. dist. rep., Columbia, Md., 1978-79, mgr. Phila. dist. office, 1979—. Active, Cub Scouts, Playa Del Rey, Calif., 1971-72; dist. coordinator United Way Campaign, Toledo, 1977. Served with C.E., U.S. Army, 1969-71. Recipient Jaycee of Yr. award Toledo Jaycees, 1978. Mem. Constrn. Specifications Inst., Producers Council (v.p. local chpt.). Republican. Episcopalian. Home: 1171 Kelly Ann Dr West Chester PA 19380 Office: 14 S Bryn Mawr Ave Bryn Mawr PA 19010

CORRADO, FRED, food co. exec.; b. Mt. Vernon, N.Y., May 20, 1940; s. Anthony E. and Rose V. (Capone) C.; B.B.A., Manhattan Coll., 1961; m. Josephine Ann Gonda, July 4, 1962; children—David, Paul, Christopher. Sr. auditor Arthur Andersen & Co., N.Y.C., 1961-65; accounting mgr. Romney Cosmetics, Stamford, Conn., 1965-68; sr. budget analyst ITT, N.Y.C., 1968-69; v.p. fin. specialty div. Kenton Corp., N.Y.C., 1969-73; asst. corporate controller Standard Brands Inc., N.Y.C., 1973-74; dir. fin. planning, controller, v.p., controller Standard Brands Foods, 1974-76, v.p. fin. and planning U.S. consumer products group, 1976-78, v.p.-corporate mgmt. info. systems, 1977-80, v.p. corporate planning and systems parent co., 1978-80, pres. Planters div., 1980—. C.P.A., N.Y. Mem. Am. Inst. C.P.A.'s, N.Y. Soc. C.P.A.'s. Home: 9 Coventry Ct Croton on Hudson NY 10520 Office: 625 Madison Ave New York NY 10022

CORRIGAN, FREDRIC H., corp. exec.; b. Grand Forks, N.D., Dec. 2, 1914; s. Thomas S. and Bertha (Wolff) C.; student U. Minn., 1933-36; m. Mary Leslie, Dec. 30, 1939; children—Leslie (Mrs. John G. Turner), Fredric Wolff, Nancy (Mrs. Kenneth B. Woodrow). Grain merchandiser Peavey Co., Mpls., 1936-43, Duluth, Minn., 1946-55, v.p., gen. mgr., Duluth, 1951-55, Mpls., 1955-58, dir., 1959—, exec. v.p., 1959-65, pres., 1965-75, chief exec. officer, 1968-77, chmn. bd., 1975-77, ret., 1977, chmn. exec. com. bd. dirs., 1977—; dir. Northwest Bancorp., Super Valu, Northwestern Nat. Bank. Pres. Duluth Bd. Trade, 1954-55, Mpls. Grain Exchange, 1967-68. Bd. dirs. United Fund Mpls., 1967-72, Mpls. YMCA, 1970-79, Mpls. Orchestral Assn., 1973-79, Mpls. Urban Coalition, 1971-74, Greater Mpls. C. of C., 1972-75, also Western, Minn. golf assns.; chmn. bd. Abbott Northwestern Hosp., Mpls., 1977-79; chmn. Farm Forum Mpls., 1977; met. chmn. Nat. Alliance Businessmen, 1976, also dir.; trustee Evans Scholars Found., 1968-72. Served with USNR, 1943-46. Methodist (trustee). Clubs: Minneapolis; Minikahda, Desert Forest. Home: 2856 Gale Rd Wayzata MN 55391 Office: 4900 IDS Center 80 S 8th St Minneapolis MN 55402

CORRIVEAU, PAUL, co. exec.; b. Grand Mere, Que., Can., Dec. 3, 1926; s. Walter and Corinne (Arseneault) C.; student Coll. Sacre Coeur Grand Mere, 1933-40; corr. courses Fin. Edn. Services, Canadian Property Mgrs. Assn., 1950-58; m. Therese Roy, June 3, 1944; children—Nelson, Paul, Raymond, Claude, Jean Pierre. With Goodyear, Toronto, 1943-46; asst. geologist Sampler Noranda Mines Ltd., 1947-63; pres. P.R.C. Distbrs. Ltd., Matagami, Que., 1964—; sec. constrn. Jean Corriveau & Fils Ltd., Matagami, 1974—; pres. J.A. Tremblay Transport Ltd., Matagami, 1978—. Mayor, Localite Joutel, Que., 1976-78. Recipient Queen award for public service, 1978. Mem. Noranda C. of C. Roman Catholic. Club: K.C. Home: 500 Boul Jontel Joutel PQ Y0Y 1N0 Canada Office: Commercial Center Matagami PQ J0Y 2A0 Canada

CORSER, SUSAN L., real estate investment co. exec.; b. Detroit, Nov. 25, 1927; d. Oliver T. and V. Lyvonne (Van Matre) Dyer; grad. Patricia Stevens Models Finishing Sch., 1949; diploma N.Y. U., 1958; student Roberts Sch. of Beauty Culture, 1960-61, Phoenix Coll., 1962-67, Ariz. State U., 1978; children by previous marriage-Sharon Sue (Mrs. John Eldridge), Lester J., Kimme Corser Wilkerson. Photographer model Galbraith Studio, Ft. Wayne, Ind., 1949-52; fashion model Patterson/Fletcher, dept. Store, Ft. Wayne, 1949-52; model for various fashion shows, Chgo., 1948-49; appeared on various fashion shows on TV, 1949-60; pres., dir. Charm and Models Finishing Sch., Lockport, N.Y., 1957-61; appeared on Nat. Biscuit Co. program Sta. WBEN, Buffalo, 1959-60; photographers model for various studios and advt. agys. in Buffalo, 1954-60, Chgo., 1949-52; sales mgr. Ray Warriner Realty Co., Phoenix, 1963-67; pres. Biwi Investments Co., Phoenix, 1967—; guest speaker to various women's clubs and civic orgns., 1949—; beauty cons., 1949-60; free-lance fashion coordinator, 1949-60. Chmn., Our Year of History Celebration, Upstate N.Y. Centennial, 1950-60. Mem. Big Sisters Ariz., Nat. Assn. Realtors, Buffalo Models Guild. Office: 4750 N Central Ave Phoenix AZ 85012

CORSON, CHARLES COLE, restaurant exec.; b. Raton, N.Mex., Apr. 13, 1949; s. Joseph Mackie and Ruth Lillian (Riggin) C.; B.A., U. Mass., Amherst, 1973; m. Susan Beth Salett, July 7, 1979. Gen. mgr. Seaside Restaurant, Beachwood, Ohio, 1978-79; sous chef Seaside Restaurant, Boston, 1977-78; gen. mgr. Patch's Backyard, Newton Centre, Mass., 1975-77; v.p. ops. Flourchild's Restaurant, Boston, 1979—; instr. food and beverage mgmt. Bunker Hill Community Coll., Boston; pres. CC Cons. Co. Mem. Food and Beverage Execs. Mass. Home and Office: 70 Withington Rd Newtonville MA 02160

CORT, ROBERT WILLIAM, motion picture co. exec.; b. N.Y.C., July 2, 1946; s. Mack and Mildred C.; B.A., U. Pa., 1968, M.A., 1970, M.B.A., 1974. Mgmt. cons. McKinsey & Co., N.Y.C., 1974-76; v.p. advt. and publicity Columbia Pictures Corp., Burbank, Calif., 1976-79; exec. v.p. worldwide advt. publicity and promotion Twentieth-Century Fox Film Corp., Beverly Hills, Calif., 1979—. Mem. Am. Film Inst., Phi Beta Kappa. Office: Box 900 Beverly Hills CA 90213

CORUM, WILLIAM MONTGOMERY, fluid milk processing co. exec.; b. Madisonville, Ky., July 14, 1942; s. Bill and Glenna B. Corum; B.S., U. Ky., 1964; m. Frances Ferguson, June 19, 1965; children—Caroline, Ashby. Purchasing agt. U.C. Milk Co., Inc., Madisonville, 1966-71, v.p., 1971-74, pres., 1974—. Bd. dirs. Hopkins County (Ky.) Fair, 1970—. Mem. Dixie Dairy Products Assn. (dir.), So. Assn. Dairy Food Mfrs. (dir.), Madisonville C. of C. (dir.). Democrat. Methodist. Clubs: Kiwanis (pres. Madisonville 1973-74), Madisonville Country, Petroleum, Shamrock. Home: 1029 Princeton Park Madisonville KY 42431 Office: 234 N Scott St Box M Madisonville KY 42431

CORWIN, WALLING, author, chemist, broker; b. Morrow, Ohio, Nov. 29, 1895; s. W.D. and Celia (Worley) C.; student Nat. Normal U., Lebanon, Ohio, 1914; B.Sc., Ohio State U., 1919, M.Sc., 1921; postgrad. U. Calif., 1923-24; grad. Martin Jensen Flying Sch., San Diego, 1925; m. Mae Johnson, Oct. 21, 1920 (dec. 1933); 1 dau., Barbara; m. 2d, Esther Helen Elliott, July 2, 1942 (dec. 1958); m. 3d, Alethea Ray, 1959. Tchr. pub. sch., Oak Ridge, 1914-15; half-time instr. Ohio State U., 1919-21; instr. vocat. agr., Millersburg, Ohio, 1921-24; instr. sci. city schs., San Diego, 1924-35; instr. vocational agr., Laurelville, Ohio, 1937-38, Bidwell, Ohio, 1938-42; chemist Dupont Remington Arms, Kings Mills, Ohio, 1942-44; chemist research div. Am. Rolling Mills, Middletown, Ohio, 1944-46; electro chemist plating lab., research dept. Nat. Cash Register Co., Dayton, 1946-48; research chemist Pollock Paper Corp., 1949-54; registered rep. Green & Ladd, brokers, mem. N.Y. Stock Exchange 1954-57; chemist Air Pollution Control Dist., Los Angeles, 1957-64. Presbyn. Mason; mem. Order Eastern Star, Grange. Home: 12018 California St Yucaipa CA 92399

CORY, PAUL RUSSELL, ins. co. exec.; b. Chgo., Oct. 8, 1926; s. Victor E. and Bernice (Tucker) C.; A.B., Wheaton Coll., 1949; postgrad. Northwestern U.; m. Carol Ann Schmitt, Apr. 3, 1976; children—Barbara Ellen, Susan Elizabeth, Tucker Paul. Dir., pres., prin. stockholder Currency Services, Inc., predecessor of Travelers Express Co., 1955-64; organizer, chmn. bd. N.J. Life Ins. Co., Saddle Brook, 1964—, now chmn. bd., chief exec. officer; sole owner, chmn. bd., chief exec. officer N.J. Life Co., NJL Services Corp., NJL Data Corp. Mem. Nat. UN Day Com. Served with USAAF, 1944-45. Mem. Nat. Assn. Life Cos. (pres. 1978-79, dir. 1979—). Presbyterian. Clubs: Upper Montclair Country; Union League (Chgo.); West Lake Country (Augusta, Ga.). Home: 6 Denison Dr E Saddle River NJ 07458 Office: Park 80 Plaza W Saddle Brook NJ 07662

COSELLI, RICHARD, title co. exec.; b. Galveston, Tex., Apr. 1, 1932; s. Frank and Beatrice (Ragone) C.; B.B.A., U. Houston, 1955, J.D., 1958; m. Mary Jo Redding, Sept. 1, 1962; children—Mary Bea, Catherine B., Richard J. Admitted to Tex. bar, 1958; real estate counsel Prudential Ins. Co., Houston, 1962-77; sr. v.p., dir. Am. Title Co., Houston, 1977—; dir. Buffalo Savs. & Loan Assn., Vetco, Inc., Barbara Robertson of Houston, Inc. Mem. Tex. Land Title Assn. (dir. 1980-81), Houston C. of C., Am. Bar Assn., Tex. Bar Assn., Houston Bar Assn. Roman Catholic. Office: 301 Esperson Bldg Houston TX 77002

COSGROVE, WILLIAM JEROME, lawyer; b. Lancaster, Pa., July 28, 1909; s. Jerome A. and Laura (Baumann) C.; student Franklin and Marshall Coll., 1926-27, Columbia, 1927-29; LL.B., St. John's Law Sch., 1932; m. Agatha Hagen, Oct. 25, 1933. Admitted to N.Y. bar, 1934, thereafter practiced in Bklyn.; partner firm Wrenn & Schmid, 1947-79, counsel, 1979—; acting city judge, Glen Cove, 1950-51; mem. adv. bd. Kings Lafayette Bank, 1973, Republic Nat. Bank N.Y., 1974-76. Pres., Glen Cove Community Chest, 1953; mem. Glen Cove Urban Renewal Com., 1956-65; pres. Glen Cove Lincoln Settlement, Inc., 1958-62; mem. Glen Cove Housing Authority, 1958-66. Served with U.S. Army, 1943-45. Mem. N.Y. State Bar Assn. (Ho. of Dels. 1976-78), Bklyn. Bar Assn. Home: 170 SW Garden St PO Box 1311 Keystone Heights FL 32656 Office: 26 Court St Brooklyn NY 11242

COSPER, NORMAN HARRY, corp. exec.; b. Birmingham, Ala., Dec. 29, 1943; s. Harry Clifford and Linnie Maude (Merchant) C.; B.A., Birmingham So. Coll., 1966; m. Vallie Lawrelle Dozier, Aug. 20, 1965; children—Kimberly Patrice, Norman Clifford. Programmer, So. Life & Health Ins. Co., Birmingham, 1966-67; internal revenue agt. U.S. Dept. Treasury, Birmingham, 1967-70; asst. controller Delwood Furniture Co., Inc., United Chair Div., 1970-73, v.p. fin. SEMCO Div., 1973-77; v.p. fin., treas. Pasquale Food Co., Inc., 1977-79; pres. The Maribud Corp., Birmingham, 1980—. Pres., PTA, 1979-80; coach Dixie Youth Baseball, 1976—. Mem. Nat. Assn. Accountants, Alpha Kappa Psi. Club: Downtown. Home: 1616 Shades Crest Rd Birmingham AL 35226 Office: 1 Independence Plaza Suite 900 Birmingham AL 35209

COSSABOOM, EWING ORVILLE, lawyer, farm mgr.; b. Millersburg, Ky., Mar. 17, 1917; s. Charles O. and Lillian (Young) C.; A.B., Transylvania U., 1939; J.D., U. Cin., 1942; m. Joy Cossaboom. Chief purchase and claims sect. real estate div. Ohio River div. U.S. Army Engrs., 1942-45; practiced in Cin., 1945—; mem. firm Dickerson, Ahrens, Cossaboom & Burns, 1954—; farm mgr. J.M. Ewing Farm, Morgan, Ky., 1952-73; sec., treas. Coll. Hill Realty Co.; v.p. Whitney Corp., 1965-67, treas., 1967—; dir. Mt. Healthy Savs. & Loan Co. Chmn., Mt. Healthy Civil Service Commn., 1968—. Bd. dirs. Hamilton County Good Govt. League, 1950-63. Mem. Christian Ch. Contbr. articles to profl. publs. Home: 1623 Madison Ave Mount Healthy OH 45231 Office: Am Bldg 30 E Central Pkwy Cincinnati OH 45202

COSTELLO, JOHN FRANCIS, tax cons.; b. Phila., June 13, 1929; s. John Thomas and Clara (Doyle) C.; B.S., LaSalle Coll., 1958; postgrad N.Y. U., 1966-67; m. Marilyn R. Lorman, Nov. 27, 1959; children—Roxanne, John T., Timothy. Cost acct. Rohm & Haas, Phila., 1958-60; inventory account supr. and tax acct. Air Products & Chems., Inc., Allentown, Pa., 1960-63; tax analyst Celanese Corp., N.Y.C. and Charlotte, N.C., 1963-69; tax mgr. Economy Fin., Indpls., 1969-73; tax cons. Bankers Life & Casualty Co., Palm Beach Gardens, Fla., 1973—; tax cons. John D. MacArthur; chmn. Bankers Life & Casualty Co., 1973-78; pres. Alamo Rent-A-Car, Inc., 1974-78, Garden Constrn. Co., 1976-78, Garden Comml. Builders, Inc., 1976-78. Bd. dirs. Palm Beach County March of Dimes, 1980—. Served with USNR, 1952-54. C.P.A., Ind. Home: 302 Riverside Dr Palm Beach Gardens FL 33410 Office: 4176 Burns Rd Palm Beach Gardens FL 33410

COSTIGAN, JOHN FRANCIS, banker; b. Derby, Conn., Aug. 6, 1930; s. William Joseph and Alice Frances (Shea) C.; grad. Nat. Sales Tng. Inst., 1955; grad. mgmt. devel. program Nat. Assn. Mut. Savs. Banks, U. Mass., 1978; m. Virginia K. Carroll, June 6, 1953; children—Ellen M., Katherine A., Virginia M., Margaret C., Mary A., Patricia S. Account rep. fin. div. Remington Rand div. Sperry Rand Corp., Bridgeport and New Haven, 1954-61; with Derby (Conn.) Savs. Bank, 1961—, v.p., corp. sec., 1973-75, sr. v.p., corp. sec., 1975—, also dir.; dir. Ansonia-Derby Water Co.; trustee F.A. Russ Fund. Trustee, Griffin Hosp., Derby, 1972—, corp. sec., 1972-78, treas., 1978-81, v.p., 1981—, chmn. audit and budget com., 1978—, chmn. by-laws com., 1979; mem. adv. bd. Cath. Family Services, Ansonia, Conn., 1980—. Served with USAF, 1950-54. Recipient Gold Seal award Valley C. of C., 1974. Mem. Am. Inst. Banking, Conn. Hosp. Assn. Roman Catholic. Clubs: Race Brook Country (Orange, Conn.); Elks (Derby). Home: 27 Fairview Terr Derby CT 06418 Office: Derby Savs Bank One Elizabeth St Derby CT 06418

COTA, ROBERT CORONADO, investment banker; b. Heber, Calif., June 27, 1941; s. Antonio Borquez and Dolores (Coronado) C.; grad. Nat. Comml. Landing Sch., Okla. U., 1973; m. Candice Rupp, Oct. 9, 1971; children—Michael, Sandra, Gregory. Credit and sales mgr. Goodyear Tire & Rubber Co., Los Angeles, 1963-66; br. mgr. Security Pacific Nat. Bank, San Clemente, Calif., 1966-71; v.p. Imperial Bank, Los Angeles, 1971-74; exec. v.p. PFO Fin. Corp., Los Angeles, 1974-79, also dir; pres. Comml. & Indsl. Fin. Services, Inc., Los Angeles, 1979—. Served with U.S. Army, 1960-63. Mem. Assn. Profl. Loan Applicant Reps. (founding dir. 1978), U.S. Small Businessman's Assn. Office: 9800 S Sepulveda Los Angeles CA 90045

COTORA, THEODORE, mfg. co. exec.; b. Detroit, Feb. 20, 1929; s. Theodore and Cornelia (Danciu) C.; B.S., U. Wis., 1953; J.D., Southwestern U., 1979; m. Dorothy Kraft, Apr. 8, 1950; 1 son, Craig. Exec. v.p. Globe Wernicke Co., Cin., 1964-69; gen. mgr. Hollowell Div. Standard Pressed Steel Corp., Santa Ana, Calif., 1969-71; pres., chief exec. officer Revcon Inc., Fountain Valley, Calif., 1971-75; pres., fluid systems div. U.S. Filter Corp., Whittier, Calif., 1976-77; exec. v.p. Verely Co., Lapeer, Mich., 1979-80; dir. Waterfront Homes, Inc. Mem. Orange County (Calif.) Citizens Direction Finding Com. Recipient citation Treasury Dept., 1974. Mem. Am. Prodn. Inventory Control Soc., Los Angeles C. of C. (energy water com.). Home: 6021 Sierra Bravo St Irvine CA 92715

COTTER, FRANCIS PATRICK, elec. mfg. co. exec.; b. N.Y.C., June 12, 1922; s. Patrick and Mary (Condron) C.; B.S., N.Y. U., 1943; LL.B. Cath. U. Am., 1955; children—John, Mary Alice, Catherine, Frank; m. 2d, Malinda Ann DuBose, Apr. 10, 1965; 1 son, Patrick. Spl. agt. FBI, 1947-52; profl. staff mem. Joint Com. Atomic Energy, 1952-56; cons., 1956—; admitted to D.C. bar, 1955; exec. asst. to v.p. atomic power div. Westinghouse Electric Corp., 1956-62, v.p. atomic def. and space group, Washington, 1963-73, v.p. govt. affairs, 1972—; dep. insp. gen. fgn. assistance State Dept., 1962-63; spl. cons. select com. astronautics and space exploration U.S. Ho. of Reps., 1958—; cons. State Dept., 1963—, AEC; lectr. tng. classes Peace Corps, 1963; mem. nat. energy study Dept. Interior. Served to capt. USMCR, 1943-46. Mem. D.C. Bar Assn. Democrat. Roman Catholic. Clubs: Univ., Congl. Country (Washington). Home: 3626 Quesada St NW Washington DC 20015 Office: 1801 K St NW Washington DC 20006

COTTER, RICHARD LAWRENCE, banker; b. Somerville, Mass., Dec. 27, 1918; s. Joseph Thomas and Mary (Coffey) C.; A.B., Syracuse U., 1943; m. Jacqueline Sipley, June 15, 1943; children—Stephanie (Mrs. Hervey Coke Parke III), Richard Lawrence, David, Mark, Bryan. Vice pres. Phila. Nat. Bank, 1955—; lectr. in field. Served with AUS, 1943-46. Mem. Am. Marketing Assn., Bank Pub. Relations Marketing Assn. Home: 3 Snowden Rd Bala-Cynwyd PA 19005 Office: Phila Nat Bank Philadelphia PA 19101

COTTER, WILLIAM STEPHEN PATRICK, investment co. exec.; b. N.Y.C., Nov. 9, 1936; s. Edward and Mary (Leonard) C.; B.S., Fordham U., 1961; m. Dolores Meier, May 6, 1961; children—William Stephen Patrick, Colleen, Stephanie, Suzanne, Deirdre. Dir. sales tng. Oppenheimer & Co., N.Y.C., 1966-70; v.p. Smith Barney & Co., N.Y.C., 1970-74, No. Trust Co., Chgo., 1974-80; pres. Am. Agrl. Investment Mgmt. Co., Inc., Bannockburn, Ill., 1980—. Nat. arts coordinator President's Council, 1969-70; pres. Madison Twp. (N.J.) Bd. Edn., 1969-71; chmn. White House Task Force on Econ. Devel., 1973. Served with U.S. Army, 1955-58. Republican. Roman Catholic. Clubs: Knollwood Country (Lake

Forest, Ill.): University (Chgo.). Editor: Social Security, The Frankenstein Monster, Vital Speeches, 1975; Social Security, Problems and Solutions, 1978. Home: 641 Tanglewood Ct Lake Forest IL 60045 Office: 2211 A Lakeside Dr Bannockburn IL 60015

COTTERILL, DAVID LEE, bank exec.; b. Rochester, N.Y., May 7, 1937; s. Henry John and Ethel May (Townsend) C.; B.S. in Indsl. Psychology, Pa. State U., 1960; m. Joan Elizabeth Royer, July 1, 1961; children—Jonathan David, Susan Elizabeth. Trainee, Mellon Nat. Bank & Trust Co., Pitts., 1961-64; pres. Wachovia Services, Inc. subs. Wachovia Corp., Winston-Salem, N.C., 1964-68, 70-72; dir. electronic data processing Wachovia Bank & Trust Co., N.A., Winston-Salem, 1968-70, sr. v.p. ops., 1972-79, exec. v.p., head adminstrv. div., 1979—; an organizer N.C. Payments System, Inc., 1973-74, dir., chmn. systems-ops. subcom., 1975, chmn. bd., 1975-77; mem. ops. adv. com. 5th Fed. Res. Dist., 1978; instr. Sch. Banking of South, also profl. courses. Served with USNR, 1954-62. Mem. Bank Adminstrn. Inst. (industry systems commn. 1974—, chmn. 1977-78, mem. exec. com. 1979-80, chmn. banking services steering com. 1979-80), Am. Bankers Assn. (payments system policy com.), Am. Nat. Standards Inst., Internat. Standards Orgn., Sigma Nu. Author articles in field. Home: Box 595 Bermuda Run Advance NC 27006 Office: Wachovia Bank & Trust Co PO Box 3099 Winston-Salem NC 27102

COTTMAN, IRYS JUANITA, mfg. co. exec.; b. Bethesda, Md., June 10, 1950; d. George Greensbury and Alice Yvette (Williams) C.; B.S., Drexel U., 1972; M.B.A. (Quaker Oats Co. fellow), U. Chgo., 1974. Mktg. asst. L'Eggs Products Inc., Winston Salem, N.C., 1974-75, asst. product mgr., 1976-78; asso. product mgr. new products Pet Inc., St. Louis, 1978-79, product mgr. Evaporated Milk div., 1979-80; new products devel. mgr. Keebler Co., Elmhurst, Ill., 1980—. Mem. Am. Mgmt. Assn., Am. Mktg. Assn., Assn. M.B.A. Execs., Nat. Assn. Female Execs., Internat. Platform Assn., Alpha Kappa Alpha. Democrat. Baptist. Home: 2004 Colebrook Dr Hillcrest Heights MO 20031 Office: 1 Hollow Tree Ln Elmhurst IL 60126

COTTON, DONALD LLOYD, lumber co. exec.; b. Sayre, Pa., May 6, 1914; s. Berton J. and Eva D. C.: B.A., Colgate U., 1936; m. Janet Crites, Oct. 21, 1939; children—Douglas Lloyd, Linda Boardman. With Cotton-Hanlon, Inc., Odessa, N.Y., 1936--, pres., chief exec. officer, 1973—; sec., Interstate Hardwood Lumber Co., Elizabeth, N.J.; dir. Glen Bank & Trust Co., Watkins Glen, N.Y., Pa. Lumbermen's Mut. Ins. Co., Phila., Security Corp., Rochester, N.Y. Bd. dirs. Scheyler Hosp., Montour Falls, N.Y. Served with U.S. Army, 1944-45. Decorated Bronze Star; recipient Silver Beaver award Boy Scouts Am., 1978. Presbyterian. Clubs: Masons, Shriners. Home: 103 Turner Park Montour Falls NY 14865 Office: Cotton-Hanlon Rd Odessa NY 14869

COTTON, JOHN CARL, bank exec.; b. Washington, Sept. 24, 1938; s. John and Marion Catherine (Hoglund) C.; B.A. (Ford Found. scholar), U. Chgo., 1959, M.B.A., 1967; m. Janet Elizabeth Hobbs, Nov. 24, 1957; children—John, Dawne, Elizabeth. Asst. cashier No. Trust, Chgo., 1964-67; v.p. Beverly Bank, Chgo., 1967-68; pres. Evanston Bank (Ill.), 1967-70, Citizens Bancorp., Vineland, N.J., 1970-74; exec. v.p., chief operating officer Patagonia Corp., Tucson, 1974-75; pres., chief exec. officer Gt. Western Bank, Phoenix, 1975—; arbitrator N.Y. Stock Exchange. Pres., Phoenix and Valley of the Sun Conv. and Vis.'s Bur., 1980; v.p., bd. dirs., mem. exec. com. Phoenix Met. C. of C.; mem. Fiesta Bowl Com., Phoenix; pres. dean's adv. council Coll. Bus., Ariz. State U. Mem. U. Chgo. Alumni Assn. (life), Ariz. Bankers Assn. (1st v.p., dir.). Clubs: Kiwanis (pres. elect), Phoenix Country. Office: 3443 N Central Ave Phoenix AZ 85012

COTTRELL, ROBERT LYMAN, retail food chain exec.; b. Cin., Sept. 11, 1932; s. William Frederick and Annice (Lyman) C.; B.S. summa cum laude, Miami U., 1954; m. Nancy Sohngen, June 8, 1954; children—Philip, Robert, Richard. With The Kroger Co., 1954—, v.p. distbn. adminstrn., Cin., 1979—; dir. Citizens Bank, Hamilton, Ohio, 1974-79. Mem. adv. council Miami U. Sch. Applied Sci., 1974-78, chmn., 1978; mem. adv. council Miami U. Sch. Bus., 1979—; trustee Miami U. Fund, 1980—, trustee Ft. Hamilton-Hughes Meml. Hosp., 1975—, treas., 1977-79. Served with USAF, 1954-57. Mem. AIIE. Republican. Presbyterian. Office: 1014 Vine St Cincinnati OH 45202

COUBA, KARL BENOIT, controller; b. Port-au-Prince, Haiti, Mar. 15, 1936; came to U.S., 1965; s. Benoit B. and Adeline (Kerlegand) C.; Licence en Droit, Faculte de Droit de Port au Prince, Haiti, 1957; B.B.A. cum laude, Bernard Baruch Coll., 1969; M.B.A. (Caldwell fellow), Columbia U., 1970; m. Juanita, Dec. 24, 1974; children—Chantalle, Tametria. Fin. analyst Gen. Foods Corp., White Plains, N.Y., 1970-71, sr. fin. analyst, 1971-72, fin. specialist, 1972-73, fin. reporting mgr., 1974-75, fin. analysis and planning mgr., 1975-76, controller North St. Capital Corp. (wholly-owned subs. Gen. Foods Corp.), White Plains, 1976—; cons. World Bank; lectr. mgmt. SUNY, Purchase; lectr. corp. fin. Manhattan Coll., N.Y. Vis. lectr. Nat. Urban League exec. exchange program. Mem. Am. Fin. Assn., Beta Gamma Sigma. Roman Catholic. Contbr. article to profl. inst. Home: 5900 Arlington Ave Apt 4W Riverdale NY 10471

COUDERC, LOUIS ARTHUR, mktg.-import exec.; b. St. Andre, France, Apr. 28, 1928; s. Arthur F. and Blanche (Daudet) C.; came to U.S., 1949; Baccalaureat, Coll. Issoire, France, 1940-46; student Ecole Superieure de Commerce, Clermont, France, 1946-49; B.S. (Fulbright scholar), King Coll., Bristol, Tenn., 1949; M.S. in Internat. Econs., Okla. State U., 1952; m. Virginia Lee Barrett, Jan. 17, 1953; children—Gary Russel, Gregg Louis, Denise Anne, Louis Arthur. With Michelin Tire Corp.-U.S.A., 1952-72, dist.-div. mgr., Oklahoma City, 1952-60, v.p. sales, Lake Success, N.Y., 1962-72; pres. P.J.F. Assos., Roslyn, N.Y., 1972-74; pres. Couderc Mktg. Systems, Roslyn, 1974—, Euro-Tire, Fairfield, N.J., 1975—; dir. Internat. Rubber Industries; cons. rubber industry, U.S., Europe. Fulbright fellow, 1950-52. Huguenot-Calvinist. Contbr. articles on European community to profl. jours. Home: 15 The Oaks Roslyn Estates NY 11576

COUGHLAN, PAUL BERNARD, hotel exec.; b. Ravelstoke, B.C., Can., Sept. 24, 1932; s. John Bernard and Etta (Walker) C.; B.A., U. Alta. (Can.), 1955; m. Phyllis P. Wheelhouse, Apr. 11, 1964; 1 dau., Janice L. Chief accountant Wilshire Oil Co. of Tex., Calgary, Alta., 1956-61; sr. accountant Dome Petroleum Ltd., Calgary, 1961-65; sr. fin. analyst Foster Assos., Inc., Washington, 1965-68, Citizens Utilities Co., Stamford, Conn., 1968-69; mgr. fin. group and asst. to v.p. fin. Gen. Public Utilities Corp., N.Y.C., 1969-77, mgr. fin. controls, Parsippany, N.J., 1977-80; owner, operator Banana Bay Inn, St. Kitts, W.I., 1980—. Bd. dirs., treas. Mental Health Assn. Stamford, Darien and New Canaan, 1969-70. Mem. Nat. Assn. Accountants, (dir. Stamford chpt. 1969-70), Am. Econ. Assn., Am. Statis. Assn., Internat. Brotherhood Magicians. Home: Basseterre St Kitts West Indies Office: Banana Bay Inn St Kitts West Indies

COUGHLIN, TIMOTHY CRATHORNE, banker; b. Evanston, Ill., June 1, 1942; s. Laurence and Mary (Crathorne) C.; B.A., Brown U., 1964; M.B.A., N.Y. U., 1969; m. Laura J. Philipp, June 10, 1967; children—Elizabeth, Timothy, Mary Blair, John. Vice-pres., div. exec. Chase Manhattan Bank, N.Y.C., 1964-78; sr. v.p. dep. gen. mgr. Banque de Paris et des Pays-Bas, N.Y.C., 1978—. Mem. Inst. Fgn. Bankers. Episcopalian. (treas. 1978—). Clubs: Racquet and Tennis, Skytop, Ridgewood Country. Home: 368 Beechwood Rd Ridgewood NJ 07450 Office: 400 Park Ave New York NY 10022

COUHIG, MARCELLE REESE, trade exec.; b. New Orleans, June 2, 1916; d. George Wilson and Marcelle Josephine (Jacquet) Reese; student Tulane U., Loyola U. of the South, Harvard U.; m. Sam A. LeBlanc, Jr., Feb. 22, 1938; children—Sam A., Marcelle LeBlanc Stephenson; m. 2d, Robert Emmet Couhig, July 15, 1948; children—Robert E., Owen Couhig Kemp, Kevin Hearsey, Mark St. John. Buyer Maison Blanche, New Orleans, 1946-48; founder Fairview, West Feliciana Parish, La., 1966; founder, pres. Asphodel Village Corp., Ltd., Jackson, La., 1968—. Mem. fin. com. La. Restoration Alliance, 1979—, now bd. dirs.; mem. La. Mental Health Bd., 1965-66; chmn. steering com. Rep. candidate for Gov., 1979; 6th dist. rep. La. Tourist Commn. Mem. Jackson Assembly, La. Travel Promotion Assn., Ladies Aux. for Nat. Pest Control. Republican. Roman Catholic. Author: Asphodel Cook Box, 1969; Asphodel Cook Book, 1980. Address: Asphodel Plantation Jackson LA 70748

COULIS, PAUL STEPHEN, mktg. exec.; b. Hammond, Ind., Aug. 2, 1950; s. Steve P. and Dena S. C.; A.B., Ind. U., 1972, postgrad. 1973; m. Diana Sue Harrer, Aug. 18, 1973; children—Dena Dae, Christian Paul. Ter. mgr. sci. products div. Am. Hosp. Supply Corp., Chgo., 1973, nat. tng. mgr., 1976, Midwest regional mgr., 1977, mktg. mgr. indsl. products, 1980—; sales tng. cons. Bd. dirs. St. Demetrios Ch. Mem. Ind. U. Alumni Assn., Nat. Assn. Sales Tng. Mgr., Phi Kappa Psi. Address: 1210 Waukegan Rd McGaw Park IL 60085

COULSON, JOHN L., banker; b. Bayonne, N.J., Nov. 21, 1916; s. William H. and Miriam (Guthrie) C.; A.B., Dartmouth Coll., 1939; postgrad. Stonier Grad. Sch. Banking, 1965; m. Mary A. Bill, June 27, 1942; children—Douglas B., Jeffrey L., Dara V. Credit trainee Mfrs. Trust Co., N.Y.C., 1940-42; credit mgr. J.H. Throp & Co., Inc., N.Y.C. 1946-58; v.p. Franklin Nat. Bank, L.I. N.Y., 1958-69; spl. asst. to commr. Bur. Indian Affairs, Dept. Interior, Washington, 1969-70; dist. v.p. Security Nat. Bank L.I., 1970-74, adminstrv. v.p., 1974—; v.p. Chem. Bank, Huntington, N.Y., 1975—. Former treas., past bd. dirs. Bay Hills Property Owners, Inc.; v.p. Suffolk County council Boy Scouts Am., 1965—, mem. fin. com., exec. bd., chmn. adv. bd., 1975-78; mem. profl. adv. com. Huntington Youth Bur., 1976—; meml. chmn. class of 1939, Dartmouth Coll., 1975—; treas. Village of Huntington Bay (N.Y.). Served to lt. comdr. USNR, 1942-46. Mem. Greater Bay Shore (v.p., dir. 1959-65), Huntington Twp. (accreditation com., dir.) chambers commerce, Robert Morris Assn., Dartmouth Alumni Assn. L.I. (pres. 1951-52), St. Andrews Soc. N.Y. (former chmn. bd. mgrs., now 1st v.p.), New Eng. Soc. N.Y., Suffolk County Grand Jurors Assn., Zeta Psi (sec., past pres., trustee ednl. found. 1965—). Republican. Presbyn. (elder, deacon, trustee). Rotarian (pres. chpt. 1963-64). Clubs: Club at Point O'Woods (N.Y.); Good Fellows Suffolk County (trustee). Home: 25 Soundview Dr Huntington NY 11743 Office: 31 W Main St Babylon NY 11702

COULSON, ROY, fuel co. exec.; b. Ernest, Pa., Jan. 7, 1922; s. Joseph and Jane (McCaw) C.; B.S. in Mech. Engring., U. Pitts., 1949; m. Bernice Bouch, June 2, 1943; children—Roy Ann, Robyn Lu. Timothy Galen. Maintenance supr., maintenance engr., maintenance foreman Rochester and Pitts. Coal Co., Indiana, Pa., 1949-55; Wyo. div. supt. Vitro Minerals Corp., Riverton, 1955-64, mgr. Alaskan operations, 1964-65; v.p. Kemmerer Coal Co., Frontier, Wyo., 1965-71, exec. v.p., 1971-72, pres., 1972—, also dir.; exec. v.p. Gunn Quealy Coal Co., 1971-72, pres., 1972-80, also dir.; pres., dir. Continental Livestock, Uinta Improvement Co., Frontier Supply Co., 1972-80; pres. Lincoln Service Co., 1977-80; dir. Bituminous Coal Research, 1st Wyo. Bank of Kemmerer. Mem. Wyo. Bd. Mines 1957-62, sec., 1958. Vice pres., mem. bd. Wyo. Council for Econ. Devel., 1961-63; mem. exec. council Wyo. State Rural Areas Devel. Com. 1962-63; mem. bd. Sch. Dist. No. 25, 1959-63, pres. bd., 1961-62; mem. Lincoln County Sch. Reorgn. Com., 1969-71. Served with USNR, 1942-45. Mem. AAAS, Am. Inst. Mining Engrs., Wyo. Mining Assn. (pres. 1961-62, dir.), Am. Mining Congress (bd. govs. 1960, 76—), Nat. Coal Assn. (dir. 1973—), Rocky Mountain Coal Mining Inst. (v.p. for Wyo. 1972-73, pres. 1974-75, dir.). Republican. Episcopalian. Mason (32 deg. Shriner), Elk. Home: Kemmerer WY 83181 Office: Kemmerer Coal Co Frontier WY 83121

COULTER, BORDEN MCKEE, JR., indsl. engr.; b. Casper, Wyo., Feb. 9, 1917; s. Borden McKee and Josephine Helen (Grother) C.; B.S., U. Calif. at Los Angeles, 1939, M.B.A., 1947; m. Emily Sawtelle, Aug. 23, 1950; children—Borden, Terry Lynn, Leigh, Richard. Research analyst Australian Nat. R.R., 1939-40; indsl. engr. Lockheed Aircraft, 1940-47, staff indsl. engr., 1948-50; with div. indsl. engring. U.S. Steel Corp., 1947; mgr. prodn. control Bakewell Products, 1947; supr. orgn. and procedures Norris Industries, 1950-53; gen. mgr. Roed Engring. Assos., 1943—; prin. The Emerson Consultants Inc., mgmt. consultants, N.Y.C., 1954-67, v.p., 1967—, also dir. Registered profl. engr., Calif. Mem. Am. Inst. Indsl. Engrs. (past pres. Los Angeles), Am. Inst. Plant Engrs., Nat. Assn. Accountants, Am. Mgmt. Assn., (speaker, chmn.), U.S. Naval Inst., Navy League U.S., Internat. Maintenance Inst., Internat. Platform Assn., Am. Arbitration Assn., Nat. Soc. Profl. Engrs., Houston Soc. Mgmt. Cons., Tex. Soc. Profl. Engrs., Inst. Mgmt. Consultants, Newcomen Soc., Blue Key, Kappa Kappa Psi, Alpha Kappa Psi, Tau Kappa Alpha, Phi Gamma Delta. Clubs: Houston, Houston Internat., Petroleum of Houston. Home: 12351 Escala Dr San Diego CA 92128 Office: 30 Rockefeller Plaza New York NY 10020

COULTER, DAVID BLAINE (SCOTTY), car rental co. exec.; b. Syracuse, N.Y., Oct. 2, 1948; s. LeRoy Edward and Eleanor Louise (Havill) C.; m. Susan Carol Durietz, Mar. 21, 1970; children—Michele Denise, Michael Fitzgerald. Night mgr., service agt. Thrifty Rent-A-Car, San Diego, 1971-72, dist. mgr., sta. mgr., Chgo., 1972-77, mgr. fleet div., Tulsa, 1977-79, v.p., 1979—. Served with USN, 1968-72. Mem. Am. Car Rental Assn. (dir.). Roman Catholic. Home: 920 W Memphis St Broken Arrow OK 74012 Office: 4606 S Garnet St Tulsa OK 74145

COULTER, HORACE ROBERT, former constrn. co. exec.; b. Charleroi, Pa., Dec. 17, 1926; s. Robert W. and Marjorie (Hill) C.; student Pa. State Coll., 1948; m. Mildred Paul, June 4, 1947; children—Karen Ann, Deborah Lynn, Cynthia Kay, Pamela Jo. Owner, H.R. Coulter Constrn. Co., Charleroi, 1950-55; chief estimator E.I. DuPont, Parkersburg, W.Va., 1955-57; chief estimator Lardner & Wich Constrn. Co., Balt., 1957-64; v.p. Paul B. Emerick Co., constrn., Portland, Oreg., 1964-69; v.p. Port City Constrn. Co., Columbia, Md., 1969-72; v.p. Med. Structures, Inc., Columbia, 1969-74; v.p. Ryland Group, Columbia, 1972-74; chief estimator Emerick Constrn. Co., Portland, 1974-77; cons. constrn. Parke-Davis, Balt., 1959, John Deere, Portland, 1965. Mem. Oreg. Adv. Council Career and Vocat. Edn., 1980—. Served with USNR, 1944-46. Mem. Am. Assn. Cost Engrs., Nat. Assn. Cost Consultants, Nat. Assn. Purchasing Agts., Assn. Gen. Contractors, Aircraft Owners and Pilots Assn., ASCE, Am. Arbitration Assn. (nat. panel arbitrators). Republican. Presbyn. Elk. Club: Multnomah Athletic (Portland). Home: 6335 SE Brownlee Rd Milwaukie OR 97222

COULTER, THOMAS HENRY, assn. exec.; b. Winnipeg, Can., Apr. 21, 1911; s. David and Sarah Anne (Allen) C.; B.S., Carnegie Inst. Tech., 1933; M.A., U. Chgo., 1935; m. Mary Alice Leach, Nov. 24, 1937; children—Sara, Anne, Jane, Thomas II. Investment analyst Shaw & Co., Chgo., 1935-36; sales engr. Universal Zonolite Insulation Co., Chgo., 1936-39, sales promotion mgr., 1939-40, gen. sales mgr., 1940-41, v.p., 1941-45; mgr. devel. div. Booz, Allen & Hamilton, Chgo., 1945-48, partner, 1948-50; pres. Am. Bildrok Co., 1950-54; chief exec. officer Chgo. Assn. Commerce and Industry, 1954—, pub. Commerce mag.; dir. Chgo.-Tokyo Bank; lectr. marketing, exec. program U. Chgo. Mem. State Dept.'s Top Mgmt. Seminar Team, Israel, 1956, Japan, 1958. Dir. Chgo. Crime Commn.; dir. Chgo. chpt. A.R.C. 1953-59; mem. Chgo.-Cook County Com. on Criminal Justice; mem. Mayor's Com. Preservation Chgo. Hist. Architecture; mem. Chgo. Com. on Urban Opportunity; mem. exec. com. Ill. Council on Econ. Edn. mem. citizens bd., council Sch. Bus. Assn.; gov. Internat. House of U. Chgo.; mem. citizens com. U. Ill.; mem. exec. council Chgo. Civil Def. Corps; mem. Dist Export Council. Bd. dirs. Better Bus. Bur. Met. Chgo., USO of Chgo., Inc.; adv. bd. Greater Chgo. Safety Council, Chgo. area Council Boy Scouts Am.; trustee Skokie Valley Community Hosp., pres. 1955-57, 66-70; dir. Hosp. Planning Council of Met. Chgo.; mem. Mayor's Commn. Rehab. of Persons, Gov.'s Council on Health and Fitness, Cook County Real Estate Tax Study Commn., Cook County Econ. Devel. Adv. Com.; mem. nat. adv. council Nat. Legal Center for Public Interest; mem. adv. council Energy Resources Center, U. Ill., Chgo.; mem. com. Chgo. Econ. Devel. Commn. mem. Northwestern U. Assos.; trustee Village of Golf, Ill., 1951-55. Decorated comdr.'s cross Order of Merit (Germany); knight Order of Merit (Italy); chevalier Nat. Order of Merit (France); 3d class Order of Sacred Treasure (Japan); recipient Silver anniversary all-Am. award Sports Illustrated, 1957, Outstanding Civilian Service medal U.S. Army, 1961, Gold Badge of Honor for Merits (Austria), 1962; Citation pub. service U. Chgo., 1954; Alumni merit award for outstanding profl. achievement Carnegie Inst. Tech., 1956; knight first class Order Lion (Finland), 1964; comdr. Royal Order Vasa (Sweden), 1972; Golden Badge of Honor for Merits, Province of Vienna, 1971; Indsl. Statesman award U.S.-Japan Trade Council, 1976; Citizen Fellowship award Inst. Medicine of Chgo., 1976; award in mktg., internat. trade in fin. in Chgo. and Ill., 1979. Mem. Nat. Sales Exec., C. of C. U.S. (banking, monetary and fiscal affairs com.), Newcomen Soc. in N. Am., Nat. Planning Assn., Mid-Am. Swedish Trade Assn., Chgo. Zool. Soc., Japan Soc. Chgo. (dir.), Midwest-Japan Assn., Chgo. Energy Policy Council, Chgo. Architecture Found., Am. Security Council (nat. adv. bd. edn. found.), Lambda Alpha. Clubs: Mid-America; Commercial, Executives (pres. 1950-51), Sales Marketing Executives (pres. 1953-54), Canadian, University, Economic (Chgo.); Glenview (Golf, Ill.). Home: 58 Overlook Dr Golf IL 60029 Office: 130 S Michigan Ave Chicago IL 60603

COUPLIN, JAMES RONALD, ret. hotel operator; b. Palouse, Wash., Aug. 31, 1909; s. Charles Allan and Madge (Callahan) C.; Ph.B., U. Chgo., 1931; m. Marie Corrine Franklyn, Aug. 3, 1936 (dec. Apr. 1980). Gen. mgr. Hotel Waldorf, Toledo, 1934-42, Hotel Chain, Chgo., 1946-60; partner, mgr. Hotel Douglas, Elgin, Ill., 1960-72; v.p., dir. Cedar State Hotel Co., 1958-72; treas., dir. Douglas Tap Corp., 1960-72. Harry S Truman Library fellow, 1974-75. Served from 1st lt. to maj. AUS, 1942-46; ETO maj. Res. ret. Decorated Bronze Star. Mem. Humane Soc. U.S., U. Chgo. Alumni Assn., Am., Ill. hotel assns., Elgin Assn. Commerce, S.A.R., Nat., N.J., Orange County geneal. socs., Conn. Soc. Genealogist (charter), Am. Legion, N.Mex. Mil. Inst. Alumni Assn. (sec.-treas. Chgo. area), Nat. Humane Soc., Soc. of Lost Chord, Mil. Order World Wars, Phi Kappa Sigma. Republican. Unitarian, Mason (32 deg., Shriner). Contbr. geneal. quars., Edsall, Winfield, Simpson, Ferris lines. Home: 1170 Dundee Ave Elgin IL 60120 Office: PO Box 1375 Elgin IL 60120

COURSEY, JOSEPH FORD, iron foundry exec.; b. Balt., Aug. 15, 1929; s. Joseph Ford and Malynda (Seymour) (Ford) C.; B.S. in Indsl. Engring., Johns Hopkins U., 1959; m. Shirley L. Boettner, Sept. 12, 1953; children—Janet Victoria, Rebecca Lynn. Supt., Large Castings Foundry, Koppers Co., Balt., 1951-64, James L. Lacy Co., Balt., 1964-66; foundry mgr. Flynn & Emrich Co., Balt., 1966-74; plant mgr. Ingersoll Rand Foundry, Painted Post, N.Y., 1974-78; pres., gen. mgr. Hamilton Foundry div. Hamilton Allied Corp. (Ohio), 1978—. Bd. dirs. Hamilton Symphony Orch. Mem. Am. Foundrymen's Soc. (past nat. dir.), Ohio Mfrs. Assn., Ohio Cast Metals Fedn. (sec.-treas., 1980—). Office: Hamilton Foundry Div 1551 Lincoln Ave Hamilton OH 45011

COURSHON, ARTHUR HOWARD, lawyer, savs. and loan exec.; b. Chgo., Feb. 21, 1921; s. Aaron H. and Beatrice (Pollak) C.; B.A., U. Fla., 1942; J.D., U. Miami, Coral Gables, Fla., 1947; m. Carol Biel, Feb. 20, 1943; children—Barbara Courshon Mills, Deanne. Admitted to Fla. bar, 1947; partner firm Courshon & Courshon and Bloom, Miami Beach, 1948—; organizer, chmn. bd. dirs. Washington Savs. and Loan Assn. Fla., Miami Beach, 1952—; dir. FMI Fin. Corp., Miami Beach; chmn. bd. Jefferson Bancorp., Inc., holding co. for Jefferson Nat. Bank of Miami Beach, Jefferson Nat. Bank, Sunny Isles, Jefferson Nat. Bank Kendall; cons. savs. and loan system in Chile, ICA, 1958—; cons. housing loans to Latin Am., 1960—, Devel. Loan Fund, Inter-Am. Devel. Bank, 1961—; cons. Govt. of Peru, 1960—; mem. U.S. Govt. task force Fed. Home Loan Bank, 1961-62; mem. savs. and loan adv. council Fed. Home Loan Bank Bd., 1969; housing finance cons. Latin Am. Affairs Subcom., Senate Fgn. Relations Com., 1960-69; mem. housing and urban devel. adv. com. AID, 1965-68; pub. mem. Adminstrv. Conf. of U.S., 1968-72. Mem. Met. Dade County Urban Renewal Agy., 1963-67. Bd. dirs. South Fla. Housing Found., Miami Heart Inst.; trustee Pub. Health Trust of Dade County. Served with USAAF, 1942-46. Recipient citation for establishment savs. and loan system in Chile, ICA, 1960. Mem. Am. (mem. savs. and loan assns. com. 1971-72), Inter-Am. (sr.), Dade County bar assns., Fla. Bar (banking liaison com.), U.S. Savs. and Loan Inst., Nat. Savs. and Loan League (pres. 1969, exec. com., legis. com.), U.S. Savs. and Loan League (atty.'s com.), Internat. Union Bldg. Socs. (devel. com., council), Miami Com. on Fgn. Relations, U.S. C. of C. (constrn. affairs com., Com. Econ. Devel. (Chmn. savs. and loan div. 1971-72), Nu Beta Epsilon, Pi Lambda Phi. Democrat. Jewish religion. Home: 5970 N Bay Rd Miami Beach FL 33140 Office: 1701 Meridian Ave Miami Beach FL 33139

COURSON, MERLE DEAN, banker; b. Anaheim, Calif., Dec. 10, 1925; s. Harold Dean and Bernice (Radke) C.; B.S. in Bus. Adminstrn., San Jose (Calif.) State U., 1972; postgrad. Santa Clara (Calif.) U., 1973; m. Mary Elizabeth Stine, June 15, 1946; children—David, Nancy, Jonathan, James. Systems analyst U.S. Nat. Bank Oreg., Portland, 1947-57; with First Nat. Bank San Jose, 1957-77, exec. v.p., 1973-77; exec. v.p. Western Bank, Coos Bay, Oreg., 1977-78, pres., chief exec. officer, 1978—; past pres. Ind. Bankers Assn. No. Calif.; exec. bd. Western States Bankard Assn.; exec. com. Asso. Oreg. Industries. Pres. Jr. Achievement Santa Clara County, 1975-76, Goodwill Industries Santa Clara County, 1975-76, S.W. Oreg. Music Enrichment Assn., 1979-80. Served with USNR, 1943-46. Mem. Am. Bankers Assn., Robert Morris Assos., Oreg. Bankers Assn. (v.p., exec. bd.). Republican. Club: Coos Bay-North Bend Rotary. Office: 290 S 4th St Coos Bay OR 97420

COURT, BRUCE EDWARD, ins. co. exec.; b. Raymond, Alta., Can., May 15, 1949; s. David D. and Doris H. (Hannah) C.; grad. Alta. Sch. Mortuary Sci., 1972; m. Kay C. Reese, July 17, 1971; children—David Spencer, John Cameron, Bruce Daniel, Robert Benjamin, Mathew Ryan. Funeral dir. Christensen-Salmon Funeral Home, Lethbridge, Alta., Can., 1970-77; life ins. agt. Paramount Life Ins. Co., Lethbridge, 1977-80; unit supr. Dominion Life Assurance Co., Lethbridge, 1980—. Mem. Life Underwriters Assn., Lethbridge Jaycees (Jaycee of Yr. 1973). Conservative. Mormon. Home: 2515 19 Ave S Lethbridge AB T1K 1E8 Canada Office: 801 Woodward Tower Lethbridge AB Canada

COURTNEY, JAMES EDMOND, mining co. exec.; b. Meadville, Pa., Dec. 28, 1931; s. Alexis James and Marian (Winans) C.; A.B. in Econs., Dartmouth Coll., 1952, M.B.A., 1954; LL.B., Harvard U., 1959; m. Eileen Alman, Nov. 2, 1970; children—Alison M., David E., Jotham C. Admitted to Ohio bar, 1960; partner firm Jones Day Reavis & Pogue, Cleve., 1959-74; v.p. internat. Hanna Mining Co., Cleve., 1974-78, sr. v.p. corp. devel., 1978-79, exec. v.p., 1979—; chmn., dir. St. John d'el Rey Mining Co., Ltd.; dir. Hollinger North Shore Exploration Co., Ltd.; mem. adv. bd. Council of Americas. Served with USN, 1954-56. Mem. Am. Iron and Steel Inst., Am. Mining Congress, Internat. Econ. Policy Assn. (dir.). Clubs: Clevelander, Union (Cleve.); Westwood Country, Rolling Rock. Home: 13834 Lake Ave Lakewood OH 44107 Office: Hanna Mining Co 100 Erieview Plaza Cleveland OH 44114

COURTNEY, THOMAS PATRICK, ins. exec.; b. Akron, Ohio, Sept. 20, 1933; s. Joseph F. and Laura (Nicklas) C.; B.S. in Mgmt., U. Akron, 1955; m. Barbara A. Royer, July 16, 1955; children—Patrick, Thomas, Deborah, Carolyn, Diane, Elizabeth, Mary, Barbara, John. With Prudential Ins. Co. Am., 1958—, beginning as spl. agt., Akron, successively div. mgr., Akron, tng. cons., Jacksonville, Fla., regional supr., Jacksonville, agy. mgr., Cin., dir. agys., Jacksonville, 1958-76, v.p. sales, Phila., 1976—. Served to 1st lt., AUS, 1955-57. C.L.U. Mem. Nat. Assn. Life Underwriters, Am. Soc. C.L.U.'s. Republican. Roman Catholic. Office: Box 388 Fort Washington PA 19034

COURTOIS, EDMOND JACQUES, lawyer, corp. dir.; b. Montreal, Que., Can., July 4, 1920; s. Edmond and Cleophee (Lefebvre) C.; B.A., Coll. de Montreal, 1940; LL.B., U. Montréal, 1943; m. Joan Miller, Oct. 23, 1943; children—Nicole, Jacques, Marc. Admitted to Que. bar, 1946, created Queen's Counsel, 1963; partner firm Courtois, Clarkson, Parsons & Tétrault, Montreal, 1953—; chmn. bd., dir. Gaz Métropolitain, inc.; pres., dir. CIIT Inc., Elican Devel. Co. Ltd., La Compagnie Foncière du Man. (1967), Limitee; chmn. bd., dir. Gaz du Québec, inc., United N.Am. Holdings, Ltd.; v.p., dir. Bank N.S.; vice chmn., dir. Trizec Corp. Ltd.; dir. Brinco Ltd., CAE Industries Ltd., Can. Life Assurance Co., Edper Investments Ltd., Le Club de Hockey Canadien Inc., McGraw-Hill Ryerson Ltd., Abitibi Asbestos Mining Co. Ltd., Norcen Energy Resources Ltd., Phoenix Steel Corp., Rolland inc., Eaton/Bay Growth Fund Ltd., Eaton/Bay Venture Fund, Ltd., QIT-Fer et Titane Inc., Eaton/Bay Commonwealth Fund Ltd., Eaton/Bay Income Fund, Eaton/Bay Internat. Fund Ltd., Eaton/Bay Leverage Fund Ltd., Eaton/Bay Viking Fund Ltd., Eaton/Bay Dividend Fund Ltd., Ritz-Carlton Hotel Co. Montreal Ltd. Served to lt. Royal Canadian Navy, 1943-45. Mem. Bar Montreal, Bar Province Quebec, Canadian Bar Assn. Office: 22d Floor 630 Dorchester Blvd W Montreal PQ H3B 1V7 Canada

COUSINS, MICHAEL ALAN, indsl. designer; b. N.Y.C., Aug. 28, 1938; s. Daniel H. and Rose (Fidel) C.; B.F.A. in Indsl. Design, R.I. Sch. Design, 1960; m. Phyllis Whitmore Mattoon, Oct. 20, 1958 (div. Mar. 1979); children—David A., Alan J. Display designer R.C. Adams Displays, Inc., N.Y.C., 1960-61; designer R.A. MacPlum Industries, N.Y.C., 1961-63; staff designer Peter Schladermundt Assos., N.Y.C., 1963-64; v.p., sec. Morison S. Cousins & Assos., Inc., N.Y.C., 1964—. Recipient numerous certificates for design excellence from various trade orgns., including Am. Inst. Graphic Arts, 1974, 77, 20 awards Indsl. Design mag., 1966-77. Mem. Indsl. Design Soc. Am., Am. Inst. Graphic Arts. Club: Centerport (N.Y.) Yacht. Contbr. articles to profl. jours.; designer Gillette Promax Compact, selected for permanent collection by N.Y. Mus. Modern Art, 1977. Home: Office: 964 3d Ave New York NY 10022

COVEY, FRANK MICHAEL, JR., lawyer; b. Chgo., Oct. 24, 1932; s. Frank M. and Marie B. (Lorenz) C.; B.S. with honors, Loyola U., 1954, J.D. cum laude, 1957; S.J.D., U. Wis., 1960; m. Patricia Ann McGill, Oct. 7, 1961; children—Geralyn, Frank Michael III, Regis Patrick. Admitted to Ill. bar, 1957, since practiced in Chgo.; admitted to U.S. Supreme Ct. bar, 1965; asso. Belnap, Spencer, Hardy & Freeman, 1959-60; asso. McDermott, Will & Emery, 1960-64, partner, 1965—, mem. exec. and mgmt. coms., 1979—; instr. Northwestern U. Sch. Law, 1958-59, Loyola U. Coll., 1958-69, 1979-80; law clk. Ill. Appellate Ct., 1959; research asso. Wis. Gov.'s Com. on Revision Law of Eminent Domain, 1958; asso. gen. counsel Union League Civic and Arts Found., 1967-69, v.p., 1969-72, 73-75, pres., 1972-73, mng. dir., 1975—; co-dir. Grant Park study team Nat. Commn. Causes and Prevention of Violence, 1968. Bd. athletics Loyola U., 1970-72, trustee, 1979—, mem. estate planning com., 1969—, mem. com. on future law sch., 1975-76, mem. citizens bd., 1979—; bd. dirs. Chgo. Bldg. Congress, 1978—. Recipient awards Conf. on Personal Finance Law, 1955, Loyola Law Alumni Assn., 1957; Lincoln award Ill. bar assn., 1963; Loyola U. Founders' Day award, 1976; medal of Excellence, Loyola Law Sch., 1979; Disting. Service award Loyola U., 1980. Mem. Am., Ill., Chgo., 7th Fed. Circuit bar assns., Catholic Lawyers Guild, Chgo. Council Lawyers, Am. Judicature Soc., North Shore Bd. Realtors (asso.), Ill. Hist. Soc., Chgo. Art Inst., Air Force Assn., Better Govt. Assn. (com. cts. and justice, com. legis. reform), Loyola U. Alumni Assn. (pres. 1965-66, chmn. law alumni fund campaign 1967-68, v.p. law alumni 1968-69, pres. 1969-70, chmn. Thomas More Club 1973-75), Chgo. Mus. Natural History, Blue Key, Phi Alpha Delta, Alpha Sigma Nu, Pi Gamma Mu, Delta Sigma Rho. Clubs: Union League (dir., chmn. house com. 1977-80), Monroe, Legal, Law (Chgo.). Author: Roadside Protection Through Access Control, 1960; (with others) Federal Civic Practice in Illinois, 1974, 78; (with others) Business Litigation I: Competition and Its Limits, 1978, Class Actions, 1979; also articles in field. Home: 1104 W Lonnquist Blvd Mount Prospect IL 60056 Office: 111 W Monroe St Chicago IL 60603

COVEY, GERALD GRANT, constrn. co. exec.; b. Euclid, Ohio, May 1, 1931; s. Gerald Grant and Edith Althea (Tiffany) C.; student Miami U., Oxford, Ohio, 1950-53, Case Inst. Tech., 1953-54, Fenn Coll., 1958-64; m. Gail Ramsdell, Dec. 28, 1963; children—Christopher R., Carrie A., Cathy L., Kellie A. Pres., Gerald G. Covey Co., Rocky River, Ohio, 1957—; v.p. Rossborough Mfg. Co., Cleve., 1973-75, Wescon Inc., Lakewood, Ohio, 1976—; gen. mgr. Esch Constrn. Co., Cleve., 1975—; owner, chief exec. officer James Hardware Co., Rocky River, Ohio, 1979—. Served with U.S. Army, 1954-57. Mem. Cleve. Builders Exchange, Greater Cleve. Growth Assn. Republican. Methodist. Clubs: Avon Oaks Country, River Oaks Racquet, Masons. Office: 19030 Lake Rd Rocky River OH 44116

COVEY, MOODY, oil co. exec.; b. Bristow, Okla., Oct. 7, 1929; s. Cyclone Davis and Lola Effie (Best) C.; B.S., Okla. State U., 1949; m. Betty Lou Gilbert, Aug. 20, 1949; 1 son, Brent Roger. With Getty Oil Co. and affiliated cos., 1950—, various assignments Drumright, Okla. and Tulsa, Houston, San Francisco, Los Angeles and Tokyo, 1950-71, corp. employee and public relations mgr., 1971, v.p., rep. dir. Mitsubishi Oil Co., Ltd., Tokyo, 1972-76; v.p. adminstrn., Skelly Oil Co., 1976; v.p. corp. adminstrn. Getty Oil Co., 1977—; dir. Getty Oil Co. Found. Mem. Am. Petroleum Inst. Republican. Presbyterian. Clubs: Jonathan, Los Angeles, Masons. Office: 3810 Wilshire Blvd Los Angeles CA 90010

COVINGTON, CHARLES J., business cons.; b. Farmington, Mo., Jan. 8, 1914; s. Mabry J. and Ethel Ann (Covington), C.; student Wichita (Kans.) U.; m. Lois Ellen Combs, Dec. 9, 1939; children—Joe J., Patricia Ann, Jon Scott. Chmn., Dowzer Electric div. Sola Basic Industries, Mt. Vernon, Ill., 1938—; pres., dir. Power Cores, Inc., 1964—; pres. Ele-Q-Solo Basic, transformer mfg., Carolina, P.R., 1974—; bus. cons., Mt. Vernon; dir. Security Bank of Mt. Vernon; chmn. bd. King City Fed. Savs. & Loan Assn., Mt. Vernon. Chmn. region 7 Boy Scouts Am., pres. Buffalo Trace council; pres. Greater Egypt Regional Planning and Devel. Commn., 1965—; vice chmn. Mt. Vernon Indsl. Devel. Commn., 1970—; trustee, pres. Rend Lake Conservancy Dist. Recipient Best Citizen award Mt. Vernon, 1954; award Nat. Elec. Mfrs. Assn., Community Service award, 1969; Outstanding Civilian Service medal Dept. Army, 1978. Mem. Nat. Indsl. Service Assn. (pres), Ill. Mfrs. Assn. (dir. 1954-64), Mt. Vernon C. of C. (pres.). Clubs: Lions (pres.), Union League (Chgo.); Mo. Athletic (St. Louis). Home: 1818 Isabella Ave Mount Vernon IL 62864 Office: First & Castleton Sts Mount Vernon IL 62864 also PO Box 2014 Carolina PR 00630 also 117 N 10th Mount Vernon IL 62864

COVINGTON, ROBERT EDWARD, oil and mining co. exec.; b. Waterloo, Iowa, Mar. 24, 1921; s. Rex S. and Jeanne S. (Stephens) C.; student Loyola U., 1941-42, Northwestern U., 1942; B.A. in Geology, U. Colo., 1947; postgrad. Colo. Sch. Mines, 1948. Geologist, Carter Oil Co., Vernal, Utah, 1948-49, Johnson & Bunn Oil Operators, 1949-54; oil cons. Caldwell & Covington, 1954-64; sec., treas., mgr. exploration Hiko Bell Mining & Oil Co., Vernal, 1964—, also dir. Served with USN, 1942-45. Fellow AAAS; mem. ASME, Wyo. Geol. Soc., Am. Inst. Profl. Geologists, Utah Geol. Soc., Geol. Soc. Am., Intermountain Assn. Petroleum Geologists, Am. Assn. Petroleum Geologists, Green Circle, Sigma Alpha Epsilon, Sigma Gamma Epsilon. Club: Elks. Contbr. articles in field to profl. jours. Home: PO Drawer AB Vernal UT 84078 Office: Zion's First Nat Bank Bldg Vernal UT 84078

COVITZ, MARTIN BERNARD, orgn. exec.; b. Oakland, Calif., Sept. 30, 1931; s. William Daniel and Gerturde (Benjamin) C.; B.S., U. Calif., Berkeley, 1954, M.S., 1958; grad. exec. program, Harvard U. Bus. Sch., 1978; m. Diane Hay-Roe, Mar. 12, 1960; children—Susan, Brian, Cynthia. Exec. dir. Hawaii Heart Assn., 1958-61; mem. faculty U. Calif. Sch. Public Health, Berkeley, 1961-64; exec. dir. San Francisco Council Alcoholism, 1964-66, San Francisco Bay Area Social Planning Council, 1966-72; exec. v.p. Greater Miami (Fla.) Coalition, 1972-73; campaign and planning dir. United Way Miami, 1973-77; exec. dir. United Way Omaha, 1977—; mem. nat. prof. adv. com., chmn. planning, allocation and public policy coms. United Way Am. Served with AUS, 1954-56. Mem. Am. Mgmt. Assn., Am. Public Health Assn. Club: Downtown Omaha Rotary. Office: 1805 Harney St Omaha NE 68102

COWAN, CHRISTINE, mgmt. cons.; b. Lansing, Mich., Nov. 2, 1952; d. David Avery and Lavonne (Evans) C.; B.S. in Econs., M.I.T., 1975; M.B.A., Harvard U., 1978. Jr. securities analyst Boston Co., 1975-76; corp. asso. Westvaco, N.Y.C., 1978-79, asso. product mgr. chem. div., Charleston, S.C., 1979-81; cons. McKinsey & Co., Cleve., 1981—. Mem. alumnae bd. Laurel Sch., Shaker Heights, Ohio. Mem. Assn. M.B.A. Execs. Republican. Episcopalian. Home: 19406-36 Van Aken Blvd #110 Shaker Heights OH 44122 Office: 100 Erieview Plaza Cleveland OH 44114

COWAN, GARY GLENN, business exec.; b. Ventura, Calif., Sept. 28, 1936; s. John F. and Phyllis M. (Dunn) C.; B.S., U. Calif. at Los Angeles, 1959, M.B.A., 1960; m. Jo Ella A. Miller, June 16, 1956; children—Gregory Gavin, Joleen Aimee. Instr., U. Calif. at Los Angeles, 1959; asso. Price Waterhouse & Co., C.P.A.'s, Los Angeles, 1960-63; treas. Networks Electronic Corp., Chatsworth, 1963-64; asst. controller, coordinator profit planning Tidewater Oil, Los Angeles, 1964-66; v.p. financial analysis and rev. Dart Industries Inc., Los Angeles, 1966-69, pres. Dart Properties div., 1969-73; exec. v.p., chief operating officer Coastland Corp., Virginia Beach, Va., 1973-77; sr. v.p., chief fin. officer Leisure Technology Corp., Los Angeles, 1977-79, Superscope, Inc., Chatsworth, Calif., 1979—. Mem. Am. Inst. C.P.A.'s. Home: 3714 Carbon Canyon Malibu CA 90265 Office: 20525 Nordoff St Chatsworth CA 91311

COWAN, MICHAEL GEORGE, mfg. co. exec.; b. Union City, N.J., May 8, 1940; s. Morris and Ann (Stern) C.; B.S. in Mgmt. Engring., U. Vt., 1962; M.S. in Mgmt. Sci., Stevens Inst. Tech., 1968; children—Marci Lee, Howard Leonard. Methods engr. Gen. Motors Co., Rochester, N.Y., 1962-63; indsl. engr. Westinghouse Corp., Jersey City, N.J., 1963-66; sr. indsl. engr., asst. engring. dept. head Gen. Foods, Hoboken, N.J., 1966-72; mgmt. cons. Touche Ross & Co., N.Y.C., Newark, 1972-79; prin. M. George Cowan Assos., Fort Lee, N.J., 1979—; v.p. mfg., gen. mgr. Durex, Inc., Union, N.J., 1979—; adj. prof. mktg. Middlesex County Coll., Edison, N.J., 1977-78. Mem. Nat. Council Phys. Distbn. Mgmt. (co-chmn., speaker ann. conf. 1978, v.p., program chmn. No. N.J. Roundtable), Am. Inst. Indsl. Engrs., Indsl. Mgmt. Club. North Hudson (v.p.). Home: Mediterranean Towers W 555 North Ave Suite 26K Fort Lee NJ 07024 Office: 5 Stahuber Ave Union NJ 07083

COWAN, ROBERT GEORGE, banker; b. Lake Linden, Mich., Feb. 25, 1905; s. William Robert and May Agnes (Harrison) C.; prep. edn. Phillips Exeter Acad.; student Mass. Inst. Tech., 2 years; B.S., N.Y. U., 1930; grad. Grad. Sch. Banking, Am. Bankers Assn., 1940; LL.D., Upsala Coll., 1955; m. Hazel Witherall Damon, May 29, 1930. Statistician in research dept., bank examiner, chief analysis div. of bank exams. div., Fed. Reserve Bank N.Y., 1927-38; cashier Nat. Newark & Essex Bank, Newark, 1938-40, pres., dir., 1940—, former chmn.; dir. Mut. Benefit Life Ins. Co., Am. Express Co. (San Francisco); mgr. Howard Savs. Inst. Past pres. Greater Newark Devel. Council; vice chmn. bd., treas. Newark Coll. Engring., Marcus L. Ward Home: trustee Newark Mus., Victoria Found.; bd. dirs. Morristown Meml. Hosp. Mem. N.J. Bankers Assn., N.J. C. of C. (dir.). Clubs: Essex (Newark); Somerset Hills Country. Home: Post Rd Bernardsville NJ 07924 Office: 744 Broad St Newark NJ 07102

COWAN, RUTH BURNS, polit. scientist, educator; b. N.Y.C., Apr. 18, 1932; d. Herman L. and Rose (Lauterstein) Burns; B.S., Cornell U., 1953; M.A., U. Ill., 1958; Ph.D., N.Y. U., 1970; m. Morris Cowan, June 27, 1957. Dir. personnel and vol. services Barnert Meml. Hosp., Paterson, N.J., 1955-57; personnel asst. Internat. Ladies Garment Workers Union, 1957-58; editorial asst. municipal services Dun & Bradstreet, 1958-59; ad hoc labor mediator N.J. Pub. Employment Relations Commn., 1976-78; arbitrator nat. labor panel arbitrators Am. Arbitration Assn., 1974—; prof. City U. N.Y., 1959-80; dir. Lifelong Learning, Marymount Manhattan Coll., 1980—; sr. research asso. Center Policy Research, 1977—; chmn. N.Y.C. Commn. on Status Women, 1976-78; vice chmn. N.Y. State Internat. Women's Year Conf. Mem. N.Y.C. Employment Planning and Tng. Council; mem. pres.'s adv. council Marymount Manhattan Coll.; adv. bd. Union Coll. Daniel J. Alpern fellow, 1951-52; N.Y. State Regents teaching fellow, 1965-66; Penfield fellow, 1968-69; U.S. Office Edn. fellow, 1971. Mem. Am., N.Y. State, Northeastern polit. sci. assns., Nat. Assn. Commns. Women (dir. Research and Devel. Fund 1977), Women's Forum, NOW, Council Mcpl. Performance. Club: Women's City (dir. 1975-80) (N.Y.C.). Author articles in field. Home: 320 Central Park W New York NY 10025

COWAN, SAMUEL JOSEPH, aerospace co. exec.; b. Kansas City, Mo., Feb. 11, 1938; s. Harold Edwin and Kathryn Elizabeth (Cline) Greenberg; B.S. in Mech. Engring., U. Calif., Berkeley, 1961, M.S., 1963; Ph.D., U. Wash., 1968; m. Marie Jeanette Johnson, Aug. 14, 1961; children—Samuel Joseph, Kathryn Anne, Michelle Dionne. Engr., Boeing Co., Seattle, 1961-62, research specialist, 1968-76, engring. mgr., 1976—. NSF trainee, 1965-68. Mem. ASME, Am. Mgmt. Assn., Pi Tau Sigma, Sigma Xi. Roman Catholic. Club: Corinthian Yacht. Patentee in field. Home: 1214 NE 105th St Seattle WA 98125 Office: PO Box 3707 Seattle WA 98111

COWAN, TERRY NOLAN, mfg. co. exec.: b. Pampa, Tex., Dec. 13, 1948; s. Herbert and Elizabeth Cowan; student public schs. Founder, 1976, since pres. Nolan Tool and Chem. Co., Inc., Alvarado, Tex. Club: Lions. Author: Auto Body Solder, 1980. Home: Box 492 Dallas TX Office: 1002 Sparks St Alvarado TX 76009

COWEN, ALLAN HOWARD, orgn. exec.; b. Pitts., Apr. 18, 1949; s. Jules and Alice Cowen; B.F.A., Kent (Ohio) State U., 1971; m. Shirley Cox, June 12, 1975; 1 son, Jonathan Aron. Adminstrv. intern Ohio Arts Council, 1972; asso. dir. Arts Council, Winston-Salem, N.C., 1973; exec. dir. Greater Louisville Fund for Arts, 1976—; nat. cons. nat. assembly Community Arts Council. Mem. Am. Council Arts. Club: Rotary. Office: 511 W Broadway Louisville KY 40202

COWEN, BRUCE DAVID, acctg. co. exec.; b. Springfield, Mass., Jan. 19, 1953; s. Irving Abraham and Pearl (Glushien) C.; B.S. in Bus. Adminstrn., Am. Internat. Coll., 1974. Audit mgr. Price Waterhouse & Co., Hartford, Conn., 1974-79; controller TRC Environ. Consultants, Inc., Wethersfield, Conn., 1979-80; treas., sec. TRC Cos., Inc., Wethersfield, 1980—; dir. Halcyon, Ltd., Hartford, Conn. Active Sammy Davis, Jr. Greater Hartford Open PGA Golf Tournament. C.P.A., Conn. Mem. Am. Inst. C.P.A.'s, Nat. Assn. Accountants, Hartford Jaycees. Republican. Jewish. Home: 922 Gilead St Hebron CT 06248 Office: PO Box 121 Wethersfield CT 06109

COWGILL, BRUCE HAYDEN, elec. products co. exec.; b. Sewickley, Pa., Jan. 15, 1945; s. Bernard Francis and Lilye (Hayden) C.; B.S. in Ceramic Engring., Alfred U., 1967; m. Patricia Ann Diehl, Aug. 12, 1967; children—Bruce William, Michael Bernard. With Gen. Electric Co., Cleve., 1967—, various positions, 1967-69, project leader photoflash, 1969-70, shop ops. supr., 1970-73, supr. program planning, 1973-75, mfg. adminstr., 1975-79, plant mgr. electronics parts mfg. facility, 1979—. Mem. Am. Ceramic Soc., Elfun Soc., Delta Sigma Phi. Episcopalian. Clubs: Rotary, Exchange, Jaycees. Home: 384 Beverly Dr Jefferson OH 44047 Office: 84 W Ashtabula St Jefferson OH 44047

COWGILL, F(RANK) BROOKS, ins. co. exec.; b. Huntington Park, Calif., Mar. 16, 1932; s. Frank H. and Henriette (Dickey) C.; A.B., Stanford U., 1954, M.B.A., 1956; m. Mary Lu Hanna, Dec. 22, 1954; children—David B., Ann M. Analyst treas. dept. Exxon Corp., N.Y.C., 1958-61; sr. analyst treas.'s dept. Dewey & Almy Chem. div. W.R. Grace, Cambridge, Mass., 1961-62; v.p., treas. New Eng. Mutual Life Ins. Co., Boston, 1962—; v.p. NEL Cash Mgmt. Trust, 1978—; v.p., treas. New Eng. Gen. Life Ins. Co., 1979—. Served to 1st, lt. U.S. Army, 1956-58. Lic. chartered fin. analyst. Mem. Inst. Chartered Fin. Analysts, Boston Security Analysts Soc. Clubs: Stanford Bus. Sch. Alumni, Treas.'s of Boston. Office: 501 Boylston St Boston MA 02117

COWIE, ROBERT PILLOW, ins. agy. exec.; b. Columbia, Tenn., Mar. 15, 1920; s. Gordon Rice and Mary Marcella (Pillow) C.; student U. Tenn., Knoxville, 1939-40; m. Catherine Elane McGuire, June 29, 1945; children—Caren Elane, Catherine Ann. Partner, Lasher-Cowie Agy., Phoenix, 1955-59, incorporated, 1959, pres., chief exec. officer, 1959—; partner Central Premium Budget Plan; founding partner Auto Ins. Mart; chmn. bd. Innkeepers Internat., Inc., 1978—, Rocky Mountain Gen. Agy., Inc., 1979—. Pres., Multiple Sclerosis Soc., 1964-74, Retinitis Pigmentosa Found., 1977-79; bd. dirs. Ariz. Humane Soc., 1968—, Ariz. Horseman's Assn., 1972-76; pres., bd. dirs. Desert Found., 1974—; mem. adv. com. YWCA. Served to maj., USAAF, 1942-45. Decorated Silver Star, D.F.C., Air medal with 11 oak leaf clusters. Mem. Maricopa County Ind. Agts. (pres.), Ariz. Ind. Agts., Nat. Ind. Agts., Phoenix C. of C., Ariz. C. of C., U.S. C. of C., Surplus Lines Assn. Republican. Episcopalian. Clubs: Univ., Los Amigos de Capa, El Dorado Polo, Pima County Polo, Scottsdale Polo (pres. 1965-79). Home: 6627 E Exeter Blvd Scottsdale AZ 85251 Office: 1807 N Central Ave Phoenix AZ 85004

COWLES, JOHN, JR., publisher; b. Des Moines, May 27, 1929; s. John and Elizabeth (Bates) C.; grad. Phillips Exeter Acad., 1947; A.B., Harvard, 1951; Litt.D. (hon.), Simpson Coll., 1965; m. Jane Sage Fuller, Aug. 23, 1952; children—Tessa Flores Cowles Radin, John, Jane Sage, Charles Fuller. With Mpls. Star and Tribune Co., 1953—, v.p. 1957-68, pres., 1968-73, chmn., 1973-79, pres., 1979—, editor, 1961-69, editorial chmn., 1969-73; pres. Harper's Mag., Inc., 1965-68, chmn. bd., 1968-72; dir. Harper & Row, Pubs., Inc., N.Y.C., 1965—, chmn., 1968-79, also chmn. exec. com.; dir. 1st Bank System, Inc., Mpls., 1964-68, Des Moines Register & Tribune Co., AP, N.Y.C., 1966-75; trustee Farmers & Mechanics Savs. Bank, Mpls., 1960-65, Equitable Life Ins. Co. Iowa, Des Moines, 1964-66. Mem. adv. bd. on Pulitzer Prizes, Columbia U., 1970—. Campaign chmn. Mpls. United Fund, 1967. Bd. dirs. Guthrie Theatre Found., 1960-71, pres., 1960-63, chmn., 1964-65; trustee Phillips Exeter Acad., 1960-65; bd. dirs. Walker Art Center, 1960-69, Minn. Civil Liberties Union, 1956-61, Urban Coalition Mpls., 1968-70, Mpls. Found., 1970-75. Served from pvt. to 2d lt. AUS, 1951-53. Named one of ten outstanding men of year U.S. Jr. C. of C., 1964. Mem. Council on Fgn. Relations, Am. Newspaper Pubs. Assn. (dir. 1975-77, mem. govt. affairs com. 1976-79), Greater Mpls. C. of C. (chmn. stadium site task force 1977—, dir. 1978—), Sigma Delta Chi. Clubs: Minneapolis, Woodhill (Mpls.); Century Assn., N.Y. Athletic (N.Y.C.). Home: 1225 LaSalle Ave Minneapolis MN 55403 Office: Rm 626 IDS Tower Minneapolis MN 55402

COX, CHARLES WESLEY, constrn. co. exec.; b. Chester, Pa., June 24, 1918; s. Wilmer and Sara Hopkins (Price) C.; ed. Drexel Inst. Tech., Phila.; m. Margaret Jill Nicholls, Dec. 16, 1976; children by previous marriage—Samuel, Charles, Barry, Christina Cox Gray, Kelle Cox Webb. Apprentice draftsman Am. Viscose Corp., Marcus Hook, Pa., 1935-38, constrn. engr., Nitro, W.Va., 1940-42, devel. mgr. staple mech. devel. dept., 1943-49, mgr. engring. machine design, Phila., 1949-51; field supt. constrn. Chemstrand Corp., Decatur, Ala., 1951-52, dir. engring., 1955-57; sr. project mgr. Daniel Constrn. Co.,

Greenville, S.C., 1957-58, sales mgr., N.Y.C., 1958-61, v.p. mgr. sales, N.Y.C., 1961-68, v.p., gen. mgr., exec. offices, Greenville, 1968-74, pres., chief operating officer, from 1974, now chmn.; vice chmn., dir. Daniel Internat. Corp., dir. Fluor Corp. Served with USNR, 1944-46. Republican. Methodist. Clubs: Green Valley Country; Greenville Country, Poinsett (Greenville). Office: Daniel Internat Corp Daniel Bldg Greenville SC 29602

COX, DONALD BRUCE, real estate exec.; b. Evansville, Ind., July 25, 1928; s. Harry and Elsie Lucille (Roll) C.; ed. U. Evansville; m. Nelda Jean VanMeter, Oct. 21, 1966; children—Jeri Haggard, Dianne Chapman, Denise Cox, Brian Rexing. With real estate and constrn. dept. So. Ind. Gas & Electric Co., 1947-66; propr. Don Cox & Assos., real estate brokerage, Evansville, 1966—; owner, sec. North Park Apts.; pres. Mid-Continent Capitol Corp.; dir. Nat. City Bank, Evansville, Investors Trust Ins. Co.; v.p., treas. Mid-Continent Ins. Agy. Bd. dirs. Welborn Bapt. Hosp., Evansville; trustee Evansville-Vanderburgh County Bldg. Authority; chmn. Vanderburgh County Republican Com., 1971-77. Named Ky. Col., 1970, Sagamore of Wabash, 1975, Ambassador of Ind., 1977. Mem. Nat. Assn. Ind. Fee Appraisers (past pres.), Nat. Assn. Real Estate Bds., Nat. Assn. Home Builders, Ind. Real Estate Assn., Evansville Bd. Realtors, Evansville C. of C. (dir. 1981-82). Baptist. Clubs: Evansville Country (pres., dir. 1981), Evansville Kennel. Home: 4029 Fairfax Rd Evansville IN 47710 Office: 1010 Sycamore St Evansville IN 47708

COX, EXUM MORRIS, investment co. exec.; b. Santa Rosa, Calif., Feb. 5, 1903; s. Exum Morris and Mary Eleanor (Anderson) C.; A.B., U. Calif., 1924; M.B.A., Harvard U., 1928; m. Elsie Margaret Storke, Sept. 6, 1934; children—Cynthia Cox Huntting, Susana More Cox Fousekis, Thomas Storke. With firm Dodge & Cox, 1933—, partner, 1933-59, pres., 1959-72, chmn., 1972-77, hon. chmn., 1977—; chmn. bd. Dodge & Cox Balanced Fund, 1933—; dir. Dodge & Cox Stock Fund. Mem. Calif. Delinquency Prevention Commn., 1963-67, San Francisco Library Commn., 1963-64; vice chmn. Citizens Adv. Com. to Atty. Gen. Calif. on Crime Prevention, 1954-58; bd. dirs., v.p. Community Chest San Francisco, 1946-48; bd. dirs. San Francisco Tb Assn., 1948-52, Bay Area Ednl. TV Assn. (KQED), 1961-70; trustee San Francisco Mus. Modern Art, Pres., 1955-60; trustee U. Calif. Hastings Law Center Found., 1974—, pres., 1979—; trustee Katherine Branson Sch., 1950-57; trustee U. Calif. Berkeley Found., 1972—, v.p., 1974-77, pres., 1977-79; Mem. Investment Counsel Assn. Am. (gov. 1955-58, 61-67), Calif. Acad. Scis. (trustee 1967—, chmn. bd. trustees 1967-73, treas. 1963-67), Sigma Chi. Clubs: Bohemian, Pacific-Union, Bankers; Anglers (N.Y.C.). Office: 3500 Crocker Plaza 1 Post St San Francisco CA 94104

COX, HARRY SEYMOUR, business exec.; b. Covington, Ky., Mar. 23, 1923; s. Harry S. and Rebecca E. (Wolfe) C.; B.A., Ohio Wesleyan U., 1947; m. Sally I. Stoneburner, Aug. 31, 1946; children—Inga C. (Mrs. Terryl Q. Walker), Sally (Mrs. Michael Sattler), Christopher. Accountant, Barrow, Wade, Guthrie & Co., Cleve., 1947-55; accountant White Consol. Industries, Inc. Cleve., 1956-68, v.p., treas., 1973—; chmn. bd. Laub Baking Co., Cleve., 1968-72. Served to lt. USNR, 1942-46. Mem. Sigma Alpha Epsilon. Methodist (chmn. trustees 1962-68). Clubs: Westwood Country (Rocky River, Ohio); Country of Ashland, Clifton (Lakewood, Ohio); Union (Cleve.). Home: 20252 Westhaven Ln Rocky River OH 44116 Office: PO Box 295 Syracuse IN 46567

COX, HUGH LENNEOUS, mech., aero. engr.; b. Greensboro, N.C., Jan. 8, 1928; s. Basil Sebastian and Mabel (Moffitt) C.; B.C.E., N.C. State U., 1949; M.S., U. Ill., 1952, Ph.D., 1953; m. Chrissa Middleton, Aug. 31, 1979; children—Craig Albert, Carmen Elisa. Exec. v.p. Structure Specialties Corp., Santa Monica, Calif., 1956-57; cons. Kirk Engring. Co., Los Angeles, 1957-59; cons. engr. H. L. Cox & Assos., Littleton, Colo., 1959-66; chief advanced ground systems Martin Marietta Corp., Denver, 1959-69; chmn. bd., pres. Electroculture Corp., Denver, 1969—; prof. U. Ala., 1955; cons. aero., aerospace and mech. engring. Served with AUS, 1954-56. Mem. Am. Inst. Aeros. and Astronautics, Aircraft Owners and Pilots Assn., Sigma Xi, Tau Beta Pi, Phi Eta Sigma, Phi Kappa Phi. Club: Pinehurst Country (Denver). Contbr. articles to profl. jours. Home: 2880 S Locust 705 N Denver CO 80222 Office: 3025 S Parker Rd Aurora CO 80014

COX, JOHN FRANCIS, public relations exec.; b. Chgo., Sept. 25, 1929; s. Roland Francis and Vera Pauline (Paisley) C.; B.S., U. Ill., 1951; M.S., Western Ill. U., 1954; m. T. Joanne Cox, Nov. 27, 1954; children—James, Thomas, Paul. Reporter, Galesburg (Ill.) Register-Mail, 1954-56; staff asst. publicity dept. United Airlines, Chgo., 1956-58; press relations mgr. Mercury Outboard Motors, Fond du Lac, Wis., 1958-60, mgr. Internat. Minerals & Chem. Corp., Chgo., 1960-68, mgr. Heublein Inc., Hartford, Conn., 1967-69; v.p. Warner Nat. Corp., Cin., 1969-72; v.p. public affairs Ky. Fried Chicken, Louisville, 1972—. Bd. dirs. Ky. Derby Festival Com., 1972-73. Served with U.S. Army, 1951-53. Mem. Public Relations Soc. Am., Public Relations Soc. Louisville, Sigma Delta Chi. Home: 2408 Chattesworth St Louisville KY 40222 Office: PO Box 32070 Louisville KY 40232

COX, JOHN JAY, bus. counselor; b. Lewistown, Mont., Mar. 9, 1938; s. John T. and Lenore (Jewart) C.; B.S. in Ceramic Engring., U. Wash., 1959; m. Alberta J. Shelton, Sept. 12, 1959; children—Jamie, Elizabeth, John M. With Gen. Electric Co., 1963-68; distbn. mgr. Sikes Corp., 1968-71; materials mgr. Stran Steel, 1971-72; bus. counselor, pres. Cox Small Bus. Counselors, Inc., Hillsboro, Oreg., 1972—. Served with USN, 1959-62. Office: PO Box 341 Hillsboro OR 97123

COX, JOHN ROGER, ins. co. exec.; b. Newburgh, N.Y., Mar. 4, 1932; s. John James and Natalie Myers (Palmer) C.; student Boston Coll., 1949-50, Valparaiso U., 1950-51, Purdue U., 1951-52; B.S., N.Y. U., 1959, postgrad. Sch. Bus., 1959-62; m. Patricia M. VanLoan, Nov. 20, 1954; children—Catherine, Patricia, John, Ellen, Susan. Acct., Pan Am. Grace Airways, N.Y.C., 1956-59; acct. Am. Home Ins. Co., N.Y.C., 1959-62, controller, 1962-65, asst. v.p., 1965-69; v.p., asst. to pres. Am. Internat. Group, N.Y.C., 1969-72; chmn., chief exec. officer Am. Life Ins. Co., Wilmington, Del., 1972-75; sr. exec. v.p. INA Corp., Phila., 1975—, pres. Property-Casualty group, 1980—; pres. Ins. Co. N.Am., 1976—; mem. underwriting bd. govs. N.Y. Ins. Exchange; pres., dir. 1792 Co., Indemnity Ins. Co. N.Am.; dir. Coll. Ins., Ins. Fedn. Pa., Inc., Am. Inst. Property and Liability Underwriters, Ins. Inst. Am., various INA cos. including Bankers Standard Ins. Co., INA Found., INA Internat. Corp., INA Internat. Ins. Co., INA Life Ins. Co., INA Reinsurance Co., INA Service Co., Investors Life Ins. Co. N.Am., Life Ins. Co. N.Am. Mem. services adv. com. U.S. Trade Rep.; mem. exec. com. U.S. council Internat. C. of C. Served with USMC, 1952-55. Asso. mem. Internat. Assn. Study of Econs. of Ins.; mem. Newcomen Soc. N.Am., Am. Legion. Clubs: Downtown Athletic (N.Y.C.), K.C. Home: 112 Shrewsbury Dr Livingston NJ 07039 Office: 1600 Arch St Philadelphia PA 19101

COX, KENNETH VICTOR, utilities exec.; b. Allison, N.B., Can., May 14, 1922; s. Charles Hilton and Hattie May (Mollins) C.; B.Sc., U. N.B., 1942; D.B.A. (hon.), U. Moncton, 1973; D.Sc. (hon.), U. New Brunswick, 1979; m. Mary MacNeill Dow, June 3, 1944; children—David R., Rodney A., Kenneth H., Marilyn L. With N.B. Telephone Co., Ltd., Saint John, 1942—, chief engr., 1956-58, gen. mgr., 1958-59, exec. v.p., dir., mem. exec. com., 1959-65, pres., 1965-77, chief exec. officer, 1965—, chmn. bd., 1977, chmn. exec. com., 1977—, chmn. bd., pres., 1979—; chief exec. officer Bruntel Holdings Ltd.; dir. Maritime Elec. Co., Ltd., Eastern Tel. & Tel. Co., Fraser, Inc., N.Am. Life Assurance Co., Bank N.S., SDL/Datacrown Inc., Telesat Can.; bd. mgmt. TransCan. Telephone Sta. Mem. Saint John Bd. Trade; chmn. N.B. Research and Productivity Council. Trustee Saint John YMCA; bd. hon. govs. Canadian Assn. Mentally Retarded. Fellow Engring. Inst. Can.; mem. Assn. Profl. Engrs. N.B., Conf. Bd., Inc. Clubs: Westfield Golf and Country, Riverside Golf and Country, Union (Saint John). Home: 216 Roderick Row Saint John NB E2M 4J8 Canada Office: One Brunswick Sq PO Box 1430 Saint John NB E2L 4K2 Canada

COX, LARRY GLEN, instrument mfr.; b. Pampa, Tex., Jan. 16, 1938; s. Odis and Dorothy Izela (Woods) C.; B.S., U.S. Naval Acad., 1960; children—Terri, David. Commd. ensign, U.S. Navy, 1960, advanced through grades to lt. comdr.; with Polaris Nuclear Submarine Service, 1960-69; engr., mgr. prodn. ops. Exxon Gas System, King Ranch Gas Plant, Gulf Coast, Tex., 1969-76; mem. mgmt. staff Prudhoe Bay Prodn. Facilities Project, Pasadena, Calif., div. supervising engr., 1976-79; v.p. ops. Williams Instrument Co., Inc. and partner U.S.A. Industries, Inc., Valencia, Calif., 1979—. Active Boy Scouts Am.; elder 1st Presbyterian Ch., Newhall, Calif. Registered profl. engr., Tex. Mem. ASME, Calif. Export Mgrs. Assn., Soc. Petroleum Engrs., Pacific Energy Assn., Pacific Coast Gas Assn. Club: Rotary. Home: 24504 W Nicklaus Dr N-4 Valencia CA 91355 Office: 25217 Rye Canyon Rd Valencia CA 91355

COX, LAWRENCE DAVID, railroad exec.; b. Takoma Park, Md., Apr. 6, 1927; s. Albert Lawrence and Joan Margaret (Edwards) C.; B.C.S., Strayer Coll., 1955; m. Priscilla Ann Crockett, Aug. 14, 1948; children—Elaine, Patricia, David, Lorene, Lawrence, Teresa, Kenneth, Kevin, Christine, Michael, Dorothy, Robert. With So. Ry. Co., Washington, 1944—, internal auditor, 1957, supr. corporate reporting, 1958-62, asst. mgr. corporate accounts, 1963-64, asst. dir. corporate accounts, 1965, mgr. corporate accounts, 1966-72, mgr. corporate accounting, 1973-79, dir. corp. acctg., 1980—; cons. on computerization, accounting and fin. reporting to various maj. transp. systems. Mem. Potomac River anti-pollution com., 1965-75. Served with USMC, 1944-45, 50-51. Mem. Nat. Assn. Accountants, Am. Accounting Assn., Phi Theta Pi. Democrat. Roman Catholic. Clubs: Potomac Walton Gun, Courts Royal Racquet. Contbr. articles in field to profl. jours. Home: 1000 Veirs Mill Rd Rockville MD 20851 Office: PO Box 1808 Washington DC 20013

COX, ROBERT GENE, cons. firm exec.; b. Liberal, Kans., June 3, 1929; s. Clarice Elden and Verene (Jones) C.; B.A. with honors, U. N.Mex., 1951, LL.B., 1955, J.D., 1968; postgrad. Fgn. Service Inst., 1956-57, Harvard Bus. Sch., 1978-79; m. Eileen Frances Hinshaw, July 10, 1953; children—Ann Rebecca, Allan Robert. Dept. mgr. Mountain States Investment Corp., Albuquerque, 1955-56; 3d to 2d sec. U.S. Embassy, Panama, 1956-58; Am. consul, Caracas, 1959-61; Korea desk officer State Dept., Washington, 1961-62, chief of staff for mgmt. planning, 1963-65; officer-in-charge State Dept. mission to Israel, 1965; staff asst. to Pres. U.S., White House, 1966-68; partner William H. Clark Assos., Inc., N.Y.C., Chgo., 1968-71; founding partner Zehnder & Clark Internat., Inc., 1970-71; sr. cons. UN Indsl. Devel. Orgn., N.Y.C., 1971-72; pres. Hennes & Cox Inc., N.Y.C., Washington and Los Angeles, 1972-75; prin., nat. dir. human resource systems Ernst & Ernst, 1975-78; dir. Arthur Young & Co., N.Y.C., 1979—; lectr. Universidad Nacional de Panama, 1957; vis. instr. in history Fla. State U., 1958; cons. on talent search Office Mayor N.Y., 1970; cons. to commn. on U.S.-Latin Am. relations, 1974; sr. adviser Commn. Orgn. Govt. for Conduct of Fgn. Policy, 1974-75; adviser exec. selection to transition staff of Pres.-elect Carter, 1976; expert witness on mil. value of Panama Canal, Ho. of Reps., 1977; dep. to county chmn. Democratic party, Albuqueque, 1954. Served to capt. USMC, 1951-55. Mem. Jonesville (Mich.) Heritage Assn., Council Fgn. Relations (chmn. study group), Am. Soc. Internat. Law, N.Y. Geneal. and Biog. Soc., Center for Study of Presidency, Royal Econ. Soc., Internat. Assn. for Religious Freedom, SAR. Unitarian. Clubs: Harvard Bus. Sch., Union League (N.Y.C.). Author: Defense Department Representation in Latin America, 1964; Choices for Partnership or Bloodshed in Panama, 1974; The Chief Executive, 1980. Home: 225 Central Park W Apt 1207 New York NY 10024 Office: 277 Park Ave New York NY 10172

COX, RUSSELL NYE, real estate exec.; b. Boston, Dec. 24, 1926; s. John Edward and Mary (Hoyt) C.; B.S. in Elec. Engring., Mass. Inst. Tech., 1949; M.B.A., Harvard U., 1951; m. Susanna Scherbaum, Aug. 16, 1974; children—Carolyn, Elizabeth, Leslie. Vice pres. Cabot, Cabot & Forbes, Co., Boston, 1953-63; pres. Linnell & Cox, Inc., Boston, 1963-71; pres. Gen. Investment & Devel. Co., Boston, 1971-77; pres. Resort Mgmt. Inc., Waterville Valley, N.H., 1977—; dir. Union Warren Savs. Bank, Commonwealth Nat. Corp., 1964-77. Chmn. finance com. Town of Weston, 1968-71, chmn. high sch. bldg. com., 1960-63; mem. vis. com. for student affairs Mass. Inst. Tech. Served with AUS, 1945-47. Mem. Young Pres.'s Orgn. (chmn. New Eng. chpt. 1971-72). Home and Office: Jennings Peak Rd Waterville Valley NH 03223

COX, WENDELL, fin. co. exec.; b. Los Angeles, Dec. 14, 1944; s. Raymond and Shirley (Miller) C.; student U. So. Calif., 1963-65; B.A. in Polit. Sci., Calif. State U., Los Angeles, 1968; M.B.A., Pepperdine U., Los Angeles, 1981; m. Valerie Woody, 1965; children—Deanna, Jeffrey, Gregory. Credit mgr. Marshall Imports Co., Los Angeles, 1967-68; asst. credit mgr. Bishop Industries, Union, N.J., 1969; mem. credit dept. United Factors (named changed to Crocker United Factors Inc., 1977), Los Angeles, 1969-73, mgmt. cons., 1973-76, asst. mgr. credit services dept., 1977-78, mgr., 1978-79, mgr. client services, 1979—. Chmn., Mayor's San Fernando Valley Adv. Com. on Transp., 1975-76, Calif. Dept. Transp., I-405 Diamond Ln. Adv. Com., 1976; mem. Los Angeles County Transp. Commn., 1977—, chmn. service coordination com., 1978—, mem. fin. rev. com., 1978—. Mem. Transp. Research Bd., Am. Pub. Transit Assn. (performance indicators com., governing bds. com.). Presbyterian. Home: 22218-2 Germain St Chatsworth CA 91311 Office: 742 S Hill St Los Angeles CA 90014

COY, FRANCIS ANDREW, mgmt. cons.; b. Cin., Mar. 9, 1914; s. John Andrew and Ellen Nettie C.; student U. Cin., 1933-34, D.C.S. (hon.), 1976; LL.D. (hon.), Wilberforce U., 1971; L.H.D. (hon.), Baldwin Wallace Coll., 1971; m. Virginia Reah Chiles, July 20, 1936; 1 son, Lawrence Andrew. Salesman, buyer Mabley and Carew, Cin., 1936-44; v.p. merchandising O'Neill's Dept. Store, Balt., 1944-51; divisional mdse. mgr. Higbee Co., Cleve., 1951-53; exec. v.p. Cleland-Simpson Co., Scranton, Pa., 1953-56; gen. mgr. May Co. stores, 1956-58; gen. mdse. mgr. May Co., Cleve., 1958-61, pres., 1961-71, chmn. bd., chief exec. officer, 1971-76, v.p. parent co. May Dept. Stores, Inc., 1976; pres. Coy & Assos., Inc., mgmt. cons., Cleve., 1976—; chmn., chief exec. officer, dir. Inarco Corp., Twinsburg, Ohio, 1978—, Internat. Artware Corp. div., Twinsburg, 1978—; dir., mem. adv. com. Nat. City Corp., Nat. City Bank of Cleve.; dir. TransOhio Fin. Corp., Russell, Burdsall & Ward, Inc., Klein Mgmt. Co., Camelback Inn Condo Assn., Grayson Pub. Co. Mem. exec. bd. Greater Cleve. council Boy Scouts Am., 1960—, mem. east central region exec. bd., 1974—, mem. nat. exec. bd., 1975—; life trustee YMCA of Cleve., 1960—; trustee Baldwin Wallace Coll., 1963—, Salvation Army, 1960—, United Torch Services, 1965—; bd. dirs., mem. exec. com. NCCJ, 1961—, Downtown Cleve. Corp., 1975-80, Billy Graham Evangelistic Assn., 1975—, Billy Graham Center, 1975—. Recipient Silver Beaver award Boy Scouts Am., 1963, Silver Antelope award, 1967; Honor award Am. Legion, 1965, Americanism award, 1974; George Washington Honor medal Freedoms Found. at Valley Forge, 1973; Disting. Service award Ohio Council Retail Mchts., 1975. Mem Greater Cleve. Growth Assn. (dir., mem. exec. com. 1966—). Republican. Methodist. Clubs: Pepper Pike Country, Kirtland Country, Canterbury Golf, Walden, Union, Cleve. Athletic, Sky Top, The 50. Home: 13415 Shaker Blvd Cleveland OH 44120 Office: 1999 Enterprise Pkwy Twinsburg OH 44087 also 725 National City Bank Bldg Cleveland OH 44114

COYNE, RAYMOND FRANCIS, city ofcl.; b. Chgo., Sept. 30, 1950; s. Raymond Francis, Jr. and Ann Marie (Sallans) C.; B.A., Reed Coll., Portland, Oreg., 1971; M.A., Northwestern U., 1972, Ph.D., 1980; m. Christine Mary Ellsworth, May 28, 1977; 2 children—Raymond Francis, IV, Kathleen Mary. Asst. to Democratic leader Ill. Senate, 1973-76; exec. dir. Ill. Econ. and Fiscal Commn., 1976-79; comptroller City of Chgo., 1979-80, asst. to mayor, 1980—, dep. commr. Dept. Health, 1980—; mem. Ins. Statutory Acctg. Principles Bd., 1980-82. Roman Catholic. Home: 3356 Newcastle St Chicago IL 60634 Office: 253 Civic Center Chicago IL 60602

CRABTREE, BARNETTE COLEY, bldg. co. exec.; b. Durham, N.C., Jan. 3, 1950; s. Leon Coley and Mary Geraldine (Couch) C.; A.B. in Chemistry, Duke U., 1972; student La. Tech. U., 1974-75; m. Cynthia Poole, Aug. 22, 1970; children—Stacy Anne, Kimberly Lynne, Matthew Coley. Co-owner, v.p., gen. mgr. Crabtree Assos., Inc., Durham, 1975—; owner, dir. ERA Crossroads Realty, Durham, 1975—; dir. First Capital Savs. & Loan Assn. Ltd., Durham, 1978—. Served to 1st lt. USAF, 1973-75. Mem. Durham-Chapel Hill Homebuilders Assn. (pres. 1980), Bd. Realtors, Merchants Assn., Sales & Mktg. Execs. Assn. Methodist (lay leader 1980). Home: 5132 N Willowhaven Dr Durham NC 27712 Office: 3101-B Guess Rd Durham NC 27705

CRAIG, BILL WILLIAM, sales exec.; b. Winston-Salem, N.C., Aug. 19, 1951; s. Walter Richard and Sadie O. (Craddock) C.; student Eastern Wash. State U., 1970-72; student in bus. adminstrn. Del. Inst. Tech., 1977-78. Sales mgr. Shelter Resources, Charlotte, N.C., 1974-75, Blue Hen Assos., Dover, Del., 1975-78; v.p. Marty's Mobile Homes, Inc., Dover, 1978—. Served with USAF, 1970-74. Mem. Del. Mobile Homes Assn., Del. Vets. Democrat. Baptist. Home: 148 Orchard Ave Dover DE 19901 Office: 1501 N DuPont St Dover DE 19901

CRAIG, JAMES WALLACE, marketing exec.; b. Parkersburg, W.Va., Feb. 14, 1935; s. George Wallace and Frances Elizabeth (Craig) C.; B.S. in Indsl. Engring., W.Va. U., 1958; m. Cynthia 21 Ann Taylor, Dec. 28, 1958; children—Brett Hayden, Julie Lynn. Vice pres. Hearin Products, Inc., Fullerton, Calif., 1969-73, Di Giorgio Corp., Fullerton, Calif., 1973-75; sales mgr. PPG Industries, Torrance, Calif., 1975-76, market mgr., Oak Creek, Wis., from 1976, now market mgr. indsl. products, Pitts. Served with Ordnance Corps, U.S. Army, 1959. Mem. Hardwood Plywood Mfrs. Assn., Imported Hardwood Plywood Assn. Republican. Presbyterian (deacon 1974-76). Clubs: Tennis. Home: 11 White Fawn Ln Fox Chapel PA 15238 Office: One Gateway Center Pittsburgh PA 15222

CRAIG, JOHN HENRY, JR., microbiologist; b. Carterville, Ill., Aug. 19, 1926; s. John Henry and Ruth (Rowatt) C.; B.A., So. Ill. U., 1950, M.S., 1955; B.S., U. Ill., 1953; m. Velma June Short, July 28, 1956. Lab. asst. So. Ill. U., 1953-55; chemist, bacteriologist Falstaff Brewing Corp., St. Louis, 1955-58; analytical chemist Allied Chem. Co., Metropolis, Ill., 1958-64; microbiologist Ill. Pub. Health, E. St. Louis, Ill., 1964-70; microbiologist, lab. mgr. State of Ill. Environ. Protection Agency, Marion, 1970—. Served with USN, 1944-46. Certified tchr., Ill. Mem. Am. Water Works Assn., Ill. Soc. Bacteriologists. Clubs: Masons, Shriners, Elks. Home: 1005 E Clark St Marion IL 62959 Office: 2209 W Main St Marion IL 62959

CRAIG, LOUIS ELWOOD, chem. co. exec.; b. Clifton Hill, Mo., Dec. 10, 1921; s. Clyde A. and Elsie (Metcalf) C; B.A., Central Coll., Fayette, Mo., 1943; Ph.D. (research fellow), U. Rochester, 1948; m. Virginia Higgins, July 17, 1943; children—James Allen, David Andrew, Margaret Louise (Mrs. Greg Price), Barbara Jean. Research chemist Am. Cyanamid Co., Stamford, Conn., 1943-46, Gen. Aniline Film Corp., Easton, Pa., 1948-54; supervising research chemist John Deere Chem. Co., Pryor, Okla., 1954-56, dir. research, 1956-61, dir. research and tech. service, 1961-63, dir. mktg. services, 1963-65; mgr. market research and devel. Kerr-McGee Chem. Corp., Oklahoma City, 1965-67, western area mktg. mgr., 1967-68, v.p. mfg., 1968-70, v.p. info. services parent co., 1970-72, v.p. chem. mfg. div. Kerr-McGee Chem. Corp., 1972-76, dir. mfg. services, 1976-77, dir. info. div. parent co., 1977—. Pres., Pryor Community Concerts Assn., 1960-63. Mem. AAAS, Am. Chem. Soc. (past chmn. Tulsa sect.), Okla. Anthrop. Soc., Oklahoma City C. of C., Mo. Archeol. Soc. Clubs: Pryor Rotary (past pres.), Pryor Quarterback (past pres.); Oklahoma City Petroleum. Contbr. articles to profl. jours., Ency. Chem. Tech. Patentee in field. Home: 4921 NW 32d St Oklahoma City OK 73122 Office: Kerr-McGee Center Oklahoma City OK 73102

CRAIG, ROBERT DON, broadcasting co. exec.; b. Lubbock, Tex., July 20, 1939; s. Thomas Bruce and Lizzette (Strickel) C.; m. Betty Ann Webber, July 20, 1957; children—Tamera Lyn, Tori Ann, Mark Alan, Spencer Todd. With Sta. KISN, Portland, Oreg., 1961-63, Sta. KCRA, Sacramento, 1963-65; co-owner Sta. KMYC, Marysville, Calif., 1965-70; gen. sales Sta. KJTV-TV, Bakersfield, Calif., 1970-72; gen. mgr. Sta. KLIQ, Portland, 1972-74; sales mgr. Sta. KUPL, Portland, 1974-75; gen. mgr. Sta. KASH/KSND, Eugene, Oreg., 1976—. Bd. dirs. Serenity Ln., hosp. for alcoholics. Mem. Nat. Assn. Broadcasters, Nat. Radio Broadcasters Assn., Oreg. Assn. Broadcasters (dir. 1980—), Eugene Broadcast Council, Radio Advt. Bur., Broadcasters Promotion Assn. Republican. Lutheran. Clubs: Mid-Oreg. Advt. (pres. 1979—), Elks. Office: 1330 Day Island Rd Eugene OR 97440

CRAIG, THOMAS E., accountant; b. Moulton, Ala., Sept. 25, 1915; s. R. Clyde and Lassie (Fretwell) C.; student pub. schs., Leon County, Tallahassee. Partner Pentland & Cowles, C.P.A.'s, Tampa, Fla., 1952-63; partner Cowles, Craig, Silverman and Wooten, C.P.A.'s, Tampa, 1963—. Served with USAAF, World War II. C.P.A., Fla. Mem. Am., Fla. Insts. C.P.A.'s. Clubs: Propellor, Univ. (Tampa). Home: 4350 W Kennedy St Tampa FL 33609 Office: Founders Life Bldg Tampa FL 33602

CRAIGHEAD, GEORGE PALMER, mgmt. cons.; b. Indpls., Oct. 22, 1929; s. George Vankirk and Janet Louise (Palmer) C.; A.B., Yale U., 1952; M.B.A., Harvard U., 1956; m. Peggy Ann Walters, Aug. 16, 1958; children—Scott, Bradford, Catherine. Sales rep. Gen. Electric Co., Bridgeport, Conn., 1956-59; dir. mktg. research C.H. Masland &

Sons, N.Y.C., 1959-61; dir. mktg. cons. services Touche Ross & Co., Detroit, 1961-66; exec. v.p. William H. Clark Assos., Inc, N.Y.C., 1966-77; pres. Egon Zehnder Internat., Inc. (U.S.A.), N.Y.C., 1977—. Pres., Assn. Exec. Recruiting Consultants, 1974-76. Served with M.I., U.S. Army, 1953-55. Clubs: Woodway Country (Darien, Conn.); Univ., Yale (N.Y.C.). Home: 6 Fox Hill Ln Darien CT 06820 Office: 645 Fifth Ave New York NY 10022

CRAIGMYLE, RONALD M., investment banker; b. Toronto, Ont., Can., June 19, 1896; s. James M. and Jessie (Gregory) C.; A.B., Columbia U., 1920, B.S. in Bus., 1921; m. Louise de Rochemont, Apr. 10, 1923; children—Ronald M., Mary Louise, Robert de Rochemont. With Minsch, Monell & Co., 1920-24; partner Burley, Peabody & Craigmyle, 1924-26, Craigmyle & Co., later Craigmyle, Pinney & Co., mem. N.Y. Stock Exchange, 1926-65; ltd. partner Fahnestock & Co., N.Y.C., 1965—; chmn. bd. Giant Portland & Masonry Cement Co. Vice pres. Intercollegiate Flying Assn., 1919-21; mayor Village of Matinecock (N.Y.), 1955-67, dep. mayor, 1967-75; trustee Columbia U., 1957-63; trustee emeritus Green Vale Sch. Mem. St. Andrews Soc. N.Y., Psi Upsilon, Republican. Episcopalian (vestryman). Clubs: Piping Rock, Creek, Met., Univ. (N.Y.C.); Everglades; Bath and Tennis. Home: Piping Rock Rd Box 321 Locust Valley NY 11560 Office: 110 Wall St New York NY 10005

CRAIN, CHARLES ANTHONY, telephone co. exec.; b. Decatur, Ill., Nov. 13, 1931; s. Archie A. and Marguerite A. (Buzan) C.; student Springfield (Ill.) Jr. Coll., 1949-51; student U. Miami, 1953; B.S. in Bus. Mgmt., U. Ill., Champaign, 1955; m. Mary Carole Bonansinga, Nov. 21, 1953; children—Charles Anthony, Richard Patrick, Michael Thomas. With Gen. Telephone Co., 1955—, mag. editor, Bloomington, Ill., indsl. relations asst., Bloomington, indsl. relations dir., Grinnell, Iowa, dir. personnel, Grinnell, mgmt. devel. adminstr. GTE Service Corp., N.Y.C., central div. mgr., Johnstown, N.Y., No. div. mgr., Johnstown, div. mgr., Erie, Pa., v.p. ops., Madison, Wis., San Angelo, Tex. and Santa Monica, Calif., v.p. mktg. and consumer service, Santa Monica, regional v.p. mktg. and customer service, Los Gatos, Calif., 1950-79, exec. v.p., Santa Monica, 1979—. Served with USAF, 1951-52; Korea. Clubs: Bel-Air Country, Porter Valley Country. Office: 100 Wilshire Blvd Santa Monica CA 90401

CRAIN, NEIL RANDALL, petroleum equipment mfg. co. exec.; b. Cameron, La., Nov. 11, 1933; s. Albert Harris and Ella Mae (Jones) C.; student Lamar U., 1962-64; m. Madeleine Ann St. Clair, Sept. 2, 1957; children—Randalin, Rosalind, Duncan. With Crain Bros., Inc., Grand Cheneir, La., 1957—, v.p., 1972—; dir. Cameron State Bank (La.). Served with USCGR, 1954-57. Mem. La. Bus. Industry Assn. (dir. 1978—). Mason (Shriner). Address: PO Box 118 Grand Chenier LA 70643

CRAMER, FRANK BROWN, coal conversion co. exec.; b. Long Beach, Calif., Aug. 29, 1921; s. Frank Brown and Clara Bell (Ritzenthaler) C.; B.A. in Chemistry, U. So. Calif., 1941, postgrad., 1942-43, 47-51; m. Pauline Gil, Aug. 3, 1973; children by previous marriage—Frieda, Eric, Lisa, Christina; stepchildren—Alfred, Consuelo, Peter. Research fellow U. So. Calif., 1947-51; with Rocketdyne div. Rockwell, Canoga Park, Calif., 1953-63; pres. Multi-Tech, Inc., San Fernando, Calif., 1962-72, Clean Energy Corp., Los Angeles, 1973-77, Adapt, Los Angeles, 1977—, ERGS Unlimited, Inc., Los Angeles, 1980—. Mem. 41st Assembly Dist. Central Republican Com., 1967-68; sec. San Fernando Valley dist. Libertarian Party of Calif., 1976-77. Served with U.S. Army, 1943-46. Mem. Am. Chem. Soc., Am. Statis. Assn., Biometric Soc., AIAA, Internat. Combustion Inst. Author: Medical Statistics, 1952; Combustion Processes, 1967; contbr. articles on combustion processes and biomed. engring. to profl. jours.; patentee in fields of fuel processing, energy mgmt., biomed engring.

CRAMER, HAROLD, lawyer; b. Phila., June 16, 1927; s. Aaron Harry and Blanche (Greenberg) C.; A.B., Temple U., 1948; J.D., U. Pa., 1951; m. Geraldine Hassuk, July 14, 1957; 1 dau. Patricia Gail. Admitted to Pa. bar, 1951; law clk. Pres. Judge Edwin O. Lewis, 1953; asso. dir. Inst. Legal Research, U. Pa. Law Sch., 1954; asso. Shapiro, Rosenfeld, Stalberg & Cook, 1955-56, partner, 1956-67; partner Mesirov, Gelman, Jaffe, Cramer & Jamieson, and predecessors, Phila., 1977—; lectr. trial adv.; pres. Theodore F. Jenkins Law Library Co. 1974—. Chmn. bd., trustee Eastern Pa. Psychiat. Inst., 1974—; trustee Pop Warner Little Scholars, Inc., United Way, Fedn. Jewish Agys., Jewish Publ. Soc.; chmn. bd. Grad. Hosp. Served from pvt. to 1st lt., AUS, 1951-53. Decorated Bronze Star Medal. Fellow Am., Phila. (trustee) bar founds.; mem. Am., Pa. (ho. of dels. 1966-75, gov. 1975—), Phila. (chmn. com. censors 1965, chmn. bd. govs. 1967-69, chancellor 1972), Korean bar assns., Am. Law Inst., Am. Arbitration Assn. (nat. panel), Jud. Conf. 3d Circuit, U. Pa. Law Alumni Soc. (bd. govs. 1959-64, sec. 1966-64, 1st v.p. 1966-68, pres. 1968-70), Order of Coif (bd. govs. 1957-65, pres. 1965-67, nat. exec. com. 1974—), Tau Epsilion Rho (chancellor 1960-62). Jewish religion (trustee congregation). Clubs: Philmont Country, Locust. Co-author: Trial Advocacy, 1968. Contbr. articles in field. Asso. editor The Shingle, Phila. Bar Jour., 1961-69, editor, 1969-70. Home: 728 Pine St Philadelphia PA 19106 Office: Fidelity Bldg 123 S Broad St Philadelphia PA 19109

CRAMTON, STANLEY CLARENCE, communications co. exec.; b. Wetaskiwin, Alta., Can., May 2, 1939; came to U.S., 1977; s. David James and Valburga (Greiner) C.; B.S. with honors in Elec. Engring., DeVry Inst. Engring. and Tech., Toronto, Ont., Can., 1963; M.S. in Communications, No. Alta. Inst. Tech., Edmonton, 1965; m. Eileen Annette Fjalestad, July 20, 1960; children—Cathy Lee, Diana Lynn, Michael James. Facilities supr. Alta. Govt. Telephones, 1963-75; sr. expert traffic engring. UN, São Paulo, Brazil, 1975-76: dir. ops. Teleconsult Inc., Washington, 1976—. Pres., Alta. and N.W. Ters. Jaycees, 1970-71; exec. v.p. Can. Jaycees, 1971-72. Named Jaycee Internat. Senator, 1969. Mem. IEEE (sr.), Armed Forces Communications and Electronics Assn., Newington Jaycees. Club: Masons. Home: 7804 New London Dr Springfield VA 22153 Office: 2555 M St NW Washington DC 20037

CRANE, KEITH, consumer products mfg. co. exec.; b. 1921. With Colgate Palmolive Co., N.Y.C., 1937—, gen. mgr., Australia, 1965-72, v.p. and gen. mgr. Far East div., 1972-74, corporate v.p., mgr. The Kendall Co., 1974-75, pres., chief operating officer, 1975-79, pres., chief exec. officer, 1979—, also dir. Served with Armed Forces, 1941-45. Office: Colgate Palmolive Co 300 Park Ave New York NY 10022

CRANE, KENT BRUCE, mgmt. services exec.; b. North Hornell, N.Y., July 25, 1935; s. Willard L. and Elizabeth (Ewart) C.; B.A. cum laude, Dartmouth Coll., 1957; postgrad. in internat. econs. Am. U., 1958; m. Catherine Ann Donnel, Dec. 31, 1976; children—Jeffrey Stuart, James Andrew. Third sec. polit. sect. U.S. Embassy, Jakarta, Indonesia, 1960-62; with U.S. Dept. State, Washington, 1963-64; vice consul in charge econ. sect. U.S. Consulate, Zanzibar, 1964-65; 2d. sec. polit. sect. U.S. Embassy, Accra, Ghana, 1965-67; sr. research asso. for fgn. affairs, sec. to task force on conduct of fgn. relations, Republican Nat. Com., 1967-68; spl. asst. to Senator George Murphy, 1968-69; nat. security affairs adv. to v.p. of U.S., 1969-72; asst. dir. for East Asia and Pacific, USIA, 1972-74; adminstrv. asst. to Rep. Peter H.B. Frelinghuysen, 1974-75; project dir. U.S. Commn. on Orgn. of Govt. for Conduct of Fgn. Policy, 1974-75; chmn. bd. Crane Pub. Co., Ridgewood, N.J., 1975—; co-chmn. Africa subcom. Rep. Nat. Com., 1978-80; pres., mng. dir. Crane Group Ltd., Washington, 1978—; pres. Ranch Devel. and Mgmt., Inc., Tex., 1980—; officer, dir. various cos. U.S. and abroad including Corona Co., Harrow Corp.; active real estate joint ventures U.S., N.Z., Spain, Africa. Served to 1st lt. U.S. Army, 1957-59, to capt. USAR. Mem. Inst. Strategic Studies (London), Nat. Rifle Assn. (dir.), Explorers Club, Game Conservation Internat. Clubs: Met. (N.Y.C.); Internat., Capitol Hill (Washington); Internat. Economists, Mt. Kenya Safari, Safari Internat. Office: 1000 Connecticut Ave NW Suite 600 Washington DC 20036

CRANE, LEO STANLEY, railroad ofcl.; b. Cin., Sept. 7, 1915; s. Leo Vincent and Blanche Gottlieb (Mitchell) C.; B.S. in Engring., George Washington U., 1938; m. Joan McCoy, Sept. 3, 1976; children by previous marriage—Pamela Blanche, Penelope Ann. With So. Ry. Co., 1937-63, 65—, test engr., 1948-56, mech. research engr., 1956-59, v.p. engring. and research, 1965-70, exec. v.p. ops., 1970-76, pres., chief adminstrv. officer, 1976-77, pres., 1977-80; chmn., chief exec. officer Con Rail, 1981—, also dir.; dir. Am. Security & Trust Co., Woodward & Lothrop. Mem. Fed. City Council; trustee George Washington U. Named Chief Exec. of Year in R.R. Industry, Fin. World mag., 1978; Man of Year, Modern Railroads mag., 1974; recipient Outstanding Mgmt. Achievement award Am. Inst. Indsl. Engrs., 1975; Research Recognition award Progressive Railroading mag., 1967. Fellow ASME, ASTM; mem. Nat. Acad. Engring., Soc. Automotive Engrs., Am. Ry. Engring. Assn., Am. Soc. Traffic and Transp. Clubs: Met., Bethesda Golf and Country, City Tavern, Internat., Biltmore Forest Country. Home: 1351 Monk Rd Gladwyne PA 19035

CRANE, ROBERT, cosmetic and toiletry mfg. co. exec.; b. N.Y.C., Aug. 18, 1927; s. David H. and Sophia (Lippet) Cohen; B.A. in Econs., Bklyn, Coll., 1949; M.S. in Mktg., Columbia U., 1950; m. Marion Segal, May 4, 1954; children—Susan, Keith. Dir. mktg. Salon div. Clairol, Inc., N.Y.C., 1964-68; dir. mktg. Revlon Profl. Hair Color div. Profl. Products Group, Revlon, Inc., N.Y.C., 1968-70, v.p. mktg. Revlon-Realistic div. Profl. Products Group, 1970-78, sr. v.p., dir. mktg. and sales Revlon Profl. Products Group, 1978—. Served with U.S. Army, 1945-47. Mem. Nat. Barber and Beauty Mfrs. Assn. (pres. 1975-76, chmn. exec. com. 1977-78, dir. 1975-80), Columbia U. Grad. Sch. Bus. Alumni Assn. Club: Dellwood Country. Home: 6 Lynhaven Ct Monsey NY 10952 Office: 767 Fifth Ave New York NY 10022

CRANSTON, DONALD MAURY, restaurant exec.; b. Champaign, Ill., Feb. 3, 1935; s. Jean Edwin and Louise (Tippins) C.; student Central YMCA Coll., 1953; m. Nancy Lee Drzal, May 17, 1969; children—Donald Michael, Stephanie. Driver, Brady Motorfrate, Chgo., 1955-65; founder, pres. C & C Offset, Inc., printing and advt., Chgo., 1962-76, dir., 1971—; mgr. sales office U.S. Carbon Products, Inc., Chgo.; pres. Brown's Chicken, fast food restaurant, Carbondale, Ill., 1976-79, Consol. Energy, Inc., 1979—, Tony's Steak House, Marion, Ill., 1979—. Served with AUS, 1953-55. Recipient Graphic Excellence award Nekoosa Edwards Paper Co. Inc., 1971. Mem. Carbondale C. of C., Aircraft Owners and Pilots Assn. Mason, Eage. Office: 105 S Market Marion IL 62959

CRANSTON, HOWARD STEPHEN, lawyer: b. Hartford, Conn., Oct. 20, 1937; s. Howard S. and Agnes H. (Carvo) C.; B.A. cum laude, Pomona Coll., 1959; LL.B., Harvard U., 1962; m. Karen Louise Youngman, June 16, 1962; children—Margaret, Susan. Admitted to Calif. bar, 1963: asso. firm Macdonald & Halsted, Los Angeles, 1964-67; partner Macdonald, Halsted & Laybourne, Los Angeles, 1968—; dir. Knapp Communications Corp., The Knapp Press, Bon Appetit Pub. Corp., Wilshire Mktg. Corp. Bd. dirs. Legal Aid Found. of Los Angeles, 1971—. Served to lt., U.S. Army, 1962-64. George F. Baker scholar, 1955-59. Mem. Am. Bar Assn., Assn. for Corp. Growth, State Bar of Calif., Am. Judicature Soc., Friends of Claremont Coll. Republican. Episcopalian. Clubs: Univ., San Marino City. Home: 1830 Lorain Rd San Marino CA 91108 Office: 1200 Wilshire Blvd Los Angeles CA 90017

CRAVEN, ANTHONY WILLIAM, publishing co. exec.; b. Townsville, Australia, May 9, 1940; came to U.S., 1978; s. Joseph and Norah Margaret (Mitchell) C.; B.A. in Econs. and Acctg., Macquarie U., Sydney, Australia, 1972; m. Julanne Carey Grant, Jan. 12, 1968; children—James, Joseph, Zoe, Thomas. Partner, Wallace Hadlow & Assos., pubs. reps., Sydney, Australia, 1968-72; founder, mng. dir. Harcourt Brace Jovanovich Group (Australia) P/L, Sydney, 1972-78; sr. v.p. Acad. Press, N.Y.C., 1978—; v.p. Johnson Reprint Corp., N.Y.C., Grune & Stratton, Inc., N.Y.C.; dir. HBJ (Australia), Acad. Press Japan, Acad. Press Brazil. Mem. Assn. Sci., Tech. and Med. Pubs. Office: 111 Fifth Ave New York NY 10003

CRAVENS, WILLIS DEAN, confectionery co. exec.; b. Ill., Dec. 26, 1935; s. Stephen A. and Jenness Margaret (Stewart) C.; B.A., Knox Coll.; m. Barbara Ann Mills, Sept. 8, 1956; children—Jill, Mitchell, Christine. Mktg. dir. Chicle Adams, S.A., Colombia, 1963-65; asst. dir. confectionery mktg. Warner-Lambert Co., 1965-68; mgr. consumer products export Pillsbury Co., 1968-70; dir. Latin-Am. ops. Life Savers, Inc., 1970-76, v.p., N.Y.C., 1976—. Bd. dirs. Youth Tennis Found. New Eng., 1980—. Mem. Am. Mgmt. Assn. Republican. Presbyterian. Club: Millbrook (Greenwich, Conn.). Office: 40 W 57th St New York NY 10019

CRAVER, WILLIAM EVERETT, JR., finance, mfg., real estate and shipping exec.; b. Columbus, Ga., Aug. 14, 1922; s. William Everett and Myrtle (Ivey) C.; student George Washington U., 1940-43; B.S., U.S. Mcht. Marine Acad., 1945; m. Jane Honour McDonald, Oct. 19, 1946; children—Virginia St. Clair (Mrs. Joseph C. Good, Jr.), Ellen Lloyd (Mrs. G. Douglas Young), Jane Honour (Mrs. Edward D. Izard), William Everett III. Adminstrv. asst. OPM, WPB, Washington, 1940-43; founder, partner Bradham-Craver Co., 1946-49; founder, owner, partner Craver & Co., pub. accountants, Charleston, S.C., 1948-58; founder, pres., dir. So. Gen. Corp. (formerly Craver Industries, Inc.), Charleston, 1949—, Carolina Gen. Corp. (formerly Cravalume, Inc.), Charleston, 1952—; Universal Financial Corp., 1962—; a founder, pres. Coastal Investers, Inc., 1955-56; founder, pres. Craver Indsl. Park, Inc., 1963-67, Beautyguard Mfg. Corp., 1962-67, Leasemasters, Inc., 1968—, Financial Resources Corp., 1973—; partner Playboy of Atlantic City, 1977—. Vice chmn. Charleston Cancer Crusade, 1965; mem. Charleston County Aviation Authority, 1970—, chmn., 1971—; mem. parents' adv. council Converse Coll., 1965-74, chmn., trustee, 1972-74; bd. dirs. Patriots Point Found., 1977—, v.p., 1979—. Served to lt. USNR, 1945-46; PTO ETO. Recipient Outstanding Bus. Achievement award U.S. Mcht. Marine Acad. Alumni, 1960, Meritorious Alumni award, 1970. Mem. Am. Soc. Metals, Hibernian Soc. (founding trustee Hibernian Soc. Found. 1976—, v.p. 1977—), Navy League (pres. Charleston council 1971-73, nat. exec. com. 1971-75, nat. dir. 1977-80), Greater Charleston C. of C., U.S. Mcht. Marine Acad. Alumni Assn. (life mem.; chpt. charter pres. 1964-65, regional gov. 1965-71), Pi Kappa Alpha. Democrat. Presbyn. (deacon). Clubs: Charleston Country, Albermarle (pres. 1965-66), Propeller of Charleston, Sertoma (past dir., chmn., life mem.) (Charleston). Patentee metal forming equipment and device field. Home: 82 Tradd St Charleston SC 29401 Office: 36 Broad St POB 1014 Charleston SC 29402

CRAWFORD, ARTHUR WALLACE, investment broker; b. Chgo., Mar. 24, 1921; s. Arthur Wallace and Elizabeth (Merrill) C.; A.B. cum laude, Harvard, 1941; m. Genevieve Byers Johnston, July 16, 1941 (div. 1976); children—Priscilla, Marie (Mrs. Charles Saale), Carol, Susan; m. 2d, Norma Silvas Myers, May 21, 1976. Market research analyst L. E. McGivena & Co., N.Y.C., 1941; exec. asst. N.Am. Aviation, Inc., Los Angeles, 1941-44, 1946-57; investment broker J. Barth & Co., Los Angeles, 1957-65, Dominick & Dominick, Inc., Los Angeles, 1965-67, White, Weld & Co., Los Angeles, 1967-73, Shields & Co., Los Angeles, 1973-75; investment broker Smith, Barney Harris Upham & Co., Inc., Los Angeles, 1975—, v.p.-sales. Served as lt. (j.g.) USNR, 1944-46; in U.S.S. Fred T. Berry. Republican. Clubs: Harvard of So. Calif., Town Hall (Los Angeles); Athletic. Lectr. on investments. Author: Practical Portfolio Management, 1971. Home: 9160 Florence Ave #303 Downey CA 90240 Office: 800 W 6th St 11th Floor Los Angeles CA 90017

CRAWFORD, BILLY RAY, chem. co. exec.; b. Kentwood, La., Nov. 1, 1942; s. Arlis Milton and Cleta Mae (Clark) C.; B.S. in Mktg., La. State U., 1970; m. Vada Lynne Blades, Dec. 5, 1962; children—Karma, Kelly. With Dow Chem. Products, Plaguemire, La., 1966-68, with plastics lab., 1968-70, salesman Baton Rouge, Chgo., 1971-76; v.p. services Coastal Chem. Co., Abbeville, La., from 1976; now pres. Chem-Vac, Inc., Houston. Served with USAF, 1960-64. Democrat. Baptist. Office: 5702 Pine Arbor Houston TX 77066

CRAWFORD, BRUCE EDGAR, advt. exec.; b. West Bridgewater, Mass., Mar. 16, 1929; s. Harry Ellsworth and Nancy (Morrison) C.; B.S. in Econs., U. Pa., 1952. With Benton & Bowles, Inc., N.Y.C., 1954-58; v.p. Ted Bates & Co., N.Y.C., 1958-61; advt. dir. Chesebrough Ponds Inc., N.Y.C., 1961-63; with Batten, Barton, Durstine & Osborn, Inc., N.Y.C., 1963—, pres., 1978—. Bd. dirs. Met. Opera Assn. Served with U.S. Army, 1947-48. Mem. Assn. Advt. Agencies Am. Republican. Clubs: Racquet and Tennis (N.Y.C.); Turf and Field. Office: 383 Madison Ave New York NY 10017*

CRAWFORD, DAVID, mfg. co. exec.; b. Charlotte, N.C., Mar. 12, 1941; s. Columbus and Margaret (Adams) C.; B.S., Johnson C. Smith U., 1963, M.A., U. N.C., 1966; m. Dorothy J. McGill, July 31, 1965; children—Davaree Yvette, Darlisa Yvonne. Digital computer analyst UTC Research Labs. East Hartford, Conn., 1967-68, exec. asst. to exec. v.p., 1979—; supr. mktg., product support info. systems Pratt & Whitney Aircraft, East Hartford, 1968-71; coordinator mgmt. devel., 1971-75, divisional supt. machine shop, mfg. div., 1975-79; advisor to Hartford rehab. workshop ops.; guest lectr. U. Conn. Prison asso. volunteer sponsor for inmates, Conn.; mem. adv. com. for admission practices to Howell Cheney Regional Vocat. Tech. Sch., 1977. Chan Gordon Meml. scholar Rotary Internat.; So. Edn. Found. fellow. Mem. Am. Mgmt. Assn., Am. Soc. for Metals. Democrat. Methodist. Home: 84 Hickory Hill Dr Somers CT 06071

CRAWFORD, DAVID LAMAR, ins. co. exec.; b. Maion, Ala., June 7, 1924; s. Roy J. and Margaret (Christenberry) C.; B.S., U. Ala., 1948; m. Dorothy Louise Hinton, Dec. 17, 1949; children—Meg, Cherry, Elon, Mary Alice, Dolly. Livestock rancher, Marion Junction, Ala., 1948—; owner, mgr. Marion (Ala.) Lumber Co., 1948-56; stock salesman So. United Life Ins. Co., Montgomery, Ala., 1956, dist. mgr., 1957, state mgr., 1958, v.p. ordinary dept., 1959-61, v.p. credit ins. dept., 1961-74, pres., 1974—, pres. subs. So. United Fire Ins. Co., 1974—, also dir.; dir. 1st Dallas County Bank, Selma, Ala.; v.p. Fordworth, Inc.; sustaining mem., bd. govs. Internat. Ins. Seminars. Served with airborne inf. U.S. Army, 1944. Recipient ins. mentor award Ala. Mem. Assn. Ala. Life Ins. Cos. (pres. 1979-81), Nat. Assn. Life Cos. (pres. 1980-81), Credit Insurers Assn. (pres. 1978-79). Methodist. Clubs: Southeastern Livestock Expositions (first v.p. 1980—), Ala. Quarter Horse Assn., Ala. Polled Hereford Assn. Office: 136 Catoma St Montgomery AL 36195

CRAWFORD, HOMER, paper co. exec., lawyer; b. St. Louis, Nov. 28, 1916; s. Raymond S. and Mary (Homer) C.; A.B., Amherst Coll., 1938; LL.B., U. Va., 1941; m. Esther Wilkinson, Oct. 4, 1944 (div. 1949); 1 dau., Candace C.; m. 2d., Sara E. Twigg, May 3, 1952; children—Georgianna, William Twigg. Admitted to N.Y. bar, 1942; asso. firm LeBoeuf, Lamb, Leiby & MacRae, N.Y.C., 1942-54, partner, 1954-56; v.p., sec. St. Regis Paper Co., N.Y.C., 1956—, dir., 1976—; sec., St. Regis (Alta.) Ltd.; sec. dir. St. Regis Paper Co. (Can.) Ltd.; dir. St. Regis Land Devel. Corp., numerous other cos. Mem. Am., N.Y. State bar assns., Am. Soc. Corp. Secs. (dir. 1965-68), Theta Delta Chi. Republican. Presbyterian. Home: 216 E 77th St New York NY 10021 Office: St Regis Paper Co 150 E 42d St New York NY 10017

CRAWFORD, HORACE RANDOLPH, petroleum engring. and fertilizer co exec.; b. Haskell, Tex., Mar. 4, 1928; s. John Milton and Annie Maud (Williams) C.; B.Ch. E., Tex. Tech. U. 1949; M.S., U. Tex., 1954, Ph.D. (Humble Oil fellow), 1958; m. Mary Louise Holcome, July 10, 1955; children—Michael Earl, Donald Kevin, Nancy Esther, Barbara Ann. Engine opr. Sun Oil Co., Rio-Grande, Tex., 1949, plant chemist, 1950, gas engr., Silver Tex., 1954-55; instr. math U. Tex. at Austin, 1956-57; research asso. Western Co., Dallas, 1957-59, research group supr., 1959-61, asst. div. mgr., 1961-63, mgr. chem. engring. dept., 1963-67, mgr. contract research and devel. dept. Richardson, tex., 1967-68; mgr. chem. engring. Enserch Corp., Dallas, 1969-72, dir. fuels sec. corp., devel. and research 1972-74, dir. Sanitech div., 1974-75; dir. process and new product devel. NIPAK; Inc., 1975-77; mgr. oil and gas sales Ensearch Exploration, Inc., 1977-78; pres. Can Gro Fertilizer, 1978—; v.p., DLAN, Real Estate, 1978; staff engr. Conoco, Inc., 1979—. Vice-chmn. finance North Trail Dist. Boy Scouts Am., 1971, chmn. fin., 1972, chmn. dist. 1973-75, chmn. relationships, 1976—; chmn. fin. Palmer Drug Abuse Program, Dallas, 1977-78. Served with AUS, 1950-52. Registered profl. engr. Recipient award of merit Boy Scouts Am., 1975, Silver Beaver award, 1978. Mem. Engring. Soc. Tex. Tech. (pres. 1948-49), Am. Inst. Chem. Engrs. (chmn. Dallas 1968), Soc. Petroleum Engrs., Am. Soc. Gas Engrs. (pres. Southwest chpt. 1972-73, nat. dir. 1972-74, Pres.'s award 1973), Nat. Solid Waste Mgmt. Assn., North Tex. Gas Mens Assn., Sigma Xi, Alpha Chi, Kappa Mu Epsilon, Tau Beta Pi, Omega Chi Epsilon (pres. Tex. chpt. 1954). Contbr. articles to profl. jours. Patentee in field. Home: 20406 Laverton Katy TX 77450 Office: 5 Greenway Plaza E Suite 2630 Houston TX 77001

CRAWFORD, JAMES LEWELLYN, mech. constrn. co. exec.; b. Kansas City, Mo., Nov. 15, 1919; s. Harold L. and Helen B. (Lacy) C.; grad. U. Okla., 1941; m. Olivia Kessler, Oct. 22, 1943; children—Jim W., Carol Crawford Stanley. With Boeing Airplane Co., Wichita, 1941-47; mech. engr. Ripstra-Turner Co., Wichita, 1947-59; pres., chmn. Central Air Conditioning Co., Inc., Wichita, 1959—; pres. CAACO, Inc. of Ariz., MCI Co.; cons. in field. Bd. dirs. Wichita Symphony. Registered profl. engr., Kans., Ga. Mem. ASHRAE. Republican. Presbyterian. Clubs: Wichita, Crestview Country. Patentee mech. systems surveilance apparatus, air conditioning energy conserver. Office: 117 W Dewey St Wichita KS 67201

CRAWFORD, OLIVER RAY, investment exec.; b. Amarillo, Tex., July 19, 1925; s. George Gordon and Bell Elizabeth (Allston) C.; student Wash. State Coll., 1943-44, S. Tex. Sch. Law, 1953-55; m. Nancy Rose Hudson, Sept. 22, 1979; children by previous marriage—Lynda Ann, Carolyn Rae, Alan Richard. Div. mgr. Phillips Petroleum Co., Midland, Tex., 1947-62; mgr. tax and tile dept. Houston Oil Co. Tex., 1952-56; asst. to gen. mgr. Southwestern Settlement and Devel. Co., Jasper, Tex., 1956-59; gen. mgr. Southwestern Timber Co., 1959-73; v.p. Eastex, Inc., 1956-73; asst. to chmn. bd. and pres. Temple Industries, Inc. div. Time Inc., 1973-74; cons. investments, real estate, govt. and pub. relations, 1974-75; pres. Austin Unltd. Inc., 1974-75; chmn. Lincoln Securities Corp.; pres. Lincoln Realty Co., Lincoln Land Mgmt. Co., Lincoln Devel. Co., 1974-75; pres., chmn. bd. Tecom Inc., 1975—, Chaparral Land and Devel., Inc., 1979—; dir. First State Bank, Jasper. Pres. So. Forest Research Inst., 1963-74; past mem. Tex. Alcoholic Beverage Commn.; dir. Tex. forest industries com. Am. Forest Products Industries. Pres. Jasper Youth Baseball Assn., 1958-74. Bd. dirs. A.R.C., Operation Orphans, Inc., Tex. Law Enforcement Found.; mem. century council, trustee research council Tex. A. & M. U.; mem. regents' devel. council Lamar U.; trustee S.W. Research Inst. Served as fighter pilot USAAF 1943-45. Named Man of Month, East Tex. C. of C., 1961; recipient hon. Lone Star Farmer degree Tex. Assn. Future Farmers; Forest Mgmt. award Nat. Lumber Mfrs. Assn.; Mr. East Texas award, operating dirs. of Tyler County Dogwood Festival, 1967; decorated Comdrs. Cross Order of Merit (Germany). Hon. life mem. Jasper Youth Baseball, Nat. Congress P.T.A., Future Farmers Am.; mem. Tex. Forestry Assn. (dir. pres. 1970-74), Sportsman's Clubs Tex. (pres. 1975-76), Jasper C. of C. (pres. 1964). Presbyn. Home: 7507 Stepdown Cove Austin TX 78731 Office: 3636 Executive Center Dr Suite 201 Austin TX 78731

CRAWFORD, STEPHEN EVERETT, fisheries biologist; b. Pawtucket, R.I., Oct. 29, 1947; s. Earl Smith and Ruth C.; B.S., U. R.I., 1970; M.S. in Zoology, U. Okla., 1979; m. Judith Ann Collins, Jan. 3, 1975. Fisheries biologist R.I. Dept. Fisheries, 1970; Peace Corps vol., Rajasthan, India, 1971-73, fisheries trainer in Nepal, Africa and India, 1973-74; mgr. Sooner Fish Farm, Washington, Okla., 1974-75; pres., mgr. Crawford's Catfish Acres, Inc., Shawnee, Okla., 1977—; fisheries cons. Am. Peace Corps. Mem. Am. Fisheries Soc. Republican. Congregationalist. Home and Office: Route 1 Box 435 Shawnee OK 74801

CRAWFORD, WILLIAM F., corp. exec., cons.; b. Chgo., Apr. 11, 1911; s. William Wilberforce and Mona (Richards) C.; student Northwestern Mil. and Naval Acad., 1925-29, U. Chgo., 1929-31; m. Ruth M. Fellinger, May 4, 1935; children—Judith Crawford Smith, Susan (dec.), Constance Crawford Dry, Barbara Crawford Boger, William Edwin. Sec., Edward Valves, Inc. (formerly Edward Valve & Mfg. Co., Inc.), East Chicago, Ind., 1931-37, v.p., 1937-41, pres., dir., 1941-63; pres., dir. Republic Flow Meters Co., Chgo., 1957-61, Valve Products, Inc., Knox, Ind., 1950-63, W.E. Bowler Co., Phila., 1954-63; v.p., dir. Rockwell Mfg. Co., Pitts., 1945-73, chmn. fin. com., 1963-73; adv. dir. Rockwell Internat., Pitts., 1973-79; v.p., dir. Chgo. Fittings Corp.; dir. U.S. Flexible Metallic Tubing Co., San Francisco, Atlantic India Rubber Works, Inc., Flex-Weld, Inc., Keflex, Inc., Tec-Line Products, Inc. (all Chgo.), Mogul Rubber Corp., Goshen, Ind., Rubbernek Fittings Ltd., Birmingham, Eng.; chmn. W.F. Crawford & Assos., Chgo.; mem. valve industry adv. com. WPB, 1941-45, 50-52. Trustee Ill. Inst. Tech., IIT Research Inst., The Crawford Found., Chgo. Mem. Valve Mfrs. Assn. (pres. 1959-61, 64-65), ASME, Art Inst. Chgo., Field Mus. Natural History, Shedd Aquarium Soc., Delta Upsilon. Republican. Congregationalist. Clubs: Union League, Tavern, Adventurers, Econ. (Chgo.); Duquesne (Pitts.). Home: 4950 Chicago Beach Dr Chicago IL 60615 also PO Box 1800 Sun Valley ID 53353 Office: 185 N Wabash Ave Chicago IL 60601

CRAWFORD, WILLIAM WAIT, securities dealer; b. Louisville, July 10, 1928; s. Malcolm Henry and Mary Louise (Webb) C.; A.B., Centre Coll. of Ky., 1950; m. Shelia Mason, Jan. 28, 1977; children—William Wait, Louise Wallis, Elizabeth Stuart, Barbara Webb. Mem. sales staff Pepsi Cola Louisville Bottlers, 1955-56, Bunte Bros. Chase Candy Co., 1957-60; partner W.L. Lyons & Co., Louisville, 1960-65; dir. J.J.B. Hilliard, W.L. Lyons Inc., Louisville, 1965—, dir. sales and mktg., 1979—, mem. exec. com., 1979—. Served with USNR, 1950-55. Bd. dirs. Ky. Ind. Coll. Found., 1979—. Mem. Nat. Assn. Securities Dealers (dist. com. chmn. 1971-73), Centre Coll. Alumni Assn. (pres. 1970, dir. 1965-71). Republican. Episcopalian. Clubs: Louisville Country, Pendennis, Jefferson, Bond (pres. 1966) (Louisville). Home: 503 Ridgewood Rd Louisville KY 40207 Office: J J B Hilliard W L Lyons Inc 535 S 3d St Louisville KY 40202

CRAWLEY, JAMES BENJAMIN, oil co. exec.; b. Simsboro, La., Aug. 5, 1926; s. John Earl and Lottie (Robison) C.; B.S., Tex. A&M U., 1947; M.B.A., Harvard U., 1956; m. Mary Colby Williamson, June 5, 1956; children—Sara Beth, Linda Sue, Martha Jane. Petroleum engr. Stanolind (now Amoco) Midland, Tex., 1947-51; asst. prodn. supt. Blackwood & Nichols, Midland, 1951-55; v.p. Consol. Prodn. Corp., Oklahoma City, 1957-71, pres., 1971-72; pres. Crawley Petroleum Corp., Oklahoma City, 1972—. Served with AC, U.S. Army, 1945. Registered profl. engr., Okla. Mem. Ind. Producers Assn. Am., Soc. Petroleum Engrs., AIME. Democrat. Presbyterian. Club: Petroleum. Home: 525 Merkle Dr Norman OK 73069 Office: 740 Hightower Bldg Oklahoma City OK 73102

CRAYS, THOMAS COLLISON, banker; b. Danville, Ill., Apr. 26, 1934; s. John Asbury and Lillian Claire (Battershell) C.; B.S., U. Ill., 1958; m. Barbara Ann Huffman, Dec. 9, 1967; children—Anne Elizabeth, Jennifer Courtney, John Forrest. Spl. rep. Fed. Reserve Bank of Chgo., 1958-62; corr. bank rep. Harris Trust & Savs. Bank, Chgo., 1962; exec. v.p. First Nat. Bank of Rossville (Ill.), 1962-66; with Palmer American Nat. Bank, Danville, Ill., 1966—, now pres., chmn. bd. dirs. Chmn., Danville United Way Campaign, 1978, bd. dirs., 1979—; bd. dirs. Center for Children's Service, 1972-79; bd. dirs. Lake View Med. Center, Danville Indsl. Park. Served with U.S. Army, 1954-56. Mem. Ill. State C. of C. (dir.), Ill. Bankers Assn., Am. Bankers Assn. Republican. Clubs: Danville Country, Elks Country, Danville Rotary. Office: 2 W Main St Danville IL 61832

CREAGER, CHARLES EDWIN, lawyer, economist, educator; b. Hagerstown, Md., Oct. 20, 1925; s. Charles Edwin and Mary Edith (Bloyer) C.; B.S., U. Balt., 1950, J.D., 1973; M.B.A., Am. U., Washington, 1959, postgrad., 1966-68; m. Alice Eleanor Hollenbach, Oct. 9, 1948 (div. Jan. 1970); children—Charles Edwin, Karen Elaine and Roger Thomas (twins); m. Dolores C. Yanuk, Nov. 1970. Traffic rep. Charlton Bros. Transp. Co., Inc., Balt., 1946-49; transp. cons., 1950—; gen. freight agt. Novick Transfer Co., Inc., Balt. 1949-58, So. div. sales mgr., Winchester, Va., 1958-59, gen. traffic mgr., 1960-62, v.p. traffic, 1962-64; dir. sales Halls Motor Transport, Sunbury, 1959-60; v.p. traffic Nat. Transport Co., Inc., Bridgeport, Conn., 1964-65, cons., 1965—; partner Germelman, Alt & Creager, 1966-68; owner Charles E. Creager & Assos., Silver Spring, Md., 1968-73; individual practice law, Hagerstown, 1974-76; pres., treas. Law Offices Creager & Newhouse, P.A., 1976—; asst. prof., dir. transp. insts. Am. U., 1965-68, practitioner ICC, 1955—; admitted to Md., D.C., U.S. Ct. of Appeals, U.S. Supreme Ct. bars; asst. prof. mktg. Lord Fairfax Community Coll. Served with USAAF, 1943-46. Bd. dirs. Middle Atlantic Conf., Washington, 1963-68. Mem. Am., Md., D.C. bar assns., Eastern Shipper-Motor Carrier Council (pres. 1964-65; chmn. exec. com. 1965-66), traffic clubs Hagerstown, Shenandoah (past pres.), Nat. Shipper Motor Carrier Conf. (chmn. exec. com. 1964-66), Assn. ICC Practitioners, Motor Carrier Lawyers Assn., Internat. Platform Assn., Phi Alpha Delta. Episcopalian. Elk. Clubs: Fountain Head Country, Rotary. Home: 133 Overhill Dr Hagerstown MD 21740 Office: Creager & Newhouse PA 1329 Pennsylvania Ave PO Box 1417 Hagerstown MD 21740

CREAN, JEREMIAH PAUL, constrn. engring. co. exec.; b. Waterbury, Conn., June 29, 1911; s. Richard Martin and Anna Catherine (Denehy) C.; B.A., Fordham U., 1933, LL.B., 1938; m. Oct. 22, 1938; children—Paula Marie, Christine Angela, Maryanne. Teller, trust dept. Guaranty Trust Co. of N.Y., 1934-42; admitted to N.Y. State bar, 1940; with M.W. Kellogg Co., N.Y.C., 1942-66, mgr. sales adminstrn., 1966; mgr. proposals and contracts, mgr. sales adminstrn. Stone & Webster Engring. Corp., N.Y.C., 1966—. Pres., Burdsall Manor Assn., N.Y.C., 1955-57, West Norwalk (Conn.) Assn., 1974-76. Mem. Bar Assn. State N.Y. Office: Stone & Webster Engring Corp One Penn Plaza 250 W 35th St New York NY 10019

CREECH, SALLY WOOD, real estate broker; educator; b. Raleigh, N.C., Apr. 10, 1939; d. Larry Faison and Harriet Alpha (Dickinson) Wood; A.B. cum laude, Salem Coll., 1961; M.A., U. N.C., 1965; postgrad. U. Oslo (Norway), N.C. State U., Duke U.; m. William Ayden Creech, Jan. 13, 1968; children—Lawrence Wood, Ezekiel Hollingsworth, Charles Alderman. Instr. dept. social scis. U. N.C., Wilmington, 1965-68, Raleigh, N.C., 1975—; Pres. Wake County Democratic Women, 1937-75; mem. Raleigh Hist. Sites Commn. Mem. LWV, Raleigh Fine Arts Soc., Raleigh Bd. Realtors, Salem Coll. Alumni Assn. (dir. 1973-74), Phi Alpha Theta. Methodist. Clubs: Jr. League of Raleigh, Twentieth Century Book. Home: 1208 College Pl Raleigh NC 27605

CREEDON, JOHN J., ins. co. exec.; b. N.Y.C., Aug. 1, 1924; s. Bartholomew and Emma (Glynn) C.; B.S. magna cum laude, N.Y. U., 1952, LL.B. cum laude, 1955, LL.M., 1962; m. Vivian Elser, Aug. 17, 1947; children—Juliette, Michele, John, David. With Met. Life Ins. Co., N.Y.C., 1942—, v.p., asso. gen. counsel, 1970-73, sr. v.p., gen. counsel, 1973-76, exec. v.p., 1976-80, pres. and dir., 1980—, chmn. bd. Met. Property & Liability Ins. Co., 1979-80; admitted to N.Y. State bar, 1955; adj. prof. law N.Y. U. Law Sch., 1962-73; bd. dirs., pres. Am. Bar Found.; chmn. bd. Met. Life Found.; trustee N.Y. U., N.Y. U. Law Center Found., Am. Coll., Practising Law Inst.; mem. legal adv. com. N.Y. Stock Exchange. Served with USNR, 1943-46. Mem. Am. (assembly del. 1972-75, chmn. sect. corp. banking and bus. law 1975-76), N.Y. State bar assns., Assn. Bar City N.Y., Assn. Life Ins. Counsel (pres. 1977-78), Life Ins. Council N.Y. (chmn.), Am. Law Inst., N.Y. State C. of C. and Industry. Editor The Bus. Lawyer, 1973-74: contbr. articles to profl. jours. Office: 1 Madison Ave New York NY 10010

CREEGER, ALLAN DAVID, equipment rental co. exec.; b. Boston, Dec. 9, 1921; s. Herbert S. and Jane S. (Nelson) C.; B.A., Columbia U., 1942; I.A. with distinction, Grad. Sch. Bus., Harvard U., 1943; m. Louise V. Rosenthal, Feb. 12, 1944; children—Lawrence A., Carol J. Pres., Creeg-Rose Corp., Richmond, Va., 1947-56, Karol Distbg. Co., Richmond, 1952-54, Handy Distbrs. Inc., Richmond, 1954—. Served to lt lt. U.S. Army, 1943-46. Mem. Am. Rental Assn. (dir. 1959-62, pres. 1972-73, chmn. 1973-75, Disting. Service award 1979), Retail Mchts. Assn. Greater Richmond (2d vice chmn.), Va. Equipment Rental Assn. (pres.). Club: Richmond Kiwanis (dir.). Contbr. articles to trade jours. Home: 43 Old Mill Rd Richmond VA 23226 Office: 2367 Staples Mill Rd Richmond VA 23230

CREEK, JOHN DENNIS, mfg. co. exec.; b. Roswell, N.Mex., Apr. 5, 1951; s. Webster Bennett and Edna Ore (Lott) C.; B.A., Tex. Tech U., 1974, postgrad., 1974-75; m. Billie Lou Kingsbery, June 19, 1976; 1 dau., Courtney A. Field technician Tait-Andritz Co., Lubbock, Tex., 1976, sales staff, 1977-78, sales mgr., 1978, dir. mktg., 1978—, v.p., 1980—, gen. mgr., 1981—; cons. U. Wis., Madison, 1978-79. Mem. TAPPI, AIME, Am. Mgmt. Assn. Republican. Baptist. Clubs: Rotary, Lubbock Country. Contbr. articles to profl. jours. Home: 4811 Tamanaco Ct Arlington TX 76017 Office: 1010 Commonwealth Blvd S Arlington TX 76063

CREEL, JAMES PEARLIE, advt. exec.; b. Conway, S.C., Mar. 6, 1939; s. John P. and Hazel M. Creel; B.S. in Indsl. Mgmt., Clemson (S.C.) U., 1961; m. Carolyn Willism, Aug. 8, 1959; children—James Pearlie, Carolyn Alicia. Mgmt. trainee Shell Oil Co., 1961; from sales dir. to v.p. Tyson & Co. Advt., Myrtle Beach, S.C., 1963-78; pres. Creel Outdoor Advt., Inc., Myrtle Beach, 1978—, Cabana I Devel. Co., Inc., Myrtle Beach, 1979—; partner T.W.C. Properties, 1969—, Bayview Acres, 1973—; sec. Fairway Corp., 1971—; dir. Standard Savs. & Loan Assn., Myrtle Beach. Co-chmn. Horry County Indsl. Council, 1967; bd. dirs. Horry County Dept. Public Welfare, 1966-71, S.C. Hall of Fame, 1973—, Jr. Achievement Horry County, 1975; chmn. dist. adv. com. Pee Dee Area council Boy Scouts Am., 1968-71; mem. Horry County Planning Commn., 1977-79; chmn. coliseum com. Myrtle Beach Auditorium, 1973; sec. Horry-Georgetown Tech. Edn. Commn., 1972; gen. chmn. United Way Horry County, 1973, bd. dirs., 1973—, v.p. agy. ops., 1975; chmn. Gov. S.C. Com. Hwy. Safety, 1980. Served to 1st lt. USAR, 1961-63. Decorated Army Commendation medal. Mem. Outdoor Advt. Assn. Am. (dir. 1978—), Inst. Outdoor Advt. (gov., exec. com. 1979—), S.C. Outdoor Advt. Assn. (pres. 1970-73), Carolina's Electric Sign Assn., Myrtle Beach C. of C. (chmn. coms.), Dunes Property Owners Assn. (v.p., dir. 1977-80), Med. Exec. Assn. (past pres.). Methodist. Clubs: Kiwanis (pres. 1967-68), Rotary (pres. 1980) (Myrtle Beach). Home: 411 Wildwood Trail Dunes Myrtle Beach SC 29577 Office: PO Box 157 Hwy 317 at 501 Myrtle Beach CA 29577

CREIGHTON, JOHN EVERETT, spl. events planner; b. Bakersfield, Calif., Oct. 23, 1931; s. John Lyon and Grayce (Mills) C.; B.S. in Animal Sci., U. Calif., Davis, 1958; m. Janice Rakestraw, Mar. 17, 1951; children—John K., Larry B., Kathrine A., Linda M. Mgr., Nev. State Fair, Reno, 1969-71, Navajo Nation Fair, Window Rock, Ariz., 1971-73; coordinator Ariz. State Fair., Phoenix, 1973-74; mgr. Ariz. Nat. Livestock Show, Phoenix, 1974-76; owner The Connection, Phoenix, 1976—. Served with U.S. Army, 1952-54. Mem. Ariz. Fairs Assn., Western Fairs Assn. Club: Ariz. Showman's. Office: PO Box 39452 Phoenix AZ 85069

CREMONA, VINCENT ANTHONY, banking adminstr.; b. Valetta, Malta, Nov. 5, 1925; s. Henry and Jane Mary (Cachia) C.; came to U.S., 1959, naturalized, 1965; B.S., Stella Maris Coll., Malta, 1945; M.S. in Finance, London Sch. Accountancy, 1950. Ships purveyor Peninsular and Oriental Steam Nav. Co., Valetta, 1945-50; asst. supr. Gen. Motors, Oshawa, Ont., Can., 1950-55; accounting supr. Ind. Groceries Assn., Toronto, Ont., Can., 1955-59; accounting mgr. Air India, N.Y.C., 1960-65; dir. adminstrn. and finance Commonwealth Services, Dhahran Internat. Airport, Saudi Arabia, 1965-66; mgr. internal audits Litton Industries, Carlstadt, N.J., 1966-67; v.p. Fashioncade, N.Y.C., 1967-68; tng. dir. FRS, Washington, 1969—. Certified internal auditor. Mem. Am. Mgmt. Assn., Inst. Internal Auditors, Assn. Govt. Accountants, Order St. John of Jerusalem. Home: Columbia Plaza Envoy 2450 Virginia Ave NW Washington DC 20037 Office: Fed Reserve System Washington DC 20551

CREQUÉ, MARCELYN ELLEN, telephone co. ofcl.; b. Cleve., Mar. 15, 1931; d. Spearman D. and P. Edwinetta (Reed) Lark; student Keller Grad. Sch. Mgmt., 1975-77; m. Carl Crequé, May 14, 1972. Long distance operator AT&T Co., Chgo., 1950-54, clerk, various depts., 1954-63, service rep., 1963-66, sales supr., 1966-73, staff supr., 1973-74, service mgr., 1974-76, ops. mgr. telegraph and radio, 1976-78, dist. engr. customer services, 1978—. Del., bd. dirs. Chgo. Conf. on Race and Religion, 1975—; mem. support com. Urban Bishops Coalition, 1977. Mem. Stony Island Assn., Dorchester Civic Assn., Chgo. Fiber Guild. Episcopalian. Home: 8732 S Dorchester Ave Chicago IL 60619 Office: 10 S Canal St 25th Floor Chicago IL 60606

CRESON, WILLIAM T., corp. exec.; b. 1929; B.S., Purdue U., 1948; M.A., U. Pa., 1950; married. With Packaging Corp. of Am. prior to 1968; sr. v.p., gen. mgr. Brown Co., 1968-75; with Crown Zellerbach Corp., San Francisco, 1976—, exec. v.p., mem. exec. com., now pres., dir. Office: Crown Zellerbach Corp 1 Bush St Box 7809 San Francisco CA 94119*

CRESWELL, DONALD CRESTON, mgmt. cons.; b. Balt., Mar. 28, 1932; s. Carroll Creston and Verna Moore (Taylor) C.; student Johns Hopkins U., 1951-52; M.B.A., U. Dayton, 1966; postgrad. bus. Stanford U., 1975; m. Terri Sue Tidwell, Dec. 27, 1958; 1 son, Creston Lee. Cons. engr. A.D. Ring & Assos., Washington, 1956-58; sales and mktg. mgr. Ampex Corp., Redwood City, Calif., 1959-68; dir. mktg., magnetic products div. RCA Corp., N.Y.C., 1968-71; staff v.p. sales and advt. Pan Am. World Airways, N.Y.C., 1971-74; mktg. v.p. Rocor Internat., Palo Alto, Calif., 1975; v.p., chief operating officer, gen. mgr., Am. AmBuCar Services, Inc., San Francisco, 1976; prin. strategic mgmt. cons. Stanford Research Inst., Menlo Park, Calif., 1977—; lectr. planning and mktg. mgmt. Am. Mgmt. Assn., 1968-69; program chmn. Grad. Bus. Assn., 1965; rep. to Electronics Industries Assn., 1968-71, to Internat. Air Transport Assn., 1971-74; spl. cons. Devtronix Organs, Inc., 1978-79. Mem. Am. Theatre Organ Soc. (dir. 1978-79). Republican. Home: 3328 Brittan Ave San Carlos CA 94070

CRETSOS, JAMES MIMIS, sci. info. co. exec., chemist; b. Athens, Greece, Oct. 23, 1929; s. Basil D. and Chrissa B. (Thomaidou) Kretsos; came to U.S., 1946, naturalized, 1955; B.S. in Chemistry, Am. U., 1960, postgrad., 1960-62; m. Barbara Ann Deitz, Mar. 10, 1952; children—Maurice William, Christopher James. Research chemist Melpar, Inc., Falls Church, Va., 1961-63, info. scientist, 1963-64, head tech. info. center, 1964-65, mgr. info. services lab., 1965-67, dir. instructional materials center, Tng. Corp. of Am., Falls Church, 1966-67; dir. info. systems lab. Litton Industries, Bethesda, Md., 1967-69; head sci. info. systems dept. Merrell-Nat. Labs., Cin., 1969—; dir. Infoflow, Inc.; cons OEO, Ohio, Ky.-Ind. Regional Library and Info. Council; lectr. U. Cin., 1973-74, U. Ky., 1976-77. Mem. Creative Edn. Found., Buffalo, 1967—. Served with M.C., AUS, 1954-56. Mem. Am. Chem. Soc., Am. Mgmt. Assn., Am. Soc. Info. Sci. (chmn. So. Ohio chpt. 1973-74, chmn. SIG/BC 1973-74, chmn. profl. enhancement com. 1974-75, chmn. 5th mid-year meeting 1976, Watson Davis award 1976, chmn. membership com. 1977, exec. com. 1979, nominations com. 1980, pres. 1979), Assn. Computing Machinery, Drug Info. Assn., IEEE Computer Soc., Am. Fedn. Info. Processing Socs. (dir. 1981—), Spl. Libraries Assn. (pres. Cin. chpt. 1974-75, consultation officer 1976-77), Pharm. Mfrs. Assn., Nat. Micrographics Assn. Club: Indoor Tennis. Editor: Health Aspects of Pesticides Abstract Bull., 1967-69; adv. bd. Chem. Abstracts Service, 1981—. Home: 10701 Adventure Ln Cincinnati OH 45242 Office: 2110 E Galbraith Rd Cincinnati OH 45215

CREW, CHARLES ANTHONY, mfg. corp. exec.; b. Balt., Mar. 23, 1943; s. Charles Albert and Nellie Elizabeth (Zurgable) C.; B.S. in Accounting and Fin., U. Balt., 1966; m. Linda Carol Bilson, Sept. 7, 1963; children—Alisa, Carol, Charles. Cost accountant Green Spring Dairy, Inc., Balt., 1963-66, cost, budget supr., 1966; sr. div. accountant Am. Trading & Production Co., Balt., 1966-69; accounting mgr. Sealtest Foods, Kraft Corp., Balt., 1969-70; plant controller Eastern Products Corp., Roper Corp., Balt., 1970-72; controller Unitote div. Gen. Instrument Co., Balt., 1972-73, fin. exec. data systems & services group, 1973-79; v.p. fin. Dur-O-Wal, Inc., Balt., 1979-80; dir. fin. Dutch Boy, Inc., Balt., 1980—. C.P.A., Md. Mem. Candlewick Community Assn. (treas. 1976-77), Md. Assn. C.P.A.'s, Nat. Assn. Accountants, Am. Mgmt. Assn. Home: 101 Talloway Ct Sykesville MD 21784 Office: 2325 Hollins Ferry Rd Baltimore MD 21230

CRICHTON, BRUCE NELSON, coal co. exec.; b. Rahway, N.J., Sept. 17, 1936; s. Harry Alan and Imelda R. Crichton; B.S. in Bus., Lehigh U., Bethlehem, Pa., 1958; s. Baily Haines, Nov. 24, 1959; children—Lissa, Douglas, Garrett. With Irving Trust Co., N.Y.C., 1959-61; pres. Crichton Co. Inc., N.Y.C., 1961-75; pres., dir. John K. Irish Co. Inc., Red Bank, N.J., 1975—; dir. Jersey Shore Bank, Long Branch, N.J. Served with USAR, 1958-64. Mem. Coal Exporters Am. (dir.), Nat. Coal Assn. Republican. Presbyterian. Clubs: Navesink Country, Saucon Valley Country, Seabright Beach, Madison Sq. Garden. Home: 6 Azalea Ln Rumson NJ 07760 Office: 176 Riverside Ave Red Bank NJ 07701

CRICHTON, JOHN HAYES, investment banker; b. Minden, La., July 21, 1920; s. Thomas and Bernard Moore (Hayes) C.; B.S., Davidson Coll., 1942; J.D., La. State U., 1949; Exec. Program, Stanford, 1970; m. 2d, Dale Cowgill, July 3, 1967; children by previous marriage—Kate, Bunnie, Lili, John Hayes. Admitted to La. bar, 1949; mem. firm Smitherman, Smitherman & Purcell, 1949-51; mng. dir. Better Hotels of La., Shreveport, 1951-61; exec. v.p., asst. to pres. Allied Properties, San Francisco, 1961-62; pres., dir. Guaranteed Reservations Inc., Palm Beach, Fla., 1962—; pres., dir. Computer Controls Corp., 1967-70; chmn., dir. Commonwealth Group Inc., 1975—; dir. Three Two Corp., Southeastern Surg. Supply Co., Inverness Corp., Nat. Assn. Merger and Acquisition Cons. Served to maj., inf. AUS, 1942-46. Decorated Bronze star with oak leaf cluster. Mem. Am., La. bar assns., Bankers Club San Francisco, Phi Delta Phi. Republican. Mem. Anglican Ch. of N.Am. Club: Bath and Tennis (Palm Beach). Home: 2411 Pacific Ave San Francisco CA Office: 601 California St San Francisco CA 94108

CRICHTON, JOHN PETER, hand tool mfg. co. exec.; b. Greenwich, Conn., Dec. 9, 1934; s. William Edward and Elizabeth (Bowen) C.; B.A., St. Michaels Coll., 1952-56; postgrad. exec. summer program Harvard U., 1970; m. Mary Ellen Horsfall, Sept. 7, 1957; children—Susan, John, Kathleen, Melissa, Matthew. Dist. sales mgr. Power Tool div. Rockwell Internat., Pitts., 1960-63, merchandising specialist, 1963-64, Can. sales mgr., 1964-66, Can. dir. mktg., 1966-69, U.S. nat. sales mgr., 1969-71, dir. mktg., 1971-73, v.p. mktg., 1973-76, dir. internat. mktg., 1976-78; pres. New Britain Tool div. Litton Industries (Conn.), 1978—; instr. Grad. Sch. Indsl. Mktg., Carnegie-Mellon U., 1979. Served with CIC, U.S. Army, 1957-60. Recipient award of merit Nat. Retail Hardware Assn., 1976. Mem. Hardware Mktg. Council. Patentee pocket socket hand tool. Home:

52 Woodmont Rd Avon CT 06001 Office: New Britain Tool Div Litton Industries South St New Britain CT 06050

CRILEY, CHARLES ALBERT, internat. mktg. and fin. co. exec.; b. Sapulpa, Okla., Aug. 20, 1936; s. Wayne and Audrey Frances (Morey) C.; student Va. Mil. Inst., 1954-55; LL.D. (hon.), London Inst. Applied Research, 1972; 1 dau., Laura Lynne. With traffic dept. Pacific No. Airlines, 1958-59, Consol. Freightways, 1959-61, Stor-Dor Forwarding Co., 1962-63, Garrett Freightlines, 1962-64, Sea-Land Service Co., 1965-66, Traffic Service Co., 1964; chmn., chief exec. officer C.A. Criley & Assos., Inc., traffic freight cons., Bellevue, Wash., 1964-80, Met. Shippers Clearings Corp., Bellevue, 1967-73, Los Angeles, 1971-73, Oak Brook, Ill., 1972-73, Hackensack, N.J., 1972-73, Trans-Action Data Systems, Inc., Bellevue, 1969-80, Taryl Resources, Inc., Bellevue, 1970—, Conaway Traffic Co., Los Angeles, 1971-73; partner Stuart Carter Internat., Seattle, 1980—. Author: The Merchants Shipper Credit Corporation Plan, 1967. Established Criley professorship of transp. computer scis., Stanford, 1972. Home: 3816 138th SE Bellevue WA 98006 Office: 1507-C Queen Anne Ave N Seattle WA 98109

CRIMMINS, MARY ELISABETH, food service mgmt. co. exec.; b. Charleston, W.Va., May 29, 1940; d. Arthur Lawrence and Marion Alberta (Crowther) C.; B.S., Ohio U., 1962; registered dietitian Mass. Gen. Hosp., 1963. Theraputic dietitian Hosp. U. Pa., 1963-64, asst. chief dietitian, 1964-68; analyst ARA Services, Inc., Phila., 1968-69, project mgr., 1969-70, dir. ops. and standards, 1970-72, v.p. sch. services, 1972—; mem. Nat. Research Council's Advisory Bd. on Mil. Personnel Supplies; chmn. Nat. Com. Child Nutrition. Mem. Am., Pa., Phila. dietetic assns., Dietitians in Bus. (sec. 1975-77), Assn. Sch. Bus. Ofcls., Am. Sch. Food Service Assn., Forum of Exec. Women, Phila. Republican. Roman Catholic. Contbr. articles in field to profl. jours. Home: 222 S Van Pelt St Philadelphia PA 19103 Office: ARA Services Independence Square W Philadelphia PA 19106

CRISAFULLI, FRANK, JR., ins. co. exec.; b. Portland, Maine, July 13, 1940; s. Frank and Inez Louise (Bowen) C.; student Bentley Coll., 1958-60; B.S. in Bus. Adminstrn., Ill. Wesleyan U., 1962: m. Janice Golden, Dec. 5, 1970; 1 dau., Amy. Acct., Peat, Marwick, Mitchell & Co., N.Y.C., 1962-64, sr. acct., 1964-66; asst. treas. Windsor Life Ins. of Am., N.Y.C., 1966-67, treas., 1967-68; controller Congressional Life Ins. Co., N.Y.C., 1968-69, v.p. adminstrn., 1970; v.p. adminstrn. Columbian Mut. Life Ins. Co., Binghamton, N.Y., 1970-78, sr. v.p. adminstrn., 1978-79, sr. v.p. ins. ops., 1979—. C.P.A., D.C. Mem. Am. Inst. C.P.A.'s, Ins. Acctg. and Statis. Assn., Alpha Kappa Psi. Methodist. Home: 420 Clarkson Dr Vestal NY 13850 Office: Columbian Mut Life Ins Co One Columbian Mut Plaza Binghamton NY 13902

CRISAFULLI, STEPHEN WILLIAM, sports apparel co. exec.; b. N.Y.C., Feb. 13, 1940; s. William Stephen and Mary Nancy (Cameleri) C.; A.B., Dartmouth Coll., 1961; M.B.A., Amos Tuck Sch. Bus. Adminstrn., 1962; m. Nancy Hill, Aug. 26, 1961; children—William Stephen, Pamela Ann. Exec. v.p. Profile Sports Corp., West Lebanon, N.H., 1967-71; pres. Slalom Skiwear, Inc., Newport, Vt., 1971—; pres. Bogner of Am., Newport, 1972-75; pres. Internat. Marine Wear, Newport, 1975—, NE Canoe Co., Newport, 1978—. Treas. North Country Hosp. Mem. Ski Industries Am. (treas.). Home: Elm St Derby Line VT 05830 Office: Slalom Skiwear Longview St Newport VT 06855

CRISP, DON DALE, engine sales and service exec.; b. Manes, Mo., Nov. 2, 1936; s. Ezra and Lucy A. (Wade) C.; ed. Joplin Bus. Coll., Kansas City Bus. Coll., U. Mo. (Kansas City); m. Rena M. Miller, Nov. 23, 1973; children—Justin, Anita, Richard, David. Sales mgr. Bormaster Furniture, Joplin, Mo., 1960-66; office mgr. Quik-Trip, Inc., Kansas City, 1966-72; owner, mgr. Central Sales & Service, Mountain Grove, Mo., 1973-77, Tree-n-Turf, Lewiston, Idaho, 1977—. Clubs: Moose, Lions, Rotary. Home: 1126 Powers St Lewiston ID 83501 Office: Box 1348 Lewiston ID 83501

CRISP, DOROTHY ROWLAND, chem. co. exec.; b. Plymouth, Mich., Sept. 2, 1927; d. Estel T. and Edith M. (Macomber) Rowland; student Ohio Wesleyan, 1944, Wayne State U., 1949; children—Gary D., Jack P. Office mgr. Hoyt Asso., 1964-67; supr. employment chem. group Olin Corp., Stamford, Conn., 1967-72, supr. personnel, 1972-73, mgr. personnel research and devel., New Haven, Conn., 1973-80, mgr. personnel tech., chems. group, Stamford, Conn., 1980—. Mem. Am. Mgmt. Assn., Am. Chem. Soc. (asso.), Mfg. Chemists Assn. (continuing edn. com.), Sigma Xi. Republican. Methodist. Club: Order Eastern Star. Home: 20-C Milford Beach Apts Shea Ave Milford CT 06460 Office: 120 Long Ridge Rd Stamford CT 06905

CRISPIN, JAMES HEWES, engring. constrn. co. cons.; b. Rochester, Minn., July 23, 1915; s. Egerton Lafayette and Angela (Shipman) C.; A.B. in Mech. Engring., Stanford, 1938; M.B.A., Harvard, 1941; grad. Command and Gen. Staff Sch., U.S. Army, 1943; m. Marjorie Holmes, Aug. 5, 1966. With C.F. Braun & Co., Alhambra, Calif., 1946-62; treas. Bechtel Corp., San Francisco, 1962-73, v.p., mem. finance com., 1967-75, mgr. investment dept., 1973-75; cons. personal investments, 1976—. Trustee, Santa Barbara (Calif.) Mus. Art, 1979—. Served to lt. col. Ordnance Corps. AUS, 1941-46. Registered profl. mech. engr., Calif. Mem. Mil. Order World Wars, Calif. Soc. SR, Soc. Colonial Wars State Calif., Baronial Order Magna Carta, Mil. Order Crusades, Am. Def. Preparedness Assn., World Affairs Council No. Calif. (treas. 1971-73, trustee 1971-76), Beta Theta Pi. Republican. Clubs: California, Chaparral (Los Angeles); Pacific-Union, St. Francis Yacht, San Francisco Golf, World Trade (dir. 1971-78, pres. 1977-78) (San Francisco); Harvard (N.Y.C.); Valley (Santa Barbara, Calif.). Home: 1340 E Mountain Dr Santa Barbara CA 93108 Office: La Arcada Bldg Suite 220 1114 State St Santa Barbara CA 93101

CRISS, JOHN WILLIAM, mathematician, physicist; b. Clarksburg, W.Va., Mar. 24, 1941; s. Benjamin Michael and Vena Jane (Bail) C.; A.B., W.Va. U., 1964; postgrad. U. Md., 1964-67; m. Judith Loree Olson, Aug. 10, 1968; children—Anne Loree, Brian William. Mathematician, engring. expt. sta. W.Va. U., Morgantown, 1964; mathematician X-ray optics br. Naval Research Lab., Washington, 1964-80; cons. applied math. X-ray spectrometry, 1966-79; pres. Criss Software, Inc., Largo, Md., 1979—; speaker seminars, workshops and symposia. Mem. Am. Math. Soc., Am. Nat. Standards Inst., Am. Phys. Soc., ASTM, Assn. Computing Machinery, Soc. Indsl. and Applied Math., Sigma Xi. Contbr. articles and papers to profl. jours. Research in applied X-ray physics and spectrometric chem. analysis. Office: 12204 Blaketon St Largo MD 20870

CRISSMAN, JAMES HUDSON, architect; b. Pitts., Apr. 28, 1937; s. Harold Eugene and Anna Martha (Logan) C.; B.Arch., Carnegie Inst. Tech., 1960; M.Arch. in Urban Design, Harvard U., 1966; m. Louisa Goddard Murray, Dec. 31, 1966; children—Charles Wright McMurtie, Sarah Wood de Coursey, William Goddard. Architect with firms in Pitts., N.Y.C. and Watertown, Mass., 1962-70; partner Crissman & Solomon Architects Inc., Watertown, 1970—, chmn. bd., treas., 1978—; mem. faculty Boston Archtl. Center, 1968-71, mem. edn. com., 1980—; vis. critic, lectr. Harvard U. Grad. Sch. Design, 1976—; prin. works include Crissman house, Hilton Head Island, S.C., 1971, Babcock Kidney Center, Boston, 1975, Dickson House, New Vernon, N.J., 1978, Littauer Center, Harvard U., 1978, Sommerville House, Wilson, N.C., 1979, Charleston (S.C.) Mus., 1980, Billerica (Mass.) Public Library, 1980. Trustee Children's Hosp. Med. Center, Boston, 1975—; mem. corp. Old North Ch., Boston; organist, choirmaster St. John's Episcopal Ch., Newtonville, Mass., 1972-74, Whitehall Ch., Pitts., 1960-64; past sec. Watertown Conservation Commn.; past sec. Sheepscot Valley Conservation Assn., Alna, Maine. Served with USAF, 1960-66. Recipient 1st prize Charleston (S.C.) Museum competition, 1976; excellence award for design Archtl. Record, 1977 (2), 1979, 81. Mem. AIA (award merit New Eng. Regional Council 1976, hon. mention 1978, honor award N.H. chpt. 1976), Mass. Assn. Architects, Boston Soc. Architects (bd. dirs., commr. edn. and research; award design excellence 1977, 79), Am. Guild Organists. Democrat. Episcopalian. Club; Harvard (Boston). Composer choral music; archtl. work pub. in Archtl. Record, House and Garden, House Beautiful, N.Y. Times, Boston Globe, others. Home: 3 Brigham St Watertown MA 02172 Office: 44 Hunt St Watertown MA 02172

CRIST, CLAUDE KENNETH, retail food co. exec.; b. Clarence, Iowa, Nov. 2, 1918; s. Harry H. and Ruth R. (Berryhill) C.; B.S. in Commerce, U. Iowa, 1940; m. Atha Kincaid, Sept. 11, 1948; children—Ron, Marlys. Auditor, Iowa Tax Commn., Des Moines 1940-42; with Hy Vee Food Stores, Inc., Chariton, Iowa, 1946—, sec., v.p., 1977—. Mem. Chariton Library Bd., 1964—, chmn., 1972-74; bd. dirs. Chariton Area Devel. Corp., 1972-75, Lucas County Jud. Magistrate Appointing Commn., 1973—; mem. Lucas County Sheriff's Posse, 1968—; bd. dirs. Lucas County chpt. ARC, 1958-79. Bd. dir. Lucas County Meml. Hosp., 1971—, chmn., 1975-77. Mem. Adminstrv. Mgmt. Soc. (Diamond Merit award 1975, pres. Des Moines chpt. 1973-74). Republican. Methodist (adminstrv. bd. 1970-76, trustee 1977-79). Mason (Shriner), Rotarian. Home: Route 5 Chariton IA 50049 Office: 1801 Osceola Ave Chariton IA 50049

CRIST, FREDERIC EUGENE, lawyer, corp. exec.; b. Dayton, Ohio, Dec. 1, 1916; s. William A. and Devone (Double) C.; LL.B., N.Y. U., 1950; m. Leta M. Clark, Apr. 8, 1939; children—Barbara D., Beverly G. Admitted to N.Y. bar, 1950, also U.S. Supreme Ct. bar; asst. to pres. Parker Hannafin Co., 1939-42; personnel dir., asst. to pres. Jaeger Instrument Co., 1942-51; indsl. adminstr. A.M.F. Inc., Co., 1951-53; sec., dir. Sun Chem. Corp., Long Island City, N.Y., 1953-57; dir. indsl. relations Barnes Group, Inc., Bristol, 1957-59, v.p., 1959-64, exec. v.p., 1964-66, dir., mem. exec. com., 1960—; pres., dir., mem. exec. com. Electronic Splty. Co., Los Angeles, 1966-68; exec. v.p., dir., mem. exec. com. Burns Internat. Security Services, Inc., Briarcliff Manor, N.Y., 1968-70, pres., 1970-72, chmn. bd., 1972-78. Bd. dirs. Barnes Group, Inc. Mem. N.Y. State Bar Assn. Clubs: Mason (K.T., Shriner), Order Eastern Star, Union League, Mt. Kisco Country, Whispering Pines, Hundred, Explorers, Heritage Hills Country. Home: 196 B Bogie Dr Whispering Pines NC 28327

CRISWELL, GARY LEE, accounting co. exec., real estate agt.; b. York, Pa., May 27, 1938; s. LeRoy F. and Lida M. (Strong) C.; B.S. in Accounting, U. Ky., 1976; m. Sadie Louise Kincaid, Dec. 23, 1957; children—Mike Wayne, Tracy Anneen. Revenue investigator dept. revenue Commonwealth of Ky., Lexington, 1960-62; sales rep. Kimberly-Clark Corp., Lexington, Huntington, W.Va., 1962-65; exec. asst. area program devel. office Commonwealth of Ky., Frankfort, 1965-67; pres. Criswells & Assos., Inc., Lexington, 1967-72; pvt. practice public acctg., Lexington, 1973—; sec., treas., dir. Day's Auto Parts, Inc.; real estate sales Wendell Tackett, broker, 1980—; instr. accounting U. Ky. Served with USAF, 1955-58. Lic. real estate agt., Ky. Mem. Nat., Ky. assns. accountants, Nat. Soc. Public Accountants (dir. 1970-74), Accreditation Council for Accountancy, Beta Alpha Psi. Presbyterian. Home: 1628 Linstead Dr Lexington KY 40504 Office: 1628 Linstead Dr Lexington KY 40504

CRITCHLOW, DAVID STEPHEN, health care cons.; b. Phila., Mar. 17, 1948; s. Harold Stephen and Adelaide (Hamlin) C.; B.A., Heidelberg Coll., 1971; M.Ed., Boston U., 1974; m. Mary Ann Regan, July 29, 1973; 1 dau., Jessica. Admitting officer Boston City Hosp., 1971-72; adminstrv. mgr. Peter Bent Brigham Hosp., Boston, 1972-74; mgr. Cambridge (Mass.) Hosp., 1975-76; v.p. Multi-Phasic Health Systems, Inc., Woburn, Mass., 1976—; mem. med. adv. bd. Aquinas Jr. Coll., Middlesex Community Coll. Mem. Council on Aging, Town of Marshfield, Mass. Mem. Mass. Med. Group Mgmt. Assn., Mass. Public Health Assn. Home: 137 Orchard Rd Marshfield MA 02050 Office: 304 Cambridge Rd Woburn MA 01801

CROCCHIOLO, ANDREW JOHN, hotel exec.; b. N.Y.C., June 7, 1935; s. Paul Andrew and Marion Veronica (Hickey) C.; B.S., Loyola U., New Orleans, 1956. Owner, operator Lafitte Guest House, New Orleans, 1965-70; mgr. Griswold Inn, Essex, Conn., 1970-73; night mgr. Waldorf Astoria Hotel, N.Y.C., 1973-75; gen. mgr. Holiday Inn Coliseum, N.Y.C., 1975—; cons. Hotel Motel Assn. Ednl. Inst. Served with Armed Forces, 1957-60. Mem. Hotel Assn. N.Y.C., Internat. Hotel Sales Mgmt., Hotel Execs. Club Inc., N.Y. State Hotel and Motel Assn. (co-chmn. cons. legis. com.). Republican. Roman Catholic. Home: Box 113 Bunny Brook Farm Beech Hill Rd Colebrook CT 06021 Office: 440 W 57th St New York NY 10019

CROCKETT, DAVID ARTHUR, JR., ins. co. exec.; b. Los Angeles, Apr. 22, 1930; s. David A. and Martha Percilla (Sherwood) C.; B.A. in Journalism, Fresno State Coll., 1957; m. Lillanbelle Hollister, Sept. 5, 1952; children—Cathleen Kimberly, David Arthur III, Stephen Glenn. Agy. service rep. Travelers Ins. Co., Fresno, Calif., 1957-58, field supr., San Francisco, 1959-61, asst. mgr., 1961-62, agy. mgr., Stockton, Calif., 1962-69, life, health and fin. services mgr., Sacramento, 1969—. Served with Intelligence, USAF, 1950-54. Recipient Spoke award Stockton Jr. C. of C., 1964; Travelers Mgmt. Leadership award 1969, 71, 74, 78; named Boss of Year Life Ins. Cashiers and Office Mgrs. Assn., 1977. Mem. Nat. Assn. Life Underwriters, Sacramento Life Underwriters Assn., Gen. Agts. and Mgmt. Assn. (past pres., nat. award 1975), Sacramento C. of C., Internat. Assn. Fin. Planners (past v.p. Sacramento chpt. 1972), Air Force Assn., VFW, Alpha Phi Gamma. Republican. Clubs: Elks, Comstock, Sacramento Exchange. Home: 3920 Orangewood Dr Fair Oaks CA 95628 Office: 555 University St Sacramento CA 95825

CROCKETT, GWENDOLYN BAILEY, lawyer, govt. ofcl.; b. Monroe, Ia.; d. Isaac and Maggie (Duncan) B.; B.A., So. U., Baton Rouge, 1954, J.D., 1958; children—John A., Jr., Donald C. Admitted to La. bar, 1958, D.C. bar, 1973, U.S. Supreme Ct., 1970; instr. law So. U. Law Sch., 1961-67; dir. Legal Aid Soc., Baton Rouge, 1967-72; atty.-adv. U.S. Dept. Labor, Washington, 1972-73; trial atty. U.S. Consumer Product Safety Commn., Washington, 1973-79, spl. asst. to commr., 1979-80; dir. planning and adminstrn. legal systems SSS, Washington, 1980—. Recipient Disting. Service award Legal Aid Soc., Baton Rouge, 1972; Chmn.'s Superior Performance award Consumer Product Safety Commn., 1978, EEO spl. citation, 1978. Mem. Nat. Bar Assn., Washington Bar Assn., D.C. Bar Assn., La. Bar Assn., Nat. Assn. Black Women Lawyers. Home: 7423 Calder Dr Capitol Heights MD 20027

CROFFORD, VERN EDWARD, engine co. exec.; b. Grandview, Mo., July 10, 1931; s. Vern and Geneva Babin (DeBose) C.; student N. Western Sch. Taxidermy, 1957; m. Margarette Louise Meadows, Feb. 7, 1953; children—Duane, Darrell Mark, Kathy Jo. Shop foreman Brewster Co., Shreveport, La.; plant mgr. Moran Tank Co., Natchez, Miss.; gen. supt. Channler Welding Service, Harvey, La.; supt. Houma Welders, Harvey; now owner, gen. mgr. Vern's Small Engine & Supply Co., Vidalia, La. Mem. Vidalia C. of C. (pres. 1979), United Assn. Steam Fitters and Plumbers. Democrat. Baptist. Clubs: Lions, Masons. Home: Ivy Rd Vidalia LA 71373 Office: 1108 Carter St Vidalia LA 71373

CROFT, ROBERT ARTHUR, mfg. co. exec.; b. N.Y.C., July 19, 1934; s. John Arthur and Jennie Doris (Robinson) C.; student Mercy Coll., 1972-73, Southwestern U., 1975-76; m. Edna Evelyn Haskins, Aug. 6, 1955; children—Jeffrey Scott, Randall Alan, Jennifer Lynn. Enlisted U.S. Navy, 1952, ret., 1974; supr. lab. diving Tarrytown (N.Y.) Labs., 1974-76; v.p. ops. Teach Tour Diving Co., Nazareth, Pa., 1976-77; mgr. tng. Turbo Machinery Div., Ingersoll Rand Co., Phillipsburg, N.J., 1977—. Chmn. fund drive Multiple Sclerosis Soc., New London, Conn., 1968. Elected to Internat. Swimming Hall of Fame; named Outstanding Young Man of Yr., Conn. Jr. C. of C., 1969. Mem. Am. Soc. Tng. and Devel., W.W. II Submarine Vets., Fleet Res. Assn. Club: Ingersoll Rand Engring. Explorer Post of Boy Scouts Am. U.S. record holder for breathhold diving. Home: 552 Roundtable Dr Nazareth PA 18064 Office: 942 Memorial Pkwy Phillipsburg NJ 08865

CROGHAN, HAROLD HEENAN, lawyer, mfg. co. exec.; b. Sioux City, Iowa, May 20, 1924; s. Edmond Harold and Marie (Heenan) C.; A.B., Lawrence U., Appleton, Wis., 1947; J.D., Cornell U., 1953; m. Mary Gertrude Murphy, Feb. 4, 1948; children—Catherine, John, Loretta, Margaret. Admitted to N.Y. bar, 1953, Mo. bar, 1953, Ohio bar, 1967; asso. firms in Kansas City, 1953-56; corp. counsel Kansas City Gas Service Co., 1956-66; house counsel, then asst. sec.-corp. counsel Philips Industries Inc., Dayton, Ohio, 1966-68, v.p., sec., corp. counsel, treas., 1968-78, exec. v.p. adminstrn., gen. counsel, 1978—, also dir.; dir. Dexter Axle Co., Winbro, Inc., Malta Mfg. Co. Served with USMCR, 1942-46, 50-52. Decorated Navy Cross, Silver Star, Bronze Star, Purple Heart. Mem. Mo. Bar Assn., Ohio Bar Assn., Dayton Bar Assn., Pvt. Carrage Conf. (dir.), Phi Beta Kappa, Phi Delta Theta, Phi Delta Phi. Roman Catholic. Clubs: Dayton City, Dayton Racquet, Chancery, Vanguard, Rockhill, Hollinger Tennis (Dayton). Home: 609 Garden Rd Dayton OH 45419 Office: 4801 Springfield St Dayton OH 45401

CROM, JAMES OLIVER, adult edn. exec.; b. Alliance, Nebr., July 31, 1933; s. James Harvey and Evalyn Grace (Robinson) C.; B.S., U. Wyo., 1955; m. Rosemary Vanderpool, Jan. 30, 1953; children—Michael Alexander, Marie Celeste, Brenda Leigh. Sales rep. Investors Diversified Services, 1955-57; dist. supt. King Merritt & Co., 1957-59; with Dale Carnegie & Assos., Inc., Garden City, N.Y., 1959—, dir. ops., all courses, 1964-67, v.p. field ops., 1967-74, exec. v.p., gen. mgr., 1974-78, pres., 1978—, v.p. Dorothy Carnegie Found. Past pres. L.I. Ednl. TV Council, Inc.; mem. L.I. Action Com. Served with USAF, 1951-52. Mem. L.I. Assn. Commerce and Industry, U.S. C. of C. Republican. Methodist. Home: Laurel Hollow NY 11791 Office: 1475 Franklin Ave Garden City NY 11530

CRONICAN, RICHARD ALAN, computer co. mgr.; b. Yonkers, N.Y., Sept. 5, 1943; s. John G. Sr., and Josephine M. (Ness) C.; student U. Ariz., 1966—; m. Dana S. Yarian, July 3, 1965; children—Kimberly and Kelly (twins), Timothy Alan. Patrolman, police dept. City of Tucson, 1966-69, detective, 1969-70, programmer, analyst dept. fin., 1970-73, sys/prog supr., 1973-74, dir. dept. computer services, 1974-81; regional mgr. Systems & Computer Technology Corp., Malvern, Pa., 1981—; guest lectr. U. Ariz., 1970—, Pima Coll., 1970—; cons. City of Phoenix, S. Tucson. Ordained deacon, Roman Catholic Ch., 1976; bd. dirs. Armory Park Found., 1977—, AMIGOS Bibliog. Council, Dallas; chmn. Diocese of Tucson Pastoral Council, 1977—, also adult religious instr.; mem. advisory council Pima Coll., Tucson, 1975—. Served with USAF, 1961-65. Mem. Am. Mgmt. Assn., Urban and Regional Info. Systems Assn. (chmn. DP mgmt. spl. interest group), Data Processing Mgmt. Assn. Club: Kiwanis. Home: 9130 E Chof Ovi Dr Tucson AZ 85715 Office: 4 Country View Rd Malvern PA 19355

CRONIN, KATHLEEN ANNE, exec. recruiter; b. Oak Park, Ill., Sept. 17, 1933; d. Brendan C. and Rose J. (Mangini) Powell; B.A., DePaul U., 1977; m. Richard J. Cronin, May 29, 1954; children—Anne, Patrick, Richard J., Edward, John, Michael, Eileen. Sec., credit asst. Hills Bros. Coffee, 1951-53; estimator Alpha Portland Cement, 1953-54; v.p. adminstrn. and research Hodge-Cronin & Assos., Inc., Rosemont, Ill., 1977—. Mem. Human Relations Com., City of Des Plaines, 1971-72; pres. St. Mary Sch. Bd., Des Plaines, 1969-71. Cert. CPR instr. Mem. Assn. Exec. Recruiter Cons., Ill. Center for Parapsychol. Research. Clubs: Meadow, Chgo. Athletic. Home: 1450 Harding Ave Des Plaines IL 60016 Office: 9575 W Higgins Rd Suite 602 Rosemont IL 60018

CRONIN, RICHARD JOSEPH, exec. search cons.; b. Chgo., Oct. 4, 1930; s. Patrick Joseph and Nell E. Cronin; B.S. in Edn., Xavier U., Cin., 1974; m. Kathleen Anne Powell, May 29, 1954; children—Anne, Patrick, Richard, Edward, John, Michael, Eileen. Personnel mgr. Admiral Corp., Chgo., 1956-58; div. mgr., employment ITT Kellogg, Chgo., 1958-63; co-founder, pres. Hodge-Cronin & Assos., Inc., Rosemont, Ill., 1963—. Pres. St. Mary's Parish PTA, 1968-69; co-chmn. Oakton Community Coll. Study Com., 1971; mem. athletic bd. Xavier U., 1980—. Served with U.S. Army, 1953-55. Accredited Am. Soc. for Personnel Adminstrn. Mem. Assn. Exec. Recruiting Consultants (dir.). Clubs: Chgo. Athletic Assn.; Meadow; Xavier U. Bus. (pres. 1975-78). Home: 1450 Harding Ave Des Plaines IL 60016 Office: 9575 W Higgins Rd Rosemont IL 60018

CRONKWRIGHT, JACK ELGIN, motor transport co. exec.; b. Simcoe, Ont., Can., Aug. 28, 1940; s. Melvin Clifford and Mabel Helen (Carpenter) C.; B.A. in Bus. Adminstrn. with honors, U. Western Ont., 1965; children—Jill Arden, Jennifer Susan, Jordan David. Student-in-accounts Clarkson, Gordon & Co., London, Ont., 1965-68; controller Cronkwright Transport Ltd., Simcoe, 1968-74, v.p. fin. and adminstrn., 1974-79, pres., gen. mgr., 1979—; pres., gen. mgr. Cronkwright Leaseholds Ltd., Rajjall Ltd. Chartered acct. Mem. Inst. Chartered Accts. Ont., Can. Inst. Chartered Accts., Ont. Trucking Assn. (owner-operator com., welfare com., taxation com.), Simcoe C. of C. (membership chmn., dir. 1972-73). Baptist. Home: 161 Maple St Simcoe ON N3Y 2G5 Canada Office: 405 Queensway W Simcoe ON N3Y 2N4 Canada

CROOKS, DONALD LAWRENCE, fin. exec.; b. Jersey City, Mar. 1, 1946; s. Vincent Lawrence and Dorothy (Blackburn) C.; B.S. in Edn., Wagner Coll., 1969, M.B.A. in Fin., 1972; Ph.D., Calif. Western U., 1980; m. Carol Ann Caldwell, Aug. 26, 1967; children—Donald Edward, Allyson Caldwell, Casey Blackburn, Brady Breheney. Sr. trader Shearson & Hammill, securities co., N.Y.C., 1969-71; sr. trader Oppenheimer & Co., N.Y.C., 1971-76, special partner, 1971-76; v.p., sr. trader Allen & Co., Inc., N.Y.C., 1976—; registered rep.; condr. industry seminars. Coach wrestling team Twp. Bernards, Basking

Ridge, N.J., 1977—. Mem. Nat. Assn. Security Dealers. Lutheran. Achieved rank of black belt in Okinawan Isshinryn Karate in record time of 8 mos.; instr. Karate for 12 yrs.; holder 4th degree black belt. Home: 56 Canter Dr Basking Ridge NJ 07920 Office: 711 Fifth Ave New York NY 10022

CROOKS, WALTER, chemist, computer co. exec.; b. Warrington, Lancashire, Eng., Jan. 8, 1931; s. Joseph and Millie (Broadhurst) C.; student Wigan and Dist. Mining and Tech. Coll., 1951-60; m. Barbara Johnson, May 7, 1954; children—Gary Walter, Kimberlee Anne. Research scientist, project leader W.Va. Pulp & Paper Co., Williamsburg, Pa., 1960-65; mem. research staff, scientist, mgr. IBM, San Jose, Calif., 1966—, mgr. materials and engring. technology Office Products div., 1969—. Served with Brit. Army, 1949-51. Recipient 8 Outstanding Invention awards IBM, 1974, 78, Invention Plateau awards, 1970, 71, 76, 79, 80. Fellow Royal Inst. Chemistry (chartered chemist); mem. Chem. Soc., Calif. Soc. Photog. Scientists and Engrs., Peninsula Soccer League (dir. 1978-79). Republican. Episcopalian. Patentee non-impact printing. Home: 119 Loma Vista Ct Los Gatos CA 95030 Office: IBM 5600 Cottle Rd San Jose CA 95193

CROOM, ESTELLE LUCKEY, life ins. co. exec.; b. Gibson, Tenn., Dec. 22, 1917; d. Fred Wilson and Corinne (Fly) Luckey; ed. high sch.; m. John Guthrie Croom, Mar. 3, 1933; children—John Harold, Wilson Buckley, Michael Luckey. Sec. Humboldt (Tenn.) 1st Baptist Ch., 1945-46; with John M. Senter & Sons, ins. and real estate, Humboldt, 1954-64; pres. Croom & Cobb Insurors, Humboldt and Bells, Tenn., 1964-69; sec. Mid-West Nat. Life Ins. Co., Nashville, 1969-71, v.p., 1971-76, exec. v.p., 1976—, also dir., mem. exec. com.; dir. Mid-West Nat. Life Co., Webster's Ency. Sales, Crusade Enterprises Inc., Am. Lab. Inst. Pres. Humboldt Band Parents Club, 1965-66. Mem. Tenn. Assn. Life Ins. Cos., Nashville Assn. Life Underwriters, Nat. Ins. Assn. (conv. co-chmn. 1976). Baptist. Club: Humboldt Bus. Women's (pres. 1963-64). Home: 135 Honeysuckle Ln Humboldt TN 38343 Office: 1161 Murfreesboro Rd Nashville TN 37217

CROSBY, DOUGLAS WEEKS, computer co. ofcl.; b. Norfolk, Va., June 28, 1953; s. Ralph R. and Joan B. (Hastings) C., Jr.; B.A. in Polit. Sci., Randolph-Macon Coll., 1975. Teller, Bank of Va., Richmond, 1976-77; sales rep. NCR Corp., Richmond, 1977-78; mktg. rep. SEC Computer Co., Richmond, 1979—. Mem. Phi Delta Theta. Club: Bank of Va. President's. Home: 6436 Primrose Pl Richmond VA 23225 Office: 6600 W Broad St Richmond VA 23230

CROSBY, GORDON EUGENE, JR., ins. co. exec.; b. Remson, Iowa, Nov. 14, 1920; s. Gordon E. and Florence (Plummer) C.; grad. Kemper Mil. Sch., 1938; student U. Mo., 1938-40; m. Betty Jo Hubbard, May 2, 1942; children—Gordon Eugene III, Douglas H. Agt., New Eng. Life Ins. Co., Knoxville, Tenn., 1945-59, agy. supr. Oakland, Calif., 1946, agy. mgr., Seattle, 1947-50, gen. agt., Seattle, 1948-59; v.p., dir. agys., U.S. Life Ins. Co., N.Y.C., 1959-62, sr. v.p., dir. agys., 1962-64, exec. v.p., 1964-66, pres., chief exec. officer, 1966-67, chmn., dir., 1967—; chmn., chief exec. officer USLIFE Corp., 1967—; chmn. USLIFE Life Ins. Co. Calif., USLIFE Credit Life Ins. Co. Ill., Gt. Nat. Life Ins. Co., Tex., Old Line Life Ins. Co. Am., Milw., USLIFE Title Ins. Co., Dallas, USLIFE Title Ins. Co. N.Y., USLIFE Systems Corp., N.Y., USLIFE Credit Corp., Schaumberg, Ill., USLIFE Equity Sales Corp., N.Y.C., USLIFE Advisers, Inc., N.Y., USLIFE Real Estate Services Corp., Dallas, USLIFE Realty Corp., N.Y., USLIFE Savs. & Loan Assn. Calif., USLIFE Real Estate Securities Corp., Dallas, All Am. Life & Casualty Co., Chgo., Gen. United Life Ins. Co., Des Moines, USLIFE Income Fund, N.Y., Lincoln Liberty Life Ins. Co. (Nebr.), Sooner Life Ins. Co., Ponca City, Okla., Security of Am. Life Ins. Co., Reading, Pa.; mem. Manhattan East Adv. Bd., Mfrs. Hanover Trust; mem. public relations and econ. policy com. Am. Council Life Ins.; trustee Coll. of Ins. Mem. dean's adv. council Coll. Bus. and Public Adminstrn., U. Mo., Columbia; adv. to Office of Chmn., Manhattan Eye, Ear and Throat Hosp.; trustee, asst. treas., mem. long-range planning com. Fifth Ave Presbyn. Ch. Served to lt. USNR, World War II; PTO. Decorated Bronze Star. Mem. Newcomen Soc., U. Mo. Alumni Assn., Sigma Chi. Clubs: Economic, India House, Anglers, Brook (N.Y.C.), Long Island. Home: 50 Sutton Pl S New York NY 10022 Office: 125 Maiden Ln New York NY 10038

CROSBY, PHILIP BAYARD, mgmt. cons.; b. Wheeling, W. Va., June 18, 1926; s. Edward Karg and Mary (Campbell) C.; student Western Res. U., 1946-49, West Liberty State Coll., 1946; Dr. Surg. Chiropody, Ohio Coll. Chiropody, 1950; postgrad. Indsl. Coll. Armed Forces, 1964; m. Shirley May Jones, May 1, 1947; children—Philip Bayard, Phylis B. With Crosley div. AVCO, Richmond, Ind., 1953-55, Bendix Co., Mishawaka, Ind., 1955-57; quality mgr. Pershing weapons system, supplier quality mgr. Martin-Orlando, Orlando, Fla., 1957-65; v.p., dir. quality IT&T, N.Y.C., 1965-79; chief exec. Philip Crosby Assos., Winter Park, Fla., 1979—. Served with M.C., USNR, 1944-46, 51-52. Recipient Dept. Def. outstanding civilian service award for creating Zero Defects concept, 1970. Mem. Internat. Acad. Quality, Am. Soc. Quality Control (pres. 1979-80). Republican. Congregationalist. Clubs: Stanwich Country (Greenwich, Conn.); N.Y. Athletic (N.Y.C.); John's Island (Vero Beach, Fla.); Bay Hill (Orlando, Fla.). Author: Cutting the Cost of Quality, 1967; The Strategy of Situation Management, 1969; The Art of Getting Your Own Sweet Way, 1972; Quality Is Free, 1978. Home: 1711 Barcelona Way Winter Park FL 32789 Office: 201 W Canton Ave Winter Park FL 32789

CROSBY, WILLIAM EVERETT, airline co. exec.; b. Mineola, N.Y., Feb. 16, 1934; s. Everett Linwood and Grace Louise (Johnson) C.; B.Liberal Arts, U. Okla., M.A., 1974; m. Jacqueline Bergel, Apr. 26, 1961; children—Maxine, Claire. Sr. systems analyst Am. Airlines, N.Y.C., 1964-66, mgr. airport passenger service, Boston, 1966-67, LaGuardia Airport, N.Y., 1967-69, mgr. ramp service, J.F. Kennedy Airport, N.Y.C., 1969-71, mgr. passenger service, Buffalo, 1971-74, mgr. services Dallas/Ft. Worth, 1974-76, gen. mgr., 1976-79, v.p. So. region, 1979—. Served with U.S. Army, 1957-59. Mem. Nat. Assn. Bus. Economists. Home: 2300 Rolling Hills Trail Arlington TX 76011 Office: PO Box 61047 Dallas/Fort Worth Airport TX 75261

CROSS, DENNIS WARD, ins. co. exec.; b. Santa Barbara, Calif., Sept. 22, 1943; s. Ward H. and Durith Ann (Stoner) C.; B.S., Ill. Wesleyan U., 1965; M.B.A., Ind. U., 1967; C.L.U., Am. Coll., 1972; m. Judith M. Marston, Feb. 5, 1967; children—Douglas, Kimberly. Dir. consultation projects Life Ins. Mktg. and Research Assn., Hartford, Conn., 1970-75; asst. v.p. sales USAA Life Ins. Co., San Antonio, 1975-78, v.p. sales, 1978—; instr., hon. faculty Army Logistics Mgmt. Center, Ft. Lee, Va., 1968-70; guest instr. U. Tex., San Antonio, 1970—, San Antonio Coll., 1978-81, sr. v.p. sales, 1981—. Served as capt. U.S. Army, 1967-70. Mem. Am. Soc. C.L.U.'s, Life Advertisers Assn., Life Ins. Mktg. and Research Assn., Am. Mgmt. Assn., Life Office Mgmt. Assn.), Am. Mktg. Assn., Am. Advt. Fedn., Army Res. Assn. Home: 7206 Winterwood St San Antonio TX 78229 Office: 9800 Fredericksburg Rd San Antonio TX 78288

CROSS, GEOFFREY R., business exec.; married. Vice pres. Sperry Rand Corp., 1958-72; pres. Internat. Computers Ltd., 1972-77; pres. GEC Enterprises Corp., 1978-79; pres., chief exec. officer A.B. Dick Co., Chgo., 1979—. Office: AB Dick Co 5700 W Touhy Ave Chicago IL 60648*

CROSS, LOUISE PORTLOCK, mfg. co. exec.; b. Norfolk, Va., Jan. 20, 1907; d. William Seth and Mary Louise (Fanshaw) Portlock; grad. high sch.; m. James Byron Cross, July 17, 1929; 1 dau., Blanche Louise. With J.B. Cross, Inc., Norfolk, 1952—, exec. pres. 1959-60, pres., chief exec. officer, 1960—. Mem. Phi Sigma Alpha (charter mem.). Episcopalian. Mem. Order Eastern Star, Oriental Shrine of N. Am. Home: 500 Pacific Ave Virginia Beach VA 23451 Office: 3797 Progress Rd Norfolk VA 23502

CROSS, MORTON DAVIDSON (DAVID), mfg. co. exec.; b. Dedham, Mass., July 16, 1938; s. Harry King and Regina (Vachon) C.; B.A. in History, Yale U., 1960; m. Suzanne Dursin, Oct. 26, 1963; children—Suzanne, Alexandra, Marilyn, Virginia. Office mgr. R.I. Tool Co., 1962-73; asst. treas. Apco Mossberg Co., Attleboro, Mass., 1973-76, plant mgr., 1976-78, pres., owner, 1978—. Corp. mem. R.I. Hosp., Women and Infants Hosp. Served to 2d lt. USAF, 1962-66. Mem. ASME, Wire Assn. Republican. Roman Catholic. Club: Agawam Hunt. All-Am. hammer throw, 1960. Office: 100 Lamb St Attleboro MA 02703

CROSS, RAYMOND JOSEPH, JR., chem. co. exec., gas co. mgr.; b. Ithaca, N.Y., July 3, 1935; s. Raymond Joseph and Janet (Cleveland) C.; B.S.M.E., Ga. Inst. Tech., Atlanta, 1958; postgrad. U. Tampa, 1961; M.S. in Indsl. Mgmt., Purdue U., Hammond, Ind., 1972; m. Marguerite Adele Ciani, Nov. 17, 1956; children—Raymond Joseph III, John Alexander, Donald James. With Linde div. Union Carbide Corp., Chgo., 1958—, product mgr., N.Y.C., 1972-74, ops. mgr., Chgo., 1974-76, region mgr. Central U.S., Cleve., 1976-77, Midwest regional mgr., Chgo., 1977—; dir. East Chicago Machine Tool Corp. Mem. tax adv. council Lake County, Ill., 1969-70; mem. adv., council businessmen Congressman Adam Benjamin, 1978-81; bd. dirs. ARC, 1972; pres. Griffith United Fund, 1967-68; treas. Lake County Young Reps., 1965-66. Served to capt. U.S. Army, 1958-59. Mem. ASME, Ga. Inst. Tech. Alumni Assn., Purdue U. Alumni Assn. Lake County, Purdue U. Lafayette Alumni Assn. Presbyterian. Author: Guided Missile Propellants, 1959. Office: 120 S Riverside Plaza Chicago IL 60606

CROSS, REX DEVERS, hardware mfg. co. exec.; b. Syracuse, N.Y., Feb. 13, 1922; s. Clarence and Mildred (Ferguson) C.; student Tulane U., 1941; m. Geneive Hinman, June 20, 1945 (div. 1955); children—Alexander, Melissa; m. 2d, Joy Thompson, Jan. 27, 1957 (div. 1967). Vice pres. Johnson Pump Co. div. Youngstown Sheet & Tube Co., 1951-53; pres. Rex D. Cross Inc., mgmt. cons., 1953-55; v.p. H.K. Porter Co. Inc., 1955-57; pres. Pomeroy Inc., Stamford, Conn., 1957—, chmn. bd., chief exec. officer, 1960—; dir., mem. exec. com. Lone Star Industries; dir., mem. exec. com. Ames Iron Works; dir. Fitzgibbons Boiler Co., Unique Sash Balance Co. Ltd., Unique Balance Co., Unique Balance Co. Eng., Unique Balance Co. Brazil. Served with USCGR, 1942-45. Clubs: Blind Brook (Purchase, N.Y.); Brook Hollow, Preston Trail (Dallas); Belair (Los Angeles); Seminole (Palm Beach, Fla.); Westchester Country (Rye, N.Y.). Office: 375 Fairfield Ave Stamford CT 06904

CROSS, ROBERT C., mfg. co. exec.; b. Naples, Italy, July 15, 1917; came to U.S., 1922, naturalized, 1927; s. Giovanni and Elvira (Vacca) Pompeo; B.A. equivalent, New Eng. Conservatory of Music; m. Phyllis Eleanor Hubert, Apr. 7, 1946; children—Virginia Elvira Cross Kolander, Robert C. Concert pianist, 1925-41; choral condr., 1938-40; tchr. High Mowing Sch., Wilton, N.H., 1946-1951, Kendall Hall Sch., Peterboro, N.H., 1947-51; pres., gen. mgr. H.J. O'Shea Assos. and Employers Service Bur., mgmt. cons., Chgo., 1951-68; dir. tng. House of Correction, Chgo., 1965-68; v.p., dir. indsl. relations KMS Industries, Inc., Ann Arbor, Mich., 1968-72; v.p. personnel and adminstrn. Advo System, Inc., Hartford, Conn., 1972-74; v.p. indsl. relations Milton Roy Co., St. Petersburg, Fla., 1975—. Served with AUS, 1941-46. Mem. Am. Mgmt. Assn. Club: Masons. Home: 7610 135th St N Seminole FL 33542 Office: Milton Roy Co 1 Plaza Place NE Saint Petersburg FL 33707

CROSS, ROBERT MICHAEL, banker; b. Eau Claire, Wis., Nov. 26, 1938; s. George H. and Dolly O. (Cross); diploma Minn. Sch. Bus., 1958-59; B.S., U. Wis., 1963; m. Judith Ann Kruse, Dec. 26, 1963; children—Michael, David. Asst. v.p. 1st. Southdale Nat. Bank, Edina, Minn., mgr. Calif. 1st. Bank, Newport, 1972-77; v.p. Citizens Bank, Costa Mesa, Calif., 1977—; pres. Bankers Investors Group Inc., 1978—; chief exec. officer ILCO Fin. Inc., 1980—; lectr. in field. Served with USNR, 1963-65. Mem. Newport Harbor (Calif.) C. of C. (dir. 1976-78), Bayside Mchts. Assn. (treas. 1974-77), Am. Inst. Banking (nat. conv. 1970—, gov. region 4 Calif. chpt.), Saddleback Valley Aquatics-Mission Viejo (pres. 1976-77, 79), Wis. Liberal Arts Soc. River Falls. Roman Catholic. Clubs: Bahia Corinthian Yacht, Elks. Home: 25276 Arcadian St Mission Viejo CA 92691 Office: 2832 Walnut Ave Suite E Tustin CA 92680

CROSS, ROBERT PORTER, mfg. co. exec.; b. Wareham, Mass., Nov. 8, 1942; s. Leslie Parker and Elizabeth Ann C.; A.S.A., Bentley Coll., 1962, B.S.A., 1969; M.B.A., Northeastern U., 1972; m. Melissa Jane Fuller, Jan. 15, 1965; children—Laurie J., Robert H., Jeffrey P., Melinda A. Staff acct. Automatic Radio, Inc., Melrose, Mass., 1966-68; asst. treas., asst. sec., clk. Tyco Labs., Inc., Exeter, N.H., 1969-72, pres., gen. mgr. subs. Mule Battery Mfg. Co., Providence, R.I., 1972-75; pres. Mule Emergency Lighting, Inc., Cranston, R.I., 1975—. Served with USAF, 1964-67. Mem. Battery Council Internat., Aircraft Owners and Pilots Assn. Club: East Greenwich Yacht. Office: 600 Park Ave Cranston RI 02910

CROSS, ROBERT ROY, ins. co. exec.; b. Kansas City, Mo., May 9, 1935; s. Mathew Forbes and Irene Virginia (Kent) C.; B.S. in Phys. Sci., Stanford U., 1957; m. Nancy Jane Beck, June 27, 1959; children—Michael Roy, Karen Kathleen. Asso. casualty dept. ERC, Kansas City, Mo., 1960-62, asst. sec., 1962-68, asst. v.p., 1968-71, dept. mgr., 1971-73, v.p., 1973-80; v.p. Centennial Life Ins. Co., Mission, Kans., 1974-78, pres., chief exec. officer, 1978—; v.p. accident and health dept. ERC Corp., 1960—. Mem. Soc. C.P.C.U.'s, Kansas City Risk Selectors Club, Assn. Casualty & Surety Underwriters, Health Ins. Assn. Am., Life Ins. Coordinating Com. Episcopalian. Club: Kansas City Actuaries. Office: 5200 Metcalf Overland Park KS 66201

CROSS, THOMAS ALLAN, paint mfg. co. exec.; b. Warren, Ohio, July 17, 1947; s. Daniel Adrian and Jane (Abbey) C.; B.S. in Chem. Engring., Case Inst. Tech., 1969; M.B.A. in Mktg., Case-Western Res. U., 1973; m. Patricia Aileen Eden, Mar. 29, 1969; 1 son, Jeffrey Allan. Process engr. E.I. DuPont de Nemours & Co., Cleve., 1969-73; product mgr. Exxon Chem. Co., Houston, 1973-75; div. mgr. Sabine Industries, Houston, 1975-77; dir. mktg. Devoe & Raynolds Co., Louisville, 1977—. Recipient article award Plant Engring., 1979. Mem. Am. Mgmt. Assn., Am. Mktg. Assn., Nat. Assn. Corrosion Engrs. Contbr. numerous articles to profl. jours. Home: 2303 Hayward Rd Louisville KY 40222 Office: PO Box 7600 Louisville KY 40207

CROSS, TIMOTHY EUGENE, banker; b. Kenosha, Wis., July 20, 1954; s. Richard C. and Iris M. Cross; student Marquette U., 1972-73; basic cert. Am. Inst. Banking, 1979, gen. cert., 1980; m. Lauren S. Vincent, Aug. 3, 1974; children—Aaron V., Kathryn L. Teller, Midtown State Bank, Milw., 1974; bank mgr. trainee Valley No. Bank, Appleton, Wis., 1974-76; asst. mgr. Valley Bank of Hortonville (Wis.), 1976-77, mgr., 1978—; mgr. Valley Bank of Dale (Wis.), 1977-78. Mem. Wis. Bankers Assn., Hortonville Comml. Club (treas. 1979—, dir. 1979—). Club: Grandview Golf. Home: 622 S Nash St Hortonville WI 54944 Office: 132 E Main St Hortonville WI 54944

CROSSEN, HENRY MORGAN, mfg. exec.; b. Detroit, May 25, 1922; s. Henry Francis and Bernice (Morgan) C.; B.M.E., U. Detroit, 1950; M.S. in Indsl. Mgmt., M.I.T., 1956; m. July 7, 1945 (div.); children—Carol A., Roderick J., Mark S., Lynne M., Henry Francis II, Scott J. Vice pres. adminstrn. J. I. Case Co., 1960-63; pres., chief exec. officer Crossen Assos., Ltd., 1963-67; v.p. N. Am. ops. E.W. Bliss Co., 1967-69; chief of staff Gulf Western Indsl. Products Co., 1969-70; vice chmn. Thomas A. Miner Assos., 1970-72; pres., chief exec. officer Beloit Coll. Center Applied Research, 1972-74; Rockford (Ill.) Bus. Mgmt. Group, Inc., 1974-78, First Ill. Investment Corp., Rockford, 1978-80, Falls Products, Inc., Genoa, Ill., 1980—; cons. in field. Active, Racine (Wis.) United Community Services, Inc., 1962-68, pres., 1967-68; bd. dirs. Family Service Council, Racine, 1964-68, Urban League, Racine, 1966-68, Racine C. of C., 1964-66; bd. regents Dominican Coll., 1964-68: mem. Econ. Opportunity Com. Racine County, 1964-65; mem. Racine County Draft Bd., 1964-68; mem. nat. ednl. com. M.I.T., 1966-67; chmn. Racine Mayor's Adv. Com., 1967-68; chmn. Racine Study Com. on Orgn. Police and Fire Depts., 1967-68. Served to lt. USAAF, 1942-45. Recipient various public service awards; Alfred P. Sloan fellow, 1955-56. Mem. Am. Mgmt. Assn., Soc. Sloan Fellows. Roman Catholic. Home: 6170 Brynwood Dr Rockford IL 61111 Office: 415 E Railroad Ave Genoa IL 60135

CROSSFIELD, HARRY BERTRAM JR., steel co. exec.; b. Nashville, Mar. 29, 1924; s. Harry Bertram and Ann (Carter) C.; B.Engring., Vanderbilt U., 1949; m. Jane Moss Gilbert, June 6, 1945; children—Rebecca Lynn, Harry Bertram, John Richard. Engr., Hibbs, Howe & Reese, Architects, Memphis, 1941-43, Va. Bridge Co., Birmingham, Ala., 1949-51; asst. contracting mgr. Am. Bridge div. U.S. Steel Corp., Birmingham, 1951-57, Atlanta, 1957-62, dist. contracting mgr., 1962-65, regional contracting mgr. So. area, 1965, regional contracting mgr. Eastern area, N.Y., 1966-69, gen. contracting mgr., Pitts., 1969-75, v.p.-gen. contracting, 1975-78, pres., 1978—. Mem. bus. com., treas. Troop 21, Boy Scouts Am., 1962-63. Served with USMCR, 1943-45. Decorated Purple Heart with 2 oak leaf clusters. Mem. Am. Inst. Steel Constrn. (dist. adviser 1961-64, dir. and mem. exec. com. 1978—), Ga. Engring. Soc., Am. Soc. Mil. Engrs., Steel Plate Fabricators Assn. (dir. 1979—), Nat. Erectors Assn. (dir. 1980—). Clubs: Rotary, Duquesne, Pitts. Field. Home: 8218 Bramble Ln Pittsburgh PA 15237 Office: PO Box 2039 Pittsburgh PA 15230

CROSSLAND, EDWARD JOHN, seismograph co. exec.; b. Okmulgee, Okla., Jan. 17, 1927; s. Samuel Hess and Iva (Jones) C.; B.S., U. Tulsa, 1954; m. Joyce Gardner, Dec. 27, 1963; children—Joy Lorraine, Iva Lynn, Lisa Pauline. Engr., Philco Corp., Phila., 1950-51; research engr. Seismograph Service Corp., Tulsa, 1951-56, mgr. new product devel., 1957-59, engring. mgr. voting machine div., 1959-65, nat. marketing mgr. voting products, 1966-68, exec. engring. cons. P.E.D./Seiscor Div., 1969—. Mem. Okla. State Bd. Registration for Profl. Engrs., 1962-67, chmn., 1966-67. Trustee Tulsa State Fair Bd., 1956-57. Served with USAAF, 1945-49. Registered profl. engr., Okla. Mem. Nat., Okla. socs. profl. engrs. Patentee in field. Home: 7022 E 64th Pl Tulsa OK 74133 Office: 6200 E 41st St POB 1590 Tulsa OK 74102

CROSSLAND, RICHARD JAMES, mfg. co. exec.; b. Marion, Ohio, Nov. 13, 1943; s. Richard James and Mary Elizabeth (Taggart) C.; B.S., Case Inst. Tech., 1965; M.B.A., Case Western Res. U., 1970; m. Joyce Matos, Sept. 25, 1965; children—Catherine Elizabeth, Christine Jane. With Lamp Div., Gen. Electric Co., Cleve., 1966-71; asst. div. mgr. Ryan Homes, Indpls., 1972; with Brush Wellman, Cleve., 1973-75: v.p. mktg. ITT Holub Industries, Sycamore, Ill., 1976-79; v.p. mktg. S.K. Wellman Corp., Bedford, Ohio, 1979—. Chmn. Indsl. Div., United Fund, Sycamore, 1977; trustee Community Hosp of Bedford. Mem. Soc. Automotive Engrs., Case Western Res. U. Alumni Assn., Beta Theta Phi. Republican. Baptist. Office: 200 Egbert Rd Bedford OH 44146

CROSSLER, DEANNA MAE, ins. agt.; b. Wenatchee, Wash., July 16, 1943; d. Bing Anthony and Dorothy Leota (Keeney) Debar; grad. Internat. Corr. Schs., 1971, Wash. Sch. Ins., 1977; m. Harold L. Crossler, Apr. 19, 1969; children—Tony, Denine. Sec., Farmers Ins., Chelan, Wash., 1976-77, ins. agt., 1977—; dep. auditor Chelan County, 1979—. Chmn. Manson (Wash.) Apple Blossom Parade, 1975, co-chmn., 1976; sec. GALS, Manson, 1977-78. Mem. Nat. Assn. Life Underwriters. Methodist. Club: Soroptomists. Home: Route 1 Box 196 Manson WA 98831 Office: 123 E Woodin St PO Box N Chelan WA 98816

CROSSON, STEPHEN THOMAS, real estate appraiser; b. Dallas, Mar. 22, 1945; s. Earl T. and Mary Frances (McCauley) C.; B.B.A., N. Tex. State U., 1968; postgrad. So. Meth. U., 1974—. Chief appraiser Oak Cliff Savs. & Loan Assn., Dallas, 1972-73; regional supr. appraisal div. First Tex. Fin. Corp., 1973-74, mgr. appraisal adminstrn., 1974-76; chief exec. officer Crosson Dannis, Inc., Dallas, 1977—. Recipient Letter of Merit, Pan Am. Appraisal Conf., 1976. Mem. Am. Inst. Real Estate Appraisers, Estate Appraisers, Soc. Real Estate Appraisers. Home: 3701 Turtle Creek Blvd 6-C Dallas TX 75219 Office: 8350 N Central Expy Suite 1140 Dallas TX 75206

CROSSWHITE, BOB HERBERT, fin. exec.; b. Kansas City, Mo., Feb. 21, 1929; s. Carleton and Esther (Herbert) C.; B.S. in B.A., Rockhurst Coll., 1955; postgrad. Am. Coll. Grad. Sch., 1971—. Vice pres. Old Security Ins. Co. and Wide World Underwriters, Kansas City, Mo., 1948-69; pres., dir. Life Ins. Co. of Kan. & Bankers Equity Underwriters, Wichita, Kans., 1969-72; pres., dir. Insured Contracts, Inc., Shawnee Mission, Kans., 1972—. Served with USMCR, 1951-52. C.L.U., Mem. Life and Health Claims Assn. (pres. 1959-60), Am. Soc. C.L.U.'s, Blue Goose Internat., Profl. Agts. Assn., Nat. Assn. Life Underwriters, Ind. Ins. Agts. Am. Presbyterian. Clubs: Kansas City Ski, Risk Selectors (pres. 1958-59). Contbr. articles to profl. jours. Home: Lake Lota PO Box 11485 Kansas City MO 64112 Office: 7301 Mission PO Box 8108 Shawnee Mission KS 66208

CROTTY, HAROLD CLIFFORD, labor union exec.; b. Oregon, Wis., Sept. 17, 1911; s. John and Alma Katherine (Christensen) C.; grade trade union program Harvard Bus. Sch., 1948; m. Josephine Helen Cavanaugh, Sept. 24, 1938. With C.&N.-W. Ry. Co., 1930-45; mem. Brotherhood of Maintenance Way Employes, 1930—, dep. grand lodge pres., 1948-49, asst. to pres., 1949-58, internat. pres., 1958-80, pres. emeritus, 1980—; dir., mem. exec. bd. Union Labor Life Ins. Co. Chmn. bd. Labor Coop. Ednl. and Pub. Soc.; chmn. Maintenance of Way Polit. League; mem. transp. dept. com. nat. bd. YMCA. Mem. Nat. Commn. Libraries and Info. Sci., 1971-76. Mem.

Ry. Labor Execs. Assn. (exec. com.). Home: 4809 Holiday Dr Madison WI 53711 Office: 12050 Woodward Ave Detroit MI 48203

CROTTY, LEO WILLIAM, textile leasing co. exec.; b. Detroit, Aug. 11, 1927; s. Fergus and Evelyn (Thorn) C.; B.S. in Bus. Adminstrn., U. Dayton, 1952; m. Marilyn Ann Hauer, Apr. 18, 1953; children—Kathleen, Daniel, Kevin, Robert, Shane, James, Brian. Service mgr. Van Dyne-Crotty, Inc., Dayton, Ohio, 1948-55, v.p. sales, 1955-63, pres., 1963—, chmn. bd., chief exec. officer, 1977—. Served with USMC, 1946-48, U.S. Army, 1952-53. Mem. Young Pres.'s Orgn., Inc., Pres.'s Assn., Inc., Linen Supply Assn. Am., Inst. Indsl. Launderers, Kex Nat. Assn., Dayton Area C. of C. (dir. 1974-77), U. Dayton Alumni Assn. (dir. 1965-71). Roman Catholic. Clubs: Dayton Country, Dayton Bicycle, Dayton Racquet. Home: 758 Plantation Ln Kettering OH 45419 Office: Van Dyne-Crotty Inc 903 Brandt St Box 442 Dayton OH 45401

CROUCH, DARYL JON, wholesale drug co. exec.; b. Pitts., Aug. 3, 1949; s. George Edward and Zeldean V. (Catlin) C.; B.A., Tex. Christian U., 1971; m. Rebecca Janece Walsh, Sept. 4, 1971; 1 dau., Sandra Janice. With Cities Service Oil Co., Atlanta, 1971-72; warehouse and sales trainee Walsh Lumpkin Drug Co., Texarkana, Tex., 1972-73, asst. to pres., 1973-75, v.p., ops. mgr., 1975-78, pres., 1979—; asso. dir. Texarkana Oaklawn Bank; dir. Security Savs. Assn. Mem. Nat. Wholesale Drug Assn., Nat. Assn. Wholesalers, Texarkana C. of C. (dir.). Methodist. Club: Rotary. Office: PO Box 1918 Texarkana TX 75501

CROUCH, RALPH EDWARD, health care exec.; b. Salem, N.J., Oct. 25, 1942; s. Paul W. and Marian D. Crouch; B.S., Elizabethtown Coll., 1964; M.B.A., U. Del., 1967; m. Margaret Weiss, June 19, 1965; children—Kim, Steven. Staff acct., audit and adminstrv. service mgr. Arthur Andersen & Co., 1967-75; dir. fin. Blue Cross and Blue Shield of Del., Inc., Wilmington, 1975-77, sr. v.p., treas., 1977—. Mem. Com. of 100. C.P.A., Del. Mem. Am. Inst. C.P.A.'s, Md. Assn. C.P.A.'s, Del. Assn. C.P.A.'s, Hosp. Fin. Mgmt. Assn. Office: 201 W 14th St Wilmington DE 19899

CROUGH, DANIEL FRANCIS, lawyer; b. Syracuse, N.Y., Feb. 2, 1936; s. Vincent Leo and Sarah Jane (McMahon) C.; A.B., LeMoyne Coll., Syracuse, N.Y., 1957; J.D., Syracuse U., 1960; m. Domenica Dolores Cappadozy, July 27, 1957; children—Sara, Deborah, Maura, Deanne, Daniel. Admitted to N.Y. bar, 1961, Pa. bar, 1969; practiced law, Syracuse, N.Y., 1961-63; staff atty. Reliance Ins. Co., N.Y., Pa., 1963-71, sec., asso. gen. counsel, Phila., 1971-72; v.p., gen. counsel Cdlonial Penn Ins. Co., Phila., 1972-74; v.p., corporate counsel Colonial Penn Group, Inc., Phila., 1974-78, sr. v.p., corporate counsel, 1978—; dir. Intramerica Life Ins. Co., Colonial Penn Life Ins. Co., Colonial Penn Ins. Co., Colonial Penn Franklin Ins. Co. Bd. dirs. Citizens Crime Commn. Phila., 1978—; vice chmn. E. Whiteland Twp. Govt. Study Commn., 1973; major gifts chmn. United Fund, Canandaigua, N.Y., 1966. Mem. Am. Bar Assn., N.Y. State Bar Assn., Internat. Assn. Ins. Counsel, Pa. Bar Assn., Phila. Bar Assn. Republican. Roman Catholic. Club: Racquet (Phila.). Home: 9 Anthony Dr Frazer PA 19355 Office: 5 Penn Center Plaza Philadelphia PA 19181

CROUSE, EARL FREDERICK, ret. publisher; b. Newton, Ill., Jan. 6, 1914; s. E. Sherman and Lillian (Smallwood) C.; B.S., U. Ill., 1938; m. Frances L. Fuson, June 25, 1939; children—Kenneth, David, Annetta, Shirley. Editor farm mgmt., v.p. in charge econ. dept. Doane Agrl. Service, Inc., 1938-58; founder, chmn., pres. Farm Bus. Council, Inc., Champaign, Ill., 1958—, Bank Services, Inc., 1967-(companies merged to form BankVertising Co. 1971, pubs. newsletters The Farm Picture, MoneyWise, Money Mgr., Farm Quar., Estate Builder. Mem. Am. Soc. Farm Mgrs. and Rural Appraisers, Am. Farm Econs. Soc., Urbana, Champaign chambers commerce. Baptist. Club: Kiwanis. Co-author: Rural Appraisals, 1956. Contbr. articles to profl. jours. Home: 606 S Pinto Ct Winter Springs FL 32708

CROW, HENRY PROCTOR, JR., book distbn. co. exec.; b. Tyler, Tex., Aug. 2, 1938; s. Henry Proctor and Janie Lloyd (Bradberry) C.; student U. Tex., 1956-59; Mus.B., Ind. U., 1960; m. Susan Elizabeth Whitelock, Apr. 11, 1964; children—Kendra Elizabeth, Thomas Gareth. With Reuter Organ Co., Lawrence, Kans., 1960-71, dir. voicing, 1967-71; gen. mgr., partner Jack Martin News Agy., Tyler, 1971—; owner, mgr. East Tex. Pipe Organ Service, Tyler, 1971—. Bd. dirs. Tyler Community Concert Assn. Mem. Ind. Mag. Wholesalers Assn. South, Mid-Am Periodical Distbrs. Assn., Council Periodical Distbrs. Assns., Am. Guild Organists (past dean). Episcopalian. Clubs: Masons, Rotary, Tyler Petroleum (Tyler); Optimist (pres. Lawrence 1967-68). Home: 1002 E Dulse Tyler TX 75701 Office: 1710 Belvedere Blvd Tyler TX 75701

CROW, JAMES SYLVESTER, banker, ry. exec.; b. Mobile, Ala., June 23, 1915; s. James S. and Elizabeth (Jackson) C.; student U. Ala., 1946-48; grad. Rutgers Sch. Banking, 1959; m. Dorothy Farwell, Sept. 21, 1974; children by previous marriage—Michele Marie, Denise Anne, Marcia Lynn, Deborah Jane. Clk., 1st Nat. Bank Mobile, 1932-41, 45-48, mgr. bond dept., 1949-50, asst. cashier, 1951, asst. v.p., 1952; sales mgr. Hendrix & Mayes, Investment Bankers, Birmingham, Ala., 1952-53; asst. cashier 1st Nat. Bank Birmingham, 1954-55, asst. v.p., 1955-56, v.p., 1957-60, sr. v.p., 1961-66, exec. v.p., 1966-67; v.p. finance So. Ry. Co., Washington, 1967-70; exec. v.p. 1st Nat. Bank Mobile, 1970-71, pres., 1971-74, chmn. bd., 1974-79; chmn. bd., pres., dir. 1st Bancgroup Ala., 1973-79; chmn. bd. Ala. Assn. Ind. Colls., 1979-80; dir. Lerio Corp., Ala. Gt. So. R.R., La. So. R.R., Ala. Dry Dock & Shipbldg. Co. Trustee So. Research Inst. Mem. Ala. Bankers Assn. (v.p. 1966-67), Newcomen Soc. N.Am. Episcopalian. Clubs: Metropolitan (Washington); Metropolitan (N.Y.C.); Birmingham Country, Downtown (Birmingham). Home: PO Box 68 Montrose AL 36559

CROWDER, EDMUND, fertilizer co. exec.; b. Drumheller, Alta., Can., July 20, 1918; s. Harry and Lizzie (Colbourne) C.; student Calgary Tech. Sch., 1937-38; B.Sc. in Chem. Engring., U. Alta., 1942; m. Josephine M. Irving, May 22, 1943; children—Joseph R., Harry E. Process engr. & maintenance engr., dept. supt. Cominco Ltd., Trail, B.C., Can., 1942-55; asst. plant mgr. Best Fertilizers Co., Lathrop, Calif., 1955-56; plant supt. NW Nitro Chems., Medicine Hat., Alta., 1956-59, plant mgr., 1960-63; gen. mgr. Border Chems. Ltd., Winnipeg, Man., Can., 1964-67; v.p., gen. mgr. Simplot Chem. Co. Ltd., Brandon, Man., 1967—, also dir.; chmn. Man. Indsl. Technologies Centre. Mem. Man. Inst. Mgmt. (dir.), Can. Mfg. Assn. (dir.), Man. Assn. Profl. Engrs. Conservative. Club: Kiwanis. Home: 2517 Rosser Ave Brandon MB R7B 0E8 Canada Office: PO Box 940 Brandon MB R7A 6A1 Canada

CROWE, BYRON DAN, food co. exec.; b. Atlanta, Jan. 14, 1939; s. William Dan and Mary Ruth (Harper) C.; B.A. in Econs., Harvard U., 1962; m. Ruth A. Hearn, Feb. 1, 1980; children by previous marriage—Byron Dan, Dean Christopher, Leslie Jeanne. Fgn. exchange trader Bankers Trust Co., N.Y., 1962-65; fin. cons. dir. various corps., 1965-74; pres. GRF, Inc., mgmt. cons., Atlanta, 1974-77; pres. Munch Corp., food mfr., Forest Park, Ga., 1977-79; pres. Whitehorse Properties, Inc., Barnesville, Ga., 1980—; dir. Whitehorse Parks, Inc. Lic. real estate broker, Ga. Mem. Ga. Cattlemen's Assn. Club: Associated Harvard. Home: Route 1 Barnesville GA 30204 Office: Old 41 Hwy North Barnesville GA 30204

CROWELL, OHMER OREAL, ins. co. exec.; b. Pulaski, Va., Oct. 2, 1924; s. Ohmer Oreal and Thelma Irene (Repass) C.; B.S., Va. Poly. Inst., 1949; m. Patsy Helen Miller, June 12, 1948; children—James Douglas, Susan Patricia, Katherine Ann. With Nationwide Ins. Co., 1949—, field underwriter, Farmville, Va., 1949-50, audit supr., Columbus, Ohio, 1950-52, underwriting serviced mgr., Canton, Ohio, 1952-54, regional underwriting mgr., Lynchburg, Va., 1954-59, regional underwriting mgr., regional adminstrn. mgr., Lynchburg, 1959-60, dir. appraisals, Columbus, 1960-62, regional mgr., Trenton, 1966, 2d v.p. Medicare, Columbus, 1966-68, v.p. Medicare, 1968-69, v.p. personnel, 1969-77, v.p. central bus. ops., 1977—. Bd. dirs., exec. com. Met. YMCA; bd. dirs. Spl. Audiences, Inc., Columbus Area Leadership Program, Columbus Cancer Clinic, Better Bus. Bur. Central Ohio, Inc.; adv. bd. Nat. Alliance Businessmen. Served with U.S. Army, 1943-45, to 1st. lt., 1950-52. Mem. Am. Soc. C.L.U.'s, Soc. Charterer Property and Casualty Underwriters. Lutheran. Clubs: Kiwanis (Columbus), Masons, Elks. Home: 3430 Sunningdale Way Columbus OH 43221 Office: Nationwide Ins One Nationwide Plaza Columbus OH 43216

CROWLEY, HUBERT CAMERON, advt. exec.; b. White Plains, N.Y., May 7, 1937; s. Hubert Gentry and Mary Estelle (Whitney) C.; B.A., Amherst Coll., 1959; postgrad. in urban planning N.Y. U., 1968-73. Account exec. Doherty, Clifford, Steers & Shenfield Inc., N.Y.C., 1959-64, Needham, Harper & Steers Inc., N.Y.C., 1965-66; product mgr. Lever Bros. Co., N.Y.C., 1966-69; account supr. Ted Bates & Co., Inc., N.Y.C., 1969-74, v.p., 1971—, account dir., 1975-79, mgmt. rep., 1980—. Served with AUS, 1961-62. Mem. Psi Upsilon. Club: Univ. (N.Y.C.). Home: Riverness Landing Hill Rd East Haddam CT 06423 Office: 1515 Broadway New York NY 10036

CROWLEY, JAMES WORTHINGTON, lawyer; b. Cookville, Tenn., Feb. 18, 1930; s. Worth and Jessie (Officer) C.; B.A., George Washington U., 1950, LL.B., 1953; m. Laura June Bauserman, Jan. 27, 1951; children—James Kenneth, Laura Cynthia; m. 2d, Joyce A. Goode, Jan. 15, 1966; children—John Worthington, Noelle Virginia. Admitted to D.C. bar, 1954; underwriter, spl. agt. Am. Surety Co. of N.Y., Washington, 1953-56; adminstrv. asst., contract adminstr. Atlantic Research Corp., Alexandria, Va., 1956-59, mgr. legal dept., asst. sec., counsel, 1959-65, sec., legal mgr., counsel, 1965-67; sec. legal mgr., counsel Susquehanna Corp. (merger with Atlantic Research Corp.), 1967-70; v.p., sec., gen. counsel E-Systems, Inc. (formerly LTV Electrosystems, Inc.), Dallas, 1970—; pres., dir. Gen. Communication Co., Boston, 1962-70; v.p., dir. Cemco, Inc., Continental Electronic Systems, Inc., TAI, Inc., Serv-Air, Inc., Houston, Tex. Mem. Am. Bar Assn., Nat. Security Indsl. Assn., Am. Soc. Corp. Secs., Omicron Delta Kappa, Alpha Chi Sigma, Phi Sigma Kappa. Republican. Methodist. Home: 15211 Preston Rd 2002 Dallas TX 75248 Office: 6250 LBJ Expressway PO Box 226030 Dallas TX 75266

CROWLEY, JOHN HARDING, advt. agy. exec.; b. Chgo., Nov. 6, 1930; s. Robert Francis and Constance Mary (Wain) C.; B.S., Marquette U. Coll. Journalism, 1952, M.A., 1956; m. Dolores Estelle Hickey, Dec. 27, 1952; children—Patrick, Eileen. Promotion asst. WTMJ and WTMJ-TV, Milw., 1956; copy dir. Carl Nelson & Assos., Inc., Milw., 1956-63; pres., creative dir. John H. Crowley & Assos., Inc., Milw., 1963-65, 1973—, Crowley/Painter & Assos., Inc., 1965-73. Instr. journalism Marquette U. Past pres. St. Bernardine Guild. Served with U.S. Army, 1952-54. Mem. Milw. Advt. Club (past sec., dir.), Milw. Assn. Advt. Agencies (pres., dir.). Home: 6600 W Tower Ave Milwaukee WI 53223 Office: 3929 N Humboldt Blvd Milwaukee WI 53212

CROWLEY, JOHN SCHAFT, bus. machine co. exec.; b. Rochester, N.Y., July 21, 1923; s. Harry Burtis and Margaret Delores (Schaft) C.; B.S., U. Rochester, 1943; M.B.A., Harvard U., 1948; married; children—John, Katherine, Margaret, Sheilah. Sr. partner, McKinsey & Co., N.Y.C., 1952-77, also dir.; exec. v.p. Xerox Corp., Stamford, Conn., 1977—, also dir. Pres., Am. Found. for Blind, Helen Keller Internat.; vice chmn. Ednl. Broadcasting Corp., Sta.-WNET/13, N.Y.C.; bd. chmn. Greenwich (Conn.) Convent of Sacred Heart; mem. trustees' council U. Rochester. Served with USN, 1944-46. Republican. Roman Catholic. Clubs: Econ. (N.Y.C.); Country of Rochester; Blind Brook (Port Chester, N.Y.); Stanwich (Greenwich); Racquet and Tennis, Genesee Valley. Office: 800 Long Ridge Rd Stamford CT 06904

CROWLEY, RICHARD LLEWELLYN, ednl. adminstr.; b. Biddeford, Maine, Aug. 22, 1930; s. Llewellyn Burton and Julia Viola (Verrill) C.; student U. Maine, 1949-51; B.A., U. Va., 1958; postgrad. Harvard U., 1971; m. Barbara Reid Smith, Aug. 15, 1952; children—Richard Llewellyn, David Burton, Mark Brian, Linda Dawn. Med. technician Worcester Found. Exptl. Biology, Shrewsbury, Mass., 1958-60; tech. rep. Fisher Sci. Co., Pitts., 1960-64; asst. purchasing agt. Brown U., Providence, 1964-66, purchasing agt., 1966-68; dir. purchasing Children's Hosp. Med. Center, Boston, 1968-72; dir. purchasing Pa. State U., University Park, 1972, asst. v.p., 1972—; faculty Burdett Coll., Boston, 1971; lectr. in field; faculty Advanced Purchasing Mgmt. Inst., 1980—. Adv., Webster (Mass.) Demolay, 1962-64; Little League coach, mgr., 1964-68; v.p. Arnold Mills (R.I.) Little League, 1968, Upper Valley Little League, 1970-71; ch. steward Arnold Mills Meth. Ch., 1970. Served with USMC, 1951-54. Decorated Purple Heart; cert. purchasing mgr. Mem. R.I. Purchasing Mgmt. Assn. (dir. 1965-68), Nat. Assn. Ednl. Buyers (edn. com. 1980—, v.p.-elect 1981), Nat. Assn. Purchasing Mgmt., Sigma Alpha Epsilon, Beta Beta Beta, Phi Sigma, Delta Phi Alpha. Clubs: Elks, Lions, Masons, Tall Cedars of Lebanon, Order Eastern Star. Home: 1030 Greenbriar Dr State College PA 16801 Office: 215 Shields Bldg University Park PA 16802

CROWLEY, WALTER LEWIS, finance co. exec.; b. Oak Park, Ill., Oct. 9, 1940; s. Walter William and Jeannette (Lewis) C.; B.S., U. Ill., 1962, LL.B., 1964; m. Carole Peterson, July 30, 1966; 1 son, Matthew Scott. Admitted to Ill. bar, 1964; asso. firm Winston & Strawn, Chgo., 1964-68; sr. v.p. Greyhound Leasing and Fin. Corp., Chgo., 1968-78; exec. v.p. Gould Fin. Inc., Rolling Meadows, Ill., 1978-80, pres., 1980—. Pres., Lincoln Sch. Edn. Council, 1976-78. Mem. Ill. State Bar Assn. Club: Meadow. Office: 10 Gould Center Rolling Meadows IL 60008

CROWNINGSHIELD, GLORIA ELAINE (MRS. JOHN F. CROWNINGSHIELD), real estate broker; b. Buffalo, Feb. 15, 1925; d. Harold Theodore and Lillian Edith (Grant) Jenkins; grad. high sch.; m. John F. Crowningshield, Oct. 3, 1967; 1 dau. by previous marriage, Janet Elaine Peart. Propr., Peninsula Realty, San Diego, 1967—. Lectr. on condominium and apt. conversions. Mem. Nat. Assn. Real Estate Bds., Calif. Real Estate Assn., Point Loma Ocean Beach Realty Assn. (dir. 1969-72, pres. 1973), Peninsula C. of C. (dir. 1968—), Sunset Cliffs Anti-Erosion Assn. Home: 1054 Devonshire Dr San Diego CA 92107 Office: 1352 Sunset Cliffs San Diego CA 92107

CROZIER, WILLIAM MARSHALL, JR., bank holding co. exec.; b. N.Y.C., Oct. 2, 1932; s. William Marshall and Alice (Parsons) C.; B.A. in Econs., Yale, 1954; M.B.A. with distinction, Harvard, 1963; m. Prudence vanZandt Slitor, June 20, 1964; children—Matthew Eaton, Abigail Parsons, Patience Wells. With Hanover Bank, N.Y.C., 1954-61, asst. sec., 1959-61; with BayBanks, Inc., Boston, 1964—, v.p. and sec., 1969-73, sr. v.p. and sec., 1973-74, chmn., dir., chief exec. officer, 1974—, pres., 1977—. Served with AUS, 1955-57. Episcopalian. Clubs: Comml.-Mchts., Economic, Harvard, Union (Boston); Yale (N.Y.C.). Office: 175 Federal St Boston MA 02110

CRUM, DARRYL GENE, investment co. exec.; b. Baton Rouge, June 5, 1948; s. Edward David and Ruth Inita (Powers) C.; B.A. in Gen. Studies, N.E. La. U., 1973, postgrad. in history, 1976-79; m. Faith Anne Deslatte, Jan. 19, 1979; 1 stepson, Kelly Patrick Reaves; 1 son, Edward David II. Salesman, Harpers Supply Co., Baton Rouge, 1974-75; counsellor VA, New Orleans, 1975—; pres. So. Philatelic Investment Co., New Orleans, 1978—. Served with U.S. Army, 1969-71. Mem. N.E. La. U. Alumni Assn., Black Cat Stamp Club. Baptist. Editor: Stamp Market Hot-Line, 1980—; contbr. articles to profl. publs. Office: PO Box 50892 New Orleans LA 70150

CRUMLING, ROBERT T., III, paint mfg. co. exec.; b. Highspire, Pa., June 30, 1940; B.S., Shippensburg (Pa.) State Coll., 1964; postgrad. Temple U., Phila., 1965, Wharton Sch., U. Pa., 1966-67; m. Margaretta Klein, Dec. 14, 1962; children—Judith A., Douglas A. Contract analyst Provident Mut. Life Ins. Co., Phila., 1965-66; personnel asst. Rockwell Mfg. Co., Pitts., 1966-68; personnel mgr. Polymer Corp. div. ACF Industries, Reading, Pa., 1968-72; with Glidden C&R div. SCM Corp., 1972—, indsl. relations rep., Cleve., 1975-77, mgr. indsl. relations, 1977—; mem. Manpower Research Council, 1972—; cons. in field. Treas. baseball program Bay Men's Club, 1976—; bd. dirs. Berks County (Pa.) Camp Fire Girls, 1969-75, Council Alcoholism, Berks County, 1973-75, AWARE Drug Abuse Program, Reading, 1971-75; v.p. Reading Jaycees, 1970. Served with U.S. Army, 1959-61, 61-62. Recipient President's award Reading Jaycees, 1971, award merit Camp Fire Girls, 1975. Mem. Indsl. Relations Research Assn., Am. Soc. Personnel Adminstrn. Clubs: Avon Oaks Country, Masons, Tall Cedars of Lebanon. Home: 31205 Kimerly Dr Bay Village OH 44140 Office: 900 Union Commerce Bldg Cleveland OH 44115

CRUMMER, ROGER NELSON, communications co. exec.; b. Essexville, Mich., Dec. 21, 1931; s. John Ernest and Ethel Linea (Nelson) C.; B.S., Mich. State U., 1957; m. Jacqueline Sue Meade, Oct. 7, 1960; children;Laura Ann, James Einar, Margaret Leigh. Sr. engr. Creole Petroleum Corp., Maracaibo, Venezuela, 1957-64; supervisory engr. Page Communications Engrs., Inc., Washington, 1964-67; v.p. Telcom, Inc., Vienna, Va., 1967-75; pres. Novacom. Inc., Fairfax, Va., 1975—. Communications systems cons. Republic of Venezuela, Fed. Mil. Govt. Nigeria, Republic of Bolivia, Jordan, Saudi Arabia. Served with USN, 1949-53. Mem. IEEE. Republican. Home: 4127 Lenox Dr Fairfax VA 22032 Office: 10720 Main St Fairfax VA 22030

CRUMP, FRANK EDWARD, investment co. exec.; b. Providence, Apr. 11, 1951; s. Yusef and Rashidah AshShaheed; bus. mgmt. degree, religion degree Franklin and Marshall Coll., 1976; m. Diana Lee Ward, Feb. 12, 1972; children—Adam Michael, Yves Lauren. Gen. distbr. Holiday Magic, Inc., Balt., 1971-73; asst. to transp. mgr. Bethlehem Steel Corp., Sparrows Point, Md., 1974-75; Western regional sales mgr. Hamilton Tech., Inc., Lancaster, Pa., 1976-78; pres., chmn. bd. United Chem-Con Corp., Lancaster, 1978-80, dir., 1978—; pres., dir., chief exec. officer, chmn. bd. Unified Progress, Inc., Lancaster, 1980—. Office: 20 Charles Rd Lancaster PA 17603

CRUMP, GIVENS LINDSAY, housing exec.; b. DeKalb, Tex., Mar. 25, 1922; s. Andrew Givens and Georgia Berry (Lindsay) C.; student Paris Jr. Coll., 1939-40, N. Tex. State U., 1941-42; B.B.A., U. Tex., Austin, 1947; m. Elza Murl Hutchinson, Jan. 31, 1943; children—Leslie, Georgia Nell. Propr. dept. stores, DeKalb and New Boston, Tex., 1947-56; with Am. Machine & Foundry Co., 1956-70, div. v.p., 1963-66; chmn. bd. dirs. AMF Australia, 1966-69; asst. group exec., indsl. products group AMF, Inc., 1969-70; v.p. Nat. Corp. for Housing Partnerships, Washington, 1971-72, 75-78, sr. v.p., 1977-79, exec. v.p., 1980—; exec. v.p. Coordinated Bldg. Systems, Inc., Cin., also pres. CBC Concrete Products, Inc., Cin., 1973-74; pres. NCHP Property Mgmt., Inc., Washington, 1978—, dir., mem. exec. com., 1978—. Mem. adv. council Nat. Rental Housing Council, Nat. Center for Housing Mgmt., Multifamily Housing Com.; mem. Fed. Housing Liaison Com. Served with USAAF, 1942-45, U.S. Army, 1951-52. Mem. Inst. Real Estate Mgmt. Republican. Club: N.Y. Athletic (N.Y.C.). Home: 1513 Snughill Ct Vienna VA 22180 Office: Nat Corp for Housing Partnerships 1133 15th St NW Washington DC 20005

CRUMP, SPENCER, editor, pub., bus. exec.; b. San Jose, Calif., Nov. 25; s. Spencer M. and Jessie (Person) C.; B.A., U. So. Calif., 1960, M.S. in Edn., 1962, M.A. in Journalism, 1968; children—John Spencer, Victoria Elizabeth Margaret. Reporter, Long Beach (Calif.) Ind., 1945-49; free-lance writer, Long Beach, 1950-51; travel columnist, picture editor Long Beach Ind.-Press-Telegram, 1952-56; pres. Crest Industries Corp., Long Beach, 1957-58; editor suburban sects. Los Angeles Times, 1959-62; editorial dir., pub. Trans-Anglo Books, Corona del Mar, Calif., 1962—; mng. dir. Person Properties Co. (now Person-Crump Industries Co.), Lubbock, Tex., 1951—; chmn. bd. Zeta Internat., 1976—; gen. cons. Flying Spur Press, 1974—; dir. Trans-Anglo Britain, Zeta Commonwealth, Briarwood East, Dallas, Cottonwood Assos., Grand Prairie, Tex., 1980—; chmn. journalism dept. Orange Coast Coll., 1966—; cons. Queen Beach Press, 1974—, So. Pacific Transp. Co., 1979-80. Mem. Los Angeles County Democratic Central Com., 1961-62. Mem. Calif. Hist. Soc., Book Pubs. Assn. So. Calif., Orange County Press Club, Fellowship Reconciliation, Soc. Profl. Journalists, ACLU. Unitarian-Universalist. Club: Masons. Author: Ride the Big Red Cars, 1962; Redwoods, Iron Horses and the Pacific, 1963; Western Pacific-The Railroad That was Built Too Late, 1963; California's Spanish Missions Yesterday and Today, 1964; Black Riot in Los Angeles, 1966; Henry Huntington and the Pacific Electric, 1970; The Fundamentals of Journalism, 1974; California's Spanish Missions, 1975; Suggestions for Teaching Fundamentals of Journalism in College, 1976; The Stylebook for Newswriting, 1979; Newsgathering and Reporting for the 1980s and Beyond, 1981. Office: Trans-Anglo Books PO Box 38 Corona del Mar CA 92625

CRUSER, RORY GIBSON, ins. co. exec.; b. Lakeland, Fla., Sept. 30, 1946; s. Conrad Seldon and Frances C.; A.A., N.E. Okla. A. & M., 1966; Indsl. Tech., Tenn. Tech. U., 1966-68; m. Carol Michelle Whited, Nov. 26, 1965; children—Autumn (dec.), Carmen (dec.). Jr. engr. Kurzynske, Green & Assos., Nashville, 1968; salesman Kit Cruser Ins. Agy., Nashville, 1969-71, v.p., 1971-75; dist. mgr. American Family Life, Nashville, 1975-76, regional mgr., 1976—. Vol., New Life, Knoxville, Tenn., 1979—. Mem. Nashville Life Underwriters Assn., Sales and Mktg. Execs. of Nashville. Home: 1992 Sunnyside Dr Brentwood TN 37027 Office: 2525 Hillsboro Rd Nashville TN 37212

CRYSTAL, GRAEF SLATER, mgmt. cons.; b. Oakland, Calif., Apr. 30, 1934; s. Louis F. and Esther D. (Harris) C.; A.B., U. Calif. at Berkeley, 1956; M.A., Occidental Coll., 1962; children—David, Allison, Matthew. Mgmt. trainee Sears, Roebuck & Co., Santa Monica, Calif., 1957-59; wage and salary analyst RCA, Van Nuys, Calif., 1959-60; compensation dir. Gen. Dynamics Corp., N.Y.C., 1960-67; dir. compensation Pfizer Internat. Inc., N.Y.C., 1968; sr. asso. Booz, Allen & Hamilton Inc., N.Y.C., 1968-69; v.p., Towers, Perrin, Forster & Crosby Inc., N.Y.C., 1969—; lectr. on exec. compensation. Mem. Am. Compensation Assn. (regional pres. 1968-69). Republican. Methodist. Club: Sky (N.Y.C.). Author: Financial Motivation for Executives; Compensating United States Executives Abroad; Executive Compensation: Money, Motivation and Imagination; also articles. Home: 60 East End Ave New York NY 10028 also 1314 Fairway Oaks Kiawah Island SC 29455 Office: Towers Perrin Forster & Crosby Inc 600 3d Ave New York NY 10016

CRYSTAL, JAMES WILLIAM, ins. co. exec.; b. N.Y.C., Oct. 9, 1937; s. I. Frank and Evelyn G. C.; B.S., Trinity Coll., 1958; m. Jean C.; children—James F., Sanford F., Jonathan F. With Royal Globe Ins. Group, N.Y.C., 1956; underwriter Home Ins. Co., N.Y.C., 1957, spl. agt., San Francisco, 1958-59; pres., chief exec. officer Frank Crystal & Co. Inc., N.Y.C., 1960—; dir. Edinburgh & Gen. Ins. Services, Inc., London. Bd. dirs. Gar Reichman Found. Mem. Nat. Assn. Casualty and Surety Agts. Republican. Clubs: World Trade Center, Harmonie, Quaker Ridge Country. Home: 33 E 70th St New York NY 10021 Office: 61 Broadway New York NY 10006

CSENDES, ERNEST, chemist, fin. exec.; b. Satu-Mare, Romania, Mar. 2, 1926; s. Edward O. and Sidonia (Von Littman) C.; B.A., Protestant Coll., Hungary, 1944; B.S., U. Heidelberg (W.Ger.), 1948, M.S., Ph.D., 1951; m. Catharine Vera von Tolnai; Feb. 7, 1953; children—Audrey Carol, Robert Alexander Edward. Came to U.S. 1951, naturalized, 1955. Asst., U. Heidelberg, 1951; research asso. biochemistry Tulane U., New Orleans, 1952; fellow Harvard, 1953; research chemist organic chems. dept. E. I. Du Pont de Nemours and Co., Inc., Wilmington, Del., 1953-56, elastomer chems. dept., 1956-61; dir. research and devel. agrl. chems. div. Armour & Co., Atlanta, 1961-63; v.p. corporate devel. Occidental Petroleum Corp., Los Angeles, 1963-64, exec. v.p. charge research, engring. and devel., mem. exec. com., 1964-68; exec. v.p., chief exec. officer, dir. Occidental Research & Engring. Corp., 1963-68; pres., chief exec. officer Tex. Republic Industries, 1968—; pres., dir. TRI Ltd., Bermuda, 1971—; chmn., dir. TRI Internat. Ltd., Bermuda, 1971—; mng. dir. TRI Holdings S.A., Luxembourg, 1971—, TRI Capital N.V., Netherlands, 1971—. Fellow A.A.A.S., Am. Oil Chemists Soc., Am. Inst. Chemists; mem. Am. Acad. Polit. and Social Sci., Soc. Plastics Engrs., Research Soc. Am., Am. Chem. Soc., N.Y. Acad. Scis., Polit. Scis., Inst. Mgmt. Scis., Am. Mgmt. Assn., AIAA, Nat. Space Inst., Am. Security Council, Explorers Club, Am. Def. Preparedness Assn., Chem. Soc. London, Faraday Soc., German Chem. Soc. Contbr. articles in field. Patentee. Research in areas of fertilizer and petrochem. processes, engring. design and constrn., feasibility studies, econ. and market devel.; regional devel. projects in natural resources and agr. in Africa, Mid East, USSR, India, Latin Am., Far East, Australia; mining and metallurgy of sulphur, potash, phosphate and iron ores; acquisitions, mergers; internat. finance and taxation, banking and ins. related to securities, leasing, real estate, financing of oil gas and coal. Home: 1601 Casale Rd Pacific Palisades CA 90272

CSOKASY, LOUIS ROBERT, mfg. co. exec.; b. Wayne, Mich., July 17, 1947; s. Louis and Leona May (Hospital) C.; B.S. in Aero. Engring., Tri-State Coll., 1969; M.B.A., Eastern Mich. U., 1974; m. Donna Faye Ambrose, June 21, 1969; children—Leslie Faye, Kelly Ann. Elec. wiring engr. Boeing Aircraft Co., Renton, Wash., 1969, design engr. Lockheed Aerospace Co., Burbank, Calif., 1970; lead design engr. systems div. Bendix Aerospace Co., Ann Arbor, Mich., 1970-72; quality control mgr. Excel Industries Calif., Riverside, 1972-74, mgr. engring., 1974-76, asst. gen. mgr., 1976-79, plant mgr., 1979—. Mem. Riverside C. of C. Patentee in field. Home: 1101 Country Club Dr Riverside CA 92508 Office: 12661 Box Springs Blvd Riverside CA 92507

CUBBEDGE, ROBERT ALLEN, mfr.'s agt. co. exec.; b. Toledo, Aug. 4, 1926; s. Robert Allen Kimberley and Marion Alice (Mulholland) C.; B.S. in Indsl. Engring., U. Ala., 1949; m. Marilyn Joan Barker, Nov. 29, 1975; children—Keith, Oticca, Kimberley, Tatjania, Kenneth, Arthur, Donald. Indsl. engr., sales engr. Acklin Stamping div. Tecumseh Products, Toledo, 1949-53; sales engr. Leake Stamping & Engring. Co., Monroe, Mich., 1953-55; sales engr., gen. sales mgr. Kiemle-Hankins Co., Toledo, 1955-71; pres. Cubbedge Controls, Inc., Toledo, 1971—. Chmn. Eagle scout bd. rev. Boy Scouts Am., Toledo, 1966-68; councilman Hope Lutheran Ch., Toledo, 1971-77; chmn. bd. Toledo YMCA Storer Camps, 1975-76. Served with USAF, 1944-45. Mem. Mfrs. Agts. Nat. Assn., IEEE, Instrument Soc. Am., Am. Inst. Indsl. Engrs. (past pres. Toledo chpt.), Toledo C. of C., Nat. Fedn. Ind. Bus., Tech. Soc. Toledo (pres. 1980-81). Clubs: Rotary, Sylvania Country, Toledo Racquet. Home: 4412 Bromley Dr Toledo OH 43623 Office: 5650 W Central Ave Toledo OH 43615

CUCCHISSI, MICHAEL SALVATORE, lawyer; b. Bklyn., Aug. 29, 1953; s. Michael Anthony and Grace Anne (Del Casino) C.; S.B., M.I.T., 1975; J.D. cum laude, U. Pa., 1978; m. Barbara V. Barbella, Apr. 12, 1980. Admitted to Calif. bar, 1978; law clk. U.S. Dist. Ct., Honolulu, 1978-79; atty. firm Gibson Dunn Crutcher, Newport Beach, Calif., 1979—. Mem. Am. Bar Assn., Orange County Bar Assn. Republican. Comment editor U. Pa. Law Rev., 1977-78; contbr. articles to profl. jours. Home: 3301 S Bear St Apt 39F Santa Ana CA 92704 Office: 660 Newport Center Dr Newport Beach CA 92663

CUELLAR, ROBERT ALEMAN, advt. exec., mgmt. cons.; b. Fresnillo, Zacatecas, Mex., Oct. 28, 1939; naturalized Am. citizen, 1963; s. Manuel R. and Lida (Aleman) C.; children—Cathlyne (Aleman) C.; B.A., N. Tex. State U., 1967, M.A., 1969; m. Mary Sylvia Cobos, Feb. 3, 1968; children—Martin Edward, Mark Andrew. Tchr. pub. schs. Mesquite (Tex.) Inds. Sch. Dist., 1967-68; asst. registrar N. Tex. State U., Denton, 1968-69; nat. dep. dir. Jobs for Progress, Inc., (chmn. Angeles, 1969-74; pres., chief exec. officer Adcom Assos., Inc., Phoenix, 1974—; dir. Nuestro Publs., Washington. Served with USAF, 1962-66. Mem. Am. Mgmt. Assn., Am. G.I. Forum of U.S., Southwestern Hist. Soc. Democrat. Roman Catholic. Author: A History of Mexican Americans in Texas, 1976; research on nat. mktg. potential of Spanish speaking population. Home: 1517 Montana Ave El Paso TX 79902 Office: Adcom Assos Inc 2626 N 7th St Phoenix AZ 85006

CUFF, WILLIAM, food mfg. co. exec.; b. Stamford, Conn., Mar. 31, 1942; s. William and Jean (Grant) C.; B.A., Yale U., 1964; M.B.A., Columbia U., 1966; m. Erin Ann Quinn, Dec. 1, 1978; children—Lisa Ann, William David. Various mktg. position Gen. Food Corp., White Plains, N.Y., 1966-77, Standard Brands, N.Y.C., 1977-79; v.p. new products and mktg. services Nestle div. Libby, McNeill & Libby, Chgo., 1979—. Mem. Beta Gamma Sigma. Home: 3930 N Pine Grove Chicago IL 60613 Office: 200 S Michigan Ave Chicago IL 60604

CUGINI, GERARD RAYMOND, architect, developer; b. Milford, Mass., Apr. 18, 1934; s. Raymond Frank and Angela Prudence C.; B.A., Middlebury Coll., 1955; M.F.A., Princeton U., 1958; m. Lois Ann Nadler, Oct. 31, 1964; children—Gregory Raymond, Angela Reva. With Pierce & Pierce, Architects, Boston, 1965-66, Edward Durell Stone, Architect, N.Y.C., 1963-66, Krokyn & Krokyn, Architects, Boston, 1960-63; designer Belglioso, Perrussitti & Rogers, Milan, Italy, 1957-58; pres. Cugini Partnership, Inc., Architects and Planners, Boston, 1958—; pres. Nat. Council Archtl. Registration Bds. Bd. dirs. Boston Ballet Soc., Mass. Center Repertory Co., Hist. Neighborhood Found. Recipient Gold Medal award Soc. Am. Registered Architects, 1970, Red medal, 1970, 1st award S.M. Hexter Co., 1971, honor award AIA, 1977. Home: 17 Fayette St Boston MA 02116 Office: 136 Boylston St Boston MA 02116

CULBERTSON, DAVID JOSEPH, publishing co. exec.; b. Paterson, N.J., Nov. 17, 1926; s. Edward and Elizabeth (McKewen) C.; B.A. in Econs., Cornell U., 1950; M.B.A., 1951; m. Helen Marie Eaton, Dec. 27, 1948; children—Amy Alizabeth, John Edward. Dir. exec. devel., adminstrv. asst. to treas. IBM World Trade Corp., 1951-68; with Xerox Corp., Stamford, Conn., 1968-80, controller, 1970-72, v.p., 1970-72, pres. Xerox edn. group, 1972-80; pres. Macmillan Inc., N.Y.C., 1980—. Served with AUS, 1945-46. Office: Macmillan Inc 866 3d Ave New York NY 10022*

CULBERTSON, HORACE COE, ins. co. exec.; b. Los Angeles, Apr. 24, 1924; s. Henry Coe and Irene A. (Blood) C.; A.B., Occidental Coll., 1949; m. Janet Ann Fadley, Dec. 27, 1949; children—Timothy Coe, Gary Dan, William Craig. With Fidelity and Deposit Co. of Md., 1949—, exec. v.p., Balt., 1966-74, dir., 1967—, pres., chief exec. officer, 1974—; dir. Md. Nat. Corp., Md. Casualty Corp. Dir. United Fund of Md., 1971-72; trustee, v.p. Community Chest of Balt., 1968-71; dir. ARC, Md., 1969-75. Served with USNR, 1943-46. Mem. Am. Ins. Assn., Surety Assn. Am., Am. Mgmt. Assn., Assn. of Gen. Contractors, Assn. of Casualty and Surety Execs., C. of C. Met. Balt. (v.p., dir. 1971-74). Republican. Presbyterian. Clubs: Md., Balt. Country, Towson Golf and Country, Center. Office: 611 Fidelity Bldg Charles and Lexington St Baltimore MD 21203

CULBERTSON, SAMUEL ALEXANDER, II, business exec.; b. Louisville, June 2, 1915; s. Alexander Craig and Florence (McFatrich) C.; student U. Va., 1934-37, Law Sch. U. Va., 1937-40; m. Nancy Madlener, June 18, 1957; children—Samuel III, Catherine, Edward. Former chmn. exec. com. Murine Co., Inc.; dir., former mem. exec. com. McIntosh Corp.; dir., former chmn. exec. com. Computer Bus. Mgmt., Inc.; chmn. bd. Investment & Capital Mgmt.; pres. 574 Corp.; pres. Utah Shale Land & Minerals Corp.; dir. Advance Ross Corp. Pres. John Howard Assn., 1950-57; chmn. Northtown Vocat. Council, North Ave. Larabee YMCA, 1954-57; mem. Ill. Bldg. Authority, 1965-68; bd. dirs. Civic Fedn., Citizens Assn., Lake Geneva (Wis.) Civic Assn.; v.p. Harris Sch., Chgo.; chmn. Chgo. Youth Centers; chmn. bd. dirs. Grant Hosp. Republican. Episcopalian. Clubs: Mason (32 deg., Shriner); Racquet, Tavern (Chgo.); Glen View; Lake Geneva (Wis.); Riomar Bay Yacht (Fla.), Augusta (Ga.) Nat. Home: 71 E Division St Chicago IL 60610 Office: 135 S LaSalle St Chicago IL 60604 Died Aug. 31, 1980

CULBERTSON, WALTER LEROY, petroleum co. exec.; b. Dederick, Mo., July 29, 1918; s. Alfred and Ethel Ida (Belong) C.; B.S. in Mech. Engring., Kans. State U., 1939; m. Wanda Marian Atkins, Sept. 30, 1940; children—Philip, Robert. With Phillips Petroleum Co., 1939—, now sr. v.p. corp. planning and budgeting, Bartlesville, Okla. Mem. ASME, Nat. Soc. Profl. Engrs., Am. Inst. Chem. Engrs. Republican. Mem. Disciples of Christ Ch. Club: Bartlesville Hillcrest Country. Office: 18 Phillips Bldg Bartlesville OK 74004

CULBREATH, BOB RAY, steel co. exec.; b. Sumner County, Tenn., Nov. 29, 1928; s. Raymond Searcy and Lela May (Martin) C.; m. Elizabeth Joseph White, Oct. 21, 1944; children—Georgia (Mrs. Charles E. Perkins III), Robert R., Elizabeth Ann Biggs. With Enterprise Iron & Fence Co., Indpls., 1944-47, foreman welding dept., 1947; with B & B Welding Co., Indpls.; with Whittington Pump & Engring. Co., Indpls., 1957-58, owner, 1958-60; partner Imperial Fabricating Co. Tenn., Portland, Tenn., 1962—, pres., 1967—, chmn. bd. dirs. 1967—; pres. Partner, Imperial Chem. Cleaning Co., 1976—; partner United Steel Fabricating Co., 1977—, Culbreath Bros., 1970—, Imperial of Tulsa, 1973—, United Farm Supply, Inc., 1974—; sec.-treas. Hydro-Systems, Inc., 1972—; sec.-treas., dir. Bank of Portland, 1977—. Mem. Sumner County Legislative Com., 1974—, Sumner County Agrl. Com., 1974—; magistrate Sumner County Ct., Tenn., 1970—, judge protem, 1973—. Bd. dirs. Portland Indsl. Park, 1971—, Portland Airport Commn., 1971—, New Deal Civic Center, 1974—. Baptist (trustee 1970—). Mason (Scottish Rite, Shriner), Rotarian (pres. 1974-75); mem. Order Eastern Star. Clubs: Indian Springs Country, Bluegrass Country. Home: Route 2 Cottontown TN 37048 Office: PO Box 70 Portland TN 37148

CULKIN, DONALD EDWARD, banker; b. N.Y.C., Jan. 27, 1934; s. Thomas Joseph and Anne Veronica (McVicar) C.; B.S., Fordham U., 1956; M.B.A., N.Y. U., 1961; student mgmt. Oxford (Eng.) U., 1970. Vice pres. Mfrs. Hanover Trust Co., N.Y.C., 1958-73; adminstrv. v.p. Security Nat. Bank, N.Y.C., 1973-75; sr. v.p., mgr. Bank fur Gemeinwirtschaft A.G., Frankfurt/Main, West Germany and N.Y.C., 1975—; tchr. Am. Inst. Banking. Served to capt., AUS, 1956-58; mem. Res., 1958-65. Mem. Bankers Assn. Fgn. Trade, Inst. Fgn. Bankers, Beta Gamma Sigma. Roman Catholic. Clubs: N.Y. Athletic, Atrium (N.Y.C.). Home: 324 E 41st St New York NY 10017 Office: 400 Park Ave New York NY 10022

CULLERS, CLEVE ALLEN, petroleum landman; b. Shawnee, Okla., June 3, 1923; s. Albert Randolph and Ora Wells (Box) C.; B.A., Abilene Christian U., 1947; m. Feb. 28, 1976; children—Nancy, Cullen, Karen, Laura, Bret. Mem. land dept. Gulf Oil Corp., 1947-50; partner Berry Brown & Co., Wichita Falls, Tex., 1950-56; organizer, pres. Cullers-Bailey & Co., Abilene, Tex., 1956-79; pvt. practice petroleum landman, Abilene, 1979—. Mem. Abilene City Council, 1961-63. Served with USNR, 1944-47. Mem. Abilene Land Assn., Am. Assn. Petroleum Landmen, Tex. Assessors Assn., W. Central Tex. Oil and Gas Assn. Mem. Ch. of Christ. Club: Kiwanis. Home: 1802 Lytle Shores Dr Abilene TX 79602 Office: Suite 4C One Energy Sq Abilene TX 79601

CULLEY, HENRY COE, govt. ofcl.; b. Las Vegas, Nev., Feb. 19, 1947; s. Paul Edward and Virginia (Chavez) C.; A.B. in Polit. Sci., Calif. State U., Long Beach, 1971; M.P.A., U. So. Calif., 1973, Ph.D. (Disting. Doctoral Student 1975), 1980; m. Susan Jessica Shaw, Sept. 12, 1970. Gen. mgr., partner Culley Bros. Prodn. Co., publishing, advt. and public relations, Long Beach, 1968-71; researcher, mem. faculty and adminstrn. U. So. Calif. Sch. Public Adminstrn., 1973-77; asst. to personnel dir., supr. mgmt. tng. and affirmative action, asst. to exec. dir., coordinator mgmt. and exec. devel. programs Port Authority N.Y. and N.J., 1977—; lectr., cons. Sch. Mgmt. and Urban Professions, New Sch. Social Research, also Grad. Sch. Public Adminstrn., N.Y. U. Mem. Am. Soc. Public Adminstrn. (exec. com. govt. bus. relations), Internat. Personnel Mgrs. Assn., Policy Studies Orgn. Home: 11 W 11th St New York NY 10011 Office: 1 World Trade Center New York NY 10048

CULLIGAN, JOHN WILLIAM, med., food and household products mfg. co. exec.; b. Newark, Nov. 22, 1916; s. John J. and Elizabeth (Kearns) C.; m. Rita McBride, Feb. 19, 1944; children—Nancy, Mary Carol, Elizabeth, Sheila, John, Neil. With Whitehall Labs. div. Am. Home Products Corp. until 1967, pres., N.Y.C., 1964-67; v.p. Am. Home Products Corp., N.Y.C., 1967-72, exec. v.p., 1972-73, pres., 1973—; trustee N.Y. Bank for Savs. Trustee, Seton Hall U., Valley Hosp., Ridgewood, N.J.; treas. Council Family Health, Washington; mem. adv. bd. St. Benedict's Prep. Sch., Newark; mem. Archbishop's Com. of Laity, Newark. Served with U.S. Army, 1943-46. Decorated Papal knight of St. Gregory, knight of Malta (Vatican). Mem. Proprietary Assn. (v.p., dir.), Serra Club. Clubs: Hackensack Golf, N.Y. Athletic, Pinnacle. Office: 685 3d Ave New York NY 10017

CULLINS, THOMAS ELDRIDGE, stock brokerage exec.; b. Mt. Vernon, Ill., Dec. 17, 1935; s. Paul Thomas and Mabel Hill (Webb) C.; B.A., U. Ill., 1957; postgrad. U. Md., 1964-65; M.B.A., U. Okla., 1970; m. Margaret Ann Dace, May 30, 1958; children—Cynthia Lynn, Thomas Scott. Field rep. Comml. Credit Corp., Mt. Vernon, Ill., 1957-58; commd. 2d lt. U.S. Army, 1957, advanced through grades to lt. col., 1973; commd. officer 7th Army, Mannheim, Germany, 1962-63; chief supply and services div., Saigon, Vietnam, 1966-67; asso. prof. mil. sci. U. Okla., 1967-70; logistics staff officer, Saigon, 1971; chief supply and services div. U.S. Military Acad., 1972-75; asst. chief staff services, Kaiserslauten, Germany, 1975-76, sec. gen. staff, 1976-78, ret., 1978; account exec. Merrill Lynch Pierce Fenner & Smith, Inc., Oklahoma City, 1978—. Coach West Point and Hudson Valley Youth Football League, 1972-74. Decorated Legion of Merit, Bronze Star medal. Mem. Am. Logistics Assn., Kappa Sigma. Baptist. Home: 603 Inverness Ct Norman OK 73069

CULLMAN, JOSEPH FREDERICK, 3D, diversified co. exec.; b. N.Y.C., Apr. 9, 1912; s. Joseph F. Jr. and Frances Nathan (Wolff) C.; A.B., Yale, 1935; 1 dau., Dorothy Cullman Treisman. Eastern sales mgr. Webster Tobacco Co., N.Y.C., 1936-41; v.p. Benson & Hedges, N.Y.C., 1946-53, exec. v.p., 1953-55, pres., 1955-61; v.p. Philip Morris Inc., N.Y.C., 1954, exec. v.p., 1955-57, pres., chief exec. officer, 1957-66, chmn. bd., chief exec. officer, 1967-78, chmn. exec. com., 1978—; pres. Philip Morris Internat., 1955; commr. Port Authority of N.Y. and N.J.; dir. Levi Strauss & Co., IBM World Trade Europe/Middle East/Africa Corp., Bankers Trust, Ford Motor Co. exec. com. Tobacco Inst., Washington, 1968-77, chmn., 1968-72. N.Y.C. chmn. United Negro Coll. Fund, 1972; dir. U.S. appeal World Wildlife Fund; pres. Internat. Atlantic Salmon Found.; chmn. U.S. Open Tennis Championships, 1969, 70, hon. chmn., 1971; trustee Am. Mus. Natural History, N.Y. State Nature and Hist. Trust; mem. nat. bd. Smithsonian Assos.; pres., bd. dirs. Whitney M. Young, Jr. Meml. Found., Colonial Williamsburg Found. Served to comdr. USNR, 1941-45. Decorated Ordre du Merite Commerciale et Industriel (France); comdr. Order Merit (Italy); named to Tobacco Industry Hall of Fame, 1966, Internat. Tennis Hall of Fame, 1977. Clubs: Yale (N.Y.C.); Century Country (Purchase, N.Y.). Office: 100 Park Ave New York NY 10017

CULMANN, LOUIS CHARLES, ins. co. exec., real estate broker; b. Indpls., Oct. 13, 1918; s. Louis Jacob and Mamie Katherine (Thomas) C.; B.B.A., In. U., 1941; m. Eulala Joy Miller, Feb. 8, 1943; 1 dau., Pamela Jo. With pension, group, acturial dept. Lincoln Nat. Life, Fort Wayne, Ind., 1946-54; gen. agt. Occidental Life Ins. Co. of Calif., Ft. Wayne, 1955—; partner Loos Ins. Gen. Lines Agy., Ft. Wayne, 1956-78; partner ins. and risk mgmt. Gen. Lines Agy., Ft. Wayne, 1978—; real estate broker Century 21 Wayne Kruse Inc., Ft. Wayne, 1979—; dir. banking, leasing and real estate mgmt. PAC Fin. Corp. 1973—; dir. Med. & Dental Inc. Mem. Govs. Ins. Com. of Ind., 1958-62; bd. dirs. Lake Luther Camp Inc., Luth. Social Services, Inc.; treas. Allen County Democratic Central Com., 1958-64. Served to maj. U.S. Army, 1941-46. Decorated Bronze Star. Mem. Nat. Assn. Life Underwriters, Internat. Accountants Soc. (life), Ind. U. Alumni Assn. (past pres. Northeast Ind.), Am. Legion, VFW (post comdr.), Res. Officers Assn., Acacia, Alpha Kappa Psi. Lutheran. Clubs: Gideons, Press, Masons. Office: 2118 Inwood Dr Room 114 Fort Wayne IN 46815

CULP, CLYDE E., III, fast food co. exec.; b. Washington, Dec. 15, 1942; s. Clyde E. and Lutie D. Culp; B.A., Coll. William and Mary, 1965; M.B.A., N.Y. U.; m. Mary Ellen Coleman, July 3, 1965; children—Kelly, Suzanne, Darby. In brand mgmt. Procter & Gamble, Cin., 1967-70; dir. mktg. Krystal Co., Chattanooga, 1970-73, v.p. mktg., 1973-77, pres. Davco Foods franchise, Annapolis, Md., 1977—; cons. Holiday Inns, Fairmont Hotels, Coca-Cola Co., M & J Foods; dir. Cosvetic Labs., Davco Food, Inc., Chattanooga, Braswell Corp., Atlanta. Bd. dirs. Chattanooga Conv. and Visitors Bur., 1976-77. Mem. Am. Mktg. Assn., Am. Mgmt. Assn., Chattanooga (v.p. 1975), Atlanta ad clubs, Mail Order Execs. Club (pres. 1974), Sales and MMktg. Execs., Young Pres.'s Assn. Republican. Congregationalist. Home: 362 Kingsberry St Annapolis MD 21401 Office: 16 Village Green Crofton MD 21114

CULPEPPER, MILTON IRVING, JR., lawyer; b. Meridian, Miss., June 14, 1929; s. Milton Irving and Margaret Medora (Brown) C.; student Spring Hill Coll., 1946-48, U. Houston, 1953-54, S. Tex. Law Sch., 1955; LL.B., Cumberland Sch. Law, 1969; m. Betty Jean Wimpee, June 4, 1949; children—Michael Irving, Donna Gene, Margaret Jane. Admitted to Ala. bar, 1969; facilities mgr. Cities Service Oil Co., Birmingham, Ala., 1955-69; spl. asst. to chmn., legal counsel dept. surgery U. Ala., Birmingham, 1969—, instr., 1971—, lobbyist to Ala. Legis., 1971; asso. legal counsel and asst. to pres. U. Ala. Health Services Found., Birmingham, 1973—, sec. 1973—, treas., 1973, mem. fin. com., 1974—; spl. lectr. in hosp. adminstrn. Sch. Community and Allied Health Resources, 1972-74; cons. Health Care Adminstrn., 1972-74. Area chmn. oil industry Community Chest Dr., 1962. Served with USNR, 1947-52. Recipient Meritorious Service award Sigma Delta Kappa, 1968, Book award Lawyers Coop. Admiralty, 1968. Mem. Am., Ala., Birmingham bar assns., Nat. Health Lawyers Assn., Am. Judicature Soc., Am. Soc. Law and Medicine, Am. Mgmt. Assn., Birmingham C. of C. (health services com. 1977-78), Relay House. Republican. Baptist (trustee local ch. 1969-70, chmn. fin. com. 1969-70). Club: Altadena Valley Golf and Country (bd. govs.). Home: 2504 Woodmeadow Pl Birmingham AL 35216 Office: 1901 7th Ave S Birmingham AL 35294

CULPEPPER, ROBERT SAMMONS, ins. agy. exec., mayor; b. Farmington, N.Mex., Aug. 23, 1927; s. Charles C. and Ethelywn (Hart) C.; student U. N.Mex., 1946-47; B.S., N.Mex. State Coll., 1951; m. Mary Eleanor Hancock, Nov. 15, 1953; children—Charles Chaisaignac II, Mary Eleanor, Robert Lee. Entomologist, Edmunds Chem. Co., Albuquerque, 1951-54; v.p. Farmington Investment Co., 1954-73; pres. Culpepper Ins. Agy., Inc., 1973—. Mem. N.Mex. Arts Commn., 1971—, vice chmn., 1972-73. Chmn., N.Mex. Arts Commn., 1973-74; mem. Farmington City Council, 1970—, mayor pro tem, 1974-78, mayor, 1978—; dir. N.Mex. Mcpl. League, 2d v.p., 1979, pres., 1980. Democratic precinct chmn., 1968-72, mem. exec. council, 1968; mem. Criminal Justice Region I Planning Com., 1976—; mem. San Juan Regional Com., 1979—, chmn., 1979-80. Served with USN, 1945-46. Mem. N.Mex. Assn. Ind. Ins. Agts. (dir. 1969-71, sec.-treas. 1972-73, v.p. 1973-74, pres. 1975-76), Farmington Insurors (pres. 1960-61), Farmington C. of C. (dir.

1959-62), Phi Kappa Tau. Episcopalian (vestryman 1970-73, sr. warden 1971-72). Clubs: Lions (Farmington pres. 1963-64), Elks (exalted ruler 1966-67). Home: 5703 Woodland Ct Farmington NM 87401 Office: 106 W Main St Farmington NM 87401

CULVER, DAVID M., aluminum co. exec.; b. Winnipeg, Man., Can., Dec. 5, 1924; s. Albert Ferguson and Fern Elizabeth (Smith) C.; B.Sc., McGill U., 1947; M.B.A., Harvard, 1949; certificate Centre d'Etudes Industrielles, Geneva, 1950; m. Mary Cecile Powell, Sept. 20, 1949; children—Michael, Andrew, Mark, Diane. With Alcan Group, 1949—, v.p. Alcan Internat. Ltd., 1956-62, pres., 1962—, exec. v.p. fabricating and sales, 1968-75, exec. v.p. N.Am. and Caribbean, 1975, also dir.; pres. Alcan Aluminum Ltd., chief exec. officer, 1979—; chmn. bd. Aluminum Co. Can., Ltd., 1977-79; dir. Canadair, MacMillan Bloedel Ltd., Am. Express Co., Am. Cyanamid Co. Chmn., Can. Japan Bus. Cooperation Com.; bd. govs. McGill U., Montreal, Que., Can. Served with Can. Inf. Corps, World War II. Mem. Alpha Delta Phi. Office: Alcan Aluminum Ltd 1 Pl Ville Marie Montreal PQ Canada

CULVER, IRVING SOUTHWICK, business exec.; b. Alameda, Calif., Oct. 7, 1893; s. Charles and Ada F. (Miller) C.; ed. pub. schs., Alameda; m. Dorothy Soule, July 24, 1918 (dec. 1956); 1 dau., Dorothy Ann Haynie; m. 2d Helen C. Adams, Sept. 2, 1957. Partner, Dodd Warehouses, San Francisco, 1919-24; mgr., partner Gibraltar Warehouses, San Francisco, 1924-71; partner Tilden & Culver, San Francisco; now co-executor Estate Charles L. Tilden, Jr. Served as ensign USN, 1917-18. Mem. bd. Asso. Warehouses, Chgo. Mem. Am. (past pres.), San Francisco (dir.), Warehousemen's assns., Distbrs. Assn. San Francisco, Federated Employers of San Francisco (gov.). Clubs: Bohemian, Rotary, Commonwealth of Cal. Home: 244 Lakeside Dr Oakland CA 94612 Office: 100 California St San Francisco CA 94111

CULVERWELL, HOWARD GLENDON, rancher; b. Concordia, Kans., May 18, 1911; s. Albert Sutcliff and Mabel Amelia (Middaugh) C.; student public schs.; m. Erma Frances Martin, Dec. 31, 1939; children—Gerald, Norman, Jon, Carolyn, Melvin, Melodie. Engaged in sheep, cattle, wheat and hay ranching, Craig, Colo., 1911—; pres. Moffat County Farm Bur., 1952-79. Pres., Dist. 13 Sch. Bd., 1955-71; bd. dirs. Colo. Assn. Sch. Bds., 1965-71. Mem. Profl. Farmers Am., Farmers Union, Nat. Farmers Orgn. Republican.

CUMBERWORTH, JAMES EMMET, bldg. material co. exec.; b. Detroit, July 7, 1917; s. Charles S. and Alice (Walsh) C.; B.S., Marist Coll., 1939; certificate in Tax Law and Investigation, U.S. Treasury Dept., 1945; m. Hazel Aline Lathrop, Dec. 24, 1938; children—Patricia Cumberworth Duchaine, Michael, Bridget Cumberworth Abbott, James, Timothy, Terence, Robert B., Colleen Cumberworth Morgan, Matthew, Margaret Cumberworth McGee, Kathleen Cumberworth Summers, Theresa Cumberworth Steinman, Daniel, Elizabeth. With Railroad Retirement Bd., Washington, 1939-43; spl. agt. intelligence div. U.S. Treasury Savannah, Ga., 1945-55; adminstrv. v.p. Moline Consumers Co. (Ill.), 1955—. Sec.-treas., dir. Settle Constrn. Co., Moline, 1967—; pres., dir. Leclaire Hotel, Moline, 1960—, Appanoose Salvage Co., Centerville, Ia.; cons. Western Ready-Mixed Co., Gem City Ready-Mix Co. (both Quincy, Ill.), Mo. Gravel Co., La Grange, Central Stone Co., Huntington, Mo., Bussen Quarry Co., St. Louis; individual practice tax law, Moline, 1955—. Trustee Leo L. Henkel Found. Served with AUS, 1943-45. Mem. Nat. Soc. Public Accountants. Home: 3702 7th St Moline IL 61265 Office: 313 16th St Moline IL 61265

CUMMINGS, BARTON A., advt. exec.; b. Rockford, Ill., Feb. 4, 1914; s. Earl M. and Myrle (Smith) C.; B.S. in Journalism, U. Ill., 1935; Trainee Swift & Co., Argentina, 1935-36; with Benton & Bowles, N.Y.C., 1936-41, Maxon Agy., 1945-47; with Compton Advt., Inc., N.Y.C., 1947—, v.p., account supr., 1947-55, pres., 1955-56, chief exec. officer, 1956-70, chmn. bd., 1963-70, chmn. exec. com., from 1970; dir. World Land Devel. Corp., Anti-Pollution Systems, Inc. Chmn. exec. com. James Webb Young Fund U. Ill.; chmn. advt. div. N.Y. Heart Assn., 1963-74; dir. Advt. Ednl. Found.; chmn. Advt. Council, 1979-81; dir. Nat. Advt. Rev. Council, 1971—, pres., 1974, 79. Served to lt. comdr. USN, 1943-45. Recipient Illini Achievement award U. Ill. Alumni Assn., 1972, I Man of Year, 1972. Mem. Am. Assn. Advt. Agys. (chmn. 1969-70, adv. council), Am. Acad. Advt. (Disting. Service award 1980), Phi Delta Theta, Pi Alpha Mu. Clubs: Adirondack League; Sky, Univ. (N.Y.C.): President's (U. Ill.). Office: 625 Madison Ave New York NY 10022

CUMMINGS, HENRY S. C., mfg. co. exec.; b. Middlefield, Mass., June 17, 1928; s. Henry S. C. and Dorothy (Smith) C.; B.S., Worcester Poly. Inst., 1950; m. Barbara Siegars, Apr. 3, 1951; children—David, Stephen, Janet. With Singer Mfg. Co., Bridgeport, Conn., 1950; with Lowell Corp., Worcester, Mass., 1955—, pres., 1961—; dir., incorporator Consumers Savs. Bank. Chmn., Heart Assn., Worcester, 1960-64; pres. Friendly House, Worcester, 1961-73; v.p. Boy Scouts, Worcester, 1962—. Trustee, Hahnemann Hosp., 1963—, Boys Club, 1968—, Becker-Leicester Jr. Coll., 1980—. Served with AUS, 1950-55. Mem. Phi Gamma Delta. Conglist. Mason. Home: 30 Harrington Dr Holden MA 01520 Office: 97 Temple St Worcester MA 01604

CUMMINGS, JOSEPH PATRICK, accountant; b. Norwich, Conn., July 20, 1919; s. Joseph Patrick and Anna C. (Maher) C.; B.S.C., U. Notre Dame, 1940; m. Miriam Lutz, Nov. 4, 1942; children—Patricia (Mrs. Edward McCarthy), Richard K., Maureen E. (Mrs. William C. Brown II), Kurt P. With Peat, Marwick, Mitchell & Co., N.Y.C., 1946-80, partner, 1955—, partner in charge profl. practice, 1966-72, dep. sr. partner, 1972-78. U.S. rep. Internat. Accounting Standards Com., 1973—, chmn., 1976. Mem. advisory council Coll. Bus. Adminstrn. U. Notre Dame. Served with USNR, 1942-45. C.P.A., N.Y. Mem. Am. Inst. C.P.A.'s (vice chmn. accounting principles bd. 1972, dir. 1976—, chmn. 1978-79), N.Y. Soc. C.P.A.'s, Beta Alpha Psi. Republican. Roman Catholic. K.C. Home: 11 Skyridge Rd Greenwich CT 06830 also Lost Tree Village North Palm Beach FL 33408

CUMMINGS, W. DEAN, grain co. exec.; b. Waynesfield, Ohio, Nov. 15, 1932; s. Walter Lewis and Bessie May (Neal) C.; B.S. in Bus. Adminstrn., Olivet Nazarene Coll., 1954; m. Naomi F. Cook, Feb. 27, 1955; children—Sheryl, Lynne, Kevin. Cost accountant Gen. Motors Corp., Columbus, Ohio, 1955-62; adminstrv. engr. Litton Industries, Los Angeles, 1962-63; pres. Cummings Grain Co., Inc., Waynesfield, 1963-79; adminstrv. dir. Real Life Ministries, 1979—; sec., treas. bd. Real Estate Investor. Served with AUS, 1956-57. Baptist (mem. bd.). Address: 7 Northway Dr Taylors SC 29687

CUMMINS, MICHAEL R., mgmt. cons., accountant; b. Carlsbad, N.Mex., July 17, 1943; s. John F. and Marjorie W. C.; B.A., Pomoca Coll., 1965; M.B.A., UCLA, 1970; m. Rebecca A. Freeman, Feb. 5, 1966; children—Julie, Owen. With Price Waterhouse & Co., Los Angeles, 1970—, audit staff acct., 1970-73, audit sr., mgmt. cons., 1973-75, sr. mgr. mgmt. services dept., 1975-79, sr. mgr. mgmt. services dept., 1979—. Served with U.S. Army, 1966-68. Decorated Bronze Star. Cert. electronic data processing auditor; C.P.A. Mem. Am. Inst. C.P.A.'s, Calif. Soc. C.P.A.'s, Electronic Data Processing Auditors Assn. Office: 1880 Century Park E Los Angeles CA 90067

CUMMINS, PAUL ZACH, II, ins. co. exec.; b. Fitchburg, Mass., May 1, 1936; s. Paul Z. and Camille M. (Hook) C.; B.S., U.S. Naval Acad., 1958, M.S., 1964; children—Paul Zach III, Colleen Elizabeth. Mgr., engring. liaison Carrier Corp., Syracuse, N.Y., 1969-73; mgr. systems, mfg. group Republic Steel Corp., Youngstown, Ohio, 1973-74, mgr., bus. planning, 1974-76; dir. administrn. planning Republic Builders Products Corp., Atlanta, 1976-77; dir. corporate planning and services Blue Cross/Blue Shield of Md., 1978—; instr. U.S. Naval Acad., Annapolis, 1964-65. Stratex Study mem. Dept. Def., 1967-68. Served with USN, 1958-69. Decorated Joint Service Commendation medal. Mem. Ops. Research Soc. Am., N.Am. Soc. Corporate Planning, Am. Inst. Indsl. Engrs. (sr.), U.S. Naval Acad. Alumni Assn. Methodist. Club: Kiwanis (past pres. Liverpool, N.Y., past pres. Camillus, N.Y.). Home: 18 Treeway Ct Apt 3C Towson MD 21204 Office: 700 E Joppa Rd Baltimore MD 21204

CUNNIFF, WILLIAM FRANCIS, mfg. co. exec.; b. Boston, Aug. 8, 1934; s. William Francis and Anne Cunniff; Bus. Mgmt., Northeastern U., 1967; postgrad. in advanced mgmt. Harvard U., 1978; m. Helen M. Mullins, Apr. 8, 1961; children—Casey, Gregory. Mgr. mgmt. info. services Barrows Industries, North Providence, R.I., 1965-67; prin. Rath & Strong, mgmt. consultants, Lexington, Mass., 1967-73; asst. controller Textron Inc., Providence, 1973-75, v.p. adminstrn. Bostitch div., East Greenwich, R.I., 1975—. Served with U.S. Army, 1955-57. Cert. in data processing. Mem. Fin. Execs. Inst. (dir. Providence chpt.), Data Processing Mgmt. Assn., Soc. for Preservation and Encouragement Barbershop Quartet Singing in Am. Club: Quidnessett Country. Home: 1260 High Hawk Rd East Greenwich RI 02818 Office: Bostitch Div Textron Inc Briggs Dr East Greenwich RI 02818

CUNNINGHAM, AUSTIN, restauranteur; b. Washington, Sept. 5, 1914; s. Austin and Clotilde (Mattingly) C.; student George Washington U., 1933-37; J.D., U. Va., 1940; postgrad. Harvard, 1943-44, U. Chgo., 1944-45; m. Jacqueline Coder, Jan. 24, 1946; children—Kathryne, Amy, Austin III. Sales mgr. Ediphone div. Thomas A. Edison, Inc., 1947-53; various exec. positions Magnavox Co., Chgo., 1953-61; pres. Product Specialties, Inc. div. Sunbeam Corp., Chgo., 1963-69, pres. Sunbeam Outdoor Co. div., Santee, S.C., 1969-75; pres. Restaurant Assos. Orangeburg, Inc. (S.C.), A & J Inc., Quality Fish Enterprises, 1975—. Chmn. budget com., trustee United Fund, Kenilworth, Ill., 1971-72. Trustee, Ravinia Festival Assn., Orangeburg-Calhoun Tech. Coll. Found. Served to 1st lt. USAAF, World War II. Mem. Outdoor Power Equipment Inst. (trustee), Orangeburg C. of C. (v.p. pub. affairs div.), Dickens Soc. (London, Eng.), Newcomen Soc., S.A.R., U.S. Indsl. Council. Presbyterian. Clubs: Rotary, Orangeburg Country. Home: 1199 Broughton St NW Orangeburg SC 29115 Office: 437 John C Calhoun Dr Orangeburg SC 29115

CUNNINGHAM, CHARLES BAKER, III, mfg. co. exec.; b. St. Louis, Oct. 1, 1941; s. Charles Baker, Jr. and Mary (Blythe) C.; B.S., Washington U., St. Louis, 1964; M.S., Ga. Inst. Tech., 1966; M.B.A., Harvard U., 1970; m. Georganne Rose, Sept. 17, 1966; children—Margaret B., Charles Baker, IV. With Cooper Industries, Houston, 1970—, v.p. corp. devel., 1978-79, pres. indsl. equipment group, 1979—, v.p. ops. corp., 1980—. Served with C.E., USAR, 1966-68. Decorated Army Commendation medal. Office: Suite 2700 2 Houston Center Houston TX 77002

CUNNINGHAM, CHARLES CLARKE, JR., banker; b. Richmond, Va., Apr. 18, 1917; s. Charles Clarke and Bessie (Bache) C.; student d. Va., 1935-39; m. Mary Peters, Sept. 24, 1941; children—Clarke III, Richard Bruce, William Kendall. With 1st & Mchts. Nat. Bank Radford (Va.), 1962—, pres., 1962—; Chmn., Radford City Sch. Bd., 1962-68, Radford United Fund; bd. dirs. New River Community Coll., 1973-79; chmn. bd. St. Albans Psychiat. Hosp., 1965—, mem. found. bd., 1977—; mem. vis. bd. U. Va., 1980—; pres. Va. Student Aid Found., U. Va., 1977-78; trustee Grove Ave. Methodist Ch., 1955-56. Served to lt. USAAF, 1941-45. Mem. Va. Bankers Assn. (pres. 1976-77), Am. Bankers Assn. (gov. council 1977-79, state v.p. 1978-79). Clubs: Farmington Country (Charlottesville); Stuart Yacht and Country (Fla.). Home: Box 3217 FSS Radford VA 24141 Office: 1100 Norwood St Radford VA 24141

CUNNINGHAM, JAMES EVERETT, energy services co. exec.; b. Cresco, Iowa, Apr. 14, 1923; s. James Franklin and Julia (Connors) C.; B.S. in Chem. Engring., U. Ala., 1946; m. Delores Ann Foytik, Jan. 31, 1959; children—Sharon Lee, Sandra Dee, Matthre Joseph, Susan Elizabeth, Michael James, Marc David. With Fluor Corp., Houston, 1947-54; pvt. practice oil bus., 1955-58; with J. Ray McDermott & Co., Inc., New Orleans, 1958—, treas., 1964-67, exec. v.p., 1967-78, vice chmn. fin. and adminstrn., 1978, vice chmn., chief exec. officer, 1979, chmn., chief exec. officer, 1979—, dir. Reading & Bates Corp. Pres. bd. regents Our Lady of Holy Cross Coll.; mem. president's council Loyola U. Served with USNR, World War II. Mem. NAM (dir.), Con. Bd., U.S. C. of C. (internat. policy com.), New Orleans C. of C. (econ. devel. council, dir.). Office: 1010 Common St New Orleans LA 70112

CUNNINGHAM, JAMES HUNTER, lumber co. exec.; b. Texarkana, Tex., Nov. 20, 1947; s. John Fletcher and Francis Lucille (Lincoln) C.; B.S. in Sociology, U. Ark., 1970; m. Catherine Ann Patterson, June 20, 1947; children—James Hunter, Catherine Brennan. Exec. trainee Champion Papers-U.S. Plywood, 1970-71; salesman Georgia Pacific, Dallas, 1971-73; owner, mgr. John Cunningham Co., Texarkana, 1973—. Mem. Tex. Lumbermen's Assn., Tex. Forest Products Assn., Texarkana Home Builders Assn., Texarkana Lumber Dealers Assn. Republican. Home: Route 3 Box 491 CA Texarkana TX 75503 Office: Box 5727 Texarkana TX 75501

CUNNINGHAM, MARCUS EDDY, engring. exec.; b. Lynn, Mass., Jan. 16, 1907; s. Daniel and Susie (Goad) C.; B.S., Yale, 1928, postgrad. Boston U., 1929; m. Mary Eloise Baird, Feb. 14, 1931 (dec. Nov. 1964); children—Charles Baird, Marcus Eddy; m. 2d, Marilyn Eneix Willis, Oct. 1, 1966. Gen. supt. Daniel Cunningham Constrn. Co., Boston, 1928-32, Austin Co., Cleve. 1932-40; pres., treas., dir. Brady Hill Co., Detroit, 1940—; pres., treas., dir. Cunningham-Limp Co., Detroit, 1948-70, chmn. bd., chief exec. officer, 1970-78; chmn. bd., pres., treas., dir. Cunningham-Limp Ltd., Toronto, Ont., Can., 1959—; chmn. bd., pres. Cunningham-Limp Internat., S.A., 1963—, Cunningham-Limp de las Americas, S.A., 1966—, Cunningham-Limp de Espana, 1966—, Cunningham-Limp (France) S.A.R.L., 1967-78, Cunningham-Limp Deutschland GmbH, 1970-78; chmn. bd., chief exec. officer, pres. Cunningham-Limp Holding Co., 1978—; v.p., dir. Gulfstream Park Racing Assn., Hallandale, Fla., 1963—; Bd. dirs. Detroit, Nat. council Boy Scouts Am. Mem. Engring. Soc. Detroit, AIM (pres.'s council). Clubs: Yale (Detroit); Bloomfield Hills (Mich.) Country; Oakland Hills Country (Birmingham, Mich.); Indian Creek Country, Indian Creek Village, Jockey (Miami Beach, Fla.); Kenilworth (Bal Harbour, Fla.); Le Mirador Country (Mont Pelerin, Lake Geneva, Switzerland). Home: 104 Brady Ln Bloomfield Hills MI 48013 also Ocean Blvd Golden Beach FL 33160 Office: 1400 N Woodward Ave Birmingham MI 48011

CUNNINGHAM, MARCUS THOMAS, supermarket chain exec.; b. Littleton, Colo., Dec. 12, 1931; s. Thomas F. and Ellen Agnes (Davin) C.; B.A., U. No. Iowa, 1953; m. Elizabeth A. Libner, Jan. 22, 1959; children—Thomas, Janine, Marcus. Asst. grocery merchandiser Kroger Co., 1953-71; zone mgr. So. div. Vescio's, Inc., Saginaw, Mich., 1971-75; dir. ops. Glossner Bros., Johnstown, Pa., 1975-80, asst. v.p. ops., 1980—. Roman Catholic. Clubs: Rotary, Elks. Home: 105 Gregory Rd Johnstown PA 15905 Office: Franklin and Locust Sts Johnstown PA 15901

CUNNINGHAM, MARILYN ALICE ENEIX, bus. and advt. exec.; b. Warren, Minn., Mar. 8, 1917; d. Frederick C. and Mary (Boman) Eneix; B.A., U. Mich., 1937; m. Marcus E. Cunningham, Oct. 1, 1966. Account supr. Grant Advt., Inc., Detroit, Chgo., N.Y.C., 1945-60; v.p., dir. Brady Hill Co., Detroit, 1960—; dir. advt. Cunningham-Limp Co., Detroit, 1960-69, v.p., dir., Birmingham, Mich., 1969-72; vice chmn. bd., v.p., dir. Cunningham-Limp Internat., 1971—; vice chmn. bd., dir. Cunningham-Limp Co., Birmingham, 1972-78, Cunningham-Limp de Las Americas, 1972—, Cunningham-Limp Ltd., 1972—, Cunningham-Limp Holding Co., 1978—. Active in civic and philanthropic activities. Mem. Fine Arts Soc. Detroit (Silver Anniversary mem.), Smithsonian Instn., Alpha Phi. Republican. Presbyterian. Clubs: Kenilworth (Bal Harbour, Fla.); Jockey (Miami Beach, Fla.); Le Mirador Country (Mont Pelerin, Lake Geneva, Switzerland). Author: The Right Plant on The Right Site for Maximum Profit, 1962; The Comprehensive Approach to Facility Expansion, 1967; Design and Engineering, 1970; The Facility Planning Services of Cunningham-Limp, 1973; Total Responsibility in Facility Expansion, 1975; Planning, Designing, Engineering and Building, 1976; Design-Engineering-Construction, 1977; Comprehensive Design, Engineering and Construction, 1978; author, pub. SCOPE mag. Contbr. articles to nat. mags., bus. publs., tech. periodicals. Home: 104 Brady Ln Bloomfield Hills MI 48013 also Ocean Blvd Golden Beach FL 33160 Office: 1400 N Woodward Ave Birmingham MI 48011

CUNNINGHAM, TIMOTHY JOHN, ins. agency exec.; b. Chgo., Sept. 28, 1949; s. James Hugh and Mary Joan (Oswald) C.; B.A., Lewis U., 1972; m. Raima Plechavicius, Dec. 28, 1974. Ins. broker James H. Cunningham Ins. Agency Inc., Oak Park, Ill., 1972—, sec.-treas., 1974—; part-time faculty Triton Coll., 1973-77; part-time faculty Morton Coll., 1977—; bd. dirs. Chgo. Bd. Underwriters, 1976—. Pres. George Halas Boys Football League, 1975-77. Mem. Ind. Ins. Agts. Am., Ind. Ins. Agts. Ill. (chmn. edn. com. 1975-79, v.p. 1979—, dir. 1975—, chmn. Midwest edn. conf. 1976—). Office: Suite 307 1515 N Harlem Ave Oak Park IL 60302

CUNNINGHAM, WILLIAM EARL, JR., business exec.; b. Webster, Mass., Jan. 13, 1945; s. William Earl and Genevieve Rita (Wajer) C.; A.S., Worcester Jr. Coll., 1968; B.S., Northeastern U., 1971; M.B.A., Western New Eng. Coll., 1974; M.S., Worcester Poly. Inst., 1975. Sr. controls engr. Riley Stoker Corp., Worcester, Mass., 1963-77; owner Cunningham Enterprises, William Cunningham & Co., Webster, 1967—; project engr. Foster Wheeler Corp., Livingstone, N.J., 1978—; mgr. applications engring. Electronics Corp. Am., 1979; sr. engr. United Engrs. & Constructors, Inc., 1979—; dir. Sr. Services, Inc., Webster. Chmn. Webster Planning Bd., 1975-77, Webster Pub. Safety Com., 1976-77; mem. Central Mass. Regional Planning Commn. Mem. ASME, Instrument Soc. Am., Assn. M.B.A. Execs., IEEE, USCG Aux. Republican. Roman Catholic. Home: PO Box 698 860 School St Webster MA 01570 Office: PO Box 698 Webster MA 01570

CUNNION, PAUL ARTHUR, food importing co. exec.; b. N.Y.C., Oct. 9, 1938; s. Arthur Jerome and Edna Marie (Curley) C.; B.S. in Mktg., Fordham U., 1965; m. Kathleen Helen McGrath, Mar. 7, 1970. Sales rep. Cheeseborough-Pond's Inc., N.Y.C., 1963-64; asst. to v.p. sales, Red V Coconut Products Co., Inc., N.Y.C., 1966-72, v.p. sales, 1972-75, exec. v.p., gen. sales mgr., 1975-78, pres., chief operating officer, 1978—, also dir.; dir. Red V Coconut Products Ltd., Smith, Bell & Co. (U.S.A.) Inc. Active, Jefferson Democratic Club, 1973-78. Served with USAR, 1961-62. Mem. Am. Mfrs. Chocolate and Confection, Nat. Confectioner's Assn., Biscuit & Cracker Mfrs. Assn., Internat. Food Technologists (N.Y. chpt.), Am. Assn. Candy Technologists, Philippine-Am. C. of C. (dir., chmn. membership com., spl. reports, 1978, 79). Democrat. Roman Catholic. Club: Met. (N.Y.C.). Elected Kettle Com., Candy & Snack Industry mag., 1979. Editor quar. newsletter, 1968-78; contbr. articles in field to trade publs. Home: 157 E 72nd St New York NY 10021 Office: 116 John St New York NY 10038

CURLEY, JOHN FRANCIS, JR., investment broker; b. Wollaston, Mass., July 24, 1939; s. John Francis and Ann (Omar) C.; A.B., Princeton U., 1960; M.B.A., Harvard U., 1962; m. Loretta Mae O'Keeffe, Oct. 20, 1962; children—William Laurance, Edward Reid, David Neil. With Paine, Webber, Jackson & Curtis Inc., N.Y.C., 1964—, v.p., asst. to chmn. bd., 1970-72, exec. v.p., dir. adminstrv. div., 1972-77, pres., 1977-80, chmn. fin. com., 1980—, also dir.; pres., dir. Cashfund Inc.; dir. Paine Webber Inc., Paine Webber Mitchell Hutchins Inc., Constitution Reins. Corp. Treas. class of 1960, Princeton U., 1970-75. Served to 1st lt. AUS, 1962-64. Mem. Securities Industry Assn. (dir., exec. com.), Investment Assn. N.Y. (past pres.), Bond Club N.Y.C. (gov.), Wall St. Planning Group. Clubs: Harvard Bus. Sch. of N.Y. (dir.), City Midday (N.Y.C.); Sleepy Hollow (Scarborough, N.Y.). Office: 140 Broadway New York NY 10005

CURLEY, WALTER JOSEPH PATRICK, JR., investment banker; b. Pitts., Sept. 17, 1922; s. Walter Joseph and Marguerite Inez (Cowan) C.; B.A., Yale U., 1944; M.B.A., Harvard U., 1948; LL.D. (hon.), Trinity Coll., Dublin, 1976; m. Mary Taylor Walton, Dec. 4, 1948; children—Margaret Curley Wiles, Walter Joseph Patrick, John Walton, James Mellon. Sect. mgr. Caltex Oil Co., India, Italy, N.Y.C., 1948-57; v.p., dir. San Jacinto Petroleum Co., N.Y.C., 1958-61; partner J.H. Whitney & Co., N.Y.C., 1961-75; dir. Curley Land Co., Pitts., Willers & Sons, Ireland, Fiduciary Trust Co. N.Y., Investment Bank Ireland, Intercontinental Energy Corp., Crane Co., N.Y. Life Ins. Co.; ambassador to Ireland, Dublin, 1975-77. Commr. pub. events, chief of protocol for N.Y.C., 1973-74. Mem. fin. com. N.Y.C. Republican Orgn., 1957-59. Served to capt. USMCR, 1943-46. Decorated Bronze Star (U.S.); Cloud and Banner (China). Republican. Roman Catholic. Author: Letters from the Pacific, 1960; Monarchs in Waiting, 1973. Home: 791 Park Ave New York NY 10021 Office: 630 Fifth Ave New York NY 10020

CURLIS, WILLIAM LEE, county ofcl.; b. Columbus, Ohio, Oct. 16, 1947; s. Billy Walter and Betty Jane (Bullock) C.; B.S., Ohio State U., 1970, M.A., 1973. Law clk. Office of the Pros. Atty., Franklin County (Ohio), Columbus, 1966-73, exec. adminstr., 1973—; tchr. social studies and English, Knox County (Ohio) Joint Vocat. Sch., Mt. Vernon, 1971-73, chmn. acad. dept., 1972-73, sec. adv. council, 1970-73. Mem. Franklin County Republican Central and Exec. Coms., 1973—; lectr. and seminar participant Ohio Republican State Com., 1976, 77; lectr. Franklin County Rep. Orgn., 1976—; bd. dirs. Leadership Columbus, 1980—; del. Nat. Fedn. of Young Reps., Memphis, 1977, Orlando, 1979. Recipient Robert A. Taft award, 1977; Named Tchr. of the Year, Knox County Joint Vocat. Sch., 1973.

Mem. Assn. of Legal Adminstrs., Nat. Council Social Studies, Nat. Archives Assn., Ohio Hist. Soc. Methodist. Author: (with Brenda Borden and Bettie Shonk) You and the Job, 1973. Home: 2668-L Cannon Point Ct Columbus OH 43209 Office: Hall of Justice Columbus OH 43215

CUROTTO, RICKY JOSEPH, lawyer, real estate exec.; b. Lomita Park, Calif., Dec. 22, 1931; s. Enrico and Nora (Giusso) C.; B.S. cum laude, U. San Francisco, 1953, J.D., 1958; m. Anne Drobac, June 12, 1954; children—Dina Lynn, John Francis, Alexis Joseph; m. 2d, Vernice Maloy, Oct. 26, 1971. Admitted to Cal. bar, 1958, asso. firm Peart, Baraty & Hassard, San Francisco, 1958-60; real estate counsel Utah Internat., Inc., San Francisco, 1960—, asst. sec. 1966—; counsel, dir. Securities Intermountain, Inc. Dir. Whitecliff Corp., 1st Capital Corp., Briggs Andrew, Pope & Co., Simco Indsl. Mortgage Co., Garden Hotels Investment Co.; sec., counsel Ross Valley Homes, Inc., Calif. Charter Mortgage Co., First Security Bank Utah. Chmn. pres.'s ambassadors and athletic bd. U. San Francisco. Served to 1st lt. AUS, 1954-56. Recipient Bur. Nat. Affairs award, 1958. Mem. State Bar Cal., San Francisco Bar Assn., Am. Arbitration Assn. (nat. panel arbitrators), U. San Francisco Alumni Assn., Am. Bar Assn., Cal. Assn. ACT. Phi Alpha Delta, Pi Sigma Alpha. Republican. Roman Catholic. Clubs: Commonwealth of Calif. (past chmn. lawmaking procedures sect., membership com.); Century (pres., dir.). Contbr. articles to law revs. Home: 399 Sail Fish Isle Foster City CA 94404 Office: 550 California St San Francisco CA 94104

CURRAN, D. PATRICK, paint mfr.; b. Kansas City, Mo., June 19, 1944; s. Desmond and Betty Ann (Cook) C.; B.A., Stanford U., 1966; M.B.A., Northwestern U., 1968; m. Janet Smith, Nov. 18, 1977; 1 dau., Josephine. With Cook Paint & Varnish Co., North Kansas City, Mo., 1968—, beginning as research technician, successively indsl. salesman fin. div., adminstrv. asst. Detroit Automotive div., adminstrv. asst. Trade Sales div., v.p. corp. planning, exec. v.p., and chief operating officer, 1968-79, pres., chmn. bd., 1979—; dir. Plaza Bank. Bd. dirs. Pembroke Country Day Sch., Kansas City Starlight Theatre. Mem. Nat. Paint and Coatings Assn. (dir.), Young Pres.'s Orgn., Mo. Golf Assn. (pres. 1978-79). Clubs: Kansas City, Kansas City Country, Detroit Athletic, River (dir.), Lyford Cay. Office: 919 E 14th Ave North Kansas City MO 64116

CURRAN, DONALD L., investment banker; b. Binghamton, N.Y., Oct. 18, 1901; s. De Lafayette and Nellie (Morey) C.; M.E., Cornell U., 1924; LL.D., Albany Law Sch., 1980. Indsl. analyst, Albany, 1924-27; broker Paine, Webber & Co., Albany, 1927-40; mgr. Merrill Lynch, Pierce, Fenner & Smith, Albany, from 1940, v.p., 1962-66, now ret.; dir. Wytex Corp.; trustee Nat. Savings Bank. Trustee, treas. Albany Law Sch.; trustee Hartwick Coll., Albany Inst. History and Art. Mem. Am. Fedn. Arts. Presbyterian. Clubs: University, Albany Country, Cooperstown Country. Home: PO Box 150 Glimmerglen Rd Cooperstown NY 13326

CURRAN, DWIGHT, wholesale lumber co. exec.; b. Santa Ana, Calif., Sept. 28, 1938; s. Frank and Nan Veronica (Mead) C.; B.S., Hayward State U., 1972; m. Linda Kemble, July 15, 1967; children—Dennis, Michael, Katie. Ops. mgr. Ga.-Pacific Co., San Jose, Calif., 1972-75; gen. mgr. wholesale div. Redwood Empire, Morgan Hill, Calif., 1976-78; founder, pres. DMK-Pacific Corp., Fremont, Calif., 1978—. Exec. bd., dir. publicity Fremont City Soccer Club. Mem. Oakland Lumbermen's Club (past pres., dir., publicity chmn.). Republican. Roman Catholic. Contbg. editor Merchant mag., 1970—. Home: 4873 Deadwood Dr Fremont CA 94536 Office: 4529 Mattos Dr Fremont CA 94536

CURRAN, JOHN CHARLES, JR., fin. co. exec.; b. N.Y.C., Aug. 21, 1932; s. John Charles and Mildred S. (Herrman) C.; B.S., Georgetown U., 1954; postgrad. N.Y. U., 1957-60; m. Valerie E. O'Donovan, Sept. 13, 1958; children—Valerie Catherine, Cinnia DeClare, Mary Christina, Sheila Mairead. Ofcl. asst. First Nat. City Bank, N.Y.C., 1957-60; asst. to pres. Sears, Roebuck Acceptance Corp., N.Y.C., 1960-62; financing mgr. Ford Motor Credit Corp., N.Y.C. and Dearborn, Mich., 1962-69; v.p., treas. Dayton Hudson Corp., Mpls., 1969-71; pres. White Motor Credit Corp., Cleve., 1972-75; v.p., treas. White Motor Corp., Cleve., 1972-75; exec. v.p., dir. Field Enterprises Ednl. Corp., Chgo., 1975-78; pres., chief exec. officer Fiat Credit Corp., 1979—. Trustee, mem. adv. bd. Woodlands Acad. of Sacred Heart. Served to 1st lt., inf. AUS, 1954-56. Mem. Fin. Execs. Inst. Clubs: Econ., Mid-Am. (Chgo.); Knollwood (Lake Forest, Ill.). Home: 844 Timber Ln Lake Forest IL 60045 Office: 2333 Waukegan Rd Deerfield IL 60015

CURREN, ARTHUR THOMAS, JR., corp. exec.; b. Paterson, N.J., Jan. 27, 1943; s. Arthur Thomas and Ella M. (Biggers) C.; B.A. in Econs., Trinity Coll., 1965; M.B.A. in Mktg., U. Pa., 1967; children—Megan, Erin. With Allen-Curren Electronics, Phila., 1967, Compton Advt., N.Y.C., 1971-73; engagement mgr. McKinsey & Co., N.Y.C., 1973-77; v.p. corp. planning Marriott Corp., Washington, 1977—. Served to lt. Supply Corps, USNR, 1968-71. Office: 1 Marriott Dr Washington DC 20058

CURRERI, ANTHONY JOSEPH, mfg. co. exec.; b. Bklyn., Feb. 6, 1935; s. Charles and Anna (Barsalona) C.; B.S., Bethany (W.Va.) Coll., 1958; M.B.A., U. Pitts., 1959. Trainee, Abraham & Strauss, N.Y.C., 1959-60; buyer cosmetics and handbags Tailored Woman, N.Y.C., 1960-63; successively asst. buyer cosmetics and handbags, buyer casual shoes, uniforms and women's dresses, buyer decorative home accessories J.C. Penney Co., N.Y.C., 1963-80; in communications Western Electric, Newark, 1980—. Served with USNG, 1960-68. Recipient award for devel. of flame retardant and static-free uniforms Chlorox Co., 1976. Mem. Two-Ten Nat. Shoe Assn., Noel Trim-a-Home Assn., 7th Ave. Dress Assn. Republican. Roman Catholic. Home: 5 Acorn Pl North Caldwell NJ 07006 Office: Gateway II Newark NJ 07102

CURREY, DAVID MARCUS, banker; b. Mt. Pleasant, Tex., Feb. 14, 1947; s. Palmore and Julia Currey; B.B.A. in Econs. and Fin., E. Tex. State U.; m. Virginia Sue Wright, Oct. 19, 1969; children—Dimitri, David Marcus, John Coulter. Nat. bank examiner, 1970-75; v.p. comml. lending Longview Nat. Bank (Tex.), 1975-79; pres. Security Nat. Bank, Austin, Tex., 1979—. Mem. Robert Morris Assos., Bank Adminstrn. Inst. (past chpt. dir.). Methodist. Clubs: Balcones Lions (charter), Town and Country Optimist. Office: 13776-A Research Blvd Austin TX 78750

CURRIE, DAVID CARL, med. supply distbg. co. exec.; b. Taungyi, Burma, May 15, 1941; came to U.S., 1958; s. Holman Carl and Eva Ruth (Longway) C.; student Atlantic Union Coll., South Lancaster, Mass., 1959-63; children—Temple, Cameo, Karmen, Korelle. Salesman, Ipco Hosp. Supply Co., Boston, 1969-71, 73-74, product mgr., 1971-72, regional sales mgr., 1972-73, gen. mgr. Midwest div., 1974-75; founder, pres. Currie Med. Co., Arcadia, Calif., 1975—; guest lectr. several univs., bus. groups, 1978—. Republican. Home: 22 Woodlyn Ln Bradbury CA 91010 Office: 416 E Live Oak Ave Arcadia CA 91006

CURRIE, GLENN KENNETH, service co. exec.; b. Stoneham, Mass., Sept. 23, 1943; s. Kenneth Aubrey and Muriel Adeline (Berry) C.; A.B., Dartmouth Coll., 1965; m. Susanne Gosnell, Feb. 6, 1971; children—Diana, Lara. Security analyst Paul Revere Life Ins. Co., 1970-72, asst. treas., 1972-73, v.p. investments, 1973-78; v.p. fin. internat. services div. Avcó Corp., Cin., 1978, v.p. internat. ops., 1979, pres. Avco Overseas Services Corp., Houston, 1979—. Served with U.S. Navy, 1965-69. Mem. Houston C. of C., N.Y. Soc. Security Analysts, Fin. Analysts Fedn., W. Houston C. of C. (dir.). Office: 17200 Park Row Houston TX 77084

CURRIE, HARRY CAMPBELL, mfg. co. exec.; b. Glasgow, Scotland, Sept. 8, 1947; s. Henry Campbell and Isabella (Andrew) C.; B. Math., U. Waterloo (Ont.), 1969; B.A. Brock U., St. Catharines, Ont., 1977. Computer programmer Stelco, Hamilton, Ont., 1969-71; programmer, analyst Can. Systems Group, Mississauga, Ont., 1971-73; data processing cons. Gosselin Cons., Mississauga, 1974-75, Quadrus Assos., Mississauga, 1975-76; data processing mgr. Gen. Tire, Welland, Ont., 1977—. Home: 6699 Water Ave Niagara Falls ON L2G 5W9 Canada Office: PO Box 1002 John St Welland ON Canada

CURRIE, ROBERT FREDERICK, banker; b. Portland, Maine, Aug. 30, 1931; s. William Otis and Helen Gertrude (Patterson) C.; student Am. Inst. Banking, 1949-56, Northeastern U., 1959; m. Eleanor M. Schattgen, May 5, 1956; children—Lisa Olive, Heidi Eleanor. Bank messenger Granite Trust Co., Quincy, Mass., 1949-52; with Norfolk County Trust Co., Brookline, Mass., 1953-63, asst. mgr., 1956-59, mgr., 1959-63; treas. Sharon Coop. Bank, Sharon, Mass., 1963-68, pres., 1968—, also dir.; dir. Coop. Central Bank, Boston; trustee Mass. Cooperative Banks Retirement Assn., 1971-78, pres., 1974—. Treas. Salvation Army, Sharon, 1958-61; bus. chmn. United Fund, Sharon, 1963; mem. warrant com., Sharon, 1966-69, mem. data processing com., 1972-74, chmn., 1972-73, mem. bd. selectmen, 1974-77, chmn., 1976—. Served with USAF, 1951-53. Clubs: Masons, Rotary (pres. 1962-63). Home: 41 Pine Grove Ave Sharon MA 02067 Office: 7 S Main St Sharon MA 02067

CURRIER, DENNIS THOMAS, hosp. fin. exec.; b. Detroit, June 10, 1944; s. Vincent James and Jean Enid (Flett) C.; B.S. in Mech. Engring., U. Notre Dame, 1966; M.B.A., U. Mich., 1967; m. Susan Kathryn Toth, Mar. 8, 1975; children—Jean Higgins, Kathryn Connor; children by previous marriage—D. Thomas, Kalin Kathleen. Staff acountant Price Waterhouse & Co., Detroit, 1967-70, cons. mgmt. advisory services, 1970-72, mgr. mgmt. advisory services, 1972-74; v.p. fin., treas. Harper-Grace Hosps., Detroit, 1974—; fin. cons. health care. Precinct del. Mich. Democratic Conv., 1966; chmn. finance com. Roman Catholic parish ch., 1970-71; trustee, treas., chmn. fin. com. and exec. com. Family Services, Detroit. C.P.A., Mich. Mem. Am. Inst. C.P.A.'s, Mich. Assn. C.P.A.'s, Engring. Soc. Detroit, Am., Mich. hosp. assns., Tau Beta Pi, Pi Tau Sigma, Beta Alpha Psi. Club: Birmingham Athletic. Home: 565 Wooddale Rd Birmingham MI 48010 Office: 3990 John R St Detroit MI 48201

CURRIN, TIMOTHY LEE, real estate broker; b. Bonham, Tex., July 27, 1948; s. Travis Lee and Arline Francis (McDonald) C.; B.B.A., Tex. Tech. U., 1970; m. Judith R. Wohler, Oct. 13, 1979. With First City Nat. Bank, Houston, 1971; asst. mgr. Young Houstonian Club, 1972; resident mgr. Columbine Condomiums, Mt. Crested Butte, Colo., 1975-77; pres. Ptarmigan Assos., Inc., realtors and property mgrs., Crested Butte, 1977—. Mem. Gunnison County Real Estate Bd. (v.p. 1979-80), Pi Kappa Alpha. Republican. Mem. Ch. of Christ. Home: Box 674 Crested Butte CO 81224 Office: PO Box 277 Crested Butte CO 81224

CURRY, ARTHUR DAN, electronics mfg. co. exec.; b. St. Louis, Oct. 4, 1921; s. Adam Samsbury and Emma Sophie (Mueller) C.; B.S. in Mech. Engring., Heald's Engring. Coll., 1961; m. Virginia Ruth Kubant, Nov. 7, 1943; children—Arthur Dan, Donna Ruth Curry Rogers. Foundry inspector Gen. Steel Casting Corp., Granite City, Ill., 1940-42; aircraft instrument mechanic Naval Air Sta. Alameda (Calif.), 1947-54; chief inspector Gen. Metals Corp., Oakland, Calif., 1954-59; quality analyst FMC Corp., San Jose, Calif., 1959-60; quality engr. Philco Western Devel. Labs., Palo Alto, Calif., 1960-61; quality assurance mgr. Huggins Labs., Sunnyvale, Calif., 1961-65; quality assurance mgr., nuclear power div. Gen. Electric Corp., San Jose, Calif. and Wilmington, N.C., 1965-69; chief procurement quality assurance Gen. Dynamics Corp., Ft. Worth, 1969-72; quality assurance mgr. Masonilson Corp., Montebello, Calif., 1972-73, Mechanics Research Corp., Los Angeles, 1973-75; owner, operator IAM Enterprises, Santa Fe Springs, Calif., 1976—. Dist. vice chmn. for adult tng. Boy Scouts Am., 1955-62; elder Hope Lutheran Ch. Served with USAAF, 1942-45. Registered profl. engr., Calif. Fellow Am. Soc. for Quality Control; sr. mem. Soc. Mfg. Engrs. (cert.). Home: 767 Virginia Ann Dr Azusa CA 91702 Office: IAM Enterprises 11823 E Slauston St Unit 28 Santa Fe Springs CA 90670

CURRY, CHARLES HENRY, advt. exec.; b. Grady, Ala., Sept. 25, 1946; s. Will Henry and Ida Belle (Guice) C.; B.S. in Bus. Adminstrn., Roosevelt U., Chgo., 1968; M.B.A. (Inland Steel Co. fellow 1969-70), Northwestern U., 1970; m. Betty Ann Chapman, Mar. 18, 1967; children—Christopher, Kelli. With Procter & Gamble Co., 1970-74, asst. brand mgr. household products, Cin., 1973-74; brand mgr. cat foods Quaker Oats Co., Chgo., 1974-76; mgr. new products Alberto-Culver Co., Melrose Park, Ill., 1976-78; account exec. Leo Burnett U.S.A., Chgo., 1978—. Deacon, past pres. ch. choir New Omega Baptist Ch., Chgo. Mem. Beta Gamma Sigma. Office: Leo Burnett USA Prudential Plaza Chicago IL 60601

CURTIN, JAMES JOSEPH, real estate exec.; b. Wakeman, Ohio, July 19, 1922; s. William James and Benedicta Ann (Strickfaden) C.; B.B.A., U. Toledo, 1948; m. Ruth Mary Cascadden, Dec. 22, 1943; children—Michael, Patricia, Timothy. Pres., Curtin & Pease, Inc., Toledo, 1948-69, Curtin & Pease div. Penton/IPC, Inc., Clearwater, Fla., 1969—, Pittway Real Estate, Inc., Clearwater, 1976—, Pittway Group, 1979—; dir. Saddlebrook Resorts, Inc., KornZaPoppin of Fla.; limited partner Revesco, Toledo. Served with A.C., USNR, 1941-42, USAAF, 1942-46. Mem. Direct Mail Mktg. Assn. (D. Stuart Webb award 1958, Darnell Gold medal 1969, Silver Mailbox 1976, Gold Mailbox 1977). Republican. Roman Catholic. Clubs: Countryside Country, Belleview Biltmore Country, Brandywine Country, Elks. Author articles in field. Office: 3040 Gulf To Bay Blvd Clearwater FL 33519

CURTIS, CHARLES EDWARD, ins. agy. exec.; b. Newburyport, Mass., Sept. 3, 1916; s. Charles P. and Sarah Ann (Heseltine) C.; student Sch. Fin., Boston U., evenings 1934-38; m. Helen W. Nason, Mar. 22, 1941; 1 dau., Marcia S. With loan dept. Haverhill (Mass.), Nat. Bank, 1934-40; with York Nat. Bank, 1941, 46; pres., treas. F.R. Smith Ins. Agy., Inc., Haverhill, 1947—: trustee, clk. of corp. Family Mut. Savs. Bank, Haverhill, 1954—. Chpt. chmn. ARC, 1950-54; pres. United Fund, 1956. Served with USAAF, 1941-46. Recipient various awards for community service. Mem. Mass. Assn. Ins. Agys., Nat. Assn. Watch and Clock Collectors. Republican. Episcopalian. Clubs: Haverhill Rotary (pres. 1955), Masons (Haverhill). Home: 48 Columbia Park Haverhill MA 01830 also Box 654A Portview Kennebunkport ME 04046 Office: 191 Merrimack St Haverhill MA 01830

CURTIS, DOUGLAS HOMER, electric co. exec., fin. cons.; b. Jackson, Mich., July 19, 1934; s. Homer K. and Luella D. (Hall) C.; B.A., Park Coll., Parkville, Mo., 1956; m. Jean Ann Breaux; children—Rebecca, Linda, Colleen, Robert. Successively fin. analyst, traveling auditor, mgr. Boston region GESCO div. Gen. Electric Co., 1958-69; v.p. fin. and adminstrn. Internat. Data Corp., 1969-80; v.p. fin. Franklin Electric Co., Inc., Bluffton, Ind., 1969—; founder, pres. Curtis Assos., Bluffton, 1980—; dir. Markhon Industries, Wabash, Ind. Pres., Wells County Hosp. Authority, 1974-75. Served with USMCR, 1956-58. Mem. Nat. Assn. Security Dealers (gov.-at-large 1978—, automated quotations and info. and exec. coms. 1976-80, chmn. fin. com. 1980), Fin. Execs. Inst. (dir. 1975). Clubs: Orchard Ridge Country, Parlor City Country. Home: Rural Route 5 Timberidge Rd Bluffton IN 46714 Office: 400 E Spring St Bluffton IN 46714

CURTIS, ELLWOOD F., farm machinery mfg. exec.; b. Mishawka, Ind., May 14, 1914; s. Warren H. and Marian (Robbins) C.; A.B., Dartmouth, 1935; m. Helen Yeomans, Apr. 12, 1936; children—Count, Don. Barron. Accountant Haskins & Sells, 1935-39; accountant Deere & Co., 1939-44, became comptroller, 1944, dir., 1951—, pres., 1964—, vice chmn., 1978-79, also chief operating officer, to 1979. Clubs: Masons, Chicago (Chgo.). Home: 4005 7th Ave Moline IL 61265 Office: Deere & Co John Deere Rd Moline IL 61265

CURTIS, JAMES THEODORE, lawyer; b. Lowell, Mass., July 8, 1923; s. Theodore D. and Maria (Souliotis) Koutras; B.A., U. Mich., 1948; J.D., Harvard, 1951; Sc.D. (hon.), U. Lowell, 1972; m. Kleanthe D. Dusopol June 25, 1950; children—Madelon Mary, Theodore James, Stephanie Diane, Gregory Theodosius, James Theodore. Admitted to Mass. State bar, 1951; asso. Adams & Blinn, Boston, 1951-52; legal asst., asst. atty. gen. Mass., 1952-53; pvt. practice law, Lowell, 1953-57; sr. partner firm Goldman & Curtis, and predecessors, Lowell and Boston, 1957—. Chmn. Lowell and Greater Lowell Heart Fund, 1967-68; mem. adv. bd. Salvation Army, sec., 1956-58; mem. Bd. Higher Edn. Mass., 1967-72; mem. Lowell Charter Commn., 1969-71; del. Democratic Party State Convs., 1956-60; trustee U. Lowell, 1963-72, chmn. bd., 1968-72; bd. dirs. U. Lowell Research Found., 1965-72, Merrimack Valley Health Planning Council, 1969-72. Served with AUS, 1943-46. Decorated Knight Order Orthodox Crusade Holy Sepulcher. Mem. Am., Mass., Middlesex County, Lowell bar assns., Am., Mass. trial lawyers assns., Mass. Acad. Trial Lawyers, Am. Judicature Soc., Harvard Law Sch., U. Mich. alumni assns., Lowell Hist. Soc., DAV, Delta Epsilon Pi. Democrat. Greek Orthodox. Clubs: Masons, Harvard of Lowell (pres. 1969-71, dir.). Home: 111 Rivercliff Rd Lowell MA 01852 Office: 144 Merrimack St Lowell MA 01852

CURTIS, RICHARD HARVEY, constrn. co. exec.; b. Balaklava, South Australia, Apr. 23, 1931; came to U.S., 1971; s. John William and Winifred Bramhall (Fidler) C.; B. Applied Sci., U. Adelaide, 1952; m. Eleanor Robson, Apr. 3, 1956; children—Robert Harvey, Helen Louise. Chem. engr. Powergas Corp. of Australia, Melbourne, 1953; chem. engr. Powergas Corp., Stockton-on-Tees, Eng., 1953-61, head devel., 1961-64, chief engr., 1964-68, div. tech. dir., 1968-71; dir. engring. Davy McKee Corp. (formerly Davy Powergas Inc.), Lakeland, Fla., 1971-72, v.p. engring., 1972-80, sr. v.p. engring., 1980—. Mem. com. Boy Scouts Am., 1975-77, merit badge counselor, 1975—. Chartered engr., U.K.; registered profl. engr., Fla., La., N.Mex., Ariz., Ohio, Oreg., Wis., Del. Fellow Inst. Gas Engrs. U.K.; mem. ASME, Am. Inst. Chem. Engrs., Fla. Engring. Soc. (sr.), Nat. Soc. Profl. Engrs. Episcopalian. Clubs: Lone Palm Golf, Lakeland Yacht and Country, Continental Country, Deep Six Scuba Diving, Univs. Lodge (Durham, Eng.). Home: 141 Skyland Dr Lakeland FL 33803 Office: PO Drawer 5000 Lakeland FL 33803

CURTIS, ROGER WILLIAM, fin. exec.; b. Buchanan, Mich., Aug. 20, 1920; s. Lloyd Norton and Gertrude (Whelan) C.; student public schs., Oakland, Calif.; m. Lula B. Current, Apr. 22, 1961; children—Linda, Susan, William, Jennie, Paul. With L.N. Curtis & Sons, Oakland, 1934—, sec.-treas., chief operating officer, 1961—, dir., 1951—. Served with USN, 1943-46. Mem. Internat. Assn. Fire Chiefs, Western Fire Chiefs Assn., Calif. Fire Chiefs Assn., Nev. Firemen's Assn., Calif. Rural Fire Assn. Republican. Club: Masons. Home: 20 Lake Pl Walnut Creek CA 94598 Office: 4133 Broadway Oakland CA 94611

CURTIS, SONDRÉ COREY, data processing co. exec.; b. New Haven, Sept. 30, 1943; d. Ellis Samuel and Myrtle Warner (Dlga) Corey; B.S. in Chem. Engring., Mich. State U., 1965; postgrad. Yale U., 1966, Tulsa U., Stanford U.; m. Kenneth Clarke Chambers, Oct. 22, 1962; children—Brett Clarke, Brian Mitchell; m. 2d, Victory John Montgomery Curtis, Nov. 20, 1968; 1 son, Todd Montgomery. Adminstrv. asst. Yale U. and Yale-New Haven Hosp., 1965-67; asst. project engr. Schick Safety Razor Co., 1967-68; sales tng. specialist, personnel mgr. Dialog Computing, Inc., Fairfield, Conn., 1968-71; pres. Curtis Assos., Inc., Stratford, Conn., 1971-74; dir. sales Automatic Data Processing Co., Inc., East Hartford, Conn., 1975-78; sales mgr. Xerox Diablo Computer Allee Office Equipment, Inc., Tulsa, 1978-79; mgr. Tulsa dist. Sun Info. Systems, 1979—; dir. Bailey System, Inc.; lectr. systematic selling techniques. Recipient various company awards. Mem. Nat. Assn. Accts., Nat. Assn. Women Accountants, Sales and Mktg. Assos., Sales and Mktg. Execs. Internat. (chpt. sec.). Republican. Home: Rural Route 1 Box 451 Terlton OK 74081 Office: 907 S Detroit Tulsa OK 74120

CURTISS, TRUMBULL CARY, banker; b. Buffalo, May 30, 1940; s. Colman and Frances Rochester (Wheeler) C.: B.A. in Am. Studies, Yale U., 1963; postgrad. U. Buffalo; m. Leslie Fisher, July 18, 1964; children—Cullen, Meredith, Emily. Dir. advt. Mfrs. & Traders Trust, Buffalo, 1963-68; asst. v.p. First Wis. Nat. Bank, Madison, 1968-69; v.p. Bank of Commonwealth, Detroit, 1969-70, BayBank Middlesex, Waltham, Mass., 1970-75: v.p. BayBanks, Inc., Boston, 1975-79, sr. v.p. mktg., 1979-80, chmn. and chief exec. officer BayBank Merrimack Valley, Andover, Mass., 1980—. Served with USMCR, 1959-60. Address: BayBank Merrimack Valley 23 Main St Andover MA 01810

CURVEN, ALFRED GUYDON, theatrical producer; b. Newark, N.J., Feb. 13, 1934; s. Arthur Whitelaw and Leah Ava (Doolittle) C.; B.A., N.Y. U., 1955; M.S. in Communication, Carnegie-Mellon U.; D.D., Faith Theol. Sem., 1968; m. Joan N. DiSarno, May 15, 1962; children—Patricia, Francys, Christofer. Vice-pres. Cyclone Advt. Agy., 1959-68; pres. Cherylaine Records, Infinity Music Pub. Co., 1959—, pres. AlCee Pub. Co., 1968—, Multi Media Advt. Agy., 1968-74, Advertiques, 1975—; chmn. bd., pres. Miracle Mountain Theatre Co., 1977—; media specialist Rutland (Vt.) Daily Herald, 1980—; country music dir. Sta. WHWB-AM-FM, Rutland, 1980—. Chmn. bd. Vt. Community Theatre, Inc., 1980—; bd. dirs. Ashley Players; vice chmn. Borderline Players. Served with USAF, 1955-59. Recipient AP award for best spot news story, Calif., 1959, award for best news photograph IDPA, 1961; award for best black and white newspaper advertisement design New Eng. Advt. Execs. Assn., 1980.

Mem. Actors Equity Assn., Screen Actors Guild, Nat. Cartoonists Soc., AFTRA. Address: Route 2 Country Club Rd Brandon VT 05733

CURY, NEAL GENE, investment and bus. cons. co. exec.; b. Norton, Va., Feb. 10, 1931; s. Dahar and Elizabeth (Haddad) C.; B.A., Va. Mil. Inst., 1953; M.B.A., U. Pa., 1955; m. Betty Jane Davis, July 11, 1953; children—James Davis, Neal Gene, Renee, Phillip Haddad. Instr., U. Pa., 1954-55, U. Md., overseas, 1955-57, Jacksonville (Fla.) U., 1961-63; pres. Cavalier Oil Co., Jacksonville, 1959-65, Sanitation Inc., Jacksonville, 1962-72, Leon Refuse Inc., Tallahassee, 1968-73, Direction Diversified, Inc., Jacksonville, 1973—. Chmn. scouting com. Grace Chapel Parish, 1963-65; asst. to chmn. Duval County Democratic Exec. Com., 1966-69. Served with USAF, 1957-59. Mem. Kappa Alpha. Episcopalian. Clubs: Bigtree Racquet, Univ., Salaam (pres. 1966, dir. 1966-69) (Jacksonville). Office: 3100 University Blvd S Jacksonville FL 32216

CURZON, ELIZABETH JEANNETTE GORE, pub. accountant; b. Alton, Ill., Oct. 15, 1911; d. Forrest Bird and Annella (Denby) Gore; A.B., U. Ill., 1932, M.S., 1934, postgrad., 1950-54; m. George J. Curzon, Jan. 6, 1930 (div. Apr. 1946); children—Marjorie A., Victoria Curzon Engelhardt, Katherine Curzon Owen. Grad. asst. U. Ill., 1932-34, library research asst. in animal nutrition, 1934-39; office mgr., accountant George J. Curzon, Champaign, Ill., 1940-46; accountant Curzon Parks Bookkeeping Service, Champaign, 1946-55; partner Peer, Hunt & Curzon, C.P.A.'s, Champaign, 1955-78, Clifton, Gunderson & Co., 1978—; sec. Clark St. Bldg. Corp., Champaign, 1958-72; dir. Clifford-Jacobs Forging Co., 1976-77, 1979—, Clark-Lindsey Inc., 1979—. Treas., Champaign County Community Chest, 1954-55, pres., 1955-56, dir., 1950-56; sec. Com. on Elm Tree Disease, 1954-55; pres. Laymon Convalescent Home, Inc., 1950-63; treas. Champaign County Estate Planning Council, 1969-70, sec., 1970-71, vice chmn., 1971-72, chmn., 1972-73. Bd. dirs. Urban League Champaign County, 1960-66, McKinley YMCA, 1960-66, 68-75; mem. Champaign County Mental Health Bd., 1977-78. Mem. Ill. Soc. C.P.A.'s (chpt. chmn. 1961-62, chpt. treas. 1960-61, profl. devel. com. 1967-68, state taxation com. 1969-71, com. ann. tax conf. 1972-74), Am. Inst. C.P.A.'s, Am. Forestry Assn., Nat. Audubon Soc., Am. Athletic Assn., Phi Beta Kappa, Phi Upsilon Omicron, Omicron Nu, Alpha Delta Pi. Baptist. Home: 617 W University St Champaign IL 61820 Office: 203 W Clark St Champaign IL 61820

CUSACK, THOMAS FRANCIS, oil co. exec.; b. Bklyn., June 4, 1918; s. John and Anna (Donohue) C.; tchrs. certificate St. Joseph's Normal Coll., 1938; grad. French Civilization Lang. and Law, Sorbonne, Paris, France, 1945; B.S. in Accounting, U. S.C., 1952; m. Margaret Martha King, June 11, 1949; children—Andrea, Jennifer. Instr. French and math. Stanislaus Coll., Bay St. Louis, Miss., 1938-39; office mgr. Metalcraft Corp., Phila., 1946-48, regional auditor, Washington, 1948-49; sec.-controller U.S. Royalty Oil Corp., Los Angeles, 1950-70, exec. v.p., 1970—, dir., 1959—; dir. Consol. Royalties Inc., Los Angeles, Clark Oil Co., Los Angeles; dir., v.p. Cabrillo Mesa Devel. Co., San Diego. Mem. nat. adv. bd. Am. Security Council. Served with AUS, 1940-45; ETO. Decorated Bronze Star medal. Democrat. Roman Catholic. K.C. Home: 14932 La Cuarta St Friendly Hills Whittier CA 90605 Office: PO Box 4631 Whittier CA 90607

CUSHMAN, ROBERT ARNOLD, wire cable mfg. co. exec.; b. Miami, Fla., Aug. 4, 1918; s. Charles Franklin and Mabel (Rorem) C.; B.S. in Bus. Adminstrn., U. Fla., 1940; M.B.A., N.Y. U., 1951; postgrad. Mich. State U., 1970; m. Helen Merle Baker, June 2, 1945; children—Lucinda, Robert. Adjuster Comml. Credit Corp., Miami, 1941; bus. mgr. research lab Gen. Cable Corp., Greenwich, Conn., 1945-51, purchasing agt., 1951-59, asst. dir. purchases, 1959—. Dist. chmn. Watchung Area council Boy Scouts Am., 1965-75. Served with USN, 1941-45; lt. comdr. Res. ret. Recipient Silver Beaver award Boy Scouts Am., 1975. Mem. Purchasing Mgrs. Assn. N.Y. (recipient certificate of honor 1974), Wire Assn., Soc. Mayflower Descs., Delta Tau Delta, Alpha Kappa Psi. Republican. Episcopalian. Home: 266 E Dudley Ave Westfield NJ 07090 Office: 411 W Putnam Ave Greenwich CT 06830

CUSHWA, CHARLES BENTON, mfg. co. exec.; b. Youngstown, Ohio, Apr. 10, 1934; s. Charles Benton and Margaret Elizabeth (Hall) C.; A.B., U. Notre Dame, 1956, M.A. in Econs., 1961; m. Joy Ellen Soarnecchia, May 4, 1963 (div.); children—Suzanne, Mara Ellen, Charles. With Comml. Shearing, Inc., Youngstown, 1961—, asst. sec., 1971-75, sec., 1975—, mng. dir., Can. subs., 1975-77, dir., 1972—; dir. Home Savs. and Loan Co., Youngstown. Gen. chmn. United Appeal, 1974; co-chmn. Goodwill Industries, 1978. Served with U.S. Army, 1957-59. Mem. Mfrs. Assn. Roman Catholic. Clubs: Youngstown Country, Chesterton. Office: 1775 Logan Ave Youngstown OH 44501

CUSHWA, WILLIAM WALLACE, mfg. co. exec.; b. Youngstown, Ohio, Aug. 15, 1937; s. Charles B. and Margaret E. (Hall) C.; A.B., U. Notre Dame, 1960; M.B.A., Case Western Res. U., 1975; m. Anna Jean Schuler, Feb. 4, 1961; children—Elizabeth A., William Wallace, Margaret L., David F., Anne J. Systems analyst Comml. Shearing, Inc., Youngstown, 1960-66, asst. to sec.-treas., 1966-69, asst. treas., 1969—, dir., 1975—, dir. corporate planning, 1978—. Mem. allocations com. Youngstown Area United Appeal, 1973-79; campaign chmn. United Negro Coll. Fund, 1979; pres. Youngstown Area Urban League, 1975-78. Mem. Youngstown Area C. of C., Notre Dame U. Alumni Assn., Case Western Res. U. Sch. Mgmt. Alumni Assn. Democrat. Roman Catholic. Office: 1775 Logan Ave Youngstown OH 44505

CUSICK, LAURENCE FRANCIS, III, restaurant exec.; b. Boston, Apr. 24, 1935; s. Laurence Francis and Edythe (Little) C.; student Cornell U. Sch. Hotel Adminstrn., 1953-55; m. Diana Gottlieb, Feb. 4, 1969; children—Craig, Nancy. Various positions in restaurants, hotels; food service Fairmont Hotel, San Francisco, 1961-63, Franciscan Restaurant, San Francisco, 1963-64; bar mgr., Breezy Point, Minn., 1964-65; owner, operator Carnival Bar, Miami, Fla., 1966-76, Cactus Restaurant, Miami, 1968-81, Cloverleaf Inn, Miami, 1976—, Lucky Duck and Lame Duck lounge/restaurants, 1978—. Bd. dirs. Biscayne Blvd. Assn. Served with U.S. Army, 1958-60. Mem. Everglades Aquarium Soc., Zool. Soc. Fla. Republican. Clubs: Racquet, Moose. Home: 4 Star Island Miami Beach FL 33139 Office: 17868 Biscayne Blvd Miami FL 33160

CUSICK, RALPH A., JR., investment banker; b. Washington, July 25, 1934; B.A. in History, Washington and Lee U., 1956; m. Jaquelin Carter Ambler, June 15, 1957; children—Ralph A., III, James Ambler, Carter Marshall. With Alex Brown & Sons, Washington, 1959—, gen. partner, 1969—. Pres. bd. Children's Hosp. Med. Research Center. Served with USNR, 1956-59. Mem. Washington Soc. Investment Analysts, Phi Delta Theta. Republican. Clubs: Metropolitan, Chevy Chase (Washington); Ponte Vedra (Jacksonville, Fla.); Coral Beach (Paget, Bermuda). Editor: Facts and Figures on Washington Securities, 1962-73. Home: 4815 Fort Sumner Dr Washington DC 20016 Office: 730 15th St NW Washington DC 20005

CUSTER, ROBERT FRED, mfg. co. exec.; b. Lincoln, Nebr., Mar. 27, 1941; s. Wilton Gerald and Stell (Rezac) C.; B.B.A., U. Mo., Kansas City, 1968; m. Alice Marie Cloughley, Aug. 12, 1978; children—Shawn, Kevin, Ben, Brad, Craig, Nathan, Beth, Michelle. Cost acctg. clk. Kenworth Trucking Co., Kansas City, 1965-68; staff acct. Ernst & Ernst, Kansas City, 1968-71; v.p. fin. Nelson Recreation Products, Inc., Lenexa, Kans., 1971—, also dir. Mem. Westwood Hills (Kans.) City Council, 1974-75. Served with USN, 1959-62. Roman Catholic. Club: K.C. Office: 14760 Santa Fe Trail Dr Lenexa KS 66215

CUTCHINS, CLIFFORD ARMSTRONG, III, banker; b. Southhampton County, Va., July 12, 1923; s. Clifford Armstrong and Sarah Penelope (Vaughan) C.; B.S.B.A., Va. Poly. and State U., 1947; grad. Stonier Sch. Banking, Rutgers U., 1952; m. Ann Woods, June 21, 1947; children—Clifford Armstrong IV, William W., Cecil V. With Vaughan and Co. Bankers (became Tidewater Bank & Trust Co.), Franklin, Va., 1947-62, pres., dir., 1962; sr. v.p. Va. Nat. Bank, Norfolk, 1963-65, exec. v.p., 1965-69, pres., chief adminstrv. officer, 1969-72, pres., chief adminstrv. officer Va. Nat. Bankshares and Va. Nat. Bank, 1972-80, chmn. bd., chief exec. officer, 1980—, also dir.; dir. Allied Bank Internat., Atlantic States Bankcard Assn., Pulaski Furniture Corp. Bd. dirs. Med. Center Hosps., Inc., Norfolk, 1967—, Hosp. Data Center Va., Norfolk, 1970—. Served with U.S. Army, 1943-46. Mem. Assn. Res. City Bankers, Assn. Bank Holding Cos. (prin. rep.). Baptist. Clubs: Princess Anne Country (Virginia Beach, Va.); Norfolk Yacht and Country, Harbor (Norfolk); Commonwealth (Richmond, Va.). Office: One Commercial Pl Norfolk VA 23510

CUTINELLO, CARL RAYMOND, cartographer; b. Chgo., Sept. 16, 1943; s. Carlo Charles and Berniece (Matz) C.; student U. Ill., 1962-63, Wright Jr. Coll., Chgo., 1967-68; m. Concetta Madonia, June 20, 1961; children—Cynthia Ann, Cherly Lynn, Christy Marie, Charlene Rene, Carl Frank. Topo draftsman, then editing supr. Chgo. Aerial Survey Co., 1962-67; cartographer Universal Map Co., and Uni-Map Co., Chgo., 1968-70; owner, mgr. Cartographics Services, Woodridge, Ill., 1970—. Address: 6008 Ross St Woodbridge IL 60515

CUTLER, DAVID HORTON, editor, publisher; b. Boston, May 26, 1934; s. Fred Abbott and Elizabeth Horton (Carnahan) C.; B.A., U. Nev., 1959; postgrad. Hastings Coll. Law, 1959-60; m. Martha Marie Emery, Dec. 6, 1959; children—Geoffrey Horton, Gregory Abbott. Editor, Stars and Stripes, 1961; with The Merchant Mag., Newport Beach, Calif., 1962—, editor-pub., owner, 1974—. Bd. dirs. Pasadena (Calif.) Planned Parenthood, 1969-74; mem. Newport Harbor Art Mus. Served in U.S. Army, 1953-55. Recipient 1st pl. editorial leadership award Western Publs. Assn., 1976; Pub. Relations award Ariz. Lumber Assn., 1974. Mem. Soc. Profl. Journalists. Republican. Episcopalian. Clubs: Newport Beach Tennis; Seaview Racquet and Swim; Masons, Shriners. Office: 4500 Campus Dr Suite 480 Newport Beach CA 92660

CUTRERA, JAMES THOMAS, govt. ofcl.; b. N.Y.C., Jan. 28, 1948; s. Vincent James and Elizabeth Mary (Mullen) C.; B.B.A. in Econs., U. Miami (Fla.), 1970; m. Sandra Lee Palmer, Aug. 19, 1978; 1 son, David Patrick. Social worker div. family services Fla. Dept. Health and Rehab. Services, Miami, 1972-73; contract adminstr. Def. Contract Adminstrv. Services Mgmt. Area, Springfield, N.J., 1973-77; contract negotiator AID, Washington, 1977—. Bd. dirs., mem. exec. com. Reston Commuter Bus, Inc. (Va.). Mem. Fgn. Affairs Recreation Assn. Home: 6104 Occoquam Forest Dr Manassas VA 22110 Office: 1735 N Lynn St Rosslyn VA 22209

CUTRONE, BENEDICT PHILIP, chemist, food co. exec.; b. Bronx, N.Y., Aug. 15, 1927; s. Santo and Rose Agnes (Catania) C.; A.B., Columbia Coll., 1948; m. Marie Louise Danet, May 20, 1972; children—Pamela, Philip, Louis. Mgr. grocery products mfg. div. Standard Brands, Inc., 1955-74; gen. mgr. oils and derivatives div. I.R.F. Matarazzo, Brazil, 1975-77; pres. Chock Full O'Nuts, N.Y.C., 1977—. Trustee Harrison Central Sch. Dist. Bd. Edn., 1979—. Served with M.C., U.S. Army, 1945-47. Office: 425 Lexington Ave New York NY 10017

CYMROT, ALLEN, real estate investment and mgmt. co. exec.; b. Bklyn., Nov. 9, 1936; s. William and Frieda (Strugatz) C.; m. Barbara Hellerman, June 12, 1960; children—Craig, Dawn, Wayne. Br. mgr. Bache & Co., N.Y.C., 1956-70; dir. retail sales Cowen & Co., N.Y.C., 1972; div. v.p. duPont Walston, N.Y.C., 1972-74; pres. Pacific Investments, San Mateo, Calif., 1974-77; pres., dir. Robert A. McNeil Corp., San Mateo, 1977—. Served with U.S. Army, 1957-59. Mem. Calif. Syndication Forum (pres. 1979), Nat. Rental Housing Council (dir. 1979—), Calif. Housing Council (dir. 1979—). Contbr. articles to profl. jours.; testified before Congress, Mar. 1980. Office: 2855 Campus Dr San Mateo CA 94403

CYPHERT, GILBERT GEORGE, equipment mfg. co. exec.; b. Milw., Jan. 8, 1943; s. Kathryan (Emler) C.; student Phoenix Coll., 1967-69, Ariz. State U., 1969; m. Dixie Davis, Apr. 11, 1968; children—Ryan Blake, Dana Lynn. New ops. mgr. Dallas Smith Services Corp., Phoenix, 1963-68; partner CIMCO Inc., Phoenix, 1969-71, Skyline Equipment Co., Phoenix, 1972; pres. Chemko Industries Inc., Phoenix, 1972-79; gen. mgr. Chemko Comml. Products, Inc. subs. The Hoover Co., 1979—. Served with Air N.G., 1964-70. Mem. Nat. Fedn. Ind. Businessmen. Home: 18625 N 9th Ave Phoenix AZ 85327 Office: 2215 W Mountain View Rd Phoenix AZ 85021

CZACHOWSKI, BERNARD EDWIN, transp. co. exec.; b. West Haven, Conn., Nov. 16, 1928; s. Walter and Victoria (Balakiewicz) C.; B.A., Brown U., 1952; m. Jane. 6, 1957; children—Joseph, Stephen, Maria. Terminal mgr. McLean Trucking Co., Winston-Salem, N.C., 1956-58; v.p. Sea-Land Service, Inc., Elizabeth, N.J., 1958-76, exec. v.p., Edison, N.J., 1976-79; v.p., gen. mgr. Mail Express, Inc., Elizabeth, 1969-79; pres. Sea-Land Industries U.S.A., Inc., Edison, 1979—; dir. numerous corps. Served with U.S. Army, 1946-48. Republican. Roman Catholic. Office: PO Box 900 Edison NJ 08817*

CZARNECKI, GERALD MILTON, banker; b. Phila., Mar. 22, 1940; s. Casimer M. and Rose-Mary (Grajek) C.; B.S., Temple U., 1965; M.A., Mich. State U., 1967; m. Lois Rae DiJoseph, July 9, 1965; 1 dau., Robin Alexandra. Mgr. methods research Continental Bank, Chgo., 1968-69, operating gen. mgr., bond ops., 1969-71, v.p., operating gen. mgr. trust ops. and gen. mgr. corp. services, 1971-79; exec. v.p. Houston Nat. Bank, 1979—; mem. faculty DePaul U., 1975-79; adj. prof. econs. Houston Bapt. U., 1979—; mem. exec. com. Houston Clearinghouse Assn.; dir. Midwest Securities Trust Co. Chmn. policy bd. Inroads Inc., Chgo., 1974-79; bd. dirs. Drug Abuse Council Ill. Served to capt., arty. U.S. Army, 1960-63, 67-68. C.P.A., Tex., Ill. Mem. Am. Bankers Assn. (chmn. trust ops. com. 1975-79), Am. Inst. C.P.A.'s, Am. Bankers Assn. (ops. and automation exec. com.), Am. Inst. Banking (chmn. Houston chpt.), Fin. Execs. Inst., Tex. Soc. C.P.A.'s, Am. Econ. Assn. Home: 13614 Perthshire Houston TX 77079 Office: 1010 Milam St Houston TX 77299

CZECH, THOMAS JAMES, investment analyst; b. Hammond, Ind., June 15, 1947; s. Walter James and Ann Marie C.; B.S. in Fin., No. Ill. U., 1969, M.B.A. in Fin., 1971. Investment analyst Blunt Ellis & Loewi, Milw., 1972-77, v.p., sr. investment analyst, 1977-80, chartered fin. analyst, 1980—. Mem. Milw. Investment Analysts Soc., Inst. Chartered Fin. Analysts, Fin. Analysts Fedn. Republican. Roman Catholic. Clubs: Milw. Athletic, Vagabond Ski. Office: 225 E Mason Milwaukee WI 53202

DAANE, ARTHUR RUSSELL, real estate broker; b. Ann Arbor, Mich., May 1, 1950; s. Russell Melville and Hildreth (VanHeitsma) D.; B.S., Ind. U., 1972: m. Pamela Louis Daane, June 21, 1980. Fin. analyst Ford Motor Co., Dearborn, Mich., 1972-74: salesman Price Corp., Holland, Mich., 1975-76: pres. Windcrest Promotions, Inc., mfr. and mktg. golf courses, Holland, 1976—; real estate broker, Holland, 1976—; fin. cons. Republican. Presbyterian. Address: 2054 Lake St Holland MI 49423

DABOVICH, THOMAS CHRIS, salt and chem. mfg. co. exec.; b. Chgo., Sept. 14, 1918; s. Chris Thomas and Sophie C. (Popovich) D.; B.S., in Pharmacy, U. Ill., 1939; m. Natalie Shaw Holmes, June 6, 1942; children—Alexandra, Christopher. Research chemist G. D. Searle, Chgo., 1939-43; tech. sales regional mgr. Sharples Chems., Chgo., 1946-52; sales mgr. indsl. div. J. T. Baker Chems., Phillipsburg, N.J., 1952-54; gen. sales mgr. chem. div. Morton-Norwich Products, Chgo., 1954-58, v.p and pres. Morton Chem. div., 1958-66, exec. v.p. salt and splty. chems., 1976—, vice chmn., 1980—; v.p., dir. Can. Salt Co., Montreal, Que., 1973—, Imperial Thermal Products, Inc. (Calif.), 1973—, Morton Bahamas Ltd., 1973—, Morton Chem., Ltd., 1966—, Morton Industries Can. Ltd., 1973—, Can. Brine Ltd., 1973—, Can. Rock Salt Co., Ltd., 1973—, Morton Terminal Ltd., 1973—, Essex Terminal Ry. Corp., 1973—; chmn. bd. Williams (Hounslow) Ltd., Eng., 1977—; dir. Como Chem. Internat. S.p.A., Italy, Morton-Williams Australia Pty., B.V. Nederlandse Kleurstofindustrie, Tokyo-Morton, Ltd., Ecuatoriana de Sal y Productos Quimicos C.A., Ecuador, Morton Chem. Co., S.A. de C.V., Mex., Morton-Chimie S.A., France. Trustee, Elmhurst (Ill.) Coll., 1979; bd. sponsors Good Shepherd Hosp., Barrington, Ill., 1978—. Served with USN, 1943-46. Mem. Am. Chem. Soc., Mfg. Chemists Assn., Chem. Industries Council-Midwest. Eastern Orthodox. Clubs: Mid-Day, Tower, Met. (Chgo.); Met. (N.Y.C.); Garden of the Gods (Colorado Springs, Colo.). Office: 110 N Wacker Dr Chicago IL 60606

DACRUZ, ANTONY ROSHAN, mktg. exec., investment cons.; b. Coimbra, Portugal, Feb. 14, 1930; s. Antonio and Sara P. (Dos Santos) DaC.; came to U.S., 1948, naturalized, 1955; student U. Lisbon (Portugal), 1946-48; B.S. cum laude in Chem. and Math., Dana Coll., 1950; M.S. in Chem. Engring. (AEC fellow), U. Minn., 1953; m. Helen D. Hassapopoulou, Dec. 19, 1952; 1 son, Antony Leslie R. Tech. ops. mgr., dir. Kodak Brasileira subs. Eastman Kodak Co., São Paulo, Brazil, 1960-66, dir., gen. mgr. Kodak Colombiana, Bogotá, Colombia, 1966-70, dir., ops. mgr. Kodak Argentina, Buenos Aires, 1970-73, mgmt. cons. to Kodak subs. U.K., London, 1973-74, internat. exec. Eastman Kodak Hdqrs., Rochester, N.Y., 1974-79; pres. Aquemar Ltd., Rochester, Impex Mktg. Internat., Inc.; cons. internat. investments. Active League Americans Residing Abroad, Brazil and Colombia, 1963-67. Served with U.S. Army, 1955-57. Recipient Distinguished Alumnus award Dana Coll., 1977. Mem. Am. Chem. Soc., Am. Soc. Mexico City, Rio de Janeiro, São Paulo, Brazil, Bogotá, Colombia, Argentina, Am. C. of C., Phi Lambda Upsilon. Clubs: Rio de Janeiro Yacht, São Paulo Athletic, San Isidro Riding, Barlovento Yacht. Pictures shown and awarded Internat. Salon Photography.

DADD, ROBERT FREDERICK, health systems agy. exec.; b. Cumberland, Md., Nov. 30, 1947; s. William Frederick and Dorothy Evelyn (Goetz) D.; B.S., U. Md., 1970, M.B.A., 1975; m. Suzanne Margaret Charland, Mar. 24, 1970; 1 son, Robert. Econ. analyst Tri-County Council for So. Md., Waldorf, 1970-73, mgmt. analyst, 1974-76; systems analyst Fairfax County, Fairfax, Va., 1973-74; dir. fin. and data adminstrn. So. Md. Health Systems Agy., Clinton, 1976—; cons. Info. Systems, 1973—; treas. Phyllis, Inc., Kensington, Md., 1979—. Mem. Urban Regional Info. Systems Assn., Ops. Research Soc. Am., Washington Ops. Research and Mgmt. Sci. Council. Home: PO Box 85 Clinton MD 20735 Office: 9131 Piscataway Rd Clinton MD 20735

DADEA, RENATO J., mining corp. exec.; b. Genova, Italy, Feb. 27, 1927; came to U.S., 1958, naturalized, 1963; s. Giuseppe and Parisina (Sacquegno) D.; Ph.D. in Chem. Engring., U. Genova, 1955; m. Gattorna Lina, Oct. 24, 1959; 1 dau., Francesca. Asst. prof. mechanics U. Genova, 1955-58; with Montedison, Milan, Italy, U.S., Mex., 1963-69; engring. group Nuovo Pignone, Agip, U.S.A., 1969-73; with Bechtel Corp., N.Y.C., 1973-76; gen. project mgr., project dir. Jamaica Bauxite Mining, Kingston, West Indies, 1976—. Served with Italian Army, 1955. Lic. profl. engr., Italy. Mem. Am. Inst. Chem. Engrs. Home: 4 Old House Ln Sands Point NY 10050 Office: City Bank Bldg Knutsen Blvd Kingston 5 Jamaica WI

DAESCHNER, RICHARD WILBUR, food co. exec., b. Preston, Nebr., July 5, 1917; s. Richard T. and Elma (Beckenhauer) D.; B.S. in Edn., Kans. State Tchrs. Coll., 1937; J.D., Washburn U., 1941; m. Prudence Armstrong, June 6, 1942; children—Richard, Rebecca, Martha. Admitted to Kan. bar, 1941; spl. agt. FBI, Washington, Boston, N.Y.C., Chgo., 1941-48; with employee relations dept. Beatrice Foods Co., Chgo., 1948—, dir. employee relations, 1963-68, dir. personnel and indsl. relations, asst. sec., 1968-73, asst. v.p., 1973-78, v.p., 1978—. Mem. Chgo. Bar Assn., Grocery Mfrs. Assn., Ill. C. of C., Chgo. Assn. Commerce and Industry, Am. Mgmt. Assn., Chgo. Better Bus. Bur. (dir.), Phi Delta Theta. Republican. Presbyn. (trustee). Elk. Clubs: Executive (Chgo.); Inverness Golf. Home: 1700 Appleby Rd Palatine IL 60067 Office: 2 N LaSalle St Chicago IL 60602

D'AGOSTINO, DONALD GERARD, ship co. exec.; b. N.Y.C., Jan. 26, 1939; s. Charles and Harriet (Miles) D'A.; B.S., Fordham U., 1960; m. Elaine Marcario, Oct. 9, 1965. Staff acct. Stockard Shipping Co., 1960-67; successively mgr. acctg., controller, treas., v.p. fin. and adminstrn. Gdynia America Line, N.Y.C., from 1967, now exec. v.p., also dir. Served with U.S.N.G., 1961-68. Mem. N.Y. Credit and Fin. Mgmt. Assn., Water Transp. Credit Group. Office: 1 World Trade Center Room 3557 New York NY 10048

DAHL, CHARLES RAYMOND, paper co. exec.; b. Bklyn., July 13, 1921; s. Oswald and Alice (Christoffersen) D.; B.M.E., Cooper Union, 1943; M.B.A., Stanford, 1947; m. Clara Joyce Glendon, Dec. 31, 1949; children—Kathleen Merle, Eric Allen, Connie Loraine. With Westinghouse Electric Co., 1947-50; with Crown Zellerbach Corp., 1950—, exec. v.p., 1969-70, pres., 1970-78, chmn., 1978—, also chief exec. officer, dir.; dir. Monsanto Co., Bank Am. N.T. and S.A., BankAm. Corp. Clubs: Pacific Union, San Francisco Golf, Commonwealth (San Francisco). Office: Crown-Zellerbach Corp 1 Bush St San Francisco CA 94119

DAHL, THOMAS MOORE, engring. and constrn. co. exec.; b. Mpls., Aug. 8, 1918; s. Walter H. and Helen (Moore) D.; m. Gail Gilje, Feb. 20, 1943; children—Susan, Janet. Vice pres. United Engrs. & Constructors Inc., Phila., 1958-71, pres., chief operating officer, 1971-76, chmn. bd., pres., chief exec. officer, 1976—; dir. Atomic

Indsl. Forum, Jackson & Moreland Internat., UE&C Internat., United Mid-East, Inc., Piccon Inc. Bd. dirs. Med. Coll. Pa. Mem. Assn. Iron and Steel Engrs., IEEE. Clubs: Aronimink Golf, Algonquin; Union League (Phila., Chgo.); Masons. Home: 901 Parkes Run Ln Villanova PA 19085 Office: 30 S 17th St Philadelphia PA 19101

DAHLBERG, KRISTINE MARIE, diversified properties mgmt. exec.; b. Rockford, Ill., May 14, 1944; d. Arthur Emanuel and Mildred Hildegard (Aronson) Sodergren; B.A., Lawrence U., 1966; M.A., U. N.C., Chapel Hill, 1970; postgrad. Inst. Edn. Mgmt., Harvard U., 1974; m. Robert Carl Dahlberg, Aug. 20, 1966. Asso. dean U. Maine, Orono, 1970-75; dir. dept. campus and community devel. Johns Hopkins Med. Instns., Balt., 1975—, also pres. Broadway Mgmt. Corp. subs. Johns Hopkins Med. Instns., 1975—. Bd. dirs. Neighborhood Housing Services, 1980; cons. community orgns. for urban redevel., 1979-80; mem. Balt. Citizens Planning and Housing Assn., 1979-80. Mem. Am. Assn. Higher Edn., Am. Assn. Med. Colls., Am. Planning Assn., Mortgage Bankers Assn., Nat. Council Philanthropy, Mortar Bd., Soc. of Janus. Research on structural and governance issues in higher edn., hotel devel., housing devel., recreation clubs devel. Home: 4014 Crescent Rd Ellicott City MD 21043 Office: 1620 McElderry St Baltimore MD 21205

DAHLQUIST, RALPH LEON, research spectroscopist; b. Springfield, Minn., Jan. 21, 1941; s. Clair W. and Elizabeth M. (Foy) D.; m. Marylyn Josephson, Mar. 1, 1968; children—Russell, Hannah, Robert. Quality assurance tech. rep. Jefferson Electronics, Santa Barbara, Calif., 1959-64; research scientist Hasler Research Center, Santa Barbara, 1964-77; research spectroscopist Applied Research Labs, Sunland, Calif., 1978-80, div. staff, analytical cons., 1980—. Recipient IR-100 award, 1975. Mem. AAAS, Soc. for Applied Spectroscopy. Contbr. numerous publs. and holder patents in field of spectrochemistry. Home: 21558 Placerita Cyn Rd Newhall CA 91321 Office: Applied Research Labs 9545 Wentworth Blvd Sunland CA 91040

DAILEY, FRED WILLIAM, hotel exec.; b. Aurora, Ill., Feb. 3, 1908; s. Louis A. and Frances (McCoy) D.; m. Elizabeth Murphy, Apr. 22, 1946; 1 son, Michael K. Builder, operator tourist resorts, 1933-42; builder, So. Calif., 1946-52; gen. partner Cal-Hawaii Assos., 1952—; pres. Riverbend Ranch, Thorobreds, Santa Ynez, Calif., Honolulu Constrn., Inc., Mokuleia Assos., Mokuleia Polo Farms, Inc. Served to maj. USAAF, World War II. Decorated Purple Heart. Mem. Hawaii Hotel Assn. (past pres.), Hawaii Horse Show Assn. (past pres.). Clubs: Army and Navy (Chgo. and N.Y.C.); Waikiki Polo (past pres.), Hawaii Polo and Racing (pres.) (Honolulu); Santa Barbara Polo; Mokuleia Polo (pres.); El Dorado Polo, Los Angeles Athletic. Author: Blood, Sweat and Jeers. Home: Waikikian Hotel Honolulu HI 96815 Office: Mokuleia Polo Club Oahu HI 96813

DAKE, LYLE LEROY, banker; b. Vinton, Iowa, Feb. 8, 1938; s. J. Harold and Erma Grace (Reid) D.; B.S. in Bus. Adminstrn., Roosevelt U., 1973, M.B.A., 1974; postgrad. in trust banking U. N.C., Charlotte, 1976, 77, Northwestern U., 1979, 80, 81; m. Marilyn C. White, Apr. 25, 1957; children—Monica, Melanie, Joel, Stephen. Served as non-commd. officer U.S. Navy, 1956-75; asst. trust officer Zion State Bank & Trust Co. (Ill.) 1975-78; head trust dept. Bank of Waukegan (Ill.), 1978-80, Citizens Nat. Bank of Macomb (Ill.), 1980—; v.p. Western Ill. Estate Planning Council, 1980—; mem. faculty Coll. of Lake County, Grayslake, Ill., 1974-80, McHenry County Coll., Crystal Lake, Ill., 1974-80, Western Ill. U., 1981—. Recipient Marathoner award Nat. Jogging Assn., 1980. Republican. Baptist. Club: Rotary. Office: 127 South Side Sq Macomb IL 61455

DALBEY, NORMAN LEE, restaurant exec.; b. Richmond, Ind., July 17, 1940; s. Oliver L. and Norma I. (Blunk) D.; student Richmond Bus. Coll., 1958, Earlham Coll., 1964; m. Sue Brown, Sept. 8, 1963; children—Andrea Kaye, Robert Christian. Asst. cashier 2d Nat. Bank, Richmond, 1962-69; restaurant mgr. W.T. Grant Co., Bedford, Ind., 1970-73; owner, mgr. Carousel Restaurant, Bedford, 1973—. Mem. Ind. Restaurant Assn. Lutheran. Clubs: Exchange, Elks, Masons. Home: 217 Westwood Dr Bedford IN 47421 Office: Carousel Plaza Bedford IN 47421

DALE, GARY CLIFFORD, advt. and mktg. exec.; b. Ellensburg, Wash., Apr. 6, 1944; s. Clifford T. and Evelyn R. D.; B.A. in Edn., Central Wash. State Coll., 1966; m. Sharon Horne, Nov. 22, 1980; children by previous marriage—Josh, Sara, Tracy. Tchr., Portland (Oreg.) Public Schs., 1966-67; sales, sales mgr. Cone Heiden Co., Seattle, 1967-75; sales Stein Co., Atlanta, 1975-76; pres. Dale Co., Seattle, 1976—. Mem. C. of C., Mcpl. League Seattle. Republican. Presbyterian. Clubs: Toastmasters, Fly Fishing of Wash. Office: 65 Marion St Seattle WA 98104

DALE, MARTIN ALBERT, mfg. co. exec.; b. Newark, Jan. 3, 1932; s. Philip D. and Lucie M. (Mintz) D.; B.A., Princeton, 1953; postgrad. (Fulbright fellow) U. Strasbourg (France), 1953-54; M.A. in Internat. Econs. with honors, Tufts U., 1955; m. Joan C. Dale, Apr. 3, 1954 (div. 1977); children—Charles, W. Gregory, Pamela, Eric; m. 2d, m. Berteline Baier, Nov. 21, 1980. Fgn. service officer U.S. Dept. State, 1955-60; pvt. counsellor, econ. adviser Prince Rainier III of Monaco, 1960-64; v.p., exec. asst. to pres. Grand Bahama Port Authority Ltd., Freeport, 1965-67; sr. v.p. fin., adminstrn. and ops. Revlon Internat. Corp., N.Y.C., 1967-72; corporate sr. v.p., dir. office strategic projects W.R. Grace & Co., N.Y.C., 1972—; dir. F.A.O. Schwarz, Inc. Trustee Lycée Francais de N.Y. Republican. Clubs: N.Y. Athletic, Princeton (N.Y.C.). Home: 40 Central Park South New York NY 10019 Office: 1114 Ave of Americas New York NY 10036

DALE, ROBERT GORDON, food and agrl. products co. exec.; b. Toronto, Ont., Can., Nov. 1, 1920; s. Gordon McIntyre and Helen Marjorie (Cartwright) D.; student Trinity Coll. U. Toronto, 1939-40, 45-46; m. Mary Austin Babcock, Apr. 3, 1948; children—Robert Austin, John Gordon. With Maple Leaf Mills Ltd., Toronto, 1947—, chmn., 1969—, pres., 1969—, chief exec. officer, 1969—, also dir.; dir. Nat. Life Assurance Co. Can., McGavin ToastMaster Ltd., Eastern Bakeries Ltd., Koppers Internat. Can. Ltd., Manpower Services Ltd., Corporate Foods Ltd., Canadian Exec. Service Overseas. Mem. adv. bd. Bloorview Children's Hosp., Toronto; trustee United Community Fund Greater Toronto. Served with RCAF, 1940-45. Decorated D.F.C., Disting. Service Order. Mem. Canadian Nat. Millers Assn., Phi Kappa Pi. Conservative. Anglican. Clubs: Rosedale Golf, Nat. Badminton and Racquet, Empire. Office: PO Box 710 Station K Toronto ON M4P 2X5 Canada

DALE, STANLEY JOHN, JR., energy resources corp. exec.: b. Yonkers, N.Y., Mar. 25, 1947: s. Stanley John and Kathleen E. Dale; B.B.A. in Acctg., Fin., Pace U., 1975; postgrad. Iona Coll.; m. Vicki Sue Garner, Jan. 21, 1978: children—Lisa Ann, Tracey Leigh. Technician, Xerox Corp., 1972-75; acct. HZI Research Co., Tarrytown, N.Y., 1975-76; taxation and fin. analysis Diversified Holdings Corp., N.Y.C., 1977-80; v.p. Aurora Energy Resources Corp., Valley Cottage, N.Y., 1980—, also sec. Committeeman, Republican Party, Rockland County, N.Y., 1975—. Mem. Nat. Assn. Security Dealers, Smithsonian Inst. Home: 126 Congress Rd New City NY 10956 Office: PO Box 291 Valley Cottage NY 10989

DALEY, FRANCIS DARNALL, JR., electronics mfg. co. exec.; b. Altoona, Pa., Mar. 9, 1938; s. Francis Darnall and Helen M. (Miller) D.; B.E.S. in Elec. Engring., Johns Hopkins U., 1960; postgrad. in elec. engring., U. Md., 1965-68; m. M. Ernestine Geist, Dec. 30, 1957; children—Francis Darnall, Christopher Michael. Design engr. Westinghouse Electric Co., Balt., 1960-65; sr. design engr. Martin Co., Balt., 1965-67; project engring. mgr. Electronic Modules Corp., Cockeysville, Md., 1967-70, sales engring. mgr., 1970-73; dir. adminstrn. Wolfe & Mann Mfg. Co., Balt., 1973-76, gen. mgr., 1976-77; dir. ops. Randolph operation Exide Electronics Inc. subs. Inco, Ltd., Randolph, Mass., 1977—. Scoutmaster, Boy Scouts Am., 1969-77, asst. dist. commr., 1978, dist. commr., 1979. Mem. IEEE, Am. Prodn. and Inventory Control Soc. Republican. Episcopalian. Patentee digital linearization methods. Home: 603 Ferry St Marshfield MA 02050 Office: 39 Teed Dr Randolph MA 02368

DALEY, JAMES ROBERT, banker; b. Fargo, N.D., July 16, 1944; s. James Robert and Shirley Marie (Quick) D.; B.A., Concordia Coll., 1966; J.D., U. Pacific, 1979. Asst. to dir. for taxes Gen. Mills, Inc., Mpls., 1969-71; dep. dir. Calif. Dept. Commerce, Sacramento, 1971-72; dir. Commn. for Econ. Devel., Sacramento, 1972-73; with Union Bank, Sacramento and Pasadena Calif., 1975-79; regional v.p. Imperial Bank, Sacramento/San Francisco, 1979—. Served with U.S. Army, 1967-69. Decorated Bronze Star. Mem. State Bar Calif., Am. Bar Assn., San Francisco Bar Assn., Sacramento County Bar Assn., Am. Judicature Soc. Lutheran. Home: 444 Wyndgate Rd Sacramento CA 95825 Office: 555 Capitol Mall Sacramento CA 95814

DALEY, PETER EDMUND, bus. services co. exec.; b. Washington, Mar. 28, 1943; s. Edmund Frances and Marie (Herbert) D.; B.S., Wheeling Coll., 1966; M.B.A., U. Md., 1968; J.D., U. Balt., 1975; m. June 27, 1970; children—Peter, Gina, Milissa, Angela. With Westinghouse Co., Balt., 1970-75, Pitts., 1975-77; corp. mgr. compensation benefits PHH Group, Hunt Valley, Md., 1977-78, corp. mgr. human resources, 1978-79, dir. human resources, 1979—. Bd. dirs. Girl Scouts Central Md., 1978-80. Mem. Md. Bar Assn., Am. Bar Assn., Am. Mgmt. Assn., Am. Assn. Personnel Adminstrs., Greater Balt. Personnel Assos., Am. Compensation Assn. Home: 411 Deaconbrook Circle Reisterstown MD 21136 Office: 11333 McCormick Rd Hunt Valley MD 21031

DALEY, RICHARD LEO, constrn. engring. co. exec.; b. Waltham, Mass., July 29, 1917; s. Richard Francis and Margarete Magdalline (O'Brien) D.; m. Rosemarie Dixon, Feb. 19, 1949; children—Richard A., Michael B., Veronica L., Victoria M., Jon P. Leadman, Leadman-Riggers-Laborers, Divers, 1947-56; field and safety engr. Morrison-Knudsen Co. Inc., Boise, Idaho, 1956-59, asst. dir. safety, 1959-70, dir. safety and environ. services, 1970—; cons. Occupational Safety and Health Adminstrn. Served with U.S. Army Air Corps, 1942-46. Decorated Air medal with 3 clusters. Registered profl. engr., Calif. Mem. Am. Soc. Safety Engrs. (pres. Snake River chpt.), Nat. Gen. Contractors Assn. Clubs: Capitol Hill, Plantation Golf, Morgans Exchange. Home: 4015 Bristol St Boise ID 83704 Office: 1 Morrison-Knudsen Plaza Boise ID 83729

DALHOUSE, WARNER NORRIS, banker; b. Roanoke, Va., June 4, 1934; s. Jefferson William and Gay-Nell (Henley) D.; B.A. in Commerce, U. Va., 1956; m. Carol Bewley, June 1956; children—Ann Lauren, Julia Lea. With First Nat. Exchange Bank, Roanoke, 1956—, sr. v.p., then exec. v.p., 1969-77, pres., chief adminstrv. officer, 1977—, dir., 1973—; exec. v.p., chief adminstrv. officer Dominion Bankshares Corp., 1977—; mem. Gov. Va. Adv. Com. Indsl. Devel. Chmn. bd. trustees Va. Western Community Coll.; vice-chmn. Roanoke City Airport Adv. Commn.; bd. dirs. Roanoke Symphony Soc.; chmn. governing bd. S.W. Va. Center Arts and Scis.; chmn. community adv. com. Roanoke Coll. Recipient Disting. Service award Roanoke Jaycees, 1970, Outstanding Citizen award, 1974. Mem. Am. Mktg. Assn. (Va. Mktg. Exec. of Yr. award 1974), Am. Banking Assn. (exec. com. mktg. div.), Assn. Bank Holding Cos., Va. Bankers Assn., Roanoke Valley C. of C. Office: PO Box 13327 Roanoke VA 24040

DALIERE, JOHN FRANKLIN, communications co. exec.; b. Cleve., May 23, 1940: s. Mark Hannah and Marie Agnus (Hellriegel) D.; B.A., Colgate U., 1962; diploma in Italian Studies, Syracuse U., 1961; B.S. (Barton Kyle Yount scholar), Am. Grad. Sch. Internat. Mgmt., 1964: diploma in Acctg., Northwestern U., 1963; m. Susan Eleanor Heitmann, Apr. 20, 1964: children—Mark, Eric, Marisa. Mgmt. trainee Continental Bank, 1963; mktg. mgr., br. mgr. Goodyear Internat., Rome, 1964-68; v.p., gen. mgr. Litart-Istituto Internazionale di Arte Liturgica, Rome and Chgo., 1968-71; mgr. internat. ops. Unistrut GTE, Wayne, Mich., 1971-74: v.p., gen. mgr., dir. GTE Unistrut Internat., Inc., Wayne., 1974—: dir., officer 6 subs., U.K., Mex., South Africa, Can., Holland, Australia, N.Z.; lectr. U. Mich., U.S. Dept. Commerce-Internat. Div.; dir. U.S. Dept. Commerce Dist. Export Council. Pres. Ann Arbor P.T.O., 1979-80. Served with U.S. Army, 1962. Mem. Manuscript Soc. Roman Catholic. Clubs: Ann Arbor Racquet (dir.), Huron Valley Tennis. Home: 3025 Provincial Dr Ann Arbor MI 48104

DALKE, CARL DONALD, orgn. exec.; b. Inman, Kans., Nov. 10, 1924; s. Peter and Helena (Heidebrecht) D.; grad. Hutchinson Jr. Coll., 1947; B.S., Kan. State U., 1950, M.S., 1950; postgrad. U. Chgo., 1950-53; m. Jeanette Harper, June 11, 1949; children—Terry Jean, Patricia Lee, Deborah Jo. Asst. mgr. automobile div. Better Bus. Bur. Met. Chgo., Inc., 1953-54, mgr. automobile div., 1954-60, v.p., 1960-63, pres., 1963-66; exec. v.p. Ill. Consumer Finance Assn., 1967-79; v.p. The Sanford Orgn., 1980—; mng. dir. Home Ventilating Inst., 1980—; conv. dir. USE, Inc., 1980—. Bd. govs. Nat. Inst. on Consumer Credit Mgmt., Marquette U., 1967-79, chmn., 1974-76; adv. com. Ill. Clergy Econ. Edn. Workshops, 1973—; trustee Ill. Council on Econ. Edn., 1970—. Served with 101st Airborne Div., U.S. Army, 1943-46. Cert. assn. exec. Mem. Am. Soc. Assn. Execs., Chgo. Soc. Assn. Execs., Phi Delta Theta. Clubs: Chicago Press, University of Chicago Track (dir. 1954—). Home: 1608 Cambridge St Flossmoor IL 60422 Office: 105 W Madison St Chicago IL 60602

DALLAIRE, RAYMOND, plastic window and door components mfg. co. exec.; b. St. Henedine, Que., Can., Feb. 16, 1932; s. Albert and Regina (Lacasse) D.; student College des Marianistes, St. Anselme, Que., 1942-45; m. Rolande Fortier, Feb. 12, 1966; children—Andree, Caroline. In various positions in constrn. industry, Que., 1947, Ont. and B.C., 1951-58; co-founder, partner Dallaire Entreprises Inc., St.-David, Que., 1958-62, Quincaillerie Panoramique, Inc., Levis, Que., 1962-71; co-founder, v.p. Futurama Plastics Inc., Lauzon, Que., 1965-71; pres. Plastiques P.H., Inc. (merger Futurama Plastics Inc. and Quincaillerie Panoramique, Inc.), Lauzon, 1971—, P.H. Plastics Inc. (name changed to P.H.-TECH Inc. 1976), Lauzon, 1971—; v.p. Les Industries Dallaire Ltee., Lauzon, 1971—; pres. Celtech Plastics Inc., Toronto, Ont., Can. Mem. Am. Mfrs. Assn., Nat. Woodworkers Mfrs. Assn., Soc. Plastic Engrs., Can. Bldg. Ofcls. Assn., Can. Mfrs. Assn., Levis C. of C., Plastic Industry Council, Soc. Plastic Industry Can. (Man of Year award 1974), Tech. Service Council, Constrn. Assn. Que., Can. Wood Door Mfrs. Assn. Clubs: Levis Golf; Nordiques Hockey (co-founder, dir.) (Quebec). Patentee window constrn. Home: 587 de la Falaise St David PQ G6W 1B2 Canada Office: PO Box 220 Levis PQ G6V 6N8 Canada

DALLAL, SALIM S., bank holding co. exec.; b. Teheren, Iran, Apr. 8, 1940; s. Salim S. and Ludmilla (Alexeioff) D.; came to U.S., 1949, naturalized, 1954; A.B., Columbia U., 1962, M.B.A., 1963; m. Eleanor Meer, Feb. 21, 1965; 1 dau., Nancy. Asst. v.p., market research mgr. Met. Div., 1st Nat. City Bank, N.Y.C., 1963-68, asst. v.p. and planning and research mgr. personal banking group, 1968-73, asst. v.p. and product devel. mgr. corporate banking group, 1973-74; v.p. personal banking div., dir. mktg. Irving Trust Co., N.Y.C., 1974-77; v.p., dir. customer services Irving Bank Corp., N.Y.C., 1977—. Bd. dirs. Gifted Child Soc., 1972—, treas., 1973-76. Mem. Bank Mktg. Assn. advt. award 1977, dir. N.Y.C. chpt.), Am. Mktg. Assn. (Effie award 1977), Fin. Advt. and Mktg. Assn. Republican. Episcopalian. Club: Indian Trails. Home: 411 Wyckoff Ave Wyckoff NJ 07481 Office: 1 Wall St New York NY 10005

DALLAS, KATHARYN TICE (MRS. JOHN W. DALLAS), owner furniture co.; b. Oshkosh, Wis., July 27, 1906; d. George Nelson and Etta J. (Ruddy) Tice; B.S., Northwestern U., 1934, M.S., 1935; m. John W. Dallas, June 6, 1936 (dec. Mar. 1962); children—John W. (dec.), Charles W. Tchr. pub. schs., West Allis, Wis., 1928-31, Hinsdale, Ill., 1931-33; with Inst. Juvenile Research, Chgo., 1932-35; dir. spl. edn. Boulder (Colo.) Pub. Schs., 1935-36; tchr. Orthogenic Sch., U. Chgo., summers 1929-31; asst. in psychology Northwestern U., 1934-35; partner Trader Jack's Pine Furniture, Denver, 1946-62. Charter mem. Rocky Mountain Kidney Found.; chmn. bd. dirs. Adams County Neighborhood Youth Corps Scholarship Fund. Mem. Am. Assn. U. Women, Pi Lambda Theta. Contbr. articles to profl. jours. Home: 3547 W 23d Ave Denver CO 80211 Office: 6606 N Federal Denver CO 80221

DALLAS, REBEKAH TAYLOR, personnel exec.; b. Kennett Sq., Pa.; d. Robert Erwin and Ann Butler (Jackson) Dallas; B.A., Goucher Coll.; M.A., Columbia, 1935. Asst. dir. Neighborhood Playhouse Sch. of Theatre, 1940-60; personnel dir. Gibbs & Cox, Inc., N.Y.C., 1942-65, v.p., 1965—. Trustee United Seamen Service, Am. Fedn. Arts, Met. Mus., Philharmonic Symphony Soc., Alumni Columbia U., N.Y. Hort. Soc. Recipient commendation USN, 1948. Mem. Am. Mgmt. Assn., AAUW. Club: Womens Univ. Home: 200 E 78th St New York City NY 10021

DALLIANIS, JEAN DEMAS, real estate co. exec.; b. Oak Park, Ill., Dec. 30, 1940; d. Charles William and Helen Alice (Kyriakopulos) Demas; B.A., Northwestern U., 1962; m. Harry T. Dallianis, Dec. 8, 1962 (div. 1979); children—Irene Lorraine, Thomas Harry. Tchr., Von Steuben High Sch., Chgo., 1962-65; sec.-treas. Ideal Real Estate & Ins. Brokerage, Inc., Chgo., 1965-72, v.p., exec. dir., 1972—, dir. corporate relocation, 1975—; dir. Ideal Realty Co. Mem. Lincolnwood (Ill.) Community Council, 1972—; treas. Lincolnwood Homeowners Assn., 1974-75. Precinct capt. Lincolnwood Citizens Action Party, 1977; mem. Lincolnwood Bicentennial Com., Lincolnwood Library Steering Com., 1978—; coordinator Ill. 15th dist. Equal Rights Amendment, 1977-78; dir. Sts. Peter and Paul Greek Orthodox Ch. Sch. Bd., 1977-79; mem. Lincolnwood PTA; den leader Cub Scout troop Boy Scouts Am., 1978-79. Cert. sr. rev. appraiser Nat. Assn. Rev. Appraisers. Mem. Nat. Assn. Realtors, Realtors Nat. Mktg. Inst., Ill. Assn. Realtors, Chgo. Real Estate Bd. (chairperson sales council 1980—), North Shore Bd. Realtors, NW Real Estate Bd., North Side Real Estate Bd., Nat. Assn. Ind. Fee Appraisers, North Suburban Chicagoland Real Estate Bd. (pres. 1976-77, dir. 1978-80), RELO/Inter-City Relocation Service (Chgo. met. area chairperson 1975-76), LWV, Zeta Tau Alpha. Contbr. articles to profl. jours. Office: 5922 N Clark St Chicago IL 60660 Mailing address: 6842 N Kostner Lincolnwood IL 60646

DALRYMPLE, GARY WAYNE, aerospace corp. exec., vocat. sch. adminstr.; b. East Orange, N.J., May 31, 1937; s. Edgar and Thelma D.; B.S. in Bus. Adminstrn., Duquesne U., 1975, postgrad.; m. Wilma L. Seabolt, Mar. 26, 1960: children—Kimber L., Kriste L. Supr. scheduling Hewitt-Robins, Passaic, N.J., 1957-59; mgr. spares and material control Martin-Marietta Corp., Cape Canaveral, Fla., 1959-66; mgr. contracts and logistics Gen. Electric Co., Valley Forge, Pa., 1966-67; with Teledyne Econ. Devel. Co., 1967—, bus. mgr., 1967-69, adminstrv. mgr., 1969-71, adminstrv. dir., 1971-73, gen. mgr., 1973-78, now v.p. Eastern Region, Pitts.; fin. cons. U.S. Dept. Labor. Served with USN, 1955-57. Mem. Am. Assn. Public Adminstrs., C. of C. Pitts., C. of C. Oakland (officer). Republican. Club: Masons (Glenshaw, Pa.). Home: 2502 College Park Rd Allison Park PA 15101 Office: Teledyne Econ Devel Co 1901 Ave of Stars Los Angeles CA 90067

DALTON, CHARLES FRANCIS, constrn. co. exec.; b. Naugatuck, Conn., Jan. 13, 1909; s. Charles F. and Gladys (Hodgeman) D.; student Mechanics Inst., 1930, Columbia, 1931; m. Mildred O'Neill, Nov. 24, 1932; children—Charles Francis, Mary Beth (Mrs. Knowlton J. O'Rielly), Barbara Ann. With John Lowry Inc., N.Y.C., 1934—, pres., 1961—. Vice pres. N.Y. Bldg. Congress, 1964-72, bd. govs., 1972—. Mem. Mayors Bldg. and Constrn. Adv. Council, N.Y.C.; bd. dirs. YMCA of Greater N.Y., 1963—, vice chmn. 1975—; bd. dirs. Am. Soc. Prevention of Cruelty to Animals, 1979—, pres., 1980—. Served with C.E., AUS, 1943-46. Mem. N.Y. C. of C. (v.p. 1968-73). Clubs: Union League (N.Y.C.), Winged Foot Golf (Mamaroneck, N.Y.), Pine Valley (N.J.) Golf, Larchmont (N.Y.) Yacht, Nat. Beagle (Aldie, Va.), So. N.Y. Beagle (pres. 1974—), Putnam Kennel. Home: 52 Mohegan Rd Larchmont NY 10538 Office: 52 Vanderbilt Ave New York NY 10017

DALY, DAVID GEORGE, graphic arts co. exec.; b. Cresco, Iowa, Oct. 7, 1936; s. Thomas William and Ellen Mary (Burgess) D.; B.B.A., State U. Iowa, 1963, postgrad., 1963; m. Kay Joan Jones, June 30, 1961; children—Kimberly, Pamela, John. Staff accountant Arthur Andersen & Co., C.P.A.'s, Chgo., 1963-66; asst. controller Josten's, Inc., Owatonna, Minn., 1966-71; v.p. finance Herff Jones Co. (now div. Carnation Co.), Indpls., 1971-74, v.p. operations, 1974—. Served with AUS, 1958-61. C.P.A., Minn. Mem. Am. Inst. C.P.A.'s, Minn. Soc. C.P.A.'s. Elk. Home: 12404 Brookshire Pkwy Carmel IN 46032 Office: 1411 N Capitol Ave Indianapolis IN 46202

DALY, ELIZABETH JANE BODNAR, microfilm co. exec.; b. Painesville, Ohio, July 27, 1944; d. Frank Andrew and Elizabeth Jane (Irish) Bodnar: student Ohio State U., 1962-63; m. David F. Daly, Nov. 29, 1963; 1 dau., Laura. With Gen. Microfilm Corp., Columbus, Ohio, 1969—, treas., 1973-78, exec. v.p., 1973-78, pres., 1978—. Mem. Nat. Micrographics Assn. (dir. Ohio chpt.). Presbyterian. Home: 1376 Lincoln Rd Columbus OH 43212 Office: Gen Microfilm Corp 37 E 5th Ave Columbus OH 43201

DALY, JOHN FRANCIS, indsl. mfg. co. exec.; b. N.Y.C., Dec. 13, 1922; s. John F. and Caroline C. (Pohl) D.; B.Mech. Engring., Rensselaer Poly. Inst., 1943; m. Casilda Boyd, July 16, 1953; children—Jo-Ann, Avis, Carol, Peter, Alexia. Exec. v.p. Hardie Mfg. Co., Hudson, Mich., 1950-56; v.p. Internat. Steel Co., Evansville, Ind., 1957-59; pres. Universal Wire Spring, Bedford, Ohio, 1959-63; v.p. Hoover Ball & Bearing Co., Ann Arbor, Mich., 1963-66, exec. v.p., 1966-68, pres., chief exec. officer, 1968-76, chmn. bd., 1976—, also dir.; dir. Nat. Bank and Trust Co., Ann Arbor, Comml. Sav. Bank, Adrian, Mich., Mich. Mut. Ins. Co., Detroit Bank. Bd. dirs. Siena Heights Coll., Adrian. Served to capt. USAAF, 1942-46. Mem. Theta

Xi. Home: 905 Berkshire Rd Ann Arbor MI 48104 Office: PO Box 1003 Ann Arbor MI 48106

DALY, JOSEPH RAYMOND, advt. exec.; b. N.Y.C., May 14, 1918; s. William C. and Mary (Hendrick) D.; A.B. Fordham U., 1940; m. Elizabeth R. Schulte, Apr. 19, 1947; children—Dorothy E., Suzanne J., Peter J., Timothy J., Mark, Andrew, Jennifer. With John A. Cairns, advt., 1946-49; with Doyle Dane Bernbach, N.Y.C., 1949—, sr. v.p. mgmt. supt., 1959-69, pres. 1968-74, chmn. bd., 1974—, also chief exec. officer. Served to lt. comdr., Air Corps, USNR, 1940-46; PTO. Decorated Navy Cross, Purple Heart, Air medal. Clubs: Turf and Field (N.Y.C.); Huntington Yacht. Office: 437 Madison Ave New York NY 10022*

DALY, THOMAS FRANCIS, lawyer; b. N.Y.C., Dec. 30, 1902; s. Thomas F. and Josephine (Walsh) D.; student William and Mary Coll.; LL.B., Columbia U., 1927; m. Isabel Hope, Apr. 12th, 1933 (dec. 1964); m. 2d, Virginia Barrett Melniker, June 16, 1966. Admitted to N.Y. State bar, 1928, N.J. bar, 1947; asso., partner firm Lord, Day & Lord, N.Y.C., 1927-75, now of counsel; practiced in N.J., 1947—. Mem. Atty. Gen.'s Nat. Com. To Study Antitrust Laws; mem. N.Y. Supreme Ct. Med. Malpractice Panel, 1971—. Bd. dirs. Monmouth County Soc. for Prevention Cruelty to Animals, 1955—, Monmouth County chpt. ARC; trustee Monmouth Mus., 1974—. Mem. Rumson (N.J.) Sch. Bd., 1960-69. Fellow Am., N.Y. State bar founds., Am. Coll. Trial Lawyers; mem. Am., N.Y. State, N.J. bar assns., Guild Catholic Lawyers (gov. 1969-71). Clubs: University, Downtown Assn. (N.Y.C.); Rumson (N.J.) Country; Root Beer and Checker (Red Bank, N.J.); Sea Bright Beach. Home: 70 East River Rd Rumson NJ 07760 Office: 25 Broadway New York NY 10004 also 105 East River Rd Rumson NJ 07760

DALY, WILLIAM JOSEPH, JR., fin. corp. exec.; b. Bklyn., Oct. 2, 1933; s. William Joseph and Gladys Irene (Weidel) D.; student pub. schs., Bklyn.; m. Carol Ann Conzelman, Apr. 8, 1956; children—Susan, Maureen, William Joseph. Supr. stock loan dept. Merrill Lynch, Pierce, Fenner & Smith, Inc., N.Y.C., 1958-63; asst. v.p. stock loan dept. Dean Witter & Co., Inc., N.Y.C., 1963-70; pres. DalGood Instl. Service Corp., N.Y.C., 1971—; mgr. broker-finder dept. Shelby Cullom Davis & Co. Served with U.S. Army, 1952-54. Mem. Assn. Stock Loan Representatives (founder, pres. 1969-70), Instl. Intermediaries Assn. (chmn. 1980—). Home: 3076 Grand Ave Baldwin NY 11510 Office: DalGood Instl Service Corp 99 Wall St New York NY 10005

D'AMATO, FRANCES LOUISE, assn. exec.; b. N.Y.C., Mar. 30, 1943; d. Frances A. D'Amato; B.S., Oswego State U., 1964; M.S., Hofstra U., 1969; m. Lewis M. Smoley, Sept. 17, 1977. Tng. cons. Chase Manhattan Bank, N.Y.C., 1971-73; asst. v.p. H.R.-CIT Corp., N.Y.C., 1973-78; v.p. human resources Am. Mgmt. Assn., N.Y.C., 1978—; instr. tng. profl. cert. program N.Y. U. Mem. Am. Soc. Tng. and Devel. (dir. N.Y. chpt.), Am. Soc. Personnel Adminstrn., Human Resource Planning Soc., Orgn. Devel. Network, Oswego State U. Alumni Assn. (dir.). Contbr. articles to Lamplighter; human resources editor Planning Rev., NE Tng. News. Home: 431 Main St New York NY 10044 Office: 135 W 50th St New York NY 10020

DA MIANO, ELIZABETH GRAHAM, export co. exec.; b. Masontown, Pa., Dec. 9, 1917; d. William L. and Estella (Sterling) Graham; student public schs.; m. Andre S. Da Miano, 1953 (dec. 1967); 1 son, Andrew S. Gen. mgr. Liggett Spring & Axle Co., Monongahela, Pa., 1942-53; pres. Da Miano and Graham Ltd., Glenview, Ill., 1953—. Mem. Internat. Trade Club Chgo., Overseas Automotive Club, Chgo. Automotive Exports Club (past pres.). Republican. Clubs: Glen View Golf (Golf, Ill.); Glenbrook Racquet. Address: 1521 Central Rd Glenview IL 60025

DAMIEN, GEORGE D., economist, social scientist, former diplomat, educator; b. Sofia, Bulgaria; came to U.S., 1954, naturalized, 1959; French baccalaureate degree, St. Augustine, Plovdiv, Bulgaria and Lyon, France; LL.B., U. Geneva, 1936, LL.M., 1938, LL.D., 1940; children—George, Sylvia-Marie, Nick Douglas. Consul gen. of Bulgaria ad interim, Paris, 1946-48; exec. v.p. Piton & Co., Ltd., Paris, 1949-52; press editor Info. Office of French Prime Minister, Paris, 1952-54; dep. dir. radio-desk and editor-writer on East Europe, Free Europe, Inc., N.Y.C., 1954-69, also fgn. areas cons., 1954-74; lectr. European affairs Columbia U., N.Y.C., 1957-67; lectr. econs. and polit. sci. N.Y. U., U. Vt., 1962-69; lectr. philosophy and phenomenology of conflict New Sch. for Social Research, N.Y.C., 1970-71, lectr. normative logic, 1973-74; adj. prof. polit. sci. U. South Fla., Tampa, 1975-76; lectr. polit. sci. and polit. economy Hillsborough Community Coll., Tampa, 1978-79; dir. and lectr. Center for Analytical Research and Consultation, Tampa, 1974—, dir. problems analysis consultation, 1979. Recipient Outstanding Achievement in Social Sci. award The Honors Registry, 1973. Mem. Am. Polit. Sci. Assn., Am. Judicature Soc., Acad. Polit. Sci., AAAS. Contbr. articles on polit. economy to scholarly jours.; introduced normative logic as new epistemological system of analytical reasoning and cognition. Home: 4015 W Fairview Heights Ave Tampa FL 33616 Office: 4015 W Fairview Heights Ave Tampa FL 33616

DAMM, ALEXANDER, airline exec.; b. Lincoln, Nebr., 1915; A.F. and A.M., U. Nebr. 1940. Asst. v.p. Trans World Airlines, 1940-59; v.p.-fin. Continental Airlines, Los Angeles, 1959-65, sr. v.p.-fin., 1965-66, sr. v.p. and gen. mgr., 1966-75, pres., chief operating officer, 1975—, vice chmn., 1980—, also dir.; dir. Crocker Nat. Bank, Crocker Nat. Corp. Office: Continental Air Lines Inc Los Angeles Internat Airport Los Angeles CA 90009*

DAMMERMAN, DENNIS DEAN, fin. exec.; b. Fairfield, Iowa, Nov. 4, 1945; s. Morris Melvin and Mary Louise (Watson) D.; B.S., U. Dubuque, 1967; m. Patricia Anne Bryk, July 9, 1967; children—Dwight David, Heather Lynne. Fin. mgmt. trainee Gen. Electric Co., 1967-69, corp. auditor, 1969-74, mgr. acquisitions analysis, lighting bus. group, 1974-76, mgr. ops. analysis, consumer products and services sector, 1976-78; v.p., comptroller Gen. Electric Credit Corp. Stamford, Conn., 1978—; dir. Trafalgar Developers, Inc., Miami, Fla., 1979—. Mem. Nat. Consumer Fin. Assn., Fin. Execs. Inst. Republican. Home: 21 Bellevale Dr Monroe CT 06468 Office: 260 Long Ridge Rd Stamford CT 06902

DAMSON, BARRIE MORTON, oil and gas exploration co. exec.; b. N.Y.C., Jan. 29, 1936; s. Harry and Ethel (Brody) D.; A.B., Harvard, 1956; LL.B., N.Y. U., 1959; m. Joan Selig, Feb. 29, 1972; children—Blair, Laura, Bethany. Admitted to N.Y. bar, 1959; practiced in N.Y.C.; pres. Damson Petroleum Corp., N.Y.C., 1963-69, Bronco Oil Corp., Midland, Tex., 1965-69, Delta Minerals Inc., Lake Charles, La., 1967-69; pres., chmn. bd. Damson Oil Corp., N.Y.C., 1969—; dir. Royalty Investments, S.A., Viking Resources Internat., N.V. Bd. dirs., co-chmn. Children's Blood Found. N.Y. Hosp. Mem. Bar Assn. N.Y., Oil Investment Inst. (pres. 1980), Ind. Petroleum Assn. Am. (dir.). Clubs: Harvard, El Morocco (N.Y.C.). Office: 366 Madison Ave New York NY 10017

DAN, MICHAEL THOMAS, security products co. exec.; b. Chgo., July 6, 1950; s. John William and Jeannette Theresa (McNamara) D.; student Morton Coll., 1968-71; m. Mary Lou Atkins, July 16, 1971; children—Michael William, Adam Joseph. Mgr., Automatic Merchandising Systems, Chgo., 1971-73; sales mgr. Security Products div. WICO Corp., Niles, Ill., 1973-76; pres. Armored Vehicle Builders, Inc., Pittsfield, Mass., 1976—; tchr./cons. operational aspects of armored vehicles. Mem. Am. Soc. Indsl. Security, Internat. Assn. Chiefs of Police, Ind. Armored Car Operators Assn., Nat. Armored Car Assn. Home: PO Box 88 Dalton MA 01226 Office: 343 Pecks Rd Pittsfield MA 01201

DANCO, LÉON ANTOINE, mgmt. cons., educator; b. N.Y.C., May 30, 1923; s. Leon A. and Alvira T. (Gomez) D.; A.B., Harvard, 1943, M.B.A., 1947; Ph.D., Case-Western Res. U., 1963; m. Katharine Elizabeth Leck, Aug. 25, 1951; children—Suzanne, Walter Ten Eyck. Asst. to div. pres. Interchem. Corp., N.Y.C., 1947-50; sales promotion mgr. Risdon Mfg. Co., Waterbury, Conn., 1950-55, mgmt. cons., Cheshire, Conn., 1955-57; prof., asso. dir. mgmt. program Case Inst. Tech., Cleve., 1957-58, lectr., 1959—; mgmt. cons. L.A. Danco & Co., 1957—; lectr. John Carroll U., Cleve., 1959-66, prof., dir. mgmt. confs., 1966—; vis. prof. econs. Cleve. Inst. Art, 1966-69, Kent State U., 1966-67; exec. dir. Univ. Services Inst., Cleve., 1967-69, pres., 1969—; pres. Center for Family Business, 1978—. Served to lt. (j.g.), USCG, 1942-46; PTO. Mem. Am. Econ. Assn. Author: Beyond Survival-A Business Owners Guide for Success, 1975; Inside the Family Business, 1980. Syndicated columnist: It's Your Business, 1973—; pub. newsletter The Family in Business, 1978—. Home: 28230 Cedar Rd Pepper Pike Cleveland OH 44122 Office: PO Box 24268 Cleveland OH 44124

DANDORA, NATHU RAM, metal fabricating and finishing co. exec.; b. Nalagarh, India, Aug. 24, 1942; s. Ragho Ram and Rameshwari Devi D.; Asso. Degree Mech. Engring., Thapar Inst. Engring. and Tech., 1961; B.S. in Mech. Engring., Inst. of Engrs., 1967; postgrad. Temple U., 1978—; m. Aruna Joshi, Nov. 25, 1968; children—Rahul, Reetu. Plant engr. Atlas Cycle Industries, Soneat, India, 1962-72; plant mgr. Chain Bike Corp., Allentown, Pa., 1972-78; v.p. mfg. Chein Industries, Burlington, N.J., 1978—. Mem. Am. Mgmt. Assn., Soc. Plastic Engrs., Am. Soc. Metals, Instn. Engrs. India (asso.), India Assn. Lehigh Valley (pres. 1977). Home: 1060 Randolf Dr Yardley PA 19067 Office: Chein Industries William St Burlington NJ 08016

DANGLER, RICHARD REISS, gambling corp. exec.; b. N.Y.C., Mar. 6, 1940; s. Edward and Gertrude (Reiss) D.; B.A., N.Y. U., 1962; LL.B., Bklyn. Law Sch., 1965, J.D., 1967; m. Lisa Frant, Feb. 1, 1968; children—Ellen Susan, Justin Todd. Asst. to pres. Bogue Elec. Mfg. Co., Paterson, N.J., 1965-68; sr. contracts adminstr./mgr. export control IT&T, N.Y.C., 1968-70; sr. v.p.-adminstrn. N.Y.C. Off-Track Betting Corp., 1970—; lectr. in field. Sponsor exec. internship program Human Resources Adminstrn., 1972-76; fin. and legal adviser Boy Scouts Am., Passaic County, N.J., 1968. Recipient Blanche White award, 1974, Outstanding Achievement award United Fund N.Y., 1975. Mem. ASME, Nat. Contract Mgmt. Assn., U.S. Naval Inst., Assn. Old Crows, Internat. Game Fish Assn., Nat. Wildlife Fedn. Clubs: Sea Horses Rod and Gun, Admiral's. Home: RFD 1 Crow Hill Path Mount Kisco NY 10549 Office: 1501 Broadway New York NY 10036

DANGO, GERRY AQUINO, air cargo co. exec., inventor; b. Philippines, Feb. 7, 1932; s. Antero D. and Irenea T. D.; came to U.S., 1969, naturalized, 1974; cert. profl. mech. engring. Cebu Inst. Tech., Philippines, 1955; cert. profl. in internat. bus. UCLA, 1977; m. Herminda Tidalgo, Nov. 15, 1958; 1 dau., Rexa T. Mktg. mgr. Bi-Rite Industries, Inc., Los Angeles, 1972-74; v.p. M.C. Industries, Inc., Glendale, Calif., 1974-76; ops. mgr. Pacific Air Cargo, Los Angeles, 1976-78; pres. Amerex Internat., Los Angeles, 1978—; inventor, internat. trade cons. Served to capt. Philippines Army, 1960-62. Recipient scientist award Philippine Govt., 1977. Mem. Soc. Am. Inventors, Export Mgrs. Assn. Calif., Philippines Assn. Inventors. Republican. Roman Catholic. Patentee in field. Home: 6110 Delphi St Los Angeles CA 90042 Office: 2700 W 3d St Los Angeles CA 90057 also Makati Metro Manila Philippines

DANIEL, CHARLES D., banker; b. Tupelo, Miss., July 16, 1923; s. Watt H. and Nellis (Hickerson) D.; student Vanderbilt U., 1940-41; B.S., U.S. Mil. Acad., 1944; m. Dorothy Stamps, Aug. 10, 1946; children—Thomas, Ann, Louise, Mary. Commd. 2d lt. U.S. Army, 1944, advanced through grades to col., 1965; ret., 1968; with 1st Nat. Bank of Washington, 1968-75, chmn. bd., pres., 1975; pres. Union 1st Nat. Bank, Washington, 1976—; dir. Datatel, Inc., 1974-75. Treas., Republican Boosters Club, 1973-78; dir. Washington Hosp. Center; past pres. Washington Opera; mem. adv. bd. Howard Univ. Hosp.; treas. Nat. Capitol area chpt. Multiple Sclerosis Soc., 1973-78; treas. fin. com. Presdl. Inaugural Com., 1981. Decorated Silver Star, Legion of Merit with oak leaf cluster, Bronze Star with oak leaf cluster, Army Commendation medal with oak leaf cluster, Air medal with 8 oak leaf clusters. Mem. D.C. Bankers Assn. (past pres.), D.C. Clearing House (asst. sec.), Washington Bd. Trade. Episcopalian. Clubs: Met., Army-Navy Country. Office: 740 15th St NW Washington DC 20005

DANIEL, DOUGLAS WALKER, computer co. exec.; b. Walters, Okla., Oct. 17, 1942; s. Delmar Lee and Vernie Ethel (Meeks) D.; B.S. in Math., Calif. State U., Hayward, 1968; M.A., 1974; m. Sherry Delight Lindley, Dec. 23, 1968; children—Jennifer Lynn, Laura Lee. Accelerator operator Lawrence Livermore (Calif.) Lab., 1966-68, mathematician, 1971-79; pres., founder Am. Microcomputer Co., Livermore, 1979—; cons. systems analysis and numerical math. Served to capt. U.S. Army, 1968-71; Vietnam. Decorated Bronze Star, Air Medal, Army Commendation Medal (U.S.), Medal of Honor (Vietnam). Mem. Res. Officers Assn., Sigma Pi Sigma. Republican. Contbr. articles to profl. jours. Home and Office: 465 Jillana Ave Livermore CA 94550

DANIEL, ELEANOR SAUER, economist, life ins. co. exec.; b. N.Y.C., Feb. 8, 1917; d. Charles Peter and Elsie Edna (Dommer) Sauer; B.A. magna cum laude (Bardwell fellow), Mt. Holyoke Coll., 1936; M.A. (Perkins fellow), Columbia, 1937; m. John Carl Daniel, Dec. 31, 1952; children—Victoria Ann, Charles Timothy. Eocnomist, U.S. Steel Co., N.Y.C., 1938; lectr. econs. Bklyn. Coll., 1939-40; with Mut. Life Ins. Co. N.Y., N.Y.C., 1940-74, asst. v.p., 1972-74, sr. econ. adviser, 1972-74; economist Fed. Home Loan Bank, N.Y.C., 1974-75; v.p., dir. Daniel Realty Cos., N.Y.C., 1975—; dir., mem. fin. com. Atlantic City Electric Co.; mem. bd. mgrs. U.S. Savs. Bank Newark; mem. Pres's. Task Force Fed. Credit Programs, 1968-69; mem. N.J. Gov's. Econ. Recovery Com., 1975-76; mem. econ. adv. bd. U.S. Sec. Commerce, 1971-73; mem. bus. research adv. council U.S. Bur. Labor Statistics, 1966—; trustee Blue Shield of N.J. Past trustee Mt. Holyoke Coll., also vice chmn., mem. fin. com. Mem. Am. Economic Assn., Am. Fin. Assn. (past dir.), Phi Beta Kappa. Author: (with J.J. O'Leary and S.F. Foster) Our National Debt and Our Savings; contbr. articles in field to profl. jours. Home: 34 North Dr East Brunswick NJ 08816

DANIEL, LAWRENCE STEVEN, banker; b. Newport, Ark., May 25, 1939; B.A., Sacramento State U., 1966; grad. Pacific Coast Banking Sch., U. Wash., 1972; postgrad. Golden Gate U., 1976; m. Lois Roper, Jan. 30, 1959; children—Steven, Brian. Vice pres., cashier Bank of Alex Brown, Walnut Grove, Calif., 1972-76, pres., dir., 1976—, chief exec. officer, 1977—. Pres. Walnut Grove P.T.A.; active Golden Empire council Boy Scouts Am. Served with AUS, 1962-64. Mem. Bank Adminstrn. Inst. (chmn. community bank council), Western Ind. Bankers Assn., Am. Bankers Assn., Calif. Bankers Assn. Clubs: Walnut Grove Rotary, Sutter (Sacramento), Comstock. Office: PO Box 38 Walnut Grove CA 95690

DANIELIAN, RONALD LAWRENCE, economist, assn. exec.; b. N.Y.C., Aug. 17, 1943; s. Noobar R. and Grace A. D.; B.A., Aurora (Ill.) Coll., 1967; m. Pamela Marie Fleming, Aug. 19, 1967; children—Edward Lawrence, Stephanie Grace, Christopher John. Asso. economist to economist Internat. Economic Policy Assn., Washington, 1967-71, exec. v.p., treas., 1974—; dir. Office of Research and Analysis, U.S. Travel Service, U.S. Dept. Commerce, Washington, 1971-73, cons., 1973-74; dir. Center for Multinat. Studies, Washington, 1974—. Vice pres., Parkwood Residents' Assn., Bethesda, Md., 1976-77, pres., 1977-78. Mem. Internat. Economic Studies Inst. (v.p., trustee 1976—). Episcopalian. Clubs: Met., Nat. Press, Internat., (Washington); Congressional Country (Bethesda). Co-author: The United States Balance of Payments: A Reappraisal, 1968; contbg. author: Raw Materials and Foreign Policy, 1976. Home: 12605 Native Dancer Pl Darnestown MD 20760 Office: 1625 Eye St Washington DC 20006

DANIELS, ALLEN JERROLD, mfg. co. mgr.; b. Bklyn., June 4, 1946; s. Irving D. and Selma C. Daniels; A.A., Miami Dade Jr. Coll., 1967; B.A., Fla. Atlantic U., 1969, M.B.A., 1971; m. Peggy; children—Brian, Scott. Teller, Washington Fed. Savs. & Loan Assn., Miami Beach, Fla., 1966-67; sr. asst. mgr. Household Fin. Corp., Miami, 1967-68; loan officer and credit analyst Hialeah-Miami Springs (Fla.) First State Bank, 1968-70; credit mgr. Mary Carter Industries, Miami, 1970-72, Cain & Bultman Inc., Miami, 1972; regional mgr. Famco Services, Inc., Miami, 1972-73; fin. services mgr. Edward Don & Co., Miami, 1973-80; credit mgr. Moss Mfg., Inc., Miami, 1980—. Mem. Nat. Assn. Credit Mgmt. (chmn. internat. com.), So. Fla. Credit Mgmt. Assn. (pres., 1977-78). Democrat. Jewish. Home: 9231 NW 32 Pl Sunrise FL 33321 Office: 7600 NW 69 Ave Miami FL 33152

DANIELS, DANIEL HOWARD, engring. cons. co. exec.: b. Albany, N.Y., Dec. 20, 1926; s. David S. and Sadie D.; B.A., Hofstra U., 1951, M.B.A., 1965; M.S., CCNY, 1953; Ph.D., Columbia U., 1969; Ed.D., London Collegiate Inst., 1976; children—Janis, Jonathan, Susan. Engring. adminstr. Hazeltine Corp., Greenlawn, L.I., N.Y., 1953-62; indsl. engring. mgr. Art Steel Co. Inc., Bronx, 1963-74; engring. cons. Diversified Mktg. Assn., Scarsdale, N.Y., 1974-76, D. Howard Daniels & Assos., Scarsdale, 1976—. Mem. ASME (cert. mfg. engr.), Internat. Material Mgmt. Soc. (cert. profl. in material mgmt., material handling), Nat. Soc. Profl. Engrs., Am. Inst. Indsl. Engrs., Am. Personnel and Guidance Assn., Am. Assn. Higher Edn. Author monographs in field. Office: PO Box 505 Scarsdale NY 10583

DANIELS, DERICK JANUARY, publishing exec.; b. Washington, Dec. 6, 1928; s. Worth Bagley and Josephine Poe (January) D.; A.B. in Journalism, U. N.C., 1950; m. Elizabeth Long Blalock, Aug. 10, 1950 (div. 1972); children—Leigh Churchill, Scott Daniels; m. 2d, Mary Jeannette Taylor. Reporter, Durham (N.C.) Herald, 1950, St. Petersburg (Fla.) Times, 1950-51, Atlanta Constn., 1951-55; sub-editor, then city editor Miami (Fla.) Herald, 1955-61; with Detroit Free Press, 1961-73; v.p., exec. editor, 1967-73; v.p. news Knight Newspapers, Inc., Detroit, 1973-74; pres. Knight News Services, Inc., 1973-76; pres., chief operating officer Playboy Enterprises, Inc., Chgo., 1976—; v.p. Knight-Ridder Newspapers Inc., 1974—; dir. News and Observer Pub. Co., Raleigh, N.C. Bd. dirs. Detroit Area Council World Affairs, United Found. Detroit; mem. founders soc. Detroit Inst. Arts. Mem. Am. Soc. Newspaper Editors (div.), Econ. Club Detroit, Alpha Tau Omega. Episcopalian. Clubs: Detroit, Adcraft (Detroit); Met. (Washington); Miami, Palm Bay (Miami). Office: Playboy Enterprises 919 N Michigan Ave Chicago IL 60611*

DANIELS, TERRENCE D., publishing co. exec.; b. St. Louis, Jan. 11, 1943; s. Edgar Martell and Mary Jane (Phelan) D.; grad. U. Va., 1966, M.B.A., 1970; m. Courtnay Sylvan, July 24, 1967; children—Courtnay, Catherine, Charles. With W. R. Grace & Co., 1970-77, asst. to chmn., chief exec. officer, until 1974, v.p. consumer service group, 1974-77; sr. v.p. corp. devel. Mattel, Inc., 1977-79; pres., chief exec. officer Western Pub. Co., Racine, Wis., 1979—; dir. Ole's Home Centers, Calif. Served to 1st lt. U.S. Army; Vietnam. Roman Catholic. Clubs: Racine Country; Summerset Hills Country (Bernardsville, N.J.). Office: 1220 Mound Ave Racine WI 53404

DANIGELIS, JOANNE STAGE, real estate co. exec.; b. Endicott, N.Y., Feb. 5, 1937; d. John Jette and Frances (Harenza) D.; A.B., Syracuse U., 1959, postgrad., 1959; m. Dean Danigelis, 1960; children—Dina Lynn, William K. II. Tchr. art public schs., Endicott, 1959-60; pres. Danigelis Imports, ready-to-wear, Brookfield Center, Conn., 1967-80; now account exec. Realtech Realtors, Danbury, Conn.; cons. to retail apparel stores, 1967—. Co-chmn. ann. festival Assumption Greek Orthodox Ch.; area chmn. ann. drive Am. Cancer Soc. Mem. Nat. Assn. Realtors, Conn. Assn. Realtors, Danbury Bd. Realtors, New Milford Bd. Realtors, LWV. Democrat. Club: Syracuse U. Alumni (N.Y.C.). Office: Realtech Realtors Old Ridgebury Rd Danbury CT 06810

DANJCZEK, WILLIAM EMIL, engring. supplies mfg. co. exec.; b. Prague, Czechoslovakia, June 4, 1913; s. Emil and Gabriele (Schich) D.; grad. St. Stevens Coll., Prague, 1931; Dr.Juris, Charles U., 1935; postgrad. Columbia, 1941, 50; m. Mary Anne Webb, Jan. 24, 1980; children by previous marriage—Helgi (Mrs. William Downes), Billie (Mrs. Mark Jorgensen), Thomas Arthur, Michael Harvey, David William. Mem. Legal and Gen. Assurance Soc., Ltd., London, 1933; market researcher Koh-inoor, Budweis, Czechoslovakia, 1935-37, Koh-inoor (Gt. Brit.), Ltd., Croydon, Eng., 1938-39; export mgr. Kohinoor, Inc., Bloomsbury, N.J., 1939-46, dir., v.p., 1947; pres. Koh-I-Noor Rapidograph, Inc. Koh-I-Noor (Can.) Ltd., Montreal, Que., 1947-75, hon. chmn. bd., 1975—; pres. Moser Jewel Co., Perth Amboy, N.J., 1970—, chmn., 1978. Decorated knight St. Gregory; recipient Disting. Citizen Salesmanship award Sales and Mktg. Execs., 1966; Gold Americanism medal DAR, 1968. Mem. Pencil Makers Assn., Inc. (past pres.), Phillipsburg C. of C. (past pres., named Outstanding Citizen 1976). Club: Rotary (dir. Rancho Bernardo, Calif., past pres. Phillipsburg, N.J.). Home: 18233 Verano Dr San Diego CA 92128 Office: 100 North St Bloomsbury NJ 08804

DANNENBERG, JOHN ERNEST, electronics co. exec.; b. San Francisco, Jan. 9, 1940; s. Hans and Elizabeth (Hirtz) D.; Victor Chem. Works scholar, M.I.T., 1957-60; B.S. in Elec. Engring., U. Utah, 1963, B.S. in Math., 1963; m. Linda Faye Braffman, Aug. 30, 1970; children—Nicole Beth, Mark Stephen. With Lockheed Missiles & Space Co., Sunnyvale, Calif., 1963-66; mktg. mgr. Applied Tech. div. Itek, Sunnyvale, 1966-73; nat. sales mgr. Antekna, Inc., Mountain View, Calif., 1973-78; dir. domestic new bus. devel. Telcom, Inc., Vienna, Va., 1979-80; pres. Guaranteed Energy Savs., Inc., Los Altos Hills, Calif., 1980—; owner Mendocino Mountain Ranch, Covelo, Calif., 1979—; mktg. cons. Chmn., Pub. Works Com., Town of Los Altos Hills, Calif., 1976—. Recipient Bausch & Lomb Sci. award,

1957. Mem. IEEE, Assn. Energy Engrs., Aircraft Owners and Pilots Assn., Assn. Old Crows. Pioneer aircraft collision avoidance system. Home: 12374 Melody Ln Los Altos Hills CA 94022

DANNER, DOUGLAS, lawyer; b. Phila., Oct. 25, 1924; s. Carl J. and Cornelia Joy (Hatmaker) D.; A.B., Harvard U., 1946; J.D., Boston U., 1949; m. Mary S. Bigelow, Aug. 19, 1950; children—David B., William B. Admitted to Mass. bar, 1949; asso. firm Powers & Hall, Boston, 1956-61, partner, 1961-71, sr. partner, 1971-79, treas., 1979—; dir. Eaton Investments, Inc., Investor's Bank & Trust Co. Bd. dirs., mem. exec. com. Jordan Hosp., 1973—, pres., 1979—; trustee Children's Hosp. Med. Center, 1979—. Served with USNR, 1942-45. Mem. Am., Mass., Boston bar assns., Am. Soc. Law and Medicine (1st v.p. 1974-78), Assn. Trial Lawyers Am., Assn. Trial Attys. Am. Club: Duxbury Yacht. Home: 32 Linden Ln Duxbury MA 02332 Office: 100 Franklin St Boston MA 02110

DANON, MORRIS, banker: b. N.Y.C., Mar. 4, 1943; s. N.B. and Victoria A. Danon; B.A., CCNY, 1964; M.B.A., Cornell U., 1966; m. Carole E. Berman, Aug. 26, 1965; children—Stacy E., Katherine V., William R.N. Vice pres. Bankers Trust Co. N.Y., 1966-76; v.p., sr. loan officer Union Bank, Los Angeles, 1976-78; regional v.p. Imperial Bank, Los Angeles, 1978—. Mem. sch. site council Las Virgenes Sch. Dist. Mem. Credit Mgrs. Assn. Los Angeles, Calif. Bankers Assn. Club: Warner Center Racquet. Office: 21945 Erwin St Woodland Hills CA 91367

DANZIG, FREDERICK PAUL, editor; b. Springfield, Mass., Sept. 17, 1925; s. Phillip and Sylvia (Levin) D.; B.A., Washington Sq. Coll., N.Y. U., 1949; m. Edith Goret, Mar. 16, 1952; children—Steven, Ellen Kay. Copy boy A.P., N.Y.C., 1943; reporter Herkimer (N.Y.) Evening Telegram, 1949; reporter Port Chester (N.Y.) Daily Item, 1950-51; reporter, columnist U.P.I., N.Y.C., 1951-62; sr. editor Advt. Age, N.Y.C., 1962-68, exec. editor, 1969—. Chmn., United Civic Orgn., Eastchester, N.Y., 1968-69. Trustee Huntley Civic Assn., Eastchester. Served with inf., AUS, 1943-46. Decorated Bronze Star medal, Purple Heart, Presdl. Unit citation with oak leaf cluster. Mem. 29th Inf. Div. Assn. Author: (with Ted Klein) How to be Heard, 1974. Office: Advertising Age 708 3d Ave New York NY 10017

DANZIG, HAL MACDONALD, watch mfg. co. exec.; b. Rochester, N.Y., Jan. 24, 1938; s. Clifford M. and Pauline (Fisher) D.; B.S. in E.E., Bucknell U., 1959; m. Carolyn King, Aug. 17, 1974; children—Linda, Carl. Sales mgr. Midland Mfg. Co., Kansas City, Kans., 1963-65; v.p. mktg. Electronic Research Co., Overland Park, Kans., 1965-70, pres., 1970-76; pres. Elgin Waltham Watch Co., Chgo., 1976—. Office: 400 S Jefferson St Chicago IL 60607

DANZIG, JEROME ALAN, mgmt. cons.; b. N.Y.C., Feb. 7, 1913; s. Jerome J. and Helen Madeline (Wolf) D.; B.A., Dartmouth Coll., 1934; m. Sarah H. Palfrey, Apr. 27, 1951; 1 son, Jerome Palfrey; 1 stepdau., Diana Dupont. Reporter, N.Y. Jour., 1934-35; comml. program mgr. Sta. WOR, N.Y.C., 1935-42; program dir. sta. WINS, N.Y.C., 1946-48; asso. dir. network programs, producer CBS-TV, 1948-55; dir. program planning and devel. NBC, 1955-56, v.p. in charge radio network programs, 1956-59, v.p. participating programs NBC-TV, 1959-61; TV-radio cons. N.Y. Republican City Com., 1961; spl. asst. to Gov., State of N.Y., 1962-69, spl. asst. to dir. communications Gov.'s staff, 1969-72, spl. asst. to Gov., 1972-74; partner Chester Burger & Co., Inc., Mgmt. Cons., N.Y.C., 1976—. Vice chmn. N.Y. State Commn. Cable TV, 1973-79, mem., 1979—; formerly trustee Jewish Bd. Guardians, N.Y.C., United Neighborhood Houses; trustee Jewish Home and Hosp. for the Aged, N.Y.C.; mem. public relations com. Fedn. Jewish Philanthropies of N.Y., 1980—. Served with USNR, 1942-46. Decorated Bronze star. Mem. Public Relations Soc. Am. (pres.-elect N.Y. chpt. 1980), Am. Arbitration Assn. (panel of arbitrators 1980—), Acad. TV Arts and Scis. Club: Quaker Hill (Pawling, N.Y.). Office: 275 Madison Ave New York NY 10016

DAOUD, GEORGE JAMIL, hotel and motel cons.; b. Beirut, Oct. 20, 1944; came to U.S., 1958, naturalized, 1970; s. Jamil G. and Shafieah E. Daoud; B.S., N.Y. U., 1967; M.P.S., Cornell U., 1969; m. Barbara A. Fisco, Apr. 30, 1972: 3 children. Gen. grm. Holiday Inn, New London and Groton, Conn., 1974-75, Centle Winds Beach Resort, St. Croix, V.I., 1975-78; pres., cons. Motor Inn Mgmt., Inc., Dayton, Ohio, 1978—; v.p. V.I. Hotel and Motel Assn., 1976. Mem. Am. Hotel and Motel Assn. (mem. Ednl. Inst., cert. hotel adminstr.), Ohio Hotel and Motel Assn., Nat. Assn. Rev. Appraisers, Cert. Real Estate Rev. Appraisers. Democrat. Roman Catholic. Club: Masons. Office: PO Box 1417 Dayton OH 45401

DAPONTE, JOHN JOSEPH, JR., lawyer; b. Bristol, R.I., May 12, 1933; s. John J. and Mary Elizabeth (Ferris) DaP.; B.A., Providence Coll., 1955; J.D., Boston U., 1962; LL.M., Georgetown U., 1966; cert. U. Muenster (West Ger.), 1968; m. Gunilla K. Tornhagen, Apr. 18, 1971; children—Karen, Karsten. Admitted to Mass. bar, 1962, D.C. bar, 1964, U.S. Supreme Ct. bar, 1976; atty. U.S. Dept. Def., 1962, Treasury Dept., 1962-67, U.S. Dept. Commerce, Washington, 1968—, exec. sec. Fgn. Trade Zones Bd., 1973. Bd. dirs. Friendship Neighborhood Coalition, D.C., 1974-78; mem. Sumner Citizens Assn., Bethesda, Md., 1978—. Served to 1st lt., U.S. Army, 1956-59. Recipient Am. Jurisprudence award, 1966, Bronze award Dept. Commerce, 1975. Mem. Mass. Bar Assn., D.C. Bar Assn., Fed. Bar Assn., Am. Soc. Internat. Law. Bd. editors Boston U. Law Rev., 1960-62; contbr. articles profl. jours. Home: 5804 Madawaska Rd Bethesda MD 20016 Office: Dept of Commerce Washington DC 20230

DAPRON, ELMER JOSEPH, JR., advt. exec.; b. Clayton, Mo., Jan. 14, 1925; s. Elmer Joseph and Susanna (Kruse) D.; m. Sharon Kay Neuling, Feb. 22, 1977. Employed in constrn. bus., Fairbanks, Alaska, 1947-48; tech. writer-editor McDonnell-Douglas Corp., St. Louis, 1948-57; free-lance writer, Paris, France, 1957; with Gardner Advt. Co., St. Louis, 1960-78, v.p. 1969-78; sr. v.p. Kenrick Advt. Inc., 1978—; pres. Cornucopia Communications, Inc., 1979—. Producer syndicated TV show Elmer Dapron's Grocery List; advt. and mktg. cons. to govt. and industry; daily commentator Mut. Radio Network. Mem. Gov.'s Energy Commn., 1977—. Served with USMCR, 1943-45; PTO; 50-51; Korea. Recipient advt. awards including New Filming Techniques award Internat.-Film Festival. Hon. fellow Harry Truman Library Inst. Mem. Nat. Agrl. Mktg. Assn. (v.p. 1970—, trustee, Miss. Valley Farm Mktg. Man of Year 1974), Marine Corps League (nat. vice comdt. 1967-69). Clubs: Media, Presidents. Democrat. Contbr. articles to publs. Home: 300 Mansion House Center St Louis MO 63102 Office: 319 N 4th St Saint Louis MO 63102

D'ARCY, ALBERT JOSEPH, mgmt. cons.; b. N.Y.C., Dec. 22, 1915; s. James J. and Ida (Etzel) D'A.; M.E., Stevens Inst. Tech., 1936; M.B.A., Columbia, 1958; m. Margaret Tangney, July 28, 1951; children—Christine, David, Karen, Steven. With White Constrn. Co., N.Y.C., 1936-37, Asiatic Petroleum Co., N.Y.C., 1937-40; purchasing agt. Union Carbide Corp., 1940-53, div. mgr. purchases, 1953-57, asst. mgr. purchases, 1957-62, mgr. purchasing services, 1962-64, dir. purchases, 1964-70, dir. purchases and material services, 1970-76, dir. planning-energy, supplies and services, 1976-78, dir. adminstrn.-energy, supplies and services, 1978-80; v.p. Barsdale Assos. Ltd., Scarsdale, N.Y., 1981—. Bd. dirs. Scarsdale-Hartsdale (N.Y.) chpt. UN Assn. U.S.A., 1977—, Friends Scarsdale Parks, 1977—. Recipient Scarsdale Mayor's Citizen Bowl award, 1978. Mem. ASME, Am. Mgmt. Assn., Nat. Assn. Purchasing Mgmt., Purchasing Mgmt. Assn. N.Y. Clubs: Princeton (N.Y.C.); Town (Scarsdale). Home: 7 Barry Rd Scarsdale NY 10583 Office: PO Box 613 Scarsdale NY 10583

D'ARIENZO, JOSEPH PAUL, petroleum co. exec.; b. Massena, N.Y., July 28, 1921; s. John and Immaculata (Memoli) D'A.; B.S. cum laude, Syracuse U., 1948; m. Gertrude Mary Denis, July 28, 1943. Dep. collector IRS, Binghamton, N.Y., 1949-51; supr. analytical accounting Arabian Am. Oil Co., Dhahran, Saudi Arabia, 1951-57; mgmt. analyst Iranian Oil Exploration Co., Tehran, Iran, 1957-59; treas. Super Mold Corp., Lodi, Calif., 1959-66; controller Reserve Oil & Gas Co., Apple Valley, Calif., 1966-71; v.p., treas. Mohawk Petroleum Corp., Inc., Bakersfield, Calif., 1971—. Vice pres., Desert Communities United Fund, Victorville, Calif., 1964-66. Served to staff sgt. USAAF, 1943-45. Decorated Air medal; recipient Frank Titus Meml. award Desert Communities United Fund, 1970. Mem. Nat. Assn. Accountants, Am. Mgmt. Assn., Beta Gamma Sigma, Alpha Beta Psi. Roman Catholic. Club: Petroleum (Bakersfield). Home: 988 Leisure World Mesa AZ 85206 Office: PO Box 1476 Bakersfield CA 93302

DARLING, GARY LYLE, carpet and furniture cleaning co. exec.; b. Passaic, N.J., Nov. 29, 1941: s. Earle Wallace and Lottie Anne (Shefcik) D.; B.A. in Bus. Adminstrn., Boston U., 1963; postgrad. Columbia U. Law Sch., 1963-64; m. Jane Constance Higgiston, Aug. 24, 1964; children—Susan Jane, Debra Ann, Eric Wallace. Data processing sales rep. Service Bur. Corp. subs. IBM, Boston, 1964-66; owner, pres. Renotex Corp., N.Y.C., 1966—. Mem. Assn. Interior Decor Specialists (pres. 1979-80), Carpet and Upholstery Cleaning Assn. (pres. 1974-76), N.Y. Rug Cleaners Inst. (dir. 1974—), Nat. Fedn. Ind. Bus., C. of C., Better Bus. Bur. Club: Englewood Field. Office: Renotex Corp 302 W 21st St New York NY 10011

DARLINGTON, DAVID WILLIAM, electronic co. adminstr.; b. Boston, Oct. 3, 1945; s. Horace and Maude Beatrice (Pfalzgraf) D.; B.S., Babson Coll., 1974, M.B.A., 1976; postgrad. Northeastern U., 1977-80; m. Nancy Elizabeth Lofgren, Nov. 25, 1967; children—Elizabeth Joy, Christine Rebecca. Planning engr. Stone & Webster Engring. Corp., Boston, 1974-75; project adminstr. Northrop Corp., Norwood, Mass., 1975-80; mgr. program adminstrn. internat. systems div. Sanders Assos., Inc., Nashua, N.H., 1980—. Served with USN, 1964-71. Mem. Am. Prodn. and Inventory Control Soc. (cert.), Assn. M.B.A. Execs., Project Mgmt. Inst., Beta Gamma. Club: Appalachian Mountain. Home: 72 Fuller Brook Rd Wellesley MA 02181 Office: Daniel Webster Hwy S Nashua NH 03061

D'ARRIGO, STEPHEN, JR., agrl. co. exec.; b. Stockton, Cal., Mar. 8, 1922; s. Stephen and Constance (Picciotto) D'A.; B.S., U. Santa Clara, 1943; m. Rosemary Anne Murphy, Aug. 20, 1949; children—Stephen III, Kathleen Anne, Joanne Marie, Michael Andrew, Dennis Patrick, Patrick Shane. Sec.-treas., D'Arrigo Bros. Co. of Cal., San Jose, 1946—, Salinas, 1962—; sec.-treas. Santa Cruz Farms (co. merged with D'Arrigo Bros. 1970), Eloy, Ariz., 1947-52, pres., gen. mgr. 1952-70, dir. 1947-70. Mem. nat. adv. bd. Am. Security Council; mem. Nat. Def. Exec. Res. Served from pvt. to 2d lt., AUS, 1943-46. Decorated Bronze Star, Combat Inf. Badge, Belgian Fouragere; recipient Distinguished Service award Santa Clara Heart Assn. Mem. Nat. Rifle Assn. (life), Springfield Armory Mus. (life), Smithsonian Assos. (nat. charter), NAM, Assn. U.S. Army, Co. Mil. Historians, Am. Soc. Arms Collectors, Tex. Gun Collectors Assn., Nat. Hist. Soc. Club: Commonwealth. Home: 2241 Dry Creek Rd San Jose CA 95124 Office: PO Box 850 Salinas CA 93901

DARROW, JOHN FRANCIS, pulp and paper industry cons., ret. trade assn. exec.; b. Poughkeepsie, N.Y., Aug. 19, 1915; s. William P. and Mary (Moran) D.; A.B. cum laude, Middlebury Coll., 1937; postgrad. Rockefeller Found., 1937-38, Am. U., 1937-38, Georgetown Law Sch., 1939-41; m. Genevieve T. Prendergast, June 4, 1977; step-dau. by previous marriage, Anne (Mrs. Jurrien Dean). Chief U.S. Dept. of Commerce, Forest Products Div., Washington, 1939-41; Washington rep. Am. Paper & Pulp Assn., 1941-42; chief gen. supplies br. Mil. Planning Div., Office Quartermaster Gen., Washington, 1942-43; asst. sec. Writing Paper Mfg. Assn., N.Y.C., 1947-61, exec. sec.-treas., 1961-66; exec. sec. printing-writing paper div. Am. Paper Inst., N.Y.C., 1966-68, v.p., 1968-71, sr. v.p., 1971-80; pulp and paper industry cons., 1980—. Mem. exec. com. Paper Distbn. Council, 1969—; mem. Adv. Com. to Congress on Revision of Title 44, 1979-80. Nat. co-chmn. Middlebury Coll. Challenge Fund., 1965-67, nat. chmn. ann. giving fund, 1967-68, mem. exec. com. alumni assn., recipient Meritorious Service plaque, 1968; pres. Lawrence Farms So. Assn., Chappaqua, N.Y., 1957-62, Huntington Recreational Assn., 1971. Served from pvt. to capt., AUS, 1943-45. Mem. Nat. Assn. Bus. Economists, Boston Paper Trade Assn., N.Y. Paper Club (exec. com. 1971-74). Clubs: Marco Polo (N.Y.C.); Army and Navy, Nat. Economists (Washington); Ponte Vedra (Ponte Vedra Beach, Fla.). Editor: The Dictionary of Paper, 4th edit., 1980. Home and office: 122 Ryder Ave Dix Hills NY 11746

DARROW, WILLIAM RICHARD, pharm. co. exec.; b. Middletown, Ohio, Sept. 7, 1939; s. Richard William and Nelda Virginia (Darling) D.; B.A., Ohio Wesleyan U., 1960; M.D., Western Res. U., 1964; Ph.D., Case-Western Res. U., 1969; m. Janet Elizabeth Swan, June 20, 1964; children—James William, Susan Elizabeth, Margaret Ellen. Intern, Univ. Hosps., Cleve., 1964; sr. clin. research asso. CIBA Pharm. Co., 1969, asst. dir. clin. pharmacology, 1969-70; dir. clin. pharmacology CIBA-GEIGY Corp., 1970-75, exec. dir. clin. research, 1975-76; sr. v.p. research, med. dir. Wallace Labs. div. Carter Wallace, Inc., Cranbury, N.J., 1976-80; med. dir. Schering Labs. div. Schering-Plough Corp., Kenilworth, N.J., 1980, v.p. med. and regulatory affairs, 1980—. Chmn. research com. N.J. Health Scis. Group, 1973-76, mem. exec. com., 1973-74, 76—, treas. 1977—; mem. Bernards Twp. (N.J.) Bd. of Health, 1979—, v.p., 1980. Recipient Roche award, 1962; USPHS postdoctoral fellow, 1965-69. Mem. AMA, Drug Info. Assn., N.J. Acad. Scis., Phi Gamma Delta, Phi Rho Sigma, Omicron Delta Kappa, Pi Delta Epsilon. Republican. Presbyterian. Home: 42 Palmerston Pl Basking Ridge NJ 07920 also 521 E Lake Rd Penn Yan NY 14527 Office: Galloping Hill Rd Kenilworth NJ 07033

DART, JUSTIN, bus. exec.; b. Evanston, Ill., Aug. 17, 1907; s. Guy Justin and Laura (Whitlock) D.; student Mercersburg (Pa.) Acad., 1924-25; A.B., Northwestern U., 1929; m. Ruth Walgreen, Oct. 9, 1929 (div. 1939); children—Justin Whitlock, Peter Walgreen; m. 2d, Jane O'Brien, Dec. 31, 1939; children—Guy Michael, Jane Campbell, Stephen. With Walgreen Co., drug store chain, Chgo., 1929-41, gen. mgr., 1939-41, dir., 1934-41; Joined Rexall Drug Co. (now Dart Industries, Inc.), 1941, v.p., dir., 1942; pres. Dart Industries Inc. (now subs. Dart and Kraft, Inc.), 1946-75, chmn., chief exec. officer, 1966—, chmn. exec. com. parent co.; dir. emeritus United Air Lines, dir. UAL, Inc. Chmn. bd. trustees U. So. Calif., 1967-71, vice chmn., 1972; trustee Los Angeles County Mus. Art, Hosp. Good Samaritan, Los Angeles; bd. dirs. Eisenhower Med. Center, Palm Desert, Calif. Republican. Clubs: Bohemian (San Francisco); Los Angeles Country, California; Cypress Point (Pebble Beach, Calif.); Eldorado Country (Palm Desert). Office: Dart Industries 8480 Beverly Blvd Los Angeles CA 90051*

DASARO, GEORGE ANTHONY, educator; b. Los Angeles, Nov. 16, 1941; s. Anthony Joseph and Virginia Ann (Roide) S.; B.B.A., Loyola U., Los Angeles, 1963; M.S., Calif. State U., Los Angeles, 1966; m. Marjorie Jay Beverung, June 22, 1968; 1 son, Christopher Michael. Div. controller Internat. Industries, Inc., Beverly Hills, Calif., 1967-71; treas. Windy Industries, Inc., Los Angeles, 1971-76; asst. prof. bus. adminstrn. Loyola Marymount U., Los Angeles, 1977—. C.P.A., Calif. Mem. Am. Acctg. Assn., Calif. Soc. C.P.A.'s. Home: 7507 Cowan Ave Los Angeles CA 90045 Office: Loyola Marymount U Los Angeles CA 90045

DASCHBACH, RICHARD JOSEPH, lawyer, govt. ofcl.; b. Columbus, Ohio, Nov. 19, 1936; s. Columbus, Ohio Nov. 19, 1936; s. Joseph Lawrence and Elizabeth (Satterfield) D.; A.B., Georgetown U., 1958, J.D., 1962; m. Virginia Brousse Holley, Sept. 6, 1958; children—Suzanne E., V. Holley, Elizabeth B. Admitted to D.C. bar, 1965; area coordinator Area Redevel. Adminstrn., Dept. Commerce, 1963-65, spl. asst. to asst. adminstr. Econ. Devel. Adminstrn., 1965-66; Washington mgr., counsel Gulf South Research Inst., 1966-68; staff atty. So. N.H. Legal Services Adminstrn., Keene, 1968-69; staff counsel U.S. Senate Commerce Com., Washington, 1969-73, maritime counsel, 1973-77; chmn. FMC, Washington, 1977-81, mem., 1981—. Democrat. Mem. Christian Ch. Office: FMC 1100 L St NW Washington DC 20573

DAUBERT, TERRANCE HARRY, retail tile co. exec.; b. Edmonton, Alta., Can., Feb. 14, 1951; s. Harry and Tess (Pilon) D.; m. Sharon E. Thompson, June 16, 1974; children—Michelle, Lori. With Century Sales and Service, Edmonton, 1966-68; salesman Edmonton Nut and Bolt Co., 1968-70; territory mgr. Kiwi Polish Co., Hamilton, Ont., Can., 1970-74; partner Dick's Auto and Indsl. Supply, Hinton and Spruce Grove, Alta., 1974-77; own(er, mgr. S & T Tile World Ltd., Edmonton, 1977—, also dir.; dir. Monarch Warehouse. Mem. Edmonton C. of C., Edmonton Constrn. Assn., Alta. Tile Terrazzo and Marble Assn. Office: 15830 111 Ave Edmonton AB T5M 2R8 Canada

DAUGHERTY, BILLY JOE, banker; b. Timpson, Tex., Jan. 31, 1923; s. David Albert and Kate (Smith) D.; grad. Tyler Comml. Coll., 1942; postgrad. So. State Coll., 1945-47; grad. Southwestern Grad. Sch. Banking, So. Meth. U., 1969; student Nat. Credit Lending Sch., U. Okla., 1969; m. Martha Carroum, May 14, 1942; children—Stephen Michael, Tony Fares, Kathryn Love. Asst. v.p., asst. trust officer First Nat. Bank Magnolia, Ark., 1947-52; plant accountant Republic Steel Corp., Magnolia, 1953-54; with Union Nat. Bank Little Rock, 1954-70, v.p., cashier, 1965-70; pres., dir., sec. to bd. dirs. First State Bank & Trust Co., Conway, Ark., 1970—; chmn. for Faulkner County Ark. State Council Economic Edn. Mem. advisory bd. Salvation Army, 1967—; bd. dirs. Met. YMCA, Little Rock, 1966-70, Goodwill Industries Ark., 1976—; chmn. Columbia chpt. ARC, Magnolia, 1952; mem. budget com. United Fund Pulaski County (Ark.), 1962-65; treas. City Beautiful Com., Little Rock, 1965-67; treas. Ark. br. Am. Assn. UN, 1965-67; pres. Heart of Ark. Travel Assn., 1971-74; pres., dir. United Fund of Faulkner County, 1972; state treas. Radio Free Europe, 1960-72; chmn. Faulkner County Heart Fund Campaign, 1971; sec. to bd. dirs., trustee Union Nat. Found.; chmn. bd. Ark. Heart Assn., 1975—; bd. dirs. Am. Heart Assn., 1976-80; trustee Baptist Med. Center System, 1965-74, sec.-treas., 1965-69; chmn. bd. dirs. Ark. Banking Sch., 1974-75. Served with USAAF, 1943-46. Mem. Little Rock Clearing House Assn. (v.p. 1969, pres. 1965-66, sec.-treas. 1967-68), Ark. Bankers Assn. (pres. jr. bankers sect. 1950; bank dirs. adv. com. 1971—; chmn. group II, 1978-79, dir. 1979—), Conway C. of C. (pres. 1975). Baptist (supt. Sunday sch.; chmn. bldg. com. 1964-66; chmn. bd. deacons 1962-63; mem. finance com. 1960-68, chmn. stewardship com. 1968). Clubs: Lions (pres. Conway Noon club 1974-75); Top of Rock (dir. 1969—); Little Rock; Conway Country; Pleasant Valley Country; Western Hills Country (dir., sec. 1968-69). Home: 22 Riviera Dr Conway AR 72032 Office: First State Bank & Trust Co Oak & Front Sts Conway AR 72032

DAUM, HUGH WARNER, frozen food brokerage co. exec.; b. Sioux Falls, S.D., Apr. 7, 1919; s. Henry Frank and Margaret Leona (Callahan) D.; student N.D. State Coll., 1936-37, U. Minn., 1937-38, U. Santa Clara (Cal.), 1941; m. Kathryn Ann Townsend, Dec. 17, 1949; 1 son, Hugh Warner. Dist. sales mgr. Union Sales Corp., Columbus, Ind., 1938-40, Libby, McNeill & Libby, Seattle, 1940-41; pres. Hugh W. Daum Co., Chgo., 1946-48; nat. sales and advt. mgr. John H. Dulany & Son, Fruitland, Md., 1949-50; pres. Hugh W. Daum Co., Crete, Ill., 1950-76; frozen food cons. Louis Hilfer Co., 1976—. Commr. Calumet council Boy Scouts Am., 1968—, mem. nat. council, 1974—, v.p., 1974-75, recipient Silver Beaver award, Good Scout award, 1975; active Ill. Assn. for Crippled. Served to maj. U.S. Army, 1941-46. Mem. Midwestern (dir., past v.p., Frozen Gavel, Igloo awards), Nat., Central States (past pres.) frozen foods assns., Merchandising Execs. Club, Nat., Chgo. food brokers assns., Aircraft Pilots and Owners Assn., Ducks Unlimited, Nat. Pilots Assn., Alpha Tau Omega. Club: K.C. Home: 585 Aberdeen Dr Crete IL 60417 Office: PO Box 74 Crete IL 60417

DAUSSMAN, GROVER FREDERICK, cons. engr.; b. Newburgh, Ind., May 6, 1919; s. Grover Cleveland and Madeline (Springer) D.; student U. Cin., 1936-38, Carnegie Inst. Tech., 1944-45, George Washington U., 1948-56; B.S. in Elec. Engring., U. Ala., 1963, postgrad., 1963-64, 77; m. Elli Margrite Kilian, Dec. 27. 1941; children—Cynthia Louise Daussman Quinn, Judith Ann, Margaret Elizabeth Daussman Davidson. Coop. engr. Sunbeam Elec. Mfg. Co., Evansville, Ind., 1936-38; engr., draftsman Phila. Navy Yard, 1941-42; elec. engr., supr. shipbldg. USN, Neville Island, Pa., 1942-45; engr. Pearl Harbor Navy Yard, 1945-48; with Bur. Ships, USN, Washington, 1948-56; with Guidance and Control Tech. Liaison, Army Ballistic Missile Agy., Huntsville, Ala., 1956-58, chief program coordination Guidance and Control Lab., 1958-60; chief program coordination Astrionics, Lab., Marshall Space Flight Center (Ala.), 1960-62, staff asst. for advanced research and tech., 1962-70; elec., aerospace and mgmt. engring. cons., 1970—; project dir. fallout shelter surveys Mil Dept. Tenn., 1971-73; head drafting dept. Alverson-Draughon Coll., Huntsville, 1974-77; instr. Ala. Christian Coll., 1977-79; draftsman Reisz Engring., 1979; chief engr. Sheraton Motor Inn, 1979; sr. engr. Sperry Support Services, 1980—. Chmn. community spl. gifts com. Madison County Heart Assn., 1965. Recipient cert. of recognition, 1945, cert. of service USN, 1946; performance award cert. U.S. Army, 1960; certs. of appreciation Am. Inst. E.E., 1960, 61, 62; award for disting. services Huntsville sect. IEEE, 1964; award for contbn. to successful launch of 1st Saturn V, George C. Marshall Space Flight Center, 1967, also award of achievement for contbn. to 1st manned lunar landing, 1969; Apollo achievement award NASA, 1969; named Engr. of Yr., 1968, 69. Registered profl. engr., Ala., Va., D.C. Mem. U. Ala. Alumni Assn., Ala. (state dir. 1962-65, 68-71, chpt. pres. 1966-67), Nat. socs. profl. engrs., Am. Inst. for Urban and Regional Affairs, IEEE (sr. mem., sect. chmn. N. Ala. sect. 1961-62; engring. mgmt. chpt. 1964-65, mem.

Region 3 exec. com. 1969-79, mem. inst. research com. 1965-67, mem. adminstv. com. of engring. mgmt. soc. 1966—, sec. soc. 1969—, regional del.-dir. S.E. region, mem. inst. bd. dirs. 1972-73), Am. Def. Preparedness Assn. (post dir. Tenn. Valley 1963-66), AAAS, Internat. Platform Assn., AIAA, Nat. Assn. Retarded Children, Huntsville Assn. Tech. Socs. (sec. 1969-70; v.p. 1970-71), Am. Soc. Naval Engrs., U.S. Naval Inst., Assn. U.S. Army, Missile, Space and Range Pioneers, NASA Retirees Assn. (pres. 1975—). Democrat. Mem. United Ch. of Christ (treas. 1959-61, ch. council 1964-66; sec. ch. council, program com. chmn. ch. council 1965-66; vice moderator Ala.-Tenn. assn. 1965-68; bd. dirs. Southeast conf. 1965-66, mem. budget and finance com. 1965-66). Home: 1910 Colice Rd SE Huntsville AL 35801

DAUT, KENNETH RICHARD, fin. exec.: b. Santa Monica, Calif., Aug. 3, 1952; s. Kenneth C. and Betty (Coggins) D.; B.A., UCLA, 1975. Account exec. Metropolitan Life Ins. Co., Torrance, Calif., 1976-77; bus. devel. officer Community Bank, Huntington Park, Calif., 1977-78; mfg. fin. analyst Northrop Corp., Hawthorne, Calif., 1978—. Mem. Youth Motivition Task Force, Los Angeles County, 1979-80. Recipient Metropolitan Life Career Booster award, 1976; Northorp Performance award, 1979. Mem. Nat. Assn. Accts. Democrat. Roman Catholic. Home: 5816 Strasmore Ave Cypress CA 91108 Office: 200 E Stanley St Compton CA 90224

DAVANT, JAMES WARING, investment banker; b. McComb, Miss., Dec. 1, 1917; s. Guy Hamilton and Em Reid (Waring) D.; student U. Va., 1939; m. Mary Ellis Westlake, Apr. 4, 1942; children—Mary Diane, John Hamilton, Patricia Jean (Mrs. Michael P. Dominick). With Paine, Webber, Jackson & Curtis, 1945—, gen. partner, 1956—, chmn. br. office com., 1963—, mem. policy com., 1963—, mng. partner, 1964—, pres., chief exec. officer, 1970-71, chmn. bd., chief exec. officer, 1971—; chmn. Paine Webber Inc., 1974—, chief exec. officer, 1974-80; dir. Bus. Mktg. Corp. for N.Y.; bd. dirs. N.Y. Stock Exchange, 1972-77. Bd. dirs. Manhattan Eye, Ear and Throat Hosp., Fresh Air Fund. Served to lt. comdr. USNR, 1940-45. Mem. Securities Industry Assn. (dir. 1971-73), UN Assn. U.S. (dir.), Assn. of Stock Exchange Firms (chmn. 1966-68), Brit.-N.Am. Com., Council Fgn. Relations. Episcopalian. Clubs: Recess, River, Links, Brook, Econ. (gov., chmn. N.Y. 1976-77), Pilgrims of U.S., Bond (gov. 1965—, pres. 1972—) (N.Y.C.); Minneapolis (Mpls.). Home: Cherrywood Locust Valley NY 11765 also 200 E 66th St New York NY 10021 Office: 140 Broadway New York NY 10005

D'AVANZO, THOMAS ANTHONY, indsl. mortgage fin. co. exec.; b. Hartford, Conn., Oct. 31, 1944; s. Thomas Anthony and Julia M. (Piccolo) D.; B.A., Amherst Coll., 1966; M.S. in Profl. Acctg., U. Hartford, 1975; m. Mary Lord Lawson, Apr. 28, 1972; 1 dau., Erica. Sales mgmt. program, fin. planning specialist Conn. Gen. Life Ins. Co., Hartford, 1966-68; investment analyst, trust new bus. rep. Conn. Bank & Trust Co., Hartford, 1968-70; treas., co-owner bus. venture, Hartford, 1970-73; mgr. fin. services Conn. Devel. Authority, Hartford, 1973-77; exec. dir. Mass. Indsl. Mortgage Ins. Agency, Boston, 1977-78; dep. dir. Mass. Indsl. Fin. Agy., Boston, 1978—; chmn. bd. dirs. Donahue & Assos., Inc., 1980—; cons. numerous states, U.S. Treasury, 1976—. Treas., mem. bd. dirs. Conn. Halfway House, Inc., 1969-70. Served with USAR, 1967-73. Home: 204 Indian Pipe Ln Concord MA 01742 Office: 131 State St Boston MA 02202

DAVENPORT, DONALD AMES, elec. engr.; b. Boston, June 11, 1916; s. Frank Ames and Doris (McKechnie) D.; student Lowell Inst. of Mass. Inst. Tech., 1935-40; m. Alma Wilton, Feb. 21, 1941; children—Donna, Alma. Resident engr. Stone & Webster Engring. Corp., 1936-49; chief engr. Herlihy Midcontinent Co., 1949-53; chief engr. Asso. Research, Inc., 1953-55; pres., chief engr. Davenport Mfg. Co., Chgo., 1955-60, gen. mgr. Davenport Mfg. div. Duncan Electric Co., Inc., 1960-62; dir. research Sola Basic Research div. Basic Products Corp., 1962-66; pres., chmn. bd. Constant Voltage Co., Chgo., 1966-68, 70-73, Electron Mfg. Co., Chgo., 1968-69, Electro-Magnetic Corp., Chgo., 1969-70; pres., dir. Micron Industries Corp., Stone Park, Ill., 1973—. Profl. elec. engr., Ill. Mem. I.E.E.E. Home: 221 Grand Blvd Park Ridge IL 60068 Office: 1830 N 32d Ave Stone Park IL 60165

DAVENPORT, DONALD LYLE, constrn. co. exec.; b. Eau Claire, Wis., Oct. 9, 1930; s. Douglas Benjamin and Leona Margaret (Fairbanks) D.; B.A. in Social Studies, Coll. St. Thomas, St. Paul, 1955; children—Ann, Martin, John, Donna, Jennifer. Adminstrv. asst. to regional mgr. Butler Mfg. Co., Mpls., 1955-58; corp. sec., gen. mgr. Spencer Corp., Eau Claire, 1958-60; sales mgr. Russell Structures Co., Madison, Wis., 1960; former pres. Bldg. Systems, Inc., Middleton, Wis., from 1960; pres. Davenport Assos., engring./real estate firm; bldg. cons. bldg. systems div. J.H. Findorff & Son, Inc., Madison. Former chmn. bd., pres. Jr. Achievement. Served with USAF, 1950-54. Registered profl. engr., Wis.; lic. real estate broker, Wis. Mem. Metal Bldg. Dealer Assn. (pres. 1971), Profl. Engrs. in Constrn., Wis. Soc. Profl. Engrs. (former pres. practice sect.), Johns Manville Dealer Council (chmn.), ARMCO Steel Corp. Dealer Council. Republican. Roman Catholic. Club: Exchange. Home: 7320 Pond View Rd Middleton WI 53562 Office: 302 S Bedford St Madison WI 53703

DAVENPORT, EDWIN LIND, real estate co. exec.; b. Pasadena, Calif., Mar. 25, 1947; s. Lind Burnett and Cleona Phonita (White) D.; student San Diego State U., 1965-67; m. Diane MacLoves, Mar. 11, 1967; children—Fawn Tiffany, Mark Edwin. Salesman, Norman Kaye Real Estate Co., Las Vegas, 1972-75; comml. mgr. Ed Post Realty, Las Vegas, 1976—; guest tchr. dept. real estate U. Nev. Served with USAF, 1967. Mem. Farm and Land Inst., Real Estate Securities and Syndication Inst., Soc. Las Vegas Exchangors (pres. 1977-78), Las Vegas Bd. Realtors (comml. investment div. sec.-treas. 1976-78, mem. faculty com. 1979-80, chmn. 1979-80), Nev. Assn. Realtors, Realtors Nat. Mktg. Inst., Nat. Assn. Realtors. Republican. Office: 2770 S Maryland Pkwy Las Vegas NV 89109

DAVENPORT, ERIC ROSS, airport mgr.; b. Tillamook, Oreg., Jan. 16, 1951; s. Ernest Elwood and Linnea Maibrit (Sword) D.; student Central Oreg. Community Coll., 1970; B.S., Oreg. Coll. Edn., 1975; m. Eleanor Faye Fritz, Jan. 14, 1978. Adminstrv. asst. City of Salem (Oreg.), 1975-76, project permit streamline coordinator, 1976-77, permit application center coordinator, 1977-80, regulatory adminstrv. cons. dir., 1978-80, tech. staff task force chmn., 1978-80; airport mgr., Pullman, Wash., 1980—; cons. in field; speaker nat. conv. Nat. Assn. Homebuilders, 1979. Departmental leader United Good Neighbors, 1975; mem. steering com. City of Silverton, 1978; U.S. Dept. Justice intern in charge minority affairs Oreg. Correctional Inst., 1974; co-chmn. central receiving Solid Waste Adv. Council, 1980; overseas del. Sister City Commn. to Vaxjö, Sweden; mem. Silverton City Council, 1979-81, chmn. planning com., 1979. Recipient Spl. Appreciation award Oreg. State Penitentiary, 1972. Home: 1211 Maple St Silverton OR 97381

DAVENPORT, ERNEST HAROLD, accountant, govt. ofcl.; b. Lima, Ohio, Apr. 12, 1917; s. William E. and Emily K. (Kennedy) D.; A.B., Morris Brown Coll., 1940; postgrad. Wayne State U., 1948; m. Lucille M. Rosemond, Mar. 1, 1944. Partner, Austin Washington & Davenport, C.P.A.'s, Detroit, 1956-71; dir. audit div. OEO, Washington, 1971-73; asst. dir. fin. and gen. mgmt. studies div. GAO, Washington, 1973—; dir. Bank of the Commonwealth, 1967-74. Bd. dirs. Jr. Achievement SE Mich., 1968-71; v.p. Fisher br. YMCA, Detroit, 1970-71, BTW Bus. Assn., Detroit, 1970; chmn. bd. trustees Plymouth Congregational Ch., Detroit, 1963-65. Served with U.S. Army, 1941-46; lt. col. ret. Decorated Air medal with 3 oak leaf clusters; recipient award for contbns. to profession Nat. Assn. Minority C.P.A. Firms, 1980; Nat. Assn. Black Accountants Achievement award, 1975, Morris Brown Coll. Outstanding Alumnus award, 1969, Mich. Minuteman award, 1968; C.P.A. Mem. Am. Inst. C.P.A.'s (chmn. minority recruitment and equal opportunity com. 1975-77, mem. state and local govt. accounting and auditing com. 1974-76, mem. council-at-large 1977-80, mem. council 1980-81), D.C. Inst. C.P.A.'s (bd. govs. 1975-80, treas. 1976, sec. 1977, v.p. 1978, pres.-elect 1979, pres. 1980), Assn. Govt. Accountants (Achievement award Montgomery-Prince George chpt. 1976, chpt. pres. 1978-79), Am. Accounting Assn., Mich. Assn. C.P.A.'s, Aircraft Owners and Pilots Assn., Res. Officers Assn. Office: 441 G St NW Washington DC 20548

DAVENPORT, JOHN WESLEY, computer software firm exec.; b. Dallas, Apr. 26, 1941; s. Claude Franklyn and Nancy Jean Davenport; B.A. in Psychology, Tex. Tech. U., 1963; M. Fin. Services, Am. Coll., 1980; m. Alicia Ann Marshaus, July 15, 1978; children—Lea Michelle, Heather Kathleen. Adminstrv. asst. Prudential Ins. Co., Houston, 1968-69; dept. mgr. Tareet Stores, Inc., Houston, 1969-70; salesman Am. Gen. Life Ins. Co., Houston, 1970-71; div. mgr. Prudential Ins. Co., St. Louis, 1971-73; dir. advanced underwriting Gen. Am. Life Ins. Co., St. Louis, 1973-79; dir. mktg. Multiple Funding Corp., N.Y.C., 1979—; guest lectr. St. Louis U.; adj. faculty St. Louis Community Colls. Mem. Nat. Tax Limitation Com., 1978—. Served with U.S. Army, 1963-68. C.L.U. Mem. Am. Soc. C.L.U.'s, Estate Planning Council St. Louis, Nat. Assn. Life Underwriters, Nat. Space Inst., Mensa. Presbyterian. Home: 1 Ozark Ln Arnold MO 63010 Office: 50 E 42d St New York NY 10017

DAVID, GEORGE, psychiatrist; b. N.Y.C., Feb. 19, 1940; s. Norman and Jennie (Danziger) D.; B.A., Yale U., 1961; M.D., N.Y. U., 1965. Intern, Children's Hosp., San Francisco, 1965; resident in psychiatry Colo. Psychiat. Hosp., Denver, 1965-66; practice medicine specializing in psychiatry, San Francisco; staff Mt. Zion Hosp., San Francisco, 1966-67, San Mateo County (Calif.) Mental Health Services, 1968-71; lectr. on application of economic theory to personal decision making. Mem. San Francisco Clin. Hypnosis (v.p. 1973-74). Libertarian. Home: 2334 California St San Francisco CA 94115 Office: 3527 Sacramento St San Francisco CA 94118

DAVID, RICHARD FRANCIS STEPHEN, electronics co. exec.; b. St. Louis, May 16, 1938; s. Richard William and Leona Marie (Schilly) D.; B.S.E.E. summa cum laude (Nat. Merit scholar 1956-60), St. Louis U., 1960; Ph.D., (Westinghouse fellow 1960-65), Johns Hopkins U., 1965; m. Marianne C. Chappuis, Nov. 22, 1962; children—Margaret, Mark, Paul, Lorena. Sr. engr. Westinghouse Surface Div., Balt., 1960-68; sect. head Martin-Marietta Corp., Denver, 1968-73; dir. engring. Teledyne Microelectronics, Los Angeles, 1973—, now v.p. engring.; adj. asst. prof. elec. engring. U. Denver, 1969-73. Mem. Internat. Soc. Hybrid Microelectronics (charter; pres. chpt. 1970), Inst. Enriron. Scis., Sigma Xi, Pi Mu Epsilon, Eta Kappa Nu. Roman Catholic. Patentee in field. Office: 12964 Panama St Los Angeles CA 90066

DAVID, VIKTOR MARK, computer services co. exec.; b. Treysa, W. Ger., July 26, 1947; came to U.S., 1954, naturalized, 1960; m. Mendel and Melanie (Rosenblatt) D.; B.E.E., CCNY, 1970; m. Susan Jane Greenberg, Aug. 15, 1976. Programmer, Ted Bates & Co., N.Y.C., 1966-69; sr. programmer Grey Advt. Inc., N.Y.C., 1969-70; sr. analyst Dyna Data Services Inc., N.Y.C., 1970-71; mgr. RDR Assos. Inc., N.Y.C., 1971-72; v.p. On-Line Software Internat., River Edge, N.J., 1972—. Author: CICS/VS Reference Handbook, 1978, rev. edit., 1980. Office: 65 Route 4E River Edge NJ 07661

DAVIDOW, STANLEY S., automotive parts corp. exec.; b. Greenville, Miss., Aug. 18, 1939; s. D. H. and Thelma L. D.; B.S., Tulane U., 1961; m. Aug. 27, 1961. Pres., Lakeshore-King Auto Inc., Jacksonville, Fla., 1963-77, King Auto Air, Inc., Jacksonville, 1967-77; pres. Car Air Components, Inc. (prior to acquisition by Standard Motor Products, Inc.) Jacksonville, 1971-79, gen. mgr. Car Air Components, Inc. subs. Standard Motor Products, Inc., 1979—. Mem. Automotive Warehouse Distbrs. Assn., Automotive Service Industry Assn., Motor Equipment Mfrs. Assn., Auto Parts Rebuilders Assn. Clubs: Ponte Vedra, Jacksonville Businessmen's (River Club). Office: 8051 Bayberry Rd Jacksonville FL 32216

DAVIDSON, DAVID DOUGLAS, mfg. exec.; b. Edinburgh, Scotland, Oct. 1, 1925; arrived Can., 1968; s. David and Mary (Ferguson) D.; ed. George Heriot's Sch., Edinburgh; M.A., Edinburgh U., 1946; m. Evelyn Turnbull, Apr. 28, 1951; children—Alistair, Neil, Lindsay. With Union Cold Storage Co. Ltd., Buenos Aires, Argentina, 1946-49; mng. dir. Zimmer Orthopaedic Ltd., London, 1950-68, chmn. and chief exec. officer, 1968-75, dir. Zimmer Orthopaedic S.A. de C.V., Mexico City, 1969-75, Zimmer Orthopaedic Australia Pty. Ltd., Melbourne, 1970-75; v.p. Everest and Jennings (Canadian) Ltd., Toronto, Ont., 1968-75, Everest and Jennings Internat., Los Angeles, 1969-75; chmn. Autocrown Corp. Ltd., Toronto, 1975—; sec.-treas. Trans-Can. Press, 1978—. Decorated Order Brit. Empire. Mem. Canadian Assn. Corp. Growth (dir. 1978—). Address: 436 Wellington St W Toronto ON M5V 1E3 Canada

DAVIDSON, GORDON BYRON, lawyer; b. Louisville, June 24, 1926; s. Paul Byron and Elizabeth (Franz) D.; A.B., Centre Coll., 1949; J.D., U. Louisville, 1951; LL.M., Yale, 1952; m. Geraldine B. Geiger, Dec. 21, 1948; children—Sally Burgess, Stuart Gordon. Asst., staff judge adv. First Army, Govs. Island, N.Y., 1952-54; law clk. Mr. Justice Stanley Reed, Supreme Ct. U.S., Washington, 1954; mng. partner firm Wyatt, Tarrant and Combs, 1954—; lectr. U. Louisville Law Sch., 1958—; dir. B. Williamson & Co., Hermitage Farm, Inc., Courier-Jour. & Louisville Times Co., WHAS, Inc., Standard Gravure Corp., Armor Elevator Co., Dixie Beer Distbg. Co., Zimmer-McClaskey-Lewis. Mem. Louisville Commn. Fgn. Relations; bd. dirs., past pres. Louisville Theatrical Assn., Louisville Central Area, Inc.; chmn. bd. dirs. Louisville Devel. Com.; bd. dirs. Macauley's Theatre, Inc., Centre Coll., Greater Louisville Fund for Arts, U. Louisville Internat. Center; bd. overseers U. Louisville; chmn. Norton Children's Hosp., Ky. Center for Arts, St. Francis High Sch.; high sch. chmn. Ky. Cultural Complex Commn. Served as cadet midshipman U.S. Mcht. Marine Acad., 1944-45; 1st lt. U.S. Army, 1952-54; Korea. Named Citizen of Year, Louisville, 1973-74. Fellow Am. Bar Found., Am. Law Inst.; mem. Am., Ky., Louisville, Fed. bar assns., Louisville C. of C. (v.p., exec. com.), Phi Delta Theta, Omicron Delta Kappa, Phi Kappa Phi. Democrat. Presbyn. Clubs: Harmony Landing Country; Pendennis; Louisville Country (dir.), Tavern; Lawyer's; Jefferson (dir.); Delray Beach. Home: 435 Lightfoot Rd Louisville KY 40207 Office: 28th Floor Citizens Bldg Louisville KY 40202

DAVIDSON, JAMES DUNCAN, employee benefit and ins. cons.; b. Chgo., Aug. 22, 1952; s. William Duncan and Marion Dorothy (Conly) D.; B.A. with high distinction in Fin., Colo. State U., 1974; m. Ellen Ann Mannix, Oct. 6, 1979; 1 dau., Alexandria Mannix. Agt., Equitable Life Ins. Co., 1974-76, asst. dist. mgr., Chgo., 1976-78; dist. mgr. 1979—; founding partner Enterprise Planning Co., Chgo., 1978—. Cert. employee benefits specialist. Mem. Nat. Assn. Life Underwriters, Chgo. Assn. Life Underwriters, Am. Inst. C.P.A.'s, Am. Soc. C.L.U.'s. Clubs: Rotary, Chgo. Athletic. Home: 327 W Belden Chicago IL 60614 Office: N Michigan Suite 606 Chicago IL 60611

DAVIDSON, JEFFREY PHILIP, mgmt. cons.; b. Hartford, Conn., Jan. 13, 1951; s. Emanuel and Shirley (Leader) D.; B.S., U. Conn., 1973, M.B.A., 1974. Mktg. rep. Burroughs Corp., East Hartford, Conn., 1974-75; sr. cons. Profiles, Inc., Vernon, Conn., 1975-77; sr. asso. Emay Corp., Washington, 1977-80; mgr. James H. Lowry & Assos., Washington, 1980—; lectr. seminars SBA; instr. Open U., Washington, 1978—. Hartford Mut. Soc. scholar, 1969. Mem. Assn. M.B.A. Execs., Inst. Mgmt. Cons. Contbr. articles to profl. jours.; book reviewer Prentice Hall, 1980—. Home: 3709 S George Mason Dr Falls Church VA 22041 Office: 1200 New Hampshire Ave NW Washington DC 20036

DAVIDSON, PHILIP HAROLD, banker; b. East Grand Rapids, Mich., Aug. 20, 1944; s. Harold Elton and Jeanne Elizabeth (Ulrich) D.; B.A., U. Mich., 1966; M.B.A., Western Mich. U., 1967; Ph.D., U. Ill., 1971; m. Kay Marie Heikkinen, Nov. 25, 1966; 1 son, Matthew Philip. Economist, research dept. Fed. Reserve Bank, Richmond, Va., 1970-73; economist Bank of Va. Co., Richmond, 1974, v.p., 1975—; mem. adj. faculty U. Richmond, 1971-74, Va. Commonwealth U., 1977-78. Bd. dirs. Housing Opportunities Made Equal, Richmond, 1975—, pres., 1977. Mem. Richmond First Club (dir. 1974-77), Am. Econ. Assn., Nat. Assn. Bus. Economists, Am. Bankers Assn. Club: Downtown (Richmond). Author: Banking Tomorrow, Managing Markets Through Planning, 1978; contbr. articles in field to profl. jours. Home: 3811 Seminary Ave Richmond VA 23227 Office: PO Box 25970 Richmond VA 23260

DAVIDSON, PHILLIP THOMAS, retail store exec.; b. New Britain, Conn., Aug. 12, 1925; s. Samuel M. and Raye L. (Levine) D.; B.S., Trinity Coll., 1948; m. Barbara Jarmon, Nov. 27, 1970; children—Merry Davidson Kelleher, Thomas, Anthony, Wendy, Philip. Pres., D & L Stores, Inc., New Britain, 1971—, Weathervane Stores, Inc., New Britain, 1971—, also dir.; dir., chmn. exec. com. New Britain Bank & Trust Co.; dir. First Bank; v.p. Conn. Bancefedn., Inc. Pres., United Way of Greater New Britain, 1962-65; bd. dirs. Central Conn. Regional Heart Assn., 1970—, Family Counseling and Children's Services of Central Conn., 1975—, Long River council Boy Scouts Am., 1975-76; corporator Wheeler Mental Health Clinic, New Britain Gen. Hosp.; econ. adviser to mayor New Britain, 1975-77. Served with USN, 1942-45. Mem. Internat. Council Shopping Centers, Nat. Retail Mchts. Assn. (v.p., dir. Zone 1), New Britain C. of C. (pres. 1972-75), Greater Hartford C. of C. (dir.). Republican. Jewish. Clubs: Westchester Country, Hopmeadow Country, New Britain, Rotary, City (New Britain). Contbr. articles to profl. jours. Home: 4 Eastview Dr Simsbury CT 06070 Office: 227 Main St New Britain CT 06050

DAVIDSON, RALPH PARSONS, publishing co. exec.; b. Santa Fe, Aug. 17, 1927; s. William Clarence Davidson and Doris Parsons Stanton; B.A. in Internat. Relations, Stanford U., 1950; postgrad. Alliance Francaise, Paris, 1951; divorced; children—William A., R. Andrew. With CIA, 1952-54; advt. salesman Life mag., 1954-56; European advt. dir. Time mag., London, 1956-62; mng. dir. Time-Life Internat., N.Y.C., 1967—; pub. Time mag., 1972-78; chmn. Time Inc.; lectr. communications Stanford U., also mem. adv. bd. profl. journalism fellowships program. Trustee, United Student Aid Funds, Nat. Urban League, N.Y.C. Ballet, Ocean Trust Found., Com. Econ. Devel.; bd. dirs. World Wildlife Fund, Keep Am. Beautiful. Served with USNR, World War II. Mem. Stanford U. Alumni Assn. (pres. 1972-73). Clubs: Explorers, River (N.Y.C.); American (London). Office: Time Inc Time and Life Bldg Rockefeller Center New York NY 10020

DAVIDSON, RANDALL WARREN ALEXANDER, entertainment safety cons.; b. Denver, Oct. 20, 1929; s. George Alexander and Olive Elise (Brodsky) D.; A.B., St. Mary's Coll., 1953; M.A., U. Denver, 1958, Ed.D., Nova U., 1976; m. Cathi Therese Seliga, June 21, 1964; children—Rebecca, David, Elizabeth, Joan. Founder, pres. Theatre Safety Assos., Riverside, Calif., 1965-73; pres., founder Internat. Safety Inst., Erie, Pa., 1973-78; loss control cons., entertainment safety specialist Alexander & Alexander, Inc., Los Angeles, 1978—; internat. cons. to entertainment industry; condr. workshops for industry and univs.; adv. doctoral candidates. Fellow U.S. Inst. Theatre Tech., Inc. (nat. commr. health and safety); mem. Union-Mgmt. Safety Com. Motion Picture, TV and Film Industry (hon.), Internat. Inst. Stage Safety, Am. Film Inst., Brit. Theatre Inst. (charter), Am. Soc. Safety Engrs. Democrat. Author, editor: National Entertainment Safety Code, 1976; contbr. numerous articles on risk mgmt. safety, loss control in entertainment industry to profl. jours. Home: 522 Citadel Ave Claremont CA 91711 Office: 3550 Wilshire Blvd Los Angeles CA 90010

DAVIDSON, THOMAS FERGUSON, II, aerospace co. exec.; b. N.Y.C., Jan. 5, 1930; s. Lorimer Arthur and Elizabeth Gael (Valentine) D.; B.S., U. Md., 1951; postgrad. George Washington U., 1949-51, Ohio State U., 1953-54; m. Nancy Lee Selecman, Nov. 10, 1951; children—Thomas Ferguson, Richard Alan, Gwyn Ann. Sr. project engr. Wright Air Devel. Center, Dayton, Ohio, 1953-57, chief tech. sect., 1958-59, dept. chief solid systems div. Air Force Flight Test Center, Edwards, Calif., 1959-60; mgr. govt. ops. Thiokol Corp., Ogden, Utah, 1960-64, dir. aerospace mktg., Bristol, Pa., 1964-67, dir. tech. planning and control, 1967-74, dir. tech. mgmt., Ogden, Utah, 1974—; mem. subcom. on lubrication and wear NACA, 1955-57; chmn. Tri-Service Working Group on solid propellants, 1959-60. Mem. Utah-Wyo. Council on Missions, 1976—; trustee Protestant Youth Center, Ogden, 1976—. Served to lt. USAF, 1951-53. Mem. Am. Newcomen Soc., Smithsonian Instn., Nat. Geog. Soc., Am. Inst. Aeros. and Astronautics, Am. Def. Preparedness Assn., Air Force Assn., Army Assn., Ogden C. of C. Republican. Methodist. Clubs: Weber (Ogden); Lago Mar (Ft. Lauderdale, Fla.). Contbr. articles to profl. jours. Home: 4206 N 350 W Pleasant View UT 84404 Office: PO Box 9258 Ogden UT 84409

DAVIDSON, WILLIAM GEORGE, III, lawyer, acctg., fin. and mgmt. cons.; b. Fr. Benning, Ga., Oct. 28, 1938; s. William George and Dorothea Kathryn (Wright) D.; B.S., U.S. Naval Acad., 1960; M.B.A. in Fin., U. Pa., 1970; J.D., Suffolk U., 1974. Electronics engr., systems analyst Phila. Naval Shipyard, 1968; fin. analyst Allied Chem. Corp., N.Y.C., 1968; fin. analyst, staff acct. Dennison Mfg. Co., Framingham, Mass., 1969-74; corp. controller Premix, Inc., North Kingsville, Ohio, 1974-78; admitted to Ohio bar, 1975, Md. bar, 1980; owner, mgr. W.G. Davidson and Assos., Inc., mgmt. and fin. cons., Rockville, Md., 1978—; dir. Polymer Engring., Inc., Lafayette, Ind.; mem. faculty Lake Erie-Garfield Coll., Painesville, Ohio, 1977-78; del. White House Conf. on Small Bus., 1980. Active Vols. in Tech. Assistance, 1970-75. Served from ensign to lt. comdr., USN, 1960-67.

Mem. Am. Bar Assn., Ohio Bar Assn., Fin. Execs. Inst., Nat. Assn. Accts., U.S. Naval Acad. Alumni Assn., Naval Res. Assn. Roman Catholic. Club: Kiwanis (past dir. Ashtabula, Ohio). Home: 4 Monroe St Rockville MD 20850 Office: PO Box 186 Courthouse Station Rockville MD 20850

DAVID-WEILL, MICHEL ALEXANDRE, investment banker; b. Nov. 23, 1932; came to U.S., 1977; s. Pierre Sylvain and Berthe Marie (Haardt) D.-W.; grad. Institut des Sciences Politiques, 1953; m. Helene Lehideux, July 20, 1956; children—Beatrice (Vicomtesse Bertrande de Villeneuve-Bargemon), Cecile, Natalie, Agate. Partner, Lazard Freres & Co., 1961-65; partner Lazard Freres & Cie, 1965—; sr. partner Lazard Freres & Co., N.Y.C., 1977—; dir. Lazard Brothers & Co., Ltd., 1965—. Chmn. bd. Eurafrance, 1972—; dir. BSN-Bervais-Danone, 1970—. Mem. Security Industry Assn. (mem. governing council 1978). Club: Knickerbocker. Office: One Rockefeller Plaza New York NY 10020

DAVIES, JAMES HOWARD, ins. broker; b. Dayton, Ohio, June 7, 1934; s. Robert Paterson and Alva (Ogsbury) D.; B.A., Ohio Wesleyan U., 1956; m. Jean Carole Travis, Apr. 23, 1960; children—Robert, James, Judith. Mem. group ins. sales staff Travelers Ins. Co., 1956-61; salesman Kemper Ins. Co., 1961-63; pres. Davies & Assos., Murray Hill, N.J., 1963—, Hazlet, N.J., 1976—; v.p. Galaxy Mgmt. Services, 1979—; dir. Galaxy Reliance. Chmn. Planning Bd. of New Providence (N.J.), 1974-78; mem. Borough Council New Providence, 1978—. Served with CIC, U.S. Army, 1957-60. Mem. Profl. Ins. Agts. Assn. (dir. 1979—), Profl. Ins. Agts. Assn. N.J. (dir. 1970—, pres. 1976-77). Republican. Episcopalian. Club: Rotary (pres. 1969) (River Edge, N.J.). Home: 64 Chestnut St Murray Hill NJ 07974

DAVIES, PAUL LEWIS, JR., lawyer; b. San Jose, Calif., July 21, 1930; s. Paul Lewis and Faith (Crummey) D.; A.B., Stanford, 1952; J.D., Harvard, 1957; m. Barbara Bechtel, Dec. 22, 1955; children—Laura, Paul Lewis III. Admitted to Calif. bar, 1957; asso. firm Pillsbury, Madison & Sutro, San Francisco, 1957-63, partner, 1963—; dir. FMC Corp., Indsl. Indemnity Co. Vice-chmn., Calif. Acad. Scis.; chmn. bd. overseers Hoover Instn.; trustee Herbert Hoover Found., Inc.; bd. regents U. Pacific; gov. San Francisco Symphony. Served from 2d to 1st lt., U.S. Army, 1952-54. Mem. State Bar Calif. (chmn. com. on corps. 1968-69), Am. (com. on fed. regulation securities), San Francisco bar assns., Phi Beta Kappa, Pi Sigma Alpha. Republican. Clubs: World Trade, Pacific-Union, Bohemian, Stock Exchange, Villa Taverna, Bankers (San Francisco); Sainte Claire (San Jose); Claremont Country (Oakland, Calif.); Explorers, Links (N.Y.C.); Metropolitan (Washington); Cypress Point (Pebble Beach, Calif.); Chicago, Mid-America (Chgo.); Farmington Country (Charlottesville, Va.). Office: 225 Bush St San Francisco CA 94104

DAVIES, RICHARD EDWARD, ins. broker; b. Mayville, N.Y., Apr. 18, 1939; s. Richard W. and Alice Nancy (Summerton) D.; m. Rosalie M. Marsala, Aug. 5, 1961; children—Kimberly Anne, David Edward, Marc Richard. Agt., Equitable Life Assurance Soc., 1960-62; sales agt., broker Westfield (N.Y.) Agy., Inc., 1962-63; v.p., 1964-78, pres., 1978—; dir. Better Baked Foods, Inc. Bd. dirs. Westfield Meml. Hosp.: trustee Village of Westfield, 1971-73, mayor, 1973-79; county legislator Chautauqua County (N.Y.), 1980—; vol. fireman, Westfield; past treas. Westfield United Way. Served with U.S. Army, 1963-64. Mem. Profl. Ins. Agts. Assn., Nat. Assn. Ind. Ins. Agts., Am. Entrepreneurs Assn., N.Y. State Suprs. and County Legislators Assn., Westfield Jaycees (past pres., past treas., recipient Disting. Community Service award 1969), VFW. Republican. Methodist. Clubs: Moose, Rotary.

DAVIN, JAMES MANSON, investment banking co. exec.; b. Allentown, Pa., Dec. 24, 1945; s. James Thomas and Louise (Manson) D.; B.S. in Bus. Adminstrn., Georgetown U., 1967; grad. Bondurant Sch. of High Performance Driving, Sonoma, Calif., 1978; m. Christine Sims, Feb. 27, 1971; 1 son, James Christian. Successively asst. to treas., asst. mgr., mgr., asst. v.p., v.p. corp. fixed income trading First Boston Corp., N.Y.C., 1969—, also dir. Served with U.S. Army, 1967-69. Counselor, Georgetown U. Mem. N.Y. Investment Assn., Securities Industry Assn. (corp. bond com.), Bond Club of N.Y., Pa. Soc. Roman Catholic. Club: Saucon Valley Country (Bethlehem, Pa.). Home: 1120 Park Ave New York NY 10021 Office: 20 Exchange Pl New York NY 10005

DAVINIC, MILAN Z., state ofcl.; b. Prague, Czechoslovakia, Feb. 27, 1930; s. Zika and Emilia (von Rheinwart) D.; B.S. in Bus. Adminstrn., U. Belgrade (Yugoslavia), 1960; postgrad. Columbia, 1965; M.B.A. in Econs. and Finance, St. John's U., 1968; m. Rada B. Kontic, Oct. 25, 1960; 1 son, Nicholas. Came to U.S., 1964, naturalized, 1969. With AID, Belgrade, 1959-64; economist Jack Faucett Assos., Inc., Silver Spring, Md., 1968-70; economist Md. Dept. State Planning, Balt., 1970—. Mem. Am. Econ. Assn., Omicron Delta Epsilon. Mem. Serbian Eastern Orthodox Ch. (trustee ch. and sch. community). Home: 15 J Old Coach Ln Owings Mills MD 21117 Office: 301 W Preston St Baltimore MD 20201

DAVIS, ADOLPHUS (AL), publisher; b. Crossett, Ark., Mar. 16, 1935; s. Opal D. (Reeves) D.; student Ariz. State Tchrs. Coll., 1955-59; m. Cheryl S. Watkins, Dec. 24, 1979; children—Sondra T., Jerry D., Kevin. Joined USAF, 1955; radar operator Elmendorf AFB, Alaska, 1955-58; flight crew, 1958-63; resigned, 1963, 1st lt. Res.; owner, operator archtl. design firm, 1963-65; counselor Job Corps., Pleasanton, Calif., 1966-68; cons. mgmt., Oakland, Calif., 1969-70; cons. bus., Oakland, 1970-72; owner, pres. Source Publs., Inc., Emeryville, Calif., 1973—; minority bus. lectr., cons.; mem. minority caucus White House Conf. Small Bus., 1980; adv. on small and minority bus. affairs State Calif., 1980. Bd. dirs. Purchasing Council, San Francisco; chmn. personnel bd. City Berkeley (Calif.), 1973-75; chmn. Minority Input, San Francisco, 1978-80; pres. U.S. Black C. of C. Recipient Outstanding Contbn. to Minority Bus. award U. Calif. M.B.A. Program, 1973. Mem. Nat. Assn. Black Mfrs. (Outstanding Contbn. to Minority Bus. Devel. award 1978), Nat. Pubs. Assn., Nat. Assn. Purchasing Mgmt. Author: California Minority Business Enterprises Directory, 1976, rev. edits., 1977-80; author profl. pamphlets. Office: 1900 Powell St Suite 1145 Emeryville CA 94608

DAVIS, AL, financial services co. exec.; b. San Antonio, Nov. 27, 1948; s. Willie H. and Ramona D. (James) D.; A.S. in Polit. Sci., Tex. So. U., 1970; B.S. in Polit. Sci., Golden Gate U., 1972. With Am. Express Co., N.Y.C., 1973—, mgr. central employment, 1977-79, dir. central employment, 1979—; career counselor; cons. compensation. Employment cons. Foutain House, N.Y.C.; bd. advs. Occupation Indsl. Center, N.Y.C. Mem. Employment Mgmt. Assn., Am. Mgmt. Assn., N.Y. Personnel Mgmt. Assn. Office: 125 Broad St New York NY 10004

DAVIS, ALLAN ISRAEL, fin. exec.; b. Columbus, Ohio, Dec. 31, 1945; s. Robert I. and Rose L. D.; B.A., U. Charleston, 1967; student Western New Eng. Coll., 1971-72; m. Eileen L. Huff, Jan. 12, 1970; children—Cindy J., Michael A. Controller, Sportscoach Corp. of Am., Chatsworth, Calif., 1974-77, LaQuinta (Calif.) Country Club, 1979—; v.p. Twin Lakes Recreational Resort Inc., Newberry Springs, Calif., 1977-80. Served with USAF, 1968-72. Mem. Nat. Assn. Accts., Desert Hospitality Accts. Assn. (pres. 1980—), Newberry Springs Water Assn. (v.p. 1978—), Alpha Sigma Phi. Home: 73260 San Nicholas Ave Palm Desert CA 92260 Office: PO Box 99 LaQuinta CA 92253

DAVIS, ALVIN GEORGE, internat. trade cons.; b. Chgo., May 10, 1918; s. Isadore and Mary (Wasserman) D.; m. Rose Lorber, Dec. 14, 1940; children—Fred Barry, Glenn Martin. With Sears Roebuck & Co., 1936-40; gen. partner, sales mgr. Ritz Mfg. Co., 1940-41; buyer hobby dept. The Fair, 1941-43; mgr. hobby div. Central Camera Co., wholesalers, 1944; pres., gen. mgr. Nat. Model Distbrs., Inc., 1945-63; dir. internat. ops. Aurora Plastics Corp., 1963-70, v.p. internat. div., 1966-70; v.p. Aurora Plastics Can., Ltd., 1963-70; mng. dir. Aurora Plastics Nederland N.V., 1964-70, Aurora Plastics Co. U.K. Ltd., Croydon, Eng.; dir. Rowe Industries H.K. Ltd., Rowe Industries, Singapore Ltd., 1967-70, Rowe Industries (Taiwan), 1967-70; internat. sr. trade cons. U.S. Comml. Service, Internat. Trade Adminstrn., U.S. Dept. Commerce, 1971—; adj. instr. internat. trade Ill. Inst. Tech., also spl. lectr. Sch. Mgmt. and Fin., 1980. Mem., chmn. People to People Com.; scoutmaster, mem. Chgo. finance council Boy Scouts Am.; dep. comdr., pub. info. officer CAP. Recipient Berkeley award, 1957, Hobbies award of Merit, Hobby Industry Assn., 1960, Peace and Commerce medal East-West Africa Market Study, 1973. Fellow Inst. Dirs. (London); mem. Nat. Rifle Assn. (life), Soaring Soc. Am., Airplane Owners and Pilots Assn., Acad. Model Aeros. (contest dir. 1936-70), Nat. Model R.R. Assn. (life), Model Industry Assn. (dir. 1952-60, sec. 1954-57, pres. 1957-59), Hobby Industry Assn. (pres. 1957-59, Meritorious award of honor 1975), Internat. Execs. Assn., Am. Soc. Internat. Execs. Mason (32 deg., Shriner). Clubs: Chgo. Press, Publicity of Chgo. Contbr. articles on merchandising to trade mags. Contbg. editor Brittanica Jr., 1949; editor Internat. Trade Handbook, 1980. Home: 5901 N Sheridan Rd Chicago IL 60660 Office: Chicago IL

DAVIS, BALEY, JR., govt. personnel adminstr.; b. Houston, Aug. 24, 1938; s. Baley and Vivian Esteen (Mosley) D.; B.B.A., Tex. So. U., 1960, M.B.A., 1978; m. Patsy Florence Frazier, June 15, 1964 (div. 1971; children—Jacqueline Sylvia, Michelle Feni (dec.); m. 2d, Pamela Lovette Joubert, Dec. 18, 1976. Accounting technician FHA, Washington, 1962-63, loan specialist, intern program, Cleve., 1963, realty loan specialist, mortgage credit analyst, Houston, 1963-66; personnel mgmt. specialist NASA Johnson Space Center, Houston, 1966-74, regional coordinator, profl. minority and female recruiting, 1974—; bd. advisers Davis Foundry, 1966-68; lectr. cons. Coll. Mainland and Houston High Schs. Recipient Apollo Achievement award NASA, 1969, Group Achievement award Lunar Landing Team, 1973, Superior Performance award, 1975, numerous others. Mem. Am. Acad. Polit. and Social Scis. Conf. Minority Pub. Adminstrs., Am. Soc. Pub. Adminstrn., Assn. M.B.A. Execs., NAACP, Nat. Urban League, Kappa Alpha Psi. Home: 4211 Charleston St Houston TX 77021

DAVIS, BRENDA ALICIA, steel co. cons.; b. Chgo., Sept. 6, 1949; d. Charles Edward and Eva Louise D.; B.S.B.A. in Indsl. Mgmt., Roosevelt U., 1977, M.B.A. in Internat. Fin., 1979; postgrad. in bus. policy analysis U. Ill., 1979—. Cons., Gt. Lakes Mgmt. & Cons., Chgo., 1972-73; auditor Cook County (Ill.) States Atty., 1973-79; cons. Inland Steel Co., Chgo., 1979—; cons. UNESCO. Mem. Am. Arbitration Assn. (lic. arbitrator), Better Bus. Bur. Chgo. (lic. arbitrator). Republican. Roman Catholic. Home: 5431 NE River Rd Chicago IL 60656 Office: 30 W Monroe Chicago IL 60605

DAVIS, CHARLES ARTHUR, investment banker; b. Burlington, Vt., Nov. 28, 1948; s. Dudley Hale and Phyllis Elmira (Lowe) D.; B.S., U. Vt., 1972; M.B.A. (acad. fellow), Columbia U., 1975; m. Marna Elizabeth Olsen, Aug. 26, 1978. With credit tng. program, mcpl. note trader First Nat. Bank of Boston, 1972-73; asso. corp. fin. Goldman, Sachs & Co., N.Y.C., 1975-79; v.p. Investment Banking Services, N.Y.C., 1979—; adj. prof. N.Y. Inst. Fin. Mem. Columbia U. Alumni Assn. (adv. bd.), Beta Gamma Sigma. Home: 1623 3rd Ave Apt 41K New York NY 10028 Office: 55 Broad St New York NY 10004

DAVIS, CHARLES EDWARD, aircraft co. exec.; b. Shreveport, La., Sept. 21, 1928; s. Thomas O. and Ellen Mary (Ellington) D.; B.S. in M.E., U. Tex. at Austin, 1951; M.S. in M.E., So. Methodist U., 1960; grad. Program Sr. Execs., Sloan Sch. Mgmt., Mass. Inst. Tech., 1977; M.B.A., U. Dallas, 1980; m. Martha Cogdill Davis, Feb. 2, 1952; children—Charles Edward, Roy Jefferson, Mary Robin. With Bell Helicopter Textron Co., various locations, 1951—, mgr. office, Bad Godesberg, Germany, 1970-71, tech. mgr., Brussels, 1971-72, project engr., chief project engr., model 214, Ft. Worth, 1972-75, dir. product assurance, 1975-79, dir. project engring., 1979—. Served with USN, 1944-45. Registered profl. engr., Tex. Mem. Am. Helicopter Soc., Nat. Soc. Profl. Engrs., U.S. Army Assn., Tau Beta Pi, Pi Tau Sigma. Episcopalian. Club: Elks. Home: 1603 Hawthorne St Arlington TX 76012 Office: PO Box 482 Fort Worth TX 76101

DAVIS, CLAY PARKER, banker; b. Sadieville, Ky., Jan. 23, 1941; s. Emery and Elmo (Hutchcraft) D.; student U. Ky., 1967, Sch. Banking, 1966, Internat. Corr. Schs., 1973, Grad. Sch. Banking of U. Wis., 1975; m. Patricia Slone, Aug. 22, 1967; 1 dau., Jodie Parker. Bookkeeper, 1st Nat. Bank, Georgetown, Ky., 1963-66, cashier, 1966-70, exec. v.p., cashier, dir., 1970-72; pres., dir. Citizens Nat. Bank, Somerset, Ky., 1973—. Pres. Scott County Jaycees, 1966-68; chmn. Scott County Jr. Miss Pageant, 1966; bd. dirs. U.S. Jaycees, 1968-69; commr. Goergetown Mpcl. Water and Sewer, 1971-72; bd. dirs. United Way of Somerset, 1974; pres. YMCA, 1976; dir. adv. bd. U. Ky., 1978; exec. bd. Boy Scouts Am., 1979. Named hon. Ky. col. Mem. Somerset-Pulaski County C. of C., Bank Adminstrn. Inst. (v.p. S.E. Ky. 1973), Ky. Bankers Assn. (sec. Group VI 1971, chmn. bd. 1980). Mem. Christian Ch. Clubs: Odd Fellows, Rotary (treas. 1970-72). Office: PO Box 760 Somerset KY 42501

DAVIS, CRAIG CARLTON, aerospace co. exec.; b. Gulfport, Miss., Dec. 14, 1919; s. Craig Carlton and Helen Lizette (Houppert) D.; B.S., Ga. Inst. Tech., 1941; J.D., Harvard U., 1949; children—Kimberly Patricia, Craig Carlton. Instr. aeros. Escola Tecnica de Aviacao, Sao Paulo, Brazil, 1946; contract adminstr. Convair, Fort Worth, 1949-51; mgr. contracts and pricing, atomics internat. and autonetics divs. N. Am. Aviation, Anaheim, Calif., 1954-62, asst. corp. dir. contracts and proposals, El Segundo, Calif., 1963-70; dir. contracts Aerojet Electro Systems Co., Azusa, Calif., 1971—. Served with AUS, 1941-45; USAF, 1951-53, to col. res., 1953-66. Mem. Am. Bar Assn., Fed. Bar Assn., D.C. Bar Assn., Town Hall Calif., Harvard U. Alumni Assn., Ga. Tech. Alumni Assn. Republican. Episcopalian. Club: Harvard. Home: 10501 Wilshire Blvd Apt 1208 Los Angeles CA 90024 Office: 1100 W Hollyvale St Azusa CA 91702

DAVIS, DONALD WALTER, mfg. co. exec.; b. Springfield, Mass., June 10, 1921; s. Donald Walter and Laura Helen (Mansfield) D.; A.B., Pa. State U., 1942; M.B.A., Harvard, 1948; m. Mary Virginia Cooper, Aug. 2, 1947; children—Randall C., Deborah M., Donald Walter III, Palmer R., Jennifer D., Ruth A. With Stanley Works, New Britain, Conn., 1948—, asst. gen. mgr. Steel Strapping div., 1960-61, v.p., gen. mgr. div., 1961-62, exec. v.p., 1962-66, pres., chief exec. officer, 1966-76, chmn., chief exec. officer, 1977—, also dir.; dir. Pitney-Bowes Co., Dexter Corp., N.E. Utilities, Conn. Mut. Life Ins. Co., Allied Chem. Corp. Regent, U. Hartford; bd. dirs. New Britain Gen. Hosp. Mem. Conn. Bus. and Industry Assn. (dir.), Phi Delta Theta. Home: 514 Shuttle Meadow Ave New Britain CT 06052 Office: Stanley Works 195 Lake St New Britain CT 06052

DAVIS, EMILY, lawyer; b. Middletown, Conn., Nov. 16, 1944; d. Carl and Beatrice Davis; B.A., U. Conn., 1966, J.D., 1969. Admitted to Conn. bar, 1969, Calif. bar, 1976, Wash. bar, 1978; atty. Aetna Life & Casualty, Hartford, Conn., 1969-71; contract analyst West Coast Life Ins. Co., San Francisco, 1971-77, asst. counsel, 1977-78; counsel No. Life Ins. Co., Seattle, 1978—. Trustee, Wash. Ins. Council, 1978. Mem. Wash. Life and Disability Guaranty Assn. (dir. 1978), Wash. Bar Assn., Calif. Bar Assn. Office: 1110 Third Ave Seattle WA 98101

DAVIS, F(RANCIS) GORDON, public relations exec.; b. Bloomfield, Ind., May 21, 1908; s. Francis Gordon and Grace (Bryan) D.; student Wayne State U., 1925-27, postgrad., 1929-30; B.A., U. Mich., 1929, postgrad., 1930, 42; postgrad. Cleve. Inst. Art, 1936-37, Western Res. U., 1938-39; m. Margaret Aletha Smith, July 13, 1931; children—Margaret Jayne (Mrs. Edward A. Johnson), Marilyn Grace (Mrs. Richard Karl Johnston). Reporter, aviation editor, editorial writer Buffalo Times, 1930-33; feature, editorial, sci. writer Cleve. Press, 1934-42; public relations dir. Mich. Blue Cross-Blue Shield, Detroit, 1942-46; exec. dir. Mich. Health Council, Detroit, 1943-46; owner F. Gordon Davis & Assos., Roscommon, Mich., 1946—. Mem. Public Relations Soc. Am., Am. Hosp. Assn. (chmn. public relations adv. com. 1965, chmn. Conf. Affilated Soc. Presidents 1969), Ohio Hosp. Assn., Am. Soc. Hosp. Public Relations (pres. 1968-69), Mich. Hosp. Public Relations Assn. (pres. 1975-76), Southeastern Mich. Hosp. Public Relations Assn. (pres. 1973-74). Club: Higgins Lake Boat (dir. 1962-65). Contbr. articles to profl. jours. Home and Office: Route 3 Box 249 Roscommon MI 48653

DAVIS, FRED PERSHING, retail jeweler; b. Dante, Va., Aug. 23, 1918; s. Zeb Grady and Blanche (Boyd) D.; student Milligan (Tenn.) Coll., E. Tenn. State U., Johnson City; m. Marguerite Clark, May 4, 1941; children—Marguerite Elaine Davis Costner, Elizabeth Clark. Owner, Fred Davis Jewelers, Elizabethton, Tenn., 1946—, Mill Race Village Apt. Complex, Elizabethton, 1976—, WIDD Radio AM-FM, Elizabethton, 1976—; chmn. Elizabethton Indsl. Commn., 1964—. Pres., Elizabethton Jaycees, 1947-48; mem. Carter County Election Commn., 1968-72. Served as officer U.S. Army, 1940-46. Named Outstanding Young Man of Yr., Elizabethton Jaycees, 1947. Mem. Jewelers Vigilance Com., Jewelry Industry Council, Tenn. Assn. Retail Jewelers (past regional dir.), Tenn. Retail Mchts. Assn. (past regional dir.), Res. Officers Assn. (past chpt. pres.), Mil. Order World Wars, VFW, Am. Legion. Democrat. Clubs: Elizabethton Golf (past pres.), Johnson City Country, Shriners, Elks. Office: 405 Elk Ave Elizabethton TN 37643

DAVIS, FREDERICK NEWTON, III, advt. exec.; b. Cin., Mar. 5, 1952; s. Frederick Newton and Marilyn Jean (Inhofe) D.; student Trinity U., 1970-72, U. Tulsa, 1972-74. Founder, Fred N. Davis and Assos., Advt., Tulsa, 1972, pres., 1972-78; owner Davis & Hall Pub. Relations, Tulsa, 1976-78; chmn. Davis & Nauser, Inc., Tulsa, 1979—, dir. U.S. Floral, Inc.; lectr. in field. Pres., Tulsa chpt. ARC, 1968-70; chmn. Young Life; bd. dirs. Jr. Achievement, Mental Health Assn. of Tulsa. Mem. SW Assn. Advt. Agys. Presbyterian. Clubs: Summit, Tulsa. Home and Office: 1820 S Boulder Pl Tulsa OK 74119

DAVIS, GILBERT KENNETH, lawyer; b. Waterloo, Iowa, Oct. 2, 1942; s. Dwight M. and Alice F. Davis; B.A., Cornell Coll., 1964; J.D., U. Va., 1969; m. Pamela Sue Saunders, Aug. 29, 1964; children—Luan, Heidi. Tchr., Iowa Community Schs., Iowa City, 1964-66; dir. Neighborhood Youth Corps, State of Iowa, 1966; dir. info. and edn. Iowa Comprehensive Alcoholism Project, Office of the Gov., 1967; admitted to Va. bar, 1969, U.S. Supreme Ct. bar, 1973, U.S. Dist. Ct. bar, D.C., 1974; asst. U.S. atty., Eastern dist. of Va., 1969-73; individual practice law, Vienna, Va., 1973-79; sr. partner firm Davis, Gillenwater, Lynch & Doane, McLean, Va., 1979—; dir. Profl. Educators, Inc., Appalchian Mineral Devel. Corp., Wayne Energy, Inc., Church and Mullins Corp. Chmn., Young Republican Fedn. Va., 1973-75. Mem. Fed. Criminal Investigators Assn. (founder, chmn. Washington chpt.), Fed., Am. bar assns., Assn. Trial Lawyers Am., Internat. Platform Assn., Delta Theta Phi. Presbyterian. Club: Optimist. Home: 2727 Wrexham Ct Herndon VA Office: 6801 Whittier Ave McLean VA 22101

DAVIS, HELEN NANCY MATSON (MRS. CHAUNCEY D. DAVIS), real estate broker, civic worker; b. Zanesville, Ohio, Nov. 18, 1905; d. Austin F. and Georgianna (Hale) Matson; grad. high sch.; m. Chauncey D. Davis, May 1, 1924; children—James Harvey, Robert Lee. Real Estate broker, South Bend, Wash., 1964—. Exec. sec. Pacific County Tb League, 1936-62; chmn. Park Bd., South Bend, 1955—; ofcl. Pacific County Bicentennial Pageant; trustee Pacific County Hist. Soc. Named Woman of Yr. Pacific County C. of C., 1949, 61. Mem. Propaelaeum Study Club, Grange, Chinook Indian Tribe (hon.), Wash. Fedn. Music Clubs, Delta Kappa Gamma. Republican. Methodist. Rebekah. Club: Garden (South Bend). Composer: Washington, My Home (ofcl. state song Wash.), 1959; Eliza and the Lumberjack (mus. play). Home: 606 W 2d St South Bend WA 98586 Office: 705 Robert Bush Dr South Bend WA 98586

DAVIS, HERBERT LOWELL, utility co. exec.; b. Douds, Iowa, Feb. 18, 1933; s. John Herbert and Edna Belle (Frazier) D.; student George Washington U., 1949-51; B.S. with distinction, U. Va., 1953; postgrad., U. Mich., 1953; m. Roberta Willey Stearns, Sept. 10, 1955; children—Michael Stearns, Elizabeth Buchanan. Sr. accountant Price Waterhouse & Co., Washington, 1957-61, mgr., 1961-66; asst. comptroller Potomac Electric Power Co., Washington, 1966-70, v.p., comptroller, 1970-72, sr. v.p., 1972-80, exec. v.p., 1980—, also dir.; dir. 1st Am. Nat. Bank of Washington. Bd. dirs. Columbia Hosp. for Women, Washington, 1970—. Served to lt. (j.g.) USNR, 1954-57. Recipient Achievement award Va. Soc. Pub. Accountants, 1953, C.P.A., Va. Mem. Met. Washington Bd. Trade, Financial Execs. Inst. (D.C. chpt. pres. 1974, dir.), Am., D.C. insts. C.P.A.'s. Episcopalian. Rotarian Clubs: Metropolitan (Washington); Belle Haven Country. Home: 506 Richards Ln Alexandria VA 22302 Office: 1900 Pennsylvania Ave Washington DC 20068

DAVIS, JAMES ELSWORTH, food co. exec.; b. Henderson, Ark., July 31, 1907; s. William M. and Ethel (Chase) D.; student U. Idaho, 1925-27, U. Ill., 1928; Stetson U., 1960; LL.D., Bethune-Cookman Coll., 1964; D.C.L., Jacksonville U., 1974. Pres., Economy Wholesale Grocery Co., 1939-42, v.p., dir., 1925-65; exec. v.p. Winn & Lovett Grocery Co., 1946-50; v.p., dir. Economy Wholesale Foods, Inc.; chmn. bd., chief exec. officer, dir. Winn-Dixie Stores, Inc.; v.p. Economy Wholesale Distbrs., Inc.; chmn. bd., dir. Am. Heritage Life Ins. Co.; v.p. Crackin' Good Bakers Inc.; pres., dir. Danov Corp.; pres. Estuary Corp., D.D.I., Inc.; v.p., dir. Deep South Products; v.p. Astor Products, Inc.; hon. dir. Barnett Nat. Bank (Jacksonville), Monterey Canning Co., Bahamas Supermarkets, Nassau. Trustee Bethune-Cookman Coll.; hon. bd. dirs. Bolles Sch.; v.p. Winn-Dixie Stores Found.; pres. J. Elsworth Davis Found.; trustee St. Luke's Hosp. Assn., Jacksonville, Fla. Served from capt. to lt. col. AUS, 1943-45; officer charge Q.M.C. Market Center, N.Y.C., 1944-45. Perishable foods ETOUSA, MTOUSA, NATOUSA. Decorated

Legion of Merit. Mem. Nat. Assn. Food Chains, Alpha Kappa Psi. Sigma Chi. Mem. Christian Ch. Clubs: Fla. Yacht, Ponte Vedra, River. Home: 3960 Ortega Blvd Jacksonville FL 32210 Office: Box B Jacksonville FL 32203

DAVIS, JAMES GORDON, consultant; b. Hartford, Tenn., Sept. 9, 1946; s. Jay N. and Peggie (Fine) D.; B.S., Drexel U., 1969, M.S. (fellow), 1970; M.B.A., U. Pa., 1971; m. Kathleen Virginia Virgilio, Aug. 12, 1977. Successively indsl. engr., sr. indsl. engr., prodn. supr., supt. ops. Mobil Oil Co., Paulsboro, N.J., 1971-73; successively cons., mgr. ops., gen. mgr. ops., v.p. Wofac Co. div. Sci. Mgmt. Corp., Moorestown, N.J., 1973-80; mng. asso. Theodore Barry & Assos., N.Y.C., 1980—. Named Outstanding Profl. of Year, Sci. Mgmt. Corp., 1976. Mem. Am. Inst. Indsl. Engrs., Am. Mgmt. Assn., Inst. Mgmt. Consultants. Republican. Contbr. articles to profl. jours. Home: 1 Bronwood Dr West Berlin NJ 08091 Office: 50 Rockefeller Plaza Suite 1035 New York NY 10020

DAVIS, JAMES GRANVILLE, steel plate fabricating co. exec.; b. Syracuse, N.Y., May 25, 1935; s. Willis E. and Thelma (Lakins) D.; student Syracuse U., 1953-57, Univ. Coll., Syracuse, 1957-60; cert. of completion sales and mktg. mgmt. program Syracuse U., 1979; m. Edith Jo Eichelberger, July 2, 1956 (div. Dec. 1962); children—Jen G., Jill G., Jody G., Jefferson G.; m. 2d, Bonnie Ann Byington, Aug. 23, 1969 (div. Jan. 1976); children—Matthew Richard, Stephen Patrick; m. 3d, Diane McColl, Feb. 20, 1976; children—Elizabeth McColl, Catherine Manroe. New bus. rep. 1st Deposit and Trust Co., Syracuse, 1956-61; asst. mgr. sales Stone Machinery Co., Manlius, N.Y., 1962; mgr. sales Trippe Mfg. Co., Chgo., 1962-67; gen. sales mgr. Fed. Sign & Signal Corp., Blue Island, Ill., 1967-71; v.p. Fed. Sign & Signal Internat., Ltd., 1971-72; regional sales mgr. Graver Tank & Mfg., East Chicago, Ind., 1972-73, mgr. mktg. and sales, 1973-78, dir. power generation markets, 1978—; v.p. Power Generation Markets, 1979—. Mem. Jr. C. of C. (past state v.p.), Internat. Trade Club, Pi Upsilon. Home: 2510 Roslyn Trail Long Beach Michigan City IN 46360 Office: 4809 Tod Ave East Chicago IN 46312

DAVIS, JEANNE LIPTAK (MRS. ROBERT A. DAVIS), real estate exec.; b. Cleve., Apr. 20, 1924; d. Duncan Lorenzo and Bessie May (Fisher) Dow; student Cleve. pub. schs.; m. James Liptak, Apr. 6, 1942 (div. 1962); children—Bruce (dec.), Tanya Maria; m. 2d, Robert A. Davis, Aug. 15, 1964. Owner, operator Ball Road Realty, Anaheim, Calif., 1959-81; bail bondswoman Davis Bail Bonds Agy., Santa Ana, Calif. Vice pres. Enchanted Village Estates, Inc., Anaheim, 1963-69; sec. Lake Elsinore Estates, Inc., Anaheim, 1963-67. Address: 515 65th Ave Dr W Bradenton FL 33507

DAVIS, JESSE DUNBAR, lawyer; b. Burden, Kan., June 19, 1908; s. Jesse Bowman and Hazel (Dunbar) D.; student U. Okla., 1926-28; LL.B., U. Tulsa, 1944; m. Frances Lou Vinson, June 19, 1929; children—Sydney (Mrs. Donald George Dove), Brett Vinson. Asst. mgr. Long-Bell Lumber Co., Muskogee, Okla., 1928-32, gen. mgr., Tulsa, 1933-48, div. mgr., Kansas City, Mo., 1949-57; admitted to Okla. bar, 1944, U.S. Supreme Ct. bar, 1950, Mo. bar, 1959, Fed. bar, 1963; v.p., dir. Tamko Asphalt Products, Inc., Joplin, Mo., 1958-59; gen. counsel Southwestern Lumberman's Assn., Kansas City, Mo., 1960-65; gen. practice law, Kansas City, Mo., Tulsa, 1960—; mgmt. cons., Tulsa, 1965—; realtor, Tulsa; v.p. Met. Bd. Tulsa Realtors, 1969-70, dir., 1970-71, treas., 1971, corporate sec., 1972—; v.p., dir. Multiple Listing Service Tulsa Reltors. Tchr. real estate law U. Tulsa, 1969-74; columnist Retail Lumberman Mag., 1962-65; cons. industry Sch. Forestry, U. Mo., 1962-65; tchr. bus. law U. Mo., 1946-65; corporate sec., dir. Southwestern Lumbermen's Assn., Kansas City, 1962-65; v.p., dir., asso. editor Retail Lumberman Pub. Co., Kansas City, 1962-65. Served to lt. USNR, 1944-46. Recipient Civic award Tulsa YMCA, 1946-47. Mem. Mid-Am. Lumbermens Assn., Nat. Lumber and Bldg. Material Dealers Assn. (past dir.) Am., Kansas City, Tulsa County, Rogers County bar assns., Tulsa County Hist. Soc. (life mem.), Am. Judicature Soc., Lawyers Assn. Kansas City, Met. Tulsa Real Estate Bd., Tulsa (Civic award 1939), Claremore (dir. 1972—, v.p. 1973-74) chambers commerce, S.A.R., U.S. Navy League, Am. Legion (life mem. Okla. dept.), Res. Officers Assn. U.S. (life mem.), Phi Delta Theta, Phi Beta Gamma. Presbyn. Republican. Kiwanian (pres. Tulsa 1941, sec.-treas. Tex.-Okla. dist. 1942). Club: University (charter) (Tulsa). Home: 3231 S Utica Ave Tulsa OK 74105 Office: 3233 S Utica Ave Tulsa OK 74105

DAVIS, JESSE EDWIN, JR., wood products exec.; b. Atlanta, Feb. 4, 1910; s. Jesse Edwin and Eufa (Swilling) D.; B.S., Ga. Sch. Tech., 1933; LL.B., Woodrow Wilson Coll., 1937; m. Sarah Etta Fitzpatrick, Apr. 7, 1938; children—Carolyn W. (Mrs. Edward W. Riser), Sarah K. (Mrs. M. Rick Taylor), Jesse Edwin III, Marion H. Admitted to Ga. bar, 1937; sales rep. Atlantic Steel Co., 1937-43, Tidewater Supply Co., 1943-49; v.p., treas. Thackston-Davis Supply, 1949-59; with Marwin Co., Columbia, S.C., 1959—, pres., treas., 1959—; pres., dir. Russell-Davis Devel. Corp., 1965— (all Columbia). Mem. Columbia Com. of 100. Chmn. religious work com. Columbia YMCA, 1956—, bd. dirs.; trustee United Community Services. Mem. Sigma Chi, Alpha Kappa Psi, Pi Delta Epsilon. Baptist (deacon). Mason (Shriner), Lion. Home: 4829 Carter Hill Rd Columbia SC 29206 Office: PO Box 9126 Atlas Rd Columbia SC 29290

DAVIS, JOHN AUSTIN, forest products co. exec.; b. Knox County, Tenn., Sept. 25, 1928; s. Hugh Harvey and Fay (Stafford) D.; B.S. in Bus. Adminstrn., U. Tenn., 1957; m. Kathleen Hamilton, Oct. 20, 1951; children—Hope, Leigh, Leslie, Susan. Supr. corporate accounting Mead Corp., Dayton, Ohio, 1966-69, wage and price controls coordinator, 1972-73, mgr. measurements and controls, 1973—; mgr. corporate acctg. Champion Internat., Hamilton, Ohio, 1970-71. Pres., Montgomery County (Ohio) Men's Republican Club, 1969; city councilman, Centerville, Ohio, 1966-73, pres. city council, 1968-69, dep. mayor, 1970-71. Served with USMC, 1946-51. Decorated Silver Star, Purple Heart (2); named hon. Lt. Gov. State of Ohio, 1973. Mem. Nat. Accounting Assn., Beta Alpha Psi. Presbyterian. Home: 6020 Culpepper Ct Centerville OH 45459 Office: Mead World Hdqrs Courthouse Plaza NE Dayton OH 45463

DAVIS, JOHN WESLEY, III, nail mfg. co. exec.; b. Washington, Aug. 17, 1942; s. John Wesley and Annie Teresa (King) D.; B.A., Guilford Coll., 1965; postgrad. in fin. N.Y. U., 1969; m. Terrie Allen, July 30, 1966; children—Virginia Allen, John Wesley IV. Mgr., Dean Witter Reynolds, Winston-Salem, N.C., 1969-72, v.p., mgr., Atlanta, 1972-75; sr. v.p. Salem Carpet Mills, Winston-Salem, 1975-78; pres. Majestic Carpet Mill, Dalton, Ga., 1978-79; chmn. Fed. Nail Mfg. Co., Winston-Salem, 1979—; mgr. Alex Brown & Sons, 1981—. Chmn. 1st TV telerama in N.C., March of Dimes, 1972; pres. YMCA, 1980—; bd. visitors Guilford Coll., 1976-80; local campaign mgr. for gubernatorial race, 1976; trustee Winston-Salem State U., 1977—; pres. Amos Cottage Hosp., 1978-80. Mem. Internat. Wire Assn., Nat. Bldg. Material Distbrs. Democrat. Methodist. Club: Rotary. Office: Fed Nail Mfg Co 715 N Cherry St Winston-Salem NC 27101

DAVIS, JOSEPH SAMUEL, dept. store exec.; b. Chgo., Jan. 27, 1930; s. Joseph and Elizabeth (Cowen) D.; student Carleton Coll., 1947-49; B.A., Columbia, 1951; M.B.A., Harvard, 1953; m. Martha Louise Gries, June 18, 1955; children—Elizabeth Louise, Katherine Ann, Mark Bennett, James Lincoln. Mgmt. trainee May D&F, Denver, 1956-57, asst. buyer, 1957-58, buyer, 1958-61; asst. div. mdse. mgr. Kaufmann's, Inc., Pitts., 1961-63, mdse. mgr., 1963-69, gen. mdse. mgr., 1969-72, exec. v.p., 1972-75; pres. G. Fox & Co., Hartford, 1975-79; pres., chief exec. officer O'Neil's, Akron, Ohio, 1979—. Bd. dirs. Akron Action Com., Akron Regional Devel. Bd., Akron Art Mus., Akron Gen. Hosp.; adv. bd. Akron Symphony Orch., Jr. League Akron. Served with USN, 1953-56. Mem. Harvard Bus. Sch. Club of Northeastern Ohio. Home: 155 Hampshire Rd Akron OH 44313 Office: 226 S Main St Akron OH 44308

DAVIS, KENNETH EUGENE, chem. co. exec.; b. Portsmouth, Ohio, Nov. 19, 1935; s. Kenneth W. and Freda L. Davis; B.Chem.Engring., Ohio State U., Columbus, 1958; m. Reba LeVally, Nov. 23, 1956; children—Jennifer, Jeffrey, Gregory. Sect. head research & devel. Wyandotte (Mich.) Chem. Corp., 1958-66; v.p., gen. mgr. SWS Silicones Corp., Adrian, Mich., 1966-75; v.p., asst. to pres. Stauffer Chem. Co., Westport, Conn., 1975-78, exec. v.p., 1978-80, pres., chief operating officer, 1980—, dir., 1979—; dir. Conn. Nat. Bank. Mem. Am. Chem. Soc., Soc. Chem. Industry, Chem. Mfrs. Assn., Am. Inst. Chem. Engrs. Clubs: Patterson, Conn. Golf. Office: Stauffer Chem Co Westport CT 06880

DAVIS, LOUIS, JR., retail chain exec.; b. Ft. Benning, Ga., July 13, 1949; s. Louis and Fannie R. Davis; student Ala. A&M U., 1967-68, Columbus Coll., 1970-72, 80—. With Ledger-Enquirer newspaper, Columbus, Ga., 1974-76, account exec., 1976; advt. mgr. Montgomery Ward & Co., Columbus, 1977—. Mem. Alpha Phi Alpha. Democrat. Office: Montgomery Ward & Co 3091 Manchester Expressway Columbus GA 31904

DAVIS, LOUIS PHIL, credit union assn. exec.; b. Chgo., July 9, 1904; s. Louis Phil and Bertha (Anderson) D.; student So. Meth. U., 1942; m. Apr. 10, 1973. With Republic Ins. Co., Dallas, 1923-27; with various ins. cos., Tex., 1927-34; with Universal C.I.T., Dallas, 1934-42; pres., gen. mgr. City Employees Credit Union, Dallas, 1942-73; treas. Nat. Credit Union Mgmt. Assn., Dallas, 1959-80; treas. Mutual Ins. Co., Dallas, 1953-63. Recipient The Bros. Keeper award, NCCJ, 1959. Mem. Am. Soc. of Assn. Execs., Meeting Planners Internat., Ins. Club Dallas. Clubs: Lakewood Country, Masons (32 deg., Shriner). Home: PO Box 140099 Dallas TX 75214

DAVIS, MARTIN SANDFORD, business exec.; b. N.Y.C. With Samuel Goldwyn Prodns., N.Y.C., 1947-55, Allied Artists Pictures Corp. N.Y.C., 1955-58; with Paramount Pictures Corp., N.Y.C., 1958-69, v.p., 1962-66, exec. v.p., chief operating officer, mem. exec. com., dir., 1966-69; sr. v.p. Gulf & Western Industries, Inc., 1967-74, exec. v.p., mem. exec. com., 1974—, also dir. Bd. dirs. Multiple Sclerosis Soc., Found. Children with Learning Disabilities, Inst. for Collective Bargaining and Group Relations, John Jay Coll. Criminal Justice. Mem. Am. Soc. Corporate Secs. Served with AUS, 1943-46. Office: 1 Gulf & Western Plaza New York City NY 10023

DAVIS, MARVIN ARNOLD, mfg. co. exec.; b. St. Louis, Nov. 16, 1937; s. Sam and Pauline (Neuman) D.; B.S. in Chem. Engring. (scholar), Washington U., St. Louis, 1959, M.B.A. in Fin. and Mktg. (fellow), 1966; m. Trudy Brenda Rein, Aug. 11, 1968; children—Julie, Jeffrey. Lead engr. Standard Oil. Calif., San Francisco, 1962-64; product mgr. Shell Chem. Co., N.Y.C., 1966-69; group controller Pfizer Inc., N.Y.C., 1969-75; exec. v.p. Good Hope Industries, New Orleans, 1975-77; pres., chief exec. officer Reed Industries, Inc., Stone Mountain, Ga., 1978—; instr. Fairleigh Dickenson U., 1968-71; lectr. Washington U., 1966, 77; also cons. Served to lt. USNR, 1959-62. Mem. DeKalb C. of C., Beta Gamma Sigma, Alpha Chi Sigma. Jewish. Club: Horseshoe Bend Country. Office: 1445 Rock Mountain Blvd Stone Mountain GA 30083

DAVIS, MELINDA B., acct.; b. Prairie Grove, Ark., Dec. 6, 1942; d. Nolan Leslie and Etta Louisa (Jones) Smith; student Draughons Sch. Bus., 1961; m. Gerald J. Davis, June 2, 1960; children—Leslie James, Teresa Louette. With Allen Canning Co., Siloam Springs, Ark., 1961—, v.p., asst. treas., 1980-81. Baptist. Office: PO Box 250 Siloam Springs AR 72761

DAVIS, MICHAEL CHARLES, plumbing co. exec.; b. Long Beach, Calif., Mar. 30, 1948; s. Charles Burnett and Bernice Irene (Russell) D.; B.A., Biola Coll., La Mirada, Calif., 1973; m. Lynette Kay Carlile, Dec. 15, 1973; children—Chelsea Elizabeth, Michael Adam. With H.L. Moe Co., Inc., Glendale, Calif., 1972—, v.p. constrn., 1978—. Bd. dirs. Glendale Babe Ruth Assn.; bd. govs. Glendale Family YMCA. Mem. USNG, 1975. Republican. Clubs: Glendale Gateway Kiwanis (dir.), Glendale Quarter Back. Home: 1206 Alma St Glendale CA 91202 Office: 310 S Brand Blvd Glendale CA 91204

DAVIS, MURRAY HAMILTON, banker; b. Kansas City, Mo., Mar. 25, 1927; s. Roger and Berenice (Radford) D.; B.S, U. Kans., 1950; m. Helen Piller Davis, July 14, 1951; children—Scott, Murray, Barbara, Matthew, Mary Catherine, Timothy. Agt., Equitable Life Assurance Soc. U.S., 1950-55; agt., asst. mgr. Northwestern Nat. Life, 1955-60; with Merc. Bank & Trust Co., Kansas City, Mo., 1960—, pres., 1977—, also dir.; dir. McGee Radio and Electronics Co., George P. Reintjes Co. Pres. bd. Marillac Childrens Center; pres. adv. bd. St. Marys Hosp., 1978-79; adv. dir. Kansas City Regional Council Higher Edn. Served to comdr. USNR. Roman Catholic. Office: PO Box 147 Kansas City MO 64141

DAVIS, NATHANAEL VINING, aluminum co. exec.; b. Pitts., June 26, 1915; s. Edward Kirk and Rhea Ada (Reineman) D.; grad. Harvard U., 1938; m. Lois Howard Thompson, 1941; children—James Howard Dow, Katharine Vining. With Alcan Aluminium Ltd. (formerly Aluminium Ltd.), 1939—, pres., 1947-72, chmn. bd., chief exec. officer, 1972-79, chmn. bd., 1979—, also dir.; dir. Can. Life Assurance Co., Toronto, Bank of Montreal. Home: Osterville MA Office: 1 Place Ville Marie Montreal PQ H3C 3H2 Canada

DAVIS, NICHOLAS HOMANS CLARK, securities co. exec.; b. N.Y.C., Dec. 1, 1938; s. Feltz Cleveland and Loraine Vanderpool (Homans) D.; grad. Pingry Prep. Sch., 1956; A.B. in Paleontology with honors, Princeton, 1961; M.B.A., Stanford, 1963; m. Carol Muriel Lowen, Apr. 26, 1972; children by previous marriages—Loraine, Helen, Alexandra, Christopher, Eleanor, Katherine, John. Instl. security analyst Fahnestock & Co., N.Y.C., 1963-67; mgr. research dept. Andersen & Co., N.Y.C., 1967-70; instl. sec. research Robert Garrett & Sons, N.Y.C., 1970-71; research partner Boettcher & Co., Denver, 1971-75, also dir.; v.p. White, Weld & Co., Denver, 1976-78; v.p. Paine Webber Jackson & Curtis, Inc., Denver, 1978—; pres., chmn. Colo. Growth Capital, Inc., Denver, 1978—; founder, dir. Colo. Life Ins. Co., Grand Junction, 1977-78. Treas., bd. dirs. Greenwich Village Montessori Sch., N.Y.C., 1965-71. trustee Bonnie Brae Farm Boys, Millington, N.J., 1969-76, Charles Emil Thenen Found., Montclair, N.J., 1965—. Chartered fin. analyst. Mem. N.Y., Denver (dir. 1973—) socs. security analysts, Chartered Fin. Analysts Soc. Clubs: N.Y. Yacht, Racquet and Tennis (N.Y.C.); Denver Petroleum, Denver Country, Mile High (Denver); Quantuck Beach (Westhampton, N.Y.). Author article. Home: 1228 E 3d Ave Denver CO 80218 Office: 1600 Broadway Denver CO 80202

DAVIS, O.C, natural gas pipeline co. exec.; b. Roseclare, Ill., May 7, 1920; s. Luther and Elizabeth (St. John) D.; B.S. in Mech. Engring., A. and M. Coll. Tex.; m. Thelma Sherry, Nov. 14, 1942; children—Henry T., Jon F. with Natural Gas Pipeline Co. Am. (now People's Energy Corp.), 1947—, v.p. charge storage, 1963-66; exec. v.p., then pres., now chmn. bd., 1977—, also dir.; chmn. bd., dir. Peoples Gas Light & Coke Co., Natural Gas Pipeline Co. Am., North Shore Gas Co., Harper Oil Co., Indsl. Fuels Corp.; dir. Amsted Industries, Harris Bancorp Inc., Harris Trust & Savs. Bank. Served to capt. USAAF, World War II. Mem. Am. Gas Assn., Am. Inst. Mining and Metall. Engrs. Clubs: Chicago, University (Chgo.). Office: Peoples Energy Corp 122 S Michigan Ave Chicago IL 60603*

DAVIS, PAMELA JO, state ofcl.; b. Miami, Fla., Oct. 9, 1943; s. Henry and Ruth Esther (Heisey) Weaver; B.B.A., U. Miami, 1965, M.Ed., 1972, now postgrad. fellow; m. J. Brower Davis III, June 12, 1965; children—Darrell Jo, J. Brower IV. Research asso. Bus. Week mag., N.Y.C., 1965; asst. to dept. accounting mgr. Dow Chem. Co., Coral Gables, Fla., 1969; asst. dir. Dade Center, Fla. Atlantic U., Boca Raton, 1970-72; spl. projects adminstr. Dade County Pub. Safety Dept., Miami, 1973-75; dir. women's detention center Dade County Corrections and Rehabs., Miami, 1976-79; asst. sec. office mgmt. and budget Fla. Dept. Corrections, Tallahassee, 1980—; dir. Wencor Corp. Inc.; project dir. numerous law enforcement adminstrn. grants; cons. exec. pre-employment screening Palm Beach County (Fla.). Mem. Pub. Schs. Adv. Council, Consumer Advocate Adv. Commn.; bd. dirs. Women's Com. of 100. Recipient Outstanding Service award Internat. Exchange Club. Mem. AAUW (v.p.), Am. Soc. Pub. Adminstrn., Am. Assn. Higher Edn., Am. Assn. Sch. Adminstrs., Am. Correctional Assn. (publs. bd.), Nat. Assn. Women Adminstrs. in Edn. Methodist. Co-author: Study of Salaries of Instructional and Administrative Personnel, 1972. Home: 2380 Pine Ridge Rd Tallahassee FL 32303 Office: 1311 Winewood Blvd Tallahassee FL 32301

DAVIS, RICHARD DAVID, mfg. co. exec.; b. Decatur, Ill., Mar. 7, 1934; s. Newton David and Anna Josephine (Vest) D.; B.S. in Indsl. Engring., Millikin U., 1963; m. Sue Ann Willoughby, Dec. 18, 1955; children—Richard David, Brandon Wells. mfg. engr., numerical control coordinator Interlake Steel Co., Chgo., 1963-67; numerical control coordinator Trans Union, E. Chicago, Ind., 1967-69; plant mgr. Metalmation, S. Bend, Ind., 1969-70; mgr. mfg. engring. Pneumo Dynamics Machine Tool Group, Windsor, Vt., 1970-72, Colt Firearms, Hartford, Conn., 1972-77; adv. mfg. engr. Web Press div. Harris Corp., Westerly, R.I., 1977-79; v.p. engring. and mfg. Stoffel Grinding Systems, Inc., Tuckahoe, N.Y., 1979—. Served with USN, 1953-57. Mem. ASME, CASA. Home: 16 Forbell Dr Norwalk CT 06850 Office: 66 Marbledale Rd Tuckahoe NY 10707

DAVIS, ROBERT HENRY, fin. exec.; b. Phila., Mar. 26, 1943; s. Robert E. and Dorothy P. (Messmann) D.; student Los Angeles Valley Coll., 1965-67, Alexander Hamilton Inst., 1965-68, Grad. Sch. of Credit and Fin. Mgmt., Stanford U., 1977-80; 1 dau., Michelle R. Fin. cons., Montepelier, Idaho, 1976-78; credit mgr. Wyo. Machinery Co., Casper, 1978-79; controller/sec.-treas. John E. Burns Drilling Co., Casper, 1979—; fin. cons. Western Energy Co., Huey's Smoked Meats, Nashville, Trans-Equip., Casper, Three Percent, Inc., Riverton, Wyo., 1979-80. Adv. bd. dirs. Highland Park Community Ch., 1980—. Served with USNR, 1961-63. Mem. Nat. Assn. Credit Mgmt. (state rep. 1979, 80), Credit Mgrs. Assn. So. Calif. (dir. bus. re-orgn. and bankruptcy 1973-74), Credit Research Found., Am. Mgmt. Assn., Stanford U. Alumni Assn. Club: Order of Demolay (sr. award 1960). Office: PO Box 9082 Casper WY 82609

DAVIS, ROBERT JOSEPH, investment co. exec.; b. St. Louis, Nov. 21, 1936; s. Joseph N. and Irene (Mraz) D.; B.S.C., St. Louis U., 1958, M.C.S., 1961; m. Jeanne A. Kuebler, Dec. 8, 1979; children—Robert, Anne Elizabeth, Timothy, Michael, Daniel, Paul. Instr., Sch. C. and F, St. Louis U., 1960, asst. to exec. v.p. Liberty Loan Corp., St. Louis, 1961-64; supt. bank agt. relations State Farm Ins. Cos., Bloomington, Ill., 1965; v.p. Michelman & Hanf, N.Y.C., 1966-67; sr. v.p. investment banking Paine Webber Jackson & Curtis, Inc., N.Y.C., 1968-79; mng. dir. Blyth Eastman Paine Webber, Inc., N.Y.C., 1980—; dir. exec. compensation com. and audit com. Acco Internat., Inc., Chgo., 1971—; dir. Thompson Steel Co., Braintree, Mass., 1974—, O.F. Mossberg & Sons, Inc., North Haven, Conn., 1976-79. Mem. adv. council Coll. Bus. Adminstrn., U. Notre Dame, 1976—; mem. pres.'s council Coll. William and Mary, 1977-79; pres. Parents' Athletic Assn. Pascack Hills (N.J.) Regional High Sch., 1976-78; active Boy Scouts Am. Mem. Securities Industry Assn. (pvt. placement com.). Clubs: Arcola Country, Wall St. Author: Finance Company Funded Debt Agreement - Analysis of Definitions and Ratios, 1960. Home: 285 Forest Glen Franklin Lakes NJ 07417 Office: 1221 Ave of Americas New York NY 10020

DAVIS, ROBERT LEE, bus. cons.; b. Galveston, Tex., Nov. 25, 1937; s. Henry and M.E. (Johnson) D.; B.S., U. Calif., Berkeley, 1972; M.B.A., Golden Gate U., 1975; m. Norma L. Rodgers, Oct. 20, 1978; children—Michael, Gary. Computer specialist Dept. of Navy, Alameda, Calif., 1968-72; mgmt. acct. Dow Chem. Co., Pittsburg, Calif., 1972-76; dir., bus. analyst Spanish-Speaking Unity Council, Oakland, Calif., 1976-78; rep.-in-charge Reno (Nev.) SBA, 1979—; bus. cons.; tutor, mem. Diamond Dist. Improvement Council, Oakland, 1976-78, Fruitvale Dist. rep., 1978; treas. United Front, Inc., Reno, 1980—. Served with U.S. Army, 1961-65. Ford Found. grantee, 1955. Mem. Nat. Assn. Accts., Assn. MBA Execs. Episcopalian. Author: Book of Happy Poems, 1957. Office: 50 S Virginia St Rm 308 Reno NV 89505

DAVIS, RONALD V., beverage co. exec.; b. Mobile, Ala., Jan. 26, 1947; s. Oliver V. and Lena A.; B.A., Calif. State U., Fullerton, 1969; M.B.A., U. So. Calif., 1971; m. Judith L. Walton, Oct. 8, 1949; children—Bryce V., Lauren K. Sales mgmt. staff Gen. Foods Co., White Plains, N.Y., 1969-73, product mgr., 1974-75, sr. product mgr., 1975-76, group product mgr., 1977-79; v.p. mktg. Great Waters of France (Perrier), Greenwich, Conn., 1979-80, pres., chief exec. officer, 1980—; pres., chief exec. officer Poland Spring Corp., Greenwich, 1980—; bd. dirs. Council of Natural Waters, Washington. Pres. Am. Landmark Springs Corp., Greenwich, 1979—. Address: 777 W Putnam Ave Greenwich CT 06830

DAVIS, SCOTT LIVINGSTON, electronics co. exec., lawyer; b. Boston, Jan. 23, 1941; s. William Francis and Marion Livingston (Morrison) D.; B.A., U. Calif., Berkeley, 1961; M.B.A., UCLA, 1965; J.D., Columbia U., 1968; m. Christina Williams, June 10, 1968; 1 son, Scott Livingston. Admitted to N.Y. bar, 1969; asso. firm Dewey Ballantine Bushby Palmer & Wood, N.Y.C., 1967-72; gen. counsel, v.p. Electro Audio Dynamics, Inc., Gt. Neck, N.Y., 1972-77, v.p. corp. devel. and legal affairs, 1978-80, group v.p. Consumer Products div., 1980—; pres., chief exec. officer IKC Internat., Inc., Canoga Park, Calif., 1980—; pres., chief exec. officer KLH Research and Devel. Corp., Westwood, Mass., 1976-78. Home: 389 Stewart Ave Garden City NY 11530 also 2271 Westshore Ln Westlake CA Office: Electro Audio Dynamics Inc 98 Cutter Mill Rd Great Neck NY 11021 also IKC Internat Inc 7930 Deering Ave Canoga Park CA

DAVIS, SIDNEY DEWITT, JR., banker; b. Indpls., Mar. 17, 1945; s. Sidney Dewitt and Inez O. D.; B.B.A., U. Miss., 1967; M.A. in Banking and Fin., U. Ala., 1975; grad. Sch. Banking of South, La. State U., 1972; m. Cynthia Jo Munson, Sept. 24, 1964; children—Dee, Brad. Asst. nat. bank examiner U.S. Treasury Dept., Jackson, Miss., 1967-69, adminstrv. asst. to Regional Adminstr. of Nat. Banks, Memphis, 1969-71, nat. bank examiner, Montgomery, Ala., 1971-74, internat. bank examiner, 1970-74; exec. v.p. Peoples Bank, Mendenhall, Miss., 1975-80, pres., 1980—. Former pres. Mendenhall Tiger Booster Club; treas., dir. Simpson County Econ. Devel. Found.; former Simpson County vice chmn. Miss. Republican Party; coach Little League, 1975—. C.P.A., Miss. Mem. Miss. Soc. C.P.A.'s, Am. Inst. C.P.A.'s, Miss. Bankers Assn., Miss. Econ. Council (v.p. Leadership Miss.), Miss. Young Bankers Assn. (exec. council 1977-78), Mendenhall C. of C. (treas., dir.), Beta Gamma Sigma. Methodist. Club: Simpson County Country (past pres.). Home: 417 Simpson Circle Mendenhall MS 39114 Office: PO Box 7 Mendenhall MS 39114

DAVIS, STUART, savs. and loan assn. exec.; b. Santa Monica, Calif., Mar. 29, 1918; s. William Arthur and Ida Mae (Honson) D.; B.S., St. Mary's (Calif.) Coll., 1938; m. Mary Young, Mar. 3, 1978; children by previous marriage—Elenor Lynn (Mrs. Arthur Alarcon), Richard Edward. With First Savs. & Loan Assn., San Francisco, 1938—, chmn. bd., 1961—; chmn. bd. Gt. Western Financial Corp., Los Angeles, Gt. Western Savs. & Loan Assn., Beverly Hills, Calif. Mem. U.S. League Savs. Assns. (pres. 1978), Calif. Savs. and Loan League (pres. 1956), Savs. and Loan Found., U.S. (dir.), Calif. (pres. 1975) chambers commerce. Office: Gt Western Savs & Loan 8484 Wilshire Blvd Beverly Hills CA 90210

DAVIS, THOMAS HENRY, airline exec.; b. Winston-Salem, N.C., Mar. 15, 1918; s. Egbert L. and Annie (Shore) D.; student U. Ariz., 1935-39; m. Nancy Caroline Teague, Oct. 28, 1944; children—Thomas Henry, Winifred (Mrs. Blackwell Pierce), George Franklin, Nancy Caroline, Juliana. Aircraft salesman Piedmont Aviation, Inc., Winston-Salem, 1940, v.p., treas., 1941-43, pres., treas., 1943—; dir., mem. exec. com. Wachovia Corp.; dir. Reliance Universal, Inc., Mid-Continent Telephone Co., Integon Corp., Duke Power Co. Trustee Wake Forest U. Recipient Winston-Salem and N.C. Jr. C. of C. Distinguished Service award, 1954, Frank Davison trophy for outstanding service to aviation in N.C., 1949, Alumni Achievement award U. Ariz., 1976; Tony Jannus award for outstanding service to airline industry, 1980. Mem. Air Transport Assn. (dir.), Nat. Aviation Club, Soaring Soc. Am., Newcomen Soc., Winston-Salem C. of C. (past pres.), Pi Kappa Alpha. Democrat. Baptist. Rotarian. Clubs: Forsyth Country, Old Town (Winston-Salem); Wings (pres.) (N.Y.C.). Home: 1190 Arbor Rd Winston-Salem NC 27104 Office: Smith Reynolds Airport Winston-Salem NC 27102

DAVIS, TRUE, banker; b. St. Joseph, Mo., Dec. 23, 1919; s. Wm. True and Helen (Marstella) D.; student Cornell U., 1937-40; L.H.D., Tarkio Coll., 1963; m. Virginia Bruce Motter, Jan. 24, 1948 (dec. Sept. 1969); children—William True, Bruce Motter, Lance Barrow. Salesman, Anchor Serum Co., South St. Joseph, 1940-42, v.p., sales mgr., 1945-50, pres., 1950-60; pres., dir. Research Labs., Inc., 1952-60, Pet's Best Co., 1954-60; v.p., dir. Phillips Electronics & Pharm. Industries Corp., N.Y.C., 1959-63; pres., dir. Philips-Roxane, Inc., N.Y.C., 1959-63, Med. Industries, Inc., 1956-63, True Davis Founds., Inc., 1956—, Carolina Vet Supply, Inc., Charlotte, N.C., 1956-60, Wilke Labs., Inc., West Plains, Mo., Wilke Labs. of Tenn., Inc., Memphis, 1956-60, Peters Serum Co., Kansas City, 1956-60, Gothic Advt., Inc., St. Joseph, 1956-60, World Health Inst., Ltd., 1958-60, Peerless Serum Co., 1956-60, Certified Labs., Inc., 1956-60, Davis Estate, Inc., Anchor Serum Co. of N.J., 1959-60, Anchor Serum Co. of Ind., 1959-60, Anchor Serum Co. of Minn., 1960-63; chmn. Thompson-Hayward Chem. Co., Kansas City, Mo., 1961-63; chmn., dir. Chemico Labs., Inc., Miami, Fla., 1960-63; U.S. ambassador to Switzerland, 1963-65; asst. sec. U.S. Treasury, 1965-68; U.S. exec. dir. Inter-Am. Devel. Bank, 1966-68; chmn. bd., dir. Nat. Bank Washington, 1968-73, pres., 1970-73; chmn. bd. Tri Internat., Bahamas, 1975—; dir. First Multi-Currency Bond Fund, Inc. Bd. dirs. Animal Health Inst., 1946-59, pres., 1954-56; mem. Nat. Serum Control Agy., 1947-58, chmn., 1954-55; chmn. U.S. Port Security Com., 1966-68, N.Y. Pier Com., 1966-68, Pub. Advisory Com. on Customs Adminstrn., 1966-68. Mem. exec. com. United Fund, 1960; mem. Advisory Council on Naval Affairs, 1958-60. Police commr. St. Joseph, 1949; bd. dirs. Little League, Nat. Assn. Boys' Clubs Am., Agrl. Hall Fame, 1969—; trustee Mo. Valley Coll., 1969-73, Coll. Mt. St. Vincent's, 1969-72, Fleming Coll. and Inst. Fgn. Affairs, Switzerland, 1969-72, Meridian House Found., Washington, 1969-75, Fed. City Council, 1970-74, D.C. chpt. Am. Cancer Soc., 1970-75, Downtown Progress Assn., D.C., 1970-74, Washington Bd. Trade, 1970-74, Am. Sch. in Switzerland, Lugano, 1966—; mem. policy bd. Internat. Health Resource Consortium, 1977—. Served to lt. USNR, 1942-45; chief test pilot Naval Air Sta., Pearl Harbor; lt. USNR. Col. staff Mo. Gov., 1949-54, 60-72, Ky. Gov., 1953. Recipient Boss of Year award St. Joseph Jr. C. of C., 1960; Exceptional Service award U.S. Treasury, 1968. Hon. fellow Consular Law Soc.; mem. NAM (nuclear energy com. 1956-63), N.Y. Acad. Scis. (life), Good Roads Assn. (dir. Jefferson City 1950-63), Am. Royal Assn. (gov. 1960—), Mo. C. of C. (dir. 1963-64), Thoroughbred Owners and Breeders Assn., Am. Legion, V.F.W. (nat. Americanism com., Mo. chmn. Americanism com., outstanding citizen award St. Joseph 1960, Nat. Gold Medal for Americanism 1967), Council on Fgn. Relations, Res. Officers Assn. (hon. life), Am. Soc. for Friendship with Switzerland (hon. life), Phi Gamma Delta. Democrat (active nat. and local). Clubs: Benton (pres. 1949-50), Keeneland, Thoroughbred of Am. (Lexington, Ky.); Minnesouri Angling (pres. Alexandria, Minn.); Met., F St. (Washington). Author: Americanism vs. Communism, 1962; The Partnership Between the Federal Government and American Universities in Financing Scientific Enquiry, 1967. Contbr. articles to various trade and farm publs. Home: 2860 Woodland Dr NW Washington DC 20008

DAVIS, VIRGINIA SUE, gen. contracting co. exec.; b. Buffalo, Mo., Mar. 2, 1936; d. Argus Dee and Gladys Hazel (Gregg) Neill; B.S. in Edn., Southwest Mo. State U., Springfield, 1958; M.S., Central Mo. State U., Warrensburg, 1973; m. Edward Davis, Aug. 8, 1958; 1 dau., Brenda Kay. Tchr., Lee's Summit (Mo.) Jr. High Sch., 1958-68; v.p. Ed Davis Constrn., Inc., Lee's Summit, 1968—. mem. citizen's adv. com. Sch. Bd.; substitute tchr. Lee's Summit Christian Ch. Mem. Mo. State Tchrs. Assn., Phi Kappa Phi. Home: 301 Lincolnwood St Lee's Summit MO 64063 Office: 212 N Main St PO Box 537 Lee's Summit MO 64063

DAVIS, WARREN EARL, assn. exec.; b. Seattle, Apr. 13, 1926; s. Earl A. and Madelyn L. Davis; B.A. in Polit. Sci., U. So. Calif., 1947; M.S. in Bus. Adminstrn., Calif. State U., Sacramento, 1968; m. Kathleen Dale Neely, Oct. 4, 1952; children—Stephen, Pamela, Julie, Jennifer. Ins. underwriter Pacific Indemnity Co., Los Angeles, 1947-51; mgr. prodn. control Aerojet-Gen. Corp., Sacramento, 1959-69; corporate planner Fairchild Camera & Instrument Corp., Mountain View, Calif., 1969-78; dir. research Semicondr. Industry Assn., Cupertino, Calif., 1978—; instr. San Jose (Calif.) State U. Sch. Bus. Served to lt. comdr. USNR, 1944-46, 51-53, 55-59. Mem. World Affairs Council of No. Calif., Army and Navy Club, Phi Delta Theta. Republican. Home: 13682 Manteca Way Saratoga CA 95070

DAVIS, WILLIAM DOYLE, JR., real estate appraiser; b. Kansas City, Mo., Sept. 24, 1934; s. Will D. and Lindalou (Turner) D.; B.S. in Agr., U. Mo., 1956, M.S. in Agrl. Econs., 1957. Partner Appraisal Assos., Kansas City, 1959—; sec.-treas. Farm Mgmt. Assos., Kansas City, 1959—; partner Bittersweet Farm, Kansas City, 1959—; partner Hart Investors, Kansas City, 1972—; instr. various realty assns.; pres., chmn. Agrl. Hall of Fame, 1975—. Served 1st lt. U.S. Army, 1957-59. Mem. Kansas City Jr. C. of C. (pres. 1967-68), Am. Inst. Real Estate Appraisers, Soc. Real Estate Appraisers, Am. Soc. Farm Mgrs. and Rural Appraisers, Internat. Assn. Assessing Officers. Disciples of Christ. Club: Masons. Author: Farm Land Prices in Six Missouri Counties, 1958. Home: Route 20 Kansas City MO 64155 Office: 1004 Baltimore Kansas City MO 64105

DAVISON, DAVID JOSEPH, accountant; b. N.Y.C., Oct. 13, 1934; s. Jack and Lillian (Shaffer) D.; B.S. in Indsl. Engring., Washington U., 1956, M.B.A., 1960; m. Abby Helene Israelow, May 29, 1977; children—Jack, Tracy, Todd, Zara. Instr., Washington U., St. Louis, 1956-58, Lafayette Coll., Easton, Pa., 1958-59; asst. prof. U. P.R., Mayaguez, 1960-62; cons. Govt. of Israel, 1962-64; staff cons. Fox & Co., St. Louis, 1965-71; pvt. practice acctg., St. Louis, 1961-75; mng. partner Davison & Co., C.P.A.'s, Bethalto, Ill., 1975—; vis. prof. acctg. So. Ill. U., Edwardsville, 1975—; dir. Rosewood Investment Corp., Alton, Ill., 1965—. Treas., Jewish Family and Children's Service, St. Louis, 1975-76. Served to 2nd lt. U.S. Army, 1959-60. Recipient Cert. of Merit, Indsl. Mgmt. Soc., 1956; C.P.A., Ill. Mem. Bethalto C. of C. (sec. 1979—), Wood River Twp. C. of C. (dir. 1978—), Am. Inst. C.P.A.'s Mo. Soc. C.P.A.'s, Sigma Xi, Beta Gamma Sigma. Clubs: Lockhaven Country, Rotary, Mason. Home: 1703 Cordell Ct Godfrey IL 62035 Office: 120 Mill St Bethalto IL 62010

DAVISON, STANLEY MARTIN, banker; b. Enderby, B.C., Can., Sept. 12, 1928; s. Ronald and Janet Grace (Livingstone) D.; grad. Banff Sch. Advanced Mfmt., 1967; m. Bette Irene Rusconi, June 12, 1957; children—Loreen Joyce, Diane Janine, Ronald James. With Bank of Montreal, 1947—, mgr., Vancouver, B.C., 1966-68, sr. v.p. Man. and Sask. div., 1968-71, exec. v.p. domestic banking, 1971-73, exec. v.p., gen. mgr. domestic banking 1973-74, exec. v.p., gen. mgr. credits and investments, 1974-76, exec. v.p., chief gen. mgr., 1976—, vice chmn., 1980—. Clubs: Saint James's of Montreal, Royal Montreal Curling, Montreal Badminton and Squash. Home: 669 Belmont Ave Westmount PQ H3Y 2W3 Canada Office: 300 5th Ave SW Suite 3000 Calgary AB T2P 3C4 Canada

DAWKINS, HERBERT PEARCE, oil field equipment exec.; b. Farmerville, La., May 6, 1923; s. Herbert Elmer and Ruth (Webb) D.; B.B.A., La. State U., 1948; m. Marilyn Cecilia Rolleigh, Aug. 22, 1953; children—Kevin Webb, James Philip, Dana Marie. Credit rep. Continental Supply Co., Houston, 1948-55; regional credit mgr. Continental-Emsco Co., Houston, 1955-61, asst. treas., Dallas, 1961-74, v.p. treasury and credit, 1974—; treas. Continental Emsco Co., C.A., Continental Emsco Internat., Inc., Continental Emsco Co. Ltd. (Can.), Continental Supply Co.; treas., dir. Continental Emsco Co. de Mex. S.A. de C.V.; asst. treas. LTV Tubular Services, Inc. Served to lt. (j.g.), USNR, 1943-46. Mem. Petroleum Equipment Suppliers Assn., Ind. Petroleum Assn. Am., Am. Petroleum Inst., Dallas Petroleum Club. Republican. Presbyterian. Office: 1810 Commerce St PO Box 359 Dallas TX 75221

DAWLEY, PATRICIA KELLY, fin. exec.; b. Seattle, July 27, 1937; d. Gail W. and Edith L. (Moore) K.; B.A., U. Wash., 1959; M.B.A., N.Y. U., 1979. With Anchor Savs. Bank, N.Y.C., 1967—, exec. v.p., sec., 1977—. Mem. Nat. Assn. Bank Women, AAUW, Delta Gamma. Office: 404 Fifth Ave New York NY 10018

DAWSON, ALEC BRUCE, counting, controlling and rec. devices mfg. co. exec.; b. San Mateo, Calif., Nov. 6, 1937; s. Lawrence G. and Alta G. (Stewart) D.; B.A., Harvard U., 1959; M.B.A., U. Hartford, 1966; m. Nancy Marshall Morton, Mar. 23, 1959; children—Bruce Stewart, David Anthony, Anne Marshall. Sales exec. Ins. Co. N.Am., Boston, 1959-60, Los Angeles, 1960-63, Hartford, Conn., 1963-66; with Veeder-Root and subsidiaries, 1966—, mng. dir. Veeder-Root Ltd., Dundee, Scotland, 1973-77, also dir., v.p. internat. div., Hartford, 1977—. Republican. Club: Univ. (Hartford). Home: 3 Eagle Ln Simsbury CT 06070 Office: 28 Sargeant St Hartford CT 06102

DAWSON, DAVID LLOYD, bus. exec., Republican nat. committeeman; b. Seattle, May 25, 1943; s. Opie Lloyd and Margaret Charlotte (Lash) D.; B.C.S. in Accounting, Seattle U., 1967; M.S. in Mgmt. Sci., Stevens Inst. Tech., 1971; postgrad. N.Y. U., 1977—; m. Nedra Marie Boyle, Feb. 16, 1963; children—Deanna, Annette, Janine, Patricia. Systems analyst Sea-Land Service, Inc., Elizabeth, N.J., 1967-71, dir. systems devel., 1971-75; dir. mgmt. info. div. Berkey Photo Inc., N.Y.C., 1975-76; dir. info. services United States Lines, Inc., N.Y.C., 1976-78, exec. mgmt. services, 1978-79; dir. systems and computer services, research and devel. Matson Navigation Co., San Francisco, 1979—; tchr. data processing related courses, 1971-75; mem. devel. group shipping operation info. systems and internat. data communications systems Maritime Adminstrn., Dept. Commerce. Mem. Republican Nat. Com. Mem. Nat. Com. Internat. Trade, Documentation Data Coordinating Com., Data Processing Mgmt. Assn., Am. Mgmt. Assn., Nat. Assn. Watch and Clock Collectors, Stevens Inst. Alumni Assn. Republican. Roman Catholic. Clubs: Commonwealth of Calif., Concord Sportman's. Home: 232 Clyde Dr Walnut Creek CA 94598 Office: 333 Market St San Francisco CA 94119

DAWSON, EDWARD JOSEPH, merger and acquisition co. exec.; b. Rochester, Pa., Apr. 1, 1944; s. Ralph Edward and Evelyn May (Riggle) D.; B.S. in Indsl. Mgmt., Carnegie Inst. Tech., 1966; M.B.A. in Fin., U. Chgo., 1968; m. Lynda Sue Weir, 1975; 5 children. Computer systems analyst, corporate fin. analyst, Tex. Instruments Corp., Dallas, 1968-70, product planning mgr. digital systems div., 1970-72, mgr. comml. equipment bus. objective, 1972-74, program mgr. electronic clocks and watches, 1974, mgr. mktg. electronic watch div., 1975-76, mgr. mktg. home video systems, 1976-77; sr. v.p. ops. and mktg. Resources Unltd. Co., Dallas, 1977-80, exec. v.p. merger ops., 1980—. Pres., coach Coppell Elementary Sch Basketball Team, Coppell, Tex., 1975-78. Lic. security broker/dealer, real estate broker. Mem. Omicron Delta Kappa, Beta Theta Pi. Mem. Church of Christ. Home: 1634 Choteau Grapevine TX 76051 Office: 1111 W Mockingbird Ln Suite 737 Dallas TX 75247

DAWSON, HANES MOORE, oil co. exec.; b. Ardmore, Okla., Aug. 31, 1918; s. David Hepburn and Pearle Juanita (Moore) D.; B.S., U. Okla., 1940; m. Jovan McCullough, July 5, 1941; 1 son, Hanes Moore. With Continental Oil Co., 1947-67, regional landman, Los Angeles, 1958-62, mgr. property acquisitions, Denver, 1962-67; owner Dawson Oil Properties, Denver, 1967—. Served with AUS, 1941-46. Mem. Am., Denver assns. petroleum landmen, Ind. Producers Assn. Am., Rocky Mountain Oil and Gas Assn., Nat., Colo., Denver bds. realtors, SAR, Okla. U. Alumni Assn., Sigma Chi. Republican. Presbyn. (deacon, elder). Clubs: Masons, Shriners, Jesters; Red Cross Constantine; Twenty Six (dir., past pres.), Pinehurst Country ;Denver Petroleum (dir., past pres.). Office: 1340 1st Nat Bank Bldg Denver CO 80293

DAWSON, JOHN HOWEL, investment dealer; b. Evanston, Ill., Dec. 30, 1944; s. John Albert and Annie Joe (Howel) D.; B.A., Oberlin Coll., 1967. Controller John A. Dawson & Co., Chgo., 1971; v.p. Charles H. Eldredge & Co., Chgo., 1971-72; pres. John Dawson & Assos., Inc., Chgo., 1972—; mem. Midwest Stock Exchange, 1981—. Mem. Chgo. Bicentennial Commn., 1973, Rogers Park Community Council. Served to lt. USN, 1968-71; lt. comdr. Res. Mem. Nat. Assn. Securities Dealers, Inc., Chgo. Assn. Commerce and Industry, U.S. C. of C., Chgo. Hist. Soc., Ill. Soc. Mayflower Descs., Ill. SAR, Soc. Colonial Wars, Naval Res. Assn., U.S. Naval Inst. Baptist. Club: Executives. Home: 7447 N Ashland Ave Chicago IL 60626 Office: 1 N La Salle St Chicago IL 60602

DAWSON, SAMUEL COOPER, JR., motel co. exec.; b. Alexandria, Va., Sept. 21, 1909; s. Samuel Cooper and Edna French (Horner) D.; grad. Episcopal High Sch., Alexandria, 1928; B.A. in Commerce, U. Va., 1932; m. Frances Margaret Boatwright, Mar. 24, 1945; children—Samuel Cooper III, Marion Boatwright. Tchr. sci. St. Christopher's Sch., Richmond, Va., 1932-36; underwriter Md. Casualty Co., Balt., 1936-39; mgr. Penn-Daw Motor Hotel, Alexandria, 1939-73; pres. Penn-Daw Hotels Corp., Alexandria, 1960-73, Penn-Daw Shopping Center, Alexandria, 1958-72; owner, operator Camp Alleghany for Girls, Lewisburg, W.Va.; bus. mgr. Episcopal High Sch. Past pres. Va. Travel Council. Served with USNR, 1942-46; capt. Res.; group comdr. 47 res. units Washington area. Recipient Hall of Fame award Hospitality magazine, 1961; Distinguished Service award Am. Motor Hotel Assn., 1964. Mem. Am. Automobile Assn. (past chmn. No. Va. adv. bd.), Va. Hotel Assn. (past pres.), Va. Motel Assn. (past pres.), Alexandria Jr. C. of C. (past pres.; Outstanding Young Man award 1942), Washington (past pres.), Nat. (dir.) restaurant assns., Am. Motor Hotel Assn. (past pres., chmn. legislative affairs com.), Washington Civil War Round Table, S.A.R. (past pres. George Washington chpt.). Episcopalian. Club: Army Navy Country (Arlington, Va.). Home: 206 N Quaker Ln Alexandria VA 22304 Office: PO Box 56 Alexandria VA 22313

DAY, G(EORGE) DAVID, banker; b. Ashtabula, Ohio, Feb. 20, 1930; s. George Frederic and Beulah (Hammond) D.; student Hanover Coll., 1947-49; B.S. in Bus. Adminstrn., Ind. U., 1951; m. Julia Ann Wurster, May 25, 1958; 1 dau., Diane Michelle. Statistician, FMC Corp., Indpls., 1951-52; sales engr. A.B. Dick Co., Indpls., 1952-54; sales rep. Champion Spark Plug Co., Terre Haute, Ind., 1954-56; market analyst Stellite div. Union Carbide Corp., Kokomo, Ind., 1956-62; sr. market analyst A.E. Staley Mfg. Co., Decatur, Ill., 1962-65; exec. v.p., dir. Andec Corp., Decatur, 1965-66; exec. v.p., dir. Midstate Machinery Co., Inc., Decatur, 1965-66; v.p. marketing Citizens Nat. Bank Decatur, 1966-67, v.p. data processing, 1968, v.p. operations, 1969-70, v.p. planning, 1971-73, v.p. automated services, 1974-80, v.p. and controller, 1981—. Instr. bus. statistics Ind. U., 1957. Adviser, Jr. Achievement, Kokomo, 1960-61; chmn. small bus. industry sect. Millikin U. capital fund drive, 1966. Vice chmn. Macon County and 22d Congl. Dist. Citizens for Goldwater, 1964. Bd. dirs. Kokomo Community Concerts, 1956-60, treas., 1957-58. Mem. Am. Marketing Assn., Decatur C. of C. (treas. 1967-68), Am. Bankers Assn., Bank Marketing Assn., Bank Adminstrn. Inst., Assn. for Modern Banking in Ill. (vice chmn. consumer banking div. 1973-74), Phi Delta Theta. Republican. Episcopalian. Rotarian. Club: Decatur. Home: 601 S Monroe St Decatur IL 62522 Office: Landmark Mall Decatur IL 62525

DAY, JOHN DENTON, wholesale indsl. sales co. exec.; b. Salt Lake City, Jan. 20, 1942; s. George W. and Grace (Denton) J.; student U. Utah, 1964-65; B.A. in Econs. and Bus. Adminstrn., Westminster Coll., 1971; m. Susan Hansen, June 20, 1971; 1 dau., Tammy Denton. With Mil. Data Cons., Inc., Los Angeles, 1961-62, Carlseon Credit Corp., Salt Lake City, 1962-65; sales mgr. sporting goods Western Enterprises, Salt Lake City, 1965-69, Western rep. PBR Co., Cleve., 1969-71: dist. sales rep. Crown Zellerbach Corp., Seattle and Los Angeles, 1971-73; pres. Dapco paper, chem., instl. food and janitorial supplies, Salt Lake City, 1973-79; dist. sales mgr. Surfonics Engrs., Inc., Woods Cross, Utah, 1976-78; rancher Rockin D Ranch, Heber, Utah, 1976—; owner, pres. John D. Day—Mfg. Reps., 1974—; dist. sales mgr. Garland Co. Inc.; sec. bd. Acquadyne, 1974-77. Group chmn. Tele-Dex fund raising project Westminster Coll. Served with U.S. Army, 1963-64. Recipient grand nat. award for engring. design and craftmanship Internat. Custom Car Show, San Diego, 1962; Key to City, Louisville, 1964. Mem. Internat. Show Car Assn. (co-chmn.), Am. Quarter Horse Assn., Utah Quarter Horse Assn. (amateur reining champion 1979), Intermountain Quarter Horse Assn. (amateur reining champion 1979), Intermountain Reining Assn. Home: care Rocken D Ranch RFD 1 Box 4 Heber UT 84032 Office: 1876 S Main St Salt Lake City UT 84115

DAY, LYMAN ROBERT, hosp. engr.; b. Fitchburg, Mass., Apr. 23, 1933; s. Odlin Hicks and Irene Cecelia (Mason) D.; B.S. in Aero. Engring., Ind. Inst. Tech., 1960; grad. Air Command and Staff Coll., 1974, Indsl. Coll. Armed Forces, 1976; m. Dorothy Elinor Reinking, May 5, 1956; children—Jonathan, Jennifer, Christopher, Benjamin. Engr., Bliss-Portland, Inc., South Portland, Maine, 1960-64, Pratt & Whitney Aircraft, East Hartford, Conn., 1964-68, Dynamic Controls Corp., South Windsor, Conn., 1968-72, Baystate Med. Center, Springfield, Mass., 1974—. Served with USAF, 1950-54, 72-73; lt. col. Res. Mem. Am. Soc. Hosp. Engrs., Res. Officers Assn. U.S., Nat. Rifle Assn. (life). Republican. Lutheran. Office: 759 Chestnut St Springfield MA 01107

DAY, MARIAN MCDONAGH, real estate exec.; b. Saginaw, Mich., Nov. 27, 1907; d. Thomas Blakely and Eleanor (Hill) McDonagh; B.S. in Home Econs., Mich. State U., 1931; m. John Edward Day, Aug. 25, 1934; children—Thomas, Patricia, John E. II, Marilyn J. Partner John Day Constrn. Co., Saginaw, 1947-65; founder, partner John Day Realty, Saginaw, 1955-76; dir., sec. treas. John Day Co., Saginaw, 1966-74, Brokers Investment Inc., Saginaw, 1968-73; dir., v.p. Saginaw Leasing Corp., 1967-72. Chmn. edn. com., bd. dirs. Women's Nat. Farm and Garden Club, Saginaw, 1963-67; co-developer real estate curriculum Delta Coll., Bay City, Mich., 1970, mem. edn. com. real estate, 1958-76. Named Realtor of Year, Saginaw Bd. Realtors, 1967. Mem. Mich. Real Estate Assn. (chmn. edn. com. 1968), Saginaw Bd. Realtors (dir. 1965-71, v.p. 1971), D.A.R. (dir. 1959-62), Home Econ. Alumni Assn. Mich. State U. (dir. 1959-65), Real Estate Alumni U. Mich. (dir. 1966-72), Soc. Mayflower Descs., Nat. Soc. Colonial Daus. 17th Century, Omicron Nu. Roman Catholic. Club: Saginaw Culture. Home: 1810 Short Rd Saginaw MI 48603 Office: 3095 Cabaret Saginaw MI 48603

DAY, MARY WINIFRED GARVEY (MRS. GEORGE EARL DAY), realtor; b. Chgo., May 5, 1932; d. William and Mary Patricia (Kennedy) Garvey; student U. Tex., 1971, Richland Coll., 1972-73, 77-78; m. George Earl Day, Jan. 15, 1955; children—Patricia Ann, Shawn Michael, Kathleen Mary. Asso. editor Bell Telephone Labs, White Sands Missile Range, N.Mex., 1961-67; city editor Richardson (Tex.) Daily News, 1968; dir. pub. relations Drs. Hosp. Found., Dallas, 1969-72; owner Mary Day/Media Design, Richardson,

1972-75; realtor Henry S. Miller Co., Dallas, 1975-77, Ebby Halliday Inc., Dallas, 1978—. Recipient Key to City Corpus Christi (Tex.), 1971. Mem. Nat. Fedn. Press Women (dir. 1970-71), Women in Communications (dir. 1973-74), Am., Tex. socs. hosp. pub. relations dirs., Profl. Photographers Am., Tex. Press Women (dir. 1966-73), Tex., Nat. assns. realtors, Greater Dallas Bd. Realtors, Women's Council Realtors, Tex. Pub. Relations Assn., Dallas Hosp. Council (mem. pub. relations com. 1969-72). Roman Catholic (bd. dirs. ch. 1974—). Clubs: Canyon Creek Country (Richardson); Press (Dallas). Home: 1614 Baltimore Dr Richardson TX 75081 Office: 14841 Coit Rd Dallas TX 75248

DAY, MAXIE STEPHEN, paper co. exec.; b. Bismarck, N.D., Apr. 29, 1942; s. Maxie N. and Dorothy V. (Anderson) D.; B.S., U.S. Naval Acad., 1964; student Northwestern Sch. Law, 1974-75; m. Haroldeen C. Wiley, Feb. 14, 1967; children—Kelley Katherine, Michael Frederick. Commd. ensign U.S. Navy, 1964, advanced through grades to lt., 1969; supply officer and main battery gun control USS Hull, South China Sea, 1965-67; dir. requirements (purchasing) Naval Supply Center, Long Beach, 1968-69; ret., 1969; mgr. systems research Zellerbach Paper Co., San Francisco, 1969-70, mgr. computer operations, 1971-72, mgr. adminstrn., Portland, 1973-75; corporate merger coordinator Crown Zellerbach Stationers Distributing Co., Ft. Worth, Tex., 1976-77; merchandising mgr. Zellerbach Paper Co., Phoenix, 1978, mgr. operating dept. So. region, Los Angeles, 1979-80, mgr. resale office products NW region, Portland, Oreg., 1980—. Mem. Nat. Assn. Bus. Economists, Naval Acad. Alumni Assn., Nat. Purchasing Mgmt. Assn. Democrat. Roman Catholic. Club: K. of C. Home: 31 Alondra Irvine CA 92714 Office: 9111 NE Columbia Blvd Portland OR 97220

DEACON, GORDON KENNETH, mgmt. cons.; b. Markham, Ont., Can., June 26, 1943; s. Kenneth Emmerson and Mary Grace (Perkin) D.; B.Sc. in Engring., U. Guelph (Ont.), 1967. With Ont. Hydro Co., London, 1967-73, mktg. exec., 1967-68, agrl. sales supr., 1968-73; asst. v.p. prodn. Simmons Ltd., Bramalea, Ont., 1974-75; pres. Mgmt. Sci. Research Assos., Toronto, Ont., 1975—; mgr. internat. sales and mktg. Cord Industries Ltd., Toronto, 1979—; lectr. farm power Centralia Coll. Agrl. Tech., Huron Park, Ont. Registered profl. engr., Ont. Mem. Assn. Profl. Engrs. Ont., Am., Canadian socs. agrl. engring., Engring. Inst. Can. Club: High Park Ski (v.p., dir. Skiing). Home: Glenburn Farms Unionville ON L3R 2G7 Canada Office: 304-44 Eglinton Ave W Toronto ON M4R 1A1 Canada

DEAN, FREDERICK, lawyer, holding co. exec.; b. N.Y.C., Sept. 21, 1927; s. Fred Carl and Loretta (Dolloff) D.; grad. Fordham Prep. Sch., 1945; B.A., Columbia U., 1950, J.D., 1953. Admitted to N.Y. bar, 1953; asso. firm Palmer and Serles, N.Y.C., 1953-59; atty. Equity Corp., N.Y.C., 1959-61; v.p., dir. Atlas Gen. Industries, Inc., 1961-64; pres. Coordinated Apparel, Inc., N.Y.C., 1967—; chmn. bd. Roydon Wear, Inc., N.Y.C., 1966—, Am. Argo Corp., N.Y.C., 1972—; chmn. exec. com. of bd. overseers Group 800 N.V. Served with AC, USNR, 1946-48. Club: Marco Polo (N.Y.C.). Home: Durham PA 18039 Office: 90 Park Ave New York NY 10016

DEAN, GEORGE W., oil co. exec.; b. Weston, W.Va., May 1, 1928; s. George W. and Amy Ellen (Wimer) D.; B.S. in Chem. Engring., 1950; m. Beatrice Adams, June 7, 1949; children—Judith, Michael, Gregory. Coal gasification researcher U.S. Bur. Mines, Morgantown, W.Va., 1949-50; various engring. positions Allied Chem. Corp., Hopewell, Va., 1950-57; with Gulf Oil and subs., 1957—, with Gulf Research & Devel., Pitts., 1957-61, various positions Gulf Chems., Pitts., 1961-67, crude oil sales mgr., Pitts., 1967-70; v.p. Gulf S. Asia, Singapore, 1970-72; v.p., regional mgr. Gulf Oil Trading, Tokyo, 1972-74; exec. v.p. Gulf Internat. Trading, Pitts., 1974-77; v.p. China trade devel., gen. mgr. project devel. Gulf Trading & Transp., 1977—; dir. Haroon Oils, 1970-72, Tsing Yi Bridge Co., Hong Kong; officer, dir. subs. Mem. Am. Mgmt. Assn., Am. Copper Council, Internat. Execs. Assn., Am. Inst. Chem. Engrs. Clubs: Pitts.; Tokyo Fgn. Corrs. Patentee miscellaneous processes.

DEAN, NORMAN M., banker; b. Heber City, Utah, Apr. 26, 1920; A.B., U. Utah, 1942; m. Bonnie Brown Dean, Sept. 6, 1971; children—Thomas, Stacey, Virginia. With Hibbs Clothing Co., 1946-57; exec. v.p. United Bank of Greeley (Colo.), 1957-64, pres., 1964—, chmn. bd.; dir. United Banks of Colo., 1st Nat. Mont. Bank. Chmn. bd. dirs. Geriatrics, Inc.; bd. dirs. U. No. Colo. Found.; treas. Longs Peak council Boy Scouts Am.; 19—; pres. Bd. Edn., Sch. Dist. #6, Greeley; mem. Community Corrections Bd. Served with U.S. Navy. Mem. Colo. Bankers Assn. (dir.), Greeley Assn. Comml. Banks (past pres.), Am. Bankers Assn. (past state v.p.), Found. Comml. Banks (past trustee), Greeley C. of C. Congregationalist. Clubs: Greeley Country, Elks. Office: 1000 10th St Greeley CO 80631

DEAN, ROBERT HAL, food co. exec.; b. Mitchell, S.D., June 27, 1916; s. Bernie Bonney and Edna May (Halladay) D.; B.A., Grinnell Coll., 1938; m. Doris Reger, Sept. 28, 1940; children—Donna (Mrs. Tom Doan), David; m. 2d, Gale H. Mullen, May 26, 1979. Mgr., Checkerboard Elevator Co., Buffalo, 1941-43; mgr. Ralston Purina Co., Circleville, Ohio, 1943-45; grain div., St. Louis, 1945-58, pres. internat. div., St. Louis, 1958-61, v.p. of co., asst. to pres., 1958-61, exec. v.p., dir., 1961-64, pres., chief operations officer, 1964-68, pres., 1968-69, chmn. bd., chief exec. officer, 1968—. Home: 4 Devon Rd Glendale MO 63122 Office: 835 S 8th St St Louis MO 63102

DEANE, FREDERICK, JR., banker; b. Boston, Aug. 5, 1926; s. Frederick and Julia (Coolidge) D.; M.B.A., Harvard, 1951; m. Dorothy Legge, Dec. 21, 1948; children—Dorothy Porcher, Eleanor Dodds, Frederick III. With Bank of Va. and Bank of Va. Co., Richmond, 1953—, now chmn. bd. and chief exec. officer of both; dir. CSX Corp., Marriott Corp., MasterCard Internat., Inc. Bd. dirs. Va. Mus. Found., Va. Found. of Ind. Colls., Federated Arts Council of Richmond, Va. Diocesan Center; trustee funds Protestant Episcopal Ch., Diocese of Va.; trustee Westminster-Canterbury Found.; mem. Conf. Bd., chmn. So. Regional Council. Served to 1st lt. U.S. Army, 1944-47, 1951-53. Mem. Richmond Soc. Financial Analysts (pres. 1963-64), Nat. Fedn. Financial Analysts Socs., Assn. Registered Bank Holding Cos. (chmn. 1979-80), Assn. Res. City Bankers. Republican. Episcopalian. Clubs: Harvard of Virginia (pres. 1969-70, v.p. 1960, pres. Bus. Sch. sect. 1960); Brook, Harvard (N.Y.C.); Metropolitan (Washington); Commonwealth, Country of Va., Hasty Pudding Inst. of 1770; Farmington Country (Charlottesville, Va.); Mid-Ocean (Bermuda). Home: 110 W Hillcrest Ave Richmond VA 23226 Office: 11011 W Broad St Rd Richmond VA 23260

DEANE, THOMAS ANDERSEN, banker; b. Los Angeles, Mar. 20, 1921; s. Thomas Clarke D. and Dorothy (Milbach) D.; B.A., Pomona Coll., 1942; M.B.A., Stanford U., 1948; m. Margaret Louise Noble, June 21, 1947; children—James C., William A. With Bank of Am. Nat. Trust & Savs. Assn., Los Angeles, 1948—, exec. v.p., 1974—. Trustee St. John's Hosp., Santa Monica, Pomona Coll. Served with USMC, 1943-46. Mem. Am. Inst. Banking (pres. Los Angeles chpt. 1961-62), Calif. Bankers Assn. (pres. 1978-79), Nat. Fgn. Trade Council, Assn. Res. City Bankers. Clubs: California, Los Angeles Country. Office: Bank of Am 555 S Flower St Los Angeles CA 90071

DEANGELIS, PETER, chem. co. exec.; b. N.Y.C., Apr. 4, 1929; s. Gilbert and Claudine DeA.; B.A. in Chemistry, Hofstra U., 1950; m. Gloria Cambria, Sept. 9, 1953; children—Steven, Lisa, Julia, Peter, Douglas. Shift supr. FMC Corp., Charleston, W.Va., 1956-66, area supt., 1966-67; project mgr. IMC Chlor-Alkali Inc., Orrington, Maine, 1967-69, plant mgr., 1969-71; plant mgr. Sobin Chems., Inc., Orrington, 1971-74, v.p., gen. mgr., 1974-76, gen. mgr., 1977—; pres. Internat. Minerals and Chem. Corp. chmn. pollution abatement task force Chlorine Inst., guest speaker, plant mgrs. seminar, New Orleans, 1974; dir. United Bank of Bangor (Maine). Bd. dirs. Eastern Maine Med. Center, United Fund, 1968-74, Pres. Cup, 1972, chmn. United Way campaign, 1977-78. Served with USAF, 1951-56. Mem. Am. Chem. Soc., Am. Mgmt. Assn. Roman Catholic. Patentee pollution control system for mercury removal from water. Home: RFD 1 Orrington ME 04474 Office: PO Box 149 Orrington ME 04474

DEANS, JAMES ELLIOTT, JR., elec. engr.; b. Velasco, Tex., July 18, 1943; s. James Elliott and Lura Finley (Coffey) D.; A.B., Austin Coll., 1965; B.S. in Elec. Engring., U. Tex., 1966, M.S. in Elec. Engring. (NDEA fellow), 1968, Ph.D., 1972; m. Catherine Upshaw, June 25, 1966; children—Christine, Emily. With Tex. Instruments Digital Systems, 1967—, design engr., Austin, Tex., 1967-70, systems engr., 1970-73, project mgr. first vector computer and advanced sci. computer installed Advanced Ballistic Missile Def. Agency, Huntsville, Ala., 1973, project mgr. Naval Research Lab. vector computer, 1976, mgr. data communications hardware devel. 990 computer systems, Austin, 1978—. Registered profl. engr., Tex. Mem. IEEE, Assn. Computing Machinery, Tau Beta Pi, Eta Kappa Nu, Phi Kappa Phi. Unitarian. Contbr. papers to publs. in field. Home: 9402 Clearock St Austin TX 78750 Office: PO Box 2909 Austin TX 78767

DEARBORN, BARRY GEORGE, sales and mktg. exec.; b. Milford, Conn., Apr. 29, 1941; s. George Martin and Bernice Kelley D.; student U. Conn., 1959-62; B.S. in Bus. Adminstrn., U. Md., 1964; m. Judith Watson, Apr. 5, 1975; children—Dewitt Barry, Kelley Cochran, Kerrey Watson. Communications cons. So. New Eng. Telephone, New Haven, 1965; western regional mgr. Electronic Futures, Inc., North Haven, Conn., 1965-68; dir. marketing H C Electronics, Tiburon, Calif., 1968-71; div. sales mgr. Avon Products, N.Y.C., 1971-74; nat. sales mgr. Rusco Electronics, Inc., Glendale, Calif., 1974-79; mktg. mgr. Wyle Distbn. Group, Wyle Labs., El Segundo, Calif., 1979-80, dir. sales, 1980—. Served with USAF, 1962-65. Recipient Certificate of Appreciation, Internat. Security Conf., 1978. Mem. Am. Soc. Indsl. Security, Am. Mgmt. Assn., Nat. Mfg. Mktg. Bd., Sales and Mktg. Execs. Los Angeles, Nat. Assn. Coll. Aux. Services. Republican. Clubs: Masons (Thomaston, Conn.); U.S. Senatorial. Office: 124 Maryland St El Segundo CA 90245

DEARDEN, WILLIAM EDGAR CHAMBERS, chocolate co. exec.; b. Phila., Sept. 14, 1922; s. William Edgar Chambers and Nellie (Maloney) D.; B.S. in Economics, Albright Coll., 1944, LL.D., 1974; postgrad. Harvard Bus. Sch., 1944-45, Temple U., 1953-54; m. Mary Kline, July 10, 1944; children—Bonnie Lynne, Pamela Kay. Sales rep. Dun & Bradstreet, Inc., Reading, Pa., 1946-50, mgr., Trenton, N.J., 1950-51; asst. bus. mgr. Milton Hershey Sch., Hershey, Pa., 1953-57, bd. mgrs., 1964—; with Hershey Foods Corp., 1957—, dir. sales and mktg., 1965-67, v.p. sales and mktg., 1967-71, group v.p., 1971-76, vice chmn., chief exec. officer, 1976—, also dir.; dir. Carpenter Tech. Corp., Sterling Drug Inc., Dun & Bradstreet Corp., Hershey Trust Co. Bd. mgrs. M.S. Hershey Found., 1964—; trustee Albright Coll., 1965—, also 2d v.p., mem. exec. com., nat. chmn. Years of Challenge capital campaign, 1974—; bd. dirs. Horatio Alger Orgn., 1978—; nat. food mfg. chmn. U.S. Indsl. Payroll Savs. Commn., 1980. Served to lt. USNR, 1943-46, 51-53. Named Alumnus of Yr., Milton Hershey Sch., 1964; Dean of Confectionery Mfg. Industry, 1972; recipient Giant of the Industry award, 1971; Disting. Alumnus award Albright Coll., 1975; Horatio Alger award, 1976; Tobacco Industry Hall of Fame award, 1978; Disting. Pennsylvanian award, 1980; Mem. Grocery Mfrs. Am. (dir.). Clubs: Masons (past pres. Hershey Shrine Club), Rotary (past pres. Hershey), Econ. of N.Y. Home: 405 Homestead Rd Hershey PA 17033 Office: Hershey Foods Corp 100 Mansion Rd E Hershey PA 17033

DEARDORFF, MARK ENGLE, civil engr.; b. Burbank, Calif., June 10, 1953; s. Harry Floyd and Sally (Swearingen) D.; B.S. in Civil Engring., U. So. Calif., 1975; M.B.A., San Diego State U., 1976; m. Pamela Ann Hofrath. Research asst. U. So. Calif., 1975-76; partner Deardorff & Deardorff, San Diego, 1976-78, pres., 1978—. Mem. resolutions com. Republican State Central Com. Calif., 1974—; mem. San Diego County Rep. Central Com., 1977—. Registered profl. engr., Calif. Mem. San Diego C. of C. (mem. research com. 1977—), ASCE, Structural Engrs. Assn., Nat. Soc. Profl. Engrs. (v.p. San Diego chpt.), David M. Wilson Assos. (dir. 1975—), Chi Epsilon. Lutheran. Clubs: Optimists (dir. 1977—), San Diego Trojan (dir. 1977—). Home: 4522 Caminito Cristalino San Diego CA 92117 Office: 9903 Businesspark Ave San Diego CA 92131

DEARING, RICHARD HALL, waste water treatment equipment mfg. co. exec.; b. Montclair, N.J., Aug. 22, 1946; s. Rogers Kennedy and Jean Hall Dearing; B.S. in Econs. and Bus. Adminstrn., Wagner Coll., 1971; m. Mary McKenna, Oct. 20, 1979. Asst. money mgr. Harris Co., N.Y.C., 1972-74; sales rep. H.D. Lee Co., Kansas City, Kans., 1974-76; exec. v.p., treas., dir. Kucher Dearing, Inc., Clinton, N.J., 1976—. Served with U.S. Army, 1966-69; Vietnam. Mem. Associated Builders and Contractors Assn., Wagner Coll. Vets. Assn. Republican. Presbyterian. Home: RD 3 Box 57 Washington NJ 07882 Office: Kucher Dearing Inc 5 Old Route 22 Clinton NJ 08809

DE ARMOND, RAYMOND TOLLIVER, JR., trade and tech. sch. exec.; b. Louisville, June 26, 1942; s. Raymond Tolliver and Ruth Vivian (Wilson) DeA.; B.S. in Indsl. Mgmt., Samford U., 1965; m. Barbara Ross, Aug. 29, 1964; children—David Robert, Elizabeth Jane. Asst. supr. acctg. U.S. Pipe & Foundry Co., Birmingham, Ala., 1965-67, supr. sales acctg., 1967-72, bus. analysis, 1972-75; dir. Herzing Inst., Birmingham, 1976-79, v.p., regional dir., 1979—. Served with U.S. Army, 1966-72. Mem. Ala. Assn. Pvt. Colls. and Tech. Schs. (founder, pres. 1979—), Nat. Assn. Trade and Tech. Schs., Assn. Ind. Colls. and Schs., Ga. Pvt. Sch. Assn., Data Processing Mgmt. Assn., Am. Mgmt. Assn. Baptist. Home: 2772 Brookcliff Landing Marietta GA 30062 Office: 120 Ralph McGill Blvd NE Atlanta GA 30308

DEATON, CHARLES, architect, indsl. designer; b. Clayton, N.Mex., Jan. 1, 1921; s. Charles Elmer and Nina Maude (Utter D.; ed. pub. schs.; children—Robert Earle, Claudia, Charlee, Snow. Aircraft illustrator, engr. Lockheed Aircraft Corp., Burbank, Cal., 1941-42, Curtis-Wright Corp., St. Louis, 1942-43; pvt. practice architecture and indsl. design, Chgo. 1943-44, N.Y.C., 1944-49, St. Louis, 1951-55, Denver, 1955—; prin. archtl. works include Wyo. Nat. Bank, Casper, 1962, sculptured house, Denver, 1965, Sports Complex Kansas City, Mo. (asso. with Kivett & Myers), 1967; prin. indsl. design includes bank vault equipment, office furniture, comml. lighting equipment; chief designer Bank Bldg. Corp., St. Louis, 1949-52; tchr. design Franklin Sch. Profl. Arts, N.Y.C., 1946-49. Patentee in field. Office: Genesee Mountain Golden CO 80401

DEAVERS, CLYDE JEROME, mfg. co. exec.; b. Corpus Christi, Tex., Apr. 23, 1924; s. Clyde Jerome and Stacie (Tackett) D.; B.M.E., U. Md., 1950; postgrad. Union Coll., 1955; m. Jean Neff Cousins, July 8, 1949; children—Patricia, Nancy, Judith. Mgr. mech. devel. Gen. Electric Research and Devel. Center, Schenectady, 1950-60, mgr. indsl. systems engring., med. systems div., Milw., 1962-69; mgr. product engring. Hotpoint Kitchen Appliance Co., Milw., 1960-62; v.p.-engring. Rotron, Inc., Woodstock, N.Y., 1969-73, v.p./gen. mgr. comml. products div., 1973-80, sr. v.p., group exec. comml. cooling products group, 1980—. Bd. dirs. Council of Industry of Southeastern N.Y.; mem. advisory bd. Ulster County Community Coll.; active Boy Scouts Am., 1971-74. Served to capt. USAF, 1942-46. Decorated D.F.C., Air medal with oak leaf clusters, Purple Heart. Registered profl. engr., Wis. Mem. ASME, Am. Product and Inventory Control Soc., Am. Mgmt. Assn., Tau Beta Pi, Phi Kappa Phi. Republican. Author: Fundamentals of X-Ray Generation and Application, 1965. Patentee in field. Home: 1 Cannon Circle Woodstock NY 12498 Office: 7 Hasbrouck Ln Woodstock NY 12498

DE BAKEY, MICHEL IBRAHIM, bus. cons.; b. Beiruth, June 13, 1947; s. Ibrahim Michel and Rosette Marie (Najjar) DeB.; H.E.C., Institut Superieur de Commerce Saint Louis, Brussels, 1973; B.S., York Coll. of Pa., 1975; M.B.A. (Scottish Rite fellow, grad. teaching fellow Sch. Govt. and Bus. Adminstrn. 1975-76), George Washington U., 1976; m. Joan Lyn Frick, July 15, 1972. With Lebanese Fgn. Service, Lebanese Embassy, Brussels, 1973; v.p. Cargo Ship Internat. Corp., Washington, 1977-78; v.p. internat. ops. Rema Inc. subs. Allerton Resources, Inc., Cin., 1978; instr. bus. adminstrn. and mktg. Prince George's Community Coll., 1977-81; cons. internat. bus., Chevy Chase, Md., 1979—. Mem. European C. of C. of Brussels (dir.), Soc. Advancement Mgmt., Am. Mgmt. Assn., Assn. M.B.A. Execs. Address: 4515 Willard Ave Chevy Chase MD 20015

DE BAROLET, FRANÇOIS, banker; b. Mulhouse, France, Aug. 5, 1933; s. Gerard and Marie-Madeleine de B.; student Hautes Etudes Commerciales, Paris, 1952-55, Centre de Perfectionnement dans l'Administration des Affaires, Paris, 1965-66; m. Marie-Jeanne Dommange, Dec. 3, 1960; children—Pascale, Laurence, Henri, Beatrice. With Banque Nationale de Paris, 1959—, sr. v.p., gen. mgr. Western region, San Francisco, 1979—. Served to lt. comdr. French Navy Res., 1955-58. Decorated Croix de Valeur Militaire, Chevalier de l'Ordre National du Mérite. Mem. French Am. C. of C. (pres. San Francisco chpt.). Roman Catholic. Office: 180 Montgomery St San Francisco CA 94104

DEBOCK, FLORENT ALPHONSE, mfg. co. exec.; b. LaLouviere, Belgium, Feb. 3, 1924; s. Benoit and Elvire (Verbeke) DeB.; Tchr. diploma, Inst. Ste. Marie, Arlon, Belgium, 1944; Accountant diploma, Inst. Professionel Superieur de Belgique, 1953; postgrad. La Salle Extension U., Chgo., 1956; m. Mary C. Murray, July 2, 1960; 1 son, Mark Steven. Came to U.S., 1954, naturalized, 1959. Govt. auditor U.S. Army Audit Agy., Engr. Procurement Center, Europe, 1946-54; auditor Touche, Ross, Bailey & Smart, N.Y.C., 1954-61; controller Armor Elevator Co. and affiliates, Queens, N.Y., 1962-64; controller subsidiary of Eaton, Yale & Towne, Dusseldorf, Germany, 1964-67; group controller bus. furnishings group Litton Industries, N.Y.C., 1967-68; controller Levitt & Sons, homebuilding div. Internat. Tel. & Tel. Co., Lake Success, N.Y., 1969-71; controller Intermodulex NDH Corp., White Plains, N.Y., 1971-74; controller Ross Watch Case Corp. div. Zale Corp., Long Island City, N.Y., 1974—. Served with inf., Belgian Army, 1945-46. Decorated War of 1940-45 Commemorative medal, 1940-45 Vol. medal. C.P.A., D.C. Mem. Am. Inst. C.P.A.'s, N.Y. State Soc. C.P.A.'s, Nat. Assn. Accountants. Home: 123 99th St Brooklyn NY 11209 Office: 21-42 44th Dr Long Island City NY 11101

DE BOISBLANC, JACQUES FELIX, transmission parts co. exec.; b. New Orleans, Dec. 24, 1944; s. Felix Joseph and Hellen (Weigand) de B.; B.S. in Mech. Engring., La. State U., 1967; M.B.A., Tulane U., 1972. Engr., Boeing Corp., New Orleans, 1967-68; salesman Gulf Plastics, New Orleans, 1969-70, Latter & Blum, New Orleans, 1973-74; chief exec. officer, pres. The Clinic, New Orleans, 1975—. Mem. Automatic Transmission Rebuilders Assn. (treas.). Roman Catholic. Club: Sea Scamps (treas.). Home: 7824 Breakwater Dr New Orleans LA 70124 Office: 2067 Poydras St New Orleans LA 70112

DE BRUYNE, DIRK, petroleum co. exec.; b. Rotterdam, Netherlands, Sept. 1, 1920; s. Dirk Eliza and Maria (Van Alphen) de B.; grad. Erasmus U., Rotterdam, 1949. With Royal Dutch/Shell Group of Cos., The Hague, 1945-55, Indonesia, 1955-58, dep. group treas., London, 1958-60, fin. mgr., The Hague, 1960-62, regional coordinator oil, Africe, London, 1965-68, dir. finance, 1970, mng. dir., 1971—, vice chmn. com. mng. dirs., 1977—; exec. v.p. Shell Italiana, Italy, 1962-65; pres. Deutsche Shell, Germany, 1968-70; dir. Shell Transport & Trading Co., Ltd., London, 1971-74; mng. dir. Royal Dutch Petroleum Co., The Hague, 1974—, pres., 1977—, vice chmn. com. mng. dirs., 1977-79, chmn., 1979; chmn. bd. Shell Oil Co., Houston, 1977—; dir. Shell Can., Ltd., Toronto, 1977, Shell Française, Paris, 1977; mem. council Trade Policy Research Centre, London, Brit.-N. Am. Com.; mem. Consultative Group on Internat. Econ. and Monetary Affairs, N.Y.C., 1978. Mem. Netherlands-Brit. C. of C. (gen. council). Clubs: Dutch (London); DeWitte (The Hague). England Office: Shell Centre London SE1 7NA England

DEBUS, ELEANOR VIOLA, fin. exec.; b. Buffalo, May 19, 1920; d. Arthur Adam and Viola Charlotte (Pohl) D.; student Chown Bus. Sch., 1939. Sec., Buffalo Wire Works, 1939-45; home talent producer Empire Producing Co., Kansas City, Mo., 1946-47; sec. Owens-Corning Fiberglas, Buffalo, 1947-49; with Niagara Falls (Ont., Can.) Theatre, 1955-57; public relations dir. Woman's Internat. Bowling Congress, Columbus, Ohio, 1959-61; sec./publicist Ice Capades, Hollywood, Calif., 1961-63; sec. to controller Rexall Drug Co., Los Angeles, 1963-67; bus. mgmt. acct. Samuel Berke & Co., Beverly Hills, Calif., 1967-75, Gadbois Mgmt. Co., Beverly Hills, 1975-76; sec.-treas. Sasha Corp. and bus. mgr. for Dean Martin, Los Angeles, 1976—; pres. Tempo Co., Los Angeles, 1976—; producer, dir. Little Theatre Group, Buffalo, 1948-49. Recipient High Single award N.Y. State Bowling Assn., 1959. Mem. Am. Film Inst., Nat. Film Soc., Nat. Notary Assn., Nat. Assn. Female Execs. Republican. Club: Order Eastern Star. Contbr. articles to profl. jours. Office: 9911 W Pico Blvd Suite 560 Los Angeles CA 90035

DECAMINADA, JOSEPH PIO, ins. exec.; b. Gebo, Wyo., Oct. 17, 1935; s. Pio and Ida (Franch) D.; B.A. magna cum laude, St. Francis Coll., 1956; J.D., St. John's U., 1959; student Advanced Mgmt. Program, Harvard U., 1979; m. Genevieve Caputo, Aug. 30, 1958; 1 son, Joseph. With Atlantic Cos., N.Y.C., 1959—, asst. sec., mgr. research and devel. dept., 1968-70, sec. research and devel. and state relations, 1970-71, corporate sec., counsel, 1971-72, v.p., sec., counsel, 1972-76, sr. v.p., sec., counsel, 1976—; adj. asso. prof. Coll. Ins., 1965—. Recipient Research Incentive award Soc. CPCU, 1973, Eugene A. Toale Meml. award, 1974. C.P.C.U., C.L.U. Mem. Am. Mgmt. Assn., Soc. Chartered Property and Casualty Underwriters (regional v.p.), Am. Soc. C.L.U.'s, Maritime Law Assn. U.S., Ins. Soc. N.Y., Soc. Ins. Research, Am. Risk and Ins. Assn. Club: World Trade Center (N.Y.C.). Contbr. articles trade jours. Home: 3 Ridgecrest N

Scarsdale NY 10583 Office: The Atlantic Cos 45 Wall St New York NY 10005

DE CAMP, IRENE FRANCES, fin. and estate planner; b. Maynard, Iowa, Oct. 2, 1928; d. Floyd L. and Effie Jane (Martin) Parker; student Rollins Coll., Winter Park, Fla., 1962-65; cert. real estate, Fla. Atlantic U., 1973; m. Gayle Schilling de Camp, July 19, 1949 (dec. Dec. 1976). Part-time tchr., Orlando, Fla., 1952-65; various secretarial positions, 1972-71; sec.-treas., dir. Toga Films, Inc., Ft. Lauderdale, Fla., 1965—; pres., dir. de Camp Enterprises, Inc., Ft. Lauderdale, 1975—, de Camp Realty, Inc., Ft. Lauderdale, 1978—; partner Royal Group, Ltd.; dir., officer Encore Yachts, Inc.; fin. and estate planner Home Life Ins. Co., 1972—; lectr. fin. seminars for women. Mem. planned gifts com. bd. trustees Boca Raton (Fla.) Community Hosp., 1976—; sec. Henderson Mental Health Center Aux., Ft. Lauderdale, 1979—; mem. Women's Advocacy for Majority/Minority, 1979—. C.L.U.; cert. profl. sec. Mem. Internat. Assn. Fin. Planners (sec. S. Fla. chpt. 1978), Nat. Assn. Life Underwriters, Broward County Assn. Life Underwriters, Million Dollar Round Table, Fla. Real Estate Commn., Nat. Assn. Securities Dealers, Cert. Profl. Secs. (service com. 1962—), AAUW, Gold Key Soc. Republican. Baptist. Clubs: Kentucky, Tower, Whale and Porpoise, Order Eastern Star. Home: 4325 NE Country Club Dr Fort Lauderdale FL 33308 Office: 5554 N Federal Hwy 4th Floor Fort Lauderdale FL 33308

DE CARBONNEL, FRANÇOIS ERIC, mgmt. cons.; b. Paris, Dec. 7, 1946; came to U.S., 1979; s. Charles Eric and Elizabeth (Chevreux) De C.; diploma Ecole Centrale, Lyon, France, 1970; M.S. in Indsl. Adminstrn. (Smith award), Carnegie-Mellon U., 1972; m. L. Vercambre, Feb. 16, 1968; children—Geoffroy, Antoine, Thomas, Matthieu. With Boston Cons. Group, 1972—, v.p., dir., Chgo., 1979—. Mellon fellow 1971. Club: Met. (Chgo.). Author: Les Mecanismes Fondamenteaux de la Competitivite, 1980. Home: 554 Longwood St Glencoe IL 60022 Office: 200 W Monroe St Chicago IL 60606

DECARIE, YVES ANDRE, mfg. co. exec.; b. Montreal, Que., Can., Aug. 30, 1941; s. Roland and Suzanne (Roy) D.; B.Commerce in Econs., Concordia U., Montreal, 1970; m. May 10, 1970; 1 dau., Licole Lebeau. Exec. v.p. Gregg Cabinets Ltd., Chambly, Que., 1974-79; pres. Eleveen Seveenteen Sales Ltd., Ottawa, Ont., 1973-79; v.p. Prodimex Bldg. Materiel, Inc., Greenfield Park, Que., 1980—. Pres., Econ. Corp. Bd. of Richelieu, Carignac, Chambly, 1979-80. Mem. Que. Kitchen Cabinet Assn. (founder, treas.). Mem. Parti Quebeçois. Roman Catholic. Home: 90 3d St Greenfield Park PQ J4V 2R7 Canada

DECARLO, DAVID JOHN, finance and mfg. co. exec.; b. Morgantown, W.Va., Sept. 2, 1945; s. Donald J. and Ida DeC.; B.S., W.Va. U., 1967; M.A., M.B.A., Wharton Sch. Fin., U. Pa., 1970; m. Peggy J. Meade; children—Natalie, Jeff, Jason, Nicole. Fin. analyst spl. projects Reynolds Aluminum Co., Richmond, Va., 1970-72; contract pricing analyst Westinghouse Electric Co., Pitts., 1972-73; asst. treas. Joy Mfg. Co., Pitts., 1973-76, gen. mgr. parts distbn., 1976—. Bd. dirs. Canonsburg Hosp., United Way Central Washington County; mem. adv. council Upper Chartiers Valley Jr. Achievement. Mem. Am. Prodn. and Inventory Control Soc., Washington County Mfrs. Assn. (trustee), Pa. Economy League, Beta Gamma Sigma. Office: Box 717 Canonsburg PA 15317

DE CARO, FRANCIS PAUL, fin. cons., educator; b. N.Y.C.; s. Francis Paul and Rose (Salmonese) DeC.; B.B.A., St. Francis Coll., 1972; M.B.A., L.I. U., 1973; Ph.D., N.Y. U. Frozen food buyer Wakefern Food Corp., Elizabeth, N.J., 1972-73; sr. budget analyst F & M Schaefer Brewing Corp., N.Y.C., 1973-74; sr. fin. analyst W.R. Grace Corp., N.Y.C., 1974-75; asso. cons. Arawak Cons. Corp., N.Y.C., 1976—; pres. Syndicated Systems, Inc., Bklyn, 1977—, Fin., Mgmt. and Computer Cons., N.Y.C., 1977—; prof. fin. St. Francis Coll., Bklyn.; adj. prof. M.B.A. program L.I. U., Bklyn, 1977—; fin. lectr. SBA, 1976—. Active Corps Execs., SBA, Washington. Mem. Acad. Mgmt., Am. Mgmt. Assn., Soc. for Advancement Mgmt., Alpha Kappa Psi (Bus. Membership award), Delta Pi Epsilon (hon. bus. educator). Office: 180 Remsen St Brooklyn NY 11201*

DECATUR, IRVING CHASE, III, securities firm exec.; b. Melrose, Mass., Apr. 28, 1950; s. Irving Chase, Jr., and Nellie Ible (Bishop) D.; B.A., Johns Hopkins U., 1972; M.S., U. Chgo., 1974, M.B.A., 1977; m. Cecile Marie DeRouin, Sept. 25, 1975. Teaching asst. U. Chgo., 1973-74; mgr. planning and fin. Am. Assn. Ins. Services, Chgo., 1974-77; mgr. banking and fin. industry group Arthur Anderson & Co. mgmt. cons. div., Chgo., 1977-80; exec. v.p. Newcom Securities Co., Chgo. and N.Y.C., 1980—. Mem. Am. Mgmt. Assn. Mem. United Church of Christ. Office: 767 Fifth Ave New York NY 10022

DE CHARETTE DE LA CONTRIE, GWEN, bus. exec.; b. Neuilly/Seine, France, Feb. 13, 1937; s. Helion and Jeanne (de Nolhac) de C.; came to U.S., 1971; diplome d'Etudes Economiques, Conservatoire des Arts et Métiers, 1967; M.B.A. in Fin., N.Y. U., 1974. Analyst, Société Générale, Paris, 1963-67; v.p. Société Crédit Immobilier du Val d'Oise, Pontoise, France, 1967-70; pres. Devinter Inc., N.Y.C., 1974—; pres. Covinter Inc., N.Y.C., 1978—; dir. Franco-Belge Foundries Am., 1978-79; v.p., dir. LTI-Transrol Inc., N.Y.C., 1980—. Served with French Air Force, 1955-60. Mem. French C. of C. in U.S., U.S. C. of C. in France. Roman Catholic. Contbr. articles in field to profl. jours. Home: 305 E 40th St New York NY 10016 Office: 70 Pine St New York NY 10270

DECKER, JAMES LEE, hosp. exec.; b. Baton Rouge, Aug. 27, 1951; s. Adrian Lee and Shirley P. (Peacock) D.; B.S. in Microbiology, La. State U., 1972, M.S. in Microbiology, 1975; M.S. in Hosp. and Health Adminstrn., U. Ala., 1977. Adminstrv. resident Fort Sanders Presbyn. Hosp., Knoxville, Tenn., 1976-77, adminstrv. asst., 1977-79; v.p. Fort Sanders Regional Med. Center, Knoxville, 1979—. Mem. adv. com. Emergency Med. Technician Program, Knoxville, 1977-80; bd. dirs. Am. Lung Assn., Mid-East Tenn., 1979-80; loaned exec. United Way Greater Knoxville, 1977-80; adv. Med. Explorers Post 654, 1979-80; bd. dirs. Ft. Sanders Hosp. Employees Credit Union, 1978-80, pres., 1980—; mem. Knoxville Area Hosp. Council, 1979-80; mem. Knoxville-Knox County Manpower Consortium, Pvt. Industry Council, 1980-81. Recipient Alumni Assn. award Grad. Program in Hosp. and Health Adminstrn., U. Ala., Birmingham, 1977. Mem. Am. Hosp. Assn., Tenn. Hosp. Assn., Am. Coll. Hosp. Adminstrs., Greater Knoxville C. of C. Baptist. Club: Sertoma (dir. 1979-81, v.p. 1980-81). Home: 1431 Cherokee Trail #1 Knoxville TN 37920 Office: 1901 Clinch Ave SW Knoxville TN 37916

DECKER, WILLIAM ROBERT, real estate devel. co. exec.; b. Jersey City, May 13, 1929; s. Emil Jon Pierre and Katherine Marie D.; student N.Y. State U., 1955-59; m. Elizabeth Gass, Sept. 3, 1950 (dec. Dec. 1974); children—Robert Paul, Virginia Beth, William George, Emil Guy, Charles Thomas; m. 2d, Bonnie Jean Spinner, May 12, 1976. Sales mgr. N.J. dist. Gen. Mills Co., 1955-59; owner, mgr. Brown Milling Co., Raldolph, N.Y., 1959-64; pres. Big D Bldg. Supply Corp., Saranac Lake, N.Y., 1964-74; gen. partner Decker Properties, Saranac Lake, 1974—; pres. Reliance Mgmt. Corp., 1977—; real estate cons. Roman Catholic. Home: 163 Park Ave Saranac Lake NY 12983 also RFD 2 Sussex NJ 07461 Office: 163 Park Ave Saranac Lake NY 12983

DECOVICH, FRANK, mfg. co. exec.; b. LaSpezia, Italy, Nov. 8, 1933; s. Sergio and Felicina (Nicoli) D.; ed. Italy, Sweden; m. July 30, 1960; children—Tina, Franco. Pattern maker, Asea, Sweden, 1948-51; foreman F.J. Murray Co., Toronto, 1951-62; owner, mgr. Cutting Tool Mfg. Co., Toronto, 1962—. Liberal. Roman Catholic. Home: 111 Firglen Ridge Woodbridge ON L4L 1H3 Canada Office: 2450 Finch Ave W Weston ON M9M 2E9 Canada

DE CRANE, VINCENT FRANCIS, constrn. co. exec.; b. Cleve., Aug. 27, 1927; s. Alfred Charles and Verona Ida (Marquard) DeC.; B.S., U. Notre Dame, 1950; m. Flora Elizabeth Friday, July 7, 1951; children—Barbara, Peter, Donna, Michael, Melinda, Melissa, Joan, Mary Jean. Field engr. Great Lakes, Dredge & Dock Co., Cleve., 1950; with Dunlop & Johnston, Inc., Cleve., 1952—, exec. v.p., sec., 1975—; gen. partner Sawmill Creek Lodge Co., Cleve., 1971—. Chmn. constrn. div. United Way Cleve., 1971-76; corp. sec. bd. trustees Brentwood Hosp., 1978—; gen. campaign chmn. Cath. Charities Corp., 1979-80, pres., 1981—. Served with U.S. Army, 1946-47, 50-52. Mem. Constrn. Industry Affairs Com. Cleve., Builders Exchange (v.p. 1980), Am. Inst. Constructors, Cleve. Engring. Soc., Constrn. Employers Assn. Cleve., Warrensville Heights C. of C. (hon. dir.). Roman Catholic. Office: 17900 Miles Ave Cleveland OH 44128

DEDEN, JOHN THORNTON, computer based word processing systems co. exec.; b. Ft. Smith, Ark., Oct. 14, 1924; s. Otto John and Laura Clyde (Taylor) D.; student Tex. A. and M. U., 1942-43, E. Oreg. State Tchrs. Coll., 1943; B.S., Aero. U., Chgo., 1948; postgrad. Washington U., 1948, U. Minn., 1950, U. Calif. at Los Angeles, 1963; m. Anna Arrington, June 2, 1946; children—Ann Elizabeth, Cassandra Louise. Sr. project engr., advanced systems, devel. and design, electronics and missiles Honeywell, Inc., Mpls. and Los Angeles, 1950-59; with TRW Systems, Inc., Los Angeles, 1959-73, Minuteman project staff, 1959-61, project engr. Vela satellite ground equipment, 1962-64, design rev. staff mgr., 1964-66, asst. program mgr., product assurance DSSO, 1966-70, staff engr., 1970-73; mgr. product assurance, reliability and quality, and components TRW Controls, Inc., Houston, 1973-78; mgr. quality, reliability and test ops. Basic/Four, Houston, 1978-80; mgr. adminstrn. Basic Four Houston Devel. Center, 1980—; pres., founder Aneco Group Inc., Reseda, Calif., 1970-72; field cons. advanced environ. tech. systems; semiar lectr. waste mgmt. U. Calif. at Irvine, 1970-72. Served with USAAF as pilot, 1943-45. Decorated Air medal with oak leaf cluster; registered profl. engr., Calif. Mem. Am. Soc. Quality Control. Home: 3162 LaQuinta St Missouri City TX 77459 Office: 10808 Fallstone Rd Houston TX 77099

DEE, AVERY EDWARD, computer co. exec.; b. Chgo., Dec. 13, 1941; s. Marvin Robert and Elizabeth Pauline (Simon) D.; B.S. in Mech. Engring., U. Ill., 1963; M.Ed., Northwestern Ill. State U., 1967; m. Carole Ann Morgan, Dec. 13, 1975; children—Edward R., Kevin R., Kristen A. Pres. I.M.I., Evanston, Ill., 1962-67; sales engr. E.S.B., Inc., Chgo., 1967-70, owner Dee Photographic Co., Nevada City, Calif., 1970-73; sales mgr., indsl. scales Howe Richardson Scale Co., Hayward, Calif., 1973-75; chmn., pres. U.S. West Investments, Inc., Carson City, Nev., 1975—; pres. A.E. Dee & Assos., Santa Clara, Calif., 1975-78; v.p. mktg. Mountain Hardware Inc., Santa Cruz, Calif., 1978—. Mem. Cook County (Ill.) Young Republicans, 1963-70; chmn. conservation com. on Anza-Borrego Desert, 1970-71. Mem. Presidents Assn., Santa Clara County C. of C., Ret. Officers Assn., ASME, Western Soc. Engrs., Internat. Materials Mgmt. Soc., Nat. Scalemen's Assn., Profl. Photographers Am., Nat. Skeet Shooters Assn., Amateur Trapshooting Assn., San Jose Trap and Skeet Club. Club: Commonwealth of Calif. One man exhbn. wildlife photographs U.S. Dept. Interior Gallery, San Francisco, 1973. Home: 22546 Summit Rd Los Gatos CA 95030 Office: 300 Harvey West Blvd Santa Cruz CA 95060

DEEG, EMIL WOLFGANG, research and devel. exec.; b. Selb, W.Ger., Sept. 20, 1926; s. Fritz and Trina (Poehlmann) D.; came to U.S., 1967, naturalized, 1975; Dipl. Physiker, U. Wuerzburg, 1954, Dr. rer. nat., 1956; m. Hedwig M.S. Kempf, Aug. 25, 1953; children—Wolfgang, Martin, Bernhard, Renate. Research asst. Max Planck Inst., Wuerzburg, 1954-59; mem. tech. staff Bell Telephone Labs., Allentown, Pa., 1959-60; research asso. Jenaer Glaswerk Schott u. Gen., Mainz, Germany, 1960, dir. research, 1960-65; asso. prof. physics and solid state sci. Am. U., Cairo, 1965-67; mgr. ceramic research Am. Optical Corp., Southbridge, Mass., 1967-71, mgr. materials research, 1971-73, dir. process and materials research, 1973-75, dir. inorganic materials research and devel., 1975-77, tech. adviser, 1977-78; sr. scientist Anchor Hocking Corp., Lancaster, Ohio, 1978-79, mgr. materials research and devel., 1979-80; mgr. glass tech. Bausch & Lomb, Rochester, N.Y., 1980—. Pres., PTA, Woodstock, Conn., 1970-71; committeeman Mohegan council Boy Scouts Am., 1967-73; trustee Woodstock Acad., 1971-78; overseer Old Sturbridge Village, Inc.; chmn. Optical Info. Center, Southbridge, 1976-77. Served with German Army, 1944-45. Fellow Am. Ceramic Soc.; mem. Internat. Commn. on Glass, Optical Soc. Am., Nat. Inst. Ceramic Engrs., Brit. Soc. Glass Tech., Soc. Advancement Materials and Process Engring. Club: Lions (pres. Woodstock chpt. 1975; zone chmn. dist. 23 C, Lions Internat. 1976-78), Contbr. chpts. to books, articles to profl. jours. Author: (with H. Richter) Glas im Laboratorium, 1966. Patentee in field. Home: 5800 Coonpath Rd Carroll OH 43112 Office: 1400 N Goodman St Rochester NY 14602

DEEGAN, WILLIAM PATRICK, investment banker; b. Bklyn., Dec. 24, 1928; s. John Joseph and Ellen Theresa (Greene) D.; B.S., Fordham U., 1958; m. Patricia Ann Collins, Apr. 18, 1953; children—William Patrick, Nancy Ellen, Kathleen Ann (dec.), Suzanne Marie, John Joseph. With L.F. Rothschild & Co., N.Y.C., 1946—, partner, 1967—. Mem. Westwood (N.J.) Planning Bd., 1969-74, chmn., 1969-71; area chmn. Am. Cancer Soc., 1965-70. Served with AUS, 1950-52. Mem. Securities Industry Assn. (municipal bond com.), Municipal Bond Club N.Y., Municipal Forum N.Y., Municipal Finance Forum of Washington, Fordham Wall Street Assn., Beta Gamma Sigma. Clubs: Wall Street, India House, Hackensack Golf. Home: 2 Gritman Ct Westwood NJ 07675 Office: 55 Water St New York City NY 10041

DEELEY, WILLIAM RADCLIFFE, retail food distbn. co. exec.; b. Mt. Vernon, Ohio, Sept. 27, 1922; s. Benjamin Charles and Frances (Radcliffe) D.; B.S., La. State U., 1948; m. Shirley Jane Edwards, June 22, 1956; 1 son, William Radcliffe II. Enlisted U.S. Army, 1942, discharged, 1945; commd. 2d Lt., 1949, advanced through grades to capt., 1954; resigned, 1957; pres., chief exec. officer Alpha Beta Co., La Habra, Calif., 1957—; v.p., dir., now vice chmn. Am. Stores Co., Salt Lake City. Episcopalian. Office: PO Box 181 Mendenhall PA 19357

DEEM, DOY C., oil co. exec.; b. Beatrice, W.Va., Mar. 2, 1927; s. Felix W. and Viola M. (Morehead) D.; B.S. in Petroleum Engring., Marietta (Ohio) Coll., 1952; postgrad. Okla. U., 1960. Petroleum engr. Sohio Petroleum Co., 1952-63; v.p. Braden Drilling Inc., Wichita, Kans., 1963-65; pres. Braden-Deem, Inc., Wichita, 1965—; cons. petroleum engr., 1963—. Bd. dirs. Wichita Met. YMCA. Served with USAAF, 1945-46. Clubs: Wichita Country, Wichita Petroleum (dir.). Home: 8 Saint James Pl Wichita KS 67206 Office: 200 E 1st St Suite 520 Wichita KS 67202

DEER, JAMES WILLIS, lawyer; b. Reading, Pa., Mar. 14, 1917; s. Irvin E. and Rosemary (French) D.; A.B. in Econs. cum laude, Oberlin Coll., 1938; J.D., U. Mich., 1941; m. Marion M. Hawkinson, July 31, 1943; 1 dau., Ann Marie. Admitted to Ohio bar, 1941, N.Y. State bar, 1948; mem. legal staff SEC, 1942-45; practiced in N.Y.C., 1948—; mem. firm Holtzmann, Wise & Shepard, 1954—; chmn. bd. Western Auto Supply Corp., 1960; sec., dir. Am. Transp. Enterprises, Inc., 1951-55; sec. Teleregister Corp., 1953-65, Dubois Chems., Inc., 1960-63, Ogden Corp., 1960—; dir. Arts Way Mfg. Co., Inc., T-Bar, Inc., Am. Diversified Enterprises, Inc., 1955—. Mem. Am., N.Y. bar assns., Phi Beta Kappa, Phi Alpha Delta. Home: 611 Shore Acres Dr Mamaroneck NY 10543 also 221 NW 17th St Delray Beach FL 33444 Office: 30 Broad St New York NY 10004

DEERING, ALLAN BROOKS, beverage co. ofcl.; b. Chappaqua, N.Y., Apr. 1, 1934; s. Clarence and Muriel (Lee) D.; B.A., Columbia U., 1956; m. Carol Ann Werle, Apr. 14, 1957; children—Peter Brooks, Andrew Werle. Systems analyst IBM Corp., White Plains, N.Y., 1956-58; EDP mgr. R. H. Donnelly Corp. N.Y.C., 1958-68; dir. systems and data processing W. R. Grace & Co., N.Y.C., 1968-76, asst. v.p., 1975, dir. info. systems SCM Corp., N.Y.C., 1976-81; dir. mgmt. info. Services PepsiCo, Purchase, N.Y., 1981—. Mem. Mayor's Industry Adv. Bd. for Data Processing, N.Y.C., 1978. Mem. Data Processing Mgmt. Assn., Soc. Mgmt. Info. Systems. Clubs: Milbrook (Greenwich, Conn.); Rocky Point, Old Greenwich Yacht. Home: 3 Perkley Ln Riverside CT 06878 Office: PepsiCo Anderson Hill Rd Purchase NY 10577

DEERING, CHRISTOPHER PAUL, mfg. co. exec.; b. Boston, Jan. 15, 1945; s. Claude V. and Helen M. (Bruno) D.; B.S. magna cum laude, Boston Coll., 1966; M.B.A., Harvard U., 1968; m. Jane VanDyke, Sept. 1, 1968. Sales planning mgr. U.S. shaving div. Gillette Co., Boston, 1970-71, product mgr. Trac II razor, 1971-72, sr. product mgr. new products, 1974-75, mktg. mgr. Good News; razor, 1976, internat. mktg. mgr. shaving div., 1977-79; mktg. mgr. Gillette Europe div. Gillette Industries Ltd., Isleworth, Middlesex, Eng., 1979—; asso., cons. McKinsey & Co., N.Y.C., 1973. Pres., Boston Waterfront Neighborhood Assn., 1975-79. Mem. Beta Gamma Sigma. Roman Catholic. Clubs: S. Boston Yacht, Harvard Bus. Sch. of Boston, Boston Bus. Assos. Inventor, patentee automatic billiard ball racking device. Home: 62 Rutland Gate Flat 10 London SW7 1PJ England Office: Gillette Industries Ltd Gillette Corner Great West Rd Isleworth Middlesex England

DEERING, FRED ARTHUR, ins. co. exec.; b. Arkansas City, Kans., Jan. 12, 1928; s. Frederick A. and Lucile (Phillips) D.; B.S., U. Colo., 1951, LL.B., 1951; m. Isabell Staufenberg, June 14, 1949; children—Anne Deering Buchanan, Kate; m. 2d, Elizabeth K. MacMillan, Apr. 12, 1979. Admitted to Colo. bar, 1951; asso. firm Gorsuch, Kirgis, Campbell, Walker & Grover, Denver, 1951-54, partner, 1954-62; v.p., gen. counsel Security Life & Accident Co., Denver, 1962-66, pres., dir., 1966—, also chief exec. officer; pres. Security Casualty Co., Denver, 1966-77; chmn. bd. Fin. Indsl. Fund, Denver, 1970—, Fin. Indsl. Income Fund, 1970—, Fin. Dynamics Fund, 1970—, Fin. Daily Income Shares, Fin. Bond Fund, 1976—; dir. Metal Fabricators, Inc., Denver, 1963—, Am. Life Ins. Assn., Washington, 1968-72, Kissinger Petroleum, Inc., Denver, 1970—, Columbia Savs. and Loan Assn., Winter Park Ranch, Inc.; instr. Am. Inst. Banking, 1953-57; lectr. Colo. Sch. Law, 1958-59. Trustee, Loretto Heights Coll., 1968-69, chmn. bd., 1968—; bd. dirs. Wallace Village for Children, 1968-74, Met. United Fund, 1969-71, Porter Hosp., 1970-78, U. Colo. Found., 1972-75; mem. adv. com. Met. Assn. for Retarded Children, Denver, 1970-71, Denver Research Inst., 1972-76. Served with U.S. Army, 1946-47. Mem. Am. Judicature Soc., Am., Colo., Denver bar assns., Assn. Life Ins. Counsel, Colo. Life Conv., Met. Denver Execs. Club (pres. 1970-71), Life Office Mgmt. Assn. (dir. 1977—), Denver C. of C., Order of Coif, Sigma Alpha Epsilon. Clubs: Cherry Hills (dir. 1973-76, pres. 1975-76) (Englewood, Colo.); Denver (dir. 1973-76), Univ., (Denver). Home: 1551 Larimer St Apt 1701 Denver CO 80202 Office: 600 Security Life Bldg 1616 Glenarm Pl Denver CO 80202 also PO Box 2040 Denver CO 80201

DEERY, HUGH GUNNER, ins. and real estate exec.; b. Calamine, Wis., Aug. 18, 1920; s. John Hugh and Minna (Gunner) D.; B.S., U. Wis., Platteville, 1947; m. Jody Mabel Hirsbrunner, Oct. 9, 1948; children—Gunner, Ted, Jack, Tom, Sue, Brad, Chuck, David. Owner, operator Hugh Deery Agy., ins., Rockford, Ill., 1957—, Rockford Speedway, 1959—, Forest Hills Lodge, Rent-A-Sign Co., Checker Flag Room, Inc., Uncle Jack's, Inc., HuJo Inc. (all Rockford); leader seminars in auto race organizing. Alderman, City of Rockford, 1961-69. Served with USNR, 1943-46. Recipient various sales and racing awards; named Auto Race Promoter of Year, 1977. Mem. Assn. Motor Sports Ill. (past v.p.), Ins. Agts. Assn. Ill. (past dir.), Profl. Ins. Agts. Assn. Ill., Nat. Assn. Mut. Agts., U. Wis. Alumni Assn., Lyran Singing Soc. Republican. Roman Catholic. Club: K.C. (4 deg.). Home: 1030 N 2d St Rockford IL 61107 Office: 2401 W Main St Rockford IL 61103

DEFAZIO, JOHN LORENZO, elec. mfg. co. exec.; b. Pitts., Aug. 10, 1923; s. Pasquale A. and Marianne (Angotti) D.; student Carnegie Inst. Tech., 1941-42, 1945-46, U. Fla., 1942-43, U. Pitts., 1947-48; m. Marian C. Scarpino, June 29, 1946; children—Patricia Marie, John Lorenzo, Therese Marie, Joann Marie, Rosemarie, Anthony A., Richard Michael. With Nuttall div. Westinghouse Electric Corp., Pitts., 1941-55, advt. staff rep., 1955-59, mgr. advt. and sales promotion, Youngwood, Pa., 1960-64, marketing communications rep., electronic components, splty. products group, Pitts., 1964-69, components and materials group, 1969-70, marketing services mgr. Semicondr. div., Youngwood, 1970-73, mgr. marketing communications Components and Materials Group, Pitts., 1973—. Maj. USAF Res. Mem. Pitts. Advt. Club, Bus./Profl. Advertisers Assn. (dir.), Air Force Assn., Air Force Hist. Soc., Italian Execs. Am., Marketing Communications Research Inst. (chmn. inquiry com.), Res. Officers Assn. Contbr. articles to profl. publs. Home: 3833 Logans Ferry Rd Pittsburgh PA 15239 Office: Westinghouse Bldg Gateway Center Pittsburgh PA 15222

DEFECHEREUX, PHILIPPE HENRY, advt. agy. exec.; b. Verviers, Belgium, Sept. 9, 1945; came to U.S., 1969; s. Henry Armand and Germaine (Lilien) D.; Licence en Sciences Economiques et Commerciales, U. Liege (Belgium), 1967; M.B.A., Columbia U., 1972; m. Martine Julia Aerts, Oct. 19, 1972 (div. Jan. 1980). Trade analyst Dart Containerline, N.Y.C., 1970; asst. brand mgr. Procter & Gamble, Cin., 1972-74; v.p., mgmt. supr. Ogilvy & Mather, Inc., N.Y.C., 1974—; investment cons. for various European firms. Mem. Columbia M.B.A. Alumni Assn. Home: 301 E 87th St Apt 21E New York NY 10028 Office: Ogilvy & Mather Inc 2 E 48th St New York NY 10017

DE FIGUEIREDO, MARIO PACHECO, food co. exec.; b. Goa, Mar. 16, 1935; s. Joao Pacheco and Maria Alcina (Rocha-Pinto) de F.; came to U.S., 1951, naturalized, 1970; S.B. in Chemistry, M.I.T., 1955, S.M. in Food Tech., 1958, Ph.D. in Food Sci. and Tech., 1962; M.B.A., U. Chgo., 1968; m. Maria Mildred Noronha Telles, Dec. 26, 1971. With Consol. Foods Corp., 1962-73, mgr. quality assurance and tech. research Kitchens of Sara Lee div., 1962-71, v.p. research Hollywood Brands div., 1967-71; v.p. research and devel., 1971-73; v.p. research and devel. Nat. Portion Control div. Hershey Foods Corp., 1973-76; dir. research Farmland Foods, Franklin Park, Ill., 1976-78; tech. dir. food enterprises div. Ralston Purina Co., St. Louis, 1979—. Calouste Gulbenkian Found. fellow, 1958-61; named outstanding new citizen of year Citizenship Council Met. Chgo., 1970. Fellow Am. Public Health Assn., Royal Soc. Health, Brit. Inst. Food Sci., Am. Inst. Chemists; mem. N.Y. Acad. Scis., Inst. Food Technologists, AAAS, Sigma Xi, Phi Tau Sigma, Phi Beta Chi. Author: Food Microbiology, Public Health and Spoilage Aspects, 1976; co-editor Jour. Food Quality, 1977—; contbr. articles to tech. jours. Home: 1887 Schoettler Valley Dr Chesterfield MO 63017

DE FOUW, EUGENE ALLEN, office systems co. exec., mech. engr.; b. Berrien Springs, Mich., Dec. 9, 1941; s. Arthur John and Myrtle Edna (Bolks) De F.; B.S. in Trade Tech. Teaching (Koh-I-Noor, Inc. scholar), Ferris State Coll., 1964; B.S.E. (Ford Motor Co. fellow), U. Mich., 1969; M.S.E., Wayne State U., 1972; m. Lucille M. Van Ess, July 12, 1968; children—Sandra Lynn, Karen Sue, Laura Jean. Product design engr. Ford Motor Co., Dearborn, Mich., 1964-66, project engr., 1969-73; sr. engr. Aeronutronic-Ford Corp., Connersville, Ind., 1973-75; chief engr. Borroughs div. Lear Siegler, Inc., Kalamazoo, 1975-79; dir. mfg. engring. Haworth, Inc., Holland, Mich., 1979—. Recipient Outstanding Leadership award U. Mich. Coll. Engring., 1968. Mem. ASME, Soc. Mfg. Engrs., Nat. Soc. Profl. Engrs., Fedn. Fly Fishermen, Trout Unltd., Delta Sigma Phi. Republican. Mem. Christian Reformed Ch. Club: Rotary Internat. Author tech. papers; patentee in field. Home: 823 Meadowbrook Ave Holland MI 49423 Office: 545 E 32d St Holland MI 49423

DEFRANCEAUX, DONALD MOSS, realty corp. exec.; b. Washington, Dec. 17, 1939; s. George W. and Ada (Moss) DeF.; student Tulane U., 1958-59; student Am. U., 1960-61; grad. Northwestern U. Sch. Mortgage Banking, 1963; m. Margaret Harper, Sept. 19, 1964; children—Deidre, Carter, Courtney, Gardner. With F.W. Berens, Inc., Washington, 1959-73, pres., 1969-73; pres. DeFranceaux Realty Group, Inc., Washington, 1973—; chmn. bd. Hicrops, 1979—. Trustee Mater Dei Sch., 1975—, Georgetown Prep. Sch., 79—; bd. dirs. Fed. City Council, 1974—. Mem. Mortgage Bankers Assn. Am., Washington Bd. Realtors (pres. 1976, Outstanding Mortgage Loan Transaction award 1963), Young Presidents Orgn., Nat. Assn. Realtors, Nat. Apt. Owners Assn., Nat. Assn. Home Builders. Clubs: Congressional Country, University, Bryce Ski and Country (dir. 1979—). Home: 10706 Burbank Dr Potomac MD 20854 Office: DeFranceaux Realty Group Inc 1909 K St NW Washington DC 20006

DEFREES, JOSEPH HUTTON, mfg. co. exec.; b. Warren, Pa., Sept. 1, 1905; m. Joseph Hutton and Anne Isabel (Stone) DeF.; C.E., Cornell U., 1929; m. Barbara Baldwin, June 30, 1945. Asst. to div. engr. Reading Co. (Pa.), 1929-32; tng. instr. Texas Co., N.Y.C., 1932-35; v.p., dir. Pa. Furnace & Iron Co., Warren, 1935-52, Tiona Mfg. Co., Warren, 1953-62, Ray Industries, Warren, 1954-62; pres., dir. Allegheny Valve Co., Warren, 1952—, Allegheny Coupling Co., Warren, 1955—; dir. Warren Bank & Trust Co. Mem. Warren Boro Council, 1937-47; dir. C.D. for Warren County, 1951-52; chmn. Warren Boro Zoning Commn., 1947-60; bd. dirs. Warren County Hist. Soc., 1962—, Council for Internat. Progress in Mgmt., 1961-74; trustee Nat. Schs. Com. for Econ. Edn., 1973-77; del. confs. Conseil Internat. pour l'Organization Scientifique, Sydney, Caracas, Tokyo, Munich; del. Internat. Humanist and Ethical Union, London, Oslo, Paris, Amsterdam, Boston; mem. Wallace Clark award com. for recognition of sci. achievement; co-founder Hospice of Warren/Forest; founder coop. grants through Research Corp. Recipient Benjamin Rush award Pa. Med. Soc., 1977. Fellow ASME; mem. Am. Welding Soc., Am. Soc. Automotive Engrs., Am. Petroleum Inst. Republican. Mem. Fellowship of Religious Humanists. Clubs: Conewango, Conewango Country (Warren); SkyTop (Pa.). Patentee in field. Home: 505 Liberty St Warren PA 16365 Office: 419 3d Ave Warren PA 16365

DEGANN, A(LAN) DAVID, cons. firm exec.; b. Bklyn., Feb. 19, 1944; s. Martin Philip and Sylvia (Hantman) D.; B.S., City U. N.Y., 1968; B.B.A., Coll. Ins., 1968; M.B.A., Pace U., 1976. Accounting clk. Manhattan Life Ins. Co., N.Y.C., 1962-64; asst. dir., dir. pensions, 2d v.p. Standard Security Life Ins. Co., N.Y.C., 1964-70, v.p., 1970-73, sr. v.p., 1973—, chief pension actuary, 1976-77, also dir.; partner Coopers & Lybrand, N.Y.C., 1978—; exec. v.p., sr. actuary Wyatt Harris Graham Cons. Actuaries; adj. asst. prof. Coll. Ins., N.Y.C., 1968—. C.L.U., 1968. Fellow Am. Soc. Pension Actuaries (chmn. edn. exam. com., dir., edn. chmn., exec. com.), Life Office Mgmt. assn.; mem. Am. Acad. Actuaries, Northeastern Pension Conf. (chmn. 1971-72), Am. Assn. Advanced Life Underwriters. Author: Historical Analysis of the Taxation of Qualified Retirement Plans, 1976; Erisa - A Lady or a Tramp, 1975; contbr. articles to profl. jours. Home: 1050 Park Ave New York NY 10028 Office: 90 Park Ave New York NY 10016

DE GASTER, ZACHARY, engring. co. exec.; b. Amsterdam, Nov. 3, 1926 (mother Am. citizen); s. Jack and Frederika (Springer) de G.; B.S., Columbia U., 1948, M.A., 1949; m. Elizabeth Philips, Dec. 20, 1952; children—Barbara, Audrey. With UN, 1948-49, Nuodex Internat. Corp., 1950-51, Radio Free Europe, 1951-53; dir. Radio Industries Corp., 1953-56, L.A. Ebasco Internat. Corp., 1956-58: pres. Interam. Standard 1958-63, Frederic R. Harris Cons. Engrs., N.Y.C., 1963-67, 68-70; v.p. Brazil ops. Frederic R. Harris, Inc., N.Y.C., 1970-79, sr. v.p. in charge Latin Am., 1979—; sr. v.p. PRC Harris Inc., PRC Engring. Inc., Europe, Middle East, Africa, Far East, 1979—; dir. F.R. Harris (Belgium) S.A., DIT-Harris S.A., Caracas, Venezuela, Harris de Brasil Ltds., Rio de Janeiro; adv. on tech. transfer to Pres. U.S., Conf. C.Am. Presidents, San Jose, Costa Rica, 1963. Served with AUS, 1944-45. Registered Kenya Engrs. Registration Bd. Mem. ASCE, Soc. Am. Mil Engrs., Am. Road Builders Assn., Am. Assn. Port Authorities, Internat. Bridge and Turnpike Orgn., Associacion Mexicana de Ingenieria Portuaria, Instituto de Ingenieros de Chile. Contbr. numerous articles on hwy. maintenance and reorgn. to profl. publs. Home: 214 Bay Ave Huntington NY 11743 Office: 300 E 42d St New York NY 10017

DEGEN, MAUREEN R., mgmt. cons.; b. N.Y.C., 1940; grad. Lenox Hill Sch. Nursing, N.Y.C., 1961; student Ind. U., 1968-70; B.A. magna cum laude, U. Philippines, 1972; M.B.A., U. Utah, 1974; doctoral candidate Golden Gate U. Commd. 1st lt. Nurses Corps, U.S. Air Force, 1965; adminstrv. acct. City of Fairfield, Calif., 1975-76; pres. Maureen R. Degen Mgmt. Cons., Vacaville, Calif., 1976—. Chairperson coordination of agys. com. Vacaville Unified Sch. Dist., 1978—; founder, chairperson Ind. Citizens' Advisory Com., 1977—; mem. fin. com., chairperson United Way Crusade, Napa-Solano Girl Scout Council, 1976-77; mem. SBA Regional Advisory Council; mem. publicity com. Napa-Solano Big Bros.-Big Sisters, 1976-77. Mem. No. Solano Bd. Realtors, Assn. M.B.A. Execs., AAUW (v.p. Vacaville br.), Inst. Certified Bus. Counselors, Nat. Assn. Realtors, Calif. Assn. Realtors, Internat. Entrepreneurs Assn., Enterprising Woman (co-founder). Office: 421 Boyd St Suite A Vacaville CA 95688

DEGEORGE, LAWRENCE JOSEPH, diversified co. exec.; b. N.Y.C., May 6, 1916; s. Frank Phillip and Frances (Cavallo) DeG.; B.E.E., Princeton U., 1936; M.S., Mass. Inst. Tech., 1938; m. Florence A. Efel, Dec. 18, 1943; children—Lawrence F., Peter R. Asso. prof. elec. engring. Columbia U., 1938-39; field engr. Radio Engring. Lab., N.Y.C., 1939-41; pres. Times Wire and Cable Co., Inc. div. Internat. Silver Co., Wallingford, Conn., 1946—, also dir., v.p. Times Wire and Cable div. (after merger in 1958) Internat. Silver Co., 1958-64, became pres., 1964; v.p. fin. Insilco Corp., 1965, exec. v.p., 1972, vice chmn. bd., 1976—; chmn., pres. Times Fiber Communications, Inc., Meriden, Conn., 1977—. Bd. dirs. Travelers Equities Fund, Inc., Hartford, Conn., Gaylord Hosp., Wallingford; past pres. Cheshire Community Theatre. Served to lt. comdr. USNR, 1941-46. Mem. IEEE, Electronic Industries Assn. (chmn. tech. com. high temperature cable). Republican. Clubs: Kiwanis, Princeton, Engrs. (N.Y.C.); Farms Country. Patentee electronic, wire and cable fields. Home: 13 Currier Ct Cheshire CT 06410 Office: 358 Hall Ave Wallingford CT 06492

DEGHETTO, ANSELM, rubber machinery mfg. co. exec.; b. Italy, Sept. 5, 1898; s. Angelo and Angela (DeLuca) DeG.; ed mech. engring.; m. Linda Zanetti, Nov. 24, 1921; children—Robert, Kenneth. Came to U.S., 1907, naturalized, 1915. In charge inspection Nat. Rubber Machinery Co., Clifton, N.J., 1919-23, gen. foreman, 1923-25, supt. 1935-39, plant mgr. 1939-59, v.p. 1943-59; pres. Getty Machine & Mold, Inc., 1960—. Registered profl. engr. Mem. N.Y. Rubber Group, Am. Ordnance Assn., ASTM, Am. Soc. Tool Engrs., N.J. Soc. Profl. Engrs., Clifton C. of C. Club: Rotary. Home: 21 Piaget Ave Clifton NJ 07011 Office: 384 Getty Ave Clifton NJ 07011

DEGOURCUFF, JEAN HERVE, pub. relations exec.; b. Tendron, France, Oct. 23, 1918; s. Herve and Daisy (de Montsaulnin) deG.; B.A., Ecole de Roches, 1936; LL.M., Faculte de Droit, 1939; m. Alix de Bartillat, June 25, 1943; children—Eric, Sylvia Diane, Alan. Sales mgr. Trans World Airlines, Paris, 1946-57, pub. relations mgr., 1957; pub. relations mgr. Sud Aviation, Paris, 1957-60; pres. Oltec, Paris, 1959-62; dir. information Eurospace, 1962-68; pub. relations mgr. Europe, Martin Co., 1962-65; Press officer Rolls Royce (France); dir. pub. relations Hispano-Suiza, 1965-68, Compagnie Internationale pour l'Informatique, 1968-70, Compagnie Generale de Constructions Telephoniques, 1970—. Served as lt. inf., 1939-43. Decorated Croix de Guerre, Knight of Malta. Mem. Internat., European pub. relations assns. Club: Jockey. Home: 45 Rue Emile Menier 75116 Paris France Office: 251 Rue de Vaugirard 75015 Paris France

DE GRADO, BETTY LOU, real estate broker; b. Burbank, Calif., Apr. 21, 1934; d. Harvey Orville and Isabel Marion (Melville) Angermeir; student pub. schs., Burbank; children—James Harvey, William Frank. Sales asso. Rich Port Realtors, Oak Brook, Ill., 1971-76, sales mgr., 1976-78, v.p., 1978—; exec. v.p. Am. Growth Real Estate Corp., Oak Brook, 1979-80, The Midwest Club, Oak Brook, Ill., 1980—. Mem. Nat. Assn. Realtors, Realtors Nat. Mktg. Inst., DuPage Bd. Realtors, Oak Brook Assn. Commerce and Industry. Republican. Home: 101 Lake Hinsdale Clarendon Hills IL 60514

DEGRANDPRE, PHILIPPE MICHEL, investment banker; b. Montreal, Que., Can., Nov. 2, 1942; s. Louis Philippe and Marthe (Gendron) deG.; B.A. Coll. Jean-de-Brébeuf, 1962; B.C.L., McGill U., 1965; M.B.A., U. Western Ont., 1968; m. Hélène Letendre, Sept. 25, 1965; children—Philippe, Vincent, Catherine. With The Power Corp. Group of Companies, Montreal, 1968-79; v.p., dir. McLeod Young Weir Ltd., Montreal, 1979—; chmn. Common Constrn. Co., Inc.; dir. Paragon Bus. Forms Ltd. Chmn., Regional Health & Social Services Council, Montreal. Served to lt. Can. Armed Forces, 1961-64. Mem. Bar of Que., C. of C. Roman Catholic. Clubs: St. Denis, Mt. Royal. Home: 64 Nelson St Outremont PQ H2V 3Z7 Canada Office: 1155 Dorchester Blvd W Montreal PQ H3B 3V4 Canada

DE GRAW, IRVING HAROLD, mfg. co. exec.; b. Englewood, N.J., May 19, 1946; s. Irving Harold and Marilyn E. (Fenn) DeG.; B.S. in Mech. Engring., U. Notre Dame, 1965; LL.B., LaSalle Law Sch., Ill., 1972; B.S. in Bus. Adminstrn., SUNY, 1978; postgrad. U. Conn.; m. Linda A. Godwin, Aug. 30, 1974; children—Lisa Marie, Ronald Patrick, Russell Joseph, Noel Edward. Programmer, Am. Express, N.Y.C., 1966-67; systems analyst Publishers Data Center, N.Y.C., 1967-69; project mgr. Research Inst. Am., Mt. Kisco, N.Y., 1969-71; bus. cons. Dictaphone Corp., Bridgeport, Conn., 1971-76; sr. bus. analyst Chesebrough-Pond's Inc., Trumbull, Conn., 1976-79; mgr. tech. services Applied Data Processing, North Haven, Conn., 1979—; asst. prof. data processing Rockland Coll., 1971-72. Human rights commr., Beacon, N.Y., 1970; cubmaster Fairfield County Council Boy Scouts Am., 1976—; bd. dirs. CPE Federal Credit Union, 1979—. Mem. Am. Inst. Indsl. Engrs. (seminar paper, 1978), Data Processing Machinery Assn., Am. Records Mgrs. Assn., Planning Execs. Inst. Club: Redding Soccer (dir.). Contbr. articles to profl. jours. Home: Simpaug Turnpike Redding CT 06896 Office: 33 Bernhard Rd North Haven CT 06473

DEGROFF, RALPH LYNN, JR., investment banker; b. Balt., Oct. 23, 1936; s. Ralph Lynn and Marion (Day) D.; A.B., Princeton, 1958; M.B.A., U. Va., 1960; m. Carol Lucinda Colman, Oct. 3, 1970. With Dillon, Read & Co. Inc., N.Y.C., 1961—, v.p., 1970-74, sr. v.p., 1974—; dir. The Ryland Group, Inc. Served with U.S. Army, 1960-61. Presbyterian. Clubs: Downtown Assn., Maryland, Rockaway Hunting, Elkridge. Home: 7 Gracie Sq New York NY 10028 Office: 46 William St New York NY 10005

DE GROOTE, PETER LELAND, public retirement corp. exec.; b. Rochester, N.Y., Jan. 19, 1940; s. Leland Peter and Lena S. DeG.; B.A., W.Va. Wesleyan Coll., 1961; cert. social studies Syracuse U., 1965; M.A. in Public Adminstrn., Am. U., 1968, postgrad. in adminstrn., 1968-69. Tchr. social studies, public schs., Syracuse, N.Y., 1965-66; dir. Project-Lichtman, Washington, 1967-68; lectr. Am. U. Sch. Govt. and Public Adminstrn., 1968-69; asso. Internat. City Mgmt. Assn., Washington, 1969-72; gen. mgr. ICMA, Retirement Corp., Washington, 1972-79, pres., 1978—. Served with U.S. Army, 1961-64. Decorated Army Commendation medal. Mem. Am. Soc. Public Adminstrn., Am. Mgmt. Assn., Internat. City Mgmt. Assn., Public Risk and Ins. Mgmt. Assn., Pi Sigma Epsilon. Contbr. articles on mgmt. to profl. jours. Office: 1101 Connecticut Ave NW Washington DC 20036

DEGRUCHY, ALAN B., cons. engr.; b. Bklyn., Oct. 4, 1932; s. William C. and Ethne L. deG.; I.E., Indsl. Mgmt. Inst., 1956; degree in Bus. Adminstrn., Temple U., 1958. Apprentice, E.G. Budd Co., 1954-58; quality control mgr. Cutler Metal Products Co., 1958-62; plant mgr. Falco Products Co., 1962-63; chief engr. Met-Pro, Inc., 1963-66; project engr. Day & Zimmerman, Inc., 1966-72; corp. cons. engr. C.S.I., Bridgewater, N.J., 1972—. Mem. Am. Inst. Indsl. Engrs., Am. Soc. Quality Control. Club: Masons. Inventor automatic process and assembly machines. Address: C S I 888 Finderne Ave Bridgewater NJ 08807

DEIHL, RICHARD HARRY, savs. and loan assn. exec.; b. Whittier, Calif., Sept. 9, 1928; s. Victor Francis and Wilma Aileen (Thomas) D.; A.B., Whittier Coll., 1949; postgrad. UCLA, 1949, U. Calif., Berkeley, 1949-50; m. Billie Dantz Beane, Mar. 24, 1952; children—Catherine Kent, Michael, Victoria, Christine. With Nat. Cash Register Co., Pomona, Calif., 1955-59; trainee Rio Hondo Savs. & Loan (Calif.), 1959-60; loan cons. Home Savs. & Loan Assn. Los Angeles, 1960-63, loan agt., supr., v.p., 1964, loan service supr., 1964, v.p. ops., v.p. loans, 1965, exec. v.p., 1966, pres., chief exec. officer, 1967—, also dir.; dir. H.F. Ahmanson Co. Mem. Charter Oak Unified Sch. Dist. Bd., 1967—; trustee Whittier Coll. Served to 1st lt. USAF, 1951-55. Decorated D.F.C., Air medal with three clusters. Republican. Club: South Hills Country (West Covina, Calif.). Contbr. articles to profl. jours. Office: 3731 Wilshire Blvd Los Angeles CA 90010

DEINES, HARRY J., agr. and livestock co. exec.; b. Loveland, Colo., Nov. 5, 1909; s. John and Mary (Maseka) D.; B.S. in Mech. Engring., U. Colo.; grad. Advanced Mgmt. Program, Harvard U.; m. Eleanor Vrooman, 1932; children—Gretchen (Mrs. Charles Langston), Mark, Katrina, Stephen. Advt. mgr. Gen. Electric Co., 1930-45; v.p. Fuller & Smith & Ross., 1943-49; gen. advt. mgr. Westinghouse Electric Corp., 1949-53; v.p. J. Walter Thompson, N.Y.C., 1953-56, Fuller & Smith & Ross, N.Y.C., 1956-59; exec. v.p., dir. Campbell, Mithun, Inc., Mpls., 1959-71; mng. partner Deines Agr. & Livestock Co., Ft. Collins, Colo., 1971—; pres. Collectors' Books Ltd. Treas. Citizens for Property Rights. Home and office: 1707 Country Club Rd Fort Collins CO 80524

DEITTRICK, HENRY LOUIS, machine co. exec.; b. Filion, Mich., Apr. 11, 1925; s. Joseph and Martha (Stotz) D.; student Detroit Coll. Applied Sci., 1948-51; m. Rita Youness, June 29, 1968; children—(by previous marriage) Paul, Krista, Matthew, Susan. Machine operator Herron Zimmers Moulding, Detroit, 1942-51; with Bertin Engring., St. Clair Shores, Mich., 1951-56; owner Crest Design, E. Detroit, 1956-57; designer Mich. Spl. Machine (merged with Bendix Corp., name now Bendix Machine Tool Corp.), Warren, 1957-60, asst. chief engr., 1960-67, chief engr., 1967-74, v.p. engring., 1974-78, staff asst., 1978—. Served with AUS, 1943-46; ETO. Lutheran. Home: 53747 Starlite Dr Utica MI 48087 Office: 23655 Hoover St Warren MI 48089

DEJARNETTE, SHIRLEY SHEA, corp. fin. ofcl.; b. Bradford, Pa., Feb. 21, 1943; d. James Harold and Jean Lorrain (Dennis) Shea; A.A., Stephens Coll., 1963; B.S. in Bus. Adminstrn., U. Mo., 1966; m. Jaquelin Harrison DeJarnette, Mar. 21, 1978; 1 dau., Shea Ann. Trust officer Boatmen's Nat. Bank, St. Louis, 1966-74; mgr. investor relations and pension funds Kraft Inc., Glenview, Ill., 1974-77; dir. investment research Cummins Engine Co., Columbus, Ind., 1977-78; asst. treas. and dir. pension fund investments Mead Corp., Dayton, Ohio, 1978—; founder So. Ohio Pension Group. Trustee, mem. fin. com. U. Dayton; mem. Oakwood Republican Council. Chartered fin. analyst. Mem. Inst. Chartered Fin. Analysts, Fin. Analysts Fedn., Investment Analysts Soc. Chgo., Cin. Soc. Fin. Analy sts, Phi Chi Theta. Episcopalian. Clubs: Dayton Racquet, Country of Va., Wintergreen Country. Home: 12 Spirea Dr Dayton OH 45419 Office: Courthouse Plaza NE Dayton OH 45463

DEJETLEY, TONY RUSSEL, corporate exec.; b. Colombo, Ceylon, Mar. 19, 1923; s. John and Marie (Ferrando) deJ.; came to U.S., 1960, naturalized, 1973; diploma Cordon Bleu Academie de Cuisine, Paris, France, 1956; m. Alberta Sophia Morita, May 31, 1968; children—David Kauiki, Tony George. Various hotel positions in Eng., 1939-49, Fiji Islands, 1949-52, 59-60, New Zealand, 1952-55, 56-59, France, 1955-56; food and beverage mgr. Halekulani Hotel, Oahu, Waiohai Hotel, Kauai, gen. mgr., Hawaii; v.p., gen. mgr. Royal Lahaina Hotel, Maui, Hawaii, 1969—, Hotel Hana Maui Hana, Hawaii, 1969—; v.p. Hana Ranch, Inc., 1969, v.p. comml. div., 1977—, also dir.; pres. Hana U Drive Co., 1973—; dir., officer Hana Land Co., Hana Water Co., Hana-Maui Transp. Co. Served with Spl. Air Service Brit. Army, 1941-45; ETO. Fellow Cookery and Food Assn. Eng.; mem. Hawaii Hotel Assn., Hotel and Catering Assn. Eng., Pacific Area Travel Assn. (asso.), Am. Hotel and Motel Assn. (blue ribbon resort com.). Address: Hotel Hana-Maui Hana HI 96713

DEKONING, JOSEPHUS BERNARDUS, elec., chem. engr.; b. Surabaya, Dutch E. Indies, Mar. 30, 1929; s. Bernardus Petrus Josephus and Johanna Elizabeth (DeRoode) DeK.; came to U.S., 1956, naturalized, 1965; B.S.E.E. & Ch.E., Hogere Technische Sch., Eindhoven, Netherlands, 1956; postgrad. in engring. U. Ill., Chgo., 1958-59; m. Corrie Nellie Vnader Linden, Sept. 14, 1954; children—Bernard L., Cornelia E., Linda H., Margaret J. Project engr. Ekco Products Co., Chgo., 1959-65, Amoco Chem. Corp., Chgo., 1965-70; area supr. Witco Chem. Corp., Chgo., 1970-72; plant mgr. Indsl. Oil & Varnish Co., Chicago Heights, Ill., 1972-74; project mgr. Chemetron Corp., Chgo., 1974-78; cons. engr. Bendek Engring. Co., Orland Park, Ill., 1978—; pres. Flying Dutchman Travel Service, Inc., Tinley Park, Ill. Chmn. adminstrv. bd. United Meth. Ch., Oak Forest, 1974—; active Boys Scouts Am., Oak Lawn Masonic Lodge 1166. Served with Royal Dutch Air Force, 1949-52. Republican. Home and Office: 15365 Orchid Ct Orland Park IL 60462

DE KOSTER, HEINZ A., technol. cons.; b. Heidelberg, Germany, Apr. 11, 1919; came to U.S., 1959; s. Godfried and Maria Elisabeth de K.; M.S.E.E., Acad. Tech. Scis. and Arts, Rotterdam, Holland, 1939; Ph.D. in Applied Physics, U. Heidelberg, 1945; m. Martha M. Hoerdt, July 27, 1942; children—Alexander P., Beatrix E. Head indsl. controls Hasler A.G., Switzerland, 1952-59; staff scientist ITT-Kellogg, Palo Alto, Calif., 1961-63; head applied physics dept. Gen. Time Corp., Stamford, Conn., 1963-68; v.p. engring., dir. Seggos Industries/Kenilworth R&D Corp., Stamford, 1968-75; technol. - cons., 1975—. Mem. IEEE (sr.), Am. Phys. Soc., N.Y. Acad. Scis. Contbr. numerous articles to profl. jours. Patentee in field (25). Address: 47 Caprice Dr Stamford CT 06902

DEKRUIF, ROBERT M., business exec. Pres., H.F. Ahmanson & Co., Los Angeles. Office: HF Ahmanson & Co 3731 Wilshire Blvd Los Angeles CA 90010*

DELAHOUSSAYE, CURTIS MARTIN, plaster contracting co. exec.; b. Lafayette, La., Dec. 28, 1925; s. John Wesley and Marie Therese (Martin) D.; grad. high sch.; m. Merry Clem Cosper, Sept. 23, 1971; children—Cynthia, Curtis, Albert, Daniel, Gregory, Don, Richard, Dominique, Andre. Pres., chief estimator J.W. Delahoussaye & Sons, Inc., Lafayette, La., 1948—; pres. C.M.D., Inc., Lafayette, 1966-74. Chmn., Lafayette Airport Commn., 1967. Served with AUS, 1944-46. Decorated Bronze Star, Purple Heart. Mem. La. Thoroughbred Breeders Assn. (dir.), Internat. Assn. Wall and Ceiling Contractors, Asso. Gen. Contractors, Am. Subcontractors Assn., Confederate Air Force, VFW. Democrat. Roman Catholic. Home: Route 1 Box 59C1F Broussard LA 70518 Office: 427 N Sterling Ave Lafayette LA 70501

DE LANCEY, WILLIAM JOHN, steel co. exec.; b. Chgo., June 2, 1916; s. John Richmond and Louise Ella (Hart) DeL.; B.A., U. Mich., 1938, J.D., 1940; m. Sally Ann Roe, July 10, 1940; children—Ann Louise, Mark Roe. Admitted to N.Y. bar, 1941; asso. firm Cravath, de Gersdorff, Swaine & Wood, N.Y.C., 1940-52; with Republic Steel Corp., Cleve., 1952—, v.p., gen. counsel, 1961-71, exec. v.p., 1971-73, pres., 1973-74, pres., chief exec. officer, 1974-79, chmn. and chief exec. officer, 1979—; dir. AmeriTrust Corp., AmeriTrust Co., Ohio Bell Telephone Co., Sherwin Williams Co., Standard Oil Co. (Ohio), Beatrice Pocahontas Co., Met. Life Ins. Co., Republic Supply Co., Res. Mining Co. trustee, chmn. Ednl. TV Assn. Met. Cleve.; active Mus. Arts Assn., Univ. Hosps., Case Western Res. U. Served with USNR, 1943-45. Decorated Commendation medal. Mem. Am. Iron and Steel Inst. (chmn., dir.), Internat. Iron and Steel Inst. (dir.). Editor: Mich. Law Rev., 1939-40. Home: 2952 Kingsley Rd Shaker Heights OH 44120 Office: 1707 Republic Bldg Cleveland OH 44101

DELANEY, FRANKLIN, broadcasting exec.; b. Magdalen Islands, Que., Can., Oct. 15, 1940; s. Albert and Claudia (Arseneau) D.; B.A., Coll. de Bathurst (N.B.), 1961; Licence in Law, U. Ottawa (Ont.), 1967; m. Genevieve Cormier, Aug. 28, 1965; children—Chantal, Danielle. Called to Que. bar, 1968; sec. Gan. Radio-television Commn., Ottawa, 1967-71; pres. Radio Inter-Cite Inc., Montreal, Que., 1971—, also pres. and dir. subsidiary companies. Mem. Can. Bar Assn. Roman Catholic. Home: 420 Strathcona Dr Mount-Royal PQ H3R 1G1 Canada Office: 1010 Ste Catherine St W Suite 920 Montreal PQ H3B 3R7 Canada

DELANEY, LOUIS M., JR., investment banker; b. Phila., Oct. 15, 1932; s. Louis M. and Rosemary C. (Wills) D.; B.S., Temple U., 1954-58; m. Margaret Kritler, Feb. 20, 1960; children—Louis M., Laura, Michelle. Importer Lotus cars, internat. team driver, 1957-60; v.p. Dehaven, Townsend, Crouter & Badine, 1960-78; with Elkins & Co., Bala Cynwyd, Pa., 1978—, gen. partner, 1980—; lectr. Investors Info. Com. of N.Y. Stock Exchange, investment seminars. Served with U.S. Army, 1952-54. Mem. Investment Assn. Phila. Republican. Roman Catholic. Club: Old York Rd. Country (Spring House, Pa.). Office: 191 Presidential Blvd Bala Cynwyd PA 19004

DE LAURENTIS, ROBERT, mfg. co. exec.; b. Pennsauken, N.J., July 22, 1940; s. Joseph and Angelina (DiPace) DeL.; B.S. with honors in Elec. Engring., Rutgers U., 1961; M.B.A., U. Pa., 1968; postgrad. in fin. and taxation Northwestern U., 1968-69; m. Frances R. Perry, Dec. 28, 1962; children—Nicole, Robert. Sr. auditor Arthur Young & Co., C.P.A.'s, San Francisco, 1968-70; asst. to v.p. fin. Envirotech. Corp., Menlo Park, Calif., 1970-71; product line controller Fairchild Camera & Instrument Corp., Mountain View, Calif., 1971-73, fgn. plant controller, 1973-76, div. controller mfg. services, 1976; v.p. fin., co-founder Diversified Mgmt. Services, Inc., 1977-79; ops. controller Measurex Corp., Cupertino, Calif., 1979-80; controller Electron Tube div. Litton Industries, San Carlos, Calif., 1980—. Mem. fin. com. City of Belmont (Calif.), 1971-72. Served to lt. USN, 1962-66. C.P.A., Calif. Mem. Am. Inst. C.P.A.'s. Republican. Roman Catholic. Club: Commonwealth of Calif. Home: 865 Somerset Ct San Carlos CA 94070

DEL CAMPO, MARTIN BERNARDELLI, architect; b. Guadalajara, Mexico, Nov. 27, 1922; s. Salvador and Margarita (Bernardelli) Del C.; B.A., Colegio Frances Morelos, Mexico City, 1941; Archtl. degree Escuela Nacional de Arquitectura, Mexico City, 1948; m. Laura Zaikowska, May 25, 1945; children—Felicia, Margarita, Mario. Came to U.S., 1949, naturalized, 1960. Partner, Del Campo & Fruiht, architects, Santa Rosa, Cal., 1955-56, Del Campo & Clark, San Francisco, 1957-63; mgr. Hotel Victoria, Oaxaca, Mexico, 1964-67; pres. Gulli-Del Campo, architects, San Francisco, 1968-70; partner Del Campo Assos., San Francisco, 1971—; pres., dir. City Fed. Savs., Oakland, Calif., 1974—. Lectr. archtl. design Coll. Environmental Design, U. Calif. at Berkeley, 1973-74. Mem. Democratic Nat. Com., 1972—. Mem. A.I.A. (sec. exec. com. 1970—). Archtl. works include: White Oaks Theatre, Carmel Valley, Calif.; Kaiser Hosp., San Rafael, Calif.; Sun Reporter Bldg., San Francisco; El Dorado Bldg., San Francisco. Address: 1601 Shrader San Francisco CA 94117

DELCHER, EDWIN G., mfg. co. exec.; b. Balt.; grad. bus. adminstrn. Loyola Coll., Balt. Controller, Martin-Marietta Corp., 1961-66; financial v.p. sec., treas. Black & Decker Mfg. 1966-78, sr. v.p. and sec., 1978—; dir. Brown & Sharpe Mfg. Co., Union Trust Co. of Md. Trustee, St. Joseph Hosp. Mem. Fin. Execs. Inst., Md. Assn. C.P.A.'s. Address: Black & Decker Mfg Co 701 E Joppa Rd Towson MD 21204

DELF, ROBERT PAUL, supermarket exec.; b. Davenport, Iowa, Oct. 13, 1938; s. Clyde and Evelyn (Strigel) D.; student data processing Auburn Community Coll.; children—Debra, Robin, Robert. Asst. store mgr. P&C Food Markets, Syracuse, N.Y., 1959-62, store mgr., 1962-65, grocery supr., 1965-66; pres. Robert Delf Inc. doing bus. as Bob's Big M, Wolcott, N.Y., 1966—. Village trustee Village of Wolcott, 1976-78, 79—, acting mayor, 1978-79, mayor, 1980—. Republican. Roman Catholic. Clubs: Lions, Elks. Home: 39 W Main St Wolcott NY 14590 Office: 1 Park Ln Wolcott NY 14590

DELGADO, JOSEPH RAMON, business exec.; b. Chgo., Mar. 4, 1932; s. Joseph Ramon and Florence (Nelson) D.; B.A. in English, U. Ill., 1958. With Campbell-Mithun Advt., Chgo., 1960-68, purchasing agent, dir. office services, 1960-66, purchasing agt., dir. office services, 1964-68; purchasing agt., asst. to pres. and treas. Maxant Button & Supply Co., Chgo., 1968-70; asst. purchasing agt., adminstrv. asst. Soiltest, Inc., 1970—. Mem. Lyric Opera Subscription Com., 1957. Observer, Joint Civic Com. on Elections, 1965, election-judge, 1968, 70. Served with AUS, 1952-54. Mem. Purchasing Agts. Assn. Chgo. (co-chmn. publicity and pub. relations com. 1963-64), U. Ill. Alumni, Illiniweks. Lutheran. Republican. Clubs: Whitehall, Barclay Ltd., Internat. (Chgo.). Dance choreographer for various groups and individuals. Home: 900 Lake Shore Dr Apt 905 Chicago IL 60611 Office: 2205 Lee St Evanston IL 60202

DELICATE, DONALD THOMAS, mining co. exec.; b. Hot Springs, S.D., June 8, 1923; s. Thomas Wesley and May P. (Phillips) D.; B.Mining cum laude, U. Minn., 1947; grad. exec. mgmt. course Columbia, 1970; m. Dorothy Jean Ross, Jan. 1, 1948; children—Ann, Thomas, Jane, Michael, Catherine. With Homestake Mining Co., 1948—, mgr. Homestake Gold Mine, Lead, S.D., 1972-78, v.p. co., 1972-78, sr. v.p., 1978—; cons., dir. Homestake Mining Co., 1979—; dir. First Nat. Bank Black Hills. Bd. dirs. Mt. Rushmore Meml. Soc. Served with inf. AUS, 1943-46. Decorated Bronze Star. Mem. AIME, Am. Mining Congress (nat. program chmn. 1978). Presbyterian (elder). Kiwanian (past pres. Lead). Home and Office: PO Box 866 Custer SD 57730

DELLA FEMINA, JERRY, advt. agy. exec.; b. Bklyn., July 22, 1936; m. Barbara Rizzi; children—Donna, Michael, Jodi. Advt. copywriter Ashe & Engelmore, 1962-64; v.p., creative dir. DKG, Inc., 1964-66; v.p., creative supr. Ted Bates & Co., 1966-67; chmn. bd. Della Femina, Travisano, & Partners Inc., 1967—. Named Advt. Exec. of Year, 1970. Author: From Those Wonderful Folks Who Gave You Pearl Harbor, 1970. Office: 625 Madison Ave New York NY 10022

DELLORFANO, FRANK JOSEPH, sports floors mfg. exec.; b. Lynn, Mass., June 2, 1934; s. Fred Michael and Olga Anna (Massa) D.; A.B., St. John's Sem., 1955; postgrad. Boston Coll., 1955-56. With Championship Sports Floors, Inc., Hingham, Mass., 1961-70, pres., 1970—. Mem. bd. overseers, mem. devel. com. Met. Center, Inc., Boston; bd. dirs. Mass. Spl. Edn. Assn., Inc. Served with USN, 1958-61. Mem. Ancient and Honorable Arty. Co. of Mass., Trustees of Reservations, Knights of Malta. Clubs: N.Y. Athletic; Boston Madison Sq. Garden. Home: 454 Jerusalem Rd Cohasset MA 02025 Office: Championship Sports Floors Inc 349 Lincoln St Hingham MA 02043

DE LOREAN, JOHN ZACHARY, automobile co. exec.; b. Detroit, Jan. 6, 1925; s. Zachary R. and Katherine (Pribak) DeL.; B.S. in Indsl. Engring., Lawrence Inst. Tech., 1948; M.S. in Automotive Engring., Chrysler Inst., 1952; M.B.A., U. Mich., 1956; m. Cristina Ferrare; children—Zachary, Kathryn. Product engr. Chrysler Corp., 1948-52; research engr., dir. research Packard Motor Co., 1952-56; dir. advanced engring. Pontiac Motor div. Gen. Motors Corp., 1956-59, asst. chief engr., 1959-61, chief engr., 1961-65, gen. mgr., 1965-69, v.p., 1965-73, gen. mgr. Chevrolet div., 1969-72, v.p., group exec. N.Am. car and truck group, 1972-73; pres. Nat. Alliance of Businessmen, 1973-74; chmn. John Z. De Lorean Corp., N.Y.C., 1974-75, De Lorean Motor Co., 1975—. Mem. Soc. Automotive Engrs. Clubs: Bloomfield Hills Country; N.Y. Athletic, The Boardroom (N.Y.C.); Augusta (Ga.) Nat. Golf (dir.); Pauma Valley Country. Author: Black Capitalism. Office: 280 Park Ave New York NY 10017

DELOZIER, DONALD EDWARD, JR., advt. co. exec.; b. Detroit, Mar. 19, 1942; s. Donald Edward and Mildred Eleanor (Tate) D.; student Mich. State U., 1959-65, Wayne State U., 1965-66, 69; m. Margaret O'Connor, Apr. 6, 1968; children—Donald Edward, Catherine. With Ross Roy Advt. Inc., Detroit, 1968—, adminstrv. v.p., 1972—. Mem. Nat. C. of C. Mem. Mich. Advt. Industry Alliance. Clubs: Detroit Athletic, Psi Upsilon. Office: 2751 E Jefferson St Detroit MI 48207

DELPH, THOMAS LEE, publisher; b. Anderson, Ind., June 26, 1933; s. Everett William and Marjorie Isabell (Cookman) D.; B.S., Ind. U., 1955; m. Marylu Merrill, June 13, 1970; children by previous marriage—Beth Delph Gifford, Carol, Deborah Delph Whitehurst, Kimberly, William, Stephanie, Angela. Asst. sports editor Bloomington (Ind.) Herald-Telephone, 1954-55; asso. editor Hardware Retailing, Indpls., 1958-61, mng. editor, 1961-64, sales promotion mgr., 1964-66, marketing mgr., 1966-68, gen. sales mgr., 1968—, dir. sales and marketing, 1973—, asso. pub., 1980—. Mem. Media Comparability Council, 1970—. Active Delaware Trails Little League, Jordan YMCA. Precinct del. Republican party, 1961-64, mem. nat. speakers' bur., 1962-64. Served with AUS, 1956-57. Recipient award for article Indsl. Marketing, 1960. Mem. Indpls. Ad Club, Am. Hardware Mfg. Assn. Young Execs., Ind. U. Alumni Assn., German Shepherd Dog Club Central Ind. (pres. 1976-77), Wabash Valley German Shepherd Dog Club (pres. 1979), German Shepherd Dog Club Am., Owners-Handlers Assn., Ind. U. Varsity Club. Methodist. Club: Toastmasters (Dist. Speaker of Year 1960). Home: 533 Quail Valley Dr Zionsville IN 46077 Office: 770 N High School Rd Indianapolis IN 46224

DEL-ROSARIO, ERNESTO, ins. co. exec.; b. Yauco, P.R., Nov. 17, 1911; s. Ulises and Josefa E. (Olivieri) Del-R.; student Yauco Comml. Coll., 1928-29; m. Josefina Masini, July 24, 1936; children—Elliette A. Del-Rosario Pico, Juan E. Asst. postmaster U.S. Post Office, Yauco, 1929-37; income tax insp. P.R. Treasury Dept., San Juan, 1937-41; pub. accountant, tax practice, San Juan, 1941-42; comptroller Coop. Azucarera Los Canos, Arecibo, P.R., 1942-62; br. mgr. Nationwide Ins. Cos., Hato Rey, P.R., 1962—, resident v.p. for P.R., 1975-77, cons., 1977-78; exec. dir. P.R. Ins. Guaranty Assns., 1977—. Hon. mem. Civic Crusade for Traffic Safety, 1975-76. Mem. P.R. Coll. C.P.A.'s, Nat. Soc. Pub. Accountants, Nat. Soc. Coop. Accountants. Roman Catholic. Clubs: Elks, Casino De P.R., Bankers Club P.R. Home: M-207 Villa Caparra Guaynabo PR 00657 Office: PO Box 272 Hato Rey PR 00919

DELUCA, RICKY ALAN, meat packing co. exec.; b. Martins Ferry, Ohio, Jan. 18, 1952; s. Lawrence P. and Mildred (Plinta) DeL.; student Ohio U., 1970-72, Jefferson County Tech. Inst., 1973-75; m. Robin Lee Conaway, June 28, 1975; 1 son, Bradley Michael. Sports writer Times-Leader, Martins Ferry, 1969-79, news reporter, writer, 1977-79; editor Company A Newsletter, Bellaire, Ohio, 1977—; with DeLuca Packing Co., Inc., Rayland, Ohio, 1970—, sec.-treas., dir., 1974—; free-lance writer, 1975-78; sports writer Times-Leader, 1969—. Pres. Warren Twp. Boys Baseball Assn., 1973-74. Served with USAR, 1972—. Mem. Am. Assn. Meat Processors, Ohio Meat Industries, Am. Meat Industry, Ohio Prep Sports Writers Assn. (award 1977, 80). Democrat. Clubs: Indian (Tiltonsville, Ohio); Forrestors (Martins Ferry, Ohio); Upper Ohio Valley Dapper Dan. Home: RD 1 Larges Hill Rayland OH 43943 Office: RD 3 Box 28 Rayland OH 43943

DE LUCCA, GREGORY JAMES, winery exec.; b. Milw., June 2, 1937; s. Anthony James and Irene Eleanor (Linski) DeL.; B.S. in Chem. Engring., U. Wis., 1959, M.B.A., 1962; m. Carol L. Enrico, Apr. 8, 1967; children—Alison, Ashley. Mgr. mktg. Pacific Coca-Cola Bottling Co., Seattle, 1967-71, mgr. ops. Western area Coca-Cola U.S.A., Burlingame, Calif., 1971-73, mgr. ops. engring. The Coca Cola Co., Atlanta, 1973-77; v.p., gen. mgr. Sterling Vineyards, Calistoga, Calif., 1977—. Trustee, Queen of the Valley Hosp. Found. Served to capt. USAR, 1959-67. Mem. Am. Soc. Enologists, Nat. Council Phys. Distbn. Mgmt., Napa Valley Vintners, Napa Valley Wine Library Assn., Upper Napa Valley Assos. Republican. Roman Catholic. Club: Meadowood Country. Home: PO Box 95 Saint Helena CA 94574 Office: PO Box 365 Calistoga CA 94515

DE LUCE, DONALD DEAN, banker; b. Steubenville, Ohio, Aug. 3, 1949; s. Dominic and Elizabeth (Miclea) DeL.; student Kent State U., 1970-73, Palm Beach Jr. Coll., 1973-76, Stonier Grad. Sch. Banking, Rutgers U., 1979-81; m. Mary Ann Borkowski, Dec. 7, 1976; children—Theresa, Joseph. Asst. mgr. comml. credit Sun Bank of Delray Beach (Fla.), 1973-75, asst. v.p., 1975-77; asst. v.p. Gulfstream Banks of Fla., Boca Raton, 1977-78, v.p., 1978-79, sr. v.p., 1979—; dir. Consumer Credit Counseling Service, 1978—. Served with USMC, 1968-70; Vietnam. Mem. Am. Bankers Assn (adv. bd. installment lending div.), Fla. Bankers Assn., Am. Inst. Banking (gov. Palm Beach chpt. 1973-75), Robert Morris Assn. Home: 3856 NW 7th Ct Delray Beach FL 33445 Office: 3900 N Federal Hwy Boca Raton FL 33432

DELZ, WILLIAM R., publishing exec.; b. N.Y.C., June 29, 1932; s. William W. and Mona M. (Hasler) D.; B.B.A., Iona Coll., 1957; m. Joan C. Breitenbach, June 29, 1957; children—Pamela J., Nicole B. Accountant, Main, Lefrentz & Co., Alexander Grant & Co. and Harris, Kerr Forster & Co., 1957-65; treas. Troy Textiles, Inc., N.Y.C., 1965-67, Royal Petroleum Corp., N.Y.C., 1967-70; v.p., controller New Eng. Petroleum Corp., N.Y.C., 1970-75, Joc Oil, Inc., N.Y.C., 1975-77; treas. Bantam Books Inc., N.Y.C., 1977-79; sr. v.p. fin. and adminstrn. Simon & Schuster, N.Y.C., 1979—. Pres. Fathers Club of Sch. of Holy Child, Purchase, N.Y., 1976-77. Served with U.S. Army, 1952-54. C.P.A., N.Y. Mem. Am. Inst. C.P.A.'s, N.Y. State Soc. C.P.A.'s, Am. Petroleum Inst. Republican. Roman Catholic. Club: Westchester Country (Rye, N.Y.). Home: Purchase St Rye NY 10580 Office: 666 Fifth Ave New York NY 10022

DE MAINE, DENNIS PAUL, agrl. equipment mfg. co. exec.; b. Pembina, N.D., Apr. 8, 1933; s. Paul and Kathryn (Matthiasson) DeM.; B.S., Calif. State Poly. U., 1961; M.B.A., U. Portland, 1976; m. Carolyn Castaneda, Sept. 9, 1956; children—Paul, Mark, David. Tchr., Los Angeles sch. system, 1962-64; with John Deere Co., San Francisco, Portland, Oreg., and Syracuse, N.Y., 1964—, spl. rep., 1964-65, ter. mgr., 1965-69, sales promotion mgr., 1969-72, divisional sales mgr., 1972-75, gen. sales mgr., 1975—; guest lectr. agr. Calif. State U., San Luis Obispo, 1969-71. Served with USN, 1952-56. Mem. Am. Mgmt. Assn., Vocat. Agr. Tchrs. Assn., Nat. Agrl. Advt. and Mktg. Assn., Agrl. Council of Am., Mensa, Phi Kappa Phi, Alpha Zeta. Democrat. Roman Catholic. Club: Elks. Home: 8823 Salt Spring Rd Chittanango NY 13037 Office: Deere and Court Sts Syracuse NY 13037

DE MANCHE, LEO MICHAEL, JR., govt. ofcl.; b. Milford, Mass., Mar. 16, 1946; s. Leo M. and Louise Martha (Ballou) De M.; cert. in labor relations Holy Cross Coll., 1970; B.A., Framingham (Mass.) State Coll., 1976; postgrad. (Grad. Senate fellow), U. Mass., 1977; M.P.A., Western New Eng. Coll., 1978; m. Carol A. Foley, Oct. 18, 1969; children—Michelle R., Christopher M. Adminstrv. asst. Mass. Ho. of Reps., Boston, 1966-70; exec. dir. Commn. on lMil. Affairs, Boston, part-time, 1971-73; chief adminstrv. asst. Mass. Senate, Boston, 1970-78; presdl. mgmt. intern U.S. Office Personnel Mgmt., Boston, 1978—, dep. area mgr., 1980—; lectr. public adminstrn. Western New Eng. Coll., 1980-81, fed. careers adv. Mem. Mass. State Bicentennial Commn. Adv. Council, 1972-75, mil. service evaluation com. Framingham State Coll., 1974-76; mem. TV public service commls., Mass. Coll. System, 1979-80. Mem. New Eng. Fed. Personnel Council, Internat. Personnel Mgmt. Assn., Am. Soc. for Public Adminstrn., Western New Eng. Coll. Alumni Assn., Framingham State Coll. Alumni Assn. Roman Catholic. Editor, Final Report of the Spl. Commn. on Mil. Affairs, 1974. Home: 12 Metcalf Ave Milford MA 01757 Office: US Office of Personnel Mgmt Boston Area Office 3 Center Plaza Boston MA 02203

DEMANN, MICHAEL MARCUS, indsl. psychologist; b. Mpls., June 1, 1932; s. George S. and Mary Hazel (Short) DeM.; B.A., U. Minn., 1955, M.A., 1958, Ph.D., 1960; m. Carol L. Knutson, Feb. 10, 1961; children—James G., Susan M., John P. Staff mem. VA Hosp., Mpls., 1960-61; cons. psychologist Rohrer, Hibler and Replogle, Mpls., 1961-65; cons. psychologist in pvt. practive, Mpls., 1965—; dir. Internat. Graphics Corp., Mpls., 1967—; cons. Social Security Adminstrn., Mpls., 1966-67. Bd. dirs. Opportunity Workshop, Mpls., 1962-69; bd. govs. St. Mary's Jr. Coll., Mpls., 1973. Served with M.C., U.S. Army, 1950-52. Mem. Am. Psychol. Assn., Minn. Psychol. Assn. (exec. council 1971-73), Am. Legion. Episcopalian. Home: 6513 Stauder Circle Edina MN 55436 Office: 6750 France Ave S Minneapolis MN 55435

DEMAREST, LEROY ERNEST, food processing machinery co. exec.; b. Patterson, La., Dec. 14, 1921; s. Ernest and Alice T. (Wiltz) D.; student Tulane U., 1939-40, La. State U., 1940-41; m. Angel Mancine, May 16, 1944; children—Charles, Paul, Arthur, Holly. Tool engr. Chrysler Corp., 1951-53; with Laitram Corp., Harahan, La., 1954-80, treas., 1963-69, mgr. mktg., 1969-80, dir., 1975-80; pvt. practice cons. to food processing industry and to designers and mfrs. equipment for processing plants; dir. Digicourse Inc., Intralox, Inc., Tuna, Inc.; mktg. mgr. Lidgroup; mem. Pres.'s Nat. Export Expansion Council, 1972—. Mem. Delta Region Preservation Commn., U.S. Dept. Interior, 1979—. Served with USNR, World War II. Mem. Nat. Fisheries Inst. (dir.), Gulf Caribbean Fisheries Inst. (dir.), Internat. Food Technologists, Am. Shrimp Breeders Assn. (dir.), La. Shrimp Assn. (dir.). Roman Catholic. Patentee machines processing shrimp. Home and Office: 130 Chateau Latour Dr Kenner LA 70062

DE MARGITAY, GEDEON, acquisitions and mgmt. cons.; b. Budapest, Hungary, Mar. 6, 1924; s. Joseph and Anne (de Bessenyei) deM.; came to U.S., 1953, naturalized, 1958; student U. Budapest Grad. Sch. Economics, 1941-44, Ecole des Scis. Politiques, Paris, 1946-48; m. Virginia Varet Martin, Dec. 30, 1963. With N.Y. Times, 1947-50, European info. div. Mut. Security Agy., 1950-53; with N.Y. Times, 1954-61; chief exec. Magnum Photos, Inc., N.Y.C., 1961-63; with Time Inc., 1964-75, dir. mktg. services Time/Life TV, 1975; dir. broadcast and corp. planning NBC, 1975-78; acquistions and mgmt. cons., N.Y.C., 1978—. Mem. N. Am. Assn. Corp. Planning, Internat. Radio TV Soc., Am. Mgmt. Assn., World Future Soc., Am. Acad. Polit. Social Sci. Republican. Presbyterian. Co-author: Broadcasting: The Next Ten Years, 1977. Address: 65 E 96th St New York NY 10028

DEMARTIGNY, FRANÇOIS LEMOYNE, publisher; b. Can., May 19, 1943; s. Camille LeMoyne and Françoise deM.; B.A., U. Ottawa (Ont.), 1963; M.A., Carleton U., 1969. Prof., Carleton U., Ottawa, 1970-72; info. officer Govt. Can., Ottawa, 1972-74; pres. François L. de Martigny, Publisher Ltd., Montreal, Que., 1977—. Author: Energy, today and tomorrow, 1973.

DE MATTEIS, FREDERICK, constrn. co. exec.; b. Bklyn., Apr. 24, 1923; s. Leon D. and Letezia (Vetere) DeM.; student N.Y. U., 1946-48, Inst. Design and Constrn., Bklyn., 1948-50; m. Jan. 5, 1947; children—Linda, Richard, Scott, Tracey Ann. Partner, Leon D. DeMatteis Constrn. Co., Bklyn., 1946-52; partner Leon DeMatteis Constrn. Corp., 1952-65, pres., 1965—; pres. Leon D. DeMatteis & Sons, Inc., Elmont, N.Y., 1953-65, chmn. bd., 1965—; chmn. bd. DeMatteis Devel. Corp., 1965—; trustee L.I. Savs. Bank. Bd. dirs. Nat. Housing Conf., Washington, St. Vincents Hall, Bklyn., 1975—, St. Francis Hosp., Roslyn, N.Y., 1972—. Served with A.C., U.S. Army, 1943-45. Decorated Air medal, Purple Heart. Named Man of Year, Real Estate Bd., 1975; recipient award for excellence City of N.Y., 1973. Mem. Downtown Lower-Manhattan Assn. (dir.), Bldg. Trades Employers Assn., Bldg. Congress. Clubs: N.Y. Athletic (N.Y.C.); Wheatley Hills Golf (Long Island, N.Y.). Office: 820 Elmont Rd Elmont NY 11003

DEMENZES, CHARLES, mortgage broker; b. N.Y.C., July 31, 1936; s. Charles and Julia (Lugo) deM.; student Westchester Community Coll., 1953-55; m. Shirley Marie Fulmer, July 8, 1961; children—April, Deborah, Craig. Sr. v.p. Dade Fed. Savs. & Loan Assn. Miami (Fla.), 1963-76; pres. Am. First Mortgage Funding Corp., Ocala, Fla., 1976—, DeMenzes Realty Inc., Ocala, 1978—. Mem. budget com. United Way, Ocala, 1979-80. Served with USAF, 1955-59. Mem. Fla. Assn. Mortgage Brokers, Nat. Assn. Mortgage Brokers, Fla. Assn. Realtors, Nat. Assn. Realtors, Ocala C. of C. Democrat. Roman Catholic. Club: K.C. Home: 1831 SE 13th St Ocala FL 32670 Office: 2137 SE Ft King St Ocala FL 32670

DEMETRAL, GEORGE DAVID, telephone co. ofcl.; b. Chgo., Mar. 23, 1927; s. William James and Emma Katherine (Hoeffling) D.; ed. high sch.; m. Shirley Wright, Mar. 17, 1949; children—David George, Ann Marie, Dawn Katherine, Dale Sharon. Apprentice cable splicer Ill. Bell Telephone Co., 1948-52, cable splicer, 1952-55, electronic technician, mobile radio and microwave, 1955-67, foreman installation repair, 1967-68, coordinator spl. projects Kincaid, Eastern Airlines, Willowcrest Cut-over (Schaumburg-Hoffman Estates), 1968-71, mgr. constrn. LaGrange, Wheaton, Hinsdale and Westmont dists., 1971-80, Villa Park dist., 1980—. First lt. Worth (Ill.) Vol. Fire Dept., 1956-69; treas. Worth Salvation Army, 1958-64; instr. 1st. aid ARC, 1959-69; active Little League, Boy Scouts Am. Served with USNR, 1945-48, 49-51; ATO, POT, Korea. Mem. Telephone Pioneers Am. (council v.p.), Ill. Firemen's Assn. Roman Catholic. Clubs: Moose, Lions. Home: 12122 Spring Dr Palos Park IL 60464 Office: 900 N Villa Villa Park IL 60181

DE MILIA, JOSEPH ANTHONY, JR., acct.; b. Tarrytown, N.Y., Dec. 1, 1946; s. Joseph Anthony and Helen (Koval) DeM.; B.B.A., Pace U., 1969; m. Mary Staffiera, Nov. 29, 1969; children—Donna, Joseph, David. Jr. acct. Hales, Dykes, C.P.A.'s, Ossining, N.Y., 1968-69; acctg. mgr. Otarion Electronics, Inc., Ossining, 1970-71, asst. controller, 1971-72; audit mgr. T.E. Hales & Co., C.P.A.'s, Tarrytown, N.Y., 1972-79; mgr. Landry, Hales and Singler, C.P.A.'s, White Plains, N.Y., 1979-80; controller, operating officer Nat. Plumbing Supply Corp., Ossining, N.Y., 1980—. Mem. Assn. Govtl. Accts., Am. Assn. Accts., Nat. Assn. Accts., Am. Mgmt. Assn. Roman Catholic. Home: 4 Ingham Rd Briarcliff Manor NY 10510 Office: 304 Spring St Ossining NY 10562

DEMING, CARL JOSEPH, comml. contractor; b. Balt., Aug. 28, 1950; s. Clyde F. and Ann H. Deming; student Montgomery Jr. Coll., 1968-70, Towson State U., 1970-71, U. Md., 1971-72; m. Marsha Diann, May 22, 1971; 1 son, Brian Joseph. Estimator, salesman Chesapeake Applicators, Inc., 1972-75; pres. Deming Bros., Inc., interior comml. contractors, Balt., 1975—; tchr. Md. apprenticeship program, 1975-76; cons. various corps. Notary public. Mem. Md. Council Gypsum Drywall Contractors, Nat. Fedn. Ind. Bus., Am. Mgmt. Assn. Republican. Roman Catholic. Home and Office: 4309 Kensington Rd Baltimore MD 21229

DE MINO, STEVEN LOUIS, fin. planner; b. N.Y.C., Aug. 19, 1935; s. Evelyn Rachel (Morra) DeM.; A.A.S. in Indsl. Mgmt., B.S. in Bus. Adminstrn., Adelphi U., m. Feb. 1, 1958; children—Steven Louis, Robert John, Adam Christopher. Indsl. mgr. Manuel San Juan Co., San Juan, P.R., 1969-70; mgr. mfg. Motorola Co., Vega Baja, P.R., 1970-71; prodn. mgr. Travelers Corp., Orlando, Fla., 1975—. Served with U.S. Army, 1954-56. Recipient citation Jr. Achievement of P.R. Mem. Nat. Rifle Assn. (life), Profl. Businessmen's Assn. Central Fla., Internat. Assn. Fin. Planners. Republican. Roman Catholic. Home: 801 North St Rolling Hills Golfview Longwood FL 32750 Office: 201 E Pine St 7th Floor Orlando FL 32750

DEMMLER, CHARLES FREDERICK, stock broker; b. Hastings-on-Hudson, N.Y., Aug. 28, 1923; s. Charles Robert and Anne Rita (Buckley) D.; student Gen. Motors Inst., 1941-43, Marquette U., 1947-48, George Washington U., 1962-63; B.A., San Diego State U., 1968; m. Clare J. O'Connor, Feb. 16, 1946; children—Robert Charles, Maryanne. Commd. ensign U.S. Navy, 1945; advanced through grades to capt., 1973; comdr. Carrier Air Wing 2, 1964-65, comdg. officer U.S.S. Forrestal, 1969-70, chief of staff 3d Fleet, 1972-73, ret. 1973; asst. v.p. Merrill Lynch Pierce Fenner & Smith, La Jolla, Calif., 1973—. Decorated Legion of Merit (3). Mem. San Diego Stock and Bond Club (dir. 1975-76), Merrill Lynch Execs., Merrill Lynch Chmns. Club. Clubs: La Jolla Country, Kiwanis, Navy League, K.C. Home: 1561 Calle de Primra La Jolla CA 92037 Office: Merrill Lynch 7722 Girard St La Jolla CA 92037

DEMORY, CHARLES WILLIAM, JR., constrn. co. exec.; b. Gaithersburg, Md., Nov. 17, 1939; s. Charles William and Erma Elizabeth (Carnes) D.; m. Judith Elaine Sebek, Aug. 18, 1962; children—Patrica Joan, Charles William, III, Michael Alan. Pres., Demory Bros., Inc., Gaithersburg, 1970-75; pres. William Demory Constrn. Corp., Gaithersburg, 1975—; v.p. Md. Montgomery Fund Inc., 1975—; sec. Demory Enterprises, 1965—; gen. partner Gaithersburg Miniature Golf Course Assn. Ltd., 1979—; pres. Demory Devel. Inc. Mem. Asso. Builders and Contractors (Wash. chpt. pres. 1970-71, sec. nat. chpt. 1972-75, named to Hall of Fame 1973, recipient award of Excellence 1974, Spl. Achievements award No. Va. chpt. 1975, certificate of Outstanding Service nat. chpt. 1975), Am. Inst. of Constructors, Gaithersburg C. of C. Republican. Methodist. Home: 20813 Apollo Ln Gaithersburg MD 20760 Office: 8135 Snouffer School Rd Gaithersburg MD 20760

DEMOS, GEORGE JAMES, mfg. co. exec.; b. Phila., Mar. 9, 1928; s. Charles Anthony and Helen Veronica (Sucauage) D.; B.S. in E.E., Drexel U., 1951; postgrad. Columbia U., 1953-54; m. Jeannette Eden, June 7, 1952; children—Barbara, Brian, Christina. Field sales engr. Leeds & Northrup Co., N.Y.C., 1951-57, resident field engr., Albany, N.Y., 1957-59, br. mgr., Balt., 1959-60, dist. mgr., Boston, 1960-65, central sales div. mgr., Phila., 1965-67, dir. sales dept., Phila., 1967, group v.p. mktg., North Wales, Pa., 1967-72, group v.p. systems, 1972-79, pres., chief exec. officer, 1980—; group exec., Gen. Signal Corp., North Wales, 1980—. Trustee Drexel U. Served with U.S. Navy, 1945-46. Mem. Instrument Soc. Am., Am. Soc. Metals, Indsl. Heating Equipment Assn., Sci. Apparatus Makers Assn. Office: Sumneytown Pike North Wales PA 19454

DEMPSEY, DAVID WILLIAM, banker; b. Dublin, Ireland, July 7, 1949; s. William P. and Mary (Murray) D.; came to U.S., 1974; B.S. in Commerce, Univ. Coll. Dublin, 1971; M.B.A. (scholar), Fordham U., 1976. Sec. gen. Aiesec, Internat., Brussels, 1971-72, internat. sr. mem., editor jour. Link 1970; with Chase Manhattan Bank, London, 1972, 2d v.p. corp. banking, N.Y.C., 1974-80; v.p. worldwide corps. group Irving Trust Co., N.Y.C., 1980—. Lic. pvt. pilot. Mem. Aircraft Owners and Pilots Assn. Chmn. conf. in field, Basel, Switzerland, 1971. Contbr. articles to profl. jours. Home: 210 E 68th St Apt 161 New York NY 10021 Office: 1 Wall St New York NY 10015

DEMPSEY, JERRY EDWARD, mfg. co. exec.; b. Landrum, S.C., Oct. 1, 1932; s. Adolphus Gerald and Willie Ceyattie (Lee) D.; B.S.M.E., Clemson U., 1954; M.B.A., Ga. State Coll., 1968; m. Harriet Coan Calvert; children—Jerri E., Harriet R., Margaret. Regional mgr. York div. Borg-Warner Corp., Atlanta, 1962-69, gen. mgr. York Can. subs., Rexdale, Ont., 1972-77, exec. v.p. York (Pa.) div., 1977-79, corp. v.p., Chgo., 1977-79, pres., chief operating officer, 1979—, also dir.; dir. Borg-Warner Corp., Nalco Chem. Co. Mem. adv. bd. Krannert Sch. Mgmt., Purdue U., 1979—. Served to 1st lt., Ordnance Corps, U.S. Army, 1954-56. Mem. NAM (dir.), ASHRAE. Registered profl. engr., Ga., Ont. Mem. Christian Ch. Clubs: Univ. (dir.), Econ. (dir.) (Chgo.); Butterfield Country; Country of York. Home: 14 Hampton Oak Brook IL 60521 Office: 200 S Michigan Ave Chicago IL 60604

DEMPSEY, JOHN NICHOLAS, mfg. co. exec.; b. St. Paul, June 16, 1923; s. Mark V. and Mabel M. (Stehly) D.; B.S., Coll. St. Thomas, 1948; Ph.D., U. Iowa, 1951; m. Marian Lind, June 5, 1948; children—Barbara (Mrs. Francis McCarrier), Mary (Mrs. Frank Santiago), Patricia. With Ethyl Corp., Detroit, 1951-52; v.p. sci. and engring. Honeywell Inc., Mpls., 1952-72; v.p. tech. services Bemis Co., Inc., Mpls., 1972—, also dir.; mem. tech. adv. com. Northwestern Nat. Bank, 1967—; mem. indsl. adv. com. Ray W. Herrick Labs., Purdue U., Lafayette, Ind., 1965-72. Bd. dirs. N. Star Research and Devel. Inst., 1964—; mem. adv. council Inst. Tech., U. Minn., Mpls., 1972—. Served with USNR, 1943-46. Decorated Purple Heart. Mem. Am. Chem. Soc., AAAS, Inst. Environ. Scis., Indsl. Research Inst., Dirs. Indsl. Research, Am. Mgmt. Assn. (mem. planning council 1966—), Sigma Xi, Phi Lambda Upsilon, Gamma Alpha. Mem. bd. dirs. Mpls. Soc. for Blind, 1970—. Editorial adv. bd. Indsl. Research Mag., 1971—. Home: 4926 Westgate Rd Minnetonka MN 55343 Office: 800 Northstar Center Minneapolis MN 55402

DEMPSEY, JOHN REXFORD, ins. broker; b. Corry, Pa., Dec. 25, 1935; s. Rexford and Lilah (Hinman) D.; B.S., Cornell U., 1957; C.L.U., 1962; m. Barbara Bentley, Aug. 13, 1960; children—Kimberly, Michael, John. Engaged in ins. bus., 1957—; pres. Jack Dempsey Assos., Inc., Ann Arbor, 1968—; speaker in field. Mem. Am. C.L.U.'s, Million Dollar Round Table (div. v.p.), Five Million Dollar Forum, Life Ins. Counselors Mich., Estate Planning and Life Underwriters Assn. Washtenaw County (past pres.), Ann Arbor C. of C. (past pres.). Republican. Presbyterian. Club: Barton Hills Country (past pres.). Home: 2171 S 7th St Ann Arbor MI 48103 Office: 1925 Pauline Plaza Ann Arbor MI 48106

DEMPSEY, NEAL, III, office equipment mfg. co. exec.; b. Butte, Mont., Mar. 20, 1941; s. Neal and Katherine Spring (Shea) D.; B.A., U. Wash., 1964; m. Janet Rae Weiss, Nov. 17, 1967; children—Sean Christian, Heather Katherine. Sales promotion coordinator Gen. Telephone/Electronics, San Carlos, Calif., 1965-67; asst. advt. mgr. Memorex Corp., Santa Clara, Calif., 1967-69; sales mgmt. positions Electronic Memories Inc., Hawthorne, Calif., 1969-73; nat. sales mgr. Intertel Inc., Burlington, Mass., 1973-74; Western regional mgr. Sanders Data Systems Group div. Sanders Assos. (acquired by Harris Corp. 1977), Los Angeles, 1974, nat. sales mgr., Nashua, N.H., 1976-77, dir. sales Harris Data Communications, Inc., 1977-79, v.p. sales data communications div., Dallas, 1979-80, v.p. mktg. data communication div., 1980—. Served to 1st lt. U.S. Army NG, 1964-70. Mem. Am. Mktg. Assn., Sales Execs. Club Dallas, Am. Mgmt. Assn. Republican. Roman Catholic. Clubs: Spring Park Racquet (dir.) (Garland, Tex.); Bent Tree Country (Dallas). Home: 2507 Spring Park Way Richardson TX 75081 Office: 16001 Dallas Pkwy Dallas TX 75240

DEMPSTER, R.V., business exec.; b. Rutherford, N.J., 1928; grad. Pace U., 1951; grad. Advanced Mgmt. Program Harvard, 1969; m. Jean Van Osten. Pres., chief exec. officer McCulloch Corp., Los Angeles; exec. v.p. Black & Decker Mfg. Co., chmn. Pacific Internat. Group. Trustee, LaVerne U. Mem. Am. Supply and Machinery Mfrs. Assn. (dir.). Clubs: Los Angeles Country; Baltimore Country; California; N.Y. Athletic. Home: PO Box 92180 Los Angeles CA 90009 Office: 5400 Alla Rd Los Angeles CA 90066

DE MURIAS, RAMON, ret. airline exec.; b. N.Y.C., Feb. 6, 1916; s. Fernando Enrique and Virginia C. (Bunce) de M.; A.B., Princeton U., 1938; LL.B., Harvard U., 1941; m. Ann-Carlin Borden, Oct. 4, 1947; children—Elena, Christopher. Vice pres. Pan Am.-Grace Airways, N.Y.C., 1946-67; v.p. internat. affairs Braniff Airways, Inc., N.Y.C., 1967-80. Bd. dirs. Southside Hosp., Bay Shore, N.Y., Pan Am. Soc. U.S. Served to lt. comdr. USNR, 1941-46. Republican. Episcopalian. Home: 74 Douglas Ave Babylon NY 11702

DENDRINOS, STEVE, JR., computer software co. exec.; b. Memphis, Nov. 25, 1938; s. Steven and Mary (Koustenis) D.; B.S. in Physics, U. Tenn., 1961; m. Mary P. Tampas, July 1, 1962; 1 son, John Steve. Staff researcher Owens Corning Fiberglas, Granville, Ohio, 1961-64; sr. engr. Brown Engring. Teledyne, Huntsville, Ala., 1964-67; mem. research staff Wyle Labs. Inc., Huntsville, 1967-69; sales engr. Digital Equipment Co., Knoxville, Tenn., 1969-71; br. mgr. Wang Labs., Inc., Knoxville, 1971-77; pres. Creative Software Devel., Knoxville, 1977—; pres., chmn. bd. Ednl. Data Systems, Knoxville, 1973--. Bd. dirs. YMCA, 1978—. Mem. Am. Phys. Soc., Acoustical Soc. Am., Data Processing Mgmt. Assn., Nat. Assn. Accountants, Wang Software Vendors Assn. (founder, pres. 1977-79). Greek Orthodox. Clubs: Knoxville, City Salesman's. Home: 8321 Chadwick Dr Knoxville TN 37919 Office: 6709B Kingston Pike Knoxville TN 37919

DE NEUFVILLE, PIERRE-FRANÇOIS, stock broker; b. Paris, Sept. 15, 1924; came to U.S., 1973, naturalized, 1978; s. Andre and Jacqueline (de Villeneuve) de N.; diploma Ecoles des Roches, Normandie, 1942; M.B.A., Sorbonne, 1946; divorced; 1 son, Olivier. Asst. v.p. La Cruz, Linares, Spain, 1947-50; liaison with U.S. Forces in France, Coca-Cola Internat., Paris, 1950-54; mgr. sales promotion France Presse, Paris, 1954-56; mgr. Hayden Stone, Paris, 1954-64; resident partner Bache, France, 1964-73; internat. sales broker Lehman Bros. Kuhn Loeb Inc., N.Y.C., 1973—. Served with Free French Forces, 1942-45. Decorated Medaille Militaire, Croix de Guerre (3). Mem. N.Y. Acad. Scis. Buddhist. Club: Yacht Club de France. Home: 23 E 74th St New York NY 10021 Office: 55 Water St New York NY 10041

DENGEL, HENRY JAMES, fin. cons. co. exec.; b. Bklyn., Mar. 13, 1913; s. Henry C. and Magdalene Dengel (Wehmuth) D.; cert. Am. Inst. Banking, 1935, Am. Mgmt. Assn.; m. Jean V. Kane, Oct. 12, 1935; children—H(enry) James, William E., H. Jane. Credit clk. Guaranty Trust Co., N.Y.C., 1929-35; credit mgr. Pa. Exchange Bank, N.Y.C., 1935-41; asst. v.p. Public Nat. Bank, N.Y.C., 1941-54; v.p., sr. lending officer Meadow Brook Nat. Bank, West Hempstead, N.Y., 1954-68, Hempstead Bank, 1968-78; pres., chief exec. officer Dengel & Assos., Melville, N.Y., 1978—; dir. N.Y. Bus. Devel. Corp., Albany, 1972—, Conesco Industries, Little Ferry, N.J., 1978—, Bullett Express, Bklyn., 1979—; thesis counselor, examiner Stonier Grad. Sch. Banking, 1968; fin. cons. corps., 1968—. Commr. water, light Village of Freeport (N.Y.), 1973—. Mem. Am. Bankers Assn. (cert. comml. lender), Robert Morris Assos., N.Y. Credit and Fin. Mgmt. Assn., Nat. Assn. Accts. Roman Catholic. Home: 281 Park Ave Freeport NY 11520 Office: Dengel & Assos 555 Broad Hollow Rd Melville NY 11747

DENICOLA, PETER FRANCIS, acctg. firm exec.; b. N.Y.C., Oct. 28, 1954; s. Louis Joseph and Nancy Eleanor (Maddi) DeN.; B.S., N.Y. U., 1976, M.B.A., 1978. Pres., founder P.F. DeNicola, Inc., N.Y.C., now Stamford, Conn., 1976—; acct. Main Hurdman & Cranstoun, N.Y.C., 1978—. Recipient Ferdinand W. Lafrentz acctg. award, 1977. Mem. Tax Soc. N.Y. U., Assn. M.B.A. Execs., Am. Mgmt. Assn., N.Y. U. Commerce Alumni Assn. (dir. 1978—, corr. sec. 1978-79, rec. sec. 1979—). Republican. Roman Catholic. Author: Legal Liability of Tax Return Preparers, 1978. Home: 39 Beaumont Circle Yonkers NY 10710 Office: P F DeNicola Inc 135 Highview Ave Stamford CT 06907

DE NINNO, JOHN LOUIS, mfg. co. exec.; b. Pitts., July 6, 1933; s. Louis Peter and Suzanne (Maurice) De N.; B.S., U. Pitts., 1956; M.S., Case Western Res. U., 1973; m. Patricia A. Gaughan, June 6, 1959; children—Karen, Lynn, Lisa, Gregory. Sr. indsl. engr. Jones & Laughlin Steel Corp., Pitts., 1956-61; mgr. indsl. engring. Cyclops Corp., steel, Pitts., 1961-65; mgr. mfg. engring. Stanley Works, New Britain, Conn., 1965-68, plant mgr. Artex div., Miami, Fla., 1968-70; dir. mfg. engring. Warner & Swasey Co., Cleve., 1970-72; pres. Reliable Products Co., Inc., Cleve., 1972-76, Crystaloid Electronics Corp., 1976-77, Investors Growth Corp., 1976—; dir. Environ. Resources Assos.; cons. Growth Planning Assn., Cleve.; lectr. bus. adminstrn. Cuyahoga Community Coll. Vice pres. Bower Hill Civic League, Pitts., 1964; pres. Library Bd. Scott Twp., Pitts., 1964-65. Served to capt. USAF, 1957-60. Mem. Am. Inst. Indsl. Engrs., Am. Soc. Die Casting Engrs., Canton C. of C. Clubs: Cleveland Athletic; Hudson (Ohio) Country; University (Pitts.). Home: 2259 Danbury Ln Hudson OH 44236 Office: 144 N Main St Hudson OH 44236

DENIS, WAYNE IGNATIUS, refrigeration and air conditioning co. exec.; b. Prince Rupert, B.C., Can., July 30, 1940; s. Ignatius Chris and Doris Ella D.; m. Dorothea Williams, Mar. 3, 1962; children—Christopher Kenneth, Kathryn Yvonne. With York Farms div. Can. Packers Ltd., 1958-62, Bristol Aircraft Corp. (Eng.), 1962-63, Tower Refrigeration Ltd., Chilliwack, B.C., 1964-67, Miller & Timmers Ltd., Sardis, B.C., 1967-71; pres. Denis Refrigeration & Air-Conditioning Ltd., Chilliwack, 1971—. Mem. Refrigeration Service Engrs. Soc. (past pres. Lions Gate chpt.), Christian and Missionary Alliance, Christian Pilots Assn. B.C., Gideons Internat.

DENISON, SCOTT ALLEN, mfg. co. exec.; b. Kansas City, Mo., Nov. 27, 1934; s. J.C. and Irene N. (Wennet) D.; B.S. in Indsl. Engring., Kans. U., 1957; postgrad. in bus. U. Iowa; m. Phyllis Elaine Rashleigh, Dec. 24, 1957; children—Scott Allen II, Blake E. Indsl. engr. U.S. Steel Co., Youngstown, Ohio, 1957-63; with Collins Radio Co., Cedar Rapids, Iowa, 1963-77; controller microelectronics div. Rockwell Internat., Anaheim, Calif., 1977—. Adv., Jr. Achievement, Youngstown and Cedar Rapids, 1960-70. Mem. Am. Inst. Indsl. Engrs. (past pres.), Am. Mgmt. Assn., Sigma Alpha Epsilon. Office: 3310 Miraloma Ave Anaheim CA 92803

DENKER, FOSTER KENNEDY, motion picture prodn. and equipment cons.; b. N.Y.C., Feb. 27, 1940; s. Peter Gilbert and Edythe (Walker) D.; A.A., Boston U., 1960; postgrad. U. So. Calif., 1960-63: m. Lynn Ellen Houston, Aug. 10, 1974: 1 dau., Ellen McNair. Founder, TECO, 1965-71; exec. v.p. Prodn. Systems, Inc., Los Angeles, 1971-77; founder Luminart Leasing Co., San Marino, Calif., 1980—. Mem. Soc. Motion Picture and TV Engrs., Am. Soc. Lighting Dirs. Republican. Presbyterian. Address: San Marino CA 91108

DENNEMEYER, JOHN JAMES, lawyer; b. Los Angeles, Feb. 17, 1921; s. Jean and Mary (Gindt) D.; Baccalaureat, Athene Grand-Ducal, 1941; student U. Munich, 1941-42; J.D., George Washington U., 1949; m. Margaret Juliette Adair, June 10, 1950; children—Paul Adair, Mary Catherine, James Eric. Admitted to D.C. bar, 1949; patents translator U.S. Patent Office, Dept. Commerce, Washington, 1949-50; fgn. patents searcher Gen. Electric Co., Washington, 1950-55, patent atty., N.Y.C., 1955-59; individual practice patent law, Washington, 1959-62; patent atty. Office Dennemeyer, Luxembourg, 1962—, also dir.; pres. S.A.B., S.A., Luxembourg: dir. Datatrust S.A., Luxembourg, Dennemeyer & Co., Ltd., Stockport, Eng., Office Hanssens, Brussels, Riccardi & Co., Milan, Italy. Served with U.S. Army, 1943-46. Mem. Assn. Internat. pour la protection dela Propriete Industrielle, Fedn. Internat. des Conseils en Propriete Industrielle, Union des Conseils en Propriete Industrielle, Assn. Luxembourgeoise des Conseils en Propriete Industrielle, Am. Patent Law Assn., Delta Theta Phi. Roman Catholic. Clubs: Am. Luxembourg Soc., Am. Bus. Men's, Golf Grand-Ducal, Tastevin St. Cunibert, Spora Football. Home: 5 rue Jean l'Aveugle Luxembourg Gr-D Luxembourg Office: 21-25 Allee Scheffer Luxembourg Gr-D Luxembourg

DENNEY, AL B., JR., motion picture producer; b. Waco, Tex., Mar. 15, 1935; s. Albert B. and Mary E. (Fason) D.; student San Antonio Jr. Coll., 1953, 57-58, Tex. Chiropractic Coll., 1953, 57-58; 1 son, Rick L. Screen writer, newsreel cameraman, Los Angeles; dir., cinematographer Ind. Artists Prodns., Northridge, Calif., 1965—, owner, producer, distbr., 1970—; owner DenReal Co., 1961—, Den-Ney Originals, 1972—. Served with USMC, 1953-56. Mem. Internat. Photographers, Internat. Alliance Theatrical Stage Employees, Dirs. Guild Am. (dir. 1978—), Am. Film Inst., Am. TV Arts and Scis., VFW. Republican. Club: Elks. Office: PO Box 5165 Sherman Oaks CA 91403

DENNEY, K. DUANE, mfg. and service co. exec.; b. Plattsburg, Ohio, May 27, 1923; s. Clark E. and Edith (Yeoman) D.; student Office Tng. Sch., Columbus, Ohio, 1942-43, Franklin U., Columbus, 1946-49; m. Patricia A. Nisley, Aug. 30, 1946; children—Susan A., Diane L. Sr. v.p. fin., chief fin. officer Automation Industries, Inc., Los Angeles, 1949—. Bd. govs. Shrine Hosp. for Crippled Children. Served with USNR, 1943-46. Decorated Bronze Star medal with 4 oak leaf clusters. Mem. Fin. Execs. Inst. (Los Angeles chpt.), Am. Mgmt. Assn., Los Angeles Treasurers Club, Los Angeles Pension Club. Clubs: Masons, Shriners, Rotary, Elks. Home: 146 Via Monte D'Oro Redondo Beach CA 90277 Office: 1901 Bldg Century City Los Angeles CA 90067

DENNIS, DONALD PHILIPS, assn. exec.; b. Kenton, Ohio, Nov. 3, 1916; s. Ray H. and Ella Maude (Snodgrass) D.; B.A., Wittenberg Coll., 1939; M.A., U. Minn., 1942; m. Helen Frances Hogue, Dec. 25, 1939; children—Donna Frances, Nancy Philips, Katherine Elizabeth Dennis Mason, Margaret Anne Dennis Toccafondi. Mgr., Kans. Assn. Municipal Utilities, 1941-42; exec. dir. Fed. Union, Inc., 1946-49; asso. exec. dir. Atlantic Union Com., 1949-52, exec. dir., 1953; bus. mgr., asst. sec.-treas. Fgn. Policy Assn., N.Y.C., 1953-79, v.p., 1980—; sec., dir. Fed. Union, Inc. Pres., Rye Forum; mem. U.S. del. to Atlantic Congress, London, 1959; chmn. assns. sect. Greater N.Y. Fund, 1958-60. Served as lt. (j.g.), staff comdr. 7th Fleet, USNR, 1943-45. Mem. Atlantic Union Com. (nat. bd., exec. com.), Assn. Internat. Relations Clubs (nat. exec. com.), Council Christian Social Action (nat. internat. relations com.), Sigma Delta Chi, Phi Mu Delta. Presbyterian (elder). Home: 9 Charlotte St Rye NY 10580 Office: 205 Lexington Ave New York NY 10016

DENNIS, HARRY ALDUS, II, engring. and constrn. co. exec.; b. West Chester, Pa., Dec. 11, 1919; s. S. Nelson and Blanche (Nicely) D.; B.S., Pa. State U., 1942; children—Harry Aldus III, Judith Lynn. Salesman Lukens Steel Co., Coatesville, Pa., Chgo., 1942-47; divisional sales mgr. Graver Tank & Mfg. Co., East Chicago, Ind., 1947-54; asst. to pres. C & I Corp., Cin., 1955-58; mng. dir. C & I/Zurich, Switzerland, 1958-61; v.p. sales C & I/Girdler Corp., Louisville, 1962-64; cons. Dennis Assos., Louisville, N.Y.C., Cin., 1964-67; v.p. sales Western Hemisphere, Sci. Design Co., Inc., N.Y.C., 1967-69, sr. v.p. sales, 1969-77, sr. v.p. govt. relations, 1977—. Mem. Am. Mgmt. Assn., Am. Inst. Chem. Engrs., Newcomen Soc. N.Am. Club: Canadian (N.Y.C.). Home: 967A S Rolfe St Arlington VA 22204 Office: 1629 K St NW Suite 800 Washington DC 20006

DENNIS, LUCINDA TIMMONS, govt. ofcl.; b. Florence, S.C., June 24, 1928; d. Lonnie DeLeon and Rosa (Brown) Timmons; grad. Cortez Bus. Coll., Balt., 1947; 1 dau., Patricia Celestine Dennis Green. Stenographer, VA, Washington, 1948-50; clk.-typist Dept. Interior, Washington, 1950-51; sec. HHFA, HUD, Washington, 1951-67; chief clk. U.S. Senate Subcom. on Intergovtl. Relations, Washington, 1967—. Recipient Freedom Bond award U.S. Treasury, 1962. Club:

U.S. Senate Staff (sec. 1975-76, pres. 1977). Home: 5006 7th Pl NW Washington DC 20011 Office: 301 1st St NE Washington DC 20510

DENNIS, RICHMOND BRAMWELL, corp. exec.; b. Mobile, Ala., Dec. 14, 1920; s. James Albert and Belva (Morris) D.; student Spring Hill Coll., Mobile, Loyola U., New Orleans; B.B.A., Tulane U., 1949; m. Barbara Anne Deasy, July 26, 1958. With Weis-Fricker Mahogany Co., Pensacola, Fla., 1949-50, Otis J. Chamberlain, C.P.A., New Orleans, 1950-51; successively audit, budget mgr., acctg. mgr., regional controller, fin. analysis mgr. Montgomery Ward & Co., Chgo., 1951-66; controller Laclede Steel Co., St. Louis, 1966, treas., 1966—, v.p., 1967-70; v.p. fin. and adminstrn. Automobile Club So. Calif., Los Angeles, 1970—; dir. ACSC Mgmt. Services, Inc. Served with USNR, 1941-46; PTO. Mem. Fin. Execs. Inst., Am. Automobile Assn. (nat. adv. bd.). Clubs: Rotary, Annandale Golf. Home: 535 S Orange Grove Blvd #8 Pasadena CA 91105 Office: 2601 S Figueroa St Los Angeles CA 90007

DENNIS, ROGER CURRIE, business cons.; b. Orlando, Fla., Jan. 18, 1944; s. Robert and Patricia Jean (Currie) D.; B.S. in Bus. Adminstrn., Oreg. State U., 1966, M.B.A., 1969. Indsl. engr. U.S. Steel Corp., Pittsburg, Calif., 1966-69; mgmt. cons. Peat, Marwick, Mitchell & Co., Portland, Oreg., 1969-70; asst. controller Columbia Plywood Corp., Portland, 1970-72; controller Clear Pine Mouldings, Inc., Prineville, Oreg., 1972-76; pres. Business Counselors, Inc., Yakima, Wash., 1976—; tchr. City Coll., Yakima, 1979. Del., White House Conf. on Small Bus., 1980. Served with USAFR, 1963-69. Mem. Nat. Soc. Public Accts., Nat. Fedn. Ind. Businesses, Nat. Small Bus. Assn. Club: Elks. Office: Business Counselors Inc 1 Crest Circle Yakima WA 98908

DENNIS, ROGER MITCHELL, ins. co. exec.; b. Hattiesburg, Miss., Mar. 10, 1939; s. Mitchell Michael and Annie Laurie (Bryant) D.; student Western Ky. State U., 1957-58; B.S., U. So. Miss., 1960; m. Merrill Flowers, Aug. 31, 1960; children—Michael Roger, Annie Laurie, Theresa Merrill, David Malcolm. Agt., N. Am. Co. for Life, Health and Accident Ins., Tallahassee, 1960-61, Franklin Life Ins. Co., Jackson, Miss., 1962; v.p. sales Coastal States Life Ins. Co., Maryville, Tenn., 1962-70; pres. Fabric King Stores, 1969-72, Crest Enterprises, Inc., Maryville, 1969—; v.p. sales Volkswagon Life Ins. Co., 1970—; sales v.p. Aquila Life Ins. Co. subs. Coastal States, Indpls., 1970—; area mgr. Franklin Life Ins. Co., Fairhope, Ala., 1975—; founder Organic Energy Corp., Inc., 1980; dir. First Nat. Bank Fairhope, 1976-79. Served with U.S. Army, 1962. Recipient Gold Plaque award Nat. Assn. Life Cos., 1966-70; Man of Month award, 1976. Mem. Omicron Delta Kappa, Pi Sigma Epsilon. Republican. Methodist. Club: President's. Home: 54 Ingleside Dr Fairhope AL 36532 Office: Professional Bldg 39 Section St Fairhope AL 36532

DENNIS, SAMUEL SIBLEY, III, lawyer; b. Boston, June 23, 1910; s. Samuel Sibley and Helen M. (Ferguson) D.; A.B., Harvard, 1932, M.B.A., 1934, LL.B., 1938; m. Lillian Elena Williamson, Aug. 19, 1938; children—Nancy Anne (dec.), Ellen Ferguson. Admitted to Mass. bar, 1938; sr. partner Hale & Door, 1951—; v.p., dir. Standex Internat. Corp., Andover, Mass., 1955—, also exec. com., gen. counsel; dir. Vaponics, Inc., Knott Tool & Mfg. Co., Augat, Inc., A.T. Cross Co. Former mem. vis. com. of bd. Overseers Law Sch., former co-chmn. bequest Com. Bus. Sch., Harvard, past mem. com. stockholder responsibility. Life trustee, pres. Roxbury Latin Sch.; mem. corp. Children's Hosp., Boston, Jordan Hosp., Plymouth; trustee Leslie Coll. Served from 1st lt. to col. C.E., AUS, 1941-45; now col. Res. Decorated Legion Merit. Mem. Am., Mass., Boston bar assns., Mil. Order World Wars, Harvard Bus. Sch. Assn., Harvard Law Sch. Assn. (former bd. govs.), World Affairs Council (dir.). Clubs: Harvard (Boston, Miami, Fla.); Duxbury Yacht; Country (Brookline, Mass.); Key Largo, Anglers, Bath, Coral Reef, Key Biscayne (Fla.) Yacht; Masons. Home: 52 Essex Rd Chestnut Hill MA 02167 also 175 Washington St Duxbury MA 02332 Office: 60 State St Boston MA 02109

DENNISON, BRUCE LESLIE, mech. engr.; b. Schenectady, Sept. 17, 1942; s. C. Leslie and Mary Evelyn (Middleton) D.; A.A.S., Hudson Valley Community Coll., 1964; B.M.E. cum laude, Western New Eng. Coll., 1971; M.S. in M.E., Rensselaer Poly. Inst., 1975; m. Claudia May Kovacs, Aug. 8, 1964; children—Timothy Leslie, Melissa May. Research technician Monsanto Co., Springfield, Mass., 1964-71; engr. advanced studies and devel. Gen. Electric Co., Schenectady, 1971-76, engr. Armature Winding devel., 1976—. Registered profl. engr., N.Y. Mem. ASME, N.Y. Soc. Profl. Engrs. Republican. Methodist. Home: RD 1 ScotchBush Rd Burnt Hills NY 12027 Office: 1 River Rd Bldg 59W-116 General Electric Co Schenectady NY 12345

DENNISON, JERRY LEE, retail office supplies exec.; b. Leitchfield, Ky., May 22, 1947; s. Ronald M. and Alice Marie D.; A.S., Western Ky. U., 1975; diploma Spencerian Coll., 1969; m. Patricia Jeanette Davis, Sept. 19, 1965; children—Sonya, Staci, Jarred. Mgr. EDP, Ky. So. Coll., Louisville, 1965-67; supr. EDP, Western Ky. U., Bowling Green, 1967-68; asst. mgr. Bank Data Center, Bowling Green, 1968-70; instr. EDP, Spencerian Coll., Louisville, 1971-72, Somerset Vocat.-Tech. Coll., 1972-77; mgr. EDP Crane Co., Ferguson, Ky., 1972-79; owner Dennison Office Supply, Russell Springs, Ky., 1979—; mem. vol. faculty Somerset Community Coll., 1972-77. Pres., Russell Springs Elem. P.T.A., 1973-74, v.p., 1974-75. Mem. Data Processing Mgmt. Assn., Nat. Office Machine Dealers Assn. Mem. Ch. of Christ. Home: Rt 1 Box 104A Russell Springs KY 42642 Office: Key Village Center Russell Springs KY 42642

DENNISON, STANLEY SCOTT, lumber co. exec.; b. Mitchelville, Md., Sept. 1, 1920; s. Ralph Stanford and Cora Adeline (Scott) D.; student Columbia Union Coll., 1936-39; B.A. in Mktg., Calif. Western U., 1976, M.B.A., 1979; m. Dorothy Gladys Willis, Aug. 7, 1939; children—Judith Dennison Tucci, Joan Dennison Daffron, Joyce Dennison Bischoff. Operative builder Dennison Co., 1939-43; traffic rep. U.P.R.R., 1943-49; v.p. Arlington Millwork (Va.), 1949-52, Internat. Filling Machine Co., Petersburg, Va., 1952-57, Atlanta Oak Flooring Co., Atlanta, 1957-62; regional mgr. Ga.-Pacific Corp., Portland, Oreg., 1962-70, v.p., 1970-78, sr. v.p., 1978—. Trustee, Oreg. Mus. Sci. and Industry; mem. Oreg. Symphony Soc.; regent U. Portland; bd. advs. Calif. Western U. Mem. Portland Art Assn., Western Forestry Assn. (charter), Alpha Kappa Psi. Democrat. Roman Catholic. Clubs: Waverly Country, Arlington (Portland). Home: 2211 SW 1st Ave #201 Portland OR 97201 Office: 900 SW 5th Ave Portland OR 97204

DENNY, EDWARD PUTNAM, utility co. exec.; b. Watertown, N.Y., Oct. 11, 1945; s. Harry S. and Dorothea M. Denny; B.A. in Bus., SUNY, Oswego, 1972, postgrad., 1980—; m. Wendy Ann Vrooman, Aug. 23, 1969. Employment interviewer N.Y. State Dept. Labor, 1972-73; with Niagara Mohawk Power Corp., Utica, N.Y., 1973—, supr. customer service, 1975-78, mgr. area office, 1978—. Adv., Jr. Achievement of Greater Mohawk Valley (N.Y.), 1978-79; mem. Herkimer-Oneida County (N.Y.) Water Quality Advt. Bd., 1978. Served with USMC, 1966-70. Mem. Nat. Assn. Accts., Assn. Systems Mgmt., Mohawk Valley C. of C., Am. Legion. Republican. Presbyterian. Club: Toastmasters. Home: 12 Jarvis Dr Manlius NY 13104 Office: 300 Erie Blvd W Syracuse NY 13202

DE NOYA, LOUIS EVERETT, govt. agy. ofcl.; b. Pawhuska, Okla., July 18, 1938; s. Louis Alexander and Mary Elizabeth (Musselwhite) De N.; B.S. in Math., Okla. State U., 1960, M.S. in Math., 1962; postgrad. Ohio State U., 1962-64. Mathematician, Babcock & Wilcox, 1964-66; mgr. mgmt. info. systems U.S. Plywood Corp., N.Y.C., 1966-72; v.p. adminstrn. Air Pollution Control div. Wheelabrator-Frye, Inc., Pitts., 1972-75; sr. ops. research analyst (planning) U.S. Govt. Printing Office, Washington, 1975-80; mgr. computer modeling div. Dept. Energy, Washington, 1980—. Mem. N. Am. Soc. Corp. Planning (pres. Washington chpt. 1978), Planning Execs. Inst., Ops. Research Soc. Am., SAR. Republican. Episcopalian. Clubs: Pitts. Univ., Capitol Hill. Home: 2601 Park Centre Dr Alexandria VA 22302 Office: Econ Regulatory Adminstrn Office Spl Counsel 12th St and Pennsylvania Ave Washington DC 20461

DENT, HARRY SHULER, lawyer; b. St. Matthews, S.C., Feb. 21, 1930; s. Hampton Nathaniel and Sallie (Prickett) D.; B.A. cum laude, Presbyn. Coll., Clinton, S.C., 1951, LL.D. (hon.) 1971; J.D., George Washington U., 1957; LL.M., George- town U., 1959; D.P.Sci. (hon.), Bapt. Coll., Charleston, S.C., 1971; m. Betty Francis, Aug. 16, 1951; children—Harry Shuler, Dolly Meggs, Virginia Brant, John R. Admitted to S.C. bar, 1957; individual practice law, Columbia, S.C., 1965; spl. counsel President Nixon, 1968-72; owner Melrose VW Inc., Nashville, 1973-76; chmn. bd. Health Investment Group, Inc., Columbia, 1977—. Chmn. S.C. Republican Party, 1965-68; gen. counsel Rep. Nat. Com., 1973-74. Served to maj. U.S. Army, 1951-53. Recipient Disting. Achievement award Presbyn. Coll., 1970. Mem. Pi Kappa Alpha. Baptist. Author: The Prodigal South Returns to Power, 1978. Home: 1120 Glenwood Ct Columbia SC 29204 Office: Box 528 1919 Gadsden St Columbia SC 29202

DENTON, ELWOOD VALENTINE, economist; b. Peoria, Ill., Feb. 14, 1912; s. George Washington and Nina (Brown) D.; B.S. in Bus., Miami U., Oxford, Ohio, 1934; M.B.A., Case Western Res. U., 1948; diploma Stonier Grad. Sch. Banking Rutgers U., 1955; m. Sara Reinartz, Sept. 17, 1938; 1 son, Elwood Valentine, II. Statistician, Armco Steel Corp., Middletown, Ohio, 1935-40; econ. analyst, asst. cashier Fed. Res. Bank, Cleve., 1940-59; adminstr. Central Nat. Bank, Cleve., 1960-65; v.p. Nat. Bank of Jackson (Mich.), 1965-69; salary adminstr. Consumers Power Co., Jackson, 1969-71, corp. economist, 1971-77, ret., 1977; econ. cons. Downtown Devel. Authority, Jackson, 1978-79; mem. Jackson Ofcls. Compensation Commn., 1971-79; chmn. Council on Econ. Edn. for Mich., 1976-77; mem. advisory council on econ. edn. Olivet Coll., 1971-78; mem. Chgo. Economists Group, Fed. Res. Bank Chgo., 1971-77. Pres. Family Service Assn. Jackson County (Mich.). Served to lt. Supply Corps, USNR, 1942-45. Decorated Navy Commendation ribbon. Mem. Nat. Assn. Bus. Economists Econ. Soc. Mich. (governing bd. 1973-79, treas. 1977-79), Family Service Assn. Cleve. (life), Phi Beta Kappa, Beta Theta Pi. Republican. Lutheran. Club: Kiwanis (pres. Bay Village, Ohio, club 1963-64). Author: What Is a Social Worker Worth?, 1957. Home: 1540 Golden Rain Rd #2 Walnut Creek CA 94595

DENTON, JOEL, aluminum co. exec.; b. Marks, Miss., Sept. 7, 1919; s. Manford Esca and Blanche (Verlyn) D.; student Millsaps Coll., 1936-38; A.B., U. N.C., 1941, J.D., 1943; m. Elizabeth Gertrude Harrell, May 23, 1947; children—Will Esca, Virginia Elizabeth (Mrs. Daniel Jonathan Ingelido), Joel, Elizabeth Lattie. Admitted to N.C. bar, 1943; law clk. to atty. gen. N.C., 1943-44; house counsel Reynolds Metals Co., Richmond, Va., 1944-60, power mgr., 1960—. Pres., Stuart Ridge Civic Assn., 1955-56. Mem. Am., N.C., Va. bar assns., Phi Delta Phi, Pi Kappa Alpha. Episcopalian. Home: 7711 Alvarado Rd Richmond VA 23229 Office: Reynolds Metal Bldg 6601 W Broad St Richmond VA 23261

DENTON, LIONEL ARTHUR, electronics co. exec.; b. Columbus, Ohio, Dec. 1, 1922; s. Arthur Samuel and Florence Nathalia (Harrington) D.; B.S., Ohio State U., 1948; m. Frances Louise Vaughan, Apr. 7, 1943. Sec.-treas. Ohio Semicondrs., Inc., Columbus, 1956-62; pres. Halmar Electronics, Inc., Columbus, 1962—; dir. Ohio Semitronics, Inc., Columbus; trustee Blue Cross Central Ohio. Vice chmn. United Way Franklin County, 1973; mem. exec. bd. Central Ohio council Boy Scouts Am.; trustee, treas. Mercy Hosp., Columbus; adv. council Columbus dist. SBA. Served with USAF, 1943-45. Mem. NAM, Ohio Mfrs. Assn., Newcomen Soc. N.Am., Columbus Indsl. Assn. (pres. 1973-74), Columbus C. of C., Ohio State U. Assn., Delta Sigma Pi. Presbyn. Rotarian. Home: 952 Amberly Pl Columbus OH 43220 Office: 900 N Hague Ave Columbus OH 43204

DENTON, THOMAS STEWART, investments co. exec., petroleum producer; b. Louisville, Oct. 12, 1945; s. Stewart Benjamin and Jane Alma (Wiggers) D.; student U. Miss., 1964-68; B.S., Murray State U., 1969, postgrad., 1974-77; m. Janet Lee Scott, Dec. 11, 1976. Asst. parts mgr. Don Corlett Volkswagen, Louisville, 1962; v.p., sec.-treas. Scoden Inc., Murray, Ky., 1979—. Mem. Public Service Research Council. Served with USAF, 1969-73. Recipient cert. of appreciation Murray State U. Super Racer Club, 1978. Mem. Murray State U. Alumni Assn., Am. Security Council, Americans Against the Union Control of Govt., Am. Hunting Union, Am. Numismatic Assn. (life). Clubs: Century (Murray State U.); Mason (Valley Sta., Ky.). Home: 812 N 20th St Murray KY 42071 Office: PO Box 1096 Murray KY 42071

DENTON, WILLIAM IRWIN, mfg. co. exec.; b. Paterson, N.J., July 5, 1917; s. Robert Fielding and Sarah (Irwin) D.; B.S., Case Inst. Tech., 1938; M.S., 1939; postgrad. Sch. Exec. Devel. New Haven Coll., 1955-59; m. Martha Elizabeth Steen, Sept. 6, 1941; children—Richard I., Robert F., William A., Kathryn E., John E. Research engr. Am. Gas Assn., Cleve., 1939-40; research engr., group leader Mobil Oil Corp., Paulsboro, N.J., 1940-53; dir. engring. services organic group, Olin Corp., Stamford, Conn., 1954-62, tech. dir. chem. group, 1962-70, dir. process tech. chem. group, 1970-75, safety and hazards mgr., 1975—; v.p. Sprayed Reinforced Plastics Corp., Cheshire, Conn., 1957-60. Mem. Cheshire (Conn.) Zoning Bd. Appeals, 1956-76, chmn., 1958, 63, 66, 69, 70, 72, 73. Treas. Cheshire Pub. Library Assn., 1959-68, trustee, 1969-77. Mem. Am. Chem. Soc. (nat. councillor, 1969—, exec. com. petroleum div. 1969—), Am. Inst. Chem. Engrs., Instrument Soc. Am. Patentee in petrochemical processes. Home: 83 Chipman Dr Cheshire CT 06410 Office: 120 Long Ridge Rd Stamford CT 06904

DENTZER, WILLIAM THOMPSON, JR., securities depository exec.; b. Rochester, Pa., Aug. 29, 1929; s. William Thompson and Elizabeth Gertrude (Campbell) D.; B.A., Muskingum Coll., 1951; postgrad. Yale Law Sch., 1953-54, U. Pa. Law Sch., 1954-55; m. Celia Caroline Hill, June 15, 1952; children—James, Susan, Ardith, William, Emily. Exec. sec. President's Com. Fgn. Econ. Assistance, AID, Washington, 1963, dir. AID Mission to Lima, Peru, 1965-68, dep. U.S. ambassador to OAS, 1968-69; exec. dir. N.Y. Council Econ. Advisors, N.Y.C., 1969-70, supt. banks, State of N.Y., 1970-72; chmn., chief exec. officer Depository Trust Co., N.Y.C., 1972—. Trustee Muskingum Coll., 1974—; elder, trustee Larchmont Ave. (N.Y.) United Presbyterian Ch., 1972—. Served with AUS, 1955-56. Home: 49 Woodbine Ave Larchmont NY 10538 Office: Depository Trust Co 55 Water St New York NY 10041

DE NUNZIO, RALPH DWIGHT, investment banker; b. White Plains, N.Y., Nov. 17, 1931; s. Frank and M. Winifred (Sandbach) DeN.; A.B., Princeton, 1953; m. Jean A. Ames, Sept. 25, 1954; children—David Ames, Peter Dwight, Thomas Richard. With KP, Inc., and predecessor, 1953—, exec. v.p., 1968, pres. and chief exec. officer, chmn. mgmt. com., 1980—, also dir.; dir. Securities Investor Protection Corp., Harris Corp., AMP, Inc.; bd. govs. N.Y. Stock Exchange, 1968—, vice chmn. bd., 1969-71, chmn. bd., 1971-72. Past trustee Vis. Nurse Service N.Y. Mem. Investment Bankers Assn. (gov.), Securities Industry Assn. (chmn. 1980-81). Republican. Roman Catholic. Clubs: Bond (officer, gov.), Wall Street, Lions (N.Y.C.); Princeton (N.J.) Quadrangle (hon. trustee); Stanwich (Greenwich, Conn.); Riverside Yacht. Home: Bridle Path Ln Riverside CT 06878 Office: 10 Hanover Sq New York NY 10005

DENYES, GORDON MACLEAN, real estate investment cons.; b. Oceanside, Calif., Sept. 3, 1943; s. Gordon Stewart and Isabel Mary (MacLean) D.; B.S. in Indsl. Engring., Stanford U., 1965; M.B.A., Columbia U., 1967; m. Kathleen Faye Glasgow, June 22, 1963; children—Nancy, Susan, Steven. Sr. cons. Touche Ross & Co., San Diego, 1967-70, dir. mgmt. services, 1969-70; treas., chief fin. officer Nat. Community Builders, San Diego, 1971-73; v.p. Shelter Equity Corp., Cardiff, Calif., 1973-75, pres., 1976-78; pres. North Coast Restaurants, Inc., 1978—. Mem. Del Mar Planning Commn., 1975-76, Del Mar Fin. Com., 1977—; chmn. Charter Revision Adv. Com., 1975, Del Mar City Council, 1979-80. C.P.A., Calif. Mem. Am. Instr. C.P.A.'s, Calif. Soc. C.P.A.'s, Nat. Assn. Accountants, Planning Execs. Inst., Am. Prodn. and Inventory Control Soc., San Diego C. of C. Club: Optimist. Home: 282 Ocean View St Del Mar CA 92014 Office: PO Box 636 Del Mar CA 92014

DEO, PATRICK A., business exec.; b. 1930; B.S., Seton Hall U., 1952; married. With Grand Union Co., 1956—, v.p., gen. mgr. suburban div., 1965-70, exec. asst. to sr. v.p. ops., 1970-71, regional v.p., N.Y., 1971-73, corp. v.p., 1973-75, sr. v.p. supermarket ops., 1975-76, exec. v.p. supermarket div., 1976-78, exec. v.p., chief operating officer, 1978-79, pres., chief operating officer, 1979—, also dir. Served with U.S. Army. Office: Grand Union Co 100 Broadway Elmwood Park NJ 07407*

DEOUL, NEAL, electronics co. exec.; b. N.Y.C., Feb. 27, 1931; s. George and Pearl (Hirschfield) D.; B.S. in Physics, Coll. City N.Y., 1952; postgrad. Rutgers U., 1954-55; LL.B., Bklyn. Law Sch., 1959; m. Bernice Kradel, Dec. 25, 1955; children—Cara Jan, Stefani Neva, Evan Craig. Engr., Signal Corps, U.S. Army, Evans Signal Lab., Belmar, N.J., 1952-55; engr. Airborne Instruments Lab., Deer Park, N.Y., 1955-56; sales mgr. FXR, Inc., Woodside, L.I., 1956-60; admitted to N.Y. State bar, 1960; pres. Microwave Dynamics Corp., Plainview, L.I., 1960-61, Paradynamics, Inc., Huntington Station, N.Y., 1961-64; mgr. Servo Corp. Am., Hicksville, N.Y., 1964-66; v.p. Trio Labs., Inc., Plainview, N.Y., 1966-69; exec. v.p. Microlab/FXR, Livingston, N.J., 1969-74; pres. Neal Deoul Assos., Owings Mills, Md., 1974—. Mem. IEEE (sr.), N.Y. State Bar Assn., Md. Bar Assn., Young Pres.'s Orgn., Profl. Group Engring. Mgmt., Am. Arbitration Assn. Home and Office: 3104 Caves Rd Owings Mills MD 21117

DEPAOLIS, JOSEPH ALEXANDER, tire co. exec.; b. Altoona, Pa., May 1, 1932; s. Alexander and Ann DePaolis; B.S., Pa. State U., 1958; postgrad. Kent State U., 1967; profl. cert. Harvard Bus. Sch., 1978; m. Shirley J. Frye, July 17, 1954; children—Mark, Michael, Jeffrey, Lisa, Tina. With Firestone Tire & Rubber Co., 1958-68, dist. mgr., Buffalo, 1967-68; pres. and chief operating officer Johnny Antonelli Tire Co., Rochester, N.Y., 1978—. Active worker various local community groups. Served with U.S. Army, 1952-54. Mem. Am. Mgmt. Assn., Nat. Tire Dealers and Retreaders Assn., Am. Retreaders Assn., Harvard Bus. Sch. Alumni Assn., Pa. State Alumni Assn., U.S. C. of C., Rochester C. of C. Roman Catholic. Home: 266 Belvista Dr Rochester NY 14625 Office: Johnny Antonelli Tire Co 156 Ames St Rochester NY 14611

DEPAOLIS, POTITO UMBERTO, food co. exec.; b. Mignano, Italy, Aug. 28, 1925; s. Giuseppe A. and Filomena (Macchiaverna) deP.; Vet. Dr., U. Naples, 1948; Libera Docenza, Minister Pubblica Istruzione (Rome, Italy), 1955; m. Marie A. Caronna, Apr. 10, 1965. Came to U.S., 1966, naturalized, 1970. Prof. food service Vet. Sch., U. Naples, Italy, 1948-66; ret., 1966; asst. prof. A titre Benevole Ecole Veterinaire Alfort, Paris, France, 1956; vet. inspector U.S. Dept. Agr., Omaha, 1966-67; sr. research chemist Grain Processing Corp., Muscatine, Iowa, 1967-68; v.p., dir. product devel. Reddi Wip, Inc., Los Angeles, 1968-72; pres. Vegetable Protein Co., Riverside, Calif., 1973-75; v.p. Shade Foods-Chocolate Internat., Belmont, Calif., 1975-77; pres. Tima Brand Co., Los Angeles, 1977—. Fulbright scholar Cornell U., Ithaca, N.Y., 1954; British Council scholar, U. Reading, Eng., 1959-60; postdoctoral research fellow NIH, Cornell U., 1963-64. Mem. Inst. Food Technologists, Italian Assn. Advancement Sci., AAAS, Vet. Med. Assn., Biol. Sci. Assn. Italy, Italian Press Assn., Greater Los Angeles Press Club. Contbr. articles in field to profl. jours. Patentee in field. Home: 131 Groverton Pl Bel Air CA 90024 Office: 8570 Wilshire Blvd Beverly Hills CA 90211

DE PASQUALE, JOHN ANTHONY, advt. agy. exec.; b. Hattiesburg, Miss., July 17, 1942; s. John Anthony and Mary Edith (Langer) De P.; B.A., U. Pa., 1964; M.B.A., Wharton Grad. Bus. Sch. U. Pa., 1967; m. Mary Welles Schlesinger. Mgmt. cons. Arthur Young & Co., N.Y.C., 1967-69; partner, pres. div. research MBA Communications, Inc., N.Y.C., 1969-74; pres., chief exec. officer D.M. Group, Inc., direct response advt. agy., N.Y.C., 1974—; mem. advisory council to Dean Wharton Grad. Bus. Sch. Mem. Direct Mail Mktg. Assn., Nat. Assn. Printers, Lithographers, Assn. Direct Mail Advertisers. Club: Univ. Research into motivational response attitudes to direct response advt. Contbr. articles to profl. jours. Home: 10 Mitchell Pl New York NY 10017 Office: 477 Madison Ave New York NY 10022

DEPASS, ERNEST T., corp. exec.; b. Memphis, Apr. 26, 1926; s. Ernest T. and Lillian (Klenke) DeP.; B.S. in Elec. Engring., U. Tenn., 1948, B.S. in Mech. Engring., 1949; postgrad. U. Ariz., 1950, Columbia, 1950-51; m. Henrietta Marie Green, May 1, 1949; 1 son, Paul Jeffrey. Asst. plant engr. Am. Finishing Co., Memphis, 1943-47; asst. to chief engr. Standard Brands, Inc., N.Y.C., 1951-53; mgr. process engring. Johnson & Johnson, New Brunswick, N.J., 1953-63; mgr. packaging machinery design and devel. Union Camp Corp., Princeton, N.J., 1963-69; v.p. mfg. and engring. Whitman's Chocolates div. Pet Inc., Phila., 1969—. Served to lt. (j.g.), USNR, 1949-51. Mem. Soc. Plastics Engrs., Soc. Mfg. Engrs. (certified), Am. Mgmt. Assn. Research in field. Home: RD 1 Woodland Terr Bound Brook NJ 08805 Office: 9701 Roosevelt Blvd Philadelphia PA 19114

DE PINGRE, MAJOR, office supply co. exec.; b. Leesville, La., May 31, 1928; s. Adrien Edward and Madeline Ethel (Kirby) deP.; B.A., La. State U., 1952; m. Patricia Lee Catron, Mar. 27, 1953; children—Benny Louis, Margaret Ann. Pres., Meadow Park Nursing Center, Shreveport, La., 1959—; pres. Major Office Supply; sec. Tremade, Inc., 1963-72. Pres. Webster Parish Tb Assn., 1958-59;

treas. New March of Dimes, 1959-60, publicity chmn., 1956-60; pres. Am. Field Service, Webster Parish chpt., 1960-61; publicity chmn. Charlie Hennigan Day, 1964; pres. Minden Little Theatre, 1964-66; chmn. comml. div. Webster United Fund, 1964; chmn. camping and activities com. Yatasi council Boy Scouts Am., 1960-61, dist. commr., 1960-61, 66; pres. chpt. A.R.C., 1965-66; publicity chmn. Webster's Centennial, 1971; v.p. Com. to Get Mus., 1974; mem. Cultural Affairs Com., 1973. Mem. Webster Parish Democratic Exec. Com., 1960-74. Bd. dirs. Webster Parish Cancer Bd., Easter Seal Soc. Served with USN, 1946-48. Recipient Outstanding Jaycee Local Pres. State La., Jr. C. of C., 1959-60, Distinguished Service award Jr. C. of C., 1969. Mem. Am. Legion (publicity chmn. 1958-59), Minden C. of C. (dir. 1961-62), Minden Jr. C. of C. (pres. 1959-60), Webster Parish La. State U. Alumni Assn. (pres. 1962-63). Baptist (deacon). Club: Tennis and Aquatic (Minden). Author: History of the First Baptist Church, 1844-1969, 1969. Home: 1001 E Chrislo Dr Minden LA 71055 Office: 116 Pearl St Minden LA 71055

DE POKOMANDY, GABRIEL, lawyer: b. Oroshaza, Hungary, July 7, 1944: s. Alexander and Irene (Czizmadia) De P.; B.A., Coll. de Levis (Que., Can.), 1965; license in Law, Laval U., 1968; s. Louise Sirois, Dec. 11, 1971; children—Erik, Alexandra. Atty. firm Rouleau, Carrier & Assos., Baie Comeau, Que., 1968-72; crown prosecutor, Sept Iles, Que., 1973; sr. partner firm De Pokomandy, Besnier & Assos., Sept-Iles, 1974—; tchr. bus. law Regional Coll., 1972-79; legal adviser Fedn. des Jeunes Chambres du Can. Francais, 1978-80. Vice-pres., Jeune Chambre de Baie-Comeau, 1971-72; pres. Jeune Chambre de Sept-Iles, 1973-74, Habitation Mingan (Sept-Iles) Inc., Mcpl. Environ. Com., Sept-Iles, 1976-78; pres. local com. P.Q. Hearth Found., Sept-Iles, 1979-80; v.p. Sept-Iles Mus., 1976-79. Mem. Barreau Du Que., Canadian Bar Assn. Roman Catholic. Club: Richelieu. Home: 11 Pampalon Sept Iles PQ G4R 3L7 Canada Office: 865 Laure Sept Iles PQ G4R 3L7 Canada

DEPPE, HENRY A., ins. co. exec.; b. S.I., N.Y., July 1, 1920; s. Herman and Marie D.; student Cornell Sch. Hotel Adminstrn., 1943; m. Florence Chieffo, Aug. 8, 1943; children—Katherine, Marliana, Lynda. Agt. Travelers Life Ins. Co., White Plains, N.Y., 1946-49; dist. mgr. Mass. Life Ins. Co., White Plains, 1949-57; gen. agt. Guardian Life Ins. Co., White Plains, 1957—; pres. Nat. Pension Service, Inc., White Plains, 1957—; mem. faculty C.L.U. Inst.; guest lectr. N.Y. State Trial Lawyers Assn., Fairleigh Dickinson Pension Inst., IRS, C.W. Post Tax Inst., various other profl. assns. and ednl. instns. Pres., Young Republicans Club of Westchester County (N.Y.), 1954-55, Ossining (N.Y.) PTA, 1963-64, Multiple Sclerosis Soc. Westchester, 1964, 65; v.p. Estate Planning Council of Westchester; founder Tax Inst., Iona Coll., co-chmn. inst., 1976-78. Served to lt., inf., U.S. Army, 1942-46. Recipient Nat. Sales Achievement award, 1966; Fred E. Hamilton award, 1975; David Ben Gurion Friendship award, 1975; Guest of Honor award United Jewish Appeal Fedn., 1978; Leadership award State of Israel, 1979. Mem. Assn. Advanced Life Underwriters, Internat. Assn. Fin. Planners, Am. Pension Conf., Am. Soc. Pension Actuaries, Am. Soc. C.L.U.'s, Life Underwriters Assn. Westchester, Nat. Assn. Pension Cons.'s and Adminstrs., Fertility Research Assn. (dir.), Nat. Assn. Health and Welfare Plans, Million Dollar Round Table (life and qualifying), Golden Key Soc. (founder), White Plains C. of C. Club: Sleepy Hollow Country. Home: 67 Ridgecrest Rd Briarcliff Manor NY 10510 Office: One N Broadway White Plains NY 10601

DEPPELER, JAMES GREGORY, cons. agency exec.; b. N.Y.C., Feb. 10, 1946; s. John Howard and Muriel Dolores (Hecker) D.; B.Engring., Stevens Inst. Tech., 1968, M.Mgmt. Sci., 1971, postgrad., 1971—; m. Wende Cyrille Somers, June 9, 1979. Engr., Jersey Central Power and Light Co., Asbury Park, N.J., 1968-71; internal cons. Gen. Pub. Utilities Corp., Morristown, N.J., 1971-73; sr. cons. Fantus Co., South Orange, N.J., 1973-77; v.p. Bus. Mktg. Corp., N.Y.C., 1977-80; chmn. Deppeler Assos., Manasquan, N.J., 1980—; dir. Econ. Geography Assos., Marlton, N.J. Environ. commr. Borough of Brielle (N.J.), 1973—, mem. bd. adjustment, 1979—. Mem. Am. Soc. Metals, AIME, Am. Assn. Econ. Developers (dir.). Club: Manasquan River Yacht (Brielle) (trustee 1974—). Researcher urban devel. problems maj. cities. Home: 407 Linden Ln Brielle NJ 08730

DEPPER, ESTELLE MARLENE, bank exec.; b. Oakland, Calif., May 13, 1942; d. Martin Samuel and Estelle Dorothy D.; A.B., U. Calif., Berkeley, 1963; J.D., Boalt Hall, U. Calif., 1967. Admitted to Calif. bar, 1967, Fed. bar, 1967; Trust adminstr., officer Wells Fargo Bank, San Francisco, 1967-74, v.p., trust officer, estate dept. mgr., 1974-80, v.p., trust officer, No. Calif. regional mgr., 1980—; lectr. Calif. Continuing Edn. Bar. Mem. Bar Assn. San Francisco (chmn. sec. probate and trust law 1979-80), Probate Attys. Assn. (dir.), Calif. Bankers Assn. (chmn. com. trust adminstrn.), State Bar Calif. (No. Calif. chmn. com. current devels. sect. estate planning, trust and probate law 1978-80, treas. exec. com. sect. 1980—), Am. Bar Assn., Nat. Assn. Women Lawyers, Calif. Woman Lawyers, Queen's Bench, Alameda County Bar Assn., St. Thomas More Soc., Women in Communications, Museum Soc., Calif. Hist. Soc., Am. Philatelic Soc., Calif. Acad. Scis., Bankers Club, Oakland Mus. Assn. Office: 464 California St San Francisco CA 94104

DEQUAINE, LESTER JOSEPH, chem. co. exec.; b. Green Bay, Wis., Mar. 15, 1930; s. Joseph John and Elsie Lily (Lhost) D.; B.S., U. Wis., 1952; LL.B., Fordham U., 1957; certificate (Fulbright scholar), U. Paris, 1958. Admitted to N.Y. bar, 1959, U.S. Supreme Court bar, 1964; asso. Hughes, Hubbard & Reed, N.Y.C., 1958-61; with Stauffer Chem. Co., Westport, Conn., 1961—, v.p. employee relations, 1969—. Bd. dirs. Fayerweather Towers Condominium Assn.; trustee Sacred Heart U., Bridgeport, Conn. Served to lt. USNR, 1952-54. Mem. Am. Bar Assn., Fordham Law Rev. Alumni Assn., Mfg. Chemists Assn. (vice chmn. indsl. relations adv. com.), Wis. Alumni Assn., Bascom Hill Soc. U. Wis. Home: 155 Brewster St Apt 4-A Bridgeport CT 06605 Office: Stauffer Chem Co Westport CT 06880

DERBES, DANIEL WILLIAM, diversified co. exec.; b. Cin., Mar. 30, 1930; s. Earl Milton and Ruth Irene (Grauten) D.; B.S., U.S. Mil. Acad., 1952; M.B.A., Xavier U., 1963; m. Patricia Ann Maloney, June 4, 1952; children—Donna Ann, Nancy Lynn, Stephen Paul. Devel. engr. Ai Research Mfg. Co., Phoenix, 1956-58, product line mgr., Los Angeles, 1967-70, asst. gen. mgr, 1970-75, v.p., gen. mgr., 1975-79; sales engr. Garrett Corp., Dayton, Ohio, 1958-63, regional sales mgr., Los Angeles, 1963-67, exec. v.p., 1979-80, also dir.; pres., dir. Signal Cos., LaJolla, Calif., 1980—; dir. UOP Inc., Mack Trucks, Inc., Golden West Broadcasters. Pres., Palos Verdes Peninsula Adv. Council, 1966-68. Served with U.S. Army, 1952-56. Mem. Atomic Indsl. Forum, Aerospace Industries Assn., Am. Pub. Transit Assn. Republican. Roman Catholic. Home: 1336 Via Milcumbres Solano Beach CA 92075 Office: 11255 N Torrey Pines Rd LaJolla CA 92037

DE RICHEMONT, PATRICK, banker; b. France, Jan. 31, 1941: came to U.S., 1978; s. Jean de Richemont; baccalaureat Coll. St. Joseph, Reims, 1960; cert. mgmt. studies Oxford (Eng.) Centre Mgmt. Studies, 1970; m. Anne Hart Green, Sept. 18, 1976. Fin. analyst Emanuel Deetjen & Co., N.Y.C. and Paris, 1967-69; with Banque de Paris et des Pays-Bas, 1971—, sr. v.p., N.Y.C., 1978—. Roman Catholic. Clubs: Jockey (Paris): Racquet and Tennis (N.Y.C.). Home: 1175 Park Ave New York NY 10028 Office: 400 Park Ave New York NY 10022

DERMER, DANIEL JAY, coatings co. exec.; b. Hartford, Conn., Jan. 4, 1950; s. Herman and Donia (Levin) D.; B.A. (Baswell scholar), Am. U., 1971; M.B.A. (Univ. fellow), Duke, 1974; m. Wendy Weisman, July 14, 1974. Staff accountant Price Waterhouse & Co., Washington, 1974-75; cons. Arthur Andersen & Co., Washington, 1975; spl. projects mgr. Coca-Cola Co., Atlanta, 1975-80, mgr. office of ops. USSR, 1978-79; dir. market devel. internat. group Sherwin-Williams Co., Cleve., 1980—. Mem. Nat. Assn. Accountants (dir.), Am. Mktg. Assn., Common Cause. Home: 23291 Greenlawn Ave Beachwood OH 44122 Office: Sherwin-Williams Co 101 Prospect Ave Cleveland OH 44115

D'ERMES, ANTHONY JOSEPH, bank exec.; b. New Rochelle, N.Y., Sept. 5, 1934; s. Anthony and Rose Margaret (Picciuto) D'E.; B.E., Bowling Green State U., 1957, B.A., 1959; m. Jacqueline D'Isa, Nov. 21, 1959; children—David, John, Mark. Tchr., Masnfield (Ohio) Pub. Schs., 1959-61; tng. specialist Ford Motor Co., Brookpark, Ohio, 1961-62, labor relations rep., 1962-65; personnel policy analyst Xerox Corp., Rochester, N.Y., 1965-68; v.p.-personnel Marine Midland Bank, Rochester, 1968-71; mgmt. cons., Washington, 1971-72; sr. v.p.-personnel Am. Security Bank, Washington, 1972—; instr. evening div. Case Western Res. U., Rochester Inst. Tech. Mem. exec. com. Human Resources Bur., Met. Washington Bd. Trade; bd. dirs. Met. Police Boys' Club. Mem. Am. Bankers Assn. (employee relations com.), Washington Bank Personnel Assn. (chmn.), Am. Soc. Personnel Adminstrn. (accredited exec. in personnel), Bank Adminstrn. Inst. (personnel commn.), Washington Personnel Assn. Office: 1501 Pennsylvania Ave NW Washington DC 20013

DE ROSA, ALFONSO MICHAEL, fin. exec.; b. Neptune, N.J., Mar. 31, 1943; s. Salvator Paul and Julia Mary (Vaccaro) DeR.; B.S. in B.A., Georgetown U., 1964; M.B.A., Am. U., 1966; m. Susan Lowe, Sept. 12, 1965; children—Christina Beth, Lisa Anne, Michael, Matthew. Account exec. Reynolds & Co., Washington, 1966-69, nat. sales devel., N.Y.C., 1969-70, mgr. regional instl. dept., Washington; v.p., resident mgr. Hayden Stone, Washington, 1971-73; v.p., resident mgr. Hornblower, Weeks, Hemphill, Noyes (merged with Shearson Loeb Rhoades), Washington, 1973—; co-chmn. Georgetown U. Alumni cons. Mem. lay adv. council Center for Applied Research in the Apostolate. Mem. John Carroll Soc. Republican. Roman Catholic. Clubs: Kenwood Golf and Country, Bond of Washington (past pres., bd. govs.). Home: 6107 Cromwell Dr Washington DC 20016 Office: 1730 Pennsylvania Ave Washington DC 20006

DEROSA, LAWRENCE ALOYSIUS, constrn. co. exec.; b. Redwood City, Calif., Apr. 12, 1927; s. Lawrence Aloysius and Annie (Mirandette) DeR.; A.A., Coll. San Mateo, 1951; m. Ann Elizabeth Robison, Sept. 14, 1968; children—Antoinette, Georgia Ann, Donald Eugene, Michelle Lynn. Auditor, various C.P.A. firms, Calif., Hawaii, 1951-58; chief accountant Jerome B. Rosenthol, Beverly Hills, Calif., 1958-61; chief accountant, asst. sec. Western Insulated Wire Co., Los Angeles, 1961-64; controller, v.p. San Jose Chems. Ltd., San Jose, Calif., 1964-66; controller, treas. Claude T. Lindsay Inc., Sunnyvale, Calif., 1966-69; controller, sec., dir. Starlite Homes, San Jose, 1969-79; pres., dir. Starbrite Industries, Inc., Sacramento, 1979—; chmn. bd. San Jose Bldg. Materials, Inc., 1976—; treas., dir. Bay Cities Sak-O-Mix Corp., 1976—. Served with AUS, 1945-47. C.P.A., Calif. Mem. Nat. Rifle Assn. (life). Republican. Roman Catholic. Home: 2021 Wright St Apt 23 Sacramento CA 95825 Office: 2717 Cottage Way Suite 15 Sacramento CA 95825

DE ROSE, LOUIS JAMES, mgmt. cons.; b. N.Y.C., May 5, 1924; s. James V. and Louise R. (Bastone) De R.; B.A., U. Rochester, 1944; B.S., Fordham U., 1946; M.B.A., N.Y. U., 1949; m. Joan Anne Gilbert, Sept. 22, 1950; children—Richard, Jeffrey. Supr. prodn. control Eagle Pencil Co., N.Y.C., 1946-48; with Phelps Time Locks, N.Y.C., 1948-50; prof. Bus. Mgmt., Fordham U., N.Y.C., 1950-59, dept. chmn., 1954-59; pres. De Rose and Assos., Inc., N.Y.C., 1960—, LaCosta, Calif., 1977—, chmn. bd., 1960-80; dir. Materials Mgmt. Inst., Carlsbad, Calif., 1968-80; feature writer, editorial cons. Purchasing World Mag., N.Y.C., 1980—; cons. editor Elec. Procurement & Aero. Procurement Mag., 1962-67; arbitrator Am. Arbitration Assn., 1950-60; mem. procurement adv. com. U.S. Senate, 1960-62. Served to 1st lt. USMC, 1944-46. Roman Catholic. Club: La Costa Country. Author: Negotiated Purchasing, 1962; Analytical Purchasing, 1963; How to Negotiate Purchase Prices, 1970: contbr. articles to profl. publs. Home and Office: 7214 Plaza de la Costa Carlsbad CA 92008

DEROULET, JOHN CLENDON, apparel co. exec.; b. Chgo., Nov. 16, 1932; s. John Nixon and Pauline Elinor (Morrison) deR.; B.S., U. Ill., 1952; m. Leah Feld, Oct. 29, 1954; children—John Clendon, Jeffrey, Jordan. Salesman, Formit-Rogers Co., 1958-64; salesman, then regional mgr. Jack Winter Inc., 1964-75, v.p., dir. sales for West, 1975—. Mem. Pacific N.W. Apparel Assn. (dir.), Seattle Opera Guild. Jewish. Clubs: Variety, Masons. Address: 2102 Seattle Trade Center Seattle WA 98121

DERR, JOHN FREDERICK, health care products co. exec.; b. Chgo., Aug. 23, 1936; s. Annette Bahlow D.; student Purdue U., 1954-58, Ind. U., 1970-71, Columbia U., 1972; m. Polly Laughlin Pease, Sept. 7, 1963; children—Deborah L., Jennifer B. Projects mgr., hosp. group product mgr., dir. hosp. market planning, dir. products and systems devel. E.R. Squibb & Sons, Princeton, N.J., 1966-74; v.p. mktg. Searle Diagnostics, Des Plaines, Ill., 1974-76, v.p. imaging mktg. products group, gen. mgr. sales/service div., 1977-79, dir. sales and service, 1979; v.p. med. systems div., mgr. nuclear and ultrasound div. Siemens Co., Iselin, N.J., 1980; sr. v.p. mktg. Nat. Med. Enterprise, Los Angeles, 1981—. Mem. exec. adv. bd. Ind. Grad. Sch. Bus., 1970—. Served with USNR, 1959-63; capt. Res. Mem. Am. Mktg. Assn., Naval Res. Assn., Pharm. Advt. Club N.Y., Soc. Nuclear Medicine, Chgo. Exec. Club. Republican. Presbyterian. Home: 213 Knoxboro Ln Barrington IL 60010 Office: 2901 28th St Santa Monica CA 90405

DERSH, RHODA ELENA, mgmt. cons.; b. Phila., Sept. 10, 1934; d. Maurice S. and Kay (Wiener) Eisman; B.A., U. Pa., 1955; M.A., Tufts U., 1956; M.B.A., Manhattan Coll. Sch. Bus., 1980; m. Jerome Dersh, Dec. 23, 1956; children—Debra Lori, Jeffrey Jonathan. Interpreter, Consul of Chile, 1954-57; various teaching and staff positions Albright Coll., Mt. Holyoke Coll., Amherst Coll., Marple Newtown Sch., 1957-64; systems designer Systems Inc., Reading, Pa., 1964-67; pres., chief exec. officer Profl. Practice Mgmt. Assos., Reading, 1976—; cons. dir. public sch. budget study project City of Reading, 1967-78, chmn. comprehensive community plan task force, 1973-75, chmn. public service cons. project, 1980—; panel chmn. budget allocations United Way, 1974-76; del. White House Conf. on Children Youth, 1970; co-founder World Affairs Council, Reading and Berks County, 1963-65; chmn. Berks County Com. for Children Youth, 1968-72. Recipient grant AAUW Ednl. Found.; Outstanding Womens award Jr. League Reading; accredited ind. cons. Mem. Inst. Community Affairs (exec. com. 1975—), League Women Voters, AAUW, Am. Mgmt. Assn., Am. Acad. Ind. Cons. (pres. 1978-80), Nat. Com. Citizens in Edn., Am. Acad. Polit. Social Sci., Nat. Assn. Female Execs., Reading and Berks C. of C. Author: The School Budget is Your Business, 1976; Business Management for Professional Offices, 1977; Improving Public School Management Practices, 1979; Part-Time Professional and Managerial Personnel: The Employers View, 1979; contbr. articles to profl. jours. Office: 606 Court St Reading PA 19601

DERWIG, HENRI GILLES, electronics co. exec.; b. Maastricht, Netherlands, Nov. 1, 1928; s. Bernardus Marie Cornelis and Marie Pauline Antoinette (Rutten) D.; Elec. Engring. Degree, Tech. High Sch. (Univ.), Heerlen, Netherlands, 1953. Elec. engr. N.V. Philips Gloeilampenfabrieken, Eindhoven, Netherlands, 1953-58, gen. mgr. lighting div. Philips Chilena S.A. Productos Electricos, Santiago, Chile, 1958-64, gen. mgr., lighting div. C.A. Philips Venezolana, Caracas, Venezuela, 1964-70, mgr. internat. project div., lighting and communication systems, Philips Electronics Industries Ltd., Toronto, Ont., Can., 1970-75, gen. mgr. internat. project div. N.Am. Philips Corp., N.Y.C., 1976—. Roman Catholic. Office: N Am Philips Corp 100 E 42d St New York NY 10017

DERZAW, RONALD MURRAY, textile co. exec.; b. Aug. 19, 1925; s. Irving and Yetta (Hager) D.; student Knox Coll., 1943-44, CCNY, 1947-50; m. Diana Diamond, Mar. 14, 1948; children—Michael Alan, Richard Lawrence. Sales agt. various textile mills, 1948-70; with Robbins Mills, 1965-67; owner, pres. Tiffany Knits Inc., N.Y.C., 1970—. Mem. Republican Nat. Com. 1980. Served with USAAF, 1943-46. Recipient Govt. Document award, 1944. Mem. Piece Goods Salesman's Assn., Textile Sales Assn., Am. Arbitration Assn. (arbitrator). Home: 10 Filmont Dr New York City NY 10956 Office: 108 W 39th St New York NY 10018

DESAI, SAMIR A., computer services co. exec.; b. Bulsar, India, May 18, 1943; s. Anant C. and Hansa A. Desai; came to U.S., 1967; B.S.M.E., U. Baroda (India), 1965; M.S. in Indsl. Engring., Ill. Inst. Tech., 1969; m. Nilima S. Desai, Jan. 20, 1972; children—Moha, Megha. Mgr. materials control Rockwell India Ltd., Udhana, 1965-67; sr. systems analyst Ill. Central R.R., Chgo., 1968-70; program mgr. Computer Identics Corp., Westwood, Mass., 1970-74; project mgr. Zayre Corp., Framingham, Mass., 1974-75; mgr. transp. systems div. Input Output Computer Services, Inc., Cambridge, Mass., 1975—; dir. Internat. Services, Inc. Mem. Transp. Research Forum, Boston, Holliston Jaycees. Hindu. Contbr. articles in field to profl. jours. Home: 56 Roy Ave Holliston MA 01746

DESAI, SAMMY NOSHIR, fin. exec.; b. Poona, India, Jan. 5, 1939; came to Can., 1970, naturalized, 1975; s. Noshir N. and Makie N. (Ghaswala) D.; B.Commerce, Brihan Maharashtra Coll. Commerce, India, 1958; m. Hirra F. Gandevia, Jan. 8, 1965; children—Darius, Farhad. Audit mgr. N.M. Marfatia & Co., Bombay, India, 1959-63; chief acct. Alta Labs., Ltd., Bombay, 1963-65; accounts officer Air India, Bombay, 1966-70; sr. auditor Touche Ross & Co., Toronto, Ont., Can., 1970-73; v.p. fin., treas. Granada TV Rental Ltd., Toronto, 1973—. Mem. Inst. Chartered Accts. of India, Nat. Assn. Accts. Zoroastrian. Home: 15 Pebble Byway Apt 76 Willowdale ON M2H 3J5 Canada Office: 100 Skyway Ave Rexdale ON M9W 3A6 Canada

DE SAPIO, MARY, fin. cons.; b. N.Y.C., Feb. 26, 1929; d. Salvatore and Florence (DeFazio) DeS.; student N.Y. U. Sch. Commerce, 1952-55, Grad. Sch. Bus., 1957-60. Jr. transp. analyst R.W. Pressprich & Co., Inc., investment bankers, N.Y.C., 1960-64; sr. transp. analyst H. Hentz & Co., stock brokers, 1964-67, Bache & Co., stock brokers, 1967-70; v.p., dir. research Carl Marks & Co., Inc., investment bankers, N.Y.C., 1970-77; fin. cons. Fed. R.R. Adminstrn., U.S. Dept. Transp., Washington, 1977-80; prin. DeSapio Research Enterprises, Washington, 1980—. Vol. worker Spence Chapin Adoption Service, N.Y.C. Mem. Fin. Analysts Fedn., N.Y. Soc. Security Analysts, Transp. Research Forum N.Y., Transp. Analysts N.Y., N.Y. Assn. Bus. Economists, Assn. Women Govt. Contractors, Women's Propeller Club U.S., Soc. Govt. Economists, Women's Transp. Seminar. Republican. Clubs: Women's Bond, World Trade Center (N.Y.C.); International (Washington). Home and Office: 2801 New Mexico Ave NW Washington DC 20007

DESCH, CARL WILLIAM, banker; b. N.Y.C., Oct. 3, 1915; s. William and Marie (Mayerhofer) D.; A.B., Columbia, 1937, M.A., 1939; m. Katharine Woerner, Aug. 31, 1940; children—Carol J. (Mrs. Russell R. Desoe), Carl William, Barbara K. (Mrs. Michael Lenihan). Vice pres. Citibank, N.A., N.Y.C., 1955-58, cashier, 1958-65, sr. v.p., cashier, 1965—; sec., treas. Citibank Overseas Investment Corp.; sec. Citicorp; dir. Citibank, N.A., Citibank (N.Y. State), N.A., Kimberley Clark Corp., SKF Industries, Inc., Hudson Ins. Co., Arlen Realty, Inc., Merc. Bank Can., Skandia Corp., Skandia Am. Reins. Corp.; mem. trust adv. bd. USIF, Real Estate. Treas., Better Bus. Bur. Met. N.Y. Bd. dirs., treas. Columbia U. Press; chmn. Greater N.Y. chpt. ARC, 1967, now bd. dirs., chmn.; alumni trustee Columbia U. Served with USAAF, also AUS, 1943-46. Mem. Am. Soc. Corp. Secs. Clubs: University, Garden City (N.Y.) Country (dir.). Home: 121 Wilson St Garden City NY 11530 Office: 399 Park Ave New York NY 10043

DESCHENY, JOHNNY, leadership and mgmt. devel. co. exec.; b. Rock Point, Ariz., Dec. 15, 1951; s. John Descheny and Daisy Descheny Badonie; B.A. in Bus. Adminstrn. (Navajo Tribe scholar 1970-74), Ft. Lewis Coll., 1974; m. Patsy R. Moses, Apr. 25, 1973; 1 son, Matthew. Supr., The Navajo Tribe, Window Rock, Ariz., 1974-75, fair dir., 1975-79, cons. to tribe, 1974-79; pres. Leadership Devel. Assos., Window Rock, 1979—. Pres. Rodeo Sponsors Assn. Named Motivator of Yr., Leadership Mgmt. Inc., 1980. Mem. Assn. Profl. Photographers, Internat. Film Assn., All Indian Rodeo Cowboy Assn. (dir., named Rodeo Person of Yr. 1978), Gallup C. of C. Lutheran. Home and Office: PO Box 78 Window Rock AZ 86515

DESCHLER, LEWIS, II, lawyer; b. Washington, Aug. 17, 1931; s. Lewis and Virginia (Cole) D.; B.S., Washington and Lee U., Lexington, Va., 1953, J.D., 1955. Admitted to Fla. bar, 1957; partner firm Deschler, Reed & Critchfield, Boca Raton, Fla., 1963—; chmn. bd. Boca Raton Savs. & Loan Assn., 1966—; adv. dir. Lawyer's Title Services, Inc., Palm Beach County, Fla. Served to lt. USNR, 1955-59. Mem. Fla. Bar Assn., Boca Raton C. of C. Episcopalian. Club: Boca Raton Exchange (past pres., dir.). Home: 2000 N Ocean Blvd Apt 205 Boca Raton FL 33432 Office: 555 S Federal Hwy Boca Raton FL 33432

DE SILVA, COLIN, financier, developer, novelist, actor; b. Ceylon, Feb. 11, 1920; s. John William and Rose Mary (Weerasinghe) de S.; came to U.S., 1962, naturalized, 1972; children—Devayani-Nolin Swaris, Cherine-Parakrama Chandrasoma. With Ceylon Civil Service, 1946-56; asst. sec. def., commr. nat. housing, Ceylon, 1948-56; mng. dir. Colombo Agys., Ltd., 1957-62; pres. Bus. Investment Ltd., Honolulu, 1964—, Econ. Devel. & Engring. Cons., Inc., 1967—; W. Coast Bus. Investment, Ltd., 1970—; pres. Calif. Bus. Investment, Ltd., 1972-77; chmn. Gen. Mgmt. Corp., 1973—; dir. Condominium Mgmt., Inc.; lectr., cons. Peace Corps, 1964-67. Past bd. dirs. Waikiki Improvement Assn.; trustee Hawaii Pacific Coll. Lic. fin. broker, Hawaii. Mem. Honolulu, Portland (Oreg.) chambers commerce, McCully Bus. and Profl. Assn. (pres. 1972-73, dir.), Screen Actors Guild. Home: 1040 Kealaolu Ave Honolulu HI 96816 Office: Pacific Trade Center Honolulu HI 96813

DE SIMONE, JAMES WILLIAM, constrn. co. exec.; b. Chgo., Jan. 3, 1932; s. James and Ellena Catherine (Lattanzia) De S.; B.S.E.E., U. Ill., 1957; J.D., De Paul U., 1961; m. Marilyn Gifford, Apr. 26, 19—; children—Deborah, Paula, Michael, John. Admitted to Ill. bar, 1962, gen. counsel IIT Research Inst., Chgo., 1959-65; patent counsel Gen. Dynamics, N.Y.C., 1965-69, corporate dir. internat. ops., 1969-73; v.p. IMODCO, Inc., Los Angeles, 1973-75; exec. v.p., chief operating officer Vinell Corp., Alhambra, Calif., 1975—, also dir. Served with U.S. Navy, 1949-53. Mem. Am. Bar Assn., Assn. Gen. Contractors, Am. Def. Preparedness Assn. Roman Catholic. Clubs: Jonathan, Crockfords, Annandale Golf. Home: 1215 Parkview Ave Pasadena CA 91103 Office: 1145 Westminster Ave PO Box 31 Alhambra CA 91802

DE SIMONE, VINCENT J., automotive research and devel. co. exec.; b. N.Y.C., Nov. 30, 1937; s. Charles and Clara F. (Riccio) DeS.; B.B.A. with honors, Manhattan Coll., 1959; m. Mary Jane Romanovitch, Oct. 15, 1960; children—Christopher, Andrew. Mgr., Peat Marwick Mitchell & Co., N.Y.C. and White Plains, N.Y., 1959-69; partner Main Hurdman & Cranston, Los Angeles, 1970-72, partner in charge, San Francisco, 1972-78, mem. nat. office profl. standards com., 1972-77, mgmt. com., 1977-78; chief fin. officer, v.p. fin. and adminstrn., dir. Rand Info. Systems, Inc., San Francisco, 1978-79; chief fin. officer, v.p. fin. and adminstrn. Minicars, Inc., Santa Barbara, Calif., 1980—. Pres., No. Calif. chpt. Multiple Sclerosis Soc. Mem. Am. Inst. C.P.A.'s, Calif., N.Y. State socs. C.P.A.'s. Roman Catholic. Clubs: Moraga Country, Univ. Home: 4 Corliss Dr Moraga CA 94556 Office: 55 Depot Rd Goleta CA 93017

DES JARDINS, PAUL ROUSSEAU, machinery co. exec.; b. Schenectady, Mar. 21, 1917; s. Arthur Joseph and Julia Angela (Breyer) Des J.; B.S., Mass. Inst. Tech., 1938; m. Madelyn Anne Shacochius, July 13, 1946; children—Arthur Charles, Peter Laurent, Steven Paul, Anne Elise. Various engring., sales and mktg. positions Worthington Pump and Machinery Corp., Harrison, N.J., 1938-68, mgr. ops. Worthington Machinery Systems Internat., 1969-70, dir. internat. projects Worthington Turbine Internat., 1970-71, dir. mktg. research Worthington Pump Internat., 1972-74, gen. mgr. Worthington Pump and Machinery Corp., 1974—; lectr. in field. Regional dir. Mass. Inst. Tech. Alumni Fund, 1973—. Served to capt. USNR, 1941-46, 51-53. Registered profl. engr., W.Va. Mem. Nat. Security Indsl. Assn., ASME (chmn. standardization com. 1967-72), Am. Chem. Soc., Inst. Mgmt. Scis., Am. Mktg. Assn., Nat. Assn. Bus. Economists, Navy League U.S. Republican. Roman Catholic. Home: 12 Surrey Ln Madison NJ 07940 Office: Worthington Pump and Machinery Corp 401 Worthington Ave Harrison NJ 07029

DE SMIDT, FRANK JOSEPH, broadcasting co. exec.; b. San Francisco, Sept. 4, 1941; s. Paul Jerome and Mary Elizabeth (Ahern) DeS.; student Peralta Coll., 1962-65. Pres., L.D.S. Enterprises Inc., restaurant operators, Milpitas, Calif., 1971—, Los Altos Broadcasting Inc., Mountain View, Calif., 1978—, also gen. mgr. Sta. KPEN-FM, Los Altos, Calif., 1978—. Mem. Milpitas C. of C. (pres. 1972-73, dir. 1972—; Distinguished Service award 1973, 78, cert. appreciation 1977). Democrat. Office: 560 N Abel St Milpitas CA 95035

DESNOES, PETER BLAISE, broadcast exec.; b. Mineola, N.Y., Mar. 24, 1943; s. Alfred Davis and Dolores (Moffitt) D.; student Colgate U., 1961-63; B.A. in Philosophy, U. Ariz., 1966; m. Carol Murphree, Feb. 7, 1973. Jr. account exec. Ogilvy & Mather, N.Y.C., 1967-68; account exec., trainee spot sales ABC-TV, N.Y.C., 1968, account exec., Chgo. and N.Y.C., 1970-73; research dir. Sta. WXYZ-TV, Detroit, 1969, sales mgr., 1973-74; gen. sales mgr. Sta. WLS-TV, Chgo., 1974-77, v.p., gen. mgr., 1979—; v.p. sales and mktg. ABC-owned stas., N.Y.C., 1977-79. Vice pres. Chgo. Area Council Boy Scouts Am.; bd. dirs. United Cerebral Palsy. Served with USAF, 1967. Recipient Maroon citation Colgate U., 1980. Mem. Nat. Acad. TV Arts and Scis. (dir. Chgo. chpt.), Ill. Broadcasters Assn. (dir.). Office: 190 N State St Chicago IL 60601

DESOER, MARC JOHN, banker; b. N.J., Feb. 28, 1953; s. Charles A. and Claudine P. Desoer; B.A., U. Calif., Berkeley, 1974, M.B.A. in Fin., 1976; m. Barbara Jean Dombkowski, June 25, 1976. Asst. to chmn. bd. Bank of Canton of Calif., San Francisco, 1975-76; comml. loan officer, then asst. v.p. Bank of Am., Concord, Calif., 1976-78, asst. v.p., head comml. dept., 1978-80, asst. v.p. corp. banking, 1980—. Mem. Am. Econs. Assn., Am. Fin. Assn., Concord C. of C., Calif. Bus. Sch. Alumni Assn., Beta Gamma Sigma. Office: 300 Pendleton Way Oakland CA 94621

DE SOFI, OLIVER JULIUS, banker; b. Havana, Cuba, Dec. 26, 1929; s. Julius A. and Edith H. (Zsuffa) DeS.; B.S. in Math. and Physics, Ernst Lehman Coll., 1950; postgrad. in agronomy U. Havana, 1952, B.S. in Aero. Engring., 1956; came to U.S., 1956, naturalized, 1961; m. Phyllis H. Dumich, Feb. 14, 1971; children—Richard D., Stephen R., Kerri L. Dir. EDP tech. services and planning Am. Airlines, N.Y.C., 1968-70; dir. Sabre II, Tulsa, 1970-72; v.p. data processing and communications Nat. Bank of N. Am., Huntington Station, N.Y., 1972-76, sr. v.p. data processing and communications, 1976-78, sr. v.p. systems and ops., 1978-79, sr. v.p. adminstrn., N.Y.C., 1979-80, exec. v.p. adminstrn. group, 1980—; lectr. program for women Adelphi Coll. Mem. Data Processing Mgmt. Assn., Computer Exec. Round Table, Am. Mgmt. Assn., Sales Execs. Club, Bank Adminstrn. Inst., Nat. Rifle Assn. Republican. Club: Masons (Havana). Office: Nat Bank of N Am 44 Wall St New York NY 10005

DE SOMBRE, ROBERT MAGNUS, publisher; b. Washington, Oct. 7, 1915; s. John William and Helena (Magnus) de S.; student pub. schs.; m. Patricia Ann Sullivan, Apr. 17, 1948; children—Diane, Patricia Ann, Joanne. With Kiplinger Washington Letters, 1942-50; with Gulf Pub. Co., Houston, 1950—, v.p., dir., from 1956, now sr. v.p.; dir. Gulf Printing Co., Houston, Internat. Tng. Co., Houston. Mem. Am. Petroleum Inst., Houston C. of C., Direct Mail Advt. Assn. (past gov.), Am. Bus. Press (past dir.), Assn. 2d Class Publishers (dir.), Bus. Profl. Audit of Circulation (dir.). Club: Houston. Home: 4410 Ingersoll St Houston TX 77027 Office: 3301 Allen Pkwy Houston TX 77019

DE SOUSA, PAULO TEIXEIRA, elec. engr., scientist; b. Nova Lisboa, Angola, Jan. 25, 1947; s. Francisco Teixeira and Liberdade Lusitana (Moita) deS.; Licenciatura Elec. Engring., U. Luanda, Angola, 1971; M.E.E., U. Mo., Columbia, 1972, Ph.D., 1976; m. Susan Gloria Allison, June 1, 1974; children—Vasco Phillip, Alexandra Allison, Andrew Nicholas. Undergrad. asst. U. Luanda, Angola, 1968-69; engr.-in-tng. Companhia Portuguesa de Electricidade, Lisbon, Portugal, 1970; lectr. U. Luanda, 1971-75; research asst. U. Mo., Columbia, 1973-74; engr., scientist Rockwell Internat., Dallas, 1976—. Mem. IEEE, Nat. Mgmt. Assn. Club: Internat. House. Home: 624 Buffalo Bend Plano TX 75023 Office: 1200 N Alma Rd MS 420 150 Richardson TX 75081

DESOUZA, IVAN XAVIER, stock broker; b. Dec. 12, 1935; s. Arthur Francis and Lillian (Pereira) DeS.; B.Commerce, 1957; M.B.A. magna cum laude, Laval U., 1959; m. Margaret Ellen Parent, June 22, 1963; 1 son, John Arthur. With DuPont of Can., Montreal, Que., 1959-64, asst. economist, 1962-63, sr. econ. cons. govt. relations, 1963-64; sr. econ. cons. Govt. of Can. Dept. Industry, Trade and Commerce, Ottawa, Ont., 1964-69, also Canadian rep. for chem. and petroleum industry to OECD, Paris; mgr. market research Esso Chems., Imperial Oil Ltd., Toronto, Ont., 1969-70; partner, dir., v.p. Canavest House Ltd., Toronto, 1970-75; dir., sr. v.p. McLeod Young Weir & Co. Ltd., Toronto, 1975—. Mem. Ont. Petroleum Inst. Clubs: Empire of Canada, Granite, Eglinton Equestrian (Toronto). Author: The Athabasca Tar Sands, 1971. Home: 78 Highland Ave Rosedale Toronto ON M4W 2A5 Canada Office: Commercial Union Tower Post Box 433 Toronto Dominion Centre Toronto ON M5K 1M2 Canada

DESTASIO, THOMAS BARTHOLOMEW, ins. co. exec.; b. Phila., Nov. 26, 1942; s. Bartholomew Thomas and Josephine Delores (Orlando) D.; B.B.A., Eureka Coll., 1965; asso. in mgmt. Meramec Coll., 1975; m. Linda Lee Mead, Dec. 20, 1966; children—Thomas Jr., Josephine D. Ops. supr. Allstate Ins. Co., Skokie, Ill., 1968-72; gen. ops. mgr. Safeco Inc. Co., Sunset Hills, Mo., 1972-75; casualty underwriting mgr. Cimarron Ins. Co. (Kans.), 1975—. Cubmaster, mem. High Plains dist. com. Boy Scouts Am. Served with U.S. Army, 1966-68. Named Supr. of Quar. Allstate Ins. Co., 1970. Mem. Underwriting Exec. Council, Phi Theta Kappa. Republican. Roman Catholic. Home: 110 Hillcrest St Cimarron KS 67835 Office: 101 Main St Cimarron KS 67835

DETTMER, ROBERT GERHART, corporate exec.; b. Parsons, Kans., Sept. 11, 1931; s. Ira Gerhart and Dema (Hinze) D.; student U.S. Naval Acad., 1949-52; B.Bus. and Engring. Adminstrn., Mass. Inst. Tech., 1955; M.B.A., Harvard U., 1957; m. Patricia Isabel York, Aug. 20, 1955; children—Stephanie, Constance, Robert Brantley. Engr., Lincoln Electric Co., Cleve., 1957-60; asso. Booz, Allen & Hamilton, Cleve., 1960-64; propr. Robert G. Dettmer, Investment Mgmt., Cleve., 1964-66; v.p. operations Tasa Corp., Pitts., 1966-68; pres. Scott Aviation div. A-T-O, Lancaster, N.Y., 1968-70, George J. Meyer Mfg. div., Milw., 1970-72; pres. N.Am. Van Lines subs. PepsiCo, Inc., Fort Wayne, Ind., 1973-76, v.p. fin. mgmt. and planning parent co., Purchase, N.Y., 1976-79, pres. Pepsi Cola Bottling Group subs., 1979—; dir. Fin., Inc., 1974-76, Pantasote, Inc., 1978—. Chmn. bd. Am. Movers Conf., 1974-76. Served with USN, 1949-52. Mem. Mass. Inst. Tech. Alumni Assn., Harvard Bus. Sch. Alumni Assn., U.S. Nav. Acad. Alumni Assn., Delta Tau Delta, Tau Beta Pi. Mason. Clubs: Harvard Bus. Sch. of Westchester-Fairfield (chmn. bd. 1977—); Harvard Bus. Sch. of Greater N.Y. (dir. 1977—, vice-chmn. 1980—). Home: 80 Round Hill Rd Greenwich CT 06830 Office: PepsiCo Inc Purchase NY

DETTWILLER, GEORGE FREDERICK, beer wholesaler; b. Memphis, Oct. 8, 1932; s. Edgar Ellis and Elsie Mai (Stroud) D.; A.B. in Philosophy, Vanderbilt U., 1954; m. Martha Ann Dietz, June 8, 1972; children—Kimberly, Sarah, George, Helene, Ann Kathryn. Pres., owner Cardett Distbg., Nashville, 1956—; pres., owner DET Distbg. Co., Nashville, 1973—. Vice pres. Muscular Dystrophy Assn., Nashville, 1978-79. Recipient Miller Masters award Miller Brewing Co., 1976, 77, 78. Mem. UN Assn. (dir. 1981, chmn. UN Day Nashville/Davidson County 1979), Tenn. Malt Beverage Assn. (v.p.). Episcopalian. Clubs: City, Cumberland, Richland Country. Home: 151 Valley Forge Dr Nashville TN 37205 Office: 301 Great Circle Rd Nashville TN 37218

DE TURK, FREDERICK WALTER, copper co. exec.; b. West Reading, Pa., May 29, 1928; s. Elmer F. and Sara M. (Snyder) DeT.; B.A., U. Mich., 1950; grad. advanced mgmt. program Harvard U. Sch. Bus., 1978; m. Carolyn Nubel, Oct. 14, 1950; children—Debi, Eric, Nancy. Mgmt. trainee Jos. G. Pollard Co., Garden City Park, N.Y., 1950; account exec. O.E. McIntyre, Inc., Great Neck, N.Y., 1951; mktg. and sales exec. Phelps Dodge Copper Products Corp., N.Y.C., 1953-63, 65-68, Phelps Dodge Elec. Products Corp., N.Y.C., 1963-65; asst. v.p. Phelps Dodge Industries, Inc., N.Y.C., 1968-69; pres. Phelps Dodge Communications Co., White Plains, N.Y., 1969-78; v.p. personnel Phelps Dodge Corp., N.Y.C., 1978-79; pres. Phelps Dodge Industries, Inc., 1979—, dir., 1978—; dir. Phelps Dodge Internat. Corp., 1980—. Served with U.S. Army, 1951-53. Mem. Soc. Mining Engrs. of AIME. Congregationalist. Clubs: Univ., Mining, Wilton Riding. Office: 300 Park Ave New York NY 10022

DETWEILER, CHARLES HENRY, banker; b. Trumbauersville, Pa., June 8, 1917; s. Robert Weidemoyer and Flora (Rotenberger) D.; gen. bus. certificate Bethlehem (Pa.) Bus. Coll., 1937; certificate Am. Inst. Banking, 1958, U. Wis. Grad. Sch. Banking, 1965, comml. bank mgmt. program, Columbia, 1970; m. Anne Hartigan, Oct. 4, 1941; children—Joanne P., Eileen P., Constance M. Sec. real estate dept. 1st Valley Bank (formerly 1st Nat. Bank Trust Co. Bethlehem), Bethlehem, 1937-40, chief clk. real estate dept., 1940-41, with bookkeeping dept., 1941, with tellers dept., 1942-49, head teller, 1953-54, asst. cashier, asst. br. mgr., 1954-55, asst. v.p., br. mgr., 1955-66, asst. to exec. v.p., 1967-68, asst. v.p. pub. relations, advt., mktg., 1969-70, sr. v.p., br. adminstr., 1971-77, sr. v.p. bldgs. div., 1977—; exec. v.p. 1st Valley Properties, Inc., 1977—. Bd. dirs., past pres., trustee YMCA, Citizenship award, 1966. Served with M.C. AUS, 1943-46, 50-53. Recipient United Fund Service award, 1968. Mem. Am. Inst. Banking, Pa., Northampton County (Pa.) (pres., dir.), Lehigh County (Pa.) bankers assns., Heritage Assn., Bethlehem Area C. of C., Bethlehem Bus. Coll. Alumni Assn. Lutheran. Home: 1548 Elm St Bethlehem PA 18017 Office: 1 Bethlehem Plaza Bethlehem PA 18018

DETWILER, HENRY SAMUEL, savs. and loan exec.; b. Souderton, Pa., May 22, 1913; s. Harry Moyer and Gertrude (Lengel) D.; student Bluffton Coll., 1930-32; B.S. in Bus. Adminstrn., Ursinus Coll., 1934; m. Beulah M. Keller, Sept. 8, 1973; children—Roger H., Janine B. Jr. accountant H.L. Frederick & Co., Souderton, 1934-36; investment salesman, Lazard Freres & Co., Phila., 1936-39; valuation clk., Pa. Power & Light Co., Allentown, 1939-40; asst. sec. Souderton Savs. & Loan Assn., 1935-48, sec., 1948-67, exec. v.p., 1967-71, pres., 1971—, dir., 1948—; pres. Insured Savs. & Loan Assns. Phila. Trustee, Bluffton Coll.; bd. dirs. N.Penn br. Southeastern Pa. chpt. ARC. Served alt. mil. duty, fgn. relief work UNRRA; 1944-46; Egypt, Europe. Mem. No. Pa. Bd. Relators, Indian Valley C. of C. Republican. Mennonite. Clubs: Indian Valley Country, Masons, Rotary (past pres.). Home: 655 Bergey Rd Telford PA 18969 Office: 15 Washington Ave Souderton PA 18964

DETWILER, PETER MEAD, investment banker; b. Detroit, June 7, 1928; s. Ward Arnold and Grace Margaret (Albert) D.; grad. St. Mark's Sch., 1946; B.A., Trinity Coll., 1950; M.B.A., Harvard, 1953; m. Helen Deming Parker, Sept. 18, 1954; children—Susan, Elizabeth, Mary. With Holly Carburetor Co., Detroit, 1953; research analyst, asst. to dir. Schroder Wagg & Co., Ltd., mcht. bankers, London, Eng., 1954-55; exec. asst. to mng. dir. and chmn. Ever-Ready Razor Products, London, 1955-57; asst. to pres. A.S.R. Products Co., N.Y.C., 1957-61; with Philip Morris, Inc., N.Y.C., 1961; v.p. E.F. Hutton & Co., Inc., N.Y.C., 1961-70, sr. v.p., 1970-72, vice chmn. bd., 1972—, dir., 1968—, mem. exec. com., mem. fin. com., 1970—; vice chmn. bd., dir., mem. exec. com. mem. fin. com. E.F. Hutton Group, Inc., 1974—; co-founder, dir., chief exec. officer HighStoy Technol. Corp., Gladstone, N.J., 1975—, chmn. 1976—; dir., mem. exec. com. Albion Malleable/Hayes Albion Corp., Jackson, Mich., 1965-72; dir., mem. exec. com. Puritan Fashions Corp., N.Y.C., 1974-76; past dir., mem. exec. com. W.R. Berkley Corp., N.Y.C.; dir., chmn. exec. com., past mem. investment com. Verex Corp., Madison, Wis., 1966-79; dir., chmn. fin. com. past mem. exec. com. Tesoro Petroleum Corp., San Antonio, 1967—; dir., chmn. fin. com., mem. exec. and audit coms. Handleman Co., Detroit, 1963-78; dir., chmn. fin. com., mem. audit com. Commonwealth Oil Refining Co., Inc., P.R., 1975-77; dir., mem. fin. com. Trinidad-Tesoro Petroleum Co., Ltd., 1969—; dir. Ferro Mfg. Corp., Detroit. Trustee Upper Raritan Watershed Assn., Far Hills, N.J., 1978—. Mem. Am. Petroleum Inst., IEEE, N.Y. Soc. Security Analysts, Am. Soc. Ultrasound Tech. Specialists, Clubs: Essex Hunt (Peapack, N.J.); Somerset Lake and Game (Far Hills, N.J.), City Midday, Knickerbocker (N.Y.C.). Home: Larger Cross Rd Gladstone NJ 07934 Office: One Battery Park Pl New York NY 10004

DETWILER, WILLIAM ARNOLD, sch. counselor; b. Altoona, Pa., Sept. 19, 1946; s. William Diehl and Alice Margaret (Arnold) D.; B.S., Pa. State U., 1964, M.Ed., 1970. With West Chester (Pa.) Area Sch. Dist., 1970—, counselor, head track coach Henderson Sr. High Sch., 1979—; supr. guidance practicuum West Chester State Coll., 1976—. ESEA Title IV grantee, 1973-75. Mem. NEA, Pa. Edn. Assn., Pa. Track and Field Coaches Assn., Phila. Track and Field Coaches Assn. Lutheran. Home: 300 E Marshall St West Chester PA 19380

DEUPREE, HARRY LINNELL, JR., banker; b. Oklahoma City, May 25, 1938; s. Harry Linnell and Dorothy Merle D.; B.A., Westminster Coll., Fulton, Mo., 1960; postgrad. Central State U., Edmond, Okla., 1963, Oklahoma City U., 1965, Okla. State U., 1971; m. Patricia Ann Page, July 3, 1969; children—Harry Linnell, Wade Chisholm, Cheyenne L., Cody. With Oklahoma City br. Fed. Res. Bank Kansas City, 1963-69; credit dept. analyst, then asst. v.p. Liberty Nat. Bank & Trust Co., Oklahoma City, 1969-72; exec. v.p. Allied Okla. Bank (formerly Shepherd Mall State Bank), Oklahoma City, 1973-75, pres., 1975—; pres. Allied Okla. Bancorp., Inc., 1974—; vice chmn. bd., chmn. discount com. Choctaw (Okla.) State Bank; mem. faculty Nat. Comml. Lending Sch., Am. Bankers Assn. Pres., trustee S.W. Am. Livestock Found.; chmn. fin. div. United Appeal Greater Oklahoma City; capt. Allied Arts Dr.; mem. adminstrv. bd. Crown Heights United Methodist Ch., trustee, chmn. fin. com., chmn. trustees endowment fund; mem. livestock com. Okla. State Fair; exec. bd. Last Frontier council Boy Scouts Am., chmn. Lamplighter div. Served to capt. USMC, 1960-63, Res., 1963-69. Mem. Oklahoma City C. of C. (chmn. agrl. div., chmn. livestock council, chmn. youth council, mem. membership com.), Oklahoma County Cattlemen's Assn. (dir.), Sirloin Club Okla. (dir., v.p.), Am. Inst. Banking, Okla. Bankers Assn. (budget com.), Ind. Bankers Assn. Okla. (dir.). Club: Oklahoma City Farm (pres., dir.). Office: PO Box 75250 Oklahoma City OK 73147

DEUTSCH, ALLEN, army officer; b. Rochester, N.Y., Oct. 26, 1950; s. Otto and Belle (Weingrad) D.; A.A.S., Alfred State Coll., 1971; B.B.A., St. John Fisher Coll., 1974; postgrad. in bus. adminstrn. Trinity U., 1975-78, Boston U., 1978—; m. Shelley Marie Rice, May 19, 1972; children—Laura, Colleen, Aaron Lee. Commd. lt. U.S. Army, 1974; budget and civilian personnel mgmt. officer Adjutant Div., Ft. Sam Houston, Tex., 1974-76, installation postal and ofcl. mail control officer, 1976-77; comdr. 125th Adj. Gen. Detachment, 1978-79; comdr. Regional Personnel Center, Mainz, 1979-80. Recipient Paul B. Orvis award Alfred State Coll., 1971. Mem. Acad. Mgmt., Sigma Iota Epsilon. Jewish. Office: COD 1st Battalion Fort Benjamin Harrison IN 46226

DEUTSCH, HOWARD, banker; b. Monticello, N.Y., July 4, 1947; s. Fred and Flora D.; B.S. in Mgmt. Engring., Rensselaer Poly. Inst., 1969: M.B.A. in Fin., St. John's U., 1978; m. Sharry Ellen Cohn, Aug. 15, 1971; children—Michael, Daniel. With Grumman Corp., Bethpage, N.Y., 1969-71, Computer Scis. Corp., Arlington, Va., 1971-72; mgr. indsl. engring. Control Data Corp., Rockville, Md., 1972-73, RCA Corp., Princeton, N.J., 1973-75; asst. treas. Chase Manhattan Bank, N.Y.C., 1975-76; v.p., mgr. indsl. engring. Bankers Trust Co., N.Y.C., 1976—; lectr. in field to profl. orgns. Mem. Omicron Delta Epsilon. Co-author book on teller staffing, 1979. Office: Bankers Trust Co 1775 Broadway New York NY 10019

DEUTSCH, OWEN CHARLES, pub. exec.; b. Chgo., Jan. 9, 1936; s. Conrad Alexander and Betty (Liebermann) D.; student U. Mich., 1956-57; B.A., Roosevelt U., 1960, postgrad., 1960-61; postgrad. Loyola U. Sch. Law, 1961-62. Advt. rep. Commerce mag., Chgo., 1962-70; advt. dir. Chicago mag., Chgo., 1970—; condr. seminars, cons. in field. Mem. Chgo. Advt. Club, Sales and Mktg. Execs. Assn. Chgo. (Distinguished Sales award 1968). Club: U. Chgo. Track. Home: 1700 E 56th St Apt 1205 Chicago IL 60637 Office: 500 N Michigan Ave Chicago IL 60611

DEV, LACHHMAN, process engr.; b. Pakistan, Mar. 5, 1938; s. Ramchand and Jamna D.: came to U.S., 1967; B.Chem.E. (Merit scholar), Delhi Polytech, 1960; M.S., U. Calif., 1968; Ph.D. (research asst.), Oreg. State U., 1972; m. Sudershana Rawal, Sept. 22, 1966; children—Sujata, Amita, Rajesh. Shift supr. Century Rayon Co., Kalyan, India, 1960-61, asst. supt., 1961-62, plant supt., 1962-65; lectr. chem. engring. Regional Engring. Coll., Srinagar, India, 1965-67; process engr. Ga. Pacific Co., Albany, Oreg., 1972-73; heat transfer specialist, sr. process engr. Weyerhaeuser Co., Tacoma, Wash., 1974—. Mem. Am. Inst. Chem. Engrs. (co-chmn. session, Chgo. 1976), TAPPI, Am. Mgmt. Assn. Contbr. publs. to profl. jours.; research in field; designer energy savs., pollution reduction process. Office: Weyerhaeuser Co Tacoma WA 98401

DEVENOW, CHESTER, mfg. co. exec.; b. Detroit, Mar. 3, 1919; s. Samuel E. and Bessie (Aronow) D.; B.A., N.Y. U., 1941; postgrad. Harvard Law Sch., 1941-42; m. Maudette H. Schachner, Dec. 17, 1978; children—Mark Stephen, Jeffrey, Sara, Susan. Chmn. bd., chief exec. officer, chmn. Sheller-Globe Corp. Mem. 1st Nat. Automotive Safety Adv. Council; former U.S. rep. to UN Council on Trade and Devel. Trustee Blue Cross Northwest Ohio, Riverside Hosp., Toledo, Toledo Labor-Mgmt.-Citizens Com., Ohio State U., Siena Heights Coll., Adrian, Mich.; bd. dirs. Nat. Energy Found. Served to 1st lt. AUS, 1942-45. Decorated Bronze Star. Mem. Toledo Area C. of C. (pres. 1978). Clubs: Glengarry Country (Holland, Ohio); Belmont Country; Toledo; Renaissance (gov.), Recess (Detroit). Home: 3000 Valleyview Dr Toledo OH 43615 Office: 1505 Jefferson Ave Toledo OH 43624

DEVERE, JAMES PATRICK, business exec.; b. N.Y.C., Aug. 7, 1916; s. Leo Bernard and Elizabeth (McCarthy) D.; B.A., U. Calif. at Los Angeles, 1941. Vice pres. Dolly Varden, Inc., Los Angeles, 1945-46; owner The Devere Co., Los Angeles, 1948-63; pres., chmn. bd. Devere Co. of So. Calif., Inc., 1963—. Served from 2d lt. to maj. AUS, 1941-45; PTO. Recipient Sporting Goods Dealer Leadership award, 1964. Mem. Sports Council (v.p. 1955-56), Asso. Western Fishing Tackle Mfrs. Reps. Assn., Nat. Sporting Goods Assn., Tackle Reps. Assn. (pres. 1968—, life mem. bd. dirs.), Hist. Soc. So. Calif., Phi Delta Theta. Democrat. Roman Catholic. Club: Portuguese Bend (Palos Verdes). Home: Portuguese Bend Club 114 Spindrift Dr Palos Verdes CA 90274 Office: 273 W 7th St San Pedro CA 90731

DEVERS, VICTOR LEE, govt. agency ofcl.; b. Topeka, Oct. 24, 1931; s. Milburn Lee and Ruth Catherine (Brooke) D.; B.S. in Bus. Mgmt., San Diego State U., 1956; M.A. in Econs., U. N.Mex., 1962; m. Constance J. Webert, Feb. 18, 1960; children—Mikel Lee, Daniel Scott. Site rep. AEC, Oak Ridge, 1967-69, chief constrn. br., budget div., Albuquerque, 1969-70, quality assurance engr., 1970-72, planning specialist, planning div., 1972-74; chief weapons evaluation branch Dept. Energy, Albuquerque, 1974—; dir. Hogares, Inc. Mem. budget com. United Way, Albuquerque, 1977-79; judge N.Mex. Sci. Fair, 1976-80; bd. dirs. Family Counseling Service. Served with USAF, 1950-54. Recipient High Quality award U.S. Dept. Energy, 1978. Mem. Delta Sigma Pi. Republican. Home: 2916 Las Cruces St NE Albuquerque NM 87110 Office: US Dept Energy Kirkland AFB Albuquerque NM 87115

DEVIG, MARVIN K., savs. and loan exec.; b. Mayville, N.D., Aug. 29, 1927; s. Erling and Clara E. (Langager) D.; B.S. in Edn., Mayville State Coll., 1950; M.S., U. N.D., 1957, postgrad., 1958-59; postgrad. U. Tex., 1957-58, Ind. U., 1970-72; m. Arlene Van Camp, Sept. 21, 1951; 1 son, Patrick M. Tchr. jr. and sr. high schs. N.D., 1951-63; faculty U. N.D., 1956-57, S.W. Tex. State U., San Marcos, 1957-58; br. mgr. Met. Savs. & Loan Assn., Fargo, N.D., 1963, mgr. Grafton (N.D.) br., 1963-71, Grand Forks (N.D.) br., 1968-71; sec.-treas., dir., chief exec. officer East Grand Forks Fed. Savs. & Loan Assn. (Minn.), 1971—; exec. v.p., dir. Am. Fed. Savs. & Loan Assn., East Grand Forks, 1972-74, pres., 1974—. Mem. citizens com. Housing and Urban Devel. Authority, 1971—; mem. citizens com. Greater Grand Forks Symphony Orch., 1971-75, pres., 1973—; pres. Indsl. Devel., Inc., East Grand Forks, 1973—; 1st v.p., dir., campaign mgr. United Way, 1974-75, pres., 1975—; bd. dirs. ARC. Served with AUS, 1946-47. Mem. East Grand Forks C. of C. (v.p., pres. 1974-75, dir. 1972—), U.S. League Savs. Assns., Savs. League Minn (dir. 1974-77, v.p. 1978, pres. 1979), Nat. Assn. Homebuilders, Nat. Savs. and Loan League, Grand Forks Bd. Realtors, Grand Forks Multiple Listing Service, Am. Legion. Methodist. Mason, Elk, Rotarian. Clubs: Grand Forks Country, Valley Country. Home: 18 Forrest Ct East Grand Forks MN 56721 Office: 124 DeMers Ave East Grand Forks MN 56721

DEVILBISS, WILLIAM ORNDORFF, JR., flour and sugar broker; b. Balt., Sept. 7, 1933; s. William O. and Virginia C. (Curtis) D.; B.B.A., Tex. Western Coll. U. Tex., 1958; LL.B., U. Balt., 1966, J.D., 1970; grad. Siebel Inst. Baking, 1969; m. Carolyn C. Cowan, Apr. 7, 1962; children—Katherine G., Jane C. Prodn. supr. Gen. Motors Corp., Balt., 1958-62; sales engr. Koppers Co. Inc., Balt., 1962-65, N.Y.C., 1963-64, Balt., 1964-65; flour broker Charles W. Cowan, Inc., Balt., 1965—, pres., 1975-76. Pres., Ringling Bros. Tent of Circus Saints and Sinners, Balt., 1975-76, pres. Nat. Saints and Sinners, 1980-81. Served with U.S. Army, 1956-57. Mem. Allied Trades of Baking Industry (Div. 3 Man of Year 1969-70, pres. 1969, Div. 4 Man of Year 1976, nat. pres. 1973-75), Am. Soc. Bakery Engrs., Potomac States (sec. 1965-75), Va. bakers assns., Bakers Assn. Carolinas, Phila. Bakers Club, S.A.R., Ducks Unltd., Balloon Fedn. Am., Wine and Food Soc. Balt., Kappa Alpha Order, Sigma Delta Kappa. Republican. Lutheran. Clubs: Balt. Country. Towson, Hub City, Masons, Shriners, Jesters. Home: 10 Tree Farm Ct Glen Arm MD 21057 Office: 7400 York Rd Towson MD 21204

DE VINE, BILLIE MACK, agrl. co. exec.; b. Gadsden, Ala., Feb. 23, 1945; s. Charles Durwood and Ida Nell (Blanton) De V.; B.S. in Acctg., Jacksonville State U., 1968; postgrad. in fin. U. S. Fla., 1970-71; postgrad. Sch. Bus. Adminstrn., Harvard U., 1978; m. Shirley Jean Pitspatrick, Mar. 16, 1966; children—Charles Durwood, Cynthia Denise. Vice pres., dir. Bay-Con Industries, Inc., Tampa, Fla., 1971-74; sec.-treas. Automatic Merchandising Inc., Tampa, 1974-75; chief fin. officer Gt. So. Equipment Co., Inc., Tampa, 1975-76; v.p., chief operating officer Am. Agronomics Corp., Tampa, 1976-77, pres., 1977—, also dir.; dir. Am. Orange Corp., Coastland Corp., Funshine Corp. Served with U.S. Army, 1966-68. Mem. Am. Acctg. Assn., Nat. Acctg. Assn., Am. Mgmt. Assn. Internat. Platform Assn., Aircraft Owners and Pilots Assn., Young Presidents' Orgn. Democrat. Clubs: Elks, Rotary. Home: PO Box 1665 Brandon FL 33511 Office: 4600 W Cypress St Tampa FL 33511

DEVINE, C. ROBERT, pub. co. exec.; b. Clarksburg, W.Va., June 13, 1917; s. James J. and Frances M. (Ryan) D.; grad. Princeton, 1938; L.H.D., Fairleigh Dickinson U., 1976; m. Louise C. Williams, Mar. 27, 1943 (div. 1958); children—Mallory C., Rodney W., Ian C.; m. 2d, Gisele Lichine, Dec. 23, 1966. Promotion, research dir. U.S. News Pub. Co., 1946-48, asst. advt. dir., 1948-55; exec. bus. dept. Reader's Digest, N.Y.C., 1955-58, advt. dir. Internat. Editions, 1958-60, asst. gen. mgr., 1960-67, v.p., 1967—; pres., dir. Internat. Fedn. Periodical Press. Bd. dirs. Met. Opera Assn.; trustee Vail-Deane Sch., Am. Hosp. Istanbul, Am. U. Cairo, Soc. for Rehab. of Facially Disfigured. Served from pvt. to maj. AUS, World War II. Decorated Bronze Star medal. Mem. Sales Exec. Club, Internat. Advt. Assn. (pres. 1962-64, chmn. 1976—), Internat. C. of C., Mil. Order Fgn. Wars, Nat. Indsl. Conf. Bd., NAM, Public Relations Soc. Am. Republican. Clubs: Union, River, Dutch Treat, Squadron A, Paris Am. (N.Y.C.); Pilgrims, Travellers (Paris). Contbr. articles to profl. jours. Home: 101 E 69th St New York NY 10021 Office: 200 Park Ave New York NY 10017

DEVINE, J(AMES) DOUGLASS, mfg. co. exec.; b. Boston, Sept. 7, 1940; s. J. James and L. Virginia Devine; A.B., Harvard U., 1962; M.B.A., UCLA, 1971; m. Tee Yarbrough, 5 children. Test pilot Lockheed Aircraft Co., Van Nuys, Calif., 1966-70; mgmt. cons., Los Angeles, 1970-1974; chief exec. officer Flight Adv. Bd., aviation cons., Los Angeles, 1974-1975; dir., chief exec. officer Sunshine Recreation Inc., Westlake Village, Calif., 1975—, Skib Inc., Chatsworth, 1978-80; lectr. in field. Trustee, Community Ch., Encino, 1977-79. Served to capt. AC, USMCR, 1962-66; Vietnam. Decorated D.F.C., Air medal with 26 oak leaf clusters. Mem. Assn. M.B.A.'s. Club: Harvard So. Calif. (treas., dir. 1974-76). Office: 31129 Via Colinas Suite 704 Westlake Village CA 91362

DE VITO, ANTHONY JOSEPH, construction co. exec.; b. Bklyn., Jan. 17, 1935; s. Daniel and Minnie De V.; student public schs., N.Y.C.; D.D. (hon.), All Faiths Clergy Ordination Center, 1979; m. Joan La Greca, Mar. 31, 1966; children—Daniel, Rickie, Taping apprentice Schmidt Taping Co., Bklyn., 1954-56; foreman Lorito Bros. Taping Co., Bklyn., 1956-58; 1954-58; sub-contractor M&R Sheet Rock Co., L.I., 1958-61; pres. Superior Taping Co., Bayside, N.Y., 1961—. Club: Elks (Queens).

DEVITO, GERALD ANTHONY, web offset press co. exec.; b. Mt. Vernon, N.Y., May 16, 1935; s. Louis Michael and Marie (Grippo) D.; B.S., U. Bridgeport, 1957; m. Martha D'Antoni, July 14, 1956; chilen—Marie, Gerard. Supr. dept. accounting Dorr-Oliver Inc., Smford, Conn., 1957-61; with George Hantscho Co., Inc., Mt. Vern, 1961—, treas., 1970-75, v.p., 1974-75, sr. v.p., 1976—, also dir. Vice chmn. Mt. Vernon Cancer Crusade, 1968. Mt. Vernon C. of C. (dir.). Roman Catholic. Home: 466 California Rd Bronxville NY

DEVITT, JAMES E., ins. co. exec.; b. St. Paul, July 23, 1920; s. Louis J. and Gertrude (Cavanaugh) D.; B.B.A., U. Minn., 1942; LL.B., Harvard, 1949; m. Judith B. Morrell, Dec. 22, 1978. Admitted to Minn. bar; practice in St. Paul, 1949-51; with Northwestern Nat. Life Ins. Co., Mpls., 1951-56, group sec., 1952-56; with Mut. of N.Y., N.Y.C., 1956—, v.p. health ins., 1965-67, v.p. underwriting, 1967-69, sr. v.p., 1969-72, exec. v.p., 1972-76, pres., chief exec. officer, 1976-78, chmn. bd., chief exec. officer, 1978—; dir. Hart Schaffner & Marx, Northwest Industries, Inc., Nat. Can Corp. Served to capt., inf. AUS, World War II. Mem. Beta Gamma Sigma. Clubs: Links, Harvard (N.Y.C.); Gardiner's Bay Country (Shelter Island, N.Y.); Blind Brook (Port Chester, N.Y.). Home: 200 E 66th St New York NY 10021 also Dinah Rock Rd Shelter Island Heights NY 11965 Office: 1740 Broadway New York NY 10019

DEVLIN, MICHAEL GERARD, lawyer; b. N.Y.C., Aug. 6, 1947; s. Hugh R. and Gertrude J. (Raubach) D.; B.S. in Mktg., St. John's U., 1970, J.D. (Thomas More scholar 1971-74), 1974; m. Eleanor Cathrine Barnett, Feb. 6, 1971; children—Kathleen Anne, Thomas Fitzmichael, Patrick Fitzmichael. Admitted to N.Y. bar, 1975; supervising tax specialist Coopers & Lybrand, N.Y.C., 1974-78; tax mgr. Dow Corning Europe, Brussels, 1978—. Dep. police commr. Village of Center Island (N.Y.), 1977-78; pres. bd. trustees Midland Montessori Sch., 1978-80. Served with USMCR, 1970-76. Mem. Internat. Bar Assn., N.Y. County Lawyers Assn., Am. Bar Assn. Home: Ave des Aubepines 175 1180 Brussels Belgium Office: Dow Corning Europe Chausee de la Hulpe 154 1170 Brussels Belgium

DEVORE, PAUL STANLEY, financial planning exec.; b. Los Angeles, Oct. 26, 1943; s. Edward and Clara (Stark) D.; B.S., U. Calif., Los Angeles, 1966, M.B.A., 1967; m. Leslie Donna Wurtzel, June 13, 1965; children—Lisa, Bryan. Life ins. agt. Pacific Mut. Life Ins. Co., Los Angeles, 1966-67, life ins. sales mgr., 1967-68, nat. dir. Coll. div., 1969-73; life ins. agt., pension cons. Pacific Mut. & Pacific Cons. Corp., Los Angeles, 1974-77, also mem. exec. council; pres. Pacific Ins. Mgmt. Corp., 1977—; guest lectr. various colls. and univs., profl. meetings and seminars throughout U.S.; cons. to law and C.P.A. firms and ins. agys. Chmn. Chancellors Honor Roll, U. Calif. Found., Los Angeles, 1976-78; trustee UCLA Found., 1977-80; seamanship lectr. U.S. Power Squadron. Named Speaker of Year, 1971, Agt. of Year, Los Angeles Gen. Agts. and Mgrs. Assn., 1979-80. Mem. Nat. Assn. Life Underwriters (Nat. Quality award 1979, 80; pres.-elect 1980), Am. Coll. Life Underwriters, Assn. for Advanced Life Underwriting, Internat. Assn. Fin. Planners, Golden Key Soc., Million Dollar Round Table (life), West Side Estate Planning Council (past pres.), Alpha Kappa Psi (Man of Year 1966). Republican. Jewish. Clubs: Masons; Braemar Country; West Valley Bruins. Contbr. articles to profl. jours., books. Home: 4626 Winnetka Circle Woodland Hills CA 91364 Office: 21031 Ventura Blvd 7th floor Woodland Hills CA 91364

DE VOS, RICHARD MARVIN, corp. exec.; b. Grand Rapids, Mich., Mar. 4, 1926; student Calvin Coll., 1945; LL.D. (hon.), Oral Roberts U., 1976, Grove City Coll., 1976, Northwood Inst., 1977, Dickinson Sch. Law, 1980, Pepperdine U., 1980; m. Helen VanWesep; 4 children. Co-owner, operator Wolverine Air Service Flying Sch., 1945-48; co-founder Ja-Ri Corp., 1949-59; co-founder Amway Corp., Ada, Mich., 1959—, now pres. Chmn., Nat. Congl. Leadership Council; chmn. Gospel Films; bd. dirs. Internat. Yr. of Disabled Person. Served with USAF, 1944-46. Mem. Grand Rapids Econ. Club, New Grand Rapids Com. (chmn.), NAM (dir.), Roundtable. Author: Believe!, 1975. Office: 7575 E Fulton Rd Ada MI 49355

DE VRIES, PAUL DAMPMAN GARRETT, food co. exec.; b. Balt., Sept. 18, 1944; s. Van Beuren Wright and Marjorie Jane (Dampman) DeV.; B.S., Yale, 1966; M.B.A., U. Pa., 1971; m. Emily Melody Doudine, June 6, 1970; children—Christopher, Matthew. Line supr. Procter & Gamble Co., N.Y.C., 1969-72; brand mgr. Quaker Oats Co., Chgo., 1972-73; mktg. mgr. Stouffer Foods Co., Cleve., 1974—. Served with AUS, 1966-68. Mem. Am. Mktg. Assn., Nat. Frozen Pizza Inst. (dir.). Republican. Home: 7109 Wilson Mills Rd Gates Mills OH 44040 Office: 5750 Harper Rd Solon OH 44139

DEW, JOHN FRANKLYN, ins. co. exec.; b. King and Queen County, Va., Nov. 5, 1901; s. John Mason and Lillian Shepherd (Segar) D., B.S., U. Va., 1952; postgrad. U. Richmond, 1942-47, Va. Commonwealth U., 1944-63; m. Annette Van Ingen, June 30, 1951; children—Jeanne Gatewood, John Franklyn, William Randolph. Security salesman Utility Securities Co., Chgo., 1928-30; agt. Acacia Life Ins. Co., Washington, 1934-38; with N. Am. Assurance Soc. of Va., Inc., Richmond, 1938—, dir., from 1940, v.p., 1942-55, pres., treas., 1955-75, chmn. bd. emeritus, 1977—, also cons. Mem. Richmond Redevel. and Housing Authority, Richmond Beautification Com., Richmond Design Com.; a founder Richmond Symphony; pres. Richmond Federated Arts Council. Recipient recognition award City of Richmond, 1972. Mem. Fin. Analysts Fedn., Acad. Polit. Sci., Va. C. of C., Va. Writers Club (trustee), Poe Soc., English-Speaking Union, Poetry Soc. Va., Acad. Am. Poets, Thomas Jefferson Alumni Soc. U. Va. (life). Episcopalian. Clubs: Va. Country, Commonwealth, Bull and Bear, Farmington Country. Author: Dragonara (poetry), 1977. Home: 5314 Tuckahoe Ave Richmond VA 23226 Office: N Am Assurance Soc of Va Inc 110 S 7th St Richmond VA 23210

DE WALT, PETER LANGLEY, glass co. exec.; b. Pitts., Nov. 13, 1936; s. Horace Edward and Ella May (Langley) DeW.; B.A., Waynesburg Coll., 1961; m. Susan Elizabeth Davis, May 18, 1963; children—Jennifer Lee, John Davis. With Pitts. Plate Glass Industries, Inc., 1962—, dir. textile mktg., 1979—. Served with USNR, 1955-57; ETO. Mem. Soc. Plastics Engrs., Soc. Plastics Industry, Boating Industry Assn., Screen Mfrs. Assn., Gummed Industries Assn., Nat. Assn. Engine and Boat Mfrs. Republican. Club: St. Clair Country. Home: 1826 Tragone Dr Pittsburgh PA 15241 Office: One Gateway Center Pittsburgh PA 15222

DEWAR, JAMES MCEWEN, agrl. cons.; b. Williamsport, Pa., Aug. 4, 1943; s. James Livingston and Margaret Ann (McEwen) D.; B.S. in Internat. Affairs, Trinity U., 1965, postgrad. internat. law, 1966, postgrad. African studies, 1965-66; children—Alec, Porter, Leah. Mgr., Dash brand Procter & Gamble Corp., Cin., 1970-72; pres. DeLair & Dewar, Inc., Tucson, 1972—; dir. Metz Constrn. Co., Marine Environ. Research Corp., Computational Analysis Corp. Bd. dirs. Casa de Los Ninos, Tucson, 1974—, Safari Club Internat., Tucson, 1974-77: mem. White House Talent Pool, 1975-76, White House Nat. Cambodia Crisis Com., 1980—; chmn. internat. bd. advs. Ariz.-Sonora Desert Mus.; bd. advs. guardian ad litem program Superior Ct. Ariz. Served to capt. USAF, 1966-70; Vietnam. Recipient Key to City Seoul (Korea), 1973, citation Pres. Korea, 1973. Mem. Am. Soc. Agrl. Cons., Dirs. Guild Am. Republican. Mem. Anglican Ch. Clubs: Mountain Oyster, Old Pueblo Court House; Australian/Asian Order Old Bastards (Sydney, Australia). Contbr. numerous articles to profl. publs. Home: PO Box 27046 Tucson AZ 85726 Office: 3690 S Park Ave Tucson AZ 85713

DEWAR, ROBERT EARL, chain store exec.; b. Traverse City, Mich., Nov. 20, 1922; s. Floyd C. and Irlene (Nash) D.; student Alma Coll., 1940-42; LL.B., Wayne State U., 1948; postgrad. U. Mich. Grad. Sch. Bus. Adminstrn., 1963; m. Nancy Jane Miller, Sept. 26, 1944; children—Robert Earl, Jane Elizabeth, John. Admitted to Mich. bar, 1948; gen. practice law, Detroit, 1948-49; with S.S. Kresge Co., 1949—, asst. v.p. finance, 1963-65, v.p. finance, 1965-66, adminstrv. v.p., 1966—, exec. v.p. adminstrn. and finance, 1968-70, pres., 1970-72, chmn. bd., 1972—, also dir. Served as pilot USNR, 1942-45. Decorated Air medal with oak leaf cluster. Office: K Mart Corp 3100 W Big Beaver Rd Troy MI 48084

DEWEES, DONALD CHARLES, securities co. exec.; b. Phila., Sept. 7, 1931; s. John Coleman and Elva (Burke) DeW.; B.S. in Commerce and Finance, Bucknell U., 1953; M.B.A., Wharton Sch., U. Pa., 1954; m. Martha V. Folk, July 31, 1954; children—Donald C., Suzanne C., Gretchen F. Data processing rep. Nat. Cash Register Co., Wilmington, Del., 1954-62; account rep. Francis I. duPont Co., investments, Wilmington, 1962-67, br. mgr., Balt., 1968; br. mgr. Butcher & Sherrerd, Wilmington, 1969-71, v.p., 1971-76, 1st v.p., 1977, sr. v.p., 1978—; dir. Mgmt. Scis. Inc., Bus. Trends Inc.; cons. in field. Active Wilmington YMCA. Served with AUS, 1954-56, 58-59; Korea. Mem. Financial Analysts Soc., Am. Philatelic Soc., Phi Kappa Psi. Republican. Methodist. Mason (32 deg., Shriner). Clubs: University (Wilmington); Turf (Delaware Park, Del.). Author sales tng. publs. Home: 6 Harlech Dr Anglesey St Wilmington DE 19807 Office: Suite 1106 Bank of Del Bldg 300 Delaware Ave Wilmington DE 19899

DEWELT, ROBERT LEO, mfg. co. exec.; b. Chgo., Nov. 11, 1942; s. Albert and Mildred M. (Oehler) DeW.; B.S. in Commerce summa cum laude, DePaul U., 1969; m. Martha Tomes, June 2, 1962; children—Robert A., Cheryl A. With U.S. Steel Corp., Chgo., 1961-67, Reynolds Metals Co., McCook, Ill., 1967-69, Sheller Globe Corp., Keokuk, Iowa, 1969-71; plant controller Allis-Chalmers Corp., Matteson, Ill. and Lexington, S.C., 1971-74, corporate mgr. cost systems and inventory control, West Allis, Wis., 1974-77, controller engine div., Harvey, Ill., 1977-80, indsl. truck div., Matteson, Ill., 1980—. C.P.A., Ill. Mem. Am. Prodn. and Inventory Control Soc., Am. Inst. C.P.A.'s, Ill. Soc. C.P.A.'s, Nat. Assn. Accountants (recipient Nat. Merit certificate, Schley Manuscript award), DePaul U. Alumni Assn. Roman Catholic. Contbr. articles to profl. jours. Home: 1854 Oak Ln Flossmoor IL 60422 Office: 21800 S Cicero Ave Matteson IL 60443

DEWEY, CHARLES SHERMAN, mgmt. cons.; b. Fairbanks, Alaska, Oct. 22, 1905; s. Sherman and Mary (Gosa) D.; Ed.D. Stanford U., 1944; m. Rebecca Arnell, Dec. 26, 1942. Instr. indsl. arts, vocat. subjects, Seattle schs., 1934-41; instr. U. Wash., 1939-40; dir. state vocat. survey, Tucson, 1938; indsl. psychologist Joshua Hendy Iron Works, Sunnyvale, Calif., 1943; tng. specialist Army Service Forces, Ft. Mason, Calif., 1943-44; indsl. psychologist Stevenson, Jordan & Harrison, Inc., Chgo., 1944-46; prin. indsl. psychologist Charles S. Dewey & Assos., cons. to mgmt., Chgo., 1946—. Fellow Am. Soc. Clin. Hypnosis Found., Am. Psychol. Assn., AAAS; mem. AIM, Ill. (pres. 1968-69), Midwestern psychol. assns., Nat. Acad. Econs. and Polit. Sci., Indsl. Relations Research Assn., Am. Acad. Polit. and Social Sci., Ill. Acad. Sci., Am. Mgmt. Assn., Am. Mktg. Assn., Soc. Am. Mil. Engrs., Internat. Assn. Applied Psychology, Inter Am. Soc. Psychology, Nat. Vocat. Assn., Nat. Inst. Social and Behavioral Sci., Chgo. Psychol. Club (sec. 1959, pres. 1960), Midwest Human Factors Soc. (pres. 1964-65), Ill. Guidance and Personnel Assn. Chgo. Guidance and Personnel Assn. (pres. 1964-65), Chgo. Soc. Clin. Hypnosis (v.p. 1965-71, dir. 1972—), Phi Delta Kappa. Mason (32 deg., Shriner). Club: City Club of Chgo. (chmn. mental health com. 1965). Contbr. articles to profl. jours. Home: 3130 Lake Shore Dr Chicago IL 60657 Office: 135 S LaSalle St Chicago IL 60603

DEWEY, REBECCA ARNELL, indsl. psychologist; b. Auburn, Wash., Oct. 11, 1902; d. John R. and Emma (Hanson) Arnell; B.A., U. Wash., 1926, M.A., 1936; Ph.D., Stanford U., 1946; m. Charles Sherman Dewey, Dec. 26, 1942. Tchr. public schs., Auburn, Aberdeen and Seattle, Wash., 1921-38; instr. Stanford U., 1941-44, U. Nev., summer 1941; asst. prof. U. Ill., Chgo., 1946-49; indsl. psychologist Charles S. Dewey & Assos., Chgo., 1946—. Fellow AAAS; mem. Am., Midwestern, Ill. (sec. 1964-69) psychol. assns., AIM, Indsl. Relations Research Assn., MLA, Am. Personnel and Guidance Assn., Internat. Assn. Applied Psychology, Inter Am. Soc. Psychology, Chgo. Psychol. Club (treas. 1951, sec. 1960-63, pres. 1964-65), Ill. Guidance and Personnel Assn., Pi Lambda Theta. Contbr. to profl. jours. Home: 3130 Lake Shore Dr Chicago IL 60657 Office: 135 S La Salle St Chicago IL 60603

DE WINDT, EDWARD MANDELL, mfg. co. exec.; b. Great Barrington, Mass., Mar. 31, 1921; s. Delano and Ruth (Church) de W.; student Williams Coll., 1939-41; m. Betsy Bope, June 21, 1941; children—Pamela, Delano II, Dana, Elizabeth, Edward Mandell. With Eaton Corp., Cleve., 1941—, gen. mgr. stamping div., 1954-59, v.p. sales, 1959-61, group v.p. internat., 1961-66, pres., 1967-69, chmn. bd., 1969—, also dir.; mem. exec. com., dir. Ohio Bell Telephone Co.; dir. UAL, Inc., Fed. Res., Dart & Kraft Inc., Sears Roebuck & Co., All State Ins. Co., United Airlines, Inc. Trustee Cleve. Ednl. Television Assn., Cleve. Clinic; bd. dirs. United Way Am., Univ. Sch., Berkshire Sch., NCCJ. Decorated comdr. Order Brit. Empire; commendatore Italian Republic. Mem. Soc. Automotive Engrs., Soc. Cin., Am. Soc. Corporate Execs., Bus. Council. Clubs: Union, Tavern, Pepper Pike Country, Kirtland (Cleve.); Bloomfield Hills (Mich.) Country; Augusta (Ga.) Nat.; Blind Brook (N.Y.); Laurel Valley, (Ligonier, Pa.); Links (N.Y.C.); Seminole, Jupiter Island (Fla.). Home: 25299 Cedar Rd Lyndhurst OH 44122 Office: 100 Erieview Plaza Cleveland OH 44114

DE WOODY, CHARLES, lawyer; b. Chgo., Oct. 18, 1914; s. Charles and Oneta (Ownby); student U. Fla., 1931-33, U. Mich., 1933-35, Columbia, 1935-36, Western Res. U., 1936-38; m. Nancy Tremaine, June 15, 1940; children—Charles, Nancy. Office atty. Oglebay, Norton & Co., Cleve., 1939-43; partner Arter, Hadden, Wykoff & Van Duzer, 1943-61; pvt. practice, 1961—; dir. Nat. Extruded Metal Products Co., Ferry Cap and Set Screw Co., Direct Digital Industries Ltd.; dir. Meteor Crater Enterprises, Inc.; gen. partner Bar-T-Bar Ranch, Mem. Am., Ohio, Cleve. bar assns., Cleve. Law Library Assn. Episcopalian. Clubs: Rancho Santa Fe Tennis; Union, Country, Cleveland Racquet (Cleve.); Chagrin Valley Hunt (Gates Mills, Ohio). Home: El Mirador Box 1169 Rancho Santa Fe CA 92067

DE WREE, EUGENE ERNEST, heat transfer equipment mfg. co. exec.; b. Fairbanks, Alaska, June 26, 1930; s. Henry Joseph and Bertha Agnes DeWree; grad. Cogswell Engring. Coll., 1955, Stanford Grad. Sch. Bus., 1978; m. Shirley May Russo, Apr. 16, 1955; children—Angela Kathryn, Mary Rebecca, Thomas Albert, Babette Gabrielle, Jane Elizabeth. Project engr. Heat & Control Co., San Francisco, 1955-59; chief applications engr., then market mgr. Wesix Electric Heater Co., San Francisco, 1959-65; account mgr. Fisher Controls, San Francisco, 1965-76; market and sales mgr. TRW Mission, Houston, 1976-80; v.p. mktg.-sales Houston Heat Exchange, 1980—; dir. Creative Capers, San Francisco and Houston. Mem. Belmont (Calif.) Personnel Bd., 1965; com. chmn. Boy Scouts Am., 1970. Served to capt., arty. U.S. Army, 1951-53; Korea. Named Outstanding Jaycee of Yr., 1966. Mem. Am. Mgmt. Assn., Am. Nuclear Soc., Valve Mfg. Assn., Water Pollution Control Fedn. Republican. Roman Catholic. Clubs: Pine Fores Country, Plaza; Engrs. (San Francisco); Elan, K.C. Home: 16203 Champions Dr Spring TX 77373 Office: PO Box 45876 Houston TX 77045 also 8310 McHard Rd Houston TX 77045

DEYER, KIRK DONALD, mfg. co. exec.; b. Berwyn, Ill., July 23, 1947; s. Donald Everett and Arlene Helen (Kirk) D.; student Miami U., 1964-66; B.S., DePaul U., 1969; M.M., Northwestern U., 1979; children—Shannon, Michael, Steven. Sr. acct. Arthur Andersen & Co., Chgo., 1968-72; divisional controller Sealed Power Corp., Muskegon, Mich., 1972-80, asst. corp. controller, 1980—. Bd. dirs. West Shore Mental Health Clinic. C.P.A., Ill., Mich. Mem. Mich. Assn. C.P.A.'s, Am. Inst. C.P.A.'s, Nat. Assn. Accts. Republican. Lutheran. Home: 411 Glen Oaks Dr 3C Muskegon MI 49442 Office: 100 Terrace Plaza Muskegon MI 49443

DE YOE, JOHN BLAINE, corporate exec., mgmt. cons.; b. Spearfish, S.D., June 14, 1941; s. Richard Albert and Jane Carolyn (Kimball) DeY.; B.S. in Elec. Engring., S.D. Sch. Mines and Tech., 1971; m. Karen Joy Olsen, Aug. 15, 1970; children—Jonathan Karl, David James. Liaison quality assurance engr. Univac, Mpls., 1968-71; dist. engr. Black Hills Power & Light Co., Rapid City, S.D., 1971-74; corporate sec., dir. engring. div., mgr. marketing Flathead Valley Contracting & Engring. Co., Polson, Mont., 1974, also dir.; owner, pres., bus. mgmt. cons. J & K Enterprises, Rapid City, 1971—; sales mgr. Tepco Corp., Rapid City, 1974-75; exec. dir. dept. community devel. City of Sturgis (S.D.), 1975-78; owner, pres., mgr. Mountain Marble, Rapid City, 1978—. Mem. Mayor's Com. on Rehab., Canyon Lake Park, 1972-74. Republican precinct committeeman, 1972-73. Served with USN, 1960-64. Mem. S.D. Assn. Housing Ofcls., S.D. Rental Owners Assn., S.D. Engring. Soc., Rapid City Jaycees (internal v.p. 1972-73, pres. 1976-77), S.D. Jaycees (regional nat. dir. 1973-74, adminstrv. nat. dir. 1974-75). Home: 2211 Lance St Rapid City SD 57701

DE ZEEUW, GLEN WARREN, ins. agt.; b. LeMars, Iowa, Jan. 2, 1948; s. Gerrit DeZ.; B.S., Iowa State U., 1969; m. Carolyn Van de Griend, June 12, 1968; 1 son, Christian Marc. Spl. agt. Northwestern Mut. Life Ins. Co., Orange City, Iowa, 1970-74, coll. unit dir., 1974-76, dist. agt., 1976—. Chmn. steering com. Tulip Festival, 1976-77; chmn. NW Days dr. Northwestern Coll., 1976; sec.-treas. Sioux County Democratic Central Com., 1976-80, county Dem. chmn., 1980—. Named Man of Year, Sioux City Underwriters, 1976, 77, 78. C.L.U. Mem. Nat. Assn. Life Underwriters, Am. Soc. C.L.U.'s, Life Underwriters' Polit. Action Com., C. of C., Orange City Jr. C. of C. (pres. 1978-79). Mem. Reformed Ch. in Am. Home: 209 Kansas St SW Orange City IA 51041 Office: 123 Albany Ave SE Orange City IA 51041

DIAL, NATHANIEL VICTOR, automotive mfg. co. exec.; b. Long Beach, Calif., June 21, 1938; s. Nathaniel Minter and Elisabeth (Porter) D.; B.A., Yale U., 1959; m. Alexandra Montgomery, Oct. 6, 1962 (div. Nov. 1979); children—Minter, Elisabeth. With Ford Motor Co. and subsidiaries, 1961—, bus. devel. mgr. Ford of Europe, Warley, Brentwood, Essex, 1970-73, chmn., gen. mgr. Ford France, Rueil-Malmaison, 1973—; chmn. bd. Credit Ford S.A. Bd. govs. Am. Hosp. of Paris, 1975—, v.p., 1976, pres., 1978. Served to lt. (j.g.) USN, 1959-61. Mem. Am. C. of C. in France (dir. 1973—, v.p. 1975-76, chmn. indsl. com. 1976), Société des Ingenieurs de l'Automobile. Clubs: American of Paris (exec. com.), Traveller's, Tir Aux Pigeons, Maxim's Bus. Home: 2 rue Octave Feuillet 75016 Paris France Office: 344 Avenue N Bonaparte 92506 Rueil-Malmaison France

DIAMOND, HARVEY JEROME, machinery mfg. co. exec.; b. Charlotte, N.C., Dec. 7, 1928; s. Harry B. and Jeanette (Davis) D.; B.S., U. N.C., 1952; m. Betty L. Ball, May 22, 1953; children—Michael, Beth, David, Abby. Sales mgr. Dixie Neon Supply House, Charlotte, 1950-61; pres., gen. mgr. Plasti-Vac, Inc., Charlotte, 1961—; pres., gen. mgr. Diamond Supply, Inc., 1971—; pres. Plastic Prodn., Inc., 1973—, PVI Internat. Corp., 1980—; mem. dist. export adv. council Dept. Commerce, 1979—; del. White House Conf. on Small Bus., 1980. Chmn. Mecklenburg Democratic Party, 1974-75, treas., 1972-74; del. Dem. Nat. Conv., 1972; bd. advisors Pfeiffer Coll., Misenheimer, N.C., 1977—; participant White House Conf. on Small Bus., 1978, White House Conf. on anti-inflation initiatives, 1978. Served with U.S. Army, 1952-54. Recipient award for Activity in U.S. Trade Mission to S.Am., Dept. Commerce, 1967; March of Dimes award, 1966. Mem. Soc. Plastic Engrs., Soc. Plastics Industry, Nat. Electric Sign Assn. Jewish. Clubs: Optimists, Masons. Author: Introduction to Vacuum Forming (manual), 1976; patentee inverted clamping frame system for vacuum forming machines, process of vacuum forming plastics with vertical oven. Home: 6929 Folger Dr Charlotte NC 28211 Office: PO Box 5543 Charlotte NC 28205

DIAMOND, IVAN MARSHALL, lawyer; b. Atlanta, Mar. 17, 1940; s. Frank E. and Helen Marie (Peltz) D.; B.A. cum laude, U. Fla., 1962, J.D., 1964; m. Priscilla Ann Seiderman, Dec. 23, 1962; children—Elizabeth A., Daniel L. Admitted to Fla. bar, 1964, D.C. bar, 1966, Ky. bar, 1969; atty. SEC, Washington, 1964-68; asso. firm Greenebaum Doll & McDonald, Louisville, 1968-70, partner, 1970—; adj. prof. securities regulation U. Louisville Law Sch., 1973-74. Mem. Am., Ky., Fla., Louisville bar assns. Jewish. Editorial bd. Fla. Law Rev., 1963-64. Office: 3300 1st National Tower Louisville KY 40202

DIAMOND, PATRICK HENRY, fin. exec.; b. N.Y.C., June 10, 1943; s. Joseph Bertram and Marie (Lynch) D.; B.C.E., Manhattan Coll., 1963; J.D., Columbia U., 1966, M.B.A., 1967; LL.M. in Taxation, N.Y. U., 1971. Admitted to N.Y., Fed. and U.S. Supreme Ct. bars; fin. planner Exxon, Inc., 1967-69; asst. to chmn. and chief exec. officer Amax, Inc., 1969-72; mem. firm Hynes, Diamond & Reidy, 1972-75; v.p. fin. Maule Industries, 1975-78; v.p. fin. Robertshaw Controls Co., Richmond, Va., 1978—, also dir.; dir. New Eng. Instruments. C.P.A.; registered profl. engr., N.Y. Mem. Fin. Execs. Inst., Internat. Liaison and Policy Com. (corp. fin. com.), Council Fgn. Relations, Econ. Club of N.Y., Newcomen Soc. N. Am., English Speaking Union. Clubs: Deep Run Hunt, Hermitage Country, Westwood Racquet. Office: 1701 Byrd Ave Richmond VA 23261

DIAMOND, RICHARD JOHN, food products and communication services co. exec.; b. Phila., Aug. 6, 1941; s. Joseph J. and Helen R. (Coonan) D.; B.S., LaSalle Coll., 1963; M.B.A., Temple U., 1970; m. Doris Gruber, June 8, 1963; children—Laura Ann, Richard John. Accounting mgr. Campbell Soup Co., Camden, N.J., 1966-69; controller Fed. Sweet & Biscuit Co., Clifton, N.J., 1969-71; v.p., treas., dir. Mickelberry Corp., N.Y.C., 1971—; pres., dir. Newcourt Industries, Inc., 1976—. Served with AUS, 1963-65. Mem. Fin. Execs. Inst., Nat. Assn. Accountants. Clubs: Univ. (N.Y.C.); Montclair (N.J.) Golf. Home: 40 Highland Dr West Caldwell NJ 07006 Office: 405 Park Ave New York NY 10022

DIAMOND, ROBERT LEMUEL, comml./indsl. real estate co. exec.; b. Savannah, Ga., Feb. 7, 1950; s. Herman and Mary Elizabeth (Hastings) D.; student West Ga. Coll., 1968-69; B.S., Ga. So. Coll., 1972; m. Miriam Latham, May 24, 1975. With Crow, Pope & Land Enterprises, Inc., Atlanta, 1972; pres., owner Diamond & Assos., Savannah, Ga., 1973—. Mem. Savannah C. of C. (mem. bus. and devel. com. 1979-80, mem. small bus. com. 1979-80), Savannah Bd. Realtors (mem. budget and fin. com., mem. library com.). Republican. Methodist. Home: 911 Oatland Island Dr Savannah GA 31410 Office: 3230 Skidaway Rd Savannah GA 31404

DIAMOND, SCOTT, home demonstration craft co. exec.; b. Phila., Mar. 2, 1952; s. Leonard and Trudy Diamond; B.S. in Textile Mktg. and Mgmt., Phila. Coll. Textiles and Sci., 1973. Mgr. retail inventory control Caron Internat., Robesonia, Pa., 1973-74, sales analyst, 1974-75, asst. to v.p. sales, 1975-76, v.p. sales and mktg. Creative Expressions div., 1976—. Recipient Excellence in Direct Selling Achievement award Sales and Mktg. Mgmt. Mag., 1978, Internat. Profl. Communications Silver Cert. award Bus. Profl. Advt. Assn., 1979. Mem. Sales Exec. Club N.Y. Office: Creative Expressions East Meadow Ave Robesonia PA 19551

DIAMOND, WALTER HENRY, economist, author; b. Syracuse, N.Y., Feb. 1, 1913; s. Samuel Clarence and Kate K. (Kabaker) D.; A.B., Syracuse U., 1934, cert. A.I.B., 1940; postgrad. N.Y. U., 1941-42; m. Dorothy Frances Blum, June 15, 1947. Dir. research Lincoln Bank, Syracuse, 1934-41; U.S. nat. bank examiner Dept. Treasury, 1941-42; fgn. analyst Fed. Res. Bank N.Y., N.Y.C., 1942-46; fgn. economist Public Nat. Bank, 1946-52; editor McGraw-Hill Am. Letter and dir. econs. McGraw-Hill Internat. Corp., N.Y.C., 1952-60; editor U.S. Investor, N.Y.C., 1960-62; dir. research Fgn. Credit Ins. Assn., N.Y.C., 1962-66; mgr. internat. taxes Peat, Marwick, Mitchell, N.Y.C., 1966-74; prin. Murphy, Hauser, O'Connor & Quinn, N.Y.C., 1974—; author numerous vols. tax and trade books, including: Foreign Tax and Trade Briefs, 1950—, International Tax Treaty Guide, 1974—, Tax Havens of the World, 1974—, Tax-Free Trade Zones of the World, 1976—, International Tax Treaties of All Nations, 1976—, Comparative State Tax Guide, 1976—, Capital Formation and Investment Incentives, 1980—; editor Internat. Bank Newsletter, 1952—; contbg. editor All States Letter, 1980—; sr. chmn. World Trade Inst.; trade adv. UN, AID; fgn. trade zone adv. to various govts., including numerous fgn. govts. Treas., Colonial Ridge Civic Assn., Hartsdale, N.Y., 1966—. Served with USNR, 1942-45. Named Matthew Bender Author of Yr., Matthew Bender & Co., 1970; recipient U.S. Treasury Fgn. Funds Control Bd. commendation, 1942, 43; cert. of honor Govt. of Honduras, 1956. Mem. Internat. Execs. Assn., Internat. Fiscal Assn., Internat. Tax Inst., Pi Delta Epsilon. Clubs: Overseas Press, Overseas Yacht, Touchdown. Home: 9 Old Farm Ln Hartsdale NY 10530 Office: 275 Madison Ave New York NY 10016

DIAMONDSTONE, LAWRENCE, paper co. exec.; b. N.Y.C., Mar. 27, 1928; s. Harry A. and Sally (Margulies) D.; B.S., U. Ill., 1950; m. Marilyn Dick, Dec. 23, 1960; 1 dau., Cynthia Ann. Founder, pres., chief exec. officer Newbrook Paper Corp., N.Y.C., 1958—, Cottonwood Converting Corp., Memphis, 1971—, Garden State Converters, Inc., Bayonne, N.J., 1973—, Triangle Mktg. Corp., N.Y.C., 1975—. Home: 650 Park Ave New York NY 10021 Office: 32 Bleecker St New York NY 10012

DIAZ-NORIEGA, JOSÉ MIGUEL, electronics component co. exec.; b. México, D.F., Mexico, May 1, 1929; s. José and Emilia deDiaz (Noriega) Diaz de la Fuente; B.A., Universidad de Oviedo (Spain), 1948; B.S., Stanford, 1951, M.S., 1952; m. María del Carmen Sotres, Aug. 22, 1953; children—María José, José Miguel, María del Carmen, Francisco Javier, Juan Ignacio, Teresa de Jesús, Ignacio. Gen. Elec. fgn. student scholar, 1952-53, electronics and elec. small appliance mgr. Gen. Electric de México, S.A., 1954-56; mgr. engring. Sylvamex Electrónica, S.A., 1956-58; mfrs. rep., 1958-62; pres., gen. mgr. Electrey, S.A., Monterrey, Mexico, 1962—. Asst. prof. Instituto Technológico y de Estudios Superiores de Monterrey. Dir. Christian Family Movement, 1964-69. Mem. I.E.E.E. (sr.), Soc. Automotive Engrs. Roman Catholic. Club: Casino del Valle Athletic (Monterrey). Patentee in field; designer test and mfg. machines for fuses and breakers. Home: 425 Rio Colorado Colonia del Valle NL México Office: Apartado 1393 Monterrey NL México

DIBBLE, GEORGE SMITH, JR., petroleum co. exec.; b. Salt Lake City, July 29, 1933; s. George Smith and Cleone (Atwood) D.; B.S. summa cum laude in Mgmt. and Acctg., U. Utah, 1954, J.D., 1960; M.B.A., Brigham Young U., 1963; m. Ilene Jensen, June 26, 1964; children—Andrea, George Smith III. Admitted to Utah bar, 1960, U.S. Supreme Ct. bar, 1971, Wyo. bar, 1974; individual practice law, Salt Lake City, 1960-66; asst. to pres., exec. asst. to chmn. bd. Husky Oil Co., Cody, Wyo., 1966-73, v.p., 1973—; co-chmn. petroleum industry task force on land use: vis. prof. various univs. Chmn. Wyo. Gov.'s Adv. Com. on Career Edn.; bd. dirs. North Absaroka Ski Patrol; legis. dir. Nat. Ski Patrol System Inc. Served with USAF, 1954-56, lt. col. Res. ret. Mem. Am. Petroleum Inst. (dir. 1977-80), Rocky Mountain Oil and Gas Assn. (pres. 1977-79), Petroleum Assn. Wyo. (pres. 1975-77). Mormon. Contbr. articles to profl. jours. Office: Box 380 Cody WY 82414

DIBLE, DONALD MEREDITH, publisher; b. Bklyn., Apr. 19, 1936; s. Henry Lincoln and Marie Magdalene (Damberg) D.; B.S. in Elec. Engring., Mass. Inst. Tech., 1962; M.S. in Elec. Engring., Stanford U., 1968; m. Alice Marie Bush, Apr. 6, 1968. Engring. mgr. Melabs, Inc., Palo Alto, Calif., 1965-69, nat. sales mgr., 1969-70; founder The Entrepreneur Press, 1971—; founder Dible Mgmt. Devel. Seminars, mgmt. topics, also Showcase Pub. Co., 1977. Served with USAF, 1954-58. Mem. IEEE, Assn. Am. Pubs., Internat. Platform Assn., Nat. Speakers Assn., Western Book Pubs. Assn. Author: Up Your Own Organization! A Handbook on How to Start and Finance a New Business, 1971, rev. edit., 1974; The Pure Joy of Making More Money, 1976; editor: Winning The Money Game—How to Plan and Finance a Growing Business, 1975; pub: How to Make Money in Your Own Small Business, 1977; Fundamentals of Recordkeeping and Finance, 1978; What Everybody Should Know About Patents, Trademarks and Copyrights, 1978; Business Startup Basics, 1978; Build a Better You—Starting Now, 1979. Home: 3422 Astoria Circle Fairfield CA 94533 Office: 1125 Missouri St Fairfield CA 94533

DIBLE, WILLIAM TROTTER, chem. co. exec.; b. Oakmont, Pa., Sept. 7, 1925; s. William T. and Lois Sarah (Croll) D.; B.S., Pa. State U., 1947; M.S., U. Wis., Ph.D., 1951; m. Sara S. Stierstorfer, Sept. 19, 1948; children—William S., John Rend, Jeffrey Croll, Charles Kendig. With Internat. Minerals and Chems. Corp., Chgo., 1950-64; with Terra Chems. Internat., Inc., Sioux City, Iowa, 1964—, pres., chief exec. officer. Pres., Siouxland United Way, 1971; bd. dirs. Sioux City Symphony Assn., 1967-72, Morningside Coll., 1977-78; asso. dir. Briar Cliff Coll., 1974; chmn. Iowa Coll. Found., Sioux City, 1974-80. Mem. Fertilizer Inst. (dir.), Iowa Mfrs. Assn. (past dir.), Am. Chem. Soc., Am. Soc. Agronomy, Soil Sci. Soc., Sigma Xi. Office: Terra Chems Internat Inc Plaza Bldg Sioux City IA 51101

DICE, CHARLES EDWARD, mfg. co. exec.; b. Boston, July 16, 1938; s. Orin Edward and Oraleah Layman (Pryor) D.; student U. Md., 1957-60, Mitchell Coll., 1961-65, Keene State Coll., 1967-68, Mt. Wachusetts Community Coll., 1970-73, Erie Community Coll., 1977—; m. Diane Elizabeth Getz, July 21, 1962; children—Charles Edward II (dec.), Scott David, Erika Lee, Keith William. Sr. cost analyst Gen. Dynamics/Electric Boat, Groton, Conn., 1962-67; supr. cost accounting Joy Mfg. Co., Claremont, N.H., 1967-68; corp. cost mgr. Kingsbury Machine Tool Corp., Keene, N.H., 1968-73; controller Allen Quimby Veneer Co., Bingham, Maine, 1973-75; controller airco welding products div. Aronson Machine Co., Arcade, N.Y., 1975—. Vice pres. Arcade Community Chest, 1979-80; bd. dirs. Marriage Renewal Inc. of Western N.Y., 1979—; mem. curriculum com. Pioneer Sch. Dist., Yorkshire, N.Y., 1979—. Served with USAF, 1956-61. Mem. Nat. Assn. Accountants, Arcade C. of C. Club: Lion. Home: PO Box 114 Arcade NY 14009 Office: Aronson Machine Co W Main St Arcade NY 14009

DICHELLO, JOHN JOSEPH, mktg. exec.; b. New Haven, Nov. 28, 1936; s. Joseph and Philomena (Vauiso) DiC.; B.A., Providence Coll., 1959; student Holy Cross Coll., 1954-56; m. Hildegarde Fleming, Oct. 15, 1966; children—Kate, Meg, John Joseph. With Sears & Roebuck Co., Hamden, Conn., 1959-61; tchr. English, creative writing St. Mary's High Sch., New Haven, 1962-66; editor-in-chief Bronx Home News. N.Y. Post Orgn., 1966-67: account exec. Josten's Am. Yearbook Co., Topeka, 1967-76; sales mgr. Wire Jour./Wire Assn., Guilford, Conn., 1977-80; pres. Breakthrough Mktg., New Haven, 1980—: cons. Arts Council of Conn., 1980—; cons., advt. sales mgr. Conn. Artists Mag., 1980—. Served with U.S. Army, 1960-66. Mem. Wire Assn. Club: Sales and Mktg. Execs. Roman Catholic. Editor, Between the Lines newsletter, 1977-80. Home: 1460 Shepard Ave Hamden CT 06518 Office: PO Box 4164 Hamden CT 06514

DICICCO, RICHARD LOUIS, research co. exec.; b. Bklyn., June 8, 1950; s. Louis Dominick and Josephine (Pietranik) DiC.; B.S. in Elec. Engring., Pratt Inst., 1972; M.E.A., George Washington U., 1975; m. Emily Lawrence Driftmier, Mar. 12, 1977. Electronics engr. IBM, Endicott, N.Y., 1968-71; dir. mktg. tech. services Control Data Corp., Mpls., 1972-79; pres. Tech. Catalysts, Inc., Arlington, Va., 1979—; cons. to numerous orgns. on transfer of corp. tech., 1979—. Vol. on developing countries to Vols. in Tech. Assistance. Mem. Licensing Execs. Soc., Am. Assn. Small Research Cos., Am. Mgmt. Assn., Info. Industry Assn., Comml. Devel. Assn. Developer new products in tech. licensing. Home: 210 S Wayne St Arlington VA 22204 Office: Technology Catalysts Inc 2323 Columbia Pike Arlington VA 22204

DICK, NEIL ALAN, archtl. and engring. services co. exec.; b. Cleve., June 15, 1941; s. Harvey L. and Rose (Flom) D.; B.Arch., Ohio State U., 1965; M.B., Cleve. State U., 1966: m. Bonnie M. Natarus, Sept. 3, 1967; 1 dau., Rory D. Exec. v.p. J.R. Hyde & Assos., Pitts., 1967-70; dir. tech. and market devel. Stirling Homex Corp., Avon, N.Y., 1970-72; sr. housing coordinator Nat. Housing Corp., Cleve., 1972-74; fin. and estate analyst Conn. Gen. Corp., Cleve., 1974-76; v.p. mktg. Cannon Design Inc., Grand Island, N.Y., 1976—, also dir. Treas., Amherst (N.Y.) Democratic Com.; zone chmn., mem. exec. com. Erie County Dem. Com. Recipient Service award Erie County Dem. Com., 1979. Mem. Soc. Mktg. Profl. Services (regional coordinator), Buffalo Area C. of C., Am. Hosp. Assn., Nat. Trust Hist. Preservation, Ohio State U. Alumni Assn., Buffalo Mus. Sci., Albright Knox Art Gallery, Alpha Rho Chi. Jewish. Home: 112 Bernhardt Dr Amherst NY 14226 Office: 2170 Whitehaven Rd Grand Island NY 14072

DICKEN, DONALD RAY, glass mfg. co. exec.; b. New Orleans, Oct. 27, 1942; s. John Raymond and Kathryn Marguart Dicken; B.S. in Mech. Engring., Kans. State U., 1965; m. Betty Anne Randall, June 12, 1965; children—Scott Randall, Kirby Kathryn. Mfg. mgmt. trainee Gen. Electric Co., Cin., 1965-66; vol. Peace Corps, Afghanistan, 1966-68; with Corning Glass Works, Corning, N.Y., 1970-76, gen. supr. forming and maintenance, 1975-76, plant mfg. engr., State College, Pa., 1977-78, plant prodn. supr., 1978-81, project dir., Greenville, Ohio, 1981—. Vice pres. Lemont/Houserville Sch. PTA, State College, 1979-80; local pack cubmaster Cub Scouts, 1978-81. Served with USAR, 1968-70. Mem. ASME. Republican. Club: Elks. Home: 1058 Buckeye Dr Greenville OH 45133 Office: Corning Glass Works Greenville OH 45133

DICKEN, WILLIAM HOWARD, JR., mfg. co. exec.; b. Columbiana, Ohio, Aug. 17, 1931; s. William Howard and Helene Lois (Crist) D.; grad. Sch. of Aviational Trades, N.Y.C., 1949; m. Myrtle Irene Capen, May 21, 1955; stepchildren—John Murrell, Robert Murrell. Supr., Nat. Can Corp., various locations, 1965-73; shift supr. Ball Metal Container Group, Findlay, Ohio, 1973-74; head dept. Owens-Ill. Metal Container, Perrysburg, Ohio and Constantine, Mich., 1974-77, mfg. specialist, 1977—. Recipient Service award, Jr. Achievement, 1977-79. Mem. Nat. Mgmt. Assn. (dir Toledo chpt. 1977-80; recipient Meritous award 1979), Nat. Metal Decorators Assn., Am. Soc. Tng. Dirs. Republican. Baptist. Clubs: Belles & Beaus Western Square Dance, Parc Del Lang Social, Mason, Shriner. Home: 61243 Timberlane Dr Jones MI 49061 Office: PO Box 218 Constantine MI 49064

DICKER, RICHARD, business exec.; b. N.Y.C., 1914; B.S., U. Pa., 1935; LL.B., Columbia U., 1938. Admitted to N.Y. bar, 1943; chmn. bd., chief exec. officer Penn Central Corp. Office: Penn Central Corp 245 Park Ave New York NY 10017*

DICKERSON, E. JAMES, corporate fin. exec.; b. South Bend, Ind., May 18, 1937; s. Edmund C. and Regina L. D.; B.S., U. Dayton, 1960; m. Roberta A., Jan. 31, 1960; children—J. Scott, Kathleen A. Systems analyst Wyandotte Chems. Corp. (Mich.), 1960-65; auditor, cons. Coopers & Lybrand, Detroit, 1965-69; controller Albert Trostel Packings, Ltd., Lake Geneva, Wis., 1969-73, Lykes Electronics Corp., Tampa, Fla., 1973-75; mgmt. cons. Tampa, 1975-78; fin. exec. Key West Hand Print Fabrics Inc. (Fla.), 1978—. Vice chmn. Fontana (Wis.) Bd. Rev., 1973; incorporator, bd. dirs. Fontana Library Civic Center Fund, Inc., 1973. C.P.A., Mich., Wis. Home: 1200 20th St Key West FL 33040

DICKERSON, MICHAEL ALBERT, banker; b. Dayton, Ohio, June 3, 1936; s. Charles E. S. and Mary Margaret (Kessler) D.; B.A., U. Omaha, 1959; grad. Stonier Grad. Sch. Banking, Rutgers U., 1972; m. Ruth Ann Fleming, Sept. 2, 1957; 1 dau., Michelle. With Nat. Central Bank, Lancaster, Pa., 1964-72; dir. mktg. Nat. Union Bank, Dover, N.J., 1972-73; v.p. Pilgrim State Bank, Cedar Grove, N.J., 1973, exec. v.p., 1973-75, pres., chief exec. officer, 1975—, also dir.; bd. dirs., mem. faculty N.J. Bankers Assn Bus. Devel. and Sales Sch., mem. faculty Human Relations Sch.; banking adv. Am. Banking Assn. Mem. Mgmt. com. Jersey Bankers Polit. Action Com., 1980; trustee Montclair (N.J.) Salvation Army, 1980; pres. Montclair State Coll. Devel. Fund, 1980; trustee Montclair 100 Club, 1980. Served with USAF, 1956-59. Mem. Comml. Bankers Assn. N.J. (pres. 1975-77), Am. Inst. Banking. Presbyterian. Office: 85-107 Pompton Ave Cedar Grove NJ 07009

DICKERSON, WILLIAM ROY, lawyer; b. Uniontown, Ky., Feb. 15, 1928; s. Benjamin Franklin and Honor Mae (Staples) D.; B.A. in Acctg., Calif. State U., Los Angeles, 1952, postgrad., 1952-55; J.D., UCLA, 1958. Admitted to Calif. bar, 1959; dep. city atty., ex-officio prosecutor City of Glendale (Calif.), 1959-62; with firm James Brewer, Los Angeles, 1962-68, firm LaFollette, Johnson, Schroeter & Dehaas, Los Angeles, 1968-73; prin. William R. Dickerson & Assos., Los Angeles, 1973—; instr. Pepperdine U., 1976, N.Mex. Soc. C.P.A.'s; arbitrator Los Angeles Superior Ct., 1979—; judge pro tem Los Angeles Mcpl. Ct. Lic. public acct., Calif. Served with U.S. Army, 1946-47. Mem. Am. Bar Assn., Soc. Calif. Accts. (com. profl. and officers and dirs. liability 1979-80, com. legal malpractice liability 1976-79), Assn. Trial Lawyers Am., Century City Bar, Fed. Bar Assn.,

Nat. Soc. Public Accts., Assn. So. Calif. Def. Counsel, Am. Film Inst. Contbr. articles to profl. jours. Home: 5006 Los Feliz Blvd Los Angeles CA 90027 Office: 3435 Wilshire Blvd Suite 2518 Los Angeles CA 90010

DICKEY, CHARLES DENSTON, JR., paper co. exec.; b. N.Y.C., Jan. 15, 1918; s. Charles Denston and Catherine Dunscomb (Colt) D.; grad. St. Paul's Sch., 1936; B.A., Yale, 1940; m. Helen Barrett Lynch, Nov. 29, 1947; children—Charles Denston 3d, Helen B., Sylvia L., Catherine S., Robert M. Spl. agt. FBI, 1941-43; with Scott Paper Co., 1946—, asst. v.p., 1956-57, v.p., 1957-67, exec. v.p., 1967-68, pres. after 1969, now chmn. bd., chief exec. officer, dir.; dir. B.C. Forest Products Ltd., Vancouver, INA Corp., Gen. Electric Co., J.P. Morgan & Co., Inc., Morgan Guaranty Trust Co. N.Y. Trustee U. Pa. Mem. Grocery Mfrs. Am. (dir.), Am. Paper Inst. (dir.), Bus. Council. Office: Scott Paper Co Scott Plaza I Philadelphia PA 19113

DICKEY, JAMES WILLIAM CALHOUN, mfg. co. exec., lawyer; b. Bessemer, Ala., May 25, 1916; s. William Calhoun and Sarah (Salter) D.; LL.B., George Washington U., 1938, LL.M., M.P.L., 1939; J.D., 1967; m. Jean Lois Round, Feb. 26, 1946; children—James, Jeanine, Jennifer, Jocelyn, Jonathan. Admitted to D.C. bar, 1939, U.S. Supreme Ct. bar; practiced in Washington, 1939—; mem. firm Dickey, Knight, Foley, Olverson & Lindsey, 1950; individual law practice, Washington, 1950—; pres. Ohio Hoist Mfg. Co., Lisbon, 1950—, chmn. bd., 1960—, also gen. counsel; past partner Dickey & DeMaris Investment Co., Miami, Fla.; owner Dickey Farms, Sykesville, Md., 1938—; pres. Cable Climber Safety Devices, Inc.; partner Coury-Dickey Land Co., Sykesville; prof. bus. law Strayer Coll., Washington, 1946-50. Active United Fund; pres. Mental Health Soc. of Dade County, 1963-64; past mem. Gov.'s Com. Employment of Handicapped, Fla., City of Miami Beautification Com.; mem. Miami Beach Com. of 100. Chmn. Republican Finance Com. of Dade County (Fla.), 1960-62. Trustee U.S. Dist. Ct., Miami, Pine Crest Sch., Fort Lauderdale; bd. dirs., chmn. budget com. Washington Internat. Horse Show Assn. Served to maj. USAAF, 1946; now maj. Res. ret. Mem. NAM (mem. nat. def. com. 1952—), Nat. Assn. Small Bus. Investment Cos. (past bd. govs.), Bar Assn. D.C., Fed., Am., Inter-Am., Md. bar assns., Am. Arbitration Assn., Am. Soc. Internat. Law, Econ. Soc. S.Fla., Miami-Dade C. of C., Nat. Hist. Soc. (founding asso.), Columbia Hist. Soc., Am. Assn. Museums, Am. Judicature Assn., Internat. Platform Assn., Nat. Legal Aid and Defenders Assn. Episcopalian. Clubs: Congressional Country (Georgetown, D.C.); Army-Navy, University (Washington), Surf, LaGorce Country, Bath (Miami Beach, Fla.), Coral Reef Yacht (Coconut Beach, Fla.), Pine Lake Trout (Cleve.), Bald Mountain (Lake Lure, N.C.); Goshen Hunt (Olney, Md.). Home: Dickey Farm 13850 Forsythe Rd Sykesville MD 21784 Office: 223 E Flagler St Miami FL 33131 also Sykesville MD 21784

DICKEY, WILLIAM L., lawyer; b. Sioux Falls, S.D., Jan. 14, 1932; s. Clarence H. and Una A. D.; B.A., Augustana Coll., 1957; J.D., George Washington U., 1962; m. Patricia Lee McCormick, June 22, 1967; children—Diane Lee, Pamala Louise. Mem. staff Sen. Karl E. Mundt, 1958-60; admitted to Va., D.C., S.D. bars, 1962; asst. prof. law U. S.D. Law Sch., 1962-63; minority counsel U.S. Senate Subcom. on Intergovtl. relations, 1963-65; spl. asst. Atty. Gen., State of S.D., 1965-66; dep. asst. sec. Dept. Treasury, Washington, 1969-72; individual practice law, Washington. Served with USAF, 1954-57. Mem. Fed., Am. bar assns., Assn. Trial Lawyers Am., Customs Bar Assn. Contbr. articles to profl. jours. Home: 7714 Crossover Dr McLean VA 22101 Office: 1200 New Hampshire Ave NW Suite 300 Washington DC 20036

DICKINSON, HUNT TILFORD, JR., investments co. exec.; b. N.Y.C., Nov. 18, 1933; s. Hunt Tilford and Betty (Gilbert) D.; B.S. in Fgn. Service, Georgetown U., 1961; m. Lis Hesse, Sept. 5, 1959; children—Scott, Gilbert, Elizabeth, Kimberly, Tripp. Sales rep. Varig Airlines, Miami, Fla., 1961-63, Braniff Airways, Dallas, 1963-65; regional mgr. Chrysler Fin. Corp., Chgo., 1966-71; asst. fin. v.p. First Mortgage Investors, Miami Beach, Fla., 1971-74; pres. H.T.D. Service Corp., Boca Raton, Fla., 1974—; owner Hunt T. Dickinson Jr. Enterprises, Boca Raton, 1974—; chmn. bd. Monitor Group, Miami, 1974-76. Trustee Hun Sch., Princeton, N.J., 1980—. Served with USMC, 1957-59. Mem. Fraternal Order Police Assos., LaGorce Island Assn. (dir. 1973—, pres. 1975-79), Miami Beach Taxpayers Assn. Episcopalian. Clubs: Union League (Chgo.); LaGorce Country, Bath (Miami Beach); Racquet and Tennis (N.Y.C.). Home: 64 LaGorce Circle Miami Beach FL 33141 Office: Spanish River Plaza 500 E Spanish River Blvd Suite 29 Boca Raton FL 33431

DICKINSON, JAMES GORDON, editor; b. Melbourne, Australia, Nov. 13, 1940; came to U.S., 1974; s. David Rushbrook and Lorna Aida (Anderson) D.; student Melbourne U., 1960-63; m. Carol Rosslyn McBurnie, Sept. 7, 1963; children—Craig, Peter, Samantha. Cadet reporter Hobart Mercury, 1957-59, Melbourne Age, 1959-63; reporter Melbourne Herald, 1963-64, TV Channel O, Melbourne, 1964-66; cons. internat. public relations, 1966-68; editor, pub. Australian Jour. Pharmacy, 1968-74; asst. exec. dir. Am. Pharm. Assn., Washington, 1975; sr. editor FDC Reports Inc., Washington, 1975-78; founder, editor Washington Drugwire, 1978-79; Washington bur. chief Drug Topics, Litton Co., 1978—; Washington corr. Scrip (U.K.), 1978—, Pharm./Cosmetic Tech., Brit. Pharm. Jour., Med. Device and Diagnostic Industry mag., Washington, cons. to drug industry; pres. Australian Monthly Newspapers and Periodicals Assn., 1972-74; founding sec. Melbourne Press Club, 1971-74. Mem. Australian Liberal Party, 1971-74; pres. Lee Forest Civic Assn., 1977-79. Mem. Periodical Corrs. Assn. Club: Nat. Press (Washington). Editor: Weekly Pharmacy Reports, 1975-78. Home: 4111 Doveville Ln Fairfax VA 22032 Office: 200 N Glebe Rd Arlington VA 22203

DICKINSON, JANE W. (MRS. E.F. SHERWOOD DICKINSON), corp. exec., club woman; b. Kalamazoo, Sept. 27, 1919; d. Charles Herman and Rachel (Whaler) Wagner; student Hollins Coll., 1938-39; B.A., Duke, 1941; M.Ed., Goucher Coll., 1965; m. E.F. Sherwood Dickinson, Oct. 23, 1943; children—Diane Jane Gray, Mrs. Vernon Vane. Exec. sec. Petroleum Industry Com., Balt., 1941-43; exec. sec. Sherwood Feed Mills Inc., Balt., 1943—, also sec. Mem. exec. com. Children's Aid Md., 1960-61; mem. bd. women's aux. Balt. Symphony Orch., 1958-60; dist. chmn. Balt. Cancer Drive, 1958; dist. chmn. Mental Health Drive, 1957; co-chmn. Balt. United Appeal, 1968. Mem. Alpha Delta Phi. Republican. Episcopalian. Clubs: Three Arts (sec. 1958-60, bd. govs., 1960-64, 67-75, pres. 1970) (Balt.); Women's (bd. govs. 1960-64) (Roland Park); Cliff Dwellers Garden. Home: 1003 Bellemore Rd Baltimore MD 21210

DICKINSON, RICHARD HENRY, accountant; b. Long Beach, Calif., June 16, 1944; s. Everett I. and Gertrude T. (Frear) D.; B.B.A., Siena Coll., 1973; m. Georgette M. Turner, Jan. 27, 1968; children—Eric, Christine, Brent. Asso. accountant Alexander Varga, C.P.A., Catskill, N.Y., 1973; controller Hocker Power Brake Co., Inc., Evansville, Ind., 1974; dep. controller Watervliet (N.Y.) Arsenal, Dept. Def., 1975-76; auditor Melvin I. Weiskopf, C.P.A., Saratoga Springs, N.Y., 1977; owner, prin. Richard H. Dickinson, C.P.A., Ballston Spa, N.Y., 1978—; accounting cons. to Town of Milton (N.Y.) and Town of Ballston (N.Y.). Served with U.S. Army, 1967-70. Decorated Silver Star, Bronze Star; C.P.A. Mem. Am. Inst. C.P.A.'s, Nat. Assn. Accts., Am. Inst. Corporate Controllers, Delta Epsilon Sigma, Alpha Kappa Alpha. Republican. Lutheran. Club: Rotary (pres. Ballston Spa chpt. 1979). Home: Frederick St Ballston Spa NY 12020 Office: 154 Milton Ave Ballston Spa NY 12020

DICKINSON, ROGER CLAIRE, computer systems devel. co. exec.; b. Poughkeepsie, N.Y., Aug. 1, 1935; s. Bruce Carpenter and Thelma Starr (Claire) D.; B.A. in Math., Hiram Coll., 1958; postgrad. U. Md., 1958, European Inst. Bus. Adminstrn., 1973; m. Uta von Rehren, Nov. 25, 1961; children—Robert, Renee (dec.), Mark, Karina. System analyst System Devel. Corp., Santa Monica, Calif., 1959-62, field site mgr., 1961-62; project leader Gen. Electric Corp., Wiesbaden, Germany, 1962-64; program mgr. ARIES Corp., McLean, Va., 1964-66, dir. plans and devel., 1966-67, dir. mktg., 1968-70; with Gemini Computer Systems Inc., The Hague, Netherlands, 1970—, pres. Pandata B.V., Dutch subs., 1970-75, v.p. for Benelux, 1974-75, exec. v.p. for European div., 1975-78, also dir. various subsidiaries; chmn., chief exec. officer, pres., founder The European Software Co. Ltd. and Subsidiaries, 1978—. Pres. Am. Assn. Netherlands, 1973-75. Recipient PANDATA, B.V., 1975. Mem. Assn. Computing Machinery, Internat. Fedn. Info. Processing Soc., Am. C. of C. in Netherlands, Fedn. Internat. Am. Clubs (charter dir., sec. 1977, 1st v.p. 1978-79, pres. elect 1979-81), Am. Club of Brussels, Data Processing Mgmt. Assn. (certified). Clubs: Hague Sqauash Racquets, Hague/Wassenaar Backgammon. Contbr. numerous articles to profl. publs. Home: Hofzichtlaan 20 2594CC The Hague Netherlands Office: Nassaulaan 21 2514 JT The Hague Netherlands

DICKOW, JAMES FRED, distbn. exec.; b. Chgo., Mar. 27, 1943; s. Fred Henry and Margaret Isabelle (Arnold) D.; B.S.M.E., Purdue U., 1965, M.S.M.E., 1967; m. Yvonne Alberta Zabilka, Aug. 20, 1966; 1 son, Michael James. Mech. engr. CPC Internat., Argo, Ill., 1965-66; engr. McDonnell Douglas Corp., St. Louis, 1967-70; project engr. Delco Electronics div. Gen. Motors Corp., Milw., 1970; mgmt. cons. Drake Sheahan/Stewart Dougall, Chgo., 1971-72; dir. distbn. planning and services Will Ross div. G.D. Searle Corp., Milw., 1972-80; mgr. phys. distbn. Gentec Healthcare, Inc., Milw., 1980—. Mem. ASME, Nat. Council Phys. Distbn. Mgmt., Internat. Materials Mgmt. Soc., Soc. Logistics Engrs., Phi Kappa Theta, Pi Tau Sigma, Phi Eta Sigma. Home: 7029 N Fairchild Circle Milwaukee WI 53217 Office: 1647 S 101st St Milwaukee WI 53214

DICKS, EDWARD PICKENS, electronics co. exec.; b. Augusta, Ga., Aug. 14, 1924; s. Edward Pickens and Tommie Emmet (Ponder) D.; B.S. in Indsl. Engring., Ga. Inst. Tech., 1953; B.B.A., Emory U., 1948; postgrad. N.Y. U., 1951-52; m. Barbara Ann Williams, May 5, 1956; children—Phillip, Dee Ann, Edward. Accountant, Price Waterhouse & Co., N.Y.C., 1948-49; accountant Am. Cyanamid Co., N.Y.C., 1949-52; indsl. engr., supr. indsl. engring. GTE Sylvania, Inc., Emporium, Pa., Shawnee, Okla., 1953-62, mgr. facilities, Mountain View, Calif., 1962—. Served with AUS, 1943-46. Registered profl. engr., Cal., Okla. Mem. Am. Inst. Indsl. Engrs., Methods Time Measurement, Assn. for Standards and Research, Mountain View C. of C. (dir.), Calif., Mfrs. Assn., Nat. Mgmt. Assn., Phi Kappa Sigma. Democrat. Baptist. Home: 20940 Pepper Tree Ln Cupertino CA 95014 Office: 100 Ferguson Dr Mountain View CA 94040

DICKSON, HERBERT JACKSON, retail food chain exec.; b. Boston, Sept. 24, 1925; s. Herbert J. and Katie Lou (Bowen) D.; B.S., U. Ga., 1949; grad. Advanced Mgmt. Program, Harvard U., 1964; m. Louise Pittman, Nov. 23, 1979; 1 son by previous marriage, Bradford C. Successively exec. v.p. Citizens & So. Nat. Bank, Atlanta; pres. Venture Industries, Inc., Atlanta, Covering Properties, Inc., Atlanta; vice chmn., chief exec. officer Farmbest Foods, Inc., Jacksonville, Fla.; now pres. Munford, Inc., Atlanta, also dir.; dir. Am. Bus. Products, Inc., Blount, Inc., Cousins Properties, Inc., Watkins Asso. Industries, Inc. Served with USCG, 1943-46. Republican. Presbyterian. Clubs: Piedmont Driving, Capital City (Atlanta). Office: Munford Inc 68 Brookwood Dr NE Atlanta GA 30309*

DICKSON, MARILYN LORRAINE, realty co. exec.; b. Kansas City, Kans., Aug. 2, 1923; d. Charles Herman and Ella Johanna (Hoefener) Neligh; ed. high sch.; m. James C. Dickson, Jan. 3, 1943; children—Kristi Lorraine, Kim BethAnne. Dept. sec. N. Am. Aviation Co., Kansas City, Kans., 1942-44; purchasing dept. Owens-Corning Fiberglass Co., Kansas City, Kans., 1945-47; corp. sec., treas., flight instr. Suburban Airpark, Bonner Springs, Kans., 1964-67; credit dept. Weyerhaeuser Co., Kansas City, Kans., 1967-71; bus. mgr.-acct., corp sec.-treas. Campbell-Leonard Realtors, Prairie Village, Kans., 1973-77; bus. mgr., corp. sec.-treas. Campbell-Derks Realtors, Prairie Village, 1977—. Vice pres. Santa Fe Trail Council, Girl Scouts U.S., 1957-75, also bd. dirs. Mem. Internat. Orgn. 99's, Aircraft Owners and Pilots Assn., Nat. Assn. Flight Instrs., All Woman Trans-continental Air Race Assn., Internat. Cessna 170 Assn. Home: 4624 Dover St Kansas City KS 66106 Office: 2210 W 75th St Prairie Village KS 66208

DICKSON, WILLIAM MASON, bank exec.; b. Second Creek, W.Va., Nov. 21, 1929; s. Edgar Farnsworth and Charlotte (Mason) D.; B.S., Va. Poly. Inst. and State U., 1952; grad. Stonier Grad. Sch. Banking, Rutgers U., 1965; m. Page Myers, Oct. 25, 1958. With First Nat. Bank, Ronceverte, W.Va., 1956—, pres., chief exec. officer, 1972—; dir. Fed. Reserve Bank of Richmond; pres. Early Am. Industries Assn., Inc., 1977-79, dir., 1977—. Served to 1st lt. U.S. Army, 1952-54. Mem. Am. Bankers Assn., W.Va., Bankers Assn. Democrat. Presbyterian. Office: PO Drawer 457 Ronceverte WV 24970

DICKSTEIN, JACK, chem. co. exec.; b. Phila., Dec. 14, 1925; s. Aaron and Anna (Anselevitz) D.; B.S., Pa. State U., 1946; M.A., Temple U., 1951; Ph.D., Rutgers U., 1958; m. Pauline M. Gothelf, Dec. 24, 1950; children—Jeffrey L., John F., Andrea E. Analytical chemist Lederle Labs., Pearl River, N.Y., 1946-48; research asso. E.R. Squibb & Sons, New Brunswick, N.J., 1951-56; group leader Borden Chem. Co., Phila., 1958-60, devel. mgr., Leominster, Mass., 1961-67, dir. research, Phila., 1967-73; group mgr. Haven Chem. Co., Phila., 1974-77; v.p. research and devel. Seal Inc., Naugatuck, Conn., 1977-78; pres. Monomer-Polymer & Dajac Labs., Trevose, Pa., 1978—; mgr. Monomer-Polymer & Dajac Labs., Phila., 1960-61; prof. chemistry Rutgers U., 1955-58, Alma White Coll., 1957-58, Bucks County Community Coll., 1970-72. Mem. Crime Commn., Phila., 1970-72. Mem. Am. Chem. Soc., AAAS, Am. Inst. Chemists, Fedn. Am. Scientists, Soc. Plastics Engrs., Franklin Inst., Smithsonian Instn., Internat. Platform Assn., T.A.P.P.I., N.Y. Acad. Scis., Phila. C. of C., Sigma Xi, Phi Lambda Upsilon, Phi Eta Sigma. Author: Polyvinyl Alcohol; Manufacture of Plastics, 1964. Contbr. articles profl. jours. Patentee in field. Home: 318 Keats Rd Huntingdon Valley PA 19006 Office: 36 Terry Dr Trevose PA 19047

DICUS, WILBUR ARTHUR, II, mining co. exec.; b. Cleve., May 26, 1937; s. Wilbur Arthur and Beatrice Leona (Friedeberg) D.; B.S. in Mining Engring., Ohio State U., 1960; m. Delores Lucielle Hyskell, Dec. 24, 1972; children—Melissa Joy, Liana Michelle. Gen. supt. UMAR Oceanics, Key West, Fla., 1960-64; v.p. WADCO Internat., Los Angeles, 1964-68, also dir.; pres. DMEX Internat., Auburn, Calif., 1968—, also dir.; chief exec. officer Internat. Mineral Services, Phoenix, 1978—; cons., investment advisor, Auburn, 1968—; chief cons. Intercoast Energy, Sacramento, 1977-79. Served with U.S. Army, 1954-56. Named to 2000 Men of Achievement, 1972; certified master diver; small ship captain; explosive expert; registered investment advisor. Mem. Soc. Mining Engrs., Am. Inst. Mining, Metall. and Petroleum Engrs., Marine Tech. Soc., World, Latin Am. dredging assns., Internat. Platform Assn., Internat. Oceanographic Found., Colo. Mining Assn. Republican. Patentee in field of mining and heavy constrn. Home: 5919 E Charter Oak Scottsdale AZ 85254

DIECK, DONALD HENRY, account exec.; b. Bklyn., Jan. 10, 1943; s. Henry Ellis and Emily Ann (Orzack) D.; B.S. in Engring., U. Mich., 1965, M.S. in Engring. (teaching fellow), 1966, M.B.A., 1967. Engr. Chrysler Corp., Detroit, 1967-70, quality cost analyst, 1971-72, engring. supr., 1972-76; corp. account exec. Merrill Lynch, Inc., 1975—; asst. prof. math. Oakland Coll., 1972, asst. prof. mgmt. Macomb Coll., 1974. Mem. Comprehensive Health Planning Council, S. Eastern Mich., 1976. Recipient aerospace engring. pin, U. Mich., 1965, cum laude, 1965, NSF fellow, 1966, Outstanding Inductee award, U. Mich., 1964; Von Darmon fellow, 1966. Mem. Am. Mgmt. Assn., Alpha Kappa Psi, Phi Kappa Phi, Tau Beta Pi. Young Republicans. Aerospace designer. Home: 34789 Maple Ln Apartment 67 Sterling Heights MI 48077 Office: Merrill Lynch Inc 26250 Northwestern Highway Southfield MI 48037

DIECKAMP, HERMAN M., utilities corp. exec.; b. Jacksonville, Ill., 1928; B.S., U. Ill., 1950. With Rockwell Internat., 1950-73, pres. Atomics Internat. div., to 1973; v.p. Gen. Public Utilities Corp., Parsippany, N.J., from 1973, pres., chief operating officer, 1974—, also dir.; pres., chief operating officer GPU Service Corp, 1974—; pres., dir. Met. Edison Co., 1980—; dir. Jersey Central Power & Light Co., Pa. Electric Co. Office: 100 Interpace Pkwy Parsippany NJ 07054*

DIEDRICH, RICHARD JOHN, ins. co. exec.; b. St. Paul, June 5, 1936; s. Carl Anthony and Alice V. (May) D.; student Macalester Coll., 1953-54; B.S., U. Minn., 1959; m. Judith Parish, Aug. 12, 1961; children—Pamela H., Stuart B., John C. With St. Paul Fire and Marine Ins. Co., 1959—, gen. mgr., Cleve., 1973-77, v.p. fidelity and surety bond dept., St. Paul, 1977-80, divisional v.p. property underwriting, 1980—. Trustee, Salem Found., 1979—; mem. exec. bd., exploring chmn. Hiawatha council Boy Scouts Am., Syracuse, N.Y., 1967-72, vice chmn. exploring, mem. exec. bd. Greater Cleve. council, 1973-77, mem. exec. bd. Indianhead council, St. Paul, 1977—; mem. exec. bd. Sci. Mus. Minn., 1980—; mem. exec. bd. Big Bros. Greater Cleve., 1975-76, Minn. Opera Co., 1978-80; trustee Oakland Cemetery Assn., 1979—. Served with USAF, 1954-58. Recipient William E. Spurgeon award Greater Cleve. council Boy Scouts Am. Mem. Surety Assn. Am. (exec. bd.). Republican. Roman Catholic. Clubs: Minn. (St. Paul); Somerset Country, Pool and Yacht, Lilydale Tennis. Home: 680 Arcadia Dr Saint Paul MN 55118 Office: St Paul Fire and Marine Ins Co 385 Washington St Saint Paul MN 55102

DIEHL, DOLORES, community relations specialist; b. Salina, Kans., Dec. 28, 1927; d. William Augustus and Martha (Frank) D.; student pub. schs., Kans., 1941-45. Bus. rep. Southwestern Bell Tel. Co., St. Louis, Kans. City, Mo., 1948-49, Mountain States Tel. Co., Denver, 1949-50; edn. coordinator public relations Pacific Tel., Los Angeles, San Diego, 1950-79; cons. Magnet Sch. Los Angeles Unified Sch. Dist., 1977—; pres. Calif. Academic Decathlon, 1979; magnet sch. cons. cons. Industry Edn. Council Calif. Dir. public relations Greater San Diego Sci. Fair, 1960-67; v.p. pub. relations San Diego Inst. Creativity, 1965-67; mem. exec. com. San Diego's 200th Anniversary Celebration, 1967. Recipient dedication to edn. award Industry Edn. Council, 1964. Mem. Los Angeles area C. of C. (dir. women's council), Calif. Magnet Sch. Consortium of Cities (chairperson), Industry Edn. Council Calif., Los Angeles, San Diego (past pres.) bus. profl. womens' clubs., Delta Kappa Gamma (hon.). Republican. Methodist. Home: 691 S Irolo St Los Angeles CA 90005 Office: 1010 Wilshire Blvd Room 516 Pacific Tel Los Angeles CA 90017

DIEHL, SAYLOR FLORY, statistician; b. Nokesville, Va., Nov. 8, 1919; s. Daniel Saylor and Vernie (Flory) D.; A.B., Bridgewater Coll., 1943; student George Washington U., 1943-45, Am. U., 1945-50; m. Nettie Ruth Mathison, Aug. 31, 1946; children—Linda Jean, Wayne Bruce. Tchr. Churchville (Va.) High Sch., 1943, Rockville (Md.) High Sch., 1943-44; agrl. statistician Census Bur. Agr. Div., Washington, 1945-47; real estate salesman Max Miller Co., Washington, 1947-48; tchr. Mt. Rainier (Md.) High Sch. 1948-49; specialist Air Intelligence, USAF, Washington, D.C. 1949-51; analyst commodity industry Nat. Prodn. Authority, Washington, 1951-53; analytical statistician Bur. Personnel, U.S. Navy, Washington, 1953-54; head work measurement br. Office Indsl. Relations, exec. office Sec. of Navy, Washington, 1954-57; supervisory survey statistician Census Bur. Washington, 1957-62; ednl. research specialist U.S. Office Edn., Washington, 1962—. Mason (32 deg., Shriner, K.T., grand master grand council Royal and Select Masters of Md.). Author: The Presiding Officer. Home: 11505 Carroll Ct Upper Marlboro MD 20870 Office: US Office Edn Washington DC 20202

DIEHL, VAL BURL, biscuit co. exec.; b. Mitchell, S.D., Sept. 4, 1916; s. Maurice Blake and Alene (Wallace) D.; B.S., Dakota Wesleyan U., 1938; student Navy Supply Corps Sch., 1943, advanced mgmt. program Harvard, 1962; m. Mary Ellen Condon, Sept. 7, 1940; children—Barbara Mae (Mrs. W. Wilson), James Maurice, Julie Ann (Mrs. G.D. Holloway). Distbr., Royal Typewriter Co., Mankato, Minn., 1940-42; with Nabisco, Inc. (formerly Nat. Biscuit Co.), 1942-43, 54—, asst. dir. internat. operations, 1955-61, chmn. Nabisco Foods Eng., 1962, asst. to pres. Nat. Biscuit Co., N.Y.C., 1962-68, v.p. internat. div., 1968, exec. v.p., now pres., chief operating officer, 1973—, also dir. subsidiary cos., Eng., France, Italy, Can., Nicaragua, Panama; dir. Gen. Pub. Utilities Corp. Trustee Council of Americas. Served to lt. USNR, 1943-45. Mem. Biscuit and Cracker Mfrs. Assn. (dir.). Republican. Roman Catholic. Clubs: Baltusrol Gold, John's Island. Office: Nabisco Inc River Rd and DeForest Ave East Hanover NJ 07936*

DIEKER, KENNETH GUS, pump mfg. co. exec.; b. Westphalia, Kans., Oct. 23, 1924; s. Lawrence T. and Kathryn A. (Weber) D.; B.S., U. Kans., 1950; postgrad. U. Santa Clara Sch. Bus., 1964-67; SCMP, Harvard U. Bus. Sch., 1975; m. Arlene; children—Sandy, Ken, Kevin. Salesman, then managerial positions Chemetron Corp., Chgo., 1951-60; mem. staff, then regional mgr. Air Products & Chems., Inc., Allentown, Pa., 1960-67; with Fairchild Camera & Instrument Corp., Mountain View, Calif., 1967-69; v.p. Adolph Blaich, Inc., Burlingame, Calif., 1969-73; pres. Fab-Knit Mfg. Co., Inc., Waco, Tex., 1973-75, Peabody Tec Tank, Parsons, Kans., 1975-79; pres. Peabody Floway and group v.p. Peabody Internat. Corp., Fresno, Calif., 1979—; partner Brown-Dieker Cons., 1967-79; part-time instr. LaLette Jr. Coll., 1976-77; dir. Peabody Tec Tank, Peabody Floway, Barnes de Colombia. Served with USAF, 1943-45. Decorated Air medal with 1 silver oak leaf cluster, 3 bronze oak leaf clusters. Mem. Hydraulic Inst., Bolted Tank Mfrs. Assn. (pres.), C. of C. Republican. Roman Catholic. Clubs: Rotary, Kiwanis. Author various bus. and sales guides. Home: 8849 N Colfax Fresno CA 93710 Office: Peabody Floway PO Box 164 Fresno CA 93707

DIENER, BETTY JANE, univ. dean; b. Washington, Sept. 15, 1940; d. Edward George and Minnie Chambliss (Feild) D.; A.B., Wellesley Coll., 1962; M.B.A., Harvard U., 1964, D.B.A., 1974. Account exec. Young & Rubicam Inc., N.Y.C., 1964-70; sr. product mgr., consumer products div. Am. Cyanamid Co., Wayne, N.J., 1970-72; asst. prof., asst. dean Sch. of Mgmt., Case Western Res. U., Cleve., 1974-79; dean Sch. Bus. Adminstrn., Old Dominion U., Norfolk, Va., 1979—; dir. Revco Drug Stores, Inc., 1975—. Mem. state coordinating com. Internat. Women's Year, 1975-77; bd. dirs. Karamu House, 1975-79, Womenspace, 1976-79, Leadership Cleve., 1977-79, Rapid Recovery, 1977-79, Woodruff Hosp., 1977-79, Va. Stage Co., 1979—, Norfolk Conv. and Visitors Bur., 1979—; commr. Norfolk Indsl. Devel. Authority, 1979—. Named Outstanding Working Woman, Glamour mag., 1979. Mem. Am. Mktg. Assn., Assn. for Consumer Research, Norfolk C. of C. (dir. 1979—). Club: Women's City (dir. 1976-79). Office: Sch of Bus Old Dominion U Norfolk VA 23508

DIENER, MARY ELEANOR MCMATH, author; b. Washington, July 20, 1929; d. Mercer Bailey and Margaret Therese (Chase) McMath; student Internat. Coll. Tokyo (Japan), 1947-48, B.A., Manhattanville Coll., 1951; M.Human Service Adminstrn., Antioch/New Eng., 1978; m. William Harrison Diener, Sept. 3, 1951; children—Eric, Paul, Lawrence, Valerie. Mem. econ. staff, reporter co. mag. The World, Gen. Motors of Brazil, Sao Paulo, 1951-52; asst. to Am. dir. Cultural Union of Brazil-U.S., Sao Paulo, 1953-54; dir.-mgr. shopping service, Sao Paulo, 1956-62; feature writer, social critique columnist Brazil Herald, Sao Paulo, 1961-65; pres. Assitencia Social de Vila Alpina, Sao Paulo, 1956-62; editor, display advt. mgr., sales mgr. The Citizen, weekly newspaper, Sarasota, Fla., 1966-67; account rep. Center for Marketing and Research, Sarasota, 1969-71; pres. Diener & Assos., Inc., Research Triangle Park, N.C., 1971—; mem. Nat. Bur. Standards Metric Speakers Bur.; chmn. N.C. del. White House Conf. on Small Bus., 1980; mem. N.C. Small Bus. Adv. Council. Fellow Internat. Acad. Poetry (founder); mem. Am. Advt. Fedn. (br. officer and dir. 1969-74), Women in Communications, Nat. League Am. Pen Women (local pres. 1972-74), U.S. Metric Assn. (regional dir.), Am. Nat. Metric Council, Nat. Assn. Women Bus. Owners (state pres., nat. dir.), Internat. Poetry Soc., So. Assn. Pub. Opinion Research, Am. Mgmt. Assn., U.S. C. of C. Republican. Roman Catholic. Author: (poetry) When The Sun Goes Down, 1969, Just Living, 1979. Contbr. poetry and bus. articles to mags. and prof. publs. Office: PO Box 12052 50 Park Dr Research Triangle Park NC 27709

DIESEL, JOHN PHILLIP, multi-nat. corp. exec.; b. St. Louis, June 10, 1926; s. John Henry and Elsa A. (Poetting) D.; B.S., Washington U., St. Louis, 1951; m. Rita Jan Meyer, June 12, 1949; children—Holly, Gretchen, John, Dana. Exec. asst. div. mgr. McQuay-Norris Mfg. Co., St. Louis, 1951-57; partner Booz, Allen & Hamilton, Inc., Chgo., 1957-61; v.p. ops. Ops. Research, Inc., Santa Monica, Calif., 1961-62; v.p., treas., dir. Mgmt. Tech., Inc., Los Angeles, 1962-63; dir. mgkt. and planning A.O. Smith Corp., Milw., 1963-65, dir. mfg. and engring., 1965-67, v.p. mfg. and planning, 1967-70, group v.p., 1970-72; chmn. bd. Armor Elevator Can., Ltd., 1970-72; chmn. bd., pres. Armor Elevator Co., Inc., 1970-72; pres., chief exec. officer Newport News (Va.) Shipbldg. & Dry Dock Co., 1972-78, chmn. bd., 1976-78; exec. v.p. Tenneco Inc., 1976-79, pres., 1979—, also dir.; dir. Cooper Industries Inc., First City Bancorp. of Tex., Inc., Aluminum Co. Am. Served with USNR, 1944-47. Methodist. Clubs: Pine Valley Golf, Seminole Golf, Metropolitan. Office: Tenneco Inc PO Box 2511 Houston TX 77001

DIETRICH, GEORGE CHARLES, chem. co. exec.; b. Detroit, Feb. 5, 1927; s. George Sylvester and Catherine Elizabeth (Cable) D.; B.S., U. Detroit; m. Dorothy Ann Flanigan, Aug. 21, 1955; children—Linda Marie, Elizabeth Ann, George Charles. Field sales mgr. Allied Chem. Co., Chgo., 1960-64; dir. sales Aerosol Research Co., North Riverside, Ill., 1964—; pres. Aeropres Corp., Chgo., 1964-65; chmn. bd., pres. Diversified Chems. & Propellants Co., Oak Brook, Ill., Chem. Distbn., Inc., Diversified CPC Internat.; chmn. bd. ChemSpec Ins. Ltd., 1st Bank Corp., Naperville, Ill.; dir. 1st Bank of Naperville, Am. Nat. Bank, De Kalb, Ill., Diversified CPC Internat., Anaheim, Calif. Served with USNR, 1945-46. Mem. Chem. Specialties Mfrs. Assn. (chmn. bd.), Chgo. Drug and Chem. Assn., Chgo. Perfumery Soap and Extract Assn., Nat. Paint and Coatings Assn., Econs. Club Chgo., Execs. Club Chgo. Roman Catholic. Clubs: Butler Nat. Golf, Olympia Fields Country, Boca Raton Hotel and Club, Broken Sound Country. Home: 1 Charleston Rd Hinsdale IL 60521 Office: 350 E Ogden Ave Westmont IL 60559

DIETRICH, HELEN RUSSELL, court reporting co. exec.; b. Birmingham, Ala., May 4, 1912; d. William Crawford and Lucy Adelaide (Powell) Russell; A.B., Newcomb Coll., Tulane U., 1933; m. Norman Edward Dietrich, July 31, 1935 (div. 1950); 1 dau., Emilie Russell Dietrich Griffin. Sr. claims clk. Liberty Mut. Ins. Co., Atlanta, 1934-35, sr. claims clk., office mgr., New Orleans, 1936-39; office mgr., YWCA, New Orleans, 1939-41; ct. reporter, sr. legal sec. U.S. Navy, 8th Naval Dist., New Orleans, 1941-42; mgr. Telephone Secretary Service, New Orleans, 1942-43; founder, pres. Dietrich and Bendix, Inc., New Orleans, 1942—, Helen R. Dietrich, Inc., New Orleans, 1965—; pres. Habersham Corp., New Orleans, 1965—, also pres. So. Writers div., 1979—; Recording sec. Le Petit Theatre du Vieux Carre, 1964-66; corr. sec. La. Hist. Soc., 1961-72; mem. C. of C. Named Hon. Col. staff Gov. John J. McKeithen, 1966. Mem. Nat. Assn. Shorthand Reporters, Internat. House, Presidents Assn.; corp. mem. Convention Services and Sightseeing Network (charter), Greater New Orleans Tourist and Conv. Commn., La. Superdome Stadium Club, La. Hotel and Motel Assn., Am. Soc. Assn. Execs., Nat. Tour Brokers Assn., Internat. Meeting Planners, Conv. Services and Sightseeing Network. Democrat. Episcopalian. Club: Newcomb Alumnae Assn. (2d. v.p., treas. 1947-51). Author: In My Day, newsletter for legal profession; pub. Of Time and Chase (Edison B. Allen), 1969, New Orleans Story (John Chase), 1967. Home: 1441 Jackson Ave Apt 5E New Orleans LA 70130 Office: Suite 1111 333 St Charles Ave New Orleans LA 70130

DIETZ, CECIL EUGENE, journalist, TV exec.; b. Cookeville, Tenn., Apr. 7, 1925; s. Harry Denney and Emma Jane (Bilbrey) D.; B.S., Tenn. Tech. U., 1950; m. Imogene Rockwell, June 29, 1946; children—Charles Harold, Cecil Burton, Brenda Carol, Wallace Wordsworth, Franz Gerald. With Nashville Tennessean, 1950-70, day city editor, 1966-68, edn. editor, 1962-70; publs. dir., journalist-in-residence Peabody Coll. Tchrs., 1970-74; pres. Dietz Enterprises, Nashville, 1974-75; exec. dir. Tenn. Pub. TV, Nashville, 1975—; exec. producer, writer films; exec. producer film The Ravaged Land, 1971; regional editor Nat. Ednl. TV, 1965-68; media cons. Nat. Seminar on Resources and Retrieval of Race Relations Info., 1974; cons. in field; Tenn. Ednl. TV Network rep. Pub. Broadcasting Service and Corp. Pub. Broadcasting. Host, writer NET spl. Of Monkeys and Men, 1967. Served with USNR, 1943-46. Recipient Tenn. Sch. Bell award, 1962. Mem. Nat. Assn. Ednl. Broadcasters (mgrs. council). Democrat. Methodist (adminstrv. bd. 1968-72). Home: 3614 Woodmont Blvd Nashville TN 37215 Office: C3-302 Cordell Hull Bldg Nashville TN 37219

DIETZ, MARY ROSSWELL, book co. exec.; b. Knoxville, Tenn.; d. Rosswell Bryan and Alice Beatrice (Fitzgerald) D.; B.A., U. Calif., Los Angeles, 1952; m. Robert Clayton Borman, Dec. 13, 1980. Mgr. textbook personnel U. Calif. at Los Angeles Student Store, 1952-54; inventory control mgr. Tech. Book Co., Los Angeles, 1954-69; acquisitions mgr., sales service mgr. Stacey div. Brodart Inc., San Francisco, 1970-72; dir. mktg. library service div. College Book Co., Los Angeles, 1972-76; owner Dietz Book Co., 1976—. Active Sunset Young Republican Clubs, 1961-62; chmn. Los Angeles County Delegation; recording sec., 1963; v.p., 1964; mem. bd. dirs., 1965-74. Mem. Nat. Women's Book Assn., Spl. Libraries Assn., Med. Library Group, Calif. Library Assn., Assn. of Western Hosps., Catholic Alumni Clubs Internat. (Los Angeles, San Francisco chpts.). Roman Catholic. Clubs: Valley Artist Guild. One woman art show Ont. Pub. Library, 1965; represented in Hollywood Bowl's Festival of Music and Art, 1966, 67. Home: 13360 Maxella Ave Apt 10 Marina del Rey CA 90291 Office: 14528 Hamlin St Van Nuys CA 91411

DIFRANGO, GERALD W., acct.; b. Wilkinsburg, Pa., Dec. 9, 1952; s. Joseph and Catherine (Caiarelli) DiF.; B.S. in Acctg., Duquesne U., 1974. Staff acct. Price Waterhouse & Co., Pitts., 1974-76; mgr. acctg. Air Repair, Inc., Pitts., 1976—. C.P.A., Pa. Mem. Nat. Assn. Accts. (chpt. dir. 1980), Pa. Inst. C.P.A.'s, Am. Inst. C.P.A.'s. Home: 3618 Forbes Trial Dr Murraysville PA 15668 Office: 1015 Center St Pittsburgh PA 15221

DIGATI, EIDO, investment cons. co. exec.; b. Milan, Italy, Aug. 2, 1941; came to U.S., 1979; s. Rosolino and Gina Sferrazza Digati; Laurea in Econs. and Bus. Adminstrn. cum laude, Rome U., 1964. Asst. to pres. Esso Italiana, Rome, 1964-72; v.p. Bastogi Internat., Rome, 1972-74; vice chmn. Ctip Engrs. and Constructors, Rome, 1974-78; pres. Sogene Contracting Corp., N.Y.C., 1979, Edge Cons. Co., N.Y.C., 1979—; asso. prof. agrarian econs. Milan U., 1972-79. Decorated cavaliere della Repubblica Italiana. Club: Rotary. Home: 310 E 46th St New York NY 10017 Office: 630 Fifth Ave New York NY 10111

DIGGINS, EDWARD PATRICK, accountant; b. Weymouth, Mass., Nov. 11, 1926; s. Joseph L. and Mary (Ryan) D.; B.S. magna cum laude, Rider Coll., 1950; m. Catherine Hulligan, Aug. 8, 1953; children—Therese, Stephen, Matthew, Timothy, Eileen, Claire, Vincent, Bernadette. Staff accountant, Arthur Andersen & Co., N.Y.C., 1950-53, mgr., 1957-64, partner, 1964-68; cons. accounting and finance; chmn. Rickay Corp.; dir. various corps. Served with USNR, 1944-46. C.P.A., N.J., N.Y. Mem. Am. Inst. C.P.A.'s, N.Y. State Soc. C.P.A.'s. Roman Catholic. Home: 2 Deer Trail Old Tappan NJ 07675

DIGIACOMO, WILLIAM ANTHONY, engr.; b. N.Y.C., Jan. 12, 1929; s. Salvatore and Lucy (De Benedetto) DiG.; B.S. in Mech. Engring., N.Y. U., 1948. With various archtl. and engring. firms, 1950-56; pvt. practice mech. and elec. engring., 1956—; mng. prin., pres. W.A. DiGiacomo Assos., N.Y.C., San Francisco and Los Angeles. Served with C.E., U.S. Army, 1948-49; capt. Res. ret. Registered profl. engr., N.Y., Calif., Ill, N.J., others. Mem. Nat., N.Y. socs. profl. engrs., Am. Soc. Heating, Refrigeration and Air-Conditioning Engrs., N.Y. Assn. Civil Engrs., Am. Cons. Engrs. Council, N.Y., Calif. assns. cons. engrs. Club: Winged Foot Golf (Mamaroneck, N.Y.). Cons. editor Heating Piping Air-Conditioning Mag. Home: 785 Fifth Ave New York NY 10022

DIGIOVANNI, MARIO MARTIN, engring. exec.; b. Italy, Dec. 20, 1911; s. Constantine and Antonetta (Raffaelo) DiG.; came to U.S., 1923, naturalized, 1928; B.S. in Mech. Engring., N.Y. U., 1935; postgrad. Princeton, 1943; Ph.D., Calif. Western U., 1976; m. Mary Cordasco, Nov. 6, 1938; children—Ann Marie (Mrs. Leonard Calabro), Martin Robert. Design engr. Glenn L. Martin Co., Balt., 1935-36; supervisory engr. Brewster Aero. Co., L.I., N.Y., 1936-42; project engr. Curtiss Wright Corp., Bloomfield, N.J., 1942-46; dean engring. Stewart Tech. Inst., N.Y.C., 1947-51; with Statham Instruments, Inc., Los Angeles, 1952-71, v.p. engring., 1958-71; v.p. engring., dir. I.C.T. Instruments, Los Angeles, 1973-79, engring. cons. Ametek Controls div., El Segundo, Calif., 1979—; adj. prof. Loyola U., Los Angeles, 1971—. Mem. Los Angeles County Economy and Efficiency Commn., 1975—. Recipient Silver medal Italian Republic, 1968, Order of Merit, 1974. Mem. AIAA, ASME, Instrument Soc. Am., Pepperdine U. Assos. Clubs: Optimist (past pres.), Unico Nat. (nat. pres. 1967-68). Author textbook on instrumentation; contbr. articles to profl. publs.; patentee in field. Home: 15400 Albright St Pacific Palisades CA 90272 Office: 605 S Douglas Blvd El Segundo CA 90245

DIGNAN, JOSEPH MICHAEL JR., transp. exec.; b. Balt., Dec. 17, 1910; s. Joseph M. and Mary E. (Bowling) D.; student evenings U. Balt., John Hopkins; m. Catherine C. Donahue, June 23, 1939; children—Catherine C. Chrismer, Corinne A. (Mrs. Muth), M. Elizabeth (Mrs. John P. Blumer), M. Patricia. Asso. with father, 1929-49, pres. Dignan Trucking, Inc. (formerly Joseph M. Dignan & Son, Inc.), Balt., 1949-71, chmn. bd., 1971—; pres. Transit Storage Co., Balt., 1968—; dir. Irvington Fed. Savs. & Loan Assn. Mem. county council Baltimore County, 1958-62; v.p. Layman's Retreat League, 1961-66; pres. adv. bd. St. Joseph's Coll., Emmitsburg, Md., 1965-66; mem. Baltimore County Welfare Bd., 1968-69. Bd. dirs. Archdiocesan Council Catholic Men, Stella Maris Hospice, St. Agnes Hosp. trustee Health and Welfare Pension Fund, Local 557 Teamsters, 1960-70. Mem. Md. Motor Truck Assn. (dir., treas. 1945-50, pres. 1950), Middle Atlantic Conf. (chmn. bd. 1972), C. of C. of Met. Balt. (dir. 1964-68). Clubs: Traffic (pres. 1956-57) (Balt.); Turf Valley Golf. Home: 9313 Meadow Hill Rd Ellicott City MD 21043 Office: Dignan Trucking Inc 6351 S Hanover Rd Baltimore MD 21227

DI IORIO, FREDERIC JULIAN, dept. store exec.; b. Pitts., May 7, 1942; s. Alfred Richard and Ann Maria (Benedict) DiI.; student U. Pitts. Sch. Retailing, 1961-63; m. Mary Ellen Haynes, Feb. 8, 1969; 1 dau., Jillian. From stock boy to jr. buyer Joseph Horne Co., Pitts., 1960-65; div. mdse. mgr. sportswear and accessories Tweed Shop, Pitts., 1965-67; with Kaufmann's, Pitts., 1968-74, 77—, vice chmn. ops., 1977-79, chmn. bd. ops., fin. and surbuban stores, 1979—; v.p., gen. mdse. mgr. gome and cosmetics, then exec. v.p. mdse. sales promotion May D & F div. May Co., Denver, 1974-77. Bd. dirs. Pitts. Opera, Pitts. Symphony; group chmn. Pitts. United Fund, 1979. Mem. Pitts. Retail C. of C. (dir.). Democrat. Roman Catholic. Clubs: Duquesne (Pitts.); Edgeworth (Sewickley). Office: Kaufmann's 400 5th Ave Pittsburgh PA 15219

DILENSCHNEIDER, ROBERT LOUIS, public relations co. exec.; b. N.Y.C., Oct. 21, 1943; B.A. in Communications Arts, U. Notre Dame, 1965; M.A. in Public Relations, Ohio State U., 1967; m. Janet Hennessy, Sept. 6, 1969. Account supr. Hill and Knowlton, Inc., N.Y.C., 1967-70, v.p., 1970-73, sr. v.p., 1973-78, mng. dir. Midwest region, sr. v.p., Chgo., 1978-80, exec. v.p., 1980—, also dir. Bd. dirs. N.Y.C. Council of Chs., 1976-78, United Charities Chgo. Recipient Big Apple award Jaycees, 1978. Mem. Public Relations Soc. Am., Nat. Acad. TV Arts and Scis., Sigma Delta Chi. Clubs: Economic, Executives, Chicago, Headline, Tavern, (Chgo.). Home: 915 Shabona Ln Wilmette IL 60091 Office: 111 E Wacker Dr Chicago IL 60601

DI LEO, FRANK JOSEPH, electronics co. exec.; b. Newark, Feb. 23, 1934; s. Frank and Rose (Dellisanti) D.; B.S. in Bus. Adminstrn., Rutgers U., 1955; m. Filomena Dominguez, Jan. 17, 1959; children—Deborah Ann, Frank Joseph III. Project controller Lummus Co., Bloomfield, N.J., 1956-59; asst. controller Sea-Land Service, Elizabeth, N.J., 1959-65; v.p. and gen. mgr. Ivers-Lee div. Becton, Dickinson & Co., Rutherford, N.J., 1965-69; asst. v.p. operational planning and group exec. W. Kidde & Co., Clifton, N.J., 1969-70; v.p. finance and adminstrn. and group v.p. Aircraft and Johnston Product group Stanray Corp., Chgo., 1970-73; gen. plant mgr. home entertainment div. Admiral group Rockwell Internat. Co., Chgo., 1973-74, v.p., controller Admiral group, 1975, v.p. mktg., sales and service Admiral group, 1976-77, group v.p. consumer electronic div., 1978-79; pres., dir. Samsung Electronics Am., Inc., 1979—. Pres., Arboretum Estates Home Owners Assn., 1974-75; pres. Stanray Found., 1970-73; trustee Chgo. Coll. Osteo. Medicine, 1976—. Served with AUS, 1956-57. Mem. Financial Execs. Inst., Planning Execs. Inst. (pres. N.J. chpt. 1969-71), Nat. Assn. Accountants, Assn. Home Appliance Mfrs. (dir.), Electronic Industries Assn. (dir.), A.I.M. Clubs: Brookwood Country, Meadows, Ill. Athletic. Home: 22 W 724 Elmwood Dr Glen Ellyn IL 60137 Office: 1701 E Woodfield Rd Schaumburg IL 60196

DILL, MELVILLE REESE, JR., material handling cons.; b. Cleve., Aug. 14, 1937; s. Melville Reese and Gladys (Frode) D.; B.S. Mech. Engring., Mich. State U., 1959; M.B.A., Harvard U. Product mgr. grocery industry equipment, asst. to pres. Lewis-Shepard Products, Inc., Watertown, Mass., 1961-66; sr. asso. material handling cons. Ganteaume & McMullen, Inc., Boston, 1966—; owner, pres. Dilltec, Inc., Boston, 1969—. Mem. Internat. Materials Mgmt. Soc., Aircraft Owners and Pilots Assn. Republican. Episcopalian. Clubs: Union Boat, Harvard (Boston). Designed world's most automated distbn. center. Home: 79 Beacon St Boston MA 02108 Office: 99 Chauncy St St Boston MA 02111

DILLARD, MAX MURRAY, drilling contractor; b. Lueders, Tex., Nov. 21, 1935; s. Alva C. and Effie Carroll (Murray) D.; B.S. in Petroleum Engring., U. Tex., 1958; m. Carol Gayle Jenkins, Dec. 28, 1957; children—Denise Gayle, Pamela Deanne, Julie Ann. Ops. mgr. Peter Bawden Drilling Co., Long Beach, Calif., 1967-69; pres. Bandera Drilling, Inc., Dallas, 1969-73, Garvey Drilling, Inc., Wichita, Kans., 1973-75, Progress Drilling, Inc., Houston, 1975-78; pres., chmn. bd., chief exec. officer Drillers, Inc., Houston, 1978—; dir. Dillco, Inc., ROC, Inc. Registered profl. engr., Tex. Mem. Internat. Assn. Drilling Contractors (dir.), Am. Petroleum Inst., Tex. Ind. Producers Assn., Nat. Soc. Profl. Engrs. Republican. Mem. Ch. of Christ. Clubs: Houston, Wichita Petroleum, Raveneaux Country. Author articles in field. Office: 5629 FM 1960 W Houston TX 77069

DILLARD, RODNEY JEFFERSON, real estate exec.; b. Short Hills, N.J., Jan. 1, 1939; s. Albert Jefferson and Anne E. (Willingham) D.; student Morristown Sch. (N.J.), 1953-55, Salisbury Sch. (Conn.), 1955-57; B.A., Rollins Coll., 1961; m. Anne Palfrey Lanston, June 10, 1961; children—Courtney Lanston, Carter Jefferson. With A.M. Kidder Co., N.Y.C., 1961-62; with Previews, Inc., N.Y.C., 1962-63, Palm Beach, Fla., 1963—, regional v.p. 1967-70, v.p., 1970—; chmn. bd., pres. Illus. Properties Inc.; v.p., dir. Sotheby Parke Bernet Internat. Realty Corp. Mem. Internat. Real Estate Fedn. Clubs: Bath and Tennis, Sailfish (Palm Beach); Wyndermere Island (Elutheria, Bahamas). Home: 315 Tangier Ave Palm Beach FL 33480 Office: 155 Worth Ave Palm Beach FL 33480

DILLEY, JERRY DALE, diversified industry exec.; b. Dallas, Nov. 24, 1931; s. Loniel Elmer and Mary Magdeline (Graves) D.; student Crozier Tech. Sch., Dallas, 1948-49, Dallas Art Inst., 1946-50; m. Carol Ann Brierton, Apr. 5, 1974; children—Marilyn Dilley Smith, Paul E., Lori Browning, Wesley C., Trey D., Cassandra K. Shopman, Welding Lab., Dallas, 1948-50, designer, 1950-51, chief engr., 1951-53; v.p., chief engr. Metal Structures Corp., Grapevine, Tex., 1954-58, v.p., gen. mgr., 1958-62; v.p., gen. mgr., dir. Rollform Corp., Dallas, 1961-63; pres., dir. Dilley Corp., 1961-65; exec. v.p., dir. Omega Industries, Inc., Grapevine, 1965—. Recipient award for painting Dallas Mus. Fine Arts, 1941. Mem. Nat. Coil Coaters Assn., Am. Mgmt. Assn., Order Foresters. Home: 1115 Hughes Rd Grapevine TX 76051 Office: 404 Dallas Rd Grapevine TX 76051

DILLEY, WILLIAM GREGORY, electronic co. exec.; b. Sterling, Colo., June 6, 1922; s. William Gregory and Ethel (Chandler) D.; B.S., U. Colo., 1951; postgrad. U. So. Calif., 1957; m. Myra Jean McCarthy, May 14, 1944; children—Gregory Dean, Karen Kay. Cons. engr., Denver, 1950-51; commd. officer U.S. Air Force, 1951-68, chief electronics engring. for Thor, Atlas D, Atlas E, Atlas F, Titan I, Titan II intercontinental ballistic missile systems, chief engring. Minutemen Engring. Test Facilities; founder, pres. Spectra Sonics, Ogden, Utah, 1968—; cons. Utah Dept. Vocational Instrn., 1970-74; cons. electronic mfg. corps. in U.S., 1968—; lectr. electronics field. Served with USAAF, 1943-46; ETO, PTO. Decorated D.F.C., Air medal with nine oak leaf clusters (U.S.); Fourraguerre (Belgium); recipient U. Colo. Disting. Engring. Alumnus award. Fellow Audio Engring. Soc.; mem. Soc. Broadcast Engrs. (sr. broadcast engr.), Soc. Registered Inventors, Soc. Motion Picture and Television Engrs., Nat. Assn. Broadcasters, Aircraft Owners and Pilots Assn., Nat. Aero. Assn., Caterpillar Club, Internat. Platform Assn., Pi Kappa Alpha. Clubs: Ogden Golf and Country. Contbr. numerous articles to profl. jours. Patentee in U.S. and fgn. countries. Office: Spectra Sonics 3750 Airport Rd Ogden UT 84403

DILLING, KIRKPATRICK WALLWICK, lawyer; b. Evanston, Ill., Apr. 11, 1920; s. Albert W. and Elizabeth (Kirkpatrick) D.; engring. student Cornell U., 1939-40; B.S. in Law, Northwestern U., 1942; student DePaul U., 1946-47, L'Ecole Vaubier, Montreux, Switzerland; Degre Normal, Sorbonne U., Paris, France; m. Betty Ellen Bronson, June 18, 1942 (div. July, 1944); m. 2d, Elizabeth Ely Tilden, Dec. 11, 1948; children—Diana Jean, Eloise Tilden, Victoria Ely, Albert Kirkpatrick. Def. work Am. Steel Foundries, East Chicago, Ind., 1942-43; admitted to Ill. Bar, 1947; mem. Dilling and Dilling, 1948—; gen. counsel Nat. Health Fedn., Am. Message and Therapy Assn.; pres. P.E.P. Industries, Ltd.; v.p. Midwest Medic-Aide, Inc.; dir. Ry. Devel. Corp., Chgo. Truck Leasing Corp., Mgmt. Info. Center, Inc., Harbil, Inc. Bd. dirs. Nat. Health Fedn., Nat. Safety Council. Served to 1st lt. AUS, 1943-46. Mem. Am., Ill., Chgo. bar assns., Am. Trial Lawyers Assn., Cornell Soc. Engrs., Am. Legion, Air Force Assn., Pharm. Advt. Club, Navy League, Delta Upsilon. Republican. Episcopalian. Clubs: Lake Michigan Yachting Assn.; Cornell University Club Chicago. Lectr. and author on pub. health law. Home: 1120 Lee Rd Northbrook IL 60062 also Casa Dorado Indian Wells CA Office: 188 W Randolph St Chicago IL 60601

DILLMAN, GEORGE FRANKLIN, mgmt. and econ. cons., operating co. exec.; b. Coronado, Cal., Sept. 5, 1934; s. Wilbur Mitchell and Meadie (Ables) D.; student Abilene Christian Coll., 1952; B.S., B.B.A., U. Tex., 1958: m. Virginia Gayle Yeary, Sept. 1, 1961; children—Leesa Gayle Mitchell Lynn, Virginia Louise, Laura Lynn. Mng. partner Dillman & Assos., Dallas, 1968—; v.p. planning and devel. Friedrich Group of Wylain, Inc.; cons. govt. agys., fin. instns., mfg. cos. Mem. univ. bd. Pepperdine U., Los Angeles, 1966—;

mem. devel. bd., bd. advs. Abilene Christian U.; past chmn. bd. dirs. Tex. Tourist Devel. Agy.; trustee Southwestern Christian Coll., 1969—. Served with USNR, 1952-55. Democrat. Mem. Ch. of Christ. Contbr. articles in field to profl. and ch. jours. Home: 13361 Peyton Dr Dallas TX 75240

DILLON, DAVID JOSEPH, corp. fin. adminstr.; b. Montclair, N.J., May 3, 1949; s. Harry David and Madeline Ann (Marusiak) D.; B.S., Bus. Adminstrn., Ohio State U., 1972; m. Deana Kay Marland, July 26, 1969; children—Keri Ann, Mathew David. Staff accountant Groner, Boyle & Quillin, Columbus, Ohio, 1972-74; mgr. fin. analysis Lamson div., Diebold, Inc., Syracuse, N.Y., 1974-77, div. controller, 1977—. Mem. Nat. Soc. Pub. Accountants, Nat. Assn. Accountants. Home: 4060 Winterpark Dr Liverpool NY 13088

DILLON, GREGORY RUSSELL, hotel corp. exec.; b. Chgo., Aug. 26, 1922; s. Gregory Thomas and Margaret Moore (Russell) D.; student Elmhurst Coll., 1941-43, 45-46; LL.B., DePaul U., 1948; m. Nancy Jane Huntsberger, Nov. 8, 1969; children—Michael Gregory, Patricia Jean, Margaret Esther, Richard Thomas, Daniel Russell. Admitted to Ill. bar, 1949; individual practice law, Chgo., 1949-63; with Hilton Hotels Corp., 1963—, sr. v.p., asst. sec., Beverly Hills, Calif., 1971-80, exec. v.p., 1980—, dir., 1977—, exec. v.p., dir. Hilton Inns, Inc., 1972; trustee Wells Fargo Mortgage & Equity Trust, San Francisco, 1975. Chmn. exec. com. Nat. Realty Com., 1979; trustee Urban Land Inst. Found., 1980. Served to 1st lt. USAAF, 1943-46. Decorated Air medal with 4 oak leaf clusters. Mem. Am. Bar Assn., Ill. Bar Assn., Chgo. Bar Assn., Am. Hotel and Motel Assn., Urban Land Inst., DePaul U. Alumni Assn., Chgo. Athletic Assn. Republican. Roman Catholic. Clubs: Bel-Air Country (Los Angeles); Marco Polo (N.Y.C.). Office: Hilton Hotels Corp 9880 Wilshire Blvd Beverly Hills CA 90210

DILLON, JOSEPH GERALD, realtor, real estate developer; b. Chgo., Sept. 1, 1934; s. Joseph Gerald and Anne (Dwyer) D.; student John Carroll U., 1952-54; B.A., Loyola U., Chgo., 1956; m. Beverly Tanty, Jan. 2, 1960; children—Joseph, Kathleen, David, Daniel. Mem. real estate staff Material Service div. Gen. Dynamics Corp., Chgo., 1959-60; v.p. Monticello Realty div. Henry Crown & Co., Chgo., 1960-67; partner Harrington, Tideman & O'Leary, Chgo., 1967-75; v.p., dir. Arthur Rubloff & Co., Chgo., 1975-79; pres. Joseph Dillon & Co., Bensenville, Ill., 1979—. Served to capt. AUS, 1956-57. Mem. Nat. Assn. Indsl. Parks (pres. Chgo. chpt. 1978), Soc. Indsl. Realtors (dir. 1975-77), Assn. Indsl. Real Estate Brokers Chgo. (pres. 1974), Urban Land Inst., Indsl. Devel. and Research Council, Chgo. Real Estate Bd. Clubs: Chgo. Athletic Assn.; Skokie Country (Glencoe, Ill.). Home: 551 Monroe St Glencoe IL 60022 Office: 631 Busse Rd Bensenville IL 60106

DILLON, PAUL ANDREW, real estate economist, pub.; b. Chgo., Mar. 21, 1945; s. Samuel David and Helen Marie (Gorman) D.; A.B., John Carroll U., 1967; M.S., No. Ill. U., 1969; postgrad. in bus. mgmt. U. So. Calif., 1969; m. Barbara Ann Kleinhenz, Aug. 30, 1969; children—Jean Marie, Timothy David, Patrick Anthony. Teaching grad. asst. No. Ill. U., 1967-68; apptd. to U.S. Diplomatic Corps, Vietnam, 1970-71; adminstrv. asst. Ill. Dept. Transp., Chgo., 1971-73; sr. cons. Lester B. Knight & Assos., Inc., Chgo., 1974-76; v.p., dir. Econ. Research div. Mid-Am. Appraisal and Research Corp., Chgo., 1976-80, chief operating officer MSA Publs. Div., 1980—; vis. lectr. in mgmt. U. Ill., Chgo.; community prof. environ. sci. Governors State U., Park Forest South, Ill. Sec., mem. Ill. Legis. Commn. for Revitalization of Midway Airport; mem. Ill. Com. to Strengthen Community Economies, 1978; vice chmn. Aviation Com., mem. Public Transp. Com., Chgo. Assn. Commerce and Industry, 1976-80; chmn. Met. Planning Orgn. Subcom., chmn. Subcom. for Revitalization of Midway Airport, Met. Housing and Planning Council of Chgo., 1977-78; commr. Village of Tinley Park Long Range Planning Commn., 1977-78. Served with USAR, 1969-71. Decorated 2 Bronze Star medals; recipient Eagle Scout award, Boy Scouts Am., 1959. Mem. Ill. 2000 Found. (chmn. Transp. Implementation Team), Transp. Research Forum (bd. dirs. Chgo. chpt. 1977-78), Am. Planning Assn., Ill. Civil Air Patrol (maj.), Ill. Aerospace Edn. Com., Nat. Eagle Scout Assn., Transp. Research Bd., Urban Land Inst., Chgo. Area Transp. Study (transp. ops. adv. com.), Northeastern Ill. Planning Commn. (pvt. sector adv.), Alpha Eta Rho. Roman Catholic. Clubs: Union League of Chgo., Irish Fellowship Club of Chgo., Execs. Club of Chgo., Aero Club of Switzerland (hon.). Contbr. articles on transp. and land use to encys.; dir. major cons. studies affecting future of Chgo., 1977-78; qualified expert witness on tax and econ. impact issues: testified transp. policy and econ. issues before U.S. Congress, 1977. Office: 180 N LaSalle St Suite 1010 Chicago IL 60601

DILLON, ROBERT MORTON, architect, research exec.; b. Seattle, Oct. 27, 1923; s. James Richard and Lucille (Morton) D.; student U. Ill., 1946-47; B.Arch., U. Wash., 1949; M.A. in Architecture, U. Fla., 1954; m. Mary Charlotte Beeson, Jan. 6, 1943; children—Robert Thomas, Colleen Marie Brown, Patrick Morton. Designer-draftsman, Williams and Longstreet, Greenville, S.C., 1949, Lyles, Bissett, Carlisle and Wolff, Columbia, S.C., 1949-50; prin. various arctl. firms, Gainesville, Fla., 1952-55; staff architect NRC, Washington, 1955-57, project dir., 1957-58, exec. dir. bldg. research adv. bd. Nat. Acad. Scis.-Nat. Acad. Engring.-NRC, 1959-77, exec. sec. U.S. nat. com. for CIB, 1962-74, also sec. U.S. planning com. 2d Internat. Conf. on Permafrost; exec. asst. to pres. Nat. Inst. Bldg. Scis., Washington, 1978—; asst. prof. architecture Clemson Coll., 1949-50; instr. U. Fla., 1950-51, asst. prof., 1951-55; lectr. structural engring. Cath. U. Am., 1957-63; professorial lectr. in engring. George Washington U., 1973-77; lectr. grad. seminars in architecture U. Mich., 1969-70; Distinguished faculty Acad. Code Adminstrn. and Enforcement, U. Ill., 1972; guest lectr. Air Force Inst. Tech., Wright-Patterson AFB, 1964-65; cons. Ednl. Facilities Labs., N.Y.C., 1959-71; mem. adv. council Ednl. Resources Info. Center/Clearing House on Ednl. Facilities, U. Wis., 1967-69; vis. prof. Grad. Sch. Architecture U. Utah, 1978; trustee Advisors to F. Stuart Fitzpatrick Meml. Award, 1969—, chmn., 1974-78; mem. adv. panel Industrialization Forum-Building: Systems constrn., Analysis, Research, U. Montreal, also Mass. Inst. Tech. and Washington U., St. Louis, 1969—; mem. basic home adv. panel HUD, 1972-77; mem. Working Groups on Bldg. for Extreme Climates and Unusual Geol. Conditions and Bldg. Materials and Components, U.S.-USSR Agreement on Housing Constrn., 1975—; mem. Nat. Adv. Council on Research in Energy Conservation, 1975-78; mem. adv. com. Council Am. Bldg. Ofcls., 1976—. Served with USNR, 1942-45. Registered architect, Fla. Mem. AIA (chmn. adv. com. on archtl. barriers 1967-68; mem. nat. com. on research for architecture 1962-67, chmn. 1969; mem. housing com. 1971-72), Md. Soc. Architects, ASCE (exec. com. tech. council codes and standards, 1976—, sec. 1978; mem. task com. cold regions engring. 1978-79, exec. com. tech. council on cold regions engring. 1979—, via chmn., 1980—), Nat. Acad. Code Adminstrn. (trustee 1976—, exec. com. 1978—, dir. 1980—), Am. Real Estate and Urban Econs. Assn., Sigma Lambda Chi (charter). Co-author: Steel Buildings: Analysis and Design, 1970, 2d edit., 1977, 3d edit., 1981; also articles in field; contbg. author Funk and Wagnall's New Ency., 1972, 73. Home: 811 Arrington Dr Silver Spring MD 20901 Office: 1015 15th St NW Suite 700 Washington DC 20005

DILLON, SALLY IRENE, forensic scientist; b. Joliet, Ill., Mar. 21, 1947; s. Thomas Eugene and Irene Louise (Castelli) D.; B.S., Coll. St. Francis, 1968. Crime lab. analyst Bur. Scientific Services, Joliet, 1969-71, criminalist, 1971-72, supervising criminalist, 1972-77, asst. lab. supr., 1977-78, dir. Maywood (Ill.) lab., 1978—. Fellow Am. Acad. Forensic Scis.; mem. Am. Soc. Crime Lab. Dirs., Am. Mgmt. Assn., Midwestern Assn. Forensic Scientists (sec.-treas.), Forensic Sci. Soc. Gt. Britain, Internat. Assn. Identification. Roman Catholic. Office: 1401 S Maybrook Dr Maywood IL 60153

DILLON, THOMAS CHURCH, advt. exec.; b. Seattle, Mar. 27, 1915; s. Thomas J. and Clarissa (Church) D.; student Harvard, 1933-36; m. Georgiana Adams, Nov. 8, 1939 (dec. May 1964); children—Thomas Adams, Victoria Caroline, George Anthony; m. 2d, Patricia Doran, 1965. With Batten, Barton, Durstine & Osborn, Inc., 1938—, copywriter, Mpls., creative chief, San Francisco, Los Angeles, 1938-48, v.p., 1948-59, mgr. Los Angeles office, 1957-58, treas., dir., 1958—, exec. v.p., 1959-64, gen. mgr., 1962-64, pres., 1964-75, chmn. bd., 1975-79, chief exec. officer, 1967-77, pres., chief exec. officer BBDO Internat., Inc., 1971-75, chmn. bd., 1971-80; pres. Muntasker, Inc., N.Y.C., 1980—. Clubs: Economic, Harvard (N.Y.C.). Home: 870 United Nations Plaza New York NY 10017 Office: 870 UN Plaza New York NY 10017

DIMARIA, ORLANDO QUINTIN, publishing exec.; b. Greensburg, Pa., Sept. 6, 1918; s. Dominic and Mary Lucy (Vitone) D.; B.A., Pa. State U., 1948; m. Betty Louise Miller, Feb. 6, 1947; children—David J., Betsy Ann. With Walworth Co., 1937-40; founder editor, pub. Club Divots, Greensburg, 1940-41; advt. mgr. Madera (Calif.) News-Tribune, 1948-50; asst. advt. mgr. Milton (Pa.) Evening Standard, 1950-51; with Wall Street Jour., 1951-64, asst. retail advt. mgr. Eastern edit., 1951-56, asso. advt. mgr. nat. edit., 1956-61; spl. projects to design and start Nat. Observer, 1961, advt. mgr. 1961-62, exec. advt. mgr., 1963-64; dir. marketing Am. Banker, 1965-66; pres. Mardee Enterprises, Inc., pub. Oceanography Newsletter, 1966—, pub. New Med. Tech., 1968—, New Pollution Tech., 1969—; pres. QD Pub., Inc., pub. bank letter, 1966—; founder, pub. Oceanside-Vista (Calif.) Observer, 1974—; pub. sci. response cards, 1974—; pres. Wall St. Newscards, 1975—; v.p. Soc. West, 1976-78; nat. advt. mgr. Los Angeles Herald-Examiner, 1978—. Trustee L.I. Library Resources Council. Served from pvt. to 1st sgt. USAAF, 1941-45; ETO, Africa. Mem. Advt. Fedn. Am., Downtown N.Y. Ad Club (organizing chmn.), Navy League U.S., Am. Soc. for Oceanography, Internat. Platform Assn., Internat. Oceanographic Found., Alpha Delta Sigma. Clubs: The Lambs; Lomas Santa Fe Country. Home: 21022 Miramar Ln Huntington Beach CA 92646 Office: Drawer 6249 Huntington Beach CA 92646

DIMMA, WILLIAM ANDREW, diversified real estate co. exec.; b. Montreal, Que., Can., Aug. 13, 1928; s. William Roy and Lillian Noreen (Miller) D.; B.A. Sc., U. Toronto, 1948; M.M.P., Harvard U., 1956, D.B.A., 1973; M.B.A., York U., Toronto, 1969. With Union Carbide Can. Ltd., 1948-69, exec. v.p., dir., 1967-69; dean Faculty Adminstrv. Studies, prof. bus. adminstrn. York U., 1973-75; pres., dir. Torstar Corp., Toronto, 1976-78, Toronto Star Newspapers Ltd., 1976-78; pres., chief operating officer A.E. LePage Ltd., Toronto, 1979—; chmn., dir. Rolysar Ltd.; dir. Continental Bank Can., IAC Ltd., Niagara Fin., Simpsons-Sears Ltd., Capstone Investment Trust, Gen. Accident Assurance Co. Can.; mem. Ont. Premier's Bus. Adv. Council, Premier's Com. on Econ. Future. Bd. dirs. Niagara Inst., Toronto Symphony; bd. govs. York U.; trustee Hosp. for Sick Children, Toronto. Sir Bertram Whindle scholar, Elmslie Meml. scholar, 1944; Can. Council fellow, 1970-73; registered profl. engr., Ont. Mem. Econ. Council Can. (exec. com.). Clubs: Canadian (dir.), Toronto, Toronto Golf, York, Granite (Toronto); Mark's (Eng.). Office: Box 100 Toronto-Dominion Bank Tower Toronto ON M5K 1G8 Canada

DIMOND, THOMAS, investment adv. co. exec.; b. Scarsdale, N.Y., Jan. 24, 1916; s. George A. and Jessie (Kennedy) D.; B.A. magna cum laude, Princeton U., 1939; M.B.A., Harvard U., 1941. Mem. faculty Wharton Sch. Fin., U. Pa., 1948; economist, account mgr. Lionel D. Edie & Co., 1948-50; economist, mgr. comml. research Youngstown Sheet and Tube Co. (Ohio), 1951-56; sr. account mgr., security analyst deVegh & Co., N.Y.C., 1956-60; pres. Humes-Schmidlapp Assos., N.Y.C., 1960—; dir. Mercer Mgmt. Corp., co-mgr. Mercer Fund, 1963-67; gen. partner HS Spl. Fund. Trustee, Humes Found., 1963—. Served to capt. USAAF, 1941-46. Mem. N.Y. Soc. Security Analysts, Motor Carrier Analysts Group. Episcopalian. Clubs: Racquet and Tennis, Down Town Assn. (N.Y.C.). Contbr. articles to profl. publs. Home: 200 E 66th St New York NY 10021 Office: 345 Park Ave New York NY 10154

DIMOPOULOS, HARRY GEORGE, chem. co. exec.; b. Istanbul, Turkey, Feb. 12, 1940; s. George Nicholas and Elizabeth (Datsis) D.; B.S., Robert Coll., 1963; M.S. in Chem. Engring., U. Ill., 1965, Ph.D. in Chem. Engring., 1967; M.B.A., Harvard, 1972; m. Carol Lee Hamilton, Feb. 25, 1967; children—George, Elizabeth, Alexandra. Research engr. Shell Oil Co., Houston, 1967-70; dir. corporate planning Air Products & Chems., Allentown, Pa., 1972-75, bus. mgr. atmospheric gases, 1976-80; dir. mktg. and Planning, Air Products Europe, London, 1980—; dir. Krikos Inc.; bd. dirs. Strategic Planning Inst. Cabot Corp. fellow, 1971; Freeport Minerals Corp. fellow, 1972. Republican. Greek Orthodox. Home: East Wissett Hook Heath Rd Woking Surrey England

DINEEN, RICHARD ALLEN, banker; b. Dayton, Ohio, May 30, 1946; s. Martin C. and Geneviene R. Dineen; B.A. in Econs., U. Cin., 1968; M.B.A., Xavier U., Cin., 1978; grad. Stonier Grad. Sch. Banking, Rutgers U., 1980; m. Susan Jane Long, June 28, 1969; children—Brian, Emily, Kevin. Mem. data processing sales staff IBM, Cin., 1968-69; with First Nat. Bank of Cin., 1969—, asst. cashier, 1972-75, asst. v.p., 1975-79, v.p., 1979—. Div. asst. chmn. United Appeal; div. capt. WCET-TV fund drive; mem. corporate fund drive team U. Cin.; bd. dirs. Dan Beard council Boy Scouts Am. Mem. Am. Bankers Assn., Am. Inst. Banking, Ohio Bankpac, Pi Kappa Alpha. Club: Cin.

DINGES, DANIEL D., mgmt. cons.; b. Chgo., Sept. 19, 1946; s. Daniel D. and Ruth (Hanrath) D.; B.A., Loyola U., Chgo., 1976; M.B.A., U. Wash., 1978; m. Krista Migala, June 18, 1969; children—Eric Paul, Jeremy Todd. Systems rep. RCA computers, Chgo., 1970-71; cons. data processing First Nat. Bank, Chgo., 1971-73, telecommunications mgr., 1973-75, funds transfer mgr., 1975-77, ops. officer, 1976-77; mgmt. cons. Touche Ross & Co., Seattle, 1979—. Served with U.S. Army, 1968-70. Mem. Omicron Delta Epsilon. Home: 14220 NE 75th St Redmond WA 98052 Office: Touche Ross & Co 2500 Financial Center Seattle WA 98161

DINGLEDINE, EUGENE W., constrn. co. exec.; b. Washington, Ill., Feb. 1, 1920; s. Walter J. and Clara E. (Hagenstoz) D.; B.S. in Civil Engring., U. Ill.; m. Doris J. Dorward, Aug. 1, 1943; children—Donald, Linda Gable, Edward, Jon. Civil engr. Patrick Warren Inst., Chgo., 1948-50, Mercury Builders, Chgo., 1950-55; with Del Constrn. Co., Washington, 1955-78, pres., 1956-78; cons. Nelson, Peters & Assos., Peoria, Ill., 1978—. Mem. Washington Sch. Bd. Served to capt. USAAF, 1942-45. Decorated Purple Heart, Air medal. Mem. Asso. Gen. Contractors Am., Central Ill. Builders. Mason (Shriner), Rotarian. Club: Washington Civic. Home: 129 Irish Ln Washington IL 61571 Office: 130 Irish Ln Washington IL 61571

DINGMAN, MICHAEL DAVID, engring. mfg. co. exec.; b. New Haven, Sept. 29, 1931; s. James Everett and Amelia (Williamson) D.; ed. U. Md.; m. Jean Hazlewood, May 16, 1953; children—Michael David, Linda Channing, James Clifford. Gen. partner Burnham & Co., investment bankers, N.Y.C., 1964-70; pres., chief exec. officer Wheelabrator-Frye Inc., Hampton, N.H., 1970—, chmn. bd., 1977—, also dir.; dir. Madison Fund Inc., Time Inc., Dominion Bridge Co., Ltd., Mellon Nat. Corp., Ford Motor Ltd., Pogo Producing Co. Trustee, John A. Hartford Found.; bd. dirs. N.H. Council World Affairs, Mem. IEEE, Sci. Museum Boston. Clubs: Recess, Links, Board Room, N.Y. Yacht (N.Y.C.); Lyford Cay (Nassau, N.Y.); Union of Boston; Basin Harbor (Vt.). Office: Wheelabrator-Frye Inc Liberty Ln Hampton NH 03842

DINING, BRUCE FRANCIS, fuels co. exec.; b. Melrose, Mass., July 14, 1934; s. Carl Moulton and Virginia Frances (Dennett) D.; B.A., U. N.H., 1953-58; m. Janet B. Taylor, Mar. 29, 1958 (div. Nov. 1974); children—Mark Taylor, Timothy Bruce, Elizabeth Joy. Pres., dir. C.M. Dining, Inc., Exeter, N.H., 1958—; founder, v.p., treas., dir. C.M. Dining (Can.), Ltd., Montreal, Que., Can., 1972—; founder, pres., treas. Xanadu, Inc., Exeter, 1973—, Dining Fuels Ltd., Montreal, 1976—; cons. Gazocean (Paris), Axel Johnson, Sea-3, Inc.; dir. Eli N. Marcotte, Inc., Moulton Investment/Leasing Corp., Exeter Clinic. Trustee, Exeter Day Sch., 1964-67, 69-75, chmn., 1965-67; mem. Rockingham County Family Planning Bd., 1973-75. Mem. Nat. (state dir. 1968-72, 78—, New Eng. dir. 1972-75), New Eng. (pres. 1974-76) LP gas assns., Newcomen Soc. Democrat. Congregationalist (trustee 1969-71). Home: RFD 1 Kingston Rd Exeter NH 03833 Office: 104 Epping Rd Exeter NH 03833

DINKELOO, JOHN GERARD, architect; b. Holland, Mich., Feb. 28, 1918; s. William and Bessie (Brouwer) D.; student Hope Coll., Holland, 1936-39; B.Arch. in Archtl. Engring., U. Mich., 1942; m. Thelma Ann Van Dyke, Jan. 30, 1943; children—Carter John, Jansje, Dirk Van Dyke, Tessa, Christian Van Dyke, Hanni, Kaaren. Designer, Skidmore, Owings & Merrill, Chgo., 1942-43, chief prodn., 1946-50; partner Eero Saarinen & Assos., Birmingham, Mich. and Hamden, Conn., 1950-66, Kevin Roche-John Dinkeloo and Assos., Hamden, 1966—; prin. works include TWA Terminal at Kennedy Airport, 1961, Dulles Airport, 1962, CBS Hdqrs. Bldg., N.Y.C., 1965, Oakland (Calif.) Mus., 1967, Ford Found. Adminstrn. Bldg., N.Y.C., 1967, Gateway Arch, Jefferson Nat. Expansion Meml., St. Louis, 1965, Morse and Stiles colls., Yale, 1963. Trustee, Hope Coll. Served as officer USNR, 1943-46. Recipient Bard award for Ford Found. Bldg., 1968. Mem. A.I.A. Devel. structural neoprene plazing gaskets, laminated metalized heat reflecting glass, exposed structural bldg. components of corrosion resistant steel. Home: 145 Blue Trail Hamden CT 06518 Office: 20 Davis St Hamden CT 06517

DINKELSPIEL, RICHARD COLEMAN, lawyer; b. Oakland, Calif., Feb. 13, 1913; s. Edward and Ellen (Gaines) D.; A.B., U. Calif., 1934, J.D., 1937; m. Miriam Cutter, Dec. 9, 1939; children—Susan (Mrs. Stern), Robin (Mrs. Miller), Joan, Anne, Richard Coleman. Admitted to Calif. bar, 1937; city judge Suisun (Calif.), 1937-42; practiced in San Francisco, 1946—; partner firm Dinkelspiel, Pelavin, Steefel & Levitt, and predecessor, 1950—. Justice of peace Suisun Twp., 1939-42; chmn. citizens adv. com. to Interim Senate and Assembly subcoms. studying lien law, 1963-68; co-chmn. Gov.'s Commn. on Family, 1966; mem. Gov.'s Adv. Com. on Children and Youth, 1966—; co-chmn. San Francisco Lawyers Com. for Urban Affairs, 1968-70; mem. exec. com., bd. dirs. Lawyers Com. for Civil Rights under Law, 1968—. Served from lt. to lt. col. AUS, 1942-46. Fellow Am. Coll. Probate Counsel, Am. Bar Found.; mem. Bar Assn. San Francisco (pres. 1968), San Francisco Bar Found. (trustee 1969-72, pres. 1972-73), State Bar Calif. (chmn. conf. com. on liens of mechanics and materialmen 1962, bd. govs. 1974-77), Internat. Bar Assn., St. Thomas More Soc. San Francisco (pres. 1960), Sigma Alpha Epsilon, Phi Delta Phi. Clubs: The Family, Commonwealth (quar. chmn. 1969, bd. govs. 1973-75, 78—), Meadow. Office: 27th Floor One Embarcadero Center San Francisco CA 94111

DIODENE, CAROL ANN, retail exec.; b. New Orleans, Feb. 16, 1947; d. John Albert and Flois (Boudreaux) D.; student Newcomb Coll., 1964-66, U. Southwestern La., 1966-67, Tulane U., 1970-72. Jr. acct. Hunt-Wesson Foods, Inc., Gretna, La., 1967-72; acct. Wells Fargo Armored Service Corp., Atlanta, 1972-73; asst. to chief fin. officer The Mayronne Co., Harvey, La., 1978-79, chief fin. officer Paneling Factory Outlet, Inc., New Orleans, also Va., 1979—. Home: PO Box 15755 New Orleans LA 70175 Office: Bldg 17 PCW Fgn Trade Zone No 2 Napoleon Ave and The River New Orleans LA 70130

DIOTTE, ALFRED PETER, pen and pencil mfg. co. exec.; b. Newport, N.H., Apr. 16, 1925; s. J. Alfred and Mary Ellen (Perry) D.; B.S., Marquette U., 1950; J.D., U. Wis., 1953, M.B.A., 1979; postgrad. Harvard U., 1961; m. Helen M. Foote, June 12, 1948; children—Cathy Diotte Scott, Cere, Peter. Admitted to Wis. bar, 1953; partner firm Fett, Murphy & Diotte, Janesville, Wis., 1953-54; with Parker Pen Co., Janesville, 1954—, v.p. adminstrn., sec., 1968-77, exec. v.p. adminstrn. 1977—, also dir.; dir. Banc Wis Corp., Bank of Wis., Janesville. Mem. adv. council U. Wis.-Rock County Campus, Marquette U. Coll. Bus.; mem. bus. adv. council U. Wis., Whitewater. Served with AC, USNR, 1943-45. Recipient Bus. Adminstrn. Man of Yr. award Marquette U., 1976. Mem. Am. Bar Assn., Wis. Bar Assn., Rock County Bar Assn., Beta Gamma Sigma. Office: 219 E Court St Janesville WI 53545

DI PERI, PHILIP TIMOTHY, publishing and mfg. co. exec.; b. N.Y.C., May 30, 1943; s. Philip John and Constance (LoDolce) DiP.; B.S. in Math., SUNY, Stony Brook, 1970; M.B.A. in Mktg. and Fin. (fellow), U. Mass., 1977; m. Claudia Degroff, Mar. 21, 1966; children—Bronwyn Sessile, Israel Justin. With Butternut Cards, Inc., Brattleboro, Vt., 1976—, pres., 1976-79, chmn. bd., 1978—; dir. Petrie Industries; cons. strategic planning to communications, electronics, paper and recreation industries, 1975—; instr. Community Coll. Vt., 1976-78, Greenfield Community Coll., 1976-78; sponsor bus. planning workshops, 1975—. Bd. dirs. Small Bus. Inst., 1973—. Served with USMC, 1967-69; Vietnam. Mem. Nat. Assn. Corp. Dirs. Author: Make It Happen, 1973; asst. editor Am. Phys. Rev.; editor, pub.: Solargram TM, 1976; Working Capital Management, 1978; Biotechnology Opportunities, 1980. Office: PO Box 266 204 Bonnyvale Rd Brattleboro VT 05301

DI PIETRO, RAYMOND JOSEPH, financing and leasing co. exec.; b. Englewood, N.J., Dec. 5, 1937; s. Ralph N. and Ida M. DiP.; B.S. in Bus. Adminstrn., Fairleigh Dickinson U., 1959; m. Phyllis J. Corey, June 3, 1961; children—Claire, Gail, Julie. Credit mgr. CIT Corp., 1960-63; with Gen. Electric Credit Corp., Boston, 1963-73, dist. credit mgr., 1966-67, dist. mgr., 1967-73; regional mgr. ITT Indsl. Credit Co., Weston, Mass., 1973, v.p., N.E. area gen. mgr., Framingham, Mass., 1974-79, sr. v.p., div. dir. ops., St. Paul, 1979—. Served with Army N.G., 1960. Mem. South Middlesex Area C. of C.,

Associated Equipment Distbrs. Club: Framingham Country. Office: 1400 N Central Life Tower Saint Paul MN 55164

DIPIETRO, WILLIAM ANTHONY, art gallery exec.; b. Phila., Nov. 4, 1948; s. William Albert and Virginia C. DiP.; student Pa. State U., 1967-71, Villanova U., 1976—. Pres., Gemex Gallery, Colmar, Pa., 1980—. Mem. U.S. Jaycees, Phila. Mus. Art, Artists Choice Mus. Republican. Roman Catholic. Office: PO Box 267 Colmar PA 18915

DIPPEL, TIEMAN HENRY, JR., banker; b. Brenham, Tex., Nov. 10, 1945; s. Tieman Henry and Evelyn (Knolle) D.; A.A., Blinn Coll., 1966; B.B.A., U. Tex., 1968, J.D., 1971; m. Katherine Elizabeth Wright, Jan. 9, 1971; children—Margaret Katherine, Tieman H. Admitted to Tex. bar, 1971; chmn. bd., chief exec. officer Brenham (Tex.) Nat. Bank, 1972—, also dir.; dir. Cable TV of Brenham, Inc.; guest lectr. Tex. A&M U., U. Tex. Sec.-treas. Brenham Indsl. Found.; trustee Nat. Livestock Merchandising Inst.; dist. sustaining membership chmn. Boy Scouts Am.; mem. governing bd. Tex. Arts Alliance, former vice chmn.; sec., legis. chmn. Tex. Commn. Arts and Humanities; chmn. U. Tex. Centennial Commn. Served to lt. comdr. JAGC, USNR, 1971-72. Mem. Tex. Ind. Bankers Assn. (dir.), Brazos Valley Bankers Assn. (pres.), Am., Tex. bar assns., State Bar Tex. (dist. admissions com.), Tex. Lyceum Assn. (pres., chmn.), U. Tex. Ex-Students Assn. (pres. Washington County chpt. 1975-76, state exec. council), E. Tex. C. of C. (pres.-elect), Alpha Kappa Psi, Beta Gamma Sigma, Phi Kappa Phi, Phi Rho Pi, Omicron Delta Kappa, Phi Delta Phi, Phi Theta Kappa, Alpha Phi Omega. Methodist. Contbr. articles to profl. and art jours. Clubs: Headliners (Austin, Tex.); Brenham Country, Washington County Rod and Gun.

DIRECTOR, HERMAN, furniture co. exec.; b. Bremen, Germany, May 15, 1915; s. Simon and Bertha (Yeserski) D.; m. Lillian Rosenzweig; children—Steven, Dennis, Toby. Came to U.S., 1934, naturalized 1939. Pres., Dir. Enterprises, Inc., Savannah, Ga., 1970—. Pres., Savannah Jewish Council, 1959-61; chmn. Israeli Bond drive, 1960-61; mem. Park and Tree Commn., 1961-66; mem. Bd. Edn., 1963-69, pres., 1969. Bd. dirs. ARC, 1960-62; pres. Dir. Found., 1979. Served with USAAF, 1942-46. Mem. Savannah Retail Furniture Assn. (pres. 1959-61), Greater Downtown Bus. Assn. (pres. 1971), Better Bus. Bur. Savannah (pres. 1976). Home: 4710 Fairfax Dr Savannah GA 31405 Office: 105 Tibet Ave Savannah GA 31406 also PO Box 13757 Savannah GA 31406

DIRKES, ROBERT FREDERICK, communications cons.; b. N.Y.C., Dec. 3, 1898; s. Herman Frank and Emilie (Back) D.; M.E., Stevens Inst. Tech., 1920; m. Eva Hutchinson, June 21, 1924. With Western Union Telegraph Co., N.Y.C., 1920—, asst. automatics engr., 1940, patron system engr., 1945, dir. operations, 1950, asst. v.p. facsimile and pvt. wire services, 1953-62, gen. mgr. systems devel., 1962-63, now communications cons.; dir. Trans Lux Corp. Mem. Brookfield Conservation Commn. Mem. Dept. Def. Exec. Res. Served with U.S. Army, 1918. Registered profl. engr., N.Y. Mem. IEEE, Sigma Phi Epsilon. Mason. Clubs: Merchants (N.Y.); Stevens Metropolitan. Patentee in field of telegraphy, optics and metallurgy. Office: Obtuse Rocks Rd Brookfield Center CT 06805

DIRKSE, DAVID LEE, auto parts mfg. exec.; b. Holland, Mich., Nov. 2, 1942; s. Alvin and Sena D.; B.S. in Bus., Ferris State Coll., 1968; m. Rachel Karen Block, June 14, 1964; children—Rachelle Renea, Karen Lee. Product mgr. automotive aftermarket ops. Bendix Corp., South Bend, Ind., 1969-73; nat. sales mgr. Tom McGuane Industries, 1973-74; owner, pres. BLD Products, Ltd., Holland, Mich., 1974—. Served with USAF, 1962-66. Mem. Ferris State Vets Assn., Chi Gamma Iota. Mem. Reformed Ch. of Am. Office: 5042 Exchange Dr Flint MI 48507

DIRUSCIO, LAWRENCE WILLIAM, advt. agy. exec.; b. Buffalo, Jan. 2, 1941; s. Guido Carmen and Mabel Ella (Bach) DiR.; m. Gloria J. Edney, Aug. 19, 1972; children—Lawrence M., Lorie P., Darryl C., Theresa M., Jack D. With various broadcast stas. and instr., adminstr. Bill Wade Sch. Radio and TV, San Diego, San Francisco, Los Angeles, 1961-69; account exec. Sta. KGB Radio, San Diego, 1969, gen. sales mgr., 1970-72; pres. Free Apple Advt., San Diego, 1972—. Fin. Mgmt. Assos., Inc., San Diego, 1979—. Served with USN, 1958-60. Mem. Nat. Acad. TV Arts and Scis. Democrat. Roman Catholic. Office: 3928 Iowa St San Diego CA 92104

DISBROW, RICHARD EDWIN, utilities exec.; b. Newark, Sept. 20, 1930; s. Milton A. and Madeline Catherine (Segal) D.; B.S., Lehigh U., 1952; M.S. in Elec. Engring., Newark Coll. Engring., 1959; M.S. in Indsl. Mgmt. (Sloan fellow), Mass. Inst. Tech., 1965; m. Patricia Fair Warner, June 27, 1953 (div. Sept. 1972); children—John Scott, Lisa Karen; m. 2d, Teresa Marie Moser, May 12, 1973. With Am. Electric Power Co., Inc., N.Y.C., 1954—, transmission and distbn. mgr., 1967-70, controller, 1970-71, v.p., controller, 1971-74, exec. v.p., 1974—, vice chmn. bd., 1974—, pres. 1979—, also dir.; pres., chief adminstrv. officer Am. Electric Power Service Corp.; instr. Newark Coll. Engring., 1959-64. Indsl. commr., Piscataway, N.J., 1960-64; mem. N.J. Engrs. Com. for Student Guidance, 1960-64. Served to 1st lt. USAF, 1952-54. Mem. Edison Electric Inst., Am. Gas Assn., Arnold Air Soc., Psi Upsilon, Eta Kappa Nu. Club: Harbor View (N.Y.C.). Office: Am Electric Power Co 2 Broadway New York NY 10004*

DISKIN, STEVEN DREW, hosp. exec.; b. Bklyn., Nov. 5, 1950; s. Charles and Muriel D.; B.S. in Psychology, SUNY, New Paltz., 1972; M.A. in Psychology, Antioch U., Keene, N.H., 1977. Staff cons. Fundashon Humanas, Curacao, Netherlands, Antilles, 1975-76; coordinator curriculum Nathaniel Hawthorne Coll., Antrim, N.H., 1977-78; orgn. devel. specialist Mary Hitchcock Meml. Hosp., Hanover, N.H., 1978—; lectr. in field. Mem. Am. Soc. Tng. & Devel., OD Inst., Am. Mgmt. Assn. Office: Mary Hitchcock Meml Hosp Tng and Edn Dept Hanover NH 03755

DISSTON, GEOFFREY WHITMORE, investment co. exec.; b. Greenwich, Conn., Apr. 30, 1933; s. Harry and Valerie (Duval) D.; B.A., Amherst Coll., 1956; m Sheila Murphy, May 31, 1972; children—Deborah W., Geoffrey W., Stuart L., Jason M. Money market specialist J.P. Morgan & Co., N.Y.C., 1956-61, Charles E. Quiney & Co., N.Y.C., 1961-62; v.p. Harris Trust & Savs. Bank, Chgo., 1962-67; pres. G.W. Disston & Co., Chgo., 1967-70; partner Bacon, Stevenson & Reeves, N.Y.C., 1969; chmn. bd. Multi-Channel Response Co., N.Y.C., 1970—; pres. Venture Capital Research, Inc., N.Y.C., 1977—. Served to capt., U.S. Army, 1957-66. Office: 440 Park Ave S New York NY 10016

DI STASIO, LYNNE ELIZABETH, lawyer; b. Bklyn., Jan. 1, 1953; d. William Ralph and Elizabeth Florence (Cohan) Di S.; B.A. in Econs., Wilson Coll., Chambersburg, Pa., 1973; J.D., Emory U., 1976. Admitted to N.Y. bar, 1977; individual practice law, Massapequa, N.Y., 1977; asst. sec., asst. gen. counsel Mgmt. Assistance, Inc., N.Y.C., 1977-79; atty. employee and union relations unit law dept. Met. Life Ins. Co., N.Y.C., 1979—. Mem. Am. Bar Assn. Phi Alpha Delta. Republican. Lutheran. Club: Eastern Star. Home: 238 Bayview Ave Massapequa NY 11758 Office: 1 Madison Ave New York NY 10010

DISTEFANO, G. PAUL, computer co. exec.; b. Baton Rouge, La., Apr. 8, 1938; s. Thomas J. and Lena H. (Hannie) D.; B.S., La. State U., 1960; Ph.D. (NSF fellow), U. Fla., 1964; m. Mary Jane Hidalgo, Apr. 12, 1960; children—Brian, Erin, John. Engr., Monsanto Co., St. Louis, 1964-66; tech. mgr. Electronic Assos., Princeton, N.J., 1966-69; regional sales mgr. Computer Complex Co., Houston, 1969-71; from Houston br. mgr. to pres. United Computing Systems, Kansas City, Mo., 1971-79, pres., 1980—; asst. prof. U. Mo., St. Louis, 1964-66; cons. on PIPETRAN computer model Am. Gas Assn. Mem. Sigma Xi. Tau Beta Pi, Pi Mu Epsilon, Phi Lambda Upsilon. Contbr. articles to profl. jours. Home: 8801 Ensley Ct Leawood KS 66206 Office: 2525 Washington St Kansas City MO 64108

DITTENHAFER, BRIAN DOUGLAS, economist; b. York, Pa., Aug. 15, 1942; s. Nathaniel Webster and Evelyn Romaine (Myers) D.; B.A., Ursinus Coll., 1964; M.A., Temple U., 1966, postgrad., 1966-71; m. Miriam Marcy, Aug. 22, 1964; 1 son, Daniel Webster. Personnel asst. Philco Corp., Phila., 1965-66; bus. economist Fed. Res. Bank, Atlanta, 1971-76; v.p., chief economist Fed. Home Loan Bank, N.Y.C., 1976-79, sr. v.p., chief fin. officer, 1980, exec. v.p., chief fin. officer, 1981—; instr. Temple U., 1966-67, research asso., 1970-71. Mem. Am. Econ. Assn., Nat. Assn. Bus. Economists, N.Am. Soc. Corporate Planning, Forecasters Club N.Y., Omicron Delta Epsilon. Office: 1 World Trade Center Fl 103 New York NY 10048

DIVERS, ALAN GERALD, banker; b. Detroit, Sept. 17, 1935; s. Earle Leland and Dorotha Evelyn (Unger) D.; B.S. in Bus. Adminstrn., U. Fla., 1957; m. Jean Bacon, Apr. 18, 1964; children—Alan Blaec, Brett Devereux. With Exchange Nat. Bank of Tampa (Fla.), 1961-75, v.p., 1967-74, exec. v.p., 1974-75, also dir.; sr. v.p. 1st Nat. Bank of Tampa, 1975-79; pres. Flagship Bank of Tampa, 1979—. Chmn., SW Fla. Blood Bank, Inc., 1970—, Fla. West Coast Public Broadcasting, 1967—; bd. dirs. Home Assn., Fla. State Fair and Gasparilla Assn.; chmn., trustee Berkeley Prep. Sch.; bd. dirs. United Way Greater Tampa, Inc. Served to lt. comdr. USNR, 1957-61. Mem. Robert Morris Assos., Am. Inst. Banking, Greater Tampa C. of C. (dir.), Phi Delta Theta. Republican. Episcopalian. Rotarian. Clubs: Merrymakers, University, Ye Mystic Krewe of Gasparilla, Tampa Yacht and Country (gov.) (Tampa); Palma Ceia Golf and Country. Home: 812 Bayside Dr Tampa FL 33609 Office: PO Box 3303 Tampa FL 33601

DIVINE, ROBERT SAMUEL, mfg. co. exec.; b. Florence, S.C., Feb. 25, 1931; s. Harris Wesley and Sara Ferguson (Smith) D.; B.S., Ga. Inst. Tech., 1952, M.S., 1953; m. Ida Mae Allen, Aug. 3, 1958; children—Cindy, Pamela, Cheryl. Vice-pres. Fuqua Industries, Inc., Atlanta, 1968-70; pres. Dahll Industries, Inc., Newport Beach, Calif., 1971-73; v.p. Guerdon Industries, Louisville, 1973-74; pres. Chinook Mobilodge, Inc., Newport Beach, 1974-76; chmn. Newport Cons. Group, 1976—; pres. Airstream div. Beatrice Foods Co., Jackson Center, Ohio, 1978-80; pres. Airstream of Calif., Inc., Cerritos, 1980—. Served with USNR, 1953-56. Office: 15939 Piuma Ave Cerritos CA 90701

DIVINO, CRAIG DOUGLAS, mgmt. cons.; b. Malden, Mass., Aug. 3, 1952; s. Louis Edward and Anne M. (MacDonald) D.; B.A., Boston Coll., 1974, M.B.A., 1976; m. Mary Jane King, June 12, 1976. Fin. analyst Data Gen. Corp., Westboro, Mass., 1976-77, sr. fin. analyst, 1977-79; cons. Pittiglio, Rabin, Todd & McGrath, Burlington, Mass., 1979-80, mgr., 1980—. Mem. Am. Prodn. and Inventory Control Soc., Small Bus. Adminstrn. New Eng., Boston Coll. Grad. Sch. Bus. Alumni Assn., Smithsonian Assos. Club: K.C. Office: 50 Mall Rd Suite 211 Burlington MA 01803

DIXON, ARTHUR JACOB, acctg. co. exec.; b. N.Y.C., Mar. 16, 1924; s. Morton W. and Estelle (Jacobs) D.; B.S. in Econs., U. Pa., 1942; J.D., N.Y. U., 1949; m. Jacqueline Marshall, Dec. 21, 1947; children—Sandra, Carol, Steven, Joel, Lisa, Matthew. From jr. acct. to partner David B. Jacobs & Co., C.P.A.'s, N.Y.C., 1946-53; admitted to N.Y. State bar, 1950; partner Oppenheim, Appel, Dixon & Co., C.P.A.'s, N.Y.C., 1953—, mng. partner, 1974—; adj. asst. prof. Sch. Continuing Edn., N.Y. U., 1969-72. Trustee, v.p., mem. and chmn. distbn. com. Fedn. Jewish Philanthropies N.Y., 1969—; trustee Jewish Guild for Blind, 1965—, N.Y. U. Law Center Found., 1978—, Beekman Downtown Hosp., 1977-80. Served with U.S. Army, 1943-46; ETO; PTO. C.P.A., N.Y. State. Mem. Am. Inst. C.P.A.'s (chmn. fed. tax div. 1977-80), N.Y. State Soc. C.P.A.'s (pres. 1974-75), Estate Planning Council N.Y.C. (pres. 1963-64). Jewish. Clubs: Harmonie, N.Y. U., Masons. Contbr. numerous articles on tax to profl. publs. Home: 59 The Hemlocks Roslyn NY 11576 Office: 750 3d Ave New York NY 10017

DIXON, FRED L., investment banker: b. Pueblo, Colo., July 18, 1922; s. Fred and Ella Alacia (Crowley) D.; A.A., U. So. Colo., 1942; B.S. in Bus., U. Colo., 1946, postgrad., 1947; postgrad. U. Pa., 1953-56; m. Frances Carolyn Princelau, Nov. 3, 1978. Field sec. Phi Gamma Delta, 1947-50; with Folger Nolan Fleming Douglas, Inc., Washington, 1951—, v.p., 1970—; vice chmn. speakers bur. N.Y. Stock Exchange, 1964-67. Nat. treas. Young Republicans, 1957, del. to NATO, 1958; chief page Rep. Nat. Conv., 1956, del., mem. rules com., 1972, 76, chief tally clk., 1980; treas. Rep. maj. of House Polit. Action Com., 1980; pres., chief exec. officer Eisenhower Meml. Center, Washington; mem. Nat. Armed Forces Mus. Adv. Bd., Smithsonian, 1975-80. Served with AC and inf. U.S. Army, 1943-45. Named Outstanding Alumnus, U. Colo., 1974. Mem. Internat. Platform Assn., Phi Gamma Delta (nat. sec. 1966-72, treas. Edn1. Found. 1974—). Roman Catholic. Clubs: Bond, Univ., Capitol Hill (Washington); Lions. Home: 2500 Que St NW Washington DC 20007 Office: Folger Nolan Fleming Douglas Inc 725 15th St NW Washington DC 20005

DIXON, GEORGE HALL, banker; b. Rochester, N.Y., Oct. 7, 1920; s. George H. and Frances (Wheeler) D.; B.S., Wharton Sch., U. Pa., 1942; M.B.A., Harvard, 1947; m. Marjorie Freeman, Apr. 3, 1948; children—George E., Andrew T., Candis H. With Brown Bros. Harriman & Co., N.Y.C., 1947-50; gen. partner Davis & Davis, Providence, 1950-56; v.p. finance, treas. Sperry & Hutchinson Co., N.Y.C., 1956-68; pres., dir. First Nat. Bank Mpls., 1968-72, chmn., pres., 1972-76; dep. sec. treasury, 1976-77; pres., dir. First Bank System, Inc., 1977—; dir. Soo Line R.R., Mpls., Donaldson Co., Mpls., Internat. Multifoods, Mpls., Northwestern Nat. Life Ins. Co., First Trust Co. St. Paul, First Nat. Bank Mpls., First Nat. Bank St. Paul. Mpls. First Computer Corp., First Bank System, Inc., Mpls. Trustee Carleton Coll. Served to capt. AUS, 1943-46. Mem. Am. Gas Assn. (banking advisory council). Assn. Res. City Bankers. Presbyterian. Clubs: Minneapolis, Minikahda, Harvard Business Sch. Alumni (Mpls.). Home: 3250 Fox St Minneapolis MN 55403 Office: 1400 1st Nat Bank Bldg PO Box 522 Minneapolis MN 55480

DIXON, HERBERT PARKER, ins. co. exec.; b. San Francisco, Dec. 13, 1931; s. Ezra S. and Eulalie M. (Miller) D.; student Wabash Coll., 1950-52; A.B. in History and Polit. Sci., Butler U., 1954, M.S. in Adminstrn., 1956; grad. Blue Cross and Blue Shield Mgmt. Devel. Inst., U. Mich., 1967; postgrad. Ind. U., Purdue U., Ball State U.: m. Jo Ann Kershner, July 21, 1956; children—Herbert Randall, Dwight Lyle. Tchr., George Washington High Sch., Indpls., 1956-57, 60-63, guidance counselor, 1960-63; dean of men N.W. High Sch., Indpls., 1963-64; physician relations rep. Ind. Blue Cross & Blue Shield, Indpls., 1964, dir. physician relations, 1964-67, v.p. profl. relations, 1967-72, v.p. Profl. Services div., 1972—, exec. asst. to pres., 1974—. Trustee, Butler U., 1976-80, pres. alumni bd., 1975-76; mem. queen selection com. 500 Festival Assos.; deacon, elder 2d Presbyn. Ch.; mem. admissions com. for grad. degree in health care adminstrn. Ind. U.; bd. dirs. Ind. Health Careers. Served as 1st lt. USAF, 1957-60. Mem. Ind. Allied Health Assn. (pres.-elect), Fellowship of Christian Athletes (adv. bd.), Butler B Men's Assn., Phi Delta Kappa, Tau Kappa Alpha, Sigma Chi. Clubs: Columbia, Econ. (Indpls.). Home: 1415 Brewster Rd Indianapolis IN 46260 Office: Blue Cross and Blue Shield of Ind 120 W Market St Indianapolis IN 46204

DIXON, JAMES THEODORE, III, med. electronics co. exec.; b. Fairfield, Ala., Aug. 28, 1940; s. James Theodore and Mildred Rosamond (Ireland) D.; B.S. in Elec. Engring. (Alcoa fellow), U. Ala., Tuscaloosa, 1963; M.S. in Engring., U. Ala., Huntsville, 1969; M.B.A., U. Ala., Tuscaloosa, 1971; diploma Chgo. Sch. Interior Decoration, 1971; m. Janice Gail Wilson, Feb. 5, 1966: children—Lara Ann, Suzanne Marie, Holly Leigh. Electronic engr. Space Craft, Inc., Huntsville, Ala., 1963-65; test engr. Motorola, Inc., Scottsdale, Ariz., 1965-66; project engr. SCI Electronics Inc., Huntsville, Ala., 1966-69; mktg. mgr. SCI Systems, Inc., Huntsville, 1970-71, asst. to pres., 1972-73, program mgr., 1973-76, sec. mgr., 1976-77; mgr. integration and test Pfizer Med. Systems, Inc., Columbia, Md., 1977-78, mgr. program mgmt., 1979-81; v.p., asst. gen. mgr. Electronics div. AVCO Corp., Huntsville, 1981—. High priest Ch. of Jesus Christ of Latter-day Saints. Registered profl. engr., Ala. Mem. Nat. Mgmt. Assn. (past chpt. pres.), Program Mgmt. Inst., Phi Eta Sigma, Pi Mu Epsilon, Chi Alpha Phi, Eta Kappa Nu, Tau Beta Pi, Theta Tau (past chpt. pres.), Omicron Delta Kappa, Delta Nu Alpha. Republican. Club: Toastmaster (past chpt. v.p.). Home: 9232 Broken Timber Way Columbia MD 21045 Office: Electronics Div AVCO Corp 4870 Bradford Dr Huntsville AL 35805

DIXON, PAUL EDWARD, mfg. co. exec.; b. Bklyn., Aug. 27, 1944; s. Paul Stewart and Bernice (Mathisen) D.; B.A., Villanova U., 1966; J.D., St. Johns U., 1972; m. Kathleen Constance Kayser, Sept. 23, 1967; children—Jennifer Pyne, Paul Kayser, Meredith Stewart. Admitted to N.Y. State bar, 1973, U.S. Supreme Ct., 1976; asso. mem. firm Rogers & Wells, N.Y.C., 1972-77; sec., asst. gen. counsel Volvo of Am. Corp., Rockleigh, N.J., 1977-79, v.p., gen. counsel, 1979—. Mem. Auto Importers Am., Bedford Hist. Soc., Am. Bar Assn., Assn. Bar City N.Y., N.Y. State Bar Assn., U.S. Supreme Ct. Hist. Soc. Club: Waccabuc Country. Office: 1 Volvo Dr Rockleigh NJ 07647

DIXON, PHILIP MORRIS, marketing exec.; b. Stoutsville, Mo., Jan. 7, 1921; s. Philip Kendrick and Oleta (Greening) D.; M.Engring., Quincy Coll., 1947; m. Mary Louis Steinkamp, May 1, 1946; children—Sharon Lee, Michael Philip. Engr. Dayton Dowd Co., Quincy, Ill., 1941-42; engr. Peerless Pump div. FMC Corp., Indpls., 1946-48, sales engr., 1948-59, dist. mgr., 1959-63, sales mgr., Oiline submersible div., Los Angeles, 1963-69, market mgr. Peerless Pump Div., Indpls., 1967—. Served with USN, 1942-46. Decorated D.F.C., Air Medals (4). Mem. AIME. Roman Catholic. Home: 4511 Cranbrook Dr Indianapolis IN 46250 Office: 2005 Northwestern Ave Indianapolis IN 46208

DIXSON, THOMAS BERTRAM, ins. exec.; b. Atlanta, Feb. 18, 1948; s. Herman R. and Margaret (Craig) D.; student Orlando Jr. Coll., 1967; m. Jodie Donohoe, May 18, 1968; children—DeAnne, Wesley. With Sun Life, 1971—, unit mgr., Orlando, Fla., 1974, br. mgr., Phoenix, 1979—, corp. officer, 1978-79. Served with USAF, 1968-71. Recipient Agt. of Yr. award, Ins. Industry award, Nat. Quality award, Nat. Sales Achievement award, 1972, 73. Mem. Gen. Agts. Mgrs. Assn., Greater Phoenix Assn. Life Underwriters. Designed C.L.U. Republican. Presbyterian. Clubs: Phoenix Civitan (dir. 1979-80, pres.-elect 1980-81), Phoenix Athletic, Scottsdale Country. Home: 2614 E Mercer Ln Phoenix AZ 85028 Office: 200 E Mitchell Dr Phoenix AZ 85012

DI ZEREGA, THOMAS WILLIAM, energy co. exec.; b. Round Hill, Va., Sept. 27, 1927; s. Augustus, Jr., and Susan Martha (Nichols) diZ.; B.A., U. Wichita, 1953; J.D., George Washington U., 1956; m. Mary Howe Glascock, Sept. 15, 1956; 1 dau., Mary Bryan. Admitted to Va. bar, 1958, D.C. bar, 1964, U.S. Supreme Ct. bar, 1965, Pa. bar, 1968, N.Y. State bar, 1971, Utah bar, 1980; v.p. Atlantic Richfield Co., Los Angeles, 1968-74; gen. counsel to exec. v.p. Northwest Energy Co., Salt Lake City, 1974-80, pres., 1980—, v.p. law Northwest Pipeline Corp., subs., 1974-80; dir. Northwest Energy Co., Energy Ventures, Inc., Houston, Devon Group, Inc., Stamford, Conn. Served with U.S. Army, 1946-47. Mem. Am. Bar Assn., Nat. Planning Assn. (Can.-Am. com.), Natural Land and Water Res. System. Office: PO Box 1526 Salt Lake City UT 84110

D'LAURO, FRANK ANDREW, JR., constrn. co. exec.; b. Phila., Nov. 11, 1940; s. Frank Andrew and Dorothy (Adams) D'L.; grad. Hill Sch., 1958; B.A., Washington and Lee U., 1962; M.Arch., U. Pa., 1965. Architect, Francis Kaufmann, Wilkinson & Pepper, Phila., 1967-68; project mgr., exec. v.p., pres. Frank A. D'Lauro Co., Phila., 1968—; pres. D'Lauro Devel. Corp., 1974—, D'Lauro Corp., 1979—; mem. regional exec. bd. Continental Bank, Phila. Chmn., Montgomery County Young Republican Fedn., 1970-72; mem. Montgomery County Rep. Finance Com., 1972—; bd. dirs. Young Republicans of Pa., 1972-74; chmn. Montgomery County Housing Authority, 1976—. Bd. dirs., v.p. Big Bros. Assn. Phila.; bd. dirs. Sacred Heart Hosp., 1980—; pres. Youth Recreation Assn. Montgomery County, 1979—. Served to capt. U.S. Army, 1965-67; Vietnam. Decorated Bronze Star with oak leaf cluster, Soldiers medal; recipient award of merit Big Bros. Phila., 1972. Mem. Gen. Contractors Assn. Pa. (gov.), Carpenters Co. Phila., Pa. Soc. S.R., Sigma Nu. Clubs: Union League, Racquet Philadelphia Cricket (Phila.). Office: 218 E Willow Grove Ave Philadelphia PA 19118

DLOUHY, JOHN ANTON, mfg. co. exec.; b. Oak Park, Ill., Aug. 10, 1930; s. Clarence O. and Ruth M. D.; B.S. in Metall. Engring., Mich. Tech. U., 1954; M.B.A., U. Chgo., 1976; m. Mary Jane Clark, June 18, 1955; children—Faye M., Mary B., Kathleen A., John C. With Emil J. Paidar Co., Chgo., 1954-73; plant mgr. to pres. Hirsh Co., Skokie, Ill., 1973-77; v.p. mfg. Bloomfield Industries div. Beatrice Foods, Inc., Chgo., 1977-78; v.p. mktg. Benton Harbor Engring. div. Koehring Co., Benton Harbor, Mich., 1979-80; v.p. ops. to pres. MPS Internat.; v.p. Prodn. Tool Corp., Chgo., 1980—; sr. partner EMPACO. Essential worker Argonne (Ill.) Nat. Lab., 1948-52; bd. dirs. ARC, Oak Park, Ill., 1963. Mem. Am. Soc. Metals, Am. Iron and Steel Engrs., Am. Prodn. and Inventory Control Soc., Chgo. C. of C. and Industry. Club: Ill. Athletic. Patentee in field. Home: 1123 Ashland Ave River Forest IL 60305 Office: 1229 E 74th St Chicago IL 60619

D'LUHY, JOHN JAMES, oil and gas exploration co. exec., investment banker; b. Passaic, N.J., Sept. 18, 1933; s. John George and Leonora (Fila) D'L.; B.A., Trinity Coll., Hartford, Conn., 1955; M.B.A., U. Pa., 1959; m. Gale Rainsford, Dec. 7, 1968. Asso., Lazard Freres & Co., N.Y.C., 1960-68; sr. v.p., partner R.W. Pressprich & Co., N.Y.C., 1968-72; dir., investment adv. Wood, Walker & Co., N.Y.C., 1972-73; pres. United States Oil Co., N.Y.C., 1973—,

D'Luhy, Sharp & Co., investment bankers, N.Y.C., 1973—. Fellow The Frick Collection, N.Y.C.; mem. nat. adv. council Hampshire Coll. Served with USN, 1955. Mem. N.Y. Soc. Security Analysts (sr. analyst), Bond Club N.Y., Am. Radio Relay League, Quarter Century Wireless Assn., Radio Club Am., Blue Hill Troupe. Roman Catholic. Clubs: Down Town Assn., University (council, treas., exec. com. 1979-81, fin. com. 1978-81) (N.Y.C.). Home: 400 E 52d St New York NY 10022 Office: 63 Wall St New York NY 10005

DOANE, JOHN PHILIP, auto supply co. exec.; b. Lincoln, Nebr., Mar. 3, 1935; s. Gilbert Harry and Susan Howland (Sherman) D.; student Mass. Inst. Tech., 1953-57; B.B.A., U. Wis., 1962, M.B.A., 1963; m. Stephanie Jay Etnier, Jan. 26, 1957; children—Charles Jay, Peter Etnier, Harry Sherman (dec.). Various positions Standard Oil Co. N.J., Exxon, various locations, 1963-73; asst. treas. Budd Co., Troy, Mich., 1973-74, treas., 1974—. Mem. Phi Beta Kappa, Beta Gamma Sigma, Delta Psi. Episcopalian. Home: 3666 Burning Bush St Birmingham MI 48010 Office: 3155 W Big Beaver Rd Troy MI 48084

DOBBELMANN, PIERRE FRANÇOIS, Netherlands diplomat; b. Nymegen, Netherlands, June 14, 1936; came to U.S., 1969; s. Reinier A. and Yvonne Y. (Perot) D.; LL.M., U. Amsterdam, 1967; m. Marita T. Slooff, Aug. 31, 1961; children—Reinier, Yvonne, Duncan. Mktg. coordinator Royal Dobbelmann Inc., Netherlands, 1967-68; sr. market analyst Am. Enka Co., Asheville, N.C., 1968-74, mgr. new ventures, mgr. mktg. research, 1977-79; bus. devel. exec. Akzo, NV, Netherlands, 1974-77; indsl. commr. of the Netherlands to U.S., N.Y.C., 1980—, diplomatic status. Served with Netherlands Army, 1957-59. Mem. Am. Mgmt. Assn., Assn. Fgn. Consuls, Smithsonian Assn. Democrat. Roman Catholic. Clubs: Kiawah I. (S.C.), Netherlands (N.Y.C.). Home: 70 Thrush Ln New Canaan CT 06840 Office: 1 Rockefeller Plaza New York NY 10020

DOBBIE, JAMES, info. storage and communications co. exec.; b. Perth, Scotland, July 10, 1930; came to U.S., 1957; s. James and Elizabeth Margaret (Morrison) D.; B.S. in Elec. Engring. with honours, Glasgow U., 1952; M.S., Ariz. State U., 1967; m. Patricia Suthers, July 20, 1957; children—Ruth Ann, Elspeth Grace, Helen Lavinia. Project mgr. Westinghouse Electric Corp., Buffalo, 1957-62; mgr. systems engring. Gen. Electric Co., Phoenix, 1961-70; dir. engring. Raytheon Data Systems Co., 1970-71; v.p. engring., then exec. v.p. Varian Data Machines Co., Irvine, Calif., 1971-74; v.p., gen. mgr. computer media div. Memorex Corp., Santa Clara, Calif., 1975-77, exec. v.p. corp., 1977-80; pres. Avantek, Santa Clara, 1980—; chmn. bd. Memorex Mini Disc Drive Corp.; dir. Memorex Fin. Co. Bd. dirs. Jr. Achievement Santa Clara County, 1978. Served as pilot officer RAFVR, 1952-57. Author, patentee in field. Office: Avantek 3175 Bowers Ave Santa Clara CA 95051

DOBBINS, DEENER EDWIN, JR., savs. and loan assn. exec.; b. Searcy, Ark., Dec. 11, 1922; s. Deener Edwin and Muda (Watson) D.; B.S. in Accounting, U. Ark., 1948; m. Betty Jo Hughes, Nov. 16, 1950. Pres., mgr. Searcy Fed. Savs. & Loan Assn., 1950—; v.p., sec. Lightle, Dobbins & Lightle, Inc., Searcy, 1948—; partner Lightle & Dobbins Developers. Mem. Searcy Democratic Twp. Com. Served with USNR, 1942-46. Mem. U.S. League Savs. Assns., Ark. Savs. and Loan League (past pres.), Searcy C. of C. (past pres., dir.). Methodist (ofcl. bd., past chmn. bd., chmn. fin. commn.). Clubs: Masons, Lions (past pres., dir. Searcy). Home: Hwy 36 W Searcy AR 72143 Office: Box 310 Searcy AR 72143

DOBBINS, JOHN STEPHEN, utility co. exec.; b. Cin., Mar. 29, 1948; s. John Albert and Ruth Fields D.; degree in adminstrv. mgmt. (scholar), U. Cin., 1975; 1 dau., Aleisha Trenai. With Cin. Gas and Electric Co., 1966—, asst. supr. mail and addressing group, 1973-74, supr. mail and addressing group, 1974-77, supr. customer services record group, 1977—, also supr. customer services. Mem. Cin. Br. Postal Customers Council, 1974-77; pres. Cin. Christian Chs. Athletic Assn., 1971. Recipient spl. recognition award Am. Businesswomen's Assn. of Greater Cin., 1976; spl. award and honor NAACP, 1979; named one of Cin.'s Black Achievers for 1980, YMCA of Cin. and Hamilton County. Mem. Cin. Gas and Electric Speakers Bur. Baptist. Home: 5107 Hawaiian Terr Cincinnati OH 45223 Office: Cin Gas and Electric Co 139 E 4th St Cincinnati OH 45202

DOBBINS, ROBERT HELM, banker; b. Louisville, June 6, 1951; s. John Dunlap and Sara (Helm) D.; B.S. with distinction, U. Va., 1973; M.B.A., Tuck Sch., Dartmouth Coll., 1978. With Mellon Bank, N.A., Pitts., 1973-76, Morgan Guaranty Trust Co., N.Y.C., 1977; v.p. nat. div. Liberty Nat. Bank, Louisville, 1978—. Vice chmn. Ky. fin. com. George Bush for Pres. Com., 1979-80. Presbyterian. Clubs: Pendennis (Louisville); Princeton (N.Y.C.). Home: 3613 Glenview Ave Glenview KY 40025 Office: PO Box 32500 Louisville KY 40232

DOBBS, DONALD EDWIN ALBERT, elec. products co. exec.; b. Ft. Wayne, Ind., Oct. 8, 1931; s. Edmund F. and Agnes (Stempnick) D.; B.S., Marquette U., 1953; m. Beatrice A. Spieker, July 27, 1957; children—Margaret L. Dobbs Herbert, Christopher E. J., Laura C. Dobbs Pribe. Reporter, Catholic Chronicle, Toledo, 1953; indsl. editor, pub. relations Nat. Supply Co., Toledo, 1955-59; employee communications exec. Prestolite Co. (formerly Electric Autolite Co.) div. ELTRA Corp., Toledo, 1959-61, dir. pub. relations, 1961—. Pres., Internat. Inst., 1970-73; pub. relations chmn. Toledo United Appeal Campaign, 1971; adv. council on vocational edn. Ohio Bd. Edn., 1974-77; past bd. mem. Nat. Council for Community Services to Internat. Visitors. Pres. adv. bd. Mercy Hosp.; v.p. Ohio Friends Library, Community Planning Council NW Ohio; chmn. bd. dirs. Salvation Army, ARC, Frederick Douglass Community Assn.; pres. Toledo Speech and Hearing Center, 1973-76; mem. bd., past pres. Cath. Interracial Council; past chmn. bd. Maumee Valley Sch. Nursing; pres., bd. dirs. Toledo Internat. Park; pres. Crosby Gardens, Citizens Devel. Forum, Toledo Council World Affairs, Toledo Life Care; past pres. Friends Lucas County Library. Served with AUS, 1953-55. Named 1 of Toledo's Outstanding Young Men, Jr. C. of C., 1967. Mem. Pub. Relations Soc. Am. (sec.), Automotive Public Relations Council (dir.), Marquette U. Alumni Assn. N.W. Ohio (past pres., area dir.), Toledo Area C. of C., Sigma Delta Chi. Democrat (past nat. com. Wis. Young Dems.). Roman Catholic. Kiwanian (past pres. Toledo club, lt. gov.). Club: Toledo Press. Home: 2433 Meadowwood Dr Toledo OH 43606 Office: 511 Hamilton St Toledo OH 43694

DOBERSTEIN, ROBERT RAYMOND, mgmt. cons.; b. Chgo., Feb. 18, 1918; s. Peter J. and Harriet (Karnowski) D.; student Northwestern U.; m. Irene A. Weckman, May 13, 1939; children—Paul R., Joan F., Donald L. Sr. asso., Griffenhagen & Assos., Mgmt. Cons., Chgo., 1947-53; sr. asso. Cresap, McCormick & Paget, Mgmt. Cons., Chgo., 1953-58, prin., 1958-62; ind. mgmt. cons., Evanston, Ill., 1962—; cons. mgmt. problems to industries and govtl. agencies, 1947—. Mem. Evanston Elementary Schs. Bd. Edn., 1960-66, pres., 1964-66. Mem. Am. Compensation Assn., Am. Mgmt. Assn. Congregationalist. Club: Thorngate Country. Contbr. articles to mags. Home: 326 Ashland Ave Evanston IL 60202

DOBSON, BRIAN GREGORY, pub. relations exec.; b. N.Y.C., Jan. 22, 1945; s. James Joseph and Rita Marie (Walsh) D.; B.A., Marist Coll., Poughkeepsie, N.Y., 1967; postgrad. N.Y. Inst. Fin., St. John's U. Grad. Sch. Bus.; m. Barbara J. Hodorowski, Nov. 13, 1970; 1 dau., Gweneth Langford. Petroleum news editor Jour. Commerce, N.Y.C., 1969; editor AP-DJ Bus. Newswire, Dow Jones & Co., N.Y.C., 1970; editor-writer Reuters Fin. Newswire, Reuter's Ltd., N.Y.C., 1971; pub. relations rep. N.Y. Stock Exchange, N.Y.C., 1973; v.p. public relations Iroquois Brands, Ltd., Greenwich, Conn., 1976-79, v.p. corp. communications, 1979—. Bd. dirs. Greenwich Red Cross, Future Bus. Leaders Am. Served with AUS, 1967-69. Mem. Nat. Investor Relations Inst., Pub. Relations Soc. Am., Internat. Assn. Bus. Communicators, Stamford Area Commerce and Industry Assn., Greenwich C. of C. Roman Catholic. Office: 41 W Putnam Ave Greenwich CT 06830

DOBSON, JOHN GORDON, mfg. co. exec.; b. Clifton, N.J., Apr. 23, 1915; s. George Gordon and Annie Beatrice (Brown) D.; M.E., Cornell U., 1936; J.D., Fordham U., 1941; m. Anne Chase, Dec. 1, 1945; children—Deborah Anne Dobson Summers, Catherine Lee Wheeler, Gregory Chase. Engr. indsl. div. Wallace & Tiernan Co., Belleville, N.J., 1936-46; mgr. chem. industry div. Foxboro Co. (Mass.), 1946-56, br. mgr. parent co., North Tonawanda, N.Y., 1958-60, asst. to pres., 1962-70, mgr. corp. market planning, 1972-77, dir. sales Foxboro Analytical div., 1977—; v.p., gen. mgr. Adsco, Inc., North Tonawanda, 1956-58; pres. Foxboro S.A. (Mexico), 1960-72; dir. Ohmart Co., Cin. Mem. ASME, Am. Inst. Chem. Engrs., Instrument Soc. Am. (sr.), AAAS (life), N. Am. Soc. Corp. Planners, Newcomen Soc. Club: Dedham Country and Polo. Contbr. articles to profl. jours.; developer process for neutralization of cyanide indsl. waste. Home: 118 Needham Ave Dedham MA 02026 Office: Foxboro MA 02035

DOBSON, JOHN JOSEPH, JR., pub. accountant; b. Kansas City, Mo., Oct. 23, 1914; s. John J. and Mattie (McPherson) D.; A.B., U. Mo., 1938, M.A., 1939; m. Phyllis Marie Land, Nov. 20, 1940; children—Bette Gae, John Joseph III. Partner, Arthur Young & Co., Kansas City, Mo., 1939-52, John Dobson & Co., South Bend, Ind., 1953—; dir. 1st Fed. Savs. & Loan Assn., South Bend. Mem. City Plan Commn., Kansas City, Mo., 1947-53. Pres. Michiana Watershed, South Bend. Served with AUS, 1942-43. C.P.A., Mo., Kan., Ind., Mich., Ill. Mem. Am. Inst. C.P.A.'s, Ind., Mich. assns. C.P.A.'s, Nat. Assn. Accountants, South Bend Estate Planning Council, South Bend C. of C. Am. Legion, D.A.V., Alpha Chi Sigma, Delta Sigma Pi, Kappa Sigma. Presbyn. Clubs: Summit, Indiana (South Bend). Home: 1628 Hoover Ave South Bend IN 46615 Office: 224 W Jefferson Blvd South Bend IN 46601

DOCES, GUST JOHN, retail furniture co. exec.; b. Oyteza, Albania, Feb. 5, 1918; s. John and Evgenia (Samesuris) D.; student Korce, Albania, 1937; student design Cornish Sch. Art, Seattle, 1943-47; student U. Wash., 1948-53, Harvard, 1956-57, Stanford, 1957-59; m. Sophie Gost, Nov. 30, 1941; children—John, Helene (Mrs. Ron Senn), Dean. Founder Doces Sixth Ave., Inc., Seattle, 1930, pres., 1964—; pres., founder Doces Enterprises, 1962—, Consumer Finance Corp., 1958—, Central Park Plaza, 1966—, Trans Am. Corp., 1968—, Doces Wholesale Contract, 1961—; pres., chmn. bd., Intercontinental, 1969—. Mem. Seattle Housing Adv. Bd., 1963—; dir. King County Safety Council. Bd. dirs. Cornish Sch. Art., Seattle Opera, Seattle Children's Home. Named Distinguished Citizen, State of Wash. Fellow Seattle Pacific Coll. Mem. King County Traffic Assn. (dir.), Retail Mchts. Assn. (exec. com. 1964—), Seattle C. of C., Young Pres. Orgn., Internat. Council Shopping Centers, Am. Mgmt. Assn., World Bus. Assn. Greek Orthodox (reader). Mason (Shriner). Clubs: Washington Athletic, Rainier, Broadmoor Golf, Harbor, Toastmasters (Seattle). Home: 4432 55th St NE Seattle WA 98105 Office: 17798 Southcenter Pkwy Seattle WA 98111

DOCKENDORFF, CHARLES HAROLD, ins. co. exec.; b. Portland, Maine, May 16, 1933; s. John Frederick and Bertha Marie (Sanders) D.; B.A., Coll. City N.Y., 1954; M.A., N.Y. U., 1958; m. Agnes B. Jesson, May 27, 1961; 1 dau., Lisa Marguerite. Agt., N.Y. Life & Equitable Co. of Iowa, N.Y.C., 1954-55; with Church Life Ins. Corp., N.Y.C., 1955—, asst. v.p., 1969-72, v.p., mgr., chief operating officer, 1972-76, sr. v.p., 1976—, also dir.; sec., dir. Church Agy. Corp., Church Finance Corp.; exec. trustee Episcopal Ch. Clergy and Employees Benefit Trust, 1978—; adj. prof. Grad. Sch., Coll. of Ins. Chmn. New Milford Mcpl. Republican Com., 1969-76; asst. treas. Bergen County Rep. Com., 1972-76; pres. New Milford Library Bd., 1975—; warden, vestryman Episcopal Ch. of Annunciation, 1970-76. Mem. Am. Econs. Assn., Am. Risk and Ins. Assn., Am. Library Trustees Assn., Life Ins. Advertisers Assn., Life Companies N.Y. (sec. 1975, pres. 1977-78), Life Ins. Council N.Y. (legis com. 1978—, dir. 1980—), Nat. Assn. Health Underwriters, Health Claims Assn. N.Y. Clubs: Church, 60 East. (N.Y.C.). Home: 636 Princeton St New Milford NJ 07646 Office: 800 2d Ave New York NY 10017

DOCKSON, ROBERT RAY, savs. and loan exec.; b. Quincy, Ill., Oct. 6. 1917; s. Marshall Ray and Letah (Edmondson) D.; A.B., Springfield Jr. Coll., 1937; B.S., U. Ill., 1939; M.S. in Fgn. Service, U. So. Calif., 1940, Ph.D., 1946; m. Katheryn Virginia Allison, Mar. 4, 1944; 1 dau., Kathy Kimberlee. Lectr., U. So. Calif., 1940-41, 45-46, prof., head dept. marketing, 1953-59, dean Sch. Bus. Adminstrn. and prof. bus. econs., 1959-69; pres., chief exec. officer Calif. Fed. Savs. & Loan Assn., Los Angeles, 1973-77, chmn., chief exec. officer, 1977—, vice chmn. bd., 1969-70, pres., 1970-73, also dir.; instr. at Rutgers U., 1946-47, asst. prof., 1947-48, dir. Bur. Bus. and Econ. Research, 1947-48; economist Western home office Prudential Ins. Co., 1948-52, Bank of Am., San Francisco, 1952-53; econ. cons., 1953-57; dir. Foremost-McKesson, Inc., IT Corp., Pacific Lighting Corp., Transam. Income Shares, Inc., Olga Co. Am. specialist for U.S. Dept. State; mem. Town Hall, 1954—, bd. govs., 1963-65, hon. bd. govs., 1965—, pres., 1961-62. Bd. dirs. So. Conf. Christians and Jews; bd. dirs. Music Center Opera Assn.; trustee John Randolph Haynes and Dora Haynes Found., Rose Hills Meml. Park Assn., Calif. Council for Econ. Edn., Com. Econ. Devel.; vice chmn. Orthopaedic Hosp., 1980—; mem. bd. regents, chmn. univ. bd. Pepperdine U. bd. councilors Grad. Sch. Bus. Adminstrn., U. So. Calif. ; mem. chancellors assos. Calif. State Colls. and U. Served from ensign to lt., USNR, 1942-44. Recipient Asa V. Call Achievement award; Human Relations award Am. Jewish Com.; Brotherhood award NCCJ; award of merit Jaycees of Los Angeles; Brandeis U. Disting. Community Service award; decorated Star of Solidarity by the Govt. of Italy, U. So. Calif. Alumni award. Mem. Calif. C. of C. (pres. 1980, dir.), Los Angeles C. of C. (past pres.), Am. Arbitration Assn., Newcomen Soc. North Am., Phi Kappa Phi, Beta Gamma Sigma. Rotarian. Clubs: Bohemian, Los Angeles, Los Angeles Country, One Hundred, Lincoln, California, Silver Dollar, Birnam Woods Golf, Thunderbird Country. Office: 5670 Wilshire Blvd Los Angeles CA 90036

DOCKSTADER, EMMETT STANLEY, constrn. co. exec.; b. Elmira, N.Y., Nov. 7, 1923; s. Roy S. and Gertrude (Everts) D.; B.C.E. cum laude, Syracuse U., 1947; m. Ruth Norma Emery, May 11, 1946; children—Deborah Ruth, David Stanley. Engr., Am. Bridge Co., Elmira, 1948-50; field engr. Sessinghaus & Ostergaard, Inc., Erie, Pa., 1950-53, project mgr., 1953-58, v.p., 1958-69; gen. mgr. constrn. div. H.H. Robertson Co., Ambridge, Pa., 1969-71; sr. v.p., sec. Sessinghaus & Ostergaard, Inc., Erie, 1972-79; constrn. exec. Gilbane Bldg. Co., Providence, R.I., 1979—. Mem. Erie Port Commn., 1967-69. Bd. dirs. Erie Civic Theatre Assn.; mem. adv. com. Erie County Tech. High Sch. Served with USNR, 1944-46. Registered profl. engr., Pa., W.Va., Ga., N.C. Mem. Pa. Soc. Profl. Engrs. (past pres.), Nat. Assn. Purchasing Agts., Erie Mannerchor, SAR. Mem. Ch. of the Covenant (trustee). Mason (32 deg.), Rotarian. Clubs: Erie Yacht, Y Mens (past pres.), Kahkwa, University (dir.) (Erie); Edgeworth (Sewickley, Pa.). Home: 6 Elton Rd Barrington RI 02806 Office: 7 Jackson Walkway Providence RI 02940

DODART, OLIVER DAVID, skin care products co. exec.; b. Long Beach, Calif., Mar. 18, 1945; s. Oliver Ulysus and Amy Jean (Wood) D.; student Brigham Young U., 1964, Weber State Coll., 1970; m. Jacqueline Marie Ritter, June 18, 1980. Regional v.p. Turner Enterprises, Ohio and Mich., 1970-72, corp. pres., W. Ger., 1972-74; dir. tng. Greentree Realty, Inc., Santa Barbara, Calif., 1974-77; pres., chief exec. officer World Wide Products, Inc., Santa Barbara, 1977—; chmn. bd. Gold Silver Exploration, Inc., Source Investments, Inc.; mem. chmn.'s com. U.S. Senatorial Bus. Adv. Bd. Republican. Mormon. Office: 1224 Coast Village Circle Santa Barbara CA 93108

DODD, EDWIN D(ILLON), mfg. exec.; b. Point Pleasant, W.Va., Jan. 26, 1919; s. David Rollin and Mary Grace (Dillon) D.; B.S. in Bus. Adminstrn., Ohio State U., 1941; postgrad. in Indsl. Adminstrn., Harvard U., 1943; LL.D. (hon.), U. Toledo, 1970, Washington and Jefferson Coll., 1972; m. Marie Marshall, Apr. 18, 1942; 1 dau., Marjorie Lee Dodd Wannamaker. Engr. airplane div. Curtiss-Wright Corp., 1941-42; pub. relations rep. Owens-Ill. Glass Co., 1946-49, pub. relations dir., 1949-54, prodn. mgr. Libbey Glass div. Owens-Ill., 1954-56, factories mgr. Libbey Glass div., 1956-58; v.p., asst. gen. mgr. Owens-Ill. Paper Products div. (formerly Nat. Container Corp.), 1958; v.p. Owens-Ill. Glass Co. (name changed to Owens-Ill., Inc. 1965), 1959-64, gen. mgr. paper products div., 1959-61, gen. mgr. forest products div., 1961-68, exec. v.p. corp., 1964-68, pres., 1968-76, chief operating officer, 1968-72, chief exec. officer, 1972—, chmn., 1976—, also dir.; pres. Forest Products Corp., 1959-68; pres., dir. Valdosta So. R.R. Co., Marinette, Tomahawk and Western R.R., 1961-68; pres. Bahamas Agrl. Industries Ltd., 1962-66, chmn. bd., 1966—; dir. Ohio Bell Telephone, Nat. Petro Chem., Toledo Trust Co., Goodyear Tire & Rubber Co., Toledo Trustcorp, Inc.; pres., dir. Sabine River & No. R.R. Co., 1966-68; pres., chmn. bd. Owens-Ill. Timber Corp., 1962-68, Angelina Plywood, 1966-68. Mem. Pres.'s Nat. Indsl. Pollution Council, 1970, Nat. Commn. on Air Quality, 1978; mem. Lucas County Republican Finance Com., 1970—; trustee Toledo Hosp., 1968-77, Toledo Mus. Art, pres. Maumee Valley Country Day Sch., 1965-67, trustee, 1962-68; past chmn. bd. dirs. Ohio State U. Devel. Fund, Am. Forest Inst., Am. Paper Inst., 1966-68; trustee Nat. Center for Resource Recovery; trustee Nat. 4-H Club Council; bd. dirs. Fourdrinier Kraft Board Inst., 1964-68, chmn., 1967-68; bd. govs. Nat. Council of Paper Industry for Air and Stream Inprovement, 1964-68; asso. trustee Toledo Boys' Club; past pres. Toledo Bd. Edn.; bd. dirs. Toledo-Lucas County Port Authority, 1962—; bd. visitors Berry Coll.; mem. council Nat. Mcpl. League, 1953-55, 57-59, 61-63, 65-67, regional v.p., 1967—; mem. Greater Toledo Corp. Served from pvt. to maj. AUS, 1943-46; PTO. Decorated Legion of Merit, 1946, Mil. Merit medal Chief of Staff, Philippine Army, 1946; recipient Distinguished Service award Toledo Jr. C. of C., 1955, Ohio Jr. C. of C., 1955; Distinguished Citizen's award Nat. Municipal League, 1959; Packaging Man of Yr. award, 1977. Mem. Fibre Box Assn. (dir. 1960-68, pres. 1964-65), Toledo C. of C. (vice chmn.), U.S. C. of C. (dir.), Nat. Paperboard Assn. (dir. 1964-65, exec. com. 1964-68), Am. Soc. Corporate Execs., Nat. Indsl. Conf. Bd., Internat. Corrugated Case Assn. (dir. 1967—, pres. 1967-68), Cum Laude Soc., Confrerie des Chevaliers, Harvard Bus. Sch. Assn. (pres. exec. council 1972-73, vis. com. 1974-80), Phi Gamma Delta. Presbyterian (trustee 1966-67, elder 1970—). Clubs: Mid-Am. (Chgo.); Toledo, Harvard Bus. Sch., Belmont Country, Toledo Country, Inverness Country (Toledo); Lyford Cay (Nassau, Bahamas); Links, Econ., Cloud (N.Y.C.); Augusta (Ga.) Nat. Golf; Muirfield Village Golf (Dublin, Ohio); Rockwell Springs Trout; Blind Brook (Purchase, N.Y.). Office: Owens-Ill Inc PO Box 1035 Toledo OH 43666

DODGE, ALFA DOROTHY MAW (MRS. HAROLD A. DODGE), aircraft tool co. exec.; b. Buffalo; d. Alfred Charles and Lillian (Beyer) Maw; grad. Chown Bus. Coll., 1916; m. Harold A. Dodge, June 8, 1922; children—Harold A., Dorothy A. (Mrs. Charles L. Plant). Sec. George A. Terry Co., 1941-44, partner, asst. mgr., 1945-62, owner, mgr. 1963—. Mem. Republican Nat. Com. Recipient award outstanding woman in industry, 1974. Mem. Buffalo Philharmonic Women's Com., Albright-Knox Art Gallery Soc., Nat., Buffalo Audubon socs., Smithsonian Instn. Assos., UN Assn. U.S.A., Am. Forestry Assn., Am. Legion Aux., Am. Mus. Natural History, Nat. Wildlife Assn., Buffalo C. of C., 500 Club WNED-TV, Buffalo Mus. Sci., Buffalo Zool. Soc., Cousteau Soc., Soc. Prevention Cruelty to Animals, Buffalo Council Chs., Buffalo Better Bus. Bur., Buffalo Goodwill Industries, Nat. Assn. Small Bus. Mem. Disciples of Christ (trustee Chatauqua assn.). Club: Zonta (dir.). Home: 4 Mona Dr Buffalo NY 14226 Office: 356 S Elmwood Ave Buffalo NY 14201

DODGE, JONATHAN WASHINGTON, investment banker; b. N.Y.C., July 24, 1933; s. Washington and Helen (Hubbard) D.; B.A., Yale U., 1955; children—Timothy Washington, Matthew Vodrey, Tyler Hubbard. Securities analyst Hayden, Stone Inc., N.Y.C., 1955-56, asso. corporate fin. dept., 1959-62, mgr. corp. fin. dept., Los Angeles, 1962-66, Schwabacher & Co., Los Angeles, 1966-67, gen. partner, 1968-69; pres. Intravest Mgmt. Corp., Los Angeles, 1969-72; v.p. Harris, Upham & Co., Los Angeles, 1972-74; treas. Flamemaster Corp., 1974-79, exec. v.p., 1979—. Served with AUS, 1956-58. Mem. Titanic Hist. Soc., Zeta Psi. Clubs: Beach (Santa Monica, Calif.); Riviera Tennis (Los Angeles). Office: 11120 Sherman Way Sun Valley CA 91352

DODGE, WILLIAM DOUGLAS, mfg., distbn. and service co. exec.; b. Savannah, Ga., Sept. 26, 1937; s. Kenneth Douglas and Betty Wilbur (Sadler) D.; B.S. in Indsl. Mgmt., Ga. Inst. Tech., 1959; M.B.A., Ga. State U., 1966; children—Gregory D., Phillip C., Warren D., Andrew L. Supervising underwriter Liberty Mut. Ins. Co., Atlanta, 1960-66; div. ins. adminstr. Lockheed-Ga. Co., Marietta, Ga., 1966-78; risk mgr. Schlumberger Ltd., Atlanta, 1978-79; v.p. ins. Fuqua Industries, Inc., Atlanta, 1979—; instr. risk mgmt. Ga. State U. Mem. exec. com. on reorganization and mgmt. improvement State of Ga., 1971. Mem. Risk and Ins. Mgmt. Soc. (past pres.). Author: The Hold Harmless Agreement, A Management Guide to Evaluation and Control, 1968. Office: 3800 FNB Tower Atlanta GA 30383

DODSON, STEPHANIE LEE, TV, film, concert prodn. co. exec.; b. Hollywood, Calif., Aug. 31, 1951; d. Harold M. and Shirley A. Samson; B.A. cum laude, U. Calif., Los Angeles, 1972; m. Norman Reynolds Dodson, July 14, 1974. Office mgr. prodn. div. Jenkins/Covington Prodns., Hollywood, 1972-74; producer, ops. dir. broadcasting div. N.W. Ayer Advt., Los Angeles, 1974-75; v.p. ops./adminstrn. Imero Fiorentino Assos., Los Angeles, 1975—; ops. cons. for various firms, Los Angeles, 1972—. Mem. Republican Nat. Com., 1976-77. Mem. Am. Film Inst., Acad. Television Arts and Scis. Author: Technical Theatre Handbook, 1974. Home: 12752 Moorpark St Studio City CA 91604 Office: 6430 Sunset Blvd #618 Hollywood CA 90028

DODSON, THOMAS LARKIN, JR., rancher, mayor; b. Ft. Worth, Dec. 24, 1919; s. Thomas Larkin and Clara Ada (Banner) D.; student Tex. Christian U., 1937-39, U. Tex., 1939-41; m. Clarabele Steele, Mar. 16, 1946; children—Thomas Larkin III, John S. Cattle rancher, Rhome, Tex., 1945—; mayor City of Fairview (Tex.), 1975—. Served with USN, 1941-45. Decorated D.F.C. with two oak leaf clusters, Air medal with three oak leaf clusters. Mem. Tex. Ind. Producers and Royalty Owners Assn. Republican. Home and office: Route 1 Box 12 Rhome TX 76078

DOEKSEN, WILBUR ALVIN, accountant; b. Rock Rapids, Iowa, Sept. 25, 1935; s. William and Rijke (Van Den Brink) D.; B.A., U. Colo., 1970; m. Lois Ruth Tolle, Aug. 2, 1955; children—Cheryl, William, Richard. Controller, Mechanex Corp., Englewood, Colo., 1962-69; staff acct. Trichak, Trainor & Tillman, C.P.A.'s, Colorado Springs, Colo., 1970-76; controller Metrix Teknika, Div. AKZO, Amsterdam, Holland, 1976; mgr. W. A. Doeksen & Co., C.P.A.'s, Denver, 1977—. Served with USAF, 1955-59. Named Denver Acct. of Yr., 1978; recipient Disting. Service award for Helping Small Bus., 1979. Mem. Aurora (Colo.) C. of C. (treas. 1980—), Nat. Assn. Accts. (dir. 1977-78, v.p. 1978-81), Colo. Soc. C.P.A.'s, Am. Inst. C.P.A.'s. Republican. Mem. Christian Reformed Ch. Club: Toastmasters. Home: 4900 W Stanford St Denver CO 80236 Office: 1602 S Parker Rd Denver CO 80231

DOENGES, RUDOLPH CONRAD, educator; b. Tonkawa, Okla., Dec. 7, 1930; s. Rudolph Soland and Helen Elizabeth (Lower) D.; A.B. magna cum laude, Harvard U., 1952, M.B.A., 1954; D.B.A., U. Colo., 1965; m. Ellen Lone Gummere, Oct. 5, 1963: children—Rudolph Conrad, John Soland, William Gummere. Mktg. analyst Ford Motor Co., 1954; mgr. Western Auto Rentals, Doenges-Long Motors, Colorado Springs, Colo., 1958-61; asst. prof. fin. U. Tex., Austin, 1964-67, asso. prof., 1967-74, prof., 1974—, asso. dean, 1972-76, chmn. dept. fin., 1976-80; dir. Doenges-Glass Motors, Bowers Auto Leasing. Served with USNR, 1954-58. Ford Found. fellow, 1963-64. Mem. Fin. Mgmt. Assn. (dir. 1973-74, 79—), Am. Fin. Assn., Southwestern Fin. Assn. (pres. 1973-74), Southwestern Fedn. Adminstrv. Disciples (pres. 1976-77). Republican. Methodist. Clubs: El Paso, Rotary. Asso. editor Finance Social Sciences Quar., 1966-74; contbr. articles to profl. jours. Home: 3500 Hillbrook Circle Austin TX 78731 Office: Dept Finance U Texas Austin TX 78712

DOEPKE, FREDERICK W., fin. services co. exec.; b. Cin., Dec. 15, 1915; s. William Leo and Ethel (Page) D.; A.B., Kenyon Coll., 1938; m. Margaret L. Lillard, Mar. 30, 1946; children—Frederick W. II, Margaret VanHook, Diane Doepke Voigt, Alice Page. Co-founder, officer Doepke Mfg. Co., 1944-59; mem. corporate staff Diamond Internat., N.Y.C., 1959-64; co-founder The Pension Selection Corp., N.Y.C., 1965-74; chmn. Webber & Doepke Inc., Fin. Services, Greenwich, Conn., 1975—; chmn. W&D Equities Corp. Mem. nat. security bd. Nat. Trust for Historic Preservation. Served with USAAF, 1941-44. Mem. C. of C., Toy Mfrs. Assn. U.S. (past pres.), Greenwich Hist. Soc., Greenwich Archaeol. Found., Alpha Delta Phi. Congregationalist. Clubs: Old Greenwich Yacht, Rocky Point (Old Greenwich); Wings (N.Y.C.); Innis Arden Golf. Home: 5 Kernan Pl Old Greenwich CT 06807 Office: 1 E Putnam Ave Greenwich CT 06830

DOERING, DAVID ANDREW, banker; b. St. Louis, Apr. 9, 1938; s. Edwin F. and Willma (Woehr) D.; B.S., St. Louis U., 1960, M.S., 1965; m. Marie E. Clark, Sept. 23, 1961; children—David Andrew, Douglas. With First Missouri Bank & Trust Co., Creve Coeur, 1963—, pres., 1978—; dir. First Missouri Banks, Inc.; dir. First Missouri Bank of Creve Coeur; dir. First Missouri Bank of West County. Served with USAF, 1962. Club: Kiwanis (past pres.). Office: First Missouri Bank & Trust Co PO Box 12570 Creve Coeur MO 63141

DOESCHER, WILLIAM FREDERICK, publisher; b. Utica, N.Y., Dec. 9, 1937; s. Frederick William and Katherine Ann (Kipp) D.; B.A. in Econs., Colgate U., 1959; M.A. in Journalism, Syracuse (N.Y.) U., 1961; postgrad. in advanced mgmt. Columbia U., 1973; m. Linda Blair, Nov. 25, 1977; children—Michele Blair, Douglas C. Doescher, Marc H. Blair, Cinda Doescher. Public relations asso., editor Chase Manhattan News, Chase Manhattan Bank, N.Y.C., 1961-65; mgr. press relations Inmont Corp., 1965-66; asst. corp. relations mgr. U.S. Plywood Corp., 1966-67; public affairs mgr. Eastern region Champion Internat. Corp., 1967-69, mgr. advt. services, then dir. corp. advt., 1969- 71; v.p. advt. and public relations Drexel Heritage Furnishings, Inc., 1971-78; v.p. communications Dun & Bradstreet, Inc., also publisher D&B Reports mag., N.Y.C., 1978—. Nat. telethon adv. Nat. Easter Seals Soc.; public relations adv. Am. Found. for Blind. Served with USAR, 1959-65. Mem. Public Relations Soc. Am. Author numerous articles in mags., periodicals. Office: 99 Church St New York NY 10007

DOHEMANN, GORDON HENRY, corp. exec., realtor; b. Fowler, Calif., Apr. 15, 1931; s. Herbert J. and Jean Pool (Bock) D.; student Stanford, 1949-50; B.S., U. Calif., Berkeley, 1957; m. Sharon R. Carwin, 1978; children—Jesse Herbert, Linda Louise, Russell Lawrence, Erik Gordon. Various positions Coldwell, Banker & Co., San Francisco, 1957-59, mgr., 1960-63; v.p. Draper Cos., San Francisco, 1963-65; owner, pres. Dohemann & Co., San Francisco, 1965—, Dohemann Fin. Corp., 1973—; founder, dir. Lincoln Nat. Bank, Santa Rosa, Calif., 1965, chmn. bd., 1968; dir. Redwood Bank, San Francisco. Served to 1st lt. U.S. Army, 1952-55. Office: 124 Beale St San Francisco CA 94105

DOHENY, DONALD ALOYSIUS, lawyer, bus. exec.; b. Milw., Apr. 20, 1924; s. John Anthony and Adelaide (Koller) D.; student U. Notre Dame, 1942-43; B.M.E., Marquette U., 1947; J.D., Harvard U., 1949; postgrad. indsl. engring. and bus. adminstrn. Washington U., 1950-56; m. Catherine Elizabeth Lee, Oct. 25, 1952; children—Donald Aloysius, Celeste Hazel, John Vincent, Ellen Adelaide, Edward Lawrence II, William Francis, Madonna Lee. Asst. to civil engr. Shipbldg. div. Froemming Bros., Inc., Milw., 1942-43; draftsman, designer The Heil Co., Milw., 1944-46; admitted to Wis. bar, 1949, Mo. bar, 1949, U.S. Supreme Ct. bar, 1970; mem. firm Igoe, Carroll & Keefe, St. Louis, 1949-51, Donald A. Doheny Attys., 1967—, Doheny & Assos., Mgmt. Counsel, 1957—; asst. to v.p. and gen. mgr., chief prodn. engr., gen. administr., dir. adminstrn. Granco Steel Products div. Granite City Steel Co., Granite City, Ill., 1951-57; asst. to pres. Vestal Labs., Inc., St. Louis, 1957-63; exec. v.p., dir. Moehlenpah Engring., Inc., Hydro-Air Engring., Inc., 1963-67; pres., dir. Foamtex Industries, Inc., St. Louis, 1967-75; v.p., dir. Seasonal Industries, Inc., N.Y.C., 1973-75; pres., dir. Mktg. & Sales Counsel, Inc., 1975—, Mid-USA Sales Co., 1976—; lectr. bus. orgn. and adminstrn. Washington U., 1950-74. Served as pvt. AUS, 1943-44; 1st lt. Res., 1948-52. Registered profl. engr., Mo. Mem. Am. Judicature Soc., Am. Mktg. Assn. (nat. membership chmn. 1959), Am., Mo., Wis., Fed. bar assns., Bar Assn. St. Louis (gen. chmn. pub. relations 1955-56, vice chmn., sec.-treas. jr. sect. 1950, 51), Marquette Engring. Assn. (pres. 1946-47), Engring. Knights, ASME, Engrs. Soc. Milw., Am. Legion, Tau Beta Pi, Pi Tau Sigma. Clubs: K.C., Notre Dame (pres. 1955, 56), Marquette (pres. 1961), Engrs., Stadium, Mo. Athletic (St. Louis). Home: 10906 Conway Rd Frontenac Saint Louis MO 63131 Office: 2284 Weldon Pkwy Saint Louis MO 63141 also 408 Olive St Suite 400 Saint Louis MO 63102

DOHERTY, ALFRED EDWARD, JR., metal fabrication co. exec.; b. Shaker Heights, Ohio, Nov. 11, 1929; s. Alfred Edward and Florence (Pylick) D.; student Dec. 24, 1949; m. Jeanette Doherty, Dec. 24, 1949; children—James Edward, Thomas Vincent, George Michael. Electronic technician, methods devel. Douglas Aircraft Corp., Torrance, Calif., 1954-59; project engr. Aerojet-Gen. Corp., Azusa and Downey, Calif., 1959-66, mgr. advanced materials tech., Downey and Fullerton, Calif., 1966-69; v.p., gen. mgr. Electro-Form, Inc., Fort Worth, 1969—; now pres. A & T Engring., Advance Mfg. Tech.; cons. to U.S. Navy. Served with U.S. Army, 1948-54. Cert. mfg. engr.; registered profl. engr., Calif. Mem. Soc. Mfg. Engrs., Nat. Fedn. Ind. Bus. Club: Ft. Worth Sertoma Breakfast (v.p. 1976). Patentee seam bonding machine, method; tube joining methods; contbr. articles to profl. jours. Home: 3601 Minot Ave Fort Worth TX 76133 Office: 3309 Winthrop Suite 208 Fort Worth TX 76116

DOHERTY, DIANA SALTER, investment co. exec.; b. South Gate, Calif., Feb. 5, 1946; d. Morris and Anna (Gvosdiff) Salter; A.A., Cerritos Coll., 1965; postgrad. U. Calif., Long Beach, 1965-67; m. John Doherty, Apr. 23, 1977; 1 dau., Heather Anne. Financial v.p. Award Meat Packing Co., South Gate, Calif., 1966-68; registered rep., research analyst Blyth Eastman Dillon, Long Beach, Calif., 1968-74, N.Y.C., 1974; registered investment adviser, v.p. Doherty & Salter, Inc., N.Y.C., 1974-76; pres. Salter Investment Co., San Francisco, 1976—. Mem. N.Y. Soc. Security Analysts (sr.). Home: 51 LaVerne Ave Long Beach CA 90803 Office: PO Box 3846 Long Beach CA 90803

DOHERTY, THOMAS ANTHONY, banker; b. Bklyn., Jan. 20, 1938; s. Joseph William and Gertrude Mary (Haggerty) D.; B.S., Fordham U., 1959; postgrad. N.Y. U. Grad. Sch. Bus., 1961-63; m. Marianne T. Hoffmann, July 23, 1960; children—Arlene, Karen, Bryan, Linda. Exec. trainee Chase Manhattan Bank, N.Y.C., 1960-64; asst. mgr. Franklin Nat. Bank, L.I., 1965-66, asst. cashier credit dept., 1966-68, mgr. credit dept., 1968-69, asst. v.p., 1970, v.p., 1971; staff Bank Suffolk County, Stony Brook, N.Y., 1971-72, exec. v.p., 1972, dir., 1972—, pres., chief exec. officer, 1972—; chmn. bd. trustees N.Y. State Bankers Retirement System, 1973—. Bd. dirs. Suffolk County Salvation Army, 1973—, L.I. div. Am. Cancer Soc. co-chmn. citizens adv. com. Stony Brook Council, State U. N.Y. at Stony Brook, 1976—. Served with N.Y. Nat. Guard, 1959. Mem. L.I. Assn. Commerce and Industry (dir.), L.I. Bankers Assn. (dir. 1975—, pres. 1978), Robert Morris Assos., Fordham U. Alumni Assn. Roman Catholic. Club: Nissequoque (N.Y.) Golf. Home: 48 Kurt Ln Hauppauge NY 11787 Office: 99 Smithtown By-Pass Hauppauge NY 11787

DOHMEN, FREDERICK HOEGER, wholesale drug co. exec.; b. Milw., May 12, 1917; s. Fred William and Viola (Gutsch) D.; B.A. in Commerce, U. Wis., 1939; m. Gladys Elizabeth Dite, Dec. 23, 1939 (dec. Sept. 1963); children—William Francis, Robert Charles; m. 2d, Mary Alexander Holgate, June 27, 1964. With F. Dohmen Co., Milw., 1939—, successively warehouse employee, sec., v.p., 1944-52, pres., 1952—, dir., 1947—, chmn. bd., 1952—. Asso. chmn. Nat. Bible Week, Laymen's Nat. Bible Com., 1968—. Bd. dirs. St. Luke's Hosp. Ednl. Found., Milw., pres., 1969-72, chmn. bd., 1972-73; bd. dirs. U. Wis.-Milw. Found., 1976-79; bd. visitors U. Wis.-Milw., 1978—. Mem. Nat. Wholesale Druggists Assn. (chmn. mfr. relations com. 1962, resolutions com. 1963, bd. control 1963-66), Druggists Service Council (dir. 1967-71, chmn. membership com. 1969), Wis. Pharm. Assn., Miss. Valley Drug Club, Nat. Assn. Wholesale Distbrs. (trustee 1966-75), Beta Gamma Sigma, Phi Eta Sigma, Delta Kappa Epsilon. Presbyterian. Clubs: University, Town (Milw.). Home: 3903 W Mequon Rd Mequon WI 53092 Office: W194 N 11381 McCormick Dr Germantown WI 53022

DOHMEN, HUBERT GERARDUS, electronics co. exec.; b. Heerlen, Netherlands, July 25, 1931; s. Jan P. and Antonia (Nicolai) D.; came to U.S., 1953, naturalized, 1955; B.S., Bernardinus Coll., 1951; m. Martha Kammandel, Nov. 21, 1956; children—Beatrix, Thomas, Shelton, Susan. Tech. supr. Sarkas Tarzian Co., Bloomington, Ind., 1957-58; prodn. mgr. Audio Devices Co., Santa Ana, Calif., 1958-59; plant mgr. Internat. Rectifier Co., El Segundo, Calif., 1959-61; supt. semicondr. mfg. Delco Electronics div. Gen. Motors Corp., Kokomo, Ind., 1961-77; v.p., gen. mgr. Galamar Industries, Palo Alto, Calif., 1977-80; dir. ops. Monsanto, St. Louis, 1978—. Served to 1st lt. Dutch Army, 1952-53; served with AUS, 1955-57. Mem. Semicondr. Equipment and Materials Inst., Am. Mgmt. Assn., Electrochem. Soc. Republican. Roman Catholic. Club: Columbia (Indpls.). Patentee crystal growth. Home: 10 Jennycliffe Chesterfield MO 63017 Office: 800 N Lindbergh Blvd Saint Peters MO 63376

DOHRING, GRACE HELEN, med. supply co. exec.; b. Detroit, May 6, 1921; d. Frederick Henry and Martha Helen Johnson; D.Chiropractic, Detroit Chiropractic, 1942: D.Naturopathic, Am. Coll. Naturopathic, 1944; D.Neuropathy, Am. Coll. Neuropathy, 1946; m. Albert A. Dohring, June 30, 1951; children—Charles, Deborah, Joan. Practice chiropractic, Detroit, 1942-47, practice naturopathy, Detroit, 1947-57; pres. Dohring Supply Center, Dearborn, Mich., 1957-71, Doctor's Supply Internat., Dearborn, 1971—; tchr. acupuncture, 1975—. Diplomate Nat. Neuropathic Bd. Mem. Internat. Entrepreneurs Assb., Nat. Small Bus. Assn., Nat. Assn. Female Execs., Acupuncture Ryodoraku Assn. (charter, trustee 1972—), Acupuncture Licensed Physicians and Hosp. Assn. (pres. 1977—), Am. Chiropractic Assn. (charter), Mich. Assn. Naturopathic Physicians (dir.). Acupuncture and Cautery Assn., Kyoto (Japan) Pain Control Inst. Club: Order Eastern Star. Author: Acupuncture Electric, 2d edit., 1974; Ear Acupuncture, 2d edit., 1974. Patentee in field. Address: 24028 Union St Dearborn MI 48124

DOHRMANN, RUSSELL WILLIAM, paper co. exec.; b. Clinton, Iowa, June 29, 1942; s. Russell Wilbert and Anita Doris Miller D.; B.S., Upper Iowa U., 1965; M.B.A., Drake U., 1971; m. Rita Marie Meade, Dec. 26, 1964 (dec.); children—Angela, Michelle, Sarah; m. 2d, M. Jean Stapleton, Aug. 18, 1979; 1 dau., Kellie. Jr. accountant Chamberlain Mfg. Corp., Clinton, 1965, sr. accountant, 1966, plant controller, Derry, Pa., 1967-68; fin. cost analyst Wheelabrator Frye Inc., Des Moines, 1968-69, cost and procedures mgr., 1969-70, acting mgr., 1970-71, v.p., controller, 1971-78, group controller Internat. div., 1974-78, v.p., controller Chem. & Coating group, 1978-80, exec. v.p., gen. mgr. Frye Copyeystem, Inc. div., 1980—. Mem. Des Moines C. of C., Am. Inst. Corp. Controllers, Nat. Assn. Accts., Nat. Audubon Soc., Am. Assn. Accts. Office: 7445 University Ave Des Moines IA 50311

DOLAN, VINCENT GERARD, communications and info. processing exec.; b. Bklyn., Oct. 12, 1927; s. Vincent Lawrence and Elizabeth Mable (Cummings) D.; B.A., St. Lawrence U., Canton, N.Y., 1955; s. Carrie Marie Knopf, Apr. 14, 1959. Trainee, Chase Manhattan bank, N.Y.C., 1956-57, asst. accounts mgr. Columbian Carbon Internat., Inc., N.Y.C., 1957-59; export credit mgr. Dorr-Oliver, Inc., Stamford, Conn., 1959-65; supr. credit/collection documentation control IGE Export div. Gen. Electric Co., N.Y.C., 1965-66; mgr. Western hemisphere credit accts. RCA Corp., N.Y.C., 1966-71; cons., analyst S.J. Rundt Assos., Inc., N.Y.C., 1971-72; credit supr. export div. Ford Motor Co., Newark, 1972-79; mgr. credit/collections Harris Corp. Info. Systems Internat. Div., Melbourne, Fla., 1979—. Served with USMC, 1945-49, 50-51. Mem. Am. Soc. Internat. Execs., Alpha Tau Omega. Roman Catholic. Home: 13 Dunham St Melbourne FL 32901 Office: 1301 Woody Burke Rd PO Box 9831 Melbourne FL 32901

DOLINGER, MILTON BRYER, r.r. exec.; b. Scranton, Pa., Oct. 11, 1921; s. Samuel and Celia (Bryer) D.; B.A. in Journalism, Pa. State U., 1943. With UPI, Cleve., 1943-53, bur. mgr., 1949-53; with C. & O. R.R., 1953—, beginning as news editor, successively gen. mgr. news div., exec. asst. to v.p. charge news and community relations, 1953-74, asst. v.p., 1974—, dir. public relations and advt., asst. v.p., 1977—. Community and univ. relations adv. com. Cleve. State U. Served as combat corr. inf., AUS, World War II. Decorated Bronze Star Medal. Mem. R.R. Public Relations Assn. (pres.), Assn. Am. R.R.'s (exec. com. public relations), Sigma Delta Chi. Office: Chessie System The Terminal Tower Cleveland OH 44101

DOLIVE, EARL, business exec.; b. 1917; married. Mgr., Charlotte ops. Genuine Parts Co., 1937-59, mgr. Mpls. ops., 1959-62, various positions, Atlanta, 1962-65, exec. v.p., 1965-73, vice chmn. bd., 1973—, also dir. Office: Genuine Parts Co 2999 Circle 75 Pkwy Atlanta GA 30339*

DOLJACK, BARBARA LYNN, pub. exec.; b. Cleve., Mar. 14, 1942; d. Rudolph Frank and Mary Jean D.; student Ohio Dominican Coll., 1960-62; grad. with honors Tobe-Coburn Sch., 1963. Exec. tng. program Bloomingdale's, N.Y.C., 1963, asst. buyer jr. dresses, 1963-64, asst. fashion dir., 1964-66; sr. merchandising coordinator Seventeen mag., N.Y.C., 1966-69, merchandising editor, 1969-71, merchandising dir., 1971-76, dir. promotion services, direct merchandising public relations and promotion depts. Seventeen mag., 1976—, Panorama mag., 1979—. Pres. exec. com. Friends of the Henry St. Settlement; mem. various coms. Floating Hosp. Recipient Mihitabel award, Tobe-Coburn Sch., 1979, T award, 1968. Mem. Mktg. Communications Execs. Internat. (dir. N.Y. chpt.), Advt. Women of N.Y., Nat. Home Fashions League, Fashion Group (membership com., v.p., gov. 1980—). Clubs: N.Y. Jr. League, Tobe-Coburn Sch. (exec. alumnae com.). Home: 310 E 70th St New York NY 10021 Office: 850 Third Ave New York NY 10022

DOLMAN, VIOLA ELIZABETH SETTER, Realtor; b. Richmond, Kans., Dec. 9, 1922; d. Christopher B. and Bertha (Miller) Setter; B.S., Kans. State U., 1944; M.S., Stanford, 1948; children—David, Laura. Faculty, Stanford Med. Sch., 1948-50, faculty biochemistry dept., 1950-53; real estate broker, Honolulu, 1958—. Pres. Hawaii Assn. for Children with Learning Disabilities, 1970; mem. profl. info. com. Am. Cancer Soc., 1967. Bd. dirs., chmn. Hawaii chpt. ARC; 1979, 80; bd. dirs. Aloha United Way, 1979; state chmn. Make Am. Better Com., 1979, 80. Public Health grantee for research, Honolulu, 1953-55. Mem. Farm and Land Brokers Assn., Traders and Exchangers Orgn., Honolulu Bd. Realtors (chmn. multiple listing service com., Realtor of Yr. 1976, sec. 1976-77, pres. 1978), Hawaii Assn. Realtors (dir. 1974-75, sec. 1976-77, vice chmn. credit union com. 1979, pres.-elect 1981), Sigma Xi. Clubs: Zonta; Oahu Country, Outrigger Canoe, Honolulu (Honolulu). Home: 1049 Waiholo St Honolulu HI 96821 Office: 210 Ward Ave Suite 100 Honolulu HI 96814

DOLNICK, LEON ALBERT, radio sta. exec.; b. Chgo., Mar. 16, 1931; s. Benjamin Isaac and Ethel (Goldman) D.; B.S. in Econs. and Psychology, U. Wis., Madison, 1954; postgrad. U. Wis., Milw., 1957-60; m. Sandra Friedman, Feb. 3, 1957; children—Randy Sue, Barrie Lynn, Amy Joan, Carol Anne. Salesman, Glen of Mich., 1954-55; pub. relations asso. Wis. Anti-Tb Assn., Milw., 1955-56; with WITI-TV, Milw., 1956-69, local sales mgr., 1959-66, gen. sales mgr., 1966-69; exec. v.p. Marx Advt. Agy., Milw., 1969-72; gen. sales mgr. Sta. WOKY, Milw., 1972-75; gen. sales mgr. Stations WISN/WLPX div. Hearst Corp., Milw., 1975—. Co-pres., Friends of Milw. Public Library, 1975-79; del. Gov.'s Conf. on Libraries and Info. Services, 1979. Served with USAF, 1951-52. Recipient writing awards Milw. Press Club, 1959, 60, 63, 69. Mem. Milw. Advt. Club (dir.), English-Speaking Union, Friends of Libraries U.S.A., Radio Advt. Bur., Nat. Assn. Broadcasters. Jewish. Clubs: Milw. Athletic, B'nai B'rith, Variety. Home: 4909 N Ardmore Ave Milwaukee WI 53217 Office: WISN/WLPX Div Hearst Corp 759 N 19th St Milwaukee WI 53201

DOMANGUE, NORRIS JOSEPH, JR., steel co. exec.; b. New Orleans, July 19, 1923; s. Norris Joseph and Kathryn (Reynolds) D.; B.A., U. Mich., 1949; m. Barbara A. Buttery, Apr. 21, 1951; children—Michelle, Norris Joseph III. With Linde divs. Union Carbide Corp., Newark, 1949-54, Essington, Pa., 1954-57; personnel asst. Lukens Steel Co., Coatesville, Pa., 1957-59, supr. employment, 1959-66, mgr. personnel adminstrn., 1966—. Chmn. bd. dirs. West Chester (Pa.) Area Day Care Center. Served to capt. USAAF, 1942-45, 51-53; ETO. Decorated D.F.C., Purple Heart, Air medal with two oak leaf clusters. Mem. Am. Soc. Personnel Adminstrn., Am. Iron and Steel Inst. (nat. chmn. safety com. 1971-73), Mensa, Indsl. Relations Greater Phila., Pa. Self-Insurers Assn., Chester County Coalition for Equal Opportunity, Brandywine Valley Assn., Coatesville C. of C. Rotarian. Club: University of Mich. (Phila.). Home: 401 Darlington Dr West Chester PA 19380 Office: Strode Ave Coatesville PA 19320

DOMBROWER, MARIO, city ofcl.; b. La Paz, Bolivia, June 26, 1941; s. Wilhelm G. Dombrower and Jenny (Feigenblatt) Gotthelf; came to U.S., 1953, naturalized, 1959; student Coll. City N.Y., 1959, Los Angeles City Coll., 1960-62; B.S. in Engring., Calif. State U. at Los Angeles, 1966; m. Beatriz Horowitz, Oct. 30, 1965; children—Michael, Shirley. With Equitable Life Assurance Co. of N.Y., 1959-60, County of Los Angeles Sheriff's Dept., Engring. Dept., 1962-65; with Bur. Engring., City of Los Angeles Dept. Pub. Works, 1965—, sr. civil engring. asst., 1969-80, civil engring. asso., 1980—; Bur. Engring. rep. Mcpl. Govt. Awareness Day, 1977. Registered profl. engr., Calif.; lic. real estate broker, Calif. Mem. ASCE, Engrs. and Architects Assn., Tau Beta Pi. Democrat. Jewish. Club: B'nai Tikvah Congregation Men's (dir.). Home: 7133 Knowlton Pl Los Angeles CA 90045 Office: Bur Engring City Los Angeles Dept Pub Works 200 N Main St Los Angeles CA 90025

DOMITRZ, JOSEPH S., ednl. adminstr.; b. Hamtramck, Mich., May 13, 1940; B.S. in Edn., Central Mich. U., 1962; M.A. in Econs., Western Mich. U., 1966; Ph.D. in Econs., So. Ill. U., 1971; m. Joan Byerwalter, Sept. 9, 1961; children—Victoria, Rita, Cheryl, Michael. Tchr., coach Lakewood Public Schs., Lake Odessa, Mich., 1962-63; Saugatuck (Mich) Public Schs., 1963-66; instr., chmn. dept. econs. Western Ill. U., 1966-76; dean Coll. Bus. and Econs., U. Wis., Whitewater, 1976—; cons. public sector. Bd. dirs. Whitewater Area C. of C., 1977—. Mem. Indsl. Relations Research Assn., Fin. Execs. Inst., Midwest Econs. Assn. Club: Rotary. Contbr. articles on public sector fin. and labor relations to profl. jours. Office: Carlson Hall Coll Bus and Econs Univ Wis Whitewater WI 53190

DOMPKE, NORBERT FRANK, photography studio exec.; b. Chgo., Oct. 16, 1920; s. Frank and Mary (Manley) D.; grad. Wright Jr. Coll., 1939-40; student Northwestern U., 1946-49; m. Marjorie Gies, Dec. 12, 1964; children—Scott, Pamela. Cost comptroller, budget dir. Scott Radio Corp., 1947; pres. TV Forecast, Inc., 1948-52, editor Chgo. edit. TV Guide, 1953, mgr. Wis. edit., 1954; pres. Root Photographers, Inc., Chgo., 1955—; elector Photography Hall Fame. Served with AC, AUS, 1943-47. C.P.A., Ill. Mem. United Photographers Orgn. (pres. 1970-71), Profl. Photographers Am., Am. Assn. Sch. Photographers (v.p. 1966-67, sec. treas. 1967-69, pres. 1969-70, dir. 1971-77), Ill. Small Bus. Men's Assn. (dir. 1970-73), Ill. Profl. Sch. Photographers Assn., Chgo. Assn. Commerce and Industry (edn. com. 1966—), Nat. Edn. Assn. Nat. Sch. Press Assn., Ill. High Sch. Press Assn., Nat. Collegiate Sch. Press Assn., Ill. C. of C. Co-founder T. Guide, 1947. Clubs: Carleton, Chgo. Press, Internat., Whitehall, Zorine's; Tonguish Creek Yacht. Home: 990 N Lake Shore Dr Chicago IL 60611 Office: 1131 W Sheridan Rd Chicago IL 60660

DONAHOE, RITA LOUISE, Realtor; b. Boston, Jan. 16, 1930; d. Franklin Augustine and Barbara Rita (Coyne) Bannister; student Boston Coll., 1948-51; m. Robert Francis Donahoe, June 15, 1957; children—Steven Francis, Christopher John. Asst. clk. Suffolk Superior Criminal Ct., Boston, 1948-57; v.p., treas. D&G Constrn. Co., Inc., Merrimack, N.H., 1964-68; broker Fisher Assos., real estate, Nashua, N.H., 1968-71; propr. R. Donahoe Assos., Bedford, N.H., 1971—; pres., treas. Century 21 Donahoe-Danais Assos., Bedford. Mem. Nashua (pres. 1976, standard and ethics com. chmn. 1978, dir. 1978-79; Realtor of Year 1977), Manchester bds. Realtors, So. N.H., (v.p. 1975—, award 1973), Greater Manchester multiple listing services, Women's Council Realtors (chpt. pres. 1974), Nat., N.H. (dir. exec. com. 1976—, chmn. pub. relations 1978) assns. realtors, Realtors Nat. Mktg. Inst., Manchester C. of C. Club: Manchester Country. Home: Davis Rd Merrimack NH 03054 Office: RFD 5 Daniel Webster Hwy Bedford NH 03102

DONAHUE, DONALD JORDAN, packaging co. exec.; b. Bklyn., July 5, 1924; s. John F. and Florence (Jordan) D.; B.A., Georgetown U., 1947; M.B.A., N.Y. U., 1951; m. Mary Meyer, Jan. 20, 1951; children—Mary G., Judith A., Donald Jordan, Thomas, Nicholas P. With Chem. Corn Exchange Bank, N.Y.C. 1947-49; with Am. Metal Climax Inc. (name changed to AMAX, Inc.), N.Y.C., 1949-75, treas., 1957-67, v.p., 1963-65, exec. v.p., 1965-69, pres., 1969-75, also dir., 1964-75; vice chmn. Continental Can Co., Inc. (name changed to Continental Group, Inc.), N.Y.C., 1975—; dir. Nat. Starch & Chem. Co., DCL Inc., United Nuclear Corp.; mem. adv. bd. Manufacturers Hanover Trust Co. Trustee Georgetown U.; v.p., trustee ICD Research Center; trustee Joint Council Econ. Edn. Served with AUS, 1943-46. Clubs: Greenwich Country, Indian Harbor Yacht (Greenwich); Stamford Yacht; Univ.; Blind Brook; River (N.Y.C.). Home: Meads Point Greenwich CT 06830 Office: One Harbor Plaza Stamford CT 06902

DONAHUE, IRVING JAMES, JR., mfg. co. exec.; b. Worcester, Mass., Feb. 14, 1922; s. Irving James and Ethel Linnea (Larson) D.; B.S., Worcester Poly. Inst., 1944; M.B.A., Harvard, 1948; m. Barbara May Grant, Sept. 14, 1946; children—Susan (Mrs. Thomas A. Falzoi), Judith. Engaged in mfg. industry, 1948-56; pres., dir. Donahue Industries, Inc., Shrewsbury, Mass., 1957—; pres., treas., dir. I.J.D. Inc., Shrewsbury, 1974—; pres., dir. Donahue Internat., Inc., Wilmington, Del., 1970—; trustee, corp. clk. Consumer Savs. Bank, Worcester. Chmn. Shrewsbury Bd. Selectmen, 1953-68, chmn. fin. com., 1968-76. Trustee, mem. exec. com., pres.'s adv. com. Worcester Poly. Inst.; trustee, pres., chmn. exec. com. Meml. Hosp., Worcester. Served to lt. (j.g.) USNR, 1944-46. Registered profl. engr., Mass. Mem. Central Mass. Employers Assn. (pres., dir. 1971-73), Worcester Area C. of C. (dir.), Small Bus. Execs. Club (chmn.), Worcester Poly. Inst. Alumni Assn. (past pres.), Phi Sigma Kappa. Republican. Conglist. Mason. Clubs: Worcester (dir.), Worcester Country (bd. govs.), Harvard, Harvard Business School (Worcester). Patentee metal-plastic grinding wheel adaptor. Home: 100 Oak St Shrewsbury MA 01545 Office: 5 Industrial Dr Shrewsbury MA 01545

DONAHUE, ROBERT FRANCIS, tax acct./cons.; b. Boston, Sept. 4, 1932; s. George Francis and Elizabeth M. (Grover) D.; B.S., Bryant Stratton Coll., 1973; m. Thelma Anne Duncan, Oct. 27, 1957; children—Mark Francis, Neale Francis. Credit mgr. Family Fin. Corp., Boston, 1953-57; asst. bank mgr. Family Indsl. Bank, Denver, 1957-58; credit office mgr. Firestone Stores, Pueblo, Colo., 1958; v.p. ops. Cape State Foods, Inc., Hanover, Mass., 1958-67; propr., tax acct./cons. R.F. Donahue Assos., Boston, Walpole, 1967—; treas./clk. I-A Assos., Inc., Walpole, 1978—; dir. Ind. Oil Co., Walpole; bus. mgr. Walpole Times, Inc. Mem. personnel bd. Town of Walpole, 1976-79; notary public, Mass., 1954—. Served with USN, 1950-53, USMCR, 1953-56. Mem. Nat. Soc. Public Accts., Am. Soc. Notaries (ethics com.), Am. Soc. Tax Cons.'s, Walpole C. of C., Walpole Mchts. Assn. Roman Catholic. Clubs: Emerald Soc., K.C., Internat. Order Alhambra. Contbr. articles to profl. jours. Home: 2224 Main St Walpole MA 02081 Office: 2224 Main St Walpole MA 02081

DONALDSON, JAMES NEILL, banker; b. Washington County, Pa., Mar. 25, 1940; s. James Reed and Mary Alice (Neill) D.; B.A. in Polit. Sci., Westminster Coll., 1962; M.Ed., U. Pitts., 1965, postgrad. in law, 1962-64; m. Wilma Jean Crankshaw, Aug. 5, 1967. Trust adminstr. Bankers Trust Co., N.Y.C., 1967-70, asst. trust officer, 1970-73, trust officer, White Plains, N.Y., 1973-76, officer-in-charge trust adminstrv. unit, 1976, v.p., 1976-78, head trust office, 1978—; dir. estate planning council Westchester County, N.Y., 1975—, Rockland County, N.Y., 1973—; lectr. estate adminstrn. Trust Div., N.Y. State Bankers Assn., 1975. Mem. Phi Kappa Tau. Presbyterian. Office: Bankers Trust Co Westchester One 44 S Broadway White Plains NY 10601

DONALSON, JAMES RYAN, real estate broker; b. Kansas City, Mo., Jan. 7, 1945; s. Joseph Elmer and Betty Lee (Cousins) D.; B.S. (Mo. Real Estate Assn. scholar), U. Mo., 1967; m. Sandra Lynn Yockey, Dec. 26, 1964; children—Kimberly Kay, Debra Lynn, Jennifer Lee. Loan officer City Wide Mortgage Co., Kansas City, Mo., 1967; interviewer personnel Panhandle Eastern Pipe Line Co., Kansas City, Mo., 1968; partner Donalson Realtors, Kansas City, Mo., 1969—; pres. Classic Homes, Kansas City, Mo., 1973—, Donalson Devel. Co. Inc., 1980—, Donalson & Assos. Realtors Inc., 1980—. Bd. dirs. Multiple Listing Service Greater Kansas City, 1971-75, treas., 1972-73. Bd. dirs. Platte County unit Am. Cancer Soc., 1973-75. Mem. Nat. Assn. Real Estate Bds., Mo. Assn. Realtors (dir. 1974-75), Kansas City Real Estate Bd. (dir. 1978-80), Homebuilders Assn. Kansas City, Platte County Bus. and Profl. Mens Assn., U. Mo. Alumni Assn. C. of C. Greater Kansas City. Baptist. Lion (dir. 1974-76). Office: 7526 NW Prairie View Rd Kansas City MO 64151

DONCHIAN, RICHARD DAVOUD, econ. analyst; b. Hartford, Conn., Sept. 21, 1905; s. Samuel B. and Armenouhi A. (Davoud) D.; A.B., Yale U., 1928; C.F.A., U. Va., 1964; m. Alma Gibbs, Feb. 9, 1957. With Hemphill Noyes & Co., N.Y.C., 1933-35, Samuel Donchian Rug Co., Hartford, 1935-38; pres. Fin. Supervision, Inc., 1938-42; econ. analyst Shearson-Hammill & Co., N.Y.C., 1946-48; investment adv., 1948-60; pres., dir. Futures Inc., N.Y.C., 1948-60; dir. commodity research, account exec. Hayden, Stone & Co. (co. named changed to Shearson Loeb Rhoades Inc. 1979), N.Y.C., 1960-69, v.p., 1970-76, sr. v.p. investments, 1976—; adv. Commodity Trend Timing Fund; dir. Donchian Mgmt. Inc., Ft. Lauderdale, Fla., Fin. Supervision, Inc., Greenwich, Conn.; mem. N.Y. Cotton Exchange, Commodity Exchange, Inc., N.Y. Futures Exchange. Served as statis. control officer USAAF, 1942-45. Mem. N.Y. Sec. Security Analysts, Am. Statis. Assn., Inst. Chartered Fin. Analysts, Fin. Forum. Republican. Presbyterian (elder). Clubs: N.Y. Commodity, Yale (N.Y.C.); Yale (Ft. Lauderdale, Fla.); Univ. (Hartford), Scarsdale Golf, Down Town Assn., Appalachian Mountain. Author articles and monographs. Home: 133 Pompano Beach Blvd Pompano Beach FL 33062 also Bomoseen VT 05732 Office: 2 Greenwich Plaza Greenwich CT 06830 also 3099 E Commercial Blvd Fort Lauderdale FL 33308

DONEHOWER, ERNEST JOHN, tourism bur. exec.; b. Wilmington, Del., June 5, 1945; s. Weston J. and Elizabeth Gladding D.; A.B., Coll. William and Mary, 1967; M.A. (East-West Center grantee), U. Hawaii, 1969; m. Kathleen Denise Hawkins, Jan. 25, 1975; 1 dau., Christina Elizabeth. Research analyst Hawaii Visitors Bur., Honolulu, 1970-73, dep. dir. research, 1973—. Mem. Hawaii Econ. Assn., Hawaii Statis. Assn. (v.p.), Am. Statis. Assn., Phi Beta Kappa, Phi Eta Sigma. Contbr. articles to profl. jours. Office: 2270 Kalakaua Ave Honolulu HI 96815

DONEHUE, JOHN DOUGLAS, newspaper exec.; b. Cramerton, N.C., July 5, 1928; s. John Sidney and Annie (Shepherd) D.; student Am. Press Inst., Columbia, 1965, 71-73; m. Mary Phelps (dec. 1964); children—Teresa Jean, Marilyn Phelps; m. Sylvia Louise McKenzie, Feb. 11, 1966 (dec. Nov. 1971); children—Hayden Shepherd, John Douglas; m. Virginia Kirkland, June 28, 1975; children—Anne Mikell, Robertson Carr. Sports writer Charleston, S.C. News and Courier, 1947, telegraph editor, 1956, state editor, 1959-62, city editor, 1962-68, mng. editor, 1968-71, promotion dir., 1971—, compiler News and Courier Style Book, 1969; sports editor Orangeburg (S.C.) Times and Democrat, 1948-50; polit. reporter Montgomery (Ala.) Advertiser, 1954-55; faculty advisor Bapt. Coll. at Charleston Student Newspaper. Spl. adviser comdt. 7th USCG dist. for establishment dist.-wide pub. information program, 1960-61; journalism lectr. Baptist Coll., Charleston, sec. 1st bd. founders, 1969. Chmn. adv. bd. Salvation Army; chmn. regional adv. council S.C. Dept. Youth Services; chmn. United Way Planning Bd.; bd. dirs. S.C. Tricentennial Parade Com., 1969—, Greater Charleston Safety Council. Served with S.C.N.G., 1948-50, USAF, 1950-54, USMCR, 1955-56, USAR, 1956-59, USCGR, 1959-66, USNR, 1966-75. Recipient Freedoms Found. award, 1969, 71. Mem. John Ancrum Soc. of Soc. Prevention Cruelty to Animals, Carolina Art Assn., YMCA, Internat. Newspaper Promotion Assn., S.C. Press Assn., Air Force Assn. (dir. Charleston council), Navy League (v.p. Charleston council), Charleston Trident C. of C. (v.p.), Toastmasters Internat. (charter mem. Okinawa club), Okinawa Soc. Episcopalian (lay reader, vestryman). Clubs: Country, Rotary (pres. 1974-75) (Charleston). Home: 66 Bull St Charleston SC 29401 Office: 134 Columbus St Charleston SC 29401

DONELAN, PATRICK MICHAEL, investment co. exec.; b. St. Louis, Jan. 10, 1940; s. Patrick J. and Kathleen Theresa (Connolly) D.; B.A., U. Mo., 1962; m. Carol Francis Luke, Sept. 21, 1963; children—Sean Michael, Elizabeth Luke, Ellen Lacey, Catherine Cunliff. Account exec. Newhard, Cook & Co., 1966-68; co-founder Donelan Phelps & Co., Inc., St. Louis, 1968, exec. v.p., sec., 1968—; chmn., chief exec. officer Kieffer Paper Mills, Inc., Brownstown, Ind.; vice chmn. bd. Brentwood Bancshares Corp., St. Louis, 1978—; dir., mem. exec. com. Am. Investment Co., 1977-80, Kieffer Paper Mills Inc., Brentwood Bank, Intercapco West, Inc.; participant Fin. Analysts Fedn., Harvard Grad. Sch. Bus., 1973. Mem. St. Louis County Historic Bldgs. Commn.; bd. dirs. Catholic Cemeteries Archdiocese St. Louis; trustee Newman Found., Washington U., St. Louis; vice-chmn. Midland dist. Boy Scouts Am. Served as officer USAF, 1962-66. Decorated Commendation medal with oak leaf cluster. Mem. Young Pres.'s Orgn., St. Louis Soc. Fin. Analysts. Clubs: Racquet, Noonday, Univ., St. Louis, Old Warson. Home: 52 Huntleigh Woods Village of Huntleigh MO 63131 Office: 7800 Bonhomme St Saint Louis MO 63105

DONER, WILFRED B., advt. exec.; b. Detroit, Nov. 5, 1914; s. Nathan and Regina (Sobel) Silberstein; A.B., U. Wis., 1936; m. Rolla Jacob Friedman, Mar. 19, 1964; children (by previous marriage)—Judith Anne (Mrs. Edward Berne), Frederick Nathan, Mary Alice. Partner Fink & Doner, 1937-43; pres. W.B. Doner & Co., advt. agy., 1943-68, chmn. bd., 1968-73, chmn. exec. com., 1973—; dir. Mich. Chandelier Co., Winkelman's, Teleco. Nat. dir. Nat. Multiple Sclerosis Soc. Clubs: Franklin Hills Country, Renaissance, Harmonica, Ocean Reef. Office: 26711 Northwestern Hwy Southfield MI 48034

DONIHUE, DAVID LEE, accounting firm exec.; b. Sturgis, Mich., Mar. 22, 1947; s. Robert Carl and Dorothy Louise (Rawles) D.; B.B.A., Western Mich. U., 1969; m. Yolanda Margarita Monroy, July 1, 1972. Audit mgr. firm Seidman & Seidman, C.P.A.'s, Grand Rapids, Mich., 1968-75; audit partner specializing in banking, firm Conley, McDonald, Sprague & Co., C.P.A.'s Milw., 1975—. Asst. treas. Camp Tall Turf, inner-city youth camp, Grand Rapids, 1970-75; co-founder, treas. Recycle Unlimited, Grand Rapids, 1972—, also dir. Bd. dirs., treas., chmn. budget, alt. del. Kent County unit Mich. Heart Assn., 1973-75. C.P.A., Mich. Mem. Am., Wis. (banking com.) insts. C.P.A.'s, Western Mich. U. Hon. Accounting Soc. Home: 2545 Brookside Ln Brookfield WI 53005 Office: 2825 N Mayfair Rd Milwaukee WI 53222

DONLEY, EDWARD, mfg. exec.; b. Highland Park, Mich., Nov. 26, 1921; s. Hugh and Frances (Gavin) D.; B.M.E., Lawrence Inst. Tech., 1943; student Advanced Mgmt. Program, Harvard, 1959; m. Inez Cantrell, Oct. 24, 1946; children—Martha Robb, Thomas, John, Vice pres. Air Products and Chems., Inc., Allentown, Pa., 1956-66, exec. v.p., 1966, pres., 1966—, chief exec. officer, 1973—, chmn. bd., 1978—, also dir.; dir. Am. Standard, Inc., Mellon Bank, N.A. Mem. corp. Lawrence Inst. Tech.; bd. overseers Coll. Engring. and Applied Sci., U. Pa.; trustee, mem. bus. adv. council Carnegie-Mellon U. Mem. Bus. Council Pa. (co-chmn. exec. com.), Conf. Bd., Bus.-Higher Edn. Forum, President's Panel. Club: Harvard Bus. Sch. of Phila. (adv. bd.). Home: 326 N 27th St Allentown PA 18104 Office: PO Box 538 Allentown PA 18105

DONLEY, JAMES WALTON, mgmt. cons.; b. Cleve., June 27, 1934; s. Howard Russell and Mary Louise D.; B.A., Denison U., Granville, Ohio, 1958; M.B.A., U. Pa., 1960; m. Frances Elizabeth Jordan, July 5, 1963; children—Dana, Eliza. Asst. to pub. Time Mag., N.Y.C., 1960-66; asst. commr. commerce City of N.Y., 1967-68; sr. v.p. Deegan Co., Los Angeles, 1969-71; asst. sec. for pub. affairs Treasury Dept., Washington, 1972-73; pres. Donley Communications Corp., N.Y.C., 1973—; adv. com. N.Y.C. Office of Telecommunications. Vice chmn. Citizens Union of N.Y.C.; bd. dirs. Greenwich (Conn.) Health Assn.; dir. Wharton Grad. Sch. Alumni. Served with AUS, 1954-56. Clubs: Univ. (N.Y.C.): Belle Haven (Greenwich). Home: 51 Dewart Rd Greenwich CT 06830 Office: 405 Park Ave New York City NY 10022

DONLON, WILLIAM JOSEPH, utility co. exec.; b. Albany, N.Y., Jan. 28, 1930; s. Charles Joseph and Margaret Mary (Shanahan) D.; B.S. in Econs., Siena Coll., 1962; m. Patricia Pommer, Apr. 26, 1952; children—Deborah, William, Robert, Susan, James, Brian. With Niagara Mohawk Power Corp., 1948—; supr. sales and services tng., Albany, 1960-62, Buffalo, 1962-64; sales mgr., Buffalo, 1964-68; comml. v.p. Western div., Buffalo, 1968-70; v.p., gen. mgr. Eastern div., Albany, 1970-76; sr. v.p., Syracuse, N.Y., 1976, now pres.; dir. Nat. Comml. Bank & Trust Co., Utilities Mut. Ins. Co. Bd. dirs. United Fund Albany Area, Albany Area ARC, Jr. Achievement Capital Dist., Better Albany Living; trustee Coll. St. Rose; bd. govs. Albany Med. Center Hosp. Served with USN, 1952-54; ETO. Mem. Capital Dist. C. of C. (pres. 1973-74). Republican. Roman Catholic. Clubs: Ft. Orange (Albany); Century (Syracuse, N.Y.). Office: Niagara Mohawk Power Corp 300 Erie Blvd W Syracuse NY 13202*

DONNELL, EDWARD S., retail chain store co. exec.; b. Cleve., Sept. 16, 1919; s. Luke and Maybell Donnell; ed. Duke, 1941; m. Rose Kueffner, Oct. 25, 1941; children—William, Ann, Sally, Mark. With B.F. Goodrich Co., 1941-46; with Sears, Roebuck & Co., 1946-62, group mgr., Los Angeles, 1961-62; v.p., Eastern regional mgr. Montgomery Ward & Co., Balt., 1962-64; exec. v.p., 1964-66, pres., Chgo., 1966-72, chmn., 1974—, pres. parent co. Marcor, Inc., 1972—; dir. Pennwalt Corp., Nortrust Corp. Mem. Pi Kappa Alpha. Clubs: Chicago, Indian Hill, Old Elm, Economic, Commercial. Home: 1207 Whitebridge Hill Winnetka IL 60093 Office: 918 Chicago Ave Chicago IL 60611

DONNELLEY, JAMES RUSSELL, printing co. exec.; b. Chgo., June 18, 1935; s. Elliott and Ann (Steinwedell) D.; B.A., Dartmouth Coll., 1957; M.B.A., U. Chgo., 1962; m. Nina Louis Herrmann, Apr. 11, 1980; children—Niel J., Nicole C. With R.R. Donnelley & Sons Co., Chgo., 1962—, v.p., 1974—, dir., 1976—, dir. fin. and electronic data sales div., 1971—. Pres., Chgo. Youth Centers, 1968-71; bd. dirs. Children's Meml. Hosp., Lake Forest Coll. Goodman Theatre, Barker Found., Latin Sch. of Chgo., 1970-76; mem. U. Chgo.'s Library Vis. Com.; bd. dirs. Chgo. Planetarium, 1965-70. Served with U.S. Navy, 1957-60. Clubs: Chgo., Commonwealth, Chgo. Yacht, Met., Tavern; Brook, Links, India House, Wall Street, Econ. (N.Y.C.); Glenview Country, Caxton, Grolier, Quadrangle. Home: 1040 Lake Shore Dr Chicago IL 60611 Office: 2223 S Martin Luther King Dr Chicago IL 60616

DONNELLY, PATRICK RAYMOND, fin. services co. exec.; b. Kincaid, Sask., Can., Sept. 28, 1942; s. Fredrick Raymond and Ruby Irene (Fizell) D.; student bus. adminstrn. Drake U., 1969; m. Donna Lynne McLeod, Aug. 25, 1962; children—Tracey Lynne, Thomas Patrick. Profl. hockey player N.Y. Rangers, 1960-69; regional claims mgr., div. sales mgr. Foremost Ins. Co., Portland, Oreg., 1969-75; owner, exec. v.p., pres. Fin. Ins. Corp., Seattle, 1976—. Republican. Roman Catholic. Home: 8518 SE 80th St Mercer Island WA 98040

DONNER, DONALD FRASER, aluminum co. exec.; b. Waseca, Minn., Mar. 25, 1930; s. Donald Fountain and Ione Bernice D.; B.S.E.E., U. Calif. at Berkeley, 1952; m. Barbara Jean Becker, June 8, 1958; children—Diana, Donara, Deborah, Devin. Elec. engr. Rheem Mfg. Co., San Pablo, Calif., 1952-56; asst. mgr. Kaiser Aluminum Co., Oakland, Calif., 1957-58; plant mgr. Hunter Engr. Co., Riverside, Calif., 1958-63; mgr. Fruehauf Corp., Decatur, Ala., 1968-75; v.p., gen. mgr. Alumax Bldg. Products, Riverside, 1975—. Mem. Calif. Bd. Registars Profl. Engrs. Mem. U. Calif. at Berkeley Alumni Assn. Decatur C. of C., (dir. 1969, v.p. 1973, chmn. edn. com. 1970-72). Presbyterian. Club: Kiwanis (dir. 1972). Address: Alumax Bldg Prdts Box 5350 Riverside CA 92517

DONOHUE, CARROLL JOHN, lawyer; b. St. Louis, June 24, 1917; s. Thomas M. and Florence (Klefisch) D.; A.B., Washington U., St. Louis, 1939, LL.B., magna cum laude, 1939; m. Juanita Maire, Jan. 4, 1943 (div. July 3, 1973); children—Patricia D. Stevens, Christine D. Smith, Deborah Lee; m. 2d, Barbara Lounsbury, Dec. 29, 1978. Admitted to Mo. bar, 1939; asso. law firm Hay and Flanagan, St. Louis, 1939-42, law firm Salkey and Jones, St. Louis, 1946-49; partner law firm Husch, Eppenberger, Donohue, Elson and Cornfeld, St. Louis, 1949—; also writer, lectr. Mayor, Olivette, Mo., 1953-56. Campaign chmn. A.R.C. St. Louis County, Mo., 1950; mem. adv. com. Child Welfare, St. Louis, 1952-55, exec. com. Slum Clearance, 1949, bond issue com, 1955, St. Louis County Bond Issue screening and supervisory coms., 1955-61, county citizen's com. for better law enforcement, 1953-56; chmn. com. on immigration policy, 1954-56. Chmn., County Bd. Election Commrs., St. Louis County, Mo., 1960-64. Served to lt. USNR, 1942-46, P.T. boats; PTO. Decorated Bronze Star, Navy and M.C. medal. Mem. Mo. Bar (bd. govs. 1948-50, 1952, 1954, 1956; chmn. ann. meeting), Am., St. Louis (pres. 1954-55, v.p. 1948-49, treas. 1951-54) bar assns., Order of Coif, Omicron Delta Kappa, Sigma Phi Epsilon, Delta Theta Phi. Clubs: Mo. Athletic (St. Louis); Creve Coeur Racquet. Office: 100 N Broadway St Louis MO 63102

DONOVAN, HEDLEY WILLIAMS, journalist; b. Brainerd, Minn., May 24, 1914; s. Percy Williams and Alice (Dougan) D.; A.B. magna cum laude, U. Minn., 1934; B.A., Oxford U. (Rhodes scholar), 1936; Litt.D., Pomona Coll., Boston U., lft. Holyoke Coll.; L.H.D., Southwestern at Memphis, Rochester U., Transylvania U.; LL.D., Carnegie-Mellon U., Lehigh U., Allegheny Coll.; m. Dorothy Hannon, Oct. 18, 1941 (dec. 1978); children—Peter Williams, Helen Welles, Mark Vicars. Reporter, Washington Post, 1937-42; writer, editor Fortune mag., N.Y.C., 1945-51; asso. mng. editor, 1951-53, mng. editor, 1953-59; editorial dir. Time, Inc., 1959-64, editor-in-chief, 1964-79, dir., 1962-79; cons., 1979—; sr. adv. to Pres. U.S., 1979-80; dir. Time-Life Books, Washington Star, Merrill Lynch. Trustee N.Y. U., Mt. Holyoke Coll., Ford Found., Nat. Humanities Center, Carnegie Endowment for Internat. Peace. Served to lt. comdr. USNR, 1942-45. Recipient Outstanding Achievement award U. Minn. Alumni, 1956. Fellow Am. Acad. Arts and Scis.; mem. Council Fgn. Relations (dir.), Phi Beta Kappa, Delta Upsilon. Clubs: University, Manhasset Bay Yacht, Century, Sands Point Golf; Met., 1925 F St. (Washington). Home: Harbor Rd Sands Point NY 11050 also 190 E 72d St New York NY 10021 Office: Time Inc Time and Life Bldg Rockefeller Center New York NY 10020

DONOVAN, JAMES ROBERT, bus. equipment co. exec.; b. Wichita, Kans., Apr. 11, 1932; s. Karl Genevay and Louise (Silcott) D.; A.B., Harvard, 1954, M.B.A., 1956; m. Ottilie Schreiber, July 2, 1955; children—Amy Louise, Robert Silcott. Mgr. sales adminstrn., market research Hickok, Inc., Rochester, N.Y., 1956-59, regional sales mgr., 1959-62, asst. nat. sales mgr., 1963-65; group program mgr. Xerox Corp., Stamford, Conn., 1965-68, mktg. mgr. spl. products, 1968-70, mgr. copier products, 1970-72, dir. corp. pricing and competitive activity, 1972-78, dir. corp. mktg. strategy and planning, 1978—. Vice pres. Family Service, Rochester, 1971-72; dir. Family and Children's Services, Stamford, 1972-79; dir. Rochester Sales Execs. Club, 1966-71; mem. mktg. adv. bd. Columbia U. Bus. Sch., 1978—; exec. com. United Way of New Canaan. Mem. Assn. Harvard Alumni (dir. 1978—). Clubs: Oak Hill Country, Harvard (pres. Rochester 1971-72, pres. Fairfield County 1976-78), Harvard Bus. Sch. (pres. Rochester 1972, chmn. Westchester/Fairfield 1973-74); New Canaan (Conn.) Field; Woodway Country (Darien, Conn.). Home: 111 Glen Dr New Canaan CT 06840 Office: Xerox Corporation Stamford CT 06904

DONOVAN, JOHN JOSEPH, JR., real estate broker and developer; b. Oakland, Calif., Mar. 10, 1916; s. John Joseph and May Ella (Coogan) D.; Ph.B., Santa Clara U., 1938; student Stanford U., 1938-40, Harvard U., 1942; m. Margaret Mary Abel, June 7, 1941; children—John Joseph III, Mary Margaret, Patricia Anne, Eileen Marie, Marian Gertrude Corrigan, George Edwin, Michael Sean. Sales mgr. Universal Window Co., Berkeley, Calif., 1940-41, v.p., 1946-49, pres., chmn. bd., 1949-66; real estate broker and developer, 1966—. Mem. aluminum window mfrs. adv. com. NPA, 1951-52; chmn. pace setters com., commerce and industry div. Alameda County United Crusade, 1961. Mem. Republican small businessmen's com., Alameda County, Calif., 1946. Bd. dirs. Providence Hosp., 1970-80, also Found., 1980—; bd. dirs. Apostleship of the Sea Center, 1968—, Hanna Boy's Center, Sonoma County, 1976-79; mem. Oakland Mayor's Internat. Welcoming Center, 1972-77; trustee, treas. Serra Internat. Found., 1980—. Served from ensign to lt. Supply Corps, USNR, 1940-46; in U.S.S. General Ballou; capt. Res. Named knight St. Gregory the Gt., Pope John XXIII, 1962 (pres. Oakland diocese 1970—), Knight of Malta, 1974; decorated Cross of Comdr. Merit, 1978. Mem. Western Archtl. Metal Mfrs. Assn. San Francisco (dir. 1956—, exec. com. 1958—, pres. 1959-60), Aluminum Window Mfrs. Assn. N.Y.C. (dir. 1950-58, 1st v.p. 1955-56), Newcomen Soc. N. Am., Naval Order U.S., Navy Supply Corps Assn. San Francisco Bay Area (2d v.p. 1970—), Father Junipero Serra 250th Anniversary Assn. (v.p., sec.), Internat. Council Shopping Centers, AIM (pres.'s council), Naval Res. Assn., Western Assn. Knights of Malta (chmn. admissions com. 1975—, dir. 1976—). Roman Catholic. Clubs: Berkeley Serra (charter mem.); Comml. (San Francisco); Monterey Peninsula Country (Pebble Beach, Calif.); Claremont Country (Oakland, Calif.). Home: 2 Lincolnshire Dr Oakland CA 94618 Office: PO Box 11100 Oakland CA 94611

DONOVAN, JOHN LEO, banker; b. Columbus, Ohio, June 2, 1936; s. Leo Daniel and Lucy Elizabeth (Bueter) D.; A.B. in History, Xavier U., 1958; postgrad. Stonier Grad. Sch. Banking, 1965-67; m. M. Michele Kane, June 20, 1964; children—Molly Marie, Abigail Suzanne, Emily Katherine. Bank examiner Office of Comptroller of Currency, Cleve., 1960-66, asst. chief nat. banks, Washington, 1967-68, regional adminstr., Boston, 1969-73; exec. v.p. Casco No. Corp., Portland, Maine, 1973—; v.p., treas. Casco Bank & Trust Co., Portland, 1976—. Mem. Fin. Commn. Topsham (Maine), 1974-79, chmn., 1978-79. Served with U.S. Army, 1958-60. Mem. Maine Bankers Assn. (dir., officer), Am. Bankers Assn. (regulatory relations task force). Roman Catholic. Home: 11 McKeen St Brunswick ME 04011 Office: One Monument Sq Portland ME 04101

DONOVAN, JOHN VINCENT, bus. and tech. transfer cons.; b. Chgo., May 13, 1924; s. Timothy Vincent and Mable Elizabeth (Hederman) D.; student Harvard U. Bus. Sch., 1944-45; A.B., DePauw U., 1947; m. Patricia Helen Hasselhorn, Dec. 29, 1950; children—James D., Timothy J., Walter C. Mem. adminstrv. staff Swift do Brazil, 1947-50; asst. treas. Mid State Corp. mobile homes mfg. co., Union City, Mich., 1951-55; sales mgr. Dole Corp., Honolulu, 1958-61; gen. mgr. Bailey Corp., cosmetics co., Chgo., 1955-58; pres. Intercon Research Assos. Ltd., Evanston, Ill., 1961—. Bd. dirs. Ind. Voters Ill., 1971. Served with USNR, World War II. Mem. Licensing Execs. Soc., AAAS, Assn. Corp. Growth, World Future Soc., German Am. C. of C., French-Am. C. of C. Clubs: Chgo. Athletic Assn., Mich. Shores, Palisades Park Country. Home: 431 Laurel Ave Wilmette IL 60091 Office: 1219 Howard St Evanston IL 60202

DONOVAN, PETER MORSE, investment co. exec.; b. Washington, Mar. 1, 1943; s. James Alport and Abbie Dagget (Morse) D.; B.A. in Econs., Goddard Coll., 1965; m. Alexandria Kujan, Nov. 1, 1969; 1 son, Aaron. Cash clk. Jones, Kreeger & Co., Washington, 1965-66; investment and econ. analyst Wright Investors' Service, Bridgeport, Conn., 1966-68; mng. editor investment publs., 1968-69, asst. v.p., 1969-71, v.p., 1971-74, sr. v.p., 1974—; dir., v.p. Wright Investment Shares, Inc., Bridgeport, 1975—; dir. Winthrop Corp. Mem. council of vis. fellows Coll. Bus. and Public Mgmt., U. Bridgeport. Mem. Fin. Analysis Fedn., N.Y. (sr), Hartford socs. security analysts. Home: 9 Gray Ln Westport CT 06880 Office: 10 Middle St Bridgeport CT 06604

DOOHAN, MICHAEL EARLE, apparel mfg. co. exec.; b. Fredericton, N.B., Can., Apr. 8, 1930; s. Thomas Earle and Mary Cathleen (Sullivan) D.; B.S., Boston Coll., 1953; M.B.A., Northeastern U., 1957; m. Winifred Anne Drobile, Apr. 11, 1959; children—Joseph Mark, Earle William, Maura Anne, Megan Agnes. Quality control mgr. Container Corp. Am., Boston, 1953-58; plant mgr. Europa Carton, Dusseldorf, Germany, 1958-59; sales engr. Dewey & Almy, div. W.R. Grace, Cambridge, Mass., 1959-63; gen. mgr. folding carton div. Boise Cascade, Spokane, Wash., 1963-68, corrugated div., West Memphis, Ark., 1968; pres., mgr. Kathleen Louise Mfg. Co., Inc., Spokane, 1968—. Bd. dirs. United Crusade, 1966; bd. regents Gonzaga U., 1980-81; trustee Fort Wright Coll., Spokane; chmn. bd. dirs. Sacred Heart Med. Center, Spokane, 1979-80. Mem. C. of C. (trustee 1964-65, 70-74). Clubs: Serra (pres. 1972-74, dist. gov. 1977-78), Spokane, City, Executive (Spokane). Home: E 10721 20th Ave Spokane WA 99206 Office: N 2726 Monroe St Spokane WA 99205

DOOLEY, DELMER JOHN, found. exec.; b. Ramona, S.D., Mar. 15, 1920; s. Frank M. and Theresa (DeRungs) D.; B.S., S.D. State U., 1948; M.S., Colo. State U., 1952; Ed.D., U. Mo., 1964; m. Thalia Elma Doty, June 12, 1952; children—Douglas John, Alan Patrick. Vocat. agr. instr., Platte, S.D., 1948-53, Lakeview, Oreg., 1953-55; agrl. advisor Near East Found., Iran, 1955-59, area dir., Jordan, 1959-61, party chief, Korea, 1962-63, overseas program dir., 1963-64, exec. dir., N.Y.C., 1964—. Exec. bd. Morris-Sussex (N.J.) council Boy Scouts Am., 1967—, dist. chmn., 1969-71, v.p., 1978—; mem. com. on continuing edn. Hanover (N.J.) Pub. Schs. Served with USAF, 1942-45. Decorated Air medal with 3 oak leaf clusters; medal of Independence, King Hussein of Jordan; recipient Silver Beaver award Boy Scouts Am. Mem. Middle East Inst., Am. Council Vol. Agys. (exec. com. 1965—, treas. 1970-75, chmn. 1981—), Soc. Internat. Devel., Internat. Platform Assn., Am. Legion, Phi Delta Kappa. Roman Catholic. Home: 116 DeForest Ave East Hanover NJ 07936 Office: 29 Broadway New York NY 10006

DOOLEY, DONALD EDWIN, fin. officer; b. Newton, Kans., Feb. 19, 1915; s. I.E. and Loretta (English) D.; B.S. in Bus., U. Kans., 1936; postgrad. Northwestern U., 1936-41; m. Helen Gordon Dodds, Aug. 29, 1941; children—John Edwin, Mary Frances (Mrs. Lowell D. Larsen), Elizabeth Ann (Mrs. Richard F. Schmalz), Margaret Caryl. Accountant, Western Electric Co., Chgo., 1936-38; underwriter Western dept. Hartford Fire Ins. Co., Chgo., 1938-39; systems designer and chief auditor Wis. Electric Power Co., Milw., 1939-49; chief auditor Weyerhaeuser Co., Tacoma, 1949-65, dir. gen. office and plantsite services, 1965-73, fin. dir. Indonesian subsidiaries, Jakarta, 1974-76; treas. Am. Fed. Savs. & Loan Assn., Tacoma, 1976-80, v.p. and treas., 1980—. Served to 1st lt. AUS. 1942-46. Recipient Bradford Cadmus Meml. award, 1969. Mem. Inst. Internal Auditors (pres. 1963-64), Am. Mgmt. Assn. (gen. services planning Council 1971-74), Delta Sigma Pi. Republican. Presbyterian. Home: 8708 Zircon SW Tacoma WA 98498 Office: 960 Pacific Ave Tacoma WA 98402

DOOLING, MICHAEL WILLIAM, ins. and securities co. exec., ins. agt.; b. Grand Junction, Colo., Nov. 30, 1932; s. Paul William and Lena Maude (Shoening) D.; B.S., U. Denver, 1954; M.B.A., U. Pa., 1958; m. Judith A. Bertolet, Feb. 21, 1958; children—Cynthia, Paige, Lane. Asst. mgr. Mut. of N.Y., Spokane, Wash and Sacramento, 1958-62; asst. mgr., field v.p. Exec. Life Ins. Co., San Francisco, 1962-65, 66-69; founder, pres. Crown Financial Services, San Rafael, Calif., 1970—. Mem. C.L.U.'s Assn., Soc. Benefit Adminstrs., Lambda Chi Alpha. Club: Rafael Racquet. Home: 55 Twin Oaks Rd San Rafael CA 94901 Office: 30 N San Pedro San Rafael CA 94903

DOOTSON, DAVID VICTOR, investment co. exec.; b. Chgo., Feb. 17, 1937; s. Paul Peter and Victoria G. (Petterson) D.; B.A., Lake Forest Coll., 1959. With City Nat. Bank & Trust, Chgo., 1960, Continental Ill. Nat. Bank, Chgo., 1961; with Allstate Ins. Co., Chgo., 1962-69; asst. treas. Allstate Investment Mgmt. Co., Allstate Enterprises Fund Sales, Inc. and Allstate Enterprises Stock Fund, Inc., Chgo., 1968-69; exec. dir. investments Sears, Roebuck & Co., Savings and Profit Sharing Fund, Chgo., 1970-75, chmn. investment com., 1975-76; dir., pres. Sears Investment Mgmt. Co., 1976—; dir. Sears Bank & Trust Co., Chgo., 1971—. Served with USMC, 1959-60. Chartered financial analyst. Mem. Inst. Chartered Financial Analysts, Investment Analysts Soc. of Chgo. Clubs: Met., Econ. (Chgo.). Office: Sears Investment Mgmt Co Sears Tower Chicago IL 60684

DORAN, ELMER, indsl. textile co. exec.; b. Eddystone, Pa., July 4, 1925; s. Joseph L. and Genevieve (Price) D.; student U. Fla., 1943-44; B.B.A., Pa. Mil. Coll., 1949; m. Ann M. Moran, Oct. 29, 1955; children—Patrick Joseph, Patricia Ann, Robert John. Accountant E. I. DuPont de Nemours & Co., 1949-57; various mgtm. positions Okonite Co., Passaic, N.J., 1957-61; sec.-treas. R.D. Wood Co., Florence, N.J., 1961-63; mdse. controller Popular Mdse. Co., Passaic, N.J., 1963-66; dir. finance and operations Lesney Products Corp., 1966-68, v.p. finance, 1968-71; v.p. finance and adminstrn. Haskell Pitts. Inc., Verona, Pa., 1971-74; pres., chief exec. officer Indutex Inc., McKeesport, Pa., 1974—. Served with AUS, 1943-45. Decorated Bronze Star, Purple Heart with 2 oak leaf clusters. Mem. Nat. Assn. Accountants, Am. Mgmt. Assn., Canvas Products Assn. Internat., Mon-yough C. of C. Club: Rotary. Home: 1112 Woodhill Dr Gibsonia PA 15044 Office: 528 Eden Park Blvd Ave McKeesport PA 15132

DORDELMAN, WILLIAM FORSYTH, food co. exec.; b. Glen Ridge, N.J., Oct. 18, 1940; s. Wilbert E. and Dorothy F. (Forsyth) D.; B.A. in Econs., U. Va., 1962; M.B.A., Harvard U., 1964; m. Barbara Ann Gaddis, Sept. 16, 1959; children—Dorothy Ann, William Edward, Patricia Lynne, Lauren Forsyth. With Gen. Foods Co., White Plains, N.Y., 1965—, advt. and merchandising mgr. Birds Eye div., 1972-73, gen. mgr. main meal strategic bus. unit, 1973-77, v.p., 1977—, pres. food products div., 1977-80, group v.p., 1980—; dir. Bailey & Alling Lumber Co. Bd. dirs. Mid-Fairfield Youth Hockey Assn., 1973-77, St. Vincent's Hosp. Mem. Am. Mgmt. Assn., Am. Mktg. Assn., Young Pres.' Orgn. Episcopalian. Clubs: Weeburn Country (Darien); Westchester/Fairfield County Harvard Bus. Sch. (dir. 1978—). Home: 9 Woodley Rd Darien CT 06820 Office: 250 North St White Plains NY 10605

DOREMUS, JOHN, radio and TV producer; b. Sapulpa, Okla., Aug. 3, 1933; s. John W. and Arie D.; B.A., U. Tulsa, 1954; m. Joellen Casler, Dec. 27, 1954; children—David, Frederick, Deidre, Paul. Announcer, newscaster Sta. KOME, Tulsa, 1951-52, Sta. KRMG, Tulsa, 1952-53, Sta. KVOO, Tulsa, 1953-54, Sta. WIND, Chgo., 1957-59, NBC AM and TV, Chgo., 1959-65, Sta. WAIT AM, Chgo., 1965-71, Sta. WGN AM, Chgo., 1971-73; founder, pres. John Doremus Inc., Chgo., 1965—; lectr. Northwestern U. Chmn., Roycemore Prep. Sch., 1967-69; mem. adv. bd. Bedside Network, 1976—; chmn. Chgo. Cerebral Palsy Drive, 1963; mem. bd. Dialogue for Blind, 1977—. Served with USMCR, 1950-51, USAF, 1954-57. Recipient Distinguished Alumnus award U. Tulsa, 1973, Chgo. Outstanding Radio Personality award Acad. Radio Arts, 1967. Mem. Chgo. C. of C., Nat. Assn. Broadcasters, Air Force Assn. Episcopalian. Clubs: Tavern, Chgo. Unlimited, Execs., Rotary, Variety. Office: 1801 John Hancock Center Chicago IL 60611

DORF, RICHARD CARL, elec. engr., educator, univ. dean; b. Bronx, N.Y., Dec. 27, 1933; s. William Carl and Marian (Fraser) D.; B.S., Clarkson Coll. Tech., 1955; M.S., U. Colo., 1957; Ph.D., U.S. Naval Postgrad. Sch., 1961; m. Joy H. MacDonald, June 15, 1957; children—Christine Joy, Renee Anne. Prof. elec. engring. U. Santa Clara (Calif.), 1963-69; v.p. Ohio U., Athens, 1969-72; prof. elec. and computer engring. U. Calif., Davis, 1972—, dean extended learning, 1972—; dir. Boyd & Fraser Pub. Co.; pres. KYLO Radio Inc., Davis, 1978—. Bd. dirs. Central Calif. TV-Channel 6. Am. Council on Edn. fellow, 1968-69. Mem. IEEE, Coll. Engring. Mgmt., Am. Soc. for Engring. Edn. Club: Rotary (dir.) (Davis). Author: Energy, Resources and Policy, 1979. Home: 1125 Bucknell Dr Davis CA 95616 Office: U Calif Davis CA 95616

DORFMAN, MYRON HERBERT, petroleum engr.; b. Shreveport, La., July 3, 1927; s. Samuel Yandell and Rose (Gold) D.; B.S., U. Tex., 1950, M.S., 1972, Ph.D., 1975; m. Bess Rich, June 29, 1947; children—Shelley Fonda (Mrs. Jeffrey Roberts), Cynthia Renee. Geologist, engr. Sklar Oil Co., Shreveport, 1950-56, mgr. prodn. and devel., 1957-59, partner, 1958-59; owner Dorfman Oil Properties, Shreveport, 1950-71, Austin, Tex., 1971—; prof. petroleum engring., chmn. dept. U. Tex., Austin, 1976—, dir. Center for Energy Studies, 1977—. Pres. Shreveport Community Council, 1966; mem. bd. La. Gov.'s Com. for Employment Handicapped, 1966-68; bd. dirs. La. Youth Opportunity Center, Shreveport, 1966-71, A.R.C., Caddo Parish, La., 1964-71; pres. La. Mental Health Center, Shreveport, 1967. Served with USNR, 1945-46; PTO, ATO. Recipient medal State of Israel, 1963. Registered profl. engr., Tex.; Disting. lectr. Soc. Petroleum Engrs., 1979-80. Fellow Geol. Soc. Am.; mem. Am. Geophys. Union, Nat. Acad. Scis., Am. Assn. Petroleum Geologists, Soc. Profl. Well Log Analysts, AIME, Shreveport Geol. Soc., Petroleum Club Shreveport, Shreveport Jewish Fedn. (pres. 1967), Pi Epsilon Tau. Club: Shreveport Skeet (pres. 1964). Contbr. articles to profl. jours. Home: 770 E Bee Cave Rd Austin TX 78746 Office: Dept Petroleum Engring U Tex Austin TX 78712

DORFMAN, PAUL MICHAEL, banker, lawyer; b. Chgo., Mar. 16, 1939; s. Isaiah S. and Lillian May (Schley) D.; A.B., Princeton, 1961; J.D., Yale, 1964; m. Janet Ruth Vogel, June 18, 1961; children—Judith Ann, Jeffrey Harris, Eric Matthew, Benjamin Kirk. Admitted to Ill. bar, 1964; atty. firm Mayer, Brown & Platt, Chgo., 1964-69; v.p. Continental Ill. Venture Capital (affiliate Continental Ill. Nat. Bank), Chgo., 1969-71; exec. v.p. JMB Realty Corp., Chgo., 1971-73; v.p. head spl. loans sect., then utilities and transp. sect. San Francisco corp. service office Bank of Am., 1973-77, head world banking client info. services dept., 1977-79, head strategic planning staff world banking div., 1979-80, head specialized industries for Europe, Middle East and Africa, div. credit adminstrn., 1980—. Mem. Phi Beta Kappa. Office: Bank of America 25 Cannon St London EC4P 4HN England

DORMANN, HENRY O., publishing exec.; b. N.Y.C., Mar. 5, 1932; s. Henry Maroni and Ivara (Soberg) D.; m. Alice Andreasen, Apr. 7, 1958; children—Kaari, Kristi. Chmn. bd. Nat. Enquirer, 1971-72; chmn. Internat. Bd. Indsl. Advisors, 1964—; pres., editor-in-chief Servicio de Information Panamericana, N.Y.C., 1966—; chmn. Haitian Devel. Corp., 1969—, Sabador, Inc. (Liberia), 1973—; pres. U.S. Tech. Devel. Co., 1969-70; pres., editor in chief Holiday Mag., 1976-77; pres., editor-in-chief Leaders Mag. Mem. adv. council Joint Legis. Com. on Met. and Regional Areas Study N.Y. State, 1969-72; chmn. N.Y. State Assembly Council on Econ. Devel., 1972—; mem. assn. bd. Mcht. Marine Acad., 1969—; founder Inst. for Study of Presidency; active mem. internat. supreme council Order DeMolay. Served with USCG. Home: 988 Fifth Ave New York NY 10021 Office: 59 E 54th St New York NY 10022

DORON, ZVI JAY, mfg. co. exec.; b. Jerusalem, Israel, Feb. 11, 1935; s. Paul Herman and Elizabeth (Kirschner) D.; immigrated to U.S., 1971, naturalized, 1977; B.Sc. with first class honors, U. London, 1958, M.Sc., 1959; m. Galia Ben-Gal, Nov. 25, 1956; children—Opher, Yael, Uri; m. 2d, Beverly Bloomfield Weisman, May 16, 1976. Engr. Israel Atomic Energy Commn., 1958-63, shift supr., 1963-65, reactor operations supt., 1965-66; with Nordostschweiz. Kraftwerke AG, Switzerland, 1966-70, sr. rep. in U.S., 1966-68, dep. head Nuclear div., 1968-70; with Westinghouse Electric Corp., Pitts., 1970—, cons., 1970-71, dir. tech. coordination, Brussels, 1971-72, dir. projects dept., Brussels, 1972-74, mgr. projects integration and strategic planning PWR Systems div., Pitts., 1974-76, mgr. strategic planning, uranium resources, Pitts., 1976-77, dir. planning and tech., uranium resources, 1977-80, sr. cons. corp. planning, 1980—. Served with Israeli Army, 1952-54. Israel Atomic Energy Commn. grad. study fellow, 1958-59. Contbr. articles in field to profl. jours. Home: 2333 Marbury Rd Pittsburgh PA 15221 Office: Westinghouse Electric Corp Westinghouse Bldg Pittsburgh PA 15222

DORRANCE, JOHN THOMPSON, JR., food processing exec.; b. Cinnaminson, N.J., Feb. 7, 1919; s. John Thompson and Ethel (Mallinckrodt) D.; grad. St. George's Sch., Newport, R.I., 1937; A.B., Princeton, 1941; m. Jean Fergusson, Nov. 19, 1966 (dec.); children—John Thompson III, Bennett, Mary Alice; m. 2d, Diana R. Dripps, Apr. 26, 1979; stepchildren—Keith Bassett, Langdon Mannion, Robert D. Dripps, 3d, Susan Stauffer. With Campbell Soup Co., 1946—, asst. treas., 1950-55, asst. to pres., 1955-62, chmn., 1962—; pres. Campbell Soup Fund, 1953-62; dir. Carter-Hawley-Hale, Los Angeles, Morgan Guaranty Trust Co. N.Y., J.P. Morgan & Co., Inc.; trustee Penn Mut. Life Ins. Co., Estate of John T. Dorrance. Trustee Ch. Farm Sch., Paoli, Pa., Dorrance Found., St. George's Sch., Hampton Inst., Inst. Med. Research, Ducks Unlimited; bd. mgrs. Wistar Inst. Served as capt. AUS, World War II. Republican. Home: Gladwyne PA 19035 Office: Campbell Pl Camden NJ 08101

DORSEY, DOLORES FLORENCE, mfg. co. exec.; b. Buffalo, May 26, 1928; d. William G. and Florence R. Dorsey; B.S. in Bus. Adminstrn., Coll. St. Elizabeth, Convent Sta., N.J., 1950. With Aerojet-Gen. Corp., 1953—, asst. to treas./mgr. cash mgmt., El Monte, Calif., 1972-74, asst. corp. treas., 1974-79, treas., 1979—. Mem. Cash Mgmt. Group So. Calif., Fin. Execs. Inst., Treasurers Club. Republican. Roman Catholic. Club: Lomas Santa Fe Country (Solana Beach, Calif.). Office: Aerojet Gen Corp 10300 N Torrey Pines Rd La Jolla CA 92037

DORSEY, JASPER NEWTON, syndicated newspaper and mag. columnist, educator; b. Marietta, Ga., Jan. 19, 1913; s. John Tucker and Annie (Coryell) D.; A.B., U. Ga., 1936, postgrad. in law, 1935-36; m. Callender Weltner, Oct. 16, 1937; children—Sally (Mrs. William Danner), John Tucker (dec.). With So. Bell Tel. & Tel. Co., Inc., 1937-61, 68-78, v.p., chief exec. Ga. operations, Atlanta, 1968-78; mgr. govt. relations AT&T, Washington, 1962-68; contbg. editor Sky mag.; adj. prof. mgmt. Coll. Bus. Adminstrn., U. Ga.; dir. Fulton Nat. Corp., Bank of South, N.A., Atlanta. Bd. dirs. Research Atlanta; mem. adv. bd. Salvation Army, Atlanta, 1970—; former sight-saving chmn. Ga.; former bd. dirs. Ga. Safety Council, West Paces Ferry Hosp., Atlanta Boys Club, Kidney Found. Ga.; mem. Ga. World Congress Center; chmn. U. Ga. Found., Atlanta; charter mem. Pres.'s adv. bd. Med. Coll. Ga.; nat. adv. bd. Gt. Am. Achievement Program; trustee Ga. Student Ednl. Fund, Athens; past bd. visitors Emory U., Atlanta; chmn. Richard B. Russell Found., Atlanta; past chmn. adv. bd. Henry Grady Sch. Journalism, U. Ga., Athens, charter mem. advisory bd. Coll. Bus. Adminstrn. Served to lt. col. inf., AUS, 1941-46. Recipient Blue Key award U. Ga., 1967, Outstanding Contbn. to U. Ga. award, 1969, Alumni Merit award, 1970; named Georgian of Year, Ga. Assn. Broadcasters, 1971; Cobb County Citizen of Year, C. of C.-Marietta Daily Jour., 1973; Outstanding Alumnus of Year, U. Ga. Sch. Journalism, 1976, Atlanta Salesman of Year, 1977, William Booth award Salvation Army, 1977, numerous others. Mem. Ga. (hon. chmn., past chmn. bd., past pres.), Atlanta (past dir.) chambers commerce, Washington Nat. Press Club, Army-Navy Club Washington, U. Ga. Alumni Assn. (nat. pres. 1967-69, chmn. bd. 1969-73), Newcomen Soc. N.Am., Soc. Colonial Wars, Blue Key, Sphinx, Gridiron, Greek Horsemen, Soc. Profl. Journalists, Sigma Delta Chi, Beta Gamma Sigma, Phi Kappa Phi, Omicron Delta Kappa, Sigma Iota Epsilon, Phi Delta Theta. Presbyn. (elder). Clubs: Peachtree Golf, Piedmont Driving, Commerce (Atlanta); President's (U. Ga.). Office: 675 W Peachtree St NE Suite 533 PO Box 3231 Atlanta GA 30302

DORSEY, JEREMIAH EDMUND, pharm. co. exec.; b. Worcester, Mass., Oct. 15, 1944; s. Jeremiah Edmund and Mary Theresa Dorsey; A.B., Assumption Coll., Worcester, 1966; M.B.A., Fairleigh Dickinson U., 1978; m. Nadia S. Vidach, Dec. 6, 1970; children—Todd Edmund, Jaime Erin, Megan Elizabeth. With Johnson & Johnson, New Brunswick, N.J., 1970—, nat. indsl. engring. mgr., 1975-76, supt. ops. and maintenance, 1976—; dir. mfg. and engring. Johnson & Johnson Dental Products Co. Active, N.J. Commn. for Discharge Up-grade, Appalachian Trail Conf.; mem. alumni bd. dirs. Assumption Coll.; mem. adv. com. U. P.R. Sch. of Pharmacy; mem. U.S. senate mil. acad. selection com. Served with U.S. Army, 1966-69; Vietnam. Decorated Bronze Star with 2 oak leaf clusters, Purple Heart with 4 oak leaf clusters, Army Commendation medal, Air medal with oak leaf cluster; Medal of Honor, Gallantry Cross (Vietnam); named Mgr. of Yr., Johnson & Johnson, 1974-75. Mem. Sierra Club, Spl. Forces Assn., Smithsonian Instn. (asso.), DAV, Soc. First Div. Roman Catholic. Clubs: K.C.; Johnson & Johnson Mgmt. Editor: Spl. Forces Assn. News. Home: 10 Eastern Dr Kendall Park NJ 08824 Office: 20 Lake Dr East Windsor NJ 08520

DORSKIND, ALBERT ALAN, motion picture exec.; b. N.Y.C., Mar. 26, 1922; s. Benjamin and Rose (Freedman) D.; B.A. with distinction, Cornell U., 1943, J.D. with distinction, 1946; m. Suzanne Mayer, Nov. 29, 1951; children—James Alan, Dorothy Ellen Dorskind Levey. Law clk. Circuit Ct. Appeals, Washington, other fed. govt. positions, 1948-50; atty. Paramount Pictures, 1950-52; with MCA Inc., Universal City, Calif., 1952—, treas., corp. v.p.; pres. MCA Devel. Co.; dir. Environ. Industries, Inc.; mem. Calif. Motion Picture Devel. Com., Los Angeles Film Devel. Com. Bd. dirs. Greater Los Angeles Visitors and Conv. Bur., Indsl. Assn. San Fernando Valley, Ralph M. Parsons Found.; bd. dirs., pres. Los Angeles Hdqrs. City Assn.; mem. Calif. Adv. Council on Econ. and Bus. Devel.; mem. Los Angeles County Econ. Devel. Council. Served to lt. (j.g.) USN, 1943-46. Recipient award for outstanding achievement in public affairs Coro Found., spl. award for service to Mexican-Am. community Nosotros. Club: Hillcrest Country. Office: 100 Universal City Plaza Universal City CA 91608

DOSTER, JEROME BROWN, airline exec.; b. Macon, Ga., Mar. 8, 1950; s. Norman Brown and Lily Lorraine (Crum) D.; B.S., Ga. Inst. Tech., 1973; M.B.A., Tulane U., 1975. Indsl. engr. Am. Airlines, Inc., N.Y.C., 1975-79, fin. analyst div. mktg. automation, Arlington, Tex., 1979—; fin. cons. to N.Y.C. Ballet, 1978-79, Opera Orch. of N.Y., 1978-79. Mem. Ga. Inst. Tech. Alumni Assn., Tulane U. Alumni Assn., Chi Phi, Omega Trust Assn. Methodist. Club: N.Y. Athletic. Home: 3610 Travis St Dallas TX 75204 Office: Am Airlines Mktg Automation 601 Ryan Plaza Arlington TX 76011

DOTO, PAUL JEROME, accountant; b. Newark, July 22, 1917; s. Anthony and Edith Margaret (Mascellaro) D.; B.S., N.Y. U., 1947. Accountant, exec. asst. John Hewitt Foundry Co., East Newark, N.J., 1941-43; accountant S. D. Leidesdorf & Co., N.Y.C., 1947-56; C.P.A., Peat Marwick Mitchell & Co., N.Y.C., 1956-64; asst. controller Lincoln Center for the Performing Arts Inc., N.Y.C. 1964-69; controller Seton Hall U., South Orange, N.J., 1969-74; cons. Controller's Office City N.Y., 1966. Bd. dirs., v.p. Parkway, 1973—. Served with AUS, 1943-46. Registered municipal accountant, N.J.; registered public sch. accountant, N.J. Mem. Nat. Police Hall of Fame. Mem. N.Y. State Soc. C.P.A.'s (chmn. govtl. accounting com. 1963-64), Am. Inst. C.P.A.'s, Catholic Accountants Guild (bd. govs. 1961-64), N.J. Soc. C.P.A.'s, N.Y. State Soc. C.P.A.'s, Am. Accounting Assn., Fin. Execs. Inst., N.Y. Assn. Profs. Home: PO Box 298 Montclair NJ 07042

DOTY, DONALD D., banker; b. Independence, Kans., June 30, 1928; s. Laton L. and Dorothy (Russell) D.; B.S., Okla. State U., 1950; postgrad. U. Wis. Grad. Sch. Banking, 1963; m. Cheri F. Montgomery, June 14, 1952; children—John Scott, Susan Dorothy, Mark Montgomery. Rancher, nr. Bartlesville, Okla., 1950-53; with First Nat. Bank, Bartlesville, 1955—, asst. v.p., 1960-62, v.p., 1962-69, exec. v.p., 1969-76, pres., 1976—, also dir.; v.p., dir. Rocking D Land & Cattle Co., Bartlesville, New Camp Minerals, Inc., Wichita, Kans.; pres. First Bancshares, Inc., Bartlesville, 1974—; chmn. First Okla. Ventures Corp., Bartlesville. Pres. Bartlesville Credit Bur., 1972—; pres. Bartlesville-Area Indsl. Devel. Co., 1970—. Chmn. trustees Jane Phillips Episcopal Meml. Med. Center, 1970—; trustee Washington County Indsl. Devel. Trust Authority, 1973—, Frank Phillips Found., Bartlesville, 1975—. Served to capt. USAF, 1953-55. Recipient Distinguished Service award Bartlesville, 1957; named Outstanding Young Man Okla., 1958. Mem. Bartlesville C. of C. (v.p., bd. dirs. 1965-70), Sigma Alpha Epsilon. Republican. Episcopalian. Clubs: Masons, Shriners, Rotary, Hillcrest Country (Bartlesville). Home: 1915 Hillcrest Dr Bartlesville OK 74003 Office: 121 W 4th St Bartlesville OK 74003

DOTY, JAMES D., electronics import co. exec.; b. Los Angeles, June 23, 1947; s. James Junior and Theresa (Blau) D.; B.S.E.E., U. Calif., 1968; B.A., George Washington U., 1970; M.A. in Econs., SUNY, 1974, Ph.D., 1979. Mgr., Grove Electronics, Garden Grove, Calif., 1965-68; tchr. North Orange County Regional Occupational Program, 1976-77; pres., chief exec. officer Cal-West Electronics Inc., Anaheim, Calif., 1971-79; sales engr. West Inc., Tustin, Calif., 1980—. Cons. to gen. planning com., Yorba Linda, Calif., 1972-73. Served with U.S. Army, 1968-70. Mem. Nat. Distbrs., Assn., Specialty Equipment Market Assn. Republican. Lutheran. Home: 2855 N Cottonwood St Apt 7 Orange CA 92665 Office: 14712 Bentley Circle Tustin CA 92680

DOUBET, EARL WESLEY, mfg. co. exec.; b. Peoria, Ill., Aug. 13, 1926; s. Earl Wesley and Julia Bertha (Petzing) D.; B.Sc., Bradley U., Peoria, 1948; grad. sr. exec. program M.I.T., 1966; m. Norma Hill, Jan. 28, 1951; children—Earl Wesley, III, Steven H. Exec. v.p. Towmotor Corp., Cleve., 1969-71; mgr. new products dept. Caterpillar Tractor Co., Peoria, 1971-72; mng. dir. lift truck ops. Caterpillar Overseas S.A., Geneva, 1972-75; pres. Caterpillar Americas Co., Peoria, 1975—; trustee Council Americas. Served with AUS, 1946-48. Mem. Constrn. Industry Mfrs. Assn., Machinery and Allied Products Inst. Republican. Office: 100 NE Adams St Peoria IL 61629

DOUBLE, PAUL BERNARD, warehousing and transp. services co. exec., sporting goods mfg. co. exec.; b. Stratford, Ont., Can., Oct. 9, 1941; came to U.S., 1952, naturalized, 1962; s. Bernard Theodore and Eleanor Marie (Nelson) D.: student St. Clair County Community Coll., 1965-68, San Diego City Coll., 1961-65; m. Norma Matar, May 11, 1968; children—John Paul, Eric Nelson, Matthew Matar, Niki. Area sales mgr. Diamond Crystal Salt Co., Winona, Minn., 1965-73; pres. Canamer Corp., Winona, 1973-80, Canamer Leasing Services, Inc., Winona, 1975-80, Cover America, Inc., Winona, 1979—; chmn. bd. Canamer Corp., Canamer Leasing Services, Inc., Cover America, Inc. Chmn. Winona Twp. Bd. Suprs., 1970-80; treas. Winona Area Ambulance Service Bd., 1975-80. Served with USN, 1959-62. Mem. Indsl. Fabrics Assn. Internat., Nat. Assn. Sporting Goods Mfrs., Am. Public Works Assn. Republican. Episcopalian. Patentee in field. Home: Two Glen Mary Rd Winona MN 55987 Office: Airport Office Plaza PO Box 38 Winona MN 55987

DOUCE, WILLIAM CLARK, petroleum co. exec.; b. Kingman, Kans., Dec. 9, 1919; s. William Thew and Grace Clark (Griswold) D.; B.S., U. Kans., 1942; m. Willene Brady Magruder, June 14, 1943; children—Terri Douce Springer, William Clark. With Phillips Petroleum Co., 1942—, chmn. operating com., 1963-66, mgr. chem. dept., 1966-69, sr. v.p., 1969-71, exec. v.p., 1971-74, pres., dir., 1977—, chief exec. officer, 1980—; dir. 1st Nat. Bank Bartlesville, 1st Nat. Bank & Trust, Tulsa. Pres., Okla. Safety Council, 1969; trustee U. Tulsa. Mem. Am. Petroleum Inst. (dir.), Okla. C. of C. (pres. 1971), U. Kans. Alumni Assn. (pres. 1975), Tau Beta Pi, Sigma Tau. Clubs: Masons, Shriners, Hillcrest Country. Presbyterian. Office: Phillips Petroleum Co 18th Floor Phillips Bldg Bartlesville OK 74004

DOUCET, DALE MARION, farmer, agrl. market analyst; b. Abbeville, La., Sept. 27, 1954; s. Roland Paul and Mildred Eve (Simon) D.; B.S. in Bus. Adminstrn., U. Southwestern La., 1976; m. Mary Virginia Thibeaux, July 21, 1979. Farmer, Lafayette, La., 1972—; mgr., market analyst Doucet Grain Elevator, Lafayette, 1976—; mgr. Doucet Grain Co., Lafayette, 1976—; cons. on commodities market, 1978—. Mem. La. Grain Dealers Assn., Top Farmers Am., Kappa Sigma. Roman Catholic. Office: Route 1 Box 117A-8 Lafayette LA 70508

DOUGHERTY, FRANCIS KELLY, computer cons.; b. Lubbock, Tex., May 15, 1953; s. Francis Kelly and Mary Anne (Odell) D.; B.A. in Math., U. Dallas, 1975, B.A. in Physics, 1975; m. Bonnie Lee Burch, June 14, 1975; 1 dau., Anne Katherine. Actuarial trainee Ranger Nat. Life Ins., Houston, 1976-77; mgr. time sharing services Phila. Life Ins. Co., Houston, 1977-81; computer cons., Houston, 1981—. U. Dallas scholar, 1971-75; Rice U. fellow, 1975-76. C.L.U.; cert. in data processing; cert. in computer programming. Fellow Life Mgmt. Inst.; mem. Data Processing Mgmt. Assn. Republican. Roman Catholic. Office: 10500 Valley Forge Suite 179 Houston TX 77042

DOUGHERTY, JEAN MCCOMRICK QUILLEN, gen. contracting co. exec.; b. Frankford, Del., Aug. 23, 1931; d. Edwin William and Margaret Evelyn (Hudson) McComrick; m. Allen John Hudson Quillen, Sept. 10, 1949 (div. 1960); children—Carol Ann, Susan Ada; m. 2d Aloysius Edward Dougherty, Nov. 25, 1977. Bus. mgr., sec.-treas. Eastern Shore Labs., Inc., Laurel, Del., 1962-70; sec., treas. property mgmt. Lindy Bros. Builders, Inc., Lindy Realty Co., North Hills, Pa., 1970-74; bus. mgr., sec., treas. Linan Contractors, Inc. and Linan Corp., Glenside, Pa., 1974—, also dir. Mem. Home Builders Assn. Phila., Pa. Builders Assn.

DOUGHERTY, JOHN CHRYSOSTOM, lawyer; b. Beeville, Tex., May 3, 1915; s. John Chrysostom and Mary V. (Henderson) D.; B.A., U. Tex., 1937; LL.B., Harvard U., 1940; diploma Inter-Am. Acad. Internat. and Comparative Law, Havana, Cuba, 1948; m. Mary Ireland Graves, Apr. 18, 1942 (dec. 1977); children—Mary Ireland, John Chrysostom; m. 2d, Bea Ann Smith, June 16, 1978. Admitted to Tex. bar, 1940; atty. Hewit & Dougherty, 1940-41; partner Graves & Dougherty, 1946-50, Graves, Dougherty & Greenhill, Austin, Tex., 1950-57, Graves, Dougherty & Gee, 1957-60, Graves, Dougherty, Gee & Hearon, 1961-66, Graves, Dougherty, Gee, Hearon, Moody & Garwood, 1966-73, Graves, Dougherty, Hearon, Moody & Garwood, 1973-79, Graves, Dougherty, Hearon & Moody, 1979—; spl. asst. atty. gen., 1949-50; hon. French consul in Austin, 1971—; lectr. on tax, estate planning, probate code, community property problems; dir. Austin Nat. Bank; mem. Tex. Submerged Lands Adv. Com., 1963-72, Tex. Bus. and Commerce Code Adv. Com., 1964-66, Gov.'s Com. on Marine Resources, 1970-71, Gov.'s Planning Com. on Colorado River Basin Water Quality Mgmt. Study, 1972-73, Tex. Legis. Property Tax Com., 1973-75. Bd. dirs. Advanced Religious Study Found., 1955-81, Grenville Clark Fund, Sea Arama, Inc.; trustee Nat. Pollution Control Found., St. Stephen's Episcopal Sch., U. Tex. at Austin Law Sch. Found. Served as capt. CIC, AUS, 1941-44, JAGC, 1944-46; now maj. Res. Recipient Médaille Française (France), Silver medal of honor Alliance Francaise. Fellow Am., Tex. bar founds.; mem. Am., Inter-Am., Travis County bar assns., State Bar Tex. (pres. 1979-80), Am. Arbitration Assn. (nat. panel arbitrators 1958—, S.W. adv. council 1965—), State Bar Tex. (chmn. sect. taxation 1965-66, pres.-elect 1978), Internat., Am. fgn. law assns., Am. Law Inst., Am. Coll. Probate Counsel, Am. Soc. Internat. Law (exec. council 1959-62), Internat. Acad. Estate and Trust Law, Cum Laude Soc., Phi Beta Kappa, Phi Eta Sigma, Beta Theta Pi. Presbyterian. Rotarian. Contbg. author: Estate Planning and Taxation, Texas Lawyers Practice Guide, 2d edit., 1971, How to Live and Die-with Texas Probate, 1968, 3d edit., 1978; Texas Estate Administration, 1975, 2d edit., 1978; bd. editors Appellate Procedure in Texas, 1964, 2d edit., 1979. Home: 6 Green Ln Austin TX 78703 Office: Austin Nat Bank Bldg PO Box 98 Austin TX 78767

DOUGLAS, HOWARD JEFFREY, corp. fin. exec., cons.; b. N.Y.C., May 8, 1946; s. Melvin D. and Shirley Ann (Rosenbaum) D.; B.S. in Indsl. Engring., Syracuse U., 1968; M.B.A. in Fin., N.Y. U., 1970, A.P.C. in Taxation, 1976; m. Frances Schwartz, June 16, 1968; children—Amy Beth, Michele Joy. Asst. fin. mgr. Gen. Foods Corp., N.Y.C., 1970-73; asst. controller W.R. Grace & Co., N.Y.C., 1973-77; dir. operational rev. and analysis Standard Brands Inc., N.Y.C., 1977—; pres. ROI Group, Ltd., 1978—, Hobar Group, Inc., Syndications and Fin. Planning, 1980—; cons. fin. and tax planning. Mem. Nat. Assn. Accts., Internat. Assn. Fin. Planners, Am. Fin. Assn. Home: 55 Buttonwood Dr Dix Hills NY 11746 Office: 625 Madison Ave New York NY 10022

DOUGLAS, JOHN JAY, ret. communications co. exec.; b. Chgo., Oct. 4, 1916; s. Charles G. and Martha (Brown) D.; Ph.B., U. Wis., 1939; m. Jeanne M. McGauran, June 3, 1944; children—Charles Gardner, John Jay, Steven Anthony, Thomas Slade, Mary Jeanne, Ann Elizabeth, Patricia Mary. With Gen. Telephone System cos., 1940—; pres. Lenkurt Electric Co., San Carlos, Calif., 1959-63, exec. v.p. fin. Gen. Telephone & Electronics Corp., N.Y.C., from 1963, vice chmn. bd., also dir., to 1980; pres. Anglo-Canadian Telephone, also dir. several subs. and affiliated cos.; dir. Allendale Ins. Co.; mem. Grand Central adv. bd. Chem. Bank N.Y. Trust Co., N.Y.C. Named Industry Man of Year, San Francisco Peninsula Mfrs. Assn., 1963. Mem. Am. Inst. C.P.A.'s, Delta Upsilon. Republican. Roman Catholic. Club: Stanwich (Greenwich, Conn.). Home: 136 Jonathan Dr Stamford CT 06903

DOUGLAS, MALCOLM ROOT, fin. exec.; b. Oak Park, Ill., Mar. 22, 1944; s. Kenneth Root and Alyce (Moehn) D.; B.A., Yale U., 1966; M.B.A., N.Y. U., 1969. Cons. cash mgmt., fin. planning No. Trust Co., Chgo., 1969-71; planning analyst Gould, Inc., Chgo., 1971-73; cash mgr. FMC Corp., Chgo., 1973-75, internat. fin. coordinator, 1975-76; asst. treas. Baxter Travenol Labs., Inc., Deerfield, Ill., 1977-79; pres. Douglas Fin. Cons. Service, Buffalo Grove, Ill., 1979—. Mem. Chgo. Cash Mgmt. Practitioners Assn., Chgo. Internat. Fin. Mgrs. Assn., Am. Mgmt. Assn. Republican. Lutheran. Author: (with Lee J. Seidler) The Management Game Players' Manual, 1969. Home: 1225 Bristol Ln Buffalo Grove IL 60090

DOUGLAS, N. JOHN, food processor; b. N.Y.C., Aug. 28, 1938; s. N. John, Sr. and Esther (Ambleman) D.; B.S., Bates Coll., 1960; M.S., Howard U., 1962; exec. program U. Va., 1978; m. Hazel J. Brown, June 14, 1964; 1 son, Gregory. Sr. scientist Lockheed Research Lab., Palo Alto, Calif., 1962-68; security analyst Bank of Am., San Francisco, 1968-69; sr. security analyst ISI Corp., San Francisco, 1969-71, Bear Stearns & Co., N.Y.C., 1971-72; mgr. Reynolds Securities, Inc., N.Y.C., 1972-73; v.p. James Capel & Co., San Francisco, 1973-75; dir. investor and pub. relations Castle & Cooke, Inc., San Francisco, 1975—; dir. Nat. Group TV, Inc. Purinton scholar, 1959-60; Travelli scholar, 1957-60; NDEA fellow, 1960-62. Mem. Nat. Investor Relations Inst. (dir., v.p. membership), San Francisco Soc. Security Analysts, Sigma Pi Sigma. Club: Commonwealth of Calif. Office: Castle & Cooke Inc 50 California St San Francisco CA 94111

DOUGLAS, RUSSELL BURLEIGH, corp. exec.; b. Seattle, Feb. 27, 1901; s. Samuel H. and Mabel (Russell) D.; A.B., U. Wash., 1923; m. Wilma Magee, Aug. 19, 1945; children—Russell B., Lawrence H. With credit dept. Standard Oil Co., 1923-25; chief accountant Johns Manville, 1925-28; pub. accountant, 1928-31; successively sec.-treas., sales mgr., v.p., gen. mgr., dir. Fernando Valley Milling & Supply Co., 1931-37; personnel dir., asst. to pres. Bireley's, Inc. div. Gen. Foods, 1937-39; nat. merchandising dir. Wine Inst. (trade assn.), 1939-44; exec. v.p., sales adv. mgr. Am. Wine Co., 1944-46; pres. Imperial Distbg. Corp., New Haven; sr. v.p. marketing, dir. Taylor Wine Co., Inc., N.Y.C., 1947—. C.P.A. Mem. C. of C. (pres.), Sales and Marketing Internat., Delta Upsilon. Clubs: N.Y. Advertising, Sales Executives; Metropolitan; Sarasota Yacht. Home: 1 Ben Franklin Dr Sarasota FL 33577 Office: 1405 Main St Sarasota FL 33577

DOUTHIT, GLEN SAMUEL, investment co. exec.; b. Clarinda, Iowa, Feb. 22, 1924; s. Calvin R. and Bessie R. (Ashwood) D.; B.S. in Bus., Denver U., 1953; married; children—Glynis J., Debra A. Owner, adminstr. nursing homes, Denver, 1949-63, Colo. and Tex., 1963-81; engaged in real estate investments, Tex. and Colo., 1968—; dir. Western Securities Mortgage Co.; pres. Denver Nursing Home Assn., 1953. Served with AUS, 1943-46. Republican. Clubs: Century (U. Denver); Longmont (Colo.) Elks. Address: 7102 S Poplar St Englewood CO 80112

DOVE, DOUGLAS JAMES ASHTON, retail exec.; b. Vancouver, B.C., Can., May 14, 1926; came to U.S., 1927, naturalized, 1945; s. Percival Ashton and Winifred Doris (Sampson) D.; student U. Wash., 1946; m. Anna-Leena Niemela, June 1, 1957; children—Alison Kathleen, Scott Douglas. Plant dept. and comml. rep. Pacific Tel & Tel, Seattle and Yakima, Wash., 1947-54; underwriter Sun Life Assurance Co. Can., 1955-56; sales rep. Sta. KBKW, Aberdeen, Wash., 1956-58; partner Feltis Dove Dever Cannon, radio and TV rep., Seattle, 1958-68; co-owner, sec.-treas., v.p. nat. and internat. sales Interstore Transfer Specialists, Inc., Edmonds, Wash., 1968—. Served with U.S. Army, 1944-46. Mem. Nat. Retail Mchts. Assn. (asso.), Yakima Jr. C. of C. (named Jaycee of Month 1954). Republican. Club: Masons (Seattle). Patentee corrugated containers. Home: 7926 192d Pl SW Edmonds WA 98020 Office: 138 Railroad Ave Edmonds WA 98020

DOVIDIO, NICHOLAS ANTONIO, mgmt. cons.; b. Bklyn., Nov. 27, 1951; s. Damiano and Anna (Ciccarello) D.; B.A., Fordham U., 1973; M.B.A., Stanford U., 1977. Systems analyst RCA Corp., 1968, 69, 72, 73-74; systems analyst Fibreboard Corp., San Francisco, 1974-75; auditor Peat, Marwick, Mitchell, N.Y.C., 1976; mgr. mgmt. cons. Arthur Young & Co., N.Y.C., 1977—. C.P.A., N.Y. Mem. Am. Mgmt. Assn., Am. Inst. C.P.A.'s, Stanford Alumni Assn., N.Y. State Soc. C.P.A.'s. Republican. Roman Catholic. Home: 2534 E 14th St Brooklyn NY 11235 Office: 277 Park Ave New York NY 10172

DOW, DONALD DOUGLAS, investment adv.; b. Portland, Maine, Apr. 13, 1942; s. Millard Harding and Marjorie Louise (Gardner) D.; student Boston U., 1961; diploma N.Y. Inst. Fin., 1964; m. Patricia Molly Towle, Dec. 28, 1968; children—Tracy Dee, Tiffany Georgia. Rep., W. E. Hutton Co., Lewiston, Maine, 1963-69, Dominick & Dominick Inc., Portland, 1969-73; pres. Dow & Dow Co. div. F. L. Putnam & Co., Inc., Portland, 1973-80; pres. Dow Corp., Falmouth, Maine, 1980—. Mem. pres's. council St. Joseph's Coll. Registered investment adv. Mem. Wildlife Conservation Trust, Timber Owners New Eng. Republican. Congregationalist. Clubs: Cumberland, Masons, Shriners. Home: Falmouth ME 04105 Office: Falmouth ME 04105

DOWD, JAMES EDWARD, stock exchange exec.; b. Cambridge, Mass., May 18, 1922; s. Bartholomew J. and Sarah E. (Connolly) D.; A.B., Boston Coll., 1944, LL.B., 1949; postgrad. Georgetown Sch. Fgn. Service, 1944; m. Marguerite A. O'Donoghue, May 5, 1951; children—Jane E. (dec.), James Edward (dec.), Ann E. Admitted to Mass. bar, 1949; practiced in Boston, 1949-50; asso. Langan, Lawless & Dempsey, 1949-50; trial atty. SEC, Boston, 1951-55, chief enforcement atty., 1957-65, regional adminstr., 1966-69; pres. Boston Stock Exchange, 1969—; dir. Boston Stock Exchange Clearing Corp., New Eng. Securities Depository Trust Co., Boston Stock Exchange Service Corp., Boseco, Inc. br. operating mgr. Westinghouse Electric Corp., N.Y.C., 1955-57. Pres., dir. Charitable Irish Soc., 1969; trustee Regis Coll. Served to 1st lt. AUS, 1943-46. Mem. Am., Fed. bar assns. Office: care Boston Stock Exchange One Boston Pl Boston MA 02108

DOWD, MERLE EDWARD, fin. exec.; b. Wellington, Kans., May 27, 1918; s. John Edward and Nellie Anna (Brown) D.; student Kans. State Coll., 1936-38, U. Wash., 1942-43; B.S. in Mech. Engring., Northwestern U., 1947, M.B.A. with distinction, 1954; m. Anne Hemenway, June 17, 1949; children—Jerry, Stephen, Richard, Timothy. Faculty Northwestern U., Evanston, 1948-52; instr. Coll. Vallejo (Calif.), 1948; home workshop editor Sci. and Mechanics, Chgo., 1952-55; founder Boeing Airliner publ. Boeing Co., Seattle, 1958-62, mgr. presentations and proposals sect. Comml. Airplane div., Renton and Seattle, Wash., 1963-68; pres., owner The Writing Works, Inc., Mercer Island, Wash., 1974—; faculty U. Wash., Seattle, 1970—; lectr. in field; registered rep. Cosse Internat. Securities, Inc., Seattle, 1974—; owner Merle E. Dowd & Assos., advt., Mercer Island. Trustee Pacific N.W. Writers Conf., 1969-73, pres., 1972. Mem. Seattle Free Lances, Am. Soc. Journalists and Authors. Presbyterian. Club: Rotary. Contbr. articles to mags. including Sci. and Mechanics, Popular Mechanics, Better Homes and Gardens, Am. Home, Reader's Digest, Mechanics Illustrated, Motor Boating, Sphere, Money, Modern Maturity; syndicated columnist Money Talk in Seattle Times, 1970—; columnist Mng. Your Money various other newspapers; author: How to Live Better and Spend 20% Less, 1966, 3d edit., 1979; How To Save Money When You Buy and Drive Your Car, 1967; How to Get More for Your Money in Running Your Home, 1968; How to Earn a Fortune and Become Independent in Your Own Business, 1971; How to Get out of Debt and Stay Out of Debt, 1971; (with W.E. Garrison) Handcrafting Jewelry; Designs and Techniques, 1972; (with Frances Call) The Practical Book of Bicycling; How to Earn More Money from Your Crafts, 1976; (with Archie Satterfield) The Seattle GuideBook. Address: 7438 SE 40th St Mercer Island WA 98040

DOWLER, ROBERT EDWARD, ins. co. exec.; b. Hempstead, N.Y., Oct. 1, 1935; s. James V. and Anna E. (Beekman) D.; A. Arts and Scis., Hofstra U., 1958; m. Allyce M. Bronner, Apr. 4, 1959; children—Christopher Scott, Colleen Yvonne, Clare Marie, Stephen Jay. Sales rep., regional credit mgr. Sinclair Refining Co., N.Y.C., 1954-62; v.p. Rollins Burdick Hunter Co., 1963—; v.p., prin. The Dowler Co., Real Estate Investments, Rockville Centre, N.Y., 1976—; mng. partner Hudson Valley Farms, 1980—; owner Am. Para-Profl. Systems of Conn., para-med. reporting firm, 1980—; adv. bd. Continental Bank N.Y.; cons. in field. Chmn. bd. mgrs., 1st v.p. Met. L.I. YMCA; fin. officer Garden City Republican Com., 1971-76; historian Hempstead Fire Dept., 1968-69, also vol. fireman; mem. Hemstead Planning Bd., 1965-70; mem. citizens adv. bd. Hofstra U.; sr. adv. Up With People. Served with U.S. Army, 1955-57. Named Man of Year, Hemstead C. of C., 1970. Mem. Nat. Assn. Ins. Agents, N.Y. State, Nassau County agts. assns. Club: Kiwanis (past sec., treas., v.p., dir.), Jaycees (chpt. founder, pres. 1967-69) (Hempstead). Home: 63-D Signal Hill Rd Madison CT 06443 Office: 450 Sunrise Hwy Rockville Centre NY 11570

DOWLING, JAMES HAMILTON, public relations exec.; b. Chgo., Oct. 20, 1931; s. Joseph Henry and Margaret (Hamilton) D.; B.J., U. Mo., 1957; m. Julie Anne Pastor, Apr. 7, 1958; children—James Jr., Kenneth Edward, Tracy Anne. Writer, editor U.P., New Orleans, 1957, Newsweek, Atlanta and N.Y.C., 1958-59, A.P., Chgo., N.Y., 1960-63; public relations staff Mobil Oil Corp., N.Y.C., 1963; with Burson-Marsteller Inc., 1964—, gen. mgr. N.Y.C., 1968-70, gen. mgr. Chgo., 1970-75, pres., N.Y.C., 1975—. Served with USMC, 1952-55. Li Found. fellow, 1957-58. Mem. Public Relations Soc. Am. Office: 866 Third Ave New York NY 10022*

DOWLING, PETER GAYLE, fgn. trade co. exec.; b. Phila., Sept. 2, 1933; s. Paul P. and Jean (Crowe) D.; A.B., Syracuse U., 1962; M.A., Western Mich. U., 1965; m. Norma Parrish, Apr. 22, 1957; children—Claudia Ann, John Paul. Educator, Kalamazoo, Mich., 1965-68, Bridgewater, N.J., 1968-80; dir. D and K Assos., Bridgewater, 1978-79; pres. PGD Internat. Inc., Bridgewater, 1980; cons. Soviet-Am. Textbrook Project, 1978—. Democratic candidate for N.J. Assembly, 1975, 77; mem. N.J. Vets. Services Council, 1975-80; mem. Battleship N.J. Commn., 1977-80. Served with USAF, 1954-63. Mem. Nat. Council for Social Studies, DAV. Roman Catholic. Home: 1975 Holland Brook Rd Somerville NJ 08876 Office: Box 6665 Bridgewater NJ 08807 also 104 Hollywood Ave Villas NJ 08251

DOWLING, RAYMOND JAMES, electronic equipment mfg. corp. exec.; b. Lake Worth, Fla., Aug. 2, 1928; s. Simon P. and Eileen M. (Tumelty) D.; B.S., M.A., Northeastern U.; m. Lucille Somers, June 12, 1954; children—David James, Dawn Marie. Corp. credit mgr. Raytheon Co., 1958-66, ops. mgr., distbr. products div., 1966-75, ops. mgr. med. electronics, 1975-77, exec. v.p. Switchcraft, Inc. subs., Topton, Pa., 1977-78, pres., chief exec. officer, 1978-80, Caloric Corp. div., 1980—. Served with AUS, 1945-48. Mem. Electronics Industries Assn. Clubs: Knollwood Country (Lake Forest, Ill.); Salem (Mass.) Country. Office: Caloric Corp Washington and Heffner Sts Topton PA 19562

DOWNER, CHARLES WEBSTER, investment banker; b. Waco, Tex., Sept. 5, 1940; s. William Webster and Marguerite Helena (Linam) D.; B.A., Harvard U., 1962, M.B.A., 1966; m. Harriette Chalifoux Draper, June 15, 1963; children—Elizabeth Burrage, Charles Webster. Pres., Weaver Internat. Corp., Boston, 1966-75, Robert A. Weaver, Jr. & Assos., Boston, 1972-75, Downer & Co., Boston, 1976—, Downers and Partners Internat., Zurich, Switzerland, 1977—; dir. Bell Western Corp., Eastern Petroleum Co., Sundown Oil & Gas (U.K.) Ltd., Sundown Exploration Co., Inc., Halifax Garden Co. Bd. dirs. Big Bro. Assn. of Boston, 1968—; mem. Mass. Minority Bus. Advisory Bd., 1968—, Gov.'s Council on Minority Bus., 1968—; mem. vis. com. bd. overseers Harvard U. Served with Ordnance Corps, U.S. Army, 1962-63. Republican. Episcopalian. Clubs: Brook (N.Y.C.); Country (Brookline, Mass.); Somerset (Boston). Office: 125 Pearl St Boston MA 02110

DOWNEY, RICHARD RALPH, lawyer, acct., mgmt. cons. co. exec.; b. Boston, Apr. 22, 1934; s. Paul Joseph and Evelyn Mae (Butler) D.; B.S., Northeastern U., 1958; M.B.A., Harvard U., 1962, J.D., Suffolk U., 1979; children—Richard Ralph, Janice M., Erin C., Timothy M. Mem. audit staff Price Waterhouse & Co., Boston, 1962-64; asso. Assos. for Internat. Research, Inc., Cambridge, Mass., 1964-68, v.p., 1968—, also dir.; admitted to Mass. bar, 1979, Fed. bar, 1980. Treas., 1580 House Condominium Trust, 1979-80. C.P.A., Mass., Mem. Am. Inst. C.P.A.'s, Mass. Soc. C.P.A.'s, Am. Bar Assn., Mass. Bar Assn., Boston Bar Assn. Club: Harvard (Boston, N.Y.C.). Home: 1580 Massachusetts Ave Unit 4D Cambridge MA 02138 Office: 1100 Massachusetts Ave Cambridge MA 02138

DOWNING, KENNETH ARGENE, ins. exec.; b. Idaho Falls, Idaho, Mar. 5, 1939; s. Kenneth Elsworth and Helen Marie (Bourassa) D.; student Eastern Wash. Coll., 1960, Mont. State Coll., 1964, Western Mont. Coll., 1965-66, Mo. State U., 1974; m. Faye Theresa Langland, Mar. 3, 1962; children—Jolene Kay, Lynn Marie, Troy Kenneth, Gary Argene. Nurse asst., musician, 1962-63; nurse aide, 1963-64; lounge mgr., 1964-66; ins. agt. Bankers Life & Casualty Co., 1966-69, supr., 1969, dist mgr., 1969-72, br. mgr., 1972-78, regional mgr., Madison, Wis., 1978—; U.S. rep. N.D. Ins. Industry 8-nation tour, 1978. Served with USAF, 1958-62. Mem. Nat. Assn. Life Underwriters, N.D. life underwriters, Life Underwriters Tng. Council, Gen. Agy. and Mgrs. Assn., Elba, C.L.U. Republican. Roman Catholic. Clubs: Nat. Rifle Assn., Elks, VFW, Moose. Home: 5886 Winchester Ave Marshall WI 53559 Office: 6414 Copps Ave Suite 213 Madison WI 53716

DOWNS, CHARLES MORTIMER, JR., paint co. exec.; b. Baton Rouge, July 15, 1919; s. Charles M. and Felicie Anna (Dupuy) D.; B.S. in Chemistry, La. State U., 1941; m. Joan Wilkes, Nov. 21, 1969; children—Susan Henry, Ruth Ryan, Charles III, Felicie Watson, Adele Sumner, Elaine Burkhardt. Jr. engr. U.S. Engr. Corp., Trinidad, 1941-42; plant supt. Flintkote Co., New Orleans, 1942-45; supr. chem. lab. Exxon Chem. Co., Baton Rouge, 1945-57; tech. sales, Chgo., 1957-60, account exec., St. Louis, 1960-66, sales mgr., Houston, 1966-69; div. mgr. indsl. coatings div. Ameron Co., Wichita, Kans., 1969—. Mem. Nat. Paint and Coating Assn. (chmn. govt. suppliers com., chem. coatings steering com.), Am. Chem. Soc. Episcopalian. Clubs: Wichita Country, Wichita, Petroleum. Patentee in field. Home: 360 N Crestway Wichita KS 67208 Office: Box 2153 Wichita KS 67201

DOYLE, JOHN STUART, advt. agy. and real estate exec.; b. Chgo., Oct. 20, 1915; s. Patrick Francis and Kathryn E. (Kelleher) D.; Ph.B., De Paul U., 1938, postgrad. Coll. Law, 1978—; M.Ed., Chgo. Tchrs. Coll., 1940; postgrad. Ill. Inst. Tech., 1942, 47-49; fellow Northwestern U., 1938-39; postgrad. Loyola U. Bus. Sch., 1950-51; m. Marie Josephine Haug, Feb. 21, 1944; children—John Stuart, Geoffrey, Donald, Susan, Charles, Deborah, Michael, Paul. Dir. religious printing div. Cuneo Press, 1941-42; commd. ensign USN, 1944, advanced through grades to lt. comdr., 1952; planning officer Nat. Security Agy., Ft. Meade, Md., 1950-51; ret., 1961; gen. mgr. Morgan Mfg. Corp., 1951-52; advt. mgr. Velsicol Chem. Corp., 1952-53; account exec. Foote, Cone & Belding, Chgo., 1953-59; v.p., account supr. Compton Advt., Chgo., 1959-66, also Edward H. Weiss & Co., Advt. Agy., 1966-68; pres. MMI Corp.; sec. Brand Group, Inc., Chgo., 1975—; dir. Rockwood & Co., Gt. Am. Industries, Superior Seal Corp., Emlin Cosmetics, others; tchr. Kelvyn Park and Wendell Phillips high schs., 1940-42, Northwestern U. Bus. and Journalism Schs., 1954-66. Vice chmn. Chgo. City Coll. Bd., 1966-70; founder, exec. sec. Council of Community Coll. Bds., 1968-71; vice chmn. Citizens Com. for Gun Control Legislation; exec. dir. Chgo. com. Ill. Sesquicentennial, 1967-68; dir. alumni relations De Paul U., 1969-71. Recipient Putnam 1st place award for most successful indsl. advt., 1955, two 1st place Toppers awards, 1954, 55, 1st place Asso. Bus. Publs. award, 1954, 55. Roman Catholic. Club: Evergreen Bath and Tennis (Evergreen Park, Ill.). Pub., DePage mag., 1969-72. Author: Christmas Interlude, 1942. Contbr. articles to mags. Home: 2031 W Hunt Ave Chicago IL 60620 Office: 910 S Michigan Ave Chicago IL 60605

DOYLE, JOHN THOMAS, fin. co. exec.; b. Kearny, N.J., Jan. 16, 1943; s. Thomas F. and Margaret G. (McCormack) D.; B.A., Rutgers U., 1971; M.B.A., Fordham U., 1973; m. Helga A. Dinzinger, Aug. 10, 1968; children—John Kevin, Kristina Anne. Adminstrv. asst. First Jersey Nat. Bank, Jersey City, 1965-69; asst. treas. Comml. Alliance Corp., N.Y.C., 1969-74; v.p. mktg. Horizon Creditcorp, Morristown, N.J., 1974-78, sr. v.p. domestic and internat. mktg., 1978—. Served with N.G., 1966-77; lt. col. U.S. Power Squadrons. Mem. Nat. Assn. Equipment Lessors, Nat. Assn. Engine and Boat Mfrs., Am. Boat and Yacht Council. Home: 10 Totty Court Florham Park NJ 07932 Office: 334 Madison Ave Morristown NJ 07960

DOYLE, MORTIMER BERNARD, trade assn. exec.; b. N.Y.C., Oct. 15, 1916; s. James Joseph and Theresa (Hanrahan) D.; student bus. mgmt. and law LaSalle Extension U., 1947-50; m. Joyce Solomon, Dec. 5, 1942; children—Stephen Paul, Kenneth Anthony. Div. traffic auditor ITT, N.Y.C., 1934-36; advt. rep. Gerlach Barklow Co., Joliet, Ill., 1945-46; asst. sales mgr. O'Sullivan Rubber Corp., Winchester, Va., 1946-47; dir. devel., mgr. Midwest div. N.A.M., 1947-57; exec. v.p. Nat. Forest Products Assn., Washington, 1957-68; pres., chmn. bd. Timber Engring. Co., Washington, 1957-68; exec. v.p. Southwest Forest Industries, Inc., Phoenix, 1968-72; chmn., chief exec. officer Internat. Snowmobile Industry Assn.; chmn. M.B. Doyle & Assos. Inc., 1972—. Chmn. lumber survey com. U.S. Dept. Commerce, 1957-65. Served with USMC, 1936-45; col. Res. ret. Decorated Navy Commendation medal, Purple Heart. Mem. U.S. C. of C. (past chmn. assn. com., Distinguished Service award 1962), Am. Soc. Assn. Execs. (chmn. elect, chmn. internat. com., Key Man award 1964), Forest Industries Council (council, past chmn. exec. com.). Club: Congressional Country (Potomac, Md.). Office: Suite 850 S 1800 M St NW Washington DC 20036

DOYLE, PATRICIA A., univ. adminstr.; b. Franklin, Mass., Jan. 13, 1937; d. Bernard J. and Mary D. Doyle; B.A., Trinity Coll., Washington, 1958; m. Charles V. Pryles. Mut. fund rep. State St. Bank & Trust Co., Boston, 1962-63; asso. Investment Trust Boston, 1963-67; v.p. John Kenney Assos., Inc., Boston, 1966-74; asst. treas. Boston U., 1974—; cons., lectr., condr. seminars in field. Adv. bd. Curry Coll., Milton, Mass.; mem. capital com. YWCA; chmn. bd. dirs. Boston U. Credit Union. Mem. Beacon Hill Civic Assn. Office: 881 Commonwealth Ave Boston MA 02215

DOYLE, RICHARD JOSEPH, investment mgmt. co. exec.; b. Chgo., Apr. 15, 1934; s. Paul Alphonsus and Adele Marguerite (Wiegand) D.; B.S. in Commerce, DePaul U., 1960; m. Kathleen Mary Miller, May 31, 1958; children—Kevin, Christopher, Daniel, David, Donna. Vice pres. Security Counselors, Inc., Chgo., 1961-66; asst. sec. Kemper Ins. Orgn., Chgo., 1966-70; sr. v.p. Kemper Fin. Services, Chgo., 1971—; del. White House Confs. on Economy, 1978, 79. Mem. fin. bd. Infant Jesus of Prague Parish, 1976-77. Served with U.S. Army, 1954-56. Mem. Investment Analysts Soc., Soc. Mcpl. Analysts. Republican. Roman Catholic. Club: Mid-Day (Chgo.). Office: 120 S La Salle St Chicago IL 60603

DOYLE, RICHARD JOSEPH, fin. services co. exec.; b. Sioux City, Iowa, May 8, 1932; s. Francis K. and Marie Margaret (Malloy) D.; grad. Kansas City U., 1955, Advanced Mgmt. Program, Harvard U., 1975; m. Donna S. Karol, Oct. 25, 1974; children—Dan, Michelle, Marie, Cindy, Richard Joseph III. With Borg Warner Acceptance Co., 1958—, v.p., Chgo., 1964-67, exec. v.p., 1967-71, pres., chief exec. officer, dir., 1971—; dir. Acradia Nat. Ins., Chgo. Served with USAF, 1950-54. Office: Borg Warner Acceptance Co 1 IBM Plaza Chicago IL 60611

DOYLE, WILLIAM JAY, II, bus. cons.; b. Cin., Nov. 7, 1928; s. William Jay and Blanche (Gross) D.; B.S., Miami U., Oxford, Ohio, 1949; postgrad. U. Cin., 1950-51, Xavier U., 1953-54, Case Western Res. U., 1959-60; m. Joan Lucas, July 23, 1949; children—David L., William Jay, III, Daniel L. With Diebold, Inc., Cin., 1949-74, asst. regional mgr., Cin., 1957-62, regional mgr., Cin., 1962-74; founder, chief exec. officer Central Bus. Systems & Security Concepts Co. div. Central Bus. Equipment Co., Inc., Cin., 1974—, dir. parent co. and divs.; speaker on bus systems, security concepts. Mem. music and auditing coms. Ch. of the Savior, Methodist ch., Montgomery, Ohio. Mem. Bus. Systems and Security Mktg. Assn. (pres. 1980-81 nat. dir.), Nat. Assn. Accountants. Clubs: Sycamore Twp. Republican, Masons, Shriners. Contbr. articles to co. and trade pubs.; developer new concepts in tng., cash and securities handling, other areas of bus. Home: 202 Shakerdale Rd Cincinnati OH 45242 Office: 10839 Indeco Dr Cincinnati OH 45241

DOZA, LAWRENCE O., accountant; b. Ste. Genevieve, Mo., June 6, 1938; s. Kenneth J. and Anna Mae D.; B.S.B.A., U. Mo., 1962; m. Lorraine M. Dickherber, July 9, 1960; children—Douglas, Jan, Dean. Various positions to audit mgr. Price Waterhouse & Co., St. Louis, 1962-72; asst. gen. controller Borden, Inc., Columbus, Ohio, 1972-74, gen. controller, 1974-77, v.p., gen. controller, 1977—. Mem. Fin. Execs. Inst. Republican. Roman Catholic. Clubs: Brookside Country, Columbus Athletic. Home: 4265 Reedbury Ln Columbus OH 43220 Office: 180 E Broad St Columbus OH 43215

DRACH, MURRAY A., financial exec.; b. N.Y.C., July 23, 1932; s. Isaak and Ethel D.; B.B.A., CCNY, 1952, M.B.A. cum laude, 1962; m. Barbara Bitterman, May 29, 1951; children—Valeri, Mitchell. Vice-pres./controller Swingline, Inc., N.Y.C., 1969-73, Litton ABS, Pinebrook, N.J., 1973-75; v.p., controller Rexel Office Products, Inc., Long Island City, N.Y., 1975-77; v.p. fin., controller Hoke Inc., Cresskill, N.J., 1977—. Served with AUS, 1953-55. C.P.A., N.Y. Mem. Nat. Assn. Accountants, Fin. Execs. Inst. Home: 98-01 67th Ave Forest Hills NY 11374 Office: 1 Tenakill Park Cresskill NJ 07626

DRAGONE, ALLAN R., mfg. co. exec.; b. Melrose, Mass., 1926; B.A., Middlebury Coll., 1950; M.B.A., Harvard U., 1952; married. Mktg. sales mgr. Champion Paper Inc., 1959-60; v.p., gen. mgr. Standard Packaging Co., 1960-66; with Celanese Corp., N.Y.C., 1966—, exec. v.p. Celanese Fibers Mktg. Co., 1970-71, corp. v.p., pres. Celanese Fibers Mktg. Co., 1971-73, group v.p. domestic fibers, pres. Celanese Fibers Mktg. Co., 1973-74, corp. group v.p. domestic fibers, 1975-80, corp. exec. v.p. fibers group, 1980—, pres., chief operating officer, 1980—, also dir.; dir. Manhattan Life Ins. Co., Millhaven-Galtex, Amcel Europe, S.A., Celanese Can. Inc., Celanese Columbiana, Celanese Mexicana, Celanese Venezolan. Office: Celanese Corp 1211 Ave of Americas New York NY 10036*

DRAKE, C. B., JR., ins. co. exec. chmn., chief exec. officer St. Paul Cos., Inc. Office: 385 Washington St Saint Paul MN 55102

DRAKE, HUDSON BILLINGS, aerospace co. exec.; b. Los Angeles, Mar. 3, 1935; s. Hudson C. and Blossom (Billings) D.; A.B., U. Calif., Los Angeles, 1957; M.B.A., Pepperdine U., 1976; m. Joan Johnson, Feb. 9, 1957; children—Howard, Paul. With Autonetics div. Rockwell Internat., Anaheim, Calif., 1957-68, proposal negotiator, 1961-65, dept. mgr. opns., 1966-68; v.p., gen. mgr. Teledyne Ryan Electronics div. Teledyne Industries, San Diego, 1972-80, pres., 1980—; cons. Ash Commn. on Exec. Reorganization, Washington, 1970; dep. undersec. commerce, Washington, 1970-71, dir. Bur. Domestic Commerce, dep. asst. sec., 1971-72; avocado rancher, Highland Valley, Calif. Bd. dirs. White House Fellows Found., 1972-75, World Affairs Council, 1979—; bd. govs. Greater San Diego Youth Sci. Fair, 1976—; mem. adv. bd. Ramona Met. Water Dist., 1977—. Served with USNR, 1953-61. White House fellow, 1968-69. Mem. Nat. Mgmt. Assn. (Silver Knight of mgmt. award 1975), Air Force Assn., U.S. Army and Navy League, Inst. Nav., Calif. Avocado Soc., White House Fellows Assn., Ramona (Calif.) Agrl. Assn., San Diego C. of C., Phi Delta Phi, Phi Delta Theta. Republican. Episcopalian. Clubs: Internat. (Washington); Stoneridge Country (San Diego). Home: 18047 Sencillo Dr San Diego CA 92128 Office: 2701 Harbor Dr San Diego CA 92112

DRAKE, JOSEPHINE ELEANOR, accounting technician, nursery and pub. co. exec., writer; b. Yellow Frame, N.J., July 20, 1931; d. John Hall and Bertha Ellen (Messler) Stickle; certificate of bookeeping and accounting, Dover Bus. Coll., 1967; certificate Pa. State U., 1969; 7 certificates (Univ. Home Econs. Extension Advisory Council scholar 1973) Rutgers U., 1970-74; certificate practical English and command of words English-Lang. Inst. Am., 1971; student in accounting Internat. Accountants Soc., 1974-77; m. Paul Edmund Drake, Aug. 17, 1952; children—Paul Edmund, Judith Ann, Patricia Ann, Robert Edmund. Aide dietary dept. Newton (N.J.) Meml. Hosp., 1950-53; partner Drake's Nursery, Andover, N.J., 1955—; accounting technician U.S. Army Armament Research and Devel. Command, Dover, N.J., 1955—; owner, operator Jo's Book Service, Andover, 1973—; author books, including: The History of Drake's Nursery, 1974; The Trail of No Return, 1974; The Geneaology of John B. Drake, 1974. Author books of poetry, including: Love Speaks, 1974; Life Races On, 1974; The Purpose of Waking in the Morning, 1974. Certified pesticide applicator, N.J. Mem. Internat. Platform Assn., ASCAP, Nat. Wildlife Fedn. (world asso.), N.J. Turfgrass Assn., Sussex County (N.J.) Soil Conservation Dist., Sussex County Assn. Retarded Citizens. Methodist. Clubs: Am. Legion Aux., No. Hills Organic Gardening. Home: Whitehall Rd Andover NJ 07821

DRAKE, THOMAS ALBERT, chem. co. exec.; b. Austin, Tex., Jan. 16, 1944; s. Albert Thomas and Lavern (Axelson) D.; B.S., U. Tex., 1966, M.S., 1968; m. Linda Joy Conte, Mar. 17, 1972; 1 son, Thomas Albert. Asso. engr. Electro Mech., Austin, Tex., 1966-68; software engr. Singer/Link, Houston, 1968-71; software group supr. N. Electric, Delaware, Ohio, 1971-73; with All State Engring., Trenton, N.J., 1973-76; project engr. E. I. DuPont De Nemours & Co., Inc., Wilmington, Del., 1976-79, supr. distributed system sect., 1979—; dir. TAD, Inc., 1977—; gen. chmn. Micro-Delcon, Wilmington, 1977. Recipient IEEE Sect. award, 1978. Mem. IEEE, Am. Mgmt. Assn., Assn. Computing Machinery. Lutheran. Contbr. articles to profl. jours. Home: 715 Foxdale Rd Wilmington DE 19803 Office: EI duPont de Nemours FB 1007 Wilmington DE 19081

DRAN, JOHN JOSEPH, educator; b. Yonkers, N.Y., May 10, 1933; s. John Joseph and Anna (Haletzky) D.; M.E., Stevens Inst. Tech., 1954; M.S., Rensselaer Poly. Inst., 1958; D.B.A. (Univ. fellow), Kent State U., 1970; m. Ellen Marie Eppolito, Feb. 1, 1964; children—Sarah Jean, Jenna Anne. Field engr. Link Aviation, Binghamton, N.Y., 1958-60; indsl. engr. IBM, Endicott, N.Y., 1961-63; systems engr. Norton Co., Watervliet, N.Y., 1964, 66; instr. mgmt. Rensselaer Poly. Inst., Troy, N.Y., 1965-66; asst. prof. finance U. Toledo, 1968-72; asso. prof. finance U. Ala. in Birmingham, 1972—; bus. and fin. cons., 1972—. Served to lt. USAF, 1954-57. Mem. Am., Eastern, Midwest, So., Southwest fin. assns., Fin Mgmt. Assn., Ala. Acad. Sci., Midsouth Acad. Economists, Beta Gamma Sigma, Phi Sigma Kappa, Omicron Delta Epsilon, Alpha Iota Delta. Mem. Russian Orthodox Ch. Home: 1548 Holly Rd Vestavia Hills AL 35226 Office: Sch Bus Univ Ala Birmingham AL 35294

DRASEN, RICHARD FRANK, mfg. co. exec.; b. Chgo., Jan. 16, 1930; s. Frank Bernard and Margaret Louise (Lindsteadt) D.; student Mich. State U., 1948-49, Northwestern U., 1954-55, UCLA, 1956-58, 60-61, Calif. State U., Northridge, 1961-63. Tchr., dir. The Acad., Los Angeles, 1959-61; mgr. communications United Parcel Service, Los Angeles, 1961-66, N.Y.C., 196-6-68; mgr. pub. relations and communications Signal Oil & Gas Co., Los Angeles, 1968-72, Houston, 1972-74; mgr. pub. affairs Burmah Oil, Inc., N.Y.C., 1974-75, Burmah Oil & Gas Co., Houston, 1975-77; mgr. pub. relations, energy R. J. Reynolds Industries, Inc., Winston-Salem, N.C., 1977-78; v.p. corp. affairs Howell Corp., Houston, 1978-80; mgr. public relations and communications MAPCO Inc., Tulsa, 1980—. Pres., Tara Homeowners Assn., Thousand Oaks, Calif., 1960. Served to 1st lt. AUS, 1951-53. Mem. Internat. Assn. Bus. Communicators, Houston Personnel Assn. Clubs: Univ., Houston, Warwick. Home: 2747 E 56th Pl Tulsa OK 74105 Office: 1800 S Baltimore Ave Tulsa OK 74119

DREBUS, RICHARD WILLIAM, pharm. co. exec.; b. Oshkosh, Wis., Mar. 30, 1924; s. William and Frieda (Schmidt) D.; B.S., U. Wis., 1947, M.S., 1949, Ph.D., 1952; m. Hazel Redford, June 7, 1947; children—William R., John R., Kathryn L. Bus. trainee Marathon Paper Corp., Menasha, Wis., 1951-52; tng. mgr. Ansul Corp., Marinette, Wis., 1952-55, asst. to v.p., 1955-58, marketing mgr., 1958-60; dir. personnel devel. Mead Johnson & Co., Evansville, Ind., 1960-65, v.p. corporate planning, 1965-66, internat. pres., 1966-68; v.p. internat. div. Bristol-Myers Co. (merger Mead Johnson Internat. div. with Bristol-Myers Co. Internat. div.), N.Y.C., 1968-77, sr. v.p., 1977-78, v.p. parent co., 1978—. Served with inf. AUS, 1943-45. Decorated Combat Inf. Badge, Purple Heart, Bronze Star. Mem. Am. Psychol. Assn., N.Y. Acad. Scis., Phi Delta Kappa. Clubs: Fox River Hunting and Fishing, Silver Springs Country. Home: 16 Old Driftway Rd Wilton CT 06897 Office: 345 Park Ave New York City NY 10022

DREFS, JEROLENE AMELIA, magazine publisher; b. Phila., Oct. 4, 1935; d. James Vincent and Mary Anna (Haury) Bizzaro; B.A., Cleve. State U., 1970, M.B.A., 1963; C.P.A., Ohio, 1970; grad. Advanced Mgmt. Program, Harvard U., 1979; m. Alfred David Drefs, Apr. 4, 1952; 1 son, Mark Allen. Controller, S.M. Hexter Co., 1971; asst. corp. controller Sherwin-Williams Co., 1971-76; v.p., controller, treas. Turbodyne Corp., 1976-79; v.p., treas. Newsweek, Inc., N.Y.C., 1979—; mem. faculty Cleve. State U., Coll. of St. Thomas, St. Paul. Mem. Am. Inst. C.P.A.'s, Fin. Execs. Inst. (past chpt. dir.). Episcopalian. Club: Board Room. Author articles in field. Office: 444 Madison Ave New York NY 10022

DRENDEL, FRANK MATTHEW, cable co. exec.; b. Paxton, Ill., Jan. 16, 1945; s. Frank Martin and Nora (Odell) D.; B.S. in Mktg., No. Ill. State U., 1971; postgrad. St. Louis U., 1972-73; m. Marilyn Beste, Dec. 21, 1968; 1 son, Matthew Clayton. Vice pres. Continental Transmission, 1970-71; v.p. ops. Cypress Communications, 1971-73; pres. Comm/Scope Co., 1973-76; pres., chief exec. officer Valtec Corp., West Boylston, Mass., 1976-80, chmn. bd., chief exec. officer, 1979—. Served with USAR, 1968-74. Mem. Calif. Cable TV Assn. (dir.), Nat. Cable TV Assn. (dir.), Catawba (N.C.) C. of C. Presbyterian. Clubs: Lake Hickory Country, Rotary. Office: 99 Hartwell St West Boylston MA 01583

DRESSEL, HENRY FRANCIS, lawyer; b. Bklyn., Apr. 11, 1914; s. Henry Philip and Ernestine (Delmar) D.; A.B., Washington Sq. Coll., N.Y. U., 1943, J.D., 1949; m. Rose Marie Valentine, Nov. 24, 1937; 1 dau., Diana (Mrs. Anthony P. Fradella). Admitted to N.Y. bar, 1949; asso. corp. law firm Chadbourne, Stanchfield & Levy (and its successors), N.Y.C., 1933-43; pvt. practice law, N.Y.C., 1950—; partner firm Dressel & Altman, profl. corp. Served from ensign to lt. USNR, 1943-46. Named hon. col. Okla., 1958, Okie, 1969. Mem. Am., N.Y. State bar assns., Assn. Bar City of N.Y., N.Y. County Lawyers, Am. Judicature Soc., Justinian Soc., Internat. Footprint Assn., Phi Delta Phi. Democrat. Episcopalian. Clubs: Danish Athletic, N.Y. University. Home: 8365 Shore Rd Brooklyn NY 11209 Office: 150 Broadway New York NY 10038

DREW, ALDEN DANA, med. indsl. optics co. exec.; b. Conway, N.H., Sept. 25, 1945; s. Frank Edward Drew; student Lowell Tech. Inst., 1973-74. Jr. accountant Am. Optical Corp., Bedford, Mass., 1968-70, sr. accountant, 1972-73, credit mgr., 1978; bus. mgr. Bio Med Spltys., LaGrange, Ill., 1978-79; mgr. adminstrn., corp. controller Melles Griot, Irvine, Calif., 1979—. Served with U.S. Army, 1965-67. Recipient Commonwealth Mass. Med. Fin. citation,

1977. Mem. Nat. Assn. Credit Mgmt. Club: Elks. Home: 1787 Orange Ave Costa Mesa CA 92627

DREW, THOMAS ARTHUR, banker; b. Milw., Aug. 29, 1945; s. Frank Emmons and Irene Louise (Wollaeger) D.; B.A., DePauw U., 1967; M.B.A., Dartmouth Coll., 1969; m. Constance C. Deckert, Sept. 9, 1978. Asso., Booz Allen & Hamilton, Inc., Chgo., 1969-76; sr. v.p., chief fin. officer First Savs. Assn. Wis., Milw., 1976—; dir. Tyme Corp., 1978—, pres., 1980—. Bd. dirs. Milw. Children's Hosp., 1980—. Mem. Fin. Execs. Inst., Fin. Mgrs. Soc. Clubs: Dairyman's Country, Milw. Athletic, Milw. Yacht, Univ. of Milw. Home: 4524 N Frederick Ave Whitefish Bay WI 53211 Office: 250 E Wisconsin Ave Milwaukee WI 53202

DREWES, WILLIAM HARRY, fin. devel. cons., mfr.; b. Honolulu, June 7, 1942; s. Harry William and Ellen Akana Drewes; A.B., Washington U., 1965; M.B.A., L.I. U., 1976; postgrad. N.Y. U., Bklyn. Law Sch.; m. Henrietta Diamond, Oct. 17, 1971; children—Alyssa Robin, Oliver Evin. With export dept. Shell Oil Corp., N.Y.C., 1965-67; unit dir. Greater N.Y. Fund, 1967-68; asst. dir. devel. N.Y. Urban Coalition, 1968-69; dir. advt. and promotion J.R. Taft Corp., Washington, 1969-71; sec.-treas., dir. Bodyscapes, Inc., 1970—; dir. fund raising Bedford Stuyvesant Restoration Corp., Bklyn., 1976-80; pvt. practice fin. devel. cons., 1980—. Mem. Direct Mail Mktg. Assn., Nat. Assistance Mgmt. Assn., Sales Execs. Club N.Y., Advt. Club N.Y. Republican. Roman Catholic. Clubs: Turtle Bay Swim and Tennis, N.Y. U. Home: 7 Lexington Ave New York NY 10010

DREXINGER, BERNARD RICHARD, dept. store exec.; b. Exeter, Pa., Aug. 8, 1928; s. Bernard John and Marie Ann (Hayes) D.; B.S. in Acctg., King's Coll., 1958; postgrad. N.Y. U., 1958-59, U. Va., 1975; m. Grace M. Leonardi, June 26, 1954; children—Bernard Richard, Gaeton. Asst. controller Klopman div. Burlington Industries, N.Y.C., 1959-66; v.p. fin. and adminstrn. Indian Head Hosiery, Indian Head, Inc., N.Y.C., 1967-75; v.p., controller Schwarzenbach Huber div. Indian Head, Inc., N.Y.C. and Charlottesville, Va., 1975-76; v.p., controller Rich's, Atlanta, 1976—. Coach, Little League Basketball, 1969-70; pres. Brookwood Community Club, 1970. Served with U.S. Army, 1951-54. Clubs: Indian Hills Country (Marietta, Ga.); Rotary. Home: 3877 Clubland Dr Marietta GA 30067 Office: 45 Broad St Atlanta GA 30302

DREYER, HAROLD EMIL, research and devel. co. exec.; b. Wayne County, Nebr., Dec. 24, 1920; s. Paul Martin and Augusta Marie (Splittgerber) D.; B.S., U. Nebr., 1942; Ph.D., M.I.T., 1952; J.D., Suffolk U., 1964; m. Irene Starkel, Feb. 19, 1943; children—Thomas Glen, Douglas Harold, James Henry. Orgn. and methods examiner VA, St. Louis, 1946-48; asst. and asso. personnel officer M.I.T., Cambridge, 1951-59, benefits officer, 1959-69, personnel officer Draper Lab., 1969-73; pvt. practice law, Belmont, Mass., 1964—, mgr. compensation, benefits and union relations Draper Lab., 1973-79, benefits cons., 1979—; mem. faculty Suffolk U., 1966—, U. Mass., 1980—. Mem. personnel bd. Town of Belmont (Mass.), 1974-77. Served with Q.M.C., U.S. Army, 1943-46. Mem. Am., Mass. bar assns., Am. Mgmt. Assn. (ins. adv. council), Am. Arbitration Assn. (labor and comml. panel arbitrators), Personnel Mgrs. Club, Greater Boston C. of C., Am. Soc. Tng. Dirs. Lutheran. Home: 5 Simmons Ave Belmont MA 02178 Office: 555 Technology Sq Cambridge MA 02139

DRIEGERT, ROBERT STEPHEN, lawyer, acctg. co. exec.; b. Jersey City, June 4, 1942; s. Robert Gustav and Aino Hilma (Watjus) D.; B.S. in Econs., U. Pa., 1964; M.B.A., U. Tex., Austin, 1967, J.D., 1970; m. Janet Hockert, Apr. 22, 1972; children—Jonathan, William. Sr. auditor Peat Marwick Mitchell & Co., Phila., 1964-66; tax mgr. Arthur Young & Co., Dallas, 1970-76; tax partner Dohm & Wolff, Dallas, 1976—. Trustee, Leukemia Soc., 1977; div. chmn. Am. Cancer Soc., 1978; chmn. Bill Clements for Gov., Richardson, Tex., 1978; chmn. 3d Congressional Dist. com. George Bush for Pres., 1980. Mem. Am. Inst. C.P.A.'s, Tex. Soc. C.P.A.'s (chmn. Dallas chpt. public affairs com. 1979—), Am. Bar Assn., Tex. Bar Assn., Richardson C. of C., Beta Gamma Sigma, Beta Alpha Psi. Republican. Lutheran. Home: 3 Shadywood Pl Richardson TX 75080 Office: 3575 1st Internat Bldg Dallas TX 75270

DRIES, DALE ANTHONY, bldg. supply co. exec.; b. Allentown, Pa., Nov. 12, 1947; s. Howard Blair and Elizabeth Rita (Kocis) D.; B.S. in Bus. Adminstrn., Rider Coll., 1969; postgrad. Lehigh U., 1968, Muhlenberg Coll., 1967; m. Lucy Ann Wittman, Oct. 31, 1970; 1 son, Darren Anthony. Retail sales mgr. Dries Bldg. Supply Co., Macungie, Pa., 1969-72, v.p., 1972—, part owner, 1979—, retail sales mgr., 1969—; owner Misty Springs Farm, 1973—; founder D.B.S. Handi-crafts, 1979; dir. First Fed. Savs. and Loan Assn., Allentown, Pa. Republican. Roman Catholic. Club: Rotary (ores. 1980) (Emmaus, Pa.). Home: RD 1 Box 508 Macungie PA 18062 Office: 44 Brookside Rd Macungie PA 18062

DRIFTMIER, JAMES LEE, realtor; b. Anacortes, Wash., Dec. 8, 1951; s. Benjamin William and Mary Jo (Raemaker) D.; student U. Wash., 1970-75; m. Linda Jane Cahoon, Oct. 11, 1975; 1 dau., Jennifer Anne. Salesman, Ewing and Clark, Seattle, 1975-76, property mgmt. mgr., 1976-77, residential div. mgr., asso. broker, 1977-79, mgr. Eastern comml. div., mem. adv. bd., 1980—. Chmn. Dean Frease for Sch. Bd. Campaign Com., 1979. Mem. Seattle Quality Listings (trustee 1977-80), mem. arbitration com. 1978-80, mem. police com. 1978-80), Delta Chi. Republican. Presbyterian. Clubs: Wash. Athletic, Key Internat. (lt. gov. 1969-70). Home: 4340 NE 56th St Seattle WA 98105 Office: 2025 5th Ave Seattle WA 98121

DRISCOLL, JOHN F., business exec.; b. Boston, Apr. 1, 1942; s. James S. and Bridget Agnes (Delaney) D.; B.Sc., Boston Coll., 1964; ed. N.Y. Inst. Fin., Canadian Inst. Mgmt.; m. Merrilyn Joy MacDonell, Apr. 6, 1968; 1 son, Shaun. Mktg. mgr. Tech. Tape Corp., 1964-67; account exec. Paine Webber Jackson & Curtis, from 1967; mgr. instl. sales and research Thomson McKinnon & Auchincloss; with Dominck Corp.; now v.p. corp. affairs, exec. asst. to pres. Acklands Ltd., Downsview, Ont., Can. Active in fund raising Progressive Conservative Party Can., UNICEF, Canadian Cancer Soc., United Way. Served with USMC, 1961-66. Mem. Canadian Inst. Mgmt., Nat. Investors Relations Inst., Automotive Warehouse Distbrs. Assn., Bd. Trade, Automotive Industry Assn. Republican. Roman Catholic. Club: Bloor Park Squash. Contbr. articles on auto parts aftermarket and phys. distbn. to profl. jours. Home: 120 Heath St W Toronto ON M4V 2Y6 Canada Office: 100 Norfinch Dr Downsview ON M3N 1X2 Canada

DRISCOLL, ROBERT SWANTON, investment co. exec.; b. N.Y.C., Jan. 12, 1912; s. Clarence Uler and Elizabeth (Pinchbeck) D.; A.B. with honors, Columbia, 1933; m. Jane Word, Sept. 30, 1936; children—Robert Swanton IV, Steven Word, David Christopher. Investment counselor, 1934-40; with Research Mgmt. Council, Inc. subs. Lord Abbett & Co., 1941-47, v.p., 1942, pres., 1944; v.p. Lord, Abbett & Co., Inc., 1948, partner, 1949, mng. partner, 1964-78, 79-80, partner, 1978-79; v.p. Lord Abbett Income Fund, Inc., N.Y.C., 1949-61, exec. v.p., 1961-64, pres., chief exec. officer, 1964-80, dir., 1949—; pres., chief exec. officer Lord Abbett Developing Growth Fund, Inc., 1973-80, dir., 1973—; v.p. Affiliated Fund, Inc., N.Y.C., 1949-61, exec. v.p., 1961-64, pres., chief exec. officer, 1964-77, chmn., 1977-78, chmn., chief exec. officer, 1979-80, dir., 1949—; pres., chief exec. officer Lord, Abbett Bond-Debenture Fund, Inc., 1971-79, chmn., chief exec. officer, 1979-80, dir., 1971—; chmn. bd., pres. Am. Utility Shares, Inc., 1975-78; pres. Lord Abbett Cash Res. Fund, Inc., 1979-80, dir., 1979—; dir. Depository Trust Co., 1974-78, Whittaker, Clark & Daniels, Inc., 1978—; former mem. Investment Co. Inst., also former mem. exec. com. and bd. govs. Commr., Westchester-Putnam council Boy Scouts Am., 1951-61, pres., 1961-64, v.p., 1964—; trustee Securities Industry Found. Econ. Edn., 1979—. Mem. N.Y. Soc. Security Analysts, Securities Industry Assn. (chmn. investment cos. com. 1977-78), Nat. Assn. Securities Dealers (past bd. govs., past chmn. arbitration com.), Amateur Fencers League (treas. 1947-52). Clubs: Fencers, Inc. (pres. 1949-58, v.p.), Broad St. (N.Y.C.); Capitol Hill (Washington); Mount Kisco (N.Y.) Country. Mem. Olympic Fencing Com., 1947-52, nat. epée champion, 1943. Home: 345 Roaring Brook Rd Chappaqua NY 10514 Office: 63 Wall St New York NY 10005

DROEGEMUELLER, ARTHUR CLARENCE, pub. accountant; b. Chgo., June 6, 1904; s. William A. and Ida W. (Lannefeld) D.; Ph.B., U. Chgo., 1925; C.P.A., U. Ill., 1930; m. Katherine H. Meyer, Nov. 19, 1927 (div.), children—Joan Louise (Mrs. Richard J. Wilke), Katherine Ellen (Mrs. R. Thomas Saether); m. 2d, Marjorie Adams Aldrich, 1954; 1 stepson, Frederick B. Aldrich. Pub. accountant, 1923—; with Frazer and Torbet, C.P.A.'s, 1930-54, partner, 1941-54; sr. partner Droegemueller, Brady & Nelson, C.P.A.'s, 1955-56; partner Main & Co., C.P.A.'s 1956-63, Main Lafrentz & Co., C.P.A.'s, 1963-65; individual practice, 1965—. Treas. Chgo. Luth. Theol. Sem., 1939-60; mem. bd. mgmt. Onward Neighborhood House (pres. 1950-51). C.P.A., Ill., Tex., Wis. Mem. Am. Inst. C.P.A.'s, Ill. Soc. C.P.A.'s (sec.-treas. 1946-48), Phi Pi Phi (nat. treas. 1933-39), Alpha Sigma Phi. Lutheran. Club: Union League. Home: 309 Tanglewood Ln Naperville IL 60540 Office: Suite 1400 100 W Monroe St Chicago IL 60603

DROSSEL, EUGENE RAYMOND, mgmt. cons.; b. Chgo., Sept. 18, 1921; s. Felix and Julia (Mroczek) D.; B.A., U. Redlands, 1952; postgrad. San Francisco State Coll., 1960-61, U. San Francisco, 1964, Columbia, 1974; m. Ruth MacIver; 1 dau. (by previous marriage), Annalee. Supr. heat treat Taylor Pipe & Forge Co., 1939-41; instrument technician Chrysler Corp., Detroit, 1946-49; with Kaiser Steel Co., Oakland, Calif., 1951-80, supr. cinematography, 1956-59, publs. mgr., 1959-64, dir. public relations, advt., 1964-74, v.p. public affairs, 1977-80; communications dir. Kaiser Industries, 1974-76; mng. dir. Drossel and MacIver, Alameda, Calif., 1976—. Served with USMC, 1942-46. Mem. Public Relations Soc. Am., World Affairs Council, Assn. Iron and Steel Engrs., Public Relations Round Table. Clubs: Press, Sierra, Commonwealth (San Francisco). Office: 615 Rock Isle Alameda CA 94501

DROZD, LEON FRANK, JR., publishing co. exec.; b. Victoria, Tex., Sept. 11, 1948; s. Leon Frank and Dorothy Lucille (Smith) D.; B.B.A., Tex. A and M U., 1971; J.D., U. Denver, 1979. Legis. asst. U.S. Ho. of Reps., also Democratic Caucus, Washington, 1971-74, chief clk. com. on sci. and tech., 1974-75; asst. to dean for devel. Coll. Law, U. Denver, 1975-79; v.p. Braddock Publs., Inc., Washington, 1975—; land rep. Chevron Shale Oil Co., 1980—. Colo. elector Anderson/Lucey Nat. Unity Campaign, 1980. Club: Nat. Democratic (Washington). Home: 1211 Vine St #905 Denver CO 80206 Office: PO Box 4001 Golden CO 80401

DROZDECK, STEVEN RICHARD, brokerage exec.; b. N.Y.C., Apr. 23, 1951; s. Frank S. and Jane (Dzingelewski) D.; student Poly. Inst. Bklyn., 1969-70; B.S. cum laude in Fin., N.Y. Inst. Tech., 1973. Pres., Unltd. Leadership Potential, S.I., N.Y., 1973-74; account exec. Merrill Lynch, Pierce, Fenner & Smith, Bklyn., 1974-78, Staten Island, 1978-80, sales trainer, N.Y.C., 1980—. Mem. Internat. Assn. Fin. Planners, Nat. Soc. Registered Reps. (charter), N.Y. Stockbrokers Club. Home: 242 Hillside Terr Staten Island NY 10308 Office: 165 Broadway 29th Floor New York NY 10080

DRUCKER, ROLF, TV sta. exec.; b. Nuremberg, Ger., Sept. 15, 1926; came to U.S., 1941, naturalized, 1945; s. Benno and Erna (Engel) D.; student CCNY, 1950; m. Olga M. Lenk, Oct. 22, 1950; children—Jane L., Robert S., Alice S. Engr., Sta. WNYC, 1946-48; tech. dirs. Sta. ABC-TV, N.Y.C., 1948-77; dir. ops. and engring. Sta. WNET-TV, N.Y.C., 1977—; owner Audio-Video Engring. Co., Merrick, N.Y., 1969—. Served with U.S. Army, 1944-46. Mem. Soc. Motion Picture and TV Engrs., Royal TV Soc., PBS Engring. Com., World Ship Soc. Home: 65 Nancy Blvd Merrick NY 11566 Office: 356 W 58th St New York NY 10019

DRUCKMAN, RICHARD ARNOLD, pharm. co. exec.; b. Hartford, Conn., Apr. 4, 1939; s. Harry and Florence (Weinstein) D.; B.A., Trinity Coll., 1961; M.B.A., Columbia U., 1962; m. Joan Phyllis Moskovitz, Aug. 12, 1962; children—Michael Neal, Gregory Wayne, Steven Edward. Mktg. analyst B.F. Goodrich Co., N.Y.C., 1962-63, Merck Internat., N.Y.C., 1963-66; mktg. research mgr. Union Carbide Corp., N.Y.C., 1966-67; dir. mktg. research E.R. Squibb Co., Princeton, N.J., 1967-77, dir. product planning and research, 1977-78, v.p. sales, 1978-80, v.p. product planning, 1980—. Mgr. Little League; active Boy Scouts Am. Mem. Assn. Internat. Med. Scis. (pres.), Am. Mktg. Assn., Nat. Pharm. Council (dir.), Am. Mgmt. Assn., Eastern Pharm. Market Research Group. Jewish. Home: 17 Benford Dr Princeton Junction NJ 08550 Office: PO Box 4000 Princeton NJ 08540

DRUMHELLER, GEORGE JESSE, motel chain exec.; b. Walla Walla, Wash., Jan. 30, 1933; s. Allen and Ila Margaret (Croxdale) D.; student Wash. State U., 1951-52, Whittier Coll., 1955-58; m. Carla Rene Cunha, May 4, 1965; 1 son, Sean M.; stepchildren—Matthew F. Mosgrove, Douglas J. Mosgrove. Asst. mgr. Olympic Hotel, Seattle, 1959; jr. exec. Western Internat. Hotels, Seattle, 1959-63; founder, pres. George Drumheller Properties, Inc., motel holding co., Pendleton, Oreg., 1963—; founder, chmn. bd. Dalles Tapadera, Inc., motel and hotel holding co., The Dalles, Oreg., 1964—; founder, pres. Lewiston Tapadera, Inc. (Idaho), motel holding co., 1970—; founder, pres. Yakima Tapadera, Inc. (Wash.), 1971—; founding partner Drumheller & Titcomb (Tapadera Motor Inn), Ontario, Oreg., 1972—, merged subs. Tapadera corps. into George Drumheller Properties, 1977; engaged in farming Eastern Wash., 1958—. Served with USCGR, 1952-55. Mem. Oreg. Hotel and Motel Assn. (dir. 1974-78), Wash. Hotel and Motel Assn. (dir. 1976-78), Wash. State Lodging Assn. (v.p., dir. 1978—), Idaho Innkeepers Assn., Wash. State Assn. Wheat Growers. Clubs: Walla Walla Country; Wash. Athletic (Seattle); La Jolla (Calif.) Beach and Tennis; Torrey. Home: 110 N Division St Walla Walla WA 99362 also 1520 Virginia Way La Jolla CA 92037 Office: George Drumheller Properties Inc 244 Marcus St PO Box 1234 Walla Walla WA 99362

DRUMMOND, FREDERICK FORD, banker, rancher; b. Enid, Okla., July 13, 1931; s. Fred G. and Grace (Ford) D.; B.S., Okla. State U., 1953; M.B.A., Stanford U., 1957; A.A., Sch. Banking, U. Wis., 1968; m. Janet Trahern, Oct. 25, 1958; children—Diana, Ann, Ford, Jane. Vice pres. United Mo. Bank, Kansas City, 1957-58; chmn., v.p. Cleveland Nat. Bank (Okla.), 1960—; sec.-treas. Pioneer Corp., Hominy, Okla., 1968—; rancher, Pawhuska, Okla., 1958—; mem. exec. com., dir. AMTA Corp., Oklahoma City; dir. Fed. Land Bank, Ponca City, Okla.; mem. nat. com. Farm Credit System, 1975—. Served with arty. U.S. Army, 1953-56. Mem. Nat. Cattlemen's Assn. (chmn. tax com. 1974-77), Osage County Cattlemen's Assn. (pres. 1970-71), Okla. State U. Alumni Assn. (pres. 1969-70). Democrat. Presbyterian. Club: Pawhuska Rotary (pres. 1972-73).

DRUMMOND, MALCOLM MCALLISTER, elec. engr.; b. London, Eng., Sept. 22, 1937; s. George James and Winifred Ethel (Jaye) D.; came to U.S., 1966, naturalized, 1977; B.S. in Elec. Engring. with honors, City U., London, 1961; m. Linda Jerome Banning, May 25, 1968; 1 dau., Heather Lynn. Engr., Brit. Fgn. Office, Cheltenham, Eng., 1964-66; sr. engr. Gen. Dynamics Corp., Rochester, N.Y., 1966-70; tech. rep. Tymshare Inc., Rochester, 1970-72; project engr. Sybron Corp., Taylor Instrument Co., Rochester, 1972—. Christian Sci. minister for VA Hosp., 1974-80. Mem. IEEE (chmn. sr., Rochester sect. 1979—, pension task force 1979— Region I PAC coordinator 1980—), Mgmt. Soc. (past chmn.), Computer Soc. (past pres.), Instrument Soc. Am., Rochester Engring. Soc. (dir. 1979—), Am. Mgmt. Assns., Inst. Elec. Engrs. (Gt. Britain). Home: 60 Marberth Dr Henrietta NY 14467 Office: 400 West Ave Rochester NY 14601

DRURY, LLOYD LEONARD, electric co. exec.; b. New Orleans, Oct. 12, 1925; s. John Joseph and Evelyn (Nebel) D.; B.S., La. State U., 1949; M.B.A., Loyola U., New Orleans, 1961; Ph.D., Rochdale Coll., 1972; D.Psychology, Pacific So. U., 1976; m. Betty Bray Byrne, July 10, 1946; children—Lloyd Leonard, David Bray, Susan Joan, Denise Ann. Marine engr. Grace Lines, Inc., N.Y.C., 1945-46; field engr. Calif. Co., New Orleans, 1949; with Gen. Electric Co., 1949—, mgr. So. dist., New Orleans, 1960—; dir. Delta Assos.; lectr., cons. in field. Active local United Fund, Jr. Achievement. Served with USNR, 1943-46. Registered profl. engr., La. Mem. Nat. Soc. Profl. Engrs., Soc. Naval Architects and Marine Engrs., Am. Soc. Indsl. Security, La. Engring. Soc., Am. Assn. Applied Psychology, Am. Astological Assn. Mem. Evang. Ch. Clubs: Metairie Country, Beau Chêne Golf and Raquet. Home: 4465 Bancroft Dr New Orleans LA 70122 Office: 1919 ITM Bldg New Orleans LA 70130

DRUSIN, SHERMAN ARTHUR, computer software co. exec.; b. N.Y.C., July 28, 1942; s. Leon and Sarah Rosalind (Peskin) D.; B.S. in Econs., Fairleigh Dickinson U., 1964; m. June Ellen Stevelman, July 4, 1963; children—Dawn Alyse, Cami Lee. Sales specialist Olivetti Underwood Corp., 1964-68; sales rep. ITT Data Services, 1968-69; systems center mgr. Info. Sci. Inc., 1969-71; founder, dir. Program Products, Montvale, N.J., 1971—, v.p. sales and mktg., 1971-78, chief operating officer, 1968-78, pres., chief exec. and operating officer, 1978-80 (became Systems Products div. Nat. CSS, Inc. 1980), v.p., gen. mgr., 1980—. Jewish. Office: 95 Chestnut Ridge Rd Montvale NJ 07645

DRY, MICHAEL POWELL, investment co. exec.; b. Chgo., Dec. 5, 1943; s. Henry and Faye (Wizner) D.; B.S. in Econs., U. Wis.-Madison, 1965; m. Joan Eileen Zisook, June 24, 1965; children—Randal, Terrence. Registered rep. Freehling & Co., Chgo., 1965-72, gen. partner, 1972—. Allied mem. N.Y. Stock Exchange, 1972—, Am. Stock Exchange, 1972—; sr. registered options prin. Chgo. Bd. Options Exchange, 1973—; asso. person Commodity Futures Trading Commn.; mem. Chgo. Merc. Exchange, 1978—, Internat. Monetary Market, 1978—. Registered investment adviser SEC. Served with AUS, 1966-71. Mem. Nat. Assn. Securities Dealers (prin.). Contbg. editor Money Maker Mag., 1979—. Home: 2440 N Lakeview Ave Chicago IL 60614 Office: 120 S LaSalle St Chicago IL 60603

DUBAIN, MYRON, ins. co. exec.; b. Cleve., June 3, 1923; s. Edward D. and Elaine (Byrne) DuB.; B.A., U. Calif., Berkeley, 1943; grad. exec. program Stanford Grad. Sch. Bus., 1967; m. Alice Elaine Hilliker, Sept. 30, 1944; children—Cynthia Lynn, Donald Aldous. With Fireman Fund Ins. Co., San Francisco, 1946—, now chmn. bd., pres., chief exec. officer; dir. Am. Express, United Calif. Bank, Pacific Gas & Electric Co., Amfac, Inc., Terra Nova Ins. Co. (Eng.); chmn., trustee AFIA Worldwide Ins., N.Y.C. Mem. adv. council SRI; bd. dirs. Bay Area Council, San Francisco Opera, Jr. Achievement Adv. Council; pres., trustee United Way of Bay Area; bd. govs. San Francisco Symphony. Served as officer USNR, 1943-46, 50-52. Mem. Nat. Assn. Casualty and Soc. Execs. (exec. com.), Property Casualty Ins. Council, Calif. (dir.), San Francisco (dir.) chambers commerce, Calif. Roundtable. Republican. Episcopalian. Clubs: Bohemian, Pacific Union, Calif. Tennis (San Francisco); Links (N.Y.C.); Lagunitas Country; Coral Beach and Tennis (Bermuda). Contbg. author: Property and Casualty Handbook, 1960; The Practical Lawyer, 1962. Office: 3333 California St San Francisco CA 94118

DUBARD, WALTER HIGHGATE, oil and gas co. exec.; b. Greenwood, Miss., Dec. 10, 1294; s. Walter Highgate and Maybelle (McDorman) DuB.; student Southwestern Coll., 1942, U. Miss., 1946; B.S., Columbia U., 1949. Owner, realtor W.H. DuBard Real Estate, Greenwood, Miss., 1961—; owner, operator W.H. DuBard Prodn. Co., N.Y.C., 1963—; v.p., dir. Pike Investments Inc., McComb, Miss., 1962-76, chmn. bd. 1976—. Served with M.C., AUS, 1943-45. Decorated Silver Star. Mem. Sigma Alpha Epsilon. Presbyterian. Club: El Morocco. Home: 55 East End Ave New York City NY 10028 Office: PO Box 698 Wall St Station New York City NY 10005

DUBBELDE, ROBERT PETER, clothing mfg. co. exec.; b. Garretson, S.D., Oct. 14, 1942; s. Francis F. and Eleanor Rose (Bucher) D.; student N.D. State Sch. Sci., 1960-61, Sioux Falls (S.D.) Coll., 1962-63, Dakota State Coll., Madison, S.D., 1963-64; m. Carole Munce, Mar. 19, 1966; children—Kimberly, Robert. Store mgr. Crawfords Inc., Sioux Falls, 1964-66; sales rep. Williamson-Dickie Mfg. Co., Ft. Worth, 1966-68; salesman Munsingwear Inc., 1968-78, v.p., regional mgr. central div., Chgo., 1978—. Recipient various sales awards. Mem. Mid-Am. Male Apparel Assn., Nat. Assn. Men's and Boys' Apparel, Nat. Rifle Assn., Izaak Walton League. Republican. Roman Catholic. Clubs: Merchants and Mfrs., Elks. Home: 337 Meadowlark Rd Bloomingdale IL 60108 Office: Chicago IL 60654

DUBIN, HOWARD SEYMOUR, publisher; b. Chgo., Aug. 16, 1933; s. Joseph and Bee (Sax) D.; B.S., Northwestern U., 1954; m. Ursula P. Lutz, Dec. 11, 1960; children—Thomas Gregory, Anne Elisabeth. Editor-in-chief Northwestern U. mag., 1953-54; mng. editor Modern Brewery Age mag., 1954-56; world traveller, free lance writer, 1957-58; pub. Ill. Mfrs. Directory, Ill. Services Directory, pres. Mfrs. News, Inc., 1958—; pres. Univ. Book Pubs., Inc., 1964-79; partner St. Clair Press Coll. Pubs., 1974-79; dir. Robert Freeman Pub. Co.; chmn. Chgo. Communications Ann. Event, 1979—. Mem. Ill. Mfrs. Assn., Ill. C. of C., Chgo. Assn. Commerce and Industry, Chgo. Better Bus. Bur., Soc. Profl. Journalists (dep. regional dir. Ill. 1978—, chmn. fin. com. 1979—), Sigma Delta Chi. Clubs: Chicago Headline (past pres., chmn. adv. bd. trustees), Chgo. Press; Deerfield Courts, Downtown Court, Execs. Home: 634 Sheridan Rd Evanston IL 60202 Office: 3 East Huron St Chicago IL 60611

DUBIN, JAMES MICHAEL, lawyer; b. N.Y.C., Aug. 20, 1946; s. Benjamin and Irene (Wasserman) D.; B.A., U. Pa., 1968; J.D. (bd. editors law rev. 1973-74), Columbia U., 1974; m. Susan Schraub, Mar.

15, 1981. Admitted to N.Y. bar, 1975; asso. firm Paul, Weiss, Rifkind, Wharton & Garrison, N.Y.C., 1974—; dir. Brandon Ct., Inc. Served with USAR, 1969-71. Decorated Army Commendation medal. Mem. Am. Bar Assn., Assn. Bar City N.Y., Phi Delta Phi. Club: Sunningdale Country. Office: 345 Park Ave New York NY 10154

DUBOW, ARTHUR MYRON, investor, cons.; b. Chgo., Sept. 18, 1933; s. David and Matilda D.; A.B., Harvard, 1954, LL.B., 1957; m. Isabella Goodrich Breckinridge, Mar. 2, 1962; children—Charles Stewart, Alexandra Breckinridge. Admitted to N.Y. bar, 1961; mem. firm Webster, Sheffield, Fleischmann, Hitchcock & Chrystie, N.Y.C., 1960-64; v.p., dir. Back Bay-Orient Enterprises, Inc., N.Y.C., 1965-68, pres., 1968-76; pres., dir. Bayorient Holding Corp., 1969-76, dir. Sulpetro of Can., Ltd., 1966-76, chmn. exec. com., 1974-76; dir. Sulpetro Internat., Ltd., 1973-76, chmn. exec. com., 1974-76; pres. Fortune Capital Ltd., Boston, Boston Co. of Tex., Houston; dir. Internat. Basic Economy Corp., Calif. Energy Corp., Inc., Santa Rosa, Castle Convertible Fund, Spectra Fund, Inc., Devel. Resources Inc., Herald Prodns., Inc., Frontier Capital of New York, Inc., vis. fellow Center for Internat. Affairs, Harvard, 1976-77. Co-chmn. New Am. Filmmakers Series, Whitney Mus., 1971-76; mem. adv. bd. Sch. Advanced Internat. Studies, Johns Hopkins U.; vis. com. dept. visual and environ. studies Harvard, 1970-76, vis. com. dept. East Asian langs. and civilizations, 1977—, agt. class of 1954; chmn. bd. dirs. Potomac Assos., Inc., 1975—; trustee Brearley Sch., 1973-76. Served with U.S. Army, 1957-59. IBM fellow Internat. Design Conf., 1979. Clubs: Harvard of N.Y., Georgica Assn. (Wainscot, N.Y.), Faculty, Harvard (Cambridge, Mass.). Home: Briar Patch Rd East Hampton NY 11937 also 21 Berkeley St Cambridge MA 02138 Office: 1212 Main St Houston TX 77002 also One Boston Pl Boston MA 02106

DUBOW, SHELDON JOEL, pub. investment advisor; b. Newark, Dec. 28, 1937; s. Henry and Ruth (Blum) D.; ed. Bloomfield Coll., 1960; postgrad. N.Y. Inst. Fin., 1965; M.B.A., Pacific Western U., 1977, Ph.D., 1978; m. Carol Taylor; children—Lauren, Jonathan. Br. mgr. Godfrey Hamilton Taylor, N.Y.C., 1962; v.p. Lincoln Equity Corp., Hawthorne, N.J., 1963; registered rep. Bache & Co., N.Y.C., 1965; exec. v.p. Valve Line Securities, N.Y.C., 1967-72; v.p. Piedmont Capital Corp., Woodland Hills, Calif., 1973-75; pres. Energy News Digest, 1977—; pres., chief exec. officer Tri Star Oil & Gas Corp.; dir. Energy News Digest; adv. faculty Pacific Western U., 1978—. Served with USAR, 1956-58. Registered investment advisor. Mem. Internat. Assn. Fin. Planners. Club: Admirals. Author: Coal, All the Things you Forgot but Now Have to Remember, 1977; Applinetics: A View Toward Self Improvement, 1972; The Rural Route to Profits, 1977. Home: 6020 Fenwood Ave Woodland Hills CA 91367 Office: 21031 Ventura Blvd Suite 501 Woodland Hills CA 91364

DUBUC, GERARD PIERRE, JR., beverage mfg. co. exec.; b. Versailles, France, Jan. 18, 1941; s. Gerard P. and Claire E. (Dobes) D.; came to U.S., 1962, naturalized, 1973; Baccalaureat, Academie Nationale Francaise, 1960, B.S. in Bus. Adminstrn., 1962; LL.B., LaSalle U., 1969. Mgr. data processing Young's Market Co., Los Angeles, 1966-72; v.p. ops., dir. Joseph J. Battle Corp., Oakland, Calif., 1973-74; dir. ops. Automatic Data Processing Co., San Francisco, 1974-75; dir. systems, gen. office mgr. Nat. Distbg. Co., Los Angeles, 1975—. Served with JAGC, U.S. Army, 1964-66. Mem. Data Processing Mgmt. Assn. (dir. 1969-72), Am. Mgmt. Assn., Townhall of Calif., Wine and Spirit Wholesalers Assn. Republican. Home: 18949 Mt Walton Circle Fountain Valley CA 92708 Office: 1650 E Nadeau St Los Angeles CA 90001

DUCIE, CHARLES JOHN, JR., banker; b. Boston, Nov. 15, 1935; s. Charles John and Catherine Loretta (Hartigan) D.; student Boston Coll., 1956, Dartmouth Inst., 1974; m. Claire A. McElhinney, Sept. 5, 1959; children—Charles John, Kristen Marie. Trainee, Old Colony Trust Co., Boston, 1957, asst. sec., 1964, asst. v.p., 1967, v.p., 1970; v.p. First Nat. Bank of Boston, 1971, div. head, 1973, 1st v.p., 1978, sr. v.p., 1979—; dir. N.E. Securities Depository. Bd. dirs. Boston YMCA, 1979—, mem. fin. com., 1979-80; mem. fund raising Children's Hosp., Boston, 1978. Mem. Am. Soc. Corp. Secs., Stock Transfer Assn. Roman Catholic. Club: W. Dennis Yacht. Office: 100 Federal St Boston MA 02110

DUDELSTON, ROBERT EUGENE, steel co. exec.; b. Hartford City, Ind., Apr. 6, 1932; s. Preston Charles and Verla Estelle (Oren) D.; B.S., Ball State U., Muncie, Ind., 1954, M.B.A., 1968; m. Ann Foster Patton, June 8, 1957; children—Deborah Patton, Jefferson Robert. Auditor, Sanford, Myers & Dewald, C.P.A.'s, Ft. Wayne, Ind., 1956-57; chief accountant, then asst. controller Ingersoll Steel div. B-W Corp., New Castle, Ind., 1957-78; asst. to v.p. fin. and adminstrn. Ingersoll Johnson Steel Co., New Castle, 1978—; cons. to small bus. Bd. dirs. New Castle Salvation Army, 1976—; chmn. bd. trustees Presbyn. Ch. Served as officer USAF, 1954-56. Republican. Presbyterian. Club: New Castle Kiwanis (treas. 1973-78). Home: Route 1 Box 57 New Castle IN 47362 Office: Ingersoll Johnson Steel Co W Broad St New Castle IN 47362

DUDLEY, DAVID BARKER, food co. exec.; b. Columbus, Ohio, Apr. 6, 1930; s. Robert Lewis and Virginia (Barker) D.; B.S., Ohio State U., 1952; m. Susan Heath, Aug. 23, 1953; children—Karen Sue, Ann Louise. With M&R Dietetic Labs., Inc., Columbus, 1954-64, dir. sales spl. products div., 1960-64; with L.K. Baker & Co., Columbus, 1964—, sec.-treas., 1964-68, exec. v.p., 1968—. Mem. city council City of Grandview Heights, Ohio, 1972—. Served to lt. Q.M.C., AUS, 1952-54. Mem. U.S. Power Squadrons, Nat. Food Processors Assn. (dir. 1971-72, 74-76), Ohio Food Processors Assn. (dir. 1968-75, 78-79, pres. 1972), Ohio Automatic Merchandising Assn. (dir. 1970—), Inst. Food Technologists, Charity Newsies, Columbus C. of C., Columbus Maennerrchor, Delta Tau Delta. Clubs: Kiwanis; The Crew's Nest (Put-in-Bay, Ohio); Nor'Easter (Catawba Island, Ohio). Home: 1117 Wyandotte Rd Columbus OH 43212 Office: 1215 W Mound St Columbus OH 43223

DUDLEY, JAMES TIM, electric utility co. exec.; b. Union Hall, Va., Aug. 13, 1916; s. William Payton and Mattie F. (Holland) D.; B.S. in Agr. Engring., Va. Poly. Inst., 1938; m. Daphne Bousman, Dec. 25, 1940; children—James Tim, Payton C., Jan. M. Engr. electric utilities, Va., 1938-40; mgr. Ft. Loudoun Electric Coop., Madisonville, Tenn., 1940-41; gen. mgr. Rural Electrification Adminstrn., Washington, 1946-48; gen. mgr. Singing River Electric Power Assn., Lucedale, Miss., 1948—; dir. Nat. Rural Utilities Coop. Fin. Corp., 1969-78, pres., 1977-78. Pres., Miss. Council Farmer Coops., 1978-79; dir. Miss. Econ. Commn.; dir. Pine Burr Area council Boy Scouts Am., Hattiesburg, Miss. Served with U.S. Army, 1941-46. Mem. S. Miss. Electric Power Assn. (dir., past pres.), Electric Power Assn. Miss. Methodist. Office: PO Box 767 Lucedale MS 39452

DUDLEY, JOHN HENRY, bus. exec.; b. Detroit, Nov. 17, 1912; s. Henry Augustus and Margaret Helen (Bigelow) D.; grad. Detroit U. Sch., 1932; B.A., Mich. State U., 1937; m. Elizabeth Baird Dean, June 21, 1940; children—John Henry, Thomas Dean. With John Henry Co., 1937—, pres., 1939-72, gen. mgr., 1939-62, chmn. bd., 1972—. Past v.p., bd. dirs., chmn. Mich. United Fund; past pres., campaign chmn. United Community Chest Greater Lansing Area; past area chmn. serving Project Hope; past Mich. dir., past pres. Ingham County unit Am. Cancer Soc.; past chmn. Ingham County Rehab. Center; past chmn. YMCA, United Negro Coll. Fund; chmn. spl. study and adv. com. YMCA-YWCA; bd. dirs. Student Loan Mktg. Assn.; mem. Mich. Gov.'s Spl. Commn. on Traffic Safety. Served from lt. (j.g.) to lt. comdr., USNR, 1942-45; ETO; PTO. Decorated Navy Marine medal, Bronze Star; named to Floriculture Hall of Fame, 1966, Fla. State Florists Hall of Fame, 1978. Mem. Soc. Am. Florists (past pres., past chmn. nat. edn. com., nat-advt. council, gold medal 1979), Soc. Am. Florists Endowment (chmn., past trustee, sec.-treas.), Florists Transworld Delivery Assn. (past dir.), All Florist Industry Congress (founder, co-chmn.), U.S. (past mem. com. econ. policy), Mich., Lansing chambers commerce, Mich. Florists Assn. (past pres., dir., chmn. awards com., mem. publs. com., membership com.), Am. Inst. Floral Designers (hon.), Wholesale Florists and Florists Suppliers Am. (past dir., treas. Lee Kintzele award 1973), Honorable Order Ky. Cols. Rotarian. Clubs: City (pres. 1959), Country (past pres.), Lansing Automobile (Lansing); Detroit, Detroit Econ.; Met. (N.Y.C.); Capitol Hill, Met. (Washington); Los Angeles Country. Home: 610 W Ottawa St Lansing MI 48933 also 875 Comstock Ave Los Angeles CA 90024

DUDLEY, WAYNE CARROLL, seed co. exec.; b. McCallsburg, Iowa, Aug. 23, 1930; s. Barrett O. and Florine Ada (Chance) D.; grad. high sch.; m. Norma Jean Johnson, Nov. 10, 1950; children—Dennis, Vicki, Jackie. With O's Gold Seed Co. Inc., Parkersburg, Iowa, 1967—, gen. mgr., 1970—, exec. v.p., 1971-74, pres., 1974—. Mem. Parkersburg C. of C., Am. Seed Trade Assn., Am. Legion, 40 and 8. Mason, Elk. Club: Parkersburg Country. Home: Dudley Rd Rural Route 1 Parkersburg IA 50665 Office: PO Box 220 Parkersburg IA 50665

DUENWEG, LOUIS, utility cons.; b. Terre Haute, Ind., July 26, 1915; s. Louis and Marie Catherine (Coons) D.; B.S. in E.E., Rose Poly. Inst., 1936; exec. devel. courses U. Mich., Columbia U.; m. Mary G. Thompson, Oct. 28, 1960. Cons. Orgn. European Econ. Coop., Paris, 1956-57; with Detroit Edison Co., 1936—, acting asst. supt. Detroit div. overhead lines, 1965, dir. tng. and communications, 1946-69, mgmt. devel. coordinator, 1970-78, cons. orgn. and mgmt. devel., 1979—; instr. Dartmouth Coll., 1952-60, U. Detroit, 1954-55, Grad. Sch. Credit Fin. Mgmt.; comdt. U.S. Army Res. Sch., Ft. Wayne, Mich., 1954-55, mem. staff and faculty Command Gen. Staff Coll. Republican precinct del., 1960-61. Served with C.E. and AGC, AUS, 1940-46. Decorated Army Commendation Medal. Registered profl. engr., Ind. Mem. Mil. Order World Wars, Am. Def. Preparedness Assn., Am. Soc. Tng. and Devel., Soc. Advancement Mgmt. (past officer), Adult Edn. Assn. U.S.A. (past bd. dirs.), Nat. Indsl. Conf. Bd., AAAS, N.Y. Acad. Scis., Detroit Inst. Arts, Alpha Tau Omega, Tau Beta Pi, Blue Key, Tau Nu Tau. Clubs: Power, Edison Bus. (past pres.), Meridian Luncheon. Contbr. articles on mgmt. to profl. jours. Home: 1111 Devonshire Rd Grosse Pointe Park MI 48230 Office: 2000 2d Ave Detroit MI 48226

DUERSON, FRANCIS WILSON, distbn. co. exec.; b. Phoenix, Apr. 22, 1930; s. John Barbour and Mary Louella (Campbell) D.; student U. Ariz., 1948-52; m. Mary Lou Stern, July 26, 1970. Salesman, Techni Builders, Inc., 1956-56, Semon Bearing, Phoenix, 1956-60; with Western Bearings, 1960-65, mgr., Grand Junction, Colo., 1964-65; mgr. Kaman Bearings, Reno, 1965-79; owner Sierra Bearing and Power Transmission, Inc., Sparks, Nev., 1979—; pres., dir. Sage Enterprises, Inc., 1975-78. Chmn. Regional Ethics in Govt. Commn., 1976; mem. Regional Planning Commn., 1977-78. Served with U.S. Army, 1952-54. Mem. Asso. Bearing and Power Transmission Distbrs. Republican. Lutheran. Clubs: Sertoma, Masons, Shriners. Home: 1643 London Circle Sparks NV 89431 Office: 1824 Deming Way Sparks NV 89431

DUESENBERG, RICHARD WILLIAM, lawyer, business exec.; b. St. Louis, Dec. 10, 1930; s. (John August) Hugo and Edna Marie (Warmann) D.; B.A., Valparaiso U., 1951, J.D., 1953; LL.M., Yale, 1956; m. Phyllis Evelyn Buehner, Aug. 7, 1955; children—Karen, Daryl, Mark, David. Admitted to Mo. bar, 1953; prof. law N.Y. U. Sch. Law, 1956-62, dir. Law Center Publs., 1960-62; sr. atty. Monsanto Co., St. Louis, 1963-70, asst. gen. counsel, asst. sec., 1975-77, v.p., sec., gen. counsel, 1977—; dir. law Monsanto Textiles Co., St. Louis, 1971-75; corp. sec. Fisher Controls Co., Marshalltown, Iowa, 1969-71; corp. sec. Olympia Industries, Inc., Spartanburg, S.C., 1974-75; vis. prof. law U. Mo. Sch. Law, 1970-71; faculty Banking Sch. of South La. State U., 1967—; mem. legal adv. council Mfg. Chemists Assn., Washington; mem. legal adv. bd. NAM, 1980—; dir. Fisher Controls Co. of Del., St. Louis, 1979-80. Bd. dirs., vice chmn. Luth. Med. Center, St. Louis, bd. dirs. Valparaiso U. also chmn. bd. visitors Law Sch.; bd. dirs. Bach Soc. of St. Louis, also pres.; mem. adv. bd. Southwestern Legal Found., Dallas, 1977—; mem. Adminstrv. Council of U.S., 1980—. Served with AUS, 1953-55. Recipient Distinguished Alumnus award Valparaiso U., 1976. Mem. Am. Law Inst., Assn. Gen. Counsel, Luth. Acad. for Scholarship, Am. Arbitration Assn. (mem. nat. panel arbitrators 1960), Am. (chmn. subcom. on sales, bulk transfers and title documents 1970-76, com. on uniform comml. code 1976-79, mem. council sect. on corps., banking and bus. law 1979—), Mo., St. Louis, Internat. bar assns., Am. Judicature Soc., Order of Coif. Lutheran. Author (with L. King) Sales and Bulk Transfers Under the Uniform Commercial Code, 2 vols., 1966, rev. edits., 1977; New York Law of Contracts, 3 vols., 1964; Missouri Forms and Practice Under the Uniform Commercial Code, 2 vols., 1966. Editor: Ann. Survey of Am. Law, N.Y. U., 1961-62; bd. contbg. editors, adv. Corp. Law Rev., 1977—; contbr. articles to law revs., jours. Home: 9124 Glencrest Dr Saint Louis MO 63126 Office: 800 N Lindbergh Blvd Saint Louis MO 63166

DUFF, JAMES GEORGE, auto credit co. exec.; b. Pittsburg, Kans., Jan. 27, 1938; s. James George and Camilla Matilda (Vinardi) D.; B.S. with distinction, U. Kans., 1960, M.B.A., 1961; m. Linda Louise Beeman, June 24, 1961; children—Michele Annette, Mark Andrew, Melissa Christine. Mgr. Fin. Studies, fin. staff, Ford Motor Co., Dearborn, Mich., 1969-70, mgr. overseas profit analysis, 1970-71, dir. product, profit, price and warranty, Ford of Europe, 1971-74, controller, Ford Div., 1974-76, controller car ops., 1976, controller car product devel. group, 1976-80, exec. v.p. ins. and spl. financing ops. Ford Motor Credit Co., 1980—; instr. U. Kans., 1961-62. Sunray Mid-Continent scholar, 1960-61, Bankers scholar, 1959-60; asst. Center for Research in Bus., U. Kans. Bd. advs. U. Kans. Sch. Bus. Mem. Beta Gamma Sigma, Alpha Tau Omega, Alpha Kappa Psi. Methodist. Club: Pine Lake Country. Home: 480 N Cranbrook Rd Birmingham MI 48009 Office: Ford Motor Credit Co The American Rd Dearborn MI 48121

DUFFIE, CORNELIUS ROOSEVELT, mfg. co. exec.; b. Jersey Shore, Pa., Aug. 20, 1919; B.S. in Chem. Engring., U. Wash., 1941; Chief engr. Pennsalt Chems., Wash., 1941-57; mgr. Albany (Oreg.) paper mill Western Kraft, 1957-60, v.p. mill div., 1960-64, v.p. prodn., 1964-71, vice-chmn., chief operating officer, 1971-72, chmn., chief exec. officer, 1972-76; pres., chief operating officer Willamette Industries, Inc., Portland, Oreg., from 1976, now vice-chmn.; dir. Fourdrinier, Kraft Termicold. Served in USN, 1943-46. Mem. Am. Paper Inst. (dir., past chmn. recovery boiler com.), Inst. Paper Chemistry (trustee, vice-chmn.), Nat. Paperboard Assn. (past chmn.). Office: Willamette Industries Inc 1300 SW 5th Ave Portland OR 97201*

DUFFIELD, CHARLES ALLEN, printing co. exec.; b. Kingsport, Tenn., Aug. 10, 1942; s. James Clyde and Nita B. (Norris) D.; B.S., E. Tenn. State U., 1972; m. Sallie Louise Gillenwater, Aug. 24, 1963; children—Sherry, Vicki, Robin. Owner electronic repair center, 1959-64; technician Kingsport Broadcasting Co., 1959-64; with Kingsport Press, 1964—, sales project specialist, 1976-77, div. supt., 1977—. Pres., Colonial Heights Service Club, Kingsport, 1976; Jr. Achievement counselor, 1973, 74; treas. Colonial Heights Girls Athletic Commn., 1979-80; chmn. Miller Perry Sch. PTA Booster Club, 1978, 79; coach Colonial Heights Girls Volleyball Team, 1979; treas. Rebel Country Athletic Commn., 1981. Recipient Pres.'s award Colonial Heights Service Club, 1976. Republican. Baptist. Club: Eagles. Address: 811 Sir Echo Dr Kingsport TN 37662

DUFFIELD, DON FORREST, bank exec.; b. Pauls Valley, Okla., Feb. 9, 1935; s. Christine Antionette Bennett; B.B.A., U. Okla., 1957; m. Carole Ann McMillan, Apr. 11, 1958; children—Anne Elizabeth, Donna Lynn. Vice pres. First Nat. Bank & Trust Co., Oklahoma City, 1960-71; sr. v.p. First Nat. Bank, Amarillo, Tex., 1971-78; pres., dir. First State Bank & Trust Co., Guthrie, Okla., 1978—; mem. thesis exam faculty Stonier Grad. Sch. Banking, 1969-79. Pres., Guthrie Found., Inc., 1979—, Greater Guthrie C. of C., 1979-80, Guthrie United Way, 1979-80. Served to comdr. USNR, 1957-60. Mem. Am. Inst. Banking, Am. Bankers Assn., Okla. Bankers Assn. Republican. Episcopalian. Clubs: Masons, Shriners. Office: PO Box 520 Guthrie OK 73044

DUFFY, EDWARD W., banker; b. Utica, N.Y., 1926; grad. Syracuse U., 1950. Chmn., chief exec. officer Marine Midland Bank, Inc., Marine Midland Bank, N.A., Buffalo; dir. Buffalo Forge Co., Utica Mut. Ins. Co., Niagara Mohawk Power Corp. Trustee Clarkson Coll. Tech., Syracuse U. Office: One Marine Midland Center Buffalo NY 14240

DUFFY, JOHN J., banker; b. Pitts.; B.S. in Bus. Adminstrn., U. Pitts.; grad. with honors Pacific Coast Grad. Sch. Banking. U. Wash.; married; 2 children. With Security Pacific Nat. Bank (formerly Security Pacific Bank), 1948—, v.p., 1961-69, sr. v.p., 1969-72, exec. v.p., adminstr. bank support group, 1972—. Bd. regents Loyola Marymount U.; mem. men's adv. com. Assistance League So. Calif. Office: Security Pacific Nat Bank 333 S Hope St Los Angeles CA 90017*

DUFFY, KEVIN PATRICK, info. systems exec.; b. Newark, July 29, 1956; s. William Joseph and Catherine Mary (McGowan) D.; B.S.B.A., Seton Hall U., 1977, M.B.A., 1979, postgrad. in law. Faculty math., bus. Seton Hall U., 1975-76, 78—, asst. athletic dir., 1976-77; dir. Info. Unltd., Maplewood, N.J., 1977—. Recipient higher edn. achievement award State of N.J., 1978; Vincent A. McIntee medallion, 1979; Garden State grad. fellow, 1978—. Mem. Am. Bar Assn. (student div.), ACLU, NAACP. Clubs: Diamond, Winners Circle, K.C. Contbg. author: Evaluating Shipping Transactions: Liquid and Dry Bulk Movements, 1979. Contbr. articles to prof. publs.; corr. Star Ledger, N.Y. Daily News, 1971—. Home: 629 Prospect St Maplewood NJ 07040 Office: PO Box 504 Maplecrest Station Maplewood NJ 07040

DU FON, JOHN L., food service co. exec.; b. Chgo., Nov. 8, 1941; s. John L. and Jean (Kubacki) DuF.; student Am. U. of Beruit, 1960-61; B.S., Loyola U., Chgo., 1963; M.B.A., U. Chgo., 1966; m. Mary Blommer, Oct. 24, 1964; children—Jack, Jim, Michelle, Frederick, Danielle. Cost analyst Kimberly Clark, Neenah, Wis., 1966-67; systems engr. IBM, Chgo., 1967-70; sr. systems engr. McDonald's Corp., Oak Brook, Ill., 1971-73, dir. fin. communications, 1973—. Treas. St. Isaac Joques Sch. Bd., Oak Brook, Ill., 1977—. Mem. Nat. Investor Relations Inst. Roman Catholic. Home: Breakenridge Farm Oak Brook IL 60521 Office: McDonald's Plaza Oak Brook IL 60521

DUGGAN, T(HOMAS) PATRICK, mgmt. cons.; b. Hartford, Conn., Mar. 17, 1946; s. Edward O. and Mildred B. (Balf) D.; A.B., Providence Coll., 1968; postgrad. in mgmt. Western New Eng. Coll., 1969-71; m. Marcia McCormack, Aug. 31, 1968; children—Mary-Christina, T. Patrick. Mgr., Travelers Mgmt. Services, Hartford, 1968-75; mgr. mgmt. cons. services Coopers & Lybrand, N.Y.C., 1975-79; prin., dir. ins. mgmt. cons. services Hay Assos., N.Y.C., 1979—. Served to 1st lt., inf. USAR, 1968-75. Mem. Human Resource Planning Soc., Am. Mgmt. Assn., Ins. Accounting and Statis. Assn. (session chmn. 1975-79). Clubs: Golf of Avon, City of Hartford (Avon, Conn.). Home: 211 W 56th St New York City NY 10019

DU HAIME, NINA LEE, oil and mining co. exec. Owner Sun Mountain Realty, Santa Fe, 1964—; co-founder, v.p., sec., dir. Atom, Inc., 1968—; active Project ICONE, Delta Rose Internat. Writer weekly oil publ. Statehouse Reporter, Austin, Tex., 1965-77. Office: 645 Camino Lejo Santa Fe NM 87501

DUKE, HAROLD BENJAMIN, JR., rubber co. exec.; b. Washington, Iowa, Jan. 11, 1922; s. Harold Benjamin and Nordica (Wells) D.; B.A., Williams Coll., 1943; m. Maud Barnard Banks, June 11, 1949; children—James Lenox, Harold Benjamin III, Peter Wells, Lester Perrin, Charles Banks. With Gates Rubber Co., Denver, 1946—, mem. exec. com., 1959—, v.p., 1960-73, exec. v.p., 1973—, dir., 1973—; dir. Gates Rubber Co. subsidiary cos. A-Bar-A Ranch, Gates Energy Products, Gates Land Co.; dir., chmn. exec. com. Vail Assos., Inc., Colo., 1965—. Mem. Denver Com. on Fgn. Relations, 1967—; mem. adv. bd. Inst. Internat. Edn., 1969—. Bd. dirs. Boys Clubs of Denver, 1960—; pres., trustee Denver Country Day Sch., Englewood, Colo., 1958-71; trustee Social Sci. Found., U. Denver, 1967-75, pres., 1972-75; trustee Denver Pub. Library Found., 1974—, pres., 1976-79. Served with U.S. Army, 1943-45. Decorated Bronze Star medal, Purple Heart. Republican. Clubs: University, Mile High, Denver Country, Country of Colo. Office: 999 S Broadway PO Box 5887 Denver CO 80217

DUKE, JUDITH SILVERMAN, researcher, writer; b. Portchester, N.Y., Mar. 27, 1934; d. Herbert Francis and Fannye (Cohen) Silverman; student U. Mich., 1951-53; B.A., Cornell U., 1955; postgrad. N.Y. U. Sch. Bus. Adminstrn., 1959-67; m. Alan Duke, Mar. 2, 1968; 1 dau., Sharon Lisa. Econ. research asst. Boni, Watkins, Jason & Co., N.Y.C., 1955; statistician Nat. Footwear Mfrs. Assn., Washington, 1956-59; head research dept. Lefcourt Realty Corp., N.Y.C., 1959-60; asst. to dir. market research dept. Life mag., Time Inc., N.Y.C., 1960-70; abstracter-indexer Morningside Assos., Pleasantville, N.Y., 1973-75; free-lance writer, researcher, Millwood, N.Y., 1976—; bus. pub. field, 1976—. Author: The Children's Literature Market, 1977-82, 1977, The Religious Communications Market, 1978-83, 1978, Children's Books and Magazines - A Market Study, 1979, The Business Information Markets, 1979-84, 1979. Address: 6 Carriage Hill Millwood NY 10546

DUKES, ROLAND EDWARD, educator; b. Amboy, Ill., Apr. 24, 1941; s. Charles Edward and Viola May (Wells) D.; B.S. in Elec. Engring., U. Ill., 1964; M.B.A., Stanford U., 1970, Ph.D. in Bus. Adminstrn., 1972; m. Phyllis Ann Gilmore, July 10, 1965; children—Peter Gilmore, Anna Catherine. Asst. prof. acctg. and fin.

Cornell U., Ithaca, N.Y., 1972-76, asso. prof., 1976-80; prof. acctg. U. Wash., Seattle, 1980—; cons. Fin. Acctg. Standards Bd., SEC, various bus. firms, 1976—. Served with USN, 1964-68. Research grantee Fin. Acctg. Standards Bd., 1977-78, Peat Marwick & Mitchell Found., 1977-80. Mem. Am. Acctg. Assn. (disting. vis. faculty doctoral consortium, 1977, program dir. doctoral consortium, 1980), Western Fin. Assn., Am. Fin. Assn. Club: Acacia. Contbr. articles to publs. in field. Office: 324 Mackinzie Hall U Washington Seattle WA 98195

DUKESS, ALFRED CARLETON, housing co. exec.; b. N.Y.C., May 11, 1930; s. Murray J. and Bessie D.; A.B., Syracuse U., 1951; LL.B., Columbia U., 1954; m. Mona N. Bernstein, Aug. 29, 1955; children—Linda, Laura, Karen. Admitted to N.Y. bar, 1954; mem. firm Demov & Morris, N.Y.C., 1954-65, sr. partner, 1961-65; co-founder, exec. v.p. Continental Wingate Co., Inc., builder, developer rehab. housing, N.Y.C., Boston, Washington and Atlanta, 1968—; vis. lectr. Columbia Law Sch., St. Johns Law Sch., New Sch. Social Research. Chmn. Com. Selection Sch. Bd. Nominees, Mamaroneck, N.Y., 1971-73; mem. task force on housing costs HUD, 1977-78; vice chmn. Citizens Adv. Com. Mamaroneck Bd. Edn., 1976; bd. dirs. N.Y.C. Citizens Housing and Planning Council, 1976-78, Nat. Realty Com., Washington, 1976-78, South Bronx Community Housing Corp., 1975-78, Nat. Housing Conf., 1977-78; mem. N.Y. State Atty. Gen.'s Adv. Panel on Condominium Law, 1964-66; mem. citizens adv. com. N.Y.C. Dept. Housing Preservation and Devel., 1977-78; del. Presdl. Econ. Summit, 1974; trustee Barnard Coll., N.Y.C., 1980—. Contbr. articles to profl. and trade jours. Home: 79 Lansdowne Dr Larchmont NY 10538 Office: 919 3d Ave New York NY 10022

DULAN, HAROLD ANDREW, educator, investment counselor; b. Bridgeton, N.J., June 28, 1911; s. Thomas Francis and Mamie (Corson) D.; B.B.A., U. Tex., 1936, M.B.A., 1937, Ph.D., 1945; postgrad. Harvard, summer 1955, U. Chgo. (Beloit, Wis.), 1956, 63; m. Bess Gunn, May 31, 1946; children—Susan Matilda Dulan Hall, Kathleen Dulan Burke, Elizabeth Dulan Dorsey. Mem. faculty Tex. A. and M. Coll., 1938-42; pub. accountant, Dallas, 1941-46; fin. economist Fed. Res. Bank, Dallas, 1944-46; faculty Dallas Coll., So. Methodist U., 1945; pvt. investment counsellor, 1938—; head dept. finance U. Ark., Fayetteville, 1946-67, prof., 1946—; co-founder Participating Annuity Life Ins. Co., Fayettesville, 1954, chmn. investment com., v.p., pres., chmn. bd., 1954-68; financial cons. Argentine bus. concern, Buenos Aires, summer 1953; lectr., moderator Southwestern Bell Telephone Co. Mgmt. Seminars, Galveston, Tex., 1956-58, Hot Springs, Ark., 1958; conferee Conf. Savs. and Residential Financing, Savs. and Loan League, Chgo., 1958; mem. Fin. Analysts Fedn. European Econ. Conf. Tour, 1964; conducted econ. studies, Australia and Orient, 1971, S. Am., 1975, Singapore, Indonesia and Malaysia, 1980; dir. First Ark. Devel. Finance Corp. Commr., Tex. Centennial Statehood, 1946; commr., vice chmn. Gov.'s Commn. Status of Women for Ark., 1964-65; fellow N.Y. Fin. Dist., 1950; mem. Ark. Econ. Devel. Study Commn., 1975-76; mem. chancellor's council U. Tex. Mem. Am. Inst. C.P.A.'s, Am. Inst. Chartered Fin. Analysts (past mem. council examiners), N.Y. Soc. Security Analysts, Am. Finance Assn., Southwestern Social Sci. Assn. (past pres. finance sect.), Ark. Soc. C.P.A.'s, Nat. Assn. Bus. Economists, Fayetteville C. of C., Beta Gamma Sigma, Beta Alpha Psi, Sigma Iota Epsilon. Methodist. Clubs: Rotary, Country of Austin, Fayetteville Country. Contbr. articles to profl. jours. Home: 414 Ila St Fayetteville AR 72701

DULL, CARL AREY, JR., ins. co. exec.; b. Winston-Salem, N.C., Jan. 5, 1918; s. Carl Arey and Nora Mae (Alspaugh) D.; B.S. cum laude, Wake Forest U., 1939; m. Mary Chitwood Cooper, June 15, 1946; children—Donna Dull Hurt, Sybil Jane Dull Edwards, Keith R. Realtor, ins. agt., Winston-Salem, 1939-41; with Integon Corp. (and predecessor cos.), Winston-Salem, 1946—, vice-pres., treas., 1961—, pres., chief exec. officer, 1979—; chief exec. officer, chmn. Integon subsidiaries. Mem. Winston-Salem Housing Authority Commn.; trustee Salem Acad. and Coll., 1969-77; trustee Denmark Loan Fund of Wake Forest U., 1965—; trustee N.C. Council on Econ. Edn., 1976—. Served to lt. comdr. USNR, 1941-46. Mem. Winston-Salem C. of C. (dir. 1976-78), N.C. Fin. Analyst Soc. Democrat. Moravian. Clubs: Forsyth Country, Rotary, Wake Forest U. Deacon. Office: 500 W 5th St Winston-Salem NC 27102

DULLES, FREDERICK HENDRIK, lawyer; b. N.Y.C., Mar. 12, 1942; s. William Winslow and Joanna (deLeu) D.; A.B. cum laude, Harvard U., 1964; J.D., Columbia U., 1968, M.B.A., 1968; m. Martine Pred'homme, Aug. 26, 1977. Admitted to D.C. bar, 1971, N.Y. bar, 1972; asso. firm Shearman & Sterling, N.Y.C. and Paris, 1971-80; counsel Philip Morris Inc., N.Y.C., 1980—; internat. exec. Assn. Internationale des Etudiants en Sciences Economiques et Commerciales, 1961-66, U.S. gen. counsel, 1977-80. Served to lt. Security Group Command, USNR, 1968-71. Decorated Navy Achievement medal. Mem. Am. Bar Assn., Assn. Bar City N.Y., Am. Mgmt. Assn. Republican. Club: Harvard (N.Y.C.). Home: 50 E 89th St New York NY 10028 Office: 100 Park Ave New York NY 10017

DULUDE, DONALD OWEN, electric co. exec.; b. Bay City, Mich., Oct. 13, 1928; s. Owen P. and Bertranda L. (LaLonde) D.; B.S. in Mech. Engring., U. Mich., 1950; m. Dorothy A. Atkinson, Feb. 21, 1980; 1 son, Timothy Donald. Design engr. Bay City Shovels, Inc., 1950-57; mech. engr. Kuhlman Electric Co., Birmingham, Mich., 1957-60; partner Barribeau-Dulude & Assos., Inc., Birmingham, 1960-68; pres., gen. mgr. Quality Spring Products, Inc., subsidiary Kuhlman Corp., Coldwater, Mich., 1968-72, also dir., now pres., dir. Kuhlman Corp.; dir. Wolverine Aluminum Corp. Bd. dirs. Howe (Ind.) Mil. Sch. Fathers Assn. Served with AUS, 1953-55. Mem. Spring Mfrs. Inst. (nat. dir.), Mich. Spring Mfrs. Assn (pres. 1972-76), Detroit, Battle Creek engring. socs., Oakland Hills C. of C. Roman Catholic. Elk. Club: Detroit Athletic. Patentee in field. Office: PO Box 288 Birmingham MI 48012

DUMAS, JAMES RANDOLPH, banker; b. Little Rock, Aug. 2, 1946; s. James Henry and Wilma Ford D.; B.A., La. Tech. U., 1967; postgrad. Georgetown U., 1974; M.B.A., Wharton Sch. Fin., U. Pa., 1977; m. Denise S. Grigaitis, Dec. 26, 1969: 1 dau., Adrienne Ford. Commd. ensign U.S. Navy, 1967, advanced through grades to lt. comdr., 1975; assigned 6th Fleet, Mediterranean, 1967-71; naval intelligence liaison officer, Washington, 1971-75, discharged, 1975; with Crocker Bank, 1976-81, regional mgr. (v.p.) So. and Eastern Europe and Africa, Crocker Bank, London, 1979-81; v.p. corp. fin. Rotan-Mosle, Inc., Houston, 1981—. Decorated Navy Commendation medal. Mem. World Affairs Council. Clubs: Wharton, Univ. (San Francisco); Wharton (London); Commonwealth, Olympic, Stock Exchange. Home: One Grosvenor Cottage Eaton Terr London SW1 England Office: 34 Great St Helen's London ECA 6EP England Rotan-Mosle Inc 1500 South Tower Pennzoil Pl Houston TX 77002

DUMAS, JEFFREY MACK, lawyer, mfg. co. exec.; b. Corpus Christi, Sept. 29, 1945; s. Glenn Irven and Virginia Louise (Jones) D.; B.S., U.S. Naval Acad., 1968; M.S.E.E., Stanford U., 1969; J.D., Harvard U., 1978; m. P. Mary Walter, June 5, 1971; 1 son. Commd. ensign U.S. Navy, 1968, advanced through grades to lt., 1975; aviator, S.E. Asia, 1970-73; asst. prof. dept. elec. engring. U.S. Air Force Acad., 1973-75; liaison U.S. Senate Com. on Armed Services, 1975; resigned, 1975; paralegal People's Legal Services, Navajo Reservation, Window Rock, Ariz., 1976; corp. counsel Boeing Co., Seattle, 1978-81; asso. McClelland Law offices, Missoula, Mont., 1981—. Fellow UN Secretariat, Arms and Disarmament Conf., 1978. Recipient George Washington medal Freedom Found. at Valley Forge, 1974; registered profl. engr., Colo., Wash. Mem. U.S. Naval Inst., AAUP, IEEE, ASME, Am. Bar Assn., AIAA, Soaring Soc. Am., Council Fgn. Relations, Nat. Audubon Soc., Sierra Club (chmn. chpt. 1974-75), Wilderness Soc., Harvard Environ. Law Soc. (chmn. 1977-78), Sigma Xi. Contbr. articles to profl. jours. Home: 3208 Queen St Missoula MT 59801 Office: PO Box 8185 Missoula MT 59807

DUMM, ROBERT JAMES, energy and electronics products co. exec.; b. Long Beach, Calif., Oct. 26, 1931; s. Howard Cabot and Helen Ida (Donahoe) D.; B.S. in Bus., UCLA, 1954; postgrad. (Sloan fellow), Stanford U., 1973; m. Karen Elizabeth Keeler, Aug. 14, 1957; children—Bonni Elizabeth, Howard Bradley. Pres. Pacific Valves Inc., Long Beach, 1972, Dummco Corp., Paramount, Calif., 1974—, Kenitic Data Corp., Paramount, 1975—; dir. Walthon Wier Pacific, Wier Pacific. Served to lt. (j.g.) USN, 1954-56. Mem. Nat. Assn. Agts., Valve Mfrs. Assn. (dir.). Republican. Home: 4523 Fairway Dr Lakewood CA 90712 Office: 15930 Downey Ave Paramount CA 90723

DU MONT, JOHN SANDERSON, mfg. exec.; b. Greenfield, Mass., Oct. 5, 1919; s. Horatio Sanderson and Leila Atkinson (Washburn) du M.; student Deerfield (Mass.) Acad., 1933-35, Salisbury (Conn.) Sch., 1935-37; m. Mary Esther Robinson, June 21, 1941; children—Susanne Waller du Mont Alexander, Mary Taliaferro Robinson du Mont Nelson, Ann Washburn. In prodn. control, asst. prodn. mgr. Millers Falls Co., Greenfield, Mass., 1939-43; sr. v.p., dir. The du Mont Corp., Greenfield, 1947-76. Mem. New Eng. Regional Export Expansion Council, 1969-76. Mem. exec. council Pocumtuck Valley Meml. Assn., 1972-76; del. N.H. Republican Conv.; trustee Wildlife Conservation Trust. Served from pvt. to cpl. AUS, 81st Inf. Div., 1943-46. Decorated Bronze Star (U.S.); knight comdr. Order St. John of Jerusalem (U.K.); recipient Pres.'s E award for export, 1967, Pres.'s E Star award, 1969. Fellow Co. Mil. Collectors and Hist. 1957—), Nat. Rifle Assn., Armour and Arms Club N.Y., S.A.R. (life mem.), Custer Battlefield Hist. Assn. (mem. exec. com.), Colonial Wars Soc., S.C.V., Order Stars and Bars, Soc. War 1812, St. Nicholas Soc., Westerners, Greenfield Library Assn. (pres. 1953-73, trustee 1953-73), Ends of Earth, S.R., Soc. Mayflower Descs., Soc. of Cincinnati (pres. gen., mem. standing com.), Order Founders and Patriots, Mass. Ruffed Grouse Soc. (vice chmn. 1972). Author: (with John E. Parsons) Firearms in the Custer Battle, 1953; du Mont and Allied Families, 1960; Samuel Colt Presents, 1961; The Custer Battle Guns, 1974; American Engraved Powder Horns, 1978; contbr. articles on antique firearms to Am. Rifleman, Gun Digest, others. Lectr. on antique firearms. Home: Brimstone Corner Rd Hancock NH 03449

DUNAWAY, FRANK ROSSER, JR., gen. mgmt. cons. co. exec.; b. Jacksonville, Fla., June 23, 1931; s. Frank Rosser and Grace Isabel (Herrick) D.; B.M.E., U. Fla., 1953; M.B.A., Kent State U., 1962; postgrad. (Sloan fellow) Stanford U., 1962-63, Air War Coll., 1976-77; m. Constance Durham, June 1, 1953; children—Frank Rosser III, Wallace Neal, Geoffrey K.A. Field engr. Babcock & Wilcox Co., Chgo., 1954-58, project engr., Barberton, Ohio, 1958-61; lectr. indsl. mgmt. Kent (Ohio) State U., 1961-62; mktg. rep. IBM, San Francisco, 1963-66; cons., v.p. Golightly & Co. Internat., Inc., N.Y.C., 1966-73, 76-77, sr. v.p., 1978—, Houston, 1973-76, also dir.; prin., partner Harbridge House, Inc., Boston, 1978—; lectr., seminar leader, 1970—. Troop and dist. leader Boy Scouts Am. Served to lt. col. USAFR, 1953-80. Registered profl. engr., Fla., Ohio; certified mgmt. cons. Mem. ASME (exec. com. 1971—), Inst. Mgmt. Consultants, N.Am. Soc. for Corp. Planning, Nat. Soc. Profl. Engrs., Air Force Assn. Episcopalian (vestryman). Clubs: Athletic (Houston); Stanford (N.Y.C.). Contbr. to Ten Years Progress in Management 1960-70, Handbook of Cost Reduction, 1975. Contbr. articles to profl. jours. Home: 108 Weyford Terr Garden City NY 11530 Office: 1 Rockefeller Plaza New York NY 10020

DUNBAR, GERALD A., mgmt. cons.; b. Flint, Mich., Dec. 12, 1935; s. Roy A. and Carrie A. (Stewart) D.; B.S. in Bus. Adminstrn., Central Mich. U., 1966; M.B.A., Ind. No. U., 1974; m. Deanna S. Beers, 1968; 1 dau., Kristin A. Staff cons. Mgmt. Assos., Grand Rapids, Mich., 1965-67; mgmt. analyst Wofac Co. div. Sci. Mgmt. Corp., Moorestown, N.J., 1967-70; indsl. engr. Zurn Industries, Inc., Kalamazoo, Mich., 1970-72; prodn. mgr. Bradford-White Corp., Middleville, Mich., 1972-73; ops. mgr. Naus & Newlyn, Inc., Paoli, Pa., 1973-74; sr. mgmt. cons. Patton Consultants, Inc., Des Plaines, Ill., 1974-79; pres. Mgmt. Planning, Inc., Traverse City, Mich., 1980—. Served with U.S. Army, 1956-58. Mem. Am. Inst. Indsl. Engrs., Am. Prodn. and Inventory Control Soc. Contbr. articles to trade jours.

DUNBAR, RONALD H., transp. services exec.; b. Detroit, Feb. 20, 1937; s. Hugh and Louella Dunbar; B.A., Mich. State U., 1959; student Wayne State U., 1959; m. Brenda Jackson, Dec. 27, 1958; children—Debra, David, Karen, Julie. With Ford Motor Co., Dearborn, Mich., 1960-65; with Xerox Corp., Rochester, N.Y., 1965-78; v.p. corp. personnel Ryder System, Inc., 1978—. Bd. dirs., mem. exec. com. Private Industry Council, Miami; bd. dirs. Consumer Credit Counseling Service, Rochester, N.Y. Presbyterian. Club: Riviera Country. Office: Ryder System Inc Box 520816 Miami FL 33152

DUNCAN, ANSLEY MC KINLEY, aerospace co. mgr.; b. Homer City, Pa., Jan. 25, 1932; s. William McKinley and Marion Melissa (Davis) D.; student U. Denver, 1955-57, Pa. State U., 1957-59. Engring. adminstr. RCA, Van Nuys, Calif., 1959-61; program evaluation coordinator N.Am. Aviation, Anaheim, Calif., 1961-66; mfg. supr., Rockwell Internat., Anaheim Calif., 1966-70, program adminstr., 1970-76, program controls mgr., 1976—. Served with USN, 1951-55. Home: 12600 Willowood Ave Garden Grove CA 92640 Office: 3370 Miraloma Ave Anaheim CA 92803

DUNCAN, BUELL GARD, JR., bank exec.; b. Orlando, Fla., July 31, 1928; s. Buell Gard and Elizabeth (Parks) D.; B.B.A., Emory U., 1950; B.M.A., Sch. Bank Mktg., Boulder, Colo., 1959; m. Patricia Ann Jones, Mar. 25, 1952; children—Buell G., Patricia Ann Duncan Gillooly, Allan Griffin, Nancy Elizabeth. Officer trainee Sun First Nat. Bank of Orlando, Fla., 1953-56, asst. cashier, 1956-60, asst. v.p., 1960-61, v.p., 1961-68, sr. v.p., 1968-72, exec. v.p., 1972-75, pres., 1975-77, chmn., chief exec. officer, 1977—; exec. v.p. Sun Banks of Fla., Inc., 1979—; dir. Sun Banks of Fla., Inc., 1976—, Sun First Nat. Bank, 1972—, Sun Bank of St. Petersburg, 1980—, Sun Bank of Jacksonville, 1980—, Sun Bank of Miami, 1980—, Sun Bank of Dunedin, 1980—; dir. Nat. Standard Life Ins. Co., 1971—; Bd. dirs. United Way of Orange County, 1966—; chmn. Downtown Devel. Bd., 1979-80; bd. dirs., treas. Central Fla. Blood Bank, 1961-80; mem. Council advs. U. Central Fla., Valencia Community Coll. Found., 1977—. Served with USAF, 1950-53. Named Sales and Mktg. Exec. of Yr., Orlando area, Fla., 1979. Mem. Bank Mktg. Assn. (pres. 1971-72), Orlando Area C. of C. (pres. 1970-71), Fla. Bankers Assn. (chmn. group V, nat. pres.), Mid-Fla. Com. of 100 (indsl. devel. commn.). Republican. Episcopalian. Clubs: Country of Orlando, Univ., Citrus, Kiwanis. Office: 200 S Orange Ave Orlando FL 32801

DUNCAN, CHARLES WILLIAM, JR., sec. Dept. Energy; b. Houston, Sept. 9, 1926; s. Charles William and Mary Lillian (House) D.; B.S. in Chem. Engring., Rice U., 1947; postgrad. mgmt. U. Tex., 1948-49; m. Thetis Anne Smith, June 10, 1957; children—Charles William III, Mary Anne. Roustabout, chem. engr. Humble Oil & Refining Co., 1947; with Duncan Foods Co., Houston, 1948-64, adminstrv. v.p., 1957-58, pres., chmn. adv. bd., 1958-64; pres. Coca-Cola Co. Food Div., Houston, 1964-67; chmn. Coca-Cola Europe, 1967-70; exec. v.p. Coca-Cola Co., Atlanta, 1970-71, pres., 1971-74; chmn. bd., dir. Rotan Mosle Financial Corp., Houston, 1974-77; dep. sec. Dept. Def., Washington, 1977-79; sec. Dept. Energy, Washington, 1979—. Served with USAAF, 1944-46. Mem. Sigma Alpha Epsilon, Sigma Iota Epsilon. Methodist. Clubs: Houston Country, River Oaks Country, Allegro (Houston). Home: 5161 Palisade Ln NW Washington DC 20016 Office: Dept Energy 1000 Independence Ave SW Washington DC 20585

DUNCAN, JOHN C., corp. exec.; b. N.Y.C., Sept. 29, 1920; s. John C. and Doris (Bullard) D.; B.A., Yale U., 1942; m. Barbara Doyle, Dec. 12, 1942; children—Wendy Duncan De Albeney, Lynn Duncan Tarbox, Craig, Gale Duncan Simmons. Exec. v.p., dir. W.R. Grace & Co., N.Y.C., 1948-70; sr. v.p., dir. St. Joe Minerals Corp., N.Y.C., 1970-71, pres., chief exec. officer, 1971-77, chmn., chief exec. officer, 1977-80, chmn., pres., chief exec. officer, 1980—; dir. Westvaco Corp., B.F. Goodrich Co., Irving Trust Co., Irving Bank Corp., CanDel Oil Ltd., Am. Mining Congress, Accion Internat. Trustee Hampton Inst.; chmn., dir. Council of the Americas; dir. AIFLD. Served to capt. U.S. Army, World War II; CBI. Mem. AIME, Council on Fgn. Relations. Clubs: Links, Round Hill, Yale, Board Room, Econ. Club of N.Y. Office: 250 Park Ave New York NY 10017

DUNDAS, GIFFORD WENDOW, owner concrete co.; b. Lewiston, Idaho, Nov. 29, 1908; s. Harry Wendow and Mamie Clarin (Gifford) D.; student U. Calif. at San Francisco, 1931-33; m. Dee Ramona Houser, Jan. 29, 1942. Pres., owner Dunclick, Inc., Lewiston, Idaho, 1945—; owner Research and Devel. Co., 1974-76. Mem. City Lewiston Water Commn., 1962-65; chmn. Planning Commn., Lewiston, 1964-65; chmn. Beautification Com., Lewiston, 1965-66. Bd. dirs. Inland Water Way, Lewiston, 1963-70. Mem. Lewiston C. of C. (dir. 1964-66). Mason (Shriner), Elk. Patentee in field. Address: 2040 Sargent Ln Clarkston WA 99403

DUNHAM, DAVID ALLAN, graphic communication exec.; b. Portland, Oreg., Mar. 26, 1938; s. Allan Miller and Helen Elizabeth (Connor) D.; student Multonomah Coll., 1962-64; B.S., Portland State U., 1967; grad. Inst. Mgmt. Sci., 1976; m. Sheree Lee Shank, July 1978. Asst. to dean bus. sch. Portland State U., 1964-66; with Dunham Printing Inc., Portland, 1967—, pres., owner, 1971—; trustee Dunham Printing Inc. Profit Sharing Plan; cons. to various printing firms. Active Jr. Achievement. Served with USN, 1957-61. Mem. Printing Industry Am. (outstanding award achievement 1978), Printing Industry Pacific (bd. govs.), Oreg. Motor Hotel Assn., Sales and Mktg. Execs. Internat. (Salesman of Year 1972), Portland Homebuilders Assn., Bus. Profl. Advt. Assn., Portland C. of C., Phi Theta Kappa. Republican. Presbyterian. Club: Rotary. Home: 4338 Botticeli Lake Oswego OR 97034 Office: 2502 SE Division St Portland OR 97202

DUNIKOSKI, FREDERICK, transp. exec.; b. N.Y.C., Aug. 1, 1925; s. Helen (Czajkowski) D.; student U. Ill.; m. Rita A. McQuade, Oct. 11, 1947; children—Susan, Fred, Donna, Robert. With Greyhound Lines, Inc., 1942—, dir. transp., 1969-70, v.p. transp., 1970-78, exec. v.p. ops., 1978-79, pres., chief operating officer, Phoenix, 1979—. Dir. Travelers Aid Soc., Cleve., 1961-69; treas. Community Orgn. for Drug Abuse Control, 1973-75. Served with USMC, 1943-45. Mem. Am. Bus. Assn. (dir.). Democrat. Roman Catholic. Office: Greyhound Tower Phoenix AZ 85077

DUNLAP, JOSEPH CHRISTOPHER, bus. machine co. exec.; b. Raleigh, N.C., June 21, 1943; s. Merle Marvin and Marian (Lorraine (Hoffa) Mowery; B.S. magna cum laude in Psychology, Duke U., 1965; M.B.A., U. N.C., 1971; m. Linda Anne Ball, June 17, 1972. Systems mktg. mgr. Olivetti Corp. Am., Richmond, Va., 1971-73, sr. systems instr., N.Y.C., 1973-74, mgr. systems edn., 1974-76; dir. manpower devel. Monroe div. Litton Industries, Morris Plains, N.J., 1976—. Vice pres. Jaycees, 1972; adv. council career devel. State of N.J. Served to lt. USN, 1965-69. Decorated Navy Cross; recipient outstanding achievement award in mktg. edn. Nat. Acad. Tng. and Devel., 1977. Mem. Am. Soc. Tng. and Devel., Nat. Soc. Sales Tng. Execs., Nat. Assn. Colls. and Univs., Phi Beta Kappa. Republican. Episcopalian. Club: Kiwanis. Author: Introduction to Basic Business Systems, 1977; Human Resources Development—Key to Productivity, 1979. Home: 81 Watnong Dr Morris Plains NJ 07950 Office: American Rd Morris Plains NJ 07950

DUNLEAVY, FRANCIS J., former communications co. exec.; b. 1914; B.B.A., Niagara U.; student Wharton Sch. Bus., U. Pa.; married; 4 children. Formerly with Crown Cork & Seal Co., Yale & Towne Mfg. Co., Communications and Control div. RCA; exec. asst. to pres. ITT, N.Y.C., 1962-63; exec. v.p. ITT Europe, Inc., 1963-64, pres., 1965-67; v.p. ITT, N.Y.C., 1964-66, exec. v.p., 1966-79, dir., 1967-79, mem. Office of Pres., 1968-79, pres., chief operating officer, mem. exec. com., 1974-77, vice chmn. bd., mem. exec. com., 1977-79; dir. Indsl. Valley Bank & Trust Co., Phila. Trustee, Niagara U., LaSalle Coll.; bd. mgrs. Germantown Hosp., Phila.; mem. nat. bds. Morality in Media, Goodwill Industries, United Negro Coll. Fund. Decorated officer Order of Crown (Belgium). Club: Econ. of N.Y. (chmn.). Office: ITT World Hdqrs 320 Park Ave New York NY 10022*

DUNLOP, RUSSELL OSCAR, printing firm exec.; b. Ashcroft, B.C., Can., Aug. 3, 1932; s. Oscar Russell and Norma Louise (Procunier) D.; grad. Woodstock (Ont.) Collegiate Inst.; children—Christopher Oscar, Sheree Irene Marshall. Asst. advt. mgr. Guelph (Ont.) Daily Mercury, 1956-59; advt. dir. Nanaimo (B.C.) Daily Free Press, 1959-70; pub., gen. mgr. Vernon (B.C.) News, 1970-73; pres. Vernon Interior Printers Ltd., 1973—; pres. Westvern Enterprises Ltd., Vernon. Mem. exec. bd. United Appeal, Nanaimo, Red Cross Soc., Nanaimo. Mem. Graphic Arts Industries Assn., Canadian Orgn. Small Bus., Vernon C. of C. Progressive Conservative. Mem. United Ch. of Can. Clubs: Gyro (pres. Vernon chpt. 1975-76, gov. internat. dist. IV 1979-80), Vernon (pres. 1980-81), Masons. Home: Rural Route 6 Okanagan Landing Rd Vernon BC V1T 6Y5 Canada Office: 2901 29th St Vernon BC V1T 5A5 Canada

DUNN, ALBERT WILKERSON, rubber co. exec.; b. Durham, N.C., Mar. 2, 1921; s. William Burwell and Maude (Wilkerson) D.; A.B. in English, Duke U., 1943; m. Jane Ballard, Oct. 23, 1943; children—Robert R., Stephen R., Christie A. (Mrs. J.P. Miller). With Goodyear Tire & Rubber Co., 1946—, mem. pub. relations dept., Akron, Ohio, 1946-48, mgr. aviation products div., Dayton, Ohio, 1948-55, aviation products mil. coordinator, 1955-57, mgr. Aviation Products div. Goodyear Internat. Corp., 1957-59, sales dir., Philippines, 1959-61, v.p., gen. mgr., 1961-71, mng. dir. Goodyear-South Africa, 1971-78, pres., chief exec. officer Goodyear

Can., Inc., Toronto, 1978—. Past pres. Am. Sch. Bd. of Manila, Am. C. of C. of Manila. Served with USAAF, World War II. Decorated Air Medal with 3 oak leaf clusters, D.F.C. *

DUNN, CHARLES WESLEY, JR., investment mgmt. exec.; b. N.Y.C., July 11, 1931; s. Charles Wesley and Alice Louise (Hafner) D.; B.A., Middlebury Coll., 1953; m. Olivia Endicott Hutchins, Dec. 5, 1959; children—Charles Wesley, III, John Endicott. Exec. trainee Chase Manhattan Bank, N.Y.C., 1954-56; charter broker William H. Muller Shipping Co., N.Y.C., 1957-59, Naess Shipping Co., N.Y.C., 1959-60; with Kidder Peabody & Co., Inc., N.Y.C., 1960—, asst. v.p., 1967, v.p., 1968—, also dir.; chmn. Kidder Peabody Employee Retirement Fund Investment Com., Kidder Peabody Employee Profit Sharing Plan Investment Com.; dir. Webster Mgmt. Co., subs. Kidder Peabody & Co. Inc. Pres. Tokeneke Tax Dist., Darien, Conn., 1973-78, bd. dirs., 1978; v.p., bd. dirs. Tokeneke Assn., 1978-79, bd. dirs., 1978—; trustee North Country Sch., Lake Placid, N.Y. Republican. Episcopalian. Clubs: Tokeneke (former gov.) (Darien); Racquet and Tennis, Downtown Assn. (N.Y.C.). Home: Siwanoy Rd Darien CT 06820 Office: Kidder Peabody Co 10 Hanover Sq New York NY 10005

DUNN, JAMES JOSEPH, mag. pub.; b. N.Y.C., July 22, 1920; s. James A. and Mary A. (Kelly) D.; B.B.A., Manhattan Coll., 1941; m. Elinor M. Hargesheimer, Aug. 30, 1943; children—Patricia Ann, Kevin James, Gregory John, Sean David, Christopher Kelly. With McCall Corp., 1946-50; with Time, Inc., 1950-66, advt. dir., N.Y.C., 1961-66; v.p., publisher Forbes, Inc., 1966—. Bd. dirs. Salvation Army; trustee Manhattan Coll. Served to lt. comdr. USNR, 1941-46. Mem. Mag. Pubs. Assn. (dir.). Clubs: Blind Brook, Winged Foot, Laurel Valley. Home: Glenville Rd Greenwich CT 06830 Office: 60 Fifth Ave New York NY 10011

DUNN, JOHANNA READ, fin. exec.; b. N.Y.C., Mar. 7, 1946; d. Joseph Mathias and Anna Helen (Judge) Hahnen; B.A. summa cum laude, Barnard Coll., 1965; M.A. summa cum laude, Columbia U., 1967, Ph.D. magna cum laude, 1970; postgrad. The Sorbonne, U. Paris, 1969-70; m. G. Leslie Fabian, Feb. 12, 1977; 1 stepdau., Barbara. Editor, McKinsey & Co., Inc., N.Y.C., 1967; mng. editor European Bus., Paris, 1969-70; co-founder, chief bus. editor Tempo Economico, Lisbon, Portugal, 1970-74; chief fin. writer for Expresso Lisbon, 1970-74; communications cons. Citicorp, 1975-76, Norton Simon Inc., 1975-76, Council of Americas, 1975-76, Donley Communications Corp., 1975-76; communications specialist N.Y. Stock Exchange, Inc., 1976-78; exec. asst. to office of chmn. N.Y. Stock Exchange, 1978-79, asst. v.p. corp. planning, 1979; v.p. market planning and support N.Y. Futures Exchange, 1980—; cons. State Edn. Dept., SUNY, 1975—. Woodrow Wilson vis. fellow, 1979. Wall St. Planning Group (v.p. 1980), Investment Assn. N.Y., Phi Beta Kappa. Democrat. Presbyterian. Author: Counterpoint: A Book of Poetry, 1966; contbr. numerous poems to lit. publs. Home: 1020 Park Ave New York NY 10028 Office: NY Stock Exchange 11 Wall St New York NY 10005

DUNN, JOSEPH FRANCES, ins. co. exec.; b. Cohasset, Mass., Feb. 27, 1924; s. Jesse and Margaret Elizabeth (Flannery) D.; A.B., Syracuse U., 1947; M.A., N.Y. U., 1953; m. Marjorie E. Moore, Dec., 1958; children—Joseph F., Karen. With Prudential Ins. Co. Am., Newark, 1947—, asso. dir. research, 1958-63, dir. planning and research, 1963-74, v.p., 1974—; dir. Sony Prudential Life Ins. Co., Ltd.; cons. Orgn. Dynamics Inc. Lic. psychologist, N.J. Mem. Am. Psychol. Assn., Life Ins. Mktg. Research Assn. (mktg. services com.), Agency Mgmt. Assn. (ins. research dirs'. group), Am. Coll. Life Underwriters (chartered). Republican. Roman Catholic. Club: Mt. Tabor Country. Home: Puddingstone Ln Millington NJ 07946 Office: Prudential Ins Co Am Prudential Plaza Newark NJ 07101

DUNN, RICHARD JOSEPH, investment counselor; b. Chgo., Apr. 5, 1924; s. Richard Joseph and Margaret Mary (Jennett) D.; A.B., Yale U., 1948; LL.B., Harvard U., 1951; M.B.A., Stanford U., 1956; m. Marygrace Calhoun, Oct. 13, 1951; children—Richard, Marianne, Anthony, Gregory, Noelle. Admitted to Tex. bar, 1952; mem. firm Carrington, Gowen, Johnson & Walker, Dallas, 1951-54; investment counselor Scudder, Stevens & Clark, San Francisco, 1956—, v.p., 1965-77, sr. v.p., 1977—, gen. partner, 1974—. Mem. Democratic State Central Com. Calif., 1962, San Francisco Dem. County Central Com., 1963-66; bd. dirs. Mercy High Sch., 1978. Served with AUS, 1943-46. Decorated Purple Heart. Mem. San Francisco Security Analyst Soc. Club: Knight of Malta. Home: 530 Junipero Serra Blvd San Francisco CA 94127 Office: 600 Montgomery St San Francisco CA 94111

DUNN, RONALD HOLLAND, engring. and mgmt. exec.; b. Balt., Sept. 15, 1937; s. Delmas Joseph and Edna Grace (Holland) D.; student U. S.C., 1956-58; B.S. in Engring., Johns Hopkins U., 1969; m. Verona Lucille Lambert, Aug. 17, 1958; children—Ronald H., Jr. (dec.), David R., Brian W. Field engr. Balt. & Ohio R.R., Balt., 1958-66; chief engr. yards, shops, trackwork DeLeuw, Cather & Co., Washington, 1966-73; mgr. engring. support Parsons-Brinckerhoff-Tudor-Bechtel, Atlanta, 1973-76; dir. railroad engring. Morrison-Knudsen Co., Inc., Boise, Idaho, 1976-78; v.p. Parsons Brinckerhoff-Centec, Inc., McLean, Va., 1978—; mem. adv. com. track engrs. U.S. Dept. Transp. Chmn., Cub Scout Pack, 1972-73, committeeman, 1973-75. Mem. Am. Mgmt. Assn., Am. Ry. Engring. Assn., ASCE, Am. Pub. Transit Assn., Soc. Am. Mil. Engrs., Roadmasters and Maintenance of Way Assn. of Am., AM. Ry. Bridge and Bldg. Assn., Ry. Tie Assn., Inst. of Rapid Transit, Phi Kappa Sigma. Methodist. Author tech. publs., profl. articles. Guest of Japan Ry. Civil Engring. Assn. observing, inspecting railroad and rail rapid transit facilities in Japan, 1972. Office: Suite 220 8301 Greensboro Dr McLean VA 22102

DUNNE, DENNIS WILLIAM, banker; b. Roundup, Mont., Aug. 30, 1928; s. William Henry and Queenie (Saby) D.; B.B.A. in Fin., U. Minn., 1950; grad. Sch. Banking U. Wis., 1959, Stonier Grad. Sch. Banking Rutgers U., 1970; m. Patricia Russell, Aug. 19, 1950; 1 son, Charles W. With Northwestern Nat. Bank of Mpls., 1946, Mont. Nat. Bank, Billings, 1950, N.W. Bancorp., 1953, Northwestern Nat. Bank of Great Falls (Mont.), 1954-59, 1st Northwestern Nat. Bank of Winona (Minn.), 1959-62, N.W. Bancorp., 1962-75; pres. 1st Nat. Bank of Duluth (Minn.), 1975—. Bd. dirs. Miller-Dwan Hosp., College St. Scholastica, Ordean Found., Courage Found.; pres. United Way of Duluth; active Duluth Downtown Devel. Corp., Lyric Block Devel. Corp. Served with USAF, 1952-53. Mem. Duluth Area C. of C. (dir.). Clubs: Northland Country, Kitchi Gammi, Rotary (Duluth). Office: 230 W Superior St Duluth MN 55802

DUNNE, GEORGE THOMAS, wholesale seafood co. exec.; b. Boston, June 16, 1935; s. George Vincent and Sarah (Carter) D.; A.B. in Econs. and Stats., Boston Coll., 1960, postgrad., 1962; m. Anne Marie Donohoe, Aug. 12, 1961; children—Beth Carter, Patrick Joseph, Christopher Brady. With IBM, 1960-63, MBI Systems, Inc., 1963-67, Arthur Young & Co., 1967-70; pres., treas. Dunne Assos., Inc., South Boston, Mass., 1970—; exec. v.p., treas. New Eng. Fillet Co., Inc., Boston, 1971-73; lectr. Northeastern U., 1962-66, Providence Coll., 1966-67. Mem. adv. com. Blue Hills Regional Vocat. Sch., 1963-69. Served with U.S. Army, 1954-56. Cert. in data processing. Mem. Systems and Procedures Assn., Data Processing Mgmt. Assn., Nat. Fisheries Inst. Democrat. Roman Catholic. Home: 22 Trowbridge Circle Stoughton MA 02072 Office: 4 Alger St South Boston MA 02127

DUNNE, JOHN EDWARD, restaurant and real estate co. exec.; b. N.Y.C., Jan. 9, 1950; B.B.A. in Acctg., Baruch Coll., 1972, M.B.A. in Taxation, 1980; m. Eileen T. Kelly, Apr. 27, 1974; children—Gregory, Timothy. Asst. staff acct. N.Y. Telephone, Berkey Photo, N.Y.C., 1969-71; staff acct. Nat. Restaurants Inc./Riese Orgn., N.Y.C., 1971-73, asst. controller, 1973-75, controller, 1975—. Democrat. Roman Catholic. Home: 12 Irvinlee Pl East Northport NY 11731 Office: 162 W 34th St New York NY 10001

DUNNIGAN, FRANK JOSEPH, pub. co. exec.; b. Westport, Conn., Dec. 15, 1914; s. Francis P. and Kathryn (Grossmann) D.; A.A., Jr. Coll. Conn., 1934; B.S., N.Y. U., 1940; hon. doctorate U. Bridgeport, 1976; m. Teresa L. Razete, Aug. 13, 1966. Accountant, Consol. Edison Co., N.Y.C., 1934-37; with Prentice-Hall, Inc., Engelwood Cliffs, N.J., 1937—, exec. v.p., 1965-71, pres., 1971-80, chmn., 1980—, also chief exec. officer. Trustee Pren-Hall Found. Served to capt. AUS, 1941-46. Recipient Madden Meml. award, 1980. Mem. Newcomen Soc., Phi Theta Kappa. Club: Manor (Mt. Pocono, Pa.). Home: 1500 Palisade Ave Fort Lee NJ 07024 Office: Prentice-Hall Sylvan Ave Englewood Cliffs NJ 07631

DUNNING, JAMES DORR, JR., publishing exec.; b. Spokane, Wash., June 7, 1947; s. James Dorr and Mary Margret (Bourne) D.; B.S., U. Pa., 1970. Pres., chief exec. officer Univ. Mktg. & Cons., Inc., Phila., 1970-73; mgr. Pubs. Clearing House, Port Washington, N.Y., 1973-76; exec. v.p., chief operating/fin. officer Straight Arrow Publs., Inc., 1977—, also dir.; dir. Nat. Samco, Inc., Phila., 1973-75, Univ. Mktg. and Cons., Inc., Phila., 1970-73; cons. in field. Republican committeeman, Phila., 1972-73. Mem. Assn. M.B.A. Execs., Am. Mgmt. Assn. Episcopalian. Clubs: N. Hempstead Country, Wharton Grad. Sch. of N.Y. Address: 301 E 52d St New York NY 10022

DUNNING, RALPH RAYMOND, bldg. materials co. exec.; b. North Andover, Mass., Mar. 9, 1918; s. John C. and Irene (Wilcox) D.; ed. Teaneck (N.J.) pub. schs., night and corr. schs.; m. Angela Lee Planchard, 1979. Apprentice, Am. Woolen Co., Skowhegan, Maine, 1937-42, supt., 1945-48; accountant Rinker Materials Corp., West Palm Beach, Fla., 1948-58, plant mgr., 1958-65, dist. mgr., 1965-75, gen. mgr., 1975-77, v.p., 1977, exec. v.p. materials div., 1978-79, pres. materials div., 1979—. Bd. dirs. Cape Canaveral Hosp., 1969-74, pres., 1973-74. Served with USAAF, 1942-45. Mem. DAV, West Palm Beach C. of C. Republican. Club: Rotary. Home: 1051 Coral Way Riviera Beach FL 33404 Office: 433 7th St West Palm Beach FL 33401

DUNSAY, RICHARD CRAIG, lawyer; b. Chgo., Sept. 13, 1940; s. Alexander Ivan and Viola Ida (Katz) D.; B.S. in Econs., Ariz. State U., 1963; J.D., DePaul U., 1964; m. Dian Elaine White, Jan. 11, 1970; children—Derek, Devin. Admitted to Ill. bar, 1964, Calif. bar, 1965; asso. firm Steinberg, Polacek & Steinberg, Chgo., 1964, Law Offices Ned Good, Los Angeles, 1965; dep. city atty. criminal div. City of Los Angeles, 1965-67; atty. Law Office Louis I. Bell, Los Angeles, 1967-70; individual practice law, Los Angeles, 1970—. Mem. Am. Bar Assn., Calif. State Bar, Ill. Bar Assn., Los Angeles County Bar Assn., Calif. Trial Lawyers Assn., Los Angeles County Trial Lawyers Assn., Am. Arbitration Assn. (arbitrator), World Affairs Council, Smithsonian Assos., Los Angeles County Art Mus. Editor-in-chief: DePaul Law Rev., 1963-64. Office: 6380 Wilshire Blvd Suite 800 Los Angeles CA 90048

DUNTON, FRANK PROUTY, fin. adminstr.; b. Melrose, Mass., Sept. 8, 1946; s. Lewis W. and Mary E. (Gable) D.; B.A. in Econs., Colby Coll., 1968; M.B.A., Suffolk U., 1980; m. Joan A. Waddell, Aug. 18, 1968; children—Brett James, Heather Elizabeth. Bursar, U. Mass., Boston, 1973—; partner, bus. mgr. Rockport (Mass.) Rascals Children's Shop, 1978—. Mem. Rockport Land Bank Com., 1978-80; treas. Sandy Bay Pre-sch., Rockport, 1979-80. Served to capt. USAF, 1968-73. Decorated D.F.C. (2), Air medal (6), others. Home: One Story St Rockport MA 01966 Office: Bursar's Office U Mass Harbor Campus Boston MA 02125

DUNWIDDIE, JAMES FOSTER, petroleum co. exec.; b. Delavan, Wis., Nov. 23, 1918; s. Ralph Sidney and Florence Emma (Waldie) D.; B.S. in Mech. Engring., U. Wis., 1940; grad. mgmt. problems for execs. course U. Pitts., 1953; m. Margaret Louise Hopkins, Nov. 17, 1945; children—Barbara Ann, Bruce Douglas. Mgr. mktg. ops. and engring. Standard-Vacuum Oil Co., Singapore, Manila, N.Y.C., 1940-60; with Mobil Oil, N.Y.C. and Bermuda, 1960-72, exec. v.p. Mundo Gas, 1970-72; mgr. spl. projects La Gloria Oil & Gas Co., 1972-74; gen. mgr. internat. trading and transp. Tex. Eastern Transmission Corp., 1974-76; pres. Tex. Eastern Internat. Services Ltd., London, 1976—, Tex. Eastern Shipping, Bermuda, 1976—; v.p. North Sea Inc., Tex. Eastern Norwegean, 1976—; chmn. bd. Iran-Tex. Engring. Co., 1976-78. Served to capt. USMCR, 1942-46. Fellow Inst. Petroleum, Royal Inst. Internat. Affairs; mem. Am. Petroleum Isnt., Am. Mgmt. Assn. Republican. Clubs: Royal Automobile, Manila Yacht; Am. (Singapore). Home: 49 Lowndes Sq London SW1 England Office: 11 Grafton London W1X 3LA England

DUPRE, DERRICK PAUL, elec. engr.; b. Middleboro, Mass., Mar. 9, 1954; s. Carl William and Gloria Anne (Giovannini) D.; B.S. in E.E., Southeastern Mass. U., 1976; m. Rosemarie Helen Harding, Oct. 8, 1977; children—Justin Monroe, Jennifer Leigh. Test engr. Instron Corp., Canton, Mass., 1976; quality control engr. Foxboro Co., East Bridgewater, Mass., 1976-78, sr. quality control engr., 1978-79, sr. test engr., Foxboro, Mass., 1979-80, chief systems engr., 1980—; prof. engring. continuing edn. div. Massasoit Community Coll., Brockton, Mass., 1981—. Mem. IEEE, Am. Soc. Quality Control, Nat. Geog. Soc., Southeastern Mass. U. Alumni Assn. Home: 29 Meadow Ln Bridgewater MA 02324 Office: D 453 Neponset Ave Foxoboro MA 02035

DUPRE, GEORGE THOMAS, mfg. co. exec.; b. Chgo., Sept. 3, 1925; s. Valentine Harry and Annette Dupre; B.S., U. Ill., 1949; m. Dolores A. Timm, Aug. 20, 1949; children—Steven Charles, Mark Valentine, Valerie Ann. With Raymond Loewy Assos., 1949-50; bus. mgr. Jack Wagner Assos., 1950-53; with Nat. Engring. Co., Chgo., 1953-62, asst. to pres., 1955-58, gen. sales mgr., 1958-62; mfr.'s rep., Ill., Iowa, Wis. and Minn., 1962-74; founder, pres. NFE Internat. Ltd., Palatine, Ill., 1969—; dir. FPI, Inc. Served with inf. U.S. Army, 1943-46. Decorated Purple Heart. Mem. Am. Foundrymen's Soc., Am. Mgmt. Assn., Lambda Chi Alpha. Clubs: 1200, Ocean Reef, Rolling Green Country. Patentee. Home: 47 Oakdene St Barrington IL 60010 Office: 300 S Hicks Rd Palatine IL 60067

DURACKA, THOMAS JOSEPH, printing co. exec.; b. Chgo., Jan. 25, 1941; s. Rudolph and Helen (Duchoslau) D.; student Moraine Valley Coll., 1974; m. Nancy Lee Costello, Apr. 25, 1964; children—Debbie, Tricia, Tommy. Asst. plant mgr. R.C.S. Press, Chgo., 1959-70; printing salesman M.H. Rosenthal, Chgo., 1970-71; owner, operator Family Press, Inc., Chgo., 1971—; pvt. pilot. Served with AUS, 1960-62. Methodist. Office: 10412 S Western Ave Chicago IL 60643

DURAN, RINE, gen. contracting co. exec.; b. San Gabriel, Calif., July 1, 1945; s. Ernest Luchini and Juanita (Lujan) D.; ed. Aims Coll. Asst. agt. Gt. Western R.R., 1967-68; pres. No. Colo. Constructors, Ltd., Greeley, Colo., also dir. Served with USAF, 1969-72. Mem. Greeley C. of C. (local affairs com., dir.), Pvt. Industry Council, Greeley Jaycees (dir.). Democrat. Mem. Assembly of God Ch. Clubs: Rotary, Exchange (dir.), Elks (Greeley). Home: 760 N 71st Ave Greeley CO 80631 Office: 6001 W 10th St Greeley CO 80631

DURAN, ROBERT SAMUEL, ins. agt.; b. McAlester, Okla., Aug. 9, 1947; s. Otis Samuel and Beatrice Evelyn (Sewell) D.; B.B.A., U. Okla., 1973; m. DeNoya Kaye Edwards, Feb. 1, 1969; 1 son, Robert Samuel. Partner, agt. Duran & Duran Ins. Agy., McAlester, 1973—. Bd. dirs. Boys' Club McAlester, 1978—; bd. dirs. Girls' Club McAlester, 1974-78, 80—, pres., 1976-77; bd. dirs. McAlester Salvation Army, 1979—, United Way, 1979—, Pittsburgh County Youth Services and Shelter, 1974-77; deacon, Sunday sch. supt., treas. Baptist Ch. Served with USAF, 1968-72. Mem. McAlester Bd. Realtors (pres. 1978), Ind. Ins. Agts. McAlester (pres. 1975, 80), U. Okla. Alumni Assn. (dir. 1978—), Mensa. Democrat. Clubs: Rotary, McAlester Golf and Country, Fin and Feather. Home: 1014 Newton Dr McAlester OK 74501 Office: 10 E Washington Suite 102 McAlester OK 74501

DURANTY, LAWRENCE, mktg. services co. exec.; b. Sturgeon Bay, Wis., Jan. 18, 1934; s. Mark Leo and Beatrice (Schneider) D.; grad. in premedicine Calif. State U.; M.B.A., Pepperdine U., 1975; m. Elizabeth Jean Stillwell, Nov. 26, 1977; children—Patricia Jean, Mark Patrick. Pres., dir. Bionics Corp., Carson, Calif., 1962—; mem. adv. bd. Am. Internat. Bank, Los Angeles, 1978—; dir. Star Systems, Inc., Las Vegas, MD Labs., Inc., Carson. Served with USN, 1953-57. Mem. Mensa. Club: Rotary (Los Angeles). Patentee in microbiology field. Office: PO Box 4547 Carson CA 90749 also 23642 Main St Carson CA 90745

DURBIN, CHARLES HAROLD, systems analyst; b. Bethlehem, Pa., Mar. 28, 1951; s. Harold Charles and Frances Gloria (Bailey) D.; B.S. in Indsl. Engring., Lehigh U., 1974; m. Rebecca Marie Mularik, May 26, 1973. Programmer-analyst Hearst Mags., N.Y.C., 1974-76; systems analyst Caloric Corp., Topton, Pa., 1976-77; sr. systems analyst Allen Products Co., Inc., Allentown, Pa., 1977—. Mem. Am. Inst. Indsl. Engrs., Lehigh U. Alumni Assn. Home: 4465 Lisa Dr Bethlehem PA 18017 Office: PO Box 2187 Allentown PA 18001

DURBIN, WILLIAM ANTHONY, ret. pub. relations firm exec.; b. Decatur, Ill., Apr. 26, 1916; s. Samuel J. and Estelle (Russell) D.; B.A., St. Louis U., 1938; J.D., 1941; m. Barbara Ann Brennan, July 10, 1947; children—David, William, Christopher, Deborah, Peggy. Spl. agt. FBI, 1942-45; dir. pub. relations St. Louis U., 1945-47; account exec. Ivy Lee and T.J. Ross, Detroit, 1947-50; dir. pub. relations Burroughs Corp., Detroit, 1950-55; dir. pub. relations Am. Cyanamid Co., N.Y.C., 1955-61; vice chmn., then chmn. Hill & Knowlton, Inc., N.Y.C., 1961-80. Mem. civilian pub. relations adv. com. U.S. Mil. Acad., 1957-80, adv. com. Center for Advancement Human Communication, Fairfield (Conn.) U., 1968-80. Trustee Chilton Meml. Hosp., St. Louis U. Mem. Equestrian Order of Holy Sepulchre of Jerusalem. Mem. Internat. Pub. Relations Assn. (council 1958-61), Pub. Relations Soc. Am. (mem. pub. relations sem. com. 1953—), Soc. Former FBI Agts., Alpha Sigma Nu. Clubs: Met. (N.Y.C.); Camelback (Ariz.). Contbr articles to profl. jours. Home: 6740 E Maverick Rd Paradise Valley AZ 85253

DURFEY, WILLARD RAYMOND, motel exec.; b. Marion, Ohio, June 15, 1917; s. Clarence Earl and Myrtle N. (Dreher) D.; B.S., Ohio State U., 1941; M.A., Columbia, 1947; m. Verda Ga-Nell Maxwell, Apr. 5, 1964; children—Phillip, Duanna, Charles. Treas. Carnegie Hall, N.Y.C., 1952-64; bus. mgr. Lakeside (Ohio) Assn., 1965-67; pres. Burr Farms, Inc., Cardington, Ohio, 1968-71; mgr. Quality Motel Clarmont, Columbus, Ohio, 1971—. Served to 1st lt. AUS, 1942-46. Mem. Columbus, Ohio, Am. hotel, motel assns., Innkeepers Assn. Am., Ohio Motel Assn. (past v.p. central Ohio region), German Village Soc., German Village Bus. Assn. Methodist. Mason; mem. Eastern Star. Home: 538 Riverview Dr Cardington OH 43315 Office: 650 S High St Columbus OH 43215

DURGIN, RICHARD LINWOOD, bus. exec.; b. York, Maine, Feb. 19, 1926; s. Harold Linwood and Sarah (Norton) D.; B.S. with distinction in Mech. Engring., U. Rochester, 1947; children—Richard E., Harold L., Deborah L. Gear engr. Gleason Works, Rochester, N.Y., 1947-52; gear lab engr. Chrysler Corp., Detroit, 1952-55; gear mfg. engr. Ill. Gear div. Wallace Murray Corp. (formerly Ill. Gear and Machine Co.), Chgo., 1955-61, v.p. sales, 1961-69, v.p., gen. mgr., 1969-77, group v.p., N.Y.C., 1977-79, exec. v.p., 1979-80, pres., chief exec. officer, dir., 1980—. Served with USNR, 1944-46. Mem. ASME, Soc. Automotive Engrs., Am. Gear Mfrs. Assn., Newcomen Soc. N.Am., Tau Beta Pi. Republican. Methodist. Mason. Elk. Office: 299 Park Ave New York NY 10017

DURHAM, LUCY ELIZABETH (MRS. DOUGLAS F. DURHAM), banker; b. Atlanta, Nov. 18, 1929; d. George Washington and Elizabeth Ganahl (Black) Sciple; student U. Ga., 1948; grad. Fla. Sch. Banking, U. Fla., 1972; m. Douglas Franklin Durham, Jan. 20, 1951; 1 dau., Sandra Elizabeth. File clk. First Nat. Bank, Atlanta, 1946-48, mgr. installment loan files, 1948-49, loan teller, 1949-51, comml. teller, drive-in teller, savs. teller, relief head teller, 1956-60; comml. teller First Nat. Bank Tampa (Fla.), 1964-66, head teller, 1967-70, asst. mgr. mil. facility, 1968-70, new accounts officer, 1968-72; asst. v.p. 1st Financial Nat. Bank Tampa, 1973-74, v.p., 1974-76; asst. v.p. and mgr. Hyde Park office First Nat. Bank of Fla., Tampa, 1977-79, v.p., mgr. Interbay Office, 1979—. Vice pres. elementary sch., Atlanta, 1961; troop leader Girl Scouts U.S.A., 1958-62; charter mem. Piedmont Hosp.'s Women's Aux.; mem. Women's Aux. Tampa Gen. Hosp., bd. dirs. 1963; finance chmn. Gulf Coast Epilepsy Found, 1974-75; treas. Hills County unit Am. Cancer Soc., 1979, bd. dirs., 1978; treas. Family Service Assn. Tampa, 1979—; adv. Foster Grandparents Project, 1979-80. Cert. consumer credit exec. Fellow Internat. Inst. Community Service (founding); mem. Am. Bus. Women's Assn. (treas. 1970-71, pres. 1971-72; Woman of Yr. award 1973), Internat. Platform Assn., Nat. Assn. Bank Women (chmn. Gulf Central Group 1975-76, Tampa Group, 1977-78, Fla. regional v.p. 1980-81), Am. Inst. Banking (dir. 1972-75), Credit Mgrs. Assn. (dir. 1974, treas. 1975-76, v.p. 1976-77, pres. 1977-78, named credit personality 1978), Smithsonian Inst., South Tampa C. of C., Historic Preservation Soc. Episcopalian. Clubs: West Coast Orchid Soc., Palma Cela Golf and Country. Home: 512 Channel Dr Tampa FL 33606 Office: PO Box 1810 Interbay Tampa FL 33601

DURHAM, PETER DEMRO, employment agency exec.; b. Louisville, June 16, 1943; s. Edward A. and Evelyn F. (Demro) D.; B.B.A., U. Buffalo, 1965; children—Peter, Christopher, Colleen. Copywriter, fin. dept. Buffalo Courier Express, 1962-63; auditor Marine Midland Holding Co., Buffalo, 1963-64; br. mgr. Manpower, Inc., Buffalo, 1964-67; pres. Durham Temporaries, Inc., Buffalo, Atlanta and Houston, 1967—, Durham Personnel Services, Inc.,

Buffalo, 1967—. Mem. Nat. Assn. Temporary Services, Ind. Office Services Inst. Republican. Roman Catholic. Contbr. articles to profl. jours. Home: 2180 N Forest Rd Williamsville NY 14221 Office: 176 Franklin St Buffalo NY 14202

DURHAM, STERLING WINSTON, data processing service co. exec.; b. Charlottesville, Va., Aug. 11, 1941; s. Connie Overton and Florine (Updike) D.; B.S. in Commerce, U. Va., 1964; M.S., U. Richmond, 1969; children—Sterling Winston II, Jonathan R. Trainee, F & M Nat. Bank, Richmond, Va., 1964-65, br. adminstr., 1966-70, v.p. comml. lending, 1971-76; chief fin. officer The Computer Co., Richmond, Va., 1977—, sr. v.p., treas., 1978—; dir. Maj. League Bowling and Recreation, Inc., 1977-79. Dir., Ch. Hill Econ. Devel. Corp., Richmond, 1972-73. Hon. life mem. Met. Richmond C. of C. Office: PO Box 6987 Richmond VA 23230

DURKIN, THOMAS ALOYSIUS, economist, educator; b. Plainfield, N.J., Aug. 8, 1945; s. Thomas A. and Helen (Raub) D.; A.B., Georgetown U., 1967; Ph.D., Columbia U., 1973; m. Carolyn I. Cramer; children—Sarah Helen, Catherine Eileen. Asst. prof. fin. Pa. State U., 1973-79, asso. prof., 1979—; vis. prof. Bd. Govs., FRS, Washington, 1977, economist, 1979—. Served with USAR, 1969-72. Mem. Am. Fin. Assn., Am. Econs. Assn., Fin. Mgmt. Assn. Roman Catholic. Author: (with Gregory Eilliehausen) The 1977 Survey of Consumer Credit, 1978; editor (with Murray E. Polakoff) and contbg. author: Financial Institutions and Markets, 1981. Home: 1949 Barton Hill Rd Reston VA 22091 Office: Pa State U 701 Bus Adminstrn Bldg University Park PA 16802

DURLEY, J. J. KUSHMER, mktg. exec.; b. Decatur, Ill., Feb. 14, 1947; d. Edward Henry and Callie (Frye) Kushmer; B.S., Nova U., 1977. Pres., 48 Motors, Inc., Decatur, 1966-70; public relations dir. Marlin Mercedes-Benz and Gunther VW, Fort Lauderdale, Fla., 1970-76; mktg. specialist FPA Corp., Pompano Beach, Fla., 1976—; pres. Forum Internat., Pompano Beach, 1978—. Named Hon. ambassador City of Fort Lauderdale. Mem. Nat. Assn. Legal Assts., Am. Mgmt. Assn., AAUW., Internat., U.S. polo assns. Home: 515 Grand Concourse Miami Shores FL 33138 Office: PO Box 530663 Miami Shores FL 33153

DURRELL, WILLIAM SANDFORD, chem. co. exec.; b. Miami, Fla., Oct. 14, 1931; s. William Eldridge and Abbie How (Newton) D.; B.S. in Chemistry, U. Fla., 1953, Ph.D., 1961; student Wright Field extension Ohio State U., 1956-57; m. Mary Jane Kusbel, June 27, 1953; children—Kathleen, Deborah, William, Patricia, Caroline. Research chemist PCR, Gainesville, Fla., 1953-55, 1961-64, Ethyl Corp., Baton Rouge, La., 1955-56; group leader devel. CIBA-GEIGY, Corp., Ardsley, N.Y., 1965-68, devel. mgr., McIntosh, Ala., 1968-69, mgr. devel. and pilot plant dept., Cranston, R.I., 1969-70, v.p. research, plastics and additives div., Ardsley, 1971-77; v.p. tech., dir. E.F. Houghton & Co., Phila., 1977-79; v.p. research and devel. Jim Walter Corp., Tampa, 1979—. Trustee Plastics Inst. Am., 1973-77. Served with USAF, 1955-57. Recipient Meritorious Service award Plastics Inst. Am., 1977. Mem. AAAS, Assn. Research Dirs., Am. Chem. Soc., Alpha Chi Sigma, Phi Kappa Phi. Contbr. articles in field to profl. jours. Patentee in field. Office: 1500 N Dale Hwy Tampa FL 33607

DURYEA, LOVEJOY REEVES, mktg. cons.; b. Bronxville, N.Y., May 7, 1944; d. Rosser and Elizabeth Lovejoy (Street) Reeves; B.A., St. John's Coll., Annapolis, Md., 1967; m. William M. Duryea, Jr., Aug. 7, 1976; children—Robert Atwell Duryea, David Rosser MacShane. Sr. copywriter Compton Advt., N.Y.C., 1967-70; copywriter Avon Products, Inc., N.Y.C., 1970-71, copychief, sales promotion, 1971-73, group coordinator sales promotion, 1973-74, mgr. sales promotion, 1974-76, nat. field ops. mgr., 1976-80; mktg. cons., 1980—; dir. Alderney Design Ltd., Boothsroy Stuart Ltd. Recipient citation Police Athletic League, Cert. of appreciation Avon Products. Mem. Achievement Rewards College Scientists Found. (founder N.Y. chpt. 1972, dir. at large 1974-76, dir. 1975-76, membership chmn. 1976-77, 1st v.p. 1978-79, chmn. exec. com. 1980—). Clubs: Fishers Island Country, Leash, Bichon Frise of Am. Home and Office: 173 E 80th St New York NY 10022

DUSSICH, VINCENT A., mktg. cons.; b. N.Y.C., May 2, 1945; s. Robert and Virginia (Varbero) D.; B.B.S., N.Y. U., 1967; m. Gayle Moran, Dec. 24, 1974; children—Jenny, Katie. Product mgr. new products Internat. Playtex, Inc., N.Y.C., 1969-73: group product mgr. Alberto Culver, Chgo., 1973-78; gen. mgr. Swift & Co., Chgo., 1978—; pres. Concepts Plus, Inc., Wooddale, Ill., 1979—. Home: 901 Georgean Ln Schaumburg IL 60193 Office: 143 Front St Wooddale IL 60191

DUTCHER, FONDA MARJORIE, stockbroker; b. Flint, Mich., July 22, 1938; d. Herbert and Cora (Hubbard) DeWitt; B.S., Central Mich. U., 1978; 1 son, Samuel Paul. Med. sec., Flint, 1954-59; bookkeeper, controller, personnel dir. S.K.S. Heat Treating Co., 1966-80, treas., corporate dir., 1974-80; stockbroker Fahnestock & Co., 1980—. Tutorial cons. Urban League Flint, 1971; gen. chmn. Cystic Fibrosis, 1967. Mem. Am. Mgmt. Assn., Nat. Assn. Credit Mgmt. Club: Quota (pres. Flint, internat. service com. 1979—, internat. bylaws com. 1980-81). Home: 517 S Franklin St Flint MI 48503 Office: 1016 Merrill St Flint MI 48503

DUTT, JAMES L., food co. exec.; b. Topeka, Feb. 11, 1925; B.S., Washburn U., 1950; M.B.A., U. Dayton, 1966. With Beatrice Foods Co., 1947—, exec. v.p. dairy and soft drink div., 1974, dir. internat. dairy ops., 1974-75, pres. internat. food ops., 1975, exec. v.p. co., 1975-77, pres., chief operating officer, 1977-79, chmn. bd., chief exec. officer, 1979—, dir., 1976—. Office: Beatrice Foods 2 N LaSalle St Chicago IL 60602

DUTTON, ROBERT WENDELL, food mfg. co. exec.; b. Marion, Ohio: s. William Ervin and Mary Juanita (Manley) D.; B.A. in Edn., Kent State U., 1960; M.B.A., Mich. State U., 1963; m. Cynthia Lynn Ledbetter, Sept. 1, 1976: children—Christopher, Jeri, Johanna, Robin, Andrew. With H.J. Heinz Co. Inc., Columbus, Ohio, Harrisburg, Pa., Phila., New Orleans and Pitts., 1960-73; dir. sales/mktg. Collins Foods Internat., Los Angeles, 1973-74; v.p. sales and mktg. J. Hungerford Smith Co., Modesto, Calif., 1974—. Served with USMC, 1954-56. Mem. Am. Mgmt. Assn., Nat. Restaurant Assn., Instl. Food Mfrs. Assn. Republican. Home: 2324 Candlewood Pl Riverbank CA 95367

D'UVA, ROBERT CARMEN, ins. and real estate broker; b. Castelpetroso, Italy, Aug. 25, 1920; s. Gabriele and Bettina (D'Uva) D'U.; brought to U.S., 1929, naturalized, 1946; student Rutgers U., 1946-47, postgrad., 1950-51; B.A. in Accounting, Seton Hall U., 1949; m. Josephine C. Del Riccio, Sept. 5, 1948; children—Robert Gary, Gary James, James Joseph. Spl. rep. Manhattan Life Ins. Co. of N.Y., 1949—; real estate sales rep. David Corhheim Agy., Newark, 1950-51; owner Robert D'Uva, ins. and real estate broker, Newark, 1951—; partner Romaine Realty Co., Newark, 1962—; gen. agt. Md. Am. Gen. Ins. Cos.; pres. Diversified Variable Annuities, Inc., Newark, 1968—; pres. Del-gior Corp., Bloomfield, N.J., 1971—, Diversified Ins. Agy., Inc., 1973—; pub. accountant. Bd. dirs. Newark Boys Club, pres. Broadway unit, 1967. Mem. Real Estate Bd. of Newark, Irvington and Hillside, N.J. Served as cpl. Q.M.C., AUS, 1942-46; PTO. Mem. N.J. Real Estate Assn., Nat. Assn. Real Estate Bd., Life Underwriters Assn., Ind. Ins. Agts. Assn., Nat. Real Estate Brokers Assn., Nat. Security Dealers Assn., Delta Sigma Pi. Roman Catholic. Lion (past pres. North Newark, dep. dist. gov. 16E 1964). Home: 27 Howland Circle West Caldwell NJ 07006 Office: 316 Mt Prospect Ave Newark NJ 07104 also 115 Bloomfield Ave Caldwell NJ 07006

DUVEEN, HENRY JULES, art gallery exec.; b. Amsterdam, Netherlands, Mar. 12, 1935; came to U.S., 1956; s. Abraham Mozes and Henriette (Frank) D.; B.A., Inst. van Praag, Amsterdam, 1955; m. Peggy R. Berkelouw, Mar. 30, 1971; 1 dau., Linda H. Founder, Merril Lynch Pierce Fenner & Smith, Amsterdam, 1960-65; asso. Francis I. DuPont Corp., Amsterdam, 1965-68; sr. v.p. Laidlaw, Adams & Peck, Brussels, 1971-78; art gallery pres. Duveen Inc., Houston, 1979—; lectr. internat. investment/art investments, 1960—. Served with U.S. Army, Germany, 1956-58. Mem. Woodlands Living Arts Council (dir. 1978-80). Clubs: Woodlands Country, Rotary. Home and Office: 37 Wakerobin Ct The Woodlands TX 77380

DU VERNAY, DAVID EVAN, fin. and leasing exec.; b. Cleve., Feb. 27, 1936; s. Gilbert and Marion L. DuV.; B.A. in Internat. Studies, Ohio State U., 1959; J.D. cum laude, Cleve.-Marshall Law Sch., 1964; m. Rae Ann Sankey, Nov. 25, 1961; children—Deirdre, Beverly, Valerie. Admitted to Ohio bar, 1964; asst. credit mgr. Nat. Acme Co., 1959-63; credit mgr. F.H. Hill Co., 1963, Gen. Elec. Credit Corp., 1963-68; mgr. transp., mgr. mktg. Gen. Elec. Credit Corp., 1968-77; sr. v.p. equipment financing Internat. Paper Credit Corp., Greenwich, Conn., 1977—. Served with USAR, 1955-62. Mem. Am. Assn. Equipment Lessors. Home: 12 Rockview Dr Greenwich CT 06830 Office: Greenwich Office Park I Greenwich CT 06830

DVORAK, DONALD FRANK, co. exec.; b. Oak Park, Ill., Feb. 28, 1933; s. Joseph and Bessie M. (Kaiser) D.; A.B. in Liberal Arts, U. Chgo., 1953, M.B.A. in Acctg., 1955; m. Gloria H. Morello, Sept. 6, 1958; children—Richard, Elizabeth, Douglas. Auditor, tax specialist, Arthur Young & Co., Chgo., 1957-61; cons., controller Tech Search, Inc., Evanston, Ill., 1961-62; controller Readers Digest Spl. Products, Inc., Chgo., 1962-63; pvt. practice mgmt. cons., Evanston, Ill., 1963-64; partner, nat. practice dir. for exec. search Peat, Marwick, Mitchell & Co., Chgo., 1964—. Guild bd. Lyric Opera of Chgo.; mem. Rehab. Inst. of Chgo. Served with USN, 1956-57. Mem. Ill. C.P.A. Soc. (mgmt. adv. services com.), Am. Inst. C.P.A.'s (chmn. exec. search task force 1974-79), Nat. Assn. Accts. Clubs: Econ. Club of Chgo., Chicago, Michigan Shores, Skokie Country. Author: An Approach to Executive Search, 1980. Office: Peat Marwick Plaza 303 E Wacker Dr Chicago IL 60601

DWIGHT, DONALD RATHBUN, newspaper pub.; b. Holyoke, Mass., Mar. 26, 1931; s. William and Dorothy Elizabeth (Rathbun) D.; A.B., Princeton U., 1953; D.Sc. (hon.), U. Lowell, 1974; m. Susan Newton Russell, Aug. 9, 1952; children—Dorothy Campbell, Laura Newton, Eleanor Addison, Arthur Ryan, Stuart Russell. Reporter, asst. to pub. Holyoke (Mass.) Transcript-Telegram, 1955-63, asso. pub., 1966-69; asso. commr. Mass. Dept. Public Works, 1963-66; commr. Dept. Adminstrn. and Fin., Commonwealth of Mass., 1969-70; lt. gov. Commonwealth of Mass., 1971-75; asso. pub., v.p. Mpls. Star and Tribune, 1975-76, pub., sr. v.p., 1976—, dir.; dir. Newspapers of New Eng., Inc., Greenfield (Mass.) Recorder, Pillsbury Co. Mem. Town Meeting, South Hadley, Mass., 1957-69; bd. dirs. Guthrie Theater Found., 1976—, chmn., 1979-81; dir. Mpls. Soc. Fine Arts, 1976—; trustee Twin Cities Public TV, 1976—; bd. dirs. Mpls. Downtown Council, 1977—. Served to lt. USMCR, 1953-55. Mem. Am. Newspaper Pubs. Assn., Sigma Delta Chi. Republican. Episcopalian. Clubs: Princeton (N.Y.C.); Chatham (Mass.) Beach and Tennis; Mpls. Office: 425 Portland Ave Minneapolis MN 55488

DWORKIN, DARRYL RICHARD, toy mfg. and retail co. exec.; b. Bklyn., May 14, 1942; s. Irvin Isidore and Pearl Paulie (Falk) D.; A.A., Los Angeles City Coll., 1962; student Calif. State Coll. at Los Angeles, 1962-66; B.S., U. So. Calif., 1968; m. Vita Petty, Jan. 18, 1975; children by previous marriage—David, Daniel. Design engr. Mattel, Inc., Hawthorne, Calif., 1968-70, mgr. liaison engring., 1970, chief engr., 1970-71, mgr. product devel., 1971-72, mgr. warranty control, 1972-73, mgr. design engring. Standard Plastic Products subs., South Plainfield, N.J., 1973-74, dir. engring. services and sales, 1974-76; exec. dir. research and devel. Knickerbocker Toy Co., Middlesex, N.J., 1976-77; v.p. product devel. CBS Toys div. CBS, Inc., Cranbury, N.J., 1977-79; v.p. ops. L.J.N. Toys Ltd., N.Y.C., 1979-80; chmn. bd. D.N.V. Inc., trading as Bright Acre, Shrewsbury, N.J., 1979—; treas., dir. Ascutney Mountain Village Condominimums, Inc. Pres., Marble Estates Homeowners Assn., 1972; trustee Temple Emanu-El, Edison, N.J., 1975—. Served with USAR, 1960. Mem. ASME, Pi Tau Sigma. Patentee toys. Home: 504 Port-Au-Peck Oceanport NJ 07757 Office: Bright Acre Route 35 Shrewsbury NJ 07701

DWORKIN, GARY STEVEN, ins. co. exec.; b. N.Y.C., July 7, 1947; s. Irving Milton and Grace Wilhelmina (Korn) D.; student Hofstra U., 1965-68, N.Y. U., 1969-71; m. Linda Lee Fuchs, Aug. 28, 1970; children—Robert Benjamin, Alexandra Tenille. Sales mgr. Chatham Blankets, N.Y.C., 1968-70; ins. agt. Travelers Ins. Co., Hartford, Conn., 1970-74; broker Dworkin Assos., Rochester, N.H., 1974-76; pres. Dworkin Assos., Inc. (DAI), Rochester, 1976—. Registered health underwriter. Mem. Nat. (state public service chmn.), Southeastern N.H. (nat. com.) assns. life underwriters, New Eng. Forum, Nat. Assn. Health Underwriters, Am. Risk and Ins. Assn. Republican. Club: Century (past chmn. life underwriters polit. action com. Southeastern N.H. chpt.). Mem. editorial adv. bd. Broker World. Home: 274 Salmon Falls Rd Rochester NH 03867 Office: Westwood Plaza 165 Charles St Rochester NH 03867

DWORKIN, HOWARD SAUL, paper converting co. exec.; b. Newark, May 20, 1939; s. Lawrence W. and Lillian (Jacoby) D.; B.S. in Econs., U. Pa. Wharton Sch., 1961; M.B.A., Fairleigh Dickinson U., 1975; m. Yvonne Gellady, Dec. 30, 1959; children—Jeffrey, James, Jill, Jonothan. Pres., owner Ajax Fibre Envelope Corp., S. River, N.J., 1961-67, Tang Binder Corp., Carteret, N.J., 1967-72; v.p. Prime Envelope Corp. div. Williamhouse-Regency, Inc., Bklyn., 1972—. Mem. Envelope Mfrs. Assn. Republican. Jewish. Home: 571 Ridge Rd Watchung NJ 07060 Office: 1710 Flushing Ave Brooklyn NY 11237

DYAS, JOHN ROBERT, bank exec.; b. Mobile, Ala., Feb. 4, 1917; s. Edmund C. and Estelle F. (Schreiner) D.; student Auburn U., 1939, George Washington U., 1954, Armed Forces Staff Coll., 1949-50, Air War Coll., 1954-55; m. Henrietta Brewer; children—Judith Ann, Joanna Lynn, John Robert (dec.). Commd. 2d lt. U.S. Army Air Force, 1941, advanced through grades to brig. gen., 1964; ret., 1971; v.p. comml. div. Colonial Mortgage Co., Montgomery, Ala., 1971-74; pres. 1st So. Mortgage Corp., Mobile, Ala., 1974—, Inter-Am. Mining Co., Panama, 1977—; chmn. bd. United Cement Co., Inc., Montevallo, Ala., 1955-60. Decorated Silver Star, D.S.M. Mem. Air Force Assn. (pres. Mobile chpt.), Home Builders Assn., Mortgage Lenders Assn., Mobile Bd. Realtors, Wings Club. Roman Catholic. Club: Lions. Home: 2901 Grant St Condo 208 Mobile AL 36606 Office: PO Box 160512 Mobile AL 36616

DYER, HUGH NELSON, III, mgmt. cons.; b. Troy, N.Y., Dec. 8, 1942; s. Hugh Nelson and Jean (Foster) D.; B.S., U. Vt., 1965; M.S., U. So. Calif., 1971; m. Kathleen Johnston, Aug. 29, 1970; children—Hugh Nelson IV, William Robert, Kathleen Caird. Account exec. Chandler & Co., Beverly Hills, Calif., 1970; sect. mgr. Avon Products, Inc., Pasadena, Calif., 1971-73; mgr. cost and schedule control Hughes Helicopters, Culver City, Calif., 1974-77, mgr. subcontractor fin. controls, 1977-79; mgmt. cons. Decision Planning Corp., 1979—; asst. prof. U. So. Calif., 1968-70. Served to lt. USNR, 1965-70. Decorated D.F.C. (2), Air Medal (13), Vietnamese Cross of Gallantry. Mem. U.S. Naval Inst., Navy League, S.R., Am. Helicopter Soc., Delta Psi. Presbyterian. Clubs: Beverly Yacht, Atlas Flyers, Los Angeles Athletic. Home: 1 Bunker Dr Belle Mead NJ 08502 Office: PO Box 102 Princeton NJ 08540

DYER, JOHN PAUL, III, mgmt. cons.; b. Grand Forks, N.D., Apr. 7, 1944; s. John Paul and Catherine Ann (Lamb) D.; student Tulane U., 1962-65; B.S., U. Fla., 1970; M.A. in Physil. Ecology and Marine Biology, U. South Fla., 1975; M.B.A. in Mgmt., Fairleigh Dickinson U., 1980; m. Lenora Stokes Birchall, May 30, 1969; children—Shannon Cay, John Paul IV. Pres., chief exec. officer Caribbean Biols. Ltd., Inc., Key West, Fla., 1973-74; internat. cons. Marine Colloids, Inc., Can., Brazil and Senegal, 1974-75, dir. ops. for S.E. Asia, Republic of Singapore, 1975-76; spl. product mktg. mgr., comml. devel. mgr. Marine Colloids div. FMC Corp., Springfield, N.J., 1976-80; program mgr. Innotech Corp., 1980—. Served with Spl. Forces, U.S. Army, 1965-69. Mem. Assn. M.B.A.'s, Chem. Mktg. Research Assn., Am. Mgmt. Assn., U.S. Inst. Diving, Spl. Forces Assn., Cousteau Soc., Common Cause, Sigma Xi, Phi Kappa Phi. Club: Copper Springs Beach and Tennis (Myersville, N.J.). Contbr. articles to profl. jours. Home: 13 Woodcrest Ave Trumbull NJ 06611 Office: 2285 Reservoir Ave Trumbull CT 06611

DYER, ROBERT BRUCE, mfg. exec.; b. Tulia, Tex., Feb. 17, 1937; s. Claud Bruce and Beulah Francis (Hall) D.; B.S. in Indsl. Engring., Tex. Tech. U., 1960; M.B.A., U. Pa., 1965; m. Judith Ann Grundy, June 10, 1961; children—Kathryn F., R. Scott, Steven J. Planning analyst Exxon Corp., Houston, 1965-66; controller C/B So. div. Cooper Industries, Inc., Houston, 1967-69, corp. sr. coordinator operational planning and analysis, 1970-72, asst. controller ops., 1972-73, dir. operational analysis, 1973-74, dir. planning and analysis, 1974-75, v.p. planning and analysis, 1975-79, sr. v.p. planning and devel., 1980—; dir. MESBIC Fin. Corp. of Houston. Bd. dirs. Houston-Harris County chpt. ARC, 1977-79, Tex. Opera Theater; deacon Meml. Dr. Presbyterian Ch., 1978-79. Served to 1st lt. USAF, 1961-63. Mem. N. Am. Soc. Corp. Planning, Fin. Execs. Inst., Nat. Assn. Bus. Economists, Assn. Corp. Growth, Houston C. of C., Phi Kappa Phi, Tau Beta Pi, Sigma Alpha Epsilon. Clubs: Lakeside Country Houston, Houstonian. Home: 335 Chapel Bell St Houston TX 77024 Office: 2700 Two Houston Center Houston TX 77002

DYER, WILLIAM PRESTON, seed co. exec.; b. Manor, Tex., Aug. 19, 1930; s. William and Arvilla Minnera (Malone) D.; A.A., City Coll., San Francisco, 1953; student U. Minn., 1953-54, Acad. Acctg., 1954-55; m. Arlene Nell Olson, Oct. 25, 1950; children—Lana Kay (Mrs. Robert Williams), Denise Arlene. Office mgr. A. Cederstrand & Co., Mpls., 1954-56; mgr. br. div. acctg. John Morrell & Co., Sioux Falls, S.D., 1956-60; asst. treas. Shelter Equipment Corp., Denver, 1960-62; acctg. mgr. Pacific Oilseeds, Inc. (name now SeedTec Internat., Inc.), San Francisco, 1962-68, office mgr., Woodland, Calif., 1968-76, v.p., treas., 1976—, dir., 1972—; dir. Pacific Seeds Internat., WAC Seed, Inc. Served with USN, 1948-52. Mem. Calif. Seed Assn., Pacific Seedsmen's Assn.. Am. Legion, Woodland C. of C. Republican. Lutheran. Clubs: Rancho Murieta Country, Woodland Lions. Home: 1609 Spruce Dr Woodland CA 95695 Office: PO Box 1008 Woodland CA 95695

DYKE, ZBIGNIEW IGOR, fire fighting equipment co. exec.: b. Poland, Jan. 1, 1921; came to U.S., 1973; s. Francis and Eleonora D.; grad. in mech. engring. Kingston Tech. Coll., Eng., 1955; m. Antonina K.S. Kozaryn, July 14, 1945; 1 son, Peter Francis. Sr. designer Atomic Energy Commn., Eng., 1949-53; asst. chief engr. Lansing Bagnall, 1953-56; export mgr. G. Angus, Wallsend, Eng., 1963-68, Dunlop Polymer Engring., Leicester, Eng., 1968-73; founder Angus Fire Armour Corp., Dorsey, Md., 1973, chief exec. officer, 1973-80; v.p. Phoenix Pyrotechnical; pres. A.T.S. Combi Holdings Corp., St. Augustine, Fla.; treas. J.J.&S. Sales, St. Augustine; mem. chmn.'s com. U.S. Senatorial Bus. Adv. Bd. Served with Polish Armed Forces, 1940-46. Decorated Order of Merit Polish Armed Forces, also Brit. and French campaign medals. Home: 36 Carrere St Saint Augustine FL 32084

DYKES, ARTHUR JACOB, public acct.; b. N.Y.C., Mar. 11, 1953; B.A. in Econs., Rutgers U., 1975, M.B.A., 1976; m. Eileen J. Meiseles, Sept. 10, 1978. With Arthur Young and Co., C.P.A.'s, Washington, 1976—, sr. acct., 1978—. C.P.A. Mem. Nat. Assn. Accts. Club: Rutgers Alumni (Washington). Office: 1025 Connecticut Ave NW Washington DC 20036

DYKSTRA, WILLIAM DWIGHT, bus. exec., cons.; b. Grand Rapids, Mich., June 15, 1927; s. John Albert and Irene (Stablekamp) D.; A.B., Hope Coll., 1949; M.B.A., Ind. U., 1950; m. Ann McGuiness, Nov. 5, 1957; children—William Hugh, Mary Irene. Asst. mgr. Ply-Curves, Inc., 1950, originator magnesium metal furniture 1951; pres. mfg. co. Dwight Corp., 1952-56; pres. W.D. Dykstra Group, 1956—; partner Dykstra Assos.; dir. Sheldon Co., Direct Transit Lines. Recipient merit award outstanding furniture, 1955; Packaging award Am. Inst. Graphic Arts, 1965, 67, Vehicle Color Design award, 1967; P.I.A. Graphic award, 1971; Am. Advt. Fedn. award, 1971, 73, 76. Mem. Am. Econs. Assn., Am. Inst. Graphic Arts, Acad. Polit. Sci., Am. Mktg. Assn., Soc. Packaging and Handling Engrs., Phi Kappa Psi, Pi Kappa Delta. Republican. Dutch Reformed Ch. (elder). Clubs: Rotary; La Coguille (Palm Beach, Fla.); Otsego Ski (Gaylord, Mich.); Charlevoix (Mich.) Yacht. Author: Management and the 4th Estate; New Profits for Management. Home: 1145 Edison St NW Grand Rapids MI 49505 Office: Old Tallmadge Grange Hall 0-1845 W Leonard Rd Grand Rapids MI 49504

DYL, EDWARD ALEXANDER, educator; b. Providence, Nov. 10, 1942; s. Walter Edward and Doris Hope (Edwards) D.; B.A., Claremont Men's Coll., 1965; M.B.A., Stanford U., 1967, Ph.D., 1973; m. Judith Alma Meyers, July 19, 1969; children—Joanna Leslie, Theodore Alexander. Asst. prof. fin. U. Tex., Austin, 1968-72; asst. prof. U. San Francisco, 1972-74; asso. prof. bus. adminstrn. U. Wyo., Laramie, 1974-78, prof., 1978—, dean Coll. Commerce and Industry, 1979—; cons. Office of Comptroller of the Currency, 1975—. Alfred P. Sloan fellow, 1965-67, Ayres fellow, 1975. Mem. Am. Fin. Assn., Fin. Mgmt. Assn., Western Fin. Assn. (v.p. 1980-81). Mem. editorial bd. Journal of Financial Education, 1978—; contbr. articles to profl. jours. Office: College of Commerce and Industry University of Wyoming Laramie WY 82071

DYSON, JOSEPH MARTIN, investment banking exec.; b. Cheyenne, Wyo., Jan. 21, 1933; s. Joseph M. and Alice F. (Baker) D.; B.S. in Acctg., Regis Coll., Denver, 1954; m. Diane L. Monson, Aug. 21, 1965; children—Lisa, Julie, Paul. Supr., Ernst & Ernst, C.P.A.'s, 1954-64; investigator SEC, 1964-65; acting Hill-Burton program dir.

HEW, 1965-73; v.p. Telco Capital Co., Chgo., 1973-75; v.p. First Am. Capital Funding Corp., La Jolla, Calif., 1975-78; v.p. Merrill Lynch, Pierce, Fenner & Smith, Inc., LaJolla, 1978—. C.P.A., Calif. Mem. Hosp. Fin. Mgmt. Assn., Am. Inst. C.P.A.'s. Roman Catholic. Office: Suite 310 7911 Herschel Ave LaJolla CA 92037

DYSTEL, OSCAR, publishing co. cons.; b. N.Y.C., Oct. 31, 1912; s. Jacob and Rose (Pintoff) D.; B.C.S., N.Y. U., 1935; M.B.A., Harvard, 1937; m. Marion Deitler, Oct. 2, 1938; children—Jane Dee, John Jay. Circulation mgr. Sports Illus. and Am. Golfer, 1937; circulation, Promotion mgr. Esquire and Coronet mags., Chgo., 1938-40; circulation mgr. Coronet mag., 1940, editor, 1940-42, 44-48; mng. editor Collier's, 1948-49; exec. staff Cowles Mags., Inc., 1949-51; editorial adviser Parents, Inst., Inc., 1951-54; pres., chief exec. officer Bantam Books, Inc., N.Y.C., 1954-78, chmn., chief exec. officer, 1978-80; cons., 1980—. Mem. Rockefeller U. Council; bd. dirs. Nat. Multiple Sclerosis Soc.; mem. adv. council Center for Strategic and Internat. Affairs, Georgetown U., 1980—. Editor of U.S.A. Mag., pub. OWI, 1942-43; engaged in psychol. warfare operations Allied Force Hdqrs., MTO, 1943-44. Decorated Medal of Freedom, 1946; Brandeis U. fellow. Mem. U.S. Alumni Assn. Club: Harvard (N.Y.C.). Author: Analysis of Paid and Controller Circulation Among Business Papers, 1938. Home: Pine Ln Rye NY 10580 Office: 666 Fifth Ave New York NY 10019

EADES, CHARLES JOSEPH, ins. co. exec.; b. Cin., July 2, 1929; s. William Leonard and Faye Elvira (Arbogast) E.; Ph.B., U. Cin., 1954; postgrad. Chase Coll., m. Doris Lee Gnimm, Aug. 5, 1978; children by previous marriage—Kathy Lynn, Charles Joseph, David Douglas. Pub. accountant, Milford, Ohio, 1956-60; with Emery Industries, Inc., Cin., 1960-78, asst. sec., 1966-78; pres. Emery Ltd., Cin., 1971-78, also dir.; pres. Tenn. Ins. Co. subs. Ingram Industries, Inc., Nashville, 1978—; dir. Corp. Ins. and Re-ins. Co. Ltd., 1977-78, Cin. Turfgrass Nursery Inc., 1968-78, Don Curless, Inc., 1966-78, Vanlandingham Bros., Inc., 1969-78. Mem. Clermont County Planning Commn., 1954-58; mem. Miami Twp. Zoning Commn., Milford, 1956-60. Mem. Clermont County (Ohio) Rep. Central Com., 1968-78; mem. Ohio Rep. Central and Exec. Coms., 1972-78; trustee Ohio Rep. Finance Com., 1973-78; trustee Ohio Rep. News, 1973-78. Mem. Miami Twp. Bd. Edn., Milford, 1954-58; trustee, sec. Clermont Care Center, Inc., 1971-78. Mem. Am. Soc. Risk and Ins. Mgmt., Captive Ins. Cos. Assn. (v.p. 1979—), Tax Execs. Inst., Council State Chambers Commerce (mem. com. on state taxation 1970-78). Mason. Office: 4304 Harding Rd Nashville TN 37205

EAGAN, DAVID LEE, retail co. mgr.; b. St. Louis, Jan. 10, 1946; s. Noel Harper ano Jenna (Lee) E.; B.S., Middle Tenn. State U., 1968; m. Janice Kay Thurston, Jan. 6, 1968; 1 son, David Lee II. With Cain Sloan Co., Nashville, 1968—, buyer, 1971-76, div. mdse. mgr., 1976—, mem. corp. steering com., 1978-79. Pres., Casco Credit Union, bd. dirs., 1980—. Served with Air N.G., 1966-72. Mem. Nashville C. of C. Republican. Mem. Ch. of Christ. Club: Masons. Home: 2116 Hartland Dr Franklin TN 37064 Office: 501 Church St Nashville TN 37219

EAGLES, JAMES BURTON, food industry exec.; b. Toronto, Ont., Can., Feb. 21, 1945; s. Burton Weller and Elizabeth (Watkins) E.; B.Sc., U. Calgary, 1967; M.B.A., U. Western Ont., 1971; m. A. Gilaine Belair, Aug. 1971; children—J.B. Miguel, Gabrielle. Group product mgr. Weston Foods Ltd., Toronto, 1973-74; asso. Kearney Mgmt. Cons. Ltd., Toronto, 1975-77; gen. mgr. Robinhood Multifoods Ltd., Toronto, 1977—. Mem. Am. Mktg. Assn., Club: Baby Point (dir.). Home: 20 Brumell Ave Toronto ON Canada Office: 243 Consumers Rd Willowdale ON Canada

EAGLESON, WILLIAM BOAL, JR., banker; b. Phila., Dec. 10, 1925; s. William Boal and Helen (Sturges) E.; B.S., Lehigh U., 1949; M.B.A., U. Pa., 1951; m. Catherine West McLean, May 28, 1960; children—Elizabeth West, John McLean. With Fed. Res. Bank Phila., 1949-51; with Girard Bank, Phila., 1951—, v.p., 1961-65, sr. v.p., 1965-67, head bank investments div., 1961-66, head banking dept., 1966-67, exec. v.p., 1967-71, pres., 1971—, also dir.; pres., dir. Girard Co., 1971—, chmn. bd., 1974—; dir. Potomac Ins. Co., Pa. Gen. Ins. Co., Camden Fire Ins. Co., Anchor Hocking Corp., Pvt. Investment Co. for Asia, Pennwalt Corp.; trustee Penn Mut. Life Ins. Co.; mem. exec. com. Gen. Accident Fire and Life Assurance Corp. Trustee Am. Found., Greater Phila. Partnership, Lehigh U., Phila. Orch. Assn. Served with USNR, 1944-46. Mem. Assn. Res. City Bankers. Episcopalian. Home: Jaffrey Rd RD 2 Malvern PA 19355 Office: Girard Bank Philadelphia PA 19101

EAGLIN, TERRY WILSON, distbn. co. exec.; b. Toledo, Nov. 8, 1945; s. Robert Mason and Patricia Ann Eaglin; B.A., Miami U., Oxford, Ohio, 1967; m. Joyce L. Trevithick, Oct. 22, 1976; children—Jennifer Lynn, Michael Patrick. With Coulter Electronics Co., 1969-80, sr. sales cons., 1976-80; pres. PX-Wolverine Co., Bellaire, Mich., 1980—. Methodist. Address: Route 3 Box 209 Bellaire MI 49615

EAMES, ALFRED WARNER, JR., ret. food corp. exec.; b. Honolulu, June 20, 1914; s. Alfred Warner and Carrie Godfrey (McLean) E.; student U. Oreg., 1932-33, 35; LL.D., Golden Gate U., 1978; m. Marion Antoinette Lucas, Feb. 17, 1938; children—Alfred Warner IV, Anthony L., Peter M., A. Christopher. With Del Monte Corp. (formerly Calif. Packing Corp.), San Francisco, from 1935, prodn. mgmt., 1942-56, prodn. v.p., 1957-65, prodn. exec. v.p., 1965-68, pres., 1968-71, chmn. bd., 1969-78, mem. mgmt. com., 1956-78, mem. exec. com., from 1977, also dir.; dir. Bank of Calif., N.A., Pacific Gas & Electric Co., Fireman's Fund Ins. Co. Hon. trustee Com. for Econ. Devel. Mem. Newcomen Soc., Chi Psi. Clubs: Menlo Country, St. Francis Yacht, Pacific Union. Office: Del Monte Corp PO Box 3575 San Francisco CA 94119

EAMES, EARL WARD, JR., mgmt. cons., business exec.; b. Morris, Minn., Oct. 22, 1923; s. Earl Ward and Camilla (Hendricks) E.; student U. Minn., 1941; S.B., Mass. Inst. Tech., 1949; m. Anyes de Horst, June 26, 1954; children—Elizabeth Anne, Earl Ward III, Erik Michael, Christopher Paul. Vice pres., then pres. dir. Consultants Inc., Boston and Amsterdam, The Netherlands, 1949-54; prodn. specialist Found. Productivity Research, Helsinki, Finland, 1955-57; pres. Gen. Mgmt. Assos., Boston, 1957-63; sr. asso. Cresap, McCormick & Paget, N.Y.C., 1963-66, v.p. operations, 1966; pres., chief exec. officer, dir. Council Internat. Progress in Mgmt., N.Y.C., 1967-69; v.p., dir. Reed, Cuff & Becker, N.Y.C., 1970-73; sr. asso. Wright Assos., N.Y.C., 1973-75, exec. cons., 1975-77; UNIDO expert U. Ife (Nigeria), 1978-80; small-scale industry adv. The World Bank, 1980—; lectr. internat. econs. Fisher Coll., 1954-55, 60-63. Mem. Gov. Com. Refugees, 1961—; chmn. trustee Nat. Service Secretariat, 1966—; rep. Internat. Council for Sci. Mgmt. to ECOSOC, 1967-69; mem. Columbia U. Sem. on Orgn. and Mgmt., 1968—; mem. ednl. council Mass. Inst. Tech., 1974—; mem. personnel commn. Met. N.Y. synod Lutheran Ch. in Am. Treas. New Eng. Opera Theatre, 1958-63; mem. com. Friends of N.Y. Philharmonic, 1967—; corporate mem. Vols. for Internat. Tech. Assistance, 1967—; nat. bd. IAESTE, 1973—. Served with USNR, 1942-46. Republican. Lutheran. Clubs: Staff (U. Ife); M.I.T. Alumni (Washington). Author: Estimation of Managerial and Technical Personnel Requirements in the Pulp and Paper Industry, 1968; Non-Woven Fabrics, 1970. Contbr. to Training Managers: The International Guide, 1969. Home: 439 15th St NE Washington DC 20002

EAMES, WARREN BAKER, interior designer; b. Gardner, Mass., June 3, 1925; s. Harold William and Ruth Sibyl (Baker) E.; A.B. magna cum laude, Harvard, 1950; diploma bus. adminstrn. Stevens Bus. Coll., 1953; m. Susan Elizabeth Cliver, Jan. 29, 1961; children—Alan Duane, Holiday. Lab. research asst. Peabody Mus. Archaeology and Ethnology, Cambridge, Mass., 1950-51, asst. archaeologist, 1950-51; asst. archaeologist in site excavation Am. Mus. Natural History N.Y., Belzoni, Miss., 1951; treas. Parker & Eames, Inc., Fitchburg, Mass., 1953-55; pres., treas. Eames Interiors, Inc., Fitchburg, 1955—; founder Templeton Ch. Decorators, 1966—, Eames Interiors, Contract Carpeting, 1966—, Eames Interiors Auditorium Planners, 1968—. Bd. dirs. Gardner (Mass.) br. Stevens Bus. Coll. Served with inf. AUS, 1943-46. Decorated Purple Heart with oak leaf cluster; Bronze Star with presdl. unit emblem; Fourragere of Croix de Guerre (France), French Fourragere of Medaille Militaire. Mem. Am. Soc. Interior Designers, Soc. 1st Inf. Div., Nat. Rifle Assn., Narragansett Hist. Soc. (asso. historian 1960—), Soc. for Preservation New Eng. Antiquities, Eastern Jaguar Group. Club: Harvard (Boston). Home: Whitney Tavern East Templeton MA 01438 Office: 1 Main St East Templeton MA 01438

EAPEN, JOHN, chem. engr.; b. Hyderabad, India, July 11, 1947; came to U.S., 1969, naturalized, 1978; s. John Pulimootil and Saramma (Eapen) T.; B.Tech., Madras U. (India), 1969; M.S. in Chem. Engring., Ga. Inst. Tech., 1970; m. Lata Cheru, Dec. 26, 1974; 1 son, Zubin John. Project engr. Bigelow-Sanford, Inc., Greenville, S.C., 1971-73; sr. research engr. Calgon Corp., Pitts., 1973-74; sr. project engr. Bigelow-Sanford, Inc., Greenville, 1974-77, corp. environ. mgr. and safety dir., 1977—. Bd. dirs. Cane Brake Homes Assn., 1979—. Mem. Am. Inst. Chem. Engrs., Water Pollution Control Fedn., S.C. Textile Mfrs. Assn. (safety and health com.), Carpet and Rug Inst. (chmn. air pollution sub com. 2nd environ. com.). Presbyterian. Home: 319 Kings Mountain Dr Greer SC 29651 Office: PO Box 3089 Greenville SC 29602

EARL, DONALD WADSWORTH, stage lighting co. exec.; b. Buffalo, May 14, 1946; s. Elmer Wadsworth and Florence (Siegrist) E.; B.F.A., Carnegie-Mellon U., 1968. Tech. dir. Tyrone Guthrie Theatre's Other Place, Mpls., 1967-68; stage mgr., lighting designer Theatre of Living Arts, Phila., 1968-70; pres. Aladdin Lighting, Inc., Phila., 1970—; sec.-treas. Auburn Devel. Corp., Phila., 1972—; vis. lectr. Towson (Md.) State Coll., 1968; adviser to Phila. '76. Bicentennial Planning Group's Cultural Activities Coordinator, 1973-74; prodn. stage mgr. Famous Artists Series, summers 1968, 69; gen. mgr. Famous Artists Series, Syracuse, summer 1970. Bd. dirs. South St. Dance Co. Recipient Grand prize Three Rivers Arts Festival Bridge Sculpture, 1968. Mem. U.S. Inst. Theatre Tech., Illuminating Engring. Soc., Am. Theatre Assn., Actors Equity Assn., Nat. Thespian Soc., Soc. Motion Picture and TV Engrs., Mensa. Home: 921 E Passyunk Ave Philadelphia PA 19147 Office: PO Box 1953 Philadelphia PA 19105

EARL, ROBERT MARTIN, gen. contractor; b. Pasadena, Calif., Oct. 24, 1946; s. Orrin Kinsley and Sarilda Katherine (Ridenour) E.; B.S.C.E., Stanford U., 1969; M.B.A., Pepperdine U., 1978; m. Nancy Lloyd Conner, Dec. 29, 1973; children—Kinsley Taylor, Conner Martin. Project mgr. Sollitt Constrn. Co., Oakland, Calif., 1972-75; project mgr., sr. estimator Nielsen-Nickles Co., Sacramento, 1975-78; exec. v.p., gen. mgr., 1978—; v.p., dir. Introlink, Inc. Bd. dirs., treas., Family Service Agy. of Sacramento, 1977, pres., 1978-79; bd. dirs. Sacramento Symphony Assn. Served with C.E., USN, 1969-72. Lic. profl. engr., Calif. Mem. Associated Gen. Contractors of Calif. Republican. Episcopalian. Clubs: Fortune 15 Investment, Stanford of Sacramento (dir.).

EARLE, DOUGLAS BARTON, leisure time products co. exec.; b. Toronto, Ont., Can., Feb. 28, 1937; s. Oliver Ronald and Donna Sara (Layton) E.; B.A., U. Western Ont., 1959; m. Elizabeth Anne Kaltenbrunner, July 28, 1962; children—Barton, Timothy. With H.A. Kidd & Co., Ltd., Toronto, 1959—, sales mgr., 1964-70, v.p., 1970-75, pres., 1975—. Mem. Young Pres.'s Orgn. Club: Royal Canadian Yacht. Office: 2 Mark St Toronto ON M5A 1T8 Canada

EARLY, HOBART FARRELL, constrn. co. exec.; b. Early, Ga., June 1, 1917; s. Phillip Henry and Mary Winefred (Battle) E.; student pub. schs.; m. Mildred Estelle Walters, Feb. 23, 1936; children—Hobart Eugene, Phillip Albert, Ronald Hoyt, Linda Ann. Constrn. supt. H.P. Little Constrn. Co., Rome, Ga., 1935-39, Ledbetter-Johnson Constrn. Co., Rome, 1941-45; owner, partner Early-Terrell Lumber Co., Rome, 1945-48; plant supt. Ga. Factory for Blind, Bainbridge, Ga., 1949-56; owner Early Contracting Co., Bainbridge, 1956-61, Smyrna, Ga., 1962-68; pres., chmn. bd. Personality Homes, Inc., Smyrna, 1968—, Personality Home Mfrs. Inc., Marietta, Ga., 1968—; pres., chmn. bd. Personality Townhouses Inc., Smyrna, 1971—, Landmark Realty Co., Smyrna, 1970—, Collateral Investment Co., Smyrna, 1970—, Consol. Apts., Ltd., Smyrna, 1971—; dir. Consol. Capital Corp. Ga. Named Bldg. Developer of Year Cobb County C. of C., 1973. Mem. Nat. Home Builders Assn. (chpt. dir. 1963—), Cobb County C. of C. (v.p. 1972-73; pres. 1974; dir. 1970—). Home: 3080 Brookview Rd SE Marietta GA 30067 Office: 1127 Shallowford Rd Marietta GA 30066

EARNEST, JACK EDWARD, pipeline co. exec.; b. Dallas, June 18, 1928; s. William Hubert and Uma Mae (Jolly) E.; student (Founders scholar), Vanderbilt U., 1944-46; B.B.A., So. Methodist U., 1948, LL.B., 1952; postgrad. Stanford U., summer 1967; m. Billie Jo Young, Aug. 1, 1953; children—Laura Ellen, Jack Edward. Admitted to Tex. bar, 1952, N.Y. bar, 1962, U.S. Supreme Ct. bar, 1957; with Mobil Oil Corp., 1946-79, asso. gen. counsel, 1966-70, v.p. natural gas for N.Am., 1970-76, v.p. natural gas worldwide, 1976-79; pres., chief operating officer Transcontinental Gas Pipe Line Corp., Houston, 1979—. Mem. Natural Gas Supply Assn. (chmn. 1979), So. Gas Assn. (dir.), Interstate Natural Gas Assn. Am. (dir.), Am. Bar Assn., N.Y. State Bar Assn., Tex. Bar Assn. Methodist. Clubs: Royal Order of Jesters, Wee Burn Country, Univ. of Houston. Office: PO Box 1396 Houston TX 77001

EARNHEART, FRANK JONES, lawyer; b. Salisbury, N.C., June 14, 1924; s. Hilbert F. and Fannie (Jones) E.; B.A. in Chemistry, U. N.C., 1947; postgrad. Duke U. Law Sch., 1947-48; J.D., George Washington U., 1951; m. Mildred Schulken, Aug. 15, 1946 (div. 1965); children—Laurie Jeanne, Gregory Steven, Barbara Susan; m. 2d, Sonia Keeble, May 6, 1967; 1 stepson, Christopher Keeble. Admitted to D.C. bar, 1951, Ark. bar, 1956, Ohio bar, 1958, Pa. bar, 1975; asso. firm Cushman, Darby & Cushman, Washington, 1948-52; asst. patent counsel Beaunit Mills Inc., N.Y.C., 1952-54; patent counsel Lion Oil div. Monsanto Chem. Co., El Dorado, Ark., 1954-56; chief patent counsel Gen. Tire & Rubber Co., Akron, Ohio, 1956-67; gen. mgr. Gen. Tire Internat. Co., 1967-69; chmn. bd. and spl. patent counsel Genitiruco, Zug, Switzerland, 1967-69; v.p. adminstrn. Interpace Corp., Parsippany, N.J., 1969-71; pres., dir. Interpace Found., 1969-71; asst. to pres., sec., corp. counsel Selas Corp. Am., Dresher, Pa., 1971-80, v.p., sec., gen. counsel, 1980—. Trustee, N.J. Citizens Hwy. Com., 1969-71; pres., counsel Plumstead Civic Assn., 1975-80. Served to lt. (j.g.) USNR, 1943-46. Fellow Internat. Acad. Law and Sci.; mem. Am. Bar Assn., Am. Patent Law Assn., Phila. Patent Law Assn., Delta Theta Phi. Republican. Lutheran. Home: Tall Trees Bergstrom Rd Doylestown PA 18901 Office: Selas Corp America Dresher PA 19025

EARNSHAW, LEIGH CONDGON, real estate broker; b. Elverson, Pa., Sept. 10, 1925; s. George D. and Elizabeth (Radcliff) E.; student Pa. State U., 1974-76, Villanova U., 1978; m. Betty Ranck, Apr. 19, 1945; children—Leigh Condgon, Patricia Ann, Theresa Mae. Owner, operator ind. garage, Morgantown, Pa., 1953; owner, broker Earnshaw's Real Estate Co., Morgantown, 1975—. Sr. mem. Variance Bd., Morgantown. Served with inf. U.S. Army, 1943-45. Decorated Purple Heart, Bronze Star. Recipient Million Dollar Sales award Berks County Greater Bd. Realtors, 1974; grad. Realtors Inst.; cert. residential specialist; cert. Farm Land Inst. Mem. Greater Reading Bd. Realtors, VFW, Am. Legion. Methodist. Club: Odd Fellows.

EARWOOD, ANTHONY DOUGLAS, retail co. exec.; b. Austell, Ga., Sept. 11, 1947; s. Spurgeon Lee and Susie Florence (Newborn) E.; B.A., Mercer U., 1969; M.B.A., N.Y. U., 1978; m. Lizbeth Ann Simmons, June 26, 1976; 1 dau., Emily Lauren. Sales rep. Procter & Gamble, Los Angeles, 1974-76; asst. mgr. Lord & Taylor, Houston, 1976-81, dir. regional ops., 1981—. Active United Way, Houston. Served to capt. USMC, 1969-73. Mem. City Post Oak Assn. (dir. 1979—), Retail Merchants Assn., Kappa Sigma. Democrat. Baptist. Home: 15603 Falling Creek Houston TX 77068 Office: 5061 Westheimer St Houston TX 77056

EASLEY, CHARLES TAYLOR, ins. co. exec.; b. Hillsboro, Tex., Oct. 24, 1930; s. Knight Homan and Ruth Crow (Lambert) E.; B.A., Tex. A. and M. U., 1951; m. Janelle Hicks, Aug. 1, 1953; children—Paul Alan, Janelle. Asso. actuary, chief underwriter Amicable Life Ins. Co., Waco, Tex., 1953-60; owner Hicks, Easley & Co. ins. agy., Waco, 1960—, now pres.; dir. Westview Nat. Bank Waco. Lectr. Am. art history Baylor U., 1971—. Bd. dirs. Historic Waco Found., Better Bus. Bur. Waco; bd. dirs. Waco Pub. Library, chmn., 1976. Served with AUS, 1951-55. Mem. Nat., Tex. assns., ins. agts. Clubs: Lake Oaks Country, Ridgewood Country, Two-man show with son, photography, Klaras Art Gallery, 1973; one-man show Birdwell Gallery, 1976, Tyler (Tex.) Mus. Art; exhbns. at Baylor U., 1973, Waco Pub. Library, 1974. Home: 5108 Lake Jackson Dr Waco TX 76710 Office: 4830 Lakewood Dr Waco TX 76710

EASLEY, GEORGE WASHINGTON, constrn. co. exec.; b. Williamson, W.Va., Mar. 14, 1933; s. George Washington and Isabel Ritchie (Saville) E.; student U. Richmond, 1952-56; m. Paula Elizabeth Pence, Jan. 3, 1970; children—Bridget Bland, Kathy Clark, Saville Woodson, Marie Alexis, Isabell Roxanne, George Washington, Laura Dean. Hwy., engr. Va. Dept. Hwys., Richmond, 1956-62; dep. city mgr. City of Anchorage, 1962-68; prin. asso. Wilbur Smith & Assos., Cons. Engrs., Los Angeles, 1969-70; commr. pub. works State of Alaska, Juneau, 1971-73; exec. v.p. Burgess Internat. Constrn. Co., Anchorage, 1974, pres., 1975; pres., chmn. bd. George W. Easley Co., Anchorage, 1976—. Recipient commendations, City of Anchorage, 1966, Greater Anchorage, Inc., 1969, Ketchikan C. of C., 1973, Alaska State Legislature, 1974, Gov. of Alaska, 1974; named Outstanding Young Man, Anchorage Jr. C. of C., 1964; Gold Pan award Anchorage C. of C., 1969, 77; registered profl. engr., Calif. Mem. Anchorage C. of C. (sec.-treas. 1976, v.p. 1977, pres. 1979), Hwy. Users Fedn. of Alaska (dir. 1972-77), Orgn. for Mgmt. of Alaska's Resources (dir. 1975-77), Alaska C. of C. (dir. 1979-80), Am. Public Works Assn., Anchorage Transp. Commn. (chmn.), Asso. Gen. Contractors (dir. 1978-80), Inst. for Mcpl. Engrs., Inst. Traffic Engrs., Am. Mil. Engrs. (v.p. 1978—), Pacific NW Waterways Assn. (regional v.p.), Internat. Orgn. Fasters, Mates and Pilots (hon.), Petroleum Club Anchorage. Democrat. Presbyterian. Club: Rotary. Home: 2219 Forest Park Dr Anchorage AK 99503 Office: 1577 C St Suite 105 Anchorage AK 99501

EAST, CHARLES ROBERT, life ins. agt.; b. Tulsa, Apr. 13, 1936; s. Robert Wendell and Geraldine Rachel (Stewart) E.; student U. Okla., 1954-55; B.A., U. Tulsa, 1959, M.A., 1962; m. Carmelita J. McDaniel, Aug. 24, 1958; children—Dawn Michelle, Heather Danielle. Placement specialist No. Natural Gas Co., Omaha, 1962-63, unit personnel adminstr., 1963-64, personnel dir., 1965; spl. agent Nat. Life Ins. Co. of Vt., Omaha, 1965-68; sales dir. New Eng. Mut. Life, Houston, Tex., 1968-79; asst. gen. agt. Mass. Mut. Life, Houston, 1979—. Bd. dirs. Unity Ch. of Christianity, Houston, 1974-75, Cypress United Meth. Ch., 1977-79; Served with U.S. Army, 1962. Recipient various life ins. mgmt., sales, quality and service awards. Mem. Houston Assn. Life Underwriters, Houston Assn. C.L.U.'s (dir. 1977-79), Am. Soc. C.L.U.'s, Houston Estate and Fin. Forum, Million Dollar Round Table, SAR, Psi Chi, Sigma Chi Alumni Assn. Republican. Methodist. Home: 18111 Mountfield Dr Houston TX 77084 Office: 1610 Bank of SW Bldg Houston TX 77002

EAST, WILLIAM JAMES, real estate exec.; b. Rochester, N.Y., Dec. 6, 1937; s. Gerald J. and Mildred I. (May) E.; A.B. cum laude, Princeton U., 1959; M.B.A. in Fin., Harvard U., 1961; children—Anne Elizabeth, William J., Jr. Controller Hoeganaes Corp., Riverton, N.J., 1963-68; dir. fin. and acctg. The West Co., Phoenixville, Pa., 1968-69; asst. corporate controller Leasco Data Processing Equipment Corp., N.Y.C., 1969-70; sec. Reed & Stambaugh Co., Phila., 1970-73, pres., 1973—; dir. Gordon Wahls Co. Treas. Soc. for Crippled Children and Adults, Phila., 1977—; sec. Bldg. Owners Labor Relations Inc., Phila., 1976—. Served with U.S. Army Security Agency, 1961. Mem. Bldg. Owners and Mgrs. Assn. (pres. 1979), Harvard Bus. Sch. Club, Big Bros. Assn. Republican. Clubs: Annapolis Yacht, Union League of Phila., Phila. Cricket, Harvard of N.Y.C. Home: 528 W Moreland Ave Philadelphia PA 19118 Office: 220 Four Penn Center Plaza Philadelphia PA 19103

EASTBURN, DAVID PLUMB, econ. cons.; b. Doylestown, Pa., Jan. 9, 1921; s. Arthur Moses and Marie (Plumb) E.; A.B., Amherst Coll., 1942; M.A., U. Pa., 1945, Ph.D., 1957; m. Phyllis Ann Groff, June 25, 1949; children—David Rodman, Stephen Frazier, Susan Barbara, Laurie Ann. With Fed. Res. Bank of Phila., from 1942, pres., 1970-81; dir. Vanguard Group, Gen. Accident Group; trustee Penn Mut. Life Ins. Co.; instr. U. Pa., summer 1945, spring 1947. Pres., Phila. Orch. Assn., 1978—. Author: The Federal Reserve on Record, 1965. Editor: Men, Money and Policy, 1970. Contbr. articles to profl. jours. Home: 75 Short Rd Doylestown PA 18901 Office: 100 N 6th St Philadelphia PA 19106

EASTBURN, RONALD JOSPEH, assn. exec.; b. Alexandria, La., Aug. 25, 1941; s. Greig William and Thelma (Breaux) E.; B.S. in B.A., U. Ariz., 1964; m. Jennylynn Bouriden, Aug. 25, 1964; children—Boyd Ronald, Beth Rene, Bret Ross, Brad Ryan. Account exec. Doyle Dane Bernbach, Inc., N.Y.C., 1965-71; v.p. Mgmt. rep. Knox Reeves Advt., Inc., Mpls., 1971-75; dir. mktg. Nordensson Advt., Tucson, 1975-77; exec. v.p. So. Ariz. Home Builders Assn., Tucson, 1977—. Mem. Citizens Adv. Sign Code Com., City of Tucson, 1979-79; mem. Pima County Bond Election Com., 1978—; Sun. sch. supt. Unity of Tucson, 1977—; bd. dirs. Tucson Youth Football, 1980. Served with N.Y. N.G., 1965-71. Recipient Am. Assn. Advt. Agencies Bus. Mgrs. Award, 1961; Seldon Hale award, Nat.

Assn. Home Builders Exec. Officers Council, 1978, 79. Mem. Am. Mktg. Assn. (pres. 1976-77), Am. Soc. Assn. Execs., Brokers Round Table. Republican. Club: Terra Del Sol Squatic (pres. 1979-80). Home: 1245 Avenida Sirio Tucson AZ 85710 Office: 2840 N Country Club Rd Tucson AZ 85716

EASTEPP, DOUGLAS DEAN, concrete co. exec.; b. Tucamcari, N.Mex., Sept. 13, 1946; s. Douglas Paul and Betty Ruth (Williamson) E.; B.B.A., Washburn U., 1969, J.D., 1972; divorced; children—Travis, Donald Paul. Comml. loan officer Topeka (Kans.) Fidelity Investment, 1973; v.p. Alex Bros. Baking Co., Topeka, 1974—; v.p. Pepsi-Cola Bottling Co. of Topeka, 1975—; pres. Colo. Concrete Mfg. Co., Colorado Springs, Colo., 1976—. Served with USAFR. Mem. Am., Kans., Colo. bar assns., Colorado Springs C. of C. (vice chmn. transp. com.), So. Colo. Masonry Assn. Republican. Baptist. Clubs: Optimists (dir. Colorado Springs chpt., v.p. Colorado Springs breakfast chpt.), Topeka, El Paso, Colorado Springs. Address: 3446 Oak Creek Dr PO Box 1086 Colorado Springs CO 80901

EASTERLIN, JAMES FINNEY, oil refining co. exec.; b. Montezuma, Ga., Nov. 11, 1949; s. William McKenzie and Florence (Finney) E.; B.S. in Commerce, B.A. in Math. summa cum laude, Washington and Lee U., 1971; postgrad. U. Cologne (W. Ger.), 1971-72; M.B.A., Harvard U., 1974. With Charter Oil div. Charter Co., 1974—, v.p. info. services, mktg. div., Hammond, La., 1977-79, v.p. ops. econs., Jacksonville, Fla., 1979—. Mem. Am. Mgmt. Assn., Phi Beta Kappa. Club: Florida Yacht. Home: 4619 Avon Ln Jacksonville FL 32210 Office: Charter Oil Co PO Box 4726 Jacksonville FL 32202

EASTHAM, WILLIAM KENNETH, chem. specialties co. exec.; b. Mineola, N.Y., Dec. 30, 1917; s. William and Alice (Watson) E.; student Am. Inst. Banking, 1936-38, N.Y. U., 1946-48; A.M.P., Harvard U., 1954; m. Dorothy Brush, Mar. 25, 1942 (dec. Dec. 1979); children—Gale Eastham Shadrick, Nancy Eastham Kaydo; m. 2d, Robin J. Ehrlich, Nov. 6, 1980. Teller, Am. Bank of Savs., N.Y.C., 1935-39; asst. advt. mgr. Whitehall Pharm. div. Am. Home Products Co., N.Y.C., 1945-51; brand mgr. soap div., advt. mgr. Good Luck div., advt. mgr. Pepsodent div. Lever Bros. Co., N.Y.C., 1951-59; asst. to pres. Am. Home Products Co., exec. v.p. div. Boyle Midway, 1959-64; v.p. household products S.C. Johnson & Co., Inc., Racine, Wis., 1964-67, exec. v.p. U.S. operations, 1967-71, exec. v.p. U.S. and European ops., 1971-72, pres., chief operating officer, 1972-79, pres., chief exec. officer, 1979-80, vice chmn., 1980—; dir. Meredith Corp.; chmn. bd. Heritage Nat. Bank of Racine, 1976—. Bd. dirs. Racine Zool. Soc. Served to maj., AUS, 1940-45. Mem. Grocery Mfrs. Am. (dir.), U.S. C. of C. (chmn. 1977-78, dir.). Clubs: Racine Country, Burning Tree, Bob O'Link Golf, Met. (Washington); Univ. (Milw.), Vets 7th Regt. Office: 1525 Howe St Racine WI 53403

EASTMAN, JACK STUART, trucking co. exec.; b. New Albany, Ind., Aug. 30, 1936; s. Webster N. and Lois (McMullen) E.; student public schs., New Albany; m. Karen Long, Aug. 14, 1976; children—Julia Lea, John Reid. Salesman, Ky. Asphalt Sales Co., Louisville, 1960-62; sales rep. Standard Materials div. Martin-Marietta Corp., Louisville, 1962-64; gen. mgr. Fischer & Arnold Trucking Co., Jeffersonville, Ind., 1964-71; salesman Ligon Spl. Hauler, Inc., Madisonville, Ky., 1971-77, regional v.p., 1978—. Mem. Western Pa. Traffic and Transp. Assn., Traffic Club N.Y. Republican. Methodist. Address: 86 Mayfair Dr Pittsburgh PA 15228

EASTMAN, THOMAS GEORGE, real estate co. exec.; b. Los Angeles, July 28, 1946; s. George Lockwood and Louisa Montgomery (Forrester) E.; A.B., Stanford, 1968; M.B.A., Harvard, 1970; m. Terry Beckley, Aug. 20, 1972. Investment analyst Systech Fin. Corp. subs. Dillingham Corp., Walnut Creek, Calif., 1971-72; mgr. acquisitions Coldwell Banker Mgmt. Corp. subs. Coldwell Banker Co., Los Angeles, 1972-74, dir. acquisitions, 1974-78, asst. v.p., 1976-78, v.p., 1978-79; v.p., dir. institutional real estate Boston Co. Real Estate Counsel, Inc. subs. Boston Co., 1979—; mgr. George L. Eastman Co. Served with USAR, 1975. Home: 16 Viles St Weston MA 02193 Office: 1 Boston Pl 38th Floor Boston MA 02106

EASTON, ROGER CONANT, internat. and domestic cons.; b. Bklyn., Apr. 13, 1930; s. Glenn Herman and Cornelia (Hanson) E.; B.B.A., U. Mich., 1953, M.B.A., 1953; postgrad. Wharton Sch. Bus., U. Pa., 1949-50; m. Roberta Calhoun Clark, Aug. 16, 1952; children—Roger Conant, George Sawyer. Mgmt. research cons. Met. Life Ins. Co., N.Y.C., 1953-54; asst. export advt. mgr. Procter & Gamble Distbg. Co., N.Y.C., 1955-58; with Avon Products, Inc., 1959-68, 71-75, internat. merchandising mgr., N.Y.C., 1959-61, merchandising mgr. Avon Cosmetics, Ltd., Northampton, Eng., 1962-64, divisional sales mgr., 1965, mktg. mgr., 1966, dir. sales promotion, advt., merchandising, 1967-68; v.p. Dart Industries, Direct Selling Group, Orlando, Fla., 1969-70; dir. market research-spl. projects Avon Products, Inc., N.Y.C., 1971-72, dir. internat. sales promotion and incentive mktg., 1973, dir. internat. market planning, 1974-75; internat. and domestic bus. cons. The Profit Adviser, Orlando, 1976—; spl. agt. Northwestern Mut. Life Ins. Co., 1977—; adj. prof. internat. mktg. Crummer Grad. Sch. Fin. and Bus. Adminstrn., Rollins Coll., 1981—; lectr. sales mgmt. Pace U., 1975. Pres., Class of 1953, U. Mich. Sch. Bus., 1952-53. Served with U.S. Army, 1950. Mem. Million Dollar Round Table, Nat. Assn. Life Underwriters (Nat. Sales Achievement awards 1978—), Central Fla. Assn. Life Underwriters (dir., Agt. of Year 1977), Am. Mgmt. Assn., Direct Selling Assn., Central Fla. World Trade Assn., Phi Delta Theta, Delta Sigma Pi. Republican. Office: 550 N Bumby Ave Orlando FL 32803

EATON, AMOS JORGE, truck co. exec.; b. Asuncion, Paraguay, Feb. 19, 1944; s. Robert James and Dorothy Iris Veronica (Kent) E.; B.A., U. Vt., 1966; m. Susan Yvonne Deslauriers, May 29, 1966; children—Amos Joseph, Catherine Veronica. Sr. programmer Aetna Life & Casualty Co., Hartford, Conn., 1969-71; sr. analyst Royal Typewriter Co. div. Litton Industries, Hartford, 1971-72; project mgr. Zayre Corp., Framingham, Mass., 1972-73; pres. Eaton-Turner Inc., North Reading, Mass., 1974—. Served to 1st. lt., U.S. Army, 1966-68. Mem. Truck Body and Equipment Assn., Phi Delta Theta. Home: 25 Lee St Stoneham MA 02180 Office: 145 Park St North Reading MA 01864

EATON, EDGAR PHILIP, JR., mfg. exec.; b. Milw., Jan. 17, 1923; s. Edgar P. and Dorothy (Morgenthau) E.; B.S. in Mech. Engring., Mass. Inst. Tech., 1944; M.S. in Bus. Adminstrn., Boston U., 1948; m. Rita Beverly Shachat, June 7, 1945 (div.); children—Richard Michael, Randall Charles; m. 2d, Helen Yansura. Asst. plant engr. Gen. Dynamics Corp., Groton, Conn., 1944-45; sales engr., supr. Allis Chalmers Mfg. Co., Boston, 1945-49, sales mgr., asst. to pres., 1949-51; exec. v.p. Carbone Corp., Boonton, N.J., 1951-56, pres., 1957—, also dir.; pres. Carbone-Lorraine Industries Corp., 1974—; chmn. bd. Advance Carbon Products, Inc., San Gabriel; chmn. Carbone Lorraine Corp., Montreal, Que., Can., Carbone-Ferraz, Rockaway, N.J., Carbons, Inc., Cedar Knolls, N.J., Carbone U.S.A. Corp.; cons. to mgmt. personnel. Active Urban League; chmn. United Fund, 1959-60, 60-61; chmn. Morris County Community Chest, 1959-60, 60-61, pres., 1963-64; chmn. Morris-Sussex Regional Health Facilities Planning Council, 1960-79; chmn. hosp. governing bds. Am. Hosp. Assn., 1968-69; bd. dirs. Morristown Mem. Hosp. Served with AUS, 1942-43. Mem. Young Pres.'s Orgn. (chmn. 1963-64), ASME, IEEE, Am. R.R. Assn., Nat. Elec. Mfrs. Assn. (treas., dir.), Assn. Iron and Steel Engrs. Club: Rockaway River Golf. Author: The Marketing of Heavy Power Equipment, 1948. Home: 30 Colonial Dr Convent Station NJ 07961 Office: Boonton NJ 07005

EATON, HENRY FELIX, pub. relations exec.; b. Cleve., Nov. 30, 1925; s. Henry F. and Stella (Simon) E.; A.B., U. Chgo., 1947; m. Barbara Feder, Aug. 28, 1950; children—Deborah, Richard, David, Susan. Asst. advt. mgr. Kromex Corp., Cleve., 1947-48; editor Material Handling Engring. mag., Cleve., 1948-52; chmn. exec. com. Dix & Eaton, Inc., Cleve., 1952—. Vice pres. adv. bd. Notre Dame Coll. Ohio. Served with AUS, 1944-46. Mem. Pub. Relations Soc. Am. (counsellors sect.), Cleve. Advt. Club, Nat. Investor Relations Inst. Clubs: Union of Cleve., Cleve. Athletic, Oakwood Country. Home: 23690 Letchworth Rd Beachwood OH 44122 Office: 1010 Euclid Bldg Cleveland OH 44115

EATON, J. D., land title ins. co. exec.; b. Stanhope, Iowa, Apr. 27, 1932; s. Herschel D. and Flossie Kathryn (Hagen) E.; A.S. in Bus. Adminstrn., Webster City (Iowa) Jr. Coll., 1952; children—Michele Lorraine, Annette Marie, Jennifer Dianne. Investigator, reporter Retail Credit Co., Des Moines, 1954-56; mgr. Iowa Employment Security Commn., 1956-60; escrow officer Lawyers Title, Phoenix, 1960-66; v.p. Stewart Title & Trust, Phoenix, 1966-74; with USLIFE Title Ins. Co. Dallas, 1974—, sr, v.p., 1980—; pres. USLIFE Title Ins. Co., Albuquerque, 1974—; v.p. USLife/Title Co., El Paso, Tex., 1978—; bd. advs. Am. Bank Commerce. Bd. advs. Loveless Bataan Med. Center, Albuquerque. Served with U.S. Army, 1952-54; Korea. Mem. Am. Land Title Assn., N.Mex. Land Title Assn., N.Mex. Mortgage Bankers, N.Mex. Savs. and Loan Assn., Albuquerque Bd. Realtors, Albuquerque Home Bldg. Assn., Albuquerque Home Contractors Assn. Clubs: Albuquerque Country, Four Hills Country. Home: 7417 Capulin Rd Albuquerque NM 87111 Office: 300 San Mateo St NE Albuquerque NM 87109

EATON, ROBERT EDWARD LEE, ret. air force officer, pub. relations and mgmt. exec.; b. Hattiesburg, Miss., Dec. 22, 1909; s. Malcolm Jasper and Sallie Lucinda (Huff) E.; student U. Miss., 1926-27, Mass. Inst. Tech., 1936-37, Command and Gen. Staff Sch., 1942; B.S., U.S. Mil. Acad., 1931; m. Jo Kathryn Rhein, Jan. 1, 1939; children—Robert Edward Lee, Sallie, Charles. Commd. 2d lt., inf. U.S. Army, 1931; trans. to Air Corps, 1933; promoted through grades to maj. gen., 1947; operations officer 5th Bomb Squadron, 1935; weather officer, 1937; comdg. officer 7th Air Base Group, 1941; regional control officer 2d Weather Region, 1941; chief weather central div. A.A.F. hdqrs., 1942; comdg. officer 451st Bomb Group, Zone of Interior and Italy, 1943-44; dep. dir. operations U.S. Strategic Air Forces, Europe, 1944-45; office asst. chief air staff personnel A.A.F. hdqrs., 1945; Office of Dir. Information, 1946; dep. dir. Office of Legislative Liaison, Office of Sec. Def., 1949; dir. Legislation and Liaison Office of Sec. Air Force, 1951-53; comdr. Sixth Allied Tactical Air Force, Izmir, Turkey, 1953-55; comdr. 10th Air Force, Selfridge AFB, Mich., 1955-59; asst. chief staff res. forces, hdqrs., 1959-62, ret.; pres. Eaton Assos., Inc., pub. relations and mgmt. consultants, Washington, 1962—. Decorated Silver Star with oak leaf cluster, Legion of Merit, D.F.C. with oak leaf cluster, Bronze Star medal, Air medal with four oak leaf clusters, D.S.M., Croix de Guerre (France). Mem. Miss. State Soc. of Washington, Am. Legion (nat. comdr. 1973-74), 40 and 8. Episcopalian. Mason. Clubs: Columbia Country, Army-Navy, Metropolitan, Burning Tree (Washington); Pine Valley Golf (Clementon, N.J.). Home: 4921 Essex Ave Chevy Chase MD 20015 Office: 1750 K St NW Suite 260 Washington DC 20006

EATON, RODERIC LEWIS, ins. co. exec.; b. Utica, N.Y., July 4, 1939; s. Jesse Bennett and Blanche Arlene (Kidney) E.; B.A., Baylor U., 1961, M.B.A., 1964; m. Barbara Ann Taylor, Oct. 18, 1975; 1 dau., Laura Anne. Vice-pres., Equitable Life Assurance Soc. U.S., N.Y.C., 1964—; dir. Equico Lessors Mpls. Served with U.S. Army, 1963-64. Mem. N.Y. Soc. Security Analysts, Am. Mgmt. Assn., Nat. Consumer Fin. Assn. Republican. Office: Equitable Life Assurance Soc 1285 Ave of the Americas New York NY 10019

EBAUGH, DAVID PAUL, econ. cons.; engr.; b. Indpls., June 22, 1930; s. Paul Edward and Gladys Rachael (Ruddick) E.; m. Betty LeTourneau, Apr. 9, 1950; children—Michael, Marcellene, Diane, Rosalie. Tool and test equipment engr. IBM, Lexington, Ky., 1956-62; sr. indsl. engr. Goodyear Aerospace Corp., Akron, from 1942 pres., 1970-81; dir. Vanguard Group, Gen. Accident Group; trustee Penn Mut. Life Ins. Co.; mfg. methods engring. AMP, Inc., Harrisburg, Pa., 1965-67; ordained to ministry Ind. Assembly of God Ch., 1968; founder, pres. David Ebaugh Bible Sch., Harrisburg, 1968—. Served with USN, 1947-52. Mem. IEEE (profl. diploma 1959), Soc. Am. Value Engrs., Am. Inst. Indsl. Engrs., Am. Soc. Tool and Mfg. Engrs. Clubs: Christian Businessmen's Com. (pres. Lexington chpt. 1960), Full Gospel Businessmen's Com. (pres. Harrisburg chpt. 1967). Author numerous publs. on religious topics. Home and Office: 102 Park Terr Harrisburg PA 17111

EBAUGH, FRANK WRIGHT, cons. indsl. engr., investments exec.; b. New Orleans, July 31, 1901; s. John Lynn and Mary (Wright) E.; B. in Chem. Engring., Tulane U., 1923; m. Elizabeth Brown, Feb. 22, 1930; 1 dau., Betty Jane (Mrs. Gordon B. McFarland, Jr.). Engr., asso. mgmt. Tex. Co., 1923-34; partner retail firm, Jacksonville, Tex., 1934-54; mgr., partner Ebaugh & Brown Investments, Jacksonville, 1955-61; prin. Frank W. Ebaugh, Profl. Engr., Cons.; dir., mem. fin. com. Palestine (Tex.) Savs. & Loan Assn. Pres. Upper Neches River Municipal Water Authority; bd. dirs. Neches River Conservation Dist., 1966-71, Tex. Indsl. Devel. Council; vice chmn. Tex. Mapping Adv. Com.; sec. Texas Coordinating Water Com.; pres. Neches River Devel. Assn., 1966-69; panel chmn. Cherokee County (Tex.) War Price and Ration Bd., 3 years; mem. Library Bd., 1976-79. Mem. regional com. Girl Scouts Am. Named Man of Month East Tex. C. of C., 1953, Man of Year, Lions Club, 1953; honored by resolution Tex. Senate, 1967, Appreciation plague Jacksonville Library, 1969. Registered profl. engr., Tex. Mem. Nat., Tex. (chmn. water com.) socs. profl. engrs., East Tex., Jacksonville (past pres., dir. chmn. water resources com.) chambers commerce, Am. Chem. Soc., A.A.A.S., Tex. Acad. Sci., Tex. Water Conservation Assn., Nat. Trust for Historic Preservation. Presbyn. (elder, trustee). Rotarian. Clubs: Headliners (Austin); Country of Jacksonville (past pres.). Patentee Ebaugh Mixer. Home: 428 S Patton St Jacksonville TX 75766 Office: Box 1031 Jacksonville TX 75766

EBBERS, TODD ALBIN, ret. food service co. exec.; b. Chgo., Nov. 14, 1914; s. Johan Albin and Ingeborg W. (Ahlstrand) E.; student Northwestern U., evenings 1935-41; Ph.D., Hamilton State U., 1973; m. Helen Sylvia Koster, Aug. 16, 1952; 1 son, Thomas Todd. Partner, Carlson & Ebbers, Chgo., 1934-38; auditor Citizens Pub. Expenditures Survey of Ill., 1938-40; asst. controller Automatic Canteen Co. Am., 1940-42; treas., 1942-57, adminstrv. v.p., 1957-59, pres. Nationwide Food Service div., 1960; v.p., dir. marketing ITT Canteen Corp., Chgo., 1960-66, group v.p., 1966-67, sr. v.p., 1967-72; chmn. bd., v.p. Comanche Oil Co., 1969-72; philatelist, propr. Kersten Stamp Co. Bd. govs. Chgo. Heart Assn., internat. del., chmn. Fund drive, 1959, mem. spl. bus. council com., 1957-59, chmn., 1959; bd. govs. Henrotin Hosp., Chgo.; trustee Nationwide Food Service Profit Sharing Fund. Mem. Am., Chgo., Brit.-N.Am., German philatelic socs., Am. Stamp Dealers Assn., Internat. Fedn. Stamp Dealers. Roman Catholic (mem. bd.). Clubs: Athletic, Yacht, Econ., Execs., Swedish, Tavern (Chgo.). Home: PO Box 745 Placida FL 33946

EBERLE, WILLIAM FRANCIS, stockbroker; b. Beallsville, Ohio, Aug. 22, 1915; s. George and Katie Beall (Hunnel) E.; B.C.S., Benjamin Franklin U., 1933-36; m. Gertrude Eloise Johnson, Sept. 3, 1937; children—John Donald and Judith Lee (twins). Mem. faculty Fenn Coll. (now Cleve. State U.), 1963-64; purchasing agt. Thomas Machine, Glenshaw, Pa., 1939-41; asst. purchasing agt. Chambersburg Engring. Co. (Pa.), 1941-42; sr. buyer Kaiser Frazer Corp., Warren, Ohio and Ypsilanti, Mich., 1942-46; with Diamond Shamrock Corp., 1946—, mgr. purchasing adminstrn., Cleve., until 1970, project purchasing mgr., La Porte, Tex., 1970-78; account exec. All Am. Mgmt. Corp., Nassau Bay, Tex., 1978—. Mem. adminstrv. bd. trustees Seabrook (Tex.) Methodist Ch. Mem. Nat. Assn. Purchasing Mgmt. (certified purchasing mgr.), Purchasing Mgmt. Assn. Houston. Clubs: Clear Lake Country, Shriners, Masons. Home and office: 2007 Back Bay Ct Nassau Bay TX 77058

EBERSHOFF, JOHN HENRY, publishing rep., ret. engine mfg. corp. exec.; b. Lafayette, Ind., Feb. 2, 1908; s. Henry John and Margaret Mary (Vaughan) E.; B.S. in Mech. Engring., Purdue U., 1930; m. Dorothy Maxine Malsbary, May 14, 1938; children—David Alfred, Janet Maxine (Mrs. Thomas McGurk, Jr.). Dist. mgr. constrn. machinery div. Chain Belt Co., Milw., 1930-39; with Briggs & Stratton Corp., Milw., 1938-76, v.p. engine sales, 1965-76; spl. rep. Miller Pub. Co., Mpls., 1977—. Mem. Phi Kappa. Clubs: Athletic, Tripoli Golf (Milw.); Hazelden Country (Brook, Ind.). Home: 2505 W Dean Rd River Hills WI 53217 Office: 3300 N 124th St Wauwatosa WI 53222

EBLEN, JAMES HAMILTON, real estate broker; b. Henderson, Ky., Oct. 2, 1929; s. Oscar Hamilton and Janet Reid (Brown) E.; A.A., Orange Coast Coll., 1971; student Lumbleau Real Estate Sch., 1968-71; m. Velma Rawlings, Dec. 13, 1952; 1 son, Paul Hamilton. Salesman, Tarbell Realtors, Fountain Valley, Calif., 1968-70, sales mgr., Garden Grove, Calif., 1971; owner Eblen Real Estate, Fountain Valley, 1972; sales mgr. Percy Goodwin Co., Fountain Valley, 1973; owner Leadership Real Estate, Huntington Beach, Calif., 1973-74; mgr. Tobin Realty Sales, Huntington Beach, 1975-76; gen. partner E & E Devel. Co., San Jose, Calif., 1976-80; pres. Eblen Industries Inc., San Jose, 1979—. Co-chmn. Citizens Against New Taxes, 1975. Mem. Am. Security Council, Calif. Assn. Realtors (32d dist. chmn. legis. com., mem. polit. affairs lecture staff 1975-76), Huntington Beach-Fountain Valley Bd. Realtors (v.p. 1975, Realtor of Year 1975). Office: 1825 De La Cruz Blvd Suite 12 San Jose CA 95050

ECCLES, SPENCER FOX, banker; b. Ogden, Utah, Aug. 24, 1934; s. Spencer Stoddard and Hope (Fox) E.; B.S., U. Utah, 1956; M.S., Columbia U., 1959; m. Cleone Emily Peterson, July 21, 1958; children—Clista Hope, Lisa Ellen, Katherine Ann, Spencer Peterson. Trainee, First Nat. City Bank, N.Y.C., 1959-60, First Security Bank, Utah, Salt Lake City, 1960-61; with First Security Bank Idaho, Boise, 1961-70, sr. v.p. until 1970; exec. v.p. First Security Co., Salt Lake City, 1970-75; pres. First Security Corp., Salt Lake City, 1975-80, pres., chief operating offier, 1980—, also dir.; v.p., dir. First Security Computer Center, Inc., Salt Lake City; First Security Life Ins. Co. of Tex., Dallas; First Security Mortgage Co., Salt Lake City; First Security State Bank, Salt Lake City; Utah Mortgage & Loan Corp., Logan; exec. v.p., dir. First Security Leasing Co., Salt Lake City; dir. Amalgamated Sugar Co., Ogden, Utah; Anderson Lumber Co., Ogden; Aubrey G. Lanston & Co., N.Y.C.; First Security Ins. Agy., Inc., Lewiston, Idaho; First Security Ins. Inc., Salt Lake City; Securities Intermountain, Inc., Portland, Orgg.; Union Pacific Corp., N.Y.C., Zion's Coop. Mercantile Instn., Salt Lake City. Mem. bd. advs. U. Utah Coll. Bus.; mem. Columbia U. Grad. Sch. Bus. Adv. Council; bd. dirs. Utah Symphony; mem. nat. adv. bd. Ballet West, Salt Lake City, Pioneer Meml. Theatre, Salt Lake City. Served to 1st lt. U.S. Army. Mem. Am. Bankers Assn., Assn. Bank Holding Cos., Assn. Res. City Bankers, Young Pres. Orgn. Office: 79 S Main St PO Box 30006 Salt Lake City UT 84125

ECKEL, EUGENE JOSEPH, communications equipment mfg. co. exec.; b. Jersey City, Feb. 24, 1924; s. John and Mary (Ficke) E.; M.E., Stevens Inst. Tech., 1951, M.S., 1956; M.S. (Sloan fellow 1961), Mass. Inst. Tech., 1962; m. Darlene Laux, May 31, 1952; children—Thomas G., Lynn M. With Western Electric Co., Inc., 1951—, asst. engr., Kearny, N.J., 1951-55, engr. planning and devel., Lawrence, Mass., 1955-56, dept. chief, Kearny, 1956-58, asst. mgr., research and devel., Princeton, N.J., 1958-62, staff mgr., Chgo., 1962-64, mgr. operating, 1964-65, dir. engring. and mfg., 1965-67, gen. mgr., Columbus, Ohio, 1967-69, gen. mgr., Chgo., 1969-71, v.p. mfg., 1971-77, v.p. Bell sales-east, 1977-79, v.p. mfg., 1979—. Mem. corporate com. United Negro Coll. Fund, 1967—; trustee N.J. Coll. Fund Assn., 1977—; v.p., trustee Greater Newark Hosp. Devel. Fund, 1977—; trustee Blue Cross N.J., 1977—; bd. overseers N.J. Inst. Tech., 1977-80; spl. gifts chmn. Stevens Inst. Tech., 1977—. Home: 70 Tanglewood Dr Summit NJ 07901 Office: A75 South St Morristown NJ 07960

ECKENFELDER, DONALD JAY, mfg. co. exec.; b. Mt. Vernon, N.Y., Apr. 27, 1941; s. William Wesley and Kathryn Matilda (Hauck) E.; B.S. in Chem. Engring., Lafayette Coll., 1962; m. Barbara Sue Greenhill, Sept. 8, 1962; children—Christina Sue, Jean Marie, Jill Ann, Todd. Fire protection engr. Factory Mutual, East Orange, N.J., 1962-66; safety mgr. Merck & Co., Inc., Rahway, N.J., 1966-75; mgr. loss prevention Chesebrough-Ponds, Inc., Greenwich, Conn., 1975—. Named Outstanding Young Alumnus, Lafayette Coll., 1977. Mem. Am. Soc. Safety Engrs. (pres. 1981-82), Nat. Fire Protection Assn., Soc. Fire Protection Engrs., Am. Inst. Chem. Engrs., Am. Indsl. Hygiene Assn. Republican. Mem. Ch. of Jesus Christ of Latter Day Saints. Home: 22 Hillcrest Pl Wilton CT 06897 Office: 33 Benedict Pl Greenwich CT 06830

ECKENRODE, ROBERT THOMAS, transp. exec.; b. Harrisburg, Pa., Nov. 12, 1927; s. Robert Thomas and Helen Gertrude (Oaster) E.; B.Ch.E., Villanova U., 1951; M.A., Fordham U., 1964; m. Isabel F. O'Leary, Sept. 29, 1951; children—Pamela Ellen Eckenrode Magyar, Robert Thomas III, David M., Cynthia A. Dir., Frankford Arsenal, Phila., 1949-56; sr. v.p. Dunlap & Assos., Inc., Darien, Conn., 1956-69; exec. v.p. Am. Stock Exchange, Inc., 1969-80; group v.p. fin. and adminstrn. Nat. R.R. Passenger Corp. (Amtrak), Washington, 1980—; adj. prof. Fairfield (Conn.) U., 1975-79; dir. Dunlap & Assos., 1975-79, Securities Industry Automation Corp., 1976-79, Amex Commodities Exchange, 1978-80, Nat. Securities Clearing Corp., 1977-80, Am. Stock Exchange Clearing Corp., 1976-80. Served with USNR, 1947-48. Registered profl. engr., Mass. Mem. Fin. Execs. Inst., N. Am. Soc. Corp. Planners, Am. Mgmt. Assn., Ops. Research Soc. Am., Inst. Mgmt. Scis., Sci. Research Soc. Am. Office: 400 N Capitol St NW Washington DC 20001

ECKERSLEY, ROBERT NEAL, accountant; b. Scranton, Pa., Dec. 18, 1919; s. Jacob and Reba (Jenkins) E.; B.A. in Econs., U. Pa., 1941; M.B.A., Marywood Coll., 1974; m. Helen Thompson Palmer, June 28, 1941; children—Bruce Loc, Richard Laurence, Tari Louise. Pub. accountant, Scranton, 1941-42; inst. accounting and econs. U.

Scranton, 1946-50; partner, C.P.A., estate tax cons. Eckersley Accounting Service, Scranton, 1949—; dir. United Penn Bank. Instr. Grad. Sch. Bus., Marywood Coll., 1966-73. Treas. Episcopal Ch. Pub. Co., 1974. Served to 2d lt. AUS, 1942-46. Mem. Pa. Inst. C.P.A.'s (counsel), Inst. Internal Auditors, Am. Accounting Assn., Am. Inst. C.P.A.'s, Am. Arbitration Assn. (nat. panel arbitrators). Home: Miller Rd RD 4 Clarks Summit PA 18411 Office: 700 Scranton Nat Bank Bldg Scranton PA 18503

ECKERT, RALPH JOHN, ins. co. exec.; b. Milw., Mar. 12, 1929; s. John C. and Vlasta (Stauber) E.; B.S., U. Wis., 1951; m. Greta M. Allen, July 11, 1953; children—Maura Eckert Benseler, Peter, Thomas, Karen, Edward. With Benefit Trust Life Ins. Co., Chgo., 1954—, pres., chief exec. officer, 1971—, chmn. bd., 1972—. Pres. bd. Ill. Life Ins. Council, 1978-79; chmn. Lutheran Ch. Council, 1979-80. Served with U.S. Army, 1951-53; Korea. Fellow Soc. Actuaries; mem. Ill. Life and Health Ins. Guaranty Assn. (chmn. 1980—), Health Ins. Assn. Am. (bd. dirs. 1980—), Am. Acad. Actuaries. Clubs: Cedar Lake Yacht; Inland Lakes Yachting Assn.; Masons. Office: 1771 Howard St Chicago IL 60626

ECKERT, ROGER REX, florist; b. Lawrence, Kans., Aug. 27, 1938; s. Rex Sexton and Frances Marie (Nichols) E.; A.A., Grossmont Coll., 1969; m. Margaret Minor, July 24, 1964. Pres., Floral Mktg. Concepts Inc., El Cajon, Calif., 1975—; tchr. advanced floral design; cons. to floral industry. Served with USMC, 1963-69. Recipient design competition awards. Mem. San Diego County Retail Florists Assn. Republican. Mormon. Office: Floral Mktg Concepts Inc 1231 Broadway El Cajon CA 92021

ECKERT, WILLIAM HENRY, lawyer; b. Pitts., Mar. 27, 1900; s. William George and Matilda (Nickel) E.; B.S. in Econs. summa cum laude, U. Pitts., 1921, LL.B. with high honor, 1924; m. Josephine B. Gibson, July 13, 1934; children—Josephine Eckert Diggs, Dorothy Eckert Grannis. Admitted to Pa. bar, 1924, since practiced in Pitts.; sr. partner firm Eckert, Seamans, Cherin & Mellott, and predecessors, 1930-75, counsel, 1976—; part-time prof. law U. Pitts. Law Sch., 1924-48; mem. Pa. Supreme Ct. Procedural Rules Com., 1945—; mem. adv. com. law decedents estates and trusts Pa. Joint Govt. Commn., 1945—, chmn., 1972—; chmn. Commonwealth Ct. Rules Com., 1973-74; mem. Pa. Appellate Rules Com., 1973-74. Mem. Rosslyn Farms Borough Council, 1942-45, Crafton Sch. Bd., 1936-40. Served with U.S. Army, 1918. Mem. Am., Pa. (pres. 1969), Allegheny County (pres. 1945-46) bar assns., Am. Law Inst. Republican. Presbyn. Home: 410 Kings Hwy Rosslyn Farms Carnegie PA 15106 Office: 42d Floor US Steel Bldg 600 Grant St Pittsburgh PA 15219

ECKHARDT, HENRY THEODORE, mfg. co. exec.; b. Somers Point, N.J., Aug. 31, 1922; s. Henry T. and Jeremiah Eliza (Greer) E.; student Carnegie Inst. Tech., 1946-49; B.A., U. Pitts., 1953, M.Litt., 1958; m. Carol Ruth Kamman, Sept. 9, 1950; children—Susan Diane, Stephen Karl, Ellen Elizabeth, Alison Lynn. Rate clk. Alcoa, Pitts., 1949-51; advt. mgr. Miller Printing Machy Co., Pitts., 1952-56; account exec. Bond & Starr, Pitts., 1957-59; account supr., v.p. Erwin Wasey, Ruthraff & Ryan, Pitts., 1960-62; dir. indsl. div. Vic Maitland & Asso. Pitts., 1962-64; with Harris Corp., Cleve., 1965—, dir. merchandising, 1968—. Trustee Theta Xi Found., 1958-62. Served to 1st lt. U.S. Army, 1940-46. Mem. Assn. Indsl. Advertisers, Graphic Arts Advertisers Council (pres. 1970-72, sec.-treas. 1975-76). Lutheran. Home: 260 B Riverbend Rd Mystic CT 06355 Office: Melbourne FL 32919

ECKHARDT, LEVI HALL, banker; b. Sylan, Wis., Oct. 21, 1905; s. Levi and Effie Euphemia (Hall) E.; B.S., U. Wis., 1927; m. Gwendolyn Mae Grimsrud, Aug. 2, 1935; children—John Hall, Sharon Lee Eckhardt Gavinski. Bookkeeper, teller 1st Nat. Bank of Virquoa (Wis.), 1927-33; v.p. 1st Nat. Bank of Baraboo (Wis.), 1933-42, pres., 1942—. Mem. lay adv. bd. St. Clare Hosp. Served with AC, USN, 1941-43. Methodist. Clubs: Kiwanis, Lions, Elks, Masons. Home: 1212 Warren St Baraboo WI 53913 Office: 502 Oak St Baraboo WI 53913

ECKHARDT, WILLIAM BOYDEN, credit union exec.; b. Bellefonte, Pa., Aug. 31, 1949; s. Boyden and Maxine Alice (Young) E.; B.S. in Bus. Adminstrn., Oreg. State U., 1971. Adminstrv. officer Alaska U.S.A. Fed. Credit Union, Anchorage, 1971-72, ops. mgr., 1972-74, asst. gen. mgr., 1974-79, gen. mgr., 1979—. Mem. Credit Union Execs. Soc. (pres. Alaska council 1975—), Alaska Credit Union League (pres. Anchorage chpt. 1979—), Credit Union Nat. Assn. (alt. dir.). Club: Elks. Home: SRA Box 4216 Anchorage AK 99502 Office: Mail Pouch 6613 777 Juneau St Anchorage AK 99502

ECKLEY, GORDON CLAYTON, electronics co. exec.; b. Lehighton, Pa., Aug. 6, 1937; s. Chester and Eloise Pearl (Kocher) E.; student Lehigh U., 1959-61; B.S. in Mech. Engring., Newark Coll. Engring., 1968; m. Patricia Ann Pattyson; children—Jeffrey, Bradley G., Kimberly Ann. Supr. engring. cosmetic making depts. Andrew Jergens Co., Belleville, N.J., 1963-65, prodn. control mgr., 1965-68; plant engr. Kimball Systems-Litton Industries, Belleville, N.J., 1968-69, plant supt., 1969-72, plant mgr., 1972-73; plant mgr. Graber-Rogg, Inc., Cranford, N.J., 1973-78; dir. ops. Mepco/Electra, Inc., N.Am. Philips Co., Morristown, N.J., 1978—. Served with U.S. Army, 1961-62. Mem. ASME, Am. Inst. Indsl. Engrs., Nat. Soc. Profl. Engrs. Home: 47 Donna Dr Fairfield NJ 07006

ECKLUND, ELVIN EUGENE, electronics and energy exec.; b. Akeley, Minn., Jan. 16, 1921; s. Carl and Ida (Bergfast) E.; B.E.E., U. Minn., 1942; M.E.E., Poly. Inst. N.Y., 1953; m. Shirley Marie Legreid, May 20, 1944; children—Ellen Eugenia Ecklund Turco, Norman Carl, Janet Marie Ecklund Mullins, Steven David. With Allen B. DuMont Labs., Inc., Clifton, N.J., 1946-47, mgr. spl. products engring. and sales mgr. engine instruments, 1952-59; pres. Bergen-Passaic Electronics, Inc., Bogota, N.J., 1947-52; bus. planning adminstr., program mgr. ITT Fed. Labs., Clifton, N.J., 1959-62; pres. Thomas Electronics, Inc., Passaic, N.J., 1962-65; dir. mktg. Electro-Optics div. Bendix Corp., Ann Arbor, Mich., 1965-68, Conductron Corp., Ann Arbor, 1969-70; pres. Performance Measurements Co., Detroit, 1970-71, Carlton Enterprises, Ann Arbor, 1970-77; staff ERDA and Dept Energy, 1975—; mem. organizing com. for internat. symposia on alcohol fuel tech.; mem. com. on alcohol applications to transp. Internat. Energy Agy.; mem. internat. ad hoc exec. com. on hydrogen-fueled aircraft; mem. coordinating research council Alternate Automotive Fuels Group; mem. com. on energy conservation and transp. demand Transp. Research Bd. Mem. exec. bd. Alhtaha council Boy Scouts Am., 1959-65, v.p., 1962-65; trustee Passaic County Legal Aid Soc., 1963-65. Served to lt. USNR, 1942-45. Fellow Am. Inst. Aero. and Astronautics (asso.); mem. IEEE (sr.), Internat. Assn. for Hydrogen Energy, Am. Def. Preparedness Assn., Assn. Old Crows. Author: Making Money in Television Servicing, 1951, Repairing Record Changers, 1955, Repairing Home Audio Systems, 1962. Home: 12907 Asbury Dr Fort Washington MD 20022 Office: 1000 Independence Ave SW Washington DC 20585

ECKMAN, JOHN WHILEY, business exec.; b. Forest Hills, N.Y., July 20, 1919; s. Samuel Whiley and Anna (Wolffram) E.; student Yale, 1937-38; B.S., U. Pa., 1943; m. Barbara Harding, Mar. 23, 1946 (div.); children—Alison Elizabeth, Stephen Keyler; m. 2d, Mary Hynson Hopkins, May 28, 1977. With Smith Kline & French Labs., Inc., Phila., 1947-52; v.p. Thomas Leeming & Co., Inc., N.Y.C., 1952-62; exec. v.p., dir. Rorer Group Inc., and predecessors, Ft. Washington, Pa., 1962-66, pres., 1966—, chmn. bd., 1976—; chmn. Fed. Res. Bank Phila.; dir. Provident Mut. Life Ins. Co. Life trustee U. Pa.; pres., bd. mgrs. Wistar Inst. Anatomy and Biology; bd. dirs. World Affairs Council, Community Home Health Services, Phila., Phila. Urban Coalition, Greater Phila. Partnership, Univ. City Sci. Center; trustee Phila. area United Way. Served from ensign to lt., USNR, 1943-46. Fellow N.Y. Acad. Sci.; mem. Pharm. Advt. Club (pres. 1960), Pharm. Mfrs. Assn. (chmn.-elect 1980), Greater Phila. C. of C. (dir.), Hist. Soc. Pa. (pres. 1980—), AAAS, Acad. Scis. at Phila., Am. Acad. Polit. and Social Sci., Pa. Soc., Wharton Sch. Alumni Assn. (dir. 1966-68, pres. 1968-70), S.R., St. Andrews Soc., Sigma Chi, Beta Gamma Sigma. Presbyn. Clubs: Union League, Phila. Cricket, Sunday Breakfast (Phila.); Nantucket (Mass.) Yacht; Yale (N.Y.C.). Home: 22 Summit St Philadelphia PA 19118 Office: 500 Virginia Dr Fort Washington PA 19034

ECKRICH, DONALD P., food co. exec.; b. 1925; B.S., U. Mich., 1948; married. With Peter Eckrich & Sons Inc. (acquired by Beatrice Foods Co.), Chgo., 1948-74, chmn., pres., chief exec. officer, to 1974; pres. meat div. Beatrice Foods Co., Chgo., 1974-75, exec. v.p. splty. meats and wholesale div., 1975-77, vice chmn. bd., pres. domestic food ops., 1977-79, pres., chief operating officer, 1979—, also dir. Office: Beatrice Foods Co 2 N LaSalle St Chicago IL 60602*

EDDY, ROBERT LEE, bus. exec.; b. Los Angeles, Nov. 17, 1934; s. Clinton Monroe and Elaine Genieve (Watson) E.; B.S., UCLA, 1956, M.B.A., 1959; m. Jeri Bechtel, June 10, 1979. Personnel asst. TRW Inc., Los Angeles, 1959-61; dir. indsl. relations Whittaker Corp., Los Angeles, 1961-72; personnel dir. Levi Strauss & Co., San Francisco, 1972-73; staff cons. Leeds & Northrup Co., North Wales, Pa., 1974-79; co-founder Leeds & Northrup Devel. Inst.; individual practice as mgmt. cons., Landsdale, Pa., 1979-80; dir. orgn. devel. UGI Corp., Valley Forge, Pa., 1980—. Chmn., Com. to Employ the Handicapped, Los Angeles, 1963. Served as lt. (s.g.) USNR, 1956-58. Mem. Am. Soc. Tng. and Devel., Internat. Speakers Platform, Beta Gamma Sigma. Club: Valley Forge Racquet. Contbr. articles to profl. jours. Home: 2101 Sycamore Circle Lansdale PA 19446

EDDY, TILLMAN LEE, med. adminstr.; b. San Angelo, Tex., Sept. 25, 1941; s. Homer Rudolph and Geneva L. (McCarty) E.; B.S., Fla. State U., 1968. Emergency procedures technologist Leon County Blood Bank, Tallahassee, Fla., 1966-68; edn. dir. St. Mary's Hosp., West Palm Beach, Fla., 1968-70, chief exec. officer clin. lab., 1970—; also real estate developer. Served with U.S. Army, 1960-65. Mem. Am. Soc. Clin. Pathology, Am. Soc. Med. Tech., Med. Group Mgmt. Assn. Home: 1501 39th St West Palm Beach FL 33407 Office: 300 Butler St West Palm Beach FL 33407

EDEL, THOMAS RAYMOND, trade assn. exec.; b. Olean, N.Y., Apr. 26, 1934; s. Raymond Alfred and Lorretta (Houghton) E.; B.S. in Bus. Adminstrn., Bowling Green State U., 1958; postgrad. Inst. Orgnl. Mgmt. at Syracuse U., 1970-71, at U. Del., 1973-74; m. Ruth F. Carls, Apr. 4, 1964; children—Dennis, Mary Alice, Elizabeth. Exec. dir. Rochester (N.Y.) Retail Merchants Assn., Rochester Downtown Promotion Council, Downtown Devel. Corp. Rochester and Henrietta C. of C., (N.Y.) 1970-75; pres. N.J. Retail Mchts., Assn., Trenton, 1975—; dir. Consumer Credit Counseling Service. Bd. dirs. Distributive Edn. Clubs Am. of N.J.; bd. advs. Channel 10 TV, Rochester. Served with U.S. Army, 1958-60. Recipient cert. of merit Distributive Edn. Clubs Am. of N.J., 1978, 80, cert. service N.J. Govs.' Job Conf., 1979; named Profl. Retail Exec. of Yr., 1978, 79, Retail Jewelers Asso. of Yr., 1978-79. Mem. Am. Retail Assn. Execs. (dir.), Am. Soc. Assn. Execs., N.J. Soc. Assn. Execs., N.J. C. of C. Execs., N.J. Press Assn., Am. Retail Fedn., Nat. Retail Mchts. Assn., Retail Jewelers Am., Nat. Conf. Retail Execs. Clubs: K.C., Rotary, Beech Aero, Forsgate Country, Elks. Office: 212 W State St Trenton NJ 08608

EDELCUP, NORMAN SCOTT, land and community devel. co. exec.; b. Chgo., May 8, 1935; B.S. in Bus. Adminstrn., Northwestern U., 1957. Public acct., sr. acct. Arthur Andersen & Co., Chgo., 1958-62; sec., treas. Acme Printing Ink Co., Chgo., 1962-65; asst. to chmn. fin. com., asst. to chmn. bd. Commonwealth Edison Co., Chgo., 1965-68; vice chmn. bd. dirs., sr. v.p. Keller Industries, Inc., Miami, Fla., 1968-76; chief fin. officer, v.p., treas. GAC Corp. (name now Avatar Holdings Inc.), Coral Gables, Fla., 1976-80, exec. v.p., chief fin. officer, dir., 1980—; pres., chief fin. officer, treas. Avatar Properties Inc., Coral Gables, 1976—, Avatar Properties Credit Inc., Coral Gables, 1976—; dir. LLC Corp. (formerly Liberty Loan Corp.), St. Louis, Nat. Bank Fla., Miami. C.P.A., Ill., Fla. Mem. Am. Inst. C.P.A.'s, Fla. Soc. C.P.A.'s, Fin. Execs. Inst., Planning Execs. Inst. (v.p.), Miami C. of C. (trustee), Coral Gables C. of C. Home: 244 Atlantic Isle North Miami Beach FL 33160 Office: 201 Alhambra Circle Coral Gables FL 33154

EDELMAN, DANIEL JOSEPH, public relations counsel; b. N.Y.C., July 3, 1920; s. Selig and Selma (Pfeiffer) E.; grad. Columbia Coll., 1940; postgrad. Columbia, 1941; m. Ruth Rozumoff, Sept. 3, 1953; children—Richard, Renee, John. Reporter, Poughkeepsie (N.Y.) newspapers, UPI, 1941-42; news writer CBS, 1946-47; staff mem. Edward Gottlieb & Assos., 1947; public relations dir. Toni Co., Chgo., 1948-52; founder, now pres. Daniel J. Edelman, Inc., Chgo., 1952—. Chmn., Chgo. chpt. Young Presidents Orgn., 1963; chmn. vis. com. U. Chgo. Library, 1976; co-chmn. sustaining fellows individual campaign Art Inst. Chgo.; bd. dirs. Ill. Children's Home and Aid Soc.; adv. bd. Children's Diabetes Found., Denver; mem. Citizenship Council of Met. Chgo. Served to 2d lt. U.S. Army, 1942-46; ETO. Mem. Public Relations Soc. Am. (past chmn. counselor sect.), Publicity Club Chgo., Phi Beta Kappa, Zeta Beta Tau. Jewish religion. Clubs: Standard, Harmonie. Home: 1301 N Astor St Chicago IL 60610 Office: 221 N La Salle St Chicago IL 60601

EDELMAN, HARRY ROLLINGS, III, contracting engrs. co. exec.; b. Pitts., Aug. 16, 1928; s. Harry Rollings and Marian (Crooks) E.; B.S., U. Pitts., 1950; postgrad., 1954-56; m. Nancy Jane McCune, Aug. 26, 1950; children—Lisa Edelman Turbeville, Harry Rollings IV, John, Amy. With Heyl & Patterson, Inc., Pitts., 1950—, exec. v.p., 1960-65, pres., gen. mgr., 1965—, chmn., 1977—; dir. Dedert Corp., Chicago Heights, Ill., Thermal Processes, Inc., LaGrange, Ill., Heyl & Patterson Internat., Inc., Pitts.; treas. Met. Broadcasting Co. Pitts. Bd. dirs. Allegheny Gen. Hosp.; past pres. Christian Assn. S.W. Pa.; vice-chmn. Presbyn. Assn. Aging; chmn. Vocat. Rehab. Center Allegheny County. Served with U.S. Army, 1952-54. Mem. AIME, World Bus. Council, Chief Execs. Forum. Clubs: Pitts. Field; Duquesne; University. Home: 101 Springhouse Ln Pittsburgh PA 15238 Office: 250 Park West Dr PO Box 36 Pittsburgh PA 15230

EDELSON, BURTON IRVING, communications co. exec.; b. N.Y.C., July 31, 1926; s. Samuel and Margaret (Raff) E.; B.S. U.S. Naval Acad., 1947; M.S., Yale U., 1954, Ph.D., 1960; m. Betty Frances Good, Aug. 30, 1952; children—Stephen, John, Daniel. Commd. ensign U.S. Navy, 1947, advanced through grades to comdr., 1963, ret., 1967; with Communications Satellite Corp., Washington, 1968—, dir. Comsat Labs., Clarksburg, Md., 1973-79, v.p. systems, Washington, 1979-80, sr. v.p. Comsat Gen. Corp., 1980—. Mem. Montgomery County (Md.) Econ. Devel. Bd., 1977-79. Decorated Legion of Merit, 1965; recipient Howe Research medal ASM, 1963; registered profl. engr., Ohio. Fellow AIAA; AAAS, IEEE. Clubs: Army Navy, Cosmos (Washington); Yale (N.Y.C.). Contbr. articles to profl. jours. Home: 116 Hesketh St Chevy Chase MD 20015 Office: Comsat Bldg 950 L'Enfant Plaza Washington DC 20024

EDELSON, LARRY MARK, equipment co. exec.; b. Bklyn., Feb. 7, 1949; s. Irving and Lillian (Resnick) E.; B.Ed., U. Toledo, 1970; m. Dale S. Levinson, Mar. 23, 1969; children—Jeffrey Alan, David Barry. Product and mktg. dir. Air-Shields, Inc., Hatboro, Pa., 1971-74; pres. RE-DE Equipment Corp. of N.J., Edison, 1974—; cons. on intensive care nursery planning State of N.J., 1974—. Mem. Aircraft Owners Pilots Assn. Democrat. Jewish. Research on sudden infant death syndrome. Office: 17 Gross Ave Edison NJ 08817

EDELSTEIN, ALAN ALBERT, aluminum refining co. exec.; b. N.Y.C., Dec. 27, 1943; s. Samuel and Frances Claire (Albert) E.; B.S., Rochester Inst. Tech., 1968; m. Donna C. Kaufmann, Mar. 20, 1965; children—Peter S., Jill L. Prodn. mgr. IMPCO, Rochester, N.Y., 1965-67; account exec. Rochester Smelting & Refining Co., Inc., 1967-73, v.p., dir., 1974—; v.p. DeRidder-Thurston, Rochester, 1973-74. Co-dir. Pittsford Mustang Youth Soccer, 1976-77; v.p. Pittsford Pop Warner Football, 1979, fin. cons., 1980—. Mem. Soc. Die Casting Engrs., Aluminum Recycling Assn. (chmn. com.). Jewish. Clubs: Tennis (Rochester); Brighton-Henrietta Racquet. Home: 12 Framingham Ln Pittsford NY 14534 Office: 26 Sherer St Rochester NY 14611

EDELSTEIN, ALAN MARTIN, lawyer, accountant; b. Boston, May 5, 1926; s. Barney and Gertrude (Lobel) E.; B.S. in Bus. Adminstrn., Boston U., 1947, J.D., 1949; m. D. Sybil Abrams, Apr. 16, 1950; children—Marcia S., David R. Admitted to Mass. bar, 1949, U.S. Tax Ct., 1949, U.S. Supreme Ct. bar, 1962; practiced in Boston, 1949—; practice accounting, Boston, 1947—; partner Alan M. Edelstein & Co.; mem. profl. liaison com. IRS, Mass. Dist., 1964-66. Founder, 1st pres. adv. com. Hillel Founds. New Eng., B'nai B'rith, Boston, 1951-52, treas. Commonwealth Lodge, 1951-53, del. Central New Eng. council, 1951-52; del. Jewish Community Council Met. Boston, 1952; area chmn. A.R.C., Brighton-Allston, Mass., 1950-51; mem. nat. alumni council Boston U., 1972—; pres. alumni bd. dirs. Sch. Mgmt., 1978-80, bd. visitors Sch. Medicine, 1980—; treas. Temple Emmanuel, Newton, Mass., 1972-78, exec. v.p., trustee, 1978—, mem. bd. Associated Synagogues Mass., 1973—, v.p., 1979—. Served with USN, 1944-45. C.P.A., Mass. Mem. Am., Mass. (pres. 1965-66) assns. attys.-C.P.A.'s, Mass. Soc. C.P.A.'s (fed. tax com. 1959-75, relations with fin. instns. com. 1978—), Am. Inst. C.P.A.'s, Boston Bar Assn. (fed. tax. com. 1954—), Am. Arbitration Assn. (nat. panel arbitrators), Jewish War Vets. (past comdr. 1951-52, past nat. dep. judge adv.). Clubs: Masons (lodge treas. 1959-62), Kiwanis (past dir. Brighton-Allston). Home: 276 Dorset Rd Waban MA 02168 Office: 1 State St Boston MA 02109

EDELSTEIN, DAVID H., bus. exec.; b. Cambridge, Mass., Jan. 29, 1936; B.S. in Econs., Temple U., 1957; LL.B., Boston U., 1960; postgrad. N.Y. U. Law Sch., 1961, JAG Sch., U. Va. Law Sch., 1962; m. Carol Slosberg, June 22, 1958; children—Lauren, John. Pres., chief exec. officer Am. Propane Corp., Waterford, Conn., 1967—; v.p. United Builders Supply Co., Inc., Westerly, R.I., 1972—, Butler Bros. Oil Co., Inc., Westerly, 1971—, Bookworks, Inc., Westerly, 1979—, Downs Patterson Corp., Stonington, Conn., 1975—; gen. partner Pawaget Devel., Westerly, 1977—; shareholder, original incorporator Pegasus Petroleum Corp., Bronco Drilling Co., Tulsa; incorporator Savs. Bank of New London (Conn.), 1977—. Bd. dirs. Pine Point Sch., Stonington, 1972-78, chmn., 1977-78; bd. dirs. Easter Seals S.E. Conn., 1977, treas., 1980; mem. L.A.M.B.S.; bd. incorporators Lawrence and Meml. Hosp., 1980—. Served to capt. JAGC, U.S. Army, 1962-65, in Res., 1965-68. Mem. Conn. Bar Assn., New Eng. LP-Gas Assn. (dir.), Nat. LP-Gas Assn. (state dir., nat. dir.). Office: PO Box 392 Uncasville CT 06382

EDELSTEIN, HASKELL, banker; b. Troy, N.Y., May 12, 1933; s. Ellis and Tilly (Kaplan) E.; B.A., Amherst Coll., 1954; J.D., Albany Law Sch., 1957; LL.M. in Taxation, N.Y. U., 1958; m. Joan Ruth Erback, Jan. 19, 1964; children—David, Benjamin. Admitted to N.Y. bar, 1957; asso. McGovern, Vincent, Connelly & Soll, N.Y.C., 1959-65, partner, 1965-68; partner Soll, Connelly & Marshall, N.Y.C., 1968-73; v.p. tax and internat. legal counsel Citicorp Leasing Internat., Inc., N.Y.C., 1973-75; v.p. Citibank, N.Y.C., 1975-78, v.p. Citicorp and Citibank, head corp. tax dept., 1978-79, v.p., gen. tax counsel, 1980—; lectr. Mem. Am., N.Y. State bar assns., Assn. Bar City N.Y. Jewish (trustee synagogue). Contbg. editor to Bur. Nat. Affairs - Tax Management and The Visual Artist and the Law, rev. edit., 1974; contbr. articles to profl. jours. Home: 340 E 69th St New York NY 10021 Office: 399 Park Ave New York NY 10043

EDGAR, JAMES MACMILLAN, JR., mgmt. cons. co. exec.; b. N.Y.C., Nov. 7, 1936; s. James Macmillan Edgar and Lilyan (McCann) E.; B. Chem. Engring., Cornell U., 1959, M.B.A. with distinction, 1960; m. Judith Francis Storey, June 28, 1958; children—Suzanne Lynn, James Macmillan, Gordon Stuart. New product rep. E.I. duPont Nemours, Wilmington, Del., 1960-63, mktg. services rep., 1963-64; with Touche Ross & Co., 1964-78, mgr., Detroit, 1966-68, partner, 1968-71, partner in charge, mgmt. services ops. for No. Calif. and Hawaii, San Francisco, 1971-78, regional mgmt. services partner, 1977-78, founder Edgar, Dunn & Conover, Inc., mgmt. cons., 1978—. Mem. San Francisco Mayor's Fin. Adv. Com., 1976—; chmn. city budget com. San Francisco C. of C., 1976-79; mem. Cornell U. Council, 1970-73. C.P.A.; cert. mgmt. cons. Mem. Assn. Corp. Growth (v.p. membership San Francisco chpt. 1979—), Am. Inst. C.P.A.'s, Calif. Soc. C.P.A.'s, Am. Mktg. Assn., Inst. Mgmt. Cons. (regional v.p. 1973-80, dir. 1975-77, v.p. bd. dirs. 1977-80), Tau Beta Pi. Clubs: Univ., Meadow (fin. com. 1980—), Commonwealth of San Francisco. Patentee nonwoven fabrics. Home: 10 Buckeye Way Kentfield CA 94904 Office: 1 Market Plaza Spear St Tower San Francisco CA 94105

EDGAR, REX E., banker; b. Hayward, Okla., June 28, 1935; s. Robert E. and Pearl M. (Craig) E.; B.B.A. in Acctg., U. Okla., 1958; M.S. in Adminstrn., Okla. State U., 1963; m. Dovie F. Hanna, Jan. 12, 1958; children—Jeffery Layne, Bryan Thomas. Vice pres. Bank Okla., N.A., Tulsa, 1966-76; exec. v.p. First Nat. Bank & Trust Co., Ponca City, Okla., 1976-78, pres., chief exec. officer, 1978—; dir. Pelton & Co.; mem. Okla. Bus. Devel. Bd., Okla. Econ. Progress Bd.; pres. Ponca City Indsl. Found. Asst. campaign dir. Ponca City United Way, 1980—; treas. Ponca City Salvation Army, 1980—; pres. Ponca City Sch. Bd., 1980—. Served as officer AUS, 1957-58. Recipient Leadership award Boy Scouts Am., 1979; named to Okla. Wrestling Hall of Fame, 1973. Mem. Am. Bankers Assn., Robert Morris Assos., Ind. Bankers Assn., Okla. Bankers Assn. Democrat. Methodist. Address: First Nat Bank & Trust Co 122 E Grand St PO Box 1151 Ponca City OK 74601

EDGAR, WILLIAM CARTWRIGHT, corp. exec.; b. Pitts., Sept. 16, 1952; s. William Dunlop and Patricia (Hegmann) E.; B.S., Robert Morris Coll., 1976; m. Kathi M. DeLuca, Apr. 29, 1978; children—Elizabeth, Robert. Owner, W.C. Edgar Photography Studio, Allison Park, Pa., 1971-76; gen. mgr. Photogroup, Huntingdon, Pa., 1976-77; asst. controller, credit mgr. Reidbord Bros. Co., Pitts., 1977-78; asst. credit and billing mgr. Copperweld Corp., Pitts., 1978-80, credit mgr., 1980—; pvt. practice acctg., 1975—. Treas., Hampton Twp. Young Republicans, 1969-70. Mem. Nat. Assn. Accts., Nat. Assn. Credit Mgmt. Presbyterian. Home: 1162 Chislett St Pittsburgh PA 15206 Office: Robinson Plaza II Pittsburgh PA 15205

EDGE, JAMES LAFAYETTE, III, mfg. co. exec.; b. Asheville, N.C., Apr. 16, 1934; s. James Lafayette and Nell Louise (Funderburk) E.; A.B., Catawba Coll., 1956; postgrad. N.C. State U., 1965, Grad. Sch. Sales Mgmt. and Mktg., Syracuse U., 1979; postgrad. exec. program Columbia, 1974, Wharton Sch., U. Pa., 1977; m. India Joan Weems, Oct. 30, 1965; children—Claudette, Tracy, Bartley, Michael, Philip. Sales supr. Atlantic Refining Co., Miami, Fla., 1956-63; salesman Ortho Diagnostics Inc., Raritan, N.J., 1963-67, mgr. export devel., 1967-70, mgr. export sales, 1970-73, dir. internat. mktg., 1973—. Mem. The Asia Soc., U.S./Arab C. of C., Far East Am. Council, Am. Mgmt. Assn., Nat. Exec. Council (Washington), Sales and Mktg. Execs. Internat., Nat. Fgn. Trade Council, N.J. Dist. Export Council, Pharm. Mfrs. Assn., N.J. Assn. Realtors, Nat. Assn. Realtors. Republican. Presbyterian. Home: Chapel View Dr Flemington NJ 08822 Office: Ortho Diagnostics Raritan NJ 08869

EDGERS, ROBERT BRUCE, wood products co. exec.; b. Seattle, May 28, 1930; s. Kenneth Barton and Lois (Heberlein) E.; B.A., U. Wash., 1952; m. Terry J. Proctor, Dec. 19, 1952; children—Enid, Robert, Peter, Tracy. Mgmt. cons., Oreg. resident mgr. Profl. Advisors, Inc., Seattle and Eugene, 1954-62; asso. Harry J. Prior & Assos., Seattle, 1962-64; with Simpson Timber Co., Seattle, 1964—, corp. staffing mgr., 1974—. Served with USAF, 1952-54. Mem. Am. Soc. Personnel Adminstrn. (pres. Seattle chpt.), Human Resource Planning Soc., Seattle C. of C. Office: Simpson Timber Co 900 4th Ave Seattle WA 98164

EDGERTON, RICHARD, restaurant/hotel owner; b. Haverford, Pa., May 2, 1911; s. Charles and Ida Bonner E.; m. Marie Lytle Page, Oct. 24, 1936; children—Leila, Margaret, Carol. Pres./owner Lakeside Inn Properties, Inc., Mt. Dora, Fla., 1935—; co-owner 19 Burger King restaurants, Pa., 1966—; gen. mgr., pres. Buck Hill Falls (Pa.) Co., 1961-65; pres., chief exec. officer Eustis Sand Co., Mt. Dora, Fla.; founding dir. Fla. Service Corp., Tampa; v.p. 1st Nat. Bank, Mt. Dora. Mem. Gov.'s Little Cabinet, 1955-61. Trustee Berry Coll.; bd. dirs. Mt. Dora Community Trust Fund. Served to lt. USNR, 1944-46; ETO. Mem. Am. (dir.), Fla. (hon., past pres.) hotel and motel assns., N.H. Hotel Assn. (past pres.), Newcomen Soc., Welcome Soc., Pa. Soc. Clubs: Miami; Mt. Dora Yacht, Mt. Dora Golf. Home: 3d and McDonald Sts Mt Dora FL 32757 Office: 234 W 3d Ave Mt Dora FL 32757

EDGERTON, WILLIAM HALSEY, retail exec.; b. Hanover, N.H., Mar. 29, 1935; s. Halsey Charles and Ada Lorraine (Sniffen) E.; B.A., Dartmouth Coll., 1957; postgrad. Harvard U. Grad. Sch. Design, 1957-59, Harvard U. Grad. Sch. Bus., 1959-60; m. Ann Omohundro Switzer, Apr. 1, 1967; 1 dau., Ann Randolph. Sales rep. Techbuilt, Inc., Cambridge, Mass., 1960-62; real estate developer, Boston, 1962-64; product mgr. McGraw-Hill Info. Systems, Inc., N.Y.C., 1964-71; pres. Constrn. Pub. Co., Inc., N.Y.C., 1971-77; pres. Mech. Music Center, Inc., Darien, Conn., 1977—; cons. in building cost, real estate and fine arts appraisal. Recognized as preservationist by Columbia U. Sch. Architecture and Planning, 1977. Mem. Am. Soc. Appraisers (sr. mem.), MBS Internat. (trustee). Republican. Club: Annisguam (Mass.) Yacht. Author: How to Renovate a Brownstone, 1970; co-author: Real Estate Valuation Cost File, 1975; compiler: Automatic Musical Instruments Pricing Guide, 1977; editor: Silver Anniversary Collection, 1974. Home: 241 Long Neck Point Rd Darien CT 06820 Office: Mech Music Center Inc 25 Kings Hwy N Darien CT 06820

EDINGTON, JACK LENOX, II, real estate broker; b. Detroit, Feb. 4, 1945; s. Jack Lenox and Minnie (Gooch) E.; B.S., Eastern Mich. U., 1972; m. Nancy Jane Bowie, Nov. 29, 1968. Asst. mgr. Dun & Bradstreet, Inc., Detroit, 1965-70; v.p., mgr. Outstate Real Estate One of Washtenaw, Ann Arbor, Mich., 1973-76; pres., treas. Wolverine Inc., Ann Arbor, 1976—; pres. Edington Assos., 1979—; v.p. Standard Securities Corp., 1979—; mem. adv. com. real estate program Washtenaw Community Coll., 1975-77; dir. real estate Sports Illustrated Ct. Clubs, 1977-79. Mem. Internat. Council Shopping Centers, Nat. Assn. Corp. Real Estate Execs., Ann Arbor Bd. Realtors, Mich. Assn. Realtors, Nat. Assn. Realtors, Realtors Nat. Mktg. Inst., Aircraft Owners and Pilots Assn. Club: Ann Arbor Town. Home: 8225 W Huron River Dr Dexter MI 48130 Office: 18311 W Ten Mile Rd Southfield MI 48075

EDMONDSON, JAMES PRESTON, county ofcl.; b. Purcellville, Va., July 20, 1933; s. Samuel Preston and Margaret Ella (Remine) E.; B.S. in Accounting, Va. Poly. Inst., 1955; M.B.A. in Mgmt., Babson Coll., 1967; grad. U.S. Army Command and Gen. Staff Coll., 1968-69, U.S. Army War Coll., 1975-76; m. Dolores Leigh Akers, June 4, 1955; children—Preston S., Lisa K., Richard D., Teresa A., Dennis N. Commd. 2d lt., U.S. Army, 1955, advanced through grades to col., 1977; acctg. officer, Ft. Wainwright, Alaska, 1959-62; instr. acctg., Ft. Benjamin Harrison, Ind., 1962-64; fin. and acctg. officer U.S. Army Adminstrn. Center, St. Louis, 1964-65; budget officer U.S. Army, Vietnam, 1967-68; fin. systems project officer Comptroller of Army, Washington, 1969-72; fin. and acctg. officer, Ft. Bragg, N.C., 1972-75; dir. combat devels. U.S. Army Adminstrn. Center, Indpls., 1976-79, ret., 1979; dir. Central Acctg., Country of Chesterfield, Va., 1979-81; owner J.W. Poff & Co., Christiansburg, Va., 1981—; instr. accounting U.S. Army Service Schs., Ft. Harrison, 1962-64; instr. acctg. Fayetteville (N.C.) State U., 1973-74. Decorated Army Commendation medal, Bronze Star, Legion of Merit with oak leaf cluster. Mem. Mcpl. Fin. Officers Assn., Am. Mgmt. Assn., Nat. Soc. Public Adminstrn., Nat. Assn. Accts., Assn. Govt. Accts. Baptist. Home: 1180 Flint Dr Christiansburg VA 24073 Office: Drawer 59 Christiansburg VA 24073

EDMUNDS, KARL DEE, sales and mktg. mgmt. exec.; b. Salt Lake City, Dec. 16, 1954; s. Paul Dee and Elizabeth Darlene (Jolley) E.; student public schs.; m. Beverly Gardner, Aug. 11, 1976; children—Megan, Zackary. Mgr., The Mattress Factory, Salt Lake City, 1978-79; v.p. Gold Standard Plan Inc., Provo, Utah, 1979—; asst. mktg. dir. The Energy Outlet, Inc., Provo, 1980—; owner, mgr. Hair Express, Provo, 1980—. Missionary, Mormon Ch., 1974-76, Sunday sch. tchr., 1980—, chmn. ward activities, 1980—, chmn. phys. activities, 1979—. Mem. Internat. Entrepreneurs Assn., Utah Mental Health Assn. Republican. Home: 3124 Hemlock St Antioch CA 94509 Office: PO Box 3702 Walnut Creek CA

EDMUNDS, SELDEN SPENCER, savs. and loan exec.; b. Roanoke, Va., Dec. 27, 1928; s. Horatio Spencer and Betsey (Sharkey) E.; A.B., Princeton U., 1950; m. Gene Brumfield Gilman, June 18, 1966; children—John Stewart Gilman, Charles Coleman Gilman, James Spencer, William Nelson. Asst. treas. Peoples Fed. Savs. & Loan Assn., Roanoke, 1950-51, pres., 1972—, also dir.; asst. cashier Mountain Trust Bank, Roanoke, 1954-59; v.p. Mortgage Investment Corp., also dir. Richmond, Va., 1959-71. Bd. dirs. Roanoke Hist. Soc., 1958-74, Soc. for Crippled of SW Va., 1960-64, Roanoke chpt. Am. Cancer Soc., 1964-66, Roanoke Symphony Soc., 1977-78; dir. Fincastle Presbytery Investment Fund, Inc.; trustee Presbyn. Sch. of Christian Edn., Richmond, 1979—. Served to 1st lt. inf. U.S. Army, 1951-53. Recipient Am. Spirit Honor medal Citizens Com. Army, Navy and Air Force, 1951; named Father of Yr. in Roanoke Valley, Roanoke Valley Mchts. Assn., 1977. Mem. Soc. Real Estate Appraisers (sr. residential appraiser), Roanoke Valley Home Builders Assn. (asso.), Va. Mortgage Bankers Assn. (pres. 1971), Roanoke Valley Merchants Assn. (dir. 1978—, pres. 1979—), Roanoke Valley C. of C. (dir. 1974-75). Republican. Presbyterian. Home: 2322 Rosalind Ave SW Roanoke VA 24014 Office: 210 S Jefferson St Roanoke VA 24011

EDMUNDS, STEPHEN ORRELL, constrn. co. exec.; b. Gretna, Va., July 17, 1919; s. John Thomas and Byrd May (Farmer) E.; B.S. in Archtl. Engring., Va. Poly. Inst., 1941; m. Norma Jeanne Parsons, July 8, 1949; children—Margaret Susan, Robert Stephen. Estimator for several gen. contractors, 1946-50; concrete contractor, estimator Spidel & Hall, Inc., Washington, 1950-52; chief estimator E.L. Daniels, Gen. Contractor, Arlington, Va., 1952-55; gen. mgr. So. Comml. Constrn., Inc., Washington, 1955-58; chief estimator Eugene Simpson & Bros., Inc., Alexandria, Va., 1959-61, v.p., 1961-72, sr. v.p., 1972—. Mem. engring. adv. com. No. Va. Community Coll., Annandale, 1968—; tchr. Fairfax County Adult Edn. Program, 1970-79; instr. George Mason U., Fairfax, Va., 1980—. Vice chmn. Fairfax County Plumbing Bd., 1968-76. Bd. dirs. Glen Forest Community Assn., 1963—, Fairfax County Vocational Ednl. Found., 1972—. Served with AUS, 1941-45; PTO. Decorated Legion of Merit; cert. profl. estimator. Mem. No. Va. Builders Assn. (dir. 1967—, pres. 1971), Am. Concrete Inst., A.I.M., Am. Soc. Profl. Estimators (Disting. Service award 1978). Baptist (treas. 1972—, chmn. bd. trustees). Home: 3308 Longbranch Dr Falls Church VA 22041 Office: POB 711 Alexandria VA 22313

EDSALL, HOWARD LINN, marketing exec.; b. N.Y.C., Nov. 17, 1904; s. John Linn and Alise (Stoughton) E.; student pub. schs. and pvt. tutoring; m. Florence S. Small, July 5, 1930; children—Florence Linn (Mrs. Robert James Whitehouse). With Marine div. RCA, 1920-25, advt. and sales promotion mgr. tube div., 1944-47; with Curtis-Martin Newspapers, Inc., 1926; marketing sales promotion exec., plans writer R.E. Lovekin Corp., 1928-34, Bridge & King, 1934-35, E. F. Houghton Co., 1935-37; co-founder, dir. G.S. Rogers & Co., Chgo., 1937-40, Ajax Metal Co. & Affiliates, 1940-44; v.p., dir. Craven & Hedrick, 1949-53; exec. v.p. Fred Wittner Advt., N.Y.C., 1953-57; sec., dir. Plastomics Products Co., Inc., 1946; pres., founder, pres. AIMS, Inc. (counselors to profl. mgrs.), 1959—; partner Bonniview Lodge, Lake Penage, Whitfish, Ont., Can. Dir. spl. events United Nations Council, 1944-45. Mem. Am. Soc. Metals (bd. editors 1944-47), Soc. Profl. Mgmt. Consultants (charter mem., v.p., dir. 1967-69), Inst. Mgmt. Cons., Inc. (founding mem.). Clubs: Pen and Pencil (Phila.); Listen-to-Me (N.J.); Morse Telegraph. Author: Borrow and Prosper, 1946; How You Can Borrow and Prosper Kit, 1972; co-author One to Ten Thousand Copies, 1963. Contbg. editor Jour. Mgmt. and Bus. Cons., 1976, Poets and Writers Directory of American Fiction Writers, 1980, Soc. Sons of Am. Revolution, 1980. Contbr. articles, fiction to mags. Inventor the Violute, 1940. Home: 39A N Mountain Ave Montclair NJ 07042

EDWARDS, BENJAMIN FRANKLIN, III, investment brokerage co. exec.; b. St. Louis, Oct. 26, 1931; s. Presley W. and Virginia (Barker) E.; B.A., Princeton U., 1953; m. Joan Moberly, June 13, 1953; children—Scott P., Benjamin F., Pamela Edwards Buan, Susan B. With A.G. Edwards & Sons, St. Louis, 1956—, pres., chief exec. officer, 1967—; dir. Jefferson Bank & Trust Co., Psychol. Assos., Inc. Served with U.S. Navy, 1953-56. Named Boss of the Year, Nat. Secs. Assn., 1980. Mem. Securities Industry Assn. (chmn. 1980). Republican. Presbyterian. Clubs: Noonday, Old Warson Country, Princeton. Office: 1 N Jefferson St Saint Louis MO 63103

EDWARDS, DEL MOUNT, bus. exec.; b. Tyler, Tex., Apr. 12, 1953; s. Welby Clell and Davida (Mount) E.; A.A. cum laude, Tyler Jr. Coll., 1974; B.B.A., Baylor U., 1976. Corp. coordinator Dillard Dept. Stores, Inc., Fort Worth, Tex., 1976-77; v.p. W.C. Supply, Inc., Tyler, 1977—; pres., owner Walker Auto Spring, Inc., Shreveport, La., 1978—; v.p. W. C. Square, Inc., 1976—. Mem. Council Fleet Specialists, Tyler Area C. of C., Smith County Hist. Soc., SCV (treas. camp 124). Baptist. Clubs: Tyler Petroleum, Willow Brook Country (Tyler). Home: 4821 Trenton Dr Tyler TX 75703 Office: WC Square Front at Bonner Sts Tyler TX 75710

EDWARDS, GEORGE LEE, mfg. and distbn. co. exec.; b. Hattiesburg, Miss., Jan. 9, 1937; s. John Bertrand and Ophelia Irwin (Sholar) E.; B.S., Ohio State U., 1965; M.A., U. Ala., 1970; m. Helen Patricia Davis, June 20, 1959; children—George Keith, Jennifer Lynn. Commd. maj. USAF, 1955, advanced through grades to maj., 1973; transp. plans officer, 1965-74, study dir. logistics, Washington, 1974-76; ret., 1976; operations systems adminstr. Am. Hardware Supply Co., Butler, Pa., 1976-79; v.p. distbn. and transp. Diversified Products Corp., Opelika, Ala., 1979—; adj. prof. U. Md., 1971-76. Edn. dir. Ch. of Christ, Zelienople, Pa., 1977—. Decorated Bronze Star, other mil. decorations. Mem. Am. Trucking Assn., Internat. Material Mgmt. Soc., Nat. Council Phys. Distbn., Pvt. Carrier Conf. (bd. dirs.), Am. Soc. Traffic and Transp. Office: Diversified Products Corp Opelika AL

EDWARDS, HARLAND LYLE, bank exec.; b. Mulberry, Kans., June 26, 1917; s. Herbert Cecil and Leona Ruth (Rambo) E.; student Pittsburg (Kans.) State U., 1934-36, U. Wis. Sch. Banking, 1951, Northwestern U., 1961; m. Lillian Catherine Buehlmann, May 30, 1942; 1 dau., Harlene Edwards Scott. With Livestock Nat. Bank, Chgo., 1936-42; pres. The Wilmette (Ill.) Bank, 1961-76; chmn. bd. dir., chief exec. officer First Nat. Bank & Trust Co., Evanston, Ill., 1976—; dir. Rust-Oleum Corp. Treas., trustee National Coll. Edn., Evanston. Served with AUS, 1942-46. Decorated Bronze Star, Purple Heart. Mem. Bankers Club Chgo., Econ. Club Chgo., Newcomen Soc. Republican. Methodist. Clubs: Westmoreland Country, Biltmore Forest Country, Rotary (pres.-elect Evanston chpt.). Office: 800 Davis St Evanston IL 60204

EDWARDS, JAMES EDWIN, lawyer; b. Clarkesville, Ga., July 29, 1914; s. Gus Calloway and Mary Clara (McKinney) E.; student U. Tex., 1931-33; B.A., George Washington U., 1935, J.D., 1946; m. Frances Lillian Stanley, Nov. 22, 1948; children—Robin Anne, James Christopher, Clare (Mrs. Ronald C. Wilkson). Admitted to Fla. bar, 1938; practiced in Cocoa, Fla., 1938-42, Ft. Lauderdale, 1951-55; divisional asst. Dept. State, 1945-50; mem. firm Bell, Edwards, Coker, Carlon & Amsden, 1956-59; pvt. practice, 1959—; asst. city atty. Ft. Lauderdale, 1961, 63-65; city commr. Coral Springs (Fla.), 1970-76, mayor, 1972-74; pres., dir. Ocean Beach Improvement Co. Chmn., Ft. Lauderdale for-Eisenhower, 1952; Rep. county parliamentarian, 1954-59; pres. Rep. Attys. Club Broward County, 1960-64. Served to lt. USCGR, 1942-45; capt. to lt. col. USAF Res., now ret. Mem. Fla., Broward County bar assns., Ret. Officers Assn., Res. Officers Assn. (state judge adv. 1960-61, state v.p. for air 1961-62), Fla. Sportsmen's Assn. (pres. 1967-68), Fla. Conservative Union (pres. Broward County chpt. 1976—), Delta Sigma Rho, Pi Gamma Mu, Phi Delta Phi, Phi Sigma Kappa. Clubs: Rotary, Broken Woods Golf and Racquet, S.E. Fla. Dressage and Combined Tng. Author: Myths About Guns, 1978. Home: 10 Covered Bridge Dr Coral Springs FL 33065 Office: Suite 510 3300 University Dr Coral Springs FL 33065

EDWARDS, JEROME MONTGOMERY, engr., health adminstrn. co. exec.; b. Knoxville, Tenn., Dec. 16, 1936; s. Bruce Montgomery and Evelyn E.; B.S., Lehigh U., 1958; M.S. in Systems Engring., U. Fla., 1965; m. Jean Elizabeth Hensley, Mar. 31, 1958; children—Charles Montgomery, Charlotte Kathleen, Staley Bruce. Indsl. engr., asst. plant mgr. Plasti-Line, Inc., Knoxville, 1958-63; project engr. Brown Engring. Co., Cape Canaveral, Fla., 1964-65; mgr. mgmt. engring. Tex. Instruments, Dallas, 1965-67; pres. Cons. Assos., Inc., Dallas, 1967-77; pres. Medex Internat. Corp., Dallas, 1978—; dir. Medex Internat. Ltd., Brit. Medex Ltd. Served with arty. U.S. Army, 1959. Mem. Am. Inst. Indsl. Engrs., Nat. Soc. Profl. Engrs., Am. Soc. Computing Equipment, Internat. Hosp. Fedn. Republican. Methodist. Home: 7443 Overdale Dr Dallas TX 75240

EDWARDS, JOHN ALLEN, mfg. co. exec.; b. Chgo., Dec. 22, 1917; s. Thomas Michael and Pearl E. (McCorkel) E.; student Northwestern U., 1948; m. Ruth S. Anderson, June 13, 1942; children—Michael K., Patricia L. With Continental Ill. Bank & Trust Co., Chgo., 1936-40; with Liquid Carbonic Corp., Chgo., 1940—, v.p., treas., comptroller, 1956-61, exec. v.p., 1961-63, pres., 1963—; vice chmn. bd. Houston Natural Gas Corp.; dir. Liquid Carbonic Gas Can. Ltd. Mem. Chgo. Council on Fgn. Relations. Served to maj. USAAF, 1941-45. Mem. Compressed Gas Assn. (mem. exec. bd. 1963, 2d v.p. 1967, 1st v.p. 1968, pres. 1969), Ill. State C. of C., Newcomen Soc. N. Am., Delta Mu Delta. Clubs: Economic, Executives, Union League, Chgo. Athletic Assn. (Chgo.); Flossmoor Country. Home: 809 Bruce St Flossmoor IL 60422 Office: 135 S LaSalle St Chicago IL 60603

EDWARDS, JOSEPH JUNIOR, labor orgn. exec.; b. Powersite, Mo., Dec. 3, 1927; s. Josiah and Mary Elizabeth (Gloyd) E.; student Sacramento Jr. Coll., 1955; m. Dorothy Jean Taylor, June 27, 1948; children—Yvonda Jean, Richard Anthony and Ronald Nathan (twins), Timothy Joseph. Rec. sec. Millwright & Machinery Erectors Local Union 1051, Sacramento, 1961-63, apprenticeship organizer, coordinator, 1963-69, fin. sec., treas., 1963-64, fin. sec., treas., bus. rep., 1964-69; bus. rep. Sacramento Area Dist. Council Carpenters, 1969—; mem. adv. com. Atty. Gen. Calif. Mem. citizens alert for crime prevention Sacramento County Sheriff Dept.; bd. dirs. Greater Sacramento Area Plan. Named hon. dep. sheriff, Sacramento County, 1970. Mem. United Brotherhood Carpenters and Joiners Am., Engrs., Carpenters, Laborers & Teamsters Assn. (dir.). Gen. Baptist (deacon, trustee). Clubs: Rosemont Cabana, Moose, Masons. Home: 9064 Goldilocks Way Sacramento CA 95826 Office: 2525 Stockton Blvd Sacramento CA 95817

EDWARDS, KENT MARTIN, business exec.; b. Enid, Okla., June 26, 1948; s. Lyman Mahlon and Thelma Imogene (Weldon) E.; B.B.A., Lamar U., 1970; m. Julia Kay Williams, June 6, 1946. Sales rep., product specialist Joseph T. Ryerson & Sons, Inc., 1970-74; sales office mgr. Encon Mfg. Co., div. Vallen Corp., Houston, 1974-75; mgr. personnel services Vallen Corp., Houston, 1975-79, mgr. adminstrv. services, 1979—. Mem. Houston Personnel Assn. Republican. Methodist. Office: 13333 Northwest Freeway Houston TX 77040

EDWARDS, LIONEL ANTONY, mfg. co. exec.; b. Didcot, Eng., Nov. 4, 1944; s. Lionel Victor and Marjorie (Hartwright) E.; came to U.S., 1968; B.Sc., U. Birmingham (Eng.), 1966; M.B.A., Harvard U., 1972. Exchange program engr. McDonnell Douglas Corp., St. Louis, 1965; prodn. engr. Aero Engine div. Rolls Royce Ltd., Derby, Eng., 1967-68; with Gen. Electric, 1968-70, 73—, operations support mgr, Lynn, Mass., 1973-74, design to cost mgr. F404 jet engines, 1975-76, product support mgr. Lynn jet engines Aircraft Engine Group, 1976-78, mgr. Aircraft Engine Field Service, Evendale, Ohio, 1978-80, mgr. aircraft engine sales operation for Far East, S.E. Asia and Australasia, 1980—; v.p. Gen. Electric Tech. Services Co.; lectr. Harvard Bus. Sch., 1972-73. Served with RAF (VR), 1963-66. Clubs: Harvard of Boston, British Officers of New Eng. Home: 4 Stonington W Fairfield OH 45014 Office: Gen Electric Co Cincinnati OH 45215

EDWARDS, PAUL ROBERT, lawyer, bus. and profl. practice cons.; b. Kansas City, Apr. 11, 1940; s. Milton Willard and Ida Rae E.; B.A., U. Mo., Kansas City, 1962, J.D., 1965; grad. Program for Urban Execs., Mass. Inst. Tech., 1969; m. Sarah Anne Glandon, Apr. 24, 1965; 1 son, Jon Scott. Admitted to Mo. bar, 1965; mem. firm Glass, Bohm, Stoup & Hirschman, Kansas City, Mo., 1965-68; coordinator intergovtl. relations, Jackson County (Mo.), 1968-69; urban specialist Inst. for Community Studies, Kansas City, 1969-70; v.p. Environmental Research and Devel. Found., Kansas City, 1970-72, pres., 1972-74; prin. Pub. Affairs Assistance, Kansas City, 1974-76; co-dir. Cathexis Inst. South, Los Angeles, 1976-77; partner Paul and Sally Edwards, Cons. and Tng., Sierra Madre, Calif., 1977—; v.p. Practice Personnel Systems, Inc. Pres. Westport Community Council, 1969-71; bd. dirs. Citizens Assn., Kansas City, 1970-75, sec., 1972-74; bd. dirs. Com. for Community Progress, Jackson County, Mo., 1971-76; mem. Kansas City Bd. Bldg. Code Examiners, 1970-72. Named Outstanding Young Man of Mo., Mo. Jr. C. of C., 1972. Mem. Am. Bar Assn., Mo. Bar Assn., World Future Soc., Am. Soc. Tng. and Devel. (dir. programs Los Angeles chpt. 1980—), Internat. Transactional Analysis Assn., Am. Mktg. Assn., Town Hall. Democrat. Author: Game Matrix, 1975; Personality Structure, 1976; Personality Functions, 1976; Driver Behavior, 1977. Home and Office: 677 Canyon Crest Dr Sierra Madre CA 91024

EDWARDS, RAY CONWAY, engring. corp. exec.; b. Belleville, Ont., Can., Sept. 1, 1913; s. Ernest Alfred and Augusta (Fee) E.; B.A., U. Calif., Los Angeles, 1935; m. Marjorie Baisch; children—David, Douglas, Ruth, Diane, Robert (dec.), Helen. Engr., Carrier Corp., Syracuse, N.Y., 1935-42; physicist Gen. Lab., U.S. Rubber Co., Passaic, N.J., 1942-46; acoustical cons., founder, chmn. bd., pres. Edwards Engring. Corp., Pompton Plains, N.J., 1947—; founder, chmn. bd. Spi-Rol-Fin Corp., 1954-58; mfr. air conditioning and refrigeration equipment, gas treatment and pollution control equipment for petroleum industry. Mem. Am. Soc. Heating and Air Conditioning Engrs., Am. Soc. Refrigerating Engrs., Theta Delta Chi. Home: 396 Ski Trail Smoke Rise Butler NJ 07405 Office: 101 Alexander Ave Pompton Plains NJ 07444

EDWARDS, ROY ANDERSON, III, banker; b. New London, Conn., Nov. 23, 1945; s. Roy A. and Joan C. (Darby) E.; B.S. in Bus. Adminstrn., U. Kans., 1968, M.B.A., 1973; m. Terry Kistler Beach, Sept. 5, 1970; children—Ross Darby, Roy Beach, Carrie Kistler. Mem. audit staff of Arthur Young & Co., Kansas City, Kans., 1973-75; fin. cons. Clay Blair Services Corp., Kansas City, 1974-75, also v.p., 1974-75; v.p. in gen. mgmt. Douglas County State Bank, Lawrence, Kans., after 1975, now pres., chief exec. officer, dir.; propr. Mitchell-Hill Seed Co., St. Joseph, Mo., 1971—; dir. Cottonwood Inc. Fin. chmn. Douglas County Republican Com., Kans., 1976-77; chmn.

Kans. U. Affairs Com., 1977-78, Kans. Spl. Olympics Com., 1977—; bd. dirs. Lawrence (Kans.) Art Center, 1976, The Lawrence Villages, 1976. Served to lt. USN, 1968-71. Mem. Young Bank Officers of Kans., Lawrence C. of C. (dir.), Lawrence Humane Soc. (chmn. 1975-77), Am. Bankers Assn. (mgmt. and tng. com. bank personnel div.), Kans. Bankers Assn., U. Kans. Alumni Assn., Phi Delta Theta, Alpha Kappa Psi. Republican. Episcopalian. Clubs: Lawrence Country, Rotarian (dir.) (Lawrence). Contbr. articles on fin. to profl. jours. Home: 1136 Hilltop Dr Lawrence KS 66044 Office: 9th St and Kentucky Ave Lawrence KS 66044

EDWARDS, SAMUEL LAWRENCE, industrialist; b. Greenwood, Miss., Jan. 15, 1937; s. Samuel and Marvalla Edwards; grad. bus. mgmt. devel. program Seton Hall U., 1976; m. Margaret Elizabeth Bishop, Feb. 24, 1955; children—Michael, Larry, Marvella, Ronold, Phyllis, Grogorey, Michell, Kenya. Formerly with Danyaic In . Mem. Invention Mktg. Inc. Patentee rocket driven vehicle transmission, aircraft with vertical take off and landing capability. Office: PO Box 1344 Newark NJ 07101

EDWARDS, THOMAS CUNNINGHAM, ins. co. exec.; b. N.Y.C., July 22, 1919; s. Thomas Cunningham and Ora (Brian) E.; A.B., U. N.C., 1941; m. Marjorie Clark Peele, Mar. 29, 1941; children—Barbara Creighton, Nancy Cunningham. Agy. asst. N.W. Mut. Co., N.Y.C., 1946-47; asst. sec. Tchrs. Ins. & Annuity Assn. Am., N.Y.C., 1948-50, asst. v.p., 1950-55, v.p., 1955-63, exec. v.p., 1963-66; pres., trustee TIAA-CREF, 1966-79, chmn., 1979—. Trustee, United Ch. of Christ Pension Bd., Russell Sage Found. Served to capt. U.S. Army, 1942-45; ETO. Decorated Verdun medal (France). C.L.U. Mem. Am. Soc. C.L.U.'s, Am. Risk and Ins. Assn. (trustee), Am. Pension Conf., Am. Council Edn., Am. Council Learned Socs. (fin. com.), Phi Beta Kappa. Contbr. numerous articles on pensions and ins. to profl. publs. Office: 730 3d Ave New York NY 10017

EDWARDS, WALTER HARRISON, JR., power plant equipment mfr.; b. Nashville, Sept. 20, 1913; s. Walter Harrison and Pearl (Williams) E.; B.S., Ind. U., 1935; m. Lucy Elizabeth Beasley, Apr. 25, 1936; children—Judith Ann Edwards Riebe, Mary Ellen Edwards Harden. Labor foreman to v.p. prodn. W.H. Edwards Engring. Corp., Indpls., 1935-42, v.p. sales, 1945-47, exec. v.p., 1947-49, pres., chief exec. officer, 1970—, chmn. bd., 1974—; exec. v.p. BECT Constrn., Indpls., 1965-70. Mem. Ind. Gov.'s Constrn. Safety Code Com., 1968-70. Served with inf. AUS, 1942-45; ETO. Decorated Silver Star, Bronze Star with oak leaf cluster, Purple Heart, Combat Inf. badge. Mem. Bldg. Contractors Assn. (dir.), Constrn. League (dir.), Masonry Contractors Assn. (past pres.), Nat. Assn. Legion of Honor (charter), Alpha Tau Omega (past state pres.). Baptist (life deacon). Clubs: Masons, Shriners, Rotary (dir.); Indpls. Athletic, So. (pres. 1951) (Indpls.). Home: 2856 Jameson Ln Indianapolis IN 46268 Office: Indianapolis IN

EDWARDS, WAYNE FORREST, paper co. exec.; b. St. Louis, Dec. 30, 1934; s. Forrest M. and Irma (Muecke) E.; B.S. in Bus. Adminstrn., Washington U., St. Louis, 1957, M.B.A., 1958; Ph.D., St. Louis U., 1965; m. Cela Ann Williams, June 14, 1958; children—Laura, Sally. With Crown Zellerbach Corp., 1957—, group controller, containers and packaging, San Francisco, 1973-76, v.p. fin., Latin Am., Crown Zellerbach Internat., 1977—; instr. M.B.A. program U. South Fla., 1961-65. Served with U.S. Army, 1954-56. Office: 1 Bush St San Francisco CA 94119

EDWARDS, WESTON EYRING, corp. exec.; b. Flushing, N.Y., May 13, 1934; s. William F. and Catherine (Eyring) E.; B.S., Brigham Young U., 1954; M.B.A. (Baker scholar), Harvard U., 1958, D.B.A. (Donald Kirk David fellow), 1961; m. Jaroldeen Asplund, Mar. 25, 1954; children—Marianna, Julia, Catherine, Charles, Christine, Robin, Carolyn, Weston, Robert, William, Jaroldeen, Patricia. Research asso. Harvard Bus. Sch., Cambridge, Mass., 1958-61; research analyst Stein, Roe & Farnham, Chgo., 1961-63; v.p. Donaldson, Lufkin & Jenrette, Inc., N.Y.C., 1963-68; sr. investment analyst Title Ins. & Trust Co., Los Angeles, 1968-69; v.p., 1969-70; pres. Ticor Relocation Mgmt. Co., Los Angeles, 1970-74; exec. v.p. corp. fin. The TI Corp., Los Angeles, 1974-77; chmn. bd., chief exec. officer Merrill Lynch Relocation Mgmt., White Plains, N.Y., 1977—, Merrill Lynch Realth Assos., Stamford, Conn., 1979—; dir. Broadcort Corp.; econ. adv. bd. Dept. of Commerce, 1972-73. Bd. trustee Ettie Lee Homes for Boys, 1975-76; exec. com. nat. adv. council grad. sch. mgmt. Brigham Young U., 1975—. Served to 1st lt., USAF, 1954-56. Recipient Disting. Service award Grad. Sch. Mgmt., Brigham Young U., 1977. Mem. N.Y. Soc. Security Analysts, Inst. Chartered Fin. Analysts. Mormon. Home: 95 Ferris Hill Rd New Canaan CT 06840 Office: One Landmark Sq Stamford CT 06901

EDWARDS, WILLIAM L., JR., business exec.; b. 1918; B.S., Grove City Coll., 1941; married. Controller, Nat. Container Corp., 1953-57, E.W. Bliss Co., 1957-62; v.p., fin., treas. UMC Industries, Inc., 1962-69; v.p. fin. Interco Inc. (formerly Internat. Shoe Co.), St. Louis, 1969-70, exec. v.p., 1970-71, sr. exec. v.p., chief fin. officer, 1971-73, sr. exec. v.p., chief adminstrv. officer, 1973-75, vice chmn. bd., chief adminstrv. officer, 1975-76, chmn. bd., chief exec. officer, 1976—, also dir. C.P.A. Office: Interco Inc 10 Broadway Saint Louis MO 63102*

EEDE, DONALD WILLIAM, accountant; b. Essex, Ont., Can., Jan. 13, 1935; s. William Richard and Alice Leone (Brackell) E.; m. Joan Charron, Mar. 31, 1979; stepchildren—M. Todd Charron, Timothy M. Charron; children from previous marriage—Christine A., Donald S., William R. Mem. auditing staff Price Waterhouse & Co., Windsor, Ont., 1953-62; controller Eastern Constrn. Co. Ltd., Windsor, 1962-65, Beauty Counselors Can. Ltd., Windsor, 1965-67; v.p., controller Sarah Coventry Can. Ltd., Mississauga, Ont., 1967-74; pres., dir. Michele Lynn Can. Ltd., Mississauga, 1974—, also dir.; dir. Michele Lynn Ltd. (U.K.), Michele Lynn Inc. U.S., Nemo Brier Ltd., Hull, Que., Can. Mem. Canadian Inst. Chartered Accts. (chartered acct.), Direct Sellers Assn. Ltd. Clubs: Credit Valley Golf and Country, Essex Golf and Country. Home: 1986 Mississauga Rd N Mississauga ON L5H 2K6 Canada Office: 6670 Campobello Rd Mississauga ON L5N 2X8 Canada

EELLS, WILLIAM HASTINGS, automobile co. exec.; b. Princeton, N.J., Mar. 30, 1924; s. Hastings and Amy (Titus) E.; B.A., Ohio Wesleyan U., 1946; M.A., Ohio State U., 1950. Asst. to dir. Inst. Practical Politics, Ohio Wesleyan U., 1948-50, asst. dir., 1952-53, dir., 1953-57; instr. dept. polit. sci., 1952-59; instr. polit. sci. Mt. Union Coll., 1950-51; coordinator Atomic Devel. Activities, State of Ohio, 1957-59; Midwest regional mgr. civic and govtl. affairs Ford Motor Co., Columbus, Ohio, 1959—. Mem. Ohio Gov.'s Cabinet, 1957-59; chmn. bd. Blue Cross, 1967-72; chmn. bd. Blossom Music Center, Cleve., 1968-76; pres. Ohio Public Expenditure Council, 1981—; chmn. Gov.'s Council on Rehab., 1966-68; mem. exec. com. Met. Opera's Nat. Council, 1967; pres. Nat. Council High Blood Pressure Research, 1975-79; mem. Nat. Council on the Arts, Nat. Endowment, 1976—, chmn. budget com.; bd. dirs. Am. Heart Assn., 1975-79; trustee Cleve. Orch., 1964—, Ednl. TV, Cleve., 1965-75, Cleve. Playhouse, 1965—, Cleve. Ballet, Cleve. Zoo, Cleve. Luth. Hosp., Cleve. Inst. Music, Ohio Arts Council, Columbus Assn. Performing Arts, 1980—. Recipient awards including USCG Disting. award, 1965, Ohio State U. Devel. award, 1967, Ohio Arts Council award, 1979, Disting. Service award Am. Heart Assn. High Blood Pressure Council, 1979. Mem. S.A.R., Ohio C. of C. (v.p.), Ohio Mfrs. Assn. (dir.), Pi Sigma Alpha, Pi Gamma Mu, Omicron Delta Kappa, Delta Tau Delta. Republican. Presbyterian. Clubs: F St. (Washington); Princeton (N.Y.); Univ., Columbus (Columbus); Cleve. Union. Author: Your Ohio Government, 1953, 6th edit., 1967. Contbr. articles to profl. publs. Home: 505 Parkview Columbus OH 43209 Office: Suite 627 Huntington Trust Bldg 37 W Broad St Columbus OH 43215

EFFINGER, CHARLES HARVEY WILLIAMS, JR., banker; b. Balt., Dec. 28, 1935; s. Charles Harvey Williams and Ann E. Effinger; B.S., Loyola Coll., Balt., 1961; LL.B., U. Balt., 1964; m. Barbara Diehl, Nov. 21, 1959; children—Brian Abbott, Peter Kirk. Adminstrv. asst. Merc. Safe Deposit & Trust Co., 1961-66; staff counsel, mortgage underwriter The Rouse Co./James W. Rouse & Co., Inc., Columbia, Md., 1966-73; mortgage officer, 2d v.p. The Equitable Trust Co., Balt., 1973-77, v.p. mortgage dept., 1977—; instr. real estate fin. Towson (Md.) State U., 1979—. Bd. dirs. Towson Recreation Council, 1978-80; commr. Towson Recreation Baseball Program, 1977. Served with USMC, 1954-57. Named Disting. Grad., Balt. Jr. C. of C., 1972. Mem. Mortgage Bankers Assn. Am. (bus. devel. com.), Md. Mortgage Bankers Assn. (gov., pres. 1978-79), Greater Balt. Bd. Realtors (comml. investment com. 1980-82), Washington Mortgage Bankers Assn. (bd. govs. 1979, 80), Nat. Assn. Indsl. and Office Parks. Republican. Episcopalian. Clubs: Center (Balt.); Country of Md.; Towson Ct. Office: PO Box 1556 Baltimore MD 21203

EFRON, SAMUEL, lawyer; b. Lansford, Pa., May 6, 1915; s. Abraham and Rose (Kaduchin) E.; B.A., Lehigh U., 1935; LL.B., Harvard U., 1938; m. Hope Bachrach Newman, Apr. 5, 1941; children—Marc Fred, Eric Michael. Admitted to Pa. bar, 1938, N.Y. bar, 1967, D.C. bar, 1949; atty. forms and regulations div., also registration div. SEC, 1939-40, Office Solicitor, Dept. Labor, 1940-42; asst. chief real and personal property sect. Office Alien Property Custodian, 1942-43; chief debt claims sect., also asst. chief claims br. Office Allen Property, Dept. Justice, 1946-51; asst. gen. counsel internat. affairs Dept. Def., 1951-53, cons., 1953-54; partner firm Surrey, Karasik, Gould & Efron, Washington, 1954-61; exec. v.p. Parsons & Whittemore Inc., N.Y.C., 1961-68; partner firm Arent, Fox, Kintner, Plotkin & Kahn, 1968—. Trustee, Meridian House Internat. Served to lt. (s.g.) USNR, 1943-46. Decorated knight 1st class Order of Lion (Finland). Mem. Am., Fed., Inter-Am., D.C. bar assns., Assn. Bar City N.Y., Am. Soc. Internat. Law, AIM (pres. council 1965), Phi Beta Kappa. Republican. Clubs: Army-Navy, Capitol Hill, Cosmos, Internat., Nat. Press, Nat. Lawyers, Univ., Harvard (Washington); Harvard, Lotos (N.Y.C.). Author: Creditors Claims Under the Trading with the Enemy Act, 1948; Foreign Taxes on United States Expenditures, 1954; Offshore Procurement and Industrial Mobilization, 1955; The Operation of Investment Incentive Laws with Emphasis on the U.S.A. and Mexico, 1977. Home: 3537 Ordway St NW Washington DC 20016 Office: Arent Fox Kintner Plotkin & Kahn Federal Bar Bldg 1815 H St NW Washington DC 20006

EGAN, JAMES PATRICK, housewares co. exec.; b. Chgo., Sept. 28, 1940; s. Edward Merle and Gertrude (Williams) E.; B.S. in B.A., U. S.D., 1962; M.B.A., Northwestern U., 1966; m. Heather Louise Bosworth, Sept. 23, 1967; children—James Bosworth, Jennifer Martin. Venture research mgr. Joseph Schlitz Brewing Co., Milw., 1966-71; bus. devel. mgr. Internat. Multi-Foods, Mpls., 1971-74; dir. corp. planning Pillsbury Co., Mpls., 1974—; dir. mktg. Wilton Enterprises div. Pillsbury Co., Chgo., 1975—. Served to 1st lt. U.S. Army, 1962-64. Mem. Am. Mktg. Assn. Home: 17 W 525 Waltham St Westmont IL 60559 Office: 2240 W 75th St Woodridge IL 60515

EGE, HANS ALSNES, securities co. exec.; b. Haugesund, Norway, Jan. 31, 1924; s. Sigwald Svendsen and Hilda Svendsen (Hansen) E.; came to U.S., 1953, naturalized, 1961; bus. degree Oslo Handelsgymnasium, 1946; spl. bus. courses City of London Coll., 1947; M.B.A., Drexel U., Phila., 1950; m. Else Mathea Lindstrom, July 11, 1953; children—Elisabeth, Anne Christine. Jr. analyst Alderson & Sessions, Mgmt. & Mktg. Cons., Phila., 1950-51; exec. asst. to U.S. ambassador to Norway, Oslo, 1951-53; asst. to pres., asst. v.p., corp. sec. A.M. Kidder & Co., Inc., N.Y.C., 1953-64; stockbroker Reynolds Securities Inc., N.Y.C., 1964-65, mgr. Ridgewood (N.J.) Office, 1965-71, mgr., resident officer, 1971-77; resident v.p. Dean Witter Reynolds, Inc., Ridgewood, 1978—; dir. Lecuno Oil Co., Jefferson, Tex. Mem. Pres.'s club Drexel U. Served with Norwegian Underground, 1942-45. Decorated War medal. Mem. Norwegian Am. C. of C., Am. Scandinavian Found., Tau Kappa Epsilon. Clubs: Royal Norwegian Yacht (Oslo); Tonsberg (Norway) Seilforening; Joe Jefferson (pres. 1966-67) (Saddle River, N.J.). Home: 877 Roslyn Rd Ridgewood NJ 07450 Office: 125 E Ridgewood Ave Ridgewood NJ 07450

EGER, CARL, JR., state govt. ofcl.; b. Holyoke, Mass., Jan. 29, 1936; s. Carl and Mary (Kosiorek) E.; B.S., U. Mass., 1977, postgrad., 1980—; m. Shirley A. Truchon, July 10, 1965. Mgr., Pauleanna's Ice Cream, Holyoke, 1957-65; in real estate, 1960-65; with Small Bus. Bur., Mass. Dept. Commerce and Devel., Springfield, 1965—, exec. officer, 1973-77, dir. Region I office, 1977—; chmn. Holyoke Indsl. Devel. Fin. Authority, Holyoke Community Devel. Corp. Bd. dirs. Soc. Prevention Cruelty to Children, 1976—; trustee Providence Hosp., Holyoke, 1977—; chmn. Connecticut River Watershed Assn., 1976-79; alderman City of Holyoke, 1964-69. Served with AUS, 1957. Mem. Mass. Econ. Devel. Council, Holyoke Taxpayers Assn., Holyoke C. of C. Roman Catholic. Club: Rotary (pres. 1978-79). Home: 1966 Northampton St Holyoke MA 01040 Office: Mass Bldg Ave of States West Springfield MA 01089

EGGERS, RICHARD AUGUST, ins. and pension exec.; b. State Center, Iowa, Apr. 24, 1943; s. Ernest and Inez C. (Hartkemayer) E.; B.S., Iowa State U., 1968; m. Verdene A. Anderson, Aug. 28, 1964; children—Shawntel, Tamara, Richard August II. Sales/service rep. Walnutgrove Products Co., State Center, Iowa, 1961-63; agt. Northwestern Mut. Ins. Co., Ames, Iowa, 1967-69; agt., supr. Conn. Mut. Life Ins. Co., Ames, 1970-72, gen. agt., Erie, Pa., 1973-78; pres. Compensation Planning Inc., Erie, 1977-79. Mem. Wekiva Presbyn. Ch., Longwood, Fla. Recipient Nat. Mgmt. award, 1977, 78. Mem. Million Dollar Round Table (life), Life Underwriters Polit. Action Com., Nat. Assn. Life Underwriters, Central Fla. Assn. Life Underwriters. Republican. Clubs: Sweetwater, Iowa State Cyclone State 250, CLU Golden Key. Home: 500 Thistlewood Court Longwood FL 32750 Office: Suite 305 Longwood Village Longwood FL 32750

EGGERT, ARTHUR CHARLES, food processing cons.; b. Milw., July 13, 1900; s. Christian F. and Bertha (Krolle) E.; LL.B., U. Wis., 1923; m. Olive Dorothy Ulbricht, Dec. 5, 1920. Pub. accounting practice, Mpls., 1926—; former cons. Old Dutch Foods, Inc., St. Paul. Active Mpls. Med. Research Found. C.P.A., Wis., Minn. Mem. NAM, Minn. Soc. C.P.A.'s, Nat. Assn. Accountants, AIM. Clubs: K.P.; Minikahda, Mpls. Home: 5107 W 44th St Minneapolis MN 55436

EGLEY, THOMAS ARTHUR, accountant; b. Aberdeen, S.D., June 23, 1945; s. Ralph Joseph and Cora Ellen E.; B.S., U. Mont., 1967, postgrad., 1967-68, 72-74. Mgr. purchasing, EDP, Mont. Merc. Co., Missoula, 1972-74; systems analyst Comml. Data Co., Missoula, 1974-77; mgr. EDP, John R. Daily Inc., Missoula, 1977-78; partner Egley & White, accountants, Missoula, 1978—; v.p., Mu Deuteron Corp., Missoula, 1976—, also dir.; cons. computers. Bd. dirs. Missoula Children's Theater Assn., 1976—; mem. Missoula Area Arts Council, 1978. Served with U.S. Army, 1968-71. C.P.A. Mem. Am. Inst. C.P.A.'s, Mont. Soc. C.P.A.'s (pres. chpt. 1979—), Nat. Assn. Accountants Mont. Data Processing Assn., EDP Auditors Assn., Phi Sigma Kappa (pres. Western Mont. 1976—). Lutheran. Clubs: S/3 & Assos. Computer, Elks. Lectr. in field. Home, office: PO Drawer 2729 Missoula MT 59806

EHLERS, NANCY LUCRETIA, community services adminstrn. co. exec.; b. Sacramento, Apr. 12, 1947; d. Charles Humphrey and June Maryann (Custino) Thompson; student Calif. State U., Sacramento, 1975-76, U. Calif., Davis, 1977-78; m. Robert Lester Ehlers, June 12, 1966. Mem. staff Sacramento Radiology Med. Group, Inc., 1969-75; ins. adminstr., office mgr. fin. dept. Inter-Tribal Council of Calif., Inc., Sacramento, 1975—. Notary public, Calif. Mem. Mewok Tribal Council El Dorado County, Nat. Notary Assn. Republican. Clubs: Sacramento Indian Athletic Assn. (mem. exec. bd. 1977-78), Nat. Rifle Assn. Am., Cap Rod and Rifle Club. Home: 3716 Kings Way Sacramento CA 95821 Office: 2220 Watt Ave C-13 951 Fulton Ave Sacramento CA 95825

EHLKE, JOHN DAVID, computer software services co. exec.; b. Appleton, Wis., Nov. 18, 1938; s. John C. and Emma D. (Peloquin) E.; B.S. in Mgmt. Sci., Case Inst. Tech., Cleve., 1961; M.B.A., Case Western Res. U., 1972; m. Jane H. McCarroll, June 4, 1977; children by previous marriage—Maria, Gretchen, Julie, Camella. Systems engr., mktg. rep. IBM Corp., Cleve., 1961-69; mktg. mgr. Republic Systems Co., Cleve., 1969; co-founder, 1969, v.p. mktg., dir. Neoterics, Inc., Cleve., 1969-80, v.p. mktg. Computer Task Group, Buffalo, 1980—. Mem. Assn. Systems Mgmt. (chpt. dir. 1971-73), Council Smaller Enterprises (dir., officer 1975-79), Soc. Sales and Mktg. Execs., Assos. Data Processing Service Companies, Greater Cleve. Growth Assn. Presbyterian. Home: 1801 E 12th St Cleveland OH 44114 Office: 1801 E 9th St Cleveland OH 44114

EHRAMJIAN, VARTKES HAGOP, fin. exec.; b. Syria, Nov. 2, 1932; came to U.S., 1959, naturalized, 1966; s. Hagop and Naomi E.; B.A., Eastern Mich U., 1962; M.B.A., Ind. U., 1963; m. Laura L. Schmoker, June 7, 1962; children—James C., Tamar M., Alyce M., Ricardo L., Kathleen Marie. Sr. fin. analyst Ford Motor Co., 1963-68; internat. financing mgr. Cummins Engine, 1968-70, regional mgr., So. Latin Am., 1970-71, pres. Cummins S.A. Brazil, 1971-72, dir. internat. bus. devel., 1972-75, asst. treas. internat., 1975-79; asst. treas. The Bendix Corp., Southfield, Mich., 1979—; lectr. Ind. U. Served with inf. Syrian Army, 1955-56. Mem. Am. Mgmt. Assn. Republican. Armenian Orthodox. Club: Harrison Lake Country. Home: 30850 Cheviot Hills Dr Franklin MI 48025 Office: Executive Offices Bendix Center Southfield MI 48037

EHRENREICH, JOSEPH WILLARD, real estate devel. co. exec.; b. N.Y.C., Dec. 21, 1920; B.B.A., CCNY, 1940; M.B.A., U. So. Calif., 1948; Ph.D., N.Y. U., 1963; m. Isabel Resler, July 4, 1949; children—Edward D., Ava M., Mark S., Beth L. With Prudential Ins. Co., 1949-64, dir. planning and research, 1959-64; prof. econs., chmn. dept. fin. and bus. econs. U. So. Calif., Los Angeles, 1964-74; chmn., pres., chief exec. officer Moraga Corp., Los Angeles, 1974—; chmn., chief exec. officer Alamand Corp., Los Angeles, 1978-80; pres. Apex Properties, 1980—; dir. Moraga Dixit Corps.; cons. to numerous orgns., 1964-74. Gov., Town Hall of Calif., 1971-76, pres., 1974. Served from ensign to lt. comdr., USNR, 1943-46. Gen. Electric Found. grantee, 1969-72; McKinsey Found. grantee, 1970; NASA grantee, 1966-74; HEW grantee, 1968-72; Social Security Adminstrn. grantee, 1969-71. Mem. Nat. Assn. Bus. Economists, Beta Gamma Sigma, Lambda Nu. Clubs: Los Angeles, Los Angeles Athletic. Office: 811 W 7th St Los Angeles CA 90017

EHRET, DAVID LAWRENCE, automotive remfg. co. exec.; b. Ft. Morgan, Colo., Jan. 14, 1945; s. Charles Wesley and Lilly May (Mills) E.; B.A., Seattle Pacific U., 1968. Multi-line claims rep. Safeco Inc. Co., Portland, Oreg., 1971-73; claims mgr. Pacific N.W. br. Fin. Indemnity Co., Portland, 1973-74; pres. Superior Machine Products, Inc., Portland, 1974—, also dir.; guest lectr. local community coll. Active Jr. Achievement, Tacoma, Wash.; campaign mgr. for candidate for Oreg. State Senate, 1972. Served with AUS, 1968-71; Vietnam. Decorated Bronze Star with oak leaf cluster, Air medal, Combat Infantryman's badge, others. Mem. Automotive Parts Rebuilders Assn., Oreg. Automotive Parts Assn., Wash. Automotive Wholesalers Assn., Portland C. of C., N.G. Assn. U.S., Assn. U.S. Army. Methodist. Clubs: Elks, Officers' Open Mess at Portland Internat. Airport. Home: 3389 NE 162d Ave Portland OR 97230 Office: 810 N Graham St Portland OR 97227

EHRLER, ROBERT RONALD, tech. publs. corp. exec.; b. Queens, N.Y., Mar. 4, 1942; s. Walter F. and Marie A. Ehrler; B.S. in Elec. Engring., Hofstra U., 1963; m. Jane M. Pelzer, Sept. 6, 1969; 1 son, Ryan Robert. With Newsday, L.I., 1963-67; elec. engr., program mgr. Grumman Aerospace Corp., Bethpage, N.Y., 1967-69; founder, pres., chief exec. officer Tech. Publs. Cons., Inc., Melville, N.Y., 1969—; dir. Tech. Communications, Inc., 1975—. Mem. Nat. Security Indsl. Assn., Soc. Logistics Engrs., Am. Def. Preparedness Assn., Huntington C. of C. Club: Masons. Address: Tech Publs Consultants Inc 535 Broad Hollow Rd Melville NY 11747

EHRLICHER, EDWARD JOHN, personnel exec.; b. Chgo., Nov. 24, 1943; s. Frederick Erasmus and Rose Rita (Meyer) E.; A.A., Kennedy-King Jr. Coll., 1968; B.A., Roosevelt U., Chgo., 1972. Clk., supr., mgr. check processing div., personnel specialist LaSalle Nat. Bank, Chgo., 1967-74; personnel asst. Nystrom div. Carnation Co., Chgo., 1974-77, asst. personnel mgr., from 1977, now personnel mgr. Mem. youth dept. bd. Jane Adams Center, Hull House Assn. Served with AUS, 1962-65. Mem. Am. Soc. Personnel Adminstrn. (accredited), Soc. Personnel Adminstr. Greater Chgo., N.W. Personnel Assn. Chgo. Home: 6238 N Winthrop Ave Apt 203 Chicago IL 60660 Office: 3333 N Elston Ave Chicago IL 60618

EICHACKER, BRUCE HARLEY, ins. co. exec.; b. Cedar Rapids, Iowa, Oct. 22, 1948; s. Henry Otto and Helen Christine (Moser) E.; student Kirkwood Community Coll., 1968, also Drake U., U. Iowa; m. Roselyn Eichacker; 1 dau., Debra. With Am. Ins. Agy., Amana, Iowa, 1966—, agy. mgr., 1968—. Advancement chmn. local Boy Scouts Am.; past pres. Amana Colonies Jaycees. Cert. ins. counselor. Mem. Nat., Iowa (past pres.; Agt. of Yr. 1981) assns. profl. ins. agts., Nat. Assn. Ind. Ins. Agts. (exec. com.). Home: PO Box 133 Amana IA 52203 Office: Merchants Nat Bank Bldg Amana IA 52203

EICHFELD, TIMOTHY JOSEPH, mfg. co. exec.; b. Camden, N.J., Sept. 22, 1946; s. Paul A. and Loretta A. (Henwood) E.; A.A.S., Camden County Coll., 1974; B.B.A. cum laude, U. Pa., 1977; m. Kathleen Patricia Stuzinski, June 7, 1969; children—Timothy Joseph 2d, Joseph Brian, Damian James, David John. Vice pres., gen. mgr.

Van Wood Mfg. Co., Inc., Cherry Hill, N.J., 1966-77; pres., chmn. bd. Disstim Corp., Pennsauken, N.J., 1977—; guest speaker Wharton Sch., U. Pa., 1978-79. Active Runnemede Youth Assn. Served with U.S. Army, 1967-69. Decorated Bronze Star, Purple Heart, Air medal; cert. in practical machining prins. Mem. VFW, DAV, Sigma Kappa Phi. Democrat. Roman Catholic. Patentee work hold down for machine tool having table and column, work hold down improvements. Home: 207 W Evesham Rd Runnemede NJ 08078 Office: 6730 Dewey Ave Pennsauken NJ 08110

EICHINGER, DAVID HERBERT, corp. ofcl.; b. Bay City, Mich., Aug. 27, 1945; s. Arnold Albert and Marie Dorthea (Nietzke) E.; B.S. in Psychology, Mich. State U., 1967; M.S. in Bus., Western Mich. U., 1976; m. Carol Elizabeth Ludford, June 7, 1969; children—Sarah, Eric, Brenda. Mgmt. cons. Occupational Health Center, Kalamazoo, 1972-74; safety and tng. dir. Georgia-Pacific Corp., Kalamazoo, 1974-80; personnel mgr. Allied Paper subs. SCM, Kalamazoo, 1980—. Served with USNR, 1967-69. Decorated Purple Heart. Winner vice president's safety award, pulp and paper divs., Georgia-Pacific, 1977, 78. Mem. Kalamazoo Personnel Assn., Am. Soc. Tng. and Devel., Indsl. Relations Research Assn. Home: 719 Homecrest St Kalamazoo MI 49001

EICHWALD, BERNARD, elec. engring. co. exec.; b. Bklyn., May 7, 1921; s. Benjamin and Amelia (Braver) E.; B.E.E., Rensselaer Polytech. Inst., 1942; m. Doris Schnackenberg, Nov. 25, 1971; children—Bethea, Bradford, Leslie. Pres., dir. B. Eichwald & Co., Inc., electric engring., constrn., N.Y.C., 1948—; pres. H.U.E. Research Corp.; sr. mem. Bernard Assos., cons.; dir. Standard Security Life Ins. Co., N.Y. Chmn., Roxbury Festival, Stamford, Conn., 1958; trustee and chmn. bd. mgmt. N.Y.U. Grad. Sch. Bus. Adminstrn. Bd. dirs., exec. bd., treas. N.Y.C. Council Econ. Edn.; trustee Inst. for Study Drug Misuse; trustee, mem. fin. com. Radio, TV, and Rec. Arts Pension Plan and Health and Welfare Plan. Served with USNR, 1942-45. Registered profl. engr., Conn. Mem. I.E.E.E., Empire State TV Guild (life), Nat. Elec. Contractors Assn., N.Y. State Elec. Contractors Assn., Internat. Assn. Elec. Insps., Elec. Contractors Assn. City N.Y., Bldg. Industry Employers N.Y. State, Bldg. Industry Trades Employers Assn., Young Presidents Orgn. (nat. dir. econ. edn. Young Pres.' Found.), Met. Presidents Orgn. (dir., past pres.), Commerce and Industry Assn. N.Y. (chmn. N.Y.C. elec. code revision com.), Def. Orientation Conf. Assn. (dir.), Am. Arbitration Assn. (nat. panel arbitration), World Bus. Council (founding), Pi Sigma Epsilon (life). Home: 143 Palmer Hill Rd Stamford CT 06902 Office: 237 E 39th St New York NY 10016

EIDSON, ROBERT ANSEL, business exec.; b. Topeka, May 30, 1921; s. O. Bain and Agnes (Ray) E.; student Kans. U., 1938-41; B.S., U.S. Naval Acad., 1944, M.S.E.E., 1953; m. Cecil Ruth King, June 10, 1944; children—Susan Lloyd Eidson Barclay, Robert Bain, John Rhodes. Commd. ensign U.S. Navy, 1944; resigned, 1959; now capt. in Res.; mgr. engring. div. Sanders Assos., Inc., Nashua, N.H., 1959-64; v.p., dir. engring. lab. Airtronics, Inc., Washington, 1964-67; dir. spl. systems Fed. Systems Center, IBM, Gaithersburg, Md., 1967-72; chmn., pres. Decisions and Designs Inc., McLean, Va., 1972—; dir. 70001 Ltd. Mem. nat. security and internat. affairs adv. council Rep. Nat. Com.; vice chmn. bd. dirs. Wolftrap; trustee U.S. Naval Acad. Found. Mem. IEEE, Am. Def. Preparedness Assn., Armed Forces Communications-Electronics Assn., Res. Officers Assn., Navy League, Sigma Chi. Republican. Presbyterian. Clubs: Congressional Country, Burning Tree (Washington); Regency Racquet (McLean, Va.). Home: 4932 Sentinel Dr Apt 106 Sumner MD 20016 Office: 8400 Westpark Dr Suite 600 McLean VA 22101

EIFERMAN, SAMUEL STANLEY, electronics corp. exec., real estate exec.; b. Bronx, N.Y., Nov. 1, 1942; s. Bernard and Beatrice (Kaufman) E.; B.E.E., Coll. City N.Y., 1967; M.B.A., Calif. State U., Northridge, 1974; m. Ellen Rosenstein, June 9, 1973; children—Carl Henry, Veronica Ivette. Elec. engr. GPL Co., Pleasantville, N.Y., 1967-69; mem. tech. staff Hughes Aircraft Co., Canoga Park, Calif., 1969-74, Fullerton, Calif., 1974-80; v.p. Sunburst Investments Corp., 1976-77; owner, broker Eiferman Realty, Anaheim, Calif., 1976—, Real Estate Stop, Anaheim, 1979—; sr. engr. Northrop Electronics Corp., Hawthorne, Calif., 1980—. Mem. IEEE. Democrat. Jewish. Clubs: Toastmasters (pres. Northrop Electronics chpt.), K.P., B'nai B'rith (pres.), K'Hillat Yisrael (pres. 1979—). Home: 1941 W Lodi Pl Anaheim CA 92804 Office: 720 S Euclid St Anaheim CA 92802

EIGEL, THOMAS JOHN, former air force officer, electronics corp. exec.; b. St. Louis, Aug. 30, 1934; s. Edwin George and Katherine (Rohan) E.; B.S.I.E., St. Louis U., 1956; M.S., San Diego State U., 1972; m. Gail Victoria Keenan, Nov. 29, 1958; children—Thomas Jr., Kathleen, Victoria, Andrea, Christina. Commd. 2d lt. U.S. Air Force, 1956, advanced through grades to lt. col., 1972; aircraft comdr. of tankers, forward air controller, Vietnam, 1968; dep. dir., configuration mgr. armament systems div., Wright Patterson AFB, Ohio, 1973-79; mgr. configuration and data mgmt. Northrop Def. Systems, Rolling Meadows, Ill., 1979—; lectr. in field. Decorated DFC, Meritorious Service medal. Mem. Am. Def. Preparedness Assn., Air Force Assn., Soc. of Logistics Engrs., Sigma Iota Epsilon, Beta Gamma Sigma. Republican. Roman Catholic. Club: K.C. Home: 772 Harvard Ct Palatine IL 60067 Office: Northrop Corp Defense Systems Div 600 Hicks Rd Rolling Meadows IL 60008

EIKREM, LYNWOOD OLAF, bus. exec.; b. Lansing, Mich., June 11, 1919; s. Arthur Rudolph and Gatha (Zupp) E.; B.S., Mich. State U., 1941; M.S., Mass. Inst. Tech., 1948; m. Margaret Rosemarie McDonough, July 13, 1946; children—Margaret, John, Marie, Jeanne. Asso. prof. chemistry La. Poly. Inst., 1946; tech. dir. Jarrell-Ash Co., Newtonville, Mass., 1949-53; project engr. Baird-Atomic, Cambridge, Mass., 1953-59; staff engr. Geophysics Corp. Am., Bedford, Mass., 1959-60; mgr. product devel. dept. David W. Mann Co. div. Geophysics Corp. Am., Lincoln, Mass., 1960-63, dir. mktg., Burlington, Mass., 1963-65; v.p. mktg. Applied Research Labs. subs. Bausch & Lomb Inc., Sunland, Calif., 1965-72; dir. mktg. Darling & Alsobrook, Los Angeles, 1972-75; prin. Darling, Paterson & Salzer, 1975-79; pres. Paterson & Co., 1979—. Fellow Am. Inst. Chemists; mem. Optical Soc. Am., ASTM, N.Y. Acad. Scis., Sales and Mktg. Execs. Assn., V.F.W. K.C. Home: 4902 Alta Canyada Rd La Canada CA 91011 Office: 1801 Ave of Stars Los Angeles CA 90067

EILANDS, INDULIS JURIS, petrochem. cons.; b. N.Y.C., Jan. 1, 1953; s. Alfred and Irene Velta (Dzelskalns) E.; B.Engring. cum laude, CUNY, 1975. Project engr. The Scientific Design Group, Halcon Internat., N.Y.C., 1975-77, operating engr. Brindisi, Italy and Port Arthur, Tex., 1977, Hale, E. Ger., 1977-78, Peking, China, 1978, process engr., N.Y.C., 1978-79; cons. the Process Assos. Cons. and Engring., Houston, 1980—. Mem. Am. Inst. Chem. Engrs. (student chpt. pres. 1974), Am. Chem. Soc., Tau Beta Pi (del. to nat. conv. 1974). Home: 3400 Ocee Apt 1702 Houston TX 77063 Office: 6776 SW Freeway Suite 370 Houston TX 77074

EINACH, CHARLES DONALD, advt. agy. exec.; b. Buffalo, July 1, 1929; s. Joseph and Esther Riva (Liner) E.; B.A., U. Buffalo, 1951; M.A., Syracuse U., 1953; m. Elen Simon, Mar. 15, 1971. Broadcast dir. Rumrill Co., Inc., Buffalo, 1954-60; advt. dir. J. Nelson Prewitt, Inc., Rochester, N.Y., 1960-63; v.p., account supr. Grey Advt., Inc., N.Y.C., 1963-71; sr. v.p. account services Nadler & Larimer, Inc., N.Y.C., 1971—. Fellow Internat. Biog. Assn.; mem. Nat. Acad. TV Arts and Scis., Museum of City of N.Y., Les Amis du Vin (life), Vintage Soc. Home: 301 E 66th St New York NY 10021 Office: 1350 Ave of Americas New York NY 10019

EISELE, WILLIAM DAVID, ins. agy. exec.; b. Iron Mountain, Mich., July 31, 1927; s. David Christian and Muriel Elizabeth (Ochstadt) E.; B.S., U. Mich., 1950; m. Helen Jeanne Holmberg, Dec. 27, 1953; children—David, Meg. Ins. agt. Employers Mut. of Wausau, Milw., 1951, West Bend, Wis., 1952-53, Watertown, Wis., 1953-56, Orlando, Fla., 1957, Tampa, Fla., 1958; pres. William D. Eisele & Co., Clearwater, Fla., 1959—. Charter pres. Heritage Presbyn. Housing Project, 1971-72; elder Presbyn. Ch. Recipient disting. alumni service award U. Mich., 1975. Mem. Fla. Assn. Ins. Agts., Clearwater-Largo-Dunedin Insurors (past pres.), U. Mich. Alumni Assn. (dir., v.p.). Clubs: Clearwater Rotary; U. Mich. (organizer, past pres. Pinellas County, Fla.). Office: 1012 E Druid Rd Clearwater FL 33516

EISENBERG, RONALD MARVIN, retail exec.; b. Cleve., May 3, 1940; s. Louis and Fannie Eisenberg; B.S. in Pharmacy, U. Toledo, 1962; m. Carol Joyce Meister, Aug. 28, 1960; children—Deanne Hope, Bradley Gregg, Adam Corey. Pharmacist, Toledo and Cleve., 1962-66; owner drug stores, Cleve., 1966-76; owner Great News Gift Stores, La Jolla, Calif., 1977—. Mem. Cleveland Heights Planning Com., 1969-70; bd. dirs. Temple Beth-El, La Jolla, 1979-80. Mem. Nat. Retail Mchts. Assn., Pacific Plaza Mchts. Assn. (v.p. 1978-79), Alpha Epsilon Pi. Office: 7063 Carroll Rd San Diego CA 92121

EISENBRAUN, DAL (IKE), ins. co. exec.; b. Tripp, S.D., June 29, 1935; s. Alvin H. and Bertha P. (Goldhammer) E.; B.S., S.D. State U., 1957, M.S., 1958; m. Carol Van Ness, Apr. 1, 1956; children—Pamela K., Michael D. Tchr., coach Brookings (S.D.) High Sch., 1959-63; agt. State Farm Ins., Brookings, 1963-66, agy. tng. dir., Santa Ana, Calif., 1966-69, agy. mgr., San Bernadino, Calif., 1969-70, agy. dir., Costa Mesa, Calif., 1970-76, exec. asst. agy., Bloomington, Ill., 1976-79, dep. regional v.p., Marshall, Mich., 1979—. Served with U.S. Army, 1958-59. Mem. Nat. Assn. Life Underwriters, Gen. Agts. and Mgrs. Assn., Soc. C.L.U.'s, Nat. Mgmt. Assn. (adv. bd.). Republican. Lutheran. Home: 131 Whisperwood Ln Battle Creek MI 49015 Office: 410 East Dr Marshall MI 49069

EISENSTADT, MARVIN ERNEST, mfg. co. exec.; b. Bklyn., Feb. 24, 1933; s. Benjamin E.; B.A., U. Vt., 1954, LL.B., 1973; m. Barbara Leah Buckwald, June 6, 1959; children—Jeffrey, Jill, Deborah, Steven. Owner, Cumberland Packing Corp., Bklyn., 1956—. Bd. dirs. Peninsula Hosp. Center, Far Rockaway, N.Y. Served with U.S. Army, 1954-56. Offered fellowship U. Vt. to do cancer research; patentee sugar substitute, air operated packing machine. Office: 2 Cumberland St Brooklyn NY 11205

EISENSTARK, RAYMOND GERALD, computer consulting exec.; b. Neuilly-sur-Seine, France, Oct. 11, 1946; s. Milton and Frida E.; student Columbia U. Sch. Engring. and Applied Sci., 1962-64. Analyst, Computer Usage Co., N.Y.C., 1965-69, Redcor Corp., N.Y.C., 1969-71; pres. Sirocco Systems, Inc., N.Y.C., 1971-77; chmn. bd. Structured Methods, Inc., N.Y.C., 1977—. Cert. in data processing. Mem. Assn. Computing Machinery, IEEE. Developed tape mount display unit, 1973. Home: 154 8th Ave New York NY 10011 Office: 7 W 18 St New York NY 10011

EISLER, JOEL ROBERT, rental co. exec.; b. Cin., Oct. 14, 1947; s. Bernard Louis and Meigh (Schatz) E.; student U. Mass., 1965; B.A., Lynchburg Coll., 1969, postgrad., 1970; postgrad. George Washington U., 1971, Bowie State Coll., 1978; m. Fredericka Schellenberg Boehm, Feb. 17, 1980. Accountant, Lynchburg (Va.) Gen. Hosp., 1967-70; asst. dir. fin. Hosp. Sick Children, Washington, 1970-72; asst. dir. housekeeping div. Macke Co., Cheverly, Md., 1972-73; accounting mgr., fuel oil burner service Amerada Hess Corp., Landover, Md., 1973-75; controller, dir. adminstrn. Cort Furniture Rental Corp. subs. Mohasco Corp., Amsterdam, N.Y., 1975-78, supervising dist. mgr. Cort Furniture Rental, Mpls., 1978—. Campaign worker city elections, Bowie, Md., 1970-76. Mem. Nat. Assn. Accountants, Bloomington C. of C. Democrat. Jewish. Club: Jaycees (past pres. Bowie, past state v.p.). Home: 7500 W 100th St Bloomington MN 55438 Office: 8925 Lyndak Ave S Bloomington MN 55420

EISNER, MICHAEL CARL, corp. exec.; b. N.Y.C., Sept. 23, 1939; s. Martin Bert and Bertie Martha (Roniger) E.; B.S., Syracuse U., 1961; postgrad. taxation Bernard M. Baruch Grad. Sch. Bus.; m. Adrianne Kobell, June 10, 1961; children—Wendy, Todd, Lori. Sr. accountant Price Waterhouse & Co., N.Y.C., 1961-66; sr. financial systems specialist Gen. Foods Corp., White Plains, N.Y., 1966-67; mgr. corporate accounting Revlon, Inc., N.Y.C., 1967-69; audit mgr. Arthur Andersen & Co., Newark, 1969-72; asst. controller Hertz Corp., N.Y.C., 1972-74; v.p., corp. controller Sony Corp. Am., N.Y.C., 1974—; speaker profl. devel. program N.J. Soc. C.P.A.'s. Pres., local civic assn., E. Brunswick, N.J., 1969-76; treas. E. Brunswick Jewish Center, 1976—. C.P.A. Mem. Am. Inst. C.P.A.'s, Controllers Inst., N.Y. Soc. C.P.A.'s, Am. Mgmt. Assn., Nat. Assn. Accts., Fin. Execs. Inst. Home: 2 Guy Dr East Brunswick NJ 08816 Office: 47-47 Van Dam St Long Island City NY 11101

EISNER, RICHARD ALAN, accountant; b. N.Y.C., Feb. 15, 1934; s. Joseph and Helen (Cohen) E.; B.A., Yale U., 1956; M.B.A., Harvard U., 1958; m. Carole Lee Swid, May 7, 1961; children—Joseph, Susan, Douglas, Michael, Hallie. Sr. acct. Eisner & Lubin, C.P.A.'s, N.Y.C., 1959-63; mng. partner Richard A. Eisner & Co., C.P.A., N.Y.C., 1964—; past dir. Wellington Mgmt. Co., Inc. Chmn. bd. Horace Mann Sch., N.Y.C., 1978—; trustee Wiltwyck Sch., 1974-80; asso. YM-YWHA's Greater N.Y., 1972, United Jewish Appeal, 1976. Served with AUS, 1958. Mem. Am. Inst. C.P.A.'s, N.Y. State Soc. C.P.A.'s. Democrat. Club: Yale. Office: 380 Madison Ave New York NY 10017

EISZNER, JAMES RICHARD, food products co. exec.; b. Chgo., Aug. 12, 1927; s. William Henry and Gertrude (Peifer) E.; student Drake U., 1945; B.S., U. Ill., 1950; Ph.D., U. Chgo., 1952; m. Joyce Carolyn Holland, Oct. 14, 1950; children—James Richard, Timothy John. Chemist, Standard Oil (Ind.), Whiting, Ind., 1952-54; market analyst Indoil Chem. Co., Chgo., 1954-57; dir. market devel. Amoco Chems., Chgo., 1957-63; v.p. marketing Ott Chem. Co., Muskegon, Mich., 1963-65, exec. v.p., 1965-66, pres., 1967-70, dir., 1965-70; sr. v.p. Indsl. div. CPC Internat., Inc., Englewood Cliffs, N.J., 1970-71, pres., 1971-76; v.p. CPC Internat., 1971-76, dir., 1975—, exec. v.p., chief adminstrv. officer, 1977-79, pres., chief adminstrv. officer, 1977-79, pres., chief operating officer, 1979—. Mem. Chgo. Bd. Trade, 1971-80. Dir. Muskegon Area Econ. Planning and Devel. Assn., 1967-70. Served with AUS, 1946-47. Mem. Comml. Devel. Assn., Corn Refiners Assn. (dir. 1971—). Republican. Presbyterian. Clubs: Econ., Univ. (N.Y.C.); Seaview Country (Absecon, N.J.); Knickerbocker Country (Tenafly, N.J.). Home: 24 Kennedy Rd Cresskill NJ 07626 Office: CPC Internat International Plaza Englewood Cliffs NJ 07632

EITELBACH, WARREN CHESTER, steamship exec.; b. N.Y.C., May 3, 1918; s. Maximmian Frederick and Lillian Burgess (Reid) E.; student U. Houston, 1950, San Jacinto Coll., 1972; m. Olive Marie Leonard, June 20, 1948; children—Leonard, Frederick, Gerrit, Elaine, Eric, Laurie. Stevedore supr. Lykes Bros. Steamship Co., Houston, 1949-56, West Gulf stevedoring mgr., 1956-71, ops. mgr. West Gulf, 1971-73, asst. v.p. West Gulf ops., 1973-79, v.p. West Gulf ops., 1979—; pres., dir. Southside Services, Inc.; pres. Terminal Services Houston, Inc.; dir. Jay's Crane Rental, Inc. Served with U.S. Maritime Service, 1934-49. Mem. West Gulf Maritime Assn., Nat. Cargo Bur., Nat. Assn. Stevedores (dir., past pres. Tex. affiliate), Nat. Rifleman's Assn. Quaker. Club: Masons. Home: Box 737 Friendswood TX 77546 Office: 6821 Ave V Houston TX 77011

EKBERG, DAVID JEROME, office equipment co. exec.; b. Mpls., May 11, 1929; s. Carl E. and Ruth E. (Olin) E.; B.B.A., B.M.E. with distinction, U. Minn., 1952; m. Joan S. McCormack, Nov. 29, 1952; children—Karen S., Elizabeth S. With Gen. Electric Co., 1952-64, test engr., Schenectady, 1955-64; sales engr. Control Data Corp., Frankfurt, W. Ger., 1964-66, European mgr., Mpls., 1966-69, gen. sales mgr., 1969; founder, v.p. mktg. Data 100 Corp., Mpls., 1969-78, also dir.; v.p., gen. mgr. Data Card Corp., Minnetonka, Minn., 1978-80; pres. Laserdyne Corp., Eden Prairie, Minn., 1981—. Mem. Colonial Ch. Club: Interlachan Country. Home: 6416 Stauder Circle Edina MN 55436 Office: 6690 Shady Oak Rd Eden Prairie MN 55344

EKERS, JOHN ANDERSON, II, mortgage banker; b. Atlanta, May 23, 1944; s. John Anderson and Jean E. (Baker) E.; B.A., Ohio State U., 1970. With Nat. Homes Acceptance Corp., Columbus, Ohio, 1971-72; loan exec. Coastal Mortgage Co., Sarasota, Fla., 1972-73; regional mgr. Community Mortgage Co., St. Petersburg, Fla., 1973-74; asst. v.p. Pan Am. Bank, Sarasota, 1974-79; pres. CFS Mortgage Corp., Columbus, 1979-80; v.p. Sunlandia West Corp., Sarasota, 1980—, 1st Fed. Savs. & Loan at Largo (Fla.), 1981—; mem. faculty St. Petersburg Jr. Coll., 1974-75, U. South Fla., 1976. Bd. dirs. Sarasota Downtown Assn., 1975-79. Served with U.S. Army, 1968. Cert. Residential Mortgage Underwriters, U.S. Profl. Tennis Assn. Mem. Nat. Assn. Rev. Appraisers (charter), Sarasota Bd. Realtors, Manatee Bd. Realtors. Home: 12800 Vonn Rd Apt 9803 Largo FL 33540 Office: 4046 Webber St Sarasota FL 33580

EKKEBUS, DANIEL ELOY, mgmt. cons.; b. Chgo., June 24, 1943; s. Eloy Daniel and Catherine Marie (Fuhrmann) E.; B.B.A., U. Notre Dame, 1965; m. Barbara Vandivier, Aug. 12, 1967 (div.). Vice pres. sales Laird, Inc., 1967-73; v.p. sales G.H. Walker, Laird, Inc., Chgo., 1973-75; v.p. Rambert & Co. Inc., Lake Bluff, Ill., 1975-77; pres. The Bardan Group, Inc., Lake Bluff, 1977-79.

EKLUND, COY GLENWOOD, life ins. co. exec.; b. Brookston, Minn., Sept. 6, 1915; s. Nels and Melba (Tester) E.; student U. Mich., 1933-34; B.S., Mich. State U., 1939, LL.D., 1973; m. Nina Wolkoff, Sept. 20, 1940; children—Melanie, Glenwood, Ronald. With Equitable Life Assurance Soc., N.Y.C., 1939—, agy. mgr., Detroit, 1947-59, v.p., asst. to pres., 1959-61, agy. v.p., 1961-64, sr. agy. v.p., 1964-69, exec. v.p., 1969-73, pres., 1973—, chief exec. officer, 1975—, also dir.; dir. Burroughs Corp., 1980—. Mem. Mich. for Eisenhower Com., 1951-52. Bd. dirs. Oakland Found., Oakland U., 1957-59; trustee Am. Coll. Life Underwriters, 1964—, Salk Inst. Biol. Studies, 1962—, Nat. Urban League; mem. bd. Ams. for Indian Opportunity. Recipient Distinguished Alumnus award Mich. State U., 1965. Served as officer AUS, 1942-46; lt. col. ret. Decorated Croix de Guerre. C.L.U. Mem. Am. Soc. C.L.U.'s, Nat. Assn. Life Underwriters (nat. v.p. 1958-59), Mich. Res. Officers Assn. (pres. 1947-48), Life Ins. Agy. Mgmt. Assn. (trustee 1965-68). Office: 1285 Ave of Americas New York NY 10019*

EKLUND, NILS OSSIAN, JR., corp. exec.; b. Portland, Oreg., June 4, 1911; s. Nils O. and Signe (Anderson) E.; student U. Oreg., 1928-30, Behnke Walker Bus. Coll., Portland, 1930; LL.D., Golden Gate U., 1977; m. Elizabeth Loukes Fairchild, July 12, 1930; children—Karin Anna, Jay Dee (dec.). Salesman, Standard Oil Co. of Calif., Portland, 1930-33, supr., 1933-38; sales mgr. Boyd Coffee Co., Portland, 1938-41; successively engr., asst. supt. and supt. assembly ops., Portland and Vancouver shipyards Kaiser Co., Inc., 1942-45; successively supt., asst. gen. supt., gen. supt. Kaiser Frazer Corp., Willow Run, Mich., 1946-48; tech. cons. Motor House, Ltd., Bombay, India, 1948; successively asst. Midwest sales mgr., Midwest sales mgr., gen. sales mgr. Kaiser Motors Corp., 1949-52, asst. exec. v.p., 1952-54; gen. mgr. Detroit engine div. Willys Motors, Inc., 1954-56; asst. v.p. Henry J. Kaiser Co., Oakland, Calif., 1956-59; v.p. Kaiser Industries Co., Oakland, 1959-72, sr. v.p., 1972-76, cons., 1976—; mem. adv. bd. Douglas Mgmt. Corp., 1977—. Pres., dir. Dist. Adminstrv. Bldg. Corp., 1966-78; gen. chmn. regional com. for better service Oakland Internat. Airport, 1971-76. Mem. Atty. Gen.'s Vol. Adv. Com., 1971-76; mem. exec. com. Gov.'s Transp. Task Force, 1967-68; chmn. Bay Area Transp. Study Commn., 1964-69, Alameda County Health Care Services Adv. Commn., 1970-72; pres. United Bay Area Crusade, 1963, 64, 66; chmn. adv. bd. Calif. State U. at Hayward, 1966-68; mem. adv. council United Community Funds and Councils Am., 1963-66; mem. nat. council Urban Am., Inc., 1965-68; co-chmn. steering com. Paramount Theatre of Arts, 1972-74; pres., chief exec. officer Oakland Symphony Orch. Assn., 1973-76; chmn. Oakland Transp. Task Force, 1972-74; mem. Bay Area civilian adv. com. to 6th U.S. Army, 1974-76; trustee, vice chmn. steering com. San Francisco Bay Area Council, 1973-76; pres., chief exec. officer, bd. dirs. Dunsmuir House Research and Ednl. Corp., 1968-72; bd. dirs. Better Bus. Bur., 1974-76; trustee Golden Gate U., 1963—, chmn. bd., 1974-77; pres., dir. Oakland Devel. Found., 1965-76. Mem. Oakland C. of C. (dir., pres. 1962-63), Navy League U.S. (v.p. Met. Oakland council 1966), Am. Ordnance Assn. (1st v.p. 1970-71, bd. San Francisco chpt.), Harold Brunn Soc. Med. Research, Sigma Phi Epsilon. Presbyn. Clubs: Bohemian; 100 (dir. 1962-65, pres. 1964). Home: 45350 Cypress Dr PO Box 253 Mendocino CA 95460 Died Oct. 31, 1980.

EKLUND, ROGER SCOTT, mfg. co. exec.; b. Everett, Wash., Nov. 12, 1945; s. Paul G. and Helen V. Eklund; B.S. in Bus. Adminstrn., Linfield Coll., McMinnville, Oreg., 1968; m. Michelle E. Fletcher, Dec. 9, 1972; children—Ryan, Megan. With E.A. Nord Co., Everett, 1970—, advt. and promotion mgr., 1972-75, v.p. mktg., 1975—, mem. exec. com., 1980—. Bd. dirs. Providence Hosp., Everett, 1977—. Recipient awards mktg. Mem. Fir and Hemlock Door Assn. (pres. 1978), Am. Mgmt. Assn., Pi Kappa Alpha. Baptist. Club: Cascade (Everett). Home: 1608 Horizon Pl Mukilteo WA 98275 Office: EA Nord Co 3d and Norton Ave Everett WA 98206

EL, WILLIAM WATSON, rec. co. exec.; b. Phila., May 7, 1939; s. William R. and Lillian Watson; student public schs., Phila.; 1 dau., Vanessa. Bus. mgr. The Intruders, singing group, 1959-72; road mgmt. Phila. Internat. Record Co., 1961-72; pres., chmn. bd. Kai Records Inc., Phila., 1975—. Active Big Bros. Served with U.S. Army, 1957-60. Mem. Am. Mgmt. Assn., Rec. Industry Assn. Am., AFTRA. Islam.

ELAD, EMANUEL, nuclear instrumentation co. exec.; b. Kutno, Poland, May 7, 1935; s. Yeshaiah and Esther Altman; B.S., Technion, Israel, 1960, M.S., 1964; Ph.D., U. Calif., Berkeley, 1968; M.B.A., U.

Tenn., 1977; m. Hanna Wakman, May 26, 1959; children—Orly, Doronne, Joel. Research engr. Atomic Energy Commn., Haifa, Israel, 1960-65; tech. dir. Nuclear Diodes, Inc., Prairie View, Ill., 1968-69; with EG&G Ortec, Oak Ridge, Tenn., 1969—, v.p., 1977-80, gen. mgr. materials analysis div., 1975—, sr. v.p., 1980—. Served with Israeli Air Force, 1953-56. Mem. IEEE, Sigma Xi, Eta Kappa Nu, Phi Kappa Phi. Jewish. Club: Oak Ridge Tennis. Contbr. articles to profl. jours. Home: 102 Canterbury Rd Oak Ridge TN 37830 Office: 100 Midland Rd Oak Ridge TN 37830

ELAM, ANDREW GREGORY, II, ins. co. exec.; b. Winchester, Va., Feb. 6, 1932; s. Andrew Gregory and Francis Clayton (Gold) E.; A.B., Presbyn. Coll., 1955; m. Rebecca Rhea Cole, Oct. 26, 1958; children—Andrew Gregory III, Philip Cole, Dawna Francis. Adminstrv. asst. Citizen's and So. Nat. Bank, Columbia, S.C., 1955-56; nat. exec. dir. Pi Kappa Phi, Sumter, S.C., 1956-59; pres. Carolina Potato Co., Inc., West Columbia, S.C., 1959-61; mem. public relations staff Kendavis Industries Internat., Inc., Fort Worth, 1961-63; dir. sales promotion Pioneer Am. Ins. Co., Fort Worth, 1963-64, dir. public relations and sales promotion, 1964-66; asst. v.p., 1966-68, v.p., mem. exec. com., 1968-71, dir., 1970-71; v.p. public relations and sales promotion Gt. Am. Res. Ins. Co. J. C. Penney Life Ins. Co., Dallas, 1972—. Mem. public relations adv. council Am. Council of Life Ins., Washington, 1971—; mem. public relations com. Tex. Life Conv., 1970—. Mem. public info. adv. com. Am. Cancer Soc., Tex. div., 1969—, chmn., 1972-78, exec. com., bd. dirs., 1972-78; vice-chmn. public relations com. Tarrant County United Fund, 1967; campaign leader Community Pride Campaign Performing Arts, 1969. Bd. dirs., treas., vice-chmn. Tarrant County unit Am. Cancer Soc., 1963-71, bd. dirs. Dallas County unit, 1972—, sec., 1977-78; bd. dirs. Fort Worth Community Theatre, 1971-72, Baylor U. Med. Center Found., Dallas, 1980—; mem. adv. bd. Sammons Cancer Center, Dallas, 1980—. Mem. Life Ins. Advertisers Assn. (dir. communications workshop 1970-71, exec. com. 1973-74, chmn. So. Round Table 1972), Public Relations Soc. Am., Tex. Public Relations Assn. (dir. 1966), Indsl. Editors Fort Worth (pres. 1968), Fort Worth C. of C. (chmn. publ. com. 1970), Dallas Advt. League, Dallas Ins. Club, Meeting Planners Inst. (pres. Dallas chpt. 1980), Soc. Preservation and Encouragement of Barbershop Quartet Singing in Am. (chpt. pres. 1978). Presbyterian (deacon 1966-68; ruling elder 1969-71). Home: 7730 Chattington St Dallas TX 75248 Office: 2020 Live Oak Dallas TX 75221

ELAM, GENE G., lumber co. exec.; b. Oklahoma City, Apr. 18, 1939; s. William Loy and Grace (Gasper) E.; B.S. in Commerce, Santa Clara U., 1961; m. Patricia J. Montrose, Apr. 27, 1963; children—Michael, Susan, Karen. Audit prin. Arthur Young & Co., San Francisco, 1962-72; v.p. finance, treas. Pacific Lumber Co., San Francisco, from 1972, now pres., dir. Served with USMC, 1961. Mem. Assn. Corp. Growth, Am. Inst. C.P.A.'s. Republican. Roman Catholic. Office: PO Box 7406 San Francisco CA 94120*

ELBERSON, ROBERT EVANS, mfg. co. exec.; b. Winston-Salem, N.C., Nov. 9, 1928; s. Charles Evans and Harriet (Branin) E.; B.S. in Engring., Princeton U., 1950; M.B.A., Harvard U., 1952; m. Helen Hanes, Aug. 17, 1979; children—Charles Evans II, Nancy Ann. With Hanes Hosiery Mills Co., Winston-Salem, 1954-65, sec. 1959-62, v.p. mfg., 1962-65, also dir.; v.p. Hanes Corp., Winston-Salem, N.C., 1965-72, pres. hosiery div., 1968-72, pres., chief exec. officer, 1972-81, dir., 1972-79; exec. v.p., dir. Consol. Foods Corp., Chgo., 1979—; dir. Charlotte (N.C.) br. Fed. Res. Bank of Richmond, 1978-80, chmn., 1979-80. Mem. bd. visitors Babcock Sch. Mgmt., Wake Forest U., 1972—; bd. dirs. United Way Forsyth County (N.C.), 1978; trustee Salem Acad. and Coll., 1980—. Served to 1st lt. USAF, 1952-54. Mem. Home Moravian Ch. Club: Old Town. Office: 135 S LaSalle St Chicago IL 60603

ELDEN, JOHN DEMARLEY, ins. co. exec.; b. Duluth, Minn., Jan. 2, 1931; s. William Elden and Amelia Josephine (Sather) E.; A.A., U. Minn., 1950; m. Joan Phyliss Tweten, Aug. 16, 1958; children—Gregory William, Julie Marie, Diana Lynn. Agt., Mut. Benefit Life Ins. Co., 1954-58, supr., 1958-63, asst. gen. agt., 1963-67; regional sales mgr. Am. States Life Ins. Co., Indpls., 1967-72; dir. marketing Wis. Life Ins. Co., Madison, 1972-76; agency dir. Fin. Security Life Ins. Co., Moline, Ill., 1976-77, agency v.p., 1977—. Served with U.S. Army, 1950-52; Korea. C.L.U. Mem. Am. Soc. C.L.U., Nat. Assn. Life Underwriters, Moline Rock Island Life Underwriter Assn. Lutheran. Clubs: Optimists, Quad City Sales Execs., Moose, Elks. Home: 48 Geneseo Hills Geneseo IL 61254 Office: 716 17th St Moline IL 61265

ELDER, ROBERT MELDRUM, engine mfg. co. exec.; b. St. Louis, Jan. 29, 1917; s. Andrew Forit and Martha Carolyn (Bohlen) E.; B.A., Westminster Coll., Fulton, Mo., 1940; postgrad. Grad. Sch. Bus. Adminstrn., Harvard U., 1942; m. Anne Louise Feild, Aug. 11, 1944; children—Laurie Anne, Martha Jane, Mary Elise. Salesman, Cummins Diesel Engines, Inc., 1945-47, br. mgr., Pitts., 1947-55, v.p. sales, Phila., 1955-66, exec. v.p., 1966-67, pres., chief exec. officer, prin. owner, 1967—. Bd. dirs. Up with People, Inc., 1970-75, mem. internat. adv. bd., 1976-80; trustee Abington Meml. Hosp., 1970-80, Westminster Coll., 1972-80; chmn. bd. trustees Abington Presbyn. Ch., 1970-76. Served to lt. comdr. USN, 1941-45. Recipient Alumni Achievement award Westminster Coll., 1975, Alumni award of merit, 1980. Mem. Soc. Automotive Engrs. Republican. Clubs: Union League (Phila.); Huntington Valley Country. Home: 1001 Delene Rd Jenkintown PA 19046 Office: 855 E Hunting Park Ave Philadelphia PA 19124

ELDERING, PAUL MARIA, pulp and paper co. exec.; b. Bloemendaal, The Netherlands, Apr. 28, 1930; naturalized Am. citizen, 1948; m. William J. and Elise A. (Van der Staay) E.; grad. St. Bonaventura, Leiden, Holland, 1946; student U.S. Army Command and Gen. Staff Coll., 1970; m. Cele J. Schames, Oct. 15, 1976; children—William W., Elizabeth M., Denise M., Mary Carol, Paula M., Harry S. Asst. office mgr. Son Bulb Farms, Foley, Ala., 1947-49; asst. div. mgr. Sears, Roebuck & Co., Mobile, Ala., 1950; supervising cost acct. St. Regis Co., Pensacola, Fla., 1953-58; asst. controller Bowaters So. Paper Co., Calhoun, Tenn., 1958-67; controller, sr. fin. officer Bowater Carolina Co., Catawba, S.C., 1967-71; corp. controller Bowater Inc., Old Greenwich, Conn., 1971-75, asst. v.p. fin., 1975—. Served to 1st lt. AUS, 1950-53. Mem. Fin. Execs. Inst. (co-chmn. conf. 1980), Planning Execs. Inst. (pres. Chattanooga chpt. 1959-60, Charlotte chpt. 1969, regional dir. 1975-77), VFW, Res. Officers Assn. Republican. Roman Catholic. Club: Elks. Home: 34 Owenoke Way Riverside CT 06878 Office: Bowater Inc 1500 E Putnam Ave Old Greenwich CT 06870

ELDRED, KENNETH MCKECHNIE, acoustical cons.; b. Springfield, Mass., Nov. 25, 1929; s. Robert Mosley and Jean (Ashton) E.; B.S., M.I.T., 1950, postgrad., 1951-53; postgrad. UCLA, 1960-63; m. Helene Barbara Koerting Fischer, May 31, 1957; 1 dau., Heidi Jean. Engr., Boston Naval Shipyard, 1951-54; supervisory physicist, chief phys. acoustics sect. U.S. Air Force, Wright Field, Ohio, 1956-57; v.p., cons. acoustics Western Electro-Acoustics Labs., Los Angeles, 1957-63; v.p., tech. dir. sci. services and systems group Wyle Labs., El Segundo, Calif., 1963-73; v.p., dir. Environ. Noise Control Tech. div. Bolt Beranek & Newman, Inc., Cambridge, Mass., 1973-77, prin. cons., 1977-81; dir. Ken Eldred Engring., 1981—. Served with USAF, 1954-56. Mem. Am. Nat. Standards Inst. (exec. standards council 1979—), NRC, Acoustical Soc. Am., Nat. Acad. Engring., Inst. Noise Control Engring. (pres. 1976), Soc. Automotive Engrs., U.S. Yacht Racing Union. Club: Bristol Yacht. Contbr. articles to profl. jours. Home: 722 Annursnac Hill Rd Concord MA 01742

ELDRED, THOMAS PROCTOR, III, banker; b. Utica, N.Y., Mar. 21, 1947; s. Thomas Proctor and Grace K. (King) E.; B.S. in Mgmt., Lehigh U., 1968; M.B.A., Pace U., 1975. Exec. trainee Marine Midland Bank, N.Y.C., 1968-70, ops. 1970-73, asst. v.p. br. ops., 1973-75; comptroller Banco Industrial de Venezuela, C.A., N.Y.C., 1976—. Mem. Inst. of Fgn. Banks, Am. Mgmt. Assn. Republican. Club: Marco Polo (N.Y.C.). Home: Amberlands 5U Croton NY 10520

ELDREDGE, EDDA ROGERS, securities transfer co. exec.; b. Deseret, Utah, Feb. 15, 1915; d. James Noah and Alice (Critchley) Rogers; student Heager Bus. Coll., 1930-31, U. Utah, 1932-35; m. Frank Aubrey Eldredge, Sept. 5, 1936; children—Frank A., Noah R., Alice Lou, Julie, Joseph U. With Gen. Petroleum Corp., 1945-55; mgr. land dept. Utah So. Oil Co., 1955-62, asst. sec., 1956-62; pres., dir. Edda R. Eldredge & Co., Inc., Salt Lake City, 1967—; pres., dir. Bonneville Petroleum Corp., 1974—. Republican. Mormon. Office: 315 Newhouse Bldg 10 Exchange Pl Salt Lake City UT 84111

ELDREDGE, FREDERICK HOMER, publishing co. exec.; b. Chgo., Sept. 13, 1912; s. Clarence Henry and Gail (Wilson) E.; B.A., Washington U., St. Louis, 1933; B.J., U. Mo., 1935; m. Delna Fielder, Aug. 13, 1935; children—Gail, Delna, Thelma. Mktg. dir. Gen. Engring. & Mfg. Co., St. Louis, 1937-39; media and account exec., D'Arcy Advt. Co., St. Louis, 1939-53; regional sales mgr. Hearst Pub. Co., St. Louis, Chgo., 1953-62; mgr. Southwest sales, Tech. Pub. Co., Chgo., Dallas, 1963—. Mem. Am. Mktg. Assn. (chpt. pres.), Bus. Profl. Advt. Assn. (dir.). Presbyterian (elder). Club: Rush Creek Yacht (commodore 1978). Author: I Quit Plan, 1961; How to Break Habits, 1962; Try Again, 1962; Gone Forever, 1963. Home: Route 1 315 Scenic Dr Forney TX 75126

ELEVELD, HENDRIK, stockbroker; b. Smilde, Netherlands, June 2, 1917; s. Klaas and Antje (Fernhout) E.; came to U.S., 1956, naturalized, 1961; ed. bus. courses; m. Anna P. Mulder, June 2, 1955; children—Ronald C., Jeffrey J., Eric H. Asst. to various tobacco plantation mgrs. in Indonesia, United Deli Cos., 1949-56; asst. to mgr. Imperial Nurseries, Conn., 1956-61; stockbroker Robert C. Buell & Co., Hartford, Conn., 1961-69, Brainard Judd & Co., 1969-75; stockbroker Coburn & Meredith Inc., 1975—, v.p., 1979—; founder, dir. Windsor Bank Trust Co., 1972-75. Fin. chmn. Windsor Republican Town Com., 1963-76, chmn., 1976—; mem. mgmt. and fin. coms. Heart Assn. Greater Hartford, 1971—; commr. Conn. Power Facility Evaluation Council, 1972-75; mem. Key Club Rep. Party of Conn.; mem. Rep. State Fin. Com.; trustee 1st Congregational Ch. of Windsor, 1974—; bd. dirs., trustee Hillside Sch., Marlborough, Mass., 1977—; bd. dirs. Windsor Public Library. Served as staff sgt. Dutch Army, 1946-49. Recipient medal for Americanism, DAR, 1972; named Rep. Man of Yr., 1972. Clubs: Windsor Exchange, Masons, Elks, Officers Conn. Contbr. articles to Windsor Jour. Home: 50 Remington Rd Windsor CT 06095 Office: 15 Lewis St Hartford CT 06103

ELFENBEIN, LEONARD, telecommunications co. exec.; b. N.Y.C., June 21, 1941; s. Melvin and Eleanor (Fried) E.; B.S., N.Y. U., 1963; m. Joyce Leventhal, Sept. 8, 1963; children—Marc, Michael, Meredith. Computer programmer Olivetti Corp., 1963-64; systems analyst N.Y. Stock Exchange, 1964-66; div. mgr., regional dir. Computer Applications Inc., 1966-68; founder, exec. v.p. Wellington Systems Inc., 1968-71; chmn., pres. Atlantic Bridge Corp., 1971-75; chmn., pres. Telecom Systems Group, Cedar Grove, N.J., 1976—; pub. World Telecommunications Directory. Office: 579 Pompton Ave Cedar Grove NJ 07009

ELFORD, GERALD GORDON, equipment co. exec.; b. Hamilton, Ont., Can., Dec. 5, 1934; s. Arthur Gordon and Hazel Louise (Lampman) E.; student Ford Motor Co. of Can. Ltd. Trade Sch., 1956, Rensselaer Poly. Inst., 1971; m. Shirley M. Sinclair, June 22, 1963; children—Arlene M., Ann M. Welder, T. H. & B. Railway, 1951; Tool and die maker Ford Motor Co., 1952-56, in quality control analysis, 1956-57, buyer, 1957-59; with Upper Can. Mfg. Ltd., Toronto, Ont., 1959—, now pres.; dir. Queenston Devels. Ltd., Upper Can. Mfg. Ltd., Williamsburg Estates Ltd. Mem. Canadian Tooling Mfrs. Assn. (past pres.). Progressive Conservative. Club: Mason. Office: 223 Evans Ave Toronto ON M8Z 1J5 Canada

ELHART, ROBERT DUANE, exec. recruiting co. exec.; b. Ashland, Oreg., Oct. 3, 1928; s. Carlton Dewey and Martha (Palma) E.; student So. Oreg. Coll., 1946-49; M.B.A., U. Chgo., 1951; children—Barbara, Penny, Carolyn, Kevin. Partner Peat Marwick & Partners, Toronto, Ont., Can., 1957-71; v.p. Booz Allen Hamilton, Toronto, 1971-73; sr. partner Caldwell Partners, Internat., Toronto, 1973—. Served with U.S. Army, 1952-54. Mem. Inst. Mgmt. Cons. Ont. Office: 50 Prince Arthur St Toronto ON M5R-1B5 Canada

ELI, JOHNNIE CARL, JR., real estate cons., dentist; b. Austin, Tex., Feb. 27, 1930; s. Johnnie Carl and Nan (Hope) E.; student La Sierra Coll., 1954-56, U. Houston, 1953-54; D.D.S., Loma Linda U., 1960; m. E. Ruth Melnechuk, Sept. 6, 1953; children—Jenell Diane, Bradley Allen. Practice dentistry, San Bernardino, Calif., 1961—; pres. Protective Care Systems, Inc., Redlands, Calif., 1976—; cons. real estate, 1975—. Pres. chpt. Nat. Assn. Seventh-day Adventist Dentists, Southeastern Calif., 1974, local elder, 1972—. Served with M.C. U.S. Army, 1951-53; ETO. Mem. Am., Calif., Tri-county dental assns., Acad. Gen. Dentistry. Democrat. Inventor in field. Home: PO Box 177 Bryn Mawr CA 92318 Office: PO Box 5902 San Bernardino CA 92412

ELIAS, PAUL S., mktg. co. exec.; b. Chgo., July 5, 1926; s. Maurice I. and Ethel (Tieger) E.; B.S., Northwestern U. Sch. Bus., 1950; hon. degree N.Y. U. Sch. Continuing Edn., 1972; m. Jennie Lee Feldschreiber, June 28, 1953; children—Eric David, Stephen Mark, Daniel Avrum. Buyer, Mandel Bros., Chgo., 1950-53; salesman Internat. Latex Corp., Chgo., 1953-56; v.p. Hy Zeiger & Co., Milw., 1957-59; exec. v.p. K-Promotions, Inc., Milw., from 1959, now pres.; dir. Carlson Mktg. and Motivation, Milw. Officer, dir. Milw. Jewish Community Center; pres. regional bd. Anti-Defamation League. Served with USAAF, 1945-46. Mem. Nat. Premium Sales Execs., Direct Mail Advt. Assn., Premium Advt. Assn. Am. Jewish. Developer inflight mail order mktg. programs for airlines. Home: 9201 N Broadmoor Rd Bayside WI 53217 Office: 3825 W Green Tree Rd Milwaukee WI 53209

ELIASON, FRANS ROBERT, ins. co. exec.; b. Wahoo, Nebr., Apr. 9, 1929; s. Bernard Emanuel and Yerda Elvira (Magnusson) E.; student Luther Jr. Coll., 1946-48; B.B.A., U. Minn., 1950; m. Eleanor Jane Lesnak, Dec. 28, 1957; children—Kent, Cinda. With Northwestern Nat. Ins. Co., 1963—, chmn., pres., chief exec. officer, 1975-77, chmn., 1977-81; pres., chief operating officer Armco Ins. Group Inc., 1980-81, pres., chief exec. officer, 1981—; exec. v.p. NN Corp., Milw., 1973-79, pres., chief operating officer, 1979-80. Bd. dirs. Friends of the Mus., Milw.; vice chmn. United Way of Greater Milw. Served with U.S. Navy, 1951-55. Mem. Nat. Soc. Chartered Property and Casualty Underwriters (v.p.). Clubs: Milwaukee, Westmoor Country. Office: 731 N Jackson St Milwaukee WI 53201

ELIASON, SVEN A., furniture co. exec.; b. Umea, Sweden, Sept. 24, 1926; s. Albin E. and Hanna (Boden) E.; B.S. magna cum laude, U. So. Calif., 1959, M.B.A., 1960; m. Siri M. Siljemo, July 29, 1950; 1 dau., Jane G. Came to U.S., 1957, naturalized, 1971. Owner, Eliasons Mobler AB, Sweden, 1949-62; pres. Eliasons Damekipering AB, Sweden, 1955-57; exec. v.p. Scandiline Industries, Inc., San Pedro, Calif., 1960-62, pres., 1962—; chmn. bd. Danica, Inc., Beverly Hills, 1971—, Setmakers Inc., Hollywood, 1971-72, Scandiline Internat., Norway, 1977—, Exotic Woods, Inc., Compton, Calif., 1977—, Brelstein Mobelfabrick A/S, Norway, 1978—. Pres., St. Eric's Ch., 1965-72, 77—; pres. Am.-Scandinavian Found., 1976-79. Decorated knight Royal Order Vasa, Vb. medal Merit (Sweden); knight Royal Order St. Olaf (Norway). Mem. Swedish Am. C. of C. Western U.S. (pres. 1971-74, hon. chmn. 1975), Norwegian Am. C. of C. (pres.), San Pedro C. of C. (dir. 1966-68), Iran Am. C. of C. (dir. 1978—). Clubs: Rotary (dir. 1967-68), Swedish, Founders, Calif. Office: 1217 W Artesia Blvd Compton CA 90220

ELICKER, PAUL H., corp. exec.; b. N.Y.C., 1923; B.S., Yale, 1944; M.B.A., Harvard, 1948; m. Jane Arnold; 2 children. With Ford Motor Co., 1949-51, Mckinsey & Co., 1952-56; with S C M Corp., 1956—, v.p. finance, 1957-70, exec. v.p., 1970-71, pres., chief exec. officer, 1972—, also dir. Office: SCM Corp 299 Park Ave New York NY 10017*

ELIEFF, LEWIS STEVEN, stockbroker; b. Sofia, Bulgaria, Aug. 2, 1929; s. Steven and Vera (Svetcoff) E.; B.B.A., U. Mich., 1953, M.B.A., 1954; m. Evanka Brown, May 25, 1958; children—Nancy Ann, Robert and Richard (twins). Statistician, tax acct. Gen. Motors Corp., Flint, Mich., 1954-60; stockbroker William C. Roney & Co., Flint, 1960-73, ltd. partner, 1973-79, gen. partner, 1979—, writer weekly stock market column Grand Blanc (Mich.) News, Tri-County News, Fenton, Mich.; tchr. stock market curriculum Flint Public Schs., 1960-68, Genesee County Community Coll., 1968-73, U. Mich. Extension and Grad. Study Center, Flint Campus. Mem. Grand Blanc Twp. Econ. Devel. Commn.; mem. regents-alumni scholarship com. U. Mich., 1977—. Served with AUS, 1954-56. Mem. U. Mich. Alumni Club and Assn. Clubs: Genesee Valley Rotary, University (Flint). Home: 6612 Kings Pointe Grand Blanc MI 48439 Office: Bristol Pl G-4488 W Bristol Rd Flint MI 48507

ELIESON, SANFRED WILLARD, estate planner; b. Salt Lake City, Apr. 5, 1915; s. Eli Walter and Lyle M. (Brimley) E.; student U. Utah; m. Virginia Shortliff, June 7, 1937; children—S. Willard, David G., V. Steven. Acct., Hogle Investment Co., The Lang Co., Salt Lake City, 1937-41, Wasatch So. Oil Co., Pleasant Grove, Utah, 1942-43, Lockheed Aircraft Co., Burbank, Calif., 1944-45; owner, mgr. Bordeaux Laundry & Cleaners, Los Angeles, 1945-50, Elieson Interiors, Los Angeles, 1950-55; agt. Cal-Western Life Ins. Co., Los Angeles, 1955-63, mgr. Utah agy., 1958-63; mgr. Dallas agy. Beneficial Life Ins. Co., 1970-75; counselor, broker Ct. So. Assn., Dallas, 1976—; dir. Tex. Commerce Trust Co. Bd. dirs. Denton Osteo. Hosp., 1971-74. Recipient citation Calif. Assembly Legislature, 1957; C.L.U. Mem. Nat. Assn. Life Underwriters, Utah Assn. Life Underwriters (sec.-treas. 1961-62, v.p. 1962-63), Am. Soc. C.L.U., Dallas Estate Planning Council. Mormon. Home: Route 1 PO Box 6 Sanger TX 76266 Office: 1710 Westminster Suite A Denton TX 76201

ELIJAH, LEO M., cons. indsl. and metall. engr.; b. Nagpur, India; came to U.S., 1949, naturalized, 1962; s. Moses and Simha (Talker) E.; B.S., U. Bombay, 1947; M.S., U. Wis., 1951; children—Danielle-Simha, Daphne-Esther. With Ford Motor Co. (Can.), Windsor, Ont., 1951-57; metall. dir. George Sall Metals, Phila., 1957-62; with IBM, N.Y.C., 1967-72; cons. indsl. and metall. engr., Denver, 1977—. Registered profl. engr., Can., Pa. Contbr. articles to tech. jours. Patentee chem. and metall. processes, metals and alloys. Address: 9080 Camenish Way #9 Denver CO 80221

ELKIN, IRVIN, business exec. Pres., Asso. Milk Producers, Inc., San Antonio. Office: Associated Milk Producers Inc PO Box 32287 San Antonio TX 87284*

ELKINS, DORIS SHUMAN, ins. agy. exec.; b. Jacksonville, Fla., Mar. 30, 1940; d. Ernest Maxwell and Doris Evelyn (Thornton) Shuman; student Draughon's Jr. Coll., Savannah, Ga., 1980—; m. James Parker Elkins, Nov. 21, 1958 (dec.); children—Douglas Edward, Steven Edward. File clk. Atlantic Mut. Fire Ins. Co., Savannah, 1958-60; ins. adjuster Edward S. DuFour & Co., Savannah, 1968-72; bookkeeper McLaughlin & Co., ins. agy., Savannah, 1975-77, personal lines customer service rep., 1977, comml. lines customer service rep., 1978-80, sec.-treas., 1975-80, office mgr., 1977-80; sec.-treas. Remer Y. Lane, Jr., Ins., Inc., 1981—. Lic. agt., Ga.; ind. ins. adjusters lic., Ga. Mem. Nat. Assn. Ins. Women (cert. profl. ins. woman), Ind. Ins. Agts. Savannah (dir. 1979-81), Savannah Claims Assn., Ins. Women Savannah (pres. 1976-77), Epsilon Sigma Alpha (life). Republican. Home: 8623 Creighton Pl E Savannah GA 31406 Office: One E Jackson Blvd PO Box 13866 Savannah GA 31406

ELKINS, JAMES ANDERSON, JR., banker; b. Galveston, Tex., Mar. 24, 1919; s. James Anderson and Isabel (Mitchell) E.; B.A., Princeton U., 1941; m. Margaret Wiess, Nov. 24, 1945; children—Elise, James Anderson, Leslie K. With First City Nat. Bank, Houston, 1941—, v.p., 1946-50, pres., 1950-60, chmn. bd., 1960—, also dir.; chmn. bd. First City Bancorp. Tex., 1971—; dir. Eastern Airlines, Am. Gen. Ins. Co., Houston, Cameron Iron Works, Freeport Minerals, Inc. Trustee Princeton U., Baylor Coll. Medicine. Episcopalian (trustee Diocese of Tex.). Home: 101 Farish Circle Houston TX 77024 Office: First City Nat Bank Houston TX 77001

ELLEDGE, BRAD RUSSELL, sanitary supply co. mgr.; b. Berkeley, Calif., July 24, 1952; s. Fred Russell and Betty May (Cicerone) E.; B.S. in Bus. Adminstrn., U. Calif., Berkeley, 1974; masters in mgmt. Northwestern U., 1976. Asst. to pres. Chemed Corp., Cin., 1976-77, field sales rep. Vestal Labs. div. Chemed Corp., Cleve., 1977-79; ops. mgr. Ariz. Janitor Supply div. Vestal Labs., Phoenix, 1979-80, br. mgr., Tucson, 1980—. Mem. Ariz. San. Supply Assn. (dir.), U. Calif. Berkeley Alumni, Northwestern Kellogg Sch. Mgmt. Alumni Assn., Delta Upsilon Alumni Assn. Republican. Office: 727 S Park Ave Tucson AZ 85719

ELLEGARD, ROY TAYLOR, indsl. products mfg. co. exec.; b. Hartford, Conn., May 26, 1927; s. Roy Edward and Helen May (Peberdy) E.; A.B., Princeton, 1951; m. Jeanette Louise Whitney, Mar. 20, 1954; children—Roy Whitney, Jan. Pres., Advancement Opportunities Inc., Hartford, Conn., 1956-66; asso. Booz, Allen & Hamilton, Inc., N.Y.C., 1966-70; v.p. Golightly & Co. Internat., Inc., N.Y.C., 1971-72; v.p. Condec Corp., Old Greenwich, Conn., 1972—. Justice Peace, West Hartford, Conn., 1965-67. Served with AUS, 1946-47. Episcopalian. Club: Princeton of N.Y. Home: 10 High Acre

Rd Weston CT 06880 Office: 1700 E Putnam Ave Old Greenwich CT 06870

ELLENBURG, WILLIAM EDWARD, JR., banker; b. Trion, Ga., Oct. 26, 1951; s. William Edward and Caroline Louise (Geise) E.; student West Ga. Coll., 1969-70, Ga. Bankers Sch., Athens, 1976-78, also Am. Inst. Banking courses; m. Jackie Blake Cook, June 8, 1973; children—Meredith Blake, Matthew Edward. With Bigelow-Sanford Carpets Co., Summerville, Ga., 1971-74; asst. v.p. Farmers & Mchts. Bank, Summerville, 1974—. Mem. lender adv. council Ga. Guaranteed Student Loan Program, 1978; chmn. fund drive ARC, Summerville, 1977, chmn. blood program, 1978. Recipient Appreciation cert. ARC, 1979. Democrat. Baptist. Club: Trion Links Golf. Home: 2 Espy St Summerville GA 30747 Office: 2 Rome Blvd Summerville GA 30747

ELLER, WARREN BERNSON, ins. agy. exec.; b. Alpena, Mich., Apr. 8, 1931; s. William Carl and Rachel Bernson E.; student U. Mich., 1954-55, Wayne State U., 1955-56; m. Marilyn Walling, Oct. 30, 1954; children—Marc William, Brian Theodore, Cynthia Marie. Agt., Northwestern Mut. Life Ins. Co., 1957-59; asst. mgr. Occidental Life of Calif., 1959; founder, pres. Warren B. Eller Agy., Inc., Farmington, Mich., 1959—. Served with USAF, 1950-54; Korea. Mem. Nat. Assn. Life Underwriters, Detroit Assn. Life Underwriters (pres. 1967-68), Life Underwriter Polit. Action Com. (trustee 1970), Risk Appraisal Forum (founder). Democrat. Lutheran. Clubs: Detroit Golf, Lakelands Country, Travis Pointe Country. Office: 31313 Northwestern St Suite 111 Farmington MI 48018

ELLIES, DAVE, indsl. design cons.; b. Washington Court House, Ohio, July 29, 1925; s. Ernest A. and Mabel B. Ellies; student Ohio State U., 1946; B.F.A., Carnegie Inst. Tech., 1950; m. Carol McCoy, June 27, 1948; children—Dianne, Lisa, Kristin, Ernest. Design cons. Butler-Zimmerman Inc., N.Y.C., 1950-54; pres., indsl. design cons. Dave Ellies Indsl. Design Inc., Columbus, Ohio, N.Y.C., Dallas and Santa Clara, Calif., 1954—; dir. Jefferson Savs. & Loan, West Jefferson, Ohio. Pres. Columbus Assn. for Performing Arts, 1978-81. Served with USAAF, 1943-46; PTO. Fellow Inst. Profl. Designers; mem. Nat. Bus. Aircraft Assn. Clubs: Wings, Rotary (pres. 1976-77), Masons, Muirfield Village Golf. Contbr. numerous articles on interior aircraft design to trade jours. Home: 4460 Langport Rd Columbus OH 43220 Office: 2015 W 5th Ave Columbus OH 43212

ELLING, JERROLD ALLEN, printing and pub. co. exec.; b. Williston, N.D., Aug. 10, 1943; s. Jerrold A. and Helen Jurene (Witt) E.; B.A., St. Olaf Coll., 1965; m. Betsey Lea Solsrud, Aug. 1, 1964; children—Michael Lee, Sonja Marie. English tchr., chmn. lang. dept. Heron Lake (Minn.) Public Schs., 1965-69; system head librarian Cumberland Public Schs., 1969-72; pres., chief exec. officer Flambeau Litho Corp., Tony, Wis., 1972—. Trustee, Mt. Senario Coll.; bd. dirs. Flambeau Valley Arts Assn. Mem. Exptl. Aircraft Assn. (pres. chpt. 631 1978-80), Printing Industries Am., Printing Industries Wis., Nat. Rifle Assn. Republican. Editor: Aeronca: Champs and Chiefs, 1979. Home: 402 Summit Ave W Ladysmith WI 54848 Office: Flambeau Litho Corp Hwy 8 Tony WI 54563

ELLINGHAUS, WILLIAM M., communications exec.; b. Balt., Apr. 19, 1922; grad. high sch.; LL.D., Iona Coll., 1974, Pace U., 1976, St. John's U., 1976, Poly. Inst. N.Y., 1976; L.H.D., Manhattan Coll., 1975; D.B.A., Curry Coll., 1978; D.Sc. (hon.), Washington Coll., 1979; m. Erlaine Dietrich, May 30, 1942; children—Marcia A. Barone, Eric J., Douglas A., Barbara E. Gurne, Raymond W., Mark D., Christopher C., Jonathan Paul. With Bell System, 1940—, comml. mgr. Chesapeake & Potomac Telephone Co. Md., Balt., 1950-51, pub. office mgr. Chesapeake & Potomac Telephone Co. Va., Norfolk, 1951-52, dist. comml. mgr., Culpeper, 1952-55, gen. comml. supr. Chesapeake & Potomac Telephone Co. W.Va., Charleston, 1955-57, div. comml. mgr., 1957, gen. accounting supr., 1957-58, comptroller, 1958-60, v.p., dir., 1960-62, v.p. accounts Chesapeake & Potomac Telephone Cos., Washington, 1962, v.p. personnel, 1962-65; asst. v.p. planning AT&T, N.Y.C., 1965-66, v.p. mktg. and rate plans, 1967-70, exec. v.p., 1970-76, vice chmn. bd., 1976-79, pres., 1979—, dir., 1976—; pres. N.Y. Telephone Co., 1970-76; dir. Bankers Trust Co., Internat. Paper Co., J.C. Penney Co., Inc., Bristol Myers Co., Pacific Tel. & Tel. Co. Trustee St. John's U., Colgate U., Hampton Inst.; mem. bd. Greater N.Y. council Boy Scouts Am.; mem. N.Y. Blood Center; mem. adv. com. bus. programs Brookings Instn.; bd. govs. United Way Am.; bd. govs. Am. Nat. Red Cross. Served with USNR, 1943-45. Mem. Am. Soc. Corp. Execs., Regional Plan Assn. (dir.), Econ. Devel. Council (dir.), N.Y.C. Chamber of Commerce and Industry (dir.), Sovereign Order Knights of Malta, Equestrian Order Holy Sepulchre of Jerusalem. Clubs: Econ., Union League, Siwanoy Country (N.Y.C.). Home: 55 Crows Nest Rd Bronxville NY 10708 Office: 195 Broadway New York NY 10007

ELLINGTON, JESSE THOMPSON, JR., film service exec.; b. Phila., Sept. 21, 1931; s. Jesse Thompson and Elizabeth Young (Turner) E.; B.S. in Commerce, U. Va., 1953; m. Nancy Cabell Meredith, July 18, 1959; children—Elizabeth C., Jesse Thompson, Keren M. Exec. producer Ellington & Co., N.Y.C., 1953-62; v.p. Young & Rubicam, N.Y.C., 1963-67, sr. v.p., Los Angeles, 1968-70; sr. asst. postmaster gen. U.S. Postal Service, Washington, 1971-76; pres. Consol. Film Industries, Hollywood, Calif., 1977—. Mem. Am. Mgmt. Assn., Soc. Motion Picture and TV Engrs., Am. Soc. Cinematographers, Acad. Motion Picture Arts and Scis., Hollywood Radio and TV Soc. Republican. Home: 1480 Charlton St San Marino CA 91108 Office: 959 Seward St Hollywood CA 90038

ELLIOT, JOHN T., filmmaker, artist; student Acad. Fine Arts, Italy, 1947-50, N.Y. U., 1951-54, Sch. of Visual Arts, 1958-59. Pres., Graphics for Industry, Englewood, N.J., 1968—; designer, producer numerous television shows and comml.s, also motion pictures; spl. cons. AT & T, Bell Labs., NASA, Nova, Ltd., Xerox, others; guest lectr. N.Y. U.; head film dept. Art Center No. N.J.; exhibited in group shows at Am. Soc. Festival, Chgo., 1974, Pastel Soc. Am., Nat. Arts Club, N.Y.C., 1977, Hunterdon Art Center 24th Annual, 1977, Somerset Art Assn. 7th Annual, 1977, Bergen County Mus., 1974, Illustrators Soc. 20th Annual, 1978, N.Y. Advt. Club, 1963, Volkswagon World Hdqrs., Englewood Cliffs, N.J., 1974, Washington Sq. Art Show, 1959; represented in permanent collections at Am. Citizens Art Council, N.Y.C., Artiste Musee Belgique, Brussels, Bilblioteque de la Republique Francaise, Paris, Chemtrade Internat., Inc., Fawcett Publs., Henry Strauss, Inc., Italia Academia de Roma, Rome, Nat. Women's Art Collectors Guild, N.Y. Lawyers Art Affiliates, Novo, Ltd., Vassar Alumnae Art Collectors League, Wharton Sch. Finance, U. Pa. Alumni Investment Group, Nat. Trust Historic Preservation, Met. Mus. Art, N.Y.C., Fogg Art Mus., Harvard, Nat. Collection Fine Arts, Smithsonian Instn., Detroit Mus. Art; paintings for childrens books include Children's Bible, Children's Day mag., Children's Almanac, The Legend of John Henry, Alexander Hamilton. Recipient 1st prizes Cannes Film Festival, 1965, 72, Gold award, 1973, Grand award, 1975, Spl. award for best film in cinemascope, 1970, Silver award, 1977 all from New York Internat. Film Festival; Chris award, 1970, Gold medal Freedom Found., 1970, Cine awards, 1965, 75, Chgo. Film Festival award, 1973, 1st prizes N.Y. Advt. Club, 1969, L.I. Art Assn., 1966. Mem. Pastel Soc. Am., Soc. Illustrators, Co-Art (pres.), others. Address: Graphics for Industry 231 Liberty Rd Englewood NJ 07631

ELLIOTT, CHARLES DEWEY, III, mgmt. cons.; b. Kansas City, Mo., Feb. 28, 1947; s. Charles Dewey and Clara Virginia (Taylor) E.; B.S. in Engring., U.S. Naval Acad., 1970; M.B.A., U. No. Colo., 1975; student U. Mo., 1965-66; m. Rodricka Ayn Ragar, June 13, 1970; children—Charles Dewey, Clayton Taylor O'Neal. Sr. research analyst Presearch, Inc., Washington, 1976-79; exec. dir. Tech. Mgmt. Corp., Washington, 1979-80; sr. partner TZ Asso., Washington, 1974—; pres. Vision Assos., Washington, 1980—; dir. Integrated Services Asso., Novex, Inc. Served with USN, 1966-76. Decorated Navy Commendation medal. Mem. U.S. Naval Acad. Alumni Assn. Republican. Methodist. Club: Masons. Contbr. articles to profl. jours. Address: 8217 Clifton Farm Ct Alexandria VA 22306

ELLIOTT, EDWARD, corp. exec.; b. Madison, Wis., Jan. 11, 1915; s. Edward C. and Elizabeth (Nowland) E.; B.S. in Mech. Engring., Purdue U., 1936; m. Letitia Ord, Feb. 20, 1943 (div. Aug. 1955); children—Emily, Ord; m. 2d, Melita Uihlein, Jan. 1, 1958; 1 dau., Deborah. Engr., Gen. Electric Co., Schenectady, 1936-37; engr. Pressed Steel Tank Co., Milw., 1937-38, N.Y.C., 1939-41, dist. sales mgr., Cleve., 1946-48 N.Y.C., 1949-54, sales mgr., Milw., 1954-58; v.p. sales Cambridge Co. div. Carrier Corp., Lowell, Mass., 1958-59; mgr. indsl. and med. sales Liquid Carbonic div. Gen. Dynamics Corp., Chgo., 1959-61; v.p. Haywood Pub. Co., Chgo., 1961-63; pres. Omnibus, Inc., Chgo., 1963-67; gen. sales mgr. Resistoflex Corp., Roseland, N.J., 1967-68; investment exec. Shearson, Hammill & Co., Inc., Chgo., 1968-74; v.p. McCormick & Co. Inc., 1974-75; v.p. Paine Webber Jackson & Curtis, Naples, Fla., 1975—. Served with USAAF, 1941-46. Decorated officer Order Brit. Empire. Mem. ASME, Air Force Assn., Phi Delta Theta. Republican. Episcopalian. Clubs: Mid-Day, Racquet (Chgo.); Shore Acres Golf (Lake Bluff, Ill.), Onwentsia (Lake Forest, Ill.); Milw. Country, Univ. (Milw.); Chenequa Country (Hartland, Wis.); Lake (Oconomowoc, Wis.); Army-Navy Country (Arlington, Va.); Lafayette (Ind.) Country; Coral Beach (Paget, Bermuda); Royal Poinciana Golf, Hole-in-Wall Golf, Racquet, Naples Athletic, Rotary (Naples, Fla.). Home: 1285 Gulf Shore Blvd N Naples FL 33940 Office: 1400 Gulf Shore Blvd N Naples FL 33940

ELLIOTT, GEORGE BYRON, security exec.; b. Berwyn, Ill., May 11, 1928; s. Joseph Grant and Clara Ruth (Powell) E.; student Latin Am. Inst., Chgo., 1949-50; m. Beverly Jean Carter; children—Judith Lynn, Susan Reene. Freelance photographer, San Diego, 1951-52, El Centro, Calif., 1952-53, Chgo., 1954-63; officer Cook County (Ill.) Sheriff's Police, 1963-66; v.p., producer Studio VII Films, Ltd., Chgo., 1966-67; investigator numerous pvt. detective agys., Chgo., 1967-75; owner, mgr. Tech. Service Co., Maywood, Ill., 1975-80; mgr. security and safety Purex Corp., Chgo., 1980—. Served with USMC, 1946-49, 50-51. Mem. Am. Soc. Indsl. Security, Nat. Rifle Assn., Nat. Assn. Chiefs Police, Internat. Assn. Bomb Technicians and Investigators, Am. Security Council, Am. Conservative Union. Lutheran. Club: Kiwanis. Office: 8825 S Greenwood Ave Chicago IL 60619

ELLIOTT, INGER MCCABE (MRS. OSBORN ELLIOTT), textile co. exec.; b. Oslo, Feb. 23, 1933; d. David and Lova (Katz) Abrahamsen; came to U.S., 1941; naturalized, 1946; A.B. in History with honors, Cornell U., 1954; postgrad. Harvard U., 1955; A.M. (Jean Birdsall fellow), Radcliffe Coll., 1957; m. Osborn Elliott, Oct. 20, 1973; children by previous marriage—Kari McCabe, Alexander McCabe, Molly McCabe. Editor, E. European Student and Youth Service, N.Y.C., 1957-60; photographer Rapho-Guillumette, U.S. and fgn. countries, 1960-73; pres. China Seas, Inc., N.Y.C., 1972—. Tchr., Newton (Mass.) Pub. Schs., 1955-56. Mem. Am. Soc. Mag. Photographers, Phi Beta Kappa. Author: Women Photographers, 1970; A Week in Amy's World, 1970; A Week in Henry's World, 1971; also portfolio in Infinity mag., 1969. Home: 10 Gracie Sq New York NY 10028 Office: 427 E 76th St New York NY 10021

ELLIOTT, JOE EDD, health care exec.; b. Seymour, Tex., Jan. 14, 1922; s. Anson Coble and Mamie Lois (Jones) E.; student Tex. Christian U., 1940-42; m. Lucy Jane Smith, Oct. 14, 1941; children—Joel Mark, Janis. Spl. projects and labor coordinator Tex. Blue Cross, 1952-58; regional mgr. Gt. Plains mktg. region Nat. Blue Cross Assn., Dallas, 1958-65, dir. Southeast mktg. region, Atlanta, also sr. dir. Southwestern and Western mktg. regions, Dallas, 1968-80; v.p. external relations Ark. Blue Cross and Blue Shield, 1965-68; cons. to nat. industries, labor, govt. agys. Served to capt. USAF, 1942-46; PTO. Decorated Air medal. Mem. Aircraft Owners and Pilots Assn., Dallas C. of C., Res. Officers Assn. Author: Methodology of Consultive Selling, 1973. Home: 6905 La Manga Dr Dallas TX 75248 Office: Suite 240 2915 LBJ Freeway Dallas TX 75234

ELLIOTT, LANE CARTER, food store exec.; b. Hamilton, Mont., June 20, 1947; s. Leo Duayne and Lorraine Marie (Lockhart) E.; B.A., Eastern Wash. U., 1974; m. Carolyn Lee Nirk, Aug. 20, 1977; children—Bret James, John Jeffrey, Meagan Marie. Sr. accountant Haden & Moran, C.P.A.'s, Spokane, Wash., 1972-75; staff accountant Roundup Co., Spokane, 1975-77; corporate controller Stein Bros., Inc., Garden Spot Food Stores, Rathdrum, Idaho, 1977—. Served with USN, 1966-70. Decorated Navy Achievement medal. Mem. Nat. Fedn. Independent Bus., Idaho Food Dealers Assn., Food Mktg. Inst., Alpha Kappa Psi (Nat. Distinguished Service medal 1974). Republican. Roman Catholic. Home: 382 Ponderosa Dr Post Falls ID 83854 Office: PO Box 165 Lakeland Mall Rathdrum ID 83858

ELLIOTT, MERLE STUART, accounting co. exec.; b. Washington County, Md., Oct. 28, 1930; s. Brant Kelso and Lydia Louise (Fiery) E.; student pub. schs., Hagerstown, Md.; m. Joann Elevia Forcino, Dec. 31, 1969; 1 dau., Judy. Staff accountant Arthur M. Moats, C.P.A., Hagerstown, 1948-56; practice accounting Merle S. Elliott, C.P.A., Hagerstown, 1956-63; partner Smith Elliott Kearns & Co., Hagerstown, 1963—. Pres., Mason Dixon council Boy Scouts Am., 1970-73, Area 1 SE region, 1973-78; pres. Hagerstown-Washington County United Way, 1973-74, Hagerstown-Washington County Indsl. Found., 1972—. Served with U.S. Army, 1953-56. Recipient Silver Beaver award Mason Dixon council Boy Scouts Am., 1974, Silver Antelope award SE region, 1976; C.P.A., Md. Mem. Am. Inst. C.P.A.'s (chmn. small bus. cons. subcom.), Md. Assn. C.P.A.'s, Am. Accounting Assn., Nat. Assn. Accountants, Hagerstown-Washington County C. of C. (pres. 1974-75), VFW, Am. Legion. Democrat. Lutheran. Clubs: Rotary, Elks, Masons, Shriners, Moose, Fountain Head Country (pres. 1971-73, 75-76). Home: 740 Fountain Head Rd Hagerstown MD 21740 Office: 25 North Ave Hagerstown MD 21740

ELLIOTT, PAUL CHARLES, oil co. exec.; b. Terre Haute, Ind., Sept. 23, 1933; s. Ross Edward and Maybelle (Reichert) E.; B.S. in Chem. Engring., Rose Poly. Inst., 1955; postgrad. Purdue U., 1955, Wharton Sch. Bus., U. Pa., 1958-59; P.M.D., Harvard U., 1971; m. Sally Nancy Sibley, Dec. 17, 1960; children—Elizabeth, Paul, Robert, Jennifer. With Socony Mobil Oil Co., Paulsboro, N.J., 1955-60, Comml. Solvents Corp., Terre Haute, 1960-62; with Marathon Oil Co., Findlay, Ohio, 1962-74; founder, pres., chief exec. officer Tampimex Petroleum Corp., Houston, 1974-78; pres., chief exec. officer Concord Petroleum Corp., Houston, 1978—. Office: 1776 Yorktown St Houston TX 77056

ELLIOTT, RICHARD HOWARD, lawyer; b. Astoria, N.Y., Apr. 30, 1933; B.S. in Bus. Adminstrn., Lehigh U., 1954; J.D. cum laude, U. Pa., 1962; m. Diane S. Schaefer, Nov. 18, 1978; children—Marc Evan, Jonathan Hugh, Eve. Admitted to Pa. bar, 1962; partner firm Clark, Ladner, Fortenbeugh & Young, Phila., 1962-75, Cotlar, Aglow & Elliott, Doylestown, Pa., 1976—. Commr., Pa. Nav. Commn., 1977—. Served with USNR, 1954-59. Mem. Am. Bar Assn., Pa. Bar Assn., Phila. Bar Assn., Bucks County Bar Assn. Democrat. Office: 1795 S Easton Rd Doylestown PA 18901

ELLIOTT, ROBERT ANDREW, food co. exec.; b. Cin., Dec. 17, 1947; s. Robert M. and Mary E. (Sullivan) E.; B.S. in Bus. Adminstrn., Marquette U., 1970; m. Rosemary Zupan. Sales rep. H.J. Heinz Corp., Indpls., 1970-73, dist. sales asst., Buffalo, 1973-74, area mgr., Syracuse, N.Y., 1974-78, spl. assignment, Pitts., 1978—. Mem. Am. Mktg. Assn. Home: 528B Guyasuta Rd Pittsburgh PA 15215 Office: PO Box 57 Pittsburgh PA 15230

ELLIOTT, SHEILA HOLLIHAN, arts co. exec.; A.B. in Physics, Vassar Coll., 1967; M.S. in Mgmt. Sci., Fairleigh Dickinson U., 1979; m. John T. Elliott; 1 son, Gilbert J. Creative dir. Graphic for Industry, Inc., Englewood, N.J., 1967-76. v.p. fin., 1976—; sr. bus. systems analyst Thomas J. Lipton, Inc., 1978—; producer (public service films) American Phenomenon, 1973, Historic Preservation, 1975, Daniel Chester French 1850-1931, 1976; (presentation film) Advertising Council, 1974. Active in the arts, public service, films and hist. preservation; rep. to Federated Art Assns. N.J., 1977. Recipient Gold award N.Y. Internat. Film and TV Festival, 1973, Bronze award, 1974, 75, Silver award, 1977. Mem. Pastel Soc. Am. (spl. advisor to bd. 1978, dir. 1978), Soc. Illustrators, Nat. Trust Hist. Preservation. Contbg. editor: Condensed Computer Encyclopedia, 1968. Office: Graphics for Industry 231 Liberty Rd Englewood NJ 07631

ELLIOTT, WILLIAM MICHAEL, mfg. co. exec.; b. Leavenworth, Kans., Apr. 18, 1934; s. James E. and Grace M. E.; B.A., U. Mo., 1959, J.D., 1962; m. Maria Esther Vega, Apr. 30, 1959; children—Carmen Marissa, Stephanie Lynn. Admitted to Mo. bar, 1962, Mich. bar, 1965, Calif. bar, 1968, Md. bar, 1975, D.C. bar, 1977; counsel Mobil Oil Co., 1962-68; gen. counsel, sec. Martin Marietta Aluminum, Bethesda, Md., 1968-77; sec. Martin Marietta Corp., Bethesda, 1974-77; sr. v.p., gen. counsel, sec. Northrop Corp., Los Angeles, 1977—. Served with USMC, 1953-56. Victor Wilson scholar. Mem. Am. Bar Assn., Los Angeles County Bar Assn., Century City Bar Assn. Office: 1800 Century Park E Los Angeles CA 90067

ELLIOTT, WILLIAM STOWE, moving co. exec.; b. Summit, N.J., June 21, 1949; came to Can., 1978; s. John Frank and Frances Gibson (Pendleton) E.; B.S., Yale U., 1971; M.B.A., Harvard U., 1976; m. Elizabeth Meyer, Oct. 6, 1979. Mgmt. cons., Boston, 1974-76; dir. ops. N. Am. Van Lines, Ft. Wayne, Ind., 1976, dir. mktg. Electronics div., 1977-78; pres. N. Am. Van Lines Can., Ltd., Whitby, Ont., 1978—; instr. Grad. Fin., St. Francis Coll., Ft. Wayne, 1978. Adv., Jr. Achievement, Ft. Wayne, 1976—. Served to lt., submarine service USN, 1971-74. Mem. Canadian Assn. Movers (dir. 1978-80), Am. Trucking Assn. Home: 45 Livingston Rd West Hill ON M1E 1K8 Canada Office: 1150 Champlain Ave Whitby ON L1N 6A8 Canada

ELLIS, ALPHEUS LEE, banker; b. Elba, Ala., Feb. 5, 1906; s. Osceola Alpheus and Lillie (Lee) E.; student U. Ala., Ala. Poly. Inst.; m. Helen Lansden, Apr. 11, 1936; 1 dau., Helen Carol Ellis Martin. Chmn. bd. dirs. Ellis Banking Corp., Tarpon Springs, Fla., Ellis 1st Nat. Bank, Tarpon Springs; pres., treas., dir. Carlen Realty Co., Tarpon Springs; dir. Fed. Res. Bank Atlanta, 1968-73, Ellis Sarasota Bank and Trust Co. Mem. Fla. Council of 100. Bd. dirs. Anclote Psychiat. Center, Tarpon Springs, Children's Home Soc. Fla.; past dir. South Fla. Mus., Bradenton; past trustee Banking Sch. of South Baton Rouge, New. Coll., Sarasota; trustee U. Tampa, Fla. So. Coll., Lakeland; mem. pres.'s council U. S.Fla. Named Citizen of Year, 1971; Champion of Higher Ind. Edn. in Fla., Presidents of Ind. Colls. and Univ. of Fla., 1973-74, Boss of Year, Am. Bus. Women's Assn., 1977; recipient award City of Tarpon Springs, numerous others. Mem. Fla. C. of C. (past dir.), Am., Fla. So. (past mem. governing council), Fla. (past mem. exec. council, past dir., pres. 1962-63), bankers assns., Theta Chi. Methodist. Mason. (Shriner, Jester), Elk. Clubs: Rotary (past pres.); University, Tower (Tampa); Tarpon Springs Yacht, Innisbrook Golf and Country, Elks (Tarpon Springs); University, Field Yacht, Longboat Key Golf and Tennis (Sarasota). Home: 518 Riverside Dr Tarpon Springs FL 33589 Office: PO Box 1225 Tarpon Springs FL 33589

ELLIS, DARRYL J., bus. exec.; b. Chgo., July 25, 1947; s. Bernard and Ethel (Maultz) E.; B.A., U. Wis., 1968; M.S., Roosevelt U., 1972; M.B.A., Northwestern U. Grad. Sch. Mgmt., 1974; m. Doreen R. Kostel, May 28, 1972. Mgmt. trainee Bank of Lincolnwood (Ill.), 1968-70; asst. to pres. Les-On-Drugs, Inc., Chgo., 1970-72; asst. dir. profit planning Baxter Labs., Deerfield, Ill., 1974, sr. fin. analyst, 1974-75; asst. dir. planning Estech, Inc., subs. Esmark, Inc., Chgo., 1975-77, dir. planning and analysis, 1976-78, mgr. strategy devel.-strategic planning op., 1978, mgr. mktg. dental systems op., 1978—; pres. Resource Tech. Devel. Corp. and prin. SRA, Milw., 1980—; adj. bus. faculty Harper Coll.; mem. faculty U. Wis. Home: 1130 E Lexington Blvd Whitefish Bay WI 53217

ELLIS, DELBERT RILEY, mortgage banker; b. Newberg, Oreg., June 11, 1932; s. Delbert Herman and Maxine Elliott (Smith) E.; B.S., Oreg. State U., 1955; m. Jessie Grace Garrick, Oct. 25, 1952; children—Debra S., Kristi Ann, Teresa Kay. Staff acct. Ernst & Ernst, Portland, Oreg., 1957-65, sr. acct., 1957-60, supr., 1960-62, mgr., 1962-65; fin. v.p. Commonwealth, Inc. (co. name changed to Amfac Mortgate Corp. 1973), Portland, 1965-69, exec. v.p., 1969-70, pres., dir., 1970—; trustee Oreg. Physicians Service. Served to capt. USAF, 1955-57. C.P.A., Oreg. Mem. Nat. Assn. Accts., Am. Inst. C.P.A.'s, Oreg. Soc. C.P.A.'s, Mortgage Bankers Assn. Am., Oreg. Mortgage Bankers (pres. 1977-78). Clubs: Arlington, Univ., Multnomah Athletic, Waverly Country. Office: Amfac Mortgage Corp 2525 SW 3d St Portland OR 97201

ELLIS, DOROTHY J. CARPENTER (MRS. GENE GREGORY ELLIS), Realtor; b. Phila., Aug. 20, 1938; d. Alfred Barrett and Dorothy Aiken (Buzby) Carpenter; student Northwestern U., 1956, U. Miami, 1963; grad. Realtor Inst., 1970; student Harper Coll., 1978—; m. Gene Gregory Ellis, Jan. 24, 1959 (dec. May 1962); children—Theresa, Laura, Kathleen. Saleswoman Boehmer & Hedlund, Park Ridge, Ill., 1966-68; saleswoman Baird & Warner, Inc., Des Plaines, Ill., 1966-70; v.p., sales mgr. Rich Port, Realtor, Park Ridge, 1970—; bd. dirs. NW Suburban Bd. Realtors. Sec., Einstein Elem. Sch. P.T.A., 1969-71; bd. dirs. Park Ridge YMCA, 1978—; dep. committeewoman, precinct capt. Elk Grove Twp. Republican Orgn.; mem. adv. bd. Oakton Community Coll. C.R.B. (cert. real estate broker), C.R.S. (cert. residential specialist. Mem. Nat. Assn. Realtors (speaker ann. conv. 1972—), Ill. Assn. Realtors (chmn. polit. action com.), Internat. Real Estate Fedn., Realtors Nat. Mktg. Inst., D.A.R., Park Ridge C. of C. Episcopalian. Contbr. articles to trade publs. Office: 800 W Higgins Rd Park Ridge IL 60068

ELLIS, GEORGE EDWIN, JR., chem. engr.; b. Beaumont, Tex., Apr. 14, 1921; s. George Edwin and Julia (Ryan) E.; B.S. in Chem. Engring., U. Tex., 1948; M.S. in Chem. Engring., U. So. Calif., 1958, M.B.A., 1965, M.S. in Mech. Engring., 1968, M.S. in Mgmt. Sci., 1971. Research chem. engr. Tex. Co., Port Arthur, Tex., 1948-51, Long Beach, Calif., Houston, 1952-53, Space and Info. div. N.Am. Aviation Co., Downey, Calif., 1959-61, Magna Corp., Anaheim, Calif., 1961-62; chem. process engr. Ai-Research Mfg. Co., Los Angeles, 1953-57, 57-59; chem. engr. Petroleum Combustion & Engring. Co., Santa Monica, Calif., 1957, Jacobs Engring. Co., Pasadena, Calif., 1957, Sesler & Assos., Los Angeles, 1959; research specialist Marquardt Corp., Van Nuys, Calif., 1962-67; sr. project engr. Conductron Corp., Northridge, Calif., 1967-68; information systems analyst City of Los Angeles Dept. Water and Power, 1969—; instr. thermodynamics U. So. Calif., Los Angeles, 1957—, engr. indsl. and systems engring., 1979—. Served with USAAF, 1943-45. Mem. Am. Chem. Soc., Am. Soc. for Metals, Am. Inst. Chem. Engrs., ASME, Am. Electroplaters Soc., Am. Inst. Indsl. Engrs., Am. Mktg. Assn., Ops. Research Soc. Am., Am. Prodn. and Inventory Control Soc., Am. Assn. Cost Engrs., Nat. Assn. Accts., Phi Lambda Upsilon, Pi Tau Sigma, Alpha Pi Mu. Home: 1344 W 20th St San Pedro CA 90732 Office: 111 N Hope St Los Angeles CA 90012

ELLIS, GILBERT R., diversified finance co. exec.; b. Mo., 1915. With Household Fin. Corp., 1935—, v.p., 1956-63, sr. v.p., 1964-66, exec. v.p., 1966-72, pres., 1972-76, chief exec. officer, 1973—, chmn. bd., 1974—, dir., 1959—; dir. First Chgo. Corp., First Nat. Bank of Chgo., Lockheed Corp., Burbank, Calif. Mem. Nat. Consumer Fin. Assn. (pres. 1975-76, chmn. exec. com. 1976-79). Office: Household Fin Corp Internat Hdqrs 2700 Sanders Rd Prospect Heights IL 60070

ELLIS, JAMES GEORGE, retail exec.; b. Tacoma, Jan. 9, 1947; s. George James and Carol Christine (Webb) E.; B.B.A., U. N.Mex., 1968; M.B.A., Harvard, 1970. Asst. to v.p. ops. Broadway Dept. Stores, Los Angeles, 1970-73, buyer housewares, 1973-76, buyer mens sportswear, 1976-77, div. mdse. mgr. young men's div., 1977-79; div. mdse. mgr. Hub Distbg. Co., Ontario, Calif., 1979—; mem. faculty Grad. Sch. Bus. Adminstrn., U. So. Calif., 1971—. Named Prof. of Year, 1974, Outstanding Young Exec. Los Angeles C. of C., 1978. Mem. Housewares Club So. Calif. (sec.), Harvard Assn. So. Calif., Blue Key. Home: 111 Waterview Playa Del Rey CA 90291 Office: Hub Distbg Co 2501 Guasti Rd Ontario CA 91764

ELLIS, JAMES RICHARD, ins. co. exec.; b. Gallipolis, Ohio, Aug. 4, 1938; s. James Glenburn and Ara Olive (Selby) E.; B.S. in Math., Ohio U., 1963; m. Judith Ann Heermans, Mar. 31, 1961; children—James Richard, Jeffrey Paul. Asst. mgr. consumer loan Ohio Valley Bank, Gallipolis, 1961-64; officer coordinator Ford Motor Credit, Miami, 1964-67; supr. brokerage Provident Life and Accident Ins. Co., Miami, Fla., 1967-70, mgr., New Orleans, 1970-72, mgr. Provident Life and Casualty, N.Y.C., 1972—. Aide to Senator Mark Hatfield, Republican Conv., Miami, 1968. R.H.U. (registered health underwriter). Mem. Nat. Assn. Life Underwriters (vice chmn. health ins. com.), N.Y. Life Underwriters Assn. (chmn. 1975, mem. exec. bd., chmn. health ins. com. 1978-79), Nat. Assn. Health Underwriters (v.p. NE region). Methodist. Club: Mason (Hartsdale, N.Y.). Contbr. articles in field to profl. jours. Home: 11 Aldridge Rd Chappaqua NY 10514 Office: 405 Lexington Ave 49th Floor New York NY 10017

ELLIS, JOHN NIGEL, safety equipment co. exec.; b. Barnsley, Eng., Jan. 19, 1942; s. Benjamin Harold and Kathleen Joan (Briault) E.; came to U.S., 1966, naturalized, 1973; B.Sc., Manchester (Eng.) U., 1963, M.Sc., 1964, Ph.D., 1966; m. Jean Hope Stewart Tillie, 1978; 1 son, John James. Research chemist DuPont, Wilmington, Del., 1966-68; sales rep. Varityper Corp., Wilmington, Del., 1968-70; pres. Research & Trading Corp., Wilmington, Del., 1970—. Mem. Am. Soc. Safety Engrs., Nat. Fire Protection Assn., Indsl. Safety Equipment Assn., Nat. Safety Council, Am. Nat. Standards Inst., Am. Mgmt. Assn. Home: 306 Country Club Dr Wilmington DE 19803 Office: 3101 N Market St Wilmington DE 19802

ELLIS, LARRY EDWARD, state exec.; b. Globe, Ariz., June 25, 1945; s. James William and Margaret Helen (Vuletich) E.; A.A., Phoenix Coll., 1973; B.S., Ariz. State U., 1976; m. Karen Anne Rogers, Oct. 22, 1977; 1 son, Christopher Ray; 1 dau. by previous marriage, Laurie Lynne. Adminstrv. asst. OEO, Chgo., 1969; mgmt. analyst Ariz. Hwy. Dept., Phoenix, 1970-72, adminstrv. asst., 1972-75, tax revenue mgr., 1975-76; adminstrv. asst. Ariz. Dept. Transp., Phoenix, 1976-80, mgmt. analyst, 1980—; instr. Phoenix Coll., 1977—. Supr. vols. Phoenix Union Adult Basic Edn. Program, 1972-73; cubmaster Cub Scouts, 1970-71; asso. adviser Explorer Scouts, 1972-73. Recipient Rural Service award OEO, 1968. Mem. Assn. Systems Mgmt., Am. Mgmt. Assn., Ariz. Edn. Assn., U.S. Chess Fedn., Sigma Iota Epsilon. Office: 1801 W Jefferson St Phoenix AZ 85007

ELLIS, PAUL ANTHONY, mfg. co. exec.; b. Cambridge, Mass., June 5, 1936; s. Joseph John and Alice Ruth (Kinsella) E.; A.B. in French, Boston Coll., 1958; m. Mary Margaret Uhlman, June 4, 1966; children—Jacqueline Marie, Catherine Mary. Tech. sales rep. Polaroid Corp., 1964-69; v.p. mktg. Vivitar Corp., Santa Monica, Calif., 1969-79; sr. v.p. Kiron Corp. subs. Kino Precision Industries Ltd., Carson, Calif., 1979—, also dir. Served to 1st lt., inf., U.S. Army, 1958-63. Republican. Roman Catholic. Club: Pasadena Bicycling. Office: 730 E Kings Hill Pl Carson CA 90746

ELLIS, PETER BEAUMONT STEPHEN, banker; b. Umtali, Zimbabwe, Oct. 22, 1953; came to U.S., 1977; s. Clifford and Dora (Middleman) E.; B.S. cum laude in Bus. Mgmt. (Alvina S. Barret scholar 1978-79), Brigham Young U., 1979; postgrad. M.I.T., 1980; m. Margaret Anne Lewis, Apr. 8, 1976; 1 dau., Norah-Anne. Asst. to traffic mgr. Salisbury (Rhodesia) United Omnibus Co., 1972; pensions clk. govt. pensions office, Salisbury, 1972-73; vol. Mormon Ch., S. Africa, 1973-75; with congressional affairs U.S. Dept. Energy, Washington, 1979; credit analyst Mich. Nat. Bank, Ann Arbor, 1980—. Served as patrol officer Brit. S. Africa Police Force, 1975-77. Mem. Beta Gamma Sigma. Democrat. Mormon. Home: 129 Pickney St Boston MA 02114

ELLIS, RAYMOND JOHN, engr., mfg. co. exec.; b. Birmingham, Eng., June 21, 1932; came to U.S., 1965, naturalized, 1974; s. George Alfred and Florence Mary (Wiggan) E.; Higher Nat. Cert. in Mech. Engring., U. Aston, Birmingham, 1956; Tech. Cert. in Plastics Tech., City and Guilds London, 1953; Diploma, Plastics Inst., Eng., 1953; M.S. in Program Mgmt., West Coast U., 1981; m. Joan Gladys Rosa Trevithick, Sept. 15, 1956; children—Karen Jane, Therese Louise. Process devel. engr. Dunlop Rubber Co., Birmingham, 1955-56; tech. service engr., asst. tech. service mgr. Resinous Chems. Ltd., Durham, Eng., 1956-64; mgr. plastics molding Industrias Unidas S.A., Mexico City, 1964-66; plant engr., chief engr. Lenox Plastics Co., St. Louis, 1966-71; plant mgr. Alladin Plastics, Inc., Gardena, Calif., 1971-73; dir. molding The Olga Co., Van Nuys, Calif., 1973—; pres. Am. Design Moldings, Inc., Van Nuys, 1973—. Served with RAF, 1953-55. Mem. Soc. Plastics Engrs., Council Brit. Socs. Anglican. Club: Mayflower.

ELLIS, ROBERT GRISWOLD, engring. co. exec.; b. Kokomo, Ind., Dec. 28, 1908; s. Ernest Eli and Ethel (Griswold) E.; A.B., Ind. U., 1934; m. Florence S. Fisher, June 28, 1966. Mem. staff Ind. U., Bloomington, 1930-34; researcher Blackett-Sample-Hummert Inc., Chgo., 1934, asst. mgr. merchandising, 1935-36; production mgr. Harvey & Howe, Inc., Chgo., 1936-37; dist. mgr. L.F. Grammes & Sons. Inc., Allentown, Pa., serving Chgo. and Midwest, 1937-45; with Ellis & Co., Chgo. and Park Ridge, Ill., 1945—, pres., chief engr., 1948—, mng. dir., chief engr. Ellis Internat. Co., Chgo. and Park Ridge, Ill., 1965—, chief engr. Ellis Engring. Co., Park Ridge, 1969—. Chmn. Citizens Com. for Cleaner and More Beautiful Park Ridge, 1957-60; trustee, treas. bd. dirs. 1st United Methodist Ch., Park Ridge, 1974-77. Recipient Civic Achievement award City of Park Ridge, 1959. Mem. Soc. Automotive Engrs., Armed Forces Communications and Electronics Assn. (life), Ind. U. Alumni Assn. (life), Quartermaster Assn. (pres. Chgo. chpt. 1957-58), Ind. Acad. Sci., Am. Powder Metallurgy Inst., Ill. Acad. Sci., Mfrs. Agts. Assn. Gt. Britain and Ireland, Internat. Union Comml. Agts. and Brokers, Am. Logistics Assn., Am. Soc. Metals, Indiana Soc. of Chgo. Republican. Clubs: Internat. Trade, Union League, Varsity (pres. 1957), Ind. U. (pres. 1956-57) (Chgo.). Home: 643 Parkwood St Park Ridge IL 60068 Office: Box 344 306 Busse Hwy Park Ridge IL 60068

ELLIS, ROBERT PEELE, III, real estate broker; b. Wilson, N.C., June 19, 1938; s. Robert Peele, II, and Ruth (Hawkins) E.; student pub. schs., Wilson, N.C.; m. Loris Ann Yelineck, Oct. 1, 1960; children—John H., Robert D., Marjorie E., Edwin B. Broker, Routh Robbins Real Estate Corp., Alexandria, Va., 1962-65, Lucey Realty Service, Madison, Wis., 1966-71; broker, McKy Ellis Realty Inc., Madison, 1972—, also v.p., sec.; dir. Bank of Shorewood Hills; mem. Wis. Real Estate Examining Bd., 1975—, chmn., 1975-79; pres. Wis. Real Estate Rev. Mem. Wis. Vets. Bd., 1974-76; vice chmn. Dane County (Wis.) Cancer Assn., 1976. Served with USAF, 1956-60. Mem. Nat. Assn. Realtors, Madison Bd. Realtors, Mendota Assn., Wis. Realtors Assn. Democrat. Roman Catholic. Office: 14 N Carroll St Madison WI 53703

ELLIS, WELDON THOMPSON, JR., mgmt. engr.; b. Portsmouth, Va., Oct. 17, 1909; s. Weldon Thompson and Ruth (Phillips) E.; B.S. in Engring., Va. Poly. Inst., 1930, M.S., 1931; M.A., Harvard U., 1933; m. Nancy Sanford Pobst, Sept. 16, 1936; children—Weldon Thompson III (dec.), Nancy M. Pvt. practice architecture, site planner City Planning Commn., Nashville, 1933-34; adminstrv. asst. Tenn. Planning Commn., 1934-35, exec. dir., 1935-39; chief adminstrv. planning Va. Div. Budget, Richmond, 1939-42; cons. Office Emergency Mgmt., Nat. Resources Planning Bd., 1941-42; adminstrv. analyst U.S. Bur. Budget, Washington, 1942, asst. budget and planning officer, 1947-48; chief fed. govt. br. Office CD Planning, Office of Sec. Def., Washington, 1948-49; adminstrv. analyst orgn. div. Hdqrs. U.S. Air Force, Washington, 1949-50, dep. dir. manpower and orgn., 1950-55; staff dir. House Subcom. Manpower Utilization, House Post Office and Civil Service Com., 1955-57; chief pub. adminstrn. adviser Govt. Bolivia, 1957-59; chief pub. adminstrn. div. Govt. Pakistan, 1959-60; sr. staff Brookings Inst., 1960-61; cons. U.S. Commn. Edn., 1961-62; dep. exec. dir. Nashville Housing Authority, 1962-64; mgmt. engr. Edwin A. Keeble Assos., Inc., Nashville, 1964-66; mgmt. cons. to USN, others, 1966-73; asst. to exec. dir. State Planning Office, 1973-74; grants coordinator planning sect. Tenn. Dept. Mental Health, 1974-76; mgmt. cons., writer, 1976—; professorial lectr. mgmt. George Washington U.; exec. sec. Air Force Com. Manpower and Personnel; cons. commn. devel. Nat. Resources Planning Bd., 1942; mem. No. Va. Regional Planning Commn., 1948-53, No. Va. Airport Authority Study Com., 1957, Hoover Commn. Staff Study Paperwork Mgmt., Hoover Commn. Work Group on Bus. Machines. Active Republican party, sr. citizens state chmn., 1972, 78; mem. Tenn. State Commn. on Aging; bd. dirs. Commn. on Mental Health, Nashville, Friends of Music, Nashville. Served to capt. AUS, 1942-46. Mem. Am. Inst. Planners (past pres. Washington chpt.), Armed Forces Mgmt. Assn. (past pres., chmn.), Pan Am. Assn. (dir. Central Tenn. chapt.), Nashville Com. Fgn. Relations, Internat. Platform Assn., Am. Soc. Pub. Adminstrn., Am. Acad. Polit. and Social Scis., Council Community Agys. (dir.), Tau Beta Pi. Presbyterian. Club: Rotary. Author articles on human relations, mgmt., sci. Inventor, patentee. Office: 57 Chowning Sq Nashville TN 37205

ELLIS, WILLIAM DONALDSON, hotel exec.; b. Buenos Aires, Argentina, Aug. 4, 1932; s. Richard Marion and Clara (Carey) E.; came to U.S., 1941; student U. Wash., 1955-57; m. Catherine Dixon, Oct. 29, 1966; 1 son, William David. Corporate auditor Westin Hotel Co., Seattle, 1951-58, regional controller, Portland, Oreg., 1963-65, v.p., controller, Seattle, 1971—; controller Hotel Benson, Portland, 1958-63; controller, asst. sec. Century Plaza Hotel, Los Angeles, 1965-71. Area finance chmn. Boy Scouts Am., 1964; bd. dirs. United Air Lines Employees Credit Union, 1975—. Served with USNR, 1949-58. Mem. Internat. Assn. Hospitality Accountants (pres. 1972-73), Hotel-Motel Accts. Assn. So. Calif. (pres. 1967). Republican. Methodist. Club: Kiwanis (pres. 1968-71). Home: 3740 NE 149th Pl Seattle WA 98155 Office: Westin Hotel Co 2001 6th Ave Seattle WA 98121

ELLISON, DONALD EARL, chem. co. exec.; b. Spanish Fork, Utah, July 28, 1947; s. John Armstrong and Willouby Elizabeth (Conder) E.; B.A., Brigham Young U., 1972; M.A., U. No. Colo., 1972; Grad. Cert., U. So. Calif., 1976; Advanced Grad. Cert., Am. U., 1980; m. Susan Ellen Lauper, Jan. 28, 1971; children—Marc John, Eric Clark, Paul Lauper, David Donald. Research asst., office instl. research Brigham Young U., Provo, Utah, 1968-70; dir. student service center for Spl. and Advanced Programs, U. No. Colo., Washington, 1971-72; cons./project safeguard mgr. EPA, Washington, 1972-76; mgr. govt. and industry relations Va. Chems. Inc., Portsmouth, 1976—; v.p. Palmyra Assos., 1972—. Mem. Portsmouth Clean Community Commn., 1977—, vice chmn. schs. com., 1977—. Recipient bronze medal for commendable service U.S. Govt., 1973; named Outstanding Young Man of Va., Va. Jaycees, 1977. Mem. Chem. Mfrs. Assn., Synthetic Organic Chem. Mfrs. Assn., Am. Indsl. Health Council, Dairy and Food Industries Supplies Assn., Drug Chem. and Allied Trade Assn., Wildlife Soc., Portsmouth C. of C., Jr. Chamber Internat. (Va. senate), U.S. Jaycees (nat. chmn.), Alexandria Jaycees (pres.). Mormon. Clubs: Toastmasters; Chemists (N.Y.C.). Home: 3709 Harding Dr Chesapeake VA 23321 Office: 3340 W Norfolk Rd Portsmouth VA 23703

ELLISON, LUTHER FREDERICK, oil co. exec.; b. Monroe, La., Jan. 2, 1925; s. Luther and Gertrude (Hudson) E.; student Emory U., 1943-44; B.S. in Petroleum Engring., Tex. A&M U., 1949, B.S. in Geol. Engring., 1950; m. Frances Z. Williams, July 17, 1948; children—Constance Elizabeth, Carolyn Williams. Jr. petroleum engr. Sun Prodn. Co., Kilgore and McAllen, Tex., 1950-52, area petroleum engr., Garcia Field, Tex., 1952-54, Delhi (La.) unit engr., 1954-60, asst. region supt., Dallas, 1960-62, dist. drilling engr., Corpus Christi, 1962-63, dist. engr., McAllen, 1963-65, supr. engring., Dallas, 1965-66, div. chief petroleum engr., 1966-70, region mgr. engring., 1970-76, region mgr., 1976-78, dir. devel., 1976-80, v.p. devel., 1981—; pres., dir., mem. exec. com. Nabors-Sun Drilling Co.; dir., mem. exec. com. East Tex. Salt & Water Disposal Co. speaker in field. Vice pres. Northwood Jr. High Sch. PTA, Dallas, 1967-68, pres., 1968-69. Served with USNR, 1943-46. Registered profl. engr., Tex., La. Mem. Tex.-Mid-Continent Oil and Gas Assn. (Outstanding Achievement award 1964, chmn. area 1964-65, mgr. north region, operating com.), Am. Petroleum Inst., Soc. Petroleum Engrs., Dallas Engrs. Club, Petroleum Engrs. Club, Dallas Petroleum Club, Parents League, Sigma Alpha Epsilon (pres. 1944-45). Presbyterian (elder). Clubs: Northwood (Dallas), Lions. Home: 3 Castle Creek Ct Dallas TX 75240 Office: 12850 Hillcrest Rd Dallas TX 75230

ELLSWORTH, SUSAN, media cons.; b. Los Angeles, May 7, 1946; d. Theodore R. and Jeanne E.; A.A. in Library Media Tech. magna cum laude, Los Angeles Valley Coll., 1976; postgrad. UCLA extension; 1 dau., Alexandra Susan Hall. Media technician Sunkist Growers, Sherman Oaks, Calif., 1976; audiovisual coordinator St. Joseph Med. Center, Burbank, Calif., 1977; adminstrv. cons., founder, dir. Media Resource Service, Los Angeles, 1977—. Mem. Nat. Micrographics Assn., Assn. Info. Mgrs., Calif. Hist. Soc. Vol. columnist Media Digest, 1978; researcher, author, pub. booklet The Handbook of Motion Picture Film Care, 1978. Home: 9043 Burroughs Rd Los Angeles CA 90046 Office: 3010 Santa Monica Blvd Suite 271 Santa Monica CA 90404

ELMAN, ANNALEE, systems analyst; b. Montreal, Que., Can., Dec. 7, 1941; d. Philip and Bessie (Katz) E.; B.A., McGill U., 1962; M.A., Stanford U., 1970, Ph.D., 1978. High sch. tchr. Protestant Sch. Bd., Montreal, 1963-69; evaluation methodologist, systems analyst Inst. Profl. Devel., San Jose, Calif., 1975-77; program evaluator San Mateo County Employment and Tng. Adminstrn., Redwood City, Calif., 1978-79; dir. data mgmt. Tech. Assistance Center, Am. Inst. for Research, Palo Alto, Calif., 1979—; dir. Job Search Workshops, Inc.; mgmt. and systems cons. ACRE, Inc. Chmn. adv. bd. San Mateo County Health and Welfare, 1979—. Fellow Can. Council, 1971-73. Mem. Am. Ednl. Research Assn., Am. Psychol. Assn., Calif. Acad. Sci. Home: 839 Cordilleras Ave San Carlos CA 94070 Office: Box 1113 Palo Alto CA 94302

ELMES, BADGLEY ALLEN, mfg. co. exec.; b. Ridley Park, Pa., Nov. 13, 1920; s. Clyde C. and Ethel Badgley) E.; B.S. in Bus. Adminstrn., Lehigh U., 1946; m. Elizabeth A. Boyer, Jan 20, 1945; children—Patricia A. (Mrs. David E. Farley), Robert B., Michael B. Salesman, Armstrong Cork Co., 1946-51; dist. mgr. Pyrene Mfg. Co., 1951-53; with Houdaille Industries, Inc., 1953-70, gen. mgr. S.M. Jones Co. div., Toledo, 1962-63, v.p. group exec. Houdaille Industries, Inc., Buffalo, 1963-70; mgmt. cons., 1971; pres., owner Riley Gear Corp., North Tonawanda, N.Y., 1972—. Served to 1st. lt. USMCR, 1942-45. Decorated Air medal. Mem. Phi Gamma Delta. Club: Orchard Park (N.Y.) Country. Presbyterian. Home: 27 Fox Meadow Ln Orchard Park NY 14127 Office: 61 Felton St North Tonawanda NY 14120

ELMS, LEONARD BROOKS, III, rubber products mfg. co. pub. relations exec.; b. N.Y.C., Aug. 27, 1939; s. Leonard Brooks and Nina (Vitale) E.; B.A., Wilmington Coll., 1961; m. Carol Lynne Mac Pherson, Mar. 9, 1968; children—Heather Lee, Leonard Brooks, IV. Gen. mgr. Maidstone Boat Yard, East Hampton, N.Y., 1962-63; sr. account exec. Sta. WLNG, Sag Harbor, N.Y., 1963-65; with Goodyear Tire & Rubber Co., N.Y.C., 1965—, now mem. corporate sr. staff, Akron, Ohio; coll. lectr. on Goodyear blimps. Committeeman United Way, Akron, YMCA, Akron; mem. Akron council Boy Scouts Am. Recipient Pub. Service awards for Goodyear blimp projects; named Hon. Mayor, City of San Antonio, 1968, adm. Tex. Navy, Ky. Col., Ark. Traveler, ambassador HemisFair, 1968. Mem. Pub. Relations Soc. Am. Episcopalian. Home: 682 Palisades Dr Akron OH 44303 Office: 1144 E Market St Akron OH 44316

ELMSTROM, GEORGE, optometrist; b. Salem, Mass., Dec. 11, 1925; s. George and Emily (Wedgewood) E.; O.D., So. Calif. Coll. Optometry, 1951; m. Nancy DePaul, Apr. 29, 1973; children—Pamela, Beverly, Robert. Pvt. practice optometry, El Segundo, Calif., 1951—; instr. So. Calif. Coll. Optometry, U. Calif.; v.p. I.P. Barker Investment Syndicate. Named Writer of Year, Calif. Optometric Assn., 1960; Man of Year, El Segundo, 1957; recipient spl. citation Nat. Eye Found., 1962. Fellow Am. Acad. Optometry, Disting. Service Found. Optometry, AAAS, S.W. Contact Lens Soc., Internat. Acad. Preventive Medicine, Am. Assn. Computer Medicine; mem. Am. Optometric Assn., Am. Public Health Assn., Flying Optometrists Assn. Am., Am. Soc. Ultrasonography, Am. Assn. Research in Vision, Optometric Editors Assn., Internat. Assn. for Ophthalmic Ultrasound, Am. Inst. Med. Climatology, Internat. Coll. Applied Nutrition. Author: Advanced Management for Optometrists, 1974; Optometric Practice Strategies, 1981; Optometric Practice Management, 1963; Legal Aspects of Contact Lens Practice, 1966; Innovative Management Concepts, 1980; contbg. editor Optometric Monthly, Rev. Optometry. Home: 306 Anderson Manhattan Beach CA 90266 Office: 502 Main St El Segundo CA 90245

ELMSTROM, PAUL VICTOR, airline exec.; b. Bklyn., Aug. 27, 1938; s. Harry Gustav and Loretta Mary (Aylward) E.; student U. Md.; m. Theresa K. D'Eredita, Dec. 7, 1963; children—Kathryn, Peter, Emily. Sales agt. Air Can., N.Y.C., 1960-61; sta. mgr. SF&O Helicopter Airlines, Oakland, Calif., 1961; tariff agt. N.E. Airlines, N.Y.C., 1961-63; interline and comml. mgr. Trans Caribbean Airlines, N.Y.C., 1963-64; rep. Air France, N.Y.C., 1964-66; mktg. mgr. N.Am. Sabena Airlines, Lake Success, 1973-74; gen. sales and traffic mgr. U.S., TAP Airline of Portugal, N.Y.C., 1966-72, 74—. Served with U.S. Army, 1955-58. Mem. Am. Soc. Travel Agts. Roman Catholic. Contbr. articles on travel and transp. to jours. Home: 254 Sequams Ln Center West Islip NY 11795 Office: 1140 Ave of Americas New York NY

ELORRIAGA, JOHN AMBROSE, banker; b. Jordan Valley, Oreg., Oct. 20, 1923; s. Ambrose and Maria (Goicoechea) E.; A.A., Boise Jr. Coll., 1949; B.B.A., U. Oreg., 1951; M.B.A., U. Pitts., 1953; grad. Pacific Coast Sch. Banking, 1959; m. Lois Corinne Newman, June 14, 1952; children—Dana W., John M., Sharon P., Steven M., Linda M., Lisa A. Vice-pres. U.S. Nat. Bank, Portland, Oreg., 1951-67; exec. v.p. Evans Products, Portland, 1967-70; pres., chief exec. officer Columbia Corp., Portland, 1970-72; pres. U.S. Nat. Bank Oreg., Portland, after 1972, now chmn. bd., chief exec. officer; dir. U.S. Bancorp; chmn. audit com. Pacific NW Bell Telephone Co.; former instr. Portland State Coll., Am. Inst. Banking, Multnomah Coll. Past chmn. bd. dirs. Jesuit High Sch.; bd. dirs. Better Bus. Bur.; mem. fin. com. Oreg. Physicians' Service; mem. adv. bd. St. Vincent Hosp. and Med. Center, devel. fund U. Oreg.; mem. bus. adv. council Coll. Bus. Adminstrn., U. Oreg. Mem. Portland C. of C. (exec. com.), Oreg. Bankers Assn., Am. Bankers Assn., Am. Inst. Banking, Phi Theta Kappa, Chi Psi. Republican. Roman Catholic. Clubs: Multnomah Athletic, Portland Golf, Arlington, Waverly Country, Eldorado Country. Home: 4011 SW Downs View Ct Portland OR 97221 Office: 309 SW 6th Ave Portland OR 97204

ELSE, WILLIS IRL, bank exec.; b. Fairbury, Nebr., Dec. 24, 1931; s. Irl Roy and Helen Gertrude (Lynch) E.; B.S., Northwestern U., 1953; M.S., U. Ill., 1958; postgrad. U. Chgo., 1959-63; m. Marion Essie Eggers, Dec. 23, 1961; children—Sharon Lee, John Frazer, Robert Irl. Asst. cashier First Nat. Bank of Chgo., 1962-67, asst. v.p., 1967-69; v.p. Citibank, N.A., N.Y.C., 1969-76; pres., chief exec. officer, dir. Akron Nat. Bank, 1977-79; pres. No. Group, BancOhio

Nat. Bank, Akron, 1979—; pres., dir. Akron Small Bus. Devel. Corp., Geneal. Systems, Inc.; dir. Else Investment Co., Fairbury, Nebr.; sec., dir. Fairbury Ins. Agy. Vice-pres., trustee Akron Regional Devel. Bd., 1977—; chmn. Akron Econ. Devel. Adv. Council, 1979—; mem. Akron Action Com.; trustee Akron City Hosp., also chmn. ins. com.; trustee Akron City Hosp. Found., U. Akron Devel. Found. Served with U.S. Army, 1953-56. Mem. Am. Bankers Assn., Am. Statis. Assn., Robert Morris Assos., Soc. Genealogists. Republican. Lutheran. Clubs: Portage Country, Cascade, Akron City. Author: A Handbook of Legal and Ethical Restrictions on Financial Advertising, 1964. Office: I Cascade Plaza Akron OH 44308 also 1404 E 9th St Cleveland OH 44114 also 155 E Broad St Columbus OH 43265

ELSEY, CLEO ADOLPHUS, cons.; b. Bartlesville, Okla., Aug. 19, 1918; s. Raymond William and Delilah Beatrice (Mickels) E.; student Tulsa Bus. Coll., 1937, Internat. Corr. Schs., 1938-40, U. Hawaii, 1944-45, Okla. State U., 1951-52, Washington U., St. Louis, 1966-67; m. Mary Martha McFarland, Feb. 22, 1941; children—Diana Cecilia, Christopher Alfred, Rose Marie, Katherine Ann. Sect. chief def. plant div. Phillips Petroleum Co., Bartlesville, Okla., 1942-43, mgr. cost estimation and cost evaluation sect., 1945-54; research and devel. Elsey Corp., Bartlesville, Okla., 1954-62; pres., mgr. Elsey Mfg. Co., Enid, Okla., 1958-62; project mgr. McDonnell Aircraft Co., St. Louis, 1962-67; cons. Commonwealth Assos., Inc., Jackson, Mich., 1968-71; cons. product devel. and mfg. oil field prodn. and natural gas industry, 1971—; devel. mgr. Ingersoll-Rand Co., Baxter Springs, Kans., 1972-77; project mgr. research and devel. Fennix & Scissons, Inc., Tulsa, 1977—. Served with USNR, 1943-45. Registered profl. engr. control systems, Calif. Mem. Instrument Soc. Am. Designer, builder environ. space chambers for testing of Gemini space capsule, valves and control items for petroleum industry. Home: 330 22d Baxter Springs KS 66713 Office: Fennix and Scisson Inc PO Box 15609 Tulsa OK 84115

ELSEY, GEORGE MCKEE, orgn. exec.; b. Palo Alto, Calif., Feb. 5, 1918; s. Howard McKee and Ethel May (Daniels) E.; A.B., Princeton U., 1939; A.M., Harvard U., 1940; m. Sally Phelps Bradley, Dec. 15, 1951; children—Anne Bradley (Mrs. Roger Kranz), Howard McKee. Mem. staff White House, 1947-53; with Nat. ARC, 1953-61, v.p., 1958-61, pres., 1970—; with various divs. Pullman, Inc., Washington, 1961-65, asst. to chmn. and pres., 1966-70; dir. Am. Security Bank, Am. Security Corp., Peoples Life Ins. Co., Security Storage Co., Perpetual Fed. Savs. & Loan. Trustee emeritus Nat. Trust for Hist. Preservation, 1976—; pres. Meridian House Found., Washington, 1961-66, vice chmn., 1967-68, trustee, 1969-71, counselor, 1971—; mem. Nat. Archives Adv. Council, 1974-79; trustee Nat. Geog. Soc., Brookings Instn., 1971—, Harry S. Truman Library Inst., George C. Marshall Research Found. Served to comdr. USNR, 1941-47. Decorated Legion of Merit, Order Brit. Empire; recipient Disting. Public Service medal Dept. Def.; medal Finnish Red Cross, Korean Red Cross Soc. Mem. English-Speaking Union, Columbia Hist. Soc., AAAS, Conf. Bd., White House Hist. Assn. (dir. 1979—), Phi Beta Kappa. Presbyterian (ruling elder). Clubs: Princeton (N.Y.); Met., City Tavern Assn. (Washington). Home: 2201 King Pl NW Washington DC 20007 Office: 17th and D Sts NW Washington DC 20006

EL SHAHAWY, SALAH, investment exec.; b. Egypt, June 27, 1929; came to U.S., 1964, naturalized, 1969; s. Ahmed Ali and Amina (Kahalil) El S.; LL.M., Ein Shas U., Cairo, 1957; 1 dau., Shireen. Research dir. Amott, Baker & Co., 1965-69; internat. petroleum specialist Bach & Co., 1969-71; v.p. D.H. Blair & Co., N.Y.C., 1971-72, Sartorious Co., N.Y.C., 1972-74, Advest Co., N.Y.C., 1974-75; pres. Shahawy Investment div. Bruns, Nordeman, Rea & Co., N.Y.C., 1975—; dir. L.I. U. Bus. Sch. Bus. Game Com.; dir. China Trade Corp. Moslem. Home: 412 E 55th St New York NY 10022 Office: 625 Madison Ave New York NY 10022

ELWOOD, JOHN PAUL, mfg. co. exec.; b. Batavia, Ill., July 23, 1944; s. John Franklin and Arleene Wilma (Kuhn) E.; B.A., Northwestern U., 1966; Ph.D., M.I.T., 1971; m. Barbara Ann Milner, Feb. 15, 1969; children—Craig Douglas, Carrie Alexis. Research mgr. Internat. Paper Co., N.Y.C., 1970-72, research planner, 1972-74, mgr. bus. analysis, 1974-76, mgr. resource recovery/solid waste policy, 1976—; adj. instr. bus. Bergen Community Coll., Paramus, N.J., 1975—. Mem. Library Bd., Greenwood Lake, N.Y., 1975-77; pres. Fathers Club of Tuxedo Park Sch., 1979-80. Mem. Am. Inst. Chem. Engrs., ASME, Am. Chem. Soc., ASTM. Clubs: M.I.T., Tuxedo, Northwestern U. Contbr. articles to profl. jours. Home: Cannon Hill Rd Tuxedo Park NY 10987

ELY, ALLEN JUDSON, JR., investment co. exec.; b. Elizabeth, N.J., Jan. 13, 1925; s. Allen Judson and Elizabeth (Fehl) E.; B.S. in Mech. Engring., Lehigh U., 1947; m. Cecilia Arroyo, June 10, 1978; children—Elizabeth Ely Morris, Margaret Ely Hixson, Allen Judson, Scott David. Engr., Standard Oil Co. N.J., Linden, 1947; engr. Taylor Forge Inc., Chgo., 1947-70, prodn. control mgr., 1954-56, mgr. engring., 1956-62, v.p. engring., 1962-64, v.p. mfg., 1964-70; pres. Tinnie Merc. Co., Roswell, N.Mex., 1970-80; chmn., pres., dir. Globe Universal Scis., Inc., El Paso, 1970; pres., dir. Hyer Boot Co., El Paso, 1970—, chmn., 1980—; pres. Cotter Corp., Golden, Colo., 1971-74; dir. Sunbell Corp., Albuquerque, Realities Inc., Denver. Served with U.S. Mcht. Marine, 1944-46. Address: Hyer Boot Co Box 9637 El Paso TX 79986

ELY, WINSTON THEODORE, clothing mfg. co. exec.; b. Detroit, Sept. 2, 1918; s. Roy Sanford and Leigh (Ryan) E.; ed. in Toronto, Ont., Can.; m. Barbara Grace Spalding, Apr. 27, 1940; children—Edward Winston, Judith Leigh, Bartlett Spalding. Mng. dir. Sunshine Uniform Supply Co., Ltd., Toronto, 1940-46; pres. Ely Corp., Detroit, 1950-67, Detroit Overall Mfg. Co., 1960-67, Winston Uniform Co., Double Springs, Ala., 1963—; chmn. bd. Garment Corp. Am., Miami, Fla., 1967—, Cadillac Mfg. Co., Mayaguez, P.R., 1968—, Cadillac Shirt Corp., Mayaguez, 1968—. Spl. hon. cons. Puerto Rican Econ. Devel. Adminstrn., 1963—. Mem. Founders Soc., Detroit Inst. Arts. Republican. Methodist. Home: 9048 SW 62d Terr Miami FL 33173 Office: Garment Corp Am 9150 SW 87th Ave Miami FL 33176 also Cadillac Industries Box 435 Mayaguez PR 00708

ELZAS, JOHN PAUL, loan co. exec.; b. Amsterdam, Holland, Oct. 16, 1917; s. Benjamin Van and Annie Cornelia (Boekman) E.; B.A., Coll. Commerce, St. Gall, Switzerland, 1935; m. Suzanne Castel, Mar. 7, 1945; children—Anne, Pauline, Albert. Pres., Peoples Fin. and Thrift Co., Beverly Hills, Calif., 1960-70; pres. Calif. Thrift and Loan, 1970-73; pres. Imperial Thrift & Loan, Beverly Hills, 1973—; chief exec. officer Imperial Plan, Inc. Pres., Hidden Valley Mcpl. Water Dist., 1960-72. Served with Royal Dutch Army, 1943-45. Mem. Calif. Assn. Thrift and Loan Cos. (dir.). Republican. Clubs: Rotary. Office: 110 N Doheny Dr Beverly Hills CA 90211

ELZE, MARTIN JAY, real estate developer; b. Lewisburg, Pa., Feb. 11, 1952; s. Warren Earl and Nora Marie (Giavelli) E.; B.S. in Mgmt., Embry-Riddle Aero. U., 1976, A.S. in Aviation Mgmt., 1976; m. Virginia Cecilia Zembrzuski, Aug. 9, 1980. Shop foreman Lahout Air Service, Lewisburg, 1971-72; data processing control specialist Olivetti Corp., Somerville, N.J., 1976-78, auditor, mgmt. cons., 1978; exec. v.p. L-Z, Inc., Lewisburg, 1978—; cons. advt., mktg., inventory control. Hon. mem. Lewisburg Mchts. Council, 1978-79. Mem. Embry-Riddle Vets. Assn., Army Aviation Assn. Am., Icarus Honor Soc., Omicron Delta Kappa. Club: Sun Corvette.

EMBER, NORMAN ALLEN, clothing co. exec.; b. N.Y.C., May 4, 1925; s. Max William and Ida (Tribijovskia) E.; B.S., Columbia, 1950, M.A., 1953; m. Susan Cohen, Feb. 14, 1974; children by previous marriage—Max, Peter, Richard. Pres. Silverstyle Dress Co., Inc., N.Y.C., 1965—, Ember Industries, Inc., N.Y.C., 1969—, The Sew-In Inc., N.Y.C., 1971—. Served with inf., AUS, 1943-46. Decorated Bronze Star medal, Purple Heart with oak leaf cluster. Clubs: Columbia U. (N.Y.C.); Knickerbocker Yacht (Manhasset, N.Y.). Contbr. articles to profl. jours. Office: 501 7th Ave New York City NY 10018

EMCH, ARNOLD F(REDERICK), mgmt. cons.; b. Manhattan, Kans., Nov. 3, 1899; s. Arnold and Hilda (Walters) E.; A.B., U. Ill., 1925, A.M., 1926; postgrad. U. Chgo., 1930; Ph.D., Harvard, 1934; m. Minna Libman, July 22, 1927 (dec. Sept. 1958); m. 2d, Eleanore Merckens, June 30, 1960; children—Arnold Devere, Frederick Bolebec. Pres., Emch Constrn. Co., Wichita, Kans., 1920-22; regional dir. Tamblyn & Brown Co., 1926-29; exec. dir. Chgo. Hosp. Council, 1936-39, asso., 1967-70; asso. dir. Am. Hosp. Assn., 1939-42, Chgo. Inst. for Hosp. Adminstrn., U. Chgo., 1939-42; mgr. Booz, Allen & Hamilton, mgmt. consultants, Chgo., 1942-48, partner, 1948-62; cons. Booz, Allen & Hamilton, Inc., 1962—. Pvt. cons., breeder Arabian horses; dir., cons. Call-Time Petroleum Corp., 1967-70; pres. North End Water Co., 1965-67, sec.-treas., 1967—; sec.-treas. Eagle Rock Ranches, 1971—. Dir. Internat. U.S.O. Survey, 1962-63. Trustee William A. White Psychiat. Found., Washington, 1945—, v.p., 1947—, pres., 1948-52; bd. dirs. Washington Sch. Psychiatry, 1946-56, Mental Health Soc. Greater Chgo., Inc., 1958-60, Council Hosp. Planning and Resources Devel., Colo., 1961—. Served with AEF, France, 1918-19; comdr. USNR, mgmt. cons. to surgeon gen. of Navy, 1942-45, hon. cons., 1945—. Recipient Wisdom award of honor and elected to Nat. Wisdom Hall of Fame, 1970. Mem. Am. Philos. Assn., A.A.A.S., Shakespearean Authorship Soc., Chi Psi. Clubs: Harvard (Chgo., Denver). Author: Uncommon Letters To A Son, 1965; A Field Guide to Life and Love, 1968; Crowded Years, 1969; also articles in profl. jours. Office: Glory Ranch Devils Gulch Rd Estes Park CO 80517

EMDEN, NARVIN IRA, savs. and loan assn. exec.; b. Cin., Nov. 5, 1921; s. Leo and Elizabeth (Orlin) E.; B.B.A., U. Cin., 1948, J.D., 1949; m. Ruth Cohen, June 4, 1950; children—Lisa, Craig, Faith, Julie. Admitted to Ohio bar, 1949; mng. officer, then exec. v.p. Found. Savs. & Loan Co., Cin., 1949-79, pres., 1979—, also dir. Served with AUS, 1942-46. Mem. Savs. and Loan League Southwestern Ohio (pres. 1974), Fin. Mgrs. Soc. Savs. Instns., Ohio Bar Assn., Cin. Bar Assn. Jewish. Office: 719 Vine St Cincinnati OH 45202

EMERICH, JOSEPH RICHARD, investment mgmt. exec.; b. Merrill, Wis.; s. Stanley Miles and Lorraine Erma (Kuester) E.; B.B.A., U. Wis., 1956; M.B.A., U. Chgo., 1959; m. Georgia Lee Giroux, Oct. 5, 1957; children—Richard, Elizabeth, James. With No. Trust Co., Chgo., 1956-72; with Dreyfus Mgmt., Inc., N.Y.C., 1972—, exec. v.p., 1977—. Treas., First Ch. of Christ, Scientist, New Canaan, Conn., 1977-79. Served with USNR, 1952-55. Chartered fin. analyst. Mem. Investment Analysts Soc. Chgo., Fin. Analysts Fedn. Home: 51 Sagamore Trail New Canaan CT 06840

EMERICK, PAUL EDWARD, contractor; b. Portland, Oreg., Oct. 18, 1924; s. Paul B. and Elva J. (Robbins) E.; B.S., Oreg. State U., 1948; m. Patricia Carol Burnett, May 12, 1967; children—Diane (Mrs. Mike Kunze), Paula (Mrs. Don Peoples), Loree (Mrs. Donald Schlanlen), Jenny (Mrs. Steven Entenman), Steven Paul, Steven Matthew Opgenorth, Carol Opgenorth. Apprentice, carpenter supr., project mgr., chief estimator, operations mgr., pres., chmn. bd. Emerick Constrn. Co., Portland, 1946—; chmn. bd. McCormack Constrn. Co., Pendleton, Oreg. Chmn. Asso. Gen. Contractors/State of Okla. Curricula; mem. Fed. Com. Apprenticeship, 1974—. Bd. dirs. Gilbert Sch. Dist., 1953-60, Mt. Hood Community Coll. Vocat. Tech. Citizens Adv. Com., 1966-68, Ore. State U. Indsl. Edn. Tchr. Edn. Program, 1970-71, Benson Poly. Indsl. Edn. Tchr. program, Career Edn. Com., Portland Pub. Schs., 1970, State of Oreg. Apprenticeship Info. Center, 1967-69, Oreg. State U. Constrn. Edn. Research Found.; trustee Nat. Laborers/Asso. Gen. Contractors Tng. Trust, Oreg. Constrn. Industry Advancement Fund. Recipient Safe Pilot award Nat. Pilots Assn., 1970; named Contractor of Yr., Oreg. Bldg. Congress, 1973, Com. Chmn. of Yr., Nat. Asso. Gen. Contractors, 1973. Mem. Nat. Asso. Gen. Contractors (dir., com. chmn., past pres. Oreg.-Columbia chpt., nat. committeeman 1979), Pacific N.W. Contractors (chmn. 1973), Portland C. of C., Am. Inst. Constructors, Oreg. Sch. Bd. Assn., Nat. Pilots Assn., Delta Sigma Rho. Clubs: Rotary, Multnomah Athletic, Columbia Aviation, Riverside Golf and Country. Home: Rt 2 Box 1355 Estacada OR 97023 Office: POB 66176 Portland OR 97266

EMERSON, ANDI (MRS. EMERSON WEEKS), sales and advt. exec.; b. N.Y.C.; d. Willard Ingham and Ethel (Mole) E.; student Barnard Coll.; m. George G. Fawcett, Jr. (div.); children—Ann Emerson II, George Gifford III, Christopher Babcock; m. 2d, Kenneth E. Weeks (div.); 1 dau., Electra Ingham. Successively account exec. Smith Hagel & Snyder, N.Y.C., pres. Emerson Assos., Inc., N.Y.C.; exec. v.p. Eugene Stevens, Inc., N.Y.C., 1956-60; pres., dir. Emerson-Weeks & Fawcett Corp., N.Y.C., 1960-78; pres., dir. Emerson Mktg. Agy., Inc., N.Y.C., 1979—; pres., dir. Mail Order Operating Co. Ltd., N.Y.C. and London, 1976—; pres., dir. Ingham Hall, Ltd., 1977—; instr. N.Y. U., 1960-65. Block chmn. fund raising ARC, Multiple Sclerosis, Nat. Found., Crippled Children, Found. for Blind, 1954-63; vol. worker Children's Ward, Meml. Hosp., 1964-66, Hosp. for Spl. Surgery, 1967; mem. adv. com. African Students League, 1965-67; bd. dirs. Violet Oakley Meml. Found., Phila., 1964—. Mem. Direct Mail Mktg. Assn., Sales Promotion Execs., Advt. Club, Mktg. Execs. Club, Mail Order Profls. Group, Soc. Profl. Writers, Direct Mktg. Creative Guild (pres. 1975—). Clubs: Ex-Mems. Squadron A, Hundred Million (treas. 1960-61), N.Y. Jr. League, Barnard. Office: 44 E 29th St New York NY 10016

EMERSON, ANDREW CRAIG, life ins. co. exec.; b. Ft. Wayne, Ind., Feb. 11, 1929; s. Kenton Craig and Lucille Katherine (Godfrey) E.; B.S., Purdue U., 1951; LL.B., Ind. U., 1953, M.B.A., 1958; m. Marilyn A. Kling, June 17, 1951; children—Daniel C., Mark S., John A., Michael A. Admitted to Ind. bar, 1953, practiced in South Bend, 1953; research asso. Ind. U. Sch. Law, 1956-58; with Indpls. Life Ins. Co., 1958—, gen. counsel, 1968-73, v.p., gen. counsel, 1973—. Pres. Broad Ripple High Sch. Assn. Parents and Tchrs., Indpls., 1973-75; chmn. Crossroads of Am. council Boy Scouts Am., 1977-78. Served with USAF, 1953-56. Mem. Assn. Ind. Life Ins. Cos. (sec.-treas.), Ind. State Bar Assn. (com. chmn.), Am. Council Life Ins., Indpls. Bar Assn., Ind. State Bar Assn., Am. Bar Assn., Estate Planning Council Indpls. Presbyterian. Club: Sertoma (pres. club 1973-74). Home: 5671 Central Indianapolis IN 46220 Office: PO Box 1230B Indianapolis IN 46206

EMERSON, DONALD MCGEACHY, JR., appraisal co. exec.; b. Clearwater, Fla., Oct. 21, 1952; s. Donald McGeachy and Ann (Parker) E.; B.S. in Bus. Adminstrn. and Real Estate, U. Fla., 1975, M.A. in Real Estate, 1976. Asso. appraiser Don Emerson Appraisal Co., Gainesville, Fla., 1973-75, v.p., 1975—; treas. Emerson Realty, Inc., 1977—. Registered real estate broker, Fla. Mem. Gainesville Bd. Realtors, Nat. Assn. Realtors, Soc. Real Estate Appraisers (asso. mem.), Southeastern Interfraternity Conf. (program dir. 1975-76), U. Fla. Interfrat. Council (pres. 1974-75), Fla. Blue Key (treas. 1976-77), Fraternity Purchasing Assn. (chmn. bd. 1979—), Order of Omega (pres. U. Fla. chpt. 1975-76), Centurion Council (pres. 1981—), Delta Tau Delta. Democrat. Roman Catholic. Home: PO Box 113 Gainesville FL 32602 Office: PO Box 882 Gainesville FL 32602

EMERSON, GEORGE HENRY, wood products mfg. co. exec.; b. Boston, Mar. 14, 1947; s. George Henry and Dorothy Fuller (Adams) E.; B.S., Norwich U., 1969; m. Susan Springer Bench, July 25, 1969; children—Wendy Susan, Jennifer Ann. Asst. retail sales mgr. Sears, Roebuck and Co., Chgo., 1972-75, sales promotional mgr., 1975-76; nat. accounts mgr. Cornwall Industries, Inc., South Paris, Maine, 1976-77, sales mgr., 1977-79, v.p., 1979—. Vestryman, Ch. of Our Savior, Elmhurst, Ill., 1976; bd. dirs. Oxford Hill YMCA, 1977-78, Child Health Center, Norway, Maine. Republican. Home: PO Box 1 Paris ME 04271 Office: PO Box 219 South Paris ME 04281

EMERY, MELISSA MILLER, consumer products co. exec.; b. Evanston, Ill., Feb. 18, 1949; d. Louis R. and Jean P. (Russell) Miller; B.S. in Bus. Econs., Purdue U., 1971; M.B.A., Northwestern U., Chgo., 1972; m. James K. Emery, Apr. 28, 1979. Asso. buyer Procter and Gamble Co., Cin., 1972-73; package devel. specialist Chesebrough-Pond's Co., Greenwich, Conn., 1973-75, asst. product mgr., 1975-76, product mgr., 1977—. Mem. Am. Mgmt. Assn., Assn. M.B.A.'s. Club: Stanwich Country. Office: Chesebrough Ponds Inc 33 Benedict Pl Greenwich CT 06830

EMERY, WALTER CARPENTER, bank exec.; b. Denver, Aug. 5, 1918; s. Roe and Jeannette (Carpenter) E.; B.S., Yale U., 1942; m. Jaynn Mann, June 23, 1944; children—Roe, Victoria Emery Wilson, Sloan E. Asst. gen. mgr. Rocky Mountain Motor Co., Denver, 1946-51; v.p. Glacier Park Transp. Co., East Glacier Park, Mont., 1951-56; investment cons., 1956-60; pres. Bank of Denver, 1960-77, chmn., chief exec. officer, 1977—. Commr., Denver Urban Renewal Authority, 1960—; mem. exec. com. Nat. Western Stock Show Assn., 1968—; trustee, Denver Found., 1976—. Served to capt. U.S. Army, 1942-46. Decorated Bronze Star with oak leaf cluster. Mem. Ind. Bankers Am. (mem. legis. com.), Ind. Bankers Colo., Colo. Hist. Soc. Democrat. Episcopalian. Clubs: Denver, Denver Country, Rotary, Masons. Office: 1534 California St Denver CO 80217

EMETT, ROBERT LYNN, ins. exec.; b. Oxnard, Calif., Aug. 9, 1927; s. Edward Lewellyn and Isabel (Vaughan) E.; student Webb Sch. Calif.; B.A., Claremont Men's Coll., 1950; children—Robert Charles, Lindy Louise, James Stewart, Michael Scott. Underwriter, Swett & Crawford, 1950; account exec. Emett & Chandler, 1951-54, office mgr., 1954-57, San Francisco mgr., 1957-60, Los Angeles dir., 1957-60, v.p., gen. mgr., 1961-62, pres., 1962-68; pres. Pinehurst Corp., Los Angeles, 1968-73, chmn. bd., 1973—; dir. Emett & Chandler, Risk Mgmt. Inc., R.L. Kautz Co., Presidio Ins. Co., Pinehurst Mgmt. Co., Ltd., Transworld Ins. Co., Ltd., N. Atlantic Ins. Co. (U.K.); underwriting mem. Lloyds of London. Bd. dirs. YMCA of Greater Los Angeles, Claremont Men's Coll. Affiliates, Calif. Congl. Recognition Project, YMCA; trustee Claremont Men's Coll., Honnold Library Soc.; past finance chmn. Calif. Republican State Central Com. Served with USNR, 1945-46: PTO; served as 1st lt. USAF, 1951-59. Mem. Music Center for Performing Arts (founder), Claremont Men's Coll. Alumni Assn. (dir., pres. 1963-64), Chief Execs. Forum, World Bus. Council. Home: 2170 Century Park E Los Angeles CA 90067 Office: 1800 Ave of the Stars Suite 1410 Los Angeles CA 90067

EMISON, JAMES WADE, petroleum co. exec.; b. Indpls., Sept. 21, 1930; s. John Rabb and Catherine (Stanbro) E.; B.A., DePauw U., 1952; m. Cornelia Coyle, July 5, 1952; children—Catherine Elizabeth, Elizabeth Ann, Thomas Weston, William Ash. Sales mgr. Oskey Bros. Petroleum Corp., St. Paul, 1960-66; v.p. mktg. Newfoundland Refining Co., Ltd., N.Y.C., 1966-69; v.p. Oskey Gasoline & Oil Co., Mpls., 1969-76; pres. Western Petroleum Co., Mpls., 1976—; founder, dir. Suburban Nat. Bank, Eden Prairie, Minn. Trustee, DePauw U. Served with USMC, 1952-56. Mem. Am. Petroleum Inst., Nat. Petroleum Council, DePauw U. Alumni Assn. (pres.). Home: 18702 Heathcote Dr Wayzata MN 55391 Office: 2950 Metro Dr Minneapolis MN 55420

EMMERICH, JOHN PATRICK, micro-computer co. exec.; b. N.Y.C., Feb. 15, 1940; s. Clifford L. and Anna V. E.; B.S., Fla. State U., 1970; M.B.A., Syracuse U., 1974. Vice pres., treas. Applied Devices Corp., Hauppage, N.Y., 1960-75; v.p., treas., gen. mgr. Ontel Corp., Woodbury, N.Y., 1976—; dir. Muncie Gear Works (Ind.), G.C. Electronics Co., Houston, G.C. Mfg. Co., Houston. Vice pres. N. Creek Property Owners Assn. (N.Y.), 1976. Recipient commendation U.S. Army, 1962, 64. Mem. U.S. Naval Inst., Am. Mgmt. Assn., Nat. Microfilm Assn., Am. Def. Preparedness Assn., Pres. Club, L.I. Assn. Bus. Commerce. Roman Catholic. Contbr. articles to profl. jours. Home: North Creek Rd Eatons Neck NY 11768

EMMETT, ROBERT, bus. valuation and fin. cons.; b. Hartford, Conn., Sept. 6, 1919; s. Max and Dora E.; B.S., CCNY, 1941, postgrad., 1941-43; postgrad. N.Y. U., 1945-47; m. Adelaide S. Kaplan, Dec. 4, 1943; children—Merrill, Craig Alan. With Standard Research Cons., N.Y.C., 1953—, v.p., 1960-73, exec. v.p., 1973—. Served with U.S. Army, 1943-45. Fellow Fin. Analysts Fedn.; mem. Nat. Assn. Bus. Economists, N.Y. Soc. Security Analysts, Am. Soc. Appraisers (sr. mem., bd. internat. examiners), Am. Arbitration Assn. (nat. panel of arbitrators), Can. Assn. Bus. Valuators, Nat. Assn. Accts. Office: 345 Hudson St New York NY 10014

EMMETT, WALTER CHARLES, bus. brokerage firm exec.; b. Lawrence, Mass., July 6, 1925; s. Walter Thornton and Agnes Owens E.; student Dartmouth Coll., 1942-43, 46-47; m. Laurel Stinnett Emmett, Nov. 21, 1975; children—Jeffrey, Nancy, Scott; stepchildren—Wayne, Victoria Dammier. Owner, pres. Emmett Bus. Brokers, Inc., Amarillo, Tex., 1978—; owner Your Graphics Are Showing, Amarillo, 1977-79; salesman Ada Realtors, Amarillo, 1976-78; salesman Stevenson Motor, 1969-74, Russell Buick, 1974-76. Bd. dirs. Maverick Boys Club; mem. adv. com. on comml. art Amarillo Coll. Served with A.C., USN, 1943-46. Mem. Nat. Assn. Realtors, Nat. Panel Consumer Arbitrators, Inst. Cert. Bus. Counselors, Center Entrepreneurial Mgmt., Tex. Assn. Realtors, Amarillo Bd. Realtors, Nat. Assn. Merger and Acquisition Cons., Inst. Bus. Appraisers. Episcopalian. Clubs: Downtown Kiwanis (bd. dirs. 1979-80). Home: 2611 Henning St Amarillo TX 79106 Office: 1616 S Kentucky St C-434 Amarillo TX 79102

EMPEY, GENE F., real estate exec.; b. Hood River, Oreg., July 13, 1923; B.S. in Animal Husbandry, Oreg. State U., 1949; masters degree in tech. journalism Iowa State U., 1950; m. Janet Halladay, Dec. 27, 1950; children—Stephen Bruce, Michael Guy. Publs. dir. U. Nev.,

Reno, 1950-55; mgr. Zephyr Cove Lodge Hotel, Lake Tahoe, Nev., 1955-65; owner Empey Co., real estate agy., Carson City and Tahoe, Nev., 1964—. Mem. Nev. Planning Bd., 1959-72, chmn., 1961-66. Served to capt., inf. U.S. Army, 1943-47; PTO. G.R.I. (grad. Realtors Inst.). Mem. Nat. Assn. Realtors (cert. comml. investment mem.; pres. Nev. chpt. C.C.I.M.'s), Real Estate Nat. Mktg. Inst., Tahoe Douglas C. of C. (pres. 1962, dir.), Carson City C. of C., Carson-Tahoe-Douglas Bd. Realtors. Republican. Clubs: Capital City, Rotary, Heavenly Valley Ski (pres. 1968). Home: PO Box 707 Zephyr Cove NV 89448 Office: 512 S Curry St Carson City NV 89701

EMSWILER, JOSEPH MICHAEL, constrn. co. exec.; b. Balt., May 4, 1947; s. Maurice Eugene and Marie Elizabeth (Semon) E.; B.S. in Acctg., Villanova (Pa.) U., 1969; M.B.A., La. State U., 1979; m. Mindy Ester Valenzuela, June 30, 1970; children—William Joseph, Mindy Lynne, David James, Michael Justin. Acct., George Hyman Constrn. Co., Inc., Bethesda, Md., 1971-73; treas. Demory Bros., Inc., Rockville, Md., 1973-75; controller Crest Inc., Beaumont, Tex., 1975-77; treasury mgr. Nichols Constrn. Corp., Baton Rouge, 1977—; pres. Acctg. Corp. Am., Baton Rouge, 1978—. Served with USAR, 1969-71; Vietnam. Decorated Air medal. Mem. Am. Mgmt. Assn., Assn. M.B.A.'s. Roman Catholic. Home: PO Box 261 Baton Rouge LA 70821 Office: PO Box 2750 Baton Rouge LA 70821

END, NANCY ELIZABETH, market analyst; b. Troy, N.Y., Dec. 9, 1949; d. William F. and June (Epple) End; A.B., Middlebury Coll., 1972; M.S. in Indsl. Adminstrn., Union Coll., 1976. Competitive analyst Norton Co., Troy, 1972-73; internat. market analyst Norton Co., Worcester, Mass., 1973-74; market research analyst Sheaffer Eaton div. Textron, Pittsfield, Mass., 1975-77; market analyst Simplex Time Recorder Co., Gardner, Mass., 1977—. Loaned exec. Nat. Alliance of Businessmen, 1975; mem. Pittsfield Urban Coalition, 1976. Mem. Am. Mktg. Assn., Friends of Old Sturbridge Village, Worcester Econ. Club.

ENDERUD, WILBUR DONALD, JR., data processing cons.; b. Pueblo, Colo., Nov. 4, 1945; s. Wilbur Donald and Loretta Faye (Jackson) E.; B.A. in Math., San Diego State U., 1967; M.B.A., Calif. State U., Long Beach, 1972; children—Cynthia. From programmer to project leader Mattel, Inc., Hawthorne, Calif., 1967-72; dir. mgmt. info. systems Audio-Magnetics Corp., Gardena, Calif., 1972-75; founder, 1975, since owner, prin. cons. Don Enderud & Assos., Diamond Bar, Calif.; founding partner New Century Leasing, Diamond Bar, 1978—. Served with USAR, 1968-69; Vietnam. Decorated Army Commendation medal. Mem. Assn. Computing Machinery, Aircraft Owners and Pilots Assn. Republican. Lutheran. Office: PO Box 4237 Diamond Bar CA 91765

ENDERVELT, JEFFREY KENNETH, diversified co. exec.; b. Bklyn., May 5, 1941; s. David S. and Belle (Slavitsky) E.; student Bklyn. Coll., 1963; LL.B., U. Balt., 1967. Admitted to Md. bar, 1968, N.Y. State bar, 1972; pvt. practice law, N.Y.C., 1967-74; legis. counsel Rep. John M. Murphy of S.I., 1968-69; adminstrv. counsel Stanley Steingut, Speaker of the Assembly, Albany, N.Y., 1969-70; asst. atty. Michael Industries, Inc., N.Y.C., 1972-73, gen. counsel, 1973, chmn. bd., pres., chief exec. officer, 1974—; vice chmn. bd. Lehigh Valley Industries, Inc., N.Y.C., 1980—. Exec. com. Nat. Com. on Am. Fgn. Policy, 1975—; bd. dirs. Bklyn. Acad. Music, 1980—. Mem. Md. Bar Assn., N.Y. Bar Assn., Young Pres.'s Orgn., Young Men's Philanthropic League. Office: 1700 Broadway New York NY 10019

ENDICK, KENNETH J., computer co. exec.; b. N.Y.C., Sept. 29, 1942; s. Irving R. and Rae (Pievko) E.; B.A., Queens Coll., 1963; J.D., Fordham U., 1966; married; children—Alysia J., Carrie J. Admitted to N.Y. bar, 1967; corp. counsel, asst. sec. Radolph Computer Corp., Greenwich, Conn., 1968-73; sec., gen. counsel DPF Inc., Hartsdale, N.Y., 1973—; arbitrator Am. Arbitration Assn. Mem. Am. Soc. Corp. Secs., Am., N.Y. State, Westchester County bar assns., Computer Law Assb. Democrat. Jewish. Address: 337 Lakeview Ln Hampton NJ 08827

ENELL, JOHN WARREN, assn. exec., educator; b. N.Y.C., June 24, 1919; s. William Howard and Cristabel (Baumann) E.; B.S., U. Pa., 1940, M.E., 1948; M. Adminstrv. Engring., N.Y. U., 1947, D. Engring. Sc., 1949; m. Anna Louise Lefferts, June 4, 1949; children—Margaret Ann, Janet Ellen, Kathryn Laurel, Mark William. Test engr., asst. project engr., sr. exptl. engr. Wright Aero. Corp. div. Curtiss-Wright Corp., Paterson, N.J., 1940-45; research asst., N.Y.U., 1946-47, instr., 1946-49, asst. prof., 1949-55, asso. prof., 1955-58, prof. mgmt. engring., 1958-59; mem. U.S. Mut. Security Adminstrn. mission to Italy, 1952-53; dir. information service and surveys Am. Mgmt. Assns., 1954-61, dir. research, 1961-67, v.p. for research, 1967—; dir. research Am. Found. Mgmt. Research, 1961-62, v.p., 1970-73; U.S. del. CIOS XV Internat. Mgmt. Congress, Tokyo, 1969, CIOS XVI, Munich, 1972; mem. AID mission to Vietnam, 1972, IESC missions to Greece, 1973, Colombia, 1978. Fellow Am. Inst. Indsl. Engrs. (nat. v.p. 1965-68, nat. pres. 1968-69, dir. 1965-71); mem. Acad. Mgmt., Am. Mgmt. Assns., ASME, Am. Soc. Quality Control, Am. Statis. Asso., Council on the CEU (dir., v.p. 1977-80, pres. 1980—), Engrs. Council for Profl. Devel. (dir. 1970-77, nat. treas. 1973-77), Engrs. Joint Council (nat. treas. 1979), Am. Assn. Engring. Socs. (sec.-treas. 1980), Sigma Xi, Alpha Pi Mu. Club: Packanack Lake Country. Author: Are Your Findings Trustworthy, 1950; (with others) Quality Control Handbook, 1951, Production Handbook, 1958, 72; (with G. H. Haas) Setting Standards for Executive Performance, 1960; editorial bd. Jour. Indsl. Engring. Home: 165 Lake Dr W Packanack Lake Wayne NJ 07470 Office: 135 W 50th St New York NY 10020

ENERSEN, ROBERT JOHN, electronic components mfg. corp. exec.; b. Detroit Lakes, Minn., Nov. 21, 1914; s. Axel Rudolph and Eliza Josephine (Anderson) E.; student U. Minn., 1934-36; m. Coralie Elna Lathrop, Oct. 3, 1936; children—Gary Robert, Kay Llona Enersen Howard, Robert John. With Honeywell, Inc., Mpls., 1933-38; cost acct., chief cost acct., 1938-56, plant controller, St. Petersburg, Fla., 1956-69; pres., dir. Hytronics Corp., Clearwater, Fla., also Gunanaja, Honduras and Alajuela, Costa Rica, 1969—. Chmn., United Fund, Honeywell, Inc., 1964, 67. Mem. Nat. Assn. Accts. (v.p. 1965-66), Stuart Cameron McLeod Soc. (pres. 1973-74), Tampa World Trade Council. Club: Masons. Home: Gulf Shores Apt 510A 100 Bluff View Dr Belleair Bluffs FL 33540 Office: Hytronics Corp 15401 Roosevelt Blvd Clearwater FL 33518

ENFIELD, MORRIS CONRAD, JR., computer systems mgr.; b. Harlingen, Tex., Oct. 28, 1938; s. Morris Conrad and Eunice Irene (Hodge) E.; B.A., Rice U., Houston, 1960; M.A., U. Tex., 1968; m. Nancy Susan Lewis, June 11, 1972. Ops. mgr. Computer Center, U. Tex., Austin, 1962-68; systems analyst SDC, Santa Monica, Calif., 1968-69; project mgr. Computer Scis. Corp., San Diego and Netherlands, 1969-73; systems cons. Control Data Corp., San Diego, 1973-75; systems mgr. Univ. Computing Co., Dallas, 1975-77; computer systems specialist Rockwell Internat. Co., Dallas, 1977-79; advanced systems architect NCR Corp., San Diego, 1979—; instr. Sch. Bus. and Computer Sci., U. Tex., Dallas, 1977—; fellow Argonne (Ill.) Nat. Lab., 1964. Mem. IEEE, Assn. Computing Machinery, AAAS, N.Y. Acad. Scis., Am. Heart Assn., Tex. Execs. Assn., So. Meth. U. M.B.A. Assn. Author tech. papers. Home: 9950 Las Conicas San Diego CA 92129 Office: 9900 Old Grove Rd San Diego CA 92131

ENG, JERRY YIT LONG, systems engr.; b. Toysan, China, Mar. 2, 1950; s. Kok Young and Gim Ying E.; came to U.S., 1955, naturalized, 1973; B.S. in Elec. Engring., Poly. Inst. Bklyn., 1974; M.B.A., Adelphi U., 1977; m. Juliana Lai Yam, May 24, 1975; children—Colleen Sue-Yen, Diana May-Yen. Asst. engr. L. I. Lighting Co., Hicksville, N.Y., 1974-77, research and tng. specialist, 1977-78; systems engr. IBM, Harrison, N.Y., 1978—. Mem. Am. Soc. Tng. and Devel. (sec. L.I. chpt. 1978-79), Poly. Inst. N.Y. Alumni Assn. (dir. 1974—). Office: 600 Mamroneck Ave Harrison NY 10528

ENGDAHL, ROGER ALAN, vehicle mfg. co. exec.; b. Mpls., Mar. 24, 1949; s. John Wallace and Dorothy Jean Engdahl; B.S. in Aero. Engring., U. Minn., 1971, M.Aero. Engring., 1973. Cons. engr., systems and research div. Honeywell, Mpls., 1973-75; pres. Recreational Engring. Inc., Fridley, Minn., 1975—. Home: 4509 Sedum Ln Edina MN 55435

ENGEL, CLARENCE EDWARD, mop mfg. co. exec.; b. Butler County, Ohio, Dec. 23, 1924; s. John Adolph and Lillian Elvena (Erven) E.; B.S. in Bus. Adminstrn., Ohio State U., 1948; m. Ann J. Hunger, Sept. 11, 1948; children—Craig, Scott. Salesman, Procter & Gamble Distbg. Co., Columbus, Ohio, 1948-55; dist. sales mgr. Willson Products div. RayoVac Co., Columbus, also Madison, Wis., 1955-57, regional sales mgr., 1957-58; dist. sales rep. Paramount Paper Products Co., Cleve., 1958; with Am. Textile Products Co., Cleve., 1959—, v.p. sales, 1979—. Mem. Cuyahoga County Republican Com., 1965-68, 72-80. Served with USMC, 1942-45; PTO. Presbyterian. Club: Kiwanis (pres. 1977-78). Home: 31500 Bexley Dr Bay Village OH 44140

ENGEL, GENE OLIVER, sales agy. exec.; b. Memphis, Dec. 23, 1943; s. Jacob Frederick and Dorothy Elizabeth (Walters) E.; student nights Memphis State U., 1972-75, U. Ala., Birmingham, 1976; children—Keith, Dawn, Wende. Restaurant mgr. Dobbs Houses, Pensacola, Ala., 1965; reservations agt. Delta Airlines, Memphis, 1966; with L.M. Berry Co., various locations, 1966—, dist. sales mgr. Birmingham, Ala., 1975-77, div. mgr. Miss., Jackson, 1977-80, dir. human resources, Dayton, Ohio, 1980—. Served with AUS 1961-64. Republican. Methodist. Home: 3226 Gambit Sq Dayton OH 45449 Office: 3170 Kettering Blvd Dayton OH 45401

ENGEL, HANS MAX, hotel exec.; b. Hamburg, Ger., June 20, 1923; came to U.S., 1950, naturalized, 1953; s. Hans Curt and Gertrude Frances (Thieme) E.; student bus. adminstrn., Hamburg State Coll., 1940-43; m. Christina Heitmann, Feb. 20, 1959; children—John Thomas, Suzanne Elizabeth, Jennifer Kathleen. Exec., German Nat. Tourist Office, N.Y.C., 1950-56; propr. H.M. Engel Hotel Reps., N.Y.C., 1956-58; merged with William P. Wolfe Orgn., 1958, owner, 1966—; pres. H.M. Engels Assos. Inc., internat. hotel reps. and cons., operating as Am. Internat. Co. and Wolfe Internat. Hotel Reps., N.Y.C., 1966—; vis. lectr. Cornell U. Hotel Sch. Named Travel Industry Hotelman of Yr., 1978. Mem. Am. Soc. Travel Agts., Caribbean Hotel Assn., Caribbean Tourism Assn., Hotel Sales Mgmt. Assn., Skal Club. Republican. Clubs: Orienta Beach, Mamaroneck, Dolphin Yacht. Home: 613 Stiles Ave Mamaroneck NY 10543 Office: 500 Fifth Ave New York NY 10036

ENGEL, VICTOR BOYNTON, constrn. industry co. exec.; b. Keokuk, Iowa, Jan. 29, 1914; s. Martin T. and Gertrude (Boynton) E.; A.A., Calif. Concordia Coll., 1935; various bus. and mil. schs.; B.A., U. Calif. at Berkeley, 1949; certificate Acad. Internat. Law, Hague, Netherlands, 1951; M.A., Grad. Inst. Internat. Studies and U. Geneva, Switzerland, 1952; m. Dorothea Ann Messner, Mar. 18, 1944. Prof. constl. law, U.S. history U. Geneva, 1950-52; exec. mgr. Assn. Plumbing and Heating Contractors of Contra Costa County, Richmond, Calif., 1952-54; exec. dir. Contra Costa Builders Exchange, Concord, Calif., 1954—; pres. Constrn. Mgmt. Services, Inc., Metro-Mgmt. Services, Inc. Pres., Internat. Builders Exchange Execs., U.S., Can., 1962-63; chmn. Builders Exchange Council, 1971-72; pres. Builders Exchanges Constrn. Industry Conf., 1969-70. Mem. Contra Costa County Devel. Assn. Served with AUS, 1941-46. Mem. World Affairs Council No. Calif., Calif. Alumni Assn., Am. Soc. Assn. Execs., No. Calif. Soc. Assn. Execs., Assn. des Anciens l'Inst. Geneva. Rotarian. Clubs: Commonwealth (San Francisco); Concord Century, Toastmasters (Concord). Author: Significant Developments in American Society, 1952. Editor: Constrn. Weekly, 1954—. Home: 10 Gran Via Alamo CA 94507 Office: 2490 Salvio St Concord CA 94520

ENGEL, WILLIAM EMANUEL, broadcasting co. exec.; b. New Orleans, Feb. 9, 1948; s. Russell Patrick and Virginia T. (Legg) E.; B.S., U. Ala., 1972; m. Susan Shepard, Dec. 20, 1969. Asst. to pres. So. Broadcasting Co., Winston-Salem, N.C., 1969-74; v.p. radio sales Arbitron Co., N.Y.C., 1974-78; gen. mgr. WTIX-Radio, Storz Broadcasting Co., New Orleans, 1978—; instr. Tulane U., 1979—. Mem. Am. Mktg. Assn. (dir. New Orleans chpt. 1980-81), La. Assn. Broadcasters (dir. 1980—), New Orleans Broadcasters Assn. (pres. 1980), Commerce Exec. Soc.-U. Ala. Republican. Roman Catholic. Club: Pass Christian Golf. Author: Research Guidelines for Programming Decision Makers, 1977. Home: 190 Trenton Dr Slidell LA 70458 Office: WTIX-Radio 332 Carondelet St New Orleans LA 70130

ENGELHARDT, JANELL SUMMERS, life ins. co. exec.; b. Kansas City, Mo., Aug. 29, 1944; d. Clarence Leonard and Dorothy Nell (Tatom) Summers; B.S. in Edn., Central Mo. State U., 1966, M.B.A., 1971; m. John L. Engelhardt, Mar. 24, 1979. Tchr. bus. Brentwood (Mo.) Public Schs., 1966-70; grad. asst., instr. Central Mo. State U., Warrensburg, 1970-72; mgmt. tng. specialist The Bendix Corp., Kansas City, 1972-74; mgmt. trainee, reins. sales asst., mgr. life ins. product planning, dir. adminstrv. planning Lincoln Nat. Sales Corp., Ft. Wayne, Ind., 1974-79, asst. v.p., dir. individual ins. mktg., 1979—. Bd. dirs. Ft. Wayne chpt. ARC, 1976—, mem. public relations com., 1979-80, youth services com., 1979-80, first aid com., 1979-80; loaned exec. United Way, 1974. Recipient Leadership award United Way, 1975; C.L.U. Mem. Nat. Assn. C.L.U., Ft. Wayne Assn. C.L.U. Home: 7117 Kebir Ct Fort Wayne IN 46815 Office: 1300 S Clinton St Fort Wayne IN 46801

ENGELHORN, RICHARD WAYNE, storage co. exec.; b. Los Angeles, July 11, 1925; s. Clarence and Virginia (Baker) E.; A.A., Riverside Coll.; student Riverside Bus. Coll., 1949, Sch. Mgmt., UCLA, 1960; m. Inez Howard Gardner, Jan. 15, 1970; children—Joanna, Gayle, Irene, Robert, Dianna, Richard Wayne II. Chief accountant, office mgr. Nat. Ice & Cold Storage Co., Riverside, Calif., 1949-53; with Poppy Food Co., Los Angeles, 1953-77, v.p. fin. and adminstrn., sec.-treas., 1968-77; exec. v.p. Pacific Cold Storage Co., Los Angeles, 1977—; trustee Temasters Food and Allied Industries Health and Welfare Fund; multiple employer union bargaining rep. and negotiator. Mem. vet. adv. council City of Riverside, 1946-47. Served with USMC, 1942-45; PTO. Decorated Purple Heart. Mem. Internat. Assn. Refrigerated Warehouse (vice chmn. Pacific chpt.), Pacific Cold Storage Warehousemen (past officer and dir.), Am. Mgmt. Assn., Fin. Execs. Inst. (past officer and dir.), Nat. Assn. Accountants (past officer and dir.), UCLA Sch. Mgmt. Alumni Assn., UCLA Alumni Assn. Republican. Mem. Ch. of Religious Science. Clubs: Los Angeles Athletic, Rotary, Elks. Home: 1360 Glen Oaks Blvd Pasadena CA 91105 Office: 3420 E Vernon Ave Los Angeles CA 90058

ENGELMAN, IRWIN, diversified co. exec.; b. N.Y.C., May 9, 1934; s. Max and Julia (Shaoul) E.; B.B.A., Coll. City N.Y., 1955; J.D., Bklyn. Law Sch., 1961; m. Rosalyn Ackerman, Nov. 24, 1956; m. Madeleine F., Marianne L. Staff, U.S. Army Audit Agy., 1955-59; pub. accountant, N.Y.C., 1959-62; controller Razdow Labs., Inc., Newark, 1962-66; various fin. mgmt. positions Xerox Corp., Rochester, N.Y., 1966-70, v.p. finance and adminstrn. Info. Systems Group, 1970-75, v.p., region gen. mgr., 1974-75, v.p., bus. area mgr., 1975-78; v.p., chief fin. officer The Singer Co., N.Y.C., 1978-81; sr. v.p. fin. Gen. Foods Corp., 1981—; asso. prof. Monroe Community Coll., 1967-68. Treas. Virginia Wilson Interracial Helping Hand Center, 1971-72; bd. dirs. Rochester Bus. Opportunities Corp., 1971-74, Citizens' Tax League, 1972—; chmn. Monroe County Met. Arts Resources Com., 1972-74. Admitted to N.Y. State bar, 1962. Served with U.S. Army, 1967. C.P.A., N.J. Mem. N.Y. State Soc. C.P.A.'s, Am. Bar Assn., Am. Inst. C.P.A.'s. Home: 12 Old Hill Rd Westport CT 06880 Office: Gen Foods Corp 250 North St White Plains NY 10625

ENGELN, FRIEDHELM PETIER, chemist; b. Duisburg, Meiderich, Ger., Jan. 15, 1936; came to U.S., 1964; s. Peter Paul and Elfriede Anna (Sonnen) E.; B.S., Obermeidlingen, 1948; Matura B/S Chemie/Philogy, 1956; M.S., Calif. State U., 1976; m. Annaliese Vanicek, Oct. 11, 1958; children—Mike, Matthew. Chemist, Standard Sample, Montreal, Que., Can., 1962-64; forest products lab. mgr. Reliance Universal, Inc., Brea, Calif., 1964—; cons. in field; Calif. clear air mgr., 1969-74. Treas., Orange County Council Boy Scouts Am., 1978-80. Mem. Internat. Graphoanalysis Soc., Los Angeles Soc. for Coatings Tech., Forest Products Soc., Grapho Soc. Republican. Roman Catholic. Home: 237 Delphia St Brea CA 92621 Office: 1215 W Lambert St Brea CA 92621

ENGLAND, WILLIAM THOMAS, lawyer, energy co. exec.; b. Manchester, Conn., Mar. 28, 1934; s. George John and Helen (Dimlow) E.; B.A., U. Conn., 1958; LL.B. with high honors, U. Conn. Sch. Law, 1963; postgrad. George Washington U. Grad. Sch. Law, 1964-65; m. Alice G. O'Rourke, Oct. 12, 1956; children—William Thomas, Jr., Kerry J., Nancy J., Kelly M. Admitted to Conn. bar, 1963; reporter Hartford (Conn.) Times, 1961-62; atty. U.S. AEC, Washington, 1963-65; chief counsel Joint Com. on Atomic Energy, U.S. Congress, Washington, 1965-70; v.p. for corporate affairs, gen. counsel Exxon Nuclear Co., Bellevue, Wash., 1970—; cons. U.S. Commn. Govt. Procurement, 1972. Served with U.S. Army, 1958-60. Recipient Author's award Fed. Bar Assn., 1967-68. Mem. Am. Bar Assn., Fed. Bar Assn., Internat. Nuclear Law Assn. Author of various legal periodicals. Home: 1609 185th Ave NE Bellevue WA 98008 Office: 777 106th Ave NE Bellevue WA 98009

ENGLE, DUANE RAYMOND, architect; b. Abilene, Kans., Sept. 2, 1936; s. Raymond Earl and Pauline Gertrude (Long) E.; B.Arch. with honors, Kans. State U., 1959; m. Marian Elizabeth Joy, Nov. 23, 1963 (div. June 1973); children—Margaret Elizabeth, David Raymond. Architect, Linder Wright & Wihte, Denver, 1959-63, Wheeler & Lewis, Denver, 1963; owner D.R. Engle, Architect, Colorado Springs, Colo., 1963-64; architect W.A. Miller, Colorado Springs, 1964-66; partner firm Miller & Engle, Architects, Colorado Springs, 1966-70; pres. Engle Asso., Inc., Arch. & Planning, Colorado Springs, 1970—. Sec., Colorado Springs Symphony Council, 1973; bd. dirs. Planned Parenthood, Colorado Springs, 1974-76, pres., 1975; bd. dirs. Rocky Mt. Planned Parenthood, 1975; bd. dirs. Energy Resource Center of Pikes Peak Region, 1980, sec.-treas., 1980. Recipient AIA Student medal, 1959; Outstanding Concrete Structure award, Am. Concrete Inst., 1979. Mem. AIA (treas. 1972-73, pres. 1975), Colo. Soc. Architects (dir. 1975, 78), Colorado Springs C. of C. Republican. Lutheran. Clubs: Colorado Springs Country, Sertoma, Pikes Peak Torch (pres. 1973-74). Home: 974 Bayfield Way Colorado Springs CO 80906 Office: 1715 N Weber St Colorado Springs CO 80907

ENGLE, FREDERICK SAMUEL, JR., lumber co. exec.; b. Lancaster, Pa., July 4, 1941; s. Frederick Samuel and Edith (Krentz) E.; B.S. in Bus. Adminstrn., Pa. State U., 1963; m. Louise L. Weaver, June 14, 1962; children—Kimberly Louise, Scott Frederick. Traffic analyst, then plant purchasing agt. Armstrong Cork Co., Lancaster, 1963-69; dir. personnel, then gen. mgr. H.M. Stauffer & Sons, Leola, Pa., 1969-78, v.p., dir. purchasing, 1978-81, also dir.; partner/owner, v.p., gen. mgr. Gerhart Bros. Lumber, Ephrata, Pa., 1981—; dir., mem. exec. com. Inter-County Hospitalization Plan, Jenkintown, Pa.; bd. dirs. Inst. Mgmt., Franklin and Marshall Coll., Lancaster, 1977, pres., 1980. Pres. Litiz Jaycees, 1967, United Way, Lancaster, 1976-80; bd. dirs. Lancaster County unit United Cerebral Palsy, 1976-80. Mem. Nat. Lumber and Bldg. Material Dealers Assn. (chmn. bus. mgmt. com. 1978), Lancaster County Lumbermen's Assn. (pres. 1973-74), Lancaster Assn. Commerce and Industry. Republican. Presbyterian. Club: Hamilton. Home: 2375 Partridge Ln Lancaster PA 17601 Office: 124 S State St Ephrata PA 17522

ENGLE, PATRICIA ANN PENDLETON, constrn. co. exec.; b. Raytown, Mo., July 30, 1931; s. Frederick Alexander and Hildred Viola (Brown) P.; student pub. schs., Raytown and Kansas City, Mo.; m. George I. Engle, Oct. 9, 1963; children—James D., Stanley M., Michelle, Rene, Garry, Catherine. With Eaton Metal Products Co., Billings, Mont., 1949, AEC, Los Alamos, N.Mex., 1949-51, Safety Drivers Ins. Co., Kansas City, Mo., 1951-52; with Mid-Western Constrn. Co. of Mo., Raytown, 1960—, co-owner, sec.-treas., 1970—; co-owner, pres. G.P. & M. Constrn. Co. Served with USNR, 1948-52. Mem. Nat. Exec. Secs. Assn., Constrn. Women's Assn. (pres. 1980-81), Am. Bus. Women's Assn., Assn. of Bus. and Profl. Women in Constrn. Home: 1701 E R D Mize Rd Blue Springs MO 64015 Office: 9814 E 53d St Raytown MO 64133

ENGLE, ROBERT LOUIS, pharm. co. exec.; b. Balt., Apr. 29, 1948; s. Robert Lee and Marie Grace (Moriconi) E.; B.S., U. Balt., 1970; M.Ed., Towson State U., 1973; m. Janice Ann Erdbrink, Nov. 26, 1969; 1 dau., Laura Marie. Tchr. pub. schs. Baltimore County, 1970-71; med. service rep. Knoll Pharm. Co., 1972-73, asst. to mgr. sales tng., 1973, mgr. sales tng., 1973-74; asst. mgr. sales tng. Ayerst Labs., N.Y.C., 1974-75, mgr. sales tng., 1975-78, mgr. sales personnel devel., 1978; mgr. sales tng. and devel. Miles Labs. Dome div., West Haven, Conn., 1978-79, nat. sales mgr. Dome div., 1979—. Mem. Am. Mgmt. Assn. Home: 54 Heatherwood Dr Madison CT 06443

ENGLER, DARLENE JO, ins. exec.; b. Crested Butte, Colo., May 24, 1938; d. Joseph Nelson and Cecelia Evelyn (Tezak) Schafer; A.A., Fullerton Coll., 1958; m. Richard F. Engler, Sept. 1, 1967. Adminstrv. asst. Sherwin Elec. Co., Los Angeles, 1966-67; acctg. supr. Caldwell-Miller, Inc., Inglewood, Calif., 1967-71; office mgr. Nat. Certified, Inc., Whittier, Calif., 1971-77; mktg. coordinator IRM Ins. Brokers, Tustin, Calif., 1977-78; ins. agt., broker, 1977—; fin. mgr. Quinlan Ins. Inc., Newport Beach, Calif. 1978-80; now ops. mgr. PMC Ins., Orange, Calif. Treas. Venture Club of Anaheim (Calif.), 1963-64; active Whittier Republican Women's Fedn. Mem. Soc. C.P.C.U.'s,

Ins. Women Orange County, Orange Empire Chpt. C.P.C.U.'s, Western Ins. Info. Service Speakers Bur. Roman Catholic. Club: Hacienda Golf. Home: 740 S Mariposa Dr LaHabra CA 90631 Office: PMC Ins 1400 E Katella Orange CA 92667

ENGLISH, PAUL KENNEDY, investment real estate broker, developer, syndicator; b. Seattle, Nov. 2, 1937; s. Myron Ralph and Margery Marie (De Champlain) E.; A.A. in Bus., Foothill Coll., 1965, cert. in indsl. mgmt., 1965; A.B. in Econs., San Jose State U., 1968; M.B.A., Harvard U., 1970; m. Mary Lou Ryan, June 23, 1962; children—Brian Kennedy, Sean Gibson. Prodn. control supr. Kaiser Aerospace & Electronics Co., Palo Alto, Calif., 1960-65; salesman Value Realty, San Jose, Calif., 1965-66; mfg. control mgr. Western Microwave Lab., Inc., Santa Clara, Calif., 1966-67; economist, subs. sec.-treas. Comml. Credit Co., Balt., 1970-74; v.p. Marcus & Millichap, Inc., Palo Alto, Calif., 1975-80; pres. PKE, Inc., 1980—; pres., chief exec. officer English Co., Los Altos, Calif., 1980—; chmn. Capital Gains Investments. Served with USCG, 1957-59. Clubs: Harvard Bus. Sch.; Harvard. Home: 386 University Ave Los Altos CA 94022 Office: English Co 167 S San Antonio Rd Suite 14 Los Altos CA 94022

ENGLISH, WILLIAM DESHAY, lawyer; b. Piedmont, Calif., Dec. 25, 1924; s. Munro and Mabel (Michener) E.; A.B. in Econs., U. Calif., Berkeley, 1948, J.D., 1951; m. Nancy Ames, Apr. 7, 1956; children—Catherine, Barbara, Susan, Stephen. Admitted to Calif. bar, 1952, D.C. bar, 1972; trial atty. and spl. asst. to atty. gen. Dept. of Justice, Washington, 1953-55; sr. atty. AEC, Washington, 1955-62; legal adviser U.S. Mission to European Communities, Brussels, 1962-64; asst. gen. counsel internat. matters COMSAT, Washington, 1965-73, v.p., gen. counsel, dir. COMSAT Gen. Corp., 1973-76; v.p. legal and govtl. affairs Satellite Bus. Systems, McLean, Va., 1976—; dir. INTERCOMSA, S.A., Panama City, Panama. Served with USAAF, 1943-45. Decorated Air medal. Mem. Am. Bar Assn., D.C. Bar Assn., State Bar Calif., Fgn. Policy Discussion Group Washington, Fed. Communications Bar Assn. Club: Met. (Washington). Office: Satellite Bus Systems 8283 Greensboro Dr McLean VA 22101

ENGLUND, ROBERT THEODORE, growing, packing, shipping co. exec.; b. McIntosh, Minn., Apr. 18, 1911; s. Godfred Theodore and Elizabeth (Conkey) E.; B.S., UCLA, 1936; postgrad. Princeton U., 1936; m. Constance Maurine Roberts, Aug. 21, 1937; children—Paul Willare, Pamela Englund Cole, Theodora Alice Englund Crewson. With Calif. Dept. Agr., 1936-37; with sales dept. Am. Fruit Growers, 1938-41; pres., owner R.T. Englund Co., Scottsdale, Ariz., 1946—; pres. R.T. Englund Equipment Corp., Salinas, 1962-78; gen. partner, mgr. Bonanza Ranches of Ariz., 1965—; pres. Mohave Copper Corp., 1959-70; dir. Pioneer Bank of Ariz., 1967-69; dir., v.p. Monterey County Ice & Devel. Co., 1953-69. Trustee U. Calif. at Los Angeles Found. Served to lt. (j.g.) USNR, 1944-46. Mem. NAM (mktg. and research coms. 1960-78), United Fresh Fruit and Vegetable Assn., U.S., Salinas (dir. 1958-59) chambers commerce, Council of Calif. Growers, Vegetable Growers Assn. of Central Ariz. (dir. 1962-63), Yuma Growers and Shippers Assn., Central Calif. Growers and Shippers Assn., Chancellors Assos. of UCLA. Republican. Mason. Clubs: Phoenix Country, Ariz. Acad., Plaza (Phoenix). Home: 41 Casa Blanca Estates Scottsdale AZ 85253 also 738 Old Stage Rd Salinas CA 93901 Office: PO Box 1705 Scottsdale AZ 85252

ENLUND, E. STANLEY, banker; b. Chgo., July 5, 1917; s. John R. and Alice E. (Schoenian) E.; J.D., DePaul U., Chgo., 1942; L.H.D. (hon.), George Williams Coll., 1973; m. Calista E. Olson, Mar. 16, 1943; 1 son, John Delos. With Continental Ill. Nat. Bank & Trust Co., Chgo., 1934-57, asst. sec., 1951-57; admitted to Ill. bar, 1942; trust officer, v.p. Sears Bank & Trust Co., Chgo., 1957-63, also dir.; exec. v.p. 1st Fed. Savs. & Loan Assn. of Chgo., 1963, pres., 1963-71, chief exec. officer, chmn. bd., 1971—; dir. No. Ill. Gas Co., Dearborn Park Corp., Chgo. Title Ins. Co., CECO Corp., NICOR. Chmn., Jr. Achievement of Chgo., 1978-79; pres. USO of Chgo., 1979; chmn. Wheatridge Found., 1979—; chmn. Ill. div. Am. Cancer Soc.; bd. mgrs. YMCA of Chgo. bd. regents St. Olaf Coll.; bd. dirs. Met. Crusade of Mercy, United Way of Met. Chgo.; trustee Glenwood Sch. for Boys, chmn., 1977—; trustee, chmn. DePaul U. Served to lt. USN, 1941-45. Recipient Outstanding Philanthropist award Chgo. Soc. Fund Raising Execs., 1977, Fin. award Dearborn Real Estate Bd., 1978, Am. Heritage award Anti-Defamation League of B'nai B'rith, 1980; decorated comdr. Royal Swedish Order North Star. Mem. Ill. Bar Assn., Chgo. Bar Assn. (chmn. liaison com.), Chgo. Assn. of Commerce and Industry (pres. 1979—), Better Govt. Assn., Cook County Council Insured Savs. Assns., Comml. Club Chgo., Legal Club Chgo., Delta Theta Phi. Lutheran. Clubs: Butler Nat. Golf (gov.), Plaza (gov.), Union League of Chgo. (Disting. Public Service award 1978). Office: 1 S Dearborn St Chicago IL 60603

ENNEKING, CLARENCE BERNARD, electronic service co. exec.; b. Melrose, Minn., Aug. 20, 1931; s. Henry John and Rose (Theilen) E.; student DeForest Coll., 1949-51, N.W. Electronics Coll., 1954-55; m. Eugenia Ann Sand, Nov. 9, 1957; children—Timothy, Todd, Sandra, Bradley, Jill. Printed circuit supr. Univac Co., St. Paul, 1955-57; plant mgr. Fabri-Tek, Amery, Wis., 1957-62, Eau Clair, Wis., 1962-65, St. Cloud, Minn., 1965-66, Hong Kong, 1966-74, circuits gen. mgr., Baldwin, Minn., 1974-76; pres. D M A Inc., Amery, 1976—; also dir.; cons. new printed circuit plants. Chmn. for fin. and spiritual com. St. Joseph's Catholic Ch., Amery. Served with USMC, 1951-54. Mem. Smithsonian Assos., Marriage Encounter Community. Club: Amery Community (pres. 1970). Home: 332 South St Amery WI 54001 Office: 119 W Birch St Amery WI 54001

ENNIS, OLIN NELSON, mfg. co. exec.; b. Mt. Morris, Mich., Nov. 3, 1917; s. George N. and Mary Jane (Goodman) E.; student Gen. Motors Inst.; m. Ruth Ann West, Dec. 27, 1963; 1 son, Olin Nelson. Mem. staff Gen. Motors Corp., 1936-45; founder, pres., gen. mgr. Ennis Mfg., Clio, Mich., 1943—. Named Automotive Man of Year, 1967. Mem. Automotive Parts Rebldg. Assn. (past pres.), Automotive Service Industry Assn. (exec. com. rebuilders div.), Inst. Water Pump Rebuilders (chmn. bd. govs.), Clio C. of C. (dir. past treas.), Automotive Warehouse Distbn. Assn. (mfrs. adv. council). Patentee rebldg. automotive water pumps. Home: Creekwood Farm Clio MI 48420 Office: G-11539 N Saginaw Rd Clio MI 48420

ENNIS, ROBERT ELLSWORTH, mining equipment co. exec.; b. Utica, N.Y., June 26, 1934; s. John Zeigler and Sarah Ann (Lauterbach) E.; B.S., Va. Poly. Inst., 1958; m. Annetta Marjorie Wainwright, Dec. 20, 1958; children—Karen, Christine. Mining engr. Humphreys Mining Co., Denver, 1958-61; sr. mining engr. Henry J. Kaiser Can., Ltd., Montreal, 1961-63; mgr. mining sales Hewitt-Robins, Inc., Litton Industries, Passaic, N.J., 1963-66, gen. mgr. mining and constrn. equipment div., Milw., 1967-68; chmn. bd., pres. Hewitt-Robins (Can.) Ltd., Montreal, 1969-70; exec. v.p., dir. Linatex Corp. Am., Stafford Springs, Conn., 1971—; dir., treas. Stafford Corp.; pres., dir. Stafford Mining & Processing Corp., 1977—. Served to USAF, 1952-54. Mem. Am. Inst. Mining, Metall. and Petroleum Engrs., Sigma Gamma Epsilon. Contbr. articles to profl. jours. Patentee in field. Home: 3 Drumlin Rd Simsbury CT 06092 Office: Linatex Corp America Stafford Springs CT 06076

ENO, JULIUS RALPH, JR., sci. products co. exec.; b. Long Beach, Calif., Mar. 29, 1929; s. Julius Ralph and Ina Coy (Hayes) E.; B.A., Whittier Coll., 1956; M.S., U. Idaho, 1958; m. Charlotte Hollywood Campbell, Oct. 21, 1961; children—Sarah, Maude, Jane, Randolph. Sr. optical engr. Cary Instruments, Monrovia, Calif., 1954-67; optical engr. John U. White, Stamford, Conn., 1968-69; chief engr. OCLI Instruments, Norwalk, Conn., 1969-70; optical designer Spex Industries, Metuchen, N.J., 1970; exec. v.p. Hamamatsu Corp., Middlesex, N.J., 1970—, dir. U.S. ops., 1971—; dir. Hamamatsu TV Co., Ltd., BHK, Inc., Mentor Marine, Inc., others. Served with USN, 1950-53. Mem. Optical Soc. Am. Quaker. Home: 120 Whitenack Rd Basking Ridge NJ 07920 Office: 420 South Ave Middlesex NJ 08846

ENOS, RICHARD MERWIN, restaurant cons.; b. Sacramento, Sept. 28, 1946; s. Joseph Franklin and Celestine (Fox) E.; B.S.C., U. Santa Clara, 1968; m. Nancy Dale McCoy, Nov. 8, 1969; children—Jeffrey, Scott. With Victoria Station Inc., San Francisco, 1972—, dir. purchasing, 1976-77, dir. ops. tng., 1978, dir. ops.-West, 1978-79; pres. RMEnterprises, San Rafael, Calif., 1980—. Bd. dirs. San Francisco Bay Area chpt. March of Dimes; mem. citizens adv. com. Dominican Coll. Served to capt. U.S. Army, 1968-71. Mem. Nat. Restaurant Assn., Guardsmen. Republican. Roman Catholic. Home: 110 Center St San Rafael CA 94901

ENSIGN, FRANK BENJAMIN, JR., mfg. co. exec.; b. Lakewood, Ohio, Aug. 30, 1930; s. Frank Benjamin and Mary Carr (Newell) E.; A.B., Harvard U., 1952, M.B.A., 1957; M. Accounting, U. So. Calif., 1962, M.S., 1964; m. Helen Bird Loring, Aug. 18, 1962; children—Katherine Newell, Brooks Loring, Frank B., Mary Elizabeth. Vice pres., controller Shaw Cotton Co. Inc., Phoenix, 1957-60; asst. to controller Security 1st Nat. Bank, Los Angeles, 1960-61; with fin. mgmt. dept. Lockheed Aircraft Corp., Burbank, Calif., 1961-71; controller EOS div. Xerox Corp., Pasadena, Calif., 1971-74; group controller Aerojet Gen. Corp., El Monte, Calif., 1974—; lectr. Calif. State U., Los Angeles, 1964—. Served to lt. (j.g.) USNR, 1952-55. Mem. Fin. Execs. Inst., Am. Accounting Assn., Nat. Assn. Accountants. Republican. Episcopalian. Home: PO Box 1269 Rancho Santa Fe CA 92067 Office: 10300 N Torrey Pines Rd La Jolla CA 92037

ENSIGN, HORACE ANGUS, mfg. co. exec.; b. Salt Lake City, Aug. 19, 1925; s. Peter Horace and Mary Alice (Shearsmith) E.; B.S., U. Utah, 1960; postgrad. U. Kans., Harvard U.; m. Emogene Raulston, June 16, 1946; children—Mary Ann, Kathryn, Patrice, Michael. With Kennecott Copper Corp., 1950—, refinery plant supt., Utah, 1974-78, gen. mgr. Kennecott Refining Corp., Balt., 1978-80; v.p. performance improvement Kennecott Minerals Co. Utah, 1980—. Served with AUS, 1944-46. Mem. Soc. Mining Engrs. Republican. Mormon. Club: Ft. Douglas-Hidden Valley Country. Home: 309 Overlook Dr Timonium MD 21093 Office: PO Box 11248 Salt Lake City UT 84147

ENSWEILER, RICHARD LAURENCE, credit union exec.; b. Milw., Dec. 1, 1940; s. Donald George and Nancy Ruth (Kulk) E.; B.S., Lakeland Coll., 1963; m. Judith Ann Johnson, Dec. 14, 1973; children—Michael, Jeffrey. Treas.-mgr. Harley Davidson Credit Union, Milw., 1965-68; field rep. Mich. Credit Union League, Detroit, 1968-71; mgr. Minn. League Credit Unions, St. Paul, 1971-73; pres. Ill. Credit Union League, Oak Brook, Ill., 1974—; treas. Mid-States Corp. Fed Credit Union, 1976—; sec.-treas. Ill. Credit Union League Service Corp., 1974—. Mem. adv. bd. Ill. State Scholarship Commn., 1977—. Mem. Credit Union Legis. Action Council (pres. 1975—), Assn. of Credit Union League Execs. (sec. 1976-77, treas. 1978-80, vice chmn. 1980—), Am. Chgo. socs. assn. execs., Lakeland Coll. Alumni Assn. (dir. 1976-79). Clubs: Masons, Lions. Home: 1340 Meyer Dr Addison IL 60101 Office: 2011 Swift Dr Oak Brook IL 60521

ENTWISTLE, SHERWOOD RAYBURN, publishing co. exec.; b. Brant Lake, N.Y., June 19, 1919; s. Raymond William and Welhemina (Lawson) E.; student pub. schs., Elmira Heights, N.Y.; m. Mary Jo McCollom, Mar. 19, 1943; children—Joan Annette Entwistle Garrett, Nancy Elaine Entwistle Banks, Jill Marie. Clk. purchasing dept. Phila. Evening Bull., 1937-39, newspaperboy contest dept. mgr., 1940-41; pub. realtions dir., circulation dir. Tex. Farm and Ranch Pub. Co., Dallas, 1946-54; with Facts Forum, pub. info. orgn., Dallas, 1955-57; circulation dir. Petroleum Engr. Pub. Co., Dallas, 1957-69; mktg. dir. Gas mag. Chilton Co., Houston, 1969-74; advt. mgr. S.W. Advt. and The Tex. Fisherman mags. Cordovan Corp., Houston, 1974-81; advt. dir. Cordovan Bus. Jours., 1981—; guest lectr. mktg. So. Meth. U., 1968-69. Served from pvt. to capt., inf., U.S. Army, 1941-45; ETO. Decorated Bronze Star, Purple Heart. Mem. Bus./Profl. Advt. Assn. Republican. Home: 8323 Hazen St Houston TX 77036 Office: 5314 Bingle Rd Houston TX 77092

EPLEY, JOHN EDWARD, landman, oil and gas operator; b. Howard County, Tex., Oct. 23, 1948; s. James Filmore and Charlotte (Willingham) E.; student Schriener Inst., 1967-69, S.W. Tex. State U., 1969-71, No. Tex. State U., 1971-72; m. Patricia Reichle, Aug. 21, 1971; children—Michale Ryan, Erin Michelle, Meagan Diane. Salesman, co-owner Continental Field Services, Inc., 1972; mgr., co-owner Epley Abstract Co., Inc., 1972-74, Epley Investments, Inc., 1974-80; co-owner Treeline Landscape Constrn., Inc., 1979-80, Epley-White, 1978-79, Kimley Corp., 1980—, Prodn. Enhancement, Inc., 1980—, Fittness Systems, Inc., 1980—. Bd. dirs. Permian Civic Ballet, 1980. Mem. Rocky Mountain Oil and Gas Assn., Petroleum Landman's Assn., Permian Basin Landman's Assn. Roman Catholic. Office: Suite 309 WTW Wall St Midland TX 79702

EPLING, MICHAEL RAY, fin. exec.; b. Slayton, Minn., Aug. 13, 1946; s. Raymond and Marie Elsie (Larsen) E.; B.S. in Bus., U. Calif., Berkeley, 1968, M.B.A., 1970; m. Julie Anne Rubini, Aug. 20, 1967; children—Nancy Marie. Staff acct. Price Waterhouse & Co., San Francisco, 1970-72; EDP audit mgr. Fireman's Fund Ins. Cos., San Francisco, 1972-75, asst. controller, 1975-77; controller GATX Fin. Services, Inc., San Francisco, 1977-80, v.p. adminstrn. and control, 1980—. Bd. dirs. Trinity Luth. Ch., San Rafael, Calif., 1981—. Mem. Am. Inst. C.P.A.'s, Calif. Soc. C.P.A.'s. Republican. Lutheran. Office: 4 Embarcadero Center San Francisco CA 94111

EPPLEY, RICHARD LEE, banker; b. Mt. Vernon, Ohio, Jan. 31, 1943; s. Walter and Martha (Hayes) E.; student Coll. of Wooster, 1961-63; B.B.A., U. Mich., 1965, M.B.A., 1966; m. Carole Catherine Klebba, Oct. 19, 1968; children—Heather, David, Jane. Bond trader Continental Ill. Nat. Bank, Chgo., 1966-68; pres. Innovest Corp., Chgo., 1968-69; with Morgan Guaranty Trust Co. of N.Y., N.Y.C., 1969—, asst. treas., 1970, asst. v.p., 1972, v.p., 1975, key v.p., 1977—. Trustee, Central Presbyn. Ch., N.Y.C., 1972-74; elder Madison Ave. Presbyn. Ch., 1978—. Republican. Home: 164 E 71st St New York NY 10021 Office: 23 Wall St New York NY 10015

EPPLEY, ROLAND RAYMOND, JR., fin. services exec.; b. Balt., Apr. 1, 1932; s. Roland Raymond and Verna (Garretson) E.; B.A., Johns Hopkins, 1952, M.A., 1953; m. LeVerne Pittman; children—Kim, Kent, Todd. Asst. chief data processing, Bethlehem Steel Co., Balt., 1958-62; pres., dir. Comml. Credit Computer Corp., Balt., 1962-68, Central Info. Processing Corp., Balt., 1968-71, Eastern States Bankcard Assn., Inc., Lake Success, N.Y., 1971—, Omniswitch Corp., Lake Success, 1973-80, Nataswitch Corp., Atlanta, 1973-80, Eastern States Monetary Services, Inc., 1977—, Eastern States Data Services, Inc., 1977—. Mem. adv. bd. St. Johns U., 1973—, also adj. prof. Served with USCG, 1953-55. Recipient Peabody award, Scott Key. Mem. Am. Mgmt. Assn., Data Processing Mgmt. Assn. (Performance award), Assn. for Systems Mgmt., Electronic Fund Transfer Assn. (bd. govs.), Interbank Assn. (ops. com.), Plandome Property Assn. (bd. dirs.), Phi Beta Kappa, Omicron Delta Epsilon, Beta Gamma Sigma, Sigma Phi Epsilon (citation). Republican. Clubs: Plandome Country, Hillendale Country, Meadow Brook Country, Madison Sq. Garden, Masons, Shriners. Home: 77 Westgate Blvd Plandome NY 11030 Office: 4 Ohio Dr Lake Success NY 11042

EPPS, JAMES VERNON, ins. agt., Realtor; b. Kingstree, S.C., Aug. 12, 1928; s. John Vernon and Opal (McKnight) E.; student U. S.C., 1946-50; m. Dot Rast, 1951; children—John, Steve, Leah. Farmer, cattleman, S.C., 1950; pres. Epps-McLendon Ins., Lake City, S.C., 1956—; Realtor, Epps Land & Cattle Co., 1962—; dir. Lake City State Bank. Mem. exec. bd. Florence County (S.C.) Econ. Opportunity Commn.; mem. Florence County Planning Council; mem. Lake City Zoning Commn.; chmn. bd. trustees Presbyterian Homes of S.C.; past pres. Lake City P.T.A.; past chmn. Lake City United Fund. Mem. S.C. Assn. Ind. Ins. Agts., Carolinas Assn. Profl. Ins. Agts. (pres. 1980—), Lake City Bd. Realtors (past pres.), Lake City C. of C. (past pres.). Presbyterian. Clubs: Lake City Band Boosters Club (past pres.); Lions (past pres., dep. dist. gov.). Home: 119 2d Ave Lake City SC 29560 Office: 249 W Main St PO Box 1348 Lake City SC 29560

EPSTEIN, EDWARD GEORGE, mktg. research exec.; b. N.Y.C., Mar. 29, 1936; s. Samuel and Mary (Neiderman) E.; B.A., Hunter Coll., 1957; M.B.A., Columbia U., 1959; m. Phyllis Gorin, June 28, 1958; children—Jeffrey Stuart, Sheryl Lynn, Brian David. Asso. dir. mktg. research J. Walter Thompson Co., N.Y.C., 1966-68; dir. mktg. services J.B. Williams Co., N.Y.C., 1969-70; pres. Action Research Centers, N.Y.C., 1970-71, Edward Epstein & Assos., Inc., Syosset, N.Y., 1971—; lectr. G.W. Post Bus. Inst.; dir. Knechtel Research Scis., Skokie, Ill. Vice pres. Syosset-Jericho Democratic Club; bd. dirs. Nassau County Civil Liberties Union; committeeman Dem. Party. Served with USAF, 1959. Mem. Am. Mktg. Assn., Phi Beta Kappa, Beta Gamma Sigma. Contbr. articles to Mktg. Rev., Viewpoints. Home: 140 Split Rock Rd Syosset NY 11791 Office: 40 Underhill Blvd Syosset NY 11791

EPSTEIN, EDWARD JOSEPH, textile co. exec.; b. Newark, N.J., Apr. 18, 1920; s. Herman and Rose Jennis E.; B.S., Lowell U., 1941; M.B.A., Seton Hall U., 1970; children—Jonathan, Judith, Robert. Vice pres. Nat. Rayon Dyeing Co., Inc., Newark, 1950-57; v.p. No. Yarn Mills, Newark, 1957-70; pres. Spacetronics Industries, Newark, 1970—. Served to lt. USN, 1942-46. Jewish. Patentee in field. Office: 548 S 11th St Newark NJ 07103

EPSTEIN, JOSEPH SAMUEL, real estate co. exec.; b. Freeport, N.Y., Oct. 28, 1943; s. Harry and Bertha Marion (Kramer) E.; B.A., Lafayette Coll., 1965; J.D., U. Cin., 1968; m. Louise Ann Fersko, June 11, 1967; children—David, Katherine. Law clk. firm Moss & Rose, N.Y.C., 1969; v.p. Prime Mortgage Co., Clifton, N.J., 1969-76; pres., dir. 1st Am. Realty Assos. Inc., Clifton, 1976—; dir. Prime Motor Inns Inc., Clifton, 1980—. Mem. Lafayette Coll. Alumni Assn. (class pres. 1965-80), Pi Lambda Phi (Sigma Club pres. 1978—), Phi Delta Phi. Jewish. Clubs: Fairfield Racquet, Detroit Men's, ORT. Home: 71 Grandview Pl Upper Montclair NJ 07043 Office: 1030 Clifton Ave Clifton NJ 07013

EPSTEIN, LAWRENCE DAVID, stainless steel products mfg. co. exec.; b. Phila., Jan. 29, 1940; s. Perez and Mary (Kaplan) E.; B.S., Pa. State U., 1961; M.B.A., Temple U., 1968. With Perry Products Corp., Hainesport, N.J., 1961—, v.p., 1965-70, pres., 1970—; v.p. Perry Equipment Co., Inc., Hainesport, 1968—, Perry Machinery Corp., Hainesport, 1970—; mng. partner Hainesport Realty Venture, 1970—; pres. Perry Products Co. of P.R., 1974—. Mem. Burlington County (N.J.) Com. of Fifty; trustee United Way of Burlington County. Mem. Assn. Builders and Contractors, Young Pres.'s Orgn., Steel Plate Fabricators Assn., Friends of the Phila. Mus. of Art, Circus Model Builders, Circus Fans Am. Club: Variety Internat. Office: Perry Products Corp 25 Mount Laurel Rd Hainesport NJ 08036

EPSTEIN, MARVIN MORRIS, internat. mktg. exec.; b. Cleve., June 2, 1928; s. Isadore E. and Rose (Gevelber) E.; student Western Res. U., 1947-49; B.A., U. Mich., 1951; m. Lois Mae DeSure, June 10, 1956; children—Deborah Leigh, David Alan. Reporter, Plain Dealer, Cleve., 1951-52; editor AP, Columbus, 1952-54; asst. mng. editor Times-Star, Cin., 1954-56; internat. editor Milw. Jour., 1956-59; sr. asso. Eden & Assos., Cleve., 1959-61; with Austin Co., Cleve., 1961—, dir. internat. sales and mktg. services, 1968—. Trustee, Am. Jewish Com., Cleve. chpt., 1973—; vice chmn. Mgmt. Action Program, 1973—. Served with AUS, 1946-47. Recipient McNaught Gold medal U. Mich., 1951. Mem. Soc. Profl. Journalists, Greater Cleve. Growth Assn., Mich. Alumni Assn. Democrat. Jewish. Clubs: Mid-day of Cleve., U. Mich. Alumni (gov. local club 1968) (Cleve.). Home: 4161 Hadleigh Rd University Heights OH 44118 Office: 3650 Mayfield Rd Cleveland OH 44141

ERB, RICHARD JOSEPH, acct., corp. exec.; b. Kittanning, Pa., Mar. 25, 1936; s. Clarence Calvin and Helen Mae (Rupp) E.; B.S., Pa. State U., 1958; m. Jean Annall Richmond, Aug. 25, 1967; children—Stephanie Jean, Elizabeth Helen, Richard Alan. Public acct. Arthur Young & Co., N.Y.C., 1960-65; with Ingersoll-Rand Co., 1965—, div. controller, Allentown, Pa., 1974-79, v.p., controller, Woodcliff Lake, N.J., 1979—. Served with USNR, 1958-60. Office: 200 Chestnut Ridge Rd Woodcliff Lake NJ 07675

ERBURU, ROBERT F., newspaper pub. co. exec.; b. Ventura, Calif., 1930; grad. U. So. Calif., 1952, Harvard Law Sch., 1955. Pres., chief exec. officer, dir. Times Mirror Co., Los Angeles. Home: 1518 Blue Jay Way Los Angeles CA 90069 Office: Times Mirror Sq Los Angeles CA 90053

ERDMAN, DARYL ALLAN, supermarket exec.; b. Rochester, Minn., June 29, 1939; s. Earl G. and Leone B. (Mertz) E.; B.A. in Math. and Bus. Adminstrn., Luther Coll., 1961; M.B.A., Mich. State U., 1962; m. Audrey N. Pederson, June 18, 1961; children—Scott Allan, Denae Diane, Laura Louise. Co-founder Erdman Supermarkets, Inc., operators 5 supermarkets, Rochester, 1962—, v.p., 1965—; v.p., past owner Minnewawa Lodge Resort, Nisswa, Minn., 1976—; part owner Aldeen's Mens Wear, Rochester, 1974—; pres. Rotab Inc., Rochester, 1976—; pres., owner Tie Rack, Rochester, 1970-76; instr. food mktg. Rochester Community Coll., 1977. Mem. adv. com. Minn. Vocat.-Tech. Schs., mem. advisory com. distributive edn., 1974—; chmn. bldg. com. Holy Cross Luth. Ch., 1969-72; mem. advisory com. mktg. Rochester Community Coll., 1976—; mem. admissions adv. council Luther Coll., 1972-76, chmn. area Pund dr., 1979; mem. council and planning com. Bethel Luth. Ch.; del. White House Conf. on Small Bus., 1980. Recipient Distinguished Service award Luther Coll., 1976. Mem. Rochester Area C. of C. (dir.), Phi Kappa Phi, Beta Gamma Sigma. Club: Sertoma. Home: 901 17th St Rochester MN 55901 Office: 1652 Hwy 52 N Rochester MN 55901

ERDMANN, MARVIN ELMER, wholesale food co. exec.; b. Milw., July 1, 1930; s. Walter and Lenora E.; student public schs., Milw., m. Lois Jean Yellick, Apr. 14, 1951; children—Mark Karter, Scott Kevin, Kim Robin. With A&P Tea Co., Milw., 1944-60, dept. mgr., 1949-51, store mgr., 1953-60; store mgr. Paulus Foods, Cedarburg, Wis., 1960-63; with Super Valu Stores, Inc., 1963—, field supr., 1964-69, sales mgr., Mpls., 1969-74, retail ops. mgr., Mpls., 1974-77, pres. Bismarck (N.D.) div., 1977—; lectr. bus. adminstrn. at high schs., colls. Served with U.S. Army, 1950-53. Decorated Bronze Star, Am. Spirit medal. Mem. N.D. Food Retailers Assn. (legis. cons.), Greater N.D. Assn. (speaker), Bismarck C. of C. (dir., mem. indsl. com.). Republican. Lutheran. Clubs: Apple Creek Country, Supreme Ct. Racquetball. Home: 1217 Crestview Ln Bismarck ND 58501 Office: 707 Airport Rd Bismarck ND 58502

EREMITA, MICHAEL, developer, contractor, investor; b. Dedham, Mass., Jan. 30, 1931; s. Marco and Mary L. (Lalli) E.; B.S. in Bus. Adminstrn., Boston U., 1953; m. Marilyn B. Giberson, June 8, 1958; children—Mark, Joseph, Lisa, Peter, Carolyn. Pres., Eremita & Valley Partnership, 1957—, Eremita & Valley, Inc., 1960—; treas. Chateau Motor Inn, Inc., Bangor, Maine, 1974—, Budget Motor Inn, Bangor, 1978—, Bangor Motor Inn, Inc., 1979—; developer, contractor, investor; dir. Brewer Savs. Bank. Bldg. com. St. Joseph Ch.; active Brewer Indsl. Devel., Brewer Housing Authority. Served with USAF, 1954-58. Home: 43 Broadlawn Dr Brewer ME 04412 Office: Bangor Motor Inn Hogan Rd Bangor ME 04401

ERFF, CHARLES GREGORY, mfg. co. exec.; b. Linden, N.J., Mar. 24, 1946; s. Charles George and Florence M. (Siegel) E.; B.A., Lebanon Valley Coll., 1969; postgrad. Ball State U., 1977-79; m. Katherine Neijstrom, Sept. 26, 1970; children—Melanie, Valerie and Carey (triplets), Gregory. Mdse. mgr., mktg. coordinator Women's Fashion div. Brown Shoe Co., St. Louis, 1969-75; v.p. mktg. MarkHon Industries, Inc., Wabash, Ind., 1975-78; pres. Charles G. Erff, Assos., Marion, Ind., 1978-79, Tru-Matic, Inc., East Stroudsburg, Pa., 1979—; dir. Phoenix-Hecht Inc., Chgo. Asso. bd. dirs. Jr. Achievement of Monroe County, 1979—; mem. 1980 Nat. UN Day Com. Served with USAR, 1969-74. Mem. Young Pres.'s Orgn., Pres.'s Assn. of Am. Mgmt. Assn., AIAA, Pocono Mountain C. of C. (chmn. crime com.). Roman Catholic. Home: West Hill Buck Hill Falls PA 18323 Office: Route 2 Box 214 East Stroudsburg PA 18301

ERFFT, KENNETH REYNDERS, ednl. cons.; b. Chgo., Nov. 14, 1908; s. Victor Athen and Ethel (Reynders) E.; A.B., No. Mich. U., 1932, LL.D., 1961; M.A., U. Richmond, 1936, D.C.S., 1967; D.Litt., MacLean Coll., 1947; m. Nancy Fontaine Creath, June 8, 1940. Tchr., Ironwood (Mich.) High Sch., 1928-30; instr. Gogebic Jr. Coll., 1930-32; bus. mgr., clk. sch. bd. Petersburg (Va.) Pub. Schs., 1935-42; bus. mgr. Furman U., 1946-54; comptroller Pa. State U., 1954-57; treas. Rutgers U., New Brunswick, N.J., 1957-62, v.p., 1958-62, treas. Rutgers U. Research and Ednl. Found., 1957-62; v.p., treas. Thomas Jefferson Med. U., Phila., 1962-65; pres. Kenneth R. Erfft Assos. Inc., ednl. cons., Phila., 1965-66; v.p., treas. Duquesne U., Pitts., 1966-71; pres. Univ. Center Va., 1974-79; chmn. bd. Carlisle-Asher Enterprises; dir. Carlisle-Asher Mgmt. Co., Afuture Fund; chmn. bd. Pennell Corp., Ken Ray Corp. Bd. assos. trustee U. Richmond. Served from lt. (j.g.) to comdr. USNR, 1942-46, 51-52. Decorated knight Sacred Order Constantinian of St. George. Mem. AAUP, Eastern Assn. Coll. and U. Bus. Officers, Middle States Assn., North Central Assn., Am. Council on Edn. (com. taxation and fiscal reporting to fed. govt.), Am. Legion, Omicron Delta Kappa, Tau Kappa Alpha, Phi Epsilon, Theta Omicron Rho, Delta Sigma Phi. Club: Torch (Pitts.). Author: (with Gerald P. Burns) The Administrators in Higher Education, 1962; editorial bd. Coll. and U. Bus. Adminstrn., 1966-68; contbr. articles to profl. jours. Home: 9501 Ground Hog Dr Richmond VA 23235

ERGER, EUGENE MERTON, broadcasting co. exec.; b. Passaic, N.J., Nov. 17, 1925; s. Edward Isaac and Marguerite (Wiemokly) E.; grad. high sch.; m. Constance Mae Ormerod, Sept. 12, 1948; children—Linda, Kenneth, Steve, Nancy. Partner, Ed Erger & Son, Los Angeles, 1948-54, O. Conger, Los Angeles, 1954-56, Continental Metal Furniture Co., Los Angeles, 1956-60; mgr. radio sta. KTOH, Kauai Island, Hawaii, 1961-64; v.p., gen. mgr. radio/TV stas. KGMB AM/FM/TV, KPUA AM/TV, Honolulu, 1965-73, exec. v.p., gen. mgr. Heftel Broadcasting, Inc., 1965-73; pres. Gene Erger Promotions Unltd., Honolulu, 1974—. Publicity chmn. Aloha council Boy Scouts Am., 1965-67, Am. Cancer Soc. Hawaii, 1970-72; bd. dirs. Cystic Fibrosis Agy., Hawaii, 1974, Variety Club Internat. Sch. for Children with Learning Disabilities. Served with USMCR, 1942-45. Decorated Purple Heart; named Hawaii Media Man of Year, Advt. Agy. Hawaii, 1967. Mem. Hawaii Assn. Broadcasters (pres. 1969). Clubs: Mid-Pacific Country (Kailua, Hawaii); Variety (dir.). Author: KO of Menehuneland, 1963. Home: 108 Kailuana Loop Kailua HI 96734 Office: 770 Kapiolani Suite 601 Honolulu HI 96813

ERICKSON, LLOYD ELWOOD, financial exec.; b. Pine County, Minn., Sept. 11, 1925; s. Henry and Ellen (Carlson) E.; student Bowling Green State U., 1943-45, U. Calif. at Berkeley, 1947-51; B.S., Golden Gate Coll., 1954; m. Dorris Berta Hicks, Feb. 22, 1947; children—Scott, Randall, Ross. With Central Bank, Oakland, Calif., 1947-51, San Francisco Bank, Hayward, Calif., 1954; navy auditor USN Audit Office, Madrid, Spain and San Francisco, 1954-57; budget and planning mgr. Western region Westinghouse Elec. Co., Sunnyvale, Calif., 1957-61, govt. contracts mgr., 1961-63, budget/planning mgr., 1963-65, finance mgr. Marine div., 1965-67, plant controller, Lester, Pa., 1967-68, controller Steam Turbine div., 1968-78, controller power generation ops., 1978—. Com. chmn., treas. Boy Scouts Am., Mountain View, Calif., 1962-65; treas. Congl. Community Ch., Sunnyvale, Calif., 1965-66; bd. dirs. Benchmark Sch., Media, Pa., 1977—; trustee YMCA, Chester, Pa., 1977—. Served with USN, 1943-47, 51-54. Mem. Nat. Assn. Accountants. Republican. Presbyterian. Home: 101 Fawn Hill Ln Media PA 19063 Office: Lester PO Box 9175 Philadelphia PA 19113

ERICKSON, RAYMOND FREDRICK, forest resource cons.; b. Spokane, Wash., Jan. 9, 1941; came to Can., 1965; s. Carl Gunnar and Ruth (Mann) E.; B.S. in Forestry, U. Wash., 1965; m. Kathleen Gulleson, Mar. 24, 1961; children—Jeffrey Stuart, Gregory Gunnar. Forest engr. Crown Zellerbach Ltd., Kitimat, B.C., 1965-67, Canadian Cellulose, Terrace, B.C., 1967-69, Wedeene River Contractors, Terrace, 1969-71; founder, operator All Trees Resources Ltd., constrn. and logging mgmt., forest industry investments, forest engring. and resource cons., Vancouver, B.C., 1971—. Address: 8006 Elliott St Vancouver BC V5S 2P2 Canada

ERICKSON, RICHARD LEE, mfg. co. exec.; b. Youngstown, Ohio, Jan. 3, 1938; s. Albin E. and Martha L. (Sandberg) E.; A.A., North Park Coll., 1957; B.S. in Elec. Engring., Northwestern U., 1959; M.S. in Engring. Adminstrn., Syracuse U., 1969; m. Jean A. Brickley, Sept. 10, 1960; children—Carolyn, Diane, David. Devel. engr. Motorola Inc., Chgo., 1958-61; project engr., engring. mgr. Gen. Electric Co., Syracuse, N.Y., 1961-71; Presdl. exchange exec. U.S. Dept. Transp., Washington, 1971-72; mgr. strategic planning Gen. Electric Co., Erie, Pa., 1972-78; v.p. products planning Purolator Inc., Piscathaway, N.J., 1978-79; dir. planning TRW Indsl. Products Group, Cleve., 1979—; dir. Albin E. Erickson Co., Youngstown, Ohio, 1960-77. Sch. dir., Liverpool, N.Y., 1970-71; mem. Millcreek Twp. Planning Commn., Erie, 1975-78, chmn., 1978; mem. County Exec. Republican Com., Erie, 1973-75; ch. chmn. Redeemer Evang. Covenant Ch., Liverpool, 1969-71; chmn. Middle East Conf. Evang. Covenant Ch. Am., 1975-78; mem. World Missions Bd., 1973-78. Mem. IEEE, Elfun Soc. (chpt. sec. 1974-75, vice chmn. 1975-76). Home: 21025 Byron Rd Shaker Heights OH 44122 Office: 20600 Chagrin Blvd Cleveland OH 44122

ERICKSON, ROLAND AXEL, financial and mgmt. cons.; b. Worcester, Mass., Sept. 8, 1913; s. Axel and Anna (Erickson) E.; A.B., Clark U., 1935; A.M., Tufts U., 1937; LL.D., Susquehanna U.; m. Roxie Erickson, Apr. 6, 1940; children—Brent, Lorna. Instr. econs. Tufts U., 1935-37; economist Norton Co., Worcester, 1937-41; v.p. Guaranty Bank & Trust Co., Worcester, 1941-47, treas., 1946-47, pres., 1947-64, dir., 1945-69; sr. v.p. Gen. Foods Corp., White Plains, N.Y., 1964-66, exec. v.p., 1966-70, dir., 1965-70; chmn. bd., dir. New Eng. High Carbon Wire Corp., 1958-73; dir. Marine Savs. & Loan Inc. Fla., State Mut. Life Assurance Co. of Am., Norton Co., Bliss & Laughlin Industries, Am. Variable Annuity Life Assurance Co., Wain-Roy Co., Inc.; vice chmn. bd. Bofors Am.; mem. adv. com. Bankers Trust Co., 1966-76. Mem. Presdl. Task Force on Prospects of Small Businesses, 1969. Trustee Clark U. Decorated knight Royal Order of Vasa 1st class, knight comdr. Royal Order of North Star (Sweden). Mem. Nat. Assn. Bus. Economists, Newcomen Soc., Swedish Council of Am., Am. Econ. Assn., Am. Acad. Polit. and Social Sci., Phi Beta Kappa. Republican. Baptist. Clubs: Masons (32 deg.); Worcester, Worcester Country, Odin, Univ.; Royal Poinciana, Port Royal (Naples, Fla.). Contbr. articles in field of corp. fin., money and banking, fiscal policy to various publs. Address: 1285 Gulf Shore Blvd N Naples FL 33940

ERICSON, KARL INGVAR, pump mfg. co. exec.; b. Stockholm, Feb. 10, 1936; s. Ragnar Karl and Margit I. (Nilsson) E.; Civ.Eng., Royal U. Engring., Stockholm, 1960; m. Kerstin Wangberg, June 19, 1960; children—Bengt, Eva. With DeLaval Co., 1960-62, Flygt Sweden, 1962-64, 67-76, Sonesson Pump Co., 1964-66; mktg. dir. Flygt USA, Norwalk, Conn., 1977—; tchr. mech. engring. Royal U., Sweden, 1960-73. Served with Swedish Army, 1955-57. Mem. Am. Soc. Swedish Engrs. Author articles in field. Home: 219 Wilton Rd Westport CT 06880 Office: 129 Glover Ave Norwalk CT 06856

ERIKSEN, JOHN GRABER, hobby and craft wholesale co. exec.; b. Tulsa, Dec. 13, 1935; s. Carl A. and Dorothy (Graber) E.; B.S., U. Kans., 1957; m. Jane Faubion, Aug. 5, 1956; children—Jeff G., Jana L. Pres., Eriksen's Crafts, Inc., Hutchinson, Kans., 1960—; dir. Northgate Nat. Bank. Mem. exec. bd. Kanza council Boy Scouts Am., 1971-79; chmn. Greater Univ. Fund, U. Kans., 1974-75. Chmn. planning commn., Hutchinson, Kans., 1968. Served to 1st lt. USAF, 1958-60. Mem. Young Presidents Orgn., Hutchinson C. of C. (dir. 1962-64, 77-80), Kans. U. Alumni Assn. (dir.), Sigma Chi, Alpha Kappa Psi. Presbyterian. Rotarian. Home: Willow Brook Hutchinson KS 67501 Office: 11th and Halstead Sts Hutchinson KS 67501

ERNEST, ALBERT DEVERY, JR., banker; b. Mobile, Ala., June 7, 1930; s. Albert Devery and Dorothy (Griffith) E.; B.A. in Econs., U. Va., 1954; grad. Advanced Mgmt. Program, Harvard U., 1974; m. Donna Barnett Sims, Nov. 20, 1954; children—Albert Devery, Lise Sims. Mgmt. trainee St. Regis Paper Co., N.Y.C., 1954, asst. to v.p. Timberlands div., 1958-61; founder, pres. Albert Ernest Enterprises, Investments and Mgmt. Cons., Jacksonville, Fla., 1961-76, Allied Timber Co., Inc., Jacksonville, 1965-73; exec. v.p. Barnett Bank of Jacksonville, 1976-77, pres., 1977—, chief exec. officer, 1979—, also dir.; dir. Barnett Mortgage Co., St. Regis Paper Co., Alpert Corp. Trustee, Jacksonville U., Jacksonville Country Day Sch., Cathedral Found.; bd. dirs. United Way, 1978—, North Fla. council Boy Scouts Am., 1978—, Cummer Gallery of Art, 1979—, Jacksonville Community Council, Inc., 1978—, Jacksonville Symphony Assn., 1979—, Leadership Jacksonville, 1978—, Arts Assembly of Jacksonville, 1978—. Mem. Am. Bankers Assn., Fla. Bankers Assn., Fla. Forestry Assn., Forest Farmers Assn., Young Pres.'s Orgn., Jacksonville Area C. of C. (gov.). Democrat. Episcopalian. Clubs: River, Harvard (N.Y.C.), Fla. Yacht, Ponte Vedra, Timuquana Country, Farmington Country, Meninak of Jacksonville (dir. 1978—), Deerwood. Home: 8070 Lakecrest Dr Jacksonville FL 32216 Office: 100 Laura St Jacksonville FL 32202

ERNEST, ROBERT C., corp. exec.; b. 1924; ed. U. Wis., M.I.T. With Kimberly-Clark Corp., 1952—, v.p. paper products, 1971, group v.p. fine paper and spltys. group, 1971, dir., 1971, exec. v.p., 1972, pres., 1978—. Office: Kimberly Clark Corp 2001 Marathon Ave Neenah WI 54956*

ERNST, JAMES WALTER, housewares importer and distbr.; b. Toledo, July 11, 1936; s. Walter Herman and Theresa Clara (Roszak) E.; B.B.A., U. Toledo, 1959, M.B.A. (Page scholar), 1963; m. Rhua Heckart, Apr. 4, 1970; children—Ronald Bruce, Erik Bernard. Spl. accounts rep. Standard Register Co., Toledo, 1959-63; br. mgr. Owens-Ill. Inc., 1963-67, nat. chain store mgr., 1967-68, mgr. design services, 1968-70, Eastern regional mgr., 1970-74; gen. sales mgr. J.G. Durand Internat., Millville, N.J., 1975-76; gen. sales mgr. Interpace Corp., Parsippany, N.J., 1976; v.p. mktg. and design services Wheaton Industries, Millville, 1976-77; v.p. mktg. Stangl Pottery div. Dorchester Industries, Millville, 1976-77; v.p., gen. mgr. Wheaton Consumer Products div. Wheaton Industries, Millville, 1977-79; pres. James W. Ernst Assos., Inc., Rosenhayn, N.J., 1979—. Pres. Democratic Com. Deerfield Twp. (N.J.), 1978; mem. Deerfield Twp. Planning Bd., 1979—. Mem. Am. Mgmt. Assn., Am. Mktg. Assn., Sigma Alpha Epsilon. Mormon. Home: RD #7 Bridgeton Ave Bridgeton NJ 08302 Office: PO Box 37 Rosenhayn NJ 08352

ERNST, JOHN LOUIS, advt. exec.; b. Pine Bluff, Ark., Dec. 24, 1932; s. Albert C. and Christine B. (Vinent) E.; B.S., Spring Hill Coll., 1954, B.S., 1954; m. Lois Geraci Ernst, June 12, 1971; children—Ann Marie, Catherine Theresa, Laura Elizabeth, Christine Margaret. Stockbroker Washington Planning Co., Washington, 1957-58; with sales exec. dept. Am. Airlines, Washington, Phila., N.Y.C., 1958-62; account exec. Ted Bates Advt. Agy., N.Y.C., 1962-65; sr. v.p., mgmt. dir. Marschalk Advt. Agy., N.Y.C., 1965-68; dir. Interpublic Service Corp., N.Y.C.; 1967-69; sr. v.p., mng. dir. McCann-Erickson Advt. Agy., N.Y.C., 1969-70; pres. Ernst-Van Praag, N.Y.C., 1970-75; chmn. bd. Advt. to Women, Inc., N.Y.C. Served to capt., USMCR, 1954-57. Home: 435 E 52nd St New York NY 10022 Office: 777 Third Ave New York NY 10017

ERNST, WALTER RICHARD, transp. cons.; b. Phila., Aug. 8, 1940; s. Walter August and Margaret Leella (Taylor) E.; B.S., Lehigh U., 1962; M.B.A., U. Wash., 1966. Asst. trainmaster, trainmaster Pa. R.R. Co., Buffalo, Renovo, Pa., Camden, N.J., 1966-69; systems analyst Penn Central Transp. Co., Phila., 1969-70, trainmaster, Selkirk, N.Y., 1970, asst. terminal supt., Selkirk, 1970-72, terminal supt., Enola, Pa., 1972, Rochester, N.Y., 1973-74; v.p. Wyer, Dick & Co., Livingston, N.J., 1974—. Mem. Greater Gotham Bus. Council, N.Y.C. Mem. Am. Mgmt. Assn., Am. Assn. R.R. Supts. Republican. Presbyterian. Home: D4 Twin Lights Terr Highlands NJ 07732 Office: 70 S Orange Ave Livingston NJ 07039

ERNST, WILLIAM H., heavy equipment mfg. cons.; b. Los Angeles, July 2, 1927; s. Franklin H. and Olive C. (Johnson) E.; student Whitman Coll., 1945, Calif. Inst. Tech., 1945-46; B.S., U. Calif., Berkeley and Davis, 1950; m. Ellouise M. Kimball, May 26, 1950; children—Sharon Louise, Jan Marie. Farmer, Tulelake, Calif., 1946-55; with Caterpillar Tractor Co., Peoria, Ill., 1956—, service rep., 1957-60, asst. mgr. Eastern div. service, 1960-64, mgr. European div. service, 1964-66, asst. mgr. parts and service dept. U.S., 1966, mgr. service dept. U.S., 1966-75, subs. cons. service engring., 1975-80, cons., 1981—. Served with USNR, 1945-46. Mem. Kappa Sigma. Home: 1204 W Woodside Dr Dunlap IL 61525 Office: Caterpillar Tractor Co 100 NE Adams St Peoria IL 61602

ERSEK, ROBERT ALLEN, physician, plastic surg. devices mfg. co. exec.; b. Ridley Park, Pa., June 19, 1938; s. Joseph M. and Theda Louise (Krommes) E.; B.S., Morris Harvey Coll., 1961; M.D., Hahnemann Med. Coll., 1966; m. Gerry Mullins, Mar. 28, 1959; children—Stephanie Louise, Cynthia Liegh. Intern, U. Minn., Mpls., 1966-67, resident, 1967-73; resident in plastic surgery Tulane U., 1975-77, U. Miss., 1978; practice medicine, specializing in plastic surgery, 1978—; chmn. bd. dirs., med. dir. Med. Gen., Mpls., 1969—; med. dir., dir. Genetic Labs., St. Paul, 1970—, Emerald Airlines, Austin. Served to maj. USAF, 1973-75. Recipient Alan Edelson prize Hahnemann Med. Coll., 1966. Mem. AMA., A.C.S., Am. Coll. Emergency Physicians. Author: Controlling Pain, 1978. Contbr. numerous articles to profl. jours. Patentee surg. devices. Home: 2300 Cypress Point W Lost Creek Austin TX 78746 Office: Bailey Square Med Center 1111 W 34th St Austin TX 78705

ERWIN, DONALD FRANCIS, ins. co. exec.; b. Bklyn., Sept. 12, 1933; s. Frank J. and Phyllis M. E.; student U. Ga., 1953, Harpur Coll., 1955; B.A., U. Puget Sound, 1958; m. Mary Lou Goodenow, Aug. 4, 1956; children—Gregory Patrick, Todd Douglas. Indsl. engr. F.S. Harmon Mfg. Co., Tacoma, 1959-60; controller Aetna Life & Casualty Co., Tacoma, 1960-64, sales supr., 1964-70, gen. agt. for Wash., Alaska, Idaho and Mont., Seattle, 1970—; instr. bus. and sales mgmt. U. Puget Sound, Seattle City Coll. Served with U.S. Army, 1953-55. Mem. C.L.U. Soc., Nat. Assn. Life Underwriters, Tacoma-Pierce County Assn. Life Underwriters (past pres.), Wash. Assn. Life Underwriters (past v.p.), Gen. Agts. and Mgrs. Assn., Gen. Agt. Elected Field Council. Clubs: Firerest Golf, Tacoma Country. Office: 627 Washington Bldg Seattle WA 98101

ERWIN, FRANK WILLIAM, mgmt. cons., pub. co. exec.; b. Elizabeth, N.J., Nov. 22, 1931; s. Frank J. and Jessie (Rugero) E.; B.A. cum laude, N.Y.U., 1957; m. Bridget E. Taddeo, June 26, 1965; children—Kristen, Bryan. With MBS, 1957-62, asst. to pres., asst. sec. to bd. dirs., 1960-62; dep. dir., div. selection, dir. recruiting operations Peace Corps, 1962-65; exec. asst. to sec. labor, 1965-68; chmn., pres. Richardson Bellows, Henry & Co., Inc., 1968—. Served with AUS, 1949-52. Mem. Am. Psychol. Assn., Am. Soc. Personnel Adminstrn., Am. Numis. Assn. Home: 1400 S Joyce St Arlington VA 22202 Office: 1140 Connecticut Ave NW Washington DC 20236

ERWIN, ROBERT GRANT, holding co. exec., publisher; b. London, Ont., Can., Feb. 28, 1944; s. Frank Middleton and Violet Dorothea (Schultz) E.; B.A. in Bus. Adminstrn. (Gold medal), Wilfrid Laurier U., 1966. Pres., chief exec. officer Edu-Media Holdings Ltd., Kitchener, Ont., 1969—; publisher, pres. Inst. for Small Bus., Inc., Kitchener; chmn. bd., chief exec. officer Futronics, Inc. Chmn., Kitchener Public Library System, 1968-74; bd. govs. Wilfrid Laurier U., Waterloo, Ont., 1970-72. Mem. Internat. Council Small Bus. (v.p. Can. chpt.), Can. C. of C. Club: Albany (Toronto). Office: 1 Adam St Kitchener ON N2H 5P6 Canada

ESCALANTE, JUDSON ROBERT, bus. cons.; b. Schenectady, Jan. 31, 1930; s. James S. and Katherine H. (Judson) E.; B.A., Union Coll., 1953; m. Charlotte D. Carpenter, June 7, 1958; children—David J., Katherine Anne. Asst. estate planning officer, Nat. Commercial Bank, Albany, N.Y., 1955-65; founder, v.p., sec., dir. Fidelity Bank of Colonie, Latham, N.Y., 1966-69; area dir., Gen. Bus. Services, Latham, N.Y., 1969—; dir. Manufacturer's Hanover Trust Co. Capital Region; instr. in field. Bd. dirs., treas. Capital Artists Opera Co., 1970-74, 79; mem. fund dr. com. Union Coll., 1979-80. Served with U.S. Army, 1953-55. Mem. Tax Cons. Assn., Colonie C. of C. (treas., dir. 1972-76), Union Coll. Alumni Soc. (pres. 1971-73; Alumni Gold medal 1978), Dutch Settlers Soc. of Albany. Republican. Episcopal. Clubs: U. of City of Albany, Exchange of Albany, Mohawk-Hudson Power Squadron. Home: 7 Vale St Latham NY 12110 Office: 1 Herbert Dr Latham NY 12110

ESCHBACHER, KENNETH HENRY, retail co. exec.; b. Cleve., Jan. 29, 1947; s. Frank Edward and Irma Freida (Mueller) E.; B.Adminstrv. Sci., Ohio State U., 1969; m. Judith Jo Donda, June 21, 1969; children—Timothy Joseph, Amanda Christina. Mgr. trainee J.C. Penney's, Mansfield, Ohio, 1970; asst. mgr., sportswear buyer Schwartz's Apparel, Dover, Ohio, 1971; store mgr., gen. merchandiser Kline Co. Inc., Dover, 1971-74; exec. v.p. Schwartz-Klines, New Philadelphia, Ohio, 1974-78, pres., 1978—, pres. subs., Wilson's Dept. Stores, Inc., Daniel's Women's Wear, Inc.; instr. retailing Kent State U., 1979. Mem. Nat. Retail Mchts. Assn., Men's Retailers Am., Dover Retail Mchts. (pres. 1972-73), Monroe Mall Mchts. Assn. (pres. 1974-75), Tuscarawas C. of C. (trustee), Aircraft Owners and Pilots Assn. Office: 1260 Monroe St New Philadelphia OH 44663

ESKRIDGE, ELBERT STANFORD, JR., transp. co. exec.; b. Raleigh, N.C., Apr. 5, 1943; s. Elbert Stanford and Eloise (Grady) E.; A.B. in English, U. N.C., 1965; m. Brenda Carol Petty, June 12, 1965; 1 dau., Meredith Grady. Pilot, salesman Holladay Aero., Richmond, Va., 1967-70; sales mgr. Cardinal Airlines, Lynchburg, Va., 1970-72; from salesman to v.p. mktg. Raleigh Durham Aviation, Morrisville, N.C., 1972-77; pres., dir. The Aviation Group, Inc., Chapel Hill, N.C., 1977—; dir. Orion Air, Inc. Home: 809 Old Mill Rd Chapel Hill NC 27514 Office: 500 Eastowne Dr Box 2809 Chapel Hill NC 27514

ESLING, HARRY ROBERT, JR., automotive parts mfg. co. exec.; b. Detroit, June 13, 1932; s. Harry Robert and Helen Frances (Moore) E.; B.S., Mich. State U., 1955, M.B.A., 1977; m. Kathryn Louise Brownyer, Aug. 4, 1962; children—Lynne Elizabeth, Karen Laurinda, Lisa Michelle. Buyer, Ford Motor Co., Dearborn, Mich., 1956-58; sales mgr. Hurd Lock & Mfg. Co., Detroit, 1958-65; sales rep. Rockwell Internat. Corp., Detroit, 1965-68; account mgr. Dura Corp., Southfield, Mich., 1968-69; v.p. sales Midland Steel Products Co., Southfield, 1969-78, pres., Cleve., 1979—; cons. Carl A. Weber Co., Detroit, 1977—. Chpt. chmn. United Found. Torch drive, 1959-61; jobs recruiter Nat. Alliance Businessman, 1968; sustaining mem. Republican Nat. Com., 1978—; mem. Automotive Orgn. Team. Served with USAF, 1950-52. Mem. Soc. Automotive Engrs., Automotive Original Equipment Mfrs. (pres. 1978), Mensa, Sigma Nu. Episcopalian. Clubs: Detroit Athletic; Avon Oaks Country; Myrtle Beach Nat. Golf. Home: 400 Sadder Rd Bay Village OH 44140 Office: 10615 Madison Ave Cleveland OH 44102

ESPOSITO, ANTHONY JOSEPH, banker; b. Bklyn., July 12, 1937; s. Joseph and Concetta Esposito; diploma Am. Inst. Banking, 1970, Brown U. Grad. Sch. Banking, 1975; m. Ann Marie Dalia, Aug. 23, 1958; children—Joanne, Anthony Joseph, Lisa, Michael, Lori.

Dir. mktg. East River Savs. Bank, N.Y.C., 1975, v.p., 1978—; dir. Am. Gold Depository Corp., Massapequa, N.Y., Solar Micro Corp., Farmingdale, N.Y. Mem. advisory bd. cultural and performing arts Town of Oyster Bay, N.Y., 1976—; mem. adv. council on banking N.Y. State Assembly; bd. dirs. Youth Environ. Services Nassau County, 1978—. Named Citizen of Year, L.I. Press Assn., 1975. Mem. Fin. Advt. Mktg. Assn. N.Y. (dir.), Savs. Banks Officers Forum, Group Interchange Assn. N.Y., Massapequa C. of C. (pres. 1975), Massapequa Hist. Soc. (dir.), Sons of Italy. Roman Catholic. Clubs: K.C., Long Island (gov.), Lions (zone chmn.). Former fin. editor and columnist L.I. Observer Group newspapers. Home: 169 Ocean Ave Massapequa NY 11758 Office: 26 Cortlandt St New York NY 10007

ESSLINGER, ANNA MAE LINTHICUM, realtor; b. Clifton, Tenn., May 29, 1912; d. Wallace Prather and Minnie P. (Bates) Linthicum; student Miss. State Coll. Women, La. State U.; m. William Francis Esslinger, Sept. 29, 1932; children—Ann Lynn (Mrs. James C. Wilcox), Susan Angie (Mrs. Heinz J. Selig). Pres. Esslinger-Wooten-Maxwell Inc., real estate, Coral Gables, Fla., 1968—. Pres. Coral Gables Bd. Realtors, 1975. Mem. Fla. (dir.), Nat. assns. realtors, D.A.R., Chi Omega. Democrat. Christian Scientist. Clubs: Coral Gables Country, Riviera Country, Coral Gables Women's, Coral Gables Garden, Coconut Grove Garden, Coral Gables Music. Home: 311 Mendoza Ave Coral Gables FL 33134 Office: 1553 San Ignacio St Coral Gables FL 33146

ESTABROOKS, THOMAS FRANK, SR., data systems exec.; b. Can., Oct. 27, 1942; came to U.S., 1962; s. Kenneth O. and Myrtle D. (Hayes) E.; A.S., Mitchell Coll., 1970; student Conn. Coll., 1972-74; m. Marianne Joan Ingersoll, Sept. 5, 1961; children—Thomas, Keirsten, Jennifer, Jason. With Pfizer Inc., N.Y.C., 1962—, mgr. sci. data systems, 1977—. Served with Can. Army, 1960-61. Mem. Data Processing Mgmt. Assn., Drug Info. Assn., Am. Med. Writers Assn. Club: Masons. Home: 583 Shewville Rd Ledyard CT 06339 Office: 235 E 42d St New York NY 10017

ESTERHAI, JOHN LOUIS, lawyer; b. Phoenixville, Pa., Jan. 26, 1920; s. Louis and Mary (Wolarik) E.; B.S.C., Temple U., 1940; LL.B., U. Pa., 1946; m. I. Louise Moyer, Nov. 13, 1943; children—John Louis, Louise Clayton (Mrs. William A. Ratcliffe). Admitted to Pa. bar, 1947; law clk. to Hon. Herbert F. Goodrich, 1946-47; asso. legal dept. Philco Corp., Phila., 1947-58, v.p., sec., dir. Philco Finance Corp., 1958-62; asst. counsel Penn Mut. Life Ins. Co., 1962-65, asso. counsel, 1965-69, asso. gen. counsel, 1970—, sec., 1971-77, dir. govt. relations, 1977—; dir. Med. Tech. Fund, Inc., Independence Sq. Properties, Inc., Penn Mut. Equity Services, Inc. Bd. mgrs. Roxborough Meml. Hosp., chmn., 1969-77, hon. chmn., 1977—; trustee delegate Am. Hosp. Assn., 1975-78. Served to lt. USNR, 1942-45. Mem. Am., Pa., Phila. bar assns., U.S. Trade Mark Assn. (pres. 1958-60), Internat. Assn. Protection Indsl. Property (treas. 1954-58), Assn. Life Ins. Counsel, Pa. Soc. Republican. Baptist. Mason. Club: Union League (Phila.). Author (with others) Trademark Management, 1955. Home: 8423 Pembrook Rd Philadelphia PA 19128 Office: Independence Sq Philadelphia PA 19172

ESTES, ELLIOTT M., automobile mfg. co. exec.; b. Mendon, Mich. Chief engr. Pontiac motor div. Gen. Motors Corp., 1956-61, gen mgr., corp. v.p., 1961-65, v.p. gen. mgr. Chevrolet, 1965-69, group exec. Car and Truck group, 1969-70, group v.p. overseas operations, 1970-72, exec. v.p. operations staff, dir., 1972-74, pres., chief operating officer, dir., 1974—; dir. Owens-Ill Inc., Kellogg Co. Address: Gen Motors Corp 3044 W Grand Blvd Detroit MI 48202*

ESTES, JAMES PAUL, ins. co. exec.; b. Fullerton, Calif., Oct. 28, 1946; s. Paul Herbert and Dorthy Jane (Fairweather) E.; B.A., Calif. State U., 1968, M.B.A., 1973; m. Denise Finley, June 7, 1968; 1 dau., Jill. Ops. div. supr. Allstate Ins. Co., Santa Ana, Calif., 1971-73; ops. mgr. Nat. Auto and Casualty Ins. Co., Los Angeles, 1973-75; mktg. specialist Metro. Property & Casualty, Orange, Calif., 1975-77; asst. v.p. Nat. Am. Ins. Co., Los Angeles, 1977-78; asst. v.p./sec. Baccala & Shoop Ins. Services, Los Angeles from 1978, now v.p. and sec.; sec. Nat. Execs. Ins. Co. Served to lt., USN, 1968-71. C.L.U. Mem. Adminstrv. Mgmt. Soc., Am. Mgmt. Soc., Chartered Property and Casualty Underwriters Assn. (chartered property and casualty underwriter), Soc. Ins. Research. Home: 730 Stillwater Ln Anaheim Hills CA 92807 Office: 2049 Century Park E Suite 2100 Los Angeles CA 90067

ESTLOW, EDWARD WALKER, newspaper exec.; b. Snyder, Colo., Mar. 20, 1920; s. Edward G. W. and Mary Rachel (McConnel) E.; A.B., U. Denver, 1942, postgrad. law sch., 1946-49; m. Charlotte Ann Schroder, Mar. 27, 1943; children—Susan Lyday, Nancy Hawes, Sally Baier, Mary Erculiani. Gen. mgr. Lovington (N.Mex.) Press, 1949-52; account exec. Rocky Mountain News, Denver, 1952-55, personnel mgr., 1955-64; v.p., bus. mgr. Denver Pub. Co., 1964-70; asst. gen. bus. mgr. Scripps-Howard Newspapers, N.Y.C., 1970-72, v.p., gen. bus. mgr., 1972-76; pres., dir., mem. exec. com. E.W. Scripps Co., 1976—, N.Mex. State Tribune, Birmingham Post Co., Herald-Post Pub. Co., El Paso, Fullerton (Calif.) Pub. Co., Denver Pub. Co.; pres., dir. Grant County News (Ky.), Leader, Inc. (Ky.); pres. Pitts. Press Co., 1975—; v.p., dir., mem. exec. com. Evansville Press Co. (Ind.), San Juan Star Co. (P.R.), Scripps-Howard Supply Co.; pres., pub., dir. Cary Publs. Inc. (Fla.); v.p., dir. Albuquerque Pub. Co.; dir., mem. exec. com. Sun Tattler Co., Hollywood, Fla., Knoxville News-Sentinel Co. (Tenn.), Memphis Pub. Co., Stuart News Co. (Fla.), Newspaper Enterprise Assn., Inc., United Features Syndicate, Inc., United Press Internat., Inc.; dir. Scripps-Howard Broadcasting Co., Newspaper Printing Corp., El Paso, Tex., United Media Enterprises, Inc., Berkley-Small, Inc., Dataway, Inc. Pres. Mile High ARC, Denver, 1965-66; bd. dirs. Denver Jr. Achievement, 1964-70, Denver Better Bus. Bur., 1968-70; trustee U. Denver, 1976—; v.p. Newspaper Advt. Bur., 1976—. Served to capt USAAF, 1942-45. Mem. U. Denver Alumni Assn. (pres. 69-71). Home: 8881 Indian Bluff Dr Cincinnati OH 45242 Office: 1100 Central Trust Tower Cincinnati OH 45202*

ESTREMERA, ROGER MICHAEL, cosmetic mfg. co. ofcl.; b. N.Y.C., Aug. 14, 1938; s. Raymond and Eliza (Liquillow) E.; student public schs., Levittown, N.Y.; m. Marlene Fredericks, May 25, 1963; children—Joseph, Michele, Jodi. Sales mgr. Miles Shoe Corp., Jersey City, 1964-66; v.p., gen. mgr. Ringwood (N.J.) Lumbar & Supply Co., 1966-69; mgr. sales and services Block Drug Co., Jersey City, 1969-75; dir. sales and services Norcliff Thayer div. Revlon Co., Tuckahoe, N.Y., 1976-80; dir. corp. travel Revlon, Inc., N.Y.C., 1981—. Mgr., Little League Baseball, Ringwood, 1972-73; cubmaster Cub Scouts Am., Ringwood, 1973-75; mem. parish council St. Catherine's Ch., Ringwood, 1977-79. Served with U.S. Army, 1961-63. Mem. Nat. Assn. Fleet Adminstrs., Meeting Planners Internat., Sales Promotion Mgrs. Assn., Sales Exec. Club N.Y. Roman Catholic. Club: K.C. (officer 1975-79) (Ringwood). Home: 354 Conklintown Rd Ringwood NJ 07456 Office: 767 5th Ave New York NY 10022

ETELSON, DORIS CAROL, restaurant chain exec.; b. N.J., May 1, 1930; d. Anthony V. and Gladys (Slater) Piserchia; B.S., State U. N.Y. at Saratoga Springs, 1975; postgrad. in Bus. Adminstrn., L.I. U.; m. Robert B. Etelson, Feb. 4, 1950; children—Robin Etelson Rivinus, Tracey. Owner/operator Indsl. Cafeteria, Jersey City, 1950-57; food supr. Howard Johnson Co., Westchester County, N.Y., 1961-64, head standards supr. Met. N.Y. region, 1964-68, area mgr., Westchester County, 1968-70, dir. standards and spl. projects Mid-Atlantic div., 1970-72, dir. adminstrn. and maintenance N.Y. div., Forest Hills, 1972-77, v.p. standards, nat. restaurant ops., Braintree, Mass., 1977—; adv. bd. hotel/restaurant sch. Cobbleskill Coll. Mem. Food Service Execs. Assn. Author manuals in field. Home: Cooper Morris Dr Pomona NY 10970 Office: 220 Forbes Rd Braintree MA 02184

ETKES, RAPHAEL, film co. exec. With MCA, Inc., 1961-73, v.p., 1978; v.p. Universal Pictures, 1973-79, sr. v.p., from 1979; pres., chief exec. officer Am. Internat. Pictures, 1980—. Office: 9033 Wilshire Blvd Beverly Hills CA 90211*

ETTER, THOMAS CLIFTON, sales agt.; b. Phila., Mar. 25, 1903; s. Samuel Howard and Elizabeth Alice (Spor) E.; student Drexel U., 1919-23; m. Mildred Evelyn Phillips, Dec. 20, 1923; children—Mildred Evelyn, Thomas Clifton. Sales agt. Hobart Corp., Phila., 1920—. Civil def. organizer, 1941-45. Republican. Methodist. Mem. S.R., Hereditary Order Descs. Loyalists and Patriots, Soc. War 1812, Hist. Soc. Pa., Geneal. Soc. Pa. Clubs: Union League, Racquet (Phila.); Bala Golf (Pa.). Home: 46 E Dartmouth Rd Bala Cynwyd PA 19004

EURICH, ALVIN CHRISTIAN, educator; b. Bay City, Mich., June 14, 1902; s. Christian H. and Hulda (Steinke) E.; B.A., N. Central Coll., 1924, Litt.D., 1949; M.A., U. Maine, 1926, LL.D., 1965; Ph.D., U. Minn., 1929; LL.D., Hamline U., 1944, Alfred U., 1949, Clarke U., 1950, Miami U., Oxford, O., 1951, Yeshiva U., 1954, Redlands U., 1960; Litt.D., New Sch. Social Research, 1952, Albion Coll., 1965; L.H.D., U. Fla., 1953, U. Miami, 1968, Fairfield U., 1971; Sc.D., Akron U., 1960; m. Nell P. Hutchinson, Mar. 15, 1953; children—Juliet Ann, Donald Alan. Instr. U. Maine, 1924-26; from asst. in ednl. psychology to prof. U. Minn., 1926-37; prof. edn. Northwestern U., 1937-38; prof. edn. Stanford U., 1938-48, v.p., 1944-48, acting pres., 1948; 1st chancellor State U. N.Y., 1949-51; v.p. Ford Fund Advancement Edn., 1951-64, bd. dirs., 1952-67; exec. dir. edn. div. Ford Found., 1958-64; pres. Acad. for Ednl. Devel., 1962—, Aspen Inst. Humanistic Studies, 1963-67, Internat. Council Ednl. Devel., Center for Public Resources; former trustee Penn Mut. Life Ins. Co.; pres. Phonemic Spelling Council; cons. U.S. govt. agys. during and following war yrs. Supr. various ednl. surveys; vis. prof. various univs.; vis. fellow Clare Coll., Cambridge U.; mem. or cons. various commns. on ednl. research, including Hoover Commn. Mem. Pres. Truman's Commn. Higher Edn., Pres. Kennedy's Task Force Edn.; chmn. Surgeon Gen.'s Commn. Nurses; chmn. U.S. Commn. for UNESCO; chmn. U.S. del. UNESCO Gen. Conf., Paris, 1968; mem. Pres. Johnson's Com. on Libraries, Washington Inst. Fgn. Affairs; cons. NASA; chmn. The Ethiopian Emperor's Com. Rev. Heile Selassie I U.; bd. dirs. Lovelace Found. Served from lt. comdr. to comdr. USNR, 1942-44, dir. standards and curriculum div. Naval Personnel. Recipient Outstanding Achievement award U. Minn., 1951, 4th Ann. award Times Sq. Club, 1953, Ann. award N.Y. Acad. Pub. Edn., 1963. Fellow AAAS (council 1941-45), Am. Psychol. Assn., Aspen Inst.; mem. Acad. Ednl. Devel. (pres.), Sigma Xi, Phi Delta Kappa. Clubs: Univ., Century, Coffee House (N.Y.C.); Cosmos (Washington); Athenaeum (London). Author: Reforming American Education, 1969; also author or co-author books and studies in edn.; also psychol. and achievement tests; editor: Campus 1980, 1968; High School 1980, 1970; contbr. to ednl. jours. and gen. mags. Home: 24 W 55th St New York NY 10019 Office: 680 Fifth Ave New York NY 10019

EUSTACE, JAMES ALBERT, ins. co. exec.; b. Nutter Ft., W.Va., Sept. 8, 1929; s. John Ross and Vivian (Hovey) E.; student U. Alaska, 1961-62, Hampton Inst., 1973; m. Cynthia Ann Kronauge, Nov. 1, 1952. Commd. officer U.S. Army, 1946-73; ret., 1973; adminstrv. mgr. Ryder Tech. Inst., Atlanta, 1973-74; sr. systems cons. Supply Line Inc. (Ryder Systems), Miami, Fla., 1974-75; systems cons. Am. Bankers Life Assurance Co. Fla., Miami, 1976, mgr. work measurement, 1976-77, asst. v.p. manual systems, 1977, v.p. operational services, 1977-78, v.p. corp. services, 1978-79, sr. v.p. corp. services, 1979—. Decorated Meritorious Service medal, UN Service medal, Bronze Star (2), Vietnam Service medal, others. Mem. Am. Mgmt. Assn. Roman Catholic. Home: 2459 Dunkerrin Ln Atlanta GA 30360 Office: 600 Brickell Ave Miami FL 33131

EVANS, BARRY CRAIG, financial planner, ins. co. exec.; b. Cin., Dec. 12, 1944; s. Tracy Warren and Dorothy (Burton) E.; B.S. in Bus., Miami U., Oxford, Ohio, 1967; m. Linda Sue Laytart, June 22, 1974. Partner, Evans & Co., fin. and estate planning, Cin., 1971—; dir. advanced underwriting and agt. devel. Massachusetts Mut. Life Ins. Co., Cin., 1978-79; guest lectr. U. Cin., Miami U., Oxford, civic groups. VIP chmn. East Seal Soc., Cin.; mem. Republican Nat. Com. Served to capt. USAF, 1967-71; Vietnam. Decorated Bronze Star, Air Force Commendation medal; recipient Silver medal as outstanding Air Force ROTC Cadet, Chgo. Tribune, 1964; Nat. Quality award Nat. Assn. Life Underwriters, 1972; named to Leaders' Club, Massachusetts Mut. Life Ins. Co., 1974, 76, 78, 79, 80, Pres's. Club, 1972—. Mem. Am. Soc. C.L.U.'s (trustee Cin. chpt., pres., C.L.U.), Million Dollar Round Table (life mem.), Nat. Assn. Life Underwriters, Cin., No. Ky. estate planning councils, Queen City Assn., Internat. Assn. Fin. Planners. Republican. Presbyterian. Clubs: Colonial Racquet, Bankers' (govt., chmn. membership); The One Hundred (Cin.), Miami U. Pres.'s and Tower. Home: 8561 Arborcrest Dr Cincinnati OH 45236 Office: 4400 Carew Tower 441 Vine St Cincinnati OH 45202

EVANS, COLIN, chem. co. exec.; b. Vancouver, B.C., Can., Aug. 17, 1924; s. Louis N.B. and Leah (Kensington) E.; B.Commerce, U. B.C., 1950; m. Sharllein Hastie, Feb. 2, 1948; children—Dory, Donny, Charie, Lyanne. Unit mgr. Procter & Gamble Inc., 1950-56; mktg. mgr. Alsto Distbrs. Ltd., Vancouver, 1956-60; sales mgr. Can., MacMillan Bloedel Ltd., Vancouver, 1960-68; v.p. Maco Industries Ltd., Vancouver, 1968-78, Guardhouse Chems. Ltd., Surrey, B.C., 1969—, Can. Woodtape Ltd., Surrey, 1969—, also dir. Served as officer, pilot RCAF, 1942-46; CBI. Mem. Nat. Bldg. Material Distbrs. Assn., Can. Bldg. Material Distbrs. Assn., Zeta Psi. Mem. Ch. of Eng. Home: Vancouver BC Canada Office: 12750 King George Hwy Surrey BC V3V 3K5 Canada

EVANS, DENNIS EARL, corp. exec.; b. Selmer, Tenn., Aug. 24, 1950; s. Lenord Earl and Imogene (Cox) E.; B.S. in Bus. Adminstrn., U. Tenn., 1972; m. Linda Beth Gerhold, May 1, 1976. Acct., RKO Bottlers, Memphis, 1973-74, controller, Blytheville, Ark., 1974, asst. group controller, Muncie, Ind., 1974; controller Great Lakes Canning, Inc., Twinsburg, Ohio, 1974-78; gen. mgr. Soft Drink Carriers, Inc., Twinsburg, 1978—, treas., 1975—. Mem. Alpha Kappa Psi, Pi Kappa Alpha. Baptist. Club: Mason. Home: 189 Benson Rd Akron OH 44313 Office: 1882 Highland Rd Twinsburg OH 44087

EVANS, EDWARD PARKER, diversified mfg. co. exec.; b. Pitts., Jan. 31, 1942; s. Thomas Mellon and Elizabeth Parker (Kase) E.; B.A., Yale U., 1964; M.B.A., Harvard U., 1967. Vice-pres., Evans & Co., Inc., N.Y.C., 1975—; chmn. bd. H. K. Porter Co., Inc., Pitts., 1976—, Fansteel, Inc., Chgo., 1977—, Mo. Portland Cement Co., 1975—, Evans Broadcasting Corp., Mo., 1977—, Macmillan, Inc., N.Y.C., 1968—; dir. Huttig Sash & Door Co., St. Louis, Joseph Dixon Crucible Co., Jersey City. Served with Air N.G., 1965-71. Clubs: Duquesne (Pitts.); River (N.Y.C.); Round Hill, Rolling Rock. Office: 300 Park Ave New York NY 10022

EVANS, EVAN, petroleum co. exec.; b. N.Y.C., May 19, 1925; s. John William, Jr. and Therese Rosemary (Guilfoyle) E.; student St. Lawrence U., 1942-43, 46, B.S., 1949; B.S., M.I.T., 1951; m. Natalie Coe Holbrook, Feb. 20, 1968; children—Megan, Meredith, Rhys, Valerie, Cynthia, David. Engr., Calif. Tex. Oil Corp., N.Y.C., 1951-55, Bahrain, 1955-57, refinery ops. asst., N.Y.C., 1957-60, Rotterdam, 1960-62, refinery plant mgr., Lebanon, 1963, refinery specialist, N.Y.C., 1963-65, refinery project mgr., King Wilkinson, Antwerp, 1966-68; v.p. United Refining Co., Warren, Pa., 1971—; dir. Can Am Oil, Syracuse, N.Y., 1969-70, Kiantone Pipeline, 1970-76, United Refining Co., 1974-76, Texoma Pipe Line, 1974-76. Chmn. Am. Sch. Rotterdam, 1961-62. Served with USN, 1943-46. Mem. Warren C. of C. Clubs: N.Y. Athletic, Conewango. Home: 1265 E 5th St Warren PA 16365 Office: Bradley & Dobson Sts Warren PA 16365

EVANS, GEORGE RUSSELL, financial co. exec.; b. Hubbard, Ohio, Apr. 25, 1910; s. Evan E. and Ellen L. (Thomas) E.; B.S. in Bus. Adminstrn., Ohio U., 1933; m. Arabelle Chute, Sept. 5, 1936; children—Jill Evans Farris, Jane Evans Hill. Case work supr. Trumble County (Ohio) Relief Commn., 1933-35; with Beneficial Corp., Wilmington, Del., 1935—, mem. exec. com., 1975—, vice chmn., dir., 1977—; sr. v.p. Beneficial Mgmt. Corp., Morristown, N.J., 1970-73, exec. v.p., 1973-74, pres., 1974-78, chmn. bd., 1978-79, also dir.; pres. Beneficial Finance Co. of Can., 1974-76, chmn. bd., 1976—, also dir.; dir., chmn. exec. com. Western Auto Supply Co., 1979—; dir. First Tex. Fin. Corp., Spiegel Co., Midland Internat. Corp., Peoples Bank & Trust Co., Beneficial Finance Internat. Corp. Trustee, Hodson Trust. Mem. Nat. Consumer Finance Assn., Nat. Second Mortgage Assn., Assn. Canadian Financial Corps., Phi Delta Theta. Republican. Presbyterian. Clubs: Masons, Shriners; Baltusrol Golf (bd. govs.). Home: 83 Tanglewood Dr Summit NJ 07901 Office: 200 South St Morristown NJ 07960

EVANS, GRACE TROUT, former realtor; b. Jacksonville, Fla., Nov. 14, 1920; d. Philip Wilbur and Leona M. (Mahin) Trout; student Fla. State U., 1938-39, U. Miami, 1939-40, U. N.C., 1940-41; m. Raymond G. Sage, Mar. 21, 1942; children—Raymond G., Mary Lee Atkins; m. 2d, Samuel F. Evans, Aug. 19, 1964. Realtor, Grand Bahama Devel. Corp., Ltd., Jacksonville, also Eleuthera Island Club Ltd., 1965-68; owner, mgr. Grace T. Evans Realtors, 1965-76; news corr. Crescent City (Fla.) Courier Jour., 1978—. Patron, Welaka Vol. Fire Dept.; del. Episcopal diocese convocation and conv., 1978-79; committeewoman, sec. exec. bd. Republican Party, Putnam County, 1980—. Mem. Putnam County Bd. Realtors, Nat. Assn. Realtors, Fla. Assn. Realtors, Brokers Co-op. Jacksonville, Inc. (v.p. 1975-76), DAR, Delta Delta. Republican. Clubs: Ponte Vedra, Welaka Women's (1st v.p. 1978-80), Garden of Welaka. Home: Thevans PO Box 255 Welaka FL 32093

EVANS, JAMES HURLBURT, corp. exec.; b. Lansing, Mich., June 26, 1920; s. James L. and Marie (Hurlburt) E.; A.B., Centre Coll. Ky., 1943; J.D., U. Chgo., 1948; LL.D. (hon.), Milliken U., 1978; children by former marriage—Eric Bertram, Carol Ruth, Joan McLeod; m. Rosemary Hall Colgate, 1972. Admitted to Ill. bar, 1949; atty., loan officer Harris Trust & Savs. Bank, Chgo., 1948-56; sec.-treas. Reuben H. Donnelley Corp., Chgo., 1956-57, v.p., N.Y.C., 1957-62, also dir.; co. merged in Dun & Bradstreet, Inc., 1961, fin. v.p., 1962-65, dir., 1962-77; pres. Seamen's Bank for Savs., N.Y.C., 1965-68, chmn. bd., 1968, trustee, 1965-78; pres. Union Pacific Corp., 1969-77, chmn., chief exec. officer, 1977—, dir., 1969—; dir. U.P. R.R., 1965—, vice chmn. bd., 1969-77, chmn. bd., 1977—; dir. AT&T, Citicorp, Citibank N.A., Gen. Motors Corp. Bd. govs. N.Y. Hosp.; trustee Union Pacific Found., Rockefeller Bros. Fund, U. Chgo., Tax Found., George C. Marshall Research Found.; chmn. bd. trustees, Centre Coll. Ky.; trustee Nat. Recreation Found., pres., 1971-75; founding chmn., life trustee Nat. Recreation and Park Assn.; found mem. Citizens Adv. Com. on Environ. Quality, 1966-70; bd. govs. ARC, 1970-76, nat. fund chmn., 1974-76; bd. dirs. Catalyst, Tri-State United Way; bd. mgrs. N.Y. Bot. Garden. Served to lt. USNR, 1943-46. Mem. Am. Bar Assn., Chgo. Bar Assn., Fgn. Policy Assn. (gov.), Am. Petroleum Inst., Nat. Petroleum Council, Bus. Roundtable, Bus. Council, Pilgrims of U.S., Phi Beta Kappa, Omicron Delta Kappa, Delta Kappa Epsilon. Presbyterian. Clubs: Down Town Assn., River, Racquet and Tennis, Links, Knickerbocker (N.Y.C.); Metropolitan (Washington). Office: 345 Park Ave New York NY 10022

EVANS, JOHANNES SANAO, bus. machine mfg. co. exec.; b. Tokyo, Mar. 10, 1927; s. Paul Yuzuru Kawai and Vicky Wichgraf-Evans; B.S. in Fgn. Service, Akademie Fuer Welthandel, Frankfurt/Main, Germany, 1954; B.S. in Bus. Adminstrn., Georgetown U., 1964; M.B.A., U. Rochester, 1970; m. Maria Johanna Langer, Mar. 10, 1947; children—Helga, Richard, Alphonse. Positions with internat. trade companies, Germany, 1948-61; jr. accountant Stanton, Minter & Bruner, Alexandria, Va., 1964; with Xerox Corp., various locations, 1964—, sr. policy planner, Stamford, Conn., 1972-77, mgr. corp. cost accounting policy, 1977—. Mem. Nat. Assn. Accountants, Am. Accounting Assn., Fin. Accounting Standards Bd. (asso.). Republican. Home: 9 Fawn Rd Bethel CT 06801 Office: Xerox Corp Stamford CT 06904

EVANS, JOHN HARVEY, ins. rep.; b. Storm Lake, Iowa, Oct. 7, 1945; s. Glenn William and Viola Marie (Madsen) E.; grad. Dale Carnegie, 1973; m. Rosalie Mae Johnson, June 29, 1969; 1 son, Nicholas John. Supermarket mgr., 1966-68; meatcutter, 1968-72; dist. rep. Aid Assn. for Lutherans, Storm Lake, 1972—, mem. pres.'s cabinet, 1976-80; course moderator Life Underwriter Tng. Council, 1975, 77, 79. Served with U.S. Army, 1963-66. Named to Million Dollar Round Table, 1976-79; recipient Sales Achievement, Nat. Quality, and Health Ins. Quality awards Nat. Assn. Life Underwriters, 1973-80. Mem. N.W. Central Life Underwriters Assn. (pres. 1978-79). Republican. Lutheran. Home: 37 Vista Dr Storm Lake IA 50588 Office: 206 W 5th St Storm Lake IA 50588

EVANS, JOHN KARRAN, business exec.; b. Portmadoc, Wales, U.K., Feb. 9, 1907; came to U.S., 1924, naturalized, 1943; s. William Henry and Katherine Kinley (Froome) E.; student schs., Wales; m. Jean Evans, June 18, 1955; children—Treflyn, Sian, Tegan, Trevor, Gareth. Trainee to resident rep. D.C. Royal Dutch Shell Group, N.Y.C. and Washington, 1933-61; cons., trader, entrepreneuer oil refineries, 1961—; cons., asso. dir. Pacific Resources, Inc., Honolulu, 1971—; pres. Hampton Roads Energy Co., Portsmouth, Va., 1973—, Reciprocal World Traders, Inc., Washington, 1965—. Pres., Nat. Welsh Am. Found. Served from pvt. to col. USAFR, 1942-64. Mem. Council on Fgn. Relations, Nat. Planning Assn., C. of C., Washington Export Council, Nat. Petroleum Refiners Assn., Am. Petroleum Inst., Am. Legion (past comdr.). Episcopalian. Clubs: Army-Navy; Nat. Press. Address: 3005 Normanstone Dr NW Washington DC 20008

EVANS, JOHN THOMAS, JR., info. processing co. ofcl.; b. Duncansville, Pa., July 28, 1941; s. John Thomas and Dorothy M. Evans; B.S., U.S. Air Force Acad., 1963; M.B.A., UCLA, 1975; m.

Sally Blair, June 1, 1964; children—Keith Mark, Kathleen M. Maintainability engr. Honeywell Info. Systems, Newton, Mass., 1967-73; dir. field engring. Computer Machinery Corp., Santa Monica, Calif., 1973-77, Lexitron-A Raytheon Co., Chatsworth, Calif., 1978-80, ARL div. Bausch & Lomb, Sunland, Calif., 1980—. Scoutmaster, troop 126, Boy Scouts Am. Served with USAF, 1959-67. Mem. Assn. Field Service Mgrs. (founder, dir.), Am. Mgmt. Assns. Club: Masons. Author: The Field Service Manager's Handbook, 1977. Office: 9600 De Soto St Chatsworth CA 91311

EVANS, THOMAS MELLON, mfg. co. exec.; b. Pitts., Sept. 8, 1910; s. Thomas M. and Martha S. Jarnagin; B.A., Yale U., 1931; m. Elizabeth Parker, June 26, 1935 (div.); children—Thomas M., Edward Parker, Robert Sheldon; m. 2d, Josephine Schlotman Mitchell, Aug. 7, 1953 (dec. May 1977). Chmn. exec. com. H.K. Porter Co., Inc., Pitts., 1939—; chmn. Crane Co., N.Y.C., 1959—, also chief exec. officer; pres. Evans & Co., Inc., N.Y.C., 1956—; dir. So. Pacific Co., San Francisco. Bd. visitors, bd. govs. St. John's Coll., Annapolis, Md.; bd. dirs. Children's Village, Dobbs Ferry, N.Y.; trustee Hirshhorn Mus., Washington, Historic Deerfield (Mass.). Republican. Presbyterian. Office: Crane Co 300 Park Ave New York NY 10022

EVANS, WILLIAM RAYMOND, trade assn. exec.; b. Oak Park, Ill., Feb. 21, 1931; s. William Raymond and Mary Theresa (Gallicchio) E.; student Monmouth (Ill.) Coll., 1949-51, Northwestern U., Chgo., 1954; m. Sept. 11, 1954; children—Bonnie Beth, William R. Salesman, Equitable Life Assurance, Chgo., 1954-63; partner LeVine, Evans & Gutstadt Ins. Agy., Inc., Chgo., 1963-67; ins. dir. Printing Industries Am., Inc., Arlington, Va., 1967—. Served with U.S. Army, 1951-53. Mem. Risk and Ins. Mgmt. Soc., Nat. Found. Health, Welfare and Pension Plans, Nat. Safety Council. Presbyterian. Created graphic arts profl. liability policy, 1970, mgmt. consol. multiple employer self insured trust, 1979. Home: 11943 Bargate Ct Rockville MD 20852 Office: 1730 N Lynn St Arlington VA 22209

EVANS, WILLIAM SAMUEL, mfg. co. exec.; b. Dayton, Ohio, Jan. 23, 1918; s. William Lewis and Della (Ferguson) E.; B.A., Harvard, 1948; M.B.A., U. Chgo., 1952; m. Eva Esterhazy, June 7, 1959; children—Alexander, Eva. Instr., Hofstra U., Hempstead, N.Y., 1954-56; economist First Nat. City Bank, N.Y.C., 1957-59; market researcher St. Regis Paper Co., N.Y.C., 1959-66; dir. bus. devel. Phelps Dodge Industries, Inc., N.Y.C., 1966—. Mem. Representative Town Meeting, Darien, Conn., 1972—. Active worker Republican Party, Darien, 1970—. Served with USAAF, 1943-46; PTO. Mem. Pan Am Soc., (dir. 1974-80), Beta Theta Pi. Clubs: Copper, Sales Execs. (N.Y.C.); Harvard (New Canaan, Conn.). Home: 105 Hollow Tree Ridge Rd Darien CT 06820 Office: 300 Park Ave New York NY 10022

EVERETT, BILLY TRAV, wholesale distbg. co. exec.; b. Ft. Worth, Sept. 20, 1936; s. William Travis and Betty Ruth (Gore) E.; B.B.A., S.W. Tex. State U., 1959; m. Betty Jo Krenek, Jan. 31, 1959; children—Michael, Lisa. Div. mgr. S.H. Leggitt Co., Marshall, Mich., 1961-64; pres. Kevco, Inc., Marshall, 1964-74, chmn. bd., Hurst, Tex., 1974—. Served with U.S. Army, 1959. Mem. Warehouse Distbrs. Assn. (v.p., dir.), Manufactured Housing Inst., Nat. Assn. Wholesaler-Distbrs. Republican. Episcopalian. Clubs: Petroleum (Ft. Worth); Century II, Masons. Office: Suite 503 Morrow Bldg II Hurst TX 76053

EVERETT, CARL NICHOLAS, mgmt. cons. exec.; b. Ardmore, Okla., June 4, 1926; s. Elmer Edwards and Cecile (Jones) E.; B.S., Columbia U., 1948; M.B.A. with distinction, Harvard U., 1951; m. Susan Blessing Lindstrom, Oct., 1975; children by previous marriages—Carl N., Karen Lee, E. Anthony. With Benton and Bowles, N.Y.C., 1951-54, asso. account exec. Gen. Foods Corp., asst. account exec. Hellmanns and Best Foods Mayonnaise; with Campbell Mithun, Mpls., 1954-56, sr. account exec. Pillsbury Mills, account exec. Pillsbury Refrigerated Products; with McCann Erickson, N.Y.C., 1956-62, bottle sales account exec. Coca Cola Co., sr. account exec. Esso. Standard Oil, accounts supr. Westinghouse Electric Corp., account dir. Liggett and Myers Tobacco, mem. marketing plans bd. and marketing and advt. cons. Coca Cola Co.; sr. v.p., dir. Western region operations Barrington & Co., N.Y.C., 1962-64; founder, pres. Everett Assos., Inc., marketing and mgmt. consultants, N.Y.C., 1964-74; founder, pres. Everett Corp., Scottsdale, Ariz., 1974—; cons. Chrysler Corp., Pepsico Inc., Michelin Tire Corp., Gen. Electric Corp., Can. Dry Corp., Allied Van Lines, Continental Airlines; co-founder, dir. Precision Investment Co., Denver, 1977—; founder, mng. partner Wilmot Properties, Scottsdale, Ariz., 1979—; dir. V&S Tooling Co., Boulder, Colo., 1977—. Served with USNR, 1944-46. Mem. Am. Mgmt. Assn., Smithsonian Assos., Sigma Alpha Epsilon. Unitarian. Clubs: Harvard, Campfire. Patentee in field. Home: 6722 N 60th St Paradise Valley AZ 85253 Office: 6991 E Camelback Rd Suite C-103 Scottsdale AZ 85251

EVERETT, ELBERT KYLE, mktg. exec.; b. Knoxville, Tenn., June 17, 1946; s. David Abraham and Lois (Hill) E.; student E. Tenn. U., 1965-67; m. Jane Harville, June 13, 1967; 1 dau., Evelyn Anne. Sales rep. Met. Life Ins. Co., Knoxville, 1968-70, Creative Displays, Knoxville, 1970-73; market mgr. central and No. Calif., Nat. Advt. div. 3M Co., Stockton from 1973, now dist. mgr. Southwestern Dist., Fresno; advt. cons. athletic dept. U. Pacific; lectr. outdoor advt. and mktg. San Joaquin Delta Coll. Mem. subcom. on tourism State of Nev.; cons. Stockton Civic Theater. Served with AUS, 1964. Recipient certificate of recognition U.S. Treasury Dept., 1977, 78; recognition award for best design Advt. Age, 1974; 2 recognition awards Outdoor Advt. Assn. Am., 1973; certificate of appreciation United Way, 1978. Mem. U. Pacific Athletic Found., Stockton C. of C., Fresno C. of C., Advt. Club Sacramento, Advt. Club Fresno, Phi Sigma Kappa. Presbyterian. Home: 6432 N Benedict Ave Fresno CA 93711 Office: 1816 S Van Ness Ave Fresno CA 93721

EVERETT, EUGENE F., banker; b. Springfield, Mo., Aug. 29, 1925; s. Eugene Francis and Helen Louise (Jacobi) E.; A.B. in Econs., Drury Coll., 1948; postgrad. Sch. Fin. Public Relations, Northwestern U., 1955; m. Juliana Johnson, June 11, 1949; children—Constance, Susan, Thomas, Diane, John. Exec. trainee Miss. Valley Trust Co., St. Louis, 1948-51; with Union Nat. Bank, Springfield, 1952-78; pres. Boatmen's Union Nat. Bank, Springfield, Mo., 1975-78, chmn. bd., chief exec. officer, 1978—, also dir.; dir. Boatmen's Bancshares, Inc., Boatmen's Bank Pulaski County, Boatmen's Bank Taney County, Boatmen's Springfield Nat. Bank; chmn. bd. Heers-Andres Investment Co., Fin. Investment Co. Pres., Mo. Public Expenditure Survey, Jefferson City; trustee Drury Coll.; pres. Better Bus. Bur. S.W. Mo. Inc. Served with AC, U.S. Army, 1943-45, to 1st lt. Intelligence Security, 1951-52, with USAR, 1948-69. Recipient Disting. Alumni Service award Drury Coll., 1979. Mem. Am. Inst. Banking, Bank Adminstrn. Inst., Mo. Bankers Assn. Office: PO Box 1157 SSS Springfield MO 65805

EVERETT, JAMES LEGRAND, III, utility exec.; b. Charlotte, N.C., July 24, 1926; s. James LeGrand and Charlotte (Keesler) E.; B.S. in Mech. Engring., Pa. State U., 1948, M.S., 1949; M.S. in Indsl. Mgmt., Mass. Inst. Tech., 1959; m. Marjorie Miriam Scherf, Sept. 3, 1947; children—James LeGrand IV, Christopher Glenn, John Keesler. Instr. mech. engring. Pa. State U., 1948-50; instr. civil and mech. engring. Drexel Evening Coll., 1950-52; head fuel sect. Atomic Power Devel. Assos., 1953-55; with Phila. Electric Co., 1950—, exec. v.p., 1968-71, pres., 1971—, also dir., mem. exec. com. parent co., dir. subsidiaries; chmn., dir. Radiation Mgmt. Corp., 1971—; dir., mem. exec. com. Phila. Nat. Bank, Fidelity Mut. Life Ins. Co.; dir. Tasty Baking Co., Martin Marietta Corp. Mem. sci. and arts com. Franklin Inst. Served to ensign USNR, 1944-46. Sloan fellow 1958-59. Recipient Outstanding Young Man of Year award Phila. Jr. C. of C., 1961; Ann. Engring. Tech. award Temple U., 1963, Disting. Alumnus award Pa. State U., 1971; named Engr. of Year, Delaware Valley, Pa., 1972; recipient numerous civic service awards; George Washington medal, 1974. Registered profl. engr., Pa. Fellow ASME; mem. Am. Nuclear Soc., Franklin Inst., IEEE, Soc. Am. Mil. Engrs., Nat. Acad. Engring., Engrs. Club Phila., Nat., Pa. socs. profl. engrs. Tau Beta Pi, Pi Tau Sigma, Pi Mu Epsilon. Office: 2301 Market St Philadelphia PA 19101

EVINRUDE, RALPH SYDNEY, outboard motors mfg. exec.; b. Milw., Sept. 27, 1907; s. Ole and Bessie (Cary) E.; student U. Wis., 1925; m. Marion Armitage, Jan. 3, 1931 (dec.); m. 2d, Frances Langford, Oct. 6, 1955. Testing mgr. Elto Outboard Motor Co., 1927-30; export sales mgr. Outboard Motors Corp., 1930-32, prodn. mgr., 1932-34, pres., 1934-36; Outboard Motors consol. with Johnson Motor Co. to form Outboard Marine & Mfg. Co., now named Outboard Marine Corp. of which became pres. and dir., now chmn. bd., chmn. exec. com. Mem. Phi Gamma Delta. Clubs: Univ., Yacht, Milw. Athletic (Milw.); Eldorado Country; Crown Colony (Bahamas); Smoky Lake Hunt and Fish, Ocean Reef, Cat Cay, Stuart Sailfish. Office: Outboard Marine Corp 100 Sea Horse Dr Waukegan IL 60085

EVIRS, HOWARD WESLEY, JR., utility exec.; b. Boston, Oct. 3, 1925; s. Howard Wesley and Inez (Harriman) E.; B.S. in Elec. Engring. with honors, Northeastern U., Boston, 1951, M.B.A., 1970; m. Helen G. Keefe, Mar. 12, 1949; children—Howard Wesley, Diane E., Patricia A. Asst. elec. engr. Exeter & Hampton Electric Co. (N.H.), 1951-52; asst. exec. engr. Brockton Taunton Gas Co. (Mass.), Concord Electric Co. (N.H.), Fitchburg Gas and Electric Co. (Mass.), Orange and Rockland Utilities, Inc. (Mass.), Springfield Gas Light Co. (Mass.), 1952-63; with Fitchburg Gas and Electric Light Co., 1963—, exec. v.p., 1969-70, pres., dir., 1970—; pres., dir. Fitchburg Energy Devel. Co.; dir. Fitchburg Fed. Savs. & Loan Assn., Concord Electric Co.; adv. dir. Worcester County Nat. Bank; instr., chmn. elec. theory Lincoln Coll., Boston, 1952-64. Mem. exec. com. New Eng. Power Pool; pres. Fitchburg Area Econ. Devel. Corp.; mem. President's Circle, Fitchburg State Coll. Bd. dirs. Jr. Achievement Montachusett Area; bd. dirs. United Fund Greater Fitchburg, v.p., 1969-71. Served with USNR, 1943-46. Recipient outstanding alumni award in sci. and tech. Northeastern U., 1979; registered profl. engr., Mass. Mem. IEEE (past chmn. Boston), Nat. Soc. Profl. Engrs., Edison Electric Inst., Am., New Eng. (dir.) gas assns., Electric Council New Eng. (dir.), Fitchburg C. of C. (past chmn., past pres.), Eta Kappa Nu (past pres.), Tau Beta Pi. Clubs: Masons, Rotary (past dir. Fitchburg); Fay (pres.); Braintree (Mass.) Yacht (past commodore); Commodores of Am. (Mass.); Down East Yacht (Maine). Home: 10 Hemlock Dr Lunenberg MA 01462 Office: 655 Main St Fitchburg MA 01420

EWALD, ROBERT FREDERICK, ins. exec.; b. Newark, May 5, 1924; s. Frederick J. and Florence M. (Reiley) E.; B.S. cum laude in Bus. Adminstrn., with spl. honors in Econs., Rutgers U., 1948; m. Jeanine Martinez, Jan. 3, 1976; children—Robert Thomas, Stephen Andrew; children by previous marriage—William F., John C., George E. Asst. corp. auditor Prudential Ins. Co., Newark, Houston, Chgo., 1948-61; audit mgr. N.Y. Life Ins. Co., N.Y.C., 1962-64; treas. Mass. Gen. Life Ins. Co., Boston, 1965-68; adminstrv. v.p., controller Res. Life Ins. Co., Dallas, 1969-70; pres. Nat. Ben Franklin Life, Chgo., 1971-77; pres. Rockford (Ill.) Blue Cross Plan, 1979—, also trustee; pres., dir. Life Ins. Assos., Inc.; trustee Communities Health Plan, Inc., North Communities Health Plan, Inc. Served with U.S. Army, 1943-46. Fellow Life Mgmt. Inst.; mem. Fin. Execs. Inst., Am. Arbitration Assn., Adminstrv. Mgmt. Soc., Mensa. Home: 12 Wisner St Park Ridge IL 60068 Office: 227 N Wyman St Rockford IL 61101

EWING, RAYMOND PEYTON, ins. co. exec., pub. relations dir.; b. Hannibal, Mo., July 31, 1925; s. Larama Angelo and Winona Fern (Adams) E.; A.A., Hannibal La-Grange Coll., 1948; B.A., William Jewell Coll., 1949; M.A. in Humanities, U. Chgo., 1950; m. Audrey Jane Schulze, May 7, 1949; 1 dau., Jane Ann. Mktg. mgmt. trainee Montgomery-Wards, Chgo., 1951-52; sr. editor Commerce Clearing House, Chgo., 1952-60; corp. communications dir. Allstate Ins. Cos. & Allstate Enterprises, Northbrook, Ill., 1960—, issues mgmt. dir., 1979—; pub. relations dir. Chgo. Mag., 1966-67, book columnist, 1968-70; staff Book News Commentator, Sta. WRSV, Skokie, Ill., 1962-70; lectr. pub. relations. Mem. Winnetka (Ill.) Library Bd., 1969-70; pres. Skokie Valley United Crusade, 1964-65. Bd. dirs. Suburban Community Chest Council, Onward Neighborhood House, Chgo., Kenilworth Inst. Served with AUS, 1943-46; ETO. Mem. Pub. Relations Soc. of Am. (accredited; Silver Anvil award for pub. affairs 1970, 72, for fin. relations 1970, for spl. event 1977), Publicity Club of Chgo. (v.p. 1967, bd. dirs. 1966-68; Golden Trumpet award for pub. affairs, 1969, 70, 72, for fin. relations 1970), Insurers Public Relations Council (pres. 1980-81), Mensa, World Future Soc., U.S. Assn. of Club of Rome, Chgo. Press Club, Chgo. Poets and Writers Found. (pub. relations dir. 1966-67). Editor Publicity Club of Chgo. Jour., 1971. Contbr. articles to mags. Home: 316 Richmond Rd Kenilworth IL 60043 Office: Allstate Plaza Northbrook IL 60062

EWING, ROBERT CLAUDE, accountant; b. Jacksonville, Fla., Oct. 12, 1942; s. Robert Claude and Hilda (Mattox) E.; B.S., U. Fla., 1964; M.B.A., U. Santa Clara, 1973; m. Leslie Sharon Kelley, Dec. 21, 1969; children—Kristine, Erin, Courtney. Mfg. cost acctg. supr. Info. Storage Systems, Cupertino, Calif., 1973-74; cost acctg. mgr. Mother's Cake & Cookie Co., Oakland, Calif., 1974-75; regional controller Nat. Health Enterprises, Oakland, 1975-79; controller Marketron, Memlo Park, Calif., 1978-79; dir. adminstrn., personnel and recruiting Arthur Andersen & Co., San Jose, Calif., 1979—. Pres. U. Santa Clara Grad. Sch. Bus. Alumni Assn., 1980—. Served to lt., USNR, 1965-71. Decorated Navy Commendation medal, 11 Air medals (U.S.), Air Gallantry Cross; Viet Nam Campaign medal (Viet Nam). Mem. Nat. Assn. Accts. (dir. Mid-Peninsula chpt.). Republican. Mem. Ch. of Christ. Club: Elks. Home: 1879 Los Altos Dr San Mateo CA 94402 Office: 99 Almaden Blvd San Jose CA 95113

EWING, SAMUEL DANIEL, JR., fin. co. exec.; b. Topeka, Aug. 9, 1938; s. Samuel Daniel and Jane Elizabeth (Smith) E.; B.Elec. Engring., U. Cin., 1961; M.S. in Elec. Engring., U. Conn., 1964; M.B.A., Harvard U., 1968. Asso. devel. engr. Norden Labs. div. United Aircraft Corp., Norwalk, Conn., 1961-62; engr. Bendix Research Lab. div. Bendix Corp., Southfield, Mass., 1962-63; staff mem. M.I.T.-Lincoln Labs., Lexington, Mass., 1964-67; security analyst, registered rep. Gruss & Co., N.Y.C., 1968-69; sr. asso. corp. fin. Salomon Bros., N.Y.C., 1969-75; v.p., dir. pvt. placement Bankers Trust Co., N.Y.C., 1975-78; dir. Fed. Savs. and Loan Ins. Corp., Fed. Home Loan Bank Bd., Washington, 1978-80; pres., chief exec. officer Broadcast Capital Fund, Inc., Washington, 1980—; research asst. U. Conn., 1963-64, asst. instr. elec. engring., 1963-64. Bd. dirs. D.C. Housing and Fin. Agy., 1980—. Recipient award Dayton Bd. Edn., 1956, Nat. Assn. Elec. Distbrs., 1956. Fellow Fin. Analysts Assn.; mem. N.Y. Soc. Security Analysts (sr.), 100 Black Men N.Y.C., Harvard Bus. Sch. Afro Am. Alumni Assn. (dir.), Urban League, Black Execs. Exchange Program, Kappa Alpha Psi. Clubs: Harvard Washington, Harvard Bus. Sch. Washington. Author: (with C. H.W. Maloney): Minority Capital Resource Handbook, 1978; contbr. articles to profl. jours. Office: 1771 N St NW Washington DC 20036

EXLEY, CHARLES ERROL, JR., mfg. co. exec.; b. Detroit, Dec. 14, 1929; s. Charles Errol and Helen Margaret (Greenizen) E.; B.A., Wesleyan U., Middletown, Conn., 1952; M.B.A., Columbia, 1954; m. Sara Elizabeth Yates, Feb. 1, 1952; children—Sarah Helen, Evelyn Victoria, Thomas Yates. With Burroughs Corp., Detroit, 1954—, controller Todd div., 1960-63, corp. controller, 1963-66, v.p., group exec., 1966-71, v.p. fin., 1971-73, exec. v.p. fin., 1973-76, also dir.; pres. NCR Corp., Dayton, Ohio, 1976—, also dir., mem. exec. com. Trustee Wesleyan U. Mem. Fin. Execs. Inst. Clubs: Grosse Pointe (Grosse Pointe Farms, Mich.); Moraine Country (Dayton), Dayton Racquet. Home: 5 Volusia Ave Oakwood OH 45409 Office: NCR World Hdqrs 1700 S Patterson Blvd Dayton OH 45479

EYRE, ALLAN LEROY, fin. mgmt. cons.; b. Hackensack, N.J., Aug. 30, 1947; s. James A. and Mildred (Wood) E.; B.S., No. Ill. U., 1969; m. Susan Melissa Perry, Aug. 17, 1968; children—Jennifer Dawn, Allan Kyle. Regional sales mgr. Fram Corp., Chgo., 1969-70, dist. mgr., 1970-72, dir. internat. mktg., Wales, Gt. Britain, 1972-74, pres. Gen. Products div., Henderson, N.C., 1974-76; exec. v.p. XM World Trade Inc., N.Y.C., 1976-78; pres. Reina Calif. Corp., Chatham, N.J., 1978—, Reinatex, Inc., Chatham, 1978—, JAE Cons., Inc., Chatham, 1978—; exec. v.p. Reina Properties Corp., Chatham, 1978—, Calabestos Mgmt. Corp., Chatham, 1978—; dir. Kala Point Devel. Co., Pressure Transport Inc. Mem. Am. Mgmt. Assn. Clubs: Masons, Elks. Home and Office: 426 Fairmount Ave Chatham Township NJ 07928

EYTON, JOHN TREVOR, lawyer, business exec.; b. Quebec, Que., Can., July 12, 1934; s. John and Dorothy Isabel (Drysdale) E.; B.A., U. Toronto, 1957, LL.B., 1960; m. Barbara Jane Montgomery, Feb. 13, 1955; children—Deborah Jane, Susannah Margaret, Adam Tudor, Christopher Montgomery, Sarah Elizabeth. Called to Ont. bar, 1962; asso. firm Tory, Tory, Deslauriers & Binnington, Toronto, Ont., Can., 1962-67, partner, 1967—. Shareholder, dir. Nat. Hees Enterprises Ltd., Astral Bellevue Pathe Ltd.; sec., dir. CFGM Broadcasting Ltd., pres., dir. Edper Investments Ltd., Winnipeg Supply & Fuel Co. Ltd.; pres., chief exec. officer, dir. Brascan Ltd.; v.p., dir. Can.-Israel C. of C.; dir. Carena-Bancorp. Inc., Foodex Ltd.; chmn., dir. Gt. Lakes Power Corp. Ltd.; dir. Hatleigh Corp., Kesmark Constrn., John Labatt Ltd., Lacana Mining Ltd., London Life Ins. Co., Silverwood Industries Ltd., Western Mines, Hume Pub. Ltd., North Can. Oils Ltd., Perma-Fleur Ltd.; gov. Olympic Trust Can.; chmn., dir. Triarch Corp. Ltd.; chmn. exec. com. Trizec Corp. Ltd. Mem. Phi Delta Theta. Mem. United Ch. Can. Clubs: Toronto Bd. Trade, Chinguacousy Golf and Country, Royal Can. Yacht, Univ., Empire, Caledoni Ski, Caledon Riding and Hunt, Caledon Mountain Trout; Coral Beach and Tennis (Bermuda). Home: Tudorcroft Rural Route 1 Caledon ON Canada also 15 Elm Ave Toronto ON M4W 1M9 Canada Office: Brascan Ltd Box 48 Commerce Ct Postal Station Toronto Canada

EZELL, JAMES KENNETH, ins. co. exec.; b. Houston, July 21, 1924; s. James William and Clara Corinne (Welch) E.; B.B.A., U. Houston, 1953; grad. Inst. Ins. Marketing, 1961; m. Dorothy Faye Cox, July 21, 1946; children—Janet K. (Mrs. William C. Naramore), Sheryl Lynn. With Nat. Life & Accident Ins. Co., Nashville, 1946-52, C&I Life Ins. Co., Houston, 1952-55; with Fidelity Union Life Ins. Co., Dallas, 1955—, sr. v.p., agy. dir., 1961—, also dir. Served with USAAF, 1942-45. Baptist (past deacon). Home: 7581 Benedict Dr Dallas TX 75214 Office: PO Box 2580 Dallas TX 75221

FABER, CHARLES PHILIP, investment adv. co. exec.; b. Sheboygan, Wis., Aug. 1, 1941; s. Charles W. and Bernetta P. (Metscher) F.; B.B.A. (Dow-Corning scholar), U. Wis., 1966, M.B.A. (Research fellow), 1967; m. Jane E. Schneider, Dec. 22, 1962; children—Charles R., David R. Field rep. Caterpillar Tractor Co., Peoria, Ill., 1967-68; mktg. mgr. Apache Corp., Mpls., 1969-72, sales rep., 1973-74; gen. mgr. Apache Programs, Inc., Mpls., 1974-76, br. mgr., Milw., 1976-77; exec. v.p., dir. Investment Search, Inc., Annapolis, Md., 1978—; dir. WFK Leasing Co., Gloucester Prodn. Co. Served with U.S. Army, 1961-63. Mem. Internat. Assn. Fin. Planners, Assn. for Continuing Edn. in Bus., Nat. Assn. Securities Dealers (licensed prin.), Beta Gamma Sigma. Club: Moose Lake Yacht. Home: W 332 N 6556 N Moose Ln Nashotah WI 53058

FABER, EBERHARD, mfg. co. exec.; b. N.Y.C., Oct. 22, 1936; s. Eberhard Lothar and Julia (Taylor) F.; B.A. magna cum laude, Princeton U., 1957; postgrad. (Fulbright scholar) U. Poitiers, 1957-58; postgrad. Princeton U., 1961-63; m. Ellen Scurria, Sept. 6, 1958; children—Eberhard Lothar, Johann George; m. 2nd Mary Louise Carey, Dec. 29, 1979. With Eberhard Faber, Inc., Wilkes-Barre, Pa., 1952—, sec., 1966, vice chmn., 1971, pres., 1971-74, chief exec. officer, 1971—, chmn. bd., 1974—; dir. Fed. Res. Bank of Phila. Bd. dirs. Wyoming Valley United Fund, Central Allocation Com. Conf. Group III, 1965-69; treas., bd. dirs. Council House of Luzerne County, 1965-69; trustee Wyoming Valley Hosp., 1971—; trustee, pres. Class of 1915 Benevolent Assn., Princeton U., 1968—; mem. pres.'s council King's Coll., 1965—, bd. dirs., 1980—; adv. bd. NPW Hosp., Wilkes-Barre, 1978—. Served with USAR, 1959-67. Fulbright Teaching fellow, France, 1958-59. Mem. U.S. Trademark Assn., Wilkes-Barre C. of C., Pencil Maker's Assn. Distbrs. Research Assn. Clubs: Princeton, Westmoreland, Dream Mile (dir. 1976-78). Contbr. articles to profl. jours. Office: Crestwood Indsl Park Wilkes-Barre PA 18773

FABER, GEORGE, radio, TV exec.; b. Mpls., June 17, 1921; s. William Maurice and Lowell Ella (Whiteman) F.; student Wis. Coll Music, Northwestern U.; m. Marjorie Knodel, June 2, 1945; children—Kathie Diane, Michael William, Patricia Dawn. Writer, announcer, actor, radio sta. WHBL, Sheboygan, Wis., 1937-39; prodn. mgr. radio sta. WMFD, Wilmington, N.C., 1939-41, columnist and author Behind the Mike series, Cape Fear Pub. Co., Wilmington, 1940-41; news editor NBC, Chgo., 1943-46; news editor, writer CBS, 1946—; now internat. dir. Viacom Enterprises. Chmn. internat. com. Hollywood Mus. Mem. Hollywood Advt. Club, Internat. Photo Journalists (hon. life), Sigma Delta Chi. Home: 10760 Cushdon Ave Los Angeles CA 90064 Office: Viacom Enterprises 9720 Wilshire Blvd Beverly Hills CA 90210

FABIAN, MORRIS SAMUEL, agrl. economist; b. Trenton, N.J., Oct. 14, 1937; s. Jesse M. and Jane M. (Vogan) F.; B.S., Rutgers U. Coll. Agr., 1959, M.S., 1961, Ed.D., 1976; m. Marilyn Ann Moorhead, June 18, 1960; children—Morris George, Mark Whitney. Dairyman, Cool Meadows Farm, Pennington, N.J., 1961-62; research asst. dept. agrl. econs. and mktg. Rutgers U., New Brunswick, N.J., 1963-64, research asso., 1965, asst. specialist mktg. Co-op. Extension Service, 1966-71, asso. specialist mktg., 1972-79, extension specialist agrl. econs. and mktg., 1980—; adv. Jersey Cert. Farm Markets, Inc., 1966—; mktg. and ednl. cons. to numerous agrl. orgns., 1966—. Co-leader Mercer County (N.J.) Lively Livestock 4-H Club, 1977-80.

Served with USAR, 1959-60. Named Hon. State Farmer, Future Farmers of Am., 1974. Mem. Am. Agrl. Econs. Assn., N.J. Co-op. Extension Specialists Assn. (treas. 1968-69, pres. 1971), Northeastern Agrl. Econs. Council, Princeton Agrl. Assn. (v.p. 1975—), Epsilon Sigma Phi, Gamma Sigma Delta, Alpha Zeta, Omicron Tau Theta. Republican. Presbyterian. Clubs: Masons, Torch of Trenton (pres. 1977-78). Contbr. articles on agrl. econs. to profl. publs. Home: PO Box 267 Pennington NJ 08534 Office: Dept Agrl Econs and Marketing PO Box 231 Cook College Rutgers Univ New Brunswick NJ 08903

FABRI, WILLIAM DAVID, ins. exec.; b. Beverly, Mass., Sept. 22, 1943; s. Settimio M. and Alba (Zanuccoli) F.; B.S., Salem State Coll., 1967; m. Marcia Fabri, June 18, 1966; children—Kristin R., William David, Jana E. Tchr., Wilmington (Mass.) High Sch., 1967-68; partner Fabri & Marciano Ins. and Real Estate Agy., Beverly, 1968-74; mktg. rep. Utica Nat. Ins. Group, Burlington, Mass., 1974-78; regional underwriting mgr., 1978—. Founder, Olde Ipswich Days Celebration, 1971; mem. Govt. Study Commn. Town of Ipswich, 1971; chmn. retail div. Heart Fund, 1971. Served with Mass. N.G., 1962-68. C.P.C.U. Mem. Ipswich C. of C. (pres. 1969-71). Home: 13 Appleton Park Ipswich MA 01938 Office: 10 New England Executive Park Burlington MA 01803

FABRIZIUS, MICHAEL PETER, oil co. exec.; b. Sycamore, Ill., Mar. 31, 1947; s. Michael Frank and Marie Helen (Hardt) F.; B.S., No. Ill. U., 1969, M.B.A., 1973; m. Katherine M. Fierz, Oct. 22, 1977. Sr. auditor Arthur Andersen & Co., Chgo., 1969, 73-75; mgr. auditing services Dekalb AgResearch Inc. (Ill.), 1975-77; mgr. corp. acctg., 1977-79; fin. v.p. Pride Oil Well Service Co., Houston, 1979—. Served with AUS, 1969-71. C.P.A., Ill., Tex. Mem. Am. Inst. C.P.A.'s, Ill. Soc. C.P.A.'s. Home: 5311 Yarwell St Houston TX 77096 Office: 1980 S Post Oak Rd Houston TX 77056

FACE, EDWARD JOSEPH, banker; b. N.Y.C., Apr. 7, 1927; s. John C.G. and Edna Mae (O'Malley) F.; B.S. in Bus. Adminstrn., U. S.C., 1953; postgrad. Am. Inst. Banking, 1966, Grad. Sch. Banking, U. Wis., 1969, Air Command and Staff Coll., 1971, Indsl. Coll. Armed Forces, 1974; m. Theresa Dean Eurey, June 13; children—Edward Joseph, John G., James M., Cheryl J. Vice pres. Comml. Lending and Community Banking divs. Bank of Va., Richmond/Petersburg, 1960—. Past pres. Pinedale Farms Civic Assn. Served with USN, 1944-48, to lt. col. USAFR, 1952-80. Mem. Sales and Mktg. Execs. Richmond (Salesman award 1971), Am. Mgmt. Assn. (lectr.), Va. Nat. Guard Assn., Nat. Guard Assn. U.S., Air Force Assn., Am. Soc. Mil. Comptrollers, Am. Inst. Banking, Lambda Chi Alpha, Alpha Kappa Psi. Presbyterian. Clubs: Masons (Scottish Rite, 32 deg.), Shriners, Optimist (past pres.); Country of Petersburg. Home: 12517 Petersburg St Chester VA 23831 Office: 20 Franklin St Petersburg VA 23803

FACKELMAN, ROBERT HENRY, newspaper exec.; b. Ponca, Nebr., Oct. 19, 1907; s. Herman Carl and Jeanette (Pomeroy) F.; student Midland Coll., 1923-25; B.J., U. Mo., 1927; postgrad. Harvard, 1941-42; m. Anna Laura Torbert, June 6, 1928; 1 dau., Ann Karen (Mrs. Frank Nixon). Editor, pub. Baxter Springs (Kans.) Citizen, 1927-28, Raymondville (Tex.) Chronicle, 1929-40; editor, gen. mgr. Winter Haven (Fla.) News-Chief, 1943-50; editor, pub. Morristown (Tenn.) Sun, 1950-52; pub. Cleveland (Tenn.) Banner, 1952-54; v.p. So. Newspapers, Inc., 1954-58; pres. Newspaper Service Co., Inc., 1953—; pres. Gulf Coast Newspapers, Inc., 1958—; pres. Ruston (La.) Pubs., Inc., Tarpon Springs (Fla.) Leader, Inc. Served in USAAF, 1941-42. Mem. So. Newspaper Pubs. Assn. (dir. 1970-73). Office: 408 S Bonita Ave Panama City FL 32401

FADELEY, HERBERT JOHN, JR., banker, lawyer; b. Ambler, Pa., Feb. 14, 1922; s. Herbert John and Jennie Miller (Lewis) F.; B.S. in Commerce, Drexel U., 1946; J.D., Temple U., 1953; diploma Stonier Sch. Banking Rutgers U., 1957; m. Eleanor A. Battafarano, Feb. 8, 1947; children—Herbert John III, Brett Duane, Theresa Jane, Scott Lewis. Asst. cashier to v.p. First Nat. Bank, Media, Pa., 1951; admitted to U.S. Supreme Ct. bar, 1957; v.p. Boardwalk Nat. Bank, Atlantic City, 1957-60, Indsl. Trust Co., Phila., 1960-62; v.p., trust officer County Trust Co. (now Bank of N.Y.), White Plains, N.Y., 1963-68; pres., chief exec. officer, trustee Troy Savs. Bank (N.Y.), 1969—; dir., past v.p. Uncle Sam Mall Corp.; lectr. banking and law Drexel U., 1962, Rockland Community Coll., Suffern, N.Y., 1964-68, Westchester County chpt. Am. Inst. Banking, 1965-68, Hudson Valley Community Coll., Troy, 1970. Vice-chmn. dist. council, Boy Scouts Am., 1969—; pres., bd. dirs. Rensselaer County unit Am. Cancer Soc., 1970—; mem. Troy Downtown Devel. Com., Tri-county Fifty Group; past commr. Troy Housing Authority; past mem. Troy Zoning Bd. of Appeals; bd. dirs. Hudon-Mohawk area United Way, chmn. fund drive, 1972; trustee Russell Sage Coll., also past treas.; past bd. mgrs. Leonard Hosp.; past v.p., trustee Mary Warren Free Inst. Served to lt. (j.g.), USNR, 1942-43, 48-59. Named Outstanding Alumnus, Drexel U., 1961; recipient trust div. sch. awards, N.Y. State Banker's Assn., 1967-68. Mem. Am. Bar Assn., Greater Troy C. of C. (dir. 1969-75), Am. Judicature Soc., Assn. U.S. Army, Internat. Platform Assn., Nat. Rifle Assn., Drexel U., Temple U. alumni assns., Rensselaer County Hist. Soc., Soc. Friends of St. Patrick (dir., pres.), Lambda Chi Alpha, Phi Alpha Delta (named outstanding alumnus 1957; chief justice Dr. Elden S. Magaw Alumni chpt. 1955-56). Episcopalian. Clubs: Masons, Shrine, Jester. Clubs: Troy, Country (Troy). Home: 37 Brunswick Rd Troy NY 12180 Office: 32 2d St Troy NY 12180

FAERMAN, DONALD STEPHEN, fin. cons.; b. Montreal, P.Q., Can., Dec. 24, 1929; came to U.S., 1965; s. Oscar and Rachael F.; student McGill U., 1949-51; B.A., Babson Inst., 1954; m. Joan Peltz Schwartz, Apr. 1, 1977; children—Lisa, Michael, Jordan. Pres., Marcus-Faerman Inc., Montreal, 1954-64, RTF Inc., N.Y.C., 1965-72; dist. mgr. IDS Inc., Fairfield, Conn., 1972-77; sr. fin. cons. Shearson Loeb Rhoades, Greenwich, Conn., 1977—. Mem. Internat. Assn. Fin. Planners, Nat. Assn. Life Underwriters. Clubs: Roxbury Tennis (Stamford, Conn.); Rotary (Greenwich). Office: Shearson Loeb Rhoads 2 Greenwich Plaza Greenwich CT 06830

FAESTEL, DAVID JOEL, investment co. exec.; b. Waukesha, Wis., July 2, 1944; s. Gerald Henry and Harriet (Kubal) F.; B.A., Marquette U., 1968; M.B.A., U. Wis., 1970; m. Catherine Delores McCormick, June 19, 1971; children—Joel, Paul, Todd. Regional mgr. Multicon Properties, Inc., Columbus, Ohio, 1970-72; fin. analyst IC Industries, Chgo., 1972-73; pres. Faestel Investments, Inc., Crystal Lake, Ill., 1973—, also dir.; pres., dir. Am. Self Storage Centers, Inc.; dir. Petren Resources Corp., Trachte Metal Bldgs. Lic. real estate broker, Ill. Mem. Self Service Storage Assn., Am. Petroleum Inst., Ind. Petroleum Assn. Am., C. of C., Am. Simmnetal Assn. Roman Catholic. Club: Kiwanis (past pres.). Office: 200 Corporate Corner 101 Virginia St Crystal Lake IL 60014

FAHEY, BRIAN ANDREW JOSEPH, auto wrecking and pub. exec.; b. Buffalo, May 13, 1947; s. Joseph Anthony and Helen (Kramek) F.; B.A., Parsons Coll., 1971. Pub., Auto Mag., 1977-79; Blue Book, 1978—; auctioneer, appraiser, 1973—; co-owner, operator Clarence Auto Parts, Inc. (N.Y.), 1979—; pub. Wheels Weekly, The Liberty Tree, Western N.Y. Blue Book. Mem. Lancaster (N.Y.) Planning Bd., 1975—. Conservative. Home: Foxhall Village 6161 Genesee Rd Lancaster NY 14086 Office: 11079 Main St Rt 5 Clarence NY 14031

FAHNER, HAROLD THOMAS, mktg. exec.; b. Detroit, Sept. 4, 1940; s. Harold L. and Beatrice H. (Craig) F.; B.S. in Econs., U. Detroit, 1962; m. Patricia A. Churchvara, Aug. 25, 1962; children—Michael, Janet Peter. With sales dept. Dun & Bradstreet, Inc., N.Y.C., 1963-67; mgr. sales tng. Blue Cross-Blue Shield, Detroit, 1967-70; mgr. sales, mgmt. tng. A. O. Smith Harvestore Products, Inc., Arlington Heights, Ill., 1970-76, dist. sales mgr., 1976-77, eastern regional mgr., 1977-79; mktg. cons., 1980—; mem. adv. bd. William Rainey Harper Coll.; instr. Internat. Sales Mgmt. Inst.; lectr. in field. Mem. Sales-Mktg. Execs. Assn. (v.p. Chgo.), Sales Mgmt. Execs. Inst. (Outstanding Performance award 1969-70), Am. Soc. Tng. and Devel., Pi Sigma Epsilon. Author: The Problem Solving Approach to Selling, 1975; The Sales Manager's Model Letter Book, 1976. Home: 2201 Foxwood Dr Orange Park FL 32073 Office: 532 Riverside Ave Jacksonville FL 32202

FAHRINGER, CATHERINE HEWSON, savs. and loan exec.; b. Phila., Aug. 1, 1922; d. George F. and Catherine G. (Magee) Hewson; diploma Inst. Fin. Edn., 1965; 1 son by previous marriage, Francis George Beckett; m. Edward F. Fahringer, July 8, 1961. Public relations clk. Dade Savs. and Loan Assn., Miami, Fla., 1958-59, asst. sec., pub. relations, 1959-61, asst. v.p., 1961-67, v.p., 1967-74, sr. v.p., 1974-75, sr. v.p., sec., 1975-79, sr. v.p., head savs., personnel and mktg. div., 1979—. Mem. Public Health Trust Dade County, Fla., 1974—, sec., 1976-79, chmn., 1979—; mem. exec. com. and council Dade County CETA Consortium, 1973—; co-chmn. United Way Panel C., Miami, 1977—, mem. priorities and allocations com., 1978—, trustee, 1980—; mem. woman's adv. bd. Fla. Internat. U., 1978; trustee, v.p. Fla. Internat. U. Found., 1979; bd. dirs. John Elliott Blood Center, 1979; trustee Dade County Vocat. Edn. Found., 1978—, Downtown Miami Mchts. Assn., 1979-80. Named Woman of Yr., Dade County Bus. Profl. Women's Club, 1974; Woman of Yr. in Fin., Zonta Internat., 1975; recipient Trailblazer award, Women's Council of 100, 1977. Mem. Inst. Fin. Edn., (past pres. Greater Miami chpt.; nat. dir.), Savs. Loan Marketing Soc. (past pres.), Am. Soc. Personnel Mgrs., Fla. Savs. Loan League, Am. Soc. Personnel Adminstrs., Internat., Nat., Fla., Dade County bus. profl. women assns. Democrat. Congregationalist. Clubs: Coral Gables Country, Bankers. Contbr. speeches and articles to profl. jours. Office: Dade Savs 101 E Flagler St Miami FL 33131

FAIGIN, MICHAEL ALAN, pub. co. exec.; b. Bklyn., Jan. 26, 1942; s. Saul Marvin and Gertrude (Hochberg) F.; B.S., Fairleigh Dickinson U., 1963; postgrad. RCA Inst., 1963-64; m. Michelle Lee Schwager, Aug. 19, 1967; children—Lisa, Robert, Richard, David., Asso. dir. WTOP-TV, Washington, 1963-64; producer, dir. CBS News, N.Y.C., 1964-69; producer sports WCBS radio, N.Y.C., 1965; sales exec. Nat. Telephone Directory Corp., Union, N.J., 1970-78; pres. Community Mktg. Corp., pubs. ind. yellow pages directories, Margate, Fla., 1978—, also dir. Served with U.S. Army, 1959-60. Recipient Project of Year award Parsippany Jr. C. of C., 1974-75. Mem. Assn. N. Am. Directory Publishers, Pompano Beach, Coral Springs, West Palm Beach, Boca Raton C. of C. Jewish. Club: Lions (dir. 1971) (Rockaway, N.J.). Office: 2333 N State Rd 7 Margate FL 33063

FAIRMAN, JARRETT SYLVESTER, retail co. exec.; b. Anderson, Ind., Feb. 22, 1939; s. Charles Lawton and Ruth (Rich) F.; B.S., Purdue U., 1961; m. Delores Rae Anderson, Nov. 13, 1960; children—Adele Suzanne, Jarrett Scott, Angela Christine. Exec. trainee, div. mgr. Sears, Marion, Ind., 1963-67, merchandise mgr., asst. store mgr., Bloomington, Ind., 1967-69, asst. retail sales mgr. sporting goods, Chgo., 1969-71, territorial mdse. mgr. sporting goods, toys and bus. equipment, Dallas, 1971-78; regional v.p. retail ops. White's Home and Auto Stores, 1978—. Served with U.S. Army, 1961-63. Republican. Lutheran. Home: 1608 Centenary St Richardson TX 75081 Office: 3910 Callfield Rd Wichita Falls TX 76328

FAIRWEATHER, OWEN, lawyer; b. Chgo., Aug. 18, 1913; s. George O. and Nellie (Dieter) F.; A.B., Dartmouth, 1935; J.D., U. Chgo., 1938; m. Sally Hallberg, May 4, 1940; children—Ellen Vail, Peter Gustav. Admitted to Ill. bar, 1938; practiced in Chgo., 1938—; asso. firm Pope & Ballard, Chgo., 1938-43, partner, 1943-45; partner firm Seyfarth, Shaw, Fairweather & Geraldson, Chgo., 1945—. Dir. Danly Machine Corp., Chgo. Mem. Am. (council sect. labor and employment law 1958—), Ill. (legal ethics com. 1943-44, labor law com. 1944-45, grievance com. 1955, 56) bar assns. Author: Labor Relations and the Law (studies 6 European countries); Practice and Procedure in Labor Arbitration. Contbr. articles to legal publs. Home: 59 Hawthorne Rd Barrington IL 60010 Office: 55 E Monroe St Chicago IL 60603

FAISON, SETH SHEPARD, ins. broker; b. N.Y.C., Jan. 18, 1924; s. John W. and Caroline (Shepard) F.; A.B. with honors and distinction, Wesleyan U., 1947; m. Susan Tyler, Apr. 14, 1956 (dec. July 1978); children—Katharine Tyler, Seth Shepard, Sarah, Ann Badger; m. 2d, Sara Williams Rose Chew, Mar. 29, 1980; stepchildren—Sara Holton Chew, Katherine Rose Chew, Arthur Duncan Chew. Personnel mgr. NBC, 1948-53; div. mgr. Am. Mgmt. Assn., N.Y.C., 1953-58; asst. v.p. Johnson & Higgins, Inc., N.Y.C., 1958-68, v.p., 1968—; trustee Kings Hwy. Savs. Bank (now Franklin Savs. Bank), 1969-71. Bd. dirs. Bklyn. Acad. Music, 1963-74, chmn., 1966-72, hon. chmn., 1979—; chmn. bd. trustees Bklyn. Inst. Arts and Scis.; vice chmn. bd. trustees Bklyn. Mus.; v.p. bd. trustees Bklyn. Hosp.; bd. dirs. Police Athletic League, 1957-73; trustee Poly. Prep., 1962-77; regent St. Francis Coll., 1961-70. Served to lt. (j.g.) USNR, 1943-46. Mem. Huguenot Soc. Am., Ins. Brokers Assn. State N.Y., Citizens Union. Unitarian (deacon). Clubs: Heights Casino, Rembrandt (Bklyn.); Bellport Bay Yacht (Bellport); Down Town Assn. (N.Y.C.). Home: 1 Pierrepont St Brooklyn NY 11201 Office: 95 Wall St New York NY 10005

FAJILAN, ROLANDO DELEON, ins. agt., bus. cons., import-export exec.; b. Manila, Philippines, Oct. 6, 1946; came to U.S., 1952, naturalized, 1962; student U. Md., 1964-67, San Jose City Coll., 1975-77, San Jose State U., 1978; m. Marianila C. Atega, Jan. 14, 1970; children—Christel Atega, Cassandra Atega, Roland Atega, Courtney Atega. Salesman, br. mgr. D & F Bosson & Assos., San Jose, 1973-75; sales mgr. Paul Revere Life Ins. Co., 1975-77; pres. R.D. Fajilan Fin. and Ins. Services, Inc., San Jose, 1977—, CAGUSAM Internat., Inc., Manila, 1979—; exec. v.p. Fajilan Devels., Ltd., Marina, Calif., 1978—; gen. partner E & F Enterprises of San Jose, 1979—. Served to capt. C.E., U.S. Army, 1968-73. Mem. Nat. Assn. Life Underwriters, San Jose Assn. Life Underwriters, Am. Soc. C.L.U.'s, Million Dollar Round Table. Republican. Roman Catholic. Home: 2480 Escalonia Ct San Jose CA 95121 Office: 1333 Lawrence Expressway Bldg 200 Suite 260 Santa Clara CA 95051

FALASCO, AUDREY ROBINSON, bus. exec.; b. Phila., Apr. 2, 1935; d. Ellwood Souder and Dorothy Mae (Lohr) Robinson; B.S. in Acctg., St. Joseph's U., Phila.; m. Eugene C. Falasco; children—Colette, Ilise. Controller, v.p. bd. Genesco, Parkerford, Pa.; also cons. Mem. citizen rev. panel, children and youth facilities Pa. Dept. Public Welfare; bd. dirs. Women Against Rape; mem. Pa. Trial Ct. Nominating Commn. Mem. Nat. Assn. Accts., Am. Soc. Women Accts., Am. Soc. Profl. and Exec. Women, Nat. Trust Historic Preservation, Women's Internat. League for Peace and Freedom, AAUW, Nat. Bus. and Profl. Women's Club, NOW, Internat. Platform Assn., Nat. Women's Polit. Caucus, LWV (dir.). Home: RD 1 Box 481 Spring City PA 19475 Office: Box 8 Linfield Rd Parkerford PA 19457

FALCK, GILBERT MARTIN, aerospace exec.; b. Mpls., Oct. 6, 1921; s. Albert Julius and Hildegarde Esther (Sommers) F.; B.M.E., U. Minn., 1949; m. Edna Kathleen Miller, June 15, 1946; children—Dennis Albert, Peter Leslie, David. With Honeywell, Inc., 1949—, environ. test supr. Aerospace div., Mpls., 1950-52, quality evaluation supr., 1953-56, chief test engr., 1957-60, program mgr., St. Petersburg, Fla., 1961-77, contracts rep., 1978—. Served with AUS, 1942-46. Methodist. Home: 2315 Indian Ave N Belleair Bluffs FL 33540 Office: 13350 US Hwy 19 St Petersburg FL 33733

FALK, MOWRY W., ins. co. exec.; b. Attleboro, Mass., Dec. 22, 1937; s. Merrill N. and Beatrice M. F.; m. Marion L. Tingley, Sept. 20, 1958; children—Derrith, James, Glenn. With Tex. Instruments nuclear div. Attleboro, Mass., 1958-62; with John Hancock Mutual Life Ins. Co., 1962—, sales and sales mgmt. mktg. staff asst., Boston, 1971-73, retirement plan cons., 1973-79, asst. supt. gen. agys., met. N.Y. div., Wayne, Pa., 1979—. Home: 315 Westtown Way West Chester PA 19380 Office: 125 Stafford Ave Bldg 3 Wayne PA 19087

FALK, NEIL RICHARD, former air force officer, real estate sales; b. Bklyn., Dec. 21, 1934; s. Nils Conrad and Viola Emily (Johnson) F.; B.A., St. Olaf Coll., 1956; m. Mary Jo Grogan, Feb. 1, 1958; children—Mark, Erica. Commd. 2d. lt., U.S. Air Force, 1956, advanced through grades to lt. col., 1972, ret., 1978; pilot Air Def. Command, 1958-60; ICBM crew duties, 1960-65; pilot SAC, 1965-70; at Air Command Staff Coll., Maxwell AFB, Ala., 1970-71; pilot elec. warfare EB66, 1971-72; staff officer future concepts Hdqrs. SAC, Offutt AFB, Nebr., 1972-75, financial, planning mgr. base support activities, Grand Forks AFB, N.D., 1975-77, emergency war order staff officer, 1977-78; real estate sales McGarvey Clark Realty, Fullerton, Calif., 1979—. Decorated D.F.C. with cluster, Air medal with 14 clusters, Meritorious Service Medal; Vietnam Gallantry Cross. Mem. Air Force Assn. Lutheran. Home: 1338 Avolencia Dr Fullerton CA 92635 Office: McGarvey Clark Realty 1431 N Harbor Blvd Fullerton CA 92635

FALKENSTERN, WILLIAM CALVIN, consumer products co. exec.; b. Rahway, N.J., June 18, 1934; s. William and Alma Palmer (Seabury) F.; B.S., Wharton Sch., U. Pa., 1955; M.B.A., Rutgers U., 1959; m. Mildred Ann Carlson, June 18, 1955; children—Peter, Carl, Carolyn. Work measurement analyst Merck Co., Inc., Rahway, 1956-63; fin. mgr. Hoffman LeRoche Co., Nutley, N.J., 1963-68; controller Standard Metals Corp., New York, N.J., 1968-71; controller Amway Corp., Ada, Mich., 1971-78, treas., 1978—, also dir., mem. polit. action com.; treas. Amway Mut. Fund, Ada, Mich., 1978; v.p., sec., dir. 1st Morris Investment Co.; guest lectr. univ. seminars in fin. Dist. fin. chmn. Boy Scouts Am.; mem. Watchung Sewer Commn.; pres. Valley Players; auditor Wilson Meml. Ch. Served with AUS, 1956. Mem. Fin. Execs. Inst. Clubs: Optimist, Elks. Home: 7576 Leonard St NE Ada MI 49301 Office: 7575 E Fulton St Ada MI 49355

FALKNER, ROBERT JERRY, investment research analyst; b. Tyler, Tex., Aug. 5, 1946; s. Robert L. and Lorene Kent F.; B.B.A. summa cum laude, U. Houston, 1968; m. Alexis Dutkin, Feb. 25, 1978; children—Anne, Cathy. With Underwood, Neuhaus, Houston, 1969—, economist, v.p., dir. research, 1972—. Chartered fin. analyst. Mem. Nat. Assn. Bus. Economists, Fin. Analysts Fedn., Houston Soc. Fin. Analysts. Presbyterian. Home: 217 Brewer St Navasota TX 77868 Office: Underwood Neuhaus 724 Travis St Houston TX 77002

FALKOWITZ, JOEL, consumer goods co. exec.; b. N.Y.C., Dec. 27, 1942; s. Charles H. and Gladys Falkowitz; B.A., Hunter Coll., 1965; postgrad. N.Y. U., 1970; m. Maureen F. Lapidus, Sept. 6, 1965; 1 son, Howard. Data processing cons. Computer Radix Corp., 1965-70; project mgr. fin. systems Dun & Bradstreet, Inc.; mgr. fin. systems Hertz Corp.; dir. data processing SuCrest Corp., N.Y.C.; dir. fin. controls SIAC; dir. adminstrv. systems Revlon, Inc., N.Y.C.; instr. Pace U.; lectr. Nat. Assn. Systems Mgmt. Mem. Nat. Micrographic Assn., Am. Mgmt. Assn. Office: Revlon Inc 767 Fifth Ave New York NY 10022

FALKOWSKI, EDWARD JOHN, mfg. co. exec.; b. Manchester, Conn., Oct. 6, 1942; s. John Edward and Mildred Camille (Mastropietro) F.; B.S. in Chem. Engring., Worcester Poly. Inst., 1965; M.A.B., Western New England Coll., 1969; m. Brenda W. Lisle, Oct. 19, 1963; children—Brenda June, Richard, Lance. Tech. sales rep. photo products E.I. duPont de Nemours, Wilmington, Del., 1965-70, market planning asst., 1970-71, product specialist export sales, 1971-72, product mgr. internat. ops., 1973-77, internat. market planning mgr., 1977-79, div. mgr., Japan, 1979—; instr. in field. Counselor Jr. Achievement, Wilmington, 1971; basketball coach St. David's Episcopal Ch., Wilmington, 1973-76. Mem. Japan Flexographic Tech. Assn. Clubs: DuPont Country, Tokyo Am. Authored and presented tech. seminars for printing industry in Peoples Republic of China, 1977-79. Contbr. articles to profl. jours. Home: 20-5 Kamiyama-Cho Shibuya-Ku Tokyo 150 Japan Office: Akasara 1 Chome Minato-Ku Kowa #2 Tokyo Japan

FALLON, GERARD C., automotive co. exec.; b. N.Y.C., July 22, 1933; s. John William and Helen Kathleen (Guinan) F.; B.A. in History, Hunter Coll., 1955; J.D., St. John's U., Jamaica, N.Y., 1961; m. Claire A. Cloonan, Nov. 17, 1956; children—John J., Gerard C. Asso. firm Reavis & McGrath, 1961-66; corp. atty. Volkswagen of Am., Inc., Englewood Cliff, N.J., 1966-78, mktg. counsel, 1978-79; v.p., gen. counsel Fiat Motors N. Am., Inc., Montvale, N.J., 1979—, also dir.; dir. Ventana Inc. Mem. Am. Bar Assn., N.Y. Bar Assn., N.J. Bar Assn., Am. Trial Lawyers Assn. Democrat. Roman Catholic. Office: 155 Chestnut Ridge Rd Montvale NJ 07645

FALLON, HARRY JAMES, electronics distbg. co. exec.; b. Bklyn., July 14, 1926; s. Harry Joseph and Agnes Marie (Murray) F.; student LaSalle Extension U., Chgo., 1962-67; m. Jacqueline Gordon, Mar. 17, 1962; children—Keith, Craig, Dorothy. Parts mgr. Motorola Inc., Chgo., 1946-49; sales mgr. Radio Electric Service Co., Phila., 1949-60; regional sales mgr. Hickok Electric Instrument Co., Cleve., 1960-70; pres. Federated Purchaser, Inc., Springfield, N.J., 1970—, also dir.; dir. Hickok Electric Instrument Co. Pres., local P.T.A. Served with USNR, 1943-46. Decorated Purple Heart. Mem. Am. Bus. Inst., Sales Mgrs. Assn. Phila., Nat. Elec. Distbrs. Assn. (past pres.), Electronic Research Inst. (past pres.). Contbr. articles to trade publs. Home: 123 Milligan Pl South Orange NJ 07079 Office: 155 Route 22 Springfield NJ 07081

FALLON, JOHN JOSEPH, lawyer; b. New Rochelle, N.Y., Feb. 2, 1923; s. Francis X. and Beatrice (Hume) F.; A.B., U. Notre Dame, 1948; J.D., Cornell U., 1951; m. Ethel Mary Schwartz, Dec. 27, 1948; children—Michael Brian, Kevin Christopher, Moira Anne, Mary

Patricia, John Hume. Admitted to Mo., Kan. bars, 1951; asso. Stinson, Mag, Thomson, McEvers and Fizzell, Kansas City, Mo., 1951-54; partner Fallon, Guffey and Jenkins and predecessor firms, Kansas City, Mo., 1955-69; counsel Popham, Conway, Sweeny, Fremont & Bundschu, Kansas City, Mo., 1970-78; partner Fallon & Jones, Kansas City, 1978—. Founding pres. Nat. Catholic Reporter Pub. Co., 1964-68; co-chmn. Kansas City region NCCJ, 1967-69; chmn. bd. councilors Avila Coll., 1978—; mem. Jackson County Bond Adv. Com., 1967-72; co-chmn. Mo. Lawyer's Com. for Re-election Pres., 1972. Served with AUS. Decorated Bronze Star, Purple Heart. Mem. Mo. C. of C. (pres. 1967-69). Home: 2029 W 96th St Leawood KS 66206 Office: 9233 Ward Pkwy Suite 200 Kansas City MO 64114

FALLON, MICHAEL CURRAN JOHN, real estate investment cons.; b. Rockville Centre, N.Y., Mar. 7, 1947; s. Peter James and Marie Agnes (Curran) F.; B.S. in Mktg., Siena Coll., 1968; grad. Am. Bankers Assn. Sch. Real Estate Fin., 1970; m. Georgiann M. Keyser, June 29, 1968; children—Ryan Michael, Tara Boyle. With Chase Manhattan Bank, N.Y.C., 1970-75, staff mktg. officer, 1972-73, loan officer mortgage loans, 1973-75; asst. v.p. mortgage loans Chem. Bank, N.Y.C., 1975-76; v.p. Investors Central Mgmt. Corp., N.Y.C., 1976-80; v.p. Howard P. Hoffman Assos., Inc. subs Lehman Bros. Kuhn Loeb, N.Y.C., 1980—; guest lectr. N.Y. U. Vol., Urban Cons. Group; vol. cons. Big Bros. Am., Albany, N.Y., 1964-68; bd. dirs. Bronx River Restoration, Inc. Served to 1st lt. U.S. Army, 1968-70. Decorated Army Commendation medal; lic. real estate broker, N.Y. Mem. Young Mortgage Bankers Assn. (chmn.), Mortgage Bankers Assn. Am., Young Men's Real Estate Assn. N.Y., L.I. Soc. Real Estate Appraisers. Home: RD 1 Goldens Bridge Rd Katonah NY 10536 Office: 100 Park Ave New York NY 10017

FALLON, MICHAEL PATRICK, research co. exec.; b. Balt., Aug. 19, 1938; s. Eugene Lee and Cecily M. (Hill) F.; B.E.E., U. Md., 1968; M.A. in Mgmt., DePaul U., 1972; Exec. M.B.A., U. Chgo., 1976; postgrad. in law Ill. Inst. Tech.; m. Alvera M. Nastase, Dec. 9, 1958; children—Kevin, Tanya, Tara. Design engr. J. Eliopolo & Assos., 1963-68; market planning analyst Square D Co., Park Ridge, Ill., 1968-72; dir. mktg. Powers Regulator Co., Skokie, Ill., 1973-75; exec. dir. Elec. Industry Study Bd., Chgo., 1976—; cons. Ford Motor Co., 1972-73; dir. Consol. Industries. Pres. Park Ridge Sports Inc., 1972-74; youth commr. City of Park Ridge, 1975-76, commr. park dist., 1978—. Named Man of Year, Hyattsville, Md., 1966. Mem. Nat. Assn. Bus. Economists, Nat. Soc. Profl. Engrs., Am. Mktg. Assn., Assn. Time Sharing Users, Park Ridge Hockey Assn., Delta Mu Delta (sec.). Clubs: Plaza, International, Park Ridge Country. Home: 300 Talcott Pl Park Ridge IL 60068 Office: One E Wacker Dr 3614 Chicago IL 60601

FALLON, WALTER ADDISON, photog. equipment co. exec.; b. Schenectady, 1918; s. Walter A. and Irene (Casler) F.; B.S., Union Coll., 1940, D.Sc. (hon.), 1972; M.S., Rensselaer Poly. Inst., 1941, D.Sc. (hon.), 1979; LL.D. (hon.), Nazareth Coll., 1978; m. Shirley Barnett, Nov. 24, 1950; children—Margaret, Martha. With Eastman Kodak Co., Rochester, N.Y., 1941—, mgr.-film emulsion and plate mfg., 1966-70, v.p. and gen. mgr. U.S. and Can. photog. div., 1970-72, pres., chief exec. officer, chmn. fin. com. and ops. com., 1972-77, chmn. bd., chief exec. officer, chmn. exec. com., 1977—; dir. Morgan Guaranty Trust Co. N.Y., Eastman Chem. Products Inc., J.P. Morgan & Co., Inc., Rochester Gas & Elec. Corp., Gen. Motors Corp.; trustee Rochester Savs. Bank. Trustee U. Rochester, Rochester Inst. Tech.; mem. council Coll. Engring., Cornell U. Recipient Herbert T. Kalmus medal Soc. Motion Picture and TV Engrs., 1968; award for excellence Carborundum Co., 1974; Man of Year award Photog. Mfrs. and Distbrs. Assn., 1977; Associated Industries/Corning Indsl. Leader of Yr., 1979. Mem. Rochester Soc. Quality Control, Bus. Council, Indsl. Mgmt. Council Rochester (dir.), Sigma Xi. Club: Genesee Valley. Office: Eastman Kodak Co 343 State St Rochester NY 14650

FALTIS, DENNIS JOSEPH, advt. exec.; b. Cedar Rapids, Iowa, Nov. 20, 1945; s. William Joseph and Helen Antonette (Michalek) F.; B.A., U. Iowa, 1968. Dir. pub. relations Bear Mfg. Co., Rock Island, Ill., 1968-70; v.p., media dir. Sperry-Boom, Inc., Chgo., 1970-75, v.p., account supr., 1975-79, also dir.; pres. Strother & Faltis, Inc., advt. agy., Dundee, 1980—; corp. sec., dir. C&L Aviation, Inc., Elgin, Ill.; guest speaker U. Iowa Sch. Journalism, dept. bus. adminstrn. Roosevelt U., Chgo. Mem. Bus. Profl. Advt. Assn., Fox Valley Ad Club, U. Iowa Alumni Assn., Aircraft Owners and Pilots Assn., Dundee Bus. and Profl. Assn., Am. Fedn. Fishermen. Republican. Club: Lauderdale Lakes Yacht. Home: 433 Cavalier Ct Apt 103B Dundee IL 60118 Office: 10 E Main St Dundee IL 60118

FAMOLARE, JOSEPH PHILLIP, JR., shoe designer and mfr.; b. Boston, June 2, 1931; s. Joseph Phillip and Merriam (Claudy) F.; student Middlebury (Vt.) Coll., 1950, Emerson Coll., Boston, 1954, Fashion Inst. Tech., N.Y.C., 1960-61; B.S., Emerson Coll., 1956; m. Sandra Burnham, Oct. 27, 1957; childrn—Bibiana, Hilary. Designer-coordinator, Capezio Shoes, N.Y.C., 1959-64; exec. v.p. Marx & Newman, N.Y.C., 1964-69; pres. Famolare, Inc., shoe design and mfg, N.Y.C., 1969—. Mem. sch. bd. Am. Sch. of Florence (Italy), 1972-77; bd. dirs. Berkshire Sch., 1977-79. Served with U.S. Army, 1955-57, Korea. Recipient Coty award, 1973. Office: 4 E 54th St New York NY 10022

FANJUL, ALFONSO GERONIMO, land co. exec., sugar producer; b. Havana, Cuba, Sept. 30, 1909; s. Higinio and Maria (Estrada) F.; came to U.S., 1959; B.A., Cath. U. Am., 1931; m. Lillian Gomez Mena, Sept. 9, 1936; children—Alfonso Jose, Lillian Fanjul Azqueta, Jose, Alexander, Andres. Vice pres. Cuban Trading Co., Havana, 1934-59, Nueva Compania Azucarera Gomez Mena, Havana, 1937-59, Manati Sugar Co., Havana, 1947-59, Francisco Sugar Co., Havana, 1945-59, Czarnikow-Rionda Co., N.Y.C., 1940-69; chmn. bd. Osceola Farms Co., Palm Beach, Fla., 1960—, New Hope Sugar Co., Palm Beach, 1961—, Flo-Sun Land Corp., Palm Beach, 1969—; dir., 2nd v.p. Fla. Sugar Cane League, 1965—. Trustee Biscayne Coll., Miami, Fla., 1963—, Palm Beach Day Sch., 1968—. Mem. Fla. Sugar Marketing and Terminal Assn. (dir. 1977—). Roman Catholic. Clubs: Everglades (gov. 1972-79), Seminole Golf, Bath and Tennis, Meadow; Bathing Corp. (Southampton). Home: 109 Wells Rd Palm Beach FL 33480 Office: 316 Royal Poinciana Plaza Palm Beach FL 33480

FANNING, JOHN ANTHONY, oilfield servicing co. exec.; b. Waterbury, Conn., Nov. 9, 1939; s. Rose F.; B.S. in Physics, Holy Cross U., 1962; M.S. in Indsl. Mgmt., M.I.T., 1965; m. Gabriella Berno, Feb. 23, 1980; children by previous marriage—Lisa, John M., Douglas, Sara. Planning analyst, fin. analyst Cabot Carbon, Pampa, Tex., 1965-68; adminstrv. asst. Western Co. N. Am., Ft. Worth, 1968, dir. corp. planning, 1968, now pres. Pres., Jr. Achievement Tarrant County, 1978-79, 80—. Mem. Young Pres.'s Orgn. (pres. W. Tex. chpt., 1979-80). Republican. Roman Catholic. Home: 1405 Westover Ln Fort Worth TX 76107 Office: 6100 Western Pl Fort Worth TX 76116

FANNING, JOHN HAROLD, chmn. NLRB; b. Putnam, Conn., Sept. 19, 1916; s. John Joseph and Eva Marie (Dumas) F.; A.B., Providence Coll., 1938; LL.B., Catholic U. Am., 1941; D. Pub. Adminstrn., Providence Coll., 1969; m. Eloise Marie Cooney, Dec. 5, 1942; children—Mary Ellen Fanning Dunn, John Michael, Ann Eloise Fanning Gallagher, Gaele Therese Fanning De Gross, Stephen Thomas. Admitted to R.I. bar; individual practice law, R.I., 1941-42; with Dept. Labor, Washington, 1942-43; legal and indsl. relations advisor depts. War, Army and Def., Washington, 1943-57; mem. NLRB, Washington, 1957—, chmn., 1977—. Mem. Cardinal O'Boyle's Com. of Laity for Washington, 1968—; bd. dirs. Cath. Youth Orgn., Washington. Recipient Ann. Career award Nat. Civil Service League, 1957; Meritorious Civilian Service medal Dept. Def., 1958. Contbr. articles to various publs. Office: Nat Labor Relations Bd 1717 Pennsylvania Ave NW Washington DC 20570*

FANSHIER, CHESTER, mfg. exec.; b. Wilson County, Kans., Mar. 2, 1897; s. Thomas J. and Nora Bell (Maxwell) F.; m. Ina Muriel Goens, Apr. 12, 1918; 1 dau., Norma Elaine (Mrs. Robert B. Rice). Gen. mgr. Bart Products Co., 1932-39; pres., gen. mgr. Metal Goods Mfg. Co., Bartlesville, Okla., 1939—. Commr. from Tulsa Presbytery to 156th Gen. Assembly, Presbyn. Ch. U.S.A., 1944; pres. Sunday Eve. Fedn. chs., 1937-38. Recipient Wisdom award Honor, 1970, Gutenberg Bible award; registered profl. engr., Okla. Mem. Nat., Okla. (charter Bartlesville chpt.) socs. profl. engrs., ASTM, ASME (life), Profl. Photographers Am., Nat. (life), Okla. rifle assns., Am. Def. Preparedness Assn. (life), Bartlesville C. of C., SAR. Presbyn. (elder). Clubs: Rotary (pres. 1956-57), Engineers (dir. 1948-49, 54-55). Patentee in field. Home: 1328 S Cherokee Ave Bartlesville OK 74003 Office: 309 W Hensley Blvd Bartlesville OK 74003

FANTAUZZI, LAWRENCE ARNOLD, fin. cons.; b. Monessen, Pa., Oct. 2, 1947; s. Lawrence Amerigo and Wilma Florence (Rajala) F.; B.S., Carnegie Mellon U., 1970, M.S. in Indsl. Adminstrn., 1970. Asst. to dir. ednl. research and devel. Carnegie Mellon U., Pitts., 1970-71, asst. to dean, 1971-72; planning asso. Asso. Corp. N.Am., South Bend, Ind. and Dallas, 1972-73, sr. corp. planning asso., 1973-74, asst. controller, 1974-75, mgr. planning, budgeting, fin. analysis, 1975-76; treas. Gary L. Palmer C.P.A., Cortland, Ohio, 1977—; pres. PRIME Info. Systems, Inc., Cortland, 1978—. Mem. Cortland Area C. of C., Jaycees (chpt. sec.), Accts. Computer Users Tech. Exchange. Club: Rotary. Home: 190 Heather Ln Cortland OH 44410 Office: 204 W Main St Cortland OH 44410

FARACLAS, JOHN ELIAS, restaurateur; b. N.Y.C., Aug. 28, 1922; s. Elias and Irene (Mesologites) F.; student N.Y. U., 1941-42, 46-47; B.S., U. Balt., 1949; postgrad. Johns Hopkins U., 1950-51; m. Mary Easton, July 28, 1965. Vice pres. Indsl. Food Service, The City Vending Co., Balt., 1947-62; v.p. Mischantons Restaurant, Balt., 1956-62; v.p., gen. mgr. Tom Ross' Charcoal Hearth, Washington, 1962-68; pres., owner Adam's Rib, Inc., Washington, 1969—. Pres. bd., Condominium Assn. Elizabeth, 1976—; mem. Washington Mayor's Overall Econ. Adv. Com., 1979—, Mayor's Spl. Com. To Promote Washington, Pvt. Industry Council, 1979-80; chmn. Com. on Expanding Employment D.C. Residents; bd. dirs. Local Devel. Corp.; mem. hotel, restaurant and instnl. mgmt. curriculum adv. com. No. Va. Community Coll., 1979—. Served with U.S. Army, 1942-45. Decorated Bronze Star Medal. Mem. Restaurant Assn. Met. Washington (pres. 1977-78; Service Restaurateur of Year 1975, Restaurateur of Yr. 1980), Am. Legion, V.F.W., United Chios Socs., Am. Hellenic Ednl. Progressive Assn. Greek Orthodox. Clubs: Kiwanis (pres. 1955), Masons (32 deg., Shriner). Home: 4601 N Park Ave Chevy Chase MD 20015 Office: 2100 Pennsylvania Ave NW Washington DC 20037

FARAGHER, THOMAS JAMES, banker; b. Seattle, May 20, 1941; s. Thomas Robert and Mary Jane (Mueller) F.; B.B.A., U. Wash., 1963; M.B.A., Stanford U., 1975; m. Cristina Cabrera, July 16, 1965; 1 son, Robert. Credit officer Wells Fargo Bank, San Jose, Calif., 1965-67; stockbroker Dean Witter & Co., San Mateo, Calif., 1967-70; Reynolds Securities Co., San Mateo, 1970-73; asst. to pres., v.p., regional mgr. nat. div. Tex. Commerce Bank, Houston, 1975-79; chmn. bd. Tex. Commerce Bank, Dallas, 1979—; dir. TACA, Inc. Served to lt. comdr., Supply Corps, USN, 1963-65. Mem. Am. Inst. Banking, Central Bus. Dist. Assn. Dallas (dir.), U. Wash. Alumni Assn., Stanford U. Alumni Assn., Stanford Grad. Sch. Bus. Alumni Assn., Zeta Psi, Alpha Kappa Psi. Republican. Clubs: Northwood, Royal Oaks Country, Plaza Athletic Club (dir.), Westside Tennis, Chaparral. Office: 300 Tex Commerce Bank Tower Pearl at Bryan Sts Dallas TX 75222

FARAH, JAMES CLIFTON, apparel exec.; b. El Paso, Tex., Mar. 30, 1947; s. William Frank and Betty Jean (Corcoran) F.; B.A., Stanford, 1968; M.B.A., U. Pa., 1970; m. Cynthia Weber, Jan. 12, 1974; 1 dau., Elise. Mgmt. trainee Farah Mfg. Co. Inc., El Paso, 1970-72, asst. to v.p. mfg., 1972-73, asst. to pres., 1973-75, v.p. fin., 1975-76, v.p., div. gen. mgr., dir., 1976-77, v.p. mktg. and sales, 1978—. Mem. Wharton Grad. Alumni Adv. Bd.; mem. adv. bd. Coll. Bus. Found. U. Tex., 1975-77; bd. dirs. Central YMCA El Paso, 1973-76, membership chmn., 1976; devel. campaign chmn. Newark Maternity Hosp.-Houchen Day Care Center, 1974-75. Mem. Wharton Grad. Alumni Assn. (dir. 1974-79). Episcopalian. Home: 233 Oleander Way El Paso TX 79922 Office: PO Box 9519 El Paso TX 79985

FARBER, BERNARD E., internat. mktg. specialist; b. Stuttgart, Germany; came to U.S., 1940, naturalized, 1943; s. Josef and Cilly (Posner) F.; B.A., U. Ky., 1948; M.A., U. Chgo., 1949; postgrad. Columbia U., N.Y. U., New Sch. Social Research and Bernard Baruch Coll., 1949-55; m. Sarah R. Sussman, June 26, 1957; children—Miriam Daphne, Sharon Lee, Rena Mindy. Asst. textile buyer Joseph H. Cohen & Sons and Stein Stores, 1952-54; export mgr. Tech. Tape Corp., Bronx, N.Y., 1954-55; export mgr. Toscony, Inc., N.Y.C., 1955-60; export mgr. Harte & Co. div. Diamond Shamrock, N.Y.C., 1960-66; internat. product mgr. Borden, Inc., Internat., N.Y.C., 1966-72, mgr. operational analysis Internat. Export dept., 1973-75; area mgr. Central and S. Am., Dominican Rep. and Haiti, N.Y.C., 1976—; tchr. langs.; multi-lingual lectr., leader internat. tech. mktg. and sales seminars; internat. cons. in mktg., fin., prodn. and machinery. Served with U.S. Army. Pepsi Cola scholar, 1948. Mem. Am. Mgmt. Assn., Council of Americas, Phi Sigma Iota, Kappa Delta Pi. Club: Lions. Home: 392 Chelsea St Paramus NJ 07652 Office: 420 Lexington Ave New York NY 10017

FARBISH, ALFRED BUCKS, rubber and plastics co. exec.; b. Phila., Sept. 18, 1923; s. Sydney Allmeyer and Rachel Levy (Bucks) F.; student Oxford (Eng.) U., 1945; B.A., U. Pa., 1948; m. Rita Ruth Fayer, Oct. 11, 1951; children—Michael B., Peter B. Civil engr. Phila. Dist., U.S. Army Engrs. Corp., 1955-57; mgr. comml. devel. Barrett div. Allied Chem. Co., N.Y.C., 1957-65; sales mgr. Am. Cyanamid Co., Wakefield, Mass., 1965-71; v.p. gen. mgr. Rubber & Plastics Compound Co., Long Island City, N.Y., 1971-74, pres., 1974—. Served with arty. U.S. Army, 1942-46, 48-53. Mem. U. Pa. Alumni Assn., Sales Exec. Club N.Y. Clubs: U. Pa. (N.Y.C.); Milford Yacht; Fencers. Patentee in field. Home: 129 Zaccheus Mead Lane Greenwich CT 06830 Office: 36 15 23d St Long Island City NY 11106

FARHA, WILLIAM FARAH, food co. exec.; b. Lebanon, Nov. 27, 1908; s. Farah Farris and Nahima (Salamy) F.; grad. U.S. Indsl. Coll., 1948; grad. Brookings Instn., 1968; m. Victoria Barkett, Apr. 15, 1934; 1 son, William George. With F & E Wholesale Grocery Co., 1929-64; pres. River Bend Shopping Center, Wichita, William F. Farha & Son Enterprises. Field adviser, nat. bd. Small Bus. Adminstrn., 14 years. Bd. dirs. Nat. Conf. Christians and Jews, Kan. Found. for Blind; trustee Met. YMCA, Antiochian Greek Orthodox Diocese of all N.Am.; bd. advisers Salvation Army; internat. bd. YMCA World Service; pres. bd. trustees St. George Ch.; chmn. Wichita Leadership Prayer Breakfast; participant prayer breakfasts Presidents Eisenhower, Johnson, and Nixon, Washington. Former mem. bd. govs. St. Jude Research Hosp., Memphis; past chmn. Wichita Police and Pension Fund; past trustee Wichita Symphony Soc.; past mem. nat. bd. Inst. Logopedicts, bd. St. Joseph's Research Hosp. Center. Named hon. col. Staff Gov. Okla., 1956; named to Wisdom Hall of Fame, 1970; recipient Gold Medalion from Antiochian Patriarch Alexander of Damascus, Syria, 1952, Antonian Gold medal of merit Antiochian Orthodox Christian Archdiocese N.Y. and all N.Am., 1972; Brotherhood award NCCJ, 1979. Mem. Wichita C. of C. (past dir.). Rotarian. Home: 8630 Shannon Way Wichita KS 67206 Office: 2220 N Somerset Wichita KS 67204

FARHA, ZACK, food co. exec.; b. Kansas City, Mo., Oct. 9, 1928; s. Zack Abraham and Jennie M. (Monsour) F.; B.S. in Mktg., U. Kans., Lawrence, 1951; m. Jeannette Leilah Naifeh, Feb. 11, 1961; children—Vincent, Christopher. Gen. mgr. Pioneer Foods Co., Hutchinson, Kans., 1951-56; owner Pioneer Sales Co., food brokerage, Wichita, Kans., 1956-59; co-founder, exec. v.p. Swiss Chalet Food Products (sold to Clorox Co. 1974), Wichita, 1970-73, sales cons., 1974—, owner, 1981—; chmn. bd. Pioneer Properties, Inc., land developers, Wichita and Toronto, Ont., Can., 1973—. Active local Boy Scouts Am.; bd. dirs. St. Jude's Hosp., Memphis, Aid to Leukemia Stricken Am. Children. Served with AUS, 1951-53. Mem. Kans. U. Alumni Assn., Sigma Phi Epsilon, Order St. Ignatius. Republican. Mem. Antiochian Orthodox Ch. Clubs: Masons, Shriners, Elks, Lions (past internat. dir.). Collaborator: (textbook) Dynamics in Marketing, 1951. Home: 509 Tallyrand Wichita KS 67206 Office: 636 N Saint Francis St PO Box 800 Wichita KS 67201

FARICY, JAMES ROLAND, truck and equipment dealer; b. Florence, Colo., Aug. 5, 1926; s. James Matthew and Elsie Fern (Price) F.; student Abbey Coll., Canon City, Colo., 1944; m. Teresa Mae Abell, July 21, 1945; children—Jerome A., H. Brian, James R., Huberta V., Melvin L., J. Kevin, Teresa Mae. Automobile and truck dealer, 1946—; pres. Rol Faricy Motor Co., Pueblo, Colo., 1968-77, Faricy Truck & Equipment Co., Pueblo, 1978—; chmn. exec. com. Abell Truck & Equipment Co., Pueblo, 1969-77; trustee, sec.-treas. Colo. Automobile Dealers Ins. Trust; mem. nat. advt. adv. council Internat. Harvester Co. truck group. A founding dir. Pueblo Devel. Found., 1963; mem. Pueblo County Democratic central and exec. com., 1960-64, advt. and campaign chmn., 1962; trustee St. Mary Corwin Hosp., Pueblo; bd. dirs. St. Joseph Hosp., Florence, Colo., 1979—; chmn. bd. trustees Colo. Automobile Dealers Ins. Trust. Served with USAAF, 1944-46. Named Truck Dealer of Year, Columbia U. Grad. Sch. Bus./Am. Truck Dealers Assn., 1981. Mem. Am. Truck Dealers Assn. (legis. chmn. Colo. 1977-78), Am. Trucking Assn., Nat. Automobile Dealers Assn., Colo. Automobile Dealers Assn. (pres. 1965), Colo. Motor Carriers Assn., Internat. Harvester Nat. Dealer Conf. Roman Catholic. Clubs: Pueblo Golf and Country, Elks, K.C. (4 deg.). Home: 12 Silverweed Ct Pueblo CO 81001 Office: 4425 N Elizabeth St Pueblo CO 81008

FARISH, R. STARR, food co. exec.; b. Piedmont, Calif., Dec. 28, 1912; s. Robert Roy and Carrie May (Edwards) F.; B.A., Wash. State U., 1935; grad. exec. seminar sales mgmt. Mich. State U., 1961; m. Barbara Jean Bequeath, Dec. 4, 1967; 1 dau., Melody Cook; children by previous marriage—R.W., J. Starr, Elaine Hopper. Food broker, New Eng., Fla. and Seattle, 1934-38; field rep. New Eng. Fish Co., Seattle, 1938-45, nat. sales mgr., 1945-52; nat. sales mgr. food div. J.R. Simplot Co., Caldwell, Idaho, 1952-66, v.p., 1966-73, exec. v.p. sales and marketing, 1973-76, sr. v.p., 1976-77, ret., 1977; cons. mktg., mgmt., advt., 1977—. Mem. Idaho Potato Commn., 1963-66. Mem. Caldwell Planning Commn. Former bd. dirs. United Fund, A.R.C. Served with USNR, 1942-45. Mem. Internat. Foodservice Mfrs. Assn. (dir. 1973-76, Sparkplug award 1972), Frozen Potato Products Inst. (past dir.), Instant Potato Products Assn. (v.p.), Caldwell C. of C. (past pres.), Alpha Kappa Psi, Phi Delta Theta. Elk, Kiwanian (past pres. Caldwell). Clubs: Caldwell Athletic Round Table (past pres.), Golf (past pres.). Home: 2111 Wyoming Ave Caldwell ID 83605

FARKAS, ANDREW E. (ED), homebuilder, land developer; b. Buckhannon, W.Va., Mar. 15, 1947; s. Andrew G. and Marjorie D. F.; student Ga. Inst. Tech., 1965-67; B.A. in Econs., U. Pitts., 1970; M.B.A., U. S.C., 1972; m. Laura L. Kelly, Aug. 27, 1971. Staff cons. statis. services U. S.C. Computer Center, Columbia, 1971-73; market research analyst Rich's, Inc., Atlanta, 1973-74; corp. planner Ryan Homes, Inc., Pitts., 1974-77; supt., sales cons. U.S. Home Corp., Houston, 1977-78, v.p., project mgr., Clearwater, Fla., 1978-79, dir. pres., Denver, 1979—. Mem. Nat. Assn. Homebuilders, Beta Gamma Sigma. Office: 12015 E 46th Ave Suite 520 Denver CO 80239

FARKAS, JONATHAN DALE, dept. store exec.; b. N.Y.C., Dec. 26, 1948; s. George and Ruth Lewis (Ambassador) F.; B.A., N.Y. U., 1971; m. Kimberly Harcleroad, Mar. 7, 1972; children—Sammantha, Blayre. Buyer, mdse. mgr. Alexander's Dept. Stores, N.Y.C., 1971-76, v.p., dir., 1976-80, v.p. services, dir., mem. mgmt. com. bd. dirs., 1980—. Bd. dirs. One to One Charity for Retarded, 1974-77; mem. N.Y. State Econ. Devel. Bd., 1978—; mem. N.Y. State Council on Internat. Bus., 1972—; spl. dep. sheriff Suffolk County. Clubs: Harmonie, Le Club, Doubles, Anabells. Office: 733 Lexington Ave New York NY 10022

FARLEY, JAMES BERNARD, mgmt. cons.; b. Pitts., Nov. 1, 1930; s. James and Marie (Wallace) F.; B.B.A., Duquesne U., 1953; M.B.A., Case Western Res. U., 1960; m. Mary Williams, Feb. 14, 1951; children—James J., Michele M., Constance M., J. Scott. Indsl. engr., econ. evaluator, supt. rail ops. subs. r.r. cos. U.S. Steel Corp., Pitts., Lorain, Ohio, Cleve., 1953-63; with Booz, Allen & Hamilton, Inc., N.Y.C., 1963—, group v.p., pres. info. systems div. and mgmt. cons. div., 1968-73, pres., dir., 1973-76, chmn. bd., chief exec. officer, 1976—; dir. Crum & Forster Ins. Cos. Trustee, Nat. Urban League, Com. Econ. Devel.; mem. adv. council Stanford Bus. Sch.; charter mem. Duquesne U. Century Club. Served with USMC, 1948-50. Mem. Conf. Bd. Clubs: Baltusrol Golf; The Links; Board Room; N.Y. Athletic. Home: 51 Taylor Rd Short Hills NJ 07078 Office: 245 Park Ave New York NY 10017

FARLEY, JOHN URBEN, II, publisher's rep.; b. Chgo., May 1, 1940; s. J. Urben and Virginia (Meis) F.; B.A. in Psychology, Loras Coll., 1963; m. Ann B. Janelli, Feb. 4, 1967; children—John U., III, Cheryl Ann, Roger Joseph. Mktg. and editorial asst. Horton Pub. Co., Evanston, Ill., 1961-62; dist. mgr. Farley Co., N.Y.C., 1965-70, dir., 1966-70, pres., 1973—; dist. mgr. Standard Rate & Data Service Co., Skokie, Ill., 1971-72; lectr. Roosevelt U., Chgo., 1974—. Pres. Young Republicans Orgn., Loras Coll., 1962; mayoral ward campaign chmn. John V. Lindsay, N.Y.C., 1965-66; city councilman Woodcliff Lake, N.J., 1970-72; chmn. March of Dimes, Bergen County, N.J., 1971-72; hon. chmn. Woodcliff Lake council Boy Scouts Am., 1971-72, cubmaster Lake Forest Pack 48, 1979-80. Served with Adj. Gen. Corps, U.S. Army, 1963-65. Mem. Internat. Advertisers Assn., Bus./Profl. Advt. Assn. (dir. 1976—, v.p. 1979—), Chgo. Bus. Pubs.

Assn., Assn. Pubs.'s Reps. (v.p. 1981—). Roman Catholic. Clubs: Univ., Winter, Exec. Address: 35 E Wacker Dr Chicago IL 60601

FARLEY, VINCENT CARROLL, bank exec.; b. N.Y.C., Apr. 18, 1924; s. James Charles and Mabel Agnes (Carroll) F.; A. in Applied Sci. Criminal Justice, St. Francis Coll., 1974, B.A., 1974; m. Mary T. McGann, Nov. 20, 1954; children—Christopher, Michael, Mary Sue, Nancy, Victoria, Patricia, Jacqueline. With N.Y.C. Police Dept., 1949-75, capt., comdg. officer of chief inspector's investigative unit and spl. ops. integrity control unit, 1972-75; asst. v.p. Citicorp/Citibank, N.Y.C., 1975—. Mem. Suffolk County Forgery and Fraud Com. Served with USMC, 1942-46. Mem. N.Y.C. Police Dept. Emerald Soc., Ret. N.Y. Detective Assn., Nat. Law Enforcement Assn., Capts. Endowment Assn., Am. Assn. for Profession Law Enforcement, Internat. Soc. Credit Card Investigators, St. Francis Coll. Alumni, Am. Legion. Roman Catholic. Home: 26 Terry Rd Northport NY 11768 Office: 2 Huntington Quadrangle Huntington Station NY 11746

FARLING, ROBERT FINLEY, banker; b. Daytona Beach, Fla., July 17, 1945; s. George Frederich and Mildred Louise (Hodges) F.; B.S. in Econs., (Marathon Oil Co. Scholar), Ball State U., 1967; M.Mgmt. in Fin., Northwestern U., 1977; m. Judith Le Baron Hambrick, June 28, 1975; 1 son, Christopher Ryan. With Continental Ill. Nat. Bank & Trust Co. of Chgo., 1970—, bond officer, 1973-74, 2d v.p., 1974-77, money market trader, 1977-79, v.p. bond dept., 1977—, govt. securities trader, 1979-80, money market trading mgr., 1981—. Served as officer USN, 1968-70; Vietnam. Republican. Club: Union League (Chgo.). Home: 2142 N Fremont St Chicago IL 60614 Office: Continental Ill Nat Bank & Trust Co of Chgo 231 S LaSalle St Chicago IL 60693

FARMER, JAMES, economist; b. Oklahoma City, Sept. 12, 1934; s. Clarence H. and Rubylea E. (Springer) F.; B.S., U. Okla., 1956; M.S., Harvard U., 1961; M.B.A., UCLA, 1962. With RAND Corp., 1960-68; dir. info. systems Calif. State Univs. and Colls., Los Angeles, 1968-72; chmn. Systems Research Inc., Washington, 1972—; cons. economist U.S. Dept. State, 1962-64; asso. in edn. Grad. Sch. Edn., Harvard U., 1976—; chmn. Sigma Group Inc., Guthrie, Okla., 1971—; dir. Am. Data Inc., Gaithersburg, Md. Served with U.S. Army, 1956-60. Mem. N.Y. Acad. Scis. Home: 1200 N 21st St Guthrie OK 73044 Office: 210 G St NE Washington DC 20002

FARMER, LEE R., ins. co. exec.; b. Alliance, Nebr., Feb. 23, 1924; s. Lee R. and Berenice (Ellis) F.; student U. Nebr., 1941-43, 46-47, U. Minn., 1948; m. Constance Audrey Lang, Sept. 18, 1954; children—Diana Lee, Lee R. III, Stuart Lang. Spl. rep. Minn. Hosp. Service Assn., St. Paul, 1948-50, dist. mgr., Duluth, 1950-55; regional mgr. Continental Casualty Co., Chgo., 1955-56, supt. group div., 1956-59, asst. v.p., 1959-61, v.p., chief operating officer of gen. group div. and ind. plans div., 1961-65; exec. v.p. Nat. Ben Franklin Life Ins. Corp. and Nat. Ben Franklin Ins. Co. affiliates of Continental Ins. Co., Chgo., 1965-68; pres. Lee R. Farmer & Assos., Inc., Hinsdale, Ill., 1969-70; exec. v.p. Continental Life & Accident Co., 1971-74; pres. Profl. Adminstrs., Inc., 1974—. Served as lt. (j.g.) USNR, 1943-45. Mem. Sigma Nu. Methodist. Mason (32 deg.). Club: Hillcrest Country. Home: 209 E Curling Dr Boise ID 83702 Office: Box 1722 Boise ID 83701

FARMER, MARJORIE ELIZABETH, electrochemist; d. Henry and Jessie (Lodewyck) Farmer; B.A., Mt. Holyoke Coll. Research electrochemist Pratt & Whitney div. United Techs. Corp., 1942-51; electrochemist The Chem. Corp., 1951-53, U.S. Navy, 1954-55; mem. tech. staff Rockwell Internat. Corp., 1957—, also lead instr. advanced career tng. program for high sch. students in conjunction with Calif. Regional Occupational Program; indsl. adv. com. Cerritos Coll., North Orange County Regional Occupational Program. Registered profl. engr. in corrosion and metallurgy, Calif. Fellow Inst. Metal Finishing (Gt. Brit.); mem. Am. Soc. Metals (chmn. Orange Coast chpt. 1980-81), Am. Electroplaters Soc. (cert.), Nat. Assn. Corrosion Engrs., Nat. Mgmt. Assn., New Eng. Antivivesection Soc., Animal Protection Inst., Humane Soc. U.S., Horse Protection Assn., Mercy League, NOW. Club: Mt. Holyoke (Los Angeles). Contbr. articles to profl. jours. Office: Anaheim CA

FARNEY, HARRIET FELDMAN, ins. co. exec.; b. Rockville, Conn., Oct. 16, 1933; d. John Fred and Flora Anna (Moser) Feldman; A.S., U. Hartford, 1963, B.S. cum laude, 1966, M.Ed., 1968, M.B.A., 1971, M.S.P.A., 1977; m. Clifford Farney, Mar. 22, 1953; children—Amber, Anne. Office mgr. Gottier's, Rockville, Conn., 1950-53; with Lewis County Trust Co., Lowville, N.Y., 1953-56; dir., treas. Nutmeg Transport, Inc., Vernon, Conn., 1956-65; tchr. bus. Rockville High Sch., Vernon, 1965-67; with Aetna Life Ins. & Annuity Co. subs. Aetna Life & Casualty Ins. Co., Hartford, Conn., 1967—, mgr. planning, 1977-78, mgr. acctg. and control, 1978-80, dir. acctg. and control, 1980—. Mem. Planning Execs. Inst. Home: 78 Hartford Turnpike Tolland CT 06084 Office: A-209 151 Farmington Ave Hartford CT 06115

FARNSLEY, CHARLES ROWLAND PEASLEE, pub.; b. Mar. 28, 1907; s. Burrel Hopson and Anna May (Peaslee) F.; LL.B., U. Louisville, 1930, A.B., 1942, LL.D., 1950; postgrad. U. Ky., 1943-44; LL.D., Wesleyan U., Middletown, Conn., 1959; m. Nancy Hall Carter, Feb. 27, 1937; children—Sally Farnsley Bird, Ann, Alexander, Burrel Charles Peaslee, Douglass Charles Ellerbe. Practiced law, 1930-48, 54-64; mem. Ky. Ho. of Reps., 1936-40; mayor Louisville, 1948-54; mem. 89th Congress from 3d Dist. Ky.; pres. Lost Cause Press, Charley Farnsley Distilling Co. Inc. Trustee U. Louisville, 1946-48, sec. bd. trustees, 1947-48, mem. bd. overseers, 1948-64; curator Transylvania U., Lexington, Ky., 1947-58; trustee Louisville Free Pub. Library, 1945-48; dir. Louisville Philharmonic Soc., 1947-48, 54—. Mem. Soc. Colonial Wars, Delta Upsilon, Omicron Delta Kappa. Democrat. Episcopalian. Mason. Clubs: River Valley, Pendennis, Wynn Stay, Filson (Louisville); Century, Grolier (N.Y.C.); Federal (Washington). Home: Glenview KY 40025 Office: Starks Bldg Louisville KY 40202

FARQUHAR, DONALD JOSEPH, computer facilities design cons.; b. Athol, Mass., Dec. 1, 1932; s. Donald Joseph and Rose Doris (Santilini) F.; A.E.E., Worcester (Mass.) Jr. Coll., 1953; m. Maryln Louise Predmore, Sept. 6, 1957; children—Patrick, Thomas, Cynthia, Michael. Asst. engr. Test Engrs. Program, Gen. Elec. Co., 1953-55, field engr. computer dept., 1959-69; mgr. facilities and real estate Computer Sci. Corp., 1969-80; sr. cons. Gottfried Cons., Inc., Los Angeles, 1980—. Mem. El Segundo (Calif.) Bicentennial Commn., 1975-76; troop chmn. Boy Scouts Am., 1972-79. Served with USAF, 1955-59. Mem. Indsl. Devel. Research Council. Roman Catholic. Home: 1400 E Walnut St El Segundo CA 90245 Office: 3435 Wilshire Blvd Suite 1910 Los Angeles CA 90010

FARQUHAR, GEORGE RALPH, commodity brokerage exec.; b. Orange, Calif., Apr. 23, 1941; s. George Shaw and Sally Ann (Campbell) F.; B.S., Calif. State U., Long Beach, 1964; M.B.A., U. So. Calif., 1965; m. Gail Tough, June 19, 1965; children—Marjorie, Rose, Karen. Sr. accountant, Price Waterhouse & Co., Los Angeles, 1965-69; sec.-treas. Trivex, Inc., Costa Mesa, Calif., 1969-73; pres. A-Mark Precious Metals, Inc. Beverly Hills, Calif., 1973—; owner Cavendish West; instr. accounting C.P.A., Calif. Mem. Calif. Soc. C.P.A.'s, Am. Inst. C.P.A.'s, Am. Numis. Assn. Presbyterian. Clubs: Town Hall, Los Angeles Athletic; Mesa Verde Country (Costa Mesa, Calif.). Home: 4150 Via Dolce #125 Marina del Rey CA 90291 Office: 9255 Sunset Blvd Los Angeles CA 90069

FARRAH, JERE TIFFIN, airline co. exec.; b. St. Thomas, Ont., Can., Sept. 5, 1916; s. James William and Nelly Emmaline (Randall) F.; came to U.S., 1934, naturalized, 1943; B.S. in Aero. Engring., B.M.E., U. Mich., 1938; m. Mary Frances Prince, Sept. 14, 1940; children—Jere Tiffin and James William (twins). With Am. Airlines, N.Y.C., 1942-57, mgr. power plant overhaul, 1955-57; with Seaboard World Airlines, Inc., Jamaica, N.Y., 1957—, v.p., Los Angeles, 1961—; designated engring. rep. FAA; lectr. air transport Oxford U., 1962-76. Pres., Red Spring Manor Civic Assn., Glen Cove, N.Y., 1964-65. Sheenan scholar, 1937-38; registered profl. engr., Wash. Fellow Royal Aero. Soc.; mem. Soc. Automotive Engrs. (chmn. met. sect. 1962-63), AIAA. Club: Alpena (Mich.) Yacht. Home: Sunview Dr Glen Cove NY 11542 Office: Flying Tiger Line Los Angeles Internat Airport Los Angeles CA 90009

FARRALL, ROBERT ARTHUR, electronics co. exec.; b. Evanston, Ill., July 2, 1932; s. Arthur William and Luella (Buck) F.; B.S. in Physics, Mich. State U., 1954; m. Nancy Mary Georgi, Dec. 22, 1955; children—John Robert, George William. Mgr. photometric engring. Gen. Electric Co., Lynn, Mass., 1954-63; exec. v.p. Clairex Corp., Mt. Vernon, N.Y., 1963-69, pres., 1969—; dir. Clairex Electronics of PR, N-Con Systems Corp. Bd. dirs. Mt. Vernon United Fund; trustee Rye Hist. Soc. Served with AUS, 1954-56. Mem. Am. Phys. Soc., Soc. Photog. Scientists and Engrs., Sigma Pi Sigma, Delta Upsilon. Club: Am. Yacht (Rye, N.Y.). Patentee photoconductive cell circuits. Home: 69 Hewlett Ave Rye NY 10580 Office: 560 S 3d Ave Mount Vernon NY 10550

FARRAR, IRWIN ELMER, property mgmt. and devel. exec.; b. nr. Camarillo, Calif., Sept. 29, 1893; s. John Leander and Mary Ann (Brubaker) F.; student U. So. Calif., 1911-12, Stanford U., 1913-16, Alexander Hamilton Inst., 1919-21; m. Lois Barbara Peebles, Nov. 28, 1917 (dec. 1970); children—Mary Elizabeth, Robert Irwin. Admitted to Calif. bar, 1916; law practice, Corona, Calif., 1916-17; sec. Corona C. of C., 1916-17; pres. La Sierra Alfalfa Co., 1919-46, Farrar-Loomis Seed Co., 1934-65, Riverside Alfalfa Growers, 1931-46; v.p. Hemet Valley Growers, 1944-72; dir. Citizens Nat. Bank of Riverside, 1952-57, mem. exec. com., 1953-57; exec. com., dir. Inland div. Security-Pacific Nat. Bank, 1957—. Bd. advisers Stanford U. Law Sch., 1955-57; trustee bd. of edn. Hemet Unified Sch. Dist., 1937-40; mem. Riverside County War Labor Bd., 1942-45; dir. Met. Water Dist. So. Calif., 1951—, mem. exec. and legal coms.; vice chmn. Water Problems Com., 1952—; mem. adv. council Water Resources Center, U. Calif., 1959-65; pres. Eastern Municipal Water Dist., 1951-59, San Jacinto River Conservation Dist., 1944-55; chmn. com. 15 on Flood Control (Riverside County), Zone 4 Commn., 1945-52; rep. Riverside County, on Water Problems and Flood Control, Washington, 1947-48; mem. 7th Ann. Global Strategy Discussions, U.S. Naval War Coll., 1955. Mem. Calif. State Bar, Am. Soc. Sugar Beet Technologists, Calif. State, Hemet (pres. 1919-21), Riverside County (pres. 1937-41) chambers commerce, Comml. Secs. Assn. Calif. (dir. 1916-17), Calif. Hay and Grain Dealers Assn. (dir. 1938-40), SAR, Phi Alpha Delta. Republican. Congregationalist (dir. Conf. So. Calif. and S.W. 1956-59). Club: Kiwanis (lt. gov. 1927, 28, pres. 1930, chmn. scholarship fund 1931-52). Author: My 79 Years in Southern California, 1973; Riverside County Water Pioneer, 1975. Home: 25661 Cornell St Hemet CA 92343

FARRAR, JACK WILLIAM, arts and crafts retail co. exec.; b. West Plains, Mo., June 2, 1936; s. Jack and Luella Belle (Maxey) F.; B.A., Drury Coll., 1959; m. Judith Ann Paul, Mar. 16, 1963; children—Paul Curtis, Matthew Grant. Fgn. prodn. mgr. Hallmark Cards, Kansas City, Mo., 1959-62; program mgr. Super Market Inst., Chgo., 1963-67; pres. A-M Food Services, Inc., div. Arden-Mayfair, Inc., Commerce, Calif., 1967-71; v.p., gen. mgr. VIP Yarns, Inc., div. Caron Internat., Robesonia, Pa., 1971-77; pres. Farrar Corp., Reading, Pa., 1977—. Served with U.S. Army, 1959. Mem. Nat. Retail Mchts. Assn., Nat. Art Needlework Assn., Nat. Art Materials Dealers Assn. Republican. Methodist. Club: Optimist. Home: 7 Bobolink Dr Wyomissing PA 19610 Office: 843 N 9th St Reading PA 19604

FARRAR, JAMES ELVIN, JR., coal co. exec.; b. Peekskill, N.Y., Aug. 31, 1934; s. James Elvin and Katherine (Throckmorton) F.; student U. Richmond (Va.), 1953-55, Va. Commonwealth U., 1956-57; m. Doris Hays, July 13, 1959; children—Robyn, Michael. Asst. v.p. A.T. Massey Coal Co., Richmond, Va., 1955-74; v.p. sales John McCall Coal Co., Bluefield, W.Va., 1974-77, Barber Paramont Coal Corp., Bluefield, 1977—. Served with AUS, 1957-59. Mem. Coal Exporters Assn. (dir.), So. Coals Conf., N.C. Coal Inst., Sales Execs. Club, Bluefield C. of C. Baptist. Clubs: Bluefield Country, Clover, University. Home: 2003 Jefferson St Bluefield WV 24701 Office: PO Box 908 Bluefield VA 24605

FARRELL, ALBERT CHARLES, economist, stock brokerage exec.; b. Iowa City, Iowa, May 2, 1940; s. Charles Raymond and Gladys Mae (Barclay) F.; B.A. in Bus. Adminstrn., Huron Coll., 1965; M.A. in Econs., U. S.D., 1966; postgrad. (NSF fellow) U. Ark., 1966, (Gen. Electric doctoral scholar), U. Chgo., 1967; m. Shirley Amanda Armfield, Aug. 5, 1967; children—Patricia Mae, Richard Spencer. Instr. econs. Yankton (S.D.) Coll., 1966-68; v.p. Dean Witter Reynolds & Co., Beverly Hills, Calif., 1968—. Mem. exec. bd. ARC, Los Angeles, chmn., Beverly Hills, 1976-78. Recipient Achievement award Wall St. Jour., 1964. Mem. Am. Econs. Assn., Mensa, Pi Gamma Mu. Clubs: Beverly Hills Bus. and Profl. Men's (pres. 1975-76), Beverly Hills Men's (pres. 1978—). Author: Economic Outlook of South Dakota: Population, Employment, Income, 1966. Home: 2302 Bagley Ave Los Angeles CA 90034

FARRELL, AUSTIN DAVID, utility exec.; b. Phila., Aug. 5, 1927; s. Austin David and Pearl Esther (Ott) F.; student mgmt. tng. Pa. State U., 1964; m. Jean Leigh Evensen, Mar. 13, 1948; children—Jill, Jack, Paul. With Phila. Gas Works, 1948—, maintenance foreman, 1954-67, tng. foreman, 1967-72, tng. supr., 1972—; speaker seminars Inst. Pub. Safety, Pa. State U. Instr. defensive driving Nat. Safety Council; councilman Bourough of Aldan (Pa.), 1972-73, mayor, 1974—; pres. Lansdowne/Aldan Home Sch. Assn.; chmn. Cancer Crusade Delaware County (Pa.). Mem. Pa. Mayors Assn. (eastern v.p.). Republican. Home: 110 Merion Ave Aldan PA 19018

FARRELL, DAVID COAKLEY, dept. store exec.; b. Chgo., June 14, 1933; s. Daniel A. and Anne D. (O'Malley) F.; B.A., Antioch Coll., Yellow Springs, Ohio, 1956. Asst. buyer, buyer, br. store gen. mgr., mdse. mgr. Kaufmann's, Pitts., 1956-66, v.p., gen. mdse. mgr., 1966-69, pres., 1969-74; v.p. May Dept. Stores Co., St. Louis, 1969-75, dir., 1974—, pres., 1975—, also chief exec. officer, dir. 1st Nat. Bank, St. Louis. Bd. dirs. St. Louis Symphony Soc., St. Louis Area council Boy Scouts Am.; chmn. fund drive Arts and Edn. Council Greater St. Louis, 1980; trustee Washington U., St. Louis; mem. Nat. Bus. Com. for Arts. Mem. Nat. Retail Mchts. Assn. Roman Catholic. Clubs: University (N.Y.C.); Duquesne (Pitts.); Bogey, Noonday, St. Louis, University (St. Louis). Office: 6th and Olive St Saint Louis MO 63101

FARRELL, GEORGE T., banker; b. 1931; B.S., U. Notre Dame; married. With Mellon Bank, N.A., Pitts., 1959—, asst. v.p. credit dept., 1962-64, asst. v.p. internat. dept., 1964-66, v.p. dept., 1966-74, sr. v.p. dept., 1974-78, exec. v.p., 1978-80, vice chmn., 1980—, also dir.; dir. Banco Bozano, Network Fin. Ltd., First Boston (Europe) Ltd., Bankers Assn. for Fgn. Trade. Served with U.S. Army. Office: Mellon Bank NA Mellon Sq and Branches Pittsburgh PA 15230*

FARRELL, JAMES SANFORD, cons., mfrs. rep.; b. Chgo., July 4, 1915; s. Francis John and Julia (Mayer) F.; grad. Campion Prep. Sch., 1932-35; student U. Cin., 1935-36, Xavier U., 1936-37; m. Eileen Joan Stuhlreyer, June 7, 1938; children—Eileen Joan, Patricia Ann, James Sanford, Frances Marie. With Internat. Harvester Co., Milw., 1937-40; sales, marketing, store mgmt. S.D. Warren Co., Boston, 1940-41, asst. sales mgr. Diem & Wing Paper Co., Cin., 1941-46; asst. sales mgr. Pioneer Pub. Co., Chgo., 1946-49; v.p. sales and mktg. Western Pub. Co., Racine, Wis., 1949-66; v.p., dir. Artists & Writers Press Inc., 1954-66, Guild Press Inc., 1954-66 (both N.Y.C.); pres., dir. RCS Press, Chgo., 1966-68; pres. Sanford Assos. Inc., Lake Forest, Ill., 1970—; pres., dir. Dean Hicks Co., Grand Rapids, Mich. Served to lt. USNR, 1942-45. Mem. Ohio Soc. of N.Y. Clubs: Knollwood (Lake Forest, Ill.); Cornell (N.Y.C.); Mchts. and Mfrs. (Chgo.); Pinehurst (N.C.) Country. Home: 775 McKinley Ave Lake Forest Dr Pinehurst NC 23874 Office: 222 Wisconsin Ave Lake Forest IL 60045

FARRELL, JOHN STANISLAUS, mfg. co. exec.; b. County Down, No. Ire., May 19, 1931; came to Can., 1931, naturalized, 1931; s. George Stanislaus and Agnes Anna (McCartney) F.; B.Sc. in Elec. Engring., U. Toronto, 1956; m. Vyra June White, Aug. 7, 1959; children—John McCartney, Lizanne Jennifer. With ITT Can., Ltd., Montreal, Que., 1962-69, dir. avionics and transmission, 1968-69; mktg. dir. Leigh Instruments, Ltd., Carleton Pl., Ont., 1969-70, gen. mgr., 1970-73; pres., chief exec. officer Gestalt Internat. Ltd., Vancouver, B.C., 1973-76; v.p. Cornat Industries, Ltd., Vancouver, 1976-78; sr. v.p. Versatile Corp., Vancouver, 1978—; chmn., dir. Versatile Farm Equipment Pty. Ltd. (Australia), Versatile Toft Ltd. (Australia), Vickers Can. Inc.; dir. Balco Industries Ltd., Kamloops, B.C. Served with RCAF, 1950-59. Profl. engr., Can. Mem. Assn. Profl. Engrs. of Ont. Club: Vancouver Lawn Tennis and Badminton. Office: PO Box 49153 3 Bentall Centre 595 Burrard St Vancouver BC V7X 1K3 Canada

FARRELL, JOSEPH MICHAEL, steamship co. exec.; b. Yonkers, N.Y., June 7, 1922; s. Joseph Michael and Mary Elizabeth (Powers) F.; B.S. in Econs., U.S. Mcht. Marine Acad., 1943; postgrad. Columbia, 1948-50, Fordham U., 1947-48; m. Cloatta Grace Pennington, Dec. 6, 1946; children—Cloatta M., Anthony J., Christopher J., Janice E. Commd. ensign, 1944; advanced through grades to capt., 1960, USN, ret. 1960; mgr. Great Lakes Service, States Marine Lines, 1960-62; European mgr. Bremerhaven, Germany, 1962-65; exec. v.p. govt. sales Waterman S.S. Corp., Washington, 1965—; v.p. Hammond Leasing Corp., Mobile, Ala., 1967—, Waterman S.S. Co. of Del.; pres. Waterman Oceanic Corp., 1974—. Mem. Propeller Club U.S. (v.p., bd. govs. 1967-68), Nat. Def. Transp. Assn., Navy League. Clubs: Congressional Country, University, Capitol Hill, George Town, Democratic, Army-Navy (Washington); Metropolitan, Whitehall (N.Y.C.); Siwanoy Country (Bronxville, N.Y.). Home: 3128 Dumbarton St NW Washington DC 20007 Office: 1133 15th St NW Washington DC 20005

FARRELL, SAMUEL DENISON, fin. exec.; b. N.Y.C., Oct. 7, 1941; s. Cecil Samuel and Viola (Saunders) F.; student Newbold Coll. Oxford U., 1962; B.A., CCNY, 1972, M.A., 1973; M.A., Fordham U., 1976; cert. in philosophy Yale U., 1977; Th.D., San Francisco Theol. Sem., 1977; m. Marguerite Annette Alexander, Dec. 26, 1966; children—Samuel Denison, Ronette. Exec. officer CCNY, 1971-75; exec. dir. Farrell Enterprises, N.Y.C., 1975-78; pres. DNR Assos., Inc., N.Y.C., 1978-80; pres., chmn. Computer Referral Services, Inc., N.Y.C., 1980—. Vice chmn. Mental Health Council of Hamilton Heights-Harlem. CCNY fellow, 1972. Mem. Black Alumni Assn. CCNY (pres. 1978-80), Alumni Varsity Assn. N.Y. (sec. 1979-80, v.p. 1980-81), Bus. Assn. Hamilton Heights (sec. 1979-80), Am. Soc. Criminology, Nat. Council Crime and Delinquency. Republican. Mem. United Ch. of Christ. Clubs: City Coll., Chemist, Caribbean. Home: 333 Broadway D32C New York NY 10031 Office: 1730 Amsterdam Ave New York NY 10031

FARRELL, THOMAS JOSEPH, ins. co. exec.; b. Butte, Mont., June 10, 1926; s. Bartholomew J. and Lavina H. (Collins) F.; student U. San Francisco, 1949; grad. Life Ins. Agy. Mgmt. Assn., 1960; m. Evelyn Irene Southam, July 29, 1951; children—Brien J., Susan M., Leslie A., Jerome T. Partner, Affiliated-Gen. Ins. Adjusters, Santa Rosa, Calif., 1949-54; agt. Lincoln Nat. Life Ins. Co., Santa Rosa, 1954-57, supr., 1957-59, gen. agt., 1959-74; pres. Thomas J. Farrell/7 Flags Ins. Mktg. Corp., 1974—; pres., dir. Lincoln Nat. Bank, Santa Rosa, San Rafael. Mem. Redwood Empire Estate Planning Council, Santa Rosa, 1966—, Sonoma County Council for Retarded Children, 1956—, City Santa Rosa Traffic and Parking Commn., 1963; pres., nat. dir. United Cerebral Palsy Assn., 1954-55; chmn. Santa Rosa Community Relations Commn., 1973-76; pres. Sonoma County Young Republicans, 1953; past dir. Sonoma County Fair and Exposition, Inc.; bd. dirs. Sonoma County Family Service Agy., Eldridge Found.; trustee Sonoma State Hosp. Mentally Retarded Children. Recipient certificate Nat. Assn. Retarded Children, 1962; C.L.U. Mem. Sonoma County Life Underwriters (pres. 1956), Nat. Assn. Life Underwriters, Redwood Empire Assn. C.L.U.'s (pres. 1974—), Gen. Agts. and Mgrs. Assn., Japanese-Am. Citizens League, Jr. C. of C. (Outstanding Young Man of Year 1961, v.p. 1955), Santa Rosa C. of C. (dir. 1974-75), Calif. PTA (life). Clubs: Commonwealth, Press (San Francisco). Home: 963 Wyoming Dr Santa Rosa CA 95405 Office: 747 Mendocino Ave Santa Rosa CA 95401

FARREN, JAMES HUGH, food co. exec.; b. Johnstown, Pa., June 24, 1928; s. J. Edward and Ann C. (Conrad) F.; B.S. in Econs., Wharton Sch., U. Pa., 1952; m. Maryette C. Winner, Feb. 14, 1953; children—J. Douglas, J. David, J. Derek. Dir. employee relations Allis Chalmers; v.p. labor relations Am. Airlines; v.p. employer relations Internat. Playtex; v.p. employer relations, dir. Swift & Co., Chgo.; dir. R.I. Thompson Assos. Served with U.S. Army, 1946-48. Mem. Am. Mgmt. Assn., Conf. Bd. Club: Knollwood. Office: 115 W Jackson Blvd Chicago IL 60604

FARRENS, ROSS, arborist; b. Decatur, Nebr., June 27, 1905; s. John L. and Elizabeth (Towne) F.; student Davey Inst. of Tree Surgery, Kent, Ohio, 1925-27; m. Nora Kathryn Reed, Nov. 2, 1929; children—Jay (dec.), Reed (dec.). Organized firm Farrens Tree Surgeons, Inc., Jacksonville, Fla., pres., 1928-65; v.p., treas. Wilson Tree Co., Inc., Shelby, N.C., 1948-52; pres. Speedicraft Boat Co., Jacksonville, 1952-58; chmn. bd., pres. Blume System Tree Experts, Houston, 1954-65; sr. partner Farrens Chem. Co., Jacksonville, 1951-58; chmn. Farrens Tree Co., Inc., San Jose, Calif., 1961—, Trees of Hawaii, Inc., Honolulu, 1967—, Utility Tree Service, Inc., Eureka, Calif., 1964—; cons. Southeastern Public Service Co. N.Y., 1965—.

Served with inf. AUS, World War II. Mem. Nat. Arborist Assn. (exec. com. 1942-47, 1950-53, pres. 1946-47), Am. Forestry Assn. (hon. v.p. 1953), Internat. Soc. Arboriculture, Am. Legion. Republican. Methodist. Mason (K.T., Shriner). Clubs: Seminole, River, Petroleum of Houston. Office: First National Bank Bldg Reno NV 89505

FARRIES, JOHN KEITH, petroleum engring. co. exec.; b. Cardston, Alta., Can., July 9, 1930; s. John Mathew adn Gladys Helen (Adams); B.S. in Petroleum Engring., U. Okla., 1955; postgrad. Banff Sch. of Advanced Mgmt., 1963; m. Donna Margaret Lloyd, Dec. 30, 1960; children—Gregory, Bradley, Kent. Engr., dist. engr., joint interest supt. Pan Am. Petroleum Corp., Calgary, Edmonton, Tulsa, Drayton Valley, 1955-65; pres. Tamarack Petroleums Ltd., Calgary, Alta., 1965-70, Canadian Well Services & Tank Co. Ltd., Calgary, 1968-70, Farries Engring. Ltd., 1970—, Wave Internat. Engring., Inc., Israel, 1975—. Mem. Am. Inst. of M.E., Canadian Inst. Mining and Metallurgy (dir. petroleum soc. 1966-68), Assn. Profl. Engrs. of Alta., B.C. and Sask., Canadian Assn. of Drilling Engrs. (pres. 1977-78). Clubs: Calgary Petroleum, Willow Park Golf and Country. Past pub. chmn. Jour. Canadian Petroleum Tech. Home: 10819 Willowglen Pl Calgary AB T2J 1R8 Canada Office: 630 6th Ave SW Calgary AB T2P 0S8 Canada

FARRINGTON, WILLIAM BENFORD, investment analyst; b. N.Y.C., Mar. 10, 1921; s. Harold Phillips and Edith C. (Aitken) F.; B.C.E., Cornell U., 1947, M.S., 1949; Ph.D., Mass. Inst. Tech., 1953; m. Frances A. Garratt, 1949 (div. 1955); children—William Benford, Phyllis Ashley, Timothy Colfax; m. Gertrude E. Eby, Jan. 3, 1979. Radio engr. Naval Research Labs., 1942-43; dir. Read Standard Corp., 1948-55; plant engr. Hope's Windows, Inc., 1950-51; instr. geology, geophysics U. Mass., 1953-54; research geophysicist Humble Oil & Refining Co., 1954-56; lectr. U. Houston, 1955-56; sr. investment analyst Continental Research Corp., N.Y.C., 1956-61; pres., dir. Farrington Engring. Corp., 1958-67; partner Farrington & Light Assos., Laguna Beach, Calif., 1967—; v.p. Empire Resources Corp., 1961-62; asst. v.p. Empire Trust Co., 1962-64; dir. Commonwealth Gas Corp., N.Y.C.; sci. dir. Select Com. on Govt. Research, U.S. Ho. of Reps., 1964-65; lectr. U. Calif. at Los Angeles, 1968-72; sr. cons. Trident Engring. Assos., Annapolis, Md., 1965—; corporate asso. Technology Assos. So. Calif., 1971—. Chmn. crusade Am. Cancer Soc., Jamestown, N.Y., 1951. Chartered fin. analyst; registered geologist, Calif. Fellow AAAS, Fin. Analysts Fedn.; mem. Am. Assn. Petroleum Geologists, Am. Inst. Mining, Metall. and Petroleum Engrs., Am. Petroleum Inst., Am. Inst. Aeros. and Astronautics, Geol. Soc. Am., Seismol. Soc. Am., N.Y. Soc. Security Analysts, Los Angeles Soc. Financial Analysts, Sigma Xi. Episcopalian. Author articles in field. Home: 1565 Skyline Dr Laguna Beach CA 92651

FARRIS, FRANK MITCHELL, JR., lawyer; b. Nashville, Sept. 29, 1915; s. Frank Mitchell and Mary Frances (Lellyett) F.; B.A., Vanderbilt U., 1937; LL.B., N.Y. Law Sch., 1939; m. Genevieve Baird, June 7, 1941; 1 dau., Genevieve Baird. Admitted to Tenn. bar, 1939, U.S. Supreme Ct. bar, 1968; conciliation commr. in bankruptcy U.S. Dist. Ct., Middle Dist. Tenn., 1940-42; partner law firm Farris, Evans & Evans, Nashville, 1946-71, Farris, Warfield & Samuels, Nashville, 1972-75, Farris, Evans & Warfield, Nashville, 1975-78, Farris Warfield & Kanaday, Nashville, 1978—; gen. counsel, trustee George Peabody Coll., Nashville, 1968-79; gen. counsel 3d Nat. Corp., Nashville, Cherokee Equity Corp., Nashville; dir. 3d Nat. Bank. Trustee, exec. com. Vanderbilt U., Nashville, 1979—; chmn. commrs. Watkins Inst., Nashville, 1953-76; chmn. bd. Oak Hill Sch., Nashville, 1968-74, 80—. Served to lt. USNR, World War II. Mem. Am. Bar Assn., Nashville Bar Assn., Tenn. Bar Assn. Presbyterian. Home: 940 Overton Lea Rd Nashville TN 37220 Office: 17th Floor Third Nat Bank Bldg Nashville TN 37219

FARRIS, JAMES LOWELL, mgmt. cons. co. exec.; b. Duquoin, Ill., Sept. 29, 1942; s. Lowell Glen and Elsie K. Farris; B.S. in Indsl. Engring., Purdue U., 1965; M.S. in Engring. Mgmt., Northeastern U., 1969; m. Carol Lynn Robertson, Jan. 30, 1965; children—Bradford, Cheryl. Indsl. engr., indsl. engring. supr., quality control mgr. Armstrong Cork Co., Braintree, Mass., 1965-70; mgr. Arthur Young & Co., N.Y.C., 1970-74, San Francisco, 1974—, prin., 1976—, dir., 1979—, dir. mgmt. services dept., 1979—. Registered profl. engr., Fla. Mem. Am. Inst. Indsl. Engrs. (sr.), Am. Prodn. and Inventory Control Soc., Mcpl. Fin. Officers Assn. Republican. Congregationalist. Clubs: Engineers (San Francisco); Fremont Hills Country. Home: 974 Yorkshire Dr Los Altos CA 94022 Office: 1 Post St San Francisco CA 94104

FARRIS, JAMES RUSSELL, geologist; b. Ft. Worth, Tex., Apr. 23, 1937; s. Maldon Floyd and Mary Helen (Anderson) F.; student Baylor U., 1955-57, M.A., 1965; student Am. Inst. Banking, Los Angeles, 1957; B.A., Hardin Simmons U., 1963; postgrad. Mesa Coll., 1973-75, Ohio U., 1976-79; m. Mava Janeece Johnston, Aug. 3, 1962; children—Gwendolyn Camille, Elizabeth Renee, Allison Nicole. Chief geologist First Worth Corp., Denton, Tex., 1965-69; sr. petrologist, mgr. mineralogy petrology lab. Lucius Pitkin Inc., Grand Junction, Colo., 1969-73; pres. Ventucross Corp., Grand Junction, 1973-74, also dir.; regional staff geologist Coastal States Energy Corp., Houston, 1974-75; chief geologist, mgr. logging div. Mineral Service Co., Grand Junction, 1975-76; sr. geologist Am. Electric Power Corp., Lancaster, Ohio, 1976-80; pres., dir. Ventio Corp., 1979—; sr. geologist Sun Tex. Co., Abilene, 1980—; dir. Crystal Minerals Corp. Active Boy Scouts Am., Abilene, 1960-63, Waco, Tex., 1963-64, Grand Junction, Colo., 1970-72, commr., Abilene, 1980—; adv. 4H, Athens, Ohio, 1978-79. Recipient Abilene Geol. Soc. award, Most Outstanding Geology Student, 1961-62, 62-63. Mem. Soc. Petroleum Engrs., Am. Mgmt. Assn., Soc. for Advancement Mgmt., Internat. Platford Assn., Geol. Soc. Am., Am. Geol. Inst., Soc. Mining Engrs. of AIME, Clay Minerals Soc., ASTM, Mineral. Soc. Am., N.Am. Thermal Analysis Soc., Coblentz Soc., Colo. Mining Assn., Soc. Econ. Paleontologists and Mineralogists, Abilene Geol. Soc., Houston Geol. Soc., Ariz. Small Mine Operators Assn., AAUP, Internat. Assn. Study of Clays. Baptist. Club: Masons. Home: 2318 Greenbriar Abilene TX 79605 Office: PO Box 2817 Abilene TX 79604

FARRUGGIA, THOMAS GEORGE, fire extinguisher co. exec.; b. Elmhurst, Ill., Sept. 10, 1955; s. Alphonse Sam and Letitia Dorothy Marie (Ratjen) F.; B.S., Valparaiso U., 1977; postgrad. in mktg. No. Ill. U., 1977—. Vice pres. Ill. Fire Extinguisher Co., Inc., Addison, Ill., 1979—. Mem. United Fire Equipment Distbrs. Assn., Nat. Assn. Fire Equipment Distbrs., Nat. Fire Protection Assn. Republican. Lutheran. Address: 702 S Route 53 Addison IL 60101

FARWELL, FRANK LESTER, ins. co. exec.; b. Worcester, Mass., May 28, 1914; s. Frank Lester and Flora Louise (Arrington) F.; B.B.A., Boston U., 1937; Advanced Mgmt. Program, Harvard, 1957; L.H.D., Boston U., 1969; m. Mary Lincoln Chambers, Sept. 24, 1938; children—Louise A. (Mrs. Charles W. Domina), Linda (Mrs. William Lange). With Liberty Mut. Ins. Co., Boston, 1934—, successively clk., asst. treas., treas., 1934-58, v.p., 1959-61, exec. v.p., 1961-62, pres., 1962—, chmn., 1974—, dir.; chmn. Liberty Mut. Fire Ins. Co.; dir. Liberty Life Assurance Co., First Nat. Bank Boston, First Nat. Boston Corp., Boston Edison Co., Dennison Mfg. Corp., Helmsman (Und.) Ltd., Liberty Mut. Ins. Co. (Mass.) Ltd. (both London, Eng.). Trustee Northeastern U. Served as officer USNR, World War II. Clubs: Wellesley Country, Algonquin, Comml. Office: 175 Berkeley St Boston MA 02117

FARWELL, HARLEIGH ELLIS, constrn. co. exec.; b. Palisades, Wash., Sept. 23, 1921; s. Harley Elmer and Cecil Nan (Johnston) F.; student public schs.; m. Suzanne Edwina Boehm, Jan. 8, 1966; children by previous marriage—E. Kay Farwell Gilbertson, Sharon A. Farwell Scriba, Marilyn Z. Farwell Gala, Ellis D., Donovan W., Daniel A. Constrn. supt., gen. supt. Bank Bldg. Corp., St. Louis, 1952-60; constrn. supt., project mgr. Howard S. Wright Constrn. Co., Seattle, 1960-73, v.p., Seattle, 1973-80, sr. v.p., 1980—; guest lectr. Pres., dir. Seattle-King County Council Alcoholism, 1967; mem. accessibility design adv. com. Easter Seal Soc. Wash., 1978—. Served with AUS, 1944-45. Decorated Purple Heart. Mem. Am. Soc. Mil. Engrs. Research on cost improvement methods, devel. and upgrading of unit price data. Home: 15715 NE 66th Pl Redmond WA 98052 Office: 414 Pontius N PO Box 3764 Seattle WA 98124

FASANO, RICHARD DENNIS, towing co. exec.; b. N.Y.C., Dec. 13, 1939; s. Amedio and Roberta Doris (Turgeon) F.; B.Sc., U.S. Mcht. Marine Acad., 1963; m. Dianne M. Newcomb, Aug. 3, 1963; 1 dau., Lisa D. Joined U.S. Mcht. Marine as 3d officer, 1963, advanced through grades to master (capt.), 1970; ret., 1974; dir. ops. G & H Towing Co., Galveston, Tex., 1974-78, v.p. ops., 1978—; cons. on license exams. USCG, Ednl. Testing Service, Princeton; lectr. Tex. A&M U., Galveston. Mem. Galveston Port Safety Council, also chmn. traffic and navigation com. Mem. Soc. Naval Architects and Marine Engrs., Naval Inst., U.S. Mcht. Marine Alumni Assn. (pres. Galveston). Republican. Roman Catholic. Clubs: Propeller, Bob Smith Yacht. Home: 8305 Crown Ct Texas City TX 77590 Office: PO Drawer 2270 Galveston TX 77550

FAUBER, BERNARD M., retail co. exec.; b. 1922; married. With K Mart Corp., 1942—, asst. mgr. So. region, 1961-65, exec. asst. to pres., 1965-66, Western regional mgr., 1966-77, v.p., 1968-77, sr. exec. v.p., chief adminstrv. officer, 1977-80, chmn., chief exec. officer, 1980—, also dir. Served with USN, 1941-45. Office: K Mart Corp 3100 W Big Beaver Troy MI 48084

FAUCHER, DARLENE, advt. exec.; b. Bell, Calif., June 3, 1944; d. Duane Orr and Maxine Brady (Schmitt) Taylor; student San Diego State U., 1962-65; m. Michael Joseph Faucher, March 14, 1970. Stewardess, Pacific SW Airlines, 1965-66, saleswoman, 1966-70; chmn. bd., pres. Faucher & Meenan Advt. and Pub. Relations, San Diego, 1970—; chmn. bd., pres. My Handy Tool Store; partner Super Prodn. Co., San Diego, 1977—; v.p. Gardner & Faucher, Advt. and Public Relations, San Diego, 1979—. Bd. dirs. Bayside Settlement House; mem. U. Calif. Chancellors Assos.; mem. alumni bd. San Diego State U. Sch. Bus.; mem. Campership Council, bd. dirs. Jr. Achievement; mem. Rep. Nat. Com./Concord Group mem. Republican State Central Com. Calif. Recipient Graphics Achievement award Fox River Paper Corp., 1974, 75; Graphic Excellence award Strathmore Paper Co., 1976; Beautification award La Jolla Town Council, 1976; named Bus. Leader of Day, Sta. KSON, 1976. Mem. Am. Mktg. Assn., Pub. Relations Soc. Am., Small Businesswomen Owners Assn. (pres.), Internat. Assn. Bus. Communicators, Nat. Assn. Women Bus. Owners. Home: 8155 Pasadena Ave La Mesa CA 92041 Office: 432 F St Suite 400 San Diego CA 92101

FAULK, NILES RICHARD, oil and land co. exec.; b. Canton, Ohio, July 22, 1920; s. Albert Roy and Freda (Sponseller) F.; B.S., Mt. Union Coll., 1944; M.S., Ohio State U., 1948; m. Melba Ann Dotson, Oct. 14, 1944. Devel. geologist California Co., Laramie, Wyo., 1948, surface geologist, Farmington, N.Mex., 1948-49, Meridian, Canton, Forest (all Miss.), 1949-50, subsurface geologist, New Orleans, 1950-53; div. geologist La. Land & Exploration Co., New Orleans, 1953-55, chief geologist, 1955-63, v.p., 1963-74, sr. v.p., 1974—; v.p. La. Land Offshore Exploration Co., Inc., 1972-76, exec. v.p., 1976—. Served from pvt. to 1st lt. USAAF, 1943-46. Mem. Am. Assn. Petroleum Geologists, New Orleans Geol. Soc., Sigma Alpha Epsilon. Republican. Methodist. Clubs: Metairie Country, Petroleum New Orleans; Tchefuncta Country (Covington). Home: 37 Pine Crest Dr Covington LA 70433 Office: PO Box 60350 New Orleans LA 70160

FAULK, RICK HYATT, real estate fin. co. exec.; b. Toledo, Nov. 1, 1949; s. Richard H. and June B. (Jones) F.; B.S., Bowling Green State U., 1969; postgrad. Harvard U., 1973; m. Jan. 24, 1970. Pres., Faulk Real Estate & Fin. Co., Inc., Andover, Mass., 1977—; cons. Donahue & Assos., 1977—. Mem. New Eng. Real Estate Assn., Real Estate Appraisers Inst., Pub. Concern Group III. Democrat. Clubs: Elks, Lions (pres. 1969—), Rotary (v.p.). Contbr. articles to profl. publs. Home and office: 3 Cherokee Circle Andover MA 01810

FAULKENBURG, CLARENCE WILLIAM, fin. exec.; b. New Albany, Ind., Apr. 21, 1920; s. Littleton Jacob and Amelia Wilhelmina (Porzig) F.; student Spencerian Coll., 1936-38; M.S., Am. Coll., 1977; m. Mary Louise Hasenstab, June 16, 1941; 1 son, John Frederick. Office mgr. Lincoln Nat. Life Ins., Louisville, 1938-41; agt. to conferee IRS, Indpls., 1942-53; pvt. practice acctg., St. Petersburg, Fla., 1953-65; asso. gen. agt. John Hancock Life Ins., St. Petersburg, 1965-69; pvt. practice fin. and tax planning, Tampa, Fla., 1969—; pres. Exec. Tax Benefits, Inc., Tampa, 1979—; lectr. in field. Mem. U.S. Senatorial Bus. Adv. Bd.; pres. West Fla. council Boy Scouts Am., 1964-66, mem. nat. council, 1977—. Served with U.S. Army, 1943-46. Recipient Silver Beaver award Boy Scouts Am., 1960. C.P.A., Ind.; C.L.U. Mem. Am. Soc. C.L.U.'s (pres. 1967-68), Am. Inst. C.P.A.'s, Ind. Soc. C.P.A.'s, Internat. Assn. Fin. Planners, Am. Soc. Pension Actuaries, Nat. Assn. Charitable Estate Counsellors. Republican. Mem. Christian Ch. Clubs: Kiwanis, Masons. Home: 917 Glen Oak Ave Clearwater FL 33519 Office: Suite 108 5700 Memorial Hwy Tampa FL 33615

FAULKNER, CLARK WOODS, ins. co. exec.; b. Lincoln, Nebr., Aug. 24, 1919; s. Albert Elsworth and Vashti Eugenia (Woods) F.; student U. Nebr., 1937-40; m. Betty Faye Smith, June 25, 1948; children—Clark Woods, Laurie Faye. With Woodmen Accident & Life Co., Lincoln, 1946—, supt. agys., 1952-58, 2d v.p. and supt. agys., 1958-61, v.p., dir. agys., 1961-77, pres., 1977—, dir., 1969—; dir. Comml. Mut. Surety Co. Trustee, Nebr. Wesleyan U., 1980. Served to lt. comdr. USN, 1940-46. Decorated Navy Cross. Mem. Life Ins. Mktg. and Research Assn. (chmn. health ins. com. 1967), Health Ins. Assn. Am., Am. Council Life Ins., Nebr. Assn. Life Underwriters, Nebr. Ins. Fedn., C. of C. (dir. 1977—), Newcomen Soc. N.Am. Republican. Presbyterian. Clubs: Lincoln Country, Univ., Nebr. Office: 1526 K St Lincoln NE 68508

FAULKNER, EDWIN JEROME, ins. co. exec.; b. Lincoln, Nebr., July 5, 1911; s. Edwin Jerome and Leah (Meyer) F.; B.A., U. Nebr., 1932; M.B.A., U. Pa., 1934; m. Jean Rathburn, Sept. 27, 1933. With Woodmen Accident & Life Co., Lincoln, 1934—, successively claim auditor, v.p., 1934-38, pres., 1938-77, dir., 1938—, chmn. bd., chief exec. officer, 1977—; pres., dir. Comml. Mut. Surety Co., 1938—; dir. First Nat. Bank, Lincoln Tel. & Tel. Co., Universal Surety Co., Inland Ins. Co. Chmn. Health Ins. Council 1959-60. Chmn. Lincoln-Lancaster County Plan Commn., 1948-68; mem. medicare adv. com. Dept. Def., 1957-71; chmn., trustee Bryan Meml. Hosp.; trustee Doane Coll., Lincoln Found., Nebraskans for Pub. TV, Nebr. Hist. Soc.; chmn. U. Nebr. Found. Served from 2d lt. to lt. col. USAAF, 1942-45. Decorated Legion of Merit, recipient Distinguished Service award U. Nebr., 1957, Nebr. Builders award, 1979; Harold R. Gordon Meml. award Internat. Assn. Health Ins. Underwriters, 1955, Ins. Man of Year award Ins. Field, 1958, Exec. of Year award Am. Coll. Hosp. Adminstrs., 1971. Mem. Am. Coll. Life Underwriters (trustee), Health Ins. Assn. Am. (1st pres. 1956), Am. Legion, Am. Life Conv. (exec. com. 1961—, pres. 1966-67), Phi Beta Kappa, Phi Kappa Psi, Alpha Kappa Psi (hon.). Republican. Presbyn. Clubs: Masons, Elks. Author: Accident and Health Insurance, 1940; Health Insurance, 1960; editor: Man's Quest for Security, 1966. Home: 4100 South St Lincoln NE 68506 Office: 1526 K St Lincoln NE 68508

FAULKNER, JAMES HERMAN, publisher; b. Lamar County, Ala., Mar. 1, 1916; s. Henry L. and Ebbie (Johnson) F.; B.J., U. Mo., 1936; m. Evelyn Irwin, Apr. 15, 1937; children—James Herman, Henry Wade. Co-owner, co-pub. The Baldwin Times, Bay Minette, Ala., 1936-74, pub. emeritus, editorial writer, 1974—; co-owner, co-pub. The Onlooker, Foley, Ala., 1967-74, Fairhope (Ala.) Courier, 1971-74; co-owner South Alabamian, Jackson, 1974-78; pres. Faulkner Radio, Inc.; owner radio stas. WLBB, WBTR, Carrollton, Ga., WBCA and WWSM, Bay Minette, WGAA, Cedartown, Ga., WAOA and WFRI, Opelika, Ala.; chmn. exec. com. David Volkert & Assos., architects and engrs., Mobile, Ala., Washington, New Orleans, Miami, Fla.; founder, pres. Loyal Am. Life Ins. Co., Mobile, 1955-57; chmn. bd. Alpine Industries, Inc., Bay Minette, 1975-79; pres., dir. Gulf Area Ins. Agy., Inc., Bay Minette, 1964-74. Mayor, Bay Minette, 1941-43; mem. Ala. Dem. Com.; mem. Baldwin County Dem. exec. com., 1936-78; del. Dem. Conv. in Phila., 1948, Chgo., 1952; Ala. state senator, 1951-55; candidate gov. Ala.; chmn. Baldwin County Hosp. Bd., 1965-73, Bay Minette Housing Authority, 1961—, Bay Minette Municipal Airport Com., 1968—, Pub. Edn., Bldg. Com. of Bay Minette, 1967—, Indsl. Devel. Bd. Bay Minette, 1968—, Ala. Devel. Bd., Montgomery, 1971—; chmn. advisory bd. James H. Faulkner State Coll., 1971—; bd. dirs. Ala. Safety Council, 1967—, pres., 1980—; bd. dirs. Ala. Crippled Children's Soc.; bd. dirs. Ala. div. Am. Cancer Soc., chmn., 1960-61; state chmn. Cancer Fund Drive, chmn. bd. dirs. Ala. Christian Coll., Montgomery, 1963—; mem. Ala. Commn. Higher Edn., 1978—. Served with USAAF, World War II. Named Man of Year, Bay Minette, 1965; named Journalist of Year (weekly newspaper), U.S. Steel Corp., 1966. Mem. Ala. Press Assn. (pres. 1939), Ala. (dir. 1947—), Newcomen Soc., Bay Minette (pres.) chambers commerce, Am. Legion, 40 and 8, Sigma Delta Chi. Rotarian. Co-pub.: Five Dollars A Scalp, 1976. Home: 705 E 5th St Bay Minette AL 36507 Office: 102 W 2d St Bay Minette AL 36507

FAULKNER, MICHAEL JOHN, ins. co. exec.; b. Glogau, Germany, July 9, 1920; s. Georg and Clara (Lewin) F.; B.S. magna cum laude, Columbia U., 1960; student Coll. Ins., N.Y.C., 1954-58; postgrad. N.Y.U. Grad. Sch. Bus. Adminstrn., 1960; m. Irene H.K. Duettmann, Nov. 3, 1951; children—Ingrid G. (Mrs. Charles R. Hatten, Jr.), Astrid E. (Mrs. Ulrich Feldmann). Chief information and records dept. civil censorship div. U.S. Mil. Govt. for Germany, Stuttgart/Esslingen, 1945-47; with Am. Internat. Underwriters (Overseas), AIG, 1948—, mgr. br. office, Weisbaden, Germany, 1948-51; fire underwriter, N.Y.C., 1951-52, mgr. for Bavaria (Germany), 1952-54, chief underwriter automobile mgmt. dept., N.Y.C. office, 1954-60, mgr. for Germany, 1960-65, legal rep. Nat. Union Ins. Co. Germany, 1963-76, dir. for Europe, Frankfurt, Germany, then Zurich, 1976—; pres., then vice chmn. Nat. Union Life Ins. Co., Frankfurt, 1971-77; partner C.V. Starr Inc., Wilmington, Del., 1970—; chmn. Am. Internat. Underwriters K.K., chief exec. officer, legal rep. AIU Ins. Co., Japan, also dir. Am. Internat. Underwriters, Germany, France, Italy, Belgium, Spain, Switzerland, Holland, Austria, Denmark and Sweden, Union Atlantique d'Assurances, Brussels, Belgium, Hellas Ins. Co., Athens, Greece, 1966-77; dir. Am. Home Assurance, N.Y.C., Am. Internat., Hong Kong, 1977—. Served with Brit. Army, Royal and Royal Canadian Navy, 1941-45; ETO. C.L.U. C.P.C.U. Mem. Am. Coll. Life Underwriters, Am. Inst. for Property and Liability Underwriters, Am. Mgmt. Assn., Am. C. of C. (Japan), Columbia U., N.Y. Coll. Ins. alumni assns. Clubs: Tokyo Am., Japan-Am. Soc., JCC (Tokyo). Home: 20—5 Ichibancho Chiyoda-Ku Tokyo 102 Japan Office: AIU-Bldg 1-3 Marunouchi 1-Chome Chiyoda-Ku Tokyo 100 Japan

FAULKNER, SEWELL FORD, realtor; b. Keene, N.H., Sept. 25, 1924; s. John Charles and Hazel Helen (Ford) F.; A.B., Harvard U., 1949, M.B.A., 1951; m. June Dayton Finn, Jan. 10, 1951 (div.); children—Patricia Anne, Bradford William, Sandra Ford, Jonathan Dayton, Winthrop Sewell; m. 2d, Constance Mae Durvin, Mar. 15, 1969 (div.); children—Sarah Elizabeth, Elizabeth Jane. Product mgr. Congoleum Nairn, Inc., Kearny, N.J., 1951-55; salesman, broker, pres. Jack White Co., real estate, Anchorage, 1956—; dir. Life Ins. Co. Alaska. Mem. Anchorage City Council, 1962-65, Greater Anchorage Area Borough Assembly, 1964-65, Anchorage Area Charter Commn., 1969-70; pres. Alaska World Affairs Council, 1967-68; treas. Alyeska Property Owners, Inc., 1973-75, Girdwood Bd. Suprs., 1977-81; pres. Downtown Anchorage Assn., 1974-75. Served with USAAF, 1943-45. Mem. Anchorage Area C. of C. (dir. 1973-74), Urban Land Inst., Bldg. Owners and Mgrs. Assn., Nat. Inst. Real Estate Brokers. Clubs: Alaska Notch, Anchorage Petroleum. Home: Mount Alyeska Girdwood AK 99587 Office: 3201 C St Anchorage AK 99503

FAUSAK, WILLIAM ARTHUR, writing instrument co. exec.; b. Jersey City, N.J., Oct. 31, 1938; s. William Otto and Eleanore Louise (Carnie) F.; B.S., U. Pa., 1961; m. Carol Jean Davis, Sept. 16, 1967; 1 son, Erik Davis. Auditor, Uniroyal, Inc., N.Y.C., 1963-66; sr. internal auditor GAF Corp., N.Y.C., 1966-68; fin. controls supr. Random House, Inc., N.Y.C., 1968-70; sr. auditor, supr. audits, mgr. audits The Singer Co., N.Y.C., 1970-75, dir. trade relations, 1975-77; dir. corporate internal auditing Parker Pen Co., Janesville, Wis., 1977—. Served with USNR, 1961-63. Cert. internal auditor. Mem. Inst. Internal Auditors. Clubs: Janesville Country, Blackhawk Curling. Home: 3207 Crystal Springs Rd Janesville WI 53545 Office: 219 E Court St Janesville WI 53545

FAUTH, JOHN MORGAN, co. exec.; b. N.Y.C., Oct. 27, 1929; s. J. Morgan and Dorothy Grace (Neilson) F.; B.S., magna cum laude, C.W. Post Coll., 1963; m. Jean Margaret Ruhle, Nov. 8, 1952; children—Douglas M., Steven G., Lisa J. Mgr. tool engring. div. Republic Aviation Corp., Farmingdale, N.Y., 1951-65; dir., chief tech. officer, dir. Singer Mfg. Co., Ltd., Clydebank, Scotland, 1965-68, gen. mgr., Diehl div. Singer Co., 1968-70, dir., product mgmt., 1970-73; sr. v.p. products and ops. Magnavox Consumer Electronics Co., Fort Wayne, Ind., 1973-79, pres. Magnavox Co. Tenn., Greenville, 1973-79; corp. sr. v.p., gen. mgr. div. Am. Biltrite Inc., Chelsea, Mass., 1979—. Council visitors Tusculum Coll., 1977-79. Served with USMC, 1946-49. Named Hon. Citizen, State of Tenn., 1975; recipient Outstanding Tennessean award Tenn. Gov., 1976. Roman Catholic. Home: 205 Sohier St Cohasset MA 02025 Office: Am Biltrite Inc 22 Willow St Chelsea MA 02150

FAUVER, JOHN WILLIAM, distbg. co. exec.; b. Detroit, Dec. 11, 1921; s. John Newton and Margaret Burns (Schofield) F.; B.S. in Mech. Engring., U. Mich., 1943; m. Margaret Miller, Dec. 7, 1943;

children—John William, Johanna, Jeffrey. Salesman, J.N. Fauver Co., Detroit, 1946-53, sales mgr., 1953-62, exec. v.p., 1962-70, pres., 1970—; mayor, city commr. City of Bloomfield Hills (Mich.), 1974—, now mayor pro tem. Pres., Boys Clubs Met. Detroit, 1973-79; trustee Fluid Power Ednl. Found.; bd. govs. Cranbrook Schs. Served to capt. Ordnance Corps, U.S. Army, 1942-46. Mem. Nat. Indsl. Distbrs. Assn. (pres. 1979). Republican. Presbyterian. Clubs: Orchard Lake Country (pres. 1975-76), Bloomfield Hills Country, Detroit Rotary (pres. 1962-63), Masons. Home: 695 Lone Pine Bloomfield Hills MI 48013 Office: 1500 Avis Dr Madison Heights MI 48071

FAVRE, ROLLAND MASCOT, JR., cons., systems engr.; b. Nyack, N.Y., Apr. 23, 1931; s. Rolland M. and Ione Lena (Burres) F.; B.E.E., Clarkson Coll. Tech., 1952; M.A. in Econs., U. Md., 1968; m. Setsuko Shinoda, Sept. 2, 1953; children—Nanette Debra, Rolland Matthew. Commd. 2d lt. U.S. Army, 1952, advanced through grades to lt. col., 1967; in Vietnam, 1964-65, 71-72; staff Dept. Army, 1968-71; JCS staff, 1973; ret., 1973; sr. systems engr. Computer Scis. Corp., Falls Church, Va., 1973-78; dir. engring. Systematics Gen. Corp., Falls Church, Va., 1978-79; v.p. Organon, Inc. Decorated Legion of Merit, Bronze Star. Mem. IEEE, Armed Forces Communications-Electronics Assn. Club: Masons. Home: 5203 Temple Hill Rd Temple Hills MD 20031 Office: PO Box 31044 Temple Hills MD 20031

FAW, MARY HELEN THOMAS (MRS. SHORTER CHARLES FAW), bank exec.; b. Dalton, Ga.; d. Raymond L. and Kate (Holtzclaw) Thomas; certificate accounting U. Chattanooga, 1958; grad. Ga. Banking Sch., U. Ga., 1970, Sch. Banking of South, La. State U., Baton Rouge, 1972; m. Shorter Charles Faw, July 21, 1961. Mem. staff 1st Nat. Bank, Dalton, 1944—, auditor, 1967-69, controller, 1969—, v.p., 1977-79, sr. v.p., controller, 1979—. Mem. Nat. Assn. Bank Women (co-chmn. N.W. Ga. group 1972-73, chmn. 1973-74, regional v.p. southeastern region 1977-78), Ga. Bankers Assn. (chmn. women's com. 1972-73, chmn. group 7 1976-77). Baptist. Clubs: Elkette (pres. Calhoun club 1972-73), Calhoun Pilot (dir. 1980). Home: 214 Victory Dr Calhoun GA 30701 Office: PO Drawer 1088 Dalton GA 30720

FAWCETT, HOWARD HOY, chem. health cons.; b. McKeesport, Pa., May 31, 1916; s. Harry Garfield and Ada (Deetz) F.; B.S. in Indsl. Chemistry, U. Md., 1940; postgrad. U. Del., 1945-47; m. Ruth Allen Bogan, Apr. 7, 1942; children—Ralph Willard, Harry Allen. Research chemist Manhattan project E.I. DuPont de Nemours & Co., Inc., Chgo., Hanford, Wash., 1944-45, research and devel. chemist organic chemistry div., Deepwater, N.J., 1945-48; cons. engr. Gen. Electric Co., Schenectady, N.Y., 1948-64; tech. sec. com. on hazardous materials Nat. Acad. Scis.-NRC, Washington, 1964-75; staff scientist, project mgr. Tracor Jitco, Inc., Rockville, Md., 1975-78; sr. chem. engr. Equitable Environ. Health, 1978—; mem. adv. com. study on socio-behavioral preparations for, responses to and recovery from chem. disasters NSF, 1977—; cons. to industry and govt. agys. Chief radiol. sect. Schenectady County CD, 1953-63. Bd. dirs. Safety sect. Schenectady C. of C., 1957-64. Recipient Distinguished Service to Safety citation Nat. Safety Council, 1966, Cameron award, 1962, 69. Registered profl. engr., Calif. Mem. Am. Chem. Soc. (sec. com. chem. safety, chmn. council com. on chem. safety 1974-77, chmn. div. chem. health and safety 1977-79, councilor 1980-82, author audio course on hazards of materials 1977), ASTM (membership sec. 1972—, sub-chmn. D-34 com.), Am. Inst. Chem. Engrs. (com. on occupational health and safety 1977—), Am. Indsl. Hygiene Assn. (dir. Balt.-Washington chpt. 1975-77), Alpha Chi Sigma. Co-editor: Safety and Accident Prevention in Chemical Operations, 2d edit., 1981; mem. editorial adv. bd. Jour. Safety Research, 1968—, Transp. Planning and Tech., 1972—; N. Am. regional editor Jour. Hazardous Materials, 1975—. Home and Office: 12920 Matey Rd Wheaton MD 20906

FAWKES, GARY SELLENS, personnel cons.; b. Kansas City, Mo., Mar. 8, 1939; s. Clio Harlan and Hilda Mary F.; B.S.B.A., U. Mo., Columbia, 1963; m. Suzanne Althouse, Aug. 14, 1960; children—Carter C., Jill K. Vice pres. Garvey, Inc., Wichita, Kans., 1967-70; account exec. E. F. Hutton, Kansas City, Mo., 1970-77; v.p. Profl. Career Devel. Inc., Kansas City, Mo., 1977-80; ops. mgr. Bus. Career Personnel Services, Houston, 1980—. Mem. Data Processing Mgmt. Assn., Nat. Assn. Personnel Consultants. Home: 103 E 4th St Cameron MO 64429 Office: care Bus Career Personnel Services 1790 Postoak Central 2000 S Post Oak Houston TX 77056

FAXON, LOUIS HENSLIE, JR., architect; b. Wadena, Minn., July 13, 1930; s. Louis Henslie and Edna Dell (McFall) F.; B.S., La. State U., 1958; m. Martha Anne Hill, Oct. 31, 1970; 1 son (by previous marriage), Louis Henslie. Designer, A. Hays Town, architect, Baton Rouge, 1958-59; architect B.G. Buquoi, architect, Baton Rouge, 1960-61, Perry L. Brown, Inc., Baton Rouge, 1961-66, v.p., 1964-66; pres. Louis H. Faxon, Inc., Architects, Baton Rouge, 1966—; asst. prof. architecture La. State U., Baton Rouge, 1966-73, spl. lectr. econs. investment architecture, 1974-76. Pres. bd. Baton Rouge Symphony Assn., 1966-67; asst. scoutmaster Istrouma Area council Boy Scouts Am., 1963-64; mem. sch. plants and facilities com. East Baton Rouge Parish Sch. Bd., 1969-71; bd. dirs. Baton Rouge Community Concert Assn.; bd. dirs., v.p. Baton Rouge Gallery; bd. dirs. Baton Rouge Area Sheltered Workshop, 1977-78; exec. officer Baton Rouge Power Squadron. Served with USAF, 1950-53. Decorated Air medal with oak leaf cluster. Mem. AIA, La. Architects Assn., Nat. Assn. Homebuilders, Council Ednl. Facilities Planners, Tau Beta Pi. Methodist. Clubs: Kiwanis; Baton Rouge Gun, Baton Rouge Rifle and Pistol, City (Baton Rouge); So. Yacht (New Orleans). Home: 2373 Baywood Ave Baton Rouge LA 70808 Office: 460 Florida St Suite 14 Baton Rouge LA 70801

FAY, ROGER JOSEPH, mfg. co. exec.; b. Dubuque, Iowa, Aug. 22, 1923; s. Rollo Joseph and Dorcas Mary (Flin) F.; B.S., Bradley U., 1948; m. Lillian Virginia Allen, Aug. 30, 1947; children—Deborah Ann, Stephen Roger. Supr. parts contact div. Caterpillar Tractor Co., 1948-50, product support mktg. rep. U.S., 1950-51, product support mktg. rep. for Mexico, Central and South Am., 1952-55, product support mktg. mgr. Latin Am. div., 1955-64, product support mktg. mgr. Canadian div., Peoria, Ill., 1964—; cons. Banff Sch. Mgmt., U. Alta. Mem. parish council Holy Family Ch., 1966-67; coach Little League baseball, 1965-67, also basketball; solicitor St. Francis Bldg. Fund, 1968. Served with USMC, 1942-46. Mem. Am. Hist. Assn., Civil War Hist. Soc. Republican. Roman Catholic. Golden Gloves champion, 1942-46. Home: 1015 Hiawatha Dr Dunlap IL 61625 Office: 100 NE Adams Peoria IL 61629

FAYE, STANLEY E., lawyer, motel co. exec.; b. N.Y.C., June 12, 1935; s. Benjamin and Beatrice Faye; A.B., Duke U., 1957, J.D., 1960; m. Marilyn Epstein, Nov. 26, 1966; children—Jodi, Robin. Admitted to N.Y. State bar, 1963, Tex. bar, 1974; pvt. practice, N.Y.C., 1961-70; with Dresser Industries, Inc., Dallas, 1970-73; v.p., sec., gen. counsel Datapoint Corp., San Antonio, 1973-78; gen. counsel La Quinta Motor Inns, Inc., San Antonio, 1978—. Bd. dirs. Ballet Soc. San Antonio. Served with USMCR, 1960-61. Mem. Am. Bar Assn., Am. Soc. Corp. Secs. Home: 9223 Bent Elm Creek San Antonio TX 78230 Office: 84 NE Loop 410 Century Bldg San Antonio TX 78216

FAZIO, JANE GOOD, mfg. co. exec.; b. Bellevue, Pa., Jan. 14, 1919; d. Frank and Anna (Huckestein) Good; B.S., Northwestern U., 1940; m. Alphonso J. Fazio, Sept. 15, 1942 (dec. 1959); children—Arthur, Frank, Donald, Nina, Paul, Alphonse, Della (dec.), Zita. Pres., Diamond Wire Spring Co., Pitts., 1959—; mem. Pa. Gov.'s Small Bus. Council; mem. adv. bd. SBA, Pitts. Mem. Smaller Mfrs. Council (dir.), Spring Mfrs. Inst. Office: 1901 Babcock Blvd Pittsburgh PA 15209

FAZIO, JOSEPH ANTHONY, co. exec.; b. L.I. City, N.Y., July 2, 1930; s. Charles and Augusta (Bilello) F.; student Farmingdale U., 1970, Hewlett Packard Seminar, 1976, Moog Hydra Point, 1973, Inst. Mgmt, 1979; m. Laura Herbold, Mar. 15, 1952; children—Rita, Irene, Joanne; m. 2d, Ruth V. Schwin, Apr. 30, 1977. Milling machinist Orenduff & Kappel, Westbury, N.Y., 1953-61; machinist Fairchild Elec. Div., L.I., 1961-62; foreman, programmer, supr. Narda Microwave Corp., Plainview, N.Y., 1962—. Served with U.S. Army, 1948-52. Mem. Moose, Am. Legion, Sons of Italy. Home: 184 Peters Ave East Meadow NY 11554 Office: 75 Commercial St Plainview NY 11803

FEARONS, GEORGE HADSALL, III, ins. adjusting co. exec.; b. N.Y.C., Dec. 22, 1927; s. George Hadsall and Alice Janssen F.; student Los Angeles City Coll., 1944-46; m. Sandra Walsh, Oct. 25, 1967; 1 son, George Thomas. Adjuster, Am. Fore Group, Nat. of Hartford Group, Md. Casualty Ins. Co., Great Am. Ins. Co., Los Angeles, 1944-54; owner Vt. Claims Service, Stowe, 1953—, Stowe Travel Service, 1955—; owner, pres. Hovercraft N.E., Stowe, 1971—. Mem. Am. Soc. Travel Agts., Nat. Assn. Ind. Ins. Adjusters. Republican. Roman Catholic. Clubs: Rotary (Stowe, Vt.); Sailfish, Yacht and Country (Stuart, Fla.); Mariner Cay Yacht); Lake Mansfield Trout; Ethan Allen (Burlington, Vt.). Club: Knights of Malta. Home: Box 249 Stowe VT 05672 Office: Main St Stowe VT 05672

FEATHERS, WILLIAM ANDREW, architect; b. Fort Scott, Kans., Jan. 30, 1925; s. William C. and Myra Marie (Prude) F.; student Santa Monica City Coll., 1942-43, Ariz. State Coll., 1943-44, Columbia U., 1944-45; B.S., U. So. Calif., 1948; m. Sally L. Pishney, July 14, 1979; children—Denise, Victor. Pub. info. officer Auto Club of So. Calif., 1950-55; dir. Seattle-King County Safety Council, 1955-60; v.p. Stiles Clements, Architect, Los Angeles, 1960-68; v.p. Welton Becket & Assos., Los Angeles, 1968-75; dir. devel. Syska & Hennessy, Engrs., Los Angeles, 1976—. Mem. Mayor's Com. Community Services, 1966-68, chmn., 1967-68; pres. Los Angeles Hdqrs. City Assn., 1966-68. Served with USNR, 1943-45. Mem. Calif. Republican League (chmn. 1963-64), Sherman Oaks Homeowners Assn. (pres. 1965). Republican. Lutheran. Kiwanian. Author: How to Choose an Industrial Site, 1965; How to Choose an Architect, 1974; History of Century City, 1977. Home 3407 Coy Dr Sherman Oaks CA 91423 Office: 1900 Avenue of Stars Los Angeles CA 90067

FECK, LUKE MATTHEW, newspaper editor; b. Cin., Aug. 15, 1935; s. John Franz and Mercedes Caroline (Rielag) F.; B.A., U. Cin., 1957; m. Gail Anne Schutte, Aug. 12, 1961; children—Lisa, Mara, Paul. Copy clk. Cin. Enquirer, 1956, reporter, 1957, TV/radio editor, 1960-62, columnist, 1962-64, asst. features editor, 1969, Sunday mag. editor, 1970, news editor, 1971, mng. editor, 1974, exec. editor, 1975, editor, v.p., 1976-80; editor Columbus (Ohio) Dispatch, 1980—; reporter Paddock Publs., Chgo., 1957-59; pres. Ackerman & Feck, 1964-69; pub. Dimension, Cin., 1965-67. Bd. dirs. Cin. Conv. and Visitors Bur., Cin. Playhouse in the Park. Served to 1st lt. U.S. Army, 1957-59. Mem. A.P. Mng. Editors Assn. (pres. Queen City chpt.), Soc. Profl. Journalists, Am. Soc. Newspaper Editors, Am. Newspaper Pubs. Assn., Cin. Hist. Soc. Clubs: Cincinnatus; Literary. Author: Yesterday's Cincinnati, 1975. Home: 2494 Sheringham Rd Columbus OH 43220 Office: 34 S Third St Columbus OH 43216

FEDE, VINCENT G., savs. and loan exec.; b. Passaic, N.J., July 8, 1937; s. Gabriel and Louise (Iapelli) F.; 1 son, Vincent J. Exec. trainee, br. mgr. Oritani Savs. & Loan Assn., Hackensack, N.J., 1959-61; chief exec. officer Park Savs. & Loan Assn., Park Ridge, N.J., 1962-68; pres., dir. Community Fed. Savs. & Loan Assn., Ramsey, N.J., 1968—. Pres. N.W. Bergen County Vis. Nurses, 1980. Served with Air Force N.G., 1957-62. Mem. Bergen County Savs. and Loan League (sec.), Nat. Soc. Controllers. Club: Ramsey Rotary. Office: Community Federal Savings and Loan Assn 161 E Main St Ramsey NJ 07446

FEDERMANN, FRANKLIN HOWARD, business exec.; b. N.Y.C., Nov. 8, 1939; s. Alfred B. and Rose (Grabinsky) F.; B.S., Bklyn. Coll., 1966; M.S., L.I. U., 1971; m. Rochelle L. Seidner, June 15, 1963; children—Barbara, Daniel, Joshua. Mem. staff Eisner & Lubin, N.Y.C., 1966-69; sr. auditor Asso. Universities, Inc., Upton, N.Y., 1969-70, chief internal auditor, 1970—. Served with USCG, 1957-66. C.P.A., N.Y. Mem. Nat. Assn. Accountants, Am. Accounting Assn., Am. Inst. C.P.A.'s, Inst. Internal Auditors, N.Y. Soc. C.P.A.'s, U.S. Power Squadrons. Club: Moose. Home: 20 Hawkins Path Coram NY 11727 Office: Bldg 134A Upton NY 11973

FEEHAN, THOMAS JOSEPH, engring. and constrn. co. exec.; b. New Orleans, Feb. 12, 1924; s. Hugh Alphonse and Rena Martha (Hill) F.; B.Engring., Tulane U., 1944; Prodn. supr. Flintcote Co., 1946-47; with Brown & Root Co., Houston, 1947—, corp. pres., chief exec. officer, 1977—, also dir.; dir. Haliburton Co., 1st City Bank Houston. Served with USMC, 1944-46. Mem. Am. Inst. Chem. Engrs., Houston Engring. Soc., Tex. Research League. Roman Catholic. Clubs: Petroleum Club Houston, Ramada Club, Sky Club N.Y., Racquet. Office: PO Box 3 Houston TX 77001*

FEEK, JAMES RICHARD, ins. cons.; b. Bremerton, Wash., Dec. 23, 1942; s. Richard James and Gladys Ann (Anderson) F.; B.A. in Zoology and Philosophy, Pacific Lutheran U., 1965; m. Kathy Page, Aug. 23, 1969; children—Garrett James, Gavin Anderson. Agt., Conn. Mut. Life Ins. Co., 1969—, supr., 1971-73, asst. gen. agt., 1973-78; pres. James R. Feek, Inc., Seattle, 1978—; founder, dir. Nat. Bank Bremerton. Bd. dirs. Pacific Luth. U. Served to 1st lt. U.S. Army, 1966-69. Mem. Nat. Assn. Life Underwriters (Man of Year 1971, 76, numerous awards), Seattle Assn. Life Underwriters (v.p.), Gen. Agts. and Mgrs. Assn., Golden Key Soc. Am. Coll. C.L.U.'s, Million Dollar Roundtable, Century Club, Seattle Seafair Commodores, Million Dollar Round Table (Wash. state chmn.). Republican. Lutheran. Contbr. articles to profl. jours. Office: 800 Plaza 600 Bldg Seattle WA 98101

FEENEY, FRANCIS PATRICK, banker; b. Hartford, Conn., Dec. 23, 1923; s. Patrick F. and Mary J. (Breen) F.; B.S. with distinction, U. Conn., 1949; grad. Stonier Grad. Sch. Banking, Rutgers U.; m. Kathryn Smith, Nov. 12, 1949; children—Christopher, David, Maryellen, Gregory, Brendan, Kathryn, Susan, Paula. Examiner, Conn. Banking Dept., 1949-53; with Dime Savs. Bank ofWallingford (Conn.), 1953—, pres., treas., dir.; dir. Fed. Home Loan Bank Boston, N.E. Datacom. Chmn. Wallingford chpt. ARC, Wallingford Family YMCA. Served to 1st lt. USAAF, 1943-45. Decorated Air medal. Mem. Wallingford C. of C. (dir.). Roman Catholic. Club: Rotary. Office: 2 N Main St Wallingford CT 06492

FEFFER, PAUL E., pub. co. exec.; b. N.Y.C., June 27, 1921; s. Joseph A. and Eve (Wax) F.; student Cornell U. Sch. Medicine, 1940-42, USCG Acad., 1944; postgrad. N.Y. U., 1963-64; m. Juliette Fein, July 30, 1964; children—Paula, Hilary, Joseph, Alison, Emily, Nicholas. Vice pres. H. M. Synder & Co., N.Y.C., 1946-55; with Feffer & Simons, Inc., subsidiary Doubleday & Co., N.Y.C., 1955—, pres., 1955—, also dir.; dir. Tabs, Ltd., London, Vakil's Feffer & Simons, Inc., India, Book Club Assos., Australia. Mem. govt. adv. com. Am. Book Pub. Council, 1963—; mem. joint internat. trade com. Am. Book Pub. Co. and Am. Textbook Inst., 1963—. Served to lt. (j.g.) USCGR, 1942-46. Home: 60 Sutton Pl New York City NY 10022 Office: 100 Park Ave New York City NY 10017

FEGAN, DAVID ALBERT, lawyer; b. Washington, July 13, 1918; s. David Bright and Elizabeth (Jost) F.; student Harvard U., 1940; LL.B., J.D., George Washington U., 1943; m. Lorraine Coyle, Aug. 14, 1943; children—David, Stephen. Admitted to D.C. bar, 1943, S.C. bar, 1943, Md. bar, 1946, U.S. Supreme Ct. bar, 1947; partner firm Morris, Pearce, Gardner & Pratt, Washington, 1943-60; individual practice law, Washington, 1960—; v.p. Calvert Bank & Trust Co., Prince Frederick, Md., 1963-77, dir., 1963—; pres., dir. Mar-Ber Devel. Corp., Bethesda, Md., 1960—, Old Line Brick & Tile Co., Inc., Buckeystown, Md., 1964—; v.p., dir. St. Leonard's Devel. Corp. (Md.), 1963—, Capitol Clay Products, Inc., Washington, 1969—. Served with USNR, 1942-43. Mem. Am. Bar Assn., D.C. Bar Assn. Republican. Roman Catholic. Clubs: Kenwood Golf and Country, Calvert County Country, Reciprocity. Home: 8709 Seven Locks Rd Bethesda MD 20034 Office: 1000 Vermont Ave NW Washington DC 20005

FEGLEY, CHARLES ROBERT, mech. engr., mfg. co. exec.; b. Reading, Pa., Apr. 28, 1926; s. Charles Samuel and Marcella E. (Schmeck) F.; B.S. in Mech. Engring., Lafayette Coll., 1964; children—Michelle Lynn, Charles Mark. Design engr. Textile Machine Works, Reading, 1944-52; chief design engr. Karl Leiberknecht, Inc., Reading, 1952-56; design engr. Binney & Smith, Easton, Pa., 1956-61; sr. staff engr. Western Electric Co., Reading, 1961—; pres. Security Control Research and Mfg. Co., Inc., Reading, 1974—. Mem. Muhlenberg Twp. Bd. Health, 1965-69; mem. Muhlenberg Twp. Sch. Dist. Sch. Bd., 1969-75, pres., 1969-70, treas., 1972-73. Mem. ASME, Aircraft Owners and Pilots Assn., Muhlenberg Twp. Taxpayers Assn. (chmn. 1968-72). Republican. Mem. United Ch. of Christ. Clubs: Green Valley Country, Reading Aero. Patentee in mech., elec., electro-mech. equipment and security devices in U.S. and fgn. countries. Home: 1606 Frush Valley Rd Laureldale PA 19605 Office: 2525 N 11th St Reading PA 19605

FEHLEN, ROBERT MATHIAS, JR., real estate broker; b. Toledo, Apr. 17, 1951; s. Robert Mathias and Mary Kay Fehlen; student U. Toledo; m. Mary Ann Wachter, June 17, 1972; children—Kristie Kay, Kevin Mathias. With Sears, Roebuck & Co., 1973-75, div. mgr., Toledo, 1975; salesman, then mgr. Neal Realty Co., Maumee, Ohio, 1976-77; mgr. DiSalle Real Estate Co., Perrysburg, Ohio, 1977; broker Baisden Realty Co., Toledo, 1979-80, Amy & Assos. Century 21, 1980—; gen. mgr. Baisden & Sons Bldg. Inc., Toledo, 1977—. Mem. Air Force N.G., 1970-76. Mem. Nat. Assn. Realtors, Nat. Assn. Home Builders, Bldg. Industry Assn., Ohio Assn. Realtors, Toledo Bd. Realtors, Maumee (Ohio) Jaycees, Theta Chi. Democrat. Roman Catholic. Home: 5-6890 1-1 Swanton OH 43558 Office: 2612 Green Valley Dr Toledo OH 43614

FEHLING, GEORGE WILLIAM, travel mktg. exec.; b. N.Y.C., July 30, 1935; s. George Edward and Helen G. (Eichenbrenner) F.; m. Sally Kathleen McCreesh, Sept. 19, 1959; children—George R., Joan A., Paul J. Mail clk. T.W.A., 1953; sales rep. N.E. Airlines, 1959-61; agy. and interline mgr. Aerolineas Argentinas, 1961-64, Alitalia, 1964-67; regional mgr. Eastern U.S., Can., Central and S. Am., Cathay Pacific, 1967-77; exec. v.p. Danor Travel, 1977; owner, pres. GWF Travel Mktg., N.Y.C., 1978—. Served with AUS, 1956-58, 61-62. Mem. Skal, Pacific Area Travel Assn. (chmn. N.Y. chpt.), East Asia Travel Assn., Soc. Preservation and Encouragement of Barbershop Quartet Singing in Am. Club: Wings. Home: 84 Abingdon Ave Staten Island NY 10308 Office: 60 E 42d St New York NY 10165

FEICHTEL, CARL JOSEPH, bank exec.; b. Allentown, Pa., Oct. 1, 1931; s. Charles J. and Laura E. (Eby) F.; cert. Pa. State U., 1955, Bucknell U., 1960; student consumer banking, comml. lending, bank mgmt., various univs., 1962-71; m. Julia Ann Green, Jan. 29, 1955; children—Denise, Carl J., Joseph, Jean. With Merchants Nat. Bank, Allentown, 1949—, sr. v.p., 1973, exec. v.p., 1973-74, pres., 1974-76, chief exec. officer, 1976—, also dir. Bd. govs. Lehigh County (Pa.) C. of C.; bd. dirs. Allentown-Lehigh County Indsl. Devel. Corp., Sacred Heart Hosp., Allentown; trustee Allentown Coll. St. Francis deSales. Served with U.S. Army, 1952-54. Mem. Am. Bankers Assn. (cert. comml. lender), Allentown/Lehigh County C. of C. (treas.). Republican. Roman Catholic. Clubs: Lehigh Country, Livingston, Rotary. Office: 702 Hamilton Mall Allentown PA 18101

FEIGEN, AARON B., fin. and econ. analysis exec.; b. Putnam, Conn., Apr. 21, 1926; s. Maurice and Anna L. F.; B.A. in Econs., U. Conn., 1949; postgrad. N.Y. U., 1953-59, N.Y. Inst. Fin., 1953-54; m. Barbara L. Lurie, Jan. 1, 1949; children—Ellen, Joseph, Daniel. Securities analyst Paine Webber Jackson & Curtis, N.Y.C., 1953-54; securities analyst Josephthal & Co., N.Y.C., 1954-56, mgr. research dept., 1958-60; securities analyst Williston & Co., N.Y.C., 1956-58; officer, dir. J.R. Williston & Beane, N.Y.C., 1960-62; officer, econ. cons. Bregman, Cummings & Co., N.Y.C., 1962-74; chief exec. Econostat Research Services, Inc., also Statigraphic Research Services, Inc., N.Y.C., 1974—; instr. N.Y. Inst. Fin., 1954-66; cons. Council Internat. Progress in Mgmt., 1964, AID, 1966, Dept. of State CENTO, 1968. Served with USNR, World War II. Chartered fin. analyst; cert. supervisory analyst N.Y. Stock Exchange. Mem. Nat. Assn. Bus. Economists, N.Y. Soc. Security Analysts, Fin. Analysts Fedn., Inst. Chartered Fin. Analysts, Internat. Industry Assn. Lectr., radio commentator on investments. Home: 1-3 Chestnut Pl Waldwick NJ 07463 Office: 120 Broadway New York NY 10005

FEIL, MICHAEL BRUCE, mgmt. analyst; b. Urbana, Ill., Apr. 30, 1949; s. Richard Anthony and Barbara June (Barnes) F.; A.A., Middlesex County Coll., 1970; B.S. in Med. Tech. with honors, Rutgers U., 1974, M.B.A., 1978; m. Dana Marie Strack, Sept. 6, 1975. With North Jersey Blood Center, East Orange, N.J., 1974-80, supr. dept. cryobiology, 1976-78, systems analyst, 1979-80; mgmt. analyst Nat. Blood Data Center, Am. Blood Commn., Arlington, Va., 1980—; cons. fin., mgmt., 1978—. Mem. AAAS, Am. Assn. Blood Banks, Am. Fin. Assn., Am. Mgmt. Assn., Am. Statis. Assn., N.Y. Acad. Scis. Republican. Lutheran. Home: 4837 W Braddock Rd Apt 3 Alexandria VA 22311 Office: 1901 N Fort Myer Dr Suite 300 Arlington VA 22209

FEINBERG, BERNARD, banker; b. Chgo., Dec. 4, 1924; s. Joseph and Bessie (Ferdinand) F.; student Ill. Inst. Tech., 1942-45. Owner, Division Mgmt. Co., Chgo., 1946; chain operator Currency Exchanges, Chgo., 1946-63; dir. Jefferson State Bank, Chgo., 1957-77, pres., chmn. bd., 1959-60, pres., 1959-77, exec. v.p., dir., 1979—; chmn., sr. partner Fleetwood Realty Corp.; vis. lectr. numismatics Roosevelt U. Chmn. N.W. Side Chgo. Real Estate Bds. Better

Neighborhood Crusade, 1958-59; pres. Joseph and Bessie Feinberg Found.; active Anti-Defamation League of B'nai B'rith; mem. Mus. Contemporary Art, Chgo. Symphony Soc. Recipient Freedom Found. award, 1960. Mem. N.W. Real Estate Bd., Nat. Inst. Real Estate Brokers, Nat. Assn. Real Estate Bds., U.S., Ill., Jefferson Park (dir., past treas.) chambers commerce, Soc. Paper Money Collectors, Field Mus. Natural History, Am., Independent, Ill. bankers assns., Am. Inst. Banking, Art Inst. Chgo. (life), North Side Bankers Club (pres. 1965), ACLU (life), Audubon Soc., Anti-Defamation League, Am. Judicature Soc., Am. Jewish Com. Jewish (trustee). Clubs: Lions, B'nai B'rith, Metropolitan. Home: 1000 Lake Shore Plaza Chicago IL 60611 Office: 200 W Jackson Blvd Chicago IL 60606 also 5245 W Lawrence Ave Chicago IL 60630 also 5301 W Lawrence Ave Chicago IL

FEINBERG, FRANK NOEL, advt. exec.; b. Chgo., Dec. 25, 1950; s. Frank Henry and Henrietta (Drolshagen) F.; B.A., U. Chgo., 1973. Asst. analyst Leo Burnett Co., Inc., Chgo., 1973-74, analyst, 1974-75, asso. research supr., 1976-77, research supr., 1978, asso. research dir., 1979; asso. research dir. Young Rubicam, N.Y.C., 1979—, v.p., 1980—. Mem. Assn. Consumer Research, Phi Beta Kappa. Office: Young & Rubicam 285 Madison Ave New York NY 10017

FEINBERG, NORMAN MAURICE, real estate exec.; b. N.Y.C., Nov. 28, 1934; s. Harry and Beatrice F.; B.S., N.Y. U., 1956, postgrad., 1957; m. Arline Itzkoff, Nov. 26, 1960; children—Mitchell, David. Exec. trainee Columbia Pictures Corp., 1956-58; exec. Columbia Pictures Corp. and Columbia Pictures Internat. Corp., 1958-61; v.p. Gateside-Corp., 1961-65; gen. partner 12 operative cos., 1965—; pres. Gateside Corp., Haverstraw Marina Corp.; dir. Noron Corp.; cons. to banks and accounting and law firms; arbitrator in real estate matters Am. Arbitration Assn. Bd. govs. Daytop Village, 1974—; bd. dirs. Assn. Mentally Ill Children, 1974—, exec. mgmt. com., 1974—; Cub Scout leader, 1971-72. Recipient Mayor's award for outstanding bldg. renovation City of White Plains (N.Y.), 1975. Mem. Young Pres.'s Orgn., Am. Arbitration Assn., Nat. Apt. Council, Del. Valley Apt. Owners Assn. Office: 150 White Plains Rd Tarrytown NY 10591

FEINBERG, ROBERT MORTON, mfg. co. exec.; b. Boston, Oct. 20, 1935; s. David H. and Rose (Jacobs) F.; B.S.E.E., Northeastern U., 1958; m. Martha E. Semans, July 14, 1957; children—Nancy, Jeffrey. With Avco Everett Research Lab., Everett, Mass., 1956—, v.p., 1978—. Served with U.S. Army, 1958. Recipient Silver medal Internat. Inst. Combustion, 1966. Mem. Am. Mgmt. Assn., Laser Inst. Am., Infrared Inst. Combusion, 1966. Info. and Analysis, AIAA. Contbr. articles to profl. jours. Home: 5 New Meadow Rd Lynnfield MA 01940 Office: 32 Cobble Hill Rd Somerville MA 02143

FEINBERG, ROBERT S., plastics mfg. co. exec., computer mktg. cons.; b. Newark, May 14, 1934; s. Clarence Jacob and Sabina (Zorn) F.; B.A. in English, B.S. in Chemistry, Trinity Coll., Hartford, Conn., 1955; M.B.A. in Mktg., Fairleigh Dickinson U., 1966; advt. diploma N.Y. Inst. Advt., 1967. Pres., Trebor Assos. and Trebor Plastics Co., Teaneck, N.J., 1961—; mktg. cons. computer software Zettler Softwear Co., Burroughs Corp.; co-chmn., partner Edgeroy Co., Ridgefield and Palisades Park, N.J., 1973—; cons. plastic formulations W.R. Grace, Endicott Johnson, Brown Shoe Co., U.S. Shoe Co., Ciba, Uniroyal. Mem. Soc. Plastics Engrs. (sr.), Sporting Goods Mfrs. Assn., U.S. Profl. Tennis Assn., Bergen County Tennis League (v.p.). Clubs: Ahdeek Tennis, Valley Tennis. Author: Olympia Shoe Co., 1966; co-inventor Edgeroy Ball Press; Polymer patentee in field. Home: 81 Edgemont Pl Teaneck NJ 07666

FEINSCHREIBER, ROBERT ANDREW, lawyer; b. N.Y.C., Apr. 18, 1943; s. Selven Frederick and Maxine (Borodkin) F.; B.A., Trinity Coll., Hartford, Conn., 1964; M.B.A., Columbia, 1967; LL.B., Yale, 1967; LL.M. in Taxation, N.Y. U., 1972; m. Nancy L. Abbott, 1979; children by previous marriage—Steven, Kathryn. Admitted to N.Y. bar, 1971; asst. prof. Wayne State U. Law Sch., Detroit, 1967-69; taxation supr. Chrysler Corp., 1969-70; dir. taxation and fin. analysis NAM, N.Y.C., 1970; asst. chief accountant Seagrams Co., N.Y.C., 1970-72; asso. Oppenheim Appel Dixon & Co., 1972-74; pvt. practice law, N.Y.C., 1972—, now partner firm Robert Feinschreiber & Assos.; dir. Marin Export Corp.; v.p. Harrison Internat., Inc.; guest lectr. in field. Mem. Am., N.Y. State bar assns., N.Y. County Lawyers Assn., Internat. Tax Inst. (dir. 1972-79), Key Biscayne C. of C., Pi Gamma Mu. Author: Tax Depreciation, 1975; Tax Incentives for U.S. Exports, 1975; International Tax Planning Today, 1977; Allocation and Apportionment of Deductions, 1978; DISC: The Domestic International Sales Corporation, 1978; co-author: Fundamentals of International Taxation, 1977; editor: Earnings and Profits—The International Aspects, 1979; co-editor: Foreign Subsidiaries and Their Tax Consequences, 1979; editor Internat. Tax Jour, 1974—, Bus. Operation Tax Jour., 1976-77, Tax Haven and Shelter Report, 1977-78; editorial advisory bd. Internat. Tax Report, 1977-78. Address: 26 Broadway New York NY 10004 also 1121 Crandon Blvd Key Biscayne FL 33149

FEINSTEIN, EDWARD, mortgage banker; b. N.Y.C., June 21, 1923; s. Robert and Bertha (Goldberg) F.; B.B.A., U. Miami, 1947; m. Shirley Klukofsky, July 12, 1963; children—Eric, Deborah, Mark, Brian. With Lawyers Mortgage & Title Co., Miami, 1960-62, Heritage Corp. of N.Y., 1962-63; founder/pres. Heritage Corp. of S. Fla., Miami, 1963—; pres. Interam. Title Corp., Miami, 1963—, F&F Properties, Miami, 1971—, Heritage Mortgage Corp., Miami, 1970—. Active Cerebral Palsy, United Way, NCCJ; pres. U. Miami M Club Varsity Athletics, also bd. dirs. Athletic Fedn. Served to lt. (j.g.) USNR, 1943-46. Cert. rev. appraiser, mortgage underwriter, mortgage banker, real estate cons. Named Fla. Mortgage Broker of Year, 1966; cert. mortgage banker. Mem. S. Fla. (past pres.), Greater Miami (past pres.) mortgage bankers assns., Soc. Mortgage Cons.'s, U. Miami Alumni Assn. (trustee), Mortgage Bankers Assn. Am., Iron Arrow. Democrat. Jewish. Home: 120 S Prospect Ave Coral Gables FL 33133 Office: 1318 NW 7th St Miami FL 33125

FEINSTEIN, PETER, film producer; b. N.Y.C., July 13, 1944; s. Lester and Jeanette (Levinson) F.; B.A. in History and English, N.Y. U., 1969; m. Miriam Weinstein, June 1973; children—Eli, Mirka. With N.Y. Times, 1965-68; asso. editor New Issue Outlook, 1969-70; founder, dir. Film Forum, N.Y.C., 1970-72; sec., treas. parent corp. Moving Image, Inc., 1972-79; dir. Univ. Film Study Center, M.I.T., 1972-76; owner, dir. Peter Feinstein Assos., Cambridge, Mass., 1976—; bd. advs. Internat. Film Seminars, Inc., 1973-79, Young Filmmakers Found., Inc., 1974—, Boston Film/Video Found., Inc., 1976—, Cambridge Arts Council, 1977-80; freelance producer film and videotape, 1976—. Recipient 1st prize Internat. Rehab. Film Festival, 1978, Blue Ribbon award Am. Film Festival, 1979. Author: The Publicist's Newsfilm Handbook, 1979; editor: The Independent Film Community, 1977. Address: 36 Shepard St Cambridge MA 02138

FEIST, LEE, retail exec.; b. Memphis, Apr. 24, 1943; s. Herbert B. and Betty B. Feist; B.A., Vanderbilt U.; M.B.A., Cornell U., 1967; m. Bobbye J. Walsh, Jan. 25, 1964; children—Samuel Edward, Tamara Leigh. Fulbright lectr., acting dir. mgmt. studies program U. W.I., Trinidad, 1967-69; product mgr. Keller Mfg. Co., Corydon, Ind., 1969-72; pres. Remnant House, Inc., Ripley, Tenn., 1972-80; sr. v.p. NMI, Inc. div. McCall's Pattern Co., N.Y.C., 1980—. Home: 16 Copper Beech Ridgefield CT 06877 Office: 230 Park Ave Suite 1305 New York NY 10017

FEIT, MELVIN I., accountant; b. N.Y.C., Feb. 26, 1931; s. Louis and Rose (Cohen) F.; A.B., Bklyn. Coll., 1952; postgrad. Baruch Sch., City Coll. N.Y., 1952-54; m. Florence Braunfotel, July 31, 1955; children—Lynette, Daniel, Kevin. Staff accountant Meyer, Wolf & Wagman, N.Y.C., 1956-59; sr. staff accountant Sidney G. Spero & Co., N.Y.C., 1959-61, Robert F. Wolman & Co., N.Y.C., 1961-62; partner Elmer Fox Westheimer & Co., C.P.A.'s, N.Y.C., 1962-79; self-employed acct., N.Y.C., 1980—; instr. paralegal tng. program L.I. U., 1977-78; adj. asst. prof. Coll. Ins., 1980—. Treas., v.p. Old Country Club Civic Assn. Flushing (N.Y.), Inc., 1963-68, pres., 1968-75, chmn., 1975—; cubmaster Boy Scouts Am., 1970-73, instl. rep., 1973-78, com. mem., 1978—. Served with U.S. Army, 1954-56. C.P.A., N.Y. Mem. Am. Inst. C.P.A.'s, N.Y. State Soc. C.P.A.'s, Tax. Inst. C.W. Post Coll., Inst. Fin. Planning. Jewish. Contbr. articles in field to profl. jours.; contbg. editor The Practical Accountant, 1968-71, The Business Owner, 1976—. Office: 122 E 42d St New York NY 10168

FELD, JOSEPH, real estate and constrn. co. exec.; b. N.Y.C., June 25, 1919; s. Morris David and Gussie (London) F.; student Coll. City N.Y., 1946-47; m. Doris Rabinor, Apr. 10, 1948; 1 dau., Elaine Susan. Builder housing, apt. projects, L.I., N.Y.C., N.J., 1948-54; pres. Kohl and Feld, Inc., builder housing devels., Rockland County, N.Y., 1955-57; pres. Feld Constrn. Corp., New City, N.Y., 1957—, Birchland Constrn. Corp., 1957-70, Ramapo Towers, Inc., 1963—; dir. Rockland County Citizen Pub. Corp., 1959-60, Peoples Nat. Bank Rockland County, Monsey, N.Y. Mem. Clarkstown Bldg. Code Com., 1959; mem. indsl. devel. adv. com. Rockland County Bd. Suprs., 1969-71; chmn. housing adv. council Rockland County Legislature; chmn. Housing Task Force, 1979—; mem., past v.p. New City Jewish Community Center, trustee, past pres. Men's Club; mem. Rockland County council Jewish War Vets., past comdr. New City post. Served to staff sgt. AUS, 1941-45. Mem. Rockland County Assn., Inc. (dir.), Rockland County Home Builders Assn. (past pres., dir., chmn. rental housing com.), Nat. (past dir.; mem. rental housing com.), N.Y. State (past dir., mem. rental housing com.) assns. home builders, Rockland County Apt. Owners Assn. (pres., dir.), Rockland County Bd. Realtors, N.Y. State Assn. Realtors (dir.), Nat. Inst. Real Estate Brokers, New City C. of C. Clubs: Masons, Lions (local pres. 1959-60; zone chmn. 1961-62), B'nai B'rith. Home: 9 Woodland Rd New City NY 10956 Office: 20 S Main St New City NY 10956

FELDMAN, ALVIN LINDBERGH, airline exec.; b. N.Y.C., Dec. 14, 1927; s. Harry and Rose (Lefkowtiz) F.; B.S. in Mech. Engring., Cornell U., 1949; S.E.P., Stanford U. Grad. Sch. Bus., 1966; m. Rosemily Petrison, Feb. 15, 1952; children—David, John, Susan. With Cornell Aeros. Lab., 1949-52; engr. Convair div. Gen. Dynamics Corp., San Diego, 1952-54; asst. gen. mgr. Liquid Rocket Co., pres. Aerojet Nuclear Systems Co., Aerojet-Gen. Corp., Sacramento, 1954-71; pres., chief exec. officer Frontier Airlines, Inc., Denver, 1971-80; pres., chief exec. officer Continental Airlines, Inc., Los Angeles, 1980—; chmn. bd., dir. Denver br. Fed. Res. Bank of Kansas City; dir. Pub. Service Co. Colo.; pub. mem. Nat. Transp. Policy Study Commn., 1976—. Recipient Man of Yr. award Sales and Mktg. Execs., 1976. Asso. fellow AIAA; mem. Assn. Local Transport Airlines (dir.), Air Transport Assn. (dir.), Denver C. of C. (dir. 1975-76). Clubs: LaJolla Country; Hiwan Golf; Aero of Washington. Home: 1077 Race St Denver CO 80206 Office: Continental Airlines Inc Los Angeles Internat Airport Los Angeles CA 90009*

FELDMAN, ELLEN SUE, food mfg. co. exec.; b. Bronx, N.Y., Aug. 27, 1951; d. Morris N. and Dorothy (Silberman) F.; B.A. cum laude (Regent scholar), Brandeis U., 1973; M.B.A. (Stein fellow 1973-74, Hunt fellow 1974-75), Amos Tuck Sch. Bus. Adminstrn., Dartmouth Coll., 1975. Research asst. analyst Leo Burnett U.S.A., Chgo., 1975-77, asst. account exec. client service, 1976-77; account exec. Needham, Harper & Steers, Chgo., 1977-79; project coordinator Gen. Foods Corp., White Plains, N.Y., 1980—. Home: 19 Colonial Rd Stamford CT 06906 Office: 250 North Ave White Plains NY 10625

FELDMAN, HOWARD JOEL, lawyer; b. Milw., Mar. 6, 1939; s. David A. and Geraldine (Kahn) F.; B.B.A., U. Wis., 1960, LL.B. cum laude, 1964; m. Clarice Rochelle Wagan, July 11, 1965; 1 son, David L. Admitted to Wis. bar, 1964, D.C. bar, 1969, U.S. Supreme Ct. bar, 1967; atty. tax. div. appellate sec. Dept. Justice, Washington, 1964-68; partner firm Becker, Feldman & Becker, Washington, 1968-73; chief counsel U.S. Senate Permanent Subcom. on Investigations, Washington, 1973-76; mem. firm Van Ness, Feldman & Sutcliffe, Washington, 1977—. Bd. dirs., exec. com. Wolf Trap Found. for Performing Arts, Washington. Served to capt. U.S. Army, 1961-69. C.P.A., Wis. Mem. Am., Fed., D.C. bar assns., Beta Gamma Sigma, Pi Lamda Phi. Contbr. articles in field to profl. jours. Home: 4455 29th St NW Washington DC 20008 Office: 1220 19th St NW Suite 500 Washington DC 20036

FELDMAN, JAY NEWMAN, holding co. exec.; b. N.Y.C., Nov. 11, 1936; s. Morris Kenneth and Della (Newman) F.; A.B. magna cum laude, Colgate U., 1958; J.D., Harvard, 1961; m. Nancy Tobias, Dec. 7, 1963; children—Nina Cheryl, Karen Elise. Admitted to N.Y. bar, 1962; asso. firm Jacobs Persinger & Parker, N.Y.C., 1961-68; sec., treas., gen. counsel Lynch Corp., N.Y.C., 1968-69; sec., counsel Kalvex Inc., N.Y.C., 1970-76, v.p., 1975-76, also dir.; sec. Allied Artists Pictures Corp., N.Y.C., 1973-74, dir., 1974—; v.p., counsel Allied Artists Industries, Inc., N.Y.C., 1976-80, sec., 1976-77, also dir.; sec., counsel, dir. PSP Inc., N.Y.C., 1970-76; sec., dir. D. Kaltman & Co., Inc., Atlantic City, 1970-79, v.p., 1977-79; sec., dir. Apollo Motor Homes, Inc., Downey, Calif., 1970-80, v.p., 1977-80, sec., dir. Vitabath Inc., 1970-72; sec., dir. Westwood Import Co., Inc., San Francisco, 1972-79, v.p., 1977-79; v.p., dir. Palmland Fashions, Inc., Miami, Fla., 1971-78; v.p., sec., dir. Allied Artists Video Corp., 1978-80; resident counsel Lorimar Prodns., Inc., 1980—. Mem. com. on criminal cts. Legal Aid Soc., 1969-72. Mem. Am. Bar Assn., N.Y. State Bar Assn., Phi Beta Kappa. Home: 61 Roger Dr Port Washington NY 11050 Office: 15 Columbus Circle New York NY 10023

FELDMAN, MARVIN, coll. pres.; b. Rochester, N.Y., May 24, 1927; s. Max and Blanche F.; student U.S. Military Acad., 1948-51; A.B., San Francisco State U., 1953; m. Dorothy Owens, July 29, 1954; children—Brian, Michael. Tchr. math. public schs., San Francisco, 1952-57; v.p. Cogswell Coll., 1958-64; program officer Ford Found., 1964-69; asst. to spl. com. Office of Edn., HEW, Washington, 1969-71; pres. Fashion Inst. Tech., N.Y.C., 1971—. Mem. President's Nat. Adv. Council on Vocat. Edn., 1972-79. Served with U.S. Army, 1944-46. Mem. Orgn. Rehab. Through Tng., President's Assn., West Point Soc. Office: 227 W 27th St New York NY 10001

FELDMAN, SUSAN LOIS, printing co. exec.; b. N.Y.C., Sept. 13, 1952; d. Murray and Myra F.; B.A. in French magna cum laude, U. Miami (Fla.), 1973. Tchr. high sch. French and Spanish, 1973; from sales trainee to sr. sales rep. info. systems group Xerox Corp., Tarrytown, N.Y., 1973-77; sales exec. R.R. Donnelley & Sons Co., N.Y.C., 1977-80, Regensteiner Press, N.Y.C., 1980—. Recipient various sales awards. Mem. Phi Kappa Phi. Home: 63 Entrance Rd PO Box 425 Roslyn Heights NY 11577 Office: One Rockefeller Plaza New York NY 10020

FELDMESSER, PHILIP, ins. co. exec.; b. Newark, May 2, 1914; s. David and Minnie (Goldkopf) F.; B.S., U. Newark, 1938; m. Feb. 18, 1939; children—Mark S., Howard S. Founder, owner Atlantic Agy., Newark and Irvington, N.J., 1938-66; founder, pres. Am. & Fgn. Agencies, Irvington, N.J., 1938-66; founder, pres. Am. & Fgn. Agencies, Irvington, 1966-70; pres. Global Am. Ins. Mgrs., South Orange, N.J., 1970—; field auditor N.J. Unemployment Compensation Commn., 1941-50; instr. Fairleigh Dickinson U., 1967-79, Coll. Ins., N.Y.C.; cons. Asso. Testing Labs., Inc. Lic. ins. broker, surplus line broker, N.J. Mem. Nat. Soc. Chartered Property and Casualty Underwriters, N.J. Soc. Chartered Property and Casualty Underwriters, Soc. Ins. Research, Ind. Ins. Agts. Am., Ind. Ins. Agts. N.J., Ins. Brokers Assn., Profl. Mut. Agts. Assn. N.J., N.J. Surplus Lines Assn., Nat. Safety Council, Am. Arbitration Assn. (panel). Contbr. articles to profl. jours. Home: 14 Troy Ct Maplewood NJ 07040 Office: 203 Irvington Ave South Orange NJ 07079

FELDON, OTTO A., publisher; b. Holyoke, Mass., Sept. 8, 1904; s. August and Martha (Schroeder) Felsentrager; student Syracuse (N.Y.) U., 1929; m. Dorothy S. Stressenger, May 31, 1929; children—Nancy Brooks Feldon Doss, Judith Banks Feldon Pierce. Dist. mgr. McGraw-Hill Pub. Co., N.Y.C., 1929-35; Western mgr. McFadden Publs., Inc., N.Y.C. and Chgo., 1935-40; pres. O.A. Feldon & Assos., Chgo., 1940-41; spl. services publisher U.S. Govt., 1941-44; pres. Drake Pub. Co., Chgo., 1946-60, Hitchcock Pub. Co., Chgo., 1960—; dir. Hawthorne Bank, Wheaton, Ill., Am. Bus. Press, Bus. Pub. Audit of Circulation, Inc. Hon. dir. Chgo. Off-The-Street Club, 1960, pres., 1945-51.

FELDSTEIN, ALAN, apparel co. exec.; b. Los Angeles, June 14, 1936; s. Sol and Betty (Goussak) F.; B.S. in Bus., U. So. Calif., 1958; m. Shirley Ellen Zenziper, Aug. 10, 1957; children—Beth, Ross. Salesman, Aileen Knitwear, 1960-63, Jonathan Logan Inc., 1963-75; pres. Saltzman-Feldstein Assos., Inc., sales agt., Chgo., 1975-79; pres. Seles Agy. for Center Stage, 1979—, Gailord Classics, 1979—. Served with AUS, 1958-59. Club: B'nith B'rith. Address: 1143 Apparel Center Chicago IL 60654

FELDSTEIN, CHARLES ROBERT, fund raising counsel; b. Chgo., Nov. 9, 1922; s. Herman and Fannie (Frank) F.; student Northwestern U., 1940-42; A.M., U. Chgo., 1944; postgrad. Harvard, 1945-46; m. Janice Ruth Josephson, Sept. 6, 1948; children—James Frank, Frances Emily, Thomas Mark. Asst. dir. Hillel Founds., Harvard U., Radcliffe Coll., Mass. Inst. Tech., 1944-45, dir. Tufts and Simmons colls., 1945-46; dir. advt. Field's Stores, Inc., N.J., 1946-48; exec. asst. to v.p. U. Chgo., 1948-51, dir. devel., 1951-55; pres. Charles R. Feldstein & Co., Inc., 1953—; pres. Chas. Frank & Co. Antiquarians, 1967—. Bd. dirs. Inst. for Psychoanalysis, Chgo. Sinai Congregation; mem. vis. com. to social service adminstrn. U. Chgo. Mem. Am. Assn. Fund-Raising Counsel, Pub. Relations Soc., Publicity Club. Clubs: Standard, Quadrangle, Cliff Dwellers, Attic; Harvard (N.Y.C.). Home: 70 E Cedar St Chicago IL 60611 Office: 135 S La Salle St Suite 1260 Chicago IL 60603

FELDSTEIN, MARTIN STUART, economist; b. N.Y.C., Nov. 25, 1939; s. Meyer and Esther (Gevarter) F.; A.B. summa cum laude, Harvard U., 1961; M.A., Oxford U., 1964, D.Phil., 1967; m. Kathleen Foley, June 19, 1965; children—Margaret, Janet. Research fellow Nuffield Coll., Oxford U., 1964-65, ofcl. fellow, 1965-67, lectr. pub. fin., 1965-67; asst. prof. econs. Harvard U., 1967-68, asso. prof., 1968-69, prof., 1969—; dir. Phoenix Mut. Life Ins. Co.; pres. Nat. Bur. Econ. Research, 1977—. Fellow Am. Acad. Arts and Scis., Econometric Soc. (council 1977—); mem. Am. Econ. Assn. (John Bates Clark medal 1977), Inst. Medicine Nat. Acad. Scis., Phi Beta Kappa. Bd. editors Am. Econ. Rev., Public Interest, Quar. Jour. Econs., Rev. Econs. and Statistics; co-editor Jour. Pub. Econs. Home: 147 Clifton St Belmont MA 02178 Office: 1050 Massachusetts Ave Cambridge MA 02138

FELICETTA, CESARE, financial cons.; b. Alexandria, Egypt, Aug. 3, 1930; s. Emanuele and Concetta (Lo Presti) F.; grad. Rome U., 1955; m. Raffaella Agostinelli, Apr. 23, 1956; 1 son, Fabio. Auditor, Price Waterhouse & Co., Rome, 1949-54; chief accountant Squibb SpA, Rome, 1954-58; systems mgr. Arthur Andersen & Co., Milan, 1958-60; controller Bowater Europea SpA, Rome, 1960-64; gen. mgr., mng. dir. Cobeva S.P.A., Rome, Pepsi Cola and Schweppes bottler, 1964-67; dir. finance and adminstrn. Warner Lambert Co. for Italy, 1967-70; for Eastern Hemisphere, 1970-71; pres. Rome Daily Am., Inc., 1964-71; dir. fin. and adminstrn. Merck Sharp & Dohme (Italia) SpA, Rome, 1971-73, Romana Calcestruzzi SpA, Rome, 1974-77; accounting expert Rome Ct. and C. of C. Revisore Ufficiale Dei Conti, 1957; mem. Collegio dei Ragionieri Del Lazio, 1956; prof. personnel adminstrn. U. Camerino. Decorated Knight of Malta, knight comdr. Order of Merit Italy, officer St. Agata of San Marino, marianer Knight Teutonic Order, Golden Cross of Lathran, comdr. Order of St. Gregorio Magno, knight comdr. Order Holy Sepulcher of Jerusalem, knight Constantinian Order of St. George, mem. Order do Cruseiro do Sul of Brasil, knight comdr. Merit of Order Holy Sepulcher of Jerusalem. Mem. Nat. Assn. Accountants (emeritus life asso.). Clubs: Brit. Horse Soc., Bath (London); Nuovo Circolo degli Scacchi, Nuovo Tennis Parioli, Circolo del Golf, Rotary Sud (Rome); Circolo della Vela (Anzio), Clubino Dadi (Milan). Home and Office: 21 Via Siracusa 00161 Rome Italy

FELION, LARRY DEAN, ins. cons.; b. Westwood, Calif., Feb. 10, 1937; s. Roderic Eugene, Sr., and Iona Viola (Butler) F.; B.A., Sacramento State U., 1955-60; m. Gertrude A. Maloney, Dec. 20, 1958 (dec.); children—Larry Dean, Brian, Ranae. Group ins. underwriter Pacific Mut. Life and Fireman's Fund Am. Life, 1961-65; v.p. group ins. ops. Pacific Nat. Life Assurance Co., 1965-72; v.p., dir. Cons. Mgrs. of Calif., Burlingame, 1972—; dir. Baine Assos., Inc. Co-chmn. Com. Against Tax Increase, Burlingame Sch. Dist., 1975; candidate Burlingame Sch. Dist. Bd. Trustees, 1977. Mem. Am. Mgmt. Assn., Calif. Farm Bur. Fedn. Roman Catholic. Club: Burlingame Rotary. Office: 1633 Old Bayshore St Suite 332 Burlingame CA 94010

FELIX, JOHN HENRY, investments exec.; b. Honolulu, June 14, 1930; s. Henry and Melinda (Pacheco) F.; student Chaminade Coll., 1947, San Mateo Coll., 1950; grad. Advanced Mgmt. Program, Stanford, 1967, Harvard, 1971; Ph.D., Walden U., 1975; m. Patricia Berry; children—Laura Marie, Melinda Susan, John Morgan, Jayne Sherry, Annette Sherry. Asst. to pres. AFL-CIO Unity House, 1955-57; exec. v.p. Hotel Operating Co. of Hawaii, 1957-60; v.p. Music Polynesia, Inc.; asst. to Gov. of Hawaii, 1960-62; pres. LaRonde Restaurants, Inc., 1962—, Hotel Assos., Inc.; dir., mem. exec. com., chmn. personnel com. Hawaii Nat. Bank; pres., chmn. exec. com. Hawaiian Meml. Park. Chmn. ARC, 1961-63, 72; del. League Red Cross Socs.; chmn. Gov.'s Jobs for Vets. Task Force, 1971-76, Honolulu Redevel. Agy., 1971, 72, Honolulu City and County Planning Com., 1959; chmn. Bd. Water Supply, 1973-75; chmn. Honolulu City County Bd. Parks Recreation; mem. City and

County Honolulu Police Commn., 1979; pres. bd. Hawaii Public Radio, 1979; bd. govs. ARC, also chmn. Pacific div.; nat. trustee March of Dimes Birth Defects Found. Served with AUS, 1952-54. Named Young Man of Year, Hawaii Jr. C. of C., 1959, Distinguished Service award Sales and Marketing Execs. Hawaii, 1968, Harriman award distinguished vol. service A.R.C., 1975, others. Mem. Young Pres.'s Orgn., Hawaii Restaurant Assn. (pres. 1967), Air Force Assn. (pres. Hawaii), C. of C. of Hawaii (life), Nat. Eagle Scout Assn. (life), CAP-U.S. Air Force Aux. (comdr. Hawaii Wing 1980). Club: Waikiki Rotary (Honolulu). Home: 4731 Kahala Ave Honolulu HI 96816 Office: 1441 Kapiolani Blvd Suite 2020 Honolulu HI 96814

FELIXSON, ROBERT JACK, lawyer, real estate co. exec.; b. Cleve., Aug. 24, 1920; s. Lewis P. and Sadye (Munitz) F.; B.A. summa cum laude, Western Res. U., 1941, J.D., 1943; m. Jane Hellman, Dec. 30, 1968; children—Carol, Nancy. Admitted to Ohio bar, 1943, Calif. bar, 1946; practiced in Cleve., 1943-44, Los Angeles, 1946—; pres. Office Bldgs., Inc., Los Angeles, 1954—, Diversified Realty Enterprises Corp., Los Angeles, 1954—; pres. Real Estate Investment div., sr. v.p. Western Mortgage Corp. div. Unionam., Inc., Los Angeles, 1973-75; chmn., pres. Growth Realty Cos. (name formerly LMI Investors), Los Angeles, 1976—; lectr. real estate UCLA Extension, 1963-68. Pres., Los Angeles Region Welfare Planning Council, 1957-58, Jewish Centers Assn. Los Angeles, 1959-62; chmn. Nat. Council on Alcoholism, Los Angeles, 1979—; bd. dirs. Community Chest, Los Angeles, 1957-60; vice chmn. Bur. Jewish Edn., Los Angeles, 1965-67; v.p. Los Angeles Recreation and Youth Services Planning Council, 1964-66; mem. Calif. Democratic Central Com., 1962-63; Dem. candidate for Congress from Calif., 1962. Mem. Am. Bar Assn., Calif. State Bar, Los Angeles Bar Assn., Beverly Hills Bar Assn., Nat. Assn. Real Estate Appraisers, Mortgage Banking Assn., Nat. Assn. Real Estate Investment Trusts, Order of Coif, Phi Beta Kappa, Delta Sigma Rho, Tau Epsilon Rho, Zeta Beta Tau. Club: Brentwood Country (Los Angeles). Office: 2029 Century Park E Suite 2000 Los Angeles CA 90067

FELKER, ERNEST SCOTT, mfg. co. exec.; b. Hood, Tex., Dec. 15, 1921; s. Ernest Alvin and Serena (Locke) F.; A.A., Gainesville Jr. Coll., 1942; B.S. in Ceramic Engring., U. Tex., 1949; Ph.D. in Bus. Adminstrn. (hon.), Hamilton State U., 1973; student Alexander Hamilton Inst. Bus., 1958-59; m. Louise Brown Meadows, Jan. 22, 1944; children—Beverly L. Felker Powell, Clinton S., Clayton D., Elizabeth Anne Felker Bronkema. Ceramic engr. Ferro Corp., Cleve., 1949-50, sales-service engr., Dallas, 1953-55, asst. div. mgr. color div., Cleve., 1955-67, gen. mgr. color div., 1967—, corporate v.p., 1974—; ceramic engr. French Saxon China Co., Sebring, Ohio, 1950-51, plant mgr., 1951-53; lectr. in field. Mem. President's Assos., Cedarville (Ohio) Coll. Served with AUS, 1942-46; PTO. Decorated Bronze Star with 4 oak leaf clusters. Mem. Am. Ceramic Soc., Sigma Gamma Epsilon. Republican. Baptist. Author: Glaze and Color Data Handbook, 1956. Home: 8408 Summer Rd Macedonia OH 44056 Office: 4150 E 56th St Cleveland OH 44105

FELL, FREDERICK VICTOR, pub. co. exec., author; b. Bklyn., May 21, 1910; s. Samuel and Victoria (Greenhut) F.; student N.Y. U., 1928-31; LL.B., Bklyn. Law Sch., 1935; m. Selma Shampain, May 18, 1975; children—Linda Fell Firestein, Nancy. Pres. Frederick Fell Pub., Inc., N.Y.C., 1943—; author: (pseudonym Vic Fredericks) Crackers in Bed, 1953; More For Doctors Only, 1953; Jest Married, 1958; For Golfers Only, 1964; Wit and Wisdom of the Presidents, 1966, also others. Trustee Long Beach Library, 1948-50; councilman City of Long Beach, 1950-54, pres. city council, 1950-52; pres. Long Beach Hosp. Club, 1949, 59; chmn. book pubs. div. crusades N.Y.C. div. Am. Cancer Soc., 1977, 78, 79. Mem. Assn. Am. Pubs., Am. Booksellers Assn. Democrat. Jewish. Club: Engrs. Country; Roslyn (L.I.); Hillcrest Country (Hollywood, Fla.). Home: 3800 Hillcrest Dr Apt 1120 Hollywood FL 33021 Office: 386 Park Ave S New York NY 10016

FELL, ROBERT BRUCE, oil co. exec.; b. Zanesville, Ohio, Feb. 12, 1930; s. Benjamin R. and Bonita (Crosby) F.; B.S. in Indsl. Engring., Ohio State U., 1955; m. Betty Jane Cary, Sept. 24, 1949; children—Robert B., James B., David A., Benjamin R. Project engr. Standard Oil Co., Cleve., 1960-64, prodn. mgr., Lima, Ohio, 1965-68, mgr. chem. mfg., 1969-71, mgr. plastics ops., Cleve., 1972-75, spl. assignment, Anchorage, 1976; exec. v.p. Sohio Pipe Line Co., Cleve., 1978—. Dist. dir. Boy Scouts Am., 1962-65; bd. dirs. Jr. Achievement, 1969-72. Mem. Am. Petroleum Inst., Assn. Oil Pipelines, Greater Cleve. Growth Assn. Lutheran. Club: Walden Golf and Tennis. Office: Midland Bldg Cleveland OH 44115

FELLER, GEORGE EDWARD, computer service co. exec.; b. Boston, July 5, 1934; s. John G. and Esther (Nelson) F.; B.S. in Math. Stats., Columbia U., 1969; m. Margret Mueller, Aug. 7, 1971; 1 child, Heike Katrina. Mgr. systems and programs Comml. Union Ins. Group, N.Y.C., 1962-69; mgr. mgmt. services Arthur Young & Co., N.Y.C., 1969-71; v.p. systems Pepsico, Tulsa, Okla., 1971-79; pres. Minimax Systems Inc., Tulsa, 1979—. Served with CIC, U.S. Army, 1958-61. Home: 1606 S Carson Ave Tulsa OK 74119 Office: PO Box 586 Tulsa OK 74101

FELLER, JACK HENRY, JR., corp. exec.; b. Benton Harbor, Mich., Apr. 30, 1933; s. Jack Henry and Louise Marie (von Getzlaff) F.; A.A., City Coll. San Francisco, 1951; B.S., Stanford U., 1954, M.S., 1956; m. Inez Mary Gutschenritter, Nov. 18, 1961; children—Jack Henry, James Bryce. Faculty, adminstr. The Kittredge Sch., San Francisco, 1954-55; asst. comdt. of cadets, asst. prof. mil. sci. and tactics San Rafael (Calif.) Mil. Acad., 1955-59; projects mgr. Dumont Corp., San Rafael, 1959-60; asst. adminstr. Westbay div. Permanante Med. Group, Kaiser Found. Med. Care Entities, San Francisco, 1960-63; mng. dir. J. H. Feller & Assos., 1963-72; pres. Cons. Services div. Stewart & Stewart, Inc., 1972-74; v.p., dir. Western ops. Rath & Strong, Inc., Burlingame, Calif., 1974-75; v.p. fin. H. Sherson, Inc., 1975—. Coordinator Mill Valley CD, 1955; mem. citizens adv. com. San Rafael City Schs., 1971-73; mem. nat. sea exploring com. Boy Scouts Am., 1969-72, nat. vice commodore tng., 1972, mem. nat. exploring com., 1973—, mem. nat. program com., 1974-79, chmn. program effectiveness com. nat. exploring program, 1974-78, mem. Western region com., 1972—, mem. regional bd., 1977—, vice chmn. Western region exploring com., 1972-77, trustee, v.p. adminstrn. Golden Gate scouting, 1973-78, mem. exec. bd. Marin council, 1968—, mem.-at-large Nat. council, 1969—, mem. Golden Gate scouting adv. council, 1978—, nat. program support com., 1979—, nat. planning and research com., 1979—, William H. Spurgeon III award, 1973, Silver Antelope award, 1975, Silver Beaver award, 1978. Mem. U.S. Yacht Racing Union (com. race mgmt. 1976—, racing rules com. 1977—, com. on judges 1977—, regional adminstrv. judge 1978—), Am. Arbitration Assn. (panel arbitrators), Better Bus. Bur. (panel arbitrators), Am. Mgmt. Assn., Inst. Mgmt. Cons.'s (founders' group, program chmn. Northwestern region 1973-74), Am. Meat Inst. (govt. relations com. 1978—, chmn. corned beef com. 1979—), Authors Guild, Calif. C. of C. (consumer affairs com. 1978—), Stanford Alumni Assn. (life), Yacht Racing Assn. San Francisco Bay (chmn. appeals com. 1968-). Democrat. Clubs: St. Francis Yacht (curator 1980—) (San Francisco); Stanford Buck (Stanford U.). Author: Yacht Racing Protests and Appeals, 1972; The Yacht Racing Rules Interpreted, 1974; mng. editor Jour. Applied Mgmt., 1977-78; contbr. articles on various subjects to mags. and jours. Home: 111 Gloria Dr San Rafael CA 94901 Office: 1955 Carroll Ave San Francisco CA 94124

FELLERMAN, ROBIN ELYSE, umbrella/rainwear import co. exec.; b. N.Y.C., July 27, 1950; s. Howard A. and Jacqueline (Heyman) F.; B.A. cum laude, Boston U., 1972; M.B.A. with honors, Adelphi U., 1980. With Estee Lauder, N.Y.C., Boston, 1970-72; pres. Boston - 'Robin Feller' Cosmetic Co., 1972-76; pres. Fellerman & Co., Inc., N.Y.C., 1977—, chief exec. officer, 1977—. Mem. N.Y. State Industries.

FELLERS, WILLIAM WARREN, actuary; b. Chgo., Mar. 9, 1917; s. Foss Luke and Elizabeth Irene (Gross) F.; A.B., Oberlin (Ohio) Coll., 1938; B.S. in Edn., Kent (Ohio) State U., 1938, M.A., 1939; m. Audrie Berdine Baker, June 29, 1940; children—Elizabeth Jayne, Martha Kay, John William. With Prudential Ins. Co., 1939-44; with Wyatt Co., Washington, 1946—, v.p., actuary, 1948-78, chmn. bd., chmn. actuarial, pension and peer rev. coms., 1950-79, cons. actuary, 1979—. Served with AUS, 1945. Fellow Soc. Actuaries; mem. Am. Acad. Actuaries. Republican. Mem. Christian Ch. (Disciples of Christ). Club: University (Washington). Co-author: Handbook For Pension Planning, 1949; Non Insured Pension Mortality, 1975. Home: 1445 Crestridge Dr Silver Spring MD 20910 Office: Wyatt Co 1990 K St NW Washington DC 20006

FELLEY, DONALD LOUIS, chem. co. exec.; b. Memphis, Feb. 7, 1921; s. Alfred and Helen Ruth (Meek) F.; B.S., Ark. State Coll., 1941; M.S., U. Ill., 1947, Ph.D., 1949; m. June Pack, Oct. 1, 1949; children—James D., Douglas C., Richard B., David L., Mary L. Tech. sales rep. Rohm and Haas Co., 1949-56, mgr. French subs., 1957-64, asst. mgr. fgn. ops., 1964-68, v.p., prodn. mgr., 1968-70, v.p., gen. mgr. internat. div., 1970-76, v.p., regional dir. N. Am., 1976-78, pres., chief operating officer, 1978—, also dir. Bd. dirs. Abington (Pa.) Meml. Hosp., 1978—. Served to capt., field arty. U.S. Army, 1942-46. Mem. Am. Chem. Soc., Soc. Chem. Industry (dir.), Greater Phila. C. of C. (dir. 1978—), Phila. World Affairs Council (dir. 1976—), Sigma Xi, Alpha Chi Sigma, Phi Lambda Upsilon. Home: 1152 Sewell Ln Rydal PA 19046 Office: Rohm and Haas Co Independence Mall W Philadelphia PA 19105

FELLONNEAU, JOHN MAURICE, JR., mfg. co. exec.; b. Chgo., June 25, 1949; s. John Maurice and Mary Margaret (Weller) F.; student Fayetteville Tech. Inst., 1970, U. Wis., 1972-73; m. Kathy Louise Maples, Sept. 7, 1970; children—Bernard William, John Maurice. Shipping supr. Internat. Harvester, Louisville, 1974-76; purchasing and traffic mgr. Louisville Scrap Material, 1976-77; v.p. Tri-City Scrap Co., Louisville, 1977—, Metals Resources Co., Louisville, 1977—; instr. Inst. Scrap Iron and Steel. Bd. dirs. DeSales High Sch., Louisville. Served with U.S. Army, 1967-73. Decorated Silver Star. Mem. Inst. Scrap Iron and Steel, Nat. Assn. Recycling Industries, Nat. Assn. Purchasing Mgmt., Louisville Assn. Purchasing Mgmt. Republican. Roman Catholic. Office: PO Box 21199 Louisville KY 40221

FELT, JOHN HAMILTON, furniture mfr.'s rep.; b. Los Alamos, N.Mex., Jan. 7, 1951; s. Gaelen L. and Margaret (Corbett) F.; B.F.A. in Environ. Design, Ariz. State U., 1974; m. Mariah Louise Anders, May 26, 1979; children—Sean Anders, Hamilton Talbot. Student intern Don Henning & Assos., Scottsdale, Ariz., 1973; with contract design/mktg. dept. Am. Furniture Co., Albuquerque, 1974-78; mktg. rep. Seal Furniture & Systems, Los Angeles, 1978-79; mfr.'s rep. Madsen/Wolfe Co., Los Angeles, 1979; spl. account mgr. James Hill & Co., Los Angeles, 1979-80; mfr.'s rep. Condi div. Pacific Furniture Co., Compton, Calif., 1980—; cons. on interior environs., 1973—. Democrat. Research on product/methods. Office: 1965 E Vista Belle Way Compton CA 90220

FELTEN, RODGER FILLMORE, life ins. co. exec.; b. Queens, N.Y., Aug. 8, 1930; s. Edward J. and Elsie M. Felten; student Hofstra U., Denver U.; m. Elizabeth Killeen, Oct. 6, 1957; children—Kenneth Dean, Jennifer Mary. From agt. to agy. mgr. Met. Life Ins. Co., 1955-66; asst. v.p. sales N. Atlantic Life Ins. Co., Jericho, N.Y., 1966-75; v.p. sales Unity Mut. Life Ins. Co., Syracuse, N.Y., 1975—. Pres. Harbour Green Civic Assn., Massapequa, N.Y., 1974, Manlius (N.Y.) Restoration ad Devel., 1977. Served with USAF, 1951-55. C.L.U. Mem. Nat. Assn. Life Underwriters, Gen. Agts. and Mgrs. Assn., Sales and Mktg. Execs. Republican. Roman Catholic. Address: 1 Unity Plaza Syracuse NY 13215

FELTENSTEIN, SIDNEY JEROME, JR., food service exec.; b. N.Y.C., Dec. 20, 1940; s. Sidney and Karolyn F.; B.S., Boston U., 1962; m. Elizabeth. With R.H. Macy Co., 1962-63, Procter & Gamble, 1963-66, Knox Reeves Advt., Inc., 1966-68, Textron, Inc., 1968-69, Candy Corp. Am., 1969-72; with Dunkin Donuts Inc., Randolph, Mass., 1972—, sr. v.p. mktg. Bd. dirs. Boston Theatre Projects; active Mayor's Office of Cultural Affairs. Office: PO Box 317 Randolph MA 02389

FELTMANN, JOHN MEINRAD, former advt. and radio exec.; b. St. Louis, Jan. 30, 1910; s. Henry Conrad and Catherine (Lake) F.; certificate in commerce and finance St. Louis U., 1938; m. Adeline A. Fiedler, Nov. 25, 1944; children—John Thomas, Mary Anne Kenney, Robert Joseph, James Anthony. Clk., Nat. Telephone Directory Co., St. Louis, 1924-36, auditor, 1936-60; sec., dir. Von Hoffmann Corp., Union, N.J., 1947-60, treas., dir., 1960-67, v.p., treas., dir., 1967-69; dir. Von Hoffmann Press, Inc., St. Louis, 1947-69, treas., dir., 1960-69; treas. dir. Publishers Lithographers, Inc., St. Louis, 1959-69; sec., treas. von Hoffmann Realty and Mortgage Corp., 1954-59; v.p., treas., dir. Victory Broadcasting Corp., Jacksonville, Fla., 1968-78; v.p. treas. Nat. Telephone Directory Corp., Union, N.J. 1968-72, dir., 1968—, exec. v.p., 1972-78; dir. Mid-State Printing Co., Jefferson City, Mo., 1947-54. Sec., treas. George Von Hoffmann Found., 1954-59. Mem. Delta Sigma Pi. Roman Catholic. Club: Mo. Athletic. Home: 7250 Christopher Dr Saint Louis MO 63129 Office: 1050 Galloping Hill Rd Union NJ 07083

FELTNER, RICHARD LEE, banker; b. Crawfordsville, Ind., Oct. 16, 1938; s. Denver D. and Marcella T. (Nees) F.; B.S., Purdue U., 1960, M.S., 1961; Ph.D., N.C. State U., 1965; m. Karen Sommer, Sept. 12, 1959; children—Richard A., Susan S. Prof. agrl. econs. Mich. State U., 1965-70; head dept. agrl. econs. U. Ill., 1970-74; asst. sec. Dept. Agr., Washington, 1974-77; pres. Fed. Intermediate Credit Bank, Louisville, 1977—. Served with U.S. N.G., 1955-61. Mem. Am. Agrl. Econs. Assn. Club: Rotary. Contbr. numerous articles on agrl. econs. to profl. jours. Office: PO Box 32390 Louisville KY 40232

FELTON, FRANK P., III, savs. and loan assn. exec.; b. Phila., Apr. 10, 1928; s. Frank P. and Margaret (Margerison) F.; student Swarthmore Coll., 1946-48; m. Doris A. Brous, Sept. 17, 1953; children—Frank P., Donna Lee, Margaret A. With J. T. Jackson Co. and predecessor firms, Phila., 1948-63, v.p., sec., 1950-60, pres., 1960-63; v.p., mortgage officer Olney Fed. Savs. & Loan Assn., 1963-68, pres., 1968—. Mem. Jenkintown Sch. Bd., 1965-76, pres., 1975-76; bd. mgrs. Abington YMCA, 1964-70, chmn., 1968-70. Mem. Pa. Savs. League (dir. 1977-79), Insured Savs. Assns. Delaware Valley (pres. 1975), N.E. Phila. Bd. Realtors. Methodist (pres. Eastern Pa. Conf. 1966-67). Clubs: Union League of Phila., Seaview Country, Mfrs. Golf and Country, Ocean City Yacht. Office: 1407 Old York Rd Abington PA 19001

FELTON, STUART I., stockbroker; b. Cin., Nov. 7, 1921; s. Harry and Mollie (Bloom) F.; B.A., U. Louisville, 1946; m. Rosalie Feldman, Sept. 26; children—Marsha Beth, Paul Mark, Sanford Alan. Pres. Researched Investments, 1951—; tax cons., commodity broker, bus. analyst Houston; mktg. dir. Houston Council Trusts; internat. investment banker and securities broker; lectr. equity trusts; lectr. in field. Served to capt. USAAF, World War II; PTO. Decorated D.F.C., Air medal with six oak leaf clusters. Mem. Internat. Assn. Fin. Planners (v.p. Houston chpt. 1967), Nat. Assn. Securities Dealers, Nat. Assn. Profl. Bankers, Investment Research Inst. (founder), Nat. Soc. Registered Reps. Republican. Christian Scientist. Author: Life Insurance Shoppers Guide. Home: 1758 E 90th Pl Indianapolis IN 46240 Office: 6430 Richmond Ave Suite 300 Houston TX 77027

FELZER, ANN LICHTER, real estate broker; b. Chgo., Dec. 19, 1914; d. Stephen and Sophia Sonya (Tibel) Lichter; student Northwestern U., 1930-31, Tex. Christian U., 1931-32, U. Okla., 1933-36; m. May 19, 1935 (div. May 1962); children—Maxine Pua (Mrs. Richard Ranicke), Pamela Donna (Mrs. Thomas McDonnell). Asst. mgr. mail order div. Sears, Roebuck and Co., Chgo., 1930-35, div. mgr., Honolulu, 1950-55; asst. mgr. Raskins Jewelers, Oklahoma City, 1935-37; purchasing-sales mgr. Woods Jewelers, Wichita, Kans., 1937-41; nurse Poly Clinic Hosp., San Francisco, 1942-43; buyer-mgr. House of Linens, Honolulu, 1943-50; broker Waikiki Realty, Honolulu, 1955-59; owner, mgr. Ann Felzer Ltd., real estate counseling and financial cons., Honolulu, 1959; pres., prin. broker Felzer & Beamer, Inc., Honolulu, 1962—; pres., dir. Pilk Apt.-Hotel, 1960—; purchasing dir. Pathology Assos. Med. Lab., 1975—; broker comml. indsl. dept. Hugh Menefee Inc., Realtors, 1974—; reporter Global-News Syndicate; pres. Women's div. Hawaii Democratic Com., 1950. Recipient Outstanding Service award A.R.C., 1950. Mem. Nat. Assn. Real Estate Bds. (women's council), Real Estate Assn. Hawaii, Internat. Platform Assn., Honolulu Realty Bd., Honolulu C. of C., Honolulu Better Bus. Bur., Multiple Listing Service, Smithsonian Assos., Waikiki Bus. and Profl. Women's Club. Jewish religion (pres. women's div. temple 1947-48). Clubs: Traders, Polo (Honolulu). Home: Hilton Lagoon Apts 2003 Kalia Rd Honolulu HI 96815 Office: Diamond Head Towers Hilton Hawaiian Village Hotel Honolulu HI 96815

FENDRICH, CHARLES WELLES, JR., environ. and energy co. exec.; b. Washington, Nov. 18, 1924; s. Charles Welles and Ellen Francis (Friel) F.; B.S. in Engring. and Sci., Dartmouth Coll., 1946, postgrad. Tuck Sch. Bus. Adminstrn., 1947-48; postgrad. N.Y. U., 1954-56; m. Roberta Knope, Sept. 8, 1948; children—Kathleen, Patricia, Charles, Anne. Sales engr. Link Belt Co., N.Y.C., 1948-54; sales engr. Mech. Handling Systems, Inc., Detroit, 1954-56; asso. Stewart, Dougall & Assos., N.Y.C., 1956-60; dir. mktg. research Walworth Co., N.Y.C., 1960-62; dir. mktg. services B.F. Goodrich Co., Akron, Ohio, 1962-67; v.p. mktg. Ohio Rubber div. Eagle Picher Industries, 1967-69; mgr. mktg. projects ITT, N.Y.C. and Brussels, 1969-73, worldwide product line mgr. pumps, compressors and indsl. products, 1973-75; sr. v.p., mem. exec. com. Research Cottrell Inc., Somerville, N.J., 1975—. Bd. dirs., vice chmn. N.J. Research and Devel. Council, Environ. Industry Council, Washington, 1975-80; trustee N.J. Sci. and Tech. Center, 1980—; mem. adv. bd. Stuart Country Day Sch., Princeton, N.J., 1976—. Served to lt. (j.g.) USNR, 1943-47. Mem. N. Am. Planning Assn. Republican. Roman Catholic. Home: 122 Gallup Rd Princeton NJ 08540 Office: PO Box 1500 Somerville NJ 08876

FENN, MICHAEL THOMAS, hotel mgr.; b. Jersey City, Aug. 13, 1942; s. George Clifton and Doreen F.; A.A.S., Paul Smith's Coll., 1962; B.A.S., Cornell U., 1964. Foods and beverage controller Nat. Restaurant Assn., 1964-67; food and beverage dir. Biltmore Hotel, N.Y.C., 1967-70; dist. food and beverage dir. parent co. Holiday Inn, 1970-72; food and beverage dir. All Americana Hotels, 1973-76; gen. mgr. Best Western Skyline Hotel, N.Y.C., 1976-80; mng. dir. Hotel Mayflower, N.Y.C., 1980—. Awarded Internat. Escoffier Gold medal, 1973. Mem. Am. Chefs Assn., Am. Hotel Assn., Am. Bus. Assn., Nat. Tour Brokers Assn., U.S. Tour Operators Assn., Ont. Motor Coach Assn. Republican. Episcopalian. Home and Office: 15 Central Park W New York NY 10023

FENOLIO, RONALD LAWRENCE, lawyer, businessman; b. Antioch, Calif., Feb. 25, 1943; B.S. in Acctg., U. Calif., Berkeley, 1964, J.D. (Robert W. Harrison scholar 1965-66), 1967; LL.M. in Taxation (tuition scholar 1967-68), N.Y. U., 1970. Accountant, Edwin J. Donahue & Assos., C.P.A.'s, El Cerrito, Calif., 1963-64; spl. agt. IRS, summer 1965; admitted to Calif. bar, 1968; asst. to gen. counsel N.Y. U., 1967-68; asso. atty. firm Miller, Starr & Regalia, Oakland, Calif., 1968-70; partner firm Rosenblum, Fenolio, Parish, Jack & Bacigalupi, and predecessors, San Francisco, 1970-79, counsel, 1979—, vice chmn., sec., 1976-79; mem. faculty Merritt Coll., Oakland, 1969-70, Contra Costa Coll., San Pablo, Calif., 1969-72, San Francisco City Coll., 1971-75; gen. partner Veedercrest-Ringsbridge Vineyard and Winery, 1974—, Painter's Mill Assos., apt. units, 1979—, River Hills Assos., apt. units, 1979—, Camino Real Assos., apt. units, 1979—, Willows Assos., apt. units, 1978—; pres., chief fin. officer Fin. Resources, Ltd., 1979—; v.p., sec. Fin. Resources Adv. Services, 1979—; mng. partner Jacuzzi Estates Cos., 1979—; dir. Internat. Mfg. Co., 1975—, Autostyles, Inc., 1978—, Dealer Products, Inc., 1978—, Barcelon-Burger Mgmt. Corp., property mgmt., 1978-79, Eugene Burger Mgmt. Corp., 1979—; lectr., seminar leader real estate law, tax shelters. Pres. San Francisco chpt. Calif. Republican League, 1972-73; a founder Performing Arts Center San Francisco, 1980. Mem. Am. Bar Assn., Nat. Assn. Realtors, State Bar Assn. Calif., Calif. Assn. Realtors (chmn. coms. 1975—), San Francisco Bar Assn., Italian Am. Bar Assn. (pres., dir. No. Calif. chpt. 1979-80), San Francisco C. of C., Internat. Wine and Food Soc., Wine Inst. Calif., Il Cenacolo, Leonardo Da Vinci Soc., Alpha Kappa Psi, Phi Alpha Delta. Clubs: Commonwealth, Olympic (San Francisco). Author booklets for real estate assns. Address: 114 Sansome St 10th Floor San Francisco CA 94104

FENSTAMAKER, RICHARD LISLE, steel fabricating exec.; b. Williamsport, Pa., Feb. 24, 1937; s. Richard Lee and Frances Elizabeth (Wilkinson) F.; A.B., Coll. William and Mary, 1959; J.D., U. Iowa, 1963; m. Andree Marie Pineau, Aug. 22, 1959; children—Richard Lisle, Ann Elizabeth, Karen Kay, Wendy Elaine. Admitted to Iowa bar, 1963, N.Y. bar, 1964, Pa. bar, 1967, Supreme Ct. U.S., 1965; asso. Pell, Butler, Curtis & LeViness, N.Y.C., 1963-65; exec. v.p. Radiant Steel Products Co., Williamsport, 1965-69, pres., dir., chmn. bd., 1969—; instr. estate and taxation law Conn. Mut. Life Ins. Co. Sub-chmn. United Way drives, 1967-70, Cancer Crusade, 1967-69; mem. Loyalsock Twp. Zoning Hearing Bd., 1970-75, also sec.; arbitrator Lycoming County Ct. System, 1968—, marital relations master, 1968-71; active fund drives Coll. William and Mary, 1969—; mem. UN Day com. UN, 1976, subchmn., 1978. Mem. Am., N.Y., Iowa, Pa., Lycoming County bar assns., Bar City N.Y. (merit service award 1966), West Branch Mfrs. Assn., Iowa Alumni Assn. (life), Nat. Assn. Ind. Businessmen, NAM, N.E. R.R. Task Force. Republican. Presbyterian. Clubs: Williamsport Country, Village Bath

(Manhasset, N.Y.), Old Capital. Home: 1621 Sheridan St Williamsport PA 17701 Office: 205 Locust St Williamsport PA 17701

FENSTERSTOCK, LYLE SUMNER, fin. cons. co. exec.; b. N.Y.C., Mar. 24, 1948; s. Nathaniel and Gertrude F.; B.A. cum laude, Brandeis U., 1969; M.B.A., (Lamont fellow), Harvard U., 1971; m. Linda Painter, Nov. 18, 1972. Vice pres. Warburg, Paribas, Becker, Chgo., 1971-75; investment banker Salomon Bros., Chgo., 1976; dir. bus. devel. Quaker Oats, Chgo., 1976-78; pres. Fensterstock & Co., Chgo., 1978—. Mem. Assn. Corp. Growth, Assn. Accts. for Coops. Club: Carlton. Home: 200 E Delaware Pl 34C Chicago IL 60611 Office: 625 N Michigan Ave Suite 1530 Chicago IL 60611

FENTON, MICHAEL STEPHEN, telephone co. exec.; b. Gloversville, N.Y., Sept. 30, 1939; s. Max I. and Ethel T. Fenton; B.B.A., Clarkson Coll. Tech., 1961; m. Marcia Heltzer, Nov. 22, 1962; 1 son, Geoffrey David. Acct., Lybrand Ross Bros., N.Y.C., 1961-62; acctg. supr. networks spl. cost study assignment AT&T Long Lines, Bridgewater, N.J., 1966-67, overseas ops. internat. service, 1967-69, ops. mgr., 1969-70, sales mgr., 1970-71, info. mgr., 1971-72, personnel mgr., benefits mgmt. tng., 1972-75, overseas ops. mgr., 1975-77, mem. nat. contract bargaining, 1977, nat. accounts mgr., 1977—. Pres., Am. Field Service, Parsippany, N.J., 1979—. Served to capt. U.S. Army, 1962-66. Decorated Def. Ribbon. Mem. Am. Mgmt. Assn., Arts Assn. N.J. Jewish. Office: 1425 Frontier Rd Bridgewater NJ 08807

FENZI, WARREN EMANUELE, mining co. exec.; b. Santa Barbara, Calif., Aug. 4, 1915; s. Camillo and Dorothy (Redfield) F.; B.S. in Civil Engring., Calif. Inst. Tech., 1937; m. Eleanor Leeds, July 12, 1940; children—Charles C., Louise R., Warren S., Joan F. and David L. (twins). With Phelps Dodge Corp., 1937-80, asst. to v.p., gen. mgr. Western div., Douglas, Ariz., 1957-59, asst. to pres., N.Y.C., 1959-62, v.p., 1962-66, exec. v.p., 1966-75, pres., 1975-80, currently dir.; dir. St. Joe Mineral Corp., 1967—. Served with USNR, 1944-46; PTO. Mem. Am. Inst. Mining Engrs. Home: 2121 Garden St Santa Barbara CA 93105 Office: 300 Park Ave New York NY 10022

FERGUSON, FRANCIS EUGENE, ins. exec.; b. Batavia, N.Y., Feb. 4, 1921; s. Harold M. and Florence (Munger) F.; student Cornell U., 1938-39; B.S., Mich. State U., 1947; m. Patricia J. Reddy, Aug. 11, 1945; children—Susan Lee, Patricia Ann. Asst. sec.-treas. Fed. Land Bank Assn., Lansing, Mich., 1947-48; appraiser Fed. Land Bank, St. Paul, 1948-50; specialist agrl. econs. Mich. State U. Extension, 1951; with Northwestern Mut. Life Ins. Co., Milw., 1951—, specialist, 1951-52, asst. mgr. farm loans, 1952-56, mgr. farm loans, 1956-62, gen. mgr. mortgage loans, 1962-63, v.p. mortgage loans, 1963-67, pres., 1967-80, chmn. and chief exec. officer, 1980—; trustee Northwestern Mut.; pres. Milw. Redevel. Corp.; dir. Ralston Purina Co., Wis. Gas Co., Oscar Mayer & Co., Inc., Rexnord, Inc., Green Bay Packaging, Inc., The Singer Co. Bd. dirs. Greater Milw. Com., Columbia Hosp., Com. for Econ. Devel.; corp. mem. Milw. Children's Hosp., Milw. Boys Club; chmn. council Med. Coll. Wis. Served to capt. USAAF, Methodist. Clubs: Milwaukee, University, Milwaukee Country. Office: 720 E Wisconsin Ave Milwaukee WI 53202

FERGUSON, JAMES FELTON, mgmt. cons.; b. Dawson, Ga., Mar. 4, 1941; s. James Felton and Daisy Evelyn (Reese) F.; B.A., Wesleyan U., 1963; grad. Program Mgmt. Devel., Harvard Bus. Sch., 1972; children—Tracy Nicole, Albert Lloyd. Mgmt. trainee Chem. Bank, N.Y. Trust Co., 1963; master of English, Kent (Conn.) Sch., 1967-69; prin. McKinsey & Co., Inc., Washington, 1969-78; dir. Ferguson, Bryan & Assos., Washington, 1978—; mem. Bd. of Trade Met. Washington. Chmn. bd. Race Relations Info. Center, 1973-75; mem. Voice of Informed Community Expression, 1974—; bd. dirs. Jr. Achievement of Met. Washington, 1977—, D.C. chpt. ARC; chmn. bd. dirs. Black Alumni, Harvard Bus. Sch. Served with U.S. Army, 1964-67. Mem. Harvard Bus. Sch. Alumni Assn. Episcopalian. Home: 2601 Park Center Dr Alexandria VA 22302 Office: 2550 M St NW Washington DC 20037

FERGUSON, JAMES LARNARD, food co. exec.; b. Evanston, Ill., Mar. 16, 1926; s. J. Larnard and Justine (Dickson) F.; A.B., Hamilton Coll., 1949; M.B.A., Harvard U., 1951; m. Elizabeth Rich, June 17, 1950; children—Deborah, John Dickson, Douglas. Asso. advt. mgr. Procter & Gamble, Cin., 1951-62; sr. v.p. account supr. Lennon & Newell Advt., N.Y.C., 1962-63; asst. to mktg. mgr. Birds Eye Div. Gen. Foods Corp., White Plains, N.Y., 1963, mktg. product devel. positions, 1963-67, gen. mgr. Birds Eye div., 1967-68, corp. v.p., 1968-70, group v.p., 1970-72, exec. v.p., 1972, pres., 1972-77, chief exec. officer, 1973—, chief operating officer, 1972, chmn., 1974—, dir., 1972—; dir. Union Carbide Corp. Trustee, Hamilton Coll. Served with AUS, 1944-46. Mem. Bus. Roundtable, Grocery Mfrs. Assn. Am. (dir., chmn.), The Conf. Bd., SRI Internat. Council, Econ. Club, Confrerie des Chevaliers du Tastevin. Episcopalian (sr. warden 1971—). Clubs: Wilton Riding; Blindbrook; Clove Valley Rod and Gun; Silver Spring Country (Ridgefield, Conn.); Links; Woodway Gun. Office: 250 North St White Plains NY 10625

FERGUSON, JOHN LESLIE, II, advt. agy. exec.; b. Glen Ridge, N.J., May 30, 1940; s. Leslie Inglis and Mary Carolyn (Jones) F.; B.A., Princeton, 1962; M.B.A., Columbia, 1968; m. Paula Cronin, June 18, 1966; children—Christopher John, Heidi Inglis, Bradley Hamilton. Product mgr. Gen. Foods Corp., White Plains, N.Y., 1968-72; sr. product mgr. Dixie Consumer Products div. Am. Can Co., Greenwich, Conn., 1972-74; v.p. 1st Nat. City Bank, N.Y.C., 1974-75; v.p. Consumer Products div. Riegel Textile Corp., Johnston, S.C., 1975-77; v.p. Hicks & Greist, Inc., N.Y.C., 1977—; career counselor Grad. Sch. Bus. Columbia. Vice pres. North Wilton (Conn.) Assn., 1970-75. Served with USN, 1962-66. Mem. Am. Mktg. Assn. Republican. Episcopalian. Clubs: Wilton Riding, Wilton Soccer Assn., Houndslake Country, Westcliff Swimming. Office: 522 Fifth Ave New York NY 10036

FERGUSON, JOHN RICHARD, publishing co. exec.; b. Columbus, Ohio, Oct. 23, 1937; s. Charles A. and A. Mildred (Weate) F.; A.A., Graceland Coll., 1957, B.L.S., 1973; student Harbor Coll., 1957, Calif. State Coll., 1965, Rockhurst Coll., 1970-71; m. Carole Mae Sturtevant, Aug. 16, 1957; children—Steven Paul, Connie Marie. Mgr. retail depts. Sears Roebuck and Co., Riverside, Calif., 1959-63, personnel mgr., 1964-66; ordained to ministry Reorganized Ch. Jesus Christ of Latter-day Saints, 1955; minister Long Beach (Calif.) Ch., 1963-64; dist. pres. Reorganized Ch. Jesus Christ of Latter Day Saints, Los Angeles, 1966-68; asst. mgr. Herald Pub. House, Independence, Mo., 1968-69, mgr., 1969—; pres. Silver Fox Ltd., realty, Ferguson Realty; dir. Standard State Bank, Sta. KMOS-TV, KCMW-FM. Pres. Independence Bd. Edn., 1970-76; bd. dirs. Health Missions Internat., Buckhorn Camp., Met. Kansas City chpt. Leukemia Soc., Independence YMCA; dir. N.W. Mo. Citizens Probation and Parole Bd.; v.p. Independence Neighborhood Councils. Named Independence Citizen of Yr., 1979. Mem. Protestant Church-Owned Publs. Assn. (dir. 1970—), Independence C. of C. (dir. 1977-79, pres. 1978-79). Clubs: Lions (charter pres. Independence 1970), Independence Rotary. Contbr. articles to religious publs. Home: 14925 E 33d St Independence MO 64055 Office: 3225 S Noland Rd PO Drawer HH Independence MO 64055

FERGUSON, KENNETH BRIAN, computer corp. exec.; b. Newark, Aug. 18, 1954; s. John Francis and Grace Louise (Reilly) F.; B.S. in Chem. Engring., Lehigh U., 1976; postgrad. U. Del., 1977—. Corp. program process engr. ICI Ams., Bayonne, N.J., 1976-77, programmer, Wilmington, Del., 1977, sci. programmer, 1977-80, sci. analyst, 1980-81; asso. process engr. ARCO Petroleum Products Co., Phila., 1981—. Mem. Am. Inst. Chem. Engrs., Sigma Xi. Roman Catholic. Club: Fall-Line Ski. Home: 13 West Court Beacon Hill Wilmington DE 19810 Office: ARCO Petroleum Products Co PO Box 7258 Philadelphia PA 19101

FERGUSON, NEIL TAYLOR, savs. and loan exec.; b. Alameda, Calif., Mar. 15, 1922; s. Hector Donald and Erna (Taylor) F.; A.A., San Francisco City Coll., 1941; B.B.A., San Jose State Coll., 1944. Founder Mut. Fund Assos., Inc., San Francisco, 1951, pres., 1951-70; v.p. Putnam Mgmt. Co., Boston, 1961-74, dir., 1961-72; chmn. bd., chief exec. officer Putnam Financial Services, Inc., San Rafael, Calif., 1971-74; chmn. Western Travelers Life Ins. Co., San Rafael, 1972-73, Centennial Savs. & Loan Assn., Guerneville, Calif.; pres. Funded Investors Inc., San Rafael, 1971-72, Union R.R. of Oreg.; chmn. Sierra Western Rail Corp.; partner Jamestown Hotel & R.R. Consultants. Mem. citizens adv. com., San Rafael, 1974—; mem. citizens adv. com., Forestville, Calif., 1973—; bd. dirs. Clear Water Ranch Children's House, Inc., Philo, Calif., 1952—, Forestville Park Devel., Russian River Renewal, Inc.; treas., mem. exec. com. President's Assos., Sonoma State U.; mem. adv. bd. Our Little Bros. and Sisters Orphanage, Mex., Ret. Sr. Vol. Program of Sonoma County. Served as lt., USNR, 1942-46. Named Citizen of the Year, Forestville, 1974. Mem. Marin County (dir. 1973-74), Forestville (dir. 1973—, pres. 1977, v.p. 1979-80) chambers commerce, Young Pres. Orgn. (sec. 1967), Nat. Assn. Security Dealers (dist. bus. conduct com. 1972-74), Grange, Cal. Acad. Sci., UN Orgn., Am. Assn. Pvt. R.R. Car Owners (v.p. 1980—). Club: Commonwealth (San Francisco). Home: 10650 Woodside Dr Forestville CA 95436 Office: Main and Church Sts Guerneville CA 95466

FERGUSON, RAY SHENDLER, paper co. sales exec.; b. Richmond, Ind., Aug. 12, 1946; s. Francis Robert and Marjorie Rhea (Shendler) F.; B.S. in Mktg., Ball State U., 1970; m. Melanie L. Garrett, Nov. 28, 1965; children—Lora E., Mark A., Peter R. Successively inventory control, buyer, salesman Schwartz Paper Co., Muncie, Ind., 1968-74, v.p. sales, 1974—. Active YMCA, United Way, local youth baseball program; gen. chmn. Delaware County fund drive Ball State U., 1979, 80; bd. dirs. Ball State U. Alumni Council. Named Outstanding Jaycee, 1978. Mem. Nat. Paper Trade Assn., Midwest Paper Assn. (2d v.p. 1979-80), Ball State U. Coll. Bus. Alumni Assn. (pres.), Muncie Jaycees (bd. dirs. 1971-73, pres. 1979-80). Methodist. Clubs: Elks, Moose. Home: 8212 N Ravenwood Dr Muncie IN 47302 Office: PO Box 2788 Muncie IN 47302

FERGUSON, ROGER NEPHI, bus. exec.; b. Ocean Park, Calif., Sept. 6, 1932; s. Byron Robert and Fawn (Christensen) F.; student Brigham Young U., 1951; m. Sybil Rae Clarke, July 10, 1952; children—Debra Kay, Michael David, Wade Clarke, Lois Christine, Julie Xarissa. Constrn. asbestos worker, 1952-72; pres. Asbestos Union, 1965-67; regional mgr. Am. Bio Chem. Co., 1972-75; pres. Diet Center, Inc., nutrition and weight reducing franchise, Rexburg, Idaho, 1971—; pres., dir. Internat. Livestock, Inc., Sybil's, Inc., Ferguson and Assos., Ferguson & Co., Print Shop, Ferguson Pharms.; co-owner Big Grassy Ranch. Mem. Rexburg C. of C., Better Bus. Bur., Nat. Fedn. Ind. Businesses, Upper Snake River Valley Hist. Soc., City Golf Assn. (dir.). Mormon. Club: Ricks Coll. Booster. Home: 401 Maple St Rexburg ID 83440 Office: Diet Center Inc 76 W Main Rexburg ID 83440

FERGUSON, SYBIL RAE, diet counselor, business woman; b. Barnwell, Alta., Can., Feb. 7, 1934; came to U.S., 1938, naturalized, 1976; d. Alva John and Xarissa (Merkley) Clarke; student public schs., Provo, Utah; m. Roger N. Ferguson, July 10, 1952; children—Debra Kay, Michael David, Wade Clarke, Lois Christine, Julie Xarissa. Founder, Diet Center, Inc., Rexburg, Idaho, 1970, with 2,500 franchises in U.S., Can. and Europe, counselor, program developer, 1970—; co-owner Big Grassy (6,000-acre potato ranch); sec., dir. Internat. Livestock, Inc., Sybil's, Inc., Ferguson and Assos., Print Shop, Ferguson Pharms., Diet Center, Inc. Recipient Bus. Leader of Yr. award Ricks Coll., 1980. Mem. Rexburg C. of C. (program dir. 1976). Mormon. Clubs: Rexburg Civic, Soroptimists (v.p., 1975, recipient award, 1979). Author, pub. books on diet and nutrition, manual for operating diet center franchise, instructional series on behavior modification, monthly newsletter on nutrition; contbr. to monthly mag. The Advantage. Home: 401 Maple St Rexburg ID 83440 Office: Diet Center Inc 76 W Main St Rexburg ID 83440

FERGUSON, WARREN MONROE, ins. co. exec.; b. Colorado Springs, Colo., Aug. 26, 1935; s. Alfred Monroe and Rosella Ethelberta Ferguson; ed. St. Martin's Coll., 1958-61, U. Wash. Law Sch., 1961-63; m. Harriet Ann Ryan, July 20, 1957; children—Jeffrey Monroe, Sharon Rose. Law clk. firm Johnson-Jonson & Innslee, Seattle, 1962-63; with Safeco Ins. Co., Seattle, 1963-75, comml. lines mgr. NW Div., 1969-72, div. mgr. group accounts, 1973-75; v.p. underwriting Hanover Ins. Cos., Worcester, Mass., 1975-80; Sr. v.p., chief operating officer Allianz Ins. Co., Los Angeles, 1981—; chmn. governing com. Wash. State FAIR Plan, 1971-72; bd. govs. Worker's Compensation Re-ins. Bur., 1975-80; mem. exec. com. Aviation Re-ins. Bur., 1975-80; bd. dirs. Ins. Services Office, 1976-79; mem. adv. com. underwriting program Ins. Inst. Am., 1977—. Served with USMC, 1953-56. Mem. Soc. Chartered Property and Casualty Underwriters. Republican. Conglist. Clubs: Plaza, Marines Meml., New Eng. AAU. Home: 23 Keep Ave Paxton MA 01612 Office: 6435 Wilshire Blvd Los Angeles CA 90054

FERGUSON, WILLIAM EMMETT, securities co. exec.; b. Quincy, Mass., Dec. 21, 1902; s. Patrick J. and Margaret F. (O'Brien) F.; m. July 6, 1935. With Thomson McKinnon Securities Inc., N.Y.C., 1919—, chmn., 1969—; dir. McKeon Constrn. Co. Mem. Chgo. Bd. Trade, Kansas City Bd. Trade. Clubs: N.Y. Athletic, Union League, Beverly Country. Office: 1 New York Plaza New York NY 10004

FERIS, DOROTHY AMELIA, aircraft corp. exec.; b. Downers Grove, Ill., Sept. 21, 1922; d. Joseph and Frances (Dvorak) Slanec; student public schs., Downers Grove, Ill.; children—Herbert Charles, Timothy Lee. Sec., Joseph T. Ryerson & Sons, Chgo., 1940-44; sec.-treas. Taylorcraft Aviation Corp., Alliance, Ohio, 1968-76, pres., 1976—. Mem. Alliance C. of C., Aircraft Owner's and Pilot's Assn., Taylorcraft Owner's Club, Exptl. Aircraft Assn. Home: 2711 S Union Ave Apt 18 Alliance OH 44601 also 32 S Wilmette St Westmont IL 60559 Office: PO Box 243 14600 Commerce St NE Alliance OH 44601

FERMAN, IRVING, lawyer, educator; b. N.Y.C., July 4, 1919; s. Joseph and Sadie (Stein) F.; B.S., N.Y. U., 1941; LL.B., Harvard U., 1948; m. Bertha Paglin, June 12, 1946; children—James Paglin, Susan Paglin. Admitted to La. bar, 1948; partner Provensal, Faris & Ferman, New Orleans, 1948-52; dir. Washington office ACLU, 1952-59; vice chmn. Nat. Civil Liberties Clearing House, 1952-54; exec. vice chmn. Pres.'s Com. Govt. Contracts, 1959-60; v.p. Internat. Latex Corp., 1960-66, cons., 1966-67; pres. Piedmont Theatres Corp., Lynchburg, Va., 1967-69; asso. prof. mgmt. N.Y. U., 1964-68; prof. law Howard U., Washington, 1968—. Chmn., D.C. Police Complaint Rev. Bd., 1965-73; mem. Am. Com. for Cultural Freedom, 1954—, Com. of Arts and Scis. for Eisenhower, 1956; mem. citizens adv. com. U.S. Commn. on Govt. Security, 1957; mem. reviewing authority HEW, 1969-79. Bd. dirs. New Orleans Acad. Art, 1948-51. Served from cadet to 1st lt. USAAF, 1942-46. Mem. Am., La., New Orleans, D.C. bar assns. Jewish. Clubs: Internat., Capitol Hill (Washington); Army-Navy Country (Arlington, Va.); Harvard, Caterpillar (N.Y.C.). Home: 3818 Huntington St Washington DC 20015 also Route 1 Sullivan Harbor ME 04682

FERNALD, CHARLES E., transp. cons.; b. Downingtown, Pa., Sept. 28, 1902; s. Joshiah Pennell and Sophia (Weltner) F.; student mech. engring. Drexel Inst. Tech., 1921-24; student Wharton Sch., U. Pa., 1926-30; m. Gertrude Marie Connell, Oct. 17, 1936; 1 son, Charles Edward. With credit dept. Notaseme Hosiery Co., 1919-22; purchasing agt. Haslett Chute & Conveyor Co., Oaks, Pa., 1922-24; sr. Partner Fernald & Co., Phila., 1924-64; sec., dir., chmn. finance com. Chem. Leaman Corp., Downington, 1964—. Active in work Republican Com. Past pres., trustee Credit Research Found. Served as lt. (j.g.) on spl. assignments USN, USCGR, World War II. C.P.A., Pa., N.J., N.Y., Ill. Mem. Am. Inst. C.P.A.'s, Pa., N.J., N.Y. Ill. socs. C.P.A.'s, Nat. Assn. Credit Mgmt. (past nat. pres.). Clubs: Union League (Phila.); Union League (Chgo.); JDM Country (Palm Gardens, Fla.). Home: 2600 N Flager Dr West Palm Beach FL 33407 Office: PO Box 179 Downingtown PA 19335

FERNANDEZ, D. RAUL petroleum mgmt. and fin. cons.; b. N.Y.C., Apr. 17, 1943; s. Delfin and Josephine (Ibarra) F.; B.B.A., Pace U., 1964, M.B.A., 1969; m. Raquel Iwrey, June 30, 1967; 1 dau., Lisa Renee. With Shell Oil Co., 1964-74, corporate auditor, Houston, 1971-74; mgr. accounting Amerada-Hess Corp., Woodbridge, N.J., 1974-75; mgr. spl. projects Hooker Chem. Corp., Houston, 1975-78; mgr. mgmt. cons. Peat, Marwick, Mitchell & Co., Houston, 1978—; cons. in field. Dir., treas. Community Civic Assn., Houston, 1972-74; trustee Norchester Maintenance Fund., Inc., Houston, 1974—; dir., treas. Huntwick Civic Assn., 1980—. Recipient Leadership in Action award U.S. Jaycees, 1974. Mem. Assn. Corp. Growth, Am. Mgmt. Assn., Petroleum Accts. Soc. Club: Toastmasters (pres. 1979). Home: 13702 Balmore Circle Houston TX 77069 Office: 4300 One Shell Plaza Houston TX 77002

FERNANDEZ, NINO JOSEPH, communications and fin. relations exec.; b. Bklyn., June 17, 1941; s. Saturnino and Anna (Santeramo) F.; B.B.A., Adelphi U., 1967; M.B.A., Pace U., 1971; children—Nino Harold, Karla Leigh. Sr. analyst fin. relations Am. Airlines, N.Y.C., 1967-70; asst. dir. investor relations Gen. Telephone & Electronics, Stamford, Conn., 1970-73; dir. communications Gen. Signal Corp., 1974—. Served with USMCR, 1959-65. Mem. Nat. Investor Relations Inst. (treas., dir.). Republican. Roman Catholic. Home: One Strawberry Hill Ave Stamford CT 06902 Office: General Signal Corp High Ridge Park Stamford CT 06904

FERNANDEZ, TELESFORO, JR., clothing industry exec.; b. San Juan, P.R., Nov. 25, 1942; s. Telesforo and Luisa (Martinez) F.; B.S. in Econs., U. Pa., 1965; m. Awilda A. Rodriguez, Nov. 23, 1967; children—Telesforo, Andres Alexis, Cristina Alexandra. Vice pres., treas. La Esquina Famosa, San Juan, 1965-68, v.p., treas., 1969-77, pres., 1977—; account exec. Young & Rubicam P.R., Inc., San Juan, 1968-69; dir., v.p., treas., prin. Telesforo Fernandez & Hermano, Inc.; dir. P.R. Electric Power Authority, Girod Trust Co.; mem. Dist. Export Council P.R. and V.I. Pres. P.R. council USO. Mem. Menswear Retailers Am., P.R. C. of C., Sales and Mktg. Assn. San Juan (mgmt. award 1972), Young President's Orgn., Audubon Soc., AFDA Frat. Republican. Roman Catholic. Clubs: N.Y. Athletic, Caparra Country, Rotary. Home: 525 Tintillo Rd Guaynabo PR 00657 Office: GPO Box G 2624 San Juan PR 00936

FERRARA, ROCCO, vocat. sch. exec.; b. N.Y.C., Jan. 2, 1924; s. Biagio and Dolores (Busco) F.; student public schs., N.Y.C.; m. Sheila Traktman, Jan. 18, 1960; children—Vincent, Paul, Robert, Gary, Linda, Rocco, Gregory. Tchr. pvt. vocat. schs., platform stylist, make-up artist, columnist, 1948-59; owner, pres. Robert Fiance Bus. Inst., N.Y.C., 1976—, Robert Fiance Hair Design Inst., N.Y.C., 1959—; examiner Nat. Cosmetology Accrediting Commn., 1973—. Mem. adv. council Westchester Bd. Coop. Edn. Services; Republican candidate for mayor and supr., Harrison, N.Y., 1979; mem. Rep. U.S. Senatorial Bus. Adv. Bd., 1981. Mem. Nat. Assn. Cosmetology Schs. Mems., Registered Bus. Sch. Assn. N.Y. State, N.Y. State Beauty Sch. Assn. (pres. 1975-77), Pvt. Vocat. Schs. Assn. N.Y. (dir. 1976-78). Author: Comprehensive Management Manual, 1977. Office: 404 Fifth Ave New York NY 10018

FERRER, GONZALO GUSTAVO, civil engr., real estate appraiser; b. Hato Rey, P.R., Aug. 2, 1936; s. Miguel and Gloria (Rincon) F.; B.C.E., Cornell U., Ithaca, N.Y., 1958; m. Maria del Pilar Viscasillas, Sept. 3, 1960; children—Pilarin, Priscilla, Monica, Gonzalo Miguel, Gustavo Xavier. Structural engr. O'Kelly, Mendez & Brunner, architects and engrs., San Juan, P.R., 1959; sec., Ramirez de Arellano & Co. Inc., San Juan, 1959-76, also dir.; partner Robert F. McCloskey Assos., San Juan, 1976—; lectr. in field. Mem. Soc. Real Estate Appraisers (sr. real property appraiser, pres. chpt. 171 P.R. 1976-77), Am. Inst. Real Estate Appraisers, P.R. Home Builders Assn. (treas. 1974-75), Colegio de Ingenieros, Arquitectos y Agrimensores de P.R., AFDA Fraternity (treas. 1973-75), Chi Epsilon. Roman Catholic. Clubs: Caribe Hilton, Swimming and Tennis. Home: 4 Meadow Ln Georgetown Guaynabo PR 00657

FERRIS, CHARLES DANIEL, govt. ofcl.; b. Boston, Apr. 9, 1933; s. Henry Joseph and Mildred Mary (MacDonald) F.; A.B., Boston Coll., 1954, J.D., 1961, LL.D. (hon.), 1978; grad. advanced mgmt. program Harvard U., 1971; m. Patricia Catherine Brennan; children—Caroline, Sabrina. Jr. physicist Sperry Gyroscope Co., Gt. Neck, N.Y.C., 1954-55; asst. prof. naval sci. Harvard U., 1958-60; admitted to Mass. bar, 1961, D.C. bar, 1969; trial atty. Dept. Justice, Washington, 1961-63; gen. counsel U.S. Senate Democratic Policy Com., U.S. Senate Majority Counselor, also gen. counsel U.S. Senate Majority Leader Mansfield, 1963-76; gen. counsel U.S. Ho. of Reps. Speaker Thomas P. O'Neil, 1977; chmn. FCC, Washington, 1977—. Served with USN, 1955-60. Mem. Mass. Bar Assn., D.C. Bar Assn. Democrat. Roman Catholic. Office: FCC 1919 M St Washington DC 20554*

FERRIS, GEORGE MALLETTE, investment banker; b. Newtown, Conn., Sept. 25, 1894; s. George B. and Bertha E. (Clark) F.; A.B., Trinity Coll., 1916, LL.D.; LL.D., Gallaudet Coll.; m. Charlotte Hamilton, Apr. 14, 1920; children—Genie, George M. Investment banker, 1920—; chmn. bd. Ferris & Co., Inc., Washington, 1933-71, chmn. bd., 1971—; sr. partner Ferris & Co., Washington, 1946—; mem. N.Y. Stock Exchange; dir. Am. Fed. Savs. & Loan Assn. Former chmn. bd. govs. Chevy Chase Village; bd. dirs. Sibley Hosp.; trustee, treas. Gallaudet Coll.; trustee emeritus Trinity Coll. Mem. Washington Bd. Trade, Alpha Chi Rho. Clubs: Masons, Rotary, Chevy Chase; Columbia; Metropolitan (Washington); Burning Tree. Home: 5810 Cedar Pkwy Chevy Chase MD 20015 Office: 1720 I St NW Washington DC 20006

FERRIS, RICHARD J., airline exec.; b. Sacramento, 1932; B.S., Cornell U., 1962; postgrad. in Bus., U. Wash. Staff analyst, restaurant mgr. Olympic Hotel; with Anchorage Westward Hotel; gen. mgr. Continental Plaza Hotel; gen. mgr. Carlton Hotel; project officer-new constrn. Western Internat. Hotels; pres. carrier's food service div., then sr. v.p.-mktg. United Air Lines, Inc., 1971-75, pres., 1975-77, chmn., 1977—, chief exec. officer, 1976—, also dir.; dir. Western Internat. Hotels. Office: United Air Lines Inc 1200 Algonquin Rd Mount Prospect IL 60007*

FERRIS, ROBERT CHARLES, nuclear chemist, lab. exec.; b. Norwood, Mass., Jan. 6, 1941; s. Mitchell and Olga Ann (Eysie) F.; B.A., St. Anselm's Coll., 1962; children—Joy Lynne, Clare Beth, Adam Michael. Application chemist Gen. Latex & Chem. Corp., Cambridge, Mass., 1962-65; v.p., site mgr. Cambridge Nuclear Corp., Billerica, Mass., 1965-71; research cons. VA Hosp., West Roxbury, Mass., 1971-72; founder, pres. Gamma Diagnostic Labs., Attleboro, Mass., 1972—. Roman Catholic. Home: 3 Commonwealth Ave Attleboro MA 02703 Office: Gamma Diagnostic Labs 50 Walton St Attleboro MA 02703

FERRO, ANTHONY MICHAEL, utility co. exec.; b. N.Y.C., May 2, 1947; s. Michael and Margaret (LaTrace) F.; B.B.A., Manhattan Coll., 1968; M.B.A. with distinction, L.I. U., 1974; m. Joanne M. Juliano, Sept. 26, 1971; children—Michael Anthony, James Matthew. Tchr. sci., history St. Francis of Paola Sch., 1968-69; with Consol. Edison Co., N.Y.C., 1969—, govtl. billing mgr., 1973-77, tariff adminstr., 1977—; speaker submetering and time of day seminars, 1979—. Sec., Williamsburg Little League, 1967-71. Pope scholar, 1960-64. Mem. Am. Mgmt. Assn., Am. Mktg. Assn. Home: 2536 Lefferts Pl Bellmore NY 11710 Office: Consol Edison Co 4 Irving Pl New York NY 10003

FERRO, DENNIS HENRY, banker; b. Yonkers, N.Y., June 20, 1945; s. Henry Albert and Helen Elizabeth (Moriarty) F.; B.A., Villanova U., 1967; M.B.A. in Fin., St. John's U., 1974; m. Elle B. McKee, Nov. 1, 1967; children—Jeffrey, Tracy. Mgmt. trainee, asst. trust officer, trust officer, v.p. investments Bankers Trust Co., Palm Beach, Fla., 1969—. Bd. dirs. J.F. and E.D.K. Found. Served with AUS, 1967-69. Decorated Bronze Star with oak leaf cluster. Mem. Fin. Analysts Soc. Miami, Miami Fin. Analyst Soc. Club: Atlantis Country. Office: 250 Royal Palm Way Palm Beach FL 33480

FERRUCCI, GABRIELE, indsl. products co. exec.; b. Amorosi, Benevento, Italy, Feb. 1, 1936; s. Giuseppe and Esterina I. (Festa) F.; B.S. in Edn., G. Guacci Coll., Italy, 1956; B.S. in Accounting, Quinnipiac Coll., Hamden, Conn., 1965; m. Maria Maddaloni, Oct. 25, 1956; children—Rina, Anna Maria, Joseph. Tchr., Latin and Italian langs. Amorosi Pub. Schs., 1956-57; machinist Precision Machine, Inc., Orange, Conn., 1958-59, controller High Percision, Inc., Hamden, Conn., 1964-71, dir., 1968-71; machinist Interstate Mfg. Co., Inc., Orange, 1959-63; accountant Sound Scriber, Inc., North Haven, Conn., 1963; controller Raybestos Manhattan Internat., 1971-72, mgr. corp. acctg. Raybestos Manhattan, Inc., Trumbull, Conn., 1973-74, v.p., 1978—, controller Raybestos Manhattan Indsl. Products Co. div., North Charleston, S.C., 1974-75, v.p. adminstrn., 1975-76, pres., 1976-80, pres., gen. mgr. internat. div., Trumbull, Conn., 1980—. Mem. Export Mgrs. Club. (officer 1971-73, pres. 1974), Nat. Assn. Accountants (dir. 1971-73, sec. 1973-74), Am. Mgmt. Assn. Roman Catholic. Home: 245 Townehouse Rd Fairfield CT 06430 Office: 100 Oakview Dr Trumbull CT 06611

FERTIG, LEONARD MARTIN, airline and communications cons.; b. Newark, Feb. 25, 1947; s. Harold Irving and Sylvia (Wiskind) F.; B.S., Columbia U., 1969, M.S., 1971, postgrad., 1972; m. Susan Arlene Schweiger, Sept. 1, 1969; 1 dau., Deborah Hope. Systems analyst Grumman Aerospace Corp., Bethpage, N.Y., 1969-71; project engr. Trans World Airlines, Inc., N.Y.C., 1972-74; dir. fin. systems devel. Am. Airlines, N.Y.C., 1974-77, sr. dir. pricing, 1977-79; v.p. product devel. Travel Network Corp., N.Y.C., 1979-80; cons., 1980—. Mem. Am. Inst. Indsl. Engrs. (sr.). Home: 890 Edison St Washington Township NJ 07675

FERY, JOHN BRUCE, paper mfg. co. exec.; b. Bellingham, Wash., Feb. 16, 1930; s. Carl S. and Margaret (Haack) F.; B.A., U. Wash., 1953; M.B.A., Stanford, 1955; m. Delores L. Carlo, Aug. 22, 1953; children—John Brent, Bruce Todd, Michael Nicholas. Asst. to pres. Western Kraft Corp., Portland, Oreg., 1955-56, prodn. mgr., Albany, Oreg., 1956-57; asst. to pres. Boise Cascade Corp. (Idaho), 1957-58, gen. mgr. paper div., Wallula, Wash., 1958-60, v.p. corp., 1960-67, exec. v.p., 1967-72, pres., chief exec. officer, 1972-78, chmn., chief exec. officer, 1978—, also dir.; dir. Albertson's, Inc., Idaho First Nat. Bank, Union Pacific Corp. Mem. adv. council Stanford U. Grad. Sch. Bus.; chmn. Am. Paper Inst.; trustee St. Alphonsus Hosp.; mem. U. Idaho Found. Served with USNR, 1950-51. Mem. The Conf. Bd. Office: 1 Jefferson Sq Boise ID 83728

FESKOE, GAFFNEY JON, mfg. co. exec.; b. N.Y.C., Feb. 21, 1949; s. George J. and Mary M. (Gaffney) F.; B.S., Boston Coll., 1971; M.B.A., Fordham U., 1976. With Mfrs. Hanover Trust Co., N.Y.C., 1971-75; asst. treas./mgr. corporate fgn. exchange adv. service European-Am. Banking Corp./European-Am. Bank & Trust Co., N.Y.C., 1975-77; asst. v.p. fgn. exchange corp. counseling dept. Citibank, N.A., N.Y.C., 1977-80; asst. treas. U.S. Filter Corp., N.Y.C., 1980—. Roman Catholic. Clubs: Union (N.Y.C.); Apawamis (Rye, N.Y.). Home: Southport CT Office: 522 Fifth Ave New York NY 10036

FEST, STEPHEN GIBSON, real estate appraiser, farm mgr.; b. Spencer, Iowa, Nov. 1, 1936; s. Thorrel B. and C. Lucille (Etzler) F.; B.S. in Farm Mgmt. and Agrl. Econs., U. Wis., 1959, postgrad., 1969-71; m. Cynthia P. Eiler, Oct. 1, 1960; children—Dawn Denise, Bradley Bruce, Michelle Marie. With Fest Farms, Inc., 1962—, pres., 1978—, dir., 1962—; treas., appraiser South Eastern Valuation Service, Inc., West Bend, Wis., 1976-77; founder, treas., dir. Appraisals Inc. of West Bend, 1977—; pres. West Kenosha State Bank, Wis., 1970-72, dir., 1970-72; pres. Heritage Bank of West Bend, 1973-76, also dir.; agrl. loan officer Production Credit Assn., Dixon, Ill., 1959-61; agrl. loan officer, farm mgr. Bank of Pecatonica (Ill.), 1961-64; agrl. loan analyst Security Pacific Nat. Bank, Los Angeles, 1964-68. Vice pres. Internat. Student Program Corp., 1978—. Am. Field Service Internat. scholar, Germany, 1954; certified assessor, Wis. Mem. Am., Wis., Ill. socs. farm mgrs. and rural appraisers, Washington County Bd. Realtors. Club: Kiwanis. Home: 3484 Paradise Dr West Bend WI 53095 Office: PO Box 858 West Bend WI 53095

FETRIDGE, WILLIAM HARRISON, publisher; b. Chgo.; s. Matthew and Clara (Hall) F.; B.S., Northwestern U., 1929; LL.D., Central Mich. U., 1954; m. Bonnie Jean Clark, June 27, 1941; children—Blakely Fetridge Bundy, Clark Worthington. Asst. to dean Northwestern U., 1929-30; editor Trade Periodical Co., 1930-31, Chgo. Tribune, 1931-34, H. W. Kastor & Son, 1934-35, Roche, Williams & Cleary, Inc., 1935-42; mng. editor Republican Mag., 1939-42; asst. to pres. Popular Mechanics mag., 1945-46, v.p., 1946; exec. v.p., 1953-59; v.p. Diamond T Motor Truck Co., Chgo., 1959-61; exec. v.p. Diamond T div. White Motor Co., 1961-65; pres. Dartnell Corp., Chgo., 1965-78, chmn. bd., chief exec. officer, 1978—; dir. Bank of Ravenswood. Pres., United Republican Fund Ill., 1967-73, 79-80, hon. pres., 1973-79; Rep. state finance chmn., 1967-74; alt. del.-at-large Rep. Nat. Conv., 1956, del.-at-large, 1968; campaign mgr. Merriam for Mayor of Chgo., 1955; chmn. Midwest Vols. for Nixon, 1960; chmn. Nixon Recount Com., 1960, Rep. Forum, 1958-60; mem. Rep. Nat. Finance Com., 1968-73; trustee Lake Forest Coll., 1969-77, Am. Humanics Found., Jacques Holinger Meml. Assn.; pres. U.S. Found. Internat. Scouting, 1971-79; vice chmn. World Scout Found., Geneva, 1978—; del. World Scout confs., Rhodes, Greece, 1963, Helsinki, Finland, 1969, Tokyo, 1971, Nairobi, Kenya, 1973, Denmark, 1975, Montreal, 1977; past pres. bd. trustees Latin Sch. Chgo.; nat. v.p. Boy Scouts Am., 1958-76. Served as lt. comdr. USNR, 1942-45. Recipient Silver Buffalo, Silver Beaver and Silver Antelope awards Boy Scouts Am., also Distinguished Eagle Scout award; Bronze Wolf, World Scout Bur., Nairobi, Kenya, 1973; Disting. Citizen's award St. Andrew Soc., 1980; Abraham Lincoln award United Republican Fund, 1980. Mem. Navy League U.S. (past regional pres.; trustee Chgo. council), Soc. Midland Authors, Grand Priory Malta (chevalier), Sovereign Order St. John of Jerusalem, Beta Theta Pi. Clubs: Chgo., Union League, Saddle and Cycle, Casino (Chgo.); Chikaming Country; Rotary/One. Author: With Warm Regards, 1976; editor: The Navy Reader, 1943; The Second Navy Reader, 1944; American Political Almanac, 1950; The Republican Precinct Workers Manual, 1968. Home: 2430 Lakeview Ave Chicago IL 60614 Office: Dartnell Corp 4660 N Ravenswood Ave Chicago IL 60640

FEUERHERD, VICTOR EDMOND, bus. exec.; b. Mineola, N.Y., Apr. 23, 1925; s. Victor Edmond and Margaret L. (O'Donnell) F.; B.S., Fordham U., 1950; Advanced Mgmt. Program, Harvard U., 1977; m. Lillian C. Dolan, June 3, 1950; children—Victor, Elizabeth, Peter, David, Stephen (dec.), Joseph, Mary (dec.), Matthew. Sr. accountant Arthur Andersen & Co., N.Y.C., 1950-54; asst. to pres. Research Inst. Am., N.Y.C., 1954-61; gen. mgr. S.D. Corp., Sioux Falls, 1961-62; v.p. investments Small Bus. Investment Co., N.Y.C., 1962-64; dir. bus. analysis Schering-Plough Corp., Bloomfield, N.J., 1967-68; dir. spl. projects SCM Corp., N.Y.C., 1964-67, staff v.p. corporate devel., 1968-70, v.p. fin. planning, 1970-73, corp. v.p. planning and acquisitions, 1973—. Treas., bd. dirs. Friends of Handicapped. Served with inf., AUS, 1943-46; ETO. C.P.A., N.Y. Roman Catholic. Home: 26 Princeton St Garden City NY 11530 Office: 299 Park Ave New York NY 10017

FEUGE, JAMES EDGAR, mgmt. cons.; b. Fredericksburg, Tex., Sept. 5, 1935; s. Edgar Carl and Anna (Spaeth) F.; A.B., U. Tex., 1958; M.Ed., S.W. Tex. State U., 1972; D.Letters, Edberhardt Karls U., Tuebingen, W. Ger., 1973; Ph.D., U. Tex., 1976. Mgr., SX Ranches, Fredericksburg, 1973—, Crawford & Assos., law, bus. and realty, Austin, Tex., 1976—; instr. German and edn. mgmt. U. Tex., Austin, 1973-78, S.W. Tex. State U., 1980—; dir. Med. Cons. Austin, 1980—. Pres., Friendswood Edn. Assn., 1968-71; Republican precinct chmn. Gillespie County (Tex.), 1974-80. Served with AUS, 1958-60. Decorated Army Commendation medal; recipient Nat. Leadership award Omicron Delta Kappa, 1974; Fulbright scholar, 1972; Adj. Gen. U.S. Distinctive scholar, 1972; Tex. Power and Light Co. scholar, 1972. Mem. Tex. Tchrs. Assn. (dist. public relations officer 1965-71). Author mgmt. guide books. Home: 4509 Merle Dr Austin TX 78745 Office: 1606 E 12th St Austin TX 78702

FEULNER, EDWIN JOHN, JR., research found. exec.; b. Chgo., Aug. 12, 1941; s. Edwin John and Helen J. (Franzen) F.; B.Sc., Regis Coll., Denver, 1963; M.B.A., Wharton Sch., U. Pa., 1974; Richard Weaver fellow London Sch. Econs., 1965; m. Linda C. Leventhal, Mar. 8, 1969; children—Edwin John III, Emily V. Confidential asst. to sec. def., 1969-70; adminstrv. asst. to U.S. Congressman Philip M. Crane, 1970-74; exec. dir. Republican study com. Ho. of Reps., 1974-77; pres. Heritage Found., Washington, also publisher Policy Rev., 1977—; vice chmn. Internat. Center Econ. Policy Studies, N.Y.C., 1977—; chmn. Inst. for European Studies, London, 1978—; guest lectr. colls. and univs. Pub. Affairs fellow Hoover Instn., 1965-67. Mem. Am. Econ. Assn., Am. Polit. Sci. Assn., Transp. Research Forum, Phila. Soc. (treas. 1964-78), Mont Pelerin Soc. (treas. 1978—), Alpha Kappa Psi Found. (v.p.). Republican. Roman Catholic. Clubs: University (Washington); Reform (London). Author: Congress and the New International Economic Order, 1976; also articles, revs., chpts. in books. Editor: China-The Turning Point, 1976. Home: 6216 Berkeley Rd Alexandria VA 22307 Office: 513 C St NE Washington DC 20002

FEY, JOHN THEODORE, ins. co. exec.; b. Hopewell, Va., Mar. 10, 1917; s. Raymond B. and Ruth (St. Fultz) F.; student Washington and Lee U., 1935-37; LL.B., U. Md., 1940; M.B.A., Harvard, 1942; J.S.D., Yale, 1952; LL.D., Middlebury Coll., 1961, Alma Coll., 1958, U. Vt., 1967; m. Jane K. Gerber, Apr. 5, 1947 (div. May 1964); 1 son, John Theodore; m. 2d, Mary Callimanopulos, Aug. 1, 1976. Admitted to Md. bar, 1940, D.C. bar, 1953, Vt. bar, 1959, N.Y. bar, 1977; county atty., Md., 1947-49; faculty George Washington U. Law Sch., 1949-53, dean, 1953-56, professorial lectr., 1956; clk. Supreme Ct. U.S., 1956-58; pres. U. Vt., 1958-64, U. Wyo., 1964-66; pres., dir. Nat. Life Ins. Co., Montpelier, Vt., 1966-74; vice chmn. bd. Equitable Life Assurance Soc. U.S., 1974-75, chmn. bd., 1975—. Mem. Md. Legislature, 1946-50. Served with USMCR, 1942-46; col. Res. Mem. Am. Coll. Life Underwriters (chmn. bd.), Order of Coif. Republican. Episcopalian. Club: Masons (32 deg.). Office: 1285 Ave of Americas New York NY 10019

FEY, MICHAEL STUART, food scientist; b. N.Y.C., Sept. 7, 1950; s. Charles Frank and Fannie Fey; B.S. in Biology, St. John's U., 1972; M.S. in Food Sci., La. State U., 1976; Ph.D. in Food Sci., Cornell U., 1979. Food product devel. scientist Procter & Gamble Co., Cin., 1979—. Served to 2d lt. Chem. Corps, U.S. Army, 1972-74. Mem. Inst. Food Technologists, Phi Tau Sigma. Home: 9108 Constitution Dr Cincinnati OH 45215 Office: Winton Hill Tech Center 6071 Center Hill Rd Cincinnati OH 45226

FEY, RICHARD SMOUSE, chem. engr.; b. Cumberland, Md., Apr. 11, 1924; s. George C. and Ruthella S. F.; student U. Louisville, 1943-44, Potomac State Coll., 1942-43; B.S., U. S.C., 1945; B.S. Ch.E., U. Md., 1948, Ph.D. Ch.E., 1953; m. Mary Louise Bender, June 7, 1953; 1 dau., Mary Beth. Research fellow U.S. Bur. Mines, 1949-51, U.S. Naval Ordnance Lab., 1951-52; instr. U. Md., 1952-53; with Hercules, Inc., Salt Lake City, 1953—, dir. propulsion products, 1980—. Served with USNR, 1943-46. Registered profl. engr., Md. Mem. Am. Chem. Soc., AIAA (Engr. of Year 1966), Sigma Xi, Tau Beta Pi, Phi Kappa Phi. Republican. Lutheran. Clubs: Masons, Shriners. Home: 2742 Saint Marys Way Salt Lake City UT 84108 Office: Hercules Aerospace Div PO Box 27408 Salt Lake City UT 84127

FIALKOV, HERMAN, investment banker; b. Bklyn., Mar. 23, 1922; s. Isidore and Pearl (Heinish) F.; student Coll. City N.Y., 1938-41; B.Adminstrv. Engring., N.Y. U., 1951; m. Elaine Dampf, Nov. 25, 1942; children—Carol Fran, Jay Michael. Engr., Emerson Radio Corp., 1941-47, MBS, 1947-49, Tele-Tone Radio Corp., 1949-51; chief engr. Radio Receptor Co., 1951-54; pres. Gen. Transistor Corp. (merged with Gen. Instrument Corp., 1960), 1954-60; v.p., dir. Gen. Instrument Corp., 1960-70, sr. v.p., 1967-68; partner Geiger & Fialkov, 1968-78; pres. Aleph Null Corp., 1979—; chmn. bd. three Dimensional Circuits, Inc.; chmn. bd. Standard Microsystems Corp., N.Y.; dir. Wells-Benrus Corp., Andover Togs, Inc., Control Transaction Corp., Q1 Corp., EMS Devel. Corp., Nat. Beryllia Corp. Panelist Am. Arbitration Assn.; trustee Adelphi U., Garden City, 1959-70. Served with AUS, 1943-46. Decorated Bronze Star medal with oak leaf cluster; Conspicuous Service Cross, N.Y. Mem. IEEE, Am. Technion Soc. (dir.), Tau Beta Pi, Alpha Pi Mu. Home: 615 Meryl Dr Westbury NY 11590 Office: One Old Country Rd Carle Place NY 11514

FICKINGER, WAYNE JOSEPH, business exec.; b. Belleville, Ill., June 23, 1926; s. Joseph and Grace (Belton) F.; B.A., U. Ill., 1949; M.S., Northwestern U., 1950; m. Joan Mary Foley, June 16, 1951; children—Michael, Joan, Jan, Ellen, Steven. Overnight editor U.P., Chgo., 1950-51; spl. project writer Sears-Roebuck & Co., Chgo., 1951-53; account exec. Calkins & Holden Advt. Agy., Chgo., 1953-56; account supr. Foote, Cone & Belding Advt. Agy., Chgo., N.Y.C., 1956-63; sr. v.p. J. Walter Thompson Co., Chgo., 1963-72, exec. v.p., mng. dir. Chgo. Office, 1972-75, exec. v.p., dir. U.S. Western div., 1975-78, dir., mem. exec. com., 1973—, pres., chief operating officer N. Am., ops., 1978-79, pres., world-wide chief operating officer, 1979—, pres. JWT Group Inc., 1980—, also mem. exec. com., dir., also trustee J. Walter Thompson retirement fund. Fund raising cons. Nat. Mental Health Assn., 1970. Communications counselor Cook County (Ill.) Republican Orgn., 1970. Trustee Salvation Army, 1973—; bd. dirs. Off-the-Street Club, Chgo., 1974—. Served with USNR, 1943-46. Recipient Five-Year Meritorious Service award A.R.C., 1963, Service award Mental Health Assn., 1970. Mem. Am. Assn. Advt. Agys. (gov. Chgo. dist.), Council Fgn. Relations (Chgo. com.), Sigma Delta Chi, Alpha Delta Sigma. Clubs: Exmoor Country (Highland Park, Ill.); Racquet (Chgo.); N.Y. Athletic. Office: 875 N Michigan Ave Chicago IL 60611 also 420 Lexington Ave New York NY 10017

FICKLING, WILLIAM ARTHUR, JR., health care co. exec.; b. Macon, Ga., July 23, 1932; s. William Arthur and Claudia Darden (Foster) F.; B.S. cum laude, Auburn U., 1954; m. Neva Jane Langley, Dec. 30, 1954; children—William Arthur, III, Jane Dru, Julia Claudia, Roy Hampton. Exec. v.p. Fickling & Walker, Inc., Macon, 1954-74; chmn. bd., chief exec. officer Charter Med. Corp., Macon, 1969—; dir. Ga. Power Co., South Ga. Ry. Co., Riverside Ford, Bob Wilson Ford; dep. chmn., dir. Atlanta Fed. Res. Bank. Mem. Macon Bd. Realtors. Trustee Wesleyan Coll., Macon. Mem. Young Pres.'s Orgn., Kappa Alpha, Delta Sigma Phi, Phi Kappa Phi. Methodist. Home: 4918 Wesleyan Woods Dr Macon GA 31210 Office: 577 Mulberry St Macon GA 31201

FIEBERT, JACK MICHAEL, fin. exec.; b. Bklyn., May 17, 1954; s. Charles and Saundra Ruth (Starr) F.; B.B.A. summa cum laude, Baruch Coll., 1976; m. Sherry Amatenstein, Oct. 22, 1977. Chief acct. Hahne & Co., Newark, N.J., 1976-78, Mature Temps, Inc., N.Y.C., 1978-78; sr. staff accountant Sterling Household Corp., N.Y.C., 1974-76; acctg. mgr. Ups 'N Downs, Inc., Secaucus, N.J., 1980—; cons. in field. mem. Am. Mgmt. Assn. Democrat. Home: W-6 Avon Dr East Windsor NJ 08520 Office: 461 8th Ave New York NY 10001

FIECHTER, RAY ALLEN, mfg. co. exec.; b. Decatur, Ind., Nov. 20, 1945; s. Homer H. and Clara M. (Schladenhauffen) F.; B.S. in M.E., Purdue U., 1970; m. Carol Marie Payne, July 18, 1965; children—Shantelle Rae, Shurell Alane, Natalie Colette. Process engr. Corning Glass Co., Bluffton, Ind., 1964-66; design engr. Detroit Diesel Allison div. Gen. Motors, Indpls., 1970-71; regional sales mgr. Schwitzer div. Wallace Murray Corp., Indpls., 1971-78; div. sales mgr. Davidson, Inc., Indpls., 1978—. Bd. dirs. Ind. chpt. Arthritis Found., 1978—. Mem. ASME, Soc. Plastics Engrs., Nat. Fluid Power Assn. Home: 226 Mill Farm Rd Noblesville IN 46060 Office: 5610 Dividend Dr Indianapolis IN 46241

FIELD, ALEXANDER C., JR., radio-TV exec.; b. Detroit, Feb. 21, 1918; s. Alexander C. and Mary (DeSaussure) F.; A.B., U. Cin., 1942; certificate wildlife conservation U. Alaska, 1949; certificate TV mgmt. U. Syracuse, 1962. Announcer, Crosley Broadcasting Co., Cin., 1939-41; mem. traffic dept. Kroger Co., Cin., 1940-42; promotion mgr. KENI, Anchorage, 1953-54; dir. spl. broadcast services, WLW, Cin., 1954-57; mgr. public affairs WGN Continental Broadcasting Co., Chgo., 1957-69, v.p. for public affairs, 1969—. Chmn., Met. Ill. Hwy. Users Council; mem. pub. affairs adv. com. Air Force Acad. Found.; mem. adv. bd. Chgo. State U.; bd. dirs. Chgo. Crime Commn., Ill. TV Commn. for Edn.; Met. Blood Bank Chgo.; mem. Gov.'s Traffic Safety Com. Served to lt. col. USAF, 1942-53. Mem. Cosmopolitan C. of C. (exec. com.), U.S. Capitol Hist. Soc., Air Force Assn. (nat. dir., Man of Yr. award 1979), Broadcast Pioneers. Reformed Episcopalian. Clubs: Ill. Athletic (bd. govs.), Brookwood Country, Valley-Lo. Home: 1806 S Cumberland Park Ridge IL 60068 Office: 2501 W Bradley Pl Chicago IL 60618

FIELD, JOSEPH M., lawyer, broadcasting exec.; b. Phila., Jan. 11, 1932; s. Sylvan H. and Hannah (Worobe) F.; B.A., U. Pa., 1952; LL.B., Yale, 1955; m. Marie H. Felber, June 28, 1959; children—David J., Nancy E. Admitted to Conn. bar, 1955, N.Y. bar, 1957, Pa. bar, 1961; law clk. to U.S. Circuit Judge Carroll C. Hincks, N.Y.C., 1955-56; asso. Roberts & Holland, N.Y.C., 1956-59; asst. U.S. atty., chmn. appellate sect. civil and tax divs. U.S. Atty's Office for So. Dist. N.Y., 1959-61; asso. firm Meltzer & Schiffrin, Phila., 1961-65, Joseph M. Field Law Offices, Phila., 1961-65; founder, pres., chmn. bd. Entertainment Communications, Inc. (Entercom), Phila., 1968—. Asst. concertmaster New Haven Symphony Orch., 1952-53; pres., 1972-75; trustee West Park Hosp., Phila., 1976—; violinist, treas. New Chamber Players Phila.; dir. Neighborhood Club Bala Cynwyd, 1977-79. Mem. Am., Phila. bar assns., Assn. Bar City N.Y., Office: One Bala Cynwyd Plaza Suite 225 Bala Cynwyd PA 19004

FIELD, MARSHALL, publisher; b. Charlottesville, Va., May 13, 1941; s. Marshall IV and Joanne (Bass) F.; B.A., Harvard U., 1963; m. Joan Best Connelly, Sept. 5, 1964 (div. 1969); 1 son, Marshall; m. 2d, Jamee Beckwith Jacobs, Aug. 19, 1972; children—Jamee, Stephanie Caroline. With N.Y. Herald-Tribune, 1964-65; dir. Field Enterprises, Inc., Chgo., 1965—, mem. exec. com., 1966—, chmn. bd., 1972—, mem. exec. com. Chgo. Sun-Times, 1965—, pub. Chgo. Sun-Times, 1969—; dir. World Book-Childcraft Internat. Inc., 1965—, pub., 1973—; dir. First Nat. Bank of Chgo., First Chgo. Corp. Co-chmn. of advisory bd. Broader Urban Involvement and Leadership Devel., Inc.; mem. adv. bd. Chgo. council Boy Scouts Am.; mem. profl. journalism adv. com. Stanford U.; mem. nat. com. Am. Land Trust; governing mem. Orchestral Assn., Chgo., Chgo. Council on Fgn. Relations; bd. advs. Presdl. Classroom for Young Ams.; bd. dirs. McGraw Wildlife Found., Chgo. Boys Club, Newspaper Advt. Bur., Field Found. Ill., Salt Water Internat. Fishing Telesis, Lincoln Park Zool. Soc., Chgo., Internat. Atlantic Salmon Found., World Wildlife Fund-U.S. Appeal, Nat. Com. for Prevention Child Abuse, Restoration Atlantic Salmon in Am., Nat. Book Com.; trustee Art Inst. Chgo., Field Mus. Natural History, Rush-Presbyn.-St. Luke's Med. Center, Mus. Sci. and Industry, Chgo., Am. Newspaper Pubs. Assn. Found., MacMurray Coll., Jacksonville, Ill.; adv. bd. Dialogue with Blind. Mem. Nat. Com. Newspaper Pubs. Clubs: Harvard,

Casino, Chgo., Hundred of Cook County, Mchts. & Mfrs., Saddle and Cycle, Mid-Am., Racquet, Tavern (Chgo.); Onwentsia (Lake Forest, Ill.); River (N.Y.C.); Jupiter Island (Hobe Sound, Fla.); McGraw Wildlife (Dundee, Ill.). Office: Field Enterprises Inc 401 N Wabash Ave Chicago IL 60611

FIELD, MARSHALL, JR., mgmt. cons.; b. Chgo., Dec. 11, 1931; s. Marshall W. and Clara F.; B.S., Western Mich. U., 1954; M.B.A., Northwestern U., 1955; m. Joan Hamlet, June 19, 1954; children—Kathleen, Matthew, Jeffrey, Stacy. Mktg. analyst Koppers Co., Pitts., 1957-60; auditor U.S. Army Audit Agy., Ford Motor Co., Detroit, 1955-57; v.p. nat. and devel. practices A.T. Kearney, Inc., Pepper Pike, Ohio, 1960—. Bd. dirs. Am. Cancer Soc.; bd. trustees Soc. Crippled Children; civic adv. bd. Nat. Cystic Fibrosis Found. Served with AUS, 1955-57. Mem. Inst. Mgmt. Consultants, Nat. Council Phys. Distbn. Mgmt. Econ. Club Chgo. Clubs: Mayfield Country, Hermit, Cleve. Racquet, Chgo., Carlton, Kiawah Island, East Bank. Office: 29425 Chagrin Blvd Pepper Pike OH 44122

FIELD, ROBERT STEVEN, acct., fin. cons.; b. Chgo., July 30, 1949; s. Marshall Harvey and Rita (Stock) F.; B.S., Ind. U., 1971; m. Ruth Ellen Teplinsky, Aug. 7, 1971; 1 dau., Lisa Michelle. Staff accountant Lester Witte & Co., Chgo., mgr. audit dept., 1971-76; fin. cons. Gustin Ins. Agy. Inc., Morton Grove, Ill., 1976; pres. Atlantic Corporate Cons.' Inc., Buffalo Grove, Ill., 1976—. C.P.A. Mem. Am. Inst. C.P.A.'s, Ill. Soc. C.P.A.'s. Mem. B'nai B'rith. Home: 501 Buckthorn Terr Buffalo Grove IL 60090 Office: 501 Buckthorn Terr Buffalo Grove IL 60090

FIELD, STANFORD, engring. cons.; b. Phila., June 3, 1929; s. Edward Feigelman and Frances Miller; B.S., Pa. State U., 1951; postgrad. U.S. Naval Postgrad. Sch., 1954-55; m. Shirley Ann Tavenner, Dec. 20, 1969; children—Glenn Alan, Julie Ann. Process devel. engr. Atlantic Refining Co., Phila., 1951-61; mgr. petrochemical process sales Hydrocarbon Research, Inc., N.Y.C., 1961-68; mgr. hydrocarbon process licensing Chem Systems, Inc., N.Y.C., 1968-71; dir. energy econs. dept. Stanford Research Inst., Menlo Park, Calif., 1971-74; prin. engr. Bechtel, Inc., San Francisco, 1974-76; mgr. spl. studies dept. Electric Power Research Inst., Palo Alto, Calif., 1976-77; engring. cons., Los Gatos, Calif., 1977—. Served with USNR, 1955-57. Mem. Am. Inst. Chem. Engrs. Contbr. articles to profl. jours. Patentee in field. Address: 105 Plazoleta Los Gatos CA 95030

FIELDING, RONALD HERBERT, fin. analyst; b. Brookline, Mass., Mar. 9, 1949; s. Herbert Charles and Edna (Rowe) F.; B.A., St. Johns Coll., 1970; M.A., 1973, M.B.A., U. Rochester, 1976. Asst. treas. Security N.Y. State Corp., Rochester, 1974-76; asst. treas., mgr. planning Lincoln 1st Banks Inc., 1976-78, asst. v.p., bond portfolio strategist, 1978-80; pres. Rochester Shares Mgmt. Co., 1980—; instr. Rochester Inst. Tech., 1975-79, Grad. Sch. Mgmt., U. Rochester, 1979—. Trustee, treas. Naples (N.Y.) Mill Sch. Arts and Crafts, 1975-77. Herbert H. Lehman fellow, 1970-73; grad. fellow Am. Inst. Economic Research, 1970-73. Mem. Rochester Soc. Security Analysts, Fin. Analysts Fedn., Bond Club Rochester. Home: 951 East Ave Rochester NY 14607 Office: 183 E Main St Rochester NY 14604

FIELDS, JOSEPH ROBERT, artist, printer; b. Montclair, N.J., May 21, 1921; s. Albert Thomas and Marie Carina (Ward) F.; student U. Mich., 1944, U. Florence (Italy), 1945, Meinzinger Art Sch., 1948, Allen Airbrush Inst., Detroit, 1949; m. Dorothy Irene Simons, Sept. 17, 1949; children—Gary Robert, Lynda Jo, Gregory Martin. Apprentice artist Van Houten Rankin, Inc., Detroit, 1946, Wards Name Plates, Inc., Detroit, 1947, Creative Displays, Inc., Detroit, 1947, George P. Johnson Co., 1948; advt. mgr. Mark's Stores, Inc., Detroit, 1948-50; owner J.R. Fields comml. artist, Canton, Mich., 1950—; owner, mgr. J-Art Co., Canton, 1962—. Served as sgt. AUS, 1942-45; ETO. Lion. Patentee sprayable pressure-sensitive wax adhesive. Address: 4565 Artley St Canton MI 48188

FIELDS-EDGERSON, CAROL INEZ, govt. ofcl.; b. Hot Springs, Ark., June 30, 1948; d. Bobbie and Helen Inez (Page) Fields; B.A. cum laude, Philander Smith Coll., Little Rock; M.A. in Mgmt., Central Mich. U., Mt. Pleasant, 1980; children—Robert Bryan, Andrea Paige. With GSA, City of Kansas City (Mo.), 1972-78; public sch. tchr., Waterloo, Iowa, 1971; communications mgmt. specialist NOAA, Dept. Commerce, Rockville, Md., 1978—; tutor Howard Community Coll., 1979-80. Recipient Crisco award, 1966, Am. Legion award, 1966. Mem. Delta Sigma Theta. Baptist. Home: 5435 Hightide Ct Columbia MD 21044 Office: 6010 Executive Blvd Rockville MD 20852

FIEN, JEROME MORRIS, accountant; b. Hartford, Conn., Dec. 26, 1921; s. Martin Herman and Frances (Chernaik) F.; B.A., Johns Hopkins U., 1943; M.B.A., N.Y. U., 1949; m. Ruth Lee Klein, Apr. 3, 1945; children—Mark Allan, Judith Anne. Sr. staff accountant Samuel Klein & Co., Newark, 1946-50, now mng. partner; v.p. N.J. State Bd. C.P.A.'s, 1965-67, pres., 1967, 78, sec., 1968-72, mem., 1976—; v.p. Northeastern region Nat. Assn. State Bds. Accountancy, 1968—, pres., 1969-70, regional dir., 1973; v.p. Nat. Assn. State Bds. Accountancy, 1972. Mem. adv. council Seton Hall U. Sch. Bus., 1968—; mem. adv. council on acctg. Rutgers U.; v.p. Florence Crittenton League, 1965-66, pres., 1967; overall chmn. Essex County Bonds for Israel, 1963-64, chmn. N.J. council, 1969-70; sec. K-F Charitable Found.; trustee Jewish Community Council Essex County, N.J., 1959-65, 70—, v.p., 1967; fellow Upsala Coll., 1974. Served with USNR, 1944-46. C.P.A. Mem. Am. Inst. C.P.A.'s, N.Y. Soc. C.P.A.'s, Pa. Soc. C.P.A.'s, N.J. Soc. C.P.A.'s, Tax Soc. N.Y. U., Registered Mcpl. Accountants Assn. N.J., C.P.A. Assos. (chmn. 1978). Club: Green Brook Country (Caldwell, N.J.). Home: 65 Speir Dr South Orange NJ 07079 Office: 1180 Raymond Blvd Newark NJ 07102

FIER, MIRIAM ROTH, pubs. mag. co. exec.; b. N.Y.C.; d. Hyman and Mollie (Asher) Roth; student Baruch Sch. Bus., 1944-49; m. Samuel G. Fier, June 8, 1947; 1 dau., Betty Anne. Office mgr., comptroller Radio City Products Co., Inc., N.Y.C., 1946-50; auditor's asst. Shedler & Shedler Accountants, N.Y.C., 1963-64; with Avant-Garde Media, Inc., N.Y.C., 1964-78, 79—, bus. dir., 1966-78, 79—, corp. sec., 1967-78, bus. dir. monthly consumer affairs 36-page tabloid Moneysworth, 1970-78, 79—, monthly tabloid Am. Bus., 1976-78, 79—, cons., cons., 1978, 79—; bus. dir. Cameo Press, Inc., 1978-79. Mem. Affiliated Young Dems. Mem. Library Assos., Bklyn. Coll., Women's Direct Response Group. Club: Hundred Million (N.Y.C.). Home: 11146 76th Dr Forest Hills NY 11375 Office: 251 W 57th St New York NY 10019

FIFE, ROBERT LEE, corp. exec.; b. Oil City, Pa., Apr. 21, 1933; s. Samuel R. and Rachel (Miller) F.; B.A., Pa. State U., 1955; B. Fgn. Trade, Am. Grad. Sch. Internat. Mgmt., 1959; postgrad. Stanford, 1974; m. Nancy Ann Newton, Aug. 29, 1959; children—Eric R., Robyn L. Office mgr. Crucible div. Colt Industries, Inc., Nassau, Bahamas, 1960-62, sales mgr., Paris, 1962-64, N. European sales dir. Copenhagen, Denmark, 1964-67; product sales mgr. Howmet Corp., Lancaster, Pa., 1967-72, dir. marketing, Greenwich, Conn., 1972-76; gen. mgr. specialty products group Gen. Portland, Inc., Dallas, 1976-77; v.p. mktg. G&W Energy Products Group, Gulf & Western Mfg. Co., Oak Brook, Ill., 1977-78, v.p., gen. mgr. Taylor-Bonney div., Southfield, Mich., 1978-80, pres. G&W Taylor-Bonney Internat., 1980—. Served with U.S. Army, 1956-58. Home: 26025 Woodlore Dr Franklin MI 48025 Office: G&W Mfg Co PO Box 999 Southfield MI 48037

FIFER, STEPHEN LAMAR, mfg. co. ofcl.; b. Fresno, Calif., Nov. 11, 1947; s. Karson Kirkland and Alma Christina (Mose) F.; student Calif. State U., Fresno, 1965-67, 71-74, A.B. in Internat. Econs., A.B. in Diplomatic History, 1974, M.Internat. Mgmt. in Internat. Econs. and Fin., Am. Grad. Sch. Internat. Mgmr., 1975; m. Mary Lorraine Joy, June 15, 1974. Export mgr. Reliance Crane and Rigging, Phoenix and Mexico City, Mex., 1975; staff Caterpillar Tractor Co., Peoria, Ill., 1976, staff Caterpillar Overseas S.A., Geneva, Switzerland, 1977, sales rep. Cat Overseas, Rome, Italy, 1978-80; sr. mktg. cons. Caterpillar Overseas S.A., Geneva, 1980—. SBA cons., 1976. Served with USN, 1967-71. Recipient award of merit SBA, 1976. Mem. Am. Econs. Assn., M.B.A. Assn. Contbr. papers, reports in field to publs. Home: Plateau de Frontenex 9C 1208 Geneva Switzerland Office: Caterpillar Tractor 118 Rue du Rhône 1206 Geneva Switzerland

FIGG, JAMES ALFRED, JR., packaging co. exec.; b. Christianburg, Va., July 14, 1925; s. James Alfred and Constance (Rigby) F.; B.A., U. Va., 1949; m. Janet Ann Leigh, Apr. 14, 1951; children—James Alfred III, Janet Ann Leigh. Sales rep. Am. Cyanamid Corp., N.Y.C., 1949-50; nat. accounts sales rep. Liquid Carbonic Corp., N.Y.C., 1950-53; sales rep. Container Corp. Am., Richmond, Va. and Balt., 1953-57, N.Y. sales mgr. Mengel div., N.Y.C., 1957-61, gen. mgr., New Brunswick, N.J., 1961-68, gen. sales mgr. corporate sales, container div., Carol Stream, Ill., 1968—. Trustee Middlesex Gen. Hosp., 1965-68. Served with USMC, 1943-46. Mem. Fibre Box Assn., Raritan Valley Regional C. of C. (pres. 1968), Huguenot Soc., S.A.R., Phi Kappa Psi. Republican. Episcopalian (sr. warden). Clubs: Meadow, Stonehenge Golf. Home: 1870 Pheasant Trail Inverness Countryside Palatine IL 60067 Office: Container Corp of America Carol Stream IL 60187

FILARDO, LILLIAN VASILAUSKAS, acctg. co. exec.; b. Norwood, Mass., May 18, 1927; d. John Anthony and Anna Theresa (Michunas) Vasilauskas; B.S., Simmons Coll., Boston, 1948; postgrad. Harvard Coll., 1948, U. Bridgeport, 1953, U. Conn., 1954; m. Feb. 25, 1960; children—Bruce Wallace, Andrew, Joseph. Div. controller Ind. Gen. Corp., Stamford, Conn., 1956-62; owner, prin. Lillian V. Filardo, C.P.A., Stamford, Conn., 1962—; pres. Branjo, Inc., Stamford, 1969—; cons. in field. C.P.A., Conn. Mem. Am. Inst. C.P.A.'s, Conn. Soc. C.P.A.'s, Nat. Assn. Accts. Democrat. Roman Catholic. Home: 114 Crestwood Dr Stamford CT 06905 Office: 114 Crestwood Dr Stamford CT 06905

FILER, JOHN HORACE, ins. co. exec.; b. New Haven, Sept. 3, 1924; s. Harry Lambert and Ehrma (Green) F.; B.A., Depauw U., 1947, LL.D., 1970; LL.B., Yale, 1950; m. Marlene Klick; children—Susan, Cynthia, Kathryn, Ann. Admitted to Conn. bar, 1950; practice in New Haven, 1950-58; law clk. Carroll C. Hincks, U.S. dist. judge, 1950-51; asso., partner Gumbart, Corbin, Tyler & Cooper, 1951-58; various positions Aetna Life & Casualty Co., Hartford, Conn., 1958-68, exec. v.p., 1968-72, chmn., chief exec. officer, 1972—, also dir.; dir. U.S. Steel Corp. Chmn. Bd. Edn., Farmington, 1963-67; mem. Conn. Commn. to Study Met. Govt., 1966-67. Mem. Conn. Senate, 1957-58. Served to ensign USNR, 1943-46. Mem. Am., Conn. Hartford County bar assns., Assn. Life Ins. Counsel, Greater Hartford C. of C. (dir.), Conn. Bus. and Industry Assn. (dir.). Episcopalian. Home: West Hartford CT Office: 151 Farmington Ave Hartford CT 06115

FILIPS, NICHOLAS JOSEPH, med. and surg. distbg. co. exec.; b. Garrett, Ind., June 10, 1925; s. John and Elizabeth (Grigore) F.; student U. Detroit, 1942-45, Ind. U., 1945-47; B.S. in Biology, Am. U., 1948; postgrad. Ind. U., 1979; m. Lucille N. Baker, July 5, 1947; children—Steven, Mary Beth, Fred John. Vice pres., mgr. Wayne Pharmacal Supply Co., Ft. Wayne, Ind., 1949-67, pres., chmn. div. Bendway, Inc., South Bend, Ind., 1955-67; v.p., gen. mgr. Karel First-Aid Supply Co., Chgo., 1967-71; pres., gen. mgr. Amedic Surg. Supply Co., Miami, 1971-78, pres., chief exec. officer Med. Supply Co., Inc., Jacksonville, Fla., 1978—. Recipient Am. Legion Leadership award, 1939. Mem. Am. Surg. Trade Assn. (recipient Distinctive Service award 1960), Fla. Sheriffs Assn. Democrat. Roman Catholic. Club: Lions. Contbr. articles in field to profl. jour. Office: 5135 NW 165th St Miami FL 33014

FILKINS, ROBERT VAUGHN, truck sales co. exec.; b. Cleve., Sept. 11, 1942; s. Robert Vaughn and Eleanore (Koehlke) F.; B.B.A., Baldwin-Wallace Coll., 1965; m. Nadia Osadtchij, Sept. 5, 1964; children—Robert W., Elaine S. Dist. mgr. Assos. Comml. Corp., Chgo., 1965-78; v.p. ops. Austin Truck Sales, Cuyahoga Falls, Ohio, 1978—. Contbr. fin. articles to trade publs. Home: 7362 LaScala Dr Hudson OH 44236 Office: Austin Truck Sales 1260 Main St Cuyahoga Falls OH 44221

FILL, DENNIS C., business exec.; b. 1929; ed. Ealing Coll., London, London U.; married. With Olin Matherson Chem. Corp.; with Squibb Corp., pres. E.R. Squibb, 1968, later corp. exec. v.p. ops. Squibb Corp., chmn. bd. internat. Squibb Asia Ltd., 1974-78, pres., chief operating officer, mem. exec. com. Squibb Corp., 1978—, also dir.; dir. Thiokol Corp. Served with RAF. Office: Squibb Corp 40 W 57th St New York NY 10019*

FILLING, J. WILLIAM, JR., ski shop exec.; b. Lancaster, Pa., Dec. 25, 1954; s. J. William and Kathryn H. Filling; B.S. in Mktg., U. Vt., 1976. Owner, mgr. Green Thumb Lawncare, Lancaster, 1975-77; mgr. Snow Shed Ski & Sport Shop, Lancaster, 1977—; condr. clinics on ski selection and care to high schs. and colls. Account exec. United Way, Lancaster, 1979; fundraiser Hempfield Ambulance Assn., 1980. Mem. U.S. Ski Assn., Ski Industries Am., Lancaster Jaycees. Republican. Lutheran. Clubs: Lancaster Ski, Lancaster Z, Lake Clarke Waterski. Home: Fern Glen Rd RD 1 Drumore PA 17518 Office: 2330 Dairy Rd Lancaster PA 17601

FILOSA, GARY FAIRMONT RANDOLPH DE MARCO, II, investor, publisher; b. Wilder, Vt., Feb. 22, 1931; s. Gary F.R. and Rosaline (Falzarano) F.; Ph.B., U. Chgo., 1954; B.A., U. Americas, 1967; M.A., Calif. Western U., 1968; Ph.D., U.S. Internat. U., 1970; m. Edith Wilson du Motier Schoenberg, Nov. 24, 1953; children—Marc Christian Bazire III, Gary Fairmont Randolph III. Account exec., editor house publs. Robertson, Buckley & Gotsch, Inc., Chgo., 1953-54; account exec., copywriter Fuller, Smith & Ross, Inc., N.Y.C., 1954-55; editor Apparel Arts mag., Esquire, Inc., N.Y.C., 1955-56; pres., chmn. bd. Filosa Publs., N.Y.C., 1956-61, pub. Teenage, Teenlife, Talent, Campus Personalities, Stardust, Mystery Digest, Rock and Roll Roundup, Rustic Rhythm mags., N.Y.C., 1956-60; pres. Montclair Sch., 1958-60; exec. asst. to Benjamin A. Javits, 1961-62; dean adminstrn. Postgrad. Center for Mental Health, N.Y.C., 1962-64; dir. Filosa Films Internat., 1964-67, now pres.; v.p. acad. affairs World Acad., San Francisco, 1967-68; asst. headmaster, instr. Latin, San Miguel Sch., 1968-69; asso. prof. philosophy Art Coll., San Francisco, 1969-70; v.p. acad. affairs, dean of faculty Internat. Inst., Phoenix, 1968-73; pres. Universite Universelle, 1970-73; v.p. acad. affairs, dean Summer Sch., Internat. Community Coll., Los Angeles, 1970-72; chmn. bd., pres. Am. Assn. Social Directories, 1970—; chmn. Social Directory of Calif., 1967—; v.p. Itel-Systemic, Newport Beach, Calif., 1979—. Chmn. Publishers for John F. Kennedy, 1960, Educators for Reelection of Ivy Baker Priest, 1970; mem. exec. com. Brown for Gov. Calif., 1974. Served with AUS, 1954-55. Recipient DAR Citizenship award, 1959. Mem. Am. Surfing Assn. (pres. 1974-78, 80—), Internat. Amateur Surfing Fedn. (pres. 1974-76), Internat. Council for Advancement of Surfing (pres. 1976—, pres. U.S. com. 1976—), Alumni Assn. U. Ams. (pres. 1967-70), United Shareowners Am., World Affairs Council San Francisco, Am. Acad. Polit. Sci., AAU (dir.), Sigma Omicron Lambda. Democrat. Episcopalian. Clubs: Chapultepec (Mexico City); KonaKai (San Diego); Commonwealth, Sierra (San Francisco); Embajadores (U. of Ams., Puebla, Mex.); Los Angeles Athletic, Town Hall (Los Angeles). Author: Technology Enters 21st Century, 1966; (with Peter Duchin) Feather Light (musical), 1968; No Public Funds for Nonpublic Schools, 1968; Creative Function of the College President, 1969; The Surfer's Almanac, 1977. Contbr. articles to profl. jours. Office: PO Box 1315 Beverly Hills CA 90213

FINAN, KENNETH EUGENE, mgmt. cons.; b. Los Angeles, Mar. 10, 1944; s. Clarence Edward and Velda (Throop) F.; A.A., Phoenix Coll., 1969; B.A., U. Ariz., 1978; m. Elizabeth Jane Gregory, Oct. 21, 1973; children—Kirk Edward, Jodie Elizabeth. Asst. mgr. Phoenix City Employees Fed. Credit Union, 1972-74, acting mgr., 1974; dental adminstr. K. A. Vinall D.D.S., P.C., Tucson, 1975-76; dental adminstr. Ariz. Dental Health Assos. P.C., Phoenix, 1976-79; cons. Planagement Services, Phoenix, 1979—. Served with USAF, 1962-66. Mem. Dental Group Mgmt. Assn. (treas. Western region 1979-81). Democrat. Roman Catholic. Home: 4119 E Almeria Rd Phoenix AZ 85008 Office: 4040 E McDowell Rd Suite 311 Phoenix AZ 85008

FINAN, THOMAS JOSEPH, mgmt. cons.; b. Norristown, Pa., Aug. 22, 1913; s. Michael Joseph and Winifred Mary (Lavin) F.; B.S., Econs., Villanova U., 1936; postgrad. U. Pa., 1949-52; m. Pearl Elizabeth Zeigler, June 3, 1939; children—Kathleen E. Finan Callan, Terence M., Thomas Joseph. Mgr. trainee, salesman B.F. Goodrich Rubber Co., Phila., 1937-41; sr. indsl. engr. RCA, Camden, N.J., 1941-45, dir. edn. and tng., 1945-55; princs. Worden & Risberg Mgmt. Cons., Phila., 1955-71; mgr. orgn. devel. SKF Industries, Inc., Phila., 1971-78; founder, pres. Fincal Assos., mgmt. cons., Audubon, N.J., 1968—; asst. prof. indsl. adminstrn. Drexel U., Phila., 1951-54; lectr. Temple U., Phila., 1948-49. Chmn. juvenile conf. com., City of Audubon, N.J., 1953-73; mem. bd. visitors Villanova U., 1975—. Mem. Am. Soc. for Tng. and Devel., Indsl. Relations Assn. Phila., Am. Arbitration Assn. (labor panel), Public Relations Council. Republican. Roman Catholic. Clubs: Vesper, K.C., Down Town, Engineers (Phila.). Home and office: 229 Park Pl Audubon NJ 08106

FINCH, JAMES AUSTIN, III, trust co. exec.; b. Cape Girardeau, Mo., Sept. 4, 1940; s. James Austin and Helen (Carroll) F.; B.S., U. Mo., Columbia, 1965; grad. trust degree Northwestern U., 1973; children—Tracy Elizabeth, Cynthia Carroll, Carrie Christine. Sr. credit analyst Merc. Trust Co., St. Louis, 1967-69; trust officer Guaranty Trust Co. Mo., Clayton, 1969, v.p., trust officer, 1970-79, pres., chief exec. officer, 1979—; dir. Intercoastal Corp., Guaranty Trust Co. Bd. dirs., treas. Block Partnership, 1968-70, New Life Center, 1973—; mem. trustees com. St. Louis Community Found., 1979—. Served with U.S. Army, 1965-67. Mem. Am. Bankers Assn., Mo. Bankers Assn., Estate Planning Council, St. Louis Jaycees (exec. v.p., dir. 1968-78). Methodist. Clubs: St. Louis, St. Louis Rotary, Knights of the Cauliflower Ear. Home: PO Box 16260 Clayton MO 63105 Office: Guaranty Trust Co 7733 Forsyth St Clayton MO 63105

FINCH, RONALD M., JR., savs. and loan exec.; b. Mpls., Jan. 21, 1932; s. Ronald M. and Lynda E. (Stapel) F.; B.Indsl. Engring., U. Fla., 1954; m. Arline Anne Atkins, Sept. 17, 1961. With 1st Fed. Savs. & Loan Assn. of Lake Worth (Fla.), 1958—, pres., 1970—, also dir.; dir. Fla. StL Services, Inc., Orlando, 1970—. Dir., Lake Worth Utilities Authority, 1969-73. Trustee Lake Worth City Employees Retirement System, 1965-69; bd. dirs., sec. Lake Worth Community Fund, 1963; bd. dirs. Lake Worth Public Library, 1967-78, Better Bus. Bur. Palm Beach County, 1973—, Palm Glades Girl Scout Council, Inc., 1978—, United Way Palm Beach County, 1978—, Econ. Council Palm Beach County, 1978—. Served to 1st lt. USAF, 1955-58. Mem. Fla. Savs. and Loan League (dir. 1976-77), Lake Worth C. of C. (past pres. and dir.), Alpha Tau Omega. Conglist. (trustee 1967). Kiwanian (past pres., dir.) (Lake Worth). Home: 413 Muirfield Dr Atlantis FL 33462 Office: 2601 10th Ave N Lake Worth FL 33460

FINCH, WALTER EDWIN, real estate exec.; b. Quincy, Mass., Nov. 25, 1938; s. Walter William and Edith Sherman (Andrews) F.; diploma chartered life underwriter, Boston U., 1968; m. Ellen M. Tenerini, June 22, 1973; children—Kimberly A., Walter E., Jr., Corinne M., Darren M., Robin J. Salesman life ins., mktg. exec. John Hancock Life Ins. Co., Boston, 1960-63; salesman, mgmt. exec. New Eng. Life Ins. Co., Boston, 1963-65; brokerage mgr. Occidental Life Ins. Co., Boston, 1967-72; pres. W.E. Finch Inc. realtors, Exeter, N.H., 1972—; dir., treas. Rockingham Bd. Realtors, Rockingham County, N.H., 1974—; treas. Comml. Investment div. State of N.H., 1977-78. Active mem. Rockingham County (N.H.) Sheriff's Mounted Posse, 1976-78, Rockingham County Bd. Realtors, Polit. Action Com., 1977-78; co-chmn. Gov. M. Thompson Com., Brentwood, N.H., 1976-77. Served with Mass. Army Nat. Guard, 1956-62. C.L.U., N.H., Mass. Mem. Rockingham, N.H., Nat. bds. of realtors, Realtors Nat. Mktg. Inst., N.H. Comml. Investment Div., Real Estate Securities and Syndication Inst., Exeter C. of C. Republican. Home: RFD-1 Brentwood Rd Brentwood NH 03833 Office: Finch Profl Plaza Exeter NH 03833

FINCHELL, ALLEN RICHARD, fin. mktg. exec., economist; b. N.Y.C., Jan. 18, 1927; s. Joseph H. and Henrietta (Fritz) F.; B.S. in Social Scis., CCNY, 1947; Doctorat-es-Lettres, U. Paris, 1951; m. Margherita Iskra, Dec. 21, 1971; 1 dau., Mayra Molne-Finchell. Pres., Greater Miami Savs. Center (Fla.), 1954-68, N. Am. Fund Mgmt. Corp., London, 1959—, N. Am. Group, London, 1961—, Noram Secured Income N.V., Amsterdam, Netherlands, 1970—, Colonial Am. Mgmt. Corp., London, 1977—, Colonial Am. Maximum Income Trust Ltd., London, 1977—; chmn. Amsterdam Am. Bank N.V., 1973-76; dir. Noram Adminstrv. Services Ltd., London, 1969—. Served with U.S. Army, 1945-46. Buddhist. Office: Noram House 22 John St London WC1 England

FINCK, WILLIAM ALBERT, chem. co. exec.; b. Balt., Feb. 1, 1926; s. William John and Elaine Vivian (De Mott) F.; B.S. in Chemistry, Western Md. Coll., 1948; m. Bonnie Gutbub, Aug. 20, 1949; children—Karen Suzanne, Kevin William. Chemist, Lever Bros. Co., 1948-51, foreman, 1951-53, shift supt., 1953-57; plant supt. Los Angeles Soap Co., 1957-60; plant mgr. Purex Corp., Omaha, 1960-63; dir. prodn. grocery products div., Washington, Calif., 1963-65, gen. mgr. mfg., Carson, Calif., 1965-68, v.p. mfg., 1968-70, group v.p., gen. mgr. indsl., instnl. comml. divs., 1970-79, exec. v.p., 1979—; dir. Purex Corp., Pacific Airmotive Corp., Air Work Corp. Served with USNR, 1942-46. Mem. Soap and Detergent Assn. (dir.). Clubs: Masons, Hacienda Golf. Office: 5101 Clark Ave Lakewood CA 90712

FINDLAY, DUNCAN MURRAY, real estate agy. exec.; b. Parkville, Mo., Aug. 3, 1900; s. Merlin C. and Isabella (McRae) F.; B.A., Park Coll., 1922; B.A., Harvard U., M.B.A., 1924; m. Eleanora Noyes, 1932; children—Ann F. Urener, Charles Noyes, Susan F.; m. 2d, Mary Harding, June 25, 1964. Vice pres., dir. Charles F. Noyes Co., Inc., N.Y.C., 1935—. Chmn., Huntington YMCA, 1945-60; trustee Park Coll., 1940—; v.p., bd. dirs. Jessie Smith Noyes Found., Inc., 1944—; mem. gen. council United Presbyterian Ch., 1942-49. Served with U.S. Army, World War I. Republican. Clubs: Harvard, Am. Yacht, Apawamis. Home: Indian Trail Harrison NY 10528 Office: Charles F Noyes Co Inc 61 Broadway New York NY 10006

FINDLEY, GERALD L. E., economist, bank mgmt. cons.; b. Truman, Ark., Oct. 27, 1920; s. Burl Clinton and Gertrude (Tolar) F.; B.S., UCLA, 1949, M.B.A., 1950; m. Myrtle L. Royer, June 11, 1948; children—Melinda Ann, Gary Steven, Pamela Ann. Head research and engring. dept. Union Bank, Los Angeles, 1950-54; Western regional mgr. Cunneen Co., Los Angeles, 1954-56; owner, pres. Gerry Findley and Assos., Temple City, Calif., 1956—; editor Findley Reports, Inc.; instr. U. Calif. Extension, 1950-53. Served with USN, 1939-45; PTO. Mem. UCLA Alumni Assn. Republican. Methodist. Clubs: Masons, Shriners. Office: 10103 E Bogue St Temple City CA 91780

FINE, ALICE ELIZABETH, banker; b. Huntsville, Ala., Apr. 9, 1931; d. Charles Marion and Allie Irene (Williams) Morgan; ed. Morristown Bus. Coll., Walters State Coll.; m. Kenneth Fine, Sept. 16, 1949; children—Sharon Yvonne Fine Johnson, Kenneth. Sec. to Fred L. Myers, atty., 1957-58; bookkeeper, sec. Nat. Bank of Newport (Tenn.), 1958-73, cashier, sec. to bd. dirs., 1973—. Office: Box 69 National Bank of Newport Newport TN 37821

FINE, BARRY K., steel drum co. exec.; b. Bklyn., May 15, 1938; s. Harry Harold and Ann (Elkind) F.; student Queens Coll., 1956-65; m. Rho Joy Stengel, Sept. 3, 1965; children—Scott Jefferson, Jill Ashley. Jr. civil engr. N.Y.C. Transit Authority, 1957-58; with Active Steel Drum Co., Long Island City, N.Y., 1958-61, pres., 1964—; founder Container Services Co., Long Island City, 1964—; pres. Able Container Corp., Bklyn., 1974—; instr. hunting safety. Served in U.S. Army, 1957-63. Mem. Gem. Nat. Rifle Assn., U.S. Power Squadron, Nat. Barrel and Drum Assn., Cooperage Industries Assn., Bur. Explosives, Assn. Am. R.R.'s, Internat. Racquetball Assn. Clubs: Masons, B'nai B'rith. Patentee in field. Home: 27 Lawrence Ln Bay Shore NY 11706 Office: 52-30 34th St Long Island City NY 11101

FINE, HAROLD DAVID, jewelry mfg. co. exec.; b. Attleboro, Mass., Nov. 2, 1923; s. Samuel Baer and Jessie G. (Baker) F.; B.S. (Textron fellow), R.I. Sch. Design, 1948; M.P.A., Harvard U., 1950; m. Anita Le Page, Apr. 29, 1961; children—Carol, Debra, David. Asst. to v.p. John Wanamaker Co., Phila., 1950-51; v.p., treas. A & Z Chain Co., Providence, 1951-70; pres. Amtel Arts Co., East Providence, R.I., 1970-78, A & Z Hayward, Inc., East Providence, 1979—. Mem. adv. council Johnson and Wales Coll., 1978—; vice chmn. exec. budget com. United Way R.I., 1964-65, chmn. capital funds com., 1966-67. Served to 1st lt., C.E., U.S. Army, 1942-46. Decorated Sword of Hagannah (Israel). Mem. Mfg. Jewelers and Silversmiths Am. (pres. 1972-74), Jewelers Bd. Trade (pres. 1976-78), Providence Jewelers Club (pres. 1966-67), Diamond Peacock Club (pres. 1968-69), Jewelry Industry Council (dir. 1963—), 24 Karat Club N.Y., Boston Jewelers Club. Jewish. Clubs: Harvard Bus. Sch. R.I. (dir. 1980—), Masons. Home: 66 Bay State Rd Rehoboth MA 02769 Office: 655 Waterman Ave East Providence RI 02914

FINE, J(AMES) ALLEN, ins. co. exec.; b. Albemarle, N.C., May 2, 1934; s. Samuel Lee and Ocie (Loflin) F.; student Pfeiffer Coll., 1957-58; B.S., U. N.C., 1961, M.B.A., 1965; m. Marie Nan Morris, Sept. 1, 1957; children—James A(llen), William Morris. Sr. accountant Haskins & Sells, C.P.A.'s Charlotte, N.C., 1961-62, Watson, Penry, & Morgan, Asheboro, N.C., 1962-64; instr. U. N.C., Chapel Hill, 1964-65; asst. prof. Pfeiffer Coll., Misenheimer, N.C., 1965-66; treas., v.p. adminstrn. Nat. Lab. for Higher Edn. (formerly Regional Edn. Lab. Carolinas and Va.), Durham, N.C., 1966-72; organizer, chief exec. officer, treas., dir. Investors Title Ins. Co., Inc., Chapel Hill, 1972—; chief exec. officer, treas., dir. Investors Title Ins. Co., Inc., Columbia, S.C., 1973—; pres., dir. Investors Title Co., Inc., Chapel Hill, 1976—; developer Carolina Forest Subdiv., Chapel Hill, 1970—, Springhill Forest subdiv., Chapel Hill, 1977—, Stoneycreek subdiv., 1978—; lectr. accounting U. N.C., Chapel Hill, 1967-70. Area officer ann. alumni giving U. N.C., Chapel Hill, 1968-69, 71-73, 75—. Served with USN, 1953-57. Recipient Haskins & Sells Found. award for excellence in accounting, 1961; N.C. Assn. CPA's award for most outstanding accounting student U. N.C., 1961. Mem. Am. Inst. C.P.A.'s, N.C. Assn. C.P.A.'s, Am. Accounting Assn., CEDAR Bus. Mgrs. (chmn. nat. exec. com. 1971), Phi Beta Kappa, Beta Gamma Sigma (treas. 1961). Home: 112 Carolina Forest Chapel Hill NC 27514 Office: Investors Title Bldg Chapel Hill NC 27514

FINE, RICHARD AARON, brokerage exec.; b. Chgo., Nov. 30, 1929; s. Michael Richard and Paula (Halperin) F.; B.S., Columbia, 1958; postgrad. New Sch. Social Research, 1960-61, N.Y. Inst. Finance, 1962; m. Mary Corinne MacKay, June 14, 1969; children—Michael Aaron, Elizabeth Lee. Financial news commentator various radio stas., N.Y.C., Boston, 1958-64; mgr. brokerage offices, 1963-73; v.p. investments and acquisitions Southtown Economist, Inc., Chgo., 1973; v.p., resident mgr. Chgo. office Stifel, Nicolaus Co., Inc., 1973-75; investment broker Dean Witter Reynolds Inc., Chgo., 1975-80; sr. v.p. Mesirow Fin. Services, Inc., Chgo., 1978—. Chmn. scholarship com. Harris Sch., Chgo. Served with USNR, 1948-49. Home: 3200 Lake Shore Dr Chicago IL 60657 Office: 135 S LaSalle St Chicago IL 60603

FINEGAN, RICHARD JOSEPH, ins. co. exec.; b. Cleve., Mar. 1, 1925; s. Franklyn J. and Mabelle R. (Hites) F.; B.S. in Elec. Engring., Kans. State U., 1948; grad. Advanced Mgmt. Program, Harvard U., 1977; m. Margret K. Reigner, Oct. 8, 1949; children—Kathleen, Maureen, Thomas, John. With Liberty Mut. Ins. Co., Detroit, Chgo., N.Y.C., 1948-73, asst. v.p., Boston, 1973-74, v.p., gen. mgr. loss prevention dept., 1974—. Served with USNR, 1944-46; PTO. Registered profl. engr., Calif.; cert. safety profl. Mem. Am. Nat. Standards Inst. (v.p., dir.), Am. Soc. Safety Engrs. Roman Catholic. Home: 18 Johnson Rd Winchester MA 01890 Office: Liberty Mut Ins Co 175 Berkeley St Boston MA 02117

FINEGOLD, RONALD, computer corp. exec.; b. Bklyn., Nov. 17, 1942; s. Herman Hearsch and Ethel (Kanner) F.; B.S., City Coll. N.Y., 1963; m. Ellen Carole Sehr, Mar. 22, 1964; children—Sherry Dawn, Edward Jon. Supr. programming Celanese Chem. Co., N.Y.C., 1962-66; v.p. marketing Automation Scis., Inc., N.Y.C., 1966-69; pres. Computer Horizons Corp., N.Y.C., 1969—, chmn. bd., 1977—, dir., 1969—; chmn. bd. Stamford Assos., Inc., N.Y.C., 1969-75; pres., dir. Rizons Brokerage, Inc., 1970-71, chmn. bd., dir., 1972-75; chmn. bd. Custom Terminals Corp., 1976—. Mem. Data Processing Mgmt. Assn., Am. Mgmt. Assn., Young Presidents Orgn., Aircraft Owners and Pilots Assn., Tau Epsilon Phi. Home: 154 Valley Forge Pl Orangeburg NY 10962 Office: 747 3d Ave New York NY 10017 also 375 Sylvan Ave Englewood Cliffs NJ 07032 also 1000 Brickell Ave Miami FL 33133

FINGER, JERRY ELLIOTT, bank exec.; b. Houston, Oct. 11, 1932; s. Hyman Elliott and Bessie Kaplan F.; B.S. in Econs., Wharton Sch., U. Pa., 1954; m. Nanette Breitenbach, June 20, 1954; children—Richard Breitenbach, Jonathan Samuel, Walter Goodman. Asst. controller Finger Furniture Co., Houston, 1956-59; partner Finger Interests, Houston, 1959—; pres. Republic Nat. Bank, Houston, 1963-75, chief exec. officer, dir., chmn., 1975—; chmn. Beaumont Savings & Loan Assn. (Tex.), 1968-76, adv. chmn., 1976—; chmn. exec. com. Reagan Commerce Bank, Houston, 1968-77; pres. Citizens & So. Life Ins. Co., Houston, 1971—; chmn. trustees S.W. Mortgage & Realty Investors, Houston, 1972—; chmn. exec. com. Gulf Republic Fin. Corp., Houston, 1972—; chmn. Colonial Nat. Bank, Houston, 1975—; adv. chmn. exec. com., The Standard Bank, Houston, 1975-79, adv. dir., 1979-80; dir. Gulf Resources & Chem. Corp., Houston, 1977—. Trustee, Meml. Hosp. Systems, 1971—; bd. dirs. Houston Clearing Assn., 1977—, Coastal Ind. Water Auth., 1968-72. Served to lt. (j.g.) USN, 1954-56. Mem. Am. Bankers Assn., Robert Morris Soc., Tex. Bankers Assn. Republican. Jewish. Clubs: Houston Racquet, Univ., Houston Yacht, Houstonian, Houston City, Met. Racquet. Office: PO Box 10816 Houston TX 77018 also 5200 N Shepherd St Houston TX 77091

FINGER, JOHN HOLDEN, lawyer; b. Oakland, Calif., June 29, 1913; s. Clyde P. and Jennie (Miller) F.; A.B., U. Calif., 1933; m. Dorothy C. Riley, Dec. 30, 1950; children—Catherine Anne, John Holden, David, Carol. Admitted to Calif. bar, 1937; pvt. practice law, San Francisco, 1937-42, 47—; chief mil. commn. sect. Far East Hdqrs. War Dept., Tokyo, 1946-47; pres. Hoberg, Finger, Brown, Cox & Molligan, San Francisco. Bd. dirs. 1st Savs. and Loan Assn. Fresno. Mem. bd. visitors Judge Adv. Gen's Sch., Charlottesville, Va., 1964-76, Stanford U. Law Sch., 1969-71. Bd. dirs. San Francisco Legal Aid Soc.; trustee Pacific Sch. Religion, chmn., pres. corp., 1969-78; Pres. Laymen's Fellowship, No. Calif. Conf. Congl. Chs., 1951-53, moderator, 1954-55. Served to maj. JAGC, AUS, 1942-46; ret. col.; comdg. officer 5th JAG detachment, 1962-64; U.S. Army judiciary, 1967-68. Decorated Legion of Merit. Fellow Am. Coll. Trial Lawyers, Am. Bar Found.; mem. Am. Bar Assn. (ho. of dels. 1970-78, council jud. adminstrn. div. 1972-77), Bar Assn. San Francisco (dir. 1960-62), State Bar Calif. (bd. govs. 1965-68, pres. 1967-68), Judge Adv. Assn. (dir. 1957—, pres. 1964-65) Lawyers Club of San Francisco (pres. 1953), Sierra Club (exec. com. def. fund), Sigma Phi Epsilon, Alpha Kappa Phi, Phi Alpha Delta. Home: 12675 Skyline Blvd Oakland CA 94619 Office 703 Market St San Francisco CA 94103

FINGON, ROBERT JAMES, data processing exec.; b. New Haven, Nov. 8, 1949; s. John J. and Helen (McDermott) F.; B.S., Northeastern U., 1973; M.S., U. New Haven, 1977; m. Joan Carroll, Apr. 22, 1977; 1 child, Shallon. Student programmer U. New Haven, West Haven, 1974-76; programmer Sperry Remington, Bridgeport, Conn., 1976-77; data processing mgr. Rockingham Meml. Hosp., Bellows Falls, Vt., 1977-78; programmer/analyst Vt. Marble Co., Proctor, Vt., 1978—. U. New Haven grantee, 1974-76.

FINK, AARON HERMAN, box mfg. exec.; b. Union City, N.J., Apr. 1, 1916; s. Jacob and Tessie (Dubow) F.; A.B., Johns Hopkins U., 1938; Ph.D. in Bus. Adminstrn. (hon.), Hamilton State U., 1977; m. Roslyn Lamb, Dec. 6, 1942; children—Elliot, Illene. Treas., Asso. Mills, 1938-45; now dir.; v.p., gen. mgr. Essex Paper Box Mfg. Co., Newark, 1945-48, pres., 1948—; pres. Internat. Gift Box Co., 1948—; U.S. del. Conf. Mfrs., Paris, 1954, Spl. Econ. Mission to Italy, 1954. Fellow Internat. Biog. Assn. (certificate of merit); mem. N.J. Paper Box Mfg. Assn. (trustee), N.J. Box Craft Bur. (pres.), Am. Soc. Quality Control, TAPPI, NAM, Am. Mgmt. Assn. (pres.'s asso.), AIM (fellow pres.'s council, adv. bd.), Nat. Soc. Bus. Budgeting, Confrerie de la Chaine des Rotisseurs, Am. Material Handling Soc., Am. Forestry Assn., Am. Soc. Advancement Mgmt., Nat. Paper Box Assn. (dir., asso. chmn. met. div., chmn. plant ops. and manpower), Am. Inst. Aeros. and Astronautics, Am. Geophys. Union, Am. Ordnance Assn., N.Y. Acad. Scis., Nat. Space Inst., Fedn. Aeronautique Internat. Clubs: Princeton, Johns Hopkins (N.Y.C.); Crestmont Country (gov.) (Great Oak); Newark Athletic; Le Mirador Country (Lake Geneva, Switzerland); Boca Raton (Fla.). Home: 20 Crestwood Dr Maplewood NJ 07040 Office: 281 Astor St Newark NJ 07114

FINK, CHARLES AUGUSTIN, behavioral systems scientist; b. McAllen, Tex., Jan. 1, 1929; s. Charles Adolph and Mary Nellie (Bonneau) F.; A.A., Pan-Am. U., 1948; B.S., Marquette U., 1950; postgrad. No. Va. Community Coll., 1973, George Mason U., 1974; M.A., Cath. U. Am., 1979; m. Ann Heslen, June 1, 1955; children—Patricia A., Marianne E., Richard G., Gerard A. Journalist, UP and Ft. Worth Star-Telegram, 1950-52; commd. 2d lt. U.S. Army, 1952, advanced through grades to lt. col., 1966, various positions telecommunications, 1952-56, teaching, 1956-58, exec. project mgmt., 1958-62, def. analysis and research, 1962-65, fgn. mil. relations, 1965-67, def. telecommunications exec., 1967-69, chief planning, budget and program control office Def. Satellite Communications Program, Def. Communications Agy., 1969-72, ret. 1972; pvt. practice cons. managerial behavior Falls Church, Va., 1972-77; pres. Charles A. Fink, behavioral systems sci. orgn., Falls Church, 1978—; leader family group dynamics, 1958-67. Adv. bd. Holy Redeemer Roman Cath. Ch., Bangkok, Thailand, St. Philip's Ch., Falls Church, Va., 1971-73. Decorated Army Commendation medals, Joint Services Commendation medal. Mem. Soc. Gen. Systems Research, Am. Soc. Cybernetics, Am. Personnel and Guidance Assn., Assn. for Counselor Edn. and Supervision, Armed Forces Communications and Electronics Assn., Assn. U.S. Army. Club: K.C. Developer hierarchial theory of human behavior, 1967—, uses in behavioral, social and biol. sci. and their applications, 1972—, behavioral causal modeling research methodology, 1974—. Home: 3305 Brandy Ct Falls Church VA 22042 Office: PO Box 2051 Falls Church VA 22042

FINK, DAVID ELIAH, rental car co. ofcl.; b. N.Y.C., Jan. 1, 1952; s. Milton and Helen (Edelstein) F.; A.A., Nassau Community Coll., 1972; B.A. in Sociology, U. Buffalo, 1974. Caseworker, VA Hosp., Buffalo, 1972-73, Wall's Meml. Headstart Program, Buffalo, 1973-74; sr. project engr. LKB Adminstrv. Systems, Syosset, N.Y., 1974-76; sales rep. Nat. Car Rental Co., N.Y.C., 1976—. Office mgr. George McGovern Campaign, 1972. Mem. Am. Tinnitus Assn. Democrat. Jewish. Club: Holiday Racquet. Home: 1018 Northfield Rd Woodmere NY 11598 Office: 95-10 Ditmars Blvd East Elmhurst NY 11369

FINK, DONALD G., engr. editor, inst. adminstr.; b. Englewood, N.J., Nov. 8, 1911; s. Harold Gardner and Margaret (Glen) F.; B.S. in Elec. Engring., Mass. Inst. Tech., 1933; M.S., Columbia, 1942; m. Alice M. Berry, Apr. 10, 1948; children—Kathleen, Stephen, Susan. Research asst. Mass. Inst. Tech., 1933-34; mem. editorial staff Electronics, 1934-52, editor in chief, 1946-52; research dept. Philco Corp., 1952-62, dir. research, 1952-58, dir., gen. mgr. research div., 1959-61, v.p. research, 1961, dir. Sci. Lab., 1962; gen. mgr. IEEE, 1963-75, exec. dir., 1972-75, exec. cons., 1975-76; TV cons., Belgium, 1952; dir. McGraw-Hill Book Co., Inc., 1947-52, cons. editor TV Series, 1949—; editor-in-chief Standard Handbook for Elec. Engrs., 1963—, Electronics Engrs. Handbook, 1970—; expert cons. Office of Sec. War, 1943-45; civilian cons. Comdr. Task Force One, Bikini atom bomb tests, 1946; adv. Dept. State, spokesman C.C.I.R. meeting, Zurich, 1949, London, 1950, Geneva, 1951, mem. Senate Adv. Com. on Color TV, 1949-50; vice-chmn. Nat. TV System Com., 1950-52; mem. Nav., Research and Devel. Bd., Dept. Def., 1948-51; mem. Nat. Stereophonic Radio Com., 1959-60, Army Sci. Adv. Panel, 1957-74; chmn. com. internat. sci. and tech. info. programs NRC, 1975-78; mem. bd. internat. orgns. and programs Nat. Acad. Scis., 1974-81; chmn. adv. bd. cable TV picture quality study U. Mo., 1975-77. Trustee, Met. Reference and Research Library Agy., 1974—. Recipient Medal of Freedom, War Dept., 1946, Presdl. Certificate of Merit, 1948, Fall Meeting award IRE, 1951; Achievement award N.Y. Inst. Tech., 1958; Outstanding Civilian Service medal U.S. Army, 1969. Fellow Am. Inst. E.E., IRE (dir., editor Proc. 1956-57, pres. 1958), Instn. Elec. Engrs. (London), IEEE (Founders medal 1978), Soc. Motion Picture and TV Engrs. (jour. award 1956, Progress medal 1979); mem. Nat. Acad. Engring., Phi Mu Delta, Tau Beta Pi, Sigma Xi, Eta Kappa Nu (eminent mem.). Clubs: Cosmos (Washington); Heritage Hills Country. Author: Engineering Electronics, 1938; Principles of Television Engineering, 1940; Microwave Radar, 1943; Radar Engineering, 1947; Television Engineering, 1952; Color Television Standards, 1955; Television Engineering Handbook, 1957; Physics of Television, 1960; Computers and the Human Mind, 1966; Standard Handbook for Electrical Engineers, 1978; Electronics Engineer's Handbook, 1981; others. Home: 103-B Heritage Hills Somers NY 10589 Office: United Engring Center 345 E 47th St New York NY 10017

FINK, JOHN FRANCIS, publishing co. exec.; b. Ft. Wayne, Ind., Dec. 17, 1931; s. Francis Anthony and Helen Elizabeth (Hartman) F.; B.A., U. Notre Dame, 1953; m. Marie Therese Waldron, May 31, 1955; children—Regina Marie, Barbara Ann, Robert Paul, Stephen Lawrence, Therese Rose, David Francis, John Noll. Asso. editor Our Sunday Visitor, Religious Pub. Co., Huntington, Ind., 1956-68, editor Family Digest, 1956-67, marketing mgr., 1967-72, exec. v.p., 1972-76, pres., 1976—; chmn. bd. Noll Printing Co., Huntington, 1978—; dir., mem. exec. com. First Nat. Bank, Huntington. Vice chmn. Religious Communications Congress, 1980. Chmn. United Fund Drive, 1963; pres. United Way of Huntington County, 1973-74, bd. dirs., 1971-74; bd. dirs. YMCA, 1969-78, Cath. Journalism Scholarship Fund, Internat. Cath. Orgns. Center, Center for Applied Research in the Apostolate; trustee Huntington Coll., 1978-81; pres. Huntington Coll. Found., 1978-81; bd. dirs. Huntington Med. Meml. Found. Served as 1st lt. USAF, 1954-56. Recipient Disting. Service award Huntington Jr. C. of C., 1960; named Outstanding Young Man of Am., 1966, Chief of Flint Springs Tribe, 1971. Mem. Internat. Fedn. Ch. Press Assns. (pres. 1980—), Internat. Cath. Union of Press (dir. and exec. com.), Catholic Press Assn. U.S. (pres. 1973-75, dir. 1965-75), Founds. and Donors Interested in Cath. Activities (bd. dirs. 1978—). Republican. Roman Catholic. Clubs: Cosmopolitan, Rotary, K.C., Knights of Holy Sepulchre, Knights of Malta. Home: Rural Route 8 Huntington IN 46750 Office: 200 Noll Plaza Huntington IN 46750

FINK, NORMA CARNEL, real estate exec.; b. Sacramento, May 23, 1929; d. Donald and Etta Grace (Rall) Carnel; B.A., U. Nev., 1951, postgrad., 1951-52; postgrad. Mich. State U., 1954; certificate Realtors Inst., 1971; m. Robert Wilbur Fink, Mar. 14, 1954; children—Marilyn, Darla Jean, Renee Alane, Nanette, Natalie. Counselor, Girl Scout camps, Denver, 1948, Portland, Ore., 1949, Spokane, Wash., 1950; dist. dir., camp dir. Girl Scouts U.S.A., Columbus, Ohio, 1953-55, Sierra-Nev. Area council, Reno 1958-61; civilian program dir. Army Service Club, Ft. Lewis, Wash., 1952-53; camp dir., dir. teen-age program Reno YWCA, 1956-58; broker-salesman Rogan Realty Co., Reno, 1965-67; broker Norma Fink Realty, Sun Valley, Nev., 1967—; pres. Norma Fink, Inc., Realtors, Sun Valley, 1970—; instr. Grad. Realtors Inst., 1971-79; mem. Reno Realtors Profl. Standard Panel, 1974-79. Chmn. Truckee Meadows Urban Transp. citizens Adv. Com., 1973-74, Washoe County Area Transp. Citizens Adv. Com., 1975-80; non-partisan dir. Sun Valley Water and Sanitation Dist., 1965-73. Mem. Nat. Assn. Realtors (named Nev. Farm and Land Broker of Year 1974; dir. 1979-81, lic. law com. 1979—, state and mcpl. legis. com. 1980—), Reno Bd. Realtors (named Realtor of Year 1974, recipient Spl. award 1969, chmn. conv. Farm and Land Inst. 1974), Women's Council of Realtors (pres. 1971), Sierra-Reno Exchangers (pres. 1975), Nev. Assn. Realtors (chmn. pub. relations 1973-74, editor newsletter 1975, chmn. policy com. 1976-78, Realtor of Year 1977, 80), Nev. State Dairy Goat Council (parliamentarian). Christian Scientist. Club: Renown Toastmistress (pres. Council VIII Sierra Nevada region 1980). Home: 245 Harmony Ln via Sparks NV 89431 Office: 5160 Sun Valley Dr Reno-Sparks NV 89431

FINKEL, BERNARD GERALD, mfg. co. exec.; b. N.Y.C., Dec. 26, 1937; s. Harry and Molly (Stern) F.; student Syracuse U., 1954-57; B.A. in Chemistry, N.Y. U., 1959; m. Natalie Peretz, May 31, 1958; children—Michelle, Susan, Karen. Mgr. diagnostics div. Warner-Lambert Pharm. Co., Morris Plains, N.J., 1960-69; pres. Sci. Spltys. Ltd., Garden City N.Y., 1969-73; pres. Clin. Scis., Inc., Whippany, N.J., 1973—; dir. Purex Labs. Instr. lab. mgmt. N.Y.C. Community Coll., 1969—. NIH grantee, 1959. Mem. Am. Assn. Clin. Chemists, Am. Soc. Microbiologists, Am. Chem. Soc. pres. N.Y. U. chpt. 1959), Downstate Soc. Med. Techs. (pres. 1968), Psi Sigma. Patentee in field. Home: 1 Brian Ln Spring Valley NY 10977 Office: 30 Troy Rd Whippany NJ 07981

FINKEL, SHELDON, concert producer; b. Bklyn., June 27, 1944; s. William and Betty (Glassman) F.; student City Coll. N.Y., 1962-64, N.Y. U., 1964-66; m. Beth Jean Rosenthal, Sept. 1, 1976. Vice pres. Cable Music Co., N.Y.C., 1970-71; pres. Cornucopia Prodns. Inc., N.Y.C., 1972-74, Cross-Country Concert Corp., N.Y.C., 1975—; cons. ASCAP. Clubs: B'nai Brith, Friars. Office: Cross-Country Concert Corp 527 Madison Ave New York NY 10022

FINKEL, STANLEY MORTON, fashion accessories co. exec.; b. Balt., May 13, 1917; s. Joseph and Dora (Hamburger) F.; student Balt. City Coll., 1931-34; A.B. (Univ. scholar), Johns Hopkins U., 1938; M.B.A. (Univ. scholar), Harvard U., 1939; m. Eileen Ershler Sandberg, May 18, 1960; children—Ann, Janet, David, Mark, Helen Robert. Merchandising mgr. Talon, Inc., N.Y.C., 1939-41; asst. to pres. Schenley Distillers Corp., N.Y.C., 1941-52; product and packaging devel. head Welch Grape Juice Co., N.Y.C., 1952-54; v.p., exec. asst. to pres. Botany Industries, Inc. and Hotel Corp. Am., N.Y.C., 1954-63; pres., chmn. bd. Baar & Beards, Inc., N.Y.C., 1963—; cons. mergers, acquisitions; condr. Making of a Pres. seminars Harvard U. Bus. Sch. Club, 1962—. Served with USN, 1942-45. Decorated Naval Commendation; recipient Disting. Service award Harvard U. Grad. Sch. Bus., 1979. Mem. Johns Hopkins U. Alumni Assn. (pres. Met. N.Y. 1977-80), Harvard Bus. Sch. Club, Am. Mgmt. Assn. (conf. chmn.). Home: 27 E 65th St New York NY 10021 Office: 15 W 37th St New York NY 10018

FINKES, WILLIAM HOWARD, banker; b. Columbus, Ohio, May 17, 1947; s. Howard William and Mary Alice F.; B.B.A. in Fin. cum laude, Ohio U., Athens, 1969; m. Barbara Louise Norris, June 28, 1969. Maintenance man Seal of Ohio Girl Scout Council, summers 1967-68; mgmt. trainee BancOhio/Ohio Nat. Bank, Columbus, 1969-70, cash position analyst cashier's dept., 1970-73, customer securities bookkeeping mgr., asst. cashier, 1973, asst. v.p., mgr. cash asset control, money transfer sect. Active Banc Ohio Corp. Govt. Awareness Assn. Mem. Am. Inst. Banking. Office: 155 E Broad St Columbus OH 43265

FINLEY, GEORGE ALVIN, III, hardware distbn. co. exec.; b. Aurora, Ill., Apr. 25, 1938; s. George Alvin, II, and Sally Ann (Lord) F.; B.B.A., So. Meth. U., 1962; postgrad. Coll. Grad. Program, Ford Motor Co., 1963; m. Sue Sellors, June 20, 1962; children—Valerie, George Alvin IV. Rep. for Europe, Finco Internat., 1959-61; trainee Ford Motor Co., Dearborn, Mich., 1962-63; v.p. mktg. Internat. Motor Cars, Oakland, Calif., 1963-64, Sequoia Lincoln lease mgr., 1965; regional mgr. Behlen Mfg. Co., Dallas, 1965-67; pres. C C Hardware Inc., Corpus Christi, Tex., 1967—; guest instr. Sch. Bus., So. Meth. U.; mem. exec. com. Pro Hardware Inc., Stamford, Conn.; dir. USSI, NBC, Inc., Taurgo Industries, Inc., BCM Marine and Indsl. Supply, AIRCO, Schmidt's Inc., Charter Savs. and Loan. Apptd. bd. mem. Nueces River Authority, 1976-82; pres. Coastal Bend Halfway Houses for Alcoholics. Recipient award for devel. full service half way houses for alcoholics, Tex., 1976-77. Mem. Nat., Tex. (past v.p.) wholesale hardware assns., Nat. Retail Hardware Assn., So. Hardware Assn., Phi Delta Theta. Democrat. Unitarian. Club: Rotary Internat. Asst. in design, engring., production, mktg. Apollo Automobile, 1963-64. Home: 3360 Ocean Dr Corpus Christi TX 78411 Office: PO Box 9153 210 McBride Ln Corpus Christi TX 78408

FINLEY, JAMES DANIELLY, textile co. exec.; b. Jackson, Ga., July 14, 1916; s. Albert C. and Kate (Danielly) F.; B.S. in Textile Engring., Ga. Inst. Tech., 1937; grad. Advanced Mgmt. Program, Harvard, 1951; m. Nancy Butler, June 7, 1941; children—James Danielly, Fred B., William G. With Firestone Tire & Rubber Co., 1938-41; with J.P. Stevens & Co., Inc., N.Y.C., 1945—, v.p., 1958-64, dir., 1961—, mem. exec. com., 1962—, exec. v.p., 1964-65, chmn. bd., 1965—, also chief exec. officer, 1969-80, chmn. exec. com., 1980—; dir. Borden Inc., Sperry Rand Corp., Bd. dirs. Am. Textile Mfrs. Inst. Served from 2d lt. to maj. Q.M.C., AUS, 1941-45. Office: 1185 Ave of Americas New York NY 10036

FINLEY, LEWIS MERREN, financial planner; b. Reubens, Idaho, Nov. 29, 1929; s. John Emory and Charlotte (Priest) F.; student pub. schs., Spokane; m. Virginia Ruth Spousta, Feb. 23, 1957; children—Ellen Annette, Charlotte Louise. With Household Finance Co., Portland, Oreg. and Seattle, 1953-56; with Doug Gerow Finance, Portland, 1956-61; pres. Family Financial Planners Inc., Portland, 1961—; realtor Peoples Choice Realty, Inc., Milwaukie, Oreg., 1977—. Standing trustee Chpt. 13, Fed. Bankruptcy Ct., Dist. of Oreg., 1979-80. Served with U.S. Army, 1951-53. Mem. Oreg. Assn. Credit Counselors (past pres.), Northwest Assn. Credit Counselors (past treas.), Am. Assn. Credit Counselors, Authors Guild. Republican. Methodist. Clubs: Masons (past master), Shriners. Author: The Complete Guide to Getting Yourself Out of Debt, 1975. Home: 3015 SE Riviere Dr Milwaukie OR 97222 Office: 1924 NE Broadway Portland OR 97232

FINLEY, SKIP, broadcasting co. exec.; b. Ann Arbor, Mich., July 23, 1948; s. Ewell W. and Mildred J. (Johnson) F.; student Northeastern U., 1966-71; m. Karen Michele Woolard, May 6, 1971; children—Kharma Isis, R. Kristen. With WHDH-TV, Boston, 1971, WSBK-TV, Boston, 1971-72, WRKO, Boston, 1972-73; account exec. Humphrey, Browning, MacDougall, Boston, 1973-74; with Sheridan Broadcasting Corp., 1974—; exec. v.p., gen. mgr. Sheridan Broadcasting Network, 1979—; guest lectr. U. Pitts., 1976, Howard U., Washington, 1979, Columbia U., N.Y.C., 1979. Adv. bd. Nat. Council Negro Women, 1979—; bd. overseers Vineyard Open Land Found.; 1980—. Mem. Nat. Assn. Black Owned Broadcasters, Am. Mgmt. Assn., Pitts. Radio-TV Club, New Eng. Advt. Club. Editor: Black Index, 1980; contbr. articles to profl. jours. Office: 1745 S Jefferson Davis Hwy Arlington VA 22202

FINN, DAVID, pub. relations exec.; b. N.Y.C., Aug. 30, 1921; s. Jonathan and Sadie (Borgenicht) F.; B.S., Coll. City N.Y., 1943; m. Laura Zeisler, Oct. 20, 1945; children—Kathy, Dena, Peter, Amy. Co-founder Ruder & Finn, Inc., 1948, pres., 1956-68, chmn. bd., 1968—; adj. asso. prof. N.Y. U. Paintings exhibited L'Orangerie, Paris, Met. Mus., N.Y.C., A. Crispo Gallery, N.Y.C., others; one man show New Sch., N.Y.C. Mem. adv. bd. Council Study Mankind; bd. visitors Coll. City N.Y.; adv. com. N.Y.C. Office Cultural Affairs. Mem. Neuberger Mus., Center for Research in Bus. and Social Policy; mem. bd. MacDowell Colony, Inst. for Future, Artists for Environment Found., Internat. Center Photography, Am. Coll. in Switzerland; trustee Jewish Theol. Sem. Am. Served to 1st lt. A.C., AUS, 1944. Mem. Am. Fedn. Arts, Am. Inst. Graphic Arts (past bd. dirs.), Internat. Pub. Relations Assn., Kappa Tau Alpha (hon.). Author: Public Relations and Management, 1956; The Corporate Oligarch, 1969. Contbr. articles to profl. jours. Photographer: (books) Embrace of Life, 1969; As the Eye Moves, 1970; Donatello: Prophet of Modern Vision, 1973. Henry Moore Sculpture and Environment, 1976; Michelangelo's Three Pietas, 1975; Oceanic Images, 1978; The Florence Baptistry Doors, 1980; Sculpture at Storm King, 1980; Busch-Reisinger Mus., 1980. Office: 110 E 59th St New York NY 10022

FINN, RICHARD HENRY, leasing co. exec.; b. Luanshya, Zambia, Nov. 23, 1934; s. Henry Reginald and Eleanor Margaret (Evans) F.; came to U.S., 1975; B.A., Oxford U., 1956, M.A., 1958; m. Rosemary Buttling, Sept. 29, 1964; children—Mark Henry, Holly Caroline, Laura Jane. Exec., Selection Trust, Ltd. and asso. cos., Africa, London, 1956-62; asso. McKinsey & Co., Inc., London, 1962-69; v.p. Europe, Integrated Container Service, Inc., London, 1969-75, pres., chief operating officer, N.Y.C., 1975—. Mem. Chartered Inst. Secs. and Adminstrs., Containerisation Inst. Clubs: Univ., Siwanoy Golf, Hurlingham, Royal Lymington Yacht, Marylebone Cricket, Royal Automobile. Home: 5 Hamilton Ave Bronxville NY 10708 Office: 522 Fifth Ave New York NY 10017

FINNEGAN, JAMES PATRICK, engring. psychologist; b. Pitts., Feb. 27, 1947; s. Regis Patrick and Edna Ann (Jesteadt) F.; B.S. in Aerospace Engring., Pa. State U., 1969; B.A. in Psychology, Chapman Coll., 1975; M.A. in Engring. Psychology, U. Ill., 1977. Design engr. Gen. Electric Co., Evandale, Ohio, 1969-70, devel. engr., 1974; research asst. Aviation Research Lab., U. Ill., Savoy, 1975-77; engring. psychologist Failure Analysis Assos., Palo Alto, Calif., 1977—; cons. in field. Served with USAF, 1970-73. Mem. Human Factors Soc., Am. Soc. Safety Engrs., System Safety Soc., Assn. Aviation Psychologists, Exptl. Aircraft Assn. Home: 9000 Alpine Rd Route 2 Box 140 LaHonda CA 94020 Office: 750 Welch Rd Palo Alto CA 94304

FINNEGAN, THOMAS JOSEPH, lawyer; b. Chgo., Aug. 18, 1900; s. Thomas Harrison and Marie (Flanagan) F.; LL.B., Chgo. Kent Coll. Law, 1923, J.D., 1969; m. Hildreth Millslagel, July 1, 1933 (dec. Mar. 1977). Admitted to Ill. bar, 1923, since practiced in Chgo.; mem. firm Fithian, Spengler & Finnegan, 1935-51, Korshak, Rothman, Oppenheim & Finnegan, 1951—. Mem. Am., Fed., Ill., Chgo. bar assns., Phi Alpha Delta. Home: 5630 Sheridan Rd Chicago IL 60660 Office: 69 W Washington St Chicago IL 60602

FINNERTY, JOHN JOSEPH, mfg. co. exec.; b. Geneva, N.Y., Nov. 25, 1939; s. Joseph John and Dorothy K. (Marshall) F.; B.S., Rochester Inst. Tech., 1970; postgrad. Pepperdine U., 1973, Harvard U., 1977, U. Va., 1978; m. Mary F. Gringeri, June 3, 1960; children—Deborah, Michelle, Mary Ellen, Colleen. Gen. supervision mfg. engring. Stromberg Carlson Co., Rochester, N.Y., 1972-73, mgr. printed circuits, 1973-75, plant mgr., Camden, Ark., 1975-76, plant mgr., Charlottesville, Va., 1976-78, gen. mgr. telephone systems center, 1978-8, pres. gen. circuits, Rochester, N.Y., 1981—. Vice pres., bd. dirs. YMCA, 1978—; bd. dirs. United Way, 1976—; bd. dirs., v.p., treas. Work Shop V, 1977—. Served with USN, 1958-62. Mem. Nat. Mgmt. Assn., Soc. for Advancement Mgmt., Va. Mfrs. Assn. Home: 3 Morningside Pk Pittsford NY 14534 Office: 95 Mt Read Blvd Rochester NY 14611

FIORAVANTI, NANCY ELEANOR, bank ofcl.; b. Gloucester, Mass., Apr. 10, 1935; d. Richard Joseph and Evelyn Grace (Souza) F.; grad. high sch. Various positions and depts. Cape Ann Bank and Trust Co. (successor to Gloucester Safe Deposit & Trust Co.), Gloucester, 1953—, with trust dept., 1959—, asst. trust officer, 1970—. Treas. art adv. com. Gloucester Lyceum and Sawyer Free Library. Mem. Nat. Assn. Bank Women. Home: 19 Harvard St Gloucester MA 01930 Office: 154 Main St Gloucester MA 01930

FIORE, JAMES LOUIS, JR., pub. accountant; b. Jersey City, Oct. 7, 1935; s. James Louis and Rose (Perrotta) F.; B.S. in Accounting, Seton Hall U., 1957; M.B.A. in Accounting and Statistics, Western Colo. U., 1978; Ph.D., Calif. Western U., 1979; m. Alberta W. Pope, July 21, 1957; children—Carolyn Leigh, James Louis, Toni Lynn. Field auditor, Trenton, N.J., 1959-60; supr. internal auditing Ronson Corp., Woodbridge, N.J., 1960-64; supr. gen. accounting Electronic Assos., West Long Branch, N.J., 1964-65; pvt. practice accounting, 1965—; pres. Bucks County Research Inst. Inc., 1972—. Bd. dirs. Brick Twp. (N.J.) Scholarship Found., 1963-67. Served to 2d lt. U.S. Army, 1957. Named Jaycee of Year, 1962; accredited Accreditation Council for Accountancy, Washington. Mem. Pa. Soc. Public Accts., Nat. Soc. Public Accts., Calif. Western U. Alumni Assn., Western Colo. U. Alumni Assn., Seton Hall U. Alumni Assn. (Crest and Century Clubs). Roman Catholic. Club: K.C. Author: (with others) Non-Absorption of Nitrofurazone from the Urethra in Men, 1976, Comparative Bioavailability of Doxycycline, 1974; contbr. articles to profl. jours. Home: Thompson Mill Rd Upper Makefield Township PA 18940 Office: 1600 Lehigh Pkwy East Allentown PA 18103

FIORITO, EDWARD GERALD, lawyer; b. Newark, Oct. 20, 1936; s. Edward and Emma (DePascale) F.; B.S. in Elec. Engring., Rutgers U., 1958; J.D., Georgetown U., 1963; m. Charlotte H. Longo, Apr. 2, 1958; children—Jeanne C., Kathryn M., Thomas E., Lynn M., Patricia A. Elec. engr. IBM Corp., Owego, N.Y., 1958-59, patent agt., Washington, 1959-63, patent atty., Yorktown Heights, N.Y., 1963-66, patent staff atty., Armonk, N.Y., 1966-69; admitted to U.S. Patent and Trademark Office, 1960, Va. bar, 1963, N.Y. bar, 1964, Mich. bar, 1970, Ohio bar, 1975; v.p. patent and comml. relations Energy Conversion Devices, Troy, Mich., 1969-71; mgr. patent prosecution Burroughs Corp., Detroit, 1971-75; gen. patent counsel B.F. Goodrich, Akron, Ohio, 1975—; dir. LIM Holding, S.A., Luxembourg, 1978—. Bd. dirs. Akron's House Extending Aid On Drugs, 1976; lay minister St. Mary Parish, Hudson, Ohio, 1976—. Mem. Am. Bar Assn. (mem. council sci. and tech. sect.), Assn. Corp. Patent Counsel, IEEE, Tau Beta Pi, Eta Kappa Nu, Pi Mu Epsilon. Roman Catholic. Clubs: Country of Hudson (Ohio), Western Res. Racket (Hudson). Home: 166 Aurora St Hudson OH 44236 Office: BF Goodrich 500 S Main St Akron OH 44318

FIRESTONE, GARY LEE, ins. agy. exec.; b. Warsaw, Ind., July 12, 1934; s. Burdette H. and Helen B. F.; B.A., DePauw U., 1956; m. Patricia Pranter, Oct. 15, 1971; children—Kathryn, Kurt, Kaye, Kristin. Agt., Coll. Life Ins. Co., 1960-67, mgr., 1967-72, regional dir. agys. 1972-76; prin. Firestone/Yott & Assos., Indpls., 1976—. Served with USAF, 1957-60. C.L.U. Mem. Million Dollar Round Table (life), Nat. Assn. Life Underwriters, Indpls. Assn. Life Underwriters, Gen. Agts. and Mgrs. Assn., Estate Planning Council. Presbyterian. Club: Kiwanis. Home: 3016 Woodshore Ct Carmel IN 46032 Office: Firestone/Yott & Assos 3500 W DePauw Blvd Indianapolis IN 46268

FISCHER, BARBARA JEAN, mgmt. cons.; b. Onawa, Iowa, Sept. 4, 1950; d. Robbins Warren and Jean Noreen (Greenawalt) F.; B.A. cum laude, Colo. Coll., 1972; M.B.A., Wharton Sch., U. Pa., 1974. Grad. intern Busch Center, U. Pa., Phila., 1973-74; color bus. area fin. analyst, corp. fin. staff Xerox, Rochester, N.Y., 1974-77; v.p. Internat. Bus. Assos., Cedar Falls, Iowa, 1977-80; comptroller Soypro of Iowa, Cedar Falls, 1977-80; mgmt. cons. Frito-Lay Inc., Dallas, 1980—; cons. in field; guest lectr. U. No. Iowa, 1977-78; mem. adv. bd. Burst Products, Inc., 1979—; Iowa del. White House Conf. Small Bus., 1980; guest speaker Wharton Women Conf., 1980. Mem. adv. bd. Kirkwood Community Coll., 1978-80. Named Iowa BPW Dist. 3 Young Career Woman of the Year, 1978. Mem. Exec. Women of Dallas, Internat. Trade Assn. Dallas, Dallas Wharton Alumni Assn., Cedar Falls C. of C. (chmn. fgn. trade com. 1977-79), World Future Soc., Phi Beta Kappa. Republican. Club: P.E.O. Sisterhood (treas. 1975-77). Contbr. articles to profl. jours. Home: 14500 Dallas Pkwy Apt 145 Dallas TX 75240 Office: Frito-Lay Tower PO Box 35034 Dallas TX 75235

FISCHER, BRUCE, securities broker; b. Phila., Jan. 10, 1943; s. Abraham and Mae (Nisman) F.; B.S. in Econs., Wharton Sch., U. Pa., 1964; postgrad. N.Y. U. Grad. Sch. Bus.; m. Nedra Kohn, Nov. 23, 1967; children—Marc, Stephanie. Trainee, Merrill Lynch, Pierce, Fenner & Smith, 1964-66; v.p., dir. Moseley, Hallgarten, Estabrook & Weeden, Inc., Phila., 1966—; dir. Athos Steel & Aluminum Co.; trustee Lower Merion (Pa.) Police Pension Fund. Pres. bd. trustees Fischer Found.; past v.p., bd. dirs. Shipley Sch. Fathers Assn., Penn Wynne Civic Assn.; past pres. Green Hill B'nai B'rith; mem. Baldwin Sch. Fathers' Assn. Registered options prin. Mem. Phila. Securities Assn., World Trade Assn. Clubs: Locust, Wharton, Masons (Phila.). Home: 234 Lloyd Ln Wynnewood PA 19151 Office: 3 Penn Center Plaza Room 317 Philadelphia PA 19102

FISCHER, JACK MARSHALL, mfg. co. exec.; b. Pitts., July 24, 1937; s. Samuel M. and Beatrice (Stewart) F.; B.S., Mass. Inst. Tech., 1959; M.B.A., U. Pitts., 1966; m. Margaret Griffin, May 13, 1961; children—Janet, Samuel, Douglas. Staff indsl. engr. Jones & Laughlin Steel Co., Pitts., 1959-65; treas. Belmont Industries Inc., Phila., 1966-75, dir., 1972-80; treas. Walbar Inc., Peabody, Mass., 1975—, also dir.; dir. Old Colony Bank and Trust Co. Essex County. Vice-pres., Temple Emanu-El, Marblehead, Mass. Served as officer AUS, 1959-62. Mem. Beta Gamma Sigma. Jewish. Club: Kernwood Country (Salem, Mass.). Home: 94 Bradlee Ave Swampscott MA 01907 Office: Walbar Inc Peabody Indsl Center Peabody MA 01960

FISCHER, KURT RONALD, mfg. co. exec.; b. Syracuse, N.Y., Dec. 23, 1954; s. Henry Johnand and Helen Ann (Viel) F.; B.A., Elmira Coll., 1976; m. Sarah Elizabeth Keyser, Sept. 9, 1978. With Corning Glass Works, various locations, 1976—, recruiting specialist, Corning, N.Y., 1978-79, supr. personnel, Danville, Ky., 1979—. Bd. dirs. Jr. Achievement, 1979-80. Mem. Central Ky. Personnel Assn., Am. Soc. Personnel Adminstrs. Presbyterian. Club: Rotary. Home: 625 Longview Rd Danville KY 40422 Office: Corning Glass Works Vaksdahl Ave Danville KY 40422

FISCHER, LAWRENCE ROBERT, metal machinery mfg. co. exec.; b. Cleve., Dec. 6, 1949; s. Hans Ferdinand and Mary Gertrude (Whitmore) F.; B.A. in Econs., U. Va., 1972; m. Deborah Rhoades, June 30, 1973; children—Mary Elizabeth, Katherine Anne. Salesman, estimator Mayfran GmbH, Duesseldorf, W. Ger., 1972-73; mfg. mgr., then mgr. ops. Am. Monorail Co., Greenville, S.C., 1973-76; pres. Install, Inc., Simpsonville, S.C., 1976-78, Fischer Industries, Inc., Cleve., 1978—; dir. Tsubakimoto-Mayfran, Osaka, Japan; adv. Bus. Sch., Clemson U., 1977. Baptist. Clubs: Poinsett (Greensville); Kirtland (Ohio). Office: 6650 Beta Dr Mayfield OH 44143

FISCHER, ROBBINS WARREN, oilseed industry cons. co. exec.; b. Turin, Iowa, Mar. 31, 1919; s. Lewis Warren and Edith (Robbins) F.; B.A., U. Colo., 1942; postgrad. U. Colo. Sch. Law, 1944-45, Rutgers U., 1954; m. Jean Noreen Greenawalt, Apr. 10, 1943; children—Barbara Jean, Martha Lou, Dorothy Ellen. Co-owner, operator Fischer Farms, Turin, 1947-53; sales promotion mgr. Payway Feed Mills, Kansas City, Mo., 1953-55; regional sales mgr. Bristol Myers Co., Kansas City, Mo., 1956-58; campaign dir. Burrell, Inc., Kansas City, Mo., 1958-59; asst. to pres. Soybean Council Am., Waterloo, Iowa, 1960-63; pres. Internat. Bus. Assos., Cedar Falls, Iowa, 1965—, Soypro Internat., Inc., Cedar Falls, 1963—; v.p. Continental Soya Corp., Manning, Iowa, 1973—; chmn., chief exec. officer Burst Products Co., Denison, Iowa, 1979—. Vice chmn. Iowa Farm Council, 1950-53; mem. Pres. Kennedy's Task Force on Internat. Trade in Agrl. Products, 1962. Mem. Cedar Falls C. of C. (past dir.), Inst. Food Technologists, Monona Harrison Flood Control Assn. (pres. 1951-54), Phi Beta Kappa, Delta Sigma Rho, Pi Gamma Mu. Congregationalist. Clubs: Rotary, Masons, Des Moines. Home: 5614 University Ave Cedar Falls IA 50613 Office: 314 Main St Cedar Falls IA 50613

FISCHER, THEODORE DAVID, hotel mgmt. co. exec., lawyer; b. Pitts., Oct. 21, 1933; s. Samuel M. and Beatrice S. (Stewart) F.; B.A., U. Pitts., 1955, J.D., 1958; m. Joan F., Aug. 29, 1954; children—Bruce, Steven, Sandra, Betsy. Admitted to Pa. bar, 1958, Fed. bar, 1958, Fla. bar, 1978; partner firm Markel, Markel, Levenson and Fischer, Pitts., 1960-69, Guren, Merritt, Sogg and Cohen, Cleve., 1979, Guren, Merritt, Fischer, Udell & Lasky, Miami, Fla., 1980—; partner Motor Inn Investors, hotel constrn. and mgmt. co., Pitts. and Shopping Center Assos., shopping center devel. co., Pitts., 1969-78; pres., chmn. bd. Suburban Lodging Corp., Miami, Fla., 1978—, also dir.; dir. Reliance Steel Products Co., Dukane Supply Co., Technoma. Mem. Pa. Bar Assn., Allegheny County (Pa.), Fla. bars, Phi Delta Phi. Contbr. articles to law revs. Home: 8305 SW 110th St Miami FL 33156 Office: Suite 400 2699 S Bayshore Dr Miami FL 33134

FISCHER, THOMAS CLARK, financial and ins. cons.; b. Kewanee, Ill., Jan. 7, 1925; s. George Lyle and Anne E. (Clark) F.; A.B., Harvard, 1948; m. Nancy Knight, Aug. 11, 1950; children—Elizabeth A., Steven K., Mary H. With Marsh & McLennan, Inc., Chgo., 1948-53, Pike Ins. Agy., Inc., Colorado Springs, Colo., 1953-56, Kenneth Murchison, Inc., Dallas, 1956-58, Bennett Shellenberger, Ltd., Colorado Springs, 1958-63; v.p., dir. J.D. Adams Co., 1963-70; pres., dir. Thomas C. Fischer, Inc., Colorado Springs, 1963—; sec., dir. Truss Plate Inst., Inc., 1968-70; financial and ins. cons., 1963—. Mem. Colorado Springs City Planning Commn., 1965-70, chmn., 1967-70; v.p., dir. Civic Theatre, 1961-64, 77-80, pres., 1980; mem. Colo. Environ. Commn., 1970-72, Colorado Springs Charter Rev. Commn., 1974-75; mem. El Paso County Bd. Health, 1977—, pres., 1977; v.p. Springs Area Beautiful Assn., 1973-75, Citizens Lobby, 1973-75. Mem. exec. com., polit. coordinator El Paso County Republican Central Com.; Rep. candidate for U.S. Ho. of Reps., 1970. Served with AUS, 1943-46, to 1st lt., 1951-52. Mem. Soc. C.P.C.U., Colorado Springs Press Assn. Republican. Episcopalian. Clubs: Rocky Mountain Harvard (dir. 1971—); Colorado Springs Rotary. Home: 2801 Country Club Dr Colorado Springs CO 80909 Office: PO Box 9153 Colorado Springs CO 80932

FISCHER, TIMOTHY PAUL, uniform mfg. co. exec.; b. Milw., June 12, 1944; s. Norman J. and Mary Patricia (Mack) F.; B.A. in Acctg. and Bus. Adminstrn., St. Ambrose Coll., Davenport, Iowa, 1962-66; m. Dorothy J. Briggs, June 15, 1968; children—Patricia Ann, JoEllen Suzanne, Timothy Briggs. Auditor, Ernst & Ernst, Milw., 1969-72; controller, gen. mgr. Dale Chevrolet Inc., Waukesha, Wis., 1972-76; pres. Medalist Stanbury Uniform Co., Brookfield, Mo., 1976—. Served with U.S. Army, 1967-69. Mem. Nat. Assn. Uniform Mfrs., Nat. Cath. Band Masters, Am. Legion. Republican. Roman Catholic. Clubs: Chillicothe (Mo.) Runners; Elks. Home: 2403 Country Club Dr Chillicothe MO 64601 Office: Medalist Stanbury Uniform Co Industrial Park W Brookfield MO 64628

FISCHMAN, MYRNA LEAH, accountant, educator; b. N.Y.C.; d. Isidore and Sally (Goldstein) Fischman; B.S., Coll. City N.Y., 1960, M.S., 1964; Ph.D., N.Y. U., 1976. Asst. to controller Sam Goody, Inc., N.Y.C.; tchr. accounting Central Comml. High Sch., N.Y.C., 1960-63, William Cullen Bryant High Sch., Queens, N.Y., 1963-66, vocational adviser, 1963-66; instr. accounting Borough of Manhattan Community Coll., N.Y.C., 1966-69; self employed accountant N.Y.C., 1960—; chief accountant investigator rackets, Office Queens Dist. Atty., 1969-70, community relations coordinator, 1970-71; adj. prof. L.I. U., 1970-79, prof. acctg. taxation and law, 1979—. Research cons. pre-tech. program Bd. Edn., City N.Y.; accountant-adviser Inst. for Advancement of Criminal Justice; accountant-cons. Coalition Devel. Corp., Interracial Council for Bus. Opportunities; treas. Breakfree Inc., Lower East Side Prep. Sch.; mem. edn. task force Am. Jewish Com., 1972—. Mem. steering com., youth div. N.Y. Dem. County Com., 1967-68, del. to Nat. Conv., Young Dems. Am., 1967, rep. assigned to women's activities com., 1967; mem. Chancellor Com. Against Discrimination in Edn., 1976—; mem. legis. adv. bd. N.Y. State Assemblyman Denis Butler, 1979—. Recipient award for meritorious service Community Service Soc., 1969. Mem. Jewish Guild for Blind, Jewish Braille Inst., Friends Am. Ballet Theatre, Friends Met. Mus. Art, Community Welfare Com. Mem. Am. Accounting Assn., Nat., Eastern (co-chmn. ann. meeting 1967) bus. edn. assns., Nat., Eastern (chmn. ann. meeting, 1968) bus. tchrs. assns., Internat. Soc. Bus. Edn., Grad. Students Orgn. N.Y. U. (treas. 1971-73, v.p. 1973-74), N.E.A., AAUP, Doctorate Assn. N.Y. Educators (v.p. 1975—), Am. Assn. Jr. Colls., Young Alumni Assn. City Coll. (mem. council), Emanu-El League Congregation Emanu-El, N.Y. (chmn. community services com. 1967-68), Delta Pi Epsilon (treas. 1976). Jewish religion. Democrat. Club: Women's City (N.Y.C.). Developed new bus. machine course and curriculum Borough Manhattan Bus. Community Coll. Home: PO Box 6241 Astoria NY 11106 Office: Zeckendorf Campus Long Island U Brooklyn NY 11201

FISHER, ALEXANDER EDWARD, ins. broker; b. Bklyn., Oct. 9, 1940; s. Aaron and Dora F.; B.S. in Econs., U. Pa., 1962; J.D., Columbia U., 1965; m. Enid Wildman, Sept. 26, 1970; children—Abby, Leigh, Ruth. Pres., A. Fisher Co., Inc., N.Y.C., 1965—, Amalgamated Programs Corp., N.Y.C., 1969—, IBIS, N.Y.C., 1978—; ins. cons.; lectr. mem. Pres.'s Club and Pres.'s Council, Guardian Life Ins. Co. Active United Jewish Appeal C.L.U.

Mem. C.L.U. Assn., Profl. Ind. Agts., N.Y. Ins. Brokers Council. Clubs: Humanity, Masons. Columnist assn. and trade periodicals. Home: 1175 Park Ave New York NY 10028 Office: 161 William St New York NY 10038

FISHER, ALLAN CAMPBELL, r.r. exec.; b. Westerly, R.I., Aug. 9, 1943; s. Arthur Chester and Norma Jean (Campbell) F.; B.A. in Econs., St. Lawrence U., 1965; M.S. in Transp., Northwestern U., 1970; m. Ellen Tryon Roop, June 14, 1969; children—Bradford Booth, Katherine Thayer. Research economist Gen. Motors Research Labs., Warren, Mich., 1969; mgmt. trainee Penn Central, 1970, asst. trainmaster, Chgo., 1970-71, trainmaster, Toledo, 1971-72, terminal trainmaster, Elkhart, Ind., 1972, trainmaster, Cleve., 1972-74, asst. terminal supt., Cleve., 1974, terminal supt., Balt., 1974-75, asst. div. supt. Chesapeake div., Balt., 1975-76, terminal supt. Conrail, Conway, Pa., 1976, div. supt. N.J. div., Elizabethport, 1977, Lehigh div., Bethlehem, Pa., 1978, regional supt. ops. improvement Central region, Pitts., 1978-80, dir. budget control, 1980—. Served with U.S. Army, 1966-67; Vietnam. Decorated Bronze Star medal. Urban Transp. fellow, 1969. Mem. Fuel and Operating Officers Assn., Internat. Platform Assn., Sigma Chi. Unitarian-Universalist. Club: Masons. Home: 418 Oak Lane Wayne PA 19087 Office: Room 1444 Six Penn Center Philadelphia PA 19104

FISHER, CHARLES J., holding co. exec.; b. 1920; B.S., M.I.T., 1946; married. Jr. engr. Hamilton Paper Co., 1947-56; v.p., gen. mgr. Wyomissing Corp., 1956-64; v.p., gen. mgr. splty. chems. div. Reliance Universal Inc., Louisville, 1969-78, pres., 1978—, chief operating officer, 1979—. Office: Reliance Universal Inc 1930 Bishop Ln Louisville KY 40218*

FISHER, CHARLES THOMAS, III, banker; b. Detroit, Nov. 22, 1929; s. Charles Thomas, Jr. and Elizabeth Jane (Briggs) F.; A.B. in Econs., Georgetown U., 1951; M.B.A., Harvard, 1953; m. Margaret Elizabeth Keegin, June 18, 1952; children—Margaret Fisher Jones, Charles Thomas IV, Curtis William, Lawrence Peter II, Mary Florence. With Touche, Ross, Bailey & Smart, C.P.A.'s, Detroit, 1953-58; asst. v.p. Nat. Bank Detroit, 1958-61, v.p., 1961-66, sr. v.p., 1966-69, exec. v.p., 1969-72, pres., chief adminstrv. officer, 1972—, also dir.; pres., dir. Nat. Detroit Corp., 1973—; dir. Internat. Bank of Detroit, Detroit Edison Co., Hiram Walker-Gooderham & Worts, Ltd., Gen. Motors Corp., Am. Airlines. Chmn., Mackinac Bridge Authority; bd. dirs. Greater Detroit Area Hosp. Council; trustee Mt. Elliott Cemetery, Detroit. Named Detroit Young Man of Year, Detroit Jr. Bd. Commerce, 1961. C.P.A., Mich. Mem. Assn. Res. City Bankers, Am. Inst. C.P.A.'s, Mich. Assn. C.P.A.'s. Clubs: Bloomfield Hills (Mich.) Country; Country of Detroit (Grosse Pointe); Detroit Athletic, Detroit, Recess, Yondotega (Detroit); Links (N.Y.C.). Office: 611 Woodward Ave Detroit MI 48226

FISHER, DAVID JUDSON, lawyer, floor covering distbg. co. exec.; b. Boone, Iowa, Dec. 7, 1936; s. Harold and Alice (Judson) F.; B.S., Grinnell Coll., 1959; J.D., U. Iowa, 1962; m. Doris Onthank, Oct. 8, 1962; children—Gregory, Anne K., Amy. Admitted to Iowa bar, 1962; with Onthank Co., Des Moines, 1962—, pres., 1971—, chmn. bd., owner, 1977—; owner, mgr. D & B Leasing Co., Des Moines, 1978—, Fisher Properties Co., Des Moines, 1980—. Bd. dirs. YMCA Boys Home. Mem. Nat. Assn. Floor Covering Distbrs. Republican. Presbyterian. Clubs: Wakonda, Univ. Athletic, Des Moines (dir.) I (pres.) (Des Moines). Home: 621 Glenview Dr Des Moines IA 50312 Office: PO Box 1462 Des Moines IA 50306

FISHER, DRURY ALEXANDER, III, ins. brokerage exec.; b. Memphis, July 26, 1946; s. Drury Alexander and Carol Dene (Christopher) F.; B.B.A., So. Meth. U., 1968. Asst. supr. Aetna Life & Casualty Co., Dallas, 1968-69; account exec. D.A. Fisher, Inc., Memphis, 1969-71; owner, operator Alexander & Co., Memphis, 1971-77, pres., chmn. bd., 1977—. C.L.U., C.P.C. U. Mem. Am. Soc. Chartered Property Casualty Underwriters, Profl. Ins. Agts. of Am., Profl. Ins. Agts. Tenn., Mensa, Internat. Platform Assn. Office: 2400 Poplar Ave Memphis TN 38112

FISHER, EUGENE ALAN, accountant; b. Balt., Aug. 2, 1943; s. Frederic H. and Marie (Sugarman) F.; B.S. in Acctg. with high honors, U. Md., 1965; J.D. with honors, Georgetown U., 1969; m. Adrienne Goldstein, June 11, 1964; children—Elyce, Paige, Wade. Field agt. IRS, 1965-68; tac mgr. Aronson, West & Greene, C.P.A.'s, Bethesda, Md., 1968-70; tax partner Aronson, Greene, Fisher & Co. Ltd., 1970—; admitted to Md. bar, 1969; asso. prof. George Washington U. Law Sch., fall 1979. Bd. dirs. Centers Handicapped, 1974—, chmn. ways and means com., 1979—; pres. Coldspring Civic Assn., 1976-77. C.P.A., Md. Mem. Am. Inst. C.P.A.'s, Md. Assn. C.P.A.'s, D.C. Inst. C.P.A.'s, Assn. Practicing C.P.A.'s (past pres.). Clubs: Potomac Tennis; Bethesda Health and Racquet. Contbr. articles to profl. jours. Home: 9912 Bluegrass Rd Potomac MD 20854 Office: 7315 Wisconsin Ave Suite 750W Bethesda MD 20014

FISHER, FRANK BERTMAN, banker; b. Lisbon, Ohio, July 11, 1921; s. Frank Bertman and Elsie (Rigby) F.; B.A., Hiram Coll., 1943; M.B.A., U. Pa., 1947; grad. Stonier Sch. Banking, Rutgers U., 1958; m. Norma M. Larsen, June 21; children—Donald, Kathryn, Jeffrey, Douglas. Exec. v.p. County Nat. Bank, Middletown, N.Y., 1950-63; pres. Cleve. region BancOhio Nat. Bank, 1963—; dir. Ohio BancLease, Inc. Chmn. fin. com. Hiram Coll.; vice chmn. bd. dirs. Ohio div. Am. Cancer Soc.; bd. dirs. Community Dialysis Center, Cleve., Singing Angels, Greater Cleve. Growth Assn., Blue Coats, Cleve. Council World Affairs, Council Smaller Enterprises. Served to lt. USN, 1941-46. Mem. Ohio Bankers Assn. (dir., chmn. group 9). Republican. Methodist. Clubs: Union of Cleve., Rotary, Country of Pepper Pike. Office: 1101 Euclid Ave Cleveland OH 44115

FISHER, FRANK X., hotels exec.; b. N.Y.C., Dec. 18, 1933; s. Frank X. and Juliet Electra (Pieri) F.; B.S., Cornell U., 1954; postgrad. Advanced Mgmt. Program, Harvard U., 1978-79; m. Eleanore L. Adam, Sept. 7, 1952; children—Laurent Ann, Frank Adam. Asst. v.p. Hilton Hotels, Waldorf Astoria, N.Y.C., 1956-68; v.p. Loew's Hotels, N.Y.C., 1968-70; area mgr. ITT Sheraton, Chgo., 1970-72; pres. Lex Hotels, Inc., N.Y.C., 1972—, dir., chief exec. officer, 1972—, dir., chief exec. officer Lex Hotels Ltd. (U.K.), 1974—; pres., chief exec. officer Kilborn and Fisher, 1978—. Served to 1st lt. AUS, 1954-56. Mem. Cornell Soc. Hotelmen (dir.). Club: Harvard (N.Y.C.). Home: 1120 Park Ave New York NY 10028

FISHER, GORDON NEIL, newspaper co. exec.; b. Montreal, Que., Can., Dec. 9, 1928; s. Philip Sydney and Margaret Linton (Southam) F.; student Lower Can. Coll., Trinity Coll. Sch., Port Hope, Ont.; B.Engring., McGill U., Montreal; m. Alison Nora Arbuckle, June 17, 1955; children—Derek A., Philip Neil, Duncan Southam. With Southam, Inc., Toronto, Ont., Can., 1958—, v.p., mng. dir., 1969-75, pres., 1975—. Bd. govs. Trinity Coll. Sch.; trustee Toronto Gen. Hosp. Mem. Can. Daily Newspaper Pubs. Assn., Can. Press. Clubs: Badminton and Racquet, Royal Can. Yacht, Mt. Royal. Office: Suite 801 321 Bloor St E Toronto ON M4W 1H3 Canada

FISHER, HAROLD ROY, mfg. co. exec.; b. Chgo., Nov. 24, 1930; s. Roy August and Ethel May (Bemis) F.; B.S. in M.E., Purdue U., 1952; M.B.A., U. Chgo., 1970; m. Marilyn Jeanne Brunson, Dec. 22, 1951. Research engr. Borg Warner, Des Plaines, Ill. and Ithaca, N.Y., 1952-56, supervising engr., 1956-58, project mgr., 1958-61, asst. chief engr., 1961-63, quality control mgr., 1963-67, mgr. mfg. engring., 1967-73; dir. engring. ITT, Rochester, Mich., 1973-75; v.p. engring. Arvin Industries, Columbus, Ind., 1975—. Trustee Village of Cayuga Heights, N.Y., 1969-73; pres. Grandview Service Utility, Columbus, 1978—. Mem. Soc. Automotive Engrs., Instrument Soc. Am., Am. Metal Stamping Assn., Soc. Mfg. Engrs. Methodist (chmn. bd. trustees). Club: Harrison Lake Country. Home: Rural Route 14 Box 194 Columbus IN 47201 Office: 1531 13th St Columbus IN 47201

FISHER, HENRY, investment banker; b. Pitts., Feb. 17, 1936; s. Henry Clayton and Dorothea T. (Smith) F.; B.A., U. Pitts., 1960; m. Ann Y., Aug. 6, 1960; children—Andrew Clayton, William Bradford. Gen. partner Singer Deane & Scribner, Pitts., 1961-69; exec. v.p. Chaplin, McGuiness & Co., Inc., Pitts., 1969-73; pres. Henry Fisher Municipals, Pitts., 1973-80, Commonwealth Securities and Investments, Inc., 1980—; mem. N.Y. Stock Exchange, 1972-74. Served with USMC, 1954-56. Mem. Bond Club Pitts., Pitts. Securities Assn., Pa. Boroughs Assn., Pa. Municipal Authority's Assn., Pitts. Builders Exchange. Clubs: Duquesne, Pitts., Pitts. Press. Office: 5985 US Steel Bldg Pittsburgh PA 15219

FISHER, JOHN ALLEN, investment banker; b. Detroit, July 28, 1948; s. Charles Thomas and Elizabeth Jane F.; B.A., Yale U., 1969; M.B.A., Stanford U., 1971; m. Dianne Louise Moloney, July 16, 1966; children—Dianne Louise, Ambrose John. Cons. mgmt. services div. Touhe Ross & Co., San Francisco, 1971-73; mgmt. asso. Office Mgmt. and Budget, Exec. Office Pres., Washington, 1973-75; v.p. corp. Planning Crocker Nat. Bank, San Francisco, 1975-78, v.p. internat. corp. fin., mcht. banking/corp. fin. div., 1978—. Mem. Atherton (Calif.) Town Council, 1978—; bd. cons. Portsmouth Abbey, Portsmouth, R.I., 1980—. Republican. Clubs: Capitol Hill (Washington); San Francisco Univ.; Menlo Circus. Office: One Montgomery St San Francisco CA 94104

FISHER, JOHN WESLEY, II, mfg. co. exec.; b. Walland, Tenn., July 15, 1915; s. Arthur Justine and Rachel (Malcott) F.; B.S., U. Tenn., 1938; M.B.A., Harvard U., 1942; LL.D. (hon.), Ball State U., 1972, Butler U.; m. Janice Kelsey Ball, Aug. 10, 1940; children—Joan Fisher Thompson, Michael, James A., Jeffrey E., Judith Fisher Hastert, Jerrold M., John Wesley. Trainee, Ball Corp., Muncie, Ind., 1941, mgr. glass factories, 1942-47, asst. sec., 1944-47, gen. mgr. container div., 1947-54, v.p. sales, 1954-63, corp. v.p. mktg. and public relations, 1963-68, corp. v.p. container div., 1968-70, vice chmn. bd., 1970, pres., 1970-78, chief exec. officer, 1970—, also chmn.; partner Blackwood & Nichols Co., Oklahoma City, 1945—; dir. Muncie Airport, Inc., Dura-Containers, Inc., Am. Nat. Bank & Trust Co., Minnetrista Corp., Muncie, Ransburg Corp., Kindel Furniture Co., Grand Rapids, Mich., Stokely-Van Camp, Inc., Indpls., Ind. Bell Telephone, Indpls., Inland Steel Co., Chgo. Mem. Ind. Gov's Commn. on Higher Edn., 1969—, Commn. on Med. Edn., 1970—; mem. Pres's U.S. Indsl. Payroll Savs. Com., 1973—; past pres., dir. Muncie Community Chest; bd. dirs., v.p. Ball Bros. Found., Muncie; bd. dirs. Ball Meml. Hosp., Muncie; trustee DePauw U., Greencastle, Ind. Mem. NAM (dir.), Conf. Bd., Muncie C. of C. (pres., dir. 1950-51), Ind. C. of C. (dir. 1959—, pres. 1966-68), Glass Container Mfrs. Inst. (pres. 1964-66), Delta Tau Delta. Republican. Clubs: Rotary, Indpls. Athletic, Muncie, Delaware Country. Office: 345 S High St Muncie IN 47302

FISHER, KENNETH RUSSELL, fiberglass mfg. co. exec.; b. Rhinelander, Wis., Jan. 11, 1933; s. Donald Kenneth and Francis M. (Day) F.; m. Margaret R. Holman, June 26, 1951; children—Russell James, Donald Scott. Founder, pres. Contemporary Products, Inc., Milw., 1963—; pres. Synergy Inc., Milw. and Madurai, India, Milw. Safety Devices Inc. Patentee in field. Co-holder Fedn. Aeronautique Internationale record speed around the world over both poles. Office: Box 18444 Milwaukee WI 53218 also 13282 W Carmen Ave Menomonee Falls WI 53051

FISHER, LAWRENCE EDMOND, cement mfg. co. exec.; b. Long Beach, Calif., Aug. 10, 1949; s. Louis Everard and Blanche Elaine (Dvorak) F.; B.S. in Engring., U. Calif., Los Angeles, 1972; M.B.A., U. So. Calif., 1976; m. Sherrie Jean Nobles, May 5, 1979; children—Andrea Jean, Michael Lawrence, Patrick Thomas. Engr., Conrad Assos., Van Nuys, Calif., 1973-74; project mgr. Los Angeles World Trade Center, 1974-76; bus. analyst Vetco Inc., Ventura, Calif., 1976; mgr. mfg. planning Vetco Offshore Group, Ventura, 1977-79; exec. v.p. Chem Tech Services, 1979—; instr. Ventura Coll., 1977. Mem. Am. Petroleum Inst., Am. Concrete Inst., Am. Prodn. and Inventory Control Soc., U. So. Calif. M.B.A., U. Calif. Los Angeles Engring., UCLA alumni assns. Republican. Home: 378 Hawthorn Ln Winnetka IL 60093 Office: 4251 Main St Skokie IL 60076

FISHER, MARSHALL DWIGHT, ret. real estate co. exec.; b. Davenport, Iowa, Aug. 27, 1925; s. Harvey Marshall and Marie (Gude) F.; B.A., U. Colo., 1950; m. Rose Clifton, July 16, 1977; children by previous marriage—Jesse, Cynthia, Heidi. Vice pres., nat. sales mgr. Pen Pal, Inc., Chgo., 1952-57; owner, operator real estate firm, 1961-68; v.p., dir. sales and mktg., tng. instr. C.J. Seibert, Inc., 1969-71; co-founder, exec. v.p., sec., dir. Century 21 Real Estate Corp., Irvine, Calif., 1971-77. Served to 2d lt. USAAF, 1943-45. Home: 453 Portlock Rd Honolulu HI 96825

FISHER, MILTON NATHAN, mfg. co. exec.; b. Newark, Nov. 25, 1921; s. Davis and Maria (Rapaport) F.; B.S. in Bus. Adminstrn., U. Fla., 1946; m. Berna Braunstein, June 9, 1946; 1 son, Jerome Peter. Pres., dir. Panelfab Internat. Corp., Miami, Fla., 1951—, Decor Internacional de Cuba, 1958-59, Dicoa Corp., 1958—, Panelfab Pacific, Inc., 1965—, Panelfab P.R., Inc., 1967—; dir. Nihon Panelfab, Ltd., Japan, Panelfab Europe, Ltd.; chmn. regional export expansion council U.S. Dept. Commerce; chmn. Fla. Export Council; mem. Adv. Com. for Trade Negotiations. Past pres., dir. Internat. Center, Greater Miami, Fla.; bd. dirs., past chmn. ARC. Served to maj. USAAF, 1942-45. Decorated D.F.C., Air medal with 3 oak leaf clusters; named Fla. Internat. Businessman of Year, 1976. Mem. SE U.S.-Japan Assn. (past chmn. Fla. del.), Tau Epsilon Phi, Beta Alpha Psi, Beta Gamma Sigma. Mason. Club: Bankers (Miami). Home: 535 Reinante Ave Coral Gables FL 33156 Office: 1600 NW Le Jeune Rd Miami FL 33126

FISHER, PAUL VICTOR, refrigerated warehouse exec.; b. Hardin County, Iowa, July 17, 1923; s. Julius and Elizabeth (Roelfs) F.; ed. pub. schs.; spl. classes Wichita State U.; m. Ruth Jean Bear, June 9, 1943; children—Julie Ann, Norman Paul, Jean Elizabeth. Farmer nr. Ackley, Iowa, 1943-49; mcht. Fisher Hardware, Boone, Iowa, 1949-56; officer, mgr. Kans. Ice & Cold Storage Inc., Hutchinson and Wichita, Kans., 1956-57; pres. United Refrigerated Services, Inc., Wichita, 1978—, United of Kans., 1980—, United of Del., 1980—. Mem. Internat. Assn. Refrigerated Warehouses (past chmn. Mo. Valley chpt., dir.), Sales and Mktg. Execs., Wichita C. of C., Allied Food Club. Republican. Presbyterian. Club: Masons. Home: 1441 N Rock Rd #1202 Wichita KS 67206 Office: 2707 N Mead St Wichita KS 67219

FISHER, ROBIN DALE, broadcast sales co. exec.; b. Canton, Ohio, Nov. 14, 1946; s. Robert D. and Jeanne E. (Lash) F.; B.S. cum laude in Communications, Ohio U., 1969. Research mgr. RKO Radio Reps., Inc., N.Y.C., 1969-73 account exec., project dir. Arbitron Broadcast Research Co., N.Y.C., 1971-73; dir. research sta. WCBS, CBS, N.Y.C., 1973-76; dir. research Maj. Market Radio, Reps., N.Y.C., 1976-79, RKO Radio Network, N.Y.C., 1979—; speaker on radio audience ratings, media analysis by computer programs; mem. goals com. Radio Advt. Bur. Dir. fund drive 350th anniversary Marble Collegiate Ch., N.Y.C., also chmn. bd. ushers Recipient award for radio programming Freedoms Found. Mem. Radio/TV Research Council, Sta. Reps. Assn., Ohio U. Alumni Assn. (v.p.). Club: Masons. Author: A Look At Year One, 1973; contbr. articles to profl. jours. Home: 435 E 86th St New York NY 10028 Office: 1440 Broadway New York NY 10018

FISHER, ROY ROBERT, real estate appraiser, counselor; b. Davenport, Iowa, Mar. 25, 1923; s. Roy Robert and Eula (Lyon) F.; B.S. in Forestry, Iowa State U., 1947; m. Joyce Day, June 10, 1944; children—Joy, Susan, Carol, Becky, Molly, Lucy, Anne. Broker, developer, appraiser Roy Fisher, Inc., Davenport, 1947-74; v.p., chief appraiser Mortgage Guarantee Ins. Co., 1974-77; dir. housing, cons. Runzheimer & Co., Inc., Rochester, Wis., 1977—; pres. Appraisal Services Internat., Ltd., 1979—. Served with USAF, 1943-45. Decorated Air medal with 5 clusters. Mem. Am. Inst. Real Estate Appraisers (Profl. Recognition award 1976, 77, 78, instr. profl. courses, designated M.A.I. appraisal inst.), Soc. Real Estate Appraisers (designated sr. real estate analyst, instr. profl. courses, pres. 1971), Soc. Real Estate Counselors (designated counselor real estate), Ednl. Found. Computer Application to Real Estate Industry (treas.). Republican. Methodist. Home: 8585 N Manor Ln Fox Point WI 53217 Office: Runzheimer & Co Inc Runzheimer Park Rochester WI 53167

FISHER, THOMAS DAILEY, bus. services co. real estate exec.; b. Lodi, Ohio, Feb. 13, 1948; s. Joseph Christopher and Lois (Stafford) F.; B.A., Baldwin Wallace Coll., 1970; grad. Grad. Realtors Inst., 1978; m. Gretchen Carol Lyons, May 5, 1975; children—Ronald David, Joseph Christopher. Sec., Lodi Electric Inc., 1969-73, pres., 1973—; owner barbershop, Lodi, 1973-74; personal lines underwriter Firemen's Fund Ins. Co., Cleve., 1970-73; office mgr. to v.p. Pearce Ins. Assos. Strongsville, Ohio, 1973-75; sales mgr. Lodi br. Gerspacher Realty Co., Medina, Ohio, 1975-80; owner, operator Fisher Investment Co., Lodi, 1977—; co-owner Sparky Oil & Gas, 1980—; instr. Wayne Gen. Coll., Akron U.; cons. in field. Mem. Medina County Bd. Realtors (Realtor of Yr. award 1979), Nat. Assn. Realtors, Ohio Assn. Realtors (Outstanding Instr. award 1980), Soc. Advancement mgmt. (life), Realtors Nat. Marketing Inst., Nat. Rifle Assn. (life), Jaycees. Clubs: Ruritan, Masons, DeMolay. Contbr. articles to profl. jours. Home: 10786 Greenwich Rd Homerville OH 44235

FISHER, WAYNE H., retail chain exec.; b. 1920; B.A., Pomona Coll., 1942; I.A., Harvard U., 1943; M.B.A., Stanford U., 1946; married. With Owl Drug Co., 1947-62, v.p., 1953-60, pres., 1960-62; v.p. Lucky Stores, Inc., 1962-68, exec. v.p., 1968-71, pres., 1971—, chmn., 1974—, also chief exec. officer, 1974-80, also dir.; dir. Transam. Corp. Served with AUS, 1943-45.

FISHLEIGH, CLARENCE TURNER, cons. engr.; b. Chgo., July 31, 1895; s. John A. and Henrietta P. (Turner) F.; B.S. in Elec. Engring., U. Mich., 1917; J.D., Detroit Coll. Law, 1939; m. Thea Holste, May 16, 1923; children—Elayne Fishleigh Bramwell, Marilyn Fishleigh Pierce. Mech. prodn. Ford Motor Co., 1919-22; exptl. motor testing, asst. prodn. mgr. Am. Car and Foundry Co., Chgo., also Rich Tool Co., Detroit, 1923-24; mgr. Clarence T. Fishleigh Co., 1924-30; asso. engr., cons. engr. Walter T. Fishleigh, 1930-47; cons. engr., Detroit, 1947-51, Chgo., 1951-73, Deerfield, Ill., 1973—; splty. automotive engr., patent experting. Served as 2d lt. USAAC, 1917-19. Decorated Croix de Guerre. Registered profl. engr., Ill., Mich., N.Y., Ohio, Fla., Tex. Mem. Soc. Automotive Engrs., ASME, Western Soc. Engrs., Engring. Soc. Detroit, Am., Mich. patent law assns., Patent Law Assn. Chgo., Ill., Mich. bar assns., Kappa Sigma, Sigma Nu Phi. Club: Union League (Chgo.). Home and office: 920 Kenton Rd Deerfield IL 60015

FISHMAN, BENSON EDWARD, advt. and pub. exec.; b. Hopewell, Va., Sept. 20, 1942; s. Carl Robert and Doris (Berg) F.; A.A., Temple U., 1963, B.S., 1967, M. Ed., 1969; postgrad. U. Pa., 1970-71; m. Lee Ann Haering, May 26, 1968; children—Andrew Ivan, Daniel Stuart. Tchr. English Phila. Bd. Edn., 1967-69; research asso., writer producer Research for Better Schs., Phila., 1969-72; pres., pub. Concert Pub., Inc. Phila., 1972—, editor, pub. Concert Mag., 1972-75, editor pub. Concert Tour Books, 1972-78; chmn. bd. Gerald Stevens Advt. Inc., Phila., 1974—; instr. in mktg. and advt. Pa. State U.; cons. in field. Bd. dirs. Logan Sq. Civic Assn., Phila., 1974, treas., 1975-76. Recipient Forefather's award local PTA, 1956. Mem. Poor Richard's Club, Art Dir's. Club (8 awards of Merit 1974-76, certificate of Excellence 1975), Mag. Pubs. Assn., Am. Mgmt. Assn. Democrat. Jewish. Clubs: Old Friends, B'nai B'rith. Producer TV pilot: Achievement Trainining, for HEW, 1971; producer documentary: Film Workshop, 1969; film editor Temple U's. documentary: Russian Tour, 1969; pub. Main Point Anniversary Book, 1975. Home: 2131-33 Cherry St Philadelphia PA 19103 Office: 1810 Ludlow St Philadelphia PA 19103

FISHMAN, ERNEST MARTIN, leasing co. exec.; b. N.Y.C., Mar. 19, 1929; s. Abraham W. and Rosabel (Siegal) F.; B.S., Phila. Coll. Textiles and Sci., 1950; M.B.A., Columbia U., 1975; m. Adele Goldstein, May 11, 1952; children—Theodore David, James Bart. Sales exec. Pacific Mills, N.Y.C., 1953-55, Cohen-Hall-Marx, N.Y.C., 1955-56; sales mgr. Tioga Texile Asso., N.Y.C., 1956-72; v.p., 1972-74; regional mgr. Techlease Inc., White Plains, N.Y., 1974-78, nat. sales mgr., 1978-80; v.p. First Comml. Corp., Mountainside, N.J., 1980—; lectr. med. leasing Greater N.Y. Hosp. Assn., 1975, St. Johns U., N.Y., 1976. Chmn. Friends of the Hunt House, 1964-68. Served to lt. U.S. Army, 1951-53. Mem. Am. Arbitration Assn., Hosp. Fin. Mgmt. Assn. Club: Columbia Bus. Sch. Home: Box 307 Scarborough NY 10510 Office: 200 Sheffield St Mountainside NJ 07092

FISHMAN, WILLIAM SAMUEL, corp. exec.; b. Clinton, Ind., Jan. 26, 1916; s. Max and Fannie (Dumes) F.; student Sch. Internship Polit. Sci., Washington, 1934-35; B.A. with highest honors in Polit. Sci., U. Ill., 1936; postgrad. U. Chgo., 1936-37; D.Bus. Adminstrn., Bryant Coll., 1968; LL.D., Lincoln Meml. U., 1969; m. Clara K. Silvian, June 28, 1936; children—Alan F., Fred B., David J. Exec. v.p. Automatic Mdsg. Co., Inc., Chgo., 1942-56, pres. 1956-59; sr. v.p. ARA Services, Inc., Phila., 1959-63, exec. v.p., 1963-64, pres., 1964-77, chief exec. officer, 1975—, chmn. bd., 1977—; dir. Versafood Services, Ltd., Can., Fidelity Bank, Phila., Fidelcor, Phila., Phila. Electric Co. Pres. Jewish Publ. Soc. Am.; fellow Brandeis U.; bd. dirs. Robin Hood Dell Concerts; trustee Com. for Econ. Devel.; bd. overseers Sch. Dental Medicine, U. Pa. Mem. Nat. Restaurant Assn., Nat. Automatic Merchandising Assn. (dir., exec. com. pres. 1958-59), Phi Beta Kappa, Phi Kappa Phi, Delta Sigma Rho. Jewish (past pres. synagogue). Clubs: Standard (Chgo.); Harmonie (N.Y.C.); Palm Beach (Fla.) Country; Locust, Philmont Country, Union League

(Phila.). Office: ARA Services Inc Independence Sq Philadelphia PA 19106

FISHPAW, CLARENCE OSCAR, wholesale druggist; b. Trenton, Md., Oct. 29, 1913; s. Clarence Edgar and Ethel May (Wisner) F.; student Western Md. Coll., 1930-32; m. Mabel Rosella Rill, July 15, 1933; 1 dau., Beverly Jane (Mrs. James Garman). With Hampstead Pub. Co., 1932-34; produce mgr. Am. Stores Co., 1934-36; with H.L. Mills Service Sta., 1936-40; founder C.O. Fishpaw Co., Westminster, Md., 1937, owner, pres., 1937—; founder C.O. Fishpaw Carnival Supply Co., Westminster, 1953, owner, pres., 1953—; dir. Hampstead Implement & Supply Co., 1960-63, v.p., 1962. Charter mem. Winfield Community Vol. Fire Co.; mem. Founders Club, Western Md. Coll. Mem. Westminster C. of C. (dir. 1953-60, pres. 1956-58), Internat. Platform Assn., Outdoor Amusement Bus. Assn., Md. State Sheriffs Assn., Md. Wildlife Fedn., Nat. Wholesale Distbrs. Assn. Lutheran (pres. council 1947-48). Elk (trustee), Lion (past dist. gov.). Clubs: Westminster Riding, Saints and Sinners Balt. (dir.). Home: 314 Stoner Ave Westminster MD 21157 Office: 1011 Baltimore Blvd Westminster MD 21157

FISHWICK, JOHN PALMER, ry. exec.; b. Roanoke, Va., Sept. 29, 1916; s. William and Nellie (Cross) F.; A.B., Roanoke Coll., 1937; LL.B., Harvard U., 1940; m. Blair Wiley, Jan. 4, 1941; children—Ellen Fishwick Martin, Anne Fishwick Posvar, John Palmer. Admitted to Va. bar, 1939; asso. Cravath, Swaine & Moore, N.Y.C., 1940-42; asst. to gen. solicitor N. & W. Ry., Roanoke, 1945-47, asst. gen. solicitor, 1947-51, asst. gen. counsel, 1951-54, gen. solicitor, 1954-56, gen. counsel, 1956-58, v.p., gen. counsel, 1958-59, v.p. law, 1959-63, sr. v.p., 1963-70, pres., chief exec. officer, 1970-80, chmn., chief exec. officer, 1980—; also dir.; chmn., chief exec. officer Erie Lackawanna Ry. Co., 1968-70; pres. Del. & Hudson Ry. Co., 1968-70, dir., 1968-71; pres. Dereco, Inc., 1968—; pres., dir. Pocahontas Land Corp., Va. Holding Corp.; dir. Akron, Canton & Youngstown R.R., Chesapeake Western Ry., N.J., Ind. & Ill. R.R., Norfolk, Franklin & Danville Ry., Winston-Salem Southbound Ry., Allied Chem. Corp., Shenandoah Life Ins. Co. Trustee Roanoke Coll., 1964-72, Va. Theol. Sem., Va. Mus. Fine Arts, Richmond, 1974-79. Served as lt. comdr. USNR, 1942-45. Mem. Assn. Am. R.R.'s (dir.). Episcopalian (former chancellor Diocese S.W. Va.). Clubs: Roanoke Country, Shenandoah (Roanoke); Commonwealth (Richmond, Va.); City Tavern Assn. (Georgetown); Met. (Washington); Duquesne (Pitts.); Union (Cleve.); Sky (N.Y.C.); Rolling Rock (Ligonier, Pa.); Hillsboro (Pompano Beach, Fla.). Office: 8 N Jefferson St Roanoke VA 24042

FISKE, GUY WILBUR, diversified industry exec.; b. Upton, Mass., Sept. 28, 1924; s. Frederick Wilbur and Daisy May (Phllips) F.; B.A., Brown U., 1946; m. Elsie Jacqueline Strachan, Sept. 2, 1949; children—Jacqui Lynne, Melinda, Melissa. Rep., Felt & Tarrant Mfg. Co., Providence, 1946-48; with Gen. Electric Co., various locations, 1948-67, nat. sales mgr. electronics div., Columbia, S.C., 1960-63, mgr. mktg. capacitor div., Glens Falls, N.Y., 1964-66, gen. mgr. computer support ops., Phoenix, 1966-68; worldwide product line mgr. controls instruments, electronic components and automotive products ITT, N.Y.C., 1968-71, group gen. mgr. automotive products, 1971, group gen. mgr., corporate v.p., 1972—; exec. v.p., dir. Gen. Dynamics Corp., St. Louis, 1977—, also chmn. bd. subsidiaries Datagraphix, Inc., San Diego, Stromberg Carlson Corp., Tampa, Fla., Am. Telecommunications Corp., El Monte, Calif., Gen. Dynamics Communications Co., St. Louis; chmn. bd. Asbestos Corp. Ltd., Montreal, Que., Can., 1977—. Founder, elder Presbyn. Ch., Havenwood, Md.; bd. dirs. Mo. Arthritis Found. Served with AUS, 1944-46; comdr. USNR (ret.). Mem. Soc. Automotive Engrs., Sigma Nu. Clubs: Metropolitan (N.Y.); Internat. Golf (Boston); Bloomfield Hills (Mich.) Country; Port Royal Country (Hilton Head, S.C.); Old Warson Country, St. Louis (St. Louis). Office: Gen Dynamics Corp Pierre Laclede Center Saint Louis MO 63105

FISTEDIS, STANLEY H., research exec.; b. June 25, 1925; s. Jordan S. and Irene S. (Karayannidis) F.; B.S., Robert Coll., 1947; M.S., Mont. State U., 1949; Ph.D., U. Mo., 1953; M.B.A., U. Chgo., 1965; postgrad. U. Louisville, 1954-55; cert. Internat. Inst. Nuclear Sci. and Engring., 1961-63. With the Babcock & Wilcox Co., Chgo., 1948-49; asst. instr. U. Mo., Columbia, 1949-51, instr., 1951-52; mech. and structural engr. Chgo. cons. firms, 1952-54; spl. assignments engr. The Girdler Co., Louisville, 1954-57; with Argonne (Ill.) Nat. Lab., 1957—, sr. research engr., mgr. Dept. Engring. Mechanics, 1971—; U.S. co-chmn. 6th Internat. Conf. on Structural Mechanics in Reactor Tech., Paris, 1981, others; rep. U.S. AEC, U.S. Energy Research and Devel. Adminstrn., U.S. Dept. Energy, various dates; lectr. in field. Bd. dirs. O'Hare Center Inc., O'Hare Center Plaza, Elk Grove, Ill., 1970—, Men's Assn. Luth. Gen. Hosp., Park Ridge, Ill., 1972-75. Recipient Commendation, U.S. AEC, 1969; Gold medal for services rendered to nuclear reactor tech., Scientific Chmn. of Conf. of Structural Mechanics in Reactor Tech., and Mayor of W. Berlin, 1971, Commemorative Medal and Commendation, U.S. AEC and Argonne Nat. Lab., 1974; Honor award and Bronze medal for disting. service in engring. U. Mo., Columbia, 1980; Most Disting. Sci. award United Hellenic Voters Am., 1981. Fellow ASCE; mem. Am. Nuclear Soc., Internat. Assn. Structural Mechanics in Reactor Tech. (v.p. 1979-81, pres. 1981-83), ASME, Am. Concrete Inst., Sci. Research Soc. Am., Ill. Soc. Profl. Engrs. Prin. editor, Internat. Jour. Nuclear Engring. & Design, 1979—; patentee in field; contbr. 85 articles to profl. jours.; compiler 5 books on nuclear technology. Address: 500 N Parkwood Ave Park Ridge IL 60068

FITCH, HOWARD MERCER, lawyer, labor arbitrator; b. Jeffersonville, Ind., Dec. 23, 1909; s. J. Howard and Kate Orvis (Girdler) F.; B.S. in Mech. Engring., U. Ky., 1930, M.S., 1936, M.E., 1939; J.D. magna cum laude, U. Louisville, 1942; m. Jane Rogers McCaw, Dec. 25, 1930; children—Catherine Mercer Fitch Druitt, Jane Rogers Fitch Butterworth. Engr., Western Electric Co., Kearny, N.J., 1930-32; joined Am. Air Filter Co., Inc. as sales engr., 1936, successively prodn. mgr., mgr. legal and patent dept., asst. to exec. v.p., became mgr. Herman Nelson div., 1953, dir. ops., 1958-63, v.p., 1954-72, mgr. mgmt. services, 1963-72; admitted to Ky. bar, 1942, Ill. bar, 1954, to practice before U.S. Patent Office, 1943; practiced Louisville, 1942—; partner Hunt & Fitch, 1945-58. Treas. Louisville Labor-Mgmt. Com.; mem. arbitration panel Fed. Mediation and Conciliation Service, Louisville Labor-Mgmt. Com. Bd. dirs. Louisville Urban League, Louisville Better Bus. Bur., Consumers Adv. Council. Registered profl. engr., Ky. Mem. ASME, Am. Soc. Heating and Air Conditioning Engrs., Am. Arbitration Assn. (panel arbitrators), Am., Ky., Louisville bar assns., Hon. Order Ky. Cols., Ky. Soc. Natural History (dir.), Louisville Photog. Soc., Louisville C. of C., Asso. Industries Quad Cities (past pres.), Am. Soc. Personnel Adminstrn., Louisville Personnel Assn., SAR. Episcopalian (vestryman). Clubs: Rotary; Filson, Pendennis, Arts. Patentee in field. Home and Office: 1704 Spruce Ln Louisville KY 40207

FITCH, JON PHILLIP, chem. oil. recovery co. exec.; b. Broken Arrow, Okla., Apr. 1, 1943; s. Harry Henry and Bettye Lou (Hart) F.; B.S., U. Idaho, 1965; m. Karen Sue Clark, Oct. 26, 1962; children—Kelley Ann, Kimberly Ann. Field engr. Water Mgmt. div. Calgon Corp., Ventura, Calif., 1965-70; field engr. Oilfield div. Betz Labs., Inc., Bakersfield, Calif., 1970-73; founder, pres. Chem. Oil Recovery Co., Bakersfield, 1973—; dir. Kelkim Corp. Active, Boys Club. Mem. Soc. Petroleum Engrs. of AIME, Am. Petroleum Inst., Prodn. Pioneers. Republican. Lutheran. Contbr. numerous articles on enhanced oil recovery to tech. publs.; patentee in field; designer, implementer systems to improve crude oil recovery. Home: 6300 Glenrock Way Bakersfield CA 93309 Office: PO Box 9666 Bakersfield CA 93389

FITTS, E. GRANT, business exec.; b. Montevallo, Ala., 1916; LL.B., U. Cin., 1940; LL.M., Harvard U., 1946. Admitted to Ala. bar, Tex. bar; asso. firm White, Bradley, Arant, All & Rose, 1946-51; partner firm Deramus, Fitts & Johnston, 1952-61; v.p., gen. counsel Am. Life Ins. Co., 1961-62; pres. Greatamerica Corp., 1962-68; chmn., pres. Gulf Life Holding Co., from 1968; with Gulf Life Ins. Co., Dallas, 1962—, chmn. bd., 1968—, pres., 1970—, also dir.; chmn., pres., chief exec. officer Gulf United Corp.; chmn. Am.-Amicable Life Ins. Co., Fin. Computer Services, Inc., Gulf Fire & Casualty Co., KYXO, Inc., WGHP-TV, Inc., WKAP, Inc., WTSP-TV, Inc., others; dir. numerous cos. Mem. Am. Bar Assn., State Bar Tex., Am. Judicature Soc. Office: Gulf United Corp 13101 Preston Rd Dallas TX 75240*

FITZ, THOMAS EDMUNDS, JR., health care cons.; b. Durham, N.C., July 24, 1949; s. Thomas Edmunds and Frances Roddey (Whitesides) F.; B.A. in Econs., Duke U., 1971; M.B.A., Mo. State U., 1975; m. Margaret Ann Murchison, Apr. 7, 1973; children—Kathryn Morgan, Anne Roddey. With Am. Med. Internat., Inc., 1976-79, Ernst & Whinney, Birmingham, Ala., 1979—; adminstrv. asst. Gordon Crowell Meml. Hosp., Lincolnton, N.C., 1976, asst. adminstr., 1976-77; asst. adminstr. Clearwater (Fla.) Community Hosp., 1977, El Cajon (Calif.) Valley Hosp., 1977-79, adminstr., Atlanta. Campaign chmn. United Way, 1977-78. Served to lt. AUS, 1971-75. Mem. Health Care Execs. Assn. Imperial, Riverside and San Diego Counties, Assn. M.B.A. Execs., Am. Mgmt. Assn., Am. Coll. Hosp. Adminstrs., Am. Acad. Med. Adminstrs., Am. Hosp. Assn., Fedn. Am. Hosps., Hosp. Council San Diego, Emergency Med. Services of San Diego, Jaycees. Republican. Presbyterian. Club: Kiwanis. Author: Labor Management System, 1978. Home: 1845 Burning Tree Circle Birmingham AL 35226 Office: Ernst & Whinney 1800 1st Nat-So Natural Bldg Birmingham AL 35203

FITZGERALD, ALBERT JAMES, III, govt. ofcl.; b. Phila., June 15, 1950; s. Albert James and Margaretta C. (O'Donnell) F.; B.S. in Math., St. Joseph's Coll., 1972; postgrad. Temple U., 1975—, Am. U., 1980—. Inventory mgr. GS-5, Aviation Supply Office, Phila., 1972-73, inventory mgr. GS-7, 1973-74, inventory mgr., GS-9, 1974-77, logistics mgr., GS-11, 1977-79; supply systems analyst GS-12, Naval Supply Systems Command, Washington, 1979-80; ops. research analyst Naval Material Command, Washington, 1980—; Navy mem. Dept. Def. Joint Service Nonconsumable Item subgroup, 1979-80. Recipient Individual Cost Reduction award NAVSUP, 1976; Sec. Navy Career fellow, 1976-77; others. Republican. Roman Catholic. Club: Main Line. Home: 9020 Giltinan Ct Springfield VA 22153 Office: Joint Aero Depot Maintenance Action Group Washington DC

FITZGERALD, FRED JOHN, JR., banker; b. Haworth, N.J., Aug. 14, 1915; s. Fred John and Grace (Johnston) F.; student Rutgers U., 1936-38, Harvard Grad. Sch. Sales Mgmt. and Mktg., 1957-58; m. Elizabeth Carson, July 6, 1940; children—Barbara, Susan, Joan. Salesman, Yardley of London, Inc., N.Y.C., 1936-53, asst. sales mgr., 1953-59, field sales mgr., 1959-60, gen. sales mgr., 1960-64, v.p., 1964-67; v.p. Dior Perfume Corp., N.Y.C., 1967-68; v.p. mktg. sales and advt. Aloe Creme Labs., Inc., Ft. Lauderdale, Fla., 1968-70, also dir.; mgr. bus. devel. Boca Raton Nat. Bank (Fla.), 1970-77, bus. devel. officer, 1977—. Active Heart Fund, New Canaan, 1958, USO, New Canaan, 1960; bd. dirs. Boca Raton United Way, YMCA, Boca Raton Center for Arts. Served to lt. comdr. USNR, World War II. Mem. Am. Legion, Chi Psi. Clubs: Masons, Kiwanis (v.p. 1976); Hundred of Palm Beach County (v.p. 1981); Boca Raton Hotel and Club; USCG Aux. (officer). Home: 1348 Sugar Plum Dr Boca Raton FL 33432 Office: Boca Raton Nat Bank Boca Raton FL 33432

FITZGERALD, GERALD FRANCIS, banker; b. Chgo., July 6, 1925; s. John Joseph and Olivia (Trader) F.; B.S., Northwestern U., 1949; m. Marjorie Gosselin, Sept. 10, 1949; children—Gerald Francis, James G., Thomas G., Julie Ann, Peter G. Sales exec. Premier Printing Co., 1949-53; partner Fitzgerald & Cooke, Chgo., 1953-59; v.p. Gardner, Jones & Crowell, 1960-64; chmn. bd. dirs. Palatine Nat. Bank (Ill.), 1961—, Cary State Bank, (Ill.), 1971—, Suburban Nat. Bank Elk Grove, Elk Grove Village, Ill., 1971—, Suburban Bank of Hoffman Estates (Ill.), 1969—, Suburban Nat. Bank of Palatine, 1968—, Suburban Nat. Bank of Woodfield (Ill.), 1974—, Bank of Rolling Meadows (Ill.), 1973—. Pres., Palatine Twp. Republican Orgn., 1960; membership chmn. United Rep. Fund of Ill., 1958. Served with Armed Forces, 1944-46. Mem. Delta Upsilon. Clubs: Chicago Athletic Assn., Inverness Golf, Executive, Bankers (Chgo.); Dairymen's Country; Meadow. Home: 1897 Stuart Ln Inverness Palatine IL 60067 Office: 50 N Brockway Palatine IL 60067

FITZGERALD, HAROLD ALVIN, former newspaper publisher; b. St. Johns, Mich., Aug. 3, 1896; s. Howard and Zylphia Irene (Shaver) F.; A.B., U. Mich., 1917; LL.D., Oakland U.; m. Elizabeth Millis, June 16, 1923; children—Howard Harold, Nancy E. Connolly, Richard Millis. With Pontiac (Mich.) Daily Press, 1919-69, telegraph editor, bus. mgr. to 1930, editor and mgr., 1930-44, pub., chmn. bd., until 1969; 1st v.p. AP, 1951-54, dir., 1955-64; v.p. Hillsdale (Mich.) News. Former trustee Kingswood Cranbrook, Brookside Schs., Bloomfield Hills; mem. Mich. Constl. Commn. Commn., 1942; vice chmn. Cranbrook Found., Bloomfield Hills, 1935-68; chmn. Mich. State U. Oakland Found., 1960-71; vice chmn. Oakland County CD, 1939-45; pres. Pontiac United Fund. Served as 2d lt. Air Service, U.S. Army, 1917-18. Mem. Am. Soc. Newspaper Editors, Inter-Am. Press Assn. (dir.), Am. Legion, Alpha Delta Phi, Sigma Delta Chi. Episcopalian (former vestryman). Clubs: Rotary (past pres.); Bloomfield Hills Country (past pres.); Orchard Lake Country; Univ. Mich. (Ann Arbor); Marco Polo (N.Y.C.). Contbr. to Sat. Eve. Post, Am. Mag., Look, others. Home: 148 Ottawa Dr Pontiac MI 48053

FITZGERALD, JAY, lawyer; b. Washington, Sept. 6, 1923; s. James V. and Alice (Tarrant) FitzG.; B.S., Georgetown U. Sch. Fgn. Service, 1948, J.D., Sch. Law, 1954; postgrad. N.Y. U., 1948-49, Fordham Law Sch., 1949-51; m. Mary Ellen Igoe, July 17, 1948; children—David W., Cynthia E., Brian C., James Andrew, Gerald Claibourne, Melanie M., Matthew M., Mary Ellen. Economist, fgn. fin. analyst Standard Oil Co. (N.J.), 1948-51; industry specialist Petroleum Adminstrn. for Def., 1951-53; spl. adviser to comdg. gen. Hdqrs. Command, USAF, 1953-57; admitted to D.C. and Md. bars, 1954; partner firm FitzGerald, Ridgway & Wilson, 1957—; gen. counsel, dir. Peoples Security Bank Md.; pres., chmn. bd. Community Savs. and Loan, Inc. Mem. bd. commrs. Md. Bldg., Savs. and Loan Commn.; active ARC, United Givers Fund; mem. Nat. Cherry Blossom Festival Com., 1954-56; pres. Montgomery County Young Democrats, 1947-48, vice chmn. N.Y. State, 1949-50; vice chmn. Young Dem. Clubs Am., 1951; bd. mgmt. Nat. Capital Area USO, 1956—, Bethesda YMCA. Served as ensign U.S. Maritime Service, 1943-46. Recipient Distinguished Service award as Md.'s Outstanding Young Man, Md. Jr. C. of C., 1954, Certificate of Distinction for outstanding contbns. to community and state D.C. dept. Am. Legion, 1954. Mem. Montgomery County Bd. Realtors, Am. Soc. Internat. Law, Am., Md., D.C. bar assns., Georgetown Alumni Assn., U.S. (dir. 1956-58), Md. (pres. 1957-58), Bethesda (pres. 1952-54) jr. chambers commerce, S.A.R., Pi Kappa Alpha, Gamma Eta Gamma. Clubs: N.Y. Athletic; Congressional Country (Md.); Potomac Rotary. Home: 11500 Beall Mountain Rd Potomac MD 20854 Office: 1 Central Plaza 11300 Rockville Pike Rockville MD 20852

FITZGERALD, JOHN CHARLES, JR., investment banker; b. Sacramento, May 23, 1941; s. John Charles and Geraldine Edith (McNabb) F.; B.S., Calif. State U. at Sacramento, 1964; M.B.A., Cornell U., 1966; m. Mildred Ann Kilpatrick, June 26, 1965; children—Geraldine Kathrine, Erec John. Dir. corp. planning Bekins Co., Los Angeles, 1966-73; mgr. corp. planning Ridder Publs., Inc., Los Angeles, 1973-75; chief fin. officer City of Inglewood (Calif.), 1975-77; treas./controller Inglewood Redevel. Agy., 1975-77, Inglewood Housing Authority, 1975-77; v.p. municipal fin. White, Weld & Co., Inc., Los Angeles, 1977-78; v.p. pub. fin. Paine Webber Jackson & Curtis, Los Angeles, 1978-79; v.p. and mgr. for Western region, mcpl. fin. dept. Merrill Lynch White Weld Capital Markets Group, Los Angeles, 1979—; instr. fin./adminstrn. El Camino Coll., Torrance, Calif., 1977—. Bd. dirs., exec. com., treas., chmn. fund raising com. Los Angeles chpt. Am. Heart Assn., 1977—; bd. dirs. Daniel Freeman Hosp., Inglewood. Mem. Fin. Execs. Inst., Municipal Fin. Officers Assn., Calif. Soc. Municipal Fin. Officers, League Calif. Cities, So. Calif. Corp. Planners Assn. (past pres.), Los Angeles Bond, Beta Gamma Sigma. Republican. Clubs: Rotary, Jonathan, Palos Verdes Country, Rancho Verdes Racquet. Home: 28424 Coveridge Dr Rancho Palos Verdes CA 90274 Office: 707 Wilshire Blvd Suite 4330 Los Angeles CA 90017

FITZGERALD, JOHN THERON, utility co. exec., ceramic store exec.; b. Ogdensburg, N.Y., Aug. 2, 1934; s. Leslie Thomas and Georgena (Amo) F.; grad. in indsl. mgmt. Lincoln Extension Inst., 1975; m. Anna Joan DeBlois, Aug. 14, 1954; children—Karen, Susan, Debra, Mary Lynn, Julie. With Niagara Mohawk Power Corp., Utica, N.Y., 1952—, asst. supr. transmission and distbn., 1972—; owner The Reel Shop, Utica, 1972—. Roman Catholic. Clubs: Moose, K. C. Home: 30 Scott St Utica NY 13501 Office: Harbor Point Utica NY 13502

FITZGERALD, JOSEPH JAMES, nuclear components mfg. co. exec.; b. Boston, Mar. 3, 1919; s. Edward J. and Mary J. (Murphy) F.; B.S., Boston Coll., 1949, M.S., 1950; postgrad. (AEC fellow) U. Rochester, 1951; m. Claire E. Whelan, Aug. 4, 1946; children—Claire Marie, Joseph Francis, Joanne Jacqueline, Edward Gerard, Francis Xavier, Kevin James. Supr. radiation chemistry and physics Gen. Electric Knolls Atomic Power Lab., Schenectady, 1951-58; asst. prof. Harvard U., Cambridge, Mass., 1958-61; pres., chmn. Cambridge Nuclear Corp., Billerica, Mass., 1961—; cons. Los Alamos Sci. Lab., 1960-70, AEC, 1960-69, HEW, 1960-73; commr. of mass AEC, 1959-64, mem. adv. com. on isotopes and radiation, 1964-67. Served with USAAF, 1942-45; ETO; NATOUSA. Cert. health physicist. Mem. Am. Nuclear Soc., Nuclear Medicine Soc., New Eng. Health Physics Soc. (pres. 1960-62), Cross and Crown Soc. Author: Mathematical Theory of Radiation Dosimetry, 1967; Applied Radiation Protection and Control, 1970; contbr. numerous articles to profl. jours., chpts. to books; patentee on radioisotope tech., nuclear powered artificial heart device, radiation dosimetry. Home: 7 Squire Rd Winchester MA 01890 Office: 575 Middlesex Turnpike Billerica MA 01865

FITZGERALD, KEVIN SCOTT, oil co. exec.; b. Providence, Aug. 1, 1947; s. Henry Scott and Arleen Meyers (Burgess) F.; student schs., Orange Park, Fla.; m. Erin Foster, July 4, 1972. Pvt. practice investments cons., San Francisco, 1971-75; chmn., chief exec. officer Highlands Energy Corp., San Francisco, 1976—. Served with USMC, 1966-70. Mem. Am. Petroleum Inst., Ind. Petroleum Assn. Am. Republican. Club: Olympic. Home: 1001 California St San Francisco CA 94108 Office: 601 California St San Francisco CA 94108

FITZGERALD, THOMAS WILLIAM, JR., banker; b. Providence, Sept. 8, 1929; s. Thomas William and Mary Elizabeth Fitzgerald; M.B.A., Loyola U., 1952, LL.D. (hon.), 1958; m. Barbara Lee Covert, Sept. 18, 1970; 1 dau., Mary Patricia. With Indsl. Nat. Bank, Providence, 1952-56, Primghar Savs. Bank (Iowa), 1956-58; pres., chief exec. officer, dir. Louis Joliet Bank, Joliet, Ill., 1958-68, with Univ. Bank and Trust Co., Cambridge, Mass., 1968-74; pres., chief exec. officer Liberty Bank and Trust Co., Boston, 1974—, also dir., chmn. exec. com. Trustee, Graham Coll.; chmn. fund drive Am. Cancer Soc., U.S. Treasury Bonds. Named hon. chief of police, Concord, Mass., 1975. Mem. Am. Bankers Assn. (loan com.), Mass. Bankers Assn. (govt. relations com.). Democrat. Roman Catholic. Clubs: Algonquin, Union (Boston). Home: 23 Hunters Ridge Rd Concord MA 01742 Office: 7 School St Boston MA 02108

FITZGERALD, WILLIAM ALLINGHAM, savs. and loan assn. exec.; b. Omaha, Nov. 18, 1937; s. William Frances and Mary (Allingham) F.; B.S.B.A. in Fin., Creighton U., 1959; grad. Savs. and Loan League exec. tng. program U. Ga., 1962, Savs. and Loan League grad. sch. program U. Ind., 1969; m. Barbara Ann Miskell, Aug. 20, 1960; children—Mary Colleen, Katherine Kara, William Tate. With Comml. Fed. Savs. & Loan Assn., Omaha, 1959—, v.p., asst. sec., 1963-68, exec. v.p., 1968-73, pres., 1974—; dir. Am. Nat. Bank. Bd. dirs. Blue Cross/Blue Shield, Omaha, NCCJ, Nebr. Ind. Coll. Found.; chmn. bd. dirs. Coll. St. Mary; bd. dirs. Regional Health Care Corp., also univ. bd. dirs. Creighton U.; pres. Neb. Found.; trustee Archbishop's com. for ednl. devel. Roman Catholic Ch.; adv. bd. Jr. League Omaha. Served to lt. Fin. Corps, U.S. Army. Mem. Omaha C. of C. (pres.), Nebr. League Savs. and Loans (pres.). Republican. Clubs: Omaha Country, Kiewit Plaza. Office: 4501 Dodge St Omaha NE 58132

FITZGERALD, WILLIAM FRANCIS, savs. and loan assn. exec.; b. Omaha, Jan. 20, 1908; s. James J. and Katherine (O'Rourke) F.; student Creighton U., 1926-27; B.S. in Mech. Engring., Iowa State Coll., 1931; m. Mary Allingham, Sept. 29, 1934; children—Mary Frances (Mrs. J. Emmet Root), William A., Katherine A. (Mrs. A. R. Grandsaert, Jr.). With Comml. Fed. Savs. & Loan Assn., Omaha, 1932—, sec., 1942-50, pres., 1950—, now chmn. bd., also dir.; dir. Hennen Realty Co., United Seed Co., Wynn Co.; vice chmn., dir. Fed. Home Loan Bank, Topeka, 1960-64. Mem. Fed. Savs. and Loan Adv. Council, Washington, 1962-63. Chmn. Creighton U. Alumni Fund drive, 1960-61. Bd. dirs. United Community Fund, Omaha, 1958-61; bd. regents Creighton U., 1961-68, mem. pres.'s council, 1968—, mem. pres.'s research council, 1967—; mem. adv. bd. Bergan Mercy Hosp., 1969—. Mem. U.S. Savs. and Loan League (bd. dirs. 1955-57), Omaha C. of C. (bd. dirs. 1958-61), Beta Gamma Sigma (hon.). Clubs: Omaha Country, Omaha; Kiwanis (charter, bd. dirs.; past pres. South Omaha). Home: 685 N 57th St Omaha NE 68132 Office: 4501 Dodge St Omaha NE 68101

FITZPATRICK, DANA G., wood products mfg. co. exec.; b. Salamanca, N.Y., Mar. 24, 1930; s. William F. and Loretto M. Fitzpatrick; A.B. in Econs., U. Notre Dame, 1952; m. Bernice Siebart, Dec. 28, 1955; children—Daniel, Marcia, Gregory, Kerry, Sheila. Sales mgr., sec.-treas. Fitzpatrick & Weller, Inc., Ellicottville, N.Y.,

1954—; dir. Salamanca Fed. Savs. & Loan, Win-Sum Corp. Mem. Ellicottville Central Sch. Bd., Cattaraugus County Indsl. Devel. Bd. Served to lt. (j.g.) Supply Corps, USN, 1952-54. Mem. Nat. Hardwood Lumber Assn. (dir.), Ellicottville C. of C. (pres.), Penn-York Lumbermans Club. Republican. Roman Catholic. Club: Crag Burn. Home: Fish Hill Rd Ellicottville NY 14731 Office: Fitzpatrick & Weller Inc Mill St Ellicottville NY 14731

FITZPATRICK, JAMES JOHN, JR., mfg. co. tax exec.; b. Catskill, N.Y., June 27, 1937; s. James John and Mary Delores (Posik) F.; B.S., Seton Hall U., 1962; postgrad. Bentley Coll., 1977; m. Charlotte Smalling, June 23, 1962; children—Eileen, Karen, Sheila, Daniel, Kelly. Tax specialist Am. Cyanamid Corp., Wayne, N.J., 1960-63; tax mgr. Control Data Corp., Mpls., 1963-73; tax dir. Honeywell Info. Systems, Inc., Waltham, Mass., 1973—. Served with U.S. Army, 1958-60. Mem. Inst. Property Taxation, Council State Chambers Commerce, Tax Execs. Inst., Internat. Assn. Assessing Officers, Computer and Bus. Equipment Mfrs. Assn. (taxation council), Soc. Auditor-Appraisers, AIM (taxation com.). Roman Catholic. Home: 6 Forest Rd Foxboro MA 02035 Office: 200 Smith St Waltham MA 02154

FITZ PATRICK, PATRICK CHARLES, profl. services co. exec.; b. Jersey City, June 8, 1939; s. Joseph and Hannah (McKeown) F.; B.S. in Engring., U.S. Naval Acad., 1961; M.B.A., Wharton Sch., U. Pa., 1971; m. Lynn Begley, May 16, 1970; children—Brendan, Rory, Conor. Vice pres. First Nat. Bank of Chgo., Ireland, Nairobi, Kenya, Chgo., N.Y., 1977-80; treas. Planning Research Corp., Washington, 1980—. Bd. dirs. Found. for Research into the Origin of Man, 1979—. Served with USN, 1961-69. Address: 1850 K St NW Washington DC 20006

FITZSIMMONS, THOMAS BRAUN, banker; b. Charleston, W.Va., Apr. 4, 1948; s. William Louis and Gerry Phyllis (Crockett) F.; B.S., Central Meth. Coll., 1972; ed. Grad. Sch. Banking, La. State U., 1975-78; m. Cathy Beth Hausman, Jan. 8, 1972; children—Catherine Nicole, Ridgley Braun. With 1st Bank of Commerce, Columbia, Mo., 1972—, beginning in credit dept., successively installment loan officer, comml. loan officer, asst. v.p. comml. loan, 1972-76, v.p. operations, 1976—, sec. to bd. dirs., 1978, exec. v.p., dir., from 1978—; now pres., chief exec. officer First Nat. Bank, Carrollton, Mo.; pres. Columbia Clearing House. Served with USNR, 1968-70; Viet Nam. Mem. Nat. Fedn. Ind. Businesses, Robert Morris Assos., Am. Inst. Banking, Columbia C. of C. (bd. dirs.). Club: Columbia Ambassador. Home: Route 7 Columbia MO 65201

FIUR, MERTON, pub. relations exec.; b. N.Y.C., Mar 5, 1932; s. Frank F. and Evette (Goechman) F.; B.S., Syracuse U., 1953; postgrad. Tchrs. Coll. Columbia, 1953-54; m. Lola Troy, Sept. 11, 1955 (div. Sept. 26, 1979); children—Michael, Jonathan; m. 2d, Suzanne Rovner, May 23, 1980. Publicity dir. Wilson, Haight & Welch, N.Y.C., 1954-55; pub. relations dir. Blaine-Thompson Advt., N.Y.C., 1955-56; account supr. Grey Pub. Relations, N.Y.C., 1956-62; pres. Merton Fiur Assos., Inc., N.Y.C., 1962-75; chmn. bd. Padilla and Speer/N.Y., 1975-78; owner Merton Fiur & Co., 1978—; founder and asso. Center for Public Communication, N.Y.C., 1979—; adj. asso. prof. mktg. Pace U., N.Y.C., 1979—; adj. asst. prof. communications N.Y. U., 1980—. Vice chmn., pub. relations dir. Young Citizens for Johnson, 1964; mem. exec. com., publicity chmn. Vol. Coordinating Council N.Y.C., 1968-69. Mem. Publicity Club N.Y. (past pres., dir.), Nat. Acad. TV Arts and Scis. Home: 429 E 52d St New York NY 10022

FIX, MEYER, lawyer; b. Manchester, Eng., July 29, 1906; s. Morris and Leah (Katz) F.; came to U.S., 1910, naturalized, 1917; A.B., U. Rochester, 1928; J.D., Harvard U., 1931; m. Elizabeth Goldsmith, July 27, 1937; children—Terry E., Brian D. Admitted to N.Y. bar, 1932, U.S. Supreme Ct. bar, 1950; mem. firms John Van Voorhis' Sons, 1936-43, Fix & MacCameron, 1943-55, Meyer Fix, 1955-61, Fix & Spindelman, 1961-74, Fix Spindelman Turk & Himelein, 1974-77; sr. partner firm Fix, Spindelman, Turk, Himelein & Schwartz, Rochester, N.Y., 1977—; chmn. bd. Extra Care Facilities, Inc. Mem. Am., N.Y. State, Monroe County bar assns., Am. Law Inst., Internat. Assn. Ins. Counsel, Fedn. Ins. Counsel, Assn. Ins. Attys., N.Y. State Trial Lawyers Assn. Clubs: Irondequoit Country, Rochester Ad, Masons, Shriners. Contbr. articles to Scribes. Home: 2501 East Ave Rochester NY 14610 Office: 2 State St Rochester NY 14614

FLACK, CHARLES ZORAH, JR., ins. co. exec., civic worker; b. Rutherford County, N.C., July 11, 1936; s. Charles Z. and Blanche (Thornton) F.; B.S., U. N.C., 1958; m. Jan Sawyer, Aug. 9, 1958; children—Charles Zorah III, Blair Thornton, Thomas Cooper. Mgr., Charles Z. Flack Agy., Inc., Forest City, N.C., 1958—; chmn. Planning and Zoning Commn., Forest City, N.C., 1968—. Vice pres. United Appeal of Rutherford County (N.C), 1976, mem. exec. com., 1974, campaign chmn., 1974, pres., 1975; treas. Rutherford County Cystic Fibrosis chpt., 1973-75; chmn. Rutherford County chpt. ARC, 1967-68; pres. Ruthgrford Vocat. Workshop, 1965-67; county chmn. John F. Kennedy Meml. Drive, 1964; treas. council Boy Scouts Am., 1973—; chmn. Clinchfield Dam Subcom. in N.C., del. to Nat. Rivers and Harbours Congress, 1972; pres. Rutherford County Young Democratic Club, 1963-64; Dem. precinct committeeman and officer, Forest City, 1971-79, treas. Rutherford County Dem. Exec. Com., 1977-79, del. to Nat. Dem. Conv., 1976; bd. dirs. Isothermal Health Council, 1973-74; bd. govs. U. N.C., 1977-84. Recipient Distinguished Service award Forest City, N.C., 1964. Mem. U.S., Forest City (pres. 1963-64) jaycees, SAR. Methodist. Clubs: Rutherford Country (pres. 1971—), Kiwanis (dir. 1974-76). Home: 122 Forest Hills Dr Forest City NC 28043 Office: PO Drawer 470 Forest City NC 28043

FLACK, JOE FENLEY, ins. co. exec.; b. Menard, Tex., Feb. 23, 1921; s. Frank H. and Evelyn (Fenley) F.; B.B.A. in Fin. with highest honors, U. Tex., 1943; m. Ann Tarry, Jan. 21, 1945; children—Kate T., Joan E., Joe Fenley. Accountant Ernst & Ernst, C.P.A.'s, Houston, 1946-47; with Am. Gen. Ins. Co., 1947—, treas., 1951—, sr. v.p., 1968—; also dir.; partner John L. Wortham and Son, Houston, 1947-65; pres., treas., dir. Knickerbocker Corp.; auditor Hawaiian Life Ins. Co.; v.p., dir. Whyburn & Co., Md. Casualty Co., Me. Bonding & Casualty Co., Robert Hampson & Son, Ltd.; v.p., treas., dir. Am. Gen. Fire & Casualty Co., Nat. Standard Ins. Co., Am. Gen. Leasing & Finance Corp., Atlas Realty Co., Am. Gen. Investment Corp., Am. Gen. Realty Co., Am. Gen. Capital Corp.; v.p. Assurance Co. Am., Marasco Co., Inc., No. Ins. Co. N.Y. Exec. bd. Boy Scouts Am. Mayor pro-tem city Bunker Hill Village (Tex.), 1959-61, mayor, 1961-65. Trustee, v.p. sch. bd. Spring Branch Ind. Sch. Dist., 1967-75; bd. dirs. Kappa Sigma Found., U. Tex., Houston chpt. Salvation Army; bd. govs. Park Plaza Hosp., Houston; mem. exec. com. U. Tex. Health Sci. Center, Houston. Served to lt. USNR, 1943-45; ETO, PTO. C.P.A., Tex. Mem. Am. Inst. C.P.A.'s. U. Tex. Ex-Students Assn. (exec. council, regional v.p.). Clubs: River Oaks Country, Petroleum (Houston). Methodist. Office: PO Box 3247 Houston TX 77001

FLAGG, DAVID CHARLES, fin. planning, pension and ins. cons.; b. Larchmont, N.Y., Aug. 22, 1926; s. Samuel Barry and Minnie (Boltz) F.; student Principia Coll., 1943-44; B.M.E. with honors, Yale U., 1946; postgrad. in bus. adminstrn. N.Y. U., 1950-51; m. Carole Henrietta Tresch, Sept. 11, 1948; children—Barry David, Donna Sue. Test engr. Gen. Electric Co., Schenectady and Bloomfield, N.J., 1946-48; design engr., fin. statistician, mktg. cons. Ebasco Services Inc., N.Y.C., 1948-51; sales rep., mgr. employee benefit dept. New Eng. Mut. Life Ins. Co., Newark, 1951-59; pres., chief exec. officer, dir. Deferred Benefits Corp., Millburn, N.J., 1959—; pres., dir. All Star Agy., Inc., d/b Asset Planning, Inc.; lectr. in field. Served with USNR, 1944-46, 51-53. Recipient Marcus Nadler Key excellence N.Y. U.; enrolled actuary IRS. Fellow Am. Soc. Pension Actuaries; mem. Nat. Assn. Pension Cons.'s and Adminstrs., Nat. Assn. Life Underwriters, Nat. Assn. Security Dealers, Am. Soc. C.L.U.'s, Million Dollar Round Table (life, div. v.p.), Nat. Assn. Charitable Estate Counsellors, Sigma Xi, Tau Beta Pi, Beta Gamma Sigma. Presbyterian. Office: 306 Main St Millburn NJ 07041

FLAGG, ROBERT FARRINGTON, advt. agy. exec.; b. Houston, Mar. 22, 1924; s. Joseph Walker and May Del (Farrington) F.; student Tex. A. and M. U., 1941-42, Tex. A. and I. U., 1942-43; B.A. with honors, Rice U., 1949; m. Nancy White, Sept., 1949; children—Robert Farrmington, Betsy, Gael, Charles. Newspaper reporter, book pub., public relations dir. Elsevier Press, Houston and Amsterdam, 1951-54; account exec. Boone & Cummings, Houston, 1954-64; pres. Flagg Advt. Agy., Houston, 1964—; pres. Compton Enterprises, Houston, 1967—; editor, pub. Flagg's Gardening Almanac, also Flagg's Gardening Newsletter, Houston, 1972—; gardening editor Houston Post, 1977—; gardening radio host KPRC, Houston, 1977—; hort. lectr. Precinct chmn., dist. and state del. Republican Party, 1960-74. Served with U.S. Army, 1941-46. Decorated Bronze Star with cluster, Combat Infantryman's badge, Purple Heart with oak leaf clusters; various campaign ribbons; recipient award State of Israel, 1976; also various advt. awards. Mem. Garden Writers Am., Houston C. of C., Houston Ad Club, Rice U. Alumni Assn., Allied Florists Houston (sec. 1964—). Episcopalian. Club: Univ. (Houston). Author: Gulf Coast Gardener, 1961, rev. edit., 1967; contbr. gardening articles to various publs. Office: 5002 Morningside St Houston TX 77005

FLAGLER, ROBERT LOOMIS, mfg. co. exec.; b. Chgo., Feb. 17, 1940; s. Holland J. and Francis Eugenia (Loomis) F.; B.A., U. Miss., 1964; children—Ann Holland, Robert Stephen. Asst. to v.p., gen. mgr. Sta. WSNS-TV, Chgo., 1967-70; v.p., gen. mgr. Telemation Prodns., Inc., Glenview, Ill., 1970-79, also dir., v.p. adminstrv. officer, 1979; pres., chief operating officer Ocenco, Inc., Northbrook, Ill., 1979—, also dir.; dir. Video Support Co., Inc., Wis. Edn. Industries. Mem. Video Tape Producers Assn., U. Miss. Alumni Assn., Am. Mining Congress, Indsl. TV Soc., Nat. Assn. Sales and Mktg. Execs. Republican. Episcopalian. Club: Lions. Home: 134 Green Bay Rd Winnetka IL 60093 Office: 400 Academy Dr Northbrook IL 60062

FLAHERTY, HUGH E., communications exec.; b. Bloomsburg, Pa., Oct. 18, 1931; grad. Villanova U., 1953; postgrad. Georgetown Law Sch.; m. Virginia Lee Purvis; 3 sons. Reporter Balt. Sun, 1956-60; polit. writer, corr. Phila. Bull., 1960-66; research asst. and speech writer Gov. Pa., 1966; sec. for legislation and pub. affairs Pa., 1967-70; asso. dir. Nat. Commn. on Marihuana and Drug Abuse, 1971; v.p. information and communications Western Pa. Nat. Bank, 1972; v.p. community Devel. Teleprompter Corp., N.Y.C., 1972-73; v.p., dir. corporate communications 1st Union Corp., Charlotte, N.C., 1974-76; dir. pub. affairs The Pittston Co., Greenwich, Conn., 1977—. Served with AUS, 1950; ETO, NATOUSA. Home: 12 Shelter Rock Rd Trumbull CT 06611 Office: One Pickwick Plaza Greenwich CT 06830

FLAMM, DONALD, real estate, investments, theatrical producer, writer; b. Pitts., Dec. 11, 1899; s. Louis and Elizabeth (Jason) F.; ed. pub. schs., N.Y.; extension courses N.Y. U.; m. Elayne Knee, Dec. 9, 1979. Pub. mags. and books, 1921-30; owner, operator radio sta. WMCA, N.Y.C., 1925-41, WPCH, N.Y.C., 1927-32; co-owner WPAT, Paterson, N.J., 1942-48; now engaged in real estate activities; founder, former owner Alpine Country Club, Alpine, N.J.; founder, pres., operating head Intercity Radio Network, 1927-41; former co-owner La Salle Apt.-Office Bldg., Washington, various other holdings; theatrical producer, N.Y.C., London; pres. Flamm Realty Corp., N.Y.; dir. Oscar Lewenstein Plays, Ltd., London, 1959-76; pres., chmn. radio sta. WMMM-AM and WDJF-FM, Westport, Conn. Former chmn. N.J. Civil War Centennial Commn.; past mem. N.Y. Mayor's Commn. on Youth Fitness, 1958-61, 76-79. Bd. dirs., v.p. Hebrew Free Loan Soc. N.Y.; mem. N.Y. exec. com., mem. nat. program com. Anti-Defamation League; former bd. dirs., officer Manfred Sakel Inst. for Brain Scis.; past pres., trustee Mt. Neboh Temple, N.Y.C. Served as spl. liaison officer O.W.I., World War II; formulated plans for Am. Broadcasting Sta. in Eng. Mem. Internat. Radio and TV Soc., Royal TV Soc. (London), Cath. Actors Guild, Jewish Theatrical Guild. Clubs: United Hunts Racing Assn., Rockefeller Luncheon, Pa. Soc. Friars, Lambs, Le Club, Alpine Country; White Elephant, Annabel's (London). Contbr. numerous articles on theatre, radio and TV to trade publs. in U.S. and Eng. Home: Closter NJ 07624 Office: 25 Central Park W New York NY 10023

FLAMMANG, ROBERT FRANCIS, oil co. exec.; b. Chgo., Oct. 29, 1927; s. Francis and Catherine Flammang; student Mich. State U., 1945; B.S. in Chemistry, De Paul U., 1951; m. Camille Faith Hamilton; children—Susan, William, Leslie, Jo-Anne. Chemist, Richfield Oil Corp., Bakersfield, Cal., 1952-59; with Magna Corp., Houston, 1959-75, mgr. internat. sales, until 1975; v.p., mgr. internat. mktg. United Chem. Corp., Hobbs, N.Mex., 1976-79, v.p. Unichem Internat., 1979—; mng. dir. TR Oil Services Ltd., Scotland, 1979—; dir. TR Oil Services (Arabia). Served with AUS, 1945-47. Mem. Houston World Trade Assn., Nat. Assn. Corrosion Engrs., Am. Inst. Mining Engrs., Am. Petroleum Inst., Brit. Inst. Petroleum, Grampian-Houston Assn. Home: 23 Hilltop Rd Cults Aberdeen AB1 9RL Scotland Office: TR Oil Services Ltd Angusfield Ln Aberdeen Scotland

FLAMSON, RICHARD JOSEPH, III, banker; b. Los Angeles, Feb. 2, 1929; s. Richard J. and Mildred (Jones) F.; B.A., Claremont Men's Coll., 1951; certificate Pacific Coast Banking Sch., U. Wash., 1962; m. Arden Black, Oct. 5, 1951; children—Richard Joseph IV, Scott Arthur, Michael Jon, Leslie Arden. With Security Pacific Nat. Bank, Los Angeles, 1955—, v.p., 1962-69, sr. v.p., 1969-70, exec. v.p. corp. banking dept., 1970, vice-chmn., 1973, pres. Security Pacific Corp., 1973, pres., chief exec. officer Security Pacific Corp. and Security Pacific Nat. Bank, 1978, chmn., chief exec. officer, 1981—. Chmn. bd. trustees Claremont Men's Coll. Served to 1st lt. AUS, 1951-53. Mem. Res. City Bankers, Robert Morris Assos., Town Hall, Stock Exchange Club. Clubs: California, Los Angeles Country; Balboa Bay, Balboa Yacht (Newport Beach, Calif.). Office: Security Pacific Corp 333 S Hope St Los Angeles CA 90071

FLANAGAN, BERNARD T., publishing co. exec. Vice pres. Dow Jones & Co., N.Y.C., also pub. Barron's. Office: Dow Jones & Co (Barron's) 22 Cortland St New York NY 10027*

FLANAGAN, LEWIS LEE, seed co. exec.; b. Abasarokee, Mont., Feb. 23, 1929; s. Lewis J. and Ida (Kitchen) F.; B.A., Mont. State Coll., 1950; postgrad. Wash. State U., 1962; m. Ruth Hamilton, Nov. 11, 1951; children—Rickey S., Michael K., Terrance D., Janice M. Pvt. agrl. cons., Billings, Mont., 1955-62; asst. mgr. Western Farmers Inc., Moses Lake, Wash., 1962-65; area mgr. Pacific Supply Coops., Walla Walla, 1965-70; Western regional mgr. Velsicol Corp., Chgo., 1970-76; chief exec. officer, gen. mgr. Ramsey Seed Inc. div. DeKalb AgResearch, Manteca, Calif., 1976—. Mem. Walla Walla (Wash.) County Republican Central Com., 1965-70. Served with AUS, 1951-55. Mem. Manteca, Walla Walla (chmn. agr. 1968-69) chambers commerce, Weed Sci. Soc. Am., Western Soc. Weed Sci., Calif. Seed Assn., Pacific Seedsmen, Am. Seed Trade Assn., Western Seedsmen. Republican. Clubs: Masons, Eastgate Lions (officer 1966-70), Spring Creek Country. Home: 435 Palomino Ct Manteca CA 95336 Office: 205 Stockton St Manteca CA 95336

FLANAGAN, PETER JOSEPH, ins. assn. exec.; b. N.Y.C., Aug. 2, 1930; s. Peter F.; A.B., Catholic U. Am., 1953; J.D., St. John's U., 1962; children—Joseph, Elizabeth, Donna, Peter, Jeremy, Arthur, John, Patrick. Admitted to N.Y. bar; spl. group underwriter Equitable Life Ins. Co., N.Y.C., 1957-59; v.p., gen. counsel U.S. Life Ins. Co., N.Y.C., 1960-75; gen. counsel Assn. N.Y. State Life Ins. Cos., N.Y.C., 1975-77; pres. Life Ins. Council N.Y., N.Y.C., 1977—. Mem. Am. Bar Assn., N.Y. State Bar Assn., N.Y. Country Bar Assn., Assn. Bar City N.Y., Assn. Life Ins. Counsel, N.Y. C.L.U.'s. Clubs: University, Rockefeller Center Luncheon (N.Y.C.); Fort Orange (Albany, N.Y.). Office: Life Ins Council NY Room 2450 630 Fifth Ave New York NY 10111

FLANDERS, DONALD HARGIS, mfg. co. exec.; b. Memphis, Apr. 26, 1924; s. Henry Jackson and Mae (Hargis) F.; student Tex. Christian U., 1943; B.B.A., Baylor U., 1947; m. Phala Kathryn Davis, Dec. 15, 1946; children-Donald Hargis, Dudley Kennedy, Phala Katherine. Dir. cost accounting, purchasing agt. McCoy-Couch Furniture Mfg. Co., Benton, Ark., 1947-50, Garrison Furniture Co., Fort Smith, Ark., 1950-54; pres., founder Flanders Mfg. Co., Ft. Smith, 1954-70, Flanders Industries, Inc., 1970—; dir. 1st Nat. Bank, Ft. Smith. Chmn. exec. com. Ft. Smith Freight Bur., 1960-61; chmn. furniture bd. govs. Dallas Market Center, 1968; mem. exec. com. Ark. Council on Econ. Edn., 1964-67; mem. Small Bus. Adv. Council, Ark., 1966-68. Chmn. Ft. Smith United Fund drive, 1962; dist. chmn. Boy Scouts Am., Ft. Smith, 1960-62, pres. Westark area council, 1963-65, regional exec. com., 1964-72, vice chmn. Region 5, 1967-69, chmn. Region 5, 1969-72, mem. nat. exec. bd., 1969-77, Silver Antelope, Silver Beaver, Silver Buffalo, Distinguished Eagle Scout awards; mem. Com. of 100, 1965—. Trustee Sparks Regional Med. Center, Hendrix Coll., Westark Coll. Found., North Ark. Conf. Meth. Ch. Served from apprentice seaman to lt. (s.g.) USNR, 1943-46. Named Industrialist of Year, Ft. Smith Realtors Bd., 1965; recipient Free Enterprise award, 1964. Mem. Southwest Furniture Mfg. Assn. (pres. 1963), Ft. Smith C. of C. (dir. 1961-63, 73—), Ark. Wood Products Assn. (dir. 1965-68), Delta Sigma Pi. Methodist (trustee conf.). Mason (K.T., 33 deg., Shriner). Home: 20 Berry Hill Rd Fort Smith AR 72903 Office: 1901 Wheeler Ave POB 1788 Fort Smith AR 72902

FLANNERY, DENNIS EDWARD, investment banker; b. Harrisburg, Pa., Oct. 7, 1946; s. John Leo and Frances Clarena (Kelly) F.; B.S. in Fgn. Service, Georgetown U., 1972. Internat. credit trainee and analyst Chase Manhattan Bank, 1972-74; asst. v.p., Euro dollar loan syndicator Bank of Am., San Francisco, 1974-77; gen. partner Kuhn Loeb Lehman Bros., Internat., 1977—. Served with U.S. Army, 1967-70. Mem. San Francisco Jr. C. of C. Democrat. Roman Catholic. Clubs: St. Francis Yacht; South End Rowing, Down Town Assn., Univ., N.Y. Yacht (N.Y.C.). Home: 956 Fifth Ave New York NY 10021 Office: 1 William St New York NY 10004

FLANNERY, JOSEPH PATRICK, mfg. co. exec.; b. Lowell, Mass., Mar. 30, 1932; s. Mary Agnes Egan Flannery; B.S. in Chemistry, Lowell Tech. Inst., 1953; M.B.A., Harvard U., 1955; m. Margaret Barrows, June 1957; children—Mary Ann, Diane, Joseph, James, David, Elizabeth. With Uniroyal Chem. Co., 1959-79, dir. mktg., 1972-75; pres., 1975-77; exec. v.p. Uniroyal, Inc., Middlebury, Conn., 1977, pres., 1977-80, chief exec. officer, 1980—, also dir.; dir. Colonial Bank. Mem. Am. Chem. Soc. Roman Catholic. Clubs: Country of Waterbury (Conn.); Vesper Country (Lowell). Home: 435 Squire Hill Rd Cheshire CT 06410 Office: Oxford Mgmt and Research Center Uniroyal Inc Middlebury CT 06749

FLANSBURGH, EARL ROBERT, architect; b. Ithaca, N.Y., Apr. 28, 1931; s. Earl Alvah and Elizabeth (Evans) F.; B.Arch., Cornell U., 1954; M. Arch., Mass. Inst. Tech., 1957; m. Louise Hospital, Aug. 27, 1955; children—Earl Schuyler, John Conant. Job capt., designer The Architects Collaborative, Cambridge, Mass., 1958-62; partner Freeman, Flansburgh and Assos., Cambridge, 1961-63; prin. Earl R. Flansburgh and Assos., Cambridge, 1963-69, pres., dir. design, 1970—; exec. v.p. Environment Systems Internat., Inc.; vis. prof. archtl. design Mass. Inst. Tech., 1965-66; instr. art Wellesley Coll., 1962-65, lectr. art, 1965-69; cons. to architects, engrs. for Boston City Hall, 1962-63; chmn. architecture com. Boston Arts Festival, 1964; chmn. design rev. bd. City of Boston; chmn. design review group City of Cambridge. Bd. dirs. Cambridge Center Adult Edn.; trustee Cornell U., 1972—, chmn. archtl. adv. com., 1972—, mem. exec. com., academic affairs com., chmn. bldg. and properties com. Served to 1st lt. USAF, 1954-56. Fulbright research grantee Bldg. Research Sta., Eng., 1957-58; design awards Progressive Architecture, 1962, 64, 68, 69, Record Houses, 1965, 66, 67, 68, 73, 75; hon. mention Copley Sq. competition Boston, 1966; spl. 1st prize Buffalo-Western N.Y. AIA, competition, 1968; design citations Am. Assn. Sch. Adminstrs.; design award ednl. bldgs. Mass. Masonry Inst. Fellow AIA; mem. Royal Inst. Brit. Architects (corp. mem.), Boston Soc. Architects (chmn. program com. 1969-71, commr. pub. affairs 1971, commr. design 1974, commr. profl. soc. 1979—, v.p., pres.-elect), Cornell U. Council, Quill and Dagger Soc., Tau Beta Pi. Archtl. works include Weston (Mass.) Sr. High Sch. addition, 1965-67, Cornell U. Campus Store, 1967-70, Cumnock Hall, Harvard Bus. Sch., 1973-75, Acton (Mass.) Elementary Schs., 1966-68, 69-71, Peabody High Sch., 1969-71, Wilton (Conn.) High Sch., 1968-71, Marlborough (Mass.) High Sch., 1972-76, 14 Story Street Bldg., 1970. Exhibited works: Light Machine I, IBM Gallery, N.Y.C., 1958, Light Machine II, Carpenter Center, Harvard, 1965, 5 Cambridge Architects, Wellesley Coll., 1969, The Work of Earl R. Flansburgh and Assos., Wellesley Coll., 1969, New Architecture in New Eng., DeCordova Mus., 1974-75. Contbr. to 50 Ville del Nostro Tempo, 1970; Interior Design, 1970; Vacation Houses, 1970; Nuove Ville, 1970; Drawings by American Architects, 1973; Interior Spaces Designed by Architects, 1974; New Architecture in New England, 1974; Techniques of Successful Practice for Architects and Engineers, 1976; Great Houses, 1976; Boston Architecture, 1976; Presentation Drawings by American Architects, 1977. Home: Old County Rd Lincoln MA 01773 Office: 77 N Washington St Boston MA 02114

FLASCHEN, STEWARD SAMUEL, multinat. conglomerate exec.; b. Berwyn, Ill., May 28, 1926; s. Hyman Herman and Ethel (Leviton) F.; B.S., U. Ill., 1947; M.S., Miami U., 1948; Ph.D., Pa. State U., 1952; m. Joyce Davies, Apr. 21, 1949; children—John, Sheryl, David, Evan. Research supr. Bell Telephone Labs., Murray Hill, N.J., 1951-59; dir.

research and devel. semicondr. div. Motorola Co., 1959-64; corp. v.p. tech. ITT, N.Y.C., 1964—; mem. faculty Miami U., 1947-49. Pace U. Bd. dirs. Nat. Retinitis Pigmentosa Found.; bd. tech. advs. Voice Found.; mem. Bd. Edn. Phoenix, 1960-64. Served with USNR, 1944-46. Office Naval Research fellow. Fellow IEEE, Am. Inst. Chemistry; mem. Electromech. Soc. Am., Am. Ceramic Soc., AAAS, Indsl. Research Inst., N.Y. Acad. Scis. Author: Search and Research, 1966; contbr. articles to profl. jours.; patentee in field. Office: 320 Park Ave New York NY 10022

FLATO, WILLIAM ROEDER, JR., petroleum chem. co. exec.; b. Corpus Christi, Tex., Apr. 20, 1945; s. William Roeder and Juanita Flato; B.B.A., U. Houston, 1967; m. Beatrice Pesl, Aug. 22, 1974. Accountant, Hughes Tool Co., Houston, 1966-67; accountant Milchem, Inc., Houston, 1967-72, accounting mgr., 1972-73, asst. controller, 1973, corp. controller, 1973-78; v.p. fin., sec.-treas. Magna Corp., Houston, 1978—. Active, Country Village Civic Assn.; state chmn. Young Ams. for Freedom, 1964; precinct chmn. Harris County Republican Exec. Com., 1966-67. Served with U.S. Army, 1968-69. Decorated Army Commendation medal. C.P.A., Tex. Mem. Am. Inst. C.P.A.'s, Tex. Soc. C.P.A.'s (Houston chpt.), Fin. Execs. Inst., Mensa. Presbyterian. Home: 11931 Drexel Hill Dr Houston TX 77077 Office: PO Box 33387 7505 Fannin Houston TX 77033

FLATTERY, THOMAS LONG, mfg. co. exec.; b. Detroit, Nov. 14, 1922; s. Thomas J. and Rosemary (Long) F.; B.S., U.S. Mil. Acad., 1947; LL.B., UCLA, 1955; LL.M., U. So. Calif., 1965; m. Gloria M. Hughes, June 10, 1947; children—Constance Marie, Carol Dianne Flattery Lee, Michael Patrick, Thomas Hughes, Dennis Jerome, Betsy Ann Flattery Bagnall. Admitted to Calif. bar, 1955, U.S. Supreme Ct. bar, 1974; with Motor Products Corp., Detroit, 1950, Equitable Life Assurance Soc. U.S., 1951, Bohn Aluminum & Brass Co., 1952; mem. legal staff, asst. contract adminstr. Radioplane Co., Van Nuys, Calif., 1955-58; successively corp. counsel, gen. counsel, asst. sec. McCulloch Corp., Los Angeles, 1957-64; sec., corp. counsel Technicolor, Inc., 1964-70; successively corp. counsel, gen. counsel Technicolor, Inc., 1964-70; successively corp. counsel, asst. sec., v.p., sec. and gen. counsel Amcord, Inc., Newport Beach, Calif., 1970-72; v.p., sec., gen. counsel Schick, Inc., Los Angeles, 1972-75; counsel, asst. sec. C.F. Braun & Co., Alhambra, Calif., 1975-76; v.p., sec., gen. counsel Automation Industries, Inc., Los Angeles, 1976—; lectr. continuing edn. program Calif. State Bar. Served to 1st lt. AUS, 1943-50. Mem. Am. Bar Assn., Calif. Bar Assn., Los Angeles County Bar Assn., Century City Bar Assn. (chmn. corp. law dept. com. 1979-80), Conn. Bar Assn., Westchester-Fairfield Corp. Counsel Assn., Am. Soc. Corp. Secs. (pres. Los Angeles regional group 1973-74), Patent Law Assn. Los Angeles, Fgn. Law Assn. Los Angeles, Lic. Exec. Soc., U.S. West Point Alumni Assn., Army Athletic Assn., Friendly Sons of St. Patrick, Phi Alpha Delta. Roman Catholic. Clubs: Los Angeles Athletic, Jonathan (Los Angeles). Contbr. articles to various jours. Office: 500 W Putnam Ave Greenwich CT 06830

FLAVIN, JOSEPH B., mfg. co. exec.; b. St. Louis, Oct. 16, 1928; s. Joseph B. and Mary E. (Toomey) F.; LL.D., U. Mass., 1978; m. Melisande Barillon, 1946; children—Patrick Brian, Shawn Elaine. Accountant, Cawley Aircraft Supply Co., 1953; with IBM World Trade Corp., 1953-67, controller, 1965-67; with Xerox Corp., 1967-75, v.p. and controller, 1967-68, group v.p., 1968-69, sr. v.p. 1969-70, exec. v.p., dir. 1970-75, also pres. internat. operations, 1972-75; chmn., chief exec. officer, dir. Singer Co., Stamford, Conn., 1975—; dir. Pfizer, Inc.; trustee Northwestern Mut. Life Ins. Co. Mem. nat. devel. bd. Columbia U. bd. dirs. United Way of Tri-State; trustee Fairfield U., Stamford Hosp., Com. for Econ. Devel., Hartman Regional Theatre, Inc., Stamford; mem. Nat. Bus. Council for ERA. Served with USMCR. Recipient Nat. Brotherhood award NCCJ, 1978. Mem. Conf. Bd. (mem. corp.), Internat. C. of C. (trustee U.S. Council), NAM (dir.). Clubs: Economic of N.Y., Blind Brook (Port Chester, N.Y.); Landmark (gov.) (Stamford); Windham Mountain. Office: Singer Co 8 Stamford Forum Stamford CT 06904

FLEISCHER, MORTON HERSCHIL, corporate fin. co. exec.; b. Dallas, Dec. 27, 1936; s. Max and Rose (Peskind) F.; B.S. in Bus. Adminstrn., Washington U., St. Louis, 1958; m. Essie Dorothy Steinfeld, Sept. 1, 1962; children—Roslyn Jeri, Jeffrey Miles. Exec. v.p. Ozark Nat. Life Ins. Co., LaFayette, La., 1965-67; partner Fleischer & Fogel, Phoenix, 1968-72; pres., dir. PFO Fin. Corp., Los Angeles, 1972-74; pres. AVR Properties, Inc., Phoenix, 1974—; pres., dir. Fleischer & Co., 1975—; pres., treas., dir. Franchise Fin. Corp. Am., 1979—; dir. TDA Industries, Inc., N.Y.C. Served with AUS, 1959. Republican. Jewish. Home: 5104 N 42d Pl Phoenix AZ 85018 Office: 3443 N Central Ave Suite 419 Phoenix AZ 85012

FLEISCHMANN, STANLEY GENE, office equipment co. exec.; b. Montreal, Que., Can., Mar. 7, 1917; came to U.S., 1947; s. Isaac and Sarah (Lowenthal) F.; student McGill U., 1938-40, Sir George Williams U., 1940-42; m. Shirley Cohen, Nov. 8, 1947; children—Rosanne Fleischmann Lapan, Marilyn Fleischmann Arensberg, Adrienne, Steven. With Steinberg's (Can.), 1931-46, exec. in charge public relations, 1944-46; self-employed efficiency expert, cons. in personnel, 1946-47; v.p. in charge ops. Keystone Packing Co., Houston, 1947-51; founder, pres. Am. Office Equipment Co., Seattle, 1951—. Bd. dirs. Federated Jewish Fund, 1970-75; active Am. Jewish Com. Recipient plaque Wash. State Penitentiary System, 1972. Mem. Nat. Office Machine Dealers Assn., Western Office Machine Dealers Assn. (pres. 1965-67), Seattle Office Machine Dealers Assn. (pres. 1970-72). Clubs: Glendale Country, Wash. Athletic, B'nai B'rith. Home: 1615 90th St NE Bellevue WA 98004 Office: 1601 2d Ave Seattle WA 98101

FLEMING, BARTLETT SAYLES, polit. scientist; b. Coshocton, Ohio, Nov. 16, 1942; s. James F. and Betty Jean (Miller) F.; B.A. in Polit. Sci., U. Ariz., 1966; m. Beth B. Fleming, June 5, 1965; children—Tricia L., Bart S.F. Account exec. E.F. Hutton Co., 1969-70; chief dep. treas. State of Ariz., 1971-73, treas., 1974-78; pres. Fiscal Policy Council, Arlington, Va., 1978—. Co-chmn. Republican Party Resolutions Subcom., Kansas City, Mo., 1976; trustee Phoenix Gen. Hosp.; chmn. bd. Maricopa County March of Dimes; state chmn. Ariz. March of Dimes; mem. lay ministry Episcopal Ch. Served to 2d lt. AUS, 1967-69. Office: 1629 K St NW Suite 700 Washington DC 20006

FLEMING, BENTON SCOTT, savs. assn. exec.; b. Houston, Apr. 12, 1922; s. Earl Hampton and Lorena Oklahoma (Stapler) F.; student U. Tex., 1940-43; LL.B., South Tex. Sch. Law, 1951; student in real estate U. Houston, 1952-53; m. Narcille Busch, Dec. 1, 1951; children—Scott, Joan, Guy, Diane. Admitted to Tex. bar, 1951; mortgage loan atty. Gen. Mortgage Corp., Houston, 1951-52; practice law specializing in mortgage loans, Houston, 1952-55; pres. Tex. Investment Corp., Houston, 1955—; pres., chmn. 1st State Bank, Point, Tex., 1961-68; pres. United Bus. Capital, Inc., Houston, 1963—; pres., chmn. bd. Bayshore Savs. Assn., La Porte, 1967—; adv. dir. Tex. Nat. Bank of Baytown. Alderman, City of Shoreacres, Tex. Served with USNR, 1943-45. Mem. Harris County League Insured Savs. Assns. (pres. 1976), Tex. Bar Assn., Tex. Savs. and Loan League (chmn. subcom. on consumer loans), La Porte C. of C. (1st v.p., dir. 1971-73), Alpha Tau Omega. Episcopalian. Rotarian. Club: Houston Yacht. Home 616 Baywood St La Porte TX 77571 Office: 1102 S Broadway La Porte TX 77571

FLEMING, CARL OTIS, JR., oil field equipment co. exec.; b. Coleman, Tex., Feb. 24, 1931; s. Carl Otis and Freda Lee (Mochell) F.; B.S., Tex. A. and M. U., 1952; m. Patsy Jane Parker, Aug. 12, 1951; children—Terilyn, Rajenia. With Otis Engring. Corp., Dallas, 1954—, mgr. data processing, 1963-67, asst. to pres. Halliburton Co., 1968, mgr. adminstrv. services, 1969-70, v.p. adminstrv. services, 1970-76, v.p. adminstrv. services and mfg., 1976—, sr. v.p. mfg. and adminstrv. services, 1977—, also dir.; dir. Dallas County State Bank. Served to 1st lt. U.S. Army, 1952-54. Registered profl. engr., Tex. Mem. Greater N.W. C. of C. (pres. 1970), Computer Aided Mfg. Internat. (dir., mem. exec. com.). Club: Rotary (pres. 1966). Address: PO Box 34380 Dallas TX 75234

FLEMING, DOUGLAS G., feed co. exec.; b. Harvey, Ill., Apr. 28, 1930; s. Harold L. and Genevieve (Hodges) F.; B.S., Mich. State U., 1954; m. Sara L. Waters, May 25, 1952; children—Christine J., James C. With Central Soya Co., 1954—, asst. mgr. field ops., Ft. Wayne, Ind., 1963-65, v.p., dir. mktg., 1965-70, exec. v.p., 1970-76, pres., 1976-79, chmn. bd., pres., chief exec. officer, 1980—, also dir.; dir. O's Gold Seed Co., Parkersburg, Iowa, Midwestern United Life Ins. Co., Ft. Wayne, Ft. Wayne Nat. Bank. Bd. dirs. United Way Allen County. Served to 2d lt. AUS, 1951-53. Mem. Am. Feed Mfrs. Assn. Clubs: Ft. Wayne Country, Summit (Ft. Wayne). Office: 1300 Fort Wayne Nat Bank Bldg Fort Wayne IN 46802

FLEMING, JOSEPH, aerospace co. exec.; b. Norristown, Pa., Mar. 11, 1929; s. James Bernard and Mary Bridgett (Corr) F.; student State U. N.Y., 1948-50; B.M.E., Syracuse U., 1954; M.B.A., U. So. Calif., 1960; m. Mary Madonna Katzer, May 29, 1965; children—Cynthia Patricia, John Michael. Asst. program mgr. Saturn propulsion systems Rockwell Internat., Canoga Park, Calif., 1960-67, sr. co. rep., Hartford, Conn., 1967-70; chief fin. and quality analysis Pratt & Whitney Aircraft, East Hartford, 1970-73; sr. adviser plans and programs Rockwell, Downey, Calif., 1973—; engring. cons. Am. Bidet Corp., Gardena, Calif., 1961-72. Recipient Apollo Achievement award NASA, 1969. Republican. Roman Catholic. Patentee in electric bidet, organic conversion system and others. Home: 15925 McDermitt St Fountain Valley CA 92708

FLEMING, MILO JOSEPH, lawyer; b. Roscoe, Ill., Jan. 4, 1911; s. John E. and Elizabeth (Shafer) F.; A.B., U. Ill., 1933, LL.B., 1936; m. Dorothea H. Kunze, Aug. 15, 1942 (dec. 1944); m. 2d, Lucy Anna Russell, June 30, 1948; step-children—Michael Bartlett Russell, Jo Ann Russell Clemens; 1 dau., Elizabeth. Pvt. practice law, 1936-42, 58-59; mem. Pallissard and Fleming, Watseka, Ill., 1942-46, Pallissard, Fleming & Oram, 1946-58, Fleming & McGrew, 1960-77, Fleming, McGrew & Boyer, 1977, Fleming & Boyer, 1977-79, Fleming, Boyer & Strough, 1980—; master in chancery, Iroquois County, Ill., 1943-44, asst. atty. gen. Ill. for Iroquois County, 1964-69. Pres., Iroquois County Devel. Corp., 1961-68; pres., dir. Belmont Water Co., 1976—. City atty. Watseka, 1949-57, 61—, Gilman, 1966-69; atty. villages of Wellington, 1961-71, Woodland, 1958-79, Beaverville, Cissna Park, Crescent City, Martinton, Milford, 1942-70, Sheldon, 1946-79, Onarga, Danforth, 1961-78, Papineau; atty. Lake Iroquois Lot Owners Assn., Central San. Dist.; also engaged in farming; a developer Belmont Acres, Iroquois County; Mem. Ill. State Employees Group Ins. Adv. Commn., 1975-78. Candidate for state rep., 1940. Trustee Odd Fellows Old Folks Home, Mattoon, Ill., 1966-71, sec., 1966-68, vice chmn., 1970, acting chmn., 1971; trustee Welles Sch. Fund, Watseka, 1978—; life mem. U. Ill. President's Council, 1979—, U. Ill. Found., 1979—. Mem. Am. (mem. subcom. on gen. obligation bonds; vice chmn. com. on ordinances and adminstrv. regulation local govt. sect. 1968-69, 73-75, chmn. 1969-72, 75-78, council of local govt. sect. 1976—), Ill. bar assns., Smithsonian Instn., Iroquois County Hist. Soc., Phi Eta Sigma, Sigma Delta Kappa. Methodist. Mason (Shriner, (32 deg.), Odd Fellow (dep. grand master Ill. 1963-64, grand master 1964-65). Home: 120 W Jefferson Ave Watseka IL 60970 Office: Odd Fellows Bldg 216 E Walnut St Watseka IL 60970

FLEMING, PATRICK EDWARD, corp. exec.; b. Blackfoot, Idaho, Aug. 15, 1940; s. David Elihue and June Arlena (Edwards) F.; student Highline Community Coll., 1968-70; m. Jeanne Alberta Bainbridge, Dec. 24, 1972; children—Leesa Anne, Jill Leanne, David Eric, Erin Lynn. Quality control technician Donor Sci. Corp., Concord, Calif., 1959; electronic repair technician Automotive Equipment Repair Service, Inc., Oakland, Calif., 1960; prodn. engr. Smith Corona Marchant Co., Albany, Calif., 1960; engring. staff cons. Pacific N.W. Bell Telephone Co., Seattle, 1967-80; exec. v.p. Security Record Systems, Inc., Lacey, Wash., 1980—. Precinct committeeman, del. Wash. Republican Conv., 1968-70; leadership and speak up counselor Firlands Correctional Center, Seattle. Served with USN, 1960-67; Vietnam. Recipient Cert. of Achievement, Pacific NW Bell Telephone, 1980. Mem. IEEE, Jaycees Internat., Wash. Jaycees (pres. 1975-76, region dir. 1976-77, Outstanding Local Pres. award 1976), Nat. Small Bus. Assn., Airplane Owners and Pilots Assn., Western Farmers Assn. Mormon. Clubs: Olympia Evergreen Gun, Elks, Masons, Toastmasters (pres. local chpt. 1970, area gov. 1971, Area Speaker award 1970, Disting. Service award 1971). Author chpt. history Kirkland Jaycees (Wash. State Henry GiessenBier award 1976). Home: 5810 Meridian Rd SE Olympia WA 98503 Office: Rowe 6 Bldg 5 4224 6th Ave SE Lacey WA 98503

FLEMING, ROBBEN WRIGHT, broadcasting exec.; b. Paw Paw, Ill., Dec. 18, 1916; s. Edmund Palmer and Emily Jeannette (Wheeler) F.; B.A., Beloit Coll., 1938; LL.B., U. Wis., 1941; LL.D. (hon.), U. Mich., 1968; also numerous hon. degrees from other colls., univs.; m. Aldyth Louise Quixley, Apr. 3, 1942; children—Nancy Jo, James Edmund, Carolyn Elizabeth. Admitted to Wis. bar, 1941; atty. reorgn. div. SEC, Washington, 1941-42; mem. War Labor Bd., Washington, 1942; dir. Indsl. Relations Center, U. Wis., 1947-52, prof. law, chancellor, 1964-67; exec. dir. nat. WSB, Washington, 1951; dir. Inst. Labor and Indsl. Relations, U. Ill., 1952-58, prof. law, 1958-64; univ. pres., prof. labor law U. Mich., 1968-78; pres. Corp. for Public Broadcasting, Washington, 1979—; exchange prof., Germany, summer 1950, Norway and Sweden, 1956; arbitrator indsl. disputes; co-chmn. task force on edn. White House Conf. on Youth, 1971; bd. dirs. Carnegie Fund for Advanced Teaching, chmn., 1978-79. Served with AUS, 1942-46. Fellow Am. Acad. Arts and Scis.; mem. Am. Arbitration Assn. (dir.), Am. Assn. Univs. (pres. 1971), Am. Council on Edn. (chmn. 1976-77), Nat. Acad. Arbitrators (pres. 1966), Order of Coif, Phi Beta Kappa (hon.), Beta Theta Phi. Presbyterian. Club: Cosmos. Co-editor: Emergency Disputes and National Policy, 1955; The Politics of Wage-Price Decision, a four country analysis, 1965; The Labor Arbitration Process, 1966; contbr. articles on indsl. relations to profl. jours. Home: 4935 Crescent St Chevy Chase MD 20016 Office: 1111 16th St Washington DC 20036

FLEMING, SAMUEL MILTON, JR., banker; b. Franklin, Tenn., Apr. 29, 1908; s. Samuel Milton and Cynthia Graham (Cannon) F.; B.A., Vanderbilt U., 1928; m. Ada Josephine Cliffe, Dec. 30, 1931; children—Joanne (Mrs. Toby S. Wilt), Daniel Milton. With N.Y. Trust Co., 1928-31; with Third Nat. Bank, Nashville, 1931—, former pres. and chmn., now chmn. trust bd.; dir. NLT Corp., Murray Ohio Mfg. Co., Genesco, Nashville & Decatur R.R. Co. Chmn. bd. trustees Vanderbilt U.; trustee Battle Ground Acad. Served as lt. comdr., USNR. Mem. Am. Bankers Assn. (past pres.). Presbyterian (elder). Clubs: Augusta (Ga.) Nat. Golf; Links, University (N.Y.C.); Belle Meade Country, Richland Country (Nashville); Garden of the Gods (Colorado Springs); Yacht, Bath and Tennis, Gulf Stream Golf (Delray Beach, Fla.); Everglades (Palm Beach, Fla.); Seminole Golf (North Palm Beach, Fla.). Home: 810 Jackson Blvd Nashville TN 37205 Office: 201 4th Ave N Nashville TN 37244

FLEMMING, JOAN ANTOINETTE, bus. exec.; b. Tulsa, Apr. 27, 1921; d. Homer Virgil and Ida Buelah (Arnold) F.; B.S., U. Tulsa, 1942. Sales mgr. Avon Products Co., Portland, Oreg., 1957-59; accountant P.I.E. Truck Transp. Co., Walnut Creek, Calif., 1959-69; supr. acctg. Western Temp. Services Co., San Francisco, 1969-75; mgr. acctg. ITEL Audatex Co., Hayward, Calif., from 1975; now mgr. billing and collections A.D.P. Collision Estimating Services, Hayward. Mem. Tulsa Art Assn., Tulsa Symphony Orch. Mem. Phi Mu (v.p. 1942), Alpha Rho Tau, Beta Sigma Phi (pres. 1955-56). Democrat. Mem. Christian Ch. (Disciples of Christ). Club: Pilot Internat. Home: 430 Taylor Ave Alameda CA 94501 Office: 2380 W Winton Ave Hayward CA 94545

FLESCHNER, ANDREW KING, publisher; b. N.Y.C., Jan. 15, 1943; s. Malcolm King and Janice F.; B.A., Harvard U., 1964, M.B.A., 1967; m. Constance Friedman, Aug. 10, 1976; children—Emily, Malcolm II. Security analyst Fidelity Mgmt. and Research Co., Boston, 1967-69; dir. research Cardinal Mgmt. Co., Boston, 1970-72; pres., chmn. Pretest Service Inc., Wallingford, Conn., 1973-79; pres. Fleschner Pub. Co., Bethany, Conn., 1979—. Office: 41 Village Ln Bethany CT 06525

FLETCHER, DEAN G., mining co. exec.; b. Cleve., Jan. 25, 1948; s. Gilbert E. and Elnora F. (Reisig) F.; B.S. in Mining Engring. (Kennecott scholar), Mich. Technol. U., 1970; m. Phyllis Young, June 20, 1970; children—Steven, Jason, Chad. Mine prodn. foreman Internat. Salt Co., Cleve., 1968; tech. aide Kennecott Copper Corp., Bingham Canyon, Utah, 1969; mine engr. Allied Chem. Corp., Green River, Wyo., 1970-71, mine engr., Jamestown, Colo., 1971-73, supt., Jamestown, 1973-74, supt. maintenance and engring., Jamesville, N.Y., 1974-76, mine supt., Cave-in-Rock, Ill., 1976-77, mgr., Cave-in-Rock, 1978; mgr. Unimin Corp., LeSueur, Minn., 1978-80, gen. mgr. Western ops., 1980—. Recipient Boss of Yr. award Shawnee chpt. Nat. Secs. Assn., 1978. Mem. Soc. Mining Engrs., Am. Mgmt. Assn., Sigma Gamma Epsilon. Republican. Home: 1065 Oak Terr North Mankato MN 56001 Office: Unimin Corp Ottawa Plant Rural Route 1 Box 119A LeSueur MN 56058

FLETCHER, DOUGLAS BADEN, investment co. exec.; b. Pleasant Ridge, Mich., Mar. 25, 1925; s. Ernest H. and Gladys (Marthan) F.; B.A., Princeton U., 1949; m. Sally Wittenberg, Sept. 9, 1950; children—David, Christopher, James, Jonathan. Security analyst Walston & Co., N.Y.C., 1949-53; mem. underwriting dept. Blyth & Co., Los Angeles, 1953-62; chmn. bd., chief exec. officer First Pacific Advisors, Inc., Los Angeles, 1962—, Angeles Corp., 1962—, Source Capital, Inc., Los Angeles, 1968—; pres., dir. Paramount Mut. Fund, Inc., Los Angeles, 1978—. Trustee Claremont (Calif.) Men's Coll., 1969—. Served with AUS, 1943-46. Mem. Inst. Chartered Fin. Analysts, Los Angeles Soc. Fin. Analysts (pres. 1960-61). Club: Princeton of So. Calif. (pres. 1962-64). Office: 1888 Century Park E Century City Los Angeles CA 90067

FLETCHER, LOUISE MARY, mfg. co. exec.; b. San Pedro, Calif., May 3, 1926; d. Jack and Vica W. (Elich) Kordich; student U. So. Calif., 1948-50; m. Jay L. Fletcher, Mar. 15, 1957; children—Jack B., William J. Owner, operator Trojan Shop, Los Angeles, 1949-51; hostess Pacific S.W. Airlines, Seattle, 1952-53; v.p. Fletcher Engring., Inc., Westminster, Calif., 1969-75; exec. v.p. Eze-Lap Diamond Products Co., Westminster, 1975—; co-owner Los Caballeros Sports Club. Recipient PTA award, 1961, Jr. Women's Club award, 1960. Office: 15164 Weststate St Westminster CA 92683

FLETCHER, MARY LEE, business exec.; b. Farnborough, Eng.; d. Dugald Angus and Mary Lee (Thurman) F.; B.A., Pembroke Coll., Brown U., 1951. Ops. officer C.I.A., Washington, 1951-53; exec. trainee Gimbels, N.Y.C., 1953-54; head researcher Ed Byron TV Prodns., N.Y.C., 1954; copywriter Benton & Bowles, Inc., N.Y.C., 1955-63; creative dir. Alberto-Culver Co., Melrose Park, Ill., 1964-66; v.p. advt. and publicity Christian Dior Perfumes, N.Y.C., 1967-71; v.p. Christian Dior-N.Y., N.Y.C., 1972-78, exec. v.p., dir., 1978—. Home: 12 Beekman Pl New York NY 10022 Office: 1370 Ave of Americas New York NY 10019

FLETCHER, PAUL LOUIE, businessman; b. Phila., Apr. 18, 1930; s. James Louie and Pearl (Lawson) F.; diploma mech. and archtl. drawing, McKee Vocat. Trade Sch., S.I., N.Y., 1958; m. Ying-Lun, Apr. 18, 1968; children—James, Raymond, Pearl, Dana, Paul Louie, England. With United Trading & Fletcher Inc., N.Y.C., 1950—, exec. v.p., 1950—, sec., 1950—; salesman Prosperity Laundry Machine Co., 1950-69; exec. v.p., sec. Canbeth Realty Corp., 1950—. Chmn., Chinatown div. March of Dimes, N.Y.C., 1960-64, Mei Wah Day Care Center, N.Y.C., 1977-80, Mei Wah Chinese Sch., 1977-80; pres. Soo Yuen Benevolent Assn., 1977-78; pres., chmn. Chinese Meth. Community Center, N.Y.C., 1977-80. Served with USAF, 1947-50. Recipient numerous community and service awards. Club: Lions (pres. Chinatown chpt., N.Y.C., 1975-76, charter pres. N.Y.C. Chinese Ams. 1978-80, dist. cabinet sec.-treas. 1980-81; numerous awards 1972—). Home: 77 Lynhurst Ave Staten Island NY 10305 Office: 162 Canal St New York NY 10013

FLETCHER, RILEY EUGENE, lawyer; b. Eddy, Tex., Nov. 29, 1912; s. Riley Jordan and Lelih (Gill) F.; B.A., Baylor U., 1950, LL.B., 1950; m. Hattie Inez Blackwell, June 11, 1954. Admitted to Tex. bar, 1950; asst. county atty. Navarro County (Tex.), 1951-52, county atty., 1952-54; pvt. practice law, Corsicana, Tex., 1955-56; asst. atty. gen. Tex., 1956-62, chief law enforcement div., atty. gen.'s dept., 1958-61, chief taxation div., atty. gen.'s dept., 1961-62; asst. gen. counsel Tex. Municipal League, Austin, 1962-63, gen. counsel, 1963-78, spl. counsel, 1978—. Lt. col. AUS Ret. Recipient Disting. Service award Tex. Mcpl. Cts. Assn., 1980. Mem. Am., Tex., Travis County bar assns., Am. Judicature Soc., Res. Officers Assn. (pres. Austin chpt. 1979-80), Assn. U.S. Army (pres. Tex. capital area chpt. 1965-66), Am. Legion, Judge Advs. Assn., Mil. Order World Wars, Austin World Affairs Council. Baptist. Clubs: Masons, K.P. Home: PO Box 1762 Austin TX 78767 Office: Texas Municipal League 1020 Southwest Tower Austin TX 78701

FLEURY, CLAUDE FLORENT, automobile dealer; b. Montreal, Que., Can., July 26, 1941; s. Antoine Tony and Yvette (Raby) F.; student U. Que., Montreal; certificat en adminstrn. U. Western Ont., London, 1971; m. Michelle Dancoste, Dec. 7, 1963; children—Ann, Eric. With Ford Can., 1959-75; pres., gen. mgr. La Diligence Ford Vente Ltee., Victoriaville, Que., 1975—; bus. mgmt. cons. several Ford dealers, 1972-75. Recipient John D. King award, 1967. Mem. Corp. des Concessionnaires Automobiles du Que. Club: Lions (Victoriaville). Home: 163 Renaud Victoriaville PQ G6P 8B6 Canada Office: 321 Notre Dame W Victoriaville PQ G6P 1S3 Canada

FLINN, THOMAS HANCE, banker; b. Hutto, Tex., Jan. 30, 1922; s. Thomas Hance and Margaret (Bowden) F.; grad. certificate Stonier Grad. Sch. Banking, 1961; B.B.A., U. Tex., 1949; m. Georgeann Atwood, May 26, 1948; children—Mary Kathleen, Michael Hance, Mark Thomas. Securities salesman various firms, San Antonio, 1949-54; v.p., M.E. Allison & Co., San Antonio, 1955-56; asst. v.p., Groos Nat. Bank, San Antonio, 1956-59; pvt. practice investment counsel, San Antonio, 1959-60; investment counsel Scudder, Stevens & Clark, Dallas, 1960-63; v.p. investments United Va. Bankshares Inc., Richmond, 1964-73, sr. v.p., corporate treas., 1973—; lectr. in field; dir. United Va. Mortgage Corp. Vice-chmn. Chesterfield County (Va.) Republican party, 1966. Served with USAAF, 1942-46. Mem. Delta Sigma Pi. Republican. Presbyterian. Clubs: Bull and Bear, Meadowbrook Country, Masons (32 deg.), Shriners. Home: 3000 Kenmore Rd Richmond VA 23225 Office: United Va Bankshares PO Box 26665 Richmond VA 23261

FLINT, ALDEN CHEDEL, distbn. co. exec.; b. Randolph, Vt., Sept. 15, 1923; s. Lewis Herrick and Jessie (Chedel) F.; B.S. in Elec. Engring., La. State U., 1945; M.S. in Indsl. Mgmt., Ga. Inst. Tech., 1948; m. Joan Brown Parker, July 2, 1945; children—Deborah Alden, Henry William. Adminstv. asst. fellow Ga., Inst. Tech. Research, Atlanta, 1947-48; adminstrv. asst. Atlantic Refining Co., Phila., 1948-53; sales engr. Livingston & Haven, Inc., Charleston, S.C., 1953-55, v.p., treas., 1955-66, pres., chief exec. officer, 1966—; pres., dir. Fluid Energy, Inc., Charlotte, N.C., 1973—, Sunbelt Distbg., Inc., Charlotte, 1975—. Served with USN, 1943-45, 50-52. Decorated Pacific Theatre ribbon. Mem. Fluid Power Distbrs. Assn. (pres. 1977-78), Am. Mgmt. Assn. Republican. Presbyterian. Clubs: Country (Charleston); Carolina Yacht, Charlotte City, Klawah Island. Patentee in textile machinery improvements. Home: 8 Guerard Rd Charleston SC 29407 Office: 11616 Wilmar Blvd Charlotte NC 28210 also 148 E Bay St Charleston SC 29402

FLINT, KEVIN EDWARD, banker; b. Fremont, Nebr., Aug. 9, 1950; s. Elmer Gerald and Nancy Jane (Hickerson) F.; student No. Ill. U., 1969-70; B.A. summa cum laude, Ohio State U., 1973, M.A. Fin., 1974; m. Philice Ann Diegel, June 14, 1980. Credit analyst in loan officer tng. program Nat. Bank Detroit, 1975-76, asst. credit officer, 1976-77, credit officer, loan rev. analyst, 1977-78, credit officer and mgr. loan control dept., 1978, loan officer internat. div., 1978-81; internat. credit mgr. Bausch & Lomb, Inc., Rochester, N.Y., 1981—; lectr. in field. Mem. Robert Morris and Assos. Office: Bausch & Lomb Inc 1400 N Goodman St Rochester NY 14602

FLINTOSH, GEORGE EDWARD, info. systems mfg. co. exec.; b. Detroit, Aug. 7, 1938; s. John William and Mary (Billy) F.; student U. Tenn., 1956, U. Md., 1958-59, Wayne State U., 1961-63; B.B.A. cum laude, U. Detroit, 1974, M.B.A., 1976; postgrad. in exec. edn. Harvard U., 1976. Systems analyst Kelsey Hayes Co., Romulus, Mich., 1963-66, Budd Co., Detroit, 1966; sr. systems analyst Montgomery Ward Co., Chgo., 1967; sr. systems analyst Rockwell Internat., Troy, Mich., 1967-73, plants systems mgr., Columbus, Ohio, 1973-74, mgr. mfg. and engring. systems, 1974-75, mgr. systems devel., 1975-76, dir. mgmt. systems automotive ops., Troy, 1977—; instr. mgmt. computer resources Marygrove Coll., Detroit, 1978—. Served with USAF, 1956-60. Republican. Roman Catholic. Home: 5556 Patterson Dr Troy MI 48098 Office: 2135 W Maple Rd Troy MI 48084

FLOM, EDWARD LEONARD, steel co. exec.; b. Tampa, Fla., Dec. 10, 1929; s. Samuel Louis and Julia (Mittle) F.; B.C.E., Cornell U., 1952; m. Beverly Boyett, Mar. 31, 1956; children—Edward Louis, Mark Robert, Julia Ruth. With Fla. Steel Corp., Tampa, 1954—, v.p. sales, 1957-64, pres., dir. 1964—; dir. Exchange Bank & Trust, Exchange Bancorp., Tampa Electric Co. Bd. dirs. mem. exec. com. United Fund Tampa; advisory com. St. Joseph's Hosp., Tampa; bd. dirs. Family Service Assn. Tampa, Jewish Welfare Fedn. Tampa; exec. com. Com. of 100, Tampa. Served with C.E., AUS, 1952-54. Mem. Am. Iron and Steel Inst. (dir.), Young Pres.'s Orgn., Fla. Engring. Soc. Jewish (bd. dirs. temple). Clubs: Rotary (bd. dirs. Tampa), University, Palma Ceia Golf and Country, Tampa Yacht, Gasparilla Krewe. Home: 4936 Saint Croix Dr Tampa FL 33609 Office: 1715 Cleveland St Tampa FL 33601

FLORAKAS, NICHOLAS EMMANUEL, mfg. co. exec.; b. Montreal, Que., June 5, 1938; s. Emmanuel Nicholas and Irene (Dondas) F.; B.Eng., McGill U., 1962, postgrad., 1963-64; postgrad. Lehigh U., 1962-63, Laval U., 1964-65; m. Elizabeth Pascal, July 3, 1965; children—Irene, Christine, Emmanuel. Gen. foreman Ralston Purina Can. Inc., Montreal, 1963-64, mgr., supt., St. Romuald, 1964-68, regional supt. Que./Atlantic Chow, now exec. v.p., dir. Chow div., also dir. parent co.; dir. Sorel Elevators Ltd. Bd. dirs. Greek Orthodox Community of Que., 1965-68, pres., 1967-68; bd. dirs. Hellenic Community of the Shouth Shore, 1977-79. Mem. Order Engrs. Que., Can. Feed Industry Assn. Office: 116 Guilbault St Longueuil PQ J4H 2T2 Canada

FLORES, FRANK FAUSTO, graphics and communications co. exec.; b. N.Y.C., Sept. 18, 1930; s. Frank E. and Marie (Navarro) F.; m. Elizabeth L. Weekes, Oct. 2, 1948; children—Donald, Stephen, Allen. Sales mgr. Marsden Offset Printing Co., Inc., N.Y.C., 1955-59, treas., 1959—; pres. Marsden Reprodns., Inc., N.Y.C., 1962—. Mem. adv. bd. Flatbush YMCA, 1968-69; chmn. adv. bd. Nat. Minority Bus. Council; bd. dirs. League United Latin Am. Citizens, Puerto Rican Dance Theatre, N.Y.C.; mem. adv. bd. Salvation Army. Mem. N.Y. Acad. Scis., Soc. Tech. Communication (past chmn.), Internat. Reprographics Assn., Nat. Assn. Photo Lithographers, Blue Printers Assn. N.Y. (treas.) Alliance of Minority Bus. Orgns. (dir.), Internat. Platform Assn., Nat. Rifle Assn. Clubs: City of N.Y. (dir.), Miramar Yacht. Home: 2301 Ave R Brooklyn NY 11229 Office: 30 E 33d St New York NY 10016

FLORES, MIGUEL ANGEL, JR., utility contractor exec.; b. Los Ebanos, Tex., Sept. 10, 1952; s. Miguel Angel and Lilia (De La Garza) F.; student Pan Am. U., 1972-74. Owner, mgr. Mike's Pump Sales and Service, Mission, Tex., 1974—. Served with U.S. Army, 1972-74. Decorated Armed Forces medal, Korean Forces medal. Mem. Nat. Rifle Assn., Nat. Fedn. Ind. Bus., Tex. Farm Bur., Contractors Indsl. Edn. Assistances, Ind. Order Foresters. Democrat. Roman Catholic. Home and Office: Route #6 Box 44-D Mission TX 78572

FLOSDORF, DAVID WELLS, bank and trust co. exec.; b. Phila., Aug. 24, 1935; s. Earl William and Esther (Wells) F.; B.A., Wesleyan U., Middletown, Conn., 1960, M.A. in Teaching, 1961; postgrad. N.Y. U., 1961-62, U. Conn., 1966-67, Am. Inst. Banking, 1968-76; m. Maria Orlando, Jan. 18, 1958; children—Glenn David, Stephen Paul, Susan Lee. Tchr. pub. schs., N.Y., 1961-62, Conn., 1962-66; with Conn. Bank and Trust Co., 1966-79, asst. sec., 1969, asst. v.p., 1972-75, v.p., 1975-79, mgr. dept. estate settlement, 1976-79; sr. trust officer New Eng. Mchts. Nat. Bank, Boston, 1979—; mem. Estate and Bus. Planning Council of Hartford. Served with U.S. Army, 1955-58. Mem. Am. Inst. Banking. Home: 2291 Washington St Newton Lower Falls MA 02161

FLOTO, WILLIAM MATHEW, recreational co. exec.; b. Los Angeles, Dec. 11, 1930; s. Frederick Francis and Addeene Lake (King) F.; A.A., Fullerton Jr. Coll., 1958; certificate in bus. U. Calif. at Los Angeles, 1963; m. Peggy Virginia Pepall, July 7, 1956; children—Cheri Virginia, William Howard, Steven Mathew. Mgr. regional sales office Beckman Instruments, Fullerton Calif., 1956-62, Toronto, Ont., Can., 1963-65; Chgo., 1965-66; mgr. prodn. planning Bourns, Riverside, Calif., 1966-67; mgr. sales prodn. adminstrn. Amax Alumninum, Riverside, 1967-69; mgr. master scheduling Day Night Payne Co., La Puente, Calif., 1969; pres. Red E Kamp, Mira Luma, Calif., 1970-71; pres. Recreational Industries, Warren, Ohio, 1971—, also dir.; v.p., dir. Toro Enterprises Inc. Bd. dirs. Y Indian Guide Program, Northbrook, Ill., 1965-66. Served with USAF, 1951-55. Mem. Am. Prodn. Control Soc. (pres. Inland Empire chpt. 1966-67) Patentee in field. Home: PO Box 861 Anna Maria FL 33501 Office: POB 3143 5232 Todd Ave Warren OH 44485

FLOTT, STEPHEN PAUL, assn. exec.; b. Washington, Aug. 25, 1943; arrived Can., 1963, naturalized, 1971; s. Allan Claude and Evelyn Mae (Simms) F.; B.A. with honors U. Waterloo (Ont.), 1967, M.A., 1968; LL.B., York (Ont.) U., 1973; m. Janet Dallas Ransom, June 15, 1968. Secondary sch. tchr. North York Bd. Edn., Toronto, Ont., 1968-70; admitted to Ont. bar, 1975; barrister and solicitor firm Weir & Foulds, Toronto, 1973-78; exec. v.p. and gen. mgr. Ont. Trucking Assn., Toronto, 1978—, exec. dir. Edn. Found., Inc., Toronto, 1978—. Mem. Motor Vehicle Safety Assn. (dir.), Law Soc. Upper Can., Canadian Bar Assn., Inst. Assn. Execs., Can. Trucking Assn. Mgrs. (chmn. 1979), Am. Soc. Assn. Execs. Roman Catholic. Office: 555 Dixon Rd Rexdale ON M9W 1H8 Canada

FLOUDARAS, ALEXANDER LOUIS, advt. agy. exec.; b. Boston, June 21, 1932; s. Leonidas and Helen Floudaras; B.S. in Bus. Adminstrn., Boston U., 1956; children—Elena, Louis, Dean. Advt. and promotion cons. A.L. Fields Co., 1958-60; advt. and sales coordinator Gen. Electric Co., Boston, 1960-65; account exec., account supr. Chirurg & Cairns Advt., Boston, 1966-73; pres. Floudaras Assos. Inc., Boston, 1973—; dir. Guardian Inc.; guest lectr. Middlesex Community Coll., 1975—. Served with U.S. Army, 1956-58. Recipient numerous awards for advt. and films; cert. bus. communicator. Mem. Bus./Profl. Advt. Assn., Small Bus. Assn. New Eng., U.S. C. of C., Mass. Businessman's Assn., Advt. Club Greater Boston. Greek Orthodox. Club: 100 of N.H. Office: 390 Commonwealth Ave Boston MA 02215

FLOWER, WALTER CHEW, III, investment counselor; b. New Orleans, Mar. 3, 1939; s. Walter Chew II and Anne Elisa (Lusk) F.; B.A. in Econs., Tulane U., 1960; M.B.A. in Fin., Harvard U., 1964; m. Ella Smith Montgomery, Dec. 21, 1966; children—Anne Stuart, Lindsey Montgomery. Cons. AID, State Dept., 1964-65; fin. analyst Delta Capital Corp., New Orleans, 1965-66; v.p., mng. partner Loomis Sayles & Co. Inc., New Orleans, 1967-78; pres. Walter C. Flower & Co., Investment Counsel, New Orleans, 1978—; dir. Lusk Shipping Co. Inc.; dir., chmn. exec. com. So. Vital Records Inc.; dir. Gt. So. Land Co., Water Maze Ltd. Bd. dirs. Preservation Resource Center, 1975—; bd. dirs., chmn. HFSM Archtl. Revolving Fund, 1976—; vestryman, mem. parish council Trinity Ch., 1978—; dir., fin. adv. Jr. League New Orleans, 1978—; fin. adv. Herman Grima House, 1978—, Beauregard House, 1979—. Served with USNR, 1960-62. Mem. Phi Beta Kappa. Clubs: Boston, Pickwick, New Orleans Lawn Tennis, So. Yacht (New Orleans). Office: 408 Magazine Cor Poydras New Orleans LA 70130

FLOWERREE, ROBERT EDMUND, paper co. exec.; b. New Orleans, Jan. 4, 1921; s. Robert E. and Amy (Hewes) F.; B.A., Tulane U., 1942; m. Elaine Dicks, Sept. 22, 1943; children—Robert E. III, Ann D., John H., David R. Vice pres. Georgia-Pacific Corp., 1956-63, exec. v.p. pulp, paper and chem. ops., 1963-75, pres., 1974-76, chmn., chief exec. officer, 1976—, also dir. Bd. visitors Berry Coll.; bd. adminstrs. Tulane U.; life trustee Lewis and Clark Coll., Portland, Oreg. Served to lt. USNR, 1942-46. Knight of Malta; recipient Disting. Alumnus award Tulane U., 1978. Clubs: Arlington, Waverley Country (Portland); Boston (New Orleans); Links, Brook (N.Y.C.); Capital City (Atlanta). Home: 02425 SW Military Rd Portland OR 97219 Office: Georgia-Pacific Corp 900 SW 5th Ave Portland OR 97204

FLOYD, MICHAEL JOHN, banker; b. Denver, June 24, 1938; s. Roy Martin and Helen Josephine (Guilfoyle) F.; B.S.B.A., U. Denver, 1961; m. Judith A. Birkett, May 6, 1961; children—Jennifer, Michael, Susan, Daniel, Margaret. Vice pres. 1st Wis. Corp., Milw., 1971-73; pres. 1st Wis. Nat. Bank of Fond du Lac, 1973-79, Bank of Spooner (Wis.), 1976—; pres., dir. Bank of Fond du Lac, 1980—; dir. Bank of Spooner, Stein Industries. Active YMCA, Marian Coll. Found., Fond du Lac Redevel. Authority. Mem. Robert Morris Assos., Am. Bankers Assn., Wis. Bankers Assn., Fond du Lac Assn. Commerce (dir.). Roman Catholic. Clubs: South Hills (dir.), Milw. Athletic. Office: 888 S Main St Fond du Lac WI 54935

FLUM, JOSEPH, lawyer; b. Phila., June 13, 1924; student Georgetown U., 1944-46; B.S., Temple U., 1947, J.D., 1951; Ph.D. in Constl. Edn., Pacific Western U., 1980. Admitted to Pa. bar, 1961, U.S. Supreme Ct. bar, 1967; owner, operator Flum's Dept. Store, Newtown, Pa., 1950—; individual practice law, Newtown, 1961—; lectr. law-related edn., world travel and cultures, 1946—. Mem. council Rock Sch. Dist. Pa., 1967-79, pres., 1971-73; chmn. legis. com. Bucks County Sch. Dirs., 1967-79; mem. com. revisions state sch. code, mem. com. on law-related edn. Pa. Dept. Edn., 1974—, mem. global edn. adv. com., 1978—. Recipient Chapel of Four Chaplains Legion of Honor award, 1977. Mem. Pa. Bar Assn. (youth edn. com. 1972), Bucks County Bar Assn., Am. Anthrop. Assn., Phila. Anthrop. Assn., Smithsonian Instn., Newtown Hist. Assn., Pa. Sch. Bds. Assn., Phi Alpha Theta. Club: Explorers. Author multimedia ednl. material on China; contbr. articles to legal and ednl. jours. Legis. editor Temple U. Law Quar., 1950-51. Office: State St at Centre Ave Newtown PA 18940

FLUOR, JOHN ROBERT, engr.; b. Santa Ana, Calif., Dec. 18, 1921; s. Peter E. and Margaret (Fischer) F.; grad. U. So. Calif., 1946; m. Lillian Marie Breaux, May 17, 1944; children—John Robert II, Peter. With Fluor Corp., 1946—, successively mgr., v.p. and gen. mgr. mfg., v.p. in charge mfg., exec. v.p., 1952-62, pres., 1962—, chmn., chief exec. officer, 1968—, pres., 1976—, also dir.; dir. Santa Anita Operating Co., Inc., Pacific Mut. Ins. Co., Calif. Can. Bank, Tex. Commerce Bancshares. Trustee, U. So. Calif., James Irvine Found. Served as 1st lt. USAAF, 1941-45. Mem. NAM (dir.). Clubs: California, San Gabriel Country; Sky (N.Y.C.); Eldorado Country (Palm Desert, Calif.); Los Angeles Country; Bohemian (San Francisco). Office: 3333 Michelson Dr Irvine CA 92730

FLYNN, KIRTLAND, JR., accountant; b. Orange, N.J., Aug. 27, 1922; s. Kirtland and Jane Elizabeth (Miller) F.; B.A., Colgate U., 1943; m. Lucy Jane Andrews, June 11, 1948; children—Patricia Carson, Gail Miller, James Kirtland. Acctg. staff Celanese Corp., Newark, Houston and Charlotte, N.C., 1947-65; sec.-treas. Little Constrn. Co., Inc., Charlotte, 1965-66; controller's staff J.P. Stevens & Co., Inc., Charlotte, 1966—. Bd. dirs., treas. Charlotte Exchange Student Program, 1979—. Served as 1st lt. USMCR, 1943-46. Decorated D.F.C., Air medals. Mem. Nat. Assn. Accts. (chpt. pres. 1966-67, nat. dir. 1971-73, nat. v.p. 1978-79). Club: Masons (Shriner, K.T.). Home: 1211 Ashcraft Ln Charlotte NC 28209 Office: PO Box 31426 Charlotte NC 28231

FLYNN, NORMAN DAVID, real estate co. exec.; b. LaCrosse, Wis., July 19, 1941; s. Percy David and Irene Ann (Polodna) F.; B.S., Wis. State U., 1963, M.S., 1967; postgrad. U. Wis., 1967-70; m. Susan Ann Romanski, June 6, 1964; children—Melanie, Andrea, David. Tchr., Aquinas High Sch., LaCrosse, 1963-67, Monona Grove (Wis.) High Sch., 1967-70; exec. v.p. Munz Investment Real Estate, Inc., Madison, 1970-78; pres. Flynn Baker Inc., investment real estate, 1978—; dir. Met. Nat. Bank, 1977—, chmn. bd., 1977—. Pres., Immaculate Heart of Mary Sch. Bd., Monona, Wis., 1971-72; trustee Greater Wis. Found., Madison, 1972-73; bd. dirs. Wis. Partners of Am., 1972-74, Wis. Jaycees Found., Appleton, 1972-74; bd. govs. Grad. Realtor Inst., 1974-77; bd. dirs. East Madison YMCA, 1975-80. Named Outstanding Young Educator of La Crosse, La Crosse Jaycees, 1966, Outstanding Young Profl., Central States Speech Assn., 1967, Outstanding Young Man in Wis., Wis. Jaycees, 1975, Realtor of Year, Madison Bd. Realtors, 1975. Mem. Wis. High Sch. Forensics Assn. (dir. 1968-70), Wis. Realtors Assn. (dir. 1975—, sec. 1980) Nat. Assn. Realtors (chmn. com. rent control 1976-78, vice-chmn. mgmt. and fin. subcom. 1980, nat. dir. 1979-81), Nat. Apt. Assn. (vice chmn. rent control 1979), Madison Apt. Assn. (sec.-treas. 1974-75, v.p. 1974-75, pres. 1975-76, dir. 1974—), Madison Builders Assn., Greater Madison Bd. Realtors (dir. 1975-77, pres. 1976), Wis. Nat. Forensics League (state chmn. 1969-70), Wis. Speech Assn. (dir. 1968-70), Monona (pres. 1969), Wis. (nat. dir. 1971, state pres. 1972) Jaycees. Roman Catholic (parish council 1969-72, v.p. 1971-72, mem. pastoral council Madison diocese 1973-75, pres. diocese 1974—). Clubs: Elks, Rotary. Home: 6209 Winnequah Rd Monona WI 53716 Office: 5708 Monona Dr Madison WI 53716

FLYNN, RICHARD JAMES, lawyer; b. Omaha, Dec. 6, 1928; s. Richard T. and Eileen (Murphy) F.; student Cornell U., 1944-46; B.S., Northwestern U., 1950, J.D., 1953; children—Richard McDonnell, William Thomas, Kathryn Eileen, James Daniel; m. Kay House Ebert. Admitted to D. C. bar, 1953, Ill. bar, 1954; law clk. to Chief Justices Vinson and Warren, 1953-54; asso. Sidley, Austin, Burgess & Smith, Chgo., 1954-63, partner, Washington, 1963-66, Sidley & Austin, 1967—. Served with USN, 1946-48. Mem. Am., Chgo., D.C., Fed., Fed. Energy bar assns., Assn. ICC Practitioners, Nat. Lawyers Club, Order of Coif, Phi Beta Kappa, Phi Delta Phi, Sigma Chi. Republican. Presbyn. (deacon 1969-72, elder 1973). Clubs: Economic of Chicago, Legal, Kenwood Golf and Country; Metropolitan (Washington). Contbr. articles to profl. jours. Home: 2342 S Queen St Arlington VA 22202 Office: 1730 Pennsylvania Ave NW Washington DC 20006

FLYNN, ROBERT EMMETT, mfg. co. exec.; b. Montreal, Que., Can., Sept. 10, 1933; s. Emmett Joseph and Pauline (Lupien) F.; B.Sc., Loyola Coll., 1955; B.Engring., McGill U., Montreal, 1957; M.B.A., Rutgers U., 1962; m. Irene Kantor, July 28, 1960; children—Donna, Darren, Diane. With Carborundum Co., 1957—, group v.p., 1976-78, sr. v.p., Niagara Falls, N.Y., 1979—; trustee Foundry Edn. Found., 1979—; bd. dirs. N.Y. State Associated Industries, 1979—. Bd. dirs. Niargara Falls United Way, 1971—; chmn. Niagara Winter Experience, 1979; mem. Grinding Wheel Inst., 1969—, Niagara Council Arts, 1979—. Served with USMCR, 1958. Mem. Buffalo C. of C. Clubs: Niagara Falls Country, Niagara. Office: Carbordundum Co Carborundum Center Niagara Falls NY 14302

FLYNN, STEPHEN ANTHONY, JR., land developer; b. Norwalk, Conn., Jan. 3, 1951; s. Stephen Anthony and Catherine Ellen (Flaherty) F.; B.S. in Real Estate and Constrn. Mgmt., U. Denver, 1974; m. Linda K. Newman, Aug. 28, 1973; 1 son, Sean Patrick. Loan mktg. rep. Empire Savs. and Loan Assn., Denver, 1975-76; dist. dir. Am. Mortgage Ins. Co., Denver, 1976-77; pres. S.A. Flynn Assos. Inc., Englewood, Colo., 1977—. Republican. Roman Catholic. Club: Denver Athletic. Office: 3531 S Pennsylvania St Englewood CO 80110

FLYNN, THOMAS CHARLES, mgmt. cons.; b. Pittsfield, Mass., July 27, 1950; s. Charles Edward and Angelina Mary (Cicurello) F.; B.S. in Mgmt., U. Bridgeport, 1972; M.B.A. in Fin., St. John's U., N.Y.C., 1975. Nat. bank examiner internat. div. Comptroller of Currency, Washington, 1973-75; asst. v.p., div. controller Citibank N.A., N.Y.C., 1975-79; mgmt. cons. Price Waterhouse & Co., N.Y.C., 1979—. Career profl. advisor St. John's U. Recipient certificate of exceptional performance Comptroller of Currency, 1975. Mem. Am. Mgmt. Assn. Home: 20 W 86th St New York NY 10024 Office: 153 E 53d St 43d Floor New York NY 10022

FOCHT, JOHN CHARLES, real estate and fin. corp. exec.; b. Lebanon, Pa., Oct. 13, 1945; s. William W. and Ethel L. F.; student Columbia Union Coll., 1968, Stetson U. Coll. Law, 1970-73; m. Lynn Templeton, Sept. 15, 1979. Pres. South Fla. Title and Guaranty Co., W. Palm Beach, 1975—, Fla. Mgmt. Enterprises, Inc., W. Palm Beach, 1974—, Mut. Funding Corp., W. Palm Beach, 1978—, Developex, Inc., real estate cons. Active Forum Club of the Palm Beaches, Better Bus. Bur. Palm Beach County. Served with USN, 1965. Lic. mortgage broker, life and health ins. agt. Mem. Title Ins. Assn. Palm Beach County, Fla. Land Title Assn., Mortgage Bankers Assn., Asso. Builders and Contractors (Gold Coast chpt.). Democrat. Club: Kiwanis (pres. Sunrise club, West Palm Beach, 1977-78). Home: 20 Country Club Rd West Palm Beach FL 33406 Office: 2831 Exchange Ct West Palm Beach FL 33409

FOERDER, STEVEN PETER, car rental co. exec.; b. N.Y.C., Sept. 25, 1940; s. Joseph and Lony F.; B.B.A. in Acctg., CCNY, 1962; M.B.A., St. John's U., 1969; m. Barbara Klausner, Apr. 7, 1963; children—David, Lori. Sr. acct. David Berdon & Co., C.P.A.'s, N.Y.C., 1962-65; with Avis, Inc., N.Y.C., 1966—, asst. to treas., 1970-71, asst. controller, 1971-73, v.p. fin. Avis Transport Can., 1973-75, v.p., internat. controller Avis Rent A Car System, Inc., 1975-77, v.p., controller Rent A Car div., 1978-79, v.p., asst. corporate controller Avis, Inc., 1979-80, v.p., dep. corporate controller, 1980—. Served with USNR, 1962-63. Mem. Fin. Execs. Inst., Nat. Assn. Accts. Home: 200 Scarborough Rd Briarcliff Manor NY 10510 Office: Avis Inc 1114 Ave of Americas New York NY 10036

FOERSTER, BRUCE SOMERNDIKE, investment banker; b. Ann Arbor, Mich., Mar. 22, 1941; s. Frederick Erwin and Vira Orswell (Somerndike) F.; A.B., Haverford Coll., 1963; M.B.A., U. Pa., 1971; m. Gail Homer Beckham, Aug. 24, 1979; 1 dau., Samantha MacRae. With Birr, Wilson & Co., Inc., San Francisco, 1972-76, H.C. Wainwright & Co., N.Y.C., 1976-77; investment banker Warburg Paribas Becker Inc., N.Y.C., 1977—; adj. prof. fin. N.Y. U. Grad. Sch. Bus., N.Y.C., 1979—; vis. lectr. U. Miami Sch. Law, 1977—. Served with USN, 1963-70. Mem. Bond Club N.Y. Presbyterian. Clubs: Recess (N.Y.C.); Army Navy Country (Arlington, Va.). Home: 36 Relihan Rd Darien CT 06820 Office: 55 Water St New York NY 10041

FOGARTY, CHARLES FRANKLIN, mining co. exec. b. Denver, May 27, 1921; s. Charles Franklin and Mabel Still F.; E.M., Colo. Sch. of Mines, 1942, D.Sc. in Geology, 1952; m. Wilma Marguerite Wells, Oct. 14, 1943; children—Charles Michael, Harry Wells, Patricia Ann Fogarty Kappus, Mary Elizabeth, Catherine Sue Fogarty Peterson, Joan Marie, Paul Thomas, Theresa Ellen. Sr. geologist exploration Socony Vacuum Oil Co., Bogota, Colombia, 1946-50; with Texasgulf Inc., 1952—, geologist, asst. mgr. exploration dept., mgr. exploration dept., 1952-57, sr. v.p., mgr. exploration dept., 1957-61, sr. v.p., 1961-64, exec. v.p., 1964-68, pres., 1968-73, chmn. bd., chief exec. officer, 1973—, also dir.; chmn., dir. Texasgulf Can. Ltd.; dir. The Greyhound Corp., The Lehman Corp., Cliffs Western Australian Mining Co. Pty. Ltd., Armco Inc., Compania Exploradora del Istmo, S.A., Sulphur Export Corp. Trustee Colo. Sch. Mines, also Research Inst.; bd. dirs. Com. Econ. Devel. Served from 2d lt. to maj. C.E., AUS, 1942-46. Recipient Distinguished Achievement medal Colo. Sch. Mines, 1962. Registered profl. engr., Tex. Mem. Chem. Mfrs. Assn. (dir.), Am. Inst. Mining, Metall. and Petroleum Engrs. (Hal Williams Hardinge award 1969), Am. Mining Congress (dir., vice chmn. 1977—), Copper Devel. Assn. (dir.), Am. Petroleum Inst., Can. Inst. Mining and Metallurgy, Am. Assn. Petroleum Geologists, Mining and Metall. Soc. Am. (pres. 1967-68), Can.-Am. Com., Zinc Inst., Nat. Acad. Engring., Sulphur Inst. (dir.), Soc. Exploration Geophysicists, Houston Geol. Soc., Newcomen Soc. N.Am., Scabbard and Blade, Tau Beta Pi, Sigma Gamma Epsilon, Kappa Sigma. Clubs: Blind Brook (Port Chester, N.Y.); Mining, Sky, University, Economic (N.Y.C.); Westchester Country (Rye, N.Y.). Office: High Ridge Park Stamford CT 06904

FOGARTY, WILLIAM EUGENE, mfg. co. exec.; b. N.Y.C., July 4, 1931; s. William Leo and Gertrude Eliose (Costello) F.; B.S. in Physics, Fairfield U., 1957; M.B.A., U. Conn., 1977; m. Nancy Ellen Meehan, Sept. 15, 1956; children—Nancy, Kathleen, William, Terence. Project engr. A.W. Haydon Co., Waterbury, Conn., 1957-63, sales engr., 1963-65; applications engr. Veeder Root Co., Hartford, Conn., 1965-69, asst. sales and mktg. mgr. instrument div., 1969-70, tech. coordinator Internat. div., 1978—; exec. asst. to commr. State of Conn. Dept. Children and Youth Services, Hartford, 1971—. Chmn., Wolcott (Conn.) Town Council, 1969-73, councilman, 1965-73; mem. Wolcott Republican Town Com., 1962—, chmn., 1978—. Served with USMC, 1951-54. Mem. Am. Mktg. Assn., Wolcott Jaycees (charter mem., dir. 1962-63), Wolcott C. of C. (pres. 1968-69), VFW (comdr. Wolcott post 1963-64). Republican. Roman Catholic. Home: 58 Charles Dr Wolcott CT 06716 Office: 28 Sargeant St Hartford CT 06102

FOGEL, IRVING MARTIN, cons. engr., author, lectr.; b. Gloucester, Mass., Apr. 15, 1929; s. Jacob and Ethel (David) F.; B.S. in Civil Engring., Ind. Inst. Tech., 1954; children—Ethan, Ronit. Pres., Fogel & Assos., Inc., N.Y.C., also Phila., Boston, Detroit, Newport Beach, 1969—. Registered profl. engr. Recipient Order Silver Slide Rule, Ind. Tech. Alumni Assn., 1976. Fellow ASCE; mem. Am. Arbitration Assn., Am. Assn. Cost Engrs., Am. Inst. Constructors, Am. Mgmt. Assn., Assn. Engrs. and Architects in Israel, Constrn. Specifications Inst., Nat. Contract Mgmt. Assn., Nat. Soc. Profl. Engrs., N.Y. State Soc. Profl. Engrs., N.Y. Bldg. Congress, Project Mgmt. Inst., Soc. Am. Mil. Engrs. Co-author: The McGraw-Hill Construction Business Handbook, 1978; Businessman's Guide to Construction, 1980; contbr. articles to profl. jours. Home: 525 E 86th St New York NY 10028 Office: 373 Park Ave S New York NY 10016

FOGEL, SEYMOUR, pub. co. exec.; b. Rochester, N.Y., July 14, 1929; s. Morris and Dora (Bloom) F.; B.S., U. Rochester, 1951; m. Joan Davis, Mar. 30, 1958; children—Linda, Deborah, Robert, David. Accountant, Am. Sugar Refining Co., N.Y.C., 1951-53, Haskins & Sells, C.P.A., Rochester, N.Y., 1953-59; v.p., treas. Lawyers Coop. Pub. Co., Rochester, 1959—, also dir., mem. exec. com.; dir. Research Inst. Am., Inc., Bancroft Whitney Co., San Francisco, Baker, Voorhis & Co., Mt. Kisco, N.Y.; mem. adv. bd. Lincoln Rochester Trust Co., 1968-71. Bd. dirs. Community Chest Rochester and Monroe County, Inc., 1972-77, Rochester Hosp. Service Corp., Freedom House, N.Y.C., 1972-75, Genesee Hosp., Jewish Community Center of Greater Rochester, 1972-77, Temple Beth El, Jewish Home and Infirmary Inc. C.P.A., N.Y. Mem. Am. Inst. C.P.A.'s, N.Y. State Soc. C.P.A.'s, Fin. Execs. Inst. (pres. 1970-71). Office: Aqueduct Bldg Rochester NY 14603

FOGLE, WILLIAM GORDON, constrn. equipment distbg. co. exec.; b. Baton Rouge, La., June 26, 1948; s. Redrick and Ruth (Murphy) F.; bus. student Southwestern U. at Georgetown, 1966-70; m. Patricia Lynne Kidson, July 11, 1970; children—Ruth Elizabeth, Rebecca Elaine, William Gordon. With Fogle Equipment Co., Houston, 1970—, dir. customer services, 1979—. Charter mem. adv. council U. Houston Coll. Bus. Tech., 1977—, chmn. adv. council, 1979, 80; mem. adv. council Tex. State Tech. Inst., Waco, 1979-80. Mem. Asso. Equipment Distbrs. Young Execs. (chmn. adv. com. 1975-76), Houston Equipment Distbrs. (pres. 1975). Unitarian. Office: 8821 Almeda Houston TX 77054

FOHL, TIMOTHY, mfg. co. exec.; b. Pitts., Apr. 21, 1934; s. Edward Zinn and Dorothy (Umbenhauer) F.; A.B., Dartmouth Coll., 1956; M.S., M.I.T., 1959, Ph.D., 1963; postgrad. exec. devel. program Whittemore Sch. Bus. and Econs., 1977; m. Nancy Lee Hattox, Apr. 15, 1961; children—Nicholas, Jeffrey, Peter. Research scientist Itek Corp., Lexington, Mass., 1962-63; research scientist Mt. Auburn Research Assos., Newton, Mass., 1963-68, prin. scientist, dir., 1968-72; with GTE Products Corp., Danvers, Mass., 1972—, mgr. new product devel. lighting group, 1977—. Pres., trustee Carlisle Conservation Found., 1972-79; v.p. Carlisle Trails Assn., 1975—; fin. chmn. Town Republican Com., 1980. Contbr. articles to profl. jours.; patentee in field. Home: 681 South St Carlisle MA 01741 Office: Lighting Center Danvers MA 01923

FOKKEN, DENIS LEROY, bank exec.; b. Sioux Falls, S.D., Feb. 1, 1950; s. Oliver and Patricia (Donahoe) F.; student Coll. St. Thomas, St. Paul, 1968-69; B.B.A., Mt. Marty Coll., Yankton, S.D., 1973; m. Deborah Ann Dose, Aug. 26, 1971; children—Jennifer, Joseph. Acct., Jerald B. Davis Co., Inc., Yankton, 1973-76; v.p., controller First Dakota Nat. Bank, Yankton, 1976—; part-time instr. acctg. Yankton Coll., spring 1978, fall 1980. Sec.-treas. Yankton Fastpitch Softball Assn., 1977; bd. dirs. Mt. Marty Coll. Booster Club, 1976—, treas., 1978—. Served in Air NG, 1969-75. C.P.A., S.D. Mem. Am. Inst. C.P.A.'s, S.D. Soc. C.P.A.'s, Yankton Jaycees. Democrat. Roman Catholic. Clubs: Elks (officer 1979—), Hillcrest Golf and Country. Home: 901 E 18th St Yankton SD 57078 Office: 201 W 3d St Yankton SD 57078

FOLEY, DANIEL EDMUND, real estate devel. exec.; b. St. Paul, Mar. 1, 1926; s. Edward and Gerry (Fitzgarld) F.; student U. Minn., 1941-43; m. Paula Evans, Apr. 1, 1946; children—Daniel, Margaret, Paula, David, Deane. Chmn. bd. Realty Partners Ltd., Los Angeles. Served with AUS, 1943-46. Home: 1255 S Oak Knoll Pasadena CA 91005 Office: 523 W 6th St Los Angeles CA 90014

FOLEY, EDWARD MINTER, mfg. co. exec.; b. Bassett, Va., Dec. 15, 1929; s. Ansley Tinsley and Mildred (Minter) F.; student U. Va., 1948-53; B.S., U. Tenn., 1960; m. Evelyn Jo Cooter, Apr. 28, 1951; children—Mildred Kathleen, Edward Minter Jr. Research physicist Union Carbide Corp., Oak Ridge, 1955-66, sr. research physicist, Greenville S.C., and Kokomo, Ind., 1966-69; sr. research engr. Stellite div. Cabot Corp., Kokomo, 1970-72, mgr. parts mfg., 1972-74, product mgr. div., 1974-80, Eastern regional mgr. Wean Tech. div., 1980—. Adult adviser Order Demoley; scoutmaster Boy Scouts Am. Served with U.S. Army, 1953-55. Recipient IR-100 award Indsl. Research Mag., 1974. Mem. Metal Powder Industries Fedn. (dir. 1975—, P/M Part of Year award 1974), Powder Metallurgy Industries Assn. (pres. 1978-80), Am. Powder Metallurgy Inst., Am. Soc. Metals, Nat. Rifle Assn. Methodist. Clubs: Masons, Shriners, Order Eastern Star (past patron). Patentee in field. Office: 1020 W Park Ave Kokomo IN 46901

FOLEY, EUGENE PATRICK, fin. cons.; b. Wabasha, Minn., Nov. 22, 1928; s. John R. and Ellen M. (Brennan) F.; B.A., St. Thomas Coll., St. Paul, 1952; LL.B., U. Minn., 1955; LL.D., Lowell Inst. Tech., 1966. Admitted to Minn. bar, 1955; partner firm Foley & Foley, Wabasha, Minn., 1955-59; legal counsel U.S. Senate Small Bus. Com., Washington, 1959-61; exec. asst. to sec. commerce Dept. Commerce, Washington, 1961-63, asst. sec. commerce for econ. devel., 1965-66; nat. adminstr. SBA, Washington, 1963-65; pres. Interore Corp. subs. Occidental Chems. Corp., N.Y.C., 1967-69; v.p. Dreyfus Corp., N.Y.C., 1969-71; fin. cons. to small and medium-sized cos., 1971—; dir. P & F Industries, Gt. Neck, N.Y., Esic Capital Corp., N.Y.C., Branch Industries, Inc., N.Y.C., Lehigh Valley Industries, Inc., N.Y.C. Trustee African-Am. Inst., N.Y.C. Served with inf. U.S. Army, 1946-48. Recipient Arthur Fleming award U.S. Govt., 1965; Internat. Boss of Yr. award Nat. Secs. Assn., 1965; Govt. Man of Yr. award Nat. Bus. League, 1966. Mem. Nat. Council for Urban Econ. Devel. (dir., Disting. Service award 1974). Author: The Negro Businessman—In Search of a Tradition, 1966; The Achieving Ghetto, 1968. Office: care Satra Corp 1211 Ave of Americas New York NY 10036

FOLEY, JOHN DANIEL, rubber and plastics co. exec.; b. N.Y.C., Apr. 4, 1916; s. John Joseph and Anna Cecelia (Dugan) F.; B.S. in M.E., N.Y. U., 1937; m. Kathleen A. Sweeney, Aug. 5, 1946; 1 dau., Ellen Gale. Supt., Remington Arms Co., Bridgeport, Conn., 1941-46; v.p. mfg. H.D. Canfield Co., Bridgeport, 1946-66; sr. v.p. Pantasote Inc., 1966-79, exec. v.p., dir. Greenwich, Conn., 1979—. Councilman, Kinnelon Borough, N.J., 1950-56, mayor, 1956-60. Mem. Am. Mgmt. Assn., Soc. Plastics Engrs. Home: 17 Brush Hill Rd Kinnelon NJ 07405 Office: Office Park IX Weaver St Greenwich CT 06830

FOLEY, PAUL FRANCIS, JR., airline food co. exec.; b. Boston, Aug. 24, 1952; s. Paul F. and Marie K. F.; B.S. in Hotel Adminstrn., Cornell U., 1974; postgrad. in bus. adminstrn. Adelphi U., 1976; m. Maureen Fitzgerald, Sept. 28, 1974; children—Emily, Shea. With Sky Chefs, 1974—, gen. mgr. Washington, 1978-79, Boston, 1979—. Vice pres. Scituate (Mass.) Jaycees. Office: Sky Chefs Logan Internat Airport Boston MA 02128

FOLEY, PHILIP SEATON, lumber co. exec.; b. Piggott, Ark., Sept. 25, 1923; s. Albert Clarence and Gertrude Dorothea (Seaton) F.; B.S., U. Mich., 1949; m. Margarethe Streschniak, Aug. 15, 1946; children—Linda S., Stephen A.T., Albert J. Supr. cabinet div. RCA, Pulaski, Va., 1949-51; sec., treas., plant supt. Penington-Foley Furniture Co., Inc., Martinsville, Ind., 1951-53; sec., mill supt. T.A. Foley Lumber Co., Inc., Paris, Ill., 1953-79, pres. and treas., 1979—; dir. Edgar County Savs. & Loan Assn. Treas. Edgar County and Paris Sesquicentennial Commn., 1972—; mem. Paris Bicentennial Commn., 1975-76. Mem. Paris Park Bd., 1967-74; commr. Pub. Property Paris, 1967-71. Served with 1st inf. div. AUS, 1944-46. Decorated Purple Heart, Bronze Star medal. Mem. U.S. C. of C., Ill. State C. of C. (exec. bd. Small Bus. Council 1981), Paris C. of C. (pres. 1965), Forest Products Research Soc. (trustee Midwest sect. 1967-68, 81-82), Soc. Wood Sci. and Tech., Ill. Tech. Forestry Assn., Soc. 1st Div., Am. Legion, Beta Phi Sigma. Episcopalian. Clubs: Society Les Voyageurs (U. Mich.), Kiwanis (pres. 1960), Elks. Home: East Twin Lakes PO Box 336 Paris IL 61944 Office: 1800 S Jefferson St Paris IL 61944

FOLEY, RAYMOND WILLIAM, advt. exec.; b. Mpls., Sept. 5, 1921; s. John J. and Theresa M. (Shandl) F.; B.A., U. Minn., 1948; m. Virginia Donna Reiling, June 19, 1948; children—Gregory, Mark, Tom. Editor, tng. Dayton's Mpls., 1948-52; dir. public relations Hennepin County United Fund, Mpls., 1952-55; v.p. Pidgeon Savage Lewis Advt. Agy., Mpls., 1955-70; exec. v.p. Colle & McVoy Advt. Agy., Mpls., 1970-74, pres., 1974—. Pres., Am. Lung Assn., Mpls., 1978—; mem. exec. com., dir. Arthritis Found., Mpls., 1960-80; exec. com., dir. Indianhead Council, Boy Scouts Am., 1978—; co-chmn. communications com. Nat. Arthritis Found., 1978—; city councilman, mem. planning commn. City of N. Oaks, St. Paul, 1976—. Served with Q.M. Corps, U.S. Army, 1942-46. Mem. Savs. Insts. Mktg. Soc. Am. (dir. 1976—), Minn. Advt. Fedn. (dir.), N.W. Council Advt. Agencies (pres. 1973-75). Roman Catholic. Clubs: Statesman's of Twin City Fed., Mpls. Athletic, N. Oaks Golf, Ticker Tape, Daybreakers Breakfast, Am. Legion, Observatory, Mpls. Downtown Council, N.W. Midwest Golfers Assn., U. Minn. CLA Alumni Assn. Home: 7 Duck Pass Rd North Oaks Saint Paul MN 55110 Office: 1550 E 78th St Minneapolis MN 55423

FOLEY, THOMAS LEO, business exec.; b. Albany, N.Y., Feb. 21, 1942; s. Thomas Leo and Helen Agnes (Hogan) F.; B.B.A., St. Johns U., 1965; M.B.A., Fordham U., 1971; m. Judith M. Collins, Apr. 29, 1978; 1 son, Thomas M. Sr. acct. Ernst & Ernst and Milligan Muller, N.Y.C., 1965-69; mgr. budgeting and analysis Sealtest Eastern Region, Kraftco Corp., 1969-72; asst. controller systems Gulf & Western, N.Y.C., 1972-75; group fin. officer, controller Consol. Foods, N.Y.C., 1975-79; corp. controller Craftex Inc., N.Y.C., 1980—. Served with U.S. Army, 1960. C.P.A., N.Y. Mem. Am. Inst. C.P.A.'s, N.Y. State Soc. C.P.A.'s, Fordham Grad. Alumni Assn. Home: 34 Phillips Ln Darien CT 06820 Office: 136 Madison Ave Ave New York NY 10016

FOLGER, JOHN CLIFFORD, former ambassador, business exec.; b. Sheldon, Iowa, May 28, 1896; s. Homer and Emma (Funston) F.; B.S., State Coll. Wash., 1917, M.S., 1918; Mary Kathrine Dulin, Nov. 2, 1929; children—John Dulin, Lee Merritt. Chmn. bd. Folger Nolan Fleming Douglas Inc., Washington, Piedmont Mortgage Co., Washington; Am. ambassador to Belgium, 1957-59; dir. Hilton Hotels Corp., Allbritton Communications Co., WJLA, Inc.; dir. emeritus IBM Corp., Hiram Walker-Gooderham Worts, Ltd. Bd. govs. N.Y. Stock Exchange. Gen. chmn. Washington Community Chest, 1940; chmn. D.C. chpt. A.R.C., 1942, now hon. chmn.; mem. Washington Cathedral. Chmn., Rep. Nat. Finance Com., 1955-57, 60-61. Pres. Investment Bankers Assn. of Am., 1943-45; mem. Nat. Inst. Social Sci., The Pilgrims. Republican. Clubs: Alfalfa, The Brook, Chevy Chase, Metropolitan, 1925 F Street (Washington); Down Town Assn. (N.Y.C.); Everglades, Bath and Tennis (Palm Beach). Home: 2991 Woodland Dr NW Washington DC 20008 Office: 725 15th St Washington DC 20005

FOLGER, LEE MERRITT, investment co. exec.; b. Washington, May 5, 1934; s. John Clifford and Mary Kathrine (Dulin) F.; A.B., Harvard, 1956; m. Nancy McElroy, 1961 (div.); children—Neil, Peter, Nicholas; m. 2d, Juliet Campbell Birmingham, Oct. 9, 1976. Sr. v.p., dir. Folger Nolan Fleming Douglas, investments, Washington, 1959-76, vice chmn., 1976—; pres. Cumberland Trust Co., Knoxville, Tenn., 1962—; v.p. Piedmont Mortgage Co., Washington, 1960—; mng. partner H.L. Dulin Co., Knoxville, 1960—; dir. Washington Star Newspaper, 1976—. Chmn. D.C. chpt. ARC, 1971-77, bd. govs.; bd. govs. Am. Nat. Red Cross, 1976—, vice chmn., 1978; vice chmn. United Way of Nat. Capital Area, 1975-78; chmn. bd. govs. St. Albans Sch., Washington, 1975-76; trustee, fin. chmn. Corcoran Gallery of Art, 1972—; mem. D.C. Fine Arts Commn., 1972-75; v.p. The Folger Fund, Washington, 1958—; mem. Protestant Episcopal Cathedral Found., 1980—; bd. dirs. Community Found. Greater Washington, Inc., 1978—, chmn. fin. com., 1980—. Served to lt. (j.g.) USNR, 1956-58. Mem. Nat. Assn. Securities Dealers (dist. com. 1971-74, vice chmn. 1973-74). Clubs: The Brook, The Downtown Assn. (N.Y.C.); Chevy Chase (Md.); Metropolitan, Federal City, 1925 F Street (Washington); Essex County (Boston). Home: 80 Kalorama Circle NW Washington DC 20008 Office: 725 15th St NW Washington DC 20005

FOLGER, MARY HELEN, mag. editor; b. Youngstown, Ohio, Sept. 10, 1929; d. Franklin Porter and Elma Christine (Bruce) Davis; student Kent State U., 1968-71; m. Leslie A. Folger, May 23, 1947 (dec. Aug. 30, 1980); children—Leslie Allen, Will Raymond, Loretta Jo, Lynette Marie. Writer, photographer, feature editor The Record-Courier, Ravenna, Ohio, 1967-73; editor The Jour., Garrettsville, Ohio, 1973-76; exec. editor Western Reserve Mag., Garrettsville, 1973—. Mem. Garrettsville Village Council, 1973-78, chmn. Parks and Recreation, 1973-78; mem. exec. com. Portage County United Way, 1969-73. Recipient numerous journalism awards. Mem. Nat. Fedn. Press Women, Ohio Press Women, Ohio Newspaper Women's Assn. Home: 8215 Water St Garrettsville OH 44231 Office: PO Box 243 Garrettsville OH 44231

FOLK, SHARON LYNN, printing co. exec.; b. Bellefontaine, Ohio, June 13, 1945; d. Emerson Dewey and Berdena Isabelle (Brown) F.; A.B., Belmont Abbey Coll., 1968. Exec. v.p. Nat. Bus. Forms Inc., Greeneville, Tenn., 1968-73, pres., chairperson of bd., 1973—; pres., chairperson of bd. Nat. Forms Co. Inc., Gastonia, N.C., 1973-79. Active YMCA Community Orch.; bd. dirs. Greeneville YMCA, 1977-80, United Way, 1980; mem. presdl. steering com. U.S. Senator Howard Baker, 1979-80. Mem. Internat. Bus. Forms Industry (chairperson indsl. relations com. 1978-81), Nat. Bus. Forms Assn., Tuesday Night Bus. Women's Bowling League, Greeneville Women's Bowling Assn. Republican. Roman Catholic. Home: 1131 Hixon Ave Greeneville TN 37743 Office: Nat Bus Forms Co Inc 100 Pennsylvania Ave Greeneville TN 37743

FOLSOM, JOHN ROY, savs. and loan exec.; b. Hartsville, S.C., Dec. 30, 1918; s. William Arthur and Flora (Newsom) F.; B.A., Furman U., 1940; m. Anita Anderson, Oct. 18, 1941; children—Anita Marie (Mrs. Harold A. Boney, Jr.), Dale (Mrs. Guy M. Tate, Jr.), John William, George Anderson. With Aiken Loan & Security Co., Florence, S.C., 1940-41, Surety Life & Liberty Life Ins. Co., Greenville and Columbia, S.C., 1941-43, 46-60; with S.C. Fed. Savs. & Loan Assn., Columbia, 1960—, pres., 1963—, also mem. exec. com., loan com., dir.; pres., dir. 1st Service Corp. S.C., 1973—, Service Mortgage Corp., 1973—; v.p., dir. S.C. Student Loan Corp., 1973-77; dir. S.C. Title Ins. Co., Investors Nat. Life Ins. Co.; dir. Seibels Bruce Inc. Mem. Richland-Lexington Airport Commn., 1973—, chmn., 1980—; financial adv. com. Erskine Coll.; mem. Am. Heart Policy Com., 1972-73. Trustee United Fund Columbia, 1966-76; past treas., vice chmn., bd. dirs. S.C. Heart Assn., 1968-73, 75—, chmn., 1968-73; bd. dirs., campaign chmn. Musical Arts, pres. Columbia Mus. Festival; trustee, v.p. Research Devel. and Ednl. Found. Richland County Meml. Hosp.; mem. citizens com., bd. adminstrs. Richland County, 1968—; adv. bd., co-chmn. Providence Hosp., 1974—; pres. adv. council Columbia Coll., 1974—, trustee, 1980—; pres. adv. council Furman U., 1976—; bd. dirs. Salvation Army, 1975-77; mgmt. fin. com. Am. Heart Assn., 1976—, bd. dirs., 1980—. Recipient Good Egg award S.C. Heart Assn. Mem. U.S. League Savs. Assns. (dir. 1973—, br. ops. com. 1979-80), S.C. League Savs. Assns. (exec. com., dir. 1979-80), S.C. C. of C. (pres. 1979-80, exec. com. 1980—), Columbia (dir. 1975—, v.p. indsl. devel.), Furman U. Alumni Assn. (pres. 1953-54, mem. athletic council 1955), Columbia Real Estate Bd., Columbia Real Estate Appraisers, Columbia Home Builders Assn., Univ. Assos. U. S.C. (pres. 1972-73, pres. Summit club 1971-76, v.p. club 1976—), Newcomen Soc. N.Am., Sigma Alpha Epsilon. Methodist (chmn. finance com., bd. dirs.). Rotarian. Clubs: Palmetto, Forest Lake, (Columbia). Home: 1515 Adger Rd Columbia SC 29205 Office: 1500 Hampton St Columbia SC 29201

FOLTZ, ROBERT EMMERT, sales cons. co. exec.; b. Polo, Ill., Oct. 11, 1910; s. Daniel Stauffer and Clara Mae (Landis) F.; M.B.A., Brown U., 1940; m. Belva Luella Magill, June 16, 1933; children—Janet, Ronald, Carol, Diane. Cost accountant Lawrence Bros. Inc., Sterling, Ill., 1930-45, sales mgr., 1946-50, v.p. sales, 1951-72, sales cons., 1973—. Trustee, Moody Bible Inst., Chgo., 1966—; elder Christian and Missionary Alliance Ch.; mem. standing com. Nat. Bur. Standards, U.S. Dept. Commerce. Fellow Internat. Biog. Assn.; mem. Builders Hardware Mfrs. Assn., Am. Inst. Mgmt., Internat. Platform Assn. Club: Rotary. Patentee builders hardware (20). Home: PO Box 2126 Sedona AZ 86336

FOMON, ROBERT M., investment co. exec.; b. Chgo., 1925; grad. U. So. Calif., 1947. Chmn. bd., chief exec. officer The E.F. Hutton Group Inc., N.Y.C., also dir.; dir. PSA Inc., Gt. Lakes Carbon Corp. Office: EF Hutton & Co One Battery Park Plaza New York NY 10004

FONDA, JOHN REAGAN, engr., mfg. co. exec.; b. Knoxville, Tenn., Aug. 25, 1917; s. Howard E. and Mabel (Reagan) F.; student Wayne State U., Mich. State U.; m. Joyce May Rupprecht, Feb. 21, 1949. With Dihydrol Co., 1946—, sec.-treas., 1950-60, pres., Highland Park, Mich., 1960—. Registered profl. engr., Mich. Mem. Nat. Assn. Corrosion Engrs., Am. Water Works Assn., Am. Soc. San. Engrs. (pres.). Baptist. Mason (32 deg., Shriner). Research in water chemistry. Patentee on equipment for chem. treatment water. Home: 30815 Billington Ct Birmingham MI 48010 Office: 150 Victor Ave Detroit MI 48203

FONNER, JULIE, editor; b. Norman, Okla., Feb. 12, 1951; d. William James and Norma June (Wilmuth) Parker; student Eastfield Coll., So. Methodist U.; m. Carl Wayne Fonner, July 12, 1969. Research asst. to mng. editor Energy Mgmt. Report, Dallas, 1969-73, mng. editor, 1973—. Home: 417 W Ave F Midlothian TX 76065 Office: 800 Davis Bldg 1309 Main St Dallas TX 75202

FONTAINE, BURT CASPAR MARIA, multi-nat. co. exec.; b. Amsterdam, Netherlands, July 15, 1928; s. Franciscus and Lamberta (Kannegieter) F.; came to U.S., 1960; student St. Ignatius Coll., Amsterdam; St. Canisius Coll., Djakarta, Indonesia, 1950-51; m. Elly van der Heijden, Aug. 4, 1958; children—Marc, Patrick (dec.), Christina, Thomas. Officer mgr. Borneo Sumatra Trading Co., Sumatra, Indonesia, 1951-57, div. supr., The Hague, Netherlands,

1957-60, with N.Y.C. office, 1960-61; first asst. to gen. purchase and sales mgr. Ocean Marine Ins., Tuteur and Co., Inc., N.Y.C., 1961-65; import mgr. E. Milten Berg, Inc., N.Y.C., 1965—, mgr. sporting goods and hardward div., 1966—, asst. treas., 1967-68; asst. v.p. fin. Brasil/FCIA Worldwide, N.Y.C., 1968; with Philipp Bros. div. Engelhard Minerals and Chems., N.Y.C., 1968—, v.p., 1979—; cons. traders, banks. Mem. steering com. parish council Roman Cath. Ch. Served as platoon comdr., commando Royal Dutch Air Force, 1948-51. Decorated Medal Order and Peace. Home: 1439 E 15th St Brooklyn NY 11230 Office: 1221 Ave of Americas New York NY 10020

FONTAINE, JEAN-LOUIS, mfg. exec.; b. Sherbrooke, Que., Can., Dec. 17, 1939; s. Alfred and Rollande (Prefontaine) F.; B.Sc. in Mech. Engring., U. Sherbrooke, 1963; M.B.A., U. Western Ont., 1977; m. Huguette Bombardier, Aug. 18, 1962; children—Diane, Sylvie, Marc, Patrick, Paule. Design engr. Sherbrooke Machinery, 1963-64; successively quality control mgr., prodn. coordinator, dir. and v.p. prodn., v.p. and gen. mgr. Ski-doo div., v.p. mfg. subs., v.p. in charge of working group, v.p. transp. products Bombardier Ltee, Montreal, Que., Can., 1964-75, v.p. corp. planning Bombardier, Inc., 1977—, also dir. Bd. dirs. Les Grands Ballets Canadiens. Mem. Association générale des anciens d l'Université de Sherbrooke (pres. 1979—), Que. Assn. M.B.A.'s, Western Bus. Sch. Club, Canadian Inst. Engrs., Order of Engrs. of Que. Home: 4 Murray Montreal PQ H3Y 2Y1 Canada Office: 800 Dorchester Blvd W Montreal PQ H3B 1X9 Canada

FONVILLE, BRYCE MCGHEE, chem. co. exec.; b. Durham, N.C., Dec. 22, 1921; s. William Bryce and Susie Ann (McGhee) F.; B.S. in Mech. Engring., Duke, 1948; m. Anne Marie Saunders, July 3, 1943; children—Kenneth, Lawrence, James, Nancy. Process engr. Union Carbide Corp., S. Charleston, W.Va., 1948-55, plant engr., Torrance, Calif., 1955-58, engring. group leader, S. Charleston, 1959-66, fin. analyst, N.Y.C., 1966-67, product mgr., 1967-69; engring. mgr., S. Charleston, 1969-78, sr. staff engr.-licensing, 1978—. Served with U.S. Army, 1943-45. Baptist. Home: 1391 Nottingham Rd Charleston WV 25314 Office: PO Box 8361 South Charleston WV 25303

FOOTE, PAUL SHELDON, educator; b. Lansing, Mich., May 22, 1946; s. Harlon Sheldon and Frances Norene (Rotter) F.; B.B.A., U. Mich., 1967; M.B.A. (Loomis-Sayles fellow), Harvard U., 1971; advanced profl. cert. N.Y. U., 1975; postgrad. doctoral program Mich. State U., 1975—; m. Badri Seddigheh Hosseinian, Oct. 25, 1968; children—David, Sheila. Br. mgr., divisional mgr. Citibank, N.Y.C., Bombay, India and Beirut, Lebanon, 1972-74; mgr. planning and devel. Singer Co., Africa/Middle East, 1974-75; instr. U. Mich., Flint, 1978-79; asst. prof. U. Windsor (Ont., Can.), 1979—; lectr. acctg. Mich. State U., East Lansing, 1977. Served to lt. AUS, 1968-69. Haskins and Sells Doctoral Consortium fellow, 1977. Mem. Am. Accounting Assn., Nat. Assn. Accountants, World Future Soc. Club: Circumnavigators. Home: 2795 Southwood East Lansing MI 48823 Office: Grad Sch Bus Adminstrn East Lansing MI 48824 also Faculty Bus Adminstrn U Windsor Windsor ON N9B 3P4 Canada

FORAN, NICHOLAS A., pump co. exec.; b. N.Y.C., Aug. 9, 1922; s. Nicholas Louis and Phyllis (Flemming) Fiorentino; B.M.E., U. N.Mex., 1948; m. Mary Elizabeth Austin, Sept. 10, 1944; 1 son, Andrew Austin. With Worthington Corp., 1948—, engr., Buffalo, 1948-52, sales engr., Phila., 1952-56, sales office mgr., Montreal, Que., Can., 1956-63, mgr. engineered products, Harrison, N.J., 1963-67, regional sales mgr., N.Y.C., 1967-71, v.p.-sales Latin Am., Mountainside, N.J., 1971—; pres. subs. Worthington, Ltd., Mountainside, 1971—; dir. Worthington Internat. Co., Inc. Served with USNR, 1942-46. Decorated Bronze Stars (2), Purple Heart. Registered profl. engr., N.Y., Can. Mem. Nat. Elec. Mfrs. Assn. Roman Catholic. Clubs: Naval Officers; Roxiticus Golf and Country (Mendham, N.J.); Palm Air Golf and Country (Pompano Beach, Fla.). Home: 28 Post Kennel Rd Bernardsville NJ Office: 270 Sheffield St Mountainside NJ 07092 Mailing Address: RFD 1 PO Box 149B Far Hills NJ 07931

FORASTIERE, MICHAEL ANTHONY, III, investment banker, lawyer; b. Yonkers, N.Y., Sept. 1, 1944; s. Michael Anthony and Alice Mary (Krushevsky) F.; B.A., Princeton, 1966; J.D., Columbia, 1969. Admitted to N.Y. bar, U.S. Supreme Ct. bar; asso. firm Lepercq, de Neuflize & Co., Inc., N.Y.C., 1969-74; v.p. Merrill Lynch, Hubbard Inc., N.Y.C., 1974-76, Merrill Lynch Leasing Inc., N.Y.C., 1976—, Merrill Lynch, Pierce, Fenner & Smith, Inc., N.Y.C., 1978—. Served with U.S. Army, 1969-70. Mem. Harlan Fiske Stone Fellowship of Columbia Law, Assn. Bar City N.Y., Am. Bar Assn., Columbia Law Sch. Alumni Assn. Clubs: Westchester Country, Princeton of N.Y. Home: Oscaleta Rd South Salem NY 10590 Office: 165 Broadway New York NY 10006

FORBES, JOHN ALEXANDER, JR., automotive parts wholesale exec.; b. New Glasgow, N.S., Can., Nov. 14, 1936; s. John Alexander and Helen Eugenie (Martin) F.; diploma in engring., St. Francis Xavier U., 1958, B.S., 1958; m. Mildred J. MacDonald, May 18, 1959; children—Penelope, John Alexander, Jill, LeeAnn, D. Francis, Jeff, Josh. Vice pres., gen. mgr. Canadian Tire Asso. Store, Antigonish, N.S., 1955-66, v.p., gen. mgr., New Glasgow, N.S., 1966-67, pres., Woodstock, N.B., 1967-70, Dartmouth, N.S., 1970-76; pres. Forbes Supplies, Ltd., Dartmouth, N.S., 1967—, Maritime Accessories Ltd., Halifax, N.S., 1979—; v.p. J.A. Forbes Ltd., 1956—. Mem. Halifax-Dartmouth Port Commn., 1976-79. Mem. Dartmouth C. of C. (mem. council 1975—), Halifax Bd. Trade, Automotive Industries Assn., Halifax Execs. Assn. Progressive Conservative. Roman Catholic. Clubs: Rotary (pres. 1978-79), St. Francis Xavier U. Pres.'s. Office: 3490 Prescott St Halifax NS B3K 5N5 Canada

FORBES, MALCOLM S(TEVENSON), publisher; b. Englewood, N.J., Aug. 19, 1919; s. Bertie Charles and Adelaide (Stevenson) F.; A.B., Princeton U., 1941; L.H.D., Nasson Coll., 1966; LL.D., Okla. Christian Coll., 1973, Am. Grad. Sch. Internat. Mgmt., 1977; Litt.D., Millikin U., 1974, Ball State U., 1980; D.F.A., Franklin Pierce Coll., 1975; Sc.D., Bryant Coll., 1976; D. Journ., Babson Coll., 1977; LL.D., Pace U., 1979, Potomac Sch. Law, 1979; D.Econ. Journalism, Lakeland Coll., 1980; m. Roberta Remsen Laidlaw, Sept. 21, 1946; children—Malcolm Stevenson, Robert Laidlaw, Christopher Charles, Timothy Carter, Moira Hamilton. Owner, pub. Fairfield Times, weekly, Lancaster, Ohio, 1941; est. Lancaster Tribune, weekly, 1942; asso. pub. Forbes Mag. of Bus., N.Y.C., 1946-54, pub., editor-in-chief, 1957—; v.p. Forbes, Inc., N.Y.C., 1947-64, pres., 1964—; pres. 60 Fifth Ave. Corp.; founder Nations Heritage, bi-monthly, pres., pub., 1948-49; pres. Forbes Trinchera Inc.; chmn. Fiji Forbes Inc., Sangre de Cristo Ranches Inc. Mem. Borough Council, Bernardsville, N.J., 1949; state senator, 1952-58; campaign chmn. A.R.C., Somerset Hills, N.J., 1949; chmn. N.J. Rhodes Scholarship Selection Com., 1976, 78; trustee St. Mark's Sch., Princeton Art Council; bd. dirs. Naval War Coll., Coast Guard Acad. Found.; Republican candidate for gov. N.J., 1957; N.J. del.-at-large Rep. Nat. Conv., 1960. Served as staff sgt. 334th Inf., 84th Div., AUS, 1942-45. Decorated Bronze Star, Purple Heart, asso. officer Order St. John; named Young Man of Year, N.J. Jr. C. of C., 1951; hon. Paramount Chief, Nimba Tribe (Liberia); recipient Harmon Trophy, 1975; Eaton Corp. award Internat. Platform Assn., 1979; award Men's Fashion Assn. Am., 1979; award Columbia U. Bus. Sch., 1980; Man of Conscience award Appeal of Conscience Found., 1980; Franklin award Printing Industries Met. N.Y., 1981; decorated Order of Merit (France). Mem. St. Andrew's Soc., 84th Inf. Div. Assn., Navy League, Assn. U.S. Army, Nat. Aeros. Assn. (dir.), Balloon Fedn. Am., N.J. Hist. Soc., Internat. Balloonists Assn., Aircraft Owners and Pilots Assn., Lighter Than Air Soc., Brit. Balloon and Airship Club, Internat. Soc. Balloonpost Specialists, Am. Motorcycle Assn., Pilgrims of U.S., Confrerie des Chevaliers du Tastevin. Episcopalian (vestryman). Clubs: Princeton; Essex Fox Hounds, N.Y. Racquet and Tennis, N.Y. Yacht; Links; Explorers; Staniel Cay. Author: Fact and Comment, 1974; The Sayings of Chairman Malcolm, 1978. Home: Timberfield Old Dutch Rd Far Hills NJ 07931 Office: 60 Fifth Ave New York NY 10011

FORBES, WALLACE FEDERATE, fin. cons. firm exec.; b. N.Y.C., May 16, 1928; s. B.C. and Adelaide S. (Stevenson) F.; B.S.E., Princeton U., 1949; M.B.A., Harvard U., 1956; m. Betty Alden Goldsmith, June 11, 1955; children—Alden Stevenson, Alexandra Elizabeth, Bruce Cameron. Research asso., mem. faculty Harvard Bus. Sch., 1956-57; asst. v.p. Baystate Corp., Boston, 1957-64; v.p. Forbes, Inc., 1964-69; pres. Forbes Investors Adv. Inst., Inc., N.Y.C., 1964-69; pres. Wallace Forbes & Partners, N.Y.C., 1969-73, Standard Research Cons., N.Y.C., 1973—; dir. Internat. Instl. Services, Inc. Trustee Anatolia Coll., Greece; mem. adv. bd. Mus. of Am. China Trade. Served to lt. USN, 1949-54. Mem. Bankers Security Life Ins. Soc. (dir.), Near East Coll. Assn. (dir.), Inst. Chartered Fin. Analysts, N.Y. Soc. Security Analysts, Assn. Mgmt. Consultants (trustee), Fin. Analysts Fedn., Assn. Corp. Growth, Newcomen Soc. in N. Am. Presbyterian. Clubs: Sleepy Hollow Country, Princeton (N.Y.C.). Contbr. articles to profl. jours. Office: 26 Broadway New York NY 10004

FORD, ERNEST EDWARD, SR., mortgage broker, ret. savs. and loan assn. exec.; b. Kinston, N.C., May 20, 1913; s. Seth Davis and Eula (Norris) F.; student N.C. State U., Sch. Savs. & Loan U. Ind., Bloomington, 1955; m. Mary Bailey Tice, May 10, 1941; children—Ernest Edward, James Tice. Salesman, Dixie Realty Co., Greensboro, N.C., 1937-41; engr. Fairchild Aircraft, Burlington, N.C., 1941-45; dist. salesman Shell Oil Co., Greensboro, 1945; v.p. Home Fed. Savs. & Loan Assn., Greensboro, 1945-66; pres. Peoples Savs. Loan Assn., Whiteville, N.C., 1966-80; owner Ernie Ford Assos., Lake Waccamaw, N.C., 1980—. Mem. exec. com. Boy Scouts Am., dir. Cape Fear council, Silver Beaver award, 1970; bd. dirs., mem. exec. com. Housing Fin. Agy. N.C. Mem. Am. Savs. Loan Inst. (dep. gov., nat. trustee), N.C. Savs. Loan League (dir.), Savs. Loan Found. (state membership chmn.), Greensboro (dir.), Whiteville (dir.) chambers commerce, Whiteville Civitan Club (gov. N.C. dist. 1970, Civitan of Yr. 1958). Democrat. Methodist (past trustee). Clubs: Whiteville Country and Golf (N.C.); Surf and Golf (N. Myrtle Beach, S.C.); Masons. Home: Lake Shore Dr Lake Waccamaw NC 28450 Office: Ernie Ford Assos Lake Shore Dr Lake Waccamaw NC 28450

FORD, FRANCES RADELL BYRD, savs. and loan exec.; b. North Wilkesboro, N.C., July 1, 1930; d. Harvey Clifton and Verna (Hall) Byrd; diploma Am. Savs. and Loan Inst., 1964, postgrad., 1966—; student Grad. Sch. Bus., Ind. U., 1968; m. Albert P. Ford, Nov. 1, 1947 (div. July 1962); children—Karen Frances Ford Brown, Teresa Catherine. With First Fed. Savs. & Loan Assn., New Smyrna Beach, Fla., 1958—, controller, 1958-63, sec.-treas., 1963-68, exec. v.p., 1968-70, pres., 1970—, chmn. bd., 1972—, dir., 1965—; instr. Daytona Beach chpt. Am. Savs. & Loan Inst., 1960-62, New Smyrna Beach Study Club, 1962—. Bd. dirs. North Coastal div. Childrens Home Soc. Fla., 1969—, mem. state legislative com., 1972—. Mem. Am. Savs. and Loan Inst. (past v.p.), Nat. Soc. Savs. and Loan Controllers. Club: Pilot (pres. 1968). Home: 101 Cunningham Dr New Smyrna Beach FL 32069 Office: 900 N Dixie Freeway New Smyrna Beach FL 32069

FORD, GORDON BUELL, acct., real estate exec.; b. Greenville, Ky., Sept. 27, 1913; s. J(ohn) Otho and Martha Jane (Newman) F.; B.S., Western Ky. U., Bowling Green, 1934; m. Rubye Ann Allen, Sept. 1, 1935; children—Gordon Buell, Gayle Ford Greene; m. 2d, Glenda Lou Cox, Oct. 10, 1974; 1 son, Gregory Newman. Sr. partner Yeager, Ford & Warren, C.P.A.'s, Louisville, 1934-60, mng. partner, 1960-70; mng. partner Coopers & Lybrand, C.P.A.'s, Louisville, Lexington and Owensboro, Ky., 1970-78, ret. mng. partner, 1978—; pres., chief exec. officer Southeastern Investment Trust, Inc., Louisville, 1960—; v.p. Vogue Furniture, Inc., Louisville, 1947-51, Sta. WSUA, Inc., Bloomington, Ind., 1948-50. Pres., chief exec. officer Gorjim Found., Inc., Louisville, 1960—; bd. dirs. Louisville Central Area, Inc., 1973—; trustee, mayor City of Mockingbird Valley (Ky.), 1949-73; trustee, treas. Ky. So. Coll., Louisville, 1963-71; trustee So. Bapt. Theol. Sem., Louisville, 1963-71, Yeager, Ford & Warren Found., Louisville, 1949-70. C.P.A., Ky., Tenn., Ind. Mem. Am. Inst. C.P.A.'s (council 1965-71, v.p. 1972-73), Ky. Soc. C.P.A.'s (pres. 1948-49). Presbyterian. Clubs: Louisville Country, Pendennis (Louisville); Harmony Landing Country (Goshen, Ky.); Delray Dunes Country (Delray Beach, Fla.); Rotary. Author: (with L. C. J. Yeager) The History of the Professional Practice of Accounting in Kentucky: 1875-1965, 1967. Home: 5915 Brittany Valley Rd Louisville KY 40222 also 107 MacFarlane Dr Delray Beach FL 33444 Office: 3600 First National Tower Louisville KY 40202

FORD, GORDON BUELL, JR., educator, author, fin. mgmt. specialist; b. Louisville, Sept. 22, 1937; s. Gordon Buell and Rubye (Allen) F.; A.B., Princeton U., 1959; M.A., Harvard U., 1962, Ph.D., 1965; postgrad. U. Olso (Norway), 1963-64, U. Sofia (Bulgaria), 1963, U. Uppsala, 1963-64, U. Stockholm, 1963-64, U. Madrid, 1963. Asst. prof. Indo-European and Baltic linguistics Northwestern U., 1965-72; prof. English, linguistics and teaching English as fgn. lang. U. No. Iowa, Cedar Falls, 1972-76; prof. linguistics Southeastern Research and Devel. Corp., Louisville, 1972—; fin. mgmt. specialist Humana, Inc., The Hosp. Co., Louisville, 1978—; vis. asst. prof. medieval Latin, U. Chgo., 1966-67, lectr. linguistics Chgo. Extension, 1966-67, 70-72; asst. prof. anthropology Northwestern U. evening divs., 1971-72. Mem. Linguistic Soc. Am., Internat. Linguistic Assn., Modern Lang. Assn. Am., Am. Philol. Assn., Am. Assn. Tchrs. Slavic and East European Langs., Mediaeval Acad. Am., Societas Linguistica Europaea, Assn. for Advancement Baltic Studies, Inst. Lithuanian Studies, S.A.R., Phi Beta Kappa. Baptist. Clubs: Harvard (Chgo.); Louisville Country; Princeton (N.Y.C.). Author: The Ruodlieb: The First Medieval Epic of Chivalry from Eleventh-Century Germany, 1965; The Ruodlieb: Linguistic Introduction, Latin Text, and Glossary, 1966; The Ruodlieb Facsimile Edition, 1967; Old Lithuanian Texts of the Sixteenth and Seventeenth Centuries with a Glossary, 1969; The Old Lithuanian Catechism of Baltramiejus Vilentas (1579): A Phonological Morphological, and Syntactical Investigation, 1969; Isidore of Seville's History of the Goths, Vandals, and Suevi, 1970; The Letters of St. Isidore of Seville, 1970; The Old Lithuanian Catechism of Martynas Mazvydas (1547), 1971; Isidore of Seville: On Grammar, 1982; Readings in Comparative Linguistic Methodology, 1981; others. Translator: A Concise Elementary Grammar of the Sanskrit Language with Exercises, Reading Selections, and a Glossary (Jan Gonda), 1966; The Comparative Method in Historical Linguistics (Antoine Meillet), 1967; A Sanskrit Grammar (Manfred Mayrhofer), 1972; Introduction to the Comparative Study of the Indo-European Languages (A. Meillet), 1981. Home: 521 Zorn Ave Louisville KY 40206 Office: 3500 First National Tower Louisville KY 40202

FORD, HENRY, II, automobile co. exec.; b. Detroit, Sept. 4, 1917; s. Edsel and Eleanor (Clay) F.; grad. Hotchkiss Sch., 1936; student Yale, 1936-40; m. Anne McDonnell, July 13, 1940 (div.); children—Charlotte, Anne, Edsel Bryant II; m. 2d, Maria Cristina Vettore Austin, Feb. 19, 1965 (div.). Dir., Ford Motor Co., 1938—, with co., 1940—, v.p., 1943, exec. v.p., 1944-45, pres., 1945, chmn., 1960-80, chief exec. officer, 1960-79, now chmn. fin. com. Mem. Bus. Council; co-chmn. Detroit Renaissance; trustee Ford Found., 1943-76; bd. govs. UN Assn. U.S.A. Office: Ford Motor Co The American Rd Dearborn MI 48121

FORD, JACOB MARION, II, bank exec.; b. St. Joseph, Mo., July 30, 1916; s. Frazer L. and Marjorie (George) F.; B.A. cum laude, Kenyon Coll., 1938; m. Hannah Bartlett, Apr. 5, 1941; children—Bartlett, John, Robert. Cashier, Farmers & Traders Bank, St. Joseph, 1938-41, also dir.; with First Nat. Bank, St. Joseph, 1946—, pres., 1954-72, chmn. bd., 1959—; dir. First Midwest Bancorp., Inc., First Trust Bank, First Stockyards Bank, Ross-Frazer Supply Co., Wire Rope Corp. Am., 1st AgCorp, Inc., St. Joseph. Trustee, Methodist Med. Center, St. Joseph, Midwest Research Inst., Kansas City, Mo., St. Joseph Grain Exchange, St. Joseph Museum, St. Joseph C. of C., St. Joseph Indsl. Found., Mt. Mora Cemetery Assn., St. Joseph. Served to capt. U.S. Army, 1942-46. Presbyterian. Clubs: Rotary, St. Joseph Country, Benton. Office: First Nat Bank 4th and Felix Sts Saint Joseph MO 64501

FORD, JAMES WILLIAM, fin. co. exec.; b. Alameda, Calif., Feb. 1, 1923; s. Shelton C. and Eunice (George) F.; A.B., Oberlin Coll., 1946; M.A. in Econs., Harvard U., 1949, PhD. in Econs., 1954; postgrad. (Fulbright scholar) 1949-51, (fellow) U. Chgo., 1958-59; m. Anne Farley, June 30, 1945; children—Julian, Amy, Carol Ford Pelham. Instr. econs. Columbia U., 1951-53; asst. prof. econs. Vanderbilt U., 1953-57; asso. prof. econs. Ohio State U., 1957-59; economist to bd. govs. FRS, 1959-61; various positions including dir. Econs. Office, asst. controller fin. staff Ford Motor Co., 1961-75, v.p., 1980—; exec. v.p. ins. and spl. fin. ops. Ford Motor Credit Co., Dearborn, Mich., 1975-77, pres., 1977-80, chmn., 1980—. Corp. mem. Detroit Osteo. Hosp. Corp., 1976-81; bd. dirs. Inner City Bus. Improvement Forum, 1979-81, Youth Living Centers, Inc., 1970-81. Served with USAAF, 1943-46. Mem. Nat. Consumer Fin. Assn. (dir.). Office: Ford Motor Credit Co The American Rd Dearborn MI 48121

FORD, JOHN CHARLES, broadcasting exec.; b. Washington, Oct. 8, 1942; s. Edgar Martin and Mary (Crowley) F.; B.A., U. Md., 1964, postgrad., 1964-65; M.A., N.Y. U., 1966; postgrad. N.Y. Inst. Finance, 1967-68, New Sch. for Social Research, 1969, Crowell-Collier Inst., 1969, Friesen-Kaye Inst., 1971, Sterling Inst., 1975, U. Wis., 1977, Colgate-Darden Sch. Bus., U. Va., 1978. TV prodn. asst. USIA, Washington, 1963-65; instr. U. Md., 1965; acct. exec. Ruder & Finn Inc., N.Y.C., 1965-66; asst. to exec. v.p., mgr. ednl. services Am. Stock Exchange, N.Y.C., 1966-70; mgr. communications and audio visual tng. Merrill Lynch, Pierce, Fenner & Smith Inc., N.Y.C., 1970-74; dir. edn. and tng. CBS Inc., 1974-77, dir. employee devel. and edn., 1977-79; pres. Travel U., v.p. Travel Network Corp. subs. ABC, N.Y.C., 1979—; mem. faculty N.Y. Inst. Fin., 1971-73, K. Gibbs Sch., 1972-74. Bd. dirs., treas. Archeus Found.; bd. dirs. Care, Inc., One-to-One; bd. overseers Emerson Coll., Boston, 1978—; mem. adv. com. dept. speech Manhattan Community Coll., CUNY; bd. dirs., v.p. 15 W 81st St. Tenants Corp., 1978-80, pres., 1979; mem. Council of West Side Coops., 20th Precinct Community Council, N.Y. Police Dept.; guest speaker Iowa Assn. for Life Long Learning. Mem. Nat. Acad. TV Arts and Scis. (bd. govs., trustee 1969—, sec. 1971—, trustee 1973—), Am. Soc. Tng. and Devel. (award 1978), Fin. Industry Tng. Assn. (pres. 1969—), AAUP, Speech Communications Assn., Eastern Communication Assn. (area chmn. 1975), N.Y. State Communication Assn. (speaker), West 70th St. Assn., Fedn. West Side Block Assns., W. 82d St. Block Assn., Internat. Radio & TV Soc., Nat. Soc. Programmed Instrn., Nat. Audio-Visual Assn., Wall Street Tng. Dirs.'s Assn., Presidents Assn. of Am. Mgmt. Assns. (seminar leader), U. Md. Alumni Assn. Greater N.Y. (dir. 1966—), N.Y. Personnel Mgrs. Assns., Internat. Platform Assn., Omicron Delta Kappa, Phi Delta Theta. Home: 15 W 81st St New York NY 10024

FORD, RICHARD FLYNN, banker; b. Bethlehem, Pa., June 29, 1936; s. John Simpson and Ruth Elizabeth (Pringle) F.; B.S. in Bus., Princeton U., 1959; postgrad. exec. program in bus. Grad. Sch. Bus., Columbia U., 1972; m. Katherine Ford. Mgr. instnl. and corp. devel. dept. Merrill Lynch, Pierce, Fenner & Smith, 1959-69; v.p. nat. accounts div. 1st Nat. Bank, St. Louis, 1969-72, sr. v.p., 1972-73, exec. v.p., 1973-76, pres., 1976—, chief operating officer, 1978—; dir. Valley Industries; adv. dir. Huttig Sash and Door. Chmn., Downtown, Inc., 1980—; trustee Webster Coll., Mary Inst. Sch., St. John's Mercy Hosp., Salvation Army, Emergency Children's Home. Served to 1st lt. USMC. Mem. Am. Bankers Assn. (chmn. comml. lending div.), St Louis Regional Commerce and Growth Assn. (dir.). Office: 510 Locust St Saint Louis MO 63101*

FORD, T. MITCHELL, corp. exec.; b. Albany, N.Y., Apr. 27, 1921; s. Clarence Edwin and Alice (Mitchell) F.; A.B., Harvard U., 1943; LL.B., Yale U., 1948; m. Mimi Parsons, Oct. 4, 1944; children—Kyle Ford Schutz, Mitchell P. Admitted to Conn. bar, 1948; with firm Becket & Wagner, Lakeville, Conn., 1948-52; asst. gen. counsel CIA, 1952-55; gen. counsel Naugatuck Valley Indsl. Council, Waterbury, Conn., 1955-58; with Emhart Corp., and predecessor Am. Hardware Corp., Hartford, Conn., 1958—, gen. counsel, 1960-64, v.p., 1964-67, pres., 1967—, chmn., 1976—, also dir.; dir. Hartford Nat. Corp., United Techs. Corp., Travelers Ins. Corp. Served with AUS, 1943-45; ETO. Office: 426 Colt Hwy Farmington CT 06032

FORD, WILLIAM F., banker, economist; b. Huntington, N.Y., Aug. 14, 1936; s. William and Margaret (Mueller) F.; B.A. summa cum laude, U. Tex., 1961; M.A. (Woodrow Wilson fellow), U. Mich., 1962; Ph.D. (NDEA fellow), 1966; m. Charlotte Diane McDonald, June 11, 1960; children—Eric, Kristin. Teaching asst. econs. U. Mich., Ann Arbor, 1962-63, instr., 1965-66; Ford fgn. area fellow, Mexico, 1964-65; economist Rand Corp., Santa Monica, Calif., 1966, cons., 1967-68, 70-71; asst. prof. econs. U. Va., Charlottesville, 1967-69; asso. prof. econs. Tex. Tech. U., Lubbock, 1969-70; prof. econs., dean Transylvania Coll., Lexington, Ky., 1970-71; exec. dir., chief economist research planning group, Am. Bankers Assn., Washington, 1971-75; sr. v.p., chief economist Wells Fargo Bank, San Francisco, 1975-80; pres. Fed. Res. Bank, Atlanta, 1980—; lectr. Harold Stonier Grad. Sch. Banking. Mem. steering com. San Francisco Bay Area Council, 1976—. Co-recipient Fred M. Taylor prize in economic theory U. Mich., 1963. Mem. Am. Econs. Assn., Phi Beta Kappa. Author: Mexico's Foreign Trade and Economic Development, 1968; contbr. articles and book revs. to profl. jours. Office: PO Box 1731 Atlanta GA 30301

FORD, WILLIAM FRANCIS, fin. corp. exec.; b. Albany, N.Y., Mar. 11, 1925; s. Patrick and Ellen F.; B.S. in Acctg., St. Michael's Coll., Vt., 1950; m. Marcia J. Whalen, Jan. 7, 1956; children—William, Michael, Timothy, Daniel, Cathleen. Vice-pres., Equitable Credit

Corp., Albany, 1950-60, Am. Fin. System, Inc., Silver Spring, Md., 1960-65, Gen. Electric Credit Corp., Stamford, Conn., 1965-74; chmn. bd., pres., chief exec. officer Security Pacific Fin. Corp., San Diego, 1974—. Served in USN, 1943-46. Mem. Nat. Consumer Fin. Assn. (dir., exec. com.). Club: Stoneridge Country. Home: 13103 Edina Way Poway CA 92064 Office: 10103 Carroll Canyon Rd San Diego CA 92131

FORDE, DOUGLAS HENDERSON, acctg. co. exec.; b. Barbados, W. Indies, Nov. 10, 1941; s. St. Clair Alonzo and Vera Montea (Rollock) F.; came to U.S., 1964, naturalized, 1976. A.A., Coll. of Virgin Islands, 1966; B.S., U. Ill., 1968; M.B.A., Bernard Baruch Coll., 1972; m. Marva Griffith, Sept. 12, 1968; children—Leslie Maria, April Lynette. Sr. accountant, tax specialist Peat, Marwick, Mitchell & Co., N.Y.C., 1968-71; asst. to v.p., corp. controller McGraw-Hill, Inc., N.Y.C., 1971-72; mgr. fin. and accounting policy Xerox Corp., Rochester, N.Y., 1972-76, mgr. capital and investment analysis, 1976—; pres. Executex, Inc., Mgmt. Cons., 1977—, D.H. Forde & Co., C.P.A., P.C., Pittsford, N.Y.; vis. prof. Black Exec. Exchange program City U. N.Y. Bd. dirs. Baden St. Settlement, Rochester, Episcopal Diocese of Rochester, United Community Chest Greater Rochester. Mem. Am. Inst. C.P.A.'s, N.Y. State Soc. C.P.A.'s, Fin. Exec. Inst., Nat. Assn. Accountants, Am. Mgmt. Assn., Fin. Mgmt. Assn. Contbr. articles in field to profl. jours. Home: 408 Garnsey Rd Fairport NY 14450 Office: 656 Kreag Rd Pittsford NY 14534

FORDER, WILLIAM ROBERT, contracting co. exec.; b. Grand Rapids, Minn., Apr. 20, 1935; s. Milton Henry and Ethel Martha (Hanson) F.; student Ely Jr. Coll., 1953-56, U. N.D., 1955-56; B.M.A. in Mech. Engring., U. Minn., 1959; m. Barbara Nan Beise, July 9, 1960; children—Robert Grant, Nancee Ann. Job capt. Ellerbe Architects & Engrs., St. Paul, 1959-66; founder, pres. Faircon, Inc., St. Paul, 1966—. Mem. ASHRAE, Nat. Soc. Profl. Engrs., Minn. Soc. Profl. Engrs., Sheet Metal, Air Conditioning and Roofing Contractors Assn. Minn. (pres. 1972). Republican. Presbyterian. Home: 5936 Halifax Pl N Minneapolis MN 55429 Office: 80 2d Ave SE Saint Paul MN 55112

FORDYCE, DONALD MICHAEL, ins. co. exec.; b. N.Y.C., Apr. 26, 1936; s. James Paul and Margaret (Monahan) F.; B.A. in Econs., U. Notre Dame, 1958; m. Ann Glascock, June 9, 1956; children—James H., Elizabeth A., Michael D. With U.S. Life Ins. Co., 1956-58; rep. Kidder Peabody & Co., 1958-60; with Manhattan Life Ins. Co., N.Y.C., 1960—, v.p. agy. adminstrn., 1969-72, exec. v.p., dir., 1972-73, pres., from 1973, chmn., chief exec. officer, 1978—; dir. Chem. Bank, No. Nat. Life Ins. Co. Trustee exploring div. Greater N.Y. council Boy Scouts Am. Mem. Am. Soc. C.L.U.'s (regional v.p.), Young Pres.' Orgn., Life Ins. Council N.Y. (past pres.), N.Y. Area Tng. Dirs. Assn. (past pres.), Bd. Trade of Greater N.Y. (past pres.). Republican. Roman Catholic. Clubs: Wee Burn Country (Darien, Conn.); University, Sky (N.Y.C.). Office: 111 W 57th St New York NY 10019

FORELL, HARLAND ELLIS, state ofcl.; b. Sterling, Colo., Aug. 25, 1926; s. Mary Edith F.; student Long Beach State U., 1960-63; m. Lois Vandelia Ashe, Oct. 15, 1964; children—Mary Lynn, Bruce Wayne, Dwight David. Sect. supr. Dept. Employment, State of Calif., Los Angeles, 1964-68, program mgr. Dept. Human Resources, Los Angeles, 1968-76, cost analyst Dept. Employment Devel., 1976-78, project mgr. cost analysis sect. Dept. Employment, Sacramento, 1978-80, mgr. field office Dept. Employment Devel., 1980—. Served with USN, 1943-63. Decorated Navy Commendation Medal with Combat V, 3 Purple Hearts. Mem. Internat. Assn. Personnel in Employment Security, Fleet Res. Assn. Clubs: Kiwanis, Masons, Shriners. Office: 510 N Main St Yreka CA 96097

FOREST, JOSEPH GERARD, food bus. exec.; b. Joliette, Que., Can., Oct. 3, 1914; s. Joseph Edward and Marie Diana (Croteau) F.; student Dale Carnegie Sch., 1946, Laval U., 1947-48; came to U.S., 1949, naturalized, 1955; m. Marie Anita Babin, Sept. 5, 1938; children—Jacques, Andre, Monique, Robert, Charles. Owner, Forest & Feeres, elec. appliances, Joliette, 1935-40; machinist war plant, Montreal, Que., 1940-44; salesman, asst. sales mgr. Internat. Stock Food Co., Ltd., Toronto, 1944-49; founder Internat. Stock Food Corp., Waverly, N.Y., 1949—, pres., 1949—, chmn. bd., 1960—, treas., 1970—; dir. Internat. Stock Food Co., Ltd., Valley Econ. Devel. Assn. Mem. Am. Inst. Mgmt., Am. Mgmt. Assn. Roman Catholic. Clubs: K.C., Elks. Inventor in field. Home: 303 Chemung St Waverly NY 14892 Office: 533 Broad St Waverly NY 14892

FORET, PIERRE G., engr., mgmt. cons.; b. Bauge, France, Dec. 18, 1922; s. Pierre E and Marie (Fayer) F.; came to U.S., 1947, naturalized, 1949; equivalent to B.S. in Mech. Engring., French Navy Tech. Sch., 1940; m. Jeanne Camoreyt, June 10, 1948; children—Pierre A., Michel L., Janine T. With Raytheon, Datamatic-Honeywell, 1954-60; mgr. engring. Sylvania Corp., Needham, Mass., 1959-61; chief engr. Midwestern Instruments, Tulsa, Natick, Mass., 1961-62, gen. mgr., 1962-64; engring., mgmt. cons. P.G. Foret Inc., Sudbury, Mass., 1964-65; pres., 1965-72; pres. Foret Systems, Inc., Falmouth, Mass., 1972—; Served with French Navy, 1940-45. Decorated Croix de Guerre, 1940. 5 internat. patents. Home: 111 Lucerne Ave Falmouth MA 02540 Office: 163-65 Worcester Park Ave Falmouth MA 02540

FORGETT, VALMORE JOSEPH, JR., arms co. exec.; b. Worcester, Mass., July 31, 1930; s. Valmore Joseph and Veron Rita (Sawicki) F.; B.S., Clemson U., 1956; m. Heidi Erika Kober, Apr. 28, 1963; children—Diana Lynn, Susan Lee, Valmore Joseph. Pres., Service Armament Co., 1957—, Navy Arms Co., Inc., 1958—, Great Am. Arms Corp., 1960—, Collectors' Arms, Inc., 1964— (all Ridgefield, N.J.); mng. dir. Ebbs/Forgett Trading Co. Ltd., Birmingham, Eng., 1969—; pres. Service Welding Co., Union City, N.J., 1970—, Classic Arms Ltd., Palmer, Mass.; cons. Ordnance Corp. Mus., Aberdeen, Md., 1958—, U.S. Arty. Sch. Mus., Ft. Sill, Okla., 1960—; spl. adviser U.S. Marine Corps Mus., 1958—, U.S. Mil. Acad., 1961—; chmn. U.S. Internat. Muzzle Loading Com. Served with AUS, 1953-55. Decorated Order of Merit (Italy). Fellow Co. of Mil. Collectors and Historians; mem. Carolina Gun Collectors Assn. (dir. 1961-62, 74—), Assn. Importers/Mfrs. Muzzle Loading (pres.), World Fedn. for Internat. Muzzle Loading Rifle Assns. (pres. 1979-80), Soc. Gun Collectors (hon. mem. Birmingham, Eng.), South African Rifle Assn. Republican. Club: Rotary (treas. Ridgefield 1961-62, pres. 1979-80). Author: (with others) Handbook of Small Arms, 1954. Home: Eagle's Roost 60 Pinecrest Dr Woodcliff Lake NJ 07680 Office: Cannon Hill Farm Box 311B Sussex NJ 07461 also 689 Bergen Blvd Ridgefield NJ 07657

FORIEST, JOSEPH LENARD, city govt. ofcl.; b. New Orleans, Dec. 10, 1946; s. J.L. and Nat Lee Foriest; B.A. in World History and Philosophy, Chgo. State U., 1971; postgrad. philosophy (grad. asst.), Oxford (Eng.) U., 1977; m. JoAnn Monier. Program adv., off campus contact agt. Chgo. City Colls., 1968-70, fin. aid coordinator, dir. fed. work study program, 1975-76; counselor Chgo. State U., 1970-71; loan officer Talman Fed. Savs. & Loan Assn., Chgo., 1972-74; accounts mgr. Alpha Marvis Enterprises, Chgo. and Atlanta, 1976-77; fin. processing officer Chgo. Dept. Planning, 1977-79, Chgo. Dept. Housing, 1980—; lectr. Chgo. State U., 1977—. Mem. Am. Theosophical Soc., Nat. Assn. Home Rehab. Officers, Afro-Am. History Club, Newberry Library. Democrat. Home: Chicago IL Office: 320 N Clark St Chicago IL 60610

FORLENZA, ANGELO CARMINE, computer co. exec.; b. Yonkers, N.Y., Jan. 5, 1937; s. Francesco and Margaret F.; A.B. magna cum laude in Econs., Hunter Coll., 1960; m. Joan Marion Smith, Aug. 10, 1958; children—Gregory, Suzanne. With IBM Corp., 1960—, dist. systems engr. mgr. N.Y. met. area, 1965-71, bus. and requirements mgr. Poughkeepsie (N.Y.) devel. labs., 1971-72, bus. and requirements mgr. Palo Alto (Calif.) devel. lab., 1973-76, ops. mgr. Menlo Park (Calif.) devel. lab., 1976—. Mem. Phi Beta Kappa, Kappa Delta Pi.

FORMAN, HOWARD IRVING, lawyer, govt. ofcl.; b. Phila., Jan. 12, 1917; s. Jacob and Dora (Moses) F.; B.S. in Chemistry, St. Joseph's Coll., 1937; LL.B., Temple U., 1944; M.A., U. Pa., 1949, Ph.D., 1955; m. Ada Pressman, Aug. 2, 1938; children—Kenneth J., Harvey R. Research chemist Frankford Arsenal, Dept. Army, Phila., 1940-44, patent atty., 1944-46, chief patents br., 1946-56; asst. dir. Pitman-Dunn Research Labs., 1955-56; admitted to D.C. bar, 1945, Pa. bar, 1973; patent atty. Rohm and Haas Co., Phila., 1956-66, trademark and internat. corp. counsel, 1966-76; dep. asst. sec. U.S. Dept. Commerce, 1976—, also dir. Office of Product Standards; counsel Weiser, Stapler & Spivak, Phila., 1974-76; sec., dir. Rohm & Haas Asia, Inc., 1973-76; v.p., gen. counsel, dir. U.S. Pharm. Corp., Bala-Cynwyd, Pa., 1970—, Brilliant Internat., Inc., Bala-Cynwyd, 1974—; sec., dir. Far East Chem. Services, Inc., Wilmington, Del., 1973-76, Rohm and Haas GmbH, Zug, Switzerland, 1975-76. Bd. dirs. Lower Moreland Twp. Sch. Bd., Montgomery County, Pa., 1969-75; bd. dirs. Eastern Montgomery County Vocational-Tech. Sch., 1969-75, sec., 1970-75; bd. dirs. Am. Nat. Standards Inst., 1977-79. Fellow Am. Inst. Chemists, ASTM (hon.); mem. Am., Fed., Phila. (sec. com. on jurimetrics, tech. and patents 1973-74, v.p. 1975) bar assns., Am. (bd. mgrs. 1970-73), Phila. (pres. 1964-66) patent law assns., Nat. Council Patent Law Assn. (chmn. 1967-68), Am. Chem. Soc., Sci. Research Soc. Am., AAAS, Nat. Lawyers Club, Licensing Execs. Soc., Association Internationale pour la Protection de la Propriete Industrielle, Sigma Xi. Author: Inventions, Patents and Related Matters, 1957; Patents-Their Ownership and Adminstration by the U.S. Government, 1957. Editor: Patents, Research and Management, 1961; The Law of Chemical, Metallurgical and Pharmaceutical Patents, 1967. Contbr. to publs. in field. Home: 1033 Corn Crib Dr Huntingdon Valley PA 19006 Office: Dept Commerce 14th and Constitution Aves Washington DC 20230

FORMAN, SANFORD, air transp. co. exec.; b. N.Y.C., Sept. 22, 1932; s. Louis and Rose (Fenster) F.; student Acad. Traffic and Transp., N.Y.C., 1957-58; B.S., Fairleigh Dickinson U., 1962; m. Marilyn Resnick, Aug. 29, 1954; children—Suzanne Myrna, Jody Lynn. Mgr. traffic ops. W.T. Grant Co., N.Y.C., 1958-69; gen. traffic mgr. Mattel, Inc., Hawthorne, Calif., 1970-79; v.p. Air Cargo Internat. and charter div. A. Cesana & Assos., Torrance, Calif., 1979—; tchr. air cargo Los Angeles Unifed Sch. Dist., 1978—. Mem. task force on deregulation U.S. Senate, 1975-79. Served with USAF, 1952-56. Cert. practioner FMC. Mem. Am. Soc. Traffic and Transp., Western Traffic Conf., Jewish War Vets. Contbr. articles on transp. to mags. and tech. jours. Home: 496 Palos Verdes Blvd Redondo Beach CA 90277 Office: 21535 Hawthorne Blvd Torrance CA 90503

FORMANEK, ROBERT JOSEPH, tire mfg. co. exec.; b. Schenectady, Dec. 25, 1922; s. Joseph Frank and Laura A. (Stock) F.; B.S. in Chem. Engring., Purdue U., 1944; m. Helen K. McKean, Nov. 30, 1946; children—Joanne, Judith. Engr., B.F. Goodrich Co., Akron, Ohio, 1944-54; mgr. textiles and testing Dunlop Tire & Rubber Corp., Buffalo, 1954-61, tech. mgr. tires, 1961-65, v.p.-tech., 1966—; dir. Am. Synthetic Rubber Corp., Louisville. Mem. Rubber Mfrs. Assn., Am. Mgmt. Assn., Buffalo C. of C. Home: 10 N Colvin Pl Buffalo NY 14223 Office: PO Box 1109 Buffalo NY 14240

FORNELLI, JOE PETE, civil engr.; b. Roseland, Kans., Dec. 8, 1915; s. Michele and Margherita (Marietta) F.; B.S. in Civil Engring., U. Kans., 1939; m. Mary Kathryn Watson, June 30, 1961; 1 son, Mike Amos. Insp., U.S. Engrs., St. Joseph, Mo., 1939-40; civil engr. Carter Oil Co., St. Elmo, Ill., 1939, 40; insp. Navy Dept., Parris Island, S.C., 1940-41; instrument man Consoer, Townsend & Quinlan, Parsons, Kans., 1941-42; party chief William S. Lozier, Inc., DeSoto, Kans., 1942-43; airways engr. C.A.A. 1943-45, 46-47; resident engr. Wilson Engrs., Salina, Kans., 1948; owner Fornelli Constrn. Co., Atwood, Kans., 1949-56; area supt. Girdler Co., Lawrence, Kans., 1953-54; civil engr. CAA, Kansas City, Mo., 1956-58, FAA, Kansas City, Mo. and DesPlaines, Ill., 1959-80. Served with AUS, 1945-46. Mem. Am. Soc. C.E., Am. Legion, Sigma Tau. Home: 16601 E 31st Independence MO 64055

FORREST, ALEXANDER TAYLOR, metals and natural resources co. exec.; b. Ferniegair, Scotland, Mar. 28, 1918; s. James and Hannah Canfield (Taylor) F.; came to U.S., 1927, naturalized, 1934; B.S. in Mech. Engring., Carnegie Inst. Tech., 1940, Mgmt. Engr., 1950; m. Olive Elizabeth Palmer, Oct. 30, 1948. Engr., U.S. Steel Corp., Homestead, Pa., 1940-46; engr. Crucible Steel Co. Am., Pitts., 1946-52, chief engr., 1952-61, gen. supt. engring. and maintenance, 1961-62, corporate chief engr., 1962-67, v.p. engring. Midland div., 1967-68; v.p. engring. Mueller Brass Co., Port Huron, Mich., 1968-74; v.p., asst. to pres. Phoenix Steel Corp., Claymont, Del., 1969-75; v.p. engring. UV Industries, Inc., N.Y.C., 1974-79; sr. v.p. mining ops. Sharon Steel Corp., 1979—; exec. v.p. U.S. Fuel Co., 1979—, Alaska Gold Co., 1979—. Served from 2d lt. to col. C.E., AUS, 1941-45; ETO. Decorated Silver Star, Bronze Star; Fourragere (Belgium). Registered profl. engr., Pa. Mem. Assn. Iron and Steel Engrs. (dir. 1967, chmn. Pitts. dist. and mech. and welding div. 1966), Am. (Kelly III award 1964), Brit. iron and steel insts., Engring. Soc. Western Pa., Pi Tau Sigma, Phi Kappa Phi. Mason (32 deg., Shriner). Clubs: Downtown (Pitts.); Black River (Port Huron); Landmark (Stamford, Conn.). Home: The Summit 241 N Vine St Apt 702W Salt Lake City UT 84103 Office: 19th Floor Univ Club Bldg 136 E South Temple Salt Lake City UT 84111

FORREST, EARL EUGENE, utility co. exec.; b. Horseheads, N.Y., Sept. 9, 1927; s. Earl and Elizabeth Jeanne F.; B.S. in Bus., Empire State Coll., 1974; student N.Y. State Maritime Coll., 1947, Rochester Inst. Tech., 1951; m. Margaret Sebring, Aug. 30, 1951; children—Mark Eugene, Brian Francis. With MooreMcCormick Lines, 1948-50; with N.Y. State Electric & Gas Corp., Binghamton, 1951—, now sr. v.p. adminstrn.; dir. regional bd. Bank of N.Y. Lic. profl. engr., N.Y. Club: Elks. Office: 4500 Vestal Pkwy E Binghamton NY 13902

FORREST, GEORGE JOSEPH, fin. exec.; b. Detroit, Nov. 15, 1928; s. Charles H. and Lillian (Reiss) F.; B.S., U. Detroit, 1955; A.M.P., Harvard Bus. Sch., 1975; m. Kathryn Jean Dilworth, Aug. 13, 1960; children—George Joseph, Ann, Michael. Acct., Ralph Genter & Co., C.P.A.'s, Detroit, 1955-60; partner Barnowski, Hart & Forrest, C.P.A.'s, Berkley, Mich., 1960-64; controller for seven corps. with common ownership, Detroit, now Guardian Industries, 1964-68; sr. v.p. Sandy Corp., Southfield, Mich., 1968—, dir., 1971—; dir. Bill Sandy Orgn. Ltd.; mng. partner Communications Center. Bd. dirs. Villa Marie, Sr. Citizen Living Complex, Livonia, 1976—; com. mem., counselor Boy Scouts Am., Detroit, 1975—. Served with U.S. Army, 1951-53. C.P.A., Mich. Mem. Mich. Assn. C.P.A.'s, Am. Inst. C.P.A.'s, Nat. Assn. Accts. Republican. Roman Catholic. Clubs: Detroit Athletic, K.C., Elks. Home: 15351 Susanna Circle Livonia MI 48154 Office: 16025 Northland Dr Southfield MI 48075

FORREST, HERBERT EMERSON, lawyer; b. N.Y.C., Sept. 20, 1923; s. Jacob K. and Rose (Fried) F.; B.A. with distinction, George Washington U., 1948, J.D. with highest honors, 1952; student Coll. City N.Y., 1941, Ohio U., 1943-44; m. Marilyn Lefsky, Jan. 12, 1952; children—Glenn Clifford, Andrew Matthew. Admitted to Va., D.C. bars, 1952, U.S. Supreme Ct. bar, 1955, Md. bar, 1959; law clk. to chief judge Bolitha J. Laws, U.S. Dist. Ct., Washington, 1952-55; practiced in Washington, 1952—; mem. firm Welch & Morgan, 1955-65, Steptoe & Johnson, 1965—; past chmn. D.C. Criminal Justice Act Adv. Bd.; past sec. com. on admissions and grievances U.S. Ct. Appeals D.C.; mem. edn. appeal bd. U.S. Dept. Edn. Past pres. Whittier Woods PTA. Served with AUS, 1943-46. Mem. George Washington Law Assn., Am. Judicature Soc., Am. (sec. adminstrv. law, liaison U.S. Regulatory Council, chmn. com. reports, chmn. com. on agy. rule making, past mem. council, mem. communications com., sec. public utility law sec. sci. and tech., internat. law, antitrust), Va. State, Fed., Fed. Commn. (del. to Am. Bar Assn. ho. of dels., mem. exec. com., past sec., past book editor Jour., chmn. legal aid com.) bar assns., Bar Assn. D.C. (past sec., chmn. com. on ct. appointments of counsel, lawyer referral service com., domestic relations com.), D.C. Unified Bar (past gov., chmn. employment discrimination referral service, chmn. task force on services to the pub., chmn. com. appointment of counsel in criminal cases), NAM (telecommunications com.), Washington Council Lawyers, Am. Arbitration Assn. (comml. panel), Legal Aid and Pub. Defender Assn., Computer Law Assn., Order of Coif, Phi Beta Kappa, Pi Gamma Mu, Artus, Phi Eta Sigma, Phi Delta Phi. Democrat. Mem. B'nai B'rith (charter mem. Bethesda-Chevy Chase), Internat. Club. Past mem. bd. advisers Duke Law Jour.; contbr. articles to profl. jours. Home: 8706 Bellwood Rd Bethesda MD 20034 Office: 1250 Connecticut Ave Washington DC 20036

FORREST, RONALD JOSEPH, geologist; b. Bklyn., Jan. 15, 1943; s. Leroy Joseph and Eloise (Witter) F.; B.A., So. Ill. U., Carbondale, 1966, M.S., 1969. Teaching asst., dept. geology So. Ill. U., 1967-69; devel. and exploration geologist Texaco Inc., Houston, 1969-72; oil devel. geologist McCulloch Oil Corp., Los Angeles, 1973; geothermal devel. exploration geologist Phillips Petroleum Co., Del Mar, Calif., from 1973, now asso. geologist, Milford, Utah. Mem. Am. Assn. Petroleum Geologists, Geothermal Resources Council. Mormon. Home: 295 E 200 N Beaver UT 84713 Office: PO Box 858 Milford UT 84751

FORRESTER, JOYCE DUNCAN, floor covering co. exec.; b. Greenville, S.C., May 27, 1939; d. John Lee and Lillian Leeomey (Wilson) Duncan; student Greenville Tech. Coll., 1975; B.S. in Mktg., U. S.C., 1979; m. Harvey C. Forrester, Sept. 28, 1957; children—Harvey, Steven. Asst. programmer Steel Heddle Mfg. Co., Greenville, 1961-64; mktg. statistician Texize Chem. Co., Mauldin, S.C., 1964-68; exec. sec. Dan River Inc., Greenville, 1968-76, mgr. spl. products sales, 1976-79; ops. mgr. L.D. Brinkman/SE, Greenville, 1979—. Pres., sec. Basketball League, Greenville, 1970-75. Mem. Greenville Community Concert Assn. Democrat. Mem. Assembly of God Ch. Home: 404 Galphin Dr Greenville SC 29609 Office: Route 2 Greenville SC 29607

FORSBERG, EDWARD CARL ALBIN, SR., fin. co. exec.; b. Bklyn., Dec. 2, 1920; B.S., U.S. Mcht. Marine Acad., 1944; m. Byrne E. Johnson, July 13, 1946; children—Edward Carl Albin, Cassandra Gayle. With Gulf Fin. Co., Atlanta, 1958—, pres., chief exec. officer, 1969—; dir. Delta Life Ins. Co., DeltaFire & Casualty Co., 1st Fin. Life Ins. Co. Served to lt. USNR, 1944-46; PTO. Mem. Nat. Consumer Fin. Assn. (chmn. bd., exec. com., v.p., adminstrn. com.). Club: Cherokee Town and Country (Atlanta). Home: 521 Hollydale Ct NW Atlanta GA 30342 Office: 4362 Peachtree Rd NE Atlanta GA 30319

FORSBERG, GREGG ALVIN, mfg. co. exec.; b. Watertown, S.D., May 2, 1947; s. Fremont G. and Lila B. (Sarempa) F.; B.A., Black Hills State Coll., 1969; m. May 30, 1969; 2 children. Salesman, Watertown (S.D.) Monument Works, Inc., 1970-72, sales mgr. Iowa div., 1972-74, gen. mgr., Watertown, 1974-77, pres., treas., 1977—; pres., treas. Owatonna Granite Works, Inc., 1977—, Aberdeen Monument Co., Inc., 1977—; sec. Casper-Watertown Monument Co., Inc., 1977—; gen. partner Concrete Dakota & Brick, 1977—; mng. partner Forsberg Leasing Co., 1978—; dir. 1st Fed. Savs. & Loan Assn. Mem. N.W. Monument Builders (pres. 1977-78), Monument Builders N. Am. (trustee 1976-79). Methodist. Clubs: Izack Walton League, Safarie Internat., Ducks Ltd., Lions, Elks. Home: 446 S Lake St Watertown SD 57201 Office: PO Box 130 Watertown SD 57201

FORSLUND, ROBERT LEE, food mfg. co. exec.; b. Harcourt, Iowa, Apr. 9, 1938; s. Monrad William and Elsie Maye (Swanlund) F.; student Drake U., 1960; m. Mary Kay Wingert, June 2, 1962; children—Robert Lee, Kristen Kay. With George A. Hormel & Co., Austin, Minn., 1962—, mktg. mgr. internat. div., 1979—; dir. Vista Internat. Packaging, Stefanutti/Homel, Santo Domingo, Dominican Republic. Served with U.S. Army, 1960-62. Republican. Presbyterian. Club: Austin Country. Home: 101 22d St NW Austin MN 55912 Office: 501 16th Ave NE Austin MN 55912

FORSTER, ANDREW JACKSON, computer and systems exec.; b. Bloomfield, N.J., Feb. 9, 1931; s. Carle Arthur and Helen Andrea (Decker) F.; B.S. in Bus. Adminstrn., Rutgers U., 1952; m. Carol Anne Roworth, Aug. 30, 1952; children—Robert, Richard, Scott. Computer methods analyst Prudential Ins. Co., 1954-60; systems engring. mgr. Sperry UNIVAC, 1960-63; dir. systems and data processing Brunswick Corp., 1963-65; asso. cons. Booz, Allen & Hamilton, 1965-67; dir. corp. systems and data processing Ingersoll-Rand Co., Woodcliff Lake, N.J., 1968—; public speaker; adj. faculty Fairleigh Dickinson U., 1962-63. Served to 1st lt., USAF, 1952-54. Mem. Am. Mgmt. Assn., Soc. Mgmt. Info. Systems, Am. Prodn. and Inventory Control Soc., Data Processing Mgmt. Assn., Internat. Data Processing Assn., SAR. Republican. Presbyterian. Clubs: Circumnavigators, Rutgers of Monmouth County, Fair Haven Sailing Assn. Contbg. author to Management Handbook, 1981; contbr. articles to procs. publs. and profl. jours. Home: 25 Beechwood Pl Fair Haven NJ 07701 Office: Ingersoll Rand Co 200 Chestnut Ridge Rd Woodcliff Lake NJ 07675

FORSTER, WILLIAM HALL, telephone mfg. co. exec.; b. Belmar, N.J., July 11, 1922; s. Hans Walter and Edith (Hall) F.; A.B., Harvard U., 1943, grad. Advanced Mgmt. Program, 1959; m. Gail Daly, July 13, 1945; children—William Daly, John Marshall, Robert Walter, Susan Hall, Frances Gail. With Philco Corp., Phila., 1943-65, dir. research solid state electronics, 1955-59, dir. semiconductor mktg. and devel. Internat. div., 1959-61, dir. engring. and research Communications and Electronics div., 1962-65; staff asst. to pres. ITT Corp., N.Y.C., 1966—, v.p., 1973—, v.p., product group mgr.-telecommunications, 1976—; v.p., tech. dir. ITT Europe,

Brussels, Belgium, 1967-75; dir. Laboretoire Centrale de Telecommunications (France), Standard Telecommunications Labs. (U.K.). Mem. John Scott Award Com., Phila., 1961—; mem. com. on sci. and arts Franklin Inst., Phila., 1964-66; bd. corporators Med. Coll. Pa., 1956-72. Fellow IEEE (chmn. Internat. Communications Conf. 1966), Phys. Soc. (U.K.), Radio Club Am.; mem. Electronic Industries Assn. (com. chmn.), Joint Electron Tube Engring. Council (chmn. semi-conductors 1953-55), Am. C. of C. in Belgium (dir. 1976), Phi Beta Kappa, Sigma Xi. Unitarian. Patentee, author tech. papers in field of electronics. Home: Mason's Island Mystic CT 06355 Office: 320 Park Ave New York NY 10022

FORSYTH, DUANE "H", movie co. exec.; b. Magrath, Alta., Can., June 3, 1922; s. Neil Snow and Chloe Roseltha (Hatch) F.; sr.dipl. edn., U. Alta., 1951; B.Sc., Brigham Young U., 1958; m. Verna Neilson, Apr. 3, 1945; children—Robert D., Mary Fassnidge, Cynthia Andelin, William James, Jerald Delbert. Tchr., Caroline, Alta., Brant, Alta., 1953, Edmonton, Alta., 1954, Nephi, Utah, 1956, Cardston area, Alta., 1956-63, Raymond, Alta., 1964-77; pres., chmn. bd. Chief Mt. Studios, Ltd., Raymond, 1968—; asso. Maxine Samuels Prodns. Ltd., Montreal, 1969—. Served to capt., Royal Canadian Air Force, 1941-45. Mem. Alta. Tchrs. Assn., Utah Edn. Assn., Nat. Tchrs. Assn. Canadian Conservative Party. Mem. Ch. of Jesus Christ of Latter-day Saints. Club: Rotary. Author: Great Men of the Mormon Church, 1981; co-author It's Alberta, 1980. Home: PO Box 6 Welling AB T0K 2N0 Canada Office: PO Box 581 Raymond AB T0K 2S0 Canada

FORT, OSMUN, printing co. exec.; b. Plainfield, N.J., Apr. 14, 1915; s. Leslie Runyon and Helen West (Osmun) F.; student Amherst Coll., 1933-35; m. Valentine Edgar, Nov. 3, 1945; children—David, Timothy, Andrew. Treas. Interstate Printing Corp., Plainfield, N.J., 1935-45, pres., 1945-77, chmn., 1977-80; v.p., dir. Equity Press, Plainfield, 1971-78; mem. adv. bd. Nat. State Bank of Elizabeth, 1966-70; bd. mgrs., Savs. Bank of Central Jersey, 1968-76. Bd. dirs. YMCA, 1952-61, v.p., 1956-60. Trustee Wardlaw Country Day Sch., 1959-71, sec., 1966-70; bd. govs. Muhlenberg Hosp., Plainfield, 1970-80, sec., 1978-79. Served to 1st lt. AUS, 1941-45. Recipient Garden Stater award N.J. C. of C. Execs., 1970; named Man of Year, Service Clubs, 1967. Mem. C. of C. (pres. 1969), Saybrook Power Squadron. Rotarian. Clubs: Plainfield Country (sec. 1959-62); North Cove (Conn.) Yacht; North Hatley (Que., Can.); Old Lyme Country. Home: 11 Cromwell Ct Old Saybrook CT 06475 Office: 400 Watchung Ave PO Box 1032 Plainfield NJ 07061

FORTH, KEVIN BERNARD, beverage distbr.; b. Adams, Mass., Dec. 4, 1949; s. Michael Charles and Catherine Cecilia (McAndrews) F.; B.A., Holy Cross Coll., 1971; M.B.A. (Benjamin Levy fellow), N.Y. U., 1973; m. Alice Jane Farnum, Sept. 14, 1974; children—Melissa Marie, Brian Paul. Div. rep. Anheuser-Busch, Inc., Boston, 1973-74, dist. sales mgr., Los Angeles, 1974-76, asst. to dir. mktg. staff, St. Louis, 1976-77; v.p. Straub Distbg. Co. Inc., Orange, Calif., 1977—, dir., 1977—. Mem. Rancho Santiago Community Coll. Dist. Adv. Bd.; bd. dirs. Santa Ana Youth Athelic Assn.; mem. Arms Found., Calif. State U. at Fullerton Athletic Found. Mem. Nat. Beer Wholesalers Assn., Calif Beer Wholesalers Assn. (dir., exec. com.), Assn. M.B.A. Execs., Holy Cross Alumni Assn., Nat. Council on Alcoholism, Beta Gamma Sigma. Roman Catholic. Home: 4333 Mahogany Circle Yorba Linda CA 92686 Office: 410 W Grove Ave Orange CA 92667

FORTHMANN, ANDREW KEATING, soap co. exec.; b. Los Angeles, Aug. 27, 1910; s. John A. and Elvira (Keating) F.; A.B., U. So. Calif., 1933, M.A., 1934; LL.B., 1939; m. Gertrude Ingli, Apr. 26, 1947; children—Andrea Marie, Andrew Keating, Christopher, DruAnne, Angele. Admitted to Calif. bar, 1946; with firm Dockweiler & Dockweiler, Los Angeles, 1946; with Los Angeles Soap Co., 1942—, chmn. bd., 1956—, also dir.; with White King Soap Co., Los Angeles, 1947—, pres., 1955—, also dir.; pres., dir. Calif. Rendering Co., 1947-62, chmn. bd., 1962-66; v.p., sec. Forthmann Estate Co., 1950-74, pres., 1974—. Served from 1st lt. to capt. USAAF, 1942-46. Mem. Am., Calif., Los Angeles bar assns., Soap and Detergent Assn. (v.p. Western div. 1954-58, 61-65, nat. pres. 1958-61), Grocery Mfrs. Am., So. Calif. Wine and Food Soc. Clubs: Los Angeles Country, California (Los Angeles), Chevaliers du Tastevin. Office: 617 E 1st St Los Angeles CA 90012

FORTIN, JEAN, mfg. co. exec.; b. Ancienne, Lorette, Que., Can., Dec. 4, 1943; s. Charles Edouard and Charlotte (Piche) F.; B.A., Seminaire de Rimouski, 1964; LL.L., U. Laval, 1969, M.B.A., 1976. Project dir. Univ. Laval, Faculty Law, 1970-72; called to Que. bar, 1970; asso. firm Brochet Fortin, barristers and solicitors, 1972—; chmn. Unibec, Inc., Que., 1976—, Unibec Equipments Inc., Drummondville, 1977—. Pres., Centre Marin des Blanchons, 1976-77. Mem. Canadian Bar Assn., Assn. Quebecoise des Transporteurs Aeriens, M.B.A. Assn. Que., Association des Gens de l'Air du Que. Club: Quebec Yacht. Office: 649 Grande Allee Est PQ G1R 2K4 Canada

FORTSON, JOHN, catering and real estate co. exec.; b. Phila., June 18, 1950; s. Mary B. Fortson; student Drexel U., 1969-76; B.B.A., Temple U., 1978, cert. Real Estate Inst., 1979. Inventory and price control clk. Drexel U., Phila., 1968-76; research asst. Temple U., Phila., 1976-78; with H. Lockings Corp., Phila., 1976—, mgr., 1978—; mgr., treas. Bus. Clinic, SBA, 1978—. Mem. Parkside Bus. Orgn., Parkside Community Assn. Baptist. Home: 2258 N 53d St Philadelphia PA 19131 Office: 4942 Parkside Ave Philadelphia PA 19131

FORTUNATO, SAMUEL FRANCIS, lawyer, ins. co. exec.; b. Bklyn., Dec. 2, 1929; s. Samuel X. and Margaret M. Fortunato; A.B., Columbia U., 1951, LL.B., 1954; m. Mary Ann O'Farrell, Dec. 26, 1953; children—Francis X., Michael A., Richard S., Mary AnnK. Admitted to N.Y. State bar, 1955; atty. Met. Life Ins. Co., 1956-66, asst. gen. counsel, 1966, asst. v.p. actuarial dept., 1966-68, v.p. variable annuities and corp. planning, 1968-71, v.p. co. property mgmt., 1971-73; v.p., then v.p., sec. Met. Property and Liability Ins. Co., Warwick, R.I., 1973-76, pres., 1976—, chief exec. officer, 1979—. Bd. dirs. R.I. Jr. Achievement mem. R.I. Public Expenditure Council, R.I. Air Study Task Force. Served with AUS, 1954-56. Mem. Greater Providence C. of C. (dir.), Alliance Am. Insurers (dir.), R.I. Commodores. Roman Catholic. Club: Monmouth Beach Bath and Tennis. Office: 700 Quaker Ln Warwick RI 02887

FORTUNOFF, ALAN MEYER, retail co. exec.; b. Bklyn., Sept. 19, 1932; s. Max and Clara (Wichner) F.; B.S., N.Y. U., 1953, LL.B., 1955, LL.M., 1974; m. Helen Finke, Nov. 25, 1953; children—Esther, Andrea, Rhonda, Louis, Ruth, David. Pres., Fortunoff Silver Sales, Inc., Westbury, N.Y., 1957—; admitted to N.Y. bar, 1956. Chmn., Nassau County Conv. and Visitors Bur.; trustee Friends Acad., Dowling Coll.; asso. trustee N. Shore Hosp.; bd. dirs. L.I. Action Com., Better Bus. Bur., Regional Plan Assn. Mem. L.I. Assn. Commerce and Industry (v.p., dir.), Victorian Soc. Am., Nat. Trust Historic Preservation, Am. Soc. Legal History, Italy-Am. C. of C., Am. Importers Assn., Fifth Ave Assn., Soc. Preservation L.I. Antiquities, Union of Am. Hebrew Congregations (long range planning com.), Beta Gamma Sigma. Jewish. Home: 7 Forte Dr Old Westbury NY 11568 Office: PO Box 132 Westbury NY 11590

FORZLEY, VICTOR GEORGE, mgmt. cons.; b. Worcester, Mass., July 16, 1918; s. Bashara Kalil and Almaza (Marina) F.; B.S., Mass. Inst. Tech., 1941, Poly. Inst. Bklyn., 1952, 57; M.B.A., N.Y. U., 1963; m. Lillian Margaret Mitchell, June 6, 1943; children—Charles Nicholas, Michele Diane, Lisa Janine. Sr. mech. engr., Am. Cyanamid Co., Stamford, Conn., 1949-55; sr. chem. engr. Ford, Bacon & Davis Inc., N.Y.C., 1955-67; pres., dir. Data Cons.; Inc., Riverside, Conn., 1967—; v.p., Stone & Webster Mgmt. Cons.'s, N.Y.C., 1971—; dir. UBAF Arab Am. Bank. Served with C.E., U.S. Army, 1943-45, Eastern Orthodox. Author books: Fourth Party Monitor for Construction Projects, 1967; Donation Economics, 1969. Patentee in field. Home: 185 Columbia Heights Brooklyn NY 11201 Office: Stone & Webster Mgmt Cons's 90 Broad St New York NY 10004

FOSS, HOWARD SAMUEL, JR., def. mfg. co. exec.; b. Pitts., May 30, 1938; s. Howard Samuel and Lois Eurilda (Mutimer) F.; B.B.A., Thiel Coll., 1960; postgrad. Cleve. State U., 1977—; m. Marie Elizabeth Muskey, Sept. 24, 1976; children—Daryl Edward, Bradley Howard; stepchildren—Paul Joseph Werner, Mary Ellen Werner Brougher, Jean Marie Werner, Jo Ann Werner, Patricia Ann Werner. Div. indsl. engr. Automatic Sprinkler div. ATO, Inc., Cleve., 1969-71; mfg. supt. Phil Mar div. Thomas Industries, Euclid, Ohio, 1971-74; asst. plant mgr. Cleve. Steel Container Corp., 1974-75; plant mgr. Air Tech. Industries, Mentor, Ohio, 1975-77; mgr. ops. support and cost estimating Gould, Inc., Ocean Systems Div., Cleve., 1977—; instr. bus. adminstrn. Lakeland Community Coll. External program dir. North Olmsted chpt. Ohio Jaycees, 1973-74; packmaster Boy Scouts Am., 1972-76. Mem. Soc. Logistics Engrs., Am. Mgmt. Assn., Alpha Chi Rho. Republican. Lutheran. Club: Edgewater Yacht (Cleve.). Home: 7296 Button Rd Mentor OH 44060 Office: 18901 Euclid Ave Cleveland OH 44117

FOSTER, CHARLES EDWARD, II, electronics co. ofcl.; b. Norfolk, Va., Apr. 5, 1944; s. Henry Herbert and Vivian Parker (Permon) F.; B.S., Clemson U., 1966; M.B.A., Harvard U., 1968; m. Alicia Stanley Turner, Apr. 16, 1977; 1 son, David Turner. Mgr. microwave equipment dept. SSE Div. Watkins-Johnson Co., Palo Alto, Calif., 1973-78; mgr. laser products mktg. IP div. Hughes Aircraft Co., Carlsbad, Calif., 1978—. Served to lt. U.S. Navy, 1968-72. Republican. Episcopalian. Home: 13070 Portofino Dr Del Mar CA 92014 Office: 6155 El Camino Real Carlsbad CA 92008

FOSTER, DAVID RAMSEY, soap co. exec.; b. London, Eng., May 24, 1920 (parents Am. citizens); s. Robert Bagley and Josephine (Ramsey) F.; student econs. Gonville and Caius Coll., Cambridge (Eng.) U., 1938; m. Anne Firth, Aug. 2, 1957; children—Sarah, Victoria. With Colgate-Palmolive Co. and affiliates, 1946-79, v.p., gen. mgr. Europe, Colgate-Palmolive Internat., 1961-65, v.p., gen. mgr. household products div. parent co., N.Y.C., 1965-68, exec. v.p., 1968-70, pres., 1970-75, chief exec. officer, 1971-79, chmn., 1975-79. Trustee, Woman's Sport Found.; mem. adv. bd. World Golf Hall of Fame; bd. govs. Desert Hosp. Served to lt. comdr. Royal Naval Vol. Res., 1940-46. Decorated Disting. Service Order, D.S.C. with bar, Mentioned in Despatches (2). Mem. Newcomen Soc. N.Am., Soc. Mayflower Descs. Clubs: Am. (London); Hawks (Cambridge U.); Royal Ancient Golf (St. Andrews, Scotland); Royal St. Georges Golf, Royal Cinque Ports Golf (life), Sunningdale Golf (U.K.); Sankaty Head Golf; Racquet and Tennis (N.Y.C.) (Palm Springs, Calif.); Baltusrol Golf, Mission Hills Country (bd. govs.). Home: 540 Desert West Dr Rancho Mirage CA 92270 also High Time Waluinet Nantucket MA 02554

FOSTER, FRED MARTIN, mfg. co. exec.; b. Berlin, Nov. 6, 1931; came to U.S., 1937, naturalized, 1944; s. Victor P. and Hanna Foster; B.S. in Mech. Engring., U. Ill., 1957; m. Faith A. Halmos, Dec. 20, 1952; children—Christine, Eric, Steven, Daniel, Julie. Project engr. Union Carbide Corp., Tonawanda, N.Y., 1951-65; project mgr. Trane Co., La Crosse, Wis., 1965-66; regional sales mgr. Airco Cryogenics, Irvine, Calif., 1966-72; gen. mgr. J.E. Watkins Co., Maywood, Ill., 1972-73, Schnacke-Grasso, Inc., Evansville, Ind., 1973—; pres. Grasso-Schnacke Internat., Evansville, 1976—; dir. Grasso-Stacon U.S.A. Served with USMC, 1951-54. Mem. ASME, ASHRAE, Air Conditioning and Refrigeration Inst., Evansville C. of C. (legis. com.). Office: 1101 N Governor St Evansville IN 47711

FOSTER, GERALD DOUGLAS, chem. co. exec.; b. Easton, Pa., June 24, 1939; s. Charles Cyril and Verna Marian (Nausbaum) F.; B.S., Davis and Elkins Coll., 1964; m. Patricia Clair Flynn, Sept. 9, 1961; children—Suzanne Marie, Douglas James. Design engr. Internat. Pipe & Ceramics Co., East Orange, N.J., 1964-65, prodn. constrn. supt., Clay, N.Y., 1965; process engr. Gen. Electric Corp., Liverpool, N.Y., 1965-68; structural engr. Sargent, Webster, Crenshaw & Folley, Syracuse, N.Y., 1968-76; constrn./project engr. Allied Chem. Corp., Solvay, N.Y., 1977—; editorial quality audit Plant Engring. mag., 1979—. Bd. dirs. Baldwinsville (N.Y.) Physicians Bldg., 1969-73. Methodist. Club: Elks (charter mem. Liverpool). Home: 6 Overbrook Ln Baldwinsville NY 13027 Office: Allied Chem Corp PO Box 6 Solvay NY 13209

FOSTER, JAMES HENRY, advt./public relations exec.; b. Kansas City, Mo., May 14, 1933; s. Wendell F. and Lillian M. (East) F.; B.A., Drake U., 1955, postgrad., 1957. Reporter, editor Des Moines (Iowa) Register, 1951-61; public relations and advt. exec. J. Walter Thompson Co., N.Y.C., 1961-73, v.p., 1970-73, sr. v.p., gen. mgr. corporate communications div., 1979—; v.p. public affairs Western Union Corp., Mahwah, N.J., 1973-79. Trustee, mem. exec. com. Inst. on Man and Sci., Rensselaerville, N.Y., 1968—. Mem. Nat. Investor Relations Inst. Presbyterian. Clubs: Econ. of N.Y., Union League, N.Y. Athletic. Office: 420 Lexington Ave New York NY 10017

FOSTER, JERALD W., porcelain co. exec.; b. Phila., Mar. 14, 1942; s. Waring V. and Margaret M. (Ferk) F.; B.A. cum laude, Glassboro (N.J.) State Coll., 1964; m. Colleen Costello, Aug. 22, 1964; children—Brigid, Amy, Dinah, Mark. Tchr. math., 1964-65; with Owens Corning Fiberglas Co., 1965-78, market mgr., Toledo, 1977-78; exec. v.p. mktg. Alliance Wall Corp., Atlanta, 1978—. Vice pres. sch. bd. St. Joseph Sch., Maumee, Ohio, 1976-78. Mem. Nat. Mineral Wool Insulation Assn. (chmn. tech. com.), Nat. Inst. Bldg. Sci. (cons. council), ASHRAE, ASTM, Mineral Insulation Mfrs. Assn. (hon.). Republican. Roman Catholic. Clubs: K.C. Home: 3715 Dunwoody Club Dr Dunwoody GA 30338 Office: PO Box 48545 Atlanta GA 30362

FOSTER, JOHN HALLETT, fin. exec.; b. Cleve., May 12, 1942; s. Hallett Phillips and Virginia (Callow) F.; B.A., Williams Coll., 1964; M.A., Ohio State U., 1965; M.B.A., Dartmouth Coll., 1967; m. Laura Laing Burbank, June 24, 1967; children—Laing Phillips, Virginia Burbank. Asst. v.p. Morgan Guaranty Trust Co., N.Y.C., 1967-72; pres. Foster Mgmt. Co., Stamford, Conn., 1972—; dir. Gen. Energy Corp., Battery Park Corp., SKY Broadcasting Corp., High Stoy Tech. Corp., The Aviation Group, Paul Hanson, Inc., Internat. Communications Scis., Inc.; chmn. Nat. Sml. Bus. Investment Co. Trustee, Pratt Inst.; chmn. adv. council to Sml. Bus. Adminstrn., 1978—. Mem. Nat. Assn. Small Bus. Investment Cos. (gov. 1978—). Episcopalian. Clubs: Links, Wadawanuck, Landmark. Home: 246 Pequot Trail Pawcatuck CT 06379 Office: 1010 Summer St Stamford CT 06905

FOSTER, LESTER ANDERSON, JR., steel co. exec.; b. Granite Quarry, N.C., Apr. 4, 1929; s. Lester Anderson and Annie Lee (Swink) F.; student Elon Coll., 1947-50; B.S., N.C. State U., 1952; m. Patricia White, July 9, 1955; children—Leslie Ann, Caroline Suzann, Lester Anderson, Samuel Timothy. With Bethlehem Steel Corp., Sparrows Point, Md., 1952—, engr., 1956-57, mech. foreman, 1957-59, asst. gen. foreman, 1959-61, asst. master mechanic, 1961-67, master mechanic, 1967—. Pres. PTA, Sparrows Point, 1963-65; mem. exec. bd. nominating com. Balt. County Sch. Bd., 1964-65; dist. field service chmn. Boy Scouts Am., Balt., 1972-78, bicentennial show program chmn., 1976; pres. 7th Dist. Republican Club, 1969-72. Served with U.S. Army, 1952-54. Recipient Silver Beaver award Boy Scouts Am., 1975. Mem. Am. Inst. Iron and Steel Engrs., Soc. Mfg. Engrs., Am. Mgmt. Assn., Soc. Advancement Mgmt., Nat. Football Found. and Hall of Fame. Republican. Lutheran. Clubs: Sparrows Point Country, Sparrows Point Engrs. Clubs: Masons, Shriners, K.T. Home: 3006 Dunmore Rd Dundalk MD 21222 Office: Bethlehem Steel Corp Steelmaking Mech Sparrows Point MD 21219

FOSTER, LOWELL WALTER, elec. co. exec.; b. Mpls., Oct. 22, 1919; s. Walter James and Ferne Constance (Edmunds) F.; grad. USCG Acad., 1944; student U. Minn., 1950, Mpls. Inst. Arts, 1953; m. Marion Jane Bjorklund, Feb. 5, 1944; children—Michael Lowell, Janette Marie, John Edward. With Honeywell, Inc., Mpls., 1946-77, successively tool designer, lead tool designer, asst. supr. tool design, lead standardization engr., sr. standardization engr., prin. standardization engr., project adminstr., sr. project adminstr., dir. corporate standardization services, dir. corp. standardization, 1974-77, dir. industry standards, 1977; pres. Tech. Concepts and Engring. Internat., 1977—; adviser drafting curriculum Mpls. Pub. Schs., 1973—; engring. cons.; tech. adviser Ferris State Coll., Big Rapids, Mich., 1970—. Active Viking council Boy Scouts Am., 1956-59, 73-77; v.p. John Ericsson Sch. P.T.A., 1971—. Bd. dirs. Am. Nat. Standards Inst. Served with USCG, 1941-46; PTO. Fellow Standards Engrs. Soc. (Leo B. Moore award 1973, Distinguished Service award Minn. sect. 1970); mem. Internat. Standards Orgn., Soc. Mfg. Engrs., Air Conditioning and Refrigeration Inst., Soc. for Advancement Mgmt., Honeywell Engrs. Club (past pres.), Am. Legion, Author 15 books, numerous articles. Home: 3120 E 45th St Minneapolis MN 55406 Office: Tech Concepts and Engring Internat Minneapolis MN 55406

FOSTER, MURRAY ALDEN, JR., state govt. ofcl.; b. Roanoke, Va., Oct. 16, 1931; s. Murray Alden and Katharine (Wentworth) F.; B.S. in Physics, Coll. William and Mary, Williamsburg, Va., 1953; m. Betty Hanson, Aug. 26, 1972; children—Allison, Amanda, Adrienne. Sales engr. Gen. Electric Co., Syracuse, N.Y., 1958, Motorola Co., Burlingame, Calif., 1960; account exec. Dean Witter & Co., San Mateo, Calif., 1964, Reynolds Securities Inc., Palo Alto, Calif., 1975, Bache & Co., Reno, 1978; dep. treas.-cashier State of Nev., Carson City, 1979—. Served with AUS, 1953-55. Mem. Fin. Planners Assn., Mensa, Omicron Delta Kappa. Republican. Methodist. Home: 4290 Garlan Ln Reno NV 89509 Office: State Capitol Bldg Carson City NV 89710

FOSTER, RAYMOND JOHN, investment banker; b. Rochester, N.Y., Apr. 23, 1941; s. John and Mary Foster; student St. John Fisher Coll., 1963-64, U. Buffalo, 1965-69; cert. fin. planner Coll. Fin. Planning, Denver, 1976; m. Patricia Catherine Reding, June 18, 1966; children—Victoria Ann, Gwendolyn Marie, Brian Charles. Registered rep. Bache & Co., Rochester, N.Y., 1970-73; v.p. Quinby & Co., Rochester, N.Y., 1973-78; sec. Foster Hickman & Zaenglein, Rochester, 1978—, also dir.; pres. Foster & Co. Equities Inc., Rochester, 1978—; dir. Rochester Shares Mgmt. Co.; mem. Boston Stock Exchange, 1980—. Bd. dirs., chmn. fin. com. Rochester Soc. for Prevention of Cruelty to Children. Served with USN, 1959-63. Registered investment adviser. Mem. Internat. Assn. Fin. Planners, Inst. Cert. Fin. Planners, Nat. Assn. Securities Dealers, Rochester Assn. Fin. Planners (past pres.). Republican. Roman Catholic. Club: Locust Hill Country (Pittsford, N.Y.); K.C. (Rochester); Rotary (Rochester). Home: 17 Crestview Dr Pittsford NY 14534 Office: 183 E Main St Rochester NY 14604

FOSTER, RICHARD JOHN, photographer; b. London, July 7, 1948; came to U.S., 1950, naturalized, 1980; s. Frederick Edward Richard and Patricia Marguerite Monica (Greenwood) F.; student Brown U., 1966-67, New Coll., 1967-69; m. Deborah Jean McMasters, Sept. 14, 1974. Disc jockey Sta. WBRU-AM-FM, Providence, 1966-67; with Sta. WYND, Sarasota, Fla., 1968; computer programming systems analyst Nat. Bus. Lists, Chgo., 1969-71; asst. photographer Alfa Studios, Chgo., 1971-73; asso. photographer Shigeta Wright, Chgo., 1973-74; head photographer Jack O'Grady Studios, Chgo., 1974-75; pres. Richard Foster Photography, Ltd., Chgo., 1975—. Active NW Community Orgn., 1972-75. Recipient numerous arts and advt. awards for photographs, art direction and creativity. Mem. Christian Ch. Home: 1479 Tower Rd Winnetka IL Office: 501 N Rush St Chicago IL 60611

FOSTER, STEPHEN KENT, banker; b. St. Louis, Dec. 14, 1936; s. John William and Josephine (Bushman) F.; B.B.A., U. Wis., 1959, M.B.A. (H.B. Earhart fellow), 1964; m. Rosanne Pleier, Sept. 13, 1958; children—John Andrew, Stephanie Mary. Asst. export mgr. Cargill Inc., Portland, Oreg., 1959-61; with First Nat. Bank Oreg., Portland, 1964—, sr. v.p., loan adminstr., 1973-75, sr. v.p.-br. and loan adminstrn., 1975-76, exec. v.p., 1976—; dir. 1st Nat. Bank of Oreg. Internat. Corp., Medford Corp. (Oreg.), Western Bancorp. Data Processing Co. Mem. audit com., capital commitments, bd. dirs. United Cerebral Palsy N.W. Oreg., 1967—; bd. dirs. Portland Opera Assn., 1970-74, United Good Neighbors, 1973-75, Oreg. Council Econ. Edn., 1970—; bd. regents U. Portland, 1976—, mem. exec. com., chmn. acad. affairs com., 1979—. Served with U.S. Army, 1958, 61-62. Recipient Leadership and Service award Oreg. Assn. Credit Men, 1973, Service to Legal Edn. award Oreg. Bar Assn., 1971, Ednl. Service award Nat. Assn. Accountants, 1974, Ednl. Service award Bank Adminstrn. Inst., 1971. Mem. C. of C., Oreg. Assn. Credit Mgmt., Am. Bankers Assn., Am. Fin. Assn., Robert Morris Assos., Nat. Assn. Accountants, Phi Beta Kappa, Phi Kappa Phi, Phi Eta Sigma, Beta Gamma Sigma. Clubs: Arlington, Waverley Country, Oswego Lake Country. Office: 1300 SW 5th Ave Portland OR 97201

FOSTER, WALTER HORTON, savs. and loan exec.; b. Bklyn., June 4, 1914; s. Louis Arthur and Clara (Gerrick) F.; student Heffley Bus. Sch., Bklyn., Am. Inst. Banking, N.Y.C., 1942, Alexander Hamilton Inst., 1950, Syracuse U., 1951; grad. Am. Savs. and Loan Inst., 1947; m. Ann J. Chianese, Jan. 19, 1936; children—Walter Horton, Claire A. (Mrs. Richard Mizerek), Arthur L. With comml. banking dept. Mfrs. Trust Co., N.Y.C., 1936-42; br. mgr. Century Fed. Savs. & Loan Assn., N.Y.C., 1942-49; exec. v.p. Glen Ridge Savs. & Loan Assn. (N.J.), 1949-56, pres., 1956-76, chmn. bd., 1977—, also dir. Mem. Vol. Fire Dept., Vol. 1st Aid Squad, Glen Ridge. Past pres. Republican Club Glen Ridge. Mem. Essex County Savs. and Loan League (past pres., dir.), N.J. Savs. League, U.S. Savs. League, Am. Savs. and Loan Inst., Soc. Residential Appraisers (sr.), Bd. Realtors Glen Ridge,

Bloomfield and Nutley, N.J. Patrolmen's Benevolent Assn. (hon.), Glen Ridge Bn. Forum. Rotarian (dir., past pres. Glen Ridge). Club: Glen Ridge Country. Home: 9 Winsor Pl Glen Ridge NJ 07028 Office: 227 Ridgewood Ave Glen Ridge NJ 07028

FOUFAS, PLATO CHRIS, lawyer, real estate developer; b. Chgo., Sept. 24, 1932; s. Chris and Urania F.; B.S., Northwestern U., 1954, J.D., 1960; m. Teddy Mouzakeotis, Sept. 10, 1965; children—Christopher, Timothy. Admitted to Ill. bar, 1960; owner, operator Plato Foufas & Co., Chgo., 1960—, Plato Foufas Investments, Inc., Chgo., 1975—, The Bayshore Co., Chgo., 1973—, also pres., chmn. bd.; developer 120 Madison Bldg., 1963, Plaza del Lago, Westerfield Sq., 1500 Sheridan Rd., 1625 Sheridan Rd., 1965-69. Trustee, treas. Roycemore Sch., Evanston, Ill. Served to lt. USAF, 1957-58. Mem. Chgo. Bar Assn., Chgo. Realty Bd., Beta Theta Pi, Delta Sigma Rho. Clubs: Tavern, Saddle and Cycle (Chgo.). Office: 1 E Wacker Dr Chicago IL 60601

FOULIARD, GEORGES GUILLAUME, mfg. co. exec.; b. Shanghai, China, Dec. 3, 1921; came to U.S., 1947, naturalized, 1951; s. Emile G. and Lucy M. (Guertz) F.; A.M.E., Lycee Mignee, France, 1938; grad. U. Breguet, 1939; postgrad. U. Wis., 1965-69, U. Ill., 1970; m. Lucie Harrison, Dec. 21, 1946; 2 children. Sales engr. Cummins Engine Co., Columbus, Ind. and N.Y.C., 1954-56; regional mgr. Latin Am., Eaton Corp., 1960-65; sales mgr. Europe and N. Africa, Allis Chalmers, 1965-69; v.p. mktg. Liebherr Am., Newport News, Va., 1970-73; dir. internat. ops. Blaw Knox Constrn., Mattoon, Ill., 1973-76; v.p. Valmet Indsl. Machinery & Products, Inc., Elmsford, N.Y., 1978—; cons., advisor to Strayer Co., Sulzer Bros., Capacity of Tex., others. Served with Free French Squadron, RAF, 1941-45. Mem. French War Vets. Assn., Soc. Automotive Engrs., Asso. Equipment Distbn. Assn., Constrn. Industry Assn., Nat. R.R. Intermodal Assn., Internat. Rd. Fedn., Internat. Execs. Assn. Chgo., Internat. Execs. Assn. Milw., Internat. Execs. Assn. N.Y., Internat. Cargo Handling and Coordination Assn. Roman Catholic. Clubs: Athletic, others. Contbr. articles to profl. jours. Home: 170 E Hartsdale Ave Hartsdale NY 10530 Office: 7 Westchester Plaza Elmsford NY 10523

FOURNIER, JAMES KAHRN, photo products mfg. and mktg. co. exec.; b. Chgo., Sept. 7, 1939; s. Leo and Helen Rosamond (Engelbach) F.; student Chafey Coll., 1971; m. Patricia Ann Maloney, Nov. 6, 1962; div.; children—James Patrick, Kristine Elizabeth. Mgr., White Front Stores, Calif., 1961-67, Schick Electric, Phoenix, 1967-69; asst. sales mgr. Kalt Corp., Santa Monica, Calif., 1969-74; pres. Fournier Ltd., Balboa, Calif., 1974—. Asst. scoutmaster, mem. council Boy Scouts Am., 1958-60. Served with USAF, 1957-61. Home: 600 E Ocean Front Balboa CA 92661 Office: PO Box 628 Balboa CA 92661

FOUST, CHARLOTTE FAE, bank exec.; b. Santa Maria, Calif., Sept. 13, 1944; d. Charles J. and Doris Ellen (Childers) Olsen; student U. Pacific, 1962-63, Sacramento City Coll., 1965-66, Calif. State U., Sacramento, 1975; children—Charles Odell, Brian David. Clk.-typist Superior Cts., Sacramento County, Calif., 1972-73; stenographer dept. justice State of Calif., 1973-74, sr. stenographer dept. consumer affairs, 1974-75; exec. asst. Bank of Alex Brown, Walnut Grove, Calif., 1975-76, corporate sec., 1976—, corporate treas., 1977—, asst. v.p., controller, 1978-79, v.p., controller, 1979—. Bd. dirs. Tierra del Oro council Girl Scouts U.S.A. Bank of Am. merit award, 1962; Calif. State scholar, 1962-63. Mem. Am. Mgmt. Assn., Nat. Assn. Bank Women, Nat. Assn. Female Execs., Sacramento C. of C. (women's council). Clubs: Comstock, Am. Mensa Ltd. Office: 7201 S Land Park Dr Sacramento CA 95831

FOUST, WILLIAM DEAN, mfg. co. exec.; b. Kokomo, Ind., Dec. 5, 1935; s. Clarence Donald and Helen (Gardner) F.; A.B. cum laude, Harvard U., 1957, A.M., 1959; m. Darlene Irene O'Harra, June 10, 1956; children—Steven, David, Diana, Suzanne. Mem. tech. staff Harvard Computation Lab., 1958-62; programmer mgr. UNIVAC, 1962-65; mgr. Computer Applications, Inc., 1965-68; dir. ITT Data Services, 1968-69; dir. HETRA, 1969-70; group mgr. RCA, 1970-71; group mgr. UNIVAC, 1972-76; pres. Advanced On-Line Systems, 1976-79; mgr. software Monroe div. Litton Industries, 1979—; vis. lectr. Lehigh U., 1975. Chair mental health com. Montgomery County, Pa.; treas. com. Boy Scouts Am.; bd. dirs. Community Counseling Services. Mem. Assn. Computing Machinery, Linguistic Soc. Am., Spl. Interest Group on Programming Langs. Democrat. Unitarian. Club: Lions. Contbr. articles profl. jours. Home: 1 Woodland Rd Mount Tabor NJ 07878 Office: 202 Johnson Rd Morris Plains NJ 07950

FOWLER, HENRY HAMILL, investment banker; b. Roanoke, Va., Sept. 5, 1908; s. Mack Johnson and Bertha (Browning) F.; A.B., Roanoke Coll., 1929, LL.D., 1962; LL.B., Yale, 1932, J.S.D., 1933; LL.D., William and Mary U., 1966, Wesleyan U.; 1966; m. Trudye Pamela Hathcote, Oct. 19, 1938; children—Mary Anne (Mrs. Roy C. Smith IV), Susan (Mrs. Fowler Gallagher), Henry Hamill (dec.). Admitted to Va. bar, 1933, D.C. bar, 1946; counsel TVA, 1934-38, asst. gen. counsel, 1939; spl. asst. to atty. gen. as chief counsel subcom. Senate Com. Edn. and Labor, 1939-40; spl. counsel Fed. Power Commn., 1941; asst. gen. counsel O.P.M., 1941, W.P.B., 1942-44; econ. advisor U.S. Mission Econ. Affairs, London, Eng., 1944; spl. asst. to adminstr. Fgn. Econ. Adminstrn., 1945; dep. adminstr. N.P.A., 1951, adminstr., 1952; adminstr. Defense Prodn. Adminstrn., 1952-53; dir. ODM, mem. Nat. Security Council, 1952-53; sr. mem. firm Fowler, Leva Hawes & Symington, Washington, 1946-51, 1953-61, 64-65; undersec. of Treasury, 1961-64; U.S. sec. of Treasury, 1965-68; gen. partner Goldman, Sachs & Co., N.Y.C., 1969—. Dir. Corning Glass Works, U.S. Industries, Inc., U.S. & Fgn. Securities Corp. Trustee Alfred P. Sloan Found., Inst. Internat. Edn., Atlantic Inst. Internat. Affairs, Lyndon B. Johnson Found.; chmn. bd. trustees Roanoke Coll.; vice chmn. Com. to Fight Inflation, Atlantic Council U.S.; co-chmn. Com. on Present Danger. Mem. Conf. Bd. (councilor), Yale Law Sch. Assn. Washington (pres. 1955), Pi Kappa Phi, Phi Delta Phi. Democrat. Episcopalian. Clubs: Recess, River, Links (N.Y.C.); Nat. Capital Democratic (pres. 1958-60), Metropolitan (Washington). Office: 55 Broad St New York NY 10004

FOWLER, JAMES BROOKS, mfrs. rep.; b. Temple, Tex., Oct. 17, 1930; s. William Brooks and Elsie Maude (Grubbs) F.; B.S., Tex. A&M U., 1952; m. Betty Jo Willetts, May 24, 1952; children—Diane, Valton. Branch mgr. Black Sivals & Bryson, Houston, 1954-59; partner Alliger & Sears, Houston, 1959-64; pres. Fowler Asso., Internat., Inc., Houston, 1964—. Served to 1st lt. USAF, 1952-54. Republican. Methodist. Home: 15615 Memorial St Houston TX 77079

FOWLER, JAMES DANIEL, JR., finance co. exec.; b. Washington, Apr. 24, 1944; s. James Daniel and Romay (Lucas) F.; student Howard U., 1962-63; B.S., U.S. Mil. Acad., 1967; M.B.A., Rochester Inst. Tech., 1975; m. Linda Marie Raiford, May 25, 1968; children—Kimberly, Scott. With Xerox Corp., Rochester, N.Y., 1971-75, coordinator grad. relations, 1973-74, mgr. personnel adminstrn., 1974-75; sr. cons. D. P. Parker & Assos., Inc., Wellesley, Mass., 1975-76; mgr. staffing ITT World Hdqrs., N.Y.C., 1976-78; v.p., dir. adminstrn. ITT Aetna, Englewood, Colo., 1978, ITT Consumer Fin. Corp., Mpls., 1978—. Trustee U.S. Mil. Acad. Served to capt. U.S. Army, 1967-71. Decorated Bronze Star with oak leaf cluster, Army Commendation medal with 2 oak leaf clusters; recipient Black Achiever award ITT, 1979. Mem. Assn. M.B.A. Execs., Am. Mgmt. Assn., Nat. Consumer Fin. Assn. Office: 300 S County Rd 18 Suite 700 Minneapolis MN 55426

FOWLER, JAMES MURAT, mktg. cons.; b. Manchester, Ky., Oct. 27, 1928; s. James David and Ruby (Lane) F.; B.A., Transylvania U., 1950; postgrad. Stetson U., 1955; m. Dorothy Savage, Dec. 30, 1949; children—Martha Lane, James Murat, Joy Shamhart, David Savage. Tchr., Winter Park (Fla.) High Sch., 1952-55; with Ayerst Labs., Jacksonville, Fla., 1955-59, Pfizer Co., Miami, Fla., 1959-65, hosp. sales mgr., 1965-70, dist. sales mgr., Toledo, 1970-71, asst. dir. tng., N.Y.C., 1971-73, product mktg. mgr., 1974-77; v.p. mktg. Curtin & Pease, N.Y.C., 1977-80; guest lectr. James Madison U., 1978. Mm. Am. Med. Writers Assn., Pharm. Advt. Council, Beethoven Soc. (founding mem.), Order Ky. Cols. Democrat. Baptist. Contbr. articles to profl. jours. Home: 220 S Euclid St Westfield NJ 07090 Office: 476 S Ave E Cranford NJ 07016

FOWLER, RAYMOND DAVID, fin. exec.; b. New Haven, Feb. 14, 1944; s. Raymour Harold and Verna Rosemary (White) F.; B.A., U. Notre Dame, 1965; M.B.A., U. N.H., 1978; m. Sallie Golightly, Nov. 10, 1971. Treas., gen. mgr. Fidelity Fin. Systems, Bridgeport, Conn., 1968-72; dist. mgr. Transcapital Fiscal Systems, Great Neck, N.Y., 1972-75; pres. Fin. and Ins. Spltys., North Haven, Conn., 1975—; fin. and ins. tng. cons. N.H. Auto Dealers Assn., 1979—. Treas., Conn. Assn. for Retarded Children, 1970—. Served to lt., USMC, 1965-68. Decorated Bronze Star medal, Purple Heart. Recipient Disting. Service award Marine Corp League, 1977; Kennedy medal for disting. service to retarded children, 1979. Mem. Marine Corp League (nat. comptroller 1977), Young Marines (nat. dir. 1978), Assn. M.B.A. Execs., Marine Corp Hist. Found. Roman Catholic. Clubs: Lions, Farms Country.

FOWLER, ROBERT DOBBS, newspaper publisher; b. Marietta Ga., Sept. 1, 1930; s. Ralph W. and Irma (Dobbs) F.; B.A., U. of South Sewanee, Tenn., 1952; m. Judith Knox Lidstone, Sept. 8, 1956; children—Nancy Adair, Elizabeth Louise. Editor, Cobb County Times, Marietta, 1956-58, Marietta Daily Jour., 1958-64; pub. Gwinnett Daily News, Lawrenceville, Ga., 1964—; v.p. North Ga. Radio, Inc., Dalton, Ga., 1961—, also dir.; pres. Gwinnett Pub. Co., Lawrenceville, 1964—, also dir.; pres. Winder (Ga.) News, Forsyth County News, Cumming, Ga.; dir. Ga. Newspaper Service. Trustee Ga. Press Ednl. Found., Atlanta; Atlanta Crime Comm. Served to 1st lt. USAF, 1952-56. Mem. Ga. Press Assn. (pres. 1966-67), Gwinnett (Ga.) C. of C., Kappa Alpha, Sigma Delta Chi. Episcopalian. Club: Kiwanis. Home: PO Box 367 Lawrenceville GA 30246 Office: 394 Clayton St NE Lawrenceville GA 30245

FOWLER, (MARION) VANCE, real estate exec.; b. Norfolk, Va., Mar. 1, 1918; s. Daniel Lee and Marian Gertrude (Forrest) F.; B.A., Coll. William and Mary, 1940; M.B.A. with distinction, Harvard U., 1952; m. Marjory Fowler, Dec. 13, 1943; children—Joan Fowler Endt, Thomas Vance, Carole. Commd. ensign U.S. Navy, 1941, advanced through grades to capt., Supply Corps, 1959; supply officer USS Forrestal, 1955-57; exec. officer Naval Supply Depot, Newport, R.I., 1957-59; supt. fiscal officer Naval Air Test Center, Patuxent River, Md., 1959-62; comdg. officer Naval Supply Corps Sch., Athens, Ga., 1962-66; ret., 1967; v.p. Sea Pines Plantation, Hilton Head Island, S.C., 1967-77; pres. Six Oaks Cemetery Corp., Hilton Head Island, 1968—, Vance Fowler Enterprises Ltd., Hilton Head Island, 1978—, Airport Co. Hilton Head, 1968-74; dir. Carswell of Carolina, ins. Chmn. bd. deacons 1st Presbyn. Ch., Hilton Head Island, 1975-76, elder, 1978—; sec. Hilton Head Community Theatre, 1977—, pres., 1981—. Mem. U.S. Tennis Assn. (stadium umpire), Theta Delta Chi. Republican. Clubs: Sea Pines (Hilton Head Island); Army-Navy Country (Arlington, Va.); Rotary (pres. Athens 1965-66). Home: 25 Isle of Pines Hilton Head Island SC 29928 Office: Sea Pines Plantation Co Hilton Head Island SC 29948

FOWLER, WILLIAM EDWARD, JR., lawyer; b. Pitts., Apr. 20, 1919; s. William Edward and Helen (Kerr) F.; B.S., Yale, 1942; J.D., U. Mich., 1948; m. Jean Louise Moore, Apr. 24, 1943; children—Mary Jane, John Moore, William Edward III, James Kerr. Admitted to Ohio bar, 1948; asso. Harrington, Huxley & Smith, Youngstown, Ohio, 1948-55, partner, 1956—. Dir. HyWay Heat Systems, Inc. Syro Steel Co. Mem. Ohio Bd. Bar Examiners, 1965-70. Active Youngstown Community Chest and other fund drives. Mem. Boardman Local Sch. Dist. Bd. Edn., 1960—. Mem. Yale Alumni Bd., 1958—. Served as lt. (s.g.), USNR, World War II. Fellow Am. Bar Found.; mem. Am., Ohio (council of dels., 1963-80, mem. exec. com. 1963-66), Mahoning County (sec.-treas. 1956-58) bar assns., Pa.-Ohio Yale Alumni Assn. (pres.). Home: 50 Forest Hill Rd Youngstown OH 44512 Office: Mahoning Bank Bldg Youngstown OH 44503

FOWLKES, WINFORD (W. C.) CALVIN, bank exec.; b. Madison, N.C., Nov. 1, 1948; s. Calvin Lee and Doris (Hylton) F.; A.A., Middle Ga. Coll., 1972; B.S. Va. Commonwealth U., 1974; postgrad. Sch. Mortgage Banking and Real Estate, Northwestern U., 1978. Mortgage loan rep. Piedmont Trust Bank, Martinsville, Va., 1974-76, mortgage loan supr., 1976-77, asst. mortgage loan officer, 1977-79, mortgage loan officer, 1979—; v.p. Lincoln Savs. & Loan Assn., Richmond, Va., 1979; lectr. Martinsville-Henry County Bd. Realtors, Va. Commonwealth U. Served with USAF, 1968-72. Named Kappa Sigma Alumni of Year, 1977. Mem. Va. Mortgage Bankers Assn. (residential com. 1980-81), Martinsville-Henry County Bd. Realtors (asso.), Martinsville-Henry County Homebuilders Assn. (asso., exec. v.p. 1980), Soc. Real Estate Appraisers, Nat. Assn. Rev. Appraisers, U.S. Jaycees, Martinsville Jaycees (dir., pres. 1980-81), Rho Epsilon, Kappa Sigma. Home: 1404 Spruce St Martinsville VA 24112 Office: Piedmont Trust Bank Ellsworth St Martinsville VA 24112

FOX, ABRAHAM HARVEY, motel and real estate exec.; b. Wausau, Wis., Oct. 6, 1918; s. Samuel and Bertha (Greenberg) F.; student pub. schs., Wausau; m. Edith Wolinsky, Oct. 18, 1942 (dec. Apr. 1973); children—Stuart Lee, Ivan Dennis, Ellen Randy. Accountant, United Air Lines, 1946; owner, mgr. Firebird Motel and Restaurant, 1946—, Fox Realty Co., 1958—, Fox Enterprises, 1961-66; pres. FFICO, Inc., 1966—; partner Fox Properties, Wausau, 1967-71, owner, 1971—; regional coordinator Friendship Inns Internat. Loan broker for Woodmen of World, 1958—. Active in Community Chest drives, other fund raising activities; Democratic precinct committeeman, 1964—. Served with AUS, 1942-45. Decorated Bronze Star. Mem. Cheyenne Motel Assn. (pres. 1961, 74), Wyo. Motor Ct. Assn. (dir. 1964—, legis. com. 1964—), Nat. Inst. Real Estate Brokers, Nat. Assn. Real Estate Bds., Am. Legion, 40 and 8 (grande chef de gare 1967-68), DAV, C. of C. (com. chmn. 1966). Clubs: Moose, Masons (32 deg.), Shriners (comdr. 1958), Elks, Order Eastern Star, B'nai B'rith (pres. 1963). Home: 1714 E 19th St Cheyenne WY 82001 Office: 1905 E Lincolnway Cheyenne WY 82001

FOX, BENTON F., JR., oil co. exec. Pres., chief exec. officer Houston Oil & Minerals Corp. Office: Houston Oil & Minerals Corp 1212 Main St Houston TX 77002*

FOX, CHARLES D'ARCY, investment co. exec.; b. St. Louis, July 29, 1936; s. Charles Smith and Helen (D'Arcy) F.; student Brown U., 1954-59; m. Juanita Cox, Dec. 20, 1975; children—Amber, Carmen, Amanda, Samuel. With A.G. Edward & Sons, Inc., St. Louis, 1960—, mgr. Western region bond dept., 1962-65, research asso., 1965-66, corp. v.p., asst. sec. dir. training and registration, 1966—. Pres., dir. Adult Edn. Council of Greater St. Louis, 1975—. Served with U.S. Army, 1959-60. Mem. Am. Soc. Training and Devel., Internat. Assn. Fin. Planners. Club: Racquet. Home: 16138 Chesterfield Lake Dr Chesterfield MO 63017 Office: 1 N Jefferson Saint Louis MO 63103

FOX, G. DOUGLAS, energy co. exec.; b. Columbus, Ohio, June 13, 1933; s. Frances Otto and Margaret Rose (Burns) F.; B.B.A., U. Okla., 1955, J.D., 1957; m. Emily Joan Wakefield, June 4, 1955; children—Judy, Larry, Mary, Kathy, Anne, Mark. Admitted to Okla. bar; asso. firm Gable, Gotwals, Rubin, Fox, Johnson, & Baker, Tulsa, 1957-60, partner, 1960-79, exec. v.p., 1970-78, pres., 1978-79; pres., dir. Midwest Energy Corp. and subsidiaries, Tulsa, 1980—; dir. Tulsa Tribune Co., Hinderliter Energy Equipment Corp., Sipes Food Markets, Inc.; lectr. oil and gas and securities law U. Tulsa, 1958-63. Chmn. Gov.'s Adv. Com. on Taxation, Okla., 1966-70; chmn. Tulsa City-County Library Commn., 1971-72; speech writer, polit strategist U.S. Sen. Dewey F. Bartlett, 1970-78. Mem. Am. Bar Assn., Okla. Bar Assn., Tulsa County Bar Assn. Republican. Roman Catholic. Editor: Oklahoma Manual for Real Estate Brokers and Salesmen, 1965; contbr. articles to profl. jours. Home: 2411 E 21st St Tulsa OK 74114 Office: Utica Tower Suite 1212 Tulsa OK 74104

FOX, HARRISON WILLIAM, JR., educator; b. Mpls., Jan. 24, 1944; s. Harrison William and Ruth Maude (Pirtle) F.; B.A., U. S.Fla., 1965; M.A., Am. U., 1969, Ph.D. (univ. fellow 1971-72), 1972; m. Lynn Ellen Hussey, Sept. 2, 1967; 1 son, Harrison William, III. Senatorial asst., 1974-75; counsel fin. com. U.S. Senate, 1975-76, counsel to co-chmn. com. to study senate com. system, 1976-77; fellow Inst. Politics, John F. Kennedy Sch. Govt., Harvard U., 1977; minority counsel reports, acctg. and mgmt. subcom., govtl. affairs com. U.S. Senate, 1977-78; prof. public adminstrn. Nat. Def. U., Indsl. Coll. Armed Forces, Ft. McNair, Washington, 1979—; cons. in field. Bd. dirs. Tuscany-Canterbury Neighborhood Assn., 1980—; mem. polit. affairs com. Greater Balt. Bd. Realtors, 1979-80. Served with USNR, 1965. Recipient Disting. Alumni award U. S.Fla., 1976; univ. fellow Dalhousie U., Halifax, N.S., Can., 1965-66. Mem. AAAS, Am. Polit. Sci. Assn., Center Study Federalism, Nat. Bd. Realtors, Nat. Capitol Area Polit. Sci. Assn., Pi Sigma Alpha. Republican. Presbyterian. Clubs: Nat. Republican, Officers (Washington). Author: Contemporary Issues in Civil Rights and Liberties, 1971, Improving Congressional Control Over the Budget, 1973, It's Your Government Too!, 1974, Congressional Staffs, 1977, How To Do Business in Washington, 1980. Office: Nat Def Univ Ft McNair Washington DC 20319

FOX, JAMES WHEELER, petroleum co. exec.; b. Boston, Dec. 12, 1937; s. Maxwell C. and Olivia T. F.; B.A., Hamilton Coll., 1959; m. Linda J. Brown, May 15, 1971; children—Timothy C., Julie Elizabeth. Group ins. underwriter Equitable Life Ins. Soc., N.Y.C., 1959-60; tech. translator Carl Freudenberg Co., Weinheim, W. Ger., 1960-62; regional mgr. Johns-Manville (West Africa) Ltd., Lagos, Nigeria, 1962-68; asst. treas. Pellon Corp., N.Y.C., 1968-76; v.p. fin. and adminstrn. Petrosil Resources Inc., Dallas, 1976-79; exec. v.p., 1979—, also dir. Mem. Fin. Execs. Inst., Dallas Geol. Soc., Psi Upsilon. Methodist. Office: Petrosil Resources Inc 2100 Two Oaks Plaza 6730 LBJ Freeway Dallas TX 75240

FOX, JOHN PHILIP, accountant; b. Chgo., Sept. 8, 1940; s. John Henry and Alice E. (Sturm) F.; B.S. in Commerce, De Paul U., 1964, M.B.A., 1967; m. Susan I. Holden, Aug. 1, 1959; children—Bridget Renee, John S. Mgr., Harris Kerr Forster & Co., Chgo., 1963-70; treas. Anvan Cos., Glen Ellyn, Ill., 1970-72; owner John P. Fox & Co., Villa Park, Ill., 1972—; fin. cons.; dir. various corps. Mem. Villa Park Traffic and Safety Comm., 1973—. C.P.A., Ill. Mem. Am. Inst. C.P.A.'s, Ill. Soc. C.P.A.'s, Villa Park C. of C., Am. Mgmt. Assn., Pi Gamma Mu. Clubs: Lions, Moose. Home: 1101 Rand Rd Villa Park IL 60181

FOX, KENNETH MALCOLM, food equipment mfg. and distbg. co. exec.; b. Kansas City, Mo., Jan. 15, 1942; s. Jack C. and Marion (Gordon) F.; student U. Okla., 1959-62. Vice pres. real estate devel. and mgmt. Jack Fox, Inc., Kansas City, 1963-66; sales rep. Leo Eisenberg & Co., Kansas City, 1966-67; hosp. product sales rep. Will Ross, Inc., Western Mo., 1967-68; in charge hosp. products sales, new product devel., market testing for So. Calif., Kimberly-Clark Corp., Los Angeles, 1968-75; pres. Juice Merchandising Corp., Kansas City, 1975—. Office: 7835 Wornall Rd Kansas City MO 64114

FOX, MICHAEL KEVIN, railroad exec.; b. N.Y.C., Jan. 9, 1946; s. Frank and Regina (Kiely) F.; B.A., U. Va., 1968; M.B.A., U. Pa., 1971; m. Elizabeth L. Holmes, Sept. 5, 1970; children—Michael K., Elizabeth M. Student indsl. engr. N.Y. Central System, Harmon, N.Y., 1967; controls analyst Penn Central, Phila., 1968; transp. asst. So. Pacific R.R., San Francisco, 1971-72, asst. trainmaster, Eugene, Oreg., 1972, service auditor, San Francisco, 1972-73, asst. mgr. intermodal service, Oakland, Calif., 1974; mgr. interstate routes U.S. Ry. Assn., Washington, 1974-76; mgr. strategic planning Consol. Rail Corp., Phila., 1976-77, asst. to pres., 1977-78, asst. to chmn. and chief exec. officer, 1978-79, div. supt., Ft. Wayne, Ind., 1979—. Office: 231 W Baker St Fort Wayne IN 46802

FOX, PETER DAVID, health care cons.; b. Los Angeles, Mar. 28, 1940; s. John Samuel and Selma (Richman) F.; B.A. with honors, Haverford Coll., 1961; M.S., Mass. Inst. Tech., 1963; Ph.D., Stanford U., 1968; m. Beverly Alice Hanson, July 31, 1965; children—David, Steven. Asso. dir. health Stanford Research Inst., Menlo Park, Calif., 1968-70; sr. staff mem. Office Mgmt. and Budget, Washington, 1970-72; dir. office of health analysis, office of asst. sec. planning and evaluation HEW, Washington, 1972-77, dir. office of policy analysis Health Care Financing Adminstrn., 1977-81; prin. Lewis & Assos. Inc., Washington, 1981—; lectr. dept. community medicine Georgetown U. Sch. Medicine, St. Thomas's Hosp. Med. Sch., London. Recipient Superior Service award HEW, 1973. Mem. Am. Pub. Health Assn., Ops. Research Soc. Am. Contbr. articles to profl. jours. Home: 8302 Loring Dr Bethesda MD 20034 Office: 1090 Vermont Ave NW Suite 700 Washington DC 20005

FOX, TERENCE J., consumer products mfg. and distbn. co. exec.; b. Bklyn., Jan. 1, 1938; s. Frank and Regina F.; B.S., N.Y.U., 1960, student Grad. Sch. Bus., 1962; student Latin Am. Inst., 1960; 1 dau., Kersten Kiely. Mgr. underwriting dept. Gruntal & Co., mems. N.Y. Stock Exchange, N.Y.C., 1959-63; sales exec. Am. Flange & Mfg. Co., N.Y.C., 1964-65; pres., chief exec. officer Iroquois Brands, Ltd., 1965—; vice chmn. Lincoln Nat. Bank Buffalo, 1968-71; chmn. bd. Aberdeen Mut. Fund, 1968-71; dir. Intervestors, Buffalo; trustee Emigrant Savs. Bank, N.Y. Mem. nominating com. Am. Stock Exchange, 1976-77, bd. govs., 1978—. Past pres., chmn. bd. Henry St. Settlement Jr. Bd. Former trustee Immaculata Coll., Hilbert Coll., Buffalo; chmn. investment bankers com. Rosary Hill Coll.; former chmn. council D'Youville Coll.; former mem. council Canisius Coll. Sch. Bus. Adminstrn.; past regional coordinator White House Conf. on Children and Youth; bd. dirs. Cath. Youth Orgn., USO. Served with AUS, 1960-61. Mem. Young Presidents Orgn., Am. Inst. Banking, Am. Ordnance Assn., Crippled Children's Guild Buffalo (life). Clubs: Goldens Bridge Hunt (North Salem); Union League, (N.Y.C.); Greenwich (Conn.), Stanwich (Greenwich, Conn). Inventor, designer, patentee Sam Snead hand strengthener. Office: 41 W Putnam Ave Greenwich CT 06830

FOX, WILLIAM GORDON, printing co. exec.; b. Evanston, Ill., Apr. 20, 1930; s. Stuart K. and Ruth (Bartels) F.; B.A. in Econs., Cornell U., 1952; m. Constance E., 1957; children—James, Mary, Gwynne. Salesman, Wallace Press div. Wallace Bus. Forms, Chgo., 1954-61, sales mgr., 1961-67, gen. mgr., 1968—, v.p., 1969-76; exec. v.p. Johnson & Quin, Chgo., 1976-78, pres., 1978—. Served to 1st lt. F.A., AUS, 1952-54. Mem. Chgo. Execs. Club, Delta Tau Delta. Club: Cornell (Chgo.). Home: 525 Lee Rd Northbrook IL 60062 Office: 5544 W Armstrong Ave Chicago IL 60646

FOXEN, GENE LOUIS, ins. exec.; b. Chgo., Mar. 28, 1936; adopted son Henry and Mary F.; student pub. schs.; children—Dan, Kathleen, Michael, Patricia, James, Karen. With New Eng. Life Ins. Co., 1957—, asso. gen. agent, 1970-73, gen. agt., Chgo., 1973—. Cubmaster DuPage council Boy Scouts Am., 1963; Midwest regional dir. Adoptees Liberty Movement Assn. Served with USMC, 1954-57. Recipient Nat. Mgmt. award Gen. Agents and Mgrs. Conf., 1976-80; named to Hall of Fame, New Eng Life Ins. Co., 1972, to Million Dollar Round Table, 1973-80. Mem. Nat. Assn. Life Underwriters, Execs. Club Chgo., Gen. Agents and Mgrs. Assn., Am. Soc. C.L.U.'s (pres. Chgo. chpt. 1977-78), Chgo. Estate Planning Council (v.p.), Am. Soc. Life Underwriters (C.L.U.). Republican. Roman Catholic. Club: Metropolitan. Home: 304 Leeds Ct Naperville IL 60540 Office: 120 S Riverside Plaza Chicago IL 60606

FOY, LEWIS WILSON, ret. steel co. exec.; b. Somerset County, Pa., Jan. 8, 1915; s. George Martin and Nellie (Speicher) F.; student Duke U., 1933-34, George Washington U., 1943-44; student Lehigh U., 1947-49, LL.D., 1975; LL.D., Moravian Coll., 1971, Valparaiso U., 1970; D.C.L., U. Liberia, 1973; m. Marjorie Werry, May 9, 1942; children—Susan Foy Heller, Jane Foy Karaman. With Bethlehem Steel Corp. (Pa.), 1936—, v.p. purchasing, 1963-70, exec. v.p., 1970, pres., 1970—, dir., 1963—, chmn., 1974-80, also chief exec. officer; dir. Communications Satellite Corp., J.P. Morgan & Co., Inc., Morgan Guaranty Trust Co. N.Y., Goodyear Tire & Rubber Co., Met. Life Ins. Co., Consol. Metals Corp. Trustee Moravian Coll., Bethlehem; bd. govs. United Way of Am. Served with AUS, 1941-46. Mem. Bus. Council, Am. Iron Steel Inst. (chmn. 1978-80). Clubs: Union League; Links; Sky; Saucon Valley Country (Bethlehem), Bethlehem; Rolling Rock (Ligonier, Pa.); Pres.'s; Seminole Golf; Everglades; Augusta Nat. Golf; Jupiter Hills. Home: The Elms Saucon Valley Rd RD 4 Bethlehem PA 18015 Office: Suite 310 437 Main St Bethlehem PA 18018

FRACKMAN, RICHARD BENOIT, investment banker; b. N.Y.C., Apr. 14, 1923; s. H. David and Ruth (Warren) F.; grad. Pratt Sch. Bus., 1941; student U. Pa., 1941-42, N.Y.U., 1946-48, N.Y. Inst. Finance, 1962-63; m. Noel Stern, July 2, 1950; 1 dau., Noel Dru. Mdse. mgr. R.H. Miller Stores, Inc., N.Y.C., 1946-49; v.p., mdse. mgr. Darling Stores Corp., N.Y.C., 1949-61; stockbroker, sr. security analyst, ltd. partner Burnham & Co., N.Y.C., 1962, corporate v.p. Drexel Burham Lambert Inc., 1972—. Pres., Greenville Community Council, 1967-70; vice chmn. Town of Greenburgh (N.Y.) Planning Bd., 1970-77; dir. N.Y. State Planning Fedn., 1975-78; mem. Westchester County Regional Plan Assn.; trustee Sarah Lawrence Coll., Bronxville, N.Y., 1979—. Served to capt. USAAF, 1942-46. Recipient Silver Box award Greenville Community Council, 1970. Mem. N.Y. Soc. Security Analysts, Fin. Analysts Fedn. Club: Metropolis Country (bd. govs. 1975—, v.p. 1977-78, treas. 1979-80, pres. 1980—) (White Plains, N.Y.). Home: 3 Hadden Rd Scarsdale NY 10583 Office: 60 Broad St New York NY 10004

FRADIN, STANLEY BERNARD, textile co. exec.; b. Balt., June 1, 1937; s. Isadore and Fannie Fradin; B.S. in Mktg., U. Balt., 1960; m. Marilynn Eileen Newhouse, June 30, 1963; children—Ivy Tamara, Darren Howard. Salesman, Bell Outdoor Advt. Co., Balt., 1959-61; advt. dir. Triangle Mfg. & Sales Inc., Balt., 1961-67; pres. Rockland Mills div. Rockland Industries, Inc., Brooklandville, Md., 1967—. Served with U.S. Army, 1957. Democrat. Jewish. Club: Beth El Mens. Office: 7100 Falls Rd Brooklandville MD 21022

FRAGNER, BERWYN N., human relations exec.; b. Uniontown, Pa., Aug. 5, 1927; s. Rudolph and Rose (Lebowitz) F.; B.A. with distinction, U. Del., 1950; M.A., Harvard U., 1952; m. Marcia Ruth Salkind, June 11, 1950; children—Robin Beth, Matthew Charles, Lisa Rachel. Vice pres. Royer & Roger, Inc., N.Y.C., 1952-62; dir. Western div. Goodway Printing Co., Los Angeles, 1962; v.p., dir. indsl. relations TRW Def. and Space Systems Group, Redondo Beach, Calif., 1963-77, v.p. human relations TRW Systems and Energy, Redondo Beach, 1977—; adv. bd. 1st Women's Bank of Calif. Chmn. Los Angeles City Pvt. Industry Council, 1979—; mem. Calif. Ednl. Mgmt. and Evaluation Commn., 1974—; chmn. bd. trustees Calif. Acad. Decathalon, 1980—; mem. bus. execs. adv. com. So. Calif. Research Council, 1979—. Served with AUS, 1944-47. Decorated Meritorious Service medal with 2 oak leaf clusters. Mem. Assn. U.S. Army, Res. Officers Assn., Internat. Assn. Applied Social Scientists (cert.). Clubs: Army and Navy (Washington); Los Angeles Athletic. Contbr. to New World of Managing Human Resources, 1979. Office: One Space Park E2 4000 Redondo Beach CA 90278

FRALIN, JAY MAXTON, textile co. exec.; b. Phila., June 19, 1947; s. Alan Simon and Rebecca (Bensignor) F.; B.S. in Textile Mgmt. and Mktg., Phila. Coll. Textiles and Sci., 1968; m. Bonnie Sue Moritz, July 30, 1972; 1 son, Eric Steven. Sales mgr. Consumer Products div. Am. Thread Co., Stamford, Conn., 1971-80; dir. sales Consumer Products div. Flash Trimming Co., Phila., 1980—. Served with USN, 1969-71. Republican. Jewish. Office: 801 Arch St Philadelphia PA 19107

FRANCESCA, CAROLE, motion picture exec., photographer; b. Phila., Dec. 4, 1950; d. John Phillip and Catherine Elizabeth (Powers) DiNardo; student Temple U., Phila., 1968-70; m. William S. Cross, June 20, 1970. Co-owner, Images Nouvelles, photog./video advt. art, New Haven, 1973-77, mktg. and lic. adminstr. Columbia Pictures, 1977-78; asst. dir. mdsg. United Artists Corp., 1978-79; dir. sales, mdsg. and lic., 1980—; co-owner Cross/Francesca Photography, advt. art, N.Y.C., 1977—. Mem. N.Y. Women in Films. Democrat. Office: 729 7th Ave New York NY 10019

FRANCIS, ERIC STEVEN, bldg. maintenance service exec., lawyer; b. Newark, Jan. 8, 1950; s. Irwin Samuel and Beatrice (Abrahamson) F.; student Seton Hall U., summers 1969-70; B.A. magna cum laude, U. Md., 1971; J.D., Villanova U., 1974; m. Frann Lauren Golden, Aug. 16, 1970; 1 dau., Meredith Sandra. Legis. aide to Joseph P. Minnish, U.S. Ho. of Reps., Washington, 1971; legal intern to U.S. atty. Eastern Dist. Pa., Phila., 1973; admitted to Pa. bar, 1974, D.C. bar, 1975, N.J. bar, 1977; atty.-adviser Office Enforcement and Gen. Counsel, EPA, Washington, 1974-76; pres., chief exec. officer, dir. Atlantic Bldg. Maintenance Corp., Newark, 1976—; exec. v.p., dir. All State Cleaning Contractors, Inc., Newark; individual practice law, Short Hills, N.J., 1976—; sr. partner Francis Enterprises, Newark, 1976—, Francis Consultants, Ltd., Newark, 1978. Pres., Cambridge Complex, U. Md., 1969, John Marshall Soc., 1971; justice U. Md. Supreme Ct., 1969-71; mem. honor bd. Villanova U. Sch. Law, 1971-72; trustee Internat. Bldg. Service Employees Pension Trust Fund, Internat. Bldg. Service Employees Welfare Trust Fund. Recipient Spl. Service commendations U. Md., 1970-71. Mem. Am., N.J., D.C., Pa. bar assns., Omicron Delta Kappa, Phi Sigma Alpha, Phi Alpha Theta. Clubs: Crestmont Country, Essex. Office: 86 Frelinghuysen Ave Newark NJ 07114

FRANCIS, JOSEPH SNELSON, consulting engr.; b. Canton, N.C., Jan. 13, 1914; s. William Lee and Iva (Snelson) F.; student Berea (Ky.) Coll. and Iowa State Coll.; B.S. in Mech. Engring., U. N.C., 1938; m. Gertrude R. Cherry Withers; children—Joseph Gregory, Roger Douglas. Design engr. J.V. Deloi Engring. Co., Durham, N.C., Chgo., Mojonnier Bros. Co., Chgo., Consol. Aircraft Corp., San Diego, Internat. Harvester Co., Chgo.; pres. The Francis Co., 1940—; pres., owner Western Research & Engring. Co. 1958—. Registered profl. engr. Ill., Okla., Ga., Tex., Colo. Mem. Soc. Automotive Engrs., Am. Soc. M.E., Army Ordnance Assn. Mason (32 deg., Shriner). Home: 1057 E 161th St South Holland IL 60473 Office: 3200 E 87th St Chicago IL 60617

FRANCIS, MARY FRANCES VAN DYKE, bus. exec., editor; b. Sedalia, Mo., Nov. 17, 1925; d. Frank B. and Mary Irene (Sims) Van Dyke; student Central Mo. State Coll.; m. Harold E. Francis, Apr. 23, 1944 (div. 1980); children—David Eugene, Lois Irene (Mrs. Edward Elbert Smith), Roland Wayne, Eric Brian. Tchr. grade sch. Pettis County, Mo., 1943-44; timekeeper Montgomery Ward & Co., Kansas City, Mo., 1944-45; instr. new operators Southwestern Bell Telephone Co., Independence, Mo., 1945-47; real estate salesman Russell Realtors, Independence, 1958-66; owner Mary Francis, Realtor, Independence, 1967—; exec. sec., editor Eastern Jackson County Bd. Realtors, 1962-68; exec. asst., pub. relations dir., editor Kansas City Realtor, 1968-71; marketing asst. S. Central region Chgo. Title Ins. Co., Kansas City, 1971-75; pres. Maranco, Inc., real estate, 1975—; v.p. Raintree Lake Realty, 1980—. Cub Scout den mother council Boy Scouts Am. Recipient Outstanding Service award Eastern Jackson County Bd. Realtors, 1964, Salesmanship award, 1965. Mem. Nat. Assn. Real Estate Bds. (charter pres. Greater Kansas City chpt., gov., pres. Mo. Women's Council), Mo. Real Estate Assn. (mem. Speakers Bur.). Club: Soroptimist (past pres., Independence). Contbr. articles to realty publs. Address: PO Box 1158 Independence MO 64051

FRANCISCO, DAVID ROBERT, bank exec.; b. Canton, Ohio, July 11, 1946; s. Robert Henry and Isabel Minerva (Moody) F.; B.B.A., Kent State U., 1968; postgrad. in banking U. Wis. Grad. Sch. Banking, 1972-75, Harvard Grad. Sch. Bus., 1979; m. Carol J. Steiger, Sept. 16, 1967; children—Christa Lee, Craig David. Asst. nat. bank examiner Comptroller of the Currency, South Bend, Ind., 1968-70; asst. v.p. First Nat. Bank, Bryan, Ohio, 1970-77, v.p., cashier, chief exec. officer, 1977-78, pres., chief exec. officer, First Nat. Bank of N.W. Ohio, Bryan, 1979—, also dir. Chmn., Williams County chpt. ARC, 1974-77; pres. Bryan Pre-Sch. Assn., 1974-77. Mem. Williams County Bankers Assn. (pres.), Bryan C. of C. (1st v.p. 1980), Bank Mktg. Assn., Bank Adminstrn. Inst., Ohio Bankers Assn., Am. Bankers Assn. Lutheran. Clubs: Rotary, Orchard Hills Country. Office: 310 S Main St Bryan OH 43506

FRANCISCO, WAYNE M(ARKLAND), petroleum mktg. co. exec.; b. Cin., June 14, 1943; s. George Lewis and Helen M. (Markland) F.; student Ohio State U., 1962-63; B.S. in Mktg. and Acctg., U. Cin., 1967; m. 2d, Paula Hicks, June 26, 1976; children—Diana Lynn, W. Michael, Lisa Kay (adopted) Shauna Deann (adopted). Unit sales mgr. Procter & Gamble, Cin., 1967-69; mktg. mgr. Nat. Mktg. Inc., Cin., 1969-70; pres. Retail Petroleum Marketers, Inc., Cin., 1970-72, chmn. bd., chief exec. officer, Phoenix, 1972—. Mem. Phoenix Bd. Appeals, 1978-80. Recipient Top Performer award for Phoenix dist. Shell Oil Co., 1979. Mem. Petroleum Retailers Ariz. (pres. 1977-79), Nat. Congress Petroleum Retailers (adv. bd.), Nat. Inst. Automotive Service Excellence (cert.), Studebaker Drivers Club, Avanti Owners Assn. (dir.). Republican. Office: 3201 E Shea Blvd Phoenix AZ 85028

FRANCO, ALBERT GABRIEL, computer co. exec.; b. N.Y.C., Aug. 10, 1935; s. Gabriel and Bessie F.; B.S., Columbia U., 1956, M.S. in E.E., 1957, E.E., 1962; m. Fanny Kligman, July 3, 1960; children—Laura S., Stephanie B. Mem. research staff IBM Corp., Yorktown Heights, N.Y., 1957-62; dep. dir. info. systems Computer Sci. Corp., Paramus, N.J., 1963-69; prin., founder, v.p. Ultimacc Systems, Inc., Maywood, N.J., 1969-77; v.p. ADP, Inc., Clifton, N.J., 1977—; adj. prof. Newark Coll. Engring. Sr. mem. IEEE. Contbr. articles to profl. jours. Office: 405 Route 3 Clifton NJ 07015

FRANK, ALAN I W, mfg. corp. exec.; b. Pitts., Mar. 6, 1932; s. Robert Jay and Cecelia F. (Moreell) F.; A.B. cum laude, Harvard Coll., 1954; LL.B., Columbia U., 1960; children—Darcy Mackay, Kimberly deVou. Spl. agt. CIC, 1955-57; pres. chmn. bd. Alan I W Frank Corp., Exton, Pa., 1962—. Gen. chmn. Columbia U. $200 Million campaign, Pitts. area, 1968-70; mem. nat. devel. bd. Columbia U., 1974—; mem. Rensselaer council Rensselaer Poly. Inst., 1974—. Mem. N.Y. Bar. Clubs: Harvard-Yale-Princeton; Mid Ocean. Inventor, patentee in field. Office: Alan I W Frank Corp Exton PA 19341

FRANK, ANTHONY MELCHIOR, financial exec.; b. Berlin, Germany, May 21, 1931; s. Lothar and Elisabeth (Roth) F.; came to U.S., 1937, naturalized, 1943; B.A., Dartmouth Coll., 1953, M.B.A., 1954; postgrad. in finance U. Vienna, 1956; m. Gay Palmer, Oct. 16, 1954; children—Tracy, Randall. Asst. to pres., bond portfolio mgr. Glendale Fed. Savs. Assn. (Calif.), 1958-61; v.p., treas. Far West Fin. Corp., Los Angeles, 1962; adminstrv. v.p., v.p. savs. First Charter Fin. Corp., Beverly Hills, Calif., 1962-66; pres. State Mut. Savs. and Loan Assn., Los Angeles, 1966-68, Titan Group, Inc., N.Y.C. and Los Angeles, 1968-70, INA Properties, Inc., 1970-71; pres. Citizens Savs. & Loan, San Francisco, 1971-73, vice chmn., chief exec. officer, 1973-74; chmn. bd., pres., chief exec. officer United Fin. Corp., 1974—, also pres.; vice chmn., pub. interest dir. Fed. Home Loan Bank San Francisco, 1972-77; trustee, treas. Blue Shield of Calif., 1976—; dir. Allianz Ins. Co. Am., Golden West Homes, Kaiser Cement Corp. Chmn., dir. Calif. Housing Fin. Agy., Sacramento, 1978—; chmn. bd. visitors Sch. Architecture and Planning U. Calif. at Los Angeles, 1971—; del. Calif. Democratic Conv., 1968. Served with AUS, 1954-56. Mem. Bankers Club, Young Pres.'s Orgn. (sec.). Clubs: Dartmouth No. Calif.; Univ. (Los Angeles). Office: 700 Market St San Francisco CA 94102

FRANK, GERALD WENDEL, investment co. exec.; b. Portland, Oreg., Sept. 21, 1923; s. Aaron M. and Ruth (Rosenfeld) F.; student Stanford, 1941-43; B.A. with honors, Cambridge U., 1948, M.A., 1953; D.B.A. (hon.), Greenville Coll., 1971. With Meier & Frank Co., Portland, 1948-53, mgr., Salem, Oreg., 1953-65; v.p. Meier & Frank Co., Inc., 1958-65; dir. U.S. Nat. Bank of Oreg., Standard Ins. Co., Am. Fed. Savs. & Loan Assn.; pres. Frank Investment Co.; now adminstrv. asst. to U.S. Senator Hatfield; mem. Culver Commn. on Operation U.S. Senate, 1975-76; mem. mgmt. com. U.S. Senate, 1978. Pres., Cascade area council Boy Scouts Am., 1959-61, mem. western regional com. 1957—, recipient Silver Beaver award, 1963; chmn. Citizens Conf. for Govtl. Cooperation, Mid-Willamette Valley of Oreg., 1958-59; dir. Portland Rose Festival Assn., 1954—, Jr. Achievement of Portland, 1953—; pres. Marion-Polk County United Good Neighbors, 1965-67; mem. Gov.'s Adv. Com. Oreg. Econ. Devel. Div., 1957-73, chmn., 1959-66; officer, mem. various other civic orgns. Trustee Willamette U.; Salem YMCA, 1960-77, St. Vincent's Hosp., 1967—; bd. dirs. Oreg. Grad. Study and Research Center, 1963-69; mem. bd. control Salem Gen. Hosp., 1955-61. Served with F.A., AUS, 1943-46, ETO. Named jr. first citizen of Salem, 1957; one of three outstanding young men of Oreg., U.S. Jr. C. of C., 1957; recipient OMSI award Oreg. Mus. of Sci. and Industry, 1961; named Outstanding Salesman Oreg., 1961, Adm. Astoria Regatta, 1964, Salem 1st Citizen 1964. Mem. Oreg. Hist. Soc. (dir. 1960-68), Am. Legion. Elk, Rotarian Clubs: Arlington, Waverly, Multnomah Athletic, Illahe. Home: 3250 Crestview Dr S Salem OR 97302 Office: Standard Ins Bldg Salem OR 97301

FRANK, LARRY AYRES, mfg. co. exec.; b. Reno, Nev., Feb. 5, 1949; s. Jack D. and Arlene V. F.; B.S. in Bus. Adminstrn., U. Nev., Reno, 1972, M.B.A., 1973; m. Jennifer L. Bruner, June 7, 1969; children—Benjamin, Jonathan. Fin. analyst Matson Nav. Co., San Francisco, 1974-75; sr. partner FOSCO, San Francisco, 1975-78; mgr. fin. planning Kennametal Inc., Latrobe, Pa., 1979—. Mem. Planning Execs. Inst., Phi Kappa Phi, Delta Sigma Pi. Author: Capital Project Financing Analysis, 1978. Home: 535 Maywood Rd York PA 17402 Office: Kennametal Inc 1 Lloyd Ave Latrobe PA 15650

FRANK, MORTON, publisher; b. Pitcairn, Pa., June 14, 1912; s. Abraham and Goldie (Friedenberg) F.; A.B., U. Mich., 1933; postgrad. Carnegie Inst. Tech., U. Pitts., Duquesne U.; LL.D. (hon.), Alfred U., 1979; m. Agnes Dodds, June 2, 1944 (div. 1957); children—Allan Dodds, Michael Robert, Marilyn Morton; m. 2d, Elizabeth Welt Pope, Dec. 31, 1963. Advt. mgr. Braddock (Pa.) Daily News-Herald, 1933-34; editor Braddock Free Press, 1934-35; advt. salesman, writer, rotogravure mgr. Pitts. Press, 1935-42, also writer, commentator Pitts. radio stas., 1935-42; corr. Printer's Ink, Billboard, Motion Picture Daily & Herald, 1938-42; v.p., bus. mgr. Ariz. Times. Phoenix, 1946; editor, pub. Canton (Ohio) Economist, 1946-58, Lorain (Ohio) Sun. News, 1949-50, Inter-County Gazette, Strasburg, Ohio, 1950-51, Stark County Times Canton, 1950-58, Farm and Dairy, Salem, Ohio, 1952-53; pres. Tri-Cities Telecasting, Canton, 1953-61, Printype, 1956-58, Property Devel. Corp., 1956-58; pub. relations dir., exec. v.p. Family Weekly and Suburbia Today, N.Y.C., 1958-65; pub., exec. v.p. Family Weekly, 1966-71, pres., pub., 1971-75, chmn., 1976, pres., pub., 1976—. Bd. dirs. Canton Symphony Orch., 1950-56; trustee Alfred U., 1968—; chmn. Commn. Ind. Colls. N.Y. State, 1976-79. Served from ensign to lt. USNR, 1942-45. Recipient award for feature writing NEA, 1954; Community Service award AHNA, 1954. Mem. Fedn. Non-Comml. Theatres (pres.), Retail Mchts. Bd., Controlled Circulation Newspapers Am. (dir.), Pitts. Fgn. Policy Assn. (dir.), Newspaper Advt. Bur. (plans com. 1974—), Internat., Am., Calif., So., Tex. newspaper pubs. assns., Nat. Newspaper Assn., Internat. Circulation Mgrs. Assn., Internat. Newspaper Promotion Assn., Internat. Newspaper Advt. Execs. Assn., Canton Advt. Club, Sales Execs. N.Y.C., Sigma Alpha Mu, Sigma Delta Chi. Clubs: Players, Overseas Press, N.Y. Deadline (pres. 1974-75). Home: 534 Rock House Rd Easton CT 06612 also 115 E 67th St New York NY 10021 Office: 641 Lexington Ave New York NY 10022

FRANK, ROBERT ALLEN, advt. corp. exec.; b. Albany, N.Y., Sept. 26, 1932; s. Edward and Marian (Kostelanetz) F.; B.A., Colby Coll., 1954; M.B.A., Amos Tuck Sch. Bus. Adminstrn., 1958. Cost control adminstr. ABC-TV, N.Y.C., 1958-59, corporate auditor CBS, Inc., N.Y.C., 1959-60, TV sales service account exec., 1961, account exec. radio network sales, 1962-69; exec. v.p., co-founder SFM Media Corp., N.Y.C., 1969—. Radio-TV cons. Nat. Kidney Fund., 1974. Active radio TV for various polit. campaigns including Robert Kennedy for Senator, 1964, Richard Nixon for Pres., 1972, Ford for Pres., 1976, Bush for Pres., 1980, Reagan for Pres., 1980; mem. Republican Nat. Com., 1980. Served to capt. USAF, 1954-56. Mem. Internat. Radio-TV Soc. (membership com. 1973-75), Amos Tuck Alumni Assn. N.Y. (pres. 1976-77, dir. 1979—), Internat. Platform Assn., Pi Gamma Mu. Club: Dartmouth (N.Y.C.). Home: 9 Hackberry Hill Rd Weston CT 06883 Office: SFM Media Corp 1180 Ave of Americas New York NY 10036

FRANK, ROBERT GREGG, life ins. co. exec.; b. Chgo., Feb. 22, 1918; s. George Charles and Estelle (Cosgrove) F.; B.S. in Finance, U. Okla., 1939; m. Patricia Walsh Shoaf, Dec. 14, 1942; children—Robert Gregg, Stephen Cosgrove, Jon Lindsay. With Equitable Life Assurance Soc., 1939-41; stockbroker Brailsford & Co., Chgo., 1945-47; regional v.p. Hugh W. Long & Co., mut. fund underwriter, Los Angeles, 1947—, chmn. sales adv. bd., 1963-66, exec. v.p. Western states, 1966-73; exec. v.p. Anchor Corp., 1973-77; pres., dir. Anchor Nat. Fin. Services, Phoenix, 1974—, Anchor Nat. Life Ins. Co., Phoenix, 1976—; dir. Washington Nat. Trust Co., Evanston, Ill; dir. Washington Nat. Corp.; chmn. Interplan Variable Account. Served to lt. col., AUS, 1941-45. Decorated Bronze Star medal with cluster. Mem. Ariz. Acad., Phi Kappa Sigma. Republican. Roman Catholic. Clubs: Camelback Country, Country of Colo., Plaza. Home: 4317 N 70th St Scottsdale AZ 85251 Office: Anchor Nat Plaza Camelback at E 22d St Phoenix AZ 85016

FRANK, ROBERT HARRY, TV and film producer; b. Balt., Aug. 1, 1948; s. Jerome and Sophie (Hurwitz) F.; A.A., Eastern Coll., Balt., 1968; J.D., Mt. Vernon Law Sch., 1970; student TV prodn., U. So. Calif., 1979. Legal analyst U.S. Congress, 1969-70, legal counsel, 1970-71; admitted to Md. bar, 1970; individual practice, Balt., 1971-73; partner firm Frank & Needleman, Balt., 1973-74; with mdsg. dept. Jonathan Logan, Inc., Atlanta, 1974-75; exec. v.p. Universal Video Systems Co., Atlanta, 1975-76; v.p. Internationale Set, Inc., Los Angeles, 1976-79; v.p. Right Bank Clothing Co., 1977-79; pres., dir. Infoset Corp., 1978-79; exec. v.p., dir. Internationale Bhan, Inc., 1977-79. Mem. Am. Film Inst. Address: 1610 N Kings Rd Los Angeles CA 90069

FRANK, STANLEY WILLIAM, retail store exec.; b. N.Y.C., May 30, 1922; s. Sidney and Frances Frank; student UCLA, 1941-43; m. Miki Kronold, May 18, 1975; 1 dau., Cara Oska. Self-employed sales rep., 1943-59; pres. Reimer, Inc., N.Y.C., 1959-71, Mista Security Devices, Bklyn., 1971—. Recipient Spl. Achievement award Locksmith's Ledger, 1961. Mem. N.Y. Locksmiths Assn. (hon.), Bklyn. C. of C., Internat. Entrepreneurs Soc., Nat. Space Inst. Patentee lock-alarm security device. Office: 163 Joralemon St Brooklyn NY 11201

FRANK, WILLIAM H., food products co. exec.; b. Chgo., Jan. 8, 1945; s. Joseph J. and Ann H. Frank; B.S., U. Ill., 1964; M.B.A., DePaul U., Chgo., 1968; m. Joyce Ann Vondra, Aug. 28, 1966; children—Steven, Jill, Jaime. Dir. fin. services, then controller consumer products Internat. Paper Co., N.Y.C., 1976-78; v.p., controller AM Internat. Co., Los Angeles, 1978-79, United Brands Co., N.Y.C., 1979—. Served as 1st sgt. USAR. C.P.A., Ill., Calif., N.Y. Mem. Am. Inst. C.P.A.'s, Calif. Soc. C.P.A.'s, Ill. Soc. C.P.A.'s, N.Y. State Soc. C.P.A.'s. Office: United Brands Co 1271 Ave of Americas New York NY 10020

FRANKE, MICHAEL WOLFGANG, railroad exec.; b. Herford, West Germany, July 31, 1948; s. Robert Wolfgang and Helena (Holak) F.; came to U.S., 1955, naturalized, 1961; B.S. in Civil Engring. (4 year scholar), Washington U., St. Louis, 1970; M.S., U. Ill., 1971; m. Jean Jester Davis, Jan. 17, 1975; 1 dau., Laura Ann. Engring. asst. N. & W. Ry., 1969-70, asst. engr. Office Chief Engr., Roanoke, Va., 1971-73; gen. mgr. Chesapeake Western Ry. Co., Harrisonburg, Va., 1972-76; v.p., gen. mgr. Winston-Salem Southbound Ry., 1976-78; v.p., gen. mgr., dir. HPT & D Ry., 1976-78; v.p. Winston Land Corp., 1976-78; gen. mgr. Norfolk, Franklin & Danville Ry. Co., Suffolk, Va., 1978-79; asst. regional engr. Norfolk & Western Ry. Co., 1979-81, engr. maintenance of way, 1981—. Recipient Wayne A. Johnson Meml. award U. Ill., 1970, grantee Burlington No. R.R., 1970-71; registered profl. engr., N.C. Mem. ASCE, Am. Ry. Engring. Assn., Acad. Sci. St. Louis, Delta Phi Alpha.

Home: 2213 Brookfield Dr SW Roanoke VA 24018 Office: Gen Office Bldg-N 8 N Jefferson St Roanoke VA 24042

FRANKE, ROBERT JOHAN, ins. brokerage co. exec.; b. Balt., Mar. 30, 1930; s. Otto Hermann and Roberta (Felty) F.; student Balt. City Coll., 1945-48; B.A., Haverford Coll., 1952; m. Joyce Black, Oct. 4, 1952; children—Elizabeth H., Robert Edward. With Conn. Gen. Life Ins. Co., 1952-55, McLean & Kochler, Balt., 1955-57; with Alexander & Alexander, N.J., 1957-78, Winston-Salem, N.C., 1978—, v.p. sales, 1964—. Past trustee Kessler Inst. Rehab., West Orange, N.J. Served with U.S. Army, 1952-54. C.P.A., Md. Presbyterian. Clubs: Rotary, N.C. Country, Baltusrol, Pinehurst Country. Home: PO Box 155 Pinehurst NC 28374 Office: Alexander & Alexander PO Box 2896 Winston-Salem NC 27102

FRANKEL, EDWARD IRWIN, fin. services co. exec.; b. Bklyn., Aug. 26, 1941; s. Paul and Anna (Pasmowitz) F.; cert. in investment analysis N.Y. Inst. Fin., 1962; student N.Y. U., 1962-66; m. Ann Ruth Weinstein, Apr. 5, 1964; children—Jennifer Lynn, Rachel Gale. Partner, Baerwald & DeBoer, mems. N.Y. Stock Exchange, N.Y.C., 1966-70; instl. account exec. Frederick & Co., N.Y.C., 1970-72; v.p., regional mgr. Variable Annuity Life Ins. Co., Los Angeles, 1973-76; chmn. United Econ. Services Inc. subs. Integrated Resources Inc., N.Y.C. Mem. Nat. Assn. Security Dealers, Profl. Ind. Mass Mktg. Adminstrs., Palos Verdes Community Arts Center, Palos Verdes Estates Ins. Com. Clubs: Palos Verdes Breakfast; Town Hall of Los Angeles. Office: 23879 Madison St Torrance CA 90505

FRANKEL, STANLEY ARTHUR, pub. co. exec., industrialist; b. Dayton, Ohio, Dec. 8, 1918; s. Mandel and Olive (Margolis) F.; B.S. with high honors, Northwestern U., 1940; student Columbia, 1940, U. Chgo., 1946-49; m. Irene Baskin, Feb. 20, 1946; children—Stephen, Thomas, Nancy. Reporter, Chgo. News Bur., 1940; publicist CBS, 1941; asst. to pres. Esquire and Coronet mags., N.Y.C., 1946-56; pres. Esquire Club, 1956-58; with McCall Corp., N.Y.C., 1958—, asst. to pres. and pub., 1958—, v.p., 1959-61; v.p., dir. corporate devel, Luria Bros. and Co., Inc., subsidiary Ogden Corp., 1961—; v.p. Ogden Corp., 1962—; dir. Internat. Terminal Operating Co., Inc., Ogden-Am. Corp., Western Canners Corp. Guest lectr. N.Y. U., 1974; adj. prof. Baruch Coll., City U. N.Y., 1974. Exec. bd. Writers for Stevenson, 1952, 56, for Kennedy, 1960; pub. relations dir. Stevenson-for-President, 1956; exec. producer Stevenson Reports TV. Mem. pres.'s adv. council Peace Corps, 1965. Bd. dirs., vice chmn. Nat. Businessmen's Council; mem. N.Y. State Gov.'s Higher Edn. Task Force-75; co-dir. pub. relations course Am. Mgmt. Assn., 1971; bd. dirs., exec. com. Nat. Council Crime and Delinquency, chmn. Loeb Award com., 1972; bd. dirs. N.Y. YMCA, 1960-72; exec. bd., v.p. YMCA of Greater N.Y.; mem. Pres.'s Youth Opportunity Council, 1966; Services; trustee Scarsdale Adult Sch.; bd. overseers Rutgers U., 1977; mem. chancellor's panel, chmn. remediation com., long range planning commn. State U. N.Y. Chmn., Writer for Humphrey, 1964; vice chmn. HHH for Pres., 1968, McGovern for Pres., 1972; mem. Vice President's Task Force on Youth Employment, 1979. Served to maj. AUS, 1940-46. Decorated Presdl. Citation, 3 Bronze Stars; recipient Alumni Merit award Northwestern U., 1964. Recipient Peabody award for Stevenson reports, 1963. Mem. Phi Beta Kappa Assos. (mem. bd.). Clubs: Overseas Press (N.Y.C.); Westchester Tennis; Scarsdale Town (gov.). Author: History of the 37th Division, 1947. Contbr. articles popular mags. Home: 109 Brewster Rd Scarsdale NY 10583 Office: 277 Park Ave New York NY 10017

FRANKLIN, LARRY DANIEL, newspaper exec.; b. Commerce, Tex., July 16, 1942; s. John Asia and Annie Mae (Castle) F.; B.B.A., East Tex. State U., 1965; M.B.A., Tex. Tech. U., 1966; m. Charlotte Anne Walker, Aug. 18, 1962; children—Kelly Leigh, Kristi Lynn. Mem. audit staff Arthur Andersen Co., Dallas, 1966-67; controller, treas. Paris Milling Co. (Tex.), 1967-69; mem. audit staff Price Waterhouse Co., Dallas, 1969-71; asst. corp. dir. acctg. Harte-Hanks Communications, Inc., San Antonio, 1971, corp. dir. fin. services, 1971-72, chief fin. officer, treas., 1972-74, v.p. fin., treas., 1974-75, v.p. fin., sec.-treas., 1975-78, sr. v.p., pres. newspaper ops., 1978-80, exec. v.p., pres. newspaper ops., 1980—, dir., 1974—; dir. First Internat. Bank, San Antonio. Mem. acctg. adv. council Tex. Tech U., Lubbock; treas. St. Thomas Episcopal Ch., San Antonio. C.P.A., Tex. Mem. Am. Inst. C.P.A.'s, Tex. Soc. C.P.A.'s, Fin. Execs. Inst. (founding dir., past pres. South Tex. chpt.), Am. Newspaper Pubs. Assn., So. Newspaper Pubs. Assn., Tex. Daily Newspaper Assn., Inst. Newspaper Controllers and Fin. Officers. Home: 16451 Los Cabin St San Antonio TX 78232 Office: Harte-Hanks Communications Inc 901 NE Loop 410 San Antonio TX 78291

FRANKLIN, PHILIP EARLE, economist; b. Detroit, Jan. 11, 1928; s. Edward Earle and Minnie (Evans) F.; B.A., George Washington U., 1949; M.A., 1956; Ph.D., Am. U., 1968; postgrad. Center for Internat. Affairs, Harvard U., 1972-73; m. Jacqueline Jo Rogers, Dec. 28, 1949; children—Debora, Janice, Stephanie, Diana, Jennifer. Bus. economist Office Bus. Econs., Dept. Commerce, 1950-51; indsl. analyst Govt. Patents Bd., Exec. Office of Pres., 1952-55; gen. economist Bur. Fgn. Commerce, Dept. Commerce, 1955-56; transp. specialist Commodity Stablzn. Service, Dept. Agr., 1956-57; transp. economist Maritime Adminstrn., Dept. Commerce, 1957-60, gen. economist Office of Area Devel., 1960-61, transp. economist Office of Under Sec. Commerce for Transp., 1961-62, Bur. Internat. Commerce, 1962-64, gen. economist, 1964-67; coordinator water resources Office of Sec. Dept. Transp., 1967-70, chief econ. and spl. projects div., 1970-73, chief, organizer internat. transp. div., 1973-78; pvt. economic cons., 1978—; cons. to UN, 1965—. Pres. Eastpines Citizens Assn., Riverdale, Md., 1955-57. Served with USAAF, 1945-47, as 1st lt. AUS, 1951-52. Mem. Am. Econ. Assn., Council Fgn. Relations, Regional Sci. Assn., Econ. History Assn., Am. Water Resources Assn., Am. Soc. Pub. Adminstrn., AAAS, Am. Acad. Arts and Scis., Transp. Research Forum, Permanent Internat. Assn. Nav. Congresses, Kappa Sigma, Delta Phi Epsilon. Home: 3734 Northampton St NW Washington DC 20015

FRANKLIN, ROBERT LOUIS, hotel exec.; b. Mt. Pocono, Pa., July 28, 1951; s. Robert Horace and Carolyn Elizabeth (Tillman) F.; B.S. with distinction, Pa. State U., 1973; m. Suzanne Brodt, Apr. 3, 1969; children—Jennifer Elizabeth, Robert Louis II. Dir. food and beverage ops. Marriott Hotel Corp., Washington, 1973, Houston, 1973-74, Dallas, 1974-75; v.p., gen. mgr. Carriage Inn, Inc., Scarborough, Maine, 1975-76; gen. mgr. Harper Hotels Inc./Holiday Inn, Plattsburgh, N.Y., 1976—. Coordinator Christian edn. United Methodist Ch., Plattsburgh. Recipient Silver award United Way Greater Portland; hon. comdr. 380th Bombardment Wing, SAC, USAF. Mem. Pa. Hotel and Restaurant Soc. (pres. 1972-73), Pa. State Club Maine (pres. 1976-78), Am., N.Y. State hotel and motel assns., Plattsburgh and Clinton County C. of C., Clinton County Tourist Bur. (dir.), Sigma Pi Eta. Clubs: Pa. State (Plattsburgh); Kiwanis, Rotary. Home: 62 S Prospect Ave Plattsburgh NY 12901 Office: Holiday Inn I-87 and NY Route 3 Plattsburgh NY 12901

FRANKLIN, WILLIAM DONALD, govt. ofcl.; b. Dacula, Ga., Nov. 26, 1933; s. Thomas Kimsey and Lora Claudia (Martin) F.; B.S., Austin Peay State U., 1961; M.S. (Univ. fellow), Tex. A. and M. U., 1963; Sc.D., U. London, 1972; grad. Advanced Mgmt. Program (fellow), Harvard U., 1973; grad. Indsl. Coll. of Armed Forces, 1971, U.S. Command and Gen. Staff Coll., 1975, Air U., 1977, Nat. Def. U., 1978; m. Elizabeth Ann Giles, Nov. 25, 1970; children—Braden, Kimette, Laura, Thomas, Amy, Holly. Data processing mgr. Boillin-Harrison, Inc., Clarksville, Tenn., 1959-61; economist Tex. A. and M. U., 1961-63, transport economist Tex. Transp. Inst., 1964-69; asst. prof. bus. Upper Iowa U., 1963-64; head dept. econs., dir. mgmt. devel. Tenn. Wesleyan Coll. and pres. Econotec Research Co., Athens, Tenn., 1969-75; dep. div. chief trade and industry analysis div. Bur. Internat. Econ. Affairs, Dept. Labor, Washington, 1975-77; industry economist Fed. R.R. Adminstrn., Dept. Transp., Washington, 1977, div. tech. assessment Fed. Hwy. Traffic Safety Adminstrn., 1977-78; chief airport and consumer affairs br. Office Noise Control, EPA, Washington, 1978-80, spl. asst. for econs. and program ops. EPA, 1981—; fed. coordinator Emergency Transp. for State Tenn., 1973-76. Mem. adminstrv. bd. Keith Methodist. Ch., Athens, Tenn., 1974-75; bd. dirs. Statewide Council Community Leadership Tenn., 1973-75, Tenn. Alcohol and Drug Aubse Higher Edn. Planning Council, 1973, Center Govt. Tng. Tenn., 1973-75; mem. Presdl. Exec. Res. Office Pres. U.S. Served to lt. col., paratroopers U.S. Army, 1953-58. Decorated Army Commendation medal; recipient certificate of achievement Dept. Def., 1958, Outstanding Achievement award, 1967. Fellow Menninger Found.; mem. Harvard Bus. Sch. Alumni Assn. Internat. Platform Assn., Am. Econ. Assn. Am. Statis. Assn., Am. Acad. Polit., Social Scis., Am. Acad. Cons., AAUP, Res. Officers Assn., Assn. U.S. Army, Am. Security Council (bd. dirs.), Phi Sigma Kappa, Phi Alpha Theta. Clubs: Harvard, Harvard Bus. Sch., Capitol Yacht, Officers of Mil. Dist. of Washington, Gaslight of Washington, Lions, Rotary. Author books, the most recent being: Highway Cost and Special Benefits, 1967; Federal Emergency Transportation Preparedness, 1968; Supervisory Management, 1972; Civil Affairs Personnel Survey, 1973; (with others) Community Leadership Development, 1975; contbr. numerous articles to profl. publs. Home: 509 Lewis St Vienna VA 22180 Office: Plans and Programs Staff EPA (ANR-471) Washington DC 20460

FRANTEL, EDWARD WILLIAM, soft drink co. exec.; b. Wauwatosa, Wis., Mar. 18, 1925; s. Edward S. and Myrtle E. (Fischer) Frantl; B.S. in Bus. Adminstrn., Marquette U., 1948; m. Charlotte Lieg, Aug. 24, 1946; 1 son, Scott. Field sales supr. H.J. Heinz Co., Milw., 1948-53; with Miller Brewing Co., Milw., 1953-79, field sales mgr., 1968-72, dir. sales, 1972-74, v.p. sales, 1974-79; pres., chief exec. officer The Seven-Up Co., Clayton, Mo., 1979—. Vice-pres. Philip Morris Inc., dir. Mission Viejo, Cheer Up Co.; Marbert, Inc., Seven-Up Bottling of Phoenix, Inc., Seven-Up Bottling Co. of Norfolk, Inc., Seven-Up Can. Ltd., Seven-Up U.S.A., Inc., Ventura Coastal Corp., Warner-Jenkinson Co. Inc., Warner-Jenkinson Co. of Calif., Warner-Jenkinson East Inc., Golden Crown Citrus Corp. Served with U.S. Army, World War II. Decorated Bronze Star with oak leaf cluster, Purple Heart with oak leaf cluster. Mem. Sales and Mktg. Execs. of Milw., Marquette U. Bus. Adminstrn. Alumni Assn. Clubs: Saint Louis, Milwaukee Athletic, Confrerie de la Chaine des Rotisseurs. Office: 121 S Meramec St Clayton MO 63105

FRANTZ, CURTIS JOHN, corp. exec.; b. Schnecksville, Pa., Dec. 11, 1931; s. Jay Claude and Carrie L.A. (Peters) F.; grad. Bethlehem (Pa.) Bus. Sch., 1960; m. Elaine B. Kuhns, Apr. 14, 1956; children—Allison E., Lori April. Supr. gen. acctg. dept. Standard Pump and Aldrich div. Ingersoll Rand Co., Allentown, Pa., 1950-70; payroll and cost dept. supr. Bonney Forge div. Gulf and Western Co., Allentown, 1970-73; v.p., controller Colonial Parking, Inc., Allentown, also Colonial Mgmt., Inc., Wilmington, Del., 1973—. Vice pres., dir. Pa. Dutch Tall Stories Event; mgr. Egypt Meml. Park Assn., 1957-70. Served with C.E., AUS, 1953-54; Korea. Profl. acct., Pa.; enrolled to practice before IRS. Mem. Nat. Assn. Enrolled Agts., Nat. Soc. Public Accts., VFW, Pa. Soc. Mem. United Ch. of Christ. Clubs: Copeechan Fish and Game, Masons, Odd Fellows. Home: 4403 Main St Egypt Whitehall PA 18052 Office: 919 Hamilton Mall Allentown PA 18101

FRANZ, DIETER, real estate co. exec.; b. Hamburg. W. Ger., July 28, 1939; came to U.S., 1965; s. Karl F.G. and Engel M. (Henn) F.; Cand.Ing., Tech. U. Hanover, 1965; B.S. in Civil Engring., Ga. Inst. Tech., 1966, M.S., 1967; m. Christine Brickley, Apr. 13, 1968. Assos., D.A. Polychrone & Assos., Atlanta, 1967-75; cons. Shenandoah Devel., Inc. (Ga.), 1975-77, chief exec. officer, gen. mgr., 1977—; asst. prof. Ga. Inst. Tech., 1973-76. Vice chmn. Atlanta Urban Design Commn., 1979, 80. Registered profl. engr., Ga. Mem. ASCE, Urban Land Inst., Nat. Assn. Fgn. Trade Zones, League New Communities, Atlanta C. of C. (internat. task force 1980—). Lutheran. Home: 1894 Wellbourne Dr NE Atlanta GA 30324 Office: Shenandoah Devel Inc PO Box 1157 6 Shenandoah Blvd Shenandoah GA 30265

FRANZ, LYDIA MILLICENT TRUC (MRS. ROBERT FRANZ), real estate exec.; b. Chgo., Jan. 11, 1924; d. Walter and Lydia (Kralovec) Truc; Mus.B., Ill. Wesleyan U., 1944; Mus.M., Northwestern U., 1949; m. Robert Franz, Aug. 27, 1952. Tchr. music pub. schs., Muskegon, Mich., 1947-48; mktg. research analyst Grant Advt. Agy., Chgo., 1949; mktg. research asst. Buchen Co., Chgo., 1949-52; asst. to dir. mktg. research Sherman Marquette Advt. Co., Chgo., 1952; asst. to pres., dir. media and research Andover Advt. Agy., 1952-55; salesman Boehmer & Hedlund, realty, Barrington, Ill., 1960-63; pres. Century-21-Country Squire, Inc., Barrington, 1963—. Mem. real estate adv. com. William Rainey Harper Coll., Palatine, Ill., 1971—. Served with WAC, 1944-46. Mem. Women in Real Estate (pres. 1966-67), Barrington Bd. Realtors (pres. 1968-69), Ill. Assn. Real Estate Bds. (dir. 1972-75, gov. Realtor's Inst. of Ill. 1972—, exec. com. 1977—), Nat. Assn. Realtors, Realtors Nat. Mktg. Inst. (bd. govs. 1979, regional gov. 1980), Barrington C. of C. (v.p. 1968-71, pres. 1974, dir. 1972-75), Am. Cryptogram Soc., Am. Contract Bridge League, Barrington Bus. and Profl. Women's Club, Sigma Alpha Iota. Republican. Home: 76 Lakeview Pkwy Timberlake Barrington IL 60010 Office: 209 Park Ave Barrington IL 60010

FRASHIER, GARY EVAN, chem. co. exec.; b. Pampa, Tex., July 2, 1936; s. Virgil G. and Hazel V.; B.S. in Chem. Engring., Tex. Technol. U., 1958; M.B.A. (Sloan fellow), M.I.T., 1970; m. Sandra J., Dec. 29, 1972; children—Brian L., Kathy A., Denise L. Chem. engr. E.I. DuPont de Nemours & Co., Inc., 1958-59; research engr. Cabot Corp., Pampa, 1959-62, plant mgr. 1963-69, mgr. prodn., 1970-71, gen. mgr., 1971-72; dir. bus. planning Rockwell Internat. Corp., Pitts., 1973; v.p. mfg. Loctite Corp., Newington, Conn., 1974-75, pres., chief exec. officer indsl. products group, 1976-80; pres. internat. ops. Millipore Corp., Bedford, Mass., 1980—, Waters Assos., Bedford, Mass., 1980—. Served as 1st lt., Chem. Corps, AUS, 1959. Registered profl. engr., Tex., La. Mem. Am. Inst. Chem. Engrs., Young Presidents Orgn., Am. Supply and Machinery Mfg. Assn. (dir. 1980—, pres.), Instrument Soc. Am. (sr.). Republican. Presbyterian. Clubs: City of Hartford; Golf of Avon. Office: Millipore Corp Bedford MA 01730

FRAUSTEIN, ROBERT JORDAN, aircraft parts mfg. co. exec.; b. Lafayette, Ind., July 18, 1948; s. Robert Guy and Mary Elizabeth F.; B.S. in Bus. Adminstrn., Calif. State U., Northridge, 1971; m. Cheryl Lynn Kraft, June 21, 1969; children—Michael Robert, Tracey Lynn, Jeffrey Brian. Internal auditor Los Angeles Dept. Water and Power, 1972-75; supr. accounts payable Western Airlines, 1975-78; internal audit mgr. Fotomat Corp., La Jolla, Calif., 1978-81; controller Machine Industries, Inc., Oceanside, Calif., 1981—. Sec.-treas., bd. dirs. Rancho Ponderosa Homeowners Assn., 1979-80; mem. sch. site council Flora Vista Elem. Sch., 1979—; ruling elder United Presbyterian Ch., 1973. Cert. internal auditor. Mem. Inst. Internal Auditors (hon. mem. Los Angeles chpt., gov. San Diego chpt.), Soc. Advancement of Mgmt. Republican. Office: Machine Industries 2141 Oceanside Blvd Oceanside CA 92054

FRAYN, ROBERT MORT, printing and pub. co. exec.; b. Faulkton, S.D., May 3, 1906; s. Newton James and Margaret (Waterman) F.; B.A., U. Wash., 1929; m. Helen Elvira Carlson, Oct. 17, 1930; children—Suzanne, Robert Mort. With Frayn Printing Co./Book Pub. Co., Seattle, 1930—, owner, 1942—, pres., chief exec. officer, 1960—, chmn. bd., 1970—; dir. Lincoln Mut. Bank, Braniff Internat.; mem. Wash. State Ho. of Reps., 1945-55, speaker, 1953. Chmn. Wash. Republican Party, 1951, 60; mem. Rep. Nat. Com., 1951-60; mem. bd. regents U. Wash., 1970—, pres., 1975—; mem. exec. com. Assn. Governing Bds. Univs. and Colls.; bd. dirs. Virginia Mason Hosp., 1946-60, U. Hosp., 1977—. Recipient Alumni Activity award U. Wash., 1977. Mem. Alumni Assn. U. Wash. Congregationalist. Clubs: Wash. Athletic, Univ., Seattle Golf, Thunderbird Golf, Rotary. Home: 2111 Parkside Dr E Seattle WA 98112 Office: 2518 Western Ave Seattle WA 98121

FRAZEE, ROWLAND CARDWELL, banker; b. Halifax, N.S., Can., May 12, 1921; s. Rowland Hill and Callie Jean (Cardwell) F.; B.Commerce, King's Coll. and Dalhousie U., Halifax, 1948; m. Marie Eileen Tait, June 11, 1949; children—Stephen, Catherine. With Royal Bank Can., 1939—, v.p., chief gen. mgr. head office, Montreal, 1972-73, exec. v.p., chief gen. mgr., dir., 1973-77, pres., 1977—, chmn., chief exec. officer, 1980—. Bd. dirs. Council for Can. Unity, Portage Program Drug Dependencies, Niagara Inst., Roosevelt Campobello Internat. Park Commn.; trustee Sports Fund for the Physically Disabled; bd. govs. McGill U. Served to maj. Canadian Army, 1939-45. Anglican. Clubs: Rosedale Golf, Toronto, Granite (Toronto); Mt. Royal, St. James's, Royal Montreal Golf, Mt. Bruno Country (Montreal); Lyford Cay (Nassau). Office: 1 Pl Ville Marie Montreal PQ H3C 3A9 Canada

FRAZIER, JOHN EARL, engring. exec.; b. Houseville, Pa., July 4, 1902; s. Chauncey Earl and Mary Ellen (Gibson) F.; B.S., Washington and Jefferson Coll., 1922; S.M., M.I.T., 1924; Sc.D., U. Brazil, 1938; m. Frances Sprague Lang, June 23, 1936; children—John Earl II, Thomas Gibson. Engr., Owens-Ill. Glass Co., 1924-26; with Frazier-Simplex, Inc., Washington, Pa., 1926—, sec.-treas., 1930-38, v.p., treas., 1938-45, pres., sec., 1945-66, pres., treas., 1966—. Keramos-Frazier Library, Pa. State U., named in his honor; recipient citation on engring. Washington and Jefferson Coll., 1953, citation of distinction Washington County Alumni Assn., Washington and Jefferson Coll., 1958, citation of appreciation Point Park Coll., 1967, citation of appreciation Japanese Ceramic Assn., 1970, Disting. Citizen award Washington (Pa.) City Council, 1960; named to Bus. and Profl. Hall of Fame, 1967; named Knight of St. Patrick, Alfred U., 1970. Fellow Am. Ceramic Soc. (pres. 1970-71, hon. life, Albert Victor Beininger Meml. award 1969, John Jeppson award 1976), Soc. Glass Tech. Eng. (life), Royal Soc. Arts of Eng. (life), Am. Inst. Chemists, AAAS (life); mem. Nat. Acad. Engring., Am. Chem. Soc. (life), AIME, ASHRAE (life), Ceramic Ednl. Council (life), Nat. Soc. Profl. Engrs., Pa. Soc. Profl. Engrs. (v.p. Washington County 1951), Ark. Soc. Profl. Engrs., Pa. Acad. Sci., N.Y. Acad. Scis. (life), Pa. Ceramics Assn. (pres. 1950, now dir.), Pa. Inst. Chemists (charter), Can. Ceramic Soc., ASTM, Solar Engring. Soc., Am. Inst. Chemists, Keramos Frat. (Greaves Walker Roll of Honor), Phi Beta Kappa, Sigma Xi, Phi Chi Mu, Kappa Sigma. Republican. Presbyterian. Clubs: Newcomen Soc. N. Am., Lions (Lion of Yr. 1970). Contbr. sci. articles to jours. Am. Ceramic Soc. and AIME, Colliers Ency., Venezuelan Govt. publs.; holder 49 patents. Office: 436 E Beau St Washington PA 15301

FRECH, RAYMOND JOSEPH, holding co. exec.; b. Jersey City, Apr. 12, 1947; s. Raymond J. and Veronica A. (Deetjen) F.; B.S. in Acctg., St. Peter's Coll., 1969; m. Frances Phyllis Cusumano, July 22, 1973; 1 son, Raymond Joseph III. Staff acct., supervising sr. acct. Peat, Marwick, Mitchell & Co., Newark, Hackensack, N.J., 1969-75; controller Alusuisse Metals, Inc., Fair Lawn, N.J., 1975-78; asst. sec., asst. treas. Alusuisse Overseas, Ltd., Fair Lawn, 1975-78; controller, asst. sec., asst. treas. Alusuisse of Am., Inc., N.Y.C., 1978—; asst. sec., asst. treas. Am. Elec. Industries, Inc., Fair Lawn, 1978—. C.P.A., N.J. Mem. Am. Inst. C.P.A.'s, N.J. Soc. C.P.A.'s, Am. Mgmt. Assn., Holy Family Lyceum. Republican. Roman Catholic. Office: 21-000 Route 208 Fair Lawn NJ 07410

FRECKA, JOHN ALLISON, steel co. exec., lawyer; b. Ironton, Ohio, Jan. 12, 1929; s. James Harold and Margaret Helene (Fowler) F.; B.S., Marshall U., 1950; J.D., Wayne State U., 1967; m. Lois Joann Williams, Sept. 23, 1950; children—Deborah, David, John, Mary Anne. Personnel mgr. Detroit Strip div. Cyclops Corp., Detroit, 1951-64, turn supt., 1964-68, gen. supt., 1969-73, gen. mgr., 1974-76; admitted to Mich. bar, 1967; v.p. Empire-Detroit Steel div. Cyclops Corp., Mansfield, Ohio, 1976-78, pres., 1979—. Mem. Mich. Bar Assn. Home: 2065 Matthes Dr Mansfield OH 44906 Office: 913 Bowman St Mansfield OH 44901

FREDERICK, CHARLES O., ins. co. exec.; b. Ala., Nov. 25, 1919; s. Luther Lee and Carrie Elizabeth (Crittenden) F.; B.A. in Bus. Adminstrn., Columbia Union Coll., 1950; m. Eldine Allen, Dec. 25, 1945; children—Cheryl Dean, Allen Lee. Gen. mgr. Gifford Ice Cream Co., Silver Spring, Md., 1950-53; bus. mgr. Spicer Meml. Coll., Poona, India, 1953-59; dir. Gencon Risk Mgmt. Service, Riverside, Calif., 1959-70; v.p., Washington, 1970-74; v.p. Internat. Ins. Co. of Takoma Park (Md.), 1974-78, pres., 1978—; tchr. bus. adminstrn. Served in USAAF, 1942-45. Mem. Risk and Ins. Mgmt. Soc., Am. Mgmt. Assn., Nat. Assn. Mut. Ins. Cos., Nat. Assn. Ind. Insurers. Club: Rotary (dir. Arlington, Calif. 1966-67, pres. 1967-68) (Silver Spring, Md.). Office: 6930 Carroll Ave Takoma Park MD 20012

FREDERICK, DOLLIVER H., investment co. exec.; b. Edmonton, Alta., Can., Apr. 2, 1944; s. Henry and Gladys (Ganske) F.; B.S., No. Alta. Inst. Tech., 1965; m. Joan B. Dickau, Aug. 28, 1965; children—Blayne Jeffrey, Tamara Lea. With Imperial Oil Ltd., Edmonton, 1965-73, sr. analyst mktg., Toronto, Ont., 1972-73; corp. devel. mgr. Kesmark Ltd. (formerly Bovis Corp. Ltd.), 1973-75, corp. v.p., 1975-79; pres., chief operating officer Gen. Supply Co. Can. (1973) Ltd., 1975-79, Equipment Fed. Que. Ltd., 1975-79; pres., chief exec. officer, dir. CanWest Investment Corp., Toronto, Ont., 1979—; chmn. exec. com., dir. Na-Churs Plant Food Co., Marion, Ohio, 1979—, Macleod Stedman, Inc., Winnipeg and Toronto, 1979—; dir. membership com. Bd. Trade Met. Toronto. Mem. Assn. Corp. Growth, Pres.'s Assn. Conservative. Clubs: Nat., Cambridge, Toronto Cricket, Skating and Curling, Bd. Trade Golf. Home: 35 Steeplechase Aurora ON L4G 3G8 Canada Office: PO Box 132 L-First Canadian Pl Toronto ON M5X 1A4 Canada

FREDERICK, MARK DEAN, mfg. engr.; b. Blossburg, Pa., Nov. 27, 1958; s. Donald and Gloria Joan (Thorsen) F.; Asso. Mech. Engring. Tech., Vt. Tech. Coll., 1978; student Central New Eng. Coll., 1979—;

m. Heather Ann Reed, June 11, 1977. Indsl. engr. Heald Machine div. Cin. Milacron Co., Worcester, Mass., 1978-79; mfg. engr. grinding machine div. Warner & Swasey, Worcester, 1979—. Mem. Soc. Mfg. Engrs. Club: Worcester Court. Office: 145 Brook St Worcester MA 01606

FREDERICKS, WARD ARTHUR, mfg. co. exec.; b. Tarrytown, N.Y., Dec. 24, 1939; s. Arthur George and Evelyn (Smith) F.; B.A. cum laude, Mich. State U., 1962, M.B.A., 1963; m. Patricia A. Sexton, June 7, 1960; children—Corrine E., Lorrine L., Ward A. Asso. dir. Technics Group, Grand Rapids, Mich., 1964-68; gen. mgr. logistics systems Massey-Ferguson Inc., Des Moines, 1968-69, v.p. mgmt. services, comptroller, 1969-73, sr. v.p. fin., dir. fin. Americas, 1975—; comptroller Massey-Ferguson Ltd., Toronto, Ont., Can., 1973-75; cons. W.B. Saunders & Co., Washington, 1962—; sr. v.p. mktg. Massey/Ferguson, Inc., 1975-80, also sr. v.p., gen. mgr. Tractor div., 1978-80; v.p. ops., Rockwell Internat., Pitts., 1980—; dir. Badger Northland Inc., Unicorn Corp., Harry Ferguson Inc., M.F. Credit Corp., M.F. Credit Co. Can. Ltd. Bd. dirs., mem. exec. com. Des Moines Symphony, 1975-79. Am. Transp. Assn. fellow, 1962-63; Ramlose fellow, 1962-63. Mem. Am. Mktg. Assn., Nat. Council Phys. Distbn. Mgmt. (exec. com. 1974), Toronto Bd. Trade, Beta Gamma Sigma. Rotarian. Author: (with Edward W. Smykay) Physical Distribution Management, 1974. Contbr. articles to profl. jours. Home: 539 Old Mill Rd Fox Chapel PA 15238 also 7877 Sendero Uno Tucson AZ Office: 400 N Lexington Ave Pittsburgh PA

FREDRICK, JEROME F., chem. co exec.; b. N.Y.C., Feb. 23, 1926; B. Sc. (Tremaine fellow in biology), Coll. City N.Y., 1949; M.Sc., N.Y.U., 1951, Ph.d., 1955; m. Miriam Macklin, June 6, 1946; children—Alan M., Naomi J., Sharona E. Instr. biology Coll. City N.Y., 1948-49; research biochemist N.Y.C. VA Hosp., 1949-51; chemist customs labs. U.S. Treasury Dept., N.Y.C., 1951-53; dir. chem. research Dodge Chem. Co., Boston, N.Y.C., 1954—; prof. Dodge Inst., Cambridge, Mass. Cons. enzymology NRC, 1957—. Chmn. Bronx Action for Clean Air Com., Bronx Council for Environmental Quality. Trustee Am. Inst. City N.Y.; pres. Am. Inst. City N.Y. Served with USNR, 1944-46. Recipient Fuller award Am. Chem. Soc., 1944. Fellow Am. Inst. Chemists (accreditation bd., bd. appeals), N.Y. Acad. Scis., Explorers Club; mem. Am. Chem. Soc., Am. Inst. Biol. Scis., A.A.A.S., Scandinavian Soc. Plant Physiologists. Author: Chelation Phenomena, 1960; Gel Electrophoresis, 1964. Editor: Plant Growth Regulators, 1968; Phylogenesis and Morphogenesis in Algae, 1971; Storage Polyglucosides, 1972. Contbr. numerous articles on exzyme and chelation chemistry and cancer chemotherapeutic agents to profl. publs. Patentee in field. Office: 3425 Boston Post Rd Bronx NY 10469

FREE, LEDGER DANIEL, constrn. forms mfg. co. exec.; b. Casper, Wyo., Dec. 24, 1921; s. Ledger Daniel and Clara Belle (Williams) F.; A.B., Harvard U., 1947; J.D., Stanford U., 1950; m. Carol Brennan Fox, June 18, 1948 (dec. Oct. 1962); children—Karen, Kenneth, Douglas; m. 2d, Dorothy Ann Clark, Nov. 12, 1966. Admitted to Calif. bar, 1951, U.S. Supreme Ct. bar, 1959; law clk. Calif. Dist. Ct. Appeal, 1951; asso. firm Landels & Weigel, San Francisco, 1953-54; asso. counsel, then counsel, asst. v.p., v.p. Bank of Am., San Francisco, 1954-65, sec.-treas. The Burke Co., San Mateo, Calif., 1965-68, v.p. fin. and adminstrn., 1968-72, pres., chief exec. officer, 1972—, chmn. bd., 1980—. Trustee, San Carlos (Calif.) Elem. Sch. Bd., 1961-67, pres. bd., 1964-66; chmn. budget com. United Bay Area Crusade, 1963-65, trustee, 1964-66. Served with U.S. Army, 1941-45, to capt. USAF, 1951-53; Korea. Decorated Bronze Star. Mem. Pres.'s Assn., Am. Mgmt. Assn. Republican. Clubs: Harvard (pres.), Univ. (San Francisco); Harvard (N.Y.C.); Foothills Tennis and Swim. Office: 2655 Campus Dr PO Box 5818 San Mateo CA 94403

FREEBORN, MARSHALL FRANKLIN, rancher; b. San Antonio, July 18, 1924; s. Sidney M. and Bella A. (Schaeffer) F.; B.S. in Agrl. Edn., Tex. A&I U., 1953; m. Mary Ann Laechelin, July 22, 1950; children—Terry Schaeffer, Jo Ann Freeborn Piant. Ranch mgr. Live Oak County, Tex., 1951; jr. high sch. tchr., Tex., 1953-56, 65-71; cattle farmer Nacogdoches County, Tex., 1956-60, San Augustine and Shelby Counties, Tex., 1960-74; mgr., owner ranch lands in Jim Wells and Duval Counties, Tex., 1950—. Active Am. Cancer Soc. Served with USNR, 1942-44. Mem. Nat. Rifle Assn. Methodist. Address: Fulton Beach Rd Box 237 Fulton TX 78358

FREEDMAN, DENNIS ALLEN, fin. and mktg. exec.; b. N.Y.C., July 24, 1944; s. James J. and Josephine Freedman; B.A. in Econs., Fairleigh Dickinson U., 1965; m. Linda Aga, July 27, 1968. Fin. analyst Dun & Bradstreet, Inc., N.Y.C., 1967-72; fin. adminstr. U.S. Trust Co. N.Y., N.Y.C., 1972-74; v.p. Physicians Properties Inc. of Nev., N.Y.C., 1974—; mgr. APPA/NARI Fed. Credit Union, N.Y.C., 1976—; v.p. Physicians Planning Service Corp. of Conn., N.Y.C., 1978—; mktg. mgr. Arden Travel Services Co., Inc., N.Y.C., 1978—. Vol. worker, sch. tchr., mem. Christian edn. com. Presbyn. Ch., Morristown, N.J., 1974—. Mem. Am. Bus. Assn. Home: 9 Rosemilt Pl Morristown NJ 07960 Office: 292 Madison Ave New York NY 10017

FREEDMAN, MICHAEL IRA, trading corp. exec.; b. New Haven, June 8, 1942; s. Louis and Mollie (Schiff) F.; B.A. with honors, Clark U., Worcester, Mass., 1964; m. Francesca Pitrelli, June 29, 1980. Sales mgr. Investors Overseas Services, Geneva, 1965-70; pres. Parlane Assos., London, 1971-72; sales mgr. Peter Pan Industries, Newark, 1972-75; pres., Gemstone Trading Corp., N.Y.C., 1976—; dir. Gemstone Trading Co. (U.K.), Ltd. Served with USAFR, 1964-65. Mem. Jewelers Vigilance Com., Jewelers Bd. Trade. Diamond Importers and Mfrs. Assn. Libertarian. Jewish. Author: Investors Guide to Diamonds, 1980; editor Gem Letter, 1976—. Office: Suite 4525 30 Rockefeller Plaza New York NY 10020

FREELAND, T. PAUL, lawyer; b. Princeton, Ind., Sept. 26, 1916; s. L. Theodore and Leona (Tryon) F.; A.B., DePauw U., 1937; LL.B., Columbia, 1940; m. Caroline Van Dyke Ransom, July 7, 1941; 1 dau., Caroline Carr. Admitted to N.Y., D.C., Mass. bars; asso. Cravath, deGersdorff Swaine & Wood, N.Y.C., summer 1939, Dunnington, Bartholow & Miller, N.Y.C., 1940-42; atty. Office Chief Counsel, Bur. Internal Revenue, 1945-48; partner Wenchel, Schulman & Manning, Washington, 1949-62, Sharp and Bogan, Washington, 1962-65, Bogan & Freeland, 1965—. Lectr. tax insts., mem. various taxation coms. Trustee Embry-Riddle Aero. U. Served as lt. USCG, 1942-45, ETO. Mem. Inter-Am., Am., Fed., D.C. bar assns., Internat. Fiscal Assn., Phi Delta Phi. Clubs: Met., Univ., Chevy Chase. Home: 5525 Pembroke Rd Bethesda MD 20034 Office: 1000 16th St NW Washington DC 20036

FREEMAN, BRADFORD MACLEAN, investment banker; b. Fargo, N.D., Mar. 11, 1942; s. Russell Otis and Louise Adams (Fuller) F.; A.B., Stanford, 1964; M.B.A., Harvard, 1966. With Dean Witter & Co., Los Angeles, 1966—, v.p., 1969-77, sr. v.p., 1977—. Mem. Beta Theta Pi. Clubs: California, Beach, Knickerbocker. Office: 800 Wilshire Blvd Los Angeles CA 90017

FREEMAN, DAVID REED, investor; b. Fredericksburg, Va., July 18, 1941; s. George Cephas and Kathryn (Reed) F.; student U. N.C., 1959-60; m. Patricia Harrison Tydings, May 2, 1977; children by previous marriage—Kimberly Rowe, David Reed; 1 stepson, Basil W. Tydings, Jr. Instl. salesman Eastman Dillon, Union Securities & Co., Washington, 1963-71; v.p. sales Blyth, Eastman Dillon, Washington, 1972-74; chmn. bd. Freeman Distributing Co., Inc., Alexandria, Va., 1973-74; pres., owner Freeman Enterprises, Easton, Md., 1974—; pres., dir. Freeman & Kagan, Inc., Realtors, Easton, 1979—; pres., owner Freeman Interiors, Easton, 1980—; chmn. bd. Tidewater Roofing and Bldg. Supply Co., Inc., 1975—; dir. Washington-Lee Savs. & Loan Assn., 1972—, chmn. adv. bd., 1976—. Bd. dirs. Historic Easton, Inc., 1975-79, Easton YMCA, 1976—; chmn. bd. deacons First Bapt. Ch., Easton, 1976—, bd. trustees, 1975—; mem. endowment com. Talbot County YMCA, 1979—. Mem. Early Am. Soc., Talbot County Hist. Soc., Victorian Soc. Am., Nat., Md. trusts hist. preservation. Republican. Editor: Historic Easton, 1979. Home: Waverly Island Farm RD 4 Box 110 Easton MD 21601 Office: 6 Glenwood Ave Easton MD 21601

FREEMAN, DONALD WILFORD, mobile home park developer; b. Brooksville, Fla., Sept. 25, 1929; s. Fred Maxwell and Dovie (Keef) F.; B.S., U. Ala., 1953, LL.B., 1953; LL.M., N.Y. U., 1957; m. Ruby Jane Lewis, Feb. 25, 1956; children—Clifton Lewis, Susan Anne. Accountant, Ernst & Ernst, Atlanta, 1953-55; admitted to Ala. bar, 1953; tax atty. Office Chief Counsel, U.S. Treasury Dept., N.Y.C., 1955-57, West Point Mfg. Co. (Ga.), 1957-58; asst. treas. Ryder System, Inc., Miami, Fla., 1958-61; v.p., dir. Henderson's Portion Pak, Inc., 1961-63; pres. Biscayne Capital Corp., Miami, Fla., 1964-66; sr. asso. Lazard Freres & Co., N.Y.C., 1967-69; pres. James A. Ryder Corp., Miami, 1969-78, Fla. Mobile Home Communities, Inc., Vero Beach, 1978—. Served with AUS, 1946-48; PTO. C.P.A., Ga. Mem. Fla. Inst. C.P.A.'s, Phi Kappa Sigma, Beta Gamma Sigma. Episcopalian. Home: 13026 Nevada St Coral Gables FL 33156 Office: 7300 State Rd 60 Vero Beach FL 32960

FREEMAN, FREDERICK ROE, lawyer, ins. and mut. fund co. exec.; b. Arkansas City, Kans., July 11, 1914; s. Claude Kenneth and Agnes (Roe) F.; A.B., Southwestern Coll., 1952; J.D., U. Mo. at Kansas City, 1954; m. Joy Parman, May 1, 1936; children—Sheryl Ann Freeman Matthews, Frederick William. Partner ins. and real estate co., 1936-40; sec.-treas. Ark. Transp. Lines, Inc., 1940-45; owner, mgr. income tax service, real estate, ins. agy., 1945-54; admitted to Mo. bar, 1954, U.S. Supreme Ct. bar, 1965; practice law, Kansas City, 1954—; sec.-treas. David L. Babson Investment Fund, Inc., Kansas City, 1959-76, v.p., treas., 1976—; sec.-treas., dir. Jones & Babson, Inc., Kansas City, 1959-65, v.p., 1965—; pres., dir. Income and Retirement Security Corp., Kansas City, 1973—. Mem. Am., Kansas City bar assns., Mo. Bar (taxation com.), Lawyers Assn. Kansas City, Nat., Kansas City life underwriters assns., S.R., S.A.R., Phi Alpha Delta. Presbyn. Club: Kansas City Athletic. Home: 6023 Wyandotte St Kansas City MO 64113 Office: G-15 2440 Pershing Rd Crown Center Kansas City MO 64108

FREEMAN, GRACE CLAUDIA, acct.; b. Buenos Aires, Argentina, Oct. 23, 1954; came to U.S., 1957, naturalized, 1963; d. Hugh Rubin and Nilda Nieves (Ferrandez) Getty; student acctg. U. No. Colo., 1971-72; student U. Ga., 1972-74, Colo. State U., 1974; 1 son, Lance Alexander. Head of fin. Young's West, Inc., Ft. Collins, Colo., 1972-74; with Hewlett Packard Co., Loveland, Colo., 1975-76; partner, sr. acct. Dickson's Acctg. Service, Ft. Collins, 1977-79; owner, mgr. G & L Assos., Ft. Collins, 1979—; lectr., cons. in field; pvt. acct. Internat. Project: Contemporary Crafts of the Ams., 1974-75; profl. acct. for Internat. Artists, 1977—. Recipient Cert. Excellence, Clarke County Sch. Dist. Mem. Nat. Soc. Public Accts., Gamma Eta Pi. Asso. editor Illiad Mag., 1972. Home: 718 E Laurel St Fort Collins CO 80524 Office: 1720 W Mulberry St Suite B-5 Fort Collins CO 80521

FREEMAN, HARRY BOIT, JR., financial exec.; b. Providence, June 14, 1926; s. Harry Boit and Theodora (Hollander) F.; A.B., Yale U., 1948; M.B.A., N.Y. U., 1952; m. Leslie Stires, June 14, 1947; children—Tracy Clark, Harry Boit. With City Bank Farmers Trust Co., N.Y.C., 1949-52; asst. treas., asso. investment officer, investment officer, v.p. Tchrs. Ins. & Annuity Assn., N.Y.C., 1952-59; gen. partner Wood, Struthers & Winthrop and predecessor, N.Y.C., 1959-67; v.p. Engelhard Hanovia, Inc., 1967-70; pres., dir. Channing Mgmt. Corp., Inc., 1970-73, Channing Mut. Funds, 1970-73; with Lord, Abbett & Co., N.Y.C., 1973—, gen. partner, 1974—, asso. mng. partner, 1977-78, mng. partner, 1978-79; asst. treas. Am.-S. African Investment Co., 1968-70. Served with USMCR, 1944-45. Mem. Am. Fin. Assn., N.Y. Soc. Security Analysts. Episcopalian. Home: 200 E 74th St New York NY 10021

FREEMAN, MILTON V., lawyer; b. N.Y.C., Nov. 16, 1911; s. Samuel and Celia (Gelfand) F.; A.B., Coll. City of N.Y., 1931; LL.B., Columbia, 1934; m. Phyllis Young, Dec. 19, 1937; children—Nancy Lois Freeman Gans, Daniel Martin, Andrew Samuel, Amy Martha Freeman Malone. Admitted to N.Y. bar, 1934; D.C. bar, 1946, bar U.S. Supreme Ct., 1943; with gen. counsel's office, SEC, 1934-42; with securities div. F.T.C., 1934; asst. solicitor, SEC, 1942-46; pvt. practice with firm Arnold & Fortas, Arnold, Fortas & Porter, Arnold & Porter, Washington, 1946—. Lectr. law schs. Hon. chmn. Internat. Law Inst., Georgetown U. Mem. Am., D.C., Fed. bar. assns. Contbr. articles to profl. jours. Home: 3405 Woolsey Dr Chevy Chase MD 20015 Office: 1200 New Hampshire Ave NW Washington DC 20036

FREEMAN, QUIEMAN EARL, computer software engr.; b. Dayton, Ohio, Aug. 11, 1954; s. Raymond Earl and Florence E. F.; grad. U. Cin., 1973-77. Programmer analyst Central Trust Co., Cin., 1977-78; sr. programmer analyst Automation Cons., Inc., Dayton, 1978-79; computer cons. Mead Corp., Dayton, 1978-79; direct access storage device mgr., mem. tech. staff Gen. Motors Dayton Info. Systems Activity, Dayton, 1979—; pres., chmn. bd. Freeman Computer Illustrations, Ltd.; teaching asst. Sinclair Coll., 1978-79; career adv. U. Cin. Named Outstanding Coll. Student, Alpha Phi Alpha, 1977; recipient Disting. Service award Def. Electronics Supply Center, USAF, 1971, work citation Wright-Patterson AFB, 1972, Ch. Scholarship award Zion Bapt. Ch., 1973. Mem. Minority Data Processing Assn. (pres.), Small Bus. Cons., Alpha Phi Alpha (pres. chpt. 1977-78). Home: 5919 Greenspoint Dr Apt 1304 Fort Worth TX 76112

FREEMAN, ROBERT PARKE, lawyer, realty co. exec.; b. Long Beach, Calif., Apr. 10, 1945; s. Charles Wellman and Carla Elizabeth (Park) F.; B.A., Stanford, 1966; J.D., Harvard, 1969; m. Sandra Ruhanen, July 9, 1966; children—Robert Parke, Saurin Clifford. Admitted to R.I. bar, 1969; asso. firm Edwards & Angell, Providence, 1969-72; gen. counsel Realty Income Trust, Providence, 1972—, pres., 1980—; mem. adv. bd. Indsl. Nat. Bank R.I., Providence, 1973-79; partner fin. cons. firm Little and Casler, 1975-79; sec., treas. Bannister's Wharf, Inc., Newport, R.I., 1976—; mem. adv. bd. R.I. Hosp. Trust Nat. Bank, Providence, 1979—; v.p., treas. Locke-Ober Co., Boston, 1978—; pres., dir. Marathon Group of Cos., Inc., 1980—. Mem. exec. com. bd. overseers Lincoln Sch., Providence, 1979—; mem. exec. com. Planned Parenthood R.I., 1972-79, v.p., 1973-79; trustee Providence Found., 1976—; bd. dirs. Smith Hill Center, 1976-78. Mem. Am., R.I. bar assns. Clubs: Hope (Providence); Agawam Hunt, Turks Head. Editor Harvard Legal Commentary, 1968-69. Home: 30 Freeman Pkwy Providence RI 02906 Office: Darol Sq Providence RI 02903

FREEMAN, ROLAND D., real estate exec.; b. Lynchburg, Va., Oct. 12, 1941; s. Reginald Duane and Frances P. F.; B.S., Carroll Coll., Waukesha, Wis., 1964; B.S., Marquette U., 1968; m. Dorothy J. Newell, June 20, 1964; children—Barton James, Laurel Anne, Bethany Marie. Pres., Nanz Mgmt. Corp., 1964-72, Roland D. Freeman Assos., 1972-75, Capital Consultants Mgmt. Corp., 1975-76; sr. v.p. Rep.-Loowi Realty Corp., Dallas, 1976—; chmn. Nat. Apt. Mgmt. Accreditation Bd.; public speaker. Sec., Waukesha Police and Fire Commn.; county campaign chmn. March of Dimes, div. leader YMCA Bldg. Fund; bd. dirs. Southeastern Wis. March of Dimes; chmn. Waukesha Republican Party. Cert. property mgr., registered apt. mgr., lic. real estate instr., Tex.; recipient Multihousing Leadership award, 1978. Mem. Inst. Real Estate Mgmt., Nat. Apt. Assn. (v.p.), Nat. Assn. Home Builders, Real Estate Fin. Execs. Assn., Apt. Assn. Tarrant County (pres., sec.), Dallas Apt. Assn. (v.p.). Author: Encyclopedia of Apartment Management, 1976; contbr. numerous articles to mags. and trade publs. Home: 6508 Briarmeade Dr Dallas TX 75240 Office: 14841 Coit Rd Suite 315 Dallas TX 75248

FREEMAN, SPENCER, cons. business engr.; b. Swansea, South Wales, 1892; student Johannesburg Coll., S. Africa (Scholarship winner); Tech. Inst., York, Pa.; m. Hilda Kathleen Toler, Mar. 6, 1924; 1 son, Brian Sidney; came to U.S., 1910. Engr. draftsman Pullman Motor Co., York, Pa., Chalmers Motor Co., Detroit, 1910-14; mng. dir. Gallite and Rubber Mfg. Co., Ltd., London, Mfrs. and Exporters Alliance, London, 1919-29; cons. bus. engr.; dir. Hosps. Trust, Ltd., Dublin, asso. Brit. Ministry Aircraft Prodn., 1940; dir. Reconstrn. Emergency Services Orgn., 1940-41; prin. dir., responsible for restoration prodn. in all munition factories, contractors to Ministry Aircraft Prodn., Ministry Supply and Admiralty, Regional and Emergency Services Orgn., 1941-44; seconded to Brit. Bd. Trade (mem. indsl. and export council) to assist reconversion; spl. assignment in reconversion of radio industry from war to peacetime production; rep. Brit. Bd. Trade on Radio Bd. (cabinet com.), Radio Planning and Prodn. Com., Radio Prodn. Exec., 1944-45. Mem. council Dublin Theatre Festival. Served in World War I, 1914; commd. 1915; founded and remained in charge of Depot for Salvage and Repair of all automotive components used by Brit. Army in France. Decorated Mons Star, mentioned in Despatches (World War I); comdr. Order Brit. Empire (World War II). Mem. Soc. Automotive Engrs. U.S.A.; Liveryman of Co. of Newspaper Makers and Stationers (a London City Co.). Author: Production Under Fire; Take Your Measure; You Can Get to the Top. Home: Knocklyon House Templeogue County Dublin Ireland Office: Hospital Bldgs 20 Merrion Rd Dublin Ireland

FREER, ROBERT ELLIOTT, JR., lawyer; b. Washington, Jan. 19, 1941; s. Robert Elliott and Alice Elizabeth (Barry) F.; B.A., Princeton U., 1963; J.D., U. Va., 1966; m. Roberta Stapleton Renchard, Dec. 31, 1972; children—Kimberly Dunlap, Robert Elliott, Ashleigh Hamilton, Daniel Renchard. Admitted to Va. bar, 1966, U.S. Dist. Ct. bar, 1968, U.S. Circuit Ct. Appeals bar, 1969, 73, U.S. Supreme Ct. bar, 1973; trial atty. Bur. Deceptive Practices, FTC, Washington, 1966-68, trial atty. Bur. Restraint of Trade, 1968-70, atty-adv. to chmn., 1970, liaison officer, asst. to gen. counsel, 1970-71; exec. asst. to gen. counsel Dept. Transp., Washington, 1971-74; v.p., Washington counsel Kimberly-Clark Corp., Washington, 1974—. Bd. dirs. Children's Hearing and Speech Center, 1980—. Recipient Disting. Service award FTC, 1971. Mem. Fed. Bar Assn. (dep. chmn. transp. council 1972-77), Am. Bar Assn., Holland Soc. N.Y., N.C. Soc. of the Cin., Order St. John (officer). Republican. Episcopalian. Clubs: Met., Chevy Chase, Princeton (N.Y.C.); Coral Beach (Bermuda). Contbr. articles to profl. jours. Office: 1730 Pennsylvania Ave NW Washington DC 20006

FREER, ROMEO HENRY, civil engr., electronics co. exec.; b. San Francisco, Aug. 25, 1921; s. Romeo Henry and Marguerite Greenfield (Bowling) F.; B.S., U. Md., 1958; B.S.E. in Civil Engring., U. Mich., 1965; m. Mary Ann Robb, Oct. 24, 1970; 1 dau., Pamela. Served as flying officer RCAF, 1941-43; commd. 1st lt. USAF, 1943, advanced through grades to lt. col., 1963; reconaissance, bomber and transport pilot and civil engr., Gt. Britain, Germany, Japan, Iceland, Taiwan, 1943-64, ret., 1964; plant engr. Bell Labs., Holmdel, N.J. and Greensboro, N.C., 1966-70; sr. engr. Western Electric Co., Cockeysville, Md., 1970—. Decorated Air medal; registered profl. engr., N.Y., N.J., Tex., Ill., Pa., Ohio, Del., Md., Va., W.Va., D.C. Fellow ASCE; mem. Nat. Soc. Profl. Engrs., Md. Soc. Profl. Engrs. (pres. Howard County chpt., state dir.), Am. Inst. Plant Engrs., Soc. Am. Mil. Engrs., Engring. Soc. Balt. Republican. Episcopalian. Clubs: Engrs. (Balt.); Army-Navy (Washington). Office: Western Electric Co 225 Schilling Circle Cockeysville MD 21030

FREESE, JAMES KING, ins. agt.; b. Bristow, Okla., Dec. 28, 1940; s. James H. and Francys K. (King) F.; student Bristow public schs.; children—James King II, Joel K., Jason K. Pres., owner Freese & Co., Inc., Tulsa, 1960—; chmn. bd. Transam. Industries, Inc., MCF Industries, Great Western Airlines, Sterling Oil of Okla., Inc., Ross Aviation. Bd. dirs. Arts and Humanities Council, Okla. Profl. Theatre Found., Tulsa Summer Musicals; com. mem. Tulsa Ballet, Tulsa Opera, Tulsa Philharmonic. Mem. Million Dollar Round Table, 1980. Mem. Tulsa Ins. Bd., Okla. Assn. Ins. Agts., Ind. Ins. Agts. Am., Petroleum Club. Republican. Clubs: Tulsa, Summit, Elks. Home: 2455 E 27th Pl Tulsa OK 74114 Office: 2121 S Columbia St Tulsa OK 74114

FREESE, ROBERT GERARD, diversified mfg. co. exec.; b. N.Y.C., Oct. 6, 1929; s. S.V. and Helen (Haverty) F.; B.B.A., Manhattan Coll., 1951; M.B.A., N.Y. U., 1953; m. Joan Ann Walsh, Sept. 6, 1952; children—Bernadette, Maryellen, John. Internal auditor Texaco, N.Y.C., 1951-56; asst. supr. Grumman Corp., Bethpage, N.Y., 1956-64, supr., 1964-65, fin. mgr., 1965-69, dir. finances, 1969-71, asst. to treas., 1971-72, treas., 1972—, v.p., 1974-80, sr. v.p. fin., 1980—, also dir.; chmn. Grumman Credit Corp., Paumanock Ins. Co. Ltd., Grumman Allied Industries, Inc.; pres., treas. Glumair Export Sales Corp.; dir. Grumman Flexible Corp.; chmn., treas. Paumanock Devel. Corp.; treas., dir. Farmhouse Dining Services, Inc.; dir. Calldata Systems, Inc., GAAC Internat. Corp., Grumman Data Systems Corp., Grumman Aerospace Corp., Grumman Emergency Products, Inc., J.B.E. Olson of Can., Ltd., Valley L.I. region Bank of N.Y. Served with AUS, 1953-55. Clubs: Indian Hills Country, Pocono Farms Country. Home: 8 Melrose Ct Dix Hills NY 11746 Office: 1111 Stewart Ave Bethpage NY 11714

FREIER, JEROLD LEWIS, investment banker; b. Washington, Mar. 10, 1945; s. Milton and Gloria Annette (Powell) F.; B.A., U. Va., 1967; M.Ed. (Mellon fellow 1967-68, Univ. fellow 1968-70), Harvard U., 1970 M. City Planning, 1970. Spl. asst. HEW, Washington, 1970-72; pres. Marlboro Sq. Restaurant Corp., Washington, 1972-73; mortgage broker Advance Mortgage Corp., Washington, 1973-74; v.p. Mergers & Acquisitions, Inc., McLean, Va., 1974-77; mgr. dept. corp. Fin. Weeden & Co., Jersey City, 1977-78; v.p. Owens & Co., Washington, 1978-80; v.p. European Am. Bank, N.Y.C., 1980—; lectr. merger/acquisition seminar Fordham U., 1977, Northwestern U. Grad. Sch. Bus. Adminstrn. Merger Tng. Week, 1977, 78. Mem.

Assn. Corp. Growth, Am. Petroleum Inst., Ind. Petroleum Assn. Am., Ripon Soc. Jewish. Clubs: Harvard, B'nai B'rith (N.Y.C.). Editorial staff Mergers Acquisitions Jour., 1974—. Home: 1161 York Ave New York NY 10021 Office: 10 Hanover Sq New York NY 10015

FREIRE, JORGE EDUARDO, photographer; b. Guayaquil, Ecuador, Nov. 29, 1949; came to U.S., 1972; s. Bolivar Absalon and Olga Irene (Murillo) F.; student N.Y. U., 1972; m. Lourdes Rodriguez, May 12, 1974; children—Alis Patricia, Valerie de Lourdes. Darkroom technician John Carras Studios, Giuayaquil, Ecuador, 1966-68, prodn. mgr., 1968-70; photography supr. S.A. Advt., Ecuador, 1970-71; free-lance photographer, various countries, 1972-74; darkroom technician Print-O-Matic, N.Y.C., 1974-75; mgr. Impact B-42, photo studio, N.Y.C., 1975-76; founder, pres., gen. mgr. Success-O-Matic, N.Y.C., 1977—. Recipient 1st prize 7-Dias mag., Ecuador, 1972; plaque Comml. Photographers Assn., 1979. Jehovah's Witness. Office: Sucess-o-Matic 1472 Broadway New York NY 10036

FREIZER, LOUIS A., radio sta. exec.; b. N.Y.C., Oct. 10, 1931; s. Morris and Celia (Blumberg) F.; B.S., U. Wis., Madison, 1953; M.A., Columbia U., 1964, postgrad., 1965-70; m. Michele Suzanne Orban, July 6, 1968; children—Sabine, Eric. Correspondent UPI Madison, 1953-54; desk asst., CBS, N.Y.C., 1956-58, newswriter, 1958-62, news editor, 1964-68; sr. news producer Radio Sta. WCBS-AM, N.Y.C., 1968-73, sr. exec. news producer, 1973—; adj. prof. Fordham U.; lectr., cons. in field. Served with U.S. Army, 1954-56. CBS News Found. fellow, Columbia U., 1962-63. Recipient Am. Legion Medal for Americanism, 1953; AMA award for radio journalism, 1965; Nat. Headliners Club award for radio journalism, 1965. Mem. Acad. Polit. Sci., Am. Acad. Polit. and Social Sci., Am. Polit. Sci. Assn., Soc. Profl. Journalists, Radio-TV News Dirs. Assn. Home: 400 Central Park W New York NY 10025 Office: 51 W 52d St New York NY 10019

FRELS, MARK EDWIN, farm bur. exec.; b. Moline, Ill., Nov. 12, 1954; s. Calvin Edwin and Lois Marian (Parnell) F.; student U. Madrid, 1968, 70; B.A., Iowa Wesleyan Coll., 1976. Farmer, Rock Island County, Ill., to 1977; technician U.S. Dept. Agr., Soil Conservation Service, Rock Island County, 1976-77; semi-profl. photographer, Galesburg, Ill., 1972—; mgr. Knox County Farm Bur., Galesburg, Ill., 1977—. Leader, 4-H Club, 1974-77; mem. Ill. Council Youth, 1970-71; dir. farm drive Knox County United Way, 1978; del. White House Conf. on Youth, 1970; baseball coach Little League, 1971-75; mem. youth council Rock Island County Coop. Extension Service, 1975-77, mem. exec. council, 1975-77. Recipient Citizenship award Ill. 4-H, 1971, state photography award 4-H Club Congress, 1973. Mem. Galesburg Jr. C. of C., Blue Key. Methodist. Club: Kiwanis (Galesburg, Ill.). Home: 2762 No 10 Springer Rd Galesburg IL 61401 Office: 180 S Soangetaha Rd Galesburg IL 61401

FREMPONG-ATUAHENE, STEPHEN, ins. co. exec., bus. cons.; b. Kumasi, Ghana, Dec. 24, 1947; s. Samuel Kojo and Yaa (Afre) A.; A.A., U. London, 1967; B.A. (Ghana Cocoa Mktg. Bd. scholar, Ghana Govt. U. Edn. fellow), U. Ghana, 1970; M.B.A. (James Naurison scholar), Western New Eng. Coll., 1975; postgrad. U. Mass., 1975; m. Agnes C. Manu, Jan. 1, 1973; 1 son, Ben. Systems analyst, acct. Mass. Mut. Ins. Co., Springfield, 1976-77; sr. analyst data base adminstrn. Aetna Life & Casualty Co., Hartford, Conn., 1977-78; data base cons. Colonial Penn Group, Inc., Phila., 1978-79; data adminstr. Penn Mut. Life Ins. Co., Phila., 1979—; pres., chmn. bd. Bus. Cons. Group, Inc., Maple Shade, N.J., 1977—. Pres., Ahafo Ano Youth Assn., 1968-73; bd. dirs. Afro-Am. Center, 1973-75. Mem. Nat. Assn. Accts., Assn. Computing Machinery, Am. Mgmt. Assn., Assn. M.B.A. Grads., Urban League, NAACP. Contbr. feature articles on nat. issues toGhanian Times, Evening News, 1967-73. Office: Penn Mutual Life Insurance Co Independence Sq Philadelphia PA 19172*

FRENCH, BENJAMIN IRWIN, JR., diversified industry exec.; b. New Castle, Pa., Jan. 6, 1924; s. Benjamin I. and Blanche Katherine (Arnold) F.; B.A., Pa. State U., 1948; m. Marjorie D. Mousley, May 28, 1949; children—Gary, Bradley, Susan. Editor AP, Harrisburg, Pa., 1948-53, Phila., 1953-55; mgr. public relations Consumer Products div. RCA, Cherry Hill, N.J., 1955-62, trade editor Corporate Staff, 1962-68, mgr. state and local govt. relations, 1968-70, dir. consumer relations, 1970—, N.Y.C., 1961—; lectr. in field. Pres. Little League Weston (Conn.), 1963. Served with Psychol. Research Unit, A.C., U.S. Army, 1943-46. Mem. Soc. Consumer Affairs Profls. in Bus. (dir., pres. N.Y. Met chpt.; Outstanding Achievement award 1976), Council Better Bus. Burs. (chmn. pub. relations adv. group 1973—), Sigma Delta Chi. Republican. Unitarian. Clubs: Nat. Press, Netherlands N.Y., Overseas Press. Author: Customer Service Manual, 1976. Home: 241 Sunrise Hill Ln Norwalk CT 06851 Office: RCA 30 Rockefeller Plaza New York City NY 10020

FRENCH, CARL BURTON, industrialist; b. Burlington, Mich.; s. Burton D. and Sarah L. (Stark) F.; B.A., Northwestern U., 1928; J.D., Kent Coll. Law, 1935; m. Ruth Maretta Arnold, June 27, 1931; children—Jean C., Carol M. Adminstr., Chgo. Daily News, 1931-35; admitted to Ill. bar, 1935; practiced law, Chgo., 1935-37; sec.-treas., dir. Eldorado Mining & Refining. Ltd., 1937-45; pres., gen. mgr. Ceebee Services, Ltd., 1959—. Bd. dirs., chmn. exec. com. Canadian Cancer Soc., 1953-56. nat. pres., 1957-61, hon. pres. North York unit; chmn. Internat. Conf. Cancer Vols., 1965; mem. nat. program control commn. Union Internationale Contre le Cancer; bd. govs. Nat. Theatre Sch., Montreal. Recipient Vermeil medal Soc. Encouragement Progress, U. Paris, 1967; Merit award Northwestern U., 1971. Mem. Arbitrators Inst. Can. (dir.), Canadian Cancer Soc. (hon. life), Phi Kappa Sigma. Phi Delta Phi, Alpha Kappa Psi. Presbyn. Clubs: National, Granite, Variety (Toronto), Eglinton Hunt, Turf, York Downs Golf and Country. Author: Manual on Fund Raising, 1972. Office: 263 Dawlish Ave Toronto ON M4N 1J4 Canada

FRENCH, CLARENCE LEVI, JR., shipbldg. co. exec.; b. New Haven, Oct. 13, 1925; s. Clarence L. and Eleanor V. (Curry) F.; B.S. in Naval Sci., Tufts U., 1944, B.S. Mech. Engring., 1947; m. Jean Ruth Sprague, June 29, 1946; children—Craig Thomas, Brian Keith, Alan Scott. Foundry engr. Bethlehem (Pa.) Steel Co., 1947-56; staff engr., asst. supt. Basic Oxygen steel plant Kaiser Steel Corp., Fontana, Calif., 1956-64; supervising engr. Bechtel Corp., Los Angeles, 1964-67; project coordinator Nat. Steel & Shipbldg. Co., San Diego, 1967-69, chief materials engr., 1969-70, mgr. engring., 1970-72, program mgr., 1972-73; dir. engring., 1973-74, v.p. engring., 1974-75, exec. v.p., gen. mgr., 1975-77, pres., chief operating officer, 1977—. Served to lt. USN, 1943-53. Mem. Soc. Naval Architects and Marine Engrs., Am. Soc. Naval Engrs., ASTM, Am. Bur. Shipping, Shipbldg. Council Am., Nat. Maritime Council. Office: 28th and Harbor Dr San Diego CA 92138

FRENCH, ROBERT LEE, mgmt. cons.; b. Middletown, Mo., Dec. 18, 1929; s. Lee and Pearl Marie F.; B.S., U. Mo., 1951, M.S. in Bus. Adminstrn., 1951; m. Barbara Gail Burks, Sept. 17, 1950; children—Carol Jean, Cynthia Ann, James Robert, John Richard. Sr. indsl. engr. Chrysler Corp., Detroit, 1951-60; chief mng. engr. Boats div. Brunswick Corp., Warsaw, Ind., 1960-63; chief indsl. engr. Arnold Engring. div. Allegheny-Ludlum, Marengo, Ill., 1963-66; v.p., dir. Mfg. Household div. Hamilton-Cosco Inc., Columbus, Ind., 1966-70; v.p., gen. mgr. Buckeye Plastics div. Buckeye Internat., Columbus, Ohio, 1970-72; v.p., gen. mgr. Buckeye Ware Inc., Regal Ware Inc., Wooster, Ohio, 1972-74; pres. R.L. French & Co., Inc., South Bend, Ind., 1974—. Pres. Bartholomew County (Ind.) chpt. ARC, 1969. Found. for Youth, Wooster, Ohio, 1973. Served with USAF, 1950-51. Mem. Assn. Mgmt. Cons., Soc. Profl. Mgmt. Cons. Republican. Mem. Christian Ch. (Disciples of Christ). Home and Office: 1240 E Irvington St South Bend IN 46614

FRENS, ARTHUR J., food co. exec.; b. Fremont, Mich., May 22, 1918; s. John B. and Johanna (Blaauw) F.; student La Salle U., 1936-40; m. Geraldyne L. Bowman, July 26, 1940; children—John Arthur, Mary Jean. With Gerber Products Co., Fremont, 1936—, v.p., asst. to pres., 1960-61, v.p. adminstrn., 1961-64, exec. v.p., 1964-71, pres., 1971-78, chmn., chief exec. officer, 1978—, also dir.; dir. Old State Bank Fremont, Rubbermaid, Inc. Trustee Nutrition Found. Served to 1st lt. AUS, 1944-46. Mem. Mich. C. of C. (dir.), Fremont C. of C., Soc. Advancement Mgmt., Nat. Food Processors Assn. Mem. Christian Reformed Ch. Office: 445 State St Fremont MI 49412

FRENZA, JAMES PASQUALE, chamber of commerce exec.; b. Detroit, Sept. 6, 1938; s. Vincent and Mary C. (Caruso) F.; A.B., Sacred Heart Coll., Detroit, 1960; m. Mary C. Gormley, May 8, 1971; 1 dau., Rosemary Jean. Ordained priest Roman Catholic Ch., 1964; asst. pastor Archdiocese of Detroit, 1964-70; mgr. community relations U. Mich., Ann Arbor, 1970-76; exec. dir. Greater Ann Arbor C. of C., 1976—; pres. Ann Arbor Econ. Devel. Corp., 1980—. Mem. Am. C. of C. Execs., Mich. C. of C. Execs. (pres. 1980). Office: 207 E Washington St Ann Arbor MI 48104

FRERKING, ROBERT GEORGE, agribus. coop. co. exec.; b. St. Louis, Aug. 16, 1931; s. Roland Franklin and Clara Martha (Kienzle) F.; B.S. in Bus. Adminstrn., U. Tenn., 1957; m. Carzell Thurman, Dec. 19, 1956; children—Katherine, Mary, William, John, James. Systems programmer U.S. Steel Corp., Birmingham, Ala. 1957-62, systems analyst Computer Center, Pitts., 1962-63; sr. systems analyst Alcoa Corp. (Tenn.), 1963-65; mgr. programming and ops. FS Services, Inc., Bloomington, Ill., 1965-70; dir. mgmt. info. services MFA, Inc., Columbia, Mo., 1970—; lectr. in field. Chmn., Empire Twp (Ill.) United Fund, 1967; mem. LeRoy (Ill.) Sch. Bd., 1969-70; pres. Daniel Boone Little League, Columbia, 1975. Served with USAF, 1950-54. Mem. Data Processing Mgmt. Assn., Beta Alpha Psi. Lutheran. Home: 901 Cowan Dr Columbia MO 65201 Office: 201 S 7th St Columbia MO 65201

FREUND, EDWARD FERDINAND, corp. exec.; b. N.Y.C., Dec. 26, 1935; s. Ferdinand Christian and Virginia F.; B.A., Wagner Coll., 1958; M.B.A., Fordham U., 1975; m. Joyce Marilyn Cooper, Nov. 1, 1959; 1 dau., Kristin Carolyn. Analyst, Credit Bankers Trust Co., N.Y.C., 1961-63; mgr. corp. credit ACF Industries, Inc., N.Y.C., 1963-69; dir. corp. fin. Gulf & Western Industries, N.Y.C., 1969-75; v.p. fin. and adminstrn. Steuber Group, Inc., N.Y.C., 1975—. Pres., Zion Luth. Ch., Stamford, Conn., 1971-72, bd. elders, 1972-78. Mem. Fin. Execs. Inst., N.Y. Credit and Fin. Mgmt. Assn., Am. Mgmt. Assn. Republican. Club: Union League (N.Y.C.). Home: 155 Winsap Rd Stamford CT 06903 Office: 330 Madison Ave New York NY 10017

FREY, DONALD NELSON, mfg. co. exec., engr.; b. St. Louis, Mar. 13, 1923; s. Muir Luken and Margaret Bryden (Nelson) F.; student Mich. State Coll., 1940-42; B.S., U. Mich., 1947, Ph.D., 1950, D.Eng., 1967; D.Eng., U. Mo. at Rolla, 1968; m. Mary Elizabeth Cameron, June 1971; children by previous marriage—Donald Nelson, Judith Kingsley, Margaret Bente, Catherine, Christopher, Elizabeth. Asst. prof. chem. and metall. engring. U. Mich., 1950-51; research engr. Babcock & Wilcox Tube Co., Beaver Falls, Pa., summer 1951; various positions Ford Motor Co., 1951-58, engr. car product engring. Ford div., 1958-59, asst. chief engr. car product engring., 1959-61, product planning mgr., 1961-62, asst. gen. mgr. Ford div., 1962-65, gen. mgr., 1965-68, co. v.p., 1965-67, v.p. for product devel., 1967-68; pres. Gen. Cable Corp., N.Y.C., 1968-71; chmn. Bell & Howell Co., Chgo., 1971—; dir. McCord Corp., Babcock & Wilcox Co., Clark Equipment Co., Twentieth Century Fox Film Corp. Active Devel. council U. Mich., 1963—. Trustee Carnegie Found. for Advancement of Teaching, 1972—; bd. dirs. Children's Meml. Hosp., Lyric Opera, Chgo. Served with AUS, 1943-46. Named Young Engr. of Year Engring. Soc. Detroit, 1953; recipient Russell Springer award Soc. Automobile Engrs., 1956; named Outstanding Alumni Coll. Engring., U. Mich., 1957; outstanding Young Man of Year Detroit Jr. Bd. Commerce, 1958. Mem. Am. Inst. Mining, Metall. and Petroleum Engrs. (chmn. Detroit 1954; chmn., editor Nat. Symposium on Sheet Steels 1956), Am. Soc. Metals, Nat. Acad. Engring. (mem. council), Am. Soc. M.E., Soc. Automotive Engrs. (vice chmn. Detroit 1958), Chgo. (dir.), N.Y. councils fgn. relations, Sigma Xi, Phi Kappa Phi, Tau Beta Pi, Phi Delta Theta. Clubs: Commercial, Chicago, Saddle and Cycle (Chgo.). Home: 1500 Lake Shore Dr Chicago IL 60610 Office: 7100 McCormick Rd Chicago IL 60645

FREY, HENRY CHARLES, systems analyst; b. N.Y.C., Aug. 6, 1933; s. Erwin and Therese (Weigl) F.; B. Indsl. Engring., N.Y. U., 1964; M.I.E., 1969; m. Brunhilde Baurick, Sept. 12, 1960; children—Helga, Ingrid. With fin. div. AT&T, N.Y.C., 1951-53; design draftsman Bell Labs., N.Y.C., 1953-56, tech. writer, 1956-58, instr., 1958-61, mem. staff, 1961-66, supr. micrographic info. systems, 1967—. Councilman, Borough of Eatontown (N.J.), 1964-70. Served with U.S. Army, 1954-56. Recipient Henry A. Cuzzens Indsl. Engring. award Indsl. Engring. Dept., N.Y. U., 1964; Founders Day award N.Y. U., 1965. Mem. Nat. Micrographics Assn. (fellow 1974, pres.), Am. Nat. Standards Assn. (chmn.), Am. Inst. Indsl. Engrs. (David G. Porter Indsl. Engring. award 1964). Republican. Presbyterian. Club: Lions. Contbr. articles on micrographics to profl. jours. Home: 353 Grant Ave Eatontown NJ 07724

FREY, THOMAS W., indsl. signaling products and systems co. exec.; b. Binghamton, N.Y., Nov. 22, 1944; s. Herman and Kathleen F.; B.S., U. R.I., 1968; M.B.A., Harvard U., 1976; m. Vanessa Haller Frey, June 17, 1978. Asst. plant mgr. Plastics div. W. R. Grace Co., Bklyn., 1976-78; v.p. mfg. Edwards Co., Inc., Farmington, Conn., 1978-79, v.p., gen. mgr. signalling products div., 1979—. Office: Edwards Co Inc 195 Farmington Ave Box F Farmington CT 06032

FRIBERG, KARL ARTHUR, mfg. co. exec.; b. Worcester, Mass., Oct. 12, 1945; s. Frank Fredrick and Mary Aurelia (Pheasant) R.; B.A., Dartmouth Coll., 1967; B.S., M.I.T., 1968; M.S. in E.E., Johns Hopkins U., 1970; M.B.A., Harvard U., 1973; m. Evelyn Jean Peterson, Feb. 27, 1971; children—Anne-Marie, Kristina Leigh. Scientist/engr. Draper Labs., M.I.T., 1967-69; research scientist Westinghouse Corp., Balt., 1969-71; v.p. internat. banking group Citibank, N.A., N.Y.C., 1974-78; chmn., chief exec. officer Motif Designs, New Rochelle, N.Y., 1978—. Mem. Harvard Bus. Sch. Club, Sigma Xi, Tau Beta Pi. Democrat. Lutheran. Club: Orienta (Mamaroneck, N.Y.). Contbr. articles in field. Home: 26 Pryer Terr New Rochelle NY 10804 Office: 15 Beechwood Ave New Rochelle NY 10801

FRICKE, RICHARD IRVIN, ins. co. exec.; b. Buffalo, Mar. 25, 1922; s. Richard F. and Julia S. (Cooper) F.; A.B., Cornell U., 1943, J.D. with distinction (editor Law Quar. 1946-47), 1947; grad. Advanced Mgmt. Program, Harvard, 1965; m. Jeanne Hines, July 22, 1943 (dec.); children—Richard J., Diane L., Kathryn J., David R.; m. 2d, Ruth Byerly Tinker, Mar. 26, 1967; children—Mark C., Michael A., Jodie P., John H. Admitted to N.Y. bar, 1947; asso. atty. Kenefick, Cooke, Mitchell, Bass & Letchworth, Buffalo, 1947-52; asst. prof., then asso. prof. law Cornell U. Law Sch., 1952-57; asso. counsel Ford Motor Co., 1957-62; v.p., gen. counsel Mut. Life Ins. Co. N.Y., 1962-67, sr. v.p., 1967-69, exec. v.p., 1969-72, chmn. bd., 1972-76; vice chmn. bd. Nat. Life Ins. Co., Montpelier, Vt., 1976-77, pres., chief exec. officer, 1977—; chmn. bd. Sentinel Group Funds, Inc.; dir. Monsanto Co. Mem. speakers bur. Buffalo Countil World Affairs, 1952; cons. N.Y. State Law Revision Commn., 1952-57. Mem. adv. council Cornell Law Sch., Cornell U. Council; trustee Champlain Coll. Served with field arty. AUS and USAAF, 1943-45. Fellow Am. Bar Found.; mem. Am., Vt. bar assns., Cornell Law Assn. (pres. 1965-67), Am. Council Life Ins. (dir.), Assn. N.Y. State Life Ins. Cos. (pres. 1974-75), Order of Coif, Am. Judicature Soc., Phi Kappa Phi, Phi Delta Phi. Clubs: Univ. (N.Y.C.); Ethan Allan, Burlington Country. Home: 349 S Willard St Burlington VT 05401 Office: Nat Life Dr Montpelier VT 05602

FRIDAY, JAMES ALFRED, ins. co. exec.; b. Gastonia, N.C., Oct. 18, 1939; s. Leonard Loy and Martha Daily (Black) F.; B.A. in Social Sci. and Bus. Adminstrn., Western Carolina U., 1962; m. Judy Gail Moore, Mar. 31, 1963; children—Lisa Ann, Jay. Claims supr. Liberty Mut. Ins. Co., Atlanta, 1962-68; ins. adminstr. Colonial Stores Inc., Atlanta, 1968-73, v.p. ins. adminstrn., 1977-79; v.p. maj. accounts div. Corroon & Black, Nashville, 1974-77; v.p. ins. Grand Union Co., Atlanta, 1979—; also sr. v.p. Rollins Burdick Hunter, multinat. ins. brokerage firm. Served with USAF, 1970-72. Mem. Risk and Ins. Mgmt. Soc. (pres., dir. Atlanta chpt.), Council Employee Benefits, Atlanta Zool. Soc. Lutheran. Club: Elks. Home: 845 Saddlehill Rd Roswell GA 30075 Office: 2251 Sylvan Rd East Point GA 30344

FRIEDEL, BERNARD, mfg. co. exec.; b. N.Y.C., Jan. 26, 1930; s. Joseph and Jeanne (Shoenbach) F.; B.S., Hofstra U., 1951, M.B.A., 1952; m. Rosalie Gertsenstein, Mar. 17, 1951 (div. 1978); children—Steven, Joyce. Pres., David Allison Co., Inc., Woodbury, N.Y., 1957—, chmn. bd., 1959—; pres., chmn. bd. Daco Internat. Corp., 1959—; pres. Kingsley Brass Co., Ltd., Woodbury, 1963-71, chmn. bd., 1963; mgmt. cons. Served to lt. USN, 1952-56. Mem. Mensa, Nat. Wood Kitchen Cabinet Assn., Am. Hardware Mfrs. Assn. Clubs: Jockey, Turnberry (Miami). Patentee hardware. Home: 24 Split Rock Dr Kings Point NY 11024 Office: 220 Crossways Park W Woodbury NY 11797

FRIEDLAND, RICHARD, mgmt. cons.; b. N.Y.C., Mar. 27, 1941; s. Leo and Rose (Blanchard) F.; B.S., U. Mich., 1963, M.B.A., 1964; m. Lois Mandiberg, Dec. 3, 1967; children—Rachel J., Benjamin H. Mng. dir. Community Systems Found., Ann Arbor, Mich., 1969-70; dir. Concord Office, 1970-72; pres. Mgmt. Systems Services, Bedford, N.H., 1972-79; sr. cons. Harris, Kerr, Forster & Co., Denver, 1979—; cons. fin. instns., major hosps. Mem. Hosp. Mgmt. Systems Soc., Am. Inst. Indsl. Engrs., Am. Hosp. Assn. Home: 8555 Double Header Ranch Rd Morrison CO 80465 Office: 400 Denver Club Bldg 518 17th St Denver CO 80202

FRIEDLEY, RANDY DEL, automobile dealership exec.; b. Waterloo, Iowa, Mar. 28, 1949; s. H. Herald and Evonthea T. (Gianoulis) F.; student Elsworth Jr. Coll., 1970; children—Tony, Jamie. Salesman Chuck Fellmer Imports, Waterloo, 1972-73, Friedley Oldsmobile, Cedar Falls, Iowa, 1973-75, U. Motors, Waterloo, 1975; gen. mgr. Friedley Lincoln-Mercury, Cedar Falls, 1976—; speaker to various sales tng. classes and seminars; cons. 21st Century Mktg., Peoria, Ill. Served with USMC, 1968-70. Decorated Purple Heart (2) winner 8 consecutive sales contests Lincoln-Mercury Corp., 1977-78; elected to Datsun Century Club for sales, 1973; winner Iowa State Champion Quarterhorse competition, 1967-68; co-owner Reserve Nat. Champion, Am. Paint Horse, 1978. Mem. Nat. Automobile, Black Hawk County dealers assns. Republican. Mem. Sunnyside Temple. Home: 102 Rebecca St Hudson IA 50643 Office: 4227 University St Friedley Lincoln-Mercury Cedar Falls IA 50613

FRIEDLIEB, LESLIE AARON, mktg. co. exec.; b. N.Y.C., Sept. 16, 1936; s. Theodore and Gertrude F.; B.S., Queens Coll., 1958; M.B.A., Baruch Coll., City U. N.Y., 1971; m. Rose Teresa, June 12, 1965; children—Katharine, Jennifer. Nat. sales staff Olivetti Co., N.Y.C., 1962-63; in mktg. devel. and sales Mosler Co., N.Y.C., account exec., asst. to pres. Fifth Ave. Letter, N.Y.C., 1965-66; mktg. services mgr. Weldotron Co., Piscataway, N.J., 1967-74; pres. Leslie Aaron Assos., Union, N.J., 1974—. Served with U.S. Army, 1959-61. Mem. Soc. Plastics Engrs., Soc. Plastics Industry, Am. Mgmt. Assn., Packaging Inst., Am. Mktg. Assn. (former editor N.J. newsletter), Bus. Publs. Audit, N.J. Bus. and Industry Assn., Queens Coll., Baruch, Sch. Visual Arts alumni assns., Sigma Alpha Mu. Democrat. Clubs: N.Y. Ad (vice-chmn. steering com. 1965-66). Contbr. articles to profl. publs. Home: 292 Clermont Terr Union NJ 07083 Office: 520 Westfield Ave Elizabeth NJ 07208

FRIEDMAN, ARTHUR MORTON, sales co. exec.; b. Yonkers, N.Y., Sept. 30, 1931; s. Isadore O. and Regina (Hertz) F.; B.S. in Mgmt., N.Y. U., 1960. Asst. dir. quality control J. P. Stevens & Co., Inc., N.Y.C., 1955-65; sales mgr. Cheraw Dyeing & Fin. Co., Cheraw, S.C., 1965; chief exec. officer, pres., chief stockholder Marcamy Sales Corp., Marcamy Sales Export Corp., N.Y.C., 1965—. Served with U.S. Army, 1952-54. Mem. N.Y. Credit Mens Assn. Clubs: Albert Gallatin Soc., N.Y. U., B'nai B'rith.

FRIEDMAN, DAVID MARTIN, govt. exec.; b. Bklyn., Mar. 30, 1947; s. Leo Monroe and Florence Friedman; B.E.E. summa cum laude, CCNY, 1969; M.E.E., Columbia U., 1971; M.B.A., George Washington U., 1977. Mem. tech. staff Bell Labs., Holmdel, N.J., 1969-72; engr. MCI Telecommunications, Washington, 1972-74; sr. mem., tech. staff Computer Scis. Corp., Falls Church, Va., 1974; electronics engr. GSA, Washington, 1974-78, dir. contract programs div., 1978—. N.Y. Cons. Engrs. scholar, 1968; recipient Blonder Tongue Found. award, 1968. Mem. Am. Mgmt. Assn., Assn. MBA. Execs., Tau Beta Pi, Eta Kappa Nu. Office: 18th and F Sts NW Washington DC 20405

FRIEDMAN, FRED JAY, fin. services exec.; b. Bklyn., July 1, 1930; s. Edward and Teresa (Belth) F.; B.A., N.Y. U., 1952; m. Linda Strong, Dec. 22, 1965; children—Erik, Adam. Sales exec. Merrill Lynch, Pierce, Fenner & Smith, Inc., N.Y.C., 1958-73, regional sales mgr., 1973-74, v.p. sales, 1974, resident sales office exec., 1974—, chmn. Merrill Lynch Pension Fund, chmn. Merrill Lynch Regional Adv. Council to Mgmt. Mem. N.Y.C. Urban Action Group, 34th St. Midtown Assn., N.Y. Urban Coalition. Served with U.S. Army, 1953-55. Recipient Fin. Exec. Award, Wharton Bus. Sch., U. Pa., 1976, Chmn.'s Club award Merrill Lynch. Mem. Am. Mgmt. Assn., Sales Exec. Club N.Y. Home: 333 E 30th St New York NY 10016 Office: Merrill Lynch Pierce Fenner & Smith Inc 1 Penn Plaza New York NY 10001

FRIEDMAN, IRVING PAUL, toy mfg. co. exec., mgmt. cons.; b. N.Y.C., Feb. 12, 1915; s. Max and Ida (Kaplan) F.; B.B.A., St. John's U., 1937; postgrad. CCNY, 1938-39; Ph.D. in Bus. Adminstrn.,

Internat. Inst. for Advanced Studies, 1980; m. Edith Levites, Mar. 22, 1942; children—Melvin Howard, Carla Rae. Controller of costs Nat. Silver Co., Bklyn., 1946-47; cons., controller Temple Tone Radio Corp., New London, Conn., 1947-48; cost. mgr., cost reduction coordinator Lightolier, Inc., Jersey City, 1948-67; corp. dir. cost Ideal Toy Corp., Hollis, N.Y., 1967—; condr. cost seminars, 1957—; lectr. Fairleigh Dickinson U., St. John's U.; vis. prof. Calif. Poly. Inst., Stevens Inst. Tech., Rutgers U., St. Peter's Coll., Am. Mgmt. Assn., Nat. Assn. Accts., 1960—. Chmn., Englewood (N.J.) Sch. Budget Com., 1957-59. Mem. Nat. Assn. Accts. (organizer Jersey City chpt., pres. 1960-61, medal 1962), AAUP, Stuart Cameron McLeod Soc. Republican. Jewish. Author: Cost Control and Profit Improvement through Product Analysis, 1966; contbr. articles to profl. jours. Home: 2444 NW 8th St Delray Beach FL 33445 Office: 184-10 Jamaica Ave Hollis NY 11423

FRIEDMAN, JOEL, oil co. exec.; b. Denver, Aug. 17, 1939; s. Israel and Josephine (Mandell) F.; student London Sch. Econs. and Polit. Sci., 1959-60; B.A. in History, Columbia U., 1961; postgrad. N.Y. Grad. Sch. Bus. Adminstrn., 1961-62; m. Elaine Doris Greenbaum, Feb. 19, 1966; children—Edward J., Jennifer C. Account exec., jr. exec. trainee Merrill Lynch, Pierce, Fenner & Smith, N.Y.C., 1961-67; registered rep. Bear, Stearns Co., N.Y.C., 1967-69; founder, dir. Metrocare Enterprises, N.Y.C., 1968-69; partner Steindecker, Friedman Co., N.Y.C., 1969-70, Haber-Friedman, Inc., N.Y.C., 1970-71; founder, pres. New Am. Industries, Inc., N.Y.C., 1971-73; founder, pres., co-chief exec. officer Kenai Corp., N.Y.C., 1973—; chmn. bd. dirs. Founders Property Corp., N.Y.C., 1975—; dir. Campanelli Industries, Inc. Bd. dirs. Asthamatic Childrens Found.; mem. bd. visitors Columbia Coll., Columbia U. Mem. Young Presidents Orgn. (exec. com. metro N.Y. chpt.). Office: 477 Madison Ave New York NY 10022

FRIEDMAN, MARTIN BURTON, chem. co. exec.; b. N.Y.C., June 21, 1927; s. William L. and Ella (Holstein) F.; student Mt. St. Mary's Coll., 1943-44, Cornell U., 1944-45; B.A., Pa. State U., 1949; m. Rita Fleischman, Mar. 19, 1950; children—Jay Edward, Ellen Jane. Mgr. advt. and promotion chems. group Sun Chem. Corp., N.Y.C., 1949-54; mgr. advt. and promotion textile chems. dept. Am. Cyanamid Co., N.Y.C., 1954-58, mgr. advt. and promotion, organic chems. div., 1958-60, gen. merchandising mgr., mgr. Fibers div., 1961-64, dir. sales, 1964-65, dir. marketing, 1965-69, asst. gen. mgr. Fibers div., 1969-72, v.p. IRC Fibers Co. subsidiary Am. Cyanamid Co., 1969-72, pres., 1980—, pres. Fibers div., 1980—; exec. v.p. Formica Corp., 1972-73, pres., 1973—; dir. Cin. br. Fed. Res. Bank Cleve., 1976—, Cyanenka S.A., Barcelona, 1980—. Served with USNR, 1945-46. Named to Textile Hall of Fame, 1958. Mem. Am. Chem. Soc., Am. Assn. Textile Chemists and Colorists. Club: Chemists (N.Y.C.). Contbr. articles to textile and tech. publs. Home: 777 Butternut Dr Franklin Lakes NJ 07417 Office: Wayne NJ

FRIEDMAN, MELVIN, real estate mgmt. and devel. exec.; b. St. Louis, Dec. 10, 1923; s. Nathan and Rose (Finschmidt) F.; student Mo. U., 1941-42, Washington U., 1942-46; J.D., St. Louis U., 1948; postgrad. in Law, Tulane U., 1948-49; m. Geri Loomstein, Nov. 23, 1952; children—Stuart H., Cindy E., Nancy Y. Admitted to Mo. bar, 1948, U.S. Tax Ct. bar; partner firm Steinberg & Friedman, 1949-57; sr. partner Friedman, Fredericks & Radloff, St. Louis, 1957—; chmn. bd. Centerco Properties, Inc., 1962—; dir., mem. exec. com. Comml. Bank of St. Louis County. Bd. dirs., gen. counsel Jewish Children's Home. Served to 1st lt. USAAF, 1942-45. Mem. Bar Assn. St. Louis County, Am. Bar Assn., Lawyers Assn. St. Louis. Clubs: Meadowbrook Country of Ballwin (Mo.) (pres., dir.), Creve Coeur Racquet, Masons. Home: 11 Upper Barnes Rd Ladue MO 63124 Office: 7730 Carondelet Ave Clayton MO 63105

FRIEDMAN, MILTON, economist; b. Bklyn., July 31, 1912; s. Jeno Saul and Sarah Ethel (Landau) F.; A.B., Rutgers U., 1932, LL.D., 1968; A.M., U. Chgo., 1933; Ph.D., Columbia, 1946; LL.D., St. Paul's (Rikkyo) U., 1963, Kalamazoo Coll., 1968, Lehigh U., 1969, Loyola U., 1971, U. N.H., 1975, Harvard U., 1979, Brigham Young U., 1980, Dartmouth Coll., 1980; Sc.D., Rochester U., 1971; L.H.D., Rockford Coll., 1969, Roosevelt U., 1975; Litt.D., Bethany Coll., 1971; Ph.D. (hon.), Hebrew U., Jerusalem, 1977. Asso. economist Nat. Resources Com., Washington, 1935-37; mem. research staff Nat. Bur. Econ. Research, N.Y., 1937-45, 1948—; vis. prof. econs. U. Wis., 1940-41; prin. economist, tax research div. U.S. Treasury Dept., 1941-43, asso. dir. research, statis. research group, war research div. Columbia, 1943-45; asso.. prof. econs. and statistics U. Minn., 1945-46; asso. prof. econs. U. Chgo., 1946-48, prof. econs., 1948-62, Paul Snowden Russell Distinguished Service prof. econs., 1962—; Fulbright lectr. Cambridge U., 1953-54; vis. Wesley Clair Mitchell Research prof. econs. Columbia, 1964-65; fellow Center for Advanced Study in Behavioral Sci., 1957-58. Mem. Pres.'s Commn. All-Volunteer Army, 1969-70, Pres.' Commn. on White House Fellows, 1971-74; vis. scholar Fed. Res. Bank, San Francisco, 1977; sr. research fellow Hoover Instn., Stanford U., 1977—. Recipient John Bates Clark medal Am. Econ. Assn., 1951; Nobel prize in econs., 1976; Scopus award Am. Friends Hebrew U., 1977; gold medal Nat. Inst. Social Scis., 1978; Pvt. Enterprise Exemplar medal Freedoms Found., 1978; named Chicagoan of Year, Chgo. Press Club, 1972, Educator of Year, Chgo. United Jewish Fund, 1973. Fellow Inst. Math. Statis., Am. Statis. Assn., Econometric Soc.; mem. Nat. Acad. Scis., Am. Econ. Assn. (mem. exec. com. 1955-57, pres. 1967), Am. Enterprise Inst. (adv. bd.), Royal Economic Soc., Am. Philos. Soc., Mont Pelerin Soc. (bd. dirs. 1958-61, pres. 1970-72). Club: Quadrangle. Author: Taxing to Prevent Inflation (with Carl Shoup and Ruth P. Mack), 1943; Income from Independent Professional Practice (with Simon S. Kuznets), 1946; Sampling Inspection (with Harold A. Freeman, Frederic Mosteller, W. Allen Wallis), 1948; Essays in Positive Economics, 1953; A Theory of the Consumption Function, 1957; A Program for Monetary Stability, 1959; Price Theory, 1962; (with Rose D. Friedman) Capitalism and Freedom, 1962; (with Anna J. Schwartz) A Monetary History of the United States, 1867-1960, 1963; Inflation: Causes and Consequences, 1963; (with Anna J. Schwartz) The Great Contraction, 1965, Monetary Statistics of the United States, 1970; (with Robert Roosa) The Balance of Payments: Free vs. Fixed Exchange Rates, 1967; Dollars and Deficits, 1968; The Optimum Quantity of Money and Other Essays, 1969; (with Walter W. Heller) Monetary vs. Fiscal Policy, 1969; A Theoretical Framework for Monetary Analysis, 1972; (with Wilbur J. Cohen) Social Security, 1972; An Economist's Protest, 1972; There Is No Such Thing As A Free Lunch, 1975; Price Theory, 1976; Tax Limitation, Inflation and the Role of Government, 1978; (with Rose D. Friedman) Free To Choose, 1980; Milton Friedman's Monetary Framework, 1974. Editor: Studies in the Quantity Theory of Money, 1956. Bd. editors Am. Econ. Rev., 1951-53, Econometrica, 1957-69; columnist Newsweek mag., 1966—, contbr. editor, 1971—. Contbr. articles to profl. jours. Office: Hoover Instn Stanford U Stanford CA 94305

FRIEDMAN, RICHARD LOESER, real estate exec.; b. Cambridge, Mass., Dec. 6, 1940; s. Aryeh Robert and Helen (Loeser) F.; B.A., Dartmouth Coll., 1963; m. Sharon Telangitz, Aug. 21, 1964; 1 son, Alex. Ski coach Harvard U., Cambridge, 1963-60; real estate broker, pres. Carpenter & Co., Inc., Boston, 1963—; corporator Boston Five Cent Savings Bank; dir. Greater Boston Real Estate Bd. Trustee, New Eng. Conservatory Music; mem. pres.'s adv. bd. Mass. Coll. Art. Served with U.S. Army, 1963. Mem. Boston C. of C., Inst. Real Estate Mgmt., Internat. Council Shopping Centers, Bldg. Owners and Mgrs. Assn. (dir.). Home: 22 Wellesley St Weston MA 02193 Office: 175 Federal St Boston MA 02110

FRIEDMAN, STANFORD JOSEPH, steel, real estate exec.; b. Cleve., June 27, 1927; s. Sol H. and Cele (Akers) F.; B.S., M.E., I.E., U. Mich., 1949; m. Louise Glatt, July 19, 1949; children—Steven James, Jonathan Richard, Sally D. Pres., dir. Solar Mid-Con, Inc. (formerly Solar Steel Corp.), Cleve., 1961—, Danstan Realty Corp., Cleve.; dir. Phillip's Syrup Corp., U-Lease Corp., Universal Container Corp. Trustee, Solar Found. Mem. ASME, Soc. Automotive Engrs., Am. Iron and Steel Inst. Clubs: Oakwood Country (Cleve.); Standard (Chgo.). Home: 5200 Three Village Dr #30 Lyndhurst OH 44124 Office: 24200 Chagrin Blvd Beachwood OH 44122

FRIEDMAN, STUART WAYNE, biomed. services co. exec.; b. Chgo., Oct. 25, 1938; s. Louis and Raye (Yablonky) F.; B.S. in Indsl. Engring., U. So. Calif., 1959; M.S. in Indsl. Engring., 1962, M.B.A. in Marketing, 1963; m. Enid Segal, June 29, 1957; children—Gregg, Janice. Engr., Hollywood Plastics, Inc. (now subsidiary Shell Oil Co., Montclair, N.J.), Los Angeles, 1958-60, mgr. tech. sales, 1960-69; pres. Physiodata, Inc., 1969-71; asso. dir. Health Systems dept. Westinghouse Electric Corp., East Orange, N.J., 1971-72; dir. bus. devel., 1972-74; gen. partner Latin Am. Med. Assos., 1970—; asst. v.p. N.J. Blue Cross Plan, 1974-76, pres. Manhattan Health Plan, 1977—. Cons. indsl. engr. on plant layout, facilities engring., 1959—; cons. health, planning and financing, 1974—. Mem. Dept. Commerce Nat. Def. Exec. Res., 1968—; pres. Mensa Edn. and Research Found. Mem. Group Health Assn. Am. (dir. 1980—), Mensa (nat. and internat. officer), Alpha Pi Mu, Tau Delta Phi. Home 37 Warren Pl Montclair NJ 07042 Office: 425 E 61st St New York NY 10021

FRIEDT, GLENN HARNER, JR., fin. cons.; b. Detroit, Nov. 23, 1923; s. Glenn H. and Lucy (Lawrence) F.; student Duke, 1941-42, Northwestern U., 1942-44; B.A. in Econs., U. Mich., 1947; J.D., Wayne State U., 1950. Admitted to Mich. bar, 1951; asst. to pres. United Platers, Inc., Detroit, 1950-53, v.p., 1953-59, pres., gen. mgr., 1959-63, chmn., 1963-65; v.p., dir. Metal Finishers, Inc., Cleve., 1959-68; asst. to chmn. Gulf & Western Industries, Inc., N.Y.C., 1965-66; dir. Am. Pres.'s Life Ins. Co., 1965-69, exec. v.p., 1966, pres., treas., 1966-68, chmn. bd., 1968-69; pres., dir. Friedt Assos. Corp., 1969—; treas., dir. Automotive Accessories, Inc.; v.p. So. United Industries, Inc.; pres., dir. Flowtrans Ltd. (Can.), Pacific Alliance Corp. Mem. Am., Mich., Detroit bar assns., World Bus. Council, Am. Electroplaters Soc. (exec. bd. Detroit 1959-66), Detroit C. of C. (past com. mem.), Am. Legion, Theta Delta Chi. Clubs: Coral Beach and Tennis, Detroit Athletic, Indian Village Tennis, Jockey, Marina City N.Y. Athletic, Palm Bay, One Hundred of Detroit, Otsego Ski, University (Detroit); Le Club (N.Y.) (Ft. Lauderdale); Masons, Shriners. Office: Suite A 15912 E Jefferson Ave Grosse Pointe MI 48230

FRIELING, GERALD HARVEY, JR., wire splty. metal mfg. co. exec.; b. Kansas City, Mo., Apr. 29, 1930; s. Gerald Harvey and Mary Ann (Coons) F.; B.S.M.E., U. Kans., 1951; m. Joan Lee Bigham, June 14, 1952; children—John, Robert, Nancy. Mfg. mgr. Madison-Faessler, Moberly, Mo., 1956-60; gen. mgr. wire dept., mktg. mgr. metall. and chem. div. Tex. Instruments, Attleboro, Mass., 1960-69; corp. v.p., pres. metall. systems div. Air Products & Chem. Corp., Allentown, Pa., 1969-79; pres., chief exec. officer, dir. Nat.-Standard Co., Niles, Mich., 1979—; instr. Brown U., Providence, 1964-67; cons. Sec. Army, 1974. Pres., bd. dirs. Kutztown (Pa.) Coll. Bd., 1974-78; v.p. Lehigh County (Pa.) C. of C., 1975-79; bd. dirs. YMCA Allentown, 1965-79, Salvation Army, Allentown, 1976-79. Served in USN, 1953-56; Korea. Recipient Medal award Wire Assn., 1966. Mem. ASME, Am. Welding Soc. Republican. Clubs: Point o'Woods Country, SIgnal Point Country, Union League. Patentee in field (6). Contbr. articles to profl. jours. Home: 514 Laurel Dr Niles MI 49120 Office: 601 N 8 St Niles MI 49120

FRIEND, CONNIE MAXINE YAGER (MRS. MERRILL B. FRIEND), bus. exec.; b. Mpls., Mar. 5, 1926; d. Jack M. and Florence (Rabinowitz) Yager; B.A., U. Minn., 1946; m. Merrill B. Friend, Sept. 7, 1946; children—Patricia Jane and Stephen Merrill (twins), Judith Ann. Pres., Friend Assos., Polit. Research Inst., Tarzana, Calif., Social Issues Research Council, Tarzana; pres. Prime Time Tours, Inc. Mem. Los Angeles County Commn. for Status of Women, Los Angeles Commn. for Charter Revision, 1968-70, Mayor's Com. on Pollution, 1970—; sec. Encino Community Center pres. League Women Voters, Los Angeles, 1965-69, Calif. Women's Equity Action League, 1976—; bd. dirs. Town Hall West, Encino Property Owners, 1969—; mem. Los Angeles County Overall Econ. Devel. Program Com. Mem. Valley U. Women. Home: 4727 Louise Ave Encino CA 91316 Office: 18345 Ventura Blvd Tarzana CA 91356

FRIEND, ROBERT NATHAN, financial exec.; b. Chgo., Feb. 2, 1930; s. Karl D. and Marion (Wollenberger) F.; A.B., Grinnell Coll., 1951; M.S., Ill. Inst. Tech., 1953; m. Lee Baer, Aug. 12, 1979; children—Karen, Alan. With K. Friend & Co. (merged into Standard Oil Co. Ind.), Chgo., 1953—, v.p., early 1960's, 1st v.p., 1964—, trustee employees' benefit trust, 1958—; active in expansion R. Friend Investments. Bd. dirs. Travel Light Theatre; admissions cons. Grinnell Coll., 1968—; admissions counselor Ill. Inst. Tech. Fellow Econ. Edn. and Research Found.; mem. Greater Chgo. Gasoline Marketers Assn. (v.p., dir.), Am. Fin. Assn., Execs. Club Chgo., Am. Acad. Polit. and Social Sci., Newcomen Soc. N. Am., Am. Econ. Assn., Econ. Time Found., So. Fin. Assn., Found. for Study Cycles, Am. Assn. Individual Investors (dir.), Chgo. Hist. Soc., Renaissance Soc., Art Inst. Chgo. (life), Sarah Siddons Soc., Vintage Soc., Acad. Polit. Sci. Clubs: Yale, Carlton (Chgo.). Home: 2801 Sheridan Rd Chicago IL 60657 Office: 222 W Adams St Chicago IL 60606

FRIERSON, T. CARTTER, EDP mgmt. cons.; b. Chattanooga, Mar. 10, 1939; s. J. Burton and Rowena Kennedy (Kruesi) F., Jr.; B.A., Dartmouth Coll., 1961; M.B.A., U. Pa., 1966; m. Patricia Browne, June 5, 1965; children—Jennifer, Eleanor, Thomas Cartter. Mfg. supr., systems analyst, systems dept. mgr. Dixie Yarns, Inc., Chattanooga, 1966-71, dir. computer services, 1971-76; founder T. Cartter Frierson & Co., data processing mgmt. cons., Chattanooga, 1977—; dir. Chattanooga Choo-Choo Co.; bd. mgrs. Provident Nat. Assurance Co., Chattanooga. Ruling elder Lookout Mountain Presbyterian Ch.; bd. dirs. Chattanooga YMCA, Salvation Army, Chattanooga, Goodwill Industries, Chattanooga, Siskin Meml. Found., Inc. Served as officer U.S. Army, 1962-64. Mem. Data Processing Mgmt. Assn., Assn. Mgmt. Cons.'s, IEEE. Republican. Clubs: Rotary, Mountain City. Office: Suite 1708 Am Nat Bank Bldg Chattanooga TN 37402

FRIES, BARRY R., civil engr.; b. N.Y.C., Mar. 17, 1947; s. George and Jeanne Fries; B.S., State U. N.Y. at Oneonta, 1969; B.S. in Civil Engring., State U. N.Y. at Buffalo, 1972; m. Ellen Feinerman, Apr. 11, 1976. Project mgr. Jan-Ro Devel. Corp., Great Neck, N.Y., 1972-73; asst. dir. ARDC Maintenance div. Arlen Realty & Devel. Corp., N.Y.C., 1973; v.p. ops. Ind. Constrn. Co. Inc., N.Y.C., 1973—; pres. B.R. Fries & Assos., Inc., designers and constructors, N.Y.C., 1979—; cons. contract adminstrn. Mem. Chi Epsilon. Home: 117 W 77 St New York NY 10024 Office: 888 7th Ave New York NY 10106

FRIESECKE, RAYMOND FRANCIS, mktg. exec.; b. N.Y.C., Mar. 12, 1937; s. Bernhard P. K. and Josephine (De Tomi) F.; B.S. in Chemistry, Boston Coll., 1959; M.S. in Civil Engring., MIT, 1961. Product specialist Dewey & Almy Chem. div. W. R. Grace & Co., Inc., Cambridge, Mass., 1963-66; market planning specialist USM Corp., Boston, 1966-71; mgmt. cons., Boston, 1971-74; dir. planning and devel. Schweitzer div. Kimberly-Clark Corp., Lee, Mass., 1974-78; v.p. corp. planning Butler Automatic, Inc., Canton, Mass., 1978-80; v.p. mktg. and planning Butler Greenwich Inc., (Conn.), 1980—, dir. Butler-Europe, Inc., Greenwich; corp. clk., v.p. Bldg. Research & Devel., Inc., Cambridge, 1966-68. State chmn. Citizens for Fair Taxation, 1972-73; state co-chmn. Mass. Young Republicans, 1967-69; chmn. Ward 7 Republican Com., Cambridge, 1968-70; vice chmn. Cambridge Rep. City Com., 1966-68. Served to 1st lt. U.S. Army, 1961-63. Mem. Am. Chem. Soc., N. Am. Soc. Corp. Planning, Am. Mktg. Assn., World Future Soc., Am. Numis. Assn., Am. Rifle Assn., Printing Industries Assn., Nat. Printing Equipment Assn. Home: 250 Hammond Pond Pkwy Chestnut Hill MA 02167 Office: 2 Soundview Dr Greenwich CT 06830

FRIESEN, JOHN EDWARD, automobile co. exec.; b. Vancouver, B.C., Can., Aug. 2, 1941; s. John V. and Mary F.; student U. B.C., 1959-63; m. Stephanie Carole Finch, children—Jed, Matthew, Bradley. Pres., B.C. Whitewood Furniture Mfg., New Westminster, 1966-80, Action Auto Auction Ltd., New Westminster, B.C., 1976—. First v.p. Edmonds Soccer Club. Mem. Western Auto Auction Assn. (pres. 1979-80), Automotive Retail Assn. (pres. 1979-80), New Westminster C. of C., B.C. Motor Dealers Assn. Club: Burnaby Tennis. Home: 5373 Buckingham Ave Burnaby BC V5E 1Z9 Canada Office: 805 Boyd Ave New Westminster BC V3L 5C3 Canada

FRISCHMUTH, ROBERT ALFRED, landscape planner; b. N.Y.C., Dec. 15, 1940; s. Alfred P. and Emma (Glas) F.; student State U. N.Y., Albany, 1958-60; B.B.A., Pace U., 1973; m. Marlis Lowenhagen, July 15, 1967 (div. 1979); children—Bettina, Malissa. Statis. analyst N.Y. Central System, N.Y.C., 1961-68; landscape planner Rosedale Nurseries, Hawthorne, N.Y., 1969—; founder RAF Prodns., 1980—; producer film Gardening: A Brief History, 1979. Served with U.S. Army, 1963-65. Certified nurseryman and pesticide applicator, N.Y. State. Mem. Am. Film Inst. Lutheran. Home: 31 Ogden Ave Peekskill NY 10566 Office: 51 Saw Mill River Rd Hawthorne NY 10532

FRISVOLD, JOHN ORVILLE, mfg. exec.; b. Milw., May 6, 1930; s. Orville John and Loretta May (Fleming) F.; A.B., Ripon (Wis.) Coll., 1953; m. Rosemary Jene Goulet, Aug. 9, 1952 (dec.); children—Craig John, Lynn Mary, Todd Michael, Eric Matthew, Julie Ann. Sales mgr. duplicating products internat. 3M Co., St. Paul, 1961-63, mgr. internat. mktg., 1965-68, dir. internat. mktg. graphic systems group, 1968-72, v.p., gen. mgr. 3M Bus. Products Sales, Inc., 1972-79, v.p. bus. products sales div., 1979, v.p. bus. communications products div., 1980, v.p. copying products div., 1981—. Vice chmn. United Fund Drive, 1962-63. Served with inf. AUS, 1954-56. Mem. Computer and Bus. Equipment Mfrs. Assn. Roman Catholic. Clubs: Edina (Minn.) Country; Normandale Racquet. Home: 6612 Gleason Rd Edina MN 55435 Office: 3M Center Bldg 220 9W Saint Paul MN 55101

FRITH, JAMES BURNESS, constrn. co. exec.; b. Henry County, Va., Jan. 29, 1916; s. Jacob Ewell and Sally Ada (Nunn) F.; B.S.C., Nat. Bus. Coll., 1937; m. Mary Kathryn Nininger, Aug. 21, 1947; children—Shelley Anne (Mrs. Wayne A. Kenas), Jacob Ewell II, James Burness. Gen. bldg. contractor, 1945—; pres., treas. Frith Constrn. Co., Inc., Martinsville, Va., 1956—; v.p., dir. Frith Equipment Corp., Martinsville; dir. Tultex Corp., Martinsville, Piedmont Trust Bank, Piedmont Bank Group, Martinsville, Hop-In Food Stores, Inc., Roanoke, Va. Bd. dirs. Patrick Henry Coll. Scholarship Found.; vice chmn., trustee Averett Coll., Danville, Va. Served with USAAF, 1942-45. Mem. Asso. Gen. Contractors Am. (state bd. dirs. 1967-72, me. exec. com. 1971-72), Martinsville-Henry County C. of C. (dir. 1973, sec. 1973, v.p. 1974). Elk, K.P., Kiwanian (pres. 1952, lt. gov. 1955). Clubs: Shenandoah (Roanoke, Va.); Chatmoss Country, Forest Park Country (Martinsville, Va.). Home: 1127 Cherokee Trail Martinsville VA 24112 Office: POB 5028 Martinsville VA 24112

FRITZ, AXEL MARVIN, biomed. instruments mfg. co. exec.; b. Mpls., Sept. 15, 1925; s. Axel Marvin and Beatrice Lily (Canfield) F.; B.A., U. Minn., 1954; M.A., U. Mich., 1955; postgrad. Yale U., 1956; m. Jo-Ann Hermann, Apr. 21, 1976; children—Eeris S. Fritz Johnson, Caara Fritz, Scott Nye, Julie Nye. Am. consulate gen., Hamburg, Germany, 1956-59; market mgr. Honeywell, Mpls., 1959; with Geophys. Spltys., Mpls., 1960-62; mfr.'s rep. AMF Assos., Mpls., 1963-66; pres. Bison Instruments, Inc., Mpls., 1966-78, Britt Corp., Mpls., 1979; pres., chmn. Sciencare Corp., Biomed. Instrumentation, Mpls., 1980—; dir. Custom Design, Wright Closers, others. Served to 2d lt. USAAF, 1943-46, with CIC, U.S. Army, 1949-52. Decorated Bronze Star, Silver Star. Mem. Am. Geophys. Union, Am. Geol. Inst., AAAS, Geol. Soc. Am., Soc. Exploration Geophysicists, European Assn. Exploration Geophysicists, Internat. Fedn. Med. and Biol. Engring., U.S. Naval Inst., Single-Handed Sailing Soc., Nat. Aviation Club. Clubs: Robert Gordon Sproul Assos., Masons. Developer seismic signal enhancement averaging instruments; author numerous articles in applied earth scis. Home: 6960 Ticonderoga Trail Eden Prairie MN 55344 Address: PO Box 175 Chanhassen MN 55317 Office: Eden 100 Bldg Mail Sta 202 5100 Eden Ave Minneapolis MN 55436

FRITZ, RICHARD MOYLE, banker; b. Grinnell, Iowa, Apr. 2, 1928; s. Samuel Clifford and Margaret (Moyle) F.; B.S., Iowa State U., 1951; student U. Va., 1959-62, U. Colo., 1974-75; m. Berneice Lauber, July 26, 1952; children—Pamela Joanne, Margaret Suzette, Richard Moyle. Vice pres. Jasper County Savs. Bank, 1954-72; head mktg. div. Hawkeye Bancorp., Des Moines, 1973; head mktg. div. Nat. Bank of Commerce, Lincoln, Nebr., 1974; pres., chief exec. officer 1st Nat. Bank and Trust Co. of Kearney (Nebr.), 1975—. Pres., YMCA-YWCA; bd. dirs. Good Samaritan Hosp., Kearney. Served with AUS. Mem. Nebr. Bankers Assn. (mem. govtl. affairs com.), Am. Bankers Assn. (chmn. communications com.). Presbyterian. Office: PO Box 578 Kearney NE 68847

FROHNHOEFER, FRANCIS WILLIAM, economist; b. Bklyn., Dec. 30, 1939; s. Francis Jacob and Elizabeth Lucille (Kent) F.; A.A., St. Joseph's Coll., 1959; A.B., Cath. U. Am., 1963; M.A., U. Pa., 1965, M.B.A., 1978. Asst. prof. Tougaloo (Miss.) Coll., 1966-68; nat. rep. Woodrow Wilson Nat. Fellowship Found., Princeton, N.J., 1968-69; asst. prof. Millsaps Coll., Jackson, Miss., 1972-79; asst. prof. econs. and bus. Cath. U. Am., Washington, 1979—; dir. Jackson Movers, Inc. Woodrow Wilson fellow, 1963-64; C.P.A., Miss. Mem. Am. Econ. Assn., Am. Acctg. Assn., Inst. Mgmt. Sci., Am. Inst. C.P.A.'s, Miss. Soc. C.P.A.'s, Inst. Mgmt. Acctg., Phi Beta Kappa. Roman Catholic. Home: 801 N Pitt St Alexandria VA 22314 Office: Catholic University of America Washington DC 20064

FROMM, ERWIN FREDERICK, ins. co. exec.; b. Kalamazoo, Oct. 24, 1933; s. Erwin Carl and Charlotte Elizabeth (Wilson) F.; student U. Mich., 1951-52, Flint Jr. Coll., 1952-53; B.A., Kalamazoo Coll., 1959; postgrad. Ill. State U., 1970-72. Underwriter, State Farm Ins., 1959-72; cons. Met. Property & Liability Ins. Co., Warwick, R.I., 1972-73, dir. underwriting and policyholders services, 1973, asst. v.p., 1973-74, v.p., 1974—; sr. v.p. Royal Ins. Co., N.Y.C., 1979—; chmn. All Industry Ins. Com. for Arson Control. Mem. adv. council Bus. Sch., U. R.I. Served to 1st lt. U.S. Army, 1953-56. C.P.C.U. Mem. C.P.C.U. Assn. N.Y., C.P.C.U. Assn. R.I., English Speaking Union. Clubs: Masons, Shriners. Home: 301 E 52d St New York NY 10022 Office: 150 William St New York NY 10038

FROMM, JOSEPH L., automobile mfg. co. exec.; b. Detroit, May 22, 1930; s. Charles and Elizabeth F.; A.B. cum laude, Princeton U., 1953; M.B.A., Harvard U., 1958; m. Beverly C. Booth, June 18, 1960; children—Charles, Laurence, Kenneth, Lisa, Brian. Research asst. Harvard Bus. Sch., 1959; asst. to pres. Gen. Electronic Labs., Cambridge, Mass., 1960-62; with Chrysler Corp., Highland Park, Mich., 1963-68; treas. Marantette & Co., Detroit, 1969; asst. treas. Am. Motors Corp., Southfield, Mich., 1970—. Instr., U. Detroit Evening Div., 1964-65. Councilman, City of Grosse Pointe Farms, 1973—; trustee Bon Secours Hosp., Grosse Pointe, 1975—. Served with AUS, 1954-56. Mem. Fin. Execs. Inst., Fin. Analysts Soc., Sentinel Pension Inst., Council on Employee Benefits, Midwest Pension Conf. Republican. Roman Catholic. Clubs: Michaywe Hills Golf, Grosse Pointe Indoor Tennis. Home: 316 Belanger Grosse Pointe Farms MI 48236 Office: 27777 Franklin Rd Southfield MI 48034

FROMMER, HENRY, fin. exec.; b. N.Y.C., July 30, 1943; s. Barney and Eleanor Jeanette (Peller) F.; B.S. in Econs., U. Pa., 1964; M.B.A., Columbia U., 1966; J.D. magna cum laude, Bklyn. Law Sch., 1976; m. Barbara Gay Hymson, Feb. 3, 1980. Asst. sec. Irving Trust Co., N.Y.C., 1968-71; asst. cashier Franklin Nat. Bank, N.Y.C., 1971-72; sr. v.p., sr. credit officer Comml. Funding, Inc., N.Y.C., 1972—. Served with U.S. Army, 1966-68. Decorated Army Commendation medal. Mem. Am. Bar Assn. Republican. Jewish. Club: Princeton (N.Y.C.). Home: 129 E 82 St New York NY 10028 Office: 230 Park Ave New York NY 10017

FROOM, WILLIAM WATKINS, banker; b. Chgo., Nov. 21, 1915; s. Edgar Albright and Gladys (Watkins) F.; student Northwestern U. Sch. Commerce, 1933-37; m. Anne Celich, Apr. 20, 1940; children—Pamela Froom Siegert, Gail Froom MacKenzie, Joan Froom Sensenbrenner. Sales mgr. soybean div. Swift & Co., Champaign, Ill., 1937-47; partner I.H. French & Co., Champaign, 1947-64, pres., 1965-74, chmn. bd., 1974-76; pres., chmn. bd. City Bank of Champaign, 1974—; dir. F & T Bldg. Corp., Champaign, Champaign Nat. Bank; v.p. Commodity Investment Fund, Mgmt. Corp. Enterprises, Cable Communications, Inc., pres. Champaign-Urbana Communications, 1974-78. Mem. Ill. Citizens Edn. Council. Presbyn. (elder). Club: Champaign Country (dir. 1965). Home: 1402 Waverly Dr Champaign IL 61820 Office: 303 W Kirby Ave Champaign IL 61820

FROOME, LLOYD WILLIAM, constrn. engring. co. exec.; b. London, Eng., July 20, 1945; came to Canada, 1946; s. Roy Arthur and Hannah (Strange) F.; grad. Archtl. program Man. Inst. Tech., Winnipeg, 1966; m. Lynda Grace Orchard, Aug. 20, 1966; children—Donovan Roy, Shelley Lynn. Dir., project mgr. Interior-West Cons. Ltd., Kamloops, B.C., Can., 1976—; pres. Saturn V Amusements, Inc., Kamloops, 1979—; gen. mgr. Spa King, Kamloops, 1979-80. Mem. Canadian Constrn. Assn., Constrn. Specifications Can., Project Mgmt. Inst. Mem. United Ch. Can. Home: 497 Laurier Dr Kamloops BC V1S 1C2 Canada Office: 257 4th Ave Kamloops BC V2C 3N9 Canada

FROST, GORDON TUCKER, lumber co. exec.; b. San Diego, May 15, 1915; s. Albert Abel and Jessie (Tucker) F.; A.B., Stanford U., 1938; postgrad. (Tarver Interfrat. scholar 19—), Heidelberg (Ger.) U., 1939; m. Adeline Jeanne Lehman, July 25, 1940; children—Alison Frost Gildred, Gordon Tucker, Susan duLaux Frost Ahlering. With Frost Hardwood Lumber Co., San Diego, 1940—, pres., 1961—; dir. San Diego Beach Co., San Diego Trust & Savs. Bank. Served as officer USCGR, 1940-46. Mem. Nat. Hardwood Lumber Assn. (past dir.), Nat. Wholesale Hardwood Distbrs. Assn. (past pres.), Pacific Coast Wholesale Hardwood Distbrs. Assn. (past pres.), Maritime Mus. Assn. San Diego (past pres.). Clubs: San Diego Yacht (staff commodore), San Diego Rotary (past pres.). Office: 347 W Market St San Diego CA 92101

FROST, PAUL ARTHUR, engr., corp. exec.; b. Hartford, Conn., Oct. 4, 1938; s. Paul Robinson and Caroline Alice (Spencer) F.; B.S.E.E., U. Conn., 1962, M.S., 1963; Ph.D., Stanford U., 1968; m. Judith Ann Hammond, Aug. 26, 1961; children—Jeffrey, Christopher. Instr., U. Conn., Storrs, 1962-64; mem. tech. staff Hughes Aircraft, Fullerton, Calif., 1964-66; asst. prof. Stanford U., 1966-69; mem. tech. staff Bell Telephone Labs., Whippany, N.J., 1969-75; pres., chief exec. officer Xybion Corp., Xybion Med. Systems Corp., Xybion Electronic Systems Corp., Cedar Knolls, N.J., 1975—. Howard Hughes fellow; NSF fellow. Mem. Am. Mgmt. Assn., IEEE, Sigma Xi, Tau Beta Pi, Eta Kappa Nu. Contbr. articles to profl. jours. Office: 7 Ridgedale Ave Cedar Knolls NJ 07927

FROST, ROBERT EARL, mfg. co. exec.; b. Eastland Tex., July 18, 1934; s. Dallas Clark and Fannie Lee (Hatton) F.; B.S., Tex. A & I Coll., 1964; postgrad Webster Coll., 1976—; m. Elaine Swedlund, Dec. 28, 1958; children—Leslie, Robert, Bert. With Gen. Electric Co., 1968—, now N.E. region mktg./sales mgr., Arkansas City, Kans.; pres. F&G Properties. Bd. dirs. Cherokee Strip Mus.; pres. Lakota Hills Homeowners Assn., 1975. Served with USMC, 1958-68. Decorated DFC, Air medal; Ky. Col. Republican. Presbyn. Club: Kiwanis. Home: RFD 3 Box 2665 Arkansas City KS 67005 Office: PO Box 797 Arkansas City KS 67005

FROST, THOMAS PEARSON, banker; b. Ormskirk, Lancashire, Eng., July 1, 1933; s. James Watterson and Enid Ella Frost; student public schs., Ormskirk; m. Elizabeth Morton, Mar. 29, 1958; children—Stuart Morton, Charlotte Jane, Emma Elizabeth. With Nat. Westminster Bank, 1950—, dep. sr. internat. exec. for Ams., 1974-75, dep. regional dir. for West End, London, 1975-76, dep. regional dir. for S.E. Eng., 1976-77, pres., chief adminstrv. officer Nat. Bank of N. Am., N.Y.C., 1979-80, pres., chief exec. officer Nat. Bank of N. Am., 1980—. Freeman, City of London. Fell Inst. Bankers (U.K.). Clubs: Apawamis (Rye, N.Y.); Marylebone Cricket. Office: 44 Wall St New York NY 10005*

FRUEHLING, DONALD L., publishing co. exec.; b. Ft. Madison, Iowa, May 29, 1931; s. Jesse W. and Elma (Fowler) F.; B.A., No. Iowa U., 1957; postgrad. Columbia U., 1969; m. Rosemary Leoni, July 23, 1969; children—Shirley, Greg, Jeffrey, Melissa. Mgr., NW Bus. Coll., Huron, S.D.; salesman Gregg div. McGraw-Hill Book Co., N.Y.C., 1958-61, field sales mgr., 1961-65, Western regional mgr., 1965-66, nat. sales mgr., 1966-67, dir. mktg., 1967-68, gen mgr., 1968-70, v.p., 1970-74, exec. v.p. sch. publishing, 1974-79, pres., 1979—. Served with U.S. Army, 1948-53. Recipient Alumni Achievement award, U. No. Iowa, 1973. Office: 1221 Ave of Americas New York NY 10020

FRUMER, LOUIS RESHIN, legal publishing co. exec.; b. Shreveport, La., Feb. 8, 1918; s. Isidor Wolf and Jennie (Reshin) F.; B.A., U. Tex., 1938, J.D., 1939; LL.M., Harvard, 1946; m. Elaine R. Dorect, July 14, 1953; children—Nancy A., John D. Admitted to Tex. bar, 1939, practiced in Kilgore, Tex., 1939-42; asst. prof. law So. Meth. U., 1946-47; prof. law Syracuse U., 1947-56; editorial dir., v.p.-editorial, Matthew Bender & Co., N.Y.C., 1956-70, exec. v.p., 1970-74, vice chmn., editor-in-chief, 1974—; adj. prof. law N.Y. U., 1970—. Served with USAAF, 1942-45; ETO. Mem. Internat., Am., N.Y. State, Fed. bar assns., Assn. Bar City N.Y. Clubs: Harvard of N.Y., Manhattan. Author various legal works, including: (with Friedman) Products Liability, 8 vols., 1960—. Home: 110 East End Ave New York NY 10028 Office: 235 E 45th St New York NY 10017

FRY, ELIZABETH O. STOCKETT (MRS. WILLIAM FINLEY FRY, JR.), mgmt. cons.; b. Los Angeles, Nov. 30, 1925; d. Lewis Oatman and Gertrude (Hogle) Stockett; student U. Ariz., 1943-46, Pitman Bus. Coll., Vancouver, B.C., 1947; m. William Finley Fry, June 3, 1951; children—Peter Finley, Stephen Stockett, Susan Elizabeth. Exec. sec. James Graham Mfg. Co., Newark, Calif., 1948-51; sec. Food Inst., Stanford, 1951-52; asst. to exec. dir. Calif. Fedn. Civic Unity, San Francisco, 1952-53; pub. Country Almanac newspaper, Woodside, Calif., 1965-81, also Redwood City (Calif.) Almanac newspaper, 1979-81; pvt. practice mgmt. cons., Portola Valley, Calif., 1981—; pres. bd. dirs. Portola Valley Pub. Corp. (Calif.), 1965—; dir. Argonaut Properties; treas. Sterling Publs. Inc., San Mateo, Calif. Pres., Portola Valley PTA, 1963-64. Mem. Pubs. Assn. San Mateo County (v.p. 1970, pres. 1971), Internat. Newspaper Promotion Assn., League Women Voters, NAACP, Calif., Calaveras, Nevada County hist. socs., Redwood City C. of C. (dir. 1980—), ACLU, Calif. Press Assn., Calif. Republican League, Internat. Wine and Food Soc., Sierra Club, Alpha Chi Omega (alumni v.p. 1957-58), Sigma Delta Chi (chpt. sec. 1971). Clubs: Calif. Book, Alpine Hills Tennis. Home and Office: 345 Golden Hills Dr Portola Valley CA 94025

FRYDENLUND, ARTHUR JORGEN, motel exec.; b. nr. Buffalo, S.D., Aug. 16, 1907; s. Olaf and Ella (Halvorson) F.; student pub. schs.; m. Elaine A. Eyler, June 25, 1934; children—Gerald, John, Karen (Mrs. Gerald Bouzek), Jane (Mrs. Elliott Moore), Eric. Barber, Prairie du Chien, Wis., 1932-51; owner Motel Brisbois, Prairie du Chien, 1951—, Moto-Miter Co., Prairie du Chien, 1959—. City chmn. Heart Fund, Prairie du Chien, 1962; mem. adv. bd. Campion Jesuit High Sch., 1970—; mem. Father Marquette Tercentenary Com., 1972—; pres. Blackhawk Com., 1974—. Mem. County Bd. Suprs., chmn. health com., 1974—, mem. social services com. Bd. dirs. Indsl. Devel., 1952-63, pres., 1963—; trustee Meml. Hosp., 1957—. Mem. Wis. Innkeepers (v.p. 1974—), Prairie du Chien C. of C. (pres. 1959, dir. 1952—), Gt. Fire Engine Race Am. (dir. 1972—). Methodist. Patentee in field. Home: 533 N Marquette Rd Prairie du Chien WI 53821

FRYE, CLAYTON WESLEY, JR., fin. exec.; b. Los Angeles, May 18, 1930; s. Clayton Wesley and Mary Virginia (Briggs) F.; A.B., Stanford U., 1953, M.B.A., 1959; m. Dorothy Dee Rumsfeld, Jan. 14, 1957; children—Carolyn Ann, Marilyn Diane. Pres., Sutter Hill Devel. Co., Palo Alto, Calif., 1962-69; gen. partner Johnson & Frye Investment Co., San Antonio, 1970-73; asso. Laurance S. Rockefeller, N.Y.C., 1973—; dir. Calif. Pacific Comml. Corp. (Palo Alto), Caneel Bay, Inc. (St. John, V.I.), Grand Teton Lodge Co. (Jackson, Wyo.), Little Dix Bay Hotel Corp. (Brit. V.I.), Rockefeller Center, Inc., N.Y.C., Rockresorts, Inc., N.Y.C., Tejon Ranch Co. (Los Angeles), Woodstock Resort Corp. (Vt.); trustee Sleepy Hollow Restorations, Inc. (Tarrytown, N.Y.). Bd. trustees Jackson Hole Preserve, Inc., South St. Seaport Mus., N.Y.C., Woodstock (Vt.) Found. Served with USNR, 1948-49. Mem. Urban Land Inst. Republican. Clubs: Knickerbocker (N.Y.C.), Univ. (N.Y.C.); Field (New Canaan, Ct.). Home: 46 Lone Tree Farm Rd New Canaan CT 06840 Office: Room 5600 30 Rockefeller Plaza New York NY 10112

FRYE, JUDITH ELEEN MINOR (MRS. VERNON LESTER FRYE), editor trade mag.; b. Seattle; d. George Edward and Eleen G. (Hartelius) Minor; student U. Cal. at Los Angeles, evenings 1947-48, U. So. Calif., 1948-53; m. Vernon Lester Frye, Apr. 1, 1954. Accountant, office mgr. Colony Wholesale Liquor, Culver City, Calif., 1947-48; credit mgr. Western Dist. Co., Culver City, 1948-53; partner in restaurants, Palm Springs, Los Angeles, 1948, partner in date ranch, La Quinta, Calif., 1949-53; partner, owner Imperial Printing, Huntington Beach, Calif., 1955—; editor New Era Laundry and Cleaning Lines, Huntington Beach, 1962—; editor New Era Mag. Mem. Laundry and Cleaning Allied Trades Assn., Laundry and Dry Cleaning Suppliers Assn., Calif. Coin-op Assn. (exec. dir. 1975—; Cooperation award 1971, Dedicated Service award 1976), Nat. Automatic Laundry and Cleaning Council (Leadership award 1972), Women in Laundry/Drycleaning (past pres.; Outstanding Service award 1977). Office: 22031 Bushard St Huntington Beach CA 92646

FRYE, PIERRE ARNOLD, lawyer; b. N.Y.C., Jan. 19, 1924; s. Lucius Arnold and Suzanne (Jaladert) F.; B.E.S., U. Paris, 1942; student Harvard U., 1942-43; J.D., Columbia, 1948; LL.M., N.Y. U., 1959; m. Annie-Vera Dysthe, July 24, 1965; children—Pierre-Christian, Vera-Ellen Suzanne. Admitted to N.Y. bar, 1950, U.S. Supreme Ct., other fed. cts.; with Hawkins, Delafield and Wood, 1948-49; asst. to L. Arnold Frye, 1949-50; pvt. practice law, 1950-52, 68-69; with 1st Nat. City Bank, 1952-54; counsel Pyrofax Gas Corp., 1954-59; mem. law dept. Union Carbide Corp., 1959-68; mem. law dept. Am. Home Products Corp., 1969-73 (all N.Y.C.); internat. counsel Grumman Corp., Bethpage, N.Y., 1973-78; sec. Grumman Internat., Inc., 1974-78; asst. gen. counsel Warnaco Inc., Bridgeport, Conn., 1978—, asst. sec., 1979—. Trustee, officer, counsel Fleming Sch., N.Y.C., 1957-58, 64-70. Served with AUS, 1943-46; now col. USAF Ret. Res. Decorated Meritorious Service medal, Bronze Star medal, N.Y. State Conspicuous Service Cross. Mem. Am. Bar Assn., Westchester-Fairfield Corp. Counsel Assn., SAR (life). Home: 17 Village Dr New Canaan CT 06840 Office: 350 Lafayette St Bridgeport CT 06602

FRYE, RICHARD CRAIG, mfg. co. exec.; b. Youngstown, Ohio, Aug. 23, 1943; s. Forrest E. and Virginia L. (Rhoads) F.; B.S. in Bus., Miami U., Oxford, Ohio, 1965; children—Carl Andrew, Matthew Philip. Media buyer Ketchum, MacLeod & Grove Inc., Pitts., 1965-67; media supr., account exec. Fuller & Smith & Ross, Inc., N.Y.C., 1967-69; with Eaton Corp., 1969—, advt. and sales promotion mgr. Indsl. Truck div., Phila., 1974-77, mgr. div. export sales, 1977-79, mgr. market devel., 1979—; cons. in field bus. publs. and non-daily newspapers. Served with USCGR, 1965-66. Mem. Internat. Trade Devel. Assn., Am. Mgmt. Assn. Republican. Methodist. Contbr. articles to bus. publs. Office: 11000 Roosevelt Blvd Philadelphia PA 19115

FRYE, VERNON LESTER, publisher; b. Niagara Falls, N.Y., Sept. 5, 1915; s. Reinhart B. and Cora B. (Carl) F.; student U. Calif. at Los Angeles, 1947-50; m. Judith Eleen Minor, Apr. 1, 1954. Accountant, McLaren, Goode & West, C.P.A.'s, Los Angeles, 1950-51; br. chief accountant Philco Corp., Los Angeles, 1951-54; chief accounting officer Centinela Valley Union High Sch. Dist., Hawthorne, Calif., 1955-60; partner Imperial Printing Co., Los Angeles, 1955-68; pub. New Era Mag., Huntington Beach, Calif., 1962—. Served with AUS, 1941-45; ETO. Mem. Laundry and Drycleaning Allied Trade Assn., Nat. Automatic Laundry and Cleaning Council, Laundry and Drycleaning Suppliers, Nat. Automatic Coin Laundry Equipment Operators, Huntington Beach C. of C. Office: 22031 Bushard St Huntington Beach CA 92646

FRYER, APPLETON, sales exec., lectr.; b. Buffalo, Feb. 25, 1927; s. Livingston and Catherine (Appleton) F.; A.B., Princeton U., 1950; m. Angeline Dudley Kenefick, May 16, 1953; children—Appleton, Daniel Kenefick, Robert Livingston, Catherine Appleton. Head interpreter Hewitt-Robins, Inc., Buffalo, 1950-51; advt. dept. Buffalo Evening News, 1953-55; field rep. Ketchum, MacLeod & Grove, Inc., advt., 1955-56; pres. Duo-Fast of Western N.Y., Inc., Buffalo, 1956—; hon. consul gen. of Japan, Buffalo, 1979—. Dep. sheriff, Erie County, N.Y., 1954-68; adv. bd. Children's Hosp. of Buffalo; mem. Community Welfare Council Buffalo and Erie County; mem. bd. Erie County Sesquicentennial Commn., 1970-71; co-chmn. Erie Bicentennial Commn., 1974-76; adviser City Buffalo Environ. Mgmt. Commn., 1973-75; trustee Theodore Roosevelt Inaugural Nat. Historic Site Found., 1969—; bd. dirs. Zool. Soc. Buffalo, 1972-78, Buffalo Fine Arts Acad., Albright-Knox Art Gallery, 1973-76; chmn. Buffalo-Kanazawa Sister Cities Com., 1978-79; pres. Arboretum of Met. Buffalo, 1977-78; bd. dirs. Maud Gordon Holmes Arboretum, 1974—, pres., 1976-78; mem. Buffalo Landmark and Preservation Bd., 1978—; mem. council Charles Burchfield Center, 1974—; mem. council Central Erie deanery Diocese Western N.Y., 1970; mem. Erie County Sesquicentennial Commn., 1970-71; mem. com. Young Life on Niagara Frontier, 1971-72; mem. planning com. Venture in Mission, 1979, mem. campaign exec. com., 1979—; chmn. sect. 3 N.Y. State am. giving com. Princeton U., 1979—. Served with USNR, 1945-46, to 1st lt. AUS, 1951-52. Mem. Niagara Frontier Indsl. Distbrs. Assn., Buffalo Area C. of C. (Buffalo Beautiful Com. 1975—), Am. Assn. Museums (trustee 1978—), S.R. (pres. Buffalo Assn. 1966-73), Soc. Mayflower Descs. (regent Buffalo colony 1961-65), Soc. Colonial Wars, Holland Soc. of N.Y. (pres. Niagara Frontier br. 1969-79), Buffalo and Erie County Hist. Soc. (bd. mgrs. 1969—, v.p. 1977—), Buffalo Soc. Natural Scis., Landmark Soc. Niagara Frontier, Outstanding award 1979 (pres. 1969-73), Old Ft. Niagara Assn. (dir. 1980—), Order. Colonial Lords of Manors, Princeton Alumni Assn. (chmn. schs. com. Western N.Y. area 1974-77). Episcopalian (warden, licensed lay reader). Clubs: Masons, Rotary of Buffalo (internat. service com. 1978—); Princeton (N.Y.C.); Princeton of Western N.Y. (pres. 1960), Saturn (vice dean 1963) (Buffalo); Nassau, University Cottage (Princeton, N.J.); Porcupine (gov. 1969-73) (Nassau). Home: 85 Windsor Ave Buffalo NY 14209 Office: 365 Nagel Dr Buffalo NY 14225

FRYKENBERG, JOHN STUART, assn. exec.; b. Worcester, Mass., Apr. 18, 1943; s. Carl Eric and Doris Marie (Skoglund) F.; B.A., Barrington Coll., 1965; M.A., U.R.I., 1968; m. Joan Ann Maugle, Jan. 22, 1966. Tchr. Bd. Edn., Norwich, Conn., 1966-67; exec. v.p. Greater Gardner (Mass.) C. of C., 1971-73, Tri-Community Area (Mass.) C. of C., 1973—. Served with USNR, 1968-71. Mem. Am., Mass. (pres.) assns. chambers commerce execs., U.S. C. of C., Mass. Commonwealth C. of C. (pres.), Gulf Atlantic Oceanographic Research Soc. Democrat. Baptist. Club: Rotary. Home: Wickaboag Valley Rd West Brookfield MA 01585 Office: 111 Main St Southbridge MA 01550

FTHENAKIS, EMANUEL, communications, electronic and space co. exec.; b. Salonica, Greece, Jan. 30, 1928; came to U.S., 1952, naturalized, 1956; s. John and Evanthia (Magoulakis) F.; diploma in Mech. and Elec. Engring., Tech. U. Athens, 1952; M.S.E.E., Columbia U., 1953; m. Hermione Jane Coates, Dec. 1972; children—John, Basil. Mem. tech. staff Bell Telephone Labs., N.Y.C., 1953-57; dir. engring. Missile and Space div. Gen. Elec. Co., Phila., 1957-61; v.p., gen. mgr. Space and Re-Entry Systems div. Philco-Ford, Palo Alto, Calif., 1961-69; pres. Aerospace div. ITT, Calif., 1969-70; chmn. bd. Intelcom Industries, Newport Beach, Calif., 1969-70; pres., dir. Am. Satellite Corp., Germantown, Md., 1973-80, chmn. mgmt. bd., 1980—; sr. v.p. Fairchild Industries, Inc.; dir. Space Communications, Inc. (Upper Saddle River, N.Y.); trustee Pacific Telecommunications Council (Honolulu); univ. tchr., govt. cons.; mem. adv. panel telecommunications study Office of Tech. Assessment, 1979-80. Recipient Bicentennial award for outstanding achievement Columbia U., 1973. Mem. IEEE (sr.), AIAA, Armed Forces Communications and Electronics Assn. (chmn. fin. com. Washington chpt.). Contbr. articles to profl. jours. Patentee in field. Office: 20301 Century Blvd Germantown MD 20767

FUCHS, OWEN GEORGE, chemist; b. Austin, Tex., June 22, 1951; s. Emil George and Hazel June (Johnson) F.; A.A., Lee Jr. Coll., 1970, A.S., 1973; B.S., U. Houston, 1972; m. Debra Ruth Roder, Jan. 10, 1975; children—Ginny Lynn, William Oberholz. Chemist, Merichem Co., Houston, 1972-73; lab. mgr. Superintendence Co., Inc., Houston, 1973-78; dir. labs. and hydrocarbon research Chas. Martin Internat., Pasadena, Tex., 1978-79; pres., chief exec. officer Alpha-Omega Labs., Inc., Crosby, Tex., 1979—. Mem. ASTM, Am. Chem. Soc., Am. Assn. Cereal Chemists, Am. Oil Chemists Soc., Nat. Cottonseed Producers Assn., Am. Fats and Oil Assn. Methodist. Home: PO Box 631 Crosby TX 77532 Office: PO Drawer L 127 Kernshan St Crosby TX 77532

FUGATE, KENDALL MORGAN, credit card co. exec.; b. Springfield, Ill., Dec. 15, 1937; s. Payton Kendall and Juliet Ellen (Morgan) F.; B.S. in Elec. Engring., U. Ill., 1961; postgrad. George Washington U., 1967; m. Lois Ann Hammett, Sept. 16, 1967; children—Deborah Irene, Kendall Donnelly. Dir. systems design Am. Express Co., N.Y.C., 1968-71, regional v.p. operations, N.Y.C. and Fla., 1971-77, v.p. systems devel., N.Y.C., 1977-79; exec. v.p. Diners Club Internat., Denver, 1979—. Served with Signal Corps, U.S. Army, 1961-68. Mem. Nat. Assn. Credit Mgrs., Am. Nat. Standards Inst. Clubs: Columbine Country; Lighthouse Point (Fla.) Yacht. Office: 10 Denver Tech Center Englewood CO 80111

FUHRER, LARRY, investment banker; b. Ft. Wayne, Ind., Sept. 23, 1939; s. Henry Roland and Wilhelmine Ellen (Kopp) F.; A.B., Taylor U., 1961; postgrad. No. Ill. U., 1965—; m. Linda Larsen, Dec. 31, 1962; 1 son, Lance. Exec. club dir. Youth for Christ, Miami, Fla., 1961; publs. mgr. Campus Life mag. Wheaton, Ill., 1962-65; asst. to pres. Youth for Christ Internat., Wheaton, 1965-66; asso. dir. devel. Ill. Inst. Tech., 1966-68; exec. asst. to pres. The Robert Johnston Corp., Los Angeles, Chgo., N.Y.C., 1968-69; pres. Compro, Inc., Glen Ellyn, Ill., 1966-72; pres. Killian Assos. Inc., Wheaton, 1973-75; chmn. Equibanque Ltd., 1973-79; dir. Fin. Services Group Ltd., Equity Realty Group Inc., Presdl. Services Inc., 1966—; ednl. mgmt. cons. numerous pvt. colls. and sems. Bd. dirs. Chicagoland Youth for Christ. Mem. Am. Mgmt. Assn., Am. Inst. Mgmt. Cons.'s, DuPage Bd. Realtors, Nat., Ill. assns. realtors, Am. Mktg. Assn., Mortgage Bankers Assn. Presbyterian. Club: Union League (Chgo.). Home: 125 W Seminary St Wheaton IL 60187 Office: 739 Roosevelt Rd Glen Ellyn IL 60137

FUJIMOTO, AKIRA, county ofcl.; b. Honolulu, June 12, 1925; s. Eiji and Yukiyo (Miyagi) F.; B.S., U. Hawaii, 1950; m. Hazel Sayoko Furutani, Mar. 24, 1951; children—Terrance B. H., Kyle W. T. Jr. civil engr. Dept. Pub. Works, County of Hawaii, Hilo, 1950-52, civil engr., 1952-57, bur. head plans and surveys, 1957-61; asst. mgr.-engr. Dept. Water Supply, County of Hawaii, Hilo, 1961-68, mgr.-engr., 1968-79; ret., 1979. Served with U.S. Army, 1945-47. Registered profl. engr., Hawaii. Named Hawaii Engr. of the Year, Hawaii Soc. Profl. Engrs., 1976. Mem. Am. Soc. Civil Engring., Hawaii Water Works Assn., Nat. Soc. Profl. Engrs., Hawaii Soc. Profl. Engrs., Am. Water Works Assn. Buddhist Religion. Clubs: Young Buddhist Assn., 442nd Vets of Hawaii, Kiwanis. Home: 152 Hoonanea St Hilo HI 96720

FUJIYAMA, WALLACE SACHIO, lawyer; b. Honolulu, Aug. 8, 1925; s. George S. and Cornelia (Matsumoto) F.; student U. Hawaii, 1943-44, 49-50; LL.B., U. Cin., 1953; m. Mildred H. Morita, Jan. 24, 1959; children—Rodney, Susan, Keith. Admitted to Hawaii bar, 1954; dep. atty. gen. Hawaii, 1954-56; examiner, atty. Hawaii Employment Relations Bd., 1956-59; individual practice law, 1956—, Honolulu, 1959—; partner Fujiyama, Duffy & Fujiyama; chmn. bd. Honolulu Corp. Mem. Hawaii Statehood Commn., 1957-59; mem. nat. platform com. from Hawaii, Rep. Nat. Conv., 1956; bd. regents U. Hawaii, 1974—, chmn., 1975-79. Served with Transp. Corps, AUS, 1946. Recipient Cin. Ct. Index award, 1953. Mem. Am. Arbitration Assn. (mediator), Am., Hawaii (pres.) bar assns., Hawaii Trial Lawyers Assn. (pres.), Internat. Savs. and Loan Assn. (sec., dir.), Order of Coif, Phi Alpha Delta. Club: Honolulu Internat. Country (dir.). Asso. editor U. Cin. Law Rev. Home: 1803 Laukahi St Honolulu HI 96821 Office: Suite 2650 Pacific Trade Center 190 S King St Honolulu HI 96813

FUKA, LYDIA, transp. co. exec.; b. Chgo., July 9, 1948; d. Anthony P. and Emma (Sholonis) L.; A.A. with honors, Chgo. City Coll., 1968; B.S. in B.A., Roosevelt U., 1970; married. Mgr. women's sportswear dept. Marshall Field & Co., Chgo., 1966-70; adminstrv. aide Office of Chancellor U. Ill., Chgo., 1970-71; sr. contractor bulk grain commodity sales Quaker Oats Co., Chgo., 1971-72; asst. mgr. personnel dept. Atchison, Topeka & Santa Fe Ry. Co., Chgo., also dir. coll. recruitment program, 1972-75, sr. pricing analyst and price quotations supr. traffic dept., 1975-78, officer-in-tng., 1978-78, price quotation supr., 1978-80, tariff pub. office mgr., 1980—; exec. on loan Nat. Alliance Businessmen, 1977. Mem. Def. Supply Assn., Am. Mgmt. Assn., R.R. Personnel Assn., Roosevelt U. Alumni Assn., Phi Theta Kappa (officer). Democrat. Lutheran. Home: 3511 W 57 St Chicago IL 60629 Office: Santa Fe Railroad Co Traffic Dept Suite 1135 80 E Jackson Blvd Chicago IL 60604

FUKUI, HATSUAKI, elec. engr.; b. Yokohama, Japan, Dec. 14, 1927; s. Ushinosuke and Yoshi (Saito) F.; grad. Miyakojima Tech. Coll. (now Osaka City U.), 1949; D.Eng., Osaka U., 1961; m. Atsuko Inamoto, Apr. 1, 1954 (dec. Apr. 1973); children—Mayumi, Naoki; m. 2d, Kiku Kato, Dec. 12, 1975. Came to U.S., 1962, naturalized, 1973. Research asso. Osaka City U., 1949-54; engr. Shimada Phys. and Chem. Indsl. Co., Tokyo, 1954-55; sr. engr. to supr. Sony Corp., semi-conductor div., Tokyo, 1955-61, mgr. engring. div., 1961-62, dep. dir. research and devel. labs., Tokyo, 1973; v.p. Sony Corp. Am., N.Y., 1973; mem. tech. staff Bell Telephone Labs., Murray Hill, N.J., 1962-69, supr., 1969-73, mem. staff, 1973—; lectr. Tokyo Met. U., part time, 1962. Mem. IEEE (sr. mem.; mem. standars com. on microwave transistors characterization of Electron Devices Soc. 1976—, editorial bd. Microwave Theory and Techniques Soc. 1980—, Microwave prize 1980), Inst. Electronics and Communications Engrs. Japan (Inada prize 1959), Inst. Television Engrs. Japan (mem. tech. steering com. 1973-75), Internat. Platform Assn. Author: Esaki Diodes, 1963; Solid-State FM Receivers, 1968; contbr. to Semiconductors Handbook, 1963; numerous patents, publs. in field. Home: 53 Drum Hill Dr Summit NJ 07901 Office: 600 Mountain Ave Murray Hill NJ 07974

FUKUNAGA, GEORGE JOJI, business exec.; b. Waialua, Oahu, Hawaii, Apr. 13, 1924; s. Peter H. and Ruth (Hamamura) F.; B.A., U. Hawaii, 1948, certificate Advanced Mgmt. Program, Harvard-U. Hawaii, 1955; m. Alice M. Tagawa, Aug. 5, 1950; 1 son, Mark H. Adminstrv. asst., dir. Service Motor Co., Ltd. (name Servco Pacific Inc. 1969), 1948-50, v.p., 1952-60, pres., 1960—; chmn. bd., dir. Pacific Internat. Co. Inc., Pacific Fin. Corp., Pacific Motors Corp., Service Finance, Ltd. (name now Servco Financial Corp.), 1960—, Am. Ins. Agy. Inc., Servco Internat. Corp., Servco Investment Corp., Servco Securities Corp., Servco Services Corp., Hawaiiana Adv. and Pub. Relations Agy. Inc.; dir. City Bank Honolulu, Am. Trust of Hawaii Inc., Island Ins., Ltd., Hawaiian Pacific Resorts, Inc. Mem. adv. bd. Advanced Mgmt. Program, U. Hawaii, 1955—; mem. Hawaii Post-Secondary Edn. Commn., 1976—; bd. govs. Iolani Sch., 1972—, Hawaii Pacific Coll., 1975—; trustee Fukunaga Scholarship Found., 1960—, U. Hawaii Found.; mem. adv. bd. Nat. Alliance Businessmen. Served from pvt. to 2d lt. AUS, 1945-47, to 1st lt., 1950-52. Mem. Hawaii (past v.p., past dir.), Honolulu Japanese (past pres., dir.) chambers commerce, Hawaii Employers Council (past dir.), Hawaii Joint Council Econ. Edn., Better Bus. Bur. (past v.p., dir.), Hawaii Econ. Study Club (past pres., dir.), Japan-Hawaii Soc., Japan-Hawaii Econ. Council. Methodist. Clubs: Rotary, Plaza (dir.), Deps., Club 200. Home: 2016 Kula St Honolulu HI 96817 Office: 900 Fort St Mall Suite 500 Honolulu HI 96813

FULGHAM, JOHN RAWLES, JR., multibank holding co. exec.; b. Windsor, Va., July 29, 1927; s. John Rawles and Gypsie Louise (Matthews) F.; B.A., Va. Mil. Inst., 1950; B.B.A., So. Meth. U., 1956; m. Betty Berger, Dec. 2, 1950; children—Emily Ann Fulgham McCullough, Virginia Fulgham Askew, Janie Rawles, John Rawles, III. With First Nat. Bank, Dallas, 1954—, sr. v.p., controller, head adminstrv. services, pres., now dir.; pres., dir. 1st Internat. Bancshares, Inc., Dallas; dir. Earth Resources Co., Republic Fin. Services, Inc., Dresser Industries, Inc.; mem. faculty Southwestern Grad. Sch. Banking; lectr. Am. Inst. Banking, Fed. Savs. and Loan Inst. Leader fund raising campaigns Wadley Research Inst., Dallas Goodwill Industries, United Fund Dallas, Presbyn. Hosp., Dallas; trustee Tex. Presbyn. Found.; bd. dirs. Children's Med. Center Dallas. Served to capt. USMCR, 1950-53. Mem. Dallas Salesmanship Club, Fin. Execs. Inst., Va. Mil. Inst. Alumni Assn. (pres. chpt. 1959), Kappa Alpha. Presbyterian (deacon). Clubs: Dallas Country (bd. govs.), Dallas Petroleum. Office: 1st Internat Bancshares Inc 1201 Elm St Dallas TX 75270*

FULGHUM, BRICE ELWIN, cons.; b. Fredonia, Kans., Aug. 27, 1919; s. Byron Harmon and Myrtle (Broderick) F.; student U. Kansas City, San Francisco State Coll.; children—Patricia B. Fulghum Mijares, Linda Lee Fulghum Sanders. Asst. to sales mgr. Gas Service Co., Kansas City, Mo., 1939-41, sales mgr. Ace Auto Rental & Sales Co., Kansas City, 1945-48; asst. mgr. Owl Drug Co., San Francisco, 1948-50; mgr. Pacific Mut. Life Ins. Co., 1950-61; v.p. Gordon H. Edwards Co., 1961-64; v.p. Federated Life Ins. Co. Calif., 1964-66; gen. mgr. Los Angeles Fulghum agy. Pacific Mut. Life Ins. Co., 1966-71; v.p. Hendrie Bonding & Ins. Corp., Huntington Beach, Calif., 1976-77; chmn. bd. PGA Ins. Services, Inc., Torrance, Calif., 1976-77; cons. Am. Health Profiles, Inc., Nashville; sr. fin. cons. Shearson Hayden Stone Inc., Newport Beach, Calif., 1977-79; cons. Penn Gen. Agys., Los Angeles and Employee Benefit Cons.'s, Santa Ana, Calif., 1979—; cons. Assn. Calif. State U. Profs. Chmn. Cancer drive; active Community Chest, Am. Heart Assn. Served with Q.M.C., U.S. Army, 1941-43. C.L.U. Mem. Am. Soc. C.L.U.'s (Golden Key Soc.), Leading Life Ins. Producers No. Calif. (life mem., pres. 1955), San Francisco Peninsula (charter), Los Angeles-San Fernando Valley (life) estate planning councils, Orange County Life Underwriters Assn. Republican. Clubs: Commonwealth, El Niguel Country. Mem. editorial advisory bd. Western Underwriter. Contbr. articles to ins. publs. Home: 30356 Via Reata Laguna Niguel CA 92667 Office: 400 N Tustin Ave Santa Ana CA 92705

FULGHUM, JOHN LAWRENCE, petroleum co. exec.; b. Crandall, Tex., Sept. 30, 1935; s. John T. and Billye (Brooks) F.; student in Engring., Tex. A&M U., 1957, in Banking and Fin., So. Meth. U., 1964-65; postgrad. N.Y. Inst. Fin., 1966; children—Scott, Chris, Julia. Project engr. Enserch Corp., Dallas, 1957-65; investment banker Rauscher Pierce Securities, Dallas, 1965-73; pres. Fulghum & Assos., Dallas, 1974-78; bus. mgr., personnel mgr. H.J. Gruy Assos., Inc., Dallas, 1979—; cons. to mgmt. Served with U.S. Army, 1959. Mem. Am. Soc. Personnel Adminstrn., Petroleum Engrs. Club Dallas. Episcopalian. Office: 150 W Carpenter Freeway Irving TX 75062

FULKS, ROBERT GRADY, computer exec.; b. Kansas City, Mo., Apr. 8, 1936; s. Hilburne Grady and Dora Elouise (Johnson) F.; B.S.E.E., M.I.T., 1958, M.S.E.E., 1959; children—Stephanie, Scott Grady. Engr., chief engr. v.p. engring. and product mktg. Genrad, Inc., Concord, Mass., 1959-73; pres. Mirco Systems, Inc., 1973-75, Omnicomp, Inc., Phoenix, 1975-80; gen. mgr. advanced tech div. (formerly Omnicomp, Inc.) Genrad, Inc., Phoenix, 1980—. Former bd. dirs., chmn. fin. com. Concord (Mass.) C. of C. Mem. IEEE, Assn. Computing Machinery, Sigma Xi. Contbr. articles tech. jours. Patentee in field. Office: 4620 N 16th St Phoenix AZ 85016

FULLARTON, WILLIAM ALAN, investment co. exec.; b. Washington, June 29, 1935; s. William Archibald and Gwendolyn Ruth (Mundhenke) F.; B.A., Wesleyan U., Middletown, Conn., 1957; M.B.A., Harvard U., 1962; m. Anne Middleton Fetterolf, Aug. 22, 1959; children—Janet Stevens, Lisa Stewart, Marissa Lord. Adminstrv. asst. Hanover Bank, N.Y.C., 1959-61; asso. Kidder, Peabody & Co. Inc., N.Y.C., 1962-74, partner, 1972-74; pres. Kidder Peabody Realty Corp., N.Y.C., 1970-74; pres. Broad St. Corp., Columbus, Ohio, 1974-79, PacAm. Corp., Columbus, 1979—, Fullarton & Lord, Inc.; v.p. The Wendward Corp., 1975-79; dir. Concrete Technology, Inc., Dayton. Mem. Real Estate Securities and Syndication Inst. (exec. com. 1973). Office: PO Box 20202 2330 Wood Ave Columbus OH 43220

FULLER, ASHLEY ELLISON, fin. cons.; b. Merced, Calif., May 13, 1930; s. Walter Simmons and Mary Roselle (Stafford) F.; B.A., Calif. State U., 1957; m. Patricia Josephine Dennis, June 23, 1951; children—Patricia, Peggy, Paulette, Jonathan. Accountant, Del Monte Corp., San Francisco and Honolulu, 1957-64; ops. accounting mgr. Levi Strauss & Co., San Francisco, 1964-71; cons., gen. mgr. Fuller Assocs., San Francisco, 1971—; lectr. in field. Served with USN, 1950-54. Mem. San Leandro C. of C. (dir. 1973-76), Nat. Assn. Accountants, Nat. Assn. Enrolled Agts., Calif. Soc. Enrolled Agts. Republican. Mem. Assemblies of God Ch. Contbr. articles in field to profl. jours. Office: 48 Williams St San Leandro CA 94577

FULLER, FRED WELDON, ins. agt.; b. Madison, Tenn., Oct. 14, 1928; s. George N. and Myrtle M. (West) F.; student So. Missionary Coll., 1951-55; m. Dorothy V. Edgmon, July 27, 1947; children—Frieda Kay, Frederick Ray, Kenneth Wayne. With Collegewood Products Co., 1947; perpetual inventory clk. So. Pub. Assn., 1948-51; gen. ins. agt. Collegedale Ins. Agy. Inc. (Tenn.), 1951-63; agt. State Farm Ins. Co., Collegedale, 1963—. Mayor of Collegedale, 1969-77; chmn. Tri Community Fire Dept. Bd., 1967-75; mem. Hamilton County Appeal Bd., 1970—; chmn. bd. Greater Collegedale Sch. System, 1971-75; chmn. Chattanooga Area Regional Council of Govts., Southeast Tenn. Devel. Dist., 1974-77; mem. Com. of 100 for So. Missionary Colls.; bd. dirs., chmn. membership com. Collegedale Seventh Day Adventist Ch. Named Citizen of Yr. for Outstanding Service. Mem. Profl. Ins. Agts. Assn., Chattanooga Underwriters Assn., Assn. Privately Owned Seventh Day Adventist Services and Industries. Club: Kiwanis (pres. E. Hamilton County 1978-79, dir.). Home: 5505 Barrington St Country Circle Collegedale TN 37315 Office: State Farm Ins Co College Plaza Center Collegedale TN 37315

FULLER, HARRY LAURANCE, oil co. exec.; b. Moline, Ill., Nov. 8, 1938; s. Marlin and Mary Hellen (Ilsley) F.; B.S. in Chem. Engring., Cornell U., 1961; J.D., DePaul U., 1965; m. Nancy Lawrence, Dec. 27, 1961; children—Kathleen, Laura, Randall. Admitted to Ill. bar, 1965; with Standard Oil Co., and affiliates, 1961—, sales mgr., 1972-74, gen. mgr. supply, 1974-77, exec. v.p. Amoco Oil Co. div., Chgo., 1977-78, pres. Amoco Oil div., 1978—. Mem. Ill. Bar Assn., Chgo. Assn. Commerce and Industry (dir.), Ill. Mfrs. Assn. (dir.). Republican. Presbyterian. Club: Mid-Am. Office: Amoco 200 E Randolph Dr Chicago IL 60601*

FULLER, JAMES WILLIAM, mktg. exec.; b. Rochester, Ind., Apr. 3, 1940; s. Raymond S. and Mildred B. F.; B.S., San Jose State U., 1962; M.B.A., Calif. State U., 1966; m. Berniece A. Mangseth, May 18, 1963; children—Kristen Anne, Glen William. Mgr. institutional sales Dean Witter & Co., N.Y.C., 1968-73; v.p., mgr. Shields & Co., investment bankers, N.Y.C., 1973-74; mgr. investment industries program Stanford Research Inst. (Calif.), 1974-77; sr. v.p. mktg. N.Y. Stock Exchange, N.Y.C., 1977-81; sr. v.p. mktg. Charles Schwab Corp., San Francisco, 1981—. Served to lt. Supply Corp, USN, 1963-67. Mem. English Speaking Union, Newcomen Soc., Sierra Club. Republican. Clubs: Commonwealth (San Francisco); Jonathan (Los Angeles); Univ. (N.Y.C.). Office: One 2d St San Francisco CA 94105

FULLER, JOSEPH DONALD, pub. co. exec.; b. Elizabeth, N.J., Oct. 17, 1945; s. Thomas William and Eleanor Alice F.; B.A., St. Francis Coll., Bklyn., 1969; M.B.A., N.Y. U., 1978; m. Mary Lou Guillen, Aug. 24, 1968; children—Andrew, Ryan. Dir. Wall St. div. United Fund Greater N.Y., 1970-72; asso. dir. Fgn. Policy Assn., N.Y.C., 1972-74; dir. Grad. Sch. Bus. Adminstrn. Alumni Fedn., N.Y. U., N.Y.C., 1974-79; coordinator coll. relations St. Francis Coll., Bklyn., 1979-80; gen. mgr. HCA Ednl. div. Harcourt Brace Jovanovich, Inc., Cherry Hill, N.J., 1980—. Republican. Home: 387 DeGraw St Brooklyn NY 11231 Office: Cherry Hill Exec Campus Bldg 2 Suite 308 Cherry Hill NJ 08002

FULLER, MORTIMER BARTINE, III, holding co. exec.; b. Scranton, Pa., May 14, 1942; s. Mortimer B. and Frances (Acker) F.; A.B., Princeton U., 1964; J.D., Boston U., 1968; M.B.A., Harvard U., 1970; m. Suzanne Miles, Aug. 29, 1964; children—Amanda, Elizabeth, Kathryn. Admitted to Mass. bar, 1968, U.S. Supreme Ct. bar, 1979; real estate analyst Conn. Gen. Life Ins. Co., Hartford, 1970-73; officer Howard Research & Devel. Corp., 1972-73; exec. v.p. M/I Schottenstein Cos., Columbus, Ohio, 1973-77, pres. M/I Homes div., 1976-77; pres., chief exec. officer Genesee and Wyo. Industries, Inc., Greenwich, Conn., 1977—; dir. Genesee and Wyo. Industries, Inc., 1973—. Trustee, Rye (N.Y.) Presbyterian Ch., 1980—, selectors com. Lawrenceville Sch., 1980-83. Mem. Young Pres.'s Orgn. Clubs: Manursing Island, Genesee Valley, Princeton of N.Y. Office: 71 Lewis St Greenwich CT 06830

FULLER, PARRISH, lumber mfr.; b. Madison, Wis., May 21, 1892; s. William Wilson and Minnie Lora (Parrish) F.; student Wabash Coll. 1910-11, M.A., 1949, LL.D. (hon.), 1954; m. Hester Porter, Oct. 18, 1919; children—Mary Margaret (Mrs. James D. Voorhees), William Porter. Gen. mgr. J.O. Parrish Lumber Co., Shelbyville, Ind., 1914-18; asst. to pres. Hillyer Deutsch Edwards, Inc., Oakdale, La., 1919-20, v.p., gen. mgr., 1920-68; v.p. Hillyer Edwards Fuller, Inc., Glenmore, La., 1923-40; gen. partner King-Edwards-Fuller Co., St. Francisville, La., 1940-47, Avoyelles Timber Co., Bordelonville, La., 1940-64, Edwards & Fuller, Oakdale, La., 1938-70, Fuller Farms, 1930-72, Shelbyville, Ind.; v.p. King Lumber Industries, Canton, Miss., 1946-50, Canton & Carthage R.R. Co., 1946-53; gen. partner Heflands Timber Co., 1961-68; pres. J.O. Parrish Lumber Co.; v.p. Porter Steel Spltys., Inc., Shelbyville, Ind., 1946-51; dir., chmn. forest lands and products com. Celotex Corp., Chgo.; dir. Canton (Miss.) & Carthage R.R. Co., 1946-53; dir. South Shore Oil & Devel. Co., New Orleans, 1946-66, Nat. Bank of Commerce, New Orleans, 1946-66, New Orleans and Lower Coast R.R., 1951-70, J.O. Parrish Lumber Co. Chmn., La. State Salvage, 1942-45, United War Fund, 1943-45; mem. La. State Bd. Edn., pres., 1952; vice chmn. La. Commn. Higher Edn., 1955-56; chmn. Citizens Adv. Com. on La. Edn., 1964; mem. coordinating council La. State Colls. and La. State U., 1948-52. Bd. visitors Tulane U.; trustee Wabash Coll.; bd. govs. Ochsner Med. Found., New Orleans; chmn. bd. dirs. St. Frances Cabrini Hosp., Alexandria, La. Decorated Benemerenti medal (Pope John Paul II); recipient Citizenship Citation, La. div. V.F.W., Distinguished Pub. Service Citation, So. U., 1952, Pub. Service Citation, La. Council Coll. Pres.'s, 1953, award of merit Wabash Coll., 1960; Silver Beaver award Boy Scouts Am., 1974; named Humanitarian of Year, Abbeville Festival, 1960. Mem. Sigma Chi. Frat. Presbyterian. Clubs: Chicago; Boston, Internat. House, Country, Plimsoll (New Orleans); Woodstock (Indpls.); Pioneer (Lake Charles, La.). Pres. Pub. Affairs Research Council of La., Inc. 1958. Office: Box 663 Oakdale LA 71463

FULLER, RICHARD LUVERNE, wine co. exec.; b. Ft. Worth, Aug. 25, 1948; s. Luverne Bernard and Dorothy Elizabeth (Day) F.; B.A. in Econs., Lamar U., 1966-70; m. Cynthia Louise Marshall, Dec. 14, 1968; children—Ashley Carole, Laura Katherine. Sales rep. Carnation Co., Oklahoma City, 1971-73, sales supr., Denver, 1973-74, area mgr., San Antonio, 1974-75, asst. dist. mgr., St. Louis, 1975-76, dist. mgr., Kansas City, Mo., 1976-77, Balt., 1977-78, gen. sales mgr., Los Angeles, 1978-80; nat. brandy sales coordinator Ernest & Julio Gallo Winery, Modesto, Calif., 1980—. Mem. Pi Kappa Alpha. Republican. Episcopalian. Club: Carroll Racquet. Home: 5121 Hensley Dr Dunwoody GA 30338 Office: 47 Perimeter Center E Dunwoody GA 30338

FULLER, SARAH WILDER, mgmt. cons.; b. Boston, Oct. 20, 1949; d. David and Nancy (Nye) Wilder; B.A., U. Pa., 1971; M.A., Harvard U., 1975; m. William C. Fuller, Jr., Sept. 15, 1973. Cons., Arthur D. Little, Inc., Cambridge, Mass., 1975—, dir. Access, computer-based strategic planning service, 1979—; non-resident tutor in bus. Kirkland House, Harvard U., 1978—. Mem. steering com. Children's Hosp. Med. Center. Club: Vincent. Home: Smith Rd Hamilton NY 13346 Office: 20 Acorn Park Cambridge MA 02140

FULLERTON, R. DONALD, banker; b. Vancouver, B.C., Can.; s. C. G. and Muriel F.; grad. U. Toronto, 1953. With Can. Bank of Commerce, 1953—, regional gen. mgr. internat., 1967, dep. chief gen. mgr., 1968-71, sr. v.p., dep. chief gen. mgr., 1971-73, exec. v.p., chief gen. mgr., 1973-76, dir., 1974—, pres., chief operating officer, 1976-80, vice chmn., pres., 1980—; dir. Am. Can of Canada Ltd., N. Am. Life Assurance Co., Calif. Canadian Bank, Canadian Eastern Fin. Ltd., AMOCO Can. Petroleum Co. Ltd. Bd. dirs. Wellesley Hosp., 1974—; bd. govs. Crescent Sch., Toronto, 1974—, Bishop Strachan Sch., Toronto; hon. treas. Royal Ont. Mus., Toronto, 1977—. Mem. Bd. Trade Met. Toronto. Clubs: York, Toronto, Rosedale, Granite, Caledon Ski, Queen's, Canadian, Empire, Harvard Bus. Sch. Toronto; Metropolitan (N.Y.C.). Address: Commerce Ct W Toronto ON M5L 1A2 Canada

FULLMER, THOMAS PATRICK, univ. adminstr.; b. Salt Lake City, Aug. 6, 1925; s. Stephen James and Ellen May (Milford) F.; student U. Calif. at Berkeley, 1945-46, Princeton U., 1945; Ph.B., U. Santa Clara, 1950; postgrad. Immaculate Conception Coll., 1956, Coll. Pacific, 1946; M.S. in Psychology, Fordham U., 1951; Ph.D. in Sociology, U. Dominicans, 1953; m. Patricia Ann Carroll Boyd, Apr. 14, 1955; children—Steven Mark, Patrick Thomas, Teresa Maria, Frances Annette, Denise Gabrielle. With Pacific Mut. Life, San Francisco, 1954-57, dist. mgr., 1955-56; brokerage mgr. E.A. Ellis Agy., San Francisco, 1956-57; asst. gen. agt. Pacific Mut. Life, 1957-58; dir. sales promotion and tng. Western Life Ins. Co., Helena, Mont., 1958; sales promotion asst. Mass. Mut. Life, Springfield, 1958-60, mgr. sales promotion, 1960; asst. supt. agys. Standard Ins. Co., Portland, Oreg., 1960-64, agy. mgr., 1964-68, mgr., Ariz., 1968—; dir. Alexander Hunt, Inc.; asst. prof. bus. U. Portland, 1967; past dir. Productivity Inst., Coll. Bus. Adminstrn., Ariz. State U., Tempe; dir. corp. productivity, research and public affairs Tanner Cos., Phoenix, 1981—. Past pres. bd. dirs. Brophy Coll. Prep. Sch., now mem. bd. regents; faculty advisor Alpha Kappa Psi. Served with USNR, 1942-46; PTO. Mem. Nat. Assn. Life Underwriters Gen. Agts. and Mgrs. Assn. (dir., past pres.). Republican. Roman Catholic. Clubs: Kiwanis, Elks, K.C. (4 deg.), Optimist (past pres.). Home: 11 W Palmaire Ave Phoenix AZ 85021 Office: PO Box 20128 Phoenix AZ 85036

FULMER, VINCENT ANTHONY, univ. ofcl.; b. Alliance, Ohio, Oct. 23, 1927; s. Anthony and Catherine (Long) F.; A.B. cum laude, Miami U., Oxford, Ohio, 1946-49; S.M., Mass. Inst. Tech., 1963; LL.D. (hon.), Suffolk U., 1971; m. Mary Alma Pineau, Dec. 27, 1950; children—Kevan, Kristine, David, Amy, Charles, Alma Leigh. Instr. econs. Williams Coll., Williamstown, Mass., 1952; indsl. liaison officer Mass. Inst. Tech., Cambridge, 1953-58, dir. indsl. liaison program, 1958-60, exec. asst. to chmn. of corp., 1960-63, v.p., 1963-73, sec. of inst., 1963—, sec. of corp., 1979—; v.p. adminstrn. William Underwood Co., Westwood, Mass., 1973-75; dir. Questar Corp., Moleculon Research Corp. Mem. planning office urban affairs Archdiocese Boston; mem. vis. com. Mus. Sch., Boston Mus. Fine Arts; chmn. bd. trustees Suffolk U., 1976—. Served with USNR, 1944-46. Mem. Am. Econs. Assn., Ops. Research Soc. Am., Inst. Mgmt. Scis., AAAS. Republican. Roman Catholic. Author articles and book chpts. in field. Home: 26 Kimball Rd Arlington MA 02174 Office: Room 3-221 MIT Massachusetts Ave Cambridge MA 02139

FULRATH, KAYE MARY, banker; b. Keota, Iowa, Jan. 14, 1922; d. Charles Alphonsus and Eva Anna (Palm) Fosdick; student Marycrest Coll., 1940; m. Thomas A. Fulrath, Dec. 26, 1944; 1 son, Douglas Kent. Asst. to purchasing agt. Penick & Ford Ltd., Inc., Cedar Rapids, Iowa, 1947-57; exec. sec. to chmn. and pres. Mchts. Nat. Bank, Cedar Rapids, 1957-65, asst. cashier, asst. v.p. compensation and employee benefits, 1965—; asst. v.p. employee benefits and compensation Blue Hills Oil Co., Cedar Rapids and Wichita, Kans., 1965—, sec.-treas., dir., 1967—; asst. sec. Banks of Iowa; Inc., Cedar Rapids, 1970—;

lectr. in field. Bd. dirs. Linn County Mental Health Assn., 1975—, Discovery Village, 1979—, Women's Community Leadership Inst.; treas., dir. United Way of Eastern Iowa, 1976—; mem. Baker scholarship com. Coe Coll., 1978-80; campaign fund solicitor Mt. Mercy Coll., 1979-80. Mem. Nat. Assn. Bank Women (regional v.p. 1977-78), Am. Inst. Banking. Clubs: Altrusa, Internat. Toastmistress (past regional sec-treas.). Home: 2601 Sue Ln NW Cedar Rapids IA 52405 Office: 222 Second Ave SE Cedar Rapids IA 52401

FULTON, CLYDE EDWARD, banker; b. Hartford City, Ind., Jan. 1, 1918; s. Ernest Clayton and Sadie Evelyn Fulton; B.S. in Accounting, Ind. U., 1940; postgrad. U.S. Naval War Coll., 1957-58; m. Mary Patricia Hynes, Nov. 5, 1946; children—Robert Kevin, Mary Lynne Fulton Vadney. Commd. ensign U.S. Navy, 1942, advanced through grades to capt., 1962; ret., 1970; now v.p. investments Dauphin Deposit Bank and Trust Co., Harrisburg, Pa. Mem. Pa. Bankers Assn. (investment com.), Am. Inst. Banking, Pa. C. of C. Decorated Navy Commendation medal (2). Republican. Roman Catholic. Home: 515 W Elmwood St Mechanicsburg PA 17055 Office: 213 Market St Harrisburg PA 17105

FULTON, NORMAN ROBERT, home entertainment co. exec.; b. Los Angeles, Dec. 16, 1935; s. Robert John and Fritzi Marie (Wacker) F.; A.A., Santa Monica Coll., 1958; B.S., U. So. Calif., 1960; m. Nancy Butler, July 6, 1966; children—Robert B., Patricia M. Fulton Fleming. Asst. v.p. Raphael Glass Co., Los Angeles, 1960-65; credit adminstr. Zellerbach Paper Co., Los Angeles, 1966-68; gen. credit mgr. Carrier Transicold Co., Montebello, Calif., 1968-70; gen. credit mgr. Virco Mfg. Co., Los Angeles, 1970-72; gen. credit mgr. Superscope, Inc., Chatsworth, Calif., 1972-79; credit mgr. J.N. Ceazan Co., Carson, Calif., 1980; asst. v.p. Inkel Corp., Carson, 1980—. Served with AUS, 1955-57. Fellow Nat. Inst. Credit; mem. Credit Mgrs. So. Calif., Nat. Notary Assn. Home: 24609 Plover Way Malibu CA 90265 Office: 17107 Kingsview Ave Carson CA 90746

FULWEILER, SPENCER BIDDLE, photog. processing cons.; b. West Chester, Pa., Aug. 26, 1913; s. Walter Herbert and Lydia Spencer (Baird) F.; S.B., Harvard U., 1937; m. Patricia Louise Platt, Oct. 5, 1946; children—Marie-Louise Fulweiler Allen, Pamela Spencer, Hull Platt, Spencer Biddle. Owner, Color Photo Lab., Phila., 1938-42; technician Product Service Lab. and film quality control Ansco, Binghamton, N.Y., 1946-48; dir. research Photofinishing Inst., N.Y.C., 1948-54; dir. process control Berkey Photo, N.Y.C., 1954-79; photo processing cons., 1979—. Tchr., St. James Ch. Sch., N.Y.C., 1958-69. Served to lt. comdr. USN, 1942-46; CBI. Mem. Nat. Assn. Photog. Mfrs. (mem. various coms.), Am. Chem. Soc., Soc. Photog. Scientists and Engrs., Soc. Photofinishing Engrs. Republican. Episcopalian. Clubs: Norwalk Yacht, St. Nicholas Soc. Patentee on silver recovery from photog. solutions. Home: 158 E 83d St New York NY 10028 Office: 77 E 13th St New York NY 10003

FUNG, FREDERICK HING LUNG, ins. co. exec.; b. Hong Kong, Aug. 5, 1936; came to U.S., 1941, naturalized, 1956; s. Reginald P.W. and Doris L. Fung; A.B., Cornell U., 1957; M.B.A., U. Pa., 1959; m. Jean Strybos, Apr. 31, 1979; children by previous marriage—Karen, Sandra, Stephanie, Linda, Frederick. Investment analyst Fidelity Bank, Phila., 1959-60; investment officer Del. Fund, Phila., 1960-63; account exec. Bache & Co., Inc., Phila., 1963-66; v.p., treas. Harleysville Ins. Cos. (Pa.), 1966—. Mem. Fin. Analysts Soc. Phila. Presbyterian. Office: 355 Maple Ave Harleysville PA 19438

FUNK, RICHARD DEAN, telephone and communications co. exec.; b. Carmen, Okla., May 14, 1931; s. William Albert and Susie Bell (Howell) F.; student Hutchinson (Kans.) Bus. Coll., 1949, Angelo State U., San Angelo, Tex., 1950; m. Dorothy Lorene McNair, Jan. 18, 1950. With Gen. Telephone Co. S.W., San Angelo, 1954-75, dir. revenues and earnings 1973-75; v.p. revenue requirements Gen. Telephone Co. Ky., Lexington, 1975-78; dir. revenue devel. GTE Service Corp., Irving, Tex., 1978—; tchr. econs. Mgmt. Devel. Center, Tampa, Fla., 1978. Active local Boy Scouts Am., YMCA. Served with USNR, 1948. Mem. Dallas County C. of C. (chmn. aviation San Angelo 1973). Mem. Christian Ch. (Disciples of Christ). Clubs: Rotary, Shriners. Home: Blake Forest Dr Roanoke TX 76262 Office: 2500 Fuller Rd Irving TX 75062

FUNKHOUSER, A. PAUL, railroad exec.; b. Roanoke, Va., Mar. 8, 1923; s. S. King and Jane Harwood (Cocke) F.; B.A., Princeton U., 1945; LL.B., U. Va., 1950; m. Eleanor R. Gamble, Feb. 4, 1950; children—John P., Eleanor K. Admitted to Va. bar, 1951; asso. firm Hunton, Williams, Anderson, Gay & Moore, Richmond, Va., 1950-52; solicitor, asst. gen. solicitor, gen. atty., asst. gen. counsel Norfolk & Western Rwy. Co., Roanoke, Va., 1952-63; asst. v.p., v.p. coal and ore traffic, v.p. public affairs, sr. v.p. passenger service, sr. v.p. sales and mktg. Pa. R.R. (later Penn Central Transp. Co.), Phila., 1963-75; sr. v.p., exec. v.p., pres. Seaboard Coast Line Industries, Jacksonville, Fla., 1975—; chief exec. officer Family Lines R.R. System, Jacksonville, 1975—; dir. Seaboard Coast Line Industries, Inc., Seaboard Coast Line R.R., L.&N. R.R., Atlantic Land and Improvement Co. Trustee Rollins Coll.; chmn. Fla. Vol. Savs. Bonds Com. Served with U.S. Army, 1943-46. Mem. Order of the Coif, Phi Beta Kappa, Delta Psi, Phi Delta Phi, Omicron Delta Kappa. Episcopalian. Clubs: Laurel Valley Golf (Ligonier, Pa.); Princeton, Union League (N.Y.C.); Metropolitan (Washington); Ponte Vedra (Fla.); Timuquana Country, Fla. Yacht, River (Jacksonville). Office: 500 Water St Jacksonville FL 32202

FUQUA, LUTHER CLARK, ins. co. exec.; b. Potter County, Tex., Mar. 13, 1935; s. James Gordon and Henrietta Claire (Clark) F.; student bus. adminstrn. Amarillo Coll., 1956-58; B.B.A., West Tex. State U., 1960; postgrad. Inst. Mcpl. Adminstrn., Chgo., 1960; m. Elaine Pulliam, Aug. 22, 1956; children—Myles, Scott. Tech. rep., multiple line spl. agt., br. mgr., mgr. large accounts dept. Cravens, Dargan and Co., Houston, 1960-69; sr. v.p. Highlands Ins. Cos., Houston, 1969-80; pres. Underwriters Spl. Risks, Inc., Houston, 1969-80, Lamar Underwriting Agy., Inc., Houston, 1969-80; pres. Resource Ins. Services, Inc., Houston, 1980—, also dir.; dir. Gulf Coast Trading Co., Houston. Served with USMC, 1954-56. Mem. Tex. Surplus Lines Ins. Assn., Houston C. of C., Gulf Coast Conservation Assn., VFW. Clubs: Warwick, Houston City, Houston Mariners. Office: Summit Tower 11 Greenway Plaza Houston TX 77046

FUREDY, JOHN PETER, ins. co. exec.; b. Yugoslavia, May 2, 1910; came to U.S., 1941, naturalized, 1943; s. Jaco and Jenny (Schrank) F.; student Pazmany Peter U., Budapest, 1929-30; grad. Life Ins. Agts. Mgmt. Assn. Sch. Mgmt., 1955; m. Lila Anne Moore, Mar. 31, 1978. Vice pres., dir. life agys. Beneficial Standard Life Ins. Co., Los Angeles, 1950-58; pres., chmn. bd. Nat. Security Ins. Agy., Inc., Los Angeles, 1958—; pres. T.W.A. Ins. Agy., Los Angeles, 1979—. Served with U.S. Army, 1943. Mem. Life Ins. Agts. Mgmt. Assn. (research com., ins. co. com.), Gen. Agts. Mgmt. Corp. (charter), Life Underwriters Assn. Club: Los Angeles Athletic. Home: 8364 Mulholland Dr Los Angeles CA 90046 Office: 3660 Wilshire Blvd Penthouse E Los Angeles CA 90010

FUREY, BRIAN THOMAS, fin. bus. systems co. exec.; b. Phila., Feb. 24, 1949; s. Dennis Francis and Anne Marie (Moore) F.; B.S. in Bus. Adminstrn., U. Notre Dame, 1971. Systems analyst Docutel Corp., Phila., 1972-74, key acct. mgr., 1974-77; corp. mktg. staff Mosler Safe Corp., 1977-79; area mgr. for Fla., N.C., S.C. TRW/Fujitsu Co., 1979—. Mem. Fla. Bankers Assn., Fla. Savs. and Loan League. Roman Catholic. Club: Notre Dame of Fla. Home: 200 Maitland Ave Apt 126 Altamonte Springs FL 32701

FUREY, JAMES JOSEPH, mfg. co. exec.; b. Pitts., Feb. 13, 1938; s. James Joseph and Kathleen (Adams) F.; B.B.A., LaSalle Coll., 1970; m. Andree Chalumeau, Dec. 2, 1958; children—Arleen, James, Renee, Philippe. Indsl. engr. Standard Pressed Steel Co., Jenkintonn, Pa., 1959-69; plant supt. Henry Troemner, Inc., Phila., 1969-70; cons. Booz, Allen & Hamilton, Inc., N.Y.C., 1970-72, asso., 1972-74, asso., Dallas, 1974-77, prin., 1977-79; v.p. mfg. Purolater Inc., Rahway, N.J., 1979—. Served with USAF, 1955-59. Republican. Roman Catholic. Home: 2800 Quail Ridge Carrollton TX 75006 also 236 White Birch Rd Edison NJ 08817 Office: 970 New Brunswick Ave Rahway NJ 07065

FURLAUD, RICHARD MORTIMER, lawyer, pharm. co. exec.; b. N.Y.C., Apr. 15, 1923; s. Maxime Hubert and Eleanor (Mortimer) F.; student Institut Sillig, Villars, Switzerland; A.B., Princeton, 1943; LL.B., Harvard, 1947; children—Richard Mortimer, Eleanor Jay, Elizabeth Tamsin. Admitted to N.Y. bar, 1949; asso. Root, Ballantine, Harlan, Bushby & Palmer, 1947-51; legal dept. Olin Mathieson Chem. Corp., 1955-56, asst. to exec. v.p. for finance, 1956-57, asst. pres., 1957-59, v.p., 1959-64, gen. counsel, 1957-60, gen. mgr., v.p. internat. div., 1960-64, exec. v.p., 1964-68, now dir.; pres., dir. E.R. Squibb & Sons, Inc., 1966-68; pres., chief exec., dir. Squibb Corp. (formerly Squibb Beech-Nut, Inc.), 1968-74, chmn., chief exec., dir., 1974—; dir. Chase Manhattan Corp., Chase Manhattan Bank, N.A., Mut. Benefit Life Ins. Co., Am. Express Co. Mem. profl. staff Ho. of Reps. Com., Ways and Means, 1954. Trustee Rockefeller U.; bd. mgrs. Meml. Sloan-Kettering Cancer Center. Served as 1st lt. Judge Adv. Gen. Corps, AUS, 1951-53. Mem. Assn. Bar City N.Y., Pharm. Mfrs. Assn. (dir. 1965—), Council on Fgn. Relations. Clubs: Links, River. Office: 40 W 57th St New York NY 10019

FURLONG, LAURENCE ALEXANDER, mfg. co. exec.; b. Toronto, Ont., Can., Aug. 4, 1929; s. Daniel Alexander and Mary Winifred (Newton) F.; grad. DeLa Salle Coll., Toronto, 1948; m. Mary Lou Doherty, May 16, 1953; children—Michael, Peter, Patricia, Susan, Lorraine. Sales rep. Kingsway Plumbing Supply, Toronto, 1950-53; pres. Waterline Products, Rexdale, Ont., Can., 1953—. Served with Canadian Army, 1948-49. Mem. Canadian Inst. Plumbing and Heating (chmn. bd. dirs. 1980-81), Canadian Retail Hardware & Houseware Assn., Toronto Bd. Trade, Royal Canadian Mil. Inst. Roman Catholic. Club: Lambton Golf. Home: 73 Edenvale Crescent Islington ON M9A 4A5 Canada Office: 117 Vulcan St Rexdale ON M9W 1L4 Canada

FURMAN, ANTHONY MICHAEL, pub. relations exec.; b. Los Angeles, Nov. 5, 1934; s. LeRoy S. and Geraldine P. F.; B.A., Bethany (W.Va.) Coll., 1957; postgrad. Columbia U. 1957-58; m. Betty Gayle Morgan, Nov. 1, 1970; 1 son, Michael Jason. Asst. account exec. Jules Beitler, Pub. Relations, Newark, 1958; account exec. Barber & Baar Pub. Relations Corp., N.Y.C., 1959-60; account exec., media dir. Sydney S. Baron & Co., Inc., N.Y.C., 1961-66; pres. Anthony M. Furman, Inc., N.Y.C., 1966—; dir. FKP Assos., Lake Placid, N.Y.; v.p., sec. Woman's Profl. Ski Championships, Inc. Served with M.C., U.S. Army, 1957-58. Mem. Pub. Relations Soc. Am. Democrat. Jewish. Exec. producer film: Floating Free, 1977 (1978 Acad. award nominee). Office: 527 Madison Ave New York NY 10022

FURSE, GEORGE RONALD, investment banker; b. Irvington, N.Y., June 26, 1921; s. William King and Annie Barton (Eddison) F.; B.A., Trinity Coll., Cambridge U., 1941; m. Charlotte Pamela Fowler, June 10, 1954; children—Rosemary Furse Taylor, Elizabeth, Diana, William. With Fiduciary Trust Co. N.Y., N.Y.C., 1946-64, London, 1964—. sr. v.p., 1978—. Served to capt. Welsh Guards, 1941-46. Clubs: Knickerbocker (N.Y.C.); Am., Cavalry and Guards (London). Home: Old House West Hoathly Sussex England also Fishers Island NY 06390 Office: Fiduciary Trust Co NY 25 Old Bulington St London W1 England

FURSTMAN, SHIRLEY ELSIE DADDOW, publishing exec.; b. Butler, N.J., Jan. 26, 1930; d. Richard and Eva M. (Kitchell) Daddow; grad. high sch.; m. Russell A. Bailey, Oct. 1, 1950 (div. Oct. 1967); m. 2d, William B. Furstman, Dec. 24, 1977. Asst. corporate sec. Hydrospace Tech., West Caldwell, N.J., 1960-62; sec. to pres. R.J. Dick Co., Totowa, N.J., 1962-63, Microlab, Livingston, N.J., 1963; asst. corporate sec. Astrosystems Internat., West Caldwell, N.J., 1963-65; corporate sec. Internat. Controls Corp., Fairfield, N.J., 1965-73; sec. to pres. Global Financial Co., Nassau, Bahamas, 1974-75; office mgr. Internat. Barter, Nassau, 1975-76; sec. to pres., corp. sec. Haas Chem. Co., Taylor, Pa., 1976-77; asst. to pres., pub. Am. Home mag., N.Y.C., 1977-78; account coordinator and sec. to account supr. public relations dept. Gilbert, Whitney & Johns, Inc., Morristown, N.J., 1979—. Home: 11A Foxwood Morris Plains NJ 07950

FURTH, ALAN COWAN, corp. exec., lawyer; b. Oakland, Calif., Sept. 16, 1922; s. Victor L. and Valance (Cowan) F.; A.B., U. Calif. at Berkeley, 1944, LL.B., 1949; grad. Advanced Mgmt. Program, Harvard U., 1959; m. Virginia Robinson, Aug. 18, 1946; children—Andrew Robinson, Alison Anne. Admitted to Calif. bar, U.S. Supreme Ct. bar; with S.P. Co., 1949—, gen. counsel, 1963—, v.p., 1966, exec. v.p. law, 1976-79, pres., 1979—, also dir.; dir., mem. exec. com. St. Louis Southwestern Ry. Co. Trustee Pomona Coll., Claremont, Calif., Merritt Hosp., Oakland, Calif.; bd. dirs. Pacific Legal Found. Served to capt. USMCR, 1944-46, 51-52. Mem. Am. Bar Assn., Calif. State Bar Assn. Clubs: Bohemian, Pacific-Union, Family, World Trade, San Francisco Golf (San Francisco); Orinda (Calif.) Country; Met., Burning Tree (Washington). Home: 54 Sotelo Ave Piedmont CA 94611 Office: So Pacific Bldg One Market Plaza San Francisco CA 94105

FUTIA, LEO RICHARD, ins. co. exec.; b. Buffalo, Aug. 27, 1919; s. Carl and Helen (Dicianne) F.; B.B.A., Canisius Coll., 1940; M.B.A., U. Pa., 1941; s. Marie Grace Giangreco, July 16, 1947; children—Carl, Mary, Leo J., Charles Elaine, Anne Marie. With Guardian Life Ins. Co. of Am., 1941—, sr. v.p., N.Y.C., 1967-70, exec. v.p., 1970-77, pres., 1977—, chmn. bd., chief exec. officer, 1980—; pres., dir. Guardian Ins. and Annuity Co., Inc.; v.p., dir. GLICOA Assos., Inc.; dir. Guardian Park Ave. Fund, Inc. Served with USCG, 1942-46. Mem. Am. Soc. C.L.U.'s (pres. 1966-67). Republican. Roman Catholic. Clubs: Greenwich Country (Conn.); Union League (N.Y.C.). Office: 201 Park Ave S New York NY 10003

FYE, RODNEY WAYNE, real estate co. exec.; b. Sutherland, Nebr., Aug. 3, 1928; s. Elmer Theodore and Pearl Gertrude (Combs) F.; grad. Chillicothe Bus. Coll., 1948; B.S., Brigham Young U., 1959; M.A., San Francisco State U., 1964; secondary teaching cert. U. Utah, 1962. Clk., Union Pacific R.R. Co., Utah, 1948-57; sec. to pres. Hughes Tool Co., Los Angeles, 1958-59; tchr. Granite Dist. High Schs., Salt Lake City, 1960-63; adminstr. Millcreek Terrace Nursing Home, Salt Lake City, 1962-63; instr. Reading Dynamics, No. Calif., 1967-75; owner, mgr. Keycount Properties, San Francisco, 1975-79; v.p. Casa Loma Properties, Inc., San Francisco, 1979—; pres. Pan Am. Investments, Inc., St. Thomas, V.I., 1980—. Pres., San Francisco Safety Council, 1980—. Mormon. Author: (musical comedy) Gandy, 1959; (dramatization) Absinthe & Wormwood, 1964; contbr. articles to mags. Office: PO Box 15308 San Francisco CA 94115

GABBE, PETER JAY, apparel mfg. co. exec.; b. Tarrytown, N.Y., Mar. 8, 1950; s. Melvin Howard and Dorothy (Rosenthal) G.; B.A., U. Hartford, 1972; student indsl. engring. Fashion Inst. Tech., 1972-74; m. Jane Ellen Holtz, Nov. 22, 1972; 1 dau., Alisa Ruth. Trainee, Cassie Cotillion, N.Y.C., 1972; asst. to gen. mgr. Sherwood Fashions, N.Y.C., 1972; asst. to prin. partner mfg. Lady Ester Lingerie, N.Y.C., 1972-73; asst. to v.p. mfg. Eastern Isles, N.Y.C., 1973-75; asst. to pres. Chevette, Inc., Christian Dior Intimate Apparel, N.Y.C., 1975-80, exec. v.p., dir., 1980—; cons. apparel mfg. domestic and import, 1975—. Mem. Am. Apparel Mfrs. Assn. (product safety com.), Tau Epsilon Phi. Club: B'nai B'rith (lodge treas. 1977-78, pres. 1978-79). Office: 135 Madison Ave New York NY 10016

GABER, BRUCE PAUL, biophys. chemist; b. Chgo., Oct. 15, 1941; s. George and Ruth Sylvia (Suekoff) G.; B.A. in Chemistry, Hendrix Coll., 1963; Ph.D. in Biochemistry, U. So. Calif., 1968; m. Sung-Suk Lee, Dec. 31, 1966; children—Mi-ai Andrea, Wha-ai Pauline. Research fellow IBM Watson Lab., Columbia U., 1968-70; research asso. IBM T.J. Watson Research Center, 1970-71; asst. prof. chemistry U. Mich., Dearborn, 1971-75; sr. research fellow chemistry U. Oreg., 1975-78; research asso. prof. biochemistry U. Va., 1978-80; staff scientist optical probes br. Naval Research Lab., Washington, 1980—; cons. Naval Research Lab., IBM Corp., Cath. U. Rio de Janeiro. Research fellow Nat. Cancer Inst., 1975-78; vis. fellow Princeton U., 1972; H.H. Rackham faculty fellow U. Mich., 1972. Mem. Am. Soc. Biol. Chemists, AAAS, Biophys. Soc., Coblentz Soc. Unitarian. Research and publs. on phys. and chem. properties of biol. membranes. Home: 12810 Peace Dr Fort Washington MD 20022 Office: Optical Probes Branch Code 6510 Naval Research Lab Washington DC 20375

GABLE, ROBERT ELLEDY, coal and lumber co. exec.; b. N.Y.C., Feb. 20, 1934; s. Gilbert E. and Paulina (Stearns) G.; B.S., Stanford U., 1956; m. Emily Brinton Thompson, July 5, 1958; children—James, Elizabeth, John. With Stearns Coal & Lumber Co. Inc. (Ky.), 1958—, asst. to pres., 1958-60, sec., 1960-70, treas., 1961-62, v.p., 1962-70, chmn. bd., 1970—, pres., 1975-78, also dir.; chmn. bd., dir. Ky. & Tenn. Ry., Stearns; chmn. bd. Lumber King Inc., Stearns; dir. Kuhn's Big K Stores Corp., Nashville, 1979—, mem. audit com., 1979—; dir. McCreary County Bank. Commr., Ky. Dept. Parks, 1967-70; mem. pub. lands com. Interstate Oil Compact Commn., 1968-70; mem. adv. com. Ky. Ednl. TV, 1971-75; past pres., past dir. McCreary County Indsl. Devel. Corp.; trustee Stearns Recreational Assn., Inc.; bd. dirs. Ky. Mountain Laurel Festival Assn., v.p., 1975; bd. dirs., mem. coms. on fin. and long-range planning Ky. Blue Cross/Blue Shield Plan; mem. McCreary County Air Bd., 1967—; mem. adv. bd. U. Ky. for Somerset Community Coll., 1965-73; mem. S.E. Regional Adv. Com. Nat. Park Service, 1973-77, sec., 1977; chmn. Ky. Republican Fin. Com., 1973-75; mem. nat. rep. fin. com., 1971-76, Ky. Rep. Central Com., 1974—; Rep. candidate U.S. Senate, 1972; Rep. nominee Gov. Ky., 1975; trustee George Peabody Coll. for Tchrs., 1970-79, mem. exec. com., 1976-79, chmn. bd. trustees, 1979. Served to lt. (j.g.) USNR, 1956-58. Named Ky. Col., Mr. Coal of Ky., 1970. Mem. Ky. Hotel-Motel Assn. (dir. 1968-70), Ky. Travel Council (dir. 1969-70), Nat. Assn. State Park Dirs., Nat. Recreation and Park Assn., Assn. Southeastern State Park Dirs. (v.p. 1969-70), Ky. Coal Assn. (dir., mem. exec. com.), Ky. C. of C. (regional v.p., dir. exec. com. 1971—), Ky. Council Econ. Edn. (founder, dir., past chmn., past pres.), McCreary County Devel. Assn. (dir. 1970), McCreary County Jaycees (past pres.), Tau Beta Pi, Alpha Kappa Lambda (past chpt. pres.). Episcopalian. Clubs: Stearns (Ky.) Golf; Frankfort (Ky.) Country; Pendennis, Jefferson (Louisville); Lafayette, Keeneland, Bluegrass Auto (Lexington, Ky.). Home: 1 Stearns Ln Stearns KY 42647 also 1715 Stonehaven Dr Frankfort KY 40601 Office: Stearns Coal & Lumber Co 303 McClure Bldg Frankfort KY 40601

GABNER, RAYMOND JOSEPH, traffic mgr.; b. Buffalo, Aug. 25, 1947; s. Joseph Albert and Arlene (Vickery) G.; A.A.S. in Bus. Adminstrn., Erie Community Coll., 1970; A.A.S. in Traffic and Transp., U. Buffalo, 1972, B.S. in Bus. Adminstrn., 1975; m. Maureen Gearin, May 25, 1968; children—Dawn Marie, Kelly Ann. Dock foreman Interstate Motor Freight, Buffalo, 1968-71; shipping and receiving supr. Worthington Compressor GEI, Buffalo, 1972-74; traffic mgr. Spaulding Fibre, Tonawanda, N.Y., 1975-78; traffic mgr. Kason Industries, Inc., Kirkwood, N.Y., 1978—. Mem. Niagara Falls Traffic Club, Triple Cities Traffic Club, Transp. Club Buffalo, Niagara Frontier Indsl. Traffic League. Office: Kason Industries Colesville Rd Kirkwood NY 13902

GABOR, FRANK, ins. co. exec.; b. Budapest, Hungary, Apr. 15, 1918; s. William and Lyvia (Nauer) G.; came to U.S., 1921, naturalized, 1928; student Boston U., 1936; m. Selma M. Cluck, Aug. 18, 1940; children—Jeffrey Alan, Ronald Steven, Cynthia B. Gabor Cushman. Ins. agt. Mut. Life Ins. Co. N.Y., Boston, 1940-44; pres. Gabor & Co., Inc., Miami, Fla., 1946—, Anglo-Am. Agrl. Underwriters, Inc., Havana, Cuba, 1950-52; pres. Variable Income Planning Co., Miami, 1965—; pres. Gabor Reins. Mgmt. Corp., Miami, 1976—; v.p., dir. Wilson Nat. Life Ins. Co., Lake City, Fla., 1957-73; dir., mem. exec. com. Stanwood Corp., Charlotte, N.C., 1975—; pres. Bent Tree Farm, Inc., Ocala, Fla., 1972—; dir. Bio-Med. Scis., Inc., 1972-74. Bd. dirs. J. Edwin Larson Ins. Edn. Found., Tallahassee, Fla., 1960-70. Served with USNR, 1944-46. Mem. Internat. (dir. 1964-68), Fla. (pres. 1960-66) assns. health underwriters, Health Ins. Soc. Fla. Mason (Shriner). Home: 600 Bitmore Way Coral Gables FL 33134 Office: 1492 W Flagler St Miami FL 33135

GADBERRY, WILLIAM FREDERIC, acctg. and tax service exec.; b. Seattle, Oct. 28, 1948; s. Billy F. and Alice M. (White) G.; B.B.A., Pacific Lutheran U., 1975; m. Robyn L. Russac, June 24, 1978; children—Billy, Karie, Leanna, Laura. Acct., bus. adv. Gadro Inc., Kent, Wash., 1973-75, dir., 1973—; tax service supr., tutor acctg. Seattle Community Coll., 1973; acct. ACI Parks Inc., Seattle and Bellevue, Wash., 1975-80, asst. controller, 1978—; cons. SBA. Served with USAR, 1968-71; Vietnam. Decorated Bronze Star, Army Commendation medal. Mem. Nat. Assn. Accts., Am. Mgmt. Assn., Nat. Hist. Soc. Address: 10127 NE 144th Pl Bothel WA 98011

GADDIS, PAUL OTTO, univ. dean; b. Muskogee, Okla., Mar. 20, 1924; s. Paul James and Ida Rose (Oerter) G.; B.S., U.S. Naval Acad., 1946; M.S., Rensselaer Poly. Inst., 1949; M.B.A., Mass. Inst. Tech., 1961; m. Martha Louise Rinker, June 28, 1948; children—Paul James, David Charles, Holly. Mgr. computer systems and finance Westinghouse Electric Corp., Pitts., 1954-68, v.p., corporate devel., Pitts., 1968-72; cons. corporate devel., prof. mgmt. Wharton Sch., sr. v.p., U. Pa., Phila., 1972-79; dean Sch. of Mgmt. and Adminstrn., prof. mgmt. scis. U. Tex., Dallas, 1979—; chmn. Globe Ticket Co., Phila.;

dir. Uni-Coll Corp., Phila., Western Savs. Bank, Phila., Wharton Econometric Forecasting Assos., Inc., Phila., Energy Reserves Group, Inc., Wichita KS; mem. nat. adv. council SBA, Washington; trustee Pa. Tax-Free Income Trust, Phila. Pres., trustee La Napoule Art Found., France. Served with USN, 1946-54. Mem. Soc. Mgmt. Info. Systems, Planning Execs. Inst. Author: Corporate Accountability, 1964; contbr. articles to Harvard Bus. Rev. Office: U Tex at Dallas Box 688 Richardson TX 75080

GAERTNER, WOLFGANG WILHELM, research co. exec.; b. Vienna, Austria, July 5, 1929; s. Wilhelm and Maria (Schuetz) G., Ph.D. in Physics, U. Vienna, 1951; Dipl. Ing., Technische Hochschule, Vienna, 1955; m. Marianne L. Weber, Feb. 22, 1955; children—Marianne P., Karin C., Christopher W. Came to U.S., 1953, naturalized, 1961. Research physicist Siemens Halske, Vienna, 1951-53, U.S. Army Signal Research and Devel. Lab., Ft. Monmouth, N.J., 1953-60; v.p. CBS Labs., Stamford, Conn., 1960-65; pres. W. W. Gaertner Research, Inc., 1965—. Fellow I.E.E.E.; mem. Am. Phys. Soc. Author: Transistors: Principles, Design and Applications, 1960; Adaptive Electronics, 1973. Contbr. articles to profl. publs. Home: 205 Saddle Hill Rd Stamford CT 06903 Office: 30 Buxton Farm Rd Stamford CT 06905 also 1492 High Ridge Rd Stamford CT 06903

GAFFNEY, NORMAN THOMAS, cons. engring. co. exec.; b. Milw., Oct. 1, 1928; s. Thomas Vernon and Mary Madeline (Harrison) G.; B.B.A., U. Wis., 1950. Sr. auditor A.O. Smith Corp., Milw., 1955-59; controller Am. Sci. Labs., Madison, Wis., 1959-62; regional dir. Peace Corps, Peru, Philippines, Washington, 1963-69; asst. adminstr. Divine Savior Hosp., Portage, Wis., 1970-72; sec.-treas. McCormick, Taylor & Assos., Inc., Phila., 1972—; cons. to savs. and loan banks, Peru, 1963-65. Mem. Profl. Services Bus. Mgmt. Assn., Phila. C. of C. Roman Catholic. Home: RD 4 Box 313 Coatesville PA 19320 Office: 1617 John F Kennedy Blvd Philadelphia PA 19103

GAGEN, HARRY EDWIN, investment banking exec.; b. Detroit, Mar. 10, 1931; s. Harry Edwin and Claire J. (Nowland) G.; B.A., U. Calif., Los Angeles, 1956, M.B.A., 1958. New products mgr. Procter & Gamble, Cin., 1958-64; mktg. mgr. Purex Co., Lakewood, Calif., 1964-73; with Loeb, Rhoades & Hornblower, 1973—; corp. services dir., 1978—. Served with AUS, 1951-53. Decorated Bronze Star with oak leaf cluster, Purple Heart. Mem. Assn. Fin. Planners, Western Pension Conf., Am. Mgmt. Assn., Municipal Treasurers Assn., Phi Kappa Sigma. Clubs: Rotary, Investment. Home: 550 Reposado Dr La Habra Heights CA 90631 Office: 2555 E Chapman Ave Fullerton CA 92631

GAGER, JOHN JAY, mgmt. cons.; b. Boston, Apr. 4, 1942; s. John Jay and Rachel Edna (Clark) G.; A.B., Boston U., 1966; M.B.A., U. R.I., 1973; m. Kathleen Ryan Carbine, Feb. 24, 1967; children—Kimberly Susan, Shawn Elizabeth. Systems analyst United Technologies, East Hartford, Conn., 1966-68, Raytheon Co., Portsmouth, R.I., 1968-73; mgr. Price Waterhouse & Co., Boston, 1973-75; cons. Deloitte Haskins & Sells, Boston, 1975-78; N.E. area adv. services mgr. Keane, Inc., Boston, 1978—; adj. asst. prof. systems analysis Bentley Coll., 1978-81. Chmn. sch. budget study com., Manchester, Mass., 1978-79. Served with USMCR, 1964. Mem. Nat. Assn. Accts., Am. Prodn. and Inventory Control Soc. Democrat. Roman Catholic. Club: Manchester Bath and Tennis. Home: 8 Crooked Ln Manchester MA 01944 Office: 210 Commercial St Boston MA 02109

GAGLIARDI, JOHN ROBERT, data processing co. exec.; b. Bklyn., Feb. 1, 1948; s. John and Antoinette M. (Miele) G.; student Hunter Coll., 1965-68; B.S. in Bus. Adminstrn., Marywood Coll., 1980; m. Constance Camp, Apr. 8, 1978. Asst. mgr. marine cargo ins. dept. Adams & Porter Brokerage, N.Y.C., 1968-69; programmer Crum & Forster Ins. Group, N.Y.C., 1969; programmer INSCO Systems, Neptune, N.J., 1969-71, systems analyst, 1971-74, sr. systems analyst, 1974-78, systems supr., 1978-79, systems staff cons., 1979—. Mem. Inst. Cert. Computer Profls. (cert. data processor). Home: 101 Atco Ct Barnegat NJ 08005 Office: 3501 Hwy 66 Neptune NJ 07753

GAINES, STANLEY FRANCIS, JR., oil co. exec.; b. Cleveland, Miss., Feb. 6, 1940; Stanley F. and Scottie (Polk) G.; B.A., Davidson Coll., 1961; m. Caroline Laudig, Dec. 29, 1962; children—Caroline Laudig, Stanley Laudig (dec.), Stanley F. III. Pres., Gaines Oil Co., Inc., Boyle, Miss., 1975—, Gaines Enterprises, Inc., Cleveland, 1974—; dir. Central Delta Warehouse, Inc., Cleveland, 1974—. Chmn., Miss. Library Commn., 1976-77; chmn. Bolivar County Library Bd., 1975-77; charter pres. Bolivar County Crosstie Arts Council, 1969-71; chmn. Cleveland-Bolivar County Indsl. Devel. Found., 1978-79; dir. Delta Council, 1970-71; chmn. adminstrv. bd. First United Meth. Ch., 1969-72; bd. govs. Miss. Inst. Arts and Letters, 1978—. Served with U.S. Army, 1962-64, capt. USAR, 1964-70. Decorated Army Commendation medal. Recipient Wall St. Jour. Achievement award, 1961, Jr. C. of C. Distinguished Service award, 1968. Mem. Miss. Library Assn. (vice chmn. 1971-72), Cleveland Bolivar County C. of C. (v.p. 1973-74, 1978-79), Nat. Oil Jobbers Assn., Miss. Oil Marketers Assn., Am. Library Assn., Omicron Delta Kappa. Methodist. Club: Exchange (pres. Cleveland chpt. 1968). Home: PO Box 278 Boyle MS 38730 Office: Gaines Hwy Boyle MS 38730

GAINES, WEAVER HENDERSON, JR., mfg. co. exec.; b. Fort Meade, S.D., Aug. 31, 1943; s. Weaver H. and Bertha (Harris) G.; A.B., Dartmouth Coll., 1965; LL.B., U. Va., 1968; m. Karen Anne Gannett, Dec. 15, 1979. Admitted to N.Y. State bar, 1969, Pa. bar, 1979; asso. mem. firm Dewey Ballantine Bushby Palmer & Wood, N.Y.C., 1971-78; sr. staff counsel INA Corp., Phila., 1979; asst. gen. counsel, sec. Indian Head Inc., N.Y.C., 1980—; mem. faculty S.C. Continuing Legal Edn., 1978-80. Bd. dirs. N.Y. Lawyers for Nixon, 1972. Served with AUS, 1968-70; Decorated Bronze Star. Mem. Am. Bar Assn., Fed. Bar Council, Pa. Bar Assn., Bar Assn. City N.Y., Am. Council on Germany. Republican. Episcopalian. Office: 1211 Ave of Americas Indian Head Inc New York NY 10036

GAIO, RAYMOND LEE, architect; b. Springfield, Ill., May 3, 1938; s. Americo and Edith E. (Bloom) G.; student Millikin U., summer 1960; profl. architecture degree U. Notre Dame, 1961. Designer, draftsman Spangler, Beall, Salogga & Bradley, Decatur, Ill., 1961-62; designer, planner, draftsman, client relations Leo A. Daly Co., Omaha, 1962-63; schematic design draftsman Perkins & Will, Washington, 1963-64; dir. Dept. of State, chpt. and student affairs A.I.A., Washington, 1964-69; mgr. client relations Vincent G. Kling & Assos., Phila., 1969-70; pres., chief exec. officer, treas. Gaio Assos., Ltd., Washington, also Los Angeles, other prin. Am. cities and London, Eng., 1970—; pres. B.I.D.S., Inc., Washington and now Springfield, Ill., C.G. Evergreene Cos. Inc.; dir. corporate devel. Gruen Assos., Los Angeles, N.Y.C., Washington, Vienna, Teheran, 1970. Lectr. various univs.; archtl. orgn. mgmt. cons. to U.S. and internat. firms. Adviser, Jr. Achievement, Omaha, 1962-63; mem. Royal Ct. of Ak-Sar-Ben, 1962-63; adviser, lectr. Heights Study House, Washington, 1965; mem. joint engring. council Notre Dame U., 1958-59, 606-1. Licensed architect, U.S.V.I. Mem. ASC-AIA (nat. pres. 1960-61), AIA (corporate mem.; co-chmn. nat. task force in student action programs), Notre Dame Alumni Assn. Republican. Roman Catholic. Author: A.I.A. Organizational Guidelines Manual; A.I.A. Student Chapter Handbook; The State Organization; Chapter Organization. Contbr. articles to profl. jours. Office: BIDS Ops Center PO Box 3344 Springfield IL 62708 also Washington DC also Los Angeles CA 90005 also London EC4Y 1HA England

GAJEWSKI, HENRY MARTIN, med. products co. exec.; b. Chgo., Aug. 18, 1925; s. Joseph and Sophia (Budnik) G.; student U. Chgo., 1947, M.B.A., 1970; B.S., Ill. Inst. Tech., 1951; m. Dorothy Schick, Apr. 28, 1956; children—Nancy Lynne, Steven Henry. Chief chemist Chgo. Rawhide Products, Elgin, Ill., 1952-60; sr. staff engr. Bunker-Ramo, Inc., Broadview, Ill., 1960-65; dir. corp. materials devel., devel. engring. Baxter/Travenol, Inc., Deerfield, Ill., 1965—, mem. chmn.'s sr. mgmt. council. Active Art Inst. Chgo., Field Mus. Natural History. Served with USN, 1943-46. Recipient Baxter engring. excellence award, 1968, inventors award, 1977, tech. achievement award, 1978. Mem. Am. Chem. Soc. (indsl. and engring. chemistry div.). Roman Catholic. Patentee U.S. and fgn. countries. Home: 187 Forest St Winnetka IL 60093 Office: Travenol Labs Box 490 Rte 120 and Wilson Rd Round Lake IL 60073

GAJEWSKI, JOSEPH CHARLES, mfg. co. exec.; b. Buffalo, Sept. 3, 1938; s. Joseph and Blanche (Gembka) G.; student Lincoln Extension Inst., 1965-67; children—Joseph Charles, Angela Karen. Meat cutter A & P Tea Co., Buffalo, 1954-56; die sinker J.H. Williams & Co., Buffalo, 1957-76; salesman Forest Lawn Cemetery, Buffalo, 1974-77; mgr. plant ops. Pu-Ro Products Inc., Buffalo, 1977-80; prodn. mgr. Reppen Hagen Roller Corp., Buffalo, 1980—; pres. United Steel Workers Am. local 5947, 1968-76. Served with USMC, 1957-60. Cert. in water safety, CPR. Roman Catholic. Club: K.C. (dir. 1973-76) (Kenmore, N.Y.). Author: So You Wanna Be A Chairman, Huh?, 1977; inventor self-regenerating direct current power supply without external motivation and fuel. Home: 505 Hinman Ave Buffalo NY 14216 Office: 817 Sycamore St Buffalo NY 14212

GAJEWSKI, PETER, economist; b. Warsaw, Poland, Jan. 30, 1932; s. Zbigniew and Ursula Ann G.; came to U.S., 1941, naturalized, 1953; B.S., U. Md., 1957, M.S., 1962; m. Lucksana Charnsetikul, Dec. 14, 1975; children by previous marriage—Gregory, Matthew. Economist, Dept. Commerce, Washington, 1957-61, NSF, Washington, 1961, Fed. Res. Bd., Washington, 1961-65; econ. adviser Thai govt., 1965-67; chief econ. policy div. AID, Bangkok, Thailand, 1967-71; v.p. Louis Berger Internat. Inc. for Asia, Middle East, Tehran, Beirut, Vietiane, Bangkok, 1971-75, v.p. internat. ops., chief economist, E. Orange, N.J., 1975—; mem. profl. working groups of UN; tchr. Indsl. Coll. of Armed Forces, Washington, George Washington U., Chulalongkorn U., Bangkok; lectr. U.S. Fgn. Service Inst. Recipient Meritorious Service Award AID, Bangkok, 1968. Mem. Am. Econ. Assn., Soc. for Internat. Devel., Asia Soc. (chmn. Iran council 1977-80). Roman Catholic. Clubs: Toastmaster (pres. Bangkok 1967). Contbr. numerous articles in field to profl. jours. Home: 126 W Mountain Rd Sparta NJ 07871 Office: 100 Halsted St East Orange NJ 07019

GALA, ANDREW ANGELO, JR., city adminstr.; b. Milford, Mass., July 6, 1944; s. Andrew and Marguerite Catherine (Consoletti) G.; B.S., Suffolk U., 1969; M.P.A., Northeastern U., 1978; m. Susan Frances Tieuli, Oct. 19, 1974; children—Jennifer, Kathryn. Ins. adjuster Craword & Co., Worcester, Mass., 1970-71; exec. sec., purchasing agt. Town of Milford, 1971-80; town adminstr. Town of Foxborough (Mass.), 1980—; sec. Milford Personnel Bd., 1978—. Served with AUS, 1964-65. Mem. Mass. Mcpl. Mgrs. Assn., Am. Soc. Public Adminstrn., Italian Am. War Vets. Roman Catholic. Club: Sons of Italy. Home: 7 Richmond St Milford MA 01757 Office: 40 South St Foxborough MA 02035

GALANTY, SIDNEY, TV and film co. exec.; b. Newark, May 15, 1932; s. Max and Bertha G.; student Seton Hall U., 1954-57, Fordham U., 1957; m. Joan R. Goldstein, Dec. 12, 1954; children—Mark Alan, Beth Michele. TV stage mgr. Bremer Broadcasting, Newark, 1950-52, TV dir., 1954-58; TV producer/dir. Teleprompter Corp., Army Missile Command, Huntsville, Ala., 1958-60; free lance TV dir., 1960; producer/dir. USIA, 1961-64, dep. chief of prodn., 1965; TV comml. producer Dancer Fitzgerald Sample, Los Angeles, 1965-68; TV dir. Hubert Humphrey Presdl. Campaign, 1968; producer/dir., pres., chmn. bd. Communications Group West, Hollywood, Calif., 1969—; chmn. bd. Pathways Prodns., 1979—; polit. media cons. Served with Signal Corps, U.S. Army, 1952-54. Recipient Superior Service award U.S. Govt., 1963; TV drama award Cannes Film Festival, 1963; Bronze award N.Y. Film Festival, 1972; Clio award, 1979. Mem. Dirs. Guild Am. Office: Communications Group West 6606 Sunset Blvd Hollywood CA 90028

GALASSO, FRANK LEONARD, transp. co. exec.; b. New Rochelle, N.Y., Sept. 3, 1951; s. Leonard R. and Mary Frances (Cassara) G.; A.Bus., Johnson and Wales Coll., 1971; m. Dolores Tedesco, Dec. 18, 1977; 2 children. Vice pres. Galasso Trucking Inc., Larchmont, N.Y. Club: N.Y. Athletic. Office: 8 Kilmer Rd Larchmont NY 10538

GALBRAITH, LYNNE EDWARD, mech. engr.; b. New Philadelphia, Ohio, Mar. 27, 1932; s. Lawrence Edward and Ada Alice (Rankin) G.; B.S., Tri-State U., 1960; m. Joanne Diehl, Mar. 30, 1958; children—Elaine Ann, Jon Edward. Draftsman, Joy Mfg. Co., 1961-64, sr. application engr., 1964-67; chief engr. Am. Coolair Corp., Jacksonville, Fla., 1967-76, v.p.-engring., 1976—; instr. indsl. ventilation conf. Mich. State U., East Lansing, 1970-80. Served with USN, 1951-55. Mem. Am. Soc. Heating Refrigerating and Air Conditioning Engrs. (bd. govs.), Air Movement and Control Assn. Methodist. Home: 1036 Lido Rd Jacksonville FL 32216 Office: 3604 Mayflower St Jacksonville FL 32205

GALE, ANDREW ROBERT, corp. exec.; b. Los Angeles, June 23, 1942; s. Myron and Clarice (Sitomer) G.; B.A., North Tex. U., 1964; M.A., New Sch. Social Research, 1966; m. Hanuska Branicka, Sept. 18, 1972. Asst. dir. program evaluation Jersey City Job Corps, 1966-68; project mgr. M.I.S. RCA Corp., N.Y.C., 1968-72; mgr. major systems mktg. and support Internat. Computers Ltd., London, 1972-74; partner Systems Devel. Internat., London, 1974-77; pres. SDI: Industry Systems, Los Angeles, 1977—; dir. I.T.M. Corp., Travel Cons. Internat. Fellow Brit. Computer Soc.; mem. Internat. Fedn. Info. Processing, Assn. Iron and Steel Engrs., Am. Mgmt. Assn., Commonwealth Soc. Office: 1543 W Olympic Blvd Suite 306 Los Angeles CA 90015

GALE, LESTER BOUTON, mfg. co. exec.; b. Middletown, N.Y., Aug. 26, 1923; s. Lester Bouton and May (Raines) G.; B.B.A., U. Houston, 1948; m. Oneida C. Fox, June 10, 1945; children—V. Susan, Michael, Phyllis. With Dresser Industries, Inc., 1945—, dir. internat. bus. planning, Dallas, 1972—. Mem. internat. adv. bd. Hankamer Sch. Bus., Baylor U.; mem. internat. com. N. Tex. Commn.; mem. exec. com. Center for Internat. Bus. Served with USMC, 1941-45, 50-51. Mem. Dist. Export Council, Internat. Trade Assn. Dallas (pres. 1978-79), Machinery and Allied Products Inst. (internat. ops. council), Dallas C. of C. (internat. com.). Republican. Baptist. Club: Lakewood Country. Home: 6434 Malcolm Dr Dallas TX 75214 Office: 1505 Elm St Dallas TX 75221

GALEN, LOUIS JOSEPH, savs. and loan assn. exec.; b. Youngstown, Ohio, Apr. 19, 1925; s. Sherley and Faye (Shulman) G.; student U. Mo., 1943-44, Santa Monica City Coll., 1946; J.D., U. So. Calif., 1951; m. Helene Caro, Dec. 31, 1975; children from previous marriage—Stafford, Janet, Kenneth, Dori, Nancy. Pres., mng. officer Great Western Escrow Co., 1951-58; founder Lynwood Savs. and Loan Assn., 1946, pres., 1959-75, chmn. bd., 1961-75; founder Trans-World Fin. Co., 1959; chmn. bd. Trans-World Bank, 1963—, Loyalty Savs. & Loan Assn., Sacramento, Calif., 1969—; pres. Trans-World Fin. Co., 1959-75, chmn. bd., 1962-75; pres., dir. Golden West Fin. Corp., Oakland, Calif., from 1975, now vice-chmn.; pres., dir. World Savs. & Loan Assn. Calif., 1975—; dir. World Savs. & Loan Assn. Colo. Chmn., So. Calif. Democratic State Fin. Com., 1962-63; mem. adv. com. U. So. Calif. Inst. Bus. and Econs.; bd. dirs. Temple Emanuel, 1963-65, chmn. religious sch. bldg. fund, 1962; bd. dirs. Reiss-Davis Clinic for Child Guidance, 1963-66, Am. Friends of Hebrew U., 1963-66, Jewish Vocat. Service, 1963-65, Nat. Kidney Disease Found., 1963-65, Park Century Sch., 1970-75; mem. Com. of 100 Jewish Welfare Fedn., 1976—. Served with AC, AUS, 1943-46. Office: Golden West Fin Corp 1970 Broadway Suite 1000 Oakland CA 94612*

GALEY, JOHN MICHAEL, computer co. exec.; b. Portland, Oreg., Feb. 12, 1936; s. John Dodge and Cecelia Patrica (Gallagher) G.; student Reed Coll., 1953-54, 58-59; children—Valerie Ann, Pamela Jean, Mark Alan; m. 2d, Amal Sedky Barkouki, Aug. 28, 1977; children—Miriam M. and Souheir M. Barkouki. Computer programmer IBM, Poughkeepsie, N.Y. 1960-64, asso. programmer, sr. asso. programmer, San Jose, 1964-68, design automation mgr., 1968-72, support mgr. microprogramming dept., 1972-75, applications support mgr., 1975-77, corp. hdqrs. staff, 1977-79, disk test engring. mgr., 1979—. Served with USMCR, 1954-58. Decorated Nat. Def. Service medal. Mem. Assn. Computing Machinery (chmn. spl. interest group microprogramming), IEEE (distinguished vis. computer soc., chmn. standing tech. program com. ann. conf., chmn. arrangements ann. conf., mem. governing bd.). Author: (with Richard Kleir) Microprogramming Textbook; contbr. articles to profl. jours. Home: 18031 Idalyn Dr Los Gatos CA 95030 Office: IBM 783/700 San Jose CA 95193

GALIFI, AUGUST ANTHONY, computer co. exec.; b. Vizzini, Italy, Oct. 25, 1944; s. Rosario Francesco and Giovanna (Giordano) G.; came to U.S., 1964, naturalized, 1973; EDP certificate Automation Inst. Am., 1968; m. Irene Koumantaris, Jan. 23, 1965; children—Roy, Frank, August Anthony. Systems programmer Info Systems & Scis., N.Y.C., 1968, 70; v.p. Guinness-Harp Corp., N.Y.C., 1970—; v.p., gen. mgr. Guinness Data Systems, Inc., Long Island City, N.Y., 1973—; dir. edn., evening classes, info. systems schs., 1968-70. Roman Catholic. Home: 30 Belmar Ave Oceanport NJ 07757 Office: 37-88 Review Ave Long Island City NY 11101

GALL, DONALD DUANE, telephone co. exec.; b. Baraboo, Wis., Feb. 4, 1924; s. Emil and Lila (Meyers) G.; student U. Wis., 1942; m. Val I. Zimmerman, June 1, 1946; children—Scott, Kim, Becky, Richard. With Gen. Telephone Co., comml. dir. Gen. Telephone Ind., pres. Gen. Telephone of Midwest, now pres. Gen. Telephone of Wis., Gen. Telephone of Ill., Bloomington; dir. First Wis. Nat. Bank, Madison, First Fed. Savs. & Loan, Bloomington. Trustee, Mennonite Hosp., Bloomington. Served with Armed Forces, 1943-46. Mem. Wis. Telephone Assn. (dir.), Ill. Telephone Assn. (dir.). Republican. Lutheran. Club: Rotary. Office: 1312 Empire St Bloomington IL 61701*

GALL, IRVING, mfg. corp. exec.; b. N.Y.C., July 25, 1921; s. Samuel and Yetta (Feder) G.; student for rabbinate Solomon Kluger Yeshiva, 1927-35, Mesiftah Tifereth Jerusalem, N.Y.C., 1935-39; m. Lena Safer, May 30, 1942; children—Martin, Ellen Roben, Barbara Norden, Alexandra. Founder, Aquarium Research Corp., Bklyn. 1950-56, merged with Gro-Wel Co., Bronx, N.Y., 1956, pres., 1956-61, merged with Metaframe and Wil-Nes into Metaframe Corp., 1961, v.p., corp. sales dir., exec. bd., Elmwood Park, N.J., 1961—; pres., partner Aqua-Stock, Petcetera, Inc., Bayonne, N.J., 1980—; bd. dirs. Pet Industry Joint Adv. Com., treas., 1974-75, pres., 1975-76; advisor bd. edn. City of N.Y., mem. animal care ednl. adv. com.; advisor animal sci. div. Assn. Tchrs. of Agr. N.Y. Mem. Port Washington Civic Assn., 1958-61. Mem. Nat. Assn. Pet Industry, Am. Pet Products Mfrs. Assn. (bd. dirs., Man of Year, 1978). Mem. K.P., B'nai B'rith. Home: 293 Alpine Dr Paramus NJ 07652 Office: 235 W 1st St Bayonne NJ 07002

GALLAGHER, ANNE TIMLIN, bank exec.; b. Wilkes Barre, Pa., Mar. 21, 1943; d. James Joseph and Ruth Brandon (MacGuffie) G.; A.B., Bucknell U., 1964. Presentation analyst A.C. Nielsen, N.Y.C., 1964; research asso. Gen. Electric Co., N.Y.C., 1965-67, sr. sales rep., 1967-69; mgr. fin. services Rapidata Co., N.Y.C., 1969; mgr. fin. markets Computer Scis. Corp., N.Y.C., 1970-73; mgmt. cons. Arthur Young & Co., N.Y.C., 1973-77; mgr. product communications, v.p. Bankers Trust Co., N.Y.C., 1978—; cons. to vol. urban cons. group. Mem. Arts and Bus. Council; bd. dirs. N.Y. Pro Arte Chamber Music Orch. Mem. Nat. Assn. Bus. Economists, Am. Statis. Assn. (asst. chmn. ann. forecasting conf. 1966, 67, past chmn. bus. econs. sect. N.Y. chpt.). Episcopalian. Home: 227 E 66th St New York NY 10021 Office: 280 Park Ave New York NY 10017

GALLAGHER, BERNARD PATRICK, editor, pub.; b. N.Y.C., Feb. 25, 1910; s. Bernard A. and Mary Helen (Fitzsimmons) G.; student Columbia U., 1928-29, Akron U., 1941-44; m. Harriet Denning, Oct. 17, 1942; 1 dau., Jill. Single-copy sales mgr. Crowell Pub. Co., 1932-34; sales mgr. charge sales tng. Stenotype Co., Inc., Chgo., 1934-39; pres. Stenotype Co. Ohio, Inc., Cleve., 1939-44; pres. World Wide Publs., Inc., N.Y.C., 1945—; pres. Gallagher Communications, Inc., 1972—; editor-in-chief, pub. The Gallagher Report, 1952—, Gallagher Presidents' Report, 1965—, mgmt., mktg., advt., sales. Served with AUS, 1944-45. Mem. Nat. Better Bus. Bur., Central Registry Mag. Pubs. Assn., U.S. C. of C., Catholic Press Assn. Clubs: Canadian, Met., Marco Polo, Overseas Press. Office: 230 Park Ave New York NY 10017

GALLAGHER, DANIEL JAMES, investment banking co. exec.; b. Wilkes-Barre, Pa.; s. Gerald Jeramiah and Elizabeth Ann (Welteroth) G.; B.S., Lycoming Coll., 1953; student U. Calif., Los Angeles, 1964, Harvard, 1976; m. Barbara B. Gallagher, Dec. 24, 1958; children—Suzanne, Steven. With Black & Decker Co., Inc., 1954-57, Lehigh Chem. Co., 1957-62; v.p. Frost & Sullivan Inc., Los Angeles, 1962-67; v.p. Goldman, Sachs & Co., N.Y.C., 1967-80; vice-chmn. Burns Fry & Timmins Inc., N.Y.C., 1980—. Mem. Newcomen Soc. Clubs: Cleve. Athletic, City Midday N.Y.C., Elks. Home: Anthony Wayne Rd Morristown NJ 07960 Office: Burns Fry & Timmins Wall St Plaza New York NY 10005

GALLAGHER, FRANCIS FELIX, data processing exec.; b. Bronx, N.Y., Jan. 21, 1943; s. James and Rose (Ryan) G.; B.B.A., St. Michael's Coll., 1964; m. Louise Pegarella, Feb. 27, 1971; 1 son, Scott. Account mgr. Sealtest Foods, 1964-67, Univac, 1968-73; sales mgr. TRW Communications and Services, N.J., 1974-77; dist. sales mgr. Raytheon Data Systems, Stamford, Conn., 1978—. Recipient Blue Vase award Sealtest Foods, 1966; named to Univac Million Dollar

Club, 1972. Mem. Am. Mgmt. Assn. Clubs: N.Y. Athletic, Elks. Office: Raytheon Data Systems Stamford CT

GALLAGHER, GERALD RAPHAEL, retail trade co. exec.; b. Easton, Pa., Mar. 17, 1941; s. Gerald Raphael and Marjorie Alice Gallagher; B.S. in Aero. Engring., Princeton U., 1963; M.B.A. (Exec. Club fellow), U. Chgo., 1969; m. Ellen Anne Mullane, Aug. 8, 1964; children—Ann Patrice, Gerald Patrick, Megan Ann. Dir. planning Metro-Goldwyn-Mayer, N.Y.C., 1969; v.p. Donaldson Lufkin & Jenrette, N.Y.C., 1969-77; v.p. planning and control Dayton Hudson Corp., Mpls., 1977-79, sr. v.p. planning and control, 1979; exec. v.p., chief adminstrs. officer Mervyn's, Hayward, Calif., 1979—. Bd. regents St. John's U., Collegeville, Minn. Served with Submarine Service, USN, 1963-67. Mem. N.Y. Soc. Security Analysts, Beta Gamma Sigma. Roman Catholic. Clubs: Princeton (N.Y.C.); Minneapolis. Office: 25001 Industrial Blvd Hayward CA 94545

GALLAGHER, HUGH PATRICK, chem. co. exec.; b. Easton, Pa., Mar. 2, 1935; s. Edward James and Bertha M. (Mayrosh) G.; B.S. in Chem. Engring., Lafayette Coll., 1957; M.B.A., U. Del., 1965; postgrad. U. Ala., 1958-59, Lehigh U., 1960; children by previous marriage—Brent P., Valerie, Shawn. Proposals engr. Air Products & Chems. Co., Allentown, Pa., 1960, gen. mgr. acetylenic chems. div., Wayne, Pa., 1971-78, gen. mgr. performance chems. div., Allentown, Pa., 1978—; project mgr. Atlas Chem. Co., Wilmington, Del., 1961-64, mgr. market devel., 1965-67, planning mgr., 1970-71; dir. planning Nashua Corp. (N.H.), 1968-70. Asst. prof. U. Del., Newark, 1965-68, 74. Served to 1st lt. AUS, 1957-60. Mem. Soc. Plastics Industry (chmn. bldg. materials com. cellular plastic 1961-67), Acad. Mgmt. Contbr. articles to profl. jours. Home: 419 N Leh St Allentown PA 18104 Office: Box 538 Allentown PA 18105

GALLAGHER, JAMES FRANCIS, ins. co. exec.; b. Pitts., Aug. 25, 1945; s. James Francis and Gertrude Helen (Hando) G.; B.A., Duquesne U., 1967; M.B.A., So. Methodist U., 1975; m. Barbara Ann Dugan, Sept. 30, 1967; children—Brian Keith, Kevin Patrick, Eric Paul. Sr. claims rep. Conn. Gen. Co., Dallas, 1969-73, asst. claims mgr., 1973-75; with World Service Life Ins. Co., Ft. Worth, 1975—, v.p., asst. dir. ops., 1978, sr. v.p., dir. ops., 1978-80, sr. v.p., dir. group ins. mktg., 1980—. Vice chmn. St. Bartholomew's Parish Council, Ft. Worth, 1977-79, chmn., 1979-80; exec. cons. Jr. Achievement, Ft. Worth, 1978-79; corp. coordinator United Campaign, Ft. Worth, 1978-79. Served to 1st lt. U.S. Army, 1967-69. Decorated Army Commendation medal; named Outstanding Young Man Am., U.S. Jaycees, 1977. Mem. Am. Mgmt. Assn., Adminstrv. Mgmt. Soc., Internat. Found. Employee Benefits, Life Office Mgmt. Assn., Dallas Soc. Claimsmen (corr. sec., exec. com.). Democrat. Roman Catholic. Club: Serra. Home: 4613 Saldana Dr Fort Worth TX 76133 Office: 307 W 7th St Fort Worth TX 76102

GALLAGHER, JAMES JOHN, pub. sch. exec.; b. Chgo., Oct. 25, 1922; s. James K. and Marie K. (Meyers) G.; B.B.A., Gen. Motors Inst., 1950; M.B.A., Western Mich. U., 1972, Ed.D. (Grad. scholar), 1976; m. Edith L. Power, May 31, 1947; children—James W., William J. Prodn. and material control supt. Gen. Motors Corp., Grand Rapids, Mich., 1950-70; dir. budget, fin. Grand Rapids Pub. Schs., 1970-73, controller, 1973-74, asst. supt. bus. affairs, 1974-78, dep. supt., 1978-79, exec. dep. supt., 1979—; instr. grad. bus. courses Western Mich U., Kalamazoo, 1977—, Grand Valley State Colls., Grand Rapids, 1978—, Wayne State U., Detroit, 1978—, Aquinas Coll., Grand Rapids, 1979—; cons. sch. bus. mgmt. Past chmn. and treas. ARC, City of Grand Rapids, 1976—. Recipient Recognition as Outstanding Vol. certificate ARC, 1971; registered sch. bus. adminstr. Assn. Sch. Bus. Ofcls. Served with USAAF, 1942-45. Mem. Am. Mgmt. Assn., Am. Assn. Sch. Adminstrs., Mich. Assn. Sch. Adminstrs., Mich. Sch. Bus. Ofcls., Assn. Sch. Bus. Ofcls., Mich. Assn. State and Fed. Program Specialists, Middle Cities Edn. Assn. (task force on bus.), Mich. Sch. Investment Assn. (past chmn.), Nat. Ski Patrol System (registered patroller). Congregationalist. Home: 2515 Union Ave SE Grand Rapids MI 49507 Office: 143 Bostwick Ave NE Grand Rapids MI 49503

GALLAGHER, JAMES JOSEPH, exec. counselor, cons.; b. Staten Island, N.Y., Mar. 12, 1930; s. James Joseph and Edith Louise (O'Brien) G.; B.A., Villanova U., 1952; M.A., N.Y. U., 1971, Ph.D., 1973; m. Christine Furler, Oct. 25, 1975; children by previous marriage—Maryanne, Maura Kathleen, MaryBeth, Serena; stepchildren—Andrew, Jennifer, Amy, Alison. Vice pres. pub. relations Palmer, Willson & Worden, Inc., N.Y.C., 1959-64; exec. dir. John LaFarge Inst., N.Y.C., 1964-68; pres. Tombrock Coll., West Paterson, N.J., 1968-70; chmn. Career Mgmt. Assos., N.Y.C., 1970—; cons. on human resource devel. to maj. U.S. corps. Adv. bd. multi-nat. corporate studies Upsala Coll., East Orange, N.J., 1977—; chmn. social relations commn. Archdiocese of Newark, 1974-76. Served with inf., AUS, 1952-54. Mem. Am. Personnel and Guidance Assn., Human Resources Planning Soc. Democrat. Roman Catholic. Clubs: Lake Valhalla, N.Y. Athletic, Sixty East. Home: 31 Stoney Brook Rd Montville NJ 07045 Office: 60E 42d St New York NY 10165

GALLAGHER, JOHN JOSEPH, assn. exec.; b. Plainfield, N.J., Dec. 13, 1946; s. Joseph Aloysius and Elizabeth Margaret (Greader) G.; B.S. in Acctg., Mount St. Mary's Coll., 1968; m. Jayne Marie Conrad, July 31, 1971; 1 son, John Joseph III. Sr. acct. Coopers & Lybrand, Washington, 1968-72; mgmt. cons. mgr. Wolf & Co., Washington, 1972-73; controller Am. Petroleum Inst., Washington, 1973—. Bd. dirs. Chi Chi Rodriguez Youth Found., Inc. Served with USAR, 1969-75. C.P.A., Md. Mem. Am. Inst. C.P.A.'s, D.C. Inst. C.P.A.'s, Am. Soc. Assn. Execs., Mount St. Mary's Coll. Alumni Assn. Roman Catholic. Contbr. articles in field to profl. jours. Home: 1490 Grandview Ct Arnold MD 21012 Office: 2101 L St NW Washington DC 20037

GALLAGHER, PHIL C., ins. exec.; b. Miami, Fla., Nov. 10, 1926; s. Phil J. and Blonda (Burrow) G.; B.B.A., U. Miami, 1949; m. Carmen Gallagher; children—Pamela Robertson, Vivien Elizabeth. With D.R. Mead & Co., Miami, 1949-72, exec. v.p., 1958-72; partner Gallagher-Cole Assos., Miami, 1972—; dir. Skylake State Bank, North Miami Beach, Fla.; underwriting mem. Lloyd's of London; past instr. Lindsey Hopkins Edn. Center. Bd. dirs. Grand Jury Assn. Fla., J. Edwin Larson Found. for Ins. Edn. Served with USNR, 1944-46. Mem. Ind. Ins. Agts. Am. (past nat. dir., past chmn. agy. mgmt. com.), Assn. Internat. Ins. Agts., Nat. Assn. Ins. Brokers, Am. Risk and Ins. Assn., Nat. Assn. Casualty and Surety Agts., Profl. Ins. Agts. Assn., Profl. Ins. Agts. Fla. and Caribbean, Fla. Surplus Lines Assn., Nat., Fla., Miami assns. life underwriters, Fla. Assn. Ins. Agts. (past pres.), Ind. Ins. Agts. Dade County (past pres.), Profl. Ins. Agts. Dade County, Greater Miami C. of C., Econ. Soc. South Fla. Clubs: Palm Bay, Jockey, Bankers (Miami); Ocean Reef, Surf, La Gorce Country. Home: 1 Palm Bay Ct Miami FL 33138 Office: 4700 Biscayne Blvd Miami FL 33137

GALLAGHER, WILLIAM, adminstrv. exec.; b. Brownsville, Pa., Feb. 27, 1932; s. Edward W. and DeLellis S. (Shannon) G.; B.S., Duquesne U., 1953; m. Nancy Cottom, Oct. 12, 1963; children—T. Scott, Nancy Ann, Partner, Am. Personnel Co., Los Angeles, 1957-59; mgr. mgmt. profl. recruiting Raytheon Co., Waltham, Mass., 1959-65; asst. dir. OEO, Exec. Office Pres., Washington, 1965-66; employment mgr. ICI Americas Inc., Wilmington, Del., 1966-74, dir. adminstrv. services, 1974—; dir. F.T. Andrews, Inc., Georgetown Investment Trust Inc., Doman Helicopters Inc., Bd. dirs. Southeastern Pa. chpt. Am. Heart Assn., 1973—, chmn., 1976-78. Served with U.S. Army, 1953-56. Recipient Outstanding Vol. award Southeastern Pa. chpt. Am. Heart Assn., 1974. Mem. Employment Mgmt. Assn. (founder pres. 1972, dir., sr. adviser), Adminstrv. Mgmt. Assn., Nat. Assn. Fleet Adminstrs., Nat. Passenger Travel Assn. Clubs: Concord Country, Radley Run Country, Elks. Office: ICI Americas Inc Administrative Services Wilmington DE 19897

GALLAGHER, WILLIAM JOSEPH, stock broker; b. Mt. Vernon, N.Y., Aug. 5, 1924; s. Joseph William and Mary Bobbie (Menagh) G.; student N.Y. U., 1941-42, Pasadena Theatre Arts Coll., 1951-52, U. So. Calif., 1959-61, U. Calif. Grad. Sch. Bus. Adminstrn., Los Angeles, 1964-65; m. Ethel Elizabeth Caucci, Oct. 19, 1947; children—John W., William Joseph, T. Clayton, Craig, Pamela, Damian, Robert. Sales mgr. Royal Distbrs., 1947-50, Bellmar Sales & Mktg. Co., 1950-54; resident mgr. Marache, Dofflemyre Co., Pasadena, 1954-68, Merrill, Luther, Kalis & Co., Pasadena, 1968-73; v.p., resident mgr. Sterling West, Inc., Pasadena, 1973-76; pres. Gallagher, Gliksman, Boylan, Robbins, Keegan & Dow, Inc., Pasadena, 1977—; pres., dir. Pasadena Mgmt. Co., Inc., dir. Barnhart-Morrow Consol. Corp., Bd. Control-United Group. Bd. dirs. Radiol. Atomic Def. Emergency Force Group, Los Angeles County, 1968-70. Served with USMCR, 1942-46; PTO. Mem. Officers Assn. Calif. State Mil. Res. (chmn. bd.), 2d Marine Div. Assn. (v.p., dir. Semper Fi council Los Angeles County), Officers Assn. Calif. N.G. Res. (pres. 1969), Am. Legion (v.p. 1949), Bus. and Profl. Mens Assn. Los Angeles, Pasadena Bond Club, Pasadena C. of C. Clubs: Optimist (pres. 1959) (Pasadena); Vaquero (v.p. 1973) (Glendale); Bond (Los Angeles). Home: 2627 Hermosita Dr Glendale CA 91208 Office: 747 E Green St Pasadena CA 91101

GALLAND, FREDERICK LEWIS, communications co. exec.; b. N.Y.C., Apr. 27, 1944; s. Sydney and Anne Naomi (Diamond) G.; B.B.A., CCNY, 1965; m. Susan Feinberg, Aug. 26, 1965; children—Amy, Neil. Accountant, Touche, Ross & Co., C.P.A.'s, and predecessor, N.Y.C., 1965-73; treas., comptroller Digital Paging Systems Co., Englewood, N.J., 1973—; chief fin. officer Graphic Scanning Corp., Englewood, N.J., 1975—, also dir. C.P.A., N.Y. State. Mem. Am. Inst. C.P.A.'s, N.Y. State Soc. C.P.A.'s. Home: 15 Belvedere Dr Syosset NY 11791 Office: 99 W Sheffield Ave Englewood NJ 07631

GALLAND, RICHARD I., oil co. exec., lawyer; b. Denver, Oct. 13, 1916; s. Raymond F. and Mabel (Wilson) G.; A.B., Yale U., 1937, LL.B., 1940; m. Alice Halstead, July 21, 1941; children—Richard I., Holley, John H. Admitted to N.Y. bar, 1940, asso. Cravath, deGersdorff, Swaine and Wood, N.Y.C., 1940-43, Cravath, Swaine & Moore, 1946-50; chief counsel Mathieson Chem. Corp., 1950-55; v.p., gen. counsel Colo. Oil and Gas Corp., 1955-58; pres. Am. Petrofina Co. of Tex., 1958—; pres. Am. Petrofina, Inc., 1969-76, chmn. bd., chief exec. officer, 1976—; dir. Tex. Industries, Inc., Petrofina, S.A., Belgium, Petrofina Can. Inc. Served as lt. (j.g.) USNR, 1943-46. Office: PO Box 2159 Dallas TX 75221*

GALLANT, SISTER FRANCETTE, religious order adminstr.; b. Worcester, Mass., July 26, 1931; d. Joseph Henry and Florence Cecelia (Dumont) G.; B.S., Villanova U., 1967; M.S., Marywood Coll., 1972; student Taylor Sch. of Bus., 1968; postgrad. Notre Dame U., 1977, Carnegie-Mellon U., 1979. Tchr. elem. schs., 1958-67; tchr. high schs., 1967-75; treas. U.S. Province, Missionary Sisters of the Most Sacred Heart of Jesus, Roman Catholic Ch., Reading, Pa., 1977—, fin. mgr., 1977—, mem. provincial council, 1972-75. Mem. Am. Mgmt. Assn., Council of Religious Treasurers. Home: St Michael Convent Hyde Park Reading PA 19605

GALLANT, WADE MILLER, JR., lawyer; b. Raleigh, N.C., Jan. 12, 1930; s. Wade M. and Sallie (Jones) G.; B.A. summa cum laude, Wake Forest Coll., 1952, J.D. cum laude, 1955; m. Sandra Kirkham, Sept. 15, 1979. Admitted to N.C. bar, 1955; asso. firm Womble, Carlyle, Sandridge & Rice, Winston-Salem, N.C., 1955-63, partner, 1963—; lectr. continuing legal edn. program N.C. Bar Found., 1966—; chmn., dir. Cayman Reef Devel. Co. Ltd., Brenner Cos., Inc., Thomas Built Buses, Inc. Pres., Forsyth County Legal Aid Soc., 1963-67, Assn. Family and Child Service Agy., Winston-Salem, 1962-65, Winston-Salem Symphony Assn., 1965-66, Forsyth Mental Health Assn., 1972-73, N.C. Mental Health Assn., 1975—; dir.-at-large Mental Health Assn. U.S., 1978—. Mem. Internat., Am., N.C., Forsyth County bar assns., Am. Law Inst., Am. Counsel Assn. (hon.), Internat. Fiscal Assn., Phi Beta Kappa, Omnicron Delta Kappa, Phi Delta Phi. Clubs: Old Town, Twin City (Winston-Salem). Home: 2534 Warwick Winston-Salem NC 27104 Office: 2400 Wachovia Bldg Winston-Salem NC 27101

GALLARD, JOHN, banker; b. Kleinliebenthab, Russia, Sept. 3, 1923; s. Michael and Matilda (Morin) Grigoriev; came to U.S., 1966, naturalized, 1980; Law Lic., U. Law Bucharest, 1949; Ph.D. in Econs., U. Perugia (Italy), 1961; m. Elivanete Silva de Almeida, July 15, 1969; children—Adzian, Fabriene, Lorraine. Orbiter, chief lawyer Ministry Industry Rumania, 1949-60; cons. Italian Govt., pres. Novostyl Industries, 1962-64; cons. Latin Am. countries, pres. Chalegard, 1964-73; chmn. London Irish Bank, 1973-74; chmn. Chalegard Bank & Trust Co., Irish Banking House, N.Y.C., 1974—. Greek Orthodox. Clubs: Curzon House, Crockfords, Sporting Internat. (London), Masons. Office: 500 5th Ave New York NY 10036

GALLEGOS, FREDERICK, auditor; b. San Bernardino, Calif., June 10, 1947; s. Frederick Reyes and Guadalupe (Aceves) G.; A.B., San Bernardino Valley Coll., 1970; B.S., Calif. State Poly. U., 1972, M.B.A., 1973; m. Susan Melinda Carney, Apr. 17, 1976. Mgmt. analyst, EDP auditor U.S. Gen. Acctg. Office, Los Angeles, 1972—; lectr. info. systems dept. Calif. State U. Poly. U., 1975—; trustee, corp. sec. EDP Auditors' Found. for Edn. and Research, 1979—. Served with U.S. Army, 1966-68. Decorated Bronze Star medal, Purple Heart medal; recipient Meritorious service award GAO, 1978, hon. award of asst. to comptroller gen. for adminstrn., 1979. Mem. EDP Auditor's Assn. (cert. data processing auditor, dir. Los Angeles chpt. 1979—), Assn. MBA Execs., Assn. Timesharing Users. Democrat. Roman Catholic. Co-author: Case Study in Business Systems Design, Case 11-Medco, Inc., 1973, The Auditor's First Steps in Applying Computer Analysis, 1978; author: Efficient Use of Timesharing Resources, 1975, Timesharing Administrator in Government, 1977; A Methodology for Reviewing Computer Software, 1979, others. Office: 350 S Figueroa St Suite 1010 Los Angeles CA 90071

GALLIGAN, EDWARD BERNARD, telecommunications co. exec.; b. Hinsdale, Ill., May 21, 1946; s. Edward B. and Catherine (Juraco) G.; B.B.A., U. Alaska, 1971, postgrad. in bus. adminstrn., 1971-77; m. Marie-Cecile S. Vanoni, July 27, 1967; children—Sarah, Benedicte. Loan officer Nat. Bank of Alaska, Anchorage, 1970-72; treas., dir. fin. planning Alascom, Inc., Anchorage, 1972—. Served with USAF, 1964-70. Roman Catholic. Clubs: Lions, Elks. Office: 949 E 36th Ave Pouch 6607 Anchorage AK 99502

GALLIGANI, CLAIRE JOSEPHINE, banker; b. Chgo., Apr. 22, 1931; d. Theodore and Josephine (Fic) Ferenc; student Northwestern U., Laney Coll., U. Calif.; m. James Galligani, Sept. 16, 1951; 1 dau., Karen. With Bank of Am., 1953—, asst. cashier, 1972-78, asst. v.p., mgr., 1978—; tchr. bus. mgmt. Active local United Way. Democrat. Roman Catholic. Clubs: Ballena Bay Yacht, Alameda Yacht. Home: 29266 Whalebone Way Hayward CA 94544

GALLIN, ALVIN LLOYD, transp. cons.; b. N.Y.C., Oct. 14, 1920; s. Henry and Elizabeth G.; B.S.E.E., U.S. Naval Acad., 1941; M.A. in Personnel Supervision, San Diego State U., 1956; m. Grace Nay, Dec. 13, 1958; 1 dau., Julia Elizabeth. Commd. ensign U.S. Navy, 1941, advanced through grades to capt., 1961; insp.-gen. Mil. Sea Transp. Service; asst. chief of staff Naval Forces Philippines; comdg. officer USS Haleakala; personnel engr. Gen. Dynamics, San Diego, 1956-57; marine dir. Panama Canal, 1967-77; with Space Shuttle Engring., Planning and Research Corp., Kennedy Space Center, 1978-79; transp. cons., 1979—; asso. prof. Ill. Inst. Tech., Chgo., 1949-51. Pres., C.Z. council Girl Scouts Am., 1968-70; v.p. C.Z. Red Cross, 1971-73; bd. dirs. YMCA, 1970-77. Decorated U.S. Army Legion of Merit, Bronze Star, Purple Heart; recipient Presdl. Mgmt. Improvement award White House, 1970; Panama Canal Outstanding Performance award, 1975, 76. Mem. Naval Acad. Alumni Assn. Clubs: Royal Oak Golf, Elks, Masons. Home: 3641 Royal Oak Dr Titusville FL 32780

GALLINARO, NICHOLAS FRANCIS, bus. exec.; b. Somerville, Mass., Feb. 25, 1930; s. Joseph Michael and Mary Marie (Valerio) G.; B.A., Boston Coll., 1952, M.B.A., 1964; B.S. in Mech. Engring., Notre Dame U., 1953; m. Inez Hanken, July 27, 1957; children—Michael J., James J., Stephen P., Robert N. With Clark Equipment Corp, Battle Creek & Benton Harbor, Mich., 1951-53; v.p., Harnischfeger Internat, Corp., Milw., Wis., 1953-63; v.p., dir. McLaughlin Equipment Corp., N.Y.C., 1963-71; v.p., dir. Prudential Internat. Corp., N.Y.C., 1971-72; pres. GAR Worldwide Corp., GAR Internat. Corp., and GAR Equipment Corp., S. Plainfield, N.J., 1972—. Trustee, Christian Brothers Acad. Served with USMC, 1949-51. Mem. N.Y. World Trade Assn., Pan Am. Soc., Am. Mining Congress, Associated Equipment Distbrs. Republican. Roman Catholic. Clubs: K.C., Navesink Country. Home: 31 Esshire Dr Middletown NJ 07748 Office: 3005 Hadley Rd S Plainfield NJ 07080

GALLO, ROBERT PETER, lighting co. exec.; b. Newark, Feb. 14, 1933; s. Joseph John and Anna (O'Boyle) G.; student Washington Coll., 1950-51; B.S., Rider Coll., 1954; m. Eleanor Prahl, May 28, 1960; children—Joseph, Susan, Eleanor, Robert, Donald. With Loomis, Suffern & Fernald, C.P.A.'s, N.Y.C., 1956-58, Lybrand Ross Bros. & Montgomery, N.Y.C., 1958-61; sr. acct. Lee Higginsons Corp., N.Y.C., 1961-63; asst. controller N. Am. Philips Corp., N.Y.C., 1963-66, controller ops. div., 1966-69, v.p., controller, 1969-79, v.p. fin., mem. exec. com., 1979—. Active Clark S.W. Civic Assn., 1964-69; county and mcpl. committeeman Clark (N.J.) Republican Club, 1965-66, treas., 1967. Served with U.S. Army, 1954-56. C.P.A., N.Y., N.J. Mem. Am. Inst. C.P.A.'s, N.J. Soc. C.P.A.'s. Roman Catholic. Home: 29 Dorset Dr Clark NJ 07066 Office: Bank St Hightstown NJ 08520

GALLOWAY, CHARLES THOMAS PEFFERS, life ins. co. exec.; b. Buckingham, Que., Can., Apr. 26, 1927; s. Andrew Scott Jubilee and Bertha Maude (Strome) G.; B.A. in Math. and Physics with honours, U. Toronto, 1950; m. Frances Alice Mackey, Oct. 26, 1956; children—Charlene, Pamela, Deborah. With Nat. Life Assurance Co. Can., 1950—, v.p., actuary, 1963-75, pres., 1975—, chief exec. officer, 1976—, also dir.; dir. Dominion Ins. Corp., Continental Ins. Co. Can. Fellow Soc. Actuaries, Can. Inst. Actuaries (pres. 1980-81); mem. Am. Acad. Actuaries. Conservative. Club: University (Toronto). Office: 522 University Ave Toronto ON M5G 1Y7 Canada

GALLUP, JOHN GARDINER, paper co. exec.; b. Bridgeport, Conn., Oct. 31, 1927; s. Prentiss Brownell and Evelyn (Crocker) G.; A.B., Dartmouth Coll., 1949; m. Paula Burgee, June 10, 1951; children—Susan, Paula, Bruce. Dept. mgr. J.B. White Co., Greenville, S.C. and Castner Knott Dept. Stores, Nashville, 1951-52; asst. store mgr. A. T. Gallup, Inc., Holyoke, Mass., 1952-55; advt. asst., mgr. prodn. planning and prodn. mgr. Strathmore Paper Co., Westfield, Mass., 1955-70, pres., div. mgr. Strathmore Paper Co. div. Hammermill Paper Co., Westfield, 1970—; dir. Third Nat. Bank, Springfield, Mass., 1979. Vice chmn. Baystate Med. Center, Springfield, 1979; bd. dirs. Jr. Achievement Western Mass., 1979, Springfield Orch., 1979; trustee Springfield Coll., 1979; mem. George Bush Campaign Com., 1979. Served with USMC, 1945-47. Mem. Boston Paper Trade Assn. (pres. 1979), Associated Industries Mass. (vice chmn. 1979), Am. Paper Inst. Episcopalian. Club: Longmeadow Country. Home: 64 Cambridge Circle Longmeadow MA 01106 Office: S Broad St Westfield MA 01085

GALLUP, ROBERT BURGESS, elec. engr.; b. Seattle, Oct. 27, 1919; s. Clarke McCullough and Lela (Tait) G.; B.S. in Elec. Engring., U. Wash., 1941; m. Rachel Hicks Maddox, Sept. 21, 1946; children—Nancy Lee, Robert Winston, Susan Carol. Engr., Rural Electrification Adminstrn., Washington, 1941-42, 46-51; with R.W. Beck & Assos., Seattle, 1951—, partner, 1954—, supervising exec. engr., 1963—, also chief cons. engr.; cons. on econs. and operation maj. hydroelectric projects, electric utility ops. Served from lt. to capt. AUS, 1942-46. Registered profl. engr. Wash., Ore., Ida., Mont., N.D. Mem. IEEE, Nat., Wash. socs. profl. engrs., Psi Upsilon. Conglist. Home: 8909 NE 16th Pl Bellevue WA 98004 Office: Tower Bldg Seattle WA 98101

GALPERIN, LEROY, fin. cons.; b. N.Y.C., Jan. 27, 1930; s. Jacob and Bertha G.; B.A., City Coll. N.Y., 1950; M.S. in Journalism, Columbia U., 1951; m. Joyce Paull, May 26, 1957; children—John Barrett, Diane. Polit. and sci. reporter, feature writer, columnist Newhouse Newspapers, 1953-60; pub. relations account exec. Tex McCrary Inc., Ruder & Finn, 1960-62; pres. Info. Specialists Inc. (merged with F.I.R. Assos. 1965), N.Y.C., 1962-65; pres., chmn. F.I.R. Assos., fin. consultants, N.Y.C., 1965—; cons. on containerization transp. and shipping, 1962—. Home: Wilshire Rd Greenwich CT 06830 Office: 30 E 42d St New York NY 10017

GALT, BARRY J., diversified co. exec.; b. Ardmore, Okla., Dec. 14, 1933; s. Monroe S. and Ethelyn (Barry) G.; B.A. (Naval ROTC scholar), U. Okla., 1955, LL.B., 1960; m. Mary Kathryn Moore, Aug. 14, 1954; children—Terri Kathryn, Carol Ann, Gayle Lyn. Research asst. to dean Law Sch., U. Okla., 1959-60; admitted to Okla. bar, 1960; asso. firm Conner, Winters, Ballaine, Barry & McGowen and predecessor firm, Tulsa, 1960-65, partner, 1966-75; sr. v.p., gen. counsel The Williams Companies, Tulsa, 1975-77, exec. v.p., 1977-78, pres., chief operating officer, 1979—. Served to lt. USNR, 1955-58. Mem. Am., Okla., Tulsa County bar assns., Order of Coif, Phi Delta Theta, Phi Alpha Delta. Presbyn. (elder 1973-75). Clubs: Southern Hills Country (Tulsa); Eldorado (Indian Wells, Calif.), LaQuinta (Calif.) Hotel Golf. Editor: Okla. Law Rev., 1959-60. Home: 6730 S Evanston St Tulsa OK 74136 Office: One Williams Center Tulsa OK 74103

GALT, THOMAS MAUNSELL, ins. co. exec.; b. Winnipeg, Man., Can., Aug. 1, 1921; s. George F. and Muriel Julyan (Maunsell) G.; student Queen's U., 1939-41, 45-46, U. Man., 1946-48; m. Helen W. Hyndman, June 15, 1942; children—Lesley Maunsell (Mrs. S. R. Brown), George Hyndman. With Sun Life Assurance Co. Can., 1948—, actuary, 1961-62, chief actuary, 1962-63, v.p., chief actuary, 1963-68, exec. v.p., 1968-72, pres., chief operating officer, 1972-73, pres., chief exec. officer, 1973-78, chmn. and chief exec. officer, 1978—, also dir.; chmn., dir. Sun Life Assurance Co. of Can. (U.K.) Ltd., Sun Life Assurance Co. of Can. (U.S.); pres., dir. other Sun Life subsidiary cos.; pres., dir. Sun Growth Fund Inc.; dir. Bank of Montreal, Liberty Life Assn. Africa Ltd., Canadian Pacific Enterprises Ltd., Canron, Inc., Steel Co. of Can. Ltd., Textron Can. Ltd. Mem. adv. bd. Salvation Army Montreal; bd. dirs. Montreal Gen. Hosp. Found., Montreal Symphony Orch., Toronto Symphony Orch., Can. Safety Council; bd. mgmt. Montreal Gen. Hosp. Corp., Victorian Order of Nurses of Can.; bd. govs. Wellesley Hosp. Research Inst. Served to flight lt., Royal Can. Air Force, 1941-45. Fellow Soc. Actuaries, Can. Inst. Actuaries; mem. Am. Acad. Actuaries, Am. Life Ins. Assn. (provincial v.p.), Am. Council of Life Ins. (dir.), Better Bus. Bur. Can. (adv. council). Clubs: Mt. Bruno Country, St. James's, Montreal Skeet, Royal Ottawa (Ont., Can.) Golf, Mt. Royal, Nat. Home: 297 Russell Hill Rd Toronto ON M4V 2T7 Canada Office: 20 King St W Toronto ON M5W 2C9 Canada

GALVIN, BETTY WEEKS, retail store exec.; b. Poinsette County, Ark., Sept. 7, 1939; d. Claybern and Lola I. (Baser) Weeks; student public schs., Marked Tree, Ark.; m. Douglas G. Galvin, Nov. 23, 1966; children—David Alan, Robert Jackson; 1 son by previous marriage, Jonathan Wayne Swan. With Bobbie Brooks Mfg. Co., Lepanto, Ark., 1963-65; billing clk. John A. Dennie Co., Memphis, 1965-67; pres. Mid-South Microwave, Inc., Columbia, S.C., 1975—; lectr. in field. Mem. Nat. Assn. Retail Dealers of Am., Internat. Microwave Power Inst. Republican. Presbyterian. Home: 1341 Railfence Dr Columbia SC 29210 Office: 2500 Decker Blvd Columbia SC 29206

GALVIN, JOHN JOSEPH, mfg. co. exec.; b. Detroit, Apr. 25, 1927; s. Don Thaddeus and Aurelia Marie (Volkman) G.; B.S., Lehigh U., 1950; m. Sharon Ann Fortin, Mar. 3, 1962; 1 dau., Mary Shaw. In sales and sales and mktg. mgmt. Carboloy Bus. and Lamp div. Gen. Electric Co., Chgo., Detroit, Cleve., 1950-72; v.p. mktg. Wallace Murray Corp., N.Y.C., 1972-73, v.p., gen. mgr. Atrax div., Newington, Conn., 1973-74; pres. Wheel Trueing Tool Co., Columbia, S.C., 1974—; chmn. CMV InterAm., Miami, Fla., 1979—, Wheel Trueing Tool Co. Can. Ltd., 1974—; group v.p. N. Am., Diamant Boart S.A., Brussels, 1981—; dir. United Diamond Drilling Services, Diamant Boart Can., Calgary, Alta. Bd. dirs. United Way, 1977—, Jr. Achievement, 1977—; mem. Econ. Devel. Commn., Richland and Lexington Counties and City of Columbia, 1977—; chmn. Wildewood Sch., 1978—. Served with USN, 1945-46; ETO. Recipient Order of Palmetto, State of S.C., 1978. Mem. Indsl. Diamond Assn. (dir. 1976-77), Diamond Wheel Mfrs. Inst., Am. Supply and Machinery Mfrs. Assn., Assn. U.S. Army, Phi Beta Kappa, Beta Gamma Sigma. Republican. Roman Catholic. Clubs: Wildewood Country, Summit, Kiwanis. Home: 13 Fox Chase Rd Columbia SC 29206 Office: Box 1317 Two Notch Rd Columbia SC 29202

GALVIN, ROBERT W., electronics products mfg. exec.; b. Marshfield, Wis., Oct. 9, 1922; student U. Notre Dame, U. Chgo.; LL.D. (hon.), Quincy Coll., St. Ambrose Coll., DePaul U., Ala. State U. With Motorola, Inc., Chgo., 1940—, now chmn. bd., chief exec. officer, dir. Bd. dirs. Jr. Achievement of Chgo.; chmn. bd. trustees Ill. Inst. Tech.; former mem. Pres.'s Commn. on Internat. Trade and Investment; trustee, mem. 12 Fellows, U. Notre Dame. Served with Signal Corps, AUS, World War II. Named Decision Maker of Yr., Chgo. Assn. Commerce and Industry-Am. Statis. Assn., 1973. Mem. Electronics Industries Assn. (pres. 1966, Medal of Honor 1970, dir.). Office: 1303 Algonquin Rd Schaumburg IL 60196

GAMBEE, ROBERT RANKIN, investment banker; b. N.Y.C., Aug. 26, 1942; s. A. Sumner and Eleanor Elizabeth (Brown) G.; A.B., Princeton U., 1964; M.B.A., Harvard U., 1966. Asso. corp. fin. White, Weld & Co., N.Y.C., 1966-71, v.p., 1971-73; v.p. Schroder Capital Corp. affiliate J. Henry Schroder Wagg-London, N.Y.C., 1973-78; v.p. Atlantic Capital Corp. affiliate Deutsche Bank, Frankfurt and Dusseldorf, Germany, 1978—; dir. Liberty Communications, Inc. Trustee Dwight-Englewood Sch. Republican. Presbyterian. Clubs: Univ., Princeton, City Midday, Downtown Athletic (N.Y.C.); Englewood. Author, photographer: Nantucket Island, 1973, rev. edit., 1974; Manhattan Seascape: Waterside Views Around New York, 1975; Exeter Impressions (intro. by Nathaniel Benchley), 1980. Home: 1230 Park Ave New York NY 10028 Office: Atlantic Capital Corp 40 Wall St New York NY 10005

GAMBLE, ALFRED JAMES, metal products mfg. exec.; b. Lansing, Mich., July 18, 1921; s. Alfred F. and Rebecca (Woodward) G.; student Mich. State U., 1939-41; children—Alfred T., Ernest M. Exec. v.p. Hartley Boiler Works, Montgomery, Ala., 1946-61; pres. Gamble's, Inc., Montgomery, 1962—; dir. Trinity Industries, Inc.; partner Woodland Hills Mobile Home Park, Montgomery; owner AG Assos., Speed Screen Sales and Service, Inc., Montgomery. Past bd. dirs. Montgomery Little Theatre. Served with USAAF, 1941-45. Mem. So. Assn. Steel Fabricators (past pres.), Sales and Mktg. Execs. Montgomery, Ala. Roadbuilders Assn. (past dir.), Men of Montgomery, Montgomery C. of C. (past dir.). Republican. Episcopalian. Clubs: Masons, Shriners, Elks; Montgomery, QB. Home: 6315 Kathmoor Dr Montgomery AL 36117 Office: 1401 N Decatur St Box 310 Montgomery AL 36101

GAMBLE, CLIFFORD NEWTON, JR., life ins. co. exec.; b. Oakland, Calif., July 11, 1945; s. Clifford Newton and Dorthea Ann (Wordyke) G.; B.S. in B us. Adminstrn., U. Santa Clara (Calif.), 1967, J.D., 1970; m. Judy Anne Helmick, July 13, 1968; children—Jenny, Gwen, Carrie. Admitted to Ariz. bar, Calif. bar; atty. firm Lewis & Roca, Phoenix, 1970-73; with Pacific Standard Life Ins. Co., Davis, Calif., 1973—, exec. v.p. mktg., 1976-78, pres., chief exec. officer, 1978—, also dir. Bd. dirs. Tierra Del Oro council Girl Scouts U.S.A. Served to capt. USAR. C.L.U. Mem. League Ariz. Ins. Cos. (dir.), Am. Bar Assn., Am. Soc. C.L.U.'s, Ariz. Bar Assn., Calif. Bar Assn. Office: 3820 Chiles Rd Davis CA 95616

GAMBLE, MICHAEL IRVING, aerospace co. exec.; b. Everett, Wash., Dec. 19, 1935; s. Paul I. and Margaret (Isacson) G.; B.S. in Physics, U. Wash., 1957; program for sr. execs. Sloan Sch. Mgmt., M.I.T., 1980; m. Charlotte A. Albrecht, Dec. 20, 1957; children—Michael Scott, Paula Michel. Asso. engr. applied physics staff Boeing Co., 1956-59, research engr. physics tech. dept., 1959-62; mgr. environ. physics dept. Tulsa div. AVCO Corp., 1962-65, mgr. engring. instrument div., mgr. program devel., 1966-69, space mktg. mgr. for govt. products group, Los Angeles, 1970-71, regional mktg. mgr., govt. products group, Albuquerque, 1972-74; laser systems mgr. Boeing Aerospace Co., Seattle, 1974-80, dep. mgr. designating optical tracker, 1980—. Served to capt. AUS, 1953-62. Asso. fellow AIAA; mem. Phi Kappa Psi, Nat. Space Club. Home: 13915 SE 241st St Kent WA 98031 Office: PO Box 3999 Seattle WA 98124

GAMBLE, MILLARD GOBERT, III, textile fibers exec.; b. N.Y.C., Mar. 8, 1919; s. Millard Gobert, Jr., and Rose McGowan (Cantey) G.; B.A. in Social Sci., Wesleyan U., Middletown, Conn., 1941; m. E. Gloria Hine, Oct. 25, 1941; children—Millard Gobert IV, Robert Hine, Lynn Hunter, Joan Foster. With Surplus Mktg. Adminstrn., Dept. of Agr., San Francisco, 1941; with Textile Fibers dept. E.I. duPont de Nemours & Co., 1945—, beginning as sales rep., successively dist. sales rep., asst. sales mgr., sales mgr., chief supr. mfg., regional mktg. mgr., mktg. dir., asst. gen. dir. mktg., dir. profit center, gen. dir. mktg., 1945-73, gen. mgr., Wilmington, Del., 1973—. Served to lt. comdr., USNR, 1941-45. Mem. Man-Made Fiber Producers Assn. (asso. dir.). Republican. Episcopalian. Clubs: Wilmington (gov.), Wilmington Country (dir.), Vicmead Hunt. Home: 23 Brandywine Falls Wilmington DE 19806 Office: DuPont Co 3410 Nemours Bldg Wilmington DE 19898

GAMBLE, RANELLE ALEASE, lawyer; b. N.Y.C., June 2, 1941; d. Albert Reginald and Everlee (Holman) G.; B.A., N.Y. U., 1966; J.D. cum laude, Cleve. State U., 1972. Caseworker N.Y.C. Dept. Social Services, 1966-68; admitted to Ohio bar, 1972; atty. FTC, Cleve., 1972-74; atty. Cleve. Electric Illuminating Co., 1974—, sr. corp. atty., 1980—. Bd. dirs. Project Friendship, Cleve., 1980-82; bd. dirs. Council Human Relations, 1980, sec. bd. trustees, 1981-82; bd. dirs. Cleve. Heights Cable TV Adv. Commn., 1979-82; trustee Legal Aid Soc. Cleve., 1981—; chmn. Democratic task force Cuyahoga Women's Polit. Caucus, 1980. Recipient YWCA/SOHIO Career Woman of Achievement award, 1979; Greater Cleve. PanHellenic Council Outstanding Service award, 1976. Mem. Cleve. Women Lawyers Assn. (pres. 1978-80), Cleve.-Marshall Law Alumni Assn. (1st v.p. 1980-81), Cuyahoga County Bar Assn. (sec., trustee), Greater Cleve. Bar Assn., Ohio Bar Assn., Nat. Assn. Women Lawyers, Black Women Lawyers Assn., Nat. Assn. Negro Bus. and Profl. Women, Cuyahoga Women's Polit. Caucus, Delta Sigma Theta (pres. chpt. 1977-81). Roman Catholic. Club: Women's City. Contbr. articles to profl. jours. Home: 1040 Helmsdale Rd Cleveland Heights OH 44112 Office: PO Box 5000 55 Public Sq Cleveland OH 44113

GAMBRELL, SARAH BELK (MRS. CHARLES G. GAMBRELL), corp. exec.; b. Charlotte, N.C.; d. William Henry and Mary (Irwin) Belk; B.A., Sweet Briar Coll., 1939; H.H.D., Erskine Coll., 1970; m. Charles G. Gambrell, Nov. 21, 1952; 1 dau., Sarah Belk. Dir. Belk Group Stores, pres. 40 stores, v.p. and dir. Belk Stores Services, Charlotte, N.C.; Disting. lectr. Grad. Sch. Bus. Adminstrn., Queens Coll., Charlotte, also bd. advs. Trustee nat. bd. YWCA; bd. dirs. YWCA N.Y.C., YWCA, Charlotte, Parkinson Found., N.Y.C.; bd. overseers, bd. dirs. Sweet Briar (Va.) Coll.; trustee Princeton (N.J.) Theol. Sem., Johnson C. Smith U., Charlotte, Brick Presbyn. Ch., N.Y.C.; hon. bd. dirs. Cancer Research Inst.; mem. exec. com. World Service Council. Mem. Nat. Soc. Colonial Dames, DAR, N.Y. Jr. League, Fashion Group. Presbyterian. Club: Cosmopolitan. Home: 580 Park Ave New York NY 10021 Office: 111 W 40th St New York NY 10018

GAMMILL, DARRYL CURTIS, investment banker; b. Milw., Jan. 20, 1950; s. Lawrence H. and Eunice G. (Birkett) G.; B.S., U. Colo., 1973; m. Maureen Mulcahy, Sept. 16, 1972; children—Rebecca, Bridgett, Maureen. Stockbroker, Douglas, Stanat, Inc., Denver, 1974; dir. research Pittman Co., Denver, 1975; option specialist B.J. Leonard & Co., Denver, 1976; v.p. research, corp. fin. Neidiger, Tucker Bruner, Denver, 1977-79; pres. G. S. Omni Corp., Denver, 1979—; partner Arrowhead Golf Course; pres., dir. Valudyne, Inc. Chmn., Gammill Found. Mem. Fin. Analysts Fedn., Nat. Assn. Security Dealers, Denver Soc. Security Analysts, Nat. Energy Assn. (nat. chmn.). Clubs: Optimists, Elks. Contbr. articles to profl. jours. Home: 9770 W Frost Pl Littleton CO 80123 Office: 1670 Broadway #3000 Denver CO

GAMORAN, ABRAHAM CARMI, mgmt. cons.; b. Cin., Mar. 15, 1926; s. Emanuel and Mamie (Goldsmith) G.; B.B.A., U. Cin., 1948; M.B.A., N.Y. U., 1950; m. Ruth Kump, Apr. 14, 1973; children—Shirley, Mary, Samuel, Benjamin, Joseph. Mem. staff Harris, Kerr Forster & Co., N.Y.C., 1949-52, 56-67, supr. mgmt. advt. services div., 1962-67; mgmt. cons. Burke, Landsberg & Gerber, Balt., 1953-54; v.p. Helmsley-Spear, Inc., N.Y.C., 1969-79. U., Cornell U., Mich. State U., Okla. State U., Am. Hotel and Motel Assn., others. Recipient medal Wall St. Jour., 1948. C.P.A., N.Y. State. Mem. Am. Inst. C.P.A.'s, Internat. Assn. Hospitality Accts., Am. Soc. Appraisers (sr.), Nat. Restaurant Assn., N.Y. State Soc. C.P.A.'s, N.Y. Real Estate Bd. Democrat. Jewish. Author articles in field, also real estate rev. portfolios. Home: 92-30 56th Ave Elmhurst NY 11373 Office: 2100 Terminal Tower Cleveland OH 44113

GANE, LEON CUMMINGS, banker; b. Bridgeport, Conn., Apr. 23, 1937; s. Harold Jordan and Beatrice (Coughlin) G.; A.B., Hamilton Coll., 1958; m. Lucinda Baker, July 23, 1973; children—Harold Jordan, Rebecca Torrey. Retail credit supr. Texaco, Inc., N.Y.C., 1959-60; mgmt. trainee United Va. Bank, Richmond, 1961-65; gen. mgr. Garey Finney Co., C.P.A.'s, Richmond, 1965-66; v.p. Chase Manhattan Bank, N.Y.C., 1967—. Recipient Vol. of Yr. award N.Y.C., 1972. Clubs: Boothbay Harbor Yacht, Williams. Office: 1 Chase Manhattan Plaza New York NY 10015

GANS, JOHN DAVID, mfg. co. exec.; b. Milw., Apr. 10, 1925; s. Samuel and Ruth R. G.; B.A., Amherst Coll., 1949; M.S., Columbia U., 1951; m. Marcia Cummings, Oct. 17, 1954; children—Thomas, Timothy, Patrick. With Lever Bros., new product div. Continental Can Corp.; merchandising mgr. Rubbermaid Inc., Winchester, Va., v.p. mktg., now pres. comml. products div.; dir. F&M Nat. Bank. Bd. dirs. Winchester Meml. Hosp., Shenandoah Coll., Boys' Clubs Am. Served to 1st lt. USAAF, 1943-46. Decorated Air medal. Office: 3124 Valley Ave Winchester VA 22601

GANS, SAMUEL MYER, temporary employment service exec.; b. Phila., June 10, 1925; s. Arthur and Goldie (Goldhirsh) G.; grad. Peirce Jr. Coll., 1949; m. Ada Zuckerman, Aug. 1, 1948; children—Gary M., Jeffrey R. Pub. accountant, 1949-55; sales exec., 1955-58; franchise owner, pres. Manpower, Inc. Delaware Valley, Pennsauken, N.J., 1958—; franchise cons.; instr. motivation courses. Mem. exec. bd., v.p. United Fund of Camden County; active So. N.J. Devel. Council, Boy Scouts Am., Camden County Bicentennial Com., Score and Ace programs, Camden, YMCA, Allied Jewish Appeal; mem. N.J. Gov.'s Mgmt. Commn., 1971. Trustee Camden County Heart Assn., Camden County Mental Health Assn.; exec. bd. Big Bros. Assn. Camden County; pub. relations com. U.S. Savs. Bonds, Camden and Trenton. Served with USNR, 1943-46. Mem. Nat. Assn. Temporary Services (chpt. relations com. 1973), Nat. Soc. Pub. Accountants, Camden County C. of C., S. Jersey Pub. Relations Assn. (pres. 1967), Better Bus. Bur. Camden County, Adminstrv. Mgmt. Soc., N.J. Assn. Temporary Services (pres. 1970-72). Jewish (exec. bd. congregation). Clubs: Masons, Lions (pres. Camden 1972-73, Lion of Yr. 1977). Home: 2128 Glenview St Philadelphia PA 19149 Office: 3720 Marlton Pike Pennsauken NJ 08105

GANSON, CHARLES MACKAY, lawyer; b. New Rochelle, N.Y., Dec. 8, 1908; s. Adam Mackay and Maria (Bull) G.; B.A., Yale U., 1932; LL.B., Harvard Law Sch., 1935; m. Caroline S. Paine, June 22, 1933; children—John P., Charles Mackay, Caroline G. Partner, Taylor, Ganson & Perrin, Boston, 1935—; admitted to Mass. bar, 1936; clk., dir., treas. George Lawley & Son Corp., Boston, 1953-57; clk., dir. Fisher-Pierce Co., Boston, 1939-55, Sigma Instrument Inc., Boston, 1943-55; clk. Photon, Inc., Wilmington, Mass., 1948-73; clk., dir. Cambridge Acoustical Assn., 1959—, Chem. Products Corp., East Providence, 1955-71, Concord Control, Inc., Boston, 1956-71, Samson Cordage Works, 1957-78; dir. Gauley Coal Land Co., 1968—. Mem. fin. com. T/Weston, Mass., 1944-50; mem. Weston Bd. Selectmen, 1951-56, commr. trust funds, 1957, town forest com., 1957-75; hon. sec.-treas. Concord (Mass.) Acad., 1958; asso. trustee N.E. Cons. Music, Boston, 1970—. Mem. Am. Bar Assn., Middlesex Bar Assn., Boston Bar Assn., Newcomen Soc. Club: Somerset, Union, The Country. Home: 118 Chestnut St Weston MA 02193 Office: 100 Franklin St Boston MA 02110

GA NUNG, GEORGE WARREN, mfg. co. exec.; b. Boston, June 1, 1928; s. Grover Henry and Ingaborg June (Hansen) GaN.; student public schs., Medford, Mass.; m. Muriel Jean Osborne; children—Kenneth, Christine, Robin, Melissa, David, Mark. Store mgr. Brigham's Inc., Boston, 1949-52; salesman, apprentice Eastern Photo-Engravers, Waltham, Mass., 1952-54; retail salesman Barclay, Brown & Jones, Boston, 1954-57; v.p. sales Atlantic Service Co., Inc., Sussex, N.J., 1957—; tchr., speaker spl. tng. clinics, 1970—. Bd. dirs. The Way Home, Inc., 1979—; mem. speaker service Christian Boys Club, Girls Club. Served with USN, 1945-49. Mem. Meat Industry Supplies Equipment Assn., N.Y. Union-Industry Safety Com. Republican. Home: 156 Conestoga Trail Sparta NJ 07871 Office: 104 Rose Morrow Rd Sussex NJ 07461

GANZ, ARNOLD MICHAEL, fin. exec.; b. N.Y.C., Jan. 19, 1933; s. Abraham and Pauline (Sternlicht) G.; B.S. in Econs., U. Pa., 1954; m. Elinor Colker, Jan. 29, 1955; children—Charles, Susan, Amy. Vice pres. investments Del. Mgmt. Co., Inc., Phila., 1963-71; pres. Arnold Ganz Assos., Inc., North Miami, Fla., 1971—; dir. Safeguard Industries, Safeguard Bus. Systems, Inc., Lion Bros. Co. Inc. Trustee, Metatherapy Inst., 1975—. Chartered fin. analyst. Mem. Fin. Analysts Miami (past pres.); fellow Fin. Analysts Fedn. Libertarian. Jewish. Home: 18051 Biscayne Blvd Miami FL 33160 Office: 12550 Biscayne Blvd North Miami FL 33181

GANZ, LEONARD ROY, stationery and printing co. exec.; b. N.Y.C., May 12, 1943; s. Jack and Sadie (Rubin) G.; B.S. in Economics, Wharton Sch., U. Pa., 1965; postgrad. Temple U., 1965-66, City Coll. N.Y., 1967; m. Harriet Landsberg, Aug. 15, 1964; children—Steven Eric, Michael Scott, Jodi Lynn. Mgmt. trainee Equitable Life Assurance Soc. U.S., Phila., 1965-66; mgmt. trainee M. Landsberg Stationery Co. Inc., N.Y.C., 1967-73, dir. ops., 1973-75, treas., 1975—. Active Little League, 1976-77. Mem. Stationers Assn. N.Y. (v.p. 1977—), Wharton Grad. Sch. Club N.Y. Republican. Jewish. Club: Crest Hollow Country. Home: 6 Split Rail Ct Dix Hills NY 11746 Office: M Landsberg Stationery Co Inc 1 E 43d St New York City NY 10017

GARABEDIAN, ROSE ARAX, mfg. engring. co. exec.; b. Manchester, Eng., Aug. 10, 1916; d. John M. and Lucia (Lusrar) Broojian; student Seton Hall U., 1957-58, Fairleigh Dickinson U., 1959-60; m. Aug. 23, 1934; 1 son, Robert Michael. Exec. sec. to pres. Nat. Conveyors Co., Inc., Fairview, N.J., 1955; office mgr., mgr. systems replacements Nat. Conveyors Co., Inc., Fairview, 1958, officer of corp., 1976—. Seal chmn. Bergen County Tb and Health Assn., Fariview, 1944-51; mem. Bergen County Ednl. Planning Commn., 1949; trustee Fairview Pub. Library, 1947-63, pres. bd. trustees, 1953-56. Recipient citation Bergen County C. of C., 1974. Mem. Am. Soc. Profl. and Exec. Women, Nat. Congress of Parents and Tchrs. Home: 200 Winston Dr Apt 111 Cliffside Park NJ 07010

GARBACZ, R(ON) RAND, diversified industries exec.; b. Summit, N.J., Nov. 20, 1938; s. George and Violette (Derbeck) G.; B.S. with highest honors, Norwich U., 1961; M.B.A. in Fin., Amos Tuck Sch., Dartmouth Coll., 1963; children—David Jodok, Christina Brewster. With Cummins Engine Co., Columbus, Ind., 1965-70, asst. corp. controller, 1966-67, dir. product planning, 1968, dir. corp. planning, 1969, pres. K2 Corp., subs., Seattle, 1969-70; asst. to chief exec. officer, dir. corp. planning Gould Inc., Chgo., 1971, dep. to chief operating officer, 1972, v.p., gen. mgr. Sonotone Corp., subs., Elmsford, N.Y., 1973; v.p. corp. planning Pullman Inc., Chgo., 1974-77; exec. dir. corp. planning FMC Corp., Chgo., 1978—; dir. Borg Erikson Corp.; instr. econs. and fin. Ind. U., 1968-70; strategic lectr. U. Va. Bus. Sch., 1970—. Served to capt. CIC/CIA, U.S. Army, 1963-65. Republican. Presbyterian (deacon). Clubs: Saddle and Cycle, Chgo. Racquet, Chgo. Yacht, Econ.; Coral Beach and Tennis (Bermuda); Manor Vail (Vail, Colo.). Home: 1120 N Lake Shore Dr Chicago IL 60611 Office: FMC Corp 200 E Randolph Dr Chicago IL 60604

GARBARINO, ROBERT PAUL, lawyer; b. Wanaque, N.J., Oct. 6, 1929; s. Attilio and Teresa (Napello) G.; B.B.A. cum laude, St. Bonaventure U., 1951; J.D. summa cum laude, Villanova U., 1956; m. Joyce A. Sullivan, June 29, 1957; children—Lynn Marie, Lisa Clare, Mark, Steven. Admitted to Pa. bar, 1957; law clk. to chief judge U.S. Dist. Ct., Phila., 1956-57; asst. counsel Phila. Electric Co., 1957-61, asst. gen. counsel, 1961-62; partner firm Kania & Gabarino, and predecessor, Bala Cynwyd, Pa., 1962—. Trustee in bankruptcy Tele-Tronics Co.; right of way cons. Edison Electric Inst., 1960-62; lectr. appraisal, right of way, utilities, real estate seminars, 1959—; mem. community leaderships seminar Fels Inst. Local and State Govt., 1961—. Chmn. bd. consultors Villanova U. Law Sch.; chmn. pres.'s adv. council St. Bonaventure U. Served with USMCR, 1951-53. Recipient Most Oustanding Bus. Student award St. Bonaventure U., 1951, Faculty award Villanova Law Sch., 1956. Mem. Am., Fed., Fed. Power, Pa., Phila., Montgomery bar assns., Assn. of Army, Thomas Moore Soc., Order of Coif. Roman Catholic. Club: Lawyers (Phila.). Contbr. articles to profl. publs. Home: 302 Conestoga Rd Wayne PA 19087 Office: 2 Bala Cynwyd Plaza Bala Cynwyd PA 19004

GARBER, DALE JAY, retail co. exec.; b. Evanston, Ill., Oct. 1, 1951; s. Alan J. and Beatrice A. (Bilsky) G.; B.S. in Bus. Adminstrn., Washington U., St. Louis, 1972, M.B.A., 1973; m. Betty J. Kahn, June 17, 1973; 1 dau., Amy Elissa. Asst. to pres. Crawford Mgmt. Corp., Chgo., 1973-74, buyer sportswear, 1975-77, mdse. mgr., 1978-79, v.p., gen. mdse. mgr., 1979—. Recipient M.B.A. Scholar award Washington U., 1973. Mem. Assn. M.B.A. Execs., Beta Gamma Sigma. Office: 2509 W Devon Ave Chicago IL 60659

GARBIS, ANDREW NICHOLAS, shipping co. exec.; b. June 26, 1936; s. Nicholas A. and Mary V. Garbis; B.B.A., Baruch Coll., 1964; m. Dana Field Blauvelt, Apr. 9, 1960; children—Paul Andrew, Elizabeth Anne. With Transoceanic Marine Co., N.Y.C., 1956-65; v.p., treas. Seatrain Lines Inc., N.Y.C., 1965-74; with Cove Shipping Inc., N.Y.C., 1974—, corp. officer 1975—; v.p. and/or dir. parent and affiliated companies. Vice chmn. Lincoln Park Twp. (N.J.) Planning Bd., 1969-70; chmn. Citizens Planning Commn., Montville Twp. (N.J.), 1973-75; chmn. Montville (N.J.) Fin. Adv. Bd., 1976-80; mem. Morris County (N.J.) Bd. Public Transp., 1976-78. Served with AUS, 1959-61. Mem. Assn. Water Transp. Ofcls. Home: 6 York St

Montville NJ 07045 Office: Suite 1630 Wall St Plaza New York NY 10005

GARCIA, FELIX TAPAWAN, wholesale co. exec.; b. Bayan Luma, Imus, Cavite, Philippines, Apr. 14, 1952; s. Jose Peres and Bellamy (Tapawan) G.; A.A.S., Camden County Coll., 1972; B.A., Rutgers U., 1978. Mgr. dept. Two Guys Dept. Store, Cherry Hill, N.J., 1972-73; dir. planning and funding Movement for a Free Philippines, Washington, 1973-77, dir. youth, 1973-80; asst. to v.p. mfg. Congoleum Corp., Kearny, N.J., 1978-79; v.p. Far East ops. Locher Corp., Wharton, N.J., 1979—. Bd. dirs. Polynesian House, Inc., Cherry Hill, N.J. Mem. Am. Soc. Internat. Law, Am. Mgmt. Assn., Assn. Energy Engrs., U. Hapkido Fedn., World Tae Kwon Do Assn. (black belt). Office: Box 394 Route 1 Wharton NJ 07885

GARCIA, FERDINAND LAWRENCE, lawyer, educator; b. Tampa, Fla., Aug. 1, 1909; s. Ferdinand Garcia and Elena (Rodriguez) A.; B.S. cum laude, N.Y. U., 1938; LL.B., Bklyn. Law Sch., 1949, J.D., 1967; LL.M., Nat. U., 1951; M.A., Fordham U., 1967; m. Grace C. Coverley, Jan. 12, 1946. Admitted to N.Y. bar 1950; practiced in Washington, 1953-61; sr. analyst Hoit, Rose & Troster, N.Y.C., 1930-42; mgr. analytical dept. R.M. Horner & Co., N.Y.C., 1946-49; prof. fin. Southeastern U., 1950-56; asst. prof. Georgetown U., 1956-61; asst. prof. Fordham U., 1961-71, asso. prof., 1971-77, adj. asso. prof. Grad. Sch. Bus. Adminstrn., 1969-74, asso. prof. emeritus, 1977—, chmn. fin. dept., 1969-72. Served to lt. col. AUS, 1942-46, 50-53. Fellow Nat. Fedn. Fin. Analysts; mem. Am., N.Y. State bar assns., Am. Fin. Assn., Met. Econ. Assn., Am. Econ. Assn., Assn. for Social Econs., N.Y. Soc. Security Analysts, Nat. Press Club, Mil. Order World Wars, Phi Delta Phi, Pi Gamma Mu, Delta Sigma Pi, Beta Gamma Sigma. Republican. Roman Catholic. Editor: Ency. Bus. and Finance, 1949—; contbr. articles on finance to profl. jours. Home: Thornycroft Garth Rd Scarsdale NY 10583 Office: Fordham U Rose Hill Bronx NY 10458

GARCIA, GASPAR VINCENT, SR., fin. cons.; b. Carolina, P.R., Jan. 7, 1946; s. Vicente and Ana Celia (Bultron) G.; A.A., Bronx Community Coll., City U. N.Y., 1967, B.A. in Econs., Queens Coll., 1971; M.B.A., Fairleigh Dickinson U., 1977; D.C.S. (hon.), Am. U., 1979; m. Maria Aurora Rivera, June 26, 1965 (div. Nov. 1979); children—Gaspar Vincent, Jillann Jo, Marc Khyyam. Adminstrv. asst. N.Y.C. Manpower and Career Devel. Agency, 1967-68, spl. asst. to dep. dir., 1968-69; adminstrv. asso. N.Y.C. Model Cities Adminstrn., 1968; project dir. Econ. & Manpower Corp., N.Y.C., 1969-72; chief investigations N.Y.C. Commn. on Human Rights, 1972; v.p. Nat. Tng. Systems Corp., Hackensack, N.J., 1972-76; pres. BLS Corp., N.Y.C., 1976—; exec. v.p. Mobicentrics Inc.; of counsel to chmn. Assembly Ways and Means Com. N.Y. State Legis.; fin. planner LRF Developers, Inc.; project dir. HEW Equal Edn. Act Program, 1976-77. Scoutmaster Troop 243 Bronx council Boy Scouts Am., 1967-68; coach Rockville Centre (N.Y.) Soccer Club, 1973; chmn. bd. dirs. Alliance for Progress, Bronx, 1977; chmn. real estate com. N.Y.C. Nat. Hispanic Housing Coalition. Recipient Scholarship Incentive award N.Y. State, 1963. Mem. Am. Mgmt. Assn., Fairleigh Dickinson U. Ann. Exec. Update. Democrat. Roman Catholic. Club: Monroe, 75th Democratic. Home: 120 Benchley Pl Apt 27K Bronx NY 10475 Office: 384 E 149th St Suite 424 Bronx NY 10455

GARCIA, JUAN ENRIQUE, fin. cons.; b. Cuba, Aug. 11, 1942; came to U.S., 1962, naturalized, 1969; s. Julio R. and Maria J. (Rodriguez) G.; grad. in bus. Sch. Commerce, Havana, 1960; B.S. in Acctg., Rutgers U., 1973; m. Frances Sanchez, June 18, 1966; children—Juan Andres, David Roberto. Adminstrv. asst. internat. dept. Chase Manhattan Bank, N.Y.C., 1962-73; v.p. internat. div., head Latin Am., Southeast First Nat. Bank, Miami, Fla., 1974-78; head Latin Am. div. Barnett Bank, Miami, 1978-80; pres., owner Coninvex, Inc., fin. services, Miami, 1980—; dir. San Marino Assos. Served with USAR, 1962. Mem. Robert Morris Assos. Republican. Roman Catholic. Office: 777 Brickell Ave Suite 608 Miami FL 33131

GARCIA, MARTIN, JR., mortgage banker; b. Yuma, Ariz., Aug. 12, 1943; s. Martin and Senaida (Villa) G.; B.S., U. Ariz., 1965. Method-time-mgmt. cons. Trans Am. Co., Los Angeles, 1965-68; mortgage banker G.E. & Co., Yuma, 1975—; fin. dir. Dan Data Co.; notary public. Served with U.S. Army, 1968-75. Banking cert., Ariz. Mem. Am. Mortgage Brokers Assn., Nat. Assn. Fin. Cons., Mcht. Brokers Exchange (London). Home: 2185 Maple Ave Yuma AZ 85364 Office: PO Box 977 Yuma AZ 85364

GARCIA-RIBEYRO, HECTOR, oil exploration and prodn. co. exec.; b. Lima, Peru, May 15, 1941; came to U.S., 1976; s. Hector and Maria (Ayulo) G.R.; B.S., U. Agraria, Lima, 1962; m. Ada Maria Belgrano, Apr. 15, 1971; children—Hector, Micaela. Indsl. relations mgr. Ford Motor Co. Peru, Lima, 1966-70, Ford Motor of Chile, Santiago, 1971, Occidental Petroleum Corp. Peru, Lima, 1971-76; adminstrn. mgr. Latin Am. ops. Occidental Exploration & Prodn. Co., Bakersfield, 1976—. Mem. Am. Mgmt. Assn., Am. Soc. Personnel Adminstrvs., Peruvian-Calif. C. of C., Peruvian Indsl. Relations Assn. (dir.). Roman Catholic. Clubs: Nacional, Lima Polo and Hunt (Lima); Casino Nautico de Ancon. Home: 5108 Annadale Dr Bakersfield CA 93306 Office: 5000 Stockdale Hwy Bakersfield CA 93309

GARDA, ROBERT ALLEN, mgmt. cons.; b. Chgo., Feb. 10, 1939; s. Arthur and Joan (Duplessis) G.; B.S.E.E. magna cum laude, Duke U., 1961; M.B.A., Harvard U., 1963; m. Annie Lewis Johnston, June 24, 1961; children—Mary Lynn, Helen Christine, Robert Allen. Asst. to treas. Aladdin Industries, Inc., Nashville, 1963-64, acting gen. mgr. Australian subs., Sydney, 1964, asst. treas., 1964, product mgr. lamp products, 1964-65, prodn. supr., 1965-66, asst. to nat. sales mgr., 1966, mktg. mgr. consumer products, 1966-67; asso. McKinsey & Co., Inc., Cleve., 1967-72, prin., 1972-78, dir., 1978—, head indsl. mktg. practice, 1976—. Trustees, chmn. planning com. John Carroll U.; bd. visitors Duke Grad. Sch. Bus. Adminstrn.; mem. adv. council and long-range planning com. Cleve. Orch. Mem. Harvard Bus. Sch. Alumni Assn., Duke U. Alumni Assn., Phi Beta Kappa, Tau Beta Pi, Omicron Delta Kappa, Pi Mu Epsilon, Eta Kappa Nu. Clubs: Country, Useppa Island, South Seas Plantation, Harvard Bus. Sch. Office: 100 Erieview Plaza Cleveland OH 44114

GARDELL, CAROL SAYER, mktg. exec.; b. Trinidad, B.W.I., Jan. 17, 1951; d. Charles S. and Shirley A. (Anderson) Walline; student No. Va. Community Coll., 1970; m. Gary T. Gardell, June 5, 1971; 1 dau., Emily C. Head bookkeeping dept. Philipsborn, Inc., Fairfax, Va., 1970; mgr. Philipsborn T/A Beydas Petites, 1971-74, Frank R. Jelleff, Arlington, Va., 1975-78; retail mktg. dir. Chas. E. Smith Mgmt., Inc., Arlington, Va., 1978-80, dir. mktg., 1980—. Sec.-treas. bd. dirs. Crystal UnderGround Mchts. Assn., 1979—; sec. bd. dirs. Blakeview Homeowners Assn., 1979—; v.p. Mosby Woods Condominium Assn., 1977-78; tchr. St. Leo's Roman Catholic Ch., Fairfax, 1979—. Mem. Internat. Council Shopping Centers. Home: 9534 Blake Ln Fairfax VA 22031 Office: 1735 Jefferson Davis Hwy Arlington VA 22202

GARDINER, ROBERT MCPHERSON, investment banker; b. Denver, Nov. 17, 1922; s. Clement E. and Margaret (McPherson) G.; student Princeton, 1940-43; m. Janet Eaton, Dec. 6, 1947 (div. 1969); children—Margaret M., Peter E., Susan N., Thomas B.; m. 2d, Elizabeth Walker Valentine, May 1975. Analyst. A.M. Kidder & Co., N.Y.C., 1946-51; partner, syndicate mgr. Reynolds & Co. (now Dean Witter Reynolds Inc.), N.Y.C., 1951-57, mng. partner, 1957-74, chmn., chief exec. officer, 1974-79, pres., chief operating officer, 1979—; bd. govs. Am. Stock Exchange, 1956-57; dir. N.Y. Stock Exchange. Mem. Nat. Assn. Securites Dealers (chmn.), Securities Industry Assn. (chmn. securities processing com. 1973—), Investment Bankers Assn. Am. (pres. N.Y. group 1967). Clubs: Bankers, Madison Square Garden (N.Y.C.); Somerset Hills Golf (Bernardsville, N.J.); Ekwanok Country (Manchester, Vt.); Essex Hunt (Peapack, N.J.). Office: 130 Liberty St New York NY 10006*

GARDNER, ELLIS BENJAMIN, III, land devel. co. exec.; b. Buffalo, July 9, 1948; s. Ellis Benjamin and Mary Elizabeth (List) G., Jr.; A.B., Princeton U., 1970; m. Judith Anne Karlen, July 9, 1977; children—Ryan Benjamin, Abigail Anne. Vice pres. constrn. Hawk Mountain Corp., Pittsfield, Vt., 1972-76, prin., v.p. fin., 1976—; commr. Vt. Housing Fin. Agy., 1977—. Town chmn. Vt. Republican Com., 1976-78, county vice chmn., 1976-78, mem. state exec. com., 1978—, county chmn., 1978-79, state fin. chmn., 1979—; corporator Rutland (Vt.) Hosp.; active Nat. Ski Patrol System. Served to lt. USNR, 1970-71. Mem. Homebuilders Assn. Vt. (pres. Central Vt. 1974-76, state pres. 1976-79). Club: Pinehurst Country. Home: 23 Cricket Hill Killington VT 05701 Office: Hawk Mountain Corp Pittsfield VT 05762

GARDNER, FREDERICK, banker; b. Englewood, N.J., Sept. 11, 1942; s. Robert A. and Margaret M. (Murphy) McKee; B.A., Jersey City State Coll., 1970; M.S.C.S., Stevens Inst. Tech., 1976; M.B.A., Fairleigh Dickinson U., 1981—; m. Meredith Susan Mardy, Dec. 21, 1969. With First Jersey Nat. Bank, Jersey City, 1965—, project officer, 1973, asst. mgr., 1976, mgr. computer research and devel., 1978—. Served with USAF, 1960-64. Mem. IEEE Computer Soc., Assn. Computing Machinery. Office: 2 Montgomery St Jersey City NJ 07802

GARDNER, RALPH DAVID, advt. exec.; b. N.Y.C., Apr. 16, 1923; s. Benjamin and Myra (Berman) G.; diploma in journalism N.Y.U., 1942, diploma in mil. adminstrn. Colo. State Coll., 1943; m. Nellie Jaglom, Apr. 9, 1952; children—Ralph, John, Peter, James. With N.Y. Times, 1942-55, copy boy, city desk, fgn. corr., started internat. edit., Paris, 1949, bur. mgr. for Germany and Austria, Frankfurt, 1950, resigned 1955; pres. Ralph D. Gardner Advt., N.Y.C., 1955—; dir. Regina Internat. Corp., others; writer, book reviewer on mil. subjects, writer, lectr., bibliographer 19th century Am. lit.; Mary C. Richardson lectr. State U. N.Y., Geneseo, 1974; mem. faculty Georgetown U. Writers Conf., 1976, 80; Hess fellow U. Minn., 1979. Bd. dirs. Fresh Air Council, 1964-68; mem.-at-large Greater N.Y. council Boy Scouts Am., 1950-60; hon. exec. com. Nat. Citizens for Public Libraries. Served as newswriter with inf., AUS, World War II, ETO; field corr. Yank mag. Recipient award for lit. Horatio Alger Soc., 1964, 72; scroll Horatio Alger Awards Com., 1978. Mem. Manuscript Soc., Bibliog. Soc. Am., Friends of Princeton U. Library, Syracuse U. Library Assos. (hon.), P.E.N., Silurians, Nat. Book Critics Circle, Children's Lit. Assn., Brandeis U. Bibliophiles (hon.), Alpha Epsilon Pi. Clubs: Overseas Press of Am.; Frankfurt Press (Germany); Grolier, Baker Street Irregulars (N.Y.C.). Author: Horatio Alger, or The American Hero Era, 1964, reissued, 1978; Road to Success: The Bibliography of the Works of Horatio Alger, 1971, rev., 1978; Introduction to Silas Snobden's Office Boy, 1973; Introduction to Cast Upon the Breakers, 1974; History of Street and Smith, Publishers for Mass Entertainment in 19th Century America, 1980; also introduction to book. Contr. to newspapers and nat. mags.; host program Ralph Gardner's Bookshelf, WVNJ-N.Y., other radio stas. Home: 135 Central Park West New York NY 10023 Office: 745 Fifth Ave New York NY 10022

GARDNER, WARREN JOSEPH, JR., ins. exec.; b. Pitts., Sept. 21, 1951; s. Warren Joseph and Elsie Clair (Da'Rin) G.; B.S. in Mgmt., Pa. State U., 1975; m. Nancy Jean Antolovich. Mgr., Windy Hill Farms, Mayport, Pa., 1975-76; trainee counselor Fidelity Union Life Ins. Co., Dallas, 1976; supr. Bankers Life Ins. Co. Nebr., Pitts., 1977-78; gen. mgr. Andrew J. Bell, Inc., Pitts., 1978-79; account exec. spl. accounts, mgmt. tng. Sentry Ins., A Mut. Co. (SIAMCO), Pitts., 1979—; tchr. in field. Committeeman, Allegheny (Pa.) County Republican Com., 1978-80. Murrysville (Pa.) Women's Club scholar, 1969; Pa. State U. scholar, 1973-75; NIH fellow, 1975; named Sentry rep. of distinction, 1980. Mem. Nat. Assn. Life Underwriters, Ind. Ins. Agts. Assn., Am. Mgmt. Assn. Republican. Clubs: Lions (dir. Monroeville), Seneca Trail, Monroeville Racquet, Oakmont Yacht, Sentry Vice President's, Triangle. Home: PO Box 125 Trafford PA 15085 Office: 7 Parkway Center Suite 385 Pittsburgh PA 15220

GARDNER, WILLIAM ALBERT, cryogenic co. exec.; b. Allentown, Pa., Sept. 10, 1930; s. Alvin John and Dorothy May (Lutz) G.; B.S., Lehigh U., 1952; m. Mignon Roscher, Sept. 25, 1965; 1 dau., Lisette Mignon. Asst. chief scientist Air Products & Chems., Inc., Allentown, 1954-60; pres. Gardner Cryogenics Corp. (merged into Air Products & Chems., Inc.), Bethlehem, Pa., 1960-70; chmn. bd. Marvell Developers, Inc., Palm Beach, Fla., 1970-76; pres. Planning Devel. Assos., Inc., Palm Beach, 1976—; dir. Asset Counsels, Inc., Palm Beach. Served with Ordnance Corps, U.S. Army, 1953-54. Clubs: N.Y. Athletic, Masons, Shriners. Developer tech., machinery, equipment, and facilities for bulk liquefaction, transport and storage of helium. Home: 1211 Fairview Ln Riviera Beach FL 33404 Office: 1202 W 54th St West Palm Beach FL 33401

GAREY, DONALD LEE, pipeline exec.; b. Ft. Worth, Sept. 9, 1931; s. Leo James and Jessie (McNatt) G.; B.S. in Geol. Engring., Tex. A. and M. U., 1953; m. Elizabeth Patricia Martin, Aug. 1, 1953; children—Deborah Anne, Elizabeth Laird. Reservoir geologist Gulf Oil Corp., 1953-54, sr. geologist, 1956-65; v.p., mng. dir. Indsl. Devel. Corp. Lea County, Hobbs, N.Mex., 1965-72, pres., 1978—, also dir.; v.p., dir. Minerals, Inc., Hobbs, 1966-72, pres., dir., 1972—, chief exec. officer, 1978—; pres., dir. Llano, Inc., 1975—, chief exec. officer, 1978—; pres., chief exec. officer, dir. Pollution Control, Inc., 1969—; dir. Hobbs Indsl. Found. Corp., 1965-76, mgr., 1965-72; cons. geologist, geol. engr., Hobbs, 1965-72; dir. Estacado, Inc., 1980—. Chmn., Hobbs Manpower Devel. Tng. Adv. Com., 1965-72; mem. Hobbs Adv. Com. for Mental Health, 1965-67; mem. exec. bd. Conquistador council Boy Scouts Am., Hobbs, 1965-76; chmn. N.Mex. Mapping Adv. Com., 1968-69; vice chmn. N.Mex. Gov.'s Com. for Econ. Devel., 1968-70; mem. Hobbs adv. bd. Salvation Army, 1967-68, chmn., 1970-72. Served to 1st lt. USAF, 1954-56. Registered profl. engr., Tex. Mem. Am. Inst. Profl. Geologists, Am. Assn. Petroleum Geologists, Am. Inst. Mining, Metall. and Petroleum Engrs., N.Mex., Roswell geol. socs., N.Mex. Amigos. Club: Rotary. Home: 315 E Alto Dr Hobbs NM 88240 Office: Broadmoor Bldg PO Box 1320 Hobbs NM 88240

GARFAT, WILLIAM JAMES, investment co. exec.; b. Windsor, Ont., Can., Mar. 21, 1915; s. Frank Edward and Hazel (Lyons) G.; grad. Dutton (Ont.) High Sch.; m. Ada M. Brown, Sept. 28, 1936; 1 dau., Marlene. With Ralston Purina, York, Simcoe and Peel Counties, Ont., Can., 1937-72, dist. sales mgr., 1937-70, advt. and promotional mgr., 1970-72; pres. Adamar Investments, Barrie, Ont., 1980—; dir. numerous agrl. cos. Campaign chmn. Barrie United Way, 1980—. Mem. Canadian Agri-Mktg. Assn. Clubs: Lions (past pres.), Masons, Shriners. Home: Rural Route 5 Barrie ON L4M 4S7 Canada Office: Route 5 Holly Wood Estates Barrie ON L4M 4S7 Canada

GARFINKEL, JOSEPH, mdse. and mgmt. exec.; b. N.Y.C., Aug. 27, 1915; s. Hyman and Jennie (Levin) G.; B.S., U. Pa., 1942; postgrad. U. Cin., 1961; m. Ruth Helen Mauer, Dec. 29, 1946; children—Barbara Louise, Robert Michael. Exec. trainee, jr. exec. merchandising L. Bamberger & Co. div. R. H. Macy Co., Newark, 1946-57; buyer L. Bamberger and Co., 1952-57; mdse. mgr. Federated Dept. Stores, Cin., 1957-63; mgmt. cons., Springfield, Mass., 1963-64; gen. mgr. Rayco Div., B.F. Goodrich Co., Paramus, N.J., 1964-70, mdse. mgr., Akron, 1970-72, dir. mktg., 1972-73, gen. mdse. mgr., 1973-80; v.p. B-Dry System, Inc., 1980—. Served to capt. AUS, 1942-46. Mem. Springfield C. of C., Nat. Indsl. Conf. Bd., Internat. Franchise Assn., Am. Mktg. Assn. Club: B'nai B'rith. Home: 2520 Brice Rd Akron OH 44313 Office: 1341 Copley Rd Akron OH 44320

GARFINKEL, MORTON ELLSWORTH, coin co. exec.; b. Kane, Pa., May 19, 1938; s. Joseph and Eva (Gruskin) G.; B.B.A., Baruch Coll., 1960; m. Judith Haimowitz, June 9, 1962; children—Jill, Douglas. Sr. accountant, S.D. Leidesdorf & Co., N.Y.C., 1961-66; controller Delmonico Internat. Corp., Maspeth, N.Y., 1966-69; treas. Childcraft Edn. Corp., N.Y.C., 1969-72; chief exec. officer, treas., dir. First Coinvestors, Inc., Albertson, N.Y., 1972—. Served with N.Y. Army NG, 1960. Mem. Am. Inst. C.P.A.'s, N.Y. Soc. C.P.A.'s. Republican. Jewish. Clubs: Lions, K.P. (chancellor comdr. 1973). Home: 234 Birch Dr Roslyn NY 11576 Office: 200 I U Willets Rd Albertson NY 11507

GARLAND, DALE WAYNE, real estate co. exec.; b. Woodstock, Ill., Aug. 29, 1940; s. Harry George and Dorothea Emma (Witt) G.; B.S. in Acctg., U. Ill., 1965; M.B.A., Roosevelt U., 1977; m. Irene Ann Peterson, Aug. 29, 1964; children—Eric Bradley, Scott Michael, Dana LeAnn. Staff auditor Main La Frentz & Co., Chgo., 1966; mgr. corp. profit planning Abbott Labs., North Chicago, Ill., 1968-73; chief fin. officer, treas. Am. Admixtures, Chgo., 1973-78; chief fin. officer, treas. Tom Fannin & Assos., Phoenix, 1979—, also dir. Mem. council Spirit of Joy Luth. Ch., Mesa, Ariz., 1979—. Served with U.S. Army, 1966-68. C.P.A., Ill. Mem. Fin. Execs. Inst. Home: 1253 W Lobo St Mesa AZ 85202 Office: 3221 N 24th St Phoenix AZ 85016

GARLAND, DAVID WINGFIELD, mfg. co. exec.; b. Atlanta, Jan. 28, 1948; s. Charles Mayo and Myrtle Ivy (Wingfield) G.; B.A., U. Va., 1970; M.B.A., Pepperdine U., 1975; m. Judith Ann Sapp, May 2, 1970; 1 dau., Emily Wingfield. Bus. mgr. Martinsville (Va.) Concrete Products Inc., 1975-77, v.p., 1977—; part-time instr. dept. bus. Patrick Henry Community Coll., 1975—. Bd. dirs., treas. Piedmont Arts Assn., 1977-80; mem. adminstrv. bd. local Methodist ch., 1980—. Served with U.S. Army, 1970-75. Decorated Army Commendation medal. Mem. Va. Concrete Masonry Assn. (pres. 1978-80). Clubs: Kiwanis (dir. 1978-80), Martinsville-Henry County Tennis Assn. (dir. and treas. 1979—). Contbr. articles to profl. jours. Home: 1104 Jefferson Davis Rd Martinsville VA 24112 Office: PO Box 3351 Martinsville VA 24112

GARLAND, JOHN LOUIS, info. systems co. exec.; b. Seattle, Sept. 18, 1928; s. Homer Alanson and Anne Margaret (Jurich) G.; A.B., St. Edward's Sem., 1950; M.S. in L.S., Cath. U. Am., 1953; J.D., Georgetown U., 1960; m. Paula Mary Joy, Feb. 19, 1955; children—Anne Frances, John Louis, Thomas Patrick. Admitted to N.Y. State bar, 1972; reference analyst CIA, Washington, 1955-58; systems analyst, def. systems dept. Gen. Electric Co., Washington, 1958-61; With fed. systems div. IBM Corp., Bethesda, Md., 1961-64, mgr. corp. info. retrieval services, Armonk, N.Y., 1965-68, mgr. advanced systems techniques, 1968-70, mgr. text processing mktg., White Plains, N.Y., 1972-75, customer exec. briefing program, 1975-77, mgr. Library and Info. Center Programs, Armonk, 1978-79, mgr. div. data mgmt., Franklin Lakes, N.J., 1979—; lectr. computers and law. Pres., St. Patrick's Sch. Bd., 1968-70; active Little League, 1968-71. Served with USCGR, 1953-55. Mem. Am. Bar Assn., Spl. Libraries Assn., Phi Delta Phi. Democrat. Roman Catholic. Contbg. author: Information Handling: First Principles, 1963. Home: 151 Fox Hollow Rd Wyckoff NJ 07481 Office: Parson's Pond Dr Franklin Lakes NJ 07417

GARLINGHOUSE, B(RADLEY) KENT, med. products mfr.; b. N.Y.C., Aug. 1, 1941; s. F. Mark and Marjorie (Beard) G.; B.A. with honors, Wesleyan U., 1963; M.B.A., Harvard U., 1965; m. Susan Horan, June 29, 1963; children—Kim, Meg, Mark, Brad, Matthew. Analyst, Irwin Mgmt. Co., Columbus, Ind., 1965-70; pres., dir. M-C Industries, Inc., Topeka, 1971—; dir. Garlinghouse Co. Pres. bd. trustees Shawnee Country Day Sch. Home: 2001 Wildwood Ln Topeka KS 66611 Office: 3601 W 29th St Topeka KS 66614

GARLOUGH, WILLIAM GLENN, marketing exec.; b. Syracuse, N.Y., Mar. 27, 1924; s. Henry James and Gladys (Killam) G.; B.E.E., Clarkson Coll. Tech., 1949; m. Charlotte M. Tanzer, June 15, 1947; children—Jennifer, William, Robert. With Knowlton Bros., Watertown, N.Y., 1949-67, mgr. mfg. services, 1966-67; v.p. planning, equipment systems div. Vare Corp., Englewood Cliffs, N.J., 1967-69; mgr. mktg. Valley Mould div. Microdot Inc., Hubbard, Ohio, 1969-70; dir. corporate devel. Microdot Inc., Greenwich, Conn., 1970-73, v.p. corporate devel., 1973-76, v.p. adminstrn., 1976-77, v.p. corporate devel., 1977-78; v.p. corporate devel. Am. Bldg. Maintenance Industries, San Francisco, 1979—. Mem. citizens adv. com. to Watertown Bd. Edn., 1957. Bd. dirs. Watertown Community Chest, 1958-61. Served with USMCR, 1942-46. Mem. Am. Mgmt. Assn., Mensa, Am. Mktg. Assn., TAPPI, Assn. Corporate Growth, Lincoln League (pres. 1958), Am. Contract Bridge League (life master), Clarkson Alumni Assn. (Watertown sect. pres. 1955). Presbyn (ruling elder). Clubs: No. N.Y. Contract (pres. 1959), No. N.Y. Transp. Home: 2557 Via Verde Walnut Creek CA 94598 Office: 333 Fell St San Francisco CA 94102

GARMANN, KETIL, steamship co. exec.; b. Sogndal, Norway, Feb. 1, 1945; grad. Royal Norwegian Naval Acad., 1964, N. European Mgmt. Inst., 1974; m. Drude M. Dahl, Mar. 25, 1971; children—Christine Benedicte, Axel Johan. Engaged in S.S. industry, 1966—; exec. v.p. Odfjell Westfal-Larsen Tankers Inc., N.Y.C., 1975—. Served as officer Norwegian Navy, 1964-66. Office: 375 Park Ave New York NY 10152

GARNAND, GARY LEE, produce mktg. co. exec.; b. Twin Falls, Idaho, Oct. 28, 1946; s. Vay Ross and Maxine Sadie (Campbell) G.; B.S., U. Idaho, 1970; m. Lori Allgaier, June 28, 1975; 1 dau., Stacy. Asst. sales mgr. Chef Reddy Foods Co., Othello, Wash., 1970-71; pres. Garnand Mktg., Inc., Firth, Idaho, 1971—, also dir.; lectr. in field; dir. Garnand Produce Co. Pres., bd. dirs. Big Bros.-Big Sisters, Moses Lake, Wash., pres., 1980-81; mem. Grant County Community Action Council, 1978-80. Mem. Produce Mktg. Assn. (dir. ins. bd. 1975—, mem. fgn. trade com., ednl. com.), United Fresh Fruit and Vegetable Assn., Am. Mktg. Assn., Sigma Alpha Epsilon (dist. pres. 1974-76, 78-82). Republican. Lutheran. Clubs: Masons, Elks, Rotary (sec. Moses Lake chpt. 1980-81); Moses Lake Toastmasters (v.p.). Home: 559 Edgewater Ln Moses Lake WA 98837 Office: PO Box 217 Firth ID 83236

GARNER, OLLIE BELLE, contracting co. exec.; b. Waynesburg, Ky., Feb. 6, 1928; d. Rufus D. and Nettie B. (Hubble) Stonecypher; attended Rogers Bus. Coll., Somerset, Ky., 1947; m. Leo M. Garner, May 26, 1947. Sec., Pulaski County (Ky.) Extension Office, Somerset, 1948-50; bookkeeper W.C. Brass & Assos., Indpls., 1951-62; sec., bookkeeper Acme Constrn. Co., Indpls., 1963-65; co-owner v.p., dir. J&O Contractors, Inc., Indpls., 1965—. Mem. Network of Women in Bus., Nat. Assn. of Women in Constrn., Internat. Platform Assn., Early Am. Soc., Marion County Art League. Home: 7515 W Mooresville Rd Camby IN 46113 Office: 3906 W Washington St Indianapolis IN 46241

GARNER, ROBERT FRANK, JR., investment co. exec.; b. Toccoa, Ga., Oct. 19, 1918; s. Robert Frank and Ella Margaret (Cooper) G.; student N. Ga. Coll., 1936-38; B.S., U. Ga., 1938-40; postgrad. Duke and U. N.C., 1948-49, George Washington U., 1951, U. Omaha (Carnegie fellow), 1961-62, Armed Forces Staff Coll., 1956-57; m. Virginia Nell Bogue, May 30, 1942; children—Robert Frank, James R., Margaret J. Commd. 2 lt. U.S. Army, 1941; commd. U.S. Air Force, 1948, advanced through grades to lt. col.; staff and faculty Armed Forces Staff Coll., 1956-60; logistician, dir. research and devel. spl. weapons, budget and fin.; ret., 1960; v.p. bus. affairs Fla. bus. affairs Fla. Presbyn. Eckerd Coll., St. Petersburg, 1960-67; pres. Cee Bee Income Properties, 1971-77; sec.-treas., dir. R.J. Fin. Corp., 1967-76; sr. v.p., sec., treas. Raymond, James & Assos., St. Petersburg, 1967-76, dir. pub. relations and advt., 1976-79; pres. Planning Corp. Am., 1972-76; counselor Fla. Fed. Savs. & Loan, 1975; mem. Investment Mgmt. & Research, Inc., 1976—; ednl. bus. cons. Sec., Fla. Boxing Commn., 1940-42; com. chmn., scoutmaster Boy Scouts Am., Va. and Fla.; mem. Mayor's Goals Com.; mem. devel. bd. Fla. Presbyn. Coll., Clearwater Christian Coll., 1968-71; mem. Pinellas Schs. Study Group. 1940-60. Decorated Bronze Star, Commendation medal; recipient Key to City, Norfolk, Va. and Toccoa, Ga. Mem. Am. Def. Preparedness Assn. (charter pres. Fla. chpt., dir. Dixie chpt.), C. of C., Symphony Soc. (v.p., pres.-elect, dir. 1964-69), St. Petersburg Civic Assn. (dir.), Lambda Chi Alpha. Republican. Baptist (deacon). Clubs: Masons, Kiwanis (pres. 1968); Toastmasters (Norfolk, Va. and St. Petersburg). Home: 6600 Pinellas Point Dr S Saint Petersburg FL 33712 Office: 6090 Central Ave Saint Petersburg FL 33707

GARNEY, CHARLES ARTHUR, constrn. exec.; b. Kansas City, Mo., Nov. 27, 1931; s. Arthur and Reba LaFaun (Wheeler) G.; B.S., U. Kans., 1953; grad. Colo. Sch. Banking, 1977; m. Patricia Ann Sargent, Dec. 31, 1966; children—Jane, Cathy, Anne, Lynda, Lisa, Julie. Partner, Garney Plumbing Co., Kansas City, Mo., 1956-61; founder, pres., chmn. Garney Cos., Inc., Kansas City, Mo., 1962—; dir. United Mo. Bancshares, Kansas City, Nat. Fidelity Life Ins. Co. Trustee, Ottawa U., 1975-77; treas. Jail Bond Drive, 1975; chmn. Clay County Devel. Commn., 1976-77; bd. dirs. Kansas City PUSH, 1978—; mem. Civic Council Greater Kansas City, Mayor's Corps of Progress; adviser YMCA; bd. dirs. Citizens Assn.; past pres. Claymont Homeowners Assn.; mem. Shang-ri-la Condominium Owners Assn. Served with USNR, 1953-56. Recipient service to youth award YMCA, 1976; Look North award, 1980. Mem. Heavy Constructors Assn. (sec.-treas., v.p., 1978-80, pres. 1980—, trustee), Young Pres.'s Orgn. (officer 1976-77, dir. internat. bd., conf. chmn. 1977, chmn. exec. com. 1979-80), Associated Plumbing Contractors (dir. Kansas City chpt. 1969, treas. 1973), Builders Assn. (labor com. 1971), Home Builders Assn., Mech. Contractors Assn., Kansas City C. of C. (econ. council), Sigma Chi. Clubs: Kansas City, Old Pike Country. Home: 507 NW 43rd St Kansas City MO 64116 Office: 1331 NW Vivion Rd Kansas City MO 64118

GAROFALO, ROY LAWRENCE, retail co. exec.; b. N.Y.C., Mar. 11, 1932; s. John S. and Angelina A. (Taibi) G.; B.A. in Econs., CCNY, 1953; m. Mary T. Minch, June 4, 1962; children—Douglas John, Cressida Anne, Gabrielle. Vice pres. research Clark, Dodge & Co., Inc., N.Y.C., 1956-69; v.p. investments E. F. Hutton & Co., Inc., N.Y.C., 1969-74, Kuhn, Loeb & Co., N.Y.C., 1974-78; v.p. investor relations F. W. Woolworth Co., N.Y.C., 1978—. Served with USNR, 1953-56. Mem. Fin. Execs. Inst., Chartered Fin. Analysts, N.Y. Soc. Security Analysts, Nat. Investor Relations Inst. Roman Catholic. Club: Alfa Romeo Owners. Home: 169 Stanwich St Greenwich CT 06830 Office: 233 Broadway New York NY 10279

GAROUFALIS, ANGELO GEORGE, hosp. sales co. exec.; b. Chgo., 1929; s. Leander and Mary (Criticos) G.; B.A., U. Chgo., 1951, M.B.A., 1956; m. Olga Visias, Oct. 29, 1960. Mgr., A.W. Fruh & Co., Chgo., 1961-63, also dir.; account exec. Uarco Inc., Chgo., 1964-67, dist. sales mgr., 1967—, div. hosp. sales mgr., 1975-78, nat. health care mktg. mgr., 1978—; cons. in field. Officer, bd. dirs. Ravenswood Med. Center; div. chmn. bd. N.W. Chgo., U. Chgo. Fund campaign; mem. adv. council Ravenswood Mental Health; chmn. selecting chief exec. nominee, sales, mktg. exec. award, Chgo. Mem. Chgo. Council Fgn. Relations, Sales and Mktg. Execs. Assn. (dir.). Clubs: Fullerton Tennis, Lake Shore Racquet. Contbr. research articles. Home: 200 E Delaware St Chicago IL 60611 Office: 1 N Wacker Chicago IL 60606

GARRETH, RALPH HIBBERT, mfg. co. exec.; b. Abington, Pa., July 15, 1943; s. Ralph and Frances Edith (Morgan) G.; B.S., U. Md., 1966; m. Jacoline M. Bickerstaff, Jan. 28, 1967; children—Jacoline Melissa, Alison Christine. With aerospace div. SPS Technologies Co., and predecessor, 1965—, nat. sales mgr., then dir. mktg., 1975-79, pres. Hallowell div., Hatfield, Pa., 1979—; dir. Remlu Savs. and Loan Assn., N. Hills, Pa. Served with USAF, 1965-66, USAR, 1967-69. Mem. Am. Mgmt. Assn., Am. Soc. Tool and Mfg. Engrs., Northampton Residents Assn., Alpha Tau Omega. Republican. Episcopalian. Clubs: Shriners, Northampton Valley Country. Home: 45 Surrey Dr Churchville PA 18966 Office: Township Line Rd Hatfield PA 19440

GARRETSON, RICHARD C., banker; b. Cleve., Apr. 2, 1923; student Yale, 1943-47; postgrad. U. Chgo., Case Western Res. U.; m. Priscilla; children—Richard C., Emily. With Soc. Nat. Bank Cleve., 1947—, v.p., 1960-68, sr. v.p., 1968-71, exec. v.p., 1971—, also dir.; dir. Farmers Nat. Bank & Trust Co. Ashtabula, Ohio; sr. v.p. Society Corp. Trustee Health Hill Hosp., Home for Aged Women. Served to lt. F.A., AUS, World War II; PTO. Mem. Robert Morris Assos. (past pres.). Home: Shaker Heights OH 44120 Office: 127 Public Sq Cleveland OH 44114

GARRETT, DAVID CLYDE, JR., airline exec.; b. Norris, S.C., July 6, 1922; s. David Clyde and Mary H. Garrett; B.A., Furman U., 1942; M.S., Ga. Inst. Tech., 1955; m. Lu Thomasson, Sept. 11, 1947; children—David, Virginia, Charles. With Delta Air Lines, Inc., Atlanta, 1946—, pres., 1971—, also dir.; dir. Travelers Corp. Served with USAAF, 1943-46. Mem. Soc. Automotive Engrs. Office: Delta Air Lines Atlanta Airport Atlanta GA 30320*

GARRETT, DENIECE SAUNDERS, fin. planning cons.; b. Washington, Pa., May 22, 1951; d. Donald Howard Saunders and Margaret Marie Saunders Marsh; student Kent State U., 1968-70; B.A. in Communications, Howard U., 1973; m. Mark Douglas Garrett, June 22, 1979. News broadcaster Howard U. Radio, Washington, 1973; editor/writer D.C. SHARE Computer Center, Washington. 1974-76; sr. fin. planning cons. Garrett & Assos. Inc., Suitland, Md., 1976—, also v.p. Mem. Nat. Assn. Security Dealers, Ind. Fin. Planners Assn., Nat. Assn. Female Execs., Howard U. Alumni Assn. Office: PO Box 9271 Suitland MD 20023

GARRETT, DONALD LYNN, pub. utilities co. exec.; b. Crawfordsville, Ind., Nov. 30, 1948; s. Harry T. and Verna (Spragg) G.; B.S. in Civil Engring., Purdue U., 1971; postgrad. U. Tenn.; m. Corliss J. Ellis, June 21, 1969; children—Todd, Ryan. Civil engr. TVA, Knoxville, Tenn., 1971-74, personnel officer engring. design div., 1974-76, tng. officer, 1976-77, supr. manpower mgmt. and devel., 1977, supr. civil engring. and design br., staff services, 1977—; lectr. U. Tenn., 1976, 77, 78. Key man leader United Way, Knoxville, 1976—. Registered profl. engr. Tenn. Mem. ASCE (mem. nat. subcom. on tech. curricula and accreditation 1978—, sec.-treas. 1979, v.p. 1980, pres. 1981, nat. coordinator energy initiative program 1980—), Am. Soc. Tng. and Devel., Nat. Mgmt. Assn. (membership chmn. Knoxville br. 1976, mgmt. devel. com. 1977, youth program chmn. 1979, awards com. 1981), Assn. Cooperatin in Engring. (mem. coordinating com. on energy 1980—). Home: 7113 Harrell Rd Knoxville TN 37921 Office: TVA 400 Commerce Ave Knoxville TN 37902

GARRETT, JOHN HUDSON, ins. and stock broker; b. Cuthbert, Ga., Apr. 17, 1952; s. George Wilbur and Margaret Maude (Hudson) G.; B.S., Columbus Coll., 1974; m. Deborah Anne Giglio, Mar. 22, 1975. Tennis coach Brookstone Sch., Columbus, Ga., 1974-76; broker Mixon, Rawls & Assos., Columbus, 1976-79; v.p. Family Savs. & Securities, Inc., Columbus, 1978-79, Mixon, Rawls & Assos.; broker Robinson-Humphrey Co., Inc., 1979—. Bd. dirs. Columbus Heart Assn. Named to Million Dollar Round Table, 1978-79. Mem. Ga., Nat. assns. life underwriters, Columbus Jaycees (dir.), Nat. Life Vt. Pres.'s Club, Life Ins. Leaders Ga. Baptist. Clubs: Green Island Country (dir.). Home: 6900 Antler Dr Columbus GA 31904 Office: Rankin Sq 1017 First Ave Columbus GA 31901

GARRETT, PAULINE, advt. exec.; b. Muscatine, Iowa, July 5, 1933; B.S., U. Iowa, 1954. Personnel mgr. Musical Masterpieces div. Crowell Collier, N.Y.C., 1955-57; placement mgr. Coll. Grad. Agy., N.Y.C., 1957-60; personnel, office mgr. Seafarer Fiberglass Yachts, N.Y.C., 1960-61; account exec. Century Advt., N.Y.C., 1961-65, Edward Weiss Advt., N.Y.C., 1965-66; pres. Tempo Advt., Inc. (merged with World Wide Advt. Agy., Inc., 1976), N.Y.C., 1966-76, regional dir. World Wide Advt. Agy., Inc. (acquired as separate div. by J. Walter Thompson 1980), N.Y.C., 1976—. Home: 140 Riverside Dr New York NY 10024 Office: World Wide Advt 551 Fifth Ave New York NY 10176

GARRETT, ROBERT, real estate corp. exec.; b. Morristown, N.J., Feb. 27, 1937; s. Harrison and Grace Dodge (Rea) G.; A.B., Princeton U., 1959; M.B.A., Harvard U., 1965; m. Jacqueline E. Marlas, July 10, 1965; children—Robert, Johnson. Vice pres. Smith, Barney & Co., N.Y.C., 1965-69, Robert Garrett & Sons, N.Y.C., Balt., 1969-71; 1st v.p. Smith Barney, Harris Upham & Co., N.Y.C., 1972-78; sr. v.p. Smith, Barney Real Estate Corp., N.Y.C., 1978—; exec. v.p. Security Capital Corp., N.Y.C., 1979—; dir. Tex. Air Corp., N.Y. Airlines, Inc., Mickelberry Corp., A.S. Abell Co., Nat. Ry. Publ. Co. Treas., Near East Found., 1976—. Served with AUS, 1959-63. Republican. Episcopalian. Clubs: University of N.Y.; Nantucket Yacht. Home: 941 Park Ave New York NY 10028 Office: Smith Barney Real Estate Corp 1345 Ave of Americas New York NY 10105

GARRETT, SAMUEL JUDSON, wholesale steel and hardware co. exec.; b. Clover, Va., July 17, 1930; s. Harry Richard and Kate (Williams) G.; B.S., Pa. Mil. Coll., 1953; m. Ruth Ann Worrilow, July 31, 1954; children—Cynthia, Andrew, Courtenay. Commd. 2d. lt. U.S. Army, 1953, advanced through grades to lt. col., 1968, asst. prof. mil. sci. U. Tex., Austin, 1957-60, office of dep. chief staff personnel U.S. Army Continental Army Command, Ft. Monroe, Va., 1962-65, advisor to Turkish Army Gen. Staff, Ankara, 1965-67, dir. storage U.S. Army Field Depot, Qui Nhon, Vietnam, 1967-68, chief supply div., dep. chief staff logistics Mil. Dist. Washington, 1968-69, post logistics officer Ft. Myer, Va., 1969-70, insp. gen. U.S. Army Materiel Command, Washington, 1970-73, ret., 1973; gen. supt. J.B. Kendall Co., Washington, 1973—. Active Lee Dist. Athletic Assn., Alexandria, Va., 1969-73, football commr., 1973. Decorated Legion Merit, Bronze Star, Air medal, Expert Infantryman's Badge. Mem. Ret. Officers Assn., Twin Centuries Mixed Bowling League (pres.). Republican. Presbyterian (elder). Home: 5444 Broadmoor St Alexandria VA 22310 Office: JB Kendall Co 2160 Queens Chapel Rd NE Washington DC 20018

GARRETTO, LEONARD ANTHONY, JR., ins. co. exec.; b. N.Y.C., Apr. 13, 1925; s. Leonard and Evenia (Egidio) G.; B.E.E., Manhattan Coll., 1951; m. Theresa Cennamo, Aug. 6, 1949; children—Deborah, Mark, Michael, Paula, David. Engr., Gen. Precision Lab. Inc., Pleasantville, N.Y., 1951-53, project adminstr., 1953-55, project mgr., 1955-58, subcontracts mgr., 1958-59; adminstrv. engr. Sperry Systems Mgmt. div. Sperry Rand Corp., Great Neck, N.Y., 1959-61, mgmt. services adminstr., 1961-63, mgmt. services mgr., 1963-65, fin. planning mgr., 1965-66, planning mgr., 1966-68, dir. adminstrn., 1968; agt. First Investors Corp., N.Y.C., 1966-69, dist. mgr., 1969-70; gen. mgr. David Gracer Co., N.Y.C., 1970-72; v.p. regional sales Somerset Capital Corp., N.Y.C., 1972-75; regional dir. Wis. Nat. Life Ins. Co., Oshkosh, 1975-77, regional sales v.p., Englewood Cliffs, N.J., 1977—. Served with U.S. Army, 1943-45; ETO. Mem. Am. Soc. Notaries, Nat. Assn. Life Underwriters, Nat. Assn. Securities Dealers. Democrat. Roman Catholic. Home: 39 Rose Hill Ave New Rochelle NY 10804 Office: 375 Sylvan Ave Englewood Cliffs NJ 07632

GARRIS, MICHAEL DENNIS, bank exec.; b. Oelwein, Iowa, July 30, 1943; s. Peter Paul and Maree Bernice (South) G.; degree in advanced acctg., LaSalle Extension U., 1975; m. Kathleen Fletcher, Feb. 3, 1968; children—Michelle, Troy, Jennifer, Erik. Insp. Retail Credit Corp., Iowa City, Iowa, 1965-70; field auditor White & White Inc., Winfield, Iowa, 1970-75; with Peoples State Bank, Winfield, 1975—, cashier, 1977—, exec. v.p., 1979—, sec., bd.; sec., treas., bd. Peoples Holding Corp. Served to 1st lt. Army N.G., 1966-73. Roman Catholic. Club: Lions (pres., 1977, 100 pres. award, 1977). Mem. Iowa Allstate Basketball team, 1961. Home: 103 N Clark St Winfield IA 52659 Office: 102 S Locust St Winfield IA 52659

GARRISON, JAMES HAMILTON, supermarket chain exec.; b. Fremont, Nebr., Feb. 6, 1936; s. Merion Weston and Ethel Pearl (Burt) G.; student public schs., also home study courses; m. Betty June Harris, June 9, 1957; children—James David, Samuel Luke, Angela Louise. From apprentice meat cutter to meat field supr. Am. Community Stores, Omaha, 1953-73; field supr., then dir. meat ops. Cullum Cos. (Tom Thumb Supermarkets), Dallas, 1973-78, v.p., 1978—. Bd. dirs. Goodwill Industries Central Nebr., 1967-68; pres. Grand Island (Nebr.) Jaycees, 1967; v.p., nat. dir. Ind. Jaycees, 1968. Served with USAR, 1957, 62. Recipient various Jaycee awards. Republican. Baptist. Home: 1721 Westridge St Plano TX 75075 Office: 14303 Inwood Rd Dallas TX 75234

GARRISON, MARIAN P., strategic planning analyst; b. Moline, Ill., Nov. 5, 1946; d. Albert Frank and Marian Louise (Hedstrom) G.; B.A., Marycrest Coll., Davenport, Iowa, 1968; postgrad. Pa. State U., 1974-77; M.B.A., Temple U., 1981. Asst. dir. Syracuse (N.Y.) office Nat. Dairy Council, 1968-72, nutrition cons. Phila. office, 1972-74; dir. mktg. S. Jersey (N.J.) C. of C., 1975-76; coordinator spl. projects Campbell Soup Co., Camden, N.J., 1976-78, sr. strategic planning analyst, 1978-81, mgr. strategic planning, 1981—. Scoutleader, Girl Scouts Am., 1970-72, adv. council Explorer Scouts, 1975-77. Mem. N.Am. Soc. Corp. Planning, Am. Fin. Assn., Assn. M.B.A. Execs., Home Economists in Bus. (past pres., adv. Phila. chpt.; Nat. Communications award 1978). Author nutrition and consumer info. materials for TV, schs. Home: 928 Meadowbrook Dr Huntingdon Valley PA 19006 Office: Campbell Pl Camden NJ 08101

GARRISON, MARION AMES, mech. engr., oil tool co. exec.; b. Indpls., July 20, 1907; s. Charles C. and Ella J. (Hilligoss) G.; M.E., U. So. Calif., 1929; m. Kathleen Goode, Aug. 23, 1933; 1 dau., Ann. Pvt. practice bottom hole oil tool design, Los Angeles, 1950-55; chief engr. Eastman Oil Well Survey Co., Denver, 1955-57; pres., chief engr. Empire Oil Tool Co., Denver, 1957-79, Williamsburg, Va., 1979—. Mem. ASME, Delta Sigma Rho, Sigma Phi Epsilon. Inventor linkage type power steering for automobiles and trucks, tire pressure warning signal, down-hole fluid powered drilling motor for oil and gas wells. Office: 104 Crownpoint Rd Williamsburg VA 23185

GARRO, BARBARA, free-lance bus. writer; b. Camden, N.J., Feb. 3, 1943; d. Dominic and Mildred Barbara (Homiak) Garro; student Phila. Art Mus., 1963-64; divorced; children—Victoria Lynne, Karen Marie. Adminstrv. asst. to v.p. sales Publicker's, Phila., 1961-62; paralegal asst. law firms in Phila., 1962-67; owner news agy., Phila., 1967-72; ins. adminstr. SGL Industries, Inc., Haddonfield, N.J., 1972-79; mem. editorial adv. panel and benefit bd. Bus. Ins., 1978—; tax cons., 1974—; freelance writer; corp. ins. adminstr./tax analyst Safeguard Industries, Inc., King of Prussia, Pa. Exec. council, regional bd. dirs. Single Parents Soc., 1974-75; exec. bd. A.S. Jenks Pub. Sch., Phila., 1967; religious educator Our Lady of Perpetual Help Roman Cath. Ch., Maple Shade, N.J., 1974-75, Mother of Divine Providence Parish, King of Prussia, 1974—. Home: A-601 Valley View 251 W DeKalb Pike King of Prussia PA 19406 Office: 630 Park Ave King of Prussia PA 19406

GARRO, JAMES FREDERICK, mgmt. cons.; b. Hartford, Conn., May 13, 1943; s. S. Fred and Mabel (Cook) G.; B.B.A., U. Conn., 1966, M.B.A., 1972; m. Claudia Elizabeth Tolles, Sept. 6, 1969; children—Nicole Melissa, Danielle Rebecca, Jonelle Patricia. Bank officer 1st Nat. City Bank, N.Y.C., 1969-70; mgr. personnel planning Xerox Edn. Group, Stamford, Conn., 1970-71; mgr. exec. compensation Xerox Corp., Stamford, 1972-73; corp. dir. compensation and benefits Bendix Corp., Southfield, Mich., 1973-75; pres. J.F. Garro & Co. Inc., La Jolla, Calif., 1975-77 (firm acquired by Wyatt Co. 1977), v.p. and nat. practice dir. exec. compensation Wyatt Co., 1977—. Recipient advanced degrees and designation Am. Coll. C.L.U.'s. Mem. Am. Compensation Assn. (dir., past pres. Eastern region), Am. Pension Conf. Clubs: Torrey, City of San Diego, Lomas Santa Fe Country. Office: 3366 N Torrey Pines Ct Suite 220 La Jolla CA 92037

GARSON, WILLIAM, banker, writer; b. Hammond, Ind., May 1, 1917; s. John Soterus and Helen Glenn (McKennan) G.; B.A., Milton Coll., 1939; postgrad. Grad. Sch. Bank Mktg., Northwestern U., 1968; m. Florence Rebecca Penstone, Sept. 21, 1974; children (by previous marriage)—Geneva (Mrs. Robert LaMay), Gary William. Mng. editor, columnist Rockford (Ill.) Register-Republic, 1952-55; pub. relations dir. Sundstrand Corp., Rockford, 1956-65; community info. officer Rockford C. of C., 1965-66; mktg. officer City Nat. Bank & Trust Co. Rockford, from 1966, now dir. spl. services, pub. relations cons. Imagination Plus, Rockford, 1955-66. Bd. dirs. Tb Assn., Heart Assn., A.R.C., 1952-54; Recipient George Washington Honor medal Freedoms Found., 1966. Mem. Am. Inter-Profl. Inst., Rockford C. of C. (Community Service award 1952), Am. Inst. Banking, Bank Mktg. Assn., Internat. Assn. Bus. Communicators, Internat. Word Processing Assn., Rockford Hist. Soc. Methodist. Author: Daddy Wore An Apron, 1974; Brother Earth, 1975; The Knight on Broadway, 1978; co-author: Political Primer, 1960; We The People..., 1976. Home: 3516 Meadow Ln Rockford IL 61107 Office: Box 3126 Rockford IL 61106

GARTENBERG, SEYMOUR LEE, rec. co. exec.; b. N.Y.C., May 27, 1931; s. Morris and Anna (Banner) G.; B.B.A. cum laude, Coll. City N.Y., 1952; m. Anna Stassi, Feb. 18, 1956; children—Leslie, Karen, Mark. Asst. controller Finlay Straus, Inc., N.Y.C., 1950-56; controller Tappin's, Inc., Newark, 1956; exec. v.p. Columbia House div. CBS, N.Y.C., 1956-73, pres. CBS Toys div., Cranbury, N.J., 1973-78; sr. v.p. CBS/Records Group, N.Y.C., 1978—. Mem. Mill Island Civic Assn. Mem. Nat. Assn. Accountants, Am. Mgmt. Assn. Office: CBS/Records Group 51 W 52 St New York NY 10019

GARTHWAIT, CLAYBORN ATLAS, III, chem. engr., mfg. co. exec.; b. Dayton, Ohio, Jan. 8, 1942; s. Clayborn Atlas and Bessie Irene (Burkett) G.; A.S. in Chem. Engring. Tech., U. Dayton, 1964, B.S. in Chem. Engring., 1977; m. Irene H. Levine, Feb. 1, 1970; 1 stepdau., Victoria Levine Belibeau. Jr. scientist U.S. Air Force, Wright Patterson AFB, Ohio, 1964-66; self-employed, Dayton, Ohio, 1966-68; chem. engring. technician Monsanto Research Corp., Dayton, 1968-77, process chem. engr., 1977—, mgr. new mfg. process line, cons. in specialized nuclear fabricated products; sr. engr. Martin Marietta Aerospace Corp., Denver, 1981—. Mem. Am. Inst. Chem. Engring., AAAS, Denver Mgmt. Assn., Epsilon Delta Tau. Clubs: Dayton Area Chess and Bridge; Edelweiss German (Englewood, Ohio). Inventor in field. Home: 1568 Nome St Apt 422 Aurora CO 80010 Office: Martin Marietta Aerospace Corp Denver Div Denver CO 80201

GARTNER, JOSEPH, economist; b. Vienna, June 2, 1929; came to U.S., 1940, naturalized, 1947; s. Israel and Molly (Landau) G.; A.A.A., L.I. Agrl. and Tech. Inst., 1951; B.Sc., U. Conn., 1954; M.Sc., U. N.H., 1955; Ph.D., Iowa State U., 1961; m. Judith Greenberg, May 30, 1956; children—Stanley, David, Barbara, Jay, Gita, Leah. Asso. prof. Kans. State U., 1961-63; research dir. Center for Consumer Affairs, vis. asso. prof. econs. U. Wis., Milw., 1963-66; research dir., asso. prof. Sch. of Mgmt., Boston Coll., 1966-79; asst. sec. Exec. Office of Econ. Affairs, State of Mass., Boston, 1979—. Chmn. planning bd. Town of Brookline (Mass.); chmn. cost/benefits adv. com. Coolidge Corner Community Corp.; bd. dirs. New Perspective Sch. Recipient Drummey award Boston Coll., 1969. Mem. Am. Econ. Assn., Am. Planning Assn., Sales and Mktg. Execs. Internat. Home: 66 Summit Ave Brookline MA 02146 Office: Exec Office of Econ Affairs State House Room 212 Boston MA 02133

GARTNER, MICHAEL GAY, newspaper editor; b. Des Moines, Oct. 25, 1938; s. Carl David and Mary Marguerite (Gay) G.; B.A., Carleton Coll., 1960; J.D., N.Y. U., 1969; m. Barbara Jeanne McCoy, May 25, 1968; children—Melissa, Christopher, Michael. Admitted to N.Y. bar, Iowa bar; with Wall St Jour., N.Y.C., 1960-74, page one editor, 1970-74. Exec. editor Des Moines Register and Tribune, 1974-76, editor, 1976—, v.p., 1975-76, exec. v.p., 1977-78, pres., chief operating officer, 1978—, also dir.; dir. Comml. Printing, Inc. Bd. dirs., mem. exec. com. Simpson Coll.; bd. dirs. Living History Farm Mus., Des Moines Ballet Assn. Mem. Assn. Bar City N.Y., Am. Bar Assn., Iowa Bar Assn., Des Moines C. of C. (dir.), Central Iowa Health Assn.

(vice-chmn.), Am. Press Inst. (dir.), Am. Soc. Newspaper Editors (dir.), Sigma Delta Chi. Clubs: Embassy, Wakonda, Des Moines (Des Moines), Garden of Gods (Colorado Springs, Colo). National syndicated columnist. Home: 5315 Waterbury Rd Des Moines IA 50312 Office: 715 Locust St Des Moines IA 50304

GARTON, CHARLES EUGENE, real estate broker and developer; b. Jane Lew, W.Va., Dec. 25, 1921; s. George Mertz and Christina Catherine (Mason) G.; student U. Okla., 1945; m. Opal Mae Dunham, May 3, 1941; children—Stephen S., Deborah Garton Gibson, Melissa Garton Wilson, Charles Gregory. Pres., gen. mgr. Garton Real Estate, Inc., Weston, W.Va., 1962—; pres. Garton Real Estate & Constrn., Inc., Weston, 1978—, GCH Devel., Inc., Weston, 1973—. Served with USNR, 1944-46. Mem. W.Va. Assn. Realtors, Lewis County C. of C., Nat. Homes Corp. (adv. com.), Am. Legion. Republican. Roman Catholic. Clubs: Deerfield Country, Moose, K.C. Home: PO Box 747 421 Main Ave Weston WV 26452 Office: PO Box 747 467 Main Ave Weston WV 26452

GARVEY, RICHARD ARTHUR, mfg. co. ofcl.; b. Poughkeepsie, N.Y., Aug. 24, 1948; s. Edward Joseph and Margret Ann (Hoke) G.; B.S. in Bus. Adminstrn. cum laude, Boston U., 1970; M.B.A. (White House Pub. Policy fellow), Wharton Grad. Sch., 1972; m. Carol Ann Battista, Dec. 5, 1970; children—Kristin, Allison, Katharin. Brand mgr. hot cereals Quaker Oats Co., Chgo., 1973-76; v.p. mktg., mem. mgmt. com. toy line LEGO Systems, Inc., Enfield, Conn., 1976—. Served with USAR, 1970. Mem. Beta Gamma Sigma. Office: 555 Taylor Rd Enfield CT 06082

GARVEY, RICHARD CONRAD, newspaper editor; b. Northampton, Mass., May 23, 1923; s. Michael Edward and Lucy Lillian (Bradford) G.; student U. Mass., 1941-42; L.H.D., 1974; m. Anne Elizabeth Vanasse, May 18, 1957; children—Philip Michael, John Bradford, Mary Agnes, Margaret Anne. Reporter, Daily Hampshire Gazette, Northampton, Mass., 1943-44; with Springfield (Mass.) Daily News, 1944—, editor, 1969—. Trustee, Springfield Instn. for Savs., 1970—; chmn. bd. trustees Springfield Coll.; trustee Mercy Hosp.; mem. U.S. Cath. Bishops Adv. Council, 1980—. Mem. Am. Cath. Hist. Assn., Am., New Eng. (pres. 1971) socs. newspaper editors. Roman Catholic. Club: Rotary. Home: 90 Macomber Ave Springfield MA 01119 Office: 1860 Main St Springfield MA 01101

GARVIN, ANDREW PAUL, info. exec.; b. N.Y.C., July 24, 1945; s. Gene and Nora (Sheldon) G.; B.A., Yale U., 1967; M.S., Columbia U., 1968; m. Sandra Kremnitzer, June 13, 1976 (div. 1980). Corr., Newsweek, N.Y.C., 1967-68; v.p. Four Elements, Inc., N.Y.C., 1968-69; co-founder, chmn., chief exec. officer Info. Clearing House, Inc., N.Y.C., 1970—; chmn. Nat. Info. Conf. and Exposition, 1979. Mem. Info. Industry Assn. (dir. 1979—), Asso. Info. Mgrs., Spl. Libraries Assn., Am. Soc. Info. Sci., Am. Mgmt. Assn., Am. Mktg. Assn., St. Elmo Soc. (treas. 1975—). Author: How to Win with Information or Lose without It, 1980. Home: 315 E 72nd St New York NY 10021 Office: 500 Fifth Ave New York NY 10036

GARVIN, CLIFTON CANTER, JR., oil co. exec.; b. Portsmouth, Va., Dec. 22, 1921; s. Clifton Canter and Esther (Ames) G.; B.S. in Chem. Engring., Va. Poly. Inst., 1943, M.S., 1947; m. Themla E. Volland. Mar. 15, 1954; children—James C., Carol Ann, Sandra Louise, Patricia Lynn. With Esso Standard Oil Co., Baton Rouge, 1947-59; with Humble Oil & Refining Co., 1960-64, v.p. central region, 1963-64; exec. asst. to pres. Standard Oil Co. (N.J.) (now Exxon Corp.), 1964-65, v.p., 1968, exec. v.p., 1968-72, pres. 1972-75, chmn. bd., chief exec. officer, 1975—; pres. Exxon Chem. Co. Inc., N.Y.C., 1965-68; dir. Citicorp, Citibank N.A., Pepsico., Inc., Sperry Corp. Vice-chmn. Bus. Council, Bus. Com. for Arts; mem. Council for Financial Aid to Edn.; trustee Conf. Bd., Sloan-Kettering Inst. for Cancer Research, Com. for Econ. Devel.; chmn. United Way Am.; mem. bd. trust Vanderbilt U. Mem. Nat. Petroleum Council, Am. Petroleum Inst. (dir.), Am. Chem. Soc., Am. Inst. Chem. Engrs., Bus. Roundtable (chmn.), Council on Fgn. Relations. Congregationalist. Home: Greenwich CT Office: 1251 Ave of Americas New York NY 10020

GARVIN, HADDEN GLENN, JR., stockbroker; b. Washington, Apr. 18, 1944; s. Hadden Glenn and Glenda Dale G.; B.B.A., Stetson U., 1966; m. July 30, 1966; children—Christopher, Jennifer. Resident mgr. Sheraton Hotel, Ft. Lauderdale, Fla., 1967-68; account exec. Bache Halsey Stuart, Ft. Lauderdale, 1968-73, sr. account exec., 1973-77, v.p., 1977-79; v.p. investments Paine Webber, Ft. Lauderdale, 1979—. Mem. headmaster's adv. council Westminster Acad., Ft. Lauderdale; bd. dirs. Floranada Little League. Served with inf. U.S. Army, 1966-67. Mem. Internat. Assn. Fin. Planners, Nat. Assn. Securities Dealers, Chgo. Bd. Trade, N.Y. Stock Exchange. Republican. Presbyterian. Office: Paine Webber 2300 E Sunrise Blvd Fort Lauderdale FL 33304

GARVIN, ROBERT FAYETTE, real estate, ins. co. exec.; b. Beaver, Pa., Nov. 28, 1896; s. John Frank and Margaret Elizabeth (Alcorn) G.; student Geneva Coll., 1915, U. Pitts., 1916-17; certificate Am. Inst. Banking, 1925; m. Viola Pearl Canuti, Aug. 30, 1922; children—Patricia Anne (Mrs. Robert E. Nunamaker), Sally Lou (Mrs. O. Howard Heckathorne, Jr.), Robert Frank, Paulette. Teller, Beaver County Trust Co., New Brighton, Pa., 1920-21, Beaver (Pa.) Trust Co., 1922-24; asst. cashier First Nat. Bank of Midland (Pa.), 1925-26; partner Carver & Garvin Ins. Agy., Beaver, 1926-30; sec., mgr. Beaver Realty & Ins. Agy., Beaver, 1930-37; owner, operator Bob Garvin, Realtor-Insuror (name changed to Bob Garvin Agy., Inc. 1968), 1937—, pres., 1968—. Mem. nat. council U.S.O., 1970—. Served with U.S. Army, 1917-19, AUS, 1942-45, to maj. USAF, 1951. Decorated Belgium War Cross; recipient Man of Year award Beaver Area C. of C., plaque Beaver County Bd. Realtors, Am. Legion citation. Mem. Nat. Assn. Realtors, Nat. Assn. Ins. Agts., Beaver County Bd. Realtors (pres. 1953-54), Beaver County Assn. Ins. Agts., (pres. 1946-50), Am. Inst. Banking (pres. Beaver County chpt. 1924-25), Am. Legion (post adj. 1927-28, post commdr. 1929-30), Vets. of World War I, Nat. Rifle Assn., 37th Div. Vets Assn., Res. Officers Assn. (pres. Gen. Brodhead chpt. 1955-56), Phi Delta Theta. Republican. Presbyn. (ch. elder). Mason (32 deg.), Rotarian. Clubs: Fort McIntosh (Beaver); Beaver Valley Country (Beaver Falls, Pa.). Home: Garvinhurst Box 267 Beaver PA 15009 Office: 877 McIntosh Sq Beaver PA 15009

GARY, ROBERT LOUIS, ins. co. exec.; b. Bronx, N.Y., Apr. 4, 1942; student Hofstra U., 1960-65; m. Marguerite Geraghty, Jan. 24, 1965; children—Kevin Michael, Kathleen Anne. With Northwestern Mut. Life Ins. Co., Garden City, N.Y., 1965-69; mem. sales staff Conn. Mut. Life Ins. Co., Woodbury, N.Y., 1969-72; v.p. The Suffolk Group, Hauppauge, N.Y., 1972—. Mem. Nassau County Democratic Com., 1969-72. C.L.U. Mem. Am. Soc. C.L.U.'s, Nat. Assn. Life Underwriters, Nat. Assn. Pension Cons.'s and Adminstrs., Estate Planning Council Suffolk County, Am. Soc. Pension Actuaries. Home: 19 Hartman Hill Rd Huntington NY 11743 Office: The Suffolk Group 330 Vanderbilt Pkwy Hauppauge NY 11787

GARZIA, RICARDO FRANCISCO, computer co. exec.; b. Buenos Aires, Argentina, Sept. 19, 1926; s. Mario Francisco and Zulema Maria (Alvarez) G.; came to U.S., 1967, naturalized, 1975; B.S. in Elec. Engring., Otto Krause Sch., 1945; M.S. in Elec. Engring., La Plata U., 1950; m. Julia Elisa Berrud, Oct. 2, 1948; children—Liliana Julia, Silvia Cristina, Mario Ricardo, Fernando Marcelo. Prof. Nat. Indsl. Sch., Buenos Aires, 1951-53; prof., Nat. Tech. U., Buenos Aires, 1954-67, chmn. elec. dept., 1964-67, dir. computer center, 1964-67; prin. engr. Gen. Dynamics/Electronics, Rochester, N.Y., 1967-69; computer scientist Computer Scis. Corp., Huntsville, Ala., 1969-71; mgr. tech. applications The Babcock & Wilcox Co., Barberton, Ohio, 1971—. Consejo Nacional de Investigacions Cientificas y Tecnicas grantee M.I.T., 1960-61. Mem. IEEE, Instrument Soc. Am., Ops. Research Soc. Am. Author: Transformada Z, 1966; Introduccion a la Computation Digital, 1968; contbg. author: Large-Scale Dynamical Systems, 1976, Rational Fault Analysis, 1977. Home: 509 Vosello Ave Akron OH 44313 Office: 20 S Van Buren St Barberton OH 44203

GASKELL, JAMES SHIELDS, JR., bank exec.; b. Evergreen, Ala., Nov. 12, 1921; s. James Shields and Anne Lois (Wiggins) G.; B.S., U. Ala., 1943; postgrad. Sch. Banking, La. State U., 1957; m. Dorothy Dale, Sept. 6, 1947; children—Dale, Barbara Anne, Lauri. With First Ala. Bank of Montgomery, now pres., chmn. bd. Served with inf. U.S. Army, 1943-46, 51-52. Decorated Silver Star, Bronze Star. Baptist. Home: 3508 Lansdowne Dr Montgomery AL 36111 Office: PO Box 511 Montgomery AL 36101

GASPER, DONALD, coal co. exec.; b. Du Bois, Pa., Oct. 3, 1927; s. Joseph and Helen (Palko) G.; student U. Pa., 1945-46; B.S., Pa. State U., 1950, M.S., 1951; m. Dorothy Dryna, June 21, 1952; children—Barbara, Therese, Dorothy, Karla. Bus. analyst Consolidation Coal Co., Pitts., 1951-61, mgr. bus. surveys, 1961-67, dir. econ. studies, 1967—. Cons. staff study com. on finance U.S. Senate Steel Imports, 1967, Nat. Fuels and Energy Study, U.S. Senate Study, 1962, Mich. Energy Study, 1966, Nat. Petroleum Council, 1969, 73-74, 76-77, Nat. Coal Policy Conf., Nat. Coal Assn. Fairmont Coal Bur.; cons. fuel allocation adv. group U.S. Dept. Interior, 1973; cons. industrywide wage negotiations Bituminous Coal Operators Assn., 1974, 77-78. Served with USNR, 1945-46. Mem. Assn. Am. Geographers, Am. Inst. Mining, Metall. and Petroleum Engrs., Assn. Iron and Steel Engrs., Internat. Assn. Energy Economists, Am. Econ. Assn. Roman Catholic. Contbr. articles to profl. jours. Home: 103 White Gate Rd Pittsburgh PA 15238 Office: Consol Plaza Pittsburgh PA 15241

GASPER, LOUIS CLEMENT, economist; b. Cin., June 13, 1943; s. George and Mary Ann Elizabeth (Rosenfeld) G.; B.S., Duquesne U., 1965; Ph.D., Duke U., 1969; m. Jo Ann Shoaf, Sept. 21, 1974; children—Stephen Gregory, Monica Elizabeth, Jeanne Marie. Asst. prof. econs. U. Ariz., Tucson, 1968-73; pvt. cons., Dallas, 1973-75; minority staff economist U.S. Ho. of Reps., Washington, 1975—. Mem. So. Econ. Assn., Assn. Social Econs., Phila. Soc., Omicron Delta Epsilon, Beta Gamma Sigma. Roman Catholic. Home: 6253 Park Rd McLean VA 22101 Office: H2-517 House Office Bldg Annex II Washington DC 20515

GASPERONI, EMIL, real estate exec.; b. Hillsville, Pa., Nov. 13, 1926; s. Attico and Rose Mary (Sarnicola) G.; diploma real estate U. Pitts., 1957; m. Ellen Jean Lias, May 28, 1955; children—Samuel Dale, Emil Attico, Jean Ellen. Owner, pres. Gasperoni Real Estate, New Castle, Pa., 1956-63, Ft. Lauderdale, Fla., 1970—; founder, chmn. bd. Fill-R-Up Auto Wash Systems Inc., Ft. Lauderdale, 1967-70; pres. Investment Property Adv. Corp., Ft. Lauderdale, 1975—. Mem. com. 100, Broward Inds 1. Bd., Ft. Lauderdale. Served with U.S. Army, 1945-46; ETO. Mem. Nat. Inst. Real Estate Brokers, Internat. Real Estate Fedn., Nat. Soc. Fee Appraisers, Fla. Assn. Mortgage Brokers. Clubs: Coral Ridge Golf and Country (Ft. Lauderdale); Lake Toxaway (N.C.) Country. Home: 4201 NE 25th Ave Fort Lauderdale FL 33308 Office: 2501 E Commercial Blvd Fort Lauderdale FL 33308

GASS, CHARLES, retail co. exec.; b. N.Y.C., June 12, 1918; s. Benjamin and Sophie (Eberlin) G.; B.B.A., Coll. City N.Y., 1940; m. Rosalyn Becker, June 23, 1945; children—Jeffrey, Marc. With Darling Stores Corp., 1946-62, asst. controller, 1956-62; controller Grayson Robinson Stores Corp., 1962-64; v.p. internal audit MMG Stores div. McCrory Corp., N.Y.C., 1966-71, v.p. McCrory Corp., 1971—, sr. v.p. ops. S. Klein Dept. Stores div., 1972-74, sr. v.p. mgmt. services McCrory Stores div., 1974-77, exec. v.p. McCrory Stores div., 1978—; pres. K.N. Distbrs., Inc., 1972-74. Served with AUS, World War II; ETO. Decorated Silver Star, Bronze Star, Purple Heart, Presdl. citation. Mem. Coll. City N.Y. Alumni Assn. Home: 2600-14 Netherland Ave Bronx NY 10463 Office: 245 Fifth Ave New York NY 10016 also 2955 E Market St York PA 17402

GASS, ROBERT LOUIS, JR., furniture co. exec.; b. Murray, Ky., Jan. 8, 1943; s. Robert Louis and Mildred (Childers) G.; student Murray U., 1961-63, Broward Community Coll., 1961-62, Am. Inst. Banking, 1967-72; m. Victoria Fuhrer, Aug. 21, 1965; children—Kimberly Ann, Kelly Elizabeth. With finance div. Gen. Electric Co., West Palm Beach, Fla., 1965-66; with trust dept. First Nat. Bank, Ft. Lauderdale, Fla., 1967-72; pres. Mar-Tec Corp., Ft. Lauderdale, 1972—; pres., chmn. Wudlite Corp., Phoenix; dir. Fla. Bank, Ft. Lauderdale. Group leader United Fund of Broward County, 1973. Mem. Ft. Lauderdale Young Republican Club, Ft. Lauderdale C. of C., S.Fla. Mfg. Assn. Club: Kiwanis. Home: 1752 NE 1st St Fort Lauderdale FL 33301 Office: 900 SW 20th Way Fort Lauderdale FL 33312

GASSE, YVON, educator; b. Carleton, Que., Can., June 7, 1943; s. Charles and Isabelle (Leblanc) G.; B.Commerce, U. Laval, 1966, M.B.A., 1967; M.A., Northwestern U., 1972, Ph.D., 1978; m. Rachele Berthelot, June 8, 1968; children—Genevieve, Marie-Stephanie. Mgr., Carleton (Que.) Golf Club, 1960-62, Carleton Park, 1963-66; prof. U. Moncton (N.B.), 1967-68; prof. U. Sherbrooke (Que.), 1968-70, dir. grad. program in adminstrn., 1973-76, dir. research div. Sch. Bus., 1976-77; prof. mgmt., asso. dean Sch. Adminstrn., U. Laval (Que.), 1977—; dir. Entraide PME, Inc.; cons. in bus. adminstrn. Mem. sch. bd., Bd. of Trade, Ste.-Foy, 1978—. Recipient Gold medal of excellence Gov.-Gen. of Que., 1962; Can. Council fellow, 1970, 71, 72, grantee, 1973, 74, 80; Que. Ministry of Edn. fellow, 1970, 71, 72. Mem. Inst. Mgmt. Scis., Acad. of Mgmt., Internat. Council Small Bus., Adminstrv. Scis. Assn. of Can., Learned Socs. of Can., French-Canadian Assn. Advancement of Sci., Can. Inst. Mgmt. Liberal. Roman Catholic. Clubs: Cap Rouge Golf, Carleton Golf. Author 2 books in mgmt., 1976, 77; contbr. numerous articles in mgmt. to profl. publs. Home: 3450 Francois Lebrun Sainte-Foy PQ G1W 2S2 Canada Office: Sch Adminstrn U Laval Laval PQ G1K 7P4 Canada

GASTON, DWIGHT MOORE, real estate broker; b. Woodward, Okla., Feb. 13, 1932; s. Virgil and Rose Emma (Savage) G.; student Washburn U., Topeka; m. Norma Lenninger, Oct. 31, 1953; children—Jane, Julie. With Halliburton Co., Duncan, Okla., 1953-57, Skelly Oil Co., Tulsa, 1957-67; real estate bus., Mission, Kans., 1967—, auctioneer, 1975—. Mem. Nat. Assn. Realtors, Kans. Assn. Realtors, Mo. Assn. Realtors, Johnson County Bds. Realtors, Am. Legion, Nat. Auctioneers Assn., Kans. Auctioneers. Baptist. Clubs: Elks, Eagles, Masons. Home: 5513 W 53d St Mission KS 66202

GASTON, W. W., business exec.; b. Chester County, S.C., 1926; ed. Presbyn. Coll., Clemson U. Chmn. exec. com., pres. Gold Kist Inc., Atlanta; dir. Central Bank for Coops., Ga. No. Ry. Co., Cotton States Life & Health Ins. Co., Cotton States Mut. Ins. Co., Nat. Council Farmer Coops., So. Bell Tel. & Tel. Co., Trust Co. Ga. Office: Gold Kist Inc 244 Perimeter Center Pkwy NE Atlanta GA 30346*

GASTON, WILLIAM DICKERSON, retail, wholesale exec.; b. Austin, Tex., Dec. 27, 1927; s. Alpheus Dickerson and Alliene (Ware) G.; B.S. in Mech. Engring., U. Tex. at Austin, 1949; M.S. Auto. Engring., Chrysler Inst. Engring., 1951; m. Eleanor Grigg, Sept. 6, 1952; children—Brian Franklin, Christy. Engr., Chrysler Engring. Co., Highland Park, Mich., 1949-51; contractor, Burnett County, Tex., 1951-53; pres. Bill Gaston Boats and Motos, Austin, 1953—; pres. Bill Gaston Inc. wholesale marine, Austin, 1954—; exec. v.p. Glastron Boat Co., mfg., Austin, 1956-76; dir. N. Austin State Bank. Mem. Nat. Boating Safety Adv. Council to U.S. Coast Guard, 1972-74, 77—. Recipient Michelob Schooner award boat safety August A. Bush, 1973. Mem. Austin C. of C. (dir., v.p.), Greater Austin Assn. (exec. com.), Boat Mfrs. Assn. (pres. 1972-73), Boating Industry Assn. (pres. 1973), Boating Trade Assn. Tex. (pres. 1960), Am. Boat and Yacht Council (pres. 1977, 78). Episcopalian. Clubs: Westwood Country, Headliners. Home: 2508 Pecos St Austin TX 78703 Office: PO Box 9577 Austin TX 78766

GASTWIRTH, DONALD EDWARD, lawyer, music pub. exec.; b. N.Y.C., Aug. 7, 1944; s. Paul and Tillie (Scheinert) G.; B.A., Yale U., 1966, J.D., 1974. Mem. advt. staff New Yorker mag., N.Y.C., 1967-68; v.p. Reader's Press, New Haven, 1968-74, dir., 1968—; exec. v.p. Mainstream TV Studio, New Haven, 1974-77, dir., 1974-79; account exec. Bache Halsey Stuart Shields Inc., New Haven, 1977-79; pres. Quasar Assos., music pub. firm., New Haven, 1979—. Trustee, Colony Found., 1975-80; v.p., bd. dirs. Friends of New Haven Shubert Theatre. Mem. Am. Mgmt. Assn., Berzelius Soc., Am. Bar Assn. (forum com. on entertainment and sports industries), Conn. Bar Assn., Assn. Trial Lawyers Am., ASCAP, Internat. Platform Assn. Democrat. Clubs: Yale (N.Y.C.); Elizabethan (New Haven). Office: 100 York St Suite 17-0 New Haven CT 06511

GATENBY, ARTHUR WHITLEY, sci. instrument mfg. co. exec.; b. B. Chelmsford, Mass., Apr. 15, 1933; s. Frederick William and Emily Maud (Whitley) G.; B.Mgmt. Engring., Rensselaer Poly. Inst., 1955; M.B.A., N.Y. U., 1961; m. Eleanor Gene Gray, July 7, 1957; children—Jennifer Elise, Jill Maud, David Arthur Gray. Sales engr. Taylor Instruments div. Sybron, 1957-61; orgn. cons. Gen. Foods Corp., White Plains, N.Y., 1961-62; dist. sales engr. Tex. Instruments, Inc., N.Y.C., 1962-63; v.p. Booz, Allen & Hamilton, Inc., N.Y.C. and Washington, 1963-69; pres. C G H Inc., Washington, 1969-76; chmn. bd., chief exec. C S C Scientific Co., Inc., Chgo., 1976—. Served with USN, 1955-57. Republican. Methodist. Office: CSC Scientific Co Inc 2600 S Kostner Ave Chicago IL 60623

GATES, BARBARA ANN, corp. exec.; b. Jerome, Ariz., June 3, 1940; d. Erma A. (Mattingly) G.; B.A., U. Hawaii, 1964. Staff analyst to v.p. bus. affairs U. Hawaii, Honolulu, 1964-65; founder, exec. v.p., pres. Computing Mgmt., Inc., Honolulu, 1965-72; v.p. mgmt. info. systems C. Brewer & Co., Honolulu, 1973-78; v.p. adminstrn. ITT Courier Terminal Systems, Inc., Tempe, Ariz., 1978—. Mem. Assn. System Mgmt. (past pres.), Hawaii Soc. Corp. Planners (dir. 1977), Ariz. Assn. Industries (dir.). Office: 1515 W 14th St Tempe AZ 85281

GATES, C. W., mortgage banker, city ofcl.; b. Pine Bluff, Ark., Aug. 13, 1923; s. Lance and Mattie (Berry) G.; student Stowe Tchrs. Coll., Washington U., St. Louis; m. Harriet Cecilia Craddock, June 14, 1947; children—Mark D., Lisa B. With C.W. Gates Realty Co., Inc., St. Louis, 1959—, pres., 1959—; pres. Gateway Nat. Bank, St. Louis, 1964—, radio sta. 1310, St. Louis, 1966—, Nat. Assurance Co., St. Louis, 1966—; vice chmn. Vbic Way Broadcasting Co., St. Louis, 1969—; v.p. Mid-Central Mortgage Co., St. Louis, 1964—. Police commr., St. Louis, 1966—. Bd dirs. Jr. Achievement, St. Louis, Boy Scouts Am., St. Louis, Cath. Charities, St. Louis, United Fund, St. Louis, Health and Welfare Council, St. Louis, Urban League, St. Louis, N.A.A.C.P.; trustee YWCA, St. Louis. Served with AUS, 1942-45; ETO. Clubs: St. Louis Press, Advertising Greater St. Louis, Media. Home: 5249 Lindell Blvd St Louis MO 63108 Office: 2921 Union Blvd St Louis MO 63115

GATEWOOD, ROBERT PAYNE, ins. exec.; b. Nebr., Mar. 4, 1923; s. Robert Harvey and Bess (Payne) G.; B.S., U.S. Naval Acad., 1946; C.L.U., Am. Coll. Life Underwriters, 1953; postgrad. La. State U., 1974; m. Marilyn Wengert, June 6, 1946; children—Robert, Lottie, Traber, Cy, Marilyn, Bess, John, Anthony, Judemarie, Anne, Tressa, Joseph, Ruth. Estate planner J.D. Marsh & Assos., 1950-56; pres. estate planning Financial Corp. Am., 1956-61; pres. Robert P. Gatewood & Co., 1961—. Bd. dirs. Sch. of Life Ins. Mktg. Found. Served with USN, 1946-50; PTO. Recipient Bernard L. Wilner Meml. award. Mem. Nat. Assn. Life Underwriters (past pres.), Assn. Advanced Underwriters, Million Dollar Round Table, Am. Soc. C.L.U.s (exec. com. 1972-77, pres. 1975-76), Five Million Dollar Forum (founder). Republican. Roman Catholic. Contbr. articles to profl. jours.; lectr. in field. Home: 3838 52d St NW Washington DC 20016 Office: 905 16th St NW Washington DC 20006

GATTEGNO, JERROLD STEVEN, acct.; b. Bronx, N.Y., Aug. 22, 1952; s. Hy and Gladys (Machalow) G.; B.S. cum laude, Herbert H. Lehman Coll., City U. N.Y., 1973; M.B.A. with distinction, Pace U., 1977; m. Karen Ford Kelly, Jan. 8, 1978. Tax mgr. Deloitte Haskins & Sells, White Plains, N.Y., 1973—. Mem. budget rev. com. City of White Plains. C.P.A., N.Y. Mem. N.Y. State Soc. C.P.A.'s (chmn. fed. and state tax com. Westchester chpt. 1978-80), Am. Inst. C.P.A.'s, Omicron Delta Epsilon, Delta Mu Delta. Clubs: Univ., Rotary (White Plains); Ridgeway Country. Contbr. articles to profl. publs. Home: White Plains NY Office: One North Broadway White Plains NY 10601

GAULKE, RAMON GEORGE, advt. exec.; b. Oak Park, Ill., Jan. 21, 1934; s. Walter George and Ann (Jaraback) G.; B.A., Elmhurst Coll., 1955. Advt. mgr. Ekco-Alcoa Packaging Co., Wheeling, Ill., 1959-63; creative dir. Lows, Inc., Chgo., 1963-65; successively exec. v.p., gen. mgr., pres., also dir. Marsteller, Inc., N.Y.C., 1965—. Trustee, Elmhurst (Ill.) Coll. Served with USNR, 1955-59; capt. Res. Mem. Advt. Council (dir.). Home: Lakeville CT Office: 4 W 58th St New York NY 10022

GAULTNEY, JOHN ORTON, life ins. agt., cons.; b. Pulaski, Tenn., Nov. 7, 1915; s. Bert Hood and Grace (Orton) G.; student Am. Inst. Banking, 1936; diploma Life Ins. Agy. Mgmt. Assn., 1948, Little Rock Jr. Coll., 1950; Mgmt. C.L.U. Diploma, 1952; grad. sales mgmt. and marketing Rutgers U., 1957; m. Elizabethine Mullette, Mar. 30, 1941; children—Elizabethine (Mrs. Donald H. McClure), John Mullette, Walker Orton, Harlow Denny. With N.Y. Life Ins. Co., 1935—, mgr., Little Rock, 1945-55, regional v.p. Atlanta, 1956-64, v.p., N.Y.C., 1964-67, v.p. charge group sales, 1967-68, v.p. mktg., 1969-80, cons., 1981—; v.p. N.Y. Life Variable Contracts Corp., 1970-80. Chmn. Downtown YMCA, Atlanta, 1963-65, bd. dirs. Vanderbilt YMCA, 1966-76, chmn. Vanderbilt, 1974-76; bd. dirs. Greater N.Y. YMCA, 1975—, mem. pub. relations com. nat. council, 1965—, mem. internat.

YMCA com., 1967-80; mem. Bronxville (N.Y.) Zoning Appeals Bd., 1973-80. Served to capt. inf. AUS, 1942-45; MTO. Decorated Silver Star, Bronze Star with 3 clusters, Purple Heart with 2 clusters; recipient Devereux C. Josephs award N.Y. Life Ins. Co., 1954; named Ark. Traveler, 1955, hon. citizen Tenn., 1956, Ky. col., 1963. C.L.U. Mem. Am., Tenn. socs. C.L.U.'s, Nat., Tenn. assns. life underwriters, Tenn. Gen. Agts. and Mgrs. Conf., Tenn. Soc. in N.Y. (pres. 1971-74), Am. Risk and Ins. Assn., Newcomen Soc. Am., N.Y. So. Soc. (trustee 1965-80), St. Nicholas Soc. N.Y., Soc. Colonial Wars, S.A.R. (dir. N.Y. 1970-80), 361st Inf. Assn. (pres. 1967-71). Mem. Reformed Ch. (elder). Clubs: Capital City (Atlanta); Rotary (Franklin, Tenn.); Am. Yacht (Rye, N.Y.); Siwanoy (Bronxville, N.Y.). Home: 5709 Cloverwood Dr Brentwood TN 37027 Office: Parkway Towers Suite 2012 Nashville TN 37219

GAUM, CARL HENRY, civil engr.; b. N.Y.C., July 29, 1922; s. Conrad and Amanda (Schultz) G.; B.S. in Civil Engring., Rutgers U., 1949; postgrad. in geology, water resources planning and exec. mgmt. U. Cin., 1962-64, U. Okla., 1965-66; m. Ruth Ellen Banks, Feb. 26, 1955; children—Virginia Lee, Carlann Ruth. With U.S. Geol. Survey, N.J. and Tex., 1949-52; prin. Gaum Profl. Engrs., Trenton, N.J., 1953-55; with U.S. Army Corps of Engrs., 1955—, hydraulic engr., Phila., 1955-60, Washington, 1960-61, bd. of engrs. rivers and harbors, Washington, 1961-62, asst. chief Ohio River Basin comprehensive study, Cin., 1962-68, chief internat. study sect. Office Chief of Engrs., Washington, 1968-70, asst. chief interagency and spl. studies br., 1970-73, chief central reports mgmt. br., planning div., 1973-80; prin. Gaum & Assos., Cons., Kensington, Md., 1980—; cons. in field, expert witness. Mem. Cin. Water and Air Pollution Commn., 1963-67; mem. Blue Ash (Ohio) Citizens Com., 1964-68; mem. Tech. and Sci. Socs. Council Cin., 1967-68. Served with USAAF, 1942-45. Registered profl. engr., Tex., N.J., Pa., Md. Fellow Am. Soc. Civil Engrs. (dir. nat. capital sect. 1973-76, pres. Trenton br. 1956-57, nat. chmn. water resources and mgmt. div. 1975-76), mem. N.J. Soc. Profl. Engrs. (pres. Mercer County 1957-58, trustee 1958-59), AAAS, U.S. Com. Large Dams, Permanent Internat. Assn. Navigation Congresses (life, chmn. publs. com. Am. sect. for XXIV Congress Leningrad 1977, XXV Congress, Edinburgh 1981), Am. Mgmt. Assn. Contbr. articles in field to profl. jours. Office: 9609 Carriage Rd Kensington MD 20795

GAUTHIER, CLARENCE JOSEPH, utility exec.; b. Houghton, Mich., Mar. 16, 1922; s. Clarence A. and Muriel V. (Beesley) G.; B.S. in Mech. Engring., U. Ill., 1943; M.B.A., U. Chgo., 1960; m. Grayce N. Wicall, July 25, 1941; children—Joseph H., Nancy M. With Pub. Service Co. No. Ill., 1945-54; with No. Ill. Gas Co., 1954—, v.p. finance, 1960-62, v.p. ops., 1962-64, exec. v.p., 1965-69, pres., 1969-76, chmn., chief exec. officer, 1971—, dir., 1965—; chmn., pres., chief exec. officer, dir. NICOR Inc., 1976—, chief exec. officer, chmn., dir. all NICOR and NI-Gas subs.'s; dir. Gas Devels. Corp., 1965-70, 76—; vice-chmn., dir. AEGIS 1978—; dir. Bank of Yorktown, Sun Electric Corp., GATX Corp., Naperville Nat. Bank & Trust Co. (Ill.), Nalco Chem. Co. Mem. citizens' bd. U. Chgo., 1972—; bd. sponsors Evang. Hosp. Assn., Oak Brook, Ill., 1977—; chmn. devel. campaign Good Samaritan Hosp., Downers Grove, Ill., 1974-77 bd. dirs. Gas Research Inst., 1977—, Mid-Am. chpt. ARC, 1962-78; trustee Council for Energy Studies, 1977—, George Williams Coll., Downers Grove, 1968-77, Ill. Inst. Tech., IITRI, 1976-80, Inst. Gas Tech., 1964-70, 71-78, chmn. bd., 1976-78; active Met. Crusade of Mercy, Chgo., 1965-77; bd. govs. Soc. Environ. Awareness, 1973—; mem. Ill. Savs. Bond Com., 1975—; mem. pres.'s council U. Ill., 1978—. Served to capt., C.E., AUS; World War II; PTO. Decorated Silver Star, Bronze Star with V; recipient Distinguished Alumnus award U. Ill. Coll. Engring., 1971, Alumni Honor award for distinguished service, 1974; Distinguished Service award Am. Gas Assn., 1976; Loyalty award U. Ill. Alumni Assn., 1977. Registered profl. engr., Ill. Mem. Am. (dir. 1970-76, chmn. bd. 1974-75), Midwest (dir. 1964-67), So. (dir. 1966-69) gas assns., Ind. Natural Gas Assn. Am. (dir. 1972-73), Internat. Gas Union (council 1970-75), AAAS, Am. Fin. Assn., Am. Mgmt. Assn., Pres.'s Assn., Newcomen Soc. N.Am., U. Ill. Found., U. Chgo. Grad. Sch. Bus. (pres. 1964-65), U. Ill. Mech.-Indsl. Engring. (dir. 1973—, pres. 1976-77) alumni assns., Northwestern U. Assos., Chgo. Council on Fgn. Relations (Chgo. com. 1974—), Ill. C. of C., Chgo. Assn. Commerce and Industry (dir. 1973-79), Sigma Pi, Beta Gamma Sigma, Tau Nu Tau, Pi Tau Sigma. Clubs: Econ., Mid-Am., Comml., Chgo. (Chgo.); Butler Nat. Golf. Contbr. articles to profl. jours. Home: 15 Lochinvar Ln Oak Brook IL 60521 Office: PO Box 200 Naperville IL 60566

GAUTHIER, T(HEOPHILE) EMIL, med. equipment co. exec.; b. Warroad, Minn., Dec. 11, 1910; s. Odilon and Mathilda (Gauthier) G.; grad. Coyne Coll., 1932; student Rochester Community Coll., 1942, U. Minn., 1943; m. Dorothy Ranney, Sept. 11, 1941; children—Janice (Mrs. Arthur Ley), Thomas, Lawrence. Gen. service worker Mayo Clinic, Rochester, Minn., 1934-37; service mgr. Sears Roebuck & Co., Rochester, Minn., 1937-40; asst. prodn. mgr. Waters-Conley Co., Rochester, 1940-46, Kepp Co., Rochester, 1946-47; organizer Rochester Products Co., 1947, mgr., 1947-66; organizer, mgr. Rochester Med. Equipment Co. (Minn.), 1966-72; organizer Gauthier Industries, Inc., sec.-treas., dir., 1974—; dir. Pine Plating Co., Pine Island, Minn., 1962-70, Ability Bldg. Center, Rochester, 1972—. Mem. Rochester (Minn.) Utility Bd., 1956-66, pres., 1956-65; chmn. com. on urban environment City of Rochester, 1974, Active Boy Scouts Am., 1924-65; pres. St. Francis P.T.A., 1953. Recipient Pres.'s award Soc. Mfg. Engrs., 1966, 71, 73. Registered mfg. engr. Mem. Soc. Mfg. Engrs., Am. Mgmt. Assn., Rochester C. of C. (chmn. indsl. com. 1953-58), Coast andGuard Aux. (flotilla vice-comdr. 1971-72), Service Core Ret. Execs. Roman Catholic. K.C., Elk. Developed plastic needle for prolonged intravenous therapy, artificial kidney machine for home patients. Home: 1210 4th St NW Rochester MN 55901 Office: Gauthier Industries Inc 300 NE 1st St Rochester MN 55901

GAVELLO, ALFRED, mortgage banker; b. Oakland, Calif., Feb. 13, 1929; s. Carlo Clemente and Leonilda Clotilda (Nicola) G.; B.S., U. Calif. at Berkeley, 1951; m. Patricia J. Hansston, Sept. 20, 1958; children—John Edward, Dana Lynn, Judi Leigh. Asst. mgr. Gen. Motors Co., Chevrolet div., Oakland, 1954-59; v.p., partner Mason McDuffie Co., Berkeley, Calif., 1959—; lectr., cons. in field. Served with M.I., U.S. Army, 1951-53. Mem. Mortgage Bankers Assn., Bay Area Mortgage Assn. Republican. Roman Catholic. Club: Colombo. Author: The ABC's of FHA, 1971; (with others) California Real Estate Finance, 1978. Home: 36 San Carlos Ct Walnut Creek CA 94598 Office: 2850 Telegraph Ave Berkeley CA 94705

GAVENDA, SAMUEL, lab. adminstr.; b. Syracuse, N.Y. Aug. 17, 1918; s. Abraham Isaac and Rose (Glinsky) G.; B.S. in Chemistry, Syracuse U., 1942; postgrad. Columbia, 1950-52; m. Beryl Norma Cohen, Nov. 26, 1969. Purchasing coordinator Sperry Rand Corp., N.Y.C., 1946-62; distbn. and warehousing mgr., Samsonite Corp., Linden, N.J., 1962-68; mgr. purchasing Cole Bus. Equipment div. Litton Industries, York, Pa., 1968-75; mgr. purchasing Red Devil, Inc., Union, N.J., 1975-77; subcontract adminstr. Plasma Physics Lab., Princeton U., 1977-80; sub-contract adminstr. Kierfott div. Singer Co., Little Falls, N.J., 1980—; instr. indsl. purchasing Pa. State U. Served to capt. Ordnance Corps, AUS, 1942-46. Decorated Bronze Star medal. Mem. Am. Production Inventory Control Soc., Purchasing Mgmt. Assn. Office: Singer Co Kierfott Div Little Falls NJ

GAVEY, JAMES EDWARD, real estate co. exec.; b. Buffalo, June 6, 1942; s. George W. and Clara E. (Hanley) G.; B.S., LeMoyne Coll., 1964; M.B.A., Columbia U., 1965; m. Joan E. Moran, June 6, 1964; children—Philip W., Peter J., John P. Acct., Peat, Marwick, Mitchell & Co., Buffalo, 1960-64; bus. cons. Arthur Andersen & Co., N.Y.C., 1965-73; pres. Gavey & Company, Inc., N.Y.C., 1973—. Chmn. com. United Fund, Bronxville, N.Y., 1970—; commr. Tuckahoe (N.Y.) Housing Authority, 1974-76, chmn., 1976—. Mem. Am. Inst. C.P.A.'s, N.Y. State Soc. C.P.A.'s, Nat. Assn. Rev. Appraisers, Nat. Apt. Assn., Nat. Assn. Home Builders. Republican. Roman Catholic. Clubs: Union League, Siwanoy Country, Cooperstown Country. Contbr. articles to profl. jours. Home: 98 Park Ave Bronxville NY 10708 Office: 80 Park Ave New York NY 10016

GAVIN, EUGENE CHARLES, lawyer, tax specialist; b. New Haven, Conn., Sept. 2, 1953; s. Eugene Charles and Gloria Dorothy (Halbig) G.; B.A. cum laude, Fordham Coll., 1975; J.D., Rutgers U., 1978, M.B.A. in Profl. Acctg., 1978; now postgrad. in taxation N.Y. U. Law Sch.; m. Cathleen L. Raggio, Apr. 2, 1978. Owner, operator Dudley & Beckwith, Guilford, Conn., 1969-73; tax intern Touche Ross & Co., Newark, N.J., 1976-77; law clerk to Judge Vincent J. Commisa, U.S. Dist. Ct., Newark, 1977-78; admitted to N.Y. State bar, U.S. Tax Ct. bar; supervising tax specialist firm Coopers & Lybrand, N.Y.C., 1978—. Mem. Am. Accounting Assn., Am. Bar Assn., Internat. Platform Assn. Roman Catholic. Home: 310 E 71st St Apt 5E New York NY 10021 Office: 1251 Ave of the Americas New York NY 10020

GAVIN, JOSEPH GLEASON, JR., aerospace co. exec.; b. Somerville, Mass., Sept. 18, 1920; s. Joseph Gleason and Elizabeth (Tay) G.; B.S., M.S. in Aeros., Mass. Inst. Tech., 1942; m. Dorothy Dunklee, Sept. 1943; children—Joseph Gleason III, Tay Anne (Mrs. Peter B. Erickson), Donald Lewis. With Grumman Aerospace Corp., Bethpage, N.Y., 1946—, chief missile and space engr., 1957-62, v.p., 1962-70, dir. Lunar Module program, 1953-72, sr. v.p., 1970-72, pres., 1972-76, chmn. bd., 1973-76, also dir.; pres., chief operating officer, dir. Grumman Corp., Bethpage; dir. Grumman Houston Corp., Grumman Internat., Inc., Grumman Data Systems Corp., Grumman Allied Industries, Inc., Grumman Credit Corp., Calldata Systems, Inc., European Am. Banking Corp., Pine St. Fund. Mem. corp. devel. com. M.I.T.; pres. Harborfields Bd. Edn., Central Sch. Dist. 6, Huntington, N.Y., 1960-64; chmn. United Fund, 1978; trustee Huntington Hosp., Poly. Inst. N.Y. Served with USNR, 1942-46. Recipient Leadership award C.W. Post Coll. of L.I. U.; Distinguished Pub. Service medal NASA, 1971. Fellow Am. Inst. Aeros. and Astronautics, Am. Astron. Soc.; mem. Aerospace Industries Assn., Nat. Acad. Engring. Home: 6 Endicott Dr Huntington NY 11743 Office: Grumman Corp 1111 Stewart Ave Bethpage NY 11714

GAVRITY, JOHN DECKER, ins. co. exec.; b. S.I., Oct. 26, 1940; s. John S. and Eleanor R. (Decker) G.; B.S., Wagner Coll., 1963; m. Jacqueline M. Cerami, Dec. 4, 1965; children—John, Joseph. With U.S. Life, N.Y.C., 1963-69, asst. actuary, 1970-71, asso. actuary, 1972-74; actuary USLIFE Corp., N.Y.C., 1975-76, 2d v.p., actuary, 1977, v.p., chief actuary, 1978, sr. v.p., chief actuary, 1979—. Fellow Soc. Actuaries; mem. Am. Acad. Actuaries. Republican. Roman Catholic. Home: 190 Maybury Ave Staten Island NY 10308 Office: 125 Maiden Ln New York NY 10038

GAW, JAMES RICHARD, motel owner; b. Owensboro, Ky., July 12, 1926; s. James William and Josephine (Thompson) G.; student Owensboro Bus. Coll., Brescia Coll.; m. Alma Irene Knott, Aug. 16, 1952; children—Stephen Thomas, Barbara, Monica, James Gerard, Angela, Teresa. Prodn. mgr. Murphy-Miller, Inc., Owensboro, 1947-48; asst. mgr. Owensboro Sportscenter, 1949-52, mgr., 1958-77; partner Elite Cigar Co., Owensboro, 1952-57. Magistrate, Daviess County, Owensboro, 1958-64. Pres., Young Democrats Daviess County, 1955; sec. exec. com. Daviess County Dem. Com., 1960-64. Bd. dirs. Spastic Home and Sch., Owensboro; bd. dirs. Ice Skating Inst. Am., pres., 1975-77. Named Ky. Col., 1955. Mem. Internat. Assn. Auditorium Mgrs., Ky. Magistrates Assn. (pres. 1960-61), Owensboro Jr. C. of C. (pres. 1954). Democrat. Roman Catholic. K.C., Elk, Moose. Home: PO Box 1 1810 Cecelia Ct Owensboro KY 42301 Office: Motor Lodge 231 1640 Triplett St Owensboro KY 42301

GAW, JOHN GOODWIN, textile mill exec.; b. Augusta County, Va., Sept. 23, 1916; s. Harry Goodwin and Lois (Boyd) G.; B.S. in Mech. Engring., N.C. State U., 1937; postgrad. U. N.C.; m. Ellen Parks Munroe, Dec. 23, 1940; children—John Goodwin, Ellen Munroe, Julia Boyd. Sales engr. Allis Chalmers Mfg. Co., West Allis, Wis., 1937-41; with Waverly Mills Inc., Laurinburg, N.C., 1946—, exec. v.p., 1965-72, pres., chief exec. officer, 1972—. Elder, First Presbyn. Ch., Laurinburg; bd. dirs. N.C. Textile Found. Served to lt. (j.g.) USNR, 1941-45. Mem. Am. Yarn Spinners Assn. (dir.), N.C. Textile Mfg. Assn. (dir.), N.C. State U. Alumni Assn. (dir.). Club: Laurinburg Rotary (pres. 1953). Home: 421 West Blvd Laurinburg NC 28352 Office: Box 309 East Laurinburg NC 28352

GAY, DAVID EDWARD RYAN, economist; b. Bryan, Tex., Sept. 19, 1945; s. John Gordon and Emma Louise (Ryan) G.; B.A., Tex. A&M U., 1968, Ph.D., 1973; postgrad. Kans. U., 1974. Asst. prof. dept. econs. U. Ark., Fayetteville, 1973-77, asso. prof., 1977—; vis. asso. prof. DePaul U., Chgo., 1979, Econs. Inst., U. Colo., 1980, Tex. A&M U., 1980-81. Mem. governing bd. Ark. Union, 1977-79. NDEA fellow, 1968-71. Mem. Am. Econ. Assn., Am. Fin. Assn., So. Econ. Assn., Western Econ. Assn., Eastern Econ. Assn., Royal Econ. Soc., Western Social Sci. Assn. (exec. council), Midsouth Acad. Economists (exec. council), S.W. Social Sci. Assn. Republican. Methodist. Club: Kiwanis (past dir.) (Fayetteville). Office: Dept Econs BA 402 U Ark Fayetteville AR 72701

GAY, E. LAURENCE, fin. cons.; b. Bridgeport, Conn., Aug. 10, 1923; s. Emil D. and Helen (Mihalich) G.; B.S., Yale U., 1947; J.D., Harvard U., 1949; m. Harriet A. Ripley, Aug. 2, 1952; children—L. Noel, Peter C., Marguerite S., Georgette A. Admitted to N.Y. bar, 1950, Conn. bar, 1959; atty. Root, Ballantine, Harlan, Bushby & Palmer, N.Y.C., 1949-51; legal staff U.S. High Commr. for Germany, 1951-52; law sec., presiding justice appellate div. 1st dept. N.Y. Supreme Ct., 1952-53; atty. Debevoise, Plimpton & McLean, 1953-58; v.p., sec.-treas. Hewitt-Robins, Inc., Stamford, Conn., 1958-65; pres. Litton Gt. Lakes Corp., N.Y.C., 1965-67; v.p. fin. Amfac, Inc., Honolulu, 1967-70, sr. v.p., 1970-74, vice chmn., 1974-78, chmn. fin. com., 1979-81, also dir.; sr. v.p. J. Alexander Securities, Inc. Trustee, Honolulu Symphony Soc., Loyola Marymount U., 1978-80, U. Hawaii Found., Chamber Soloists of San Francisco, San Francisco Conservatory Music, Hawaii Council for Culture and Arts. Served as 2d lt. AUS, 1943-46. Mem. Phi Beta Kappa. Roman Catholic. Home: 199 Ridgeway Rd Hillsborough CA 94010 Office: 1105 Burlingame Ave Burlingame CA 94010

GAY, LAWRENCE ALVIN, word processing co. exec.; b. Cocoa Beach, Fla., Nov. 12, 1951; s. Gibson Stancel and Catherine (Flaherty) G.; A.A. in Gen. Mgmt., Broward Community Coll., 1972; B.B.A. in Bus. Adminstrn., Fla. Atlantic U., 1974; m. Judith Allean Fleming, Oct. 9, 1976. Salesman, Curtis 1000, Balt., 1975-77, Vydec Inc., Balt., 1977-79; dist. mgr. COMDOC, Inc., Birmingham, Ala., 1979—. Mem. Internat. Word Processors Assn. Republican. Office: 3430 Independence Dr Birmingham AL 35209

GAY, MARJORIE LOUISE ANDERSON, Realtor; b. Tampa, Fla., Oct. 18, 1909; d. Louis Markham and Bertha Marjorie (Graham) Anderson; student Agnes Scott Coll., 1926-27; B.S., Fla. State Coll. of Women, 1930; postgrad. U. Tampa, 1942, Drake U., 1961, U. Fla., 1962; m. Forrest Theodore Gay, Jr., July 23, 1932; children—Forrest Theodore III, Marjorie Anderson (Mrs. Russell Tuck, Jr.). Tchr., Woodrow Wilson Jr. High Sch., Tampa, 1930-32, St. Petersburg (Fla.) High Sch., 1938-45; saleswoman W.H. Toole & Sons, Tampa, 1962-63; pres. Marjorie Gay Realty, Tampa, 1964—. Bd. dirs. Fla. Gulf Coast Symphony, St. Joseph's Hosp. Devel. Council; mem. Downtown Council of Tampa. Mem. Nat., Fla. assns. realtors, Tampa Bd. Realtors, Realtors Nat. Mktg. Inst., Women's Council Realtors, Greater Tampa C. of C., Grad. Realtors Inst., Nat. Assn. Real Estate Bds., Alpha Delta Pi. Presbyterian (deacon). Clubs: Coral Gables (Fla.) Jr. Women's, St. Petersburg Jr. Women's, Edgebrook Woman's (Chgo.); Des Moines Woman's; Village Garden, Tower, Tampa Yacht and Country, Carrollwood Village Golf and Country (Tampa). Office: 100 Madison St Bldg Suite 202 Tampa FL 33602

GAY, PAUL EDWARD, real estate exec.; b. Charleston, W.Va., July 18, 1938; s. Nathan Ray and Nadia (Young) G.; ed. U. S.C., 1961. Vice-pres. L.B. Kaye Assos., Ltd., N.Y.C., 1967-70; v.p. William B. May Co., Inc., N.Y.C., 1970-71; pres. Paul Gay & Co., Inc., N.Y.C., 1971-77; pres., chmn. James N. Wells' Sons, Inc., N.Y.C., 1977—. Bd. dirs. McBurney YMCA, N.Y.C.; mem. property mgmt. com. of bd. dirs. YMCA of Greater N.Y.; pres. Twenty-Third St. Assn., N.Y.C.; founder, trustee Chelsea Community Ch., N.Y.C.; bd. dirs. Washington Sq. Music Festival, N.Y.C.; bd. deacons First Presbyterian Ch., N.Y.C., 1969-72; mem. Housing Task Force Presbytery of N.Y., 1970-73. Mem. Real Estate Bd. N.Y.C., Young Men's Real Estate Assn. N.Y., N.Y. Bd. Trade, N.Y. State Assn. Realtors, Nat. Assn. Realtors, Mcpl. Art Soc. N.Y.C., N.Y. State Preservation League, Cooper-Hewitt Mus., N.Y. Landmarks Conservancy, Hundred Yr. Assn., Nat. Arts Club, Chi Psi, Phi Mu Alpha Sinfonia. Republican. Office: 340 W 23d St New York NY 10011

GAY, WILSON A., chem. co. exec.; b. Saginaw, Mich., June 30, 1928; s. Harry H. and Kittie Gay (Wilson) G.; B.A., Mich. State U., 1952; m. Kathleen Conley, Apr. 9, 1977; children—James W., David S. With Dow Chem. Co., Midland, Mich., 1957—, staff asst., then asst. treas., 1967-76, treas., 1976—; treas. Dow Chem. Internat. Inc., Dow Chem. Internat. Ltd., Dow Chem. Inter-Am. Ltd., Dow Chem. Overseas Capital N.V.; fin. dir. Dow Chem. A.G., Dow Chem. N.V (C); dir. Bank Mendes Gans N.V., Amsterdam, Midland Pipeline Co., Dorintal Reins. Ltd., Dorinco Reins. Co., Dow Chem. Overseas Mgmt. Co., Dow Chem. Overseas Capital N.V., Dow Chem. Internat. Inc. (Del.). Mem. Freeland (Mich.) Sch. Bd., 1974-75; mem. econ. adv. council Mich. Dem. Party, 1979—. Served to lt. comdr. USNR, 1952-55. Mem. Internat. C. of C. (internat. monetary com. U.S. Council 1980—). Home: 1124 Holyrood St Midland MI 48640 Office: 2030 Dow Center Midland MI 48640

GAZIANO, JOSEPH SALVATORE, diversified mfg. co. exec.; b. Waltham, Mass., Apr. 2, 1935; s. Salvatore and Carmela (Gangi) G.; B.S.E.E., M.I.T., 1956; m. Anne Marie Bradley, Sept. 8, 1962; children—Christopher, Cara, Mary Elizabeth. Mgr. maj. space systems Raytheon Co., Lexington, Mass., 1960-67; v.p., gen. mgr. Allied Research Assos., Concord, Mass., 1967-69; pres. Prelude Corp., Westport, Mass., 1969-73; chmn. bd., pres. Tyco Labs., Inc., Waltham, 1973—; dir. Mobil Tyco Solar Energy Corp., New Boston Garden Corp. Trustee Berwick Acad., South Berwick, Maine, St. Anselm's Coll., Manchester, N.H. Republican. Roman Catholic. Clubs: Brae Burn (Newton, Mass.); Board Room, Met. (N.Y.C.); Duquesne (Pitts.); York (Maine) Harbor Golf and Tennis. Office: Tyco Park Exeter NH 03833

GEBHARDT, FRANK HERMAN, communications co. exec.; b. Monango, N.D., May 20, 1931; s. John and Wilhelmina (Nehls) G.; student public schs., Monango; m. Margaret Ann Bruty, Dec. 28, 1957; children—John W., Denise W., Matthew F., Margaret M., Anne Michelle, Christopher M., Jennifer Jo. With G.T.E. Automatic Electric Co., Northlake, Ill., 1956-64; communications contractor, 1964-72; supt. central office Northwestern Telephone Systems, Kalispell, Mont., 1972-75; pres. Alamon Telco Inc., Kalispell, 1975—; pres. Altel Inc.; v.p. P.G.A. Investment Co.; pres. Alamon Tng. Center. Trustee Sch. Dist. 3, Kalispell, 1980—. Mem. Kalispell C. of C. Republican. Lutheran. Home: 530 Middle Rd Kalispell MT 59901 Office: 298 Sullivan Crossroads Columbia Falls MT 59912

GE BORDE, LINDLEY (DON), financial cons.; b. Guyana, Jan. 18, 1943; s. Thomas Syarka and Margaret Magena (Sutherland) GeB.; came to U.S., 1968; divorced; children—Dion, Troy, Delise. Sales mgr. for Caribbean, Combined Ins. Co. Am., 1964-68; v.p. Rasmussen Assos., E. Orange, N.J., 1968-72; pres. Estate Econs. Corp., Am., E. Orange, 1972—. C.L.U., cert. fin. planner. Mem. Million Dollar Roundtable (life), Nat. Assn. Securities Dealers, Am. Soc. C.L.U., Nat. Assn. Life Underwriters, N.J. Assn. Realtors. Address: Rural Route 2 Box 751 Route 206 Chester NJ 07930

GEE, EDWIN AUSTIN, paper co. exec.; b. Washington, Feb. 19, 1920; s. Edwin S. and Marie J. Gee; B.S., George Washington U., 1941; M.S. in Phys. Chemistry, 1944; Ph.D. in Chem. Engring., U. Md., 1948; m. Genevieve R. Riordan, Aug. 26, 1944; children—J. Michael, William S., David S. Lab. asst. U.S. Naval Research Lab., Anacostia, D.C., 1941-42; chemist, then asst. chief metallurgist Bur. Mines, Tenn., Md. and Washington, 1942-48; with DuPont Co., 1948-78, gen. mgr. photo products dept., 1968, sr. v.p., 1970-78; pres. Internat. Paper Co., N.Y.C., 1978-80, chmn. and chief exec. officer, 1980—; v.p., trees. Buck Hill Falls Co.; dir. Am. Home Products Co. Bd. dirs. New Castle County (Del.) YMCA, 1978—, Episcopal Ch. Home Found., 1978—; treas. Episcopal Diocese Del., 1978—. Republican. Co-author: Managing Innovation, 1976; author tech. papers. Address: 77 W 45th St New York NY 10036

GEEDEY, HARRY MICHAEL, poultry co. exec.; b. Lewistown, Pa., Mar. 26, 1951; s. Harry Alton and Thelma Jean (Gearhart) G.; B.S. in Math., Clarion State Coll., 1973; m. Glenda Gay Webb, Aug. 19, 1972; children—Shelly Ann, Andrew Michael. Indsl. engr. United Parcel Service, Bethlehem, Pa., 1973-76; export sales mgr. Empire Kosher Poultry, Mifflintown, Pa., 1976—; participant Pa. Internat. Trade Conf., 1980, 81. Active Juniata County Tax Payers Assn., Fayette Fire Co. Mem. Nat. Rifle Assn., Juniata Sportsman's Assn., Sons of Am. Legion. Democrat. Methodist. Home: RD 2 McAlisterville PA 17049 Office: RD 3 Box 165 Mifflintown PA 17059

GEENTIENS, GASTON PETRUS, JR., constrn. mgmt. cons. co. exec.; b. Garfield, N.J., Apr. 6, 1935; s. Gaston Petrus and Margaret (Piros) G.; B.S. in Civil Engring., The Citadel, 1956; m. Barbara Ann Chamberlain, Oct. 14, 1960; children—Mercedes Frith, Faith Piros. Plant engr. Western Elec. Co., Inc., Kearny, N.J., 1956-58, owner's rep., N.Y.C., 1960-64; v.p. Gentyne Motors, Inc., Passaic, N.J., 1958-60; project engr. Ethyl Corp., Baton Rouge, La., 1964-65; mgr. Timothy McCarthy Constrn. Co., Atlanta, 1965; asst. to v.p. A.R.

Abrams, Inc. and Columbia Engring., Inc., Atlanta, 1965-66; supr. engring. and constrn. Litton Industries, N.Y.C., 1966-71; pres. G.P. Geentiens Jr., Inc., Charleston, S.C., 1971—; gen. partner Engineered Enterprises Co., Charleston, 1973-76; dir. Cayman Broadcasting Assos., Cayman Islands, B.W.I., 1977—. Mem. Ramapo (N.Y.) Republican Com., 1961-64. Served to 1st lt. C.E., AUS, 1956-58. Registered profl. engr., 13 states. Mem. ASCE, Charleston C. of C., S.C. Indsl. Developers Assn. Club: Charleston Yacht. Home: 7 Fort Royal Dr Charleston SC 29407 Office: 4 Carriage Ln Charleston SC 29407

GEER, EDWARD DOUGLAS, constrn. cons.; b. Portland, Oreg., June 9, 1929; s. Lester John and Leona (Andrews) G.; B.S. in Engring., Oreg. State U., 1952; postgrad. U. So. Calif., 1955-61; m. Marylou Damewood, Mar. 15, 1951; children—Steven Douglas, Lynda Diane, Tricia Ellen. Field engr. Bethlehem Steel Co., Los Angeles, 1955-57; project engr. H.E. Robertson Co., Los Angeles, 1958-61; exec. v.p. Calif. Erectors Constrn. Co., Los Angeles, 1963-65; projects mgr. Murphy Pacific Corp., San Francisco, 1966-71; mgr. steel constrn. Allied Structural Steel Corp., Mpls., 1972-74, mng. dir. European operation, London, 1975—; mng. dir. Tokola Offshore (U.K.); v.p. Tokola Offshore, Inc.; pres. Columbia Bridge & Geer; chmn. Willamette Bridge Ltd.; dir. Fabcon Norway. Served to lt. col. U.S. Army, 1952-54, Korea, 1961-62, Berlin. Mem. ASCE, Am. Soc. Mil. Engrs., Oreg. Hist. Soc. Republican. Presbyterian. Home: 18311 Lothlorien Way Lake Oswego OR 97034 Office: Tokola Offshore Ltd 103/105 Jermyn St London SW1 Y6EE England United Kingdom

GEERDES, HENRY EVERETT, chem. co. exec.; b. Lakota, Iowa, Mar. 11, 1923; s. George I. and Mina Elizabeth (Geerdes) G.; B.S., U. Minn., 1949; postgrad. U. Mich., 1955; m. Violet Esther Erdahl, July 21, 1942; children—Patti Geerdes Hildebrandt, Bonnie, Carole. Exam. agt. IRS, 1949-56; accountant Bertram Cooper, C.P.A., also Broeker & Hendrickson, C.P.A.'s, St. Paul, 1956-63; treas., controller Peck, Inc., St. Paul, 1963-66; individual practice acctg., 1966-68; dir. taxes H.B. Fuller Co., St. Paul, 1968—; pres., dir. N.W. Pioneer Corp., Mpls., 1966—; sec., dir. Star Crown Industries, Inc.; dir. Atsatt Co., N.W. Pioneer Corp.; chmn. MicroComm Corp. Served with AUS, 1944-46. Mem. Am. Inst. C.P.A.'s, Minn. Soc. C.P.A.'s, Am. Legion. Home: 6817 Lyndale Ave S Minneapolis MN 55423 Office: 2400 Kasota Ave St Paul MN 55108

GEERY, MICHAEL JAMES, electronics co. exec.; b. Missoula, Mont., July 15, 1937; s. Glenn Leroy and Rhye (Ward) G.; B.S. in Aero. Engring., Northrop U., 1960; m. Carole Ann Gibbs, Feb. 27, 1965; children—Laura Lynn, Patricia, Melanie, Angela, Jeffrey, Jill, Holly. Electronic design engr. N. Am. Aviation, Los Angeles, 1960-62; electronic project engr. Lockheed Electronics, Los Angeles, 1962-64; biomed. electronic design engr. Space Labs Inc., Chattsworth, Calif., 1964-65; mktg. staff exec. TRW, Los Angeles, 1965-73; western area mgr. Gates Energy Products Co., Los Angeles, 1973-78; chief exec. officer Xenotronix Systems, Torrance, Calif., 1978—; cons. Mem. Ch. of Scientology. Home: 1327 Curtis Ave Manhattan Beach CA 90266 Office: 2909 A3 Oregon Ct Torrance CA 90503

GEESLIN, WILLIAM FLEMING, r.r. co. exec.; b. Macon, Ga., June 16, 1919; s. William F. and Louise (Wynn) G.; A.B., Mercer U., 1940; m. Mary E. Timmerman, May 18, 1946; children—William Fleming, John Warren, Christopher Lee. Spl. agt. FBI, 1942-47; account exec. Young & Rubicam, Inc., N.Y.C., 1947-60; exec. v.p. Manatee County (Fla.) C. of C., 1961-63; v.p. First Nat. Bank, Bradenton, Fla., 1963-64; asst. v.p. So. Ry. System, Washington, 1967—. Mem. R.R. Pub. Relations Assn., Pub. Relations Soc. Am., Am. Mktg. Assn. Episcopalian. Clubs: Traffic, Nat. Press, Chevy Chase, City Tavern. Home: 5351 MacArthur Blvd NW Washington DC 20016 Office: PO Box 1808 Washington DC 20013

GEHRING, FRANCIS PENTLARGE, JR., textile co. exec.; b. N.Y.C., June 23, 1931; s. Frank P. and Gertrude E. (Steiger) G.; B.Mech. Engring., Villanova U., 1954; M.B.A., Columbia, 1966; m. Anne Ferrebee, Dec. 22, 1968; children—Francis III, Moira, Arthur, Alexandra, Samantha. Plant mgr. Helmont Mills, St. Johnsville, N.Y., 1957-63; v.p. Millitex Corp., N.Y.C., 1963-69; pres. Gehring Textiles, 1966-69; asst. to pres. Bangor div. Collins/Aikman, 1969-71; exec. v.p. Liberty Fabrics of N.Y., N.Y.C., 1971-79, also dir.; exec. v.p. mktg. Dan River Knits, N.Y.C., 1979—; trustee Inst. Textile Tech., Charlottesville, Va. Mgr. various charitable campaigns upstate N.Y., L.I. Served with USN, 1954-57. Mem. ASME, Am. Arbitration Assn., Tau Beta Pi. Clubs: Cooperstown Country; N.Y. Athletic; Boars Head Racquet. Home: 1833 Westview Dr Charlottesville VA 22902 Office: 111 W 40th St New York NY 10016

GEHRKE, JUDITH ANN, housewares mfg. co. exec.; b. Waterloo, Iowa, May 9, 1948; d. Paul Albert and Margaret Louise (Jessen) G.; B.A., Northwestern U., 1969; M.S. in Design, Pratt Inst., 1971; M.B.A., Harvard U., 1973; m. Jose Luis Rodriguez, Nov. 1, 1979. Sr. product mgr. Dansk Designs, Mt. Kisco, N.Y., 1973-76; sr. mktg. analyst Internat. Paper Co., N.Y.C., 1976-78; founding pres. Design Lines, Inc., N.Y.C., 1977—. Baker scholar, 1973; Laurence Rockefeller scholar, 1971-73. Office: 450 W 31st St 4th floor New York NY 10001

GEIGER, LEO, hosp. adminstr.; b. Gladstone, N.D., Dec. 9, 1928; s. Peter and Tillie Gieser; student Dickinson (N.D.) State Coll., 1949-50; diploma hosp. adminstrn. U. Minn., 1972; m. Alvina Anderson, July 10, 1952; children—Marianne, Gregory, Edward. X-ray technician Harrisburg (Ill.) Med. Found. Hosps., 1950-61; adminstr. Mc Intosh County Meml. Hosp., Ashby, N.D., 1961-70; adminstr. St. Aloisius Hosp., Harvey, N.D., 1970-79; corp. adminstr. Sisters of Mary of the Presentation, Valley City, N.D., 1979—; trustee Rolla (N.D.) Community Hosp., 1978—; bd. dirs. S. Central Mental Health Center. Mem. Am. (del. 1979—), N.D. (pres. 1975, dir. 1970—) hosps. assns., Am. Coll. Hosp. Adminstrs., Hosp. Fin. Mgmt. Assn. Roman Catholic. Clubs: Elks, Kiwanis, Eagles. Home: 1435 2d Ave NE Valley City ND 58072 Office: Sisters of Mary of the Presentation Route 1 Maryvale Valley City ND 58072

GEIGER, RICHARD LAWRENCE, venture capital co. exec.; b. N.Y.C., Apr. 18, 1917; s. Jerome C. and Ruth (Alton) G.; B.S., Coll. City N.Y., 1935; Indsl. Engr., N.Y. U., 1951; m. Emmy L. Epstein, Feb. 2, 1946; children—Ellen Catherine, James Lawrence. Prodn. control mgr. Eagle Pencil Co., N.Y.C., 1947-50; indsl. relations dir. Maidenform, Bayonne, N.J., 1950-51; controller Am. Aluminum Co., Newark, 1951-55; gen. mgr. Telautograph Corp., N.Y.C., 1955-56; asso. N.W. Levin & Co., financial advisers, N.Y.C., 1956-60; pres. de Vegh Internat. Corp., N.Y.C., 1960-64; financial cons., N.Y.C., 1964-68, 78—; gen. partner Geiger & Fialkov, venture capital, N.Y.C., 1968-77; pres. RLGCCC Corp., Summit, N.J., 1978—; chmn. bd. Micro Semiconductor Corp., Santa Ana, Calif., Vega Labs. Inc., Tucson; dir. Metrocare Inc., St. Petersburg, Fla., Standard Microsystems, Hauppage, N.Y., Apollo Lasers, Los Angeles, Geotel, Inc., Amityville, N.Y., Franchise Mktg. Assos., Boston, Sentinel Resources, East Orange, N.J. Adviser, J.M. Kaplan Fund, 1964-68. Served to capt. USNR, 1940-47. Registered profl. engr., N.J. Mem. Tech. Socs. Council N.J. (past pres.), Am. Phys. Soc., Financial Analysts Fedn., N.Y. Soc. Security Analysts, Alpha Pi Mu. Club: Army-Navy (Washington). Home: 133 Whittredge Rd Summit NJ 07901

GEIGERMAN, CLARICE FURCHGOTT, pub. relations and ins. co. exec.; b. Charleston, S.C., Sept. 24, 1916; d. Melvin and Doreta (Brown) Furchgott; student Draughan Sch. Commerce, 1934-35, U. Ga., 1935, 36, Am. Inst. Banking, 1936-41, Ga. Inst. Real Estate, 1972; m. Henry David Geigerman, July 4, 1941 (dec. 1967); children—Henry David, Robert M. Sec. to v.p. investment dept. Citizens and So. Nat. Bank, Atlanta, 1935-41; personnel dir. Atlanta Ordnance Dept., 1941-43; pub. relations counselor in pvt. practice, Atlanta, 1944—; agt. Nat. Life Ins. Co., Atlanta, 1968—; real estate agt. First Atlanta Equity, 1972—. Bd. dirs. So. Regional Opera, 1968-75, pres., 1968-69; dir. Active Voters, 1965—; pres. Atlanta Playhouse Theatre, 1973—; pres. Atlanta Civic Ballet, 1962-64, bd. dirs., 1962-67; mem. Atlanta Ballet Assos., 1962—; mem. adv. bd. Muscular Dystrophy Assn., 1968—; mem. bd. sponsors Atlanta Symphony Guild, 1969—, v.p., women's bd., 1966-68, mem. policy bd., 1966—; bd. dirs. Atlanta Youth Symphony, 1974—, Altanta Funds Rev. Bd., 1973-75, Atlanta Music Club, 1972—; trustee Atlanta Press Club, 1974—. Mem. Pub. Relations Soc. Am., Victorian Soc. Am., Nat. Council Jewish Women, Marquis Library Soc., Nat. Acad. Television Arts and Scis., Am. Women in Radio and TV, Women's C. of C., English Speaking Union, Epicurean Soc. Am., Italian Cultural Soc., Atlanta Hist. Soc., World Assn. Women Journalists. Jewish. Clubs: Atlanta Music (dir. 1973—), Oaks, Standard, Ga. Writers. Contbr. articles on arts and music to mags.; co-editor Atlanta Music Club Newsletter and Atlanta Music Club Mag., 1973—; contbg. editor Arts Mag., 1962-63, TV Digest, 1961-62; contbr. articles So. Israelite Newspaper. Home: 620 Peachtree St NE Atlanta GA 30308 Office: 151 Ellis St Atlanta GA 30308

GEIKEN, ALAN RICHARD, contractor; b. Toledo, Aug. 24, 1923; s. Martin Herman and Herta Regina G.; B.S. in Engring., Iowa State U., 1950. Engr., sec. Hot Spot Detector, Inc., Des Moines, 1950-53, sales engr., asst. gen. mgr., 1953-60; pres., owner Alan Geiken Co., San Francisco, 1960—; cons. on grain storage. Served with USAAF, 1943-45. Mem. Am. Soc. Agrl. Engrs., Calif. Warehousemens Assn., Calif. Grain and Feed Assn., Grain Elevator and Processing Soc. Lutheran. Developed electronic system to maintain healthful condition of stored grain and bulk foods. Address: 2115 Van Ness Ave San Francisco CA 94109

GEIL, JOHN, bus. and computer systems cons.; b. Mound City, Mo., Sept. 21, 1921; s. Henry and Zella G.; B.S. in Econs., U. Oreg., 1947; m. Marilyn Marie Beers, Mar. 12, 1971; children—Carl, Pamela. Bus. systems designer, 1948-55; head systems and procedures dept. Boeing Corp., Wichita, Kans., 1955-58; dir. computerization program Montgomery Ward, Chgo. and Kansas City, Mo., 1958-60; pres., chmn. bd. Bus. Technicians, Inc., Health Data Internat., Inc., Specification Technology, Inc. and Internat. Systems, Inc., Santa Ana, Calif. and Kansas City, 1961-74; cons. Region IV Edn. Service Center, Houston, 1974-79; dir. data processing City of Shreveport (La.), 1980—. Mem. adminstrv. bd. 1st Methodist Ch., Houston, 1977-80. Served with C.E., U.S. Army, 1942-46. Patentee computer software system. Contbg. author: Business Systems, 1962. Address: 7800 Youree Dr Apt 219 Town Oak S Shreveport LA 71105

GEISE, HARRY FREMONT, ret. meteorologist; b. Oak Park, Ill., Jan. 8, 1920; student U. Chgo., 1938-39, Meterorol. Service Sch., Lakehurst, N.J., 1943-44; m. Juanita Calmer, 1974; children—Barry, Gary, Harry (triplets); children by previous marriage—Marian Frances, Gloria Tara. Pioneered in extending pvt. weather services in Chgo., 1937; chief meteorologist Kingsbury Ordnance, 1943; meteorologist radio sta. WLS, and Prairie Farmer Newspaper, 1941, 42, 46; asso. Dr. Irving P. Krick, metorol. cons., 1947-49; Army Air Corps research, 1948-49, developed new temperature forecasting technique; condr. weather and travel shows WBKB-TV, Chgo., also radio sta. WOPA, Oak Park, 1950-51; developed radio and television shows, San Francisco and San Jose, Cal., 1954-55; dir. media div. Irving P. Krick Assos., 1955-59; produced, appeared on weather programs Columbia Pacific Radio and TV Networks, also weatherman KNXT, Hollywood, Calif., 1957-58; comml. weather service, 1962-80; instr. meteorology Santa Rosa Jr. Coll., 1964-66, Sonoma State Coll., 1967-68; weather dir. WCBS-TV, 1966-67, established weather center for CBS, N.Y., 1966-67. Research relationship between specified solar emission and major change in earth's weather patterns, tornado forecasting and long-range forecasting up to 2 years in advance. Meteorologist, Nat. Def. Exec. Res., 1968-74. Served with USMC, 1944-45. Mem. Am. Meterol. Soc., Royal Meterol. Soc. (life fgn. mem.). Author articles in field, contbr. to newspapers and mags. Contbr. long range forecasts. Home: 1780 Avenida del Mundo Coronado CA 92118

GEISER, KARL FREDERICK, lawyer; b. New Hampton, Iowa, June 6, 1903; s. Mathias Edgar and Belle (Rowe) G.; student Oberlin Coll., 1921-22; A.B., State U. Iowa, 1925, J.D., 1927; m. Jane Schoentgen, June 6, 1928; children—Karl Frederick, Gretel Geiser Stephens. Admitted to Iowa bar, 1927, Calif. bar, 1946, U.S. Supreme Ct.; partner Geiser, Donohue & Geiser, New Hampton, 1927-29; exec. v.p. E. H. Lougee, Inc., 1929-30; partner Tinley, Mitchell, Ross, Everest & Geiser, 1930-42; pvt. practice, Beverly Hills, Calif., 1945-78. Served from lt. to comdr. USNR, 1942-45. Mem. Am., Iowa, Calif., Los Angeles bar assns., Order of Coif, Phi Delta Phi, Sigma Alpha Epsilon. Republican. Home: 6271 Paseo Canyon Dr Malibu CA 90265

GEISINGER, WILLIAM ROBERT, mgmt. cons., economist; b. Fredericksburg, Va., Oct. 21, 1908; s. William M. and Glada (Hawthorne) G.; A.B., Dartmouth Coll., 1930; student George Washington U., 1952; Ph.D. in Bus. Adminstrn. (hon.), Hamilton State U., 1973; m. Verna Cragg, June 20, 1931 (div. 1946); children—Harry C., William Robert. With Central Trust Co., Cin., 1930-40; economist Montgomery Ward & Co., 1940-49; mktg. and forecasting exec. Kroger Co., Cin., 1949-54; mgmt. cons., 1954—; tchr. U. Cin. evening sch., 1937-40, Am. Inst. Banking, 1938-40; lectr. Miami U., Oxford, Ohio, 1939-40, Northwestern U., 1948, Am. Coalition Patriotic Socs. Seminar, 1954. Examiner, RFC, 1938-39; chief food and restaurant div. statistics OPS, 1952; Dept. State (ICA) mktg. and distbn. specialist to Germany, 1955. Mem. Trans-Atlantic council Boy Scouts Am., 1955, Cin. council, 1953-54. Mem. Am. Econ. Assn., Am. Mgmt. Assn., Am. Statis. Assn., Found. Study Cycles, AAAS, Waco Hist. Soc. (historian). Republican. Presbyterian. Clubs: Masons, Shriners, Lions. Published Chart on Major War Cycles in U.S.A., 1948-49, Geisinger Indicator U.S.A., Forecasting Business Activity, 1954—. Office: 108 S Monroe St PO Box 279 Troy OH 45373

GEISLER, NATHAN DAVID, stockbroker; b. Kokand, Russia, Jan. 22, 1946; s. Leon and Esther (Korn) G.; B.A., Ohio State U., 1968; J.D., U. Toledo, 1970. Account exec. Merrill Lynch Pierce Fenner & Smith, Toledo, 1973—. Served to capt. USAF, 1971-73. Mem. Air Force Assn., Ohio Air N.G. Assn., Ohio State Alumni Assn., U. Toledo Alumni Assn., Phi Alpha Delta. Home: 5906 Cresthaven Ln Apt C-2 Toledo OH 43614 Office: 300 Madison Ave Toledo OH 43604

GEIST, GLENN WILLIAM, television exec.; b. Topeka, Kans., Jan. 29, 1921; s. William F. and Mytle Mae (Hardisty) G.; student pub. schs.; m. Jane R. Mol, Apr. 6, 1961; children—Daniel W., Steven W. Vice pres. Television Engrs. Inc., 1947-51, pres., 1951-57; pres. Certified TV Service Inc., 1957-80, Certified Computer Services Inc., 1972-80, Certified Electronic Distbr. Inc., 1959-80; with Geist-Swislow Ltd., Chgo., 1979—; chmn. bd. Andre & Co. Inc., Universal Lamp Co., Inc., 1967-70 (all Chgo.). Served with AUS, 1942-45. Decorated Purple Heart, Bronze Star (U.S.); Croix de Guerre with palm (France). Lion. Home: 6846 N Mendota Ave Chicago IL 60646 Office: 5048 W Fullerton Ave Chicago IL 60639

GEIST, JERRY DOUGLAS, electric utility co. exec.; b. Raton, N.Mex., May 23, 1934; s. Jacob D. and Jessie Kathleen (Wadley) G.; student U. Mo., 1952-54; B.E.E., U. Colo., 1956; m. Sharon Ludell Kaemper, June 9, 1956; children—Douglas, Bruce, Robert. With Public Service Co. N.Mex., Albuquerque, 1960—, v.p. engring. and ops., 1970-71, v.p. corporate affairs, 1971-73, exec. v.p., 1973-76, pres., 1976—, also dir., mem. exec. com.; sr. v.p. Western Coal Co., 1972—, also dir., mem. exec. com.; dir. Bank Securities, Inc., Lectrosonics Inc., Reddy Communications, Inc. Associated Electric and Gas Ins. Ltd., Resources for the Future. Bd. dirs., past chmn. Western Regional Council; chmn. adminstrv. bd. First United Methodist Ch.; mem. Nat. Public Lands Adv. Council; bd. dirs. St. Joseph's Hosp. Served with USN, 1952-59. Registered profl. engr., N.Mex. Mem. Albuquerque C. of C. (pres. 1972-73), Tau Beta Pi, Sigma Tau, Eta Kappa Nu, Pi Mu Epsilon. Clubs: Four Four Hills Country, Albuquerque Country, Albuquerque Petroleum. Home: 1312 Cuatro Cerros Trail SE Albuquerque NM 87123 Office: Public Service Co NMex Alvarado Sq Albuquerque NM 87158

GELB, RICHARD LEE, business exec.; b. N.Y.C., June 8, 1924; s. Lawrence M. and Joan F. (Bove) M.; student Phillips Acad., 1938-41; B.A., Yale, 1945; M.B.A. with distinction, Harvard, 1950; m. Phyllis L. Nason, May 5, 1951; children—Lawrence N., Lucy G., Jane E., James M. Chmn. bd., chief exec., dir. Bristol-Myers Co.; dir. Bankers Trust Co., Bankers Trust N.Y. Corp., Charter Corp., Cluett, Peabody & Co., Inc., N.Y. Times Co. Trustee, Nat. Council Crime and Delinquency, Conf. Bd.; chmn. N.Y. State Crime Control Planning Bd.; mem. Bus. Council, Bus. Roundtable, Bus. Com. for Arts; bd. dirs. Lincoln Center for Performing Arts, Council on Fgn. Relations; trustee Com. Econ. Devel., N.Y.C. Police Found., Inc., N.Y. State Racing Assn.; charter trustee Phillips Acad.-Andover. Home: 1060 Fifth Ave New York NY 10028 Office: 345 Park Ave New York NY 10022

GELBAUM, DENNIS JAY, audio visual co. exec.; b. N.Y.C., Mar. 31, 1950; s. Harold and Ruth (Flender) G.; B.S. in Broadcast Journalism, Am. U., 1970; M.S. in Communications, Syracuse (N.Y.) U., 1971; m. Stacy Lynn Klein, May 11, 1975. Writer, producer J. Walter Thompson Co., N.Y.C., 1973-75; pres., exec. producer D.J.G. Communications Inc., N.Y.C., after 1975; now sr. TV producer Compton Advt., N.Y.C. Recipient U.S. Indsl. Film Festival award, 1978, Bronze medal N.Y. Internat. Film and TV Festival, 1979; Grand award N.Y. Film Festival, 1979; Best TV Commercial of Yr. award Utah Film Festival, 1979; producer 1 of 100 Best Commercials of Yr., 1979; Andy award of Merit (2), 1980; One Show award, 1980. Mem. Screenwriters Guild Am., Nat. Assn. Broadcasters, Dirs. Guild Am., Nat. Assn. Media Educators. Jewish. Club: B'nai B'rith. Author: One Solitary Life, 1979; also children's books, communications articles. Home: 2500 Johnson Ave #16L Riverdale NY 10463 Office: 154 W 57th St Studio 810 New York NY 10022 also 625 Madison Ave New York NY 10022

GELFAND, IVAN, investment advisor; b. Cleve., Mar. 29, 1927; s. Samuel and Sarah (Kruglin) G.; B.S., Miami U., Oxford, Ohio, 1950; postgrad. Case-Western Res. U., 1951; grad. Columbia U. Bank Mgmt. Program, 1968; certs. Am. Inst. Banking, 1952-57; m. Suzanne Frank, Sept. 23, 1956; children—Dennis Scott, Andrew Steven. Acct., Central Nat. Bank Cleve., 1950-53, v.p., mgr. bank and corp. investments, 1957-75; chief acct. Stars & Stripes newspaper, Darmstadt, Germany, 1953-55; account exec. Merrill, Lynch, Pierce, Fenner & Smith, Inc., Cleve., 1955-57; chmn., chief exec. officer Gelfand, Quinn & Assos., Inc., Cleve., 1975—; pres. Lindow, Gelfand and Quinn, Inc., 1976—; co-editor Gelfand-Quinn/Liquidity Portfolio Mgr. Newsletter, 1978—; money market columnist Nat. Thrift News, 1976-78; instr. investments adult div. Cleve. Bd. Edn., 1956-58, Am. Inst. Banking, 1958-68; lectr. in econs., bank portfolio mgmt., 1972—; chmn. Bus. in Action, 1978—. Mem. investment com. United Torch Cleve., 1972-74; study-rev. team capt. Lake Erie Regional Transp. Authority, 1973-77; mem. Cuyahoga County Republican Fin. Com.; mem. exec. bd. Cleve. chpt. Am. Men's Orgn. Rehab. and Tng., 1968-76, asst. sec., 1970-72. Served with AUS, 1945-47. Mem. Greater Cleve. Growth Assn., Cleve. Soc. Security Analysts, Les Politiques. Republican. Clubs: Mid-day, Commerce (Cleve.); Univ., Oakwood, Masons. Home: 2900 Alvord Pl Pepper Pike OH 44124 Office: Leader Bldg Cleveland OH 44114

GELINAS, JOHN GERALD, pub. affairs cons.; b. Stroudsburg, Pa., Feb. 24, 1929; s. Anthony J.F. and Margaret E. (Morris) G.; A.A., Keystone Jr. Coll., 1951; B.S. in Public Communication, Boston U., 1953, M.S. (fellow), 1954; m. Barbara Ann Link, Sept. 6, 1958; children—Cynthia A., John Gerald, Amy Elizabeth, Gregory J., Garrick M. Public relations intern Young-Alleghany-Kirby Ownership Bd., 1954; public relations staff asst. N.Y. Central R.R., 1955-56, Mobil Corp., 1956-58; public relations adviser Mobil Oil Nigeria Ltd. and Mobil Exploration Nigeria, Inc., 1958-62; sr. public relations adviser Mobil Internat., 1962; account exec. Thomas J. Deegan Co., Inc., 1962-65, asst. v.p., 1965, v.p., 1965-67; dir. corp. communication Nat. Union Electric Corp., 1967-68, exec. asst. to chief exec. officer, cons. public relations, 1968-71; exec. v.p. and chief operating officer Thomas J. Deegan Co., Inc., 1971-73, vice chmn., 1973; sr. v.p., dir. fin. services Edward Gottlieb & Assos., Ltd., 1973-76; dir. Pilot Radio Corp., 1970-72; internat. public affairs cons., pres. John G. Gelinas Assos., Inc., N.Y.C. Mem. planning bd. Town of Eastchester, N.Y., 1975-78; mem. exec. bd. Westchester-Putnam council Boy Scouts Am., 1977—, chmn. quality control program of long range planning com., mem. exec. council Greater N.Y. Councils, chmn. public relations com., 1967-72; mem. Nat. Alumni Council, Boston U., 1971—; exec. coordinator Am. Cancer Soc. Athlete of Decade Awards Program, 1979—. Served with U.S. Army, 1947-48. Recipient Robert R. Young award Boston U., 1954; Gold Key award PR News, 1970. Mem. Investors Relations Inst. (charter mem.), Internat. Inst. Communications, Nat. Press Club of Nigeria (life), Ave. of Americas Assn. (mem. public relations com.), Tau Mu Epsilon. Clubs: Classic Car of Am. (dir.), Explorers. Contbr. articles to profl. jours. Home: 96 Puritan Dr Scarsdale NY 10583 Office: Pan Am Bldg 200 Park Ave New York NY 10017

GELLASCH, DENNIS KEITH, electronic monitoring co. exec.; b. Detroit, Sept. 7, 1938; s. Reno Arthur William and Dorothy Ermina (Stead) G.; A.A.S., Mohawk Valley Community Coll., 1964; B.S., Utica Coll. Syracuse U., 1967; M.B.A., Rochester Inst. Tech., 1972; m. Nancy Cromwell Curtis, Aug. 27, 1966; children—Tara L., Tyler E. Customer engr. IBM, Rochester, 1963-65; dir. residence hall Syracuse U., Utica, 1965-67; product planner Eastman Kodak, Rochester, 1967-69; sr. sales adminstr. Itek Bus. Products div., Itek

Corp. Rochester, 1969-70; product mgr. Castle Co., Rochester, 1970-72; sales mgr. ophthalmic instruments Bausch & Lomb, Rochester to 1976; product sales mgr. Rochester Instrument Systems, Inc., 1976—; cons. minority bus. Served with USMCR, 1957-62. Mem. Am. Marketing Assn. (pres. 1971-72, dir. 1968-72), Instrument Soc. Am. (sr. mem.; edn. chmn. Rochester sect. 1977), IEEE (chmn. sub-com. 1978-80), Rochester Sales and Mktg. Execs. Club (edn. com. 1979-80), Mohawk Valley Community Alumni Assn. (nat. bd. dirs. 1971-72), Phi Kappa Phi. Home: 33 Meadow Dr Webster NY 14580 Office: 255 N Union St Rochester NY 14605

GELLERSTED, HARRY WALTER, JR., investor; b. Chgo., Jan. 30, 1922; s. Harry W. and Mildred D. (Wilson) G.; grad. Ill. Wesleyan U., 1942; m. Marilyn Skillman, June 26, 1976; children—Diane C., Richard H. Pvt. investor, Chgo., 1972—. Served with USCG, 1942-46. Sigma Chi Alumni Assn. Chgo. Clubs: Bond, Rotary One Chgo., Execs. (Chgo.), Westmoreland Country, Tavern. Home: 570 Winnetka Ave Winnetka IL 60093

GELVEN, MICHAEL PAUL, retail liquor exec.; b. Boston, June 4, 1946; s. Abraham and Sarah Rebecca (Glick) G.; student Boston State Coll., 1964-66, Northeastern U., 1969-71; certificate Southeastern Mass. U., 1978; m. Wendy Ellen Tanzer, Oct. 20, 1968; children—Marc Ian, Shana Lee. Mgr. trainee Contan Liquors, Inc., Somerville, Mass., 1967-68, mgr., 1968-73; mgr. Tanza Liquors, Inc., Somerville, 1973-74; pres., chief exec. officer Perry's Liquor Inc., N. Dartmouth, Mass., 1974—; pres. GTC Assos. Inc., North Easton, Mass., 1978—; pres. DeRoy's Package Store, Chicopee, Mass., 1979-80; cons. Tanza Wine Assn., 1977—; instr. wine appreciation Bristol Community Coll., 1979—. Served with Army N.G., 1966. Mem. Mass. Beverage Assn., Soc. Wine Educators, Les Amis DuVin, La Confrerie Saint-Etienne d'Alsace. Democrat. Jewish (pres. temple 1978-80, dir. 1980—). Clubs: Mensa, Lions, Masons, K.P., B'nai B'rith (pres. 1973-74). Home: 18 Guinevere Rd North Easton MA 02356 Office: 17 Faunce Corner Rd North Dartmouth MA 02747

GELZER, RANDELL EDWIN, millwork co. exec.; b. Summerville, S.C., July 14, 1943; s. George Edward and Caryl Mary (Smith) G.; B.S., The Citadel, 1965; m. Kathleen McLeod, Dec. 29, 1966; children—Margaret, Randell. Asst. to pres., gen. mgr. Driwood Moulding Co., Murray Mitchell Bldg. Supply, Murray Mitchell Lighting Co., Florence, S.C., 1971—. Mem. Quinby (S.C.) City Council, 1980—. Served as pilot USAF, 1966-71. Mem. Archtl. Woodwork Inst. Presbyterian. Home: 13 Bayswater Rd Quinby SC 29501 Office: PO Box 1729 Florence SC 29503

GENDRON, DONALD ROGER, quality control engr.; b. Southbridge, Mass., Sept. 19, 1936; s. Albert Elzard and Gertrude Florence (Tetreault) G.; Diplomas, Mgmt. Tng. Program, Worcester Jr. Coll., 1969, Quality Control, Northeastern U., 1970; m. Loretta G. LaBonte, Feb. 2, 1957; children—MaryLou, Maria, Paul, Donna. Supr. quality control Mosaic Fabrications div. Bendix Corp., Sturbridge, Mass., 1966-72; supr. quality control Galileo Electro-Optics Corp., Sturbridge, 1972-75, mgr. quality control, 1975-77, dir. product assurance, from 1977; now sr. quality engr. CTI Cryogenics div. Helix Corp., Waltham, Mass. Elected mem. Bay Path Regional Vocat. Sch. Com., Charlton, Mass.; mem. Mass. Assn. Sch. Coms., 1976—; mem. Sturbridge Lions Club, 1969-72; asso. mem. Southbridge Town Democratic Com., 1976—. Served with USAF, 1956-60. Registered profl. quality engr., Calif. Mem. Am. Soc. Quality Control (sr., quality control, tech. conf. 1977), Nat. Soc. Profl. Engrs., Worcester Engring Soc., Aircraft Owners and Pilots Assn., Bay Path Archery, Air Force Sgts. Assn. Roman Catholic. Lic. pvt. airplane pilot single engine land; certified 2d. class radiotelephone, FAA. Home: 332 Morris St Southbridge MA 01550 Office: 266 Second Ave Waltham MA 02154

GENEEN, HAROLD SYDNEY, communications co. exec.; b. Bournemouth, Eng., Jan. 22, 1910; s. S. Alexander and Aida (DeCrucian) G.; brought to U.S., 1911, naturalized (derivative), 1918; B.S. in Accounting and Fin., N.Y. U., 1934; grad. Advanced Mgmt. Program, Harvard U.; LL.D. (hon.), Lafayette Coll., PMC Colls.; m. June Elizabeth Hjelm, Dec. 1949. Accountant and analyst Mayflower Assos., 1932-34; sr. accountant Lybrand, Ross Bros. & Montgomery, 1934-42; chief accountant Am. Can Co., 1942-46; controller Bell & Howell Co., Chgo., 1946-50; v.p., controller Jones & Laughlin Steel Corp., Pitts., 1950-56; exec. v.p., dir. Raytheon Mfg. Co., Waltham, Mass., 1956-59; pres. ITT, 1959-73, chief exec., 1959-77, dir., 1959—, chmn. bd., 1964-79, chmn. exec. com., 1974-80, chmn. emeritus, 1980—, also dir. fgn. subsidiaries, affiliated cos.; advisory com. Uptown br. Bankers Trust Co. Bd. dirs. Internat. Rescue Com.; mem. nat. council Salk Inst. Biol. Studies, 1977—; treas. Voice Found. Decorated grand officer Order of Merit (Peru); comdr. Order of the Crown (Belgium); Grand Cross of Civil Merit, Grand Cross of Isabella Cath. Mother of the Americas (Spain); co-recipient 5th ann. Communications award ICD Rehab. and Research Center, 1976. C.P.A., N.Y., Ill. Mem. Am. Inst. C.P.A.'s, Fin. Execs. Inst., Soc. C.P.A.'s, Nat. Assn. Accountants, Internat. C. of C. (trustee U.S. council), Voice Found. Episcopalian. Clubs: Duquesne (Pitts.); Links, Oakmont Country, Braeburn Country, Oyster Harbors, Union League (N.Y.C.); Harvard (Boston). Office: ITT World Hdqrs 320 Park Ave New York NY 10022*

GENEMATAS, GEORGE NICHOLAS, real estate developer, resort owner; b. Detroit, Jan. 5, 1923; s. Nicholas William and Marie Maud (Seguin) G.; student Athens Coll. (Greece), 1938-39, U. Ariz., 1941-42, Wayne State U., 1942-43; m. Patricia Ann Frazer, Sept. 16, 1953; children—Nicholas, Gene Marie, James, Robert. Pres., dir. Marathon Linen Service, Detroit, 1947-57; pres., dir. Oracle Foothills Estates, Tucson, 1957-61; owner, operator Catalina Foothills Lodge, Tucson, 1963—; developer Casa Blanca Villa, Tucson, 1968—; developer, owner Casa Blanca Plaza, Tucson, 1969—. Chmn. Tucson Crime Commn.; bd. dirs. St. Odilia's Bldg. Com., Tucson, 1964—. Served with AUS, 1943-46. Decorated Bronze Star. Mem. Tucson Symphony Soc., Sun. Eve. Forum, Tucson Festival Soc., Audubon Soc., Tucson Ariz. Sonora Desert Mus., C. of C. Republican. Roman Catholic. Clubs: Rotary (dir. 1978-79), Oro Valley Country (Tucson). Home: 325 Canyon View Dr Tucson AZ 85704 Office: 5250 N Oracle Rd Tucson AZ 85704

GENGE, WILLIAM HARRISON, advt. exec., writer; b. Warren, Pa., May 7, 1923; s. Valleau Francis and Beatrice (Badger) G.; B.A., U. Pitts., 1948; grad. Internat. Marketing Inst., Harvard, 1967; m. Beverly Ann Milway, June 23, 1945; children—Deborah Ann, William Dean. Writer, Bull. Index, Pitts., 1947-48; editor Gulf Oil Corp., 1948-53; with Ketchum, MacLeod & Grove, Inc., 1953—, sr. v.p., 1965-68, exec. v.p., 1968-70, pres., 1970—, chmn., chief exec. officer, 1979—, also dir.; dir. Botsford-Ketchum, Inc., Pitts. Met. Broadcasting Corp. Bd. dirs. Nat. Chamber Found., Allegheny Gen. Hosp., Pitts. Symphony Soc.; pres., bd. dirs. Pitts. Youth Symphony, Pitts. Ballet Theatre, Civic Light Opera Assn., United Way of Allegheny County. Served to 1st lt. USAAF, 1942-46; prisoner of war, 1944-45. Decorated Purple Heart, D.F.C. with oak leaf cluster. Mem. Am. Assn. Advt. Agys., U.S. C. of C. (dir.), Citizen's Choice (dir.), Phi Gamma Delta. Republican. Presbyn. (elder). Clubs: Pitts. Golf, Duquesne, University, Fox Chapel, Rolling Rock (Pitts.); River Oaks (Houston); Laurel Valley (Ligonier, Pa.). Home: 725 Devonshire St Pittsburgh PA 15213 Office: 4 Gateway Center Pittsburgh PA 15222

GENGER, ARIE, retail co. exec.; b. Tel Aviv, Israel, July 10, 1945; s. Shraga and Dora (Menkes) G.; B.B.A. in Econs. with honors, Bernard Baruch Coll., 1971, M.B.A., 1972; m. Dalia Cohen, July 23, 1967; children—Sagi, Orly. Asst. to chmn. bd. Rapid-Am. Corp., N.Y.C., from 1972, v.p., exec. asst. to chmn., 1976—; exec. v.p., dir. McCrory Corp., 1977—; dir. KGA Industries, Kenton Corp. Served as sgt.-maj., Israeli Army, 1966. Office: Rapid-Am Corp 888 Seventh Ave New York NY 10019

GENTHE, WALTER ALFRED, automotive components mfg. exec.; b. Ludwigshafen, Germany, Mar. 20, 1926; s. Max Ferdinand and Hildegard (Ebbecke) G.; came to U.S., 1953, naturalized, 1958; Baccalaureat, Heidelberg (Germany) U., 1948; student Wayne State U., 1960; m. Marga Schimmer, July 24, 1945; children—George, Peter J., Michael W. Prodn. engr. Fisher Body div. Gen. Motors Corp., 1953; mgr. Meldrum Tool & Mfg. Co., 1953-59; v.p., gen. mgr. Worman Pillifant Co., automobile accessories, Warren, Mich., 1959-63; gen. mfg. mgr. Paramount Fabricating Co., automobile parts, Detroit, 1963-67; v.p. Sparton Corp.; v.p., gen. mgr., dir. Sparton Mfg. Co., Flora, Ill., 1967-78; pres. Hella N.Am., Inc., Flora and Troy, Mich., 1978—. Mem. Flora High Sch. Bd. Edn., 1971-73; mem. vocat.-tech. occupations adv. com. Ill. Eastern Jr. Colls. Mem. Ill. Mfrs. Assn. (fgn. trade com.), Soc. Automotive Engrs., Automobile Service Industry Assn., Flora C. of C. Republican. Lutheran. Clubs: Clay County Country, Fairlane, Elks. Patentee automotive luggage carrier. Home: RFD 2 Flora IL 62839 Office: Box 493 Flora IL 62839

GENTILE, ANTHONY, coal co. exec.; b. Aquila, Italy, Nov. 1, 1920; s. Gregorio and Antonietta (Duronio) G.; student Youngstown Coll., 1939-42; L.H.D. (hon.), Coll. Steubenville, 1977; m. Nina Angela DiScipio, Mar. 4, 1943; children—Robert Henry, Anita Marie, Rita Ann, Thomas Gregory. Co-owner Pike Inn-Restaurant, Bloomingdale, Ohio, 1946-52; asst. to owner Huberta Coal Co., Steubenville, Ohio, 1952-55; gen. mgr. Half Moon Coal Co., Weirton, W.Va., 1955-57; gen. mgr. Ohio River Collieries Co., Columbus, 1957-59, pres., 1959—; pres. Lafferty Coal Mining Co., Eastern Ohio Coal Co., 1959—; v.p. Big Mountain Coals, Inc., Prenter, W.Va., 1962—, chmn. bd., 1962—; pres. Bither Mining Co. W.Va.; v.p. N & G Constrn., Bannock Land Co.; mem. exec. com., dir. Mining and Reclamation Council Am., Washington; dir. Union Bank, Steubenville. Mem. 1st Ohio Trade Commn. to Europe, 1965; mem. adv. bd. St. John Med. Center, Steubenville; trustee Coll. Steubenville, Ohio Valley Hosp., Steubenville. Served to 1st lt. AUS, 1942-45. Decorated Purple Heart, Silver Star; recipient Citizen of Year award Wintersville C. of C., 1976; Conservation award for Ohio River collieries from Gov. Ohio, 1977. Mem. Am. Mining Congress (mem. adv. council coal div. 1965). Home: 4 Normandy Dr Wintersville OH 43952 Office: Ohio River Collieries Co Box 128 Bannock OH 43972

GENTRY, FENTON ALLEN SEVIER, ins exec.; b. Chattanooga, Mar. 12, 1910; s. Thomas Gray and Evelyn (Sevier) G.; B.S., U. Va., 1932, M.S., 1933; B.A. (Rhodes scholar), Oxford (Eng.) U., 1936, M.A., 1937; m. Barbara Fulton, Apr. 17, 1941; 1 son, Fenton Allen Sevier. Vice pres. So. Title Ins. Co., Knoxville, Tenn., 1941-46, pres. dir., 1946-77; pres., dir. Gentry Enterprises, Knoxville, 1977—. Mem. Knoxville Civil Service Bd., 1948-77, former chmn. Served to lt. comdr. USNR, 1942-46. Mem. Nat. Assn. Ind. Insurers (pres. 1961-62, gov.), Phi Beta Kappa. Clubs: Cherokee Country, Club LeConte (Knoxville). Home: 7914 Gleason Rd Apt 1118 Knoxville TN 37919 Office: PO Box 10187 11020 Kingston Pike Knoxville TN 37919

GENTRY, LEE C., landscape contractor, investment co. exec.; b. Little Rock, Nov. 8, 1935; s. Henry C. and Eva Cross Gentry; student U. Ark., 1954-60; m. Merle Harris, Sept. 4, 1957 (div. 1975); children—Perry, Todd, Tracy. Owner, operator Mico Landscape Co., Orange County, Calif., 1964-79; owner, mgr. Gentry Assos., Anaheim, Calif., 1977—. Recipient local and state awards Calif. Landscape Contractors Assn. Mem. Calif. Landscape Contractors Assn. (dir. 1968-77, pres. 1973-74, Man of Yr. award 1971). Baptist. Club: Elks (Garden Grove, Calif.). Home and Office: 6033 E Prado St Anaheim CA 92807

GENTRY, WILLIAM NORTON, safety cons.; b. Greenwood, Ark., May 29, 1908; s. William Fred and Lola (Caudle) G.; B.S. in Bus. Adminstrn., U. Ark., 1929; m. Margaret Sue Whaley, May 25, 1938 (dec.); children—Susan Margaret, William David. Wire chief SW Bell Telephone Co., Hope, Ark., 1932-34, constrn. foreman, 1935-40, exchange engr., 1940-42, 46-50, plant tng. supr., 1950-57, plant personnel and tng. supr., 1958-67, plant tng. and employment supr., 1967-73; safety cons. Little Rock Mcpl. Water Works. Div. leader Community Chest, Little Rock, 1949-52; pres., del. from Ark., Pres.'s Conf. on Occupational Safety, 1958; organizing pres. United Cerebral Palsy of Central Ark., 1959-60; chmn. Little Rock Safety Commn., 1970-71, mem., 1966—; bd. dirs. Little Rock Central YMCA, 1972-74; worker, mem. organizing bd. Contact Inc., Crisis Prevention Center, Little Rock, 1968-76; mem. Gov.'s Com. on Employment of Handicapped, Ark., 1973-80; del. to Pres.'s Conf. on Employment of Handicapped, Washington, 1977; chmn. work area on evangelism First United Methodist Ch., Little Rock, 1980, lay speaker, 1980-81. Served with Signal Corps, U.S. Army 1942-46. Recipient W.H. Sadler trophy Community Chest of Little Rock, 1950, 51, Service award United Cerebral Palsy of Central Ark., 1969, Safety award of commendation Ark. Dept. Labor, 1973. Mem. Am. Soc. Safety Engrs. (charter mem. Ark. chpt., sec. 1974-80, vice chmn. 1959-60, gen. chmn. 1960-61, chmn. annual safety inst. 1972-76), So. Safety Conf. (pres. 1968-69, exec. dir. 1969-72, dir. 1962—). Democrat. Club: Hilltop Kiwanis (program chmn., v.p. 1980-81). Only hearing mem. of Kiwanis Club for the deaf. Address: 12524 Colleen Dr Little Rock AR 72212

GEOFFRION, H. WILLIAM, lantern mfg. co. exec.; b. Endfield, Conn., Nov. 30, 1931; s. Harvey H. and Violet Elizabeth (Miller) G.; B.A., U. N.H., 1955; M.B.A., Northeastern U., 1963; m. Shirley Gibson, Aug. 19, 1955; children—Sandra E., Sarah A. Sr. engr. Bay State Abrasives, Mass., 1959-62; corp. staff engr. Sanders Assos., N.H., 1962-64; chief indsl. engr. Internat. Packins Corp., N.H., 1964-67; sr. cons. Booz, Allen & Hamilton, Ill., 1967-71; pres. Comnet Corp., Mass., 1968-/1; co-owner, chief exec. officer Heritage Lanterns, Yarmouth, Maine, 1968—. Served with USAF, 1955-58. Mem. New Eng. Mail Order Assn., Direct Mail Assn., Am. Lighting Inst., Metal Finishing Assn. Club: U. N.H. 100. Research on computer applications, hydraulic systems, low pressure-high temperature systems, antique reprodn. lighting fixtures. Office: 70A Main St Yarmouth ME 04096

GEOHAGAN, LARRY JEROME, automobile dealership exec.; b. Andalusia, Ala., Nov. 10, 1945; s. Winfred and Willie Lois (Peters) G.; B.B.A., U. North Fla., 1975; m. Alicia Elizabeth Mott, Feb. 24, 1968; children—Tamela Lynn, Kimberly Renee. Dist. mgr. Chevrolet Motor div. Gen. Motors Corp., Miami, Fla., 1969-74, merchandising mgr., 1974-75, distbn. mgr., 1975-76, regional merchandising and distbn. mgr., 1976-77; pres. Tallahassee Chrysler-Plymouth, 1977—, Larry Jay Chevrolet, Charlotte, N.C., 1980—. Bd. dirs. Sr. Citizens Planning Council. Served with U.S. Army, 1966-71. Mem. Nat. Automobile Dealers Assn., Orlando Chrysler-Plymouth Dealer Advt. Assn. (dir.), Dist. Dealers Council (rep.). Democrat. Office: 2415 W Tennessee St Tallahassee FL 32304 also 8101 South Blvd Charlotte NC

GEORGATOS, JERRY FRANK, computer systems exec.; b. Argostoli, Greece, Jan. 1, 1943; s. Fotios K. and Mary F. (Miliaresis); came to U.S., 1955, naturalized, 1961; B.S. in Math., Calif. State U., Hayward, 1965; M.S. in Statistics, Stanford U., 1968; m. Esther Peters, Dec. 1, 1968; children—Nicholas, Philip, Staci. Mathematician, Lawrence Radiation Lab., Livermore, Calif., 1965-67; sr. ops. research analyst Inter-Am. Devel. Bank, Washington, 1973-75, chief mgmt. systems sect., 1975—; mem. faculty Am. U., 1971-73. Served to capt. USAF, 1967-73. Mem. Am. Math. Soc., Am. Soc. Info. Scis., Ahepa. Greek Orthodox. Author articles. Home: 3916 Colonel Ellis Ave Alexandria VA 22304 Office: 801 17th St NW Washington DC 20577

GEORGE, ERNEST THORNTON, III, ins. exec.; b. Charleston, S.C., Dec. 29, 1950; s. Ernest Thornton and Bettye (Long) G.; student U. Miss., 1969-71; B.S. in Mktg., Miss. State U. 1973; estate planning cert. La. State U., 1975; student U. Southwestern La. and Inst. of Ins. Mktg. Dynamics Lab., 1975; m. Frances Thomson, Sept. 30, 1977; children—Andrew Neal, Ernest Thornton. With Mutual of N.Y., Mississippi State, Miss., 1974—, ins. and investment counselor, 1977—; pres. Ernie George & Assos., Fin. Services Co., Mississippi State, 1977—. Chmn. mchts. solicitation com. United Fund, Starkville, Miss., 1977-78; exec. membership com. Boy Scouts Am., Starkville, 1975-77; adv. bd. Pace Setter Agy. of Miss., 1977-80. Recipient Nat. Quality award Nat. Assn. Life Underwriters, 1977-80, Nat. Sales Achievement award, 1977-80, Health Ins. Quality award, 1976-80. Mem. Nat. Assn. Life Underwriters, Miss. Assn. Life Underwriters, Internat. Assn. Fin. Planners, Nat. Assn. Security Dealers, Sigma Chi, Pi Sigma Epsilon. Republican. Presbyterian (deacon, Sunday sch. tchr.). Clubs: Men of Ch. (pres.), Rotary, 100, Pres., Million Dollar Round Table. Contbr. articles to profl. jours. Home: 502 N Montgomery St Starkville MS 39759 Office: PO Box 1033 Mississippi State MS 39762

GEORGE, JERRY VANCE, petroleum co. exec.; b. Hillsboro, Tex., July 18, 1927; s. Van Theodore and Mayna (Weir) G.; B.S., Tex. A. and M. Coll., 1948; m. Joan Daisy Stoney, Apr. 29, 1960; children—Allen Van, Eric Van. Petroleum engr. Magnolia Petroleum Co., Lake Charles, La., 1949-53, Carmi, Ill., 1953-55; dist. supt. Tex.-Canadian Oil Corp., Paintsville, Ky., 1955-63, R. C. Davoust Co., Paintsville, 1964—; petroleum engr. Quasar, Inc., 1964-66; petroleum cons., Paintsville, Ky., 1967-70; mgr. ops. Guernsey Petroleum Corp., Claysville, Ohio, 1970-81; with Enterprise Energy Corp., Cambridge, Ohio, 1981—. Served with USNR, 1945-46. Registered profl. engr., Ky. Mem. Am. Inst. Mining, Metall. and Petroleum Engrs. (chmn. East Ky. sect. 1964), Soc. Petroleum Engrs. Republican. Methodist. Club: Ky. Cols. Home: 943 Somers St Zanesville OH 43701 Office: Enterprise Energy Corp PO Box 516 Cambridge OH 43725

GEORGE, PATRICK JOSEPH, profl. services co. exec.; b. Worcester, Mass., Aug. 30, 1951; s. Joseph Patrick and Lucy J. (Zarette) G.; student U. Dijon (France), 1968, Worcester State Coll., 1969-72; m. Debra Ann Pelczar, Oct. 26, 1974; children—Kristen Lee, Sherilyn Ann. Editor, the Pacesetter, 1968-69; editor Recorder Group Publs., Worcester, 1969-73; pub. Night Life Mag., 1973-74; pres. Campus Services, Inc., Spencer, Mass., 1968—, also dir.; pres. Roadwork, Inc., Worcester, 1978—, also dir. bd. dirs. Spencer (Mass.) Youth Commn. Mem. Center for Entrepreneurial Mgmt. Office: 172 Main St Spencer MA 01562

GEORGE, RICHARD GERARD, mfg. co. exec.; b. Waterbury, Conn., Mar. 27, 1950; s. Richard Ferris and Sadie Elizabeth (Wihbey) G.; B.S. in Acctg., Bentley Coll., 1972; M.B.A., U. New Haven, 1978. Cost accountant Uniroyal, Inc., Phila., 1972-73, sr. cost accountant, Oxford, Conn., 1974-75, accounting supr., 1975-76, divisional fin. accountant, 1976-77, mktg. economist, 1977-78, mktg. specialist, 1978-79, mgr. mktg. services and sales policy, 1979—; cons. in field. Trustee, treas. Watertown (Conn.) Library Assn., 1975-78; advisor Jr. Achievement, Waterbury, Conn., 1977-78. Recipient Outstanding Service award Nat. Assn. Acctg. 1977. Mem. Nat. Assn. Accts., Am. Mgmt. Assn., Nat. Acctg. Assn. (treas., v.p. mktg., mem. New Eng. regional council), Council Internat. Econs., Am. Mgmt. Assn. Clubs: Oxford Men's, League of Women Voters, Watertown Land Trust. Author: Marketing and the Law, 1979. Home: 31 Wheeler St Watertown CT 06795 Office: Benson Rd Oxford CT 06749

GEORGE, ROBERT JACOB, publisher; b. Boston, Aug. 11, 1944; s. George J. and Dorothy E. (Glick) G.; B.A., Mo. U., 1967; m. Pamela Jones, June 24, 1968. Founder, pres. United Media Internat., Inc., pub. variety books and periodicals, Boston, 1971-79; v.p. Harcourt Brace Jovanovich (merged with United Media Internat., Inc.), Boston, 1976-79; pres. Harcourt Brace Jovanovich Press, 1976-79; now pres. Boston Pub. Co.; cons. Mass. Consumers Council, Atty. Gen.'s Office. Served with USMC, 1967-71. Decorated D.F.C., Air medal. Mem. Nat. Aero. Inst. (pres.). Episcopalian. Clubs: Tennis and Racket, Somerset (Boston); Knickerbocker (N.Y.C.). Editor PSRO Update. Home: 60 Washington Sherborn MA 01770 Office: 306 Dartmouth St Boston MA 02116

GEORGE, ROBERT LEE, bus. cons.; b. Blytheville, Ark., Sept. 16, 1945; s. Lloyd Richard and Helen Juanita (Wicecarver) G.; B.A., Vanderbilt U., 1967; M.B.A., U. Tenn., Chattanooga, 1973; m. Mary Lou Cooke, Sept. 30, 1967; children—Lauri Ann, Sarah Elizabeth. Vice pres. Cooke Mfg., Cleveland, Tenn., 1971-77, treas., 1973-77; pres. George Acctg. Services, Cleveland, 1977—; dir. Hiwassee Memory Assn., Inc.; prof. bus. Bryan Coll. Pres., Hiwassee Audubon Soc., 1976-80; v.p. Bradley County Hist. Soc., 1978-79, pres., 1980—; active Meth. Men's Club. Served with USN, 1967-71. C.P.A.; cert. mgmt. acct. Mem. Am. Inst. C.P.A.'s, Tenn. Soc. C.P.A.'s, Inst. Mgmt. Accts., Am. Assn. Accts. Republican. Club: Sertoma (pres. 1976-77; Sertoman of Year 1976). Contbr. chpt. to History of Bradley County. Home: 3705 Northwood Dr Cleveland TN 37311

GEORGE, STEPHAN ANTHONY, mfg. co. exec.; b. Waterloo, Iowa, Sept. 20, 1946; s. Leon E. and Marie (Weires) G.; A.B., Bellarmine Coll., 1969, M.A., 1972, postgrad., 1969-76; m. Lucy Lynch, June 7, 1969. Field service engr. Hewlett Packard Co., Indpls., 1977, product support engr., Avondale, Pa., 1977-78, tng. specialist, 1978-79, European product mgr., 1980—. NSF fellow, 1969-71. Home: 713 Painters Crossing Chadds Ford PA 19317 Office: Hewlett Packard Route 41 and Starr Rd Avondale PA 19311

GEORGE, W. H. KROME, aluminum co. exec.; b. St. Louis, Mar. 27, 1918; s. Robert J. and Anne (Krome) G.; S.B., Mass. Inst. Tech., 1940; D.Sc. (hon.), Clarkson Coll.; m. Jean Murphy, May 4, 1946; children—Doyle Krome, Robert Charles, Peter Gillham. With Aluminum Co. Am., 1942—, v.p. charge econ. analysis and planning, 1964-65, v.p. fin., 1965-67, exec. v.p., 1967-70, pres., 1970-75, chief operating officer, 1972-75, chmn. bd., chief exec. officer, 1975—, chmn. exec. com., 1977—; dir. TRW, Inc., Mellon Bank N.A., Mellon

Nat. Corp., Norfolk and Western RR Co. Mem. corp. Mass. Inst. Tech; trustee Allegheny Health, Edn. and Research Corp.; bd. dirs. Internat. Primary Aluminum Inst., Nat. Center for Resource Recovery, Internat. Exec. Service Corps, Pa. Economy League, United Way Southwestern Pa.; trustee Conf. Bd., Tax Found. Inc.; chmn. bd. Bus. Com. for Arts, Indsl. Policy Adv. Com., Nat. Adv. Council on Minorities in Engring.; mem. adv. council Jr. Achievement SW Pa.; mem. bus. and profl. friends com. Nat. Center for State Cts.; mem. adv. council Columbia Grad. Sch. Bus.; bd. visitors Grad. Sch. Bus. Adminstrn., Duke U.; trustee U. Pitts.; mem. U.S. council Internat. C. of C.; mem. corp. Woods Hole Oceanographic Inst.; trustee Found. Ind. Colls.; bd. dirs., mem. exec. com. Bd. Pennsylvanians for Effective Govt.; adv. bd. Center for Strategic and Internat. Studies; former met. chmn. Nat. Alliance Businessmen; dir. U.S.-USSR Trade and Econ. Council, Inc.; mem. exec. com. Allegheny Conf. on Community Devel. Recipient Corporate Leadership award Mass. Inst. Tech., 1976; Businessman of Yr. award Pitts. Jaycees, 1977. Mem. Bus. Council, Mgmt. Execs. Soc., Engrs. Soc. Western Pa., Council Fgn. Relations, Pa. Soc., Aluminum Assn. (mem. chmn.'s adv. council, past chmn.), Bus. Roundtable, World Affairs Council Pitts. Clubs: Allegheny, Duquesne (Pitts.); Rolling Rock (dir.); Laurel Valley Golf (dir.); Harvard-Yale-Princeton; Edgeworth; Allegheny Country; Links, Economic (N.Y.C.); F Street, Internat. (Washington). Office: 1501 Alcoa Bldg Pittsburgh PA 15219

GEORGE, WILFRED RAYMOND, investment co. exec.; b. Grinnell, Iowa, Apr. 1, 1928; s. Raymond Lawrence and Doris Love (Durey) G.; B.S., U. Iowa, 1950; M.B.A, Harvard U., 1955; Ph.D., Golden Gate U., 1979; m. Katherine Elizabeth Shaughnessy, Aug. 14, 1971; children by previous marriage—Winifred Doris, Kathryn Gwen; stepchildren—Grace Mary Bruns, Denise Creedan Bruns. Engr., Westinghouse Electric Co., Pitts., 1950-51; budget supr., sales and employment adminstr. Lockheed Missile and Space Div., Sunnyvale, Calif., 1955-59; registered rep. Hooker and Fay, Inc., Redwood City, Calif., 1959-63, Shearson Hammill & Co., Menlo Park, Calif., 1963; mgr. instl. sales Bache & Co., Inc., San Francisco, 1964-70; v.p., mgr. Instl. br., 1970-72; v.p., account exec. Bache Halsey Stuart Inc., San Francisco, 1972—; pres., investment adviser Stanford Investment Mgmt., Palo Alto, Calif., 1962. Served to lt. (j.g.), USNR, 1951-52. Mem. Authors Guild, Nat. Assn. Bus. Economists, Tech. Securities Analysts San Francisco, St. Andrew's Soc. (trustee 1979), Brit. Benevolent Soc. (trustee 1979). Clubs: San Francisco Bond, Harvard Bus. Sch., Commonwealth, Marines Meml. Author: The Profit Box System of Forecasting Stock Prices, 1976; inventor paper grate. Home: 16 Bonita Ave Piedmont CA 94611 Office: 350 California St San Francisco CA 94104

GEORGE, WILLIAM BROOKS, indsl. co. exec.; b. Stuart, Va., Dec. 21, 1911; s. T.J. and Minnie Lou (Handy) G.; B.S., Coll. William and Mary, 1932, L.H.D. (hon.), 1972; postgrad. Va. Mechanics Inst., 1935-36, T.C. Williams Sch. Bus. Adminstrn., 1937-38; m. Elizabeth Harman Simmerman, Nov. 24, 1934; children—William Brooks, Henry H. Asst. to auditor Larus & Brother Co., Inc., Richmond, Va., 1937-39, controller, 1939-51, asst. to pres., 1951-54, exec. v.p., 1954-62, pres., 1962-66, pres., chief exec. officer, 1966-68, chmn. bd. Larus & Brother Co., Inc. T/A House of Edgeworth, Richmond, 1968—; v.p. Rothmans of London, Inc., Richmond; dir. Bank of Va. Co., Bank of Va.-Central, Lawyers Title Ins. Corp., Life Ins. Co. Va.; mem. bd. dirs. Tobacco Tax Council, Asso. Tobacco Mfrs., Tobacco Inst., Inc.; mem. Nat. Tobacco Adv. Com. Mem. devel. council Coll. William and Mary, 1976—, mem. and rector bd. visitors, 1966-68, trustee Endowment Assn., bd. dirs. Sponsors of Sch. Bus. Adminstrn.; pres. Richmond, Henrico & Chesterfield United Givers Fund, 1969, bd. govs., 1973—; dir., v.p. Richmond Eye Hosp.; chmn. bd. Central Va. Ednl. TV; bd. dirs. Richmond Symphony; dir. Nat. Tobacco Festival, 1954-74, pres., 1972; mem., elder First Presbyterian Ch., Richmond. Named Man of Year, Richmond Jr. C. of C., 1947; recipient Distinguished Service award Va. Jr. C. of C., 1947, Alumni medallion Coll. William and Mary, 1954. C.P.A., Va. Mem. Tobacco Mchts. Assn. (pres., dir.), Phi Beta Kappa, Beta Gamma Sigma (charter), Kappa Sigma, Omicron Delta Kappa. Clubs: Commonwealth (sec. bd.), Forum, Newcomen Soc. Am., Country Club Va. Established Elizabeth S. George scholarship fund, Coll. William and Mary. Home: 106 Berkshire Rd Richmond VA 23221

GEORGEN, W. DONALD, accountant; b. Chgo., June 1, 1929; s. Michael A. and Lauretta M. G.; B.S., U. Notre Dame, 1951; J.D., Northwestern U., 1953; m. Eleanor J. Hays, Sept. 15, 1956; children—Susan M., Lauretta M., Catherine J., Sarah A., William D. Admitted to Ill. bar, 1953; with Touche Ross & Co., 1953—, partner, Chgo., 1966-69, dir. audit operations, 1969-72, nat. dir. accounting and auditing, 1972-79, partner-in-charge N.J. offices, 1979—, vice-chmn. bd. dirs., 1979—. Served with U.S. Army, 1954-56. Mem. Am. Inst. C.P.A.'s (mem. exec. com. SEC practice div.), Ill. Soc. C.P.A.'s, N.J. Soc. C.P.A.'s, N.Y. Soc. C.P.A.'s, Beta Alpha Psi. Roman Catholic. Clubs: Spring Brook Country, Essex, Baltusrol Golf. Home: Morristown NJ 07960 Office: Touche Ross and Co Gateway 1 Newark NJ 07102

GEORGETTE, FRANCES, cons. co. exec.; b. Los Angeles; B.A. magna cum laude, U. So. Calif., 1956, Ph.D., 1977; 1 dau., Jane L. Watson. Cons. clin. psychology, vocat. psychology, vocat. edn. and mgmt. selection Reiss-Davis Child Study Inst., Los Angeles, 1959-63, Los Angeles Psychiat. Service, 1963-66, Child Guidance Centers, Los Angeles City Sch. System, 1963-66, Washington Sch. Psychiatry, 1966-70; cons. Georgetown U. Sch. Medicine and Internat. Health, 1966-70; pres. Frances Georgette Watson Assos., Washington, 1969-72, Planning & Human Systems, Inc., 1972—; vol. staff Small Bus. Guidance and Devel. Center of Howard U. Bd. trustees Women's Equity Action League, 1978; active NOW. Mem. Am., D.C. psychol. assns., Soc. Internat. Devel., U. So. Calif. Alumni Assn. (Service award 1977), Mensa, Phi Beta Kappa. Club: U. So. Calif. Alumni (pres. Washington 1970-76). Office: 3201 New Mexico Ave NW Suite 200 Washington DC 20016

GEORGITSIS, NICOLAS MIKE, mfg. co. exec.; b. Chios, Greece, Sept. 2, 1934; s. Michael George and Angelika D. (Latina) G.; B.S. in Elec. Engring. (Fulbright scholar, Honor scholar), Washington U., St. Louis, 1958, B.S. in Indsl. Mgmt., 1962, B.S. in Engring. Sci., 1963; postgrad. in Econs., St. Louis U., 1964-65; m. Iro Kaliroe Lazou, July 5, 1964; children—Melina A., Michael Nicolas, Ares Panos. Field engr. Wagner Electric Corp., St. Louis, 1959-62, sales mgr., 1962-65, dir. internat. div., 1965-66; pres. Bendix do Brazil, São Paulo, 1967-70; v.p. Bendix Internat., N.Y.C., 1970-71, sr. v.p., 1971-72, exec. v.p., 1972-73; pres. Bendix Europe, Paris, 1974-78; v.p. Latin Am. and Far East, Am. Can Internat., Greenwich, Conn., 1978—; group v.p. Am. Standard, automotive products Mem. Greek Orthodox Ch. Clubs: São Paulo (Brazil); Royal Yacht (Athens, Greece); Golf Saint-Nom La Breteche (Paris). Contbr. articles on internat. mgmt., internat. trade and liquidity to profl. jours. Home: 13 Av de Wagram 78600 Maison Laffitte France Office: Tour Albert 1er 65 Av de Colmar 92500 Rueil Malmaison France

GERAGHTY, RICHARD BANKS, banker; b. Upper Darby, Pa., July 14, 1945; s. John Joseph and Sarah (Williston) G.; B.A., Hamilton Coll., 1968; m. Barbara Elaine Max, Oct. 6, 1967; children—Jennifer Fox, Cassandra Starr. Vice pres. S.E. First Nat. Bank of Miami (Fla.), 1974—, mgr. nat. dept., 1977-78, European rep., 1978—; asst. treas. Morgan Guaranty Trust Co., N.Y.C., 1968-72; v.p., mgr. Nat. div. Continental Mortgage Investors, Coral Gables, Fla., 1972-74. Mem. Interracial Council for Bus. Opportunity, Capital Resources Com., Bankers Club Miami, Overseas Bankers Club (London), Lombard Assn. (London), Woolnoth Soc. (London), European-Atlantic Group (London), London Chamber Commerce and Industry (N.Am. com.), Alpha Delta Phi. Home: 26 Pelham Crescent London SW7 England Office: Stock Exchange Bldg Old Broad St London EC2N 1ED England

GERAN, GEORGE PATRICK, accountant; b. Marion, Ohio, Nov. 18, 1943; s. Robert S. and Mary A. (Gallagher) G.; B.S., Ferris State Coll. 1966; M.B.A., U. Detroit, 1968; m. Kay Taylor, Sept. 27, 1969; children—Laura Claire, Julia Carter. Computer operator, Am. Motors Corp., Detroit, 1966-68; systems accountant, First Va. Bankshares Corp., Falls Church, Va., 1971-75; operations systems coordinator, First & Merchants Corp., Richmond, Va., 1975-76, mgr. cost accting., 1976-77; v.p. and controller First Nat. Bank of Brevard, Merritt Island, Fla., 1977-79; asst. fin. mgr. Greater Orlando Aviation Authority, 1979-80, fin. mgr., 1980—. Dist. bd. dirs. Merritt Island Library, 1980—. Served with U.S. Army, 1968-71. C.P.A., Fla. Mem. Mcpl. Fin. Officers Assn., Am. Inst. C.P.A.'s, Fla. Inst. C.P.A.'s, Nat. Assn. Accountants, Assn. U.S. Army, Nat. Rifle Assn. Republican. Roman Catholic. Home: 65 Via De La Reina Merritt Island FL 32952 Office: PO Box 80004 Orlando FL 32862

GERARD, ROGER LAWRENCE, indsl. relations exec.; b. Gardner, Mass., Sept. 20, 1936; s. Reginald McLeod and Genevieve Sally (Danisienka) G.; B.S. (Alpha Kappa Sigma scholar), Northeastern U., 1959, M.B.A., 1969; postgrad. Detroit Coll. Law, 1960-62; m. Joyce Ann Howard, Nov. 28, 1970; children—Scott, Lisa. Personnel adminstr. Ford Motor Co., Dearborn, Mich., 1957-63, Vickers Inc., Troy, Mich., 1963-65, Gen. Electric Co., Lynn, Mass. and Providence, 1965-69; dir. personnel and bus. planning Foto-Mem Inc., Natick, Mass., 1969-71; pres. Infotrieve Systems, Inc., Southboro, Mass., 1971; internat. indsl. relations dir. Fairchild Camera Corp., South Portland, Maine and Mountainview, Calif., 1971-79; v.p. adminstrn. Atari, Inc., Sunnyvale, Calif., 1979-80; corp. dir. compensation and benefits Intel Corp., Santa Clara, Calif., 1980—. lectr. U. Maine, 1972-73. Mem. adv. bd. Indsl. Health Counseling Service, Nat. Council on the Aging, 1972-74, Nat. Alliance of Businessmen, Maine, 1971-73; mem. Gov's. Council on Manpower Affairs, Maine, 1972, Joint Action Commn. on Univ. Goals and Direction, U. Maine, 1972. Served to capt. AUS, 1959-60. Recipient Mgmt. Proposal commendations Ford Motor Co., 1960-62. Mem. Electronic Personnel Assn. Boston, So. Maine Personnel Execs. Council (v.p. 1972-73), Northeastern U. Alumni Assn. (pres. 1972-73), South Portland Bd. Industry, Greater Portland C. of C., Personnel Mgrs. Club, Personnel Club, Middlesex County C. of C., Personnel Interchange Group of Bus. Internat., Alpha Kappa Sigma (pres. local chpt. 1958-59). Home: 101 Belhaven Dr Los Gatos CA 95030 Office: 3065 Bowers Ave Santa Clara CA 95051

GERBER, HENRY CLAY, banker; b. Guymon, Okla., Jan. 10, 1909; s. Henry U. and Madge M. (Cutler) G.; student Southwestern Coll., 1928-30; m. Lurline Adele Weitzel, Apr. 19, 1931; children—Loren Alan, Arita Loree (Mrs. Joe F. Simpson), Lonnie Lynn, Deanna Gayle (Mrs. C. Lee Dyer). Mgr. Security Elevator Co., Liberal, Kans., 1932-42; farmer, nr. Rolla, Kan. and Guymon, Okla., 1935—; owner, operator H.C. Gerber Realty Co., Colorado Springs, Colo., 1949-56; chmn. bd. Am. Heritage Bank & Trust Co. (formerly Southgate State Bank), Colorado Springs, 1959-74; owner-operator H.C. Gerber Realty Co.; chmn. bd., chief exec. officer Liberty Indsl. Bank, Colorado Springs; pres. Colorado Springs Ins. Agy. Inc.; chmn. bd. Centennial Financial Services, Inc., Colorado Springs; dir. Farmers Alliance Mut. Ins. Co., McPherson, Kans. Recipient Free Enterprise Champion award for Pikes Peak region Salesmen with a Purpose Club, 1968. Mem. Air Force Assn. (life), Assn. U.S. Army (life), Internat. Platform Assn., Internat. Footprint Assn. Mason (32 deg., Shriner), Lion. Club: Am. Sportsmans. Home: 14 W Oak Ave Colorado Springs CO 80906 Office: 1776 S Nevada Ave Colorado Springs CO 80906

GERBETH, JOHN, merchandising co. exec.; b. Germany, July 7, 1930; s. Albin and Margaret (Smith) G.; came to U.S., 1949, naturalized, 1952; grad. Advanced Mgmt. Program, Harvard, 1959; m. Dorothy Collette Herman; 1 dau., Deirdre Catherine. Plant mgr. Popular Club Plan, Passaic, also Fairlawn, N.J., 1955-59; controller Carr's Dept. Store, West Orange, N.J., 1959-60; mgr. diversification Popular Merchandising Co., Inc., Passaic, 1961-62, corporate comptroller, 1962-68; v.p. finance Popular Services, Inc., 1968-72; exec. v.p., dir. Stuart McGuire, Salem, Va., 1972-76; chief fin. officer, dir. Vornado, Inc., Garfield, N.J., 1976—; dir. Am. Garden Products, Boston; mem. adv. bd. Bank of Passaic & Clifton. Bd. dirs. Popular Services, Passaic. Served with USAF, 1951-52. Mem. Passaic Area C. of C. (dir. 1972—). Home: 85-1 Mountaintop Rd Bernardsville NJ 07924 Office: Passaic St Garfield NJ 07026

GERBRACHT, RICHARD EDWIN, advt. and mktg. co. exec.; b. Erie, Pa., Jan. 2, 1932; s. Edwin Jacob and Ursula (Schulze) G.; B.A., U. Notre Dame, 1954; grad. advanced mgmt. program Harvard U.; m. Shirley Ann Dillon, Jan. 22, 1955; children—Robert, Thomas, Elizabeth, John, Patrick, Kathleen, Richard. Pres., chief exec. officer Griswold-Eshleman Co., Cleve., 1974—; with Interpub. Group of Cos., 1954-74, v.p. Interpub. (N.Y.), 1973; sr. v.p., area mgr. McCann-Erickson Europe, 1974; exec. v.p., gen. mgr. Marschalk Co., Cleve., 1967-73. Chmn. pub. relations United Torch Dr., Cleve., 1970-73. Trustee Raphael Corp., Cleve., 1965-69, Welfare Fedn., Cleve., 1969-72, Children's Aid Soc., Cleve., 1969-72, Cleve. Ballet, 1979—; mem. exec. com. St. John Coll., Cleve., 1971-73, also trustee. Mem. Cleve. Advt. Club (pres. 1978-79), Greater Cleve. Growth Assn. (dir. 1972). Clubs: Union, Mentor Harbor Yachting, Harvard of N.Y. Home: PO Box 232 Fox Hill Dr Gates Mills OH 44040 Office: Griswold-Eshleman Co 55 Public Sq Cleveland OH 44113

GERBRICK, WILLIAM JOHN, paper co. exec.; b. Neenah, Wis., Jan. 5, 1920; s. William Kurtz and Flossie (Hanson) G.; student U. Wis., 1937-39, Ripon Coll., 1939-40; m. Jane Claire Strange, Sept. 22, 1943; 1 son, John Chapman (dec.). Order clk. Central Paper Co., Menasha, Wis., 1940-41, 1945-46, salesman, 1946-49, prodn. mgr., 1950-55, v.p., gen. mgr., 1956-58, pres., 1958—; dir. First Nat. Bank, Menasha, Wis. Dir. Wis. Paper Group, 1963-68, pres., 1966-67. Bd. dirs. Goodwill Industries, 1962—, pres. 1966, 73-74; chmn. bus. and industry div. Winnebago County unit Muscular Dystrophy Assn. Served with USCGR, 1942-45. Mem. Nat. Paper Trade Assn., Gummed Industries Assn. (dir. 1966-69, 75—, pres. 1966-67), Wis. Paper Mfrs. Traffic Assn. (dir., pres. 1978-79). Episcopalian, Elk. Clubs: North Shore Golf (Menasha, Wis.), Chicago Athletic Assn. (Chgo.). Home: 121 Poplar Ct Neenah WI 54956 Office: 741 4th St Menasha WI 54952

GERDING, PAUL AUGUST, mining co. exec.; b. Ottawa, Ill., Nov. 17, 1921; s. Carl T. and Margaret M. (Bretag) G.; B.S. in Mech. Engring., U. Ill., 1943; m. Patricia A. Geschwind, May 19, 1956; children—Barbara H., Paul August, Richard C. Plant engr. Ottawa (Ill.) Silica Co., 1946-50, chief engr., 1950-56, asst. gen. mgr., 1956-59, v.p., 1959-62; pres., owner, dir. Bellrose Silica Co., Ottawa, 1962—; dir. 1st Nat. Bank of Ottawa; silica mining and processing cons. with glass industry, U.S., Jamaica, Dominican Republic. Pres. bd. trustees Ryburn Hosp., 1957-62; bd. trustees Ottawa High Sch., 1975—, YMCA Future Devel. Bd., 1975—; chmn. bd. trustees Camp Fire Girls, 1960-64; gen. chmn. Community Hosp. Fund Drive, 1967-69; pres. Community Hosp., 1976-78, Mental Health Bd. LaSalle County, 1971-77; mem. U.S., Ill., Ottawa Chambers Commerce. Served to capt. AUS, 1943-46. Recipient Distinguished Citizen award, U.S. Jr. C. of C., 1958. Mem. Am. Inst. Mining Engrs. (v.p. 1969, 71), Ill. Mfrs. Assn., Nat. Assn. Mfrs., Nat. Indsl. Sand Assn., Nat., Ill. socs. profl. engrs. Republican. Presbyterian. Clubs: Ottawa Boat, YMCA Century, Wide Waters Yacht, Ottawa Airman's. Home: 725 Congress St Ottawa IL 61350 Office: Box 460 Ottawa IL 61350

GERDING, THOMAS GRAHAM, mfg. co. exec.; b. Evanston, Ill., Feb. 11, 1930; s. Louis and Helen Francis (Graham) G.; student U. Notre Dame, 1948-49; B.S., Purdue U., 1954, M.S., 1954, Ph.D., 1960; m. Beverly Ann Starnes, June 18, 1955; children—Mark, David, Gail, Gene Ann. Tech. dir. Glenbrook Labs. div. Sterling Drug Inc., N.Y.C., 1964-66, dir. product devel. Sterling Winthrop Research Inst. div., Rensselaer, N.Y., 1966-71; v.p. research and devel. Calgon Consumer Products div. Merck & Co., Inc., Rahway, N.J., 1971-77; v.p., dir. Research div. Johnson & Johnson Products Inc., New Brunswick, N.J., 1977—; asst. prof. Purdue U. Vice chmn. Johnson & Johnson unit United Fund, 1979, chmn., 1980. Served with AUS, 1954-56. Mem. Am. Chem. Soc., Am. Pharm. Assn., Soc. Chem. Industry, Am. Mgmt. Assn., Assn. Research Dirs. Republican. Roman Catholic. Clubs: Union League of Chgo.; Shrewsbury River Yacht (Fair Haven N.J.). Office: 501 George St New Brunswick NJ 08903

GEREND, ROBERT PAUL, real estate co. exec.; b. Memphis, Feb. 7, 1938; s. Joseph J. and Herta Frieda (Mueller) G.; B.S. in Mech. Engring. with honors, U. Wis., 1961; M.S., Seattle U., 1968; children—Steven, Laura. Pres., Pace Corp., Bellevue, Wash., 1977—, Pace Securities Corp., Bellevue, 1978—; sec./treas. Sound Comml. Devel. Corp., 1978—; lectr. real estate investment; realtor, broker; comml. flight instr. Mem. Real Estate Securities and Syndication Inst. (pres. Wash. chpt. 1981). Republican. Home: 14877 SE 50th St Bellevue WA 98006

GERG, CARL ARTHUR, business exec.; b. Niagara Falls, N.Y., Feb. 19, 1947; s. James Arthur and Marjorie Louise (Jorgensen) G.; student Ind. U., 1965-67; B.S., Duquesne U., 1973; M.B.A., U. Denver, 1974; m. Joanne S. Bozoukoff, Aug. 4, 1967; 1 son, James B. Unit mgr. Plastic Applicators, Inc., Harvey, La., 1976-77; indsl. engr. Ingalls Shipbuilding div. Litton Industries, Pascagoula, Miss., 1977-78; corp. sec. Polydimensional Service Systems, Inc., Oceans Springs, Miss., 1978; project adminstr. Northrop DSD Corp., Rolling Meadows, Ill., 1978-79; lead fin. systems analyst G.D. Searle & Co., Skokie, Ill., 1979-80; sr. fin. systems analyst N. Am. Philips, Itasca, Ill., 1980, Underwriters Labs., Northbrook, Ill., 1980—. Pres., Hickory Hill Country Club Homeowners Assn., 1977-78. Served with USN, 1967-70. Mem. Am. Mgmt. Assn., Assn. M.B.A. Execs., Omicron Delta Epsilon. Home: 2002 E Crabtree Dr Arlington Heights IL 60004 Office: 333 Pfingsten Rd Northbrook IL 60062

GERHARD, HARRY E., JR., shipping co. exec.; b. Phila., Aug. 7, 1925; s. Harry E. and Frances Jane (Edwards) G.; student Muhlenberg Coll., 1943-44; A.B., George Washington U., 1968, M.A., 1969; m. Barbara McDonald, Dec. 27, 1947; children—Marjorie Chasteen, Jane Tehan, Susan Jillson, John, Nancy, Barbara. Commd. ensign U.S. Navy, 1943, advanced through grades to rear admiral, 1971, test pilot, 1955-57, ret., 1976; exec. v.p. Costa Line Cargo Services, Inc., N.Y.C., 1976—. Decorated Silver Star, D.F.C. (2), Air Medals (16), Navy Commendation Medals (2). Mem. Am. Mgmt. Assn., Assn. Naval Aviation, Retired Officers Assn., Order of Daedalians, Tailhook Assn., Am.-Arab Assn. for Commerce and Industry, N.Y. Shipping Assn., U.S.-Italy Spain/Portugal/Mexico/Arab chambers commerce. Republican. Lutheran. Clubs: Union League, Wings, Army Navy Country, N.Y. Yacht. Home: 109 Deer Trail N Ramsey NJ 07446 Office: 26 Broadway Suite 1122 New York NY 10004

GERING, ROBERT LEE, research co. exec.; b. Parker, S.D., Feb. 18, 1920; s. John J. and Pauline (Graber) G.; A.B., U. Utah, 1947, M.A., 1948, Ph.D., 1950; m. Rose Elaine Kaufman, Nov. 24, 1945; children—Lee Maxwell, John Charles. Chmn. biology dept., natural sci. div. Bethel Coll., 1948-53; asst. dir. ecol. research Dugway (Utah) Proving Grounds, 1953-54; chmn. biology dept. Wells Coll., 1954-65; pres. Info. Applications, Inc., Penfield, 1966—. Vis prof. biology U. Rochester, 1965-66; prof. biology Rochester Inst. Tech., 1966-68, coordinator computer assisted instrn. Nat. Tech. Inst. for Deaf, 1968-69. Served with AUS, 1940-46. Mem. AAAS, Am. Inst. Biol. Scis., N.Y. Acad. Sci., Nat. Soc. for Programmed Instrn. Former asst. mng. editor Am. Biology Tchr. Home and Office: 2169 Baird Rd Penfield NY 14526

GERINGER, MICHAEL JAMES, household products and apparel mfg. co. exec.; b. N.Y.C., Nov. 26, 1941; s. Murray and Elizabeth (Beigel) G.; B.A. magna cum laude, Hebrew U., 1966, M.A., 1967; m. Nurit Getzler, Aug. 29, 1967; children—Liat, Shira, Matan. Fin. mgr. bus. devel. Gen. Telephone & Electronics Corp., Stamford, Conn., 1975-77; gen. mgr. Tiffany div. U.S. Industries Inc., Clifton, N.J., 1977-78, pres. Jan Colby div., N.Y.C., 1978, chief fin. officer Consumer Group, N.Y.C., 1978—. Served with AUS, 1960-62. Mem. Fin. Execs. Inst. Home: 16 Stanwick Pl Stamford CT 06905 Office: Consumer Group div US Industries Inc 350 Fifth Ave New York NY 10001

GERLA, MORTON, bus. and engring. exec., cons.; b. Bklyn., July 11, 1916; s. Harry and Jennie (Levy) G.; B.Mech.Engring., City U. N.Y., 1937; postgrad. George Washington U., 1940-41, Calif. Inst. Tech., 1944, N.Y. U., 1953, New Sch. Social Research, 1953-57; m. Miriam Kleeger, Oct. 14, 1939; children—Harry Seymour, Lisa Joy. Asst. to Arnold Weisselberg, M.E., cons. engr., N.Y.C., 1937-38; ordnance engr. U.S. Naval Gun Factory, Washington, 1938-45; asst. chief engr. Industro-Matic Corp., cons. engrs., N.Y.C., 1945-47; v.p. Superior Devel. Corp., N.Y.C., 1947-50; mgr. electro-mech. design engring. W.L. Maxson Corp., N.Y.C., 1950-55; v.p. Lalin Constrn. Corp., Nassau County, N.Y., 1955-65; mgr. machine design Anaconda Wire & Cable Co., N.Y.C., 1965-71; mgr. systems and standards Addressograph-Multigraph Corp., Cleve., 1972-76; cons. engr. Scott & Fetzer Co., Cleve., 1976-77; cons. engr., engring. standards and metrication coordinator, staff engr. Ocean Systems div. Gould Inc., Cleve., 1977—; cons. Maschinenfabrik Herborn, Herborn, Dillkreis, West Germany, 1968-71; cons. engr. Soltam, Haifa, 1974-79, Albar Ltd., Kfar Sava, 1979—. Sec., Hillside Civic Assn., New Hyde Park, N.Y., 1948-50. Bd. dirs. New Sch. Assos., N.Y.C., 1954-57, Jamaica Estates Assn., N.Y.C., 1968-72. Recipient Civilian Commendation, Navy Dept., 1945. Registered profl. engr., N.Y., Ohio. Mem. ASME (life; dir. D.C. sect. 1943-45), Am. Rocket Soc. (pres., dir. N.Y. sect. 1948-50), Am. Nat. Standards Inst. (exec. standards council 1974-75), Standards Engring. Soc., Am. Soc. Metals (life), Tau Beta Pi. Jewish (adult edn. commn. United Synagogue 1958-60). Club: Masons. Contbr. to profl. publs. Home: 764 Pipe's Ct Northfield OH 44067

Office: Gould Inc Ocean Systems Div 18901 Euclid Ave Cleveland OH 44117

GERLACH, CLINTON G., diversified mfg. co. exec.; b. Rosemont, Nebr., June 18, 1926; s. Herman F. and Lena (Knigge) G.; B.S. in Bus. Adminstrn., U. Denver, 1949; m. Juanita R. Sowers, Aug. 29, 1953; children—Kimberlee Ann Gerlach Deterville, Clinton G. II. With Arthur Andersen & Co., Chgo., 1949-52; controller Penn-Union Electric Corp., Erie, Pa., 1952-58, pres., 1958-67; group exec. in charge 15 cos. Teledyne Co., 1967-79; founder, chmn. bd. Tennetics, Inc., Erie, 1969—; dir. Zero Corp., Security Peoples Trust Co. C.P.A., Colo. Mem. Am. Inst. C.P.A.'s, Beta Gamma Sigma. Presbyterian. Clubs: Masons, Shriners. Office: 700 1st Nat Bank Bldg Erie PA 16501 also 4676 Admiralty Way Suite 534 Marina del Rey CA 90291

GERMANETTI, HUGH FENTON, constrn. co. exec.; b. Saratoga Springs, N.Y., Oct. 28, 1932; s. Leo and Anne Byrd (Fenton) G.; B.A. in Physics, Williams Coll., 1954; B.S. in Civil Engring. with great distinction, Clarkson Coll. Tech., 1966; m. Nancy Davison Mann, Jan. 7, 1955; children—Michele Anne, Gail Lee, William David. Owner, mgr. Parmeter Co., Saratoga Springs, 1954-55, Coordinated Homes, Saratoga Springs, Massena, N.Y., 1955-58; majority stockholder, pres. Germanetti & Ryan, Inc., Massena, 1958—; owner, pres. Sherman Heavy Hauling Corp., 1979—; owner Conquip Constrn. Equipment Co., Inc., 1979—; chmn. bd., trustee North Country Savs. Bank. Trustee, pres. Massena Central Sch. Bd. Edn., 1965-76; class agt., vice-chmn., chmn. Williams Coll. Alumni Fund, 1972—; trustee Laborer's Joint Welfare Adminstrn. Fund, 1973—, Laborer's Local 322 Pension Fund, 1973—. Recipient Young Man of Yr. Distinguished Service award Massena Jaycees, 1968. Registered profl. engr., N.Y. State, Fla. Mem. Nat., N.Y. State socs. profl. engrs., No. N.Y. Builder's Exchange, Gen. Bldg. Contractors N.Y. State, Bldg. Industry Employers N.Y. State, Asso. Gen. Contractors Am., Am. Arbitration Assn. (nat. panel arbitrators 1968—), Tau Beta Pi, Delta Phi. Congregationalist. Clubs: Massena Monday Luncheon, Massena Country. Home: 39 Sherwood Dr Massena NY 13662 Office: PO Box 330 Massena NY 13662

GERMANN, RICHARD P(AUL), chemist, bus. exec.; b. Ithaca, N.Y., Apr. 3, 1918; s. Frank E. E. and Martha Mary Marie (Knechtel) G.; B.A., Colo. U., 1939; student (Naval Research fellow) Western Res. U., 1941-43, Brown U., 1954; m. Malinda Jane Plietz, Dec. 11, 1942; 1 dau., Cheranne Lee. Chief analytical chemist Taylor Refining Co., Corpus Christi, Tex., 1943-44; research devel. chemist Calco Chem. div. Am. Cyanamid Co., 1944-52; devel. chemist charge pilot plant Alrose Chem. Co. div. Geigy Chem. Corp., 1952-55; new product devel. chemist, research div. W. R. Grace & Co., Clarksville, Md., 1955-60; chief chemist soap-cosmetic div. G.H. Packwood Mfg. Co., St. Louis, 1960-61; coordinator chem. product devel. Abbott Labs., North Chicago, Ill., 1961-71; internat. chem. cons. to mgmt., 1971-73; pres. Germann Internat. Ltd., 1973—; real estate broker, 1972—; Am. Inst. Chemists rep. to Joint Com. on Employment Practices, 1969-72. Fellow Am. Inst. Chemists (chmn. com. employment relations 1969—), Chem. Soc. (London), A.A.A.S.; mem. Am. Chem. Soc. (chmn. membership com. chem. marketing and econs. div. 1966-68, chmn. program com. 1968-69, del. at large for local sects. 1970-71, councilor 1971—, chmn. 1972-73; chmn. Chgo. program com. 1966-67, chmn Chgo. endowment com. 1967-68, dir. Chgo. sect. 1968-72; chmn. awards com. 1972-73; sec. chem. marketing and econs. group Chgo. sect. 1964-66, chmn. 1967-68), Internat. Sci. Found., Sci. Research Soc. Am., Comml. Chem. Devel. Assn. (chmn. program com. Chgo. conv. 1966, mem. finance com. 1966-67, ad hoc com. 1968-69, co-chmn. pub. relations Denver conv. 1968, chmn. membership com. 1969-70), Chem. Market Research Assn. (mem. directory com. 1967-68, employment com. 1969-70), Midwest Planning Assn., Midwest Chem. Marketing Assn., Internat. Platform Assn., Lake County (Ill.) Bd. Realtors, World Future Soc., Sigma Xi, Alpha Chi Sigma (chmn. profl. activities com. 1968-70, v.p. Chgo. chpt. 1967-68, pres. Chgo. chpt. 1968-70). Episcopalian. Clubs: Lions (sec. Allview, Md. 1956-57, Gurnee, Ill. 1975—), Kiwanis, Rotary, Masons. Chemists (N.Y.C., Chgo.). Patentee in organic and pharm. field. Home and Office: 6 Vinewood Dr Norwalk OH 44857

GERMANY, JAMES WALTER, r.r. exec.; b. Ennis, Tex., Oct. 17, 1921; s. John Warren and Icie Elizabeth (Bledsoe) G.; student in transp. mgmt. Stanford, 1957; grad. Advanced Mgmt. Program, Harvard, 1967; m. Linda O. Curnow, May 18, 1974; 1 son, John Richard; children by previous marriage—Carol Bettis, Kimberly Ann. Transp. insp. So. Pacific Co., 1946-47, trainmaster, 1947-50, operating officer, 1950-67, gen. mgr., 1967-72, v.p., San Francisco, 1972—; pres., dir. TOPS On-Line Services Inc. Served with USAAF, 1941-46. Decorated D.F.C., Air medal. Named Railroad Man of Year, Modern Railroad mag., 1972. Mem. Assn. Am. R.R.'s (chmn. data systems div. 1974-75). Clubs: World Trade, Olympic, Comml. Office: 1 Market Plaza San Francisco CA 94105

GERMOND, JOHN LOUIS, banker; b. Adrian, Mich., Oct. 28, 1929; s. Louis F. and Vera E. (Cottrell) G.; student U. Mich., 1947-48, also banking schs.; m. Mary Patricia Hermes, June 23, 1951; children—David, Steven, Patrick, Janet, Daniel. Asst. cashier Comml. Savs. Bank, Adrian, 1954-59, asst. v.p., 1959-61, v.p., cashier, 1961-69, pres., chief exec. officer, dir., 1969—; dir. Adrian Steel Co., Merillat Industries; pres., dir. Comml. Bankshares Corp. Trustee, pres. E.L. Bixby Hosp.; treas. Greater Adrian Devel. Corp., 1979, pres., 1976-79; mem. Adrian Coll. Bd. Assos.; mem. pres.'s adv. bd. Siena Heights Coll. Served with USNR, 1948-50. Recipient Disting. Service award Jaycees, 1956, Outstanding Jaycee Pres. in Mich. award, 1953, Disting. Citizen award Adrian Coll. Sesquicentennial, 1975. Mem. Mich. Bankers Assn., Adrian Area C. of C. (Maple Leaf award 1974). Republican. Roman Catholic. Clubs: Rotary, Lenawee Country. Office: Commercial Savings Bank Box 249 Adrian MI 49221

GERNERT, HIAL BURROWS, JR., oil and gas co. exec.; b. Kemmerer, Wyo., May 15, 1938; s. Hial Burrows and Helen Gardner (Mason) G.; B.B.A., U. Okla., 1960; m. Patricia Ann Cunningham, Dec. 18, 1960; children—Lori Kay, Gregory Scott. Mgmt. trainee Republic Nat. Bank of Dallas, 1963-64; loan officer United Bank of Denver, 1964-68; asst. to chmn. bd. King Resources Co., Denver, 1968-69; fin. v.p. Delhi Internat. Oil Corp., Dallas, 1969-74; asst. to pres. Forest Oil Corp., Denver, 1974—; dir. Energy Enterprises, Dionysus, Inc., Forest Energy, Inc., Forest Energy, Ltd., Forest Exploration, Inc. (all Denver), Loch Exploration, Inc., Gainesville, Tex. Served with arty. U.S. Army, 1961-63. Mem. Rocky Mountain Oil and Gas Assn., Ind. Petroleum Assn. Am. (dir.), Am. Petroleum Inst., Nat. Petroleum Council. Clubs: Columbine Country, Denver Met. Execs., Denver Petroleum. Home: 6721 S Lamar St Littleton CO 80123

GEROMETTA, ROBERT KENNETH, constrn. exec.; b. Gary, Ind., Apr. 1, 1922; m. Marcello and Marie Edith (Clericy) G.; B.S. in Architecture, U. Ill., 1948; m. Marjorie M. Rowe, Aug. 9, 1944; children—Robert M., John S., Kathryn Gerometta Bloom. Owner, Gerometta Constrn. Co., Gary, 1948-52; pres. Gerometta Constrn. Co. Inc., Gary, 1952-75, Gerometta Constrn., Inc., also Gerometta Builders Corp., 1954-75, S.E.I. Corp., 1971—; exec. v.p. Calumet Mgmt. Corp., Hammond, Ind., 1976-78; pres. The Gerometta Group, Archtl. and Constrn. Cons.'s, Chesterton, Ind., 1978—; v.p. MRM Constrn. Corp., 1975-76; dir., mem. exec. com. 1st Fed. Savs. & Loan Assn. Gary. Former bd. dirs. Gary Indsl. Found. Served with AUS, 1942-46. Decorated Silver Star, Bronze Star, Purple Heart, Combat Inf. Badge; registered architect, Ind.; lic. real estate broker, Ind. Mem. Asso. Gen. Contractors, Gary C. of C. (past dir.), Am. Arbitration Assn., Delta Upsilon. Republican. Episcopalian. Club: Gary Country (past dir.). Home: Box 1217 Ogden Dunes Portage IN 46368 Office: 423 S Roosevelt St Chesterton IN 46350

GERRAUGHTY, RICHARD GERARD, banker; b. Newton, Mass., June 18, 1940; s. John J. and Dorothy T. (Moran) G.; certificate in accounting Bentley Coll., 1963; m. Sally A. Deveaux, June 23, 1962; children—Brian, John, Cheryl. Asst. v.p. Guaranty Trust Co., Waltham, Mass., 1959-69; cashier 1st Nat. Bank Greenfield, Mass., 1969-70; v.p., treas. Garden City Trust Co., Newton, 1970-73; sr. v.p., controller Shawmut Mchts. Bank, Salem, Mass., 1973—; chmn. ops. com. Shawmut Corp., Boston. Mem. Northboro Housing Com., 1972-73; treas. Support Our Servicemen, 1965-69. Mem. Am. Bankers Assn., Salem C. of C. (treas.), Bentley Coll. Alumni Assn. Republican. Roman Catholic. Office: 253 Essex St Salem MA 01970

GERRISH, HOLLIS G., confectionery co. exec.; b. Berwick, Maine, June 23, 1907; s. Perley G. and Grace (Guptill) G.; A.B., Harvard, 1930, postgrad. Harvard Bus. Sch., 1930-31; m. Catherine G. Ruggles, Sept. 10, 1946. With Squirrel Brand Co., mfg. confectioners, 1931—, pres., 1939-42, 46—; trustee Cambridge Savs. Bank. Bd. dirs. Middlesex-Cambridge Lung Assn., Cambridge YMCA, East End House, Cambridge Home for the Aged; trustee Lesley Coll., Cambridge, Mass.; corp. mem. New Eng. Deaconess Hosp. Served as lt. comdr. USNR, 1942-46; capt. Res. Mem. Am. Soc. Candy Technologists, Cambridge Hist. Soc., Nat. Tax Assn., Mass. Audubon Soc. Episcopalian (trustee). Clubs: Harvard, Faculty, New England Confectioners, Norfolk Trout, Cambridge, Economy, Rotary. Home: 207 Grove St Cambridge MA 02138 Office: 10-12 Boardman St Cambridge MA 02139

GERRISH, ROBERT GRANT, investment banking co. exec.; b. Boston, Feb. 9, 1921; s. John Jordan and Alice (Grant) G.; student Tufts Coll., 1938-39; Boston U., 1939-42; children—Grant T., Gail V., Conrad J., Thomas R. Salesman, Whiting, Weeks & Stubbs, Boston, 1945-50; mgr. syndicate and municipal bond depts. G.H. Walker & Co., Providence, 1950-59; partner Oscar E. Dooly & Co., Miami, Fla., 1959-64; pres. Dooly, Gerrish & Co., Inc., 1964-70; account exec. Dean Witter Reynolds Inc., Miami, 1970—; dir. Mil. & Computer Electronics Corp., Ft. Lauderdale, Fla., Millers Falls Paper Co. (Mass.); mem. Boston Stock Exchange, Phila.-Balt. Stock Exchange; mem. investors info. com. N.Y. Stock Exchange. Mem. R.I. Pub. Expenditures Council, Providence, 1956-59, Com. State Budget, 1957-59, Taxation Com., 1957-59, Met. Govt. Com., 1957-59; past pres. United Way Fla.; bd. dirs. United Health Found. Dade County, Big Bros. Greater Miami, Hearing and Speech Center Dade County, Crime Commn. Greater Miami; bd. dirs. Fla. com. U.S. Olympic Com.; bd. dirs., trustee United Way Dade County. Served with USNR, 1942-45. Mem. Investment Bankers Assn. Am. (edn. com.), R.I. Assn. Investment Firms (founder 1959), Nat. Security Traders Assn. (edn. com.), Fla. Security Dealers Assn. (past pres.), Security Dealers Assn. Greater Miami (past pres.). Clubs: Boston Investment (founder 1946, pres. 1946-48); Country (Coral Gables, Fla.); Miami, Com. 100 (Miami). Home: 547 NE 59th St Miami FL 33137 Office: 700 Brickell Ave Miami FL 33131

GERRITY, EDWARD JOSEPH, JR., communications co. exec.; b. Scranton, Pa., Jan. 3, 1924; s. Edward Joseph and Helen T. (Walton) G.; B.S., U. Scranton, 1946, also LL.D.; M.S., Columbia U., 1948; m. Katharine Casey, Sept. 22, 1956; children—Katharine, Edward Joseph III. Editorial staff, columnist Scranton Times, 1948-58; with ITT, 1958—, v.p., dir. pub. relations, 1961-64, sr. v.p., dir. corporate relations and advt., 1964—, dir. subsidiaries. Chmn. pub. relations com. Cardinal's Com. for Laity of Cath. Charities, Archdiocese of N.Y.; bd. dirs. Cath. Big Bros., Fifth Ave. Assn. Served with U.S. Army, 1942-45; ETO. Decorated knight Order Holy Sepulchre, Silver Star, Bronze Star with cluster. Named PR Profl. of Year, Pub. Relations News, 1971. Mem. Pub. Relations Soc. Am., Internat. Pub. Relations Assn., Am. Mgmt. Assn., Pa. Soc., Internat. Econ. Policy Assn. (dir.), Sigma Delta Chi. Clubs: Overseas Press (N.Y.C.); Metropolitan, Federal City, Nat. Press (Washington); Westchester Country (Rye, N.Y.). Knight of Malta. Office: ITT World Hdqrs 320 Park Ave New York NY 10022

GERSCH, SETH JONATHAN, fin. exec.; b. N.Y.C., Sept. 2, 1947; s. Howard K. and Sarah (Seibel) G.; B.B.A., Pace U., 1970; student Pratt Inst. 1964-67; m. Barbara Curczinski, Aug. 10, 1969; 1 son, Jordan. Vice pres. Oppenheimer & Co., N.Y.C., 1969-77; v.p. Morgan Stanley, N.Y.C., 1977-79, Chgo., 1979—. Club: Mid-Day. Office: 115 S LaSalle St Chicago IL 60603

GERSHMAN, NORMAN HERBERT, finance co. exec.; b. Jersey City, Aug. 14, 1932; s. Albert Edward and Pearl (Baumgarten) G.; B.S., N.Y. U., 1954; m. Carol Lipman, June 5, 1955; children—Leslie, Eric, Roger. Account exec. Merrill Lynch & Co., N.Y.C., 1957-65, sales mgr., 1965-69, asst. v.p., mgr., 1969-70, v.p., mgr., 1970-75, v.p., options tax shelters, 1975-76; nat. sales mgr. Josephthal & Co., N.Y.C., 1976—; pres. Norman H. Gershman Assos., Securities Brokers, Norman H. Gershman Search Cons., Norman H. Gershman Photog. Art Gallery. Bd. dirs. Nat. Council to Combat Blindness. Served to capt. USAF, 1954-57. Mem. Ethical Culture Soc. (dir. 1972—). Contbr. articles to trade pubis. Home: 131 E 83d St Apt 3D New York NY 10028 Office: Josephthal Co 120 Broadway New York NY 10005

GERSHOWITZ, SONYA ZIPORKIN, med. care adminstrv. exec.; b. Bronx, N.Y., July 30, 1940; d. David and Rose Ziporkin; R.N., Sinai Hosp., Balt. 1960; B.S. in Nursing, U. Md., 1973, M.S. in Nursing, 1978; m. Irvin Gershowitz, Mar. 30, 1960; children—Benjamin, Sharon. Staff nurse Sinai Hosp., 1960-63; evening supr. Happy Hill Convalescent Home, Balt., 1963-64; dir. nurses Ashburton Home, Balt., 1963-64, Mt. Sinai Nursing Home, Balt., 1968-71, 73-74, Multi-Med. Convalescent and Nursing Center, Balt., 1974-75; owner-adminstr. Greater Pa. Ave. Nursing Center, Balt., 1975-76, adminstrv. dir., 1978—; owner-adminstr. Lafayette Sq. Nursing Center, Balt., 1976-78, adminstrv. dir., 1978—; owner, adminstrv. dir. Fed. Hill Nursing Center, Balt., 1978—; chmn. subcom. innovation survey procedures Md. Dept. Health and Mental Hygiene; mem. labor market adv. com. Mayor Balt. Office Manpower Resources, 1978—; mem. White House Conf. Aging, 1971, Md. Task Force Nosocomial Infection, 1974—; mem. Washington Legal Found., 1980-81; mem. Gov.'s Conf. on Aging, 1980. Fellow Am. Coll. Nursing Home Adminstrs. (chmn. edn. com. 1977, pres. elect com. 1978); mem. U. Md. Alumni Assn., New Stoneybrook Improvement Assn. (pres. 1974), League Md. Horsemen (past dir.), Md. Law Enforcement Officers Inc., Am. Fedn. Police. Jewish. Home: 2307 Hidden Glen Dr Owings Mills MD 21117 Office: 1400 Johns St Baltimore MD 21217

GERSON, ELISABETH, communications co. exec.; b. Los Angeles, Feb. 6, 1924; d. Sidney and Nell Gerson; A.B. in Psychology summa cum laude, UCLA, 1946; div.; children—Dean Hunter Rolston, Matthew Russell Rolston. Radio and TV exec., 1949-56; pvt. practice ednl. psychology, 1946-71; founder Intercom Internat., Inc., Princeton, 1978, pres., 1978-80; founder, pres. Internat. Fellowship Authors, Artists and Filmmakers; cons. to corps. in design and implementation of communications. Recipient 1st prize N.J. Poetry Soc., 1974. Mem. Am. Film Inst., Graphic Artists Guild, Internat. Soc. Artists, Princeton C. of C. Club: Women's Club (Princeton). Editor: Einstein As I Knew Him (by Alan W. Richards), 1979; creator 30 radio programs, 15 major film prodns., also consumer products for children, designs for timepieces, TV programs, others. Home and office: Eden West 30 Nassau St Princeton NJ 08540

GERSON, MYLES ZACHARY, tube co. exec.; b. N.Y.C., Aug. 15, 1925; s. Samuel and Pauline (Farber) G.; student Bordentown (N.J.) Mil. Inst., 1940; grad. Tilton Sch., 1942; m. Albine Roberta Gutterman, Dec. 19, 1948; children—Roger, David, Elizabeth. Mgr., Smith Transport, Ltd., N.Y.C., 1946-48; regional mgr. B. & E. Transp., Secaucus, N.J., 1948-51; v.p. Hayes Freight Lines, Springfield, Ill., 1951-56; gen. mgr. Gen. Expressways, Chgo., 1956-63; v.p., gen. mgr. Spl. Commodity div. Navajo Freight Lines, Chgo., 1964—, v.p., Gary, Ind., 1965-73; v.p. adminstrn. Allied Tube & Conduit Corp., Harvey, Ill., 1973—. Mem. Com. hwys., N.Y., 1951-53, Ill., 1961-69. Bd. dirs. Pitts. Symphony., 1954-55; chmn. adv. bd. Prairie State Coll., Work Edn. Council of S.Chgo. Served with AUS. 1943-46; PTO. Decorated Purple Heart, Bronze Star. Mem. N.Y., Chgo. traffic clubs. Jewish. Club: Ravisloe Country. Home: 630 Argyle Rd Flossmoor IL 60422 Office: 16100 Lathrop St Harvey IL 60426

GERSTEIN, MEL, research and mktg. exec.; b. N.Y.C., Jan. 30, 1936; s. Frank and May (Brown) Gerstein; B.B.A., Pace Coll., 1955; postgrad. Columbia U., 1957; m. Gayle; children—Teddy, Madeline, Amy. Vice pres. research and devel., treas., dir. Thermwell Products Co., Inc., Paterson, N.J., 1957—; v.p. research and devel., sec., dir. Lever Mfg. Corp., N.Y.C., 1958—; treas., dir. Eagle Lamp Corp., Spiral Bagging Machine Corp.; dir. L&M Vending Corp., Woodlowe Realty Corp., Vogue Studios, Inc., Belleville, N.J., Royal Crown Bottling Co., Newark, Lever Mfg. Corp. Co-chmn. N.J. Cultural Center; trustee Barnert Meml. Hosp. Center, Paterson. Mem. Am. Mgmt. Assn., N.J., Paterson chambers commerce. Developer houseware and hardware products. Home: Buckingham Dr Alpine NJ 07620 Office: 150 E 7th St Paterson NJ 07524

GERSTENMAIER, JOHN HERBERT, rubber co. exec.; b. St. Paul, Aug. 24, 1916; s. Walter and Alma (Lindenberg) G.; B.M.E., U. Minn., 1938; M.Indsl. Mgmt., Mass. Inst. Tech., 1952; m. Lois Rolfing, Dec. 28, 1939; children—John Herbert, Jan Lee McClennan, JoEllen. With Goodyear Tire & Rubber Co., 1938-63, 67—, plant mgr., Logan Ohio, 1963, exec. v.p., dir., Akron, Ohio, 1971-74, pres., chief operating officer, 1974-78, vice-chmn., 1978—; pres. Motor Wheel Corp., Lansing, Mich., 1964-67. Mem. Soc. Automotive Engrs., Sigma Nu. Lutheran. Club: Portage Country (Akron). Office: Goodyear Tire & Rubber Co 1144 E Market St Akron OH 44316*

GERSTIN, STANLEY, ret. publishing co. exec.; b. Washington, June 6, 1908; s. Jacob and Mary (Pollack) G.; student George Washington U., 1927-29, Coll. City N.Y., 1929, 30, N.Y. U., 1931; m. Ethel Hecht, Dec. 22, 1930; Reporter, Washington News, 1928-1929; night editor Asso. Press, N.Y.C., 1930-31; mng. editor Chilton Pub. Co., Phila., 1932-35; feature editor Fawcett Publs., N.Y.C., 1937-40; editor FM Bus., N.Y.C., 1946-47; asst. pub. Electronic Industries, N.Y.C., 1948-50; gen. mgr. U.S. Electronic Publs., Hicksville, N.Y., 1951-58, pres., 1958-69, chmn. bd., 1969-76; dir. Charter Communications, Inc., N.Y.C.; chmn. bd. USEP Services, Inc., Hicksville, 1969-76; pub. and editorial cons., 1976—. Served as lt. col. AUS, 1942-45. Decorated Legion of Merit; recipient Medal of Merit for outstanding pub., editorial and mgmt. skill. Home: 14 Yankee Hill Rd Westport CT 06880

GERSTNER, LOUIS VINCENT, JR., fin. services co. exec.; b. Mineola, N.Y., Mar. 1, 1942; s. Louis V. and Marjorie (Rutan) G.; B.A., Dartmouth Coll., 1963; M.B.A., Harvard U., 1965; m. Elizabeth Robins Link, Nov. 30, 1968; children—Louis, Elizabeth. Dir., McKinsey & Co., N.Y.C., N.Y., 1965-78; exec. v.p. Am. Express Co., N.Y.C., 1978—, dir., 1979—; dir. Am. Express Internat. Banking Corp., 1979—, Jewel Cos., Inc., 1980—. Mem. bd. mgrs. Sloan Kettering Cancer Center, 1978—; trustee, mem. exec. com. Joint Council Econ. Edn., 1975—; bd. dirs. Internat. Golf Assn., 1979—, Bus. Com. for Arts., 1980—; mem. Dartmouth Coll. Alumni Council, 1974-77. Clubs: Blind Brook, Round Hill, Links, Sky. Office: 125 Broad St New York NY 10004

GERTLER, ALFRED MARTIN, pub. relations co. exec.; b. N.Y.C., Nov. 15, 1922; s. Harry and Peggy L. (Weinberg) G.; B.S. in Journalism, U. Ill., 1947; m. Claire O. Gruenberg, Oct. 19, 1951; children—Eric, Jonathan, Richard. With Harshe-Rotman & Druck, Inc., Chgo., 1948—, sr. exec. v.p., 1973—, chief operating officer, 1977—, pres. and chief operating officer, 1979—, also dir.; reporter, editor Peoria (Ill.) Star, 1947; account exec. Ridings & Ferris, Inc., Chgo., 1948; lectr. U. Ill., 1975, counselor, 1974-75. Served with USAAF, 1942-45. Decorated D.F.C., Air medal with 5 oak leaf clusters. Mem. Pub. Relations Soc. Am. (accredited), Publicity Club Chgo., Sigma Delta Chi. Democrat. Jewish. Contbr. articles to profl. jours. Home: 1450 Ridge Rd Highland Park IL 60035 Office: 444 N Michigan Ave Chicago IL 60611

GERTZ, JOSEPH BARRY, bus. and fin. exec., fin. and mgmt. cons., philanthropist; b. Detroit, May 7, 1942; s. Harold Morris and Geneva Rice (Skirvin) G.; A.B., Stanford U., 1964; M.B.A., U. Calif. at Los Angeles, 1966, C.Phil., 1970; m. Dorinda Donohoe DeWitt, Dec. 31, 1978; 1 dau., Lindsey Dene. Investment analyst Bank of Am., Los Angeles, 1961-63; officer tng. program Shearson Hammill & Co., Los Angeles, 1965; research asso. fin. U. Calif. at Los Angeles, 1966-68; asst. prof. fin. U. Tex., 1968-71; owner J.B. Gertz & Co., N.Y.C., 1969—, Faubion Ranch, Leander, Tex., 1970-73, Town Lake Apts., Austin, 1971-73; pres. No. Trust Co., Panama, 1973—, Am. Land Investors Corp., Columbia, S.C., 1973—, Combined Deposits Fund, Inc., Los Angeles, 1974—, Carolina Nat. Cons., Inc., Carolina Tax Planning, Inc., Desert Oil Corp., Nat. Resources Corp. and predecessor firms; chmn. bd., chief exec. officer AMTAX Cons.'s, Palm Springs, Calif., 1977—, Columbia Nat. Cons.'s Alaska, Inc., Anchorage, 1978—; state dir. S.C. Energy Crisis Assistance Program, 1979-80, S.C. Low Income Energy Assistance Program, 1980; cons. Competitive Capital Corp.; editorial cons. on investments to pubs.; lectr. investment banking and portfolio mgmt.; dir. Innovation Research Assos. of Prescott (Ariz.) Coll. Trustee, Endowment for Commonwealth, Gertz Found. Named Ky. col. Mem. Econometric Soc., Am. Econ. Assn., Am. Fin. Assn., Am. Mgmt. Assn., Inst. Mgmt. Sci., Am. Judicature Soc., Los Angeles World Affairs Council, Beta Gamma Sigma, Delta Sigma Pi. Clubs: Los Angeles Athletic, Town Hall, Rotary (former chief fin. officer), Ephebian Soc. Los Angeles (past pres.). Author numerous articles on mergers, acquisitions, investment and fin. Home: PO Box 4051 Columbia SC 29240 Office: 2875 E Baristo Rd Palm Springs CA 92262

GERUNDA, ARTHUR BENEDICT, engring. co. exec.; b. N.Y.C., Apr. 8, 1938; s. Benedict John and Antonina (Rizzuto) G.; B.S. in Chem. Engring., Ind. Inst. Tech., 1959; M.Chem. Engring., N.Y. U.,

1970; m. Margaret Edelmann, Feb. 19, 1959; 1 son, Arthur Benedict. Process design engr. M.W. Kellogg Co., Inc., N.Y.C., 1963-66; staff cons. Chem. Systems, Inc., N.Y.C., 1966-71; cons., N.Y.C., 1971-75; v.p. comml. devel. The Heyward Robinson Co., Inc., N.Y.C., 1975—. Leader, committeeman Suffolk County council Boy Scouts Am., Medford, 1971-74; dir. Community Bd., West Islip, N.Y., 1976-79. Mem. Comml. Devel. Assn., Licensing Execs. Soc., Chem. Industry Assn., AICE. Home: 225 Oak Neck Ln West Islip NY 11795 Office: 1 World Trade Center New York NY 10048

GESSLING, ROBERT FRANCIS, engring. exec.; b. N.Y.C., Mar. 18, 1923; s. Clarence and Minnie; grad. Marine Engring., State U. of N.Y. Maritime Coll., 1945; M.S.M.E., N.Y. U., 1949; m. Margaret M. Dennin, Nov. 5, 1949; children—Margaret, Patricia, Anne. Thermodynamics specialist Combustion Engring. Corp., N.Y.C., 1947-50; cons. engr. Visco Franzblau Assos., N.Y.C., 1950-52; mgr. mech. engring. GTE Sylvania, Williamsport, Pa., 1952-62, dir. GTE facilities devel., Woburn, Mass., 1962—. Served to lt. USNR, 1945-47. Registered profl. engr., 14 states; licensed marine engr. Mem. ASME, Am. Assn. Cost Engrs., Nat. Soc. Profl. Engrs. Home: 5 Tamarack Ln Peabody MA 01960 Office: 300 Unicron Park Dr Woburn MA 01801

GETTINGER, HAROLD SEYMOUR, confectionery co. exec.; b. N.Y.C., Sept. 21, 1930; s. Abraham and Fannie (Noble) G.; B.B.A., CCNY, 1952; M.S., Stevens Inst. Tech., Hoboken, N.J., 1958; m. Charlene Penner, Sept. 14, 1952; children—Kenneth Paul, Michael Aaron. Civilian statistician U.S. Naval Supply Logistics Research, Bayonne, N.J., 1954-56; sr. statistician Rayco Auto Seat Covers Co., Paterson, N.J., 1956-58; ops. research engr. research and devel. Bulova Co., Woodside, N.Y., 1958-60; group head analytic studies Systems Devel. Corp., Paramus, N.J., 1960-64; ops. research mgr. M&M/Mars Co., Hackettstown, N.J., 1964-66, indsl. engring. dir., then ops. research dir., 1966-72, v.p. (comml.) purchasing, 1975—; v.p. service and fin. Uncle Ben's Foods, Houston, 1972-75; bd. mgrs. N.Y. Coffee, Sugar and Cocoa Exchange, 1978—; instr. Grad. Sch. Bus., CCNY, 1962. Served with USNR, 1952-54. Mem. Am. Inst. Indsl. Engrs., Ops. Research Soc. Am., Inst. Mgmt. Scis. Jewish. Club: Odd Fellows. Home: 22 Armstrong Rd Morristown NJ 07960 Office: High St Hackettstown NJ 07840

GETTY, WILLIAM PATTON, former steel co. exec.; b. Pitts., Mar. 26, 1910; s. William Fleming and Bertha A. (Keefe) G.; B.S., U. Pitts., 1932; m. Betty Ann Cochran, Nov. 23, 1938; children—Judith Ann Getty Treadwell, William Patton III. With Weirton Steel Co., 1932-36; with Jones & Laughlin Steel Corp., 1936-70, asst. v.p. prodn., 1953-63, v.p. prodn., 1963-67, exec. v.p., 1967-68, pres., chief operating officer, 1968-70, also dir.; cons. to steel industry, 1970—; dir. H.H. Robertson Co., Salem Corp., Pa Engring. Corp., Birdsboro Corp., Ry. Service Corp. Chmn. bd. trustees Winchester-Thurston Sch., 1961-67; trustee United Fund; mem. exec. council, v.p. Allegheny Trails council Boy Scouts Am. Mem. Am. Iron and Steel Inst. (chmn. mfg. problems com. 1966-68), Brit. Metals Soc., AIME, Am. Soc. Metals, Am. Welding Soc., Soc. Automotive Engrs., Coal Mining Inst. Am., Eastern States Blast Furnace and Coke Oven Assn., Assn. Iron and Steel Engrs., Engrs. Soc. Western Pa. Clubs: Duquesne, Longue Vue Country (Pitts.); Laurel Valley Golf (Ligonier, Pa.); Ponte Vedra, Boca Raton, Quail Ridge (Fla.). Home: 107 Hawthorne Rd Fox Chapel Pittsburgh PA 15238

GEWIRTZ, MORRIS, city ofcl.; b. Bklyn., July 18, 1915; s. Henry and Lena (Wilner) G.; B.A., Bklyn. Coll., 1937; postgrad., 1937-41; B.Engring., N.Y. U., 1962, postgrad., 1942-43, 46-48; m. Frances Yvonne Wigler, Oct. 7, 1939; children—Joan Susan, Lawrence Herbert. With U.S. Navy, 1948-73, facilities mgmt. coordinator Third Naval Dist., Eastern Div., Naval Facilities Engring. Command, N.Y.C., 1963-66, dir. mgmt. services div. U.S. Naval Facilities Engring. Command, Alexandria, Va., 1966-73; chief human resources adminstrn. revenue sect., office of budget and fiscal affairs N.Y.C. Human Resources Adminstrn., 1979—. Vice chmn. local sch. bd. Dist. 14 Bklyn., 1963-64, chmn., 1965; chmn. subcom. on budget N.Y.C. Bd. Edn., 1965. Served with U.S. Army, 1943-45. N.Y. State War Service Scholar, 1946; registered profl. engr., Mass. Mem. Inst. Mgmt. Scis., Am. Soc. Public Adminstrn., Am. Inst. Indsl. Engrs. (sr.), Soc. Am. Mil. Engrs., N.Y. State Soc. Profl. Engrs., Nat. Soc. Profl. Engrs., N.Y. Acad. Scis. Club: N.Y. U. Home: 1311D Brightwater Ave Apt 5D Brooklyn NY 11235 Office: NYC Human Resources Adminstrn 200 Church St Room 503 New York NY 10013

GHAI, PARSHOTAM LAL, civil engr.; b. Akbar, Sialkote, India, Oct. 2, 1936; s. Gopal Das and Parkash Vati (Rakhrai) G.; came to U.S., 1968, naturalized, 1975; B.A. with honors, Panjab U., India, 1956, B.Sc. in Civil Engring., 1960, M.S., 1968; postgrad. U. Pitts., 1968-69; m. Indra Bhalla, June 21, 1961; children—Prabodh, Simmi, Neeraj. Lectr. civil engring. Nat. Inst. Engring., Hoshiarpur, India, 1960-61; design engr. Hydroelectric Designs Directorate, Chandigarh, India, 1961-68; grad. research asst. U. Pitts., 1968-69; civil engr. Pa. Dept. Transp., Clearfield, 1969-72; project engr. Pa. Power & Light Co., Allentown, 1972-77, sr. project engr., 1977—; adj. instr. hydraulics engring. Lehigh County Community Coll., 1980—. Founding mem., dir., sec. India Assn. of Lehigh Valley, 1974-75, 76-77; v.p. Bhartiya Cultural Soc., 1976-78, pres., 1978—; trustee, sec. Hindu Temple Soc. Registered profl. engr., Pa. Mem. ASCE, Speakers Bur. Pa. Power & Light Co. Hindu. Contbr. articles to tech. jours. Home: 4 Fugazzotto Dr RD 3 Allentown PA 18104 Office: 2 N 9th St Allentown PA 18101

GHAREEB, GEORGE SALEM, indsl. and automotive parts mfg. exec.; b. Aita-El-Fokhar, Lebanon, Mar. 25, 1949; s. Salem M. and Nabiha G.; came to U.S., 1967, naturalized, 1973; M.B.A., U. Toledo, 1976. Internat. fin. specialist 1st Nat. Bank of Toledo, 1971-76; internal auditor Dana Corp., Toledo, 1976—, accountant, 1979—; cons. fgn. banking, investments; instr. Davis Bus. Coll., Toledo. Bd. dirs. St. George Cathedral. Mem. Internal Auditor Inst., Nat. Assn. Accountants. Republican. Greek Orthodox. Club: Spring Meadows Racquetball. Home: 2261 Lehman Rd Toledo OH 43611 Office: 4500 Dorr St Toledo OH 43615

GHENTS, JOHN HENRY, oil co. exec.; b. Bklyn., May 7, 1916; s. Frederick Michael and Mary Cecilia (O'Malley) G.; B.B.A., St. John's U., Bklyn., 1942; m. Ruth Heig, Jan. 10, 1943; children—Pamela May (Mrs. Bulkley), Bonnie Ruth (Mrs. Flaherty), Michelle Ann. With Asiatic Petroleum Corp., N.Y.C., 1936-76, asst. treas., 1954-62, controller, 1962—, treas., 1963—, v.p., dir., 1965-76, chmn. exec. com., 1971-74; pres., dir. Shell Funding Corp., 1971-76, Greater N.Y. Terminal, Inc., 1969-74; dir. Res./2d Res. Terminals, 1962-74, v.p., 1969-74; v.p., dir. Scallop Holding Inc., Scallop Nuclear Inc. Bd. dirs. Nat. Hemophilia Found., 1972-76. Mem. Econ. Club N.Y., Am. Petroleum Inst., Newcomen Soc., Am. Mgmt. Assn., Tax Inst. Clubs: Internat. (Washington); New Canaan (Conn.) Field; Metropolitan, Rockefeller Center Luncheon (gov.) (N.Y.C.). Home: 97 Sturbridge Hill Rd New Canaan CT 06840 Office: 1 Rockefeller Plaza New York City NY 10020

GHIGLIONE, LOREN FRANK, editor, publisher; b. N.Y.C., Apr. 5, 1941; s. William John and Norma Rae (Whitney) G.; A.B., Haverford Coll., 1963; J.D., Yale, 1966, M.Urban Studies, 1966; Ph.D., George Washington U., 1976; m. Nancy Ellen Geiger, Feb. 24, 1968; children—Jessica, Laura. Planning officer Nat. Endowment for Humanities, 1967-68; editor, pub., pres. Evening News, Southbridge, Mass., 1969—; pres. Worcester County Newspapers Webster (Mass.) Times, 1973—, Auburn (Mass.) News, 1973—, Blackstone Valley Tribune/Advertiser, Whitinsville, Mass., 1976—, Wick-Qua-Boag-Weekly and New Leader, Spencer, Mass., 1977—; vis. prof. English, U. Mass., 1973; media commentator Sta. WGBH-TV, Boston, 1972-75; mem. Nat. News Council, 1973—; dir. Mass. Daily Newspaper Survey, 1971, New Eng. Daily Newspaper Survey, 1973-74. Bd. overseers Old Sturbridge Village, 1976—. Recipient Haverford prize, 1974; Newspaper Fund fellow, 1962; Congl. fellow, 1966-67; Winston Churchill traveling fellow, 1974. Mem. Am. Soc. Newspaper Editors (chmn. bull.), Internat. Press Inst., New Eng. Soc. Newspaper Editors (pres. 1978-79), Nat. Conf. Editorial Writers, Mass. Press-Bar Com. (co-chmn. 1980-81), UPI New Eng. Press Assn. (bd. govs., Allan B. Rogers meml. award 1977), Mass. Newspaper Pubs. Assn. (dir.), New Eng. Press Assn. (sec.-treas.), New Eng. Daily Newspaper Assn., Soc. Profl. Journalists (award 1974), Am. Antiquarian Soc. Editor: Evaluating the Press: The New England Daily Newspaper Survey, 1974. Home: 56 Woodland St Southbridge MA 01550 Office: 25 Elm St Southbridge MA 01550

GHIRALDINI, JOAN, paper co. exec.; b. Bklyn., Mar. 31, 1951; s. Robert and Anne (Centineo) G.; B.A., Smith Coll., 1972; M.B.A., U. Pa., 1975. Intern, N.Y.C. Econ. Devel. Adminstrn., 1971; econ. specialist Western Electric Co., N.Y.C., 1975-76; sr. fin. analyst Internat. Paper Co., N.Y.C., 1976-78, mgr. strategic planning, 1978—. Mem. Am. Fin. Assn., N.Am. Soc. for Corp. Planning, Fin. Women's Assn. N.Y., Murray Hill Civic Assn. Clubs: Wharton Bus. Sch. (v.p.), Smith Coll. N.Y. Home: 155 E 38th St New York NY 10016 Office: 220 E 42d St New York NY 10017

GHOLSON, CECIL JACK, diversified energy co. exec.; b. Haskell, Tex., Sept. 25, 1927; s. Jesse White and Beulah Harriet (Foy) G.; B.B.A. with highest honors, Tex. Tech. U., 1949; m. Bettye Jo Lynch, Sept. 16, 1956; 1 dau., Twyla Lynn. With Pioneer Corp., Amarillo, 1949—, asst. v.p., 1964-69, v.p. fin., 1969—, dir. subs.'s.; vis. lectr. W. Tex. State U., 1958-60. Bd. dirs. Panhandle Baptist Found. Mem. Amarillo Area Fin. and Econ. Council. Served with U.S. Army, 1947-48, 50-53. Mem. Am. Inst. C.P.A.'s. Baptist. Clubs: Amarillo, Amarillo Country. Home: 1508 Bowie Amarillo TX 79102 Office: 301 Taylor Amarillo TX 79163

GHUBLIKIAN, JOHN RICHARD, design, engring. and constrn. co. exec.; b. Boston, Nov. 7, 1917; s. Dickran H. and Santook (Kasparian) G.; B.S. in Chem. Engring., Tufts U., 1939; cert. Center for Mgmt. Devel., Northeastern U., 1963; m. Leona A. Laskowski, Aug. 21, 1943; children—John Richard, Ann K. Lab. supr., process engr., sr. process engr. E.B. Badger & Sons Co., Boston, 1940-51; process supr. Badger Process div. Stone & Webster Engring. Co., 1951-53; process supr. The Badger Co., Inc., Cambridge, Mass., 1953-60, mgr. process dept., 1960-67, engring. mgr., 1967-68, v.p. Western Hemisphere, 1975-77, sr. v.p. Western Hemisphere, 1977—, also dir.; dep. mng. dir. Badger B.V., Holland, 1968-70, mng. dir., 1970-75, now dir.; pres., dir. Badger Am., Inc., Cambridge, 1975—; v.p., dir. Badger Energy, Inc., Badger Plants, Inc.; v.p. Can. Badger, Chem. Process Corp.; pres., dir. Badger Pan Am. Corp. mem. Wentworth Inst. Tech. Recipient Outstanding Leadership award ASME, 1976; registered profl. engr., Mass. Mem. Am. Chem. Soc., Am. Inst. Chem. Engrs. Clubs: Algonquin, Univ. (Boston); New Seabury (Mass.) Tennis. Contbr. articles to profl. jours.; patentee in field. Home: 192 Commonwealth Ave Boston MA 02116 Office: One Broadway Cambridge MA 02142

GIACCO, ALEXANDER FORTUNATUS, diversified chem. co. exec.; b. St. John, Italy, Aug. 24, 1919; s. Salvatore J. and Maria Concetta (de Maria) G.; B.S. in Chem. Engring., Va. Poly. Inst., 1942; postgrad. in mgmt. Harvard U., 1965; D.Bus. (hon.), William Carey Coll., Hattiesburg, Miss., 1980; m. Edith Brown, Feb. 16, 1946; children—Alexander Fortunatus, Richard John, Mary P. Giacco Walsh, Elizabeth B., Marissa A. With Hercules Inc., Wilmington, Del., 1942—, gen. mgr. polymers dept., 1968-73, dir., 1970—, gen. mgr. operating dept. Hercules Europe, 1973, v.p. parent co., 1974-76, mem. exec. com., 1974—, exec. v.p., 1976-77, pres., chief exec. officer, chmn. exec. com., 1977—, chmn. bd., 1980; dir. Del. Trust Co., Texasgulf Inc. Mem. U.S. Com. on New Initiatives in East-West Co-op., 1976—, chmn. Cath. Diocese of Wilmington 2d ann. appeal; chmn. United Fund, Wilmington, 1963-66; hon. chmn. bd., mem. nat. bd. dirs. Jr. Achievement Del., 1975; trustee, bd. dirs., mem. exec. com. Wilmington Med. Center, 1975—; trustee, bd. visitors Va. Poly. Inst., 1979; bd. dirs. Greater Wilmington Devel. Council; chmn. bd. Grand Opera House, Wilmington. Named One of Ten Outstanding Chief Exec. Officers, Fin. World, 1980. Mem. Chem. Mfrs. Assn. (bd. dirs.), Soc. Chem. Industry, Soc. Plastics Industry, Soc. Automotive Engrs., Man-Made Fiber Producers Assn., Del. Round Table (chmn. econ. devel. com.), Am. Ordnance Assn. (past dep. chmn.). Clubs: Wilmington, Wilmington Country, Vicmead Hunt, Bidermann Golf, Hercules Country, Rehoboth Beach Country. Patentee in field. Office: 910 Market St Wilmington DE 19899

GIALANELLA, PHILIP THOMAS, publishing co. exec.; b. Binghamton, N.Y., June 6, 1930; s. Felix and Frances (Demuro) G.; B.A., Harpur Coll., 1952; M.A., State U. N.Y., 1955; m. Marie Amelia Davis, May 1, 1953; 1 son, Thomas Davis. Promotion dir. Evening Press and Sta. WINR-TV, Binghamton, 1957-62; v.p., gen. mgr. Daily Advance, Dover, N.J., 1962-66; v.p. Hartford (Conn.) Times, 1966-70; pres., pub. Newburgh (N.Y.) News, 1970-71; exec. v.p. Hawaii Newspaper Agy., Honolulu, 1971-73, pres., 1974—, also dir.; pub. Honolulu Star-Bull., 1975—; sec.-treas. Newspaper Prodn. Co., Shreveport, La.; sec., asst. treas. Newspaper Printing Corp., Newspaper Realty Corp., El Paso, Tex.; pres. Gannett Southwest and Pacific Newspaper Group; v.p., dir. Gannett Pacific Corp.; dir. Tucson Newspaper Inc., Capital Investment Co., Guam Publs., AP Assn. Calif., Ariz., Hawaii and Nev. Bd. govs. Pacific Asian Affairs Council; bd. dirs. Aloha United Way; pres. Hawaii Newspaper Agy. Found. Served with AUS, 1952-54. Mem. Am. Newspaper Pubs. Assn. Hawaii Pubs. Assn., Nat. Alliance of Businessmen (exec. com.), Hawaii-Japan Econ. Council. Roman Catholic. Home: 143 Hanapepe Loop Honolulu HI 96825 Office: 605 Kapiolani Blvd Honolulu HI 96813

GIANCARLO, SAMUEL SALVATOR, engring. and constrn. co. exec.; b. Buffalo, June 11, 1942; s. Guy Paul and Josephine Helen (Alessi) G.; student Cleve. State U., 1960-62; B.S. in Chem. Engring., SUNY, Buffalo, 1965, M.B.A., 1968; m. Heather Andrea Murphy, Jan. 15, 1966; children—John Paul, Matthew Christopher. Engr. trainee Rep. Steel Corp., Buffalo, 1961-63; devel. engr. Allied Chem. Corp., Buffalo, 1965-67; mgr. engring., asst. sales mgr. Luwa Corp., Charlotte, N.C., 1968-73; contract engr. engring. and constrn. J.F. Pritchard & Co., Kansas City, Mo., 1973; project mgr. M.W. Kellogg Co., Houston, 1973-74; engring. and constrn. sales exec. A.G. McKee & Co., Houston, 1974-79; v.p., gen. mgr. GKN Birwelco (U.S.) Inc., Houston, 1979-80; v.p. sales and mktg. Davy McKee Corp., Chgo., 1980—. Pack exec. com. Boy Scouts Am.; cub master Cub Scouts, leader Webelos, 1975-77; active YMCA Indian Guide Program, 1973-77. Licensed profl. engr., Tex. Mem. Am. Inst. Chem. Engrs., Nat., Tex. socs. profl. engrs., U. Buffalo Alumni Assn., Beta Gamma Sigma, Tau Kappa Epsilon. Roman Catholic. Clubs: University, Houstonian (Houston). Home: 12927 Taylorcrest St Houston TX 77079 Office: 10 S Riverside Plaza Chicago IL 60606

GIANNINOTO, FRANK ANTHONY, indsl. designer; b. Sicily, Jan. 5, 1903; came to U.S., 1917; s. Sebastiano and Carmela (Nicosia) G.; student Art Students League and Parsons Sch. Design, 1923-24; children—Patricia, Gordon, James, Art dir. BBD&O, N.Y.C., 1925-32; pres. Gianninoto Assos., N.Y.C., 1932—; lectr. design schs. and colls. Recipient numerous design awards Am. Inst. Graphic Arts, Packaging Inst., European Packaging Fedn. Founder, fellow Am. Soc. Indsl. Designers (design awards), Package Designers Council (design awards). Club: Redding (Conn.) Country. Contbr. articles to bus. and profl. periodicals. Home: 80 Lonetown Rd West Redding CT 06896 Office: 133 E 54th St New York NY 10022

GIANNINOTO, ROBERT, mgmt. cons. co. exec.; b. Bklyn., May 25, 1937; s. Joseph and Lola (Renzetti) G.; B.B.A., CCNY, 1962; M.B.A., Hofstra U., 1968; m. Elizabeth Alfano, May 2, 1959; children—Daria, Deanna, Dorene. Controller, Bogart Mfg. Corp., 1959-63, Amperex Electronics Corp., 1963-72; gen. mgr., corp. planner Electra/Midland Corp., Morristown, N.J., 1972-75; controller E. R. Squibb & Sons, Inc., Princeton, N.J., 1975-77; v.p. McCormick & Co., Scarsdale, N.Y., 1977—. Mem. Hauppauge (N.Y.) Bd. Edn., 1969-72. C.P.A., N.Y. State, N.J. Mem. Am. Inst. C.P.A.'s. Republican. Home: 15 Laurel Wood Dr Lawrenceville NJ 08648 Office: Two Overhill Rd Scarsdale NY 10583

GIANNONE, RAYMOND LOUIS, computer systems co. exec.; b. Auburn, N.Y., Nov. 19, 1952; s. Raymond Joseph and Lillian Giannone; B.S. in Bus. Adminstrn., Alfred U., 1975. Computer sales rep. NCR Corp., Syracuse, N.Y., 1977-79; computer sales rep. comml. systems Hewlett Packard Co., Pitts., 1979-80; computer sales rep. Pertec Computer Corp., Phila., 1980—. Mem. Am. Mgmt. Assn., Am. Prodn. and Inventory Control Soc. Home: 1416 Lincoln Dr W Ambler PA 19002 Office: 111 Presidential Blvd Suite 213 Bala Cynwyd PA 19004

GIANNUZZI, GREGORY ADRIANO, florist; b. Bari, Italy, Jan. 18, 1949; came to Can., 1965, naturalized, 1970; s. Giuseppe Domenico and Filomena Giovanna (Sportelli) G.; B.A. summa cum laude, Loyola U., Montreal, Que., Can., 1973; M.A., U. Wis., 1975, Ph.D., 1977; m. Naomi Lakritz, May 5, 1977. Tchr., U. Wis., 1973-77; owner, mgr. Giannuzzi Florist Co., Montreal, 1977—, Fleuriste St. Remi, Montreal, 1977—. Mem. Florist Transworld Delivery, Montreal Flower Market. Liberal. Contbr. articles to profl. jours. Home: 9002 Nobel St Saint Leonard PQ H1P 2Y5 Canada Office: 6249 Henri Bourassa E Montreal North PQ H1G 2V3 Canada

GIBBON, SAMUEL YOUNG, ret. mfg. exec.; b. Phila., Apr. 8. 1905; s. John Heysham and Marjorie Gwendolyn (Young) G.; B.A., Princeton U., 1924; m. Virginia Newbold, Apr. 29, 1930; children—Samuel Young, Virginia G. (Mrs. J. Daniel Nyhart). With Am. Tube & Stamping Co., Bridgeport, Conn., 1924-26, Battles & Co., investment bankers, Phila., 1926-32; with W.H. Newbold's Son & Co., mem. N.Y. Stock Exchange, Phila., 1933-42, partner in charge trading and investment counsel div., 1936-42, ltd. partner, 1967-74; founder, pres., chmn. Air-Shields, Inc., Hatboro, Pa., 1946-66. Mayor Town of Longboat Key (Fla.), 1969-74, mem. Longboat Key Town Commn., 1968-76; pres. Longboat Key Art Center, 1978—. Served to capt. USAAF, 1942-45. Clubs: Princeton (N.Y.C.); Philadelphia; Sarasota (Fla.) Yacht, University (Sarasota). Patentee in field infant incubators, other breathing equipment. Home: 641 Rountree Dr Longboat Key FL 33548 Office: 10 S Adams Dr PO Box 908 Sarasota FL 33578

GIBBONS, EDWARD F., retail co. exec.; b. Boston, 1919; grad. Bentley Coll., 1948; married. With McCord Corp., 1965-66; v.p. finance United Brands Co., 1966-73; v.p. fin. F. W. Woolworth Co., N.Y.C., 1973-74, exec. v.p., 1974-75, pres., 1975—, also dir., chief exec. officer, 1977—, chmn. bd., 1978—. Office: 233 Broadway New York NY 10279

GIBBONS, MRS. JOHN SHELDON (CELIA VICTORIA TOWNSEND), editor, publisher; b. Fargo, N.D.; d. Harry Alton and Helen (Haag) Townsend; student U. Minn., 1930-33; m. John Sheldon Gibbons, May 1, 1935; children—Mary Vee, John Townsend. Advt. mgr. Hotel Nicollet, Mpls., 1933-37; contbg. editor children's mags., 1935—; partner Youth Assos. Co., Mpls., 1942-65; pub., art dir. Mines and Escholier mags., 1954-65; founder Bull. Bd. Pictures, Inc., Mpls., 1954, pres., 1954—; founder Periodical Litho Art Co., Mpls., 1962, pres., 1962-65. Republican chairwoman Golden Valley, Minn., 1950; alt. del. Hennepin County Rep. Conv., 1962. Mem. Mpls. Inst. Arts, Ft. Lauderdale Mus. Arts, Art Guild Boca Raton, Delta Zeta. Clubs: Woman's, Minikahda. Home: 1416 Alpine Pass Tyrol Hills Minneapolis MN 55416 Office: 1057 AIA Hillsboro Beach FL 33062

GIBBONS, JOSEPH JOHN, former mill equipment co. exec.; b. Wheatland, Wyo., Mar. 18, 1906; s. Michael and Edith (D'Arcy) G.; student Crane Jr. Coll., 1925-26; Ph.B., U. Chgo., 1930; postgrad. Northwestern U., 1931-33, De Paul U., 1933-35; m. Hazel Bisson, Jan. 1, 1930; children—Betty Louise Gibbons Smith, Albert J., Robert J. Tax supr. U.S. Steel Corp., Duluth, Minn. and Pitts., 1941-50; mgr. tax and ins. dept. Mine Safety Appliances Co., 1950-52; with Blaw-Knox Co., Pitts., 1952-69, treas., 1967-68, v.p. finance, 1968-69; treas. Corde Co., Pitts., 1962-68, pres., 1968-69; controller Cleve. Builders Supply Co., 1969-71. Mem. Am. Inst. C.P.A.'s, Tau Kappa Epsilon, Alpha Kappa Psi. Presbyn. (elder). Home: Hillsboro Colonnade 1161 A1A Hillsboro Beach FL 33062

GIBBONS, PATRICK THOMAS, real estate investor; b. Louisville, Jan. 16, 1940; s. Harold J. and Ann M. (Culter) G.; A.B., U. Mo., 1962; M.B.A., Harvard U., 1969; m. Dorathy Dreeben; children—Merideth, Pamela, Sylvan Lang, Ellen Lang, Nathan Lang. Asst. to pres. ARA Services, Inc., Phila., 1971-72, 73-74; v.p. adminstrn. Carl A. Morse, Inc., N.Y.C., 1972-73; sr. v.p., dir. La Quinta Motor Inns, Inc., San Antonio, 1974-80, chief operating officer, 1976-80; real estate investor, 1980—. Chmn., Bonds for Israel campaign, San Antonio, 1975, 76; bd. dirs. Jewish Fedn. San Antonio, 1977—. Served to capt. USAF, 1964-71. Decorated Bronze Star. Clubs: Harvard (N.Y.); Argyle (San Antonio). Office: Texian Devel Co 1635 NE Loop 410 Suite 603 San Antonio TX 78209

GIBBS, FREDERICK WINFIELD, communications co. exec.; b. Buffalo, Mar. 22, 1932; s. Walter and Elizabeth (Georgi) G.; B.A. cum laude, Alfred U., 1954; m. Josephine Janice Jarvis, Dec. 20, 1954; children—Michael, Mathew, Robyn. With N.Y. Telephone Co., 1954-65; with ITT, 1965—, mng. dir. ITT Standard Electrica, S.A., Rio de Janeiro, Brazil, 1971-75, chief exec. officer ITT Brazil, Rio de Janeiro, 1975-77, exec. dir. ops. ITT COG, 1977, corp. exec. v.p., 1977—, also exec. dir. telecommunications and electronics, 1978—; pres. U.S. Tel. & Tel. Corp., N.Y.C., 1980—. dir. System 12. Served with USMC, 1954-56. Office: 320 Park Ave New York NY 10022

GIBERSON, HARRY FRANCIS, mfg. co. exec.; b. Medford, Mass., Feb. 13, 1938; s. Kenneth Brown and Ethel Marie (Glazer) G.; B.S. in Chem. Engring., Northeastern U., 1961, M.S. in Engring. Mgmt.,

1966; m. Doris Marie Mietzner, Oct. 14, 1961; children—Linda Lee, Kimberlee Ann, Amanda Marie. Design engr. Pratt & Whitney Co., West Palm Beach, Fla., 1961-62; design specialist Air Products & Chems. Co., Allentown, Pa., 1962-63; project engr., then sr. engr. Gen. Foods Corp., Woburn, Mass., 1963-68; from sr. engr. to mgr. maintenance constrn. and utilities Norton Co., Worcester, Mass., 1968-79, plant engr., dir. security constrn. products div., Gainesville, Ga., 1979—. Mem. West Boyeston (Mass.) Planning Bd., 1969-79, chmn., 1976-77; mem. Hall County (Ga.) Community Partnership Council, 1979—; mem. steering com. Hall County Jr. Achievement, 1980; v.p. bd. dirs. N.E. Ga. Jr. Achievement, 1980—. Registered profl. engr., Mass. Mem. Nat. Soc. Profl. Engrs. pres. Lanier chpt. 1980, pres. Central Mass. chpt. 1971), Am. Inst. Chem. Engrs., Am. Soc. Indsl. Security. Club: Masons. Home: 3461 Point View Circle Gainesville GA 30501 Office: PO Box 2898 Gainesville GA 30503

GIBLIN, EDWARD JOSEPH, mfg. co. exec.; b. N.Y.C., Oct. 7, 1917; s. Peter and (Logan) G.; B.S. in Accounting, Fordham U., 1941; M.B.A. in Fin., N.Y. U., 1950; m. Josephine Fischer, May 24, 1923; 1 son, Robert. With Peat, Marwick, Mitchell & Co., Chgo., prior to 1953; joined Ex-Cell-O Corp., Detroit, 1953, asst. sec., 1954-55, asst. treas., 1955-60, treas., 1960-65, dir. corp. devel., v.p., 1965-69, exec. v.p., 1969-70, pres., 1970-77, chmn., chief exec. officer, 1978—, also dir.; dir. Detroit Bank & Trust Co., Tecumseh Products Co., Detroit Edison Co. Served to capt. USAAF, 1942-46. Home: 1341 Indian Mound Rd W Birmingham MI 48010 Office: Ex-Cell-O Corp 2855 Coolidge Troy MI 48084

GIBSON, EMMETT WAYNE, investment co. exec.; b. Norfolk, Va., Nov. 16, 1952; s. Marion Haywood and Elizabeth Hobgood G.; B.A., U. N.C., Chapel Hill, 1974, M.B.A., 1976. Asst. to pres. Tarrytown Assos., Inc., Rocky Mount, N.C., 1976, asst. v.p., 1976-77, v.p. fin., 1977-79, exec. v.p., 1979-80, pres., 1980—, dir., 1976—; dir. Mr. Dunderbak, Inc., Tastee Donuts, Inc., M.D. Inc. Founding mem. planning bd. Marketplace Ministry. Cert. activity vector analysis analyst. Home and Office: PO Box 912 Rocky Mount NC 27801

GIBSON, GEORGE WARRINER, JR., automotive mfg. co. exec.; b. Detroit, Oct. 23, 1922; s. George Warriner and Vivian E. (Schulte) G.; B.S. in Elec. Engring., Washington U., St. Louis, 1947; M.Automotive Engring., Chrysler Inst. Engring., 1949; m. Betty Ann Doyle, June 14, 1947; children—Anne Marie, Michael Doyle, Celia Marie, Lisa Marie. Chief engr. Dodge div. Chrysler Corp., Highland Park, Mich., 1958-63, dir. corp. product planning, 1963-68; v.p., dir. product devel. and ops. staff Chrysler Internat., Eng. and Switzerland, 1968-73; v.p. engring. Monroe Auto Equipment div. Tenneco Inc., Monroe, Mich., 1973-80; v.p., dir. corp. devel. Newcor, Inc., Warren, Mich., 1980—; asst. dir. Grad. Sch., Chrysler Inst., 1951-53; asst. prof. elec. engring. Lawrence Inst. Tech., 1948-54. Bd. dirs. Monroe County (Mich.) Sr. Citizens. Served with U.S. Army, 1943-46. Recipient Disting. Service medal Xavier U., Cin., 1980; registered profl. engr., Mich. Mem. Soc. Automotive Engrs., Nat. Soc. Profl. Engrs., Mich. Assn. of Professions, Am. Soc. for Engring. Edn., Engring. Soc. Detroit. Club: Country of Detroit. Home: 41 Stonehurst Rd Grosse Pointe Shores MI 48236 Office: Newcor Corp Devel Office 12434 Twelve Mile Rd Warren MI 48093

GIBSON, MICHAEL HERRING, energy resource co. exec.; b. Derby, Eng., July 28, 1943; s. George Harrison and Queenie May (Herring) G.; came to U.S., 1969; B.Sc. with honors, U. London, 1966; Asso. Royal Sch. Mines, London, 1966; M.S. (Henry DeWitt Smith scholar), Stanford U., 1970, M.B.A., 1972. With New Market Zinc Corp. (Tenn.), 1964, Zinc Corp., Broken Hill, Australia, 1965; mineral processing engr. Sierra Leone Devel. Co. (West Africa), 1966-67, asst. mill supt., 1967-68, acting mill supt., 1969; research asst. Stanford, 1970-71; mgmt. intern Kerr-McGee Corp., Oklahoma City, 1972-74, supr. engring. Kerr-McGee Nuclear Corp., Oklahoma City, 1974, mgr. engring., 1974-79, asst. mgr. engring., planning and services, Church Rock, N.Mex., 1979—. Chmn. vocat. edn. adv. com. Gallup-McKinley County (N.Mex.) Schs.; trustee McKinley County Hosp., Gallup. Mem. Soc. Mining Engrs. of Am. Inst. Mining Engrs., Instn. Mining and Metallurgy (London). Unitarian. Club: Gallup Country. Home: 3702 Dulce Ct Gallup NM 87301 Office: Kerr-McGee Corp PO Box 28 Church Rock NM 87311

GIBSON, RALPH DODGE, plastics co. exec.; b. Melrose, Mass., Oct. 1, 1924; s. Robert and Jane Lydia (Bartlett) G.; A.B., Bowdoin Coll., 1950; m. Sarah Hollenbeck Mitchell, June 15, 1951; children—Marden, Christopher, Robert, Daniel, Ralph. Traveling internal auditor Gen. Motors Corp., Detroit, 195—55; sales mgr. Gen. Tire & Rubber Co., Lawrence, Mass., 1955-69; v.p., gen. mgr. Ind. Plastic Sheet div. Schott Industries, Elkhart, Ind., 1969-73; gen. mgr. Paragon Plastics, Mansfield, Tex., 1973—. Served with USAAF, 1943-47. Decorated Air medal. Mem. Soc. Plastics Engrs., Soc. Plastics Industry, Nat. Rifle Assn., Amateur Trapshooting Assn. Republican. Presbyterian. Club: Ft. Worth Gun. Address: 4201 Sparkford Ct Arlington TX 76013

GIBSON, WILLIAM EDWARD, publisher; b. Farragut, Idaho, Apr. 11, 1944; s. William E. and Lucille E. (Dickehut) G.; A.B., U. Chgo., 1964, M.A., 1965, Ph.D., 1967; m. Judith TenBrock. Economist, Fed. Res. Bank of Chgo., 1966-67, now cons. Fed. Res. System; asst. prof. econs. UCLA, 1967-71; sr. staff mem. Brookings Instn., Washington, 1973-75; sr. staff economist President's Council Econ. Advisers, 1971-73; v.p., dir. monetary affairs Chase Manhattan Bank, N.Y.C., 1975-76; 1st v.p., dir. fixed-income research Smith Barney, Harris Upham & Co., Inc., N.Y.C., 1976-80; sr. v.p. econs. and fin. policy McGraw-Hill, Inc., N.Y.C., 1980—; dir. V'Soske Rug Corp.; adj. prof. fin. Amos Tuck Sch., Dartmouth Coll. Chartered fin. analyst. Mem. Fin. Mgmt. Assn. (dir.), Am. Econ. Assn., Am. Fin. Assn., Bond Club N.Y.C., Fin. Analysts Fedn. Clubs: University (N.Y.C.); Cosmos (Washington); Woodstock (N.Y.) Country. Asso. editor: Jour. Money, Credit and Banking; author papers in field. Office: McGraw-Hill Inc 1221 Ave Americas New York NY 10020

GIDEON, RICHARD WALTER, broadcast mgmt. cons.; b. Phila., Nov. 23, 1928; s. Walter Richard and Amelia Molly (Ebinger) G.; B.S. in Econs., U. Pa., 1952; m. Yolanda Elena Josefe, Jan. 12, 1957; children—Richard E. and Michael J. (twins). Statis. clk. Triangle Pubs. Inc., Phila., 1952-55, research mgr., 1955-62; asst. dir. media research Young & Rubicam, N.Y.C., 1962-63; with John Blair & Co., N.Y.C., 1963-75, dir. research, 1967-75, v.p., 1969-73, v.p., dir. sales strategy div., 1973-75; pres., owner Dick Gideon Enterprises, Cherry Hill, N.J., 1975—. Dist. leader Westchester County (N.Y.) Republican Com., 1974-76; mem. adv. com. N.Y. State Assemblyman Gordon Burrows, 1974-76. Served with USMC, 1946-48. Mem. TV and Radio Club Phila., Broadcast Pioneers Assn., Sigma Phi Epsilon. Club: Wharton (Phila.). Editor: Statistical Trends in Broadcasting, 1970—. Home and Office: 113 Antietam Rd Cherry Hill NJ 08034

GIDNEY, JOHN ARCHIBALD, accountant; b. Buffalo, Apr. 19, 1920; s. Ray M. and Jean Ellison (Brock) G.; A.B., Dartmouth, 1941; B.B.A., Western Res. U., 1948; m. Margaret J. Dempster, Aug. 4, 1945 (div. Oct. 1962); 1 dau., Martha J.; m. 2d, Frances A. Merrell, Dec. 4, 1962. Partner firm Haskins & Sells, C.P.A.'s, Cleve., Pitts., Buffalo, 1945-62, Paulus & Gidney, C.P.A.'s, Reno, 1963-72; propr. John A. Gidney, C.P.A., Reno, 1972-73; pres. John A. Gidney, Ltd., C.P.A.'s, Reno, 1973-80, Gidney, Quinn & Summers, Ltd., Reno, 1980—; pres. Estate Planning Council, Reno, 1976-77. Pres., Fairway Villas Condominium Assn. Inc., 1972-73; treas. Nev. Opera Guild, 1974-78, Unitarian Fellowship No. Nev., 1976-77. Served with AUS, 1942-45. C.P.A., Ohio, Pa., N.Y., Calif., Nev., Utah, N.C. Mem. Am. Inst. C.P.A.'s (council 1976, 79—), Nev. Soc. C.P.A.'s (pres. 1976-77), Mountain States Conf. C.P.A.'s (chmn. 1978—), Beta Alpha Psi. Clubs: Rowfant (Cleve.); Hidden Valley Country (pres. 1979), Elks, Prospector's (Reno). Home: 2670 Tamarisk Dr Reno NV 89502 Office: 1 E 1st St Reno NV 89501

GIERING, RICHARD HERBERT, computerized information systems co. exec.; b. Emmaus, Pa., Nov. 27, 1929; s. Harold Augustus and Marguerite (Bruder) G.; B.S. in Engring. Math. U. Ariz. 1962; m. Carol Alice Scott, Aug. 16, 1959; children—Richard H. Jr. Scott K. Joined U.S. Army, 1947, commd. 2d lt., 1963, advanced through grades to capt., 1963, 1965, sect. chief data processing Def. Intelligence Agy., Washington, 1965-67; ret. 1967; with Data Corp. (name changed to Mead Tech. Labs. 1968), Dayton, Ohio, 1967—, v.p. tech. ops., 1970-71, dir. advanced programs, 1971-77; pres., chief exec. officer DG Assos., Inc., 1974—; sr. partner Infotex Assos., Dayton, 1977—; instr. data processing U. Ariz., Tucson, 1962-63. Mem. Assn. Computing Machinery, Am. Soc. Information Scis. Home: 5460 Royalwood St Dayton OH 45429 Office: 1476 Route 725 Dayton OH 45459

GIESE, ROBERT JOSEPH, corp. exec.; b. N.Y.C., June 16, 1934; s. Emil Joseph and Noreen (Black) G.; student Bklyn. coll., 1952-57, N.Y.U., 1968-69; m. Dolores J. Moran, Nov. 19, 1960; 1 dau., Lara. Archtl. draftsman Ebasco Services, Inc., N.Y.C., 1952-53, adminstrv. asst. to supt. design, 1953-56, engring. coordinator on pulp and paper projects, 1956-57, adminstrv. asst. to engring. mgr., 1957-60, mgr. advt. and publicity, 1960-73, mgr. corp. communications, 1973-78, dir. mktg. and corp. communications, 1978-80, dir. govtl. relations, 1980, exec. asst. to chmn. bd., 1980—; spl. investigator N.Y. Atty. Gen's office, N.Y.C., 1959-61. Served with USNR, 1951-59. Mem. Advt. Club, N.Y. Alumni Assn., N.Y. Chamber Commerce and Industry, U.S. C. of C. Clubs: World Trade Center, Kwan Yin, Forsgate. Roman Catholic. Home: 314 Pinebrook Rd Englishtown NJ 07726 Office: 2 World Trade Center New York NY 10048

GIESEN, HERMAN MILLS, indsl. mgmt./engring. co. exec.; b. San Antonio, Sept. 22, 1928; s. Herman Iglehart and Emeline Barbara (Frey) G.; student Tex. A. and M. U., 1946-47; B.S. in Engring., U.S. Naval Acad., 1951; M.S. in Elec. Engring., USAF Inst. Tech., 1960; M.S. in Ops. Mgmt., U. So. Calif., Los Angeles, 1966; m. Linda B. Williams, Aug. 9, 1979; 1 son, Jonathan Williams; children by previous marriage—John Herman, David Douglas, Amy Lynn. Commd. 2d lt. USAF, 1951, advanced through grades to maj., 1966; served as aircraft maintenance mgr., 1954-56, flight instr., 1957-59, research and devel. program officer, 1960-63, aircraft, flight commdr., 1963-64, elec. engr.-analyst, 1964-66, resigned, 1966, now col. Res.; exec. adviser in program control McDonnell-Douglas Corp., Huntington Beach, Calif., 1966-68; sr. bus. planner E-Systems, Inc., Greenville, Tex., 1968-71; pres. Giesen & Assos., Inc., indsl. mgmt. engring. cons., Dallas, 1971-72, 78—; plant engr. Dixie Metals of Tex., Dallas, 1972-73; plant engr. Murph Metals Div., R.S.R. Corp., Dallas, 1973-74, ops. maintenance/engring. mgr., 1974-76; mfg. mgr. Ferguson Industries, Dallas, 1976-78. Decorated Air medal, USAF Commendation medal. Registered profl. engr., Tex.; certified as flight instr., advanced instrument ground aircraft instr. FAA. Mem. Nat., Tex. socs. profl. engrs. Contbr. article to profl. jour. Home: 3636 Shenandoah Dallas TX 75205

GIESEN, RICHARD ALLYN, pub. co. exec.; b. Evanston, Ill., Oct. 7, 1929; s. Elmer J. and Ethyl (Lillig) G.; B.S., Northwestern U., 1951; m. Jeannine St. Bernard, Jan. 31, 1953; children—Richard Allyn, Laurie J., Mark S. Research analyst new bus. and research depts. Glore, Forgan & Co., Chgo., 1951-57; asst. to pres. Gen. Dynamics Corp., N.Y.C., 1957-60, asst. treas., 1960-61, asst. v.p. operations and contracts, 1961-63; fin. cons. IBM Corp., 1963, exec. asst. to sr. v.p., 1964-65; treas. subs. Sci. Research Assos., Inc., Chgo., 1965-66, v.p. fin. and adminstrn., 1966-67, exec. v.p., chief operating officer, 1967-68, pres., chief exec. officer, 1968—, also dir.; dir. Sci. Research Assos. (Can.), Ltd., Sci. Research Assos., Ltd. (U.K.), Sci. Research Assos. (Pty.) Ltd. (Australia), Société de Recherche Appliquée à l'Education (France), Stone Container Corp. Mem. bus. adv. council Chgo. Urban League. Trustee, Chgo. Ednl. TV Assn., Roosevelt U., Chgo.; mem. pres.'s council Nat. Coll. Edn. Mem. Young Pres.'s Orgn., Chief Execs. Forum, Alpha Tau Omega, Beta Gamma Sigma. Clubs: Chicago; Glen View (Golf, Ill.). Home: 301 N Sheridan Rd Lake Forest IL 60045 Office: 155 N Wacker Dr Chicago IL 60606

GIFFORD, CHARLES LEVI, mining and chem. co. exec.; b. Cissna Park, Ill., Dec. 26, 1920; s. Jesse Junior and Lora (Smith) G.; certificate Bryant and Stratton Coll., Chgo., 1941; m. Willie Claire Phillips, Mar. 8, 1947; children—Charles Robert, Pamela May, Margaret Elizabeth. Office mgr. Chgo. Switchboard Co., 1941-42; accounting mgr. Edgar Bros. Co., Metuchen, N.J., 1946-54; asst. controller Minerals & Chems. Corp. Am., Menlo Park, N.J., 1954-60; controller Minerals & Chems. Philipp Corp., Menlo Park, 1960-67; v.p., controller minerals and chems. div., asst. treas. Engelhard Minerals & Chems. Corp., Menlo Park, Edison, N.J., 1967-74, sr. v.p. and asst. to pres. minerals and chems. div., also asst. treas. corp., 1974—; dir. Commonwealth Bank, Metuchen, N.J., Res-Net Corp., Whippany, N.J. Trustee, v.p. John F. Kennedy Med. Center. Served with USAAF, 1942-46; PTO. Mem. Nat. Assn. Accountants. Presbyn. Clubs: Metuchen Country, River North Golf and Country. Home: 63 Beacon Hill Dr Metuchen NJ 08840 Office: Menlo Park Edison NJ 08817

GIFFORD, NELSON SAGE, mfg. co. exec.; b. Newton, Mass., May 3, 1930; s. Gordon Babcock and Hariette Rose (Dooley) G.; A.B., Tufts Coll., 1952; m. Elizabeth Barrett Brow, Nov. 12, 1955; children—Susan Helen, Ian Christopher, Diane Brow. With Dennison Mfg. Co., Framingham, Mass., 1954—, controller, 1964, gen. mgr., 1965-67, v.p., 1967-72, pres., 1972—; dir. John Hancock Mut. Life Ins. Co., First Nat. Boston Corp., M/A COM, Inc., NYPRO, Inc., Reed & Barton, Mass. Bus. Roundtable, A.I.M. Chmn. Wellesley Personnel Bd., 1971-73; dir. N.Eng. Colls. Fund; trustee Newton Wellesley Hosp. Served with USN, 1952-54. Clubs: Algonquin, Brae Burn Country, Commercial, Beverley Yacht, Kittansett. Office: 275 Wyman St Waltham MA 02254

GIGLIO, FRANK E., mortgage banker; b. Phila., Sept. 29, 1934; s. Francisco A. and Anna (D'Elia) G.; B.A., U. Pa., 1966; grad. diploma Northwestern U., 1968, U. Pa., 1970, Brown U., 1971, U. Mass., 1976; m. Theresa Grab, May 2, 1970. Supr., Western Savs. Bank, Phila., 1953-64, asst. mortgage officer, 1964-67, mortgage officer, 1967-71, sr. mortgage officer, 1971-73, asst. v.p., 1973-77, v.p., 1977-80; v.p. Kennedy Mortgage Co., Cherry Hill, N.J., 1979—, Lomas & Nettleton Co., Phila., 1980—; lectr. adult edn. Mem. Am. Mgmt. Assn., Nat., Phila. M.B.A. assns. Roman Catholic. Home: 116 Yorktown Dr Mount Laurel NJ 08054 Office: Lomas & Nettleton Co 121 N Broad St Philadelphia PA 19107

GILBANE, THOMAS FREEMAN, constrn. co. exec.; b. Providence, Nov. 4, 1911; s. William Henry and Frances Virginia (Freeman) G.; Ph.B., Brown U., 1933, A.M. (hon.), 1958; m. Jean A. Murphy, Sept. 12, 1946; children—Thomas Freeman, Robert V., Richard T., Jean Marie, John D., James M. Head varsity football coach Westminster Coll., New Wilmington, Pa., 1935; head freshman coach for football Brown U., Providence, 1936-40; sec. Gilbane Bldg. Co., Providence, 1933-50, supt., 1933-39, pres., treas., 1939-75, chief exec. officer, 1975—, chmn. bd., 1975—; exec. v.p., treas. B.T. Equipment Co., Providence, 1943-75, pres., treas., 1975—; pres. Gilbane Internat. Corp., Ltd., 1958—, Downtown Realty Corp., Providence, 1964—, Gilbane-McShain Hotel Corp., 1964—; trustee Indsl. Found. of R.I., 1959-75, HNC Mortgage and Realty Investors, 1971-77, Westport Co., 1977—. Chmn. parents com. Harvard U., 1972-73; mem. Harvard-Radcliffe Parents Com., 1978-79; chmn. friends com. Pine Manor Jr. Coll., 1972-73; mem. corp. Roger Williams Gen. Hosp., Emma Pendleton Bradley Hosp., Sophia Little Home, Women and Infants Hosp., South County Hosp.; mem. Narragansett council Boy Scouts Am., 1924—, past pres. N.E. region; bd. govs. R.I. Commodore Commn., 1968—; bd. dirs. Butler Hosp., 1955-56, R.I. chpt. Am. Heart Assn., 1974-80, R.I. Philharmonic Orch., 1980—; mem. R.I. Soc. Prevention of Blindness, 1972-73, 78-79, Coast Guard Acad. Found., 1976—; trustee Brown U., 1954-61, emeritus, 1961—. Nat. AAU shot-put champion, 1934; recipient award of Merit, Jewish War Vets. U.S.A., 1956; Silver Antelope award Boy Scouts Am., 1972, Disting. Eagle award, 1975, Silver Buffalo award, 1980; Honor award Nat. Jewish Hosp. and Research Center, 1975; inducted into Brown Hall of Fame, Brown U., 1971, R.I. Heritage Hall of Fame, 1977. Mem. Associated Gen. Contractors Am. (pres. R.I. chpt. 1947-48), Providence C. of C. (pres. 1954-56), Nat. Eagle Scout Assn. (chmn. nat. com. 1974-76), Brown Football Assn. (dir. 1973—), Am. Soc. of Concrete Constrn. (dir. 1974-75). Roman Catholic. Clubs: Univ., Turks Head, Point Judith Country, Providence Gridiron (pres. 1945-47, inducted Hall of Fame 1971), Saunderstown Yacht, Serra, Dunes, Brown (R.I. and Palm Beach), Beach (Palm Beach), Knights of Malta, Knights of Holy Sepulchre. Editorial bd. Bldg. Design and Constrn., 1974—. Home: 151 Grotto Ave Providence RI 02906 Office: 7 Jackson Walkway Providence RI 02940

GILBERT, HAROLD WENDELL, record co. exec.; b. Murray, Ky., Jan. 24, 1939; s. Vernon and Martha (Walls) G.; student Miss. Vocat. Coll., 1956-58, Wayne State U., George Peabody Coll., Austin Peay State U.; B.S., Tenn. A. and I. U., 1958-62; m. Jean Farley, Sept. 7, 1958; children—Kenneth, Keith, King, Kim, Kleetha. Tchr., Hampton High Sch., Dickson, Tenn., 1960-65; pres. Hitsburgh Music Co. & Rec. Co., Gallatin, 1964—; chmn. bd. Hal and Jean Enterprises, Inc.; pres. So. City Records; staff songwriter Cape Ann Music Co., 1971-72, Moss Ross Music Co., 1963, Tree Pub. Co., 1962-63; resource specialist Clarksville-Montgomery Sch. System, Clarksville, Tenn.; work adjustment coordinator Tenn. Div. Vocat. Rehab. Served with USAF, 1958-60. Named Mid-Tenn. High Sch. Band Dir. of Year, 1969. Mem. Nat., Tenn., Clarksville-Montgomery edn. assns., Council for Exceptional Children, U.S. Olympic Soc. Club: Mystery Men Soc. (treas.). Author: A History of Black American Music. Home: 157 Ford Ave Gallatin TN 37066 Office: Hitsburgh Music Bldg Ford Ave Gallatin TN 37066

GILBERT, JOAN STULMAN, petroleum co. exec.; b. N.Y.C., May 10, 1934; d. Julius and Paula Stulman; student Conn. Coll. for Women, 1951-53; m. Phil E. Gilbert, Jr., Oct. 6, 1968; children—Linda, Dana, Patricia. Br. coordinator Vol. Service Bur., Westchester, N.Y., 1970-72; pub. relations dir. Westchester Lighthouse, 1972-76; exec. dir. Westchester Heart Assn., 1976-77; community relations mgr. Texaco Inc., White Plains, N.Y., 1977—. Bd. dirs. Teatown Lake Reservation of Bklyn. Bot. Garden, 1975—, Coll. Careers, Lend-A-Hand, Corp. Community Jobs Project; mem. adv. council Econ. Understanding Found. Westchester. Mem. Women in Communications, Sales and Mktg. Execs., Pub. Relations Soc. Am. (chpt. pres. 1977), Advt. Club. Home: The Croft Spring Valley Rd Ossining NY 10562 Office: 2000 Westchester Ave White Plains NY 10650

GILBERT, RALPH EUGENE, lumber co. exec.; b. Shoals, Ind., Mar. 17, 1924; s. Homer Charles and Lydia Mae (Earl) G.; B.S., Ind. State U., 1950; m. Asta Pihlakas, Aug. 24, 1945; children—Linda Gilbert Wendt, Mary Ann Gilbert Keegan. With Quaker Maid Co., Terre Haute, Ind., 1950-58; asst. sec.-treas. Arketex Ceramic Corp., Brazil, Ind., 1958-65; sec.-treas. Miller Lumber Co., Miller Sash & Door Co., Kalamazoo, 1965-69, pres., 1969—. Bd. dirs. Kalamazoo County Jr. Achievement, 1977—. Served in U.S. Army, 1943-46; ETO. Decorated Bronze Star. Mem. Kalamazoo County C. of C. (dir. 1978—), Nat. Sash and Door Jobbers Assn. (dir. 1972-74), Nat. Assn. Accts., U.S. C. of C., Mich. C. of C., Am. Nat. Metric Council. Republican. Lutheran. Club: Rotary. Home: 1119 Romence Rd Kalamazoo MI 49002 Office: 1919 Factory St Kalamazoo MI 49001

GILBERT, ROBERT, mfg. co. exec.; b. Newark, Aug. 19, 1944; s. Nathan and Annie (Horne) G.; A.S. in Bus. Mgmt., Essex County Coll., Newark, 1972; B.S. in Bus. Adminstrn., Seton Hall U., 1977; m. Constance A. Harrell, Nov. 9, 1968; children—Adonna, Raqui Gilbert and Rashaan (twins). Operator Taxi Service Co., 1968-72; ednl. sales rep. Lafayette Acad., Queens, N.Y., 1972-74; chem. ops. BASF Wyandotte Co., South Kearny, N.J., 1974-78; union steward, safety coordinator United Rubber Workers Local 234, South Kearny, N.J., 1974-78; plant personnel mgr. Walter Kidde & Co., Inc., Belleville, N.J., 1978—. Served with U.S. Army, 1965-67. Mem. Am. Soc. Safety Engrs., Am. Soc. Personnel Adminstrn., N.J. Personnel Group, Am. Soc. Indsl. Security, N.J. Tool, Die and Precision Machining Assn. Baptist. Office: 675 Main St Belleville NJ 07109

GILBERTSON, ERIC E., tire mfg. co. ofcl.; b. Menomonie, Wis., Mar. 31, 1931; s. Elmer G. and Margaret (Burkart) G.; B.S., Beloit Coll., 1953; m. Donna H. Hoffe, Aug. 22, 1954; children—Amy, Jay, Kurt. Indsl. engr. Uniroyal Inc., Eau Claire, Wis., 1957-60, labor relations mgr., 1960-64, mgmt. systems mgr., 1964-70, prodn. foreman, 1971-73, factory acct., 1973-74, mgr. mfg. fin., 1974—; dir. Blue Cross-Blue Shield Wis. Bd. dirs. Public Expenditure Survey Wis., 1979—; vice-chmn. Wis. Council Safety, 1978—. Served with CIC, U.S. Army, 1953-55. Mem. Wis. Mfrs. and Commerce Assn. (dir.). Home: 308 Heather Rd Eau Claire WI 54701 Office: 799 Wisconsin St Eau Claire WI 54701

GILDEN, MORTON CHARLES, mfg. co. exec.; b. Balt., Nov. 17, 1924; s. Herman Louis and Rose (Bank) G.; B.S., Loyola Coll., 1949; m. Ann Hanover, Aug. 17, 1952; children—Marc, Karen. Sales mgr. Md. Match Co., Balt., 1949-53; plant mgr. Md. Paper Products Co., Balt., 1953-59; gen. mgr. Md. Cup Corp., Owings Mills, 1959—, v.p. ops., 1976—; exec. v.p. Sweetheart Cup, Owings Mills, 1972—; dir. Sweetheart Monocn, N.V., Holland, Sweetheart Internat., U.K., Strike Rite Matches, Ltd., Can. Active Jr. Achievement, 1975-78. Served with USAAF, 1943-46. Recipient cert. of honor European Single Service, 1977. Mem. European Single Service Assn. (pres. 1974-77), Single Service Inst. U.S.A. (pres. 1979, cert. of honor 1979). Home: 3 Swanhill Dr Pikesville MD 21208 Office: 10100 Reisterstown Rd Owings Mills MD 21117

GILES, ALEXANDER WETHERAL, JR., electronics co. exec.; b. Hackensack, N.J., Jan. 26, 1935; s. Alexander Wetheral and Mildred Giles; B.S., U.S. Merchant Marine Acad., 1956; M.B.A., N.Y. U., 1963; m. Evelyn M. Exley, Dec. 12, 1959; children—Alexander Wetheral III, Jennifer Garret. Adminstrv. asst. Chubb Corp., N.Y.C., 1959-61, budget dir., 1966-68; asst. to zone controller Allstate Ins. Cos., White Plains, N.Y., 1961-63, regional controller, Hartford, Conn., 1963-66; with Gen. Host Corp., N.Y.C., 1968-74, controller, 1973-74, v.p. adminstrn., 1974; v.p. fin. Caron Internat., Inc., N.Y.C., 1974-76; sr. v.p. fin. Modular Computer Systems, Inc., Ft. Lauderdale, Fla., 1976-79, pres., chief exec. officer, 1979-80, chmn. bd., chief exec. officer, 1980—, also dir.; dir. Modular Computer Services, Inc., Modcomp Internat., Inc., Modcomp Bus. Systems, Inc., Modular Computer Systems GmbH, Modcomp France Sarl, Infomark, Inc., La Coquille Villas, Inc. Served to lt. USN, 1957-59. Mem. Fin. Execs. Inst. Republican. Episcopalian. Clubs: La Coquille (Palm Beach, Fla.); Met. (N.Y.C.). Office: 1650 W McNab Rd Fort Lauderdale FL 33309

GILES, BENJAMIN FRANKLIN, hosp. adminstr.; b. Moultrie, Ga., Oct. 17, 1937; s. B. Frank and Mamie G.; B.S.I.M., Ga. Inst. Tech., 1959, M.S.I.M., 1964; m. Beverley Hall, 1960; children—David, Michael. Systems analyst U.S. Dept. Navy, Charleston, S.C., 1964-67; dir. data processing Med. Coll. S.C., Charleston, 1967-70; controller Clayton Gen. Hosp., Riverdale, Ga., 1970-73, Peak Textiles, Inc., Americus, Ga., 1973-74, L. W. Blake Meml. Hosp., Bradenton, Fla., 1974—; cons. U. S.C., 1971. Served with USAF, 1964. Fellow Hosp. Fin. Mgmt. Assn. Republican. Baptist. Club: W. Bradenton Kiwanis (sec.). Home: 4114 19th Ave W Bradenton FL 33505 Office: L W Blake Meml Hosp 2020 59th St W Bradenton FL 33505

GILES, EDWARD MORGAN, security analyst; b. Buffalo, Sept. 8, 1935; s. Walter Arthur and Alice Elaine (Depew) G.; B.S.E.E. in Chem. Engring., Princeton U., 1957; S.M. in Indsl. Mgmt., M.I.T., 1959; m. Patricia Venable, Dec. 5, 1959; children—Walter, Carolyn, Stephen, Jeanne. With F. Eberstadt & Co., N.Y.C., 1959—, partner, 1966—, dir. research, 1969-77, exec. v.p., 1977-79, pres., 1979—, security analyst chem. industry, 1959—; trustee Williamsburgh Savs. Bank, Bklyn. Mem. Soc. Chem. Industry. Club: Manhasset Bay Yacht.

GILES, JEAN HALL, former bus. exec.; b. Dallas, Mar. 30, 1908; d. C. D. and Ida (McIntyre) Overton; m. Alonzo Russell Hall, II, Jan. 23, 1923 (dec.); children—Marjorie (Mrs. Kenneth C. Hodges, Jr.), Alonzo Russell III; m. 2d, Harry E. Giles, Apr. 24, 1928 (div. 1937); 1 dau., Janice, Ruth; adopted dau., Marjean. Owner Los Angeles Real Estate Exchange, ret.; partner Tech. Contractors, Los Angeles. Ret. Capt., comdg. officer S.W. Los Angeles Women's Ambulance and Def. Corps, 1942-43, maj., nat. exec. officer, 1944-45; coordinator War Chest Motor Corps, 1943-44; dir. Los Angeles Area War Chest Vol. Corps and Motor Corps, 1945-46; capt.-dir. unit orgn., nat. staff Communications Corps U.S., 1951, dir. field ops. and unit orgn., 1952. First v.p., program chmn. Mothers Club Pepperdine Coll. Mem. AIM, Hist. Soc. So. Calif., Opera Guild So. Calif., Assistance League So. Calif., Town Hall, Los Angeles Art Assn., Los Angeles World Affairs Council. Clubs: Los Angeles Garden, Los Fiesteros De Los Angelos, Los Angeles Athletic; Pacific Coast (Long Beach, Calif.), Riviera Country. Office: Box 36474 Wilshire-La Brea Sta Los Angeles CA 90036

GILES, TERRY D., banker; b. Rochester, N.Y., Nov. 22, 1942; s. Harold J. and Eleanor L. (Duncan) Giles; B.S., U. Rochester, M.B.A., 1966; m. Marilyn Walker, Aug. 5, 1967; children—Todd, Erin. Fin. analyst Lincoln First Banks Inc., Rochester, N.Y., 1969-71, asst. v.p., 1971-73, v.p., asst. treas., 1973-74, treas., 1974-79, sr. v.p. fin., 1980—. Bd. dirs. YMCA, U. Rochester River Campus. Served with USN, 1966-69. Mem. U. Rochester Monroe County Alumni. Home: 9 Tall Tree Ln Rochester NY 14450 Office: Lincoln First Banks Inc One Lincoln First Sq Rochester NY 14643*

GILKESON, JAMES WILLIAM, JR., constrn. co. exec.; b. Fisherville, Va., Oct. 9, 1925; s. James William and Zanie Julia (Winchester) G.; B.S. in Civil Engring., Va. Poly. Inst., 1950; m. Emily Thomas Scott, June 27, 1953; children—J. Scott, Julia R., David T., Emily Page. Foreman, Va. Asphalt Paving Co., Inc., 1950-55, mgr. no. dist., 1955-56; v.p. engring., safety dir. Nielsen Constrn. Co., Inc., Harrisonburg, Va.; also dir.; Shen Valley Corp., 1968-71. Mem. gen. adv. com. Massenutten Vocation Tech. Center, 1970—; mem. exec. com. bldg. div., constrn. sect. Indsl. Dept., Nat. Safety Council, 1970—; chmn. activities com., dir. Stonewall Jackson Area council Boy Scouts Am., 1970-74, v.p., 1974—; mem. local Price Stblzn. Bd., 1970—; mem. Christian edn. com. Lexington Presbytery, Va., 1959-67, pres. ch. Sch. Supts., 1961-62, with Christian edn. com. Synod. of Va. Presbyn. Ch., 1961-63; commr. Gen. Assembly Presbyn. Ch. U.S., 1965, mem. mission to society ministry group Synod of Vas., 1977; missions leader Desmios Community House Ch., 1972-73, pastoral leader, 1973-76; mem. corrections adv. com. Va. State Crime Commn., 1973—; mem. Va. Task Force Criminal Justice Goals and Objectives, 1975—. Mem. Planning Commn., City of Harrisonburg, Va., 1969—, vice-chmn., 1971-72, chmn., 1973-77; bd. dirs. Va. Safety Assn., Inc., 1970—. Bd. dirs. Homes Found. Served with USNR, 1943-46. Recipient dist. award merit Stonwall Jackson area council Boy Scouts Am., 1971, Silver Beaver award, 1973. Mem. Am. Soc. C.E. (asso. mem.; mem. exec. council, program chmn. Blue Ridge chpt. Va. sect. 1971), Asso. Gen. Contractors Am. (co-chmn. safety com. Va. br. 1967), Harrisonburg Rockingham C. of C. (chmn. safety com. 1968-73), Va. Poly. Inst. Alumni Assn. (v.p. Massanutten chpt. 1967-68), Order Arrow Boy Scouts Am. (Vigil honor 1972). Presbyn. (elder 1961—). Home: 1048 S Dogwood Dr Harrisonburg VA 22801 Office: PO Box 591 State Route 988 Harrisonburg VA 22801

GILKESON, ROBERT FAIRBAIRN, utility co. exec.; b. Phila., June 26, 1917; s. Fairbairn and Helen L. (Geiger) G.; E.E., Cornell U.,1939; m. Marie L. Whitwell, Apr. 26, 1941; children—Katharine, Richard, Thomas, David, Elizabeth. Jr. engr. Phila. Electric Co., 1939-40, engr., 1946-51, operating dept., 1953-60, mgr. engring. and research, 1960, v.p. engring. and research, 1961-62, exec. v.p., 1962-65, pres., 1965-71, chmn. bd., 1971—; engr. Westinghouse Electric Corp., Idaho Falls, Idaho, 1951-53; pres., dir. Susquehanna Power Co., Phila. Electric Power Co., Susquehanna Electric Co.; dir. First Pa. Bank N.A., Penn Mut. Life Ins. Co.; bd. mgrs. Germantown Savs. Bank. Served from 2d lt. to capt. AUS, 1940-45. Registered profl. engr., Pa. Mem. IEEE, Engrs. Club Phila., Sigma Alpha Epsilon. Republican. Episcopalian. Clubs: Philadelphia Country, Union League (Phila.), Masons. Home: 1084 Broadview Rd Wayne PA 19087 Office: 2301 Market St Philadelphia PA 19101

GILL, CYNTHIA-ANN CARNEVALE, credit union exec.; b. Providence, June 26, 1947; d. Thomas Salvatore and Frances (LaVigne) Carnevale; student U. North Fla., 1978—; m. Terry Daniel Gill, June 4, 1977; 1 son, Jason Thomas. From clk. to supr. market research Speidel Inc. div. Textron, Providence, 1971-73; acct. Longlife Dairy Products div. Beatrice Foods Inc., Jacksonville, Fla., 1973-76; asst. controller wholesale office supply div. Lewis Bus. Products Inc., Jacksonville, 1976-78; acctg. supr. Jax Navy Fed. Credit Union, 1978-80; asst. gen. mgr. Fla. USDA Fed. Credit Union, Gainesville, 1980—; tax and fin. cons. Republican. Episcopalian. Home: 618 SW 69th St Gainesville FL 32601 Office: PO Box 1162 Gainesville FL 32602

GILL, DAVID LEE, ins. co. exec.; b. Peoria, Ill., June 27, 1943; s. William Clement and Dorothy Marie (Turner) G.; B.S., Purdue U., 1965; postgrad. Blackhawk Jr. Coll., 1978; m. Virginia Sendelbach, July 8, 1967; 1 dau., Andera Marie. Owner, mgr. Wyoming Ins. Agy., Wyoming, Ill., 1976—; farmer, Speer, Ill.; advisory bd. Central Ill. Light Co., 1976. Ill. rural chmn. McGovern for Pres., 1972. Served with USAF, 1966-71. Lic. real estate asso., Ill. Mem. Ill. Independent Ins. Agts. Assn., Ill. Mutual Ins. Agts., Wyo. C. of C. (pres. 1978-79), Ill. Agr. Assn., M-P Farm Bur. (dir. 1975-78), Am. Legion. Democrat. Roman Catholic. Clubs: Lions, 4-H (council pres. 1976-77, advisor 1974). Home: Rural Route 1 Speer IL 61479 Office: 122 E Williams St Wyoming IL 61491

GILL, EARL GROVER, JR., elec. constrn. co. exec.; b. Balt., Aug. 2, 1919; s. Earl Grover and Margaret (Karfgin) G.; grad. Balt. Poly. Inst., 1937; B.E. in Elec. Engring., Johns Hopkins U., 1940; m. Katherine Corban Bauer, Apr. 25, 1942; 1 dau., Barbara Gill Odell. Test engr. Gen. Electric Co., Lynn, Mass., 1940-41; elec. engr. Gill-Simpson, Inc., Balt., 1946-55, pres., 1956—. Served from 2d lt. to maj. Signal Corps, U.S. Army, 1942-46. Mem. IEEE, Nat. Elec. Contractors Assn. (pres. Md. chpt. 1962-64), Bldg. Congress and Exchange of Balt., Balt. C. of C., Engring. Soc. Balt., Alumni Assn. Johns Hopkins U., Sigma Phi Epsilon Alumni, Tau Beta Pi (treas. Md. Alpha 1939-40). Republican. Lutheran. Club: Johns Hopkins. Office: Gill-Simpson Inc 1119 E 30th St Baltimore MD 21218

GILL, ELMORE AUGUSTUS, mortgage banking co. exec.; b. Oklahoma City, Feb. 1, 1912; s. Elmore Augustus and Minnie Terrisa (Finerty) G.; student U. Okla., 1929-31, U. Tex. Sch. Law, 1938, U. Miami, 1965, Mich. State U., 1966, Fla. Internat. U., 1976; m. Rosarii Marie Sammon, May 26, 1961. With Gill Cos., San Antonio, 1932—, v.p., 1942—; pres. Elmore A. Gill Co., Miami, Fla., 1974—; exec. v.p. Nat. Title Ins. Co., Miami, 1968-74; v.p. Lon Worth Crow Mortgage Co. (name changed to SE Mortgage Co.), Miami, 1966-68, J.I. Kislak Mortgage Corp., Miami, 1960-66; vis. lectr. comml. loans U. Miami, 1969, 70, 71. Mem. Mortgage Bankers Assn. Greater Miami, Miami Builders Exchange, S.Fla. Builders Assn. Democrat. Roman Catholic. Author articles on comml. loans. Home: 7934 SW 146th Ct Miami FL 33143 Office: Suite 3 Gill 9703 S Dixie Hwy Miami FL 33156

GILL, GEOFFREY YOUNG, tool mfg. co. exec.; b. Salem, Mass., May 10, 1943; s. Warren Everist and Betty Ada (Young) G.; B.S.E.E. (Gen. Motors scholar), M.I.T., 1965; M.S. in Indsl. Adminstrn. (Ford fellow), Carnegie Inst. Tech., 1967; m. Linda Wilson, July 8, 1978; 1 stepdau., Laura L. Wilson; children—Laura M., Sarah D. Material control analyst Foxboro Co., 1967-69; mgr. advanced materials, aerospace instrument bus. sect., Gen. Elec. Co., 1969-70; data processing mgr. Vt. Research Corp., 1970-72; sales engr., sales mgr. Muskegon Tool Industries (Mich.), 1972-75, v.p., 1976—. Budget com. Muskegon County United Way, 1973-79, bd. dirs., 1979—; pres. Webster House for Runaways, 1977-79, mgmt. bd., 1977—. Mem. Soc. Mfg. Engrs., Cutting Tool Mfg. Assn. Republican. Club: Masons. Patentee spl. trepan-boring tool; developer high speed tape Brailler. Home: Rt 3 Hart MI 49420 Office: 1000 E Barney St Muskegon MI 49443

GILL, JAMES JOSEPH, mfg. co. exec.; b. Platteville, Wis., Aug. 18, 1931; s. Percy Edward and Esther LaSetta (Weist) G.; B.S.C.E., U. Wis., 1957; M.B.A., U. Toronto, 1971; m. Virginia Karen Gotsche, Aug. 11, 1956; children—Susan, Grant, Gretchen. Gen. mgr. mktg., constrn. equipment div. J. I. Case Co., Racine, Wis., 1972-75, v.p. agrl. equipment div., 1975-77, v.p. constrn. equipment div., 1977-79, corp. exec. v.p., 1979—. Mem. adv. council Boy Scouts Am., 1977—. Served to 2d lt. USAF, 1951. Mem. Farm and Indsl. Equipment Inst. (dir.). Republican. Clubs: Masons, Kiwanis (membership chmn. 1978-79). Office: 700 State St Racine WI 53404

GILL, JEANETTE THERESA HARPENAU, bus. equipment co. exec.; b. Tell City, Ind., Mar. 24, 1937; d. Francis L. and Frances Harpenau; B.S., Ind. State U., 1959; Am. Mgmt. Assn. cert. in bus. mgmt. Calif. State U. Consortium, 1980; m. John Thomas Gill, Dec. 30, 1961. Tchr. math. Cin. Pub. Schs., 1959-60; engring. technician Gen. Electric Co., Cin., 1960-61; engr. Space div. N.Am. Aviation, Downey, Calif., 1962-66, Nortronics div. Northrop Corp., Anaheim, Calif., 1966-68; sr. applications programmer Collins Radio, Newport Beach, Calif., 1968-69; sr. programmer analyst MDM div. Control Data Corp., Santa Ana, Calif., 1969-71; lead programmer, applications programming mgr., standard systems programming mgr., mgr. customer programming AM Documentor div. AM Internat., Inc., Santa Ana, 1971—. Office: 2921 S Daimler St Santa Ana CA 92711

GILL, JOHN BERNARD, transp. exec.; b. Barnes, Eng., July 25, 1946; immigrated to Can., 1968, naturalized, 1979; m. Victoria Heise, June 16, 1972; children—Zoe Victoria, Randy Jonathan. Pres., Concord Freight System Ltd., Vancouver, B.C., Can., 1969-80; chmn. Concord Group of Cos., Vancouver, 1980—; dir. various cos. Mem. Canadian Internat. Freight Forwarders Assn. (past dir. and pres.). Contbr. articles to trade publs., U.S., U.K., Japan, China. Office: PO Box 23456 Vancouver AMF BC U7B 1W1 Canada

GILL, MERWYN CARLYLE, plastics co. exec.; b. Terril, Iowa, July 30, 1910; s. Carl Eugene and Maude Zella (Smith) G.; A.A., Estherville Jr. Coll., 1929; student U. Minn., 1930-33; A.B. in Chemistry, U. So. Calif., 1936, B.S. in Chem. Engring., 1937; m. Ellen Vonice Wildy, May 21, 1939; children—Stephen Edward, Phillip Carl, Debaney Dianne. Asst. quality control foreman U.S. Rubber Co., Los Angeles, 1937-42; research and devel. chem. engr. A.O. Smith Corp., Los Angeles, 1942-45, Swedlow Aeroplastics Corp., Glendale, Calif., 1945; pres., chmn. bd. M.C. Gill Corp., El Monte, Calif., 1946-47, 51—; head corrosion lab. Aerojet Engring. Corp., Azusa, Calif., 1947-51. Home: 1385 El Mirador St Pasadena CA 92103 Office: M C Gill Corp 4056 Easy St El Monte CA 91731

GILL, MICHAEL DOUD, corp. exec.; b. San Antonio, Dec. 14, 1935; s. Richard and Frances (Doud) G.; ed. U. Va.; m. Elizabeth Gay Fletcher, Aug. 23, 1975; 1 son, Fletcher Doud: children by previous marriage—Julia, Gordon, Michael Doud. Asst. to pres. Air Transit Services, Inc., 1954-58; dir. Wells Industries Corp., North Hollywood, Calif., 1956-58; asst. to bd. chmn. Decker Corp., Oxy-Catalyst Co. and Nat. Aero. Assn., 1962-65; gen. agt. Am. Heritage Life Ins. Co., 1963-65; v.p. Internat. Expns. Corp., N.Y. World's Fair, 1961-63; adminstr. asst. chmn. Republican Nat. Com., 1958-60; gen. mgr. Bahamas Oceanographic Soc., 1964-68; chmn. bd., v.p., exec. dir. Film Am. Found., 1965; pres. Michael Doud Gill Africa, Ltd., Zambia, 1969, Michael Doud Gill & Assos., Inc., Washington, 1969, Mgmt. Systems & Sales, Inc., Washington, 1971; exec. v.p. United Continental Corp., 1976; pres. G.M. Homes, Inc., 1977. Del. 2d Atlantic Conf. NATO, 1960, Eric Johnston Conf. Mut. Security, 1959, Pres.'s Conf. Reciprocal Trade, 1959; nat. vice chmn. Friends of Korea Com., Nat. Citizens for Columbus Day; exec. staff Inaugural Com., 1975; active Nat. Found., Heart Found.; steering com. D.C. Com. of Eisenhower Presdl. Library; nat. com. Boy Scouts Am., 1964—; bd. dirs. Project HEALTH, 1974—; mem. D.C. platform com. Rep. Nat. Conv., 1964; mem. nat. exec. com. Young Rep. Nat. Fedn., 1956-64; asst. nat. chmn. United Citizens for Nixon/Agnew, 1968; mem. D.C. Rep. Com., 1972—, vice-chmn. fin. com., 1976, chmn. fin. com., 1977-80, mem. exec. com., 1976—; del. Rep. Nat. Conv., 1976,cons. subcom. on program, 1980; vice chmn. D.C. Pres. Ford Com., 1976; asst. to chmn. Rep. Nat. Com., 1959-60, mem. fin. com., 1977—, mem. Nat. Com., 1980—, mem. exec. com., 1981. Served with USMCR, 1954-62. Named 1 of 10 outstanding young men in politics Nat. Rep. Women's Club of N.Y., 1957; recipient citation for outstanding achievement and contbn. 2d Atlantic Conf. of NATO, 1960. Mem. Washington Bd. Trade, Jaycees, Internat. Platform Assn., Am. Acad. Polit. and Social Sci., Am. Legion, Sigma Alpha Epsilon. Clubs: Toastmasters, Pisces, Capitol Hill (Washington); Jockey (Miami, Fla.); St. Hubert Soc. Am. (N.Y.C.); Bethesda (Md.) Country; Country of Guadalajara (Mex.); St. Anthony (San Antonio); Club of Ocean Pines (Md.). Home: 4201 Cathedral Ave NW Washington DC 20016

GILL, STANLEY C., mfg. co. exec.; b. Phila., May 21, 1942; s. Robert Lee and Dorothy (Irvella) G.; B.B.A. (State of N.J. grantee), George Washington U., 1972; m. Judith Ann Specker, July 12, 1969; children—Denise Joy, Francine Leigh. Sales mgr. Marchant Calculator div. SCM Corp., Trenton, N.J., 1960-62; regional salesman Cottrell div. Harris Intertype, Phila., 1972-73; sales and mktg. mgr. HED Industries div. Am. Gen. Energy, Ringoes, N.J., 1973—; cons. in field. Served with U.S. Army, 1966-68. Mem. Am. Mgmt. Assn., Am. Legion, VFW, Am. Newspaper Assn. Roman Catholic. Club: Elks. Home: Skyview Dr Hopewell NJ 08525 Office: Route 31 PO Box 246 Ringoes NJ 08551

GILLAM, JAMES KENNEDY, pub. exec.; b. Cleve., Apr. 30, 1922; s. Frank Benson and Clara Louise (Koenig) G.; student DePauw U., 1940-42, Western Res. U., 1946-48; m. Ruth A. Geddes, Nov. 7, 1974; children from previous marriage—Richard B., Diane L., David W., James Kennedy. Asst. pub. Tooling and Prodn. mag., 1946-49; Eastern sales mgr. Jenkins Publs., 1949-52; dist. mgr. Steel mag., 1952-55, regional mgr., 1955-64, sales mgr., 1964-67, bus. mgr., 1967-68, pub. Industry Week mag., 1968-75; group v.p. Penton Pub. Co., Cleve., 1972-75, v.p. pub. Penton/IPC, Inc., 1975-78, sr. v.p., 1978—. Div. chmn. Cleve. United Torch Drive, 1972-73. Served with USNR, 1942-46. Mem. Bus./Profl. Advertisers Assn. (v.p. Cleve. chpt. 1961-62, internat. v.p. 1973-74), Delta Chi, Alpha Phi Omega. Presbyn. (deacon). Clubs: Hermit, Mayfield Country (Cleve.). Home: 29600 Edgedale Rd Pepper Pike OH 44124 Office: 1111 Chester Ave Cleveland OH 44114

GILLAN, JOHN TERRY, pub. relations exec.; b. Peoria, Ill., Oct. 20, 1937; s. Floyd George and Blanche (Kincaid) G.; student U. Md., 1955-56; B.S. in Journalism, Bradley U., 1963; m. Judith Alane Wright, Jan. 14, 1961; children—Julia Maureen, David Brian. Reporter, NBC-TV, WEEK, Peoria, 1962-63; pub. relations writer Continental Casualty Co., Chgo., 1964-65; mng. editor Bowling Proprs. Assn. Am., Park Ridge, Ill., 1964-66; pub. relations exec. Gen. Electric Co., Chgo., 1966-67, Peitscher, Janda/Assos., Chgo., 1967-69, Robertson Advt., Chgo., 1969; product news mgr. Ampex Corp., 1970-71; asst. dir. pub. relations Zenith Radio Corp., 1971-72; asst. dir. consumer products pub. relations Motorola Inc., Franklin Park, Ill., 1972-74; dir. communication programs Am. Soc. Safety Engrs., Park Ridge, 1974-77; pub. relations dir. Bunker-Ramo Corp., Oak Brook, Ill., 1977—. Served with USAF, 1954-58. Recipent Presdl. All-Sch. Extra Curricular award Bradley U., 1963. Mem. Chgo. Headline Club, Imperial Drum and Bugle Corps (dir.), Sigma Delta Chi, Kappa Alpha Mu. Unitarian. Author: Changes in Types of City Governments, 1963; also numerous articles. Home: 8030 N Lockwood Skokie IL 60077 Office: 900 Commerce Dr Oak Brook IL 60521

GILLENWATER, DONALD LEE, chem. engr.; b. Ft. Madison, Iowa, Mar. 24, 1929; s. Chauncie James and Hazel Ada (Farr) G.; B.S. in Chem. Engring., U. Mo., Rolla, 1958; m. Patricia Louise Riley, June 18, 1950; children—Russell Lee, Richard Louis. Standards mgr. duPont Co., Ft. Madison, 1947-51; chem. engr. A.E. Staley Mfg. Co., Decatur, Ill., 1958-62; chem. engr. Grain Processing Corp., Muscatine, Iowa, 1962—, project mgr. new product devel., 1970-78, product engr. plant engring., 1978—; cons. spray drying. Active local Boy Scouts Am. Served with AUS, 1951-54. Archer Daniels Midland Co. grantee, 1957. Mem. Am. Assn. Cereal Chemists, Am. Inst. Chem. Engrs. Republican. Club: Wilton Rifle. Author articles in field. Home: 1800 Hammann Ave Muscatine IA 52761 Office: 1600 Oregon St Muscatine IA 52761

GILLESPIE, DAVID ELLIS, mfg. co. exec.; b. Chgo., Dec. 18, 1933; s. Davis Ellis and Helen Leota (Andrews) G.; B.A., Wayne State U., 1955; postgrad. U. Tex. Market research mgr. Gen. Steel Wares, London, Ont., Can., 1955-58; market research mgr. KLM Royal Dutch Airlines, Montreal, Que., Can., 1958-60; media dir. Comcore Communications Ltd., Toronto, Ont., 1960-61, v.p., 1961-62, exec. v.p., 1963-65, pres., chief exec. officer, 1965-73; chmn. bd., chief exec. officer Glaser Bros., Los Angeles, 1974—; chmn. bd., pres. Glaser Brothers Holding Corp., Los Angeles; dir. Miss Saylors Candy Co., Long Beach, Calif., Seeeman Co., San Francisco, Gardena Seed & Feeding Co., Los Angeles. Mem. Nat. Assn. Tobacco Distbrs. (dir.), Calif. Assn. Tobacco and Candy Distbrs. (dir., treas.). Republican. Episcopalian. Club: Ontario (Toronto). Home: 135 N Rossmore St Los Angeles CA 90004 Office: 3130 Leonis Blvd Los Angeles CA 90058

GILLESPIE, ROXANI MANOU, ins. co. exec.; b. Athens, Greece, Apr. 19, 1941; came to U.S., 1964, naturalized, 1969; d. Pericles Constantine and Helen (Zavitsianou) Manos; law student U. Athens, 1959-64; J.D., Boston Coll., 1967; m. J. Christopher Gillespie, Dec. 2, 1963; children—Margaret, Constantine. Admitted to Mass. bar, 1969, Calif bar, 1971; with Indsl. Indemnity Co., San Jose, Calif., 1970—, v.p., sec., corp. counsel, 1976-78, v.p., div. mgr., 1978—. Mem. Calif. Ins. Guarantee Assn. (sec. 1976-78), Calif. Bar Assn., Am. Bar Assn. Club: Stock Exchange (San Francisco). Office: 1999 S Bascom Ave San Jose CA 95150

GILLETT, LESLIE DILL, consumer package goods mfg. co. ofcl.; b. Wilmington, Del., Mar. 5, 1951; d. Colby and Betty Anne (Utter) Dill; B.A., St. Lawrence U., 1973; m. Antony William Hamilton Gillett, June 29, 1974. Sales rep. Noxell Corp., Buffalo, 1974-79, sales services mgr., Balt., 1979-80, mgr. sales service, 1981—. Mem. Exec. Woman's Network. Republican. Episcopalian. Clubs: Yorktowne Racquet, Padonia Swim. Office: Noxell Corp PO Box 1799 Baltimore MD 21203

GILLETT, VICTOR WILLIAM, JR., title ins. co. exec.; b. El Paso, Tex., Feb. 4, 1932; s. Victor William and Alice Cecelia (Kemper) G.; B.B.A., Tex. A. and M. U., 1953; m. Anita Johanne Dexter, Mar. 1, 1975; children—Victor William, III, Blake Andrew. Vice pres., dist. mgr. Stewart Title Guaranty Co., Corpus Christi, Tex., 1955-61; pres., chief exec. officer Stewart Title & Trust Co., Phoenix, 1961-77, dir., 1965-77; sr. v.p., nat. mktg. dir. Stewart Title Guaranty Co., Houston, 1977—; dir. Stewart Title Co. Tex., 1955-65. Bd. dirs. Ariz. Heart Assn., 1970-73; bd. dirs., sec. Phoenix Civic Improvement Corp., 1974-76. Served with AUS, 1953-55. Mem. Am. Land Title Assn.

(gov. 1969-71), Tex. Land Title Assn., Nat. Assn. Corp. Real Estate Execs., Mortgage Bankers Assn. Am., Nat. Assn. Indsl. and Office Parks, Internat. Council Shopping Centers, Nat. Assn. Real Estate Investments Trusts, Assn. U.S. Army (pres., dir. 1968), Navy League, Newcomen Soc. N.Am., Former Students Assn. Tex. A&M U. Episcopalian. Clubs: Houstonian; Sugar Creek Country (Sugar Land); Aggie (Tex. A&M U.). Home: 2803 Fairway Dr Sugar Land TX 77478 Office: 2200 W Loop S Suite 840 Houston TX 77027

GILLETTE, HALBERT SCRANTON, publisher; b. Chgo., June 29, 1922; s. Edward Scranton and Clarabel (Thornton) G.; B.S., Mass. Inst. Tech., 1944; m. Mary Livingston, Feb. 12, 1949 (dec. Jan. 1962); children—Anne Livingston, Susan L.; m. 2d, Karla Ann McCall, June 8, 1963; children—James McCall, Halbert G., Edward S. II. Space buyer Andrews Agy., 1946-48; advt. mgr. Good Roads Mach. Co., Minerva, Ohio, 1948; exec. v.p. Gillette Pub. Co., Chgo., 1949-72, Scranton Pub. Co., Chgo., 1972-76, Ins. News, Inc., Phoenix; pres. Scranton Gillette Communications, 1978—; chmn. bd., pres. Publisher's Paper Co., Inc., Ednl. Screen Inc., Diapason, Inc., Piano Trade Mag., 1972-77; chmn. bd. Occidental Life Ins. Co. N.C., 1973-74; chmn. bd. McMillen Co., Jacksonville, Fla., 1974-75; chmn. bd. Peninsular Life Ins. Co., Jacksonville, 1974-76, Occidental Fire & Casualty Co., Denver, 1974-77. Mem. Lake Forest (Ill.) City Council, 1978—. Served to ensign USNR, World War II. Mem. Phi Gamma Delta. Club: Onwentsia (Lake Forest). Home: 255 Foster Pl Lake Forest IL 60045 Office: 380 North-West Hwy Des Plaines IL 60016

GILLETTE, LEROY OWEN, interior furnishings co. exec.; b. Arlington, Va., Nov. 27, 1922; s. Leroy Otto and Annetta Ethel (Owen) G.; B.S. in Indsl. Engring., Va. Poly. Inst., 1947; m. Jane Ann Kirk, Sept. 18, 1948; children—Leroy Kirk, Thomas Lloyd, William James, Barbara Jane. With Armstrong World Industries, Lancaster, Pa., 1947—, gen. mgr. quality control, 1964-71, dir. indsl. engring. and quality assurance, 1971-81, dir. indsl. engring., 1981—. Served to 1st lt. C.E., U.S. Army, 1943-46. Fellow Am. Inst. Indsl. Engrs. (pres. 1980-81); mem. Am. Soc. Quality Control (sr.), Council on Indsl. Engring. Republican. Home: 1114 Country Club Dr Lancaster PA 17601 Office: Armstrong World Industries Lancaster PA 17604

GILLEY, JAMES RAY, retail food co. exec.; b. Surry County, N.C., Apr. 25, 1934; s. William Hassel and Delsie May (Brinkley) G.; B.A., Wake Forest U., 1957, M.B.A., 1972; m. Sylvia Ray Messick, Mar. 28, 1954; children—William Michael, Elizabeth Dale, Nita Ann. Pres., 7-11 Food Store N.C., Inc., Winston Salem, 1959-61, Stop & Shop N.C., Inc., Winston Salem, 1957-66, Gilley Leasing Co., Inc., Winston Salem, 1966-69, Convenient Systems, Inc., Winston Salem, 1969-73; exec. v.p., chief fin. officer Washington Group, Inc., Winston Salem, 1973-75, pres., 1975—; pres., chmn. bd., chief exec. officer Hungry Bull Assos.; dir. Integon Corp., Northwestern Bank, Salem Carpet Co., Piedmont Fed. Savs. & Loan Assn., Winston Salem. Trustee, Wake Forest U., 1975—, Gardner Webb Coll., 1969-74; chmn. bd. dirs. Better Bus. Bur, Winston Salem, 1974—; bd. visitors Babcock Sch. Mgmt., Wake Forest U., 1973—; mem. mayors commn. recreation parks, Forsyth County, N.C. Recipient Distinguished Alumni Service citation Wake Forest U., 1974. Mem. Fin. Execs. Inst., Newcomen Soc., Greater Winston Salem C. of C. (dir. 1974—). Baptist. Home: 2712 Bartram Pl Winston Salem NC 27106 Office: 3069 Trenwest Dr PO Box 1015 Winston Salem NC 27102

GILLIAM, LANCE CLARK, real estate exec.; b. Lufkin, Tex., Sept. 12, 1956; s. Robert Wilson and Janet (McFaddin) G.; B.B.A. in Real Estate, So. Meth. U., 1977, postgrad., 1978-79; postgrad. in acctg. U. Houston, 1978; m. Karen Brookshire, July 7, 1979. Retail leasing agt. McFaddin Kendrick, Dallas, 1976-77, sr. v.p. real estate, Houston, 1978—; mortgage loan analyst First Mortgage Co. of Tex., Houston, 1977-78. Recipient award Dallas Bd. Realtors, 1977; lic. broker, Tex. Republican. Episcopalian. Clubs: Univ., Downtown. Office: 1900 Yorktown 100 Houston TX 77056

GILLIAM, THOMAS WEST, JR., fin. co. exec.; b. Lynchburg, Va., June 16, 1938; s. Thomas West and Mary (Truett) G.; B.A. magna cum laude, Washington and Lee U., 1960; M.B.A., Harvard U., 1962; m. Diane McKay, Aug. 19, 1960; children—Thomas, Connally, Robert. Vice pres. Blyth Eastman Dillon Co., Washington, 1968-73; v.p. fin. Builders Resources Corp., Washington, 1974-77; sr. v.p. Amvest Leasing and Capital Corp., Charlottesville, Va., 1977-80; pres. Petroleum Funding Corp., 1980. Served to 1st lt. U.S. Army, 1962-64. Decorated Army Commendation medal. Mem. Am. Assn. Equipment Lessors, Sigma Alpha Epsilon. Presbyterian. Clubs: University (Washington); Torch. Home: 206 Rowledge Rd Charlottesville VA 22901 Office: One Village Green Circle Charlottesville VA 22901

GILLIAND, MERLE ELLSWORTH, banker; b. Pitcairn, Pa., Dec. 21, 1921; s. Walter M. and Elsie N. (Dean) G.; B.S. in Bus. Adminstrn. cum laude, Duquesne U., 1948; m. Olive Lee Henry, June 11, 1954; 1 son, Mark. With Albert A. Logan, C.P.A., Pitts., 1948-53; with Pitts. Nat. Bank, 1953—, exec. v.p., 1965-67, pres., 1967-70, pres., chief exec. officer, 1970-72, chmn. bd., chief exec. officer, 1972—; dir. Pitts. Nat. Corp., Kissell Co., Bell Telephone Co. Pa., Cooper Tire and Rubber Co., Wean United, Inc., USAir; instr. accounting Duquesne U., 1948-53; mem. fed. adv. council Fed. Res. System. Mem. exec. council Allegheny Conf. on Community Devel.; bd. dirs. Pitts. Opera, Duquesne U., Pa. Economy League, Inc., Pitts. Theol. Sem.; mem. exec. com. Penn's Southwest Assn.; trustee and bd. visitors Grad. Sch. Bus. Adminstrn., U. Pitts.; bd. visitors Grad. Sch. Bus. Adminstrn., Duke U. Served with AUS, 1942-46. C.P.A., Pa. Mem. Bank Adminstrn. Inst., Pa. Inst. C.P.A.'s, Financial Execs. Inst., Assn. Res. City Bankers. Presbyn. (elder). Clubs: Duquesne, Fox Chapel Golf, Churchill Valley Country, Allegheny (Pitts.); Belleview Biltmore Country (Belleair, Fla.); Laurel Valley Golf (Ligonier, Pa.); Rolling Rock. Home: 300 Fox Chapel Rd Apt 518 Pittsburgh PA 15238 Office: Pittsburgh Nat Bank Pittsburgh PA 15230

GILLILAN, WILLIAM J., III, constrn. co. exec.; b. Pitts., June 20, 1946; s. William J., II and Sara Parker (Wynn) G.; B.S. in Indsl. Engring. with honors, Purdue U., 1968; M.B.A., Harvard U., 1970; m. Susan Woodyard, June 20, 1970; children—William J., Mary, John C., Mark. With Centex Homes, Inc., 1974—, exec. v.p. ops. Centex Homes Midwest, Inc., Palatine, Ill., 1978, pres., 1978—. Served to lt. USNR, 1970-74. Mem. Delta Tau Delta. Republican. Presbyterian. Clubs: Meadows (Rolling Meadows, Ill.); Westmoreland Country (Wilmette, Ill.). Home: 452 Buckthorn Ct Buffalo Grove IL 60090 Office: 887 E Wilmette Bldg B Palantine IL 60067

GILLILAND, PAUL MICHAEL, farm exec., city ofcl.; b. Brewer, Maine, Dec. 10, 1932; s. William Lester and Lucile (Cartmell) G.; B.S. in Chemistry, Purdue U., 1958, M.A. in English, 1964; M.A. in L.S., Ind. U., 1966; cert. Advanced Study, U. Chgo., 1969; m. Lorraine Elizabeth Amidei, June 2, 1962; children—Laura Christine, William Dean. Research chemist DeSoto Chem. Coatings, Chgo., 1961-62; librarian Purdue U., 1962-68; asst. prof. library sci. McGill U., Montreal, Can., 1969-71; sec.-treas. Gilliland Farms, Inc., Harrington, Wash., 1971—; mayor City of Harrington, 1980—; mem. Wash. State Library Commn., 1978—; del. Wash. Gov.'s Conf. Library and Info. Service. Committeeman, Wash. State Democratic Com., 1977—. Served with U.S. Army, 1952-55. Mem. ALA, Am. Chem. Soc., AAAS, Wash. Library Assn., Wash. Assn. Wheat Growers, Air Force Assn., Nat. Trust Historic Preservation, Beta Phi Mu. Mem. Ch. of Christ. Home and Office: PO Box 421 Harrington WA 99134

GILLIS, CHRISTINE DIEST-LORGION, stockbroker; b. San Francisco; d. Evert Jan and Christina Helen (Radcliffe) Diest-Lorgion; B.S. in Bus. Adminstrn., U. Calif.; M.S., U. So. Calif., 1968; children—Suzanne and Barbara (twins). Account exec. Winslow, Cohu & Stetson Inc., N.Y.C., 1963-64, Paine, Webber, Jackson & Curtis, N.Y.C., 1964-65; sr. investment exec. Shearson, Hammill, Beverly Hills, Calif., 1966-72; cert. fin. planner E.F. Hutton & Co., Los Angeles, 1972—; instr. investment classes UCLA, U. So. Calif. Sec., dir., mem. bd. govs. Town Hall of Calif., 1975-80. Cert., Inst. Cert. Fin. Planners. Mem. Women Stockbrokers Assn. (founder, pres.), Women of Wall St. West (founder, pres.), AAUW (life mem., founder Palos Verdes br., trustee Nat. Edn. Fellowship Found.), Bus. and Profl. Women's Club, Navy League (life mem., dir. Bel Air Council). Home: 1495 Pegfair Estates Dr Pasadena CA 91103

GILLIS, DONALD JOSEPH PETER, constrn., bldg. spltys. co. exec.; b. Halifax, N.S., Apr. 5, 1935; s. Ernest Joseph and Viola Geraldine (Lavers) G.; student St. Mary's U., 1953; m. Brenda Lou Smith, Sept. 17, 1956; children—Christopher, Andrew, John, Gregor. Salesman, The Gillis Co. Ltd., Halifax, 1957-61, v.p., 1966-71, pres., 1971—; v.p. Overhead Door Sales, Halifax, 1962-65; pres. G&M Steel Bldgs. Ltd., Dartmouth, 1979, D&B Gillis Holdings, Dartmouth, N.S., 1979; dir. and vice chmn. Halifax Metro Centre; dir. N.S. Place Ltd. Chmn., bd. dirs. Halifax Visitors and Conv. Bur. Mem. Constrn. Assn. N.S. (past chmn.), Design and Constrn. Inst. N.S. (past pres.), Canadian Constrn. Assn., Halifax Bd. of Trade (dir., 2d v.p. exec. com., recipient Exec. award 1977). Mem. Royal United Services Inst., North Brit. Soc., Maritime Comml. Travellers Assn., Naval Officers Assn. Can. Roman Catholic. Clubs: Joe Howe Festival, Waegwoltic, Her Majesty Can. Ship Scotian (wardroom, hon. life mem.). Home: 27 Downs Ave Halifax NS B3N 2Z1 Canada Office: 15 Borden Ave Dartmouth NS B3B 1C7 Canada

GILLIS, ELSBETH HANNA, textile printing and 3-dimensional photo transparencies co. exec.; b. Basel, Switzerland, Oct. 3, 1921; d. Benjamin and Sophie (Senn) Baumann; came to U.S., 1947, naturalized, 1953; student schs., Switzerland; m. Jan Richard Gillis, June 24, 1951; children—Peter B., Jacqueline H., Robert A.; 1 stepson, Jan Richard. Asst. to bookkeeper Columeta A.G., Basel, 1940; sec. to personnel dir. Schweizerische Treuhand Gesellschaft, Basel, 1940-41; asst. bookkeeper Schweizerische Werkzeuggesellschaft, Basel, 1941-46; sec.-5 langs. Otto Keller & Co., Zurich, 1946-47; sec. J.B. Ellis & Co., N.Y.C., 1947-48; exec. sec.-3 langs. Leon Bergl & Co., N.Y.C., 1948-51; pres. Am. Art Textile Printing Co., Inc., N.Y.C., 1959—, also Janprint, Inc., Gilstripe, Inc., Dynoptics, Inc. Mem. Elmsford-Greenburgh C. of C. (pres. 1980). Christian Scientist. Home: 18 Bayberry Rd Elmsford NY 10523 Office: 95 Morton St New York NY 10014 also 1 Westchester Plaza Elmsford NY 10523

GILLIS, HARVEY NEAL, banker; b. Pitts., Feb. 8, 1946; s. Martin David and Lillian Baseman; B.S., Carnegie Mellon U., 1968; M.B.A., Stanford U., 1970, M.S. in Ops. Research, 1971; postgrad. Pacific Coast Banking Sch., U. Wash., 1979; m. Wendy Anne Rushbrook, May 24, 1973; children—Gavin Brian, Rebecca Anne. Mgr. ops. research and analysis Memorex Corp., Santa Clara, Calif., 1971-72, mgr. corp. planning, 1972-73; mgr. fin. planning Raychem Corp., Menlo Park, Calif., 1973-74; asst. v.p., mgr. fin. analysis Seafirst Corp., Seattle, 1974-75, v.p., mgr. fin. reports and analysis, 1975-76, v.p., controller, 1976-79, sr. v.p., controller, 1976-79, exec. v.p., chief fin. officer, 1979—. Tchr., cons. Jr. Achievement; mem. Citizens Budget Adv. Com., Seattle, 1979. Mem. Bank Adminstrn. Inst. (acctg. and fin. commn.), Chgo. C. of C., Fin. Execs. Inst., Fin. Mgmt. Assn., Am. Banking Assn. (acctg. policy com.). Clubs: Rotary, Wash. Athletic, Rainier. Home: 8042 116th Ave SE Renton WA 98055 Office: Box 3586 Seattle WA 98124

GILLIS, JOHN WINFRED, architect; b. Chgo., July 13, 1947; s. Winfred John and Veronica (Marinko) G.; student Ill. Inst. Tech., 1965-66, Frank L. Wright Sch. Architecture, 1966-67, U. Ill., 1968-69. Designer, architect Taliesin Asso. Architects, 1966-67, Paul Rudolph, Architect, 1970-72; prin. John Gillis Architects, 1973—; gen. partner Anthem Properties. Registered architect, N.Y., N.J.; cert. Nat. Council Archtl. Registration Bds. Mem. Met. Mus. Art, Ford Hall Forum, Pa. Acad. Fine Arts. Designer, developer of methods to recycle bldgs. worthy of preservation into revitalized urban housing and comml. environments. Home and Office: 25 Joralemon St Brooklyn Heights NY 11201 Office: 36 W 62d St New York NY 10023

GILLIS, KENNETH ROBERT, cattle co. exec.; b. Ithaca, N.Y., Aug. 15, 1950; s. Marvin Bob and Helen (Reed) G.; B.S., Colo. State U., 1972; M.A., U. Colo., 1973; m. Ann Louise Conde, Oct. 26, 1974; 1 son, Reed Kenneth. Econ. analyst Great Western Sugar Co., Denver, 1974-76, mgr. fin. planning, 1977-78; mgr. fin. planning Foxley & Co. and Flavorland Industries, Denver, 1978-79, v.p. fin., 1979—. Mem. Am. Econs. Assn., Am. Agrl. Econs. Assn. Home: 1198 Fairfax St Denver CO 80220 Office: Box 7000 Englewood CO 80110

GILLIS, MARVIN BOB, chem. and mining co. exec.; b. Treutlen County, Ga., Apr. 5, 1920; s. Bob Lee and Pearl (Gillis) G.; B.S.A., U. Ga., 1940; Ph.D., Cornell U., 1947; m. Helen Reed, Dec. 23, 1946; children—Margaret Susan, Marvin Reed, Kenneth Robert. Research asso. Cornell U., 1947-51; with Internat. Minerals and Chem. Corp., 1947—, asst. dir. research, 1956-57, dir. research, 1957-64, dir. animal health and nutrition, 1964-66, div. v.p., 1966-70, corp. v.p., 1970—, sr. v.p., 1972—, pres., dir. IMC Chem. Group, Inc., 1976-78; pres. Animal Products Group, 1978—; dir. Dynapol; sec. Agrl. Research Inst., Nat. Acad. Scis.-NRC, 1958-59, v.p., 1960-62, 1966-67; pres., 1962-63, 68-69, mem. Agrl. Bd., 1962-67; bd. dirs. Animal Health Inst., 1966-69. Served to 1st lt. USAAF, 1942-45. Decorated D.F.C. with oak leaf cluster, Air medal with 3 oak leaf clusters. Mem. Am. Chem. Soc., Mfg. Chemists Assn., Am. Inst. Nutrition, Sigma Xi, Gamma Alpha, Alpha Zeta, Phi Kappa Phi. Baptist. Clubs: North Shore Country; Bent Tree (Jasper, Ga.); Lone Palm (Lakeland, Fla.). Patentee in field. Author numerous papers in field. Editorial adv. com. Jour. Agrl. and Food Chemistry, 1962-65. Home: 2116 Larkdale Dr Glenview IL 60025 Office: IMC Plaza 2315 Sanders Rd Northbrook IL 60062

GILLISON, ROBERT WILLIAM, III, mfg. co. exec.; b. Irvington, N.J., Oct. 28, 1935; s. Robert William and Jessie E. (Gillanders) G.; B.A., Cleve. State U., 1960; m. Marvis E. Esko, June 20, 1959; children—Robert W., Elizabeth A., Maura L., James E. With Eaton Corp., 1956—, asst. gen. mgr. axle div., 1972-73, gen. mgr. dispenser div., 1973-74, div. mgr. axle div., 1975-78, pres. truck components group, Cleve., 1978—. Trustee Euclid Gen. Hosp., 1979—. Mem. Western Hwy. Inst. (dir.), Heavy Duty Truck Mfrs. Assn. (dir.), Cleve. Council World Affairs. Clubs: Clevelander, Detroit Athletic. Office: 100 Erieview Plaza Cleveland OH 44114

GILMAN, ELISA AMBROSINA, fin. exec.; b. Locarno, Switzerland, Sept. 1, 1929; came to U.S., 1930, naturalized, 1947; d. Mario A. and Ida Elisa (Fantoni) Ferrari; B.S., N.Y. Inst. Fin., 1955; children—Gary R., Sandra K. Kanahele. With Paine Webber, Santa Barbara, Calif., 1953-55; cashier/broker Shearson Hammil, Santa Barbara, 1955-69; stockbroker, sr. investment exec. Reynolds Securities, Santa Barbara, 1970-79, v.p., 1976; account exec., v.p. Dean Witter Reynolds, Santa Barbara, 1979—; cons. Com. for Status Am. Women, 1974—. Mem. grants com. Dir. Relief Found., 1980. Republican. Club: Coral Casino. Home: 5100 Camino Floral Santa Barbara CA 93111 Office: 200 E Carrillo St Santa Barbara CA 93101

GILMAN, JOHN RICHARD, JR., cons.; b. Malden, Mass., July 6, 1925; s. John Richard and Philomene (Gradie) G.; A.B., Harvard, 1945; postgrad. Georgetown U., 1945-46; m. Julia Streeter, Feb. 6, 1960; children—Derek, Susan. Dir. publicity John H. Breck, Inc., Springfield, Mass., 1949-53, asst. advt. mgr., 1950-53, dir. new products, 1955-56, tech. dir., 1956-63; dir. new products Acco Labs., Am. Cyanamid Co., Wayne, N.J., 1963; treas., exec. v.p. August Sauter of Am., Inc., N.Y.C., 1964, pres., 1965-79, also chief exec. officer; pres. John R. Gilman Inc., N.Y.C., 1980—; dir. Slee Internat., Inc., N.Y.C., Finex Mining Co., Reno. Trustee, Sculpture Center, N.Y.C., 1977—; budget com. Town of Tiverton (R.I.), 1977-79. Served with USNR, 1943-46. Mem. Soc. Cosmetic Chemists, N.Y. Acad. Scis., Am. Pharm. Assn., Soc. Photog. Scientists and Engrs., Profl. Photographers Am., Art Students League. Clubs: Chemists; Harvard (N.Y.C.). Film maker: Water, 1950; Dear Nancy, 1953; co-pub. Arcadia Press, N.Y.C., 1979—. Home: 395 Punkateest Neck Rd Tiverton RI 02878 Office: 80 Fifth Ave New York NY 10011

GILMAN, PAUL C(ROSBY), bank trust officer; b. Haverhill, Mass. July 21, 1934; s. Ernest Paul and Helen M. (Crosby) G.; B.S. in Gen. Bus., Lehigh U., 1957; LL.B., U. Colo., 1962; m. Lilian P., June 29, 1957; children—Nancy, Paul C., Barbara, Peter. Admitted to Colo. bar, 1962; trust officer Colo. Nat. Bank, Denver, 1962-72, estate and trust adminstr., 1962-70, head new bus. devel., 1970-72; trust officer, sr. v.p. First Nat. Bank, Boulder, 1972—. Chmn. exec. com. and adminstrv. com. Boulder County United Way, 1979, pres., 1980—; treas. for several Republican candidates, state and local campaigns, 1974-80. Served to 1st lt. U.S. Army, 1957-59. Recipient Citizenship award Boulder County United Way, 1979. Mem. Am. Bar Assn., Colo. Bar Assn., Boulder County Bar Assn. (chmn. sect. unauthorized practice law 1977-78), Boulder County Estate Planning Council (pres. 1978), Nat. Rifle Assn., Browning Collectors Assn. Lutheran. Club: Boulder Country. Home: 360 Kiowa Pl Boulder CO 80303 Office: PO Box 59 Boulder CO 80302

GILMAN, SUMNER DEAN, ins. exec.; b. Cambridge, Mass., June 10, 1946; s. Justin Morton and Helen Pearl (Roffer) G.; B.S., U. Tenn., 1967; m. Joanne Helen Levine, Oct. 3, 1971; 1 dau., Marla Joy. Sales mgr. New Eng. div. Motor Club Am. Cos., 1967-77; pres. Economy Ins. Agy., Inc. and Economy Ins. Agy. of Holyoke, Inc., Springfield, Mass., 1977—. Mem. Mass. Auto Ins. Agts. Assn. (pres.), Profl. Ins. Agts. Assn., Ind. Ins. Agts. Mass. Home: 71 Sheri Ln Agawam MA 01001 Office: 1691 Main St Springfield MA 01103

GILMER, FRANK BARNETT, JR., bus. edn. specialist; b. Albuquerque, July 13, 1928; s. Frank Barnett and Pattie Snoddy (Harris) G.; B.S. in Edn., U. N.Mex., 1955; M.B.A., U. Denver, 1959. Circulation clk. Albuquerque Pub. Co., 1944-47, display advt. salesman, 1948-50, 53; classroom tchr. Valley High Sch., Albuquerque, 1955-64, Del Norte High Sch., Albuquerque, 1964-65; bus. edn. specialist Albuquerque Public Schs., 1965—. Served with arty., AUS, 1950-52. Mem. Mountain-Plains Bus. Edn. Assn. (pres. 1969, leadership award 1974), Internat. World Processing Assn., Am. Vocat. Assn., Nat. Bus. Edn. Assn., Nat. Assn. Suprs. Bus. Edn. (pres. 1975), Delta Pi Epsilon, Phi Delta Kappa (life, service key 1975). Democrat. Baptist. Contbr. to Yearbook of Nat. Bus. Edn. Assn., 1969. Home: Suite 1401 Park Plaza 1331 Park Ave SW Albuquerque NM 87102 Office: 725 University Blvd SE Albuquerque NM 87106

GILMONT, ERNEST RICH, mfg. co. exec.; b. Boston, July 1, 1929; s. Bernard I. and Ethel (Rich) Goldberg; A.B., Middlebury (Vt.) Coll., 1951, M.Sc., 1952; Ph.D. (Bristol overseas fellow), M.I.T., 1956; m. Joy L. Pasternack, Oct. 23, 1965. Sr. chemist, then group leader FMC Corp., Princeton, N.J., 1956-61; dir. research U.S. Peroxygen Co., Richmond, Calif., 1961-62; with Millmaster Onyx Corp., 1962-66; tech. dir. div. A. Gross & Co., 1970-78; gen. mgr. Copygraphics, Fairfield, N.J., 1978—; Robert A. Welch Found. lectr., 1975. Recipient Honor scroll N.J. Inst. Chemists, 1974, Disting. Service award Assn. Cons. Chemists and Chem. Engrs., 1977. Fellow AAAS. Patentee organic perodides. Home: 146 Central Park W New York NY 10023 Office: 134 Clinton Rd Fairfield NJ 07006

GILMORE, ROBERT EUGENE, earthmoving machinery co. exec.; b. nr. Peoria, Ill., May 4, 1920; s. Myron E. and Lillian G. (Mallm) G.; grad. high sch.; m. Marguerite A. Best, May 1, 1948; children—Christine Ann, Scott Eugene. With Caterpillar Tractor Co., Peoria, 1938—, pres. Caterpillar France, Grenoble, 1963-68, gen. mgr. worldwide mfg. and facilities planning, 1968, gen. mgr. U.S. mfg. plants, 1968-69, v.p. U.S. mfg. plants, 1969-73, exec. v.p., 1973-77, pres., chief operating officer, 1977—, also dir.; dir. Santa Fe Industries, Security Savs. & Loan Assn., Peoria. Bd. dirs. Proctor Hosp., SME Mfg. Engring. Edn. Found. Served to 1st lt. USAAF, 1943-45; ETO. Decorated Air medal with 4 oak leaf clusters. Mem. Soc. Automotive Engrs., NAM (dir.), Nat. Exec. Service Corps. (mem. council). Republican. Lutheran. Clubs: Peoria Country; Union League (Chgo.); Masons. Office: 100 NE Adams St Peoria IL 61629*

GILMORE, WILLIAM FREDRICK, govt. ofcl.; b. Omaha, Feb. 21, 1944; s. Henry Carson and Dorothy Elizabeth (Graff) G.; B.S. in B.A., Creighton U., 1972; m. Marion Lynn Burkholder, Sept. 5, 1971; 1 son, Christopher William. Budget and internal control dir. City of Omaha Fin. Dept., 1972-78; exec. dir., adminstr. Public Bldg. Commn. Omaha, 1978—; pres. Gilmore & Assos., Omaha, 1976—. Sec.-treas., Douglas County Sheriff Res., 1979-81; bd. dirs., treas. Omaha Arts Festival, 1980-81. Served with USAF, 1964-68. Decorated Air Force Commendation medal. Mem. Nat. Assn. Accts., Bldg. Owners and Mgmt. Assn., Leadership Omaha, Fed. Employees Credit Union. Republican. Presbyterian. Address: 1819 Farnam St Omaha NE 68118

GILPATRICK, RALPH BENJAMIN, JR., banker; b. McKeesport, Pa., Mar. 26, 1924; s. Ralph Benjamin and Katherine J. (Smith) G.; B.A., Amherst Coll., 1949; M.B.A., Harvard U., 1951; m. Dorothy Olga Werlinich, Sept. 3, 1955; 1 son, David A. With Mellon Bank, N.A., Pitts., 1951—, v.p., 1966-73, sr. v.p., 1973-78, exec. v.p., 1978-80, vice-chmn. bd., 1980—; dir. Pennzoil Co., Dravo Corp., Western Pa. Devel. Credit Corp., Pitts. Trustee, Shadyside Hosp., Pitts., 1978—; bd. dirs. Pitts. Regional Planning Assn., 1979—. Served with USAF, 1942-45; ETO. Decorated Air medal with two oak leaf clusters, Purple Heart. Mem. Am. Bankers Assn., Assn. Res. City Bankers, Robert Morris Assos. Clubs: Duquesne, Longue Vue (Pitts.); Rolling Rock, Laurel Valley Golf (Ligonier, Pa.). Home: 405 Buckingham Rd Pittsburgh PA 15215 Office: Mellon Bank NA Mellon Sq Pittsburgh PA 15230

GILSTRAP, JOE JACKSON, ins. exec.; b. Pickens, S.C., Apr. 21, 1923; s. Luther Hubbard and Ethel Bulah (Massey) G.; B.A., Furman U., Greenville, S.C., 1948; m. Esterlene Burroughs, Dec. 22, 1945; children—Carol, Donald. Asst. treas. Liberty Life Ins. Co., Greenville, 1948—; ins. mgr. Liberty Corp., Greenville, 1970-75, asst. v.p., 1975—. Served with USNR, 1943-46. Fellow Life Office Mgmt. Assn., Risk and Ins. Mgmt. Soc. Methodist (chmn. coms., tchr.). Mason (Shriner). Home: 34 Lockwood Ave Greenville SC 29607 Office: PO Box 789 Greenville SC 29602

GIMLIN, ROBERT CHARLES, mfg. co. exec.; b. Chgo., Jan. 11, 1921; s. Guy M. and Corinne (Koch) G.; B.S. in Mech. Engring., Purdue U., 1942; m. Jane Elizabeth Haltom, Apr. 19, 1942; children—Hal, Gail. Various mgmt. positions to v.p. merchandising U.S. Gypsum Co., Chgo., 1946-66; v.p. Abitibi Paper Co. Ltd., Toronto, Ont., Can., 1966-69, group v.p., 1974-76, pres., chief operating officer, 1978-79; pres. Abitibi Corp., Birmingham, Mich., 1969-74; chmn. Abitibi-Price Sales Corp., N.Y.C., 1976-78, pres., chief exec. officer Abitibi-Price Inc., Toronto, 1979—, also dir.; dir. The Price Co. Ltd., Interprovincial Pipe Line Ltd. Served to lt. s.g. USN, 1942-45. Clubs: York, Toronto, Toronto Hunt, Mt. Royal, Pinehurst Golf and Country (N.C.). Office: Toronto-Dominion Centre Toronto ON M5K 1B3 Canada

GIMMA, JOSEPH ANTHONY, investment banker; b. Bari, Italy, Apr. 12, 1907; s. Giovanni Batiste and Maria (DiBenedetto) G.; came to U.S., 1913, naturalized, 1932; grad. high sch.; m. Licia Albanese, Apr. 7, 1945; 1 son, Joseph Anthony. Trader, Herrick, Berg & Co., N.Y.C., 1924-37, B. M-P Murphy & Co., N.Y.C., 1937-43; with Hornblower & Weeks-Hemphill, Noyes, N.Y.C., 1942—, partner, 1950—, sr. mng. dir. Shearson-Loeb Rhoades (formerly Loeb Rhoades, Hornblower), 1978-79, sr. v.p. investments, 1979—; dir. Lionel Corp. Mem. Cardinal's Com. of Laity Catholic Charities, 1950—; mem. N.Y. State Racing Commn., chmn., 1965-73; mem. joint legis. task force to study and evaluate pari-mutual racing and breeding industry; mem. Commn. on Review Nat. Policy Toward Gambling; chmn. N.Y. Republican County Com., 1962-63; mem. adv. bd. Marymount Coll., N.Y.C., 1967—; trustee Nat. Mus. Racing Saratoga, Loyola Sch., N.Y.C.; bd. dirs., pres. Bagby Found., Mus. Arts, N.Y.C.; bd. dirs. Eymard Found., St. Peter's Coll., Rome; pres. Puccini Found., N.Y.C. Decorated Knight of Malta, knight Grand Cross Holy Sepulchre. Mem. Nat. Hunts Racing Assn., Turf and Field, U.S. Navy League. Club: Met. Opera. Home: 800 Park Ave New York NY 10021 Office: 14 Wall St New York NY 10005

GIMPEL, RONALD MARK, fin. systems mgmt. exec.; b. N.Y.C., June 25, 1943; s. Benjamin and Anna G.; B.B.A., Coll. City N.Y., 1965; M.B.A., Fairleigh-Dickinson U., 1977; m. Roberta Jane Ostrov, July 6, 1968; children—Ross Bradley, Brent Stuart. Regional data center dir. Zeinitron Corp., N.Y.C., 1968-70; mgr. tech. services Computer Horizons Corp., N.Y.C., 1970-74; systems group supr. A.T. & T., N.Y.C., 1974-77; dir. systems devel. Am. Express, N.Y.C., 1977-80; v.p. Barron Systems Group, Ltd., N.Y.C., 1980—; adj. instr. bus. systems Middlesex Coll. Mem. Hazlet Twp. Zoning Bd. Mem. Data Processing Assn., Assn. Computing Machinery. Home: 18 Kildare Dr Hazlet NJ 07730 Office: 301 E 68th St New York NY 10021

GINADER, GEORGE HALL, investment banker; b. Buffalo, Apr. 5, 1933; s. George Edward and Meredith (Hall) G.; B.A., Allegheny Coll., 1955; M.S. in L.S., Drexel U., 1964. Asst. buyer Lord & Taylor, N.Y.C., 1957-59; job analyst Ins. Co. N. Am., Phila., 1959-60; asst. buyer John Wanamaker, Phila., 1960-61; acting curator Automobile Reference Collection, Free Library Phila., 1961-63; librarian, N.Y. C. of C., N.Y.C., 1964-66; chief librarian N.Y. Stock Exchange, N.Y.C., 1966-67; exec. dir. Spl. Libraries Assn., N.Y.C., 1967-70; dir. research library Morgan Stanley & Co., N.Y.C., 1970—; coordinator libraries, London, Tokyo, Paris, Montreal. Mem. N.Y. State Geneal. Soc., N.Y. C. of C., Records Mgrs. and Adminstrs., Phi Delta Theta. Republican. Episcopalian. Home: 45 S Main St Cranbury NJ 08512 Office: Morgan Stanley & Co Inc 1251 Ave of Americas New York NY 10020

GINDER, CHARLES RICHARD, mining equipment co. exec.; b. Pitts., June 23, 1941; s. John Cope Stanton and Jean Ann (Buttermore) G.; B.B.A., U. Notre Dame, 1963; m. Bonnie Shirley Thomson, Aug. 26, 1967; children—Richard Charles, Timothy Wallace. Sales rep. Terex div. Gen. Motors Corp., 1968-70; sales rep. Lake Shore Inc., Phoenix, 1970-73, gen. sales mgr., 1973-76; founder, pres., chief exec. officer, chmn. bd. Ginco, Raton, N.Mex., 1976—. Pres., Raton Cath. Sch. Bd., 1977—. Served to capt. U.S. Army, 1964-68. Decorated Purple Heart with two oak leaf clusters, Bronze Star with oak leaf cluster, Army Commendation medal. Mem. Am. Mining Congress, Rocky Mountain Mining Assn., Raton C. of C. (dir. 1979—). Republican. Roman Catholic. Club: Raton Country, Pueblo Country. Home: 1114 Nelson Rd Raton NM 87740 Office: Ginco York Canyon Rd Raton NM 87740

GINGERICH, JOHN CHARLES, mfg. co. exec.; b. Macomb, Ill., Mar. 4, 1936; s. Arbon Jacob and Amy Evelyn G.; B.S. in Elec. Engring., U. Ill., 1958; postgrad. U. Md., 1959; m. Judith Ann Caldwell, July 22, 1961; children—Jana, Tracy, Brian. Elec. engr. Nat. Security Agy., Ft. Mead, Md., 1958-59; sales engr. Elec. Assos., Inc., Los Angeles, 1959-62, dist. mgr., Palo Alto, Calif., regional mgr., 1968-70; area mgr. Measurex Corp., Santa Clara, Calif., 1970, area mgr., Portland, Oreg., 1970-71, regional mgr., Atlanta, 1971-74, dir. mktg. and service, Cupertino, Calif., 1974-77, dep. dir. Europe, Reading, Eng., 1977, v.p. Europe, 1977-79, v.p. So. and Western divs., U.S., 1980-81, v.p. nat. sales and service, 1981—. Mem. Paper Industry Mgmt. Assn., TAPPI. Republican. Office: Measurex Corp One Results Way Cupertino CA 95014

GINN, H(ORACE) MARVIN, publishing co. exec.; b. Miller, Mo., Jan. 17, 1914; s. Horace Maynard and Jurley (Ward) G.; student S.W. Mo. State Coll., 1934-35, Northwestern U., 1947; m. Laura Marie Birzele, Apr. 16, 1942; children—Marcia Eleanor, Sheila Margaret, Sandra. Tchr., Union Hall Sch., Halltown, Mo., 1936-38; salesman Crowell-Collier Pub. Co., N.Y.C., 1939-42; promotion mgr. Opportunity Mag., Chgo., 1946-50, Irving-Cloud Pub. Co., Chgo., 1950-55; sales mgr. Pubs. Devel. Corp., Skokie, Ill., 1955-61; chmn., pres. H. Marvin Ginn Corp., Chgo., 1961—. Served with inf. AUS, 1942-46; PTO. Decorated Bronze Star, Iwo Jima citation. Mem. Chgo. Assn. Bus. Pubs., Internat. Assn. Fire Chiefs. Fire Equipment Mfrs. and Services Assn. Clubs: Box 15 Fire Service, Chicago Advt., Masons (32 deg.), Shriners. Author: How to Be An Executive Salesman, 1953. Home: 1959 W Hood St Chicago IL 60660 Office: 625 N Michigan Ave Chicago IL 60611

GINTELL, BURTON, distillery exec.; b. N.Y.C., May 11, 1935; s. William and Lillian (Krieger) G.; B.B.A., City U. N.Y., 1956. Div. pres. Seagram Co., Ltd., N.Y.C., 1965-74; bus. devel. cons., 1974-75; v.p. fin. and adminstrn., treas. Am. Distilling Co., N.Y.C., 1975-78; chmn. William Whiteley & Co., London, 1978—. Served with U.S. Army, 1957. C.P.A., N.Y. State. Mem. Am. Mktg. Assn., Am. Inst. C.P.A.'s, Internat. Wine and Food Soc., French Inst.-Alliance Franciase. Club: Savile (London). Home and Office: 57 A Catherine Pl London SW1E 6HA England UK

GINZBURG, SOL, sales exec.; b. Vilna, Poland, May 15, 1937; came to U.S., 1951, naturalized, 1956; s. Samuel and Ida (Schub) G.; A.A.S., N.Y. Inst. Tech., 1959, B.S. in Elec. Engring., 1963; m. Nina Bar, Oct. 1, 1963; children—Betty, Samuel. Test engr. Liton Industry, New Rochelle, N.Y., 1963-64; design engr. Gen. Dynamics, Rochester, N.Y., 1964-65; distbr., regional sales mgr. Corning Glass Works/Signetics, Woodbury, N.Y., 1965-75; dist. sales mgr. Intersil, N.Y.C., 1975-77; sales mgr. Harvey Electronics, Woodbury, 1977-78; nat. sales mgr. Veeco Instruments, Plainview, N.Y., 1978—. Mem. IEEE, Am. Vacuum Soc. Democrat. Jewish. Home: 23 Amherst Ln Smithtown NY 11787 Office: Veeco Instruments Terminal Dr Plainview NY 11803

GIOFFRE, JOSEPH DOMINIC, savs. and loan exec.; b. Port Chester, N.Y., June 18, 1943; s. Joseph B. and Rose Gioffre; student U. Vt., 1961-63; diploma Inst. Fin. Edn., 1970; m. Kathryn R. Woodward, Oct. 10, 1964; children—Joseph, Kimberly. Supr. accounting dept. Westchester Fed. Savs. & Loan, New Rochelle, 1967-69; treas. Greenwich Fed. Savs. & Loan (Conn.), 1969-74, v.p., controller, 1974-76, exec. v.p., 1976—, chief adminstrv. officer, 1980—, also dir. Mem. fin. com. ARC, Greenwich, 1977—; bd. dirs. Jr. Achievement, 1977—. Mem. Fin. Mgrs. Soc. (pres. 1973-74). Roman Catholic. Clubs: Milbrook, Kiwanis. Home: Bruce Park Dr Greenwich CT 06830 Office: 28 Havemeyer Pl Greenwich CT 06830

GIOVACCHINI, ROBERT PETER, toxicologist, mfg. co. exec.; b. Fresno, Calif., June 2, 1928; s. Robert and Olga (Mencarini) G.; B.S., Creighton U., 1948, M.S., 1954; Ph.D., U. Nebr., 1958, D.Sc. (hon.), 1980; grad. Advanced Mgmt. Program, Harvard Grad. Sch. Bus., 1969; m. Gertrude Joan Stech, June 18, 1949; children—Mary Joan, Diane Marie, Karen Denise. Instr., U. Nebr. Med. Sch., 1957-58; asso. dept. anesthesia Bishop Clarkson Meml. Hosp., Omaha, 1957-58; research histopathologist Gillette Co., Rockville, Md., 1958-60, supr. toxicol. evaluations, 1960-62, asst. med. dir., 1962-64, dir. med. evaluations, 1964-70, pres. med. evaluations, 1970-74, v.p. corp. product integrity, 1974—. Recipient award Cosmetic Industry Buyers and Suppliers, 1974; Gold Medal award Soc. Cosmetic Chemists, 1975. Mem. Am. Acad. Dermatology, Am. Acad. Clin. Toxicology, Am. Coll. Toxicology, Acad. Toxicol. Scis. (chmn.), Am. Toxicology Soc., European Toxicology Soc., Am. Indsl. Hygiene Assn., N.Y. Acad. Scis., Va. Dermatology Soc., Sigma Xi. Club: Harvard (Boston). Contbr. articles to profl. jours. Home: 2518 Fernwood Dr Vienna VA 22180 Office: 1413 Research Blvd Rockville MD

GIOVANNANGELO, FRANCIS ANTHONY JOSEPH, fin. ops. cons.; b. Boston, Aug. 16, 1938; s. Antonio and Margaret Sarah (Izzo) G.; B.S. in Bus. Adminstrn., Boston Coll., 1967; M.B.A., Suffolk U., 1977. With State St. Bank & Trust Co., Boston, 1958-67; cost and pricing analyst Aerospace Systems div. RCA (now Automated Systems), Burlington, Mass., 1967-69; bank examiner Dept. Bank and Banking, Commonwealth of Mass., Boston, 1969-78; field cons. Credit Union League of Mass., Inc., Chestnut Hill, 1978-79; pvt. practice fin. ops. cons., Belmont, Mass., 1980—; speaker in field. Lt., Belmont Spl./Aux. Police Dept. Served with U.S. Army N.G., 1961-67. Mem. Assn. M.B.A. Execs., Inc., Boston Coll. Alumni Assn., Suffolk U. Alumni Assn. Roman Catholic. Home: 27 Chester Rd Belmont MA 02178

GIOVANNUCCI, DANIEL LUCIEN, jewelry mfg. co. exec.; b. Providence, Dec. 13, 1919; s. Salvatore and Michelina (Paolilli) G.; B.A. summa cum laude in Acctg. and Fin., Bryant Coll., 1947; m. Livia A. Pagliarini, May 18, 1946; children—Lorraine L., Kathleen, Daniel Lucien. With Annex Glass & Novelty, Inc., Johnston, R.I., 1947—, treas., 1947-55, pres., 1956—. Served with U.S. Army, 1941-45. Mem. Frat. Order Police (asso.), Johnson C. of C. (dir.). Roman Catholic. Club: Johnston Lions. Office: 1340 Hartford Ave Johnston RI 02919

GIRDLER, REYNOLDS, JR., art materials co. exec.; b. N.Y.C., Aug. 15, 1935; s. Reynolds and Barbara (Kitchel) G.; grad. Phillips Acad., Andover, Mass., 1953; B.A., Yale, 1957; m. Jean Abernathy, Aug. 30, 1958; children—Amy, Faith, Reynolds Edward. With Binney & Smith Inc., N.Y.C., 1957—, ednl. sales mgr., 1970-71, v.p. marketing, 1972-76, v.p. corporate relations, 1976—; dir. Canada Crayon Co., Ltd., Binney & Smith (Europe), Ltd. Mem. Greenwich (Conn.) Representative Town Meeting, 1965; chmn. RTM Social Services Com., 1972—; chmn. Greenwich Community Action Devel. Plan, 1970—. Trustee N.Y. Sch. Art League. Mem. Ednl. Industries Assn. (pres. 1978, dir.), Nat. Sch. Supply and Equipment Assn. (chmn. 1977; dir. mfrs. sect., pres. Ednl. Exhibitors sect. 1978). Clubs: Yale (N.Y.C.); Rocky Point (Old Greenwich, Conn.). Author: Crayon Techniques, 1967. Home: Binney Ln Old Greenwich CT 06870 Office: 201 E 42d St New York NY 10017

GIRDNER, ALLEN JAMES, state ofcl.; b. Tucson, Apr. 28, 1949; s. Alwin James and Marjorie Jo (Wilson) G.; B.A., U. N.Mex., 1971, M.B.A., 1974; m. Clarice Lucille Campbell, Sept. 5, 1970; children—Aaron Jason, Matthew Steven. Owner, mgr. Gimubes Janitorial Service, Albuquerque, 1965-71; mgr. supply dept., editor publ. N.Mex. Credit Union League, Albuquerque, 1973-75; bus. adminstr. health services div. Dist. 2 N.Mex. Health and Environment Dept., Santa Fe, 1975—; mem. ad hoc com. tax expenditures for human services City Santa Fe. Served with USN, 1971-72. Recipient Appreciation certificate N.Mex. Swine Influenza Program, 1976. Republican. Methodist. Home: Route 4 Box 81-G Santa Fe NM 87501 Office: PO Box 4397 Santa Fe NM 87502

GIRDNER, ALWIN JAMES, credit union exec.; b. Albuquerque, Oct. 10, 1923; s. Glen Clark and Marie Ellen (Holcomb) G.; B.S. in Bus. Adminstrn., U. Ariz., 1948, M.A., 1950; m. Marjorie Jo Wilson, Sept. 1, 1946; children—Allen James, Sharon Lynn, Kennan Eugene, Mari Jo. Sales adminstrn. RCA Victor, Camden, N.J., 1952-53; purchasing dept. Temco Aircraft Co., Dallas, 1954-58; asst. dir. edn. Tex. Credit Union League, 1958-61; asst. mng. dir. N.Mex. Credit Union League, 1961-64, mng. dir., 1964-73; treas. N.Mex. Central Credit Union, 1963-73; pres. NMCUL Service Corp., 1971-73, Tenn. Credit Union League, 1973—, TCUL Service Corp., 1973—; dir. Southeast Corp. Fed. Credit Union, 1976-78; chmn. Tenn. Central Credit Union, 1978-79; lectr. in field. Chmn. Credit Union Legis. Action Council, 1972-73. Mem. Assn. Credit Union League Execs. (sec. 1968-72), Credit Union Nat. Assn. (dir. 1966, Founders Club award 1962, world extension com. 1967-70, European bank study team 1978), Am. Soc. Assn. Execs., Internat. Platform Assn. Republican. Methodist. Author: Navaho-U.S. Relations, 1950; Chapter Leader's Handbook, 1959; Credit Union Informational Manual, 1960. Home: 7829 Parkshore Circle Chattanooga TN 37343 Office: 1317 Hickory Valley Rd Chattanooga TN 37421

GIRGUS, SAMUEL DANIEL, engr., investment co. exec.; b. Elizabeth, N.J., Mar. 21, 1932; s. Nicholas and Mary (Makara) G.; A.A., Union Coll., N.J., 1955; B.S. in Elec. Engring., Rutgers U., 1957; m. Lequetta Sue Tacker, Sept. 7, 1952; children—Mark Daniel, Glen Samuel, Todd John. Lab. dir. Avionics div. ITT, Nutley, N.J., 1957-70; v.p. intelligence Kuras-Alterman Corp., Fairfield, N.J., 1970-74; pres. mfg. K-A South, San Antonio, 1974-79; chmn. bd. Shield Investment Corp., San Antonio, 1979—; dir. Competitive Bus. Forms, Mil-Com Electronics Corp., Community Nursery. Elder, Bethany Presbyn. Ch., Bloomfield, N.J. Served with USAF, 1948-52. Recipient Tex. Gov.'s award, 1975. Mem. AIM (pres.'s council), Am. Inst. Indsl. Engrs. (sr.), Air Force Assn., Soc. Logistics Engrs., Electronic Def. Assn., San Antonio C. of C. (chmn. govt. contracting task force 1976-78, mem. econ. devel. steering com. 1978), North San Antonio C. of C. (charter), Rutgers U. Alumni Assn., Assn. Old Crows. Contbr. articles on electronic intelligence to classified publs.; developer Aero Gate complex, San Antonio, 1978, Energy Plaza, San Antonio, 1979. Home: 600 Paseo Canada San Antonio TX 78232 Office: 8820 Broadway San Antonio TX 78217

GIRI, AMAR, food technologist; b. Janakpur, Nepal, Nov. 19, 1938; s. Bikram and Sarswati G.; came to U.S., 1971, naturalized, 1976; M.Sc. Agr., Washington State U., 1962; Ph.D. Food Tech., W. Pakistan Agrl. U., 1967; m. Meena; 1 dau., Pallavi. Sr. food technologist Food Research Lab., Nepal, 1966-67; cons. in food tech., Canning Co., Nepal, 1968-70; dir. quality control and product devel. Catelli Habitant Inc., Manchester, N.H., 1973-76; mgr. quality assurance Channel Fish Co., Boston, 1976-77; mgr. quality control Good Servings Co., Manchester, 1977-78; mgr. quality assurance Victor F. Weaver, Inc., New Holland, Pa., 1978—. Mem. Inst. Food Techs. Contbr. articles to profl. publs. Home: 428 Longmeadow Rd Lancaster PA 17601 Office: 403 S Custer Ave New Holland PA 17557

GIRLING, WILLIAM FRANK, mktg. co. exec.; b. Winnipeg, Man., Can., Sept. 23, 1932; s. Frank Robert and Dorothy Francis (Hughes) G.; grad. St. Paul's Coll., Winnipeg, 1949; m. Apr. 30, 1965; children—Patricia, Jeffery, Steven, Gillian. Sales mgr. Kellogg Co., 1955-58, Mennen Co., 1958-60; nat. sales mgr. sta. CJAY-TV, 1960-63; mktg. dir. Kiddie Kastle, 1963-64; TV film sales mgr. Warner Brothers, 1964-66; nat sales mgr. sta. KCND-TV, Winnipeg, 1966-68; owner, mgr. Imperial Travel Co., Winnipeg, 1968-70; asso. v.p. Darragh & Assos., Toronto, Ont., Can., 1970-78; co-owner, chmn., sec. Girling Wade Mktg. Inc., Toronto, 1978—; pres., Fam-Mar, Inc., Newport Beach, Calif., 1980—. Served with Can. Army, 1949-55. Mem. Toronto Sales and Mktg. Execs. Clubs: Variety of Ontario, Cambridge, Royal Canadian Mil. Inst. Toronto. Office: 12 Sheppard St Suite 301 Toronto ON M5H 3A1 Canada

GIRVIN, RICHARD ALLEN, film co. exec.; b. Chgo., Feb. 10, 1926; s. Harry J. and Esther (Easter) G.; Mus.B., Chgo. Music Coll., 1950, Mus.M., 1954; D.F.A., Ga. Tchrs. Coll., 1954; m. Sharon Hillertz, June 9, 1968; children—Gregory, Kimberly, Scott. Instr. in music Bob Jones U., 1950-52; tchr. music Chgo. Pub. High Schs., 1954-56; dir. radio and TV, NBC, Chgo., 1956-57; asst. prodn. dir. Coronet Instructional Films, Chgo., 1957-62; producer, editor Gilbert Altschul Prodns., Chgo., 1962-64; free lance producer, writer, Chgo. and Hollywood, Calif., 1964-65; instr. Columbia Coll., 1970—; author screenplay Wine of Morning, 1957 (Cannes Film Festival award 1957); v.p. Zenith Cinema Service (now div. Dick Girvin Prodns.), Chgo., 1965-73, owner, 1973—, pres. Dick Girvin Prodns. Inc., Chgo., 1967—, owner numerous subsidiaries including Timbrewood Prodn. Music, Timbrewood Pub., Sharilda Pub., Zenith Camera, Typing Unltd., Phase 5 Prodns., db Studios. Served to lt. USAAF, 1943-45. Recipient Indsl. Arts award, 1964, 74, Cine Golden Eagle award USIA, 1964, 67, Atlanta Silver award, 1971, Freedom's Found. award, 1961. Fellow Brit. Internat. Audio Soc.; mem. Audio Engring. Soc., Nat. Assn. TV Arts and Scis., Nat. Assn. Rec. Arts and Scis., Soc. Motion Picture Technicians and Engrs., Aircraft Owners and Pilots Assn., Internat. Brotherhood Magicians. Composer: The Seventh Psalm, 1953; composer film scores: Macbeth, 1951, Pound of Flesh, 1952; composer music for Wild Kingdom TV show, 1973—, also composer indsl. and ednl. film scores, film library program music scores. Office: 676 N LaSalle St Chicago IL 60610

GITTELSON, BERNARD, pub. relations cons., writer, columnist, lectr.; b. N.Y.C., June 13, 1918; s. Sam and Gussie (Lefand) G.; B.A., St. Johns U., 1939; m. Rosalind Weinstein, Mar. 1, 1945; children—Louise Barbara, Steven Henry. Cons. on race relations N.Y. State War Council, 1939-41; cons. N.Y. Com. on Industry & Labor Relations, 1941-42; dir. N.Y. State Legis. Com. Discrimination, 1943-45; asso. coordinator Com. Community Inter-relations, 1945-46; pub. relations counselor European Common Market; pres. The Roy Bernard Co., Inc., 1946-64, chmn. Roy Bernard Co., Ltd. (London), 1955-64; dir. Time Pattern Research Inst., N.Y.C., 1965-74; pres. Biorhythm Computers Inc., N.Y.C., 1975—, Med. News Service, Inc.; pub. Biorhythm Newsletter, Med. Hot Line. Recipient Order Merit, Fed. Republic Germany. Mem. Authors Guild, Am. Soc. Journalists and Authors, Internat. Biorhythm Research Assn., Institut Ely du Biorhythme, Instituto de Biopscioenergetica de la Argentina. Author: Biorhythm A Personal Science; Biorhythm Sports Forecasting; syndicated columnist Your Personal Biorhythm. Home: 96 Division Ave Summit NJ 07901 Office: 119 W 57th St New York NY 10019

GITTLEMAN, ALLAN MORRIS, investment co. exec.; b. Providence, June 23, 1942; s. Sidney Allan and Dorothy Foster (Green) G.; B.S., Northeastern U., 1968; grad. Brown U., 1964; m. Ellen Kaplan, May 28, 1966; children—Danielle, Rachel. Vice pres. Michael Investment Co., Providence, 1966-68, pres., 1968—; v.p. F.L. Putnam & Co., Inc., Boston, 1973—; chmn. bd. Gen. Magnaplate Co., Linden, N.J., 1970-71; pres. Foster, Brown & Ballou, Inc., Providence, 1974—. Mem. exec. com. Nat. Jewish Hosp., Denver; mem. R.I. Public Expenditure Council. Mem. Am. Numis. Assn., Newcomen Soc., Nat., Boston securities traders assns., Soc. Paper Money Collectors, Bond and Share Soc., Providence Soc. Fin. Analysts. Author: Scripophily-A Guide to Collecting Antique Stock and Bond Certificates, 1980. Office: 7 Trappers Ln East Greenwich RI 02818

GITTLEMAN, MORRIS, cons. metallurgist; b. Zhidkovitz, Minsk, Russia, Nov. 2, 1912; s. Louis and Ida (Gorodietsky) G.; came to U.S., 1920, naturalized; B.S. cum laude, Bklyn. Coll., 1934; postgrad. Poly. Inst. Bklyn., 1946-47; m. Clara Konefsky, Apr. 7, 1937; children—Arthur Paul, Michael Jay. Metall. engr. N.Y. Naval Shipyard, 1942-47; chief metallurgist, chemist Pacific Cast Iron Pipe & Fitting Co., South Gate, Calif., 1948-54, tech. mgr., 1954-57, tech. and prodn. mgr., 1957-58; cons. Valley Brass, Inc., El Monte, Calif., 1958-61, Vulcan Foundry, Ltd., Haifa, Israel, 1958-65, Anaheim Foundry Co. (Calif.), 1958-63, Hollywood Alloy Casting Co. (Calif.), 1960-70, Spartan Casting Co., El Monte, 1961-62; Overton Foundry, South Gate, Calif., 1962-70, cons., gen. mgr., 1970-71; cons. Familian Pipe & Supply Co., Van Nuys, Calif., 1962-72, Comml. Enameling Co., Los Angeles, 1963-75, Universal Cast Iron Mfg. Co., South Gate, Calif., 1965-71; pres. MG Coupling Co., 1972, 79—; instr. physics Los Angeles Harbor Coll., 1958-59; instr. chemistry Western States Coll. Engring., Inglewood, Calif., 1961-68. Registered profl. engr., Calif. Mem. Am. Foundrymen's Soc., AAAS, Am. Soc. Metals, Internat. Solar Energy Soc., Am. Solar Energy Soc., N.Y. Acad. Scis. Contbr. to tech. jours. Inventor MG coupling. Home: 8232 Blackburn Ave Los Angeles CA 90048 Office: 17044 Montanero St Carson CA 90746

GITTLIN, A. SAM, industrialist, banker; b. Newark, Nov. 21, 1913; s. Benjamin and Ethel (Bernstein) G.; B.C.S., Rutgers U., 1938; m. Fay Lerner, Sept. 18, 1938; children—Carol (Mrs. Alan H. Franklin), Regina (Mrs. Peter Gross), Bruce David, Steven Robert. Partner, Gittlin Cos. Inc. (formerly Gittlin Bag Co.), Fairfield, N.J., 1935-40, v.p., dir., 1954—, chmn., 1963—; v.p., dir. Abbey Record Mfg. Co.,

Newark, 1958-60; partner Benjamin Mission Co., Los Angeles, 1960-64; chmn. Barrington Industries, N.Y.C., 1963-72; vice chmn., dir., chmn. exec. com. Falmouth Supply, Ltd., Montreal, Que., Can., Ascher Trading Corp., Newark, Aptex, Inc., Newark; vice chmn. bd. Peninsula Savs. and Loan Assn., San Mateo and San Francisco, 1964-67, chmn., 1967-68; chmn. First Peninsula Cal. Corp., N.Y.C., 1964-68; chmn. Pines Shirt & Pajama Co., N.Y.C., 1960—, Pottsville Shirt & Pajama Co. (Pa), 1960—, Wall-co Imperial, Miami, 1965—, Levin & Hecht, Inc., N.Y.C., 1966-72, Wallco of San Juan (P.R.), Brunswick Shirt Co., N.Y.C., 1966-72, Fleetline Industries, Garland, N.C., 1966-72, All State Auto Leasing & Rental Corp., Beverly Hills, Calif., 1968-72, Packaging Ltd., Newark, 1970-76, Kans. Plastics, Inc., Garden City, 1970—, Bob Cushman Distbrs., Inc., Phoenix, 1972—, Wallpaper Supermarkets, Phoenix, 1976-80, Wallco Internat., Inc., Miami, 1976, Overwrap Equipment Corp., Fairfield, 1978—; chmn., treas. Packaging Products & Design Co. (now PPD Corp.), Newark and Glendale, Calif., 1959-71, chmn. exec. com., treas., 1972—; chmn. bd., treas. Bob Cushman Painting & Decorating Co. (now Wallco West), Phoenix, 1972—; pres. Covington Funding Co., N.Y.C., 1963—; treas., dir. Flex Pak Industries, Inc., Atlanta, 1973-76, Ploy Plax Films, Inc., Santa Ana, Calif., 1973-76; sec., chmn. exec. com. Zins Wallcoverings, Newark; partner Benjamin Co., N.Y.C., Laurel Assos. (Md.), Seaboard Realty Assos., Miami, 1980—, GHG Realty Assos., N.Y.C., 1980; partner, investors cons. Mission Pack, Inc., Los Angeles; dir. Harris Paint & Wall Covering Super Marts, Miami, Morgan Hill Mfg. Co., Reading, Pa.; dir., financial cons. Ramada Inns, Phoenix, Realty Equities Corp. N.Y., N.Y.C. Mem. com. to review dept. of banking and ins. N.J. Commn. on Efficiency and Economy in State Govt., 1967—. Chmn. N.C. Com. B'nai B'rith, 1940; treas. N.C. Fedn. B'nai B'rith Lodges, 1941-43, v.p., 1943-44, pres., 1944-47. Trustee BAMA Master Retirement program, Benjamin Gittlin Charity Found., Newark, Rutgers U. Hillel Found.; bd. visitors Franklin and Marshall U. Jewish (trustee, pres. Onai Abraham, Livingston, N.J.). Club: Greenbrook Country (Caldwell, N.J.). Home: 59 Glenview Rd South Orange NJ 07079 Office: 60 E 42d St New York NY 10165

GIUDICE, ANGELO RAPHAEL, fin. planning cons.; b. Balt., Oct. 28, 1940; s. Raphael angelo and Mamie (Armetta) G.; B.S., U. Md., 1963; J.D., U. Balt., 1973; m. Barbara Ann Bejvan, Apr. 19, 1968; children—Michael, Monica. Asso. broker Poor Bowen Bartlett & Kennedy, Inc., Balt., 1964-68; cons. Modern Am. Co., Balt., 1968-71; pres. Fringe Benefits, Inc., Balt., 1971—, Profl. Pension Planners, Balt., 1978—; dir., organizer 1st Women's Bank Md. Trustee, Md. Kidney Found., 1978—. Served with Army N.G., 1963-64. Mem. Am. Soc. Pension Actuaries, Estate Planners Council, Five Million Dollar Forum, Internat. Found. Employee Benefit Plans, Million Dollar Round Table, Nat. Assn. Securities Dealers, Purdue U. Pension and Profit Sharing Inst., Practising Law Inst. Home: 1 Old Sound Rd Joppa MD 21085 Office: 204 E Joppa Rd Penthouse One Baltimore MD 21204

GIUFFRIDA, RICHARD THOMAS, carpet mfg. co. exec.; b. N.Y.C., Jan. 8, 1943; s. Nickloas S. and Faye I.G.; student Rockland Community Coll., 1965-67; m. Sheila Screder, Sept. 30, 1966; children—Margaret, Elizabeth. With Ekisiman's Carpets, Nanuet, N.Y., 1965-70; salesman Bigelow Carpets, N.Y.C., 1970-72, mgr., 1972-75; v.p. sales Central div. Coronet Industries, Southfield, Mich., 1975—. Served with USAF, 1961-65. Mem. Detroit Floor Covering Club. Republican. Home: 1952 Portlock Ave Union Lake MI 48085 Office: Coronet Industries 18280 W 10 Mile Rd Southfield MI 48075

GIUSTI, GEORGE WILLIAM, bedding co. exec.; b. San Mateo, Calif., July 13, 1953; s. George Dominic and Marie Emma (Heppler) G.; B.S., San Francisco State U., 1975; m. Margot Marie Fourie, Sept. 11, 1976. Vice pres. King Koil Sleep Products, Emeryville, Calif., 1975—. Mem. Nat. Assn. Bedding Mfrs., Nat. Assn. Accts. Republican. Roman Catholic. Home: 215 Lassen Dr San Bruno CA 94066 Office: 1327 Park Ave Emeryville CA 94608

GIUSTI, GINO PAUL, natural resources co. exec.; b. New Kensington, Pa., May 31, 1927; s. Peter Paul and Rose (Bonadio) G.; B.S. in Chem. Engring., U. Pitts., 1949, M.S., 1953, Ph.D. in Bus. and Econs., 1959; m. Ruth Marie Greblunas, May 4, 1957; children—Paul, Susan, Patricia, John, Christopher. Texasgulf research fellow Mellon Inst. Indsl. Research, Pitts., 1948-57; asst. to pres. Texasgulf Inc., Stamford, Conn., 1958-61, mgr. market research, 1962-64, corp. personnel mgr., 1965-71, v.p. employee relations and adminstr., 1972-77, v.p. agrl. chems. div., 1978-79, sr. v.p., 1979; pres. Texasgulf Chems. Co., 1979; pres., chief operating officer Texasgulf Inc., 1979—, also dir. Texasgulf Can. Ltd.; dir. Sulphur Export Corp., Union Trust Co., N.E. Bancorp, Inc., Phosphate Chems. Export Corp. Mem. metals and minerals unit Nat. Def. Exec. Res., Dept. Interior, 1962—; bd. dirs. Potash and Phosphate Inst., Fertilizer Inst.; trustee Stamford Hosp. Served with USAAF, 1945-46. Registered profl. engr., Pa. Mem. Am. Chem. Soc., Am. Econs. Assn., Am. Inst. Chem. Engrs., Chem. Market Research Assn., Soc. Mining Engrs., AIME, Newcomen Soc. N. Am. Roman Catholic. Clubs: Woodway Country, Landmark, Sky. Office: Texasgulf Inc High Ridge Park Stamford CT 06904

GJERTSEN, EDWARD WALTER, design cons. co. exec.; b. Chgo., Nov. 19, 1941; s. Edward John and Berniece (Branfalt) G.; M.B.A., U. Chgo., 1973; m. Carol J. Kortas, Dec. 29, 1962; children—Joyce, Janice, Edward Walter. Personnel supr. Household Fin. Corp., Chgo., 1963-68; v.p. ISD Inc., Chgo., 1969-77; pres. Interiors Inc., Chgo., 1977—; dir. Planning Systems, Inc., Chgo. Commr., Met. Sanitary Dist. Greater Chgo., 1979—. Served with U.S. Army, 1960-63. Mem. Ill. State C. of C., Chgo. Assn. Commerce and Industry. Republican. Club: Lions (pres.). Home: 658 S Elm St Palatine IL 60067 Office: 224 S Michigan Ave Chicago IL 60604

GLADSTEIN, MICHAEL FALK, distbn. cos. exec.; b. McAlester, Okla., Jan. 27, 1935; s. Irvin A. and Margaret (Falk) G.; B.B.A., U. Okla., 1957; m. Bobett Beatus, Dec. 23, 1956 (div. Oct. 1980); children—Mark Beatus, Margaret Rose. Pres., Economy Housing Developers, McAlester, 1968—; v.p., sec. Welding Supplies, Inc., McAlester, 1964—, also dir.; v.p., sec. Gladstein Co. and Gladstein Co. of Ada, Inc., McAlester, 1966-72, pres., 1972—, also dir.; v.p., sec. Out Products, Inc., Hominey, Okla., 1970-73, also dir.; mng. partner Gladco Devel., McAlester, 1966—; pres. M & D Devel. Co., Tulsa, 1966-70; pres. the Gladstein Co. of Shawnee (Okla.), 1978—; partner M & E, E & M. Treas., Citizens for Better McAlester; active United Fund; chmn. active Indian Nations council Boy Scouts Am.; chmn. Okla. Aeros. Commn.; mem. Interstate Commn. Airport Authority; mem. McAlester Mayor's Com. for Handicapped Workers; trustee Okla. Trauma Research Com.; mem. Task Force Com. City of McAlester, 1977-78. Mem. Am. Supply Assn., Nat. Assn. Wholesale Distbrs., McAlester Jaycees (pres., Leadership award), McAlester C. of C. Jewish religion. Clubs: Navy League, McAlester Country, Elks, Okla. Alumni of Pittsburg County (dir.). Home: 1837 S 14th St McAlester OK 74501 Office: 403-25 S Main St McAlester OK 74501

GLASCOCK, RAY D., engring. services co. exec., office furniture and equipment co. exec.; b. Auxausse, Mo., Apr. 1, 1922; s. Joseph Ewing and Mildred Hazel (Thomas) G.; B.S., U. Ill., 1949, M.S., 1950; m. Norma E. Howard, Jan. 17, 1941; 1 dau., Barbara Joan Glascock Bourland; m. 2d, Dorothy E. Pullen, Sept. 4, 1954; 1 son, Donald Ray; stepchildren—Arthur Richard Pullen, Charles A. Pullen; m. 3d, Martha G. Greene, Nov. 18, 1977; stepchildren—Larri Anne Greene, William K. Greene. Group leader Norair div. Northrop Corp., Hawthorne, Calif., 1951-59; sec. head communications div. Hughes Aircraft Co., Los Angeles, 1959-63; sect. head aeronutronic div. Philco Ford Corp., Newport Beach, Calif., 1964-65; owner/mgr. Engring. Corp. of Am.-Orange County div., Anaheim, Calif., 1966—, Glascock Enterprises, Anaheim, 1976—. Served with U.S. Maritime Service, 1943-46. Mem. IEEE, Eta Kappa Nu. Home: 111 S Broadview St Anaheim CA 92804 Office: 210-A/B N Crescent Way Anaheim CA 92801

GLASE, PAGE BENTLY, mfg. co. exec.; b. Elkhart, Ind., Sept. 10, 1925; s. Paul William and Georgia E. (Page) G.; B.A., DePauw U., 1950; m. Joan Dorothy Wolter, July 23, 1949; children—Page Kevin, Thomas Bently, Scott Richard. Prodn. control mgr. U.S. Rubber Co., Mishawaka, Ind., 1950-58, asst. supt., 1958-60; inventory control mgr. Clark Equipment Co., Buchanan, Mich., 1960-70, dir. purchasing and transp., 1970—, corp. v.p., 1973—; instr. Ind. U., South Bend, 1953-54, 56. Served with USN, 1943-46. Mem. Nat. Assn. Purchasing Mgrs., Nat. Assn. Mfrs., Nat. Mgmt. Assn., Machinery and Allied Products Inst. Purchasing Council. Episcopalian. Clubs: Orchard Hills Country, Elks. Home: 3510 E Sorin St South Bend IN 46615 Office: Clark Circle Dr Buchanan MI 49107

GLASER, ALVIN mfg. co. exec.; b. B. New Bedford, Mass., Jan. 8, 1932; s. Morris and Jennie (Brody) G.; student pub. schs. New Bedford; m. Rosalyn S.F. Clasky, Jan. 20, 1963; children—Iris, Linda, Marjorie, Jeffrey. Mgr., Morris Glaser Glass Co., New Bedford, 1949—; treas. Glaser Inc., 1964—; corporator New Bedford Five Cents Savs. Bank. Mem. Dartmouth (Mass.) Youth Commn. Mem. Nat. Glass Dealers Assn., New Bedford C. of C. Clubs: Masons, Order Eastern Star, Shriners, B'nai B'rith, Moose. Home: 2 Ann Ave North Dartmouth MA 02747 Office: 1265 Purchase St New Bedford MA 02740

GLASGOW, CLARENCE OGDEN, oil equipment mfg. co. exec.; b. Fairview, Okla., Sept. 26, 1908; s. Arthur W. and Floy (McCowan) G.; B.S. in Mech. Engring., Okla. State U.; 19—; m. Elizabeth McClung, Feb. 15, 1938; children—Edsel, Melvin. Vice pres., dir. engring. CE Natco Co., Tulsa, 1961—; pres., owner Custom Engring. & Mfg. Corp., Tulsa, 1961—. Owner, Spring Valley Ranch, Locust Grove, Okla., 1946—; dir. Tulsa Rubber Co., 1956—. Bd. regents Oral Roberts U., 1968-74. Registered profl. engr., Okla. Mem. Am. Soc. Mech. Engrs., Nat. Soc. Profl. Engrs., Okla. Inventers' Congress, Okla. Soc. Profl. Engrs., Phi Kappa Phi, Sigma Tau, Pi Tau Sigma, Acacia. Republican. Methodist. Clubs: Petroleum, Manufacturing (Tulsa). Patentee in field. Home: 2620 S Yorktown St Tulsa OK 74114 Office: Box 50391 Tulsa OK 74150

GLASMANN, ROBERT VERN, printing co. exec.; b. Ogden, Utah, Aug. 9, 1925; s. William Wiese and Juanita Richards G.; student Weber State Coll., 1946-48; A.A., U. Calif., 1949; m. LaRue Nielsen, Nov. 14, 1949 (div.); children—Robert V., Jill Glasmann, Kim, Kelly. Personnel specialist U.S. Air Force, 1950-59; advt. salesman Ogden Standard-Examiner, 1959-60; mgr., chief exec. officer Western Arts Photoengravers Co., Ogden, Utah, 1961—; dir. Standard Corp., Standards Bldgs., Inc., Examiner Realty Co., Standard Examiner Pub. Co., Orpheum Corp. Served with USNR, 1943-46. Decorated Purple Heart. Mem. Western States Photoplatemakers (dir.), Internat. Assn. Photoplatemakers, Printing Platemakers Assn. Republican. Mormon. Clubs: Ogden Advt. (pres.), Ogden Exchange, Weber (pres. elect), Ogden Golf and Country, Elks. Home: 474 South 40 East Farmington UT 84025 Office: 2538 Washington Blvd Ogden UT 84401

GLASS, ARTHUR GENE, savs. and loan co. exec.; b. Schulenburg, Tex., Nov. 20, 1944; s. John H. and Pearlie M. (Warren) G.; B.B.A., Tex. So. U., 1971. Mgmt. trainee Western Savs. & Loan Assn., Phoenix, 1971-72, asst. br. mgr. fin. center office, 1972, br. mgr., 1972-75; br. mgr., v.p. San Diego Fed. Savs. & Loan Assn., 1975—. Bd. dirs. William J. Oakes br. Boys' Club of San Diego, Merit award, 1976; community rep. parents policy council San Diego Headstart; active United Way, Merit award, 1976. Recipient Merit awards United Way of Tempe (Ariz.), 1972, 73, 74, Community Service award NAACP, 1977. Mem. Am. Mgmt. Assn., NAACP (treas. 1977-78, 3d v.p. and chmn. Freedom Fund 1979-80, 2d v.p. and chmn. Freedom Fund 1981-82), Savs. and Loan Inst. of Fin. Edn. (chpt. dir.). Clubs: Rotary of SE San Diego (award, sec. 1977-78), Variety of San Diego. Home: 4600 Lamont 4-220 San Diego CA 92109 Office: 3511 National Ave San Diego CA 92113

GLASS, CHARLES LEE, airline exec.; b. Jacksonville, Fla., Dec. 15, 1939; s. Charles E. and Martha S. (Peters) G.; A.B., Duke U., 1961; m. Wanda K. Galbreath, June 24, 1961; children—Martha, Stephen, Deborah. Asst. treas. Eastern Air Lines, N.Y.C., 1970-72, v.p. investor relations, Miami, Fla., 1972-76, asst. treas., 1976-77, v.p., treas., 1977—. C.P.A., N.C. Mem. Am. Inst. C.P.A.'s, Fin. Execs. Inst., Phi Beta Kappa. Baptist. Office: Eastern Air Lines Inc Miami Internat Airport Miami FL 33148

GLASS, GARRETT RICHARD, banker; b. Chgo., Sept. 17, 1950; s. George A. and Marianne (Fiedler) G.; B.A., Northwestern U., 1972, M.B.A., 1974. Asst mgr., spl. asst. to dept. head internat. banking dept. 1st Nat. Bank Chgo., 1974-76, asst. mgr. Singapore br., 1977-78; asst. mgr. First Chgo. Internat., Los Angeles, 1978, asst. v.p. and mgr. fgn. exchange mktg. First Chgo. Internat. Banking Corp., N.Y.C., 1978-80, v.p. and mgr. Latin Am. and Asian central bank Eurocurrency and fgn. exchange mktg., 1980—. Mem. Northwestern Alumni Assn. N.Y., Mensa. Democrat. Roman Catholic. Home: 58 W 58 St New York NY 10019 Office: 767 Fifth Ave New York NY 10153

GLASS, ROBERT JAMES, apparel mfg. co. exec.; b. Detroit, July 3, 1934; s. Roy Burns and Lois Margaret (Soldal) G.; B.S., Central Mich. U., 1956; postgrad. U. Detroit, 1960; m. Barbara Wisser, May 22, 1971; children—Robert, Kirk, Gavin, Darin, Arin. Sales mgr. Cosmetic div. Chesebrough Ponds, Inc., N.Y.C., 1961-69; region mgr. Philip Morris U.S.A., N.Y.C., 1969-72; sr. v.p. No Nonsense Fashions div. Kayser Roth, N.Y.C., 1972-79; pres. Kayser Roth Branded Products, Greensboro, N.C., 1979—. Served with arty. U.S. Army, 1957-59. Recipient cert. Pres.'s Assn., 1980. Mem. Nat. Assn. Chain Drug Stores, Food Mktg. Inst., Sigma Tau Gamma. Republican. Club: Sedgefield Country. Home: 4602 Trailwood Dr Greensboro NC 27407 Office: PO Box 7057 Greensboro NC 27407

GLASS, THOMAS REAKIRT, newspaper editor and pub.; b. Lynchburg, Va., May 13, 1928; s. Carter and Ria (Thomas) G.; student Va. Mil. Inst., 1945-46; B.A. in Journalism, Washington and Lee U., 1949; m. Julia Marguerite Thomason, Sept. 29, 1951; children—Julia Eastham, Mary Byrd, Laura Binford, Blair Thomas. Pub., News and Daily Advance, Lynchburg, 1977—; pres. Carter Glass & Sons, Pubs., 1977-79; v.p., exec. editor, asso. pub. Carter Glass Newspapers, Inc., 1979—; dir. Fidelity Nat. Bank. Mem. Va. Hwy. Commn., 1969-79; mem. Va. State Bd. Community Colls., 1966-68, vice chmn., 1968; mem. Va. Ho. of Dels., 1958-66; bd. dirs. Salvation Army; trustee Lynchburg Coll., 1972—. Served to 1st lt. USAF, 1951-53; Korea. Mem. So. Newspaper Pubs. Assn. (dir. 1975-79), Va. Press Assn. (treas. 1955-57), Lynchburg Hist. Soc., Ams. for Effective Law Enforcement (adv. com. Va. chpt. 1971—), Sigma Delta Chi, Phi Delta. Episcopalian. Clubs: Masons, Shriners, Elks, Lions, Odd Fellows; Commonwealth (Richmond), Boonsboro Country (Lynchburg). Home: 3130 Landon St Lynchburg VA 24503 Office: PO Box 10129 Lynchburg VA 24506

GLASSCOCK, JAMES CLIFFORD, fence co. exec.; b. Carl Junction, Mo., Aug. 21, 1919; s. James A. and Goldie M. (Cooley) G.; grad. Ft. Smith (Ark.) Jr. Coll., 1952; B.S. in Indsl. Engring., U. Ark., 1954; m. Bette Geneva Allen, July 2, 1939; children—Philip Allen, Nancy Jane. Heavy equipment operator Mississippi Valley Constrn. & Engring. Co., Fort Smith, 1951; salesman United Fence Co., Inc., Fort Smith, 1951-54, mgr., 1954-60, pres., chmn., gen. mgr., 1960—; owner Glasscock Real Estate Rentals. Served with USN, 1941-51. Mem. Internat. Fence Industry Assn. (dir. 1967-76, pres. 1974, Ambassador award 1972, Service award 1973), ASTM, Ret. Mil. Assn. Republican. Methodist. Home: 3200 S Thompson St Springdale AR 72766 Office: 2110 N O St Fort Smith AR 72901

GLASSCOCK, MICHAEL EMMANUEL, real estate broker, cons.; b. N.Y.C., Feb. 26, 1913; s. Michael Emmanuel and Rosa Marie (Valerio) G.; B.S. in Speech, LL.B., Cumberland U., 1933; M.B.A., Calif. Western U., 1976, Ph.D., 1978; m. Martina Taylor, Feb. 18, 1932; children—Michael E. III, Patrick T. Owner, operator ranch, Utopia, Tex., 1933-42; owner Glasscock Aviation and Glasscock Constrn., Corpus Christi, Tex., 1945-49; mktg. researcher Glasscock Assocs., San Antonio and Dallas, 1949-55; real estate investor, cons., fin. advisor, 1955-63; investor, cons., fin. advisor, realtor, 1963—; pres. Marmont Investment Properties; faculty West Los Angeles Coll., 1976-78; now instr. real estate appraisal, continuing edn. div. U. So. Calif.; advisor, cons. liaison Smith County Bank, Carthage, Tenn.; appraiser banks, corps. and individuals. Pres., Sabinal (Tex.) Jr. C. of C., 1938; chmn. aviation com. Corpus Christi (Tex.) C. of C.; aide de Camp, Gov. of Tenn., 1965. Served to comdr., USN, 1942-45. Recipient Certificate of Appreciation, Los Angeles Jr. C. of C., 1978; certified mortgage underwriter, rev. appraiser, fine arts appraiser, constrn. estimator; lic. real estate broker, Tex. Mem. Nat. Calif. assns. realtors, Los Angeles, Beverly Hills bd. realtors, Am. Assn. Mortgage Underwriters, Real Estate Certificate Inst. (chmn. 17th dist. 1977, chmn. dist. investment div.), 1977-78), Calif. Inst. Real Estate (pres.), Calif. Assn. Real Estate Tchrs., Nat. Inst. Investment Seminars (pres.), Am. Soc. Profl. Estimators, Am. Soc. Fine Arts Appraisers, Nat. Assn. Review Appraisers, Internat. Assn. Fin. Planners, U.S. Navy League (life), Sigma Delta Kappa. Roman Catholic. Clubs: Athletic (Los Angeles); Rotary (pub. relation chmn., chpt. dir.) (West Hollywood, Calif.). Author: Real Estate Investments; Real Estate—The Last Brass Ring. Contbributing editor, Apt. Owner/Builder mag., 1974-78. Home and Office: 2622 29th St Santa Monica CA 90405

GLASSER, JAMES JAY, leasing co. exec.; b. Chgo., June 5, 1934; s. Daniel D. and Sylvia G. Glasser; A.B., Yale, 1955; J.D., Harvard, 1958; m. Louise D. Rosenthal, Apr. 19, 1964; children—Mary, Emily, Daniel. Admitted to Ill. bar, 1958; asst. states atty. Cook County, Ill., 1958-61; mem. exec. staff GATX Corp., Chgo., 1961-69, pres. and chief operating officer, 1974-78, chmn. bd. and chief exec. officer, 1978—; gen. mgr. Infilco Products Co., 1969-70; v.p. GATX Leasing Corp., San Francisco, 1970-71, pres., 1971-74; dir. Harris Bankcorp, Inc., Harris Trust and Savs. Bank, GATX Corp., Mut. Trust Life Ins. Co. Trustee, Michael Reese Hosp. and Med. Center, Chgo. Zool. Soc.; bd. dirs. Northwestern Meml. Hosp.; governing life mem. Art Inst. Chgo.; governing mem. Glenwood Sch. for Boys; mem. Chgo. Crime Commn. Mem. Chgo. Assn. of Commerce and Industry (dir.), Econ. Club Chgo., Chi Psi. Clubs: Casino, Chicago, Racquet, Tavern (Chgo.); Lake Shore Country (Glencoe, Ill.); Onwentsia, Winter (Lake Forest, Ill.). Home: 644 E Spruce Ave Lake Forest IL 60045 Office: 120 S Riverside Plaza Chicago IL 60606

GLASSER, JOSEPH, co. exec.; b. Phila., May 17, 1925; B.S. in Econs., U. Pa., 1947, M.B.A., 1948. Examiner, NLRB, Phila., 1949-51; internal mgmt. cons. Nat. Indsl. Laundries, N.J., 1953-54; mem. faculty Sch. Bus., U. Conn., Storrs, 1955—; pres. Eljen Devel. Corp., Storrs, 1970—. Mediator Conn. Bd. Edn.; fact finder Conn. Bd. Mediation; arbitrator Am. Arbitration Assn., Fed. Mediation and Conciliation Service, Nat. Mediation Bd.; rev. officer FAA, Nat. Def. Exec. Res., Office of Pres. U.S. Served with AC, U.S. Army, 1943-45, USAF, 1951-52, lt. col. Res. Decorated Air medal with 4 oak leaf clusters, Air Force commendation medal. Mem. Indsl. Relations Research Assn., Am. Arbitration Assn., Soc. Profls. in Dispute Resolution. Author: Fundamentals of Applied Industrial Management, 1975; also numerous articles. Office: 15 Westwood Rd Storrs CT 06268

GLASSMAN, MARVIN, mfg. co. exec.; b. N.Y.C., May 20, 1930; s. Aaron Harry and Goldie (Haberman) G.; student CCNY, 1949-51; m. Sheila B. Young, Oct. 23, 1955; children—Lawrence Ira, Lisa Merril. Founder, chief exec. officer Marglo Packaging Corp., Plainview, N.Y., 1961—; salesman Waldbaum & Cipes, N.Y.C., 1953-55; product mgr., salesman Kleartone Trans. Product Co., Westbury, N.Y., 1955-61. Served with U.S. Army, 1951-53. Decorated Bronze Star. Mem. Flexographic Tech. Assn. Club: K.P. (dep. grand chancellor 1978-79; Pythian of Year, N.Y. State 1980). Office: 1522 Old Country Rd Plainview NY 11803

GLATZ, AUGUST WILLIAM, food brokerage exec.; b. Bloomington, Ill., Sept. 24, 1923; s. August F. and Myrtle L. (Cullers) G.; student Kemper Mil. Coll., 1940-42; m. Dale L. Lacy, Jan. 13, 1946; children—Jay A., Debora L., Janet S. Salesman, Glatz Bros., Inc., Peoria, Ill., 1946-58, pres., 1962—; v.p., sec., treas. Chgo. Mktg. and Merchandisers, Inc., Riverside, Ill.; nat. sales mgr. J.L. Read Foods, Streator, Ill., 1958-62. Dir., Gray Y Clubs YMCA, 1947-50; elder 1st Presbyterian Ch., Peoria. Served with USNR, 1943-46; PTO. Mem. Ill. Food Brokers Assn. (pres. 1948-58), Buyers Sellers Club (sec. treas. 1949-55), Nat. Food Brokers Assn. Republican. Home: 5913 Roxbury Ln Peoria IL 61614 Office: 826 SW Adams St Peoria IL 61602

GLAUBINGER, LAWRENCE DAVID, textile co. exec.; b. Newark, Nov. 26, 1925; s. Samuel I. and Pauline (Sandler) G.; B.S. with honors, Ind. U., 1949; M.B.A., Columbia U., 1977; m. Lucienne Lefebvre, Nov. 11, 1967. Adminstrv. asst. to pres. Ronson Inc., Newark, 1949-51; mdse. mgr. United Mchts., N.Y.C., 1951-65; v.p. Marietta Silk Mills (Pa.), 1965-66; pres., chief exec. officer Channel Textile Co. Inc., Bradford, Vt., 1966-75; chmn. bd., chief exec. officer Stern & Stern Textiles Inc., N.Y.C., 1977—, also dir.; pres. Lawrence Cons. Inc., Hallandale, Fla., 1977—; dir. Lawrence Cons. Inc., Leucadia Nat. Corp., Leucadia, Inc. Served with USCGR, 1943-46. Mem. Hoosier Hundred, Ind. U. Dean's Assos., Columbia U. Bus. Assos., Am. Arbitration Assn., Beta Gamma Sigma. Republican. Jewish. Clubs: Princeton (N.Y.); Green Brook Country, Sugarbush Country. Home: 401 Golden Isle Dr Hallandale FL 33009 Office: Stern & Stern Textiles Inc 1290 Ave of Americas New York NY 10104

GLAVIN, WILLIAM FRANCIS, bus. equipment co. exec.; b. Albany, N.Y., Mar. 29, 1932; s. John J. and Lillian C. (Slattery) G.; B.S. in Acctg., Coll. Holy Cross, 1953; M.B.A., U. Pa., 1955; m. Cecily Elizabeth McClatchy, Sept. 24, 1955; children—Joanne, William, Patricia, Christine, Thomas, Cecily, Richard. With IBM, 1955-68, corp. dir. market requirements planning, Armonk, N.Y., 1966-68, v.p. ops. subs. Services Bur. Corp., N.Y.C., 1968-70, pres. Xerox Data Systems, El Segundo, Calif., 1970-72, group v.p. Xerox Corp. and pres. bus. devel. group, Rochester, N.Y., 1972-74, mng. dir. and chief exec. officer Rank Xerox Ltd., London, 1974-80, exec. v.p. Xerox Corp., Stamford, Conn., 1980—. Trustee, Coll. Holy Cross, 1976—; mem. exec. council Wharton Grad. Sch. Bus., U. Pa., 1979; adv. trustee St. John Fisher Coll., Rochester, 1973. Mem. Computer and Bus. Equipment Mfrs. Assn. (dir.), Am. C. of C. (U.K.) (dir.). Clubs: Country of Rochester (N.Y.); Stanwich Country; Belle Haven Yacht. Office: Xerox Corp Stamford CT 06904

GLAZE, CLINTON DAVIS, real estate co. exec.; b. Athens, Ala., July 1, 1905; s. Clinton Dillard and Willie Julia (Davis) G.; student Auburn U., 1922-24; m. Helen Morgenthau, Sept. 18, 1948; 1 son, R. Jeff. Pres., So. Devel. Co. Inc., Mobile, Ala., 1946—, Colonial Devel. Corp., Sarasota, Fla., 1965, Fed. Devel. Co. Inc., Greenville, Miss., 1955-67, Fed. Land Co. Inc., Pensacola, Fla., 1956-68; mem. Ala. State Oil and Gas Bd., 1965-70. Served with USMC, 1942-44. Democrat. Clubs: Mobile Country, Dauphin Island Country, Bienville of Mobile. Home: 5358 Moffat Rd Mobile AL 36618 Office: PO Box 16348 Mobile AL 36616

GLAZER, GUILFORD, real estate exec.; b. Knoxville, Tenn., July 17, 1921; s. Aaron Oscar and Ida (Bressoff) G.; student George Washington U., 1938-39, U. Louisville, 1944-45; m. Francoise Wizenberg, Apr. 29, 1956 (div. 1964); children—Emerson Upton, Erika Jane; m. 2d, Diane Pregerson, Jan. 29, 1967. Organizer, Glazer Steel Corp., Knoxville, 1945, Sun Constrn. Corp., gen. contractors, 1949, Shelbourne Towers, Inc., 1949, Glencoe, Inc., 1953, Mayfair Village Corp., 1949, Colonial Village Corp., 1949, Troy Constrn. Corp., 1950, Barbizon Terrace, Inc., 1953, Jerome Corp., 1952, G. & K. Machinery Corp., 1952, Allied Constrn. Corp., 1954, Builders Investment, Inc., 1954, also Gen. Devel. Corp., 1954; developer, owner Del Amo Fashion Square, Torrance, Calif., builder Glencoe Homes, housing project, Oak Ridge, Tenn., 1953-54; developer, builder, propr. comml. dist. Downtown Oak Ridge, 1955—, Swifton Center, shopping center, Cin., 1956—; developer Park Shopping Center, Parkersburg, W.Va., 1956; now pres., chmn. Oak Ridge Properties, Inc., Tenn. Investment Corp., Champion, Inc., Downtown Mgmt. Corp., City Mgmt. Corp.; organizer Tenn. Western Corp., Knoxville, 1959; v.p. Del Amo Properties Co. Active with Great Smoky Mountain council Boy Scouts Am.; chmn. Knoxville Jewish Welfare, 1950; dir. Knoxville Community Chest, 1951, Jewish Community Center, 1952, Boys Club, 1952; organizer Aaron Glazer Charitable Found., 1953; dir. Inst. Cancer Research and Leukemia, Los Angeles; co-chmn. Bonds for Israel Com., Los Angeles; pres. Prime Minister's Club Israel Bonds, 1976; bd. govs. Tel Aviv U., bd. dirs. Inst. for Strategic Studies. Served as warrant officer USNR, 1942-45. Mem. Am. Legion, Jewish War Vets., Knoxville Symphony Soc. (past dir.), C. of C. (past dir.). Mason (32 deg.); mem. B'nai B'rith. Club: Hillcrest Country (Los Angeles). Office: 1901 Ave of Stars Los Angeles CA 90067

GLEASON, RICHARD DUNN, career cons.; b. Grand Rapids, Mich., Nov. 13, 1911; s. Raymond B. and Emma L. (Burdick) G.; A.B., U. Mich., 1933; m. Beverly J. Driscoll, July 14, 1939; children—Jeanne Louise, David Richard, Robert Edward. Sales div. Bissell Inc., Grand Rapids, 1934-41; asst. to pres. (sales, advt. and indsl. relations) Robert Reis & Co., N.Y.C., 1941-46; employee relations mgr. Gen. Electric Co. and affiliates, 1946-51; marketing mgr. Toledo Scale Co., 1951-52; v.p. W. L. Stensgaard & Asso., Chgo., 1952-54; chmn. Gleason Assos., Man-Marketing Services, Inc., 1954-76; cons., writer, lectr., 1978—. Mem. Alpha Kappa Psi. Rotarian. Author: The Answer to Your Job Problems—Plan Your Career by Objectives. Home: 1314 N Illinois Ave Arlington Heights IL 60004

GLEIBER, STUART ANDER, lumber mfr.; b. Bklyn., July 20, 1942; s. Ira and Anita Jean (Ander) G.; B.B.A., N.Y.U., 1964; m. Jill Ann Fairberg, Aug. 30, 1964; children—Joshua Daniel, Gary Stephen, Douglas Ross. Vice pres., sales dir. Am. Metal Spinning & Stamping Co., N.Y.C., 1964-70; pres., chmn. bd. Abbot & Abbot Box Corp., Long Island City, 1970—; also pres. Simglib Realty, Inc., Long Island City. cons. in packaging. Mem. Police Chiefs Assn. N.Y. State. Contbr. article to profl. jour. Home: 5 Kristi Ct Greenlawn NY 11740 Office: 28-31 Borden Ave Long Island City NY 11101

GLEN, WILLIAM B., foam mfg. co. exec.; b. Providence, Aug. 13, 1932; s. William F. and Rosanna (Boulay) G.; B.A. in Chemistry, Brown U., 1958; postgrad. Am. Mgmt. Assn., 1977; m. Joan B. Ellis, Apr. 11, 1964; children—Douglas S., Laura J. Chemist, C.P.L. Corp., East Providence, R.I., 1958-66; plant mgr., purchasing mgr. Engineered Yarns Inc., Coventry, R.I., 1966-75; gen. mgr. Oxford Mills, Compton, Calif., 1975-77; dir. purchasing United Foam Corp., Compton, 1977—; sec. urethane group U. So. Calif.; cons. in polyvinyl chloride and polyurethane, 1975—. Chmn. bldg. com. Calvin Presbyn. Ch., Cumberland, R.I., 1971-74, also elder. Served with C.E., U.S. Army, 1952-54. Mem. Am. Chem. Soc., Soc. Plastics Engrs., Bur. Urethane Info. (steering com.). Club: Masons (32 deg.). Patentee plastic printing plate. Home: 630 Green Acre Dr Fullerton CA 92635 Office: 2626 Vista Industria Compton CA 90221

GLENN, MELVILLE DAVIES, steel co. exec.; b. Toronto, Ont., Can., Oct. 3, 1917; s. William Ephram and Margaret (Davies) G.; student Malvern Coll., 1932-36; student Shaw Bus. Coll., 1937-38; m. Joan Constance Lutes, Oct. 15, 1949; children—Rosemary, Nancy, Kathryn. With Russelsteel, Downsview, Ont., 1939—, sales mgr., 1948-62, div. mgr., 1962-63, v.p. sales, 1964-65, v.p. ops., 1966-67, pres., 1968—; dir. Hugh Russel Inc., Downsview, 1962-80, v.p., 1970—. Served to capt., Royal Canadian Infantry, 1942-46. Mem. Canadian Steel Warehouse Assn. (v.p. 1960-65), Canadian Steel Service Center Inst. (dir. 1965-70, exec. com. 1965-80). Clubs: Mt. Stephen, Beaconsfield, Bd. Trade Country. Office: PO Box 5009 Downsview ON M3M 3B5 Canada

GLENN, NORMAN ROBERT, publisher, editor; b. Chicago Heights, Ill., Sept. 3, 1909; s. Max and Jennie (Wechsler) Goldman; student U. Chgo., 1927-30; m. Elaine Lee Couper, June 14, 1945 (dec.); children—Robin Day, Geoffrey Merrit; m. 2d, Roberta Hope Brewster, Oct. 27, 1972. Promotion mgr. radio sta. WLS, Chgo., 1932-36; bus. mgr. Broadcasting mag., Washington, 1937-43; pres., pub. Sponsor mag., N.Y.C., 1946-65; pres., pub., editor Media Decisions mag., N.Y.C., 1966—, also Encyclomedia, 6-vol. ann. media library; chmn. Decisions Publ. Inc., N.Y.C.; vis. lectr. Syracuse U., 1961; dir. ComCor Publs., Green Mountain Enterprises, Inc. Served from pvt. to 1st lt. USAAF, 1943-45. Decorated Army Commendation ribbon; recipient Polk award for distinguished journalism. Mem. Radio and TV Execs. Soc. (v.p.), Broadcast Pioneers, Mag. Pubs. Assn. Christian Scientist. Club: Yale. Author: (with Irving Settel) Television Advertising and Production, 1953. Home: Forest Rd North Haven NY 11963 Office: 342 Madison Ave New York City NY 10017

GLENNIE, DONALD MORGAN, seed co. exec.; b. Missouri Valley, Iowa, Mar. 23, 1923; s. James and Anne McPherson (Morgan) G.; B.A., U. Iowa, 1949; m. Gloria Agnes Satterlee, Sept. 1, 1946; children—Elizabeth Ann, Donald Lachlan, Mary Irene, James M. Retail sales mgr. Am. Field Seed Co., Chgo., 1949-56; regional sales mgr. Berry Seed Co., Clarinda, Iowa, 1956-62; v.p. sales Lowe Seed Co., Kankakee, Ill., 1962-71; v.p. mktg. Jacques Seed Co., Prescott, Wis., 1971—. Served with USNR, 1942-46. Mem. Am. Seed Trade Assn., Sales and Market Execs. Assn., Nat. Agrl. and Mktg. Assn., Internat. Platform Assn. (Gold Key award 1979), Am. Mktg. Assn., St. Andrew's Soc. Presbyterian (elder). Home: 407 Lake St Prescott WI 54021 Office: 720 St Croix Prescott WI 54021

GLIDEWELL, WILLIAM ELDRED, engring. co. exec.; b. Mineral Wells, Tex., Mar. 21, 1942; s. Eldred Davis and Ruth Ellen Glidewell; B.S. in M.E., Tex. Tech. Coll., 1965; M.B.A., So. Meth. U., 1971; m. Shirley Ann Sowards, June 5, 1967; children—Edward Blaine, Jennifer Lynn. Power service engr. Dallas Power & Light Co., 1965-70; project engr. McCally Co. Mech. Contractors, Dallas, 1970-73; dir. mktg. Olin-Am. Properties, Inc., Dallas, 1973-74; pres. William E. Glidewell Inc., Dallas, 1974-78, Thomas Systems, Inc., Ft. Worth, Tex., 1978—. Served with USNR, 1966-67. Registered profl. engr., Tex. Mem. ASME, Mensa. Presbyterian. Club: Inter-Tel. Office: PO Box 18629 Fort Worth TX 76118

GLOSSER, ALVIN M., business exec.; b. Johnstown, Pa., 1923. Pres., chief operating officer Glosser Bros., Inc., Johnstown. Office: Glosser Bros Inc Franklin and Locust Sts Johnstown PA 15901*

GLOVER, DALE DELOYD, purchasing exec.; b. Ithaca, N.Y., May 6, 1928; s. Fred M. and N. Carmileta (Hammond) G.; A.B., Columbia, 1949; M.B.A., N.Y.U., 1959; m. Betty Lou Kanouse, Jan. 22, 1955; children—Scott T., Charlene M. With Am. Sugar div. Amstar Corp., N.Y.C., 1949—, beginning as buyer, successively sr. buyer, asst. mgr. purchasing dept., mgr. purchasing dept., dir. purchasing, 1949-76, v.p. purchasing, 1976—. Served with Signal Corps, AUS, 1950-52. Nat. Assn. Purchasing Mgmt. (certified purchasing mgr.), Purchasing Mgmt. Assn. N.Y. (dir. 1977-79). Home: 69 Stevens Ave Old Bridge NJ 08857 Office: 1251 Ave of Americas New York City NY 10020

GLUCK, ADRIAN, computer co. exec.; b. Bucharest, Romania, Dec. 18, 1947; s. Jack and Sonya (Meyer) G.; B.Applied Sci., U. Toronto, 1970; M.B.A., 1971; m. Susan Terry Kelman, May 17, 1970; 1 child, Leslie. Computer analyst Imperial Oil Co. Ltd., Toronto, Ont., Can., 1970-73; computer dept. mgr. Reed Shaw Stenhouse, Toronto, 1973-75; v.p. Fortrex Systems Corp., Markham, Ont., 1975-76, pres., 1976—. Registered profl. engr. Mem. Assn. Profl. Engrs. Ont., Can. Info. Processing Soc. Office: 480 Denison St Markham ON L3R 1B9 Canada

GLUCKSMAN, LEWIS R., business exec. Chmn. operating com., mng. dir. Lehman Bros. Kuhn Loeb, Inc., N.Y.C. Office: Lehman Bros Kuhn Loeb Inc 1 William St New York NY 10004*

GO, HOWARD TIANG, mgmt. cons.; b. Solo, Indonesia, Nov. 15, 1933; s. Joe Gwan and Erkien (Oei) G.; Dr.Eng., U. Tech., Delft, Netherlands, 1958; Ph.D., Calif. Western U.; m. Mary Thouw, July 22, 1960; children—Joan Maychu, Brian Mingtao. Product assurance con. Westinghouse Space and Def. Center, Balt., 1963-66; dir. product assurance Fairchild Hiller Corp., Germantown, Md., 1966-68; pres. Interscience Mgmt. Corp., Columbia, Md., 1968-70; pres. Mgmt. Adv. Services, Inc., Columbia, Md., 1971—; asso. prof. econs. and fin. U. Md. Sch. Medicine, 1974—; mem. faculty Johns Hopkins U. Grad. Adminstrv. Sci. Program, 1970—. Mem. Am. Mgmt. Assn., Am. Soc. Quality Control, Soc. Advancement Mgmt., AAUP. Methodist. Contbr. articles to profl. jours. Office: Suite 216 10221 Wincopin Circle Columbia MD 21044

GOBAR, ALFRED JULIAN, econ. cons. co. asso. educator; b. Lucerne Valley, Calif., July 12, 1932; s. Julian Smith and Hilda (Millbank) G.; B.A. in Econs., Whittier Coll., 1953, M.A. in History, 1955; postgrad. Claremont Grad. Sch., 1953-54; Ph.D. in Econs., U. So. Calif., 1963; m. Sally Ann Randall, June 17, 1957; children—Wendy Lee, Curtis Julian, Joseph Julian. Asst. pres. Microdot Inc., Pasadena, 1953-57; regional sales mgr. Sutorbilt Corp., Los Angeles, 1957-59; market research asso. Beckman Instrument Inc., Fullerton, 1959-64; sr. marketing cons. Western Mgmt. Consultants Inc., Phoenix, Los Angeles, 1964-66; partner, prin., chmn. bd. Darley/Gobar Assos., Inc., 1966-73, also pres.; pres., chmn. bd. Alfred Gobar Assos., Inc., 1973—. Asst. prof. finance U. So. Calif., Los Angeles, 1963-64; asso. prof. bus. Calif. State U., Los Angeles, 1963-68, 70—; asso. prof. Calif. State U. at Fullerton, 1968-69; marketing, financial adviser 1957—. Mem. Am., Western econ. assns., Western Finance Assn., Artus. Contbr. articles to profl. publs. Home: 1100 W Valencia Mesa Dr Fullerton CA 92633 Office: 207 S Brea Blvd Brea CA 92621

GOBERNI, JOSEPH MICHAEL, mgmt. cons.; b. Uniontown, Pa., Oct. 9, 1948; s. Paul J. and Sophia E. G.; B.S., California (Pa.) State Coll., 1970; M.S., W.Va. U., 1972, Ed.D., 1977; m. Bonnie A. Nara, Nov. 12, 1977. Dir. safety and tng. Hillman Barge & Constrn. Co., Brownsville, Pa., 1972-79; adminstr. corp. loss prevention Hillman Co., Pitts., 1976-79; owner, operator J.M. Goberni Assos., mgmt. cons., Connellsville, Pa., 1979—. Vice chmn. occupational health hazards com., marine sect. Nat. Safety Council; mem. exec. bd. West Moreland-Fayette council Boy Scouts Am., 1974—; vice chmn. Fayette County Pvt. Industry Council, 1979-80; bd. dirs. Fayette County Bd. Assistance, 1980. Mem. Am. Soc. Safety Engrs., Nat. Safety Mgmt. Soc., Propeller Club U.S., River Terminal Operators Assn. Republican. Roman Catholic. Contbr. articles to profl. jours. Office: 1303 Concord Dr Connellsville PA 15425

GOBLE, STEVEN CRAIG, mgmt. cons.; b. Terre Haute, Ind., Mar. 23, 1949; s. Robert Wood and Charlotte Elaine (Newlin) G.; B.S. in Math., Rose-Hulman Inst. Tech., 1971, B.S. in Physics, 1971; M.B.A. in Fin., U. Chgo., 1974. Engr., Inland Steel Co., East Chicago, Ind., 1971-74; fin. analyst FMC Corp., Chgo., 1974-75, staff asst. to dir. mgr., Houston, 1975-76, materials mgr., 1976-79; mgmt. cons. Booz Allen & Hamilton, Dallas, 1979—. Mem. Am. Prodn. and Inventory Control Soc. (cert fellow), Phi Gamma Delta, Tau Beta Pi. Republican. Methodist. Home: 15539 Preston Rd #1039 Dallas TX 75248 Office: 1700 One Dallas Centre Dallas TX 75201

GODBEHERE, WALTER, mfg. co. exec.; b. Montreal, Que., Can., June 8, 1924; s. Horace William and Elsie Scott; student Sir George Williams U. Extension, 1940-42, McGill U., 1943-44; m. Frances Mary Willett, June 2, 1945; children—Walter Wayne, Ann Frances. With No. Telecom, various locations, 1940-74, mng. dir. subs., Istanbul, 1972-74; sr. v.p. ops. BXK Machinery Internat. Ltd., Toronto, Ont., Can., 1974-77; pres., chief exec. officer Enheat Inc., Sackville, N.B., Can., 1977—, also dir.; pres., dir. Airco Products, 1977—; dir. Thompson & Sutherland Ltd. Served with Can. Army, 1942-45. Fellow Cert. Gen. Accts. Assn. (past pres.); mem. Can. Foundry Assn. (dir.). Liberal Anglican. Home: 283 Orleans St Dieppe NB E1A 1W8 Canada Office: Lusby St Amherst NS B4H 3Y7 Canada also 100 Main St E Sackville NB E0A 3C0 Canada

GODBOLD, PERCY ELLIS, JR., banker; b. Pine Hill, Ala., Feb. 5, 1913; s. Percy Ellis and Kathleen (Davie) G.; B.S., U. Ala., 1933; M.B.A., Jacksonville State U., 1978; m. Grace Fuller, Sept. 16, 1937; 1 son, Leonard William. Agt. Internal Revenue Service, Birmingham, Ala., 1945-50; partner Kirkland, Godbold & Smith, C.P.A.'s, Birmingham, 1951-63; self-employed mgmt. cons., Anniston, Ala., 1964—; pres. People's Bank, Anniston, 1973-74; chmn. bd. Comml. Bank, Douglasville, Ga., 1961-75, Bank of Pine Hill (Ala.), 1972—. Trustee Stringfellow Meml. Hosp., Anniston. Served with AUS, 1943-45, C.P.A., Ala. Mem. Am. Bankers Assn. Baptist. Kiwanian. Club: Country (Anniston). Home: 2105 Henry Rd Anniston AL 36201

GODBOUT, JAMES (MICHAEL), cellulosic plastics mfg. co. exec.; b. Conn., June 22, 1945; s. Arthur R. and Elizabeth A. (Desmond) G.; B.S.B.A., Georgetown U., 1967; m. Katherine O'Keefe, June 29, 1968; children—Kara, John, Katie, Bridgid. Field service rep. Pratt & Whitney, United Techs. Corp., 1967-68; sales rep. Permacel div. Johnson & Johnson, 1968-71; mfg. rep. Connors Sales Co., Wethersfield, Conn., 1971-74; owner, pres. Product Mktg. Inc., indsl. mktg. and sales cons., Kensington, Conn., 1974—; owner, pres. Universal Inc. doing bus. as Universal Spltys., Kensington, Conn., 1975—. Mem. YMCA, Parent Tchr. Bd. West Hartford, Berlin C. of C., Conn. Bus. and Industry Assn., Soc. Plastics Engrs. Club: Georgetown. Office: PO Drawer 128 Kensington CT 06037

GODFREY, JILES MARTY, retailer; b. McCaysville, Ga., Sept. 4, 1947; s. Jiles Edward and Marie (Curtis) G.; student John Marshall Law Sch., 1965-67; B.S. in Bus. Adminstrn., U. Tenn., 1973; m. Beverly Harper, June 15, 1969; 1 dau., Jill Suzanne. Cost acct. Cities Service Co., Copperhill, Tenn., 1973-74; mgr. Blue Ridge br. Home Fed. Savs. and Loan, Gainesville, Ga., 1974-76; owner Piggly Wiggly Supermarket, pres. Godfrey Enterprises, Blue Ridge, Ga., 1976—. Chmn., County Heart Fund, 1974; co-chmn. Hosp. Expansion Com., 1975-76; county coordinator Gov. George Busbee campaign, 1974, 78; mem. State Council on Developmental Disabilities, 1976-78; pres. Fannin County Assn. Retarded Citizens, 1977-78; chmn. county finance dr. Boy Scouts Am., 1979; mem. City Council Blue Ridge, 1976-78, police commr. and mayor pro-tem, 1976-78; bd. dirs. Fannin County Assn. Retarded Citizens, 1975-78, Community Action Agy., 1974-75. Served with U.S. Army, 1966-68. Mem. Food Mktg. Inst., Polk-Fannin C. of C. (dir. 1975-76), Fannin County Indsl. Devel. Commn. Baptist. Club: Kiwanis (dir. Blue Ridge 1976-78). Contbr. articles to hobby mags. Office: Piggly Wiggly Food Store Hwy 5 Blue Ridge GA 30513

GODFREY, OLLIN, oil and banking exec.; b. Cin., Dec. 10, 1930; s. Ollin and Mattie (Clemmons) G.; student Edward Waters Jr. Coll., Jacksonville, Fla., 1949, Malcolm-King Coll., N.Y.C., 1968-71; m. Joan Jarboe, June 10, 1953; children—Ollin, Mark, David. Vice pres. East Harlem Community Corp., N.Y.C., 1969-71; pres. United Leadership Consultant Services, Inc., N.Y.C., 1972—; now exec. cons., Cin.; cons. Massive Neighborhood Devel. Corp., 1970-72. Past bd. dirs. Malcolm King Coll. Served with U.S. Navy, 1950-53. Recipient certificate of appreciation Republican Nat. Com., 1977. Mem. Am. Security Council (adv. bd.), Nat. Rep. Congressional Com. (sponsor), Nat. Rep. Senatorial Com. Baptist. Host; Minorities Sta. WNYC, N.Y.C., 1970-73. Address: 825 William Howard Taft Rd Cincinnati OH 45206

GODFREY, RICHARD GEORGE, real estate appraiser; b. Sharon, Pa., Dec. 18, 1927; s. Fay Morris and Elisabeth Marquerite (Stefanak) G.; B.A., Ripon Coll., 1949; m. Golda Fay Goss, Oct. 28, 1951; children—Deborah Jayne, Gayle Rogers, Bryan Edward. Vice-pres. 1st Thrift and Loan Assn., Albuquerque, 1959-61; pres. Richard G. Godfrey and Assos., Inc., Albuquerque, 1961—. Mem. Am. Inst. Real Estate Appraisers, Soc. Real Estate Appraisers, Am. Right of Way Assn., Am. Soc. Real Estate Counselors. Baptist. Club: Elks. Home: 1700 Columbia Dr SE Albuquerque NM 87106 Office: 457 Washington St SE Albuquerque NM 87108

GODFREY, ROBERT R., mgmt. co. exec.; b. Sweetwater, Tex., May 22, 1947; s. Ross R. and Lillian L. (Bradford) G.; B.B.A., Tex. Tech. U., 1969, postgrad. in bus. adminstrn., 1969-71; m. Diane M., June 30, 1972. Underwriter, Aetna Life and Casualty Co., Lubbock, Tex. and Hartford, Conn., 1969-72; teaching fellow Tex. Tech. U., 1969-71, Central Conn. State Coll., 1972; asst. mgr. Gulf Ins. Group, Dallas, 1972-76; asst. v.p. Scor Reins. Co., Dallas, 1976-79; pres. Rollins Burdick Hunter Mgmt. Co., N.Y.C., 1979—; dir. Rollins Burdick Hunter (Cayman). Served with U.S. Army, 1970. Club: Union League (N.Y.C.). Office: 605 3d Ave New York NY 10016

GODFREY, TED JACK, rancher; b. Dimmitt, Tex., Apr. 6, 1937; s. John W. and Pauline C. (Dinkins) G.; grad. high sch.; m. May 19, 1955; children—Jayne, Dalene, Charlie, Julie. Farmer, Spearman, Tex., 1955—; pres. Godfrey Farms, Spearman, 1980—; Tex. del. Am. Agr. Movement, 1970-80. Mem. Wheat Assn., Farmers Grain and Livestock Assn. (dir. 1979-80), Hansford County Grain Sorghum Producers Assn. (pres. 1980-81), Farmers Union.

GODFREY, WESLEY LYNN, nuclear services co. exec.; b. Washington, Jan. 24, 1939; s. Wesley Edward and Dorothy Lyngby (Garff) G.; B.Engring. Sci. in Chem. Engring., Brigham Young U., 1961; m. Annette Batty, Dec. 28, 1959; children—Nicole, Wesley Lance, Piper, Miles York. Research engr. Am. Potash & Chem. Co., Henderson, Nev., 1961-63; Gen. Electric Co., Richland, Wash., 1963-65; sr. engr. Isochem, Inc., Richland, 1965-66, Atlantic Richfield Hanford Co., Richland, 1966-72; gen. mgr. Mountain Breeze Produce, Pasco, Wash., 1972-74; chief engr. radio-active waste Allied-Gen. Nuclear Services, Barnwell, S.C., 1973—; pres. Elk Mountain Shooters Supply, Inc., 1969—, chmn. bd., 1971—; mem. subcom. on radioactive waste Atomic Indsl. Forum; chmn. com. on high level radioactive waste storage Am. Nat. Standards Inst. Served with various coms. Boy Scouts Am., 1963-69. Mem. Nat. Rifle Assn., Am. Inst. Chem. Engrs., Am. Soc. Photogrametry, Am. Chem. Soc., Am. Nuclear Soc. Mem. Ch. of Jesus Christ of Latter-day Saints (mem. bishoprics and high councils). Contbr. articles in field to profl. jours. Patentee in field. Author: The 30-'06, 1974; the .243 & 6 mm, 1978. Home: 2405 Jackson St Barnwell SC 29812 Office: Allied-Gen Nuclear Services PO Box 847 Barnwell SC 29812

GODIN, WILLIAM NEAL, mfg. co. exec.; b. N.Y.C., Dec. 4, 1936; s. Maurice and Berenice (Siegal) G.; B.S., Lehigh U., 1958; M.B.A., N.Y.U., 1963; Ph.D., State U. N.Y. at Buffalo, 1972; m. Lenore Diane Leinwand, Aug. 30, 1959; children—Seth Warren, Marjorie Beth, Emily Ruth. Prodn. planner Ford Instrument Co., N.Y.C., 1958; indsl. engr., sales adminstr. Sonotone Corp., Elmsford, N.Y., 1959-63; div. controller Carborundum Co., Niagara Falls, N.Y., 1964-66; v.p. finance Moog, Inc., East Aurora, N.Y., 1967-79; pres. Hard Mfg. Co., Inc., Buffalo, 1980—, also dir.; dir. Mohawk Industries, Inc.; adj. prof. State U. N.Y. at Buffalo; also various mgmt. assns. Mem. adv. bd. Sch. Mgmt., SUNY, Buffalo; bd. dirs. Studio Arena Theatre, pres., trustee; v.p., exec. com. United Way Buffalo and Erie County, campaign chmn., 1978; mem. exec. bd. Buffalo chpt. NCCJ. Mem. Am. Mgmt.

Assn., Soc. Mfg. Engrs., Assn. M.B.A.'s, Buffalo C. of C. Clubs: Buffalo Racquet (past treas., dir.); Westwood (Amherst, N.Y.); Crag Burn (East Aurora). Home: 46 Dan Troy Williamsville NY 14221 Office: 230 Grider St Buffalo NY 14215

GODLESKI, VINCENT ALTON, bus. exec.; b. Brookline, Mass., Mar. 13, 1937; s. Vincent and Margaret (Stockwell) G.; B.S. in Mech. Engring., Tufts U., 1959; M.B.A., Dartmouth Coll., 1962; m. Barbara Van Wagner, July 9, 1960; children—Eric Alton, Kevin Vincent, Kristin Ann. Engr. Sylvania Data Systems, Needham, Mass., 1959-61; project mgr. Astro Electronics div. RCA, Hightstown, N.J., 1962-65; mgr. adminstrn. ITT Mackay Marine, Clark, N.J., 1965-69; mgr. ITT Mobile Communications, 1969-73; mktg. mgr. ITT Ice Rinks, Midland Park, N.J., 1974-78; mgr. nat. accounts ITT Terryphone, Harrisburg, 1979-80; prodn. mgr. ITT USTS, N.Y.C., 1980—. Fin. com. Middlesex County (N.J.) Republican Orgn., 1965-67; campaign com. chmn. Tewksbury (N.J. Republican Club, 1971-74, pres., 1980—. Mem. ASHRAE (tech. com.), Ice Skating Inst. Am. (mem. tech. com.), Nat. Ice Hockey Ofcls. Assn. (pres. N.J. chpt. 1965-79), Am. Hockey Assn. U.S. (referee-in-chief dist. 4, 1975—). Republican. Roman Catholic. Club: Essex Hunt. Contbg. author on ice rink design and constrn. ASHRAE Applications Guide, 1978. Office: One Whitehall New York NY 10004

GODOMSKY, CHESTER JOHN, restaurant exec., real estate broker; b. Stonington, Conn., Sept. 14, 1931; s. Alex and Helen (Symcyk) G.; real estate broker certificate Lee Inst., Brookline, Mass., 1966; m. Elizabeth Ann Geyer, Jan. 17, 1952; children—Patricia Lynn, Diana Marie. Chem. operator Charles Pfizer, Inc., Groton, Conn., 1952-57; chef Mystic-Oral Sch., Mystic, Conn., 1957-62; owner, mgr. Sailor Ed's Restaurant, Stonington, 1964—; real estate broker, Mystic, 1966—. Bd. dirs. Mystic Community Center, 1973-74. Served with U.S. Army, 1950-52. Roman Catholic. Clubs: Lions (treas. 1969-72), V.F.W. (charter life), Mystic Rod and Gun (Mystic); Elks, Westerly Yacht. Home: Montauk Ave Stonington CT 06378 Office: Sailor Ed's Restaurant Old Stonington Rd Stonington CT 06378

GODSMAN, MITCHELL SIDNEY, pump mfg. co. exec.; b. Burlington, Colo., Mar. 25, 1923; s. Sidney Paul and June (Mitchell) G.; B.S. in Civil Engring., U. Denver, 1949; m. Katherine Gulos, Oct. 16, 1944; children—Frances Charlotte Doolittle, Paul Bromley II, Cornelia Mitchell Stearns, Elizabeth Allen, William Pickett, Thomas Gregory. Engr., then sales Standard Oil Co. (Ind.), 1949-57; spl. agt. Prudential Ins. Co., 1958-61; service mgr. Bennett Pump Co., Muskegon, Mich., 1961-72, dist. mgr., Richmond, Va., 1972—; chmn. asso. membership com. Nat. Conf. Weights and Measures, 1971, also speaker; speaker all regional and state assns. weights and measures. Pres. Central-Elliott Sch. PTA, Grand Haven, Mich., 1964; del. county and state Republican convs., 1962—, 1965—; mem. Henrico County Rep. Com., 1965-72, Ottawa County Rep. Com., 1973—; asst. Ottawa (Mich.) dist. chmn. Boy Scouts Am., 1963-67; vestryman Episcopalian Ch., 1957-60, lay leader, 1965—, key man, 1959, jr. warden, 1960. Served with USAAC, 1942-45, USAF, 1951-52; ETO. Decorated Air medal; recipient honor award Nat. Conf. Weights and Measures, 1971, 78, spl. recognition award Western Conf. Weights and Measures, 1973. Mem. Va. Oil Men's Assn., Va. Weights and Measures Assn. (chmn. industry relations com. 1979-80), N.C. Oil Jobbers Assn., Md. Petroleum Council, Western Weights and Measures Assn. (chmn. industry com. 1966-72), Mich. Weights and Measures Assn. (chmn. industry com. 1964-72), Gasoline Pump Mfg. Assn. (weights and measures com. 1981), VFW, Am. Legion. Republican. Clubs: Masons, Kiwanis (pres. 1961, 67). Home: 1504 Westshire Ln Richmond VA 23233 Office: 1501 Santa Rosa Rd Suite B-14 Richmond VA 23288

GOEBEL, HANK JOHN, steel co. exec.; b. Detroit, Dec. 7, 1951; s. John H. and Eleanor (Rejc) G.; B.B.A., Bowling Green State U., 1974; m. Mary Jo Welborn, Mar. 31, 1978. Personnel trainee Chrysler Corp., Detroit, 1974; employee devel. specialist Massey-Ferguson, Inc., Detroit, 1975, hourly employment supr., 1975-76; personnel mgr. Fed. Mogul Corp., Mendon, Mich., 1976-77; employee relations mgr. Baron Drawn Steel Corp., Toledo, Ohio, 1977—. Mem. Am. Soc. Personnel Adminstrn., Toledo Personnel Mgmt. Assn., Am. Compensation Assn., Toledo Employers Assn., Indsl. Relations Group. Home: 2024 Sandown Toledo OH 43615 Office: 1400 Hastings St Toledo OH 43607

GOEBEL, ROBERT ANTHONY, woodworking co. exec.; b. Milw., Jan. 26, 1943; s. Anton and Flora Marie (Kirsh) G.; student Marquette U., 1961-63; m. Linda Lee Torke, Dec. 10, 1977; 1 dau., Ellen; children by previous marriage—Michael, Richard, Anmarie; stepchildren—Reed, LeAnn. Owner, pres. Goebel Woodwork Inc., Port Washington, Wis. Mem. sch. bd., choir St. Mary's Sch., 1979—; mem. Port Washington City Band; treas. pack Boy Scouts Am. Mem. Square Dance Callers Assn. (treas. Milw. area 1979-80). Roman Catholic. Club: K.C. (2 deg.). Home: S 528 N Port Washington Rd Grafton WI 53024 Office: Goebel Woodworking Inc Route 1 Box 734 Port Washington WI 53074

GOEL, RADHEY S., mfg. co. exec.; b. Ganaur, India, Jan. 5, 1944; came to U.S., 1971, naturalized, 1978; s. Ram Swaroop and Pathori (Devi) G.; B.S. in E.E., Birla Inst. Tech. & Sci., India, 1964; M.B.A., Seton Hall U., 1978; m. Kanta Kumari, Mar. 6, 1967; children—Sangita, Sunjay, Neeraj. Quality control and testing engr. Indsl. Cables (I), Ltd., India, 1965-70; quality control mgr. Vanguard Plastics, Inc., Hawthorne, N.J., 1971-72; sr. quality control engr. Engelhard Industries div. Englehard M. & C. Corp., N.Y.C., 1973-77, plant process control supr., 1978-79, sr. product assurance engr., 1980—. Registered profl. engr., Calif. Sr. mem. Am. Soc. Quality Control cert. quality engr.); mem. Am. Mgmt. Assn. Home: 21 Stratford Dr Manalpan NJ 07726 Office: Englehard Industries Div Englehard M & C Corp 70 Wood Ave S Iselin NJ 08830

GOEL, VIRENDRA SINGH, material scientist; b. Jhansi, U.P. India, Mar. 8, 1927; s. Shyam and Buglee (Devee) L.; B.S. in Physics, U. Allahabad, 1946; M.E., Roorkee Engring. U., 1949; B.S. in M.S., U. Colo., 1959; Ph.D., U. Calif., Berkeley, 1964; m. Saroj, May 15, 1966; 1 dau., Meera. Sr. sci. officer Council Sci. and Indsl. Research, New Delhi, 1949-57; instr. U. Colo., Boulder, 1957-58, Occidental Coll., Los Angeles, 1958-60; research engr. Laurence Livermore Lab., Berkeley, 1960-64; sr. research scientist Martin Marietta Corp., Denver, 1965-69; staff scientist Honeywell, Inc., Denver, 1969-70; pvt. cons., 1970-73; staff engr. Nuclear Regulatory Commn., Washington, 1974—; gen. chmn. Internat. Conf. on Nondestructive Evaluation in Nuclear Industry, 1975. Mem. ASME, Am. Soc. Nondestructive Testing, Am. Soc. Metals. Democrat. Hindu. Home: 4708 Topping Rd Rockville MD 20852 Office: Office Standards Nuclear Regulatory Commn Washington DC 20555

GOERGEN, ANTHONY JOSEPH, glass decorating co. exec.; b. Chgo., May 18, 1942; s. Michael A. and Virginia (Rodger) G.; B.B.A., Western Mich. U., 1966; m. Joan Condon, Jan. 18, 1969; children—Brian, Gina. Acct., FMC Corp., Chgo., 1966-71; internat. acctg. mgr. Fedders Corp., Edison, N.J., 1972; asst. controller Concrete Plank Co., North Arlington, N.J., 1972-74; controller SGL Modern Creative, Elmwood Park, N.J., 1974—. Served with U.S. Army, 1966-68. Office: SGL Modern Creative 35 Market St Elmwood Park NJ 07407

GOERGEN, ROBERT BLYTH, investment banker; b. Buffalo, June 30, 1938; s. Anthony T. and Alice M. (Blyth) G.; A.B. cum laude, U. Rochester, 1960; M.B.A., U. Pa., 1962; m. Pamela M. Tart, Nov. 30, 1968; children—Robert Blyth, Todd Andrew. Sr. account exec. McCann-Erickson Inc., N.Y.C., 1963-66; asso. McKinsey & Co. Inc., N.Y.C., 1966-70, prin., 1970-73; exec. v.p., dir. Donaldson, Lufkin, Jenrette & Co. Inc., N.Y.C. and mng. gen. partner Sprout, N.Y.C., 1973-79; pres. Ropart, Inc., N.Y.C., 1979—; dir. Clopay Corp., Devon Group; chmn. bd. Candle Corp. Am., N.Y.C., HammerBlow Corp., Tennis Lady, Inc., MWM Dexter Industries Inc. Bd. dirs. Citizens for Clean Air, N.Y.C., 1966-69; mem. trustee council U. Rochester, 1973—. Served with U.S. Army, 1962-63. Clubs: Yale, N.Y. Racquet, Quogue Field. Home: 11 Rockridge Ave Greenwich CT 06830 Office: Ropart Inc Suite 1211 230 Park Ave New York NY 10017

GOERNER, BASIL STEVEN, paper co. exec.; b. N.Y., Sept. 23, 1932; s. Alfred and Mary Margaret (Popp) G.; B.S., N.Y. State Coll. Forestry, Syracuse U., 1954; postgrad. U. Houston, 1971; m. Mary Patricia Avery, Mar. 14, 1949; children—Katherine Mary, Christine Ann, Mary Alice. Various operating and tech. positions Champion Internat. Corp., Tex., Ohio and Brazil, now v.p. mfg. Champion Papel e Celulose S.A. subs., Mogi Guacu, Brazil. Mem. TAPPI, Paper Industry Mgmt. Assn., Associacao Brasileira de Celulose e Papel, Inst. of Paper Chemistry, U.S. Am. Chamber for Brazil, Sociedade Hipica de Campinas. Home: 519 H Humberto Bertani 13100 Campinas SP 13100 Brazil Office: Champion Papel e Celulose SA 377-8deg Libero Badaro Sao Paulo 01002 Brazil*

GOETSCH, EDWARD JOSEPH, mfg. co. exec.; b. Hinsdale, Ill., July 22, 1924; s. Edward Joseph and Jennie Mildred (Putts) G.; B.S. in Mech. Engring., Ill. Inst. Tech., 1945; M.B.A., U. Wash., 1951; m. Marilyn Frances Terry, Aug. 20, 1949; children—Terry Jean, Lori Margaret, Karen Lee, David Edward. Structural test engr. Boeing Airplane Co., Seattle, 1946-48, indsl. engr., 1951-52; mgmt. trainee Brunswick Corp., Muskegon, Mich., 1952-56; planning and scheduling mgr. Trailmobile, Inc., Cin., 1956-59; processing supr. J.I. Case Co., Bettendorf, Iowa, 1959-62, chief indsl. engr., 1962-63, prodn. control mgr., 1963-66, mfg. mgr., 1966-69, gen. plant mgr., 1969-72, dir. corp. mfg., Racine, 1973—; pres. Asso. Employees of Quad Cities, Moline, Ill., 1973; pres. Bettendorf C. of C., 1968. Vice chmn. United Way of Quad Cities, 1973; pres. Bettendorf Community Theatre, 1960-70. Served with USN, 1943-46. Mem. Tau Omega, Beta Gamma Sigma. Republican. Methodist. Club: Meadowbrook Country (Racine). Home: 1505 Crabapple Dr Racine WI 53405 Office: 700 State St Racine WI 53404

GOETZ, CARL, JR., sporting goods co. exec.; b. N.Y.C., Dec. 14, 1943; s. Karl and Marie (Unger) G.; B.S., SUNY Maritime Coll., 1965; M.B.A., Baruch Coll., 1970; m. Jean A. Radlein, July 21, 1966; children—Erika J., Carla J. Ship's officer in maritime industry, 1965-70; various mgmt. positions Internat. Bowling Group, AMF, Inc., N.Y., 1970-77; dir. internat. and govt. sales Rawlings Sporting Goods Co., St. Louis, 1977-80; dir. Mktg. Fred Perry Co., St. Louis, 1980—. Mem. World Trade Club. Clubs: Masons, Shriners, Jesters, Brookdale Swim and Tennis (pres.). Home: 11741 Summerhaven Dr Creve Coeur MO 63141 Office: 2300 Delmar Blvd Saint Louis MO 63166

GOFF, STEPHEN CHARLES, retail/real estate exec.; b. St. Paul, Sept. 21, 1945; s. Stillman Reese and Marion Emma (Zinsmeister) F.; B.S., Bradley U., 1967; M.B.A., No. Ill. U., 1969; m. Donna Jean Domnick, Mar. 9, 1969; children—Dale, Donald. Grad. resident adv. No. Ill. U. DeKalb, 1968-69; cons. Thorolf Gregerson A/S, Oslo, Norway, 1968; market research dir., planner Nash Finch Co., retail trade, St. Louis Park, Minn., 1969-78; mktg. dir. Musicland Group, Am. Can Corp., St. Louis Park, 1978—; pres. U.S. Renovation Corp., Mpls., 1980—; v.p. U.S. Devel. Corp., Inc., 1980—; guest lectr. U. Minn., Ohio State U. Adv. HELP, minority bus. cons., St. Paul Model Cities, 1971-73; faculty Met. State U., 1975—. Pres., Social Innovations, Mpls., 1971—; pres. Bldg. Block Nursery Sch. and Day Care Center, Mpls., 1971—. Del. local precinct Republican Party, 1972. Mem. Am. Mktg. Assn. (nat. minority bus. assistance com.), North Central Corp. Planning Soc. (officer 1978), Nat. Assn. Edn. Young Children, Nat. Assn. Retail Grocers (conv. lectr.), Internat. Shopping Center Council, Nat. Assn. Record Mfrs., Minn. Minority Bus. Cons., Food Mktg. Inst. (adv. bd.; conv. lectr.), Food Distbn. Research Soc. (conv. lectr.), Day Care and Child Devel. Council Am., Greater Mpls. Day Care Assn., Greater St. Paul Council Coordinated Child Care, Minn. Assn. Edn. Young Children, Minn. Jr. C. of C. (state dir. drug edn. 1971-72), Golden Valley Jr. C. of C., Minn. Wine Tasting Soc. (pres. 1973), Sigma Chi. Author: Computerized Food Shopping, 1974; Super Marketing in Japan, 1977; Super Marketing in Soviet Union, 1978; Need for Strategic Market Planning, 1978; Super Marketing in South America, 1979. Home: 1820 Du Pont Ave S Minneapolis MN 55403 Office: 7500 Excelsior Blvd St Louis Park MN 55426

GOFMAN, HERBERT BURTON, banker; b. New Rochelle, N.Y., Feb. 13, 1931; s. Samuel and Pauline (Cooper) G.; B.B.A., N.Y. U., 1957, M.B.A., 1961; m. Judith Safier, Nov. 22, 1958; children—Steven N., Sheryl B. Asso. mgr. investment adv. service Bache, Halsey, Stuart & Shields, N.Y.C., 1961-68; mgr. investment supervisory service Hertz, Warner & Co., N.Y.C., 1968-69; v.p., div. head investment mgmt. services No. Trust Co., Chgo., 1969—; faculty Elmhurst Coll., Mundelein Coll., Lake Forest Coll., part-time 1972—. Served with AUS, 1953-54. Chartered Fin. Analyst. Mem. Investment Analysts Soc. Chgo., Fin. Analysts Fedn. Club: Union League of Chgo. Home: 1912 Smith Rd Northbrook IL 60062 Office: No Trust Co 50 S LaSalle St Chicago IL 60675

GOHRBAND, ROGER, chem. co. exec.; b. Portland, Oreg., May 21, 1930; s. Ernest and Pauline (Tompkins) G.; B.S. in Chem. Engring., Oreg. State U., 1951; M.B.A., Harvard U., 1956; m. Virginia Maude Harmon, June 21, 1953; children—Christopher, Lezlie, Gregg. With Dow Chem. U.S.A., 1956—, dir. purchasing and fin. services, Midland, Mich., 1975-76, dir. planning, 1977-79, gen. mgr. inorganic chems., 1979—; dir. Nat. Minority Purchasing Council, 1976. Pres. Lake Huron Area Council Boy Scouts Am., 1976-78, v.p., 1978—; advisor Jr. Achievement, 1966-67; mem. bd. tax equalization Lake Jackson, Tex., 1963-64; bd. dirs. S. Tex. C. of C., 1965-66. Served with U.S. Army, 1951-54. Decorated Bronze Star, Air Medal. Mem. Am. Inst. Chem. Engrs., Phi Kappa Phi, Tau Beta Pi, Sigma Tau, Phi Lambda Upsilon. Presbyterian (elder, deacon). Clubs: Midland Country, Rotary. Home: 1806 Norwood Dr Midland MI 48640 Office: 2020 Dow Center Midland MI 48640

GOIZUETA, ROBERTO CRISPULO, food co. exec.; b. Havana, Cuba, Nov. 18, 1931; came to U.S., 1961; s. Crispulo D. and Aida (Cantera) G.; B.S., B.Engring. in Chem. Engring., Yale, 1953; m. Olga T. Casteleiro, June 14, 1953; children—Roberto S., Olga M., Javier C. Process engr. Indsl. Corp. Tropics, Havana, 1953-54; tech. dir. Coca-Cola Co., Havana, 1954-60, asst. to sr. v.p., Nassau, Bahamas, 1960-64, asst. to v.p. research and devel., Atlanta, 1964-66, v.p. engring., 1966-74, sr. v.p., 1974-75, exec. v.p., 1975-80, pres., chief operating officer, dir., 1980, chmn. bd., chief exec. officer, 1980—, mem. corp. operating com., 1975-80; mem. exec. office, mem. office of chmn., mem. retirement plan and thrift coms., 1978-80, vice chmn., 1979-80; dir., mem. exec. com. Coca-Cola Export Corp., 1978—; dir. Aqua-Chem. Inc. Bd. visitors Emory U., 1979—, trustee, 1980—; trustee The Am. Assembly, 1979—, Engring. Found. Ga., 1979—. Mem. Tau Beta Pi. Clubs: Capital City (bd. govs.), Piedmont Driving (Atlanta). Home: 4620 Jettridge Dr NW Atlanta GA 30327 Office: Coca-Cola Co 310 North Ave Atlanta GA 30304

GOLASKI, WALTER MICHAEL, machinery co. exec.; b. Torrington, Conn., Aug. 12, 1913; s. Paul and Helen (Kulesza) Golaszewski; M.E., Drexel U., 1946, completing B.S. degree; D.Sc., Alliance Coll., 1968; m. Helene D. Ambrose, Sept. 5, 1942 (dec. Aug. 1968); 1 dau., Michelle; m. 2d, Alexandra Budna, Oct. 25, 1969; children—Alexandra Maria, John Paul, Edmund Walter. With The Torrington Co., 1928-45; partner Bearing Products Co., Phila., design and manufacture spl. machinery, 1945-47, owner-mgr., 1947-63, pres., mgr., 1963—; pres., treas. Overbrook Knitting Corp., Phila., 1956—; pres. Golaski Labs., Inc., 1967—; former chmn. bd. Nowy Swiat newspaper; dir. 3d Fed. Savs. & Loan Assn. Nat. chmn. Kosciuszko Found. Ball, 1960, 76; chmn. bd. trustees Kosciuszko Found. Recipient Gold medal Drexel U., 1953, alumni citation, 1961; George Washington medal, 1972; named Alumni Man of Year Drexel Evening Coll., 1961. Mem. Pa. Soc., AAAS, N.Y. Acad. Scis., Am. Soc. Artificial Internal Organs, Polish Nat. Alliance, ASTM, Pa. Mfrs. Assn., Sigma Delta. Club: Polish Intercollegiate (alumni pres.). Invented processes converting hosiery machinery to finer gauges, and for making neckties and sweaters, machinery for mfr. blood vessels. Contbr. papers to profl. lit. Patentee in field. Home: 6445 Drexel Rd Philadelphia PA 19151 Office: 4567 Wayne Ave Philadelphia PA 19144

GOLD, AARON ALAN, fin. co. exec.; b. Phila., Oct. 4, 1919; s. Lewis and Rose (Kroll) G.; student Temple U., 1940-42; hon. degree Jewish Theol. Sem., 1975; m. Claire Halpern, Oct. 18, 1942; children—Ross Michael, Joshua S. and Julie B. (twins). Pres., chmn. bd. Oxford First Corp., Phila., 1950—; regional dir. Continental Bank, Phila.; v.p., agt. Qualidine, Inc., 1978-80; v.p., dir. Metro Products of Israel, 1978-80; exec. vp Bio/Trim Inst. lectr. Small Bus. Opportunities Corp., 1970—, Temple U., 1970-78, other instns. Trustee Lower Kensington Environ. Drug Addiction Center, 1968—, Opportunities Industrialization Center, 1963—, Allied Jewish Appeal, 1965—, Adath Jeshurun Synagogue, 1965—; bd. dirs. Am. Jewish Com., 1975—, Fedn. Jewish Agys., 1970—; chmn. Kensington Hosp., Phila., 1969—. Served with AUS, 1942-45. Recipient cert. appreciation Fedn. Allied Jewish Appeal, 1975, United Shareowners Am. Mgmt. award, 1966-72, Cyrus Adler Community Service award, 1974, B'nai B'rith Internat. Humanitarian award, 1979. Mem. Am. Technion Soc. (dir. 1969—), Am.-Israel C. of C. (dir.), Pa. Assn. Sales and Fin. Cos. (Leadership and Service award 1959-62), Pa. Indsl. Bankers, Pa. Consumer Fin. Assn. Clubs: Locust (Phila.); Meadowlands Country (Blue Bell, Pa.). Office: Oxford First Corp 6701 N Broad St Philadelphia PA 19126

GOLD, ELIJAH HERMAN, pharm. co. exec.; b. N.Y.C., May 22, 1936; s. George A. and Esther E. (Brandler) G.; B.S. cum laude, CCNY, 1957; M.S., Yale U., 1958, Ph.D., 1963; m. Lorraine F. Berger, June 22, 1962; children—Benjamin Zev, Tova Malka. Postdoctoral research fellow Columbia U., N.Y.C., 1963-64, Israel Inst. Tech., Haifa, 1964-66; sr. scientist Schering-Plough, Bloomfield, N.J., 1966-69, prin. scientist, 1969-70, sect. leader, 1970-73, mgr., 1973-74, asso. dir. medicinal chem. research, 1974—. NIH fellow, 1958-63, 64-66. Fellow Am. Inst. Chemists; mem. Am. Chem. Soc., N.Y. Acad. Sci., Am. Mgmt. Assn., Sigma Xi, Phi Beta Kappa, Phi Lambda Upsilon. Contbr. articles to profl. jours.; patentee in field. Office: 60 Orange St Bloomfield NJ 07003

GOLD, FRED L., pharmacist, drug chain exec.; b. Phila., Feb. 28, 1933; s. Al and Henryetta (Zehring) G.; B.S. in Pharmacy, Temple U., 1955; m. Rose L. Drossner, Sept. 2, 1956; children—Mona, Marc, Neil. Pharmacist, Suburban Pharmacy, Portsmouth, Va., 1957-58; pharmacist, mgr. Cambria Pharmacy, Inc., Phila., 1958—. Vice pres. Congregation Shaare Shamayim. Served with USNR, 1955-57. Registered pharmacist, Pa. Mem. Nat. Assn. Retail Druggists, Am. Pharm. Assn. Home: 486 Pinewood Pl Philadelphia PA 19116 Office: 2860 N 5th St Philadelphia PA 19133

GOLD, JEFFREY MARK, diversified mfg. and pub. co. exec.; b. Bronx, N.Y., Jan. 7, 1945; s. Samuel L. and Sylvia E. Gold; B.B.A. in Acctg., Pace U., 1967; m. Lenore N. Epstein May 29, 1966; children—Brian, Steven, Samuel. Sr. acct. Main Hurdman & Cranstoun, C.P.A.'s, N.Y.C., 1967-71; v.p., corp. controller Nat. Patent Devel. Corp., N.Y.C., 1971-78; v.p. fin. and corp. devel. Esquire, Inc., N.Y.C., 1978—. Mem. transp. task force Chappaqua (N.Y.) Sch. Bd. Club: Willowbrook Swim and Tennis. Home: 48 North Way Chappaqua NY 10514 Office: 488 Madison Ave New York NY 10022

GOLD, JOEL L., investment banker; b. Bklyn., Sept. 26, 1941; s. Henry and Pearl (Frank) G.; B.S. in Acctg., Bklyn. Coll., 1963; M.B.A., Columbia U., 1964; J.D., N.Y. U., 1967; m. Miriam Greenbaum, Mar. 25, 1969; children—Rochelle Lynne, Elliott Ernest, Tanya H., Henry. Admitted to N.Y. State bar, 1967, U.S. Supreme Ct. bar, 1969; asso. corp. fin. Bache & Co., N.Y.C., 1967-69, Thompson & McKinnon, N.Y.C., 1969-71; first v.p. corp. fin. Drexel Burnham Lambert, N.Y.C., 1971—; dir. Action Industries, Mich. Gen. Corp. Bd. dirs. Young Israel of Boro Park, 1980; v.p. Congregation Agudath Sholom, Flatbush, 1978. Mem. Am. Bar Assn., Columbia Bus. Sch. Alumni, Bklyn. Coll. Alumni. Home: 1675 45th St Brooklyn NY 11204 Office: 60 Broad St New York NY 10004

GOLDBACH, JOSEPH V., bank exec., rancher, developer; b. Burlington, Iowa, Feb. 9, 1930; s. Joseph and Evelyn Louise (Snyder) G.; B.A. in Econs., State U. Iowa, 1952; m. Dorothy M. Walker, June 8, 1952; children—Joseph C., James D. Officer, dept. bank and bankers Iowa Des Moines Nat. Bank, 1952-58; v.p. Ill. Nat. Bank, Springfield, 1958-61; chmn., pres. Nat. Bank of St. Petersburg, Fla., 1961-74; pres. Pinellas Bank, St. Petersburg, 1974—; cons. in field. Mem. bd. dirs. Pinellas United Way, 1977—. Mem. Fla. Bankers Assn. Presbyterian. Club: St. Petersburg Yacht. Office: PO Box 14273 Saint Petersburg FL 33733

GOLDBERG, ARTHUR ABBA, lawyer, investment banker; b. Jersey City, Nov. 25, 1940; s. Jack Geddy and Ida (Steinberg) G.; A.B. with honors, Am. U., 1962; LL.B., Cornell U., Ithaca, N.Y., 1965; m. Jane Elizabeth Gottlieb, Aug. 10, 1968; children—Ari Matthew, Shoshana Eve, Benjamin Saul, Talia Akiva. Admitted to N.J. bar, 1965, Conn. bar, 1966, U.S. Supreme Ct., 1968; intern, staff mem. to senator, 1962; law clk. DeSevo & Cerutti, Jersey City, 1964; practiced in Jersey City, 1965—; asst. prof. law U. Conn. Sch. Law, 1965-67; cooperating atty. NAACP Legal Def. Fund, 1965—; adminstrv. asst. to congressman Ohio, 1966-67; dep. atty. gen. N.J., counsel Dept. Community Affairs and Housing Fin. Agy., 1967-70; exec. v.p., dir., mgr. municipal fin. dept. Matthews & Wright, Inc., N.Y.C., 1970—; v.p. Alfus Corp., 1958—, Basow Corp., 1965—, KDS Builders, Hudson Mgmt. Services; mng. partner Bank Bldg. Assos.; partner Shayna Enterprises; dir. Titan Industries, 1975-80; vis. lectr. Rutgers

U., Practising Law Inst., Hunter Coll., Inst. for Profl. and Exec. Devel., New Sch. for Social Research. Mem. exec. com. N.J. Commn. Discrimination in Housing; chmn. Nat. Leased Housing Assn., from 1973, now chmn. emeritus; bd. dirs. South Bronx Community Housing, Inc.; mem. urban adv. council Anti-Defamation League; spl. cons. on exclusionary zoning Nat. Com. Discrimination in Housing; mem. adv. bd. Housing and Devel. Reporter; cons. scholarship edn. Def. Fund for Racial Equality; gen. counsel N.J. chpt. Mcpl. Fin. Officers Assn., N.J. chpt. Nat. Assn. Housing and Redevel. Ofcls.; mem. Settlement House Fund; pres. Met. N.Y. Com. on Soviet Jewish Resettlement; chmn. Com. for Absorption of Soviet Emigres, Mus. Soviet Unofcl. Art; co-pres. The New Synagogue, 1974-80; treas. Hebrew Free Loan N.J.; bd. dirs. Yeshiva of Hudson County, 1977—; pres. Case Community Devel. Corp., 1977—; active Boys Club of Jersey City. Mem. Conn. Assn. Municipal Attys. (exec. com., editor Newsletter), Nat. Housing Conf., Am. (local govt. sect.), N.J. (chmn. com. on housing and urban renewal), Conn., Hudson County bar assns., Am. Polit. Sci. Assn., Nat. Acad. Polit. and Social Sci., Pub. Securities Assn. (legis. com.), Council Jewish Orgns. Jersey City (treas.), Omicron Delta Kappa, Pi Gamma Mu, Pi Sigma Alpha, Pi Delta Epsilon. Author: Financing Housing and Urban Development, 1972; Zoning and Land Use, 1972; Tax-Exempt Financing of Industrial Development and Pollution Abatement Facilities, 1973; contbr. articles to law revs.; chmn. New Am. Newspaper, 1980—. Home: 83 Montgomery St Jersey City NJ 07302 Office: Matthews & Wright Inc 14 Wall St New York NY 10005

GOLDBERG, ARTHUR H., lawyer, fin. services co. exec.; b. N.Y.C., May 13, 1942; s. Irving and Pearl (Rubin) G.; B.S. cum laude, N.Y. U., 1963, J.D., 1966; m. Hedy Krauss, June 6, 1963; children—Jill Marla, Mia Joy. Admitted to N.Y. State bar, 1966; asso. firm Javits & Javits, N.Y.C., 1966-69; exec. v.p. Integrated Resources, Inc., N.Y.C., 1969-73, pres., 1973—; chmn. Resources Life Ins. Co., N.Y.C., 1978—. Trustee, Children's Med. Center, N.Y.C., 1978, Jerusalem Inst. Mgmt., 1980—. Mem. Young Pres.'s Orgn., Order of Coif, Beta Gamma Sigma. Mem. N.Y. U. Law Rev., 1965-66. Home: 55 Sunset Rd Kings Point NY 11024 Office: 295 Madison Ave New York NY 10017

GOLDBERG, CHARLES HAROLD, real estate co. exec., textile mfg. co. exec.; b. Marinette, Wis., Jan. 3, 1903; s. David Charles and Harriet Ruth (Lewin) G.; student Marquette U., 1922; m. Viola Forester, Mar. 17, 1975. Propr., mgr. Goldberg's Men's Store, Inc.; dir. WMAM-TV, Green Bay, Wis., 1965; v.p. Harmon Knitting Mill Co., Marinette, 1960—; pres. Charles Enterprises, Inc., Marinette, 1940—, Marinette Downtown Corp.; dir. Guild Film Inc., 1958—, Farmers and Mchts. Bank, 1960—, Green Bay Packer Football Corp., 1952—, Gale Builders, Coral Gables, Fla. Mem. Gov.'s Trade Mission Com. Bd. dirs. Marinette Youth Center, 1969—, Day Care Center, 1963—; pres. Marinette County Gen. Hosp., 1961-75. Named Wis. Retailer of Year, 1967; Man of Year, Marinette Am. Legion, 1966. Mem. Wis. Apparel Assn. (pres.), Wis. State C. of C. Clubs: Rotary, Masons, Elks, Riverside Country (pres.), Twi-Cees Men's (pres. 1952). Home: 2829 Riverside Ave Marinette WI 54143 Office: 2100 Hall Ave Marinette WI 54143

GOLDBERG, EDWARD MARTIN, holding co. exec.; b. N.Y.C., June 26, 1933; s. Benjamin and Gertrude (Stertzer) G.; grad. Dickinson Coll., 1954; postgrad. N.Y. U., 1957; m. Myrna Siegel, June 27, 1954; children—Stuart, Gayl. Pres. Berkeley Capital, N.Y.C., 1972-74; pres., chmn. Northampton Mfg. (Mass.), 1973-79; chmn. bd. Gen. Corrosion Services, Atlanta, 1977-79, Fed. Funding Corp., N.Y.C., 1980—. Office: 9 W 57th St New York NY 10019

GOLDBERG, FREDERICK IRA, architect; b. N.Y.C., Mar. 11, 1943; s. Morris and Rose (Weinstein) G.; B.Arch., Pratt Inst., 1965, M.S. in Environ. Design, 1972; m. Judith Fellner, June 12, 1965; children—Alan Bradley, Taryn Wendy. Head design dept. D. Salvati & Son, Bklyn., 1965-67; dir. Builderamic Research and Devel. div. Lefrak, Inc., Forest Hills, N.Y., 1967; design architect Dallek Design Group, N.Y.C., 1968—; architect Environ. Research and Devel., N.Y.C., 1969; owner Frederick Goldberg Architect, N.Y.C., 1969—; pres. Design Derivatives Inc., 1970; adj. asst. prof. grad. environ. design dept. Pratt Inst., 1969—. Recipient cert. of merit Nat. Inst. Archtl. Edn., 1965; 1st prize bldg. awards program Queens C. of C., 1979; cert. Nat. Council Archtl. Registration Bds.; registered architect, N.Y., N.J., Vt. Mem. Am. Inst. Architects. Patentee in field. Home: 86 The Serpentine Roslyn Estates NY 11576 Office: 201 E 56 St New York NY 10022

GOLDBERG, HARLEAN FADER, weight reduction orgn. exec.; b. Bklyn., June 1, 1932; d. Moe and Marjorie (Cullens) Fader; student Bklyn. Coll., 1949-51; m. Leonard Goldberg, Mar. 30, 1969; children—Terry, Janet, Randi, Warren. Pres., Weight Watchers of S.I. Inc., 1965-69; v.p. Weight Watchers of Syracuse Inc. (N.Y.), 1968—; sec. Select-A-Size Ltd., Syracuse, 1972—; pres. Shape Shoppes Inc., Syracuse, 1974—; v.p. Skeleton Foods, 1976—. Dir. W.W. Franchisee Assn. Inc., N.Y.C., 1972-73, mem. purchasing com., 1971-73, chmn. emergency fund com., 1972-74. Bd. dirs. Jewish Family Service Bur., Syracuse, 1973-78; bd. dirs. Inter-Agy. Com. for Diabetes Edn., also co-chmn. finance com., 1975-77; bd. dirs. nutrition adv. com. Syracuse City Schs., 1980—. Mem. Am. Diabetes Assn. (treas. Upstate N.Y. chpt., dir. 1977-79). Club: Syracuse University Hardwood (dir. 1973—, corr. sec. 1972-78, 1st v.p. 1978-79, pres. 1980—). Home: 5263 Jamesville Rd Dewitt NY 13214 Office: 5858 E Molloy Rd Suite 112 Syracuse NY 13211

GOLDBERG, LEE WINICKI, furniture co. exec.; b. Laredo, Tex., Nov. 20, 1932; d. Frank and Goldie (Ostrowiak) Winicki; student San Diego State U., 1951-52; m. Frank M. Goldberg, Aug. 17, 1952; children—Susan Arlene, Edward Lewis, Anne Carri. With United Furniture Co., Inc., San Diego, 1953—, corporate sec., dir., 1963—, dir. environ. interiors, 1970—; founding partner, v.p. FLJB Corp., 1976—. Den mother Boy Scouts Am., San Diego, 1965; vol. Am. Cancer Soc., San Diego, 1964-69; chmn. jr. matrons United Jewish Fedn., San Diego, 1958; del. So. Pacific Coast region Hadassah Conv., 1960, pres. Galilee group San Diego chpt., 1960-61. Recipient Hadassah Service award San Diego chpt., 1958-59. Mem. Nat. Home Furnishings Inst. Democrat. Jewish. Address: 1472 Point Loma Way San Diego CA 92106

GOLDBERG, MERYL (ANN), hosp. purchasing exec.; b. N.Y.C., Mar. 19, 1948; d. Louis and Emma (Gordon) Gerber; m. Jack A. Goldberg, Jan. 28, 1975; 1 son, Glenn Robert. Asst. supr. customer relations Burlington Industries, N.Y.C., 1971-72; dept. adminstr. Monroe Knitting Industries, N.Y.C., 1972-75; legal researcher litigation research firm Hughes Hubbard & Reed, N.Y.C., 1968-70; purchasing agt. Calvary Hosp., Bronx, N.Y., 1979—. Mem. Hosp. Purchasing Agts. Assn., Am. Hosp. Assn., Am. Mgmt. Assn. Internat. Material Mgmt. Soc., East Ramapo Civic Orgn. Republican. Office: 1740 Eastchester Rd Bronx NY 10461

GOLDBERG, MORRIS, personnel service co. exec.; b. London, Nov. 11, 1925; s. Solomon and Nina (Portsch) G.; B.B.A., City U. N.Y., 1963, postgrad., 1963-65; m. Susan L. Goldberg, June 4, 1950 (dec. Aug. 1975); m. 2d, Elizabeth M. Kowal, Dec. 13, 1980. Plant supt. Lewyt Corp., L.I., 1949-60; plant mgr. asst. Standard Motor Products, L.I., 1960-64; plant mgr. Alloys Unltd., Inc., Melville, N.Y., 1964-68; pres. Electronic Metals & Aloys, Inc., North Attleboro, Mass., 1968-72, Rita Personnel System of N. Am., Providence, 1972—. Served with RAF, 1946-48. Mem. Nat. Assn. Personnel Cons. (founder, R.I. chpt. first pres. 1973), Mu Gamma Tau. Clubs: Kiwanis, Masons. Office: 1 Weybosset Hill Providence RI 02903

GOLDBERG, NORMAN, advt. agy. exec.; b. Washington, Nov. 7, 1940; s. Reuben and Jean Elaine (Smith) G.; B.S., U. Wis., 1962; m. Sandra L. Chazin, Aug. 9, 1964 (div. 1976); children—Allan Mark, Amy Carla. Clk. prodn. dept. Kal, Ehrlich & Merrick Advt., Washington, 1963-64; copy chief W.A. Lemer Advt., Washington, 1965-68; creative dir. Lemer & Goldberg, Washington, 1969-70; pres. Goldberg/Marchesano & Assos., Inc., Washington, 1970—, chmn. bd., 1980—. Mem. Met. Washington Bd. Trade, Met. Washington Advt. Club, Internat. Platform Assn., Zeta Beta Tau. Office: 1910 Sunderland Pl NW Washington DC 20036

GOLDBERG, PAUL MORTON, real estate exec.; b. Boston, May 27, 1939; s. Nathan and Tillie (Steinberg) G.; A.B., Dartmouth Coll., 1960; J.D., U. Wash., 1967; Ph.D., Mass. Inst. Tech., 1971; m. Margie Ann Campbell, Oct. 5, 1968; children—Zachary, Nathanael, Judd. Admitted to Mass. bar, 1968; individual practice law, Boston, 1968-71; sr. research asso. Abt Assos., Inc., Cambridge, Mass., 1968-71; dir. forward planning Paul Properties, Great Neck, N.Y., 1971-74; pres. Terrex Internat., Glen Head, N.Y., 1974-79; pres. Sunrise Devel. Co., subs. Forest City Enterprises, Inc., Cleve., 1979—; mem. faculty Sloan Sch. Mgmt., Mass. Inst. Tech., 1968-71. Bd. dirs. Mass. Inst. Tech. Alumni Fund. Served with USNR, 1960-64. Ford Found. fellow, 1970-71. Mem. Urban Land Inst. Office: 10800 Brookpark Rd Cleveland OH 44130

GOLDBERG, RAY ALLAN, educator; b. Fargo, N.D., Oct. 19, 1926; s. Max and Anne Libby (Paletz) G.; A.B. cum laude, Harvard U., 1948, M.B.A., 1950; Ph.D., U. Minn., 1952; m. Thelma Ruth Englander, May 20, 1956; children—Marc Evan, Jennifer Eve, Jeffrey Lewis. Officer, dir. Experience, Inc., Mpls.; dir. Internat. Basic Economy Corp., Green Giant Co.; lectr. bus. and agr. Harvard Grad. Sch. Bus. Adminstrn., 1955-57, asst. prof. bus. adminstrn., 57, 60, asso. prof., 1966-70, prof., 1970—, Moffett prof. agr. and bus., 1970—; dir. Tri/Valley Growers, 1973—; adviser John Hancock Agribus. Investment Com., INCAE, Managua, Nicaragua, 1973—, IPADE, Mexico City, 1973—; chmn. New Eng. Fed. Regional Council Conf. on Food, Nutrition and Health, 1978—; chmn. panel on food processing Nat. Commn. Productivity, 1972, Mass. Gov.'s Commn. on Food, 1974; co-chmn. panel on nutrition and food availability Select Com. on Nutrition and Human Needs, U.S. Senate, White House Conf. Food and Nutrition, 1974; gov. Internat. Devel. Research Centre Can. Bd. dirs. Internat. Devel. Found., Agribus. Mgmt. for Developing Countries, 1973; bd. govs. Internat. Devel. Research Center Can., 1978—; asso. trustee New Eng. Conservatory of Music, 1978—; trustee Roxbury Latin Sch., Beth Israel Hosp., 1978—. Recipient Uhlmann Grain award, 1952. Mem. Agrl. Econs. Assn., Am. Dairy Sci. Assn., Canadian Agrl. Econs. Soc., Mpls. Grain Exchange, Am. Soc. Animal Prodn. Clubs: Harvard (Boston) (N.Y.C.) (N.D., sec.); Oakridge Country, Harvard Bus. Sch. (Mpls.). Author: The Soybean Industry, 1952; Agribusiness Coordination, 1968; Agribusiness Management for Developing Countries-Latin America, 1974; (with others) A Concept of Agribusiness, 1957, Brand Strategy in U.S. Food Marketing, 1967; (with Lee F. Schrader) Federal Income Taxes and Farmers Cooperatives, 1974; (with others) The Lessons of Wage and Price Controls—The Food Sector; editor: Agribusiness Management for Developing Countries: Southeast Asia Corn System and American and Japanese Trends Affecting It (Ray A. Goldberg and Richard C. McGinity), 1979; editorial council Am. Jour. Agrl. Econs.; series editor Research in Domestic and International Agribusiness Management, a research ann., 1980. Home: 5 Rangeley Rd Chestnut Hill MA 02167 Office: Harvard Bus Sch Boston MA 02163

GOLDBERG, ROBERT IRVING, mktg. cons., educator, indsl. design co. exec.; b. Bklyn., Dec. 30, 1919; s. David and Rose (Maslow) G.; B.A., Bklyn. Coll., 1941; M.A., Columbia U., 1948; student Coll. City N.Y., 1941-42, Washington U., St. Louis, 1943-44, N.Y. U., 1949-50; Ph.D., Philathea Coll. (Can.), 1972; m. Leah Mishkin, Mar. 27, 1948; children—Marsha Sue, Mark George. Sr. indsl. designer Emerson Electric Mfg. Co., St. Louis, 1942-44; chief indsl. designer Display House, Phila., 1946; chief indsl. designer N.Am. Shipbldg. & Repair Corp., N.Y.C., 1946-47; partner, chief indsl. designer Robert I. Goldberg Assos., N.Y.C., 1946-56; pres., chief indsl. designer Associated Indsl. Designers, Inc., N.Y.C., 1956—; exhibited watercolor painting in group shows: Honolulu Art Mus., Indsl. Designers Inst., Springfield Mus. Fine Art, Am. Inst. Graphic Artists Show, others; prof. mktg. and package design Sch. Commerce N.Y. U., 1952-69; dir. N.Y. U. Seminars in indsl. design, color and package design; dir. workshop in package design Pratt Inst. Art Sch., 1952-69, also prof. packaging; dir. Center Profl. Packaging Edn., New Sch., N.Y.C., 1967-69; pres. Center for Packaging Edn., Inc., N.Y.C., 1969—; asso. prof. mktg. and bus. mgmt. St. Francis Coll., Bklyn., 1970—; lectr. on packaging USIA, Zagreb, Belgrade, Yugoslavia, Budapest, Hungary, 1969; lectr. export mktg. World Trade Center, UN Indsl. Devel. Orgn.; lectr. Am. Mgmt. Assn.; cons. govt. indsl. commns. Israel, Brazil, Spain; lectr. export mktg., Israel, 1976. Active Boy Scouts; bd. dirs. United Community Centers, Inc. Served to lt. (j.g.) USNR, 1944-46. Fellow Package Designers Council (founding mem.); mem. Indsl. Designers Soc. Am. (exec. bd.), Am. Mktg. Assn., Inter Soc. Color Council, Inst. Bus. Designers, Packaging Inst., Execs. Assn. N.Y. (dir.), Chi Beta Nu (founding pres.). Author numerous articles in field; contbg. editor: Modern Packaging Ency., Marketing Handbook, Playthings mag.; packaging editor Toys and Novelties Mag. Home: 29 Lawrence St New Hyde Park NY 11040 Office: 157 W 57th St New York NY 10019

GOLDBERG, ROBERT LINN, coal co. exec.; b. Boston, June 19, 1946; s. M. Melvin and Adeline (Linn) G.; B.S. in Bus. Adminstrn., Babson Coll., 1968; m. Elaine Levine, June 22, 1968; children—Robin, Pamela. With Spaulding & Slye Corp., real estate devel., Boston, 1968; investment property officer, broker Data Realty Corp., Brookline, Mass., 1969-72, advt. dir., 1972; owner, mgr. real estate acquisition, mgmt. and devel. co., Boston, 1973-76; founder, pres. NRG Coal Corp., Boston, 1977—, also dir. Served with U.S. Army, 1973. Recipient real estate advt. awards New Eng. Real Estate Jour., Boston Herald Am. Office: One Federal St Suite 1800 Boston MA 02110

GOLDBERG, STANLEY IRWIN, real estate exec.; b. Newport News, Va., May 13, 1934; s. David and Sara (Levy) G.; student Coll. William and Mary, 1952-54, U. Va., 1954-55; m. Marilyn Levin, Nov. 22, 1963 (dec. Oct. 1970); 1 son, Andrew Garfield; m. 2d, Carol Firestone, May 27, 1973 (div. 1975). With Bedding Supply Co., Inc., Newport News, 1956-73, v.p., 1956-59, exec. v.p., 1960-61, pres., 1962-73; pres. Mut. Realty Corp., 1975—; dir. Goldkress Corp. Served with USAF, 1957-58. Mem. Va. Mfrs. Assn., Def. Supply Assn., Nat. Assn. Realtors. Jewish religion (trustee temple). Club: Elks. Home: 19 Hopemont Dr Newport News VA 23606 Office: 11100 Jefferson Ave Newport News VA 23601

GOLDBLATT, ROBERT EUGENE, film processing co. exec.; b. Newark, July 18, 1940; s. Sol D. and Mina; B.S., Villanova U., 1966; M.B.A., U. Pa., 1968; m. Judith Belle Arbeiter, June 9, 1962; children—David, Daniel, Douglas. Various positions RCA, 1963-68, mgr. personnel adminstrn., Joseph Bancroft & Sons, Del., N.Y., 1968-73; dir. personnel, adminstrn. Simplicity Pattern Co., N.Y.C., 1973-77; v.p. personnel, indsl. relations Berkey Film Processing, Paramus, N.J., 1977—; speaker N.Y. Personnel Assn., 1972-73. Mem. Indsl. Council, 1970-72, Sports/Recreation Com., 1979—; soccer, baseball coach, 1975—. Mem. Am. Soc. Personnel Adminstrn., N.J.-N.Y. C. of C. (chmn. industry com. 1970—). Office: Berkey Photo Inc 40 Eisenhower Dr Paramus NJ 07652

GOLDEN, BALFOUR HENRY, food service co. exec.; b. Bangor, Maine, Aug. 23, 1922; s. Samuel Henry and Helen (Rybier) G.; A.B. cum laude, Bowdoin Coll., 1944; postgrad. Columbia U., 1945-47; m. Emma Jane Krakauer, June 22, 1956; children—Peter Balfour, Betsy Jane, Robert Henry. Pres., Golden Food Services Corp. of N.Y., 1951-70, of N.J., 1951-70, of Iowa, 1951-70, Golden Co. of Maine, 1952-70, Golden Base Services Corp., 1952-70, Plaza Eats, Inc., 1958-70, Dubonnet Restaurant Corp., 1960-70; food service cons., 1970-74; pres. Guardian Food Service Corp., N.Y.C., 1974—. Served with AUS, 1943-45. Mem. New Eng. Soc. in N.Y.C., N.Y. Restaurant Assn., Phi Beta Kappa. Club: Williams. Home: 325 Beechwood Rd Ridgewood NJ 07450 Office: 630 Fifth Ave New York NY 10020

GOLDEN, JAMES ANDREW, leasing co. exec.; b. Barnstable, Mass., Dec. 6, 1946; s. Jackson J. and Irene G.; B.S., Boston U., 1970. Service mgr. Colonial Car Lease Co., Inc., Plymouth, Mass., 1969-71, sales rep., 1971-73, sales mgr., 1973-74, v.p., 1974-75, pres., chief exec. officer, 1975—. Mem. Jewish Big Brother Assn. Served with AUS, 1968-70. Mem. Car and Truck Rental and Leasing Assn. Mass. (pres. 1975-76, dir. 1974—), Nat. Car and Truck Rental and Leasing Assn. (dir. 1976-78, exec. com. 1977-78), Am. Auto Leasing Assn. (dir. 1980—), Nat. Assn. Fleet Adminstrn., Am. Car Rental Assn. Home: 379 Commonwealth Ave Boston MA 02115 Office: Colonial Car Lease Co Samoset St Plymouth MA 02360

GOLDENBERG, GEORGE, pharm. co. exec.; b. N.Y.C., Mar. 12, 1929; s. Gersh and Rose (Kolpacci) G.; student Bklyn. Coll., 1946-47; B.S., Bklyn. Coll. Pharmacy of L.I. U., 1951; m. Arlene Sandra Yudell, May 22, 1955; children—Steven Alan, Heidi Michele, Jeffrey Evan. Pharmacist, Dolcorts Pharmacy, N.Y.C., 1951-56; export mgr. Chem. Specialties Co., Inc., N.Y.C., 1956-58; sales mgr. Syntex Chem. Co., Inc., N.Y.C., 1958-60; asst. to pres. Syntex Labs., Inc., N.Y.C., 1960-61; gen. sales mgr. Panray-Parlam Corp., Englewood, N.J., 1961-63; v.p. Ormont Drug & Chem. Co., Inc., Englewood, 1963-64, exec. v.p., dir., 1964-66, pres., dir., 1966—; sec., dir. Goldleaf Pharmacal Co., Inc., Englewood, N.J., 1966—; dir. A-G Pharms. Inc., 1971—; dir. Fed. Pharmacal Co., Ft. Lauderdale, Fla., Bedford Acme Surg. Co., Inc., Bklyn., Lawton Labs., Inc., Englewood, Ormont Diagnostics Ltd., London. Trustee L.I. U., Bklyn. Coll. Pharmacy. Mem. Bklyn. Coll. Pharmacy Alumni Assn. (pres.), Fedn. Alumni Assns. L.I. U. (pres.), Am. Pharm. Assn., Englewood Jr. C. of C., Young Pres.'s Orgn., Am. Mgmt. Assn., Drug and Allied Trades Assn., Delta Sigma Theta. Club: B'nai B'rith. Home: 21 Carol Ct Demarest NJ 07627 also 3070 N 34th St Hollywood FL Office: 520 S Dean St Englewood NJ 07631

GOLDENSON, LEONARD HARRY, motion picture, radio, TV exec.; b. Scottdale, Pa., Dec. 7, 1905; s. Lee and Ester (Broude) G.; ed. Harvard, 1927, Harvard Law Sch., 1930; m. Isabelle Weinstein, Oct. 10, 1939; children—Genise, Loreen, Maxine. Admitted to N.Y., Pa. bars, 1930, pvt. practice N.Y.C., 1930-33; asst. to Y. Frank Freeman, in charge theatre operations, Paramount Pictures, N.Y.C., 1937-38, in charge theatre operations, 1941, v.p., Paramount Pictures, N.Y.C., 1942-50, dir. Paramount Pictures, Inc., 1944-50; pres., dir. United Paramount Theatres, Inc., 1950-52; pres., dir. Am. Broadcasting-Paramount Theatres, Inc. (name changed to Am. Broadcasting Cos., Inc.), 1953-71, chmn. bd., chief exec. officer, 1971—; mem. Uptown adv. com. Bankers Trust Co. Founder, pres., United Cerebral Palsy Assn., Inc., 1949-53, chmn. bd., 1954—, vice chmn. bd. dirs. Bd. dirs. United Cerebral Palsy Research and Ednl. Found.; mem. adv. com. Nat. Cultural Center, Nat. Com. for Voluntary Action. Bd. dirs. Will Rogers Meml. Hosp., Daus. of Jacob Geriatric Center, N.Y.C.; trustee Children's Research Found. of Children's Med. Center, Boston. Mem. Advt. Council (dir.), Internat. Radio and TV Soc. Club: Harvard. Office: 1330 Ave of Americas New York NY 10019*

GOLDFARB, MURIEL BERNICE, gold products mfg. co. exec.; b. Bklyn., Mar. 29, 1920; s. Barnett Goldfarb and May (Steinberg) Goldfarb Oshman; B.A., U. Miami, Coral Gables, Fla., 1942; postgrad. Coll. City N.Y., 1950. Advt. mgr. Majestic Specialities Co., N.Y.C., 1942-43; pub. info. asst. UNESCO, Paris, 1946-47; retail promotion mgr. Glamour Mag., 1955-61; advt. dir. Country Tweeds Co., N.Y.C., 1961-65; advt. dir. S. Augstein & Co., N.Y.C., 1966-72, Feature Ring Co., Inc., Gotham Ring Co., Inc., Fidco Inc., N.Y.C., 1972-78; dir. advt. and promotion Wasko Gold Products Corp., N.Y.C., 1979—. Served to lt. WAVES, 1943-46. Mem. Fashion Group N.Y. Inc. Jewish. Home: 340 52d St New York NY 10022

GOLDFEDER, HOWARD, retail store exec.; b. N.Y.C., 1926; grad. Tufts U., 1947; married. Exec. v.p., pres. May Co. div. May Dept. Stores, 1967-71; with Federated Dept. Stores Inc., 1947-67, 71—, pres. Bullock's div., 1971-73, chmn., chief exec. officer, 1973-77, vice chmn. corp., 1977-80, pres., chief operating officer, 1980-81, pres., chief exec. officer, 1981—, also dir.; dir. Champion Internat. Corp., Conn. Mut. Life Ins. Co. Office: Federated Dept Stores Inc 7 W 7th St Cincinnati OH 45202

GOLDFIELD, ROBERT SAUL, corp. exec.; b. Phila., Aug. 4, 1927; s. James Edward and Minna (Mellen) G.; B.S., Drexel Inst. Tech., 1948; m. Florence P. Berg, Sept. 14, 1948; children—David S., Burton M., Danny J. Technician elec. photometric research Naval Research Labs., Washington, 1944-45; customer service mgr. lab. and photog. equipment dept. Williams, Brown & Earle, Inc., Phila., 1948-55; sec.-treas., sales mgr. Albern Color Research, Phila., 1955-60; v.p., nat. sales mgr. Perfect Photo, Inc., Phila., 1960-62, asst. to pres. and v.p., 1962-66, pres., 1966-71; v.p. GAF Corp., N.Y.C., 1971-72; pres., chief exec. officer CGS Sci. Corp., Concordville, Pa., 1973-76, pres., chief exec. officer, chmn. bd., 1977—. Mem. Phila. C. of C., Sales and Mktg. Execs. Internat., U.S. C. of C., Pa. Mfrs. Assn., Phi Kappa Phi. Home: 213 Stonehouse Ln Wyncote PA 19095 Office: Concord Industrial Park Lacrue Ave PO Box 222 Concordville PA 19331

GOLDFRANK, LIONEL, III, investment co. exec.; b. N.Y.C., Sept. 5, 1943; s. Lionel and Jean (Mann) G.; B.A., Yale U., 1965; 1 dau., Adelaide S. With Goldman, Sachs & Co., N.Y.C., 1965-69, arbitrage trader, 1965-69; pres. Am. & Overseas Asset Services Corp., N.Y.C., 1969—; gen. partner Allied Founders Co.; dir. Intermarket Fund I. Mem. Real Estate Bd. N.Y., Inc. Clubs: Yale (N.Y.C.); Century Country (Purchase, N.Y.). Office: 345 Park Ave New York NY 10154

GOLDMACHER, IRVING, communications co. exec.; b. Samarovo, USSR, Jan. 1, 1943; came to U.S., 1960, naturalized, 1965; s. Matt and Yadviga G.; B.S., City U. N.Y., 1964; M.S. in Elec. Engring., Poly.

Inst. N.Y., 1966; M.A. in Physics, SUNY-Stony Brook, 1967; m. Jacqueline Lewis, June 22, 1980. Engr. missile systems div. Raytheon Co., Bedford, Mass., 1968-69; sr. engr., project mgr. Norden div. United Technologies Corp., Norwalk, Conn., 1969-72; cons., 1972-76; founder Meadows Communications, Fresh Meadows, N.Y., 1976—; partner Goldmacher/Mitchell Communications, Flushing, N.Y., 1979—. Jewish. Writer tng. programs for various cos. Patentee in field of radar systems. Home: 188-02 64th Ave Fresh Meadows NY 11365 Office: PO Box 447 Flushing NY 11365

GOLDMAN, DAVID HARVEY, bowling center and import co. exec.; b. Auburn, N.Y., Mar. 30, 1929; s. Samuel and Bertha (Winnick) G.; B.B.A., Ohio State U., 1951; m. Marilyn Kenyon, Mar. 5, 1955; children—Marjorie, Robert, Amy. Sales exec. I.C. Issac & Co., Balt., 1952-58; a founder Am. Bowling Enterprises, Rochester, N.Y., 1958, chmn. bd., pres., 1958-63; a founder Rochester Elton Corp., 1963, pres., 1963-72; pres. Reltron Corp., Rochester, 1972—, Vanguard Products, Berkely Springs, W.Va.; founder, pres. Elton Internat., Hong Kong, 1973—, Spitz 7 Ltd., Hong Kong, 1973—. Patron U. Rochester, 1964—. Club: Irondiquoit Country (Rochester). Home: 200 Georgian Ct Rd Rochester NY 14610 Office: 45 Gould St Rochester NY 14610

GOLDMAN, ELLIOT LEONARD, fin. exec.; b. Providence, Mar. 16, 1936; s. Harry Isaac and Rebecca Thelma (Katz) G.; B.A. cum laude, Harvard U., 1957; M.B.A., Wharton Sch., U. Pa., 1959; m. Muriel Freedman, June 17, 1961; 1 son, Arthur David. Group controller Teledyne Co., Burlington, N.J., 1961-68; treas. CGS Sci. Corp., Southampton, Pa., 1968-70; controller Metalstand Co., Phila., 1970-74; fin. cons., 1974-76; v.p. fin. Life Assurance Co. Phila., 1976-78; v.p. fin. Am. Health Programs, Phila., 1978—. Recipient award of Merit Nat. Contract Mgmt. Assn. Mem. Fin. Execs. Inst., Am. Mgmt. Assn. Club: Harvard (Phila.). Home: EE 1023 Green Hill Apts Philadelphia PA 19151 Office: Am Health Programs One Neshaminy Interplex Suite 106 Trevose PA 19047

GOLDMAN, HARVEY JOE, mgmt. cons.; b. Newark, June 7, 1946; s. Morris J. and Sylvia (Gordon) G.; B.A. in Accounting, Duke U., 1968; M.B.A., Harvard U., 1970; m. Judith Kusnitz, June 22, 1969; children—Mark Daniel, Cari Beth. Sr. accountant, staff cons. Peat, Marwick & Mitchell & Co., Boston, 1969-72; controller, financial v.p. Miralin Co., Hudson, Mass., 1972-74; prin. Arthur Young & Co., Worcester, Mass., 1972-74, Newark, 1974—, dir. fin. planning and control consulting N.J. offices, 1979—, partner, 1980—; nat. coordinator services to EPA grantees; expert witness on fin. impact of EPA regulations Congressional Com. on Environ. Pollution. Mem. adv. bd. William Paterson Sch. Bus., Paterson, N.J.; treas., bd. dirs. Authorities Assn. of N.J. Woodrow Wilson fellow, 1970. C.P.A., N.J., Mass., N.C.; lic. pub. sch. accountant, N.J. Mem. Am. Inst. C.P.A.'s, N.J. State Soc. C.P.A.'s, Planning Execs. Inst., Municipal Finance Officers Assn. Club: Harvard Bus. Sch. Author: Making Cost Control Work: Handbook of Business Problem Solving, 1980; contbr. articles to profl. jours. Home: 2 Bernard Dr Holmdel NJ 07733 Office: 520 Broad St Newark NJ 07102

GOLDMAN, LEONARD, mgmt. corp. exec., lawyer; b. Phila., June 18, 1937; s. Joseph and Gertrude (Cherry) G.; B.S., Temple U., 1959, J.D., 1962; m. Marilyn Dee Singer, Apr. 15, 1962; children—Jeffrey, Michael, David. Admitted to Pa. bar, 1963, Md. bar, 1978; individual practice law, Phila., 1963-64; asst. gen. counsel Am. Acceptance Corp., Phila., 1965-68, GAC Fin., Inc., Allentown, Pa., 1969-72; house counsel, asst. sec. Jerrold Electronics Corp., Horsham, Pa., 1972-77; counsel, v.p., sec. Am. Fin. Mgmt. Corp., Silver Spring, Md., 1977-79; atty. Computer Scis. Corp., Falls Church, Va., 1980—. Mem. Nat. Consumer Fin. Assn. (law com.), Am. Bar Assn., Phi Alpha Theta. Feature editor Temple Law Reports, 1962. Home: 17 Blueberry Ridge Ct Potomac MD 20854 Office: Computer Scis Corp 6565 Arlington Blvd Falls Ch VA 22046

GOLDMAN, MARSHALL IRWIN, economist; b. Elgin, Ill., July 26, 1930; s. Sam and Bella (Silvian) G.; B.S., U. Pa., 1952; M.A., Harvard U., 1956, Ph.D., 1961; m. Merle Rosenblatt, June 14, 1953; children—Ethan Harris, Avra Lea, Karla Ann, Seth Abraham. Instr., Wellesley Coll., Boston, 1958-61, prof. econs., 1968—; vis. asst. prof. Brandeis U., 1961; asst. dir. Russian Research Center, Harvard U., Boston, 1975—; cons. U.S. State Dept., Gulf Oil, Atlantic Richfield, Continental Bank & Trust. Mem. Wellesley Town Meeting, 1974-77, Wellesley Democratic Town Com., 1962-70. Served with U.S. Army, 1953-55. Fulbright-Hayes fellow to Soviet Union, 1977. Mem. Am. Econ. Assn., Council Fgn. Relations N.Y. Jewish. Club: Econ. of Boston. Author: Soviet Foreign Aid, 1967; Soviet Marketing: Distribution in a Controlled Economy, 1963; The Enigma of Soviet Petroleum: Half Empty or Half Full, 1980; Detente and Dollars: Doing Business with the Soviets, 1975; The Spoils of Progress: Environmental Pollution in the Soviet Union, 1972; The Soviet Economy: Myth and Reality, 1968. Home: 17 Midland Rd Wellesley MA 02181 Office: Harvard Univ Russian Research Center Cambridge MA 02138

GOLDMAN, MAYNARD, lawyer, fin. cons., retail co. exec.; b. Boston, Aug. 8, 1937; s. Sumner S. and Harriette F. Goldman; B.A., U. Mich., 1959; LL.B., Harvard U., 62; m. Margery Loewenberg, June 12, 1967 (div.); 1 son, Derek Anthony. Admitted to Mass. bar, 1962; sr. cons. Harbridge House, Inc., Boston, 1963-67, Arthur D. Little Inc., Cambridge, Mass., 1968-69; asst. to pres. ITT Sheraton Corp. Am., Boston, 1970-71; chmn., treas. Goldman Del Rossi & Co., Inc., Boston, 1973—; pres. Hurok Concerts Inc., 1976-77; prin., gen. mgr. Charles Sumner, Inc., Boston, 1977—; dir. various cos.; fin. cons., 1963—; exec. dir. Nat. Def. Edn. Inst., 1965-67. Bd. dirs. Boston Zool. Soc., Center for Internat. Visitors, Crime and Justice Found.; bd. overseers Met. Center; bd. visitors Sch. Theatre Arts, Boston U. Mem. Am. Bar Assn., Am. Arbitration Assn. Clubs: Belmont (Mass.) Country; Harvard (Boston). Home: 375 Beacon St Boston MA 02116 Office: 16 Newbury St Boston MA 02114

GOLDMAN, ROBERT SORRELL, mgmt. cons.; b. Buffalo, Oct. 19, 1933; s. Jack and Annette (Rudin) G.; B.S. in Econs., U. Pa., 1955; m. Janet Lavner; children—Dale Sue, Jay Alan. Indsl. engr. Morrison Steel Products, Buffalo, 1955-57; mgr. indsl. engring. Merck, Sharp & Dohme, West Point, Pa., 1959-65; adminstr. mgmt. systems & procedures RCA, Moorestown, N.J., 1965-67; dir. mgmt. controls Rheingold Corp., Bklyn., 1967-68; sr. cons. bus. systems and computing, Xerox Corp., Stamford, Conn., 1968-70; pres. R.S. Goldman Assos., Phila., 1970-72; prin., mgmt. cons. Coopers & Lybrand, Phila., 1972-80; pres. Asso. Internat. Mgmt. Corp., Phila., 1980; pres. R.S. Goldman Assos., Phila., 1980—. Scoutmaster, Boy Scouts Am., Buffalo, 1955-57. Served to adj. gen. U.S. Army, 1957-59. Cert. mgmt. cons. Mem. Inst. Mgmt. Cons., Am. Inst. Indsl. Engrs. (dir. nat. conf. procs. 1964), Am. Prodn. and Inventory Control Soc. Contbr. articles to profl. jours. Office: Philadelphia PA

GOLDNER, HERMAN WILSON, lawyer; b. Detroit, Nov. 12, 1916; s. Michael and Ethel (Wilson) G.; student Ohio State U., 1934-35; B.S., Miami U., Oxford, O., 1939; LL.B., Case-Western Res. U., 1942; M.B.A., Harvard, 1948; m. Winifred Herlan Munyan, Nov. 3, 1938; children—Brian Early, Michael Herlan. Admitted to Ohio bar, 1942, Mass. bar, 1947, Fla. bar, 1949; founder firm Goldner, Cramer (name changed to Goldner, Reams, Marger, Davis, Kirnan 1976), St. Petersburg, Fla., 1949, pres., 1949-78, of counsel, 1978—; v.p. All Advt. Assos., St. Petersburg, 1979—; bd. dirs. Central Plaza Bank & Trust Co., St. Petersburg, 1973—. Mayor City of St. Petersburg, 1962-68, 1971-73; exec. bd. U.S. Conf. Mayors, 1963-68, chmn. Bi-Racial Commn., 1963; founder, chmn. Tampa Bay Regional Planning Council, 1964-68; mem. president's bi-racial com. President's Adv. Commn. Intergovtl. Relations, 1966-68. Served with U.S. Navy, 1942-46; PTO. Recipient Good Govt. Award State of Fla., C. of C., 1968. Mem. Alumni Assn. Case Western Res. U., St. Petersburg Bar Assn., Fla. Bar Assn., Am. Bar Assn. Republican. Jewish. Clubs: Yacht, Commerce (St. Petersburg, Fla.); Lakewood Country; Mason (Shriner). Contbr. articles to various publs. Office: 5665 Central Ave Saint Petersburg FL 33710

GOLDSBERRY, RONALD EUGENE, chem. co. exec.; b. Wilmington, Del., Sept. 12, 1942; s. Clifford Isaacs and Constance (Wright) G.; B.S. summa cum laude, Central State U., 1964; Ph.D., Mich. State U., 1969; M.B.A., Stanford U., 1973; m. Betty Sanders, June 19, 1965; children—Ryan, Renee. Instr., U. Calif., San Jose, 1969-71; research chemist NASA Ames Research Center, Moffett Field, Calif., 1969-72; mktg. mgr. Hewlett Packard Co., Palo Alto, Calif., 1972-73; mgmt. cons. specializing in corp. strategy Boston Cons. Group, 1973-75; dir. corp. planning ops. Gulf Oil Corp., Pitts., 1975-78; v.p. planning and bus. devel. Occidental Petroleum-Hooker Chem. Co., Houston, 1978—. Served to capt. AUS, 1969-71. Mem. Comml. Devel. Assn., Assn. Corp. Growth, Nat. Orgn. Black Chemists and Chem. Engrs., Am. Mgmt. Assn., Am. Chem. Soc., Forum Club Houston, Omega Psi Phi. Patentee ultraviolet and thermally stable polymer composition. Office: 1980 S Post Oak Houston TX 77201

GOLDSCHMIDT, CHARLES, advt. agency exec.; b. N.Y.C., June 15, 1921; s. Harry and Adele (Safir) G.; B.A., N.Y.U., 1941; m. Patricia Nevins, Jan. 17, 1951; children—Richard Walter, Jane, Peter. Advt. copywriter Warner Bros. Pictures Co., 1946-48, Buchanan & Co., N.Y.C., 1948-49, Ray Austrian Asso., N.Y.C., 1949-52; a founder, partner Daniel & Charles, Inc., advt., N.Y.C., 1952—, chmn. bd., 1959—; dir. Mickelberry Corp., N.Y.C. Served to lt. USNR, 1941-46. Democrat. Clubs: Harmonie (N.Y.C.); Beach Point (Mamaroneck, N.Y.). Author fiction, play, articles. Office: 261 Madison Ave New York NY 10016*

GOLDSCHMIDT, LESTER ALLAN, cosmetic co. exec.; b. N.Y.C., May 31, 1945; s. Joseph and Isabelle (Allweiss) G.; B.S., Columbia U., 1968; M.S., Bklyn. Coll. Pharmacy, 1970; m. Edith Kremer, Nov. 1, 1970; children—Jessica Marlene, Sharon Rachelle. Resident, Mercy Hosp., Rockville Centre, N.Y., 1968-69, staff pharmacist, 1969-70, supr., 1970-73; dir. pharmacy services St. Joseph's Hosp., Elmira, N.Y., 1973-79, dir. poison control center, 1973-79; sales mgr. Joseph Goldschmidt Cosmetics, Inc., St. James, N.Y., 1979—; mem. faculty Albany Coll. Pharmacy, 1974-79, Elmira Coll., 1975-79. Bd. dirs. Congregation Shomray Hadath, Elmira, 1974-79, v.p., 1978-79; bd. dirs. Jewish Community Center, Elmira, 1977-79. Mem. Am. Pharm. Assn., Am. Soc. Hosp. Pharmacists, So. Tier Soc. Hosp. Pharmacists (past pres.), Am. Coll. Apothecaries, N.Y. State Council Hosp. Pharmacists. Home: 11 Stanley Pl Hauppauge NY 11787 Office: 110 Drew Dr Saint James NY 11780

GOLDSMITH, CLIFFORD HENRY, tobacco co. exec.; b. Leipzig, Germany, Sept. 6, 1919; s. Conrad and Elise (Stahl) G.; grad. Bradford (Eng.) U., 1939; m. Katherine W. Kaynis; children—Corinne Elizabeth (Mrs. Philemon Dickinson), Audrey Jane (Mrs. David Kubie), Alexandra Eve. Came to U.S., 1940, naturalized, 1943. Technologist Glenside Mills Corp., Skaneateles, N.Y., 1940-41; supt. Falls Yarn Mills, Woonsocket, R.I., 1941-42, Aldon Spinning Mills, Talcotville, Conn., 1942-43; with Benson & Hedges Co., 1943-53, plant mgr., 1945-53; with Philip Morris, Inc., 1954—, now pres., dir.; dir. Central Fidelity Banks, Inc. Bd. dirs. Nat. Multiple Sclerosis Soc. Served with inf. AUS, 1943-45. Asso. mem. Textile Inst. (Manchester, Eng.). Clubs: Commonwealth, Downtown (Richmond). Office: Philip Morris Inc 100 Park Ave New York NY 10017*

GOLDSMITH, PETER STEVEN, data processing exec.; b. N.Y.C., May 21, 1943; s. Alfons and Lotte (Abeles) G.; B.B.A., CCNY, 1964; M.B.A. in Fin. with honors, St. John's U., 1978; m. Joyce Marilyn Kahan, June 24, 1973; 1 son, Matthew Harris. Mgr. adminstrv. services CBS Inc., N.Y.C., 1967-70, asst. dir. fin. mgmt., 1970-73, dir. ops., Los Angeles, 1973-75; asst. to v.p. devel. Grumman Data Systems, Woodbury, N.Y., 1975—, tchr. fin. analysis course, 1978—. Vice pres. Old Forge Civic Assn., 1979—. Served with U.S. Army, 1964-65. Mem. Beta Gamma Sigma, Pi Sigma Epsilon. Jewish. Home: 44 Farmington Ln Dix Hills NY 11747 Office: 150 Crossways Park Dr Woodbury NY 11797

GOLDSMITH, RICHARD PHILIP, nursing home exec.; b. Balt., Jan. 26, 1954; s. Theodore Harold and Sheila Fay (Price) G.; B.S., U. Balt., 1976; m. Lynne Karen Gerber, July 31, 1975. Analyst, Hosp. Cost Analysis Services Inc., Balt., 1975-77; dir. fin. Jenkins Meml. Inc., Balt., 1977—. Vol., Jewish Community Center Greater Balt.; vice chmn. fin., bd. dirs. B'nai B'rith Youth. Mem. Md. Health Roundtable (citation 1979). Democrat. Club: B'nai B'rith (lodge treas. 1979—). Home: 701 Sturgis Pl Pikesville MD 21208 Office: 1000 S Caton Ave Baltimore MD 21229

GOLDSTEIN, FREDERICK ARYA, mktg. and opinion research co. exec.; b. Chgo., Mar. 21, 1931; s. Irving and Lillie (Ginsberg) G.; B.A., Williams Coll., 1952; M.B.A., U. Pa., 1956; m. Edwen Leyens, July 11, 1954; children—Dana Eve, Peter Bron, Joanna. Asst. dir. market research Fortune mag., N.Y.C., 1956-61; account research mgr., J. Walter Thompson, 1961-63; research mgr. Morse Internat. div. Richardson-Merrell Co., 1963-64; creative research mgr. Cunningham & Walsh, 1964-68; dir. market research and devel. Liggett & Meyers, N.Y.C., 1968-70; pres. Goldstein/Krall Mktg. Resources, Inc., N.Y.C., 1970—, New Products Mktg. Corp., N.Y.C., 1972—; v.p., dir. Internat. Mktg. Research Corp., 1980—, Survey Tab, Inc., 1980—; dir. New Products Europe Corp. Bd. dirs. Mental Health Assn., Stamford, Conn., 1968-70, Temple Sinai, Stamford, 1975-77, Jr. Achievement Stamford, 1976—. Served with AUS, 1952-54. Mem. Am. Mgmt. Assn., Am. Mktg. Assn., Am. Assn. for Public Opinion Research, Brit. Market Research Soc., European Soc. for Opinion and Mktg. Research, Mktg. Research Assn. Democrat. Club: Williams of N.Y. Office: Goldstein/Krall Mktg Resources Inc 25 3d St Stamford CT 06905

GOLDSTEIN, JACK, steel co. exec.; b. Lincoln, Nebr., Oct. 3, 1916; s. Samuel and Mollie (Stine) G.; m. Sept. 11, 1980. With Steel & Pipe Supply Co., Inc., Manhattan, Kans., 1933—, chmn. bd., 1954—; chmn. bd. Manhattan Bldgs., Inc., Bus. Bldgs., Inc., Bldg. Investment Co., Inc., Kans. Indsl. Products, Inc.; dir. Union Nat. Bank, Manhattan. City commr. Manhattan, 1967-69; bd. dirs. St. Mary Hosp., 1977; mem. exec. com. Kans. State U. Found. Served with USAAF, 1942-45. Mem. Manhattan C. of C. (pres. 1980—), Assn. U.S. Army (trustee 1978—, pres.-elect chpt.). Clubs: Rotary (pres.) (Manhattan); Masons, Shriners. Home: 222 Pine St Manhattan KS 66502 Office: 205 Osage St Manhattan KS 66502

GOLDSTEIN, MANFRED, cons.; b. Vienna, Austria, Jan. 30, 1927; s. Isadore and Anna (Hahn) G.; student Manhattan Trade Center, 1947; E.E., Capitol Radio Engring. Inst., 1963; student L.I. U., 1961, Indsl. Coll. Armed Forces, 1967-68; m. Shirley Marie Lavine, Aug. 27, 1950; children—Cindy Marie, Lynn Alyse. Came to U.S., 1939, naturalized, 1945. Sr. technician Bklyn. Radio, 1953-55, Budd Stanley, Inc., Long Island City, 1955; lead engr. telephone equipment Precision Indsl. Design, Newark, 1955-57; project engr., contract adminstr., sales mgr. Lieco, Inc., Syossett, N.Y. 1957-65, v.p., 1964-65; mgmt. and engring. cons., 1965—; pres. Positive Consultants Inc., Bellmore, N.Y., 1967—. Owner Lake Luzerne (N.Y.) Seaplane Base, 1969—. Mem. small bus. adv. com., chmn. fed. procurement subcom. Congressman Thomas J. Downey of N.Y. Served with AUS, 1945-46. Mem. Soc. Plastics Engrs., I.E.E.E. (sr.), Am. Def. Preparedness Assn. (exec. bd. mgmt. div.), Nat. Contract Mgmt. Assn. (dir.), Air Force Assn., Capitol Radio Engr. Inst. Alumni (sr.), Nat. Pilots Assn., Aircraft Owners and Pilots Assn., L.I. Assn. Commerce and Industry, Civil Air Patrol, Internat. Platform Assn., Lake Luzerne C. of C. (chmn. indsl. devel. com.). Inventor torpedo fire control cable and connector for Polaris, high pressure seals for Polaris submarine antennae. Office: 2255 Arby Ct Wantagh Bellmore NY 11710

GOLDSTEIN, MARK KINGSTON LEVIN, business exec.; b. Burlington, Vt., Aug. 22, 1941; s. Harold Meyer and Roberta Olga (Butterfield) Levin; stepson Frank Goldstein; B.S. in Chemistry, U. Vt., 1964; Ph.D. in Chemistry, U. Miami, Coral Gables, Fla., 1971; m. Beverly Twilley, June 16, 1971; children—Geoffry, Allision. Founder, pres. IBR, Inc., Coral Gables, 1971-74; group leader Brookhaven Nat. Lab., Upton, N.Y., 1974-77; sr. researcher East-West Center, Honolulu, 1977-79; sr. tech. advisor JGC Corp., Tokyo, 1979—; cons. in field. NSF fellow, 1963, 64. Mem. Am. Nuclear Soc., Friends of East West Center, Inst. Nuclear Materials Mgmt., Am. Chem. Soc., AAAS, Sigma Xi. Club: Hawaii Yacht. Home: 31 Negishi Asahi Dai Naka-Ku Yokohama Japan Office: 14-1 Bessho 1-chome Minamiku Yokohama Japan also care JGC Corp 2-1 Ohtemachi-2 chome Chiyoda-ku Tokyo Japan

GOLDSTEIN, STANLEY, corp. exec.; b. Bklyn., Aug. 20, 1937; s. Max and Fannie (Eisner) G.; student N.Y.C. Community Coll. Pres. T.J. Menners, Inc., Bklyn., 1976—. Office: 2855 Ocean Ave Brooklyn NY 11235

GOLDSTEIN, WILLIAM ALLAN, investment banker; b. Chgo., June 24, 1939; s. Jack E. and Marion B. (Peskind) G.; B.S., Purdue U., 1961; m. Anne B. Frank, Aug. 19, 1962; children—Deborah, Catherine. Instl. sales mgr. Midwest region Hornblower & Weeks-Hemphill Noyes, Chgo., 1962-70; exec. v.p., dir., stockholder Chesley & Co. Inc., Chgo., 1970-74; exec. v.p., dir., stockholder Burton J. Vincent, Chesley & Co., 1974—; mem. Midwest Stock Exchange; allied mem. N.Y. Stock Exchange; cons. in field. Mem. campaign com. young peoples div. Chgo. United Jewish Fund drive, 1968-70. Served with AUS. Mem. Alpha Epsilon Pi. Mem. B'nai B'rith. Clubs: Bond, Covenant (Chgo.). Home: 1621 Kirk St Evanston IL 60202 Office: 105 W Adams St Chicago IL 60603

GOLDSTONE, GEORGE RONALD, real estate broker; b. Phila., Apr. 29, 1932; s. David and Lena (Horowitz) G.; B.S. in Econs. cum laude, Temple U., 1954; m. Jacqueline Yentis, June 5, 1955; children—Jeffrey, Mark, Debra. Pres. Herbert Yentis & Co., Phila., 1960—; dir. Commonwealth Holding & Devel. Co., Yale Realty Co., Harvard Realty Co., Jeff-Mark Corp.; advisor Gov.'s Energy Council, State of Pa., 1977-78; lectr. Harcum Jr. Coll., Drexel U., Phila., 1972-78. Vice pres. Temple Beth Hillel, Wynnewood, Pa., 1978—; bd. dirs. Jewish Youth Center, Phila., 1977—; pres. Yentis Found., 1965—. Served with U.S. Army, 1954-56. Cert. sr. resdl. appraiser, cert. property mgr. Mem. Inst. Real Estate Mgmt. (pres. Del. Valley chpt. 1977-78), Phila., Main Line, West Phila. bds. Realtors, Pa. Realtors Assn., Beta Gamma Sigma. Jewish. Clubs: 32 Carat, Masons. Home: 455 N Highland Ave Merion PA 19066 Office: 7300 City Line Ave Philadelphia PA 19151

GOLDSTROM, JERALD MARTIN, financial adviser; b. Des Moines, Mar. 29, 1942; s. Bernard Lester and Betty Ruth (Schlanger) G.; B.S. in Fin., U. Nebr., Omaha, 1965; M.B.A., U. Iowa, 1970; m. Kathryn Ann Yoerg, Feb. 7, 1964; 1 son, Jeffrey. Mgr. real estate and office personnel Progressive Corp., Cleve., 1968-69; specialist, systems design and computers Singer Friden Bus. Machines, Cleve., 1969-72; real estate developer Soltesz Realty, Cleve., 1972; pres. Internat. Energy Co., Cleve., 1972-74; partner, dir. Trans-World Energy, Cleve., 1973-76; fin. planning cons., 1976-77; pres. Fin. Planning Group, Beachwood, Ohio, 1977—. Home: 4101 Verona Rd South Euclid OH 44121

GOLICZ, LAWRENCE JOHN, appraisal corp. exec.; b. Detroit, Feb. 21, 1944; s. Anthony John and Estelle Ann (Rogowski) G.; B.A. (regents scholar), U. Mich., 1966; M.A. (teaching asst.) Wash. State U., 1968; Ph.D. (teaching asst., grad. sch. scholar), U. Maine, 1973; spl. student U. Wis., 1970-72; m. Peggy L. Erickson, Aug. 3, 1968; children—Eric John, Karl Peter, Mark Joseph. Pres., Am. Appraisal Feasibility Corp. Madison, Wis., 1973—; part-time time tchr. real estate Madison Area Tech. Coll., U. Wis. Extension; pres. Total Realty Inc.; mng. partner Total Enterprises, Madison Mut. Investors. Social Sci. Research Council grantee. Mem. Soc. Real Estate Appraisers, Am. Inst. Real Estate Appraisers, Madison Bd. Realtors, Urban Land Inst., Internat. Council Shopping Centers. Clubs: Optimists, Exchange. Home: 1619 Elderwood Circle Middleton WI 53562 Office: 6510 Schroeder Rd Madison WI 53711

GOLLIVER, ROBERT RUSSELL, energy co. exec.; b. Silver Lake, Ind., May 22, 1935; s. Norman and Helen (Hankins) G.; B.S. in Engring., Purdue U., 1957; LL.B., Ind. U., 1960; m. Joy J. Gadbury, June 26, 1955; children—Gregory, Guy, Pamela. Aditted to Ind. bar, 1960; with Stone & Webster, mgmt. cons.'s, N.Y.C., 1960-65; from dir. indsl. relations to exec. v.p. Wash. Natural Gas Co., Seattle, 1965-80, pres., chief operating officer, 1980—, also dir. Bd. dirs., chief Seattle council Boy Scouts Am. Mem. Am. Gas Assn., Pacific Coast Gas Assn. Clubs: Rainier, Rotary, Overlake Golf and Country, Wash. Athletic. Office: 815 Mercer St Seattle WA 98111

GOLUB, JERRY DAVID, fin. and tax cons.; b. Bronx, N.Y., Jan. 31, 1952; s. William and Sylvia (Barrow) G.; B.S. summa cum laude, SUNY, Binghamton, 1974; M.B.A., U. Chgo., 1976; diploma N.Y. U. Acctg. and fin. specialist IBM Corp., 1977-78; asst. research analyst Kidder, Peabody & Co., N.Y.C., 1978-79; ind. cons. taxation and fin., Whitestone, N.Y., 1979—; cons. portfolio and trust acctg., operational controls, fin. analysis Paine, Webber Jackson & Curtis, Inc., 1980-81; lectr. Latin Am. Inst. Leon Carrol Marshall fellow, 1974-76. C.P.A., N.Y. Mem. Am. Inst. C.P.A.'s (adv. grading service), Nat. Assn. Accts., Nat. Assn. Bus. Economists, Am. Fin. Assn., Fin. Mgmt. Assn., Am. Acctg. Assn., N.Y. U. Fin. Club, Amnesty Internat. Address: 24-17 Parsons Blvd Whitestone NY 11357

GOLZ, RONALD ALFRED, banker; b. Fall River, Mass., Feb. 4, 1934; s. Alfred E. and Irene F. (Thibault) G.; A.B., Bowdoin Coll., 1956; M.A., Villanova U., 1963; m. Geraldine Torpey, Nov. 22, 1958; children—Heidi, Erik, Gretchen. Dist. mgr. Bell Telephone Pa.,

Phila., 1956-65; mktg. mgr. IBM, Wilmington, Del., Boston, 1965-73; v.p. mktg. ADP, N.Y.C., 1973-74; sr. v.p. State St. Bank & Trust Co., Boston, 1974—. Served with AUS, 1957-59, 62. Mem. Internat. Found., Ednl. Conf. Health, Welfare Pension Plans. Author articles and speeches on pensions. Home: 27 Curve St Sherborn MA 01770 Office: State Street Bank Trust Co 1776 Heritage Dr Quincy MA

GOMES, NORMAN VINCENT, indsl. engr., Realtor; b. New Bedford, Mass., Nov. 7, 1914; s. John Vincent and Georgianna (Sylvia) G.; B.S. in Indsl. Engring. and Mgmt., Okla. State U., 1950; M.B.A. in Mgmt., Xavier U., 1955; m. Carolyn Moore, June 6, 1942. Asst. chief engr. Leschen div. H.K. Porter Co., St. Louis, 1950-52; staff mfg. cons. Gen. Electric Co., Cin, 1952-57; lectr. indsl. mgmt. U. Cin., 1955-56; vis. lectr. indsl. mgmt. Xavier U. Sch. Bus. Adminstrn., 1956-57; staff indsl. engr. Gen. Dynamics, Ft. Worth, 1957-60; chief ops. analysis Ryan Electronics, San Diego, 1960-64; sr. engr., jet propulsion lab. Calif. Inst. Tech., Pasadena, 1964-67, mgr. mgmt. systems, 1967-71; industry rep. and cons. U.S. Commn. on Govt. Procurement, Washington, 1970-72; adminstrv. officer GSA, Washington, 1973-78, program dir., 1979; now engaged in real estate and investments. Served as 2d lt. to maj. C.E., AUS, 1941-46; engring. adviser to War Manpower Bd., 1945. Registered profl. engr., Calif., Mo., Tex.; lic. real estate broker, Tex. Mem. Am. Inst. Indsl. Engrs. (nat. chmn. prodn. control research com., 1951-57; bd. dirs. Cin., Fort Worth, San Diego, Los Angeles chpts. 1954-71, pres. Los Angeles 1970-71, nat. dir. community services 1969-73), Nat., Calif. socs. profl. engrs., Soc. Am. Mil. Engrs., Nat. Mgmt. Assn., Ret. Officers Assn. U.S. (chpt. pres. 1968-69, recipient Nat. Pres. certificate Merit 1969), Mil. Order World Wars, Nat. Security Indsl. Assn. (mgmt. systems subcom. 1967-69), San Antonio Bd. Realtors, Tex. Assn. Realtors, Am. Assn. Realtors. Republican. Roman Catholic. Club: K.C. Home and Office: 2719 Knoll Tree San Antonio TX 78247

GOMPELS, JOOST ARIE, oil co. exec.; b. Capetown, South Africa, Mar. 15, 1927; came to U.S., 1962, naturalized, 1978; s. Meyer and Adele G.; B.Sc. in Chem. Engring., U. Witwatersrand, 1949, B.S. in Law and Econs., 1952; m. Annette Elizabeth Hamlyn Harding, Aug. 30, 1952; children—Mark, Janet, Ursula, Elizabeth. Successively process engr., chief process engr., head planning and econs., planning various and supply mgr. Mobil Oil Corp. affiliates, N.Z., Singapore, S. Am., and U.K., 1952-67, joint venture negotiator, 1968-73, mgr. product sales internat., N.Y.C., v.p. sales Mobil Sales & Supply Corp, subs., 1974—. Episcopalian. Clubs: Marco Polo, N.Y. Yacht (N.Y.C.); Tanglin (Singapore). Home: 31 Sheffield Rd Summit NJ 07901 Office: 150 E 42d St New York NY 10017

GOMPF, JOHN LAWRENCE, oil co. exec.; b. Casper, Wyo., May 10, 1922; s. Carl Herbert and Nina Margaret G.; B.M.E., Ohio State U., 1944; m. Elaine Sebastian, June 19, 1948; children—Becky, Lynne, John Lawrence. With Marathon Oil Co., 1944-60, beginning as refinery engr., successively purchasing analyst, sect. head wage and salary, analyst wage and salary adminstrn., chief analyst orgn. dept., buyer purchasing dept., 1944-69, asst. purchasing agt., 1959-60; purchasing and traffic agt. Oasis Oil Co., N.Y.C., 1960-78, asst. v.p., sec., 1978—; dir. materials div. Region I, Petroleum and Gas Exec. Res., 1966-72. Served with USNR, 1946-48. Registered profl. engr., Ohio. Mem. Nat. Assn. Purchasing Mgmt., Purchasing Mgmt. Assn. N.Y., Petroleum Industry Buyers Group (chmn. 1966-67). Republican. Methodist. Home: 45 Belmont Dr Livingston NJ 07039 Office: 1270 Ave of Americas New York NY 10020

GONCALVES, KAREN PIERCE, mktg. cons.; b. St. Johnsbury, Vt., Feb. 5, 1950; d. Ralph Wallace and Betty (Tilton) Pierce; B.S. with honors, Northeastern U., 1973, M.B.A. with honors, 1975; m. Humberto F. Goncalves, Apr. 15, 1970; 1 dau., Michelle Pierce-Ferreira. Asst. dir. Inst. for New Enterprise Devel., Belmont, Mass., 1974-78; sr. staff cons. Arthur D. Little, Inc., Cambridge, Mass., 1978—. Mem. Bus. Women's Forum in Boston. Office: 25 Acorn Park Cambridge MA 02140

GONDER, ROBERT ANDRE, constrn. co. exec.; b. Sheridan, Wyo., Feb. 20, 1937; s. Robert Charles and Ruth (Morrison) G.; student No. Wyo. Community Coll., 1956-58; m. Carolina Mae Olheiser, June 3, 1961; children—Robert Edward, Carol Jean, Roger Wayne. With Hank's Auto Repair, Sheridan, Wyo., 1954-56, Fair's Home & Auto Supply, Sheridan, 1956-57, Storm Vulcan, Dallas, 1957-58, Weber Auto Body, Denver, 1958-59, Bob Jones Skyland Ford, Denver, 1959, Western Nuclear Mining & Constrn., Rawlins, Wyo., 1959-61, Gilpatrick Constrn. Co., Riverton, Wyo., 1961-62, Morningstar Dairy, Riverton, 1962-64, Vitro Minerals, Healy, Alaska, 1964, Yukon Equip., Anchorage, 1964-65, Bernard Stewart Excavating Co., Anchorage, 1965, No. Comml. Machinery, Anchorage, 1965-66, Steve Cooper Constrn. Co., Delta Junction, Alaska, 1966, Aspeotis Constrn. Co., Anchorage, 1967-71, Chris Berg, Inc., Anchorage, 1971, Studnix, Anchorage, 1971-72, Greater Anchorage Area Borough, 1972-75; builder, landlord and mgr. house and trailer rentals, Riverton, Wyo., 1963-64; owner, operator heavy equipment co., Anchorage 1971; builder, property mgr., developer Robert A. Gonder Enterprises and Gonder-Kelly Enterprises, Anchorage, 1968—. Mem. Ad hoc com. Alaska Landlord and Property Mgrs. Assn. to Anchorage Mcpl. Assembly, 1977. Mem. Am. Fedn. Bus., Whittier Boat Owners Assn., Coast Guard Aux., Internat. Union of Operating Engrs., United Fisherman of Alaska. Home and Office: 1460 W 26 Ave Anchorage AK 99503

GONSIOR, GARY EUGENE, mfg. co. exec.; b. Genoa, Nebr., Sept. 23, 1946; s. Charles and Dorothy Elizabeth (Beck) G.; student archtl. engring. Nettelton Tech. Inst., Columbus, Nebr., 1966-67; m. Pauline Marie Cave, May 9, 1970; children—Christopher, Jennifer. With Behlen Mfg. Co., Columbus, 1967—, comml. and indsl. account mgr., 1972-75, dist. mgr. comml. and indsl. bldg. sales, 1975—. Recipient various sales awards. Mem. Metal Bldg. Dealers Assn. Democrat. Roman Catholic. Home: 3417 36th St Columbus NE 68601 Office: Box 569 East Hwy 30 Columbus NE 68601

GONZALES, ANTHONY C., retail exec.; b. Santa Fe, Mar. 25, 1929; s. C. and Phylis (Roybal) G.; A.A., Sacramento State U., 1950; m. Dorothy C. Huffaker, June 14, 1957; children—Keith M., Karen S., Kurtis E. Pres., chmn. bd. A & A Builders Supply of Gonzales Enterprises, Inc., Sacramento, 1954—; chmn. bd. Benning McPherson, Inc. Bd. dirs. Capitol Christian Center. Served in USAF, 1950-54. Mem. Sacramento Bd. Realtors, Industry Inst., Sacramento Symphony Assn. Democrat. Home: 7245 Morningside Dr Loomis CA 95650 Office: 6700 Folsom Blvd Sacramento CA 95819

GONZALEZ, CARLOS MANUEL, internat. banker; b. Havana, Cuba, Nov. 12, 1946; came to U.S., 1961, naturalized, 1972; s. Carlos Manuel and Teresa (Pujol) G.; B.A. in Internat. Bus. Adminstrn., Portland State U., 1975, cert. in Latin Am. Studies, 1975. Asst. fgn. exchange trader internat. banking div. 1st Nat. Bank Oreg., Portland, 1966-68, ops. officer, comml. loan officer, internat. loan officer, asst. v.p. Latin Am. Region, 1970-78; asst. v.p. Latin Am. Region internat. banking Seattle-1st Nat. Bank, 1978-79; v.p. and mgr. Latin Am. Region internat. banking div. Sun Bank NA, Orlando, Fla., 1979—; dir. Latin Am. C. of C. of Oreg., 1976-79. Served with U.S. Army, 1968-70; Vietnam; USAR, 1975—. Decorated Army Commendation medal. Republican. Home: 112 Wild Holly Ln Longwood FL 32750 Office: Internat Banking Div Sun Bank NA PO Box 3833 Orlando FL 32897

GONZALEZ, EUGENE ROBERT, investment banker; b. Boston, Dec. 5, 1929; s. Eugenio Tomas and Alice Marie (Macdonald) Gonzalez-Mandiola; B.A., Yale U., 1952; postgrad. Institut pour l'Etude des Methodes de Direction de l'Enterprise, Lausanne, Switzerland, 1967. Civil engr., Dept. Public Works, Commonwealth of Mass., Boston, 1952; econ. officer Dept. Def., Washington, 1954-57; gen. fin. officer Devel. Loan Fund (now AID), Washington, 1957-58; fin. mgr. RCA Internat., N.Y.C., 1958-61; devel. bank specialist Interamerican Devel. Bank, Washington, 1961-62, fin. officer, 1962-63, dep. regional rep. for Europe, Paris, 1964; exec. v.p. Adela Investment Co., Luxembourg, 1969-74, mng. dir., 1974-75; pres., chief exec. officer, 1975-76; advisor Morgan Stanley Internat., N.Y.C., 1977—. Served with U.S. Army, 1952-54. Fellow Internat. Bankers Assn.; mem. Internat. Exec. Service Corps (dir.), Accion Internat. (dir.), Internat. Assn. Fin. Planners, Center for Interamerican Relations, Spanish Inst. Clubs: Overseas Bankers (London); Banqueros, Industriales (Mexico City); Metropolitan (Washington); Brook, River, Racquet and Tennis, Meadow (N.Y.); Union (Santiago, Chile), Nacional (Lima, Peru), Baur Au Lac (Zurich). Home: 137 E 66th St New York NY 10021 Office: 1251 Ave of the Americas New York NY 10020

GONZALEZ, JANE ALINE, city ofcl.; b. Berkeley, Calif., July 11, 1943; d. Kary Kirby and Lois Lillie (Woods) Taylor; student Oakland City Coll., 1961-64; m. Santiago A. Gonzalez III, Dec. 23, 1967 (dec. Nov. 1976); children—Constance, Mercedez, Santiago A. IV. Mail clk. U. Calif. at Berkeley, 1964-65; sec. Bay Area Urban League, Oakland, Calif., 1964-67; personal sec. ITT Continental Baking Co., San Francisco, 1967-74; adminstrv. sec. pub. works City of Concord (Calif.), 1974—; beauty cons. Mary Kay, 1978—. Active Democratic party, League Women Voters. Mem. Am. Soc. Public Adminstrs., Calif. Women in Govt. (dir. 1980-81, area coordinator 1980-81), Black Family Assos. Central Contra Costa. Democrat. Methodist. Office: City of Concord 1950 Parkside Dr Concord CA 94518

GONZALEZ, JOAQUIN ANTONIO, tire distbg. co. exec.; b. San Jose de las Lajas, Cuba, Aug. 16, 1943; s. Antonio and Georgina Gonzalez (Perez) G.; came to U.S., 1962, naturalized, 1975; B.A., Inst. Luz Caballero, San Jose de las Lajas, Cuba, 1957, postgrad., 1960; m. Maria A. Carmona, Mar. 19, 1966; children—Antonio Rafael, Georgina Armelia, Joaquin Antonio. Pres., TCM Internat., Inc., Miami, Fla., 1970—, TCM Automotive Center, Miami, 1978—, Toca Inc., Miami, 1972—, Giant Mart, Miami, 1976—, TMF Investment, Miami, 1976—, Wide World Import & Export, Miami, 1978—. Pres., Comite Por Rincon a San Lazaro. Mem. Nat. Tire Dealers Retreaders Assn., Fla. Tire Retreaders Assn., Asociacion Interamericana de Hombres de Empresa, Camacol. Club: Kiwanis. Office: 3466 N Miami Ave Miami FL 33127

GONZALEZ, JUANA ANTONIA, banker; b. P. del Rio, Cuba, Oct. 14, 1928; came to U.S., 1961, naturalized, 1970; d. Juan and Natividad (Roberto) G.; B.S. cum laude, Montclair State Coll., 1979. Acct. various cos., Havana, 1953-61; staff officer Citibank N.A., N.Y.C., 1968—. Mem. Nat. Assn. Accts., Am. Soc. Notaries, AAUW. Republican. Roman Catholic. Home: 7112 Blvd East North Bergen NJ 07047 Office: 399 Park Ave New York NY 10043

GONZALEZ, OSWALDO, ins. co. import, export firm exec.; b. Matanzas, Cuba, Dec. 26, 1932; s. Estanislao and Felicita (Rodriquez) G.; came to U.S., 1965, naturalized, 1974; J.D., Havana U., 1959; m. Teresa, Nov. 8, 1950; children—Teresita, Osualdo. Admitted to Havana (Cuba) bar, 1959; pres. Silver Paint Co., Havana, 1954-62, Concveseal Co., Havana, 1957-62, Estrella de Plata, Havana, 1957-62, Argon Trading Co., Havana, 1959-62; pres. Comput Income Inc., Union City, N.J., 1969—; internat. advisor bus. financing in Latin Am. countries. Mem. Cuban Lawyers Assn. Roman Catholic. Clubs: Latin Am. Press of N.Y. (founder), UN Lions. Author: Murallas de Silencio, 1961. Research in art field. Home: 6600 Boulevard E West New York NJ 02093 Office: Comput Income Inc 2000 Bergenline Ave Union City NJ 07087

GOOD, DANIEL JAMES, investment banker; b. Lake Forest, Ill., Apr. 4, 1940; s. A.C. and Lillian E. (Senft) G.; B.A., DePaul U., 1961; postgrad. U. Chgo., 1964; m. Marlene E. Breithaupt, Oct. 14, 1961; children—Julie Ann, Laura. Asso. to mng. dir. Warburg Paribas Becker, Chgo., 1964—, also dir. Mem. pres.'s com. Lyric Opera Chgo., 1966—; mem. jr. bd. Chgo. Symphony Orch., 1971—; mem. sustaining fund com. Ravinia Festival Assn., 1968—; mem. Chgo. Crime Commn., 1975—; mem. Chgo. Council Fgn. Relations, 1975—. Mem. Lincoln Park Zool. Soc. (dir., exec. com.). Episcopalian. Clubs: Econ. N.Y.; Econ. Chgo., Chgo., Winter, Lake Forest. Home: Lake Forest IL Office: 2 1st Nat Plaza Chicago IL 60603

GOOD, RAYMOND F., mfg. co. exec.; b. Torrington, Conn., 1928; B.B.A., U. Conn.; M.B.A., Harvard U.; married. With Standard Oil Co. Ohio, 1953-60, McKinsey & Co. Inc., 1960-66; pres. Heinz U.S., H.J. Heinz Co., 1967-76; exec. v.p. Pillsbury Co., 1976-79; pres. Munsingwear Inc., Mpls., 1979, pres., chief exec. officer, 1980—, also dir. Office: Munsingwear Inc 718 Glenwood Ave Minneapolis MN 55405*

GOOD, ROY SHELDON, ins. mfg. co. exec.; b. Cleve., Dec. 13, 1924; s. Julius and Sally (Sharpe) G.; B.B.A., Western Res. U., 1948, M.B.A., 1951; children—Jeri Good Rollin, Michael. Mgr. tax dept. Touche, Ross & Co., 1952-61; asst. controller Am. Motors Corp., 1961-68; mgr. employee benefits financial adminstrn. Chrysler Corp., Detroit, 1968-77, mgr. investment rev., 1977-78, mgr. investment rev. and spl. fin., 1978-80; internat. benefit cons. Alexander & Alexander Services, Inc., Detroit, 1981—; lectr., author employee benefits and pension fund investment mgmt., 1970—. Served with AUS, 1943-46; ETO. C.P.A., Mich., Ohio. Mem. Am. Inst. C.P.A.'s, Mich. Assn. C.P.A.'s, Midwest Pension Conf., Beta Alpha Psi. Republican. Jewish. Club: Beverly Hills Racquet. Home: 24435 Evergreen Rd Southfield MI 48075 Office: 600 Fisher Bldg Detroit MI 48202

GOODACRE, KENNETH ROBERT, real estate exec.; b. San Antonio, Jan. 21, 1943; s. Robert Edward and Lorraine Allison G.; B.S., Ariz. State U., 1970; m. Cinda C. Poarch, Sept. 9, 1972; 1 stepson, Donald Ray Bouthillier. Asst. dir. property mgmt. O'Malley Investment Co., Phoenix, 1970; mgr. residential properties Del E. Webb Realty & Mgmt., Phoenix, 1970-76, gen. mgr. Dewguard div., 1974-76; pres., chief exec. officer, co-founder Camelback Mgmt. Co., Phoenix, 1976—. Mem. Ariz. Gov.'s Sports Council, 1978—; mem. legal arbitration panel State Bar Ariz., 1979—. Served with AUS, 1966-68. Mem. Inst. Real Estate Mgmt. (cert. property mgr.), Phoenix Bd. Realtors, Am. Mgmt. Assn., Phoenix C. of C. Republican. Club: Guardian Angels Ariz. State U. Home: 5124 E Desert Park Ln Paradise Valley AZ 85253 Office: 2515 N 3d St Phoenix AZ 85004

GOODE, RICHARD HARRIS, investment banker; b. Chgo., Sept. 13, 1939; s. William Richard and Lois May (Harris) G.; S.B. in Chem. Engring. and Indsl. Mgmt., M.I.T., 1961, S.M. in Chem. Engring. and Indsl. Mgmt. (Pullman-Kellogg Inc. scholar), 1965; m. Eleanor Louise, June 26, 1965; 1 son, James Scott. Mgt. internat. sales Pullman-Kellogg Inc., N.Y.C., 1961-69; v.p., mgr. sales Davy Internat. Inc., N.Y.C., 1969-73; internat. sales mgr. Mitchell, Hutchins Inc., N.Y.C., 1973-75; v.p., mgr. internat. dept. Spencer Trust Inc., N.Y.C., 1975-77; sr. v.p. internat. div. Lehman Bros. Kuhn Loeb Inc., N.Y.C., 1977—. Mem. task force on energy crisis and alt. fuels FPC, 1970-73; admissions officer M.I.T. Alumni Ednl. Council; mem. Vol. Urban Cons. Group, Harvard U.-M.I.T., N.Y.C. Mem. M.I.T. Alumni Center. Home: 81 White Oak Ridge Rd Lincroft NJ 07738 Office: 55 Water St New York NY 10041

GOODELL, JOHN CARLETON, aerospace co. exec.; b. Chgo., Nov. 7, 1913; s. Robert Hosea and Ellen (Hanlon) G.; A.B., Princeton, 1937; M.B.A. with Distinction, Harvard, 1951; m. Dorothy Coy, Nov. 28, 1945; children—Amy (Mrs. Robert Spitzmiller), Robert Justin. Asst. to pres. Scott Aviation, Lancaster, N.Y., 1953-55; v.p. Firewel Corp., mil. life support systems, Buffalo, 1955-60; founder, pres. Carleton Controls Corp., pneumatic controls, East Aurora, N.Y., 1960—; mem. adv. bd. Mfrs. and Traders Trust Co., East Aurora, 1964-74; dir. Moog, Inc., East Aurora. Mem. Iroquois Central Sch. Bd., Elma, N.Y., 1963-66. Served to lt. col. USAF, 1941-51. Decorated D.F.C., Air medal, Purple Heart; recipient Apollo Achievement award NASA. Republican. Presbyterian (elder). Clubs: Country of Buffalo, Harvard (Buffalo); Princeton (Buffalo and N.Y.C.); Beach (Osterville, Mass.). Home: 160 Bridle Path Orchard Park NY 14127 Office: Jamison Rd East Aurora NY 14052

GOODELL, JOHN DEWITTE, motion picture dir., producer; b. Omaha, Sept. 20, 1909; s. Edwin DeWitte and Vera (Watts) G.; Ph.D., U. Lodz, 1953; m. Bernadette Michel, Apr. 30, 1943; children—Mary, John, Thomas, Caroline, Daniel. Cons. engr. Disc Recording, 1930-35; cons. engr. Goodell Electronics Corp., 1936-41; engring. cons. to officer in charge Detroit Signal Lab. AUS, 1941-43; pres. Minn. Electronics Corp., 1946-51; pres. Inst. Applied Logic, 1950-53; cons. engring., 1953-55; mgr. new products dept. Brown & Bigelow, 1955-57; mgr. new product devel. CBS Labs., 1957-59; pres. Robodyne Div. U.S. Industries, Silver Spring, Md., 1960-62, corporate tech. dir., 1962-64; ind. documentary motion picture dir. and producer, 1964—; producer, dir. Always a New Beginning, Insights, others; pres. Goodell Motion Pictures. Served with USNR, 1943-46. Mem. Numerical Control Soc., Inst. Applied Logic (past pres.), IEEE, Audio Engring. Soc., Inst. Symbolic Logic, Assn. Computing Machinery, Soc. Motion Picture and TV Engrs. Author: The World of Ki, 1957. Editor Jour. Computing Systems, 1955-56. Patentee in field. Office: 355 Kenneth St St Paul MN 55105

GOODELL, JOSEPH EDWARD, JR., mfg. exec.; b. El Paso, Tex., Aug. 18, 1937; s. Joseph Edward and Grace Ellen (Beck) G.; B.S., M.I.T., 1959; M.B.A., Harvard U., 1967; children—Marian Grace, Margaret Ann, Martha Jean, Maryellen Rives. Vice pres. Chase Brass & Copper Co., 1971-76; group v.p. Chase Brass & Copper Co., 1976-79; v.p., gen. mgr. Pangborn Worldwide Ops., Carborundum Co., Hagerstown, Md., 1979-80; group v.p. Pangborn Worldwide Ops., Kennecott Engineered Systems Co., 1980—; dir. Nitto Metals Industries, Tokyo, 1973-79; chmn. bd. Citizens Fin. Co. (El Paso); bd. advisors 1st Nat. Bank of Md., Hagerstown. Area dir. Boy Scouts Am.; bd. dirs. Bryan (Ohio) and Newtown (Conn.) Montessori Schs. Club: Hagerstown Rotary. Home: 9420 Hickory View Pl Gaithersburg MD 20760 Office: Pangborn Div PO Box 380 Hagerstown MD 21740

GOODENOUGH, RICHARD WHITE, ins. co. exec.; b. Waterbury, Conn., Feb. 16, 1931; s. Robert deLancey and Alice (Abajian) G.; B.S. in Commerce, Grove City Coll., 1954; M.B.A., Nat. U., 1978; m. Geraldine Mildred Grimaldi, May 21, 1955; children—Keith Alden, Gwynneth Franklin, Darcie White. Ins. broker Goodenough Ins. Inc., Coronado, Calif., 1956—, pres., 1980—; vice chmn. bd. dirs. Bank of Coronado. Active San Diego County council Boy Scouts Am., Coronado; chmn. Coronado Planning Commn., 1972-74. Served with U.S. Army, 1954-56. Mem. Nat. Assn. Ins. Agents, Am. Inst. C.P.C.U.'s, State Assn. Ins. Agts., S.D. Assn. Ins. Agents, Calif. Banking Assn. Republican. Episcopalian. Clubs: Rotary, Masons. Office: PO Box 578 Coronado CA 92718

GOODHUE, NEIL BRUCE, real estate exec.; b. Oakland, Calif., June 7, 1954; s. Neil Ostrander and Mary Lee (Herd) G.; student Calif. State U., 1972-73; St. Mary's Coll., 1974; B.S., Lone Mountain Coll., 1975; m. Diane Christine De Lucchi, 1980. Properties mgr. Nat. Mgmt. Corp., Lafayette, Calif., 1972-73; pres. Bonanza Bldg., Inc., Lafayette, 1972-74; pres., pub. Claremont Press, Inc. (Calif.), 1971-74; pres. NBG Enterprises, Inc., Oakland, 1974-77; v.p. 1200 Lakeshore Inc., Oakland, 1977—; gen. partner Laketowers, 1979—; dir. Hill Castle Properties, NBG Enterprises, Inc., Calif. Investors. Res. police officer City of Oakland, 1975-78; dir. Lafayette Youth Adult Council, Inc., 1971-73; bd. dirs. Oakland YMCA; mem. Mayor's Task Force on Rent Control, on Rental Constrn. Recipient award of merit No. Calif. Industry-Edn. Council, 1973, advt. award Future Bus. Leaders Am., 1973; accredited real estate mgr. Inst. Real Estate Mgmt. Mem. Bldg. Owners and Mgrs. Assn., Oakland C. of C., Oakland Mus. Assn. Republican. Roman Catholic. Clubs: Athenian-Nile, Commonwealth of Calif., San Francisco Press, Wash. Athletic, Oakland Athletic. Home: 170 Sandringham Rd Piedmont CA 94611 Office: 1200 Lakeshore Ave Oakland CA 94606

GOODIN, MAURICE E., publisher; b. Louisville, Sept. 30, 1913; s. Edward C. and Bertha (Vorhies) G.; student U. Colo., 1932-34; m. Shirlee Anderson, July 12, 1947; children—Phillip, Michael, Carl. With Sinclair Oil & Gas Co., Casper, Wyo., 1936-46; pres. Petroleum Information Corp., Denver, 1946-76, chmn. bd., 1976-79, emeritus, 1979—; chmn. bd. Petroleum Information Exchange, Calgary, Alta., Can., 1969—; dir. A.C. Nielson Co., Chgo. Commr., Denver Centennial Authority, 1957-59, Colo. Centennial Authority, 1958-59. Served to capt. USAAF, 1941-46. Mem. Rocky Mountain Oil and Gas Assn. (dir. 1949—), Am. Landmens Assn., Am. Petroleum Inst., Ind. Petroleum Assn. Am., Denver C. of C., (dir. 1958-61). Colo. Petroleum Council (dir. 1959—), Rocky Mountain Assn. Geologists (hon.), Assn. Petroleum Writers (pres. 1977-78). Clubs: Cherry Hills Country (dir. 1959-62), Denver Petroleum (pres. 1948, 55), Denver, Denver Athletic, Garden of Gods (Denver). Home: 3165 Floyd Dr Denver CO 80210 Office: 1375 Delaware St Denver CO 80201

GOODIN, WILLIAM CHARLES, publisher; b. Louisville, Sept. 18, 1917; s. Edward C. and Bertha (Vorhies) G.; B.A., U. Colo., 1941; m. Emily E. Percefull, Sept. 8, 1946; children—Sue Ellen, Charles W. Former pres., now chmn. Petroleum Information Corp. subsidiary A.C. Nielsen Co., Denver, 1946—; dir. A.C. Nielsen Co. Past mem. Colo. Oil & Gas Conservation Commn. Served to 2d lt. M.I. Corps, USAAF, 1942-44; to 1st lt. CIC AUS, 1944-46. Mem. Rocky Mountain Assn. Geologists (life hon. mem.), Denver Landmens Assn., Rocky Mountain Petroleum Pioneers, Assn. Petroleum Writers. Presbyterian. Clubs: Denver Petroleum (life mem., past pres., dir.), Denver Athletic, Cherry Hills Country (Denver). Home: 11 Parkway Dr Englewood CO 80110 Office: 1375 Delaware St Denver CO 80204

GOODKIN, SANFORD RONALD, real estate analyst; b. Passaic, N.J., Feb. 8, 1929; s. Robert and Lillian (Ellman) G. Pres., chmn. bd. Sanford R. Goodkin Research Corp., Del Mar, Calif., Ft. Lauderdale, Fla., Santa Fe, Tucson and Los Angeles, 1957—; pub., writer The

Goodkin Report, also real estate editor Calif. Bus. Mag.; contbg. editor, columnist writer column Real Estate Dynamics in Profl. Builder Mag.; syndicated columnist Winning in Real Estate 26 newspapers; cons. to industry; author Web Apt. Reporter; contbg. editor San Diego Home/Garden mag.; condr. real estate seminars; lectr. colls. and univs.; adv. Solar Energy Inst.; sr. fellow Hubert Humphrey Sch. Social Ecology, Ben Gurion U., Israel. Founder, bd. govs. Ben-Gurion U., Negev, Israel; exec. bd. and internat. adv. bd. World Congress of Engrs. and Architects. Recipient Medal of Valor, State of Israel, 1975, Max C. Tipton Meml. award for mktg. excellence, 1974; named 1 of 24 of West's most distinguished citizens Sunset Mag., 1973; elected to Inst. of Residential Mktg. Apt. Assn. San Fernando Valley (dir.), Lambda Alpha Land Economics Frat. (historian). Author: The Goodkin Guide to Winning in Real Estate, 1977. Address: 2190 Carmel Valley Rd Del Mar CA 92014

GOODLOE, NORMAN MALLORY, JR., constrn. and real estate exec.; b. Richmond, Va., Aug. 26, 1936; s. Norman Mallory and Ann Franklin (Bradley) G.; B.S., U. Richmond, 1959. Sec.-treas. Robert R. Marquis, Inc., Portsmouth, Va., 1960—; pres. E.G. Realty, Inc., 1965, R.R. Marquis Leasing, Inc., 1970, G & W Enterprises, 1965; chmn. Joint Apprenticeship Carpenters Council, 1978. Treas. Jaycees, 1959-72. Recipient various Jaycee awards. Mem. Asso. Gen. Contractors Am., Nat. Fedn. Ind. Bus., Builders and Contractors Exchange, Tidewater Asso. Gen. Contractors (pres. 1981), Portsmouth C. of C. (legis. chmn. 1969). Clubs: Cavalier Golf and Yacht, Norfolk Boat, Circus Saints and Sinners, Cape Henry Billfish; Racquet (Miami, Fla.). Office: 2229 County St Portsmouth VA 23704

GOODMAN, FRANKLIN LEE, JR., diversified investment exec.; b. Stratford, Tex., June 22, 1931; s. Franklin Lee and Billie (Bryan) G.; B.S., Abilene Christian U., 1955; grad. Inst. Orgn. Mgmt., Houston, 1958; m. Carolyn Colville, Mar. 9, 1952; children—Gary Lee, Gregory Franklin, Gay Ann. Asst. mgr. Santa Gertrudis Ranch, Waco, Tex., 1955; mgr. Taylor (Tex.) C. of C., 1956-57, McAllen (Tex.) C. of C., 1958; exec. dir. Life Line Found., Washington, 1959, Downtown Ft. Worth Assn., 1960-71; owner Lee Goodman Enterprises, Ft. Worth, 1972; partner Overcash Goodman Enterprises, Ft. Worth, 1972—; dir. numerous corps. Bd. dirs. Ft. Worth Christian Coll., 1962-70, Ft. Worth Opera Assn., 1967, Ft. Worth Symphony, 1967, Longhorn council Boy Scouts Am., 1960—. Served with USAF, 1951-55. Named Outstanding Young Man Ft. Worth, Ft. Worth Jaycees, 1966, One of 5 Outstanding Texans, Tex. Jaycees, 1967. Mem. Tex. Christian U. Round Table. Mem. Ch. of Christ. Clubs: Ft. Worth Downtown Rotary (v.p. 1966), Met. Dinner (pres. 1967-78), Ft. Worth (Ft. Worth); Century 11, Woodhaven Country. Home: 5905 End O'Trail Fort Worth TX 76112 Office: 2630 W Freeway Suite 102 Fort Worth TX 76102

GOODMAN, GERALD MALCOLM, mfg. co. exec.; b. Bklyn., Sept. 24, 1945; s. Irving and Florence (Rosenfeld) G.; B.S., Columbia U., 1966; M.S. in Indsl. Engring., U. Calif., Berkeley, 1967; m. Susan Rachelle Terner, June 30, 1972; children—Cyd Terner, Martin Terner, Jamie Terner. Indsl. engr. RCA, Camden, N.J., 1968-70; mgmt. cons. Booz, Allen & Hamilton, N.Y.C., 1971-72; sr. indsl. engr. McGraw Edison Co., Canonsburg, Pa., 1972-74, sr. prodn. control systems analyst, 1975—. Mem. Am. Inst. Indsl. Engrs., Am. Prodn. and Inventory Control Soc., Tau Beta Pi, Alpha Pi Mu. Republican. Jewish. Club: B'nai Brith. Home: 108 Beechmont Rd Pittsburgh PA 15206 Office: PO Box 440 Canonsburg PA 15317

GOODMAN, JACQUELYN LOUISE, optical co. exec.; b. Altanta, June 30, 1949; d. Arnold Frankling and Gladys Louise (Camp) G.; student Ga. State U., 1969-70. Various clerical positions, 1967-75; engaged in sales of eyeglass framees Tura, Inc., Great Neck, N.Y., 1975, McGee Eye Fashions, Atlanta, 1976-79; founder, v.p. Illusion Optics, Longwood, Fla., 1979—. Pres., Brookwood Neighbors Assn., 1978. Mem. Ga. Soc. Dispensing Opticians. Democrat. Mem. Christian Ch. Home: 30 Alden Ave NW Atlanta GA 30309 Office: Illusion Optics 103 E Church Ave Longwood FL 32750

GOODMAN, SAM RICHARD, electronics co. exec.; b. N.Y.C., May 23, 1930; s. Morris and Virginia (Gross) G.; B.B.A., Coll. City N.Y., 1951; M.B.A., N.Y. U., 1957, Ph.D., 1968; m. Beatrice Bettencourt, Sept. 15, 1957; children—Mark Stuart, Stephen Manuel, Christopher Bettencourt. Chief accountant John C. Valentine Co., N.Y.C., 1957-60; supr. budgets and analysis Gen. Foods Corp., White Plains, N.Y., 1960-63; budget dir. Crowell Collier Pub. Co., N.Y.C., 1963-64; v.p., controller Nestle Co., Inc., White Plains, N.Y., 1964-73; chief fin. officer Aileen, Inc., N.Y.C., 1973-74, Ampex Corp., Redwood City, Calif., 1974-76; exec. v.p. fin. and adminstrn. Bake & Taylor div. W.R. Grace, N.Y.C., 1976—; exec. v.p. fin. and adminstrn. Magnuson Computer Systems, Inc., San Jose, Calif., 1979—; lectr. N.Y. U. Mgmt. Inst., 1964-67; prof. mktg. Pace Coll. Grad. Sch. Bus. Adminstrn., 1967-74; prof. fin. Golden Gate U., 1974—. Served to lt. (j.g.) USNR, 1951-55. Mem. Fin. Execs. Inst., Nat. Assn. Accountants, Am. Statis. Assn., Am. Econ. Assn., Planning Execs. Inst. Author: Techniques of Profitability Analysis, 1970; Financial Managers Manual and Guide, 1971; The Marketing Controller, 1972; Treasurers and Controllers Encyclopedia, 1974; Controller's Handbook, 1978; Financial Analysis for Marketing Decisions, 1978; contbr. articles to profl jours. Home: 11566 Arroyo Oaks Los Altos CA 94022 Office: 2902 Orchard Park Way San Jose CA 95134

GOODMAN, SIDNEY RICHARD, computer co. exec.; b. Cleve., June 29, 1940; s. David H. and Rose (Woolman) G.; B.S. in Bus. and Acctg., Miami U., 1962; m. Diane Susan Katz, Oct. 12, 1962; children—Martin, Wendy, Tracey. Acct., Ernst & Ernst, 1962-65; exec. v.p. Becker C.P.A. Rev. Course, 1965; asst. to controller Foseco, Inc., Cleve., 1966-68; controller Arby's Northfield Systems, Cleve., 1968-69; pres. DatAssistance Corp., Cleve., 1969-71, Mgmt. Reports, Inc., Beachwood, Ohio, 1971—. Bd. govs. Temple Emanuel, 1973-76, treas., 1975, v.p., 1976. C.P.A., Ohio. Mem. Am. Inst. C.P.A.'s, Ohio Soc. C.P.A.'s, Internat. Platform Assn. Jewish. Patentee in field. Home: 32400 Chestnut Ln Pepper Pike OH 44124 Office: 23945 Mercantile Rd Beachwood OH 44122

GOODRICH, GARDNER ANTHONY (TONY), trucking co. exec.; b. Evanston, Ill., Jan. 15, 1937; s. James Gardner and Tilo (Jones) G.; student Lewis and Clark Coll., 1955-56, Portland State Coll., 1959-60; m. Sharlene Mae Goodrich, July 19, 1960; children—Victoria Lyn, Brian Scott. Sales mgr. so. pine div. Ga. Pacific Corp., Crosset, Ark., 1966-68; sales mgr. so. pine div. Hearin Forest Industries, Portland, Oreg., 1968-71; v.p., gen. mgr. Hearin Transp., Inc., Portland, 1971-78, DG Transport, Inc. subs. Digiorgio Corp., Portland, 1978—; teaching cons. Acad. One, Inc., Beaverton, Oreg. Pres., chmn. bd. dirs. South Shore Sch. for Mentally Retarded, 1968-70; asst. coach Pop Warner Football Program, 1969-74, head coach, 1975-79; mem. Republican precinct com., 1968-72. Served with USNR, 1956-58. Home: 8965 NW Sherry Ct Portland OR 97229 Office: 8700 SW Elligsen Rd Wilsonville OR 97070

GOODWIN, GERALD LOUIS, finance co. exec.; b. Elmira, N.Y., Feb. 5, 1943; s. Elmer James and Ervene (Snover) G.; A.B. (acad. scholar), Lafayette Coll., Easton, Pa., 1965; M.B.A. (acad. scholar), N.Y. U., 1968; m. Christine Gail Wilsey, June 21, 1969; children—Alexander Gerald, Carrie Christine. Portfolio mgr. Merrill Lynch, N.Y.C., 1967-68; with F. Eberstadt & Co. Inc., N.Y.C., 1968—, v.p. 1971—, portfolio mgr., 1973—; sr. v.p. Anchor Pension Mgmt. Corp., 1976-77; pres. Goodwin, Alexander Inc., investment advisors and venture capitalists, 1978—. Pres. Knickerbocker Republican Club; mem. N.Y. State Rep. Com., 1974—; staff advanceman Pres. Ford, 1976; mem. com. on compaign services Rep. Nat. Com., 1978—. Cert. fin. analyst; registered rep. N.Y. Stock Exchange. Mem. N.Y. Soc. Security Analysts, Nat. Assn. Security Dealers (registered prin.), Phi Kappa Psi. Methodist. Clubs: University (N.Y.C.); Capitol Hill (Washington). Home: 444 E 82d St New York NY 10028 Office: One W 54 St New York NY 10019

GOODWIN, HAZEL JEAN THOMAS, cons.; b. St. Louis, Apr. 15, 1946; d. Albert Wendell and Ollie Bell (Matthews) Thomas; B.S. in Bus., Eastern Ill. U., 1969. Computer programmer, instr. McDonald-Douglas Automation Co., St. Louis, 1968-72; computer programmer, sr. data processing instr. Xerox Corp., Webster and Rochester, N.Y., 1972-74; computer tng. coordinator Potomac Electric Power Co., Washington, 1974-79; tng. mgr. N.E. Utilities Service Co., Wethersfield, Conn., 1979-80; cons. Deltak, Inc., Oak Brook, Ill., 1980—. Active Explorer Scouts, St. Louis, 1970-72. Mem. Am. Soc. for Tng. and Devel., Hartford Area Trainers Assn. Baptist. Office: Deltak Inc Oak Brook IL

GOODYEAR, JOHN LEE, ins. brokerage co. exec., cons.; b. Snowshoe, Pa., Sept. 15, 1936; s. Willis Lee and Anne Rose Goodyear; B.A. cum laude (Christian Schmidt scholar), Villanova U., 1958; postgrad. Sch. Law, U. Miami, 1962-64; m. Rose Marie Toner, Oct. 24, 1959; children—Jeanne, John Lee II, James, Judith, Jeffrey. Regional group mgr. for N.E. U.S., Provident Mut. Life Ins. Co., N.Y.C., 1961-75; dep. mng. v.p. Alexander & Alexander, Inc., N.Y.C., 1975-80, prodn. coordinator Greater N.Y. region, 1980—; cons. employee benefit plans, 1975—. Chmn. gift campaign Boy Scouts Am., 1975-80; basketball coach Cath. Youth Orgn.; mem. industry com. Am. Cancer Crusade. Served to capt. USMC, 1958-61. Recipient Alumni award Police Athletic League 1956. C.L.U. Mem. Am. Soc. C.L.U.'s (chmn. employee benefits sect. N.Y. chpt. 1978-79), N.Y. Group Mgrs. Assn., Pa. Soc., Delta Epsilon Sigma, Delta Theta Phi. Clubs: Sleepy Hollow Country (gov.); N.Y. Athletic. Home: 2 Highview Rd Ossining NY 10562 Office: 1185 Ave of the Americas New York NY 10036

GOOR, DAN, digital equipment co. exec.; b. Palestine, Jan. 16, 1933; s. Amihud Y. and Shifra (Smilansky) G.; came to U.S., 1951, naturalized, 1958; B.S. in Physics, Colo. State U., 1955; student Sr. Exec. Program, Mass. Inst. Tech., 1969; D.Math., Hebrew U., 1961; A.M., Tufts U., 1973, Ph.D., 1975; m. E. Patricia Robison, Aug. 28, 1953; children—YaDean Asaf Grant, Diana Lynn, Elizabeth Rena, Jacqueline, Sharon Patricia. Project engr., heavy mil. electronics dept. Gen. Electric, Syracuse, N.Y., 1959-63; gen. mgr. advanced components and comml. systems Lab. for Electronics, Inc., Waltham, Mass., 1963-67; pres. Goor Assos., Inc., Lincoln, Mass., 1967-74; mem. faculty Tufts U. Engring. Sch., 1973-74; dist. mgr. tech. assessment, mem. corp. research and advanced devel. com. Digital Equipment Corp., Maynard, Mass., 1974-77, tech. assessment mgr. digital equipment, 1977-80, mgr. storage-media devel., 1980—; cons. in field. Certified mfg. engr. Mem. Nat. Soc. Profl. Engrs., IEEE, N.Y. Acad. Scis., Soc. Automotive Engrs., AIAA, Computer Soc. India, Brit. Inst. Mgmt. Jewish. Club: Jewish War Vets. U.S.A. Patentee in field. Home: 1090 C Fontmore Blvd Colorado Springs CO 80904 also 5019 Mortier Ave Orlando FL Office: Digital Equipment Corp 146 Main St Maynard MA 01754

GORALNIK, OLIVER AARON, chain store exec.; b. Newark, June 13, 1907; s. Abe and Anna (Krugman) G.; B.S., Washington U., 1930; m. Alma Hirsch, Oct. 27, 1935; children—Barbara (Mrs. Bernard G. Kohm), Jane Ellen (Mrs. Hans Levi), Mary Beth (Mrs. Joseph Henry Mohrman, Jr.). Accountant C. B. Adams, C.P.A.'s, St. Louis, 1930-31; asst. sales mgr. Weilkalter Mfg. Co., St. Louis, 1931-36; store mgr. P. N. Hirsch & Co., Retail Jr. Dept. Stores, St. Louis, 1936-44, div. merchandise mgr., 1944-46, treas., 1946—, also dir. Bd. dirs. Jewish Employment and Vocational Service. Mem. Beta Gamma Sigma. Omicron Delta Gamma. Jewish. Home: 14 Lake Forest St St Louis MO 63117 Office: 2001 Walton Rd St Louis MO 63114

GORANS, GERALD ELMER, accountant; b. Benson, Minn., Sept. 17, 1922; s. George W. and Gladys (Schneider) G.; student Lower Columbia Jr. Coll., 1941-43, Whiteman Coll., 1943-44; B.A., U. Wash., 1947; m. Mildred Louise Stallard, July 19, 1944; 1 dau., Gretchen. With Allen R. Smart & Co., 1947, Touche, Niven, Bailey & Smart, 1947-60, partner, 1957-60; partner Touche, Ross & Co., 1960—, partner in charge Seattle office, former Western region coordinating adminstrn. partner, mem. policy group, adminstrv. com., bd. dirs., 1974—, sr. partner, 1979—. Vice pres. budget and finance Seattle Worlds Fair; chmn. budget and finance com. Century 21 Center, Inc.; mem. citizen's adv. com. Seattle License and Consumer Protection Com.; head profl. div. United Good Neighbor Fund campaign, 1963, 64, advanced gifts div., 1965, exec. v.p., 1966, pres., 1967, also bd. dirs.; mem. adv. bd. Salvation Army, 1965-79, treas., 1974-79; mem. finance com. Bellevue Christian Sch.; mem. citizens adv. bd. on pub. affairs KIRO, Inc. (TV); bd. dirs. Citizens Council Against Crime, 1972-80, treas., 1972-75, pres., 1976, 77; bd. dirs., exec. com. N.W. Hosp. Found., 1977—; bd. dirs. N.W. Hosp., 1980—; mem. bd. U. Wash. Alumni Fund, 1969-71, chmn., 1971. Served to lt. (j.g.) USNR, 1943-45, Mem. Am. Inst. C.P.A.'s (chmn. nat. def. com.), Wash. Soc. C.P.A.'s, Seattle C. of C. (chmn. com. on taxation, dir. 1970-73, 74-78), Nat. Office Mgmt. Assn. (past pres.). Clubs: Harbor, Seattle Golf; Wash. Athletic (bd. govs. 1971-77, treas. 1973-74, pres. 1975—), U. Wash. Presidents (bd. dirs. 1980—), Rainier (treas. 1976-77), Quarterback, 101; The Family (San Francisco). Home: 9013 NE 37th Pl Bellevue WA 98004 Office: 1111 3d Ave Seattle WA 98101

GORCHOW, NEIL, computer sci. exec.; b. Sioux City, Iowa, June 23, 1925; s. Joseph and Doris (Shapiro) G.; B.S., U. Iowa, 1948, postgrad., 1949; m. Roslyn Wein, Oct. 23, 1955; children—Julie Beth, Bruce David, Jonathan Ross, Sheryl Lynn. Managerial positions Sperry Univac Co., St. Paul, 1956-60, Washington, 1960-65, v.p. systems programming, Bluebell, Pa., 1965-70, v.p. worldwide mktg. support, 1970-74, v.p. product strategy and requirements, 1974—; dir. Nippon Univac, Tokyo; lectr. Univac Exec. Center, Rome, Nippon Univac Exec. Center, Izu, Japan; panelist Nat. Security Analysts Bicentennial Conf., N.Y.C., 1976; speaker Nat. Computer Conf., Anaheim, Calif., 1976. Mem. Nat. Def. Exec. Res., 1971—; vice pres., chmn. edn. Beth Sholom Congregation, Elkins Park, Pa., 1975-78, pres., 1978—; mem. adv. bd. Grad. Sch. Bus., Temple U., 1980—. Served to lt. (j.g.) USNR, 1943-46. Recipient Letter of Appreciation from asso. adminstr. Manned Space Flight, NASA, 1969. Mem. Assn. Computer Machinery, Assn. for Systems Mgmt., Jewish War Vets. (past comdr.). Club: B'nai B'rith. Contbr. articles to profl. jours. Home: 1245 Imperial Rd Rydal PA 19046 Office: Sperry Univac Co Bluebell PA 19422

GORCYCA, RAYMOND MYRON, valve mfg. co. exec.; b. Pitts., Jan. 19, 1942; s. Adam Raymond and Rose (Latanzio) G.; B.A., Duquesne U., 1964; m. Carolyn Faith Babb, May 10, 1980; children by previous marriage—Raymond Adam, Michelle Ann, Paul Norman, Jodi Lynn. Labor relation rep. Ford Motor Co., Mahwah, N.J., 1966-67; mgr. employee relations Allied Chem. Co., Toledo, 1967-72; v.p. employee relations DeZurik Corp., Sartell, Minn., 1972-75, v.p. mfg., from 1975; now v.p. mfg. Henry Pratt Co., Aurora, Ill.; speaker employee relations seminars. Bd. dirs. Consumer Relations Bur., St. Cloud, Minn. Served with inf. AUS, 1964-66. Mem. Am. Soc. Personnel Adminstrn., St. Cloud Area C. of C. (chmn. polit. edn. div. 1974, chmn. transp. div. 1975). Club: St. Cloud Country. Office: Henry Pratt Co 401 S Highland Ave Aurora IL 60507

GORDANA, JOHN KENNETH, fin. exec.; b. Teaneck, N.J., July 31, 1942; s. Samuel and Vivienne (Wunderlich) G.; B.A., Seton Hall U., 1964, LL.B., 1970; m. Sylvia Bradley, July 23, 1976. Pres., Equitable Adjustment Service, Inc., Clifton, N.J., 1965—, D'Lorenzo Mens' Shop, Clifton, 1974—, Great Am. Fin. Corp., East Orange, N.J. 1973—; Dollar Savs. & Loan Assn., Newark. Served as 2d lt. U.S. Army, 1964-65. Mem. Comml. Law League of Am., Am. Comml. Collectors Assn. (charter mem.), N.J. Assn. of Credit Execs. Home: 45 Swiss Terr Wayne NJ 07470 Office: 9 Furler St Totowa NJ 07512

GORDEVITCH, IGOR, publishing co. exec.; b. Kaunas, Lithuania, Dec. 17, 1924; s. Alexander Michael and Militsa (de Nikitin) G.; came to U.S., 1950, naturalized, 1955; ed. Institut Sillig, Vevey, Switzerland, 1937-38, Royal U., Rome, 1939-40; m. Margaret Boomer; children—Alexandra, Tatiana; m. 2d, Carin Roechling, Oct. 7, 1960. Sr. adminstrv. asst. Allied Mil. Govt., Europe, 1944-45; corr. N.Y. Herald Tribune, 1945-50; Washington bur. chief Vision Inc., N.Y.C., 1950-56, editor, 1957-64, chief exec. officer, Sao Paulo, Brazil, 1964-67, pub., exec. v.p., dir. Vision Group of Cos., N.Y.C., 1967-76, mng. dir., chmn. Vision/Europe, Paris, 1970-76; pres. Publi-Communications Inc., N.Y.C., 1976-79; exec. v.p., dir. Gruner & Jahr USA, Inc., N.Y.C., 1979—; also mng. dir., pub. GEO mag.; publishing cons.; lectr. in field. Mem. Pan Am. Soc. U.S., Council of Ams., Akin Hall Assn. Republican. Eastern Orthodox. Clubs: Knickerbocker (N.Y.C.); Quaker Hill Country (Pawling, N.Y.); Coral Beach and Tennis (Bermuda); Nat. Press (Washington). Home: 1105 Park Ave New York NY 10028 Office: 450 Park Ave New York NY 10022

GORDILLO, GILBERT AL, stock brokerage exec.; b. Tampa, Fla., Oct. 18, 1944; s. Alfred and Concha (Palomino) G.; B.B. A., U. Miami, 1971; m. Janice M. Gill, June 29, 1968; children—Christopher M., Nicole. Stock broker Bache & Co., Miami, 1970-72, Walston & Co., Coral Gables, Fla., 1972-75; asst. mgr., 2d v.p. Shearson, Hayden Stone, Coral Gables, Fla., 1977-80, v.p., resident mgr. Shearson, Loeb Rhoades, 1978-81, Miami Beach, Fla., 1981—. Served with U.S. Army Res., 1964-71. Mem. Alpha Kappa Psi. Democrat. Mem. Coral Gables C. of C. Home: 2200 Segovia Circle Coral Gables FL 33134 Office: Shearson Loeb Rhoades 111 Lincoln Rd Miami Beach FL 33139

GORDON, ALBERT HAMILTON, investment banker; b. Scituate, Mass., July 21, 1901; s. Albert Franklin and Sarah Veronica (Flanagan) G.; A.B., Harvard, 1923, M.B.A., 1925; LL.D. (hon.), St. Anselm's Coll.; grad. (hon.) Winchester Coll., Eng.; m. Mary Farwell Rousmaniere, Oct. 5, 1935; children—Albert F., Mary A. Gordon Roberts, Sarah F. John R., Daniel F. Analyst, Goldman, Sachs & Co., N.Y.C., 1925-31; partner Kidder, Peabody & Co., Inc., N.Y.C., 1931-56, pres., 1956-57, chmn. bd., 1957—; dir. Allen Group, Inc., Deltec Panam. S.A., Carnation Co. Active Council on Fgn. Relations; dir. Nat. Rep. Finance Com., 1969-77; bd. dirs. Center for Inter-Am. Relations; trustee, chmn. Roxbury Latin Sch.; bd. overseers, bd. mgrs. Meml./Sloan Kettering Cancer Center, N.Y.C. Clubs: Harvard (N.Y.C.); Links; Racquet and Tennis. Home: 10 Gracie Sq New York NY 10028 Office: 10 Hanover Sq New York NY 10005

GORDON, BARON JACK, stock broker; s. George M. and Rose (Salsbury) G.; B.S., Lynchburg Coll., 1953; m. Ellin Bachrach, Aug. 20, 1954; children—Jonathan Ross, Rose Patricia, Alison. Vice pres. Consol. Ins. Agy., Norfolk, 1948-55; asst. treas. Henry Montor Assos., Inc., N.Y.C., 1956; v.p., sec. Propp & Co., Inc., N.Y.C., 1957-58; partner Koerner, Gordon & Co., N.Y.C., 1959-62; sr. partner Gordon, Kulman Perry (and predecessor firm), N.Y.C., 1962-71, pres., chmn. bd., 1971-74; pres., chmn. bd. Palison, Inc., mems. N.Y. Stock Exchange, N.Y.C., 1974—; chmn. bd. Rojon, Inc., real estate and investments, Williamsburg, Va., 1978—. Mem. Harrison (N.Y.) Archtl. Rev. Bd., 1970-72, Harrison Planning Bd., 1975-77. Served to lt. USNR, in U.S.S. Midway, 1953-55. Mem. U.S. Naval Acad. Alumni Assn. (life). Clubs: N.Y. Stock Exchange Luncheon; Poinciana (Palm Beach, Fla.); Piedmont (Lynchburg, Va.). Home: Westchester Ave Purchase NY 10577 Office: 7 Corporate Park Dr White Plains NY 10604

GORDON, CATHERINE ANN, constrn. co. exec.; b. Jacksonville, Fla., Jan. 16, 1953; d. Robert E. and Annette (Willcox) G.; A.A., Fla. Jr. Coll., 1973; student U. North Fla., 1974—. Various office and clerical positions bond portfolio dept. Barnett Bank of Jacksonville (Fla.), 1973-76; sales rep. Travelers Ins. Co., Jacksonville, 1976-77; partner Gordon Constrn Co., Jacksonville, 1974-81, v.p., 1974—; prin. Catherine A. Gordon, agri-bus. ins. agt., 1976—. Mem. Am. Bus. Women's Assn., Am. Soc. Profl. and Exec. Women, Am. Farm Bur. Fedn., Fla. Forestry Assn., Am. Forestry Assn., Am. Quarter Horse Assn., Beta Sigma Phi. Baptist. Home: 17901 Lem Turner Rd Jacksonville FL 32218 Office: PO Box 18044 Jacksonville FL 32229

GORDON, CHARLES FOX, JR., health care exec.; b. Somers Point, N.J., Aug. 4, 1935; s. Charles F. and Evelyn (Grig) G.; B.A., Brown U., Providence, 1958; m. Marylyn G. Gordon, Nov. 4, 1960; children—Charles F. III, Holly Lynn, Christin Grig. With Chrysler Corp., 1961-62, Amchem Products, 1962-64; dir. sales of patient care div. Johnson & Johnson, New Brunswick, N.J., 1964—. Vice pres. Hunterdon County Little League, 1974-76; chmn. Ind. Citizens Polit. Action Group, 1975-77, Raritan Twp. Park and Recreation Com., 1974-76. Served with C.I.C., AUS, 1959-61. Republican. Presbyterian. Home: Box 446G RD 5 Flemington NJ 08822 Office: Johnson & Johnson 501 George St New Brunswick NJ 08903

GORDON, CHARLES LEWIS, fin. exec.; b. Beech Grove, Ind., Mar. 27, 1938; s. Charles O. and Anna Mae (McPherson) G.; B.S., Ind. U., 1961; postgrad. U. Mich., 1963-65; m. Lydia J. Phelps, July 8, 1961; children—Jeffrey D., Kimberly A. Asst to 2d v.p. City Mortgage Dept., Equitable Life Assurance Soc. of N.Y., Detroit, N.Y.C., 1962-69; asst. v.p. comml. mortgage dept. Bank of the Commonwealth, Detroit, 1969-71; v.p. Real Estate Investments-Multi-Vest, Inc., Southfield, Mich., 1971-74; partner Monetary Investment Group, Southfield, 1974—; chmn. bd. MIG Constrn. Co., Inc., Southfield, 1974—; pres., chief exec. officer, trustee Monetary Realty Trust, Southfield, 1974—. Active, Boy Scouts Am., Huntington Woods, Mich., 1972-78, YMCA, 1974-78. Served with U.S. Army, 1961-62. Mem. Real Estate Securities and Syndication Inst., Am. Inst. Real Estate Appraisers, Soc. Real Estate Appraisers, Nat. Assn. Real Estate Bds., S. Oakland County Bd. Realtors, Nat. Assn. Real Estate Investment Trusts, Urban Land Inst. Presbyterian. Club: Grosse Pointe Yacht. Office: 23777 Southfield Rd Southfield MI 48075

GORDON, DAVID WILLIAM, advt. exec.; b. Niagara Falls, N.Y., May 25, 1954; s. Lawrence and Jeanne Eleanor (Monrian) G.; B.A., U. Vt., 1976. Sales rep. Northland Food Brokers, Buffalo, 1974-76; sales mgr. Muzak, Buffalo, 1977-79; dir. sales and mktg. In-Store Broadcast Advt., Buffalo, 1979—; ski instr. Kissing Bridge Corp., Glenwood, N.Y., 1976—. Mem. Frozen Food Assn. Western N.Y., Food Industry Sales Execs. of Buffalo. Methodist. Clubs: Univ., Brookfield Country. Home: 346 Lafayette Ave Buffalo NY 14213 Office: 1227 Main St Buffalo NY 14209

GORDON, EDGAR GEORGE, lawyer, business exec.; b. Detroit, Feb. 27, 1924; s. Edgar George and Verna (Hay) G.; A.B., Princeton, 1947; postgrad. Harvard Bus. Sch., 1945; J.D., Harvard U., 1950; m. Alice J. Irwin, Feb. 4, 1967; children—David A., J. Scott. Admitted to Mich. bar, 1951, also U.S. Supreme Ct. bar; asso. Poole, Warren & Littell, 1950-54; partner Poole, Warren, Littell and Gordon, Detroit, 1954-63; exec. corporate counsel Hygrade Food Products Corp., 1963-69, sec., 1966-69, v.p., 1968-69; v.p., sec., counsel City Nat. Bank Detroit, 1969—; v.p., sec., counsel No. States Bancorp., 1971—; pres. Kelly Mortgage & Investment Co., 1978—; dir., 1979—; dir. 1st Nat. Bank of Plymouth, 1979—, 1st Citizens Bank in Troy, 1979. Bd. dirs. Inner-City Community Clinic, 1961-69, 74—. Served as lt. (j.g.) USNR, 1943-46. Mem. Am., Detroit (chmn. corp. com. 1970—), Mich. bar assns., Am. Judicature Soc., Am. Soc. Corporate Secs., Founders Soc. Detroit Inst. Arts, Detroit Hist. Soc. Presbyn. Clubs: Detroit, Economic, Country (Detroit). Home: 210 Lothrop Rd Grosse Pointe Farms MI 48236 Office: Suite 3900 Tower 400 Renaissance Center Detroit MI 48243

GORDON, EDWIN FREDERICK ROBERT, metal fabricating co. exec.; b. Oak Park, Ill., Jan. 4, 1921; s. Edwin C. and Alice (Heller) G.; B.S., Concordia Coll., 1942; M.A., Northwestern U., 1945; Ph.D., Purdue U., 1951; children—Dawn Alice, Denise Ann, E. Robert F., Allen D., Roger M., James Adams, John Robin, Jana Amanda. Chmn. bd., dir. Geuder, Paeschke & Frey Co., metal fabricating co., Milw., 1955—; dir. Gordon-Hoover & Assos., Inc., mgmt. cons., Chgo., Capital Investments, Inc., Milw.; chmn. bd. Boyer-Rosene Moving & Storage Co., Inc., Arlington Heights, Ill., Gordon Studios Inc., Hillsboro Beach, Fla.; pres. Hillsboro Land Mark, Inc., Hillsboro Beach, Fla. Mem. Am. Psychol. Assn., Sigma Xi. Home: 1021 Hillsboro Mile Hillsboro Beach FL 33062 Office: 324 N 15th St Milwaukee WI 53201

GORDON, ELLEN R., candy co. exec.; b. N.Y.C., May 29, 1931; d. William B. and Cele H. Rubin; student Vassar Coll., 1948-50; B.A., Brandeis U., 1965; postgrad. Harvard U., 1968; m. Melvin J. Gordon, June 25, 1950; children—Virginia L., Karen D., Wendy J., Lisa J. Vice-pres. product devel. Tootsie Roll Industries, Inc., Chgo., 1974-77, corp. sec., 1974-77, sr. v.p., 1977-78, pres., 1978—. Office: 7401 S Cicero Ave Chicago IL 60629

GORDON, GEOFFREY NEIL, telephone co. exec.; b. N.Y.C., July 23, 1946; s. Jacob Isaac and Myrna G.; B.A., U. Va., 1968; Ed.M., Rutgers U., 1972, Ed.D., 1981; m. Karen Deborah Gordon, Aug. 2, 1980. Tchr. public schs., Manalapan Twp., N.J., 1968-72; adminstrv. asst. Rumson-Fair Haven Regional High Sch., 1972-78; asst. staff mgr. 195 Broadway Corp., Bell System, N.Y.C., 1978-79, project coordinator, 1980—. Recreation dir. Manalpan Twp., 1972-74; recreation dir. Colt Neck Twp., N.J., 1978. Mem. Nat. Recreation Assn., N.J. Recreation Assn., Kappa Delta Pi. Office: 295 N Maple Ave Basking Ridge NJ 07920

GORDON, HAROLD, book pub. co. exec.; b. Bklyn., Oct. 24, 1926; s. Herman and Beatrice (Posner) G.; B.B.A. cum laude, City U. N.Y., 1956, M.B.A., 1964; m. Madeline R. Tragerman, Apr. 1, 1958; 1 son, Scott Jay. Mgr. accounts receivable Pocket Books, Inc., N.Y.C., 1956-60, credit mgr., 1960-65; v.p. Affiliated Pubs., Inc., N.Y.C., 1966-67; divisional v.p. Simon & Schuster, Inc., N.Y.C., 1967-71, corp. v.p., 1971—, also dir.; pres., dir. Total Warehouse Services Corp., Bristol, Pa., 1976—. Served with USAAF, 1945-46. Mem. Beta Gamma Sigma. Home: 35 Seacoast Terr Brooklyn NY 11235 Office: 1230 Ave Americas New York NY 10020

GORDON, JACK D., savs. and loan exec., state senator; b. Detroit, June 3, 1922; s. A. Louis and Henrietta (Rodgers) G.; B.A., U. Mich., 1942; m. Barbara Yaffey, Dec. 20, 1951; children—Andrew Louis, Deborah Mary, Jonathan Henry. Real estate, ins. agt., Miami Beach, Fla., 1946-52; founding dir., pres., chief mng. officer Washington Savs. & Loan Assn., Miami Beach, 1952-80, vice chmn. bd., 1980—; founding dir. Jefferson Nat. Bank, Miami Beach, 1962-77, past chmn. exec. com.; mem. Fla. Senate, 1972—; housing finance cons. Dept. State; expert cons. UN Tech. Assistance Program in Costa Rica, Nicaragua, Panama, Ethiopia, Somali Republic, 1959-63; cons. Eastern Nigerian Housing Corp., 1963; contract supr. AID Housing Guarantee Program in Latin Am., 1966-69. Chmn., Miami Beach Housing Authority, 1947-56; mem. Dade County Bd. Public Instrn., 1961-68. Served with AUS, 1943-46. Democrat. Jewish. Office: 1701 Meridian Ave Miami Beach FL 33139

GORDON, LEWIS ALEXANDER, electronics exec.; b. Milw., Oct. 4, 1937; s. Lewis Alexander and Verna Alma (Stocker) G.; B.S. in Mech. Engring., Purdue U., 1959; postgrad. RCA Insts., 1962, No. Ill. U., 1967-68; m. Frances Rita Dziadzio, June 4, 1960; children—Robert Alan, Richard Alan, Pamela Ann. Process engr. Ill. Tool Works, Elgin, 1959-63; chief engr. Norcon Electronics, Elgin, 1963-65; v.p. Midland Standard, Inc., Elgin, 1964-78, chmn. bd., 1967-78; pres., chief exec. officer Gt. Lakes Industries, Elgin, 1978—; del. Joint Electronics Industry Conf.; mem. adv. bd. Electronics mag., 1976—. Vice pres. bd. trustees Gail Borden Pub. Library Dist., 1971—, v.p., bd. dirs. North Suburban Library System, 1971—. Bd. advisers Easter Seal Assn., Elgin, 1971-74; adv. bd. Elgin Community Coll., 1977—. Registered profl. engr., Ill., Mich. Mem. Ill. C. of C., Elgin Assn. Commerce, A.L.A., Ill. Library Assn. (automation com. 1975—), Ill. Soc. Profl. Engrs., Nat. Brit. Horological Inst., So. Calif. Computer Soc., Ill. Mfrs. Assn., Assn. Watch and Clock Collectors, Mensa, Agent-Aeronca Champion Club, Kane County Farm Bur., Pi Tau Sigma. Lutheran. Contbr. articles to profl. jours. Patentee in field. Home: 705 Diane Ave Elgin IL 60120 Office: PO Box 801 Elgin IL 60120

GORDON, MELVIN TRUSSELL, JR., apparel mfg. co. exec., publisher; b. Atlanta, Feb. 24, 1943; s. Melvin Trussell and Lettie Lenora (Houseworth) G.; E.E., Ga. Inst. Tech., 1963; B.B.A. in Mgmt., Ga. State U., Atlanta, 1967; m. Camille Elizabeth Henderson, Aug. 27, 1966; children—Michael, Dennis, Nicole Renee. Adminstrv. staff mdse. specialist Rich's, Inc., Atlanta, 1966-67; adminstrv. mgr., zone sales support Dover Elevator Co., Atlanta, 1967-69; bus. systems analyst Blue Bell, Inc., Greensboro, N.C., 1969-70, adminstrv. services mgr., 1970-73, dir. micrographics systems/services and spl. projects, 1973-79, mgr. data processing adminstrv. support, micrographics systems/ops., 1980—; pub., editor Mentor Communiqué, 1981—. Mem. Nat. Micrographics Assn. (co-founder chpt., treas. 1977-79, dir. newsletter 1980—), Am. Mgmt. Assn., Internat. Diamond Distbrs. Assn., Am. Entrepreneurs Assn., Newsletter Assn. Am. Republican. Patentee in pet product field. Home: 5107 Amberhill Dr Greensboro NC 27405 Office: PO Box 21488 Greensboro NC 27420

GORDON, MICHAEL JOHN DAVID, accountant; b. London, Eng., Apr. 29, 1935; s. Nathan and Yetta (Goldrich) G.; student pvt. schs. (London, Eng.). Came to U.S., 1960. Accountant, Gane, Jackson, Jefferys & Freeman, London, Eng., 1953-60, Alexander Grant & Co., C.P.A.'s, N.Y.C., 1960; sr. supr. accountant Ernst & Ernst, C.P.A.'s, Oakland, Calif., 1960-63; systems engr. IBM Corp., San Francisco, 1963-65; pres. PBI Research, Inc., San Francisco, 1966-80, Inner Circle, San Francisco, 1968-80, Travelsphere, Inc., 1970-80, Bay Area Lifestyle, 1972-80. Mem. Inst. Chartered Accountants in Eng. and Wales (asso.), Inst. of Taxation (U.K.) (asso.) Am. Inst. C.P.A.'s (asso.), Calif. Soc. C.P.A.'s.

GORDON, ROBERT SALAWAY, bus. exec.; b. Boston, Oct. 6, 1916; s. Isaac and Minnie (Salaway) G.; B.S., Mass. Inst. Tech., 1938; postgrad. Stanford Sch. Bus. Adminstrn., 1963; m. Joan Williams, Feb. 24, 1946; children—Richard W., Kathleen M. Gordon Mulqueeney, Carol J. Gordon Witt. Asst. prodn. supt. Stanwood Hillson Corp., Brookline, Mass., 1938-41; indsl. engr. Libby, McNeill & Libby, Honolulu, 1946-49, chief indsl. engr., 1949-52; with Castle & Cooke, Inc., Honolulu, 1952—, dir. indsl. engring., 1958—, asst. treas., 1961-65, v.p., 1965-74, sr. v.p., 1974—; v.p., dir. Kohala Corp. Hawi, Hawaii, Waialua Sugar Co. (Hawaii), Castle & Cooke Merchandising Corp. (Calif.), Kohala Ditch Co., Ltd., Hawaii; pres., dir., treas. Kawaihae Terminals, Inc.; chmn. bd. Hawaiian Equipment Co., Oahu Transport Co., Ltd., (both Honolulu), Arneson Products Inc., Calif., Castle & Cooke Terminals Ltd., Hawaii, Thai Asia Steel Pipe Co., Bangkok, Malaysian Rock Prodn., Sdn Bhd, Malaysia, Intervest, Inc., Singapore. Served from ensign to lt. comdr. USNR, 1941-45. Mem. Soc. Advancement Mgmt., Am. Inst. Indsl. Engrs. Home: 153 Pauahilani Pl Kailua Oahu HI 96734 Office: PO Box 2990 Honolulu HI 96802

GORDON, SAUL, ednl. center exec.; b. N.Y.C., Nov. 29, 1925; s. Abraham Isaac and Mary (Warschaw) G.; B.S., Ohio State U., 1946, M.S., U. Ky., 1949, Ph.D. in Chemistry, 1951; children—Scott, Alan, Jody, Arthur. Chemist, Picatinny Arsenal, Dover, N.J., 1951-52, group leader, 1952-55, chief basic chem. research unit, 1955-59, staff chemist specialist Pyrotech Lab., 1959-61; asst. prof. chemistry Fairleigh Dickinson U., Florham-Madison campus, 1960-62, asso. prof., 1962-64, prof., 1965-67, chmn. dept. chemistry, 1963-67, dir. ann. thermoanalytical insts., 1962-67; founder, pres. Center for Profl. Advancement, continuing edn. in sci. and tech., East Brunswick, N.J., 1967—; cons. to govt., industry. Fellow Am. Inst. Chemists; mem. AAAS, Am. Chem. Soc., Am. Soc. Tng. and Devel., Am. Soc. Engring. Edn., N.J. Acad. Sci., N.Y. Acad. Sci., N.J. C. of C., Raritan Valley C. of C. Home: 393 B Hystrix Plaza Cranbury NJ 08512 Office: PO Box H East Brunswick NJ 08816

GORDON, STEWART G., business exec.; b. Searcy, Ark., 1937; grad. U. Mich., 1959. Formerly exec. v.p. Reed Paper Ltd. (Can.); exec. v.p. for ops. ITT Rayonier, Inc., Stamford, Conn., 1979—. Office: ITT Rayonier Inc 1177 Summer St Stamford CT 06904

GORDON, THOMAS FRANCIS, candy and tobacco co. exec.; b. Bklyn., Jan. 24, 1949; s. Francis Gerard and Helen Paticia (Granger) G.; B.A. in Psychology, Hofstra U., 1973; m. Andrea Ruzansky, Aug. 19, 1972; 1 son, William Thomas. Order clk. Capitol Candy Co., Hartford, Conn., 1973-74, salesman, 1974-75, sales mgr., 1975-76, v.p. sales and mktg., 1976—. Served with U.S. Army, 1967-70. Mem. Nat. Assn. Candy Wholesalers, Nat. Assn. Tobacco Distbrs., Conn. Assn. Candy and Tobacco Distbrs. Republican. Roman Catholic. Office: Capitol Candy Co 750 Wethersfield Ave Hartford CT 06101

GORDON, TRINA DRU, cons.; b. Alliance, Ohio, Dec. 9, 1954; d. Rodger W. and Beatrice B. Gordon; B.S., Auburn U., 1975, M.P.A., 1976; m. Richard A. McCallister, Sept. 1, 1979. Grad. asst. Ala. Supreme Ct., Auburn, 1975-76; cons. William H. Clark Assos., Inc., Chgo., 1976—. Asso., Jr. League Chgo., 1980—; mem. fraternity housing com. Northwestern Univ., 1979-80. Mem. Indsl. Relations Assn. Chgo., Mortar Bd. Alumni Assn., Pi Beta Phi, Omicron Delta Kappa. Republican. Clubs: Racuqet (Chgo.); Glen View. Office: 200 E Randolph Dr Suite 7912 Chicago IL 60601

GORE, BURTON DOUGLAS, hotel co. exec.; b. Lansdale, Pa., Nov. 28, 1942; s. Burton Ira and Beatrice (Grosse) G.; student Ohio State U., 1964, 66; m. Nancy Joan Hankin, Apr. 17, 1971. Mgr., Beverlee Dr. Inns, Columbus, Ohio, 1964-70, John F. Davis Co., 1970-71; pres. Easton (Md.) Manor Inn, 1971-76; gen. mgr. Ramada Inn, Lakeland, Fla., 1976-78, Cadillac Motel, Bar Harbor, Maine, 1978-80; with Truck Stops Am., Duncan, S.C., 1980—; pres. Gore Enterprises. Mem. Lakeland Mayor's Airport Adv. Com., 1976, Warrant Com. Bar Harbor, 1978. Served in USAF, 1961-64. Mem. Md. Hotel-Motel Assn. (dir.), Fla. Restaurant Assn. (dir.), Maine Mid Coast Route 1 Assn. (dir.), Maine Publicity Bur., Maine Hotel-Motel Assn. Republican. Baptist. Club: Lions. Author tng. manuals.

GORE, CHARLES MINOR, lawyer; b. Johnson City, Tenn., Oct. 26, 1910; s. Benjamin Stone and Helen (Hayward) G.; A.B., Vanderbilt U., 1933; postgrad. Harvard Law Sch., 1933-34; LL.B., U. Tenn., 1936; m. Mildred Anne Smith, June 20, 1937; children—Charles Smith, Anne Hayward. Admitted to Tenn. bar, 1936; mem. firm Gore & Gore, attys., 1937-54, Gore, Gore & McIntyre, Bristol, Tenn., 1954-63, Gore & Gore, 1963-65, Gore, Gore & Ladd, 1965-67, Gore, Ladd & Gillenwater, 1968-71, Gore, Ladd, Gillenwater and Hillman, 1976-77, Gore, Gillenwater and Hillman, 1977-78, Gore and Hillman, 1978—; spl. justice Tenn. Supreme Ct., 1976; sec., dir. Appalachian Broadcasting Corp., WCYB-TV, 1946-74, dir., asst. sec., 1977—; sec., dir. Strong-Robinette Bag Co., Inc., 1953—; dir., mem. exec. com. Gen. Shale Products Corp. Johnson City. Mem. Tenn. Democratic Exec. Com., 1971-74; bd. dirs. United Fund, 1957-59. Served from lt. (j.g.) to lt. USNR, 1943-46. Mem. Am., Tenn., Bristol bar assns., Sixth Circuit Jud. Conf. (life mem.). Presbyn. Home: Lick Branch Rd Bristol TN 37620 Office: Central Bldg Bristol TN 37620

GORE, JEROME SIDNEY, clothing co. exec.; b. Chgo., Dec. 17, 1919; s. Alex Samuel and Rebecca (Spector) G.; B.S., U. Ill., 1941; m. Shirley Faye Zax, June 15, 1941; children—Stanley Norman (dec.), Lawrence Steven. With Hart Schaffner & Marx, Chgo., 1941—, successively auditor, retail controller, asst. treas., 1955-60, v.p., 1960-67, group v.p. retail store adminstrn., 1967, exec. v.p., 1968-70, pres., 1970—, chief exec. officer, 1976—, also dir.; dir. Ill. Bell Telephone Co. Mem., past chmn. businessmen's adv. council Coll. Bus. Adminstrn., U. Ill. Circle Campus; mem. Council on Grad. Sch. Bus., U. Chgo.; bd. dirs. U. Ill. Found., United Way Met. Chgo., NCCJ, Jewish Fedn. Met. Chgo. Served with USNR, 1943-46. Mem. Chgo. Assn. Commerce and Industry (dir.), Clothing Mfrs. Assn. U.S.A. (dir.), Northwestern U. Assos., Beta Gamma Sigma (dirs.' table). Jewish religion. Clubs: Execs., Standard, Tavern, Mid-Day, Commerical, Mid-America, Economic (Chgo.). Home: 1040 N Lake Shore Dr Chicago IL 60611 Office: 36 S Franklin St Chicago IL 60606

GORE, JOHN MOSES, assn. bus. officer; b. Orangeburg, S.C., June 14, 1917; s. William Arthur and Laura Elizabeth (Whitfield) G.; B.S., U.S. Naval Acad., 1939; student U.S. Armed Forces Staff Coll., 1951; M.Ed., Am. U., 1966; m. Sarah Emily Fenn, June 9, 1941; children—Anne Whitfield, Jane Lucile, Suzanne Legare, John Bryan. Commd. ensign U.S. Navy, 1939, advanced through grades to capt., 1957; fin. control officer Aviation Supply Office, Phila., 1952-56; comptroller Def. Atomic Support Agy., Washington, 1962-66; chief logistics Nat. Security Agy., 1966-67; ret., 1967; comptroller Ret. Officers Assn., Washington, 1967—. Chmn. mil. edn. nomination com. Rep. J.L. Fisher, 1975-80. Mem. Am. Soc. Assn. Execs., Am. Mgmt. Assn., U.S. Naval Inst., Air Force Assn., Order St. Luke the Physician. Episcopalian. Home: 2021 Rhode Island Ave McLean VA 22101 Office: 201 N Washington St Alexandria VA 22314

GORHAM, EUGENE TIMOTHY, conveyor co. exec.; b. Chgo., May 2, 1935; s. Sidney Smith and Corinne (McVoy) G.; B.M.E., Stanford, 1957; m. Barbara Francis Steinke, Nov. 26, 1966; children—Jonathon Lewis, Eugene Timothy, Brooke Lee, Whitney Ann. Indsl. engr. U.S. Rubber Co., Chgo., 1959-60, Oscar Mayer Co., Chgo., 1960-61; sales engr. Olson Conveyor Co. (now div. ACCO), Franklin Park, Ill., 1962-67; v.p. sales Automotion, Inc. (Ill. Corp.), Alsip, Ill., 1967-73, pres. Automotion Inc. (Del. Corp.), Alsip, 1973-78, also dir., v.p. Automation Inc. (Del. Corp.), 1978—; partner AW & H Leasing Corp. Served with AUS, 1957. Mem. Internat. Material Mgmt. Soc., Material Handling Equipment Distbrs. Assn. (chmn. engineered products com. 1971-75), Am. Material Mgmt. Soc., Chi Psi. Clubs: Pentwater (Mich.) Yacht; Saddle and Cycle, Tavern (Chgo.). Home: 1201 Chatfield Rd Winnetka IL 60093 Office: 11743 S Mayfield Ave Alsip IL 60482

GORMAN, CORNELIUS FRANCIS, JR., mfg. co. exec.; b. N.Y.C., Aug. 13, 1952; s. Cornelius Francis and Madonna I. (Riendeau) G.; B.S., Marquette U., 1974; m. Rita Elaine Iris, May 21, 1974; 2 children. Sales rep. Robertson, Inc., Milw., 1975-76, Surg. div. Parke-Davis, Madison, Wis., 1976-77, IPCO Hosp. Supply, Chgo., 1977-78, Medi, Inc., Chgo., 1978-80; regional rep. William Harvey Research Corp. Mem. Assn. Practitioners in Infection Control, Jaycees (v.p. internal affairs 1976, SPOKE award 1976). Roman Catholic. Home: 28423 Raleigh Crescent New Baltimore MI 48207 Office: PO Box 39 New Baltimore MI 48047

GORMLEY, DAVID FRANK, marketing exec.; b. Swampscott, Mass., Feb. 10, 1934; s. Ernest Raymond and Cathrine (Maitland) G.; B.A., U. Mass., 1956; m. Mary Lou Carroll, Aug. 22, 1954; children—Kathleen, David, John, Nancy, Robert, Patrick. With Sentry Ins. Cos., 1958-75, v.p. sales, 1970-73, v.p. sales and marketing, 1973-75; v.p., sr. mktg. officer United Am. Life Ins., Denver, 1975-78; pres., chief exec. officer Am. Health and Life Ins. Co., Balt., 1978—. Instr., U. Wis. Alumni trustee U. Mass. Served to capt. USMC, 1956-58. Mem. Am. Soc. Life Underwriters, Nat. Assn. Life Underwriters, Md. Life Underwriters, Nat. Assn. Health Underwriters, Kappa Sigma. Clubs: Balt. Mchts., Balt. Center, Elk, K.C. Home: 1 Ascot Ct Baldwin MD 21013 Office: 300 St Paul Place Baltimore MD 21202

GORMLEY, ELIZABETH ADELA, mfg. co. ofcl.; b. Georgetown, Ky., July 22, 1951; d. Frederick James and Adela (Martinez) G.; B.Sc., St. Francis Xavier U., N.S., Can., 1972; M.B.A., U. Tex., Austin, 1978. Morgage officer Can. Imperial Bank of Commerce, Toronto, Ont., 1972-73; editor Holt, Rinehart and Winston of Can., Ltd., Toronto, 1973-74; editor Copp Clark Pub. Co., Toronto, 1974-75, U. Tex., Austin, 1975-76; planner dept. econ. and employment devel. City of San Antonio, 1973-78; editorial asst. San Antonio Express News Corp., 1978-80; actuarial analyst U.S. Automobile Assn., San Antonio, 1980; prodn. control supr. tech. publs. Cypress plant Tex. Instruments Inc., Houston, 1980—. Mem. Common Cause. Office: Tex Instruments Inc PO Box 1444 MS7878 Houston TX 77001

GORNICK, ALAN LEWIS, lawyer; b. Leadville, Colo.; s. Mark and Anne (Grayhack) G.; A.B., Columbia U., 1935, J.D., 1937; m. Ruth L. Willcockson, 1940 (dec. May 1959); children—Alan Lewis Jr., Diana Gornick Richard, Keith Hardin; m. 2d, Pauline Martoi, 1972. Admitted to N.Y. bar, 1937, Mich. bar, 1948; practiced with Baldwin, Todd & Young, N.Y.C., 1937-41, Milbank, Tweed, Hope & Hadley, 1941-47; asso. counsel, charge tax matters, Ford Motor Co., Dearborn, Mich., 1947-49, dir. tax affairs, tax counsel, 1949-64; pres. Perry-Davis, Inc., Meadow Brook Park Devel. Co.; v.p., dir. Bloomfield Centers, Inc.; dir. Brooks Perkins, Inc., Detroit; v.p. Seagate Hotel, Inc., Delray Beach, Fla.; lectr. N.Y. U. Inst. Fed. Taxation, 1947, Am. Bar Assn. and Practising Law Inst. courses in continuing legal edn., 1950; spl. lectr. Sch. Bus. Adminstrn. U. Mich., 1949, 53; adv. editor Nat. Tax. Jour., 1952. Pres. Mich. Assn. Emotionally Disturbed Children, 1962; v.p. Archives Am. Art; mem. Columbia Coll. Council, Columbia U., N.Y.C.; trustee Council World Affairs, Detroit. Recipient Gov's. Spl. award State Colo., 1952. Author: Divorce, Separation and Estate Taxes, Estate Tax Handbook, 1952; Arrangements for Separation or Divorce, Handbook of Tax Techniques, 1952; Taxation of Partnerships, Estates and Trusts, 1952; contbr. articles on taxation to profl. jours. Home: 150 Lowell Ct Bloomfield Hills MI 48013 Office: 1565 Woodward Suite 8 Bloomfield Hills MI 48013

GORSKI, EDWARD JOSEPH, iron foundry exec.; b. Kansas City, Kans., Feb. 13, 1944; s. Stance C. and Edith Marie (Oberforcher) G.; B.S., U. Kans., 1968. Programmer, Goodyear Tire & Rubber Co., Akron, 1968-72; mgr. data processing Perfect Equipment, Murfreesboro, Tenn., 1972-76; mgr. systems EDP, Cutler Hammer Corp., Cleveland, Tenn., 1976-78; mgr. data processing U.S. Industries Agri-Bus. Co., Atlanta, 1978-79; dir. data processing Columbus (Ga.) Foundries, Inc., 1977—. Served with U.S. Army, 1968-70. Decorated Bronze Star. Lic. pvt. pilot. Mem. Data Processing Mgmt. Assn., Am. Prodn. and Inventory Control Soc., Mensa. Club: Columbus Exchange. Home: 1216 Autumnridge Dr Columbus GA 31904 Office: PO Box 4201 Columbus GA 31904

GORUP, GREGORY JAMES, banker; b. Kansas City, Kans., Mar. 27, 1948; s. Mike and Helen F. Gorup; B.A. in Econs., St. Benedict Coll., 1970; M.B.A., U. Pa., 1972. Market analyst product planning and devel. dept. Citibank, N.Y.C., 1972-73, market planning officer corp. product mgmt. div., 1973-74, product mgr. securities services, 1974-75; asst. v.p., dir. product devel. Irving Trust Co. N.Y.C., 1975-78, v.p., 1978—, mgr. product mgmt. dept., 1980—. Mem. fund raising com. Big Bros. of N.Y. 1975-77. Mem. Am. Mgmt. Assn. Roman Catholic. Club: Lions. Home: 245 E 63d St New York NY 10021 Office: One Wall St New York NY 10015

GOSLINE, ANDREW JACKSON, V, computer systems exec.; b. Clearfield, Pa., Apr. 16, 1940; s. Andrew J. and Margaret E. (Gross) G.; B.S., Ind., U. Pa., 1962; M.M.S., Stevens Inst. Tech., 1970; postgrad. Rutgers U.; m. Mary Leffler, Nov. 18, 1961; children—Andrew, Matthew. Mgr. ops. research Fairless (Pa.) works U.S. Corp., 1964-67; dir. data processing Native Textiles, 1967-73; mgr. Hosp. Systems Devel. Corp., Hackensack, N.J., 1973-79; pres. Atlas Computer Systems, Inc., 1979—. Mem. Hosp. Fin. Mgmt. Assn. Home: 51 Abbott Ave Ocean Grove NJ 07756 Office: 401 Hackensack Ave Hackensack NJ 07601

GOSLINE, CARL ANTHONY, assn. exec.; b. Beloit, Wis., Feb. 11, 1921; s. Carl Anthony and LaRene (Halls) G.; B.A. in Zoology, U. Iowa, 1941; M.B.A., Alexander Hamilton Inst., 1953; postgrad.

Stanford, 1967-68; m. Carol Tiffany, June 18, 1941; children—Carl Dennis, Charles Michael. Observer, U.S. Weather Bur., Rock Springs, Wyo., 1942-43; group leader Manhattan Project, U. Chgo., 1943-44; sr. supr. prodn. Hanford Engr. Works, E.I. duPont de Nemours & Co., Inc., 1944-46, research engr. engring. dept., Wilmington, Del., 1946-48, cons., cons. supr., 1948-52, cons. mgr., 1952-53, mgr. plant tech. sect. Chambers Works (N.J.), 1953-56, group supr. Corp. Engring. Test Center, Wilmington, 1956-58, dir., 1958-62, new venture marketing mgr. devel. dept., 1962-66; exec. v.p. Hexcel Products Inc., Dublin, Calif., 1966-67; dir. marketing services Fibreboard Corp., San Francisco, 1967, v.p. mktg. and planning, 1967-68; corporate exec. v.p. Univ. Patents, Inc., Chgo., 1969-70; pres., founder, treas. MGA Tech., Inc., 1970-72; pres., chief exec. officer Rollins Environ. Services, Wilmington, Del., 1972-74; founder, pres. Gosline Assos. Inc., 1974—; exec. v.p., dir. Systems Assos., 1974-75; asst. tech. dir. environ. div. Chem. Mfrs. Assn., Washington, 1975-79, dir. Hazardous Waste Tech. Center, 1979—. Contbg. author: McGraw Hill Handbook of Air Pollution Abatement; contbg. author Colliers Ency. Editor: MCA Air Pollution Abatement Manual. Contbr. 21 articles on air pollution control, technology transfer, venture mgmt. and regulation impacts to tech. jours. Home: 1515 S Jefferson Davis Hwy Arlington VA 22202

GOSLINE, NORMAN ABBOT, realtor; b. Gardiner, Maine, Nov. 6, 1935; s. Arthur N. and Katherine R. (Wardsworth) G.; B.A., U. Maine, 1957; children—Lee Gosline Fairbairn, Jeffrey Crosman, Mark Abbot; m. Shirlene Heath Hoch; Feb. 19, 1977; stepchildren—Jolene Hoch, Ellen Hoch, William K. Hoch, Jr. Pres., gen. mgr. Gosline's Dairy, Inc., Gardiner, Maine, 1957-59; realtor, Gardiner, 1959—; mem. faculty (part-time) U. Maine, Augusta, 1973—; cons. in real estate to various agys. and firms in No. New Eng. area, 1965—. Past mem. Gardiner Planning Bd. Named Outstanding Young Man, Gardiner, Maine, 1965, Realtor of the Year, Kennebec Valley Bd. Realtors, 1967. Mem. Am. Inst. of Real Estate Appraisers (dir. chpt. 1973—), Soc. of Real Estate Appraisers (pres. Maine chpt. 1975-76), Nat. (dir. 1967), Maine (pres. 1967) assns. of realtors, Kennebec Valley Bd. Realtors (pres. 1963-64). Episcopalian. Clubs: Masons, Rotary. Home: 87 W Hill Rd Gardiner ME 04345 Office: Two Central Plaza Augusta ME 04330

GOSS, THOMAS HAYDEN, restaurant exec.; b. Queens, N.Y., Aug. 30, 1950; s. George Hayden and Mildred (Wadkins) G.; B.A. in English and Philosophy, U. Va., 1972; M.P.S., Cornell U., 1975. Gen. mgr. Restaurant Mgmt. Inc., Washington, 1975-76; v.p., gen. mgr. GRG Assos., Washington, 1977—. Mem. Cornell Soc. Hotelmen, U. Va. Alumni Assn., D.C. Lic. Restaurant Group. Republican.

GOSSETT, OSCAR MILTON, advt. exec.; b. N.Y.C., May 27, 1925; s. Oscar Percival and Helen (Deutsch) G.; student Stevens Inst. Tech., 1943-44, 46-47, Columbia, 1947-48; m. Anna C. Scheid, May 29, 1949; children—Susanne, Michael, Thomas, Lorraine, James M. With Compton Advt., Inc., 1949—, pres., 1968—, chief exec. officer, 1975—, chmn., 1977—. Chmn. bus. and advt. sect. Am. Cancer Soc., N.Y.C.; chmn. council ministries United Methodist Ch., Ridgefield, Conn. Served with USNR, World War II. Mem. Am. Assn. Advt. Agencies. Inventor mobile of solar system. Office: 625 Madison Ave New York City NY 10022

GOTTEMOELLER, MEG, banker; grad. with honors U. Mich.; masters degree in communications Temple U. Mgr. employee communications Ins. Co. N.Am., Phila., until 1975; sr. producer internat. video network Merrill Lynch, Pierce, Fenner and Smith, Inc., 1975-78; with Chase Manhattan Bank NA, N.Y.C., 1978—, v.p., mgr. Chase Trade Info. Corp., 1980—; mem. faculty Grad. Sch. Corp. and Polit. Communication, Fairfield (Conn.) U. Bd. dirs. Saving Families for Children. Contbg. author: The Handbook of Private Television, 1981. Office: Chase Manhattan Bank NA 1 World Trade Center Suite 7800 New York NY 10048

GOTTFRIED, SAMUEL, physicist, investment co. exec.; b. Lampertheim, W.Ger., July 16, 1946; s. Isadore and Bronia (Engelmaier) G.; came to U.S., 1949, naturalized, 1962; B.S., Cornell U., 1967, M.E.E., 1968; E.E., N.Y. U., 1972; Ph.D., Poly. Inst. N.Y., 1977; m. Anna Kreiner, Nov. 17, 1973. Mem. tech. staff Bell Telephone Labs., Holmdel, N.J., 1967-79; mng. gen. partner Salar Assos., pvt. investment co., N.Y.C., 1979—; mem. Am. Stock Exchange, 1979—. Mem. Cornell U. Secondary Schs. Com., 1968—. Mem. IEEE, Optical Soc. Am., Am. Inst. Physics, Sigma Xi, Tau Beta Pi, Phi Eta Sigma, Eta Kappa Nu, Tau Epsilon Phi. Club: B'nai B'rith. Office: Salar Assos Rm 900 115 Broadway New York NY 10006 also Am Stock Exchange 86 Trinity Pl New York NY 10006

GOTTLIEB, LESTER M., data processing co. exec.; b. N.Y.C., May 3, 1932; s. Samuel and Eva (Schoenfeld) G.; B.A., Coll. City N.Y., 1954; postgrad. N.Y. U.; m. Sarah Dean Tompkins, Dec. 4, 1967; children—Cynthia Anne, Curtis Tompkins; children by previous marriage—Mark, Alyssa, Adine. With IBM, 1956-69, mgr. bus. planning for systems devel. div., 1967-69; pres. Data Dimensions, Inc., Norwalk, Conn., 1969—; adj. asst. prof. dept. econs. U. Bridgeport (Conn.); nat. lectr. Assn. Computing Machinery. Pres. Woodlands-Worthington Taxpayers Assn., 1962-68; bd. dirs. Center for Internat. Mgmt. Studies, Nat. Bd. YMCA's, Greater N.Y. YMCA, North Greenwich Assn., 1973-74. Served with AUS, 1954-56. Fellow Am. Sociol. Soc.; mem. Acad. Polit. Sci., Pres.'s Assn. Republican. Clubs: Landmark (charter mem.) (Stamford, Conn.); Masons; Bailiwick (Greenwich). Mem. editorial bd. Jour. Computer Ops., 1965-69. Home: 21 Calhoun Dr Greenwich CT 06830 Office: 50 Washington St Norwalk CT 06854

GOTTLIEB, ROBERT ADAMS, publisher; b. N.Y.C., Apr. 29, 1931; s. Charles and Martha (Keen) G.; B.A., Columbia, 1952; postgrad. Cambridge (Eng.) U., 1952-54; m. Maria Tucci, Apr. 26, 1969; children—Roger, Elizabeth, Nicholas. Editor-in-chief, v.p. Simon & Schuster, 1955-68; editor-in-chief Alfred A. Knopf, Inc., N.Y.C., 1968—, exec. v.p., 1968-73, pres., 1973—. Bd. dirs. N.Y.C. Ballet. Mem. Phi Beta Kappa. Office: 201 E 50th St New York NY 10022

GOTTSCHALK, NORMAN EDWARD, JR., steel co. exec.; b. Harmarville, Pa., Apr. 25, 1944; s. Norman Edward and Helen Ruth (Burrows) G.; A.A. magna cum laude in Acctg., Robert Morris Coll., 1966; m. Patricia Ann Koehler, Dec. 22, 1962; children—Laura L., Lisa Lynne, Norman Edward, Charles Anthony. From acctg. clk. to acct. Internat. Harvester Co., Leersdale, Pa., 1965-68; acct., acctg. supr., mgr. acctg., asst. controller Tubular Service Corp., Springdale, Pa., 1968-70; asst. controller Marmon/Keystone Corp., Butler, Pa., 1971-78, controller, 1978—, asst. sec., 1979—, mem. exec. com., 1978—; tax cons., 1971-76. Mem. Am. Assn. Controllers, Steel Service Center Inst. Home: 116 Wagon Wheel Ln Pittsburgh PA 15238 Office: 225 E Cunningham St Butler PA 16001

GOTTSCHALK, OLIVER ALVIN, bus. broker mergers and acquisitions, cons.; b. Roslyn, S.D., Apr. 5, 1922; s. Forrest Milton and Helga (Monshaugen) G.; student U. S.D., 1940-42; m. Eunice Faye Packernigg, May 16, 1943; children—Marcia, Mark, Maureen. Owner, operator grocery store, Lake Preston, S.D., 1946-47; agt. Equitable Life Assurance Soc., Lake Preston, 1947-50; owner, mgr. Gottschalk Co., Brookings, S.D., 1950-57, pres., 1957—; pres. Negotiators, Inc., Brookings, 1969-76; v.p. Brookings Bowling Corp., 1962-65, sec.-treas., 1965-79; pres. Am. Bus. Brokers and Exchange, Sarasota, Fla., 1977—; mayor Brookings, 1962-64. Pres. Brookings C. of C., 1961-62. Served with USAAC, 1942-46. Named S.D. Realtor of Yr., 1970; recipient award of merit C. of C., 1970. Mem. Am. Legion, Inst. Cert. Bus. Counselors. Republican. Lutheran. Clubs: Masons, Rotary, Shriners, Elks. Leader seminars, lectrs. in field; founder bus. brokerage mktg. network. Home: 2981 Hardee Dr Sarasota FL 33581 Office: 630 S Orange Ave Sarasota FL 33577

GOTTWALD, BRUCE COBB, chem. co. exec.; b. Richmond, Va., Sept. 28, 1933; s. Floyd Dewey and Anne Ruth (Cobb) G.; B.S., Va. Mil. Inst., 1954; grad. student U. Va., also Inst. Paper Chemistry, Appleton, Wis.; m. Nancy Hays, Dec. 22, 1956; children—Bruce Cobb, Mark Hays, Thomas Edward. With Albemarie Paper Mfg. Co., 1956-62; v.p., sec. Ethyl Corp., 1962-64, coll. exec. v.p., sec., 1964-70, pres., 1970—; dir. Richmond Engring. Co., James River Corp. Chmn. bd. dirs. Va. Gov.'s Adv. Bd. on Indsl. Devel., Va. Council on Econ. Devel.; trustee Va. Mus. Fine Arts, Med. Coll. Va. Found., Randolph Macon Woman's Coll. Presbyn. Clubs: Chemists (N.Y.C.); Commonwealth (Richmond). Home: 4203 Sulgrave Rd Richmond VA 23221 Office: 330 S 4th St Richmond VA 23217

GOTTWALD, FLOYD DEWEY, chem. co. exec.; b. Richmond, Va., May 22, 1898; s. William H. and Mary A. Gottwald; student William and Mary Coll.; m. Anne Cobb, Nov. 17, 1919; children—Floyd Dewey, Bruce Cobb. Asst. paymaster Richmond Fredericksburg & Potomac R.R. Co., 1917-18; with Albemarle Paper Co., Richmond, 1918-68, successively export mgr., asst. sec., sec., prodn. mgr., v.p., exec. v.p., pres., vice chmn. bd.; chief exec. officer, now vice chmn. exec. com., dir. Ethyl Corp., Richmond; dir. emeritus First & Mchts. Nat. Bank Richmond. Trustee U. Richmond. Mem. Richmond C. of C. (dir.). Baptist. Clubs: Commonwealth, Masons, Country of Va.; Princess Anne Country (Norfolk, Va.). Home: 3907 Sulgrave Rd Richmond VA 23221 Office: 330 S 4th St Box 2189 Richmond VA 23217

GOULD, BENJAMIN Z., lawyer; b. Chgo., July 27, 1913; s. Samuel and Fanny (Tendrich) G.; A.B., U. Chgo., 1935, J.D. cum laude, 1937; m. Shirley Handleman, Nov. 22, 1942; children—Fredrick G., Edward S., Barbara F. Admitted to Ill. bar, 1937, since practiced in Chgo.; asso. firm Gould & Ratner, and predecessors, 1937-49, sr. partner, 1949—; sec., gen. counsel, dir. Henry Crown & Co., Univ. Exchange Corp., Century-Am. Corp., Burton-Dixie Corp., Central Enterprises, Inc., Monticello Realty Corp., Follansbee Metals Co.; sec., gen. counsel Material Service Corp. subs. Gen. Dynamics Corp., Marblehead Lime Co., Freeman United Coal Mining Co. Div., Material Service Corp., Aberdeen Mfg. Corp., Finkel Outdoor Products, Inc.; sec., gen. counsel, v.p., dir. Exchange Bldg. Corp., Standard Forgings Corp.; sec., gen. counsel Univ. Village Golf Course, Univ. Village Plaza, Santa Barbara Research Park, Thomas B. Bishop Co., divs. Univ. Exchange Corp., San Francisco, SCNO Barge Lines, Inc., SCNO Terminal Corp., Oils, Inc., Lemont Shipbldg. & Repair Co. divs. Exchange Bldg. Corp., Mills-Am. Envelope Co., Utah Marblehead Lime Co., Nat. Aircrafts Inc., Henderson Camp Products Co., Arie and Ida Crown Meml. Bd. dirs. Hebrew Theol. Coll., Chgo. Loop Synagogue. Served with USCGR, World War II. Mem. Am. Arbitration Assn. (nat. panel), Chgo. Council Fgn. Relations, Am. Soc. Corporate Secs., Am. Soc. Internat. Law, Internat., Am., Ill., Chgo. bar assns., Navy League U.S., Am. Judicature Soc., Phi Beta Kappa. Jewish (dir. Chgo. congregations). Clubs: Exec., Standard, Hundred of Cook County (Chgo.). Home: 1170 Michigan Ave Wilmette IL 60091 Office: 300 W Washington St Chicago IL 60606

GOULD, CLIO LAVERNE, electric utility co. exec.; b. Madison, S.D., Feb. 20, 1919; s. Howard Bennett and Moneta Kay (Herrick) G.; student Walla Walla Coll., 1948, U. Wash. Extension, 1954, U. Calif. at San Diego Extension, 1962, Capital Radio Engring. Inst. Corr., 1958-62; diploma elec. engring. Internat. Corr. Schs., 1958; m. Mildred May Newell, Apr. 13, 1942; children—George Marcus, Deanna May (Mrs. Terry L. Paxton). With astronautics div. Gen. Dynamics Corp., San Diego, 1957-66, sr. design engr. research and devel. Atlas and Centaur space vehicles, 1958-66; supt. power and pumping depts. Wellton Mohawk Irrigation & Drainage Dist., Wellton, Ariz., 1966-76, gen. mgr., 1976—, treas. Liga Internat., Inc., San Diego, 1964-65. Dir. exec. com. Agri-Bus. Council Ariz. Served with AUS, 1941-45; PTO. Recipient Performance award Gen. Dynamics Corp., 1963. Registered profl. engr., Ariz. Mem. IEEE (sr.), AIAA, Nat., Ariz. (pres. chpt. 1977-78) socs. profl. engrs., Photog. Soc. Am., Nat. Water Resources Assn., Ariz. State Reclamation Assn. Republican. Seventh-day Adventist (elder 1956—, chmn. bldg. com. 1970-73). Home: Route 1 Box 4 Wellton AZ 85356 Office: Route 1 Box 19 Wellton AZ 85356

GOULD, DONALD EVERETT, chem. co. exec., b. Concord, N.H., May 19, 1932; s. Everett Luther and Gladys (Wilcox) G.; B.S. in Chem. Engring., U. N.H. 1954; postgrad. math. Rutgers U., 1955-59; m. Marilyn Bachelder, June 13, 1953; children—Barbara, Allen, Douglas. Devel. chem. engr. chems. and plastics div. Union Carbide Co., Bound Brook, N.J., 1954-59, tech. service engr., Bound Brook and Wayne, N.J. 1959-64, mgr. tech. service indsl. bag dept., Wayne, 1964-66, mgr. tech. services indsl. fabricated products dept. 1966-67, marketing mgr. indsl. bags, 1967-69, sr. packaging engr., 1969-72, mgr. packaging, 1972-75, mgr. distbn. safety and regulations, 1975-79, staff packaging engr., 1980—. Mem. Packaging Inst. (chmn. films, foils and laminations com. 1964-66, sect. leader bottle containers 1967-69, chmn. bag com. 1975-78), Soc. Plastics Engrs., Am. Soc. Quality Control, Alpha Chi Sigma. Club: Packanack Lake Country. Contbr. articles profl. jours., also to Ency. Engring. Materials and Processes. Home: 98 Lake Dr E Wayne NJ 07470 Office: River Rd Bound Brook NJ 08805

GOULD, FRANK NELSON, JR., banker; b. Mpls., May 19, 1926; s. Frank Nelson and Ella (Exe) G.; B.A., Mont. State U., 1950; m. June Marilyn Beach, Sept. 1, 1948; children—Howard Nelson, Gregory Jay, Tracy Dee. Asst. v.p. Metal Bank & Trust Co., Butte, Mont., 1958-60; with United Calif. Bank, Los Angeles, 1960—, now sr. v.p. Bd. dirs. Oakland Boys Club; mem. adv. bd. Nat. Alliance Bus., Displaced Homemakers Center. Served with USNR, 1944-46. Republican. Lutheran. Home: 409 Birchwood Dr Moraga CA 94556 Office: United Calif Bank 14th and Broadway Oakland CA 94612

GOULD, HARRY EDWARD, JR., mfg. exec.; b. N.Y.C., Sept. 24, 1938; s. Harry E. and Lucille (Quartucy) G.; student Oxford U., 1958; B.A. cum laude, Colgate U., 1960; postgrad. Harvard Bus. Sch., 1960-61; M.B.A., Columbia, 1964; m. Barbara Clement, Apr. 26, 1975, children—Harry Edward III, Katharine Elizabeth. Asso. in corporate finance dept. Goldman, Sachs & Co., N.Y.C., 1961-62; exec. asst. to sr. v.p. ops. Universal Am., N.Y.C., 1964-65; sec., treas. Young Spring & Wire Corp., Detroit, 1965-67, exec. v.p., chief operating officer, 1967-69, also dir.; v.p. adminstrn. and finance Universal Am. Corp., 1968-69; mem. exec. com., v.p., sec.-treas. Daybrook-Ottawa Corp., Bowling Green, Ohio, 1967-69; dir., mem. exec. com. Am. Med. Ins. Co., N.Y.C., 1966-74; pres., chmn. bd., dir., chief exec. officer Gould Paper Corp., N.Y.C., 1969—; chmn. bd., dir. Samuel Porritt & Co., East Peoria, Ill., 1969—; chmn. bd., dir. Ingalls Mfg., Inc., Ceres, Calif., 1971—, McNair Mfg., Inc., Chico, Calif., 1972—, Computer Copies Corp., N.Y.C., 1970-73, Hawthorne Paper Co., Inc., Kalamazoo, 1974, Weiss Mfg., Inc., Chico, 1974—, Vrisimo Mfg., Inc., Ceres, 1974—; pres., dir. Carlyle Internat. Sales Corp., N.Y.C., 1975—; Ltd. partner Hardy & Co., mem. N.Y. Stock Exchange, N.Y.C., 1973-78; dir. Reinhold-Gould GmbH, Hamburg, Germany, 1969—, Lewis and Gould Paper Co., Inc., Chgo., 1975-78. Co-chmn. Pacesetter's com. Boy Scouts Am., 1966-69; bd. dirs. Nat. Multiple Sclerosis Soc., 1977—; pres. Harry E. Gould Found., N.Y.C., 1971—; participant as U.S. Pres.'s rep. UN E.-W. Trade Devel. Commn., 1967; mem. nat. council Colgate U., 1973-76, trustee, 1976—, mem. budget, devel., fin. and student affairs com., 1976—; bd. dirs. Ophthal. Found. Am., 1973—, United Cerebral Palsy Research and Ednl. Found., 1976—; mem. U.S. Pres.'s Export Council, 1979—, mem. exec. com., chmn. export expansion subcom., mem. export promotion subcom.; mem. N.Y. Gov.'s Task Force on N.Y. State Cultural Life and Arts, 1975—; nat. trustee Nat. Symphony Orch., Washington, mem. exec. com., 1978—; mem. Mayor's Citizens Com. 1976 Democratic Nat. Conv.; dir. N.Y.C. Housing Devel. Corp., 1977—; mem. Dem. Nat. Fin. Council, 1974—, vice chmn. exec. com., chmn. budget and audit coms.; mem. chmn.'s council N.Y. State Dem. Com., 1975—, treas. 1976-77; adv. bd. Columbia U. Grad. Sch. Bus., 1980—, bd. dirs. alumni assn., 1980—; bd. dirs. Cinema Group, Inc., Los Angeles, chmn. exec. com., 1980—. Mem. Paper Mchts. Assn. N.Y. (dir. 1972—), Nat. Paper Trade Assn. (dir., mem. printing paper com. 1973—), Paper Club N.Y., Financial Execs. Inst., Young Presidents' Orgn., Phi Kappa Tau. Clubs: President's (co-chmn. assos., div. 1964-68), Harvard, Harvard Business, Friars, Marco Polo, City Athletic (N.Y.C.); Rockrimmon Country (Stamford, Conn.); Les Ambassadeurs (London). Home: 25 Sutton Pl S New York NY 10022 also Cherry Hill Farm 429 Taconic Rd Greenwich CT 06830 Office: 145 E 32d St New York NY 10016

GOULD, STEPHEN, paper mfg. exec., writer; b. N.Y.C., Dec. 25, 1909; s. Jacob and Fannie (Schwartz) G.; D.F.A., Geneva Theol. Coll., 1969; D.Integral Philosophy, World U.; Ph.D. in Psychology, Clayton (Mo.) U., 1979; m. Marlene Ossias, Aug. 24, 1941; children—Phyllis Jane, Roberta Louise, Debra Elaine. Columnist, Port & Terminal Publs., 1931-36, cons., 1940—. Bd. dirs. Purdue U.-Extension Packaging and Handling, mus. dir. Nova Tamarac Symphonic Pops Orch., Fla. Recipient H. De Bellis Sculpture award, 1970. Fellow Am. Assn. Humanistic Psychology; mem. Am. Humanist Assn., Nat. Soc. Arts and Letters (life), N.Y. Acad. Scis. (life), Soc. Indsl. Packaging and Handling Engrs. Clubs: Salmagundi, Forsgate Country, Masons. Home: 4905 Bayberry Ln Tamarac FL 33319

GOULD, SYD S., publisher; b. Boston, Dec. 16, 1912; s. Charles M. and Cecelia (Duke) G.; student Coll. William and Mary, 1934; m. Grace Leich, May 22, 1938; 1 dau., Nancy Hamilton (Mrs. Lucien M. Gex, Jr.). Radio bus., Buenos Aires, Argentina, 1934, 36; advt. dept. Call-Chronicle Newspapers, Allentown, Pa., 1936-42; v.p. adv. dir. Baytown (Tex.) Sun, 1943-55; pub.-owner Cleveland (Tenn.) Daily Banner, 1955—; pres. Cleveland Newspapers, Inc., 1956-67; exec. v.p. Southern Newspapers, Inc., 1963-69; pres. Syd S. Gould Assos., 1966—, Bolivar Newspapers, Inc., 1967—, Ironton Tribune Corp. (O.), Franklin Newspapers, Inc. (La.), Comet-Press Newspapers, Thibodaux, La., Milton Newspapers, Inc. (Fla.). Mem. Regional Small Bus. Adv. Council. Sec., Bradley County (Tenn.) Indsl. Devel. Bd., 1961—; bd. dirs. Providence Hosp.; pres. Bradley County Heart Assn., 1960-61. Served with USNR, World War II. Mem. Newspaper Advt. Execs. Assn., Tenn. Press. Assn., Bur. Advt., Am. Newspaper Pubs. Assn., USCG Aux., U.S. Power Squadron, U.S. Naval Inst., Navy League, Eagle Scout Assn., Sigma Delta Chi. Episcopalian. Clubs: Bayou Country, Mobile Big Game Fishing, Isle Dauphine Country, Capitol Hill, Yachting of Am., Internat. Trade, Bienville, Athelstan. Home: Route 1 Box 146 Theodore AL 36582 Office: Route 1 Box 146 Theodore AL 36582

GOULD, WILLIAM EVERETT, exec. search cons.; b. Watertown, N.Y., Oct. 23, 1932; s. Leslie Albert and Hazel (Overacker) G.; B.A., Williams Coll., 1957; M.B.A. with distinction, Harvard U., 1965; m. Sharon Lynn Abley, June 20, 1958; children—William, John A., Whitney H., Nicholas C.R. Sales engr. Carborundum Co., Niagara Falls, N.Y., 1958-61; mktg./sales Varcum div. Reichhold Chems., Niagara Falls and Hamburg, Ger., 1961-65; gen. mgr. Am. Metal Climax/Amax Aluminum Ltd., Aston Clinton, Eng., 1965-69; v.p. Heidrick & Struggles, Inc., N.Y.C., 1969-73; chmn. Gould & McCoy, Inc., N.Y.C., 1973—; career counselor Harvard Bus. Sch. Served with U.S. Army, 1953-55. Mem. Inst. Dirs. (London), Am. Mgmt. Assn., Personnel Mgmt. Assn. Clubs: Harvard Bus. Sch.; Wilton Riding. Patentee in field. Home: 195 Branch Brook Rd Wilton CT 06897 Office: 375 Park Ave New York NY 10152

GOULD, WILLIAM RICHARD, utility exec., engr.; b. Provo, Utah, Oct. 31, 1919; s. William Gilbert and Pauline Eva (Faser) G.; B.S. in Mech. Engring., U. Utah, 1942; postgrad. Mass. Inst. Tech., U. Calif. at Los Angeles, U. Idaho; m. Erlyn Arvilla Johnson, Mar. 20, 1942; children—Erlyn Sharon, William Richard, Gilbert John, Wayne Raymond. With So. Calif. Edison Co., 1948—, mgr. engring., 1962-63, v.p. engring., constrn., planning, 1963-67, sr. v.p., 1967-73, exec. v.p., 1973-78, pres., 1978—, chmn. bd., 1980—, also dir.; dir. Union Bank, Aerospace Corp., Kaiser Steel Corp., Energy Services, Inc., Mono Power Co., Electric Systems Co., Project Mgmt. Corp., Breeder Reactor Corp., Asso. So. Investment Co., Beckman Instruments. Chmn., Calif. Tech. Services Adv. Council; pres. U.S. nat. com. Internat. Congress Large Electric Systems; past chmn. bd. Atomic Indsl. Forum. Mem. sci. and engring. com. U. Redlands; bd. councilors Sch. Engring., U. So. Calif.; mem. energy adv. bd., trustee Calif. Inst. Tech.; mem. nat. regulatory commn., exec. com. Assembly Engring.; mem. nat. adv. bd. U. Utah; mem. adv. com. electric certificate program U. Calif. at Los Angeles. Trustee, Long Beach Community Hosp.; bd. dirs. Nat. Energy Found., Electric Power Research Inst., Eyring Research Inst., Los Angeles World Affairs Council, Los Angeles Philharm. Assn. Served to lt. USN, 1942-47. Registered profl. engr., Utah, Calif.; recipient George Westinghouse Gold Medal award Assn. Mech. Engrs., 1979. Fellow ASME, Inst. Advanced Engring. (chmn. bd., Engr. of Year 1970); mem. Nat. Acad. Engring., Newcomen Soc. N. Am., Edison Electric Inst. (dir., chmn. exec. adv. bd. policy com. on nuclear power, mem. policy com. on research), Los Angeles Council Engrs. and Scientists (adv. com.), Pacific Coast Elec. Assn. (dir.), Los Angeles C. of C. Mem. Ch. of Jesus Christ of Latter Day Saints. Club: California. Home: 6441 Shire Way Long Beach CA 90815 Office: 2244 Walnut Grove Ave Rosemead CA 91770

GOURLEY, JAMES LELAND, editor, publisher, business exec.; b. Mounds, Okla., Jan. 29, 1925; s. Samuel O. and Lodema (Scott) G.; B.Liberal Studies, U. Okla., 1963; m. Vicki Graham Clark, Nov. 24, 1976; children—James Leland II, Janna Lynn Frazer, Kelly Clark, Brandon Clark. Editor, pub., pres. Daily Free-Lance, Henryetta, Okla., 1946-73; editor Friday, 1974—; pres. Nichols Hills Pub. Co., 1974—; pres. radio sta. KHEN, KHEN-TV, Henryetta, 1955-71; pres. Hugo (Okla.) Daily News, 1953-63; chief of staff gov. Okla., 1959-63; chmn., pres. State Capitol Bank, 1962-69; v.p. radio sta. KXOJ Sapulpa, 1972-75; treas. Okla. Radio Co., Inc., 1962-67. Mem. Pres. Nat. Pub. Advisory Com. to sec. commerce, 1963-66; exec. dir. Gov's

Comm. Higher Edn., 1960-61; chmn. Okla. Lake Redevel. Authority, 1960-63; dist. chmn. Boy Scouts Am. 1962-64. Democratic candidate for gov. Okla., 1966. Bd. dirs. So. Regional Edn. Bd., 1959-67, Okla. Symphony Soc., 1976—. Served to maj. AUS, 1941-46. Decorated Bronze Star. Recipient 13 Best Small Town Daily Newspaper Okla. awards, Best Large City Weekly newspaper awards (4), 1977, 78, 79, 80; inducted Okla. Journalism Hall of Fame, 1980. Mem. UP Internat. Editors Okla. (pres. 1958-59), Okla. Disciples of Christ Laymen (pres. 1964-65), Inter-Am. Press Assn., Suburban Newspapers Am. (dir.), Okla. Press Assn., Oklahoma City C. of C. (dir.), Sigma Delta Chi, Pi Kappa Alpha. Democrat. Club: Rotary (dir.). Home: 1605 W Wilshire Oklahoma City OK 73116 Office: 10801 N Quail Plaza Dr Oklahoma City OK 73156

GOUSSELAND, PIERRE LEOPOLD, mining co. exec.; b. Tonnay-Charente, France, Jan. 14, 1922; s. Edmond and Marthe (Lemarre) G.; Ingenieur Civil des Mines, Ecole Nationale Superieure des Mines, Paris, 1947; LL.B., Sorbonne, Paris, 1947; postgrad. Mass. Inst. Tech., 1947-48. With AMAX Inc., 1948—, pres. Climax div., 1970-75, exec. v.p., 1975, pres., 1975-77, chmn. bd., chief exec. officer, Greenwich, Conn., 1977—, also dir.; dir. Am. Internat. Group, Inc., French Am. Banking Corp. Mem. Brit. Iron, Steel Inst., Societe Francaise de Metallurgie, Verein Deutscher Eisenhuttenleute, Soc. Automotive Engrs., French-Am. C. of C. in U.S., U.S. (pres.), Am. Soc. Metals, Metall. Soc. Office: AMAX Center Greenwich CT 06830

GOUW, ANDY SIOE-SAN, sporting goods co. exec.; b. Djakarta, Indonesia, Mar. 5, 1944; came to U.S., 1962, naturalized, 1980; s. Leo Chin-Sian and Katherine Wie-Bwee (Tan) G.; B.Sc. in M.E., San Jose State U., 1968, M.Sc., 1971; m. Peggy Beng-yoe Oei, Oct. 3, 1971. Field engr. Eichleay Corp., Santa Clara, Calif., 1968-70; owner, mgr. Artifacts Oriental, San Jose, Calif., 1970-71; owner, mgr. Unikus Gifts, Monterey, Calif., 1971-74; owner Solely Yours, Santa Clara, 1975-79; partner, gen. mgr. Santa Teresa Sporthaus, San Jose, 1979—. Mem. ASME. Roman Catholic. Clubs: U.S. Badminton Assn. (dir. 1972), No. Calif. Badminton Assn. (dir. 1979), Peninsula Badminton (pres. 1978-79). Editor, No. Calif. Badminton Assn. Newsletter, 1979—. Home: 1740 Grace Ave San Jose CA 95125 Office: 7128 Santa Teresa Blvd San Jose CA 95139

GOW, JAMES THOMAS, JR., food retailing co. exec.; b. Columbus, Ohio, Dec. 7, 1937; s. James Thomas and Rhoda Roberts (Dresser) G.; B.S.B.A., Babson Coll., 1959; P.M.D., Harvard U., 1973; children—James Thomas III, Michael James. Vice pres. Supermarkets Gen. Corp., Woodbridge, N.J., 1968-75; pres. G. Tamblyn Ltd., Toronto, Ont., Can., 1975-77; corp. v.p. Gt. Atlantic & Pacific Tea Co., Montvale, N.J., 1977—. Mem. Food Distbn. Research Soc., Nat. Assn. Accts., Am. Prodn. and Inventory Control Soc. Office: 2 Paragon Dr Montvale NJ 07645

GOWER, FRANK HERBERT, JR., petroleum co. exec.; b. Denver, Dec. 14, 1923; s. Frank Herbert and Mildred Caro (Ward) G.; B.A., U. Colo., 1950; m. Marie Patricia Pedersen, June 12, 1947; children—Steven, Michael, Mark, Jeannette, Mathew. With F.H. Gower Oil Properties, Denver, 1949-56; mgr. Gower Oil Co., Denver, 1956-65, owner, 1965—; tres. Chaparral Resources, Inc.; pres. Minnelusa Corp. D.B.A. Deep Lagoon Marina. Bd. dirs. Harmony Found., Inc. Served with AUS, 1942-45. Mem. Am. Assn. Petroleum Geologists, Rocky Mountain Assn. Geologists, Denver Petroleum Landmans Assn., Ind. Petroleum Assn. Am., Ind. Petroleum Assn. Mountain States, Rocky Mountain Oil and Gas Assn. (dir.), Rocky Mountain Petroleum Pioneers, Wyo. Geol. Assn., Assn. Profl. Geol. Scientists, Am. Petroleum Inst., Sigma Alpha Epsilon. Clubs: Petroleum, Garden of the Gods, Cherry Hills Country, Landings Yacht and Golf. Home: 3300 E Floyd Dr Denver CO 80210 also 4666 S Landing, Dr. Fort Meyers FL 33907 Office: 5660 S Syracuse Circle Englewood CO 80111

GOZONSKY, EDWIN S., investment broker; b. Laconia, N.H., Mar. 31, 1930; s. Archie and Ida G.; B.A., Yale U., 1952, M.B.A., Harvard U., 1954; m. Dorothy Adelson, Feb. 28, 1965; children—Judith, Diane. With Eastman Dillon, Union Securities (merged with Paine Webber 1980), Boston, 1959—, v.p. Boston office, 1971—; pres. Variable Annuities Provide Personal Security, 1979—; lectr., publicist variable annuities, 1979—. Served with U.S. Army, 1954-56. Mem. Bulldog Soc. (provisional dir.). Home: 118 Irving Ave Providence RI 02906 Office: Paine Webber One Federal St Boston MA 02110

GRABSKE, WILLIAM JOHN, corp. exec.; b. Chgo., Jan. 31, 1943; s. Edward Walter and Helen Julia G.; B.S. in Civil Engring., U. Ill., 1965; postgrad. U. Ill. Sch. Bus., Columbia U. Grad. Sch. Bus., 1969; m. Judith Elaine Benz, Apr. 12, 1969; children—Gretchen, Bradford, Lindsay. Operating mgmt. trainee, N.Y. Central System, N.Y.C., 1965-66, asst. supt. shops, E. Rochester, N.Y., 1966-67, prodn. mgr. Beech Grove Works, Indpls., 1967-68; gen. supt. Harmon Diesel and Elec. Shops, Penn Central Transp. Co., Croton-on-Hudson, N.Y., 1968-69, system mgr. planning and devel., Phila., 1969-70, dir. intermodal ops., Phila., 1970-71; sr. asso., dir. transp. ops. Booz, Allen and Hamilton, Phila., 1971-73; dir. bicentennial transp. programs City of Phila., 1973-74, dep. mayor, 1974-76; v.p. Boston and Maine Corp., Boston, 1976—; dir. Springfield Terminal Co. Chmn. Mayor's task force for transp. qualtiy, Phila., 1974-76; mem. Market St. East Council, 1974-76, Delaware Valley Council, 1974-76; Delaware Valley Regional Planning Commn., 1974-76. Recipient spl. recognition award for bicentennial planning, Phila., 1976. Mem. ASCE, ASME, Transp. Research Forum., U. Ill., Alumni Assn. (life), Illini Club Phila. (v.p.). Republican. Contbr. research paper to profl. publ., paper to internat. transp. conf., Montreal, Que., Can., 1974, U. Chgo., 1976. Home: Holly Hill Dr Amherst NH 03031 Office: 150 Causeway St Boston MA 02109

GRACE, CHARLES MACDONALD, fin. exec.; b. Manhasset, N.Y., Sept. 13, 1926; s. Joseph P. and Janet (MacDonald) G.; A.B., Mount St. Mary's Coll., 1951; M.B.A., Columbia U., 1959; m. Margaret Mary VanDerpool, July 3, 1954; children—Maureen, Charles Macdonald, James V., Joseph E. Cons., investment analyst Marine Midland Grace Trust, N.Y.C., 1968-69; pres. CMG Enterprises, Marina del Rey, Calif., 1969—. Vice pres., dir. Madison Sq. Boys' Club; bd. mgrs. Lincoln Hall; chmn. Internat. Fund for Monuments; bd. dirs., chmn., Center for Applied Research; trustee Fordham U., Conservation Found., U. San Diego, LaSalle Coll., Seton Hall U., Talladega Coll., N.Y. Cancer Research Inst., Sacred Heart U., Marymount Coll. Va.; hon. trustee Anna Maria Coll. Recipient Caritas medal Niagara U., 1967. Mem. N.Y. Soc. Security Analysts, N.Y. U. Men-in-Fin. Club, The Conf. Bd. Clubs: Union League, Met. Univ., Century Assn., Knights of Malta, Knights of Holy Sepulcher. Office: 330 Washington St Suite 310 Marina del Rey CA 90291

GRACE, HAROLD STEPHEN, JR., business exec.; b. New Orleans, Aug. 25, 1942; s. Harold Stephen and Adele Elizabeth (Graham) G.; B.S. in Indsl. Engring., Lamar U., Beaumont, Tex., 1964; M.B.A., U. Chgo., 1966; Ph.D., U. Houston, 1970; m. Phebe Marie Dore, Dec. 26, 1964; children—Michelle, Stephen. Instr. U. Houston, 1968; financial asst. to pres. Ennis Bus. Forms, Inc. (Tex.), 1969; asso. prof. finance, acting head dept. Tex. So. U., Houston, 1970-77; adv. dir. Small Bus. Devel. Center, 1971-72; now v.p. fin. Century Corp., Houston; cons., lectr. corporate planning and finance; dir. economic profile project Model Cities Project, 1971. Named Outstanding Tchr. in Sch. Bus., Tex. So. U., 1971. Mem. Am., Southwestern (adv. bd. to pres. 1972-73) finance assns., Financial Mgmt. Assn., Financial Execs. Inst. (dir. Houston 1973-76, treas. Houston 1980-81, dir. So. Area 1980-81), Houston C. of C., Omicron Delta Epsilon, Alpha Phi Mu. Author research papers. Office: Five Greenway Plaza E Suite 1700 Houston TX 77046

GRACE, WILLIAM FRANCIS, ins. co. exec.; b. Louisville, Sept. 10, 1913; s. Albert Clement and Cecile Jeanne (LeBesque) G.; student Tulane U., 1930-32; m. Helen Meyers, July 26, 1941; children—Josephine Grace McCloskey, Cecile Grace Ballard, William Francis, Elizabeth Manning. Loan officer, bank, New Orleans, to 1941; with John Hancock Mut. Life Ins. Co., New Orleans, 1945—, gen. agt., 1953—. Treas. citizens council Pub. Sch. Survey; active United Fund; chief fund raiser Sara Mayo Hosp., 1970; bd. dirs. ARC. Recipient award Juvenile Ct. New Orleans. Mem. New Orleans Life Underwriters Assn. (past pres.), John Hancock Mut. Life Ins. Co. Gen. Agts. Assn. (past pres.), New Orleans Gen. Agts. and Mgrs. Assn. (past pres.), Nat. Assn. Life Underwriters, Million Dollar Round Table. Clubs: Stratford, Lake Shore, New Orleans Country, Boston, La., Pickwick. Home: 1328 Octavia St New Orleans LA 70115 Office: 809 Howard Ave New Orleans LA 70113

GRAD, MARCIA LYNNE, research firm exec.; b. Albany, N.Y., Nov. 17, 1942; d. Gerald Dean and Bernice Elizabeth (Ferguson) Bouton; B.A., U. Denver, 1969, M.A., 1976; 1 dau., Blys Lien Grad. Exec. asst. Daru Brokerage, N.Y.C., 1962-66; adminstrv. asst., editor dept. mass communications U. Denver, 1967, research asst., 1967-69; instr. history Trinity Coll., Burlington, Vt., 1971-72; research asst. spl. edn. program U. Vt., Burlington, 1971-73; writer Behavior Assos., Tucson, 1973-74; research social scientist Denver Research Inst., 1975-79; owner, mgr. M.L. Grad Cons., contract research firm, Chgo., 1979—; cons. in field. Mem. ICONE Internat. Steering Com. Mem. Product Devel. and Mgmt. Assn. Contbr. articles to profl. jours. Home and Office: 3930 N Pine Grove Ave Chicago IL 60613

GRAD, VINSON WINFIELD, lawyer; b. Haverhill, Mass., Nov. 23, 1912; s. Benjamin and Eva Elizabeth (Sandler) G.; A.B., Cornell U., 1934; J.D., Harvard U., 1937; m. Bessie Wilner, Nov. 23, 1938; children—Jeffrey Stuart, William Lewis. Admitted to Mass. bar, 1937; atty. Boston Legal Aid Soc., 1937-38; individual practice law, Haverhill, 1938-41, 77—; with Gen. Electric Co., Lynn, Mass., 1941-45; labor relations Grad's Splty. Shops, Haverhill, 1945-77; dir. Haverhill Nat. Bank. Mem. Haverhill Indsl. Commn.; bd. dirs. Haverhill Indsl. Found., 1971—; mem. adv. bd. Haverhill Schs., Plaistow (N.H.) Schs.; pres. Temple Emanu-El, 1969-71, treas., 1971—. Recipient Disting. Service award B'nai B'rith, 1972. Mem. Am. Bar Assn., Mass. Bar Assn., Am. Jurisprudence Assn., Am. Arbitration Assn., Haverhill C. of C. (Pres. 1965-70). Club: Masons. Home: 14 Eastland Terr Haverhill MA 01830 Office: 25 Kenoza Ave Haverhill MA 01830

GRADY, JOHN EDWARD, JR., investment banker; b. Boston, June 15, 1915; s. John Edward and Catherine Agnes (Connolly) G.; A.B., Harvard U., 1956, M.B.A., 1965; m. Angela Loretta McDonnell, July 10, 1965 (div.); children—John Edward III, Robert Emmet McDonnell, Douglas Anderson. Account exec. Merrill Lynch, Pierce, Fenner & Smith, N.Y.C., 1960-63; sr. asso. Cresap, McCormick and Paget, N.Y.C., 1965-69; v.p. Investment Mgmt. and Research, Inc., St. Petersburg, Fla., 1969-70; v.p. fin., treas. Suncoast Highland Corp., Clearwater, Fla., 1970-74, v.p. fin.-ops., sec.-treas., 1974-76, also dir.; dir. corp. fin. Raymon James & Assos., Inc., St. Petersburg, Fla., 1976—. Regional chmn. Harvard Bus. Sch. Fund, 1971-73; mem. pres.'s roundtable Eckerd Coll., 1971—; trustee Canterbury Sch. Fla., St. Petersburg, 1973—, treas., 1974-75, chmn., 1975-76; mem. com. on social service allocations City of St. Petersburg, 1978; bd. dirs. Fla. Gulf Coast Symphony, St. Petersburg, 1979—. Served to lt. (j.g.) USNR, 1956-60. Clubs: Lakewood Country, Harvard Bus. Sch. West Coast (dir. 1976—), Harvard West Coast (pres. 1976-78)(St. Petersburg-Tampa, Fla.); Harvard Bus. Sch. (sec. 1969)(N.Y.C.); St. Petersburg Yacht; Suncoast Tiger Bay, Rotary. Home: 5910 Bayou Grande Blvd NE Saint Petersburg FL 33703

GRAEBNER, LINDA SUSAN, mfg. co. exec.; b. Lakewood, Ohio, Mar. 28, 1950; d. Herman F. and Marilynn J. (Baumer) G.; B.S., Purdue U., 1972; M.B.A., Stanford U., 1974. Analyst, IRS, Washington, 1971-72; asso. Griffenhagen Koreger Inc., San Francisco, 1974-75; asso., mgr. Booz, Allen & Hamilton, Inc., San Francisco, 1975-79; bus. planning mgr. Crown Zellerbach Corp., San Francisco, 1979—. Mem. Regional Transit Productivity Commn., San Francisco, 1978—. Mem. Corp. Planners Assn., World Affairs Council, Bay Area Profl. Women's Network. Club: San Francisco Bay. Contbr. articles to profl. jours. Office: 1 Bush St San Francisco CA 94104

GRAESE, CLIFFORD ERNEST, acct.; b. Canova, S.D., Jan. 5, 1927; s. Arthur Edward and Alma Matilda (Neugebauer) G.; B.S., U. S.D., 1949, LL.D., 1980; m. LaVonne Marie Bohn, May 3, 1953; children—Diane Graese, Sally Graese Daugherty, Susan Graese Alfirevic, Larry. With Peat, Marwick, Mitchell & Co., 1949—, partner in charge mgmt. cons., N.Y.C., 1963-75, vice chmn. acctg. and auditing, 1975—. Trustee, U. S.D. Found.; v.p. Saddle River (N.J.) Bd. Edn., 1972-78. Served with U.S. Navy, 1945-46. Mem. Am. Inst. C.P.A.'s (past chmn. div. profl. ethics), Am. Acctg. Assn., Accts. Club Am. Republican. Lutheran. Clubs: Ridgewood Country, Board Room. Office: 345 Park Ave New York NY 10022

GRAF, JOHN RICHARD, JR., transp. exec.; b. Abington, Pa., Nov. 14, 1943; s. John Richard and Eleanor (Lyle) G.; student Boston U., 1962-63; I.E., Lowell U., 1965; m. Barbara Hope Bearse, July 1, 1967; children—Cathrine Anne, Cheryl Elaine, Sharleen Hope. Propr., Graf Products Co., Phila. and Lowell, Mass., 1961-63; asst. to pres., dir. engring. Panelucent Corp. and Penn Box Co., Warrington, Pa., 1966-68; pres. G & G Assos., Doylestown, Pa. and Orleans, Mass., 1968-73, Integrated Concepts Corp., Hyannis, Mass., 1970—, Aviation Concepts & Transp., Inc., Hyannis, 1974—; cons. Served to lt. USAR, 1961-68. Mem. Metal Bldg. Mfrs. Assn., Airplane Owners and Pilots Assn., Am. Fedn. Musicians. Republican. Episcopalian. Club: Lions. Inventor riot control foam gun, 1968, solid state wireless audio switcher, 1979, electronic Frisbee for the blind, 1980. Home: 24 Powder Horn Way Centerville MA 02632 Office: PO Box 1261 Hyannis MA 02601

GRAF, JOSEPH CHARLES, petroleum corp. exec.; b. Jersey City, Sept. 10, 1928; s. John Bernard and Margaret Cecilia (Toomey) G.; B.S., Seton Hall U., 1949, M.B.A., U. Pa., 1954; children—Claire, Joseph Charles, Michelle, Mary Ellen, Thomas, Richard. Trainee, Prudential Ins. Co., Newark, 1954-55, systems analyst, 1955-56, asst. research analyst, 1956-58, research analyst, 1958-61, investment analyst, 1961-63, sr. investment analyst, 1963-64, Houston, 1964-67; v.p. So. Nat. Bank, Houston, 1967-69; financial advisor Quintana Petroleum Corp., Houston, 1969-79, investment mgr., 1979—; dir. Linbeck Constrn. Middle East Ltd. (Cayman Islands), Internat. Bank of Finance (Cayman Islands), Terrain King Corp., Tapco Internat. Inc., Quintana Oil and Gas Co., Outdoor Leisure Products Inc., Southland Enterprises, Inc.; mem. investment com. trust dept. Cullen Center Bank & Trust. Cons. research com. Houston C. of C., 1966-71. Exec. sec. Cullen Found., 1974; bd. govs. Center for Retarded, Inc., Houston. Served with AUS, 1951-53. Mem. Houston Fin. Analysts (pres. 1973-74, dir. 1974-77). Clubs: Houston, Houston Racquet. Home: 11711 Memorial #139 Houston TX 77024 Office: 601 Jefferson St Houston TX 77002

GRAFF, JOHN FREDERIC, ins. agy. exec.; b. Highland Park, Ill., Dec. 1, 1933; s. Karl Von and Bernice Mildred (Mattes) G.; B.A. in Econs., DePauw U., 1955; children—Barbara Lynn, Karen Sue. Agt., Provident Mut. Life Ins. Co., Chgo., 1958-61; mem. mgmt. devel. program, Phila., 1961-62, agy. mgr., Chgo., 1962-73; owner, propr. John F. Graff & Assos., Chgo., 1973—; pres. United Corp. of Am., Inc., 1973—, Ill. Bus. Corp., 1976—. Past officer New Trier Republican Orgn.; past chmn. Village Party, Wilmette, Ill.; charter mem., pres. Greater Chgo. Ins. Council of City of Hope, 1980—. Served to lt. (j.g.) USN, 1955-58. Named Ins. Man of Yr., City of Hope, 1978; C.L.U.; registered health underwriter Nat. Assn. Health Underwriters. Mem. Nat. Assn. Life Underwriters, Chgo. Estate Planning Council, Chgo. Assn. Life Underwriters (pres. 1975-76, Disting. Service award 1979), Chgo. Chpt. Chartered Life Underwriters (pres. 1976-77, Huebner Scholar-Disting. Service award 1979), Ill. Life Underwriters Assn. (pres. 1977-78), Chgo. Assn. Health Underwriters (dir. 1975—, Edward H. O'Connor Disting. Service award 1977), Chgo. Gen. Agts. and Mgrs. Assn. (nat. com.). Republican. Methodist. Clubs: Univ. (Chgo.); Westmoreland Country. Contbr. articles to trade mags. Home: 2556 Prairie Ave Apt 15 Evanston IL 60201 Office: United Corp Am 223 W Jackson Blvd Suite 1108 Chicago IL 60606

GRAGG, WILLIFORD, ins. co. exec.; b. Memphis, June 11, 1914; s. Ovvie H. and Ruth Graves (Williford) G.; student Southwestern U., 1931-32; LL.B., U. Tenn., 1936; m. Grace Clement Bailey, Oct. 19, 1940; children—Frances Ann. Uhlenhoff. Admitted to Tenn. bar, 1936; practice in Memphis, 1936-37; agt. FBI, 1942-43; with U.S. Fidelity & Guaranty Co., Balt., 1937-42, 46—, v.p., 1956-59, exec. v.p., 1959-63, sr. exec. v.p., dir., 1963-70, pres., 1970-72, chmn. bd., pres., 1972-78, chmn. bd., chief exec. officer, 1978-80, now ret.; dir. First Nat. Bank, Provident Savings Bank, Del Mar Co., Am. Stores Co., Noxell Corp., Fidelity & Guaranty Life Ins. Co., Fidelity & Guaranty Ins. Underwriters, Inc. Trustee Presbyn. Eye, Ear and Throat Hosp., Balt., Greater Balt. Med. Center, Goucher Coll. Served to capt. USMC, 1944-46. Mem. Alpha Tau Omega. Presbyterian (elder). Clubs: Maryland, Center, Balt. Country (Balt.). Home: 109 Churchwardens Rd Baltimore MD 21212 Office: US Fidelity & Guaranty Co Baltimore MD 21203

GRAHAM, ANN MAUREEN, bus. devel. co. exec.; b. Mich., Aug. 14, 1938; d. John C. and Madeline M. Zemke; B.A. with honors, U. Hawaii, 1960; M.A. (Danforth Found. fellow 1965-67), Stanford U., 1967; SCMP, Harvard U. Bus. Sch., 1980; m. Otis L. Graham, Jr., Sept. 5, 1959; children—Ann Kathryn Graham Lakin, Wade Livingston. Project dir. Dir. Securities Inc., Santa Barbara, Calif., 1974-75; v.p., broker Greentree Realty Inc., Santa Barbara, 1976-77; v.p. The Littlestone Co., Santa Barbara, 1978—; pres. The Graham Corp., 1980—; vice chmn., founder County Savs. and Loan Assn., Santa Barbara. Bd. dirs. Citizens Planning Assn., Santa Barbara, 1974-77, Santa Barbara Symphony Assn., 1977—. Mem. Santa Barbara Bd. Realtors (dir. 1976-77), League Women Voters. Democrat. Clubs: Jr. League, Santa Barbara Tennis, Coral Casino Beach. Home: 112 Olive Mill Rd Santa Barbara CA 93108 Office: 132 E Carrillo St Santa Barbara CA 93101

GRAHAM, CARL FRANCIS, chem. products co. exec., chemist; b. Limon, Colo., Jan. 2, 1915; s. Karl and Edith (Nesselrode) G.; B.S., Baker U., 1938; postgrad. U. Kansas City, 1938-39; m. Marjorie Ruth Killebrew, Apr. 27, 1941; children—David Carl, Nancy Lou (Mrs. J.R. Flink), Carol Ann. Head of lab. Procter and Gamble Mfg. Co., Kansas City, Kans., 1938-41; sect. head research dept. J.B. Ford Co., Wyandotte, Mich., 1941-43; supr. analytical research Wyandotte Chems. Corp. (Mich.), 1943-56, mgr. analytical research, 1956-57; dir. research and devel. Turco Products Inc., Wilmington, Calif., 1957-65; adminstrv. asst. to v.p. chem. research Purex Corp., Ltd., Wilmington, 1964-66; mgr. research and devel. Amway Corp., Ada, Mich., 1967-70, mgr. industry and govt. tech. relations, 1970-72, sr. adviser legis. and regulatory standards, 1970-76, mgr. govt. affairs, 1976—. Cons. to Chem. Corps., U.S. Army, 1952-62, Chem.-Biol.-Radio. Agy., Edgewood (Md.) Arsenal, 1962-63. Fellow Am. Inst. Chemists; mem. Am. Chem. Soc. (com. nat. def. 1963-70), ASTM (councilor Detroit dist. 1955-57, councilor So. Calif. dist. 1962-66), Soap and Detergent Assn. (legal com. tech. and materials div. 1970-74, legis. subcom. legal com. 1974—, chmn. eutrophication task force 1980-81), Cosmetic, Toiletry and Fragrance Assn. (govt. relations com. 1972—), Chem. Specialties Mfrs. Assn. (chmn. div. com. legis. standards 1971-77, bd. govs. 1976-78, 81—, chmn. public affairs com. 1979; vice-chmn. detergents and cleaning cos. div. 1979-80, div. chmn. 1981—), Am. Def. Preparedness Assn. (tech. com. on surface preservation 1958-66), Chemist Club of N.Y. Home: 4212 Oak Forest Ct SE Grand Rapids MI 49506 Office: 7575 E Fulton Rd Ada MI 49355

GRAHAM, CHRISTINE ROGERS, savs. and loan assn. exec.; b. Winner, S.D., July 31, 1944; d. Harry Bernard and Mildred V. (Tideman) Rogers; B.A., Calif. State U., San Diego, 1967, M.A., 1975; divorced. Adminstrv. asst. to pres. Percy H. Goodwin Real Estate Co., San Diego, 1967-69; research asst. econ. research and site and mktg. research Security Pacific Nat. Bank, Los Angeles, 1970-73; research analyst Am. Savs. & Loan Assn., Beverly Hills, Calif., 1973-74; v.p., dir. br. devel. and mktg. research Calif. Fed. Savs. & Loan Assn., Los Angeles, 1974—. Recipient cert. achievement YMCA Leaders Club, 1978. Mem. Nat. Assn. Bus. Economists (exec. com. 1977-79), Savs. Instn. Mktg. Soc. Am. (vice chmn. research com. 1980, speaker convs. 1977-81). Calif. Savs. and Loan League (chmn. industry devel. com. 1977-78), Los Angeles C. of C. Office: 5670 Wilshire Blvd Los Angeles CA 90036

GRAHAM, DONALD EDWARD, publisher; b. Balt., Apr. 22, 1945; s. Philip and Katharine G.; B.A., Harvard U., 1966; m. Mary L. Wissler, Jan. 7, 1967; children—Liza, Laura, William. Patrolman, Met. D.C. Police Dept., 1969-70; reporter, writer, Newsweek mag., 1973-74; with The Washington Post, 1971—, asst. mng. editor/sports, 1974-75, asst. gen. mgr., 1975-76, exec. v.p. and gen. mgr., 1976-79, pub., 1979—; dir. The Washington Post Co., Bowaters Mersey Paper Co., Ltd. Trustee, Fed. City Council, 1976; bd. dirs. Am. Press Inst., 1976. Served with Air Cavalry, U.S. Army, 1967-68; Vietnam. Office: Washington Post Co 1150 15th St NW Washington DC 20071

GRAHAM, FLOYD, mfg. co. exec.; b. Lake City, S.C., July 6, 1929; s. Jimmy Clinton and Mattie Bell (Player) G.; student Lee Coll., 1950, Memphis State U., 1963, Broward Community Coll., 1973; m. Dolores Elizabeth Cook, Dec. 6, 1952; children—Richard Allen, Michael Lee, Sandra Ann. Enlisted in USMC, 1948; advanced to sgt., 1965, ret., 1968; tech. tng. instr. RCA, Palm Beach Gardens, Fla., 1968-71; asso. engr. Photon, Inc., Delray Beach, Fla., 1971-72; tech. publ. specialist Systems Engring. Labs., Inc., Ft. Lauderdale, Fla., 1972—; pres., owner Graham Realty, Ft. Lauderdale, 1977—. Vice pres., Sunrise Taxpayers Assn., 1979—; bd. dirs. Palm Beach Gardens

Youth Athletic Assn., 1971. Mem. Am. Mgmt. Assn., Am. Legion, Fleet Res. Assn. Democrat. Contbr. articles to profl. jours. Office: 6901 W Sunrise Blvd Fort Lauderdale FL 33313*

GRAHAM, GARY JONATHAN, jewelry mfg. co. exec.; b. Forest Hills, N.Y., Oct. 14, 1954; s. Robert T. and Jody (Feher) G.; student U. Denver, 1972; B.A. in History, U. Miami, 1976. Asst. buyer Sanger Harris, Dallas, 1976-78; exec. v.p. Jubilee Diamonds, N.Y.C., 1978—. Mem. Sigma Chi. Jewish. Club: Friar's (N.Y.C.). Office: Jubilee Diamonds 580 Fifth Ave New York NY 10036

GRAHAM, GEORGE A., hardware mfrs. agt.; b. Englewood, N.J., Jan. 5, 1909; B.S., Princeton U., 1933; m. Emily Bayless, July 6, 1934. With John H. Graham & Co. Inc., Oradell, N.J., 1933—, pres., 1955—, chmn. bd., 1975—. Clubs: Englewood Men's, Englewood Field. Home: 514 Anderson Ave Closter NJ 07624 Office: 617 Oradell Ave Oradell NJ 07649

GRAHAM, GEORGE ANDREW, JR., banker; b. Bakersfield, Calif., Dec. 7, 1930; s. George Andrew and Mary Pearl (Sandidge) G.; B.A., U. Redlands, 1952; B.D., Andover Newton Theol. Sch., 1956; M.A., Boston U., 1956; S.T.M., Union Theol. Sem., 1957; postgrad. U. Chgo., 1957-60; Ph.D., Marquette U., 1974; grad. Sch. Banking, U. Wis., 1978; advanced program in orgnl. devel. Columbia U., 1980; m. Patricia Anne Phillips, June 19, 1953; children—George Andrew, Ronald Glen, Holly Anne. Ordained to ministry Am. Bapt. Ch., 1956; asst. for young adult work Old South Ch., Boston, 1952-55; minister edn. First Bapt. Ch., Mt. Vernon, N.Y., 1955-57; sch. psychologist Lab. Sch., U. Chgo., 1957-60; minister, univ. chaplain First Bapt. Ch., Iowa City, Iowa, 1960-63; chaplain to univ., asst. prof. religion U. Redlands (Calif.), 1963-70; asso. McGinley & Co., Milw., 1970-73; dir. employment and devel., asst. v.p. First Wis. Nat. Bank, Milw., 1973-77, v.p., 1977—. Vis. prof. Hebrew, Augustana Sem., Rock Island, Ill., 1962, 63; vis. lectr. Bus. Sch., U. Wis.-Milw., 1976—; asso. chaplain VA Hosp., Iowa City, 1961-63; chaplain, cons. San Bernardino County (Calif.) Juvenile Home, 1964-69; pres. Wis. Epilepsy League, 1976-77, pres. bd. dirs. Lad Lake, 1979—, Kettle Moraine Sch. Dist., Wales, Wis., 1973-74, Wis. Leukemia Soc., 1977—, Epilepsy League Milw., 1977—; chmn. sustaining membership campaign Potowatomi council Boy Scouts Am., 1977—. Danforth U. chaplain fellow, 1969-70. Mem. Am., Wis. psychol. assns. Clubs: Masons; Univ. (Milw.). Home: N8 W30095 Woodcrest Dr Waukesha WI 53186 Office: 777 E Wisconsin Ave Milwaukee WI 53202

GRAHAM, KATHARINE, newspaper co. exec.; b. N.Y.C., June 16, 1917; d. Eugene and Agnes (Ernst) Meyer; student Vassar Coll., 1934-36; A.B., U. Chgo., 1938; m. Philip L. Graham, June 5, 1940 (dec. 1963); children—Elizabeth Morris Graham Weymouth, Donald Edward, William Welsh, Stephen Meyer. Reporter, San Francisco News, 1938-39; mem. editorial, Sunday, circulation depts. Washington Post, 1939-45, pub., 1968-79; pres. Washington Post Co., 1963-73, 77, chmn. bd., 1973—; dir. Bowaters Mersey Paper Co., Ltd., AP. Trustee Conf. Bd., Urban Inst., Fed. City Council, George Washington U., U. Chgo.; mem. adv. com. Inst. Politics, John Fitzgerald Kennedy Sch. Govt., Harvard U. Mem. Washington, Nat. press clubs, Am. Newspaper Pubs. Assn. (dir.), Am. Soc. Newspaper Editors (mem. ind. commn. on internat. devel. issues), Sigma Delta Chi. Clubs: 1925 F St., Nat. Press, Washington Press (Washington); Cosmopolitan (N.Y.C.). Office: 1150 15th St Washington DC 20071*

GRAHAM, LESLIE RIDGWAY, oil co. exec.; b. Cin., Nov. 1, 1933; s. Leslie C. and Della Jane (Ridgway) G.; B.S. in Chem. Engring., Purdue U., 1956; M.B.A., U. Chgo., 1967; m. Elizabeth Ann Bauman, June 1, 1956; children—Leslie B., John E., Debra E., Ronald S. With Union Carbide Corp., N.Y.C., 1956-57, Emery Industries, Cin., 1960-63; with Lawter Chems., Inc., Northbrook, Ill., 1963-80, v.p., 1968-80, dir., 1971-80; pres., chief exec. officer Calumet Industries Inc., Chgo., 1980—, also dir.; dir. Gen. Binding Corp., 1980—. Served to capt. USAF, 1957-60. Mem. Northwestern U. Assos., Economic Club Chgo., Chgo. Printing Production Club, Exec. Program Club (U. Chgo.). Episcopalian. Clubs: Chgo.; Onwentsia (Lake Forest, Ill.); Indian Creek (Miami Beach, Fla.). Office: Calumet Industries Inc 400 N Michigan Ave Suite 916 Chicago IL 60611

GRAHAM, PEARSON, economist, mfg. co. exec.; b. Mt. Pleasant, Mich., Dec. 18, 1929; s. J. Elmer and Hannah Elizabeth (Pearson) G.; B.S. in Engring., U. Mich., 1950; M.S. in Engring., 1955; M.A. in Economics, Cleve. State U., 1973; m. Joan Norris, July 26, 1958; children—Jennifer Susan, Jeffrey Bruce. Engr., Gen. Motors, Detroit, 1950-57, Thompson Ramo Wooldridge Inc., Cleve., 1957-64; bus. cons. Elmendorf & Co., Cleve., 1964-69; dir. capital planning TRW Inc., Cleve., 1969—; lectr. econs. Cleve. State U.; mem. com. natural resources Internat. Economic Policy Assn. Trustee Glen Oak Sch. Author: Managerial Economics, 1976. Office: TRW Inc 23555 Euclid Ave Cleveland OH 44117

GRAHAM, ROBERT CECIL, mfg. co. exec.; b. Richmond, Va., Oct. 23, 1936; s. Raymond V. and Adalena Deane Graham; B.S., Hampton Inst., 1958; cert. exec. program Colgate U., 1969, Stanford U., 1972; m. Barbara Roy Graham, Oct. 23, 1971. Supr. student accts. Fla. A&M U., Tallahassee, 1958-60; mgr. data processing, instr. Va. State Coll., Petersburg, 1960-64; systems engr. IBM Corp., N.Y.C., 1964-68; mgr. equal opportunity programs IBM Corp., White Plains, N.Y., 1968-70, br. mgr., Washington, 1970-73; mgr. service ops. planning and analysis Xerox Corp., Rochester, N.Y., 1973-75, service ops. mgr., Washington, 1975-76, region mgr. tech. service, 1976-78, nat. service mgr., Rochester, 1978-79, v.p. nat. service, field ops., 1979-80, v.p. nat. service ops., 1980—. Office: Xerox Sq Rochester NY 14644

GRAHAM, ROBERT KLARK, lens mfr.; b. Harbor Springs, Mich., June 9, 1906; s. Frank A. and Ellen Fern (Klark) G.; A.B., Mich. State U., 1933; B.Sc. in Optics, Ohio State U., 1937; children (by previous marriage)-David, Gregory, Robin, Robert K., Janis, Wesley; m. 2d, Marta Ve Everton; children—Marcia, Christie. With Bausch & Lomb, 1937-40; Western mgr. Univis Lens Co., 1940-44, asst. sales mgr., 1945, sales mgr., 1945-46; v.p., dir. research Plastic Optics Co., 1946-47; pres., chmn. bd. Armorlite, Inc., 1947—; dir. Advanced Concepts Tech.; lectr. optics Loma Linda U. Trustee, Found. Advancement of Man; bd. dirs. Inst. for Research on Morality; bd. dirs. Intra-Sci. Research Found., v.p., 1980. Recipient Herschel Gold medal Germany. Fellow AAAS; mem. Am. Inst. Physics Profs., Optical Soc. Am., Am. Acad. Optometry, Mensa, Sigma Xi. Author: The Evolution of Corneal Contact Lenses; The Future of Man; also articles in sci. publs. Inventor variable focus lens, hybrid corneal lens; directed devel. hard resin lenses. Home: 3024 Sycamore Ln Escondido CA 92025 Office: 130 N Bingham Dr San Marcos CA 92069

GRAHAM, (HARVARD EUGENE) SKIP, fin. exec.; b. Oakland, Calif., Nov. 16, 1926; s. Harvard Eugene Sr. and Blanche Alice (Belisle) G.; grad. Oakland (Calif.) public schs., 1944; m. Beverly Jean Maudlin, May 2, 1973; children—Kenneth E., Debbie, Peggy; step-children—Rick and Kevin Maudlin. Laborer to office mgr. Pacific Gas & Elec. Co., Santa Rosa, Calif., 1947-63; sales exec. Mut. of N.Y. Ins. Co., Santa Rosa, 1963-75; owner, supr., trainer Fin. Planning Services, Santa Rosa, 1975—; pres. H. E. Graham & Assos., Inc. and regional v.p. Unimarc, Inc., 1980—. Served with U.S. Merchant Marine, 1944-46. Mem. Internat. Assn. Fin. Planners, Caller Lab. Republican. Christian. Condr. numerous seminars, insts. in field. Home: 3630 Holland Dr Santa Rosa CA 95404 Office: Fin Planning Services PO Box 2505 2345 4th St Santa Rosa CA 95405

GRAHAM, STEPHEN SHAFTON, lawyer, exec., securities and commodities trader; b. Chgo., July 10, 1938; s. Sidney G. and Phyllis (Shafton) G.; A.B. cum laude, Harvard U., 1960, J.D., 1963; m. Ruth Vogel, 1967 (div. Oct. 1980); children—Justin Vogel, Charles Spencer. Admitted to Ill. bar, 1964; exec. trainee Office of Sec. Def., Washington, 1963-65; v.p., sec. dir. Nat. Soda Straw Co., Chgo., 1966-75; mem. Chgo. Bd. Trade, 1977—, mem. new products com., 1979—; mem., market-maker Chgo. Bd. Options Exchange, 1974—, mem. securities com., 1976—, pres., dir. Pacesetter Industries, Inc. Chgo., 1968-80; pres., dir. Optec Investments, Ltd., 1976—. Mem. Com. on Ill. Govt. 1966-74, mem. edn. and housing task forces, 1966-67, bd. dirs., 1970-72; mem. exec. bd. Expt. in Internat. Living, Chgo. Council, 1966-70; mem. central com. Cook County Young Democrats, 1966-70; exec. bd. Ill. State Young Dems., 1966-70. Mem. Fed., Ill., Chgo. bar assns., Council Fgn. Relations, Com. on Fgn. Affairs, Chgo. Bd. Options Exchange Market Makers Assn., Chgo. Assn. Commerce and Industry, Harvard Law Sch. Assn. Club: Harvard (Chgo.). Office: Chgo Bd Options Exchange 7th Floor Box 253 141 W Jackson Blvd Chicago IL 60604

GRAHAM, WILLIAM B., pharm. exec.; b. Chgo., July 14, 1911; S.B. cum laude, U. Chgo., 1932, J.D. cum laude, 1936; LL.D., Carthage Coll., 1974; m. Edna Kanaley, June 15, 1940; children—William J., Elizabeth Anne, Margaret, Robert B. Admitted to Ill. bar, 1936; patent lawyer Dyrenforth, Lee, Chritton & Wiles, 1936-40; mem. firm Dawson & Ooms, 1940-45; v.p., mgr. Baxter Travenol Labs., Deerfield, Ill., 1945-53, pres., chief exec. officer, dir., 1953-71, chmn. bd., chief exec. officer, 1971-80, chmn. bd., dir., 1980—; dir. Bell & Howell Co.; dir., mem. exec. com. N.W. Industries, First Nat. Bank Chgo.; dir. Deere & Co., Field Enterprises, Borg Warner Co.; dir. Nat. Council for U.S.-China Trade. Bd. dirs. Lyric Opera Chgo., Chgo. Hort. Soc.; past pres. Community Fund, Chgo.; trustee Crusade of Mercy, Evanston Hosp., U. Chgo. Recipient VIP award, 1963; Distinguished Citizen award Ill. St. Andrew Soc., 1974; Decision Maker of Year award Am. Statis. Assn., 1974; Marketer of Year award AMA, 1976; named to Professorial chair Weizmann Inst., 1978. Mem. Am. Pharm. Mfrs. Assn. (past pres.), Ill. Mfrs. Assn. (past pres., dir.), Pharm. Mfrs. Assn. (dir., past chmn.), Phi Beta Kappa, Sigma Xi, Phi Delta Phi. Clubs: Chgo., Commonwealth, Commercial, Mid-America; Old Elm; Indian Hill (Winnetka, Ill.); Casino, University, Links (N.Y.C.). Home: 40 Devonshire Ln Kenilworth IL 60043 Office: One Baxter Pkwy Deerfield IL 60015

GRAHAM, WILLIAM PIERSON, mgmt. services co. exec.; b. E. St. Louis, Ill., Feb. 19, 1935; s. William Schley and Opal Elizabeth (Gray) G.; B.S., U. Ill., 1956; m. Margaret Newton McDowell, Sept. 30, 1961; children—Lisa, Heather, Jennifer; guardian of Cassandra Dickson, Caroline Dickson. With IBM Corp., 1956-69, asst. to pres., 1967-68, dir. mktg. comml. industries, data processing div., 1968-69; exec. v.p. EDP Tech., Inc., Washington, 1969-71, pres., chief exec. officer, 1971-73; pres. Washington Profl. Group, 1973—, also Capitol Venture Group, Inc., real estate devel., chmn. bd. Daisy Prodns., Inc., entertainment. Asst. for domestic programs White House, Washington, 1966-67; pres. White House Fellows Found., 1973-74; chmn. bd. dirs. Congressional Mgmt. Found.; mem. fgn. service profl. devel. rev. group Dept. State, 1976; mem. U.S. Adv. Com. Vocat. Edn., 1968-69, U.S. Fed. Adv. Com. Employment Security, 1968-71; panel cons. Edn. Professional Devel. Act, HEW, 1969-71; del. German Am. Forum, Bonn, Berlin, 1975; chmn. parents assn. Sidwell Friends Sch., Washington, 1976-78; vice chmn. fin. adv. com. Nat. Com. for Effective Congress, 1976-77. Served with AUS, 1957. White House Fellow, 1966-67. Mem. White House Fellows Assn. (pres., 1973-74). Home: 9030 Congressional Pkwy Potomac MD 20854 Office: 3062 M St Washington DC 20007

GRAINGER, DAVID WILLIAM, elec. equipment distbn. co. exec.; b. Chgo., Oct. 23, 1927; s. William Wallace and Hally (Ward) G.; grad. Phillips Exeter Acad., 1945; B.S. in Elec. Engring., U. Wis., 1950; m. Juli Ann Plant, June 15, 1949. With W.W. Grainger, Inc., Chgo., 1952—, chmn. bd., 1968—, pres., 1974—. Served with USAAF, 1946-47. Office: 5500 Howard St Skokie IL 60077

GRALA, WILLIAM LEON, pharm. co. exec.; b. Hazleton, Pa., Sept. 29, 1922; s. William Leon and Mary Magdalene (Demschick) G.; B.S., Haverford Coll., 1943; m. June Wilkins, Nov. 5, 1943 (div. Mar. 1961); m. 2d, Babette Liversidge Jensen, Nov. 22, 1963; 1 son, Christopher Wells. Copywriter, John F. Arndt, Inc., Phila., 1946; indsl. relations asst. ACF-Brill Motors Co., Phila., 1946-48; with SmithKline Corp., Phila., 1948—, v.p. corporate pub. relations, 1971-73, v.p. pub. affairs, 1973—. Exec. sec. SmithKline Found., 1970-75, trustee, 1971—, pres., chief exec. officer, 1978—; exec. sec. C. Mahlon Kline Meml. Found., 1970-78. Chmn., Pharm. Information Com. Greater Phila., 1960-65. Asst. sec. Pennsylvanians for Effective Govt., 1973—; div. chmn. United Fund, 1973-74; gen. chmn. ann. dr. Phila. Police Athletic League, 1975-76, also bd. dirs.; mem. exec. bd. Phila. council Boy Scouts Am., 1967-69, chmn. pub. relations com.; trustee Child Study Center Phila., 1965-69; bd. dirs., sec. North City Corp., 1968-75; bd. dirs., vice-chmn. emergency med. services Council of Phila. Health Mgmt. Corp., 1973—, chmn. bus. and industry com., 1974—; bd. dirs. Del. Valley Council, 1968-78, mem. exec. com., 1975-77; bd. dirs. Eastern region Pa. Economy League, 1971—, mem. exec. com., 1975—; bd. dirs. Phila. Urban Coalition, 1976—, Hahnemann Med. Coll. and Hosp., 1978—; mem. Phila. Commn. Effective Criminal Justice, 1975-77; bd. dirs. Burn Found. Greater Delaware Valley, 1975—, chmn. exec. com., 1976-78, chmn. bd., 1978—; bd. dirs., chmn. communications and pub. relations com. Area Council for Econ. Edn., 1975—, mem. exec. com., 1976—, v.p., 1976—; mem. pub. info. com. Joint Council on Econ. Edn., 1975—; mem. pub. relations com. S.E. Phila. chpt. ARC, 1978-79; mem. Phila. adv. com. Moton Center for Ind. Studies, 1975-77; bd. dirs., Consumer Council Greater Phila., 1975-76, vice chmn., 1976; bd. dirs. Southeastern Pa. Emergency Health Services Council, 1975-76, Phila. Sch. Dist. Adv. Council for Career Edn., 1975-76, NCCJ, 1976-78, Pa. Environ. Council, 1977—, Citizens Crime Commn. Phila., 1978—, Jr. Achievement of Greater Delaware Valley, 1979—, Pa. Acad. Fine Arts, 1980—; pres. and bd. dirs. Friends of Benjamin Franklin, 1979—; mem. adv. com. Internat. Assn. Students in Econ. and Comml. Scis., The Wharton Sch., U. Pa. Served with AUS, 1943-46. Fellow Coll. of Physicians of Phila.; mem. Pub. Relations Soc. Am. (past dir. Phila. chpt.), Phila. Pub. Relations Assn., Pa. C. of C. (dir. 1976—), Mfrs. Assn. Delaware Valley (dir. 1978—), Am. Pub. Health Assn., Am. Acad. Polit. and Social Sci., Acad. Polit. Sci., Pa. Soc., Hist. Soc. Pa. (dir. 1979—). Club: Union League (Phila.). Home: 360 Conestoga Rd Wayne PA 19087 Office: 1500 Spring Garden St Philadelphia PA 19101

GRAMLING, JAMES THOMAS, machine mfg. co. exec.; b. Wichita, Kans., Feb. 3, 1944; s. Gaylord Trussel and Avis Elaine (Franklin) G.; student U. Mo., Kansas City, 1969; m. Romala Kay Warren, July 25, 1963; children—James Warren, Lori Elaine, Richard Thomas, Steven Douglas. Tool and die maker Gramling Tool and Die, Inc., Kansas City, Kans., 1966-68, machinist designer, 1968-71, mgr., 1971-75; v.p. Preco Industries, Inc., Shawnee Mission, Kans., 1975—, also dir.; cons. in field. Served with USAF, 1962-66. Republican. Inventor Preco press, Gramling rotary engine, digital to analogue converter. Home: Route 1 Box 24W Basehor KS 66007

GRAMMATER, RUDOLF DIMITRI, former constrn. co. exec.; b. Detroit, Nov. 29, 1910; s. D.M. and Amelia (Busse) G.; student accountancy and bus. adminstrn., Pace Inst., 1928-32; LL.B., Lincoln U., 1937; m. Fredricka W. Cook, Aug. 18, 1943; 1 son, Douglas. Admitted to Calif. bar, 1938; with Bechtel Corp., San Francisco, 1941-73, treas., v.p., 1955-62, v.p., 1962-71, dir., 1960-73, cons., 1973—, v.p., dir. subsidiaries, 1955-71. Mem. C.P.A., Calif. Mem. Am., San Francisco bar assns., State Bar Calif., Am. Inst. C.P.A.'s, Calif. Soc. C.P.A.'s, C. of C. Club: Menlo Country (Redwood City). Home: 50 Mounds Rd Apt 302 San Mateo CA 94402

GRAMMES, MARK RONALD, bank exec.; b. Miami, Fla., Nov. 19, 1942; s. Mark Elmer and Rose (Chaykovsky) G.; B.B.A., U. Miami, 1964, Fla. State U., 1968, postgrad. Wharton Sch. Fin., 1972-74. Sr. auditor Coopers & Lybrand, N.Y.C., 1964-67; sr. v.p. money mgmt. div. Southeast First Nat. Bank of Miami, 1968—; mem. investment com. Fla. Bankers Assoc., 1973—, chmn., 1975-76. Bd. dirs. Fla. Lighthouse for Blind, 1974—, chmn. fin. com., treas. exec. com., 1976—. Mem. Dealer Bank Assn. (dir., dir. funds mgmt. com. 1980-81), Public Securities Assn. Republican. Lutheran. Clubs: Bankers, Miami Bond, Miami. Office: 100 S Biscayne Blvd Miami FL 33131

GRANATA, ROBERT JOHN, pub. co. exec.; b. Jersey City, N.J., Nov. 17, 1934; s. Sam and Florence (Rosso) G.; B.S. in Acctg., Fairleigh Dickinson U., 1957, M.B.A, 1961; m. Margaret Anne Supple, Oct. 26, 1957; children—Elizabeth, Robert, David, Kathleen. Mgr. long range planning Singer Co.; dir. acquisitions devel. CBS, Inc., N.Y.C., 1968-75; v.p. fin. and planning CBS Pub. Group, 1976-78; v.p. Fawcett Books, N.Y.C., 1978—, gen. mgr., 1978-80, mng. dir., 1981—. Mem. Am. Assn. Pubs. Office: 1515 Broadway New York NY 10036

GRANDOFF, ANTHONY BERNARD, SR., investments co. exec.; b. Tampa, Fla., June 13, 1911; s. John Baptiste and Theresa Agnes (Cantwell) Gandolfo; grad. Jesuit high sch., Tampa; m. Frances Evelyn Kidd, Mar. 4, 1930; children—Elizabeth Joan, Anthony Bernard. Gen. mgr. parcel delivery service, 1928-33; pres. taxicab and city bus. cos., 1933-42; pres. Rent-A-Car Service in 15 cities in 3 states, 1942-57; v.p., Southeastern mgr. Hertz Corp., Tampa, 1957-60, dir., 1960-67; pres., dir. Grandoff Investments Inc., Tampa, 1944—; dir. Hertz Corp., Landmark Bank Tampa. Bd. dirs. Tampa Port Authority, Jesuit High Sch. Found., St. Leo Coll. Recipient award for services on Port Authority, Propeller Club Tampa, 1967; award for contbns. to transp. Sales and Mktg. Execs., 1965. Mem. Tampa C. of C. (chmn. taxation com., chmn. downtown art show com.; recipient Pres.'s award 1965), So., Fla. seniors golf assns. Roman Catholic. Democrat. Clubs: Waynesville (N.C.) Golf, Palma Ceia Golf and Country (Tampa), Univ. (Tampa). Home: Box 20 Route 1 Trenton FL 32693 Office: 412 Madison St Tampa FL 33602

GRANGAARD, DONALD R., banker; b. 1918; B.S. in Commerce, U. N.D., 1939; LL.B., William Mitchell Coll. Law, 1948; married. With 1st Bank System, Inc., Mpls., 1939—, formerly v.p. 1st Nat. Bank of Fairmont, v.p., dir. 1st Nat. Bank of Austin, v.p., liaison officer Eastern div. parent co., 1959-68, sr. v.p. adminstrn., 1968-69, pres., chief exec. officer, 1969-77, chmn. bd., chief exec. officer, 1977—, also dir. Served with AUS, 1942-46. Office: 1400 First Nat Bank Bldg 120 S 6th St Minneapolis MN 55402

GRANSTON, DAVID WILFRED, fin. exec.; b. Schenectady, N.Y., Dec. 5, 1936; s. Arnold Andrew and Edna (Nickerson) G.; B.A., Colgate U., 1958; M.B.A., Syracuse U., 1960; m. Priscilla Day, June 10, 1961; 1 son, David Wilfred. Supr. E. I. DuPont De Nemours & Co., Inc., Parlin, N.J., 1961-62; sr. fin. analyst Bendix Corp., N.Y.C., 1963-69; controller Allied Chem. Corp., N.Y.C., 1969-71; v.p. fin. Thomas Borthwick Sons, Ltd., N.Y.C., 1972-78; group controller N.Y. Times Corp., N.Y.C., from 1978, now v.p. and chief fin. officer N.Y. Times Syndication Sales Corp. Served with USCGR, 1960. Colgate U. War Meml. scholar, 1954-58. Mem. Phi Delta Theta, Sigma Iota Epsilon. Clubs: Colgate U. Alumni (L.I.) (pres. 1975-76); Creek (Locust Valley, N.Y.); Northport (Maine) Yacht (vice commodore); Windham (N.Y.) Mountain. Home: Box 368 Piping Rock Rd Locust Valley NY 11560 Office: 200 Park Ave New York NY 10017

GRANT, BROOKE, finance co. exec.; b. Pitts., Aug. 27, 1935; s. Van Hatch and Mildred Larkin (Blood) G.; student U. Calif., Los Angeles, 1953-55, U. Utah, 1956-57; B.A., Stanford, 1958, J.D., 1960; m. Sara Jane Moyle Creer, Dec. 30, 1957; children—Preston, Elizabeth, Gregory, Allison, Pamela. Mgr., Van Grant & Co., Salt Lake City, 1955-57; auditor, tax accountant Touche Ross & Co., San Francisco, 1960-62, mgr. mgmt. services, 1968-69; asst. legal counsel Varian Assos., Palo Alto, Calif., 1962-65, mgr. mktg., 1965-68; pres., chmn. bd. Tracy Bancorp., Salt Lake City, 1969-71; asst. prof. Brigham Young U., 1971-73; owner, operator Hanover Ltd., Salt Lake City, 1971—; chmn. bd., chief exec. officer Intermountain Pipe & Welding Co., Inc., 1971—, James Talcott, Inc. and Talcott Nat. Corp., N.Y.C., 1976-77, Uintah Nat. Corp., Salt Lake City, 1977-79. Bd. dirs. Utah Symphony. Clubs: Alta; Ft. Douglas. Home: Salt Lake City UT Office: 900 Kennecott Bldg Salt Lake City UT 84133

GRANT, EDWIN RANDOLPH, mfg. co. exec.; b. Stoneham, Mass., Oct. 6, 1943; s. Lauris Levi and Dorothy Hall (Lewis) G.; B.F.A., Denison U., 1966; M.B.A., Syracuse U., 1969; m. Ruth Louise Kennedy, June 24, 1967. Trainee, Sears, Roebuck & Co., Springfield, Mass., 1968-69; asst. to pres. Kennedy Bros., Inc., Vergennes, Vt., 1969-70, v.p., 1970-72, exec. v.p., 1972-74, pres., treas., 1974—, partner Vergennes Shopping Center; dir. Chittenden Trust Co., 1980—. Mem., incorporator, dir. Addison County Devel. Corp., Vergennes Devel. Corp., dir. Vt. Attractions Assn., 1975-77, v.p., treas., 1977-78, pres., 1978-80; mem. Vt. Travel-Advisory Council, 1978-80; mem. Addison County Exec. Bd.; trustee Burlington (Vt.) Coll., 1980—. Served to 2d lt. USAR, 1969-73. Mem. Vergennes Area (pres. 1976—), Vt. State (dir. 1977-78), Addison (dir. 1975-76), Lake Champlain chambers commerce (dir. 1977—), Asso. Industries Vt. Clubs: Charlotte-Shelburne (Vt.) Rotary; Green Mountain Transp. (pres. 1976-77); Lake Champlain Yacht. Home: RD 3 Box 284 Shelburne VT 05482 Office: 11 Main St Vergennes VT 05491

GRANT, JANE H., constrn. co. exec.; b. Fort Wayne, Ind., Apr. 23, 1930; d. Arthur Lee and Mildred Inez (Markley) Haycoz; student Ind. U., 1947-53; m. Joseph Anthony Grant, Sept. 13, 1958; children—Carolyn Jane, Joseph Andrew. Ins. agt. People's Trust and Savs. Co., Fort Wayne, 1950-53; sec. to bd. chmn. Kemper Ins., Chgo., N.Y.C., also aide to ambassador to Brazil, 1954-58; mgr. Garten Assos., Caldwell, N.J., 1960-67; pres. Squire Hill Enterprises, Inc., North Caldwell, N.J., 1970—. Vice-pres. bd. trustees Jr. Essex Troop; trustee Jr. Cavalry Am., Girls Mounted Troop Cavalry, West Orange, N.J. Mem. Builders Assn. Met. N.J., Nat. Assn. Home Builders, N.J.

State Builders, N.J. State Fedn. Women's Clubs (trustee), Alpha Omicron Pi (trustee). Address: 6 Robin Hill Rd North Caldwell NJ 07006

GRANT, JOHN GALLERY, publisher; b. Chgo., June 11, 1933; s. Gerald and Rosemary (Gallery) G.; A.B., Princeton U., 1957; m. Madelyn Ann Stephenson, Dec. 9, 1961; children—Bruce, Gillian. Dist. mgr. McGraw-Hill, various locations, 1957-72, regional mgr., Houston, 1972-76; publ. mgr. Petroleum Engr. Internat. Mag., Dallas, 1976-78, pub., 1978—. Served with U.S. Army, 1954-56; Korea. Decorated Presdl. Unit Citation (Republic of Korea). Mem. Nomads, Petroleum Engr.'s Club. Clubs: Dallas Petroleum, North Dallas Racquet. Office: PO Box 1589 Dallas TX 75221

GRANT, WILLIAM ALEXANDER, JR., coal co. exec.; b. Richmond, Va., Nov. 7, 1918; s. William Alexander and Louise (Hooper) G.; B.A. U. Richmond, 1941; m. Marion Louise Bankhead, Aug. 27, 1945; children—William Alexander III, Blossom Grant, Walter Bankhead. Sec.-treas. Bankhead Mining Co. Inc., 1953-80; sec. Tri W Broadcasting Inc., Jasper, 1 1965—, Franklin Broadcasting Inc., Russellville, Ala., 1965-80, Bankhead Devel. Ltd., Jasper, 1960—, Live Line Inc., Jasper, 1968-80; pres. GMC Broadcasting, Inc., Tuscaloosa, 1976-80; chmn. bd. Gatorland Broadcasting Inc., St. Augustine, Fla., 1969-80; pres. Chattanooga Sound Inc., 1978-80; gen. partner Pinewood Devel. Ltd.; mng. partner Cobb Coal Co., Automated Accounting Systems, Jasper, 1973-80; owner Easy Clean Center, Jasper, 1964-80; dir. Viking Oil Co., Jasper, Energy Exploration Inc., Birmingham. Chmn., March of Dimes, 1955; bd. assos. U. Richmond. Served as lt. (s.g.) USNR, 1942-46. Decorated Navy Cross, D.F.C., Air Medal with gold star. Mem. Nat. Assn. Accountants, Theta Chi, C. of C. (dir. 1956). Clubs: Northriver Yacht, Downtown (Birmingham); Musgrove Country, Rotary (pres.). Home: 912 9th Ave Jasper AL 35501 Office: Box 990 Jasper AL 35501

GRANT, WILLIAM ROBERT, advt. agy. exec.; b. Evanston, Ill., Aug. 11, 1943; s. Will C. and Mary Julia (Waller) G.; B.A., Duke U., 1965; M.B.A., Am. Grad. Sch. Internat. Mgmt., 1967; m. Carol E. McGregor, Apr. 10, 1971; 1 dau., Elizabeth Mary. Account supr. Grant Advt., Inc., N.Y.C., 1965-66; pres., Grant Advt. Panama, S.Am., 1968-69; exec. v.p. Grant Advt., Inc., Chgo., 1969-71; exec. v.p. Grant Advt. Internat., Inc., Chgo., 1972—, also dir.; pres., dir. W.R. Grant, Inc., 1974—; commodity broker Chgo. Bd. Trade; producers rep. computer animation Image West Ltd. Bd. dirs. Travelers Aid Soc., Midwest chpt., 1974—. Mem. Internat. Advt. Assn. (dir. Midwest chpt. 1973—), Advt. Assn. Panama (v.p. 1967-68). Clubs: Indian Hill Country (Chgo.), McCullom Lake Sport. Home: 2148 Beechwood S Wilmette IL 60091 Office: Chgo Bd Trade LaSalle St and Jackson Blvd Chicago IL 60604

GRANTHAM, JOHN RICHARD, energy co. exec.; b. McGregor, Tex., Aug. 8, 1917; s. John Richard and Myrtle Naomi (Kirkpatrick) G.; B.S., Tex. A&M U., 1939; m. Mary Lois McWhirter, June 23, 1944; children—Gail Grantham LaGrone, Becky Grantham Schwedland, Susan Grantham Goodman, James W. Tng. coordinator Exxon Co., 1946-47, coordinator indsl. relations research, 1947-48; owner, mgr. pvt. bus., 1948-53; asst. mgr. employee relations Phillips Petroleum Co., 1953-56, mgr. employee relations, 1956-58; dir. indsl. relations Apco Oil Corp., Oklahoma City, 1958-67, v.p. indsl. relations, 1967-75, v.p. adminstrn., 1975, sr. v.p. adminstrn., 1975-77; v.p. adminstrn. N.W. Energy Co., Salt Lake City, N.W. Pipeline Corp., 1977-81. Bd. dirs. United Way of Greater Oklahoma City Area, 1967-77, gen. campaign chmn., 1967, pres., 1970-71; bd. dirs. Oklahoma City Cultural Devel. Found., 1972, Community Council Central Okla., 1967-77, St. Anthony Hosp. Adv. Bd., Oklahoma City, 1976-77; gen. campaign chmn. Oklahoma City Jr. Achievement, 1977; trustee, v.p. Ballet West, 1978-81, mem. exec. com., 1978-81; bd. dirs. United Way of Gt. Salt Lake Area, 1978-81, campaign cabinet mem., 1979-81. Served to maj. C.E., AUS, 1942-46. Mem. Am. Gas Assn., Am. Mgmt. Assn., Tau Beta Pi (Eminent Engr. 1977). Republican. Presbyterian. Clubs: Alta, Fort Douglas-Hidden Valley Country, Masons. Office: N W Energy Co PO Box 1526 Salt Lake City UT 84110

GRANTHAM, JOSEPH MICHAEL, JR., hotel exec.; b. Smithfield, N.C., Aug. 23, 1947; s. Joseph Michael and Anne Laurie (Hare) G.; student Oak Ridge Mil. Inst., 1965-66, E. Tenn. State U., 1966-70; m. Wilsie Moss Hartman, Nov. 3, 1973; children—Molly Meade, Joseph Michael III. With Grand Hotel, Mackinac Island, Mich., 1966—, v.p. sales, 1973-74, v.p. and mgr., 1974-79; dir. resort ops., gen. mgr. Pinehurst (N.C.) Hotel and Country Club, 1978—. Vice chmn. No. Mich. Conv. and Visitors Bur., Mackinac Island; commr. scouting Boy Scouts Am., Pinehurst, 1978—. Served with USNG, 1970-76. Mem. Mackinac Island C. of C. (dir. 1976-79), Mich. Lodging Assn. (dir. 1976-79), Meeting Planners Internat., Hotel Sales Mgmt. Assn. Internat., Am. Hotel and Motor Hotel Assn., Nat. Tour Brokers Assn., Chgo. Assn. Execs., N.C. Innkeepers Assn. (dir. 1978—), Travel Council of N.C. (dir. 1978—), Kappa Alpha. Methodist. Home: PO Box 1582 Pinehurst NC 28374 Office: Pinehurst Hotel and Country Club Pinehurst NC 28374

GRANVILLE, CHARLES N., JR., business exec.; b. N.Y.C., Dec. 10, 1905; s. Charles N. and Mary (Clark) G.; ed. U. Ill., 1930; m. Mary R. Coyle, Oct. 16, 1936; children—Charles III, Richard, Judith. Formerly gen. mgr. Eastern div. George B. May Co., Chgo., also asst. to pres. Marshall Field and Co., Chgo.; chmn. bd., treas. Celeste Industries Corp., Easton, Md. Exhibited paintings one-man show, Madison Hotel, Washington, 1973. Mem. Phi Kappa Psi. Clubs: Talbot Country (Easton, Md.); N.Y. Yacht. Home: Tred Avon Apts Oxford MD 21654 Office: Clifton Industrial Park Easton MD 21601

GRANVILLE, MAURICE FREDERICK, petroleum co. exec.; b. La Grange, Tex., Oct. 26, 1915; s. Maurice Frederick and Dorathea (von Rosenburg) G.; B.S. in Chem. Engring., U. Tex., 1937; Sc.M. in Chem. Engring., Mass. Inst. Tech., 1939; m. Janet Knotts, Jan. 13, 1945; children—Carol McCoy (Mrs. Peter Blyberg), Frederick Lloyd. With Texaco Inc., 1939—, organizer chem. div., Port Arthur, Tex., 1955-58, gen. mgr. petrochem. dept., 1958-60, v.p. petrochem. dept., 1960-67, v.p. strategic planning and asst. chmn., 1967-70, pres., dir., 1970-71, chmn. bd., 1971—, chief exec. officer, 1972—; dir. Gen. Telephone & Electronics Corp.; trustee Mut. Life Ins. Co. of N.Y., U.S. sect. of Brazil-U.S. Bus. Council. Mem. adv. bd. Met. Opera Assn.; bd. dirs. Am. Petroleum Inst.; trustee Presbyn. Hosp., N.Y.C.; mem. governing bd. corp. Mass. Inst. Tech. Mem. Conf. Bd. (sr. mem.), Tau Beta Pi, Delta Kappa Epsilon, Phi Lambda Upsilon. Conglist. Clubs: Round Hill (Greenwich, Conn.); Links (N.Y.C.); Links Golf (Manhasset, N.Y.). Office: 2000 Westchester Ave White Plains NY 10650

GRANVILLE, RICHARD COYLE, mfg. co. exec.; b. Chgo., July 10, 1942; s. Charles Norman and Mary R. (Coyle) G.; A.B., Hamilton Coll., 1964; m. Susan Crosby Young, Dec. 3, 1966; children—Steven Charles, Emily Lloyd, David Westerlund, Richard Coyle Jr. Br. mgr. Dictaphone Corp., Springfield, Mass., 1966-67; div. mgr. Celeste Industries Corp., Wilton, Conn., 1967-69, exec. v.p., Easton, Md., 1970-73, pres., 1973—, also dir.; pres., dir. Celeste Export Corp., Easton, 1974—; chmn. bd., pres. Celeste Industries Corp., 1980—. Mem. AIAA, ASTM. Clubs: Squadron A (N.Y.); Miles River Yacht (St. Michaels, Md.); Tred Avon Yacht (Oxford, Md.); Talbot Country (Easton). Home: Goose Neck Rd Royal Oak MD 21662 Office: Clifton Indsl Park Easton MD 21601

GRASHEIM, EDMUND, ins. broker; b. N.Y.C., Feb. 9, 1918; s. Joseph and Johanna (Teller) G.; ed. Sch. Commerce, N.Y. U., 1938-42; m. Elinor K. Krieger, July 5, 1976; 1 dau. by previous marriage, Marilyn Grasheim Richter; 1 stepson, Michael P. Krieger. Agt., Conn. Mut. Life Ins. Co., 1956—, agy. supr., 1973-78, asst. dir. brokerage, N.Y.C., 1978-79, dir. brokerage sales, 1980—. Served with USAAF, 1942-46. Recipient Nat. Quality awards Life Underwriters Assn.; C.L.U. Mem. Am. Soc. C.L.U.'s, Life Underwriters Assn. N.Y.C. (dir. 1965-76), Am. Begonia Soc. (nat. dir.), Indoor Light Gardening Soc. Am. (nat. dir.), Mus. Modern Art N.Y. (asso. dept. prints and illustrated books). Home: 132 E 35th St New York NY 10016 Office: Conn Mut Life Ins Co 551 Fifth Ave New York NY 10176

GRASSLE, PAUL ALBERT, JR., corp. exec.; b. Rochester, Minn., July 20, 1920; s. Paul Albert and Evangeline Rosella (Linstrom) G.; A.A., U. Minn., 1941; m. Marie H. Williamson, Jan. 17, 1942; children—Paul A., Linda M. With Carlton Hotel, Rochester, 1934-75, asst. mgr., 1941-42, 45-50, mgr., 1950-75; dir. tng. Kahler Corp., Rochester, 1975-80, mng. dir. Clinic View Motel, 1980—. Mem. dist. bd. Boy Scouts Am., 1950—, Gamehaven Area Found., 1979—; bd. dirs. Nat. Found. Infantile Paralysis, 1955-60; bd. dirs. Sr. Citizens Services, 1978; mem. human resources com. of bd. trustees St. Mary's Hosp., 1980—. Served with USAAF, 1942-45; lt. col. Res. (ret.). Mem. Am. Mgmt. Assn., Am. Soc. Tng. Dirs., Rochester Personnel Assn., Res. Officers Assn., Rochester C. of C., Air Force Assn. Episcopalian. Clubs: Elks, Lions. Home: 1307 9th St SW Rochester MN 55901 Office: 20 2d Ave SW Rochester MN 55901

GRASTORF, DENNIS JEFFRY, publisher; b. Canandaigua, N.Y., Dec. 4, 1946; s. Clifford Glenn and Rosemary Autumn (Stillwell) G.; A.A.S., Rochester Inst. Tech., 1967, B.S. in Printing with honors, 1969. Prodn. asst. prodn. coll. textbooks Holt, Rinehart & Winston, N.Y.C., 1967; typographic researcher RCA, Dayton, N.J., 1968; gen. mgr. Cal Industries, N.Y.C., 1970-73; cons. in printing and free lance designer, N.Y.C., 1973—; pres., owner Angelica Press, N.Y.C., 1974—; v.p., partner Grastorf & Lang, Ltd., pubs., N.Y.C., 1978—; lectr. Syracuse U., Rochester Inst. Tech., Typophiles, Bibliographic Soc.; exhibited in one-man shows: Am. Inst. Graphic Arts, N.Y.C., 1975, Art Dirs. Ann. Exhbn. (2 design awards 1977, NYCTA design award 1977). Chmn. bd. Happy Spot, day care center, N.Y.C., 1974-75. Mem. Printing Hist. Assn. U.S.A., Printing Hist. Soc. (London), Grolier Club, Typophiles. Presbyterian. Author: Wood Type, 1976; designer, printer: Wasp in A Wig, 1977. Home and Office: 920 Broadway New York NY 10010

GRAUPNER, MICHAEL ERNEST, co. exec.; b. N.Y.C., Mar. 17, 1950; s. Ernest Arnold and Gabriella (Ledorf) G.; B.A., Gettysburg Coll., 1972; m. Suzanne Frederick Skeats, Oct. 2, 1976; 1 dau., Christina Marie. Supr. advt. and sales promotion Uniroyal Inc., N.Y.C., 1972-74, mgr. brand advt. and sales promotion, 1974-78, advt. dir., 1978-80; dir. mktg.-tobacco Culbro Corp., N.Y.C., 1980—. Served with AUS, 1972-78. Mem. Kappa Delta Rho. Lutheran. Home: 308 Washington Rd Woodbury CT 06798 Office: Culbro Corp 605 3d Ave New York NY 10017

GRAVEL, PIERRE RODOLPHE, mfg. exec.; b. Montreal, Que., Can., July 31, 1937; s. Marcel and Jeheanne (Thibodeau) G.; B.A., Querbes Acad., 1955; postgrad. in engring. U. Montreal, 1956-59; m. Marielle Beland, Mar. 4, 1960; children—Francois, Marc, Marie-Josee, Marie-France. Nat. mktg. mgr. Addressograph of Can., Montreal, 1960-74; gen. mgr. Dymo Graphics Systems, Toronto, 1974-77; pres. and dir. Alphatype Can., Inc., North York, Ont., 1977—. Mem. Canadian C. of C., French C. of C. of Can., Bd. of Trade. Roman Catholic. Club: Richelieu. Home: Rural Route 3 Newmarket ON L3Y 4W1 Canada Office: 105 Scarsdale Rd North York ON M3B 2R5 Canada

GRAVES, DARLA JEAN, accountant; b. Creek County, Okla., Dec. 1, 1933; d. William Hulbert and Ella Elizabeth (Wiseley) Glimp; B.S.B.A., Okla. State U., 1974; m. Robert L. Graves, Aug. 3, 1952; children—Karen, Ronald, Barbara. Staff acct. Clifford C. Schmidt, C.P.A., Mineral Wells, Tex., 1968-69; owner, mgr. Darla J. Graves Bookkeeping & Tax Service, Drumright, Okla., 1971-76; sec.-treas. Triplex Well Service, Drumright, 1974—; owner, mgr. Darla J. Graves, C.P.A., Drumright, 1976—; partner Wash House Laundry, Drumright, 1974—; partner Glimp Prodn. Co., Drumright, 1978—. Mem. bus. and office adv. com., data processing adv. com. Central Area Vo-Tech., Drumright; treas., bd. dirs. United Community Action Program; pres. Head Start Policy Council. C.P.A. Mem. Am. Inst. C.P.A.'s, Am. Women's Soc. C.P.A.'s, Okla. Soc. C.P.A.'s, Drumright C. of C. (pres. 1978), Nat. Assn. Female Execs. Republican. Ch. Christ. Club: Desk & Derrick Club of Cushing. Home: Route 1 Drumright OK 74030 Office: 129 E Broadway Drumright OK 74030

GRAVES, DOUGLAS EVENSEN, aerospace co. exec.; b. Great Falls, Mont., Jan. 15, 1918; s. Paul and Evelyn (Evensen) G.; B.S. in Civil Engring., U. Wash., 1940; bus. student Northwestern U., 1962; m. Ruth Frances McBride, Aug. 27, 1943; children—Kathleen, Douglas. With The Boeing Co., Seattle, 1940—, mgr. Atlantic Test Center, 1961-64, space propulsion system mgr., 1964-65, AWACS program mgr., 1965-71, info. systems mgr., 1971-73, v.p. Boeing Aerospace Co., 1973—. Lic. profl. aero engr. Mem. AIAA, Am. Def. Preparedness Assn., Boeing Mgmt. Assn. Republican. Episcopalian. Club: Sand Point Country. Author articles in field. Office: PO Box 3999 Seattle WA 98124

GRAVES, EARL GILBERT, publisher; b. Bklyn., 1935; s. Earl Godwin and Winifred (Sealy) G.; grad. Morgan State Coll., Balt., 1958, LL.D., 1973; LL.D., Rust Coll., 1974; m. Barbara Kydd, July 2, 1960; children—Earl Gilbert, John, Michael. Adminstrv. asst. to Senator Robert F. Kennedy, 1965-68; owner mgmt. cons. firm, 1968-70; pub. Black Enterprise mag., N.Y.C., 1970—; pres. Earl G. Graves Ltd., Earl G. Graves Pub. Co., Inc., Earl G. Graves Assos.; dir. ITT, Liggett & Myers Tobacco Co. Mem. McGovern Commn., 1968. Mem. nat. bd., exec. com. Interracial Council for Bus. Opportunity; mem. adv. council U. Notre Dame Center Civil Rights; mem. Commn. Reform Relationship between Govt. and Pvt. Philanthropy; mem. exec. com. Greater New York council Boy Scouts Am. Trustee Tuskegee Inst. Served to capt. U.S. Army, 1958-60. Recipient Horace Suddoth Spl. award Nat. Bus. League, 1970, Scroll of Honor, Nat. Med. Assn., 1971, Bus. Achievement award Black Retail Action Group, Inc., 1971, Interam. Travel Agts. Soc. award, 1972, R.R. Wright award Black Travel Agts. Soc., 1972, Nat. award of excellence, 1972. Silver Beaver award Boy Scouts Am., 1969, Publisher for Freedom award Operation PUSH; listed as one of 100 influential Blacks in Am. Ebony mag.; named One of Ten Most Outstanding Minority Businessmen in Country by Pres. Nixon, 1973, Outstanding Citizen of Year, Omega Psi Phi, 1974, also one of 200 Future Leaders of Country, Time mag., Outstanding Black Businessman Nat. Bus. League. Mem. NAACP, Young President's Orgn. Home: 8 Heathcote Rd Scarsdale NY 10583 Office: 295 Madison Ave New York NY 10017

GRAVES, GEORGE GARLAND, indsl. designer; b. Salem, Ind., June 17, 1908; s. John T.J. and Leota (Cauble) G.; B.S., Ind. U., 1930; B.F.A., Art Inst. Chgo., 1935; postgrad. Columbia, 1946-49; m. Estelle Madeline Mull, Sept. 18, 1948 (dec. Oct. 1973). Indsl. designer Iannelli Studios, Park Ridge, Ill., 1936, Sterling B. McDonald, Chgo., 1937, Dunbar Furniture Mfg. Co., Berne, Ind., 1938-40, John H. Hopkins, Chgo., 1941-42, Murrill Co., N.Y.C., 1946-57, Simmons Co., N.Y.C., 1957-73. Served to lt. comdr. USNR, 1942-46. Mem. Indsl. Designers Soc. Am., Indsl. Design Inst. (past chmn.), Am. Watercolor Soc. (asso.), Delta Phi Delta, Delta Sigma Pi, Alpha Tau Omega. Methodist. Club: Salmagundi. Contbr. articles to profl. jours. Home: 26 Cove Rd Huntington NY 11743 also PO Box 54 Halesite NY 11743 Office: 1 Park Ave New York NY 10016

GRAVES, JOHN HARVEY, lumber co. exec.; b. Akron, Ohio, Sept. 18, 1929; s. Harold Elton and Almeda (Bolton) G.; B.S., Mich. State U., 1951; m. Patricia Kipple, May 21, 1959; children—Dianne Louise, Mary Ann, John Harvey. Salesman, Empire Wholesale Lumber Co., Akron, 1951-53, buyer, 1953-54, v.p., 1954-63, pres., owner, 1963—. Served as 2d lt. AUS, 1951. Mem. N.Am. Wholesale Lumberman's Assn., Nat. Assn. Wholesaler-Distbrs., Phi Delta Theta. Republican. Episcopalian. Clubs: Akron City, Portage Country (Akron). Home: 525 St Andrews Akron OH 44303 Office: Empire Wholesale Lumber Co Miami and Gault Sts Akron OH 44311*

GRAVES, MARY JO, landscape contractor; b. Beirne, Ark., Aug. 26, 1928; d. Wells Albert and Stella Mae (Baker) Wright; student Henderson (Ark.) State Tchrs. Coll., 1946-48, La. Landscape Sch., 1968-71; extension student Ark. State Tchrs. Coll. Conway, 1948; m. Cleve Verlon Graves, Mar. 5, 1949; children—Cleve Verlon, Sandra Lyn Graves Lindsay. Tchr., Glenrose, Ark., 1947-49, England, Ark., 1950; partner N. Caddo Drug Co., Vivian, La., 1954—; propr. N. Caddo Landscape, Vivian, 1973—; city horticulturist, 1973—. Mem. bd. Caddo-Bossier Conv. and Tourists Bur., 1975—, vice chmn., 1977—; chmn. N.W. La., Gov.'s Clean-up and Beautification Com., 1975-76. Chmn. N. Caddo Parish Bicentennial Com., 1973-76, museum renovations furnishings chmn., 1970-76; organizer Redbud Festival, 1964, pres., 1965-67; pres. Vivian Garden Club, 1963-65. Recipient award of appreciation from gov. La., 1974, 75; grantee La. Bicentennial Com., 1973; various other honors. Masters accredited flower show judge. Mem. Landscape Design Critics Council, Council State Garden Clubs, La. Garden Club Fedn. (judges council, pres. 1979), NW La. Hist. Soc. Presbyterian. Club: North Highlands Garden (pres. 1975-77). Co-author: Monterey?, 1973. Designer, builder Bicentennial Fountain and Mini Park. Home: 311 W Mary St Vivian LA 71082 Office: 144 W Louisiana St Vivian LA 71082

GRAVITZ, SIDNEY ISAAC, aeropace co. exec.; b. Balt., June 28, 1932; s. Philip Benjamin and Sophie (Korim) G.; B.S. (scholar), Mass. Inst. Tech., 1953, M.S., 1954, Aero. Engr. (fellow), 1957; m. Phyllis Bilgrad, June 14, 1964; children—Deborah Anne, Elizabeth Ellen. Research engr., aero. engring. dept. Mass. Inst. Tech., Cambridge, part-time 1952-57; dynamics group engr. N.Am. Aviation, Columbus, Ohio, 1957-60; with Boeing Co., Seattle, 1960—, mgr. flight ops. for inertial upper stage program, 1976-80, mgr. systems analysis and evaluation for 757/767 flight mgmt. system, 1980—; mem. NASA-Industry Space Shuttle Design Criteria working group. Loaned exec. King County United Good Neighbor Fund, 1968; regional chmn. Mass. Inst. Tech. Alumni Fund Dr., 1970; mem. Mass. Inst. Tech. Ednl. Council, 1974—. Served with USAF, 1954-56. Mem. ASME, Am. Inst. Aeros. and Astronautics, AAAS, Sigma Xi, Sigma Gamma Tau, Mass Inst. Tech. Alumni Club. Contbr. articles in field to profl. jours. Home: 8428 S E 62d St Mercer Island WA 98040 Office: Boeing Co Seattle WA 98124

GRAY, CHARLES AUGUSTUS, banker; b. Syracuse, N.Y., Sept. 16, 1928; s. Charles William and Elizabeth Marie (Koch) G.; certificate Am. Inst. Banking, 1958, Sch. Bank Adminstrn., 1961. With Mchts. Nat. Bank & Trust Co. of Syracuse, 1946-77, auditor, 1959-77, v.p., 1970-77; N.Y. State dir. Bank Adminstrn. Inst., 1970-72; regional auditor Central N.Y. region Irving Bank Corp., 1977—. Treas. Upper N.Y. Synod Luth. Ch. in Am., 1966—, Luth. Found. Upper N.Y., 1972—; pres. Interfrat. Alumni Council, Syracuse U., 1980-81. Chartered internal auditor. Mem. Bank Adminstrn. Inst. (pres. central N.Y. chpt. 1970-72), Inst. Internal Auditors (treas. central N.Y. chpt. 1974-76). Republican. Clubs: Lions (pres. local club 1973-75), Masons, Shriners. Home: 1321 Westmoreland Ave Syracuse NY 13210 Office: 220 S Warren St Syracuse NY 13201

GRAY, CHARLES ELMER, lawyer; b. Elvins, Mo., July 23, 1919; s. Grover P. and Martha Elizabeth (Sullivan) G.; student Flat River Jr. Coll., 1937-38, U. Hawaii, 1940-41; LL.B., Washington U., St. Louis, 1947; m. Beulah Hennrich Gray, July 4, 1942; children—Karen Lee, Cecelia Jean, Bette Sue, Marsha Dawn. Admitted to Mo. bar, 1947, since practiced in St. Louis; partner firm Gray & Ritter; sec., gen. counsel Don V. Davis Co.; pres. Don-Ite Corp., dir. United Mo. Bank St. Louis. Mem. Mo. Appellate Jud. Commn.; mem. rules com. Mo. Supreme Ct. Served to capt. USAAF, 1939-45. Fellow Internat. Acad. Trial Lawyers (dir. 1964-70; sec.-treas.), Am. Coll. Trial Lawyers; mem. Am., Mo. (bd. govs.), St. Louis bar assns., Lawyers Assn. St. Louis (v.p. 1954, bd. govs., award of honor 1977), Internat. Soc. Barristers (Mo. chmn. 1966, dir. 1970—). Phi Delta Phi. Home: Apt 1003 625 S Skinker Saint Louis MO 63105 Office: 900 Locust Bldg 1015 Locust St St Louis MO 63101

GRAY, DAVID MACDONALD, polit. scientist, coll. adminstr.; b. Richwood, W.Va., Mar. 20, 1931; s. Harry M. and Charlotte M. (Erhart) G.; B.A., U. Pa., 1952, M.A., 1954, Ph.D. (Penfield fellow), 1965; m. Patricia Ann Delano, June 28, 1952; children—Alison, Jonathan. Instr. polit. sci. U. Pa., Phila., 1956-59, research fellow, 1963-64; asst. prof. polit. sci. Drew U., Madison, N.J., 1959-63; asso. prof. polit. sci., dir. internat. programs Beaver Coll., Glenside, Pa., 1964-68, v.p. adminstrn., dir. internat. programs, 1969-71, exec. v.p., 1972—; dir. Health Tech. Labs., 1979—, U.C.T., Inc. Bd. dirs. United Colls. Fgn. Study, 1967-72; mem. exec. com. Pa. Council Internat. Edn., 1970—, pres., 1972-74, exec. dir., 1976—; chmn. bd. trustees Stevens Sch., 1972-75; trustee Theater Sch., 1975—. Am. Council Edn. fellow, 1968. Mem. Internat. Studies Assn., Am. Assn. Higher Edn., Internat. Polit. Sci. Assn., Soc. Coll. and Univ. Planning, Nat. Council Univ. Research Adminstrs., Phila Art Alliance, Phi Kappa Psi. Author: Foreign Policy Formulation in Emerging African Nations, 1962; editor: Rising Influence in Tropical Africa, 1956. Office: Beaver Coll Glenside PA 19038

GRAY, DORA EVELYN, accountant; b. Smith County, Tex., Mar. 26, 1924; d. H. Esten and Mattie E. (Payne) Clyburn; grad. Fed. Inst., 1944; m. Harvie A. Gray, Dec. 22, 1945 (dec.); children—Dennis H., Ladell L. Gray Green. Treas., asst. mgr. Wagner Office Equipment, 1948-61; asst. treas. Pool. Co., San Angelo, Tex., 1962-72; loan officer, acting mgr. Concho Educators Fed. Credit Union, San Angelo, 1972-75; warehouse accountant M System Food Stores, Inc., San Angelo, 1976—. Precinct del. county convs., 1976—; active various community drives; active in legislation regarding ERA, 1959—. Mem. Bus. and Profl. Women's Club (local pres., dist. chmn. for personal devel., legislative chmn., past state bd. dirs.), Internat. Platform Assn. Democrat. Mem. Ch. of Christ. Home: 915 N Adams St San Angelo TX 76901

GRAY, GEORGIA NEESE, banker; b. Richland, Kans.; d. Albert and Ellen (O'Sullivan) Neese; A.B., Washburn Coll., 1921, D.B.A. (hon.), 1966; student Sargent's, 1921-22; L.H.D., Russell Sage Coll., 1950; m. George M. Clark, Jan. 21, 1929; m. 2d, Andrew J. Gray, 1953. Began as actress, 1923; asst. cashier, Richland State Bank, 1935-37, pres., 1937—; pres. Capital City State Bank & Trust Co., Topeka; treas. of U.S., 1949-53. Mem. Commn. on Jud. Qualifications for Supreme Ct. Kans. Democratic nat. committeewoman, 1936-64; hon. chmn. Villages project C. of C. Bd. dirs. Kans. Am. Automobile Assn., 1950—; bd. dirs., former chmn. Kans. div. Am. Cancer Soc.; mem. bd. exec. campaign and maj. gifts com. Georgetown U.; bd. dirs. Seven Steps Found., Harry S. Truman Library Inst.; bd. regents Washburn U.; chmn. Alpha Phi Found., 1962-63; mem. nat. bd. Womens Med. Coll. Pa.; treas. Girls Club of Topeka; bd. dirs. Florence Crittenton Service. Recipient Distinguished Alumni award Washburn U., 1950. Mem. Am. Bus. Women's Assn., Nat. Assn. Bank Women, Shawnee County Hist. Soc. (pres.), Topeka C. of C., Met. Bus. and Profl. Womens Club, Alpha Phi (nat. trustee), Alpha Phi Upsilon, Theta Sigma Phi. Clubs: Soroptomist (hon. life), Met. Zonta, Topeka Country. Home: 2331 Mayfair Pl Topeka KS 66611 Office: 2709 W 29th St Topeka KS 66614

GRAY, HARRY JACK, business exec.; b. Milledgeville Crossroads, Ga., Nov. 18, 1919; B.S. with honors, U. Ill., 1941, M.S., 1947; LL.D., Trinity Coll., Conn., 1976, U. Hartford, 1978; m. Helen Buckley; children—Pam, Vicky Lynn. Instr., U. Ill., 1946-47; sales mgr. truck div. Esserman Motor Sales, Chgo., 1947-50; exec. salesman Platt, Inc., Chgo., 1950-51; exec. v.p., gen. mgr. Greyvan Lines, div. Greyhound Corp., Chgo., 1951-54; pres. U.S. Engring. div. Litton Industries, Van Nuys, Calif., 1956; v.p. Litton Industries, Beverly Hills, Calif., 1958-61; group v.p., 1961-64, sr. v.p. components, 1964-65, sr. v.p. for finance and adminstrn., 1965-67, exec. v.p., 1967-69, sr. exec. v.p., 1969-71, also dir.; pres. United Technologies Corp. (formerly United Aircraft), Hartford, Conn., 1971—, chief exec. officer, 1972—, chmn., 1974—, pres., 1974-79, also dir.; dir. Carrier Corp., Essex Group, Otis Elevator Co., Mostek Corp., Turbo Power & Marine Systems, Inc., Pratt & Whitney Aircraft of W.Va., Inc., United Technologies Internat., Inc., Pratt & Whitney Aircraft of Can. Ltd., Citicorp, Citibank, N.A., Aetna Life & Casualty Co., Hartford, Exxon Corp., Greater Hartford Corp., Carrier Corp., Syracuse, N.Y. Corporator Hartford Hosp., Inst. of Living, Hartford; bd. dirs. Old State House Assn., Hartford, Odyssey House, N.Y.C. Served to capt. AUS, 1941-46. Decorated Silver Star, Bronze Star. Mem. Bus. Council Washington (bd. dirs.), Conf. Bd. N.Y.C., IEEE, Aerospace Industries Assn. (gov.), Nat. Sales Exec. Club, Navy League U.S., Alpha Delta Sigma, Kappa Tau Alpha. Clubs: Hartford, Hartford Golf; Econ., Wings (N.Y.C.); Burning Tree (Washington); Lost Tree (North Palm Beach, Fla.). Office: United Technologies Corp Hartford CT 06101*

GRAY, JACK DONNELLY, banker; b. Fort Worth, Tex., July 9, 1944; s. Jack D. Vinsant and Thelma Louise (Flory) G.; B.A., U. Tex., at Austin, 1966, M.B.A., 1968; m. Dorothy Porcher Deane, Dec. 9, 1972 (div. 1978). Asso., McKinsey & Co., N.Y.C., 1968-70; v.p. Goldman Sachs & Co., N.Y.C., 1970-79; pres., chmn. 1st Nat. Bank of Cobb County, Marietta, Ga., 1979—; founder, dir. First Houston Group Inc., Parts of Fla. Inc.; pres. Bilo Inc. Trustee, Leukemia Found. Served to 1st lt. USAFR, 1967. Mem. Am. Finance Assn., Newcomen Soc., Cobb County C. of C. (dir.), Young President's Orgn. Clubs: Union League (N.Y.C.); Creek; Capital City, Commerce (Atlanta); Shoal Creek, Mountain Brook. Home: 722 Beauregard Dr Marietta GA 30064 Office: 100 Cherokee St Marietta GA 30061

GRAY, JAMES LARRY, metals co. exec.; b. Southmayd, Tex., Dec. 17, 1932; s. Cecil Lawray and Coquese Adeline (Cee) G.; student Tex. Tech. U., 1954, So. Meth. U., 1956; M.B.A., Pepperdine U., 1978. Sales engr. Simplex Wire & Cable, Cambridge, Mass., 1958-63; pres. Integral Corp., Dallas, 1963—. Served with U.S. Army, 1956-58. Mem. IEEE, Sigma Alpha Epsilon. Republican. Club: Toastmasters (pres. 1966-67), Jaycees (v.p. 1969-70). Home: 3534 Fairmount St Dallas TX 75219 Office: 6218 Cedar Springs Dallas TX 75235

GRAY, JAMES WESLEY, JR., investment broker; b. East Orange, N.J., Jan. 14, 1932; s. James Wesley and Kathryn Wolf (Nash) G.; B.S. in Elec. Engring., Va. Mil. Inst., 1953; M.B.A., U. Pa., 1957; m. Elizabeth Blantern Thomas, Apr. 19, 1958; children—Susan, James Wesley, Joyce. Engring. tng. program, systems engr. and sales engr. Def. Electronics div. Gen. Electric Co., Syracuse, N.Y., 1957-67, sales mgr. advanced manned space programs Space div., Valley Forge, Pa., 1967-69, sales devel. specialist Info. Services div., Bethesda, Md., 1969-71; account exec. Paine Webber Co., Washington, 1971-76; asst. v.p. Kidder Peabody Co., Washington, 1976-79, Merrill Lynch Pierce Fenner and Smith, Washington, 1979—. Mem. investment com. Episcopal Diocese of Washington. Served to 1st lt. U.S. Army, 1953-55. Mem. IEEE, Pres. Club (Merrill Lynch). Republican. Clubs: Darnestown Swim and Racquet (treas.), Quince Orchard Swim and Tennis, Washington Squash Racquets. A developer 1st optical data transmission system using infra-red light emitting diodes. Home: 13100 Chestnut Oak Dr Gaithersburg MD 20760 also Calypso #604 Ocean City MD Office: 1111 19th St NW Washington DC 20036

GRAY, JOHN DELBERT, apparel co. exec.; b. Petersburg, Ind.; s. John Daniel and Emma Louise (Rudolph) G.; m. Ruth Josephine Campbell, Dec. 31, 1936 (dec. 1966); children—John Douglas, Thomas Campbell, Andrew Michael, Stephen Joseph; m. 2d, Ann Milligan, May 1, 1971. Divisional mdse. mgr. Mandel Bros., Chgo., 1931-42; pres. Baskin Stores, Chgo., 1945-48; pres. Wallachs, Inc., N.Y.C., 1948-61; chmn. bd. Hart Schaffner & Marx, 1960—; dir. W.T. Grant Co., First Nat. Bank of Chgo., The First Chgo. Corp., Northwest Industries Inc., Sunbeam Corp., Nat. Can Corp.; trustee Mut. Life Ins. Co. N.Y. Bd. dirs. Better Bus. Bur. Met. Chgo., Jr. Achievement, Chgo., Mid-Am. chpt. A.R.C., Evanston Hosp., Lyric Opera Chgo.; trustee Better Govt. Assn., Chgo. Orchestral Assn., Com. Econ. Devel.; asso. Northwestern U.; chmn. Chgo. Council Fgn. Relations, The Chgo. Com. Served as maj., spl. asst. to dep. dir. spl. services div. AUS, World War II. Named Man of Year, Asso. Men's Wear Retailers, 1950; Golden Fleece award Nat. Assn. Wool Mfrs., 1958. Mem. Clothing Mfrs. Assn. (dir.), Ill. Mfrs. Assn. (dir.), U.S. C. of C. (dir.), Chgo. Assn. Commerce and Industry (dir.). Presbyn. Clubs: Pere Marquette Rod and Gun; Mid-America; Glen View, Chicago Curling, Mid-Day, Commercial, Economic, Tavern, Old Elm, Eldorado, Chicago; Links (N.Y.C.). Office: Hart Schaffner & Marx 36 S Franklin St Chicago IL 60606*

GRAY, RICHARD G., diversified investment co. exec. Pres., chief exec. officer Investors Mut. Inc., Mpls. Office: Investors Mutual Inc Roanoke Bldg Minneapolis MN 55402*

GRAY, ROBERT TAYLOR, mgmt. cons.; b. Cuba, Ill., May 14, 1927; s. Ned Taylor and Doris Katherine (Howerter) G.; B.S. in Sci., Kans. State U., 1953, postgrad. (Grad. fellow), 1954; m. Shirley Jean Sapp, July 29, 1969; children—John Stephen, Mark Robert, Todd Douglas; stepchildren—Wendy, Margot, Lori (Peterson). With Kaiser Aluminum and Chem. Co., 1954-65; dir. labor relations Tex. Instruments Co., 1965-69; dir. indsl. relations Litton Industries, 1969-72; sr. v.p., chief adminstrv. officer Wheelabrator-Frye, Inc., 1972; exec. v.p., dir. Wylain Co., Inc., Dallas, 1972-76; founder, pres. Gray & Assos. Inc., Dallas, 1976—; program mgr., dir. Black Diamond Mining Corp.; v.p. adminstrn. Gulf & Western Industries, Inc., Nashville. Served with USNR, World War II. Mem. NAM, Am. Mgmt. Assn., Labor Policy Assn., Sigma Chi. Club: Tanglewood Country (Dallas). Home: 6254 Emeraldwood Pl Dallas TX 75240 Office: 1845 Place One Ln Garland TX 75042

GRAYER, MERYL ROMAINE, ins. co. exec.; b. Mar. 7, 1933; d. Harry and Betty (Hurwick) G.; B.S., N.Y. U., 1948, M.A., 1949, Ph.D., 1980; C.L.U., Am. Coll., 1969; children—Melody Anderson, Morgan Meredyth Held. Asst. v.p. Standard Security Life Ins. Co., N.Y.C., 1959-69; corporate asst. sec. Asso. Madison Cos., Inc., N.Y.C., 1969-71, Madison Life Ins. Co., 1969-71; industry liaison cons. Met. Life. Ins. Co., N.Y.C., 1972—; adj. asst. prof. Coll. of Ins., N.Y.C., 1973—; vis. cons., lectr. Scarsdale (N.Y.) Sch. System, 1976—. Chmn. membership enrollment Greater N.Y. council Boy Scouts Am., 1978; mem. steering com. Easter Seal Soc. Telethon, 1979-81. Recipient Outstanding Achievement award Myopia Internat. Research Found., 1977; Explorers award Boy Scouts Am., 1977, 79; Outstanding Achievement award Women Leaders Round Table, 1974, 77, Boy Scouts Am., 1978. Mem. Bus. and Profl. Women's Clubs of N.Y. State, Inc. (dir., legislation chmn. 1976-77, 2d v.p. 1978-79, 1st v.p. 1979-80 pres.-elect 1980-81), Nat. Fedn. Bus. and Profl. Women's Clubs (nat. legis. com. 1976—), N.Y. League Bus. and Profl. Women (pres. 1975-76, dir. 1972-76), N.Y. Soc. Chartered Life Underwriters (chpt. sec. 1974-75, dir. 1972-75, program chmn. 1976-78, chmn. pub. relations 1977-81), Nat. Assn. Life Underwriters (chmn. N.Y.C. legislation com. 1974—, dir., 1977—), N.Y. Soc. Ins. Women (bylaws chmn.), Gen. Agts. and Mgrs. Conf., N.Y. C. of C. and Industry, New York Press Women (v.p. 1975-76, 78-81), Women in Communications (job chmn. 1977-78), Nat. Council Women in U.S., Nat. Assn. Female Execs., AAUW, N.Y. U. Alumni Fedn., Accts. for Public Interest, Inc. (nat. dir. 1980—). Clubs: N.Y. U. Alumnae (dir. 1976-79, corr. sec. 1980—); Zonta of N.Y. (dir. 1975—, membership chmn. 1975-76, program chmn. and rec. sec. 1976-77, 2d v.p. 1977-78, pres. 1978-80); N.Y. U.; Touchdown of Am. (dir. 1980—); N.Y. U. Fin. Author: Why Not a Career in Life Insurance?, 1974; The Career Path in Sales, 1975; The Career Path in Sales Management, 1975; editor, columnist Life Underwriters Bull., 1973—; contbr. articles to newspapers and mags. Home: 130 E 18th St New York NY 10003 Office: Metropolitan Life Ins Co One Madison Ave New York NY 10010

GRAYSON, DAVID STUART, stockbroker; b. Newark, Sept. 1, 1953; s. Edward Lee and Lois Edwina G.; student U. No. Colo., 1971-72, U. Denver, 1973-76. Pres., Serenity Hill, Naples, Maine, summers 1974, 75; dir. activities Latin Quarter Apts., Denver, 1975-76; pres. Mile Hi Control Systems, Denver, 1975-76; v.p. Discount Brokerage Corp., N.Y.C., 1977—, Tweedy Browne Clearing Corp., 1977—. Mem. Cunningham Vol. Fire Dept., Denver, 1974-75. Office: 67 Wall St New York NY 10005

GRAYSON, EDWIN MILTON, Realtor; b. Pocatello, Idaho, Dec. 20, 1931; s. William Thomas and Marjorie Jane (Wilcox) G.; student Idaho State Coll., 1955-56, Grimms Sch. Bus., 1956-57; m. Elaine Diane Mooney, Oct. 20, 1957; children—Christine (Mrs. Keith Harding), Michelle (Mrs. Kent Morris), Brenda, Cindy (Mrs. Alan Rowbury), Marjorie (Mrs. Mike Carpenter), Jolene. Salesman, Shattuck Agy., Idaho Falls, Ida., 1957-65; owner Grayson Real Estate & Builders, 1965-73; owner, dir. Grayson Builders, Inc., Idaho Falls, 1973—. Mem. Ida. Real Estate Commn., 1957—, Idaho Falls Realty Bd., 1957—; pres. Idaho Falls Multiple Listing Bur., 1960. Mem. Idaho Gov.'s Pub. Assistance Bd.; Republican precinct committeeman, 1968-70. Bd. dirs. Key Club-Skyline High Sch. Served with USN, 1950-54; PTO. Mem. Nat. Assn. Realtors. Presbyn. Mason (Shriner), Elk, Kiwanian (Distinguished Service awards 1969, 73, 74). Home: 3170 E Iona Rd Idaho Falls ID 83401 Office: 458 Lomax St Idaho Falls ID 83401

GRAYSON, JOHN CHARLES, retail business forms and equipment co. exec.; b. Savannah, Ga., Jan. 22, 1947; s. John Gugle and Lois Imogene (Greenwaide) G., Jr.; A.A., Brewton-Parker Jr. Coll., 1967; B.S. in Edn., U. Ga., 1970. Sales trainee Burroughs Co., Savannah, 1970-71, sr. sales rep., 1971-72, sales mgr., 1972-75; propr., mgr. Systems Bus. Forms & Equipment Co., Savannah, 1975—; profl. model, appeared in various TV shows and movies, 1975—; condr. sales seminars, office seminars, 1972—. Recipient Addy award Ga. Advt. TV Comml. Dirs., 1979. Mem. Ind. Forms Distbrs., '80 Ga. (hon.), Ga. Bulldog Club, U. Ga. Alumni Assn. Democrat. Roman Catholic. Clubs: Savannah Quarterback, K.C. (chancellor, com. chmn.). Home: 5 Cardinal Rd Savannah GA 31406 Office: 5105 Paulsen St Suite 140 Savannah GA 31405

GRAYSON, MELVIN JAY, public relations exec.; b. N.Y.C., May 29, 1924; s. Sydney and Rose (Sherman) G.; B.Litt., Rutgers U., 1947; M.S., Columbia U., 1948; m. Gloria Medof, Aug. 24, 1947; children—Scott Alan, Cathy Ann. Reporter, A.P., Trenton, N.J., 1948-50; feature writer Newark Star-Ledger, 1950-51; rewrite man, asst. night city editor N.Y. Herald Tribune, 1951-53; copywriter Batten, Barton, Durstine & Osborn, N.Y.C., 1953-55; promotion writer Look mag. Look div. Cowles Communications, Inc., N.Y.C., 1955-60, promotion mgr., 1960-67, dir. promotion, 1967-70, v.p. sales promotion, 1970-71; dir. editorial services Conoco, 1971; spl. asst. to Vice Pres. of U.S., 1972; v.p. Outdoor Advt. Assn. Am., N.Y.C., 1972-73, exec. v.p., 1974-75; pres. Grayson & Woodhouse, Inc., public relations firm, N.Y.C., 1976-80; dir. public relations Nabisco, Inc., N.Y.C., 1980—. Chmn. printing-pub. sect. Heart Fund, N.Y. Heart Assn., 1966-71, head dr. for printing sect., 1967-71. Served with AUS, 1943-46; ETO. Decorated Bronze Star. Mem. Mag. Promotion Group (pres. 1962-63, v.p. 1964-65), Sales Promotion Execs. Assn. Author: The Disaster Lobby, 1973; Executive Sweeties, 1973. Home: 16 Clive Hills Rd Edison NJ 08817 Office: 485 Lexington Ave New York NY 10017

GRAYSON, WALTON, III, lawyer; b. Shreveport, La., Aug. 18, 1928; s. Walton and Mary Alice (Lowrey) G.; A.B., Princeton, 1949; LL.B., Harvard, 1952; m. Bennetta Purse, May 20, 1955; children—Walton IV, Mark, Bennett, Dwight. Admitted to Tex. bar, 1952; practice law, Dallas, 1952—; asst. counsel Gt. Nat. Life Ins. Co., Dallas, 1954-69; partner Atwell, Grayson & Atwell, Dallas, 1961-69, Grayson & Simon, Dallas, 1969-73; of counsel Simon & Twombly, 1973—; v.p., gen. counsel Southland Corp., Dallas, 1961-72, exec. v.p., 1972—, also dir. Served with USNR, 1952-54. Mem. Am., Tex., Dallas bar assns. Home: 10525 Strait Ln Dallas TX 75229 Office: 2828 N Haskell Ave Dallas TX 75221

GRAYSON, YALE AVROM, data processing co. exec.; b. Albany, N.Y., May 24, 1930; s. Max and Sophie (Cohen) Greenberg; A.A.S., SUNY at Morrisville, 1951, student, 1953-55; student U. Tex., 1952-53; m. Leslie Drew, May 9, 1970; children—William S.B., Yale A., Scott A., Dina L. With Gen. Electric Research Labs., 1950-56, IBM Corp., 1956-59; dir. software devel. Gen. Precision Labs., Tarrytown and N.J., 1959-62; mktg. rep. RCA, N.Y.C., 1962-64; pres. Grayson Consultronics, Rye, N.Y. and N.Y.C., 1966-67; dir. systems and programming ITT Worldcom, 1967-69; pres. Benetronics, Inc., White Plains, N.Y., 1969-77; v.p. merger and acquisitions E.T.C., Newburgh, N.Y., 1977-78; v.p. mktg. New Eng. Digital Corp., Norwich, Vt., 1978; pres. Country Programmers Internat., Inc., White River Junction, Vt., 1978—, also dir.; chmn. bd. Country Programmers Internat., Inc.; cons. IBM, DEC, Univac, Honeywell, Exxon, Bell Labs. Served with USAF, 1952-54. Mem. Soc. Naval Architects and Marine Engrs., Assn. for Computing Machinery, IEEE, Profl. Air Traffic Controllers Assn., Data Processing Mgrs. Assn. Democrat. Episcopalian. Clubs: Orienta Yacht, Sheldrake Yacht. Author 2 ltd. edit. books, articles. Home: Vershire VT 05079 Office: Holiday Inn Dr White River Junction VT 05001

GREANOFF, CHARLES SAMUEL, mfg. co. exec., cons.; b. Cleve., May 30, 1915; s. Percy Richard and Flora (Bowden) G.; A.B., Baldwin-Wallace Coll., 1937; postgrad. Case Western Res. U., 1950-51, Cleve. State U., 1952-53; m. Virginia M. Taylor, Jan. 30, 1945; children—Susan, Beverly, Janet, Charles II. Mgmt. cons. Cleve. office Arthur Young & Co., C.P.A.'s, 1944-61; v.p., dir. Bomgartner Mfg. Co., 1954-56; dist. supr. mgmt. services div. Ernst & Ernst, C.P.A.'s, Cleve., 1961-66; asst. to pres. Ryan Industries, Inc., 1966-67; exec. v.p., treas., gen. mgr. Gilmore Industries, Inc., Cleve., 1967-72; pres., treas. Motor Rim Mfrs. Co., Inc., Cleve. and Akron, Ohio, 1968-72; with Cerro Corp., Cleve., 1972-75; partner Control Property Group, Cleve., 1975—; bus. mgr., asst. treas. Cleve. Yachting Club, Inc., Rocky River, Ohio, 1979—. Mem. ednl. safety panel Nat. Safety Congress, 1960; chmn. Nat. Safe Boating Week Com., 1958-60; sponsor Girl Scout Troop for Handicapped, Cleve. Served with USCG, 1943-45; mem. USCG Aux., 1943—, nat. commodore, 1958-60, mem. nat. bd. dirs., 1958-60. Recipient USCG certificate of merit, 1960. Registered profl. engr., Ohio. Mem. Am. Inst. Indsl. Engrs. (dir.), Nat. Assn. Accountants, Soc. Advancement Mgmt. (pres., mem. nat. research com.), Nat. Soc. Profl. Engrs., Cleve. Engring. Soc., Cleve. C. of C., Baldwin-Wallace Coll. Nat. Alumni Assn. (pres. 1965-66), Alpha Tau Omega. Clubs: Jackson Park Yacht (Chgo.); Hawaii Yacht (Honolulu). Home: 1536 Arthur Ave Cleveland OH 44107 Office: 19109 Detroit Rd Cleveland OH 44116

GREASOR, RUSSELL EARL, telephone co. exec.; b. Logansport, Ind., May 25, 1926; s. Virgil Elmer and Margaret Ruth (Shaw) G.; student Valparaiso (Ind.) U., 1962; m. Jeanette Elizabeth Rupenthal, Jan. 20, 1951; children—Pamela Jean, Patricia Ann, Charles Russell, Roger Allen. With Gen. Telephone Co., 1947—, plant service mgr., Elkhart, Ind., 1972, customer relations mgr., Terre Haute, Ind., 1972—. Chmn. bd. United Way Wabash Valley, 1980; pres. Jr. Achievement Wabash Valley, 1980; v.p. Wabash Valley chpt. Honor Am., 1979; Vigo County chmn. Wabash Valley council Boy Scouts Am., 1979-80; chief staff Ind. Guard Res., 1977-79; zip area coordinator U.S. Mil. Acad., 1976—. Served with AUS, 1944-46; mem. Ind. N.G., 1955-64. Decorated Bronze Star, Combat Inf. badge, Ind. N.G. Commendation medal with oak leaf cluster; recipient award merit Wabash Valley Central Labor Council, 1979. Mem. Ind. Telephone Pioneer Assn. (club pres.), Telephone Pioneers Am., Ind. Telephone Assn., Home Builders Assn. Wabash Valley, Terre Haute C. of C. Democrat. Clubs: Wabash Valley Press, Rotary (past pres. Terre Haute). Home: 61 Canterbury Dr Terre Haute IN 47805

GREAVES, KENNETH WILLIAM, corporate engring. devel. exec.; b. N.Y.C., Mar. 13, 1941; s. Edward Thomas and Valeria Elizabeth (Hossu) G.; B.S. in Engring. (Douglas Aircraft scholar), Rensselaer Poly. Inst., 1962; M.S. in Engring., U. So. Calif., 1967; M.S. in Mgmt. (Henry Ingram Engring. Mgmt. scholar), Vanderbilt U., 1971; m. Antoinette Marie Spanier, Nov. 11, 1962. Engring. asst. Applied Physics Lab., Silver Spring, Md., 1961; sr. research engr. Rocketdyne Div. N.Am. Rockwell, Canoga Park, Calif., 1962-70; fellow Von Karman Inst., Belgium, 1965-66; research fellow U. Tenn. Space Inst., Tullahoma, 1968-69; coordinator cost systems, steam turbine div. engring. Westinghouse Corp., Lester, Pa., 1970-72, mgr. budgeting and control, 1972-78, mgr. advanced engring. dept., 1978—; instr. advanced edn. program N.Am. Rockwell, 1966-68; internal cons., zero-based budgeting Westinghouse Electric Co., Mgmt. Analysis Corp., 1975-76. Vice chmn. Garnet Valley (Pa.) Taxpayers Assn., 1976. Republican. Contbr. articles in field to profl. jours. Home: 26 Bullard Ln Millis MA 02054

GREAVES, PERCY LAURIE, JR., economist; b. Bklyn., Aug. 24, 1906; s. Percy Laurie and Grace I. (Dodge) G.; B.S. in Bus. magna cum laude, Syracuse U., 1929; postgrad. econs. Columbia, 1933-34, N.Y.U., 1950-69; m. Edith Leslye Platt, Aug. 23, 1930; children—Richard L., Muriel A., Charles Flint; m. 2d, Bettina Herbert Bien, June 26, 1971. Bookkeeper, Am. Trading Co., 1923-24; exec. trainee, asst. advt. mgr. Gillette Safety Razor Co., 1929-32; advt. tng. with Batten, Barton, Durstine & Osborn, 1930; instr. econs. and fgn. trade YMHA, 1933-34; financial editor, research economist U.S. News, 1934-36; advt. mgr. European subsidiaries Pet and Carnation Milk cos., 1936-38; advt. and pub. relations exec. Met. Life Ins. Co., 1938-43; asso. research dir. Republican Nat. Com., 1943-45; chief minority staff Joint Congl. Com. on Investigation Pearl Harbor Attack, 1945-46; exec. dir. Found. for Freedom, Inc., 1946-48; expert House Com. on Edn. and Labor, 1947; econ. cons., writer, lectr., 1948—; econ. adviser, columnist Christian Freedom Found., 1950-58; guest lectr. econs. Freedom Sch., Inc., 1957-61; guest lectr. Found. Econ. Edn., 1961-67; Armstrong prof. econs. U. Plano, 1965-71; pres. Free Market Books, 1974—. Mem. exec. bd. Am. Party, 1976—, presdl. candidate, 1980. Mem. Am. Econ. Assn., Am. Hist. Assn., Beta Gamma Sigma, Phi Kappa Phi. Episcopalian. Author: Operation Immigration, 1947; Understanding the Dollar Crises, 1973; Mises Made Easier, 1974; also numerous articles on econs., politics, pub. affairs. Contbr. to Perpetual War for Perpetual Peace, 1952; On Freedom and Free Enterprise, 1956; Essays on Liberty, Vols. III, VI, XII, XIII, Toward Liberty, 1971; Free Market Economics: A Basic Reader, 1975; On the Manipulation of Money and Credit, 1978. Home: 19 Pine Ln Irvington-on-Hudson NY 10533 Office: PO Box 298 Dobbs Ferry NY 10522

GRECO, CHARLES PAUL, fin. exec.; b. Bklyn., May 18, 1943; s. Charles Paul and Frances (LaManna) G.; B.S., St. John's U., 1970; children—Mark, Paul, Ian, Corey. Asst. controller B. Gertz, Inc., N.Y.C., 1965-72, Alexander's, N.Y.C., 1972-74; asst. controller Hecht Co., Washington, 1974-80, dir. internal audit, 1980—. Mem. Am. Mgmt. Assn., Nat. Retail Mchts. Assn. Home: 4849 Connecticut Ave Washington DC 20008 Office: Hecht Co Fenton St and Ellsworth Dr Silver Spring MD 20010

GRECO, MARVIN MEREL, state govt. ofcl.; b. Rupert, Idaho, Nov. 10, 1946; s. McKay Z. and Winifred (Masters) G.; B.A. cum laude, U. Mass., Amherst, 1974; M.S. (research asst. 1974-76), SUNY, Stony Brook, 1976; m. Marie L. Cianci, June 27, 1971; children—Brian, Christina. Adminstrv. analyst Office Instl. Research, Fairleigh Dickinson U., 1976-77; asst. dir. Office Mgmt. Systems, then exec. asso. Office Fiscal Affairs, N.J. Dept. Higher Edn., Trenton, 1977-80, acting dir. Office Mgmt. Systems, 1980—, dir. computer policy and planning, 1980—; bd. dirs. N.J. Ednl. Computer Network. Served with USAR, 1966-70. Mem. Assn. Instl. Research, Am. Mgmt. Assn., Allentown (N.J.) Jaycees. Home: 6 Allen Dr Allentown NJ 08501 Office: 225 W State St Trenton NJ 08625

GREELEY, ROBERT CHARLES, banker; b. Coeur d'Alene, Idaho, July 27, 1948; s. Gerald William and Letha Mae (Serrette) G.; B.S., U. Idaho, 1970; m. Celeste Marie Meyer, May 17, 1980. Asst. mgr. Burlingame (Calif.) office Wells Fargo Bank, 1975-77, asst. v.p., mgr., br. officer tng. dept., 1977-80, br. mgr. West Berkeley (Calif.) office, 1978-80, loan supr., asst. v.p. Oakland region, 1980—. Treas., Berkeley-Albany Industries Assn., 1979-80. Mem. Alpha Kappa Psi, Theta Chi. Clubs: Lions, Kiwanis, Bay, Commonwealth of Calif. Office: 1333 Broadway 3d Floor Oakland Region Oakland CA 94612

GREELEY, WILDER JOSEPH, service co. exec.; b. Southington, Conn., Sept. 17, 1906; s. Daniel W. and Elizabeth (Belser) G.; student Bates Coll., 1924-25; m. Benita Pape, July 15, 1933; 1 dau., Benita (Mrs. Peter J. Sherwood). Actor, The Jitney Players, A Trip to Scarborough, The Wonder, Murder in the Red Barn, 1929-30; with So. New Eng. Telephone Co., 1930-44; engr. charge G-23, OWI, Cambridge, Eng., 1944-45; asst. mgr. radio sta. WBRY, 1946-50; pres., treas. Paper Delivery, Inc., Waterbury, Conn., 1950—, Waterbury Motor Lease, Inc., 1960—; pres. Catrala of Conn., 1976-78, v.p. car leasing, 1978—; treas., gen. mgr. Woodbridge Skating Rink, Inc. (Conn.), 1938-72. Mem. Republican Town Com., 1946—. Vice pres. finance Mental Health Assn. Central Naugatuck Valley, 1966-71; mem. finance com. Conn. Mental Health Assn., 1972—; chmn. Woodbridge (Conn.) Bd. Police Commrs., 1972—. Mem. New Eng. Fedn. Men's Glee Clubs (pres. 1964—), Waterbury, Naugatuck C. of C. Republican. Conglist. Mason (33 deg., K.T.), Kiwanian (past pres., lt. gov. div. 1-West). Club: Waterbury. Home: 826 Fountain St Woodbridge CT 06525 Office: 456 Meadow St Waterbury CT 06702

GREEN, BERNARD JULIAN, automobile parts mfg. co. exec.; b. N.Y.C., Sept. 18, 1918; s. Maurice S. and Ella P. Green; B.S., U. Va., 1939; M.B.A., Harvard U., 1941; m. Reba June Long, Apr. 21, 1965; children—Patricia, Richard. Asst. to v.p. sales Fairchild Camera and Instrument Corp., 1946-49; pres. Plumbium Mfg. Corp., Bristol, Tenn., 1949—; dir. Airvert, Ltd., Wheel Weights (Pty.) Ltd. Served to 1st lt. AUS, 1941-46. Mem. Soc. Automotive Engrs. (asso.), Motor and Equipment Mfrs. Assn., Automotive Warehouse Distbrs. Assn., Nat. Tire Dealers and Retreaders Assn., Am. Retreaders Assn., Greater Bristol Area C. of C. (pres. 1972), Raven Soc. Patentee in field. Home: 2201 King College Rd Bristol TN 37620 Office: 8 Boswell Dr Bristol TN 37620

GREEN, CYRIL KENNETH, retail co. exec.; b. Portland, Oreg., June 11, 1931; s. Lionel and Nora Evelyn G.; student public schs., Portland; m. Beverly Ann Hutchinson, July 24, 1950; children—Kenneth James, Teri Ann Green Quinby, Tamara Jo Green Easton, Kelly Denise. With Fred Meyer Inc., Portland, 1947—, v.p., dir. ops., 1970-72, pres., prin. operating officer, 1972—, also dir. Mem. Western Assn. Food Chains (dir.). Republican. Office: 3800 SE 22d Ave Portland OR 97242

GREEN, ERNA JANE, exec. recruiting co. exec.; b. Norwalk, Conn., May 14, 1936; d. Allen A. and Bess R. Feldman; B.B.A. in Fin., U. Miami, 1958; M.A. in History, U. Bridgeport, 1972; m. Leonard Green, May 14, 1961. With stats. and adminstrv. depts. A.G. Becker & Co., Inc., N.Y.C., 1958-61; tchr. secondary schs., Fairfield County, Conn., 1961-68; teaching asst. U. Bridgeport, 1968-69; sr. asso. Charles Irish Co., Inc., exec. recruiting consultants, N.Y.C. Mem. New Canaan (Conn.) Town Council, 1975-79. Mem. Phi Alpha Theta. Home: 210 Main St New Canaan CT 06840 Office: 420 Lexington Ave New York NY 10170

GREEN, GERALD MILTON, lawyer; b. Cambridge, Mass., Dec. 20, 1945; s. Manning J. and Estelle (Liberman) G.; B.S., Boston U., 1967; J.D., Am. U., 1971. Admitted to D.C. bar, 1971, Md. bar, 1973; staff atty. Neighborhood Legal Services, Washington, 1971-72; asst dir. D.C. Law Students in Court program, 1972-73; atty. Laborers Legal Services Program, Washington, 1973-75; partner Cramer & Green, Washington, 1975-77; partner firm Reuss, Mc Connville, King & Green, 1978—; mayoral appointee D.C. Bd. of Appeals and Rev., 1979—; law instr. Am. U., Cath. U. Pres., Barney Neighborhood House, 1976-78; treas. Mt. Pleasant Neighbors Assn., 1976-78; bd. dirs. Ayuda, Inc., 1977—, sec., 1978—. Served with Peace Corps, 1968-70. Mem. Am. Bar Assn., D.C. Bar, Md. Bar. Home: 1854 Ingleside Terr NW Washington DC 20010 Office: 2021 K St NW Washington DC 20036 also 4720 Montgomery Ln Bethesda MD 20014

GREEN, HAROLD JAMES, corp. economist; b. Youngstown, Ohio, July 20, 1948; s. Harold Wallace and RuaBelle (Hays) G.; B.A. in Econs., Youngstown State U., 1971, M.A. in Econs., 1972, M.B.A. in Mktg., 1977; m. Janet Clare Timko, Aug. 1, 1970; children—Tiffany Laura, Allyson Tara, Bryan Harold. Asst. mgr. econ. research Ohio Bell Telephone Co., Cleve., 1972-74; supr. market research and planning Copperweld Steel Co., Warren, Ohio, 1974-75; economist Borden, Inc., Columbus, 1975—; cons. to small bus. on improvement mktg. and ops. techniques. Mem. Nat. Assn. Bus. Economists, Am. Mktg. Assn., Omicron Delta Epsilon. Researcher changing aspect of velocity of money. Home: 578 Michael Ave Westerville OH 43081

GREEN, JACK LEONARD, fin. exec.; b. Pittsfield, Mass., Sept. 28, 1933; S. Abraham and Bella Ruth (Hymanson) G.; student Bklyn. Coll., 1956; m. Florence Schwartz, Sept. 5, 1954; children—Ian Allen, Staci Lynne. Regional mgr. D. Strauss Co., Inc., N.Y.C., 1954-61; sr. field mgr. Savin Bus. Machines, N.Y.C., 1961-67; nat. mktg. dir. FloraMir Corp., N.Y.C., 1967-69; asst. to pres. and chmn. bd. F. Chusid & Co., N.Y.C., 1969-71; founder, pres., chief exec. officer Dyna-Lease Corp., N.Y.C., 1971-74; pres., chief exec. officer Florian Fin. Group, Plainview, N.Y., 1974—; lectr. Hastings Industries, 1978-79, Internat. Systems Dealers Assn., 1978—. Served with USN, 1951-54; ETO. Mem. Am. Acad. Cons., Writers Guild. Republican. Clubs: Met. Rod and Sporting, K.P. Author: Leasing-Principles and Methods, 1978; contbr. articles to profl. jours. Address: 9 Dee Ct Plainview NY 11803

GREEN, JAY PATRICK, JR., graphics arts exec.; b. Searcy, Ark., Feb. 14, 1949; s. Jay Patrick and Mary Virginia (Bates) G.; student Brandywine Coll., 1967, 68, 69, 79, U. Del., 1969; student Grand Valley State Coll., 1973; student W. Shore Community Coll., 1974; m. Judith Eileen Rineer, Jan. 15, 1968; children—Brent Patrick, Patrick Christopher, Regina Marie, Sarah Lynn. Graphics plant mgr. Religious Book Discount House, Inc., Grand Rapids, Mich., 1965-69; pres. Plywood Market Inc., Byron Center, Mich., 1969-72; pres., gen. mgr. LKS Modular Components, Inc., Lowell, Mich., 1970-72; owner, gen. mgr. LKS Constrn., Grand Rapids, 1969-74; gen. mgr. New Religious Book Discount House, Wilmington, Del., 1975-77; prodn. mgr. Asso. Pubs. & Authors, Inc., Lafayette, Ind., 1978-79; gen. mgr., v.p. Book Factory, Inc., Lafayette, Ind., 1980—; dir. Lit. Discovery, Inc., Wilmington, 1976-78. Served with USN, 1968-69. Mem. Nat. C. of C., Am. Entrepreneurs Assn., Internat. Entrepreneurs Assn. Republican. Baptist. Office: 408 North St Lafayette IN 47901

GREEN, JEFFREY CHARLES, investment banker; b. Dearborn, Mich., Nov. 25, 1952; s. Bruce Wilmont and Dorothy Beatrice (Morris) G.; student Harvard U., 1972; B.A., Miami U., Oxford, Ohio, 1975; M.B.A., U. So. Calif., 1979; m. Mary Anne Beckerman, Dec. 16, 1977. Legis. aide U.S. Ho. of Reps., Washington, 1974; asst. to pres. Miami U., 1974-75; head municipal securities regulation Fed. Res. Bank of San Francisco, 1975-77; investment banker United Calif. Bank, Los Angeles, 1977-79; investment banker in charge mcpl. debt. repurchase Goldman, Sachs & Co., N.Y.C., 1979—. Mem. campaign com. Nat. Republican Com., 1974-76. Mem. N.Y. Bond Club, World Affairs Council, Soc. Fin. Analysts, Phi Kappa Phi, Omicron Delta Kappa. Episcopalian. Clubs: Downtown Athletic, Toppers. Home: Indian Hill Rd Pound Ridge NY 10576 Office: Goldman Sachs & Co 55 Broad St New York NY 10004

GREEN, JOHN LAFAYETTE, JR., univ. exec.; b. Trenton, N.Y., Apr. 3, 1929; s. Edith (Howell) G.; B.S. Miss. State U., 1955; M.Ed., Wayne State U., 1971; Ph.D., Rensselaer Poly. Inst., 1975; m. Harriet Hill, Nov. 8, 1965; 1 son, John L. Vice-pres. bus. and fin. U. Ga., Athens, 1965-70; v.p. adminstrn. and budget Rensselaer Poly. Inst., Troy, N.Y., 1971-76; exec. v.p. adminstrn. and fin. U. Miami, Coral Gables, Fla., 1976-79; sr. v.p. adminstrn. and fin. U. Houston System, 1979—; past dir. Marine Midland Bank-Eastern, Troy, First Nat. Bank of Athens; dir. Blue Shield, Albany, N.Y., 1970-71. Served with U.S. Army, 1951-53. Mem. Planning Execs. Inst., NAM, Fin. Execs. Inst., Fin. Mgmt. Assn., Pi Kappa Alpha, Phi Delta Kappa, Beta Alpha Psi. Presbyterian. Clubs: Miami, Riviera Country, Standard. Home: 12310 Broken Arrow Houston TX 77024

GREEN, JOHN MARKHAM, investment banker; b. Dallas, Aug. 30, 1943; s. James William and Dorothy Maxine (Cooke) G.; B.B.A., U. Tex., 1965; M.B.A., So. Meth. U., 1966; m. Cheryl Jean Wright, Dec. 29, 1973; 1 son, Andrew Markham. Regional mgr. investment banking Merrill Lynch Pierce Fenner & Smith, N.Y.C., 1967-73, v.p., 1970-73; v.p. Goldman Sachs & Co., N.Y.C., 1973—. Bd. dirs. Counseling and Human Devel. Center, N.Y.C.; asso. vestryman St. Bartholomew's Ch., N.Y.C. Mem. Chi Phi. Episcopalian. Home: 1150 Park Ave New York NY 10028 Office: 55 Broad St New York NY 10004

GREEN, JOSEPH HAROLD, mfg. and sales co. exec.; b. Detroit, July 30, 1925; s. Joseph Clarence and Esther Helen (Groehn) G.; student mech. engring. Lawrence Inst. Tech., 1948; B.S. in Bus., Wayne State U., 1950. Founder, pres. J.H. Green Co., Dearborn, Mich., 1957—, Greenco Corp., Dearborn, 1970—, J.H. Green Sales, Inc., Dearborn, 1979—, Tri-Motion Industries, Inc., 1980—, Green Group Internat., Inc., 1980—; pres. Parts Handling Corp., Dearborn, 1976—. Served with USN, 1944-46; to lt. USAF, 1950. Republican. Methodist. Club: Masons. Home: 30315 Ledgecliff Westland MI 48185 Office: 7330 Greenfield Dearborn MI 48126

GREEN, JOSHUA, III, bank exec.; b. Seattle, June 30, 1936; s. Joshua and Elaine (Brygger) G.; B.A. in English, Harvard U., 1958; grad. Pacific Coast Banking Sch., 1967; m. Pamela K. Pemberton, Nov. 1, 1974; children—Joshua IV, Jennifer Elaine, Paige Courtney. Trainee, Citibank, N.A., N.Y.C., 1959-60; with Peoples Nat. Bank of Wash., Seattle, 1960—, sr. v.p., 1970-72, exec. v.p., 1972-75, pres., 1975-79, chmn. bd., chief exec. officer, 1979—; dir. Joshua Green Corp., Peoples Nat. Bank of Wash. and subs. Bd. dirs. Joshua Green Found., U. Puget Sound, Seattle Found.; hon. consul of Belgium, 1968—. Mem. Res. City Bankers Assn. (sr. bank mem.), Seattle C. of C. (v.p. 1979-81), Downtown Seattle Devel. Assn., Econ. Devel. Council. Republican. Episcopalian. Clubs: Seattle Tennis, Wash. Athletic, Rainier. Office: Peoples Nat Bank 1414 4th Ave Seattle WA 98171

GREEN, LAWRENCE THEODORE, aircraft co. exec.; b. Los Angeles, Feb. 21, 1934; s. Regnold William and Aurania (Westman) G.; B.S. in Bus. Adminstrn., U. Calif. Los Angeles, 1956; M.B.A., U. So. Calif., 1967; m. Doris Lorraine Lindstrom, June 25, 1961; 1 dau., Deborah Ann. Pricing, budgeting analyst Douglas Aircraft Co., Santa Monica, Calif., 1958-63; with Hughes Aircraft Co., Culver City, Calif., 1963—, accounting supr., 1971—; instr. accounting El Camino Coll., Torrance, Calif., part-time 1976-78; enrolled agt. IRS. Chmn., Day Sch. Commn., Westchester Luth. Ch., 1979-80. Served with U.S. Army, 1956-58. Life mem. U. So. Calif. Alumni Assn., UCLA Alumni Assn. Club: Hughes Aircraft Co. Mgmt. Home: 12212 Herbert St Los Angeles CA 90066 Office: Bldg E40 Mail Sta G193 2101 E El Segundo Blvd El Segundo CA 90245

GREEN, LEE, fin. planner; b. N.Y.C., May 9, 1947; s. Leroy A. and Louise W. (Jones) G.; B.A., Hampton (Va.) Inst., 1969; m. Valerie J. Burton, Nov. 27, 1976; children—Akiba, Briana, Candace. Fin. dir. Robeson Multi-Media Center, Washington, 1972-75; broker, mgr. Employee Benefits, Inc., Alexandria, Va., 1975-79; pres. Capitol Planning Corp., Washington, 1979—; dir. Archway Realty, Inc. Recipient Western Res. Fin. Services award, 1979. Mem. Am. Mgmt. Assn., Internat. Assn. Fin. Planners. Mem. Full Gospel Businessmen's Internat. Evang. Temple. Office: 1511 Pennsylvania Ave Washington DC 20003

GREEN, MARVIN HOWE, JR., TV prodn. co. exec.; b. Syracuse, N.Y., Mar. 30, 1935; s. Marvin Howe and Evelyn (Hougan) G.; student Bowdoin Coll., 1957; m. Catherine Anne Curwain, Nov. 23, 1971; children—Marvin Howe III, Melissa Perkins, Alexandra Victoria, Allegra Victoria Hougan. Salesman Hallmark Greeting Cards Co., N.Y.C., 1957-60; salesman Visualscope, Inc., N.Y.C., 1960-65, v.p. mktg., 1965-70, pres. 1970-75; chmn. Reeves Communications, Inc., N.Y.C., 1976—; dir. Masterworks Theater. Served with U.S. Army, 1955-57. Mem. Young Pres.'s Orgn., TV, Acad. Arts and Scis., New Eng. Soc. (dir.). Presbyterian. Clubs: N.Y. Yacht, Stamford Yacht (vice commodore), Ox Ridge Hunt, River, Royal Bermuda Yacht. Home: 435 Ocean Dr West Stamford CT 06902 Office: 605 3d Ave New York NY 10017

GREEN, RAYMOND FERGUSON ST. JOHN, broadcasting co. exec.; b. Phila., Aug. 15, 1950; Raymond Silvernail and Rose Dorathea (Basile) G.; B.A. in Psychology, Lafayette Coll., 1972; postgrad. Temple U., 1972-75; m. Lisa Rose Wardzinski, June 24, 1972. Prodn. asst. Franklin Broadcasting Co., Phila., 1972-73, asst. sec., 1973-75, v.p. corp. affairs, 1975-78, exec. v.p., 1978—, chief operating officer, 1979—, also dir. Mem. advisory bd. Good Shepherd Home for Girls, 1976—. Mem. TV Radio Advt. Club, N.G. Assns. of U.S. and Pa., Phila. Art Alliance. Roman Catholic. Club: Union League (Phila.). Office: 8200 Ridge Ave Philadelphia PA 19128

GREEN, WARREN HAROLD, publisher; b. Auburn, Ill., July 25, 1915; s. John Anderson Logan and Clara Christina (Wortman) G.; student Presbyn. Theol. Sem., 1933-34, Ill. Wesleyan U., 1934-36; B.Mus., Southwestern Conservatory, Dallas, 1938; M.Mus., St. Louis Conservatory, 1940, Ph.D., 1942; m. Joyce Reinerd, Oct. 8, 1960. Prof. voice, composition and aural theory St. Louis Conservatory, 1938-44; program dir. USO, Highland Park, Ill., Brownwood, Tex., Orange, Tex., Waukegan, Ill., 1944-46; community service specialist Rotary Internat., Chgo., 1946-47; editor in chief Charles C. Thomas, Pub., Springfield, Ill., 1947-66; pub., pres. Warren H. Green, Inc., St. Louis, 1966—; sec. John R. Davis Assos., Chgo., 1955—; exec. v.p. Visioneering Advt., St. Louis, 1966—; mng. dir. Publishers Service Center, St. Louis, Mo. and Longview, Tex., 1967—; chief exec. officer Affirmative Action, Inc., 1974—. Cons. to U.S. and European publishers, profl. socs.; lectr. med. pub. and Civil War. Mem. Mayor's Com. on Water Safety; mem. Met. St. Louis Art Mus., Mo. Bot. Gardens. Recipient Presdl. citation outstanding contbn. export expansion program U.S., 1973. Mem. Civil War Round Table (v.p. 1969—), Am. Acad. Criminology, Am. Acad. Polit. and Social Sci., Am. Med. Pubs. Assn., Am. Judicature Soc., Am. Acad. Criminology, Great Plains Hist. Soc., Co. Mil. Historians, Am. Soc. Personnel Adminstrs. Nat. Small Bus. Assn., University City C. of C. (pres. 1979—), Internat. Assn. Chiefs of Police, Nat. Rifle Assn. Clubs: Mo. Athletic, World Trade, Direct Marketing (St. Louis), Elks. Contbr. articles and books on Civil War history, writing and editing to profl. jours. Home: 12120 Hibler Dr Creve Coeur MO 63141 Office: 8356 Olive Blvd St Louis MO 63132

GREEN, WILLIAM PAUL, educator, corp. exec.; b. Rayne, La., Sept. 7, 1930; s. Murphy Joseph and Verl Russia (Butler) G.; B.S. in Bus. Adminstrn., U. Colo., 1963, M.B.A. in Fin., 1964; Ph.D. in Bus. Adminstrn., U. N.C., Chapel Hill, 1968; m. Margaret Phyllis Lapleau, July 9, 1961; children—Philip Lee, Larre Paul, Sara Margaret. Mgmt. trainee Johns-Manville Corp., Denver, 1951-52; owner, mgr. Green's Hardware and Machinery Co., Inc., Crowley, La., 1952-63; prof. finance, U. Tex. at Arlington, 1967—; chmn. bd., chief exec. officer Teltex Corp. Mem. Am., So., Southwestern fin. assns., Fin. Mgmt. Assn., Am. Inst. Decision Scis., Fin. Execs. Inst., M.B.A. Assn., Beta Gamma Sigma. Methodist (adminstrv. bd.). Home: 4000 Fairway Ct Arlington TX 76013 Office: 602-B Coll Bus Adminstrn U Texas Arlington TX 76019

GREEN, WILLIAM TRIMBLE, credit co. exec.; b. Laurel, Miss., Feb. 6, 1947; s. George Gardiner and Eleanor (Trimble) G.; B.S. in Bus., Centenary Coll. La., 1971; m. Barbara Brown Treat, Dec. 19, 1970; children—L. Trimble, Catherine T. Trainee, Comml. Nat. Bank, Shreveport, La., 1971-74; treas. Central Oil Co., Laurel, 1974-75, Green Lumber Co., 1974—, Miss. Investments, Inc., 1974—, The Gardiner Co., Laurel, 1974—; sec.-treas. Central Credit Corp., Laurel, 1975—. Treas., chmn. crusade Am. Cancer Soc., 1977; advance gifts chmn. United Way, 1979. Mem. Nat. Consumer Fin. Assn., Am. Forestry Assn., Miss. Forestry Assn., Kappa Alpha. Episcopalian. Clubs: Rotary; Univ. (Jackson, Miss.); Princeton (N.Y.C.). Office: PO Box 2097 Laurel MS 39440

GREENAWALT, KENNETH WILLIAM, lawyer; b. Town of Wall Street, Colo., Oct. 9, 1903; s. William Eckert and Cora May (Cornell) G.; pre-law student in arts and scis. Cornell U., LL.B., 1927; m. Martha Frances Sloan, Sept. 3, 1929; children—William Sloan, Robert Kent, Ann Cornell (Mrs. William Beven Abernethy), Kim Chandler. Admitted to N.Y. bar, 1929, U.S. Supreme Ct. bar, various Fed. cts.; practiced in N.Y.C., 1929—; asso. firm Sackett, Chapman, Brown & Cross, 1927-30, Davies, Auerbach & Cornell, 1930-44, mem. firm, 1944-49, and successor firms including Windels, Marx, Davies & Ives, 1949—. Mem. Met. Opera Guild; mem. Gen. Council, Congl. Christian Chs., 1952-58; mem. Edgemont Sch. Dist. Bd. Edn., Scarsdale, N.Y., 1957-62; bd. regents L.I. Coll. Hosp. Recipient Woodford prize Cornell U., 1927, Am. Bar Assn. Gavel award, 1962, George Washington Honor medal Freedoms Found., 1962. Fellow Am. Coll. Trial Lawyers, Soc. for Values in Higher Edn. (dir.); mem. Acad. Polit. Sci., Am. Acad. Polit. and Social Sci., Am. (coms.), N.Y. State (coms.) bar assns., Am. Judicature Soc., Bar Assn. City N.Y. (coms.), Cornell Law Assn., N.Y. State Vet. Med. Soc. (hon.), Vet. Med. Assn. N.Y.C. (hon.), Sigma Delta Chi, Phi Sigma Kappa, Phi Delta Phi, Sphinx Head (Cornell). Independent Democrat. Congregationalist (trustee). Clubs: Cornell of N.Y.C. and Westchester County; Westchester County Tennis (past pres.); Fox Meadow Tennis (Scarsdale, N.Y.); Harbor View (N.Y.C.). Contbr. to legal publs.; guest participant radio and TV programs. Home: 65 Highridge Rd Hartsdale NY 10530 Office: Windels Marx Davies & Ives 51 W 51st New York NY 10019

GREENBAUM, JOSEPH, mcht., furniture mfg. co. exec.; b. Paterson, N.J., Apr. 5, 1929; s. Maurice Nathaniel and Rose Greenbaum; B.S. in Bus. Adminstrn., N.Y. U., 1951, postgrad., 1951-53; student ecns. Oxford (Eng.) U., summer 1950; m. Ellen Lou Krasner, June 18, 1961; children—Susan L., David Marc. Asst. mgr. Main Furniture Co., Paterson, 1947-51; with prodn. control dept. Curtis Wright Co., 1951-52; co-owner, pres., mgr. Greenbaum Bros., Paterson, 1952—; co-owner Greenbaum Interior Design Center, Paterson, 1952—; sec., treas. Country Mile House Inc., Morristown, N.J., 1975—. Trustee North Jersey Jewish Fedn., 1975-77; bd. dirs. Downtown Mall. Served with inf. U.S. Army, 1946-47. Recipient award Jewish Fedn. North Jersey, 1978, N.J. chpt. Am. Soc. Interior Design, 1979. Mem. Nat. Retail Furniture Assn., N.Y. U. Alumni Assn., Daus. of Miriam, Paterson C. of C. (trustee retail div.). Home: 134 Heller Way Upper Montclair NJ 07043 Office: 101-109 Washington St Paterson NJ 07505

GREENBERG, FRANK BRUCE, real estate exec.; b. Port Chester, N.Y., Apr. 30, 1947; s. Samuel and Sylvia (Levy) G.; B.S., N.Y. U., 1974; m. Sherrill Anne Hammond, Sept. 29, 1975; child—Rachel Marie. Salesman, J. Rodman Realty Co., N.Y.C., 1974-76; owner, operator N. Heights Gallery, Bklyn. Heights, 1976-77; property mgr. Middagh St. Assocs., Bklyn. Heights, 1976-77; property mgmt. exec. N. Heights Real Estate & Mgmt. Co., Ltd., Bklyn. Heights, 1977—. Pres., Somerset Art Assn., Bernardsville, N.J., 1978; chmn. public relations Rutherford (N.J.) Mus., 1979—. Mem. N. Hts. Merchants Assn. (treas. 1977), Bklyn. Arts and Cultural Assn., Mu Gamma Tau. Club: N.Y. U. Club. Creator, producer community art, talent shows, fund raising events; contbr. research paper on NYC Taxicab Industry, 1974. Home: 612 Ridge Rd North Arlington NJ 07032 Office: 50 Hicks St Brooklyn Hts NY 11201

GREENBERG, FRANK S., textile co. exec.; b. 1929; Ph.B., U. Chgo., 1949; married. Asst. to pres. Charm Tred Mills, 1949, v.p., 1953, pres., 1953-59; v.p. Charm Tred Mills div. Burlington Industries, Inc., 1959-61, pres. Charm Tred Mills div., 1961-62, pres. Monticello Carpet Mill div., 1962-70, group v.p., mem. mgmt. com. parent co., Greensboro, N.C., 1970-72, exec. v.p., 1972-78, pres., 1978—, also chief operating officer. Served with AUS, 1951-53. Office: Burlington Industries Inc 3330 W Friendly Ave Greensboro NC 27410*

GREENBERG, MAURICE RAYMOND, ins. co. exec.; b. N.Y.C., May 4, 1925; s. Jacob and Ada (Rheingold) G.; pre-law certificate U. Miami (Fla.), 1948; LL.B., N.Y. Law Sch., 1950; m. Corinne Phyllis Zuckerman, Nov. 12, 1950; children—Jeffrey W., Evan G., Lawrence S., Cathleen J. Admitted to N.Y. bar, 1951; with Continental Casualty Co., 1952-60; v.p. C.V. Starr & Co., Inc., 1961-66, exec. v.p., 1966-68, pres., dir. 1968—; pres., dir. Am. Internat. Group, 1967—, also chief exec. officer; chmn., dir. Transatlantic Reins. Co., N.Am. Mgrs., Inc., Bank of N.Y. Trustee, N.Y. Law Sch., N.Y. U., N.Y. Hosp. Served to capt. AUS, World War II, Korea. Decorated Bronze Star. Mem. Council Fgn. Relations, N.Y. Bar Assn., Adv. Com. Trade Negotiations, Fgn. Policy Assn., Sigma Alpha Mu. Clubs: Georgetown; City Athletic, Sky (N.Y.C.); India House. Home: 1001 Park Ave New York NY 10028 Office: 70 Pine St New York NY 10005

GREENBERG, PAUL, pub. co. exec.; b. Indpls., Aug. 4, 1921; s. Louis and Ida (Schwartz) G.; B.S. in Chem. Engring., Purdue U., 1949; m. Janet R. Sussman, May 5, 1957; children—Beth, Amy. Research and devel. engr. Reilly Tar & Chem. Co., Indpls., 1949-51; with RCA, 1951-75, dir. quality assurance record div., 1957-59, gen. plant mgr., 1970-73, ops. mgr., 1973-75; corp. dir. quality Revlon, Inc., N.Y.C., 1959-60; group dir. ops. ITT Pub. Co., Indpls., 1976—.

Served to 1st lt. USAAF, 1942-46. Home: 211 Pine Dr Indianapolis IN 46260 Office: 4300 W 62d St Indianapolis IN 46268

GREENE, ALAN STEVEN, printing co. exec.; b. N.Y.C., Mar. 6, 1930; s. Herman L. and Jean O. (Davis) G.; B.S., N.Y.U., 1957, M.B.A., 1960; m. Joyce Rosenthal, June 13, 1965; children—Sanford, Roger, David. Prodn. man L.W. Froelich & Co. Inc., N.Y.C., 1949-51, 54; account exec. Doyle/Dane/Bernbach, N.Y.C., 1954-57; advt. prodn. mgr. Geigy Pharms., N.Y.C., 1957-62; salesman Printing Corp. Am., N.Y.C., 1963-66; founder, pres. Grenex Inc., N.Y.C., 1967-68; with Froelich/Greene Litho Corp., N.Y.C., 1969—, pres., 1973—. Chmn., Bd. of Adjustment of North Caldwell (N.J.), 1973; mem. Planning Bd. of North Caldwell. Served as officer U.S. Army, 1951-54. Mem. Printing Industries Met. N.Y., Met. Lithographers Assn. Republican. Club: Greenbrook Country. Home: 253 Park Ave North Caldwell NJ 07006 Office: Froelich/Greene Litho Corp 250 Hudson St New York NY 10013

GREENE, ALVIN, distbn. co. exec.; b. Pitts., Aug. 26, 1932; s. Samuel David and Yetta (Kroff) G.; B.A., Stanford U., 1954, M.B.A., 1959; m. M. Louise Sokol, Nov. 11, 1977; children—Aaron, Sharon, Ami, Ann, Daniel. Asst. to pres. Narmco Industries, Inc., San Diego, 1959-62; adminstrv. mgr., mgr. mktg. Whittaker Corp., Los Angeles, 1962-67; sr. v.p. Cordura Corp., Los Angeles, 1967-75; chmn. bd. Sharon-Sage, Inc., Los Angeles, 1975-79; exec. v.p., chief operating officer Republic Distbrs., Inc., Carson, Calif., 1979-81, also dir.; dir. Sharon-Sage, Inc., True Data Corp.; vis. prof. Am. Grad. Sch. Bus., Phoenix, 1977—. Served to 1st lt., U.S. Army, 1955-57. Mem. Direct Mail Assn., Safety Helmet Mfrs. Assn. Office: 1640 5th St Suite 214 Santa Monica CA 90401

GREENE, ANTHONY STORM, constrn. equipment mfg. co. exec.; b. Aurora, Ill., Apr. 28, 1925; s. William Bertram and Eva Jane (Smith) G.; B.S. in Mech. Engring., UCLA, 1948; m. Barbara Jane Anderson, Aug. 31, 1946; children—Christopher, Kimberly. With Barber-Greene Co., Aurora, 1948—, v.p. internat. ops., 1963-69, dir., 1966—, exec. v.p., 1969-71, pres., 1971—, chief exec. officer, chmn. bd., 1976—; sec. Barber-Greene Can., Toronto, Ont., 1956-63, pres., 1956-63; dir. Growth Industry Shares, Inc., Belden Corp. Active Boy Scouts Am. Served with USMC, 1942-46. Mem. Constrn. Industry Mfrs. Assn., Internat. Road Fedn. (dir.), Ill. C. of C. (dir.), Valley Indsl. Assn. (dir.), Aurora C. of C. Republican. Congregationalist. Clubs: Union League, Aurora Country, Rotary. Home: 17 Buckingham Dr Prestbury Aurora IL 60504 Office: 400 N Highland Ave Aurora IL 60507

GREENE, BARRY STEVEN, lawyer, leisure co. exec.; b. N.Y.C., Mar. 22, 1946; s. George and Pearl G.; B.S., U. Pa., 1967; J.D., Columbia U., 1970; m. Carolyn Rose, Sept. 24, 1972; children—Jordin Sara, Brian Robert. Admitted to N.Y. State bar, 1971, Fla. bar, 1978; asso. firm White & Case, N.Y.C., 1970-77; v.p., gen. counsel, sec. Chris-Craft Industries, Inc., N.Y.C., 1977—. Mem. Fla. Bar Assn. Club: Woodmont Country (Tamarac, Fla.). Office: 555 SW 12th Ave Pompano Beach FL 33060

GREENE, CLYDE CORNELIUS, JR., physician, corporate med. dir.; b. Charlotte, N.C., June 14, 1917; s. Clyde Cornelius and Ellen (White) G.; B.S., Wake Forest Coll., 1937; M.D., Jefferson Med. Coll., 1941; m. Jean H. Eisenhower, Dec. 30, 1972; children—Nancy Ellen Greene Thomas, Ralph Chapman Greene, Clyde Cornelius Greene, III, Anne Eisenhower, Lyn Eisenhower. Intern, Jefferson Hosp., Phila., 1942; asst. resident in medicine Stanford U. Hosp., San Francisco, 1946-47; practice medicine specializing in internal medicine, San Francisco, 1947-75; examining physician Pacific Telephone Co., San Francisco, 1947-48, asst. med. officer, 1948-57, gen. med. dir., personnel, 1957-75, corporate med. dir., personnel, 1975—; mem. staff Pacific Med. Center; former cons. pharmacy related programs Spl. Research and Devel. Projects Div., HEW. Trustee, former v.p. bd. dirs. San Francisco Hearing and Speech Center; former trustee Calif. Coll. Podiatric Medicine; elder Calvary Presbyn. Ch., San Francisco, 1975—. Served to maj M.C., U.S. Army, 1942-46. Recipient Distinguished Alumni award Wake Forest U., 1971. Fellow A.C.P., Am. Occupational Med Assn.; mem. Am. Soc. Internal Medicine (historian, former pres.), AMA, Calif. Med. Assn., San Francisco Med. Soc., Calif. (former officer), San Francisco (former trustee) socs. internal medicine, Am. Acad. Occupational Medicine, Calif. Acad. Medicine, Jefferson Med. Coll. Alumni Assn. (v.p. Calif.), Alpha Omega Alpha, Phi Chi, Kappa Alpha. Republican. Presbyterian. Home: 2757 Green St San Francisco CA 94123 Office: 140 New Montgomery St Room 816 San Francisco CA 94105

GREENE, EDWARD FRANKLIN, retail co. exec.; b. Davidson County, N.C., Oct. 13, 1929; s. Stokes Whitehead and Leona Elizabeth (Koontz) G.; A.B. in Biology, Catawba Coll., 1951; m. Sara Frances Curlee, Aug. 7, 1954; children—Richard Edward, Stephen Brian, Katharine Ann. With Lowe's Cos., Inc., North Wilkesboro, N.C., 1954—, mgr. Lowe's of Sparta, Inc. (N.C.), 1956-57, other br. managerial positions, 1957-66, mgr. mktg. control, 1966-68, mktg. mgr., plumbing heating, 1968-72, v.p. mktg., 1972-76, sr. v.p. mgmt. devel., 1976—, chmn. Lowe's Bus. Mgmt. Group, 1976—. Served with AUS, 1951-53. Republican. Methodist. Home: Box 67 Rte 4 Wilkesboro NC 28697 Office: Box 1111 PO North Wilkesboro NC 28659

GREENE, HENRY VINCENT, III, mfg. co. exec.; b. Newton, Mass., Aug. 9, 1946; s. Henry Vincent and May (Hewitt) G., Jr.; B.S. in Acctg., Utica Coll., 1969; M.B.A., Western Caroline U., 1979; m. Madeleine A. Rudy, Sept. 27, 1969. Staff auditor Coopers & Lybrand, N.Y.C., 1971-75; internal auditor Talley Industries, Mesa, Ariz., 1975-76, controller Stencel Aero Engring. Corp. subs., Arden, N.C., 1976-79, gen. mgr., 1979—. Served as pilot USN, 1969-71. Mem. Nat. Assn. Accts. (treas.). Republican. Roman Catholic. Home: 312 Vanderbilt Rd Asheville NC 28803 Office: PO Box 1107 Arden NC 28704

GREENE, HERBERT BRUCE, lawyer; b. N.Y.C., Apr. 13, 1934; s. Joseph Lester and Shirley (Kasen) G.; A.B., Harvard U., 1955; J.D., Columbia U., 1958; m. Judith Jean Metricks, Dec. 31, 1958; children—Pamela S., Scott L. Admitted to N.Y. bar, 1959, Conn. bar, 1975; asst. U.S. atty. So. dist. N.Y., N.Y.C., 1958-61; asso. firm Kaye, Scholar, Fierman, Hays & Handler, N.Y.C., 1961-66; asst. to gen. counsel CIT Fin. Corp., N.Y.C., 1966-67; group gen. counsel Xerox Corp., Rochester, N.Y., 1967-75, v.p. adminstrn. Xerox Edn. Group, Stamford, Conn., 1967-69, sr. v.p., 1970-75; v.p., sec., gen. counsel, Lone Star Industries, Inc., Greenwich, Conn., 1976-79, sr. v.p. and asst. to chmn., 1979—; dir. Lone Star Fla., Inc., Lone Star Hawaii, Inc., Lone Star Properties, Inc., Portland Cement Co. of Utah, Kaelepulu Co., Inc., KCOR Corp., Cement Fin. Corp. Mem. Am., N.Y. State bar assns., Conn. Bar Assn., Bar Assn. City of N.Y., Assn. Asst. U.S. Attys for So. Dist. N.Y., Am. Mgmt. Assn. Republican. Home: 44 N Bulkley Ave Westport CT 06880 Office: 1 Greenwich Plaza Greenwich CT 06830

GREENE, HOWARD PAUL, communications exec.; b. N.Y.C., Mar. 18, 1931; s. Jack and Esther (Platt) Greenberg; B.B.A. cum laude, CCNY, 1952; m. Lorna Patrox, Aug. 10, 1952; children—Marc David, Jeffrey Glenn. Publicity dir. Popular Library, Inc., N.Y.C., 1956-58; promotion dir. Macfadden Publs., N.Y.C., 1958; v.p. Barkas and Shalit Pub. Relations, N.Y.C., 1958-65; pres. Medivox Prodns., N.Y.C., 1965-67; pres. Greene Inc. Communications, N.Y.C., 1965—; exec. v.p., partner, Infocom Broadcast Services Inc., N.Y.C., 1976—. Vol. Cerebral Palsy of Nassau County campaigns, 1963, 64, local Dem. polit. campaigns, 1976, 77; active Broadcast Service to Youth, Boy Scouts Am. Served to lt. (j.g.) USNR, 1952-56. Recipient Stroock prize Alumni Varsity Boxing award CCNY, 1952; Mass Media award NCCJ, 1978. Mem. Public Relations Soc. Am. Jewish. Producer first nat. syndicated stereo radio program The Best of the Month, 1966, Margaret Truman nat. syndicated radio series, 1966-73, Dr. Norman Vincent Peale on The American Character, nat. syndicated radio series, 1978—. Home: 272 Heather Ln Hewlett Harbor NY 11557 Office: 71 Park Ave New York NY 10016

GREENE, LEHMAN OTHO, aluminum co. exec.; b. Savannah, Ga., Nov. 15, 1924; s. Jeff Otho and Lenora (Glover) G.; B.S., Wake Forest Coll., 1948; postgrad. U. Richmond, 1951-52; m. Ann McCollum, Nov. 24, 1948; children—Ann Robin, Lehman Otho. Pub. accountant Baker, Brydon, Rennolds and Whitt, Richmond, Va., 1951-54; exec. v.p., gen. mgr. Lock Vent, Inc., Richmond, 1954-55; gen. mgr. Orma Corp., Beltsville, Md., 1955-58, Alumaroll, Inc., Rutherford, N.J., 1958-61; exec. v.p., gen. mgr. Security Aluminum Co., Detroit, 1961-67, dir. 1963-67; gen. mgr. constrn. materials div. Phelps Dodge Aluminum Corp., Jackson, Miss., 1967-68; gen. mgr. bldg. systems div. Phelps Dodge Industries, Yonkers, N.Y., 1969-73; sales dir.-indsl. Phelps Dodge Brass Co., Dayton, N.J., 1974-75; v.p., gen. mgr. Lord & Burnham div. Burnham Corp., Irvington, N.J., 1975-79. Served with USNR, 1943-45. Mem. Nat. Assn. Bldg. Mfrs. (dir.), Industrialized Bldg. Congress (adv. com.). Baptist. Mason (32 deg., Shriner). Home: 158 Locust Rd Briarcliff Manor NY 10510 Office: Burnham Corp Irvington NY 10533

GREENE, LEWIS FRANKLIN, fin. exec.; b. Portland, Oreg., Jan. 28, 1936; s. William Clark and Perla (Dobberstein) G.; student Falls Bus. Coll., 1956-59; m. Mary Sue Biggs, Aug. 13, 1955; children—Debra, Donna, Vickey, Jeff, Dana. Terminal mgr. Tenn-Caro Transp., Cookeville, Tenn., 1963-66; claim and safety dir. White Motor Express, Nashville, 1966-69; pres., owner Owensboro (Ky.) Express, 1969-78; fin. broker Transco Fin. Services, Owensboro, 1979—. Served with paratroopers U.S. Army, 1953-56. Mem. Am. Trucking Assn., Ky. Motor Transp. Assn. Democrat. Lutheran. Club: Owensboro Transp. Home: 4031 Greenfield Ln Owensboro KY 42301 Office: Swiss Plaza Center Owensboro KY 42301

GREENE, MARK FRANK, accountant, investment syndicator; b. Bklyn., Apr. 1, 1925; s. Samuel and Kate (Frank) Greenberg; A.B., Bklyn. Coll., 1948. M.B.A., CUNY, 1950; m. Estelle Levy, Feb. 1, 1948; children—Robert, Randi, Joanne. Partner, Klempner & Greene, acctg., N.Y.C., 1952-76; pres. M.F. Greene & Co., P.C., N.Y.C., 1976—; dir. Ewen-Parker X-Ray Corp., Indsl. Gasket Corp. Served with AUS, 1943-46. Decorated Bronze Star, Purple Heart, Combat Inf. badge. Clubs: Muttontown, Yale, Masons. Author: Purple Testament, 1947. Office: 6 E 45th St New York NY 10017

GREENE, PHILIP ELLIS NATHANIEL, III, subscription agy. exec.; b. N.Y.C., Dec. 7, 1943; s. Philip Ellis Nathaniel and Barbara (Baker) G.; B.A., Rutgers U., 1966; m. Audrey Nadeau, Oct. 5, 1964; children—Kimberly, Jonathan, Chandler. Sales rep. Allegheny Ludlum Corp., 1966-68; wage and salary analyst Charles Pfizer Co., 1968-69; v.p. Turner Subscription Agy., N.Y.C., 1969-71; regional sales mgr. Universal Periodical Service, Ann Arbor, Mich., 1973-74; gen. mgr. EBSCO Subscription Service, Red Bank, N.J., 1974—; v.p. EBSCO Industries, 1981—; lectr. Rumson Community Edn. Program, 1978-79; guest lectr. library sci. Mem. Rumson (N.J.) Bd. Edn., 1973—, chmn. negotiating and policy coms., 1978-79, pres., 1979—. Mem. ALA, Spl. Library Assn., Med. Library Assn., N.J. Library Assn. Republican. Episcopalian. Club: Sea Bright Anglers (pres. 1970-73). Home: Nicol Terr Rumson NJ 07760 Office: EBSCO Bldg Red Bank NJ 07701

GREENE, ROBERT LEROY, investment broker; b. Muskegon, Mich., June 29, 1947; s. Raymond Aaron and Alma Marie (Hoekenga) G.; A.S., Muskegon Community Coll., 1970; B.S.E., U. Mich., 1972; M.B.A., Tulane U., 1976; m. Maureen Theresa Clark, Oct. 18, 1980. Indsl. engr., Sealed Power Corp., Muskegon, 1973; estimator, Dresser Industries, Muskegon, 1973-74; market research mgr. Interstate Motor Freight, Grand Rapids, 1976-77; competitive research analyst Union Pacific R.R., Omaha, 1977-78; owner, mgr. Wash on Wheels of Chgo., 1978-79; investment broker Dean Witter Reynolds, Chgo., 1979-80, Oberweis Securities, Aurora, Ill., 1980—. Served with AUS, 1966-69. Mem. U. Mich. Club Chgo., Am. Mktg. Assn., Mensa Assn., Republican. Mem. Reformed Ch. in Am. Home: 138 E Bailey Rd Naperville IL 60565 Office: 841 N Lake St Aurora IL 60506

GREENE, SHELDON, motel-hotel broker; b. Bklyn., June 25, 1933; s. Morris and Jean (Kessler) Greenberg; B.B.A., CCNY, 1954; m. Lila Marilyn Greene, Apr. 2, 1960; (dec.); children—Susan Dana, Joel Mathew. Vice pres. Futterman Corp., N.Y.C., 1956-66; v.p. Elk Realty, Inc., N.Y.C., 1964-66, Keyes Nat. Investors, Miami, Fla., 1968-70; founder, owner Sheldon Greene & Assos., Inc., Miami, 1971—. Served with U.S. Army, 1954. Mem. Nat. Assn. Ind. Fee Appraisers, Motel Brokers Assn. Am., Fla. Motel Brokers (pres.), Miami Beach Bd. Realtors (dir.). Jewish. Club: Elks. Home: 7441 Wayne Ave Miami Beach FL 33141 Office: Sheldon Greene & Assos Inc 1720 79th Street Causeway Miami FL 33141

GREENE, THEODORE RICHARD, internat. freight forwarding co. exec.; b. Germany, May 7, 1921; s. Richard and Erna (Kaufmann) Gruenebaum; student Coll. City N.Y., 1947-48, Pohs Inst. Ins., N.Y.C., 1948-49; m. Erna Wolf, Oct. 24, 1948; children—Janet, Marian. Export traffic mgr. Boehr Shipping Co., Inc., N.Y.C., 1947-52; co-founder, pres. Triangle Forwarding Corp., N.Y.C., 1952, chmn. bd., 1952—; dir. Consol. Forwarders Intermodal Corp., N.Y.C. Vice pres. Temple Emanu-El of Queens Aux., 1964-65; v.p. Brotherhood Habonim, N.Y.C., 1974-76, pres., 1977-79. Served with AUS, 1942-46. Mem. Greater N.Y. Ins. Brokers Assn. Inc., N.Y. Fgn. Freight Forwarders and Brokers Assn. (gov. 1978—). Clubs: Foreign Commerce, World Trade N.Y. Inc. (N.Y.C.). Home: 112-20 72d Dr Apt D21 Forest Hills NY 11375 Office: 11 Broadway St New York NY 10004

GREENE, WILLIAM DONALD, mfg. co. exec.; b. Jersey City, N.J., Nov. 19, 1942; s. Brossy Donnell and Katherine Louise (Stansbury) G.; B.A., Bellarmine Coll., 1965; m. Carole Ann Murphy, Nov. 28, 1964; children—Daniel, Donald, Dennis, Mary Carole. Asst. purchasing agt. Am. Saw and Tool div. Vt. Am. Corp., 1965-69; sr. buyer Am. Air Filter Co., Louisville, 1969-74; purchasing mgr. Kingsford Co. div. Clorox Co., Louisville, 1974—. Mem. Louisville Minority Purchasing Council. Democrat. Roman Catholic. Club: Glendale Optimists (pres.). Home: 2574 Taylorsville Rd Louisville KY 40205 Office: 1700 Commonwealth Bldg Louisville KY 40202

GREENE, WILLIAM HARRIS, finance corp. exec.; b. Boone, N.C., Mar. 28, 1936; s. Thomas Grant and Ruth Ellen (Day) G.; B.A., Lenoir Rhyne Coll., 1958; m. Tonita Lewis; children—Pamela Denise, Mary Elizabeth, Ellen Anita. Mgr., supr. Domestic Loans, Mt. Airy, N.C., 1958-64; supr. Continental Acceptance Corp., Rocky Mountain, N.C., 1964-68, asst. v.p., 1968-70; asst. v.p. TranSouth Fin. Co., Florence, S.C., 1970-75; pres. Greene Fin. Corp., Mt. Airy, 1975—. Pres., Mt. Airy Mchts. Assn., 1980-82; bd. dirs. Mt. Airy C. of C., 1980-81. Mem. N.C. Consumer Fin. Assn. Lutheran. Clubs: Mt. Airy Country (dir. and sec. 1980-81), Shriners (v.p. club), Masons, Elks (treas. 1977-78, 79-80, exalted ruler 1980-81). Home: 1003 Lakeview Dr Mount Airy NC 27030 Office: 115 N Main St Mount Airy NC 27030

GREENFIELD, HELEN MEYERS, publishing co. exec., insp. and test service exec.; b. Albany, N.Y., Aug. 4, 1908; d. Stephen and Catherine (Bronkov) Meyers; grad. Baker's Bus. Sch., 1924; m. Frank L. Greenfield, Apr. 1, 1929; children—Stuart Franklin, Val Shea. Accounts supr. George G. McCaskey Co., N.Y.C., 1924-29; spl. assignments purchasing dept. McCall's Pub. Co., 1929, Fgn. Affairs Publs., Inc., 1929-31; with purchasing dept. Glidden-Buick Corp., 1931-32; interviewer Civil Works Adminstrn., supr. filing and payroll systems Houston St. Project Center, 1933-36; with dept. accounting Reuben H. Donnelley Co., 1936-37; supr. layouts, makeup prins. of semi-monthly publs. Tide Publs., Inc., 1939-41; asst. to purchasing agt., supr. maintenance perpetual inventory Hopeman Bros., 1941-43; with money order div., corr. dept. U.S. Govt., P.O. Dept., N.Y.C., 1943-44; v.p. Frank L. Greenfield Co., Inc., N.Y.C., 1945-59; v.p. All Purpose Chair Corp., 1950-55; pres. VAL Equipment, Inc., 1950-62; v.p. Am. Testing Labs., Inc., 1950-63; supr. personnel, purchases Irving Lampert Co., 1951-52; account assignment coordinator, advt. contracts dept. Newsweek, N.Y.C., 1970-78; owner, operator Princess Helen Antiques, Helen M. Greenfield Realty Corp. active New York Heart Assn.; hostess ann. banquet Mt. Laurel Chapel, 1960—. Named Hon. princess Cherokee Tribe by Chief Rising Sun of Richmond, Va. Club: Order Eastern Star (past matron). Home: 4500 Arthur Kill Rd Staten Island NY 10309

GREENHAUS, ARTHUR MICHAEL, computer software co. ofcl.; b. N.Y.C., Sept. 18, 1950; s. Emanuel and Irma G.; B.S. in Elec. Engring., Columbia U., 1971; M.B.A., St. Johns U., 1974; m. Brenda Garber, Aug. 7, 1977. Data base adminstr. N.Y. Telephone Co., N.Y.C., 1972-78; sr. systems analyst RCA Americom, Piscataway, N.J., 1978-79; tech. mktg. mgr. Info. Builders Inc., N.Y.C., 1979—. Mem. Assn. Computing Machinery, IEEE, Theta Tau, Beta Gamma Sigma. Jewish. Home: 224 Doxey Dr Park Ridge NJ 07656 Office: 254 W 31st St New York NY 10001

GREENHAUS, LAWRENCE ROY, mfg. co. exec.; b. N.Y.C., Dec. 25, 1920; s. Harry V. and Sadie (Diamond) G.; B.S. in Chem. Engring., Carnegie Inst., 1941, M.S., 1942; m. Gwen Davies, Mar. 30, 1947; children—James, Jody, Michael. Head group design Hudrocarbon Research Co., N.Y.C., 1951-60; sales mgr. Luria Engring. Co., N.Y.C., 1951-60; exec. v.p., dir. mktg., dir. Fisher & Porter Co., Warminster, Pa., 1960-64; dir. mktg. Joy Mfg. Co., Michigan City, Ind., 1965-67, v.p., gen. mgr. air power div., 1967-72, group v.p., 1972-74, sr. v.p., 1974-78, exec. v.p., Montgomeryville, Pa., 1978—. Bd. mgrs. Franklin Inst., Phila.; bd. dirs. Franklin Research Corp., Phila. Served to lt. (j.g.) USNR, 1943-46. Home: Windy Hill Farms Dark Hollow Rd Pipersville PA 18947 Office: Joy Mfg Co Montgomeryville PA 18936

GREENHOUSE, DENNIS EDWARD, mortgage banker; b. Wilmington, Del., Jan. 17, 1950; s. Bernard and Sylvia (Chesler) G.; B.A., Fairleigh Dickinson U., 1972; m. Adelaide Elizabeth Donovan, Feb. 2, 1979. Asst. v.p. ops. Home Fed. Savs. & Loan Assn., Wilmington, 1973—; mem. Ednl. Resources, Inc. Mem. Mayor's Subcom. for Urban Lending, Wilmington, 1978-79; Democratic candidate for Del. State Auditor, 1980; bd. dirs. Head Start of New Castle County. Mem. Del. League of Savs. Assn. Democrat. Jewish. Club: Masons (pastmaster). Developer FlexiLoan mortgage plan for Del. Home: 407 S Broad St Middletown DE 19709 Office: 201 W 9th St Wilmington DE 19801

GREENLAW, DAVID SUTTON, photog. co. exec.; b. Norway, Maine, Dec. 16, 1919; s. Norman U. and Bernice H. Greenlaw; B.S., U. Maine, 1951; M.S., M.I.T., 1957; m. Wilma Louise Thomas, Dec. 25, 1941; children—Thomas H., Deborah A., Martha L. With Eastman Kodak Co., Rochester, N.Y., dir. advanced planning, asst. v.p., from 1972, pres. Eastman Tech., Inc., from 1972, v.p. Eastman Kodak Co., 1979—, also v.p. corp. comml. affairs. Mem. Monroe County Planning Council, 1958-70; mem. Town of Mendon (N.Y.) Planning Council, 1958-70; v.p. dir. Rochester Assn. of UN, 1977—. Mem. N.Y. Acad. Scis., Photog. Soc. Am., AAAS, Alpha Chi Sigma, Tau Beta Pi. Republican. Presbyterian. Clubs: U. Rochester Faculty, Tennis. Office: 343 State St Rochester NY 14650

GREENLEAF, RAYMOND ROSS, ins. agy. exec.; b. Boothbay Harbor, Maine, Dec. 23, 1923; s. Lewis Sheldon and Jessie Florence (Boston) G.; student U. Maine, U. Ill., U. Wis., Northeastern U.; B.S. in Bus. Adminstrn., Suffolk U.; m. Patricia Ann Spaulding, May 17, 1952; children—Cynthia Ann, Debra Lee, Robert Sheldon. Driver, Frank L. Sample & Son, Boothbay Harvor, 1941; asst. to dir. tng. Bath Iron Works (Maine), 1941-42; patrolman Boothbay Harbor Police Dept., 1948-53; pres., treas., J. Edward Knight & Co., Boothbay Harbor, 1953—, dir. WIMS Inc.; chmn. eastern adv. bd. Canal Nat. Bank, Portland, Maine. Mem. Boothbay Harbor Water Commn., 1953-55; mem. Maine Ho. of Reps., 1954-57; dir. Lincoln County CD, 1954-57; trustee St. Andrews Hosp., Boothbay Harbor, 1967—, Boothbay Regional YMCA. Served with U.S. Army, 1943-46, USAF, 1951-52. Mem. Nat., Maine ind. ins. agts. assns., Profl. Ins. Agts. Assn., Boothbay Region C. of C. (past pres., dir.). Republican. Methodist. Clubs: Lions (pres. 1973-74), Masons, Shriners, K.P. Home: West Boothbay Harbor ME 04575 Office: 1 Townsend Ave Boothbay Harbor ME 04538

GREENLEE, HOWARD NOBLE, JR., book publisher; b. Vincennes, Ind., Nov. 29, 1935; s. Howard Noble and America (Brown) G.; B.A., DePauw U., Greencastle, Ind., 1958; m. Martha Nelson, May 3, 1979; children—Amy, Charles. With advt. dept. Wall St. Jour., Chgo., 1958, Indpls. Star-News, 1959-60; v.p. Franklin Orgn., Chgo., 1960-62; account exec. E.H. Weiss Advt., Chgo., 1962-65; v.p. Sta. WAOV, Vincennes, Ind., 1965-70; pres. Fun Pub. Co., 1970—; part-time instr. Maricopa County Community Coll. Mem. Screen Actors Guild. Democrat. Conglist. Inventor ednl. toy Learning Talking Machine, 1965. Home: 3520 Creighton Ct Scottsdale AZ 85251

GREENWALD, MARTIN, publishing co. exec.; b. Bronx, N.Y., Apr. 25, 1942; s. David and Jean (Kaufman) G.; A.B., Lafayette Coll., 1963; M.B.A., Columbia U., 1965; m. Beth Susan Fishman, Feb. 7, 1965; children—Karen Sue, Craig Mitchell. Mgr. acquisition planning, financial analyst Macmillan, Inc., N.Y.C., 1965-69; new bus. devel. analyst Holt div. CBS, N.Y.C., 1969-70; bus. mgr. trade div. Macmillan Pub. Co., N.Y.C., 1970-72; v.p., gen. mgr. Hagstrom Co. Inc., N.Y.C., 1972-76; pres. Paddington Press Ltd., N.Y.C., 1976-79; dir. mktg. Facts On File Inc., N.Y.C., 1980—. Vice pres. Green Acres Library Bd., 1976—; mem. Republican County Com., 1973—; v.p. Green Acres Civic Assn., 1976—. Mem. Assn. Am. Pubs. (mktg.

group 1979—). Republican. Jewish. Home: 80 Riverdale Rd Valley Stream NY 11581 Office: 119 W 57 St New York NY 10017

GREENWALD, RUTH ANDERSON, advt. and sales promotion co. exec.; b. Charlotte, N.C., July 24, 1926; d. William Turner and Ruth Thomas (Stanfield) Anderson; student Mary Baldwin Coll., 1944-46, Queens Coll., Charlotte, 1946-47; certificate Famous Artist Sch., Westport, Conn., 1962; B.Profl. Studies, Pace U., 1975; m. Robert Clark Greenwald, Jr., June 14, 1947; children—Robert Clark III, William Anderson, Jeffrey Alan, Kenneth Edward. Artist, John Berryman Studio, Briarcliff, N.Y., 1966-67; asst. art dir. Ednl. Audio Visuals, Inc., Pleasantville, N.Y., 1967-68; freelance artist, 1968-69; sole propr. GRA Assos., Mt. Kisco, N.Y., 1969-72; pres. GRA Concepts Inc., Pleasantville, 1972—; pres. SON-A-Vision Inc., Pleasantville, 1978—; instr. graphic arts Westchester Community Coll., 1976-77. Chmn. communications United Way, Westchester, N.Y., 1975-77, bd. dirs., 1976-78. Mem. Advt. Club Westchester (treas. 1971-73, pres., 1973-74, dir. 1974-75, sec. 1980), Am. Advt. Fedn. (dir. 2d dist. 1973-74, treas. 1976—), Chi Omega. Republican. Episcopalian. Club: Soroptimist Internat. Office: 110 Washington Ave Pleasantville NY 10570

GREENWAY, JACK WILLIAM, real estate broker; b. Norman, Okla., Aug. 28, 1926; s. Will and Artie Lula G.; m. Mary Ellen Kees, Jan. 24, 1947; children—Jack W., Cheryl Ann. Owner, mgr. State Farm Ins. Agy., Bozeman, Mont., 1968-69; sales asso. Mecklenberg Realty, 1969-70; mng. parter Greenway-Heath, Bozeman, 1970-71; owner, mgr. Greenway & Assos., Bozeman, 1971-76; mgr. real estate dept., prin. United Agencies, Bozeman, 1976—, dir.; dir. Downtown Devel. Corp. Served with USMC, 1942-46, U.S. Army, 1950-68. Decorated Purple Heart, Silver Star, Bronze Star, Legion of Merit; named Mont. Realtor of Yr., 1980. Mem. Mont. Assn. Realtors (pres.), Mont. Assn. Real Estate Exchangers, Internat. Real Estate Exchangers, Farm and Land Inst., Inst. Certified Bus. Counselors. Democrat. Clubs: Shriners, Riverside Country, Masons, Elks. Home: 22 Riverside Dr Bozeman MT 59715 Office: 1612 W Main St Bozeman MT 59715

GREENWOOD, DONALD BENSON, real estate co. exec.; b. N.Y.C., Feb. 7, 1937; s. Quentin Edward and Louise (Benson) G.; B.A., Brigham Young U., Provo, Utah, 1961; M.B.A., Northwestern U., 1962; children—Travis, Suzanne, Tamela. Exchange mgr. Pacific Telephone Co., 1963-67; So. Calif. sales mgr. container div. Boise Cascade Corp., Torrance, 1967-71; pres. Greenwood & Co., real estate devel. and leasing, Los Angeles, 1971—. Served with U.S. Army, 1961-62. Mem. Los Angeles C. of C. (dir.). Address: 1888 Century Park East Los Angeles CA 90067

GREENWOOD, IVAN ANDERSON, physicist; b. Cleve., Jan. 31, 1921; s. Ivan A. and Mabel (Harlow) G.; B.S., Case Inst. Tech., 1942; postgrad. Mass. Inst. Tech., N.Y.U., Columbia; m. Jean Elizabeth Siebrecht, June 18, 1949; children—Kyle Ann, Hilary (dec. Oct. 8, 1978). Asst. group leader Radiation Lab., Mass. Inst. Tech., 1942-46; mgr. research dept., asso. dir. research and advanced devel. GPL div. Gen. Precision Systems Inc., 1946-69; research mgr. physics research center Kearfott div. Singer Co., 1969—; cons. on med. research project N.Y.U. Bellevue Med. Center, 1956-60, Albert Einstein Coll. Medicine, Yeshiva U., 1960-64; incorporating dir. Bio-Instrumentation Inst., Inc., 1962—; dir., exec. com. Glen Ellen Corp., 1962-70; partner Bus. Trends Publs., Cleve., 1947-49; dir., exec. com. Syntha Corp., Greenwich, Conn., 1965—. Past mem. bd. dirs. Conn. Ski Council; v.p., incorporator Vt. Recreation Center, Inc., 1971—. Mem. Am. Phys. Soc., Am. Inst. Physics, IEEE, Inst. Nav., Fedn. Am. Scientists, AAAS, Am. Chem. Soc. (asso.), Case Alumni Assn., Tau Beta Pi, Theta Tau, Sigma Alpha Epsilon. Presbyterian. Clubs: River Hills Ski; Cove Island Yacht (exec. com. vice commodore 1979—). Patentee in field. Home: 6 Weed Circle Stamford CT 06902 Office: 1225 McBride Ave Little Falls NJ 07424

GREENWOOD, JOHN ORVILLE, transp. co. exec.; b. Mpls., June 18, 1935; s. Orville Francis John and Florence Agnes Greenwood; B.S. in Bus. and Econs., Valparaiso (Ind.) U., 1957; M.B.A. in Transp., Northwestern U., 1958; m. Jane Ellen Coffman, Feb. 23, 1963; children—Holly Gates. With Cargo Carriers, Inc., 1958-69, mgr. Cleve. office, 1959-69; adminstrv. asst. Pickands Mather & Co., Cleve., 1970-75, asst. to v.p., 1975-80, asst. v.p., 1980—; founder, dir. Freshwater Press, Inc., pubs. Gt. Lakes shipping books and directories, Cleve., 1961—; dir. Tomlinson Fleet Corp., 1963-70. Served with U.S. Army, 1959. Mem. Soc. Naval Architects and Marine Engrs., Marine Hist. Soc. Detroit, Lake Carriers Assn., Gt. Lakes Hist. Soc., Gt. Lakes Maritime Inst., Toronto Marine Hist. Soc., St. Mary's River Marine Soc. Republican. Lutheran. Clubs: Propeller U.S., Cleve. Athletic, Shaker Heights Country. Author: Namesakes of the Lakes, 1970, Namesakes II, 1972, New Namesakes of the Lakes, 1975, Namessakes 1930-1955, 1978; Namesakes of the 80's, 1980; Greenwood's Guide to Great Lakes Shipping, ann. publ., 1959—. Office: 1100 Superior Ave Cleveland OH 44114

GREENWOOD, MORGAN ALLEN, mfg. co. exec.; b. Painesville, Ohio, Dec. 20, 1915; s. Ross Allen and Katherine (Morgan) G.; A.B. in Econs., Hiram Coll., Ohio, 1937; student Cleve. Law Sch., 1938; m. Barbara Harvey, Nov. 28, 1942; children—Pamela Dean, Timothy Morgan. Merchandising mgr. T. A. O'Laughlin & Co., Newark, 1947-48; advt. mgr. comml. laundry and dry cleaning div. Philco Corp., Phila., 1948-59, gen. mgr., 1948-63; v.p. Knox Glass Inc. (Pa.), 1963-68; pres. tech. services div. The Williams Cos., Tulsa, 1968-70; pres., dir. Resource Sciences Corp., Tulsa, 1970-79; sr. v.p., asst. to chmn. U.S. Filter Corp., Tulsa, 1979—; dir. Shaw Pipe Industries, Ltd., Rexdale, Ont., Can., No. Resources, Inc., Billings, Mont., Resource Sciences-Arabia Ltd., Tulsa, Holmes & Narver, Inc., Orange, Calif. Co-founder, dir. Am. Golf Hall of Fame, Foxburg, Pa.; trustee U. Tulsa; mem. exec. com. Indian Nations council Boy Scouts Am. Served to capt. USAAF, 1941-45. Mem. Am. Petroleum Inst., Energy Advocates, Am. Gas Assn. Republican. Episcopalian. Clubs: Tulsa, So. Hills Country (Tulsa). Office: US Filter Corp 6600 S Yale Ave Tulsa OK 74177

GREER, DOROTHY LUCILLE LEECH, business exec.; b. Fort Morgan, Colo., Nov. 5, 1921; d. Laurance Blakely and Lucille Otis (Gill) Leech; student Mills Coll., 1939-40; B.A., San Diego State Coll., 1943; m. Thomas Keister Greer, Jan. 9, 1943; children—Nancy Tallaferro (Mrs. William Nelson Alexander II), Giles Carter, Celeste Claiborne. Tchr., Franklin County Schs., Rocky Mount, Va., 1944-45, 48-49, Roanoke (Va.) City Schs., 1949-51; dir., sec.-treas. Franklin County Times, Inc., Rocky Mount, 1968—; v.p. Greer Investment Corp., 1977—. Mem. central com. Assistance League So. Calif., Los Angeles, 1952-54; mem. patrons com. Internat. Debutante Ball, 1969-71. Mem. D.A.R., Internat. Platform Assn. Christian Scientist. Clubs: Willow Creek Country (sec.-dir. Rocky Mount 1962-64); Roanoke Country; San Diego Yacht. Home: The Grove Rocky Mount VA 24151

GREER, PHILIP, journalist; b. Bklyn., Nov. 10, 1930; s. Jacob and Mary Rose Greenberg; B.A., Bklyn. Coll., 1952; m. Joyce Phyllis Shaffer, Mar. 25, 1956; children—Jonathan Austin, Karen Elise. Copywriter, Kleppner Co., N.Y.C., 1956-58; account exec. Brand, Grumet & Seigel, Inc., N.Y.C., 1958-63; account exec. Shearson, Hammill & Co., N.Y.C., 1963-65; Wall St. reporter N.Y. Herald Tribune, 1965-66; New York fin. corr. Washington Post, 1966-75; fin. commentator Group W Westinghouse Broadcasting Co., 1968-72; bus. editor NBC Radio News, 1975-76; co-author Greer/Kandel Report, N.Y.C., 1976—; fin. corr. ABC News, 1980—. Served with U.S. Army, 1952-54. Recipient G.M. Loeb Column Editorial award, 1971. Mem. Soc. Am. Bus. and Econ. Writers, Soc. Profl. Journalists, N.Y. Fin. Writers Assn. Contbr. to Grolier Ency. Yearbooks, 1967-73, The Anatomy of Wall Street, 1968. Home: 209-80 18th Ave Bayside NY 11360 Office: 1926 Broadway New York NY 10023

GREER, RANDALL DEWEY, fin. analyst; b. Balt., Apr. 29, 1951; s. James Walter and Ruth Virtue (Cooper) G.; B.S. in Psychology, U. Nebr., Lincoln, 1973; M.B.A., U. Fla., 1975; m. Beverly Ann Smeal, May 31, 1974. Research analyst Kirkpatrick, Pettis, Smith, Polian Inc., Omaha, 1975-76, asst. v.p., 1977-78, v.p., dir. research, 1979—. Vice chmn. Nebr. Muscular Dystrophy Telethon Com., 1980. Chartered fin. analyst. Mem. Fin. Analysts Fedn., Omaha-Lincoln Soc. Fin. Analysts. Republican. Presbyterian. Clubs: Plaza, Omaha Country. Home: 9911 Pratt St Omaha NE 68134 Office: 1623 Farnam St Omaha NE 68102

GREER, ROBERT STEPHENSON, ins. exec.; b. Baton Rouge, Apr. 2, 1920; s. Fred and Nannie (Stephenson) G.; B.S., La. State U., 1941; m. Patricia Pettry, Oct. 1, 1944; children—Robert S., John P. With Union Nat. Life Ins. Co., Baton Rouge, 1941—, dist. mgr., 1945-48, v.p., 1948-56, exec. v.p., 1956-70, pres., chief exec. officer, 1970—, also dir.; dir. La. Nat. Bank, Baton Rouge Savs. & Loan Assn., Union Nat. Fire Ins. Co. Pres., Better Bus. Bur., 1962-63; campaign chmn. United Way, 1977, pres., 1981; pres. Council for a Better La., 1981; pres. YMCA, 1958, 62. Served to lt. USN, 1941-45. Mem. Life Insurers Conf. (chmn. 1979-80, exec. com. 1980-81), La. Insurers Conf. (exec. com. 1980-81), Life Underwriters Assn., Kappa Sigma, Beta Gamma Sigma, Baton Rouge C. of C. (pres. 1972-73), La. State U. Alumni Fedn. (pres. 1979-80). Clubs: Rotary (pres. 1975-76), City (past gov.), Baton Rouge Country (pres. 1978). Office: 8282 Goodwood St Baton Rouge LA 70806

GREGG, JOHN NATHAN, fibers corp. exec.; b. Charlotte, N.C., Jan. 11, 1934; s. James Murphy and Nancy Olive (Watkins) G.; B.S., N.C. State Coll., 1955; A.M.P., Harvard U., 1975; m. Nancy Carpenter, July 23, 1955; children—Miriam Ashley, Nancy Elizabeth, John Nathan, Mary Kathryn. Salesman. mgr. So. regional sales Am. Viscose Corp., Charlotte, N.C., 1957-68; mgr. fiber sales ops., fiber div. FMC Corp., Phila., 1968-69, dir. sales, fiber products, 1969-71, div. v.p. mktg., 1971-75; chmn., pres. Avtex Fibers Inc., Valley Forge, Pa., 1976—. Trustee Phila. Coll. of Textiles and Sci.; bd. dirs. N.C. Textile Found., Inc. Served with U.S. Army, 1955-57. Mem. Man-Made Fiber Producers Assn. (dir.). Episcopalian. Clubs: Aronimink Golf (Newtown, Square, Pa.), Harvard (N.Y.C.), Country of N.C., Union League of N.Y.C. Office: 9 Executive Mall Valley Forge PA 19482

GREGG, RONALD SCOTT, pub. co. exec.; b. Denver, Apr. 28, 1944; s. Harry W. and Millicent G. (Glover) G.; B.S. in Acctg. and Finance, San Jose State U., 1966; m. Dorinda Gene Wood, June 7, 1965; children—Jennifer, Michael. Budget dir. IBM, San Jose, Calif., 1967-68; sr. acct. Touche, Ross & Co., San Jose, 1968-71; v.p. fin. and adminstrn. Joseph George Distbr., Santa Clara, Calif., 1971-80; chief fin. officer J.R. Anderson Enterprises, Mountain View, Calif., 1980—. Vice pres. Santa Clara County Taxpayers Assn., 1978; coach Almaden Youth Athletics, 1974-79; bd. dirs. Santa Clara YMCA, 1978. C.P.A., Calif. Mem. Am. Inst. C.P.A.'s, Calif. Soc. C.P.A.'s, Nat. Assn. Accts., Am. Inst. Corp. Controllers. Republican. Club: Almaden Cabana (treas. 1979). Home: 7045 Elmsdale Dr San Jose CA 95120 Office: J R Anderson Enterprises 1400 Stierlin Rd Mountain View CA 94043

GREGG, THEODORE M., JR., coal co. exec.; b. Feb. 28, 1944; B.S. with high distinction in Bus. Adminstrn., Pa. State U., 1970, M.B.A., 1971; 1 son. Acct., auditor Peat, Marwick, Mitchell and Co., Bethlehem, Pa., 1971-73; co-founder, v.p., dir. Macro Enterprises, Inc., Lancaster, Pa., part-time 1969-73, 73-74; asst. controller Westmoreland Coal Co., Phila., 1974-75, corp. controller, 1975—. Served with U.S. Army, 1964-68. C.P.A., Pa. Mem. Am. Inst. C.P.A.'s, Pa. Inst. C.P.A.'s, Beta Alpha Psi, Beta Gamma Sigma, Phi Kappa Phi. Office: 2500 Fidelity Bldg Philadelphia PA 19109

GREGG, WILLIAM KIRKER, railway rolling stock mfr.; b. Hackensack, N.J., July 11, 1921; s. Otis Tiffany and Juliette Belle (Kirker) G.; student Lehigh U., 1941-42, Carnegie Inst. Tech., 1943-44; m. Louis Lydecker, June 28, 1947; children—Susan, Juliette, Janet, Dorothy. Sales engr. Gregg Co. Ltd., N.Y.C., 1945-47; adminstr. Societe Gregg d'Europe, S.A., Lot, Belgium, 1947-55, 69-79; v.p. Gregg Co., Ltd., Hackensack, 1955-63, pres., 1963—, chmn. bd. dirs., 1969—. Bd. dirs. YMCA of Greater Bergen County (N.J.), pres., 1966-68; trustee Hackensack Hosp. Assn., 1963—, v.p., 1974-77. Served with AUS, 1942-45. Decorated Bronze Star. Mem. Ry. Progress Inst., N.Y. R.R. Club, North Jersey C. of C. and Industry. Republican. Episcopalian. Rotarian (pres. Hackensack 1970-71). Clubs: Lawyers (N.Y.C.); American (Brussels, Belgium); Arcola Country. Home: 15 Hollis Dr Ho-Ho-Kus NJ 07423 Office: 15 Dyatt Pl Hackensack NJ 07602

GREGORCYK, WALLIS JAMES, appliance co. exec.; b. Beeville, Tex., Sept. 23, 1937; s. Albert Hubert and Irene Minnie (Mussman) G.; B.B.A., Tex. A&I U., 1960; m. Frances Carol Sralla, Aug. 25, 1958; children—Michael Scott, Vicky Ann, Sharon Gaye. Br. mgr. Gen. Electric Credit Corp., Corpus Christi and Beaumont, Tex., 1961-68; pres., dir. Conn Credit Corp., treas., dir. Conn Appliances, Inc., Beaumont, 1968—. Bd. dirs. Retail Mchts. Assn. Port Arthur, 1978-80. Cert. consumer credit exec. Mem. Internat. Consumer Credit Assn., Credit Mgmt. Assn. Tex., Soc. Cert. Consumer Credit Execs., Credit Mgmt. Assn. Beaumont (pres. 1972). Roman Catholic. Clubs: Business and Profl. Mens, Young Men's Bus. League. Home: 5920 Tangledahl St Beaumont TX 77706 Office: Conn Credit Corp Conn Appliances Inc 195 N 11th St Beaumont TX 77702

GREGORY, ALEXANDER GEORGE, banker; b. State College, Pa., Nov. 11, 1925; s. George John and Catherine G. (Columbus) G.; B.A., Rollins Coll., Wonter Park, Fla., 1951; m. Lilian Stamathioudakis, Aug. 11, 1954; children—George, Natasha, Alexander George. Chmn. bd. Federated Home & Mortgage Co., Inc., State College, 1961—, Nat. Capital Cos., State College, 1976—; pres. Alex Gregory Assos., State Coll., 1955-76; founder-dir. Capital Bank, Miami Beach, Fla. Bd. dirs. Centre County March of Dimes, 1955-60. Served with AUS, 1944-46. Recipient various service awards. Mem. Greek Orthodox Ch. Clubs: Everglades, Bal Harvour, Surf, Palm Bay, La Gorce Country (Miami Beach); Elks. Office: Suite 405 City Nat Bank Bldg 300 71st St Miami Beach FL 33141

GREGORY, ARTHUR CHARLES, JR., heating, air conditioning and ventilation co. ofcl.; b. Chgo., Oct. 12, 1932; s. Arthur Charles and Elizabeth Gertrude (Husch) G.; B.S.C., DePaul U., 1958; m. Doris Ann Sheehan, Sept. 7, 1957; children—Sharon, Thomas, Edward, Colleen, Kathleen. Salesman, Equitable Life Assurance Co., Chgo., 1958; tchr. St. Christopher Sch., Midlothian, Ill., 1959; service mgr., hydronics mgr., salesman Anderson Heating Co., Chgo., 1960-63; salesman Accurate Cooling Corp., Chgo., 1964-68; salesman, sales mgr. Reedy Industries, Chgo., 1968-78; sales mgr. service and indsl. Midwest Trane Corp., Willowbrook, Ill., 1978—. Bd. dirs. Home Improvement Assn., 1966-67, Oak Lawn YMCA, 1969-71; pres. St. Geralds Holy Name Soc., 1970-72, St. Vincent Aux., 1978-79, Oak Lawn Babe Ruth, 1974-75. Served with Signal Corps, U.S. Army, 1953-55. Roman Catholic. Clubs: Builders Tee; Elks (Man of Yr. 1964) (Oak Lawn). Home: 172 Heatherwood Ct Lockport IL 60441 Office: Midwest Trane Corp 540 Executive Dr Willowbrook IL 60521

GREGORY, LOWELL DEAN, aerospace co. exec.; b. Chickasha, Okla., Feb. 19, 1918; s. Simeon Roscoe and Pearl (Robinson) G.; B.A. in English, U. Okla., 1940, M.A. in Math., 1950; Ph.D. in Math. Statistics, So. Meth. U., 1968; m. Marian Gavin, May 27, 1939; children—Gavin George, Lynn. Instr., math. U. Okla., Norman, 1947-51; sr. analyst Chance Vought Aircraft, Dallas, 1951-55, devel. project engr., 1955-57, supr. advanced weapon systems analysis, 1957-59, chief reliability astro. div., 1959-62; mgr. reliability engring. astro. div. Ling-Temco-Vought Dallas, 1962-64, supr. operations analysis, 1964—. Served to 1st lt. F.A., AUS, 1940-42, to capt. USAAF, 1942-45. Ling-Temco-Vought Doctoral fellow So. Meth. U., 1966. Mem. Aerospace Industries Assn. (mem. reliability com. 1964—), Am. Astronautical Soc. (sec. SW. chpt. 1964, sr. mem.), Operations Research Soc. Am., N. Tex. Operations Research Soc. (dir.), Phi Mu Epsilon. Home: 1300 W 2d St Arlington TX 76013 Office: PO Box 225907 Dallas TX 75222

GREGORY, VINCENT LEWIS, JR., chem. co. exec.; b. Oil City, Pa., June 10, 1923; s. Vincent Louis and Celia Viola (Whitling) G.; B.A., Princeton U., 1949; M.B.A., Harvard U., 1949; m. Marjorie Gladys Scott, Feb. 16, 1946; 1 son, Vincent Louis. Fin. asst., asst. plant controller Rohm & Haas Co., Phila., 1949-52; fin. mgr. Minoc S.A.R.L., Paris, 1952-55; asst. to mng. dir. Lennig Chems., Ltd., 1955, asst. mng. dir., 1956-58, mng. dir., 1958-64, chmn., 1964-68, dir. European ops., London, 1964-68, asst. gen. mgr. fgn. ops., Phila., 1968-70, pres., chief exec. officer, 1970-78, chmn., chief exec. officer, 1978—; dir. H.B.S. Assos., Mead Corp., Rohm and Haas Can., Indofil Chems. Ltd., Modipon Ltd. Served with USAAF, 1942-46. Mem. Inst. Dirs. (London), Soc. Chem. Industry (chmn.), Phi Beta Kappa. Clubs: Harvard, Princeton (Phila.). Home: 321 S 3d St Philadelphia PA 19106 Office: Independence Mall W Philadelphia PA 19105

GREIDER, BOB, oil co. exec.; b. Wichita, Kans., July 8, 1918; s. Melvin Chester and Bonnie Willis (Chunn) G.; student U. Wichita, 1936-39; Degree in Geol. Engring., Colo. Sch. Mines, 1943; m. Mary P. Stinius Aug. 7, 1943; children—Bob, Bradley William. Geologist, geophysicist Calif. Co., 1946-53, dist. geologist, Midcontinent and Gulf Coast Regions, 1953-56; supt. exploration div., 1956-58; supt. exploration div. Chevron Oil Co., Denver, 1958-67, supt. exptl. div., Jackson, Miss., 1967-69, asst. mgr. minerals, San Francisco, Denver, 1974—; v.p. Chevron Greece, 1973—; supt. exptl. div. Standard Oil Tex., Oklahoma City, 1969, geol. cons. Standard Oil Calif., San Francisco, 1969-74; exec. v.p., dir. Intercontinental Energy Corp., 1977-79; pres. Geothermal Resources Internat., 1979—; pres. Geothermal Resources Council and U.S. Organizing Com., Inc.; cons. NSF, Dept. of Energy, U. Calif. Lawrence Berkely Labs.; mem. exec. com. UN 2nd Internat. Geothermal Symposium; U.S. del. to Internat. Atomic Energy Agency Internat. Symposium, 1974, 76; conf. leader 1st China-U.S. geothermal conf., Tianjin, China, 1981; mem., NSF grantee, USAF Advanced Research Projects; cons. U.S. Energy Resources Devel. Adminstrn. Certified profl. engr., Colo., Miss.; registered geologist, Calif. Republican. Episcopalian. Contbr. articles to profl. jours. and books. Home: 7875 S Wabash Ct Englewood CO 80112

GREIF, J. H., fin. exec.; b. Leipzig, Germany, May 1, 1934; s. Georg Roan and Magdalena (Wahrendorff) G.; student Free U., Berlin, Germany, 1953, Northwestern U., 1953-54; M.B.A., U. Chgo., 1956, postgrad., 1956-58. Came to U.S., 1953, naturalized, 1963. Instr. econs. U. Chgo. Grad. Sch. Bus., 1957-58; financial analyst treas.'s dept. Standard Oil Co. (N.J.), N.Y.C., 1958-60, head portfolio mgmt. sect., 1961-62, mgr. Far East sect. treas.'s dept. Esso Internat. Inc., N.Y.C., 1963-65, head market planning sect., marine sales dept., 1965-67, mgr. Europe/Africa div., treas.'s dept., 1967-69, asst. treas., 1969-71; risk mgr. Exxon Corp., N.Y.C., 1971-73; v.p. finance Exxon Nuclear, Bellevue, Wash., 1973-77; chief exec. The Griffin Group, Seattle and Honolulu, 1977—. Served with AUS, 1959-60, 61-62. Ford Found. fellow, 1957-58. Mem. Am. Econ. Assn., Am. Finance Assn., Fin. Execs. Inst. Home: 4714 E Mercer Way Mercer Island WA 98040 Office: Professional Center Bldg Mercer Island WA 90840

GRENARD, JACK, publisher; b. Springfield, Ill., July 15, 1933; s. Edward Merrill and Jane (Ashmore) G.; B.S. with high honors in Journalism, Mich. State U., 1955; m. Andrea Saxer, Dec. 21, 1977; children—Mark Edward, Elizabeth Ann. Free-lance writer, 1958-59; writer James P. Chapman, public relations co., Detroit, 1959-60; asst. editor Shamie Publs., Detroit, 1960-61; pub. Detroit Publ. Cons.'s, St. Clair Shores, Mich., 1959—, Worldwide Yacht Charter Guide, 1970—. Served with USN, 1956-58. Mem. Soc. Publ. Designers, Am. Soc. Bus. Press Editors, Engring. Soc. Detroit. Club: Detroit Yacht. Editor Detroit Engr. mag., 1971—; contbr. numerous articles to boating publs. Office: 25875 Jefferson St Saint Clair Shores MI 48081

GRENELL, JAMES HENRY, mfg. co. exec.; b. Mpls., Feb. 19, 1924; s. Harrison Morton and Harriet Elizabeth (Kuch) G.; B.B.A., U. Minn., 1947; grad. Advanced Mgmt. Program, Harvard, 1974; m. Naomi Betty Callerstrom, Sept. 15, 1945; children—Bonita Grenell Wolfe, Suzanne Naomi, Andrea Grenell Mendes. With Honeywell, Inc., Mpls., 1951—, accountant, 1951-56, div. controller, 1956-58, group controller, 1968-71, asst. corporate controller, 1971-74, v.p., controller, 1974—; mem. faculty Inst. Mgmt., U. Wis., 1960-69, Inst. Tech., U. Minn., Mpls., 1963-65; asso. dir. Mgmt. Center, Coll. St. Thomas, St. Paul, 1959-69. Bd. dirs. Mpls. Soc. for Blind, 1963-71, pres., 1970-71. Served to 1st lt. AUS, 1943-46; ETO. Mem. Fin. Execs. Inst., U. Minn. Coll. Bus. Adminstrn. Alumni Bd. (dir.), Alpha Kappa Psi. Republican. Congregationalist. Clubs: Harvard (Minn.); Edina (Minn.) Country. Contbr. articles to profl. jours. Home: 6200 Wyman Ave Edina MN 55436 Office: Honeywell Plaza Minneapolis MN 55408

GRESHAM, BATEY MOORE, JR., architect; b. Lebanon, Tenn., Apr. 5, 1934; s. Batey Moore and Elisabeth (Doak) G.; B.Arch., Auburn U., 1957; m. Edna Ann Weaver, Nov. 6, 1967. With U.S. Army Corps Engrs., 1957-59, 61-62; designer, draftsman Clemmons & Gingles, Nashville, 1959-65, Sam H. McLean, architect, Nashville, 1965-66; partner McLean & Gresham, Nashville, 1966; self-employed as architect, Nashville, 1967; partner Gresham & Smith, Nashville, 1967—; chmn. bd. Gresham & Smith Internat. Corp.; dir. Plusmedia, Inc.; partner Cumberland Office Bldg., Rivergate Towers, Bon-Ann Co., Highland Devel., Hart St. Devel., 3310 West End Partnership. Bd. dirs. Castle Heights Found.; trustee Cumberland Coll. Recipient Castle Heights Mil. Acad. Outstanding Alumnus award. Mem. A.I.A., Nashville C. of C. (bd. govs.), Young Pres.'s Orgn., Auburn Alumni Assn., U.S. Tennis Assn., Blue Key, Scarab, Kappa Sigma. Clubs: Nashville Racquet, Nashville City. Home: 330 Lynwood Blvd Nashville TN 37205 Office: 3310 West End Ave Nashville TN 37203

GRESOV, BORIS (VLADIMIR), economist; b. St. Petersburg, Russia, Aug. 7, 1914; s. Paul Vladimir and Maria de Suzor G.; B.A. with honours, Cambridge (Eng.) U., 1938, M.A. with honours, 1952; m. Letitia Coxen Graham, June 21, 1945; children—Winston Graham, Christopher Leo. With office Economic Warfare, Unit of War Prodn. Bd.; prodn. mgr. Compania Nacional Minera de Taxco S.A., Mex., 1941-45; v.p. Industrias y Minas S.A., Mex., 1945-49; cons. economist Shields & Co., N.Y.C., 1949-52, G.H. Walker & Co., N.Y.C., 1952-58, E.W. Axe & Co., N.Y.C., 1957-61; dir., mem. exec. com. Western Devel. Co. Del., Santa Fe, 1954-61; mem. adv. bd. Axe Sci. & Electronic Corp., N.Y.C., 1957-61; dir., chmn. bd., chief exec. officer Shattuck Denn Mining Corp., N.Y.C., 1958-60, dir., chmn. exec. com., 1962; founder, pres. Excelsior Fund, Inc., 1963—; chmn. Standard Metals Corp., 1963—, pres., chief exec. officer, 1965—; dir. Flying Tiger Line, Inc., Burbank, Calif., 1957-65, Axe-Templeton Growth Fund of Can., Ltd., N.Y.C., 1958-61, Internat. Oil & Gas Corp., Denver, 1961-66. USLIFE Income Fund Inc., N.Y.C. 1976—. Mem. Confrerie de la Chaine des Rotisseurs (chevalier), N.Y. Soc. Security Analysts, N.Y. Assn. Bus. Economists, AIM (pres.'s council), Union Soc. (Cambridge, Eng.). Roman Catholic. Clubs: Univ., Econ., Met., Met. Opera (N.Y.C.); Nat. Economists (Washington); Westhampton Country (Westhampton Beach, N.Y.); L.I. Country (Eastport, N.Y.); Surf (Quoque, L.I.); La Coquille (Palm Beach, Fla.); Le Mirador Country (Lake Geneva, Switzerland). Home: 900 Fifth Ave New York NY 10021 Office: Olympic Tower 645 Fifth Ave New York NY 10022

GREY, JOHN ROBERT, oil co. exec.; b. Burbank, Calif., 1922; A.B. in Chem. Engineering, Stanford U., 1943; married. Engr., Standard Oil Co. Calif., El Segundo, 1944-57, chief engr., 1965-66, corp. v.p., 1969-74, pres., dir., 1974—; mgr. Salt Lake Refining Co. subs. Standard Oil Co. Calif., 1957-61, chief engr., 1965-66, corp. v.p., San Francisco, 1969-74, pres., 1974—, also dir.; v.p. mfg. Standard-Western Ops., Inc., 1966-69; v.p. western div. Chevron Oil Co., Salt Lake Pipe Line Co., 1961-65; dir. Bank Am. Mem. Am. Petroleum Inst. (dir.). Office: Standard Oil Co Calif 225 Bush St San Francisco CA 94104*

GREY, WILLIAM LEON, lawyer; b. Bklyn., Mar. 24, 1916; s. Joseph Charles and Theresa Charlotte (Olsen) G.; B.S. in Mech. Engring., N.Y. U., 1937; J.D., Bklyn. Law Sch., 1950; grad. Advanced Mgmt. Program, Harvard U., 1957; m. Marguerite Felicia Kefer, Aug. 31, 1940; children—Richard William, Carol Lynne. Admitted to N.Y. bar, 1951; with Anaconda Wire & Cable Co., Hastings-on-Hudson, N.Y. and N.Y.C., 1939-72, pres., chief exec. officer, 1966-72; v.p. Boyden Assos., N.Y.C., 1973; mng. partner Pennie & Edmonds, N.Y.C., 1974—; dir. Handy & Harman, N.Y.C., 1971—; mem. nominating com. Am. Stock Exchange, 1980. Mem. Am. Bar Assn. Episcopalian. Clubs: Scarsdale Golf (past gov.) (Hartsdale, N.Y.); Harvard, Union League (N.Y.C.). Address: Pennie & Edmonds 330 Madison Ave New York NY 10017

GRIBBLE, CHARLES EDWARD, publishing co. exec.; b. Lansing, Mich., Nov. 10, 1936; s. Charles Percy and Elizabeth Keturah Gribble; B.A., U. Mich., 1957; A.M., Harvard U., 1958, Ph.D., 1967; postgrad. Moscow State U., 1960-61. Instr., asst. prof. Russian, Brandeis U., Waltham, Mass., 1961-68; asst. prof. Slavic langs. Ind. U., Bloomington, 1968-75; asso. prof. Slavic langs. Ohio State U., Columbus, 1975—; pres., editor Slavica Pubs., Inc., Columbus, 1966—; vis. asso. prof. Slavic langs. U. Va., 1977. Woodrow Wilson fellow, 1957-58; Am. Council Learned Socs. fellow, 1972; Internat. Research and Exchanges Bd. grantee, 1960-61, 72. Mem. Am. Assn. Advancement of Slavic Studies, Am. Assn. Tchrs. of Slavic and E. European Langs., Linguistic Soc. Am., Modern Lang. Assn., Linguistic Soc. Europe, Am. Assn. S.E. European Studies, Phi Beta Kappa. Author: Russian Root List, 1973; A Short Dictionary of 18th-Century Russian, 1976; editor-in-chief Folia Slavica, 1977—; editor: Studies Presented to Professor Roman Jakobson by His Students, 1968; Medieval Slavic Texts, Vol. 1, 1973; contbr. articles to scholarly jours. Office: PO Box 14388 Columbus OH 43214

GRIDLEY, JOHN ARTHUR, real estate broker; b. N.Y.C., July 27, 1946; s. Arthur and Antonette (DiGirolamo) G.; ed. spl. courses Adelphi U., Posh Inst., Nassau Community Coll., St. Leo Coll.; m. Rosemarie Quattrochi, Oct. 2, 1971; 1 dau., Maria. Rental agt. and broker Ibar Realty Corp., N.Y.C., 1967--, Anjomi Realty Corp., 1967—; owner, broker Jag Realty Co., Floral Park, N.Y., 1976—; arbitrator Am. Arbitration Assn., for Home Owners Warranty Corp. Greater N.Y. Former capt. hook and ladder Floral Park Fire Dept.; mem. S. Side Civic Assn. Named Fireman of Year, F. & M. Schaefer Brewing Co., 1975. Republican. Roman Catholic. Club: Floral Park Kiwanis. Office: 242 Jericho Turnpike Floral Park NY 11001

GRIER, GERALD ARTHUR, research center exec.; b. Balt., May 3, 1942; s. Raymond Fredrick and Margaret I. G.; A.A., San Jose Community Coll., 1975; B.S. in Bus., San Jose State U., 1977; m. Shirley Ann Hauser, June 13, 1964; children—Tammy Lynn, Heather Dee. Analog computer technician Astrodata Inc., Langley Research Center, NASA, Hampton, Va., 1965-68, shift supr. analog computer maintenance, 1968-69, supr. analog computer maintenance Ames Research Center, Moffett Field, Calif., 1969-70, dept. mgr. systems maintenance Computer Scis. Corp., Ames Research Center, 1970—. Organizer, Stonegate Home Owner Assn., 1972. Served with USAF, 1960-64. Mem. IEEE (asso.). Republican. Club: San Jose Coin. Home: 4188 Forestwood Dr San Jose CA 95121 Office: 1101 San Antonio Rd Suite 202 Mountain View CA 94040

GRIEVE, PIERSON MACDONALD, diversified co. exec.; b. Flint, Mich., Dec. 5, 1927; s. P.M. and Margaret (Leamy) G.; B.B.A., Northwestern U., 1950; postgrad. U. Minn., 1955-56; m. Florence R. Brogan, July 29, 1950; children—Margaret, Scott, Bruce. With Caterpillar Tractor Co., Peoria, Ill., 1950-52; staff engr. A.T. Kearney & Co., mgmt. cons., Chgo., 1952-55; pres. Rap-in-Wax, Mpls., 1955-62; exec. Questor Corp. (formerly Dunhill Internat., Inc.), Toledo, 1962—, pres., chief exec. officer, 1967—. Mem. adv. council J.L. Kellogg Grad. Sch. Mgmt., Northwestern U. Served with USNR, 1945-46. Mem. Kappa Sigma. Episcopalian. Clubs: Econ. (N.Y.C.); Toledo; Shadow Valley; Chevaliers du Tastevin. Home: 2105 Orchard Rd Toledo OH 43606 Office: One John Goerlich Sq Toledo OH 43691

GRIFFIN, ALPHONSO, architect, devel. co. exec.; b. Norfolk, Va., Feb. 11, 1951; s. Richard Artelia and Mary Louise G.; student Norfolk State U., 1969-71; B.Arch., Hampton Inst., 1975; m. Alfreda K. Shaw, Sept. 18, 1976. Archtl. draftsman Little Creek Naval Amphibious Base, Norfolk, summer 1971, U.S. Army C.E., Norfolk, 1973-74; architect Pa. Dept. Gen. Services, Harrisburg, 1975-76; pres. Oaktree Devel. Corp., Chesapeake, Va., 1979—. Mem. Constrn. Specifications Inst., Chesapeake C. of C., Gamma Epsilon Theta. Patentee disalinization system. Home and Office: 2625 Hemple St Chesapeake VA 23324

GRIFFIN, CARLETON HADLOCK, accountant; b. Richmond Heights, Mo., Oct. 30, 1928; s. Merle and Bernice (Edwards) G.; B.B.A., U. Mich., 1950, M.B.A., 1953, J.D., 1953; m. Mary Lou Goodrich, Dec. 26, 1953; children—Julia, Anne. With Touche Ross & Co., 1955—, nat. dir. ops., N.Y.C., 1972-74, nat. dir. resource devel., 1977-80, chmn. bd., 1974—. Sr. warden St. Paul's Episcopal Ch., Darien, Conn., 1979—; trustee Barrington (R.I.) Coll., 1980, Opera Orch. N.Y., 1980; mem. bus. adv. council Carnegie Mellon U., 1979-80. Served in Fin. Corps, U.S. Army, 1953-55. Mem. Am. Inst. C.P.A.'s, N.Y. Soc. C.P.A.'s, Colo. Soc. C.P.A.'s (pres. 1970-71). Republican. Club: Univ. (N.Y.C.). Contbr. articles to legal and acctg. jours. Office: 1633 Broadway New York NY 10019

GRIFFIN, DONALD JOHN, legis. cons., former title ins. and trust co. exec.; b. Anamosa, Iowa, Sept. 11, 1917; s. John George and Cecelia Catherine (Kelly) G.; student Columbia, 1935-36, U. Chgo., 1957; m. Maureen Margaret Moes, Sept. 11, 1940; children—Michael John, Kathleen Ann (Mrs. Dennis M. Sampson). Mgr. automotive advt. Rockford Newspapers Inc. (Ill.), 1940-48; exec. v.p. Rockford Real Estate Bd., Inc. (Ill.), 1948-53; with Chgo. Title & Trust Co. (Ill.), 1953-80, v.p. customer relations, 1963-80. Chmn. finance sect. Mayor's Summer Jobs for Youth, Chgo., 1968-70; chmn. real estate sect. Crusade of Mercy, Chgo., 1964. Bd. dirs. Booth Meml. Hosp., Chgo.; bd. chmn. Mercy Halfway House Inc., Chgo., 1970—. Served with AUS, 1945-46. Mem. Pub. Relations Soc. Am., Chgo. Real Estate Bd., Chgo. Assn. Commerce and Industry (chmn. govtl. affairs council 1971-79), Rockford Bd. Realtors (hon. life), Chgo. Mortgage Bankers, Ill. State C. of C., Chgo. Athletic Assn. (dir. 1971—, pres. 1978—). Roman Catholic. Clubs: Executives (hon. life, pres. 1969-70, chmn. exec. com. 1970-71), Chicago Yacht (Chgo.). Home: 1350 Buttonwood Ln Glenview IL 60025 Office: 111 W Washington St Chicago IL 60602

GRIFFIN, GARY ARTHUR, high tech. devel. co. exec.; b. Yonkers, N.Y., Nov. 23, 1937; s. William Edmund and Madeline (Lane) G.; student Manhattan Coll., 1956-57, Westchester Community Coll., 1957-62; diploma LaSalle Extension U., 1968; m. Jacqueline Cahill, June 21, 1958; children—Lynn, Elizabeth, Margaret. Engring. cons. IBM Corp., Yorktown, N.Y., 1960-61; engring. cons. Perkin Elmer Corp., Norwalk, Conn., 1961-63; product devel. mgr. Technicon Corp., Tarrytown, N.Y., 1963-69; chmn., pres. Dynacon Research Corp., Rockland, N.Y., 1969-72; with Nat. Patent Devel. Corp., New Brunswick, N.J., 1973—, corp. v.p. new product mktg., 1977—, pres. Hydromed Scis. div., 1978—, pres. NDP Dental Systems, Inc., 1979—, pres. NPD Epic Systems, Inc., 1979—, pres., dir. Amalgamated Fin. Services, Inc., 1979—, v.p., dir. NPD Productos Médicos, S.A., 1979—, Washburn Ltd., 1979—. Served with USNR, 1954-62. Mem. Am. Prodn. and Inventory Control Soc., Am. Mgmt. Assn., Ieee, Am. Assn. Advancement of Med. Instrumentation, Am. Entrepreneurs Assn., Internat. Entrepreneurs Assn., Smithsonian Assos., N.Y. Vet. Police Assn. Republican. Roman Catholic. Office: 783 Jersey Ave New Brunswick NJ 08902

GRIFFIN, JOSEPH WAYNE, investment co. exec.; b. Greensboro, N.C., Dec. 10, 1937; s. Joseph Hassell and Ila Mae (Sawyer) G.; B.A., Greensboro Coll., 1963; postgrad. U. N.C. Law Sch., 1964-65, Pace U. Exec. Program, 1969; m. Betty Gail Fuller, Aug. 10, 1965; 1 son, Michael Joseph. With Hayden, Stone Inc., 1968-70, Paine Webber Jackson & Curtis, Inc., N.Y.C., 1971-74, Wall, Patterson, McGrew & Richards, Inc., Atlanta, 1974; gen. partner Century Capital Assos., N.Y.C., 1975—. Active fund raising, trustee Walden Sch., 1980; mem. pace-setter group Greensboro United Fund, 1963-64. Served with AUS, 1956-59. Republican. Episcopalian. Home: 245 E 87th St New York NY 10028 Office: Century Capital Assos 777 3d Ave New York NY 10017

GRIFFIN, LLOYD MARCUS, electric utility exec.; b. Oakland, Calif., Nov. 23, 1917; s. Lloyd Marion and Louise (Frizell) G.; B.S., Va. Mil. Inst., 1939; m. Marie Bowen, May 31, 1941; children—Judith Elizabeth, Mark Lloyd, Wayne Bowen. Asst. dir. research Chesapeake & Ohio Ry. Co., Cleve., 1945-50; sr. asso. Booz, Allen & Hamilton, Chgo., 1950-58; dir. govt. sales Cummins Engine Co., Columbus, Ind., 1958-61; v.p. So. div. Pub. Service Co. Ind., Inc., Columbus, 1961-68, v.p. ops., Plainfield, 1968-78, sr. v.p. customer services, 1978—; past chmn. and dir. Food and Energy Council; chmn. Mktg. Execs. Conf. Mem. adv. bd. Central Ind. Jr. Achievement. Served to lt. col. USAAF, 1941-45. Decorated D.F.C., Air medal with four oak leaf clusters; recipient Disting. Service award Electric League Ind. Mem. Kappa Alpha. Clubs: Crooked Stick Golf, Indpls. Athletic. Office: 1000 E Main St Plainfield IN 46168

GRIFFIN, MADELYN JEAN, credit card co. ofcl.; b. Greenwood, S.C., Jan. 18, 1952; d. Frank Marvin and Lorraine Page (Varney) G.; A.S. in Bus. Mgmt., U. S.C., B.A. in Journalism, 1974, B.S. in Psychology, 1974. Relocation mgr. TICOR Inc., White Plains, N.Y., 1974-75; sales rep. Am. Express Co., N.Y.C., 1975-76, sr. ter. mgr. Card div., L.I., N.Y., 1977-78, ter. mgr., 1976-77, regional sales mgr., Los Angeles, 1978—; cons. mktg. strategies to travel agts. and tour operators, 1978—. Mem. Am. Mgmt. Assn., Am. Soc. Travel Agts. Republican. Baptist. Home: 8211 San Angelo Dr Huntington Beach CA 92647 Office: Am Express Co 21515 Hawthorne Blvd Suite 1200 Torrance CA 90503

GRIFFIN, MELVIN WILLIAM, distilling co. exec.; b. Winnipeg, Man., Can., Mar. 16, 1923; s. Aylmer and Elma G.; B.Sc., U. Man.; Profl. Engr., Queen's U.. Kingston, Ont.; m. Kathleen Ann Devine, Oct. 27, 1947; children—Lorna Griffin Smith, Patrick, Richard, Bruce, David. With Defence Industries Ltd., 1944; with Distillers Corp., Ltd., Jamaica, W.I., 1945-63, dir. Can. ops. 1963-67, v.p., dir., 1967-70, exec. v.p., chief operating officer, 1970-75; pres. House of Seagram Ltd. Montreal, Que., Can., 1975-78, exec. v.p. mfg. The Seagram Co. Ltd., 1978—, pres. Joseph E. Seagram & Sons Ltd., 1978-80, chief exec. officer, 1980—, also dir.; dir. The Seagram Co. Ltd., Rowett, Legge & Co. Ltd., Montreal Baseball Club Ltd., Glenlivet Distillers Ltd., Donwood Inst. Mem., Montreal Bd. Trade. Mem. Canadian Council, Internat. C. of C., Province of Que. C. of C., Winnipeg C. of C., La Chambre de Commerce du District de Montreal, Queen's U. Alumni. Roman Catholic. Clubs: Royal Montreal Golf, Montreal Amateur Athletic Assn. Office: Seagram Co Ltd 1430 Peel St Montreal PQ H3A 1S9 Canada

GRIFFIN, MICHAEL DANIEL, investment counselor; b. New Haven, May 26, 1939; s. Michael F. and Mae S. G.; B.A., Yale U., 1960; M.B.A., Columbia U., 1962; m. Alice Nowak, June 15, 1963; children—Michael S., Peter G., Geoffrey S. Gen. partner Scudder, Stevens & Clark, N.Y.C., 1963—. Pres., United Fund of Bronxville, N.Y., 1977-78; bd. govs. Lawrence Hosp., Bronxville, 1979—; mem. Bronxville Bd. Zoning Appeals, 1977—. Clubs: Field (Bronxville); Univ. (N.Y.C.). Home: 3 Hawthorne Rd Bronxville NY 10708 Office: 345 Park Ave New York NY 10022

GRIFFIN, RICHARD ALLEN, telephone service co. exec., leasing co. exec.; b. Rocksdale, W.Va., Feb. 22, 1938; s. Clarence Everett and Louise Alberta G.; student Manchester (Ohio) Pub. Schs.; spl. seminars Akron U., Kent State U., SBA; m. Mary Jane Sifritt, Oct. 29, 1966; stepchildren—Donna Brodsky, Gail Rice, Jack Rice; 1 dau., Virginia Louise. Contractor, 1957-69; pres. Underground Service Co., 1969-75; mgr. W.Va., S.E. Ohio, Ky. area High Voltage Systems Inc., Toledo, 1975; pres., chmn. bd. Telecom Corp., Meadowbrook, W.Va., from 1975; pres., chmn. bd. Tuner Leasing Co., Inc., Meadowbrook, 1978—; master plumber and electrician. Chmn. Northampton Twp. Water Bd.; active polit. campaigns. Mem. N.Am. Telephone Assn., U.S. C. of C. Methodist. Home: 799 Long St Bridgeport WV 26330 Office: Route 19 N Meadowbrook WV 26404

GRIFFIN, STEPHEN JAMES, consumer products co. exec.; b. Woburn, Mass., 1916; married. With The Gillette Co., 1941—, asst. to pres., v.p. Gillette Safety Razor Co. div., 1960-64, v.p. corp., 1964-66, asst. to chmn. bd., 1966, sr. v.p., 1967, exec. v.p. internat. ops., 1970, pres. Gillette Internat., 1971-76, also dir.; pres., dir. Gillette Co., 1976—, vice chmn. bd., 1981—; dir. Shawmut Bank of Boston. Bd. dirs. Nat. Fgn. Trade Council. Address: The Gillette Co Prudential Tower Bldg Boston MA 02199

GRIFFIN, WILLIAM JULIAN, II, machinery mfg. co. exec.; b. Indpls., Feb. 10, 1925; s. Frank Julian Cox and Mary (Williams) G.; student Butler U., 1942-43, The Citadel, 1943-44; grad. Ind. Bus. Coll., 1948; m. Mary Jane Noel, Apr. 24, 1953; children—William Julian III, Kevin L., Kirk E., Kerry J. Buyer. Griffin Realty Corp., 1946-47; prodn. mgr. Griffin Engring. Co., Worthington, Ind., 1949-51; sec.-treas., gen. mgr. Imperial Machinery & Tool Corp., Worthington, 1952-53; v.p., gen. mgr., dir. So. Ind. Machine Co., Inc., Worthington, 1954-60, pres., gen. mgr., dir. Griffin Engring. div., 1961—; pres., dir. GBF Dodge, Inc., Casa Grande, Ariz., 1964—; owner, mgr. Griffin Audit Service, 1965—. Bd. dirs. Hulen Meml. Youth Center. Served with AUS, 1943-46, 50. Mem. Am. Ordnance Assn., Am. Legion (past local comdr.), V.F.W., DAV. Mem. Disciples of Christ Ch. Mason (Shriner), Elk. Home: 774 Cholla Casa Grande AZ 85222 Office: Southern Ind Machine Co Inc 3d and Williams Sts Worthington IN 47471 also GBF Motors 841 Gila Bend Hwy Casa Grande AZ 85222

GRIFFIN, WILLIAM MARTIN, savs. and loan exec.; b. Steubenville, Ohio, Feb. 24, 1943; s. John Joseph and Anna Mary (Burke) G.; B.A., Coll. Steubenville, 1965; M.B.A., Loyola Coll., Balt., 1971; postgrad. Grad. Sch. Savs. and Loan, 1975; m. Mary Laura Muse, Sept. 9, 1967; children—John, Amy, Eileen. With Martin-Marietta Corp., 1965-67, Fairchild Industries, 1967-70; spl. asst. to dir. Office of Exams. and Supervision Fed. Home Loan Bank Bd., Washington, 1971-73; exec. v.p. Central Pa. Savs. Assn., Shamokin, Pa., 1973-80; chief exec. officer Cecil Fed. Savs. & Loan Assn., Elkton, Md., 1980—; chmn. bd., dir. Fin. Acctg. Services, Inc., Pitts.; adj. faculty Susquehanna U. Mem. Susquehanna Valley Mgmt. Soc. (past pres.). Home: 325 Hermitage Dr Elkton MD 21921 Office: 27 North St Elkton MD 21921

GRIFFIN, WILLIAM MARVIN, ins. co. exec.; b. Hartford, Conn., June 20, 1926; s. Samuel M. and Florence E. (Smith) G.; A.A., U. Hartford, 1949; B.S., U. Pa., 1952; m. Shirley Klotzbaugh, May 1, 1954; 1 dau., Martha. Sec. investments Conn. Gen. Life Ins. Co., Hartford, 1952-64; sr. v.p. Hartford Fire Ins. Co., 1964-73, exec. v.p., chmn. fin. com., 1973—, also dir., dir. subsidiaries; pres. Hartford Securities Co., Inc., Hartford Real Estate Co.; dir. Tex. Utilities Co., Eaton & Howard, Vance Sanders mut. funds. Chmn. bd. regents U. Hartford, 1980—; bd. dirs., chmn. fin. com. Inst. of Living. Served with AUS, 1945-46. Mem. Am. Fgn. Ins. Assn. (finance com.). Club: Hartford Golf. Office: Hartford Plaza Hartford CT 06115

GRIFFITH, DANIEL BOYD, bus. exec.; b. Albuquerque, Aug. 30, 1934; s. Reese Humphrey and Faye (Boyd) G.; B.S., Oreg. State U., 1956; m. Patricia Dawn Mosley, July 26, 1956; 1 dau., Leann Dawn. Pres., Burns Bros., Inc., Portland, Oreg., 1959-61, 69—; mgr. Ga. Pacific Corp., 1961-69; dir. Nat. Tire Corp. Bd. dirs. Oreg. Contemporary Theater. Served with USAF, 1956-59. Mem. Aircraft Owners and Pilots Assn., Phi Gamma Delta. Republican. Presbyterian. Clubs: Lake Oswego Country, Mountain Park Racquet, Rotary. Office: 621 SE Union Ave Portland OR 97214

GRIFFITH, DARLENE INEZ, real estate fin. planner; b. South Gate, Calif., June 14, 1938; d. John Joseph and Sarah Inez (Ritchey) G.; student Compton Jr. Coll., 1958-59, Cerritos Jr. Coll., 1960-61, Rio Hondo Jr. Coll., 1966-67, U. Calif., Berkeley, 1972-74, also investment courses; m. John Baca Lopez, Oct. 15, 1966; children—David Richard Haberbush, John Robert Haberbush. Profl. dancer, choreographer, Hollywood, Calif., 1954-62; mgr., trainer Weaver Airline Personnel Sch., Kansas City, Mo., 1962-67; owner mgr. co., Whittier, Calif., 1967—; pvt. practice real estate fin. planner, bus. counselor, Whittier, 1976—; tchr. Downey (Calif.) High Sch., 1972-76. Grad. Realtors Inst., cert. bus. counselor. Mem. Whittier Dist. Bd. Realtors, Los Angeles Bus. Mktg. Assn. (sec.), Calif. Assn. Realtors, Nat. Assn. Realtors, Realtors Nat. Mktg. Inst., Real Estate Securities and Syndication Inst., Nat. Council Exchangors, Internat. Exchangors Assn. Home: 14130 Caswood St Whittier CA 90602 Office: 13400 E Whittier Blvd Whittier CA 90605

GRIFFITH, JOHN GORDON, investment co. exec.; b. Council Bluffs, Iowa, Dec. 16, 1934; s. Frank Leroy and Geneva O. Griffith; B.S., Iowa State Coll., 1954; m. Patricia Jean Milnor, Apr. 22, 1978; children—Stephen John, Jessica Geneva. Salesman, Kraft Foods Co., Miami, Fla., 1954-58; animal biol. and chem. products salesman Dow Chem. Co., Los Angeles, 1958-66; sr. sales rep. Coldwell Banker Co., Newport Beach, Calif., 1966-73; founder, chmn. bd., pres. Centurion Investment Corp., Newport Beach, 1973—; agrl. devel. cons. to various cos. Mem. tax com. Garden Grove (Calif.) Sch. Bd., 1968. Served with USAF, 1953. Mem. Calif. Bd. Realtors, Commerce Assos. U. So. Calif. Republican. Home: 4 Tahoe St Irvine CA 92715 Office: 4041 MacArthur Blvd Suite 140 Newport Beach CA 92660

GRIFFITH, P. LEROY, cons. engr.; b. Havana, Cuba, July 24, 1908; s. Percy L. and Kathryn E. (Dreyfuss) G.; B.S., Columbia U., 1929, M.S. in Indsl. Engring., 1931; m. Dorothy G. Salle, Aug. 3, 1935; children—Allan L., Richard S. Cons. Ebasco Services, N.Y.C., 1931-41; asst. v.p. Gilbert Assos., N.Y.C., 1941-50; origination mgr. Union Securities, N.Y.C., 1950-52; new bus. mgr. Sanderson & Porter, N.Y.C., 1952-54; sec., dir. indsl. devel. Walter Kidde Constrn., N.Y.C., 1954-59; v.p. James King & Son, Inc., N.Y.C., 1959-67, pres., dir. 1967-77; cons. Pope Evans & Robbins, N.Y.C., 1977—; cons. in financing, engring. and mgmt. Chmn. Urban Redevel. Agy., Montclair, 1961-65; mem. Planning Bd., Montclair, 1960-65; mem. Montclair Def. Council, 1960—. Fellow ASME (chmn. civic affairs com. 1968-70); mem. ASCE Soc. Am. Mil. Engrs., Columbia Alumni Assn. (pres. Essex County 1955-60), Phi Delta Theta. Clubs: Columbia (pres., dir. 1968-70) (N.Y.C.); Montclair Golf; Union League. Co-inventor Braketrol (automatic brake device). Home: 59 Prospect Ave Montclair NJ 07042 Office: 59 Prospect Ave Montclair NJ 07042

GRIFFITHS, EDGAR H., corp. exec.; b. Phila., 1921; grad. St. Joseph's Coll., 1943. With RCA Corp., 1948—, treas., controller, 1957-63, v.p. internat. fin. div., 1963-66, exec. v.p. services 1971-72, exec. v.p., 1972-76, pres., chief exec. officer, 1976—, also dir.; v.p. comml. service div. RCA Service Co., 1966-68, pres. 1968-71. Served with U.S. Army, 1943-45. Office: RCA Corp 30 Rockefeller Plaza New York NY 10020*

GRIFFITHS, JOHN BRITTAIN, mfg. co. exec.; b. San Diego, Mar. 10, 1937; s. Cuthbert Ambrose and Marion Claire G.; B.S., U.S. Naval Acad., 1958; M.B.A., Harvard U., 1966; m. Donna Lee Truog, July 21, 1961; children—Christina, Margaret, John Brittain, Kent. Cons.,

Rand Corp., Santa Monica, Calif., 1965; asst. to chmn. FMC Corp., San Jose, Calif., 1966-68; cons. Touch Ross & Co., San Diego, 1968-70; exec. v.p. C.H. Tripp Co., San Diego, 1970-75; v.p., gen. mgr. Mobex Corp., Fullerton, Calif., 1976-78; div. mgr. FMC Corp., Houston, 1978—; dir. C.H. Tripp Co., Master Distbrs. Inc. Served with USN, 1958-64. C.P.A., Calif. Mem. Harvard Bus. Club Assn. (pres. 1972-73), Calif. C.P.A. Soc. Republican. Club: Army Navy Country (Arlington, Va.). Office: 10516 Old Katy Rd Houston TX 77024

GRIGG, DON ALFRED, advt. and public relations co. exec.; b. Charlotte, N.C., Jan. 14, 1945; s. Vernon Castle and Sadie (Cautheu) G.; B.S. in Aerospace Engring., N.C. State U., 1967; M.B.A., U. N.C., Chapel Hill, 1969. Cons., Mgmt. Analysis Center, Boston, 1973-74; spl. rep. So. Ry. System, Washington, 1974-77; owner Bus. Writers Assos., Washington, 1977-78; pres. Washington, Inc. APR, Washington, 1979—. Publicity dir. Common Cause Md., 1974-77; treas. Montgomery County (Md.) Democratic Caucus, 1978—. Served to capt. USAF, 1969-73. Mem. Am. Mktg. Assn., Public Relations Soc. Am., Ad Club Washington, Nat. Press Club. Presbyterian. Club: Georgetown Prep. Author: A Primer in Amateur Motor Car Racing in the U.S., 1974; The PR Cookbook, 1978. Office: 910 17th St NW Washington DC 20006

GRIGGS, JACK ALLEN, banker; b. Brownfield, Tex., July 22, 1942; s. Thomas Jackson and Ruth (Allen) G.; B.S., Abilene Christian U., 1964; M.B.A., U. Tex., Austin, 1967, Ph.D., 1971; m. Ann Faubus, Aug. 9, 1963; children—Angela, Julie, Ashlie, Jackson Overton. Auditor, Arthur Andersen & Co., Dallas, 1964-66; asst. to dean M.B.A. program U. Tex., Austin, 1967-69; asst. prof. Tex. Tech. U., Lubbock, 1971-73; v.p. 1st Nat. Bank San Antonio, 1973, exec. v.p., 1974-77, pres., 1977—, dir.; dir. Sanderson State Bank, TransWorld Leasing Corp., Kent Oil Co., Kent Distbg. Co. Bd. dirs. Am. Heart Assn.; pres. San Antonio Research and Planning Council, 1979; trustee Abilene Christian U.; mem. fin. adv. bd. Tex. Tech. U. Mem. Am. Inst. C.P.A.'s, Tex. Soc. C.P.A.'s, San Antonio Soc. C.P.A.'s. Mem. Ch. of Christ. Club: Oak Hills Country. Office: 6243 Northwest Expressway San Antonio TX 78213

GRIGOROFF, LOUIS, real estate corp. exec.; b. Niagara Falls, Ont., Can., Nov. 19, 1932; s. Grigor Lambeff and Marika (Tsvetcoff) G.; diploma Mexico City Coll., 1957; m. Lidia Cass-Ramirez, June 14, 1958; children—Michael George, Brenda Yvonne. With Norton Abrasives Co., Chippawa, Ont., 1951-55; night editor Mexico City Daily News, 1956-58; supplementary editor, staff writer Niagara Falls Evening Rev. 1958-66, writer column Niagara Outdoors, 1962-66; gen. mgr. N.P.H.B. Land Devels., Ltd., St. Catharines, Ont., 1967-71; sec.-mgr., sec.-treas., bd. dirs. Niagara Peninsula Home Builders Assn., 1967-70; devel. dir. Paramount Properties, St. Catharines, 1971-74; pres. Grigoroff Mgmt. Services Inc., 1975-80, Multiplex Securities Ltd., 1977—, Ultrafax Equities Ltd., 1981—. Founding pres. Niagara Falls Bus. and Indsl. Growth Agy., Inc., 1976-78; chmn. Mayors Com. on Housing Niagara Falls, 1967-73; past pres. Welland County br. Canadian Mental Health Assn.; mem. Niagara Falls Planning Bd., 1972-75. Served to lt. Royal Canadian Arty., 1960-65. Recipient B.F. Goodrich award Western Ont. Newspaper Awards, 1962. Mem. C. of C. Clubs: Niagara Falls, St. Catharines Golf and Country, Kiwanis. Home: 4110 Glenayr Ave Niagara Falls ON L2E 6J9 Canada Office: 21 Elizabeth St St Catharines ON L2R 2K8 Canada

GRIMES, ALDEN, assn. exec.; b. Mpls., Aug. 28, 1918; s. Gordon and Margaret H. (Grimes) G.; A.B., U. Minn., 1939, B.B.A., 1940; m. Rochelle Berry; children—Mary Elizabeth, Jeffrey David, Judith Ann, Susan Margaret. Market research cons., 1939-41; advt. account exec. McCann-Erickson, Inc., 1947-49; v.p., dir. Campbell-Mithun, Inc., Chgo., 1949-68; exec. v.p. HEAR (Hearing Edn. and Research Found.), Evanston, Ill., 1968-70; v.p. Dairy Research, Inc., Rosemont, Ill., 1970-74; v.p. United Dairy Industry Assn., Rosemont, 1974—; exec. v.p., gen. mgr. Am. Dairy Assn., Rosemont, 1974—; chmn. bd. KAAA Communications, 1969-74; dir. Reynolds-United Properties. Served sgt. to maj. U.S. Army, 1941-46. Home: 832 Ingleside Pl Evanston IL 60201 Office: 6300 N River Rd Rosemont IL 60018

GRIMES, SHERRILL DEANE, savs. and loan exec.; b. Pascagoula, Miss., Apr. 11, 1947; d. George Mallison and Lizzie Kate (Haden) Rose; A.A., Hinds Jr. Coll., 1967; student Ga. Inst. Tech., 1970, U. So. Miss., 1972-73, Miss. Coll., 1979—; m. Eddie Grimes, June 26, 1971. Dir. personnel and public relations Rankin Gen. Hosp., Brandon, Miss., 1969-76; adminstrv. asst., dir. staff devel. Miss. State Hosp., Whitfield, 1976-79; asst. v.p., dir. personnel Unifirst Fed. Savs. & Loan Assn., Jackson, Miss., 1979—; cons. public relations and staff devel. Miss. State Hosp.; dir. guidance dept. Jackson State U. Bd. dirs. Mental Health Assn. Miss.; vice chmn. adv. council Hinds Jr. Coll. Notary public Rankin County. Mem. Inst. Fin. Edn., Nat. Assn. Nurse Recruiters, Am. Soc. Personnel Adminstrs. (accredited), Am. Hosp. Soc. Personnel Adminstrn., Miss. Hosp. Assn. Soc. Personnel Adminstrs., Am. Hosp. Soc. Edn. and Tng., U.S. Savs. and Loan League (personnel com.). Methodist. Office: PO Box 1818 Jackson MS 39205

GRIMM, JAY VAUGHN, stockbroker; b. Sabetha, Kans., Jan. 28, 1926; s. Benjamin W. and Emma Marie (Hunzeker) G.; B.A., U. Kans., 1949; LL.B., Yale U., 1952; m. Teresa McGarry, July 29, 1956; children—Katherine, Cordelia, Jay Vaughn. Admitted to N.Y. State bar, 1952; practiced in N.Y.C., 1952-56; founder, pres. Grimm & Davis, Inc., N.Y.C., 1962—. Served with USN, 1944-45. Decorated Purple Heart. Mem. N.Y. Soc. Security Analysts, Chartered Fin. Analysts, Phi Beta Kappa. Democrat. Episcopalian. Clubs: Down Town Assn., Yale. Home: 950 Park Ave New York City NY 10028 Office: 76 Beaver St New York NY 10005

GRIMMITT, HARRY LEROY, bus. exec.; b. Maury City, Tenn., Apr. 3, 1942; s. Brown C. and Margaret Akin G.; B.S., Tenn. Tech. Coll.; m. Patsy Ball, Aug. 16, 1963; children—Lee Grimmitt, Tracy. Pres., Smith Enterprises, Inc., Rock Hill, S.C., 1980—. Home: 707 Ottawa Dr Rock Hill SC 29730 Office: PO Drawer 12006 Rock Hill SC 29731

GRISSOM, LEE ALAN, assn. exec.; b. Pensacola, Fla., Sept. 7, 1942; s. Levi Aaron and Virginia Sue (Olinger) G.; B.A., San Diego State U., 1965, M.City Planning, 1971; m. Sharon Kay Hasty, May 14, 1966; children—David, Jonathan, Matthew. Sr. research asso. Western Behavioral Scis. Inst., La Jolla, Calif., 1965-73; mgr. planning div., then gen. mgr. San Diego C. of C., 1973-75, exec. v.p., gen. mgr., 1975—; instr. urban planning U. Calif., San Diego, 1973; host TV program The City Game, 1972-75. Chmn., Boy Scout Fair, San Diego, 1977-78; mem. pres.'s adv. bd. San Diego State U.; trustee COMBO, 1975-78, San Diego council Boy Scouts Am.; trustee, v.p., mem. exec. com. Western Behavioral Scis. Inst.; mem. Gov. Calif.'s Planning and Adv. Assistance Council, 1977-79; mem. integration com. San Diego City Schs.; bd. dirs. Econ. Devel. Corp. Named Outstanding Young Citizen, San Diego Jaycees, 1976, Calif. Jaycees, 1977, U.S. Jaycees, 1978. Mem. Am. Soc. Planning Ofcls., San Diego County Cultural Heritage Commn., Am. Inst. Planners (award recognition Calif. chpt. 1973), Calif. Assn. C. of C. Execs. Club: San Diego Rotary. Author articles in field. Office: 233 A St San Diego CA 92101

GRIST, JOHN, govt. ofcl.; b. Havana, Cuba, Nov. 17, 1928 (father Am. citizen); s. John Rivers and Raphaela Matilda (Santiesteban) G.; came to U.S., 1945; B.S., Ga. Inst. Tech., 1958; m. Ana Dolores D'Almonte, Nov. 22, 1961; children—Anna Cecilia, John Alexander, Paul Steven. Aircraft indsl. engring. cons. Parr Engring., Atlanta, 1958; food mfg. indsl. engring. cons. U.S. Dept. Agr., Washington, 1958-60; postal mechanization indsl. engr. U.S. Post Office Dept., Washington, 1960-62; hosp. indsl. engr. cons. VA, Washington, 1962-64; bldgs. mgmt. indsl. engr. cons. GSA, Washington, 1964-65; parks mgmt. sr. mgmt. analysis cons. Nat. Park Service, Washington, 1965-71; sr. indsl. engring. cons. U.S. Postal Service, N.Y.C., 1971-74, sr. indsl. engring. cons. Western Mass., Springfield, Mass., 1974—; internat. bilingual export-import tech. cons., 1958—. Pres., parents council Arlington (Va.) Pub. Schs. Deaf Edn. Program, 1970-71; mem. Parents' Council, Lexington Sch. for Deaf, Queens, N.Y., 1972-74; mem. fund raising com. Clarke Sch. for Deaf, Northampton, Mass., 1975-76. Served with USAF, 1951-55. Mem. Am. Inst. Indsl. Engrs., Ga. Inst. Tech. Nat. Alumni Assn. Roman Catholic. Home: 131 Rolling Ridge Rd Amherst MA 01002 Office: Main PO Box 2702 Springfield MA 01101

GRIVAS, WILLIAM LOUIS, electronics mfg. co. exec.; b. Pitts., Oct. 8, 1954; s. William and Patricia Jean (Pollock) G.; student public schs., Pa., 1971; 1 son, Billy. Pres., Grivas Industries, Inc., Vista, Calif., 1975—, S.W. Gen. Industries, Inc., Vista, 1975—. Served with USMC, 1971-78. Mem. Nat. Alliance Bus., U.S. Parachuters Assn.

GRODBERG, MARCUS GORDON, pharm. co. exec.; b. Worcester, Mass., Jan. 27, 1923; s. Isaac and Rosalie (Hirsch) G.; A.B., Clark U., 1944; M.S., U. Ill., 1948; m. Shirley Florence Merkle, Apr. 15, 1951; children—Joel David, Kim Gordon, Jeremy Daniel. Jr. research chemist Schenley Labs., Inc., Lawrenceburg, Ind., 1944-47; research and devel. chemist Marine Products Co., Boston, 1948-50, Brewer & Co., Inc., Worcester, 1950-55; tech. dir. Gray Pharm. Co., Inc., Newton, Mass., 1955-58; dir. research and devel. Davies Rose Hoyt pharm. div. Kendall Co. (now Hoyt Labs. div. Colgate-Palmolive Co.), Needham, Mass., 1958—. Mem. Internat. Assn. Dental Research, Internat. Coll. Pediatrics, Acad. Dentistry for Handicapped, N.Y. Acad. Scis., Am. Soc. Dentistry for Children, Orthopedic Research Soc., Am. Pharm. Assn., ADA, AAAS, Acad. Pharm. Scis. Patentee in field. Home: 111 Hyde St Newton MA 02161 Office: 633 Highland Ave Needham MA 02194

GRODEN, WALTER STEVEN, ins. exec.; b. Bronx, N.Y., Feb. 14, 1939; s. Nathan and Yetta (Fuchsman) G.; B.B.A., Adelphi U., 1960; m. Marjorie Alice Wolf, Feb. 21, 1961; children—Elisabeth, Neil. Trainee, Sears, Roebuck & Co., Bklyn., 1960-61, mgr. catalog/sales div., 1961-62; partner Lawrence Excess, Ltd. and H.S.W. Agy., Inc., Lawrence, N.Y., 1962-74; pres., owner David C. White Agy., Inc., Lynbrook, N.Y., 1975—; sec.-treas. Internat. Guaranty Ins. Co., 1978—; dir. Exec. Ins. Co.; charter broker N.Y. Ins. Exchange, 1980—. Treas., The Brandeis Sch., Lawrence, N.Y., 1975-77. Mem. N.Y. Excess and Surplus Lines Assn. (pres.-elect 1980-81, dir.), Nat. Assn. Profl. Surplus Lines Offices (chmn. scholarship, edn. and contingency fund com. 1979, 80, 81), Ind. Agts. Assn., Council Ins. Brokers of Greater N.Y. Republican. Jewish. Office: 8 Freer St Lynbrook NY 11563

GROEBER, RICHARD FRANCIS, meteorologist; b. Springfield, Ohio, Apr. 20, 1944; s. Paul Joseph and Catherine Agnes (Walsh) G.; A.A., Urbana Coll., 1966. Meteorologist, Sta. WBLY, Springfield, 1956-62, Sta. WEEC, Springfield, 1962—; owner, operator Dicks Weather Service, Springfield. Mem. Am. Meteorol. Soc. (voting privilege), Am. Geophys. Union (supporting mem.). Democrat. Roman Catholic. Home and Office: 1452 N Limestone St Springfield OH 45503

GROETKEN, EDWARD LEONARD, truck parts dealer; b. LeMars, Iowa, June 3, 1914; s. Henry Francis and Mary Adelade (Franklin) G.; grad. St. Joseph's High Sch., LeMars, 1931; m. Marilyn Rose Knapp, Oct. 6, 1979. Field serviceman Hobson & Co., Kansas City, Mo., 1945-49; master mechanic Peter Kiewit Sons, Omaha, 1949-58; service mgr. Leased Trucks, Inc., Sioux City, Iowa, 1958-62; owner, mgr. N.W. Truck and Trailer Service, Sioux City, 1962—. Mem. Sioux City Better Bus. Bur., Sioux City C. of C. Democrat. Roman Catholic. Home: 3101 N Martha St Sioux City IA 51105 Office: 3114 Hwy 75 N Sioux City IA 51105

GROFF, RICHARD LAMARR, investment counseling co. exec.; b. Lancaster, Pa., Aug. 6, 1925; s. Frank L. and Martha E. Groff; B.S. in Econs., Franklin and Marshall Coll., 1950; M.Letters in Retail Sci., U. Pitts., 1951; m. Elizabeth Mastrocolo, May 25, 1974. Buyer, The Higbee Co., Cleve., 1951-61, mgr. suburban store, 1961-71, gen. mgr. Splty. Shop div., 1971-79; investment counselor, broker Smith Barney Harris & Upham, Cleve., 1979—. Served with USAAF, 1944-46. Mem. Am. Mgmt. Assn., Sales and Mktg. Execs. Cleve. Clubs: Rotary, Masons. Home: 390-2 Windward Ln Aurora OH 44202 Office: 1300 E 9th St Cleveland OH 44114

GROGAN, ROBERT HARRIS, lawyer; b. Bklyn., Feb. 25, 1933; s. Robert Michael and Nora Howarth (Johnson) G.; A.B., Harvard U., 1955; LL.B., U. Va., 1961; m. Delia Ann Grossi, Dec. 23, 1967. Admitted to Va. bar, 1961, N.Y. bar, 1962, Ill. bar, 1977; asso. firm Milbank, Tweed, Hadley & McCloy, N.Y.C., 1961-66; counsel Anaconda Co., N.Y.C., 1966-68; asso. firm Shearman & Sterling, N.Y.C., 1968-75; v.p., gen. counsel staff Citibank, N.Y.C., 1975-76; partner firm Mayer, Brown & Platt, Chgo., 1976—; lectr. in field; sec., dir. 3d Equity Owners Corp., coop. housing corp., 1975-77. Served with U.S. Army, 1956-58. Mem. Am., Ill., N.Y. (exec. com. banking, corp. bus. law sect. 1977—, mem. bus. law com. 1975—), Va. bar assns., Phi Delta Phi. Clubs: Union League (Chgo.); Harvard N.Y.C. Contbg. author: The Local Economic Development Corporation, 1970. Home: 525 E 86th St New York NY 10028 Office: Mayer Brown & Platt 277 Park Ave New York NY 10017

GROMAN, MARGARET ELAINE, farm and heavy equipment co. exec.; b. Alliance, Ohio, May 6, 1955; d. Frank and A. Elaine G.; B.A. in Bus. Adminstrn., Muhlenberg Coll., 1977; M.B.A. in Mktg., Syracuse U., 1978. Retail sales rep. Internat. Harvester Co., Balt., 1979-80, govt. bid coordinator, Washington, 1980—. Mem. Assn. of Grad. Bus. Students, Assn. M.B.A.'s, Phi Alpha Theta. Home: 4701 Rouge Ct Apt 201 Alexandria VA 22312 Office: Internat Harvester Co 1707 L St NW Washington DC 20036

GROSS, DAVID, corp. ofcl.; b. Bronx, N.Y., July 20, 1942; s. Charles and Shirley G.; B.A. in Mktg., Fordham U., 1966; m. Ellen Levenson, Mar. 23, 1963; 1 son, Richard Heath. Dist. mgr. Apeco Corp., 1961-67; sales engr. Memorex Corp., 1967-74; br. mgr. Saxon Bus. Products, Union, N.J., 1974-77; nat. supply mgr. Sharp Electronics, Paramus, N.J., 1977-78; Eastern zone sales mgr. Apeco Corp., Elk Grove Village, Ill., 1978-81; v.p. sales and mktg. Castelli Furniture Inc., N.Y.C., 1981—. Mem. Am. Mgmt. Assn. Home: 82-46 135th St Kew Gardens NY 11435 Office: Castelli Furniture Inc 950 3d Ave New York NY 10022

GROSS, JENARD MORRIS, investment exec., investor; b. Nashville, Oct. 7, 1929; s. Edward and Anna Madeline (Rubenstein) G.; B.A. magna cum laude, Vanderbilt U., 1950; fellow Brandeis U., 19—; m. Gail Marilyn Meyrowitz, July 11, 1973; children—Jay, Stephanie, Amy, Dawn, Shawn. Investment builder; pres. Gross Builders, Inc., Houston, 1959—, Nationwide Apartment Mgmt. Corp., 1967-76; chmn. bd. Gulf Coast Savs. Assn., 1977—; bd. dirs. Spring Branch Bank, 1973—, mem. loan com., 1974—, investment com., 1977—; bds. dirs. Capital Title Co., 1974—, Tex. Mortgage Investors, 1974—; dir. Delta Lloyds Ins. Co., 1971—, Robstown Savs. and Loan Assn., 1969-76, San Jacinto Underwriters, Inc., 1968-71, Central Nat. Bank of Houston, 1969-71; mem. Lloyd's of London, 1978—, World Bus. Council, 1979; lectr. U. Houston, 1973-75. Treas. San Jacinto council Girl Scouts U.S.A., 1979—, fin. com., 1976; bds. dirs. Houston Grand Opera, 1977—, Houston Symphony Orch., 1979—, March of Dimes, 1979—; gen. chmn. United Jewish Campaign of Houston, 1970; local chmn. Brandeis U., 1970, mem. president's council, 1972—; mem. mayor's citizens' adv. com. of Housing, Houston, 1969-71, mayor's urban renewal com., 1967-68; exec. com. Citizens for Decent Housing; vice chmn. president's com. of UN Day of UN Assn., 1972—; v.p. Jewish Community Council, 1972; co-chmn. bicentennial week Temple Emanu El, 1976; active Rice Assos., 1971—, Constrn. Industry Council, 1969-70. Served with U.S. Army, 1953-54. Mem. Houston Apt. Assn. (pres. 1968, bd. dirs. 1967-76), Nat. Apt. Assn. (pres. 1969-70, bd. dirs. 1968-73, regional v.p. 1968-69, exec. com. 1968-69), Tex. Apt. Assn. (bd. dirs. 1967-69), Vanderbilt Alumni Club of Houston (pres. 1965, class agt. 1972-75, chmn. Living Endowment Drive of Vanderbilt 1966), Greater Houston Alumni Chpt. Phi Beta Kappa (pres.1975),cC (pres. 1975), C. of C. (govtl. affairs com. 1975, housing com. 1975-78). Clubs: University, Raquet, Houstonian, Westwood Country (dir. 1968-75, pres. 1971). Speaker profl. assns.; interview Today Show, 1969; testimony U.S. Ho. of Reps., U.S. Senate. Office: 1670 Transco Tower Houston TX 77056

GROSS, JOHN C(HARLES), broker, industrialist; b. N.Y.C., Apr. 2, 1904; s. Edward H. and Anna Catharine (Muelhaus) G.; student pub. schs., N.Y.C.; m. Helen Victoria Newman, Sept, 26, 1926; 1 dau., Jean Anne. Pres., treas., dir. John C. Gross, Inc.; treas., dir. Artifacts Recovery Corp.; pres. New Smyrna Subcontractors Corp.; pres., treas., dir. Yacht Club Island Corp., Yacht Club Island Estates, Yacht Club Island Apts.; pres., treas. Ponce de Leon Corp.; reorganized, merged various companies. Mem. Com. of 100 of New Smyrna Beach; chmn. S.E. Volusia Area Devel. Council; mem. Edgewater (Fla.) Planning Bd. Bd. dirs., treas. Visual Arts Acad., Inc.; exec. bd. Boy Scouts Am. Mem. Nat. Assn. Security Dealers, New Smyrna Beach C. of C. Lutheran (council). Rotarian. Home: 404 N Riverside Dr Edgewater FL 32032 Office: PO Box 596 New Smyrna Beach FL 32069

GROSS, NELSON BOON, investment banker; b. Los Angeles, Nov. 27, 1929; s. Nels and Wilhelmina (Boon) G.; B.S., U. So. Calif., 1955; m. Susie Sutton Raddon, Sept. 3, 1954; children—Susan Wilhelmina, William Nelson Raddon. Pres. Gross and Co., Inc., Los Angeles, 1956—, G.R. Capital, Inc., Los Angeles, 1970—, Freeway Comml. Properties, Los Angeles, 1973—, Municipal Improvements Acceptance Corp., financing, Los Angeles, 1974—; dir. Walker Scott Co., San Diego, Morgan, Olmstead, Kennedy & Gardner, mem. N.Y. Stock Exchange. Served with USAF, 1950-53. Mem. Los Angeles Security Analysts Soc. Club: Jonathan (Los Angeles). Home: 536 Harbor Island Dr Newport Beach CA 92660 Office: 359 San Miguel Dr Suite 102 Newport Beach CA 92660

GROSS, NORMAN, mfg. co. exec.; b. N.Y.C., Apr. 10, 1935; s. Jacob and Anna (Feld) G.; A.A., Los Angeles City Coll., 1956; m. Rochelle Barbara Katz, Mar. 25, 1956; children—Michael Alan, Susan Beth, Jamie Illaina. Expediter, Beckman Instruments, Fullerton, Calif., 1956-58; mfrs. rep. Barney Weingard Assn., Los Angeles, 1958-62; owner, pres. Norman Gross & Asso., Los Angeles, 1962-67; pres. Sunshine Leisure, Chatsworth, Calif., 1967—. Mem. Ken Wolf chpt. City of Hope. Licensed real estate broker, Calif. Mem. Nat. Sporting Goods Assn., Asso. Surplus Dlrs. Assn., Tau Epsilon Phi. Jewish. Office: 20310 Plummer St Chatsworth CA 91311

GROSS, PATRICK WALTER, computer services co. exec.; b. Ithaca, N.Y., May 15, 1944; s. Eric T.B. and Catharine B. (Rohrer) G.; student Cornell U., 1962-63; B. Engring. Sci., Rensselaer Poly. Inst., 1965; M.S.E. in Applied Math., U. Mich., 1966; M.B.A., Stanford, 1968; m. Sheila Eve Proby, Apr. 12, 1969; children—Geoffrey Philipp, Stephanie Lovell. Cons. info. mgmt. operation Gen. Electric Co., Schenectady, 1965-67; sr. staff mem. Office Sec. Def., Washington, 1968-69, spl. asst., 1969-70; founder, mng. dir. Am. Mgmt. Systems, Inc., Arlington, Va., 1970—; cons. Rand Corp., 1973-75. Trustee, Washington Hosp. Center, 1977—, Sidwell Friends Sch., 1980—. Mem. Nat. Economists Club, Am. Econ. Assn., President's Assn., UN Assn. (Econ. Policy Council), Fgn. Policy Assn. (gov., dir. exec. com. 1977), Council on Fgn. Relations, World Affairs Council Washington (dir., vice chmn. 1980—), Internat. Inst. Strategic Studies, Washington Inst. Fgn. Affairs, Sigma Xi, Tau Beta Pi. Club: Mid-Atlantic Club Washington. Home: 7401 Glenbrook Rd Bethesda MD 20014 Office: 1515 Wilson Blvd Arlington VA 22209

GROSS, PEGGY EILEEN KNUTSON, lumber mfg. co. exec.; b. Mpls., Sept. 26, 1947; d. Edwin Walter and Barbara M. (Schneider) Knutson; B.A., Coll. of St. Catherin, 1969; postgrad. (NSF grantee) U. Minn., 1970-72; m. Harvard William Gross, Jr., Mar. 29, 1969; children—Kevin, Timothy, Brian, Jeffrey, Colleen Erin. Tchr. Am. history St. Louis Park (Minn.) High Sch., 1969-70; exec. sec., translator CEA Carter Americas, Inc., Mpls., 1975-77; youth dir. YWCA, Wausau, Wis., 1977-78; adminstrv. asst. to pres. Crestline, Inc., Wausau, 1979—. Mem. Minn. Select Com. Judicial Reform, 1974-77. Vol. counselor Hotline, 1971-72; v.p. Mpls. Jaycees Convs., Inc., 1972-74; bd. dirs. Outreach Community Center, 1974-77, Wausau Newcomers, 1977-78; mem. Wausau Area Coalition for Marital Property Legis. Reform, 1979-80. Mem. LWV (state dir. 1973-76), U.S. Jayceettes (exec. com. 1976—, programming v.p. 1977-78, parlimaentarian 1978-80, govtl. affairs program mgr. 1980-81, named Outstanding Nat. Officer of the Year 1979), Wis. Jaycettes (dir. 1977—, v.p. programming 1980-81, Presdl. award 1978, 79, named Outstanding State Officer 1980), AAUW, Wausau Jaycettes (dir. 1977-78), Wausau Hockey Assn., Wausau C. of C. (mem. firm prevention com. 1977-79), NOW, Women's Polit. Caucus, Coll. of St. Catherine Alumnae Assn. (class chmn. 1969-77) Pi Delta Phi, Pi Gamma Mu. Author: (with others) Minnesota Judiciary, Structure and Procedure, 1972; Today's Woman, 1976. Home: 410 Kent St Wausau WI 54401 Office: Crestline 910 Cleveland Ave Wausau WI 54401

GROSS, SPENCER, lawyer; b. Hartford, Conn., Dec. 22, 1906; s. Charles Welles and Hilda (Welch) G.; B.A., Yale, 1928, LL.B., 1931. Admitted to Conn. bar, 1931; practice law Gross, Hyde & Williams, Hartford, Conn., 1931—, partner, 1936—; dep. judge City Ct. Hartford, 1945-47; corporator Mechanics Savs. Bank, dir., 1941-79; dir. Nat. Fire Ins. Co., Transcontinental Ins. Co. Mem. Adv. Council on Banking. Treas. distbn. com. Hartford Found. for Pub. Giving, 1945-68; mem. Met. Dist. Commn., 1940-50, 52-54, City Planning

Commn., 1936-45, Bd. Park Commrs., Hartford, 1939-48; sec. Wadsworth Atheneum, 1943-66; corporator Am. Sch. for Deaf, 1940—, Children's Mus. Hartford, 1940—, Hartford Hosp., St. Francis Hosp.; trustee Howard and Bush Found., YMCA Met. Hartford. Fellow Am. Coll. Probate Counsel; mem. Zeta Psi, Phi Delta Phi. Democrat. Conglist. Clubs: University, Wampanoag Country, Twentieth Century (Hartford). Home: 229 Kenyon St Hartford CT 06105 Office: 799 Main St Hartford CT 06103

GROSS, STUART ALAN, computer software exec.; b. Bridgeport, Conn., Feb. 8, 1946; s. Andrew and Ethel W. (Weiner) G.; student Northeastern U., 1963-65; B.S., U. Bridgeport, 1967; M.S., U. New Haven, 1969; M.B.A., U. Conn., 1971; m. Carol Guice, Sept. 6, 1969; children—Aimee Mellissa, Kristin Michelle. Chief corp. acct. Downe Communications, N.Y.C., 1971-73; asst. controller Triangle Pacific Corp., New Haven, 1973-75; controller Lubin Bus. Interiors, New Haven, 1975-78; pres. Info Systems, Inc., Orange, Conn., 1978—. Mem. Assn. M.B.A. Execs., U. Conn. Alumni Assn. Club: Probus (v.p. 1979-80). Office: 380 Boston Post Rd Orange CT 06477

GROSSEL-ROSSI, MARION NICHOLAS, lawyer, corp. exec.; b. New Orleans, June 22, 1931; s. Arthur and Helen G. (Troyanovich) G-R.; B.S., Tulane U., 1955, J.D., 1962; m. Sandra Sue Cason, 1975. Geologist, Forest Oil Corp., Lafayette, La., 1955-59; admitted to La. bar, 1962; with firm Jackson & Hess, New Orleans, 1962-63; partner firm Leach & Grossel-Rossi, New Orleans, 1963-68, Leach, Grossel-Rossi & Paysse, 1968-77; of counsel Leach, Paysse & Baldwin, 1977—; exec. v.p. Tex. Sch. Book Depository, Inc., Dallas, 1977—; sec., treas. Elisan Corp., New Orleans. Bd. govs. Southeastern Admiralty Law Inst. Mem. Am., Fed., La. bar assns., Maritime Law Assn. U.S., Am. Judicature Soc., La. Hist. Soc., Am. Arbitration Assn., Upper Audubon Assn. (pres. 1971-72), Nat. Rifle Assn. (life), Internat. Oceanographic Found., Audubon Soc. Clubs: Essex, Sports Car of America (pres. Delta region 1965), Dallas Woods and Waters, Brookhaven Country, Dallas Gun. Home: 8901 Douglas St Dallas TX 75225 Office: 8301 Ambassador Row Dallas TX 75247

GROSSER, FRANK THOMAS, mfg. co. exec.; b. N.Y.C., Dec. 6, 1946; s. Frank T. and Gladys M. (Barnes) G.; B.A. in Econs., Lafayette Coll., 1968; m. Jutta Roethke, Aug. 1, 1971; children—Kristen Lynn, Jeffrey Thomas. Sales mgr. Aluminum Co. Am., Atlanta and Chgo., 1968-77, mktg. mgr., 1978-79; v.p. mktg. and sales Hose & Couplings div. Gould Inc., Manitowoc, Wis., 1979—. Served to 1st lt. U.S. Army, 1969-71. Mem. Phi Delta Theta. Club: Branch River Country. Home: 807 Manistee Ct Manitowoc WI 54220 Office: 1440 N 24th St Manitowoc WI 54220

GROSSHAUSER, PETER, mfg. co. exec.; b. Bremen, Germany, May 5, 1936; came to U.S., 1957, naturalized, 1962; s. Klemens and Anna (Honisch) G.; degree in Bus. Adminstrn., Bremer Bildungs Zentrale; M.B.A. in Gen. Mgmt. with honors, St. Mary's Coll. of Calif., Moraga, 1977; m. Doris C. Martinez, Oct. 10, 1959; children—Ana Cecilia, Doris Maria, Peter Michael. Asst. controller Napko Corp., Houston, 1966-72, treas. West Coast ops., Fremont, Calif., 1972-78, asst. to pres., Houston, 1978-79, mgr. materials and distbn., 1980—; dir. Napko S.A., Monterrey, Mex. Former dir., sec. Brownsville (Tex.) Jaycees. Mem. Am. Prodn. and Inventory Control Soc. Republican. Roman Catholic. Home: 518 Lorie Ln Seabrook TX 77586 Office: 5300 Sunrise St Houston TX 77021

GROSSJUNG, THOMAS LEE, banker; b. Jackson, Miss., July 13, 1947; s. Charles G. and Marjorie L. (Carnal) G.; A.S., Miami-Dade Community Coll., 1967; B.A., U. South Fla., 1970; M.B.A., U. Miami, 1977; postgrad. La. State U. Sch. Banking, 1975, Nat. Comml. Lending Grad. Sch., 1979; 1 dau., Shelley Inez. Mgmt. trainee S.E. 1st Nat. Bank Miami (Fla.), 1970-71, personal banker, 1971-76, v.p., asst. dept. head, 1976-77; adminstr. corp. bus. devel. S.E. Banking Corp., 1977-78, seminar lectr., 1975—; sr. v.p., mgr. downtown br. 1st Nat. Bank Greater Miami, 1978-79, sr. v.p., dir. mktg., dir. br. expansion and devel., mem. sr. loan com., 1979-80; exec. v.p., dir. Hanover Bank of Fla., Plantation, 1980—; adj. prof. fin. Fla. Internat. U., 1979—; mem. adv. bd. exec. M.B.A. program U. Miami, 1977—; instr. Am. Inst. Banking, 1975—. Bd. dirs., chmn. fin. com. Goodwill Industries South Fla.; ann. mem. United Way Dade County. Served with USAR, 1970-76. Mem. Am. Inst. Banking, Fla. Bankers Assn., Bank Mktg. Assn., Greater Miami C. of C. Democrat. Methodist. Clubs: Bankers, University (Miami); Brickell Bay. Home: 3687 E Citrus Trace Fort Lauderdale FL 33328 Office: 1380 N University Dr Plantation FL 33322

GROSSMAN, ANNE RAFSKY, interior decorator; b. N.Y.C., Dec. 20, 1922; d. Henry A. and Bertha (Fischel) Rafsky; student Adelphi Coll., 1940-42; B.S., Columbia U., 1944; m. Harry Grossman, Aug. 6, 1950; children—Sandra Kay, Ilene Hope. Partner interior decorating firm Jo-Ann Designs, N.Y.C., 1957-67; owner Anne R. Grossman Interiors, 1967—. Trustee, treas. Henry A. Rafsky Research Fund, Inc. Mem. Nat. Council Jewish Women, N.Y. chpt. WAIF, Am. Soc. Interior Designers. Clubs: B'nai B'rith, Alpine Country. Office: 25 Sutton Pl S New York NY 10022

GROSSMAN, HARRY, lawyer; b. N.Y.C., Oct. 30, 1911; s. Isaac and Anna (Hoffman) G.; B.S., N.Y. U., 1933; LL.B., Columbia U., 1936; m. Barbara J. Solomon, Aug. 9, 1942 (div.); 1 dau., Patricia Joyce; m. 2d, Anne E. Rafsky, Aug. 6, 1950; children—Sandra Kay, Ilene Hope. Admitted to N.Y. bar, 1937, D.C. bar, 1948; dep. collector IRS, 1937-40; partner Grossman & Grossman, N.Y.C., 1950-63, Grossman, Grossman & Feigen, N.Y.C. and Washington 1964-68, Grossman, Feigen & Rossetti, 1968-69; counsel Automobile Driving Schs. Assn., Inc., 1949-54, Eastern Dry Cleaning and Laundry Machinery Distbrs. Assn. Inc., 1961-64, Tri-State Machinery Distbrs. Council, 1964-67, Westchester Asso. Stationers, Inc., 1967-68; lectr. Columbia. Practicing Law Inst., Delehanty Inst., Collegiate Inst. Pres., Atlantic Beach Property Owners Assn., 1954-55; past chmn. campaign Nat. Found. Infantile Paralysis; trustee Harry and Jane Fischel Found. Served from 2d lt. to maj. AUS, 1942-46; lt. col. Res. Decorated Commendation medal; recipient N.Y. Conspicuous Service award, 1946. Mem. Am., N.Y. bar assns., Assn. Bar City N.Y., N.Y. County Lawyers Assn., Fed. Bar Council, Am. Acad. Polit. and Social Scis., Res. Officers Assn., Mil. Order World Wars, Jewish War Vets., Am. Legion, Grand Street Boys' Assn., Zeta Beta Tau. Democrat. Clubs: Alpine Country, Elks, B'nai B'rith. Contbr. articles to periodicals. Home: 25 Sutton Pl S New York NY 10022 Office: 418 Park Ave S New York NY 10016

GROSSMAN, JACK, mktg. exec.; b. N.Y.C., Mar. 22, 1925; s. Benjamin R. and Sarah Dora (Bennett) G.; B.Sc., N.Y. U., 1950, M.B.A., 1952; m. Esther Arline Goldman, Nov. 23, 1949; children—Barbara Ruth, Neil David. Research analyst Biow Co., Inc., N.Y.C., 1951-52, economist, 1952-53, mgr. sales research dept., 1954-56; mgr. sales/media research William Esty Co., Inc., N.Y.C., 1956-62, mgr. research dept., 1962-65, v.p. research, 1966-72, v.p. research, partner, 1972-74, sr. v.p. research, dir., 1974—; asst. adj. prof. mktg. Pace U., 1962-72. Bd. dirs. L.I. Cons. Center, 1979—. Served with U.S. Army, 1943-47. Decorated Purple Heart, Bronze Star with oak leaf cluster. Mem. Am. Mktg. Assn., Advt. Agy. Research Dirs. Council, World Future Soc. Jewish. Home: 1025 Fifth Ave New York NY 10028 Office: 100 E 42 St New York NY 10017

GROSSMAN, MARK IRA, corporate systems exec.; b. Newark, July 13, 1945; s. Sidney and Nettie G.; B.S. in Applied Math., Mass. Inst. Tech., 1967; M.S. in Physics, Rutgers U., 1969, M.S. in Statistics, 1974; m. Susan Helene Cohen, Nov. 22, 1969; children—Jennifer Dara, Jonathan David, Jaclyn Dyan. Ops. research analyst RCA Corp., Princeton, N.J., 1969-73, sr. analyst, 1973-74, mgr., mgmt. info. systems adminstrn., N.Y.C., 1974-75, mgr. mgmt. info. systems fin. and adminstrn., Cherry Hill, N.J., 1975-76, mgr. mgmt. info. systems RCA Am. Communications, Inc., Piscataway, N.J., 1976-78; dir. bus. systems devel. RCA Corp., Princeton, N.J., 1978-79, dir. fin. systems, corp. staff, 1979—. Exec. com. Princeton United Jewish Appeal, 1973—. Mem. Ops. Research Soc. Am., Inst. Mgmt. Scis., Am. Statis. Assn., Sigma Xi. Research presentations. Home: 12 Wallingford Dr Princeton NJ 08540 Office: RCA David Sarnoff Research Center Princeton NJ 08540

GROSSMAN, N. BUD, business exec.; b. Mpls., 1921; grad. U. Minn., 1941. Chmn., pres. Gelco Corp., Eden Prairie, Minn.; chmn. Denver Airport Hilton Inn, Dyco Petroleum Corp., Scottsdale Hilton Hotel; dir. Artic Enterprises, Inc., Econs. Lab. Inc., Northwestern Nat. Bank Mpls., No. States Power Co., Toro Co., Gen. Mills Inc. Office: Gelco Corp One Gelco Dr Eden Prairie MN 55343*

GROSSMAN, OSCAR LAWRENCE, banker; J.D., Harvard U., 1936; m. Hermine Margon; children—Joan Constance, Margaret Ann. Admitted to N.Y. State bar, Calif. bar, also U.S. Supreme Ct., fed., dist. and circuit bars; chief atty. NLRB, Cin., 1937-41; labor relations cons. Sears, Roebuck & Co., Chgo., 1941-42; v.p., dir. Stokes Industries, Cin., 1942-46; pres., chmn. bd. Columbia Supply Co., Los Angeles, 1946-49, Dunster Corp., 1949-54, Washington Savs. & Loan Assn., 1957-58; pres., chmn. bd. dirs. Surety Nat. Bank, Encino, Calif., 1964-79; practice law, Los Angeles, 1954—; cons. savs. and loan banking legislation, 1958-63. Mem. regional adv. com. 14th region U.S. Comptroller Currency, 1973-75; mem. Los Angeles Dist. Atty.'s Adv. Council, Calif. Atty. Gen.'s Adv. Council. Trustee Los Angeles Art Assn. Recipient award of commendation County and City of Los Angeles. Mem. State Bar Calif., Am., N.Y., Los Angeles County bar assn., Am. Judicature Soc., Am., Calif., Ind. bankers assns., Am. Acad. Polit. and Social Sci., A.I.M. (fellow pres.'s council), Clubs: Los Angeles; Harvard of Southern Calif. Office: 17777 Ventura Blvd Encino CA 91316

GROSSMAN, ROBERT ALLEN, railcar leasing co. exec.; b. Port Jervis, N.Y., July 24, 1941; s. George and Helen (Garson) G.; student Cornell U., 1959-60, U. Pa., 1960-62; m. Joan Ward, June 15, 1962; children—Jeffrey, Wendy. Mgr. fin. div. North Shore Packing Co., Inc., North Bellmore, N.Y., 1962-64; mgr. refin. and legal dept. Coburn Corp. Am., Rockville Centre, N.Y., 1964-67; stock broker Weis, Voison & Cannon, Inc., N.Y.C., 1967-69, Nadel & Co., N.Y.C., 1969-70; chmn. bd., chief exec. officer Emons Industries, Inc., York, Pa., 1970—; dir. Interallied Resources Corp., N.Y.C. Mem. York Area C. of C. (dir. 1978—). Office: 490 E Market St York PA 17403

GROSSMAN, ROBERT ERICH, mfg. co. exec.; b. Chgo., Mar. 24, 1937; s. Maurice Orrington and Nettie (Belitsky) G.; B.S., Northwestern U., 1964; M.B.A., U. Calif., 1965; m. Karen Ann Peterson, Oct. 16, 1973; 1 dau., Brooke Rana. Auditor, Arthur Anderson, Chgo., 1965-67; mgr. corp. devel. Kaiser Aluminum & Chem., Oakland, Calif., 1967-70; internal mgmt. cons. ITT, N.Y.C., 1970-75; dir. mgmt. cons. Coopers & Lybrand, Los Angeles, 1975-77; asst. chmn. bd., chief fin. officer Rodac Corp., Carson, Calif., 1977—; dir. Rodac Corp., Action Leather Craft Corp., J.B. Realty Corp. Mem. Am. Inst. C.P.A.'s, Am. Soc. Mgmt. Cons. Club: Sombrero Yacht and Golf. Home: 1257 Westgate Los Angeles CA 90025 Office: 1005 Artesia Blvd Carson CA 90746

GROTE, EDWIN O., fin. co. exec.; b. Evansville, Ill., Mar. 16, 1924; student Evansville Coll. Formerly exec. v.p. ops. Chrysler Fin. Corp., Troy, Mich., pres., chief operating officer, 1980—. Office: Chrysler Financial Corp 900 Tower Dr Troy MI 48908*

GROTE, OTTO FREDERICK, stock broker; b. Boston, Dec. 20, 1930; s. Friedrich Franz Graf and Rachel Derby (Smith) G.; A.B. cum laude, Harvard U., 1953, M.B.A., 1957. Asso. corp. fin. dept. Hornblower & Weeks-Hemphill, Noyes, N.Y.C., 1961-67; research sales mgr. J. & W. Seligman & Co., N.Y.C., 1967-72; prin. Van Bergen & Co., Inc., N.Y.C., 1972-78, chmn., 1975-78; prin., pres. Derby Securities, Inc., N.Y.C., 1978—. Served to 1st lt. USAF, 1954-56. Club: River (N.Y.C.). Office: Derby Securities Inc 120 Broadway New York NY 10271

GROTH, ROGER PETER, real estate exec.; b. Mpls., Mar. 7, 1935; s. Clarence William and Ethyl Ann (Copeland) G.; B.A., U. Idaho, 1957; cert. basic engring. sci., U. Minn., 1964, postgrad. Sch. Bus., 1964-67; m. Marcia Jean Thornton, Sept. 13, 1958; children—Randall T., Whitney C., Cynthia L. Successively instr., supervising tech. writer, sr. systems design engr. Sperry Rand Univac, St. Paul, 1960-70; mfrs. rep., Bloomington, Minn., 1970-73; sales asso. Bermel-Smaby Realty, Inc., Mpls., 1973-77; pres., chief exec. officer Paladin, Inc., Realtors, Bloomington, 1977—; instr. real estate investments, contracts. Bd. dirs. Bloomington Conv. Bur., 1977-79, Bloomington Devel. Council, 1980—; mem. Bloomington Promotion and Devel. Comm., 1977-79. Served to lt. (j.g.) USNR, 1957-60; comdr. Res. Cert. resdl. specialist. Mem. Nat. Assn. Realtors, Realtors Nat. Mktg. Inst., Minn. Assn. Realtors, Greater Mpls. Area Bd. Realtors, U.S. Naval Inst., Navy League, Naval Res. Assn., Res. Officers Assn., Aircraft Owners and Pilots Assn. Republican. Presbyterian. Club: Rotary (Paul Harris fellow 1980). Contbr. articles to profl. jours. Home: 8429 Little Rd Bloomington MN 55437 Office: NW Financial Center 7900 Xerxes Ave S Bloomington MN 55431

GROTHE, FRANCIS DONALD, fin tube coil mfg. co. exec.; b. St. Louis, Apr. 19, 1928; s. Francis Bartholomew and Margaret Helen G.; B.S. in Air Conditioning and Refrigeration Engring., Calif. State Poly. Coll., 1954; children—Carol Ann, Nancy Elizabeth. Application engr. Kennard Corp., St. Louis, 1954-58; chief engr. Chgo. Steel Furnace, Elk Grove, Ill., 1958-61; sales engr. Sweiger-Davidson Co., Chgo., 1961-64; owner, mgr. F.R. Grothe & Assos., Chgo., 1964-66; chief engr. Anderson-Snow Corp., Schiller Park, Ill., 1966—, v.p., 1973—. Served with USN, 1946-48, 51-52. Mem. ASHRAE. Republican. Roman Catholic. Club: Mission Hills Country. Home: 1621 E Mission Hills Rd Northbrook IL 60062 Office: 9225 Ivanhoe St Schiller Park IL 60176

GROTKOWSKI, EDWIN ADAM, cons. engring. co. exec.; b. Sexsmith, Alta., Can., Jan. 30, 1950; student U. Alta., 1968-70; diploma in bus. adminstrn. No. Alta. Inst. Tech., 1972; m. Patricia A. Grotkowski, Aug. 19, 1972; children—Shelene, Cameron. With Imperial Oil Ltd., 1972-74, Luscar Ltd., 1974-76, Asso. Engring. Services Ltd., Edmonton, Alta., 1976-77; with Cheriton and Assos., Ltd., Edmonton, 1977—, now v.p. fin./adminstrn.; dir. pres. Assembly Devels. Ltd.; instr. No. Alta. Inst. Tech. Mem. Cert. Gen. Accts. Assn. (cert. gen. acct.). Home: 71 Broadview Crescent Saint Albert AB T8N 0B1 Canada

GROVE, BARRY, theatre mgmt. cons.; b. Madison, Conn., Nov. 19, 1951; s. Herbert Frank and Cecelia Irene (Sullivan) G.; A.B., Dartmouth Coll., 1973; m. Rosemary Barnsdall Blackmon, Oct. 8, 1973. Prodn. stage mgr. Shakespeare & Co., Eng. and U.S., 1973; gen. mgr. New Repertory Project, also Theatre Dept., U. R.I., Kingston, 1973-75; mng. dir. Manhattan Theatre Club, Inc., N.Y.C., 1975—, now cons.; theatre panelist N.Y. State Council on the Arts, 1979—, chmn., 1980—; cons. in field. Recipient Tony awards, 1978, Time Mag. award, 1977, 78, Drama Desk award, 1978, Obie award, 1976-79, James N. Vaughan award, 1978. Mem. Off-Off Broadway Alliance (dir. 1976—), League of Off-Broadway Theatre and Producers, Actor's Equity, Dartmouth Alumni Assn. N.Y. Congregationalist. Club: Yale. Producer plays and musicals including: The Runner Stumbles, 1975; The Last Street Play, 1977; Ashes, 1977; Rear Column, 1978; Ain't Misbehavin', 1978; Mass Appeal, 1980. Office: 321 E 73d St New York NY 10021

GROVE, ERNEST L., JR., utility exec.; b. Martinsburg, W.Va., 1924; B.A., Denison U., 1947; M.B.A., U. Pa., 1949; J.D., U. Conn., 1959; married. Vice pres., chief fin. and acctg. officer Conn. Light & Power Co., 1965-66, All N.E. Utilities Systems Co., 1966-72; exec. v.p. N.E. Utilities Service Co., 1972-75; sr. exec. v.p. fin., dir. Detroit Edison Co., 1975—; v.p., dir. Midwest Energy Resources Co., St. Clair Energy Corp., Edison Illuminating Co. Detroit, Peninsular Electric Light Co., Washtenaw Energy Corp.; dir. Asso. Electric and Gas Services Ltd. Office: Detroit Edison Co 200 2d Ave Detroit MI 48226*

GROVES, CHARLES FRANCIS, mfg. co. ofcl.; b. N.Y.C., June 2, 1949; s. Charles Xavier and Mary Catherine (McNicholas) G.; B.S., City U. N.Y., 1973; m. Joann T. Murphy, Sept. 16, 1971; children—Timothy Patrick, Sean Michael. Supr., Nat. Distillers & Chem. Co., N.Y.C., 1972; asst. supr. Union Carbide Corp., N.Y.C., 1972-73; budget mgr. Interphoto Corp., N.Y.C., 1973-74, asst. controller, 1974-79; dir. fin. and adminstrn. Keel Mfg. div. Pickwick Internat., Inc., Hauppauge, N.Y., 1974-79; controller PRC Recording Co., Compton, Calif., 1979-80, plant mgr., 1980—. Served with U.S. Army, 1969-71. Mem. Am. Mgmt. Assn., Nat. Assn. Accts. Roman Catholic. Home: 20530 Anza Ave Apt 217 Torrance CA 90503 Office: 18700 Laurel Park Rd Compton CA 90220

GROVES, FRANKLIN NELSON, hwy. constrn. co. exec.; b. Mpls., Dec. 28, 1930; s. Frank Malvon and Hazel Olive G.; B.B.A., U. Minn., 1954; m. Carolyn Thomas, July 31, 1954; children—Catherine Mary Groves Gangelhoff, Franklin Nelson Jr., Elizabeth Ann. Sec. treas. S.J. Groves & Sons., Co., Mpls., 1954-57, treas, 1957-69, v.p., 1964-69, pres., 1969—, chmn. bd., 1971—, dir., 1964—. Founder, bd. dirs. Groves Learning Center, 1972—; trustee Mpls. Soc. Fine Arts, 1977—; pres., trustee Groves Found., 1971—. Served to lt. USAF, 1954-56. Mem. Moles, Beavers, Am. Saddle Horse Breeder Assn., Thoroughbred Club. Am. Club: Mpls. Athletic. Home: 1482 Hunter Dr Wayzata MN 55391 Office: PO Box 1267 Minneapolis MN 55440

GROVES, RICHARD HUGH, communications exec.; b. Detroit, Dec. 18, 1929; s. Charles Paul and Viola Emma (Kreger) G.; student Miami U., 1948-50; B.A., U. Mich., 1952, M.B.A. cum laude, 1953; m. Mary Ann Wilkinson, Feb. 1, 1952; children—Richard Hugh, Charles Paul, Virginia Ellen. Mktg. and sales mgr. Gen. Electric, N.Y.C. and Detroit, 1953-58; sales mgr. Iron Age mag., Phila., 1958-67, pub., 1967-70; pub., v.p. Chiltonco, Phila., 1970-73, exec. v.p., 1973—; dir. Newton Falls Paper Mill. Co-chmn., Heart Fund Delaware County, 1978. Served with USN, 1953-55. Mem. Phila. C. of C., Am. Bus. Press, Mag. Pubs. Assn., Bus. and Profl. Advt. Assn., Sigma Alpha Epsilon, Beta Gamma Sigma, Phi Kappa Phi. Republican. Episcopalian. Clubs: Aronimink Golf, Pine Valley Golf, Merion Cricket, Detroit Athletic. Home: 442 Margo Ln Berwyn PA 19312 Office: Chilton Way Radnor PA 19089

GROVES, RICHARD NEWLAND, JR., mfg. co. exec.; b. Syracuse, N.Y., Sept. 11, 1936; s. Richard Newland and Charlotte (Johnston) G.; B.S., U.S. Mil. Acad., 1958; M.S.E., Purdue U., 1963, Ph.D., 1968; m. Margaret E. Barnhill, June 6, 1958; children—Charlotte E., Kelly A. Commd. 2d lt. U.S. Army, 1958; advanced through grades to maj., 1966; asst. prof. U.S. Mil. Acad., West Point, N.Y., 1963-66; aircraft maintenance officer 1st Air Cavalry Div., Vietnam, 1966-67; resigned, 1967; pres. Midwest Applied Sci. Corp., West Lafayette, Ind., 1967-71; group v.p. Bell & Howell Co., Pasadena, Calif., 1971-75; v.p. Profl. Assos. Inc., Irvine, Calif., 1975-77; sr. exec. v.p. Zenith Labs., Northvale, N.J., 1975-78; pres. Century Indsl. Assos., Irvine, 1975-77; chmn., chief exec. officer Belvac Internat. Industries, Inc., Long Island City, N.Y., 1976, Effective Packaging Inc., Irvine, 1975-77, Century Industries Corp., Sierra Madre, Calif. and N.Y.C., 1977—; chmn., pres., chief exec. officer Internat. Election Systems Corp., Beverly, N.J., 1978—, CCA Electronics Corp., Cherry Hill, N.J., 1978—; vis. prof. Prudue U., 1968-71; cons. in field. Decorated Air medal, Bronze Star. Mem. Am. Mgmt. Assn., ASME, Am. Inst. Aeros. and Astronautics, Tau Beta Pi. Republican. Episcopalian. Clubs: Kiwanis, Tof Roses, Mason, Elks. Contbr. articles to profl. jours. Patentee electric barbecue and cool range. Home: 624 Arbolada Dr Arcadia CA 91006 Office: 49 S Baldwin Ave Sierra Madre CA 91024

GROW, DONALD LELAND, ins. co. exec.; b. Los Angeles, June 20, 1938; s. Leonard W. and Dorothy G. (Engberg) G.; student El Camino Coll., 1958-63, UCLA Extension, 1962-67; A.A., Cypress Coll., 1979; m. Shirley Ann Voyda, Aug. 22, 1970; children—Charles Leonard, Kevin Matthew, Kristi Lynn. Collection mgr. Casualty Ins. Co. Calif., Los Angeles, 1957-65, Transit Casualty Co., Los Angeles, 1967-69, Swett and Crawford Co., Los Angeles, 1972-74; collection supr. Mission Equities Ins. Co., Los Angeles, 1965-67; office mgr. Gen. Accident Group, Los Angeles, 1969-72; regional credit mgr. Employers Ins. Wausau, Los Angeles, 1974—; co-editor, tchr. company premium accounting and collections course Ins. Ednl. Assn. and Ins. Credit Mgrs. Assn Los Angeles. Pres. La Palma (Calif.) Homeowners Assn., 1974; mem. La Palma Traffic Safety Com., 1975—. Mem. Ins. Credit Mgrs. Assn. Los Angeles (pres. 1971, 81), Gardena Jaycees (Jaycees of Month 1969, Jaycee of Quarter 1970, state dir. 1969) La Palma C. of C. (dir. 1976). Republican. Presbyterian. Home: 5954 Thelma St La Palma CA 90623 Office: 3130 Wilshire Blvd Los Angeles CA 90010

GRUBB, LOUIS EDWARD, bus. exec.; b. Passaic, N.J., Apr. 17, 1912; s. William Henry and Nettie Ralph (Arnold) G.; B.A., Wesleyan U., Middletown, Conn., 1934; LL.D., Marshall U., 1976; m. Catherine Adelaide Swartz, May 15, 1936; children—Nancy Southwick (Mrs. David Lee Byrd), William Henry. With INCO, Inc. (Internat. Nickel Co., Inc.), N.Y.C., 1934-77, v.p., 1961-64, asst. v.p. parent co., 1964-67; dir. Internat. Nickel, Ltd., U.K., 1964-71, mng. dir., 1967-68, chmn., 1968; mng. dir. Henry Wiggin & Co., Ltd., 1964-67, chmn., 1968; v.p. Inco Ltd., 1968-71, exec. v.p., dir., 1971, pres., chief officer, 1972-74, chmn., chief officer, chmn. exec. com., 1974-77; ret., 1977; dir. Ashland Oil, Inc., Canada Life Assurance Co., Moore Corp. Mem. Am. Inst. Mining, Metall. and Petroleum Engrs., Pilgrims of U.S., Canadian Inst. Mining and Metallurgy, Metals Soc. U.K. Clubs: Toronto, Rosedale Golf, York, Toronto Hunt (Toronto); New York Yacht, Union League, India House, University (N.Y.C.); Baltusrol Golf (N.J.); Rumson (N.J.) Country; Sea Bright Beach; Royal

Mid-Surrey Golf (Eng.); Royal Cork Yacht (Ireland). Home: 3 Ave of Two Rivers S Rumson NJ 07760 Office: One New York Plaza New York NY 10004

GRUBMAN, WALLACE KARL, chem. co. exec.; b. N.Y.C., Sept. 12, 1928; B.S. in Chem. Engring., Columbia U., 1950; M.S. in Chem. Engring., N.Y. U., 1954; m. Ruth Winer, July 29, 1950; children—James W., Steven L., Eric P. Pres., chief operating officer, dir. Nat. Starch & Chem. Corp., Bridgewater, N.J., 1950—; dir. United Nat. Bank, Plainfield, N.J. Mem. Chem. Mfrs. Assn., Soc. Chem. Industries, Am. Inst. Chem. Engrs. Office: National Starch & Chemical Corp 10 Finderne Ave Bridgewater NJ 08807

GRUBSTEIN, JOSEPH FREDERICK, leather co. exec.; b. Newark, Jan. 30, 1911; s. Charles and Esther (Katz) G.; A.B., Yale U., 1932; m. Sibyl Jean Herzog, Oct. 21, 1946; children—Leigh Grubstein Fenwick, Peter Sulzberger Herzog. Pres., Am. Leather Mfg. Co., Rahway, N.J., 1950-80, chmn. bd., 1980—. Served to lt. USNR, 1942-47. Decorated Bronze Star; Croix de Guerre (France). Clubs: Yale (N.Y.C.); Yale (Central N.J.); Essex Hunt, Kenwood Country. Home: Bernardsville NJ 07924 Office: 2195 Elizabeth Ave Rahway NJ 07965

GRUEN, MARK DENNIS, mktg. exec.; b. Chgo., Apr. 26, 1951; s. Alfred J. and Lotte G.; B.A. with honors, Drake U., 1973. Copywriter, Age Advt., Inc., 1973-74, copy editor, 1974-75; catalog mgr. Spiegel, Inc., Oak Brook, Ill., 1976-77; v.p. creative and client relations RPG & Assos., advt. agy., Lincolnwood, Ill., 1978; co-founder Norman Rockwell Mus., Inc., Northbrook, Ill., 1979, v.p. mktg., 1979—; cons. mktg., Chgo., 1979—; speaker direct mktg. Mem. Direct Mail/Mktg. Assn., Chgo. Assn. Direct Mktg. (direct mail mktg. awards 1979-80), Am. Mktg. Assn., Nat. Assn. Ltd. Edit. Dealers (distinctions), Collector's Plate Makers Guild. Author: Limited Edition Dealers Guide to Successful Print Advertising; also trade jour. columns.

GRUENWALD, WILLIAM RONALD, electronics mfg. co. mktg. exec.; b. N.Y.C., Feb. 13, 1936; s. William Frederick and Mary (Massimi) G.; B.S.E.E., U. Mo., Rolla, 1958; m. Diane P. Garcia, Apr. 8, 1958; children—Kathi Lynn, William G., Cindy Lee. Design engr. Emerson Electric Co., 1958-60; product mgr. Gen. Electric Co., Valley Forge, Pa., 1960-72; v.p. engring. Simmonds Precision, Inc., Vergennes, Vt., 1972-75; v.p. mktg. RF Communications div. Harris Corp., Rochester, N.Y., 1975-78; v.p. mktg. N.E. Electronics div. No. Telecom, Concord, N.H., 1978—. Mem. U.S. Ind. Telephone Assn., Am. Electronics Assn. Home: 40 Random Rd RFD 5 Bedford NH 03102 Office: No Telecom Airport Rd Concord NH 03301

GRUETZMACHER, ALFRED H., commodities trader; b. Chgo., Apr. 14, 1919; student Central YMCA Coll., Chgo., Ripon (Wis.) Coll.; m. Marcella. Ind. trader Chgo. Bd. Trade, 1953-61, partner Geldermann & Co., Chgo., 1961-69; v.p., dir., 1969—; dir. Chgo. Bd. Trade, 1960-65, 2d vice-chmn, 1965, vice-chmn., 1966-67, now chmn. bd. Mem. Nat. Grain Dealers Assn., Calif. Grain and Feed Dealers Assn. Office: Suite 1115 141 W Jackson Blvd Chcago IL 60604

GRUM, CLIFFORD J., publishing exec.; b. Davenport, Iowa, Dec. 12, 1934; s. Allen F. and Nathalie (Cate) G.; B.A., Austin Coll., 1956; M.B.A., Wharton Sch., U. Pa., 1958. Formerly with Republic Nat. Bank, Dallas; former v.p. finance Temple Industries, Diboll, Tex.; with Time, Inc., N.Y.C., treas., 1973-75, v.p., 1975—; publisher Fortune mag., 1975-78. Office: Time Inc Time and Life Bldg Rockefeller Center New York NY 10020

GRUND, CLARENCE B., JR., elec. utility exec.; b. Portland, Oreg., July 31, 1925; s. Clarence B. and Frances (Eckert) G.; B.E.E., Ala. Poly. Inst., 1951, M.E.E., 1952; m. Marilyn Grace Hornsby, May 2, 1948. Engr. system planning Ala. Power Co., Birmingham, 1953-58; engr. rate dept. So. Services, Inc., Birmingham, 1958-63; supr. research rate dept., 1964-67, asst. mgr. rate dept., 1967-69, mgr. rate dept., 1969-72, asst. v.p., 1972—; instr. Ala. Poly. Inst., 1951-52, extension center U. Ala., 1952. Pres., Rocky Ridge Vol. Fire Dept., 1957-58, bd. dirs., 1956-62. Served with USAAF, World War II. Registered profl. engr., Ala., Miss. Mem. IEEE, Nat. Soc. Profl. Engrs., Birmingham Soc. Engrs., Newcomen Soc. N. Am., Internat. Platform Assn., Am. Legion, Phi Kappa Phi, Tau Beta Pi, Eta Kappa Nu. Contbr. articles to profl. jours. Home: 3421 Cruzan Dr Birmingham AL 35243 Office: Southern Services Inc 64 Perimeter Center E PO Box 720071 Atlanta GA 30346

GRUNEWALD, RICHARD OTTO, mfr. farm and truck equipment; b. Milw., Dec. 28, 1928; s. Otto W. and Paula Anna (Weerts) G.; B.S. in Agr., U. Wis., 1952; m. Sue Jorgensen, Jan. 2, 1954; 3 children. Mgr. tng. and edn. Allis-Chalmers Corp., 1968-73; mgr. mktg. services White Farm Equipment Co., 1973-75; v.p. mktg. Schwartz Mfg. Co., div. Chromalloy Am. Corp., Lester Prairie, Minn., 1975—. Served with AUS, 1952-54. Mem. Nat. Agrl. Mktg. Assn., Farm and Indsl. 1st. Republican. Methodist. Club: Shriners. Home: 4380 Shady Ln Mound MN 55364 Office: 129 Pine St Lester Prairie MN 55354

GRUNSETH, JON RIEDER, mfg. co. exec.; b. Nov. 11, 1945; s. Rieder J. and Louise (Brunsdale) G.; B.A. in History and Polit. Sci., Luther Coll., 1967; postgrad. (Bush Found. Leadership fellow) Georgetown U., 1975; m. Katharine S. Winston, Apr. 3, 1971; children—Nina, Lucia, Katharine. Dist. dir. Minn. Republican Com., Cold Spring, 1971-74, vice-chmn., 1975-76; farmer, Granite Ledge, Minn., 1972-76; v.p. Paulsen Advt. Agy., Sioux Falls, S.D., 1976; adminstrv. asst. to Larry Pressler, Washington, 1976-78; v.p. govt. relations Econs. Lab. Inc., St. Paul, 1978—; mem. faculty Inst. Applied Politics, Westminster Coll., Salt Lake City, 1980—. Rep. candidate for Congress from 6th Dist. Minn., 1974. Served with U.S. Army, 1968-70. Mem. Soap and Detergent Assn., Chem. Spltys. Mfrs. Assn. (dir.), NAM. Home: 17940 Blackbird Trail Hastings MN 55033 Office: Osborn Bldg 370 Wabasha St Saint Paul MN 55102

GRUTSCH, RALPH JOSEPH, JR., mfg. co. exec.; b. St. Louis, Sept. 18, 1932; s. Ralph Joseph and Lucile M. (MacManemin) G.; B.S., U.S. Naval Acad., 1955; postgrad. M.I.T.-Sloan Sch., 1974; m. Winifred Mary Saviori, June 11, 1955; children—Leigh Ann, Ellen Marie. With Allis-Chalmers Mfg. Co., 1955-64, sales engr., Washington, 1956-61, mgr. marine sale, 1961-63, product mgr. marine equipment, 1963-64; sales engr. Solar Turbines Internat., Washington, 1964-65, mgr. application engring., 1965-70, product mgr., 1970, dir. product mgmt., 1970-74, dir. bus. planning and mgmt., 1974-77, dir. total quality assurance, 1977, v.p. tech. ops., 1977-79, v.p. internat. ops., San Diego, 1979—. Bd. dirs./ltd. grant com. planning, allocation and resource council/funding policies task force United Way of San Diego, 1976-80. Served with USMC, 1950-51. Mem. Am. Soc. Naval Engrs., ASME. Office: PO Box 80966 San Diego CA 92138

GRYCNER, EDWARD, moped mfg. co. exec.; b. Wilno, Poland, May 1, 1924; came to U.S., 1951, naturalized, 1956; s. Robert and Victoria Von Grutzner; M.B.A., Sch. Econs., London U., 1949, B.S. in Fgn. Trade, Sch. Fgn. Trade, 1949; m. Iris Lila Kehr, May 1, 1956; children—Henry, Richard, Gregory, Pamela, Nancy, April, Michelle. Export traffic mgr. George Wehry Co., N.Y.C., 1951-55; export controller U.S. Borax Corp., 1956-66; mgr. internat. ops. Ingersoll Rand, N.Y.C., 1966-67; dir. internat. ops. Revell, Inc., 1967-70; pres. Grycner Toys Internat., Grycner Leisure Group, and Grycner Moped Corp., Palm Springs, Calif., 1970—, chmn. bd., pres. Grycner Moped Corp., 1977—; lectr. fgn. trade state univs. Calif., 1978—. Recipient cert. Am. Soc. Internat. Execs., 1967. Mem. Fgn. Trade Assn. So. Calif., Los Angeles C. of C., Palm Springs C. of C., Am. Sporting Goods Assn., Am. Hobby Assn. Club: Los Angeles Internat. Contbr. numerous articles on internat. trade to mags. Home: 796 N Via Miraleste Palm Springs CA 92262 Office: PO Box 1987 Palm Springs CA 92263

GSCHWIND, ALFRED EDWARD, reins. exec.; b. LaCrosse, Wis., Oct. 19, 1932; s. Alfred James and Mary Elizabeth (Donahue) G.; B.S. in Commerce and Fin., U. Notre Dame, 1954; M.B.A., U. Pa., 1960; m. Marilyn Frances Martin, Aug. 23, 1958; children—Christina Marie, Mark Alfred, Theresa Ann, Andrew Martin. Vice-pres. reins. Carpenter Mgmt. Corp., N.Y.C., 1965-71; exec. v.p. Worexco Corp., N.Y.C., 1971-75, pres., dir., 1975—; pres., dir. Am. Overseas Mgmt. Corp., N.Y.C., 1979—, also Am. Overseas Reins. Co., Underwriting Mgmt. Services (Bermuda), Ltd.; dir. Tower Hill Ins. Co., Victor O. Schinnerer & Co., Inc. Served with USNR, 1955-58. C.P.C.U. Mem. Ind. Reins. Underwriters Assn. (chmn., dir.)., Drug and Chem. Club. Republican. Roman Catholic. Office: 40 Wall St New York NY 10005

GUAGLIANONE, ROBERT ANTHONY, acct.; b. Collingswood, N.J., Apr. 18, 1952; s. Anthony Thomas and Alice Teresa G.; B.S. in Acctg., Drexel U., 1977, M.B.A. in Fin., 1980; m. Jacquelyn Alice Wadsworth, Sept. 22, 1973. Loan collector 1st Peoples Bank, Westmont, N.J., 1970-72; acct. Bob Scarborough Inc., Marlton, N.J., 1972-74, sr. staff acct., 1974-76, controller, 1976—. Home: 4 Addington Ct Voorhees NJ 08043 Office: PO Box 387 Marlton NJ 08053

GUANCIALE, DAN, Realtor, real estate developer; b. Colellongo, Italy, Apr. 6, 1928; s. Domenic and Carolina (Mancini) G.; student St. Francis de Sales, Newark, 1948, Franklin Inst., 1949, Internat. Corr. Schs., 1950-52, Dennison U., 1952-56; m. Patricia Sue McCann, Aug. 26, 1950; children—Patrick Donato, Robin Sue, Tina Marie, Dino Adam. Process devel. project engr. Owens Corning Fiberglas Co., Newark, Ohio, 1950-58; plant engr. Weakley Mfg. Co., Newark, 1958-59, plant mgr., 1959-61; v.p. Newark Trust Co., 1961-69; v.p. Arkay Homes, Newark, 1969-71; pres. Woeste Real Estate, Inc., Newark, 1971-78; prin. Patrick D. Guanciale, Real Estate, Newark, 1978—. Life senator, Jr. C. of C. Internat., 1963—; treas. Newark Catholic Athletic Assn., 1965—; bd. dirs. Licking County council Boy Scouts Am., 1963—; mem. Licking County (Ohio) Starlight Sch. Bd., 1962—; bd. dirs. United Way, Newark, 1972—; bd. dirs. Mid-Ohio Multiple Sclerosis Soc.; chmn. Licking County Multiple Sclerosis Soc. Recipient Distinguished Service award Newark Jaycees, 1961, 62, 63; named Licking County Outstanding Young Man of Yr., C. of C., 1963. Mem. Licking County Bd. Realtors, Nat. Assn. Real Estate Bds. Republican. Roman Catholic. Republican. Clubs: Moundbuilders Country, K.C. Home: 700 Tall Oaks Dr Newark OH 43055 Office: 40 N 2d St Newark OH 43055

GUARNIERI, FRED RAYMOND, JR., retail wine and liquor exec.; b. Warren, Ohio, Apr. 24, 1940; s. Fred Raymond and Carolyn Elizabeth (Van Huffel) G.; B.A., Youngstown U., 1962; m. Patricia Ann Pape, Apr. 22, 1967; children—Elizabeth Carolyn, Patricia Anne. Owner, mgr. Freddy's Liquor Shop, Westmont, N.J., 1967—. Served to lt. USNR, 1962-66. Mem. U.S. Package Store Assn., N.J. Package Store Assn. (dir. 1979), S. Jersey Package Store Assn. (exec. v.p. 1979), Les Amis du Vin, Wine Connoisseurs Calif., Le Comite National des Vins de France. Republican. Roman Catholic. Clubs: Rotary (pres. 1972-73), Tavistock Country, K.C. Office: Freddy's Liquor Shop 570 W Cuthbert Blvd Westmont NJ 08108

GUAS, RENE, constrn. co. exec.; b. Havana, Cuba, Jan. 24, 1949 (mother Am. citizen); s. Mariano W. and Lillian (Kemp) G.; B.S. in Indsl. Engring., La. State U., Baton Rouge, 1971; M.B.A., U. New Orleans, 1976; m. Minia F. Fein, Mar. 4, 1978; 1 dau., Stephanie Renee. Estimator, project engr. T.L. James Co., New Orleans, 1972-74; project engr. J.A. Jones Constrn. Co., New Orleans, 1974; cost engr. Fremin-Smith Services Co., 1975-76, comptroller, 1976-77, v.p. fin., 1977-81; v.p. Poydras Services & Devel., 1981—; mem. faculty U. New Orleans; cons. in field. Chmn. fin. com. Big Bros. New Orleans, 1972-73. Served to capt. USAR, 1971-72. Registered profl. engr., La. Mem. Asso. Builders and Contractors, Asso. Gen. Contractors. Republican. Roman Catholic. Clubs: Ormond Country, River Ridge Good fellows (pres. 1979-80). Home: 1301 Rural St River Ridge LA 70123

GUBANC, DAVID MICHAEL, steel co. exec.; b. Toledo, Oct. 31, 1949; s. Robert David and Louise Marie (Soule) G.; B.S. in Chem. Engring., Northwestern U., 1971; M.B.A., Cleve. State U., 1979. Combustion technologist Republic Steel Corp., Independence, Ohio, 1975-77, staff environ. engr., Cleve., 1977-79, solid waste mgmt. engr., 1979—. Trustee, Garden Valley Neighborhood House, 1976-80; mem. Parma Heights (Ohio) Planning Commn., 1979—. Served with USN, 1971-75. Registered profl. engr., Ohio. Mem. Am. Inst. Chem. Engrs. (chmn. govt. interaction Cleve. sect. 1977-79), Northwestern U. Alumni Club Cleve. (trustee 1977-79), Water Mgmt. Assn. of Ohio, Assn. Iron and Steel Engrs. (vice chmn. planning com. Parma Heights 1979—). Republican. Presbyterian. Club: Masons. Home: 3359 W 31st St Cleveland OH 44109 Office: PO Box 6778 Room 523R Cleveland OH 44101

GUBBINS, PAUL GORDON, lawyer, business exec.; b. Quincy, Ill., Aug. 20, 1921; s. George H. and Edna (Wottman) G.; B.S., Northwestern U., 1942; LL.B., Harvard U., 1945; m. Corinne King, Apr. 8, 1950; children—Michael D., Paula E. Admitted to Ill. bar, 1946, Conn. bar, 1956; asso. firm Scott, MacLeish & Falk, Chgo., 1945-48; asst. gen. counsel Western claims dept. Hartford Accident and Indemnity Co., Chgo., 1948-52; v.p., gen. counsel F.H. McGraw & Co., N.Y.C., 1952-63; asst. gen. counsel Colt Industries, Inc., N.Y.C., 1963—, gen. counsel Hartford Divs. (Conn.), also Holley Carburetor (Mich.), 1963—; dir. Hartford et Cie, Paris, France, Pratt, Whitney & Herbert, Coventry, Eng. Mem. Am. Ordnance Assn., Am. Helicopter Soc., Am., N.Y., Conn. bar assns., Am. Rifle Assn., Nat. Skeet Shooting Assn., A.M.A. Elk. Clubs: Wampanoag Country; Hartford. Home: 156 Westmont West Hartford CT 06117 Office: Charter Oak Blvd West Hartford CT 06101

GUCKENHEIMER, DANIEL PAUL, banker; b. Tel Aviv, Oct. 10, 1943; s. Ernest and Eva Guckenheimer; came to U.S., 1947, naturalized, 1957; B.B.A. in Fin., U. Houston, 1970; cert. hosp. adminstrn., Trinity U., San Antonio, 1973; m. Helen Sandra Fox, Dec. 21, 1969; children—Debra Ellen, Julie Susan. Asst. adminstr. Harris County Hosp. Dist., Houston, 1970-76; pres. Mid Am. Investments, Kansas City, Kans., 1976; exec. dir. Allen County Hosp., Iola, Kans., 1977-78; comml. loanofficer Traders Bank, Kansas City, Mo., 1979-80, v.p. and mgr. installment loans, 1980—; v.p., mgr. Traders Ward Parkway Bank, 1980—. Bd. dirs. United Way, Iola, Kans., 1977-78; adv. bd. Country Side Estate Nursing Home, Iola, 1977-78; clinic adminstr. 190th USAF Clinic. Served with USAF, 1962-66, maj. Res. Mem. Am. Coll. Hosp. Adminstrs., Am. Hosp. Assn., N.G. Guard Assn. Clubs: Iola Rotary; Kansas City. Home: 10259 Caenen Lake Rd Lenexa KS 66215 Office: 1125 Grand Ave Kansas City MO 64106

GUDIS, MICHAEL LAURENCE, mgmt. cons., county ofcl.; b. Bklyn., May 29, 1936; s. Henry and Ruth (Cohn) G.; B.A., George Washington U., 1958, postgrad., 1961. Auditing supr. Sears Roebuck & Co., Washington, 1953-57; sr. accountant Tepper & Kozlow, C.P.A.'s, Washington, 1958-59; asst. controller Pascal, Inc., Washington, 1959-60; systems acct. Treasury Dept. Washington, 1960-65, P.O. Dept., Washington, 1965; pres. mgmt. cons. firm Michael L. Gudis & Assos., Washington, 1965-71; adminstrv. partner acctg. firm Gudis, Hillman & Kriegsfeld, 1971—. Lectr. acctg. and finance Dunbarton Coll., Washington, 1966-68; lectr. acctg. and taxation U. Md., 1970-75, mem. Speakers bur., 1975—; pres. Transcontinental Data Processing of Greater Washington, Inc.; cons. Dept. Labor, Dept. Interior, USPHS. Auditor, B'nai B'rith Youth Orgn., Washington; pres. co-ed singles unit B'nai B'rith, 1977-78; past pres. B'nai B'rith Gudelsky Lodge; mem. finance com. Montgomery County Day Care Centers, 1970; pres. Jewish Single Adult Council Washington, 1973-77. Mem. exec. bd. Montgomery County Young Democrats, 1967—, pres., 1969-71; fin. adviser Montgomery County Democratic State Central Com., 1967-71; chmn. precincts, 1970, 73-78; campaign treas. Dem. party Montgomery County, 1974; com. mem. various task forces Montgomery County Council, mem., 1978—, liaison to Md. Legislature, 1978—; mem. legis. com. Md. Assn. of Counties, 1978; mem. human resources com. Met. Washington Council Govts.; mem. steering com. fin. and taxation Nat. Assn. of Counties, 1979—. Enrolled agt. IRS. Mem. Fed. Govt. Accountants Assn. (nat. dir. 1965-67), Soc. Advancement Mgmt. (dir. 1964-65), Am. Accounting Assn., Systems and Procedures Assn., Nat. Soc. Pub. Accountants (state dir. D.C. 1974-78), Appalachian Finance Assn., Washington Jr. C. of C. (dir. 1964-66), Silver Spring C. of C. (dir. 1974—). Home: 14809 Old Columbia Pike Burtonsville MD 20730 Office: 4708 Wisconsin Ave NW Washington DC 20015 also 10750 Old Columbia Pike Silver Spring MD 20901

GUENON, JACQUARD WELSH, computer software cons.; b. Waynesboro, Pa., Jan. 19, 1949; s. William A. and Dorothy Elizabeth (Welsh) G.; B.S. in Math., Allegheny Coll., 1971; M.S. in Computer Sci., Mich. State U., 1975. Programmer analyst Coll. Human Medicine, Mich. State U., 1975-77, systems analyst, 1977-79, sr. systems analyst, 1979—, dir. long-term care archive, 1978—, dir. quantitative services, 1980—; pres. LAM Cons., Inc., East Lansing, Mich., 1977—. Mem. AAAS, Assn. Computing Machinery. Home: 521 Cornell Ave East Lansing MI 48823 Office: Com Health Sci Mich State U East Lansing MI 48823

GUERNSEY, JOHN BERTRAND, steel co. exec.; b. Middletown, Ohio, Oct. 2, 1929; s. Bertrand Ulay and Ruth (Whitehead) G.; Met.E., U. Cin., 1952; postgrad. Carnegie Inst. Tech., 1954-56; m. Betty Denninger, Dec. 22, 1951; children—Sue Ann, Michael John, Mary Francis. Research metallurgist Lunkenheimer Co., Cin., 1952-53, Rem-Cru Titanium, Inc., Midland, Pa., 1953-56; chief metallurgist Precision Parts div. Ex-Cell-O Corp., Lima, Ohio, 1956-60; research metallurgist Crucible Steel Corp., Midland, Pitts., 1960, successively mgr. process devel., mgr. titanium research, asso. dir. research, 1968-71; with Jessop Steel Co., Washington, Pa., 1971—, v.p. tech. services, 1972—. Mem. Am. Soc. Metals (chmn. Pitts. chpt. 1977-78), Am. Iron and Steel Inst. (chmn. tech. com. stainless steels), ASTM (chmn. subcom. E46-10 quality assurance), Sigma Xi (asso.), Tau Beta Pi. Republican. Contbr. articles to tech. publs.; patentee in metal processing. Office: 500 Green St Washington PA 15301

GUERRA, MICHAEL VICTOR, banker; b. San Jose, Calif., Sept. 24, 1945; s. Michael and Victoria G.; B.S.C., U. Santa Clara, 1967; m. Aug. 12, 1967; children—Thomas, Amy, Suzanne, Lisa. Escrow officer Valley Title Co., San Jose, 1967-69; comml. loan officer Norris Beggs & Simpson, 1969-71; with Guerra Realty Co., 1971-75; pres. Pioneer Fed. Savs. & Loan Assn., San Jose, 1975—, also dir. Mem. Santa Clara C. of C. (dir. 1980—), Calif. Savs. and Loan League, Conf. Fed. Savs. and Loan Assns., San Jose Real Estate Bd., Nat. Savs. and Loan Found., Italian Am. Heritage Found. Republican. Roman Catholic. Clubs: San Jose Civic, Exchange (dir.), Elks. Office: 2730 Homestead Rd Santa Clara CA 91051

GUERRERO, SAM NAHULU, wholesale and retail co. exec.; b. Honolulu, May 9, 1921; s. Sam Philip and Magdalena Elia (Nahulu) G.; student public schs., Honolulu; m. Vivian Mello, Nov. 18, 1944; children—Sam Nahulu, Leslie K. Welder, Hawaiian Plumbing and Sheet Metal Co., Honolulu, 1940-48; customer engr. IBM, Honolulu, 1948-59; pres., mgr. Simplex Internat. Time Equipment, Inc., Honolulu, 1959—; pres. Samlena, Inc., Honolulu, 1973—, Global Industry, Inc., Honolulu, 1978—. Pres., mgr. Kamehameha Alumni Glee Club, 1964-76. Mem. Hawaiian Businessmen's Assn., Honolulu C. of C., Hawaii Visitors Bur. Clubs: Waialae Country, Mid-Pacific Country. Home: 114 Kakahiaka St Kailua HI 96734 Office: 935 Makahiki Way Honolulu HI 96826

GUERRIERI, VINCENT RICHARD, telephone co. mgr.; b. Pitts., Oct. 5, 1942; s. Gabriel and Inez Mary (Zecca) G.; B.A., Duquesne U., 1965; M.B.A., George Washington U., 1973; m. Kathleen Cannon, June 23, 1973. Foreman, C & P Telephone Co., Kensington, Md., 1968-70, staff asso. rate planning, 1970-74; pricing analyst AT&T, N.Y.C., 1974-77; product mgr. C & P Telephone Co., 1977—. Pres., Rock Creek Hills Citizens Assn., Kensington, 1980. Served with AUS, 1966-68. Decorated Air medal, Army Commendation medal with 3 oak leaf clusters. Republican. Roman Catholic. Home: 9806 Hill St Kensington MD 20795 Office: 8701 Georgia Ave Silver Spring MD 20910

GUEST, CHARLES LUTHER, lawyer, banker; b. Yazoo City, Miss., Dec. 13, 1935; s. Roland P. and Bernice E. (Jones) G.; B.S. in Elec. Engring., Miss. State U., 1960; postgrad. Miss. Coll., 1972-73; J.D. cum laude, Jackson Sch. Law, 1977; m. Rubye L. Perkins, Apr. 8, 1962; children—Charles Luther, Daryl Parker, Scott Hardin. Customer engr. IBM, Jackson, Miss., 1960-63, systems engr., New Orleans, 1964; owner, operator Rental Service, Inc., Greenville, Miss., 1964-66; systems/program mgr. Lamar Life Ins. Co., Jackson, Miss., 1966-69; br. adminstr. Computer div. RCA Corp., Jackson, 1969-70; exec. dir. Miss. Central Data Processing Authority, Jackson, 1970-75; admitted to Miss. bar, 1977; sr. v.p., sr. trust officer 1st Miss. Nat. Bank, Hattiesburg, 1975—; instr. Am. Inst. Banking, 1979—. Active Boy Scouts Am., United Way Campaign; bd. dirs. Friends of Kamper Park. Cert. in data processing. Mem. Miss. State Bar Assn., Data Processing Mgmt. Assn. (pres., dir.), Am. Inst. Banking, Assn. Trial Lawyers, So. Miss. Estate Planning Council, Estate Planning Council Miss., Pension Study Group. Presbyterian. Clubs: Rotary, Masons, Shriners. Home: 3000 Tiltree Rd Hattiesburg MS 39401 Office: PO Box 1231 Hattiesburg MS 39401

GUFFEY, JAMES ROGER banker; b. Kingston, Mo., Sept. 11, 1929; s. John W. and Elsie M. Guffey; B.S., U. Mo., 1952, J.D., 1958; advanced mgmt. program Harvard Bus. Sch., 1974; m. Sara Katherine Carmack, Feb. 7, 1959; children—James Michael, Sara Elizabeth. Admitted to Mo. bar, 1958; asso. firm Knipmeyer McCann & Millett,

Kansas City, Mo., 1958-64; partner firm Fallon Guffey & Jenkins, Kansas City, Mo., 1965-68; gen. counsel Fed. Res. Bank Kansas City (Mo.), 1968-70, sr. v.p., 1970-76, pres., 1976—. Bd. dirs. Greater Kansas City YMCA, 1975—, Greater Kansas City Fgn.-Trade Zone, Inc., 1977—, St. Luke's Hosp., 1978—, United Way, 1977—; asso. mem. Civic Council Greater Kansas City, 1976—. Served in U.S. Army, 1952-54. Recipient cert. of merit U. Mo., Columbia, 1980. Mem. Greater Kansas City C. of C., Mo. Bar Assn. Episcopalian. Club: Mission Hills Country (Kans.). Office: 925 Grand Ave Kansas City MO 64198

GUHA, MANOJ K., materials engr., chemist, economist, energy cons.; b. Bangladesh, India, June 23, 1940; s. Dwijendra M. and Bibha R. (Ghosh) G.; came to U.S., 1963, naturalized, 1976; B.S. with honors in Chemistry, U. Calcutta, India, 1959, B.A. in Econs., 1961, B. Engring. in Metallurgy (NSF scholar), 1963; M.S. in Materials Sci., Brown U., 1965, postgrad. (fellow), 1965-67; m. Sipra Ghosh, Nov. 21, 1973. Sr. research engr. Westinghouse Elec. Corp., Pitts., 1967-70; prin. engr. Ebasco Services Corp., N.Y.C., 1971-74; staff engr. Am. Elec. Power Service Corp., N.Y.C., N.Y., 1974—; cons. energy conversion processes; cons. Rand Corp.; spl. cons. Dept. Energy; mem. U.S.-USSR Joint Com. on Sci. and Tech. Devel.; assos. vis. prof. City U. N.Y. 1971-73. Fellow AAAS; mem. Am. Mgmt. Assn., Inst. Mgmt., Smithsonian Instn., AIME, Am. Soc. Metals, Am. Inst. Aeros. and Aeronautics, Cultural Assn. India. Club: Brown Univ. Contbr. short stories to various publs. and articles on energy conversion to tech. jours.; mem. rev. com. numerous sci. jours. Home: 233-19 39th Rd Douglaston NY 11363 Office: 2 Broadway Room 1032 New York NY 10004

GUI, JAMES EDMUND, architect; b. Wooster, Ohio, Aug. 13, 1928; s. Harry Ludwig and Mabel Josephine (Olson) G.; B.Arch., Ohio State U., 1954; m. Anne Louise Outram, Oct. 15, 1955; children—Linda Anne, Jeffrey Allen. Asso. firm Charles F. McKirahan & Assos., Architects, Ft. Lauderdale, Fla., 1958-63; chief specifications Architects Collaborative, Cambridge, Mass., 1963-67; propr. James E. Gui, Archtl. and Specifications Cons., Belmont, Mass., 1967—. Cons., Architects Collaborative, Benjamin Thompson & Assos., Cambridge Seven Assos., Pietro Belluschi, Harvard, Mass. Inst. Tech., U. Baghdad (Iraq), Hotel Intercontinental, others. Chmn. folk music com., dir. Stone Arch folk music series Belmont Music Sch. Mem. Constrn. Specifications Inst., AIA, Boston Soc. Architects, Mass. Assn. Architects. Cons. on Juilliard Sch. Music, Lincoln Center, N.Y.C.; U.S. Pavillion Expo 67, Montreal; New Eng. Aquarium; Children's Hosp. Med. Center; Harvard U. Law Sch. Complex (2d award Constrn. Specifications Inst.); Harvard Gutman Library, Harvard Obs.; Kirkland Coll.; Berkshire Community Coll.; Tufts U. Dental Health Center; Independence Nat. Hist. Park Visitors Center; Wilmington Jewish Community Center (1st award Constrn. Specifications Inst.). Address: 965 Concord Ave Belmont MA 02178

GUIDO, LOUIE, mfg. co. exec.; b. Oakland, Calif., Apr. 15, 1931; s. Frank and Vintz (Prinzo) G.; B.S. in Bus. Mgmt., San Diego State U., 1960; m. Joan McGregor, Sept. 2, 1954; children—Donald E., Linda D., David A., Lorraine D. Sales coordinator Brown Engring. Co., 1956-58; engring. writer Ryan Aero. Co., 1958-60; gen. mgr. Hamilton Electro Sales Co., San Diego, 1960-69; co-founder, 1969, since v.p., sec., dir. Celtec Co., Irvine, Calif.; co-founder, 1977, since sec.-treas., dir. Bishop Electronics Corp., Pico Rivera, Calif.; co-founder, 1979, since partner Lectro Lease, Mission Viejo, Calif. Active Boy Scouts. Am. Served with USN, 1950-54; Korea. Republican. Mormon. Home: 24351 via Santa Clara Mission Viejo CA 92692 Office: 3729-B San Gabriel River Pkwy Pico Rivera CA 90660

GUIDO, MICHAEL FLETCHER, mfg. cons.; b. Munich, Mar. 7, 1948; s. Constantino Michael and Margaret Ontee (Crawford) G.; B.S., San Jose State Coll., 1970; M.B.A., U. Calif., Berkeley, 1972, B.S. in Indsl. Engring., 1972. Indsl. engr. Colgate Palmolive Co., Berkeley, 1970-72; dir. systems and planning Raychem Co., Menlo Park, Calif., 1970-75; cons. Booz Allen Co., San Francisco, 1975-77; mfg. cons. Peat Marwick & Mitchell, Los Angeles, 1978—; dir. Good Earth Assos., Colorado Springs. Recipient Zurich Goss award U. Bonn, 1976. Mem. Am. Inst. Indsl. Engrs. Republican. Roman Catholic. Office: #3 Embarcadero San Francisco CA 91111

GUILARTE, PEDRO MANUEL, utility co. exec.; b. Cuba, May 19, 1952; s. Miguel G. and Emma G.; B.S. in Indsl. Engring. (scholar), Northwestern U., 1975; M.B.A., Washington U., St. Louis, 1977; cert. systems dynamics MIT, 1978; m. Zulima Piedra, May 26, 1979. Market analyst Cummins Engine Co., Columbus, Ind., 1976; planning analyst Fla. Power & Light Co., Miami, 1977—. Consortium for Grad. Study in Bus. fellow, 1975-77. Mem. Northwestern U. Alumni Admission Council (dir. S. Fla. region 1979—), Planning Execs. Inst. Republican. Methodist. Home: 13232 SW 12th Ln Miami FL 33184 Office: PO Box 529100 Miami FL 33152

GUILD, GEORGE HERBERT, wood turning co. exec.; b. Nashua, N.H., May 4, 1919; s. Walter R. and Ruth L. (Wells) G.; B.S., U. N.H., 1940; m. Lucille I. Follett, Sept. 7, 1946; children—Stephen G., Jonathan R. With Allen-Rogers Corp., Laconia, N.H., 1940—, pres., treas., dir., 1973—; dir. Hale Brook Co., Inc., 1952—. Mem. Laconia City Planning Bd., 1960-66, chmn., 1963-65; mem. Laconia Housing and Redevel. Authority, 1966-76, chmn., 1974-76; chmn. Laconia Sch. Bldg. Com., 1973-77. Served with AUS, 1941-45. Mem. Wood Turners and Shapers Assn. (dir. 1964-66, 68-73, pres. 1970-71), Bus. and Industry Assn. N.H. (dir. 1977—, mem. exec. com. 1978, chmn. membership com. 1979). Republican. Club: Rotary. Home: 18 Clark Ave Laconia NH 03246 Office: Allen-Rogers Corp 54 Water St Laconia NH 03246

GUILD, MONTAGUE, JR., fin. exec.; b. Los Angeles, June 6, 1942; s. Montague and Dorothy (Duncan) G.; B.A., U. Calif. at Santa Barbara, 1964; M.B.A. in Fin., Calif. State U., 1968; m. Andrea Taylor Cole, Dec. 19, 1973. Fin. analyst Security Pacific Nat. Bank, Los Angeles, 1968-69; securities analyst, portfolio mgr. Taurus Partners, Los Angeles, 1969; gen. partner The Himalaya Fund, Malibu, Calif., 1969—; founder, pres. Guild Investment Mgmt., Inc., Malibu, 1969—, Calif. Ranch Properties, 1979—. Tchr., Transcendental Meditation Program, 1969—; trustee World Plan Exec. Council, 1974—; bd. dirs. Am. Found. for Sci. of Creative Intelligence, 1973—. Served with Calif. Air N.G., 1966-67. Mem. Internat. Platform Assn., Phi Kappa Phi, Delta Tau Delta. Club: Bel Air Bay. Office: 23410 Civic Center Way Suite E-10 Malibu CA 90265

GUILFOYLE, JOHN W., communications co. exec.; b. Burbank, Calif., ed. Wilson Jr. Coll., Northwestern U. With ITT, 1951—, v.p., indsl. relations dir., then v.p. ops. Fed. Electric Corp., 1956-59, pres., 1959-64, pres. Am. Cable and Radio Corp., 1964, group exec. U.S. Def./Space Group, 1964-66, v.p., 1966-79, group exec. Far East and Pacific Group, 1966-68, Latin Am. Group, 1968-78, Africa and Middle East Group, 1978-79, pres. ITT Europe, 1979—, sr. v.p. parent co. 1979-80, exec. v.p., 1980—. Served with U.S. Army, World War II. Mem. NAM (past vice chmn. nat. def. com.), Council of Americas (dir., exec. com.), Navy League, Air Force Assn., Nat. Aviation Club. *

GUILLAUME, BERNARD GEORGE, realtor; b. Guernsey, Channel Island, July 11, 1910; s. Stephen Osmond and Jessie May (LePage) G.; student LaSalle Extension U., 1940, Loyola U., Chgo., 1941, Northwestern U., 1942; m. Ethylle Marie Perkins, Aug. 27, 1938; 1 son, Stephen B. Controller Pickard, Inc., Antioch, Ill., 1945-54; owner, mgr. Ebb Tide Motel, Treasure Island, Fla., 1954-70; real estate broker Guillaume Realty Co., Seminole, Fla., 1958—. Chmn. Seminole Action Bicentennial Com., 1975-76; mem. City Commn., Treasure Island, 1960-70; mem. Pinellas County Planning Council, 1964-71, chmn. council, 1968; chmn. Seminole City Annexation Com., 1980—; mem. Pinellas County Charter Commn., 1971-72, Holiday Isles Devel. Council, 1973-75, Central Pinellas County Citizens Transit Involvement Com., Central Pinellas Transit Authority, pres. Republican Club Greater Seminole, 1972-75. Mem. Nat., Gulf Beach-Seminole Bd. Realtors (pres. 1968, v.p., dir. 1969-74, dir. 1980—), Nat. Assn. Realtors, Fla. Assn. Realtors (dist. 6th v.p. 1979), Greater Seminole Area C. of C. (v.p. 1974-75, pres. 1975-76), Farm and Land Brokers, Am. Master Appraisers (hon. dir.). Republican. Methodist (chmn. adminstrv. bd.). Mason (32 deg.). Home: 11331 80th Ave N Seminole FL 33542 Office: 8000 Seminole Blvd Seminole FL 33542

GUILLORY, WEBSTER JAMES, county govt. ofcl.; b. Pasadena, Calif., Apr. 21, 1944; s. Webster and Bertha (Houston) G.; B.S. in Aerospace Engring., Northrop U., Inglewood, Calif., 1966; M.S. in Civil Engring., U. So. Calif., 1972; m. Yolanda Marie Brown, June 5, 1971; 1 son, Dax Bainsworth. Engr./scientist McDonnell Douglas Corp., Huntington Beach, Calif., 1966-73; project mgr. Holmes & Narver, Inc., Orange, Calif., 1973-76; mgr. Orange County Dept. Assessor, Santa Ana, Calif., 1976—; mem. sci. and tech. task force Nat. Assn. Counties, 1978; cons. in field. Dir., program cons. Orange County Youth Motivation Task Force, 1975-78, chmn., 1980-81. Recipient various certificates appreciation. Mem. Am. Inst. Aeros. and Astronautics (Achievement award 1967), Nat. Assn. Rev. Appraisers, Los Angeles Maintainability Assn. (dir. 1974-76), Nat. Assn. Black County Ofcls. (dir. for West 1980-81, chmn. Com. on cable TV 1980-81). Home: 1820 E Altadena Dr Altadena CA 91001 Office: 630 N Broadway Santa Ana CA 92702

GUIMOND, FRANCOIS XAVIER, pulp and paper cons.; b. Campbellton, N.B., Can., Mar. 6, 1911; s. Z. Amedee and Lauza (Cormier) G.; B.Sc. with honors, U. N.B., 1932; m. Gladys A. Powers, Nov. 14, 1934; children—E. Anne (Mrs. Robert Griffin), M. Lucille (Mrs. Mark J. Scanlon), Jean-Francois. Chief chemist Que. North Shore Paper Co., Baie Comeau, Que., Can., 1937-40; gen. supt. Can. Internat. Paper, Gatineau, Que., 1940-52, Temiskaming, Que., 1952-56; mgr. pulp mfg. Brown Co. Ltd., Berlin, N.H., 1956-60; sr. tech. cons. Parsons, Whittemore, Lyddon Co. Ltd., London, Eng., 1960-66; v.p. operations Prince Albert Pulp Co. Ltd. (Sask., Can.), 1966-69; sr. v.p. operations Canadian Cellulose Co., Ltd., Vancouver, B.C., Can., 1969-74, sr. v.p. engring. and devel., 1974-76; exec. v.p., chief operating officer pulp mfg. Rayonier Que. div. ITT Industries Can. Ltd., Port Cartier, v.p., dir. Les Industries ITT du Canada Ltse, 1976-77; sr. tech. advisor ITT Rayonier Corp., N.Y.C., 1977-78; ind. tech. cons. forest products, pulp and paper, 1978—. Home: Suite 112 The Gables 4675 Valley Dr Vancouver BC V6J 4B7 Canada

GUIMOND, JEAN, mktg. exec.; b. N.Y.C., Nov. 12, 1932; arrived Can., 1936, naturalized, 1942; s. Wilfrid Camille Georges and Zenda Carmen G.; LL.B., Blackstone Sch. of Law, Chgo., 1955; m. Pierrette Viau, June 16, 1956; children—Joseph, Jean, Roma, C. Michel. Pvt. practice mgmt. cons. representing German interests in Que., 1965-72; engaged in mktg. of pianos and organs region of Eastern Can., 1972—. Address: CP 178 Duvernay Laval PQ H7E 4P5 Canada

GUIST, FREDRIC MICHAEL, minerals and chems. corp. exec.; b. Homestead, Pa., Oct. 8, 1946; s. Thomas John and Clara Hertha (Orend) G.; student in chemistry Juniata Coll., 1964-66; B.S. with high honors in Bus. Adminstrn., U. Md., 1968; m. Barbara Jean Hill, Aug. 4, 1972; children—Heidi Margit, James Fredric. Rate analyst Dow Chem. Co., Midland, Mich., 1968-69, inside sales rep., Saddlebrook, N.J., 1969-70, sales rep. for splty. chems., Chgo., 1970-73, field salesman, 1973-74; product specialist for indsl. chems. Nalco Chem. Co., Oakbrook, Ill., 1974, product mgr. for indsl. chems., 1974-75; mktg. mgr. Engelhard Minerals & Chems. Corp., Edison, N.J., 1975-78, dir. new bus. devel., 1978-79, dir. mktg. and sales worldwide for petroleum catalysts, 1979—. Mem. Nat. Petroleum Refiners Assn. (rep. to bd. dirs. 1979—), Am. Petroleum Inst., Phi Kappa Phi. Home: 13 Polktown Rd RD 2 Glen Gardner NJ 08826 Office: Engelhard Minerals & Chems Corp Menlo Park Edison NJ 08817

GUITAR, EARL BEAL, JR., oil co. exec.; b. San Angelo, Tex., Nov. 20, 1929; s. Earl Beal and Anita (Grissom) G.; student Stanford U., 1949-50; B.A., U. of South, 1951; J.D., U. Tex., 1957; m. Margaret Ann Mackay, Oct. 5, 1963; children—Brandon, Allison, Carolyn, Sandra, John. Admitted to Tex. bar, 1957, Okla. bar, 1958; staff atty. Phillips Petroleum Co., Bartlesville, Okla., 1957-67; v.p., gen. counsel Phillips Petroleum Europe Africa, Brussels and London, 1967-71, sr. v.p., London, 1971-74; mgr. adminstrn. internat. affairs Natural Resources group Phillips Petroleum, Bartlesville, 1974-76, mng. dir. Europe Africa div., London, 1976—; dir. various subs. Served to lt. comdr. USN, 1951-55; Korea. Mem. Okla. Bar Assn., Tex. Bar Assn., Am.-U.K. C. of C. (dir.), Phi Delta Theta, Phi Alpha Delta. Club: Am. (dir.) (London). Home: 1 Bristol Gardens London SW15 England Office: Phillips Petroleum EA Portland House Stag Pl London SW1 England

GUITON, HENRIETTA FAYE BRAZELTON (BONNIE), mfg. co. adminstr.; b. Springfield, Ill., Oct. 30, 1941; d. Henry Frank and Zola Elizabeth (Newman) Brazelton; B.A., Mills Coll., 1974; M.S., Calif. State U., Hayward, 1975; postgrad. U. Calif., Berkeley, 1975—; m. Harvie Guiton Jr., Aug. 21, 1966; 1 dau., Nichele Monique. Sec. to pres.'s spl. asst. Mills Coll., Oakland, Calif., 1969-72, adminstrv. asst. to asst. v.p., 1972-74, student services counselor, adv. to resuming students, 1974-75, asst. dean of students, interim dir. ethnic studies, lectr., 1975-76; exec. dir. Marcus A. Foster Ednl. Inst., Oakland, 1976-79; adminstrv. mgr. Kaiser Aluminum & Chem. Soc., Oakland, 1979—; v.p., gen. mgr. Kaiser Center, Inc. Community adv. Jr. League of Oakland East Bay, Inc., 1977—; bd. dirs. Univ. YWCA, Berkeley, 1976-77, Oakland Symphony Orch. Assn., 1977—, Pacific Children's Center/Pacific Child and Family Counseling Center, 1977—. Mem. Nat. Soc. Fund Raising Execs., Devel. Execs. Roundtable, Am. Mgmt. Assn., LWV, Pi Lambda Theta. Club: Oakland Athletic. Office: One Kaiser Plaza Oakland CA 94643

GUITTAR, LEE JOHN, newspaper exec.; b. St. Louis, May 4, 1931; s. LeRoy and Edna Mae (Johnston) G.; A.B., Columbia U., 1953; M.B.A., U. Mass., 1962; m. Joan Mayo, Sept. 13, 1952 (div. 1979); children—David Lee, Stephen Joseph, Mitchell John, Jeanne Marie, Richard Laughran. With Gen. Electric Co., Schenectady, 1955-63, mgr. community and govt. relations programs, N.Y.C., 1963-65; mgr. employee and public relations Tidewater Oil Co., N.Y.C., 1965-66; dir. personnel, circulation dir. Miami (Fla.) Herald Pub. Co., 1967-72; v.p., bus. mgr. Detroit Free Press, Inc., 1972-74, v.p., gen. mgr., 1974-75, pres., dir., 1975-77; pub. Dallas Times Herald, 1977—. Bd. dirs. Dallas Citizens Council, Goals for Dallas, ARC, United Way, Central Bus. Dist. Assn. Served to lt. j.g. USNR, 1953-55. Mem. Am. Mgmt. Assn., Am. Newspaper Pubs. Assn., Dallas C. of C. (dir.), Am. Press Inst., Phi Beta Kappa. Republican. Roman Catholic. Clubs: City, Lancers, Bent Tree Country (Dallas). Office: 1101 Pacific St Dallas TX 75202

GULBRANDSEN, DONALD ALAN, mfg. co. exec.; b. Rockford, Ill., Feb. 11, 1941; s. Yul M. and Pearl M. (Butler) G.; B.S.B.A., Rockford Coll., 1964; m. Maureene D. Schafer, Aug. 4, 1962; children—Donald, Dana, Robert, Sara. Insp., Rockford (Ill.) Clutch div. Borg Warner Corp., 1962; prodn. control coordinator Eclipse Fuel Engring. Co., Rockford, 1962-63, chief cost acct., 1963-66; internal auditor Sundstrand Corp., Rockford, 1966-69, div. controller Sundstrand Fluid Handling div., Denver, 1969-76, group controller Air Comfort Products Europe, London, 1976-77, chief fin. officer Sundstrand Europe, London, 1977-78, dir. fin. adminstrn. Sundstrand Hydro-Transmission div., Ames, Iowa, 1978—; dir. Sundstrand Pumpar, A.B. (Sweden), Sundstrand U.K., Sundstrand Italiana, 1977-78. Mem. Fin. Execs. Inst., Internat. Mgmt. Assn. Republican. Lutheran. Home: Rural Route 2 Ames IA 50010 Office: 2800 E 13th St Ames IA 50010

GULHATI, KAVAL, tng. firm exec.; b. Lahore, India, Dec. 26, 1936; came to U.S., 1969, resident, 1976; d. Qurban and Bhajan Singh; M.A. in Social Work, Delhi U., 1959; cert. in mgmt., Oxford U. Eng., 1977, D.Phil. candidate; m. Ravi Gulhati, Aug. 31, 1959. Project dir., corp. v.p. Center for Population Activities, Washington, 1975-80, pres., exec. dir., 1980—. Bd. dirs. Orgn. Renewal, Inc., Women's Internat. Health Coalition. Mem. Am. Soc. Tng. and Devel., Women in Corp. Founds. and Philanthropy, Am. Public Health Assn., Indian Soc. Study of Population, Soc. Internat. Devel. Research on demographic trends, health needs, urbanization problems, Third World women. Office: 1717 Massachusetts Ave NW Washington DC 20036

GULLEDGE, THOMAS RAYFIELD, JR., educator; b. Lancaster, S.C., Oct. 24, 1947; s. Thomas R. and Cora M. (Goude) G.; B.S., U. S.C., 1975; M.S., Clemson (S.C.) U., 1977, Ph.D., 1980; m. Jo Marie Lewis, Oct. 26, 1968; 1 dau., Kristin Marie. Agt., Travelers Ins. Co., 1972-75; with LACIE project NASA, 1975-78; instr. mgmt. and mgmt. sci. Clemson U., 1978—; ind. mgmt. cons., econ. forecaster. Served with Army N.G., 1967-73. Mem. Ops. Research Soc. Am., Econometric Soc., Omega Rho (past chpt. pres.), Omicron Delta Epsilon (past chpt. pres.). Home: 36-L Morrison Rd Clemson SC 29631 Office: 110 Sirrine Hall Clemson Univ Clemson SC 29631

GULLEY, WILBUR PAUL, JR., savs. and loan assn. exec.; b. Little Rock, Aug. 8, 1923; s. Wilbur Paul and JaJa Douglas (Ashburn) G.; A.B. in Bus. Adminstrn., Duke, 1947; m. Mary Elizabeth Bragg Hunt, Mar. 13, 1971; children by previous marriage—Wilbur Paul III and William H. (twins), James Ransom, Michael. With Gulley Ins. Agy., Little Rock, 1947, partner, mng. officer, 1947-58; with Pulaski Fed. Savs. & Loan Assn. (name now Savers Fed. Savs. and Loan Assn.), Little Rock, 1947—, sec., 1948-52, v.p., 1952-58, pres., 1959—, also dir. Pres. Better Bus. Bur. Ark., 1962; gen. chmn. United Fund campaign, Pulaski County, Ark., 1963-64; v.p. Little Rock Boys Club, 1970-71, pres., 1971-72. Trustee, pres. George W. Donaghey Found., 1969-72; trustee, chmn. bd. Ark. State U., 1969, sec., treas. trustees, 1971; trustee Savs. and Loan Found., 1977—. Served with USNR, 1943-46. Mem. Southwestern Savs. and Loan Conf. (pres. 1960-61), Savs. Assn. Retirement Fund (trustee 1960-65), U.S. Savs. and Loan League (mem. exec. com. 1963-66), Pulaski County Savs. and Loan League (pres. 1964), Ark. Savs. and Loan League (pres. 1965-66), Little Rock C. of C. (pres. 1968), Phi Beta Kappa, Sigma Alpha Epsilon, Beta Omega Sigma. Methodist (bd. stewards). Clubs: Country, Little Rock, Capital (Little Rock). Home: 2 Sunset Dr Little Rock AR 72207 Office: Capitol at Spring Sts Little Rock AR 72201

GULMI, HENRY CHARLES, cons.; b. Cleve., Feb. 24, 1921; s. James and Justine (Marchiano) G.; B.S. in Edn., Wittenberg U., 1943; m. June Doris Singleton, Dec. 24, 1943; children—James, Susan, Sally. With Gen. Electric Co., various locations, 1945-79, mgr. fin., machinery apparatus ops., Schenectady, 1959-67, mgr. fin. services shops dept., 1967-75, mgr. fin. East Central apparatus service dept., Cleve., from 1975; now cons. bus. mgmt., Sanford, N.C.; treas. Middle East Engring. Ltd., Bahrain, J.B. Van Wijnsberge en Zoon, Rotterdam, Netherlands, G.E. Reconstruccion Co., Ponce, P.R. Pres., Niskayuna High Sch. PTA, 1963-64; asst. treas. Red Feather Drive. Served with USAF, 1943-45; ETO; POW, 1944-45. Decorated Purple Heart. Mem. Elfun Soc., Blue Key, Delta Phi Alpha, Kappa Phi Kappa. Republican. Episcopalian. Club: Carolina Trace. Address: 3055 Bourbon St Carolina Trace Sanford NC 27330

GULYWASZ, GEORGE EDWARD, motel co. exec.; b. Passaic, N.J., June 9, 1949; s. George Theodore and Helen (Marut) G.; B.A., Montclair (N.J.) State Coll., 1972; M.B.A. cum laude, Fairleigh Dickinson U., Rutherford, N.J., 1974. Jr. acct. Cooper Labs., Inc., Wayne, N.J., 1972-73; staff acct., then asst. controller Prime Motor Inns, Inc., Clifton, N.J., 1973-76, corp. controller, 1976—. Served with USNR, 1966-72. Home: 18 Brandon Rd Midland Park NJ 07432 Office: 1030 Clifton Ave Clifton NJ 07013

GUM, JON W., mfg. co. exec.; b. Mt. Vernon, Mo., May 21, 1942; s. J. B. and Faye G.; B.S., U. Mo., 1964, M.S. in Aerospace Engring., 1967, M.S. in Engring. Mgmt., 1971; m. Sue T. Bradsher, Nov. 11, 1970. Flight test engr. McDonnell Douglas, St. Louis, 1964-69; sales engr. Clifton Precision, Maryland Heights, Md., 1969-71; sales engr. Midwest Meridian, Maryland Heights, 1971-77; v.p. mktg. Clifton Precision, Clifton Heights, Pa., 1977—. Mem. Tau Beta Pi, Sigma Pi Sigma. Office: Marple at Broadway Clifton Heights PA 19018

GUND, GEORGE, III, profl. hockey team exec.; b. Cleve., May 7, 1937; s. George and Jessica (Roesler) G.; student Western Res. U., Menlo Sch. of Bus.; m. Mary Theo Feld, Aug. 13, 1966; children—George IV, Gregory. Cattle rancher nr. Lee, Nev., 1967—; partner Calif. Seals, San Francisco, 1976-77; pres. Ohio Barons, Inc., Richfield, 1977-78; chmn. bd. Northstar Fin. Corp., Bloomington, Minn., 1978—, Minn. North Stars, 1978—; dir. Ameritrust of Cleve., Gund Investment Corp., Princeton, N.J., Sun Valley Ice Skating Inc. (Idaho). Bd. dirs. Calif. Theatre Found., San Francisco, Bay Area Ednl. TV Assn., San Francisco, Sierra Club Found. Nat. Adv. Council, San Francisco Art Inst., Cleve. Health Mus., George Gund Found., Cleve., Cleve. Internat. Film Festival, Sun Valley Center for Arts and Humanities, Collectors Com. of Nat. Gallery Art, Washington, Mpls. Film Festival, Internat. Council Mus. Modern Art, N.Y.C., U. Nev. Reno Found.; chmn. San Francisco Internat. Film Festival. Served with USMC, 1955-58. Clubs: Calif. Tennis, Univ., Olympic (San Francisco); Union, Cleve. Skating, Cleve. Athletic, Rowfant (Cleve.); Rainier (Seattle). Office: 1821 Union St San Francisco CA 94123

GUNDLACH, HEINZ LUDWIG, retail exec.; b. Dusseldorf, Ger., July 6, 1937; s. Heinrich and Ilse (Schuster) G.; LL.M., U. Heidelberg (Ger.), 1961, dr. juris prudentiae 1962; divorced; children—Andrew, Annabelle. Vice pres., partner Loeb, Rhoades & Co., investment bankers, N.Y.C., 1967-75; vice chmn. bd. FedMart Corp., San Diego, 1976—. Office: 3851 Rosecrans San Diego CA 92110

GUNHEIM, CLAYTON EARL, indsl. corp. exec.; b. Holt, Minn., Apr. 9, 1919; s. Charles Hans and Christine (Lein) G.; B.A., Concordia Coll., Moorhead, Minn., 1940; m. Martha Gneiding, May 20, 1954; children—Clayton, Charles, John. Economist U.S. Dept. Navy, Washington, 1944-46, Dept. Justice, Washington, 1946-48, corp. economist U.S. Occupation Govt., Far East Command, Tokyo, Japan, 1948-50; with Progress Lighting, div. Walter Kidde Corp., 1954—, sr. v.p., 1969-75, chmn., chief exec. officer, 1975—; dir. Walter Kidde Ltd., Can. Lutheran. Home: 3654 Wyola Dr Newtown Square PA 19073

GUNN, GEORGE R., JR., advt. agy. exec.; b. Abington, Pa., Dec. 10, 1939; s. George R. and Grace Marion (John) G.; student Charles Morris Price Sch. Advt. and Journalism, 1958; B.S., Temple U., 1962, M.B.A., 1971; m. Ruth A. Wallace, Nov. 25, 1966; children—George, Kimberly. With Lewis & Gilman, Inc., Phila., 1966—, sr. v.p., 1979—; guest lectr. TV-Radio Advt. Club. Served with USN, 1962-65. Presbyterian. Club: Union League of Phila. Home: 1105 Donna Dr Fort Washington PA 19034 Office: 1700 Market St Philadelphia PA 19103

GUNTER, WILLIAM DAWSON, JR., state ofcl.; b. Jacksonville, Fla., July 16, 1934; s. William Dawson and Tillie G.; B.S.A., U. Fla., 1956; m. Teresa Arbaugh, June 26, 1971; children—Bartlett D., Joel S., Rachel D. Mem. Fla. senate, 1966-72; mem. 92d Congress from Fla., 1973-74; sr. v.p. Southland Equity Corp., Orlando, Fla., 1975-76; pres. Southland Capital Investors, Inc., Orlando, 1975-76; state treas., ins. commr. State of Fla., Tallahassee, 1976—. Deacon, Baptist Ch.; active Central Fla. Fair Assn., Orange County Farm Bur., United Appeal. Served with U.S. Army, 1956-58. Elected to U. Fla. Hall of Fame, 1956. Mem. Fla. Jr. C. of C. (Good Govt. award 1972). Democrat. Clubs: Kiwanis, Masons. Office: The Capitol Plaza Level Tallahassee FL 32301

GUNZBURGER, GERARD JOSEF, plastics co. exec.; b. June 26, 1931; s. Ernest and Alma (Gutman) G.; B.S., Colegio Americano, Bogota, Colombia, 1948; Chemist, Universidad Nacional de Colombia, 1952; C.P. in English, U. Mich., 1953; M.S. in Chem. Engring., M.I.T., 1955; M.B.A., U. Detroit, 1961; m. Suzanne Nathan, Apr. 10, 1960. Chem. engr., supr. Wyandotte Chem. Corp. (Mich.), 1955-63; plant tech. mgr. Nat. Distillers & Chem. Corp., Stratford, Conn., 1962-67; v.p., gen. mgr. Smartpak Industries, Inc., Miami, Fla., 1967—, 2d treas., sec., dir.; chmn. plastics and chems. U.S. Cons. for Israeli Industry. Bd. dirs. Com. Quality Edn. Broward County, 1969-70; planning com. Jewish Fedn. South Broward; treas. Nova High Sch. Debate Fund. Mem. Soc. Plastics Engrs. (sr.), Beta Gamma Sigma. Office: 19401 W Dixie Hwy Miami FL 33180*

GUPTA, SATISH K., engr., electronics corp. exec.; b. Karnal, India, Sept. 10, 1942; s. Shyam Lal and Vidya G.; came to U.S., 1970, naturalized, 1978; B.A. in Applied Math., Panjab U. (India), 1962; B.S. in Mech. Engring., Punjabi U. (India), 1968; M.S. in Indsl. and Mgmt. Engring., City U. N.Y., 1973; M.B.A., Monmouth Coll. N.J., 1978; m. Purnima Aggarwal, July 11, 1970; children—Arpita, Atul. Asst. engr. Jai Bharat Auto Industries, Karnal, India 1968; mech. engr. Bharat Carpets Ltd., Faridabad, India, 1969-70, plant engr., 1970; maintenance engr. N.Y. Telephone Co., N.Y.C., 1971-73; plant indsl. engr., mgmt. engr. Everlon Fabrics Corp. div. Nabisco, Inc., Rio Grande, N.J., 1973-80; assembly mechanization engr. Tex. Instruments, Inc., Lubbock, 1980—; cons. in field. Registered profl. engr., N.J., N.Y. Mem. ASME, Am. Inst. Indsl. Engrs., Inst. Engrs. (India). Home: 4505 80th St Lubbock TX 79424 Office: PO Box 10508 MS 5838 Lubbock TX 79408

GURA, MARTIN PAUL, public relations co. exec.; b. N.Y.C., Jan. 20, 1933; s. Louis and Sue (Donner) G.; B.A., N.Y. U., 1953; m. Judith Bette Jankowitz, Mar. 27, 1960; children—Meryl, Jeremy. Account exec. Grey Advt. Agy., N.Y.C., 1953-55; product mgr. Lever Bros. Co., N.Y.C., 1959-70; mktg. mgr. Beecham Products Co., Clifton, N.J., 1971-73; new product devel. mgr. Am. Can Co., Greenwich, Conn., 1973-74; owner, mgr. Gura Public Relations Inc., N.Y.C., 1974—. Served with U.S. Army, 1956-58. Mem. Nat. Home Fashions Assn. (industry colleague). Jewish. Home: 321 W 78th St New York NY 10024 Office: 22 E 60th St New York NY 10022

GURASH, JOHN THOMAS, ins. holding co. exec.; b. Oakland, Calif., Nov. 25, 1910; s. Nicholas and Katherine (Restovic) G.; student Loyola U. Sch. Law, Los Angeles, 1936, 38-39; m. Katherine Mills, Feb. 4, 1934; 1 son, John N. With Am. Surety Co. N.Y., 1930-44; with Pacific Employers Ins. Co., 1944-53; pres., organizer Meritplan Ins. Co., 1953-59; exec. v.p. Pacific Employers Ins. Co., 1959-60, pres., 1960-68, chmn., bd., 1968-76, also dir.; v.p. Ins. Co. N. Am., 1966-70; exec. v.p., dir. INA Corp., 1968-69, chmn., pres., chief exec. officer, 1969-74, chmn., chief exec. officer, 1974-75, chmn. bd., 1975, chmn. exec. com., 1975-79, also dir.; chmn. bd. Certain-Teed Corp., also dir., dir. Purex Industries Inc., Household Fin. Corp., Certain-teed Corp., MGIC Investment Corp., Lockheed Corp. Trustee Occidental Coll., Los Angeles; vice chmn., trustee Orthopaedic Hosp., Los Angeles; mem. nat. Council Pomona Coll., Claremont, Calif. Mem. Pa. Soc., Knights of Malta. Clubs: California (Los Angeles), Pine Valley (N.J.) Golf, Los Angeles Country, Sr. Golf Assn. of So. Calif., Anandale Golf (Pasadena). Office: 1600 Arch St Philadelphia PA 19101 also 4050 Wilshire Blvd Los Angeles CA 91105

GURNEE, ROBERT FRANCIS, fin. co. exec.; b. Bklyn., Dec. 3, 1927; s. Robert Philip and Florence Catherine (O'Brien) G.; B.B.A. in Fin., St. John's U., Jamaica, N.Y., 1955; grad. Consumer Fin. Program Columbia U., 1963, Aspen Inst. Humanistic Studies, 1969; m. Arline Catherine Degen, May 21 1950; children—Patricia, Barbara, Robert. Staff credit and comml. paper depts. Goldman, Sachs & Co., N.Y.C., 1951-58; with Sears Roebuck Acceptance Corp., Wilmington, Del., 1958—, exec. v.p., 1967-72, pres., chief exec. officer, 1972—, also dir.; dir., chmn. exec. com. Farmers Bank of State of Del., 1976—. Bd. dirs. Boys Club of Wilmington, 1972—, United Way, Wilmington, 1972-73, NCCJ, 1973-77; bus. chmn. Del. Heart Assn. Fund Raising, 1976-77. Served with USN, 1945-48, 51-52; Korea. Mem. Wilmington Money Market Club, Del. Fin. Assn., Assn. R.R. Treas's., Am. Mgmt. Ass., Newcomen Soc., Assn. State Treas.'s, Del. World Affairs Council. Roman Catholic. Clubs: Downtown Athletic (N.Y.C.); Univ. (Wilmington). Home: 617 Black Gates Rd Wilmington DE 19803 Office: One Customs House Sq Wilmington DE 19899

GURNEY, FLETCHER BARNES, mfg. co. exec.; b. Chgo., Sept. 24, 1931; s. James Granville and Patricia Flora (Early) G.; B.A., Beloit (Wis.) Coll., 1955; postgrad. Northwestern U., 1961; m. Ruth Margaret Rodgers, Oct. 15, 1966; children—James, Peter, Burke, Geoffrey; stepchildren—Adrian, Robin, Heather. Sales engr. Belden Mfg. Co., Chgo., 1956-58; sales rep. Standard Oil Co., Chgo., 1959-60; spl. agt. Prudential Ins. Co. Am., 1960-61; western regional sales mgr. Teledyne McKay Co., Chgo., 1962-79; nat. sales mgr. Taylor Chem. Co., Inc., Hammond, Ind., 1979-80; nat. sales mgr. alloy products Swedish Wire Corp., Muskegon, Mich. and Chgo., 1980, nat. sales mgr. chain div., 1980—. Mem. USNR, 1951-58. Mem. Chgo. Dist. Tennis Assn., Am. Mgmt. Assn., Sigma Chi. Home: Unit 5E 500 W Barry Chicago IL 60657 Office: 255 Laura Dr Addison IL 60101

GUSLER, RICHARD NOEL, recreational franchise co. exec.; b. Burlington, N.C., Dec. 2, 1948; s. Noel and Margaret Elgin G.; B.A. in Polit. Sci., N.C. State U., Raleigh, 1972, M.P.A., 1980; m. Doris Wells, July 16, 1972. Tchr., Bertie County Schs., Windsor, N.C., 1972-75; residential mgr. Albemarle Mental Health Center, Elizabeth City, N.C., 1975-77; v.p., gen. mgr., Gusler Enterprises, Inc., Virginia Beach, Va., 1977—, also dir. Mem. Am. Soc. Public Adminstrn., Virginia Beach C. of C. Democrat. Unitarian. Home: 917 Method Rd Raleigh NC 27606 Office: Gusler Enterprises Inc 2900 Baltic Ave Virginia Beach VA 23451

GUSTAV, ROBERT JACK, real estate planner and developer; b. Seattle, Nov. 25, 1921; s. Samuel and Beatrice (Gordon) G.; grad. in archtl. design and constrn. devel. U. Wash., 1939; m. Letty Janet Cole, Oct. 30, 1969; children—Steven, Susan, Richard. With Gustav Co., 1944-51, Gustav Developers, Inc., Seattle, 1951-76; pres., gen. mgr. Sportscene, Inc., 1975-77; owner, pres. The Lebo Co., Palm Springs, Calif., 1977--. Mem. Nat. Assn. Home Builders, Bldg. Industry Assn. So. Calif. Republican. Jewish. Clubs: Racquet, Wash. Athletic, Cathedral Canyon, Swedish, Bellevue (Wash.) Athletic, Country, Elks. Home: 355 N Ave Caballeros Palm Springs CA 92262 Office: 121 S Palm Canyon Dr Palm Springs CA 92262

GUTH, HERBERT HALL, box-making machinery dealer; b. Chgo., Dec. 14, 1928; s. Karl Walter and Mildred Adeline (Hall) G.; student Wilson Jr. Coll., Chgo., 1947-49; m. Darlene Knarr, Sept. 16, 1950; 1 son, David Scott. Clk., Boldt's Food Store, Chgo., 1943-49; with traffic dept. Hills Bros. Coffee Co., Chgo., 1949-50; salesman, supr. Standard Oil Co., Chgo., 1952-62; pres. Reliable Converted Machinery Co., Lansing, Ill., 1962—. Treas., United Presbyn. Ch., 1958-67; mem. adv. council Sch. Dist. 151 Sch. Bd., 1968; active Jr. Achievement. Served with AUS, 1950-52. Mem. TAPPI, Lansing C. of C., Am. Legion. Republican. Clubs: Lansing Sportsman's, Elks, Masons, Shriners. Home: 634 E 162d Pl South Holland IL 60473 Office: 18503 Torrence Ave Lansing IL 60438

GUTHRIE, DAVID WILLIAM, lawyer; b. Colorado Springs, Colo., Sept. 18, 1947; s. James William and Ruth Virginia (Murchison) G.; B.A., Claremont Men's Coll., 1969; J.D., Bklyn. Law Sch., 1979; m. Nancy S. Harrison, Aug. 23, 1977; 1 son, William Jon. Systems analyst, N.Y.C., 1972-76; instr. N.Y. U., 1976-77; pvt. practice data processing cons. to utilities, mfg. corps. and airlines, N.Y.C., 1978-80; admitted to Calif. bar, 1979, U.S. Dist. Ct. bar, 1979; owner, asso. firm Traveling Atty., San Diego, 1980—; instr. data processing U. Calif., San Diego, extension div., 1980—. Mem. State Bar Calif., Am. Bar Assn., ACLU. Democrat. Home: 2373 Seaside St San Diego CA 92107 Office: 1200 3d Ave Suite 1200 San Diego CA 92101

GUTHRIE, GEORGE RALPH, JR., real estate devel. corp. exec.; b. Phila., Mar. 12, 1928; s. George Ralph and Myrtle (Robertson) G.; B.S. in Econs., U. Pa., 1948; m. Shirley B. Remmey; children—Mary Elizabeth, Brenda Ann. With I-T-E Imperial Corp., Phila., 1948-70, controller, fin. planner, 1960-68, treas., 1968-69, v.p. fin., 1969-70; pres. N.K. Winston Corp., N.Y.C., 1970-76; exec. v.p. Urban Investment and Devel. Co., Chgo., 1976-78, pres., 1978—. Mem. Am. Mgmt. Assn. (fin. planning council 1970-75), Fin. Execs. Inst., Urban Land Inst., Cosmopolitan C. of C., Chgo. Assn. Commerce and Industry. Republican. Clubs: Union League (Phila.); Econ., Execs., Carlton (Chgo.); Westmoreland Country; Jupiter Hill. Office: 845 N Michigan Ave Chicago IL 60611

GUTHRIE, ROBERT DAVID, distbn. co. exec.; b. Winnipeg, Man., Can., Mar. 11, 1943; s. Robert Dewar and Elizabeth Jean (McGill) G.; B.A., U. Wash., 1965; M.B.A. (Commerce Assos. scholar), U. So. Calif., 1971; m. Ruth Lynd Weisel, Oct. 12, 1968; children—Scott David, Robin Elizabeth. Coordinator and staff asst., Mgmt. Info. Systems, div. Naval Reactors U.S. AEC, Washington, 1966-68; systems coordinator Naval Supply Center, Long Beach, Calif., 1968; EDP cons. and servicer, Los Angeles, 1969-70; asst. v.p., EDP mgr., Coldwell Banker & Co., Los Angeles, 1971-74; v.p., head, EDP and gen. services divs., Advance Mortgage Corp., Southfield, Mich., 1974-79; v.p., EDP and computer equipment sales/leasing Detroit Ball Bearing Co., 1979—; instr. Long Beach City Coll., 1969-71. Served with USNR, 1965-68. Mem. Commerce Assos., SE Mich. Computer Orgn., Beta Gamma Sigma, Delta Tau Delta. Contbr. articles in field to tech. jours. Home: 2956 London Wall Bloomfield Hills MI 48013 Office: 1400 Howard St Detroit MI 48216

GUTHRIE, WILLIAM ALLEN, accountant; b. Steubenville, Ohio, Feb. 25, 1943; s. William McElvain and Mildred Lucille (Thompson) G.; B.S., Ariz. State U., 1972; m. Constance Sue Baxley, Jan. 4, 1964; children—Craig Allen, Susan Jayne, Geoffrey Adam. Sr. acct. Deloitte Haskins & Sells, Los Angeles, 1972-75; mgr. fin. planning Kobe, Inc., Huntington Park, Calif., 1975-77; v.p. fin. Baker Sand Control Co., Houston, 1977—. Served with USAF, 1961-69. Mem. Am. Inst. C.P.A.'s, Calif. Soc. C.P.A.'s, Tex. Soc. C.P.A.'s, Beta Gamma Sigma. Republican. Presbyterian. Office: 1010 Rankin Rd Houston TX 77073

GUTKIN, ROBERT HIRAM, mail order lab supply co. exec.; b. Rochester, N.Y., Mar. 25, 1942; s. Phillip and Betty (Goronkin) G.; student public schs., Rochester, N.Y.; m. Rochelle Rosenbaum, Sept. 3, 1961; children—Paula, Jeffrey, Laura. With Dynalab Corp., Rochester, 1961—, pres., 1967—; cons. in field. Bd. dirs. Jewish Community Center, Rochester, 1978—, Genesee Valley chpt. Am. Heart Assn., 1977-80. Mem. Scientific Apparatus Makers Assn. Jewish. Clubs: Masons, Irondequoit Country (pres. 1977-79). Office: 350 Commerce Dr Rochester NY 14601

GUTMAN, I. CYRUS, business exec.; b. Perth Amboy, N.J., Mar. 28, 1912; s. Leon and Jennie (Levine) G.; B.S. in Econs., Johns Hopkins U., 1932; m. Mildred B. Largman, July 21, 1940; children—Harry L., Peggy Sheren, Richard J.S. Dist. mgr. Motor Freight Express, Inc., Phila., 1933-40; v.p., treas., gen. mgr. Modern Transfer Co., Inc., Allentown, Pa., 1940-67, dir. nat. sales, 1967-70; dir. Eastern Industries, Inc., Wescosville, Pa., 1967-76. Pres., Lehigh County Indsl. Devel. Corp., 1959—, Lehigh's Econ. Advancement Project, Inc., 1960—; chmn. Lehigh County Indsl. Devel. Authority, 1966—; mem. adv. com. Central Pa. Teamsters Pension and Health and Welfare Funds, 1969-76; mem. nat. resources com., nat. alumni schs. com. Johns Hopkins; mem. Lehigh-Northampton Counties Joint Planning Commn., 1962—; chmn. Allentown Sch. Dist. Authority; mem. Lehigh and Northampton Transp. Authority, 1972-74; chmn. Allentown Non-Partisan Com. for Local Govt.; mem. Eastern Conf. Joint Area Com.; asso. mem. Nat. Jewish Welfare Bd.; exec. com. Citizens for Lehigh County Progress, 1965—; chmn. central campaign planning com. Lehigh Valley Hosps.; adv. com. Good Shepherd Workshop; adv. bd. Allentown citadel Salvation Army, treas., 1971-80; pres. bd. assos. Muhlenberg Coll., v.p., 1971-73, pres. 1974-76; bd. assos. Cedar Crest Coll., 1972—; gen. adv. com. Lehigh County Vocat.-Tech. Sch., Lehigh County Community Coll., 1977; mem. Lehigh County Republican Exec. Com.; trustee Allentown Hosp., 1970—, Swain Sch., 1977-80; bd. dirs. Lehigh Valley Jr. Achievement, United Fund, Allentown, Jewish Fedn. Allentown, 1953-60, Wiley House, 1969-80, Lehigh Valley Public TV, Sta. WLVT, 1980—; past trustee Rabbi Louis M. Youngerman Found., Internat. Assn. Machinists Local 1099 Dist. Pension Plan, Phi Sigma Delta Found; hon. adv. bd. Lehigh Valley Assn. for Retarded Children, 1969-70; mem. adv. bd. Lehigh Valley Center for Performing Arts, 1975—. Recipient St. Patrick's Day award Lehigh Valley, 1961, Civic Service commendation Whitehall C. of C.; Golden Deeds award Allentown Exchange Club, 1972; Distinguished Citizens Sales award Sales and Mktg. Execs., Allentown and Bethlehem, 1976; Outstanding Service award Lehigh Valley Traffic Club, 1978. Mem. Allentown C. of C. (Distinguished Service award 1967, past-dir.), Traffic and Transp. Assn. Pitts., Met. Traffic Assn. N.Y., Central Pa. Motor Carriers Assn. (v.p., exec. com.), Am. Trucking Assn. (gov. Regular Common Carrier Conf. 1968), Eastern Labor Adv. Assn. (v.p.), Hon. First Defenders, Johns Hopkins Alumni Assn. (past sec., past pres. Phila. area), Lehigh County Hist. Soc. (exec. com. 1968-71), Nat. Fedn. Temple Brotherhoods, Omicron Delta Kappa, Pi Delta Epsilon, Zeta Beta Tau. Jewish (past dir. temple). Clubs: Masons, B'nai B'rith (founder lodge scholarship (com.); Berkleigh Country (hon. dir., past pres.) (Kutztown, Pa.); Lehigh Valley (Allentown); Locust Midcity, Traffic and Transp., Traffic (Phila.); Traffic (Balt.); N.Y. Traffic (N.Y.C.); Livingston. Home: 1824 Turner St Allentown PA 18104 Office: 462 Walnut St Allentown PA 18102

GUTTMAN, JERRY G., cons. firm exec.; b. Dresden, Germany, May 14, 1932; came to U.S., 1950, naturalized, 1953; s. Jacques and Clara (Kiebetz) G.; B.S. in Econs. and Indsl. Mgmt., U. Pa., 1960; m. Avie Silver, Feb. 28, 1958; children—William, Claudia. Pres., IDR Co., Phila., 1960-73, Fimaco, Inc., Riverton, N.J., 1973-75, MTA Group, Dresher, Pa., 1975-77; v.p. Decision Scis. Corp., Jenkintown, Pa., 1977—. Served with U.S. Army, 1953-55. Mem. Am. Mgmt. Assn., Fulfillment Mgmt. Assn. Jewish. Club: U. Pa. Contbr. to Folio and Zip mags. Home: 501 General Patterson Dr Glenside PA 19038 Office: PO Box 1010 Jenkintown PA 19046

GUY, CHARLES WILLIAM, mgmt. cons. co. exec.; b. Fairfield, Ohio, Mar. 23, 1945; s. Charles William and Helen S. (Ogle) G.; student Harvey Mudd Coll., 1963-64, Foothill Coll., 1964-65; B.A. in Economics, Calif. State U. at Northridge, 1967; m. Katherine Elba Hambright, June 16, 1967; children—Robert William, Cynthia Eva. Asst. to v.p. Viking Inds., Inc., Chatsworth, Calif., 1964-67; adminstrv. asst. to chief of police Burbank, Calif., 1967-69; pres., Environ. Mktg., Los Angeles and St. Louis, 1969-74; dir. hospitality and real estate recruiting Wells Mgmt. Corp., N.Y.C., 1974-75; sr. asso. Korn/Ferry & Assos., Los Angeles, 1975-77; v.p., partner Paul R. Ray & Co., Inc., Fort Worth, 1977-79; v.p., mng. partner Los Angeles office Barton Sans, Inc., 1979—; past chmn. Bank Advisory Bd.; lectr. various colleges and univs., orgns. Active, Sister City Program, Symphony Assn., World Affairs Council; pres. Outreach Love, internat. philanthropic orgn., 1979-80; mem. adv. bd. Adventure Unlimited, internat. youth orgn. Named life mem. Calif. Scholarship Fedn., 1963. Mem. The Travel Research Assn. (dir. So. Calif. chpt.), Am. Environ. Assn. (past pres.), Advt. Club of Los Angeles, Alpha Gamma Sigma. Clubs: Kiwanis (bd. dirs. local chpt.), Masons (affiliate). Home: 4023 Alcove Ave Studio City CA 91604 Office: 2049 Century Park E Suite 3050 Los Angeles CA 90067

GUY, JOHN ALBERT, mech. contractor; b. Columbus, Ohio, June 1, 1917; s. Maurice Albert and Esther Marion (Holliday) G.; student exec. mgmt. Ohio State U., 1966; m. Hermanna M. Groeniger, June 1, 1939; children—John Albert II, William H., Barbara Ann. Founder, pres., chmn. bd. J.A., Guy, Inc., Dublin, Ohio, 1953—; dir. Ohio State Bank. Active Boy Scouts Am., P.T.A. Mem. Mech. Contractors Assn. Central Ohio (pres.), Heating and Ventilating Engrs. (pres. Central Ohio chpt.), Ohio State U. Assn. (life). Mason (Shriner). Club: Brookside Country. Home: 7192 Dublin Rd Dublin OH 43017 Office: 5810 Shierrings Rd Dublin OH 43017

GUYTON, RALPH JOSEPH, corp. exec.; b. Franklin, Pa., May 7, 1924; s. Joseph Henry and Mary Agusta (Kroell) G.; B.S. in Acctg., Grove City Coll., 1949; postgrad. Memphis State U., 1950; M.B.A., U. Pitts., 1951; m. Mary Catherine Flecken, Aug. 19, 1944; children—Ralph J., Robert, Patrick, Dianne, Rene, Nancy, Joseph, Gregory. Spl. agt. FBI; store mgr. Joseph Horne Co., 1951-57; pres., dir. Raton, Inc., Pitts., 1951-60; owner, chief exec. officer, dir. Linden Creek Farms, Inc., 1960—; v.p., dir. Johnson Bros. Co., 1957—. Bd. dirs. Mercyhurst Coll., Meadows Standardbred Owners Assn., Brentwood-Whitehall Mchts. Assn., 100,000 Pennsylvanians; chmn. TriBoro Young Republicans. Served with USAAF, 1942-45; PTO. Decorated Air medal with 7 oak leaf clusters; recipient Meritorious Service award Mt. Lebanon C. of C., citation J. Edgar Hoover, 1963; Ky. col.; Tenn. squire. Mem. Nat. Rifle Assn., U.S. Trotting Assn., Wash. Legal Assn., Dapper Dans Found., Whittington Center, Ont. Harness Horseman Assn., Ducks Unltd., Mt. Lebanon C. of C. (pres.), Ex-F.B.I. Agts. (chmn. Pitts. chpt., chmn. award), Painting and Decorating Contractors Am. (pres. Pitts. chpt.), Am. Legion. Republican. Roman Catholic. Clubs: Univ., Valley Brook Country (dir.), Pitts. Athletic Assn., Igloo, Govs., Elks, Moose, K.C., Fraternal Order Police, Pitts. Sportsmen, Red Carpet, U.S. Senatorial, Safari, South Hills Kiwanis (dir.). Home: RD 1 Box 113A Linnwood Rd Canonsburg PA 15317 Office: Box 666 Pkwy W Pittsburgh PA 15205

GWINN, ROBERT P., elec. appliance mfg. exec.; b. Anderson, Ind., June 30, 1907; s. Marshall and Margaret (Cather) G.; Ph.B., U. Chgo., 1929; m. Nancy Flanders, Jan. 20, 1942; children—John Marshall, Richard Herbert. With Sunbeam Corp., Chgo., 1936—, successively in sales dept., asst. sales mgr., sales mgr., v.p. sales, 1936-55, pres., gen. mgr., dir., now chmn. bd., chief exec. officer; pres. Sunbeam Appliance Service Co., Chgo., 1952—; chmn. bd., chief exec. officer Ency. Brit.; chmn. bd. Titan Oil Co., Exploration, Inc.; dir. Sunbeam Corp., Ltd. (Can., U.K., Mex.); Continental Casualty Co., CNA Fin., 1st Nat. Bank Chgo., Riverside Nat. Bank, Continental Assurance Co. Trustee Hanover Coll., U. Chgo., U. Chgo. Cancer Research Found. Mem. Alpha Sigma Phi. Clubs: Riverside Country (Ill.); Mid-Am., Wine and Food Soc., Chicago, Univ., Comml., Econ. (Chgo.); Confrerie des Chevaliers du Tastevin; Mill Reef. Home: 144 Fairbanks Rd Riverside IL 60546 Office: 5400 Roosevelt Rd Chicago IL 60650

GYEMANT, ROBERT ERNEST, indsl. corp. exec., accountant, lawyer; b. Nicaragua, Jan. 17, 1944; s. Emery and Magda (Von Rechnitz) G.; came to U.S., 1949, naturalized, 1954; A.B., magna cum laude, U. Calif. at Los Angeles, 1965; J.D. (John Woodman Ayer fellow), U. Calif. at Berkeley, 1968; m. Ina Stephannie Levin, Feb. 28, 1970; children—George, Scott, Robert Ernest II, Anne Elizabeth. C.P.A. firm Ernst & Ernst, Oakland, Calif., 1966-68; admitted to Calif. bar, 1968; with firm Orrick, Herrington, Rowley & Sutcliffe, San Francisco, 1968-69, Skornia, Rosenblum & Gyemant, San Francisco, 1969-74; individual practice law, San Francisco, 1975-77; sec., dir., gen. counsel Topps & Trowsers, San Francisco, 1971—, exec. v.p. fin., 1977—; sec. Advanced Micro Devices, Inc., 1973-75; gen. counsel, dir. Comml. Bank of San Francisco, 1974-77; dir. Fidelity Nat. Bank, 1977; v.p., dir. M.A.R.C., Inc., 1975—; dir. Comdial Corp., 1977—; instr. U. Calif. Extension, 1969-76. Mem. Calif. Council Criminal Justice Task Force, 1971-73; commr. San Francisco Juvenile Justice Commn., 1976-78; mem. Republican State Central Com. Calif., 1971—. C.P.A., Calif. Mem. Am. Inst. C.P.A.s, State Bar Calif. (spl. com. on juvenile justice 1976), Am. Bar Assn., Calif. Soc. C.P.A.s. Republican. Episcopalian. Club: N.Y. Athletic. Mem. Calif. Law Rev.; contbr. articles to profl. jours. Office: 681 Market St San Francisco CA 94105

HAAG, CAROL ANN GUNDERSON, food co. exec.; b. Mpls.; d. Glenn Alvin and Genevieve Esther (Knudson) Gunderson; B.J., U. Mo., 1969; postgrad. Roosevelt U., Chgo., 1975—; m. Lawrence S. Haag, Aug. 30, 1969. Reporter, Waukegan (Ill.) News Sun, summers 1966-69; pub. relations writer, advt. copywriter Am. Hosp. Supply Corp., Evanston, 1969-70, also free-lance editor Lake County (Ill.) Circle weekly newspaper; asst. dir. pub. relations Rush-Presbyn.-St. Luke's Med. Center, Chgo., 1970-71; asst. mgr. pub. and employee communications Quaker Oats Co., Chgo., 1971-72, mgr. editorial communications, 1972-74, mgr. employee communications programs, 1974-77, mem. corp. office planning com., 1972-77; mgr. pub. relations Shaklee Corp., San Francisco, 1977—. Mem. adv. bd. dirs. San Francisco Spl. Olympics. Recipient 1st Place Certificate award Printing Industry Am., 1972, 74, 1st Place Spl. Communication award Internat. Assn. Bus. Communicators, 1974, First Place Citation for Outstanding Editorial Achievement award Chg. Assn. Bus. Communicators, 1974. Mem. Nat. Acad. TV Arts and Scis., Indsl. Communication Council, Public Relations Soc. Am. Presbyterian. Home: 133 Fernwood Dr Moraga CA 94556 Office: 444 Market St San Francisco CA 94111

HAAN, HENDRIK MARIE, diversified mfg. co. exec.; b. Leyden, Netherlands, July 22, 1924; s. Theodorus Antonius and Theresa Catarina (Fles) H.; Baccalaureate, U. Delft, 1947; diploma in mech. engring. Gen. Motors Inst., Flint, Mich., 1949; m. Frieda Ruytenbeek, May 21, 1950; children—Henry M., Roland V., Elizabeth A. Engr. power and indsl. products Gen. Motors Continental, Antwerp, Belgium, 1949-51; tech. mgr. NAHV (Lindeteves), Elizabethville, Zaire, 1951-55; dist. mgr. Ford Motor Co., Teheran, Iran, 1956-58; liaison exec. Bendix Corp., Paris, 1959-62; merchandising mgr. Chrysler Corp., Geneva, 1963-68; chief exec. officer subs. Fuqua Industries of Atlanta, Brussels, 1968-70; project exec. ITT, Brussels, 1971-73; adviser to pres. G & W Industries, Geneva, 1973-75; dir. internat. ops. Condec Corp., Old Greenwich, Conn., 1975-78; founder, pres., chief exec. officer Internat. Bus. Bur. (I.B.B.), bus. devel. cons., 1978—. Served with RAF, 1945. Mem. Am. Mgmt. Assn., Gen. Motors Alumni Assn., Brussels C. of C., Smithsonian Assos. Club: Swissair Travel. Home: 106 Peconic Hills Dr Southampton NY 11968

HAAP, FREDERICK, aviation co. exec.; b. Torrington, Conn., Apr. 7, 1939; s. Frederick and Hedwig Emma (Litke) H.; B.S., The Citadel, 1961; m. Diana Lee Stoner, July 4, 1964; children—Elizabeth Ann, Patricia Lynn. Pilot, U.S. Air Force, 1961-70, advanced through grades to maj., 1970; maj. Res.; pilot Gen. Electric Co., 1970-75; pilot Mead Corp., Vandalia, Ohio, 1975-76, mgr. aviation dept., 1976—. Decorated Air Medal (4). Mem. Nat. Bus. Aircraft Assn. (vice chmn. mgmt. com.), Aircraft Owners and Pilots Assn. Home: 1769 Furnas Rd Vandalia OH 45377

HAAS, EDWARD LEE, accounting firm exec.; b. Camden, N.J., Nov. 9, 1935; s. Edward David and Mildred (Wynne) H.; B.A., LaSalle Coll., 1958; postgrad. Temple U., 1960-62; m. Mary Ann Lind, Dec. 27, 1958; children—John Eric, Gretchen Lind. Mgr. systems devel. RCA Corp., Cherry Hill, N.J., 1966-71; mgr. computer tech. services The Gen. Tire & Rubber Co., Akron, Ohio, 1971-74; mgr. computer applications research and devel. Ernst & Whinney, Cleve., 1974-75, dir. nat. systems group, 1976, nat. dir. data processing and software products, 1977, nat. partner, 1978—. Mem. Greater Cleve. Growth Assn. Served to 1st lt., arty., U.S. Army, 1958-59. Mem. Soc. Cert. Data Processors, Data Processing Mgmt. Assn., Assn. for Systems Mgmt., Assn. for Computing Machinery, Republican. Roman Catholic. Clubs: Cleve. Athletic, Hudson Country, Western Res. Racquet, Hudson Tennis, Mid-day, Cotillion Soc. Cleve. Home: 111 Old Orchard Dr Hudson OH 44236 Office: 2000 National City Center Cleveland OH 44114

HAAS, FREDERICK CARL, chem. co. exec.; b. Buffalo, Feb. 16, 1936; s. Karl A. and Marie S. (Shilling) H.; B.S. in Chem. Engring., Purdue U., 1957; M.S. in Nuclear Engring., Rensselaer Poly. Inst., 1959, Ph.D., 1960; student Advanced Mgmt. Program, Harvard U., 1978; m. Dorothy Wittlief, Aug. 31, 1957; children—Kenneth, Laurence, Sandra. With Cornell Aero Lab., Buffalo, 1960-63; tech. dir. Westvaco Corp., Luke, Md. and N.Y.C., 1963-72, plant mgr., Tyrone, Pa., 1972-74, gen. mgr. mfg., Charleston, S.C., 1974-76, v.p., corporate research dir., Laurel, Md., 1979—; asst. prof. Potomac State Coll. of W.Va. U., 1967-68. U.S. AEC fellow, 1958-60. Mem. Am. Inst. Chem. Engrs., Am. Chem. Soc., TAPPI, N.Y. Acad. Sci., AAAS. Methodist. Clubs: Bearded Collie of Eng., Bearded Collie of Am. Contbr. articles to profl. jours. Office: Corporate Research Center Johns Hopkins Rd Laurel MD 20810

HAAS, JOSEPH SANDERS, JR., fin. exec.; b. Bryn Mawr, Pa., Jan. 12, 1953; s. J. Sanders and Betty Katherine (Hardeman) H.; B.S., U. N.H., 1976. Night watchman Loon Mt. Ski Area, Lincoln, N.H., summers, 1969-71; pvt. detective Missing Heirs of Am., Lincoln, 1972—; pastor Cathedral of the Beechwoods, Lincoln, 1976—; pres. The Meteorite Found., Lincoln, 1978—; landlord Odd Fellow Block, Ashland, N.H., 1978—. Town chmn. Lincoln Mosquito Control com., 1975—; N.H. notary pub. Mem. Soc. for Investigation of the Unexplained, Lincolnwood C. of C. Republican. Club: Blue Hill Country. Contbr. articles to profl. jours. Address: 7 N Main St Ashland NH 03217

HAAS, KARL ALAN, platics co. exec.; b. Englewood, N.J., June 6, 1933; s. Karl and Martha (Osterman) H.; B.Mgmt. Engring., Rensselaer Poly. Inst., 1959, M.Mgmt. Engring. (fellow), 1960, Ph.D. (Ford fellow), 1968; m. Jacqueline Crawford, Jan. 27, 1962; children—James Andrew, Susan Jennifer, David Reid, Peter Crawford. Instr. Sch. Mgmt. Rensselaer Poly. Inst., Troy, N.Y., 1960-62; asso. prof. dept. indsl. engring. and ops. research N.Y.U., N.Y.C., 1963-70; dir. mgmt. services Plymouth Rubber Co., Canton, Mass., 1970-72, v.p. adminstrn., 1972-75, group v.p., 1975—, group v.p. Plyroof div., 1979—; dir. Time Sharing Scis., Inc., cons. bus. and govt. N. and S. Am., 1961-70. Mem. Am. Inst. Indsl. Engrs., Sigma Xi, Tau Beta Pi, Epsilon Delta Sigma, Alpha Pi Mu. Presbyterian. Clubs: Indian Harbor Yacht (Greenwich, Conn.); Met. (Chgo.). Home: 42 Partridge Hill Rd Weston MA 02193 Office: 104 Revere St Canton MA 02021

HAAS, PAUL RAYMOND, investor; b. Kingston, N.Y., Mar. 10, 1915; s. Frederick J. and Amanda (Lange) H.; A.B., Rider Coll., 1934, LL.B., 1976; postgrad. U. Tex., 1939; m. Mary F. Diedrick, Aug. 30, 1936; children—Rheta Marie, Raymond Paul, Rene Marie. Accountant, Arthur Andersen & Co., C.P.A.'s, N.Y.C., and Houston, 1934-41; with La Gloria Oil & Gas Co. (now subsidiary Tex. Eastern Transmission Corp.), Corpus Christi, Tex., 1941-59, v.p., treas., dir., 1947-59; adminstrv. v.p. Tex. Eastern Transmission Corp., 1958-59; pres., chmn. Prado Oil & Gas Co., Corpus Christi, 1959-66; pres., dir. Wiltex Corp., 1950-65, Garland Co., 1956-65; chmn. bd., pres., dir. Corpus Christi Oil & Gas Co. and asso. cos., 1967—, Metal sales, Inc., 1970-72; ltd. partner Salomon Bros., 1973—; partner Price Cattle Co., 1959-68; dir. Houston Natural Gas Corp., Tex. Commerce Bankshares, Inc., Kaneb Services, Inc., Corpus Christi Nat. Bank. Mem. Tex. Gov's Com. on Edn., 1966-69; commr. Edn. Commn. of States, 1966-68; mem. Tex. Bd. Edn., 1962-72, trustee Corpus Christi Ind. Sch. Dist., 1951-58, v.p., 1952-56, pres., 1956-58. Trustee Rider Coll., 1959-67, Commn. on Pvt. Philanthropy and Pub. Needs, 1973-76, Moody Found., 1966-73, Found. Center, 1968-75, Paul and Mary Haas Found., 1954—, Council on Founds., 1970-76. C.P.A. Presbyterian (elder). Home: 36 Hewit Dr Corpus Christi TX 78404 Office: The Six Hundred Bldg POB 779 Corpus Christi TX 78404

HAAS, PETER EDGAR, mfr.; b. San Francisco, Dec. 20, 1918; s. Walter A. and Elise (Stern) H.; student Deerfield Acad., 1935-36; A.B., U. Cal., 1940; postgrad. Harvard, 1943; m. Josephine Baum, Feb. 1, 1945; children—Peter E., Michael Stern, Margaret Elizabeth. Asst. prodn. mgr. Levi Strauss & Co., San Francisco, 1946-51, v.p., dir., 1951-58, exec. v.p., 1958-70, pres., 1970—, chief exec. officer, 1976—; dir. Crocker-Citizens Nat. Bank, Am. Tel. & Tel. Co. Bd. dirs. Jewish Welfare Fedn.; trustee Stanford U., United Bay Area Crusade, San Francisco Bay Area Council; mem. citizens adv. commn. Golden Gate Nat. Recreation Area. Named a leader of tomorrow Time mag., 1953. Mem. Calif. Acad. Scis. (vice chmn., trustee), Calif. Alumni Fedn. (trustee). Republican. Jewish. Home: 313 Maple St San Francisco CA 94115 Office: Two Embarcadero Center San Francisco CA 94106

HAAS, ROBERT TERRY, chem. co. exec.; b. Norwood, Mass., Nov. 22, 1947; s. Albert Frederick and Miriam (Godley) H.; B.S., U. Rochester, 1969; M.S., Naval Postgrad. Sch., 1970; m. MaryElisa Pettinicchio, June 20, 1970. Systems mgr. Air Products and Chems., Inc., Allentown, Pa., 1975—. Served to lt. Supply Corps, USN, 1969-75. Cert. in data processing Inst. for Certification of Computer Profls. Mem. Am. Prodn. and Inventory Control Soc. (exec. v.p. Lehigh Valley chpt., cert. fellow inventory mgmt.), Data Processing Mgmt. Assn., Antique Automobile Club Am., Model A Ford Club Am. Office: Air Products and Chems Inc PO Box 538 Allentown PA 18105

HAAS, WALTER ABRAHAM, JR., apparel co. exec.; b. San Francisco, Jan. 24, 1916; s. Walter Abraham and Elise (Stern) H.; B.A., U. Calif., 1937; M.B.A., Harvard U., 1939; m. Evelyn Danzig, 1940; children—Robert D., Elizabeth Haas Eisenhardt, Walter J. Chmn. bd. Levi Strauss & Co., San Francisco; dir. Bank of Am., BankAm. Corp., United Airlines, Inc. Trustee Ford Found., Nat. Urban League, Com. for Econ. Devel.; mem. SRI Council, Trilateral Commn. Served in Mil., World War II. Named a Leader of Tomorrow, Time mag., 1953; Chief Exec. Officer of Yr., Fin. World mag., 1976; Jefferson award Am. Inst. Public Service, 1977; Alumni Achievement award Harvard Grad. Sch. Bus., 1979. Office: Levi Strauss & Co Two Embarcadero Center San Francisco CA 94106

HABA, LEONARD ALLEN, mfg. co. exec.; b. Carrington, N.D., Aug. 11, 1931; s. Martin and Agnes Haba; B.A., U. Wash., 1956; postgrad. U. Pitts., 1972; m. Sherry Marie Kearney, May 19, 1962; children—Linda, Cindy, Matthew, Steven. Sr. auditor Ernst & Ernst, Seattle, 1956-65; with PACCAR Inc., Bellevue, Wash., 1965—, chief internal auditor, 1965-70, controller Kenworth Truck div., 1970-72, v.p., corp. controller, 1972—; dir. Paccar Fin. Corp., Truck Acceptance Corp., Kenworth Mexicana; exec.-in-residence U. Wash., Seattle, 1978. Bd. dirs. Am. Diabetes Assn., 1977—; trustee Diabetic Trust Fund, 1979—; pres., chmn. Am. Diabetes Assn., Wash. affiliate, 1974-76, bd. dirs., 1979—. Served with USAF, 1950-52. C.P.A., Wash. Mem. Am. Inst. C.P.A.'s, Wash. Soc. C.P.A.'s, Fin. Execs. Inst., Am. Inst. Corp. Controllers. Home: 6531 82nd Ave SE Mercer Island WA 98040 Office: 777 106th Ave NE Bellevue WA 98004

HABACK, PETER LEE, real estate exec.; b. N.Y.C., July 25, 1951; s. Harry J. and Leah (Mintz) H.; B.A., Am. U., 1973; postgrad. John Marshall Law Sch., 1974-76. Office leasing cons. Helmsley-Spear, Chgo., 1976, bldg. mgr., 1976-79, asst. v.p., 1979-80, v.p., 1980—. Registered real estate broker, Ill. Mem. Bldg. Owners and Mgrs. Assn., Bldg. Mgrs. Club. Democrat. Jewish. Office: Suite 210 One N Dearborn St Chicago IL 60602

HABERECHT, ROLF REINHOLD, electronic co. exec.; b. Germany, June 4, 1929; came to U.S., 1956, naturalized, 1962; Ph.D., U. Berlin, 1956; M.B.A., So. Meth. U., 1967; m. Ute Schwarz, Aug. 18, 1961; children—Michael, Caroline. Dept. head research and devel. P.R. Mallory & Co., Indpls., 1956-61; with Tex. Instruments Inc., Dallas, 1962—, v.p. mgr. U.S. semicondr. group, 1975—. Trustee St. Mark's Sch. Tex., Episc. Sch. Dallas. Mem. Beta Gamma Sigma. Contbr. articles to profl. jours. Patentee in field. Home: 10984 Crooked Creek Dr Dallas TX 75229 Office: 10500 N Central Expressway Dallas TX 75222

HACHEY, MARILYN, camera mfg. co. exec.; b. Ayer, Mass., July 21, 1953; d. Harry L. and Marianne (Farrall) Wood; B.L.S., Boston U., 1977; M.Ed., Northeastern U., 1980. Exec. sec. Polaroid Corp., Cambridge, Mass., 1973-77, edn. and tng. specialist, 1977-80, sr. edn. and tng. specialist, 1980—. Mem. bus. tech. adv. bd. Shawsheen Valley Vocat. High Sch., 1978—. Mem. Am. Mgmt. Assn., Nat. Bus. Edn. Assn., Kappa Delta Pi. Office: 750 Main St Cambridge MA 02139

HACKER, DONALD WILBUR, mail advt. exec.; b. Ionia, Mich., June 18, 1914; s. Herman F. and Helena (Steinke) H.; grad. Chgo. Acad. Fine Arts, 1937; student U. Ga., 1942-43; m. Ruby Elaine Simonson, Sept. 28, 1943; children—Eve Rulaine, David Kent, Donna Kathleen. Asst. advt. mgr. Gen. Furniture Co., Inc., Chgo., 1937-39; advt. merchandising mgr. Franc's, Davenport, Ia., 1939-42; owner Lettercraft Co., Detroit, 1946—; pres. D. W. Hacker Co., Inc., Detroit, 1950—, Hacker-Stutz Corp., 1963—, Univ. Type Corp., 1964—. Active community drives; v.p. Detroit Cerebral Palsy Center. Vice pres. United Cerebral Palsy Assn. Mich.; pres. United Cerebral Palsy Found. Served as dir. pub. relations U.S.A. Engr. Corps, AUS, 1944-46. Mem. Mail Advt. Service Assn. Internat. (pres. 1954-57), Mail Advt. Service Assn. (pres. Detroit chpt. 1947-52), Advt. Fedn. Am. (dir., 1954—), Detroit Execs. Assn. (dir.), Classic Car Club Am. Lutheran. Clubs: Forest Lake Country (Bloomfield Hills, Mich.); Recess (Detroit); Innisbrook Golf and Country, Innisbrook Resort (Tarpon Springs, Fla.); Rolls Royce Owners; Club at Crayton Cove (Naples, Fla.). Home: 4778 Lahser Rd Bloomfield Hills MI 48013 also 1817 Cliff Rd Point Aux Barques MI 48467 also 4001 Gulfshore Blvd N Naples FL 33940 Office: 2180 E Milwaukee Ave Detroit MI 48211

HACKETT, MARY MILAM STEVENSON (MRS. RALPH C. HACKETT), banker, farmer; b. Chelsea, Okla., May 16, 1916; d. Jesse Bartley and Elizabeth (McSpadden) Milam; B.A., U. Okla., 1937; m. George Joseph Stevenson, Jr., Nov. 5, 1938 (dec. Apr. 1962); children—George Joseph III, Gelvin Lee, Mark Milam, Elizabeth Ellen; m. 2d, Ralph C. Hackett, Mar. 22, 1970. Bookkeeper, Phillips & Milam, 1937-38; mgr. grain and livestock farm, Tarkio, Mo., 1962—; former v.p., now chmn. bd. Farmers & Valley Bank; pres. Water Supply Co., Inc., Chelsea, Okla.; partner Phillips & Milam Oil Co., Chelsea, 1949-72, Miller & Stevenson Ins. Co., Tarkio, Mo., 1962-75, M. & S. Trailer Rental Co., Harlingen, Tex., 1962-67. Mem. children and youth com. N.W. div. Mo. Assn. Social Welfare; bd. dirs. Midland Empire council Girl Scouts U.S.A., 1959-67, dist. chmn., 1960-65; bd. dirs. Atchison County chpt. A.R.C., 1957—, water safety chmn., 1955-60; mem. finance com. Tarkio Coll.-Community Farm Project; mem. bd. Mo. Soc. Crippled Children and Adults; bd. dirs. Tarkio Coll., 1962-76, asso. bd. dirs., 1976—, sec., 1962-68, asst. treas., 1969-76, exec. bd., 1965-68, 72-76; pres. Tarkio Coll. Mule Barn Theater Guild, 1976-78, v.p., 1980-81. Mem. Nat. Assn. Bank Women, Okla. Hist. Soc., Cherokee Nat. Hist. Soc., League Democratic Women Voters, Am. Legion Aux., Daus. Am. Colonists, P.E.O. (past pres.), Kappa Alpha Theta. Presbyterian (elder, past pres. Presbyn. Women's Assn.). Home: 902 Park St Tarkio MO 64491 Office: 512 Main St Tarkio MO 64491

HACKMAN, RICHARD PAUL, lawyer; b. Brighton, Mass., May 30, 1946; s. Howard Thomas and Catherine Ann (Russell) H.; B.A., Holy Cross Coll., 1968; J.D., Coll. of William and Mary, 1974; postgrad. Temple U., 1977—; m. Martha Jane Craig, Sept. 29, 1973; children—Mary Brennan, Brooke Ellis. Asso. firm Delk & Barlow, Smithfield, Va., 1974-75; admitted to Va. bar, 1974, Pa. bar, 1976; asso. firm Robert D. Stuart, Esq., Exton, Pa., 1976; div. counsel Litton Industries, Inc., Drexel Hill, Pa., 1976-79; staff atty. RCA Corp., Camden, N.J., 1979—; asst. sec. Litton Systems, Inc., 1977-79; def. counsel Pa. Army N.G., 1979—. Served with U.S. Army, 1968-71; Vietnam. Decorated Bronze Star. Mem. Pa. Bar Assn., Va. Bar Assn., Am. Bar Assn. Democrat. Roman Catholic. Home: 752 Rugby Rd Bryn Mawr PA 19010 Office: RCA Corp Front and Cooper Sts Camden NJ 08102

HACKNEY, JAMES ACRA, III, engr., mfg. co. exec.; b. Washington, N.C., Sept. 27, 1939; s. James Acra and Margaret Dunston (Hodges) H.; B.S. in Mech. Engring., N.C. State U., 1961, B.S. in Indsl. Engring., 1962; m. Constance Garrenton, June 5, 1961; children—Kenneth Ross, Jane Mather. With Hackney & Sons, Inc., Washington, N.C., 1961—, chief engr., 1961-63, asst. gen. mgr., 1963-65, exec. v.p., gen. mgr., 1965-70, pres., chief exec. officer, 1970—; also pres. subs. Hackney & Sons (East) Inc., Washington, Hackney & Sons (Midwest), Inc., Independence, Kans.; dir. N.C. Nat. Bank, Washington; mem. So. adv. bd. Am. Mut. Ins. Co., 1975—. Pres., East Carolina council Boy Scouts Am., 1976-77, mem. exec. bd. S.E. region, 1978—; chmn. bus. curriculum adv. com. Beaufort County Tech. Inst., 1969-72; mem. engring. adv. council N.C. State U., 1973-76, chmn., 1975-76; pres. Coastal Plain Devel. Assn., 1969; vice chmn. Zoning and Planning Commn., Washington, 1966-73; v.p., bd. dirs. N.C. Engring. Found., 1977—; mem. adminstrv. bd. local Methodist Ch., 1976—; bd. dirs. N.C. Citizens Assn., 1979—; chmn. bd. trustees Beaufort County Hosp., 1975-77; trustee N.C. State U., 1979—; mem. policy panel for statewide outdoor recreation program State of N.C., 1980—. Served to 1st lt., Ordnance Corps, AUS, 1963-65. Recipient Distinguished Service award (young man of year), Washington Jr. C. of C., 1970; named N.C. Small Businessman of year U.S. SBA, 1971, Outstanding Young Engr. N.C., Profl. Engrs. N.C., 1970-71, Young Engr. of Yr., Nat. Soc. Profl. Engrs., 1971, Outstanding Young Alumnus, N.C. State U., 1975; registered profl. engr., N.C., Kans. Mem. Truck Body and Equipment Assn. (dir. 1970-72, 79—), Beverage Body Mfrs. Assn. (pres. 1969-70, 78-79), Washington C. of C. (pres. 1972-74), Eastern N.C. C. of C. (exec. com. 1981—), Am. Inst. Indsl. Engrs. (chpt. pres. 1967-68), Profl. Engrs. N.C. (pres. Eastern Carolina chpt. 1971-72), N.C. Soc. Engrs., N.C. State U. Alumni Assn. (dir. 1976-80). Rotarian (pres. 1978-79). Home: 220 Alderson Rd Washington NC 27889 Office: 400 Hackney Ave Washington NC 27889

HADDAD, WILLIAM GEORGE, stockbroker; b. Cedar Rapids, Iowa, Mar. 8, 1925; s. David Joseph and Sadie Haddad; B.S., UCLA, 1949; m. Mary Rose Attyah, July 11, 1953; children—Benjamin Albert, David John, Rose Marie. Stockbroker, v.p. E.F. Hutton & Co., Los Angeles, 1949-78; stockbroker/vice chmn. Petra Capital Corp., Los Angeles, 1978—. Served to 1st lt. USAAF, 1943-45. Republican. Mem. Eastern Orthodox Ch. Clubs: Wilshire Country, Masons, K.T. Home: 191 S Hudson Ave Los Angeles CA 90004 Office: 800 W 6th St Los Angeles CA 90017

HADDAWAY, JAMES DAVID, ins. co. ofcl.; b. Louisville, July 25, 1933; s. Charles Montgomery and Viola (Sands) H.; B.Sc., U. Louisville, 1961; M.B.A., Xavier U., 1973; m. Myrna Lou Harris, June 5, 1954; children—Peggy Ann, Robert Marshall, Susan Gayle. Ins. cons. Met. Life Ins., Louisville, 1955-59; supt. Byck Bros. & Co., Louisville, 1959-61; dir. purchasing Liberty Nat. Bank, Louisville, 1961-63; v.p., mgr. gen. services adminstrn. Citizens Fed. Bank, Louisville, 1963-79; mgr. human resources Ky. Farm Bur. Ins. Co., 1979—. Founder, chmn. emeritus Kentuckiana Expn. of Bus. and Industry, 1973—. Served with U.S. Army, 1953-55. Named Boss of Year, Louisville chpt. Nat. Secs. Assn., 1978, 79. Cert. adminstrv. mgr., purchasing mgr. Mem. Assn. M.B.A. Execs., Internat. Adminstrv. Mgmt. Soc. (dir. 1979-81), Adminstrv. Mgmt. Soc. Louisville (past pres.), Adminstrv. Mgmt. Soc. Found. (charter), Purchasing Mgmt. Assn. Louisville (past pres.), Louisville Personnel Assn., Nat. Eagle Scout Assn., Hon. Order Ky. Cols. Baptist. Clubs: Masons, Shriners, Caravan Internat. Home: 4015 Wimpole Rd Louisville KY 40218 Office: 120 S Hubbard Ln Louisville KY 40207

HADDOCK, BRUCE LASHER, holding co. exec.; b. Cleve., June 13, 1930; s. T. M. and Daisy (Lasher) H.; B.A., Syracuse U., 1953; M.B.A., Harvard U., 1956; m. Leah Marie Goguen; children—Cheryl Ann, Melissa Ann. Pres., Ram Industries, Auburn, Ohio, 1960-70; v.p. Challanger Industries, Ravenna, Ohio, 1970-75, Polymer Industries, Middlefield, Ohio, 1975—; pres., chief exec. officer Gemini Products Corp., Chagrin Falls, Ohio, 1975—; v.p. Once Upon A House; gen. partner I North Franklin Investments, Island Properties, Oahu, Hawaii, Historic Properties, Savannah, Ga. Co-chmn. Geauga County Republican Party, Chardon, Ohio, 1960-64. Served with U.S. Army, 1953-56. Fellow Public Relations Soc. Am. (Writing Excellence award 1960); mem. Cleve. Advt. Club, Automotive Parts and Accessories Assn., Splty. Equipment Mktg. Assn., Performance Warehouse Assn., Am. Mktg. Assn., Advt. Splty. Inst. Clubs: Cleve. Athletic, Hill Brook, Chagrin Valley Racquet, Tanglewood Country, Bath, Balboa Bay, Hilton Head Plantation. Office: 6 W Washington St Chagrin Falls OH 44022

HADDOCK, GARTH DEWITT, ins. and real estate exec.; b. Kellogg, Idaho, Jan. 6, 1921; s. Herbert Massed and Inez Marguerite (Roland) H.; B.S., U. Idaho, 1948; m. Margie Agnes Erickson, Jan. 16, 1944; 1 son, Randy Garth. Adminstrv. asst. Bunker Hill and Sullivan Mining Co., Kellogg, 1948-52; owner Shoshone Ins. Co., Kellogg, 1952—; dir. mining cos. Pres. No. Idaho Econ. Devel. Assn., 1961-62; nat. pres. Vandal Boosters U. Idaho, 1973-74. Served as pilot USMC, 1942-46. Decorated D.F.C., Air medal, Purple Heart. Mem. Idaho Assn. Ins. Agts. (pres. 1958), Kellogg C. of C. (pres. 1958), Am. Legion (comdr. 1961-62). Republican. Episcopalian. Clubs: Masons, Shriners, Gyro Internat. (dist. gov. 1964-65). Home: Route 3 Box 427 R2 Coeur d'Alene ID 83814 Office: 125 McKinley Ave Kellogg ID 83837

HADDOX, JEROME BLISS, ins. co. exec., lawyer; b. Cedar Falls, Iowa, Apr. 19, 1933; s. Homer C. and Helen M. (Daum) H.; B.S., Ohio State U., 1955, J.D., 1959; m. Donna Doyle, Sept. 13, 1958; children—Jeffrey, Stephen, Michelle, Amy, Owen, Eric. Admitted to Ohio bar, 1960; atty. Nationwide Ins. Co., Columbus, Ohio, 1960-64; corp. counsel Indsl. Nucleonics Corp., Columbus, 1964-66; asso. counsel Western-S. Life Ins. Co., Cin., 1966-68; with J.C. Penney Casualty Ins. Co., Westerville, Ohio, 1968—, v.p., sec., counsel, 1974—; chmn. Ohio Insurers Polit. Action Com., 1978-80. Served to lt. USMCR, 1955-57. C.P.C.U., C.L.U.; recipient Merit award Ohio

Legal Center, 1968. Mem. Am. Bar Assn., Ohio Bar Assn., Ohio Ins. Fedn., Fedn. Ins. Counsel, Columbus Bar Assn., Nat. Assn. Life Underwriters, Ohio Assn. Life Underwriters, Columbus Assn. Life Underwriters, Columbus Health Underwriters Assn., Am. Soc. C.L.U.s, Am. Judicature Soc., Am. Trial Lawyers Assn., Ohio Assn. Civil Trial Attys. Office: JC Penney Casualty Ins Co 800 Brooksedge Blvd Westerville OH 43081

HADFIELD, JAMES PETER, mktg. exec.; b. Milw., Oct. 16, 1945; s. James John and Jeannette (Pierson) H.; B.S., U. Wis., Milw., 1972; M.B.A., U. Chgo., 1979; m. Mary Ellen Goelz, Sept. 16, 1972; 1 son, James Arnold. Asso. engr. Westinghouse Electric Corp., Lester, Pa., 1972-74; customer service rep. Gen. Cable Corp., Des Plaines, Ill., 1974-76, account mgr., 1976-79, mktg. mgr., OEM sales, St. Louis, 1979—. Served with USAF, 1965-69. Mem. Tau Beta Pi, Beta Gamma Sigma. Republican. Roman Catholic. Home: 1 Marche Dr Lake Saint Louis MO 63367 Office: 502 Earth City Plaza Suite 311 Earth City MO 63045

HADLEY, JOHN BART, r.r. assn. exec.; b. Oil City, Pa., Feb. 17, 1942; s. James Edward and Genevieve A. (Rowley) H.; B.A., Hiram Coll., 1964; M.B.A., (Samuel S. Fels scholar), U. Pa., 1967. Fin. analyst Westinghouse Electric Corp., Bloomington, Ind., 1967-69, mgr. fin. planning, Pitts., Tucson, Richmond, Va., 1969-71, staff asst. corporate fin. planning, Pitts., 1971-74, sr. fin. analyst, 1974; bus. analyst Farah Mfg. Co., El Paso, Tex., 1974-75, fin. analyst (Treasury), 1975-76, div. controller young men's and boys' div., 1976-77; chief agy. and fin. rev. U.S. Ry. Assn., Washington, 1977-79, chief fin. analysis, 1979-80, spl. asst. to dir. fin. analysis, 1980—. Mem. Nat. Assn. Accountants, Transp. Research Forum, Chi Sigma Phi. Episcopalian. Clubs: Circle K (sec. 1963), Propeller (publicity coordinator 1966-67), Wharton Sch. Home: 1400 S Joyce St Apt C 608 Arlington VA 22202 Office: 955 L'Enfant Plaza North SW Washington DC 20595

HADLEY, PAUL ROBERT, JR., industrialist; b. Woodstock, Ont., Can., May 9, 1920 (parents Am. citizens); s. Paul Robert and Isabelle (Montgomery) H.; B.S., Ithaca Coll., 1948, B.F.A., 1948; M.B.A., U. Ky., 1953; grad. Inst. Orgn. Mgmt., U. Colo., 1977; grad. Acad. Orgn. Mgmt., U. Notre Dame, 1977; m. Alice Churchill, Nov. 25, 1942; children—Alice Anne, Paul Robert III, Patricia E., Kim. Prodn. supr. Rural Radio Network, Ithaca, N.Y., 1948-49; v.p., gen. mgr., dir. Churchill Weavers, Berea, Ky., 1949-60; dir. arts, crafts div. Dept. Econ. Devel., State of Ky., 1960-64; v.p., dir. Ky. Metalcrafters, Inez, 1961; pres., dir. Pink Pig, Inc., Frankfort, Ky., 1961—; v.p., dir. Tradewater Craft Center, Providence, Ky.; sec. JADA Corp.; dir. Sunliner div., dir. marketing services, marine group Am. Comml. Lines; v.p., gen. mgr. Marine div. Kayot, Inc., Mankato, Minn., 1969-70; exec. v.p. Mankato Area C. of C., 1970-77; v.p. devel. Taylor Corp./Carlson Cratt, 1977—; dir. Ky. Mountain Crafts, Jackson; tourist, travel cons. Gov's. Tourist Commn.; cons. houseboat industry, 1967; indsl. developer, 1970—; instr. communications and bus. adminstrn. Mankato State U., 1976—. Dir. Madison County Air Bd., 1961-64; sec. Berea Planning, Zoning Commn., 1958-60, Mankato Area Airport Commn., 1970—, Mankato Parking Adv. Commn.; commr. Minn. Region 9 Recycling Center, 1978—; mem. Minn. N.G. Adv. Commn., 1973—, Region 9 Indsl. Safety Council. Bd. dirs. So. Highlands Handcraft Guild, Asheville, N.C., Mankato Area Humane Soc., Mankato Area Vocational Tech. Sch. Adv. Com. Named Man of Year, C. of C., 1960; Ky. col. Mem. Soc. Safety Engrs., Louisville Personnel Assn., Am. Craftsmen Council, Ky., Berea, Clark County (exec. v.p.) (exec. dir.) chambers commerce, Internat. Houseboat Mfrs. Assn. (pres.), Boat Mfrs. Assn. (dir. 1968-70), Am. Bur. Yacht Council (tech. mem.), Pub. Relations Soc. Am. (v.p. Blue Cross chpt.), Am. (certified chamber exec.), Minn. (dir. 1974-77) chamber commerce execs., Am. Indsl. Devel. Council (certified indsl. developer), Minn. Assn. Chambers Commerce (regional exec. v.p. 1972—), N. Mankato Civic and Commerce Assn. (exec. v.p. 1978), Outdoor Writers Assn. Mason (Shriner), Rotarian. Contbg. editor Houseboating Mag.; houseboat editor Motorboat Mag., 1976—. Home: 1501 Lor Ray Dr North Mankato MN 56001 Office: Taylor Corp 1750 Tower Blvd North Mankato MN 56001

HADREAS, JAMES DEMETRIOS, motel exec.; b. LaCrosse, Wis., Aug. 29, 1910; s. John Demetrios and Anna (Rozakis) H.; student U. Calif., Berkeley, 1947-49; m. Catherine Mountanos, Dec. 6, 1942; children—John J., Peter J. Pres., Md. Hotel Bldg. Corp., San Diego, 1946-51, Los Gables Apt. Hotel, Salt Lake City, 1951-57, Sundial Motor Lodge of Redwood City (Calif.), 1960-67, Sundial Motor Lodge, Inc., Hillsborough, Calif., 1967—, Republican candidate for Congress from 13th Dist. Calif., 1974. Mem. Redwood City C. of C. Club: Commonwealth. Home: 903 Tournament Dr Hillsborough CA 94010 Office: 316 El Camino Real Redwood City CA 94062

HAEFLINGER, CHARLES FRED, JR., educator, coll. fin. adminstr.; b. High Point, N.C., Dec. 11, 1933; s. Charles Fred and Lucile Anderson H.; B.S., Fla. State U., 1958; M.Ed., Fla. Atlantic U., 1965; m. Jane Haskell Lewis, Sept. 1, 1958; children—Charles Fred III, Sarah Jane, Lewis Anderson. Auditor, Fla. Auditing Dept., Tallahassee, 1958-62; sr. acct. Fla. Atlantic U., Boca Raton, 1962-65; asst. comptroller Vassar Coll., Poughkeepsie, N.Y., 1965-69; bus. mgr. Brenau Coll., Gainesville, Ga., 1969-70; trust officer U. S.C., Columbia, 1970-74; v.p. bus. and fin. Midlands Tech. Coll., Columbia, S.C., 1974-80; prof. fin., v.p. fin. affairs Converse Coll., Spartanburg, S.C., 1980—; cons. coll. fin. Bd. dirs. dist. Council on Ministries Methodist Ch., also mem. dist. council. Served to 1st lt. U.S. Army, 1952-55. Mem. Nat. Assn. Coll. Bus. Officers, Eastern Assn. Coll. Bus. Officers, So. Assn. Coll. Bus. Officers. Clubs: Kiwanis, Sertoma. Office: Converse Coll Spartanburg SC 29301

HAEGER, PHYLLIS M., profl. assn. mgmt. co. exec.; b. Chgo., May 20, 1928; d. Milton O. and Ethel H.; B.A., Lawrence U., 1950; M.A., Northwestern U., 1952; Midwest editor TIDE mag., Chgo., 1952-55; exec. v.p. Smith, Bucklin & Assos., Inc., Chgo., 1955-78; pres. P.M. Haeger and Assos., Inc., Chgo., 1978-80; exec. v.p. Nat. Assn. Bank Women, Inc., Chgo., 1980- . Mem. Am. Soc. Assn. Execs., Chgo. Soc. Assn. Execs., Inst. Assn. Mgmt. Cos., Nat. Assn. Women Bus. Owners, Chgo. Fin. Exchange, Chgo. Network. Club: Executives (Chgo.). Office: 500 N Michigan Ave Chicago IL 60610

HAEHL, JOHN GEORGE, JR., utility exec.; b. Bklyn., Aug. 16, 1922; s. John George and Madeline (Hamilton) H.; B.S. in Accounting cum laude, U. So. Calif., 1949; m. Alice Norton; children—Constance, Victoria. Mgr., Price Waterhouse & Co., C.P.A.'s, N.Y.C., Rochester and Syracuse, N.Y., 1949-61; with Niagara Mohawk Power Corp., Syracuse, 1961—, controller, from 1965, v.p., 1968-73, exec. v.p., from 1973, pres., 1973-80, chief exec. officer, 1973—, chmn., 1980—, also dir.; dir. Key Bank of Central N.Y., Canadian Niagara Power Co., Ltd., Crouse-Hinds Co., Utilities Mut. Ins. Co., Empire State Power Resources, Inc., Morris Pumps Inc. Bd. dirs. N.Y. State Coll. Forestry; trustee Canal Mus., Syracuse U. Served with USNR, 1942-46, C.P.A., N.Y. Mem. Am. Inst. C.P.A.'s, NY. State Soc. C.P.A.'s, Gyro Internat. Episcopalian. Club: Onondaga Golf and Country (Fayetteville, N.Y.). Office: 300 Erie Blvd W Syracuse NY 13202

HAERR, ROBERT KNAUS, instrumentation co. exec.; b. Great Falls, Mont., May 14, 1929; s. George Lester and Eula (Knaus) H.; B.S. in B.A., U. Utah, 1951; postgrad. UCLA Extension, 1954-65; m. Helen Louise Schultz, May 10, 1957; children—Robert Kenneth, Kenneth Paul. Mgr. pricing and planning, asst. to exec. v.p. Hycon Mfg. Co., Pasadena, Calif., 1954-58; mgr. contracts adminstrn. Consol. Systems Corp., Monrovia-Pomona, Calif., 1958-64, SDS Data Systems, Pomona, 1964-67; dir. adminstrn., aerospace div. Perkin-Elmer Corp., Pomona, 1967—; cons. in govt. procurement. Served to lt. U.S. Army, 1951-54. Cert. profl. contracts mgr. Mem. Nat. Contract Mgmt. Assn. (nat. dir. 1963-65), Pomona C. of C., Sigma Nu. Club: Masons. Address: 2771 N Garey Ave Pomona CA 91767

HAERRI, HERMANN J. M., aluminum co. exec.; b. 1928; ed. Swill Comml. Sch.; married. Mgr. fin. and ops. Bulova Watch Co. Inc., 1951-61; dir. internat. ops. Tektronix Internat., 1961-67; pres. R.J. Reynolds Tobacco Internat. S.A., Geneva, 1967-77; sr. v.p. corp. planning Consol. Aluminum Corp., St. Louis, 1978-79, pres., chief exec. officer, 1979—. Office: Consol Aluminum Corp 11960 Westline Indsl Dr Box 14448 Saint Louis MO 63178*

HAERTLING, GENE HENRY, ceramics engr.; b. Old Appleton, Mo., Mar. 15, 1932; s. Herbert Oswald and Dorothy (Schaefer) H.; B.S., U. Mo., 1954; M.S., U. Ill., 1960, Ph.D., 1961; m. Lois Ann Klein, June 22, 1958; children—Mark Allen, Barbara Ann, Carol Lynn. Mem. staff Sandia Labs., Albuquerque, 1961-64, div. supr., 1965-72; pres. Optoceram, Inc., Albuquerque, 1973-74; resource mgr. ceramics Motorola, Inc., Albuquerque, 1975-77, mgr. ceramic research and devel., 1978—. Served with U.S. Army, 1955-57. Fellow IEEE, Am. Ceramic Soc.; mem. Nat. Inst. Ceramic Engrs. Republican. Lutheran. Patentee in field. Home: 3624 Colorado Ct NE Albuquerque NM 87110 Office: 3434 Vassar NE Albuquerque NM 87107

HAFFER, LOUIS PAUL, lawyer, assn. exec.; b. Boston, May 19, 1914; s. George and Laura (Yager) H.; LL.B. cum laude, Boston U., 1937; m. Hilda Elizabeth Thompson, Aug. 8, 1941; children—Laura S. (Mrs. David Braddock), Douglas P. Admitted Mass. bar, 1937, U.S. Supreme Ct. bar, 1945, D.C. bar, 1949; sec. to justices Mass. Supreme Jud. Ct., 1937-39; atty. Wage and Hour Adminstrn., 1939-42, FDA, 1942; trial atty. Dept. Justice, 1942-48; practiced in Washington, 1948—; exec. v.p., counsel Air Freight Assn. Am. (formerly Freight Forwarders Assn.), Washington, 1956—. Lectr., Catholic U. Sch. Law, 1955-64, Am. Inst. Banking, 1953-54. Recipient John Ordronaux prize Boston U., 1937. Mem. Am. Bar Assn. (anti-trust com. adminstrv. law com.). Democrat. Clubs: Internat. Aviation, Wings. Editor-in-chief Boston U. Law Rev., 1937. Home: 4711 MacArthur Blvd NW Washington DC 20007 Office: 1730 Rhode Island Ave NW Washington DC 20036

HAFFORD, DAVID GORDON, ins. broker; b. San Francisco, Oct. 18, 1924; s. Samuel John and Ethel Lucille (Turner) H.; student U. Calif., 1946-49, Golden Gate Coll., 1952-54; B.S., UCLA, 1955; m. Thelma Mae Busick, Jan. 17, 1976. Fire ins. underwriter Phoenix Ins. Co., San Francisco, 1949-54, mgr. fire dept., Los Angeles, 1954, multiple line spl. agt., San Diego, 1955-57; account exec. Willis H. Fletcher Co., San Diego, 1957-65; pres. Snapp Ins. Agy., Inc., El Cajon, Calif., 1965—; instr. ins. part-time, various colls. and schs., San Diego, 1955-75. Served with USNR, 1943-52. C.P.C.U. Mem. Soc. C.P.C.U.'s (chpt. pres. 1964, 70), Ind. Ins. Agts. Assn. E. San Diego County (pres. 1965-66), Western Assn. Ins. Brokers, El Cajon C. of C. (pres. 1976-77). Republican. Clubs: Rotary (pres. El Cajon 1973-74), Masons. Home: 1069 Rippey St El Cajon CA 92020 Office: 333 W Lexington El Cajon CA 92020

HAFKUS, PETER LUDWIG, mfg. co. exec.; b. Geesthacht, W. Ger., Nov. 12, 1945; came to U.S., 1974; s. Ludwig Carl and Ludwina (Roth) H.; B.S. (German NSF fellow 1967-69), U. Berlin, 1969; M.S., U. Paris, 1973; M.B.A. (Inst. of Internat. Edn. fellow 1974, ITT Internat. fellow 1975), La. State U. and Am. Grad. Sch. Internat. Mgmt., 1975; m. Alexandra L.Y. Pérès, Oct. 21, 1976; children—Catherine Julia, Jennifer Elizabeth. Asst. prof., cons. U. Munster (W. Ger.), 1970-71; asst. comml. dir. Siimex SARL, Paris, 1971-74; product mgr. Air Products & Chems., Inc., Allentown, Pa. and Paris, 1976-78; v.p., gen. mgr. Lampi Corp., Huntsville, Ala., 1969—. UNESCO fellow, 1970; NATO fellow, 1971. Mem. Am. Mgmt. Assn., Am. Soc. Personnel Adminstrn., Am. Soc. Metals, Am. Soc. Mining Engrs., Nat. Elec. Mfrs. Assn., Illuminating Engring. Soc., Assn. Technique du Traitment Thermique (France), Nat. Hardware Assn./Home Center Inst. Home: 2705 Briarwood Dr Huntsville AL 35801 Office: PO Box 26 Huntsville AL 35804

HAFNER, THEODORE, physicist, lawyer; b. Vienna, Austria, Oct. 4, 1901; s. Mathias and Rose (Kohl) H.; Ph.D. in Physics and Math., U. Vienna, 1926; J.D., Fordham U., 1946; m. Renee Schwarz, May 6, 1950; 1 dau., Erika (Mrs. Marvin Kalisch). Came to U.S., 1941, naturalized, 1947. Research on sound and video AEG and Telefunken, Berlin, Germany, 1927-33; asst. to pres. Brit. Acoustic Films and Technicolor, London, Eng., 1933-37; mng. dir. Mole-Richardson, Paris, France, 1937-41; design engr. N.Y. Eagle Electric, N.Y.C.-Internat. Resistance, Phila., 1941-43; patent counsel Internat. Tel. & Tel. Co., N.Y.C., 1943-45; with internat. patent operations dept. RCA, N.Y.C., 1945-49; admitted to N.Y. bar, 1947, U.S. Patent Office bar, 1946; practiced in N.Y.C., 1949—. Pres., Surface Conduction, Beam Guidance Inc., Guided Space Transmissions (all N.Y.C.). Mem. Fed. Bar Assn. (com. atomic energy), Assn. Bar City N.Y., Patent Law Assn. (com. profl. ethics), I.E.E.E. (sr. mem.), Carl Neuberg Soc. Internat. Sci. Relations. Contbr. lectrs. and articles to profl jours. Patentee single-wire transmission line, laser resonator-light transmission line. Home: 265 Riverside Dr New York NY 10025 Office: 1501 Broadway New York NY 10036

HAGAN, ARTHUR SPRINGER, sporting goods co. exec.; b. N.Y.C., Oct. 31, 1938; s. Arthur Springer and Eleanor (Reinhardt) H.; B.S., Colo. State U., 1960; m. Suzanne Marie Cooper, Aug. 27, 1960; children—Scott Arthur, Clark John. Staff, Mountain region J.C. Penney Co., Denver, 1960-70; pres. Aspen Leaf, 15 sporting goods stores in 3 states, Denver, 1970-80, also dir.; pres. Hagan Sports, Denver, 1980—. Mem. Mayor's Com. for Greater Denver, 1978—; mem. Chancellor's Soc. U. Denver, 1977—. Mem. Nat. Sporting Goods Assn. (dir. 1978—), Ski Retailers Internat. Assn. (dir. 1978—), Nat. Retail Mchts. Assn., Colo. Tennis Assn., Intermountain Tennis Assn. Tennis World, Sigma Alpha Epsilon. Republican. Clubs: Denver Athletic, Denver Tennis, Rotary, Pinehurst Country, Masons (32 deg.). Home: 5798 E Powers Ave Englewood CO 80111 Office: 2553 S Colorado Blvd Denver CO 80222

HAGAN, EILEEN, lighting co. exec.; b. Paterson, N.J., July 27, 1930; s. Thomas A. and Ruth J. (Conlon) H.; 1 son, Mark Fusco. Asst. to sales mgr. C. N. Burman Co., Paterson, 1955-61, asst. to pres., 1961-67, design coordinator, 1967-73, v.p. mktg. and design, dir., 1973—; dir. Heldak Lighting Products, Paterson Shade, Univ. Lamp, Certified Shade Co. Bd. dirs. YWCA, Paterson, 1949-53. Mem. Decorative and Fine Arts Soc. Bergen County, Nat. Assn. Variety Stores, Assn. Gen. Mdse. Chains, Paterson C. of C. Office: 781 River St Paterson NJ 07524

HAGAN, FRANK MARTIN, ins. exec.; b. Wichita, Kans., Sept. 26, 1918; s. John L. and Julia P. (Murphy) H.; B.S. in Commerce, U. Santa Clara, 1940; m. Anne Wardlaw, Sept. 18, 1942. With Johnson & Higgins, San Francisco, 1946-54; with Miller & Ames, San Francisco, 1954-68, pres., 1964-68; v.p., dir. Corroon & Black Corp., N.Y.C., 1968-75, pres., chmn. exec. com., 1975-78, dir., chmn. exec. com., 1978—, also mng. dir. Western region, San Francisco, 1978—; pres. Corroon & Black-Miller & Ames, San Francisco, 1968-75. Served to lt. comdr. USNR, 1942-45. Decorated Bronze Star. Home: 43 Faxon Rd Atherton CA 94025 Office: 50 California St San Francisco CA 94111

HAGAN, JOHN M., ednl. adminstr.; b. Cambridge, Mass., June 21, 1939; s. Charles G. and Beatrice H.; B.A. in History, Providence Coll., 1961; M.A., Catholic U., 1964; postgrad. U. Md., 1965-70; m. Eleanor Niles, Aug. 17, 1963. Tchr. social studies Prince George County (Md.) pub. schs., 1964-71; vice prin. Douglass Sr. High Sch., Upper Marlboro, Md., 1971-74; prin. Kent Jr. High Sch., Landover, Md., 1975-76; prin. Bowie (Md.) Sr. High Sch., 1976—. Named Outstanding Young Educator, Bowie Jaycees, 1970. Mem. NEA, Md. Tchrs. Assn., Nat., Md. assns. secondary sch. prins., Prince Georges County Educators Assn., Phi Delta Kappa. Club: Kiwanis (pres. 1977-78). Home: 4001 Wakefield Ln Bowie MD 20715 Office: 15200 Annapolis Rd Bowie MD 20715

HAGAN, WARD STANLEY, mfg. co. exec.; b. nr. Sioux City, Iowa, June 11, 1920; s. Edward Ensley and Katherine (Dimmel) H.; B.A. in Econs. and English, Princeton, 1947; m. Patricia Kelly, Dec. 16, 1950; children—Susan Kay, Tracey Pauline. Salesman, Goodyear Tire & Rubber Co., Boston, 1947-49; asst. account exec. Young & Rubicam, Inc., N.Y.C., 1949-50, account exec., London, 1950-53, dir. all client service, asst. gen. mgr., London, 1953-56, dir., Germany, 1953-56, gen. mgr., Can., 1956-58, v.p., N.Y.C., 1958-61; mgr. internat. devel. Drackett Co., London, 1961-62; dir. marketing European div. Colgate-Palmolive Co., 1962-64, gen. mgr. Colgate-Palmolive Benelux, Brussels, 1964-65; dir. mktg. Household Products, N.Y.C., 1965-68, v.p., gen. mgr., 1968-70; sr. exec. v.p., dir. U.S. ops., mem. exec. com., pres. consumer products group Warner-Lambert Co., Morris Plains, N.J., 1970-74, pres., chief exec. officer, 1974—, chmn., 1979—; dir. Parke-Davis, Am. Optical Co. Bd. dirs. United Way Morris County (N.J.), Advt. Council, Inc.; trustee Solebury Sch. (Pa.). Served with USAAF, 1941-44; PTO. Clubs: Cottage (Princeton); Royal Mid-Surrey Golf (London). Office: Warner-Lambert Co 201 Tabor Rd Morris Plains NJ 07950*

HAGELMAN, RONALD RUDOLPH, ins. co. exec.; b. Houston, June 23, 1926; s. Charles W. and Anna Marie (Griffin) H.; B.A., M.A., U. Tex., 1948; m. Rebecca O'Bannon, Nov. 25, 1953; children—Ronald Rudolph, Carl Frederick, Curt Rudolph, Christa Marie, Claus Edward. Agt. New Eng. Mut. Life Ins. Co., Houston, 1952-54; asst. to v.p. Am. Gen. Life Ins. Co., Houston, 1954-56; asst. dir. agys. Union Nat. Life Ins. Co., Lincoln, Nebr., 1956-57; pres. So. Heritage Life Ins. Co., Charlotte, N.C., 1957-59; chief exec. officer, v.p. Zurich Life Ins. Co., Chgo., 1959-60; pres. Delphi Cons.'s; chmn. Delphi Realty, Delphi Brokerage, Tucson, 1980—; pres., dir. Inland Life Ins. Co., Chgo., 1960; pres., dir. Guardsman Life Ins. Co., 1962-80, exec. cons., 1980—; pres., dir. Guardsman Equity Corp., West Des Moines; dir. Engring. Enterprises, Houston, Nat. Life and Accident Ins. Co., Nashville, NORED Corp., Adair, Iowa; non-resident fellow Inst. Higher Studies, Santa Barbara, Calif. Served with USNR, 1944-45, to 1st lt. AUS, 1950-52. C.L.U. Episcopalian. Clubs: Univ., Mid-Am. (Chgo.); Mirador (Switzerland). Home: 6225 Calle Alta Vista Tucson AZ 85715 Office: 6835 Camino Principal Tucson AZ 85715

HAGEN, RAYMOND EUGENE, banker; b. Sioux City, Iowa, Mar. 24, 1933; s. William E. and Mabel M. Hagen; B.S., Morningside Coll., 1959; postgrad. Stonier Grad. Sch. Banking, Rutgers U., 1971; m. Carla Ashman, Nov. 25, 1955; children—Sally Jo, Gregory Stewart. With Security Nat. Bank, Sioux City, 1958—, v.p., 1969-76, sr. v.p., 1976-77, exec. v.p., 1977-79, pres., 1979—, also dir.; dir. Security Nat. Corp., Northwestern State Bank, Orange City, Iowa. Bd. dirs. Morningside Coll.; mem. exec. bd. Boy Scouts Am., Sioux City; treas. Indsl. Devel. Council. Served with U.S. Army, 1953-55. Mem. Iowa Bankers Assn. (dir. Iowa transfer system). Republican. Methodist. Clubs: Sioux City Country, Masons, Shriners. Home: 3606 Pawnee Pl Sioux City IA 51104 Office: Security Nat Bank 6th and Pierce Sts Sioux City IA 51102

HAGER, CHAUNCEY WILLIAM, real estate exec.; student U. Kans., Lawrence, 1947-49, Wayne State U., 1954-55; B.A., Mich. State U., M.A., Sch. Bus. Adminstrn., 1958; m. Ruth Hager; children—Mary, Michele, Grant. With Ford Motor co., Detroit, 1953-56, Sears, Roebuck & Co., Dayton, Ohio, 1958-59; market research analyst Chrysler Corp., Dayton, 1959-61; with Ohio Bur. Employment Services, Dayton, 1961-73; pres., owner Classics Realty, Inc., Dayton, 1973—; pres., treas., dir. Mi-Val Buc Credit Union, Dayton, 1965-72; instr. Patterson Coop. Adult Night Sch., Dayton, 1965-66. Pres., Clayton (Ohio) Citizens Assn., 1965-68, Oakwood Hist. Soc., Dayton, 1978-79. Served in U.S. Army, 1951-53. Mem. Mich. State U. Alumni Assn. (chpt. pres. 1965-66), Nat. Trust Hist. Preservation. Methodist. Club: Oakwood Optimists.

HAGERTY, JEAN GEIER, exec. seach co. exec.; b. Pearl River, N.Y., May 12, 1946; d. Louis James and Eleanor A. Geier; student Lab. Inst. Merchandising, N.Y.C., 1964-66; U. N.C., 1970-71; m. Clark G. Hagerty, Feb. 28, 1970. Asst. buyer J.C. Penney Co., N.Y.C., 1966-68; asso. buyer Almart Stores, N.Y.C., 1968-70; merchandiser Dacona Industries, Gastonia, N.C., 1970-72; recruiter Wells Recruiting Systems, Chgo., 1972-73, retail mgr., 1973-74, div. mgr., 1974-75; v.p., div. mgr. Bus. Careers, Inc., Chgo., 1975—. Mem. women's bd. Lincoln Park Zoo. Mem. N. Michigan Ave. Council, Ill. Retail Mchts. Assn., Fashion Group. Club: Carlton. Home: 1555 N Astor St Chicago IL 60610 Office: 444 N Michigan Ave Chicago IL 60611

HAGESTAD, DOUGLAS DEAN, r.r. co. exec.; b. Chgo., Sept. 13, 1943; s. Walther Ferdinand and Marian May H.; B.S. in Indsl. Mgmt., Washington and Lee U., 1965; M.B.A., Northwestern U., 1966; m. Dorothy Ann Pechtel, Feb. 20, 1971; children—James Douglas, Timothy Allen, William Michael. Asst. indsl. engr. C. & O. Ry./Balt. & Ohio R.R., Balt., 1966-67; service planning analyst Ill. Central R.R., Chgo., 1969-70; system mgr. Piggyback Terminals, Ill. Central R.R., Chgo., 1970-71, asst. to pres., 1971-72, dir. mktg., Chgo., 1972-75, asst. v.p. market devel., 1975-79, v.p. market devel., 1979—; mem. Task Force on Rail Transp. Served with AUS, 1967-69. Mem. Am. Ry. Devel. Assn., Nat. Def. Transp. Assn., Transp. Research Forum, Western R.R. Club, Traffic Club Chgo., Nat. Council Phys. Distbn. Mgmt. Republican. Lutheran. Club: Calumet Country. Office: 27th Floor 233 N Michigan Ave Chicago IL 60601

HAGEY, WALTER REX, banker; b. Hatfield. Pa., July 24, 1909; s. Justus T. and Martha (Mabel) H.; student U. Pa., 1931-36; LL.B., La Salle Extension U., 1938; S.T.B., Temple U., 1943; grad. Stonier Grad.

Sch. Banking Rutgers U., 1951; LL.D., Muhlenberg Coll., 1963; m. Dorothy E. Rosenberger, Oct. 17, 1931; 1 son, Donald C. With Fidelity Bank (formerly Fidelity-Phila. Trust Co.), 1929—, asst. sec., 1948—, asst. v.p., 1957-66, v.p., 1966-74. Supply pastor Eastern Pa. Synod Lutheran Ch. Am., 1950—, treas., 1950-80, now Luth. Synod S.E. Pa.; treas. Luth. Synod Northeastern Pa., 1969-70; pres., dir. Phila. Luth. Social Union; treas. Luth. Laymens Movement for Stewardship of United Luth. Ch.; mem. bd., exec. com. Luth. Council in U.S.; mem. bds., treas. home missions, inner missions, Christian edn. Eastern Pa. Synod, Luth. Ch. Am., 1950-69; vice chmn. adminstrn. and fin. Luth. Ch. in Am., 1972-78, mem. bd. pensions, 1978—, v.p. Bd. Am. Missions, 1972-78; bd. dirs., adv. bd. Muhlenberg Med. Center; bd. dirs., chmn. Prosser Found., 1968—; bd. dirs., treas. Luth. Retirement Homes, 1978—; bd. dirs. Silver Springs-Martin Luther Sch.; treas. Bethesda House, 1950-69. Mem. Am. Inst. Banking, Phila. Estate Planning Council, Pa. Council Chs. (dir. 1954-70), Pa. Soc., Luth. Hist. Soc. Eastern Pa., Men of Mt. Airy Sem. (pres. 1976—), Pa. Bible Soc. (treas., sec., dir. 1971—). Clubs: Rotary. Elm (sec. 1951-63); Midday, Anglers (Phila.). Home: 510 E Lawn Ave Lansdale PA 19446 Office: 2900 Queen Ln Philadelphia PA 19119

HAGFORS, RICHARD HAROLD, electronics co. exec.; b. Mpls., Aug. 31, 1951; s. Harold Ted and Dorothy Helen (Jansen) H.; E.E., U. Minn., 1973; m. Kimberly Kay Saunders, Nov. 27, 1971; children—Kristen, Adam. Project engr. Amoco Plastic Products Co., Mora, Minn., 1971-78; founder, pres. Hagfors Electronics Co., Braham, Minn., 1978—. Address: 500 N Cherry Ave Braham MN 55006

HAGGIS, FLORENCE LAWLOR, acct.; b. St. Albans, L.I., N.Y., Sept. 19; d. William Henry and Margaret Mary (O'Brien) Lawlor; B.S. magna cum laude, Fairleigh Dickenson U., 1966; M.B.A. magna cum laude, Seton Hall U., 1969; m. Theodore Haggis, May 24; children—Louis, Alexis, Theodore, Alexander, Alena, William. Audit mgr. Touche Ross & Co., N.Y.C., 1970—; instr. advanced acctg. Upsala Coll., East Orange, N.J., 1973—. C.P.A., N.J. Mem. N.J. Soc. C.P.A.'s (practice rev. com.), Am. Woman's Soc. C.P.A.'s (nat. pres.), Am. Soc. Women Accts. (founder N.J. chpt.), Seton Hall U. Alumni Assn. (dir.), Phi Zeta Kappa, Phi Omega Epsilon. Contbr. chpt. to Accountant's Handbook, 1981; rev. SEC Accountants Handbook, 1978. Office: 1633 Broadway New York NY 10019

HAGLER, JOHN CARROLL, III, iron works exec.; b. Augusta, Ga., Feb. 14, 1923; s. John Carroll and Susan (Barrett) H.; B.S., U. Ga. 1946; m. Mary Anne Tyler, Oct. 16, 1948; children—Mary Anne, John Carroll IV, Richard Belton, Katharine Waterman, Elizabeth Tyler. Chmn. bd. Ga. Iron Works Co., 1947—; pres., chief exec. officer GIW Engineered Systems; chmn. bd. GIW Industries, Inc., pres., treas. H & T Brass & Aluminum Foundry, Inc., Thomson, Ga., 1965—, Winfield Hills, Inc., Augusta, Ga., 1967—. Mem. Augusta Aviation Commn., 1962—. Trustee, pres. Historic Augusta, Inc., 1971-74; bd. dirs. Richmond County Hist. Soc. Served with A.C., AUS, 1943-45. Mem. Am. Foundrymen's Soc., Am. Inst. Mining, Metall. and Petroleum Engrs., ASTM, Am. Soc. for Metals, NAM, Aircraft Owners and Pilots Assn., Quiet Birdmen, Ducks Unltd. (chmn. Augusta area 1971), Ga. Trust for Hist. Preservation (exec. com.), Augusta Coll. Alumni Assn. (bd. dirs.), Sigma Alpha Epsilon. Republican. Roman Catholic. Clubs: Rotary, Augusta Country, The Pinnacle, Ponte Vedra. Home: 999 Highland Ave Augusta GA 30904 Office: POB 626 Grovetown GA 30813

HAGOPIAN, LOUIS THOMAS, advt. exec.; b. Pontiac, Mich., June 1, 1925; s Thomas and Sarah (Uligian) H.; student Northwestern U., 1944; B.A. in Bus. Adminstrn., Mich. State U., 1947; m. Joanne Kelly, Dec. 31, 1955; children—Susan, Thomas, Matthew. With Pontiac Motor Car Co., 1948-53, successively service rep., dist sales mgr.; with Chrysler Corp., 1953-60, sales and promotion exec. Dodge div. 1953-56, dir. advt. and sales promotion Plymouth div., 1956-60; account supr. NW Ayer ABH Internat., 1960-62, vp., 1962-66, Detroit mgr., 1963-66, exec. v.p. gen. mgr., N.Y. region, 1967-73, vice chmn., 1973-76, chmn., chief exec. officer, 1976—. Bd. dirs. N.Y.C. div. Am. Cancer Soc.; mem. exec. com. Hwy. Users Fedn. for Safety and Mobility; chmn. Automotive Safety Found., 1978. Served to lt. (j.g.) USNR, World War II. Recipient Disting. Alumnus award Mich. State U., 1978. Mem. Adcraft Club Detroit (dir.), Am. Assn. Advt. Agys. (nat. dir. 1979—, chmn. Eastern region 1978), Internat. Radio and TV Soc. (gov.), Kappa Sigma. Clubs: Wee Burn Country; Pine Valley Golf; University. Home: 5 Meadowbrook Rd Darien CT 06820 Office: 1345 Ave of Americas New York NY 10019

HAHN, ALAN THEODORE, computer cons.; b. S. Amboy, N.J., Nov. 18, 1950; s. Donald Joseph and Helen Ann (Marcey) H.; A.B. in History Edn. magna cum laude, Mt. St. Mary's Coll., 1972; M.B.A. summa cum laude, Loyola Coll., Balt., 1979; m. Maureen Annette Hinke, June 1, 1974. Consumer credit trainee Md. Nat. Bank, Balt., 1973, credit supr., 1973-74; programmer/analyst, supr. USF&G Ins. Cos., Balt., 1974-80; computer cons. DP Assos. Inc., Balt., 1980—. Econ. advisor for Christopher Smith, Rep. candidate U.S. Ho. Reps., 1978, 80; dir. basketball Cath. Youth Orgn., St. Dominic's Ch., Balt., 1973-79; basketball coach USF&G Ins. Cos., Balt. Bankers League champions, 1975-79. Mem. Nat. Capital History Soc., Assn. M.B.A. Execs., Alpha Sigma Nu, Phi Alpha Theta. Republican. Roman Catholic. Club: K.C. (dep. grand knight MSM council 1971-72). Home: 3119 Hiss Ave Baltimore MD 21234 Office: 205 Village Sq Village of Cross Keys Baltimore MD 21202

HAHN, JOHN WILLIAM, ins. co. exec.; b. N.Y.C., July 12, 1940; s. Ferdinand J. and Evelyn H. H.; B.A., Queens Coll., 1962; P.M.D., Harvard Bus. Sch., 1973; m. L. Dale Mazza; children—Nancy, John. With Atlantic Mut. Ins., N.Y.C., 1963—, v.p. adminstrv. services, 1974-78, Roanoke, Va., 1978-80, sr. v.p., 1980—. Served with USMCR, 1959-66. Mem. Am. Mgmt. Assn., Ins. Acctg. Statis. Assn. Clubs: Harvard of N.Y.; Roanoke Country, Kiwanis, Hidden Valley Country (Roanoke). Office: PO Box 4657 Roanoke VA 24015

HAHN, RAYMOND MARTIN, tree harvesting equipment mfg. co. exec.; b. Hines, Minn., Feb. 16, 1923; s. Lowell Otis and Zella Mae (Lingenfelter) H.; student pub. schs. Mizpah, Minn.; m. Carolyn June Bursack, Aug. 30, 1945; children—Carole, Nancy Hahn Olsen, Beverly Hahn Bright, Sharon. Owner, operator Raymond Hahn Co., Schroeder, Minn., 1945-75; owner Hahn Machinery, Inc., Two Harbors, Minn., 1972—. Patentee in field. Home: PO Box 244 Two Harbors MN 55616 Office: PO Box 220 Two Harbors MN 55616

HAHN, RICHARD THOBE, computer peripheral equipment and media products co. exec.; b. Lakewood, Ohio, Sept. 16, 1954; s. Walter F. and Sally H.; B.S., Ohio State U., 1976. Sr. accountant Alexander Grant & Co., C.P.A.'s, Chgo., 1976-79; sr. internal auditor Memorex Corp., Santa Clara, Calif., 1979-80, fin. mgr. corp. phys. distbn. group, 1980, mgr. budgets and planning, consumer products group, 1980—. Mem. Am. Mensa. Republican. Congregationalist. Club: Decathelon (Santa Clara). Home: 1462 Dartshire Ct Sunnyvale CA 94087 Office: Memorex Corp San Tomas at Central Santa Clara CA 95052

HAHN, THOMAS JOSEPH, automobile dealer and leasing co. exec.; b. Cleve., July 3, 1928; s. Joseph Thomas and Frances Bernadette (Englert) H.; B.S. Chem. Engring., Purdue U., 1950; M.B.A., U. Pa. Wharton Sch., 1954; m. Dorothy Lillian Toboy, Sept. 4, 1954; children—Michael Joseph, Carolyn Mary, Christine Frances, Timothy John. Project engr. Nat. Bur. Standards, Washington, 1950-52; prodn. and quality control engr. Pennsylvania Salt Co., Wyandotte, Mich., 1952-54; quality control engr. jet engine div. Gen. Electric Co., Evendale, Ohio, 1955; dir. plant quality control, asst. plant supt. Dow Co., Ironton, Ohio, 1956-58; indsl. engr. in product devel. Internat. Latex Co., Dover, Del., 1958-60; pres. Clairmont Cadillac Co., West Caldwell, N.J., 1974—, Bradford Leasing Inc., West Caldwell, 1964—, Gen. Car Accessories, West Caldwell, 1979—; partner Bradford Agy., 1979—; condr. seminars in statis. quality control; mem. N.J. Motor Vehicle Inspection Study Commn. Trustee Essex County (N.J.) Better Bus. Bur., 1969-74; founding trustee Montclair (N.J.) Urban Coalition, 1970-75; v.p. Montclair 100 Club, for police and firemen benefits, 1973-75; founding trustee Hahn Family Found., Clairmont Cadillac Employees Profit-Sharing Plan & Trust. Served with U.S. Army, 1950-52. Recipient Time mag. quality dealer award. Mem. N.J. (pres. 1975-76), Nat. automobile dealers assns., Essex County Auto Trade Assn. (pres. 1970-73), Montclair C. of C. (pres. 1967-68), West Essex C. of C., Am. Chem. Soc., Am. Inst. Chem. Engrs., Am. Inst. Indsl. Engrs., Am. Soc. Quality Control, Beta Gamma Sigma, Pi Kappa Phi. Roman Catholic. Clubs: Essex Fells Country, Montclair Country. Designer variables sampling slide rule, 1955. Office: 1220 Bloomfield Ave West Caldwell NJ 07006

HAHN, THOMAS MARSHALL, JR., forest products co. exec.; b. Lexington, Ky., Dec. 2, 1926; s. Thomas Marshall and Mary Elizabeth (Boston) H.; B.S., U. Ky., 1945; Ph.D., Mass. Inst. Tech., 1950; LL.D. (hon.), Seton Hall U., 1976; m. Margaret Louise Lee, Dec. 27, 1948; children—Elizabeth Lee, Anne Hahn Clarke. Asso. prof. physics U. Ky., 1950-52, prof., 1952-54; head dept. physics Va. Poly. Inst. and State U., 1954-59, pres., 1962-75; dean arts and scis. Kans. State U., 1959-62; exec. v.p. Georgia-Pacific Corp., Portland, Oreg., 1975-76, pres., 1976—, also dir.; pres. So. Assn. State Univs. and Land-Grant Colls., 1965-66; chmn. Va. Met. Areas Study Commn., 1966-68; mem. exec. com. So. Regional Edn. Bd., 1972-74; mem. Nat. Sci. Bd., 1972-78. Mem. bd. visitors Air U., 1966-69; Chmn. Va. Cancer Crusade, 1972, Salvation Army Nat. Capital and Va's. Divisional Advisory Bd., 1972-74. Recipient Outstanding Citizen award State of Va., 1966. Fellow Am. Phys. Soc.; mem. Phi Beta Kappa, Sigma Xi, Omicron Delta Kappa, Sigma Pi Sigma, Pi Mu Epsilon. Republican. Methodist. Clubs: Waverley Country, Shenandoah, Capital City. Office: 900 SW 5th Ave Portland OR 97204

HAIDON, MICHAEL WILLIAM, energy mgmt. co. exec.; b. Syracuse, N.Y., Sept. 26, 1947; s. Hubert Louis and Delia Anne (LaBoda) H.; A.A.S., Alfred State Coll., 1972; B.S., Mercy Coll., 1980; m. Mary Susan Schmitt, June 16, 1972. Contract account supr. Carrier Corp., N.Y.C., 1974-80; dist. sales engr. Flack & Kurtz Energy Mgmt. Corp., N.Y.C., 1980—. Served with USN, 1968-69. Democrat. Office: 475 Fifth Ave New York NY 10017

HAIGH, GEORGE WHYLDEN, banker; b. Toledo, Aug 4, 1931; s. Frederick Dwight and Annette (Lipe) H.; B.A., Dartmouth, 1953; postgrad. Fgn. Service Sch., Georgetown U., 1953-54; m. Joan DuBois Haigh, Oct. 15, 1954; children—Constance, Stephen. With DeVilbiss Co., Toledo, 1956-76, v.p., gen. mgr., 1970-72, pres., 1972-76; pres., chief exec. officer Toledo Trust Co., 1976—, Toledo Trustcorp, Inc., 1976—; dir. Champion Spark Plug Co., Toledo, LST Corp., Inc. Pres., Family Services of Greater Toledo, 1971-72; mem. Ottawa Hills Sch. Bd., 1973-75; chmn. Toledo Econ. Planning Council, 1977—; bd. dirs. ARC, Toledo Mus. Art; trustee Toledo Hosp. Served with Signal Corps., AUS, 1954-56. Mem. Toledo C. of C. (pres. 1977, dir.). Republican. Episcopalian. Clubs: Toledo Country, Toledo (trustee), Belmont Country (Toledo); Carranor Hunt and Polo (Perrysburg, Ohio). Home: 4206 Bonnie Brae Circle Toledo OH 43606 Office: 245 Summit St Toledo OH 43603

HAINES, EDWARD HENRY, food co. exec.; b. Binghamton, N.Y., May 12, 1931; s. Lee Wilson and Leona Evelyn (Lessing) H.; B.S. in Agr., Purdue U., 1953; B.S. in Chem. Engring., U. Wis., 1957, B.S. in Naval Sci., 1957; m. Wanda Williamson, Nov. 28, 1957; children—Patricia Lynn, Steven Mark. Mgr. quality control Campbell Soup Plant, Modesto, Calif., 1965-68, Sumter, S.C., 1968-72, Sacramento, 1972-74, dir. quality control, Camden, N.J., 1974-77, dir. quality control Canned Food div., 1977-79, dir. quality control Swanson div., 1979—. Served to lt. USN, 1953-55; Korea. Mem. Inst. Food Technologists. Home: 105 Cobblestone St Mount Laurel NJ 08054 Office: Campbell Place Camden NJ 08101

HAINES, LULA ALLISON, ins. co. mgr.; b. Birmingham, Ala., June 20, 1926; d. Boatman and Jeffalonie (Armstrong) Allison; B.S. in Music, Ala. State Tchrs. Coll., 1947; postgrad. Adelbert Coll., 1962, Cuyahoga Community Coll., 1977; m. John W. Haines, Nov. 27, 1965; children—Berry Hill, Jefferecia Poindexter, Ronald Hill (by previous marriage). Substitute tchr. Cleve. Bd. Edn., 1949-57; mathematician E.M. Klein & Associates, Cleve., 1957-62, supr. ins. dept., 1963-76, asst. account exec., 1977; sales rep. Met. Ins. Co., Cleve., 1977—. Dir. youth and adult choirs Starlight Bat. Ch., Cleve., 1957-59, Mt. Nebo Bapt. Ch., Cleve., 1960-62, Holy Trinity Bapt. Ch., Cleve., 1962-64. Cert. elem. tchr., Ohio. Mem. Nat. Assn. Life Underwriters, Bus. and Profl. Women of Cleve., NAACP, Forest City Vol. Assn. (pres. 1978—), Ala. State U. Alumni (treas. 1976—), Delta Sigma Theta. Democrat. Clubs: Women's City (Cleve.); Alacrity. Contbr. poetry to lit. publs. Office: 3659 Green Rd Beachwood OH 44122

HAINSWORTH, DAVID JAMES, food mktg. and supply co. exec.; b. St. Louis, Nov. 29, 1941; s. Joseph C. and Anna M. Hainsworth; student Coll. of Sch. Ozarks, 1960-63, Forest Park Community Coll., 1967-68, U. Mo., 1968-69; m. Beverly Ann Berner, Oct. 25, 1969; children—Lorry Ann, Jessica Nicole. Purchasing agt. Anheuser-Busch, Inc., St. Louis, 1967-70; asst. to v.p. mktg. D & D Bean Co., Greeley, Colo., 1970-77; asst. mgr. Outwest Bean, Inc., regional mktg. coop., Englewood, Colo., 1977-78, gen. mgr. and treas., 1978—; dir. Nat. Council Farmers Coops., Washington, 1981—; sec. adv. bd. Wichita (Kans.) Bank for Coops., 1980-81; participant Mktg. and Internat. Trade Conf., 1980. Active choirs and youth orgns. Oak Hill Presbyn. Ch., St. Louis, 1958-69, First United Meth. Ch., Greeley, 1969-78; supply pastor Hollister (Mo.) Presbyn. Ch., 1961-63; mem. citizen's budget rev. com. Arapahoe County Dist. 6 Sch. Dist., 1980-81. Served with USAF, 1963-67; Vietnam. Mem. Rocky Mountain Bean Dealers Assn. (dir. 1979—, v.p. 1981), Englewood C. of C., Traffic Club of Denver. Republican. Methodist. Home: 6540 S Washington St Littleton CO 80121 Office: 770 W Hampden Englewood CO 80150

HAIR, GILBERT MARTIN, exec. recruiter; b. Manila; Mar. 16, 1941; s. John Martin and Jane Mary (McMahon) H. (parents Am. citizens); student Internat. Sch. Bangkok, 1958-60; B.A., Am. U., 1966; m. Susan Jane Christian, Mar. 15, 1969 (div. Nov. 1978); 1 dau., Nicole. With U.S. Govt., Washington, 1963-65; various mgmt. positions Pan Am. World Airways, N.Y.C., 1966-67, Chgo., 1967-71; sr. cons. Welt Internat. Co., Chgo., 1971-72; mgr. mktg. Micronesia and Far East, Continental Airlines, Los Angeles, 1972-75; pres., chief exec. officer Westlake Mgmt. Services Inc. (Calif.), 1975-80; exec. recruiter The Westlake Group, 1980—; ambassador West Valley Com. Rep. Govt., 1975. Advisor Village Homes Homeowner's Assn. Served with USMC, 1960-62. Mem. Calif. Notary Assn., Nat. Small Bus. Assn., Westlake C. of C., Better Bus. Bur., Calif. Landscape Contractors Assn. (pres. Ventura chpt.), Asso. Landscape Contractors Am., Pacific Area Travel Assn., Alpha Tau Omega, Republican. Roman Catholic. Clubs: Field House; Shadow Mountain Tennis; Kiwanis, Silver Dollar, Westlake Tennis and Swim, Royal Bangkok Sports. Home: 109 Padua Circle Newbury Park CA 91320 Office: Suite 218 650 Hampshire Rd Westlake Village CA 91361

HALABY, RURIK BENDALY, investment banker; b. Jaffa, Palestine, May 20, 1940; s. Bendaly Jacob and Vera (Debbas) H.; S.B., M.I.T., 1962, S.M., 1964; M.B.A., Stanford U., 1969; m. Cynthia Jean Petre, Mar. 27, 1964; children—Michael George Rurik, Nicholas Alexander. Engr., Bechtel Corp., San Francisco, 1964-67; asso. corp. fin. dept. Paine Webber Jackson Curtis Inc., N.Y.C., 1969-73; v.p. corp. fin. dept. Hornblower Weeks-Hemphill Noyes Inc., N.Y.C., 1973-76; pres. Crescent Diversified Ltd., N.Y.C., 1976—. Mem. ASCE, Assn. for Corp. Growth. Republican. Eastern Orthodox. Clubs: Downtown Assn., Univ. (N.Y.C.). Home: 374 Evergreen Pl Ridgewood NJ 07450 Office: 505 Park Ave New York NY 10022

HALANYCH, NICHOLAS, nurse anesthetist, vending and office coffee service co. exec.; b. Dowdentown, Pa., Oct. 7, 1934; s. John and Tessie (Huron) H.; student U. Md., 1966-68; diploma Sch. Anesthesia, Jefferson Med. Coll. Hosp., 1956; R.N., Pa. Hosp., 1955; m. Shirley Mae Williams, July 29, 1961; children—Kimberly Ann, Kenneth Michael, Jennifer Marie. Pres., King Manor Co., Inc., Reisterstown, Md., 1974—; sr. nurse anesthetist, Sinai Hosp., Balt., 1956—; pvt. anesthesia practice, Reisterstown, 1964—. Trustee, St. Peters Episcopal Ch., 1970-72. Served with USAF, 1956-58, to lt. col. USAFR, 1956—, now chief nursing service Br. 22 d MSES, Andrews AFB. Mem. Am., Md. (pres. 1961-62) assns. nurse anesthetists, Am., Md. nurses assns., Res. Officers Assn. Democrat. Episcopalian. Home and office: 6503 Deer Park Rd Reisterstown MD 21136

HALASI-KUN, ADAM TIBOR, utility co. mgr.; b. Budapest, Hungary, Nov. 29, 1943; came to U.S., 1952, naturalized, 1961; s. Tibor and Eva (Metzger) H.; B.S., N.Y. U., 1966; M.B.A., St. John's U., 1973; m. Karen M. Cherubin, Oct. 17, 1970. Mgr., dir. food service Saga Admin. Corp., Menlo Park, Calif., 1968-70; orgn. devel. cons. Con Edison, N.Y.C., 1973-80, mgr. mgmt. orgn. devel., 1980—; adj. prof. Adelphi U. Served with U.S. Army, 1966-68. Mem. ASTD Orgn. Devel. Network, Res. Officers Assn., Civil Affairs Assn., Republican. Roman Catholic. Club: Weantinogue Heritage. Office: 4 Irving Pl New York NY 10003

HALBERSTADT, PAUL EDWARD, JR., trucking co. exec.; b. Charlottesville, Va., July 7, 1944; s. Paul Edward and Grace Dyer (Howard) H.; B.S. cum laude, U.S. Naval Acad., 1966; m. Sheridan Rowe Lowery, Mar. 13, 1973. Dir. transp. Standard Trucking Co., Charlotte, N.C., 1971-72, v.p., 1973—. Served to lt. USN, 1966-71. Mem. N.C. Motor Carriers Assn. (past chmn. maintenance council), Am. Trucking Assn., Soc. Automotive Engrs. Clubs: Charlotte Athletic; River Hills Country (Clover, S.C.). Developed computer program series for motor vehicle inventory control and history analysis. Home: 21 New River Trace River Hills Plantation Clover SC 29710 Office: Standard Trucking Co Inc PO Box 30725 Charlotte NC 28230

HALBERSTAM, SINAI, mgmt. efficiency specialist, city adminstr., clergyman; b. Jerusalem, Mar. 1, 1945; came to U.S., 1948, naturalized, 1955; s. Israel and Bella (Tal) H.; B.A. in Acctg. and Econs. magna cum laude (Alpha Sigma Lambda fellow), Queens Coll., 1968; Morah Ho'raeh in Yeshiva Torah Vodaath, Talmudical Sem., N.Y.C., 1964; Yorah Yodin in Talmudic Law, Mesiftha Tifereth Jerusalem, N.Y.C., 1969; m. Chava Lisz, May 29, 1969; children—Rochma, Yosef, Yitzchok, Nachum, Yehudis, Chaim Boruch. Sr. acct. John Addison & Co., N.Y.C., 1968-70; sr. state auditor N.Y. State Comptroller's Office, N.Y.C., 1970-71; dir. contracts adminstrn. and voucher audit N.Y. State Urban Devel. Corp., N.Y.C., 1971-74; asst. dir. Office Auditor-Gen., N.Y.C. Bd. Edn., 1974—; ordained rabbi, 1969; bd. dirs. Congregation Divrei Chaim, Bklyn., 1968—, rabbi, 1976—; prof. ethics and philosophy Shevet Y'hudah Inst., 1971-74; lectr. in law Mesivta Heichal Hatorah, Bklyn., 1975—; asst. prof. bus. and fin. Touro Coll., 1977—; mem. faculty N.Y. State Soc. C.P.A.'s Found. Acctg. Edn.; mem. Bd. Edn., Jewish Boys High Sch., 1976—; lectr. in field. C.P.A., N.Y. State. Mem. Am. Inst. C.P.A.'s, N.Y. State Soc. C.P.A.'s, Igud Harabonim, Rabbinical Alliance Am., Chasidei Tzanz, Gorlicz, Zmigrod, Alpha Sigma Lambda. Author: Succoth Code of Law, 1963; Pesach Hagadah, 1964; Passover Code of Law, 1977; New York City Board of Examiners: Financial and Operating Practices, 1979; contbr. articles to profl. publs.; editor: Achilas Matzohs K'hilchosa, 10 vols., 1976-78; Achilas Tarnigolim K'hilchosa, 1979; Sholom Larochok V'lakorov: Passover Laws of Medicine, 1978. Home: 1770 E 18th St Brooklyn NY 11229 Office: 65 Court St Brooklyn NY 11201

HALBERT, MURRAY LESTER, bus. services co. exec.; b. Phila., Apr. 13, 1934; s. Isadore and Bette (Glestein) H.; B.S., Temple U., 1956, M.B.A., 1959. Sr. staff cons. Fry Cons.'s Inc., N.Y.C., 1964-67; sr. asso. Cresap, McCormick & Paget, N.Y.C., 1967-69; mgr. office Technomic Research Assos., N.Y.C., 1969-71; pres. Strategic Futures Inc., N.Y.C., 1971—; lectr. in field. Mem. Am. Mktg. Assn., Assn. Graphic Arts Cons.'s. Editor: Marketing Manual for Printers, 1975, also contbg. author. Home: 220 E 60th St New York NY 10022 Office: Strategic Futures Inc 595 Madison Ave New York NY 10022

HALCOTT, KENNETH EARL, mfg. co. exec.; b. Middletown, N.Y., Aug. 23, 1931; s. Leslie E. Halcott; B.A., U. Bridgeport (Conn.), 1959; B.D., Duke U., 1963; m. Shirley Mae Lewis, June 3, 1950; children—Kenneth Earl, Terri, Donna, Roberta, Pi. Mgr. tng. Pitney Bowes Inc., 1965-67; mgr. employee relations Gen. Time Inc., 1967-69; mgr. personnel adminstrn., then mgr. compensation SGM Corp., N.Y.C., 1969-74, dir. personnel services, 1974—. Past pres. Walnut Beach Sch. PTA, Milford, Conn., Stanford (Conn.) Jaycees. Served with USN, 1948-53; Korea. Decorated Silver Star, Purple Heart. Mem. Assn. Labor Mgmt. (council on alcoholism), Am. Soc. Personnel Adminstrs., Am. Mgmt. Assn., Internat. Soc. Preretirement Planners. Republican. Methodist. Office: 299 Park Ave New York NY 10017

HALE, CLAYTON GOULD, business exec.; b. Cleve., Mar. 27, 1902; s. Jesse G. and Edith M. (Clayton) H.; A.B., U. Mich., 1924; B.B.A., Fenn Coll. (now Cleve. State U.), 1932, LL.D., 1956; LL.D., Baldwin-Wallace Coll., 1975; student econs., 1946; m. Laura Barlett, Oct. 8, 1927; children—Sally L. (Mrs. Thales Bowen, Jr.), William C. Property ins. agt. and broker, 1924; licensed in eleven states and Province of Ont.; mng. partner Hale & Hale Co., Cleve., 1939-63, pres., 1963-67, chmn., 1967-76; pres. Basic Investments, Inc., 1961—; prof. ins. Grad. Sch. Bus. Adminstrn., U. Mich., Ann Arbor, 1949-56, lectr., 1935-49; editorial cons. for interpretation ins. statistics and trends, on staff The Spectator, 1948-52; asst. chief ins. div. Navy Dept., 1942-43; ins. cons. office sec. def., 1950-62; mem. bd. ins. advisers Munitions Bd., 1950-53; ins. cons. to Ohio Turnpike

Commn., 1953-58; dir. several corps. Invited del. White House Com. Hwy. Safety, 1954-58. Life Trustee Cleve. Met. YMCA; chmn. bd. trustees Fenn Ednl. Found., 1967-69; mem. vis. com. U. Mich. Grad. Sch. Bus. Adminstrn.; trustee Western Res. Hist. Soc. Fellow Ins. Inst. Am.; mem. Ins. Soc. N.Y., Am. Risk and Ins. Assn. (com. on gen. ins. terminology), Order Founders and Patriots Am., S.A.R., Chi Phi. Republican. Conglist. Clubs: Clifton (Lakewood, Ohio); Westwood Country (Rocky River, Ohio); Union (Cleve.); University (Chgo.); University (Ann Arbor). Author: An Approach to Fire Insurance, 1933. Cons. editor Property and Casualty Ins. Handbook, 1962-66. Contbr. tech. articles to various jours. Home: 1056 Kirtland Ln Lakewood OH 44107 Office: The Arcade Cleveland OH 44114

HALE, GERALD ALBERT, corp. exec.; b. Kalamazoo, May 9, 1927; s. Edwin M. and Helen M. (Hinrichs) H.; B.S., Western Mich. U., 1952; m. Emma Jean Hamilton, Aug. 22, 1953; children—Jeffrey, Kathleen, John. Salesman, Edgar Bros. Co., Metuchen, N.J., 1952-56; with Engelhard Minerals & Chems. Corp., and predecessors, 1956-78, v.p. sales minerals and chems. div., 1964-66, corp. v.p., 1965-69, asst. sec., 1967-69, exec. v.p. Minerals & Chems. div., 1967-69, pres. Minerals & Chems. div., 1969-78, exec. v.p. corp., 1970-78; exec. v.p., pres. gen. industry group, dir. Allegheny Ludlum Industries, Inc., Pitts., 1978-80; pres. Hale Resources, 1980—; dir. Sci. Mgmt. Corp., N.J. Mfrs. Ins. Co., Summit & Elizabeth Trust Co., Lenox Inc. Served as meteorologist USAAF, 1945-47. Mem. N.J. Bus. and Industry Assn. (trustee), Delta Upsilon. Mason. Clubs: Union League (N.Y.C.); Duquesne (Pitts.); Baltusrol Golf (Springfield); Beacon Hill (Summit, N.J.); Little Egg Harbor Yacht (Beach Haven, N.J.); Ocean Reef (Key Largo, Fla.). Home: 11 Glendale Rd Summit NJ 07901 Office: Hale Resources PO Box 6 Summit NJ 07901

HALE, IRVING, investment exec., writer; b. Denver, Mar. 22, 1932; s. Irving, Jr. and Lucile (Beggs) H.; B.A., U. Colo., 1964; m. Joan E. Domenico, Dec. 29, 1954; children—Pamela Joan, Beth Ellen. Security analyst Colo. Nat. Bank, Denver, 1955-58; asst. sec. Centennial Fund, Inc., Second Centennial Fund, Inc., Gryphon Fund, Inc., Meridian Fund, Inc., 1959-68; portfolio mgr. Twenty Five Fund, Inc. (formerly Trend Fund, Inc.), Denver, 1969—; v.p. Alpine Corp., Denver, 1971-72, Forum Investment Counsel, Inc., 1971-72; dir. research Hanifen, Imhoff & Samford, Inc., Denver, 1973-77; v.p. research 1st Fin. Securities, Inc., Denver, 1977—; Instr., Head Start Adult Edn. Program, 1968-69. Denver affiliate Santa Fe Opera Guild, 1971; lectr. community talent Denver Public Schs., 1975—; bd. dirs. Community Resources, Inc., 1981—. Mem. Denver Soc. Security Analysts, Radio Hist. Assn. Colo. (pres. 1977-78), Beta Sigma Tau. Republican. Episcopalian. Contbr. articles to profl. jours. Home: 1642 Ivanhoe St Denver CO 80220 Office: 1624 Tremont Pl Denver CO 80202

HALE, ROGER LOUCKS, mfg. exec.; b. Plainfield, N.J., Dec. 13, 1934; s. Lloyd and Elizabeth (Adams) H.; B.A., Brown U., 1956; M.B.A., Harvard U., 1961; m. Sandra Johnston, June 10, 1961; children—Jocelyn, Leslie, Nina. With Tennant Co., Mpls., 1961—, v.p. systems and corporate devel., 1965-67, dir., 1967—, v.p. internat., 1972-75, pres., chief operating officer, 1975, pres., chief exec. officer, 1976—; dir. 1st Nat. Bank of Mpls., Valspar Co., Donaldson Co., St. Paul Cos. Sec. Minn. Democratic Farm Labor Party, 1968-70; mem. Met. Planning Commn., 1965-67, Citizens League, 1961—; bd. dirs. Walker Art Center, 1971—, pres., 1976-78. Served to lt. (j.g.) USN, 1956-59. Congregationalist. Club: Mpls. Office: 701 N Lilac Dr Minneapolis MN 55440

HALE, SELDON HOUSTON, automobile dealership mgr.; b. Jefferson, Tex., June 11, 1948; s. Woster Seldon and Geraldine Leston (Sacra) Hale, Jr.; student U. Tex., Arlington, 1972-76; m. Kay Ellen Moler, Aug. 7, 1970; children—Emily Michelle, Denise Kathleen. Asst. mgr. service center Phillips Petroleum Co., San Antonio, 1968-69; asst. youth dir. N.W. YMCA, San Antonio, 1969-70; youth dir. Greenville (Tex.) YMCA, 1970-71; asst. mgr. men's and boy's dept. Watson's Arlington, 1971-76; gen. mgr. Pate's San Antonio, 1976-77; bus. mgr. Bruce Lowrie Chevrolet, Ft. Worth, 1977-80; fin. mgr. Late Chevrolet Co., Richardson, Tex., 1980—. Vice chmn. Greenville 4th of July Celebration, 1971; chmn. youth com. Arlington YMCA, 1973-75, sec. bd., 1976. Recipient Dedicated Service award Arlington Fellowship of Christian Athletes, 1975-76, Membership Producer award, 1975; Dedicated Service award, Arlington YMCA, 1976; Outstanding Service award Tex. State Youth and Govt. Program, 1970-71. Mem. Am. Mgmt. Assn., U.S. Golf Assn., Arlington Fellowship of Christian Athletes (pres.-elect 1976), Chevrolet Soc. Sales Execs. Methodist. Home: 111 Hidalgo Ln Arlington TX 76014 Office: 800 N Central Expy Richardson TX 75080

HALE, SHADRACH PAYNE, real estate lawyer; b. Trenton, Ga., Jan. 13, 1912; s. Shadrach Jerome and Clara (Street) H.; LL.B., Chattanooga Coll. Law, 1931, LL.M., 1934; m. Margaret Virginia Ashworth, Apr. 16, 1937; children—S. Jerome II, Patricia Elaine. Admitted to Ga. bar, 1931, Tenn. bar, 1936; mem. firm Hale & Hale, Trenton, 1931-36; mem. firm McClure, McClure & Hale (formerly McClure & McClure), Chattanooga, 1936-41, Hale & Ellis, Chattanooga, 1942-80, Hale, Hale & McInturff, Chattanooga, 1980—; sec. Milligan-Reynolds Guaranty Title Agy., Inc., 1941—, exec. v.p., 1975, chmn. bd., chief exec. officer, 1976—, dir., 1944—. Mem. Am., Tenn., Chattanooga bar assns., Sigma Delta Kappa. Methodist. Clubs: Chattanooga Golf and Country, Mountain City, Kiwanis. Home: 1624 Hillcrest Rd Chattanooga TN 37405 Office: 724 Cherry St Chattanooga TN 37402

HALEGUA, ABE, electronic parts distbr.; b. N.Y.C., Nov. 13, 1934; s. Max and Rachel H.; student pub. schs.; m. Barbara Halegua (div.); children—Michael, Steven; 1 stepson, James. Spl. products mgr. West Instrument Co., Schiller Park, Ill., 1959-64; salesman Pace Electronics, Schiller Park, 1964-67; v.p. Ohm Electronics, Palatine, Ill., 1967-70; pres. Advent Electronics, Inc., Rosemont, Ill., 1970—. Served with U.S. Army, 1955-58. Mem. Nat. Electronics Distbr. Assn., Young Tigers. Democrat. Jewish. Home: 1248 Somerset Deerfield IL 60015 Office: 7110 N Lyndon St Rosemont IL 60018

HALEY, MARTIN RYAN, pub. affairs and govt. relations co. exec.; b. Hibbing, Minn., Feb. 24, 1929; s. Martin Thomas and Bertha Madeline (Ryan) H.; student Coll. of St. Thomas, St. Paul, 1949-50. Vice pres. Walter Butler Cos., St. Paul, Miami and Washington, 1954-59; pres. Walter Butler Engring. Co., St. Paul and Washington, 1957-59; pres. Martin Ryan Haley & Assos., Inc., N.Y.C., 1949—; chmn. Martin Haley Cos., N.Y.C., 1975—; chmn. Fed.-State Reports, Inc., Falls Church, Va., 1974—; chmn. SEIREGO, Rome, 1975—; chmn. World Affairs Co., N.Y.C., 1975—; chmn. exec. com. Pub. Affairs Analysts, Inc. Decorated knight of Malta, knight comdr. Holy Sepulchre of Jerusalem. Mem. Internat., Am. assns. polit. consultants, Internat., Am. polit. sci. assns., Soc. Surveyors and Engrs., Internat. Pub. Relations Assn., Pub. Relations Soc. Am. Roman Catholic. Clubs: Met. (N.Y.C.); Capitol Hill, Nat. Capital Dem., George Town (Washington); Algonquin of Boston; Minn., Athletic, Univ. (St. Paul). Contbr. articles to profl. jours. Office: 40 Central Park S New York NY 10019

HALF, ROBERT, personnel agy. exec.; b. N.Y.C., Nov. 11, 1918; s. Sidney and Pauline (Kahn) H.; B.S., N.Y. U., 1940; m. Maxine Levison, June 17, 1945; children—Nancy Half Asch, Peggy Half Silbert. Staff accountant S.D. Leidesdorf & Co., 1940-43; office and personnel mgr. Kayser-Roth Corp., 1943-48; chmn. bd. Robert Half, Inc., 1948—; pres. R-H Internat., Inc., Accountemps Inc., various offices U.S., Can., Eng. 1964—; guest speaker Am. Mgmt. Assn., N.Y.C., Chgo., Nat. Assn. Accountants; expert witness subcoms. U.S. Senate. Mem. Bd. Appeals Village of Saddle Rock, Great Neck, N.Y., 1956-62. C.P.A., N.Y. Mem Am. Accounting Assn., Assn. Personnel Cons. N.Y. (pres. 1963-64, dir. 1960-65), Nat. Assn. Personnel Cons., Nat. Assn. Accountants, N.Y. State Soc. C.P.A.'s, Am. Inst. C.P.A.'s, Am. Mgmt. Assn. Pioneer in specialized personnel agys. Office: 522 Fifth Ave New York NY 10036

HALFACRE, EDWARD JOSEPH, ins. co. exec.; b. Danville, Ill., Oct. 27, 1925; s. Edward Joseph and Ruth Irene H.; B.S., N.C. Central U., 1975, M.B.A., 1977; m. Barbara Lamare Williams, Aug. 7, 1949; children—Xenia Irene, Albert Edward. Vice pres., agy. dir. Unity Mut. Life Ins. Co., Chgo., 1961-62; asst. agy. dir. N.C. Mut. Life Ins. Co., Durham, 1962-70, regional agy. dir., 1970-78, dir. group sales and gen. agy., 1978—; tchr. mgmt. course Nat. Ins. Assn., 1969-74. Past bd. sec. Cosmopolitan C. of C., Chgo.; bd. dirs. Altgeld Nursery, Chgo., Elliott Donnelly Youth Center, Chgo. Served with USAAF, 1944-46. C.L.U.; Cert. Am. Coll. Agy. Mgmt.; recipient award of achievement Chgo. Ins. Assn., 1962; award Asst. Agy. Dir. Zone Contest, N.C. Mut. Life Ins. Co., 65, others. Fellow Life Office Mgmt. Inst.; mem. Life Office Mgmt. Assn., Soc. Life Underwriters. Roman Catholic. Clubs: Nomads, Original Forty. Office: NC Mut Life Ins Co 411 W Chapel Hill St Durham NC 27701

HALL, ALBERT RICHARDSON, mfg. co. exec., elec. engr.; b. Wilmington, Del., Apr. 13, 1946; s. Rodger William and Eunice Elizabeth (Richardson) H.; student U.S. Navy Tech. Schs., 1967-71; B.S.E.E., U. Del., 1975. Assembler, mechanic, Newark (Del.) Assembly Plant, Chrysler Corp., 1964-75; technician U. Del. Inst. Energy Conversion, 1973-75; field service engr. engring. service office Westinghouse Corp., Buffalo, 1975-77, supt. Miami Apparatus Service Center (Fla.), 1977-80; mgr. facilities and tech. services Latin Am. ops. Westinghouse Industry Services, Miami, 1980—. Served with USN, 1967-71. Mem. IEEE, Am. Mgmt. Assn. Office: 3525 NW 51st St Miami FL 33142

HALL, CALVIN JAMES, mfg. co. exec.; b. Chgo., June 5, 1941; s. James Calvin and Theresa (Wilson) H.; B.B.A., U. Iowa, 1972, M.A., 1974, Ph.D., 1978; m. Loleta Carter, Apr. 28, 1975; children—Talin Kirk, Steven, Cherell. Admissions rep. U. Iowa, Iowa City, 1972-73, personnel rep., 1973-74, coordinator fin. aid Coll. Medicine, 1974-75; mgr. affirmative action Collins div. Rockwell Internat., Cedar Rapids, Iowa, 1975-77; occupational analyst Am. Coll. Testing Corp., Iowa City, 1977-79; dir. instnl. policy evaluation Nat. Inst. Cost Conscious Compliance Cons. Firm, Iowa City, 1979—. Teaching certificate, Iowa. Home: 1318 Bristol Dr Iowa City IA 52240 Office: PO Box 390 Iowa City IA 52240

HALL, EDWARD CHRISTIAN, aviation and marine tng. services co. exec.; b. Huntington, N.Y., Feb. 15, 1941; s. Robert Leicester and Rhoda Christine (Halvorsen) H.; grad. Deerfield Acad., 1959; B.S.E., Princeton, 1963, M.B.A., Harvard, 1967; m. Stephanie Gene Meister, Apr. 25, 1970; children—Rebecca Katharine, Robert Christian. Engr., Grumman Aircraft Co., Bethpage, N.Y., 1963-65; group devel. staff TRW Indsl. Opns., Los Angeles, 1967-71; dir. finance Itel Corp., San Francisco, 1971-72, treas., 1972-77, v.p., treas. transp. service group, 1977—; v.p. fin. Itel Nav., Inc., 1978-79, Flight Safety Internat., Inc., 1979—. Mem. San Francisco Treas. Club (pres. 1976-77). Clubs: Univ. (N.Y.); Cruising of Am.; Noroton Yacht. Home: 56 Allwood Rd Darien CT 06820 Office: Flight Safety Internat Marine Air Terminal LaGuardia Airport Flushing NY 11371

HALL, ELIZABETH MERRICK, ins. co. exec.; b. Easton, Md., Nov. 2, 1945; d. Charles Percival and Elizabeth Talbott (Chaney) Merrick; B.A., Denison U., 1967; M. Computer Sci., Tex. A. and M. U., 1972; m. Roy F. Spalding, Mar. 27, 1965; 1 son, Arthur Follansbee Spalding; m. 2d James M. Hall, Jr., Feb. 25, 1977. Jr. programmer Duke U., Durham, N.C., 1967-68; programmer Tex. A. and M. U., College Station, 1970-71; project leader Md. Casualty Co., Balt., 1972-77; dir. systems planning and analysis Monumental Life Ins. Co., Balt., 1977-79; project coordinator Blue Cross of Md., Balt., 1979—. Active Boy Scouts Am., 1975-77; PTA, 1973—; pres. Acolyte Mothers, 1979—. Democrat. Episcopalian. Contbr. articles in field to profl. jours. Home: 2422 Ellis Rd Baltimore MD 21234 Office: 700 E Joppa Rd Baltimore MD 21204

HALL, EUGENE THOMAS, petroleum co. exec.; b. Calgary, Alta., Can., June 18, 1926; s. T. T. and Ellen (Gallagher) H.; student commerce U. Alta., 1946-49; m. L. C. Johnstone, 1954; children—Karen, Kevin, E. Thomas, Steven. With Sparling & Davis, Leduc, Alta., 1948, Falcon-Seaboard, Redwater and Leduc, 1949, Phillips Petroleum Co., Calgary, 1950, Western Leaseholds, Calgary, 1951, Amurex Oil Co., Calgary, 1952-55, Murphy Corp., Billings, Mont. 1955-56; mgr. office and land dept. Signal Oil & Gas Co., Calgary, 1957-60; pres. Parkman Petroleums Ltd., Calgary, Alta., Can., 1961—; mgr. land dept. Ashland Oil Can., 1972-77; pres. Hottah Ridge Minerals Ltd., 1967—. Served with Can. Navy, 1944-45. Mem. Can. Assn. Petroleum Landmen, Am. Assn. Petroleum Landmen. Conservative. Roman Catholic. Clubs: Calgary Golf and Country, Calgary Petroleum, United Services, Royal Can. Legions, Home: 54 Waskatenau Crescent SW Calgary AB T3C 2X6 Canada Office: Parkman Petroleums Ltd Box 6840 Station D Calgary AB T2P 2E9 Canada

HALL, HAROLD HENRY, r.r. exec.; b. Andrews, N.C., Apr. 30, 1926; s. Odell and Myrtle (Rowland) H.; student Northwestern U., Am. U.; grad. Advanced Mgmt. Program, Harvard U.; m. Mary Elizabeth Abernathy, Sept. 1, 1947; children—Gregory, Martha. Train dispatcher So. Ry. Co., 1948-57, trainmaster, 195761, asst. supt., 1961, supt., 1961-66, gen. mgr. Eastern lines, 1966-68, Western lines, 1968-70, v.p.-transp., Washington, 1970-76, sr. v.p.-ops., 1976-78, exec. v.p.-ops., 1978-79, pres., 1979—, chief adminstrv. officer, 1979-80, chief exec. officer, 1980—; dir. Riggs Nat. Bank, Washington, Fla. East Coast Ry. Co., Richmond Fredericksburg & Potomac R.R. Co. Mem. Fed. City Council, Washington. Served with AC, USN, 1944-47. Clubs: Congl. Country, Burning Tree, Internat. (Washington). Office: 920 15th St NW Washington DC 20005

HALL, HARRY CHARLES, diversified corp. exec.; b. Pittsfield, Mass., Oct. 1, 1927; s. Ted and Florence C. (Shaw) H.; B.B.A., Manhattan Coll., 1951; postgrad. N.Y. U., 1951-52, Calif. State Coll., Long Beach, 1960-61; m. Pauline Harriet Greeley, Aug. 4, 1951; children—Candice B., Susan M., Melinda L., Stacy A., Tracy R., Troy E. Supr. personnel adminstrn. Caltex Petroleum Co., Sumatra, Indonesia, 1955-58; v.p. adminstrn. Transworld Mgmt. Corp., Long Beach, 1959-61; supr. compensation research Philco-Ford Co., Phila., 1961-67; dir. compensation and benefits, ITT European Hdqrs., Brussels, 1967-72; dir. adminstrn. ITT Automotive Products Group, Brussels, 1972-78; v.p., dir. adminstrn. ITT Grinnell, Providence, 1979—. Served with USN, 1945-46. N.Y. State war service scholar, 1947-48. Mem. Greater Providence C. of C. Episcopalian. Office: ITT Grinnell 260 W Exchange St Providence RI 02840

HALL, JAMES WILLIAM, advt. agy. exec.; b. Atlanta, Nov. 19, 1941; B.S., U. Ga., 1960; M.S., U. Colo., Colo. Springs, 1968; m. Nechie Tesitor, Nov. 25, 1967; 1 dau., Meridith Elyse. Ski mgr. Broadmoor Hotel, Colorado Springs, 1965-66; with Wolfe Research computer team NORAD, Colorado Springs, 1967-69; pres. Praco Ltd., Colorado Springs, 1970—; lectr., cons. in field. Mem. exec. com. Citizens Com. for Conv. Center; bd. dirs. Jr. Achievement, YMCA Booster Club, Pikes Peak, 1975—. Served with USAF, 1960-64. Decorated Purple Heart (2), Air medal with 2 clusters; recipient numerous regional, nat. awards, creative dir. in advt. field. Mem. Pikes Peak Advt. Fedn. (dir. 1972-77), Sales and Mktg. Execs. Internat., Bank Mktg. Assn., Colo. Bankers Assn. Republican. Roman Catholic. Home: 3198 Breckenridge Dr W Colorado Springs CO 80906 Office: 923 W Colorado Ave Colorado Springs CO 80905

HALL, JOHN RICHARD, oil co. exec.; b. Dallas, Nov. 30, 1932; s. John W. and Agnes (Sanders) H.; B.Chem. Engring., Vanderbilt U., 1955; m. Donna Stauffer, May 10, 1980. Chem. engr. Esso Standard Oil Co., Balt., 1956-58, Ashland Oil Co. (Ky.), 1959-63, coordinator carbon black div., Houston, 1963-65, exec. asst. v.p., 1965-66, v.p., 1966-68, sr. v.p., 1970-71, also dir.; pres. Ashland Chem. Co., 1971-74; exec. v.p. Ashland Oil, Inc., 1974-79, vice chmn. chief operating officer, 1979—, group operating officer, 1976-79, chief exec. officer petroleum and chems., 1978-79. Trustee Franklin U., Columbus, Ohio; mem. com. visitors Vanderbilt U. Engring. Sch., Nashville. Served as 2d lt., Chem. Corps, AUS, 1955-56. Mem. Mfg. Chemists Assn., Nat. Petroleum Refiners Assn., Am. Petroleum Inst., Ky. Soc. Profl. Engrs., Tau Delta Pi, Sigma Chi, Delta Kappa. Republican. Home: 2610 Central Pkwy Ashland KY 41101 Office: PO Box 391 Ashland KY 41101

HALL, JUDSON EDWARD, telecommunications co. exec.; b. Hartford, Conn., Jan. 2, 1942; s. Albert James and Evelyn Elizabeth H.; B.A. in Liberal Arts and English, Norwich U., 1964; m. Daryle Mae Detamore, Feb. 6, 1965; 1 dau., Elizabeth Mae. Programmer analyst Aetna Ins. Co., Hartford, 1967-70; mgr. planning and scheduling dept. Hartford Nat. Bank & Trust, 1970-72; mgr. telecommunications support Travelers Ins. Co., Hartford, 1972-74; sr. bus. analyst Conn. Gen. Ins., Bloomfield, 1974-77; data processing staff mgr. and mgr. corp. telecommunications strategic planning GTE Service Corp., Tampa, Fla., 1977—. Served with U.S. Army, 1965-67. Decorated Army Commendation medal. Office: GTE Service Corp PO Box 1548 Tampa FL 33601

HALL, LARRY THOMAS, real estate broker; b. Lakeland, Fla., Oct. 22, 1940; s. Jerry Kenneth and Sabrina Evelyn (Brown) H.; B.S.B.A. in Fin., U. Fla., 1966; postgrad. Sch. Banking of South, La. State U., 1971; m. Karen Gail Kremer, May 2, 1964; children—John Thomas, Steven Travis, Brian Trevor. Asst. cashier loans 1st Nat. Bank Gainesville (Fla.), 1969-70; asst. v.p. Indian River Citrus Bank, Vero Beach, Fla., 1970-76; pres. Sebastian River Bank (now SE Bank Sebastian) (Fla.), 1971-76; pres., chief exec. officer SE Nat. Bank of Cocoa, Cocoa Beach, Fla., 1977-78; pres. Larry T. Hall, Inc., registered real estate broker, Vero Beach, Fla., 1978-79; pres. Assos. Realty of Indian River, Inc., 1979—; instr. Bert Rodgers Schs. Real Estate, Inc., Orlando, Fla. Chmn. bd. Sebastian River Med. Center, Inc., 1973-74, dir., 1974-76, asst. treas., 1974-75, treas., 1975-76; Served with USAR, 1960-68. Fla. Bankers Assn. scholar, 1965-66; recipient F.C. Oschner award Am. Cancer Soc., 1973. Mem. Am., Fla. bankers assns., Alpha Kappa Psi. Democrat. Baptist. Club: Riomar Bay Yacht. Home: 3895 Indian River Dr Vero Beach FL 32960 Office: 95 Royal Palm Rd Vero Beach FL 32960

HALL, MICHAEL TIMOTHY, real estate devel. exec.; b. San Diego, May 7, 1941; s. Dayton William and Mary Jane (St. John) H.; A.B., San Diego State U., 1968; M.B.A., Pepperdine U., 1972; M.P.A., U. So. Calif., 1977, Ph.D., 1978; m. Bineke Verschuur, Jan. 29, 1966; children—Kimberly Michele, Kirsten Yvonne, Brian Timothy. Dir. field ops. Housing Resources Inc., Beverly Hills, Calif., 1970-71; exec. v.p. Creative Housing Inc., Los Angeles, 1971-74; gen. mgr., resident partner Gerald D. Hines Interests, Newport Beach, Calif., 1974-77; founder, mng. partner Hall Partners, 1977—; founder, pres. LaCosta Schs., Inc. (Montessori), San Juan Capistrano, Calif., 1969-74. Served to capt. USMC, 1963-68; Vietnam. Decorated D.F.C., Air medal (7), Purple Heart; Vietnamese Cross of Gallantry. Mem. Urban Land Inst., Aircraft Owners and Pilots Assn., Air Force Assn., Mensa, U. So. Calif. Scapa Praetor Soc. Republican. Episcopalian. Clubs: Balboa Bay, Laguna Niguel Tennis. Home: 2321 South Coast Hwy Laguna Beach CA 92651 Office: 610 Newport Center Dr Newport Beach CA 92660

HALL, MILES LEWIS, JR., lawyer; b. Ft. Lauderdale, Fla., Aug. 14, 1924; s. Miles Lewis and Mary Frances (Dawson) H.; A.B., Princeton, 1947; J.D., Harvard, 1950; m. Muriel M. Fisher, Nov. 4, 1950; children—Miles Lewis III, Don Thomas. Admitted to Fla. bar, 1951, since practiced in Miami; partner Hall & Hedrick, 1953—; admitted to U.S. Supreme Ct. bar, 1959; dir. Gen. Portland, Inc., Dallas, 1974—. Vice pres. Orange Bowl Com., 1961-63, pres., 1964-65, dir., 1966—; mem. Fla. Council of 100, vice chmn., 1961-62; exec. bd. S. Fla. council Boy Scouts Am., 1966-67; vice chmn., dir. Dade County chpt. ARC, 1961-62, chmn., 1963-64, dir., 1967-73, nat. fund cons., 1963, 66-68; pres. Dade County Bar Assn. Ednl. Found., 1967-68; mem. adv. bd. Salvation Army, 1968—; bd. dirs. Coral Gables War Meml. Youth Center, 1967—, v.p., 1968-69, pres., 1969-72; mem. citizens bd. U. Miami, 1961-66; pres. Ransom Sch. Parents Assn., 1966; chmn. S. Fla. Gov.'s Scholarship Ball, 1966; mem. nominating com. Dade County Met. Ct., 1968-72; chmn. nominating commn. Dist. Ct. Appeal 3d Dist. Fla., 1972-75; mem. Biltmore Devel. Bd., City of Coral Gables, 1971-73; mem. bd. visitors Coll. Law Fla. State U., 1974—. Served to 2d lt. USAAF, 1943-45. Mem. Am. (Fla. co-chmn. membership com., sect. corp. banking and bus. law 1968-72), Dade County (dir. 1964-65, pres. 1967-68) bar assns., Fla. Bar, Am. Judicature Soc., Miami-Dade County C. of C., (v.p. 1962-64, dir. 1966-68), Harvard Law Sch. Assn. Fla. (dir. 1964-66), Alpha Tau Omega. Methodist (steward). Clubs: Princeton So. Fla. (past pres., dir.); Harvard of Miami; Cottage; The Miami; Kiwanis. Author: Titles, Ejectment and Election of Remedies, Vol. VIII, Fla. Law and Practice, 1958. Home: 2907 Alhambra Circle Coral Gables FL 33134 Office: Greater Miami Federal Bldg Suite 1104 200 SE 1st St Miami FL 33131

HALL, PATRICIA LYNN, chem. co. exec.; b. Washington, Mar. 28, 1954; d. George John and Virginia Marie (Kingston) H.; B.S., Shepherd Coll., 1976; postgrad. So. Ill. U.; Asst. head resident, asst. to dean women Shepherd Coll., Shepherdstown, W.Va., 1973-75; nuclear med. technologist Oscar B. Hunter Meml. Lab., Doctor's Hosp. and Sibley Meml. Hosp., Washington, 1976-78; tech. rep., NIH govt. sales specialist New Eng. Nuclear Corp., Boston, 1978-80; NIH govt. sales specialist Waters Assos. Inc., Milford, Mass., 1980—. Mem. Am. Soc. Clin. Pathologists, Soc. Nuclear Medicine (awards com. 1977-78), Soc. Nuclear Medicine Technologists, Am. Soc. Med. Technologists, Nat. Assn. Material Mgrs., Clin. Radioimmunoassay Soc., N.C. Health Physics Soc. Democrat. Roman Catholic. Home:

9312 Fernwood Rd Bethesda MD 20034 Office: 34 Maple St Milford MA 01757

HALL, RICHARD GORDON, fin. exec.; b. Yorkshire, Eng., Mar. 23, 1941; came to U.S., 1974; s. Gordon H. and Esme H.; B.A. in Engring. and Law, Corpus Christi Coll., Cambridge U., 1963, M.A., 1966; m. Jacquelin Brown, Oct. 8, 1966; children—Matthew, Sally, Katie. Group treas. EMI, Ltd., London, 1970-73; sr. v.p. Rolls Royce, Inc., N.Y.C., 1974-76; v.p. fin. EMI Tech., Inc., Stamford, Conn., 1976-79; fin. dir. Inmos Internat., Ltd., Colorado Springs, Colo., 1979—; v.p. fin. and adminstrn. Inmos Corp. Served with U.K. Territorial Army, 1960-74. Recipient Territorial Decoration. Fellow Inst. Chartered Accts. Club: Colo. Country. Home: 350 Oakhurst Ln Colorado Springs CO 80906 Office: PO Box 16000 Colorado Springs CO 80935

HALL, RICHARD SHAW, corp. exec. b. S.I., N.Y., Apr. 21, 1921; s. Raymond Peter and Blanche (Shaw) H.; student Wagner Coll., 1946-48; m. Alice Mary Baker, Feb 12, 1944; children—Richard Shaw, Gregory H. Sales rep. Doyle & Roth Mfg. Co., Inc., Bklyn., 1947-54, sales mgr., 1954-63, v.p., 1963-70; v.p. Walster Corp., Simpson, Pa., 1962-70; asso. Chem-Pro Marketing Services, S.I., 1966-70; v.p. Chem-Pro Assos., Ltd., 1970—; pres. Richard S. Hall & Assos., 1970—. Served to lt. (j.g.), USNR, 1942-46. Decorated Air medal (Navy), D.F.C. Mem. Chemists Club. Home: 72 Roman Ave Staten Island NY 10314 Office: 145 Cortlandt St Staten Island NY 10302

HALL, ROBERT, swimming pool mfg. corp. exec.; b. Milw., Mar. 24, 1930; s. Joseph and Emily (Savich) Savatovich; student public schs.; m. Bernice Krainovich, July 30, 1955; children—Robert, Bonnie, Michael, Tom. Vice pres. King's Awning Corp., Addison, Ill., 1957-60, Gen. Pool Corp., Addison, 1960-66; pres., chief exec. officer Hallmark Pool Corp., Rolling Meadows, Ill., 1966—, pres. Hallmark Pool Mfg. and Hallmark Pool Corp. Can. Ltd., 1969—. Active Chgo. Better Bus. Bur., 1971—. Recipient numerous sales awards and certs. Mem. Nat. Swimming Pool Inst. (pres. 1978, Man of Yr. award 1976, Algy award 1969), Spa and Hot Tub Assn., U.S. C. of C., Rolling Meadows C. of C. Republican. Mem. Serbian Orthodox Ch. Club: Moose, Masons. Author booklets and slide presentations on sales techniques. Home: 4604 Sycamore Ln Rolling Meadows IL 60008 Office: Hallmark Pool Corp 2785 Algonquin Rd Rolling Meadows IL 60008

HALL, ROBERT CHAMBERS, communications co. exec.; b. Ames, Iowa, May 20, 1931; s. Harry and Martha S. Hall; B.S.M.E., Iowa State U., 1955; m. Joan S. Hall, July 9, 1955; children—Ellen Hall McEllin, Kathryn, Elizabeth, Timothy, Laura, Margaret, Edward, Jean. With Stewart-Warner Corp., 1955-56, Sunstrand Corp., Denver, 1956-61; with Control Data Corp., 1961-72, v.p., group exec. computer systems, 1970-72; pres., chmn., chief exec. officer Securities Industry Assn. Corp., N.Y.C., 1972-77; exec. v.p. N.Y. Stock Exchange, Inc., 1977-79; pres. Satellite Bus. Systems, McLean, Va., 1979—. Bd. dirs. United Fund of Mpls., 1971-72. Served with USAF, 1951-52. Mem. Am. Mgmt. Assn. Clubs: Apawamis, Manursing Island (Rye, N.Y.). Office: 8382 Greensboro Dr McLean VA 22102

HALL, ROBERT EMMETT, JR., investment banker, realtor; b. Sioux City, Iowa, Apr. 28, 1936; s. Robert Emmett and Alvina (Faden) H.; B.A., State U. S.D., 1958, M.A., 1959; M.B.A., U. Santa Clara, 1975. Mgr. ins. dept. asst. mgr. installment loan dept. Northwestern Nat. Bank of Sioux Falls (S.D.) (formerly N.W. Security Nat. Bank), 1959-61, asst. cashier, 1961-65; asst. mgr. Crocker Citizens Nat. Bank, San Francisco, 1965-67, loan officer, 1967-69, asst. v.p., asst. mgr. San Mateo br., 1969-72; v.p., Western regional mgr. Internat. Investments & Realty, Inc., 1972—; owner Almaden Oaks Realtors, San Jose, Calif., 1975—; instr. real estate, fin. industry and mgmt. West Valley Coll., Saratoga, Calif.; instr. real estate fin. and investments Grad. Sch. Bus., U. Santa Clara. Treas. Minnehaha Leukemia Soc., 1963, Lake County Heart Fund Assn., 1962, Minnehaha Young Republican Club, 1963; active Palo Alto Young Reps. Mem. Am. Inst. Banking, San Mateo C. of C., Beta Theta Pi. Roman Catholic. Clubs: Elks, Rotary (past pres.), Kiwanis, K.C., Shadow Brook Country, Almaden Country. Home: 6951 Castlerock Dr San Jose CA 95120 Office: 6501 Crown Blvd San Jose CA 95120

HALL, ROBERT HARDY, JR., ins. co. exec.; b. Petersburg, Va., July 5, 1928; s. Robert Hardy and Kathryn Mabel Hall; student Va. Commonwealth U., 1946-47, U. Richmond, 1960-63; m. Evelyn McFarland, Nov. 5, 1949; children—Linda Evelyn, Robert Wayne, Brenda Gail, Mark Kevin. With Equitable Life Assurance Soc. U.S., 1954—, agy. mgr., Springfield, Ill., 1965-70, Charleston, W.Va., 1970—. Bd. dirs. ARC, Petersburg, Va., 1963-65, United Fund, Petersburg, 1962-65. Recipient President's Trophy, Equitable Life Assurance Soc., 1975, 78, 80, Silver award, 1979, numerous other awards. Mem. Charleston Life Underwriters Assn., Nat. Assn. Life Underwriters, Am. Soc. C.L.U.'s (past pres.), Charleston Estate Planning Council (pres. 1972-73), Charleston Area C. of C. Republican. Mem. Christian Ch. Club: Kiwanis (pres. Springfield 1969-70). Home: 6 Birch Tree Ln Charleston WV 25314 Office: 1110 Commerce Sq Charleston WV 25301

HALL, ROBERT WAYNE, real estate appraiser and counselor; b. Phila., June 22, 1924; s. Irvin Kay and Emma (Cronin) H.; B.S., Temple U., 1949; m. K. Clarice Hamilton, Apr. 13, 1946; children—Robert H., James A., Kathleen E. Exec. v.p. Nessen Co., Phila., 1949-52; owner, operator Robert W. Hall and Assos., Real Estate Appriasers and Counselors, Glen Mills, Pa., 1952-77; v.p. Dickinson, Inc., Realtors, Chadds Ford, Pa., 1977—; adj. asst. prof. Widener Coll.; guest lectr. various colls. Served with U.S. Army, 1943-46. Named Realtor of Yr., Chester Real Estate Bd., 1958. Mem. Am. Inst. Real Estate Appraisers (instr. 1967—, Profl. Recognition award 1976-81), Soc. Real Estate Appraisers, Realtors Nat. Mktg. Inst., Am. Right-of-Way Assn. (sr.), Lambda Alpha. Republican. Methodist. Contbr. articles to Appraisal Jour. Home: Box 265 RD 2 Glen Mills PA 19342 Office: PO Box 175 Chadds Ford PA 19317

HALL, ROGER ALLEN, engring. and constrn. co. exec.; b. Calhoun County, Ala., Sept. 20, 1945; s. Alton Coolidge and Ernestine (Owen) H.; B.C.E., U. Ala., 1967, M.S., 1968; m. Charlotte Ray Hall, Oct. 7, 1967 (div.); 1 son, Zachary Dylan. Civil engr. Internat. Paper Co., Mobile, 1968-70, Ala. Power Co., Birmingham, 1970-73; pres. Constructo Corp., Inc., Birmingham, 1973-79, also dir.; cons. agrl. areas, 1979—; cons. on water quality, supply problems Farm Fresh Catfish Co., Greensboro, Ala. NASA fellow, 1968. Registered profl. engr., Ala. Mem. Sigma Xi, Tau Beta Pi, Omicron Delta Kappa. Home and office: 901 Centerville St Greensboro AL 36744

HALL, ROLAND MEREDITH, Realtor, gen. contractor, real estate developer; b. Shreveport, June 20, 1947; s. Charles Thaxter and Ruth Lucille (Bouanchaud) H.; B.S., La. State U., Baton Rouge, 1969; m. Phyllis Charlene Felts; children—Roland Meredith, Allison Courtney, Jennifer Mason. Pres. Hall & Co., real estate, Hall-Robi Gen. Contractors Co. Inc.; pres. Hall Land Co., Inc., Hall Devel. Corp.; sec. 70th Jewella Corp.; appraiser various cos. Mem. Nat., La. realtors assns., Shreveport-Bossier Bd. Realtors, Metal Bldg. Dealers Assn., Sigma Chi (life). Republican. Baptist. Clubs: Shreveport Racquet/Tennis Indoor; Pierremont Oaks Tennis. Home: 7515 Millbrook Dr Shreveport LA 71105 Office: 1941 E 70th St Shreveport LA 71105

HALL, ROY DOUGLAS, III, real estate co. exec.; b. Glen Ridge, N.J., Mar. 29, 1941; s. Roy Douglas and Dorothy (Wheildon) H., Jr.; B.A. in Econs., Yale U., 1963; m. Susan E. Dodge, Feb. 2, 1968; children—Lisa Susan, Sarah Elizabeth. Mortgage loan officer John Hancock Mut. Life Ins. Co., Boston, 1965-70; mgr. real estate financing Ford Motor Credit Co., Dearborn, Mich., 1970-74; sr. v.p. Bay Colony Property Co., Boston, 1974-79, pres., 1979; pres. Bay Fin. Corp., mems. N.Y. Stock Exchange, Boston, 1979—. Chmn., Manchester (Mass.) Fin. Com.; vice chmn. Manchester Capital Plans Com. Mem. Urban Land Inst., Nat. Assn. Office and Indsl. Parks. Home: 5 Running Ridge Rd Manchester MA 01944 Office: 2 Faneuil Hall Marketplace Boston MA 02109

HALL, WARREN ESTERLY, JR., lawyer; b. Atlanta, Dec. 22, 1910; s. Warren Esterly and Martha (Haygood) H.; student Ga. Sch. Tech., 1929-30, 31-32; LL.B., Atlanta Law Sch., 1938; m. Pauline Lewis, Feb. 3, 1934; children—Martha Hall Byrne, Warren Esterly III (dec. 1958). Engring. work B.M. Hall & Sons, Atlanta, 1926-32; various positions including sales, office mgmt. and govt., 1932-37; admitted to Ga. bar, 1937, Fla. bar, 1954, also U.S. Supreme Ct. bar, U.S. Ct. Appeals 5th Circuit bar, D.C. bar; partner firm Prestwood & Hall, Atlanta, 1937-42; labor relations adviser to OPA adminstr., Washington, also regional atty. and asst. regional adminstr. Southeastern states, Atlanta, 1942-45; partner Poole, Pearce & Hall, Atlanta, 1946-61, Hall, Sweeny & Godbee, DeLand, Fla., 1955-60, Adams, Hall, Sweeny & Godbee, Ft. Lauderdale, Fla., 1958-60, Holland, Bevis & Smith, Bartow, Fla., 1961-64, Holland, Bevis, Smith & Kibler, Bartow and Lakeland, 1964-65, Holland, Bevis, Smith, Kibler & Hall, Bartow also Lakeland, 1965-68, Holland & Knight, Bartow, Lakeland, Tallahassee, Bradenton and Tampa, Fla., 1968—; gen. solicitor Econ. Stblizn. Agy., Washington, 1950-51; legal adviser to under sec. of navy Washington, 1951; instr., lectr. labor law various law schs. Mem. Am., Ga., 10th Jud. Circuit, Atlanta, Fed. bar assns., Fla. Bar (del. jud. conf. 5th circuit 1964-71, chmn. subcom. on appellate rules 1964-67), Am. Judicature Soc., Am. Arbitration Assn. (nat. panel), Scribes, Phi Delta Theta. Episcopalian. Clubs: Lawyers (Atlanta); Bartow Golf and Country; Peace River Country. Mem. bd. editors Fla. Law and Practice. Contbr. articles to law jours. Office: 245 S Central Ave Bartow FL 33830*

HALL, WESLEY JAMES, JR., genetic seed supply and land devel. co. exec.; b. Des Moines, Oct. 23, 1929; s. Wesley James and Juanita Farrel (Woody) H.; student public schs.; m. Fay Lois King; children—Lynn James, Merle Gene, David Wayne. Grain farmer, Urbandale, Iowa, 1945-48; with Armstrong Tire and Rubber Co., Des Moines, 1949-53; with Pioneer Hibred Internat. Inc., Des Moines, 1953—, dir. bldg. maintenance subsidiary Green Meadows Ltd., 1975—. Cert. chief engr. Nat. Inst. Uniform Lic. Power Engrs. Mem. Nat. Assn. Power Engrs. (dir. region 6). Republican. Mem. Evang. Ch. Office: 5608 Merle Hay Rd Des Moines IA 50323

HALL, WILFRED MCGREGOR, engring. exec.; b. Denver, June 12, 1894; s. Frederick Folsom and Annie (Thompson) H.; B.S., U. Colo., 1916; D. Engring., Tufts U., 1955; m. Anne Gertrude Jones, Apr. 4, 1921 (dec. Dec. 1976); children—Frederick Folsom, Anne Hall (dec.); m. 2d, Louise Hull Claire, June 23, 1978. Asst. res. engr. Chas. T. Main, Inc., Boston, 1916-17, field and res. engr., 1920-22, dir., 1943—, v.p. 1953-57, pres., chief exec. officer, 1957-72, chmn. bd., chief exec. officer, 1972—, also dir.; chmn. bd., chief exec. officer Chas. T. Main Internat. Inc., Chas. T. Main of N.Y., Inc., Chas. T. Main of Mich., Inc., Chas. T. Main of Va., Inc., Tech. Services Co., Inc., Buerkel & Co. Inc.; field and asst. engr. J.A.P. Chrisfield Contracting Co., 1919-20; supt. constrn., engring. U.G.I. Contracting Co., Phila., 1922-28; supt. constrn. Electric Bond & Share Co., N.Y.C., 1929-31, cons., sales rep., 1931-33; engr. in charge constrn. TVA, Knoxville, Tenn., 1933-37; engr. in charge constrn. P.R. Reconstrn. Adminstrn., 1937-41; partner Uhl, Hall & Rich, 1953-62, mng. partner, 1962-80; Former bd. dirs. Mass. Heart Assn. Mem. U.S. Com. on Large Dams. Served as 2d lt. U.S. Coast and Heavy Arty. Corps, 1918. Fellow Am. Soc. C.E., Royal Soc. for Encouragement Arts, Manufactures and Commerce; mem. AIM (pres.'s council), Cons. Engrs. Council New Eng. (past dir). Am. Inst. Cons. Engrs. (past sect. pres.), Mass. Soc. Profl. Engrs., Am. Mgmt. Assn., Newcomen Soc. (trustee, chmn. New Eng. com.), Tau Beta Pi, Alpha Sigma Phi, Sigma Tau. Clubs: Country (Brookline, Mass.); Algonquin, Hamilton Trust (past pres.), Rotary (past dir.) Boston, Engineers (gov.); Metropolitan (N.Y.C.). Home: Penthouse D Fairfield Prudential Center Boston MA 02199 Office: 4600 Prudential Tower Boston MA 02199

HALL, WILLIAM DWIGHT, mfg. co. exec.; b. Boise, Idaho, Aug. 30, 1918; s. Almon Jacob and Sarah Grace (Mann) H.; Aero. Engr., Curtiss Wright Tech. Inst., 1938; postgrad. evenings U. Cin., Columbus Art Sch., U. N.C.; m. Mary Frances Shoemaker, Mar. 30, 1940 (div.); children—James Almon, William Dwight, Sarah Grace. Aero. engr., chief engr. Aeronca Aircraft Co., Middletown, Ohio, 1938-44; farmer, Urbana, Ohio, 1946-50; quality control mgr. Grimes Mfg. Co., Urbana, 1950-60; pres. The Hall Co., Urbana, 1960—, pres. 1960-78, treas., 1978—. Served with USN, 1944-46. Mem. Mensa. Republican. Club: Lions (pres. 1973-74) (Urbana). Patentee aircraft lighting designs. Home: PO Box 38158 Urbana OH 43078 Office: The Hall Co 420 E Water St Urbana OH 43078

HALL, WILLIAM RICHARDSON, mktg. cons.; b. Princeton, N.J., July 27, 1935; s. Willard M. and Mildred E. (Sidwell) H.; B.S.B.A., Yale U., 1958; m. Barbara M. Bradley, June 1, 1957; children—R. Lacey, W. Bradley, Catherine L. Staff engr., brand mgr., asso. advt. mgr. Procter & Gamble, 1957-65; v.p. Glendinning Assos., 1965-70; div. v.p., group v.p., mem. chmn.'s staff Rapid Am. Corp., 1970-79; pres. Mktg. and Adminstrv. Services, Inc., Katonah, N.Y., 1979—. Served with U.S. Army, 1954-58. Mem. Phi Beta Kappa, Sigma Xi, Tau Beta Pi. Club: Stanwich Country (Greenwich, Conn.). Office: PO Box 211 Katonah NY 10536

HALLER, JOHN C., comml. banker; b. Erie, Pa., Jan. 18, 1945; s. John C. and Jean B. Haller; B.A., Allegheny Coll., 1967; m. Claudia P. Spampinato, June 22, 1968; 1 dau., Jennifer. From mgmt. devel. program to banking officer Mellon Bank, Pitts., 1968-75; v.p., area mgr. Marine Bank, Erie, 1975-77, sr. v.p. in charge retail banking div., 1977—; dir. Trisach. Treas., Hospice of Met. Erie; bd. dirs. N.W. Pa. Heart Assn., Boy Scouts Am., Erie. Served with U.S. Army, 1967. Cert. comml. lender Am. Bankers Assn. Mem. Erie Area C. of C. (treas.). Clubs: University (Erie); Kahkwa. Office: Marine Bank 901 State St Erie PA 16501

HALLEY, GILBERT ROY, wholesale bldg. materials co. exec.; b. Seattle, Mar. 13, 1938; s. James Dewey and Elizabeth D. (Drake) H.; B.A., U. Wash., 1963, B.A. in Prodn. Mgmt. and Acctg., 1970; m. Betty E. Walker, Mar. 17, 1962; children—Mark A., Karen Anne. Prodn. mgr. Mattel, Inc., Hawthorne, Calif., 1963-65; budget supr. Boeing Co., Seattle, 1965-71; tax acct. Weyerhaeuser Co., Federal Way, Wash., 1971-72; sec.-treas., chief fin. officer, dir. Palmer G. Lewis Co., Inc., Auburn, Wash., 1972—. Served with U.S. Army, 1958-64. C.P.A., Wash. Mem. Am. Inst. C.P.A.'s. Republican. Roman Catholic. Office: 525 C St NW Auburn WA 98002

HALLIDAY, WILLIAM JAMES, JR., mfg. exec.; b. Detroit, Nov. 16, 1921; s. William James and Katherine Elizabeth (Krantz) H.; A.B. (scholar), U. Mich., 1943, J.D., 1948; m. Lois Jeanne Streelman, Sept. 6, 1947; children—Carol Lynn Halliday Murphy, Richard Andrew, Marcia Katherine, James Anthony. Admitted to Mich. bar, 1948; asso. firm Schmidt, Smith & Howlett and successors, Grand Rapids, Mich., 1952-56, partner, 1956-66; sec. Amway Corp. Ada, Mich., 1964—; gen. counsel, 1966-71, v.p., 1970-79, exec. v.p., 1979—, also dir.; asst. pros. atty., Kent County, Mich., 1949-51; twp. atty., Wyoming Twp., Mich., 1955-57; city atty., Wyoming, Mich., 1961-66. Served with M.I., U.S. Army, 1943-46, with JAGC, 1951-52. Decorated Bronze Star; recipient William Jennings Bryan award, U. Mich., 1943. Mem. Am., Mich., Grand Rapids bar assns., Phi Beta Kappa, Phi Kappa Phi, Delta Sigma Rho, Phi Eta Sigma. Republican. Presbyterian. Club: Kiwanis. Home: 2096 Robinson Rd S E Grand Rapids MI 49506 Office: Amway Corp 7575 E Fulton Rd Ada MI 49355

HALLIER, GERARD EDOUARD, hotel co. exec.; b. Casablanca, Morocco, July 19, 1941; came to U.S., 1965; s. Marcel E. and Yvette S. (Rousseau) H.; grad. Coll. Scis. Economiques, Paris, 1965, Sch. Hotel Adminstrn., Nice, 1963; m. Michele Smadja, Sept. 10, 1964; children—Laurent, Brigitte, Isabelle. Mgr. trainee Hotel Corp. of Am., Washington and London, 1965-67, asst. gen. mgr., 1967-68; hotel mgr. Grand Hotel, Paris, 1968-70; devel. dir. Esso Motor Hotels, Europe, 1970-72; div. v.p. Ramada Inns, Inc., Phoenix, 1972-79, exec. v.p., dir., 1979—. Office: 3838 E Van Buren St Phoenix AZ 85008

HALLIGAN, SIDNEY JAMES, fin. co. exec.; b. Ft. Dodge, Iowa, Mar. 29, 1930; s. Raymond A. and Anne M. H.; B.A., B.S., U. No. Iowa, 1958; M.B.A., Boston U., 1980; m. Virginia Kier, 1956; children—Lisa, Sara, Nora, Mary, Jerald. European mktg. dir. Honeywell, Ltd., London, 1965-69; co-founder, v.p. sales Prime Computer, 1970-74; co-founder, v.p. Computer Store, 1974-78; pres. Boston Mgmt. Group, Wellesley, Mass., 1980—; cons. Mem. IEEE. Home: 14 Revere Rd Sudbury MA 01776

HALLORAN, T. WILLIAM, bus. devel. exec.; b. Jamaica, N.Y., Apr. 3, 1931; s. Thomas and Alyce (Conway) H.; B.E.E., Northeastern U., 1957, M.S., 1967; m. Lorraine Mildred Smith, Nov. 15, 1952; children—Sandra Lee, Lou Ann, Tracy Marie. Engring. asst. Trans-Sonics, Inc., Burlington, Mass., 1953-57; engr. Radiation Labs., Maynard, Mass., 1957-58; engring. mgr. Avco Corp., Wilmington, Mass., 1958-68; product line mgr. Electronic Resources, Inc., Los Angeles, 1968-70; comml. prodn. mgr. Aerojet Corp., El Monte, Calif., 1970-75; dir. Western new bus. devel. Grumman Data Systems Corp., Encino, Calif., 1975-80; co-founder, pres. Nat. IMS Corp., 1979—. Served in USAF, 1950-53; Korea. Mem. Am. Mgmt. Assn., Soc. Flight Test Engrs., Tech. Mktg. Soc. Am., Soc. Old Crows, Soc. Exptl. Test Pilots. Roman Catholic. Home: 533 Sunset Rd Glendale CA 91202 Office: 109 E Harvard St Glendale CA 91205

HALLSTROM, GERALD LINCOLN, newspaper exec.; b. Worcester, Mass., Dec. 29, 1947; s. Lincoln A. and Mary A. H.; student San Francisco City Coll., 1969; m. Colleen Margaret Farrell, Sept. 1, 1967; 1 dau., Heather Aileen. Advt. rep. Tahoe Daily Tribune, South Lake Tahoe, Calif., 1969, mgr. classified advt., 1969-73; mgr. classified advt. Antioch (Calif.) Daily Ledger, 1974-75; dir. classified advt. Contra Costa Times, Walnut Creek, Calif., 1975-79; gen. mgr. Valley Times, Pleasanton, Calif., 1979—. Served with USMC, 1965-69; Vietnam. Mem. No. Calif. Classified Advt. Mgrs. Assn. (dir. 1977-79), Assn. Newspaper Classified Advt. Mgrs., Western Classified Advt. Mgrs. Assn., Calif. Newspaper Pubs. Assn. Office: 122 Spring St Pleasanton CA 94566

HALM, PATRICK EUGENE, mech. engr.; b. Chgo., July 30, 1939; s. John William and Ellen Myrtle (Cain) H.; student U. Ill., 1957-60, Ill. Inst. Tech., 1960-63; m. Marianne Reinert, June 17, 1961; children—Lisa Marie, Julie Ann. Plant engr. Argonne (Ill.) Nat. Labs, 1961-66; design engr. Engrs. Collaborative, Chgo., 1966-71; v.p. Environ. Systems Desigr,, Chgo., 1972—. Registered profl. engr., Ill., Mich., Ind., N.C. Mem. ASHRAE, Nat., Ill. socs. profl. engrs., Am. Soc. Plumbing Engrs. Project engr. Rush Med. Coll., Chgo., Am. Center, Southfield, Mich., Continental Ill. Nat. Bank Computer Center, Chgo., Motorola Communications Group Bldg., others. Home: 16 Bonnie Brae Rd Hinsdale IL 60521 Office: Environmental Systems Design Inc 35 E Wacker Dr Chicago IL 60601

HALPERIN, EDWARD ALEXANDER, ins. co. exec.; b. N.Y.C., Jan. 5, 1936; s. Leopold A. and Jeanne N. H.; B.S. in Acctg., Temple U., 1966, M.B.A. in Ins. and Risk Mgmt., 1972; m. Marlene F. Becker, Dec. 24, 1958; children—Sondra Lynn, Allison Beth, Lee Alexander. With Phila. Life Ins. Co., Phila., 1958—, mgr. actuarial dept., 1968-70, asst. treas., 1970-74, controller, 1974—. Served with U.S. Army Res., 1958-64. Fellow Life Office Mgmt. Assn.; mem. Health Ins. Assn. Am. (cert. 1978), Ins. Acctg. and Statis. Assn. Home: 5805 Wharton Circle Bensalem PA 19020 Office: 111 N Broad St Philadelphia PA 19107

HALPERN, MERRIL MARK, investment banker; b. Bayonne, N.J., May 4, 1934; s. Samuel and Belle (Schwartz) H.; B.S., Rutgers U., 1956; M.B.A., Harvard, 1962; m. Phyllis Goldstein, June 14, 1960; children—Belle Linda, Jennifer, Samuel, Irving. With Ernst & Ernst, N.Y.C., 1956-60, sr. accountant, 1958-60; with McDonnell & Co., Inc., 1962-68, v.p., 1967-68; partner H. Hentz & Co., N.Y.C., 1969—, dir. corporate finance, 1969-70; prin. Merril M. Halpern & Co., N.Y.C., 1970-73; pres. Charterhouse Group Internat., Inc. subsidiary Charterhouse Group Ltd., London, 1973—; pres., dir. Arista Graphic Arts Corp., N.Y.C.; chmn. bd. Paco Pharm. Services Inc., 1975—; v.p., dir. Tempo Devices, Inc., Plainview, L.I., N.Y.; dir. Dreyer's Grand Ice Cream, Inc., 1977, Marathon Enterprises, Inc., 1979—, Carleton Woolen Mills, Inc., 1979—. Served with AUS, 1957-58. Home: 1 Halsey Pl South Orange NJ 07079 Office: 477 Madison Ave New York NY 10022

HALPERN, NATHAN LOREN, industrialist; b. Sioux City, Iowa, Oct. 22, 1914; s. Aaron and Lena (Robin) H.; B.A., U. So. Calif., 1936; LL.B. cum laude, Harvard, 1939; m. Edith Kessel, Oct. 7, 1938; 1 son, Michael. Admitted to Calif., D.C. bars, 1939; asst. to chmn. SEC, Washington, 1939-41; exec. asst. to dir. WPB, Washington, 1941-42; exec. asst. to dir. USIS, France, 1945; asst. to pres. CBS, N.Y.C., 1945-49; pres. TNT Communications, Inc., N.Y.C., 1949—. Pres. Internat. Center of Photography, East Hampton Beach Preservation Soc.; mem. corp. Met. Mus. Art. Served with USNR, 1942-44. Mem. Soc. Motion Picture and TV Engrs., Phi Beta Kappa. Clubs: Harvard, Players. Contbr. articles on closed-circuit TV to tech. jours. Home: 993 Fifth Ave New York NY 10028 Office: 575 Madison Ave New York NY 10022

HALPIN, IGNATIUS (NACE) EMANUEL, aluminum co. exec.; b. Crosby, N.D., June 24, 1928; s. Edward John and Caroline Louise (McNerny) H.; B.S.C., U. N.D., 1950; P.M.D., Harvard U., 1965; m. Donna Claire Rehor, Apr. 19, 1950; children—Steven, Erin, Melissa, Frederick. Store mgr. Gambel Skogmo, Charles City, Iowa, 1950-53;

ops. supt. Kaiser Aluminum & Chem. Corp., Trentwood, Wash., 1953-70; pres. Maralco Aluminum, Seattle, 1971—; treas. Aluminum Recycling Corp., Spokane, Wash., 1979—; partner Halpin-Lyon Co., Seattle, 1973—, Accord Leasing Co., Spokane, 1979—. Registered profl. engr., Calif. Mem. Am. Inst. Indsl. Engrs., Am. Foundry Soc., Soc. Die Casting Engrs., AIME. Republican. Club: Rainier Golf and Country. Home: 20715 Marine View Dr SW Seattle WA 98166 Office: 6760 W Marginal Way SW Seattle WA 98106

HALPIN, JOHN MICHAEL, food service co. exec.; b. Kalamazoo, Mich., Sept. 20, 1941; s. Donald Cass and Blanche Marie (Welter) H.; B.S. in B.A., Xavier U., Cin., 1963. Staff accountant Peat Marwick Mitchell & Co., Toledo, 1965-70; personal tax adviser, clients accounting dept. Wood, Struthers & Winthrop, Inc. subs. Donaldson, Lufkin & Jenrette, Inc., N.Y.C., 1970-73; asst. treas. Gladieux Corp., Toledo, 1973—. Served to 1st lt. U.S. Army, 1963-65. C.P.A., Ohio. Mem. Catholic Alumni Clubs Internat. (internat. treas., 1970, pres. Toledo chpt. 1969), Am. Inst. C.P.A.'s, Ohio Soc. C.P.A.'s. Republican. Roman Catholic. Home: 4160 Garrison Rd Toledo OH 43613 Office: 2630 Laskey Rd Toledo OH 43697

HALSEY, JIM, theatrical producer, talent mgr.; b. Independence, Kans., Oct. 7, 1930; student Independence Community Coll., 1948-50, also Kans. U.; children—Sherman Brooks, Gina Halsey. Producer shows for auditoriums, fairs, rodeos, celebrations in various cities U.S., Can., 1950—; pres. Thunderbird Artists, Inc., Independence, 1952—, Jim Halsey Co., Inc., Jim Halsey Lighting & Sound Co., Jim Halsey Agy., Jim Halsey Radio Mgmt., James Halsey Property Mgmt., Silverline-Goldline Music, Inc., Proud Country Entertainment (stas. KTOW Tulsa, KGOW-FM Tulsa), Cyclone Records, Tulsa Records; gen. partner Parker Ranch, Tulsa; pres. Otter Creek Music, Pencil Music, Quill Music, Palo Duro Music, Brazos Valley Music, Parker Lane Music, Open Air Music, Town Crier Music, Fish Music, Palo Mesa Music; producer Tulsa Internat. Music Festival; dir., producer Kans. Celebration Neewollah, Independence, 1958—; v.p. country and Western div. Gen. Artists Corp., Beverly Hills, Calif., 1966-67, Singin' T Prodns., NERECO Prodns.; dir. Mercantile Bank & Trust, Tulsa, Farmers & Mchts. Bank, Mound City, Kans., Roy Clark Celebrity Golf Classic; personal mgr. various entertainment personalities; dir. Blucher Boot Co., Fairfax, Okla. Mem. Kans. Centennial Commn., 1960-61; mem. Independence Park Bd., 1969-72; trustee Philbrook Art Center, Tulsa. Served with AUS, 1954-56. Recipient Distinguished Service award U.S. Jr. C. of C., 1959. Mem. Independence C. of C. (dir. 1958-61), Country Music Assn. (dir. 1963-64, 70-71), Acad. Country Music (Jim Reeves Meml. award 1977; dir. 1969-70, 73-74, v.p. 1975-76). Episcopalian. Clubs: Rotary, Elks (trustee). Home: 801 W Beech St Independence KS 67301 Office: 3225 S Norwood St Tulsa OK 74135

HALSEY, WANDA PHILPOTT, utility exec.; b. Winding Gulf, W.Va., Apr. 26, 1932; d. Larkin Shelton and Julia Edith (Spasiuk) Philpott; student Sullins Coll., 1949-50, W.Va. U., 1950-51; A.B. cum laude in Journalism, U. N.C., 1953; m. Stephen Simmons Halsey, Feb. 11, 1956 (div. 1966); children—Alexandra Simmons, Nicholas Van Rensselaer. Buyer, Bloomingdales, N.Y.C., 1953-54; asst. dir. pub. relations and fashion coordination Julius Garfinckel & Co., Washington, 1954-56; dir. editorial and spl. services Burson-Marsteller, N.Y.C., 1971-72, account exec., 1972-75; mgr. media relations Continental Group, Inc., N.Y.C., 1975-77, dir. media relations, 1977-78; mgr. communications Union Pacific Corp., N.Y.C., 1978-79; exec. v.p. Public Policy Group, N.Y.C., 1979-80; dir. corp. communications Orange and Rockland Utilities, Inc., 1980—. Chmn. Washington Nat. Symphony Ball, 1965; mem. Presdl. Innaugural Com., 1961, 1965; bd. dirs. Children's Convalescent Hosp., 1962-65; mem. Cherry Blossom Festival Com., 1960. Mem. Publicity Club N.Y., Indsl. Communications Council, Nat. Council Career Women, Paper Industry Pub. Relations Group (chmn.), Wall Street Irregulars, Fgn. Press Assn., Alpha Psi Omega, Theta Sigma Phi. Democrat. Home: 446 E 86th St New York NY 10028 Office: One Blue Hill Plaza Pearl River NY 10965

HALSTED, DONALD M., JR., cement co. exec.; b. Glen Ridge, N.J., Feb. 27, 1927; s. Donald M. and Barbara (Harris) H.; A.B. in Econs., Princeton U., 1950; m. Helen Trent Harvey, June 14, 1950; children—Donald M., Amy M. With Atlantic Cement Co., Inc., Stamford, Conn., subs. Newmont Mining Corp., N.Y.C., 1961—, asst. v.p. mktg., 1961-63, v.p., gen. sales mgr., 1963-65, v.p. mktg., 1966-67, pres., chief exec. officer, dir., 1967-79; pres., chief operating officer Lone Star Industries, Inc., Greenwich, Conn., 1979—; dir. Bancroft Convertible Fund, N.Y.C., 1970—, Trust Bd., Union Trust Co., Stamford, Hydraulic Co., Bridgeport, Conn. and subs. Bridgeport Hydraulic Co., 1975. Mem. Tower Fellow, U. Bridgeport. Served with USAAF, 1945-46, to 2d lt. U.S. Army, 1949-58. Clubs: Landmark (Stamford), Mining (N.Y.C.), Nassau (Princeton, N.J.), Country Club of New Canaan, Aspetuck Hunt and Fish (Easton, Conn.). Office: 1 Greenwich Plaza Greenwich CT 06830

HALSTED, DONALD MERWIN, investment adviser, broker; b. Bklyn., Nov. 6, 1898; s. William Moore and Nettie (Hutchinson) H.; A.B., Princeton, 1920; m. Barbara Avery Harris, Mar. 7, 1925; children—Marilla Avery (Mrs. Edward Lee Ives, Jr.), Donald Merwin. Asso. various investment firms, 1921-40, pres. Donald M. Halsted & Co., Inc., Jersey City, 1940-75, Halsted Adv. Corp., N.Y.C., 1975-78; asso. Whitney, Goadby, Inc., N.Y.C., 1979—. Congregationalist. Home: 10 Crestmont Rd Montclair NJ 07042 Office: 48 Wall St New York NY 10005

HALT, WALLACE ARTHUR, JR., electronics co. exec.; b. Chester, Ill., Nov. 20, 1922; s. Wallace A. and Elda (Gerlach) H.; student Air U., Air Command and Staff Sch., 1946-48; m. Dorothy Myers, Sept. 16, 1942; children—Judith, Daniel. Served as enlisted man U.S. Air Force, 1940-44; commd. 2d lt. U.S. Air Force, 1944, advanced through grades to maj., 1953; dir. tng., dept. officer communications, 1953, resigned, 1953; mem. sales and service staff, two-way communications products Motorola, Inc., 1953-65, v.p., gen. mgr. Europe, 1974-79; v.p., midwest area mgr. Motorola Communications & Electronics, Inc., 1965-73; v.p., dir. subsidiaries Motorola Communications Internat., Schaumburg, Ill., 1980—. Mem. Armed Forces Communications and Electronics Assn. (pres. Weisbaden, W. Ger. 1975-76, mem. exec. bd. Wiesbaden/Frankfurt). Home: 195 Crest Rd Glen Ellyn IL 60137 Office: Motorola Inc 1301 Algonquin Rd Schaumburg IL 60194

HALVARSSON-DEWITT, MISHA, archtl. and glass design/gen. contracting co. exec.; b. Oakland, Calif., May 25, 1951; d. Carl Maurice and Ruth Beckner (Ayres) Halvarsson; student World Campus Afloat, Chapman Coll.; B.A. in Design and Journalism, Union U., Jackson, Tenn., 1971; m. Dennis Craig DeWitt, Dec. 31, 1979. Sr. designer Halvarsson Design, Oreg., 1975-79, pres., 1978-79; v.p. Icefire Glassworks, Inc., Oreg., 1976-78, corp. gen. mgr., 1977-78; design cons. Van Workshop, Inc., Oreg., 1978-79; pres., archtl. and glass designer, gen. contractor Halvarsson, DeWitt & Assos., Inc., Duvall, Wash., 1979—; acting dir. Images & Reflections, Inc., Duvall, 1979—; promotional cons. Marawood Devel. Corp., 1981—; cons. archtl. glass and Victorian renovation, mktg. cons. Mem. Oreg. Land Conservation and Devel. Com., 1976-79; chmn. Duvall Revitalization Com., 1981—. Mem. Nat. Trust Hist. Prevervation. Editor: Scratchbook Cookery Series, 1980-81. Office: PO Box 136 Duvall WA 98019

HALVERSON, GYLE ODEAN, mktg. cons.; b. Havre, Mont., Feb. 14, 1922; s. Herman N. and Clara M. (Haugen) H.; m. Harriet Irene Lee, Apr. 17, 1948; children—Lesley Gayle, Gregory Wallen, Steven Gyle, Jon Eric. Radio announcer, engr. Sta. KYAK, Yakima, Wash., 1947-50; regional mktg. dir. Gen. Distbrs., Spokane, Wash., 1950-55; owner Consumers Electric, Spokane, 1955-58; sales mgr. Culligan, Inc., Spokane, 1958-59, regional mgr., 1959-62; mktg. mgr. Western dist. A to Z Rental Centers, San Francisco, 1962-69; prin., sales-mktg. cons. Profit Centers, Gresham, Oreg., 1970—. Served with USN, 1943-46. Mem. Direct Mktg. Assn., Nat. Car Wash Assn. Republican. Lutheran. Clubs: Lions, Masons, Shriners. Home: 1915 NE Hood Ct Gresham OR 97030 Office: 225 Burnside E Gresham OR 97030

HALVERSON, ROGER MICHAEL, ins. co. exec.; b. Manitowoc, Wis., May 3, 1940; s. Erwin Joseph and Wilma H.; B.S. in Econs., U. Wis., 1964; m. Deanna C. Durben, June 17, 1961; 1 son, Troy. Supr. checking dept. Allstate Ins. Co., Milw., 1965, supr. steno dept., 1965-66; asst. mgr. customer service Surg. Care Blue Shield, Milw., 1966-67, asst. mgr. Wis. Medicaid, 1967-68, mgr. Wis. Medicaid, 1968-70, mgr. Blue Shield claims, 1970-74, v.p. Blue Shield ops., 1974-77; asst. v.p., instl. benefits adminstr. Blue Cross and Blue Shield of Greater N.Y., 1977-80; v.p. claims and govt. programs Blue Cross of N.W. Ohio, Toledo, 1980—. Mem. Adminstrv. Mgmt. Soc. Home: 5843 Winslow Rd Whitehouse OH 43591 Office: Blue Cross of NW Ohio 3737 Sylvania Ave Toledo OH 43656

HALVERSTADT, ROBERT DALE, engr., mfg. co. exec.; b. Warren, Ohio, Jan. 25, 1920; s. Roscoe B. and Dorothy (Grubbs) H.; B.S. in Mech. Engring., Case Inst. Tech., 1951; m. Maryella Greene, Dec. 31, 1941; children—Marta Jean (Mrs. Michael Carmen), Linda Anne (Mrs. Gary Orelup), Sally Jo. Journeyman machinist Republic Steel Corp., Cleve., 1939-51; design engr. Gen. Electric Co., Evendale, Ohio, 1951-53; supr. Metalworking Lab., 1953-58, corporate cons., N.Y.C., 1958-59, mgr. Thomson Engring. Lab., Lynn, Mass., 1959-63; gen. mgr. engring. Continental Can Co., N.Y.C., 1963-64; group v.p. Booz, Allen & Hamilton Inc., N.Y.C., 1964-73, chief exec. Foster D. Snell Inc. subsidiary, 1964-72, pres. Design & Devel., Inc. subsidiary, 1966-70; v.p. tech. Singer Co., 1973-74; pres. Spl. Metals Corp., subsidiary Allegheny Ludlum Industries, Inc., New Hartford N.Y., 1974-81, pres. Materials Tech. Group, 1981—, mng. dir. Allegheny Ludlum Industries Ltd.; dir. Titanium Metals Corp. Am. Pres., Industry, Labor and Edn. Council Mohawk Valley, Inc. Served with USCGR, 1942-45. Registered profl. engr., N.Y., Ohio. Fellow Am. Soc. Metals; mem. ASME, Am. Inst. Chem. Engrs., Am. Ordnance Assn., Regional Plan Assn., Am. Water Resources Assn., N.Y. Acad. Scis., Mohawk Valley C. of C. (dir.), Chemists Club, Sigma Xi, Tau Beta Pi, Theta Tau. Mem. United Ch. of Christ. Clubs: Toastmasters; Yahnundasis Golf; University (N.Y.C.); Ft. Schuyler. Patentee in field. Home: 7 Old Willow Rd New Hartford NY 13413 Office: New Hartford NY 13413

HAMAI, JAMES YUTAKA, business exec.; b. Los Angeles, Oct. 14, 1926; s. Seizo and May (Sata) H.; B.S., U. So. Calif., 1952, M.S., 1955; postgrad. bus. mgmt. program industry exec., U. Calif., Los Angeles, 1963-64; m. Dorothy K. Fukuda, Sept. 10, 1954; 1 dau., Wendy A. Lectr. chem. engring. dept. U. So. Calif., Los Angeles, 1963-64; process engr., sr. process engr. Fluor Corp., Los Angeles, 1954-64; sr. project mgr. central research dept. Monsanto Co., St. Louis, 1964-67, mgr. research, devel. and engring. graphic systems dept., 1967-68, mgr. comml. devel. New Enterprise div., 1968-69; exec. v.p., dir. Concrete Cutting Industries, Inc., Los Angeles, 1969-72; pres., dir. Concrete Cutting Internat., Inc., Los Angeles, 1972—; cons. Fluor Corp., Los Angeles, 1972—; dir. Nippon Concrete Cutting Co. Ltd., Tokyo, Nippon Continental Drilling Co. Ltd., Tokyo, Dry Print Systems Co. Ltd., Tokyo; internat. bus. cons. Served with AUS, 1946-48. Mem. Am. Inst. Chem. Engrs., Am. Mgmt. Assn., Tau Beta Pi, Phi Lambda Upsilon. Club: Rotary. Home: 6600 Via La Paloma Rancho Palos Verdes CA 90274 Office: 20963 Lamberton Ave Long Beach CA 90810

HAMANN, JOHN RIAL, utilities exec.; b. Chgo., Jan. 1, 1915; s. Louis and Zoe (Rial) H.; B.S., Mich. State U., 1937; m. Lois Agnes Sherman, Aug. 6, 1938; children—Joan (Mrs. Terry Mountford), Rial, John, Steven. With Detroit Edison Co., 1937—, v.p., 1971-73, exec. v.p. ops., 1973-74, sr. exec. v.p. ops., 1975-79, pres., chief operating officer, 1975-79, vice chmn. bd., 1979—; dir. Midwest Energy Resources Co., Nat. Detroit Corp. Councilman, City of Grosse Pointe, 1967-71. Mem. Lawrence Inst. Tech. Served to lt. col. AUS, 1940-45. Registered profl. engr., Mich. Fellow ASME, Engring. Soc. Detroit; mem. Am. Nuclear Soc., Assn. Edison Illuminating Cos., Mich. Electric Assn. (pres. 1978), Edison Electric Assn. (dir.), Greater Detroit C. of C. (chmn. 1979), Mich. State U. Engring. Alumni Assn. (dir.). Clubs: Detroit Athletic; Lochmoor. Home: 441 Rivard Blvd Grosse Pointe MI 48230 Office: 2000 2d Ave Detroit MI 48226

HAMANO, MICHIYA, x-ray products mfg. co. exec.; b. Chiba, Japan, June 25, 1938; came to U.S., 1971; s. Yosuke and Chizue (Hori) H.; B.Polit. Sci., Waseda U., Tokyo, 1963; m. Hisako Shimizu, Apr. 5, 1965; 1 dau., Kumiko. With Japan Aviotronic Co., 1963-68, overseas dept. TEAC Corp., Tokyo, 1968-71; exec. asst. to pres. Teac Corp. Am., Los Angeles, 1972-74; asst. to pres. Rigaku Corp., Tokyo, 1974-76; treas. Rigaku/USA, Inc., Danvers, Mass., 1976—. Home: 6 Worthington Ave Danvers MA 01923 Office: 3 Electronics Ave Danvers MA 01923

HAMAR, RUDOLF, business exec.; b. Tartu, Estonia, Jan. 27, 1925; s. Rudolf and Marta (Ainson) H.; came to U.S., 1955, naturalized, 1960; grad. Am. Inst. of Banking, 1959; m. Ingrid Swars, July 1, 1950; children—Vaike R., Anja K. Bank clk. 1st Nat. City Bank, N.Y.C., 1955-59; loan officer Broad & Wall Corp., N.Y.C., 1960-61; stockbroker Gude, Winmill, Prescott, Merrill, Turben & Co., N.Y.C., 1962-74; pres. Wm. Sander Co., N.Y.C., Conn and N.J. 1974—, Auto Sound Specialists Inc., 1979—. Lutheran. Clubs: Sibelius Lodge, various Estonian organizations. Editor, collaborator in philatelic literature. Office: 12 Bi-State Plaza Old Tappan NJ 07675

HAMBLET, NEWMAN, retail chain co. exec.; b. Winchester, Mass., Aug. 20, 1914; s. Abel Martin and Marcia Leavitt (Coburn) H.; A.B., Dartmouth, 1935; m. Mae Catherine Moynahan, Jan. 17, 1942; children—Barbara, Carolyn, Janice, Kenneth, Doreen, Shirley. Sales clk., supr., mgmt. exec. Macy's Dept. Store, N.Y.C., 1935-48; selling service mgr. Bloomingdale's Dept. Store, N.Y.C., 1948-50; asst. gen. mgr. ops. Lord & Taylor, N.Y.C., 1950-54; v.p. Thalhimer Bros. Inc., Richmond, Va., 1954, then sr. v.p., now exec. v.p., also dir., dir. subsidiaries; dir. Met. Nat. Bank, 1966—, Golden Skillet Corp., Richmond, and subsidiaries. Mem. Richmond Downtown Devel. Commn., 1974—; sec.-treas. Met. Econ. Devel. Commn., 1977—; chmn. Unted Givers Fund, 1962; mem. Richmond City Planning Commn. Served to lt. comdr. USNR, 1942-45. Mem. Met. Richmond (chmn. 1976—), Va., U.S. chambers commerce, Nat. Retail Mchts. Assn. Republican. Presbyterian. Clubs: Kiwanis, Hermitage Country, Duck Woods Country (Kitty Hawk, N.C.); Commonwealth, Bull and Bear. Home: 11807 Sussex Square Dr Richmond VA 23233 Office: 601 E Broad St Richmond VA 23219

HAMBLETT, DAVID TARLTON, lighting co. exec.; b. Newport, Vt., June 30, 1946; s. Robert Horton and Joan Patricia Hamblett; A.A., Rochester Inst. Tech., 1966, B.A., 1968; m. Patricia June Walts, June 29, 1968; 1 son, Jonathan David. Graphic arts tech. rep., ter. mgr., tech. rep. E.I. DuPont, Inc., 1968-73; computer circuit tech. sales mgr., mgr. research and devel., prototype product mgr. Spectra Lighting Inc., Endicott, N.Y., 1973-75, pres., 1975—; distbr. and mfr. energy saving lighting devices, mfrs.' rep., pres. Hamblett Assos., Endicott, 1975—. Mem. Broome County Energy Council; indsl. ambassador of Broome Council; mem. solicitor and allocations com. United Way of Broome County; mem. Johnson City Econ. Adv. Bd.; bd. dirs. Broome County Indsl. Incubator Program. Home: 205 Groveland Ave Endwell NY 13760 Office: 43 Washington Ave Suite 202 Endicott NY 13760

HAMEL, LOUIS REGINALD, systems analysis cons.; b. Lowell, Mass., July 23, 1945; s. Wilfred John and Angelina Lucienne (Paradis) H.; A.A., Kellogg Community Coll., 1978; m. Roi Anne Roberts, Mar. 24, 1967 (dec.); 1 dau., Felicia Antoinette; m. 2d, Anne Louise Staup, July 2, 1972; 1 dau., Shawna Michelle. Retail mgr. Marshalls dept. Stores, Beverly, Mass., 1972-73; tech. service rep. Monarch Marking Systems, Framingham, Mass., 1973-74; employment specialist Dept. Labor, Battle Creek, Mich., 1977-78; v.p. corp. Keith Polygraph Cons. and Investigative Service, Inc., Battle Creek, Mich., 1978-79; systems analysis cons., 1975—. Mem. Calhoun County Com. on Employment of Handicapped, Battle Creek, Mich., 1977-78. Served with USN, 1963-71; Vietnam. Recipient Services to Handicapped award Internat. Assn. Personnel in Employment Security, Mich. chpt., 1978. Mem. Nat. Geog. Soc., Mich. Assn. Concerned Vets. (dir.), Nat. Assn. Concerned Vets. Democrat. Roman Catholic. Home and Office: 12240 Assyria Rd Bellevue MI 49021

HAMERNICK, RAPHAEL (RAY) HUBERT, stamp dealer; b. Little Falls, Minn., Nov. 2, 1925; s. John Cyril and Anna Mary H.; student public schs. Little Falls; m. Betty Mae Barrett, May 10, 1945; children—Lawrence, Daniel, Rebecca. Carpenter, contractor, until 1964; partner Hamernick Stamp Co., St. Paul, 1964-79, pres., owner, 1979—. Served with USN, WW II. Mem. Am. Stamp Dealers Assn. Twin City Stamp Dealers Assn., Trans Miss. Philatelic Soc., Maplewood Stamp Club, VFW, Am. Legion. Roman Catholic. Office: 522 Rice St St Paul MN 55103

HAMILTON, ALEXANDER DANILE, mfg. co. exec.; b. Montreal, Que., Can., Nov. 13, 1917; s. Daniel Evoy and Isobel (Stewart) H.; B.Engring., McGill U., 1940; m. Frances McLeod, Feb. 25, 1942; children—Sandra, Joanne, Stewart, Kirk, Alex. With Ont. Paper Co., Thorold, Can., 1946-55, asst. div. mgr., 1960-61; supt. Que. N. Shore Paper Co., Baie Comeau, 1955-60; v.p. B.C. Forest Products Ltd., Vancouver, Can., 1964-67, pres., chief exec. officer, 1967-68; pres. Domtar Pulp & Paper Products Ltd., Montreal, 1968-74, pres., chief exec. officer Domtar Inc., 1974—, also dir.; dir. Can. Imperial Bank of Commerce, Dominion Textile Inc., Drummond McCall & Co. Ltd., Total Petroleum (N.AM.) Ltd., Centraide. Bd. dirs. C.D. Howe Research Inst. Served with RCAF, 1941-45. Mentioned in dispatches. Bd. mgmt. Montreal Gen. Hosp.; mem. gov. body Trinity Coll. Sch.; bd. govs. McGill U., Conseil du Patronat du Que., Douglas Hosp. Corp., Jr. Achievement Que. Clubs: University, Mount Royal, Royal Montreal Golf, Montreal Indoor Tennis, Canadian, Laurentian Golf and Country (Montreal); Toronto, Coral Beach and Tennis. Office: Domtar Inc 395 de Maisonneuve St W Montreal PQ H3C 3M1 Canada

HAMILTON, ALLAN CORNING, oil co. exec.; b. Chgo., June 9, 1921; s. Daniel Sprague and Mildred (Corning) H.; B.S. in Econs., Haverford Coll., 1943; m. Edith Johnson, June 3, 1950; children—Kimball C., Scott W., Dean C., Gail W. With Standard Oil Co. (N.J.), 1946-51, Esso Export Corp., 1951-56; treas. Internat. Petroleum Co., Ltd., Coral Gables, Fla., 1956-61, Esso Internat. Inc., 1961-66; with Exxon Corp., 1966—, treas., prin. financial officer, 1970—. Mem. vis. com. U. Chgo. Sch. Bus.; mem. council Inst. Adminstrn. and Mgmt., Union Coll. Served to lt. (j.g.) USNR, 1943-46. Clubs: Explorers, Woodway Country. Office: Exxon Bldg New York NY 10020*

HAMILTON, ARTHUR THOMAS, mfg. co. exec.; b. N.Y.C., Dec. 18, 1947; s. Thomas R. and Margaret G. (Greco) H.; B.S.E.E., M.I.T., 1969; m. Henrietta Jalbert, Aug. 23, 1969; children—Stacey, Lynn, Cheryl Gayle. Engr., Honeywell Info. Systems, Framingham, Mass., 1969-72; chief engr. Applied Magnetics Corp.-Okidata Corp., Santa Barbara, Calif., 1972-76; sales mgr. Xebec Systems, Santa Clara, Calif., 1976-78; product mktg. mgr. Nat. Semicondr., Santa Clara, 1978-79; product mgr. Okidata Corp., Santa Barbara, 1979—; chief fin. officer, dir. Bonanza Seed, Gilroy, Calif., 1978—. Mem. IEEE. Republican. Lutheran. Home and office: 7223 Shea Ct San Jose CA 95139

HAMILTON, EARL HADEN, JR., bank exec.; b. Rock Hill, S.C., May 31, 1942; s. Earl Haden and Frances (Ford) H.; B.B.A., Wake Forest U., 1964; m. Brenda Jean Hewitt, Nov. 14, 1964; children—Alison Jean, Stephanie Ann. Quality control supr. Burlington Industries, High Point, N.C., 1965-67; asst. v.p. First Union Nat. Bank, Charlotte, N.C., 1967-73; v.p. Security Bank & Trust Co., Monroe, N.C., 1973; pres., chief exec. officer Bank of Isle of Wight, Smithfield, Va., 1973—. Mem. Smithfield C. of C. (pres. 1977, 78), Va. Bankers Assn., Am. Bankers Assn., Ind. Bankers Assn. Va., Bank Mktg. Assn. Clubs: Rotary, Ruritan. Office: PO Box 429 Smithfield VA 23430

HAMILTON, ELIZABETH VERNER, publisher; b. Charleston, S.C., Nov. 24, 1908; d. Ebenezer Pettigrew and Elizabeth Quayle (O'Neill) Verner; A.B., Coll. Charleston, 1930; postgrad. U. N.C. Sch. Library Sci., U. Philippines Sch. Library Sci.; m. John A. Hamilton, Aug. 29, 1931; children—Andrew, David, Ward, Pettigrew. Pres. Tradd St. Press, Charleston, 1966—. Bd. dirs. Home Health Nursing Charleston. Mem. Charleston Jr. League, Ladies Benevolent Soc. Democrat. Episcopalian. Author: (poetry) Tall Houses, 1968; (fiction) When Walls Are High, 1972. Home: 38 Tradd St Charleston SC 29401 Office: 38 Tradd St Charleston SC 29401

HAMILTON, JAMES S., banker; b. Moundsville, W.Va., Feb. 7, 1942; s. Woodrow Wilson and Ruby Glea (Roberts) H.; B.S., Ohio State U., 1965; postgrad. U. Pitts., 1966-67, Sch. Internat. Banking, 1972, Grad. Sch. Banking, 1977-79; m. Mary Margaret Wiedle, Sept. 12, 1964; children—Michael James, Rebecca Marie. Mgmt. trainee Pitts. Nat. Bank, 1965-69; with Equibank, 1969—, asst. v.p. regional banking, Pitts., 1971-77, v.p., mgr. fin. instns. group, 1977—. Bd. dirs. Golden Triangle YMCA, 1976—, Youth Guidance, Inc., 1970; treas. Franklin Twp. Mcpl. San. Authority, 1976-81. Mem. Pa. Bankers Assn. (sec. group 8), Ohio State U. Alumni Assn., Pitts. Econ. Club. Presbyterian. Club: Oakmont Country. Home: 3643 Sardis Rd Murrysville PA 15668 Office: 2 Oliver Plaza Pittsburgh PA 15222

HAMILTON, JOSEPH HEBERLING, textile co. exec.; b. Iowa City, Aug. 8, 1920; s. Clair E. and Prudence M. (Heberling) H.; B.A., Harvard U., 1946, M.B.A., 1948; m. Joan Van Gonsic, Oct. 8, 1952; children—Holly Heberling, Joseph Jeffrey. Asst. to chmn. bd. Burlington Industries, Greensboro, N.C., 1948-55; pres. Burlington

Throwing Co., High Point, N.C., 1955-60; v.p. Madison Throwing Co. (N.C.), 1960-63; founder Textured Fibres, Inc. (name changed to Texfi Industries Inc. 1969), Greensboro, 1963, now chmn., chief exec. officer. Served to lt. USNR, 1942-45. Episcopalian. Home: 617 Blair St Greensboro NC 27408 Office: 1400 Battleground Ave Greensboro NC 27420

HAMILTON, LYMAN CRITCHFIELD, JR., diversified co. exec.; b. Los Angeles, Aug. 29, 1926; s. Lyman Critchfield and Lorraine (Gluck) H.; B.A., Principia Coll., Elsah, Ill., 1947; student U. Redlands, 1944-45; M.P.A., Harvard U., 1949; m. Mary Shepard, June 25, 1949; children—William, Richard, Douglas, David. With Bur. Budget, 1950-56, U.S. Civil Adminstrn. of Ryukyu Islands, 1956-60, IBRD, also Internat. Fin. Corp., 1960-62; with ITT, 1962-80, treas., 1967-76, v.p., 1968-73, sr. v.p., 1973-74, exec. v.p., 1974-77, pres., 1977-79, chief operating officer, 1977, chief exec., 1978-79, also officer, dir. affiliated cos.; chmn., pres. Tamco Enterprises Inc., N.Y.C., 1980—; dir. Eur-Am Banking Corp., St. Joe Minerals Corp., Equitable Life Mortgage & Realty Investors, Central Bancorp., Inc., C.C.B., Inc., Eur-Am Bank and Trust Co. Mem. vis. com. John F. Kennedy Sch. Govt., Harvard U. Served to ensign USNR, 1944-46. Office: Tamco Enterprises Inc 645 Fifth Ave New York NY 10019

HAMILTON, MABEL ESTELLE, banker; b. Clinton, Mass., Sept. 15, 1922; d. Newman James and Jennie Hamilton; student McGill U., Montreal, Que., Can., 1939-41; grad. Sch. Banking, Williams Coll., 1967. With Shawmut Bank Boston, 1942-76; pres., chief exec. officer Conn. Women's Bank, Greenwich, 1976—. Bd. dirs., mem. allocations com. United Way Greenwich; bd. dirs., v.p. fin. Greenwich Philharmonia; exec. bd. Greenwich council Boy Scouts Am.; fin. com. Greenwich YWCA. Mem. Nat. Assn. Bank Women, Am. Bankers Assn., Am. Mgmt. Assn., Conn. Bankers Assn., Gamma Phi Beta, Beta Gamma Sigma (hon.). Congregationalist. Office: 100 Mason St Greenwich CT 06830

HAMILTON, MILO CHARLES, newsletter pub.; b. Columbia, Mo., June 4, 1945; s. Milo Fowler and Katherine (Miller) H.; B.A., Stanford U., 1967; B.S. cum laude, U. Mo., 1974; M.S., U. Minn., 1976; m. Janice Auwaerter, Mar. 3, 1973; children—Laura Jennifer, Renee Christine, Scott Matthew. Farm mgr. Green Top Farms Inc., Richmond, Mo., 1972; research asst. agrl. econs. U. Minn., St. Paul, 1974-76; mng. editor Commodities mag., also editor Commodities Report, Cedar Falls, Iowa, 1976-80; futures portfolio advisor, editor, pub. Center for Futures Edn. and asso. dir., sr. partner Futures Portfolio Index Services, Cedar Falls, 1980—; cons. Served with U.S. Army, 1969-72. Mem. Stanford Alumni Orgn., Internat. Fin. Futures Assn., Acad. Polit. Sci., Rate Watchers. Democrat. Rotarian. Author: Multiply Your Profits Through Commodity Speculation, 1979. Asso. editor Pro Farmer, Corn Pro, Pork Pro, Soybean Profits, Soybean Digest, 1976-80. Home: 2520 Alameda St Cedar Falls IA 50613 Office: PO Box 849 Cedar Falls IA 50613

HAMILTON, MUNROE HORACE, lawyer; b. Cumberland, Maine, Apr. 2, 1906; s. Horace Bradford and Marion (Lockwood) H.; B.Chem. Engring., Northeastern U., 1931; LL.B., Boston U., 1945, LL.D., 1979; m. Mary Adelaide, Nov. 25, 1939; children—John, William, David. Admitted to Mass. bar, 1945, U.S. Supreme Ct. bar, 1980; individual practice law, Boston, 1933-76; sr. mem. firm Hamilton, Brook, Smith & Reynolds, Lexington, Mass., 1976—; pres. Long Reach Mountain Corp., 1967—. Home: 66 Robbins Rd Lexington MA 02173

HAMILTON, RICHARD, advt. exec.; b. N.Y.C., June 11, 1938; s. Harry and Constance (Doucet) H.; student Art Students League, 1956-58; m. Noreen Cribbin, Oct. 7, 1961; children—Mark, Ann, Eve. Boardman, Planet Art Service, N.Y.C., 1956-58; boardman to sr. art dir. Maxwell Sackheim Advt., N.Y.C., 1958-65; art dir. Rapp & Collins Advt., N.Y.C., 1965-66; sr. art dir. Franklin & Joseph, Inc., N.Y.C., 1966-70; owner, operator advt. art service, 1970—; profl. photographer, illustrator. Mem. Soc. Illustrators, Graphic Artist Guild. Photog. illustrator, designer, photographer nat. advertisers. Home and Office: 139 Beach 91st St Rockaway Beach NY 11693

HAMILTON, ROBERT APPLEBY, JR., ins. co. exec.; b. Boston, Feb. 20, 1940; s. Robert A. and Alice Margaret (Dowdall) H.; B.S. in Mktg. and Fin., Miami U. (Ohio), 1962; m. Ellen Kuhlen, Aug. 13, 1966; children—Jennifer, Robert Appleby, III, Elizabeth. With Travelers Ins. Co., Hartford, Conn., Portland, Maine and Phila., 1962-65; with New Eng. Mut. Life Ins. Co., various locations, 1965—, regional rep., Boston, 1968-71, Midwest regional mgr., Chgo., 1972—. Mem. Republican Town Com., Wenham, Mass., 1970-72, Milton Twp., Ill., 1973-75; mem. Wenham Water Commn., 1970-72. C.L.U. Mem. Midwest Pension Conf., Chgo. Council Fgn. Relations, Am. Soc. Pension Actuaries (asso.), Am. Soc. C.L.U., Alpha Epsilon Rho. Republican. Club: Essex (sec. 1971-72). Home: 2 S 110 Hamilton Ct Wheaton IL 60187 Office: 10 S Riverside Plaza Chicago IL 60606

HAMILTON, STANLEY WILLIAM, assn. exec.; b. Grand Island, Nebr., Jan. 13, 1934; s. Robert Wylie and Margaret Olive (Stanley) H.; B.S., U. Kans., 1955; m. Frances Anne Webster, Mar. 9, 1974; children—Susan, Robert, Jennifer, Arthur. Copy editor Kansas City (Mo.) Star, 1955-57; Congl. editor Traffic World, Washington, 1957-67; dir. publs. Dept. Transp., Washington, 1967; dir. public affairs Am. Bus Assn., Washington, 1968-76; exec. dir. Common Carrier Conf.-Irregular Route, Washington, 1976—. Dir., Transp. Vols. for Nixon-Agnew, 1968; mem. Nat. Democratic Club. Mem. Sigma Delta Chi. Clubs: Capitol Hill, Nat. Press; Internat. (Washington). Republican. Presbyterian. Home: 2240 Cathedral St NW Washington DC 20008 Office: Common Carrier Conf-Irregular Route 1616 P St NW Washington DC 20036

HAMILTON, WILLIAM VICTOR, strategic planning and govt. relations cons.; b. Terre Haute, Ind., May 17, 1931; s. Clyde Abraham and Helen Elizabeth (Camp) H.; B.S. in Bus. and Econs., U. Nebr., Omaha, 1961; M.B.A., George Washington U., 1973; m. Betty Lou Haynes, Dec. 4, 1955; children—Kimberly, Mark Haynes. Commd. 2d lt., U.S. Air Force, 1951, advanced through grades to maj., 1967; ret., 1971; asst. to pres. Morris Cafritz Hosp., Washington, 1972-73; sr. cons. LMC, Inc., Washington, 1973-75; partner Polaris Data Systems, Arlington, Va., 1975; cons. hosp. planning, Washington, 1975-77; sr. cons. govt. mktg. Blue Shield Assn., Washington, 1977-78; govt. relations cons. Optimum Systems, Inc., Washington, 1978-79; pres. W.V. Hamilton & Assos., Arlington, 1980—; treas. AMC, Inc. Vol. John Connally for Pres. Nat. Hdqrs., 1980. Decorated Air Force Commendation medal. Mem. Am. Mktg. Assn., Am. Coll. Hosp. Adminstrs., Hosp. Fin. Mgmt. Assn. Unitarian. Club: George Washington U. Home: 3430 N Randolph St Arlington VA 22207

HAMISTER, DONALD BRUCE, electronics co. exec.; b. Cleve., Nov. 29, 1920; s. Victor Carl and Bess Irene (Sutherland) H.; A.B. cum laude, Kenyon Coll., 1947; postgrad. Stanford U. 1948-49, U. Chgo., 1957; m. Margaret Irene Singiser, Dec. 22, 1946; children—Don Bruce, Tracy. Application engr. S.E. Joslyn Co., Cin., 1947-48; regional sales mgr. Joslyn Mfg. & Supply Co., St. Louis, 1950-52, mktg. mgr., Chgo., 1953-55, asst. to pres., 1956-57, mgr. aircraft arrester dept., 1958-62, gen. mgr. electronic systems div., 1962-71, v.p., gen. mgr., dir., Goleta Calif., 1973-78, group v.p. indsl. products, 1974-78, pres., chief exec. officer, 1978—, chmn. bd., 1979—; dir. Porcelanas Pinco, Mex., Joslyn Can. Industries Ltd., Little, Haugland and Kerr Ltd., Can. Served to lt. USNR, 1942-46. Mem. IEEE, Airline Avionics Inst. (pres., chmn. 1972-74). Club: Univ. (Chgo.). Home: 1141 Camino Del Rio Santa Barbara CA 93110 Office: PO Box 817 Coleta CA 93017

HAMLET, KENNETH B., hotel co. exec.; b. N.Y.C., May 24, 1944; s. Henry K. and Hilde S. H.; B.S., Cornell U.; postgrad. Boston U.; m. Linda Jensen, June 1967; children—Channing, Brendan. Sr. v.p. hotel group, Holiday Inns, Inc., Memphis, 1975—. Mem. Chaine des Rotissieurs, les Amies D'Escoffier. Club: Skal. Office: Holiday Inns of Am 3742 Lamar Ave Memphis TN 38118

HAMM, CHARLES JOHN, advt. co. exec.; b. Bklyn., May 11, 1937; s. Frank Coleman and Lisbeth (Higgins) H.; B.A., Harvard, 1959, M.B.A., N.Y. U., 1965; m. Irene M. Frail, Aug. 14, 1960; children—Charles William, Liza Higgins. Advt. account mgr. Benton & Bowles, Inc., N.Y.C., 1961-67; mgmt. supv., Wells, Rich, Greene & Co., Inc., N.Y.C., 1967-74; sr. v.p. Foote, Cone & Belding, Inc., N.Y.C., 1974-75; pres. chief operating officer F. William Free & Co., Inc., N.Y.C., 1975-77; exec. v.p. Worldwide, dir. McCann-Erickson, Inc., N.Y.C., 1977-79, vice chmn. McCann-Erickson, U.S.A., 1979—; trustee Independence Savs. Bank, N.Y.C., 1975—; adviser 4 to Go Publ. Co., N.Y.C., 1974—. Bd. dirs. United Way, Bronxville, Eastchester, Tuckahoe, N.Y., 1971-74; gov. Childrens Service and Adoption Agency, Westchester, N.Y., 1974-75. Served to 1st lt. U.S. Army, 1959-61. Clubs: University, Bronxville Field, Mason's Island Yacht, Mashomak Fish and Game Preserve. Home: 6125 River Chase Circle Atlanta GA 30328 Office: 615 Peachtree St NE Atlanta GA 30308

HAMM, DONALD EDWARD, banker; b. Poplar Bluff, Mo., Nov. 25, 1930; s. Samuel Gilbert and Myrtle Frances (Haley) H.; student U. Wis., 1964; m. Irene Ruth Gaebler, Nov. 25, 1950; children—Brenda Irene, Steven Douglas. With Commerce Bank, Poplar Bluff, 1950—, pres., 1973—, also dir. Pres., Poplar Bluff (Mo.) Industries, 1970; chmn. bd. dirs. Drs. Hosp.; bd. dirs. Blue Cross. Served with USNR, 1948-50. Recipient Distinguished Service award Jr. C. of C., 1964. Mem. Mo. C. of C. (dir. 1974—). Lutheran (elder 1973). Lion. Home: 1415 Sylvan Dr Poplar Bluff MO 63901 Office: 101 S Main St Poplar Bluff MO 63901

HAMMER, ARMAND, petroleum co. exec.; b. N.Y.C., May 21, 1898; s. Julius and Rose (Robinson) H.; B.S., Columbia U., 1919, M.D., 1921; LL.D. (hon.), Pepperdine U., 1978, Southeastern U., Washington, 1978; m. Olga von Root, Mar. 14, 1927; 1 son, Julian A.; m. 2d, Angela Zevely, Dec. 19, 1943; m. 3d, Frances Barrett, Jan. 26, 1956. Pres., Allied Am. Corp., N.Y.C., 1923-25, A. Hammer Pencil Co., N.Y.C. and London, 1925-30, Hammer Galleries, N.Y.C., 1930—, United Distillers Am., Inc., N.Y.C. and J.W. Dant Distilling Co., N.Y.C. and Dant, Ky., 1943-54; chmn. bd., pres., chief exec. officer Occidental Petroleum Corp., Los Angeles, 1957—; pres., chmn. bd. MBS; co-owner Knoedler and Co., N.Y.C., 1971—; dir. First Bank & Trust Co., Perth Amboy, N.J., City Nat. Bank, Beverly Hills, Calif., Canadian Occidental Petroleum Ltd., Calgary, Alta., Belgische Petroleum Raffinaderij N. V. (RBP), Antwerp, Belgium; hon. dir. Fla. Nat. Bank, Jacksonville. Mem. Pres. Truman's Citizen's Food Com., 1945-47; chmn. Am. Aid to France, 1947; mem. Adv. Bd. Inst. Peace, 1950-54; mem. Com. of Laity for Catholic Charities, 1946-48; bd. govs. Monmouth Hosp.; bd. govs. MCOSS-Family Health and Nursing, 1949-61; patron mem. Am. Soc. of French Legion of Honor, 1978; exec. mem. Energy Research and Edn. Found., 1978; charter mem. Nat. Vis. Council of Health Scis. Faculties, 1978; bd. govs. Eleanor Roosevelt Cancer Found., Eleanor Roosevelt Meml. Found.; mem. Adv. Com. on U.S. Trade Policy, 1968; trustee U. N.Africa Assn.; mem. exec. com. Los Angeles Econ. Devel. Bd., 1968—, mem. adv. com. Com. for Greater Calif., from 1969; donor Armand Hammer Center for Cancer Biology, The Salk Inst., 1969; mem. Los Angeles Bd. Municipal Art Commrs.; mem. adv. bd. Los Angeles Beautiful, Inc., from 1969; bd. dirs. Los Angeles World Affairs Council; founder mem. Los Angeles Music Center, 1969—; trustee, chmn. exec. com. Salk Inst. Biol. Studies, 1969; mem. vis. com. U. Calif. at Los Angeles, from 1947; trustee, exec. com., acquisition com. Los Angeles County Mus. Art; trustee U. Calif. at Los Angeles Found., from 1973; bd. govs. Ford's Theatre Soc., from 1970; bd. dirs. U.S.-USSR Trade and Econ. Council, from 1973; mem. Americana com. Nat. Archives, from 1974; trustee Nat. Symphony, from 1977; mem. nat. fin. council Democratic Nat. Com., 1977; mem. adv. com. Fogg Art Mus. and Fine Arts Library, 1977, The Friendship Force, 1977; trustee United for Calif., 1977; pres., founder Internat. Inst. Rights of Man, Geneva, 1977. Decorated comdr. Order of Crown (Belgium), 1969; Spl. award Los Angeles Econ. Devel. Bd., 1969; comdr. Order of Andres Bellos (Venezuela), 1975; Humanitarian award Eleanor Roosevelt Cancer Found., 1962; commendation Mayor Los Angeles, 1968; Aztec Eagle award, 1977; Distinguished Honoree of Year, Nat. Art Assn., 1978; Order of Friendship Among Peoples, USSR, 1978. Mem. Royal Acad. Arts (London) (hon. corr.), Asn. Harvard Bus. Sch. (dir. 1975—), Am. Petroleum Inst. (dir. 1975—), Calif. Roundtable (dir. 1976—), Pepperdine Assos., UN Assn. U.S.A. (bd. govs. 1976—), Calif. Gas Producers Assn. (pres. 1961—), AMA, N.Y. County Med. Soc., Alpha Omega Alpha, Mu Sigma, Phi Sigma Delta. Club: Los Angeles Petroleum. Author: Quest of the Romanoff Treasure; subject of two biographies. Office: 10889 Wilshire Blvd Los Angeles CA*

HAMMER, GUY SAINT CLAIR, II, elec. and biomed. engr.; b. Elkins, W.Va., Oct. 3, 1943; s. Guy Saint Clair and Ethyl Marie (Miller) H.; B.S. with high honors in Elec. Engring., U. Md., 1974; postgrad. Johns Hopkins U. Med. Sch., 1975-80; m. Jean Heather Weir, Dec. 29, 1976; children—Jennifer, Guy III, Thomas. Math. aid U.S. Weather Bur., 1963-64; pres. Instant Rain, Inc., 1964-66; research staff mem. elec. engring. dept. U. Md., College Park, 1970-72; cons. Hammer Electronics, Greenbelt, Md., 1972-74; cons. clin. engr. VA Hosp., Washington, 1973-78; mgr. tech. devel. Assn. for Advancement of Med. Instrumentation, Arlington, Va., 1975-78; dir. biomed. engring. dept. Washington Hosp. Center, 1978-80, cons. engr., 1980—; lectr. elec. engring. dept. U. Md.; cons. Georgetown U. Hosp., 1978. Organizer Washington Monument Laser Light Show for Bicentennial, 1976; judge Washington Soc. Engrs. Engring. Fair, 1976. Served with U.S. Army, 1966-69. Recipient Outstanding Achievement award, Biomed. apprenticeship U. of Md., 1974, Nat. Capital Outstanding Young Engr. award, 1979. Fellow Washington Acad. Sci.; mem. IEEE (sr.), Engring. in Medicine and Biology Soc., Nat., D.C. socs. profl. engrs., Standards Engrs. Soc. (certificate of appreciation 1976), Assn. for Advancement Med. Instrumentation, Nat. Inst. Technol. Art (pres. 1976), Wash. Soc. Engrs. (pres. 1979), D.C. Council Engring. and Archtl. Socs. (sec. 1980), Phi Kappa Phi, Tau Beta Pi, Eta Kappa Nu. Roman Catholic. Tech. editor Med. Instrumentation, 1975-78; staff contbr. Standards Engring., 1975-78; contbr. articles to profl. jours., chpts. to books. Home and office: 8902 Ewing Dr Bethesda MD 20034

HAMMER, HAROLD HARLAN, oil co. exec.; b. Chgo., May 23, 1920; s. B. James and Frances (Halbren) H.; B.S., Nortwestern U., 1941; M.B.A., N.Y. U., 1950, J.D., 1955; m. Hannah Richmond, Mar. 1, 1956; children—John, Elizabeth. Accountant, U.S. Steel Corp., 1941-42; asst. sec.-treas. Duraloy Co., Scottdale, Pa., 1945-48; financial analyst, asst. controller Port of N.Y. Authority, 1948-50; investment counsel, N.Y.C., 1950—; admitted to N.Y. State bar, 1955, since practiced in N.Y.C.; v.p. finance, dir. Control Data Corp., Mpls., 1966-72; chmn. finance com., dir. Gen. Refractories Co., 1963-66; with Gulf Oil Corp., Pitts., 1972—, sr. v.p., 1972-73, exec. v.p., 1973—; dir., 1979—, also mem. corp. sr. exec. com.; dir. Northwestern Nat. Bank, Foxboro Corp., Data 100 Corp., North Central Cos., LaSalle Steel Co.; bd. govs. Midwest Stock Exchange. Bd. dirs. Northwestern Hosp., Western Pa. Hosp., Jr. Achievement of Western Pa. Served as lt. USNR, World War II. Mem. Am. Bar Assn., N.Y. State Bar Assn., Fin. Analysts Fedn., N.Y. Soc. Security Analysts, Fin. Execs. Inst., V.F.W., Am. Legion, Phi Alpha Delta. Methodist. Clubs: Duquesne, Fox Chapel Golf, Pitts. Golf, Univ. (Pitts.); Laurel Valley Golf, Coral Beach and Tennis, Hillsboro. Author: Financing the Port of New York Authority, 1957; also articles in field. Office: PO Box 1166 Pittsburgh PA 15230

HAMMER, ROBERT EARL, drill mfg. co. exec.; b. Chgo., Sept. 27, 1914; s. Ben and Frances (Halperin) H.; B.A.B.A., Northwestern U., 1940; m. Marjorie Colef, Aug. 10, 1940; children—Mark, Suzanne, Jeff. Acct., Chgo.-Latrobe Drill Co., 1934-40; asst. chmn. bd. Avildsen Tools Co., Chgo., 1940-49; founder, chmn. bd. N.Y. Twist Drills Co., Melville, N.Y., 1949—. Bd. dirs. Guttman Inst. Breast Cancer Research, N.Y.C. Club: Longboat Key Tennis (Sarasota, Fla.). Office: NY Twist Drill Co 25 Melville Park Rd Melville NY 11747

HAMMERLUND, NORMA JEAN, hotel exec.; b. Mobile, Sept. 16, 1942; d. James Gilbert and Mary Jo (McSwain) Barber; student Kilgore (Tex.) Jr. Coll., 1961-62, So. Methodist U., nights 1973-74. Various secretarial and clerical positions; purchasing agt. Crow Hotel Devel. Co., div. Dallas Market Center, 1971—. Recipient various certs. of achievement. Republican. Roman Catholic. Home: 3201 High Plateau Garland TX 75042 Office: 2050 Stemmons Freeway Dallas TX 75207

HAMMETT, EARL DONALD, foundry co. exec.; b. St. Louis, Jan. 31, 1928; s. Earl Falkner and Pearl Irene (Schlief) H.; student Marquette U., 1945-46, Stanford U., 1949-51; m. Mary Celeste Marcy, Sept. 15, 1956; children—Elizabeth Anne, Michael Frederick, David Kevin. Long-distance trucker, 1951-54; sales mgr. Wertch Motor Co., Oshkosh, Wis., 1954-56; gen. mgr. Community Motors, La Crosse, Wis., 1956-59; sales mgr. Watry Industries Inc., Sheboygan, Wis., 1959-62, v.p., 1962-71, pres., 1971—, also dir.; cons. to permanent mold foundry industry. Bd. dirs. Sheboygan Community Players, 1972-77, pres., 1974-76. Served with U.S. Army, 1946-48. Mem. Am. Soc. Metals, Am. Foundryman's Soc., Nat. Foundryman's Soc., Asso. Industry and Mfrs., U.S. C. of C., Wis. Conservation Assn. (affiliate). Republican. Episcopalian. Club: Elks. Home: Route 2 Box 5610 Oosburg WI 53070 Office: Watry Industries Inc 3312 Lakeshore Dr Sheboygan WI 53081

HAMMITT, JOHN MICHAEL, data processing mgr.; b. Chgo., Sept. 21, 1943; s. John Melvin and Catherine (Ivanuski) H.; B.S. in Chem. Engring., Ill. Inst. Tech., 1970; M.B.A., U. Chgo., 1976; m. Kathryn Logan, Sept. 9, 1972. Engring. and research technician Moffett Research Lab., CPC Internat., 1962-67, mgr. process control computer Argo plant, 1968-70; sr. systems analyst Morton-Norwich Products, Inc., Chgo., 1970-72, mgr. corp. info. services, 1972-79, dir. corp. info. services, 1979-81, dir. info. mgmt., 1981—; cons. use of computers in lab. automation, 1968-71. Mem. Am. Inst. Chem. Engrs., Soc. Mgmt. Info. Systems, Chgo. Council Fgn. Relations, Chgo. Geog. Soc., Phi Theta Kappa. Clubs: Young Execs., Union League. (Chgo.). Home: 10 Valdon Rd Rural Route 1 Mundelein IL 60060 Office: 110 N Wacker Dr Chicago IL 60606

HAMMOND, GEORGE, pub. relations co. exec.; b. Bklyn., Nov. 29, 1907; s. William G. and Sara (Ragan) H.; A.B. (Pulitzer scholar), Columbia, 1928; m. Genevieve Nelson, Oct. 19, 1933; children—Wendy (Mrs. Jasper M. Evarts), Victoria Craigie (Mrs. Richard L. Bell). With editorial dept. N.Y. Sun, 1924-35; with Carl Byoir & Assos., Inc., N.Y.C., 1932—, chmn. bd., 1965—. Bd. dirs. George Jr. Republic. Recipient Am. Acad. Achievement award, 1973. Mem. Pub. Relations Soc. Am., Internat. Pub. Relations Assn. Office: 380 Madison Ave New York NY 10017*

HAMMOND, LEE CUSTER, mfg. co. exec.; b. Bristol, Pa., Aug. 19, 1910; s. W. Custer and Mabel E. (Lee) H.; A.B., U. Mich., 1932; m. Hazel M. Hinga, Aug. 25, 1934; children—Steven L., Robert E. Vice pres. Hammond Machinery, Inc., Kalamazoo, 1932-41, pres., 1941—; dir. Am. Nat. Bank & Trust Co., Am. Nat. Holding Co. (both Kalamazoo). Co-trustee Hammond Found.; past trustee Bronson Methodist Hosp., Kalamazoo. Mem. Kalamazoo C. of C.

HAMMOND, STUART LINDSLEY, pub. co. exec.; b. Orange, N.J., May 6, 1922; s. Caleb Dean and Alice (Lindsley) H.; B.A., Lehigh U., 1944; m. Doris Fitchette, Apr. 6, 1946; children—Gail, Jean, Dana, Katherine Brooke. With Hammond, Inc., Maplewood, N.J., 1946—, v.p., 1958-61, exec. v.p., 1961-67, pres., 1967-76, pres., chief exec. officer, 1976—. Served to 1st lt. USAAF, 1943-45. Decorated Air medal. Mem. Assn. Am. Publishers, C. of C. (dir.). Republican. Office: Hammond Inc 515 Valley St Maplewood NJ 07040

HAMPTON, CLYDE ROBERT, lawyer, oil co. exec.; b. Worland, Wyo., May 10, 1926; s. Clyde E. and Mabel (Lasley) H.; B.A., Columbia U., 1949; LL.B., U. Colo., 1952; m. Dorothy Laura Gaebelein, June 3, 1949; 1 dau., Dorothy Norma. Admitted to Colo. bar, 1952; oil and gas atty., sr. counsel legal dept. Continental Oil Co., Denver, 1952-69, counsel, 1969-77, sr. counsel, 1977—; lectr. on environ. legal concerns. Chmn. adv. com. on rules and regulations Com. on Air and Water Conservation Am. Petroleum Inst.; chmn. Colo. Air and Water Conservation Com. Colo. Petroleum Council. Bd. dirs., past pres. Colo., Denver assns. for retarded citizens; bd. dirs. Denver Bapt. Sem.; chmn. bd. Denver Bd. for Mentally Retarded and Seriously Handicapped. Served as capt. USNR. Recipient Distinguished Service award Colo. Petroleum Council, 1966, 68, 70. Mem. Am. Petroleum Council (Leadership award 1969), Am. (chmn.-elect natural resources sect.), Denver, Colo. bar assns., Rocky Mountain Oil and Gas Assn., Sigma Chi, Phi Alpha Delta. Republican. Clubs: Columbia Alumni of Colo.; Law, Petroleum (Denver). Author: Oil Industry and Environmental Concerns in the Rocky Mountain Region, 1970. Co-author legal handbook. Contbr. articles to profl. jours. Home: 14830 E Jefferson Ave Aurora CO 80014 Office: 555 17th St Denver CO 80202

HAMPTON, PHILIP MICHAEL, civil engr.; b. Asheville, N.C., Sept. 5, 1932; s. Boyd Walker and Helen Reba Hampton; A.B., Berea (Ky.) Coll., 1954; m. Chris Coross, July 7, 1951; children—Philip Michael, Deborah Lynn, Greg Ashley. With Johnson & Anderson, Inc., Pontiac, Mich., 1955-76, exec. v.p., 1974-76; v.p. Spalding-Decker & Assos., Inc., Madison Heights, Mich., 1976—, Jaylen Internat., 1971-73; co-founder, 1976, since owner My World Shops, Madison Heights, Hampton-Tvedten Galleries, Ltd., Madison Heights; pres. HMA Cons. Inc., 1977; mem. public adv. panel GSA, 1977. Pres. Waterford (Mich.) Bd. Edn., 1969-71; mem. resolutions com. Mich. Democratic Party Conv., 1974; trustee Environ. Research Assos., 1970—, pres., 1971-73. Fellow Am. Cons. Engrs. Council (chmn. coms.); mem. Nat. Water Well Assn. (chmn. tech. div. 1969-71), Am. Arbitration Assn. Club: Detroit Lions Quarterback (co-founder, sec. 1975-77). Office: 655 W 13 Mile Rd Madison Heights MI 48071

HAMPTON-KAUFFMAN, MARGARET FRANCES, banker; b. Gainesville, Fla., May 12, 1947; d. William Wade and Carol Dorothy (Maples) Hampton; B.A. summa cum laude with honors, Fla. State U., 1969; student U. Nice (France), summer 1969; M.B.A., Columbia U., 1974; m. Kenneth L. Kauffman, May 12, 1973. Bd. govs. Fed. Res. System, Washington, 1974-75; asst. v.p., banking industry specialist, corp. fin. dept. Mfrs. Hanover Trust Co., N.Y.C., 1975-76; v.p., dir. corp. planning and research, sec. asset and liability mgmt. and strategic planning coms. Nat. Bank Ga., Atlanta, 1976—; dir. Accent Enterprises, Inc., Atlanta; guest lectr. Ga. Inst. Tech.; dir. TOMAK, Inc., Atlanta; bus. adv. Accent in Tango Restaurant, Atlanta. Comptroller, Angel Flight, 1967-68, liaison officer, 1966-67, del. area and nat. conclaves, 1966-68; trustee Ga. chpt. Leukemia Found.; mem. Atlanta Women's Forum. Alcoa Found. fellow, 1973; Dorothy Shaw Leadership award finalist. Mem. Planning Execs. Inst., Inst. Mgmt. Scis., Am. Inst. Banking, Inst. Fin. Edn., Am. Fin. Assn., Phi Beta Kappa, Beta Gamma Sigma, Mortar Board, Garnet Key, Phi Kappa Phi, Alpha Lambda Delta, Pi Delta Phi (v.p.), Alliance Française, Alpha Delta Pi (exec. bd., efficiency chmn., scholarship chmn.), Kappa Sigma (treas. Little Sisters, pres., snow ball queen). Democrat. Episcopalian. Home: Atlanta GA Office: 34 Peachtree St Atlanta GA 30301

HAMRA, SAM FARRIS, JR., lawyer, food service co. exec.; b. Steele, Mo., Jan. 21, 1932; s. Sam Farris and Victoria H.; B.S. in Bus., U. Mo., 1954, LL.B., 1959; m. June Samaha, Apr. 1, 1956; children—Sam Farris, III, Karen E., Michael K., Jacquelline. Admitted to Mo. bar, 1959, practiced in Springfield, Mo., 1959—; mem. firm Miller, Fairman, Sanford, Carr and Lowther, 1959-65, individual practice law, 1965—; spl. asst. to atty. gen. Mo., 1966-68; pres., chmn. bd. Wendy's of Mo., Inc., 1977—. Chmn., United Fund Kickoff Campaign, 1966; mem. Mo. Savs. and Loan Commn., 1977-83; chmn. 7th Dist. Democratic Com., 1970-72; del. Dem. Nat. Conv., 1972, 80; mem. vestry St. James Episcopal Ch., Springfield, 1962-64, 69-71, then clk. Served as 1st lt., arty. U.S. Army, 1954-56. Named Springfield's Outstanding Young Man of Year, 1966, Mo.'s Outstanding Young Man of Year, 1967. Mem. Mo. Bar Assn. (mem. corp. com. 1963-80), Am. Bar Assn., Greene County Bar Assn. (dir. 1974-77), Springfield C. of C. (dir. 1971-77, chmn. sidewalk and st. improvements bond issue com. 1977-78, chmn. bldg. fund dr. 1979), Legal Aid Assn. (pres. 1976-77), Springfield Jaycees (pres. 1963-64), Phi Delta Phi (pres. 1958-59). Clubs: Masons, Shriners, Hickory Hills Country (chmn. bldg. renovation com. 1979-80); Rotary (pres. 1967-68). Home: 3937 Saint Andrews Dr Springfield MO 65804 Office: 2-200 #2 Corporate Sq Springfield MO 65804

HAMRICK, CLAIR PAGE, III, lawyer; b. Clarksburg, W.Va., June 24, 1944; s. Clair Page, Jr. and Agnes E. (Lover) H.; B.S. in Acctg., W.Va. U., 1966, J.D., 1968; postgrad. W.Va. Coll. Grad. Studies; m. Elizabeth Faye McCune, June 30, 1973; children—E. Courtney, Clair Page, IV. Admitted to W.Va. bar, 1969; atty. W.Va. Dept. Hwys., 1969; acct. Touche Ross & Co., C.P.A.'s, Washington, 1970-73; asst. atty. gen. State of W.Va., 1973-77; individual practice law, Charleston, W.Va., 1977—; counsel jud. com. W.Va. Senate, 1979, 80, 81; adj. instr. acctg. W.Va. Coll. Grad. Studies, 1977-78; speaker W.Va. Tax Inst., 1975-77. C.P.A., W.Va. Mem. Am. Inst. C.P.A.'s, Am. Assn. Atty.-C.P.A.'s, W.Va. State Bar, W.Va. Bar Assn., W.Va. Soc. C.P.A.'s, Phi Delta Phi, Beta Theta Pi. Episcopalian. Home: 1437 Long Ridge Rd Charleston WV 25314 Office: 1701 Charleston Nat Plaza Charleston WV 25301

HAMRICK, THOMAS DANIEL, real estate exec.; b. Freeport, Tex., Feb. 11, 1928; s. Floyd James and Marion Fay Hamrick; B.B.A., Sam Houston State Coll., Huntsville, Tex., 1950; grad. Realtors Inst., 1976; m. Dolores Anne Weeks, Mar. 7, 1980; children—Lisa Marie, Lauren Ann. Commd. ensign U.S. Navy, 1946, advanced through grades to comdr., 1966; service in World War II, Korea, Vietnam; ret., 1972; pres. Guardian Brokers, San Diego, 1973—, Strand-Crown, Realtors, Coronado, 1976; v.p., dir. E-Z 8 Motels, Inc. Decorated Army Commendation medal, Navy Commendation medal, Navy Achievement medal. Mem. Nat., Calif. assns. realtors, Realtors Nat. Mktg. Inst., San Diego, Coronado bds. realtors, San Diego C. of C., VFW. Republican. Roman Catholic. Home: 900 Glorietta Blvd Coronado CA 92118 Office: 2565 Camino del Rio S Suite A San Diego CA 92108

HANAHAN, JAMES LAKE, ins. co. exec.; b. Burlington, Iowa, Aug. 27, 1932; s. Thomas J. and Clarice P. (Lorey) H.; B.S., Drake U., 1955; postgrad. George Williams Coll., 1956; m. Marilyn R. Lowe, Dec. 27, 1952; children—Bridget Sue Bahlke, Erin Rose Hoff. Phys. dir. Monmouth (Ill.) YMCA, 1955-56; mem. community relations staff Caterpillar Tractor Co., Peoria, Ill., 1956-57; rep. Conn. Gen. Life Ins. Co., Des Moines, 1957-59, asst. mgr., 1959-63, mgr. group ins. ops., Tampa, Fla., 1963-80; pres. Wittner Hanahan & Peck, Inc., 1980—, J & H Cons. Group Inc., 1980—; instr. certified property casualty underwriters courses; seminar leader C.L.U. workshop; cons. ins. seminar Fla. State U. Bd. dirs. Tampa Sports Found., Jr. Achievement. Recipient Double D award Drake U., 1978. Mem. Sales Mktg. Execs. Tampa (pres.), Tampa Commerce Club, Nat. Risk Mgmt. Soc., Greater Tampa C. of C., Minerat Soc. U. Tampa, Tampa Sports and Recreation Council (bd. dirs.), Com. of 100, Phi Sigma Epsilon. Democrat. Roman Catholic. Clubs: 7th Inning (chmn.), Nat. D (Drake U.) (v.p., dir.). Home: 8012 W Hiawatha St Tampa FL 33615

HANAS, STEPHEN, banker; b. Derby, Conn., June 27, 1950; s. Stephen Louis and Wanda (Zybort) H.; B.S. in Econs., U. Tampa (Fla.), 1972. With Bank of Am., 1975—, comml. loan officer, Santa Ana, Calif., 1977-79, asst. v.p. comml. fin., Newport Beach, Calif., 1979-80; asst. v.p. internat. fin. Bank Am. Internat., Miami, Fla., 1980—. Served to 1st lt. USMC, 1972-75. Mem. Orange County Bank Am. Officers Speaking Group (treas. 1979-80). Republican. Home: 230 Camilo Ave Coral Gables FL 33134 Office: 1000 Brickell Ave Miami FL 33131

HANAU, KENNETH JOHN, JR., packaging co. exec.; b. Montclair, N.J., Feb. 27, 1927; s. Kenneth John and Elizabeth (Oliver) H.; B.A., Wesleyan U., Middletown, Conn., 1951; m. Carol Lee Rossner, July 30, 1949; children—Holly Elizabeth, Jill Ann, Lori Carol, Kenneth John. Salesman, Union Bag-Camp Paper Co., N.Y.C., 1951-53; sales rep. Gibraltar Corrugated Paper Co., North Bergen, N.J., 1953-56; pres. K. & H. Corrugated Case Corp., Walden, N.Y., 1956—, Vt. Container Corp., Bennington, 1960—, K & H Containers, Inc., Wallingford, Conn., 1966—; dir. U.S. Pipe and Foundry Co., Birmingham, Ala., 1961-69, mem. exec. com., 1962-69; dir., mem. exec. com. Furntec Industries, Easton, Pa., 1971-73; dir. Jim Walter Corp., Tampa, Fla., 1969-76, chmn. audit com., 1975-76; dir. Corp. Leaders Am., Englewood, N.J., 1961-69, Nytronics Corp., Phillipsburg, N.J., 1962-65, Bennington County Indsl. Corp., 1964-67, Stover Plywood Corp., Greenville, Maine, 1964-68, Lexington Corporate Leaders, Englewood, 1964-69, United Concrete Pipe Corp., Baldwin Park, Calif., 1966-69, J.B. Schaefer Industries, S.I., N.Y., 1966-71, Lexington Income Fund, Brentwood, Calif., 1973-80, Tingue Brown, Englewood, 1973-80, Lexington Growth Fund, Brentwood, 1973-80, Lexington Research Fund, Brentwood, 1973-80, Lexington Tax Free Fund, Englewood, 1977-80, Lexington Money Market Trust, Englewood, 1977-80; dir. U.S. Home Corp., Houston, 1976—, chmn. audit and nominating coms., 1977—; dir. Empire Nat. Bank, New City, N.Y., 1977-80, Foster Mfg., Wilton, Maine, 1978-80. Eastern regional chmn. Nat. Multiple Sclerosis Soc., 1965. Served with USNR, 1945-46. Clubs: Upper Montclair (N.J.) Country; Madison (Conn.) Beach (gov. 1970, treas. 1972-76, pres. 1976-77); Yale (N.Y.C.); Windermere Island (Bahamas). Home: 239 Edgewood Rd Franklin Lakes NJ 07417 also 18 Fairview Ave Madison CT 06443 Office: POB 301 Walden NY 12586

HANCOCK, JOE IREY, ins. exec.; b. Grantsboro, N.C., Feb. 2, 1947; s. Joseph Ira and Mattie (Price) H.; B.S. in Psychology, U. N.C., 1972; LL.B., LaSalle Extension U., 1977; m. JoAnn Freeman, Nov. 22, 1975; 1 dau., Maria Nicole. Vice pres. exec. sales and service Ward & Bosely Ins. Agency Inc., Bel Air, Md., 1972—, pres. subs. IFC, Inc.; lectr. estate and fin. planning. Served as capt. U.S. Army, 1965-69; Vietnam. Decorated Silver Star, Bronze Star, Army Commendation medal, Purple Heart. Mem. Am. Mgmt. Assn., Nat. (Harford-Cecil County chpt.) Assn. Life Underwriters, Nat. Assn. Casualty Writers, Nat. Inst. Fin. Planning, N.G. Assn., Aircraft Owners and Pilots Assn., Greater Bel Air Bus. Assn. (chmn. fin. com. 1977-78, chmn. ways and means com. 1978-79, v.p. 1978-79). Republican. Roman Catholic. Club: Lions. Home: 110 Victory Ln Bel Air MD 21014 Office: 1 Bel Air S Bel Air MD 21014

HANCOCK, WILLIAM FRANK, JR., business exec.; b. Richmond, Va., Jan. 4, 1942; s. William Frank and Gladys Elizabeth (George) H.; B.B.A., U. Iowa, 1964; M.B.A., U. Pa., 1966; m. Donna G. Hosmer, May 18, 1968; children—Peter James, Jeffrey William, Jennifer Beth. Exec. asst. to exec. v.p. John Hancock Mutual Life Ins. Co., Boston, 1966-69; mgmt. cons. Keane Assos., Boston, 1969-74, regional mgr., 1974-75; v.p., gen. mgr. comml. systems SofTech, Inc., Waltham, Mass., 1975-79; dir. internat. sales and field ops. Nixdorf Computer Co., Burlington, Mass., 1979—; mgr. mktg. and strategic planning Digital Equipment Corp., 1980—; instr. acctg. and fin. Grad. Sch. Bus., Northeastern U., Boston, 1966—. Treas., Pilgrim Ch. Served with U.S. Army, 1967-72. C.P.A., C.L.U., C.P.C.U., C.M.A., C.D.P. Mem. Data Processing Mgmt. Assn., Nat. Assn. Accountants, Assn. Computing Machinery, Boston C. of C. Presbyterian. Clubs: Executive (Boston); U. Pa. Alumni; Wharton; U. Iowa Alumni. Home: 24 Dexter Dr Sherborn MA 01770 Office: 129 Parket St Maynard MA 01754

HANCOX, ROBERT ERNEST, ins. co. exec.; b. Newark, Apr. 6, 1943; s. Ernest E. and Laverne (Bruguiere) H.; B.A., Lycoming Coll., 1965; M.B.A., Fairleigh Dickinson U., 1970; Ph.D., Pace U., 1981; m. Judith Hale, Aug. 6, 1966; children—Jennifer Susan, Elizabeth Jane. Coordinator mgmt. devel. State Farm Ins. Cos., Wayne, N.J., 1965-66, asst. personnel mgr., 1968-70, personnel supt., 1970-72, regional personnel mgr., 1972-76, regional personnel dir., 1976—; adj. asso. prof. Fordham U., 1974—, Seton Hall U., 1970—; counselor Family Counseling Service, Wayne, 1973—. Mem. Community Affairs Group North Jersey, 1973—; mem. Gov.'s Adv. Com. N.J. Employment Service, 1974—. Mem. Am. Soc. Personnel Adminstrn. (accredited personnel exec.), Acad. Mgmt., Assn. Measurement and Evaluation in Guidance, Am. Compensation Assn., Am. Personnel and Guidance Assn., Assn. Specialists Group Work, Indsl. Relations Research Assn., Am. Soc. Tng. and Devel. Republican. Methodist. Home: 60 Dryden Rd Bernardsville NJ 07924 Office: State Farm Ins Cos 1750 Route 23 Wayne NJ 07470

HAND, HORACE DELOS, metals lab. exec.; b. Dillon, Mont., Dec. 18, 1934; s. John William and Ida Barbara (Hartwig) H.; student Mont. Sch. Mines, 1952-57; m. Virginia Lee Stefonic, June 17, 1956; children—Kevin, Danial, Pamela, Randall, Ronald, Tamarilla. Mining engr. Hand Mine, Dillon, 1956-59; chemist, lab. technician Minerals Engring. Co. of Colo., Dillon, 1960-61; owner, exec. Metals Assay Western Labs., Helena, Mont., 1961—. Mem. small miner's advisory com. State of Mont., 1971-73; mem. architecture and rev. com. Helena Urban Renewal Project, 1970-71; mem. South Area Neighborhood Council, Helena, 1970-71. Mem. Helena C. of C. (chmn. environ. com.), Am. Inst. Mining, Metal. and Petroleum Engrs., Southwestern Mont. (pres. 1971), Western (pres. 1972), Mont. (pres. 1973, exec. sec. 1975), Colo., Northwestern mining assns. Clubs: Rotary (pres. 1977-78, sec. 1979—), Montana. Home: 130 Greenwood Dr Helena MT 59601 Office: PO Box 5359 Helena MT 59601

HAND, NANCY TALLY, architect, resort exec.; b. Lincoln, Nebr., Sept. 14, 1940; d. Gerald M. Tally and Ruth Hester Byrd; student Grinnell Coll., 1958-61; B.A., Mich. State U., 1962; postgrad. Concord Inst. Tech., 1977-78; m. James Henry Hand, June 9, 1961; children—David, Kristin. Owner, mgr. Sandybeach of Newfound (N.H.), 1972—; free-lance architect, Bridgewater, N.H., 1972—. Pres. LWV, Plainfield, N.J., 1966-72, Bristol Community Center, 1974—; mem. pub. relations com. United Fund, Plainfield, 1969-70; bd. dirs. Center for Human Resources, 1974-76; del. N.H. Democratic Conv., 1976, 78. Mem. Newfound Region C. of C. (dir., sec.-treas. 1972—). Clubs: Bristol Women's, Pasquaney Garden. Home and office: Whittemore Point Rd Bridgewater NH 03222

HAND, WILLIAM JESSUP, investment banker; b. Washington, Aug. 18, 1936; s. Alfred and Elizabeth A. (Grant) H.; B.A., Yale U., 1958; m. Nancy Ann Dube, Nov. 22, 1969; children—Caroline Dube, William Alfred. With internat. div. Chem. Bank, N.Y.C., 1958-68; v.p. A.G. Becker and Co., N.Y.C., 1968-77; v.p. Smith Barney Harris Upham, N.Y.C., 1977—. Mem. Mcpl. Bond Club N.Y. Home: 233 Pondfield Rd Bronxville NY 10708 Office: 1345 Ave of Americas New York NY 10019

HANDEL, MORTON, leisure product mfg. co. exec.; b. N.Y.C., Apr. 12, 1935; s. Benjamin and Mollie (Heller) H.; B.A., U. Pa., 1956; student N.Y. U. Grad. Sch. Bus., 1957-59; m. Irma Ruby, Aug. 5, 1956; children—Mark, Gary, Karen. Vice pres. Dale Plastic Playing Card Corp., 1955-57; gen. mgr. Handel Nets & Fabrics Corp., 1957-62; pres. A.M. Industries, Inc., 1962-68; pres. Allan Marine, Inc., 1969-71; chmn. bd. Marlowe Yacht Corp., 1969-71; v.p. finance, sec., treas. Aurora Products Corp. subsidiary Nabisco, Inc., 1971-73, sr. v.p., sec., chief financial officer, 1973-74; v.p. fin. Rowe Industries, Inc., 1971-74; chief fin. officer Coleco Industries, Inc., 1974—, v.p., 1974-78, sr. v.p., 1978—, also dir.; dir. Aurora Nederland (N.V.), Johnson Electric Singapore, Ltd. Pres. Rochdale Village Civic Assn., 1964-65, Coleco Industries Pension Fund, 1974—; bd. dirs., v.p. Symphony Soc. of Hartford, Jewish Children's Service Orgn., 1976-78. Mem. Am. Mgmt. Assn., Fin. Execs. Inst., Planning Execs. Inst., Alpha Epsilon Pi. Home: 21 Vardon Rd West Hartford CT 06117 Office: 945 Asylum Ave Hartford CT 06105

HANDEL, WILLIAM KEATING, advt. and pub. relations exec.; b. N.Y.C., Mar. 23, 1929; s. Irving Nathaniel and Marguerite Mary (Keating) H.; B.A. in Journalism, U. S.C., 1959, postgrad., 1959-60; children—William Keating II, David Roger. With Packaging div. The Mead Corp., Atlanta, 1960-64, Ketchum, MacLeod & Grove, Pitts., 1964-67, Rexall Drug & Chem. Corp., Los Angeles, 1967-68; owner Creative Enterprises/Mktg. Communications, Los Angeles, 1968-71; creative dir., sales promotion mgr. Beneficial Standard Life Ins., Los Angeles, 1971-72; mgr. advt. and pub. relations ITT Gen. Controls, Glendale, Calif., 1972-80; mgr. corp. recruitment advt. Hughes Aircraft Co., Los Angeles, 1980—; pub. relations counsel Calif. Pvt. Edn. Schs., 1978—; chmn. exhibits Mini/Micro Computer Conf., 1977-78. Bd. dirs. West Valley Athletic League; pub. relations cons. Ensenada, Mexico Tourist Commn., 1978; chmn. U.S. Marine Corps Birthday Ball, Los Angeles, 1979, 80, 81. Served with USMC, 1950-53. Decorated Silver Star, Bronze Star, Purple Heart (4), Navy Letter of Commendation with V and medal. Recipient Pub. Service award Los Angeles Heart Assn., 1971, 72, 73. Mem. Bus. and Profl. Advt. Assn., 1st Marine div. assns., Navy League, Sigma Chi. Republican. Roman Catholic. Clubs: Nueva España Boat, Ensenada Fish and Game (Baja, Mexico). Home: 23731 Candlewood Way Canoga Park CA 91307 Office: 5250 W Century Blvd Los Angeles CA 90009

HANDELSMAN, HAROLD SAMUEL, hotel exec.; b. N.Y.C., Oct. 1, 1946; s. Milton B. and Lois H.; B.A., Amherst Coll., 1968; LL.B. (Jane Kent scholar), Columbia U., 1973; children—Joshua, Amy. Admitted to N.Y. bar, 1974; atty. U.S. Ct. Appeals, Bridgeport, Conn., 1973-74; atty. firm Wachtell, Lipton, Rosen & Katz, N.Y.C., 1974-78; sr. v.p. Hyatt Corp., Rosemont, Ill., 1978—; dir. Hyatt Hotels Corp., Roland Internat. Corp.; v.p. Elsinore Corp. Served with U.S. Army, 1968-70. Mem. Am. Bar Assn., N.Y. State Bar Assn. Contbr. articles to profl. publs. Office: 9700 W Bryn Mawr Ave Rosemont IL 60016

HANDLEY, HELEN MULLINS, computer billing, credit-collections co. exec.; b. Trafford, Ala., Nov. 18, 1921; d. James Oliver and Carrie Frances (Abel) Mullins; student Massey Bus. Coll., 1940-41; m. Thomas Harley Handley, Feb. 7, 1941; children—Hetty Patricia Handley Nevin, Thomas Harley, Mary Catherine. Owner, mgr. Anderson County Adjustment Co., Oak Ridge, 1961—; bd. dirs. Better Bus. Bur. Knoxville, 1978—. Founder, chmn. Arthritis Clinic for Anderson and Roane Counties, 1969—; co-chmn. 3d Dist. Rep. Com., 1972—; committeewoman Tenn. Republican Com., 1974—; chmn. Anderson County Republican Com., 1977-78. Named Hidden Heroine, Girl Scouts U.S.A., 1976; recipient plaque Anderson County Rep. Com., 1978. Mem. Associated Credit Burs., Nat. Fedn. Ind. Bus., Oak Ridge C. of C. (membership com. 1976—), Am. Bus. Women's Assn. (pres. 1979-80), Oak Ridge Bus. and Profl. Women (corr. sec. 1980-81), Am. Collectors Assn. (nat. dir. 1969-70, nat. legis. com. 1975—), Tenn. Collectors Assn. (pres. 1968-69, pub., editor Tenn. Collector 1968—). Baptist. Clubs: Oak Ridge Women's, Lady of Elks. Home: 103 Delaware Ave Oak Ridge TN 37830 Office: 210 Town Hall Bldg Oak Ridge TN 37830

HANDLEY, KENNETH G., business exec.; b. 1906; B.A., Brigham Young U., 1928; M.B.A., N.Y. U., 1931; married. Vice pres. Mfrs. Hanover Bank, 1930-57; partner J.A. Hogle & Co., 1959-64; with Imperial Corp. Am., San Diego, 1961—, chmn. bd., chief exec. officer, 1979—, also dir.; dir. Olson Farms Inc., Met. Water Dist. Office: Imperial Corp Am 8787 Complex Dr San Diego CA 92123*

HANDLIR, GREGORY FRANK, univ. ofcl.; b. Balt., Jan. 22, 1947; s. John and Sylvia (Finnerty) H.; B.S. in Econs., Loyola Coll., Balt., 1969, M.B.A., 1973; m. Ina L. Hagerman, Apr. 27, 1968; 1 son, Jason. Adminstrv. asst. Office of the Dean, U. Md. Sch. Medicine, Balt., 1971-73, asst. dean for fiscal affairs, 1973—; asst. dir. for finance U. Md. Hosp., Balt., 1974-75. Mem. Assn. Am. Med. Colls. Group on Bus. Affairs, Assn. Am. Med. Colls. (group on instl. planning), Soc. Research Adminstrs., Am. Mgmt. Assn. Home: 8809 Littlewood Rd Baltimore MD 21234 Office: 655 W Baltimore St Baltimore MD 21201

HANDREN, ROBERT THEODORE, architect, engr.; b. West Hoboken, N.J., May 1, 1907; s. John William and Sarah J. (Curtis) H.; student Pratt Inst., 1925-27; B.Arch. magna cum laude, N.Y. U., 1938; m. Theresa C. Hanaway, June 9, 1939; children—Robert Theodore, Edward P. Archtl. practice, 1922-42; v.p. Park & Tilford Distillers Corp., 1942-55; asso. Ketchum and Sharp, Architects, N.Y.C., 1955-58, partner, 1958-61; partner Sharp & Handren, architects, 1962-67; sr. partner Handren, Sharp and Assos., 1967-73; propr. Robert Handren, Architect, 1973—. Mem. industry adv. com. WPB, adv. com. Dept. Agr., RFC. Vice pres., dir., treas. Distilled Spirits Inst., 1942-55; mem. pub. adv. council Gen. Services Adminstrn., 1969—. Recipient F. B. Morse medal Alpha Soc., A.I.A., Scholarship award. Fellow Soc. Am. Mil. Engrs.; mem. Am. Def. Preparedness Assn., A.I.A., N.Y. State Assn. Architects, Nat. Rifle Assn. (life). Clubs: Westchester Country, Pendennis. Home: Buttonwood Ln Harmony NJ 08865

HANDS, H. WILLIAM, mfg. co. exec.; b. N.Y.C., Apr. 15, 1913; s. William H. and May Louise (FitzGerald) H.; A.B., Dartmouth, 1935; M.B.A., Amos Tuck Sch., 1936; m. Alice Macdonald, Feb. 6, 1937; children—Geoffrey W., Deirdre M. Buyer, B. Altman & Co., N.Y.C., 1936-40; gen. mgr. Flowerfield Bulb Farm, N.Y., 1940-45; S.Am. mgr. Atlas Supply Co., 1948-54; gen. sales mgr. Peru, Standard Oil Co. N.J., 1954-58; v.p. Internat. Am. Hosp. Supply Co., Evanston, Ill., 1958-61; European v.p. Abbott Labs., Chgo., 1961-64; dir. internat. mktg. H.K. Porter Co., Inc., N.Y.C., 1965-80; gen. mgr. U.S.A., GeoTrade, S.A., 1980—. Trustee Barat Coll., Lake Forest, Ill., 1961-72. Mem. Internat. Exec. Assn. (dir.). Roman Catholic. Clubs: University (N.Y.C.); Old Lyme Country, Old Lyme Beach. Home: Honey Hill Ln Lyme CT 06371 Office: PO Box 428 Old Lyme CT 06371

HANDWERKER, SY, public relations exec.; b. Chgo., Apr. 5, 1933; s. Alex and Bella (Schwartzberg) H.; B.S., U. Ill., 1954; postgrad. DePaul U. Coll. Law, 1954-56; m. Marilyn Iris Parker, Aug. 6, 1961; children—Jaye, Dana, Steven. Reporter, asst. radio news editor City News Bur. Chgo., 1951-54; asst. dir. pub. information U. Ill., Chgo., 1954-59; owner Sy Handwerker Pub. Relations, Chgo., 1959-61; pub. relations account exec. Aaron D. Cushman Assos., Inc., Chgo., 1961-64, Cooper & Golin Inc., Chgo., 1964-67; v.p. Bernard E. Ury Assos., Inc., Chgo., 1967-69; v.p. pub. relations Data Transformation, Inc., Skokie, Ill., 1969-70; pres., partner Hanlen Orgn., Inc. Vice pres. Highland Park Hockey Assn. Served with AUS 1956-58. Recipient Honor award Publicity Club Chgo., 1962, 63, 79, Shaughnessey award, 1979, Golden Trumpet award, 1980. Clubs: Elms Swim and Tennis (pres. 1978); Turnberry Isle Country. Home: 1637 Sherwood Rd Highland Park IL 60035 Office: 401 N Michigan Ave Chicago IL 60611

HANDY, ARTHUR ALVIN, JR., mgmt. cons.; b. Springfield, Mass., Jan. 8, 1926; s. Arthur Alvin and Lillian J. (Rhoades) H.; B.S. in Bus. Adminstrn., Am. Internat. Coll., Springfield, 1949; m. Joan F. Reilly, Dec. 17, 1959; children—Arthur Alvin, 3d, Christopher J., Keith B., Leigh P. Personnel asst. Springfield Bell & Marine Ins. Co., 1949-57; mgr. compensation Mitre Corp., Lexington, Mass., 1958-62; dir. compensation and personnel services Honeywell Inc., Wellesley Hills, Mass., 1962-67; dir. compensation and benefits Kaiser Aluminum Co., Oakland, Calif., 1967-73; dir. personnel Kaiser Industries, Oakland, 1974-77, Kaiser Steel Corp., Oakland, 1977-79; pres. Handy & Wajda Cons. Group Inc., Oakland, 1979—; instr. Golden Gate Coll., San

Francisco. Served with USAAF, 1943-45. Mem. Am. Compensation Assn. (life mem., course leader, past pres., chmn. bd.), Am. Soc. Personnel Adminstrs., No. Calif. Indsl. Relations Council. Republican. Congregationalist. Home: 9415 Alcosta Blvd San Ramon CA 94583 Office: 333 Hegenberger Rd Oakland CA 94621

HANES, RALPH PHILLIP, JR., textile co. exec.; b. Winston-Salem, N.C., Feb. 25, 1926; s. Ralph Philip and Dewitt (Chatham) H.; student U. N.C., 1944-46; B.A., Yale U., 1949; m. Joan Audrey Humpstone, Jan. 14, 1950. With Hanes Dye & Finishing Co., Winston-Salem, 1950—, pres., 1965-68, chmn. bd., 1968—; chmn. bd. Ampersand, Inc., 1976—, Hanes Converting Co., 1978—. Founder, dir. Gallery Contemporary Arts (now Southeastern Center for Contemporary Arts), 1956-58; founder Winston-Salem Arts Council, 1963-64; dir. Moravian Music Found., 1963-65; vice chmn. Winston-Salem Total Devel. Commn., 1960-62; mem. Nat. Council on Arts, 1965-70, mem. advisory music panel, 1970-72; pres. Arts Councils Am., 1964-68, Fgn. Art Study Fedn. N.C., 1974-78, Student Creative Arts Fedn. N.C., 1974-78; chmn., founder N.C. State Arts Council, 1964-67; vice chmn., founder Am. Council Arts, 1966-69; mem. nat. advisory com. Am. Crafts Council, 1970-72; chmn. com. on music Yale U. Council, 1970-73; bd. visitors Barter Theater, State Theater Va., 1967-75; bd. dirs. Nat. Cultural Center, 1962-65, Nat. Endowment Arts, 1965-72, Forsyth Econ. Devel. Corp., 1969-71, Winterthur, 1972-77, Nat. Audubon Soc., 1972-78, John W. and Anna H. Hanes Found., 1973—, S. Appalachian Highlands Conservancy, 1974-78, Old Salem, Inc., 1974-77, Nature Conservancy, 1975-79; Nat. Mus. Art (formerly Nat. Collection Fine Arts, 1976—, Alliance Arts Edn., 1976-79, Gov.'s Bus. Council Arts and Humanities, 1977—, Salzburg (Austria) Seminars Am. Studies, 1978, Spoleto Festival, 1979—, Bus. Com. for Arts, 1980—; trustee, mem. exec. com. N.C. Sch. for Arts; trustee Salem Coll., 1961-64, Am. Land Trust, 1976-78, Nat. Collection Fine Arts Com., 1976—, Renwick Gallery, 1976—; bd. dirs. Kennedy Center for Performing Arts, 1975-80, Nat. Council Friends of Kennedy Center, 1975-78; mem. Chief Exec. Forum, 1975-78, World Bus. Council, 1976-78, Bus. Com. on Arts, 1977; mem. exec. com. Nat. Council Arts and Edn., 1976-79; mem. adv. council on arts Fed. Res. Bank of Richmond (Va.), 1977-78, fine arts com. Fed. Res. Bank Washington, 1979—; mem. adv. bd. Pauline Koner Dance Consort, 1977—; mem. internat. council Mus. Modern Art, 1978—; bd. devel. N.C. Dance Theatre, 1978—. Served to lt. USNR. Recipient Young Man of Year award N.C. Jaycees, 1958; Arts Council award, 1960, Gov.'s award for preservation of natural areas, 1969, N.C. Pub. Service award, 1976, Morrison award for the arts, 1977, numerous others. Life fellow Royal Soc. Arts, Pa. Acad. Fine Arts, Council on Founds.; mem. Walpole Soc., Jargon Soc. (pres. 1968-74), Am. Symphony Orch. League (dir. 1958-61), N.Am. Mycological Assn., Sierra Club (life), Appalachian Trail Conf. (nat. advisory com. 1973—), Wilderness Soc. (life), Ducks Unltd., Izaak Walton League Am. (dir. 1974—, life), Am. Forestry Assn. (life), Nat. Wildlife Fedn. (life), East African Wildlife Soc. (life), So. Appalachian Highlands Assn. (life), Appalachian Consortium (life), Potomac Appalachian mountain clubs, S.E. Council Founds. Clubs: Rotary, Currituck (Jarvisburg, N.C.); Cane River (Burnsville, N.C.); Old Town, Roaring Gap (N.C.); Century Assn., Yale (N.Y.C.); Met. (Washington); Peale for Visual Arts (Phila.). Home: Box 749 Winston-Salem NC 27102 Office: Hanes Dye & Finishing Co Buxton St Winston-Salem NC 27102

HANES, ROGER ALLEN, rubber mfg. co. exec.; b. Claremore, Okla., May 7, 1947; s. Ernest Roosevelt and Flena (Cartwright) H.; B.S., U. Tulsa, 1970; m. Cynthia A. Brock, May 20, 1973; children—Roger A., Travis G. Cost acct. W.C. Norris div. Dover Corp., Tulsa, 1972-73; chief acct. Dorsett Electronics div. LaBarge, Inc., Tulsa, 1973-74; controller Vulcan Tank Corp., 1974-75; v.p. fin. Unarco Rubber Prodn. Div. Unarco Industries, Inc., Tulsa, 1975—. Served with U.S. Navy, 1970-72. Home: 7710 E 25th Pl Tulsa OK 74125 Office: PO Box 15647 Tulsa OK 74112

HANFORD, LARRY PAUL, mfg. co. exec.; b. Canon City, Colo., July 21, 1947; s. Charles Edwin and Helen Inez (Klattenburg) H.; B.S., U. So. Colo., 1970; m. Larre Elaine Sauer, Aug. 28, 1971; children—Jason Todd, Ryan Scott, Stephan Frederick. Sr. acct. Great Western Cities, Colorado City, Colo., 1968-75; controller Vanco, Inc., Colorado City, 1975-76; controller Do-Ray Lamp Co., Inc., Colorado City, 1976—, sec., 1977—. Chmn. Colorado City Met. Recreation Dist., 1975. Baptist. Club: Jaycees.

HANGEN, WILLIAM J., elec. products mfg. co. exec., b. St. Louis, Mar. 28, 1931; s. William M. and Mabel Josephine (Jinkerson) H.; student Washington U., St. Louis, 1948-51; B.S., U. Mo., 1953; postgrad. Wayne State U., 1957-62; m. Shirley Mae Diebal, June 13, 1953; children—William Eric, Lori Jean Hangen Young, Jill Marie, Kurt David. Chemist, pigments dept. E. I. duPont de Nemours & Co., Newark, 1955-56; materials engr. missile div. Chrysler Corp., Detroit, 1956-64; engring. and mgmt. positions, elec. products and advanced products divs. G. T. Schjeldahl Co. (name now changed to Sheldahl, Inc.). Northfield, Minn., 1964—, v.p., gen. mgr. elec. products div., 1970-76, sr. v.p., gen. mgr. indsls. group, 1976-80, exec. v.p., chief operating officer, 1980—. Corp. rep. Inst. Printed Circuits, 1970—, bd. dirs., 1974-76, treas., 1976-78, v.p., 1978-80, pres., 1980—, mem. program com., 1975-79, chmn., 1977-79, chmn. fin. com., 1978, chmn. long range planning com., 1978-80. Served with Ordnance Corps, AUS, 1953-55. Mem. Am. Chem. Soc., Walter's Lake Property Owner's Assn. (pres. 1962-64), Alpha Chi Sigma. Republican. Lutheran (past trustee, past sponsor Luther League). Clubs: Optimist (v.p. Waterford, Mich. 1963-67); Northfield Golf, Northfield Hockey Assn. Contbr. to profl. jours. Home: Route 5 Old Dutch Rd Northfield MN 55057 Office: Box 170 Northfield MN 55057

HANHAUSER, JOHN FRANCIS, dept. store exec.; b. Abington, Pa., Aug. 4, 1947; s. George Joseph and Marjorie Marion (McCaughn) H.; B.S. in Bus. Adminstrn., Bryant Coll., 1970. Sales mgr., carpet specialist, asst. buyer floor coverings Macy's, N.Y.C., 1970-75; divisional sales mgr., buyer floor coverings Shillito's, Cin., 1975-79; v.p., gen. mgr. Chgo. Carpet Warehouse, 1979; group buyer floor coverings Rich's, Atlanta, 1980, asst. store mgr., merchandising, 1980—. Mem. steering com. Federated Dept. Stores, 1975—. Mem. So. Floor Covering Assn. Home: 174 Elysian Way NW Atlanta GA 30327 Office: Rich's 45 Broad St SW Atlanta GA 30302

HANIGAN, JOHN LEONARD, mfg. co. exec.; b. N.Y.C., Aug. 15, 1911; s. John P. and Winifred L. (Brennan) H.; student Stevens Inst. Tech., 1930-33; grad. Advanced Mgmt. Program, Harvard, 1944; m. Elsa L. Stelter, Jan. 17, 1953; children by previous marriage—Joan C., John F. With R. H. Macy & Co., N.Y.C., 1933-35, Corning Glass Works (N.Y.), 1937-62, v.p., 1953-62; pres. Corning Glass Works Can., Ltd., 1957-61; exec. v.p. Dow Corning Corp., Midland, Mich., 1962-63, dir.; chief exec. officer, chmn. bd., mem. exec. com. Brunswick Corp., Chgo., 1963-76, chmn. bd., chmn. exec. com., 1976-77; chmn., chief exec. officer Genesco, Inc., Nashville, 1979—, pres., 1979-80, also dir.; dir. Sherwood Med. Industries, Inc., Clark Oil & Refining Corp. Mem. Pres.'s Export Council. Served as 1st lt., inf. U.S. Army Res., 1935-37. Mem. Sigma Nu. K.C. Office: 111 7th Ave N Nashville TN 37202*

HANKES, WILBUR RAY, mech. engr.; b. Canton, Ohio, Apr. 17, 1921; s. Cecil Clarence and Emma Anna (Rufle) H.; B.S. in Mech. Engring., Case Inst. Tech., 1942; m. Ann Jeanette McKimmey, May 13, 1942; 1 dau., Sue Elaine; m. 2d, Marlene Rose DeKay, July 7, 1954; children—Katherine Kim, Casey Kathleen. Dir. Washington office Kollsman Instrument Corp., 1946-54; dir. Navy customer relations AVCO Corp., 1955-58, dir. mil. relations AVCO Research Labs., 1958-60; research sales mgr. link div. Gen. Precision, Inc., 1960-61; mgr. research marketing Vertol div. Boeing Co., Morton, Pa., 1961-62; sales mgr. reentry and space systems Missile div. Chrysler Corp., Detroit, 1963-64, gen. sales mgr. space div., New Orleans, 1964-67, asst. gen. mgr. computer div. Geo Space Corp., Houston, 1967-68; marketing mgr. re-entry systems Lockheed Missiles & Space Co., 1968-69, corp. staff new bus. devel., 1970-76; pres., Dr. Personnel of Houston, 1976—. Served as lt. USNR, 1943-45. Registered profl. engr. D.C., Ohio. Mem. Nat. Aviation Club. Club: Congressional. Home: 5251 Memorial Dr Houston TX 77007 Office: Doctors Center Med Profl Bldg 7000 Fannin St Houston TX 77030

HANKINS, MALLOY, tax service exec.; b. Trion, Ga., Mar. 18, 1941; s. James Henry and Rebecca (Wilson) H.; student N.E. Ala. Jr. Coll., 1975-76; m. Carolyn June Grubbs, Apr. 16, 1966; children—Stuart, Matthew. Agt., Interstate Life, Rome, Ga., 1966-71; mgr. Globe Life & Accident Ins. Co., Trion, Ga., 1971-76; owner Ga. Franchise H & R Block, Summerville, 1971-76, Fla. franchise, Stuart, 1977—; faculty Floyd Jr. Coll., Rome, 1968-69. Served with USN, 1959-66. Recipient Jr. C. of C. award, 1976. Mem. C. of C., Better Bus. Bur. Democrat. Baptist. Clubs: Masons (Shriner), Order Eastern Star. Home: 1050 SE Salerno Rd Stuart FL 33494 Office: 207 W Ocean Blvd Stuart FL 33494 also Jensen Beach FL also 4326 S Federal Hwy Stuart FL

HANKINSON, COE FOGLE LONG, mfg. co. exec.; b. St. Matthews, S.C., Aug. 5, 1938; d. John Robert and Kathryn McLain (Smoak) Fogle; student (scholar) Columbia Coll., 1956-57; B.S. in Bus. Adminstrn., U. S.C., 1976; m. John Crimmins Hankinson, Jr., Sept. 6, 1975; children—Mary Kathryn Long, George Robert Long. Sec. to personnel dir. S.C. Dept. Mental Health, Columbia, 1957-66; asst. to pres. The State-Record Co., Columbia, 1966-72; asst. corp. sec. Shakespeare Co., Columbia, 1972-78, corp. sec., 1978—, corp. risk mgr., 1972—; chmn. S.C. mktg. assistance S.C. Ins. Commn., 1977—. Mem. Hist. Columbia Found., 1968-70, Richland County Preservation Commn., 1968-70; sec. S.C. Gov.'s Hwy. Adv. Com., 1969-70; div. chmn. United Way, 1976, chmn. agy. relations, mem. exec. com., 1977-80; pres. bd. dirs. Carolina Ballet Co., 1971-72; rep. Miss S.C. Pageant, 1956. Mem. Am. Soc. Corp. Secs., Risk and Ins. Mgrs. Soc. (nat. chmn. govtl. affairs), S.C. C. of C., S.C. Textile Mfrs. Assn. (legis. com.). Presbyterian. Clubs: Palmetto, Spring Valley Country. Home: 5 Sims Alley Columbia SC 29205 Office: PO Box 1 1501 Lady St Columbia SC 29202

HANKINSON, JOHN CRIMMINS, JR., state adminstr.; b. Waynesboro, Ga. Oct. 14, 1933; s. John Crimmins and Sara (Blount) H.; B.S., Clemson U., 1955; grad. Sch. Banking of South, La. State U., 1964, S.C. Bankers Sch., 1965; grad. Nat. Comml. Lending Grad. Sch., U. Okla., 1979; m. Coe Fogle, Sept. 6, 1975; children—Mona Lane, Ann Crimmins. Mgmt. trainee S.C. Nat. Bank, Greenville, 1957-59, administry, asst., Sumter, 1959-60, asst. cashier, Cheraw, 1960-63, asst. v.p., sr. officer, Bennettsville, 1963-67, v.p. internat. banking div., Columbia, 1967-71, v.p., adminstr. nat. banking div., 1971-80; dep. dir. S.C. State Devel. Bd., 1980—. Pres., Bennettsville Parking and Devel. Co., 1965-67; chmn. Pee Dee Area chpt. Nat. Found. March Dimes, 1966-67; chmn. S.C. edn. funds crusade S.C. div. Am. Cancer Soc., 1969-70; vice chmn. S.C. Regional Export Expansion Council 1969-73. Served with AUS, 1956. Mem. S.C. Bankers Assn. (pres. Young bankers div. 1973-74). Presbyn. Home: 5 Sims Alley Columbia SC 29205 Office: 1301 Gervais St PO Box 927 Columbia SC 29202

HANKS, DONALD ANTHONY, fin. co. exec.; b. San Antonio, Dec. 31, 1944; s. Edward Francis and Theodora Martha (Pajon) H.; A.A. in Police Sci., Mt. San Antonio Coll., 1971; A.A. in Real Estate, Fullerton (Calif.) Coll., 1976; M.A. in Psychology, Calif. State U., Fullerton, 1973; postgrad. Western States Law Sch. Pres., Am. Fin. Services Co., Newport Beach, Calif., 1973-75; v.p. J.R. Anderson Fin. Services Co., Newport Beach, 1978—, also dir.; v.p., dir. Lenders Appraisal Service Co., Newport Beach, 1979—; chief fin. officer Founders Funding Group, Newport Beach, 1979, chmn. bd., 1979—, also dir.; pres., chmn. bd. Equity Securities Inc., Newport Beach, 1975; dir. Dandylion Wine Co., 1972—. Mem. Laguna Beach (Calif.) Fin. Planning Com., 1974-75. Mem. Covina Valley Bd. Realtors. Club: Laguna Beach Rotary. Home: 237 San Miguel Circle Placentia CA 92670 Office: 901 Dove St Suite 295 Newport Beach CA 92660

HANKS, LARRY BERKLEY, life ins. co. exec.; b. Idaho Falls, Idaho, Sept. 25, 1940; s. Victor Franklin and Marjorie (Burke) H.; A.B., Brigham Young U., 1964; m. Georgia Lee Gammett, Dec. 29, 1965; children—Tiffany, Berkley, Colli, Andrea, Rachel, Jared, Cyrus. Owner, mgr. Larry B. Hanks, C.L.U., ins. and employee benefits, Boise, Idaho, 1969—; pres. Am. Pension Adminstrs. Inc., Boise, 1978—; gen. agt. Mass. Mut. Life Ins. Co., Boise, 1980—; instr. C.L.U. classes Am. Coll., Bryn Mawr, Pa., 1975—. Served with C.E., U.S. Army, 1968-69. Mem. Am. Soc. C.L.U. (dir. Magic Valley chpt.), Nat. Assn. Life Underwriters, Am. Soc. Pension Actuaries, N.E. Idaho Assn. Life Underwriters (dir., officer), Million Dollar Roundtable, Estate Planning Council Idaho Falls. Republican. Mormon. Home: 5669 Fieldcrest Dr Boise ID 83704 Office: 1471 Shoreline Dr Boise ID 83707

HANLEY, JOHN WELLER, mfg. co. exec.; b. Parkersburg, W.Va., Jan. 11, 1922; s. James P. and Ida May (Ayers) H.; B.S. in Metall. Engring., Pa. State U., 1942; M.B.A., Harvard, 1947; D.Eng. (hon.), U. Mo., Rolla, 1974; LL.D. (hon.), Maryville Coll., 1979, U. Pacific, 1980; m. Mary Jane Reel, June 26, 1948; children—John Weller, Michael James, Susan Jayne. Metall. engr. Allegheny Ludlum Steel Corp., 1942-43; with Procter & Gamble Co., 1947-72, mgr. case soap products, 1961-63, v.p. household soap products div., 1963-67, corp. v.p., group exec., 1967-70, exec. v.p., 1970-72, also dir.; pres., chief exec. officer Monsanto Co., St. Louis, 1972—, chmn. bd., 1975—, also dir.; dir. Citicorp., May Dept. Stores Co., So. Pacific R.R. Mem. Bus. Council, Washington, Bus. Roundtable, N.Y.; trustee Conf. Bd.; vice chmn. bd. govs. United Way Am., Alexandria, Va.; bd. dirs. Harvard Bus. Sch. Assos., Boston; vis. com. Harvard Med. Sch. and Sch. Dental Medicine; mem. nat. adv. council Salvation Army; mem. council Stanford Research Inst.; mem. St. Louis Civic Progress Assn.; trustee Washington U., St. Louis; mem. Nat. Council U.S.-China Trade. Served to lt. (s.g.) USNR, 1943-46; PTO. Recipient Distinguished Alumnus award Pa. State U., 1972; Merit award Urban League St. Louis, 1975. Home: 801 S Skinker Blvd Saint Louis MO 63105 Office: 800 N Lindbergh Saint Louis MO 63166

HANLEY, RICHARD LAWRENCE, investment banker, stock broker; b. Poughkeepsie, N.Y., June 17, 1947; s. Harry Vincent and Marie Joan H.; A.B., Georgetown U., 1968; M.B.A., Columbia U., 1971. Asso. Merrill Lynch, N.Y.C., 1971-72, Faulkner Dawkins & Sullivan, N.Y.C., 1972-74; v.p. Baird, Patrick & Co., N.Y.C., 1975-77; dir. research, sr. v.p. Ross Stebbins, Inc., N.Y.C., 1978-79; sr. v.p. Prescott, Ball & Turben, N.Y.C., 1979—. Mem. N.Y. Soc. Security Analysts. Republican. Roman Catholic. Club: Princeton N.Y. Home: 56 Sagamore Rd Bronxville NY 10708 Office: Prescott Ball & Turben One World Trade Center New York NY 10048

HANLIN, HUGH CAREY, ins. co. exec.; b. Chattanooga, Mar. 16, 1925; s. Hugh Carey and Irene Larrimore (Thompson) H.; student Emory U., 1942-44, 46-47; B.A., U. Mich., 1948; m. Wilma Jean Deal, June 23, 1951; children—Timothy Carey, Chris Allan. With Provident Life and Accident Ins. Co., Chattanooga, 1948—, exec. v.p., 1973-77, pres., 1977-79, pres., chief exec. officer, 1979—, also dir.; dir. Provident Gen. Ins. Co., 1974—; dir. Am. Nat. Bank & Trust Co. Active numerous civic orgns.; pres. Cherokee area council Boy Scouts Am., 1980; trustee U. Chattanooga Found., 1977—; bd. dirs. Tenn. Ind. Colls. Fund Assn., 1979-81, Chattanooga YMCA, 1980, United Fund, Chattanooga, 1980. Served to lt. (j.g.) USNR, 1943-46. Fellow Soc. Actuaries; mem. Southeastern Actuaries Club (pres. 1956-57), Chattanooga C. of C. Clubs: Rotary, Mountain City (dir. 1977—), Chattanooga Golf and Country. Office: Provident Bldg Fountain Sq Chattanooga TN 37402

HANNA, COLIN ARTHUR, trade exchange exec.; b. Abington, Pa., Dec. 3, 1946; s. Arthur and Jean Victoria (McClure) H.; A.B., U. Pa., 1968; m. Anne Price Hemphill, Dec. 28, 1967; 1 dau., JeanPrice. Account exec. CBS Radio Spot Sales, N.Y.C., 1969-70; mgr. creative services CBS-Viacom Group, N.Y.C., 1970-71; account exec. CBS Radio Spot Sales, N.Y.C., 1971-72, sales mgr., Phila., 1974-76; account exec. WCAU Radio, Phila., 1972-74; dir. sales devel. WCAU-TV, Phila., 1976; pres. Hanna & Wile Advt., Wayne, Pa., 1976-77, Tri-State Trade Exchange, Inc., West Chester, Pa., 1978-80, Hanna Enterprises Ltd., 1980—; dir. devel. Tradex Eastern Corp., Boston, 1980—, also dir. Served with USNR, 1968-69. Mem. Shakspere Soc. Phila., Am. Vets. Assn. (dir.), Soc. Coll. U. Pa. (dir.). Republican. Episcopalian. Clubs: Racquet (Phila.); Radley Run Country (West Chester). Home and Office: 603 Fairway Dr West Chester PA 19380

HANNA, FRANK JOSEPH, credit co. exec.; b. Douglas, Ga., Apr. 20, 1939; s. Frank Joseph and Josephine (Nahoom) H.; B.B.A., U. Ga., 1961; m. Vail Deadwyler, Sept. 15, 1960; children—Frank, Lisa, David. Credit mgr. Sears, Roebeck & Co., Atlanta, 1961-63, Gen. Motors Corp., Atlanta, 1963-65; gen. mgr. Rollins Acceptance Corp., Atlanta, 1965—; real estate developer, 1968—. Mem. Nat. Assn. Consumer Credit, Consumer Credit Assn., Atlanta Credit Club. Roman Catholic. Office: 2170 Piedmont Rd Atlanta GA 30324

HANNA, HENRY HARLAN, III, Realtor; b. Salisbury, Md., Feb. 15, 1947; s. Henry Harlan and Mable M. (Brown) H.; B.A., U. Va., 1969; M.B.A., So. Ill. U., 1980; m. Dara Lee Cragg, Oct. 21, 1972. Sales rep. Hanna Real Estate, Inc., Salisbury, Md., 1970-73; pres. Henry H. Hanna Real Estate Co., Inc., Salisbury, 1974-76; exec. v.p. Ahtes & Hanna Partners-Realtors, Inc., Salisbury, 1977—; mem. adv. bd. 2d Nat. Savs. and Loan Assn. Pres., Mid-Delmarva YMCA. Mem. Nat. Assn. Realtors, Nat. Assn. Home Builders, Salisbury C. of C. (dir.), Md. Assn. Realtors (dir. 1976-78). Democrat. Episcopalian. Home: 712 Burning Tree Circle Salisbury MD 21801 Office: Box 228 1 Plaza East Salisbury MD 21801

HANNAFORD, PETER DOR, pub. relations exec.; b. Glendale, Calif., Sept. 21, 1932; s. Donald R. and Elinor (Nielsen) H.; A.B., U. Calif., 1954; m. Irene Dorothy Harville, Aug. 14, 1954; children—Richard Harville, Donald R. II. Account exec. Helen A. Kennedy Advt., 1956; v.p. Kennedy-Hannaford, Inc., San Francisco and Oakland, Calif., 1957-62; pres. Kennedy, Hannaford & Dolman, Inc., 1962-67, Pettler & Hannaford, Inc., 1967-69; v.p. Wilton, Coombs & Colnett, Inc., 1969-72; pres. Hannaford & Assos., 1972-74; on leave as asst. to gov., dir. pub. affairs Gov.'s Office Calif., Sacramento, 1974; v.p. Deaver & Hannaford, Inc., Los Angeles, 1975-76, chmn. bd., chief exec. officer, 1977—. Pres., Mut. Advt. Agy. Network, 1968-69. Mem. Piedmont Park Commn., 1964-68; mem. Republican Central Com., Alameda County, 1966-74; mem. Rep. Central Com. Cal., 1968-74; pres. Alameda County Rep. Alliance, 1968-69; sec. Bay Area Rep. Alliance, 1970; Rep. nominee for congress 7th dist. Calif., 1972; bd. dirs. Childrens Hosp. Med. Center, Oakland, 1967-70, Oakland Symphony Orch. Assn. 1963-69, Calif. Roadside Council, 1965-69, San Francisco Opera Guild Talent Bank Found., 1967-75, Coro Found., 1973-74; elder Pasadena Presbyn. Ch., 1980—. Served to 1st lt. Signal Corps, AUS, 1954-56. Mem. Advt. Club Oakland (pres. 1961-62), Theta Xi. Clubs: Univ. (San Francisco); Univ. (Washington); Overseas Press (N.Y.C.); Guardsmen. Office: 10960 Wilshire Blvd Los Angeles CA 90024

HANNAHS, JAMES ROGER, lab. exec.; b. Columbus, Ohio, Dec. 23, 1942; s. James Harvey and Dorothy (Limes) H.; B.S. in Welding Engring., Ohio State U., 1967; m. Mary E. Hemmert, Jan. 7, 1967; children—Tricia, Michael. Welding engr. Hobart Bros. Co., Troy, Ohio, 1966-73; mgr. Bowser-Morner Testing Labs., Dayton, Ohio, 1973-79; pres. Midwest Testing Labs., Piqua, Ohio, 1979—, also dir; instr. U. Dayton, Edison State Coll., Hobart Sch. Welding Tech. Mem. Garfield Skill Center Adv. Com., Dayton; mem. adv. com. Western Ohio Youth Center, Troy; chmn. adv. com. Edison State Coll., Piqua; mem. adv. com. Upper Valley Joint Vocat. Sch., Piqua. Registered profl. engr., Ohio; cert. welding insp. Mem. Am. Welding Soc. (awards; past sect. chmn.), Am. Soc. Metals (awards; sect. treas.), ASME, ASTM, Nat. Soc. Profl. Engrs., Central Ohio Metallographic Sc., Theta Tau. Club: Ohio State U. Welding Engring. Alumni (dir.). Author: Porta-Slag Welding, 1970; contbr. articles to profl. jours.; patentee in field. Office: 8598 Industry Park Dr Piqua OH 45356

HANNAN, MYLES, diversified holding co. exec., lawyer; b. Rye, N.Y., Oct. 14, 1936; s. Joseph and Rosemary (Edwards) H.; A.B., Holy Cross Coll., 1958; LL.B., Harvard, 1964; m. Maureen Ann Ronan, June 24, 1961; children—Myles, Paul F., Thomas J. Admitted to N.Y. bar, 1964, Mass. bar, 1970; asso. firm Cadwalader, Wickersham and Taft, N.Y.C., 1964-69; v.p., gen. counsel, sec. High Voltage Engring. Corp., Burlington, Mass., 1969-73; v.p., sec. The Stop and Shop Cos., Inc., Boston, 1973-79; group v.p. law and adminstrn. Delaware North Cos., Inc., 1979—; dir. Anderson Power Products, Inc., Boston, Payment and Transfer Services, Inc., Lewiston, Maine. Served to lt. USNR, 1958-61. Home: 1240 Delaware Ave Buffalo NY 14222 Office: 700 Delaware Ave Buffalo NY 14209

HANNON, JOHN WILLIAM, JR., banker; b. N.Y.C., Apr. 22, 1922; s. John William and Leonora (King) H.; A.B., St. Lawrence U., 1946; m. Vivien Gardner, July 26, 1944; children—Bruce, Elizabeth, Christine. With Comml. Nat. Bank, N.Y.C., 1946-51; with Bankers Trust Co., N.Y.C., 1951—, adminstrv. v.p., 1970-75, pres., 1975—; dir. Consumers Power Co. Treas., chmn. finance com. local A.R.C.; mem. finance com. Community Blood Council. Trustee, treas. St. Lawrence U. Served as officer USAAF, 1942-45. Decorated Air medal. Office: Bankers Trust NY Corp 280 Park Ave New York NY 10017

HANNUM, WILLIAM EVANS, II, banker; b. Balt., Mar. 20, 1939; s. Ellwood and Lillian Victoria (Brown) H.; B.A., U. of South, 1961; M.A., U. Va., 1963, Ph.D., 1972; m. Susan Hathaway White, June 9, 1962; children—William Evans, Kirke Hathaway. Faculty, Washington and Lee U., Lexington, Va., 1964-65, Bates Coll., Lewiston, Maine, 1967-73; dir. personnel Canal Nat. Bank, Portland, Maine, 1973-79; asst. v.p., trust office Maine Nat. Bank, Portland, 1979—. Bd. dirs. Portland Symphony Orch., 1979—; mem. mus. com. Portland Art Mus., 1979—; mem. annual fund com. Maine Med. Center, 1979—. Club: Rotary. Address: 400 Congress St Portland ME 04104

HANRATTY, LAWRENCE CHARLES, mfg. co. exec.; b. Balt., June 30, 1935; s. Lawrence Bernard and Ruth Margaret (Willinger) H.; B.S., Johns Hopkins, 1967, M. Liberal Arts, 1970; m. E. Catherine Todd, Aug. 25, 1971; children—Ann, Sabrina, Colleen. Div. controller Roper Corp., Chattanooga, Tenn. and Hagerstown, Md., 1967-72; group controller Handy & Harman, N.Y.C. and Balt., 1972-74; v.p. fin. and adminstrn. Boyles Galvanizing Co., Hurst, Tex., 1974-78, also dir.; exec. v.p. Lake River Corp., Hinsdale, Ill., 1978—; instr. econs. Tarrant County Jr. Coll., Hurst. Organizer, fund raiser John F. and Robert F. Kennedy presdl. campaigns; active ACLU, Balt. Symphony Found., Cub Hill Riding Acad. (Md.), Abby Downs Riding Acad. (Tex.); scholarship trustee Johns Hopkins. Served with U.S. Army, 1953-62. C.P.A., N.Y., Md. Mem. Am. Inst. C.P.A.'s, Johns Hopkins Alumni Assn., Delta Sigma Pi. Democrat. Roman Catholic. Clubs: Balt. Alumni; Woodhaven Country; Hopkins. Author: Deferred Pay-Outs in the Tax-Free Corporate Acquisition, 1972; Capitalization Vs. Expense - A Critique of Critical Determinations, 1973. Contbr. articles to profl. jours. Address: 6 E 8th St Hinsdale IL 60521

HANS, PAUL CHARLES, fin. exec.; b. N.Y.C., Oct. 10, 1946; s. Charles Sigmund and Eleanore Lydia (Knorowski) H.; B.S. in Materials Sci. Engring., Brown U., 1968; M.B.A., U. Pa., 1972; m. Cynthia L. Troha, Dec. 22, 1977. Mktg. and tech. analyst advanced planning dept., Pratt & Whitney Aircraft div. United Technologies Corp., East Hartford, Conn., 1968-70; adminstr. fin. analysis and devel. Fairchild Space and Electronics Co. div. Fairchild Industries, Inc., Germantown, Md., 1972-74, mgr. fin. analysis parent co., 1974; dir. fin. analysis and planning Arvin Industries, Inc., Columbus, Ind., 1974-79, asst. treas., 1979-80; corp. mgr. comml. bus. devel. Gen. Dynamics Corp., St. Louis, 1980—. Mem. AIAA. Club: Indpls. Ski. Home: 16068 Clarkson Woods Dr Chesterfield MO 63017 Office: Pierre Laclede Center Saint Louis MO 63105

HANSEN, CHARLES MEDOM, chemist; b. Louisville, Sept. 16, 1938; s. Kristian and Alma H.; B.Chem. Engring., U. Louisville, 1961; M.S., U. Wis., 1962; Teknisk Licentiat, Techn. U. Denmark, 1964, Teknisk Doktor, 1967; m. Kirsten Lyck, June 23, 1967; children—Susan, Kristian, Michael. With PPG Industries, 1968-76; dir. Scandinavian Paint and Printing Ink Research Inst., Copenhagen, 1976—. Mem. Am. Chem. Soc., AAAS, Fedn. Soc. for Coatings Tech. Office: Scandinavian Paint and Printing Ink Research Inst Agern Alle 3 2970 Horsholm Denmark

HANSEN, DONALD WALDEMAR, distbn. and mfg. cos. exec.; b. Washington, Oct. 16, 1927; s. Waldemar Conrad and Muriel (Bruggman) H.; B.S., Purdue U., 1951; M.S., Iowa State U., 1952; m. Janet Eleanor Lines, Sept. 6, 1952; children—Kimberly, Philip, Jeffrey. Vice pres. Stamats Pub. Co., Cedar Rapids, Iowa, 1953-62; gen. mgr. PDI Internat. (A.B.), Time Inc., London, 1962-67; v.p., dir. Crosfield Electronics Inc., N.Y.C., 1967-68; with W.W. Grainger, Inc., Chgo., 1970—, v.p., 1973-76, v.p. ops., 1976-77, v.p. adminstrn. and planning, 1978—, dir., 1975—; pres. Doerr Electric Corp., W.W. Grainger, Inc., Wis., 1975-76; dir. Doerr Electric Corp., Roberts & Porter, Inc. Served with USN, 1946-47. Mem. Econ. Club Chgo., Sigma Alpha Epsilon, Sigma Delta Chi. Clubs: Lansdowne, Am. (London); Barrington Hills (Ill.) Country. Office: 5959 Howard St Chicago IL 60648

HANSEN, GLENN CHARLES, savs. and loan exec.; b. Oak Park, Ill., Nov. 11, 1947; s. Clarence Charles and Bernice Mary (Och) H.; B.S., Loyola U., Chgo., 1970, M.B.A., 1972; m. Mardelle Mary Garrity, Sept. 20, 1969; children—Liane Kathryn, Lauren Annie. Mgr., First Nat. Bank of Morton Grove (Ill.), 1969-71; analyst Fed. Home Loan Bank of Chgo., 1971-73; asst. v.p. mktg. First Fed. of Chgo., 1973-80, v.p. corp. planning, 1980—. Adj. faculty mem. William Rainey Harper Coll., Palatine, Ill. Mem. dean's adv. bd. Loyola U. Recipient Disting. Service award Loyola U., 1979. Home: 104 Fallstone St Lincolnshire IL 60045 Office: First Fed of Chgo 1 S Dearborn St Chicago IL 60680

HANSEN, HERBERT EDWIN, oil co. exec., lawyer; b. Cleve., Oct. 29, 1920; s. Marius and Romaine (Christman) H.; B.A. summa cum laude, Oberlin Coll., 1942; M.B.A. with distinction, Harvard, 1946, J.D., 1949; m. Marietta Grider Hewitt, Jan. 5, 1946; children—Marian Romaine, Donna Hewitt, David Christman. Admitted to Mo. bar, 1949; asso. firm Dietrich, Tyler and Davis, Kansas City, Mo., 1949-52; zone landman Gulf Oil Corp., Tulsa, Okla., also Wichita, Kans., 1952-56; adminstrv. asst. to gen. mng. dir. Iranian Oil Operating Co., Teheran, Iran, 1956-62; coordinator govt. agreements Eastern Hemisphere Gulf Oil Co., London, Eng., 1962-69; v.p. Gulf Oil Corp., Pitts., 1969-75; v.p. Gulf Oil Exploration and Prodn. Co., Houston, 1975-80, sr. v.p. internat. govt. relations, 1980—. Bd. govs. Middle East Inst., Washington; mem. adv. bd. Georgetown U. Program for Internat. Bus. Diplomacy, Houston World Trade Assn., Center for Internat. Bus., Houston and Dallas. Served to lt. comdr. USNR, 1943-46; PTO. Mem. Mo. Bar Assn., Harvard Law Sch. Assn., Houston Com. on Fgn. Relations, Asia Soc., Conf. Bd., Phi Beta Kappa. Republican. Methodist. Clubs: Houston, Harvard (Houston). Contbr. to Jour. Energy and Devel. Home: 11839 Durrette St Houston TX 77024 Office: Box 2100 Houston TX 77001

HANSEN, JAMES ALLEN, banker; b. West Point, Nebr., Jan. 10, 1939; s. Walter J. and Dorothy A. Hansen; B.A., Wayne State Coll., 1965; m. Rebecca A. Boyer, Nov. 27, 1975; children—Jeffrey, Cara, Elizabeth, Christopher. Acct., Dinklage Cattle Co., Wisner, Nebr., 1958-65; cashier 1st Nat. Bank, Wisner, 1965-69; v.p. Farmers State Bank, Aurora, Nebr., 1969-72; pres., dir. Farmers State Bank & Trust Co., Lexington, Nebr., 1972-80, 1st Savs. Co. of Lexington, 1979-80, North Side Bank, Omaha, 1980—. Pres. Bd. Edn., Lexington, 1976-80; mem. Council for Indsl. Devel., 1974—; bd. dirs. Bus. Devel. Corp. of Nebr., 1979-80; treas. Greater Lexington Corp., 1974-80; treas., bd. dirs. Lexington Meals on Wheels. Rotary Club Exchange exec. to Australia, 1970. Republican. Presbyterian. Clubs: Masons, Shriners, Rotary. Office: 31st and Ames Ave Omaha NE 68111

HANSEN, KIM DANIEL, chem. co. ofcl.; b. Bogota, Colombia, Jan. 20, 1950; s. Ole Daniel and Grete Heide (Jensen) H.; came to U.S., 1971; B.S. in Bus. Adminstrn., Babson Coll., Wellesley, Mass., 1974; m. Susan Marie MacKinnon, July 8, 1972; 1 dau., Kristina Marie. Sales rep. Nat. Merchandising Co., Natick, Mass., 1974, Dun & Bradstreet Inc., Boston, 1974; export mgr. Arne Vittrup, Cia Ltda., Bogota, 1975; sales rep. Dow Chem. Co. USA, Dallas, 1976—. Soccer coach Plano (Tex.) Sports Authority, 1978—. Served with Danish Marines, 1969-71. Mem. Soc. Petroleum Engrs., Nat. Paint and Coating Tech. Assn., Dallas Paint and Coating Assn. Lutheran. Clubs: Los Rios Country, Toastmasters (past chpt. v.p.). Home: 2605 Lemmontree Ln Plano TX 75074 Office: 12700 Park Central Dallas TX 75251

HANSEN, LAWRENCE LEROY, JR., ins. co. exec.; b. Bronxville, N.Y., Oct. 2, 1945; s. Lawrence LeRoy and Mildred R. H.; student C.W. Post Coll., 1963-65; B.S. in Indsl. Mgmt., U. New Haven, 1968; Asso. in Risk Mgmt., Ins. Inst. Am., 1977; m. Janet Susan Goodale, June 10, 1967; children—Lawrence LeRoy, Eric Reed. Asst. safety cons. Employers Ins. of Wausau, Syracuse, N.Y., 1968-70, safety cons., Albany, 1970-76, coordinator field safety services, Syracuse, 1976-77, regional safety and health mgr., 1978—. Cert. safety profl.; cert. product safety mgr. Mem. Am. Soc. Safety Engrs., Nat. Safety Mgmt. Soc. Home: 13 Gettman Dr Baldwinsville NY 13027 Office: PO Box 4834 Syracuse NY 13221

HANSEN, PETER J., import and export co. exec.; b. Los Angeles, Oct. 7, 1931; s. Charles Lawrence and Agnes Mary (Hanifan) H.; B.A., Fullerton Coll., 1953; m. 1967; 1 son. Civil engr. State of Calif., 1955-58; real estate devels. with numerous bldg. corps. throughout Calif., 1958-70; pres. Advance Components Corp. DBA Clark Electronics, Irvine, Calif., 1970—; pres. Peter Hansen & Assos., Inc., Las Vegas, developers. Served with USNR, 1950-62. Club: Balboa Bay. Home: 832 San Luis Rey Coronado Island San Diego CA 92109 Office: 555 Paularino Ave Costa Mesa CA 92626 also Suite 617 300 S 4th St Las Vegas NV 89101

HANSEN, THOMAS HAROLD, health care cons. co. exec.; b. Omaha, June 27, 1943; s. Harold Robert and Dorothy Jennette (Lingenfelder) H.; A.A., Allan Hancock Coll., 1969; student U. Md., 1965-67; standard cert. Am. Inst. Banking, 1972; m. Joan Marie Steiner, Dec. 26, 1967; children—Laura Ann, Tracy Lynn. Asst. br. mgr. First Trust & Deposit Co., Syracuse, N.Y., 1969-72; br. mgr. Seneca Fed. Savs. & Loan, Baldwinsville, N.Y., 1972; v.p. subs. Am. Hosp. Supply Corp., Evanston, Ill., 1972-77; sr. v.p. Med. Care Systems, Inc., Alstead, N.H., 1977-79; pres. IMPAC, Inc., Walpole, N.H., 1979—; sec., dir. Hosp. North, Inc., North Syracuse, N.Y., 1971-72. Fund raiser Boy Scouts Am., Syracuse, 1972; mem. United Health Systems Agy., Concord, N.H., 1977-80. Served with USAF, 1964-68. Mem. Am. Acad. Med. Adminstrs., Am. Hosp. Assn., N.H. Hosp. Assn. Republican. Office: PO Box 667 Walpole NH 03608

HANSEN, WALDEMAR HENRY, banker; b. Bklyn., Oct. 5, 1931; s. Walter Hans and Emily (Parola) H.; B.Chem. Engring., Bklyn. Polytech. Inst., 1953; M.B.A., Temple U., 1961; m. Mary Elizabeth Wilson, Sept. 11, 1954; children—David, Craig, Todd. Research chem. engr. Mobil Oil Co., Paulsboro, N.J., 1955-62; project mgr. Mobil Chem. Co., N.Y.C., 1962-65; mgr. market research Nat. Distillers & Chem. Co., N.Y.C., 1965-68; asst. v.p., then v.p. Irving Trust Co., N.Y.C., 1968—. Served with AUS, 1953-55. Mem. Bank Adminstrn. Inst., Am. Inst. Chem. Engrs., Am. Chem. Soc., Chem. Marketing Research Assn. Home: 13 Birchwood Ln Westport CT 06880 Office: One Wall St New York NY 10017

HANSEN, WALTER EUGENE, ins. exec.; b. Woodland, Wash., May 15, 1929; s. August Hans and Esther Johanna (Johnson) H.; grad. high sch.; m. Donna Carol Phillips, Aug. 1, 1953; children—Larry, Monty, Gena, Martin, Lori, Bradley, Walter Eugene. Laborer lumbering field, 1943-51; service mgr. Sears Roebuck & Co., Los Angeles, Portland, Oreg., 1951-57; agt. various ins. cos., 1957-63, dist. mgr., 1960-61, state mgr., 1963-65, regional mgr., 1963-72; owner Pacific N.W. Ins. Service, Portland, 1963—, Am. Pacific Agys., Portland, 1970—, Am. Pacific Services, Portland, 1970—, Nat. Research Assos., Seattle, 1968—; farmer, Woodland, 1962—. Active Boy Scouts Am.; chmn. Community Bicentennial Commn., 1976. Mem. Internat. Platform Assn., Nat. Assn. Life Underwriters, Accident and Health Underwriters Assn. Club: Elks. Home: PO Box A Woodland WA 96874 Office: PO Box 12225 Portland OR 97212

HANSFORD, LARRY CLARENCE, air force officer, beekeeping supplies and honey mfg. co. exec.; b. La Porte, Ind., Oct. 15, 1945; s. Curtis Edgar and Eva Maree (Owens) H.; B.E.E., Ga. Inst. Tech., 1975; m. Mabel Darlene Miller, June 27, 1970; 1 son, Patrick Robert. Asst. purchasing agt. Dobbs House, Inc., Atlanta Airport, 1963-65; enlisted man U.S. Air Force, 1965-75, commd. 2d lt., 1975, advanced through grades to capt., 1979; computer systems analyst Mil. Airlift Command, Scott AFB, Ill., 1976-80, Air Force Communications Command, 1980—; pres., chmn. bd. Milk-N-Honey Acres, Inc., Baldwin, Ill., 1978-79, owner, 1980—. Supt. edn. Skyland United Meth. Ch., Atlanta, 1973-75; sec. enlistment 1st United Meth. Ch., Sparta, Ill., 1978—. Mem. Am. Beekeeping Fedn., Am. Dairy Goat Assn., Ill. State Beekeepers Assn. Republican. Home: Rural Route 1 Box 156 Baldwin IL 62217 Office: 2199 CPUSS/ADT Scott AFB IL 62225

HANSON, CARL DWAYNE, oil co. exec.; b. Fredericktown, Pa., May 31, 1927; s. John Lawrence and Mildred (Cook) H.; B.S. in Petroleum Engring., Pa. State U., 1950; m. Nellda L. Bynum, June 1, 1953; children—Carl Dwayne, Lisa Ann, Jon Bynum. With Forest Oil Corp., 1950—, gen. prodn. mgr., Denver, 1966-73, v.p. prodn., 1973—. Served with USNR, 1945-46. Registered prof. engr., Colo. Mem. AIME, Am. Petroleum Inst., Rocky Mountains Oil and Gas Assn., Ind. Petroleum Assn. Am. Methodist. Clubs: Cherry Hills Country, Columbine Country, Petroleum. Home: 4580 Sumac Ln Littleton CO 80123 Office: 1500 Colorado Nat Bldg Denver CO 80202

HANSON, FRED T., lawyer; b. Wakefield, Nebr., Feb. 25, 1902; s. Peter H. and Hannah Ulrika (Anderson) H.; LL.B., U. Neb., 1925; m. Helen Elizabeth Haddock, Nov. 12, 1928; 1 son, John Fredrik. Admitted to Nebr. bar, 1925, since in pvt. practice; probate judge, 1931-42, pros. atty., 1927-30, 51-54; spl. asst. to U.S. atty. gen., 1954-62; life mem. Nat. Conf. of Commrs. Uniform State Laws from Nebr., com. on uniform probate code. Bd. dirs. Nebr. dist. Lutheran Ch.-Mo. Synod; mem. editorial bd., contbr. Lay Voice Nebr. Lutherans. Served as capt. AUS, 1942-46. Mem. Am. Judicature Soc., Am. Coll. Probate Counsel (regent), Am., Nebr., local bar assns., Am. Legion. Office: 316 Norris Ave McCook NE 69001

HANSON, JOHN NILS, elec. equipment co. exec.; b. Berwyn, Ill., Jan. 22, 1942; s. Robert and Stephanie Ann (Kazluskas) H.; B.S., M.I.T., 1964, M.S. (Sloan fellow), 1965; Ph.D., Carnegie Mellon U., 1969; m. Stephanie Morgan, June 5, 1965; children—Laurel, Mark Nils. Sr. scientist Westinghouse Electric, Bettis Atomic Power Lab., W. Mifflin, Pa., 1965-70, mgr. advanced test core, 1971-73; exec. asst. to Sec., U.S. Dept. Labor, Washington, 1970-71; asst. to pres. Gould, Inc., Chgo., 1973-74, pres. electric motor div., St. Louis, 1974-78, group v.p. elec. products, Rolling Meadows, Ill., 1978—. Active U.S. Right to Work Com., 1977—, White House Fellows Assn., 1971—; dir. White House Fellows Found., 1973; mem. vis. com. on sponsored research M.I.T., 1979—. White House fellow, 1970. Mem. Nat. Elec. Mfrs. Assn. (bd. govs. 1980). Sigma Xi, Phi Sigma Kappa. Republican. Contbr. articles in field to profl. jours. Office: 10 Gould Center Rolling Meadows IL 60008

HANSON, MARLON FAYE, newspaper exec.; b. Breckenridge, Minn., Jan. 25, 1948; s. Martin and Ferne Marie (Dunn) H.; B.B.A., Pace U., 1977; M.B.A., Adelphi U., 1980; m. Carmela D'Elia, July 6, 1968; children—David Joseph, Alexander Anthony. With N.Y. Daily News, 1970—, statistician, 1974-76, sr. statistician, 1977-79, mgr. Mgmt. Info. Systems, 1980—. Served with USAF, 1966-70. Republican. Home: 8 Grand Canyon Ln Coram NY 11727 Office: 220 E 42d St New York NY 10017

HANSON, MICHAEL FREDERICK, radio sta. exec.; b. Saskatoon, Sask., Can., Mar. 11, 1940; s. Francis John and Elva Pearl (McLean) H.; B.A., U. B.C., 1962, M.B.A., 1963; m. Sharon Dawn McDonald, Dec. 21, 1963; children—Michael Gregory. Newscaster, CFUN, Vancouver, B.C., 1963, sales promotion mgr., 1964-66; retail sales mgr. CHSC-AM-FM, St. Catharine, Ont., 1967-70, gen. sales mgr., 1971-74, gen. mgr., 1975-79; v.p., gen. mgr. CHSC and CHRE-FM, St. Catharines, also CHNR, Simcoe, Ont., 1980—; chmn. Radio Bur. Can., 1979—; instr. bus. adminstrn. Brock U.; pres. Press Theatre Inc., 1979—. Mem. Central Can. Broadcasters Assn. (pres. 1976-77), St. Catharines Advt. and Sales (pres. 1974). Club: Rotary (pres. St. Catharines South 1980). Office: Sta CHSC 36 Queenston St Sainte Catharines ON L2R 7C7 Canada

HANSON, NOEL RODGER, mgmt. cons.; b. Los Angeles, Jan. 19, 1942; s. Albert and Madelyne Gladys (Pobanz) H.; B.S. in Indsl. Mgmt., U. So. Calif., 1963, M.B.A. in Fin., 1966; m. Carol Lynn Travis, June 17, 1967; 1 son, Eric Rodger. Asst. dir. alumni fund, then dir. ann. funds U. So. Calif., 1964-66; asst. to Walt Disney for Cal-Arts, Retlaw Enterprises, Glendale, Calif., 1966-68; asst. dir. joint devel. Claremont U. Center, 1968-69; v.p. adminstrn. Robert Johnston Co., Los Angeles, 1969-70; partner Hale, Hanson & Co., Pasadena, Calif., 1970—; dir. Pasadena Fin. Cons., Inc. Trustee Oakhurst Sch., Pasadena, 1973-75; bd. advisers Girls Club Pasadena, 1977—; mem. U. So. Calif. Assos., 1979—, U. So. Calif. Commerce Assos., 1965—. Republican. Presbyterian. Club: Jonathan (Los Angeles). Address: 1051 LaLoma Rd Pasadena CA 91105

HANSON, NORMAN MARK, computer services co. exec.; b. Omaha, June 22, 1937; s. Richard Emmanuel and Margaret Elsie (Gautier) H.; B.S.Ed. (Ford Found.-M3 fellow), U. N.Mex., 1964; M.S. in Math., U. Houston, 1968; m. Cheryl Elaine Perkins, Nov. 1, 1976; children—Norman Mark, Rodney Emerson. Research mathematician Shell Oil, Houston, 1964-69; staff cons. Asso. Computer Services, Houston, 1969-71; mgr. tech. services-process control, 1971-72; staff cons. Biles & Assos., Houston, 1972-77; cons. SETPOINT, Houston, 1977, v.p. product devel., 1977—. Served with USN, 1956-60. Sr. mem. Instrument Soc. Am. Designer, developer process control software packages, Music, 1965-69, Prose/Aim, 1973-77, SETCON, 1979-80. Office: SETPOINT Inc 901 Threadneedle Suite 150 Houston TX 77079

HANSON, ROBERT ARTHUR, agrl. equipment exec.; b. Moline, Ill., Dec. 13, 1924; s. Nels A. and Margaret I. (Chapman) H.; B.A., Augustana Coll., Rock Island, Ill., 1948; m. Patricia Ann Klinger, June 25, 1955. Various positions Deere & Co., Moline, 1950-62, gen. mgr., Mexico, 1962-64, gen. mgr., Spain, 1964-66, dir. mktg. overseas, 1966-70, v.p. overseas ops., 1972, sr. v.p. overseas div., 1973, dir., 1974—, exec. v.p., 1975-78, pres., 1978—, chief operating officer, 1979—; dir. Davenport Bank & Trust Co. (Iowa), Dun & Bradstreet; internat. council Morgan Guaranty Trust Co., N.Y.C. Adv. com. bus. programs Brookings Instn. Bd. dirs. Augustana Coll., Rock Island. Served with USMCR, 1943-46. Home: 2200 29th Avenue Ct Moline IL 61265 Office: John Deere Rd Moline IL 61265

HANSON, ROBERT CARL, III, bus. exec., industrialist; b. Detroit, Sept. 15, 1928; s. Robert Carl and Grace (Morris) H.; student Valparaiso U., 1945-49; B.S. in Mech. and Indsl. Engring., Purdue U., 1951; postgrad. U. Mich., 1958; m. Betty Jean Hastings, June 16, 1951; children—Robert Clayton, Bettina, Erik Brian. Indsl. engr. Alcoa, Lafayette, Ind., 1951; exec. officer (ops.) and chief control office U.S. Army Missile Test and Evaluation Directorate, White Sands Missile Range, 1951-61; asst. to v.p. research and engring. Gen. Dynamics Corp., N.Y.C., 1961-66; v.p., gen. mgr. Reflectone, Inc. subs. Otis Elevator Co., Stamford, Conn., 1966-69; cons. gen. mgmt., corp. planning and mktg., 1969-73; v.p. ops. Greenwich Mills Co., Secaucus, N.J., 1973—. Served with U.S. Army, 1946-48, 51-55. Recipient Lion of Yr. award Lions Club, El Paso, Tex., 1960; Packaging Pioneer award St Regis Paper Co., 1976, Package of Year awards, 1976, 79. Mem. Am. Inst. Indsl. Engrs. (sr.), Metric Conversion Panel, Nat. Coffee Assn. U.S.A., Pi Tau Sigma, Tau Kappa Epsilon. Lutheran. Club: Smoke Rise. Home: 735 Ridge Rd Smokerise Kinnelon NJ 07405 Office: 520 Secaucus Rd Secaucus NJ 07094

HANSON, ROBERT EUGENE, state ofcl.; b. Jamestown, N.D., Aug. 26, 1947; s. Louis J. and Kathlene A. (Wilmart) H.; B.S. in Bus. Adminstrn., N.D. State U., Fargo, 1968; m. Melody R. McFall, May 11, 1974; children—Jason Paul, Jamie Beth, Kristen Anne. Campaign scheduler N.D. Democratic-Non-Partisan League Party, Bismarck, 1968-70, campaign mgr., 1970; legis. aide Dem. Non-Partisan League Legislators, Bismarck, 1971; youth coordinator State of N.D., Bismarck, 1971, also manpower planner N.D. Employment Security Bur.; spl. asst. Office N.D. Gov. William L. Guy, Bismarck, 1971-73; dep. state treas. State of N.D., Bismarck, 1973-79, state treas., 1979—; chmn. State Investment Bd., 1979—. Vice chmn. Central Regional Conf. Nat. Conf. State Liquor Adminstrs., 1975, exec. sec.-treas., 1976-79, v.p., 1979—; chmn. Vets. Day, 1977; chmn. U.S. Savs. Bond, N.D., 1978-79; treas. N.D. Heritage Center Found., 1979—; Dem. candidate for State Pub. Service Commr., 1978; bd. dirs. Easter Seal Soc., N.D. PTA. Served with U.S. Army, 1968-70. Decorated Bronze Star medal with oak leaf cluster; recipient Pi Omega award, 1968. Mem. Am. Soc. Pub. Adminstrs., Am. Legion, VFW, Blue Key. Roman Catholic. Clubs: Elks, Lions, N.D. Century. Author: Minutes of the National Conference of State Liquor Adminstrators, 1976, 77, Official Directory of State Liquor Administrators, 1978. Home: 304 Teton Ave Bismarck ND 58501 Office: State Treas Office Bismarck ND 58501

HANSON, ROBERT LEONARD, office products co. exec.; b. Chgo., May 19, 1937; s. James L. and Thyra (Johnson) H.; A.A., Northwestern Mich. Coll., 1956; B.S., Ferris Inst., 1958; m. Mary Frances Filomeno, Nov. 18, 1961; children—Linda, Michael, Jeffrey, Karyn, Tracy. Mem. sr. staff Arthur Andersen & Co., Chgo., 1958-66; v.p. finance ACCO div. Gary Industries, Chgo., 1966-69, v.p., gen. mgr. ACCO Canadian Co. Ltd., Toronto, Ont., Can., 1969-72, v.p. materials mgmt., asst. to pres. ACCO Internat., Wheeling, Ill., 1972—. Mem. Wheeling Indsl. Devel. Bd., 1977—; scouting chmn. Skokie Valley Dist. council Boy Scouts Am., 1976-77; mem. Northbrook (Ill.) Vol. Pool, 1977—; bd. dirs. Northwest Community Hosp. Found. Served with U.S. Army, 1961. Paul Harris fellow Rotary Internat., 1977—. Mem. Wheeling Area Chamber Commerce and Industry (pres. 1977-78, dir.), Assn. Internal Mgmt. Consultants, Adminstrv. Mgmt. Soc., Assn. Systems Mgmt., Am. Mgmt. Assn., Windham Homeowners Assn. (pres. 1979-80, dir. 1977—). Clubs: Rotary of Wheeling (pres. 1980-81, dir.); North Suburban Jr. Varsity Hockey League (gen. mgr. 1978—); Scarboro Golf and Country (Toronto). Home: 3010 Margo St Northbrook IL 60062 Office: 770 S ACCO Plaza Wheeling IL 60090

HANSON, WILLIAM ALBERT, mfg. co. exec.; b. Boston, May 12, 1921; s. Albert Jarvis and Reina Ellen (Brackett) H.; student Boston U., 1939-40, Milw. Sch. Engring., 1941-44, U. Wis., 1943-44; Ph.D., Calif. Western U., 1979; children—Maren L. Malhas, Priscilla L. Silverman, Royal A. Devel. engr., lab. research dir. Lee Found. for Nutritional Research, Milw., 1940-52; founder Hanson Research Corp. and subs. Enzyme Process Co., Northridge, Calif., 1952—, pres., chief exec. officer, 1968—; cons. engr. Pres., Joint Bd. of Westlake Village, 1973; pres. Westlake Lake Mgmt. Assn., 1974-76; pres. Acad. Aquatic Ecosystems, 1977—. Served with Signal Corps, U.S. Army, 1945-46. Registered profl. engr., Calif., Wis. Mem. Am. Acad. Environ. Engrs., Am. Arbitration Assn., Nat. Soc. Profl. Engrs., Instrument Soc. Am., Acad. Aquatic Ecosystems. Unitarian. Clubs: Westlake Yacht (commodore 1979), Masons (Shriner). Author: (with Royal Lee) Principles of Cell Regulation, 1947; contbr. articles to profl. jours.; patentee in field. Home: 2546 Northlake Circle Westlake Village CA 91361 Office: 19727 Bahama St Northridge CA 91323

HANSON, WINSTON ROBERT, JR., computer co. exec.; b. Sacramento, June 15, 1944; s. Winston Robert and Virginia M. Hanson; B.S., Calif. State U., Northridge, 1971; M.B.A., U. So. Calif., 1976. Purchasing agt. R.V. Weatherford Co., 1972-73; buyer Xerox Corp., 1973-76; corp. purchasing agt. Davis Walker Corp., Los Angeles, 1976-79; inventory control mgr. Pertec Computer Corp., Chatsworth, Calif., 1979—. Served with U.S. Army, 1967-71. Office: 9600 Irondale Ave Chatsworth CA 91311

HANWAY, JOHN, II, multinational co. exec.; b. Mt. Vernon, N.Y., Oct. 23, 1924; s. John Howard and Marie Theresa (Fenlon) H.; grad. Hill Sch., 1942; B.A., Yale, 1948; m. Elena Gracia, May 8, 1950; children—John III, David Howard (dec.), Robert William, Linda, Thomas Edward. With A.D. McKelvy Co., also Prince Matchabelli, Inc., 1948-53, Robert Heller & Assos., 1953-63; with Internat. Tel. & Tel. Corp., 1963—, v.p. adminstrn., 1964—, also sr. v.p., 1964—. Served to 1st lt., pilot USAAF, 1942-45; PTO. Office: ITT Corp 320 Park Ave New York NY 10022

HARBECK, WILLIAM JAMES, chain store exec.; b. Glenview, Ill., Dec. 16, 1921; s. Christian F. and Anna (Goethe) H.; student Lake Forest Coll., 1942-43; B.A., Wabash Coll., 1947; J.D., Northwestern U., 1950; m. Jean Marie Allsopp, Jan. 20, 1945; children—John, Stephen, Timothy, Mark, Christopher. Admitted to Ill. bar, 1950; land acquisition atty. Chgo. Land Clearance Commn., 1950-51; real estate negotiator Montgomery Ward & Co., Chgo., 1951-56, real estate mgr. South Central region, Kansas City, Mo., 1957-64, North Central region, Chgo., 1964-68, asst. to pres., dir. corporate facilities, 1968-70, v.p., dir. facilities devel., 1970—; pres., chief exec. officer Montgomery Ward Properties Corp., Chgo., 1974—; v.p. Montgomery Ward Devel. Corp., 1972—; dir. Randhurst Corp.; instr. Bethel Bible Coll., 1975—. Chief crusader Chgo. Crusade of Mercy, 1976-78; bd. dirs. Greater N. Michigan Ave. Assn., 1979—; chmn. constrn. com. Chgo. United, 1979-80; bd. dirs. Internat. Council Shopping Centers, mem. law and govt. affairs com., mem. pub. relations com., mem. exec. com., lectr.; mem. Pres.'s Council Concordia Coll., 1969—; div. chmn. Cerebral Palsy Campaign, 1977-78; corporate chmn. U.S. Bond Dr., 1976; bd. dirs. Luth. Found., 1975-76; bd. dirs., chmn. devel. com. Lawson YMCA, Chgo. Served to lt. (s.g.) USNR, 1942-46. Life mem. Field Mus. Natural History, Patrons of Lyric Opera. Mem. Ill., Chgo. bar assns., Chgo. Symphony Orch. Soc., Phi Alpha Delta, Alpha Sigma Chi, Pi Alpha Chi. Republican. Lutheran (Laymen's League, youth dir.; mem. mission study commn. 1974-75; mem. task force on constn., by-laws and structure Mo. synod 1976—). Editorial bd. Legal Publs. Sch. Law Northwestern U. Contbr. articles to profl. jours. Home: 470 E Linden St Lake Forest IL 60045 Office: 1 Montgomery Ward Plaza Chicago IL 60671

HARBIN, WAYNE DEWITT, mfg. co. exec.; b. Donna, Tex., Apr. 29, 1925; s. Jesse Mathuews and Lela (Bettes) H.; B.B.A., U. Tex., 1949; postgrad. Harvard, 1962; m. Elinor Victoria Tolish, Apr. 17, 1946; children—Kenneth Wayne, Richard Wayne. With Arthur Young & Co., N.Y.C., also Houston, 1959-68, adminstrv. partner, 1959-68; pres., chmn. bd. Marathon Mfg. Co., Houston, 1968-73; pres., chmn. bd. Richmond Tank Car Co., Houston, 1973—; dir., mem. exec. com. Crutcher Resources Corp., Houston. Mem. adv. council U. Tex. Bus. Sch., 1963—, mem. chancellors com., recipient distinguished alumni award; mem. Pres.'s council Baylor U. Served with USN, 1942-46. C.P.A., N.Y., Tex. Mem. Am. Inst. C.P.A.'s, Tex. Soc. C.P.A.'s (past dir.), Tex. Assn. Bus. (past dir.), Tex. Mfrs. Assn. (past dir.). Baptist. Mason. Clubs: Harvard Business (Cambridge, Mass.); Petroleum, Coronado, River Oaks Country (Houston). Home: 3994 Inverness St Houston TX 77019 Office: 1700 West Loop S Suite 1500 Houston TX 77027

HARBISON, EARLE HARRISON, JR., chem. co. exec.; b. St. Louis, Aug. 10, 1928; s. Earle Harrison and Rose (Hensberg) H.; student Harvard U., 1960; A.B., Washington U., St. Louis, 1949, LL.B., 1957; m. Suzanne Groves Siegel, Nov. 18, 1952; children—Earle Douglas, Keith Siegel. With CIA, Washington, 1949-67; dir. mgmt. info. systems dept. Monsanto Co., 1967-73, dir. corp. orgn. and mgmt. devel. dept., 1973-75, gen. mgr. specialty chems. div., 1975, gen. mgr. plasticizers div., 1976-77, gen. mgr. detergents and phosphates div. and plasticizers div., 1977, v.p., mng. dir. Monsanto Comml. Products Co., 1977, mem. corp. adminstrv. com., 1977, group v.p., mng. dir. Monsanto Indsl. Chems. Co., St. Louis, 1979—. Bd. dirs., pres. Mental Health Assn. St. Louis, 1973-78; mem. long-range planning com. United Way of Am., 1976—, mem. personnel devel. com., 1973-75, chmn. agy. relations subcom., 1977, mem. program evaluation com., 1977—, chmn. subcom. on youth and voluntarism, 1979—; bd. dirs. Bethesda Gen. Hosp., 1979—. Served with AUS, 1950-65. Mem. Fed. Bar. Clubs: Old Warson Country, Ponte Vedra (Ponte Vedra Beach, Fla.). Office: 800 N Lindbergh Blvd Saint Louis MO 63166

HARD, ARNE MAYNARD, savs. and loan exec.; b. Kiron, Iowa, Jan. 21, 1921; s. Perry A. and Hannah E. (Nilsson) H.; student Am. Inst. of Bus., 1937-40; m. Shirley C. Eckman, Apr. 22, 1944. With Am. Fed. Savs. and Loan Assn., Des Moines, 1946-61, asst. v.p., 1950-61; with Hawkeye Savs. and Loan Assn., Boone, Iowa, 1961—, pres., 1971-80, chmn., 1980—; dir., past chmn. First Central Service Corp.; dir. Mid-Iowa Security Corp., Mid Central Service Corp. Trustee Am. Inst. of Bus.; bd. dirs., pres. Boone County YMCA, 1970-76; past bd. dirs., past chmn. Boone County chpt. ARC; bd. dirs. United Fund, 1965, Madrid Home for Aging, 1980; trustee Mamie Eisenhower Restoration Com.; bd. dirs. Augustana Luth. Ch., 1977—, treas., 1980. Served with USAAF, 1942-46. Named Boss of Yr., Boone Jr. C. of C., 1965, Am. Bus. Women's Assn., 1975. Mem. C. of C. (pres. 1965). Clubs: Lions, Boone Country, Armes Country. Home: 1128 Country Club Dr Boone IA 50036 Office: Hawkeye Savs and Loan Assn 8th and Arden Sts Boone IA 50036

HARDAGE, SAMUEL ALTON, real estate co. exec.; b. Jackson, Miss., Mar. 14, 1939; s. Samuel Alton and Alice (Woodfin) H.; B.S. with distinction, U.S. Air Force Acad., 1961; M.B.A., Harvard, 1968; m. Allison Price, Dec. 24, 1969; children—Briarly, Adam. Asst. to v.p. and gen. mgr. Boise Cascade Corp. (Idaho), 1968-69; asst. to pres., mgr. ops. Am. Mobilehome Corp., Los Angeles, 1969-73; pres. U.S. Communities, Inc., Los Angeles, 1973-76, Wichita, Kans., 1976—; pres. Hardage Enterprises, Inc., 1976—; dir. Wichita Area Devel., Inc., mem. exec. com., 1974—. Cons. to Ford Found. sponsored Bus. Assistance Program, Harvard Bus. Sch., 1966-68. Bd. dirs. Wichita Festivals, Inc., 1974—. Served to capt. USAF, 1961-66; Vietnam. Mem. Wichita C. of C. (chmn. indsl. devel. com. 1973-74). Methodist (pres. youth fellowship 1955-57). Rotarian. Clubs: Wichita Country, Wichita, Wagonmasters, Finance (pres. 1967-68). Home: 236 North Crestway Wichita KS 67208 Office: 100 S Main St Wichita KS 67202

HARDESTY, CHARLES HOWARD, JR., lawyer, oil co. exec.; b. Fairmont, W.Va., Jan. 18, 1922; s. Charles Howard and Elizabeth (Miller) H.; grad. Mercersburg (Pa.) Acad., 1939; B.S., Duke, 1943; LL.B., W.Va. U., 1949; m. Doris Wilson, Apr. 24, 1946; children—Sarah Elizabeth, Charles Howard III. Admitted to W.Va. bar, 1949, since practiced in Fairmont as partner Furbee & Hardesty; state tax commr., W.Va., 1961-62; gen. counsel Consolidation Coal Co., 1963-68, v.p., sec., 1965-66, exec. v.p., 1966-68; sr. v.p. Continental Oil Co., 1968-72, exec. v.p., 1972-74, pres. Eastern Hemisphere Petroleum div., 1974-75, vice chmn., 1975-77, also dir.; partner firm Rose, Schmidt, Dixon, Hasley, Whyte & Hardesty, Washington, 1978—; chmn., pres., chief exec. officer Commonwealth Oil Refining Co., San Antonio, 1979—; dir. Purolator Inc., NCR Corp., Consol. Natural Gas Co. Trustee Duke. Served with USNR, 1943-46. Mem. Am., Pa., W.Va. (pres. 1964) bar assns. Democrat. Office: 1575 I St NW Washington DC 20005

HARDIMAN, PAUL WORTHINGTON, telephone co. exec.; b. Concord, N.H., Feb. 1, 1943; s. John Patrick and Phyllis Pearl H.; A.S., Grahm Jr. Coll., 1966; B.S. in Bus. Adminstrn., Boston U., 1968; m. Judith Virgin, Sept. 2, 1967; children—Leigh Ann, Sara, Abbe. Asst. mgr. bus. office New Eng. Telephone Co., Claremont, N.H., 1969-72, staff mgr. rates and tariffs exec. dept., 1972-74, mktg. cons., 1974-76, account exec., 1976-78, account exec. II (state mgr.), 1978—; condr. ann. N.H. State Police Communications Seminars, 1978—; propr. Olmec Motor Lodge, Meredith, N.H. Pres., Concord Boys' Club, 1979—. Served with USNR, 1964-66; Vietnam. Lic. real estate salesman, N.H.; justice of peace; notary public. Mem. Am. Mgmt. Assn., N.H. Good Roads Assn., Indsl. Mgmt. Club. Republican. Roman Catholic. Clubs: Concord Athletic, Concord Country. Office: 143 N Main St Concord NH 03301

HARDIN, GEORGE CECIL, JR., petroleum cons.; b. Oakwood, Tex., Oct. 6, 1920; s. George Cecil and Pearl (Moore) H.; B.S. in Geology and Petroleum Engring., Tex. A. and M. U., 1941; Ph.D. in Geology (Van Hise fellow), U. Wis., 1942; m. Virginia Howard, Nov. 21, 1942; children—George Howard, Susan. Mining engr. Victory Fluorspar Mine, Cave in Rock, Ill., 1942; geologist U.S. Geol. Survey, 1942-45, party chief, 1944-45; geologist Carter Gragg Oil Co., Palestine, Tex., 1945-46; geologist, petroleum engr. M.T. Halbouty Cons., Houston, 1946-51; exploration and prodn. mgr. M.T. Halbouty Oil and Gas Interests, Houston, 1951-59, gen. mgr., 1959-61; exec. v.p. Halbouty Alaska Oil Co., 1957-61; partner Hardin & Hardin, cons. geologists, Houston, 1961-64; mgr. oil and gas exploration Kerr-McGee Oil Ind., Inc., 1964-65; v.p. N.Am. Oil & Gas Exploration, 1965-67, v.p. oil, gas and minerals exploration, 1967-68, group v.p. exploration, 1968; v.p. Kerr-McGee Argentina, 1967-68, Kerr-McGee Can., Ltd., 1967-68, Kerr-McGee Australia, Ltd., 1967-68; pres., chief exec. officer Royal Resources Corp., Houston, 1968-70; pres. Ashland Exploration Co. div. Ashland Oil, Inc., Houston, 1970-80, also sr. v.p. parent co.; petroleum cons., 1980—; dir. Continental Bank & Trust Co., Houston, 1956—, mem. exec. com., 1956-62, chmn. auditing com., 1962—; dir. North Side State Bank, Houston, Ashland Oil Can. owner Poverty Ridge Farm, Oklahoma City, 1966—. Registered profl. engr., Tex., Okla. Fellow Geol. Soc. Am., A.A.A.S.; mem. Houston Geol. Soc. (pres. 1961-62), Soc. Econ. Paleontologists and Mineralogists, New Orleans, South Tex. geol. socs., Gulf Coast Assn. Geol. Socs. (pres. 1959), Am. Assn. Petroleum Geologists (sec.-treas. 1964-66), Soc. Exploration Geophysicists Am. Inst. Profl. Geologists. Clubs: Petroleum, Plaza, River Oaks Country (Houston); Brazos River Hunting and Fishing, Columbia Lakes Country (West Columbia, Tex.). Contbr. articles to profl. jours. Home: 204 Arborway Houston TX 77057 Office: 1115 Barkdull Houston TX 77006

HARDING, EDWARD LLOYD, real estate broker; b. Washington, N.C., Feb. 22, 1953; s. Henry Champion and Dorothy Ann (Lloyd) H.; B.S., Atlantic Christian Coll., 1976. Spl. rep. Pilot Life Ins. Co., Washington, 1977-80; crew chief Rodman & Waters Land Surveying & Civil Engring., Washington, N.C., 1980—. Block capt. Citizens Crime Watch; Fund raising chmn. Beaufort County Heart Fund, 1976-77. Mem. Washington Jr. C. of C. (Presdl. award of Honor, 1976-77, dir. 1977-78, sec. 1979-81; Speak Up award 1976-80, Spoke award 1976). Democrat. Episcopalian. Home: 615 Bank St Washington Park Washington NC 27889 Office: 137 N Market St Washington NC 27889

HARDING, JOHN CHARLES, III, mfg. co. exec.; b. Fall River, Mass., Feb. 28, 1937; s. John Charles and Alice (Wallace) H.; B.S., Lehigh U., 1959, M.B.A., 1961; m. Elizabeth Katherine Donovan, Sept. 3, 1960; children—John Christopher, Elizabeth Ann, Daniel Joseph, Katherine Patricia, Margaret Mary, Richard Daniel, Christina Ann, Jennifer Kathleen, Laura Christine. With Price Waterhouse & Co., Boston, 1961-64, Plimpton Press div. McCall Corp., Norwood, Mass., 1964-66; asst. controller The Dyson-Kissner Corp., a N.Y. holding co., 1966, v.p., controller, 1967-72; dir., pres., chief exec. officer Bickford Corp. (formerly LaTouraine-Bickford's Foods, Inc.), Brighton, Mass., 1972—; dir. Pneumo Corp., Boston, Kearney-Nat. Inc., N.Y.C. Trustee, Newton-Wellesley Hosp., Newton, Mass.; 1st v.p. Francis Ouimet Caddie Scholarship Fund, Weston, Mass., 1977—. Mem. Am. Inst. C.P.A.'s, Nat. Restaurant Assn., Beta Gamma Sigma, Pi Gamma Mu, Beta Alpha Psi. Republican. Roman Catholic. Clubs: Kittansett, Charles River Country, Algonquin. Office: 1330 Soldiers Field Rd Brighton MA 02135

HARDING, WAYNE EDWARD, III, business exec.; b. Topeka, Sept. 29, 1954; s. Wayne Edward and Nancy M. (Gean) H.; B.S. with honors in Bus. Adminstrn., U. Denver, 1976; m. Janet O'Shaughnessy, Sept. 5, 1979. Partner, HKG Assos., Denver, 1976-77; staff auditor Peat, Marwick, Mitchell & Co., Denver, 1976-78; auditor Marshall Hornstein, P.C., Wheat Ridge, Colo., 1978-79; sr. auditor Touche Ross & Co., Denver, 1979-80; controller Mortgage Plus, Inc., Englewood, Colo., 1980—; dir., sec., treas. Sunlight Systems Energy Corp., 1980—; dir. Harding Transp., Crown Parking Products; formerly instr. Nat. Coll. Bus. extension, Denver. Class agt., mem. alumni council Phillips Exeter Acad., Exeter, N.H., 1973—; bd. dirs. Legal Center for Handicapped Citizens, Denver. Lic. real estate broker, Colo. Mem. Am. Inst. C.P.A.'s, Colo. Soc. C.P.A.'s, Beta Alpha Psi, Pi Gamma Mu, Beta Gamma Sigma. Republican. Home: 6029 S Kenton Way Englewood CO 80111 Office: 5680 S Syracuse Circle Suite 106 Englewood CO 80111

HARDIS, STEPHEN ROGER, mfg. co. exec.; b. N.Y.C., July 13, 1935; s. Abraham I. and Ethel (Krinsky) H.; B.A. with distinction, Cornell U., 1956; M.P.A., Princeton U., 1960; m. Sondra Rolbin, Sept. 15, 1957; children—Julia, Andrew, Joanna. Asst. to controller Gen. Dynamic Corp., Rochester, N.Y., 1960-61; exec. v.p. fin. and planning Sybron Corp., Rochester, 1961-79; exec. v.p. fin. and adminstrn. Eaton Corp., Cleve., 1979—; dir. Gilford Instrument Labs. Inc., Schlegel Corp., Central Nat. Bank of Cleve. Mem. Cleve. Council on World Affairs, 1980. Bd. dirs. Cleveland Opera Co. Served with USNR, 1956-58. Woodrow Wilson Nat. fellow, 1958. Mem. Fin. Execs. Inst., Machinery and Allied Products Inst., Phi Beta Kappa. Clubs: Clevelander, Cleve. Racquet. Office: 100 Erieview Plaza Cleveland OH 44114

HARDISON, LESLIE CLAIRE, pollution control co. exec.; b. Chgo., Feb. 16, 1929; s. William Leland and Lyda Sue (Sims) H.; B.S. in Mech. Engring., Ill. Inst. Tech., 1950; m. Dolores Wachdorf, June 14, 1952; children—William, John, Patricia, Susan, Janet, James, Paul. Asst. bldg. supt., research project engr. Ill. Inst. Tech. Research Inst., Chgo., 1950-53; process engr., supt. ops., asst. mgr. process devel., dir. research and devel., tech. dir. Universal Oil Products Co., Des Plaines, Ill., 1953-70; v.p. Air Resources, Inc., Palatine, Ill., 1970-78, chmn., pres., 1978—; chmn., pres. Nat. Seal Co., Palatine, 1979—. Bd. dirs. Greater Chgo. Com. To Use Energy Wisely. Registered profl. engr., Ill., Pa., Colo.; cert. Nat. Bd. for Cert. Profl. Engrs. Mem. Am. Chem. Soc., Am. Inst. Chem. Engrs., ASME, Air Pollution Control Assn., Am. Mgmt. Assn. Republican. Contbr. articles to profl. jours.; patentee in field. Home: 233 Apple Tree Ln Barrington IL 60010 Office: 600 N First Bank Dr Palatine IL 60067

HARDY, ROBERT SAYRE, fin. co. exec.; b. Bklyn., May 4, 1933; s. Reginald Sayre and Mae Estelle (Sculthorp) H.; A.B. in Sociology with honors, U. Pa., 1954; postgrad. in Sociology, U. Conn., 1954-55; m. Barry Eisenhower, June 11, 1955; children—Suan C., Virginia M., Janet L. Br. mgr. Stromberg Datagrphix; sr. v.p., chief operating officer DCL Inc., 1969-73; pres. Robert S. Hardy Assos., N.Y.C., 1973-77; v.p., treas., dir. Computer Financial, Inc., Hackensack, N.J., 1977-80; pres. No. Telecom Fin. Corp., Nashville, 1980—; past chmn. Diebold Computer Leasing S.A., Paris; past dir. Diebold Computer Leasing Ltd., London; dir. DCL Capital Corp., Rathmines Midland Fin., Birmingham, Eng., Malvern Fin., Worcestershire, Eng., Chem. Cleaning Services, London, Danea Chao Travel Inc., N.Y.C., Computer Fin., Inc., N.J., No. Telecom Acceptance Corp., Nashville; cons. NSF, 1976. Served as spl. agt. CIC, U.S. Army, 1956-59. Am. Assn. Equipment Leasors. Republican. Episcopalian. Clubs: Saddle River Valley; White Elephant; Acad.; Swim and Tennis; Skytop (Pa.) Lodge. Author: Glossary of Leasing Terminology, 1981. Home: 15 Barnfield Ct Upper Saddle River NJ 07548 Office: 219 Cumberland Bend MetroCenter Office Park Nashville TN 37228

HARDYMON, JAMES FRANKLIN, tool co. exec.; b. Maysville, Ky., Nov. 11, 1934; s. Kenneth Thomas and Pauline (Strode) H.; B.S. in C.E., U. Ky., 1956, M.S. in C.E., 1958; m. Rebecca Gay Garred, June 25, 1960; children—Jennifer, Frank. Vice pres. planning and devel. Borwning div. Emerson Electric Co., 1970-73, exec. v.p. Browning div., 1973-76, pres. spl. products div., 1976-79, group v.p., Chgo., 1979—, pres. Skil Corp. subs., 1979—; dir. State Nat. Bank, Maysville, Ky., 1975-76. Bd. dirs. Mason County Airport Authority, 1973-76, Maysville Community Coll., 1974-76. Served with U.S. Army, 1958-59, 1961-62. Recipient Corp. Devel. award ASME, 1976. Mem. Ky. Profl. Engrs., Power Tool Inst. Republican. Mem. Christian Ch. Club: Knollwood Country. Office: 4801 W Peterson Ave Chicago IL 60646

HAREN, JAMES HARRISON, bus. exec.; b. Denton, Tex., Mar. 25, 1935; s. William Harrison and Effie E. (Jones) H.; B.S., Va. Poly. Inst. and State U., 1955; M.A., N.Mex. State U., 1968; postgrad. Tex. Tech. U., 1958-59; children—James Harrison II, David M., Susan J., Jeffrey W., Gregory P., Jamie L. Tchr., coach Washington Lee High Sch., Arlington, Va., 1958-60; pres. Safe Baby Products Co., Washington and Pitts., 1960-72; pres. Internat. Inventors, Inc. East, Alexandria, Va., 1972—; pres. Internat. Bartending Inst., Alexandria, 1977—. Served with U.S. Army, 1956-58. Mem. Va. Assn. Pvt. Career Schs., Better Bus. Bur., Washington C. of C. Home: 1884 St Andrews Place Longwood FL 32750 Office: 113 Robin Rd Altamonte Springs FL 32701

HARGADON, BERNARD JOSEPH, JR., mfg. mgr.; b. Ardmore, Pa., Dec. 27, 1927; s. Bernard Joseph and Anna Mendenhall (Lancaster) H.; B.S., Drexel U., 1952, M.B.A., 1959; m. Lee Jones, June 13, 1953; children—Geoffrey, Robert, Louise, Lawrence, David. Auditor, Gen. Motors Corp., 1955-57; instr. acctg. Drexel U., 1957-59; prof., cons. AID, Colombia, 1960-64; with Foremost-McKesson, San Francisco, 1964—, pres. Foremost-McKesson Internat. div., 1980—; adj. prof. internat. bus. Golden Gate U. Served with USN, 1945-48. Mem. Am. Acctg. Assn. Clubs: San Francisco Tennis; Boundary Oaks Tennis (Walnut Creek, Calif.). Author: Principles of Accounting (Spanish), 1964; Principles of Cost Accounting (Spanish), 1971. Home: 17 Mi Elana Ct Walnut Creek CA 94598 Office: 1 Post St San Francisco CA 94104

HARGITT, EDWIN FORRY, investment advisor; b. Indpls., Aug. 12, 1934; s. Paul Lee and Caroline Malott (Forry) H.; B.A., Wabash Coll., 1956; B.S., Purdue U., 1960, M.B.A., 1961; m. Verma Lee Steely, Nov. 26, 1966; children—Edwin Forry, Charles Victor, Russell Cushing, Danlee Malott, Marea Eden, David Edmond. Treas. Dahl Corp., Lafayette, Ind., 1961-67, Fin. Services, Inc., Lafayette, 1967-72, Dunn & Hargitt, Inc., Lafayette, 1972-73; pres. Dunn & Hargitt Investment Mgmt., Inc., Lafayette, 1973—; gen. partner Financial Futures Fund, Denver; dir. Dunn & Hargitt Research S.A., Brussels. Pres., West Lafayette High Sch. PTA; sec. West Lafayette Sch. Bldg. Corp.; co-chmn. West Lafayette Swimming Pool Com.; chmn. SME Sycamore council Girl Scouts U.S.A.; cubmaster Boy Scouts Am.; pres. Lafayette Youth Hockey; deacon, elder Covenant Ch. Registered investment adviser SEC, commodity trading advisor, commodity pool operator Commodity Futures Trading Commn. Mem. Nat. Assn. Futures Trading Advisors (founding dir.), Market Tech. Assn., Fin. Analysts Fedn., Am. Fin. Assn., Phi Delta Theta. Republican. Clubs: Rotary, Elks. Editor, pub. Market Guide, 1962—, Commodity Service, 1965—, Growing Child, 1971—, Growing Parent, 1971—, Option Charts, 1973—. Home: 128 Mohican Ct West Lafayette IN 47906 Office: 22 N 2d St Lafayette IN 47902

HARGRAVE, ALEXANDER DAVIDSON, banker; b. Canandaigua, N.Y., Mar. 17, 1920; s. Thomas J. and Catherine (Davidson) H.; A.B., Princeton U., 1941; LL.B. cum laude, Harvard U., 1948; m. Marcia Van Der Voort; children—Susan Hargrave Hopeman, Alexander M., Charles C., Margaret Hargrave Mariner. Admitted to N.Y. State bar, 1948; partner firm Nixon, Hargrave, Devans & Doyle, 1948-63; exec. v.p. Lincoln First Bank of Rochester (N.Y.), 1963-68, pres., 1968-74, chief exec., 1970-74; pres., chief exec. Lincoln First Banks Inc., Rochester, 1974-78, chmn. bd., 1975—, chief exec., 1978—, also dir.; chmn. bd., chief exec. Lincoln First Bank, N.A., Rochester, 1979—, also dir.; dir. Bausch and Lomb Inc., Gleason Works, Rochester Telephone Corp., Visa Internat., Sybron Corp.; chmn. bd. VISA U.S.A. Inc. Trustee Internat. Mus. of Photography, George Eastman House, Rochester Inst. Tech.; bd. dirs. Automobile Club of Rochester, Rochester/Monroe County Conv. and Publicity Bur., Inc.; founder Rochesterians. Served to lt. comdr., USN, 1941-45. Recipient Disting. Eagle award Otetiana Council Boy Scouts Am., 1977. Mem. Am. Bar Assn., N.Y. State Bar Assn., Monroe County Bar Assn. Clubs:

Country of Rochester; Genesee Valley; Princeton of N.Y. Office: 1 Lincoln First Sq Rochester NY 14643

HARGRAVE, GLENN MORTIMER, former interior designer; b. Sulphur Springs, Tex., Sept. 7, 1908; s. Joseph Wheeler and Belle (Healy) H.; student N.Y. Sch. Interior Design, 1955; m. Cecille Terry, Oct. 9, 1937. Constrn. supt. Spencer Constrn. Co. and others, 1937-40; salesman Browning-Ferris Machinery Co., Dallas, 1940-42; owner Hargrave Machinery Co., McKinney, 1946-53; co-owner, partner, mgr. contract dept. Interiors by Cecille (now Glenn & Cecille Hargrave, interior designers, consultants, specifiers), Dallas, Texas, 1953-70; interior designers Gt. So. Life Ins. Co. Offices, Dallas, Italian Village Restaurant, Dallas, Gt. Commonwealth Life Ins. Co. Offices, Dallas, Uarco Printing Co. Offices, Paris, Tex. Melrose Hotel, Dallas, U.S. Aviation Underwriters, Inc., Teeling Mtg. Co., lobby Western Hills Hotel, Ft. Worth; co-designer interior Garland (Tex.) City Hall, Midway Park Elementary Sch., Euless, Tex., also many residences. Lectr. (with wife) Career Day clinics, schs. and colls. Served with USMC, 1927-31, World War II; PTO; with Shanghai Vol. Corps, China, 1932-33. Recipient (with wife) Instns. mag.'s Interiors award for interior design Sam Rayburn Meml. Student Center, E. Tex. State U., 1964. Mem. Soc. Animal Protection, DAV, VFW, 6th Marine Div. Assn., Arthritis Found. Home: 6938 Winchester St Dallas TX 75231

HARGRAVE, ROBERT WEBB, banker; b. Evansville, Ind., May 8, 1920; s. William Jasper and Erma Christina (Fabian) H.; B.S. in Acctg., U. Notre Dame, 1942; m. Florence I. Molyneaux, Nov. 11, 1944; children—Robert Webb, Christine, Thomas, Susan, John, Michael, Jane. With Haskins & Sells, Chgo., 1945-47, Bell & Gossett Heating Equipment, Morton Grove, Ill., 1947-48; with Citizens Nat. Bank, Evansville, 1948—, pres., 1978—. Pres. St. Mary's Med. Center Found., 1979-80; mem. Vanderburgh County Sheriff Merit Bd., 1961—. Served with USNR, 1942-45. Mem. Evansville C. of C., Ind. Bankers Assn., Am. Bankers Assn., Evansville Petroleum Club. Republican. Roman Catholic. Clubs: Evansville Country, Evansville Kennel. Office: 19 NW 4th St Evansville IN 47708

HARGREAVE, JOHN HAROLD, III, advt. exec.; b. Wilkes-Barre, Pa., Sept. 10, 1910; s. John H. and Elizabeth (Weismer) H.; student Ind. State Coll., 1929-30; B.S., Temple U., 1935; m. Marilyn J. Caunitz, Nov. 26, 1965; children—Daryl Anne (Mrs. Robert Mahon), Pamela (Mrs. Joseph T. Carrigan), Leslie. Pres. mktg. research firm J.H. Hargreave Assos., Phila., 1935-39, Albany, N.Y., 1939-44; now pres. Hargreave Assos., Advt., pub. relations and mktg.; sales cons. Dearstyne Bros., Albany, 1946-53; theme park cons. and designer Rips Retreat, Haines Falls, N.Y., 1954-61; pres. Land of Rip Van Winkle, Inc., Saugerties, N.Y., 1954-61; cons., gen. mgr. Wonder Mountain Park, Liberty, N.Y., 1961-62; v.p. Bass & Co., N.Y.C., 1961—; pres. Big Bear Ski Bowl, Inc., Vega, N.Y., 1962—; pres. lab. div. Hargreave Assos.; dir. Man Machine & Music, Inc., Woodstock, N.Y., Vibroscope Co., Inc., Glenford, N.Y.; adj. asst. prof. bus. adminstrn. Greene-Columbia Community Coll. Chmn., Cancer drive, Saugerties, N.Y., 1957; mem. men's com. Japan Internat. Christian Found. Sec., Albany Republican Club, 1940. Served with USNR, 1944-46. Mem. United Comml. Travelers, Internat. Platform Assn., Geneal. Soc. Pa., Sigma Phi Epsilon. Mem. Dutch Ref. Ch. (deacon, elder). Mason, Odd Fellow. Clubs: Temple University (N.Y.C.); Varsity, Quarterback, Temple U. Assos. (Phila.). Contbr. articles to profl. jours. Home: Box 62 Woodstock NY 12498 Office: Box 62 Woodstock NY 12498 also 111 Broadway New York City NY 10006 also 259 Smith Ave Kingston NY 12401

HARGROVE, ROBERT CLYDE, lawyer; b. Shreveport, La., Dec. 13, 1918; s. Reginald Henry and Hallie (Ward) H.; B.A., Rice U., 1939; LL.B., Yale, 1942; m. Marjorie Clare Chinski, June 17, 1941; children—Robert Clyde (dec.), Reginald Henry II. Admitted to La. bar, 1946, D.C. bar, 1975; partner Hargrove, Guyton, VanHook & Hargrove, 1946-56; asst. gen. counsel Tex. Eastern Transp. Corp., 1953-55; sec., counsel J.B. Beaird Co., 1954-56; partner Hargrove Oil & Gas Co., 1948—, v.p. Bechtel Internat. Corp., 1958-61; practiced in Shreveport, 1961—; of counsel firm Hargrove, Guyton, Ramey & Barlow, Shreveport, 1978—. Life asso. Rice U.; past mem. alumni bd. govs. Sewanee (Tenn.) Mil. Acad.; trustee U. of South, Sewanee. Served to capt. AUS, 1942-45. Decorated D.S.C., Purple Heart. Mem. Am., D.C., La., Fed. Energy bar assns., Wolf Trap Found., Met. Opera Assn. (nat. council). Democrat. Episcopalian. Clubs: Shreveport; Met. (Washington); Hawkeye Hunting (Center, Tex.). Home: 614 Oakhill Dr Shreveport LA 71106 Office: Commercial Nat Bank Bldg Shreveport LA 71101

HARHAY, WARREN CHARLES, electric vehicle mfg. co. exec.; b. Cleve., Aug. 3, 1943; s. Joseph Stephen and Hedwig (Krucke) H.; student Kent State U., 1962-66; B.A., Cleve. State U., 1969; m. Marcia Lee Gibson, June 10, 1967; children—Matthew, Marshall, Mitchell. Field service engr., Ohio Sound Systems, Northeast Ohio, 1964-67; broadcast studio and transmitter engr., Stas. WERE, WJW, WMMS, Cleve., 1967-69; sr. instr. electronics, Normandy High Sch., Parma, Ohio, 1969-73; pres. Electric Vehicle Assos., Inc., Cleve., 1973—, also chief exec. officer; apptd. mem. nat. battery adv. council U.S. Dept. Energy. Ordained deacon, ruling elder, chmn. stewardship com. United Presbyterian Church. Mem. IEEE, Soc. Automotive Engrs., Cleve. Engring. Soc. Club: Rotary. Expert witness, U.S. Congress, 1974, 79, Dept. Transp., 1977; contbr. tech. papers to confs.; patentee electric vehicle drives. Home: 6374 Fry Rd Brook Park OH 44142 Office: 9100 Bank St Cleveland OH 44125

HARKINS, PETER BOWERS, assn. exec.; b. Upper Darby, Pa., Feb. 7, 1941; s. John G. and Elizabeth Bowers H.; A.B., U. Pa., 1963, M.G.A. (Samuel S. Fels fellow), 1967; m. Donna Jean Lovett, Dec. 30, 1971; children—Karen Lia, Peter Barnaby. Legis. counsel Nat. League of Cities and U.S. Conf. of Mayors, Washington, 1967-70; exec. dir. Md. Municipal League, Annapolis, 1970-73; spl. asst. to mayor of Indpls., 1973-76; dir. program devel., bd. dirs., govtl. cons. Nat. League of Cities, Washington, 1976; exec. dir. Dealer Bank Assn., Washington, 1976—; pres. Municipal Fin. Forum of Washington, 1969. Active Westbriar (Va.) Civic Assn. Served with USN, 1963-65. Mem. Internat. City Mgmt. Assn., Am. Soc. Assn. Execs., Am. Soc. Pub. Adminstrn., Am. Polit. Sci. Assn. Clubs: Univ. (Washington), Westwood Country (Va.). Home: 1009 Country Club Dr Vienna VA 22180 Office: Dealer Bank Assn 1800 K St NW Suite 1014 Washington DC 20006

HARLAN, LEONARD MORTON, real estate developer, cons.; b. Newark, June 1, 1936; s. Harold Robinson and Doris Harriet (Siegler) H.; B.M.E., Cornell U., 1959; M.B.A. with distinction, Harvard U., 1961, D.B.A., 1965; m. Elizabeth Nan Kramon, Aug. 27, 1969; children—Joshua, Noah. Security analyst Donaldson, Lufkin & Jenrette, Inc., 1965-69, v.p., 1968-69; founder, chmn. bd. The Harlan Co., Inc. (formerly Harlan, Betke & Myers Inc.), N.Y.C., 1969—; dir., co-owner San Luis Central R.R., 1970-78; gen. partner Real Estate Partnerships, 1971—; co-owner HBM Properties, Inc., 1976-78; founder, co-owner Mich. Interstate Ry. Co., 1977—; dir. Quidnet Capital Corp., guest lectr. Harvard and Columbia U. grad. schs. bus. adminstrn., 1968—, others; adj. asso. prof. N.Y. U. Real Estate Ist., 1968—, Grad. Sch. Bus. Adminstrn., 1976-80; adj. prof. bus. adminstrn. Columbia U. Grad. Sch. Bus. Adminstrn., 1980—. Mem. Pres.'s Com. on Indsl. Innovation, 1978-80; mem. exec. com. N.Y. chpt. Am. Jewish Com., 1975—, Central N.J. chpt. Recipient Charles B. Shatuck Meml. award Am. Inst. Real Estate Appraisers, 1967; Disting. Tchr. award N.Y. U., 1979; Ford Found. fellow, 1964-65; Zurn fellow, 1962-63. Lic. real estate broker, N.Y., N.J. Clubs: Harvard, Harvard Bus. Sch. (admissions com. 1973-75, v.p. 1977-79) (N.Y.C.). Editorial bd. Real Estate Inst. Jour.; contbr. articles to profl. jours. Office: The Harlan Co Inc 150 E 58 St New York NY 10155

HARLAN, NORMAN RALPH, builder; b. Dayton, Ohio, Dec. 21, 1914; s. Joseph and Anna (Kaplan) H.; indsl. engring. degree U. Cin., 1937; m. Thelma Katz, Sept. 4, 1955; children—Leslie Anne, Todd. Pres., Am. Constrn. Corp., Dayton, 1949—, Mainline Investment Corp., 1951—; pres. Harlan, Inc., realtors; treas. Norman Estates, Inc. Mem. Dayton Real Estate Bd., Ohio Real Estate Assn., Nat. Assn. Real Estate Bds., C. of C., Pi Lambda Phi. Home: 303 Glenridge Rd Kettering OH 45429 Office: 2451 S Dixie Dr Dayton OH 45409

HARLAN, RIDGE LATIMER, mgmt. cons.; b. Pilot Grove, Mo., Feb. 25, 1917; s. George B. and Dale (Latimer) H.; B.J., U. Mo., 1939; postgrad. Harvard, 1943, Colo. U., 1945-46, Stanford U. Grad. Sch. Bus., 1965; m. Barbara Hawley, Oct. 7, 1939; children—Brooke, Holly Ann, Robert Ridge; m. 2d, Marjory Folinsbee, June 4, 1976. Pres. Barnes-Hind Pharms., Inc., 1972-76; prin. Harlan & Clucas, Inc., San Francisco, 1968—; pres. Charila Found., 1969-73; chmn. bd., pres. Flores de las Americas, 1979—; chmn. Millenium Systems, Inc., 1978—; dir. Am. Microsystems, Inc., Velo-Bind, Inc., Tech. Equities, Inc., Impulflor de Mexico. Served to lt. (j.g.) USNR, 1943-46. Mem. Nat. Investor Relations Inst. (dir.), Assn. for Corporate Growth (dir.), Alpha Delta Sigma, Kappa Tau Alpha. Clubs: Olympic, The Family, Commonwealth (San Francisco). Home: 839 Seabury Rd Hillsborough CA 94010 Office: 155 Montgomery St San Francisco CA 94104

HARLAN, ROSS EDGAR, utility co. exec.; b. Poteau, Okla., July 11, 1919; s. Edgar L. and Leola (Carter) H.; student Southeastern State Coll., Okla., 1937-38, Eastern Okla. A. and M. Coll., 1938-39; B.S., Okla. State U., 1941; m. Margaret Burns, May 31, 1942; children—Raymond Carter, Rosemary, Marvin Allen, Scott Lee. With Okla. Gas & Electric Co., 1946—, v.p., Oklahoma City, 1964—, sr. v.p., 1978—. Mem. adv. bd. Okla. State U. Tech. Inst.; pres. adv. council Okla. State U. Coll. Bus.; mem. Okla. Council Econ. Edn. Served with Okla. N.G., 1937-38, 47; to lt. col. USAAF, 1941-46. Recipient George Washington Honor medal Freedoms Found., Valley Forge, Pa., 1969; named to Okla. State U. Coll. Bus. Hall of Fame. Mem. Oklahoma City C. of C., Nat. Wrestling Hall of Fame (gov.), Beta Gamma Sigma. Methodist. Club: Beacon (Oklahoma City). Author: Strikes, 1947. Home: 2639 Eagle Lane Oklahoma City OK 73127 Office: 321 N Harvey St Oklahoma City OK 73101

HARLAN, STEPHEN DONALD, accountant; b. St. Louis, Oct. 24, 1933; s. Stephen Donald and Mary Edith (Baker) H.; B.S. in Accounting, U. Mo., 1959; m. Mary Joan Heath, 1958; children—Ann, Donald. Mem. staff PMM & Co., St. Louis, 1959-67, partner, 1967-70, partner charge of audit Long Range Planning and Research Group, 1970-75, mng. partner, Washington, 1975—; speaker. Served with AUS, 1953-56. Recipient certificate of merit U. Mo., 1976. Mem. Am. Inst. C.P.A.'s, Met. Washington Bd. Trade, D.C., N.Y. socs. C.P.A.'s, Nat. Accountants Assn. Clubs: Internat., Univ., George Town, Columbia Country. Home: 11113 Bellavista Dr Potomac MD 20854 Office: 1990 K St NW Washington DC 20001

HARLEY, LEWIS KENNETH, mgmt. cons.; b. N.Y.C., Feb. 3, 1953; s. Sydney K. and Louise E. (Kelly) H.; B.Sc. in Chem. Engring., U. W.I., 1974; M.B.A., L.I. U., 1980. Market analyst GAF Corp., N.Y.C., 1974; sales engr. Stauffer Chem. Co., Westport, Conn., 1974-78; mgmt. cons. Charles H. Kline & Co., Fairfield, N.J., 1978—. Mem. Am. Soc. Lubrication Engrs., Chem. Mktg. Research Assn. Democrat. Roman Catholic. Home: 313 Richard Ct Pomona NY 10970 Office: 330 Passaic Ave Fairfield NJ 07006

HARLING, JOHN A., banker; b. Woodland, Calif., Sept. 17, 1935; s. Robert D. and Elizabeth (Allen) H.; B.S., Iowa State U., 1960; postgrad. U. Nebr., Omaha, 1954, 62-64, Creighton U., 1963; m. Nancy K. Rose, Nov. 4, 1978; children—Kimberly, Vicky, Penny, Douglas, Stephanie. Farmer, Lucas County, Iowa, 1960-62; acct. Jay G. Quick, C.P.A., Omaha, 1962-64; bus. analyst Omaha Bank for Coops., Omaha, 1964-67, asst. v.p., 1967-69, v.p., 1969-73, pres., 1973—. Bd. dirs. Presbyn. Theol. Sem., Omaha, Nebr. Meth. Hosp. Served with AUS, 1954-56. Mem. U.S. Feed Grains Council (dir.), Agrl. Builders Nebr. (chmn. mktg. com.), Omaha C. of C. (v.p. agrl. council). Republican. Presbyterian. Clubs: Rotary, Omaha (dir.). Office: 206 S 19th St Omaha NE 68102

HARLOW, ARTHUR ALLEN, electric utility exec.; b. Thompson Falls, Mont., Feb. 20, 1935; s. Paul Kidder and Margaret (Barto) H.; B.A. with distinction, Stanford U., 1957, M.A., 1959; m. Michele Lynn Leitch, June 4, 1966; children—Margaret Erin, Melinda Catherine. Agrl. statistician U.S. Dept. Agr., Washington, 1959-62; economist Bonneville Power Adminstrn., Spokane, Wash., 1962-72, area power mgr., 1973—. Bd. dirs. Youth Employment Service, Spokane, 1976—, pres., 1978—; bd. dirs. United Way of Spokane County, 1974-76, chmn. planning and allocation div., 1975; bd. dirs. Spokane Fed. Credit Union, 1974—, pres., 1975-78. Earheart fellow, Stanford U., 1958; recipient Am. Farm Econ. Assn. award for best pub. research, 1962. Mem. Hist. Auto Soc. Spokane and Inland Empire (dir. 1974-77, pres. 1976). Contbr. articles to profl. jours. Home: S 1130 Wall St Spokane WA 99204 Office: W 920 Riverside Ave Spokane WA 99201

HARMA, RISTO, agrl. economist; b. Liminka, Finland, Aug. 8, 1924; came to U.S., 1961; s. Paavo and Tyyne H.; M.S. in Econs., U. Helsinki, 1949; Ph.D. in Econs. of Agr., Cornell U., 1954; m. Rosemary Irene Sander, July 15, 1967; children—Risto Frederick, Saara Elizabeth, Joanna Catherine. Grad. asst. Cornell U., 1952-53; research and extension officer Agrl. Work Efficiency Assn. Finland, 1954-55; sec. Govt. Com., Finland, 1955-56; dir. Mktg. Research Inst., Pellervo Assn., Finland, 1955-59; editor Quar. Econ. Rev. of Kansallis-Osake-Pankki, Finland, 1959-60; with World Bank, Washington, 1961—, sr. agrl. economist, 1971—; vis. lectr. U. Md., 1977-78. Served with Finnish Army, 1943-45. Lutheran. Home: 9218 Aldershot Dr Bethesda MD 20034 Office: 1818 H St NW Washington DC 20433

HARMAN, CODY, JR., mining equipment co. exec.; b. Richlands, Va., July 24, 1949; s. Cody and Reva H.; student Bluefield (W.Va.) State Coll., 1972; m. Connie DeReene Horne, Apr. 5, 1969; children—Julia DeReene, Jennifer Renee, Richard Wade. Engr., Pittston Group Coal Co., Lebanon, Va., 1967-69; research and devel. designer S & S Corp., Richlands, 1970-75; pres., owner Triangle Mining Equipment Co., Inc., Cedar Bluff, Va., 1975—, sec.-treas. subs. Mine Controls Co. Inc., Cedar Bluff, 1975—; v.p. Messick Br. Coal Co., Cedar Bluff, 1977—; owner Julie Coal Co., Cedar Bluff. Bd. dirs. Richlands Christian Acad., Va. Penecostal Youth Camps. Home: Cedar Bluff VA 24609 Office: PO Box 225 Cedar Bluff VA 24609

HARMAN, ROBERT MAX, real estate devel. co. exec.; b. Salt Lake City, Dec. 9, 1929; s. Kenneth Hemenway and Ada Lerona (McDonald) H.; student Ariz. Sch. Bus. Adminstrn., 1952-55; m. Charlene Suzanne Larson, Nov. 5, 1966; children—Scott Hemenway, Penny Lee, Suzan Elizabeth. Treas., K.T. Realty & Investment, Glendale, Ariz., 1955-65; real estate broker, Glendale, 1965-72; pres. La Olla Devel. Corp., Phoenix, 1972—; treas. Family Bldg. Investment, Inc., Phoenix, 1965—; pres. Biltmore Realty, Inc., 1978—; sec. Geothermal Energy Corp., Phoenix, 1976—, Manor Energy Corp., 1979—. Served with USCG, 1949-52. Republican. Mormon. Home: 17610 Foothill Dr Sun City AZ 85372 Office: 6842 N 58th Dr PO Box 748 Glendale AZ 85311

HARMAN, WILLIAM ALEXANDER, computer co. exec.; b. Toronto, Ont., Can., Oct. 27, 1947; s. Norman M. and Bernice (Brewer) H.; B.A.Sc. (Mech. Engr.), U. Toronto, 1972; m. Elisabeth Haavind, Aug. 28, 1970; children—Karin, Amanda, Andrea, William Alexander. Pres., owner W.A. Harman Holding Co. Ltd., Milton, Ont., 1977—, DataWise Computing Services Ltd., Mississauga, Ont., 1976—, Computer Clearinghouse Ltd., Mississauga, 1977—, Hawk Land Computers Ltd., Milton, 1977—. Mem. Ch. Jesus Christ of Latter Day Saints.

HARMELIN, WILLIAM, ins. co. exec.; b. Newark, N.J., Sept. 1, 1916; s. Arnold and Clara (Bartel) H.; B.S., N.Y. U., 1940; m. July 31, 1942; children—Stephen C., Marjory. Pres., Bus. and Estate Planning Consultants, Inc., N.Y.C., 1955—, The Harmelin Agy., Inc., 1956—; dir. Dyna-Lease Corp., N.Y.C.; instr. ins. N.Y. U., 1968; faculty advanced health ins. conf. Purdue U., Lafayette, Ind., 1961-71, Life Ins. Marketing Inst., 1960-67; sr. moderator Life Underwriter Tng. Council for Life and Health Ins., 1954-60, mem. nat. exam. bd., 1961-62; guest speaker various colls., univs. and profl. groups, 1960—; faculty U. Conn., Storrs, 1977, C.L.U. Inst., Boulder, Colo., 1977, Stetson U., Deland, Fla., 1978, U. Ariz., 1978. Served with U.S. Army, 1942-46. Recipient Distinguished Service award Internat. Assn. of Health Underwriters, 1959. Mem. Nat. Assn. of Pension Consultants and Actuaries (dir. 1978—), N.Y.C. Life Underwriters Assn. (dir. 1956-58), Assn. of Risk and Ins., Am. Coll. of Life Underwriters, Estate Planning Council, Nat. Jogging Assn. (dir. 1972—), N.Y. U. Edn. Alumni (dir. 1973—). Club: N.Y. U. Author: Life Insurance Course, 1957; contbr. over 300 articles on ins. to profl. jours.; editor Supervision, 1955-56; editorial bd. Leader's Mag., 1968; columnist Phot Industry News, 1969-71, Ins. Advocate Mag., 1977—. Home: 12 Hunters Ln Roslyn NY 11576 Office: Business and Estate Planning Cons 30 Vesey St New York NY 10007

HARMON, DORSEY ALLAN, constrn. co. exec.; b. Wichita, Kans., Mar. 7, 1901; s. Joel Allan and Edith (Reeves) H.; student Fairmount Coll., 1919-21, in civil engring., U. Kans., 1921-23; m. Dorothy Maude Baugh, Oct. 15, 1928; children—Virginia Maude Harmon Gohrband, Tom A. Estimator-bookkeeper H.W. Underhill Constrn. Co., Wichita, 1923-24, br. mgr., Oklahoma City, 1925-26; partner Harmon & Mattison Constrn. Co., Oklahoma City, 1927-34; owner Harmon Constrn. Co., Oklahoma City, 1934-57, chmn. bd., 1971—; dir. Okla. Brick Corp.; chmn. bd. dirs. local fed. savs. and loan assn., 1977-78, dir., 1966-78, asso. dir., 1978—. Bd. dir. Better Bus. Bur., 1970-73. Mem. Midwest Christian Coll. Adv. Bd., 1973-75. Mem. Am. Inst. Constructors (hon. life dir.), Asso. Gen. Contractors Am. (chmn. builders div. 1964), Oklahoma City C. of C., Kans. U. Alumni Assn. (life), Cons. Constructors Council Am., Phi Gamma Delta. Mem. Christian Ch. (elder 1972-74). Clubs: Petroleum, Beacon, Oklahoma City Golf and Country, Oklahoma City Men's Dinner (exec. com. 1975-78). Home: 6820 NW Grand Blvd Oklahoma City OK 73116 Office: PO Box 25414 Oklahoma City OK 73125

HARMON, GEORGE OLEN, computer co. exec.; b. Hunter, Mo., Mar. 18, 1923; s. George Olen and Mary Mae (Taylor) H.; student George Washington U., 1941-42, Bakersfield (Calif.) Coll., 1946-48; m. Nina Lorene Curtman, Mar. 24, 1945; children—Sharyn Suzanne Harmon Moore, Timothy Olen. Dir. mgmt. systems IBM Corp., White Plains, N.Y., 1952-68; pres. Comma Corp., N.Y.C., 1968-71; v.p. NCR Corp., Dayton, Ohio, 1971-75; pres. Sorbus, Inc., King of Prussia, Pa., 1975-76; v.p., gen. mgr. service Pertec Computer Corp., Los Angeles, 1976—. Adv. bd. Abilene Christian U., 1974—, pres. Circle, 1975-77. Served with USNR, 1942-46. Mem. Assn. Field Service Mgrs. (nat. pres. 1977-78). Republican. Mem. Ch. of Christ. Home: 3119 Adirondak Ct Westlake Village CA 91361 Office: 12910 Culver Blvd Los Angeles CA 90066

HARMON, LEON GAIL, banker; b. Lincoln, Kans., Sept. 17, 1925; s. Amos E. and Aggie Olive (Shafer) H.; student Colo. Sch. Banking, U. Colo.; m. Dorothy Lois Morrison, Aug. 18, 1967; children—Steven, Gail (Mrs. Larry Patton), Kent. With Planters State Bank, Salina, Kans., 1946-48; asst. nat. bank examiner U.S. Treasury, 1948-49; with Casper Nat. Bank (Wyo.), 1949-51; asst. cashier First Nat. Bank, Riverton, Wyo., 1951-52, cashier, 1952-55, v.p., 1955-56, pres., 1957-63; pres., chief exec. officer N.Mex. Bank & Trust Co., Hobbs, 1963—; contact banker for U.S. Rep. Harold Runnels, 1972—. Vice pres. Conquistador council Boy Scouts Am., 1965-75; mem. Gov.'s Com. for Econ. Devel., 1967-71; pres., bd. dirs. Jr. Achievement, 1974-76; active N.Mex. Bd. Ednl. Fin., 1976-80; bd. dirs. Indsl. Devel. Corp. of Lea County; treas., trustee Coll. of S.W.; trustee Llano Estacado Med. Center, 1974-77. Served with USN. Recipient Disting. Service award Riverton Jr. C. of C. Mem. Am. (v.p. N.Mex. 1968-69), N.Mex. (pres. 1978-79) bankers assns., N.Mex. Taxpayers Assn. (dir. 1973-75), Hobbs C. of C. (pres. 1966). Methodist. Clubs: Masons (32 deg.); Shriners; Hobbs Rotary. Home: 1002 Jicarilla Hobbs NM 88240 Office: Box 400 220 W Broadway Hobbs NM 88240

HARMS, ROY CARL, state ofcl.; b. Dubuque, Iowa, Nov. 3, 1926; s. Frank William and Catherine Elizabeth (Hohnecker) H.; B.S., U. Md., 1963; M.B.A., Fla. Atlantic U., 1973; m. Helene Wunder, Oct. 20, 1948; children—Heide Helene, Heli Regina, Holli Catherine. Enlisted in U.S. Army, 1944, advanced through grades to lt. col., 1965; duty in U.S., Europe, Far East, 1944-67; ret., 1967; exec. dir. S.C. Consumer Fin. Assn., Columbia, 1967-74; dep. adminstr. S.C. Dept. Consumer Affairs, Columbia, 1974—. Mem. planning div. United Way of Midlands; chmn. medic care adv. com. S.C. Dept. Social Services. Decorated Silver Star, Bronze Star with V, Purple Heart. Mem. Am. Council on Consumer Interest, Am. Conf. Uniform Credit Code States (pres.). Club: Forest Acres Rotary. Contbr. chpt. to Jäger in Deutschland, 1964. Office: 2221 Devine St Columbia SC 29250

HARNDEN, WILLARD JOE, oil and gas prodn. co.; b. Medicine Lodge, Kans., Nov. 30, 1928; s. Willard G. and Mildred R. (Orr) H.; B.S., Kans. State Tchrs. Coll., 1951; m. Ethel A. McNeill, July 9, 1950 (div. 1969); children—Willard J., Jeffrey N.; m. 2d, M. Ann Barley, Sept. 6, 1969; 1 son, Andrew E. Asso., Bonicamp, Koelling & Smith, Wichita, Kans., 1953-54, Denver, 1954-58, partner, 1958-69; pres., dir. Premier Resources, Ltd., Denver, 1969-75, Domestic Hydrocarbons, Inc., 1977—; owner Harnden Prodn. Co., 1976—. Active Boy Scouts Am. Served with USMCR, 1946-47, 51-53; col. Res. (ret.). Mem. Am. Inst. C.P.A.'s, Colo. Soc. C.P.A.'s, Marine Corps Res. Officers Assn., Res. Officers Assn., Marine Corps Assn., Navy League, Kappa Sigma Epsilon. Republican. Clubs: Lions (dir.),

Falcon Quarterback (dir.), Denver Petroleum (sec.-treas., dir.), Pinehurst Country. Editor: Colo. C.P.A. Report. Home: 7182 S Poplar St Englewood CO 80112 Office: 7200 E Dry Creek Rd #G-207 Englewood CO 80112

HARNER, JAMES LEROY, exec. search cons.; b. Great Falls, Mont., Nov. 9, 1929; s. Lawrence Harold and Sadie Margaret (Olson) H.; B.A., UCLA, 1952; m. Lois Elizabeth Whitsett, Aug. 6, 1969; children—Kathleen Ann, Christopher Robey. Orgn. planning mgr. Rohr Corp., Chula Vista, Calif., 1955-62; prin. Arthur Young & Co., Los Angeles, 1962-69; v.p. planning John Graham Co., Architects, Seattle, 1969-71; v.p. corp. planning AVCO Community Developers, La Jolla, Calif., 1971-73; mgmt. cons. J.L. Harner & Assos., San Diego and Los Angeles, 1973-80; v.p. Eastman & Beaudine, Inc., Los Angeles, 1980—. Bd. dirs. Nat. Council on Alcoholism, Los Angeles county, 1981—. Served with USN, 1953-55. Mem. Am. Mgmt. Assn., Commerce Assos., UCLA Alumni Assn. Club: Sons of Norway. Office: 2049 Century Park E Los Angeles CA 90067

HARNESS, EDWARD GRANVILLE, soap products mfr.; b. Marietta, O., Dec. 17, 1918; s. Lewis Nye and Mary (McKinney) H.; A.B., Marietta Coll., 1940; m. Mary McCrady Chaney, Aug. 7, 1943; children—Frances Ann (Mrs. Daniel J. Jones), Edward Granville, Robert R. With Procter & Gamble Co., Cin., 1940—, v.p. paper products div., 1963-66, v.p.-group exec., dir., 1966-70, exec. v.p., 1970-71, pres., 1971—, chmn. bd., 1974—; dir. Exxon Corp., Caterpillar Tractor Co. Chmn. bd. dirs. Marietta Coll.; trustee Ohio Found. Ind. Colls. Served with USAAF, 1942-46. Mem. Bus. Roundtable, Bus. Council, Conf. Bd. (vice chmn.). Clubs: Carmargo, Commercial, Queen City, Commonwealth (Cin.).

HARNETT, JOSEPH DURHAM, oil co. exec.; b. Paterson, N.J., Aug. 23, 1917; s. James Harold and Emily (Steele) H.; B.S., Purdue U., 1939; m. Wilhelmina Nordstrom, June 21, 1941 (dec. July 1958); children—Gordon D., Linda C., Ralph H., David S.; m. 2d, Nancy Beam. With Consol. Edison Co., N.Y.C., 1939, Worthington Pump & Machinery Corp., 1940; with Standard Oil Co. (Ohio), 1941—, v.p., 1957-68; sr. v.p., 1968-70, exec. v.p., 1970-77, pres., 1977—, also dir.; pres., dir. Mountaineer Carbon Co., BP Oil Inc., Vistron Corp. Mem. Am. Petroleum Inst. (dir.). Presbyterian. Clubs: Mentor Harbor Yacht, Country, Union, Pepper Pike (Cleve.); Univ. (N.Y.C.). Home: 2799 Lander Rd Pepper Pike OH 44124 Office: Midland Bldg Cleveland OH 44115

HARNETT, THOMAS AQUINAS, ins. co. exec.; b. Bronx, N.Y., Mar. 22, 1924; s. William Joseph and Katherine Cecelia (Farrell) H.; student Fordham U., 1940-43, LL.B., 1949; LL.D., Coll. of Ins., 1977; m. Doris Mary Van Dien, Dec. 2, 1950; children—Dorisanne, Thomas A., William Arthur, Kathleen Anne. With law dept. Nat. Surety Corp., N.Y.C., 1950-52; asso. firm Bingham, Englar, Jones & Houston, N.Y.C., 1952-54; asso. firm Watters & Donovan, N.Y.C., 1954-59, partner, 1959-64; founding partner firm Harnett & Reid, N.Y.C., 1964-69; sr. partner firm Hart & Hume, N.Y.C., 1969-75; supt. N.Y. State Ins. Dept., 1975-77; sr. v.p., counsel Travelers Corp., Hartford, Conn., 1977—. Parish council pres. Sacred Heart Ch., Suffern, N.Y., 1966-70, dir. religious edn., 1966-70; mem., then chmn. Devel. Easement Acquisition Commn., Town of Ramapo (N.Y.), 1966-75. Served with USAAF; PTO. Decorated Air medal. Fellow Internat. Acad. Trial Lawyers, Am. Bar Found.; mem. Am. Bar Assn., N.Y. State Bar Assn. (del. 1974-75), Am. Judicature Soc., Internat. Assn. Ins. Counsel. Democrat. Roman Catholic. Clubs: Boca Raton; Glastonbury Hills; Univ. (Albany, N.Y.); Drug and Chem., Manhattan (N.Y.C.); Nat. Lawyers (Washington). Contbr. articles to profl. jours. Home: 110 Millstone Rd Glastonbury CT 06033 also 875 E Camino Real Boca Raton FL 33432 Office: Travelers Corp 1 Tower Sq Hartford CT 06115*

HARPER, CHARLES LITTLE, steel co. exec.; b. Evanston, Ill., Mar. 23, 1930; s. H. Mitchell and Margaret (Little) H.; B.S., Princeton, 1952; m. Alice Patterson Fall, Oct. 19, 1955; children—Charles, Margaret, Greta, Alice, Serena, Paisley. Successively metall. engineer process metallurgy, prodn. control, cost control The H.M. Harper Co., Morton Grove, Ill., 1954-68; with ITT Harper, Inc., 1968—, pres., 1972-78, also dir.; pres. C.L. Harper Co., Winnetka, Ill., 1978—. Served to lt. USNR, 1952-54. Mem. Am. Soc. Metals, Am. Inst. Mining Engrs., Midwest Indsl. Mgmt. Assn. (dir.), Newcomen Soc. Clubs: Economic of Chicago, Executive; Glen View (Golf, Ill.). Home: 644 Pine Ln Winnetka IL 60093 Office: 8200 Lehigh Ave Morton Grove IL 60053

HARPER, CHARLES MICHEL, basic foods co. exec.; b. Lansing, Mich., Sept. 26, 1927; s. Charles Frost and Alma Anna (Michel) H.; B.S.M.E., Purdue U., 1949; M.B.A., U. Chgo., 1950; m. Joan Frances Bruggema, June 24, 1950; children—Kathleen Harper Wenngatz, Carolyn Harper Wherry, Michel, Elizabeth Ann. Sr. methods engr. Oldsmobile div. Gen. Motors Corp., 1950-54; dir. indsl. engring. The Pillsbury Co., 1954-60, dir. engring., 1960-65, corp. v.p. research and devel., 1965-70, group v.p. poultry and food service, 1970-74; pres., chief exec. officer ConAgra, Inc., Omaha, 1976—; dir. Omaha Nat. Bank, Valmont Industries, Diamond Crystal Salt. Mayor Village of Excelsior, Minn., 1974; bd. dirs. Creighton U., Nebr. Ind. Coll. Found. Served with AUS, 1944-46. Mem. Greater Omaha C. of C. (chmn. 1979). Clubs: Omaha Country, Mpls., Ak-Sar-Ben (Gov.). Office: 200 Kiewit Plaza Omaha NE 68131

HARPER, DAVID EDWIN, mgmt. cons.; b. Omaha, Nebr., Sept. 12, 1939; s. Howard North and Neitha Lorraine (Senift) H.; B.S. in Bus. Adminstrn., U. Nebr., 1961; m. Oct. 7, 1972; 1 son by previous marriage, David Edwin. Systems cons. John L. Marley & Co., 1965-70; mgmt. cons. A.T. Kearney Inc., Chgo., 1970-79; mng. dir. Kearney Internat., Amsterdam, Netherlands, 1979—. Bd. dirs. Guide Internat., Inc. Served to capt. USAF, 1962-66. Mem. Am. C. of C. in Netherlands (dir.). Episcopalian. Club: Chgo. Athletic Assn. Home: Berg Weg 70 Blaricum Netherlands Office: Kearney Internat Herengracht 499 Amsterdam Netherlands*

HARPER, DONALD JACQUES, holding co. exec.; b. Knoxville, Tenn., June 30, 1928; s. Raymond James and Pauline Jean (Huffstuttler) H.; student Wichita (Kan.) State U., 1946-47, Kansas City Coll. Engring., 1948; Indsl. Engr., U. Okla., 1950; m. Jayne Combs; children—Nancy Lynn Harper Mehl, Danial Ray, Larry Fred, Lenny Gene, Lindsay Jon. Indsl. engr. Coleman Co., Ins., Wichita, 1953-56; agt. Penn Mut. Life Ins. Co., Wichita, 1956-60; gen. agt. Crown Life Ins. Co., Wichita, 1960-63; pres. Financial Unification Corp., holding co., Scottsdale, Ariz., 1963—. Bd. dirs. Scottsdale Symphony Orch. Served with USNR, 1942-45. Mem. Am. Soc. Bus. and Mgmt. Cons., Internat. Assn. Fin. Planners, Ariz. Law Soc., Ariz. Central Estate Planning Council, Scottsdale C. of C. Home: 4448 W Solano Dr N Glendale AZ 85301 Office: PO Box 33970 Phoenix AZ 85067

HARPER, EDWIN LELAND, mfg. co. exec.; b. Belleville, Ill., Nov. 13, 1941; s. Horace Edwin and Evelyn Ruth (Wright) H.; B.A. with honors, Principia Coll., Elsah, Ill., 1963; Ph.D., U. Va., 1968; m. Lucy Davis, Aug. 21, 1965; children—Elizabeth Allen, Peter Edwin. Guest scholar Brookings Instn., Washington, 1965-66; lectr. Rutgers U., 1966-68; with Bur. Budget, Exec. Office Pres., 1968-69; sr. cons. Arthur D. Little, Inc., Washington, 1969; spl. asst. to Pres. of U.S., 1969-72; asst. dir. Domestic Council, White House, 1970-72; v.p. INA Corp., Phila., 1973-74; pres., chief exec. officer Air Balance, Inc., Chgo., 1975—; sr. v.p. strategic planning chief adminstrv. officer Certain Teed Products Corp., Valley Forge, Pa., 1976-78; v.p. Emerson Electric Co., St. Louis, 1978—; dir. Carver Assos., Phila., SWECO, Inc., Los Angeles. Mem. Pres.'s Commn. on Personnel Interchange, Washington, 1976-79; mem. nat. adv. bd. Goodwill Industries, 1977—; mem. Com. of 70, Phila., 1977-78; mem. policy adv. bd. Harvard-M.I.T. Joint Center, 1976-78. Recipient Louis Brownlow award, 1969; NDEA fellow, 1963; Ford Found. grantee, 1965. Fellow Am. Soc. Public Adminstrn.; mem. Am. Polit. Sci. Assn., So. Polit. Sci. Assn., U.S. C. of C. (anti-trust policy com. 1976—), Omicron Delta Kappa. Clubs: Raven, Racquet. Contbr. articles to profl. jours. Home: 1170 Hampton Park Dr Saint Louis MO 63117 Office: Emerson Electric Co 8100 W Florissant Ave Saint Louis MO 63136

HARPER, GLENN S., business cons.; b. Phila., Apr. 19, 1940; s. Glenn Samuel and Minnie Marie Harper; student U. Dayton (Ohio), 1961-65; m. Mary Linda Weaver; children—Christopher, Trish. Br. mgr. Household Fin. Corp., Dayton, 1965-69; mgmt. cons. A.B. Cassidy & Assos., Ridgefield, Conn., 1969-70; v.p. sales Lin Conselyea, Inc., Medway, Ohio, 1970-72, exec. v.p., treas., dir., 1972-77; founder Val-Pak Promotions, Inc., Dayton, 1974-77, pres., chief exec. officer, 1977-79; founder Metro Maid, Inc., Dayton, 1978-79, pres., chief exec. officer, 1979—; dir., exec. v.p. San Sal Villas, San Salvador, Bahamas, 1978—; dir. Carousel Mountain Amusement Park, Owego, N.Y. Mem. Ch. of Brethren. Address: Metro Maid Inc 4336 Gorman Ave Englewood OH 45322

HARPER, JAMES CUNNINGHAM, banker; b. Lenoir, N.C., Feb. 17, 1893; s. George Finley and Frances (Cunningham) H.; student Culver Naval Sch.; B.S., Davidson Coll., 1915, L.H.D., 1965; M.A., U. N.C., 1916; postgrad. Duke, 1928, Lenoir Rhyne Coll., 1930, Columbia, 1932; m. Charlotte Critz, Mar. 19, 1927 (dec.); children—Lucy Harper Grier, James Cuningham, George F., Charlotte C. (Mrs. George E. Stone). Band dir. Lenoir High Sch., 1924-58; tchr. summer sch. Appalachian State U., 1955, Davidson Coll.; chmn. bd. Lenoir br. First Union Nat. Bank N.C., Lenoir, 1958—. Served from 2d lt. to capt. U.S. Army, 1917-18. Recipient Mac award for sch. band dirs. Sch. Musician mag., ann. 1st Chair Am., 1960; Goldman award Am. Sch. Band Assn., 1965. Mem. Am. (pres. 1955, chmn. bd. dirs. 1956, hon. life pres. 1956—), N.C. (pres. 1943-44) bandmasters assns., Phi Mu Alpha Sinfonia, Phi Beta Mu (hon.). Home: 203 Norwood St Lenoir NC 28645

HARPER, JAMES WELDON, III, fin. cons.; b. Frederick, Md., Mar. 3, 1937; s. James Weldon, Jr. and Mildred Mary (Conaway) H.; student Duke U. Coll. rep. Time, Inc., 1955-59; jr. exec. trainee Merrill Lynch Pierce Fenner and Smith, N.Y.C., 1959-60; v.p. fin. planning Haight and Co. Inc., Washington, 1961-72; pres. fin. cons. Weldon Enterprises Ltd., Washington, 1972—; pres. U.S. Energy Conservation Service, Inc.; v.p. Culiban Prodns. Ltd.; cons. Aries Corp. Served with U.S. Army, 1959. Mem. Apt. Office Builders Assn. Republican. Methodist. Author three manuals on consulting. Office: PO Box 1061 Main Station Washington DC 20013

HARPER, JOHN DICKSON, aluminum mfg. co. exec.; b. Louisville, Tenn., Apr. 6, 1910; s. Lafayette Rodgers and Mary Alice (Collier) H.; B.S., U. Tenn., 1933; m. Samma Lucille McCrary, Oct. 21, 1937; children—Rodgers McCrary, John Dickson, Thomas William. With Aluminum Co. Am., 1925—, v.p., 1960-62, exec. v.p., 1962-63, pres., 1963-70, chief exec. officer, 1965-75, chmn., 1970-75, chmn. exec. com., 1966—; dir. subsidiaries; chmn., dir. Communications Satellite Corp., Crutcher Resources, Coke Investors and subs.'s, Paribas N.Am., Met. Life Ins. Co., Procter & Gamble Co., AEA, Inc. Mem. nat. council, past pres. Northeast region Boy Scouts Am.; devel. bd. U. Tenn.; vice chmn. Com. for Econ. Devel.; life trustee Carnegie-Mellon U.; founding mem. Rockefeller U. Council; adv. com. Woodrow Wilson Internat. Center for Scholars. Recipient Pa. Soc. gold medal, 1970; knight's cross Royal Order St. Olav. Mem. IEEE (life, past v.p.), ASME, Bus. Council, Nat. Acad. Engring., Am. Soc. for Metals (Distinguished life), Internat. Aluminium Inst. (past chmn.), Aluminum Assn. (hon., past pres.), Nat. Alliance Businessmen (dir.), Bus. Roundtable (past chmn.), Conf. Bd. (trustee), Tau Beta Pi, Eta Kappa Nu, Beta Gamma Sigma. Clubs: Allegheny, Duquesne, St. Clair Country (Pitts.); Rolling Rock; Links, Sky (N.Y.C.); Internat. (Washington); Rolling Rock (Ligonier, Pa.). Office: 1501 Alcoa Bldg Pittsburgh PA 15219

HARPER, NOLAN SIDNEY, lawyer, bus. exec.; b. Jackson, Miss., June 22, 1940; s. Robert William and Elizabeth (Brame) H.; B.A., Miss. State U., 1962; J.D., U. Miss., 1965; m. Elizabeth Cary, June 27, 1972; 1 dau., Elizabeth Christine. Admitted to Miss. bar, 1965, since practiced in Jackson; sec.-treas. Harper Supply Co., 1965-73; pres. Harper Foundry & Machine Co., 1971—; pres. Harper & Co., 1966—, Miss. Valley Leasing Corp., 1964—; adv. dir. Century Nat. Bank, New Orleans. Mem. Am., Miss., Hinds County bar assns., Sigma Phi Epsilon. Presbyterian. Club: Jackson Country. Home: 5445 Briarfield Rd Jackson MS 39205 Office: 103 E Rankin St Jackson MS 39205

HARPER, PAUL CHURCH, JR., advt. agy. exec.; b. Coblenz, Germany, Dec. 16, 1920 (parents Am. Citizens); s. Paul Church and Anne Lindsay (White) H.; B.A., Yale, 1942; m. Eleanor Emery, Jan. 3, 1947; children—Diana, Jessica, William, Lindsay, Samuel, Charles. With Needham, Harper & Steers, Inc. (formerly Needham, Louis & Brorby, Inc.), N.Y.C., 1946—, exec. v.p., 1958-60, pres., 1960-67, chmn. bd., chief exec. officer, 1967—. Trustee Beloit Coll., Fountain Valley Sch., Inst. Internat. Edn.; mem. bus. com. Mus. Modern Art. Served as maj. USMC, 1942-45. Decorated Bronze Star; recipient Human Relations award Am. Jewish Com., 1977. Mem. Am. Assn. Advt. Agys. (dir. 1960-61, co-chmn. interchange), Council Fgn. Relations (v.p., dir. exec. com.), Newcomen Soc. Clubs: Chgo., Mid-Am., Economic (Chgo.); Yale, Knickerbocker, Board Room, Univ. (N.Y.C.). Office: 909 3d Ave New York NY 10022*

HARPER, ROGER WESLEY, consumer products co. exec.; b. Youngstown, Ohio, July 11, 1933; s. Harry Edward and Helen Marjorie (Young) H.; B.A., Wittenberg U., 1956. Sales rep. Shell Oil Co., Cleve., 1958-62, Chicopee Mills, Inc., N.Y.C., 1962-64; sales rep. H.H. Cutler Co., Grand Rapids, Mich., 1964-68; exec. v.p. Scharp Contemporary, Inc., Columbus, Ohio, 1968-77, now dir.; chmn., pres. Am. Leather Village, Inc., Columbus, 1977—; dir. Scharp Contemporary, Inc., Columbus. Serveo with U.S. Army, 1956-58. Lutheran. Home: 622 Indian Mound Rd Columbus OH 43213 Office: 2163 S James Rd Columbus OH 43227

HARPSTER, JAMES ERVING, lawyer, business exec.; b. Milw., Dec. 24, 1923; s. Philo E. and Pauline (Daanen) H.; Ph.B., Marquette U., 1950, LL.B., 1952. Dir. info. services Nat. Cotton Council Am., Memphis, 1952-55; dir. pub. relations Christian Bros. Coll., 1956; mgr. govt. affairs dept. Memphis C. of C., 1956-62; exec. v.p. Rep. Assn. Memphis and Shelby County, 1962-64; practice law, 1965—; partner Rickey, Shankman, Blanchard, Agee & Harpster, 1965-80; partner Harpster & Baird, 1980—; pres. Duncan Devel. Co., 1966, Scenic Hills Apts., Inc., 1967-70. Mem. Shelby County Tax Assessor's Adv. Com., 1960-61; editor, asst. counsel Memphis and Shelby County Charter Commn., 1962, chmn. Scenic Hills Planning Com., 1964-66; a founder Lions Inst. for Visually Handicapped Children, 1954; chmn. E.H. Crump Meml. Football Game for the Blind, 1956; pres. Siena Student Aid Found., 1960; v.p. Nat. Council Rep. Workships, 1967-69; pres. Rep. Workshop of Shelby County, 1967, 71, 77; candidate Tenn. Gen. Assembly, 1964; pres. Republican Assn. Memphis and Shelby County 1966-67; mem. Shelby County Election Commn., 1968-70; mem. Tenn. Bd. Elections, 1970—, sec., 1971-72, 75—, chmn., 1974—; co-chmn. Shelby County Rep. Exec. Com. 1968-70 col., aide-de-camp to gov. Tenn., 1971-75. Served with USAAF, 1942-46. Mem. Memphis Pub. Affairs Forum, Citizens Assn. Memphis and Shelby County, Am., Tenn., Wis., bar assns., Am. Legion, Animal Protection Assn. (chmn. bd. 1981), Cardinal Mindszenty Found., Una Voce in U.S., Caths. United for Faith, Am. Security Council (asso.). Roman Catholic. Clubs: Tenn. Home: 3032 E Glengarry Rd Memphis TN 38128 Office: Suite 3217 100 N Main Bldg Memphis TN 38103

HARRELL, SAMUEL M., grain co. exec.; b. Indpls., Jan. 4, 1931; s. Samuel Runnels and Mary (Evans) H.; B.S. in Econs., Wharton Sch. U. Pa., 1953; m. Sally Bowers, Sept. 2, 1958; children—Samuel D., Holly Evans, Kevin Bowers, Karen Susan, Donald Runnels, Kenneth Macy. Chief exec. officer, treas., chmn. bd., chmn. exec. com. Early & Daniel Industries; pres., chmn. bd., chmn. exec. com. Gen. Grain, Inc., Indpls.; chmn. bd., pres., exec. com. Early & Daniel Co. Cin.; chmn. bd., chief exec. officer, treas., mem. exec. com. Tidewater Grain Co., Phila.; dir. Wainwright Bank & Trust Co., Wainright's Abstract Co., Nat. Grain Trade Council, U.S. Feed Grains Council, N.Am. Export Grain Assn.; mem. Chgo. Bd. Trade, Buffalo Corn Exchange, St. Louis Mchts. Exchange, Mpls. Bd. Trade. Trustee Hanover Coll., YWCA, Indpls.; bd. overseers Wharton Sch., U. Pa. Served with AUS, 1953-55. Mem. Young Pres's. Orgn., U. Pa. Alumni Assn. (pres. Ind. chpt.), Terminal Elevator Grain Mchts. Assn. (dir.), Millers Nat. Fedn. (dir.), Assn. Operative Millers, Am. Soc. Bakery Engrs., Am. Finance Assn., Council Fgn. Relations, Financial Execs. Inst., Delta Tau Delta (pres. Ind. alumni). Presbyterian. Clubs: Masons, Shriners, Rotary; Columbia, Indpls. Athletic, Woodstock, Dramatic, Players, Lambs (Indpls.); Racquet (Phila.). Home: 5858 Sunset Ln Indianapolis IN 46208 Office: 902 W Washington Ave Indianapolis IN 46204

HARRELL, SAMUEL RUNNELS, business exec.; b. Noblesville, Ind., Nov. 25, 1897; s. Samuel and Vivian (Voss) H.; B.S. in Econs., U. Pa., 1919; LL.B., Yale, 1924; L.H.D., Combs Coll., Phila., 1973; m. Mary Robertson Evans, Oct. 10, 1925 (div. Mar. 1972); children—Evans Malott, Mary Eleanor, Samuel Macy. First employed, Land Title & Trust Co., Phila.; admitted to Ind. bar, 1922; former chmn. bd., chmn. exec. com. Gen. Grain, Inc., now hon. chmn., adviser; pres. Acme Evans Co., Inc. 1945-59, chmn. bd., 1954—; pres. Acme Goodrich, Inc., 1947-52, chmn. bd., chmn. exec. com., 1952—; pres., chmn. bd. Tidewater Grain Co., Phila.; chmn. exec. com., chmn. bd., dir. The Early & Daniel Co., Cin., from 1946, now hon. chmn., adviser; dir. Cleve. Grain Co., 1950-58, pres., chmn. bd., 1955-58; pres. Harrell & Co.; dir. Terminal Elevator Grain Mchts. Assn., N.Am. Export Grain Assn., Indpls. Union Ry. Co.; chmn. bd. dirs. Indpls. Bd. Trade; mem. Chgo. Bd. Trade. Co-chmn. Ind. adv. com. on commerce, industry, agr., pub. relations. Served with Naval Aviation Pilot Div. of Naval Res., 1918. Chmn., trustee Nat. Found. for Edn. in Am. Citizenship; trustee U. Pa., 1940-50, Wharton Sch. Finance and Commerce, 1950-54; chmn. bd. trustees Combs Coll.; mem. vis. com. Harvard Grad. Sch. Edn., 1941-56; mem. adv. com. U.S. Banking and Currency Com.; del. Am. Legion to Paris, 1937. Mem. exec. council, nat. treas. Am. Heart Assn., 1947-48; founder Ind. Heart Found., Sagamores of Wabash; founder, charter mem. Acropolitan Research and Cultural Center. Mem. Ind. Millers Assn., (pres.), Am. Bar Assn., Am. Econ. Assn., Am. Polit. Sci. Assn., Acad. Polit. Sci., Am. Acad. Polit. and Social Sci. Am. Soc. for Pub. Adminstrn., Citizens Com. Hoover Commn., S.R., S.A.R., Delta Tau Delta, Phi Delta Phi. Presbyn. Mason (32 deg.). Clubs: Racquet, Sharswood Law (Phila.); Harvard Faculty (Cambridge); University (Chgo., N.Y.); Contemporary, Athletic, Lawyers, Literary, Pioneer, Pennsylvania, Yale (Indpls.); Queen City (Cin.); Pendennis (Louisville). Chmn. and editor Nat. Found. Press. Publisher: Fundamental American Principles. Home: care Valley Forge Farms Route 4 Noblesville IN 46060 Office: 902 Washington Ave Indianapolis IN 46204

HARRINGTON, BENJAMIN FRANKLIN, III, bank exec.; b. Princess Anne, Md., Dec. 8, 1922; s. Benjamin Franklin and Etta Maurice (Dashiell) H.; student Beacom Coll., 1939-40; A.A., Salisbury State Coll., 1951; LL.B., LaSalle U., Chgo., 1954; m. Jean Cameron Gilliam, July 21, 1962; children—Benjamin Franklin IV, Charles Macalaster. Examiner, Fed. Reserve Bank, Richmond, Va., 1951-61; exec. v.p. Truckers & Savs. Bank, Salisbury, Md., 1961-69; pres. Peoples Bank, Elkton, Md., 1969—. Chmn., United Fund of Cecil County, Md.; dir., chmn. fin. com. Union Hosp.; treas. Delmarva council Boy Scouts Am.; treas., dir. Md. Gov.'s Pvt. Industry Council; dir. Cecil County Assn. for Retarded. Served with USNR, 1942-43. Mem. Cecil County Hist. Soc. (dir.), Ind. Bankers Assn., Md. Bankers Assn. Office: Peoples Bank 130 North St Elkton MD 21921

HARRINGTON, ELIZABETH DALLAS, advt. exec.; b. Jackson, Miss., Nov. 9, 1942; d. William Lee and Louise Landis (Crowder) Dallas; B.A., Cornell U., 1965; m. Robert William Harrington, Aug. 21, 1965; children—Elizabeth Brooke, Kristen Robin (dec.). Fashion coordinator, commentator Marshall Field Co., Chgo., 1965; asst. brand mgr. Procter & Gamble Co., Cin., 1966-68; account exec. J. Walter Thompson Co., Chgo., 1968-72, account supr., 1972-76, v.p., 1973—, v.p. mgmt. supr., 1976-79; v.p. advt., pres. Ad Com subs. Quaker Oats Co., Chgo., 1979—; instr. advt. Barat Coll., Lake Forest, Ill., 1977-79. Bd. dirs. Am. Advt. Fedn., children's advt. rev. unit Nat. Better Bus. Bur. Recipient Family Circle Nutrition award for commls. for children, 1973; named Outstanding Young Bus. Woman of Yr., Glamour mag., 1977; Chgo. Advt. Woman of Yr., 1980; recipient YWCA Leadership award, 1977. Mem. Chgo. Advt. Club, Women's Advt. Club Chgo. Office: Quaker Oats Co Mdse Mart Plaza Chicago IL 60654

HARRINGTON, HERBERT HARRINGTON, accountant; b. Meadville, Pa., Sept. 19, 1946; s. Herbert H. and Sara F. (Rogers) H.; student Kent State U., 1964-69; B.S., Memphis State U., 1975; M.S. in Criminal Justice, Dyersburg State U., 1977. Transp. dir. West Tenn. Easter Seal Soc., 1972-75; comptroller So. Trucking Inc., 1976-77; acct. Central So. Inc., 1978-79; comptroller Wonder div. ITT Baking Corp., 1980—; cons., Covington, Tenn., 1973—. Served with USN, 1963-67. Mem. Covington C. of C. Republican. Episcopalian. Clubs: Lions, Good Fellows, Optimists, Rotary. Author 3 textbooks on acctg. procedures and practice. Home and office: PO Box 402 Covington TN 38019

HARRINGTON, JOHN ALLEN, lawyer; b. Moncure, N.C., Nov. 10, 1914; s. Thomas Jackson and Cornelia Clair (Lawrence) H.; LL.B., Duke U., 1951; m. Geraldine Frances Young, Sept. 6, 1952 (dec.); children—John Allen, Steven Young; m. 2d, Lucille Cox Gibson, Nov. 15, 1980. Employed in various positions, 1931-36; with Continental Life Ins. Co., 1936-39; salesman R.J. Reynolds Tobacco

Co., various locations in S.W., Va., 1939-42; admitted to N.C. bar, 1951; spl. agt. FBI, 1951-53; practice of law, Sanford, N.C., 1953—; partner firm Harrington, Shaw & Gilleland, 1977—; dir., gen. counsel The Pantry, Inc.; gen. counsel Carolina Bank, Lee-Moore Oil Co., Neapolitan Constrn. Co., Hoover Johnson Constrn. Co. Mem., past chmn. Selective Service, Lee County; chmn. Lee County Bd. Elections; mem. N.C. Bar Rev. Commn. 11th Jud. Dist. Served to capt. U.S. Army, 1942-46. Mem. N.C. State Bar, N.C. Bar Assn., Lee County Bar Assn. (past pres.), 11th Jud. Bar Assn. (past pres.), Delta Theta Phi (pres. coll. chpt.). Democrat. Methodist. Clubs: Exchange (pres. 1965-66). Elks, VFW. Home: 901 Ferndell Path Sanford NC 27330 Office: 1410 Elm St Sanford NC 27330

HARRIS, ARNOLD STUART, univ. ofcl.; b. Troy, N.Y., Dec. 6, 1947; s. Jacob A. and Pauline (Davidoff) H.; B.A., SUNY, Oneonta, 1969; M.P.A., Syracuse U., 1970; m. Jane Regan, May 21, 1977. Sr. planner Capital Dist. Regional Planning Commn., Albany, N.Y., 1971-73; dir. planning City of Troy, 1973-75; policy analyst Office of Speaker, N.Y. State Assembly, Albany, 1975-76; dir. mgmt. tng. continuing edn. project SUNY, Albany, 1976—; mem. vis. faculty Hudson Valley Community Coll., 1974—; tng. cons. N.Y. State Dept. Civil Service, 1975—. Chmn., Troy City Planning Commn., 1973—; mem. Troy Urban Agy., 1975-78, Troy City Charter Revision Commn., 1979—. Mem. Am. Mgmt. Assn., Am. Soc. Public Adminstrn., NEA. Democrat. Club: Troy. Home: 1727 Tibbits Ave Troy NY 12180 Office: 135 Western Ave Albany NY 12205

HARRIS, BARBARA GOEBEL, real estate exec.; b. Anniston, Ala., Apr. 2, 1927; d. Victor Albert and Lynne (Greene) Goebel; student N. Ga. Coll., 1946, Crawford W. Long Sch. Nursing, Atlanta, 1949, U. Ga. at Atlanta, 1950, Auburn U., 1950, U. Ala. at Huntsville, 1964-65; m. Robert B. Harris, Jr., Aug. 28, 1950 (div. 1975); children—Barbara Lynne (Mrs. Edwin Thomas Horton), Robert Burns, III. R.N., hostess Silver Comet, seaboard railroad Birmingham, Ala., to N.Y.C., 1949-50; night supr. nurses Auburn U., 1950-52; realtor Macon Realty Co., Birmingham, 1957-60, Eula Brooks Realty Co., Huntsville, 1960-65, Oceanside Builders Inc., Freeport, Bahamas, 1965-68; broker Heritage Realty Co., Birmingham, 1969-76; realtor Village Realtors, Birmingham; pres. Custom Built Homes, Inc., 1978—; v.p. Hermitage Realtors, 1978—. Mem. Million Dollar Club, 1973. Mem. Birmingham Bd. Realtors, Ala., Nat. assns. realtors, Birmingham Assn. Homebuilders, Nurses Registry Ga. Baptist. Address: 1306 Branchwater Ln Birmingham AL 35216

HARRIS, BARRY CLIFFORD, economist; b. N.Y.C., Oct. 14, 1948; s. George Donald and Judith Bomser H.; B.A. in Math., Lehigh U., 1970; M.A. in Econs., U. Pa., 1972, Ph.D. in Econs., 1979; m. Sandra Lee Smuckler, Aug. 14, 1977. With econ. policy office, antitrust div. Dept. Justice, Washington, 1974-79; sr. economist Office of Policy and Analysis, ICC, Washington, 1979—. Mem. Am. Econ. Assn. Home: 6001 Cobalt Rd Bethesda MD 20016 Office: ICC Bldg 12th and Constitution St NW Washington DC 20433

HARRIS, BOBBY JOE, oil co. exec.; b. Frankston, Tex., May 23, 1926; s. Jessie Houston and Amanda Elizabeth (Tipton) H.; B.B.A., U. Houston, 1955; m. Martha Jenkins, May 17, 1952; children—Laura, David. With Stanolind Oil & Gas, Alvin, Tex., 1948-55, Continental Oil Co., Temple, Tex., 1955-59, agt., Cleburne, Tex., 1959-68; pres. Bob Harris Oil Co., Cleburne, 1968—; dir. First State Bank of Cleburne. Served with USN, 1944-46. Mem. Tex. Oil Marketers Assn. Office: 903 05 S Main St Cleburne TX 76031

HARRIS, CHARLES EDGAR, wholesale grocery co. exec.; b. Englewood, Tenn., Nov. 6, 1915; s. Charles Leonard and Minnie (Borin) H.; m. Dorothy Wilson, Aug. 20, 1938; children—Charles Edgar, William John. With H.T. Hackney Co., Knoxville, Tenn., also Athens and Greenville, Tenn., 1948—, treas., 1958-72, v.p., 1964-71, pres., chief adminstrv. officer, 1971-72, pres., chief exec. officer, 1972—, also dir.; pres., dir. Appalachian Realty Corp., Knoxville, Carolina Oil and Gas Co., Bryson City, N.C.; chmn. bd., dir. Valley Oil Co., Athens, Tenn., Hackney Carolina Co., Murphy, N.C., Hackney Harlan Co., Harlan, Ky., Hackney Jellico Co., Harlan, Haywood Wholesale Grocery Co., Waynesville, N.C., Maryville Wholesale Grocery Co. (Tenn.), Brink's, Inc., Knoxville, Testoil Co., Harlan, Park Oil Co., Alcoa, Tenn., Knoxoil Co., Knoxville, Pride Markets, Inc., Knoxville, Central Oil Co., Mid State Investment Corp. (both McMinnville, Tenn.), Carolina Oil & Gas Co., Bryson City, N.C., Foodservice Distbrs., Inc., Knoxville; chmn. bd. Jellico Wholesale Grocery Co., Tri-State Wholesale Co.. Middlesboro, Ky.; dir. Park Nat. Bank. Mem. Southeastern Regional Oil Jobbers Council, Atlanta, 1969-70. Mem. exec. bd. Great Smoky Mountain council Boy Scouts Am., 1956-57; bd. dirs., exec. com. Met. YMCA, Knoxville, 1971-77, asst. treas., 1971-74, treas., 1974-75; bd. dirs., mem. exec. com. U.S. Indsl. Council, 1975—; deacon Baptist Ch., 1957—; treas. Knox County Bapt. Assn., 1964-67, chmn. fin. com., exec. bd. 1973—; mem. exec. bd. Tenn. Bapt. Conv. Mem. Knoxville Wholesale Credit Assn. (dir. 1955-58, pres. 1956-57), Tenn. Taxpayers Assn. (dir. 1976—) Greater Knoxville C. of C. (dir. 1973-76, v.p. 1975-76), Nat. Assn. Wholesalers (trustee 1976—), Downtown Knoxville Assn. (dir., v.p. 1977—). Rotarian (dir. 1973-74, v.p. 1975-76). Home: 7709 Westland Dr Knoxville TN 37919 Office: Fidelity Bldg Knoxville TN 37902

HARRIS, CHARLES FREDERICK, JR., printing co. exec.; b. Worcester, Mass., Feb. 17, 1949; s. Charles Frederick and Louise (Ramey) H.; B.A., Washington and Lee U., 1971; M.A., U. Ga., 1972; m. Margaret Carolyn Fleenor, Sept. 8, 1973; children—Carolyn Ramey, Charles Adam. Reporter, Richmond (Va.) Times-Dispatch, 1968-71; reporter, music critic Worcester Telegram & Gazette, 1967-68; account exec., dir. communications Goudelock Advt. Agy. Inc., Greenville, S.C., 1972-73; v.p. account services Prentiss Ct. Advt., Greenville, 1973-75; pres., chief exec. officer Upper Valley Press, Inc., Bradford, Vt., 1975—; seminar asso. Amos Tuck Sch. Bus., Dartmouth Coll., 1977—. Served with U.S. Army, 1971-72. Mem. New Eng. Press Assn., Printing Industries Am., Printing Industries New Eng., Sigma Delta Chi. Republican. Episcopalian. Clubs: Sertoma, Lions. Home: Benton Rd North Haverhill NH 03774 Office: Upper Valley Press Inc Route 25 PO Box 305A Bradford VT 05033

HARRIS, CHARLES MEREDITH, fruit packing and storage co. exec.; b. Wenatchee, Wash., Nov. 2, 1917; s. Ardenvoir and Cleta (Meredith) H.; B.A. in Econs. and Bus., U. Wash., 1939; m. Kilbourne Jane Hastie, June 22, 1944; children—Nancy Kilbourne, Barbara Beatrice. Jr. acct. Price Waterhouse, Los Angeles, 1939-40; sr. acct. Barrow, Wade, Guthrie, Seattle, 1940-41, 42-43; sr. acct. C.W. Franklin, C.P.A., 1942-43, 43-44; v.p. Mad River Orchard Co., Inc., Entiat, Wash. and C.A. Harris & Son, Inc., Entiat, 1939-55, pres., 1955—; sec.-treas. Harris Orchard Co., Inc., 1939—; dir. Growers Credit Corp. Regent, U. Wash., Seattle, 1953-58; trustee N.W. Christian Coll., Eugene, Oreg., 1959-78; chmn. Chelan County Rep. Central Com., 1950-54; pres. Entiat Valley Credit Union, 1976-79. Named Honor Citizen, Entiat Valley C. of C., 1972; C.P.A., Wash. Mem. Nat. Forest Products Assn., Western Wood Products Assn., Wash. Hort. Assn., Am. Inst. C.P.A.'s, Wash. Soc. C.P.A.'s, Wenatchee Soc. C.P.A.'s. Republican. Christian Ch. Club: Elks. Home: PO Box 456 Entiat WA 98822 Office: PO Box 477 Entiat WA 98822

HARRIS, DAVID JOHN, investment banker; b. Chgo., June 13, 1913; s. David John and Harriet (Aurelius) H.; B.A., U. Chgo., 1935; m. Evelyn Carr, Dec. 19, 1936; children—Carol Ann, Glenn Carr, John Corydon. Sales positions Sills, Minton & Co., investment bankers, 1935-43; chief cost accountant United Drill & Tool, 1943; pres. Sills, Fairman & Harris, Inc., 1944-56; asso. N.Y. Stock Exchange, 1949—, allied mem., 1965; resident partner Bache & Co., 1956-64; pres. Chgo. Corp., 1964-69, chmn., chief exec. officer, 1969—; dir. Sentry Ins., Stevens Point, Wis., CIC Financial Corp., 1972—. Gov. Midwest Stock Exchange, 1959—, chmn. exec. com. 1962-63, chmn., 1963-65, mem., 1964—; mem. Am. Stock Exchange, 1968—, N.Y. 60604 1954-57; chmn. Highland Park Community Chest, 1958. Trustee Highland Park Hosp., 1970—; bd. dirs. Arthritis Found., 1978—, treas., 1980. Mem. Investment Bankers Assn. (chmn. Central States group 1955, gov. 1956-59, v.p. 1960-63, pres. 1963-64), Assn. Stock Exchange Firms (gov.), Securities Industry Assn. (gov. 1977-80, dir. 1978-81), Chgo. Bd. Options (gov. 1977), Ill. Srs. Golf Assn. (gov. 1971-74), Western Golf Assn. (dir. 1971—), Delta Kappa Epsilon. Clubs: Bond, University, Chicago, Attic (Chgo.); Exmoor Country (gov. 1957-59, pres. 1969-71) (Highland Park). Home: 142 Central Ave Highland Park IL 60035 Office: 208 S LaSalle St Chicago IL 60604

HARRIS, DIANE CAROL, optical products mfg. co. exec.; b. Rockville Centre, N.Y., Dec. 25, 1942; d. Daniel Christopher and Laura Louise (Schmitt) Quigley; B.A., Catholic U. Am., 1964; M.S., Rensselaer Poly. Inst., 1967; m. Wayne Manley Harris, Sept. 30, 1978. With Bausch & Lomb, Rochester, N.Y., 1967—, dir. applications lab., 1972-74, dir. tech. mktg. analytical systems div., 1974-76, bus. line mgr., 1976-77, v.p. planning and bus. programs, 1977-78, v.p. planning and bus. devel. Soflens div., 1978-80, corp. dir. planning, 1980—; dir. Bausch & Lomb Ins. Co. Pres., Rochester Against Intoxicated Driving, 1979—; bd. dirs. Rochester area Nat. Council on Alcoholism, 1980—; mem. long-range planning com. Health Assn. Rochester and Monroe County. NSF grantee, 1963; recipient Disting. Citizen's award Monroe County, 1979. Mem. Newcomen Soc. N. Am., Am. Mgmt. Assn., Am. Chem. Soc., Planning Execs. Inst., Phi Beta Kappa, Sigma Xi, Delta Epsilon Sigma. Contbr. articles to profl. jours. Home: 123 Blue Ridge Rd Penfield NY 14526 Office: One Lincoln First Sq Rochester NY 14601

HARRIS, DOUGLAS HERSHEL, research co. exec.; b. Indpls., Oct. 7, 1930; s. Douglas H. and Letha Mae (Baker) H.; B.S., Iowa State U., 1952; M.S. (fellow), Purdue U., 1957, Ph.D., 1959; m. Cynthia Ann Brodeur, July 17, 1976; children by previous marriage—Kimberly Ann, Robin Lin. Project dir. Human Factors Research, Inc., Los Angeles, 1958-62; group scientist Rockwell Internat. Corp., Los Angeles, 1962-69; lectr. U. So. Calif., 1962-72; pres. Anacapa Scis., Inc., Santa Barbara, Calif., 1969—. Served with underwater demolition USNR, 1952-55; Korea. Fellow Human Factors Soc. (Jack Kraft award 1975); mem. Am. Psychol. Assn. Republican. Author: Human Factors in Quality Assurance, 1969; editorial bd. Human Factors Jour., 1969—; contbr. articles to profl. jours. Home: 334 E Padre Santa Barbara CA 93105 Office: PO Drawer Q Santa Barbara CA 93102

HARRIS, EWING JACKSON, lawyer; b. Sylvia, Tenn., Mar. 17, 1901; s. John Chastain and Sarah Frances (Walker) H.; LL.B., Cumberland U., 1928; m. Lena Sue Hartman, Mar. 28, 1931; children—Frances Ann Harris (Mrs. Frank Avent), Marjorie Sue Harris (Mrs. Dean Lucht), Ewlene Harris. Admitted to Tenn. bar, 1928, practiced in Bolivar, 1932—; city atty. Bolivar, 1942—; county atty. Hardeman County, 1942-70; dir. Bank of Bolivar. Pres., State Bd. Elections, 1949-53, state Democratic exec. com., 1949-51, 1953-55; mem. Tenn. Senate, 1937-39; del. Tenn. Constl. Conv., 1965. Fellow Am. Coll. Probate Counsel; mem. Am. (ho. dels. 1973—), Tenn. (bd. govs. 1959-62), Hardeman County bar assns., Am. Judicature Soc., C. of C. (pres. 1958), Phi Beta Gamma. Democrat. Methodist (trustee). Clubs: Masons, Rotary (Paul Harris fellow), Elks. Home: 608 S Union St Bolivar TN 38008 Office: Bank Bolivar Bldg Bolivar TN 38008

HARRIS, FREDERICK EARL, II, investment advisor; b. Los Angeles, Aug. 9, 1940; s. Frederick F. and Maxine (Solomon) H.; grad. UCLA, 1960; m. Susan Margaret Priest, May 11, 1968. Real estate salesman Santa Monica Investment Co. (Calif.), 1964-66; underwater archaeologist Council Underwater Archaeology, San Francisco, 1966-69; land developer Mustique Island and St. Vincent, West Indies, 1969-71; investment advisor various trusts, 1972—. Bd. dirs. Santa Monica chpt. Am. Cancer Soc.; pres. Palisades Beach Property Owners Assn. Served with USCGR, 1958-66. Mem. CG Aux. (flotilla and div. staff officer), U.S. Yacht Racing Union, West Indies Yachting Assn. Clubs: Royal Ocean Racing, Ocean Cruising, Transpacific Yacht, Calif. Yacht, Los Angeles Yacht, Grenada Yacht. Patentee flesh-color bandages. Office: PO Box 1859 Santa Monica CA 90406

HARRIS, FREDERICK MILO, securities co. exec.; b. Ottawa, Kans., Nov. 26, 1915; s. Fred Milo and Helen (Janes) H.; B.A., U. Kans., 1936; m. Josephine Elizabeth Burrow, Nov. 21, 1936; children—Fred Milo III, Nancy (Mrs. Ronald Lee Chandler), Cynthia Ann, David Christopher. With Chanute (Kans.) Tribune, 1936-52, 73—, asso. editor, 1942-48, pub., 1948-52, 73-80; promotion-publicity dir. KMBC-TV and Radio, Kansas City, Mo., 1955-59; mgr. S.E. Kans. Westam. Securities, Inc., Chanute, 1959-71; div. mgr. Internat. Securities Corp., Chanute, 1971-75; resident mgr. Weinrich Zitzmann Whitehead Inc., investment securities, 1975—; pres. Chanute Pub. Co., 1973-80, chmn., 1980—; pres., Mid-Am., Inc., 1967-68, chmn., 1968-69. Chmn. Kans. Adv. Commn. on Alcoholism; mem. Kans. Adv. Commn. on Drug Abuse; mem. Commn. on Alcoholism and Drug Abuse, Kans. Episcopal Diocese. Mem. Chanute City Commn., 1964-67; mayor Chanute, 1966-67; mem. Kans. Ho. of Reps., 1968-76, chmn. transp. and utilities com., 1973-76. Chmn., Neosho Meml. Hosp. Endowment Found., Chanute; bd. advisers Gladys A. Kelce Sch. Bus. and Econ. Devel., Pittsburg (Kans.) State U.; trustee William Allen White Found., Sch. Journalism, U. Kans. Served to lt. (j.g.) USNR, 1943-46. Mem. Chanute C. of C. (past dir., pres.), Kans. Assn. Commerce and Industry (past dir.), Am. Legion (past comdr.), V.F.W., Nat. Council Alcoholism, Sigma Delta Chi, Phi Kappa Psi. Republican. Episcopalian. Home: 1208 W 14th St Ct Chanute KS 66720 Office: 4 W Main St Chanute KS 66720

HARRIS, GEORGE CARLETON, govt. ofcl.; b. Dublin, Ga., Oct. 14, 1941; s. Cephas Willard and Eloise (Chapman) H.; B.A., U. Ga., 1961, M.A. (grad. research asst. 1965-66), 1966, postgrad. (teaching asst.), 1967-69; m. Doris Jean McCormick, July 7, 1979. Asst. prof. polit. sci. The Citadel, Charleston, S.C., 1968-69; civilian chief employee, career devel. and employee relations Loring AFB, Maine, 1971-77; personnel specialist Air Force Systems Command Hdqrs., Andrews AFB, Washington, 1977—; cons., lectr. in field. Served with USNR, 1961-63, 70. Mem. Am. Soc. Personnel Adminstrn., Naval Inst. Author: On Target. . .You Can Get There From Here, 1978. Home: PO Box 42 Cheltenham MD 20623

HARRIS, GODFREY, mgmt. cons.; b. London, June 11, 1937; s. Alfred and Victoria H.; came to U.S., 1939, naturalized, 1945; A.B. with gt. distinction, Stanford U., 1958; M.A., UCLA, 1960; m. Linda Berkowitz Harris, Dec. 21, 1958; children—Gregrey, Kennith, Mark. Teaching asst. UCLA, 1958-60; lectr. Rutgers U., 1961-62; fgn. service officer, U.S. Dept. State, 1962-65; mgmt. analyst Office of Mgmt. and Budget, Washington, 1965-67; spl. asst. to pres. IOS Devel. Co., Geneva, Switzerland, 1967-68; pres., chief exec. officer Harris/Ragan Mgmt. Corp., Los Angeles, 1968—. Mem. dist. advisory com. on gifted Santa Monica United Sch. Dist., 1976-79, chmn. dist. advisory com., 1978-79. Served to 1st lt. U.S. Army, 1960-62. Decorated Army Commendation medal. Fellow Am. Acad. Consultants; mem. Assn. of Mgmt. Cons.; Los Angeles World Affairs Council, London C. of C. and Industry (membership sec. N. Am. chpt.), Stanford U. Alumni Assn., Phi Beta Kappa. Author: History of Sandy Hook, New Jersey, 1962; (with Frances Fielder) The Quest for Foreign Affairs Officers, 1966; Panama's Position, 1973; founder, editor Almanac of World Leaders, 1957-62, Consultants Directory, 1975—. Office: 9200 Sunset Blvd Los Angeles CA 90069

HARRIS, HENRY SCOTT, mgmt. cons.; b. N.Y.C., Feb. 12, 1928; B.A., New Eng. Coll., 1949; M.A., Columbia, 1951; m. Shirley; children—Randal, Susan, David, Heidi. Founder, Interpub. Ventures, N.Y.C., 1952, pres., 1952-62; v.p. Madison Life Ins. Co., N.Y.C., 1962-63, exec. v.p., 1964; pres. Am. Mayflower Life Ins. Co. N.Y., N.Y.C., 1965-70; chmn. bd. F.M. Guide Inc., N.Y.C., 1970-72; founder, pres. See and Sound Ltd., N.Y.C., 1972—; dir. Grammercy Funding Corp., N.Y.C.; chmn. bd. Edn. & Leisure Systems, Inc., N.Y.C., 1968-72. Lectr., U. Conn., 1960—, N.Y. U., 1960—. Mem. N.Y.C. Mayor's Scholastic Adv. Com., 1964—; pres. Better Bus. Bur. South Fla., 1980—; bd. dirs. Internat. Labor Exchange, 1963. Served as lt. (j.g.) USNR, 1944-46; PTO. Decorated D.F.C., Silver Star, Purple Heart; recipient Letter of Commendation, State of Israel, 1977; Community Affairs award NOW, 1977; Heritage award City of Hope, others. Mem. Mensa. Contbr. articles to profl. jours., newspapers and mags.; pub. FM Guide, The Boatowner. Home: 1061 NE 179 St North Miami Beach FL 33162

HARRIS, HOWARD H., lawyer, oil co. exec.; b. Cushing, Okla., Dec. 7, 1924; s. Oscar H. and Gertie Lee (Stark) H.; student Okla. Baptist U., 1942-43; B.S., U. Okla., 1949, J.D., 1949; A.M.P., Stanford U., 1971; m. Gwendolyne J. Moyers, Dec. 31, 1945; children—Howard S., Rodney C. Admitted to Okla. bar, 1949, Ohio bar, 1963; atty. Marathon Oil Co., Tulsa, 1954, div. atty., 1955-63, staff atty. Marathon Internat., Findlay, Ohio, 1963-65, Germany, 1965-70, mktg. atty., Findlay, 1970-72, asso. gen. counsel, 1972-74, v.p. corp. external affairs, 1974—. Served with AUS, 1943-45. Decorated Bronze Star. Mem. Findlay C. of C., Am. Petroleum Inst., Am. Bar Assn., Okla. Bar Assn., Ohio Bar Assn., Findlay Bar Assn., Order of Coif, Beta Gamma Sigma. Episcopalian. Club: Rotary. Office: 539 S Main St Findlay OH 45840

HARRIS, HOWARD JEFFREY, printing co. exec.; b. Denver, June 9, 1949; s. Gerald Victor and Leona Lee (Tepper) H.; B.F.A. with honors, Kansas City Art Inst., 1973; M. of Indsl. Design with honors, Pratt Inst., 1975; postgrad. Graphic Arts Research Center, Rochester Inst. Tech., 1977; m. Michele Whealen, Feb. 6, 1975; 1 dau., Kimberly. Indsl. designer Kivett & Myers, Architects, 1970-71; indsl. designer United Research Corp., Denver, 1971-72; indsl. designer, asst. to v.p., pres. JFN Assos., N.Y.C., 1972-73; dir. facility planning Abt & Assos., Cambridge, Mass., 1973-74; v.p. design, prodn. and research Eagle Printing Co., Denver from 1974, now v.p. design, research and devel.; lectr. corp. and organizational communications. Bd. dirs. Friends of Nat. Center for the Prevention and Treatment of Child Abuse and Neglect, Denver. Mem. Indsl. Designers Soc. Am., Graphic Arts Tech. Found., Design Methods Group, The Color Group, Cable TV Adminstrn. and Mktg. Soc., Am. Advt. Fedn., Nat. Assn. for Children. Democrat. Jewish. Home: 929 Washington St Denver CO 80203 Office: Eagle LithoGraphics 5105 E 41st St Denver CO 80216

HARRIS, HUGH MALVERN, drilling co. exec.; b. Colorado Springs, Colo., Mar. 6, 1924; s. William Franklin and Marion Maxine (Magruder) H.; student U. Denver, 1946-48; m. Angeline A. Block, Feb. 19, 1955; children—Patrick Michael, Kathleen A. Engaged in drilling bus., 1956—; pres. Hugh M. Harris Drilling Co., Stevens and Harris Drilling Co., Maxfield and Harris Drilling Co., Toler and Harris Drilling Co. (all Poway, San Diego), 1956—. Served with USN, 1942-46. Mem. Internat. Assn. Geophys. Contractors, Nat. Water Well Assn., Mining Club of S.W., Inc. (charter). Club: Stoneridge Country. Office: 11650 Iberia Pl Suite N-1 San Diego CA 92128

HARRIS, JAMES HENRY, JR., casket mfg. co. exec.; b. Commerce, Ga., May 19, 1925; s. James Henry and Bertha Mae (Luthi) H.; B.B.A., U. Ga., 1949; m. Marilyn Diane Morse, Mar. 6, 1952; children—James Henry III, Jeffrey A. With Toccoa Casket Co. (Ga.), 1950—, pres., 1978—, also dir.; pres. J.H. Enterprises, Inc., Toccoa, 1974—, also dir.; dir. Citizens Bank, Franklin Discount Co. Served with USN, 1942-45; ETO. Decorated Purple Heart. Mem. Casket Mfrs. Assn. Am., Ga. Funeral Supply Assn., S.C. Funeral Supply Assn., N.C. Funeral Supply Assn., Toccoa C. of C. (dir.), Sigma Chi. Clubs: Toccoa Country, Kingwood Country, Shriners, Elks. Home: 167 Valley Rd Toccoa GA 30577 Office: 726 W Currahee St Toccoa GA 30577

HARRIS, JAY, govt. budget ofcl.; b. Balt., June 14, 1941; s. Robert David and Bessie Lucille (Mazeroff) H.; B.A. U. Md., 1969; m. Charna Silverstein, July 16, 1967; children—Eric Michael, Jeffrey Ira. Contract specialist Navy Dept., Washington, 1966-68; contracting officer Westinghouse Electric Corp., Balt., 1968-70; contract specialist U.S. Postal Service, Washington, 1970-72; budget analyst Social Security Adminstrn., Balt., 1972—; dir. promotions and sales Balt Metros Profl. Basketball Team. Mem. Balt. County Commn. on Aging, 1974—; bd. dirs. Balt. County Fair, 1976; bd. dirs. Poison Prevention, Inc., Randallstown Jaycees Found.; pres. bd. dirs. Vol. Action Center, Balt., 1979-80; exec. dir. Md. Jr. Miss, 1979—. Mem. Randallstown Jaycees (pres. 1975-76 chmn. bd. 1976), Md. Jaycees (pub. relations dir. 1976-77, exec. dir. 1977—), Nat. Jaycees (pub. relations dir. presdl. campaign com., internat. senator). Democrat. Jewish. Club: B'nai B'rith (pres. 1980). Home: 9053 Meadow Heights Rd Randallstown MD 21133 Office: Social Security Adminstrn 6401 Security Blvd Baltimore MD 21235

HARRIS, JEFFREY DALE, accountant; b. Albuquerque, Dec. 8, 1947; s. Joe D. and Freda (Champion) H.; B.B.A. in Acctg., U. N.Mex., 1969; m. Aletha Boggs Corbin, June 14, 1969; children—Aletha Brynn, Thomas Joe. Audit mgr. Arthur Andersen & Co., Houston, 1969-77; v.p. fin. Superior Homes, Inc., 1977-79; v.p., controller Mitchell Devel. Corp. of S.W. subs. Mitchell Energy & Devel. Corp., Houston, 1979—. Bd. dirs. Woodlands (Tex.) Community Assn. C.P.A., Ariz., Tex. Mem. Am. Inst. C.P.A.'s, Ariz. Soc. C.P.A.'s, Tex. Soc. C.P.A.'s (dir. Houston chpt.), U. N.Mex. Alumni Assn. (dir.). Episcopalian. Home: 3858 Villa Ridge St Houston TX 77068 Office: 2201 Timberloch St The Woodlands TX 77380

HARRIS, JOHN ANDREW, real estate corp. exec., recreation cons.; b. Washington, Mar. 28, 1936; s. Milton and Carolyn (Wolf) H.; A.B. in History, U. Mich., 1958, M.B.A. in Mktg., 1960; m. Nancy Rosenthal, Mar.9, 1968; children—Brian Scott, Nicole. Mktg. trainee General Electric Co., various locations, 1960-62; account exec. Merril

Lynch, Fenner and Smith, Washington, 1962-65; fin. officer Upward Bound Program, OEO, 1965-67; v.p., gen. mgr. Greater Chgo. Indoor Tennis Clubs, Inc., 1967-69; pres. Potomac Ventures, Inc., Washington, 1971—; player major U.S. tennis tournaments including Forest Hills, Pan Am. Maccabiah Games, Brazil, 1966; bd. dirs. Washington Area Tennis Patrons Found., Inc., 1962-67, exec. sec., 1970—; promoter tennis exhbns. including Davis Cup preview matches, 1966, co-chmn., 1968, 69; mem. Pres.'s Com. Youth Opportunity; bd. dirs. Chgo. Tennis Patrons, 1968-69, Chgo. Dist. Tennis Assn., 1968-69; co-chmn. Washington Star Tennis Championships, 1969—; hon. chmn. Virginia Slims Women's Classic, Washington, 1972-73; tournament dir. Xerox Tennis Classic, 1974; U.S. Tournament Dirs.'s rep. Men's Internat. Profl. Tennis Council, 1977-79; cons. corps. tennis industry, 1972—; dir. recreational activities Charles E. Smith Co., 1972—. Served with U.S. Army, 1960. Mem. Washington Bd. Trade, N.Am. Tennis Tournament Dirs. Assn. (founder, pres.), Nat. Indoor Tennis Assn. (founder, steering com., v.p. 1971-72, dir. 1971-73), U.S. Tennis Assn. (facilities com. 1968-75, chmn. Men's Grand Prix Tournament). Office: 3300 Whitehaven St NW Washington DC 20007

HARRIS, JOHN MALCOLM (RED), chem. co. exec.; b. Clearwater, Fla., Jan. 4, 1921; s. Delmar C. and Eunice (Avery) H.; B.S., Rollins Coll., 1944; postgrad. Oberlin Coll., 1944; m. Margaret Parsons, Aug. 16, 1946; children—John M., William D., Donna M. Personnel mgr. W.R. Grace & Co., Bartow, Fla., 1946-49, prodn. supt., 1949-51, asst. mgr., 1951-55, mgr., 1955-56, asst. div. mgr. chem. div., Balt., 1956-61; pres. Best Fertilizers, Lathrop, Cal., 1961-64, Occidental Corp. Fla., 1964-66; v.p. Occidental Petroleum, Los Angeles, 1966-67; exec. v.p. Occidental Chem. Co., Houston, 1967-78; v.p., dir. Cambridge Systems, Houston, 1979—. Served to lt. (j.g.) USNR, 1944-46. Mem. Am. Inst. Mining, Metall. and Petroleum Engrs., Kappa Alpha. Democrat. Clubs: Ponte Verde (Fla.); University, River Oaks Country (Houston). Home: 2928 Del Monte Dr Houston TX 77019 Office: 2400 Augusta Suite 240 Houston TX 77057

HARRIS, JOHN RICHARD, advt. co., pub. relations exec.; b. Choteau, Mont., Mar. 7, 1932; s. Hugh Delbert and Retta Madge (Kirkpatrick) H.; student U. Wyo., 1950-52; B.A., U. Mont., 1956, M.A., 1959; m. Ann Laurah Mitchell, June 25, 1953; children—John Richard, David Bennitt. Dir. photography Seattle World's Fair, 1961-62; asst. to pres., dir. pub. relations Palomar (Calif.) Jr. Coll., 1962-63; account supr. Rumrill-Hoyt Advt. and Pub. Relations, N.Y.C., 1964-70; v.p. Grant Advt. Internat., N.Y.C., 1970-73; exec. v.p., dir. Comcore Public Relations, Ltd. (Can.), Toronto, Ont., also N.Y.C., 1972-78; pres., chief exec. officer Jon-R Assos., public relations and mgmt. cons. firm, N.Y.C., 1950—; exec. v.p., dir. Pro-Gramo, Inc., N.Y.C., 1965—; pres., chief exec. officer, dir. Harris-Grant Inc., N.Y.C., 1973-75; mem. exec. com. Grant Advt. Internat.; London, Eng., Panama, Santiago, Chile, Caracas, Venezuela, 1969-75; lectr. photo-journalism, 1962—; mng. dir. Nat. Council Affiliated Advt. Agys., 1975-77; exec. v.p. Mast Advt. Assos., Inc., N.Y.C., 1976-77. Spl. dep. sheriff Missoula County, Mont., 1960-62. Served with USMC, 1952-55. Recipient Struckman Meml. award Mont. State U. Sch. Journalism, 1955; President's Outstanding Service award Seattle World's Fair, 1962. Mem. Mont. Inst. Arts (dir. fine arts photography 1961-62), Caribbean Travel Assn., Nat. Audio Visual Assn., Pub. Relations Soc. Am., Internat. Advt. Assn., Internat. Graphic Arts Edn. Assn. Unitarian. Elk. Club: Squadron A (N.Y.C.). Co-inventor audio-visual system, abacus teaching machine. Contbr. articles to profl. publs. Home: 174 Broadway Pleasantville NY 10570 Office: 7 W 44th St New York NY 10036

HARRIS, JOHN WOODS, banker; b. Galveston, Tex., Sept. 23, 1893; s. John Woods and Minnie (Hutchings) H.; LL.B., U. Va., 1920; m. Eugenia Davis, June 14, 1917; children—Eugenia (Mrs. Archibald Rowland Campbell, Jr.), Anne (Mrs. Donald C. Miller), Joan (Mrs. Alvin N. Kelso), Florence (Mrs. Marshall McDonald, Jr.) (dec.). Admitted to Tex. bar, 1920, practiced as atty. and mng. agt. oil, farm, ranch properties in Tex., 1922—; dir. Hutchings Sealy Nat. Bank; chmn. exec. com., chmn. bd. First Hutchings Sealy Nat. Bank (merged into First Internat. Bancshares), Galveston, 1960-74; pres. Hutchings Joint Stock Assn., 1936—; dir. Galveston Corp., Cotton Concentration Co., Gulf Transfer Co., Tex. Fiberglas Products Co. Vice pres., chmn. land com. Sealy and Smith Found. for John Sealy Hosp.; pres. bd. Rosenberg Library, Galveston Orphans Home, Galveston Found.; bd. dirs., v.p., chmn. fin. com. George Ball Charity Fund; trustee Galveston Ind. Sch. Dist., 1927-30. Served as aviator USN, 1918. Mem. Am. Judicature Soc., Early and Pioneer Naval Aviators Assn., Sons of Republic Tex., Am. Legion, Delta Kappa Epsilon. Episcopalian. Clubs: Galveston Artillery; Farmington Country (Charlottesville, Va.); Bob Smith Yacht. Home: 2603 Ave O Galveston TX 77550 Office: First Hutchings-Sealy Nat Bank Bldg Galveston TX 77550

HARRIS, LEE KELLY, banker; b. Genoa, Nebr., June 22, 1935; s. Frederick Charles and Gwendolyn Arlene H.; B.S., U. Nebr., 1956; M.S. in Mgmt., U.S. Naval Postgrad Sch., 1966; m. Ruby Lee Hill, Apr. 21, 1962; children—Lee Kelly, Bradford William. Salesman, Phillips Petroleum Co., 1958-61; pres. Bank of Monroe (Nebr.), 1968-69; v.p. United Calif. Bank, Los Angeles, 1969-80, Am. City Bank, Los Angeles, 1980—. Bd. dirs. Mission Viejo (Calif.) Little League, 1970—; zone fund chmn. Boy Scouts Am., 1971. Served with USN, 1956-58, to lt. comdr., 61-68; Vietnam; capt. USNR. Mem. Sigma Chi. Republican. Clubs: Lions, Univ. Athletic. Home: 27581 Tres Vistas Mission Viejo CA 92692 Office: 2743 East Coast Hwy Corona del Mar CA 92625

HARRIS, NATHANIEL CARROLL, JR., banker; b. Hackensack, N.J., Jan. 1, 1941; s. Nathaniel Carroll and Susan M. (Satterwhite) H.; B.S., Hampton Inst., 1964; M.B.A., Pace U., 1979; m. Frazeal Larrymore, Feb. 1, 1969; 1 dau., Courtney. Engring. account mgr. Aetna Life & Casualty, Newark, 1966-68; with Citibank, N.A., N.Y.C., 1968-80, asst. v.p. mktg./planning real estate industries div., 1979-80; v.p., urban lending project mgr. Chase Manhattan Bank, N.Y.C., 1980—. Bd. dirs. Coop. Assistance Fund, Washington, 1980—; chmn. fin. com., bd. dirs. Energy Task Force, Nat. Urban League Black Exchange Program, 1975-80. Served with U.S. Army, 1964-66. Mem. Nat. Assn. Housing and Redevel. Ofcls., Omega Psi Phi. Home: 264 Highland Ave Orange NJ 07050 Office: 40 Wall St New York NY 10005

HARRIS, PETER ANGELO, retail co. exec.; b. Boston, July 19, 1918; s. Angelo P. and Antonia (Carlton) H.; B.B.A., Northeastern U., 1943; M.B.A., Babson Coll., 1969; m. Irene P. Carr, Aug. 1, 1943; 1 dau., Donna. Sec.-treas. Southwest Hardware Co., Los Angeles, 1965-69; comptroller Mal's Dept. Stores, Newton, Mass., 1969-73, Zayne Corp. div. Bell Nugent, Framingham, Mass., 1973—; comptroller, tax and acctg. specialist S.J. Balsama Corp., Brockton, Mass., 1973—. Served to lt. USNR, 1943-47. Notary public, Mass.; public acct., Mass. Mem. Nat. Soc. Public Accts. Home: Falmouth MA Office: SJ Balsama Corp 365 Westgate Dr Brockton MA 02401

HARRIS, RICHARD FOSTER, JR., ins. co. exec.; b. Athens, Ga., Feb. 8, 1918; s. Richard Foster and Mai Audli (Chandler) H.; B.C.S., U. Ga., 1939; m. Virginia McCurdy, Aug. 21, 1937 (div.); children—Richard Foster, Gaye Karyl Harris Law; m. 2d, Kari Melandso, Dec. 29, 1962. Bookkeeper, salesman 1st Nat. Bank, Atlanta, 1936-40; agt. Vol. State Life Ins. Co., Atlanta, 1940-41; asst. mgr. N.Y. Life Ins. Co., Atlanta and Charlotte, N.C., 1941-44; mgr., agt. Pilot Life Ins. Co., Charlotte and Houston, 1944-63; mgr., agt., bus. planning div.; city agy. Am. Gen. Life Ins. Co., Houston, 1963—; dir. Fidelity Bank & Trust Co., Houston, 1965-66. Chmn. fund drive Am. Heart Assn., Charlotte, Mecklenburg County, 1958-59, chmn. bd., 1959-61; gen. chmn. Shrine Bowl Promotion, Charlotte Shriners, 1955; v.p., dir. Myers Park Meth. Ch. Men's Class, 1956-59, bd. stewards, Charlotte, 1959-61. Recipient Pres.'s Cabinet award Am. Gen. Life Ins. Co., 1964-67, 69, 71, 77, 78, 79; Disting. Salesman award Charlotte Sales Exec. Club, 1955, 57-59; Bronze Medallion award Am. Heart Assn., 1959; Nat. Quality award Life Ins. Agency Mgmt. Assn. and Nat. Assn. Life Underwriters, 1976-79; C.L.U. Mem. Assn. Advanced Life Underwriters, Am. Soc. C.L.U.'s, Nat. Assn. Life Underwriters, SAR (sec. chpt. 5, Tex. Soc. 1974—), Sertoma Internat. (life, v.p., dir. Charlotte chpt.), Life Underwriters Polit. Action Com. (life), Ky. Cols., Houston Estate and Fin. Forum, English Speaking Union, Mensa Internat., Houston Assn. Life Underwriters, Lone Star Leaders Club, Tex. Leader's Round Table (life), Million Dollar Round Table, Tex. Assn. Life Underwriters, Am. Security Council (nat. adv. bd. 1979—), Nat. Platform Assn., Tex. Crime Prevention Assn., Pi Kappa Phi. Republican. Episcopalian. Clubs: Warwick, Napoleon, 100, Kiwanis (dir. 1979—), Houston Knife and Fork, Masons (32 deg.), Shriners. Contbr. articles to profl. jours. Home: 2701 Westheimer Rd Houston TX 77098 also Dunbar Ln Sea Island GA 31561 Office: Am Gen Tower 2727 Allen Parkway Suite 500 Houston TX 77019

HARRIS, RICHARD HENRY, machinery and instrument mfg. co. exec.; b. Worcester, Mass., July 23, 1926; s. Percy Henry Guy and Helen Elizabeth (Hult) H.; S.B., M.I.T., 1948, S.M., 1949; D.Econs. (hon.), Central New Eng. Coll., 1978; m. Rosemary Marble, Nov. 5, 1949; children—Jonathan, Candace, Susan, Leslie, Andrea. Fin. and acctg. exec. Norton Co., Worcester, 1949-69; dir. corp. devel. Curtis & Marble Corp., Worcester, 1969—, also pres. Served with USNR, 1944-46. Mem. Am. Textile Machinery Assn. (pres.). Republican. Unitarian. Club: Worcester. Home: 26 South St Grafton MA 01519 Office: 72 Cambridge St Worcester MA 01603

HARRIS, RICHARD TENNEY, ins. exec.; b. Worcester, Mass., June 8, 1938; s. William H. and Ruth E. (Howe) H.; A.B., Brown U., 1962; m. Nancy G. Clarke, June 23, 1962; children—Christopher, Jonathan, Nathaniel, Jeremy. Engaged in ins. bus., 1962—; mng. dir. internat. div. Allendale Ins. Co., 1970-72; v.p. Johnson & Higgins, 1972-77; pres., chief exec. officer Rollins Burdick Hunter Pa., Phila., also div. dir., corp. v.p. Rollins Burdick Hunter, 1977—; bd. dirs. Nat. Acad. Conciliators, Washington. Served with USMCR, 1956-58. Republican. Congregationalist. Clubs: Union League, Merion Cricket, Merion Golf, Corinthian Yacht. Home: 8 Welwyn Rd Wayne PA 19087 Office: 756 Public Ledger Bldg Philadelphia PA 19106

HARRIS, ROBERT ALFRED, chem. co. exec.; b. Perrysburg, Ohio, June 8, 1916; s. Arthur Benjamin and Grace Ellen (Martin) H.; student Adelbert Coll., Western Res. Coll.; m. Lois West Harris, Oct. 25, 1965; children—Joan, Robert, Laurence, Barbara, Cheryl, David, Joseph. With ordnance dept. Standard Oil of Ohio, 1938-39; with Hilton-Davis Chem. Co., Cin., pres., 1975—. Mem. Cin. Council World Affairs; deacon, elder Presbyn. Ch. Mem. AAAS, Engring. Soc. Cin., Am. Chem. Soc., Sigma Xi. Presbyterian. Club: Bankers. Office: 2235 Langdon Farm Rd Cincinnati OH 45237

HARRIS, ROBERT BRUCE, lab. exec.; b. Lincoln, Nebr., Feb. 8, 1945; s. Lewis Elden and Antonietta E. (Synovac) H.; B.S., U. Nebr., 1968, postgrad., 1968-70; children—Matthew, Theodore. With Harris Labs., Inc., Lincoln, 1960—, v.p., 1970-76, chmn. bd., 1977—; founder, prin. R.B. Harris Co., Lincoln, 1975—; founder, pres. Harris Sci., Inc., Lincoln, 1973—; dir. PSA, Inc., Sci. Devel. Corp., FSI, Inc., SDI, Inc. Mem. Am. Platform Assn., Assn. Systems Mgmt., Nebr. Assn. Commerce and Industry, Fertilizer Inst., Nat. Fertilizer Solutions Assn., Am. Council Ind. Labs., Council Soil Testing and Plant Analysis, Am. Advt. Fedn., Am. Soc. Agrl. Engrs., Council Agrl. Sci. and Tech., Newcomen Soc., others. Republican. Presbyterian. Contbr. articles to profl. jours. Home: 2829 S 31st St Lincoln NE 68501 Office: 624 Peach St Lincoln NE 68501

HARRIS, ROBERT FRANKLIN, holding co. exec.; b. Bklyn., Aug. 9, 1943; s. Abram B. and Pearl R. (Rudaw) H.; B.S. Investment Banking, N.Y. U., 1965; D.C.S. (hon.), London Inst. Applied Research, 1972; m. Laura Irene Schoenfeld Dec. 19, 1974; 1 dau., Sharon. Sr. sci./technology analyst Orvis Bros. & Co., N.Y.C., 1969-70; mgr. corporate devel. Med. Analytics Inc., N.Y.C., 1970-71; pres. Research Analytics, East Meadow, N.Y., 1971-74; treas., dir. Standard Container Transport Corp., Elizabeth, N.J., 1974-75; account exec., corporate devel. Merrill Lynch Pierce Fenner & Smith, Inc., Garden City, N.Y., 1975-78; v.p. corp. devel. Dynetel Group Ltd., Gt. Neck, N.Y., 1978-79; exec. v.p., treas., dir. NRX Techs. Inc., N.Y.C., 1979—; v.p., dir. Hastings Industries, Inc., Great Neck, N.Y., 1979—. Mem. Nassau County Rep. Com., 1976—; mem. East Meadow Rep. Committeemen's Council, 1976—; Rep. committeeman, 31st Election Dist., 1976—; mem. legis. adv. com. N.Y. State Assembly, 1978—. Served with M.I. U.S. Army, 1965-71. Fellow Fin. Analysts Fedn.; mem. N.Y. Soc. Security Analysts (sr.), L.I. Assn. Commerce and Industry, Am. Numismatic Assn., L.I. Brokers Club, Tau Delta Phi. Contbr. articles to profl. jours. Office: PO Box 246 East Meadow NY 11554

HARRIS, ROBERT WESLEY, hosp. adminstr.; b. Buffalo, June 2, 1934; s. Gordon Clifford and Florence E. (Palmquist) H.; B.S. in Phys. Therapy, Ithaca Coll., 1960; M.H.A., U. Toronto, 1965; m. Nancy Jean La Point, Feb. 14, 1969; children—Keirstan J., Alissa L. Hosp. cons. N.Y. State Health Dept., 1965-66; exec. asst. N.Y. State Commr. Health, 1967-69; asso. adminstr. Geneva Gen. Hosp., 1969-72; exec. dir. Western N.Y. Hosp. Assn., 1972-73; v.p. Medico Assos., 1973-76; adminstr., chief exec. officer Jones Meml. Hosp., Wellsville, N.Y., 1977—. Served with U.S. Army, 1954-56. Mem. Am. Coll. Hosp. Adminstrs. Home: 150 Scott Ave Wellsville NY 14895 Office: 191 N Main Wellsville NY 14895

HARRIS, TEDRIC ALAN, ball and roller bearings mfg. co. exec.; b. Phila., Feb. 25, 1932; s. Philip Hall and Bella (Rosenberg) H.; B.S.M.E., Pa. State U., 1953, M.S.M.E. (Hamilton Standard fellow), 1954; m. Selma Bette Fine, June 6, 1954; children—Philip Lee, Barbara Ann. Devel. test engr. Hamilton Standard div. United Aircraft Corp., Windsor Locks, Conn., 1953-55; analytical design engr. Bettis Atomic Power Lab., Westinghouse Electric Co., Pitts., 1955-60; supr. bearing tech. SKF Industries, 1960-67, mgr. analytical services, 1969-71, dir. corp. data systems, Phila., 1971-73, pres. Splty. Bearings div., Phila., 1977-79; mng. dir. SKF Engring. and Research Centre B.V., Nieuwegein, Netherlands, 1980—; cons. engr. Jones & Harris, Newington, Conn., 1968; v.p. info. systems Aktiebolaget SKF, group hdqrs., Gothenburg, Sweden, 1973-77. Recipient Deutsch award Am. Soc. Lubrication Engrs., 1965, Hodson award, 1968. Fellow ASME (exec. com. lubrication div. 1971-72, mem. research com. on lubrication 1970-71). Clubs: Masons, Rotary. Author: Rolling Bearing Analysis, 1966; contbr. numerous articles to profl. publs.; patentee in bearings field. Home: Vermeerlaan 8 Bilthoven Netherlands Office: SKF Engring and Research Centre BV Postbus 50 3430AB Nieuwegein Netherlands

HARRIS, WILLIAM GIBSON, II, investment banker; b. Washington, Mar. 18, 1944; s. William Gibson and Jane (Hardy) H.; B.A., Yale U., 1966; M.B.A., U. Pa., 1968; m. Pamela Dixon, June 24, 1972; children by previous marriage—Helen K., Christopher H.; children—William Gibson III, Barbara Dixon. Vice pres. Smith Barney Harris Upham Co., N.Y.C., 1968-77; sr. v.p. Blyth Eastman Dillon Co., N.Y.C., 1977-80; mng. dir. Blyth Eastman Paine Webber and Co., N.Y.C., 1980—; dir. Victor F. Weaver, Inc. Mem. Bond Club N.Y.C. Episcopalian. Clubs: Round Hill (Greenwich, Conn.); Country of Va. (Richmond); Yale (N.Y.C.). Home: 47 E 88th St New York NY 10028 also 14 Willow Rd Riverside CT 06878 Office: 1221 Ave of Americas New York NY 10020

HARRIS, WILLIAM ROBERT, retail exec.; b. Fayetteville, Ga., Aug. 16, 1914; s. Lenord Alexander and Millie Lilla (Boyd) H.; grad. Young Harris Jr. Coll., 1935; m. Gertrude G. Goss, Nov. 31, 1940; children—Sally Sue, William Robert. With F.W. Woolworth Co., N.Y.C., 1935-42, 45—, v.p., 1965-70, exec. v.p., from 1970, dir., mem. exec. com., 1977—, vice-chmn. bd., from 1976, pres. U.S. Woolworth-Woolco operating div., 1975-78, corp. pres., chief operating officer, 1978—; dir. F.W. Woolworth Ltd. Can., Kinney Shoes, Richmond Bros. Clothier; chief exec. officer Charles K. Campbell, Inc. Served with U.S. Army, 1942-45. Mem. Am. Retail Fedn. (dir.), Nat. Retail Mchts. Assn. (dir.). Methodist. Clubs: Greenwich (Conn.) Country; Seaview Country (Absecon, N.J.); John's Island Country (Vero Beach, Fla.); Walden Country (Montgomery, Tex.). Home: 212 Island Creek Dr Vero Beach FL 77356 Office: 1616 W Loop S #212 Houston TX 77027

HARRISON, BILL CLARK, environ. co. exec.; b. Roseland, La., Feb. 22, 1933; s. Nathaniel and Zular Mae (Williams) H.; B.S. with honors, So. U., 1956; M.S., Wash. State U., 1966; M.B.A., Babson Coll., 1977; m. Mona L. Chambers, Aug. 22, 1970; 1 son, W. Clark. Commd. 2d lt., U.S. Army, 1959, advanced through grades to lt. col., 1974; air pollution engr. Wash. State U., 1956-58; chem. comdr./advisor, Ger., 1961-64; research asso., Ft. Detrick, Md., 1966-68; comdr. McNamara Electronic Wall team, South Vietnam, 1967-68; dep. comdr. Night Vision Research and Devel. Command. Ft. Belvoir, Va., 1968-71; chem advisor Hdqrs. 1st U.S. Army, Ft. Meade, Md., 1972-74; comdr. Materials and Mech. Research Center, Watertown, Mass., 1975; dep. lab. chief materials lab., Watertown, 1976-78; ret., 1979; mgmt. cons., pres. Med. Bus. Services, Boston, 1977-78; founder, pres., chmn. bd. WCH Industries, Inc., Waltham, Mass., 1978—. Asst. Watertown Conservation Commn. and Watertown Hist. Soc., 1975. Decorated Bronze Star, Air medal, Meritorious Service medal, Army Commendation medal; recipient Outstanding Achievement Momento, 1977. Mem. Am. Assn. Small Research Cos., Nat. Tech. Assn., Assn. Blacks in Energy, Assn. M.B.A. Execs., Water Pollution Fedn., New Eng. Solar Energy Assn., Black Corp. Pres's of New Eng., Alpha Kappa Mu, Eta Chi Sigma, Phi Sigma, Sigma Xi. Mem. Ch. of God in Christ. Home: 42 Tillotson Rd Needham MA 02194 Office: 24 Crescent St Waltham MA 02154

HARRISON, EARLE, real estate devel. cons.; b. Rainsville, Ala., May 20, 1905; s. Robert Lee and Sarepta Ophelia (Hansard) H.; A.B., Northwestern U., 1929, postgrad. bus. adminstrn., 1942; LL.B., Chgo.-Kent Coll. Law, 1935; m. Joan Mary Jackson, Jan. 24, 1942. With Marshall Field & Co., Chgo., 1929-68, div. operating mgr., 1959-60, v.p. ops., 1960-64, v.p., treas., 1964-68; owner Greenbrier Farm, Libertyville, Ill.; pres. Condell Meml. Hosp., Libertyville, 1973-77, chmn. bd., 1977-78, now dir.; cons. to real estate developer, 1978—. Formerly mem. Lake County Bd. Suprs.; chmn. Lake County Planning and Zoning Com., 1970—; commr. Northeastern Ill. Plan Commn., pres., 1973-74; bd. dirs. Credit Bur. Cook County, Chgo., 1949—, pres., 1958-69, chief exec. officer; bd. dirs., pres. Family Financial Counseling Service Greater Chgo., 1969. Mem. Phi Delta Phi. Episcopalian. Home: Deerpath House Apt 2E 501 Oakwood Lake Forest IL 60045 also 2712 Chrysler Dr Roswell NM 88201 Office: Condell Meml Hosp Stewart and Cleveland Libertyville IL 60048

HARRISON, EDWARD GIBSON, banker; b. Newtown, Pa., May 15, 1934; s. L.G. and Harriet Harrison; B.S. in Acctg., Pa. State U., 1958; postgrad. La. State U. Grad. Sch. Banking, 1972; m. Cynthia Elizabeth Parker, Oct. 15, 1960; children—Scott, Todd. Cost analyst, acctg. supr. Pitts. Plate Glass Co., 1958-62; v.p., loan officer, corr. banking officer First Union Nat. Bank, Charlotte, N.C., 1962-76; v.p., city exec. Bank N.C., Charlotte, 1976-80; pres. Metrolina Nat. Bank, Charlotte, 1980—. Bd. dirs. Kidney Found. Mecklenburg, 1970-75; treas. Nature Mus. Charlotte, 1970; chmn. Better Bus. Bur. Greater Mecklenburg, 1977. Served with AUS, 1953-55. Mem. Bank Adminstrn. Inst. (chpt. dir. 1979). Clubs: Charlotte Athletic (past dir.), Myers Park Country. Office: Metrolina Nat Bank Bldg Independence Blvd Charlotte NC 28212

HARRISON, JAMES PENNOCK, nursing home exec.; b. Coatesville, Pa., Dec. 28, 1926; s. James P. and Blanche A. (Carlin) H.; B.S., Millersville State Coll., 1950; Ed.M., Temple U., 1956, Ed.D., 1965; postgrad. Columbia U., 1965; m. Katherine Shockley, Aug. 12, 1951; children—Ellen, James, Jeffrey. Supt., Glassboro (N.J.) pub. schs., 1962-66; supt. schs. Nether Providence Twp., Wallingford, Pa., 1966-71, Wallingford-Swarthmore Sch. Dist., 1971-77; pres. J.P. Harrison, Inc., Moylan, Pa., 1978—; ednl. cons. Pres., Community Arts Center, Wallingford, 1971; bd. dirs. Ethel Mason Day Care Center, Media, Pa., 1973-75. Served with U.S. Army, 1945-47. Mem. Health Facilities Assn. Md., Am. Health Facilities Assn., Phi Delta Kappa. Clubs: Nassawango Country, Rose Valley Folk, Masons. Contbr. articles to profl. jours. Home: PO Box 122 Rose Valley PA 19065

HARRISON, JAMES WILLIAM, banker; b. Winder, Ga., June 18, 1939; s. James Thomas and Kathryn Marjie (Jones) H.; B.S., Ga. Inst. Tech., 1962; M.B.A., Ga. State U., 1967; m. Ina Sue Hunter, Sept. 1, 1962; children—James William, Mark Hunter, Amy Lynn. Sales rep. Burroughs Corp., 1962-63; sr. adminstr. Trust Co. Ga., 1964-65; sr. mktg. research analyst Lockheed-Ga. Co., 1966-70; asst. prof., chmn. undergrad. studies Calif. State U., Sacramento, 1971-75; asst. v.p. Bank of Barrow, Winder, Ga., 1975—; owner, operator Harrison Farms, Harrison Ethanol & Gasohol Plant, Auburn, Ga. Deacon, vice chmn., chmn. 1st Christian Ch., Winder. Served with U.S. Army, 1960-66. Democrat. Clubs: Pine Shore, N. Am. Hunting. Home: 107 Olevia St Route 1 Sherwood Forest Winder GA 30680 Office: PO Drawer 627 Winder GA 30680

HARRISON, JOHN ALEXANDER, leasing co. exec.; b. Lakeland, Fla., Jan. 22, 1944; s. William Henry and Aileen Helen (Jarvi) H.; B.I.E. with highest honors, Ga. Inst. Tech., 1966; M.B.A. (J. Spencer Love fellow), Harvard, 1968; m. Susan Leigh Smart, May 9, 1970; children—Kathryn Leigh, Jane Elizabeth. With Baxter Travenol Labs., Inc., Deerfield, Ill., 1968-78, asst. to v.p. fin., 1970-71, asst. treas., domestic, 1971-74, asst. treas., internat., 1974-76, fin. dir. Europe, Brussels, 1976-77, v.p. fin. and adminstrn. internat., 1978; v.p. fin. N.Am. Car Corp. subs. Tiger Internat., Inc., 1978—, also v.p.

fin. Tiger Leasing Group, 1980—. Bd. dirs. Youth Guidance, 1979-80. Mem. Harvard Bus. Sch. Club Chgo. (dir. 1970-71), Am. Club Brussels, Tau Beta Pi, Phi Kappa Phi, Phi Eta Sigma, Tau Kappa Epsilon. Home: 794 Walden Rd Winnetka IL 60093 Office: N Am Car Corp 33 W Monroe St Chicago IL 60603

HARRISON, RICHARD ALAN, mfg. co. exec.; b. New Haven, Apr. 12, 1948; s. Edward Joseph and Rose Ann (Szirbik) H.; A.S., Post Jr. Coll., 1972; B.B.A. magna cum laude (Baker scholar), Hofstra U., 1974; m. Elizabeth Joan Fanelli, June 22, 1974. Sr. auditor Coopers & Lybrand, New Haven, 1974-76; asst. comptroller Acme United Corp., Bridgeport, Conn., 1976-78; corporate controller Dual-Lite Inc., Newtown, Conn., 1978—. Served with USN, 1966-70. Recipient Academic Achievement award Greater Waterbury (Conn.) Area Group C.P.A.'s, 1971; C.P.A., Conn. Mem. Am. Inst. C.P.A.'s, Conn. Soc. C.P.A.'s, Beta Gamma Sigma. Office: Dual-Lite Inc 63 S Main St Newtown CT 06470

HARRISON, ROY, trade assn. exec.; b. N.Y.C., July 8, 1927; s. George L. and Irene H.; student Hunter Coll., 1947-49, N.Y. U., 1949-51; m. Doris Jean Fitzimons, May 22, 1976; children—Thomas, Ann, Suzy, James, Kathleen. With Mitchell Beck & Co., Inc., N.Y.C., 1952-55; pres. Am. Inst. Food Distbn., Inc., Fair Lawn, N.J., 1955—. Served with USN, 1944-46. Mem. Am. Soc. Assn. Execs., Food Distbn. Research Soc. Club: Watchung Lions (pres.). Home: 241 Ridge Rd Watchung NJ 07060 Office: 28-06 Broadway Fair Lawn NJ 07410

HARRISON, RUSSELL EDWARD, banker; b. Grandview, Man., Can., May 31, 1921; s. Edward Smith and Annie L. (Purvis) H.; ed. U. Man.; m. Nancy Doreen Bell, Oct. 18, 1944; 2 children. With Canadian Imperial Bank of Commerce (formerly Canadian Bank of Commerce), from 1945, asst. mgr., Hamilton, Ont., 1953-55, asst. mgr., Toronto, Ont., 1956, head of ops. in Que., Montreal, 1956-69, exec. v.p., chief gen. mgr. Head Office, Toronto, 1969-73, dir., 1970—, pres., chief operating officer, 1973-76, chmn., chief exec. officer, 1976—; dir. United Dominions Corp. (Can.) Ltd., Western Assurance Co., Calif. Canadian Bank, Royal Ins. Co. Can. Ltd., TransCan. PipeLines Falconbridge Nickel Mines, Can. Life Assurance Co., Can. Eastern Fin. Ltd., Can. Exec. Service Overseas, Dominion Realty Co., Ltd., Edifice Dorchester-Commerce Realty Ltd., Imbank Realty Co. Ltd.; dir., mem. fin. and gen. purposes com. ROINS Holding, Ltd. bd. govs., vice chmn. Massey Hall, Toronto; hon. mem. Stanford Research Inst.; mem. adv. bd. Bus. Sch., U. Western Ont.; mem. devel. bd. Centre for Conflict Studies, U. N.B.; bd. dirs. C.D. Howe Research Inst., Conf. Bd. in Can. Served with Canadian Army, World War II. Mem. Bus. Council on Nat. Issues, Can. Com. Clubs: Albany, Toronto, York, Rosedale Golf, Ont. Jockey, Ont. (Toronto); Mt. Royal, St. James's (Montreal); Ranchmen's (Calgary). Office: Can Imperial Bank Commerce Commerce Ct W Toronto ON M5L 1A2 Canada

HARRISON, STANLEY EARL, profl. services firm exec.; b. Northup, Ohio, Nov. 19, 1930; s. Stanley Mervin and Helen Mildred (Northup) H.; B.S. in Elec. Engring., Ohio State U., 1958; M.S. in Elec. Engring., U. N.Mex., 1962; m. Doris Ann Powell, June 21, 1953; children—Brenda Kay Harrison Ruysen, Anne Elizabeth, David Stanley, Anita Lynn. Mem. tech. staff Sandia Corp., Albuquerque, 1958-63; supr., program mgr. nuclear div. Martin-Marietta Corp., Balt., 1963-68; dir. western ops. BDM Corp., Albuquerque, 1968-72, v.p. ops., Vienna, Va., 1972-74, exec. v.p., 1974-78, exec. v.p., chief operating officer, McLean, Va., 1978—, also dir.; exec. v.p. BDM Services Co., McLean, 1971—; pres., dir. Zapex Corp., McLean, 1975—; chmn. Com. for Tomorrow, Ohio State U. Served with USAF, 1948-52. Named Distinguished Alumnus, Ohio State U.; registered profl. engr. Ohio. Mem. Assn. U.S. Army, IEEE (sr. mem.), Nat. Council Tech. Service Industries (dir.), Am. Mgmt. Assn., Am. Def. Preparedness Assn. (dir. Washington chpt.), Ohio State U. Assn. (life), Navy League U.S., U.S. Air Force Assn., Armed Forces Communications and Electronics Assn., Smithsonian Assos., Wolf Trap Found. (bd. dirs.), Eta Kappa Nu, Pi Mu Epsilon. Methodist (past chmn. ofcl. bd.). Mason (Shriner, Scottish Rite); mem. Order Eastern Star. Clubs: Westwood Country (Vienna, Va.); Presidents (Ohio State U.); Internat. (Washington). Contbr. profl. jours. Home: 1417 Montague Dr Vienna VA 22180 Office: 7915 Jones Branch Dr McLean VA 22102

HARROLD, WILLIAM NEAL, hosp. ofcl.; b. Elkhart, Ind., Aug. 11, 1943; s. John Woodrow and Olive Ann (Brewer) H.; grad. Ft. Wayne (Ind.) Comml. Coll., 1962; m. Joyce Ann Zimmerman, May 30, 1965; Br. mgr. Pacific Fin. Loans, New Castle, Ind., 1966-69; staff acct. Am. Water Work, Inc., Richmond, Ind., 1969-75; rep. Equitable Life Assurance Soc. U.S., Richmond, 1976-79; bus. office mgr. Jay County Hosp., Portland, Ind., 1979—. Commr., Crossroads of Am. council Boy Scouts Am. Mem. Nat. Assn. Life Underwriters, Ind. Hosp. Fin. Mgmt. Assn. Republican. Clubs: Kiwanis, Rotary. Home: 618 N Western Ave Portland IN 47371 Office: 505 W Arch St Portland IN 47371

HARSHBARGER, RICHARD B., economist; b. Lafayette, Ind., May 6, 1934; s. Albert E. and Olive Harshbarger; B.S., Manchester Coll., 1956; M.A. (fellow), Ind. U., 1958, Ph.D. (NSF fellow), 1964; m. Jane Newcomer, Aug. 24, 1958; children—Lisa, Jon. Mem. faculty Manchester (Ind.) Coll., 1960—, prof. econs., 1973—, chmn. dept., 1965—; vis. prof. Eastern Nazarene Coll., 1977-78, Pasadena Coll., 1968-69; lectr. labor edn. program Ind. U., 1972-77. Mem. Manchester Community Sch. Bd., 1972-76; mem. North Manchester Park Bd., 1972-76. Mem. Midwestern Econ. Assn., Am. Econ. Assn., Ind. Acad. Social Scis. Mem. Ch. of Brethren. Club: Rotary. Home: 400 Kohser Ave North Manchester IN 46962 Office: Dept Econs Manchester Coll North Manchester IN 46962

HART, ALDEN SHERBURNE, mfg. co. exec.; b. Bklyn., Sept. 14, 1924; s. Henry T. and Avis A. (Sherburne) H.; B.A., Colgate U., 1944; J.D., Harvard, 1949; m. Harriet Ruffner Stone, Feb. 26, 1955; children—Alden Sherburne, Pamela W., Marcia A., Cynthia R. Admitted to N.J. bar, 1950, N.Y. bar, 1957; pvt. practice law, N.J., 1949-54; asst. U.S. Atty., Fed. Dist. N.J., Newark, 1954-56; atty. Union Carbide Corp., N.Y.C., 1956-71, asst. dir. Law Dept., 1971-73, asso. gen. counsel, 1973-76, v.p. in charge of public affairs, 1976—. Served with USNR, 1943-46. Mem. Am., N.J., N.Y. bar assns., Internat. Eon. Policy Assn. (dir. 1977—). Clubs: Baltusrol Golf; Sawgrass; Silver Spring. Home: Danbury Rd Ridgefield CT 06877 also Sawgrass Lake Julia Dr Ponte Vedra Beach FL 32082 Office: Old Ridgebury Rd Danbury CT 06817

HART, ALEX WAY, data processing co. exec.; b. Meadville, Pa., June 4, 1940; s. Alex William and Rosemary (Brown) H.; A.B., Harvard U., 1962; m. Fyanne Edwards, July 1, 1961; children—Alex, Michael, Gregory, Suzanne. Lumber broker Webb Lumber Co., Cleve., 1963-69; asst. v.p. Ohio Nat. Bank, Columbus, 1969-73; sr. v.p. First Nat. Bank Chgo., 1973-78; pres., chief exec. officer Western Bancorp Data Processing Co., Los Angeles, 1978—. Mem. Bank Mktg. Assn. (dir. Chgo. 1978—). Club: Harvard of So. Calif. Office: 21505 Hawthorne Blvd Torrance CA 90503

HART, DAMON CECIL, computer software co. exec.; b. Lexington, Ky., Mar. 28, 1945; s. Damon C. and Helen L. (Ecklar) H.; B.A. in Math. (Nat. Merit scholar, Tyng Found. scholar), Williams Coll., 1967; M.S. in Mgmt. Tech. (Tyng Found. scholar), Am. U., 1971; m. Louisa Booker Goff, Sept. 9, 1967; children—Benjamin Howland, William Hathaway. Systems programmer U.S. Govt., Washington, 1967-68; project mgr. Naval Intelligence Processing System Support Activity, Arlington, Va., 1970-72; v.p. RLG Assos., Inc., Reston, Va., 1972-76; pres. Lexico Enterprises, Inc., Washington, 1976—. Served with USNR, 1968-70. NSF scholar, U. N.D., 1961, Fla. State U., 1962. Mem. IEEE (cons. on test lang. standardization, vice chmn. Atlas com.), Assn. for Computing Machinery. Contbr. articles to profl. jours. Home: 5008 Worthington Dr Bethesda MD 20016 Office: 1333 New Hampshire Ave NW Suite 510 Washington DC 20036

HART, DONALD RAY, publisher; b. Kansas City, Kans., Aug. 13, 1943; s. Isaac Newton and Lulu Irene (Rollins) H.; B.A., Colo. State U., 1966; m. Jane Marie Vondy, Mar. 13, 1971; children—Bradley Ray, Michael Allan. Founder, operator Photo-By Hart Studio, Ft. Collins, Colo., 1962-65; founder, editor, pub. The Campus Tayle, Ft. Collins, 1965-66; salesman Petroleum Pubs., Inc. subs. Bell Publs. Co. (acquired by Data Services Inc. 1970), Denver, 1967-70, pub., 1970-73, editor, 1972-73; founder, pres., editor, pub. Western Oil Reporter and Rocky Mountain Petroleum Directory, Hart Publs., Inc., Denver, 1973—, editor, pub. Drill Bit mag., 1976—. Mem. Colo. Elephant Club; pres. Russellville Homeowners and Property Owners Assn., 1980. Mem. Rocky Mountain Oil and Gas Assn., Ind. Petroleum Assn. Mountain States, Assn. Oilwell Servicing Contractors, Rocky Mountain Gas Men's Assn., Assn. Petroleum Writers. Baptist. Clubs: Denver Petroleum, Pinery Country. Home: 1601 Gold Camp Rd Franktown CO 80116 Office: PO Box 1917 Denver CO 80201

HART, GURNEE FELLOWS, investment counselor; b. Chgo., Apr. 26, 1929; s. Percival Gray and Marguerite May (Fellows) H.; B.A. cum laude, Pomona Coll., 1951; M.B.A., Stanford U., 1955; m. Marjorie Walker Leigh, Apr. 23, 1966. With Willis & Christy, Los Angeles, 1955-65; investment counsel Scudder, Stevens & Clark, Inc., Los Angeles, 1965-67; partner Scudder, Stevens & Clark, N.Y.C., 1967—. Bd. dirs. N.Y. Pharmonic; chmn. Friends of N.Y. Philharm.; bd. dirs., v.p. Berkshire Farm Center and Services for Youth. Served to lt., inf. U.S. Army, 1951-53; Korea. Decorated Bronze Star. Mem. N.Y. Soc. Security Analysts, St. Andrew's Soc. State of N.Y., Phi Beta Kappa. Republican. Episcopalian. Club: Univ. Home: 133 E 64th St New York NY 10021 Office: Scudder Stevens & Clark 345 Park Ave New York NY 10154

HART, HARRY JAMES, paper mcht.; b. Chgo., June 17, 1918; s. Robert J. and Peggy (Slutzker) H.; grad. Francis W. Parker Sch., Chgo., 1935; B.S., Northwestern U., 1939. Br. mgr. Nat. Bond & Investment Co., Chgo., 1939-41; with Schwarz Paper Co., Chgo., 1946—, v.p., 1967—, also dir. Underwriting mem. Lloyd's of London Sturge Syndicate, 1973—. Trustee Harry J. Hart Found. Bd. dirs., v.p. Sr. Centers Met. Chgo. Served to capt. AUS, 1941-46; PTO. Mem. Paper Club Chgo. (pres. 1965-66), Cercle Universitaire Franco-Americain, Alliance Francaise de Chicago. Clubs: Lake Shore Country (Glencoe, Ill.); Monroe, Execs., Plaza. (Chgo.). Home: 2321C N Geneva Terr Chicago IL 60614 Office: Schwarz Paper Co 8338 N Austin Ave Morton Grove IL 60053

HART, HORACE, graphic arts cons.; b. Rochester, N.Y., Sept. 14, 1910; s. Leo and Ethel Mae (Steuerwald) H.; B.A., Harvard, 1933; m. Joan Ruth Stein, May 30, 1934; children—Karen Gail, Nancy Joan Hart Wartow. Pres., Leo Hart Co., Rochester, 1933-55; partner Playtime House, Rochester, 1939-56; dir. Printing and Pub. Industries div. Dept. Commerce, 1957-63; pres. Lanston Monotype Co., Phila. and Monotype Co. of Can., Ltd., 1963-66; cons. to graphic arts industry, Springwater, N.Y., 1966—; asst. to pres. Printing Industry Met. N.Y., 1974—; edn. adviser Nat. Printing Equipment Assn., 1966-69; tchr. Rochester Inst. Tech., 1949-50; U.S. del. Internat. Conf. Printing and Pub. Execs., Milan, Italy, 1959; chmn. U.S. del. Tripartite Tech. Meeting for Printing and Allied Trades, Geneva, 1962. Chmn. N.Y. area Nat. Def. Exec. Res. Assn., 1972-74; trustee U. Rochester Libraries Friends; mem. vis. com. U. Rochester Libraries, 1979—; hon. mem. Gutenberg Mus., Mainz, Germany. Recipient Elmer G. Voight award Edn. Council Graphic Arts Industry, 1961, Silver medal Dept. Commerce, 1962; established Horace Hart award Edn. Council Graphic Arts Industry, 1962. Fellow Pierpont Morgan Library; mem. Nat. Press Club, Am. Inst. Graphic Arts, Wynken de Worde Soc. Eng., Type Dirs. Club, The Typophiles, Printing Industry Rochester (pres. 1937-40, 42-49), Printing Industry Am. (dir. 1944-49, chmn. coms. on edn., gen. mgmt., Pres.'s Conf. 1952-56), Nat. Printing Equipment Mfrs. (dir. 1966-68), Advt. Council Rochester (dir. 1942-52), Graphic Arts Assn. Execs. (hon.), Direct Mail Advt. Assn. Washington (hon.), Printing Industry Washington (hon.), Goudy Soc. (pres. 1968-74, 78—). Republican. Jewish. Author: Bibliotheca Typographica, 1934; Printing: Industrial Giant, 1944; A Mid-Century Review of Printing in the U.S.A., 1959. Home and Office: 6219 Canadice Hill Rd Springwater NY 14560

HART, JAY ALBERT CHARLES, real estate broker; b. Rockford, Ill., Apr. 16, 1923; s. Jabez Waterman and Monty Evangeline (Burgin) H.; student U. Ill., 1941-42, U. Mo., 1942-43, U. Miami (Fla.), 1952-56, Rockford Coll., 1961-62; m. Marie D. Goetz, July 16, 1976; children—Dale M. (Mrs. Richard Peel Jr.), Jay C.H. Exec. v.p. Hart Oil Co., Rockford, 1947—; pres. Internat. Service Co., Pompano Beach, Fla., 1952-58; v.p. Ipsen Industries, Inc., Rockford, 1958-61; owner Hart Realtors, Rockford, 1961—; lectr. in field; trustee, sr. analyst Anchor Real Estate Investment Trust, Chgo., 1971—. Dir. Winnebago County (Ill.) CD, 1975. Chmn. Rock River chpt. ARC, 1973, nat. nominating com., 1971, disaster chmn. Illiana div., 1972—; bd. counselors Rockford Coll., 1974—; emergency coordinator 9th Naval dist. M.A.R.S., USN, 1960-68, civilian adv. council, 1968—. Office mgr. Citizens for Eisenhower, Chgo., 1952. Served with USAAF, 1943-46. Mem. Rockford Air Guild (pres. 1974, 76-77), Tamaroa Watercolor Soc. (v.p. 1974—), Rockford Boys Club Assn. (dir.), Exptl. Amateur Radio Soc. (pres. 1960—), Internat. Council Shopping Centers, Nat. Assn. Real Estate Appraisers, Soc. Indsl. Realtors, Nat. Assn. Realtors, Phi Eta Sigma. Mason (Shriner). Clubs: Rockford Country, Mid-Day, Gaslight. Author: Real Estate Buyers and Sellers Guide, 1961. Paintings in pvt., pub. collections; illustrations in numerous publs. Home: 2406 E Lane Rockford IL 61107 Office: 3701 E State St Rockford IL 61108

HART, JOANNE MARIE, caterer; b. Boston, Jan. 9, 1931; d. Patrick Joseph and Josephine Hanna (Casey) Sullivan; student Brookline (Mass.) pub. schs.; m. Maurice Edmund Hart, Sept. 10, 1955; children—Charleen, Michael, Mary, Joseph, Brenda, Kathleen, Paul. With Fed. Res. Bank, 1949-55; treas., mgr. Hart Bros. Caterers, Randolph, Mass., 1955—, Lantana, Mass., 1971—; corporator Quincy Savs. Bank (Mass.). Bd. dirs. Braintree Family Counseling and Guidance Center; mem. South Shore Bus. and Indsl. Polit. Action Commn. Mem. South Shore C. of C. (dir.), Wedgewood Soc. Roman Catholic. Club: Old Colony Tennis (Hingham, Mass.). Home: 99 Atlantic Ave Cohasset MA 02025 Office: 43 Scanlon Dr Randolph MA 02368

HART, JOHN TERRENCE, advt. exec.; b. St. Louis, June 22, 1916; s. Luke Edward and Catherine Jane (O'Connor) H.; A.B., St. Louis U., 1938; m. Gladys Kletzker, July 31, 1945; children—Sally Ann, John Terrence, Daniel Shay, William Luke. Account exec. D'Arcy Advt. Co., St. Louis, 1938-53; v.p. Lynch & Hart Advt. Co., St. Louis, 1953-60; pres. Hart & Johnson Air Terminal Advt. Co., St. Louis, 1960-75, chmn. bd., 1975-80; chief exec. officer H & H Sales Corp., 1980—. Served with USNR, 1941-45. Decorated Air medal. Roman Catholic. Clubs: Old Warson Country (St. Louis); San Antonio (Tex.); K.C. Home: 9 Exmoor St Saint Louis MO 63124

HART, JOHN WALLACE, utilities exec.; b. Anderson, S.C., Sept. 2, 1930; s. James Luther and Lola Irene (Rhouda) H.; B.E.E., Clemson U., 1958; m. Barbara Jean Kline, Nov. 24, 1955; children—John Kline, Stephanie Charlene, Angela Jeannine. With Fla. Power & Light Co., 1958—, emergency service supr., Sarasota, 1969, dist. supr., 1969-72, No. div. transmission and distbn. mgr., Daytona Beach, 1972-79, mgr. eastern div., W. Palm Beach, Fla., 1979—. Organizer, Miami Home Assn., 1963; Palmetto rep. Dade County Sch. Bd., 1964-65; Cotillion sponsor, 1968-69; active Ringling Art Mus., 1970-72, Sarasota Playhouse, 1970-72, Mus. Arts and Scis., 1972—, Daytona Symphony Soc., 1972-74, Civic Mus., 1972-74, Daytona Playhouse, 1972—. Served with USN, 1950-54; PTO. Recipient Dir. of Year award FBC of Daytona Beach, 1975. Mem. IEEE. Democrat. Baptist. Home: 12763 Westport Circle West Palm Beach FL 33411 Office: Drawer D West Palm Beach FL 33402

HART, JOSEPH ADRIAN, machinery mfg. co. exec.; b. Hicksville, Ohio, June 27, 1920; s. Laurence E. and Leah E. (Hilliard) H.; A.B., Kent State U., 1960; M.B.A., U. Chgo., 1960; m. Mary Anne Bail, June 23, 1949; children—Anne Marie Hart Roberts, Jo Alice Hart Moody, Larence K., Karen Hart Bruketa. With Internat. Harvester, 1948—, plant mgr. tractor works Payline div., Chgo., successively mgr. source and facilities planning Truck div., Chgo., mgr. mfg. ops. agrl. equipment, Chgo., v.p. mfg. and employee relations Internat. Harvester of Can., Hamilton, 1965-77, v.p. mfg. planning Components Group, Chgo., 1977—; dir. Iowa Indsl. Hydraulics. Served with USAAF, 1942-45; ETO. Republican. Roman Catholic. Clubs: Internat. Harvester Mgmt., 401. Office: 401 N Michigan Ave Chicago IL 60611

HART, JOSEPH MONTRAVILLE, JR., banker; b. Davenport, Nebr., Aug. 24, 1921; s. Joseph Montraville and Bessie Ann (Sien) H.; student U. Nebr., 1940; grad. U. Wis. Sch. Banking, 1961; m. Wilma H. Stutt, June 9, 1946; children—Charles, Robert, Jeannine. With North Side Bank, Omaha, 1945—, chmn. bd., chief exec. officer, sec. to bd. dirs., dir., 1980—. Mem. Omaha Charter Study Conv., 1965; mem. Omaha Bd. Edn., 1968-73, pres., 1971-73; exec. bd., 2d v.p. Nebr. Hist. Soc.; bd. dirs., treas., Nebr. Ind. Coll. Found., Douglas County Hist. Soc.; trustee, v.p. Florence Home for Aged; pres. Met. Tech. Community Coll. Found.; bd. dirs., asst. treas. Western Heritage Soc.; past chmn. Omaha Landmarks Heritage Preservation Commn.; mem. Nebr. Preservation Commn.; chmn. Mormon Pioneer Nat. Trail Project. Served with USAAF, 1942-45; CBI. Recipient Sch. Bell award Omaha Edn. Assn., 1972; hon. life mem. PTA. Mem. Bank Adminstrn. Inst. (past chpt. pres.), Am. Inst. Banking (past chpt. v.p.), Omaha Bankers Assn. (past pres.), Presidents' Assn., Robert Morris Assos. (past gov. chpt.), Soc. Fin. Analysts, Nebr. Bankers Assn. (exec. council), Westerners, Omaha Com. Fgn. Relations, Newcomen Soc. N. Am., Am. Legion, VFW, N. Council C. of C. (pres. 1980—). Republican. Mem. Ch. of Christ. Clubs: North Omaha Kiwanis (past pres.), North Omaha Comml. (past pres.), Omaha. Office: North Side Bank 31st and Ames Ave Omaha NE 68111

HART, KYLE MCNUTT, ins. co. exec.; b. Knoxville, Tenn., Jan. 23, 1925; s. Cowan McNutt and Hazel (Brown) H.; B.S., U. Tenn., 1952, M.S., 1953; m. Ruby Jean Russell, Aug. 12, 1970; children—David Kyle, Diana Jean. With Ernst & Ernst, 1953-55; treas. Tenn. Life & Service Ins. Co., 1955-58; sr. v.p. Lincoln Am. Life Ins. Co., 1958-64; pres. Nat. Savs. Life Ins. Co., Murfreesboro, Tenn., 1964—; dir. Thomas Nelson Pub. Co., Murfreesboro Bank & Trust Co. Mem. meml. com. Carroll Reece Meml. Library, East Tenn. State U.; chmn. Washington County Heart Fund, 1965. Served with USAAF, 1942-46. C.P.A., Tenn. Mem. Tenn. Assn. Life Ins. Cos. (v.p.), Tenn. Soc. C.P.A.'s, Am. Inst. C.P.A.'s, Nat. Assn. Life Cos., Beta Alpha Psi. Clubs: Stones River Country, Ponte Vedra. Home: 1823 Riverview Dr Murfreesboro TN 37130 Office: Hwy 2315 Murfreesboro TN 37130

HART, LOUIS IRELAND, JR., lawyer, oil co. exec.; b. Nunn, Colo., May 14, 1922; s. Louis Ireland and Kathryn (Kirby) H.; LL.B., U. Colo., 1946; children—Timothy, Eric, John, Daniel. Admitted to Colo. bar, 1946; practiced in Denver, 1946-65; legal and mining cons., 1946-65; pres. Internat. Mineral Engrs., Denver, 1965-73, Western Tar Sands, Inc., Denver, 1974-81; mem. Colo. Ho. of Reps., 1950. Mem. Colo. Moffat Tunnel Commn., 1952-56. Served to lt. USNR, 1942-45. Mem. Colo. Bar Assn. Republican. Episcopalian. Clubs: Denver Athletic, Tower Athletic. Patentee process to extract tar from tar sand by mixing and ultrasonics. Home: 1020 15th St Apt 37E Denver CO 80202 Office: 818 17th St Suite 804 Denver CO 80202

HART, MARIE MOONEY, real estate broker; b. Montgomery, Ala., Jan. 20, 1913; d. Charles France and Marie (Kidd) Mooney; B.S. in Bus., Ind. U., 1939; student U. Wis., summer 1938; m. Arthur Leland Hart, Nov. 20, 1941; children—Jeffrey Mooney, John Scot, Anne Leslie. High sch. tchr. bus., St. Paul, Ind., 1939-41; with USAAF, Army Ordnance and IRS, 1941-50; cofounder Hart Realty Co., Evansville, Ind., 1964-74; owner, mgr. rental housing. Exec. bd. Dexter Sch., 1964. Mem. VFW Aux. Republican. Presbyterian. Club: Central Turners (Evansville). Home: 2919 Washington Ave Evansville IN 47714

HARTCH, FRED ERNEST, business exec., found. exec.; b. N.Y.C., Aug. 26, 1908; s. Paul Fred and Fanny (Hartel) H.; A.B., Cornell U., 1931; M.B.A., N.Y. U., 1934; LL.B., Bklyn. Law Sch., 1939, J.S.D., 1941; m. Florence Ruth Ferguson, Aug. 11, 1933; 1 son, Thomas Ferguson. Admitted to N.Y. bar, 1941; bank examiner FDIC, N.Y.C., 1933-42; treas., trust officer Greenwich Trust Co. (Conn.), 1942-46; dep. chief, chief property control and external assets Office Mil. Govt., Berlin and Wiesbaden, Germany, 1946-49; chief rev. examiner Fed. Res. Bank N.Y., 1949-52; v.p., treas., gen. mgr. Maher Bros. Corp., Greenwich, 1952-56; pres., dir. Home Oil Co. Greenwich, Inc., Fairfield Oil Heating Co., Inc.; chmn. bd. Fairfield Home Oil Co., Inc., Greenwich, 1953-71; pres. Vianda Playter Williams Found., Greenwich, 1969—; chmn. bd. Gen. Equities Corp., Flemming Rutledge Oil Corp., 1959—; dir. spl. mgmt. studies RCA, N.Y.C., 1958-62; sec.-treas., v.p. Rawlings Corp., Rawlings Sporting Goods Co.; v.p., treas., dir. Overseas Sports Co., Inc., Anasco Sports Co., Inc., Caribe Sports Co., Inc.; asso dir. State Nat. Bank Conn. Financial cons.; admitted to N.Y. bar. Asst. adminstr. Gen. Services Adminstrn., Washington, 1956, commr. transp. and pub. utilities, 1957. Bd. dirs. Greenwich YMCA, 1943—, pres., 1956-57; trustee Brunswick Sch., Greenwich, 1956-57. Mem. Phi Delta Phi. Home: 491 Lake Ave Greenwich CT 06830

HARTEIS, GERALD JOSEPH, mktg. co. exec.; b. Ebensburg, Pa., Dec. 24, 1946; s. Larence Aloyisis and Ruth Matilda (Bodenschatz) H.; B.S., Delaware Valley Coll., 1968; M.Ed., Pa. State U., 1975; m. Paulette Helene Skalek, Aug. 21, 1971; children—Jennifer, Tara. Tchr., coach Western Wayne Sch. Dist., 1969-78; pres. Harteis Assos., Moscow, Pa., 1974—; speaker in field. Named to Diamond Level, Amway Co., 1980; named Dist. 12 Wrestling Coach of Yr., Wrestling Coaches Assn., 1976, Outstanding Tchr., N.E. Pa. Tchrs. Assn., 1976. Mem. Amway Distbrs. Assn., Pa. Wrestling Ofcls. Assn. Democrat. Roman Catholic. Clubs: Lions, K.C. Home and Office: RD 6 Box 24 Moscow PA 18444

HARTER, BENEDICT THOMAS, ednl. adminstr.; b. Irvington, N.J., Aug. 15, 1917; s. Benedict Alexander and Mary Katherine (Grimm) H.; B.S., Fordham U., 1939; postgrad. in bus. Harvard U., 1943-44; J.D., Georgetown U., 1949; m. Anna Mae Graves, Nov. 27, 1943; children—Barbara, Suzanne, Benedict Thomas, Jeanne, Patricia, Richard. Admitted to D.C. bar, 1949, U.S. Supreme Ct. bar, 1953, Ohio bar, 1955; asst. comptroller Bur. Ships, Dept. Navy, 1949-52; budget dir., gen. auditor C&O Ry. Co., 1953-56; fin. exec. W.R. Grace & Co., 1956-58; controller communications div. ITT, N.Y.C., 1958-60; sr. v.p. adminstrn., chief fin. officer, dir. Becton Dickinson & Co., Paramus, N.J., 1960-79; dean Bus. Schs., Fordham U., 1979—. Treas., bd. trustees Overlook Hosp., Summit, N.J., 1969-75; bd. govs. Jersey Shore Med. Center, Neptune, N.J.; trustee Immaculate Conception Sem., Mahwah, N.J., Marymount Coll., Tarrytown, N.Y., 1969-75. Served to lt. comdr. USNR, 1941-46. Mem. Fin. Execs. Inst. Roman Catholic. Club: Univ. (N.Y.C.). Office: Fordham U at Lincoln Center New York NY 10023

HARTFIELD, DAVID, JR., lawyer; b. N.Y.C., May 25, 1919; s. David and Barbara (Mayer) H.; B.A., U. Va., 1941; LL.B., 1943; m. Freda L. Burling, Nov. 21, 1964. Admitted to N.Y. bar, 1943; asst. U.S. atty., 1943-45; mem. firm White & Case, N.Y.C., 1945—, partner, 1955—. Mem. Am., Fed. bar assns., Am. Law Inst., Am. Soc. Internat. Law, Am. Judicature Soc., N.Y. County Lawyers Assn. Republican. Clubs: Recess, (N.Y.C.); Farmington Country (Charlottesville, Va.); Card Sound Golf (Key Largo, Fla.). Home: 530 E 72d St New York NY 10021 Office: 14 Wall St New York NY 10005

HARTFORD, DONALD HAROLD, broadcasting co. exec.; b. Edmonton, Alta., Can., Jan. 24, 1919; s. Harold Hunter and Mabel Irene (Younge) H.; ed. pub. schs.; m. Jean Emilie Skogland, Dec. 1, 1973; children from previous marriage—Donald Leigh, Douglas Wayne, Diane Leslie; stepchildren—Fred Skogland, Kari Skogland. Announcer, sales mgr. Sta. CFAC, Calgary, Alta., 1945-48, sta. mgr., 1948-60, v.p., gen. mgr., 1960-65; v.p., gen. mgr. Sta. CFRB, Toronto, Ont., Can., 1965-69, pres., gen. mgr., 1970—; pres. radio div. Standard Broadcasting Corp., Ltd.; pres., dir. CFRB Ltd., CJAD Ltd., St. Clair Prodns., Ltd.; founding mem. Radio Bur. Can.; dir. Standard Broadcasting Corp., Toronto, Standard Broadcast Prodns., Ltd., Toronto, Standard Sound Systems, Montreal. Council mem. Bd. Trade Met. Toronto; dir. Canadian Nat. Sportsmen Show; past pres. Ont. Safety League, Canadian Nat. Exhbn., Toronto; trustee Clark Inst. Psychiatry, Toronto. Recipient Humanitarian award Internat. B'nai B'rith, 1978. Mem. Broadcast Execs. Soc. (founding), Canadian Assn. Broadcasters (vice-chmn.), Western Assn. Broadcasters (pres. 1960-63). Clubs: Granite, Bd. Trade Met. Toronto, Variety, Goodwood. Home: 65 Harbour Side Harbour Sq Toronto ON M4S 1E1 Canada Office: 2 St Clair Ave W Toronto ON Canada

HARTFORD, JAMES BEVERLY, shipping co. exec.; b. Owen Sound, Ont., Can., May 18, 1932; s. James Joseph and Bertha Elizabeth (Miersch) H.; ed. various marine colls. and univs., Can. and U.K.; m. Alice Louise Barnecott, Mar. 21, 1973. Jr. and sr. officer various ships Upper Lakes Shipping Ltd., Toronto, 1952-66, master various ships, 1966-71, shore capt., 1971-72, v.p. ops., 1973-77, v.p., gen. mgr. shipping, dir., 1977—; dir. Gt. Lakes Grain Inc., Hagerstown, Md., Naviteck Co., Nassau; dir. Gt. Lakes Pilotage Authority, 1974-79; vice chmn. Nat. Adv. Council Marine Tng., Central region, 1974; adv. Open Bulk Carriers Ltd., Hamilton, Bermuda, 1977—. Adv. Georgian Coll., Barrie, Ont., 1973, Niagara Coll., St. Catharines, Ont., 1980. Sr. transp. mgmt. cert. Can. Ministry Transport. Mem. Soc. Naval Architects and Marine Engrs. (life), U.S. Naval Inst. (life), Am. Mgmt. Assns., Inst. Nav. Progressive Conservative. Clubs: Manitoba, Bd. of Trade, Order of Alhambra, K.C. (4 deg.). Home: 5 Vicora Linkway Suite 1916 Don Mills ON M3C 1A6 Canada Office: 49 Jackes Ave Toronto ON M4T 1E2 Canada

HARTFORD, TERRENCE JAMES, mgmt. cons.; b. Massena, N.Y., Dec. 14, 1930; s. John D. and Maefred Ester (Stacey) H.; B.A., St. Lawrence U., 1952; M.P.A., N.Y. U., 1958; m. R. Leona Calderone, Sept. 10, 1953; children—Kevin James, Kathleen Anne, Terrence Leonard. Personnel asst. Westchester County, N.Y., 1953, staff asst. Recreation Dept., 1953; personnel staff Massena (N.Y.) Works, Aluminum Co. Am., 1956; training staff Alcoa, Edgewater, N.J., 1957, tng. dir., New Kensington, Pa., 1958-61, indsl. relations staff hdqrs., Pitts., 1962-70, head resource mgmt. devel., 1971; dir. mgmt. program for execs. U. Pitts. and faculty, 1971-75; pres. Cons. for Performance Improvement, New Kensington, 1971—; adminstr. Continuing Edn. Evening Sch., Pa. State U., New Kensington campus, 1960; cons., lectr. in field. Pres., PTA, Kiski Area Sch. System, 1960-61, supt. adv. com., 1978-79. Served with U.S. Army, 1954-56. Mem. Pitts. Personnel Assn. (dir. 1965-70), Am. Soc. Tng. and Devel., Am. Psychol. Assn., Am. Mining Congress, Am. Mgmt. Assn. Republican. Roman Catholic. Clubs: Hillcrest Co try, Pitts. Press, Pitts. Golden Panthers. Contbr. articles to profl. jours. Originator, developer JKS process, performance improvement program for orgns. Home: 114 Woodland Dr New Kensington PA 15608 Office: Terrace Ave Leechburg PA 15656

HARTGROVE, BILLY RAY, ins. co. exec.; b. Beaumont, Tex., Sept. 10, 1931; s. L.B. and Virginia (Ledenham) H.; student McNeese State Coll., Lake Charles, La., 1949-52, U. Houston, 1959-60; m. Evelyn Summers, Mar. 31, 1955; children—Billy Ray, Brian Lee. Vice pres. Great Midwest Life Ins. Co., Oklahoma City, 1962-64; v.p., sec. Security Brokers Investment Corp., Oklahoma City, 1964-66, Great Midwest Life Ins., 1967-69; v.p., sec. United Investors, Inc., 1969-73, pres., 1974-80; v.p., sec. Mid-American Investors Life Ins. Co., Oklahoma City, 1969-71, pres., 1971-72 (merged into Investors Life), pres. Investors Life, 1973-75, Liberty Investors Life, 1975—; dir. City Nat. Bank, Oklahoma City. Served to lt. (j.g.) USNR, 1952-57. Club: Oak Tree Golf, Home: 3101 Castle Rock Rd Villa 27 Oklahoma City OK 73120 Office: 4001 Lincoln Blvd Suite 407 Oklahoma City OK 73105

HARTLEY, EDITH LEE BOONE (MRS. JAMES NEAL PARKER), business exec.; b. Osceola, Tex., Feb. 20, 1928; d. Robert Lee and Ida (Weatherred) Boone; student Eastern N.Mex. U., 1945-46; grad. St. Mary's Sch. Radiologic Tech., 1962; m. James Robert Hartley, June 28, 1946 (dec. Apr. 1959); children—James Lynn, Lee Anne; m. 2d, James Neal Parker, Feb. 14, 1968. X-ray technologist St. Mary's Hosp., Tucson, 1962-64; asst. instr. St. Mary's Sch., 1963-64; owner Lee Anne Dress Shoppe, Tucson, 1964-66; v.p., sec. Swan Drug Store, Inc., Tucson, 1967—. Mem. Am. Soc. Radiologic Technologists, Am. Registry Radiologic Technologists. Methodist. Home: 6939 Crestline Dr Tucson AZ 85715 Office: 4817 E Speedway Tucson AZ 85716

HARTLEY, FRED L(LOYD), petroleum exec.; b. Vancouver, B.C., Can., Jan. 16, 1917; s. John William and Hannah (Mitchell) H.; B.Sc. in Applied Sci., U. B.C., 1939; m. Margaret Alice Murphy, Nov. 2, 1940; children—Margaret Ann, Fred Lloyd. Came U.S. 1939, naturalized, 1950. Engring. supr. Union Oil Co. Calif., 1939-53, mgr. comml. devel., 1953-55, gen. mgr. research dept., 1955-56, v.p. charge research, 1956-60, sr. v.p., 1960-63, exec. v.p., 1963-64, pres., 1964—, chmn. bd., 1974—, also dir.; dir. Rockwell Internat., Union Bank. Bd. dirs. Los Angeles Philharmonic Assn.; asso. U. So. Calif. Mem. Am. Petroleum Inst. (exec. com., dir.), Am. Inst. Chem. Engrs. (chmn. So. Calif. 1942), Nat. Petroleum Council (dir.), Calif. C. of C. (past pres., dir.), Am. Chem. Soc. Clubs: California, Los Angeles (Los Angeles); Palos Verdes Breakfast (past pres.); Jonathan, Bohemian, Pacific-Union. Office: PO Box 7600 Los Angeles CA 90051

HARTLEY, JOSEPH WILLARD, textile exec.; b. Jacksonville, Fla., Dec. 27, 1942; s. Cromwell Alexander and Kathleen Lucille (Midgette) H.; B.S., Fla. State U., 1966; m. JoAnn Louise Zirkel, Aug. 22, 1964; children—Kevin Alan, Kenneth Alexander. Mfg. mgr. worsted div. Burlington Industries, Raeford, N.C., 1966-69, mfg. overseer, yarn div., Oxford, N.C., 1969-71, quality control mgr., Wilson, N.C., 1971-72; div. materials quality control mgr. Hanes Hosiery, Winston-Salem, N.C., 1972-74; div. tech. mgr. Texfi Industries, Rocky Mount, N.C., 1974-77; dir. quality control Kayser-Roth Hosiery, 1977-78; v.p. men's mfg. Kayser-Roth Hosiery, Inc., Greensboro, N.C., 1978—; mem. cotton dust standard com. Occupational Safety and Health Adminstrn. Served with U.S. Army, 1961-64. Mem. Nat. Assn. Hosiery Mfg. (socks and anklets adv. com.), Am. Soc. Quality Control, Am. Mgmt. Assn. Democrat. Roman Catholic. Clubs: K.C., Sedgefield Country, Cardinal Country. Home: 5906 Muirfield Dr Greensboro NC 27410 Office: PO Box 77077 Greensboro NC 27407

HARTLINE, CHRISTINE ELIZABETH, mfg. co. exec.; b. Menard County, Ill., May 20, 1934; d. Elzie Logan and Christy Evelyn (Edwards) Forbis; student U. Calif. at Los Angeles, 1970-73, bus. adminstrn. Am. Grad. U., Covina, Calif., 1978—; m. John Leopold Hartline, June 6, 1952; children—John Edward, Richard Leopold, James Logan. Contract analyst Consol. Systems Corp., Monrovia, Calif., 1957-63; contract adminstr. Ordnance Assos., Rialto, Calif., 1963-65; purchasing agt. Spaulding Instruments, Pasadena, Calif., 1965-73; material mgr. Jennings Co. div. ITT, Monrovia, 1973-75; sr. subcontract adminstr. Honeywell Inc., West Covina, Calif., 1975—. Home: 1021 Witherill St San Dimas CA 91773 Office: 1200 E San Bernardino Rd West Covina CA 91790

HARTLINE, JOHN EDMOND, r.r. exec.; b. Bloomington, Ind., Dec. 25, 1925; s. Clyde E. and Clara K. (Johnson) H.; m. Loretta Laverne Hartline, Dec. 13, 1945; children—Terry L., Janet, Donald, Sidney, Randy, James, Richard. With Ky. & Ind. Terminal R.R., gen. agt., Louisville, 1979—. Mem. Internat. Assn. Car Service Officers, So. Assn. Car Service Officers (pres. 1974), Louisville Freight Agts. Assn. (v.p. 1979, pres. 1980), Rail Club Louisville (dir. 1980). Office: 2910 NW Pkwy Louisville KY 40212

HARTMAN, A. SCOTT, printing co. exec.; b. Boston, Feb. 28, 1942; s. Ben M. and Barbara H.; B.S., Calif. State U., Northridge, 1963; M.A., UCLA, 1964; m. Estelle Lyon, 1966; children—Dale Scott, Holly. Mgr., Far West Communications, Los Angeles, 1963-64; mgr. Stark Printing Co., Los Angeles, 1964-67; v.p., sec. Tax Forms Printing Co., Los Angeles, 1967—; v.p. United Nat. Industries, Inc. Mem. Nat. Bus. Forms Assn., Nat. Office Products Assn., Data Processing Mgmt. Assn. Office: 9700 Topanga Canyon Pl Chatsworth CA 91311

HARTMAN, BERNARD, electronics engr.; b. Poland, Nov. 3, 1923; s. Jack and Fannie H.; came to U.S., 1928; B.S.E.E., Am. TV Inst., 1948; M.S.M. Lake Forest Coll., 1976; m. Beatrice Weinstock, Jan. 1, 1950; children—Fern Anne, Alan Brian. With Motorola, Inc., 1949-76, head dept. mfg. research, 1974-76; mgr. sect. component design Zenith Radio Corp., Glenview, Ill., 1976—. Served with AUS, 1942-46. Author: Fundamentals of Television, 1975. Office: 7344 Lake St Morton Grove IL 60053

HARTMAN, CHARLES DALE, food mfg. co. exec.; b. Chgo., July 30, 1935; s. Joseph F. and Elsa H.; B.A., Monmouth Coll., 1957; M.B.A., U. Ind., 1958; m. Patricia Ann Skarada, June 24, 1967; children—Susanne, Brian. Product asst. Helene Curtis Industries, 1960-62; with H.J. Heinz Co., Pitts., 1962—, v.p. processed foods, 1979—, pres. Camargo Foods div., 1979—. Chmn., United Way, 1979-80. Served with AUS, 1959-60. Republican. Clubs: Fox Chapel Golf, Allegheny. Office: 1062 Progress St Pittsburgh PA 15212

HARTMAN, CHARLES HENRY, found. exec.; b. Red Lion, Pa., Feb. 1, 1933; s. Earl Eugene and Jeannette (Kline) H.; B.S., Millersville (Pa.) State Coll., 1954; M.A., Mich. State U., 1958, Ed.D., 1962; m. Catherine M. Wheeler, June 7, 1975; children—Elizabeth Jean, Amy Joan, Eric Michael, Jennifer Leigh, David Wheeler. Asso. prof. edn. Ill. State U., Normal, 1959-62; vis. lectr. edn. U. Wis., Madison, 1962-63; dir. edn. Automotive Safety Found. and Hwy. Users Fedn., Washington, 1964-70; dep. adminstr. Nat. Hwy. Traffic Safety Adminstrn., Dept. Transp., Washington, 1970-73; pres. Motorcycle Safety Found., Linthicum, Md., 1973—. Bd. dirs., vice-chmn. traffic conf. Nat. Safety Council, 1976-79; vice-chmn. Hwy. Safety Adv. Panel, Hwy. Users Fedn., 1977-80; Presdl. appointee Nat. Hwy. Safety Adv. Com., 1977-80. Served with U.S. Army, 1954-56; ETO. Named Traffic Safety Educator of Yr. in Wis., 1972; recipient Sec.'s award U.S. Dept. Transp., 1973; certified assn. exec. Mem. Am. Driver and Traffic Safety Edn. Assn., Am. Acad. Safety Edn., Am. Soc. Assn. Execs., Soc. Automotive Engrs., AAUP, NEA, Millersville State Coll., Mich. State U. alumni assns. Republican. Home: Box 51 RD 2 Delta PA 17314 Office: 780 Elkridge Landing Rd Linthicum MD 21090

HARTMAN, LILA JEAN, packaging co. exec.; b. Oldham, S.D., Dec. 23, 1929; d. Aly and Sofie (Darouge) Hamway; student Toledo U., Owens Tech. Sch.; m. Mar. 27, 1948; children—Kathy Maurine, Donald William. Bookkeeper, Keeshin Truck Line, Toledo; sec., office mgr. sales office Lincoln Elec. Co., Toledo; now pres., owner, mgr. Perfect Packaging Co., Perrysburg, Ohio. Bd. dirs. Health Clinics Internat. Mem. Spl. Packaging and Handling Engrs. (past pres., service award), Internat. Trade Assn. (dir. Toledo Area). Home: 25700 W River Rd Perrysburg OH 43551 Office: 26615 Eckel Rd Perrysburg OH 43551

HARTMAN, STEWART EUGENE, JR., dairy and restaurant exec.; b. York, Pa., May 30, 1931; s. Stewart and Florence (Chronster) H.; B.S., Franklin and Marshall Coll., 1952; m. Joann R. Rutter, June 7, 1952; children—Terry S., Scott E. Accountant, York Shipley, York, 1952-53; C.P.A., Harry Ness & Co., York, 1955-59; officer, owner Rutter's Dairy, Farm Stores, Restaurants, York, 1959—. Pres. PTA, Central Sch. Dist., York, 1965-67; active YMCA; bd. dirs. York YMCA, 1980—, March of Dimes, 1980—. Served in USMC, 1953-55; Korea. C.P.A., Pa. Mem. Nat. Assn. Convenience Stores, Milk Industry Found., York County Milk Dealers Assn. (past pres.), York C. of C. (dir. 1980—). Republican. Lutheran. Clubs: Rotary, Masons. Home: 1973 Tulip Tree Ln York PA 17402 Office: 2100 N George St York PA 17404

HARTMANN, DONALD H., business exec.; b. 1927; B.S. in Mech. Engring., 1949. Dir. diesel engine div. Gen. Motors Corp., 1949-51; mgr. govt. and indsl. products and planning, Packard Motor Car Co., 1951-57; v.p. Dura Corp., 1957-61; exec. v.p. Heath div. Daystrom Electric, Inc., 1961-63; with Dresser Industries, Inc., Dallas, 1963-71, pres. Lane Wells div., 1963-66, pres. Magcobar div., 1966-67, v.p. petroleum and minerals group, 1967-69, exec. v.p., 1969-71, also dir.; pres., chief exec. officer Crutcher Resources Corp., Houston, 1971-75, pres., chief exec. officer Ramteck Industries, Inc., Houston, 1975—, also subs. F-H Maloney Co., Houston, The Rochester Corp., Culpeper, Va.; dir. Peninsula Resources Corp., Corpus Christi, Tex. Served with USNR, 1945-47. Office: 1212 Main St Suite 1500 Houston TX 77002

HARTNACK, CARL EDWARD, banker; b. Los Angeles, Apr. 9, 1916; s. Johannes C. and Kate (Schoneman) H.; grad. Pacific Coast Banking Sch., Seattle, 1950; grad. (honor certificate) Am. Inst. Banking, 1949; m. Roberta DeLuce, Sept. 6, 1939; children—Richard C., Robert D., Gretchen. With Security Pacific Nat. Bank, Los Angeles, 1934—, v.p., 1959-61, sr. v.p., 1961-69, pres., 1969-78, dir., 1969—, chief operating officer, 1973-78, chmn. bd., 1978—; dir. Pacific Indemnity Co., Superior Farming Co. Chmn., Los Angeles met. area Nat. Alliance Businessmen JOBS program, 1972, nat. chmn., 1975-76. Mem. Am. Bankers Assn., Assn. Res. City Bankers. Clubs: La Jolla Country; Stock Exchange, Los Angeles Country, Calif. (Los Angeles). Office: 333 S Hope St Los Angeles CA 90071

HARTNAGEL, RICHARD LEE, mfg. co. exec.; b. Belleville, Ill., Apr. 14, 1937; s. Albert Adolph and Mildred Evelyn (Lucas) H.; B.S. in Fire Protection and Safety Engring. (Western Actuarial Bur. scholar), Ill. Inst. Tech., 1961; m. Catherine Claire Hotz, Aug. 29, 1959; children—Richard Dale, Gregory Joseph, Catherine Lynn, Maureen Anne, Kristin Elizabeth. Insp., Mo. Inspection Bur., St. Louis, 1963-66; safety engr. McDonnell Aircraft Co., St. Louis, 1966-71, sr. safety engr., 1972-74; asst. safety dir. Granite City Steel Co. (Ill.), 1971-72; pres. Edwardsville Machine & Welding Co. (Ill.), 1974—. Ins. chmn. Edwardsville Little League, 1966-72; treas. Edwardsville Investment Club, 1966-70; pres. Dunlap Lake Property Owners Assn., Edwardsville, 1969. Served with USAF, 1960-63. Mem. Res. Officers Assn. Democrat. Roman Catholic. Clubs: Edwardsville Gun, Edwardsville Quarterbacks. Home: 574 E Lake Dr Edwardsville IL 62025 Office: 1509 Troy Rd Edwardsville IL 62025

HARTNETT, JOHN FREDERICK, accountant; b. Stamford, Conn., Feb. 19, 1947; s. Richard Joseph and Jane Elizabeth (Berg) H.; B.A., Hiram Scott Coll., Scottsbluff, Nebr., 1970; M.B.A., U. Conn., 1980; m. Carol Ann Gedney, Aug. 13, 1969 (div. Nov. 1974); m. 2d, Antonia Colucelli, Sept. 26, 1980. Accountant, L.L. Daly, P.A., Scottsbluff, 1970, System Feed Lots, Minatare, Nebr., 1970-71, Lockwood Corp., Gering, Nebr., 1971-73; self-employed, Omaha, 1973-74; asst. controller Executrans Internat., Greenwich, Conn., 1974-75; mgr. gen. accounting Homequity Inc., Wilton, Conn., 1975-77, sr. accountant, 1978—; dir. fin. Uinimin/Unisil, Greenwich, 1977. Mem. Stamford Aux. Fire Dept. Mem. Nat. Assn. Accountants, Am. Accounting Assn., Inst. Internal Auditors. Republican. Roman Catholic.

HARTOGENSIS, STEPHEN, internat. exec.; b. N.Y.C., Aug. 28, 1931; s. Alwyn M. and Ethel M. (Schutt) H.; B.S., Lehigh U., 1952; m. Diane Baker, Dec. 5, 1964; 1 dau., Andrea; children by previous marriage—Karen, George, James. Controller Gen. Foods, Europe, 1967-70; v.p. Technicon Corp., 1970-75; v.p. internat. Branson Sonic Power Co., Danbury, Conn., 1976—. Served to lt. (j.g.), USNR, 1953-55. Mem. Fin. Execs. Inst. Home: 70 Cedar Rd Wilton CT 06897 Office: 10 Eagle Rd Danbury CT 06810

HARTSON, MAURICE JOHN, JR., ins. agt.; b. New Orleans, Jan. 20, 1906; s. Maurice J. and Marguerite (Calongne) H.; ed. Loyola U. South, 1922-26; m. Elizabeth Freret, June 6, 1929; children—Lise Anne (Mrs. J. Parham Werlein, Jr.), Maurice J. III, Elizabeth. Entered ins. bus., 1924; owner agy., New Orleans, 1937—; v.p. Columbia Homestead Assn.; past pres. New Orleans Ins. Exchange. Past pres. New Orleans Fire Prevention Bd., New Orleans United Fund; organizer, past pres. New Orleans Area Health Planning Council; pres. New Orleans Community Chest; pres. St. Mary's Orphan Boys Asylum; chmn. devel. council, mem. bd. adminstrs. St. Mary's Dominican Coll.; bd. dirs. Mercy Hosp., New Orleans Speech and Hearing Center, Maison Hospitaliere, Jesuit High Sch.; chmn. Archbishop's Community Appeal; mem. pres.'s council Cath. U. Am. Recipient citation for outstanding service La. Assn. Ins. Agts.; Weiss Brotherhood award NCCJ; Order of St. Louis, 1975; Knight of St. Gregory, 1977. Mem. Nat. Assn. Ins. Agts. (exec. com., recipient presdl. citation), New Orleans C. of C. (past chmn. civic affairs), Soc. War of 1812, Blue Key, Sigma Alpha Epsilon. Roman Catholic. Most Loyal Gander of Blue Goose. Clubs: Pickwick (past pres.); Serra (past pres. New Orleans; dist. 11 gov. 1965-67; New Orleans Country, Southern Yacht; Stratford, Orleans. Home: 1528 Webster St New Orleans LA 70118 Office: 332 Carondelet St New Orleans LA 70130

HARTUNG, HAZEL JANE SPRINGER (MRS. DONALD NORMAN HARTUNG), advt. exec.; b. Youngstown, Ohio, Feb. 19, 1918; d. Homer Edward and Cora (Nichols) Springer; student pub. schs.; m. Donald Norman Hartung, July 18, 1937; children—Donald Glenn, Daniel Richard, James Lee. Newspaperwoman, Muskegon (Mich.) Chronicle, 1953-56; indsl. editor Muskegon Piston Ring Co., 1956-57; account exec. Studio 5 Advt. Agy., 1957-59; personnel, pub. relations dir. Hardy-Herpolsheimer's Dept. Store, 1959-61; dir. advt., pub. relations Nat. Lumberman's Bank, 1961-65; advt., pub. relations dir. Farmers Nat. Bank & Trust Co., 1965-66; mgr. advt., promotion Fasson Products Corp., 1966-67; pub. service dir. McKay-Dee Hosp. Center, Ogden, Utah, 1967-69; dir. pub. relations Lima (Ohio) Meml. Hosp., 1969—. Free-lance writer trade, religious mags., 1953—. Advt., pub. relations dir. Greater Muskegon's Seaway Festival, 1963; pub. relations com. United Way, 1972-80, individual/ministerial div. chmn. 1980-81; mem. Juvenile Writer's Workshop; chmn. pub. relations com. United Way, 1977-78; bd. dirs. PACT; bd. dirs. Child and Family Agy., Lima, pres., 1977-79, 80-81. Recipient Outdoor Advt. award for creation and execution billboards, 1963; Advt. Woman of Year award Advt. and Sales Club Western Mich., 1964; Layout and Editor award Intermountain Assn. Indsl. Editors, 1969, Outstanding Achievement in Editing award, 1969. Mem. Internat. Assn. Bus. Communicators, Greater Muskegon C. of C. (dir. women's div. 1961-64), Zonta (v.p., 1962-63, treas. 1963-64). Mem. Reorganized Ch. of Jesus Christ of Latter-day Saints (women's leader 1961-63, 74 NW Ohio regional pastoral care dir.). Clubs: Lima Advt. (dir.), West State Press (charter). Home: 3138 Clifford Dr Lima OH 45805

HARTUNG, JOHN THOMAS, securities exec.; b. Tarentum, Pa., Apr. 8, 1929; s. Albert Paul and Janet Claire (Campbell) H.; student acctg. Robert Morris Sch. Bus., Pitts., 1949; B.A. in Econs. (Mellon

Bank scholar), Muskingum Coll., New Concord, Ohio, 1952; postgrad. Harvard Grad Sch. Bus., 1968, N.Y. Inst. Fin., 1970; m. Katherine Kennedy, Dec. 18, 1954; children—Johanna, Elizabeth. Divisional mgr. H.J. Heinz, Pitts., 1954-60; gen. sales mgr. Jet Spray Corp., Boston, 1960-70; account exec. Merrill Lynch, Clearwater, Fla., 1970-76; v.p., mgr. Smith Barney Harris Upham, Clearwater, 1976-79, Dean Witter Reynolds, Clearwater, 1979—; presenter radio stock market reports, 1970—. Adviser, Council of Chs.; v.p., dir. Community Sailing Bd., 1968-70; active polit. campaign coms. Served with C.I.C., AUS, 1952-54. Named Producing Mgr. of Year, Smith Barney Harris Upham, 1977; registered prin. fin., option prin., mgr. fin., commodity prin. Republican. Presbyterian. Clubs: Wellesley Sailing, Countryside Country, Masons, Shriners, Rotary (dir. internat.). Home: 1415 Monte Carlo Dr Clearwater FL 33516 Office: 2560 Enterprise Rd E Clearwater FL 33515

HARTUNG, RODERICK LEE, petroleum co. exec.; b. Albion, Mich., July 25, 1935; s. Clarence Roy and Evelyn Anna (Young) H.; B.S. in Chem. Engring., U. Mich., 1958, M.S. in Chem. Engring. 1959; m. Evelyn Ludy, Jan. 3, 1959; children—Katherine, Victoria, Robert. Project engr. Standard Oil Co., San Francisco, 1959-62; foreman asst. supt. Western Ops. Inc., Richmond, Calif., 1963-66, supt. mfg. ops., Honolulu, 1967-69; dir. Chevron-Latin Am., (Refineria Conchan), Lima, Peru, 1969-72; refinery mgr. Chevron West Salt Lake Refinery (Utah), 1972-74, asst. chief engr. corp. engring. dept., San Francisco, 1976; gen. mgr. Pascagoula Refining and Petrochm. Complex (Miss.), 1977—. Mem. Am. Inst. Chem. Engrs., Miss. Mfrs. Assn. (dir.), Pascagoula C. of C. (pres.). Club: Rotary (pres. Pascagoula). Home: 1909 Beach Blvd Pascagoula MS 39567 Office: Chevron-USA PO Box 1300 Pascagoula MS 39567

HARTWIGSEN, BRUCE, architect; b. Jersey City, Mar. 10, 1931; s. George Lewis and Ester Mary (Keely) H.; B.Arch., Cornell U., 1954; m. Rosemary Eleanor Murphy, Apr. 7, 1956; children—Bruce Scott, Susan Marie, Brian George. Prin., Bruce Hartwigsen, Architect, N.Y.C., 1960-62; architect J.C. Penny Co., N.Y.C., 1962-64; partner Kiff, Voss & Franklin, Architects, N.Y.C., 1964-74; partner Rogers, Butler & Burgun, Architects, N.Y.C., 1974-77; asso. Rogers, Lovelock & Fritz, Architects & Engrs., Winter Park, Fla., 1977—. Chmn. Rye (N.Y.) City Bd. Archtl. Rev., 1968-77; mem. Rye City Planning Adv. Bd., 1974-77. Served with USNR, 1954-56. Mem. AIA (pres. Westchester, N.Y. chpt. 1970), N.Y. State Assn. Architects (pres. 1976), Fla. Assn. Architects (dir. 1980), Am. Assn. Hosp. Planning, Am. Hosp. Assn. Roman Catholic. Clubs: Skytop (Pa.), Union League (N.Y.C.). Prin. works include: St. Barnabas Hosp., Bronx, N.Y., 1978, Naval Regional Med. Center, Orlando, Fla., Med. Center at Princeton, N.J., 1978. Office: 145 Lincoln Ave Winter Park FL 32789

HARTWIGSEN, NELSON LEROY, rubber co. exec.; b. Nanticoke, Pa., Mar. 4, 1941; s. Norman L. and Anna (Rowland) H.; B.S., Wilkes Coll., 1963; m. Lucille Bartish, June 11, 1963; children—Dawn Marie, Deborah Ann, Eric Norman. Trade service asst., mech. rubber goods div. UniRoyal, Inc., Buffalo, 1963, salesman, 1964, inside salesman, Pitts., 1964-65, salesman, Balt., 1965-68, asst. mgr. hose sales, Passaic, N.J., 1968-69, dist. sales mgr., Detroit, 1969-70; v.p., gen. mgr. Md. Rubber Corp., Balt., 1970-71, pres., 1971—; pres. Keystone Rubber Corp., York, Pa., 1974—. Served with Md. Army N.G., 1965-71. Home: 1506 Donegal Rd Bel Air MD 21014 Office: 6350 Frankford Ave Baltimore MD 21206 also I-83 Industrial Park York PA 17405

HARVEY, ERIC LEE, mgmt. cons. firm exec.; b. Chester, Pa., Apr. 20, 1946; s. Harry William and Hildegarde M. (Bobb) H.; B.B.A., U. Tex., 1971; m. Nancy H. Garwacke, Apr. 29, 1969; children—Nicole, Erika. Personnel dir. Champion Internat. Corp., 1971-74; tng. mgr. Johnson & Johnson Corp., Somerville, N.J., 1974-76; dir. human resource devel. Am. Medicorp, Dallas, 1976-78; exec. v.p. Performance Systems Corp., Dallas, 1978—; mem. adj. faculty U. Tex. Head vol. probation officers Somerset Juvenile Probation Dept. Served with U.S. Army, 1969-71. Mem. Am. Soc. Tng. and Devel., Tex. Soc. Hosp. Educators, Am. Soc. Manpower Edn. and Tng. Republican. Home: 106 Addison Dr Lewisville TX 75067 Office: 2925 LBJ Freeway Suite 281 Dallas TX 75234

HARVEY, JAMES ROSS, diversified service co. exec.; b. Los Angeles, Aug. 20, 1934; s. James Ernest and Loretta Bernice (Ross) H.; B.S., Princeton U., 1956; M.B.A., U. Calif., Berkeley, 1963; m. Charlene Coakley, July 22, 1971; children—Kjersten Ann, Kristina Ross. Engr., Standard Oil Co. (Calif.), San Francisco, 1956-61; acct. Touche, Ross & Co., 1963-64; pres., dir. Transamerica Corp., San Francisco, 1965—; chmn. bd. United Artists Corp., Budget Rent a Car Corp., Transamerica Delaval Inc., Transamerica Film Service Corp.; dir. Occidental Life Ins. Co., Transamerica Fin. Corp., Transamerica Airlines, Transamerica Ins. Co., Transamerica Title Ins. Co. Trustee Calif. Hist. Soc., 1978; bd. dirs. U. Calif. Bus. Sch.; trustee West Coast Cancer Found.; bd. regents St. Marys Coll. Served with U.S. Army, 1958-59. Mem. San Francisco C. of C. (dir.). Clubs: Bohemian (San Francisco); Union League (N.Y.C.). Home: PO Box 3775 San Francisco CA 94119 Office: 600 Montgomery St San Francisco CA 94111

HARVEY, JOHN FRANCIS, fin exec.; b. Jefferson City, Mo., Aug. 1, 1922; s. William Walter and Exie Marie (Lindley) H.; S.B., Harvard U., 1943, M.B.A., 1947; m. Mary Jane Shaw, Jan. 24, 1959; children—Mary Lindley, Laura Treat, Thomas Shaw. Comptroller, Time Inc., N.Y.C., 1957-71, v.p., 1963-71, sec., 1967-71, asst. to pres., 1971; v.p.-fin., treas. Schering-Plough Corp., Kenilworth, N.J., 1971-74; v.p.-fin., treas. Times Mirror Co., Los Angeles, 1974-77; sr. v.p., treas., chief fin. officer Summa Corp., Las Vegas, Nev., 1978—. Trustee, S.W. Mus., Los Angeles, 1976—; mem. Bus. Advisory Council for Mgmt. Improvement in N.Y. State, 1969-71; mem. Cardinal's Com. for Edn., Catholic Archdiocese N.Y., 1969—. Served in U.S. Army, 1944-46. Mem. Fin. Execs. Inst. Clubs: Annadale Golf (Pasadena); Mill Reef (W.I.). Home: 7127 LaPuebla St Las Vegas NV 89120 Office: PO Box 14000 Las Vegas NV 89156

HARVEY, LOUIS SAMUEL, cons. co. exec.; b. Puerto Barrios, Guatemala, Oct. 26, 1942; s. Cyril Percival and Beryl Cynthia (Hawthorne) H.; came to U.S., 1963; B.S. in Physics, U. West Indies, 1961; m. Clover Allen, June 4, 1964; children—Shelley, Ann. Systems engr. IBM, Kingston, Jamaica, 1961-63, Mgmt. Assistance Inc., N.Y.C., 1963-68; project mgr. John Wiley & Sons, Inc., N.Y.C., 1968-70; v.p. Bradford Trust Co./Bradford Nat., N.Y.C. and Boston, 1970-76; pres. Dalbar Fin. Services, Inc., N.Y.C., 1976—. Home: 159 W 53d St New York NY 10019 Office: 545 Madison Ave New York NY 10022

HARVEY, RICHARD DUDLEY, mktg. cons.; b. Atlanta, Sept. 24, 1923; s. Robert Emmett and June (Dudley) H.; B.A., U. Denver, 1947; postgrad. various bus. seminars Harvard U., Stanford U.; m. Donna Helen Smith, Oct. 12, 1944; 1 dau., Louise Dudley. Various positions in sales, sales promotion and mktg. The Coca-Cola Co., St. Louis, Denver and Atlanta, 1948-60, v.p., brand mgr., mktg. mgr., mktg. dir., Atlanta, 1965-70, v.p. orgn. and mktg. devel., 1970-75; sr. v.p. mktg. Olympia Brewing Co., Olympia, Wash., 1975-78; dir. Lone Star Brewing Co., San Antonio. Mem. mayor's housing resources com., Atlanta, 1968-70; program chmn. United Way, Atlanta, 1969; vice chmn. Episcopal Radio-TV Found., Atlanta, 1975—. Served with USAAF, 1942-45. Mem. Am. Mktg. Assn., Mktg. Communications Execs. Internat., Assn. for Corp. Growth, Assn. Mgmt. Consultants, Seattle C. of C., Phi Beta Kappa, Omicron Delta Kappa. Democrat. Episcopalian. Clubs: Piedmont Driving (Atlanta), The Rainier (Seattle). Home: 3837 E Crockett St Seattle WA 98112 Office: Sound Mktg Services Inc Suite 402 Grosvenor House 500 Wall St Seattle WA 98121

HARVEY, ROBERT GEORGE, transp. co. exec.; b. Lintlaw, Sask., Can., Jan. 13, 1943; s. Harold Earnest and Elizabeth Julie (Schmidt) H.; m. Marcia Marian Pidmurny, July 4, 1970; 1 dau., Tahnee Lee. Regional mgr. Thomas Meadows & Co., Hamiton, Ont., Can., 1965-67; Customs mgr. Pacific Customs Brokers, Vancouver, B.C., Can., 1968-69; v.p. Concord Air Freight System Ltd., Vancouver, 1969-75; v.p. Concord Freight System Ltd., Vancouver, 1975-80, pres., Toronto, 1980—; v.p. Starlife Internat. Inc.; v.p. Concord Mortuary Services Ltd. Mem. Internat. Air Shippers Assn., Canadian Internat. Freight Forwarders Assn., Canadian Importers Assn., Canadian Exporters Assn. Office: PO Box 274 Malton ON L4T 3B6 Canada

HARVEY, WILLIAM HEATH, health services co. exec.; b. Columbus, Ga., July 7, 1913; s. Walter Forest and Edna Louise (Heath) H.; student U. Calif. at Los Angeles, Northwestern Med. Sch.; m. Dorothy Hudson, June 30, 1968; children—Betty Jo (Mrs. William E. Anderson), Peggy (Mrs. Bruce Bullard). Pres. Harvey's, Inc., Columbus, 1943—, Macon, Ga., 1964—; pres. Heath Harvey's Inc. Ala., 1972—. Mem. Am. Orthotic and Prosthetic Assn. (pres., dir. region 4 1974) Phenix City, Columbus chambers commerce, Mchts. Assn., Prescription Shoe Assn., Internat. Soc. Orthotists and Prosthetists, Am. Acad. Orthotists and Prosthetists, Ga. Soc. Orthotists and Prosthetists (pres. 1964, 80). Clubs: Masons, Elks, Lions. Home: 350 Cumberland Rd Columbus GA 31904 Office: 1306 Broadway Columbus GA 31901

HARVILL, ELEANOR K., pub. relations research exec.; b. Yonkers, N.Y., Dec. 31, 1919; d. Peter K. and Anna (Rodak) Harvill; B.A., Barnard Coll., Columbia U., 1941; M.A., Tchrs. Coll., Columbia, 1942. Sec., researcher Hill & Knowlton, Inc., N.Y.C., 1946-48, research asst., 1948-49, research supr., 1949-52, research dir., 1952-56; research asst. U.S. Steel Corp., N.Y.C., 1956-68, Pitts., 1969; mgr. corporate research, fin. relations dept. Gulf and Western Industries, Inc., N.Y.C., 1970—. Tchr., Riverdale (N.Y.) Country Sch. for Boys, 1942-43. Served with WAC's 1943-46. Mem. Pub. Relations Soc. Am. (chpt. dir. 1967-68; chmn. research com. 1966-68). Contbg. author: Handbook of Public Relations, 1971. Editor Reflections, 1966-68; contbg. editor Public Relations Jour., 1968-70. Contbr. articles to profl. jours. Home: 5552 Netherland Ave Apt 2C Riverdale NY 10471 Office: 1 Gulf and Western Plaza New York City NY 10023

HARVIN, WILLIAM CHARLES, lawyer; b. San Francisco, Feb. 15, 1919; s. William Charles and Irma Beth (Hawkins) H.; B.A., U. Tex., 1940, LL.B., 1947; m. Ruth Helen Beck, Nov. 30, 1942; children—David Tarleton, Susan Elizabeth Harvin Lawhon, Andrew Richard. Admitted to Tex. bar, 1946; with firm Baker & Botts, Houston, 1947—, partner, 1956—, mng. partner, chmn. exec. com., 1972—; dir. Tex. Commerce Bancshares, Inc., 1975—; lectr. legal insts. and law schs.; chmn. U.S. circuit judge nominating commn. Western Fifth Circuit. Bd. dirs. Tex. Med. Center, Inc., St. Luke's Episcopal Hosp., U. Tex. Health Scis. Center, Houston, San Jacinto History Mus., St. John's Sch., Houston, Episc. Theol. Sem. S.W. Fellow Am. Coll. Trial Lawyers, Am., Tex. bar founds.; mem. Am. Law Inst., Am. Bar Assn., Fedn. Ins. Counsel (pres. 1969-70), Def. Research Inst. (dir. 1969-72), Houston C. of C. (dir.). Contbr. articles to legal periodicals. Office: Baker & Botts Law Firm 3000 One Shell Plaza Houston TX 77002

HARWAY, MAXWELL, real estate exec.; b. N.Y.C., Mar. 7, 1913; s. Samuel and Esther (Steinbook) H.; B.S. in Econs., Coll. City N.Y., 1940; grad. Indsl. Coll. Armed Forces, 1951; M.A. in Internat. Relations, Georgetown U., 1952; m. Georgette Nadelar, Dec. 1, 1945 (dec.); children—Michele, Philip A., Danielle S. Tchr., econs. research dir. WPA, 1935-38; wage hour insp. Dept. Labor, 1941, economist, 1941; chief econs. processed food rationing OPA, 1942; dir. transp. div. Nat. Housing Authority, 1946; fgn. affairs officer Dept. State, 1947-53; owner import-export bus. North Africa, 1954-56; corr. for mags., 1954-57; fgn. corr. McGraw Hill World News, 1956-59; asst. to pres. Continental Ore Corp., 1959-65; program officer SBA, 1965; cons. Office Econ. Opportunity, 1965; internat. economist Commerce Dept., 1966; with AID, 1967-78; chief comml. import div. Supporting Assistance Bur., 1967-78, prgs. Warrenton Realty Co., Inc., N.Y.C., Waterloo (Va.) Enterprises, 1978—; dir. Waterloo Enterprises, Warrenton, Va. Chmn. internat. relations com. N.Y.C. LWV; mem. Pres.'s Task Force on War Against Poverty, 1964. Served with USAAF, 1943-46. Mem. Nat. Assn. Bus. Economists, Soc. Internat. Devel., Fauquier Hist. Soc. Overseas Press Club. Home: 132B Fairfield Dr Warrenton VA 22186 Office: 301 E 45th St New York NY 10017

HARWOOD, LEE, oil co. exec.; b. New London, Conn., Oct. 9, 1901; s. Pliny LeRoy and Rowena (Lee) H.; student Dartmouth Coll., 1920-23; m. Ann Elizabeth Kiesewetter, Jan. 19, 1931 (dec. 1959); m. 2d, Alison McDaniel Bisgood, 1960. Bond trader Remick, Hodges & Co., mem. N.Y. Stock Exchange, 1924-27, Schwabacher & Co., 1927-29; registered rep. several N.Y. Stock Exchange firms including W. E. Hutton & Co., 1929-41; exec. v.p., dir. Enesco Corp., N.Y.C., 1941-47; N.Y. account exec. LaRoche & Ellis, 1947-50; v.p., chmn. devel. com. Robert W. Orr & Assos. Inc., 1950-57; v.p. Orr div. Fuller & Smith & Ross, Inc., 1957-63; pres. Harwood & Harwood, Inc., 1961-63; v.p. Market Planning Corp., N.Y.C., 1963-67; v.p., dir. McRae Oil Corp., 1967-69, sr. v.p., dir., 1969—; sr. v.p., dir. subs. Petrofunds, Inc.; sr. v.p., dir. McRae Oil & Gas Co., Inc. Mem. Ex-mems. Assn. Squadron A (gov.), Soc. Mayflower Descs., S.R., Pilgrims of U.S., Psi Upsilon. Republican. Episcopalian. Clubs: Knickerbocker, Squadron A (gov.), River (N.Y.C.); Charleston, Yeamans Hall (Charleston, S.C.). Home: 23 Tradd St Charleston SC 29401 Office: 800 Dresser Tower Houston TX 77002

HARWOOD, RICHARD ADRIAN, rancher; b. Chgo., Feb. 6, 1945; s. Thomas S. and Martha L. Harwood; student Chapman Coll., Orange, Calif., 1966. Owner, mgr. Brushy Creek Cattle Co., Round Rock and Jarrell, Tex., 1977—. Chmn., Williamson County Child Welfare Bd., 1979; mem. Big Bros. Austin. Served with U.S. Army, 1966-68. Mem. Nat. Cattlemen's Assn., Tex. and Southwestern Cattle Raisers Assn., Santa Gertrudis Breeders Internat., Mid-Coast Santa Gertrudis Assn., Williamson County Livestock Assn. Republican. Methodist. Club: Round Rock Sertoma (sec.). Home: 1206 Glen Cove St Round Rock TX 78664 Office: PO Box 143 Round Rock TX 78664

HARWOOD, RICHARD MAURICE, indsl. properties exec.; b. Chgo., Nov. 21, 1928; s. Robert S. and Lilian (Feuerlicht) H.; student U. So. Calif., 1946; m. Beth Daniels, Feb. 27, 1955; children—Brooke Ann, Robert L. Publicity dir. Bishop & Assos., Los Angeles, 1952-53; advt. mgr. Gilbar Sales Co., Los Angeles, 1954-56; advt. supr., mgr. advt. and sales promotion Hotpoint div. Gen. Elec. Co., Los Angeles, Chgo., 1956-62; advt. and sales promotion mgr. RCA Distbg. Corp., Des Plaines, Ill., 1962-70, sales mgr., 1968-70; nat. sales promotion mgr. Toyota Motor Sales USA Inc., Torrance, Calif., 1970-76, nat. merchandising mgr., 1977-78; indsl. properties sales and leasing, 1978—. Chmn., Pub. Relations Com. Elk Grove, 1965-70. Served with AUS, 1950-52. Mem. Marketing Communications Execs. Internat., Point of Purchase Advt. Inst., Am. Marketing Assn. Developer Hotpoint Plan-A-Kitchen, 1961. Home: 1804-D Esplanade Redondo Beach CA 90277

HARWOOD, ROBERT GEORGE, inventor; b. Clifton, N.J., Apr. 4, 1939; s. Frank William and Marjorie Elva (Ackerman) H.; B.S. in Mech. Engring., Newark Coll. Engring., 1964; m. Elsie Marie Happ, Apr. 25, 1965; children—Heidi Christina, Stacey Jennifer. Reliability engr. Gen. Electric Re-entry systems div., Phila., 1965-68; supervisory engring. positions AMP Inc., Harrisburg, Pa., 1968-72, mgr. devel. engring. PACOM div., 1972-78, mgr. advanced devel. lab. AMP Inc., Largo, Fla., 1978—. Mem. IEEE, Soc. Automotive Engrs., U.S. Tennis Assn. Holder nine patents in field of fiber optics and electronic components; contbr. articles on fiber optic tech. and connector design to profl. jours. Home: 700 Wild Oak Ln Palm Harbor FL 33563 Office: 230 Commerce Dr Largo FL 33540

HARZ, KARL JOSEPH, fin. co. exec.; b. Paterson, N.J., July 10, 1950; s. Karl Oscar and Vera Marie (Gennaro) H.; B.S., Fairleigh Dickinson U., 1972, M.B.A., 1974; m. Marilyn Lee Kindred, Mar. 3, 1974; children—Alexa Marie, Tiffany Ann. Regional dir., life and disability agt. Lincoln Nat. Life Ins. co., Los Angeles, 1974-76; registered rep. Nat. Plan Coordinators, Inc., Long Beach, Calif., 1976-77; pension cons., fin. planner Mut. Benefit Life Ins. Co., 1977-78; pres., founder Pension Home Loan Corp., 1978—; Realtor. Recipient cert. of achievement AAU, 1972. Real estate broker, Tex., Calif. Mem. Nat. Assn. Realtors, Nat. Notary Assn., Rolling Hills Bd. Realtors, others. Clubs: N.Y. Athletic (life); Los Angeles Athletic (profl.). Office: 21535 Hawthorne Blvd Suite 300 Torrance CA 9503

HASEK, JOSEPH KAREL, internat. trade, fin. and econs. cons.; b. Prague, Czechoslovakia, Apr. 2, 1911; s. Frantisek and Eliska (Skolek) H.; came to U.S., 1948, naturalized, 1954; Dr. in Law and Economics, Charles U., Czechoslovakia, 1934; student London Sch. Econs., 1937; m. Karla Policka, Apr. 19, 1938 (div. 1948); children—Eliska Hasek Coolidge, Jan Hasek. Rep. of Czechoslovak Export Inst., 1938; pres. Hasek & Co., Bankers, Prague, 1945-48; asst. to judge Appellate Comml. Ct., Prague, 1935; atty. with Eduard Schwartz, Prague, 1936, N.M. Rothschild & Sons, Bankers, London, 1936, Bank of Manhattan Co., N.Y.C., 1938; dir. Czechoslovak-Am. C. of C., Prague, 1946-48; pres. Combined Agencies Corp., Washington, 1948—; exec. in charge of export financing Internat. Bank of Washington, 1951-53; cons., lectr. on internat. econs., trade and fin., 1938—; dir. Aeromaritime, Inc., Washington, 1960-71; pres. Kenwood Devel. Corp., Washington, 1957—; chmn. export sub-com. Washington Bd. Trade, 1960-67; apptd. to U.S. Export Expansion Councils, 1968-74. Mem. Am. Soc. Internat. Execs., Czechoslovak-Am. Edn. Council (pres. 1975—), Czechoslovak Nat. Council Am. (co-chmn. fgn. affairs com. 1965—). Clubs: City Tavern, Kenwood Golf and Country. Author: (with J. Allen) Foreign Exchange Restriction, 1938; (with A. Faltus and C. Jesina) Birth of Czechoslovakia, 1968; contbr. articles on internat. econs. to profl. publs. and newspapers. Home: 4207 45th St NW Washington DC 20016 Office: 910 17th St NW Washington DC 20006

HASELMANN, JOHN PHILIP, mgmt. cons.; b. Summit, N.J., Feb. 25, 1940; s. John and Elizabeth H.; B.S. in Elec. Engring., N.J. Inst. Tech., 1961; M.B.A., U. Pa., 1963; children—Terri Lee, Karen Lynn, Guy Philip. Asst. dir. Behavior Systems Co., Phila., 1961-63; mgr. mgmt. sci. Western Electric Co., Princeton, N.J., 1970-73; mgr. mktg. sci. AT&T Long Lines, Bedminster, N.J., 1974-78; pres. Info. Mgmt. Group, Inc., Morristown, N.J., 1978—. Mem. Am. Mgmt. Assn. Office: Info Mgmt Group Inc 25 Airport Rd Morristown NJ 07960

HASELTINE, ORAN LEE, oil exploration co. exec.; b. Springfield, Mo., Oct. 24, 1925; s. J. Bryan and Mary Gladys (Brown) H.; B.S. in M.E., U. Calif., 1950; m. Doris Jean Keith, June 17, 1949; children—Claudia Sewell, Jeffrey Haseltine, William. Vice pres. So. Union Gas Co., Dallas, 1972-74; v.p., gen. mgr. So. Union Exploration Co., Dallas, 1974, pres., 1979—. Served with USN, 1943-46. Registered profl. engr. Tex. Mem. AIME, Am. Petroleum Inst., Am. Gas Assn. Republican. Ch. of Christ. Club: Dallas Petroleum. Office: Suite 400 1217 Main St Dallas TX 75202

HASELTON, WILLIAM RAYMOND, paper co. exec.; b. Glens Falls, N.Y., Jan. 11, 1925; s. Raymond Richard and Mary Frances (Vanderwerker) H.; B.S. in Chem. Engring., Rensselaer Poly. Inst., 1949; M.S. in Chemistry, Lawrence U., 1951; Ph.D., Inst. Paper Chemistry, 1953; m. Frances Crooks, July 10, 1948; children—Susan Lizbeth Haselton Barr, Judith Haselton Ferguson, June Ann. Tech. dir. Rhinelander Paper Co. div. St. Regis Paper Co. (Wis.), 1953-54, v.p. ops., 1957, v.p., gen. mgr., 1958-61; gen. mgr. St. Regis Paper Co., Tacoma, 1961, v.p., 1962, v.p., gen. mgr. Forest Products div., 1963-69, sr. v.p. timberlands and forest products, N.Y.C., 1969-70, sr. v.p. pulp, paper, forestry and land mgmt. group, 1970-71, exec. v.p. ops., 1971-73, pres., 1973-79, pres., 1979-81, chief exec. officer, 1979—, chmn., 1981—. Served with USNR, 1943-46. Presbyterian. Clubs: Pinnacle, Sky (N.Y.C.); Woodway Country (Darien, Conn.); Blind Brook (Purchase, N.Y.); Rolling Rock (Ligonier, Pa.). Office: St Regis Paper Co 150 E 42d St New York NY 10017

HASINGER, DAVID JOHN, mfg. co. exec.; b. Indiana, Pa., Mar. 15, 1915; s. Paul Burns and Lucy (Taylor) H.; student pub. schs.; m. Jane E. Thompson, June 8, 1939. Accountant, Rochester & Pitts. Coal Co., Indiana, Pa., 1937; sec., treas. Whiteman & Co., Inc., 1938-40, v.p. and gen. mgr., 1940-46; gen. mgr. Paul & Beekman, Inc., Phila., 1946, v.p., 1947, pres., 1948—, also dir. Pres., bd. trustees West Park Hosp., 1969—. Served on U.S. Maritime Commn., 1943-45. Recipient Smithson Benefactor medallion Smithsonian Instn., 1973. Clubs: Huntington Valley Country, African Safari (pres. Phila. 1967); English Setter of Am. (pres. 1967); Shikar Safari Internat.; Quaker City Gun (dir.); Nat. Red Setter Field Trial. Home: Stafford House Wissahickon and Chelton Aves Philadelphia PA 19144 Office: 1801 Courtland St Philadelphia PA 19140

HASKELL, ARTHUR JACOB, steamship co. exec.; b. Newark, Apr. 16, 1926; s. Isidore David and Elena (Greenbaum) H.; B.S., U.S. Naval Acad., 1947; Naval Engr., Mass. Inst. Tech., 1950-53; m. Amparo Serrano, Dec. 31, 1958 (div. 1979); children—Amparo Rocio, Vincent Isidore, Joaquin Arthur. Commd. ensign U.S. Navy, 1947, advanced through grades to comdr., 1966; ret., 1970; sr. procurement engr. Nat. Bulk Carriers Co., N.Y.C., 1956-62; asst. plant mgr. Western Gear Corp., Belmont, Calif., 1962-63; sr. v.p. Matson Navigation Co., San Francisco, 1973—; dir. San Francisco Marine Exchange, 1975-78, v.p., 1976-77, pres., 1977-78. Mem. Soc. Naval Architects and Marine Engrs. (chmn. Calif. sect. 1971-72, mem. research steering com. 1972-74, nat. v.p. 1973—, exec. com. 1977-80), Sigma Xi. Home: 24 Via Cheparro Greenbrae CA 94904 Office: 333 Market St San Francisco CA 94105

HASKELL, JOHN HENRY FARRELL, JR., investment banker; b. N.Y.C., Jan. 24, 1932; s. John Henry Farrell and Paulette (Heger) H.; B.S., U.S. Mil. Acad., 1953; M.B.A. with distinction, Harvard U., 1958; m. Francine G. Le Roux, June 30, 1955; children—Michael J., Christopher E., Diana F.T. Asso., Dillon, Read & Co. Inc., N.Y.C., 1958-61, mgr. European Office, Paris, 1961-66, v.p., N.Y.C., 1964-75, mng. dir., 1975—; chmn., dir. Dillon Read Overseas Corp.; pres., dir. Scandinavian Securities Corp.; dir. ASA Ltd., Dynalectron Corp.; mem. adv. council Overseas Pvt. Investment Co., 1972-75. Bd. dirs., exec. v.p. Friends of New Cavell Hosp., Inc. Served with U.S. Army, 1953-56. Decorated croix de chevalier l'Ordre National du Mérite (France). Mem. Securities Industry Assn. (internat. fin. com.), Council on Fgn. Relations, French-Am. C. of C. (dir.). Clubs: Links, Recess (N.Y.C.); Piping Rock (Locust Valley, N.Y.). Home: 120 East End Ave New York NY 10028 Office: 46 William St New York NY 10005

HASKELL, RICHARD KENT, cons. co. exec.; b. Tulsa, Okla., July 3, 1925; s. Richard Marsden and Helen (Dickson) H.; grad. Yale U., 1951; m. Jennifer Larkin, Nov. 15, 1952; children—Richard Kent, Rebecca K., Helen D. With Alcoa, 1951-56, Pitts. Plate Glass Co., 1957; v.p. adminstrn. Olin Corp.-Squibb Corp.-Beechnut Inc., N.Y.C., 1957-71; corporate v.p.-personnel Booz Allen, Chgo., 1968; pres. U.S. of MSL Internat. Cons.'s Ltd., N.Y.C., 1971—. Served to 2d lt., USAAF, 1943-45. Republican. Presbyterian. Clubs: Yale, Union League. Home: 425 E 50 St New York City NY 10022 Office: MSL Internat Cons's Ltd 1 Dag Hammarskjold Plaza New York City NY 10017

HASKINS, GEORGE ALLEN, savs. and loan assn. exec.; b. Springfield, Mass., Feb. 22, 1933; s. Ralph Warner and Hilda Marie (Allen) H.; A.B., Dartmouth Coll., 1954; M.B.A., Ind. U., 1955; m. Barbara Eike, June 28, 1958 (dec. June 1977); children—Scott Warner, Steven David, Kimberly Beth; m. 2d, Sheila Seide Gerling, Mar. 1, 1980; children—Robert C. Gerling, James A. Gerling. Loan counselor Eastman Savs. & Loan Assn., Rochester, N.Y., 1957-60, appraiser, 1960-70, mgr. appraisal dept., 1965-70, br. adminstr., 1970-76, loan officer, v.p., 1976—. State committeeman N.Y. Republican Com., 1975-76, town leader Webster Rep. Com., 1972-76; chmn. Webster Zoning Bd. Appeals, 1964-71. Served with USAF, 1955-57. Mem. Soc. Real Estate Appraisers (sr. residential appraiser; dist. gov. 1977—), N.Y. State Soc. Real Estate Appraisers, Rochester, Webster chambers commerce. Republican. Office: 377 State St Rochester NY 14650

HASKINS, GEORGE LEE, lawyer, educator; b. Cambridge, Mass., Feb. 13, 1915; s. Charles Homer and Clare (Allen) H.; Classical Diploma, Phillips Exeter Acad., 1931; A.B. summa cum laude, Harvard, 1935, LL.B., 1942, M.A. (hon.) U. Pa., 1971; Henry fellow, Merton Coll., Oxford U., 1935-36. Jr. fellow Soc. of Fellows, Harvard, 1936-42, lectr. dept. sociology, 1937-38; Lowell lectr., Boston, 1938; asso. Herrick, Smith, Donald & Farley, Boston, 1942; admitted to Mass. bar, 1943, ICC bar, 1951, Pa. bar, 1952, U.S. Supreme Ct. bar, 1952, U.S. Ct. Appeals, 3d circuit, 1953, 1st circuit 1969, Maine bar, 1968; ofcl. observer and War Dept., rep. U.S. del. to UN Conf., San Francisco, 1945; with office of spl. asst. to sec. of state, 1946; asst. prof. Law U. Pa., 1946-48, asso. prof., 1948-49 prof., 1949—, Algernon Sydney Biddle prof. law, 1974—; spl. atty. legal dept. Pa. R.R., 1951-54, cons. counsel, 1955-71, asst. reporter Supreme and Superior Cts. of Pa., 1970-72; v.p., dir. Pa. Mut. Fund (N.Y.), 1961-68. Apptd. to Permanent Commn. on Oliver Wendell Holmes' Devise, 1956; mem. council, mem. editorial bd. Inst. Early Am. History and Culture, Williamsburg, Va., 1968-71; mem. Council Humanities TV Sta. WHYY, Phila.; mem. Adv. Com. for Papers of Chief Justice Marshall, Justice Bradley project Rutgers U.; univ. seminar asso. Columbia U., 1971-73, 77—; permanent mem. Jud. Conf. U.S. 3d Circuit; mem. Hancock (Maine) Bicentennial Commn., 1976, Sesquicentennial Commn., 1977-80; appeared on Phila. Bicentennial NBC Today Show, 1976. Served from pvt. to cpl. CAC, 1942-43; from 1st lt. to capt. AUS, 1943-46; maj. Res., 1946-54. Recipient Army Commendation medal with oak leaf clusters, 1946; Demoblzn. award Social Sci. Research Council, 1946. John Simon Guggenheim fellow, 1957. Fellow Royal Hist. Soc. Am. Soc. Legal History (hon.; pres. 1970-74), Societe Jean Bodin Pour l'Histoire Comparative des Institutions (Belgium); mem. Internat. Law Soc., Soc. Colonial Wars, Am., Maine, Mass., Pa., Phila. bar assns., Assn. Bar City N.Y., Am. Judicature Soc., Colonial Soc. Pa. (council 1977—), Internat. Soc. for Study Medieval Philosophy (titular), Internat. Assn. for History Law (council 1971—), Am. Antiquarian Soc., Am. Soc. Eighteenth-Century Studies, Am. Mgmt. Assn., Swedish Colonial Soc., Sharswood Law Club, Am. Acad. Polit. Sci., Am. Hist. Assn., Am. Law Inst., Assn. I.C.C. Practitioners, Juristic Soc., Brit. Records Assn., Mediaeval Acad. Am. (council 1958-60), Soc. Comparative Legislation, Colonial Soc. Mass., Selden Soc., S.R., Soc. War of 1812, New Eng. Land Title Assn., Mass., Maine, Va. hist. socs., Am. Arbitration Assn. (nat. panel), Phila Art Alliance, Mil. Order Fgn. Wars of U.S., Library Co. Phila., U.S. Ct. Tennis Assn., Soc. Mayflower Desc., Century Assn. (N.Y.C.), Order of Coif, Phi Beta Kappa. Clubs: Somerset (Boston); Pilgrims (N.Y.C.); Metropolitan (Washington); Racquet, Harvard, Legal (Phila.); Royal Automobile (London). Author: The Statute of York and the Interest of the Commons, 1935; The Growth of English Representative Government, 1948; American Law of Property (with others), 1952; Pennsylvania Fiduciary Guide (with M.P. Smith), 1957, 62; Law and Authority in Early Massachusetts: A Study in Tradition and Design, 1960, 68, 77; John Marshall: Foundations of Power, 1981; articles in U.S. and fgn. periodicals. Contbr. to Ency. Brit. Editor Phi Beta Kappa series, 1934-37 John Dickinson's Death of a Republic, 1963; co-editor: History of Hancock, Maine, 1828-1978. Adv. bd. editors Speculum, 1949-69, William and Mary Quar., 1968-70, Studies in Legal History, 1972—. Home: Box 760 Paoli PA 19301 also Hancock ME 04640 Office: 3400 Chestnut St Philadelphia PA 19104

HASLEY, ROBERT NATHAN, income tax preparation co. exec.; b. Newport Twp., Ohio, Apr. 2, 1933; s. Nathan and Nellie (Williamson) H.; student Marietta Coll., 1951-52; m. Thelma Marie Cottrill, Apr. 18, 1954; children—Deborah Marie Hasley Wallace, Vicky Diane Hasley Lentz, Roberta Nell, James Paris, Jeffrey Robert. Asst. mgr. Broughton Dairy Store, Marietta, 1952-59; owner, mgr. Piplate Cafeteria, Marietta, 1959-67, Piplate Drive Inn, Belpre, 1963-64; office mgr., city asst. H & R Block, Columbus, Ohio, 1965-66, office mgr., 1967, Parkersburg W.Va., 1967, dist. mgr., satellite dir., Greensburg, Pa., 1967—. Mem. Luxor Vol. Fire Dept., 1971—. Recipient regional awards of recognition for pub. relations, 1970, 71, 74-76. Mem. Central Westmoreland C. of C., Internat. Platform Assn. Clubs: Three-Thirteen CB, Moose. Home: RD 8 Box 96 Hasley Ln Greensburg PA 15601 Office: Suite 2A 128 E Pittsburgh St Greensburg PA 15601

HASNER, ROLF KAARE, food equipment mfg. co. exec.; b. Oslo, Norway, Mar. 15, 1919; s. Harald Alexander and Henny (Christensen) H.; grad. Norwegian Mil. Acad., 1939; M.B.A., Norwegian U. Commerce and Sci., 1943, U. Chgo., 1947; m. Edel Jensen, May 26, 1956; children—Richard, Nina. Clk., Nat. Bank of Norway, Oslo, 1940-41; economist A.S. Lilleborg Fabrikker, Oslo, 1943-45; bus. cons., Oslo, 1947-51; bus. cons.; newspaper corr., N.Y.C., 1951-57; v.p. Globe Slicing Machine Co., Inc., Stamford, Conn., 1957-65, exec. v.p., 1965—, also dir.; dir. Globe Slicing Machine Co. Ltd. (Can.), Stimpson Computing Scale Co. Inc., Louisville. Bd. dirs. Norwegian Am. Mus., Decorah, Iowa. Served with Armed Forces, Norway, 1940-45. Rockefeller Found. scholar, 1946-47. Mem. Norwegian-Am. C. of C. (dir., mem. exec. com. 1958—). Lutheran. Clubs: Landmark (Stamford); Skytop (Pa.); Greenwich Country, Greenwich Skating, Greenwich Rotary (pres. 1978-79, dir.). Home: Bobolink Ln Greenwich CT 06830 Office: PO Box 1217 Stamford CT 06904

HASSELBACHER, HAROLD HARDY, elec. engr.; b. Downers Grove, Ill., Jan. 6, 1922; s. Harold Hardy and Zella Mae (Bird) H.; B.E.E., Ill. Inst. Tech., 1948; m. Helen Louise Hubbard, Mar. 4, 1944; children—Carol Ann Lamos, Catherine Jane McMullen, Susan Helen. Design engr. RCA, Camden, N.J., 1948-49; v.p. engring. McCleery Engring. and Mfg. Co., Chgo., 1950-61; founder, pres. Control Masters Inc., Downers Grove, Ill., 1961—. Deacon, Congl. Ch. Downers Grove, 1952-55. Served with USAAF, 1943-45. Decorated Air medal. Republican. Clubs: Lions (pres. 1972-73), Good Samaritan (Downers Grove); Country of Naples (Fla.). Home: 648 61st St Downers Grove IL 60515 Office: 5013 Chase St Downers Grove IL 60515

HASSELL, MORRIS WILLIAM, lawyer; b. Jacksonville, Tex., Aug. 9, 1916; s. Alonzo Seldon and Cora (Rainey) H.; A.A., Lon Morris Coll., 1936; LL.B., U. Tex., 1942; m. Mauriete Watson, Sept. 3, 1944; children—Morris William, Charles Robert. Tchr., Cherokee County Pub. Schs., 1937-38; admitted to Tex. bar, 1942; pvt. practice since 1946, mem. firm Norman, Hassell, Spiers, Holland & Thrall; sec. S.W. Title & Guaranty Co. Tex.; dir. First State Bank of Rusk; chmn. bd. Swift Oil Co.; v.p., dir. H & I Oil Co., Citizens Indsl. Life Ins. Co. County atty. Cherokee County, Texas, 1943-46; mayor Rusk, 1959-63. Democratic nominee for County atty., 1942, 44. Mem. state adv. com. Wesley Found., Austin, Tex.; bd. devel. Lon Morris Coll.; scoutmaster Boy Scouts Am., 1944-45. Fellow Am. Coll. Probate Counsel, Am. Bar Found., State Bar Tex. Found.; mem. C. of C. (pres.), Am., E. Tex. bar assns., State Bar Tex. (dir., chmn. gen. practice sect. 1967-68, chmn. profl. ethics com. 1970—). Methodist (steward). Odd Fellow, Mason, Kiwanian (dist. lt. gov.). Office: First State Bank Bldg Rusk TX 75785

HASSETT, CHANDLER JEROME, constrn. co. exec.; b. Kansas City, Mo., Apr. 13, 1938; s. Chandler O. and Mary Margaret (Hogerty) H.; B.S., Ariz. State U., 1961; postgrad. in law U. Ariz., 1962; m. Patricia Ann Lowe, Jan. 30, 1963; children—Michael Jerome, Eden Colleen, Shannan Kathleen, Patrick Jerome. Pres., C.J. Hassett Corp., Phoenix, 1964—, Hassett Devel. Corp., 1977—. Served with USAFR, 1961-67. Mem. Asso. Gen. Contractors Am. (dir. Ariz. bldg. chpt. 1978—, pres. chpt. 1979-80), Am. Inst. Constructors, Republican. Roman Catholic. Clubs: Kiva, Plaza, Phoenix Country; Univ. (Houston). Home: 41 W Marlette St Phoenix AZ 85012 Office: 110 W Camelback Rd Phoenix AZ 85013

HASSON, JAMES KEITH, JR., lawyer; b. Knoxville, Tenn., Mar. 3, 1946; s. James Keith and Elaine (Biggers) H.; B.A. with distinction in Econs., Duke U., 1967, J.D. with distinction, 1970; m. Loretta Jayne Young, July 27, 1968; 1 son, Keith Samuel. Admitted to Ga. bar, 1971; asso. firm Sutherland, Asbill & Brennan, Atlanta, 1970-76, partner, 1976—; dir. House-Hasson Hardware Co., Knoxville; adj. prof. law Emory U., Atlanta, 1973—. Trustee, Met. Atlanta Crime Commn., 1978—. Served to 1st lt. USAR. Mem. Am. Bar Assn., State Bar Ga., Atlanta Bar Assn. (gen. counsel 1976-80, President's Disting. Service award 1980), Nat. Health Lawyers Assn., Nat. Assn. Coll. and Univ. Attys. Presbyterian. Club: Lawyers (Atlanta). Home: 3185 Chatham Rd NW Atlanta GA 30305 Office: 3100 1st National Bank Tower Atlanta GA 30383

HAST, EDNA F., lawyer, business exec.; b. Indpls., Dec. 3, 1940; d. William D. and Elizabeth (Franck) H.; B.A., Ind. U., 1961; J.D., U. Chgo., 1964. Admitted to Ill. bar, 1964, U.S. Supreme Ct. bar, 1969; asso. firm White & Smith, Chgo., 1964-67; individual practice law, Chgo., 1967—; asst. counsel Borg-Warner, Chgo., 1974-78, gen. counsel, 1978—, asst. sec., 1980—, also dir. Trustee Latin Sch. Chgo., 1978—; bd. dirs. Newberry Library. Mem. Am. Bar Assn., Ill. State Bar Assn., Chgo. Bar Assn., Am. Judicature Soc. Clubs: University, Saddle and Cycle. Home: 210 4th St Wilmette IL 60091

HASTEN, MICHAEL VAUGH, state commerce commn. ofcl.; b. Chgo., Sept. 16, 1946; s. Erwin Joseph and Kathryn Olivia (Vaughn) H.; B.A., St. Mary of the Lake U., 1968; J.D., Loyola U., 1974; m. Sara J. Hasten, Oct. 16, 1971. Successively counsel Ill. State Bd. Elections, asso. firm Burditt & Calkins, Chgo., gen. counsel, asst. dir. Ill. State Dept. Ins., spl. asst. to Gov. James R. Thompson, Springfield, Ill.; now chmn. Ill. Commerce Commn., Chgo. Mem. Am. Bar Assn., Ill. State Bar Assn., Chgo. Bar Assn. Roman Catholic. Club: Athletic. Office: 160 N LaSalle Chicago IL 60601

HASTINGS, CAROLE ANNE, personnel exec.; b. Allentown, Pa., June 2, 1949; d. Joseph Andrew and Irene Cecelia (La Buda) Mullen; student U. Del., 1967-69; B.S. cum laude, Keene State Coll. (U. N.H.), 1975, M.Ed., 1980; doctoral candidate Vanderbilt U.; m. Marcus W. Hastings, Dec. 18, 1976. With E.I. Du Pont De Nemours & Co., Inc., Newark, 1969-72; classification analyst/asst. dir. personnel Harford County Govt., Bel Air, Md., 1975-77; mgr. personnel services N.H. Sch. Adminstrv. Unit 29, Keene, 1977—; lectr., cons. in field. Bd. dirs. United Way, 1978-79; mem. Harford County Human Rights Commn., 1976-77. Recipient Gold award Monadnock United Way, 1978, 79, 80; citation for service to community, Harford County, Md., 1977. Mem. Am. Mgmt. Assn., Am. Assn. Sch. Personnel Adminstrs. Office: 34 West St Keene NH 03431

HASTINGS, JAMES C., business cons.; b. Delight, N.C., Aug. 1, 1943; s. J.C. and Selma Jane (Short) H.; B.S., Appalachian State U., 1966, M.A., 1968; m. Karen Blalock, July 5, 1963; children—K. Michaele, J. Cory. Recreation dir. Town of Boone (N.C.), 1967-70; field dir. N.C. chpt. Nat. Cystic Fibrosis Found., 1970-72; field. dir. Com. To Reelect Pres., 1972; tourism dir. State of N.C., Raleigh, 1973-75; dir. new franchise sales Hardees Food Systems, Rocky Mount, N.C., 1975-77; pres. Hastings & Key Assos., Boone, 1977—; v.p., dir. Regency Investment Inc., Boone, 1976—, Regency Restaurants Inc., Boone, 1978—, Dermox, Inc., of W.Va., Boone, 1977—. Bd. dirs. N.C. Zool. Council. Mem. Nat. Assn. Zoos and Parks, N.C. Zool. Soc., Internat. Platform Assn., U.S. Restaurant Assn., U.S. Jaycees (v.p. 1974-75, Upson award 1974, Dunnigan award 1975), N.C. Jaycees (pres. 1973-74). Republican. Methodist. Home and office: PO Box 2101 Boone NC 28607

HASTINGS, MERRILL GEORGE, JR., publisher; b. Dedham, Mass., May 12, 1922; s. Merrill G. and Emita E. (Zeil) H.; grad. Taft Sch., 1940; ed. Bowdoin Coll.; m. Priscilla G. Brayton, July 31, 1948; children—William and Deborah. Pres., Skiing Pub. Co., Denver, 1950-64; pres. Colo. Mag., Inc., Denver, 1964-77, Mountain Bus. Pub., Denver, 1972-77; pres. Hastings, Johnson & White, mktg. cons., Vail, Colo., 1979-80; pres. Energy Pub. Co., Denver, 1980—. Served with Brit. Army, 1944-45. Recipient Austrian IX Winter Olympic medal. Mem. Colo. Press Assn. Club: Denver. Home: Sunnyvail Angus Ranch McCoy CO 80463 Office: 10488 W 6th Pl Denver CO 80215

HASTINGS, ROBERT DEAN, editor; b. Effingham, Ill., July 5, 1925; s. Cecil and Ethel (Butler) H.; student Northwestern U., 1944, Coll. Mortuary Sci., 1948, Springfield Jr. Coll., 1951; m. Beverly Jo Gregory, Dec. 6, 1953; children—Gregory, Craig, Tracy Lynn, Randy, Eric. Funeral dir., embalmer Waddington Funeral Home, Tuscola, Ill., 1949; pub. relations and license supr. Sec. State Ill., 1950-54; asst. cashier Tuscola (Ill.) Nat. Bank, 1954-56; editor, pub. Tuscola Review, 1957—. Twp. clk., Tuscola, 1965—; dep. coroner Douglas County (Ill.), 1977-80. Served with USNR, 1943-46. Recipient Pub. Service award Nat. Police Officers Assn. Am., 1965. Mem. Soc. Profl. Journalists, Am. Legion (comdr. 1968-69), VFW, Sigma Delta Chi. Mason, Elk, Rotarian (pres. 1973-74), Kiwanian. Club: Am. Business (pres. 1965-66) (Tuscola). Home: 36 Hillcrest Dr Tuscola IL 61953 Office: 115 W Sale St Tuscola IL 61953

HASTINGS, ROBERT LAWRENCE, mortgage ins. co. exec.; b. Kenosha, Wis., May 18, 1925; s. H. Lawrence and Priscilla Esther (Rahel) H.; B.S. in Econs., U. Wis., 1949, postgrad. Grad. Sch. Banking, 1964; m. Jean Dell Bieler, Sept. 10, 1949; children—Heather, Thomas, Heidi. With Hastings Realtors & Insurors, Kenosha, 1949-58; asst. v.p. 1st Nat. Bank of Kenosha, 1958-65; exec. v.p. Continental Mortgage Ins. Co., Madison, Wis., 1965-72; partner Hastings, Schienle & Assos., Madison, 1972-73; pres. Foremost Guaranty Corp., Madison, 1973—, also dir. Mem. Kenosha Bd. Edn., 1955-61, pres., 1958, 60; m. Shorewood Hills Plan Commn. Served with USAAF, 1943-45; ETO. Decorated Air medal with two oak leaf clusters. Mem. Soc. Real Estate Appraisers (internat. pres. 1978), Am. Inst. Real Estate Appraisers Mortgage Ins. Cos. Am., Trade Assn. (exec. com.). Republican. Congregationalist. Club: Downtown Rotary (Madison). Home: 3549 Lake Mendota Dr Madison WI 53705 Office: 131 W Wilson St Madison WI 53703

HASTINGS, SAMUEL DAVID, r.r. exec.; b. Trenton, Feb. 25, 1928; s. Samuel Alexander and Marie Veronica (Gunning) H.; A.A. in Acctg., U. Pa., 1960; m. Marie A. Vetter, Nov. 8, 1952; children—Samuel Robert, Elizabeth Ann. With Pa. R.R., 1947-68, supr. gen. acctg., Indpls., 1961-62, Phila., 1963-65, supr. budget and analysis, 1966-67, mgr. budget adminstrn., 1968; regional comptroller Penn Central Transp. Co., Phila., 1969-72, mgr. acctg. ops., 1972-74; mgr. corp. acctg. Consol. Rail Corp., Phila., 1974-77, dir. corp. acctg., 1977—. Served with U.S. Army, 1946-47. Mem. Assn. Am. Railroads. Democrat. Roman Catholic. Home: 6 Thistle Rd Levittown PA 19056 Office: 6 Penn Center Plaza Room 806 Philadelphia PA 19104

HASTY, JAMES ALLEN, mfg. co. exec.; b. Moline, Ill., June 8, 1947; s. Edward James and Margaret Ivalee (Johnson) H.; B.A., N. Park Coll., 1969; A.A., Black Hawk Coll., 1967; postgrad. No. Ill. U., 1974; m. Janice Ruth Enderton, June 21, 1969; children—Jason Richard, Jodine Suzzanne, Jennine Danielle. Sta. attendant, bookkeeper Hasty's Mobil Inc., East Moline, Ill., 1958-69; auditor McGladrey, Hansen, Dunn & Co., Moline, 1974-76; treas. Swords Veneer & Lumber Co., Rock Island, Ill., 1976—, Swords Internat. Corp., 1976—, Genwove U.S. Ltd., Indian Trail, N.C., 1977—, also dir. Bd. dirs. Youth for Christ, Rock Island, 1976—; deacon Elim Covenant Ch., 1976-78. Served with USAF, 1969-73. C.P.A., Ill. Mem. Am. Inst. C.P.A.'s, Ill. Soc. C.P.A.'s, Nat. Assn. Accts. Republican. Home: 5001 48th St A Moline IL 61265 Office: 37th and 7th St Rock Island IL 61265

HATALA, ROBERT JOHN, major capital equipment mfg. co. exec.; b. N.Y.C., Nov. 9, 1935; s. John and Marie H.; B.S., Fordham U., 1957; M.B.A., Fairleigh Dickinson U., 1965; m. Mary Jo Sturges, July 19, 1958; children—Karen, Thomas, Elaine, Ellen, James, Robert, Peter, John. Mgr. mgmt. systems Kearfott, Little Falls, N.J., 1960-68; project mgr. GAF Corp., N.Y.C., 1968-69; dir. mgmt. systems Standard & Poors, N.Y.C., 1969-70; dr. info. mgmt. systems, Research-Cottrell, Somerville, N.J., 1970—; mem. adj. faculty Somerset County Coll., Somerville. Served to capt. U.S. Army, 1958. Mem. U.S. Power Squadron (comdr.). Home: RD 4 Box 87-B Haytown Rd Lebanon NJ 08833 Office: PO Box 1500 Somerville NJ 08876

HATCH, (ALDEN) DENISON, advt. copywriter, designer, author; b. N.Y.C., Aug. 15, 1935; s. Alden R. Hatch and Ruth Brown Hatch Elwell; student Kenyon Coll., 1953-54; A.B. in English, Columbia, 1958; m. Margaret Cook, July 12, 1970. Sales mgr. Franklin Watts, Inc., Pubs., N.Y.C., 1961-64; mem. staff advt. sales Library Jour. mag., N.Y.C., 1965-66; copywriter, dir. new products Grolier Enterprises, N.Y.C., 1966-68; dir. book club Crowell Collier and Macmillan, N.Y.C., 1968-69; dir. book clubs Meredith Corp., Manhasset, N.Y., 1970-71; v.p., account exec. Walter Weintz & Co., Stamford, Conn., 1972-75; pres. Denison Hatch Assos., Inc., direct response advt. copy and design, 1976—. Served with AUS, 1959-61. Mem. Delta Kappa Epsilon. Episcopalian. Clubs: Players (N.Y.C.); Nutmeg Curling (Darien, Conn.). Author: Statuary Rape, 1961; Statues of Limitations, 1962; Cedarhurst Alley, 1970; The Fingered City, 1973; The Stork, 1977. Home: 210 Red Fox Rd Stamford CT 06903

HATCH, FRANCIS ERWIN, pharmacist; b. Northwood, Iowa, June 14, 1927; s. Francis Erwin and Wilma Beatrice (Palmer) H.; student U. Minn., 1946-47; B.S., U. Colo., 1950; m. Mary Lulu Ganschow, June 27, 1952. Mgr., Hatch Drug Co., Denver, 1951-62; operator, owner Super Drug Co., Denver, 1963—, Happy Canyon Super Drug Co., Denver, 1972—, Yosemite Super Drug Co., Denver, 1975—. Served with USNR, 1945-46. Republican. Home: 14 Sunrise Dr Englewood CO 80110 Office: 1665 S Colorado Blvd Denver CO 80222

HATCH, JAMES HENRY, III, steel fabricating co. exec.; b. N.Y.C., Dec. 6, 1922; s. James Henry, Jr. and Velma Frances (Davis) H.; B.S. in Mech. Engring., U. Mo., Columbia, 1947; m. Dorothy Louise Stickrod, Oct. 11, 1947; children—Steven Warren, James Scott, Carol Louise. Engr., Kansas City Structural Steel Co. (Kans.), 1947-51; prodn. mgr. Rock Island Bridge & Iron Works (Ill.), 1951-54; founder, 1954, since pres. Shawnee Steel Co. (Okla.); guest lectr. in field; bd. dirs. Okla. Council Econ. Edn., Shawnee Indsl. Found. Bd. dirs. Pottawatomi County chpt. A.R.C. Served to 1st lt. USAAF, 1943-45. Named Kiwanis Shawnee Citizen of Year, 1968, Shawnee Jaycee Boss of Year, 1970; registered profl. engr., Okla., Kan. Mem. Shawnee C. of C. (dir.), Assn. Industries Okla. (dir.), Central Fabricators Assn. (dir.), Okla. Steel Fabricators Assn., Am. Inst. Steel Constrn., Asso. Gen. Contractors (asso.), U.S. C. of C., Okla. C. of C., Shawnee C. of C., Sigma Chi. Republican. Presbyterian. Clubs: Rotary (Shawnee Rotarian of Year award 1977), Elks. Home: 2111 N Minnesota St Shawnee OK 74801 Office: PO Box 1344 Shawnee OK 74801

HATCH, JOHN ALVA, semicondr. co. exec.; b. Helper, Utah, June 14, 1933; s. Thorit and Janet (Freeman) H.; B.S., U. Utah, 1955, U. Wyo., 1969; m. Jo Elizabeth Dawn, June 13, 1954 (div. 1972); children—Carol, Susan; m. 2d, Josephine Reyna, May 31, 1980. Commd. 2d. lt. U.S. Air Force, 1955, advanced through grades to capt., 1968; ret. 1968; engr. Collins Radio Co., Cedar Rapids, Iowa, 1969-71; mgr. engring. Nat. Semicondr. Corp., Santa Clara, Calif., 1972-79; engring. mgr. Advanced Micro Devices, SDN BHD,

Penang, Malaysia, 1979—. Recipient Commendation medal. Mem. Am. Contract Bridge League (life master), Sigma Tau. Republican. Episcopalian. Inventor in field. Home: 2A Lorong Gajah Tan Jone Bungah Penang Malaysia Office: care AMD Penang 901 Thompson Pl Sunnyvale CA 94086

HATCHER, HARRIS HICKOX, ins. agt.; b. Springfield, Ill., Oct. 14, 1950; s. Robert Evans and Jeanne (Hickox) H.; A.B. in English Lit., Washington U., St. Louis, 1973, M.A., 1974; m. Sharon Lynn Starkey, Nov. 27, 1976; 1 dau., Tracey Lynn. Asst. underwriter Continental Ins. Cos., St. Louis, 1975-76; field rep. Home Ins. Cos., St. Louis, 1976-77; spl. agt. N.H. Ins. Group, Springfield, Ill., 1977-79; mktg. mgr. Am. Internat. Group, Springfield, 1979-80; asso. R.W. Troxell & Co., ins. brokerage, Springfield, 1980—. Chester Sikking scholar, 1977. Episcopalian. Clubs: Masons (32d degree), Shriners. Home: 1412 Noble Ave Springfield IL 62704 Office: 300 S Grand Ave W Springfield IL 62704

HATCHER, WILLIAM C., mfg. co. exec.; b. Breeker, Ala., 1922; married. With Genuine Parts Co., 1940—, sales mgr. Birmingham br., 1949-52, mgr. New Orleans ops., 1952-61, in charge Atlanta ops., 1961-65, exec. v.p. ops., 1965-73, pres., 1973—, also dir.; dir. Munich Am. Reassurance Co., Nat. Service Industries. Office: Genuine Parts Co 2999 Circle 75 Pkwy Atlanta GA 30339*

HATFIELD, CHARLES HOWARD, JR., economist; b. Shreveport, La., Dec. 28, 1937; s. Charles Howard and Thelma E. (Carruth) H.; B.A., U. N.Mex., 1961, M.B.A., 1963; M.A., So. Methodist U., 1967; m. Sarah E. Richardson, June 19, 1965; children—Charles Howard, III, Elizabeth Ann. Economist, Del Monte Corp., San Francisco, 1963-65; sr. ops. research analyst Gen. Dynamics Corp., Fort Worth, 1967-73; mgr. ops. research Dresser Industries, Dallas, 1973—; dir. Hatfield Hardware & Lumber Co.; instr. econs. So. Meth. U., 1965-66. Mem. Am. Econs. Assn., Econometric Soc., Omicron Delta Epsilon, Phi Delta Theta. Home: 313 High Brook Dr Richardson TX 75080 Office: 1505 Elm St Dallas TX 75221

HATFIELD, ROBERT SHERMAN, hosp. exec.; b. Utica, N.Y., Jan. 16, 1916; s. Albert R. and Mary (Sherman) H.; student Cornell U., 1937; LL.B., Fordham U., 1945; grad. Advanced Mgmt. Program Harvard U., 1954; m. Roberta Sullivan, May 8, 1937; children—Roberta A. (Mrs. Alexander M. Williamson), Suzanne S. (Mrs. John A. Miele), Molly J., Robert Sherman. With Continental Group, Inc., N.Y.C., 1936-81, exec. v.p., 1962-69, sr. exec. v.p., chief operating officer, 1969-71, chmn. bd., chief exec. officer, 1971-81, also dir.; pres., chief exec. officer N.Y. Hosp., N.Y.C., 1981—; dir. Kennecott Corp., Eastman Kodak Co., Citicorp/Citibank, N.A., Gen. Motors Corp., Johnson & Johnson, Standard Brands, Inc., N.Y. Stock Exchange. Trustee Cornell U., Conf. Bd.; mem. Bus. Council; chmn. Internat. Exec. Service Corp. Clubs: Pinnacle, Cornell, Links (N.Y.C.); Blind Brook (Port Chester, N.Y.); Pine Valley (N.J.); Augusta Nat. (Ga.). Home: Greenwich CT 06830 Office: 633 3d Ave New York NY 10017

HATFIELD, RONALD LEWIS, data processor; b. Balt., Mar. 31, 1951; s. Charles Reed and Lillian (Blackburn) H.; high sch. diploma U.S. Armed Forces Inst., 1970. Mgr. data processing English/Am. Tailoring, Balt., 1971-78; customer support rep. Sperry Univac, Balt., 1978-79; mgr. data processing Publ. Press, Balt., 1979—. Served with U.S. Army, 1968-71. Cert. first-aid instr. ARC. Mem. Am. Legion. Home: 4022 Roland Ave Baltimore MD 21211 Office: 200 N Bentalou St Baltimore MD 21223

HATFIELD, W. C., bank exec.; b. Denison, Tex., Aug. 18, 1926; s. Roy E. and Henretta (Biggerstaff) H.; B.S., Austin Coll., Sherman, Tex., 1950; M.B.A., Tex. A&M U., 1951; m. Wilma Leura Nichols, July 5, 1953; children—David Lee, Sharon Linn, Amy Dawn. Acct., Peat, Marwick, Mitchel & Co., Dallas, 1951-57; with Republic Nat. Bank Dallas, 1957-74, sr. v.p., 1970-72, exec. v.p., 1972-74; exec. v.p., chief fin. officer Republic of Tex. Corp., bank holding co., Dallas, 1974-77, pres., 1977-78, vice chmn. bd., 1978—, also dir.; dir. Halliburton Oil Producing Co., Stewart Office Supply Co.; pres. Exchange Nat. Life Ins. Co.; chmn. bd. Republic Exchange Co. Chmn. bd. dirs. Christian Edn. Found., Dallas; trustee Harding U., Abilene Christian U.; bd. dirs. Community Council Greater Dallas. Served with U.S. Army, 1944-46; Philippines. C.P.A., Tex. Mem. Tex. Soc. C.P.A.'s (treas. 1972-73, pres. Dallas chpt. 1967-68), Tex. Bank Holding Cos. (treas.), Res. City Bankers, Am. Inst. C.P.A.'s, Dallas County Public Health Services, Dallas Symphony Assn. Mem. Ch. of Christ. Club: Breakfast (Dept. Commerce). Contbr. numerous tax and estate planning articles to profl. jours., 1960's. Office: PO Box 222105 Dallas TX 75222

HATHAWAY, ARTHUR JUSTIN, printing co. exec.; b. Dallas, Jan. 11, 1953; s. Herbert Hoover and Dawn (Leggett) H.; student S.W. Tex. State U., 1976-77; m. Delia Sanchez, Mar. 31, 1977; 1 son, Brian Patrick. Print shop mgr. BBA Advt., San Antonio, 1969-72; prodn. mgr. Pacesetter Pub. Co., San Antonio, 1972-73; print shop mgr. Sherwood Van Lines, San Antonio, 1973-75; vocat. printing instr., supr. Gary Job Corps., San Marcos, Tex., 1975-78; prodn. mgr. Bennett Printing Co., Dallas, 1978—; gen. mgr. Multicopy Printing Co., San Antonio, 1980—; coordinator graphic communications Woodcreek Resort, Wimberly, Tex., 1977-78. Bd. dirs. Miss. Black San Antonio Beauty Pagent, 1976-77. Recipient cert. of Achievement, Eastman Kodak Co., 1979, Dallas Sch. Printing Papers, 1979. Mem. Internat. Graphic Arts Edn. Assn., Council Reprographics Execs., Graphic Arts Tech. Found., Am. Printing History Assn., Internat. Club of Printing House Craftsmen, San Antonio Litho Club. Democrat. Baptist. Club: Dallas Litho. Home: 131 Claremont Ave San Antonio TX 78209 Office: 307 E Nakoma St San Antonio TX 78216

HATHAWAY, LOUIS EDMUND, III, ins. co. exec.; b. Springfield, Mass., Sept. 16, 1936; s. Louis Edmund Jr. and Edith (Weeks) H.; B.A., Brown U., 1960; m. Judith Ann Rowand, Aug. 15, 1964; children—Holly Ann, Lisa Jane, Louis Edmund IV. Asst. treas., asst. sec. Union Dime Savs. Bank, N.Y.C., 1960-66, asst. v.p., 1966-68, asst. v.p., asst. mortgage officer, 1968-72, 3d v.p., sr. mortgage officer, 1972-77; v.p. charge real estate and mortgages Manhattan Life Ins. Co., N.Y.C., 1977—; mem. adv. com. N.Y. U. Mortgage Inst. Served with U.S. Army, 1958-59. Fellow Nat. Assn. Cert. Mortgage Bankers; mem. Mortgage Bankers Assn. Am., Mortgage Bankers Assn. N.Y., Real Estate Bd. N.Y. (chmn. mortgage com.), Am. Arbitration Assn. Methodist. Clubs: Middlesex (Darien, Conn.), Masons. Home: 39 Leeuwarden Rd Darien CT 06820 Office: 111 W 57th St New York NY 10019

HATHWAY, CLIFFORD NEWTON, former machinery mfg. co. exec.; b. Waukesha, Wis., Mar. 12, 1918; s. Clifford W. and Maude (Bierkenheier) H.; ed. pub. schs.; m. Ruth Hammond, June 1, 1940; children—Stephen Dallas, John Hammond, Michael Wilson, Deborah Nell, Clifford Newton. With Caterpillar Tractor Co., Peoria, Ill., 1935—, v.p. domestic plants, 1964-69, v.p. personnel and labor relations, 1969-80. Bd. dirs., past pres. Creve Coeur council Boy Scouts Am.; bd. dirs. Central Ill. Jr. Achievement, trustee, past chmn. bd. Eureka Coll.; trustee Lakeview Mus. Mem. Ill., Peoria chambers commerce, Navy League. Club: Peoria Country. Home: 507 W Northgate Rd Peoria IL 61614 Office: 100 NE Adams St Peoria IL 61629

HATTA, RYUTARO, cons. mech. engr.; b. Aizu-Wakamatsu, Japan, May 30, 1912; s. Kichihei and Tokiko (Watanabe) H.; B.Engring., Tokyo Imperial U., 1936; m. Kazuko Ishikawa, Nov. 14, 1939; children—Masako Hatta Suzuki, Hiroshi, Susumu, Tomoko. Asst. mem. Aero. Research Inst. Tokyo Imperial U., 1936-38; engr. Nakajima Hikoki Co., Tokyo, 1938-45; chief designer Watanabe Seikosho, Tokyo, 1947-51; chief mfg. div. Honda Motor Co., Tokyo, 1952-59; asst. mgr. Yamaha Tech. Research Inst., Hamamatsu, Japan, 1960-62; sr. mng. dir. TEAC Corp., Tokyo, 1962-71, exec. v.p. TEAC Seiki Corp., 1971-72; pres. Tokyo Met. Tech. Coll., 1973-79; cons. mech. engr., 1979—. Mem. Soc. Automotive Engrs. Japan, Japan Soc. Mech. Engrs., Internat. House Japan. Home: 834 Oizumigakuen-machi Nerima-ku Tokyo Japan

HATTIS, ALBERT D., business and found. exec.; b. Chgo., Oct. 12, 1929; s. Robert E. and Victoria C. (Kaufman) H.; B.S. with highest distinction, Northwestern U., 1948, M.B.A., 1950; m. Fern Hollobow; children—Kim Allyson, Kay Arlene, John Elmore, Michael Allen, Sharon Beth. Vice-pres., sec.-treas. Robert E. Hattis Engrs., Inc., Hattis Service Co., Inc., Deerfield, Ill., 1950-73; co-mng. dir. Robert E. Hattis Engrs., Inc. AB, Robert E. Hattis Engrs., Inc. BV, 1950-73; v.p., sec.-treas. Servbest Foods, Inc., Highland Park, Ill., 1973-78; v.p., sec.-treas., dir. W.D. Allen Mfg. Co., Sterling Products Co., Inc., Gearex Inc., Dinachrome, Inc., Fulton Machine Co., Inc., A.C. Equipment Co., 1978-80; v.p., sec.-treas. Prime Packing Co., Inc., Haitian Am. Meat and Provision Co., Spanish-Am. Foods, Inc., Packers Provision Co., Inc., Servbest Foods of P.R., Inc., 1973-78; pres., chief exec. officer Frigidmeats, Inc., Chgo., 1978-80; pres., dir. Gits Enterprises, Inc., 1978-80, Double K Bar J Ranch, Inc., 1968—; exec. dir. The Lambs, Inc. Trustee Orphans of the Storm Found., 1972-74, Cobblers Found., 1972-74; mem. advisory bd. Northwestern Psychiat. Inst., Beta Gamma Sigma. Served to capt. USAF, 1946-48, 50-52. Republican. Roman Catholic. Club: Lions. Home: 1720 N Waukegan Rd Lake Forest IL 60045 Office: Junction Tri-State Tollway I-94 and Ill Route 176 Libertyville IL 60048

HAUCK, EARL WILLIAM, indsl. laundry controls co. exec.; b. New Orleans, Oct. 2, 1920; s. Joseph George and Emma Marie (Stopper) H.; B.S., Kingspoint Maritime Acad., 1940; B.S. in M.E., Mich. U., 1949, M.S., 1954, Ph.D., 1956; B.A., U. Hawaii, 1972; m. Dorothea E. Hauck, Aug. 12, 1976; children by previous marriage—Diana, Margaret, Rose Marie, Susan, Joseph, Earl, Karl James. Commd. ensign, U.S. Navy, 1940; advanced through grades to capt., 1960; served in PTO, Korea, Vietnam; ret., 1960; port capt. Calif. Stevedore & Ballast Co., 1968-70; marine surveyor John Mullen & Co., Honolulu, 1970-73; v.p. Fred S. James & Co., Los Angeles, 1974-76; dir. ins., safety and personnel Work Wear Corp., Encino, Calif., 1976—; cons. in field. Decorated Purple Heart, Silver Star. Mem. Safety Soc. Assn., Assn. Profl. Engrs., Soc. Advancement of Sci., Sigma Sigma. Democrat. Roman Catholic. Clubs: New Orleans Athletic, Kobe Wrestling, Elks, K.C., Knights of Lazarus.

HAUG, LOUISE CATO SMITH, publisher; b. LaGrange, Ga., June 27, 1929; d. Clifford Levi and Nora (Tidwell) Cato; student public schs.; divorced; 1 son, Ralph Anthony Marrs. With Publishers Asso. Service, Greenwich, Conn., 1949-57, Boone Publs., Lubbock, Tex., 1957-59; owner Smith Pub. Co., Lubbock, 1959—. Mem. Nat. Assn. Female Execs., Internat. Entrepreneurs Assn. Club: University City. Office: 1713 Ave K Lubbock TX 79408

HAUGE, GABRIEL, ret. banker; b. Hawley, Minn., Mar. 7, 1914; s. Soren Gabrielson and Anna B. (Thompson) H.; A.B., Concordia Coll., Moorhead, Minn., 1935, LL.D., 1957; George Christian fellow, Harvard, 1936-38, M.A., 1938, Social Sci. Research Council fellow, 1946, Ph.D., 1947; LL.D., Bryant Coll. 1958, Muhlenberg Coll., 1959, Gettysburg Coll., 1960; L.H.D., Pace Coll., 1969; m. Helen Landsdowne Resor, Nov. 6, 1948; children—Ann Bayliss, Stephen Burnet and John Resor (twins), Barbara Thompson, Susan Lansdowne, Elizabeth Larsen, Caroline Clark. Asst. dean of men, coach forensics Concordia Coll., 1935-36; budget examiner Office Commr. Budget, State of Minn., 1938; instr. econs. Harvard, 1938-40; sr. statistician Fed. Res. Bank of N.Y., summer 1939; instr. econs. Princeton, 1940-42; chief div. research and statistics, N.Y. State Banking Dept., 1947-50; mem. tech. commn. Joint N.Y. Legislative Com. on Interstate Cooperation, 1949-50; editor Trend editorial, Bus. Week Mag., asst. chmn. exec. com. McGraw-Hill Pub. Co., Inc., 1950-52; research dir. Citizens for Eisenhower, 1951-52; research dir. personal campaign staff Dwight D. Eisenhower, 1952; adminstrv. asst. to Pres. of U.S. for econ. affairs, 1953-56, spl. asst. to Pres. of U.S. for econ. affairs, 1956-58; dir., chmn. finance com. Mfrs. Trust Co., N.Y.C., 1958-61; vice chmn. bd. Mfrs. Hanover Trust Co., 1961-63, pres., 1963-71, chmn. bd., 1971-79; pres. Mfrs. Hanover Corp., 1969-71, chmn. bd., 1971-79; dir. N.Y. Life Ins. Co., Amax, Inc., Chrysler Corp., Royal Dutch Petroleum, Scandinavian Airlines N.Am. Inc., Mfrs. Hanover Corp., N.Y. Telephone Co., Discount Corp. N.Y., Bklyn. Union Gas Co., Am. Home Products Corp. Mem. Council Harvard Found. for Advanced Study and Research, 1959-64; mem. adv., vis. coms. Harvard Center for Internat. Affairs, 1964-70. Bd. dirs. Religion Am. Life, Inc., 1961-70; Greater N.Y. Fund, 1965; trustee Juilliard Mus. Found., 1963-79, Bus. Com. for Arts, 1968-79, Nat. Bur. Econ. Research, Carnegie Endowment Internat. Peace, United Fund Greater N.Y., 1964-79, Council for Latin Am., Com. for Econ. Devel.; vis. com. to dept. econs. Harvard, 1968-73. Served from ensign to lt. comdr. USNR, 1942-46; ret. lt. comdr. Res. Decorated comdr. Royal Order of Phoenix (Greece), Gran Cruz de Isabel la Catolica (Spain); knight comdr. Order Brit. Empire; comdr. Order St. Olav (Norway). Mem. Council Fgn. Relations (dir.) N.Y.C., Assn. Res. City Bankers, Pilgrims U.S., Am. Am. Econs. Assn., Am. Bankers Assn. (mem. found. for edn. in econs. 1966-68), Norwegian-Am. Hist. Assn. Lutheran. Clubs: Univ., Links, Century Assn. N.Y. Athletic (N.Y.C.). Home: 950 Park Ave New York NY 10028 Office: 350 Park Ave New York NY 10022

HAUGEN, ORRIN MILLARD, lawyer; b. Mpls., Aug. 1, 1927; s. Oscar M. and Emma (Moe) H.; B.S. in Chem. Engring., U. Minn., 1948, LL.B., 1951; m. Marilyn Dixon, June 17, 1950; children—Melissa, Kristen, Eric, Kimberly. Admitted to Minn. bar, 1951; patent lawyer Honeywell, Inc., Mpls., 1951-59, Univac div. Sperry Rand, 1959-63; pvt. practice specializing in patent law, Mpls., 1963—; partner Adams, Cwayna & Haugen, Mpls., 1966-68; individual practice, 1968-78; partner firm Haugen & Nikolai, 1979—. Pres., Arrowhead Lake Improvement Assn., Inc., Mpls., 1958-79. Served with USNR, 1945-46. Mem. Am., Minn. bar assns., Minn. Patent Law Assn., Minn. Acacia Alumni Assn. (pres. 1961-63), Acacia. Methodist. Kiwanian. Home: 6612 Indian Hills Rd Edina MN 55435 Office: Midwest Plaza Bldg Minneapolis MN 55402

HAUGH, JAMES CALVIN, investment exec.; b. Omaha, Aug. 28, 1920; s. Jesse Lee and Edith Melissa (Applegate) H.; A.B. cum laude, Stanford, 1942; m. Sarah Breuner, Feb. 11, 1950; children—Jesse B., Sarah E., David F., Charles V. Mechanic, Interstate Transit Lines, Omaha; asst. mgr. (Gt. Falls City Lines (Mont.), 1945; mgr. Burbank City Lines (Calif.), 1945, Everett City Lines (Wash.), 1945-47; v.p., gen. mgr. Western Transit Systems, Inc., San Diego, 1947-53; v.p., gen. mgr. San Diego Transit System and San Diego & Coronado Ferry Co., 1953-65, pres., 1965-70; pres. Calif. Motor Express Ltd., San Diego, 1965-70; chmn. bd. Haugh Enterprises, San Diego, 1971—; dir. First Fed. Savs. & Loan. Mem. Calif. Council on Intergovtl. Relations, State Transp. Systems Evaluation Project. Bd. dirs., pres. Sharp Hosp., Children's Hosp.; bd. dirs. San Diego Chamber Pres.'s Council; bd. govs. Stanford Assos. Served with AUS, 1942-45. Named Young Man of Year, Everett Jr. C. of C., 1948. Mem. San Diego C. of C. (past dir.), Stanford Alumni Assn. (past dir.), Am. Transit Assn. (past dir.), Calif. Bus. Assn. (past v.p. and dir.), Phi Beta Kappa, Tau Beta Pi, Delta Tau Delta. Republican. Episcopalian. Mason, Rotarian. Clubs: Scholia, San Diego Yacht, Stanford, University, San Diego Country (San Diego). Home: 887 Golden Park Ave San Diego CA 92106 Office: PO Box 1271 San Diego CA 92112

HAUGH, LOUIS JOHN, mktg. services co. exec.; b. Menomonie, Wis., Aug. 22, 1939; s. Francis John and Lucille Marie (Zahradka) H.; B.A., U. Wis., 1961, M.A., 1965; m. Judith Farley, Dec. 26, 1964; children—Meredith Lee, Amanda Marie, Daniel Louis. Teaching fellow U. Wis., 1964-65; reporter, copy editor Chgo. Tribune, 1965-67; news editor Business Ins., Chgo., 1967-69; editor Advt. & Sales Promotion, Chgo., N.Y.C., 1969-74; sr. editor Advt. Age, N.Y.C., 1974-78, columnist, 1978—; mng. partner Westport Mktg. Group (Conn.), 1978—; mem. panel of experts Boardroom Reports. Served from ensign to lt. (j.g.) USN, 1961-64. Mem. Wis. Alumni Assn., Naval Res. Assn., Sigma Delta Chi. Roman Catholic. Office: Westport Mktg Group 50 Riverside Ave Westport CT 06880

HAUGHT, DANIEL DEFOREST, ins. co. exec.; b. Fairmont, W.Va., Feb. 21, 1932; s. Cleo DeForest and Bessie (Belle) H.; B.S. in Bus. and Commerce, Fairmont State Coll., 1953; M.S. in Pub. Relations, Boston U., 1966; m. Virginia May House, June 6, 1953; children—David DeForest, Jennifer Ann. Rep. group sales, asst. dir. tng. John Hancock Mut. Life Ins. Co., Boston, 1958-62; exec. sec. Ins. Inst., Boston U., 1962-66; sr. cons. Life Ins. Mktg. Research Assn., Hartford, Conn., 1966-69; v.p. sales Educators Mut. Life Ins. Co., Lancaster, Pa., 1969—. Past mem. bd. dirs. Ephrata Community Hosp.; past trustee Moravian Ch. Mem. Nat. Assn. Life Underwriters, SAR. Clubs: Sales Mktg. Execs. (past dir.). Home: 2 Ridge Dr Lititz PA 17543 Office: 2490 Lincoln Hwy E Lancaster PA 17604

HAUGHTON, RONALD WARING, govt. ofcl., arbitrator; b. Toronto, Can., July 20, 1916; s. Herbert J. and Lilian J. (Strachan) H.; brought to U.S., 1927; naturalized, 1927; B.A., U. Wash., 1937; M.A., U. Wis., 1938; m. Anne Fletcher, Feb. 23, 1952; children—Jan, Patricia, Leslie, John. Assembly worker Gen. Electric Co., 1936-37; chief contested claims Wash. State Unemployment Compensation Div., 1938-40; Rockefeller research grant, 1940; tech. adviser U.S. Social Security Bd., 1941-42; successively disputes dir. Detroit Regional War Labor Bd., dir. strike div. Nat. War Labor Bd., 1942-45; asst. to dir. U.S. Conciliation Service, 1945-47; spl. asst. dir. Inst. Indsl. Relations, U. Calif. at Berkeley, 1947-50; impartial arbitrator Ford Motor Co. and United Automobile Workers, 1950-55; prof. mgmt., co-dir. Inst. Labor and Indsl. Relations, U. Mich., Wayne State U., 1956-79, v.p. urban affairs, 1972-79; chmn. Fed. Labor Relations Authority, Washington, 1979—; pres. Bd. Meditation for community disputes, N.Y.C., 1970-71; permanent arbitrator labor disputes bus. firms and unions, 1948-78; chmn. Ford Motor Co.-United Auto Workers Joint Pension Bd., 1950-78; cons. to Sec. of Labor, 1960, 63, to USAF, 1961, to govt. agys., 1960-62, to UN, Minsk, Russia, 1964, to Mayors of Detroit, Boston, Newark, Phila., San Francisco, 1967, 71, 73, 74. Mem. adv. com. on Pres.'s Com. Equal Employment Opportunity; chmn. Presdl. Fact Finding Bds. in maritime, r.r. and airline industries, 1962-64; 64; fact finder for govs. Mich., Calif., 1966—; lectr. U. Stockholm, 1966; cons. Cost of Living Council, Washington, 1973. Mem. Am. Arbitration Assn. (dir.), Nat. Acad. Arbitrators (past sec.), Indsl. Relations Research Assn., Am. Econ. Assn. Mem. Soc. of Friends. Office: Fed Labor Relations Authority Washington DC 20424*

HAUSER, JON WILLIAM, indsl. designer; b. Sault Ste. Marie, Mich., June 8, 1916; s. Kenneth and Arlie (Hershey) H.; m. Jean MacCallum, Aug. 30, 1939; 1 son, Jon William II. With United Motors Co., 1936; stylist Gen. Motors Corp., 1936-41, Chrysler Corp., 1941-43, Budd Mfg. Co., 1939; dir. design Sears, Roebuck & Co., 1943-45; designer Dave Chapman, Chgo., 1945-46, Barnes & Reinecke, 1946-49, Reinecke Asso., 1949-52; pres. Jon W. Hauser, Inc., St. Charles, Ill., 1952—; vis. prof. U. Ill., 1978-79; dir. State Bank St. Charles. Del., Internat. Council Socs. Indsl. Design, 1963-65, 67; chmn. judging com. Design in Housewares awards, 1966; chmn. judging com. Wescon Indsl. Design Awards, 1968, 69; lectr. indsl. design. Trustee Delnor Hosp., 1973-77, pres. bd. trustees, 1977—. Furnished two designs named in Best 100 Designs History, 1959. Mem. Indsl. Designers Soc. Am. (chmn. bd. 1968), Indsl. Designers Inst. (award 1956, pres. 1962-64, chmn. bd., fellow, men. nat. exec. com., trustee Chgo. chpt); Quiet Birdmen. Clubs: St. Charles Country, Fox Valley Shrine, Masons. Home: 3N981 Rt 31 Saint Charles IL 60174 Office: 10 State Ave Saint Charles IL 60174

HAUSPURG, ARTHUR, utilities co. exec.; b. N.Y.C., Aug. 27, 1925; s. Otto and Charlotte (Braul) H.; B.S.E.E., Columbia U., 1945, M.S.E.E., 1947. Asst. v.p. Am. Electric Power Corp., 1968; v.p. Consol. Edison Co. N.Y., Inc., 1969-73, sr. v.p., 1973-75, exec. v.p., chief operating officer, 1975, pres., chief operating officer, 1975—, also dir.; pres., dir. Empire State Electric Energy Research Corp.; dir. Helium Breeder Assn., Chancellor High Yield Fund, Inc., Chancellor Tax-Exempt Daily Income Fund, Inc., Chancellor High Yield Mcpls., Inc., Chancellor New Decade Growth Fund, Inc. Mem. adv. com. on energy facility sitting NSF; mem. adv. council Faculty of Engring. and Applied Sci., Columbia U.; rep., mem. exec. com. N.E. Power Coordinating Council; bd. dirs. Illuminating Engring. Research Inst., Regional Plan Assn., Com. Econ. Devel., N.Y. Constrn. Users Council, N.Y.C. Partnership, N.Y. Power Pool, Electric Power Research Inst., Econ. Devel. Council N.Y.C. Served with USNR, 1943-46. Fellow IEEE; mem. Nat. Acad. Engring., Chamber Commerce and Industry (dir.). Patentee in field. Contbr. articles to profl. jours. Office: 4 Irving Pl New York NY 10003

HAVENS, CHARLES WILLIAM, III, ins. co. exec.; b. Mar. 22, 1936; s. Charles William and Jessie May H.; A.B., Franklin and Marshall Coll., 1958; LL.B., U. Va., 1961; m. Lucille Bowman, June 3, 1957; children—Charles William IV, Jessica Madaline. Admitted to D.C. bar, Md. bar, U.S. Supreme Ct. bar; asso. firm Covington & Burling, Washington, 1961-66; spl. asst. to gen. counsel Dept. Def., Washington, 1966-67, asst. to asst. sec. def. for internat. security affairs, 1967-69, spl. asst. to dep. sec. def., 1969-79; v.p., gen. counsel Reins. Assn. Am., Washington, 1970-74, pres., 1974—. Recipient Meritorious Civilian Service award Sec. Def., 1969. Mem. Am. Bar Assn., D.C. Bar Assn., Am. Soc. Internat. Law (panel on humanitarian problems and internat. law 1970-72), Am. Arbitration Assn. (comml. panel 1975), Fedn. Ins. Counsel (chmn. com. excess and surplus lines and reins), Internat. Assn. Ins. Counsel. Clubs: Met., Kenwood Country. Home: 4641 Garfield St NW Washington DC 20007 Office: 1025 Connecticut Ave NW Suite 512 Washington DC 20036

HAVERTY, CHARLES F., mfg. co. exec.; b. Bayside, N.Y., Aug. 12, 1931; s. Charles F., Sr., and Marguerite (Murphy) H.; student SUNY, 1949-51; m. Mary A. Heigold, Dec. 6, 1952; children—Charles F., Patrick, Marianne, Timothy. Salesman, Picker X-Ray, 1955-57; N.E. regional indsl. X-Ray sales supr., X-ray div. Westinghouse Co., 1957-59; nat. sales mgr. Ilford, Inc., 1959-64; mktg. mgr., v.p., pres. Profexray div. Litton Industries, 1964-72; v.p. med. subs. Xonics, Inc., Des Plaines, Ill., 1972-77, chmn., chief exec. officer, pres., chief operating officer, 1977—. Served with USAF, 1951-55. Office: 515 E Touhy Des Plaines IL 60018

HAVRANEK, JERRY O., JR., savs. and loan exec.; b. Astoria, N.Y., Feb. 27, 1929; s. Jerry O. and Anna D. (Heins) H.; ed. spl. courses Hofstra U., Ind. U., Am. Inst. Banking, real estate courses; m. Edythe S. Deutsch, July 1, 1948; children—Gary, Allan. With Jamaica Nat. Bank, 1947-48, Title Guarantee & Trust Co., 1948, Jamaica Savs. Bank of N.Y., 1948-61, N.Y. State Banking Dept., 1955; v.p. to exec. v.p. Roosevelt Savs. & Loan Assn., 1961-73; sr. v.p., exec. v.p., now pres., chief exec. officer, chmn. exec. com. Heritage Fed. Savs. & Loan Assn., Huntington, N.Y., 1973—. Bd. overseers Adelphi U. Mem. Sr. Real Estate Appraisers, Columbia Soc. Real Estate Appraisers, Am. Soc. Real Estate Appraisers, L.I. Soc. Real Estate Appraisers, Fin. Mgrs. Group. Republican. Episcopalian. Office: 24 W Carver St Huntington NY 11743

HAWE, DAVID LEE, health care co. exec.; b. Columbus, Ohio, Feb. 19, 1938; s. William Dole and Carlyon Mary (Hassig) H.; m. Margret J. Hoover, Apr. 15, 1962; children—Darrin Lee, Kelly Lynn. Project mgr. ground antenna systems W.D.L. Labs., Philco Corp., 1960-65; credit mgr. for Western U.S., Am. Hosp. Supply Corp., Burbank, Calif., 1965-74; owner, mgr. Hoover Profl. Equipment Co., contract health equipment co., Guasti, Calif., 1974-75; pres. Baslor Care Services, owners convalescent homes, Santa Ana, Calif., 1975—; dir. Mesdis Co., Casa Pacifica, Broadway Assos. Bd. dirs. Santa Ana Community Convalescent Hosp., 1974-79, pres., 1975-79. Served with USN, 1954-56. Lic. real estate broker, Calif. Mem. East Orange County Bd. Realtors. Republican. Roman Catholic. Club: Kiwanis. Home: 18082 Hallsworth Circle Villa Park CA 92667

HAWKES, ROBERT HOWIE, tobacco co. exec.; b. Toronto, Ont., Can., Mar. 9, 1930; s. Robert Kelvin and Agnes (Howie) H.; B.A., Victoria Coll. of U. Toronto, 1951; LL.B., Osgoode Hall Law Sch., 1955; m. Joan May Lepard, May 6, 1960; 1 son, Robert Scott. Student-at-law firm MacKenzie, Wood & Goodchild, 1953-55; called to Ont. bar, 1955, created Queen's Counsel, 1969; asst. to gen. counsel Swift Can. Co., Toronto, 1955-58; gen. counsel, sec. Rothmans of Pall Mall Can. Ltd., Toronto, 1958-70, v.p., gen. counsel, 1970-72, pres., chief exec. officer, 1972—; dir. Rothmans Investments Ltd.; pres. Craven Found., House of Craven, Rock City Tobacco Co. Ltd., Alfred Dunhill of London, Ltd.; gov. North York Gen. Hosp.; exec. com. Rothmans Internat. Ltd.; mem. Bus. Council on Nat. Issues, Ont. Bus. Adv. Council, Can. Tobacco Mfrs. Council. Mem. Can. Bar Assn., Law Soc. Upper Can., Patent and Tradesmark Inst. of Can. Progressive-Conservative. Mem. United Church. Clubs: Empire, Lawyers (Toronto), Granite, National, Hidden Valley, Highlands Ski, Port Sydney Yacht. Office: 1500 Don Mills Rd Don Mills ON M3B 3L1 Canada

HAWKINS, DOLORES DANNER, answering and secretarial service co. exec.; b. Chgo., Aug. 28, 1942; d. Fred A. and Violet L. Danner; B.A. summa cum laude, So. Methodist U., 1978; divorced. Exec. sec. to pres. Rollex Corp., Elk Grove Village, Ill., 1961; pres. Keystone Park Secretarial & Answering Service, Inc., Dallas, 1972—; pres. A Better Answer, Inc., Dallas and Houston, 1979; owner Lakewood Answering Service, Secretarial Center; tchr. Parrish Day Sch., Richardson, Tex., 1978. Coach McKinney (Tex.) YMCA boys and girls soccer teams. Mem. Asso. Telephone Answering Exchanges, Tex. Assn. Telephone Answering Services, Nat. Assn. Female Execs., AAHPER, Tex. Assn. Health, Phys. Edn. and Recreation, Dallas C. of C., East Dallas C. of C., Richardson C. of C., Lakewood-Skillman Bus. and Profl. Assn., Dallas Solar Energy and Conservation Club. Clubs: Willowbend Polo and Hunt, Am. Racquetball (Dallas); Dallas-Ft. Worth Ski. Cons. editor: (J.R. Hawkins) Transpluto, or Should We Call Him Baachus, 1976. Address: 401 Keystone Park Dallas TX 75243

HAWKINS, GEORGE OLIVER, animal feed co. exec.; b. Antioch, Ill., Apr. 13, 1920; s. Arthur McKinley and Harriet Gertrude (Miller) H.; student U. Ill., 1938-39; m. Virginia Mae Ames, Nov. 23, 1942 (dec. 1946); 1 son, Arthur; m. 2d, Sally Elizabeth Welch, June 28, 1948; children—Lark, Scott. Owner, operator Mount Hatcheries, Antioch, 1947-57; sales mgr. FS Services, Inc., Bloomington, Ill., 1952-65; owner, operator Shoes By George, Antioch, 1960-68; v.p., gen. mgr. Hales & Hunter Co., Inc., Chgo., 1965-69; pres. Pioneer Pellets, 1967-69; gen. mgr. Nixon Feed div. ConAgra, Inc., Omaha, 1969-74; pres. Honeggers & Co., Fairbury, Ill., 1974—; pres. several subs.'s; dir. Honegger Feeds. Bd. dirs. Immigrant Service League, Chgo., 1966-70, Travelers Aid Soc., Chgo., 1968-70; past bd. mem., mem. sch. bd., mem. ch. vestry Episcopal Ch. Served with USAAF, 1942-46. Mem. Am. Feed Mfrs. Assn. (dir.), Fairbury Assn. Commerce (pres. 1980). Republican. Clubs: Lions (pres. 1959) (Antioch); Moose (life), Masons. Contbr. articles to profl. publs. Home: PO Box 297 Antioch IL 60002 Office: 201 W Locust St Fairbury IL 61739

HAWKINS, JAMES V., banker; b. Coeur d'Alene, Idaho, Sept. 28, 1936; s. William Stark and Agnes (Ramstedt) H.; B.S. in Bus. Adminstrn., U. Ida., 1959; Diploma, Am. Savs. and Loan Inst., 1966; m. Gail Ruth Guernsey, June 19, 1959; children—John William, Nancy Clare. Mgmt. trainee Gen. Telephone Co. of the Northwest, 1959; asst. mgr., asst. sec. 1st Fed. Savs. and Loan Assn., Coeur d'Alene, 1960-67; exec. v.p. Southwest Devel. Co., 1967; v.p., mng. trust officer 1st Security Bank Idaho, Boise, 1968-72, pres., gen. mgr., 1972—; pres. Statewide Stores Inc., 1972—; dir. United 1st Fed. Savs. Loan Assn., Boise, Chandler Corp. Bd. dirs. Idaho Council Economic Edn., 1978—, St. Alphonsus Hosp. Found.; chmn. adv. bd. Coll. Bus. Adminstrn. and Econs., U. Idaho, 1976—; mem. U. Idaho Found., 1975—; bd. dirs. Boise United Fund. Named One of Three Outstanding Young Men, Idaho Jaycees, 1967. Mem. Am. Inst. Banking, Boise Art Assn. (dir.), U. Idaho Alumni Assn. (dir.), Phi Gamma Delta. Episcopalian. Rotarian. Clubs: Arid, Crane Creek Country (Boise). Home: 1900 Harrison Blvd Boise ID 83702 Office: PO Box 8477 Boise ID 83707

HAWKINS, JOSEPH DALE, cons. actuary; b. DeKalb, Tex., July 5, 1937; s. Wilbur H. and Crystelle R. (Lewis) H.; B.A., U. Tex., Austin, 1963; m. Lisa Ann Owens, Aug. 25, 1979; children—J. Marc, Brian Joel, Christopher Stark. Vice pres. Blue Cross & Blue Shield, Dallas, 1968-75; ins. commr. State of Tex., Austin, 1975-77; owner S.W. Ins. Cons., Dallas, 1977—; chmn. bd. Continental Bankers Fin. Corp., Dallas, 1980—. Served with USAF, 1954-57. Mem. Am. Acad. Actuaries. Methodist. Address: 327 Columbia Dr Rockwall TX 75087

HAWKINS, JOSEPH KEY, communications co. exec.; b. Pomona, Calif., Aug. 13, 1926; s. Joseph Key and Helen Ethel (Hourigan) H.; student Lingnan U., Canton, China, 1948-49, Benares (India) U., 1949-50; B.Sc., Stanford, 1951, M.S., 1952; J.D., Western State U., 1979; m. Kathryn Annette McColl, June 21, 1953 (div. July 1977); children—Ann Patrick, Torrey Sue, Gale Britta. Dir. engring. Alwac Corp., Hawthorne, Calif., 1954-58; dept. mgr. Philco-Ford Co., Newport Beach, Calif., 1959-68; pres. Robot Research Inc., San Diego, 1968—; admitted to Calif. bar, 1979; lectr. digital computer design UCLA, 1961-66. Served with AUS, 1946-48. Mem. Am. Bar Assn., State Bar Calif., IEEE, Mensa, Phi Beta Kappa. Author: Circuit Design of Digital Computers, 1968; (with Kovalevsky, Muroga, Pankhurst, Watanabe) Advances in Information Systems Science III, 1970. Editor: Pattern Recognition, 1970. Asso. editor Pattern Recognition Soc. Journal, 1968-76. Contbr. numerous articles to profl. jours. Home: 7329 Caminito Cruzada La Jolla CA 92037 Office: 7591 Convov Ct San Diego CA 92111

HAWKINS, OLIVER JERRY, mfg. co. exec.; b. Flora, Miss., Nov. 12, 1941; s. Emory Lee and Josie Ethel (Harrell) H.; B.B.A., U. So. Miss., 1966; m. Ann Broome, Nov. 22, 1965; children—Jason, Heather, Taylor. Marketing rep. Armstrong Cork Co., Lancaster, Pa., 1967-68; v.p. Commodore Corp., Omaha, 1968-69; pres. Brougham Industries, Inc., Chino, Calif., 1969—. Served with U.S. Army, 1960-63. Office: 14320 Ramona Ave Chino CA 91710

HAWLEY, JEFFREY LANCE, fin. exec.; b. Shreveport, La., Aug. 28, 1948; s. Eugene Elvin and Opal Marie (Hitchcock) H.; B.S., La. Tech U., 1970; M.B.A., N.E. La. U., 1978; m. Pamela Haley, Mar. 7, 1970; children—Suzanne Marie, Allison Jean. Sr. acct. Peat, Marwick, Mitchell & Co., Houston, 1970-74; fin. planner Olinkraft, Inc., West Monroe, La., 1974-77; v.p., treas., chief fin. officer Palomar Fin., Monroe, La.; dir. First Fidelity Mortgage Co., C.P.A., Tex., La. Mem. Am. Inst. C.P.A.'s, Soc. La. C.P.A.'s (sec.-treas. Monroe chpt.), Mortgage Bankers Assn. Am. (internal mgmt. com.). Republican. Baptist. Clubs: Chauvin Racquet, Optimist (sec.-treas., dir.). Home: 3023 River Oaks Dr Monroe LA 71201 Office: Palomar Fin 1803 Tower Dr Monroe LA 71203

HAWLEY, PHILIP METSCHAN, retail exec.; b. Portland, Oreg., July 29, 1925; s. Willard P. and Dorothy (Metschan) H.; B.S., U. Calif., Berkeley, 1946; grad. Advanced Mgmt. Program, Harvard U., 1967; m. Mary Catherine Follen, May 31, 1947; children—Diane Johnson, Willard, Philip Metschan, John, Victor, Edward, Erin, George. Pres., chief exec. officer, dir. Carter Hawley Hale Stores, Inc., Los Angeles; dir. Atlantic Richfield Co., BankAmerica Corp., Pacific Tel.&Tel. Co., Walt Disney Prodns. Mem. vis. com. Harvard U. Grad. Sch. Bus. Adminstrn., U. Calif. at Los Angeles Grad. Sch. Mgmt.; Trustee Conf. Bd., Com. Econ. Devel., Aspen Inst., Huntington Library and Art Gallery, Calif. Inst. Tech.; chmn. Los Angeles Energy Conservation Com., 1973-74. Served to ensign USNR, 1944-46. Named Calif. Industrialist of Year, Calif. Mus. Sci. and Industry, 1975; recipient award of Merit, Los Angeles Jr. C. of C., 1974, Coro Pub. Affairs award, 1978; decorated hon. comdr. Order Brit. Empire, knight comdr. Star Solidarity, Republic of Italy. Mem. Bus. Council, Bus. Roundtable Phi Beta Kappa, Beta Alpha Psi, Beta Gamma Sigma. Clubs: Calif., Jonathan, Los Angeles Country (Los Angeles); Pacific Union (San Francisco); Newport Harbor Yacht (Newport Beach); Multonomah (Portland). Office: 550 S Flower St Los Angeles CA 90071

HAWRYLIW, ADRIAN OLEH, banker; b. Boryslaw, Ukraine, June 19, 1936; came to U.S., 1950, naturalized, 1957; s. George and Theodosia (Wytwycka) H.; B.A., LaSalle Coll., 1958; M.B.A., Temple U., 1975; m. Dorothy J. Crussard, May 21, 1966; children—Christine, Michael. With Liberty Fed. Savs. & Loan Assn., Phila., 1964—, controller, 1970—, treas., 1978—. Served with AUS, 1959-62. Mem. Fin. Mgrs. Soc. (Nat. Merit award 1977, pres.). Republican. Ukrainian Catholic. Clubs: Ukrainian Am. Sport, Ukrainian Nat. Soccer. Office: 202 N Broad St Philadelphia PA 19102

HAY, ANDREW MACKENZIE, mcht. banking and commodities co. exec.; b. London, Apr. 9, 1928; came to U.S., 1954, naturalized, 1959; s. Ewen Mackenzie and Bertine (Buxton) H.; M.A. in Econs., St. John's Coll., Cambridge U., 1950; m. Catherine Newman, July 30, 1977. Engaged in commodity trade, London and Ceylon, 1950-53; v.p. Calvert Vavasseur & Co. Inc., N.Y.C., 1954-61, pres., 1962-78, pres. Calvert-Peat Inc., N.Y.C., 1978—, Andrew M. Hay, Inc.; chmn. Barretto Peat Inc., N.Y.C., 1974—; radio and TV appearances. Mem. adv. com. on tech. innovation Nat. Acad. Scis., 1978; bd. dirs. Winston Churchill Found. Served to capt. Brit. Army, World War II. Decorated comdr. Order Brit. Empire. Mem. Am. Importer Assn. (pres. 1977-79), Brit. Am. C. of C. (pres. 1966-68), Philippine Am. C. of C. (pres. 1977-79), St. George's Soc. (dir.), St. Andrew's Soc. (dir.). Episcopalian. Clubs: Recess, Downtown Assn. (N.Y.C.). Author: A Century of Coconuts, 1972. Home: 162A E 64th St New York NY 10021 Office: Wall St Plaza New York NY 10005

HAY, GERALD ROBERT, real estate devel. exec.; b. San Diego, Dec. 14, 1935; s. Horace Russell and Alice Lenora (Peacock) H.; B.A., San Diego State Coll., 1957; cert. U. Paris, 1957; diploma advanced mgmt. Stanford U., 1978; m. Constance Jeannine Reynolds, Sept. 6, 1969; children—Clinton Patrick, Jeannine Suzanne. Leasing mgr. Oak Cliff Bank & Trust Co., Dallas, 1960-64; project mgr. David H. Murdock Devel. Co., Orange, Calif, 1964-66; dir. mktg. Del Amo Fin. Center, Torrance, Calif., 1968-71; v.p. City Mgmt. Corp., Orange, 1971-73; dir. sales Grubb & Ellis Co., Los Angeles, 1971-73; v.p., then exec. v.p. Dillingham Devel. Co., Los Angeles, 1973-75, pres., chief exec. officer, 1975-79; exec. v.p., chief operating officer G. L. Lewis Co., Grange, 1979-80; pres. The Hawkins Devel. Co., Santa Ana, Calif., 1981—. Chmn. bd. dirs. Insight for Living, non-profit Christian radio broadcasting orgn. Served with AUS, 1958-60. Mem. Central City Assn. Los Angeles (dir.), Nat. Realty Com., Urban Land Inst., Internat. Council Shopping Centers, Calif. Council Econ. and Environ. Balance. Republican. Mem. 1st Evang. Free Ch. of Fullerton (Calif.). Home: 7331 Stone Creek Ln Anaheim CA 92807 Office: 2001 E 1st St Santa Ana CA 90705

HAY, JOHN WOODS, JR., banker; b. Rock Springs, Wyo., Apr. 23, 1905; s. John Woods and Mary Ann (Blair) H.; A.B., U. Mich., 1927; m. Frances B. Smith, Dec. 28, 1948; children—Helen Mary, John Woods III, Keith Norbert, Joseph Garrett. Pres., dir. Rock Springs Nat. Bank, 1947—, Rock Springs Grazing Assn., 1939—, Blair & Hay Land & Livestock Co., Rock Springs, 1949—; dir. Mountain Fuel Supply Co. Trustee, v.p. William H. and Carrie Gottsche Found. Mem. Sigma Alpha Epsilon. Republican. Episcopalian. Mason (33 deg., Shriner, Jester), Rotarian. Home: 502 B St Rock Springs WY 82901 Office: 333 Broadway Rock Springs WY 82901

HAY, RAYMOND A., duplicating equipment co. exec.; b. L.I., N.Y., July 13, 1928; B.S. in Econs., L.I. U., 1949; M.B.A., St. John's U., 1960; m. Grace Mattson; children—John Alexander, Susan Elizabeth. Mgr., Northeastern div. Monroe Calculating Machine Co. (now Monroe-Sweda), 1958-61; with Xerox Corp., Rochester, N.Y., 1961-75, br. mgr., N.Y.C., 1961-62, zone mgr. Western region, also asst. dir. sales ops. and dir. mktg., 1962-68, group v.p. and gen. mgr. info. systems, 1968, exec. v.p., to 1975; pres., chief operating officer LTV Corp., Dallas, 1975—, also dir.; dir. First City Bancorp. Tex., Diamond Shamrock Corp. Bd. govs. Kennedy Center for Performing Arts; trustee Dallas Mus. Fine Arts, Dallas Symphony Orch.; bd. dirs. Dallas Civic Opera Assn. Mem. Am. Mgmt. Assn., Nat. Sales Execs. Club, Dallas C. of C. (council steering com.). Home: 4312 Bordeaux Dallas TX 75205 Office: LTV Corp PO Box 225003 Dallas TX 75265

HAYANY, ADNAN TAWFIK, engring. telecommunications cons., bus. broker; b. Aleppo, Syria, Mar. 10, 1928; came to U.S., 1947, naturalized, 1964; s. Tawfik Bashir and Fayha Aisha H.; B.S.E.E., U. Mo., Columbia, 1951; m. Ethel Lee Headrick, Aug. 10, 1949; 1 dau., Mayla Adnan. Dept. head Syrian Telephone Adminstrn., Damascus, 1951-54; elec. design engr. H.N.T.B., DeRigne & Assos., Turnbull-Novak, 1954-59; sr. microwave engr. Western Elec. Co., Kansas City, Mo., 1959-75; pres. Hayany Investment & Engring. Corp., Kansas City, 1975—; cons. engr., investment and bus. broker, inventor. Recipient Publ. award Western Elec. Co., 1965, Outstanding Engring. Achievement award, 1974. Mem. Nat. Soc. Profl. Engrs., Mo. Soc. Profl. Engrs., Profl. Engrs. in Pvt. Practice, Kansas City C. of C. Moslem. Contbr. articles to tech. jours. Inventor high power amplifier, microwave local oscillator and dielectric waveguide circuits. Home: 1276 W 72d Terr Kansas City MO 64114

HAYASHI, HAJIME, trading com. exec.; b. San Mateo, Calif., Apr. 13, 1925; s. Kiyoichi and Masue H.; B.A. Doshisha U., 1947; student Stanford U., 1949; B.A., San Francisco State U., 1952; m. Emiko, Feb. 4, 1953; 1 dau., Mami. Dir. Matsushita Electric Trading Co., Ltd., Osaka, Japan, 1953—, pres. numerous subsidiaries including Matsubo Electronic Instrument Co., Matsubo Electronic Components Co., Matsubo Spl. Project Co., Matsubo Credit Sales Co., Matsubo Engring. Co., Tokyo and Osaka, Japan, 1975—. Mem. Japan Machinery Import Assn. Home: 700 Okadaura Sennan-City Osaka 590-05 Japan Office: 48 Andojibashi-Dori 4-Chome Minami-ku Osaka 542 Japan also One Panasonic Way Secaucas NJ 07094 also 400 Bldg Suite 302 400 18th Ave NE Bellevue WA 98004

HAYASHI, KEIICHIRO, mech. engr.; b. Tottori, Japan, Aug. 11, 1929; s. Tomoyuki and Kaoru (Hirotomi) H.; B.S., U. Tokyo, 1953; M.S., U. Ill., 1956; postgrad. Mass. Inst. Tech., 1956; m. Mitsuko Kometani, Dec. 11, 1957; children—Masanari, Shigenari. Came to U.S., 1957. Engr., George G. Sharp, Inc., N.Y.C., 1957-58, Bechtel Assos., N.Y.C., 1958-65, Exxon Research & Engring. Co., Florham Park, N.J., 1965—. Mem. Am. Soc. M.E., Am. Soc. C.E., Welding Research Council (pressure vessel research com.), Am. Petroleum Inst., Sigma Xi. Research on brittle fracture propagation in steel plate, refinery equipment and future energy sources. Home: 31 Carol Rd Westfield NJ 07091 Office: care Exxon Research & Engring Co Florham Park NJ 07932

HAYDEN, LUKE STEPHEN, banker; b. Bklyn., Dec. 26, 1918; s. Luke Patrick and Mary Elizabeth (Acer) H.; B.S., M.I.T., 1941; M.B.A., Syracuse U., 1950; m. Dorothy M. Karb, May 1, 1943; children—Suzanne Mayden Gallup, Patricia Hayden Hodgson, Mimi, Luke. With Syracuse Savs. Bank (N.Y.), 1948-59, v.p., sec., 1957-59; pres. City Savs. Bank, Pittsfield, Mass., 1959—; dir. Drayton Co. Ltd.; v.p., asst. treas. Savs. Bank Investment Fund. Chmn. investment com. Berkshire County Home for Aged Women, 1977—; bd. dirs. Berkshire Art Assn., 1971—. Served to lt. USNR, 1943-46. Mem. Savs. Banks Assn. Mass., Mut. Instns. Nat. Transfer System (dir.), Nat. Assn. Mut. Savs. Banks. Democrat. Roman Catholic. Office: 116 North St Pittsfield MA 01201

HAYDEN, NEIL STEVEN, newspaper pub. exec.; b. N.Y.C., May 23, 1937; s. Aaron Alvin and Selma H. (Turtletaub) H.; student U. Fla., 1955-58, U. Miami, Coral Gables, Fla., 1958; m. Elaine Charlotte Lawson, July 3, 1960 (div. 1975); children—Stephanie, Jennifer, Aaron Alexander II; m. 2d, Carolyn Sue Smith, May 8, 1975; 1 stepson, Michael Sean. Copy staff Miami Herald, 1958; reporter Albany (Ga.) Herald, 1959, Hickory (N.C.) Daily Record, 1959-60; editor Jackson Herald, Jefferson, Ga., 1960-62; editor, pub. Hartwell (Ga.) Sun, pres. The Sun, Inc., 1962-67; pub. Athens (Ga.) Banner-Herald & Daily News, 1967-72; pres., pub. Huntington (W.Va.) Herald-Dispatch & Huntington Advertiser, 1972-76; pres., pub. Oreg. Statesman & Capital Jour., Salem, 1976-79, Courier-Post, Camden, N.J., 1979-80, Bulletin, Phila., 1980—. Bd. dirs. Mission Mill Mus., 1976-79, Marion-Polk United Way, 1976-79, Salem Symphony, 1977-79, Boys' Club of Salem, 1977-79, Oreg. Symphony Soc., 1977-79, Phila. Police Athletic League, World Affairs Council of Phila.; bd. dirs. Cascade council Boy Scouts Am., 1977-79, mem. exec. bd. Camden County council, 1979—; mem. long-range planning com. Salem Art Assn., 1977-79; adv. bd. Phila. Orch. Council, Haddonfield (N.J.) Symphony Soc., 1979—; bd. mgrs. Cooper Med. Center, 1979—; bd. dirs. United Way of Camden County, 1979—; trustee S. Jersey Chamber Found., 1980—; chmn. Salem Multi-Purpose Center Feasibility Task Force, 1978, YMCA Capital Devel. Program, 1978; mem. Citizens for CPR, 1978-79; chmn. funding com. Oreg. Newspaper Found., 1978-79. Recipient numerous nat., state journalism awards, 1961; named Outstanding Young Man of Yr., Huntington Jr. C. of C., 1972. Mem. Am. Newspaper Pubs. Assn., Am. Soc. Newspaper Editors (bull. com. 1976-77, freedom of info. com. 1977-78), Nat. Newspaper Assn., Am. Council on Edn. for Journalism, N.J. Press Assn. (chmn. prodn. com. 1980), N.J. State C. of C., S. Jefsey C. of C. (dir. 1979—), Cherry Hill C. of C. (dir. 1980—), Women in Communication, Sigma Delta Chi (pres. N.E. Ga. chpt. 1969-70, regional dep. dir. 1970). Office: The Bulletin Philadelphia PA 19101

HAYDEN, PAUL A(NTHONY), investment banking and brokerage co. exec.; b. Akron, Ohio, Apr. 26, 1936; s. Paul A. and Clare C. (Yahner) H.; student John Carroll U., 1954-57, Fenn Coll., 1960-61, U. Akron, 1962-63; m. Catherine M. Pittenger, June 28, 1958; children—Julia Barbara, Stephen, Frances, Patrick, Andrew. Owner, pres. Fund. Ways of Summit County, Cuyahoga Falls, Ohio, 1962-67; supr. Goodyear Aerospace Corp., Akron, 1964-67; account exec. Merrill Lynch Pierce Fenner & Smith, Akron, 1967-76; v.p., br. mgr. Butcher & Singer, Inc., Akron, 1976—. Scoutmaster, Troop 152 Gt. Trail council Boy Scouts Am., 1977-80; mem. Democratic Precinct Com., Summit County, Ohio, 1980. Served with U.S. Army, 1957-60. Mem. Summit Sportsmen's Assn. (pres.). Roman Catholic. Clubs: Briar Hill Hunting and Fishing, Kiwanis (club officer and dir.), Loyola of the Lake Retreat Center (officer, dir. and chmn. Friends of Loyola). Home: 807 Washington Ave Cuyahoga Falls OH 44221 Office: Quaker Sq 120 E Mill St Akron OH 44308

HAYDEN, RALPH FREDERICK, public accountant, corp. exec.; b. N.Y.C., Jan. 15, 1922; s. Fred T. and Thrya (Ohlson) H.; B.B.A., Pace Coll., 1951; m. Gloria McCormick, Feb. 27, 1943; children—Craig, Glen. Vice pres., sec., dir. King Kullen Grocery Co., Inc., Westbury, N.Y., 1948—; sr. partner Hayden & Hayden, accountants and auditors, Huntington, N.Y., 1941—. Vice pres. Bi-County Devel. Corp.; pres. L.I. YMCA; bd. dirs. L.I. Com. for Crime Control; vice chmn. Citizens Adv. Com. to Suffolk County Airport. Served with USCGR, 1942-45. Mem. Empire State Assn. Pub. Accountants, Aviation Council L.I. (treas.), Nat. Soc. Pub. Accountants, N.Y. Assn. Ind. Pub. Accountants, USCG Aux., C.W. Post Tax Inst., Real Estate Inst. Clubs: Kiwanis (past pres.), Met. Office: 43 Prospect St Huntington NY 11743

HAYDEN, SPENCER JAMES, mgmt. cons.; b. N.Y.C., Sept. 18, 1922; s. Thomas Churchill and Anna May (Forshay) H.; B.S., St. John's Coll., 1942; M.A., Columbia U., 1946; Ph.D., Fordham U.,

1951; m. Erica Bannister, Feb. 18, 1950; children—Lisa, Christopher, Robert, Wendy. Cons., Booz, Allen & Hamilton, Genoa, Italy and N.Y.C., 1957-61; v.p., sec. Richardson, Bellows, Henry & Co., Inc., N.Y.C., 1961-63; pres. Spencer Hayden Co., Inc., N.Y.C., 1963—; prof. mgmt. Rensselaer Poly. Inst., 1967-70. Trustee Knickerbocker Hosp., N.Y.C., 1963-70. Served to lt. USAAF, 1942-45. Mem. Am. Inst. Indsl. Engrs., Am. Soc. for Microbiology, Am. Psychol. Assn., AAAS. Clubs: Union League (bd. govs. 1980—), Engrs., Columbia U. (N.Y.C.). Author: Solving the Problems of International Operations, 1970. Home: 166 Farrington Ave North Tarrytown NY 10591 Office: 485 Lexington Ave New York NY 10017

HAYDEN, VIRGIL O., actuary; b. Marcola, Oreg., Oct. 17, 1921; s. Albert O. and Bessie (Mortimer) H.; student Oreg. Coll. Edn., 1939-42; B.S., Boston U., 1947; m. Norma F. Colby, May 12, 1946; children—Susan, Sally Ann, Robert. With Mut. Benefit Life Ins. Co., Newark, 1947—, v.p., mathematician, 1966-72, sr. v.p., mathematician, 1972-73, sr. v.p., chief actuary, 1973—; sec.-treas., dir. Retirement Plan, Inc., 1976-80. Trustee, Heart Research Inst., St. Michael's Med. Center, Newark, Served to lt. (j.g.) USN, 1942-46. Fellow Soc. of Actuaries; mem. Am. Acad. Actuaries (charter), Internat. Actuarial Assn. Club: Canoe Brook Country (Summit, N.J.). Office: Mut Benefit Life Ins Co 520 Broad St Newark NJ 07101

HAYDEN, VIRGINIA EVA, pharm. co. cons.; b. Midland, Mich., May 20, 1927; d. Robert James and Altheda Mae (Wood) H.; B.A., Mich. State U., 1949; m. Donald Conrad, Feb. 14, 1952 (div.) Audit clk. City of Midland, Mich., summers 1945-49; stock inventory clk. Dow Chem. Co., 1949-50; budget clk. Upjohn Co., Kalamazoo, 1950-52, budget analyst, 1952-57, accountant, 1957-65, accounting specialist, 1965-69, budget coordinator, 1969-72, budget mgr, 1972-78, exec. devel. cons., 1978—; lectr. local colls.; co-founder, advisor Grow, Orgn. for Upjohn Women; advisor Center for Women's Services, Western Mich. U.; co-founder Kalamazoo Network. Team leader Community Communication Project. Recipient Upjohn award, 1970. Mem. Planning Execs. Inst., Am. Soc. for Tng. and Devel., Kalamazoo Personnel Assn., Audubon Soc., Nat. Wildlife Assn. Clubs: Altrusa of Kalamazoo (pres.), Kalamazoo Nature Center, Mich. State Univ. Alumni. Home: 8207 Bruning Kalamazoo MI 49002 Office: 7000 Portage Rd Kalamazoo MI 49001

HAYERS, PAUL HUGH, lawyer; b. Wichita Falls, Tex., Dec. 2, 1942; s. Carl Edward and Emogene (Wagoner) H.; B.B.A., So. Meth. U., 1964; J.D., Georgetown U., 1967; m. Jannis Baker, Aug. 16, 1964; children—Stephanie Laura, Christopher Mark. Admitted to Tex. bar, 1967; partner McKelvey & Hayers, Electra, Tex., 1968—; city atty. City of Electra, 1976-80; atty. Electra Hosp. Dist., 1973-80; atty. Electra Ind. Sch. Dist., 1973-78. City commr. City of Electra, 1972-75, 80—, mayor pro-tem, 1973-75; dir. Electra Service Corp., 1973-77; sec. Wichita County Tax Appraisal Bd., 1980—. Mem. Electra C. of C. (pres. 1970), Tex. Bar Assn., Wichita County Bar Assn. Democrat. Methodist. Clubs: Lions, Rotary. Home: 200 Southland St Electra TX 76360 Office: 109 N Main St Electra TX 76360

HAYES, BETTINE J. (MRS. M. VINSON HAYES), investment exec.; b. Boston, Sept. 6, 1928; d. Reginald W. P. and Ethel (Thomas) Brown; B.A., Wellesley Coll., 1950; m. M. Vinson Hayes, June 10, 1961; children—M. Vinson III, Juliet Dorothy. Security analyst Merrill Lynch, Pierce, Fenner & Smith, Inc., N.Y.C., 1950-60, 76—, portfolio analyst, 1960-73, Canadian research coordinator, 1967-69; mgr. N.Y. Wellesley Club, 1973-74; researcher Nat. Information Bur., Inc., N.Y.C., 1974-76. Mem. D.A.R. (chpt. treas. 1958-59, historian 1961-62, rec. sec. Colonielles 1961-71, 73-77, treas., 1971-73), N.Y. Soc. Security Analysts. Club: New York Wellesley. Home: 39 Gramercy Park New York City NY 10010 also 11 Spring Close Ln East Hampton NY 11937 Office: One Liberty Plaza New York NY 10080

HAYES, DAVID JOHN, mfg. co. exec.; b. Indpls., July 30, 1943; s. Alfred Henry and Jean Alexander (Morrison) H.; grad. Phillips Exeter Acad., 1961; A.B., Boston U., 1965; M.B.A., Cornell U., 1967. Mgmt. trainee Westinghouse Broadcasting Co., Chgo., Norwalk, Conn., Boston, 1967-71; nat. sales rep. NBC, Chgo., 1971-72; pres. Dana Enterprises, Chgo., 1972-75; v.p. mktg. Micron Industries Corp., Stone Park, Ill., 1975—; dir. New Orleans Hotel Corp. Mem. Assn. M.B.A. Execs., Ill. State Hist. Soc. Clubs: Cornell of Chgo., Boston U. of Chgo., Execs. (Chgo.). Home: 807 Wenonah Ave Oak Park IL 60304 Office: 1830 N 32d Ave Stone Park IL 60165

HAYES, ERNEST A., ins. investment sales; b. New London, Iowa, Jan. 20, 1904; s. Alonzo D. and Margaret E. (Ferrell) H.; student Iowa Wesleyan Coll., 1921-24, H.H.D. (hon.), 1964; A.B., Washington Univ., 1924, M.S., 1926; m. Ruth Anita Irons, Feb. 13, 1937; children—Ruth Jo Ann (Mrs. Edmund J. Farrell), Janet Elizabeth (Mrs. Richard A. Dougherty). President of Central States Mutual Insurance, Assn., 1929-59; chmn. bd. Capitol Savs. & Loan Assn., 1937-77; pres. Hillsboro Savs. Bank (Iowa), 1950-76, Henry County Indsl. Devel. Corp.; chmn. bd. New London State Bank, 1945-76, Town & Country Bank, Quincy, Ill., 1974-76; dir. Hawkeye Bank & Trust Co., Burlington, Iowa, Hawkeye Ban Corp., Des Moines; pres. Hawkeye Nat. Investment Co., 1964-78; vice chmn. Hawkeye Nat. Life Ins. Co. (both Des Moines); dir. Henry Co. Savs. Bank (Mt. Pleasant); vice chmn. Iowa Bus. Devel. Credit Corp.; chmn. bd. Iowa Blue Cross; dir. Iowa Blue Shield; mem. Nat. Adv. Council Hosp. Governing Bds. Mem. exec. com. S.E. Iowa council Boy Scouts Am.; vice chmn. Iowa Hosp. Found., Des Moines; mem. U.S. Hist. Adv. Com., Washington, Hoover Found.; chmn. Iowa Devel. Commn., 1962-78; regional Dir. U.S. Savs. Bond Div.; Republican State Finance Chmn., 1961-69; mem. Nat. Rep. Finance Com., 1961-69; chmn. bd. dirs. Henry County Meml. Hosp., Iowa Wesleyan College; trustee Midwest Research Inst., Kansas City. Recipient S.E. Iowa Man of Yr., 1961. Mem. Iowa Assn. Ind. Ins. Agts., Internat. Livestock Assn. (sec., dir.), Navy League, Sigma Phi Epsilon, Delta Sigma Pi, Omicron Delta Gamma. Methodist. Mason (Shriner). Moose, Elk. Clubs: Kiwanis, Des Moines, Lincoln (Des Moines). Home: 400 Broadway Mount Pleasant IA 52641 Office: Hayes Bldg Mount Pleasant IA 52641

HAYES, JAMES LOUIS, assn. exec.; b. Binghamton, N.Y., Sept. 25, 1914; s. James C. and Margaret (Sullivan) H.; A.B., St. Bernard's Coll. and Sem., 1936; M.A., St. Bonaventure U., 1937; postgrad. Columbia, 1938; D.Bus. Adminstrn. (hon.), Theil Coll., St. Joseph's Coll., U. Cin.; m. Pauline Jacobus, Sept. 1, 1941; children—Elizabeth, James C. With St. Bonaventure U., 1936-59, successively instr. social sci. 1936-38, prof. econs., 1941-59, head dept. bus. adminstrn., 1941-59, coordinator vet. affairs, dir. guidance, 1946-59; dean Duquesne U. Sch. Bus. Adminstrn., Pitts., 1959-70; exec. v.p. devel. Am. Mgmt. Assn., N.Y.C., 1970-71, pres., chief exec. officer, 1971—, also mem. exec. com.; trustee affiliate Am. Grad. Sch. Internat. Mgmt.; pres. Council for Internat. Progress in Mgmt.; dir. Bklyn. Savs. Bank, Equibank, N.A., Levinson Steel Corp., Pitts., Marsteller Inc., Litco Corp., L.I. Trust Co., Nabisco Inc., May Dept. Stores Co. Instr. Am. Inst. Banking, 1941-59; prin. lectr. Am. Mgmt. Assns., N.Y.C., 1956—; mem. faculty Stonier Grad. Sch. of Banking, Rutgers U., 1961—, lectr. Presidents Assn., N.Y.C., 1960—. Mem. Mgmt. Adv. Bd. for N.Y.C. Trustee St. Bonaventure U., 1973—, now vice chmn.; bd. dirs. Greater N.Y. council Boy Scouts Am.; nat. bd. dirs. Nat. Symphony Orch., Washington, 1976—. Recipient Bronze Pelican award Cath. Com. Scouting, Silver Beaver award, also St. George award Boy Scouts Am.; hon. award Order of Cedars of Lebanon; Taylor Key award Soc. Advancement of Mgmt., 1976. Fellow Internat. Acad. Mgmt., Am. Mgmt. Assn. (trustee), Acad. Mgmt.; mem. Newcomen Soc., Fgn. Service Inst., Jr. Achievement N.Y., Council Post Secondary Sch. Accreditation (trustee), Am. Assn. Collegiate Schs. Bus. (newsletter editorial advisor), Omicron Delta Epsilon (nat. honoree 1973), Delta Sigma Pi, Beta Gamma Sigma. Roman Catholic. Home: 400 E 56th St New York NY 10022 Office: 135 W 50th St New York NY 10020

HAYES, PHILIP LOUIS, ins. co. exec.; b. Watertown, N.Y., Sept. 30, 1934; s. Louis Neville and Lorene (Kerr) H.; B.S. cum laude, Syracuse U., 1960, M.B.A., 1962; m. Catherine M. Sears, June 5, 1955. Dist. credit supr. Eastman Kodak Co., Rochester, N.Y., 1962-64; sr. financial analyst Indsl. Indemnity Co., San Francisco, 1964-66, asst. mgr. financial analysis, 1967, mgr. financial analysis, 1968-71, asst. treas., 1971-74, asst. v.p., asst. treas., 1974-76, v.p., asst. treas., 1976—, v.p. numerous subs. cos., 1973—. Chmn. grad. alumni ann. giving campaign Syracuse U. Sch. Mgmt., 1978; bd. dirs. Marin County Republican Com., treas., 1973-76. Served as 2d class petty officer USCG, 1952-56. Mem. Ins. Acctg. and Statis. Assn., Belvedere Sailing Soc., Syracuse U. Alumni Assn. (nat. dir.), San Francisco Mus. Modern Art, M.H. deYoung Meml. Mus., San Francisco Symphony Assn., Marin Symphony Assn., Beta Gamma Sigma (chpt. v.p. 1961), Phi Kappa Phi (chpt. v.p. 1960), Alpha Kappa Psi (chpt. social chmn. 1960). Clubs: Syracuse U. San Francisco Bay Area Alumni (pres. 1967-77), Scott Valley Swim and Tennis, Tiburon Peninsula Tennis and Swimming, San Francisco Engineers, Commonwealth of Calif. (San Francisco); San Francisco Rotary. Home: 104 Sugarloaf Dr Tiburon CA 94920 Office: 255 California St San Francisco CA 94120

HAYES, SAMUEL BANKS, III, bank exec.; b. Morristown, N.J., Nov. 30, 1936; s. Samuel Banks and Alden (Bailey) H.; student Yale U., 1959, Harvard U., 1970; m. Kathryn Hannam; children—Alden Catherine, Ruth Crokett, Samuel Banks. Mem. exec. tng. program Citibank, N.A., 1960-62, mem. nat. div., 1962-63, mem. petroleum dept., 1963-70, head wholesale retail trade dept., 1970-73, area supr. brs. Lower Manhattan, N.Y.C., 1973-74, div. mgr. brs. Bklyn., Queens, S.I., Nassau, Suffolk, 1974-75, regional credit officer Austrailian br., 1976-77; pres., chief operating officer Bank of Okla., N.A., Tulsa, 1977—. Bd. dirs. United Way, Arts & Humanities Council of Tulsa; trustee Children's Med. Center, Metro-YMCA. Served with U.S. Army. Mem. Tulsa Clearing House (past pres.), Harvard Bus. Assos., Tulsa C. of C. Office: PO Box 2300 Tulsa OK 74192

HAYES, THOMAS RICHARD, telephone co. exec.; b. Tacoma, July 5, 1926; s. Richard and Mabel Emily (Edgar) H.; student Highline Community Coll., 1970-71; m. Dolores Mae Lane, June 19, 1948; children—Joan, John, Thomas, Elizabeth, Richard, Juliette, Gwendolyn, Mary. With Pacific N.W. Bell Co., Seattle, 1947—, plant staff asst., 1974-77, staff specialist, 1977—. Capt., Federal Way Fire Dept., 1957-67, fire commr., 1969-72; dep. sheriff, Palisades, Wash., 1960-64; mem. Des Moines Design Commn., 1980—, Whatcom County Emergency Services Com., 1972-74. Served with USN, 1944-47. Mem. N.W. Inductive Coordination Com. Telephone Pioneers.

HAYES, WILLIAM RUPERT, JR., mfg. co. exec.; b. Los Angeles, Sept. 19, 1943; s. William Rupert and Gertrude W. Hayes; student public schs., Verdugo Hills, Calif.; m. Sandra S. Blackard, Sept. 19, 1964 (div.); children—William Rupert, Robin L. Pres., Hayes Bolt & Supply, Inc., San Diego, also Hawaii Nut & Bolt, Inc., Honolulu. Mem. S.W. Fastener Assn., San Diego C. of C. Club: Propeller of U.S. Office: Hayes Bolt & Supply Inc 2986 National Ave San Diego CA 92113

HAYFORD, WARREN JOSEPH, mfg. co. exec.; b. Ft. Sill, Okla., July 21, 1929; s. Warren and Mabel (Moll) H.; B.S., U.S. Mil. Acad., 1952; m. Marylou Meyer, June 14, 1952; children—Warren, Mary Beth, David, Lisa, Laura, Susan, Michael. Formerly with Continental Can Co., Stamford, Conn., 1955-79, exec. v.p., dir., 1975-79; pres. Internat. Harvester Co., Chgo., 1979—; dir. Norton Co., Burlington No. R.R., No. Trust Co. Active Chgo. United. Served to 1st lt., inf., AUS, 1946-48, 52-55. Mem. Machinery and Allied Products Inst. (dir.). Republican. Roman Catholic. Clubs: Indian Hill, Greenwich Country, Sky, Chgo., Univ. Patentee in field (2). Office: 401 N Michigan Ave Chicago IL 60611

HAYNES, AMANDA HARRIS, investment adv.; b. N.Y.C.; d. Justin Obrien and Evelyn (Green) H.; student N.Y. U., 1969-70. Asst. to editor-in-chief Vogue mag., N.Y.C., 1971-72; acct. rep. dept. merchandising Hoechst Inc., N.Y.C., 1973-74; fashion editor Town & Country mag., N.Y.C., 1974-75; portfolio money mgr. Wertheim & Co., Inc., N.Y.C., 1976-79; pres., investment adv. Haynes & Co., N.Y.C., 1980—. Republican. Episcopalian. Clubs: River, Maidstone. Home: Rivercourt 429 E 52d St New York NY 10022 Office: Suite 450 Park Ave New York NY 10022

HAYNES, FREDERICK LESLIE, indsl. engr.; b. Portsmouth, N.H., Oct. 27, 1934; s. James Edwin and Elizabeth (Crankshaw) H.; B.S., Northeastern U., 1960; M.B.A., Am. U., 1968; m. Patricia Marie Griffith, July 29, 1960. Indsl. engr. Alcoa, Edgewater, N.J., 1962-64; sr. indsl. engr. U.S. Air Force Mgmt. Engring. Program, Pentagon, 1964-72; asst. dir. U.S. Gen. Acctg. Office, Washington, 1972-79; dir. office coop. generic tech. U.S. Dept. Commerce, Washington, 1979—; lectr. in field. Served with USN, 1955-57, U.S. Army, 1960-62. Decorated U.S. Army Commendation medal. Registered profl. engr., Mass. Fellow Am. Inst. Indsl. Engrs.; mem. Soc. Mfg. Engrs., World Future Soc. Contbr. articles to profl. jours. Home: 3806 Fort Hill Dr Alexandria VA 22310 Office: US Dept Commerce Washington DC 20230

HAYNES, HAROLD JEAN, oil co. exec.; b. Ft. Worth Sept. 29, 1925; s. Jean Calvin and Hallie May (Badgett) H.; B.S. in Civil Engring., Tex. A. and M. U., 1947; m. Reta Katheryn Adams, Mar. 14, 1945; children—Sharon, Karen, Toya. Engr., Cal. Co., 1947-56; v.p. Richmond Exploration Co., 1958-60; v.p. Standard Oil Co. Cal., Western Operations, Inc., 1963-65, pres., 1965-66; v.p., dir. Standard Oil Co. of Calif., 1966-69, pres., 1969-74, chmn., 1974—, also chief exec. officer; dir. Citicorp, Citibank, Boeing Co., Carter Hawley Hale Stores. Mem. Bus. Council, Bus. Roundtable. Bd. dirs. Am. Petroleum Inst., Stanford Research Inst.; Am. Enterprise Inst. Served with USNR, 1944-46. Clubs: San Francisco Golf, Stock Exchange, Bohemian, Pacific-Union (San Francisco); Burlingame (Calif.) Country; Augusta Nat. Golf; Cypress Point (Monterey, Calif.); Thunderbird Country (Rancho Mirage, Calif.); Burning Tree, International (Washington). Office: 225 Bush St San Francisco CA 94104

HAYNES, HAROLD WALTER, aviation mfg. co. exec.; b. Snoqualmie, Wash., Jan. 23, 1923; s. Ralph and Bertha I. (Sewell) H.; B.A., U. Wash.; m. Barbara J. Tatham, Oct. 11, 1943; children—Christine, Steven, Kevin. With Touche Ross & Co., Seattle, 1948-54; with Boeing Co., Seattle, 1954—, now exec. v.p., chief fin. officer, and dir.; dir. Pacific Nat. Bank Wash., Peabody Holding Co. Served with USMC, 1942-45. Mem. Fin. Execs. Inst., Fin. Execs. Council (Conf. Bd.). Republican. Episcopalian. Clubs: Seattle Golf, Springy, Ranier, Wash. Athletic. Office: PO Box 3707 MS 10-14 Seattle WA 98124

HAYNES, JOHN MABIN, utility co. exec.; b. Albany, N.Y., Apr. 22, 1928; s. John Mabin and Gladys Elizabeth (Phillips) H.; B.S., Syracuse U., 1952; m. Marion Enola Hamilton, Apr. 7, 1956; children—John David, Douglas Hamilton, Robert Paul. Acct., Price Waterhouse & Co., N.Y.C., 1953-56, Syracuse, N.Y., 1956-61; auditor Niagara Mohawk Power Corp., Syracuse, 1961-63, adminstrv. asst., 1963-67, asst. treas., 1967-71, treas., 1971-73, v.p., treas., 1973-80, sr. v.p. charge fin., money mgmt., pension fund mgmt. and investor relations, 1980—; dir., treas. NM Uranium, Inc., 1976—, Can. Niagara Power Co., Ltd.; 1971—; treas. Moreau Mfg. Corp., 1973-80, St. Lawrence Power Co., 1971-80; pres. Beebee Island Corp., 1972-77, now dir. Mem. Westhill Central Sch. Bd. Edn., 1968-73, pres., 1969-71; bd. dirs. N.Y. Bus. Devel. Corp. Served with U.S. Army, 1945-47. Mem. Nat. Assn. Accts., Fin. Execs. Inst., Am. Gas Assn. (fin. com.), Edison Electric Inst. (fin. com.), Bond Club Syracuse. Club: Masons. Office: 300 Erie Blvd W Syracuse NY 13202

HAYNES, ROBERT LEROY, pump mfg. co. exec.; b. Detroit, June 22, 1928; s. Richard LeRoy and Eva Hatfield (Brooks) H.; B.S., Va. Poly. Inst., 1950; m. Nan Catherine Cox, Dec. 30, 1950; children—Robin Lee, Lynn Catherine, Drew Loren. Sr. Metall. engr. Am. Standard Corp., Louisville, 1950-62; mgr. Wichita Falls Foundry and Machine Co., 1962-64; v.p. ops. Dixie Foundry & Machine Co., Marksville, La., 1964-65; dir. corp. devel. Vulcan Inc., Latrobe, Pa., 1965-73; pres., dir. Metcast Internat. Inc., Harrison, N.J., 1973—; v.p., dir. Worthington Pump Corp., Mountainside, N.J., 1973—; pres. Haynes Assos., Inc., 1978—; dir. Metcast, S.p.A. (Italy), Westmoreland Plastic Co., Hydro Carbide Corp., Vulcan Engring. Co. Mem. Am. Soc. Metals, Nat. Foundry Assn., Am. Foundrymen's Soc. Clubs: University, Raritan Valley Country. Patentee metal forming method. Home: Pattenburg Rd Pattenburg NJ 08802 Office: 401 Worthington Ave Harrison NJ 07029

HAYS, HERSCHEL MARTIN, elec. engr., b. Neillsville, Wis., Mar. 2, 1920; s. Myron E. and Esther (Marquardt) H.; E.E., U. Minn., 1942; grad. student U. So. Calif., 1947; children—Howard Martin, Holly Mary, Diane Esther, Willet Martin Hays II. Elec. engr. City of Los Angeles, 1947-60; pres. Li-Bonn Corp. Served as radio officer, 810th Signal Service Bn., U.S. Army, 1942-43; asst. signal constrn. officer, E.T.O., 1943-45, tech. supr. Japanese radio systems, U.S. Army of Occupation, 1945-46; mem. tech. staff, Signal Corps Engring. Labs., U.S. Army, 1946; col. U.S. Army, ret. Signal Officer Calif. N.G. 1947-50. Registered profl. engr. Calif. Mem. Eta Kappa Nu, Pi Tau Pi Sigma, Kappa Eta Kappa. Republican. Episcopalian. Home: 1211 SE 11th St Fort Lauderdale FL 33316

HAYS, JOHN EDWARD, hotel exec.; b. Saratoga Springs, N.Y., Sept. 9, 1948; s. John E. and Norma M. H.; B.S. in Hotel Adminstrn. and Indsl. Relations, U. Mass., 1976; m. Teresa J. Condraski, Jan. 28, 1978. Mgmt. trainee Hyatt Hotels, San Francisco, 1976-77; asst. dir. personnel Hyatt Regency O'Hare, Rosemont, Ill., 1977; dir. personnel Hyatt Lincolnwood (Ill.), 1977-78, Hyatt Pitts., 1978-80, Hyatt Del Monte, Monterey, Calif., 1980—; instr. Oakton Community Coll., Morton Grove, Ill., 1977-78. Mem. Employers Council on Youth, Pitts., 1979-80, Employers Adv. Council to Pa. Employment Service, Pitts., 1979-80. Served with U.S. Army, 1967-69. Decorated D.F.C., Army Commendation medal with V device and 2 oak leaf clusters, Air medal with 8 oak leaf clusters; Vietnamese Cross of Gallantry with palm leaf cluster. Mem. Am. Soc. Personnel Adminstrn., Am. Soc. Tng. and Devel. Office: Hyatt Del Monte 1 Old Golf Course Rd Monterey CA 93940

HAYS, KAY I., mgmt. cons.; b. Arapahoe, Nebr., Mar. 15, 1940; d. LaVerne Joseph and Mildred Elaine Hays; B.A. in Psychology, Central Mo. State U., 1970, M.B.A., 1980; M.Ed. in Reading, U. Del., 1972. Tchr. schs. in Mo. and Kans., 1960-68; dir. Longview Community Coll., Kansas City, Mo., 1968-70; mgmt. cons. Internat. Reading Assn., Newark, Del., 1970-77, membership specialist, 1977—. Mem. Nat. Fedn. Bus. and Profl. Women's Clubs (rec. sec. Newark 1976-78), Internat. Reading Assn., Nat. Assn. Female Execs., Psi Chi. Author papers in field. Home: 420 Willa Rd Newark DE 19711 Office: 800 Barksdale Rd PO Box 8139 Newark DE 19711

HAYWOOD, WILLIAM THOMAS, coll. ofcl.; b. Columbia, Tenn., May 25, 1928; s. William Thomas and Frances (Stone) H.; student Millsaps Coll., 1945-46, Bowling Green Bus. U., 1948-49; B.B.A., U. Miss., 1951; postgrad. Tulane U., 1958-60; LL.D., Atlanta Law Sch., 1969; m. Sylvia Anne Graham, Nov. 25, 1954; children—William Thomas, Sylvia Annette, Robert Alton, Susan Lynne. Bus. mgr., instr. accounting and econs. East Central Jr. Coll., 1951-58; purchasing agt. Tulane U., 1958-59, chief accountant, 1959-60; bus. mgr., instr. econs. Mercer U., Macon, Ga., 1960-65, sec., 1960-79, v.p. bus. and fin., 1965-79; v.p. for bus. affairs, treas. Skidmore Coll., 1979—. Instr. econs. Miss. State U., 1954-56; cons. Ford Found., N.Y.C., 1963-64. Sec., Walter F. George Sch. Law Found., Macon, 1963-79; mem. adv. council Ga. Dept. Labor, 1972-79; bd. govs., mem. exec. com. Ga. Region V, Health Systems Agy., 1975-79; mem. nat. adv. council on fin. aid to students U.S. Office Edn., 1976-77. Trustee Common Fund for Non-profit Instns., N.Y.C., 1969—, v.p., 1969-72, vice chmn., 1976-80. Served with USNR, 1946-48. Mem. So. (pres. 1968-69), Nat. (pres. 1972-73) assns. coll. and univ. bus. officers, Am. Council on Edn. (taxation com. 1971—), Saratoga Springs C. of C. (dir. 1980—), Nat. Assn. Ednl. Buyers (pres. 1967-68) Beta Alpha Psi, Lambda Chi Alpha, Delta Sigma Pi. Contbr. articles to profl. publs. Home: 12 3d St Saratoga Springs NY 12866

HAZELTINE, HERBERT SAMUEL, lawyer; b. Huntington Beach, Calif., Dec. 12, 1908; s. Herbert Samuel and Emma (Phelps) H.; A.B., Stanford, 1931; LL.D., Harvard U., 1934, U. So. Calif., 1979; m. Frances Sue Coffin, Aug. 5, 1936; children—Susan Connell, Ann Hyde, Lynn. Admitted to Calif. bar, 1935; asso. mem. firm Evans & Boyle, Pasadena, Calif., 1935-42; partner firm Adams, Duque & Hazeltine, Los Angeles, 1945—; dir. Norris Industries, Los Angeles. Trustee U. So. Calif., 1970—. Served with USN, 1942-45. Mem. Am. Bar Assn. Republican. Clubs: Calif. Annandale Golf, Valley of Montecito, Cypress Point. Home: 495 Orange Grove Circle Pasadena CA Office: 523 W 6th St Los Angeles CA 90014

HAZELTON, BRUCE WINSTON, constrn. equipment co. exec.; b. Chester, N.H., Nov. 2, 1927; s. Robert Carroll and Margaret L. (McComb) H.; student Phillips-Exeter Acad., 1944-46, Dartmouth, 1946-50; m. Avalon L. Crosby, June 30, 1950; children—Gweneth, Robert, Janet, Lisa. With R.C. Hazelton Co., Inc., Cumberland, Maine, 1950—, dir., 1953—, pres., 1959—; pres. B&R Equipment Rental Corp.; treas. N.H. Services, Inc. Chmn. div. Maine missions, bd. dirs. Maine Conf. United Ch. of Christ; trustee Bangor Theol. Sem., 1978—; mem. standing com. Maine Hist. Soc., 1978—; mem. Interconf. Com. for Regional Sem. Support, 1977—. Mem. Maine Good Roads Assn., Asso. Equipment Distbrs., Asso. Gen. Contractors, Am., Maine, N.Mex. (life), Hawaiian, philatelic socs.,

Am. Philatelic Congress Inc., Maine Hist. Soc. (life), Postal History Soc., U.S. Cancellation Club, Am. Topical Assn., Penn., Conn. postal history socs., Collectors Club (N.Y.), Maine Philatelic Soc. (pres. 1973-74), Portland Stamp Club (pres. 1973-74), Cumberland Hist. Soc. (pres. 1974-76), Confederate Stamp Alliance, Am. Revenue Assn., U.S. Classics (life), Philatelic Found. Club: Masons. Home: PO Box 67A Cumberland Center ME 04021 Office: 199 Middle Rd Cumberland ME 04104

HEABERG, GEORGE THOMAS, III, real estate investment co. exec.; b. Jackson, Tenn., Oct. 31, 1930; s. George Thomas, Jr. and Evelyn Elizabeth (Thomas) H.; student Lambuth Coll., 1948-51, U. Miss., 1959-60, Temple U., 1965-66, Fairfield U., 1970-71; m. Grace Elaine Zazzie, Apr. 20, 1968; children—Patrick, Michael, Lisa, Sara. Rep., Smith Kline & French, 1956-60, regional mgr., 1960-65, personnel mgr., 1965-69, v.p. adminstrn. and finance Branson subs. 1969-70; v.p. personnel Smith Kline Corp., Phila., 1971-79; pres. Coventry Corp., Jackson, Tenn., 1979—. Bd. dirs., v.p., mem. exec. com. Child Devel. Center; bd. dirs. Hilltop Sch.; chmn. adminstrv. bd. Berwyn (Pa.) United Meth. Ch., 1968, pres. adult fellowship, 1969, mem. council membership and evangelism Southeastern Pa. conf., chmn. personnel com., 1973—; exec. com. Indsl. Relations Assn. Phila., 1975-77; mem. labor relations council U. Pa., mem. multi-nat. advisory group, 1977—; mem. devel. council Lambuth Coll., 1977—. Served to capt. USAF, 1951-55. Mem. Pharm. Mfrs. Assn. (personnel com.). Methodist (chmn. bd.). Home: 984 Country Club Ln Jackson TN 38301 Office: 573 Old Hickory Blvd Jackson TN 38301

HEABERLIN, DAVID ALLEN, banker; b. Kirksville, Mo., Aug. 12, 1949; s. James Claude and Loraine Frances (Cain) H.; B.A. in Acct., St. Ambrose Coll., 1971; m. Nancy Lee Odell, June 5, 1971. Auditor, Arthur Young & Co., Chgo., 1971-73, auditor supr., 1973-76, audit mgr., 1976-77; 1st v.p., comptroller Exchange Nat. Bank of Chgo., 1977-78, 1st v.p., chief fin. officer, 1978-79, sr. v.p., chief fin. officer, 1979—; treas., chief fin. officer Exchange Internat. Corp., parent co. of Exchange Nat. Bank, 1978—. Recipient Scholarship award state of Iowa, 1969, Acct. Achievement award Ernst & Ernst, 1970; C.P.A., Ill. Mem. Am. Inst. C.P.A.'s, Ill. Soc. C.P.A.'s, Bank Adminstrn. Inst., Am. Bankers Assn. Roman Catholic. Office: Exchange Nat Bank LaSalle and Adams Sts Chicago IL 60603

HEALEY, JAMES HENRY, mgmt. cons.; b. Winsted, Conn., May 21, 1920; s. Henry J. and Elizabeth (Hartnett) H.; B.S. in Bus. Adminstrn., U. Conn., 1942, M.S., 1944; Ph.D. in Industry, U. Pa., 1953; m. Marjorie Jean Tate, Jan. 18, 1944; children—Carol Lee, Deborah Lynn, Jamie Ellen, Jon Christopher. From instr. to asst. prof., U. Conn., 1942-46; asst. to wage adminstr. Veeder-Root, Inc., 1944-45, Pratt & Whitney Aircraft, 1945; instr. Wharton Sch., 1946-47; asso. prof. Ohio State U., 1947-56; vis. asso. prof. U. Calif., 1955-56; adj. prof. Miami U., 1972—; mgmt. cons. Coop. League U.S.A., 1956-58; owner-mgr. Mgmt. and Bus. Services, Inc., 1958—, pres., 1972—; mem. team Operation Jefe, Chile, 1959-61, team leader, 1960-61. Mem. Am. Mgmt. Assn, Acad. Mgmt., Beta Gamma Sigma. Author: (with Maynard, Weidler, others) Introduction to Business Management, 1951; Executive Coordination and Control, 1956; co-author: Power Management, 1962. Home: 3780 Patricia Dr Columbus OH 43220 Office: 1085 Fishinger Rd Columbus OH 43221

HEALEY, VINCENT PATRICK, undersea and aerospace co. exec.; b. N.Y.C., Mar. 13, 1918; s. John William and Katherine Mary (Clancey) H.; B.S., U.S. Naval Acad., 1940; M.S.E.E., M.I.T., 1949; m. Helen M. Clarke, Oct. 27, 1945; children—Dominic, John, Mary, Jane, Peter. Commd. ensign U.S. Navy, 1940, advanced through grades to rear adm., 1967; comdr. Cruiser Destroyer Flotilla, 1967-69; dir. undersea and strategic warfare devel., 1969-72; ret., 1972; cons. research and devel., 1972-74; gen. mgr. EDO Corp., Washington, 1974—; tech. program chmn. Electronics and Aerospace Conf., IEEE, 1975, gen. chmn., 1976. Pres. St. Dominic's Parish Council. Decorated Legion of Merit, Bronze Star. Mem. IEEE, Nat. Security Indsl. Assn., Am. Def. Preparedness Assn., Sigma Xi. Roman Catholic. Home: 1259 Delaware Ave SW Washington DC 20024 Office: 2001 Jefferson Davis Hwy Arlington VA 22202

HEALY, JOEL WATRES, JR., ins. co. mgr.; b. Kansas City, Mo., July 11, 1930; s. Joel Watres and Eleanor Francis (Nuckolls) H.; student Tex A. and M. U., 1949-50; B.S., Stetson U., 1956; m. Norma C. Smith, May 5, 1956; children—Robert W., Kimberly C. Home office rep., group div. Aetna Life & Casualty Co., Lynchburg, Va., 1956-58, home office rep., group div., Tampa, Fla., 1958-65, asst. mgr., group div., Tampa, 1965—. Served with USMC, 1948-49, 50-52. Decorated Purple Heart. Mem. Greater Tampa C. of C. (com. 100). Republican. Methodist. Clubs: Univ., Tower. Home: 13025 Whisper Sound Dr Tampa FL 33624

HEALY, JOSEPH FRANCIS, JR., lawyer; b. N.Y.C., Aug. 11, 1930; s. Joseph Francis and Agnes (Kett) H.; B.S., Fordham U., 1952, J.D., Georgetown U., 1959; m. Patricia A. Casey, Apr. 25, 1955; children—James C., Timothy, Kevin, Cathleen M., Mary, Terence. With gen. traffic dept. Eastman-Kodak Co., Rochester, N.Y., 1954-55; air transport examiner CAB, Washington, 1955-59; admitted to D.C. bar, 1959; practiced in Washington, 1959-70, 1980—; mem. firm C. Edward Leasure, 1959-63, Chadbourne, Parke, Whiteside & Wolff, 1963-66; asst. gen. counsel Air Transport Assn. Am., Washington, 1966-70; v.p. legal Eastern Air Lines, Inc., N.Y.C., Miami, Fla., 1970-80, corp. sec., 1977-80; partner firm Ford, Farquhar, Kornblut & O'Neill, Washington, 1980—. Served to lt. USAF, 1952-54. Mem. Am., Fed., Internat. bar assns., Nat. Aero. Assn., Am. Irish Hist. Soc., Beta Gamma Sigma, Phi Delta Phi. Clubs: Internat. Aviation, Univ. (Washington); Wings (N.Y.C.). Home: 9602 Cable Dr Kensington MD 20795 Office: 5028 Wisconsin Ave NW Washington DC 20016

HEALY, WALTER FRANCIS XAVIER, diversified energy co. exec.; b. N.Y.C., Sept. 15, 1941; s. Walter Patrick and Helen (Fischer) H.; A.B. in Philosophy, St. Joseph's Coll., Yonkers, N.Y., 1963; LL.B., Fordham U., 1966; m. Margaret O'Hanlon, Nov. 26, 1966; 1 dau., Katherine Siobahan. Admitted to N.Y. State bar, 1967, Pa. bar, 1980; asso. firm Dewey, Ballantine, Bushby, Palmer & Wood, N.Y.C., 1966-76; corp. counsel Singer Co., N.Y.C., 1976; corp. sec., asst. gen. counsel Studebaker-Worthington, Inc., N.Y.C., 1976-79; v.p., gen. counsel UGI Corp., Valley Forge, Pa., 1979—. Mem. Am. Bar Assn., Am. Soc. Corp. Secs., N.Y. State Bar Assn., Pa. Bar Assn., Assn. Bar City N.Y. Roman Catholic. Home: 611 Morris Ave Bryn Mawr PA 19010 Office: Box 858 Valley Forge PA 19482

HEANEY, ROBERT C(ECIL) C(URTIS), lawyer; b. Big Rapids, Mich., Jan. 22, 1906; s. Herbert Melville and Harriet Irene (Emmons) H.; student Grand Rapids Jr. Coll., 1924-26; A.B., U. Mich., 1928, LL.B., J.D., 1930; m. Barbara Helen Patton, Feb. 14, 1931; children—Robert Daniel (dec.), Brian Richard, Marilyn Jean. Admitted to Mich. bar, 1930, practiced in Grand Rapids, 1930-73; practiced in Tucson, 1973—. Treas., Mich. Republican Central Com., 1949-57. Bd. dirs. Grand Rapids YMCA, 1935-73, emeritus, 1973—; past pres. Mich. chpt. Arthritis Found., past pres., bd. dirs. So. Ariz. chpt., Tucson. Mem. Am. Judicature Soc., Am., Mich. Grand Rapids, Ariz., Pima County bar assns., Tucson C. of C., Phi Sigma Kappa, Phi Alpha Delta. Presbyterian. Clubs: U. Mich. Alumni (past pres.), U. Mich. President's; Tucson Nat. Golf; Garden of the Gods (Colorado Springs, Colo.); Rotary. Home: 7902 N Casas Cameo Tucson AZ 85704 Office: 7110 N Oracle Rd Suite 106 Tucson AZ 85704

HEAPS, MARVIN DALE, mgmt. services co. exec.; b. Boone, Iowa, June 26, 1932; s. Donald and Mary Isabel (Robson) H.; B.A. in Econs., Whitworth Coll., 1953; postgrad., George Washington U., 1957; M.B.A. (Achievement scholar), U. Pa., 1959; m. Martha Coleman Davis, July 4, 1957; children—Mitchell, Matthew, Martha. Asso., McKinsey & Co., mgmt. cons., Washington, Geneva, Switzerland, N.Y.C., 1960-66; dir. service systems engring. Automatic Retailers of Am., Phila., 1967, v.p., 1968; sr. v.p. ARA Services, Inc., Phila., 1969-71; pres. ARA Food Services Co., 1971-75; exec. v.p. ops. ARA Services, Inc., 1975-78, pres., chief operating officer, 1978—, also dir.; dir. VS Services, Ltd. (Can.), Morse/Diesel Inc.; cons. to Office Edn., HEW; mem. food service industry adv. com. Exec. Office of Pres., 1969—. Bd. dirs. Young Life Campaign, chmn., 1976; bd. dirs. YMCA, Greater Phila. C. of C. Tourism and Conv. Bur.; trustee Whitworth Coll. Served to lt. USNR, 1955-59. Mem. Am. Mgmt. Assn., Soc. Personnel Adminstrn., Assn. Internat. Devel., Nat. Automatic Mdse. Assn. (chmn., dir.), Conf. Bd., Greater Phila. C. of C. (dir.), Wharton MBA Alumni Club. Republican. Presbyn. (elder). Club: Metropolitan (Washington); Union League, Downtown (dir.) (Phila.). Home: 301 Elm Ave Swarthmore PA 19081 Office: Independence Sq W Philadelphia PA 19106

HEARD, JOHN HOWELL, funeral dir.; b. Atlanta, Oct. 1, 1948; s. Howell Crane and Mary Catherine (Shipp) H.; student Norman Coll., Norman Park, Ga., 1966-68; grad. Dallas Inst. Mortuary Sci., 1969; m. Diane S. Mueller, June 27, 1971. Funeral dir. Ward's Funeral Home, Gainesville, Ga., 1969-71; asst. mgr. McGowens, Inc., Funeral Dirs., Valdosta, Ga., 1971-72; mgr. Henderson Funeral Home, Moultrie, Ga., 1972-74; pres. Oxley-Heard Funeral Home, Fernandina Beach, Fla., 1974—. Treas., Eight Flags Hist. Museum, Fernandina Beach, 1979. Lic. funeral dir., Ga., Fla. Mem. Fla. Funeral Dirs. Assn., Ga. Funeral Dirs. Assn., Nat. Funeral Dirs. Assn., Ga. Acad. Grad. Embalmers. Democrat. Baptist. Clubs: Rotary (dir. 1977-78), Masons, Shriners (pres. Fernandiana Beach chpt. 1976), Elks. Home and Office: 1305 Atlantic Ave Fernandina Beach FL 32034

HEARD, ROSE NELL, energy equipment group exec.; b. Havana, Ark., Aug. 20, 1930; d. Edgar Earl and Birtia Louisa (Benefield) Buckman; student Met. Bus. Coll., 1949, also UCLA; m. Paul J. Adams; children—Allen G. Mobley, Phillip D. Mobley. Sec., Firestone Tire & Rubber Co., South Gate, Calif., 1949-50, Century Metalcraft, Los Angeles, 1950-51, Pioneer-Flintkote Los Angeles, 1955-56, Byron Jackson Pump Div., Verona, Calif., 1957-75; ins. adminstr. Borg-Warner Corp., 1961, ins. and benefits adminstr., 1970, mgr. ins. and benefits, Energy Equipment Group, Los Angeles, 1976—. First v.p. Long Beach Republican Women's Fedn., 1979—; bus. adminstr. New Life Center Ch., Downey, Calif., 1978—. Mem. Byron Jackson Pum Div. Mgmt. Assn. Mem. Assemblies of God Ch. Office: 800 W 6th St Suite 950 Los Angeles CA 90017

HEARD, WILLIAM ROBERT, ins. co. exec.; b. Indpls., Apr. 25, 1925; s. French and Estelle (Austin) H.; student Ind. U.; m. Virginia Ann Patrick, Feb. 6, 1951; children—Cynthia Ann, William Robert, II. With Grain Dealers Mut. Ins. Co., 1948, exec. v.p., Indpls., 1978-79, pres., chief exec. officer, dir., 1979—; pres., chief exec. officer, dir. Companion Ins. Co., 1979—; vice chmn., dir. Alliance Am. Insurers; chmn., exec. com. IRM; pres., dir. Grain Dealers Mut. Agy., Inc. Served with USNR, 1942-46. Mem. Assn. Mill and Elevator Ins. Cos. (vice chmn., dir.), Ins. Inst. Ind. (dir., exec. com.), Mut. Reins. Bur. (dir.), Excess of Loss Assn. (vice chmn., dir.), Sales and Mktg. Execs. Indpls. (past pres.), Sales and Mktg. Execs. Internat. (past dir.), Fla. 1752 Club (past pres.), Am. Legion, Pi Sigma Epsilon. Office: 1752 N Meridian St Indianapolis IN 46202

HEARST, RANDOLPH APPERSON, pub. exec.; b. N.Y.C., Dec. 2, 1915; s. William Randolph and Millicent (Willson) H.; student Harvard, 1933-34; m. Catherine Campbell, Jan. 12, 1938; children—Catherine, Virginia, Patricia, Anne, Victoria. Asst. to editor Atlanta Georgian, 1939-40; asst. to pub. San Francisco Call-Bull., 1940-44, exec. editor, 1947-49, pub., 1950-53; asso. pub. Oakland Post-Enquirer, 1946-47; pres., dir., chief exec. officer Hearst Consol. Publs., Inc. and Hearst Pub. Co., Inc., 1961-64, 72—; pres. San Francisco Examiner; chmn. exec. com. The Hearst Corp., 1965-73, chmn. bd., 1973—, also dir. Bd. dirs. Hearst Found., 1945—, pres., 1972—; bd. dirs. Wm. Randolph Hearst Found., 1950—. Served as capt., Air Transport Command, USAAF, 1942-45. Roman Catholic. Clubs: Piedmont Driving (Atlanta), Burlingame Country; Pacific Union; Press (San Francisco). Office: 110 5th St San Francisco CA 94103

HEATH, STRATTON ROLLINS, JR., mfg. co. exec.; b. Balt., Dec. 28, 1937; s. Stratton Rollins and Dorothy Frances (Ornstil) H.; B.B.A. in Mktg., U. Wis., 1959, J.D., 1961; m. Josephine Ellen Ward, Aug. 27, 1961; children—Stratton Rollins, III, Kristin Elisabeth, Joel Ward. Admitted to Wis. bar, 1961, U.S. Supreme Ct. bar, 1968, Colo. bar, 1974; v.p., dir. contracts, corp. atty. Chaparral Industries, Inc. subs. Armco Steel Corp., Denver, 1970-73; asso. corp. counsel Johns-Manville Corp., Denver, 1973-76, v.p. purchasing, 1976-80, v.p., gen. mgr. filtration and minerals div., 1979—; instr. procurement law JAG Sch., Charlottesville, Va. Served to maj. U.S. Army, 1961-70. Decorated Army Commendation medal with oak leaf cluster, Meritorious Service medal. Mem. Colo. Bar Assn., State Bar Wis., Am. Mgmt. Assn., Nat. Assn. Purchasing Mgmt. (certified purchasing mgr.), U.S. Army Res. Officers Assn. Unitarian. Office: PO Box 5108 Denver CO 80217

HEATON, ELDON CARLYLE, book distbg. co. exec.; b. St. Louis, Sept. 5, 1928; s. Otto John and Madeline Irvin (Hill) H.; B.S. in Physics, M.I.T., 1951, B.S. in Bus. Adminstrn., 1955; postgrad. Washington U., St. Louis, 1953-54; m. Nancy Louise Kellogg, July 5, 1952; children—Stuart Alan, Phillip Randall. Tchr. physics Washington U., 1953-54; research engr. North Am. Aviation, Downey, Calif., 1955-57; engring. supr. Hallamore Electronics, Anaheim, Calif., 1957-62; mem. tech. staff Lear Siegler, Inc., Santa Monica, Calif., 1962-64; research and radiation effects specialist Autonetics, Anaheim, 1964-76; pres. Living Books, Inc., Riverside, Calif., 1976—; cons. in field. Served to 1st lt. USAF, 1951-53. Mem. Am. Physics Soc., IEEE, Nat. Fedn. Independent Businessmen, Calif. Assn. Independent Businessmen. Republican. Contbr. articles in field of radiation effects on electronics. Home: 4060 Cedar Ave Norco CA 91760 Office: 12155 Magnolia Ave Riverside CA 92503

HEATZIG, WILLIAM GRANT, oil exploration and prodn. co. exec.; b. Boston, July 11, 1935; s. William B. and Eleanor Eunice (Grant) H.; B.S. in Geology, Rensselaer Poly. Inst., 1957; m. Anita S. Dalen, Sept. 8, 1962; children—Eric W., Marina K. With Metcalf & Eddy, Greenland, 1957-58; v.p. ops. H. Wassall & ASC/Petroconsultants, S.A., Havana, 1958-59, Geneva, 1956-69; exec. v.p., dir. Comoro Exploration Ltd., Geneva, 1969-73; mgr. European ops. Van Dyke Oil Co., London, 1973-76; pres., chief exec. officer, chmn. bd. Sigma Resources, Inc., London, 1976—; dir. Gexco Ind., Houston, Internat. Petrogas N.V., Geneva, Hadson Onshore U.K. Ltd., London. Mem. corp. Kings Coll. Sch., London. Mem. Am. Assn. Petroleum Geologists, Petroleum Exploration Soc. Gt. Britain, Conservative. Episcopalian. Clubs: Nautique de Morge (Switzerland); Lansdowne, Wimbledon Squash (London); Princess Water Ski. Co-editor N. African sect. Ann. Am. Assn. Petroleum Geologists Bull., 1967-68; contbr. articles to profl. jours. Home: Stonecourt 63 Murray Rd Wimbledon London SW19 England Office: Sigma Resources Inc 30 New Bond St London W1Y 9HD England

HEAVEN, BRYAN TERENCE, machine tool co. exec.; b. Coventry, Eng., July 10, 1921; came to U.S., 1979; s. Terence H. and Susan Mary (Doherty) H.; cert. Coventry Tech. Coll., 1934-40, 46-50; m. June 6, 1942; 1 dau. Engring. apprentice Dunlop Ltd., Coventry, Eng., 1934-40, prodn. engr., 1946-48; prodn. engr. Wickman Ltd., Coventry, 1948-50, sales engr., 1950-52, sales engr. Wickman Scrivener Ltd., Birmingham, Eng., 1952-60, sales dir., 1960-65, mng. dir., 1965-79; pres. Wickman Machine Tools, Inc., Elk Grove, Ill., 1979—. Served with Royal Navy, 1940-46. Mem. Machine Tool Trade Assn. (regional chmn.). Ch. of Eng. Clubs: Earls Ct. Lodge, St. John's Lodge. Home: 145A Indian Trail Barrington IL 60010 Office: 950 Morse Ave Elk Grove IL 60007

HEBDEN, JAMES H., fin. co. ofcl.; b. Providence, Oct. 6, 1950; s. Lael Aubrey Wharton and Muriel Avis H.; student Tenn. Tech. U., 1968-70, U. Tenn., Nashville, 1970-73; m. Janice Diane Turnbow, June 1, 1973. Mgr., Avco Fin. Services, Lexington and Louisville, Ky., Knoxville, Tenn., 1972-75; mgr. CIT Fin. Services, Smyrna, Tenn., 1975-77; asst. v.p., loan officer First Nat. Bank Rutherford County, Smyrna, 1977-78; mgr. CIT Fin. Services, Lebanon, Tenn., 1978-80, Security Pacific Fin. Money Center, Inc., Nashville, 1980—. Vice-pres. Rutherford County Heart Unit, 1977-78, 78-79; chmn. N. Rutherford County Heart Fund Drive, 1977, 78, 79, 81. Mem. Smyrna C. of C. Episcopalian. Clubs: Rotary (dir. 1976-78), Lions, Exchange. Home: 1B Frank St Smyrna TN 37167 Office: 4537 Nolensville Rd Nashville TN 37211

HEBDEN, WILLIAM ERNEST, mfg. co. exec.; b. Ashland, Mass., Nov. 15, 1934; s. Charles Ernest and Anne (MacNeil) H.; m. Barbara Ann Ward, Sept. 22, 1954. Sales mgr. Walenar Inc., Holliston, Mass., 1959-60, MacKenzie Machinery Co., Worcester, Mass., 1960-64; pres. Spray Engring. Co., Nashua, N.H., 1964—; v.p. Lechler GmbH & Co. KG, Fellbach, W. Ger. Served with USMC, 1953-56. Mem. Am. Nuclear Soc., Iron and Steel Inst. Home: Fieldstone Dr Hollis NH 03049 Office: Spray Engring Co Two E Spit Brook Rd Nashua NH 03060

HEBEL, ROBERT WILLIAM, elec. equipment mfg. co. exec.; b. Detroit, Oct. 2, 1923; s. Alvin J. and Agnes (Winkel) H.; B.S.E., U. Mich., 1949, M.S.E. (fellow), 1950; m. Helen I. Knap, June 14, 1948; children—Claudia, Kurt, Susan. Cons., mgr. A.E. Bishop & Assos., Detroit, 1956-59; chief engr., Airborne Accessories Corp., Hillside, N.J., 1959-66; v.p. mktg. Power Equipment div. Lear Siegler Inc., Cleve., 1966-75, pres., Maple Heights, Ohio, 1980—, pres. Romec div., Elyria, Ohio, 1975-80. Bd. dirs. Jr. Achievement Lorain County, 1976—; bd. govs. Assoc. Industries of Cleve., 1980—. Served with USN, 1943-46. Mem. Elyria C. of C. (mfg. council), Am. Mgmt. Assn., Greater Cleve. Growth Assn., Am. Def. Preparedness Assn., Cleve. Machine Trades Assn., Soc. Automotive Engrs. Club: Elyria Country. Home: 32840 Creekside Dr Pepper Pike OH 44124 Office: 17600 Broadway Maple Heights OH 44137

HEBERT, DONALD RAY, health facilities cons.; b. Kaplan, La., Dec. 5, 1935; s. Lennis J. and Pearl (Kibodeaux) H.; B.S. in Bus. Adminstrn., U. Southwestern La., 1971, M.B.A., 1977; m. Connie Ann Deshotels, Dec. 25, 1955; children—Steven, Craig, Donna, Gerard. Consumer fin. bus. mgr. and supr. X-L Fin. Co., Lafayette and Lake Charles, La., 1959-64, Lake Charles and New Iberia, La., 1965-68; sales mgr. Vermillion Creamery, Abbeville, La., 1964-65; successively bus. mgr., asst. adminstr., chief exec. officer Our Lady of Lourdes Hosp., 1968-79; fin. mgr., chief exec. officer Health Care Cons. Services, Inc. and Health Plan, Inc., Lafayette, 1978-79, pres., 1979—. Served with USAF, 1955-59. Recipient Cert. of Appreciation, La. Hosp. Assn.; lic. nursing home adminstr., La. Mem. Am. Coll. Hosp. Adminstrs., Am. Hosp. Assn. (council on mgmt.). Democrat. Roman Catholic. Home and Office: 114 Omega St Lafayette LA 70506

HEBERT, HOWARD JOSEPH, investment cons.; b. Cheyenne, Wyo., Apr. 16, 1930; s. Leon Eldridge and Howardine Eleanor (Donehue) H.; student public schs., Cheyenne; m. Catherine Lois Ward, May 31, 1950; children—Richard Lee, William Leon, Suzanne Marie. Vice pres. Boyer-Hebert & Wake & Co., Cheyenne, 1959-62; account exec. Bosworth Sullivan & Co., Cheyenne 1962-64; account exec., mem. mgmt. adv. bd. Hornblower & Week, Hemphill & Noyes, Denver, 1964-73; pres. Newhard Cook Adv. Services, Inc., Denver, 1979—; gen. partner Quan Tech Ltd., Denver, 1979. Mem. Market Technicians Assn., Denver Soc. Security Analysts. Roman Catholic. Club: Denver Athletic. Home: 13456 W Center Dr Lakewood CO 80228 Office: Newhard Cook Adv Services Inc 1580 Lincoln Suite 610 Denver CO 80203

HECK, DANIEL CURTIS, mfg. co. exec.; b. Bethlehem, N.Y., Nov. 18, 1923; s. Nicholas Joseph and Josephine Elizabeth (Curtis) H.; B.B.A., N.Mex. State U., 1949; M.B.A., U. Chgo., 1959; m. Jeanne Elizabeth Andersen, Dec. 21, 1946; children—James Curtis, Patricia Lynn, Daniel Curtis. Mgr. pipe, valves and plastics Crane Co., Chgo., 1949-60; owner, mgr. Ridge Plastics Co., injection molding and extrusion, Jonesboro, Ark., 1960-64; regional sales mgr. Fastex div. Ill. Tool Works, Inc., Des Plaines, 1964—. Served with USNR, 1943-46. Republican. Presbyterian. Patentee in field. Home: 385 Paula Ct Deerfield IL 60015 Office: 195 Algonquin Rd Des Plaines IL 60016

HECKER, GEORGE ERNST, lab. dir.; b. Hamburg, Germany, Sept. 10, 1939; s. Hanns E. and Wilhelmine K. (Corinth) H.; came to U.S., 1948, naturalized, 1954; B.S. in Engring., Yale U., 1961; M.S., Mass. Inst. Tech., 1962; m. Mary Frances Iacobelli, Dec. 29, 1962; children—Steven, Suzanne. Research engr. TVA, Norris, Tenn., 1962-68; sr. hydraulic engr. Stone & Webster Engring. Corp., Boston, 1968-70; asst. dir. Alden Research Lab., Worcester (Mass.) Poly. Inst., 1970-75, dir., 1975—, asst. prof., 1970-75, asso. prof., 1975—. Mem. Internat. Assn. Hydraulic Research, Internat. Assn. for Great Lakes Research, ASCE (certificate appreciation), Tau Beta Phi, Chi Epsilon, Sigma Xi. Contbr. articles to engring. jours. Office: 30 Shrewsbury St Holden MA 01520

HECKMAN, HENRY TREVENNEN SHICK, steel co. exec.; b. Reading, Pa., Mar. 27, 1918; s. H. Raymond and Charlotte E. Shick H.; A.B., Lehigh U., 1939; m. Helen Clausen Wright, Nov. 28, 1946; children—Sharon Anita, Charlotte Marie. Advt. prodn. mgr. Republic Steel Corp., Cleve., 1940-42, editor Enduro Era, 1946-51, account exec., 1953-54, asst. dir. advt., 1957-65, dir. advt., 1965—; partner Applegate & Heckman, Washington, 1955-56; advt. mgr. Harris Corp., 1956-57. Permanent chmn. Joint Com. for Audit Comparability, 1968—; chmn. Media Comparability Council, 1969—; chmn. indsl. advertisers com. Greater Cleve. Growth Assn., 1973-76; chmn. publs. com. Lehigh U., 1971-76; pres.'s adv. council Ashland

Coll., 1966-76; advt. adv. council Kent State U., 1976—; exec. com. Cleve. chpt. ARC, 1968-74; mem. Republican Fin. Exec. Com., 1966—. Served to comdr. USNR, 1942-46, 51-53; Korea. Named to Advt. Effectiveness Hall of Fame, 1967; Advt. Man of Yr., 1969; recipient G.D. Crain, Jr. award, 1973; Disting. Alumnus award Lehigh U., 1979. Mem. Indsl. Marketers Cleve. (past pres., Golden Mousetrap award 1968), Bus./Profl. Advt. Assn. (pres. 1968-69, Best Seller award 1966), Assn. Nat. Advertisers (chmn. shows and exhibits com. 1966-74, dir. 1969-72), Am. Iron and Steel Inst. (com. chmn. 1961-69), Steel Service Center Inst. (advt. adv. com. 1965-77), SAR (pres. 1979), Mil. Order World Wars (comdr. 1980), Early Settlers, Cleve. Advt. Club (pres. 1961-62, Hall of Fame 1980), Center for Mktg. Communications (chmn. bd. 1965). Clubs: Cheshire Cheese, Women's Advt., Cleve. Grays, Mid-Day, Cleve. Skating. Home: 13700 Shaker Blvd Cleveland OH 44120 Office: Republic Bldg Cleveland OH 44101

HEDBERG, ALLAN EDWARD, cosmetic co. exec.; b. Bronx, N.Y., Jan. 1, 1933; s. Anton and Mae (Durkin) H.; B.B.A., St. Johns U., 1958; M.B.A., U. Bridgeport, 1971; m. Anne M. Jones, Feb. 19, 1955; children—Regina, Marianne, Allan, Christine. Vice pres. internat. fin. Estee Lauder Inc., N.Y.C., 1974-77, v.p., controller, 1977-79, v.p. fin., 1979—; dir. Ronald House. Trustee Village of Manorhaven (N.Y.), 1960-64. Served with U.S. Army, 1952-54. C.P.A., Ind. Mem. Am. Inst. C.P.A.'s, Fin. Execs. Inst., Ind. Soc. C.P.A.'s. Roman Catholic. Home: 32 Inness Pl Manhasset NY 11030 Office: Estee Lauder Inc 767 Fifth Ave New York NY 10022

HEDBERG, HERBERT JOHNSTON, engring. exec.; b. Worcester, Mass., July 7, 1951; s. Stephen Emmanuel and Elizabeth Wells (Johnston) H.; B.S. in Elec. Engring., Worcester Poly. Inst., 1973; M.B.A., Northeastern U., 1980. Product engr. Tex. Instruments, Attleboro, Mass., 1973-74; design engr. Frost Controls, Cumberland, R.I., 1974-75; propr. Research Engring., South Attleboro, Mass., 1975; design engr. Waters Assos., Milford, Mass., 1975-76, product engr., 1976-77, project mgr., 1977-79, mgr. test engring., 1979—. Home: 28 High St North Attleboro MA 02760 Office: 34 Maple St Milford MA 01757

HEDGE, JAMES DALE, contracting co. exec.; b. Chicago Heights, Ill., Sept. 28, 1947; s. Amanda Elizabeth Hedge; student parochial sch., Hammond, Ind.; m. Priscilla Kay Tolson, July 31, 1966; children—Patrick Alan, Brian Michael, Penny Sue, David Eugene, James Scott. Laborer, Youngstown Sheet & Tube Co., Indiana Harbor, Ind., 1966-67, locomotive engr. inner plant r.r., 1967-72; foreman N & L Contracting Co., Merrillville, Ind., 1972-78; pres. J & P Contracting Co., Inc., Hammond, 1978—. Baptist. Home and Office: 932 Michigan St Hammond IN 46320

HEDRICK, HAROLD MELVIN, II, mfg. co. exec.; b. Torrance, Calif., Oct. 26, 1942; s. Harold Melvin and Enid Jessica (Terpstra) H.; B.A. in Math., Calif. State U., Long Beach, 1968; m. Carol DePierri, Oct. 28, 1978; 1 dau., Amanda. Pres., Apache Abrasives, Inc., Houston, 1973—; pres. Hedrick-Apache, Inc., Cerritos, Calif., 1973—; pres. Apache-Blast, Inc., Copperhill, Tenn., 1980—. Served to lt. USCG, 1969-73. Mem. Nat. Assn. Corrosion Engrs., Sigma Pi. Republican. Methodist. Office: 10690 Shadow Wood Dr Suite 112 Houston TX 77043

HEEBNER, A(LBERT) GILBERT, economist, banker; b. Phila., Mar. 7, 1927; s. Albert and Julia (Zwada) H.; A.B., U. Denver, 1948; A.M., U. Pa., 1950, Ph.D., 1967; m. Dorothy Mae Kiler, Aug. 16, 1952. Instr. econs. Coll. Wooster (Ohio), 1950-52; with Phila. Nat. Bank, 1952—, economist, 1960—, asst. v.p., 1961-64, v.p., 1964-70, sr. v.p., 1970-74, exec. v.p., 1974—; spl. asst. to chmn. Council Econ. Advisers, 1971-72; vis. prof. economics Swarthmore Coll., 1976. Served with USNR, 1945-46. Mem. Am. Econ. Assn., Am. Fin. Assn., Nat. Assn. Bus. Economists (pres. 1975-76), Am. Bankers Assn. (chmn. econ. adv. com. 1978-80), Conf. Bus. Economists. Baptist. Clubs: Union League, Sunday Breakfast. Home: 7 Blackwell Pl Philadelphia PA 19147 Office: Broad & Chestnut Sts Philadelphia PA 19101

HEERWAGEN, HERBERT ALFRED, lawyer; b. Newark, Nov. 20, 1910; s. Arthur and Margaret (Juban) H.; student Dickinson Coll., 1928-30; A.B., Cornell U., 1932, J.D., 1934; m. Doris Louise Richardson, May 26, 1939 (div. 1965); children—Peter D., David R., Nancy L., John R.; m. 2d, Margaret Knoll Anderson, Dec. 17, 1977. Admitted to N.Y. bar, 1934, since practiced in N.Y.C.; asso. Davies, Hardy & Schenck, 1934-44, 46-57, partner, 1958-68; sr. partner Davies, Hardy, Ives & Lewther and predecessor, 1968-77, Windels, Marx, Davies & Ives, N.Y.C., 1978—. Mem. New Castle (N.Y.) Recreation Commn., 1957-69, vice chmn., 1962-65, chmn., 1965-67; Republican committeeman, 1958-67; sec., trustee Ox Hollow Found., Inc., Bar Harbor Festival Corp., 1975—; hon. trustee, former sec. Big Bros., Inc., N.Y.C., past chmn. Manhattan council. Served with AUS, 1944-46. Recipient McKinney prize, 1934, Boardman prize, 1933 Cornell Law Sch. Mem. Am., N.Y. State bar assns., Am. Judicature Soc., Acad. Polit. Sci., Cornell Law Assn., Nat. Council Juvenile Court Judges (asso.), Nat., Bedford Audubon socs., Order of Coif, Phi Beta Kappa, Phi Kappa Phi. Episcopalian. Asso. editor Cornell Law Quar., 1932-33, editor-in-chief, 1933-34. Home: 133 Parker Ave Maplewood NJ 07040 Office: 51 W 51st St New York NY 10019

HEFFNER, RICHARD LOUIS, mgmt. cons.; b. St. Louis, Apr. 9, 1933; s. Edward Louis and Esther (Herter) H.; A.B., Columbia, 1955; M.B.A. cum laude, U. Tenn., 1965; m. Charlotte Anne Maclellan, Sept. 2, 1961; children—Richard Louis, Thomas Maclellan. Asst. advt. mgr. Richardson-Merrell, Inc., N.Y.C., 1957-60; new products market mgr. Chattem Drug & Chem. Co., 1960-64; v.p. marketing, corp. planning Dorsey Corp., 1964-69; dep. adminstr. Bus. and Def. Services Adminstrn., U.S. Dept. Commerce, 1969-70; pres., chief exec. officer, dir. Chattanooga Glass Corp., subsidiary Dorsey Corp., 1970-73, v.p., asst. sec. parent co., 1970-73; exec. v.p., mem. exec. com. Hamilton Bancshares, Inc., 1973-75; regional secretarial rep. of Sec. Commerce for 8 Southeastern states U.S. Dept. Commerce, 1975-77, mem. Fed. Regional Council, 1975-77; mgmt. cons., 1977—. Vice chmn. Southeastern States Regional Export Expansion Council, 1971-74; mem. nat. mktg. adv. com. U.S. Dept. Commerce, 1971—; trustee Glass Container Industry Research Corp. U.S., 1971-73; mem. Ky.-Tenn. dist. export council, 1974-75; regional chmn. Rep. Nat. Fin. Com., 1979—. Mem. allocations com. Chattanooga United Fund, 1961-72; bd. dirs. Chattanooga Tb and Respiratory Diseases Assn., 1962-76, pres., 1969-70; v.p. Allied Arts Fund, 1969-70; bd. dirs. Family Service Agy., 1968-69, Travelers Aid Soc., 1968-69, Jr. Achievement, 1971-74, Chattanooga Symphony Assn., 1973-74, Orange Grove Sch. for Retarded, 1973-74; bd. dirs., mem. exec. com. YMCA, 1974-76. Served to lt. USNR, 1955-57. Mem. NAM (mktg. com. 1967-70), Nat. Alliance Businessmen (met. chmn. 1970-71), Chattanooga C. of C. (dir. 1971-74), Newcomen Soc. N.Am., Sigma Alpha Epsilon. Presbyterian. Clubs: Sea Island (Ga.) Cottage, Capital City, Rotary. Home: 3655 Randall Hall NW Atlanta GA 30327

HEFNER, HUGH MARSTON, mag. pub.; b. Chgo., Apr. 9, 1926; s. Glenn L. and Grace (Swanson) H.; B.S., U. Ill., 1949; m. Mildred M. Williams, June 25, 1949 (div.); children—Christie A., David P. Subscription promotion writer Esquire mag., 1951; promotion mgr. Pubs. Devel. Corp., 1952; circulation mgr. Children's Activities mag., 1953; chmn. bd., chief exec. officer HMH Pub. Co. Inc., (now Playboy Enterprises, Inc.), 1953—, editor, pub. Playboy mag., 1953—; pres. Playboy Clubs Internat., Inc., 1959—; editor, pub. VIP mag., 1963-75, Oui mag., 1972—. Served with AUS, 1944-46. Office: 919 N Michigan Ave Chicago IL 60611*

HEFNER, JOE DENSON, ins. agy. exec.; b. Atlanta, Tex., Sept. 20, 1930; s. Byron Denson and Marcele (Johnson) H.; B.A., North Tex. State U., 1954; m. Julie Gregory, Oct. 25, 1979; children—Jerri Lynn, Julie Cecile, Debra Jo. Div. mgr. Continental Oil Co., Ft. Worth, 1954-63; pres. Compensation Systems, Inc., Dallas, 1964—; chmn. bd. Nat. Trust Corp., financial planners, Dallas, 1971—; dir. Commonwealth Nat. Bank, Dallas. Vice pres. Tex. div. Am. Cancer Soc., 1971—. Served to capt. 49th Armored Div., AUS, 1961-63. Mem. Million Dollar Round Table (life), Nat., Dallas (dir. 1970—) assns. life underwriters, Assn. for Advanced Life Underwriters, Internat. Assn. Financial Counsellors, Nat. Assn. Securities Dealers, Dallas Estate Council. Contbr. articles to profl. jours. Home: 6255 W Northwest Hwy Unit 104 Dallas TX 75225 Office: 4525 Lemmon Ave Dallas TX 75219

HEFNI, MOHAMED OMAR, aerospace/electronics co. exec.; b. Alexandria, Egypt, Mar. 7, 1933; s. Omar Hefni Moosa and Badreya (Soloman); came to U.S., 1958, naturalized, 1963; B.Commerce, U. Alexandria, 1955; M.B.A., U. So. Calif., 1961, D.B.A., 1969; m. Toussi Khonsary, Sept. 22, 1965; children—Nadia, Fadia. Head acctg. Shell Oil of Egypt, Alexandria, 1955-58; asst. controller Community Redevel. Agy. City of Los Angeles, 1960-67; head internal audits, corp. fin. Hughes Aircraft Co., Los Angeles, 1967-74, mgr. corp. econ. forecasting, 1974-80, chief economist, 1980—; instr. mgmt. UCLA; grad. faculty advisor U. Redlands. Mem. Planning Execs. Inst., Acad. Mgmt., So. Calif. Corp. Planners Assn., Nat. Assn. Bus. Economists, Am. Econ. Assn., Nat. Contract Mgmt. Assn., Inst. Internal Auditors. Republican. Moslem. Home: 1534 Stradella Rd Los Angeles CA 90024 Office: PO Box 90515 Los Angeles CA 90009

HEGARTY, CHRISTOPHER JOSEPH, mgmt. cons.; b. Jersey City, Dec. 29, 1934; s. Michael John and Catherine Mary (Morrissey) H.; student Youngstown U., 1958-61; Doctorate in Edn., Creative Devel. Inst., Philippines, 1977; m. Marion Ann Mike, Nov. 1976; children—Mahren, Cahlil, Michael. Investors exec., zone mgr. Investors Diversified Services, Mpls., 1960-65; pres. Hegarty & Co., N.Y.C., 1965-67; sr. v.p. Competitive Capital Corp., San Francisco, 1967-69; pres. Charter Street Corp., San Francisco, 1969-71; pres. C.J. Hegarty & Co., Novato, Calif., 1971—; mem. faculty for continuing edn. U. So. Calif.; cons. SRI Internat.; founder, regent Coll. Fin. Planning. Recipient Top Preview Speaker of Yr. award Internat. Platform Assn., 1972; Spokesman of Yr. award Internat. Assn. Fin. Planners, 1974; Spl. award Sci. Found., 1977; Leadership and Communications award Toastmasters Internat., 1978, 79; Innovative Mktg. award Sales and Mktg. Assn., San Francisco, 1979; Outstanding Speaker award Am. Soc. Tng. and Devel., 1980; Legion of Honor award Nat. Chaplains Assn., 1981. Mem. Nat. Speakers Assn. (founding dir.; Continuare Professos Articulatus Excellere award 1977), Sales and Mktg. Execs. Internat. Club: Commonwealth. Author: How to Manage Your Boss, 1980. Home: 2038 El Dorado Ct Novato CA 94947 Office: C J Hegarty & Co PO Box 1152 Novato CA 94947

HEGEMAN, JAMES ALAN, corp. exec.; b. Indpls., Jan. 8, 1943; s. Frank Anderson and Helene Anne (Sudbrock) H.; B.S. in Acctg. cum laude, U. Tenn., 1973; M.B.A., Harvard U., 1975; m. Catherine Louise Mallers, May 1, 1966 (div. 1973); 1 son, Christopher Scott. Pres., chmn. Nat. Rent-A-Cycle, Inc., Indpls., 1964-68, Fairfield Electronics Corp., Indpls., 1965-68; gen. mgr. H & R Block, Inc., Knoxville, Tenn., 1967-73; asst. controller Rohm & Haas, Inc., Knoxville, 1973-75; v.p. Gerson Co., Middleboro, Mass., 1975-76; controller Acton Corp. (Mass.), 1976-79; chief exec. officer Acton Films, Inc., N.Y.C., Telaction Phone Corp., Palisades Park, N.J., 1976—; v.p. fin. Audio Specialists, Inc., Newington, Conn., 1979—; fin./mgmt. cons. Standex Internat. Corp., Salem, N.H., 1979—; pres. LWC Industries, Inc., Miami, Fla., also dir.; dir. Window Corp. Am. Mem. Ind. Republican Central Com., 1967-68; bd. govs. U. Tenn., 1975—. Named to Tenn. Gov.'s staff, Tenn. Col. Continental Grain Co. fellow, 1973; Cabot fellow, 1974. C.P.A., Tenn. Mem. Am. Film Inst., Am. Inst. C.P.A.'s, Tenn. Soc. C.P.A.'s, U. Tenn. Alumni Assn. (pres.), Beta Alpha Psi. Lutheran. Club: Harvard (Boston). Home: 37 Scott Dr Bloomfield CT 06002 Office: Standex Internat Corp Manor Pkwy Salem NH 03079

HEIDELBAUGH, WARREN REDDING, retail exec.; b. Altoona, Pa., Sept. 22, 1934; s. Emlen Cresse and Marian (Redding) H.; B.S. in Econs., Lebanon Valley Coll., 1958; M.B.A., Temple U., 1968; m. Helen Louise Felty, Aug. 18, 1962; children—Deborah Renee, Michael Alan, Matthew Thomas. Commd. ensign U.S. Navy, 1958, advanced through grades to lt. comdr., 1978, ret., 1978; accountant Hershey Foods Corp. (Pa.), 1969-73; mgmt. cons. Leventhal & Harwath, Harrisburg, Pa., 1973-75; sec.-treas. Heidelbaugh Enterprises, Inc., Harrisburg, 1973—, owner accountant Stretch & Sew franchise, 1973—. Bd. dirs. Linglestown Baseball Assn.; bd. dirs., scheduler Holy Name Youth Hockey. Mem. Nat. Assn. Accountants, Pa. Retailers Assn., Harrisburg C. of C., Union Deposit Center Mchts. Assn. (dir., past treas.), Train Collectors Club Am. Republican. Clubs: Colonial (Harrisburg); Rotary, Masons, Shriners. Home: 4486 Olde Salem Rd Harrisburg PA 17112 Office: 1070 Union Deposit Center Harrisburg PA 17111

HEIDELL, JAMES MARTIN, investment banker; b. N.Y.C., Sept. 20, 1915; s. Irving and Rena (Sinn) H.; B.S., Harvard, 1935, J.D., 1938; M.S., Columbia, 1948; Ph.D., N.Y. U., 1960; m. Flora Ann Siegel, June 26, 1952; children—Elizabeth, Pamela, James A. Admitted to N.Y. bar, 1939, U.S. Supreme Ct. bar, 1961; practiced in N.Y.C., 1939-40; controller Ladenburg, Thalmann & Co., N.Y.C., 1946-63; asso. prof. U. Bridgeport (Conn.), 1963-66; asso. prof. Fordham U., N.Y.C., 1966-69; v.p. First Manhattan Co., N.Y.C., 1969—; sec. Guerdon Industries, 1961-63. Lectr. investments Baruch Sch. City Coll. N.Y., evenings, 1963; guest lectr. Savs. Bank Assn. Conn., 1964-66. Mem. Scarsdale Town Club Fiscal Affairs Com., 1971-72. Served from pvt. to capt. AUS, 1941-46; ETO. Mem. Municipal Finance Officers Assn. (nat. com. on student recruitment 1968-69), N.Y. County Lawyers Assn., Am. Econ. Assn., Am. Finance Assn., Municipal Forum N.Y. Club: Harvard (N.Y.C.). Author: The Purchasing of Tax-Exempt Bonds By Individuals In The 1946-1956 Decade, 1960. Home: 14 Fenimore Rd Scarsdale NY 10583 Office: 380 Madison Ave New York City NY 10017

HEIDEMAN, GEORGE JOHN, carbide tool co. exec.; b. Union, Ill., Apr. 9, 1912; s. George E. and Mathilde (Schmidt) H.; B.S., U. Ill., 1934; postgrad. Yale U., 1935-36; married. Instr. acctg. Yale U., 1935-36; accountant Arthur Andersen & Co., N.Y.C., 1936-38, Detroit, 1938-41, Cleve., 1946-55; treas. Kennametal Inc., Latrobe, Pa., 1955-68, v.p., 1968-77, sr. v.p., 1977—; also dir. Served with AUS, 1941-42, to comdr. USNR, 1942-46. Mem. Am. Inst. C.P.A.'s, Ohio Soc. C.P.A.'s, Nat. Mgmt. Assn. Republican. Club: Latrobe Country, Ligonier Country. Home: 2 Franklin Rd Ligonier PA 15658 Office: PO Box 231 Latrobe PA 15650

HEIDER, DAVID ARTHUR, mgmt. cons.; b. Oconomowoc, Wis., Mar. 30, 1941; s. Maynard Laverne and Marcella Florence (Schneider) H.; B.A., Swarthmore Coll., 1964; M.B.A., Harvard, 1966; m. Ann Mueller, July 30, 1966; children—Daniel Arthur, Kathryn Anne. Instr. Harvard Bus. Sch., Boston, 1966-69; asso. in bus. adminstrn. Harvard Med. Sch., Boston, 1969-72; cons. bus. mgmt. Peter Bent Brigham Hosp., Boston, 1969-72; pres., dir. Gambles Continental State Bank, St. Paul, 1972-76; asst. v.p. Gamble-Skogmo, Inc., Mpls., 1976-77, v.p., 1977-80; asso. Merrimac Assos., Inc., Mpls., 1980—; pres. Heider Research Assos., Newton, Mass., 1967-70; asso. Trident Growth Services, N.Y.C., 1970-72; research dir. Inst. for Ednl. Adminstrn., Harvard U., Boston, 1969-71; v.p., treas., dir. Specialized Legal Publs., Inc., St. Paul, 1980—; chief exec. officer Rhino Internat. of N.D., Inc., Grand Forks, 1980—; v.p., dir. Bluff House Holdings, Ltd., Bahamas; dir. Aristar, Inc., John Alden Life Ins. Co., Gambles Credit Corp. Mem. City St. Paul Bd. Appeals and Rev., 1974-79. Chmn. governing bd. Samaritan Hosp., St. Paul, 1974-79; exec. com. E. Met. Hosp. Trustees Council, St. Paul, 1977-79. Mem. Harvard Bus. Sch. Assn. Minn. (v.p., dir. 1973-79). Episcopalian (regional bd.). Clubs: Moss Creek Golf. Author: (with others) Selective Insect Control, 1966; Income Bonds Through the Looking Glass, 1974. Editor: Business and the Urban Environment, 1969. Home: 776 Fairmount Ave St Paul MN 55105 Office: 715 Florida Ave S Minneapolis MN 55426

HEIDER, FRED CLARENCE, profl. golfer; b. Denver, Feb. 22, 1923; s. Fred August and Marie Barbara (Froman) H.; B.G.E., Municipal U. of Omaha, 1965; m. Chisato Hazi, Dec. 3, 1958; children—Anna Marie, Renee Jean. Asst. golf profl. to Bob Carr, Class A golfer, 1939-41; surveyor U.S. Geol. Survey, Alaska, 1948-49; asst. golf profl. Orange Brook Golf Club, Hollywood, Fla., 1953-55, Philmont Country Club, Philmont, Pa., 1955; enlisted U.S. Air Force, 1955, advanced through grades to master sgt., 1969, ret., 1969; franchise and regional dir. for Career Acad., S.D. and Nebr., 1969; head golf profl. Skyline Golf Club, Omaha, 1970, Platteview Country Club, Omaha, 1971-72; teaching profl. Fun Fairways Driving Range, Omaha, 1973-74; with Custom Golf Corp., Omaha, 1974; cons. to engr. Bucaneer Bay Golf Course, Plattsmouth, Nebr., 1974; golf dir. Buccaneer Bay Golf Course, Bellevue, Nebr., 1974—. Served with USN, 1942-45, U.S. Army, 1949-52. Decorated D.F.C., Air Medal with five oak leaf clusters. Mem. Sr. Profl. Golfers Assn. (pres. N.D., S.D. and Nebr. sect. 1979), Golf Club Repair and Fitting Assn., DAV, Nebr. Golf Course Supts. Assn., Profl. Golfers Assn. (class A) Precision Measurement Assn. Republican. Club: Kiwanis. Home: 3206 Wallace Ave Bellevue NE 68005 Office: PO Box 69 Bellevue NE 68005

HEIDINGER, HELMUT, banker; b. Graz, Austria, Oct. 25, 1922; s. Josef and Gertrude (Ipsen) H.; Dr. rer. pol., U. Graz, 1954; m. Annemarie Goedel, Oct. 25, 1947; children—Gertrude (Mrs. Karl Haertl), Reinhold, Hartmut, Wolfram. Export bookkeeper firm Leonardo Graz, 1949-53; sales mg. Binder & Co., 1953-56; rep. proxy br. Austrian Credit Inst. Corp., Graz, 1956-59; rep., dir. Bank Financial Trade and Industry, 1959-63; mgr. Savs. Bank of Leibnitz, 1963-69; chmn. bd., dir. Steierm Sparkasse in Graz, 1970-73; mem. governing council Girozentrale & Bank der Österreichen Sparkassen, 1976—, Austria-Ferngas GmbH, 1977—, Beteiligungs-Finanzierungs-AG; chmn. Steiermärkischen Bank GmbH, 1973—; dir., mem. governing council Steirischen Ferngas GmbH, 1976—. Del., Styria Land Parliament, 1966—. Bd. dirs. Styria Econs. Assn., 1966—. Served with Austrian Army, 1940-45. Mem. Liszt Assn., Styria Farmers Union. Lion. Home: 15 Grottenhof Kaindorf/Sulm 8430 Leibnitz Austria Office: Landhausgasse 14-18 8010 Graz Austria

HEIDRICK, GARDNER WILSON, mgmt. cons.; b. Clarion, Pa. Oct. 7, 1911; s. R. Emmet and Helen (Wilson) H.; B.S. in Banking and Finance, U. Ill, 1935; m. Marian Eileen Lindsay, Feb. 19, 1937; children—Gardner Wilson, Robert L. Indsl. dist. sales mgr. Scott Paper Co., Chester, Pa., 1935-42; dir. personnel Farmland Industries, Kansas City, Mo., 1942-51; asso. Booz, Allen & Hamilton, Chgo., 1951-53; partner Heidrick & Struggles, Inc., Chgo., 1953—, now chmn. bd.; dir. Internat. Exec. Service Corp., N.Y.C. Bd. dirs. U. Ill. Found., Keller Grad. Sch. Mgmt., Chgo. Served with USNR, 1945-46. Recipient President's award U. Ill. Found., 1979. Mem. Chgo. Assn. Commerce, Ill. C. of C., U. Ill. Alumni Assn. (past pres.; Achievement award 1980), Phi Kappa Sigma. Clubs: Chicago, Tower (Chgo.); Hinsdale (Ill.). Golf (past pres.); University (N.Y.); Country of Fla., Ocean (Delray Beach). Home: 101 S County Line Rd Hinsdale IL 60521 Office: 125 S Wacker Dr Chicago IL 60606

HEIDT, JOHN MURRAY, banker; b. Oceanside, N.Y., Dec., 1931; s. Horace M. and Adaline (Sohns) H.; A.B., Stanford U., 1954; postgrad. Pacific Coast Banking Sch., 1965; M.B.A., U. So. Calif., 1969; m. Mary Ann Kerans, June 18, 1953; children—John K., Ann A. With the Union Bank, Los Angeles, 1959—, exec. v.p., 1971-75, pres., 1975—, also dir.; dir. Union Venture Corp. Trustee St. John's Hosp., Marlborough Sch. Served as spl. agt. USAF, 1954-57. Recipient Man of Hope award City of Hope, 1978. Mem. Am. Bankers Assn., Calif. Bankers Assn., Assn. of Res. City Bankers. Clubs: Los Angeles Country; California. Office: 445 S Figueroa St Los Angeles CA 90071

HEIECK, PAUL JAY, wholesale distributor co. exec.; b. San Francisco, Aug. 6, 1937; s. Erwin N. and Ann C. (Retchlees) H.; student Golden Gate Coll., 1957-58; m. Kathleen Pawela, Oct. 14, 1967; children—Valerie, Yvonne, Elizabeth, Krista, Justin. Salesman, Heieck & Moran, San Francisco, 1958-63; sec.-treas. Heieck Supply, San Francisco, 1963-76, pres., 1976—, also dir.; pres., dir. Eureka Supply (Calif.), 1972—, Heieck Supply, San Jose, Calif., 1980—, Heieck Supply, Sacramento, 1980—. Bd. dirs. San Francisco Boys Club, 1972—; dir. San Francisco Bd. Trade, 1978—, v.p., 1980—. Served with U.S. Army, 1955-57. Mem. Nat. Assn. Wholesalers, Am. Supply Assn., No. Calif. Suppliers Assn. (dir. 1980—). Republican. Episcopalian. Clubs: Rotary, Olympic, Ingomar, Sharon Heights Country, San Mateo Country Mounted Posse. Office: 1111 Connecticut St San Francisco CA 94107

HEIKER, VINCENT EDWARD, mfg. co. adminstr.; b. St. Louis, Apr. 21, 1942; s. Anthony E. and Muriel E. (Evans) H.; student St. Louis U., 1960-62; B.S. with honors in Systems and Data Processing, Washington U., St. Louis, 1972; M.B.A., So. Ill. U., Edwardsville, 1974; m. Sheryl Ann Bunevac, Sept. 13, 1969; children—Stacie Marie, Vincent Edward. Russian interpreter U.S. Army Security Agy., 1962-65; successively asst. sales mgr., market research mgr., systems analyst, order entry supr., product line mgr. Emerson Elec. Co., St. Louis, 1966-73; systems analyst Mallinckrodt, Inc., St. Louis, 1973-74; dir. mgmt. info. systems Permaneer Corp., St. Louis, 1974-77; info. systems mgr. Boise Cascade Corp., St. Louis, 1977—; cons. to small bus.; career counselor, speaker. Served with AUS, 1962-65. Cert. data processor. Mem. Assn. Systems Mgmt., Am. Prodn. and Inventory Control Soc., Miss. Valley Telecommunications Assn., Mensa Internat. Republican. Reviewer EDP books; contbr. articles profl. jours. Home: 6027 Hageman Rd Mehlville MO 63128 Office: 13300 Interstate Dr Saint Louis MO 63042

HEILMAN, JOHN EDWARD, engr.; b. Chgo., Mar. 20, 1936; s. Frederick John and Kathryn Grace (Schnider) H.; B.S. in Food Engring., Ill. Inst. Tech., 1961; m. Virginia Lois Anderson, Jan. 28, 1956; children—Wayne John, Warren Wesley. Engr. grocery products div. Armour & Co., Chgo., 1959-61, lab. technician, 1958, foreman, 1958-59; process engr. Central Soya Co., Inc., Ft. Wayne, Ind., 1962-65, supt., Chgo., 1965-68; sr. process engr. Continental Grain Co., Chgo., 1966-75, dir. engring. process div., N.Y.C., 1975-77, asst. v.p. process div., 1977-79, v.p. process div., 1979—. Mem. Nat. Soybean Processors Assn. (chmn. tech. com.), Nat. Fire Protection Assn. (sectional com. solvent extraction), Am. Oil Chemists Soc. (tech. engring. com. nat. program planning com.), Am. Assn. Cereal Chemists. Republican. Methodist. Home: 22 Sugarbush Ct Wilton CT 06897 Office: Continental Grain Co 277 Park Ave New York NY 10017

HEILWEIL, MARC S., investment counselor, lawyer; b. Greensboro, N.C., Dec. 18, 1945; s. Murray and Charlotte Heilweil; B.A. magna cum laude, Yale U., 1967, J.D., 1974. With U.S. Dept. State, 1969-70; admitted to Ga. bar, 1974; asso. firm Arnall, Golden & Gregory, Atlanta, 1975-77; pres. Profl. Asset Mgmt., Inc., Atlanta, 1977-80; treas. Ga. Lawyers Investment Co., Decatur, 1980—. Fulbright Scholar, 1967-68. Mem. Phi Beta Kappa. Home: PO Box 1141 Decatur GA 30031

HEIMANN, JOHN GAINES, comptroller of currency; b. N.Y.C., Apr. 1, 1929; s. Sidney M. and Dorothy V.B. (Gainesburg) H.; A.B., Syracuse (N.Y.) U., 1950; m. Margaret E. Fechheimer, Dec. 2, 1956; children—Joshua Gaines, Eliza Faith. Vice pres. Smith, Barney & Co., N.Y.C., 1955-66; sr. v.p., dir. E.M. Warburg, Pincus & Co., Inc., N.Y.C., 1967-75; N.Y. State supt. banks, 1975-76; N.Y. State commr. housing and community renewal, 1976-77; mem. N.Y. State Banking Bd., 1976-77; comptroller of the currency, Washington, 1977—; dir. FDIC, 1977—, Neighborhood Reinvestment Corp., 1977—; chmn. Fed. Fin. Instns. Exam. Council, 1979—; mem. Depository Instns. Deregulation Com., 1980—; lectr. Harvard U. Bus. Sch., 1969, U. Calif., Berkeley, 1970; adviser, cons. in field. Trustee New Lincoln Sch., N.Y.C.; mem. corp. adv. council Syracuse U., 1968-75. Served with AUS, 1951-53. Named Housing Man of Year, Nat. Housing Conf., 1976. Fellow Lambda Alpha; mem. Nat. Businessmen's Council (dir.), Fgn. Policy Assn. (asso.), Fed. Nat. Mortgage Assn. (dir.). Democrat. Jewish. Clubs: 1925 F St. (Washington); Ft. Orange (Albany, N.Y.). Office: 490 L'Enfant Plaza E SW Washington DC 20219

HEIMANN, ROBERT KARL, tobacco co. exec.; b. N.Y.C., Sept. 22, 1918; s. Charles and Elizabeth (Quinan) H.; A.B. summa cum laude, Princeton, 1948; M.A., N.Y.U., 1949, Ph.D., 1953; m. Charlotte Parker, Feb. 19, 1950; children—Mark, Karla. Editor, Nation's Heritage, 1948-49; mng. and exec. editor Forbes mag., 1949-53; with Am. Brands Inc. (formerly Am. Tobacco Co.), 1954—, exec. v.p., 1966-69, pres., chief operating officer, 1969-72, chmn., chief exec. officer, 1973—, also dir. Served to capt. AUS, 1942-46. Fellow Am. Sociol. Soc.; mem. N.Y. Security Analysts Soc., N.Y. Financial Writers. Author: Tobacco and Americans, 1960, also articles. Office: Am Brands Inc 245 Park Ave New York NY 10167

HEIMBOLD, CHARLES ANDREAS, JR., mfg. co. exec.; b. Newark, May 27, 1933; s. Charles Andreas and Mary Joseph (Corrigan) H.; B.A. cum laude, Villanova U., 1954; LL.B. cum laude, U. Pa., 1960; LL.M., N.Y. U., 1966; postgrad. Hague Acad. Internat. Law, 1959; m. Monika Astrid Barkvall, Sept. 22, 1962; children—Joanna, Eric, Leif, Peter. Admitted to N.Y. bar, 1962; asso. mem. firm Milbank, Tweed, Hadley & McCloy, 1960-63; with Bristol Myers, N.Y.C., 1963—, dir. corporate devel., 1970-73, v.p. planning and devel., 1973—. Bd. dirs. Sheltering Arms Childrens Service, Putnam-Indian Field Sch. Served with USN, 1957-60. Mem. Assn. Bar City N.Y. Clubs: The Board Room (N.Y.C.); Riverside (Conn.) Yacht. Home: Leeward Ln Riverside CT 06878 Office: 345 Park Ave New York NY 10022

HEIN, DAVID LEON, diversified industry exec.; b. Cleve., Feb. 4, 1939; s. Oscar Gustave and Helen Rose (Gruss) H.; B.S., Bowling Green State U., 1961; m. Judith Ann Diemert, July 27, 1963; children—Susan, Cathleen, David, Matthew. Audit supr. Ernst & Whinney, Cleve., 1961-65, tax acct., 1963-65, mgmt. cons., 1965-70; v.p. fin. Brewer-Chilcote Paper Co., Cleve., 1970-75, treas., 1972-75, also dir.; v.p. finance Chilcote Co., Cleve., 1970—, treas., 1975, also dir.; dir., cons. Cleve. area small businesses; mem. faculty Cleve. State U., 1965-67. Adviser Great Lakes Shakespeare Festival, 1964-67; pres. Rocky River Figure Skating Club, 1977, dir., 1976; chmn. and vice chmn. Greater Cleve. Council Figure Skating Clubs, 1978-79. Bowling Green State U. grantee, 1958-61; C.P.A., Ohio. Mem. Ohio Soc. C.P.A.'s, Alpha Tau Omega, Beta Alpha Psi. Republican. Roman Catholic. Clubs: Cleve. Athletic; Cleve. Skating. Home: 21298 Endsley Ave Rocky River OH 44116 Office: 2140 Superior Ave Cleveland OH 44114

HEIN, ILENE LACKEMEYER, pub. co. exec.; b. Buffalo, Nov. 25, 1919; d. William and Nellie (Stewart) Lackemeyer; R.N., Deaconess Hosp., 1940; m. William Sylvester Hein, May 15, 1941 (dec. 1976); children—Susan, Bonnie, William. Nurse, 1941-60; with William S. Hein & Co., Inc., Buffalo, 1960—, v.p., chmn. bd., 1976—. Mem. Am. Assn. Law Librarians, Nurses Alumnae Assn. Deaconess Hosp. Republican. Compiler: Hein's Legal Periodical Checklist, vol. 1, 1977, vol. 2, 1978. Office: William S Hein & Co Inc 1285 Main St Buffalo NY 14209

HEINECKE, ERNST ARTHUR, ins. co. agt.; b. Sheboygan, Wis., Apr. 17, 1926; s. Ernst F. and Lydia (Guehlstorf) H.; B.A. in Bus., Valparaiso U., 1950; m. Nadine L. Bundy, Sept. 1, 1975; children—Thomas, Steven, Timothy, Ins. agt. Phoenix Mut., 1959, dist. rep. Aid Assn. Luths., West Bend, Wis., 1959-63, gen. agt., 1963—. Mem. Planning Commn., Town Kronenwetter, 1980—; chmn. Marathon County March of Dimes, 1970-71, Marathon County Heart Fund, 1965-66; bd. dirs. N. Wis. dist. Luth. Ch.-Mo. Synod, 1965-71, mem. bd. fin., 1973—. Served with U.S. Army, 1944-46. C.L.U. Mem. Gen. Agts. and Mgrs. Assn. (dir. 1980—), Wisconsin Valley Assn. Life Underwriters (pres. 1965-66), Wis. Assn. Life Underwriters (pres. 1970-71). Club: Lions (pres. 1976); Wausau Country. Home: 1737 McAddoe Pl Mosinee WI 54455 Office: 2420 Stewart Sq Wausau WI 54401

HEINEMAN, BEN WALTER, lawyer; b. Wausau, Wis., Feb. 10, 1914; s. Walter Ben and Elsie Brunswick (Deutsch) H.; student U. Mich., 1930-33; LL.B., Northwestern U., 1936, LL.D., 1967; LL.D., Lawrence Coll., 1959, Lake Forest Coll., 1966, Northwestern U., 1967; m. Natalie Goldstein, Apr. 17, 1935; children—Martha Heineman Field, Ben Walter. Admitted to Ill. bar, 1936; chmn. bd. dirs. Four Wheel Drive Auto Co., 1954-57; chmn. C. & N.-W. Ry., 1956-72, chief exec. officer, dir.; pres. Northwest Industries, Inc., 1968—; chmn. exec. com., dir. 1st Nat. Bank Chgo., 1st Chgo. Corp.; dir. Field Enterprises, Inc.; trustee, mem. investment com. Sears Roebuck Savs. and Profit Sharing Fund, 1967-71. Chmn., Ill. Bd. Higher Edn., 1961-69; mem. Presdl. Task Force on Housing and Urban Devel., 1965; chmn. White House Civil Rights Conf., 1966, Chgo. Civil Rights Summit Conf. on Housing, 1966, Presdl. Com. on Govt. Orgn., 1966-67, Pres.'s Commn. on Income Maintenance Programs, 1967-69. Trustee U. Chgo.; trustee Rockefeller Found., 1972-78; hon. life dir. Lyric Opera of Chgo., Chgo. Orchestral Assn.; mem. vis. com. dept. econs. Harvard, 1966-71. Fellow Am. Bar Found. (life), Am. Acad. Arts and Scis.; mem. Am. Law Inst., Am., Ill., Chgo. bar assns., Transp. Assn. Am. (hon. life), Art Inst. Chgo. (life), Order of Coif, Phi Delta Phi. Clubs: Chicago, Casino, Standard, Quadrangle, Chicago Yacht, Executives, Mid-Am., Metropolitan, Carlton, Commercial, Commonwealth, Wayfarers (Chgo.); Ephraim (Wis.) Yacht; Great Lakes Cruising. Home: 180 E Pearson St Chicago IL 60611 Office: 6300 Sears Tower Chicago IL 60606

HEINER, DENNIS GRANT, mfg. co. exec.; b. Ogden, Utah, Aug. 18, 1943; s. Grant and Mary (Stoker) H.; B.A., Weber State Coll., 1969; M.B.A., Brigham Young U., 1971; m. Margo Proctor, Dec. 17, 1970; children—Shalayna, Bryce James, Jillian. Vice pres. mktg., exec. v.p., gen. mgr. Sportplay, Inc., Salt Lake City, 1971-72; mgr. mktg. adminstrn., dir. fin. Sno Jet, Inc., Burlington, Vt., 1972-75; v.p. fin. and adminstrn. Glastron Boat Co., Austin, Tex., 1975-79; v.p. fin. Liken Home Furnishings div. Beatrice Foods Co., Huntington Beach, Calif., 1979—. Bd. dirs. Austin Jr. Achievement, 1978—, fundraising chmn., 1978. Mem. Beta Gamma Sigma. Mormon. Home: 2731 N Rockridge Circle Orange CA 92667 Office: 7150 Fenwick Ln Westminster CA 92683

HEINRICH, DANIEL JAY, retail exec.; b. Hillsboro, Oreg., June 15, 1951; s. John C. and Joyce (Voges) H.; student Portland State U., 1969-73; m. Linda Diane Smith, July 28, 1969; children—Christopher, Michael, Lesley. Mem. staff Heinrich Datsun-GMC, Hillsboro, 1966—, office mgr., 1972, bus. mgr., 1973—; sec. treas., founder Heinrich Leasing Inc., 1973—; partner, founder Men-a retail clothing, Portland, 1976—. Leader, United Way. Mem. Nat., Oreg. automobile dealers assns., Datsun Accountants Club, Datsun Century Club. Republican. Lutheran. Clubs: Rock Creek Country. Home: 20040 NW Nestucca Portland OR 97229 Office: PO Box 479 Hillsboro OR 97123

HEINS, JAMES EDWARD, telephone co. exec.; b. Lee County, N.C., Nov. 17, 1930; s. Max Thomas and Eunice (Blue) H.; B.S. in Bus. Adminstrn., U. N.C., 1953, M.B.A., 1959; m. Carroll Butts, July 9, 1960; children—James Edward, Cooper Corinne. Sales rep. Anaconda Wire & Cable Co., 1959-60; product mgr. Whitney Blake Co., 1960-63; exec. v.p. Heins Telephone Co., Sanford, N.C., 1963-71, pres., 1971—; dir., chmn. exec. com. Carolina Bank, Sanford; dir. Trion Corp., Sanford; active in formation and devel. N.C. Sch. Telephone, Sanford; commr. N.C. Agy. Public Telecommunications. Past chmn. bd. dirs. and chmn. fund raising com. N.C. Heart Assn.; past chmn. Sanford community guidance com. N.C. Dept. Corrections; mem. Lee County Recreation Commn., 1964-68, chmn., 1970-76; pres. Lee County Young Democratic Club, 1964-65; bd. dirs. N.C. Citizens Assn.; deacon, mem. planning council 1st Presbyn. Ch., Sanford. Served with U.S. Army, 1955-56. Named Young Man of Yr., Sanford Jaycees, 1964, Rotarian of Yr., Sanford, 1980, Sanford Citizen of Yr., Sanford Herald, 1977. Mem. U.S. Ind. Telephone Assn. (pres. 1979-80, chmn. advt. and public relations com. 1975-79), N.C. Ind. Telephone Assn. (dir., pres. 1969-70), Sanford C. of C. (pres. 1967), R.R. House Hist. Assn. (pres. 1968-69). Club: Sanford Rotary. Home: 1906 Windmill Dr Sanford NC 27330 Office: 106 Gordon St PO Box 1209 Sanford NC 27330

HEINS, M. JACK, accountant; b. Cedar Rapids, Iowa, June 19, 1928; s. John C. and Martha R. (Faverty) H.; B.S.C. in Acctg., State U. Iowa, 1950; m. Jacqueline A. Englebert, Nov. 2, 1962; children—Charlie, Ann. Staff acct. Thor Power Tool Co.; office mgr. Cedar Rapids Block Co. (Iowa); partner McGladrey Hendrickson & Co., Cedar Rapids. Served with U.S. Army, 1951-53. Recipient Man of Yr. award Nat. Assn. Accts.; C.P.A. Mem. Am. Inst. C.P.A.'s, Iowa Soc. C.P.A.'s, Cedar Rapids C. of C. (legis. com.). Republican. Congregationalist. Clubs: Cedar Rapids Country, Pickwick, Optimist, Univ. Athletic, Elks. Office: Merchants National Bank 10th Floor Cedar Rapids IA 52401

HEINSOHN, WILLIAM BISHOP, chem. co. exec.; b. St. Louis, Apr. 28, 1929; s. Frank Otto and Marjorie (Bishop) H.; B. Mech. Engring., Cornell U., 1953; M.B.A., U. Pa., 1958; m. Susan Jean Medinger, June 20, 1964; children—Jean Elizabeth, Katharine Parr, William Bishop. Project engr. DuPont Co., Gibbstown, N.J. and Buffalo, 1953-57; sr. fin. analyst Phila. Electric Co., 1958-64; asst. to treas. and economist Shell Can. Ltd., Toronto, Ont., 1964-67; asst. to treas. Internat. Utilities, Phila., 1967-70; asst. treas. ICI Ams. Wilmington, Del., 1970-77, corp. economist, 1977—; treas. financing subs.; dir. Econ. Council Del., Ams. for Competitive Enterprise, Wilmington Bus. Opportunities. Past chmn. suburban businessmen com. United Way; steering com. Del. Humanities Forum; monetary com. Global Interdependence Center, Phila.; trustee Westminster Presbyterian Ch. Served to lt. U.S. Army, 1954-56. Chartered fin. analyst. Mem. Nat. Assn. Bus. Economists (chmn. Wilmington chpt.), Fin. Analysts Fedn. Clubs: Cornell; Wharton. Home: 505 Rothbury Rd Woodbrook Wilmington DE 19803 Office: ICI Americas Wilmington DE 19897

HEINZ, EDWARD N., JR., flavor and fragrance mfg. co. exec.; b. Chgo., Nov. 27, 1914; s. Edward N. and Adeline M. (Kelly) H.; B.S. in Chem. Engring., Ill. Inst. Tech., 1937; m. Laurette F. Higgins, Oct. 22, 1943; children—Edward, Raymond, James, Pamela, Laurette, Joan, Mary. Vice pres., dir. Food Materials Corp., Chgo., 1937-67; pres. dir. Wm. M. Bell Co., Melrose Park, Ill., 1967—. Served with Chem. Corps AUS, 1943-46. Mem. Flavor and Extract Mfrs. Assn. U.S. (pres. 1958-60), Am. Chem. Soc., Inst. Food Technologists, Am. Assn. Cereal Chemists. Clubs: North Shore Country (Glenview, Ill.); Lake Shore Athletic (Chgo.). Home: 22 Meadowview Dr Winnetka IL 60093 Office: 3312 Bloomingdale St Melrose Park IL 60160

HEINZ, HENRY JOHN, II, food co. exec.; b. Sewickley, Pa., July 10, 1908; s. Howard and Elizabeth (Rust) H.; grad. Shadyside Acad., 1927; A.B., Yale, 1931; student Trinity Coll., Cambridge, 1931-32; LL.D., Bowling Green U., 1943, Allegheny Coll., 1944, U. Pitts., 1960; m. Joan Diehl, June 18, 1935 (div.); 1 son, Henry John III; m. 2d, Drue English Maher, Aug. 22, 1953. With H. J. Heinz Co., 1933—, pres., 1941-59, chmn., 1959—. Head spl. fgn. ops. adminstrn. mission to Pakistan, 1954; pub. adv. mem. U.S. del. to 12th session Gen. Agreement Tariffs and Trade, Geneva, 1957; chmn. U.S. del. Econ. Commn. for Europe, 1958-60. Bd. dirs. Bus. Com. for Arts, Pitts. Regional Planning Assn., Pitts. Symphony Soc., World Affairs Council; trustee Nutrition Found., Carnegie Inst., Carnegie-Mellon U., Com. Econ. Devel., Food and Drug Law Inst.; gov. bd. Yale U. Art Gallery; mem. Yale U. Econ. Growth Center; mem. exec. com. Allegheny Conf. Community Devel.; chmn. Agribus. Council Inc.; bd. dirs. Sarah Heinz House. Mem. Internat. C. of C. (trustee U.S. council), Order St. John. Republican. Presbyterian. Clubs: Duquesne, Allegheny Country, Rolling Rock (Pitts.); Brook, River (N.Y.C.); Bucks, White's (London, Eng.). Home: Goodwood Sewickley PA 15143 Office: H J Heinz Co Pittsburgh PA 15230

HEINZE, JAMES HENRY, ins. co. exec.; b. Clarksburg, W.Va., Sept. 4, 1914; s. H. Arthur and Helene (Devore) H.; A.B., W.Va. U., 1936, LL.B., 1938; A.A. (hon.), Kalamazoo Valley Community Coll., 1972; m. Mary Frances Gibbs, Aug. 12, 1939; children—Frances (Mrs. William P. Winslow), Margaret Jane. Admitted to W.Va. bar, 1938, Ind. bar, 1946, Mich. bar, 1963; practice law, West Union, W.Va., 1938-42; gen. counsel Secured Group Ins. Cos., Indpls., 1946-54, v.p., 1949-54, pres., 1954-64; sec., gen. counsel Wolverine-Riverside Ins. Cos., Battle Creek, Mich., 1964-80, dir., 1972-80; Midwest counsel, asst. sec. Transamerica Ins. Group, 1968-80; ltd. pvt. practice law, Battle Creek, 1980—. Pres., Calhoun County Community Action Com., 1965-67; chmn. Mich. Legislative Retirement Com., 1968-70, Gov.'s Task Force Drinking Driver, 1973-74. Pres. Battle Creek Policemen's and Firemen's Retirement Bd., 1962-76; mem. Mich. Ho. of Reps., 1967-72. Served to lt. USNR, 1942-45. Recipient honor certificate award Freedoms Found. at Valley Forge, 1968. Mem. Am., W.Va., Ind. bar assns., State Bar Mich., Battle Creek C. of C. (pres. 1976-77), Phi Beta Kappa. Mason, Lion. Presbyn. (trustee 1966-68; 78—). Home: 130 Edgebrook Dr Battle Creek MI 49015 Office: Great Lakes Fed Savs & Loan Bldg Suite 200 Battle Creek MI 49016

HEISE, ARTHUR GUSTAV, bank holding co. exec.; b. Luebeck, Germany, Aug. 8, 1948; came to U.S., 1952, naturalized, 1960; s. Friedrich and Christine (Matt) H.; B.B.A. in Acctg., U. Wis., Milw., 1971; m. Annemarie Osti, Aug. 21, 1971. Sr. auditor First Wis. Corp., Milw., 1971-77; dir. audit Valley Bancorp., Appleton, Wis., 1977—; mem. faculty Bank Adminstrn. Inst. Bd. dirs. Voice of Hope Outreach, Inc., Dallas; sec. Calumet County (Wis.) Republican Party, state del., 1979—. C.P.A., Wis. Mem. Inst. Internal Auditors, Am. Inst. C.P.A.'s, Wis. Soc. C.P.A.'s. Home: Rt 1 PO Box 294N Menasha WI 54952

HEISEY, WILLIAM LAWRENCE, publisher; b. Toronto, Ont., Can., May 29, 1930; s. Karl Brooks and Alice Isobel (Smith) H.; B.A., Trinity Coll., U. Toronto, 1952; M.B.A., Harvard U., 1954. Mktg. asst. Procter & Gamble, Toronto, 1954-67, mgr. advt. prodn. div., 1967; exec. v.p. Standard Broadcasting Sales, Toronto, 1967-71; pres. Harlequin Enterprises, Ltd., Don Mills, Ont., 1971—, also dir.; dir. Torstar Corp. Bd. govs. Toronto French Sch., 1966-73. Mem. Assn. Canadian Advertisers (dir. 1964-66), B.B.M. Bur. Measurement (dir. 1963-69), Zeta Psi. Conservative. Mem. United Ch. Can. Clubs: Granite, Badminton and Racket. Office: 225 Duncan Mill Rd Don Mills ON M3B 3K9 Canada

HEISKELL, ANDREW, publishing exec.; b. Naples, Italy, Sept 13, 1915; s. Morgan and Ann (Hubbard) H.; ed. in Switzerland, Germany, France; student Harvard U. Bus. Sch., 1935-36; LL.D., Shaw U., 1968, Lake Erie Coll., 1969, Hofstra U., 1972, Hobart and William Smith Colls., 1973; D.Litt., Lafayette Coll., 1969; m. Cornelia Scott, Nov. 12, 1937 (div.); children—Diane, Peter; m. 2d, Madeleine Carroll (div.); 1 dau., Anne M.; m. 3d, Marian Sulzberger Dryfoos, 1965. Reporter, N.Y. Henald-Tribune, 1936-37; asso. editor Life mag., 1937-39, asst. gen. mgr., 1939-42, gen. mgr., 1942-46, pub., 1946-60; v.p. Time, Inc., 1949-60, chmn. bd., 1960-69, chmn. bd., chief exec. officer 1969-80, also dir.; dir. Am. TV & Communications Corp., Book-of-the Month Club, Inland Container Corp., Temple-Eastex, Inc. Vice chmn., chmn. exec. com. Brookings Inst.; bd. advisers Dumbarton Oaks Research Library and Collection; mem. Pan Am. Internat. Adv. Bd.; bd. dirs. Internat. Exec. Service Corps, N.Y. Urban Coalition; trustee Trust for Cultural Resources, N.Y.C.; vice chmn. N.Y. Pub. Library; fellow Harvard Coll. Home: Darlen CT Office: Time Inc Rockefeller Center New York NY 10020

HEISLER, HAROLD REINHART, JR., utilities mgmt. cons.; b. Chgo.; s. Harold Reinhart and Beulah Mary (Schade) H.; B.M.E., U. Ill., 1954. Mgmt. cons. Ill. Power Co., Decatur, 1954—, mem. Nuclear Power Group Inc., breeder reactor design div. Argonne (Ill.) Nat. Lab., 1955-57; chmn. fossil fuel com. FPC, w. central region, Chgo., 1966-68; chmn. evaluation com. Coal Gasification Group Inc., 1971-75; dir. Indsl. Water Supply Co., Robinson, Ill., 1975-77; chmn. bd. Decatur Marine Inc., 1964-66; mem. Ill. Gov's. Fuel Energy Bd., 1970; mem. fuel energy bd. Ill. Commerce Commn., 1971-75, mem. power plant productivity com., 1977—; mem. coal study panel Ill. Energy Resources Commn., 1976—. Served as marine engring. officer USNR. Conceptual designer power plant sites and recreational lakes, Baldwin, Ill., 1959, Clinton, Ill., 1967. Home: 1375 W Main St Decatur IL 62522

HEISLER, MICHAEL BRUCE, foundry exec.; b. Ravenna, Ohio, Nov. 2, 1951; s. Bruce Lowry and Beverly (Roberston) H.; student in mktg. Ohio State U., summer 1973; B.A. in Econs., Ohio Wesleyan U., 1974; postgrad. in mktg. and fin. Kent State U., 1978-79; m. Diana Lynn Ross, Aug. 27, 1977; children—Michael Bruce, Nathan. With A.C. Williams Co., Ravenna, 1975—, v.p. sales, 1977-78, pres. Iron div., 1978-80, v.p. Iron Foundry Group, 1980—, also dir. Advisor, Jr. Achievement, Ravenna, 1977; mem. campaign com. United Way of Portage County, 1979. Mem. Am. Foundrymen's Soc. Republican. Congregationalist. Clubs: Elks, Rotary. Home: 1139 Pin Oak Dr Kent OH 44240 Office: 267 Hazen St Ravenna OH 44266

HEIST, LEWIS CLARK, forest products co. exec.; b. Bridgeport, Conn., June 6, 1931; s. Floyd L. and Gladys M. (Hall) H.; B.A. in Econs., Yale U., 1953, M.Forestry, 1957; m. Mary E. Lyman, Feb. 5, 1954; children—Jane, William, Peter, Matthew. With U.S. Plywood, Hartford, Conn., 1957-61, sales mgr., Pitts., 1961-64; v.p. bus. planning U.S. Plywood-Champion Paper, N.Y.C., 1970-75; exec. v.p. Timberlands div. Champion Internat., Stamford, Conn., 1976—; v.p., dir. Lyman Farm Inc., Middlefield, Conn., 1975—. Bd. dirs. Greenwich (Conn.) United Way, 1977—, Old Greenwich Community Center, 1973-77. Served to 1st lt. USMC, 1953-55. Mem. Soc. Am. Foresters, Am. Forestry Assn., Nat. Forest Products Assn. Presbyterian. Club: Rocky Point. Home: 187 Shore Rd Old Greenwich CT 06870 Office: One Champion Plaza Stamford CT 06921

HEITKAMP, ROBERT FRED, packaging co. exec.; b. Cin., Oct. 25, 1936; s. Walter August and Margaret (Denek) H.; B.B.A. in Mktg., U. Cin., 1960; m. Charlotte Grace Kelly, Dec. 22, 1961; children—Eric, Kelly. Product mgr. Phillips Films div. Phillips Petroleum Co., Cin., 1961-65, nat. mktg. mgr., 1966-70; mktg. mgr. Norfilm div. No. Petrochem. Co., Williamstown, Ky., 1970-73; founder, v.p. Pak-Sher, Inc., Kilgore, Tex., 1973-76; mktg. mgr. Midwest Films, Chgo., 1976-79; owner, operator Packaging Plus, Longview, Tex., 1979—; mem. adv. staff, printing tech. Kilgore Coll. Served with U.S. Army, 1960. Mem. Nat. Flexible Packaging Assn. (Break Through award 1968), S.W. Paper Suppliers Assn., Sigma Chi. Episcopalian. Club: Oak Forest Country. Home: 1610 Willowview St Longview TX 75604 Office: Suite 412 Cargill Towers 208 N Green St Longview TX 75601

HEITMANN, WILLIAM JOSEPH, mfg. co. ofcl.; b. N.Y.C., July 19, 1942; s. William Vincent and Mary Frances (Barrett) H.; student Mich. State U., 1965-67, Pace U., 1976; m. Carole M. Gustavson, June 24, 1967; children—William Henry, Shirley Mary. With Sears Roebuck and Co., White Plains, N.Y., Denver, 1968-69, Sexauer Co., White Plains, 1970; with Pitney Bowes Co., White Plains, 1971-76, Albany, N.Y., 1976-78, Lexington, Ky., 1978—, br. mgr., 1979—. Served with U.S. Army, 1962-65. Decorated Purple Heart. Mem. Postal Customer Council (pres.), Sales and Mktg. Execs. (Disting.

Salesman's award 1975), Lexington C. of C. Clubs: Kiwanis, Sin The Sport Center. Office: 210 E Reynolds Rd Lexington KY 40503

HEJNA, MICHAEL JAMES, financial specialist; b. St. Louis, Jan. 7, 1954; s. Paul A. and JoAnn J.; B.S., U. Mo., Columbia, 1977; M.A. (Coro Found. fellow), Occidental Coll., 1977; m. Lynn Jacobs, Sept. 8, 1978. Legis. asst. to Congressman Gephardt of Mo., 1977-78; fin. specialist City of St. Louis, 1978-80; partner Mgmt. Services Group, 1979—; Bd. dirs. Maplewood Local Devel. Co.; active Renaissance Soc., Maplewood, Mo. Named Outstanding Young Man Am., 1977. Home: 3127 Edgar St Saint Louis MO 63143 Office: 1300 Del Mar Saint Louis MO 63103

HELAL, ANDREW, hotel exec.; b. Princeton, W.Va., Apr. 26, 1950; s. Fortunato Hussein and Badia HeL.; student W.Va. Inst. Tech., 1968-71. Banquet mgr. Royal Coach Inn, Dallas, 1973-74; asst. mgr. Dallas Hyatt House, 1974-75; asst. food and beverage mgr. Playboy Resort, Lake Geneva, Wis., 1971-72, rooms div. mgr., 1975-76, resident mgr., 1976-77, mng. dir. Playboy Resort and Country Club, Lake Geneva, 1977—. Mem. Mem. Lake Geneva C. of C. (dir.), Geneva Lake Area Hotel/Motel Assn. (dir.), Nat. Restaurant Assn., Geneva Lake Area Mktg. Group (chmn.). Home and Office: Playboy Resort and Country Club Lake Geneva WI 53147

HELANDER, ROBERT CHARLES, lawyer, internat. devel. exec.; b. Chgo., Oct. 30, 1932; s. William E. and Grace (Pedderson) H.; B.A. magna cum laude, Amherst Coll., 1953; J.D., Harvard, 1956, Program Mgmt. Devel., 1971; m. Betty Jane Vinson, Apr. 8, 1961; children—Diana Chaffin, Alexander Christian, Nicholas Charles. Instr. gen. semantics and pub. speaking Tufts U., 1954-55; admitted to D.C. bar, Ill. bar, N.Y. bar; with firm Isham, Lincoln & Beale, Chgo.; resident rep. Iricon Agy. Ltd., Tehran, Iran, 1962-65; pvt. practice, Tehran and Beirut, Lebanon, 1961-65; acting mng. dir. Skerkat Sehami IBEC, Iran, 1964; counsel, cons. Iranian operations IBEC (Internat. Basic Economy Corp.), 1961-65, asst. to regional v.p., Peru, 1965-69, v.p., area mgr., Peru, 1968-71, v.p. devel. and adminstrn., 1971-73. group v.p., N.Y.C., 1973-76; pres., vice chmn. bd., IBEC Housing Internat., Inc., 1973-76; chmn. AOFC, Inc., 1972-76; of counsel firm Surrey & Morse, 1976—; dir. various cos. Pres. Am. C. of C. of Iran, 1962-63; dir. Am. C. of C. of Peru, 1966-70, chmn. civic action com. 1968-69, pres., 1970; founding dir., mem. exec. com. Accion Comunitaria del Peru, 1968-71; bd. dirs., pres. Accion Internat., 1973—; bd. dirs. Fund for Multinat. Mgmt. Edn., 1971—, vice chmn., 1978—; bd. dirs. Nr. East Found., 1977—, exec. com., 1979—; chmn. spl. com. to organizer 2d conf. Peruvian-U.S. relations Adlai Stevenson Inst. Internat. Affairs, 1970; mem. Eisenhower Fellowship Selection Bd. for Peru, 1969-71; vice chmn. adv. bd. Council of Ams., 1979—; bd. dirs. Internat. Partnership for Econ. Devel., 1980—. Trustee Mohammad Reza Shah Pahlavi U., 1964-65; bd. dirs. Fulbright Commn., Iran, 1964-65, Peru, 1969-71, Inst. Met. Lima, 1969-70, Asociacion Cristiana de Jovenes Lima, 1969-71, Iran Am. Soc., 1962-65, John Woodruff Simpson fellow in law, 1953-54; Amherst fellow in Middle East, 1960-61; recipient Medal of Merit, Lima, 1971, also Medal of merit from students univs. in Lima, 1970. Mem. Am. Bar Assn., Am. Soc. Internat. Law, Iran-Am. (founder 1965), Inter-Am. bar assns., Le Cercle Francais (Tehran), Am. Soc. (Lima), Pan Am Soc. U.S. (v.p. 1979—), Council Fgn. Relations, Phi Beta Kappa, Alpha Delta Phi. Episcopalian (vestry 1973—, warden 1979—). Clubs: Century Assn.; Harvard of Boston; Le Circle Francais (Tehran), Tehran; Villa Country (Lima); Echo Lake (Westfield, N.J.). Home: 534 Tremont Ave Westfield NJ 07090 Office: 485 Madison Ave New York NY 10022

HELAVA, UUNO VILHO, research co. exec.; b. Kokemaki, Finland, Mar. 1, 1923; s. Uuno N. and Jenny (Peltonen) H.; came to U.S., 1967; B.Sc., Helsinki U. Tech., 1945, M.Sc., 1947, Dr. h.c., 1978; m. Liisa Maire Inkeri Virolainen, Dec. 25, 1942; children—Katri Inkeri, Heikki Ilmari, Jussi Vilhotapio. Photogrammetric engr. Nat. Bd. Surveying, Helsinki, 1947-53; research officer NRC Can., Ottawa, 1953-65; cons. Ottico Meccanica Italiana, Rome, 1965-66; cons. scientist Bendix Research Labs., Southfield, Mich., 1967-79; pres., chief scientist Helava Assos., Inc., Southfield, 1979—; mem. faculty Helsinki U. Tech., 1951-53, Ottawa U., 1954-59. Served with Finnish Army, 1944-45. Recipient Brock Gold medal Internat. Soc. Photogrammetry, 1972, Alexander von Humboldt Sr. Am. Scientist award, 1977. Mem. Am. Soc. Photogrammetry (Photogrammetric award 1964), IEEE, Can. Inst. Surveying, Sigma Xi. Lutheran. Patentee in field; contbr. articles to profl. jours. Home: 5267 Wright Way E West Bloomfield MI 48033 Office: 21421 Hilltop St Southfield MI 48034

HELBLING, ROBERT JAMES, metalworking plant exec.; b. Chgo., Aug. 12, 1945; s. James V. and Jeanne Russell (Rowbotham) H.; B.S., Purdue U., 1968, M.B.A. Wharton Sch., 1969; m. Madeline Kiefer, July 17, 1971; children—Lisa, James, Edward. Ops. research analysts Acme Markets, Phila., 1968-69; systems analyst DuPont, Wilmington, Del., 1969-70, bus. and fin. analyst, 1970-71; auditor Rockwell Internat., Pitts., 1972, audit exec., 1972, asst. to v.p. mfg. Miehle div., 1973; asst. plant mgr. Parker Hannifin, Sebring, Ohio, 1973-74, Plant agr., 1974-78, ops. mgr. Gould Fluid Components div., Niles, Ill., 1978—. Recipient Joseph Wharton fellowship. Home: 811 Waverly St Arlington Heights IL 60004 Office: Niles IL

HELD, MARGARET J. DUNKLEY, Realtor; b. Washington, Sept. 11, 1911; d. Randolph Lee and Susie (Engelke) Jennings; student Am. U., 1946, Southeastern U., 1944-47; m. Charles W. Dunkley, Aug. 30, 1937 (dec. July 1954); m. 2d, Emil C. Held, Aug. 20, 1955. Real estate broker, Md., D.C., Va., 1936—; owner, pres. Margaret J. Dunkley Realtor, Bethesda, Md., owner, dir. Margaret J. Dunkley, Interior Designers, 1953—, Margaret J. Dunkley Ins. Agy., Inc., 1961—; v.p. Fed. Supply Co., Inc., Washington, 1955-70, pres., gen. mgr., 1970—. Mem. women's fitness bd. YMCA, Bethesda; trustee Montgomery County Crippled Childrens Soc., 1956-58; mem. com. United Givers Fund, 1961—; past realtor chmn. Montgomery County Heart Assn. Named Realtor of Year, Montgomery County, 1956, 57. Mem. Montgomery County (Md.) Bd. Realtors (pres. 1954-55), Bethesda-Chevy Chase C. of C. (v.p. 1956, 58), Montgomery County C. of C. (past v.p.), Nat. Assn. Real Estate Bds. (past pres. Md. women's council), Nat. Inst. Brokers (gov. 1957-59), Md. Real Estate Assn. (gov. 1957-60), Internat. Real Estate Fedn. (del. to internat. congress Geneva, Switzerland, Vienna, Austria, 1954). Active in Woman's Aux. for Cancer Research, Womans Aux. Washington Bible Coll. Clubs: Congressional Country (Bethesda); Pinehurst (N.C.). Home: 8613 Fenway Dr Bethesda MD 20034 Office: 4804 Moorland Ln Bethesda MD 20034 also 1108 K St NW Washington DC 20005

HELDRIDGE, RICHARD WALLACE, banker; b. Wessington Springs, S.D., Sept. 18, 1918; s. Alvin A. and Helen H. (DeMaranville) H.; ed. U. Iowa; m. Shirely Ann VanDecar, Jan. 5, 1943; children—Kathryn Helen Heldridge Tyson, Michael W., Dan Richard, Sarah Elizabeth. Vice-pres. Northwestern Nat. Bank, Mpls., 1946-59; exec. v.p. Crocker Nat. Bank, San Francisco, 1960-75; pres., chief exec. officer Community Bank San Jose (Calif.), 1975-80, also dir.; pres., chief exec. officer Ammex Holding Co., 1978-80. Served to lt. col. U.S. Army. Decorated Bronze Star. Mem. Calif. Bankers Assn. (dir., treas. 1974-75). Republican. Clubs: Stock Exchange, La Rinconada Country.

HELFANT, SEYMOUR MEYER, assn. exec.; b. N.Y.C., May 8, 1916; s. Henry and Esther (Alteresku) H.; B.S., Coll. City N.Y., 1937; J.D., St. John's U., 1941; M.S., N.Y. U., 1947; m. Thelma (Kurinsky), Dec. 21, 1947; children—Ronald, Michael, Richard. Co-owner, Del Fant Shoes, Far Rockaway, N.Y., 1940-57; mgr. smaller stores div. also splty. stores div. Nat. Retail Mchts. Assn., 1957-67, v.p., mgr. ind. stores div., 1967-69; dir. edn., mgmt. and promotion services Internat. Council Shopping Centers, 1969—; lectr. Coll. City N.Y., 1947-70, Bklyn. Coll., 1951-72; adj. asso. prof. Adelphi U., 1974—; dir. seminars in shoe fitting and therapy, fashion, buying and merchandising; co-dir. Top Mgmt. Seminar; dir. Basic and Advanced Inst. for Shopping Center Mgrs. and Promotion Dirs., Mgmt. Inst., dir. seminar on increasing retail productivity; mem. N.Y. State adv. council U.S. Small Bus. Adminstrn. Mem. Am. Mktg. Assn., Am. Soc. for Tng. and Devel., Eta Mu Pi. Mason. Author: Problems of Smaller Stores, 1959; Retail Shoe Sales Training Manual, 1960; Operations Manual for Smaller Stores, 2 vols., 1960; The Successful Future of the Independent Retailer, 1960; Profitable Ideas for Smaller Stores, 1961; Increasing Profitability in Today's Retailing, 1963; Training and Motivating Retail Sales People, 1969; Person to Person Selling, 1969; co-author: Retail Merchandising and Management with Electronic Data Processing; Small Store Planning for Growth, 1966; Management Manual for Independent Stores, 1969; Planning Your Store for Maximum Sales and Profits, 1969. Home: 810 A Fairview Rd Columbia MO 65201 Office: Columbia Coll Columbia MO 65216

HELFER, HERMAN HYMAN, glass co. exec.; b. Chgo., Dec. 6, 1919; s. Harry and Sarah (Kurlansky) H.; student Herzl Jr. Coll., 1941; certificate U. Ill. Coll. Pharmacy, 1946; B.S. in Mktg., Roosevelt U., 1973, M.B.A., 1977; m. Frieda Hershkopf, Nov. 16, 1947; children—Joel, Harvey, Gail, Gina. With Novelty Glass & Mirror Co., Chgo., 1946—, gen. mgr., sec.-treas., 1960—; pres. Columbia Glass Co., Chgo., 1969—; pres. Energipane Insulating Glass Corp.; pres. Insulating Glass Ednl. Inst., 1980-81. Instr. Boys State, Springfield, Ill., 1966; chmn. Glazier's Pension and Welfare Funds, Chgo., 1969-73. Served with USAAF, 1943-46. Mem. Am. Legion (post comdr. 1967-68), Assn. Glazing Contractors (pres. 1957-73), Nat. Glass Dealers Assn. (exec. com., pres. 1978-80, rep. to Consumer Safety Products Commn.), Flat Glass Marketing Assn. (dir.), Nat. Assn. Store Fixture Mfrs. (asso.), Am.-Israel C. of C. Jewish (sec., treas. synagogue). Mem. B'nai B'rith. Mason (Shriner). Home: 8937 Forest View Rd Evanston IL 60203 Office: 4716 W Lake St Chicago IL 60644

HELFER, ROBERT GREGG, credit bur. exec.; b. Rochester, N.Y., Nov. 16, 1946; s. Robert P. and Colleen (Beard) H.; student Monroe Community Coll., 1965-67, Grad. Sch. Credit and Fin. Mgmt., Princeton U., 1973; m. Diane Rieflin, Feb. 24, 1979. Field service rep. Electronics div. Gen. Dynamics Corp., Rochester, 1967-68; exec. v.p. Credit Bur. Rochester, 1968—. Mem. Am. Mgmt. Assn., Asso. Credit Burs. N.Y. State (state legislation chmn. 1978, v.p. 1979-80, pres. 1980-81), Rochester Credit and Fin. Mgmt. Assn. (sec.). Club: Irondequoit Rotary. Office: 19 Prince St Rochester NY 14607

HELFERT, ERICH ANTON, forest products co. exec.; b. Aussig/Elbe, Sudetenland, May 29, 1931; came to U.S., 1950; s. Julius and Anna Maria (Wilde) H.; B.S., U. Nev., 1954; M.B.A. with high distinction, Harvard U., 1956, D.B.A. (Ford fellow 1956), 1958. Newspaper reporter, corr., Neuburg, W. Ger., 1948-52; research asst. Harvard U., 1956-57; asst. prof. bus. policy San Francisco State U., 1958-59; asst. prof. fin. and control Grad. Sch. Bus. Adminstrn., Harvard U., 1959-65; internal cons., then asst. to pres., dir. corp. planning Crown Zellerbach Corp., San Francisco, 1965-78, asst. to chmn., dir. corp. planning, 1978—; cons., lectr. in field. Exchange student fellow U.S. Inst. Internat. Edn., 1950. Mem. Am. Acctg. Assn., Am. Econs. Assn., Am. Fin. Assn., Assn. Corp. Growth (pres., dir. San Francisco chpt. 1980-81, Corp. Planners Assn. (past pres., dir.), Phi Kappa Phi. Roman Catholic. Clubs: Commonwealth, Commercial, Harvard Bus. Sch. No. Calif. (past pres., dir.). Author: Techniques of Financial Analysis, 1963, 5th edit., 1981; Valuation, 1966; co-author: Case Book, 1963; Controllership, 1965; contbr. articles to profl. jours. Office: 1 Bush St San Francisco CA 94104

HELFRICH, CHARLES HENRY, transp. co. exec.; b. Passaic, N.J., Oct. 3, 1945; s. Karl H. and Barbara (Clarke) H.; student Ohio Wesleyan U., 1965-66; B.A. cum laude, Bloomfield Coll., 1973; postgrad. Seton Hall U., 1974—. Fin. analyst Mut. Benefit Life Ins. Co., Newark, 1973-75, project leader advanced planning, 1976, fin. analyst fin. and cash mgmt., 1977-79; mgr. corp. and div. analysis Prudential Lines, Inc., N.Y.C., 1980—. Loaned exec. United Way of Essex and West Hudson, 1975-76; co-dir. acad. advising Bloomfield (N.J.) Coll., 1977-79. Served with U.S. Army, 1967-70. Republican. Episcopalian. Home: PO Box F Cedar Grove NJ 07009 Office: One World Trade Center New York NY 10048

HELITZER, MORRIE, publisher; b. N.Y.C., June 8, 1925; s. Abraham and Ethel (Lifschutz) H.; B.S. in Elec. Engring., Cornell U., 1945; A.M. in Polit. Sci., U. Chgo., 1948; postgrad. (Council on Fgn. Relations press fellow) Columbia U., 1960-61; m. Irene Rodman, Sept. 29, 1974; children—Jonathan Aaron, Cynthia. Reporter, U.P., Madison, Wis., 1946-47; reporter Internat. News Service, Chgo., 1947-48, Paris, 1948, Berlin, 1948-49, Frankfurt, W. Ger., 1949, bur. chief, Vienna, 1949-50, Belgrade, Yugoslavia, 1950; free-lance writer, Los Angeles, 1950-53; fgn. corr. NBC, India, 1954; news editor ABC, N.Y.C., 1955-56; news editor McGraw-Hill, London, 1956-57, bur. chief, Bonn, W. Ger., 1957-60; asst. to pres. McGraw-Hill Book Co., Washington, 1961-66, v.p. pub. affairs, N.Y.C., 1966-73; mkgr. mgr. McGraw-Hill Pub. Co., N.Y.C., 1974-76, gen. mgr., 1976-78; pres. Helitzer Communications, Inc., Sea Cliff, N.Y., 1979—. Mem. exec. bd. Princeton Jewish Center, 1970-71. Served with USN, 1945-46. Jewish. Club: Nat. Press. Author: The Cold War, 1977; contbr. articles to various publs. Home and Office: 72 DuBois Ave Sea Cliff NY 11579

HELLEBRONTH, HARRY, mfg. co. exec.; b. Berlin, May 25, 1929; s. Heinrich and Hildegardh Henrietta (von Dell) H.; came to U.S., 1958, naturalized, 1965; B.A., U. Berlin, 1952, M.A. summa cum laude in Econs., 1953; postgrad. in Advanced Econs., U. Chgo., 1959-60. Asst. sales mgr. Mercedes-Benz Argentina, Buenos Aires, 1953-55, sales mgr., Montevideo, Uruguay, 1955-56; mgr. Borg-Warner Uruguay, Montevideo, 1956-58; from automotive export sales mgr. Latin Am. to sales mgr. internat. Borg-Warner Internat. Corp., Chgo., 1958-62, mgr. European program, 1963-64, gen. mgr. Borg-Warner Internat. GmbH, Hamburg, Germany, 1964-65, gen. mgr. Borg-Warner de Mex., Mexico City, 1965-67; mng. dir. Teves-Thompson GmbH, Société de Mécanique de Pringy (France), Société Métallurgique G. Jeudy, Schirmeck (France); dir. Dresdner Bank AG, Hannover, Germany. Named Automotive Exec. of Year, Mex., 1966. Mem. German Assn. Automotive Mfrs. (dir.). Home: 107 Geibelstrasse 3 Hanover 1 Federal Republic of Germany Office: Teves-Thompson GmbH 3013 Barsinghausen Federal Republic of Germany

HELLENBRAND, SAMUEL HENRY, diversified industry exec.; b. N.Y.C., Nov. 11, 1916; s. Louis H. and Fannie (Cohen) H.; LL.B., Bklyn. Law Sch./St. Lawrence U., 1941, LL.M., 1942; children—Kathy Hellenbrand Rocklen, Linda Hellenbrand Silberstein. Admitted to N.Y. bar, 1942; with N.Y. Central R.R., 1942-68, dir. taxes fin. dept., 1956-63, v.p. planning and devel., 1963-64, v.p. real estate, 1964-68; v.p. indsl. and real estate Penn Central Co., 1968-70, v.p. real estate and taxes, 1970-71; pres. Pa. Co., 1970-71; v.p., exec. asst. to pres., dir. real estate affairs ITT, N.Y.C., 1971—. Mem. N.Y. State C. of C. (past exec. com., chmn. taxation and city affairs coms.), Am. Bar Assn., N.Y. State Bar Assn., Assn. Bar City N.Y. Patentee heart diagnostic unit. Office: 320 Park Ave New York NY 10022

HELLER, FREDERICK, mining co. exec.; b. Detroit, May 6, 1932; s. Robert and Lois Mouch H.; B.A., Harvard U., 1954; m. Barbara Ann McGreevy, Nov. 22, 1979; children—Thomas M., John G., Cynthia R. With Hanna Mining Co., 1957—, v.p. sales, 1973-76, sr. v.p. sales and transp., Cleve., 1976—. Trustee, mem. exec. com. Cleve. Inst. Art, 1977—; trustee, mem. fin. com. McGregor Home, 1978—. Served with U.S. Army, 1954-56. Mem. Ferroalloys Assn. (dir.), Am. Iron and Steel Inst., Am. Mining Congress, Am. Iron Ore Assn., Soc. Mining Engrs. Republican. Episcopalian. Clubs: Union, Kirtland Country, Pepper Pike, Tavern, Duquesne. Home: 2942 Fontenay Rd Shaker Heights OH 44120 Office: 100 Erieview Plaza Cleveland OH 44114

HELLER, STEVEN ANTHONY, mktg. exec.; b. Budapest, Hungary, Sept. 1, 1938; s. Gedeon and Elizabeth (Spitzer) H.; came to U.S., naturalized, 1939; B.S. in Econs., Wharton Sch., U. Pa., 1961, M.B.A., 1977; m. Peggy Grace Fulton, June 30, 1968; children—Thomas Charles, Emily Elizabeth, George Fulton. Media planner, buyer Benton & Bowles, Inc., N.Y.C., 1962-64; account exec. Compton Advt., Inc., N.Y.C., 1964-67; brand mgr. Bristol Myers Co., Inc., N.Y.C., 1967-71; dir. mktg. I.U. Internat., Phila., 1971-75; v.p. mktg. and communications Phila. Savs. Fund Soc., 1975-78; v.p. mktg. services and planning Block Drug Co., Inc., Jersey City, 1978—. Served with AUS, 1957-58. Club: Beacon Hill. Home: 95 Druid Hill Rd Summit NJ 07901 Office: 257 Cornelison Ave Jersey City NJ 07302

HELLIWELL, MICHAEL GEORGE, educator; b. Jersey City, Feb. 13, 1945; s. Leo George and Alicia Agnus (Moore) H.; B.S., St. Peter's Coll., 1966; M.B.A., Rutgers U., 1971, Ed.D., 1981; M.A. in Teaching, Montclair State Coll., 1973; m. Kathleen Reginia Wulff, Oct. 28, 1967; children—Kerri Ann, Margaret Mary, Elizabeth Anne. Retail sales mgr. Firestone, 1966; mem. Peace Corps, 1966-67; salesman Gen. Foods Co., Clifton, N.J., 1969-71; tchr. Jersey City Bd. Edn., 1971-73, Bayonne (N.J.) High Sch., 1973-77; coordinator/instr. mktg. and retailing programs Passaic County Community Coll., Paterson, N.J., 1977-78, chmn. bus. div., 1978-80; prof. mktg. mgmt. Coll. Bus. Adminstrn., Fordham U., Bronx, N.Y., 1980—; adj. prof. mgmt. and mktg. Hudson County Community Coll., Jersey City, 1975-80, Montclair (N.J.) State Coll., 1979—. Served with U.S. Army, 1967-69; Vietnam. Mem. Am. Vocat. Assn., Am. Mgmt. Assn., Am. Mktg. Assn., Nat. Assn. Mktg. and Mgmt. Edn., N.J. Bus. Edn. Assn. Republican. Roman Catholic. Club: K.C. Home: 192 Santiago Ave Rutherford NJ 07070

HELLMAN, GABRIEL, diversified co. exec.; b. N.Y.C., Nov. 4, 1927; B.S., L.I. U., 1948; M. in Ednl. Psychology, N.Y. U., 1950; m. Audrey; 1 son, Jerrold. With United Piece Dye Works, N.Y.C., 1956—, v.p. merchandising, 1972-74, pres. UPD div., 1974—; textile account rep. Old Dominion Freight Line, N.Y.C., 1978-79; dir. textile div. Thurston Motor Lines, N.Y.C., 1979—; textile industry rep. U.S. Consumer Product Safety Commn. Mem. Textile Salesmen's Assn. (bd. govs.), Textile Distributors Assn. (quality control com.), Am. Arbitration Assn. Club: Weavers' (bd. govs.). Home: 15 Rose Tree Terr Ridgefield NJ 07657 Office: The United Piece Dye Works 111 W 40th St New York NY 10018 also Thurston Motor Lines 49 W 37th St New York NY 10018

HELLMAN, MERLIN JOHN, estate and bus. planning co. exec.; b. Fort Madison, Iowa, Sept. 1, 1935; s. William G. and Cecilia (Sanders) H.; student Regis Coll., Denver, 1953-57; m. Theresa A. Arndt, Feb. 1, 1958; children—Rita, Dorothy, William, Tony, Paul, Barbara, Anita, Martha, Joan, Mary Sara, John, Sue. With Hellman Trucking Co., 1958-61; salesman life ins. K.C., Houghton, 1962-63; agt. Conn. Gen. Life Ins. Co., Burlington, Iowa, 1963—; dir. Fort Madison Bank & Trust. Mayor, Houghton, Iowa, 1970-74, mem. town council. Served with U.S. Army, 1961-62. C.L.U. Mem. Iowa State Assn. Life Underwriters (past pres.), Southeast Iowa Assn. Life Underwriters (past pres.), Nat. Assn. Life Underwriters, Am. Soc. Chartered Life Underwriters, Million Dollar Round Table (life). Republican. Roman Catholic. Clubs: Elks, K.C. Home: Blackhawk Heights Fort Madison IA 51627 Office: 706 F & M Bank Bldg Burlington IA 52601

HELLMUTH, JAMES GRANT, banker; b. Washington, July 31, 1923; s. William F. and Sybel M. (Grant) H.; B.S., Yale U., 1948; LL.B., George Washington U., 1953; m. Daphne S. Preece, Nov. 21, 1959; children—James Grant, Timothy P. Asso. William A.M. Burden, N.Y.C., 1958-60; v.p. Bank of N.Y., N.Y.C., 1960-67; v.p. J.P. Morgan & Co., N.Y.C., 1967-71; v.p. Bankers Trust N.Y. Corp., N.Y.C., 1971—; pres. BT Capital Corp., N.Y.C., 1980—. Treas., N.Y. Republican State Com., 1967-78. Served to 1st lt. U.S. Army, 1943-46. Clubs: Lawrence Beach, Rockaway Hunt, Yale of N.Y. Editor: Modern Trust Forms, 1960; Atomic Energy Law Jour., 1955-65. Home: 1105 Park Ave New York NY 10028 Office: 280 Park Ave New York NY 10017

HELLMUTH, PAUL FRANCIS, lawyer; b. Springfield, Ohio, Dec. 7, 1918; s. Andrew Alfred and Clara Elizabeth (Link) H.; A.B., U. Notre Dame, 1940; LL.B., Harvard, 1947; spl. courses Mass. Inst. Tech., Harvard Grad. Sch. Pub. Adminstrn. Admitted to Ohio bar, 1947, Mass. bar, 1952, mem. Hale & Dorr, Boston, 1947-76, partner, 1952-56, sr. mng. partner, 1956-76, now ret. partner; chmn., chief exec. officer Maynard H. Murch Co., Cleve.; dir. A-T-O, Inc., Pioneer Western Corp., Robbins & Myers, Inc., United Screw & Bolt Co., W.R. Grace & Co., Bessemer Securities Corp., Computer Systems Am., Ritz Carlton Hotel Co.; chmn., dir. Am. Energy Services Inc.; trustee Boston Five Cent Savs. Bank. Hon. trustee Mus. Sci. Boston; mem. adv. council Notre Dame Law Sch.; bd. govs. New Eng. Aquarium; trustee, fellow U. Notre Dame; bd. govs. Children's Hosp. Med. Center; trustee Univ. Hosp.; trustee, vice chmn. Boston U. Med. Center; trustee Boston Mus. Fine Arts, Boston Ballet, J. Frederick Brown Found., Noonan Found., W.G. Moore Ednl. Found.; mem. corp., trustee Retina Found.; mem. corp. Mass. Inst. Tech.; fellow Brandeis U.; bd. dirs. United Way Mass. Bay. Served from pvt. to 2d lt., AUS, 1941-42, advanced to lt. col. USAAF, 1945. Decorated Legion of Merit, Bronze Star; French Croix de Guerre. Mem. Harvard Law Sch. Assn. (treas.). Clubs: Harvard, Badminton and Tennis, Union, Somerset Commercial (Boston); Country, Polo (Springfield). Home: 100 Memorial Dr Cambridge MA 02142

HELLON, MICHAEL THOMAS, polit. and mgmt. cons.; b. Camden, N.J., June 24, 1942; s. James Bernard and Dena Louise (Blackburn) H.; B.S., Ariz. State U., 1972. Ins. investigator Equifax, Phoenix, 1968-69; asst. exec. v.p. Phoenix Met. C. of C., 1969-76; v.p. Londen Ins. Group, 1976-78; pres. Hellon Mgmt. Co., 1978—. Mem. Ariz. Occupational Safety and Health Adv. Council, 1972—, Phoenix Urban League, 1972-73, Area Manpower Planning Council, 1971-72, Phoenix Civic Plaza Dedication Com., 1972. Precinct capt.

Republican party, 1973—; campaign mgr. State Rep. James Skelly, 1972, 74, 76, State Senator John Roeder, 1974, others; cons. Rep. State Com. of Ariz., 1978; mem. adv. com. Ariz. Citizens for Reagan, 1976, campaign mgr., 1980; Ariz. campaign dir. Reagan for Pres., 1980; alternate del. Rep. Nat. Conv., 1980; bd. dirs. Vis. Nurse Service, Inc., 1976—, pres., 1978-79. Served with USAF, 1964-68. Decorated Bronze Star medal, Purple Heart. Recipient George Washington Honor medal Freedom's Found., 1964. Mem. U.S. C. of C. (pub. affairs com. western div. 1974—), Am. C. of C. Execs., Ariz. C. of C. Mgrs. Assn. (bd. mem. 1974—), Conf. Ariz. Employer Assns. (sec. 1972). Clubs: Kiwanis, Trunk 'N Tusk. Home: 2209 E Cactus Wren Phoenix AZ 85020 Office: 4808 N 22d St Phoenix AZ 85016

HELLWEGE, JOHN PHILIP, orgn. exec.; b. St. Louis, Apr. 5, 1934; s. Oscar Albert and Leona Katherin (Mueller) H.; B.S. in Bus. Adminstrn., Washington U., 1955, M.S. in Bus. Adminstrn., 1962; m. Shirley Wanda Dueker, June 27, 1959; children—Judith Lynn, John Philip. Office mgr. William A. Straub, Inc., St. Louis, 1958-61; supr. engring. budgets McDonnell-Douglas Corp., St. Louis, 1961-67; asst. controller Photronix, Inc., St. Louis, 1967-68; treas. St. Paul Title Ins. Corp., St. Louis, 1968-70; v.p. fin. YMCA of Greater St. Louis, 1970—; chmn. chief fin. officers group from 25 largest YMCA's in N. Am., 1975-80. Pres., Eagle Scout Assn. St. Louis, 1969; treas., bd. dirs. Mo. dist. Lutheran Ch., Mo. Synod, 1970-78; pres. congregation Glendale Luth. Ch., St. Louis, 1969-72; bd. dirs. Luth. Med. Center, 1980—. Mem. Nat. Assn. Accts. (recipient Socio-Economic Program award 1974, pres. St. Louis chpt. 1979-80, nat. public relations com. 1980—). Club: Washington U. Home: 11542 Templar Dr Creve Coeur MO 63141 Office: YMCA 1528 Locust St St Louis MO 63103

HELM, JOHN LESLIE, mech. engr.; b. Red Wing, Minn., Apr. 10, 1921; s. Leslie Cornell and Dora (McGuigan) H.; B.S. in Mech. Engring., Columbia U., 1943, M.S., 1944; postgrad. in Nuclear Engring., U. Conn., 1956-57; m. Nancy Ellen Molle, May 15, 1954; children—John Leslie, Juli-Ann, Catherine Marie. Asst. in mech. engring. Columbia U., 1943-44; process engr. Metals Disintegrating Co., Elizabeth, N.J., 1944-45; project engr. Aero Manuscripts Inc., 1945-46; staff engr., central engring. dept. Gen. Foods Corp., White Plains, N.Y., 1946-52; with Gen. Dynamics Corp., Groton, Conn., 1952-74, spl. tech. asst. Office of Pres., Electric Boat div., 1965-72, gen. mgr. Gen. Dynamics Energy Systems, 1972-74; founder, pres., chief exec. officer Proto-Power Mgmt. Corp., Groton, 1974—, also dir. Mem. Groton Bd. Edn., 1967-77, chmn., 1971-72. Recipient citation for work on Manhattan Project, War Dept., 1945; registered profl. engr., N.Y. Mem. ASME. Republican. Roman Catholic. Clubs: Shonnecosset Yacht, Off Soundings. Home: 116 Tyler Ave Groton CT 06340 Office: 591 Poquonnock Rd Groton CT 06340

HELM, WILLIAM LLOYD, JR., fuel co. exec.; b. N.Y.C., June 21, 1923; s. William Lloyd and May (Kelly) H.; B.S.E.E., Princeton U., 1949; postgrad. Mgmt. Devel. Program, Northeastern U., 1963; Sloan fellow Stanford U., 1972; m. Eleanor Lloyd, Feb. 16, 1952; children—Pamela Kelly, Peter Lloyd, David Belknap, William Lloyd III. Test engr. Gen. Elec. Co., 1949; tech. cadet Boston Gas Co., 1950-51, staff engr., 1952, asst. supt. elec. dept., 1952-55, mgr. elec. dept., 1955-64, v.p. mktg., 1967-69, dir., 1968-69; asst. to sr. v.p. Eastern Gas & Fuel Assn., Boston, 1964-65, exec. asst. to pres., 1965-67, controller, 1969-72, v.p. fin. planning, 1972-73, v.p. corp. services, 1973-74; asst. gen. mgr. Phila. Coke div., 1974-75, gen. mgr., 1975-76; pres. Phila. Coke Co., Inc., 1976—. Water commr. Town of Weston (Mass.), 1960-67, mem. fin. com., 1968-71, 72-75; trustee Meadowbrook Sch., Weston, 1965-74; sec. Eastern Asso. Found., Boston, 1964-70; bd. dirs. Northeastern Hosp., Phila., 1977—, Phila. Health Plan, 1978—. Registered profl. engr., Mass. Mem. IEEE, Am. Coke and Coal Chems. Inst. (dir.). Club: Phila. Cricket. Office: 4501 Richmond St Philadelphia PA 19137

HELMS, JACK EDWIN, reins. co. exec.; b. Grafton, W.Va., Jan. 19, 1927; s. George Franklin and Hester May (Poling) G.; student George Washington U., 1950-52, Ins. Soc. N.Y.C. Ins. clk. to office mgr. State Farm Ins. Co., Washington, 1946-55, state office mgr., Clifton, N.J., 1955-57; asst. v.p. reins. underwriter Agy. Mgrs. Ltd., N.Y.C., 1957-70; v.p., reins. underwriter Constn. Reins. Corp., N.Y.C., 1970-73; exec. v.p., reins. underwriter E.D. Sayer Inc., Princeton, N.J., 1973-78, pres., 1978-79, also dir.; sr. v.p. Placers, Inc., Convent Station, N.J., 1979—. Served with USNR, 1945-46. Mem. Drug and Chem. Club N.Y.C. Republican. Methodist. Home: PO Box 187 Hopewell NJ 08525 Office: 334 Madison Ave Convent Station NJ 07961

HELMS, JAMES WILLIAM, furniture mfg. co. exec.; b. Morganton, N.C., July 14, 1941; s. Jefferson Bivins and Doris Elizabeth (McCollum) H.; B.A., U. N.C., Boone, 1966; m. Alice Ann McNeely, Aug. 11, 1968. Salesman, Drexel Furniture Co., Chgo. and Milw., 1966-70, Founders Furniture Co., N.Y.C. and N.J., 1970-73; salesman Thomasville Furniture Co., Ga. and S.C., 1973-75, salesman South Fla., 1975—, also design cons.; organizer, prin. James Wm. Helms & Assos., 1979—. Served with USNR, 1960-62. Republican. Clubs: Tuxedo (Tuxedo Park, N.Y.); Quail Ridge (Boynton Beach, Fla.). Home: Quail Ridge 3768 Partridge Pl S Boynton Beach FL 33436

HELMS, JOHN BENJAMIN, furniture accessories mfg. co. exec.; b. Monroe, N.C., June 18, 1946; s. Lester Lee and Mary Emiline (Smith) H.; B.S. in Bus. Adminstrn., U. N.C., Chapel Hill, 1968; postgrad. Young Execs. Inst., 1973, Harvard U., 1980; m. Anne Bonnell Rushing, July 17, 1976; 1 son, Paul Christopher. With Maleck Industries, Inc., Wingate, N.C., 1968—, exec. v.p., 1973-75, pres., 1975—; dir. N.C. Nat. Bank, Monroe; instr. Mgmt. Devel. Inst., 1975-76; N.C. del. White House Conf. on Small Bus., 1980. Mem. social planning council United Way, 1978—; dist. chmn. Boy Scouts Am., 1978; bd. overseers, com. on bus. Wingate Coll.; adv. bd. Wingate Elem. Sch. and Union County Career Center. Served with U.S. Army Res., 1968-74. Mem. U. N.C. Alumni Assn., Mensa, Phi Kappa Sigma. Clubs: Lake Norman Yacht, Rotary. Home: PO Box 305 Wingate NC 28174 Office: PO Box 247 Wingate NC 28174

HELMS, JOHN WALKER, med. supply co. exec.; b. Hattiesburg, Miss., June 21, 1944; s. Jack Edwin and Nancy Rebecca (Walker) H.; B.A. in Econs., La. State U., 1966; M.B.A., U. Utah, 1972; m. Linda H. Lewis, Dec. 9, 1977; children—John Wesley, Rebecca Anne. Product planning mgr. Motorola, Chgo., 1973-75; product mgr. Magnavox Consumer Electronics Co., Ft. Wayne, Ind., 1975-77; new product devel. mgr. Westclox div. Talley Industries, LaSalle, Ill., 1977-78; asso. mgr. mktg. communications Am. Hosp. Supply Corp., Evanston, Ill., 1978-80, mgr. corp. mktg. services, 1980—. Served with USAF, 1966-73. Decorated Bronze Star. Mem. Am. Mktg. Assn. Home: 2245 Beechwood Ave Wilmette IL 60091 Office: Am Hosp Supply Corp One American Plaza Evanston IL 60201

HELMS, JONEE LYNN, aircraft co. exec.; b. DeQueen, Ark., Mar. 1, 1925; s. Benjamin Franklin and Mamie (Johnson) H.; m. Lorraine Rose Bisgard, Mar. 16, 1947; children—Jon Lynn, Lora Lyn, Carole Diane, Zackary Craig. Dir sales N. Am. Aviation, Columbus, Ohio, 1955-63; gen. mgr. Bendix Corp., Ann Arbor, Mich., 1963-65, group v.p., 1966-70; pres. Norden div. United Aircraft, Norwalk, Conn., 1970-75; pres., chmn. bd. Piper Aircraft, Lock Haven, Pa., 1974—; dir. Ark. Bank. Chmn. Columbus unit Am. Cancer Soc., 1960-63. Served to col. USMC, 1943-55. Office: 820 Bald Eagle Lock Haven PA 17775

HELTON, THOMAS JOE, retail co. exec.; b. Ft. Wayne, Ind., Aug. 15, 1944; s. Vernon L. and Isabelle E. (Price) H.; A.B. in Sociology, Ind. U., 1968, M.B.A., 1970; m. Karen Sue Anderson, Dec. 4, 1965 (div. 1978); children—Thomas Vernon, Heather Lee; m. 2d, Mary E. Martin, Feb. 12, 1979; 1 dau., Amity Rae. Staff, Touche Ross & Co., Chgo., 1970-73, audit supr., 1973-75; asst. controller Sanger-Harris div. Federated Dept. Stores, Dallas, 1975-76; dir. store control May Dept. Stores, St. Louis, 1976-78, dir. fin. public relations, 1978-79; controller Things Remembered div. Cole Nat., Highland Heights, Ohio, 1980—; lectr. accounting Loyola U., Chgo., 1975. C.P.A., Ill. Mem. Nat. Assn. Accountants (past dir. pub. relations Dallas chpt.), Am. Inst. C.P.A.'s, Ill., Mo., Tex. socs. C.P.A.'s, EDP Auditors Assn., Ethical Soc. St. Louis. Home: 3751 Bridgeview South Euclid OH 44121 Office: 5340 Avion Park Dr Highland Heights OH 44143

HELZER, JAMES ALBERT, mail order mktg. co. exec.; b. Cheyenne, Wyo., Sept. 11, 1946; s. H. Albert and Bernadette J. (Stalker) H.; B.A. with honors, Yale, 1968; m. Mary Elizabeth Clark, Mar. 15, 1969; children—Katherine, John. An organizer Unicover Corp., Cheyenne, mail order marketer collectibles, 1968, pres., chief exec. officer, 1968—; pres. Unicover Graphics Corp., Cheyenne, 1972—; dir. 1st Nat. Bank & Trust Co. Wyo., First Bankshares of Wyo., Wyo. State Bank. State co-chmn. Campaign for Yale, 1975-78; chmn. Wyo. Bus. Conf. on Arts, 1979; mem. Bus. Com. for Arts; bd. dirs., chmn. fin. com. DePaul Hosp. Recipient Silliman Cup for contbns. to coll. Yale U., 1968; asso. fellow Silliman Coll. Yale, 1976—; recipient citation Am. Stamp Dealers Assn., 1976. Mem. Indsl. Devel. Assn. Cheyenne (dir. 1973-76, v.p. 1974-75), Assn. Yale Alumni (Wyo. del. 1973-75), Direct Mail Mktg. Assn., Am. Stamp Dealers Assn., Cheyenne C. of C. Clubs: Young Men's Lit. (Cheyenne), Rotary. Author: (with Chester O. Harris) A Philatelic Portfolio of America's National Parks, 1972. Editor-in-chief: The Standard First Day Cover Catalog, 1969, 76, 79. Home: 4021 Carey Ave Cheyenne WY 82001 Office: 1 Unicover Center Cheyenne WY 82008

HEMANN, RAYMOND GLENN, aerospace co. exec.; b. Cleve., Jan. 24, 1933; s. Walter Harold Marsha Mae (Colbert) H.; B.S., Fla. State U., 1957; postgrad. U.S. Naval Postgrad. Sch., 1963-64, U. Calif. at Los Angeles, 1960-62; M.S. in Systems Engring., Calif. State Coll. at Fullerton, 1970; M.A. in Econs., Calif. State U. at Fullerton, 1972; m. Leslie K. Lewis, May 23, 1980; children—James Edward, Carolyn Frances. Aero. engring. aide U.S. Navy, David Taylor Model Basin, Carderock, Md., 1956; analyst Fairchild Aerial Surveys, Tallahassee, 1957; research analyst Fla. Rd. Dept., Tallahassee, 1957-59; chief Autonetics div. N. Am. Rockwell Corp., Anaheim, Calif., 1959-69; v.p., dir. Ralph E. Manns Co., Wilmington, Calif., 1969-70; mgr. avionics design and analysis dept. Lockheed Aircraft Corp., Burbank, Calif., 1970-72, mgr. program devel., 1976—; gen mgr. Western div. Arinc Research Corp., Santa Ana, Calif., 1972-76; instr. ops. analysis dept. U.S. Naval Postgrad. Sch., Monterey, Calif., 1963-64, Calif. State Coll. at Fullerton, 1964-71, Monterey Peninsula Coll., 1963; pres. Asso. Aviation, Inc., Fullerton, Calif., 1965-74. Served with AUS, 1950-53. Recipient numerous profl. and civic awards. Fellow A.A.A.S.; mem. Ops. Research Soc. Am., IEEE, AIAA, N.Y. Acad. Scis., Air Force Assn., Assn. Old Crows, Air Force Assn., Nat. Assn. Remotely Piloted Vehicles (founding mem.; dir. Los Angeles chpt.), Soaring Soc. Am., Phi Kappa Tau. Episcopalian. Author numerous tech. articles and reports. Home: 2333 Midlothian Dr Altadena CA 91001 Office: PO Box 551 Burbank CA 91520

HEMBRE, JOHN IVER, advt. exec.; b. Baker, Mont., Dec. 31, 1926; s. Julius O. and Cora (Lanning) H.; B.B.A., U. Minn., 1951; m. Florence M. Wilson, July 19, 1953; children—Jane Cora, Julie Florence, Ellen Ruth. Vice pres. Nat. Outdoor Advt. Bur., various locations, 1952-62; supr. outdoor and transit media Young & Rubicam, Inc., N.Y.C., 1962-64; sr. v.p., dir. mktg. and sales, mem. exec. com. of bd. dirs. Transp. Displays, Inc. subs. ITT, N.Y.C., 1964-72; pres., chmn. bd. The Hembre Co., Inc., Huntington, N.Y., 1972—; founder, chmn. bd. D-Cube Inc., Huntington, N.Y., 1976—. Home: 2 Hardwick Dr Huntington NY 11746 Office: 55 Wall St Huntington NY 11743

HEMBREE, HUGH LAWSON, III, diversified holding co. exec.; b. Fort Smith, Ark., Nov. 16, 1931; s. Raymond N. and Gladys (Newman) H.; B.S. in Bus. Adminstrn., U. Ark., 1953, LL.B., 1958; m. Sara Janelle Young, Sept. 1, 1956; children—Hugh Lawson, Raymond Scott. In middle mgmt. Ark.-Best Freight System, Inc., Fort Smith, 1958-61, dir. finance, 1961-64, v.p., 1964-66; pres. Ark.-Best Corp., Fort Smith, 1966-73, chief exec. officer, 1966—, chmn. bd., 1973—, also dir.; dir., exec. com. Nat. Bank of Commerce, Dallas, 1967-75; chmn. 1st Bankers Real Estate Investment Trust, 1969-73; pres. Sugar Hill Farms, Inc., Ft. Smith; dir. Mid-Am. Industries, Inc., Mchts. Nat. Bank, Ft. Smith, Comml. Nat. Bank, Little Rock, First Fed. Savs. and Loan Assn., Ft. Smith. Sec., Fort Smith/Sebastian County Joint Planning Commn., 1959-74; Ark. chmn. Radio Free Europe Program, 1968-69; mem. dean's adv. com. sch. bus. U. Ark., 1969-73; mem. Ark. Adv. Bd. on Higher Edn., 1975—; mem. Democratic Central Com. Ark., 1968—; pres. Westark area council Boy Scouts Am., 1966-67, area S. Central Region, 1974—; trustee U. Kans. Found.; chmn. bd. trustees Edwards Mercy Hosp.; chmn. bd. trustees, mem. devel. council St. Edward Regional Med. Center; bd. dirs. Western Ark. Emergency Med. Services, 1970-76; chmn. devel. council U. Ark., 1972-74, chmn. exec. com., 1974—; exec. com., treas. Western Ark. Planning and Devel. Dist., 1965-73; chmn. Ark.-Okla. Livestock and Fair Bd., 1974—. Served to lt. USAF, 1953-55. Recipient Silver Beaver award Boy Scouts Am., 1969, Silver Antelope award, 1975; Ark. Leadership award, 1970, 75. Mem. Nat. Assn. Devel. Orgns. (chmn. adv. com.), Ark. (1st v.p. 1971-73, pres. 1973-75, chmn. bd. 1975—), Ft. Smith (pres. 1970-73) chambers commerce, NAM (regional v.p., exec. com. 1974-75), Nat. Assn. Devel. Dists. (chmn. 1971-73), Young President's Orgn., U. Ark. Alumni Assn. (dir., mem. bldg. com.), Am. Trucking Assn. (nat. accounting and fin. council, dir.), NAM (dir., exec. com., regional v.p.), Ark. Arts Center, Sigma Alpha Epsilon, Delta Theta Phi, Phi Eta Sigma, Beta Gamma Sigma, Scabbard and Blade. Episcopalian (vestryman, co-chmn. ch. fin. com.). Clubs: Chaparral, Lancers, Econ. (Dallas); N.Y. Athletic; Fianna Hills Country, Fort Smith Hardscrabble Country, Town (Ft. Smith). Home: 3220 Park Ave Fort Smith AR 72901 Office: 1000 S 21st St Fort Smith AR 72901

HEMINGWAY, TIMOTHY TRUESDALE, transp. equipment mfg. co. exec.; b. Auburn, N.Y., Feb. 6, 1946; s. David Stuart and Lucy Truesdale H.; B.S. in Bus. Adminstrn., Babson Coll., 1970; M.B.A., Suffolk U., 1971; m. Anne McIlwaine, Dec. 28, 1968; children—Kristen Truesdale, Graham Stuart. With Ultragaz SA, Sao Paulo, Brazil, 1971-76, supt. comml. activities and planning, 1973-76; asst. gen. mgr. Holland Pacific Hitch, Milpitas, Calif., 1977-79, v.p., gen. mgr., Wylies, Tex., 1979—. Served with USAF, 1966. Mem. C. of C. (pres. econ. devel.) Presbyterian. Club: Lions. Office: 1301 Martinez Ln Wylie TX 75098

HEMKER, PAUL WILLIAM, oil co. exec.; b. LaCrosse, Wis., Mar. 2, 1940; s. Bernard William and Esther Lillian (Sprain) H.; B.B.A., U. Wis., 1963; m. Marilyn Jean Ikert, Sept. 30, 1967; children—Carrie Lynn, Patricia Ann. Pres., chmn. bd. Gen. Energy Co., Inc., Tulsa, 1976—, Mid-Am. Refinery, Chanute, Kans., 1976-79, Hemker Oil Co., Inc., LaCrosse, 1963—; officer, part owner, dir. Linnmar, Inc., Lithographics, Inc., HMML, Inc., Black River Enterprises, Medary Co., Janmar, Inc., Risman Enterprises, Host Enterprises, Wis. Tool, Inc., Total Services, Inc., Hoenig Transp., Phoenix Co., Gas N Go, Inc., Smorgy's Inc. Served with USAR, 1963-69. Mem. Nat. Petroleum Refiners Assn., Beta Theta Pi. Lutheran. Club: LaCrosse Country. Home: 1577 E Young Dr Onalaska WI 54650 Office: 83 Milwaukee St LaCrosse WI 54601

HEMMING, WALTER WILLIAM, soft drink co. exec.; b. Vineland, N.J., Oct. 2, 1939; s. Percy Albert and Marguerite (Smith) H.; B.S. magna cum laude, Syracuse U., 1961; m. June 10, 1961; children—Cynthia, Catherine, Walter William. Prin., Arthur Young & Co., Stamford, Conn., 1961-72; v.p., controller Soft Drink div. Coca-Cola Bottling Co. N.Y., N.Y.C., 1972-74, corp. controller, Hackensack, N.J., 1974-78; exec. v.p., chief operating officer KW Inc., Manchester, N.H., 1978—. Treas., Clinton (Conn.) Methodist Ch., 1969-72, Ridgefield (Conn.) Meth. Ch., 1974-77, Hollis Congregational Ch., 1981—. Recipient Haskins & Sells Found. award, 1961; C.P.A., N.Y., Conn. Mem. N.H. Soft Drink Assn. (treas. 1979—), Am. Inst. C.P.A.'s, Conn. Soc. C.P.A.'s, N.Y. Soc. C.P.A.'s. Republican. Home: PO Box 141 123 Worcester Rd Hollis NH 03049 Office: 80 Stark St Manchester NH 03101

HEMSEL, WILLIAM FREDERICK, mfg. engr.; b. Elizabeth, N.J., Oct. 19, 1935; s. Charles Edward and Edna Elizabeth-Marie (Gray) H.; student Coll. Engring., Rutgers U., 1958-60; m. Olga Betty Benda, Aug. 26, 1961; children—William Charles, Kathryn Anne. Draftsman, Bell Telephone Labs., Inc., Murray Hill, N.J., 1960-64; design engr. Mitronics, Inc., Murray Hill, 1964-67; staff engr., alkaline battery div. Gulton Industries, Inc., Metuchen, N.J., 1967-68; methods engr. Precision Circuits, Inc., Farmingdale, N.J., 1968-69; mfg. engr., mgr. tech. services Trimpot div. Bourns, Inc., Riverside, Calif., 1969—. Served with USN, 1954-57. Registered profl. engr., Calif. Mem. Soc. Mfg. Engrs. (certified mfg. engr.), Am. Ceramic Soc. Home: 41095 Academy Dr Hemet CA 92343 Office: 1200 Columbia Ave Riverside CA 92507

HENCLEY, RICHARD LEROY, mfg. co. exec.; b. Seattle, June 4, 1927; s. Fred James and Inez Emily (Finley) H.; B.S. in Indsl. Engring., U. Wis., 1952; postgrad. U. Minn., 1952-53; m. Murcille D. Hofkes, June 16, 1948; children—Kathleen, Richard E., Robert E., Denise G., Peggy A. Engring. mgr. Rohr Corp., San Diego, 1958-60; group mgr. Sperry Univac Co., St. Paul, 1960-69; sr. v.p. Data Card Corp., Mpls., 1969-79; sr. v.p. Micro Component Tech., Inc., St. Paul, 1979—, also dir.; dir. Teleproducts Corp., Turtle Mountain Corp., Moores Ins. Agy., Intercontinental Communications Corp.; mem. mech. engring. adv. council U. Minn. Served with USN, 1944-46; PTC. Mem. Am. Mgmt. Assn., Assn. for Corp. Growth. Republican. Patentee in field. Office: 599 Cardigan Rd PO Box 43013 Saint Paul MN 55164

HENDERSON, BRUCE D(OOLIN), mgmt. exec.; b. Nashville, Apr. 30, 1915; s. John B. and Ceacy (Doolin) H.; B.S., Vanderbilt U., 1937; m. Frances Fleming, Sept. 5, 1949; children—Asta, Bruce Balfour, Ceacy, Bruce Alexander. Trainee, Frigidaire div. Gen. Motors Corp., 1937-38; sales Leland Electric Co., 1938-39; attended Harvard Bus. Sch., 1940-41; buyer Westinghouse Electric Corp., 1941, asst. purchasing agt., Lima, Ohio, 1942, purchasing agt., Newark, 1943-46, mgr. purchases, stores, Sharon, Pa., 1946-49; asst. to v.p. Westinghouse Electric Co., Pitts., 1950, gen. purchasing agt., 1951, gen. mgr. purchases and traffic, 1952, v.p. purchases, 1953-55, v.p., gen. mgr. transformer div., 1955, air conditioning div., 1956-59; sr. v.p. in charge mgmt services div. Arthur D. Little, Inc., 1959-63; v.p. charge of mgmt. cons. div. Boston Safe Deposit & Trust Co., 1963-66, sr. v.p., 1966-67; pres. The Boston Cons. Group, Inc.; chmn. Boston Consulting Group Ltd., Eng. Clubs: Farmington Country (Charlottesville, Va.); Duquesne (Pitts.); Union League (N.Y.); St. Croix Country (Virgin Islands); Bay, Harvard, Harvard Faculty (Boston). Home: 163 Hampshire Rd Wellesley MA 02181 Office: 1 Boston Pl Boston MA 02106

HENDERSON, BRUCE LESLIE, real estate broker; b. Atlanta, Nov. 12, 1951; s. Herbert Clay and Doris Virginia (Powell) H.; B.B.A. in Real Estate, Ga. State U., 1975. Sales asso. Barton & Ludwig Realtors, Atlanta, 1976-78, Realty Specialists, Inc., Marietta, Ga., 1978; broker G.M.A. Realty & Investments, Inc., Atlanta, 1978-79; broker, propr. Henderson Properties, Atlanta, 1979—. Mem. Million Dollar Club, 1980. Mem. Nat. Assn. Realtors, Apt. Owners and Mgrs. Assn., Ga. Assn. Realtors, Cobb County Bd. Realtors, Cobb County Council Young Realtors (past pres.), Cobb County Jaycees. Office: 1000 Circle 75 Pkwy S-10 Atlanta GA 30339

HENDERSON, DAVID EARL, heating and air conditioning contractor; b. Oklahoma City, Mar. 23, 1939; s. John R. and Dora B. (Bryant) H.; B.S. in Bus., Oklahoma City U., 1963; m. D. Darlene Brand, Dec. 20, 1957; children—Danny, Debbie, Diana. With J.R. Henderson Co., Oklahoma City, 1957—, sales rep., 1961-63, v.p., 1963-66, pres., 1966—. Bd. dirs. Found. Sr. Citizens; pres. Baptist Men's Group. Mem. ASHRAE, Sheetmetal and Air Conditioning Contractors Nat. Assn. Democrat. Office: 4820 N Santa Fe St Oklahoma City OK 73118

HENDERSON, GEORGE TRUMBULL, ret. airline co. exec.; b. Toledo, Feb. 4, 1919; s. C. Clyde and Elsie (Norwood) H.; B.S., Purdue U., 1940; m. Norine Moody, Sept. 20, 1941; children—Larry, Tod, Linda Noshay. With United Airlines, Chgo., 1940-79, airline pilot, 1940-55, flight mgr., 1955-63, flight ops. mgr., 1963-66, dir. flight ops. devel., 1966-79. Mem. asso. bd. Community Meml. Gen. Hosp., LaGrange, Ill., 1972—; mem. pres.'s council Purdue U., W. Lafayette, Ind., 1975—; trustee, vice chmn. No. Bapt. Theol. Sem. Fellow Am. Inst. Aeros. and Astronautics; mem. Internat. Air Transport Assn. (chmn. aircraft noise and emissions adv. com. 1974-79), Soc. Automotive Engrs., Delta Chi. Baptist. Club: Masons (Shriner). Home: 208 Briarwood Pass Oak Brook IL 60521

HENDERSON, HENRY LORENZO, former food products co. exec.; b. Greenville, S.C., Dec. 10, 1915; s. John Clyde and Lydia (Ross) H.; certificate Carolina Sch. of Commerce, 1936; student N.Y. U., 1951-53; advanced mgmt. program Harvard Grad. Sch. Bus., 1964; m. Eugenia McMahan, Sept. 21, 1940; children—Michael L., Richard R. Office mgr. Nabisco Inc., N.Y.C., 1940-43, auditor, 1946-50; plant mgr., Atlanta, 1954-59, gen. mgr. Chgo. bakeries, 1959-69, dir. mfg., 1969-72, corp. v.p. new products div., 1972, pres. spl. products div., 1973-78; chmn. bd. Nabisco-Astra Corp., 1973-78; ret., 1978; now horse farmer, Piedmont, S.C. Dir. Cereal Inst., Pet Foods Inst. Served to capt. AUS, 1943-46. Mem. Ill. State C. of C. (dir. 1965-69, chmn. exec. com. 1966-69), Am. Mgmt. Assn. Republican. Methodist (steward 1955—, trustee 1967-69). Clubs: Harvard of Chgo., Harvard Bus. Sch. of S.C., Palmetto Dunes Golf and Country, Hilton Head Island. Address: Belle Terre Farms Box 566 Route 6 Piedmont SC 29673

HENDERSON, JAMES ALAN, engine co. exec.; b. South Bend, Ind., July 26, 1934; s. John William and Norma (Wilson) H.; A.B., Princeton, 1956; Baker scholar, Harvard, 1961-63; m. Mary Evelyn Kriner, June 20, 1959; children—James Alan, John Stuart, Jeffrey Todd, Amy Brenton. With Scott Foresman & Co., Chgo., 1962; staff mem. Am. Research & Devel. Corp., Boston, 1963; faculty Harvard Bus. Sch., 1963; asst. to chmn. Cummins Engine Co., Inc., Columbus, Ind., 1964-65, v.p. mgmt. devel., 1965-69, v.p. personnel, 1969-70, v.p. ops., 1970-71, exec. v.p., 1971-75, exec. v.p., chief operating officer, 1975-77, pres., 1977—, also dir.; dir. Cummins Engine Found., Ind. Bell Telephone Co., Indpls., Inland Steel Co., Chgo., Hayes-Albion Corp., Jackson, Mich. Pres., Jr. Achievement, Columbus, 1967-69; gen. chmn. Bartholomew County United Fund Campaign, 1970; pres. Hoosier Hills council Boy Scouts Am., 1970-72, Culver Legion, Culver Alumni Assn., 1971-72; mem. selection com. Rockefeller Pub. Service awards, 1978-79; Co-mgr. Rockefeller for Pres. Campaign, 1968; trustee Princeton U.; bd. dirs. Culver Ednl. Found., Heritage Fund of Bartholomew County, Inc. Served to lt. USNR, 1956-61. Mem. NAM (dir.), Columbus Area C. of C. (pres. 1973, adv. com. 1974). Presbyn. (elder). Author: Creative Collective Bargaining, 1965. Office: Cummins Engine Co 1460 N National Rd Columbus IN 47201*

HENDERSON, JAMES BROOKE, oil and chem. co. exec.; b. Washington, Feb. 26, 1926; s. Robert Neel and Dorothy (Brooke) H.; B.S., Purdue U., 1946, Ph.D., 1949, m. Joan Yvonne Niksch, Feb. 3, 1948; children—Jan, Robert Brooke. With Shell Chem. Co., Houston, 1949-72, gen. mgr. Synthetic Rubber div., 1965-66, gen. mgr. Indsl. Chems. div., 1966-69, v.p., 1969-72, pres., 1979—; with Shell Oil Co., Houston, 1972-77, v.p. mktg., 1974-75, v.p. oil products, 1975-77, v.p., 1979, exec. v.p., dir., 1979—; mktg. coordinator oil Shell Internat. Petroleum Co., London, 1977-79, dir., 1978-79; dir. Nat. Gypsum Co. Bd. govs. Purdue Found.; vice chmn., dir. Am. Indsl. Health Council. Named Disting. Engring. Alumnus, Purdue U., 1975. Mem. Am. Inst. Chem. Engrs., Am. Chem. Soc., NAM (dir. 1973-77, vice chmn. So. div. 1979—), Am. Petroleum Inst. (dir.), Chem. Mfrs. Assn. (dir., exec. com.), Sigma Xi, Tau Beta Pi, Omega Chi Epsilon, Phi Lambda Upsilon. Clubs: Heritage; Sunningdale Golf (Eng.). Houston Athletic, Lochinvar Golf, Lakeside Country (Houston). Office: Shell Oil Co PO Box 2463 Houston TX 77001

HENDERSON, JAMES HARRIS, fin. exec.; b. Jackson, Miss., Dec. 12, 1944; s. Raymond Harris and Carrye Lee (Ashford) H.; B.A., Vanderbilt U., 1967; B.S., Am. Grad. Sch. Internat. Mgmt., 1970. With State Dept., Iran, 1968; with Harris-Upham & Co., N.Y.C., 1970-72, Fin. Execs. Inst., N.Y.C., 1972-73, Naarden Internat., N.Y.C., 1974-75; dir. mktg. fin. and info. services Citicorp., N.Y.C., 1976—. Mem. Am. Mgmt. Assn., Am. Banking Assn., Bank Adminstrn. Inst., Am. Mktg. Assn. Home: 320 E 49th St New York NY 10017 Office: 399 Park Ave New York NY 10043

HENDERSON, RICHARD, JR., computer services co. exec.; b. Columbia, S.C., Aug. 12, 1935; s. Richard and Claire S.; A.B. with honors, Grove City Coll., 1959; M.B.A., N.Y. U., 1960; m. Janet DeVonis, Apr. 2, 1964. Dir. spl. products, office products div. IBM Corp., 1969; v.p. Fairchild Camera & Instrument Corp., Mountain View, Calif., 1969-72; sr. v.p. Engelhard Industries, Murray Hill, N.J., 1972-75; v.p. Boeing Computer Services Co., Morristown, N.J., 1975—. Served with AUS, 1954-55. Home: 30 Bradwahl Dr Convent Station NJ 07960 Office: Boeing Computer Services Co 177 Madison Ave Morristown NJ 07960

HENDERSON, WILLIAM DIEMER, agrl. machinery mfg. exec.; b. Davenport, Iowa, June 3, 1946; s. William Joseph and Barbara Jane (Diemer) H.; B.A., Denison U., 1968; M.B.A., U. Va., 1975; m. Sherry Lee Bousman, Nov. 7, 1970; children—Scott, Mark. Asst. to group v.p. FMC Corp., Chgo., 1975-76, mgr. bus. devel. agrl. machinery div., Jonesboro, Ark., 1976-77, works mgr., Ocoee, Fla., 1978-79, gen. mgr. Jonesboro (Ark.) operation, 1979—. Adv. bd. Sch. Bus., Ark. State U. Served to lt. USN, 1968-73. Club: Jonesboro Country. Home: 1401 White Oak St Jonesboro AR 72401 Office: Agrl Machinery Div FMC Corp 5601 E Highland Jonesboro AR 72401

HENDERSON-FOREHAND, RONI KAYE, sales exec.; b. Mt. Vernon, Ohio, Mar. 4, 1947; d. Darrell Austin and Margaret Frances (Furman) Branson; student in biology U. Tex., 1966-69; m. Michael Ray Forehand, June 3, 1978. Tech. support staff First of Ft. Worth (Tex.), 1969-71, First of Dallas, 1972-73; ind. cons., 1971-72; system mktg. rep. The Service Bur. Co., Dallas, 1973-75, mktg. rep., 1975-77; mktg. rep. Prime Computer Inc., Dallas, 1977-79; mgr. market devel. Lloyd Bush & Assos., Dallas, 1979—; cons. in field. Vol. Republican Com., 1980. Named Rookie of the Yr. Service Bur. Co., 1975, Prime, 1977. Mem. Data Processing Mgrs. Assn., Assn. for Systems Mgmt., Women in Bus. Republican. Office: 14679 Midway Rd Dallas TX 75234

HENDLIN, DAVID, microbiologist; b. Harbin, China, Mar. 8, 1920; came to U.S., 1923, naturalized, 1928; s. Louis and Minna (Halpern) H.; B.A., Bklyn. Coll., City U. N.Y., 1941; M.Sc. (Research fellow 1941-43), Iowa State U., 1943; Ph.D., Rutgers U., 1949; m. Ruth Maltz, Jan. 2, 1944; children—Susan Hendlin Mooallem, Harriet. Research microbiologist Merck Sharp & Dohme Research Labs., Merck & Co., Inc., Rahway, N.J., 1943-48, head nutrition sect., 1948-53, mgr. dept. microbiology, 1953-56, asst. dir. microbiology, 1956-57, dir. bacteriology, 1967-69, dir. basic microbiology, 1969-74, sr. dir. devel. microbiology, 1974—. Fellow Am. Acad. Microbiology, N.Y. Acad. Sci.; mem. Am. Soc. Microbiology (pres. N.J. chpt. 1956-57, nat. councilor 1957-59), Am. Chem. Soc., Soc. Indsl. Microbiology, Brit. Soc. Gen. Microbiology, AAAS. Contbr. articles to profl. jours.; patentee in field. Office: Merck & Co Inc Rahway NJ 07065

HENDON, ROBERT CARAWAY, cons., ret. transp. and mfg. exec.; b. Shelbyville, Tenn., Jan. 13, 1912; s. William Oscar and Anna Bertha (Caraway) H.; B.J., U. Mont., 1931, J.D., 1934; m. Ruth Perham, Apr. 23, 1936; children—Robert Caraway, Elizabeth Anne Hendon Dunbar. Admitted to Mont., Tenn. bars, 1934; gen. law practice, Monterey, Tenn., 1934-35; spl. agt., spl. agt. in charge FBI, 1935-39; insp., adminstrv. asst. to dir., exec. com. 1939-47; exec. rep. to pres. Ry. Express Agy. (name changed to REA Express), 1947, various exec. positions, 1947-50, v.p. personnel and indsl. relations, 1953-55, v.p. ops., 1955-64, v.p. exec. dept., 1964-68; v.p. Consol. Freightways, Inc., 1968-77, ret., 1977; asst. to pres., dir. personnel Mathieson Chem. Corp., 1950-52; dir. REA Leasing Corp. 1961-68, pres., 1964-67, vice chmn., 1967-68; pres., dir. REA Express Seven Arts Transvision Inc., 1965-68, TOFC Leasing Corp., 1966-68; dir., chmn. exec. com. Fast Service Shipping Terminals, 1961-68; dir., mem. exec., nominating, examination and audit coms. Manhattan Life Ins. Co.; dir., mem. exec., nominating, examination and audit coms. Manhattan Life Corp.; dir., exec. com., chmn. audit com. No. Nat. Life Ins. Co. Del., Atty. Gen.'s Conf. Juvenile Delinquency, 1946; mem. U.S. Com. for Security of War Info., 1942; mem. prevention com. Assn. Am. R.R.'s, 1947-50; trustee, mem. exec. com., past pres. U. Mont. Found.; bd. mgrs., vice chmn. Grand Central YMCA, 1953-68; trustee, past pres. Center for Environ. and Resource Analysis; bd. dirs., chmn. awards com. Nat. Safety Council, 1963-68. Recipient Distinguished Service award U. Mont., 1967. Mem. Soc. Former Spl. Agts FBI, Transp. Assn. Am. (policy implementation and facilitation coms. 1969-77), Nat. Indsl. Conf. Bd. (asso.), Phi Sigma Kappa, Sigma Delta Chi. Episcopalian (past vestryman, warden). Clubs: Univ. (Larchmont, N.Y.); Congressional Country, Propeller (Washington); Grizzly Riders Internat. (Mont.). Author: Frontiers in Labor-Management Relations, 1956; Seniority: First In, Last Out, 1958; also articles. Address: 134 Harpeth Trace Dr Nashville TN 37221

HENDREN, MERLYN CHURCHILL, furniture co. exec.; b. Gooding, Idaho, Oct. 16, 1926; d. Herbert Winston and Annie Averett Churchill; student U. Idaho, 1944-47; m. Robert Lee Hendren, June 14, 1947; children—Robert Lee, Anne Aleen. With Hendren's Furniture Co., Boise, 1947-69; co-owner, v.p. Hendren's Inc., Boise, 1969—. Bd. dirs. Idaho Law Found, 1978—; chmn. Coll. of Idaho Symposium, 1977-78; pres. Boise Council on Aging, 1959-60; mem. Gov.'s Commn. on Aging, 1960, Idaho del. to White House Conf. Aging, 1961. Mem. Boise C. of C. Republican. Episcopalian. Home: 3504 Hillcrest Dr Boise ID 83705 Office: 516 S 9th St Boise ID 83706

HENDREN, ROBERT LEE, JR., furniture co. exec.; b. Reno, Oct. 10, 1925; s. Robert Lee and Aleen (Hill) H.; student U. Idaho, 1943-44, 46-47; m. Merlyn Churchill, June 14, 1947; children—Robert Lee IV, Anne Aleen. Owner, Hendren's, Inc. (formerly Hendren's Furniture Co.), Boise, Idaho, 1947—, now pres. Trustee Coll. of Idaho; chmn. bd. Southwestern Idaho Multiple Sclerosis Assn.; mem. Ada County Welfare Bd.; mem. bd. Marriage Counseling Service; exec. com. Mountainview council Boy Scouts Am.; trustee, chmn. bd. Boise Independent Sch. Dist.; mem. council Ada County Dept. Pub. Assistance; mem. Boise City Planning Commn.; charter dir. Boise Valley Indsl. Found.; chmn. bd. trustees Coll. of Idaho. Served with AUS, 1944-46. Mem. Ida. Council Retailers (v.p.), Boise Valley Carpet and Furniture Retailers (pres.), Boise Retail Mchts. (chmn.), C. of C. (pres., dir.), Am. Inst. Interior Designers. Mason (K.T., Shriner), Rotarian. Home: 3504 Hillcrest Dr Boise ID 83705 Office: 516 S 9th St Boise ID 83706

HENDRICK, ANTHONY STUART, energy mgmt. cons.; b. Rockville Centre, N.Y., Sept. 8, 1934; s. Stuart Augustus and Edith Eleanor (Hamilton) H.; B.M.E., Rensselaer Poly. Inst., 1956; M.B.A., Harvard U., 1961. Test engr., Gen. Electric Co., Schenectady, also Pittsfield, Mass., 1954-55; computer devel. engr. IBM, Poughkeepsie, N.Y., 1956-60; mgr. pacemaker mfg. and engring. Gen. Electric Co., Milw., 1961-64, mgr. transducer engring., Phoenix, 1964-66; mgr. advt. bus. planning Western Union Telegraph Co., Mahwah, N.J., 1966-71; pvt. indsl. mktg. cons., Rockville Centre, 1971-77; cons. FCC, 1977; prin. investigator energy conserving controls in bldgs. U.S. Dept. Energy, 1977—, Brookhaven Lab., 1977—. Served with USAF, 1958. Mem. Harvard Bus. Sch. Club Greater N.Y., Tau Beta Pi. Author: Energy Conservation and Home Improvement, 1977; Consumer Protection in the U.S., 1977; Portable Energy Sources, 1977; Consumer Markets for Magnetic Recording Products, 1977; Energy Transmission and Transportation, 1975; Solar Energy 1975-2000, 1975; Office Equipment Markets, 1974; Data Telecommunications Progress Report, 1974; Plastics and Pollution, 1972; New Forces in Telecommunications, 1972. Inventor composite silver/stainless steel heart electrode for implantable cardiac pacemaker. Home: 36 Cumberland St Rockville Centre NY 11570 Office: 81 Cornell St B-120 Upton NY 11973

HENDRICKS, JOHN ALOYSIUS, bank exec.; b. New Brunswick, N.J., Oct. 3, 1940; s. Aloysius John and Dorothy Elizabeth (Rupp) H.; A.B. (State scholar), Rutgers U., 1962; M.B.A., U. Pa., 1966; m. Kathleen Mary O'Grady, Aug. 12, 1972; children—Maureen, Sean, Christine. Programmer, ITT, Paramus, N.J., 1962; supervising internal auditor N.Y. Telephone Co., N.Y.C., 1966-70; asst. to v.p., sec. Coca-Cola Bottling Co. of N.Y., Hackensack, N.J., 1970-75; asst. v.p. Horizon Bancorp., Morristown, N.J., 1975—; sec. Horizon Creditcorp, Morristown, 1975—; treas. Horizon Trust Co., N.A., 1981—. Dir. Hanover Twp. Town Meeting, 1976. Served with AUS, 1962-64. Ashton scholar, 1964-66. Mem. Am. Inst. Banking, Nat. Investor Relations Inst., N.Am. Soc. Corporate Planning, Assn. MBA Execs., Hanover Twp. Jaycees (chmn. 1977-79), Rutgers U. Alumni Assn., Scarlet R Round Table. Roman Catholic (dist. rep., pres. Parish Council). Home: 72 Fairchild Pl Whippany NJ 07981 Office: 65 Madison Ave Morristown NJ 07960

HENDRICKS, ROBERT MICHAEL, ins. co. exec.; b. St. Louis, Aug. 23, 1943; s. Chester Eugene and Reba Eileen (Leake) H.; B.A., U. Calif., Berkeley, 1965; m. Yvonne Sharon McAnally, Sept. 18, 1971; 1 son, Robert Christian. Dist. mgr. Am. Gen. Life Ins. Co., Los Angeles, 1965-70; gen. partner Hendricks & Assos., Los Angeles, 1970-75; v.p. mktg. U.S. Life Corp., Los Angeles, 1975-76; dir. agys. Bankers United Life Assurance Co., Los Angeles, 1976-77; gen. partner Assurance Distbg. Co., Inc., Los Angeles, 1977-80; pres., chief exec. officer ADCO Re Life Assurance Co., Santa Ana, Calif., 1980—; dir. Assurance Distbg. Co., Inc.; instr. C.L.U. and Life Underwriter Tng. Council programs. Recipient various awards in field. Mem. Nat. Assn. Life Underwriters, C. of C. Republican. Clubs: Rotary, Masons, Shriners. Office: ADCO Re Life Assurance Co 1010 N Main St Suite 525 Santa Ana CA 92701

HENDRICKSON, CHARLES DANA, employee benefits cons.; b. Middletown, Ohio, Jan. 15, 1951; s. Charles W. and Gladys Emma (Horn) H.; B.S., Ohio State U., 1974; m. Valerie Elizabeth Jamra, Aug. 26, 1977. Agt., Penn Mut. Ins. Co., Phila., 1973-78; dir. mktg. Benefit Communicators, Columbus, Ohio, 1978-79; pres. Hendrickson & Hendrickson, Inc., Columbus, 1979—. C.L.U. Republican. Methodist. Home: 2856 McCoy Rd Columbus OH 43220

HENDRICKSON, JEROME ORLAND, assn. exec., lawyer; b. Eau Claire, Wis., July 25, 1918; s. Harold and Clara (Halverson) H.; student Wis. State Coll., 1936-39; J.D., U. Wis., 1942; m. Helen Phoebe Harty, Dec. 27, 1948; children—Jaime Ann, Jerome Orland. Admitted to Wis. bar, 1942, U.S. Supreme Ct. bar, 1955; pvt. practice, Eau Claire, 1946; sales and advt. mgr. Eau Claire Coco-Cola Bottling Co., Inc., 1947-48; exec. sec. Eau Claire Community Chest, 1948-49; in charge dist. office Am. Petroleum Inst., Kansas City, Mo., 1950-53, Chgo., 1953-55; exec. dir. Nat. Assn. Plumbing-Heating-Cooling Contractors, 1955-64; sec. Joint Apprentice Text, Inc., 1955-64; exec. v.p. Cast Iron Soil Pipe Inst., Washington, 1964-74; pres. Valve Mfrs. Assn., McLean, Va., 1975—. Treas., Wis. Community Chest, 1948-49. Treas., All-Industry Plumbing & Heating Modernization Com., 1956-57; co-sec. Joint Industry Program Com., 1958-64. Served from ensign to lt. USNR, 1943-46. Mem. Am., Wis. bar assns., Am., Washington socs. assn. execs., Wis. State Soc. Washington (pres. 1966-68), Nat. Conf. Plumbing-Heating-Cooling Industry (chmn. 1967-69), U. Wis. Alumni Assn., U. Wis. Law Sch. Alumni Assn. Washington (pres. 1970-74), C. of C. of U.S., NAM, Gamma Eta Gamma (pres. Upsilon chpt. 1941-42). Episcopalian. Mason (32 deg., Shriner). Clubs: Washington Golf and Country, Internat. (Washington). Home: 8370 Greensboro Dr McLean VA 22102 Office: 6845 Elm St Suite 711 McLean VA 22101

HENDRIX, DENNIS RALPH, gas transmission co. exec.; b. Selmer, Tenn., Jan. 8, 1940; s. Forrest Ralph and Mary Lee (Tull) H.; B.S., U. Tenn., 1962; M.B.A., Ga. State U., 1965; m. Jennie L. Moore, Dec. 28, 1960; children—Alisa Lee, Natalie Moore, Amy Louise. Staff accountant, cons. Arthur Andersen & Co., Atlanta, 1962-65; faculty Ga. Inst. Tech., 1965-67; sr. cons. Touche, Ross & Co., Memphis, 1967-68; asst. to pres. Tex. Gas Transmission Corp., Owensboro, Ky., 1973-75, pres., 1976-78, pres., chief exec. officer, 1978—; pres. United Foods, Inc., Memphis, 1968-73; dir. First Ky. Nat. Corp., Stokely-Van Camp, Inc.; dir. Ky. Center for Energy Research; trustee Inst. Gas Tech. Vice pres., dir. Jr. Achievement, Owensboro; bd. dirs. U. Tenn. Devel. Council. C.P.A., Ga. Mem. NAM (dir.). Presbyterian. Clubs: Owensboro Country; River Oaks Country, Ramada (Houston). Office: 3800 Frederica St Owensboro KY 42301*

HENDRIX, ERIC THOMAS, economist; b. Los Angeles, June 10, 1948; s. Thomas Russell and Clara Sonia (Arusell) H.; student Dickinson Coll., 1966-68; B.A., Johns Hopkins U., 1971; postgrad. London Sch. Econs. and Polit. Sci., 1973-74; M.B.A., U. Chgo., 1975. Securities auditor, ops. analyst Alex, Brown & Sons, Balt., 1968-73; econ. analyst, intelligence officer Office of Econ. Research, CIA, Washington, 1975—. Mem. U. Chgo. Grad. Sch. Bus. Alumni Assn. Home: 10201 Grosvenor Pl Apt 1125 Rockville MD 20852

HENDRY, JAMES E., lawyer, automobile club exec.; b. Perry, Fla., Nov. 7, 1912; s. Wesley Alonzo and Mae (Weaver) H.; student St. Petersburg Jr. Coll., 1930-32; J.D., U. Fla., 1935; m. Frances Swope, June 25, 1948; children—James E., Jayne L., Thomas S., John W., David F. Vice pres. Hendry Lumber Co., 1935-42, sec., treas., 1946-60; partner, mgr. Hendry Bldg. Co., 1946-60; practice law as James E. Hendry, atty., 1961—; pres. Gulf Housing Corp., 1946; sec.-mgr. St. Petersburg A.A.A. Motor Club, 1962-67, exec. v.p., gen. mgr., 1967—; v.p. Club Ins. Agy., Inc., 1962—; dir. Guardian Bank; admitted to U.S. Supreme Ct. bar. Mem. City Planning and Zoning Bd., 1948-57, Pinellas County Sch. Bd., 1957-66, Pinellas Co. Airport Com., 1952, St. Petersburg Planning Commn., 1973-74. Mem. citizens adv. com. St. Petersburg Jr. Coll., 1948-68, bd. govs., 1938-48, chmn. dist. bd. trustees, 1968-75, bd. dirs. Devel. Found.; pres. bd. dirs. YMCA, 1951; mem. Mound Park Hosp. Bd., 1951-52; mem. bd. Pinellas County chpt. Am. Cancer Soc., chmn. Cancer Drive, 1962; pres. Fla. Sch. Bd. Assn., 1964; sec.-treas. Southeastern Conf. AAA Motor Clubs, 1964, v.p., 1965, pres., 1966; exec. com. Continuing Ednl. Council Fla., 1964; mem. Pinellas Com. of 100, State Community Coll. Council. Past pres. St. Petersburg Jr. Coll. Found. Lt. comdr. USCG Res. Recipient award of honor Wisdom Soc., 1970; Top Mgmt. award St. Petersburg Sales and Mktg. Execs., 1980. Mem. Am., St. Petersburg bar assns., Fla. Bar, Am. Judicature Soc., Fla. C. of C., Nat. Assn. Home Builders (past dir.), Contractors and Builders Assn. of Pinellas County (pres. 1953), Fla. Home Builders Assn. (v.p. 1955), Eastern (treas. 1970-72, vice chmn. 1972-74, chmn. 1975-77), Fla. (chmn. 1974, 79, 80) confs. AAA Motor Clubs, U.S. C. of C., St. Petersburg C. of C. (gov.), Phi Delta Theta, Phi Alpha Delta. Democrat. Methodist. Clubs: Rotary, St. Petersburg Yacht, Skal, Quarterback, Commerce, Circumnavigators, Suncoasters, Feathersound Country. Home: 409 Snell Isle Blvd Saint Petersburg FL 33704 Office: 1211 1st Ave N Saint Petersburg FL 33705

HENDRY, PATRICK RYON, gem dealer; b. Jacksonville, Fla., Jan. 13, 1950; s. James Benjamin and Betty Elaine (Pacetti) H.; A.A., U. Fla., 1973; m. Mary Cecelia Toomey, Feb. 24, 1973; 1 son, David Benjamin. Motion picture dir.-producer Barton Film Co., Jacksonville, 1973-75; sales mgr. Asandro Jewels, Inc., Miami, Fla., 1975-76; pres. The Royal Stone Corp., Coral Gables, Fla., 1976—; dir. Internat. Music Mktg.; lectr. on precious stones, 1976—. Mem. Retail Jewelers Am., Coral Gables C. of C., Met. Mus. Art, Viscayans. Democrat. Club: Coral Reef Yacht. Home: 4200 Monserrate St Coral Gables FL 33146 Office: 255 Alhambra Circle Suite 255-260 Coral Gables FL 33134

HENINGTON, CLARENCE DAYLE, bus. exec.; b. Bartlett, Tex., Mar. 2, 1931; s. Clarence William and Ora (Robbins) H.; B.A. in Econs., U. Nebr., 1964. Enlisted U.S. Air Force, 1951; commd. 2d lt., 1952, advanced through grades to maj., 1966; ret., 1971; adminstrv. asst. to Congressman W.R. Poage, U.S. Ho. of Reps., 1971-77; v.p. govt. relations Chgo. Merc. Exchange, Washington, 1977—. Decorated D.F.C., Air Medal with eight oak leaf clusters. Democrat. Universalist. Clubs: Masons, Shriners. Office: 1101 Connecticut Ave NW Washington DC 20036

HENKE, FRANK XAVIER, III, banker; b. Chgo., May 8, 1941; s. Frank Xavier and Mary Frances (Crane) H.; B.A., Northwestern U., 1963; J.D., Tulsa U., 1967; m. Mary Elizabeth "Bonnie" Creekmore, Oct. 6, 1961; children—Allyson Brooke, Melissa Anne, Frank Xavier. Sr. v.p., trust officer 4th Nat. Bank, Tulsa, 1971-73, exec. v.p., sr. trust officer, 1973-77; pres. 4th Nat. Corp., Tulsa, 1973-77, vice chmn., chief operating officer, 1977—; dir. Deutsche Fin. Service Corp. Bd. dirs., pres. Tulsa council Campfire Girls; bd. dirs. YMCA, Salvation Army, Tulsa Citizens Crime Commn., Jr. Achievement, Tulsa. Mem. Am. Bar Assn., Okla. Bar Assn., Tulsa County Bar Assn. Presbyterian. Clubs: So. Hills Country, Tulsa, Summit, Philcrest Hills Tennis, Downtown Tulsa Rotary. Office: PO Box 2360 Tulsa OK 74101

HENKEL, ARTHUR JOHN, JR., investment banker; b. Bklyn., Aug. 27, 1945; s. Arthur John and Catherine Rita (Burns) H.; A.B., U. Conn., 1969; M.B.A., U. Chgo., 1971. USPHS trainee U. Chgo. Hosps. Clinics, 1969-71, adminstrv. asst. fiscal affairs, 1971; cons. Booz, Allen Hamilton, Inc., N.Y.C., 1972-74; asst. dir. ambulatory ops. New Eng. Med. Center Hosp., Boston, 1974-75, dir. ambulatory care, 1975-77; asso. mcpl. fin. dept. Kidder, Peabody and Co., Inc., N.Y C., 1977-78, asst. v.p., 1978-79, v.p., 1979-80, mng. officer health fin. group, 1980—; instr. community health Tufts U. Sch. Medicine; mem. exec. com. alumni council U. Chgo. Program Hosp. Adminstrn., 1972-76; spl. teaching cons., fin. evaluation hosp. capital projects HEW, 1973. Chmn. investmenfs com. Better Boys Found./Nat. Football League Players Assn. Awards Barnquet, 1978. Recipient Mary Bachmeyer award U. Chgo., 1971; citation Commonwealth Mass., 1976. Office: Kidder Peabody and Co Inc 10 Hanover Sq New York NY 10005

HENKLE, RALPH HAROLD, real estate devel. co. exec.; b. San Francisco, Jan. 7, 1933; s. Ralph Harold and Eleanor (Birmingham) H.; B.A. in Econs., Coll. William and Mary, 1958; M.B.A., U. Pa., 1960; m. Dorothy Lee Benson, July 25, 1964; children—Kurt, Heidi, Krista, Gretchen. With James W. Rouse & Co., Washington, 1961-62; v.p. Treadway Faherty Co., New Orleans, 1962-65, Lawrence Eustis Mortgage Co., New Orleans, 1965-68, J.H. Harris Mortgage Co., New Orleans, 1968-69, Pacific Western Mortgage Co., Los Angeles, 1969-70; pres. Henkle Devel. Co., Inc., Pacific Palisades, Calif., 1970—. Served with U.S. Army, 1954-56. Mem. Nat. Assn. Homebuilders, Building Industry Assn. So. Calif., Delta Tau Delta. Republican. Lutheran. Clubs: Bel Air Bay, Riviera Tennis, Berkeley Tennis, Optimist. Home: 648 Ocampo Dr Pacific Palisades CA 90272 Office: 16801 Pacific Coast Hwy Pacific Palisades CA 90272

HENLEY, JOSEPH OLIVER, mfg. co. exec.; b. Sikeston, Mo., June 25, 1949; s. Fred Louis and Bernice (Chilton) H.; B.S.B.A., U. Mo., 1972; M.B.A., Mich. State U., 1973; m. Jane Ann Rhodes, Aug. 21,

1971. Operations analyst Midland-Ross, Inc., Cleve., 1974, prodn. control mgr., 1974-75, engring. systems mgr. Cameron-Waldron div. Somerset, N.J., 1976; prodn. control mgr. ICM div. Massey Ferguson, Inc., Akron, Ohio, 1976-77, prodn. planning and mfg. systems mgr., 1977-78; sr. audit specialist (mfg.) United Techs. Corp., Hartford, Conn., 1978—. Served with Mo. Army N.G., 1970-72. Mem. Am. Mgmt. Assn., Assn. M.B.A. Execs., Beta Gamma Sigma, Sigma Iota Epsilon, Omicron Delta Epsilon. Presbyterian. Home: 25 Duncaster Ln Vernon CT 06066 Office: Airport Office Annex 400 Main St East Hartford CT 06108

HENLEY, PRESTON VANFLEET, bus. and fin. cons.; b. Fort Madison, Iowa, July 7, 1913; s. Jesse vanFleet and Ruth (Roberts) H.; student Tulane U., 1931-34, Loyola U. (New Orleans), 1935-36; A.B., Calif. State Coll. at Santa Barbara, 1939; postgrad. U. Wash., 1939-40, N.Y. U., 1946; m. Elizabeth Artis Watts, Mar. 31, 1940 (div. June 1956); children—Preston Edward vanFleet, Stephen Watts, John vanFleet; m. 2d, Helena Margaret Greenslade, Nov. 29, 1964; 1 adopted son, Lawrence D. Teaching fellow U. Wash., 1939-40; sr. credit analyst, head credit dept. Chase Nat. Bank, 45th St. br. N.Y.C., 1942-49; Western sales rep. Devoe & Reynolds, Inc., N.Y.C., 1949-51; v.p., comml. loan officer, mgr. credit dept. U.S. Nat. Bank, Portland, Oreg., 1951-72; v.p. Kanabec State Bank, Mora, Minn., Citizens State Bank of Montgomery (Minn.), Park Falls State Bank (Wis.), Montello State Bank (Wis.), all 1972; Wis. loan adminstr. Voyageur Bank Group, Eau Claire, 1972-73; v.p. Nev. Nat. Bank, sr. credit officer So. Nev. Region, 1973-75; bus. and fin. cons., 1975; adv. cons. dir. Vita Plus, 1978—; exec. dir. Nev. Minority Purchasing Council, 1979-80; instr. Am. Inst. Banking, Portland, 1952-65, Multomah Coll., Portland, 1956-62, Portland State U., 1961-72, Mt. Hood Community Coll., 1971-72, Clark County Community Coll., 1979—; treas., dir. Consumer Credit Counselling Service Ore., 1965-72. Treas., Oreg. chpt. Leukemia Soc., 1965-66; mem. Menninger Found. Served with USNR, 1943-45. Mem. Oreg. Bankers Assn., Robert Morris Assos. (pres. Ore. chpt. 1959-60, nat. dir. 1961-64), Nat. Assn. Credit Mgmt., Credit Research Found., Inst. Internal Auditors, S.A.R., Leaf and Scarab, Portland C. of C., Oreg. Retail Council, Am. Legion, Navy League, Alpha Phi Omega, Beta Mu. Republican. Episcopalian. Clubs: Internat., Elks, Masons, Shriners. Contbr. articles to profl. jours. Home and Office: 4235 Gibraltar St Las Vegas NV 89121

HENN, CECIL BENNETT, mech. engr., mfg. co. exec.; b. Dayton, Ohio, Apr. 22, 1930; s. Owen Carl and Anna Mae (Bennett) H.; B.S. in Bus. Adminstrn., Ind. U., 1980; A.A. in Mech. Engring. Tech., U. Dayton, 1961; m. Donna Marlene Liles, June 14, 1950; children—David, Rhonda, Conna. Project engr. Bendix Corp., Dayton, Ohio, 1963-66; with Ex-Cell-O Corp., Berne, Ind., 1966—, sales mgr., 1966-68, chief engr., 1968-73, mfg. mgr., 1973-75, gen. mgr., 1975—. Mem. Nat. Soc. Profl. Engrs. Republican. Mennonite. Club: Rotary (past pres.). Home: 406 Schug St Berne IN 46711 Office: 525 Berne St Berne IN 46711

HENNAGE, JOSEPH HOWARD, pub., printing co. exec.; b. Washington, Jan. 2, 1921. Organizer, pres. Hennage Creative Printers, Washington, 1945—; pres. Jonage Investment Corp., Washington, 1958—, Highland House Pubs. Inc., Washington, 1969—; adv. bd. 1st Nat. Bank Washington, 1963-69, Am. Security & Trust Co., Washington, 1969—; dir. Graphic Arts Mut. Ins. Co., N.Y.C., United Ins. Co. Ltd., Hamilton, Bermuda. Chmn. joint govt.-industry adv. bd. Govt. Printing Office, 1972-79. Exec. com., Potomacland ambassador Washington Bd. Trade, 1970; mem. fine arts com. U.S. Dept. State; mem. bus. adv. bd. George Washington U., 1967-75; chmn. Americana com. Nat. Archives, 1972-77. Bd. dirs. Boys Club Washington, 1949-79, recipient award for disting. service, 1951, Alumni award, 1959; chmn. Printing Mgmt. Edn. Trust Fund, 1972—; trustee D.C., Am. Cancer Soc.; chmn. bd. dirs., pres., trustee Carlyle House Found., 1978-79; bd. dirs. Gadsby's Tavern. Served with USNR, 1942-45. Recipient Freedom Found. award, 1976; citation Brit. Fedn. Master Printers, 1971; U.S. Pub. Printers Distinguished Service award, 1972; Bronze medal Boys Clubs Am., 1976; named Graphic Arts Man of Yr., 1971. Mem. Master Printers Am. (pres. 1967-69, Man of Yr. 1969), Printing Industries Am. (dir. 1964-76, exec. com. 1966-76, chmn. bd. 1969-70, v.p. public relations 1971-76), Printing Industry Washington (pres. 1964-65, dir. 1960-75, disting. service award 1969), Creative Printers Am. (pres. 1963-64), Master Printers Washington (pres. 1960-61), Met. Washington Bd. Trade (dir.-at-large 1972, 78), Supreme Ct. Hist. Soc. (trustee, chmn. acquisitions com. 1975-79), Optimists Internat. (gov. 1957-58, dir. Leonard Cheshire Found., Disting. Gov. award 1958). Methodist (dir. 1966-70). Clubs: Nat. Capital Optimist (pres. 1953-54), City Tavern of Georgetown (Washington); Columbia Country (Chevy Chase, Md.); Farmington Country (Charlottesville, Va.); Metropolitan (N.Y.C.); La Coquille (Palm Beach, Fla.); Chatmoss (Martinville, Va.); Mid Ocean (Bermuda); Confrerie des Chevaliers du Tastevin. Home: 6211 Highland Dr Chevy Chase MD 20015 Office: 814 H St NW Washington DC 20001

HENNEBACH, RALPH L., non-ferrous metal co. exec.; b. Garfield, Utah, May 2, 1920; s. Leo and Consuelo (Herrerias) H.; Metall. Engr., Colo. Sch. Mines, 1941; M.S. in Indsl. Mgmt. (Sloan fellow), M.I.T., 1953; m. Mary Louise Johnston, Sept. 14, 1946; children—Mark Leo, Anne Louise, Margo Lynnne. With ASARCO, Inc., 1941—, asst. to v.p. smelting and refining, 1958-63, v.p. smelting and refining, 1963-66, exec. v.p., 1966-71, pres., 1971—, also dir.; dir. Crompton & Knowles, So. Peru Copper Co., So. Peru Copper Sales Co., Indsl. Minera Mexico, Capco Pipe Co., Federated Metals, Enthone, Lac D'Amiante du Quebec, Neptune Mining, Bolivia Lead Co. Served to lt. (j.g.) USNR, 1944-46. Recipient Distinguished Achievement medal Colo. Sch. Mines, 1965. Mem. AIME, Mining and Metall. Soc., Colo. Sch. Mines Alumni Assn., Sigma Alpha Epsilon, Theta Tau. Clubs: Mining, Pinnacle, Wall St. (N.Y.C.); Canoe Brook Country (Summit, N.J.); Economic. Home: 33 Tennyson Dr Short Hills NJ 07078 Office: 120 Broadway New York NY 10005

HENNELLY, EDMUND PAUL, lawyer, oil co. exec.; b. N.Y.C., Apr. 2, 1923; s. Edmund Patrick and Alice (Laccorn) H.; B.C.E., Manhattan Coll., 1944; postgrad. Columbia; J.D., Fordham U., 1950; m. Josephine Kline; children—Patricia Anne Hennelly Melborne III, Pamela Jeanne Hennelly Farley. Instr., Manhattan Coll., 1947-50; admitted to N.Y. bar, 1950; litigation asso. law firm Cravath, Swaine and Moore, 1950-51, sr. litigation asso. 1953-54; asst. gen. counsel CIA, Washington, 1952-53; asso. counsel, Time, Inc., N.Y.C., 1954-56; asst. legislative cons. Mobil Oil Corp., N.Y.C., 1956-60, legislative cons., 1960-61, mgr. domestic govt. relations dept., N.Y.C., 1961-67, mgr. govt. relations dept., 1967-73, gen. mgr. govt. relations dept., 1974-78, gen. mgr. pub. affairs dept., 1978—; dir. Citroil Enterprises, Citroil Aromatic, South Cay Trust; trustee, mem. exec. com. Hamburg Savs. Bank, N.Y.C. Mem. adv. com. N.Y. State Legislative Com. on Higher Edn.; mem. White House Conf. on Natural Beauty, 1963; mem. N.Y. State Def. Council; mem. Nassau County Energy Commn., Nassau County Subcom. on the Economy, L.I. Citizens' Com. for Mass Transit; mem. Nassau County Overall Econ. Devel. Plan; co-chmn. Public Affairs Research Council. Trustee Am. Good Govt. Soc., Austen Riggs Center; trustee, vice chmn. bd. Marymount Coll., Tarrytown; bd. dirs., v.p. West L.I. council Navy League; bd. dirs. Nat. Council on Aging. Served from ensign to lt. USNR, 1943-46; PTO, ETO. Mem. Nat. Sales Execs. (dir.), N.A.M., Am. Petroleum Inst., N.Y. Chamber Commerce and Industry, Am., Fed. bar assns., Assn. Bar City of N.Y., N.Y. C. of C. (v.p., dir.), Assn. Petroleum Writers, Conf. Bd., Acad. Polit. and Social Scis., U.S. C. of C., Tax Council (dir.), Naval Order U.S. (dir.), Pi Sigma Epsilon, Delta Theta Phi. Clubs: Internat. (Washington), Metropolitan, Nat. Republican, Army-Navy, Capitol Hill, Southward Ho Country, Babylon Yacht, Explorers. Contbr. articles on engring. and law to profl. publs. Home: 84 Sequams Ln E West Islip NY 11795 Office: 150 E 42d St New York City NY 10017

HENNES, ROBERT TAFT, mgmt. cons. exec.; b. Jamestown, N.Y., Mar. 8, 1930; s. Theodore Preston and Lucille (Kane) H.; A.B., Harvard, 1951; M.B.A., Wharton Sch., U. Pa., 1952; m. Frances Walker Pratt, May 9, 1953 (div. 1962); children—Robert Taft, Duncan Pratt, Margaret Nickerson, Theodore Preston II; m. 2d, Grace Margaret Bruton, Oct. 9, 1971. With Lummus Co., N.Y.C., 1952-62; exec. v.p., dir. Conahay & Lyon, Inc., advt. N.Y.C., 1962-70; sr. v.p. Cole & Assos., Boston, 1970-72; chmn., dir. Hennes & Cox Inc., N.Y.C., 1972-77; v.p., prin. Spencer Stuart & Assos., N.Y.C., 1977—; dir. Oldwyck Industries, Inc., N.Y.C. Mem. Harvard Soc. Scientists and Engrs. Club: Harvard. Home: 40 E 84 St New York NY 10028 Office: 437 Madison Ave New York NY 10022

HENNESSEY, HUBERT DAVID, indsl. mktg. cons.; b. Waterbury, Conn., June 18, 1951; s. John Francis and Ella Rita (Korhman) H.; B.S. in Bus. Adminstrn., Norwich U., 1972; M.B.A., Clark U., 1974; postgrad. N.Y. U., 1979—. Sr. pricing analyst Am. Can Co., Greenwich, Conn., 1972-74; mgr. mktg. Interpace Corp., Parsippany, N.J., 1974-79; pres. McDade & Hennessey Co., Bklyn., 1978—; instr. mktg. mgmt. Mem. Am. Mktg. Assn., Am. Acad. Advt. Home and Office: 1120 Church Ave Brooklyn NY 11218

HENNESSY, DEAN MCDONALD, lawyer, mfg. co. exec.; b. McPherson, Kans., June 13, 1923; s. Ernest Weston and Beulah A. (Dunn) H.; A.B. cum laude (Sheldon fellow), Harvard U., 1947, LL.B., 1950; M.B.A., U. Chgo., 1959; m. Marguerite Sundheim, Sept. 6, 1946 (div. Sept. 1979); children—Joan Catherine Hennessy Wright, John D., Robert D., Scott D. Admitted to Ill. bar, 1950; asso. firm Carney, Crowell & Leibman, Chgo., 1950-53; atty. Borg-Warner Corp., Chgo., 1953-62; asst. counsel Emhart Corp., Hartford, Conn., 1962-64, asst. sec., 1964-67, sec., gen. counsel, 1967-74, v.p., sec., gen. counsel, 1974-76, v.p., gen. counsel, 1976—; dir. Emhart Industries, Inc., Emhart Internat. Corp., USM Corp. Sec., chmn. citizens activities Ill. Citizens for Eisenhower, 1952; vice chmn. Jr. Achievement, Chgo., 1959; trustee West Hartford (Conn.) Bicentennial Trust, Inc., 1976-77, Friends and Trustees of Bushnell Meml., Hartford, 1978—. Served to lt. (j.g.) USN, 1943-46. Mem. Am. Bar Assn., Am. Soc. Corp. Secs., Machinery and Allied Products Inst. (mem. law council). Republican. Presbyterian. Club: Farmington (Conn.) Country. Home: 315 Brittany Farms New Britain CT 06053 also Wagner Rd Shelter Harbor Westerly RI 02891 Office: PO Box 2730 Hartford CT 06101

HENNESSY, EDWARD LAWRENCE, JR., chem. co. exec.; b. Boston, Mar. 22, 1928; s. Edward Lawrence and Celina Mae (Doucette) H.; B.S., Fairleigh Dickinson U., 1955; postgrad. N.Y. U., Law Sch.; m. Ruth Frances Schilling, Aug. 18, 1951; children—Michael E., Elizabeth R. Asst. controller Textron Inc., 1950-55; group controller Eastern Electronics, Lear Siegler Inc., 1956-60; with ITT, 1962-64; dir. fin. Europe, Middle East and Africa, Colgate Palmolive Co., 1964-65; v.p. fin. Heublein Inc., Hartford, 1965-68, sr. v.p. adminstrn. and fin., 1969-72; sr. v.p. fin. and adminstrn. United Technologies Corp., Hartford, 1972-77, exec. v.p., group v.p. Systems and Equipment, chief fin. officer, 1977-79; chmn., chief exec. officer Allied Chem. Corp., Morristown, N.J., 1979—, also dir.; dir. Fed. Res. Bank N.Y., Automatic Data Processing Inc., Travelers Ins. Co. Bd. dirs. USCG Acad. Found.; trustee Fairleigh Dickinson U., St. Joseph Coll., Hartford. Mem. Nat. Assn. Accts., Fin. Execs. Inst., Econ. Club N.Y. Roman Catholic. Clubs: Cat Cay (Bahamas); N.Y. Yacht; Ocean Reef Yacht (Key Largo, Fla.). Office: Allied Chem Corp Morristown NJ 07960

HENNESSY, JOHN FRANCIS, cons. engr.; b. N.Y.C., July 18, 1928; s. John F. and Dorothy (O'Grady) H.; B.S. in Physics, Georgetown U., 1949; B.S. in Engring., Mass. Inst. Tech., 1951; m. Barbara McDonnell, Oct. 24, 1953; children—John III, Kathleen, James, Kevin, Peter, David; m. 2d, Bruce Rial, Dec. 30, 1971 (div. 1975). With Syska & Hennessy, Inc., N.Y.C., 1951—, exec. v.p., 1955-66, pres., 1967—, chmn., 1973—, chief exec. officer, 1977—; dir. Franklin Soc. Fed. Savs. & Loan. Mem. exec. bd. Greater N. Y. council Boy Scouts Am. 1958—; mem. Battery Park City Authority; chmn. architect-engr. com. Cardinal's Com. on Laity; Trustee N.Y. Hall Sci., Clark Coll., Atlanta; bd. dirs. N.Y. Heart Assn. Served with USAF, 1951-52. Registered profl. engr., N.Y., Conn., Va., D.C., N.J., Ill., Fla., Mass., N.H., R.I., Calif., Ga., Colo., Ohio, Ind., Oreg. Mem. N.Y. Assn. Cons. Engrs. (pres. 1959-60), N.Y. Bldg. Congress, N.Y., Conn. socs. profl. engrs., Soc. Am. Mil. Engrs., ASME. Clubs: University, Links, River (N.Y.C.); Federal City, Metropolitan (Washington); Lyford Cay (Nassau); Nat. Golf Links; Shinnecock; Seaview Country; Marks (London); Traveler's (Paris). Office: 11 W 42d St New York NY 10036

HENNESSY, RICHARD EDWARD, fin. exec.; b. Buffalo, Mar. 16, 1938; s. Edward William and Elsie (Busch) H.; A.S.E.E., Worcester Jr. Coll., 1966; B.S., Northeastern U., 1970; m. Helen Rose Lerro, May 12, 1962; children—Linda, Timothy, Christina, Richard, Michael. Staff engr. Concord Control, Inc., Brighton, Mass., 1966-71; systems programmer Computek, Cambridge, Mass., 1971-73; systems mgr. Datatrol, Inc., Hudson, Mass., 1973-74; mgr. info. systems Lincoln First Banks, Inc. Rochester, N.Y., 1974-75; product mgr. ATM's, Incoterm/Honeywell, Wellesley, Mass., 1975—. Parish Council pres. Roman Cath. Ch., Marlborough, Mass., 1974, 76, 77. Served with USAF, 1956-61. Recipient Incoterm Annual Mgmt. award, 1978. Roman Catholic. Club: Ancient Order Hibernians (recording sec. 1980). Patentee in field. Home: 24 Girard St Marlborough MA 01752 Office: 65 Walnut St Wellesley Hills MA 02181

HENNING, JEAN NORMA, food service exec.; b. Gainesville, Tex.; d. Mertle William and Johnnie Lee (Hayworth) Gibbs; student in mgmt., Hawaii Employers Council, 1968; dietetic asst. diploma, Kapiolani Community Coll., 1974; m. Edward E. Henning, Aug. 7, 1954 (dec.); children—Vicki, Terri, Ron, Shell, Ward, Sunni. Staff FHA loan dept., Bank of Am., Los Angeles, 1951-53; mgmt. tng. various food service ops., Los Angeles, 1950-63; mgmt. trainee Spencecliff Corp., Honolulu, 1964-67; dir. food services, Arcadia Retirement Residence, 1967. Mem. Chefs de Cuisine Assn. (sec.), Internat. Food Service Execs. Assn., Hosp., Instl. and Ednl. Food Service Soc. (pres.). Office: Arcadia Retirement Residence 1434 Punahou St Honolulu HI 96822

HENRICHS, MILTON JOHN, pharm. co. exec.; b. Lena, Wis., Mar. 3, 1923; s. John and Emma (Nooyen) H.; B.S. in Pharmacy, U. Wis., 1944; m. Betty Ann Murphy, Aug. 16, 1947; children—Thomas, Timothy, Christopher, Mary. Sales rep. Abbott Labs., Des Moines, 1947-54, Rockford, Ill., 1954-61, dist. sales mgr., Davenport, Iowa, 1961-63, mgr. pricing, North Chicago, Ill., 1963-65, dir. U.S. govt. operations, 1965-69, v.p. sales hosp. products, 1969-71, v.p. sales and marketing pharm. products, 1971-72, corporate v.p. and pres. pharm. operations, 1972—. Dir. Nat. Pharm. Council. Bd. dirs. Am. Found. Pharm. Edn., Abbott Found., Condell Meml. Hosp., Libertyville, Ill. Served to 2nd lt. infantry AUS, 1944-47. Mem. Am., Ill. pharm. assns., Ill. C. of C., Rho Chi, Pi Lambda Upsilon, Alpha Chi Sigma. Home: 217 Homewood Dr Libertyville IL 60048 Office: 1400 Sheridan Rd North Chicago IL 60064

HENRY, ANDREW FREDRICK, mfg. co. exec.; b. Shelby, Ohio, Jan. 2, 1924; s. Andrew Jackson and Merl Lela (Hammond) H.; student Bowling Green (Ohio) State U.; m. Velma Ilene Brooke, Oct. 13, 1947; children—Andrea Lynn, Teresa Merl, Andrew Fredrick. Mgr. data processing, then mgr. systems and procedures Fed. Mogul Corp., Coldwater, Mich., 1955-67; mgr. systems and data processing div. Joy Mfg. Co., Franklin, Pa., 1967-69; dir. systems and data processing Nat. Forge Co., Irvine, Pa., 1969—; speaker, lectr. in field. Eucharistic minister, lector Holy Redeemer Roman Catholic Ch., Warren, Pa., 1972—. Served with USNR, 1942-46. Mem. Am. Prodn. and Inventory Control Soc., Data Processing Mgmt. Assn. (past chpt. pres.), S.P.E.B.S.Q.A. (past chpt. pres.), Am. Legion. Republican. Club: Elks. Editor: Job Recording and Shop Floor Control, 3d edit., 1979. Home: 611 Conewango Ave Warren PA 16365 Office: 1 Front St Irvine PA 16329

HENRY, JAMES ROBERT, fin. exec.; b. Dubach, La., Apr. 14, 1930; s. Reginald Thomas, Sr., and Lula Willie (Robinson) H.; student Tulane U., 1947-48, La. State U., 1954-55; B.S. in Bus. Adminstrn., La. Tech. U., 1954. Mgmt. trainee Calif. Bank, Los Angeles, 1955-56; asst. div. controller Olin Corp., 1956-65; mgr. corp. accounting and budgeting Schlumberger, Ltd., 1965-68; div. controller Cone Mills Corp., 1968-70; sr. cons. Peat, Marwick, Mitchell & Co., 1970-71; v.p. fin., asst. sec. Carousel Fashions, Inc., 1971; pvt. cons. fin., 1971-72; asst. corp. controller MacMillan, Inc., 1972-74; v.p. fin., treas. Curtis Corp., Sandy Hook, Conn., 1974-76; chief exec. officer Hook 'n Needle, Westport, Conn., 1976—. Active Little Theatre of Monroe, United Givers, Community Art and Symphony Assn., Boy Scouts Am. Served to 1st lt. USAF, 1950-53. Mem. Fin. Execs. Inst., Nat. Assn. Accountants, Planning Execs. Inst., Am. Accounting Assn., SAR, Huguenot Soc. Am., Pi Kappa Alpha. Democrat. Methodist. Home: 34 Codfish Ln Weston CT 06883 Office: 1869 Post Rd E Westport CT 06880

HENRY, JOAN LOGUE, broadcasting exec.; b. Richmond, Va., Oct. 26, 1943; d. John Thomas and Helen (Harvey) Logue; B.A., Adelphi U., Garden City, N.Y., 1964; cert. in edn., Mercy Coll., Dobbs Ferry, N.Y., 1971; cert. in bus., N.Y. U., 1974; m. Lowell A. Henry, Jr., Oct. 6, 1963; children—Lowell A. III, Catherine D., Christopher Logue. Adminstrv. asst. to dist. office mgr. U.S. Census Bur., N.Y.C., 1970; tchr. social studies, Yonkers, N.Y., 1971-75; spl. cons. KLM Royal Dutch Airlines, N.Y.C., 1976; dir. public relations Nat. Black Network, N.Y.C., 1976—; exec. dir. World Inst. Black Communications, 1978—; cons. in field. State del. nat. conv. N.Y. State Women's Polit. Caucus, 1975, pres. Black caucus, 1976-77; del. White House Conf. on Small Bus., 1980. Mem. Advt. Women N.Y., Am. Women in Radio and TV, Public Relations Soc. Am., 100 Black Women, Nigerian-Am. Friendship Soc. (past dir.), Westchester Civil Liberties Union (past dir.).

HENRY, JOSEPH PATRICK, chem. co. exec.; b. Mansfield, Ohio, Mar. 3, 1925; s. Harold H. and Louise A. (Droxler) H.; student Bowling Green State U., 1943-44; B.S., Ohio State U., 1949; m. Jeanette E. Russell, Oct. 26, 1957; 1 dau., Jeanette Louise. Ohio sales mgr. NaChurs Plant Food Co., Marion, Ohio, 1949-55; organizer, pres. Growers Chem. Corp., Milan, Ohio, 1955—, Sandusky Imported Motors, Inc. (Ohio), 1958—; pres. Homestead Motors, Inc., 1978—; co-owner Homestead Inn Restaurant, Homestead Farms; v.p. Homestead Inn, Inc. Motels, South Avery Corp. Motels; dir. Erie County Bank, Vermilion, Ohio. Served with USMCR, 1943-46; PTO. Mem. Nat. Fedn. Ind. Bus. (nat. adv. council), Ohio Farm Bur. Fedn., Milan C. of C., Aircraft Owners and Pilots Assn., Internat. Flying Farmers, Ohio Restaurant Assn., Ohio Motel-Hotel Assn., Ohio Licensed Beverage Assn., Am. Horse Show Assn., Nat. Trust for Historic Preservation, N.A.M., Internat. Platform Assn., Huron County Hist. Soc., Ohio Farm Bur., (pres.), Ohio, Internat. (dir. 1978—) Arabian horse assns. Clubs: Antique Automobile Am., Sports Car Am., N. Am. Yacht Racing Union, Sandusky Yacht, Sandusky Sailing. Home: 128 Center St Milan OH 44846 also Homestead Farms Route 1 Milan OH 44846 Office: Growers Chem Corp Box 1750 Milan OH 44846

HENRY, RENE ARTHUR, JR., pub. relations exec.; b. Charleston, W.Va., June 13, 1933; s. Rene A. and Lillian E. (Reveal) H.; A.B., William and Mary Coll., 1954; postgrad. W.Va. U., 1954-56; children—Deborah Marie, Bruce Rexford. Sports publicity dir. William and Mary, 1953-54, W.Va. U., 1954-56; account exec. Flournoy & Gibbs, Toledo, 1956-59; publicity dir. Lennen & Newell, Inc., San Francisco, 1959-67; sr. v.p., dir. Daniel J. Edelman, Inc., 1967-70; pres. Rene A. Henry, Jr., Inc., Los Angeles, 1970-74; partner Allen, Ingersoll, Segal & Henry, Inc., 1974-75; partner ICPR, Los Angeles, 1975—; exec. sec. to bd. dirs. Council Housing Producers, 1968-78; adv. bd. Apt. Builder/Developer Conf. and Expn., 1971-76, Indsl. Bldg. Congress and Expn., 1971-73; ofcl. del. Pres. Ford's Conf. on Inflation, 1974, Pre-econ. Summit Conf. on Housing and Constrn., Atlanta, 1974. Served with AUS, 1956-58. Named San Francisco Bay Area Pub. Relations Man of Yr., 1963; recipient Pub. Relations award Excellence San Francisco Bay Area Publicity Club, 1966. Mem. Pub. Relations Soc. Am. (disting. citizen award Los Angeles chpt. 1979), Football Writer's Assn. Am., Nat. Assn. Real Estate Editors, U.S. Basketball Writers' Assn., Acad. TV Arts and Scis. (chmn. bldg. com.), Acad. Motion Picture Arts and Scis., Assn. Internationale de la Presse Sportive, Sigma Nu. Republican. Episcopalian. Club: South Bay Yacht Racing. Author: How to Profitably Buy and Sell Land, 1977. Home: 809 S Bundy Dr Los Angeles CA 90049 Office: 9255 Sunset Blvd 8th Floor Los Angeles CA 90069

HENRY, ROBERT MELVIN, fin. exec.; b. Bronx, N.Y., Feb. 22, 1947; s. Zoltan and Helen (Farkowitz) H.; B.S. in Acctg./Econs., Herbert H. Lehman Coll., 1969; J.D., Bklyn. Law Sch., 1974; m. Lynne Hertzog, Aug. 22, 1970; children—Jason Mark, Douglas Allen. Admitted to N.Y. State bar, 1975; staff auditor Eisner & Lubin, C.P.A.'s, N.Y.C., 1969-71; acct. Avon Products, Inc., 1971-73, supr. nat. expense acctg., 1973-75, mgr. accounts payable and inter-co. acctg., 1975, mgr. internal auditing, mgr. fin. Family Fashions by Avon, 1976-78, regional controller Morton Grove/Glenview, Ill. facility, 1978—. Mem. Eagle Scout Recognition Day Com., Greater Chgo. council Boy Scouts Am., 1980, mem. luncheon fund raising com., 1980; chmn. local Avon community relations subcom., 1979-80. Served with U.S. Army Res., 1968-74. Mem. N.Y. State Bar Assn., Fin. Execs. Inst. Home: 1303 Oxford Ct Libertyville IL 60048 Office: 6901 Golf Rd Morton Grove IL 60053

HENSARLING, WILLIAM A., JR., savs. and loan exec.; b. Jourdanton, Tex., July 25, 1921; s. William A. and Mary Ella (Winn) H.; student U. Tex., 1938-42; m. Bobbie Melba Pytel, Feb. 16, 1943; children—James L., Gary A., Robert G. Pres. dir. Garner Abstract & Land Co., Uvalde, Tex., 1946—; owner Hensarling Ins. Agy., Uvalde,

1948—; chmn. bd., pres., chief exec. officer First Savs & Loan Assn., Uvalde, 1949—. Mem. Planning Bd., City of Uvalde, 1948-50; past pres. Uvalde Area Devel. Found.; bd. dirs. Uvalde Meml. Hosp., 1956-62, chmn., 1962. Served to lt. col. USAF, 1942-46. Mem. U.S. League Savs. Assns., Tex. Savs. and Loan League (past dir.), Uvalde C. of C. (past dir.). Democrat. Baptist. Clubs: Rotary, Masons. Home: 900 Cherry St Uvalde TX 78801 Office: 400 N Getty St Uvalde TX 78801

HENSEL, GEORGE ROBERT, real estate and driving sch. exec.; b. Los Angeles, Mar. 20, 1924; s. John and Jean Ruth (Shannon) H.; B.B., Woodbury U., 1953; m. Catherine Pizer, Dec. 15, 1965; children—Vern, Colleen, Ann Cinders Mullenax, Jan Cinders, Raymond Cinders, Cinnia Easley. Pres., Calif. Safety Center Inc., Los Angeles, 1953—, San Francisco, 1972—; v.p. Country Club Investment Corp., 1964—; dir. Rio Hondo Pub. Co.; owner Hensel Investment Co. Mem. Planning Commn. Montebello, 1970-76; past pres. Beverly Community Hosp. Found.; bd. dirs. Woodbury U.; candidate Calif. senate, 1978. Served with U.S. Mcht. Marine, 1942-50; PTO. Recipient Man and Woman of Year award City of Hope, 1975. Mem. Driving Sch. Assn. Am. (pres. 1974-75), Driving Sch. Assn. Calif. (past pres.). Clubs: Rotary, Toastmasters. Office: 111 W Pomona Blvd Monterey Park CA 91744

HENSHAW, GUY RUNALS, banker; b. Moscow, Idaho, Sept. 27, 1946; s. Paul Carrington and Helen Elizabeth (Runals) H.; B.A., Ripon Coll., 1968; M.B.A., U. Pa., 1970; m. Susan Siegel, Dec. 29, 1967; children—Christine Elizabeth, Victoria Kathryn. With Security Nat. Bank, Walnut Creek, Calif., 1970-80, dir. mktg., 1972-75, v.p. investments, 1975-77, v.p. corporate devel., 1977-79, v.p. real estate, 1979-80; v.p. real estate Hibernia Bank, 1981—. Bd. dirs. Seven Hills Sch., Diablo Symphony. Served with U.S. Army, 1968-76. Mem. Am. Bankers Assn., Mortgage Bankers Assn., Calif. Mortgage Bankers Assn. Republican. Episcopalian. Clubs: Reform, R.A.C. (London); Commonwealth of Calif.; Diablo Country. Contbr. articles to profl. jours. Home: 149 Arlene Dr Walnut Creek CA 94595

HENSHAW, PAUL CARRINGTON, mining co. exec.; b. Rye, N.Y., Nov. 15, 1913; s. R. Townsend and Clara A. (venable) H.; A.B. magna cum laude, Harvard, 1936, student Advanced Mgmt. Program, 1958; M.S., Calif. Inst. Tech., 1938, Ph.D., 1940; m. Helen Elizabeth Runals, May 25, 1939; children—Sydney Parker (Mrs. Paul W. Nordt III), Guy Runals, Paul Carrington. Head geologist Cerro Corp., Morococha, Peru, 1940-43; geologist Consorcio Minero del Peru, Mina Calpa, Peru, 1943-45; cons. geologist Compania Peruana de Cemento Portland, Lima, Peru, 1945; geologist Day Mines, Inc., Wallace, Idaho, 1945-46; asso. prof., acting head geology U. Idaho, Moscow, 1946-47; chief geologist San Luis Mining Co., Tayoltita, Dgo, Mexico, 1947-53; chief geologist, asst. to pres. Homestake Mining Co., San Francisco, 1953-60, v.p., 1961-69, exec. v.p., 1969-70, pres., dir., 1970—, chief exec. officer, 1971-79, chmn. bd., 1976—. Trustee Alta Bates Hosp., Berkeley, Calif.; vis. com. div. geol. and planetary scis. Calif. Inst. Tech.; mem. Research Inst., Colo. Sch. Mines. Mem. Am. Inst. Mining and Metall. Engrs., Geol. Soc. Am., Soc. Econ. Geologists (past pres., councilor), Geo-Chem. Soc., World Affairs Council, Mining and Metall. Soc., Am. Geol. Inst., Societe de Geologie Appliquee, Canadian Inst. Mining and Metallurgy, Prospectors and Developers Assn., Phi Beta Kappa, Sigma Xi. Clubs: Commonwealth of Calif., Bankers, Le Conte Geological, Harvard, Harvard Business School, Pacific Union, World Trade (San Francisco), Engineers of San Francisco; Mining of N.Y.; Harvard Varsity (Cambridge, Mass.). Home: 875 Arlington Ave Berkeley CA 94707 Office: 650 California St San Francisco CA 94108

HENSKE, JOHN M., corp. exec.; b. Omaha, 1923; B.S. in Chem. Engring. and Indsl. Adminstrn., Yale U., 1948. Vice-pres., dir. Dow Chem. Co., 1948-69; group v.p.-chems. Olin Corp., Stamford, Conn., 1969-71, sr. v.p. and pres.-chems group, 1971-73, pres., dir., 1973—, also chief exec. officer; dir. Am. Precision Industries, Inc., N.E. Bancorp, Inc., Scovill Mfg. Co. Served with U.S. Army, 1942-43. Mem. Chem. Mfg. Assn. (chmn. (chmn., dir.). Office: Olin Corp 120 Long Ridge Rd Stamford CT 06904*

HENSLER, WILLIAM ARTHUR, lumber co. exec.; b. Saginaw, Mich., Oct. 20, 1929; s. Arthur W. and Caroline F. (Schwarzott) H.; B.S., Ferris State Coll., 1951; m. Shirley A. Marten, Nov. 17, 1951; children—Randy A., Nancy A. Mgmt. trainee Chevrolet div. Gen. Motors, Saginaw, Mich., 1953-60; with corp. treasury dept. Wickes Credit, Saginaw, 1960-63, dir. budgeting, 1963-67; regional controller Wickes Lumber, Akron, Ohio, 1967-68, controller, Saginaw, 1968-72, v.p. fin./adminstrn., 1972-76, v.p. ops., 1976-79, area v.p., Indpls., 1979—. Served with Fin. Corps, U.S. Army, 1951-53. Lutheran. Clubs: Saginaw Country, Germania. Home: 12968 Wembly Rd Carmel IN 46032 Office: 3226 Lafayette Rd Indianapolis IN 46222

HENSON, JOHN PORTER, equipment co. exec.; b. Girard, Kans., Sept. 25, 1922; s. John Porter and Gladys (deVenny) H.; B.S. in Mech. Engring., Purdue U., 1946; m. Sarah Winslow Hodgdon, Sept. 27, 1947; children—Christena Margaret, John Winslow, David deVenny. Regional mgr. Bendix Westinghouse Air Brake, 1946-59; account exec. Dana Corp., Toledo, 1959-60, sales mgr., 1960-61, asst. gen. sales mgr., 1961-64; sales mgr. Kaydon Engring. Co., Muskegon, Mich., 1964-65; product planning mgr. Clark Equipment Co., Buchanan, Mich., 1965—; exec. engr., 1965-66, v.p. engring. axle div., 1966-72, v.p. mktg., 1972-75, sales mgr. N.Am., axle and transmission divs., 1975-77, cons., 1977—; cons. Transmisiones y Equipos Mechanicos S.A., Queretaro, Mex., 1977—. Served to 2d lt. USMC, 1942-46. Mem. Am. Ordnance Assn., Soc. Automotive Engring., Tau Beta Pi, Pi Tau Sigma, Sigma Chi. Home and office: 1105 Plym Rd Niles MI 49120

HENSON, PAUL HARRY, utility co. exec.; b. Bennet, Nebr., July 22, 1925; s. Harry H. and Mae (Schoenthal) H.; B.S. in Elec. Engring., U. Nebr., 1947, M.S. 1950; m. Betty L. Roeder, Aug. 2, 1946; children—Susan Irene Flury, Lizbeth Ann Barelli. Engr., Lincoln (Nebr.) Tel. & Tel. Co., 1941-42, 1945-48, div. mgr. 1948-54, chief engr. 1954-59; v.p. United Telecommunications Inc., Kansas City, Mo., 1959-60, exec. v.p., 1960-64, pres., 1964-73, chmn., 1966—, dir. 1960—; dir. Kansas City So. Industries, Duke Power Co., Fed. Res. Bank of Kansas City, Armco Inc. Trustee Tax Found.; bd. dirs. Nat. Legal Center Pub. Interest. Served from pvt. to capt. USAAF, 1942-45. Hon. consul of Sweden; registered profl. engr., Nebr. Mem. Nat. Soc. Profl. Engrs., IEEE, Armed Forces Communications Electronics Assn., U.S. Ind. Telephone Assn. (dir. 1960-76), Sigma Xi, Eta Kappa Nu, Sigma Tau, Kappa Sigma. Clubs: Chicago, Kansas City Country, River, Kansas City, Mission Hills Country, Burning Tree, Surf, Masons, Shriners. Home: 3505 W 64th St Shawnee Mission KS 66208 Office: 2330 Johnson Dr Box 11315 Kansas City MO 64112

HEPBURN, JOHN ANTHONY, investment dealer; b. Kirkcaldy, Fife, Scotland, Sept. 4, 1936; s. John Harley and Helen Campbell (Ritchie) H.; came to Can., 1960, citizen, 1966; C.A., Edinburgh U., 1960; m. Patricia Mary Hepburn, Feb. 26, 1970; children—Tony, James. With Price Waterhouse, Montreal, Que., 1960-63, Vancouver, B.C., 1963-68; pres., chief exec. officer Odlum Brown TB Read Ltd., Vancouver, 1978—; gov. Vancouver Stock Exchange. Mem. Investment Dealers Assn. Can. (dir.), Inst. Chartered Accts. Scotland, Inst. Chartered Accts. B.C.; fellow Fin. Analysts Fedn. Can. Club: Vancouver. Home: 3160 W 57th Ave Vancouver BC V6N 3X6 Canada Office: PO Box 10012 Pacific Centre 700 W Georgia St Vancouver BC V7Y 1A3 Canada

HERBERT, JAMES HALL, II, bank exec.; b. Columbus, Ohio, July 30, 1944; s. James Hall and Joanne (Moore) H.; B.S.B.A., Babson Coll., 1966; M.B.A., N.Y. U., 1969; m. Cecilia A. Healy, Dec. 18, 1976. Asst. treas. Chase Manhattan Bank, N.Y.C., 1966-69; asso. corp. fin. Newburger, Loeb & Co., N.Y.C., 1969-71; v.p. Citizens Fin. Corp., Cleve., 1971-73; pres. Herbert & Assos., Arlington, Tex., 1973-76; pres., owner Soda Pop Systems, Inc., Richmond, Va., 1976-78, Bay Beverages, Inc., San Francisco, 1978-79; Western regional mgr. Pop Shoppes Am., Denver, 1978-79; pres., dir. San Francisco Bancorp, 1980—; adj. prof. fin. Va. Commonwealth U. Served with USMCR, 1963-69. Republican. Clubs: Univ. (N.Y.); 2300 (Richmond); N.Y. Yacht. Address: 1075 Broadway San Francisco CA 94133

HERBERT, JOHN RUGGLES, bank exec.; b. Boston, Nov. 30, 1908; s. Charles John and Evelyn Estes (Harvey) H.; B.S., Boston U., 1931, L.H.D., 1969; D.Journalism, Suffolk U., 1958; m. Elsa O. Johnson, Dec. 15, 1934; children—John A., Robert M. Mng. editor Patriot Ledger, Quincy, Mass., 1936-52, editor, 1952-67; editor Boston Herald Traveler, 1967-72, exec. editor, 1972-74; exec. dir. Mass. Newspaper Pubs. Assn., 1974-75; pres. Quincy Co-op. Bank, 1975—, also dir.; pres. Squanto Corp., Quincy, 1976—. Decorated grand ofcl. Order Duarte, Sanchez and Mella (Dominican Republic); recipient Cabot award Columbia U., 1962. Mem. Inter-Am. Press Assn. (recipient Tom Wallace award, 1961), Bostonian Soc., World Peace Found., Am. Soc. Newspaper Editors, Brotherhood Green Turtle, Acad. New Eng. Journalists, Pan Am. Soc. New Eng. (past pres.), Navy League (dir. 1977—), Sigma Delta Chi (Yankee Quill award 1964). Republican. Clubs: Union, Rotary (dir.) (Boston); Overseas Press; Neighborhood (Quincy). Home: 181 Bellevue Rd Quincy MA 02171 Office: 1259 Hancock St Quincy MA 02169

HERBST, LAWRENCE ROBERT, investment adviser, tax cons., economist, promoter; b. Haverhill, Mass., Aug. 8, 1946; s. Morton and Ruth I. (Cooper) H.; student U. Calif., Los Angeles, Alexander Hamilton Bus. Inst., D.V.M., N.Am. Sch. Animal Scis.; D.D., Missionaries of New Truth, Chgo. Owner Total Sound Records, Lawrence Herbst Records, Beverly Hills Music Pubs., 1975—; founder Future World Stores, Larry's Family Restaurant, Heavenly Waterbed Showrooms, 1978. Mem. Broadcast Music, Inc., pres. Lawrence Herbst Farms, producer Spacee the Lion Cartoon. Pres., adminstr. Lawrence Herbst Found., Lawrence Herbst Investment Trust Fund. Mem. Nat. Acad. TV Arts and Scis., Los Angeles Press Club, Internat., Hollywood, Los Angeles chambers commerce, Internat. Platform Assn., Pres.'s Assn., Nat. Club Assn., Rec. Industry Assn. Am., Epsilon Delta Chi. Author: (book and movie) Legend of Tobby Kingdom, 1975; The Good, The Bad, The True Story of Lawrence Herbst; news columnist World of Investments, 1976. Designer 1st mus. electronic amplifier with plug in I.C.'s; inventor one-man air car. Office: PO Box 1659 Beverly Hills CA 90213

HERBST, RICHARD WARREN, banker; b. Chattanooga, Feb. 10, 1949; s. Warren Larry and Caroline Barbara (Dickert) H.; B.S. in Indsl. Mgmt., Ga. Inst. Tech., 1972; m. Elizabeth Nelson, May 13, 1975. Trainee credit dept. N.C. Nat. Bank, 1972-74, mem. ops. staff internat. div., 1974-75, with div. account office, 1975-76, with div. London office, 1976, v.p., dir. Carolina Bank Ltd. subs., London. Served with USMC, 1969. Democrat. Roman Catholic. Home: 8 Blithfield St London W8 England UK Office: Carolina Bank Ltd 14 Austin Friars London EC2 England UK*

HERDEG, JOHN ANDREW, bank exec.; b. Buffalo, Sept. 15, 1937; s. Franklin Leland and Susannah Estelle (Clark) H.; B.A., Princeton, 1959; LL.B., U. Pa., 1962; m. Judith C. Carpenter, June 24, 1961; children—Judith Leland, Andrew Carpenter, Fell Coolidge. Personal asst. to trustee New Haven R.R., N.Y.C., 1962-63; with Wilmington Trust Co., Wilmington, Del., 1963—, asst. sec., 1964-66, trust officer, 1966-68, asst. v.p., 1968-71, v.p., 1971-75, sr. v.p., 1975—, sec., 1975-79, head trust dept., chmn. trust com., dir., 1977—. Trustee Henry Francis duPont Winterthur Museum., 1969—; trustee v.p., 1973-77, pres., 1977—; trustee Woodlawn Trustees, Inc., 1967-77, Wilmington Med. Center, Inc., 1975—; bd. dirs. Pilot Sch., Inc., 1969-72; supr. Pennsbury Twp., Pa., 1968-74. Mem. Del., Conn. bar assns. Presbyterian. Clubs: Vicmead Hunt, Wilmington, Walpole Soc. Home: Hillendale Rd Mendenhall PA 19357 Office: Wilmington Trust Co 10th and Market Sts Wilmington DE 19899

HERGET, CHARLES EDWARD, JR., actuarial cons. co. exec.; b. Balt., May 29, 1939; s. Charles Edward and Kathleen (Freeney) H.; B.A. in Bus. Adminstrn., Loyola Coll., Balt., 1962; m. Mary Elizabeth Barringer, Sept. 29, 1973; children—Melissa, Stacey, Kelly Kathleen. Broker's asst. Lloyds of London (Eng.), 1959-60; pres., chief exec. officer Herget & Co., Inc., Balt., Ft. Lauderdale, Fla. and Pitts., 1966—; dir. Capital Savs. Loan Assn., Balt., Arundel Corp. Chmn. bd. Loyola Coll.; mem. Mayor's Council Bus. Advisors; trustee Villa Julie Coll., St. Paul's Sch. for Girls; mem. Md. Province devel. council Soc. Jesus. Mem. Am. Soc. Pension Actuaries (dir.), Am. Mgmt. Assn., Pres.'s Assn., Young Pres.'s Orgn., N.Am. Soc. Corp. Planning, Profit Sharing Council Am. Clubs: Balt. Country (pres.), Center, Mchts., Md., Wiltondale Gun. Home: 8207 White Manor Dr Lutherville MD 21093 Office: 204 E Lombard St Baltimore MD 21202

HERGET, JAMES PATRICK, exec. search exec.; b. Cleve., Oct. 21, 1944; s. Louis E. and Dorothy R. (Whearty) H.; A.B., Holy Cross Coll., 1966; M.B.A., Case Western Res. U., 1969. Analyst, Cleve. Trust Co., 1966; sales rep. Xerox Corp., Cleve., 1967, cons., 1968-70, product mgr., Washington, 1971, social service leave, 1972, regional cons. mgr., 1973-75, mgr. sales and sales mgmt. programs, Rochester, N.Y., 1975-76; product mgr. Forward Products, Rochester, 1977-78, asst. to v.p. mktg., 1979—; v.p. Spencer Stuart & Assos., 1980—; cons. Nat. Minority Purchasing Council, Inc., 1973-76; instr. mktg. Cleve. State U., 1970; dir. mktg. Interracial Council for Bus. Opportunity, 1972; treas. Urban Small Bus. Cons., 1970. Co. location chmn. United Way, Arlington, Va., 1973-76; active Big Bros., Washington, 1972-75; v.p. Genesee Valley Arts Found., Rochester, 1977-78. Recipient Nat. citation Nat. Center for Voluntary Action, 1971; Ace award SBA, 1970. Republican. Roman Catholic. Designer, producer 3 tng. programs for office of minority enterprise Commerce Dept., 1973-76. Mem. Vols. in Partnership, Mensa, Internat. Platform Assn. Club: Univ., Playhouse, City (Cleve.). Home: 2178 Harcourt Dr Cleveland Heights OH 44106

HERGET, RICHARD PHILIP, JR., ins. co. exec.; b. Washington, Apr. 19, 1939; s. Richard Philip and Mary E. (Barlow) H.; grad. U.S. Mil. Acad. Prep., 1958; m. Mary Mel French, Nov. 7, 1975. Asso., Ford and Herget Ins. Agy., Paragould, Ark., 1960-69; v.p., sec. Cobb, Atkins, Boyd & Eggleston, Inc., Little Rock, 1972-79; sec., treas. Ark. All Risks, Inc., Little Rock, 1975—; exec. v.p., sec., treas. Atkins Ins. Corp., Little Rock, 1976—. Master, East Ark. council Boy Scouts Am., Paragould; mem. vestry All Saints Episcopal Ch., Paragould; chmn. Parks and Recreation Commn. City of Paragould; mem. vestry, sr. warden Trinity Episcopal Cathedral, Little Rock, trustee Day Sch., 1969-74; trustee Ark. State U., 1975—, chmn., 1979-80; mem. Democratic State Com., 1974; campaign organizer, mem. fin. com. Gov. David H. Pryor, 1974, 76; campaign mgr. re-election campaign Gov. Bill Clinton, 1980. Recipient Ark. Cert. of Merit, 1976; Ark. Community Devel. award State C. of C., 1977. Mem. Ark. Assn. Ins. Agts. (exec. v.p. 1969-72). Club: Lions. Office: 1400 Worthen Bank Bldg Little Rock AR 72201

HERKNESS, LINDSAY COATES, III, securities broker; b. N.Y.C., Feb. 8, 1943; s. Lindsay C. and Harriett H. (Richard) H.; B.A., Trinity Coll., Hartford, Conn., 1965. With Reynolds Securities Inc. (merged with Dean Witter & Co. 1978), N.Y.C., 1965-78; v.p. investments Dean Witter Reynolds, Inc., N.Y.C., 1978—. Clubs: Union, Downtown Assn. (N.Y.C.); Bath and Tennis (Palm Beach, Fla.); Rockaway Hunting; Piping Rock. Home: 160 E 65th St Apt 30-B New York NY 10021 Office: Dean Witter Reynolds Inc Five World Trade Center New York NY 10048

HERLIHY, JOANNE JAAP, fashion industry exec.; b. Kansas City, Mo., Sept. 23, 1925; d. Nelan Herbert and Virginia (Springer) Jaap; student pub. schs.; m. John Edward Herlihy, Jr., Sept. 20, 1956 (div. Jan. 1959). With Ziegfield Follies, 1943; toured for U.S.O. in Dough Girls, 1944; model Harry Conover, N.Y.C., 1945; featured in stage plays Duchess Misbehaves, 1946, Sweet Bye and Bye, 1946, Angel Street, summer 1947; sales/fashion coordinator Sam Freidlander, N.Y.C., 1950-51, Ben Zuckerman, N.Y.C., 1951-54, 56-59; asst. sales mgr. Christian Dior, N.Y.C., 1954-56, sales mgr., 1959-64, v.p., 1964-68; mng. dir. Design-Thai for U.S. div. Internat. Basic Economy Corp., 1969-73; exec. v.p. Design Thai (U.S.A.) Inc., N.Y.C., 1973-76; v.p. mktg. wholesale div. Roberta di Camerino, N.Y.C., 1976-78; prin. Joanne Jaap, Ltd., wholesale mfrs. cons., N.Y.C., 1979—. Mem. Fashion Group of N.Y. Home and office: 50 E 68th St New York NY 10021 Office: 550 7th Ave New York NY 10022

HERLONG, JAMES HERBERT, citrus processing co. exec.; b. Leesburg, Fla., Feb. 15, 1922; s. Albert Sydney and Cora (Knight) H.; student The Citadel, 1939-43; m. Ruby Elizabeth Prevatt, Feb. 21, 1946; children—Cora Nelle, James Herbert. With A. S. Herlong & Co., Leesburg, 1946—, field mgr., 1948-50, asst. sales mgr., 1950-52, mgr. Fresh Fruit and Processing div., 1952—; pres. Herlong Industries, Inc., Leesburg, 1959—; sec. A.S. Herlong & Co., 1967—, pres., 1979—, also dir.; dir., mem. exec. com. B & W Canning Co., Groveland, Fla., 1963—; dir. 1st Fed. Savs. & Loan Assn., Leesburg, Sun 1st Nat. Bank of Lake County, Lake County Service Corp. Served to capt., inf., AUS, 1943-46. Methodist. Elk. Club: Silver Lake Golf and Country (Leesburg). Home: 6526 N Silver Lake Dr Leesburg FL 32748 Office: 2d and Meadow Sts Leesburg FL 32748

HERMAN, ALEX CHARLES, mfg. co. mgr.; b. Ellwood City, Pa., Sept. 14, 1946; s. Alex and Edith Irene (Maffei) H.; B. Mech. Engring., Youngstown (Ohio) State U., 1969; postgrad. Fairleigh Dickinson U., Rutherford, N.J.; m. Lora Jane Guesman, May 13, 1972; 1 son, Alex William. Project and application engr. Mathews conveyor div. Rexnord, Inc., Ellwood, 1970-74, sales engr., Memphis, 1974-77; dist. sales mgr. Litton Unit Handling Systems, Florence, Ky., 1977-78, gen. sales mgr. pre-engineered products, 1978—. Roman Catholic. Club: Summit Hills Country. Home: 8840 Valley Circle Dr Florence KY 41042 Office: 7100 Industrial Rd Florence KY 41042

HERMAN, ELVIN EUGENE, aerospace industry exec.; b. Sigourney, Iowa, Mar. 17, 1921; s. John Lawrence and Martha (Conner) H.; B.S., State U. Iowa, 1942; m. Grace Winifred Eklund, Sept. 29, 1945; 1 dau., Jane Ann. Electronic engr. Naval Research Lab., Washington, 1942-51; head radar circuits sect. Nat. Bur. Standards, Corona, Calif., 1951-53; with Hughes Aircraft Co., Culver City, Calif., 1953—, head airborne radar subsystems dept., 1955-60, mgr. signal processing and display lab. 1960-68, asst. mgr. research and devel. div., 1963-70, tech. dir. radar systems group, 1970—. Recipient Meritorious Civilian Service award U.S. Navy, 1945; Lawrence A. Hyland Patent award Hughes Aircraft Co., 1970. Fellow IEEE; mem. Sci. Research Soc. Am., Eta Kappa Nu. Patentee in field. Home: 1200 Lachman Ln Pacific Palisades CA 90272 Office: Hughes Aircraft Co 2000 E Imperial Hwy El Segundo CA 90245

HERMAN, GERALD EVERETT, fin. co. exec.; b. Hays, Kans., Jan. 29, 1947; s. Henry Everett and Bertha (Dreiling) H.; student Ft. Hays (Kans.) State Coll., 1965-67; B.S., Kans. State U., 1973; m. Dianne Lee Nance, June 27, 1974; children—Stacia Lynn, Chad, Tara Lee. Auditor, Elmer Fox & Co., acctg., Wichita, 1974-76, sr. auditor, 1976; v.p. sec./treas. Becker Corp., El Dorado, Kans., 1976—. Treas., mem. fin. bd., adminstrv. bd. 1st United Meth. Ch., El Dorado, 1979—. Served with U.S. Army, 1967-72; Vietnam. Decorated Bronze Star, Army Commendation medal with cluster, Air medal with 25 clusters; C.P.A. Mem. Kans. Soc. C.P.A.'s, Am. Inst. C.P.A.'s, Nat. Acctg. and Fin. Council, Am. Trucking Assn., VFW (life), Phi Kappa Phi. Republican. Clubs: Rotary (dir. 1980-81), El Dorado Country (dir.). Home: 730 Post Rd El Dorado KS 67042 Office: Becker Corp 131 N Haverhill Rd El Dorado KS 67042

HERMAN, MICHAEL EDWARD, pharm. co. exec.; b. N.Y.C., May 31, 1941; s. Harris Abraham and Sally (Ruzga) H.; B.Metall. Engring., Rensselaer Poly. Inst., 1962; M.B.A., U. Chgo., 1964; m. Karen May Kuivinen, May 29, 1966; children—Jolyan Blake, Hamilton Brooks. Sr. bus. analyst W.R. Grace & Co., N.Y.C., 1964-66; asst. to pres., v.p. corp. devel. Nuclear Fuel Services subs. W.R. Grace & Co., Washington, 1966-68; v.p. Laird, Inc., N.Y.C., 1968-70; founding gen. partner Dryden & Co., N.Y.C., 1970-74; sr. v.p., chief fin. officer, dir. Marion Labs., Inc., Kansas City, Mo., 1974—; dir. Janus Fund, Boatmen's Bank of Kansas City; asso. prof. Rockhurst Coll. Grad. Sch. Bus.; vis. lectr. Kans. U. Grad. Sch. Bus.; trustee Kansas City Royals Baseball Club Profit Sharing Trust. Chmn. fund raising Lower and Middle Sch., Sunset Hill Sch., 1978. Mem. Assn. for Corp. Growth, Pharm. Mfrs. Assn. (mem. fin. steering com.), Fin. Analysts Fedn. Jewish. Clubs: Kansas City; N.Y. Athletic; Lake Quivira Country. Home: A Lake Shore Dr E Lake Quivira KS 66106 Office: Marion Labs Inc 9221 Ward Pkwy Kansas City MO 64114

HERMAN, ROBERT LEWIS, cork co. exec.; b. N.Y.C. July 16, 1927; s. Nat W. and Ruth (Stockton) H.; A.B., Columbia, 1948, B.S., 1949; m. Susan Marie Volper, Dec. 10, 1966; children—Candia Ruth, William Neal. Vice pres. Joseph Samuels & Sons, Inc., Whippany, N.J., 1953-62; pres. Dependable Cork Co., Inc., Morristown, N.J., 1962—; chmn. bd. Badger Cork & Mfg. Co., Trevor, Wis., 1980—. Served to comdr. C.E. Corps, USNR, 1949-53. Mem. N.J. Mfrs. Assn., Naval Res. Assn., U.S. C. of C. Clubs: Navy League; Columbia University, Princeton (N.Y.C.). Inventor Corticiera natural cork wallcovering. Home: Gaston Rd Washington Valley Morristown NJ 07960 Office: POB 1102R Morristown NJ 07960

HERMAN, SUMNER WILFRED, ins. agy. exec.; b. Worcester, Mass., Mar. 20, 1928; s. Jesse I. and Dorothy E. (Fine) H.; B.S. in Mech. Engring., Worcester Poly. Inst., 1950; m. Lois Fielding, June 13, 1954; children—Laura Beth, Peter Howard. Asst. to mgr. N.E. Fire Ins. Rating Assn., Boston, 1950-57; partner Harold Fielding Ins. Agy. Inc., Worcester, 1957-69; pres. Ins. Mktg. Agys., Inc., Worcester, 1969—; chmn. communique panel St. Pauls Ins. Cos.;

mem. agts. adv. panels Crum & Forsters Ins. Co., Aetna Casualty and Surety. Dir. Jewish Community Center of Greater Framingham, 1971-77; fin. com. Temple Beth Am.; active YMCA. Served with U.S. Army, 1946-48. Named Man of Year, Aetna Casualty Ins. Co., 1978; notary public. Mem. Ind. Ins. Agys. Am., Profl. Ins. Agts. Am., Worcester Ins. Soc., Ind. Ins. Agts. of Greater Worcester, Ins. Mktg. Services, Am. Mgmt. Assn., Am. Contract Bridge League. Clubs: Sudbury River Tennis, Clearbrook Swim (dir.). Home: 135 Oak Crest Dr Framingham MA 01701 Office: 1200 Mechanics Tower Worcester MA 01608

HERMISTON, GEORGE JAMES, credit union exec.; b. Boston, Mar. 17, 1935; s. George J. and Josephine H.; A.B., Stonehill Coll., 1957; M.Ed., Boston State Coll., cert. in Advanced Edn. specialization; m. Maureen T. Moroney, June 26, 1965; children—Nancy, Andrew, George. Treas., editor Share, Credit Union Digest, Westwood, Mass.; pres. Educators Credit Union, 1967-74, mng. dir., treas., 1974—. Mem. Credit Union Dirs. Soc. (founder), Credit Union Execs. Soc. Home: 81 Cedar Ln Westwood MA 02090

HERNANDEZ, JAIME MANUEL, businessman; b. Mexico City, July 29, 1944; came to U.S., 1952, naturalized, 1958; s. Luis A. Hernandez and Dolores Hernandez Perez Castro; B.S. in Marine Engring., U.S. Mcht. Marine Acad., 1966; m. Lois Grace Hart, Dec. 3, 1966; children—Delores Grace, Debra Ann, Jaime Manuel. Marine engr. Marine Engrs. Beneficial Assn., Los Angeles, 1966-69; field and prodn. engr. Worthington Corp., La Mirada, Calif., 1969-73; project supr. Gen. Electric, Anaheim, Calif., 1974-75; area mgr. Mexico, C.Am., Caribbean, Dresser Industries, Mexico City, 1975—. Mem. Mexican Petroleum Engrs. Assn., Soc. Naval and Marine Architects. Roman Catholic. Club: Raqueta Brittania (Mexico City). Home: 9 Bosque Rio Frio Mexico 10 DF Mexico Office: 85-4 Dinamarca Mexico 6 DF Mexico

HERNANDEZ, JOHN GONZALO, cosmetics co. exec.; b. N.Y.C., Nov. 18, 1932; s. Gonzalo Hernandez and Ines (Moreno) H.; B.A., CCNY, 1953; m. Margarita Maria Sanchez, Mar. 30, 1959; 1 dau., Margarita Roxanne. Asst. bus. mgr. CBS-TV, N.Y.C., 1954-57; gen. mgr. Gillette Co., Cali, Colombia, 1957-59, San Jose, Costa Rica, 1959-63, Santiago, Chile, 1963-67, area mgr. Latin Am. JAFRA Cosmetics Co. div. Gillette Co. (Brazil), 1975—; dir. internat. bus. devel. R.J. Reynolds Industries, Winston-Salem, N.C., 1969-72; dir. internat. new ventures Kendall Co., Boston, 1972-74; asst. v.p. Latin Am. div. Colgate Co., N.Y.C., 1974-75. Named Hon. Citizen, Chile, 1965, Costa Rica, 1961; recipient Congl. citation Costa Rica, 1960. Developed first bus. census in Costa Rica, 1960. Home: 200 Rua Joao Borges 20000 Rio de Janeiro RJ Brazil Office: 156 Rua Hermes Fontes 20.000 Rio de Janeiro RJ Brazil

HERO, BYRON A., JR., investment banker; b. N.Y.C., Aug. 3, 1950; s. Byron A. and Angela C. (Constantinides) H.; B.A. magna cum laude, Tufts U., 1972, M.A., 1973; J.D., Columbia U., 1976. Admitted to N.Y. bar, 1976; asso. firm Winthrop, Stimson, Putnam and Roberts, N.Y.C., 1976-79; staff atty. mergers and aquisitions dept. Oppenheimer & Co., Inc., N.Y.C., 1979-80; founding partner Wolsey & Co., N.Y.C., 1980—. Mem. Assn. Bar City N.Y. Clubs: Racquet and Tennis (N.Y.C.); Meadow (Southampton, N.Y.); Lyford Cay (Bahamas). Home: 419 E 57th St New York NY 10022 Office: 919 3d Ave New York NY 10022

HEROLD, HOPE ANNE, systems analyst; b. N.Y.C., Aug. 10, 1954; d. Harry and Grace Catherine (McGurn) H.; B.S., St. John's U., 1976. Mortgage dept. clk. Anchor Savs. Bank, N.Y.C., 1973; work measurement analyst Chase Manhattan Bank, N.Y.C., 1975-76; systems analyst Morgan Guaranty Trust Co., N.Y.C., 1976-79, sr. systems analyst, 1979-80, project mgr., 1980—; systems cons. Recipient Pres.'s medal for loyal and disting. service St. John's U. Mem. Am. Mgmt. Assns., St. John's U. Alumni Assn., Nat. Assn. Female Execs. Roman Catholic. Club: Conca D'oro Swim. Mem. Lambda Kappa Phi, Alpha Psi Omega. Home: 11 Presley St Staten Island NY 10308 Office: 30 Broad St New York NY 10015

HERRERA, ALBERTO, mgmt. cons.; b. Guatemala, Jan. 11, 1941; s. Alberto and Rosario (Guzman) H.; came to U.S., 1965; B.A. in Mathematics and Computer Scis., N.Y. U., 1970; postgrad. in mgmt. Clayton U.; m. Beatriz Otero, May 19, 1977; 1 son, Alberto. Sr. systems analyst Am. Express Co., N.Y.C., 1965-69; mgmt. cons. Booz, Allen & Hamilton, N.Y.C., 1969-72; research and devel. dir. Gamboa & Schlesinger, Venezuela, 1972-74; pres. Kohoutek Inc., N.Y.C., 1974—; v.p., fin. dir. Kexar Internat. Corp., N.Y.C.; dir. edn. div. Beke, Santos y Asociados, Venezuela, 1980. Mem. EDP Auditors Assn., Am. Mgmt. Assn., Assn. Computing Machinery. Author articles in field. Office: 97-45 Queens Blvd Rego Park NY 11374

HERRICK, TRACY GRANT, fin. cons.; b. Cleve., Dec. 30, 1933; s. Stanford Avery and Elizabeth Grant (Smith) H.; B.A., Columbia U., 1956, M.A., 1958; postgrad. Yale U., 1956-57; M.A., Oxford U. (Eng.), 1960; m. Maie Kaarsoo, Oct. 12, 1963; children—Sylvi Ann, Alan Kalev. Economist, Fed. Res. Bank, Cleve., 1960-70; sr. economist Stanford Research Inst., Menlo Park, Calif., 1970-73; v.p., sr. analyst Shuman, Agnew & Co., Inc., San Francisco, 1973-75; v.p. Bank of Am., San Francisco, 1975—; lectr. Stonier Grad. Sch. Banking, Am. Bankers Assn., 1967-76; commencement speaker Memphis Banking Sch., 1974; dir. C.D. Anderson & Co., Inc., Stickney & Herrick, Inc., Palo Alto Cons. Group, Inc.; editor Money Analyst. Bd. dirs. Planned Parenthood Assn., Cleve., 1967-70. Mem. Columbia Coll. Alumni Assn. (dir. 1973—), Nat. Assn. Bus. Economists, San Francisco Bus. Economists Assn., San Francisco Soc. Security Analysts. Republican. Congregationalist. Author: Bank Analysts Handbook, 1978; Timing, 1981; contbr. articles to profl. jours. Home: 1150 University Ave Palo Alto CA 94301 Office: 555 California St San Francisco CA 94137

HERRMAN, LETTIE MARIE, lumber co. exec.; b. Milan, Mo. Nov. 18, 1902; d. Ira Richard and Daisy Maude (Myers) Franklin; B.A., Stephens Coll., 1923; m. Cecil Loran Herrman, Sept. 15, 1926. Asst. editor Appleton (Mo.) City Jour., 1923-30; with Herrman Lumber Co., Fort Scott, Kans., Rolla, Mo., 1930—, Pres., 1976—. Mem. Democratic State Com. 8th Congl. Dist., 1963-64, 65-66; mem. Country Com., Rolla, 1966-72. Mem. Mo., Rolla chambers commerce, Mid-Am. Lumbermen's Assn., Meramec Basin Assn. Democrat. Methodist. Home: 803 W 13th St Rolla MO 65401 Office: 117 W 8th St Rolla MO 65401

HERRMANN, JAMES ANDREW, financial analyst; b. Dallas, Aug. 28, 1950; s. Frederick Alvin and Alicemarie (Collins) H.; B.S. in Engring. Mgmt., U.S. Air Force Acad., 1972; M.B.A. in Fin., Ga. State U., 1975; m. Karen M. Cliffgard, Oct. 17, 1980. Commd. 2d lt. U.S. Air Force, 1972, advanced through grades to capt., 1976; fin. analyst Air Force contract mgmt. div. Lockheed-Ga. Co., Marietta, Ga., 1972-76; internal mgmt. cons. hdqrs. Air Force contract mgmt. div., Kirtland (N.Mex.) AFB, 1976-77; resigned, 1977; research fellow Logistics Mgmt. Inst., Washington, 1977-78; fin. analyst Harris Corp., Melbourne, Fla., 1978-80; supr. contract pricing practices Harris Semiconductor, Melbourne, 1980—. Mem. Assn. M.B.A. Execs., Condominium Homeowners Assn. (pres. 1975), Nat. Contract Mgmt. Assn. Roman Catholic. Home: 2308 Colonial Dr S Melbourne FL 32901 Office: Harris Semiconductor PO Box 883 Melbourne FL 32901

HERRMANN, JOHN A, JR., investment banker; b. N.Y.C., July 30, 1935; s. John A and Marjorie Sarah (Kiam) H.; B.A., Yale U., 1957; M.B.A., Harvard U., 1961; m. Anne Day, Aug. 7, 1976; children—John Day, Francis Tim. Asso., Lehman Bros., 1961-70; v.p. New Court Securities Corp., 1970-74; v.p. Kuhn Loeb & Co., 1974-77; mng. dir. Lehman Bros. Kuhn Loeb, Inc., N.Y.C., 1977—; dir. Cornelius Co. Pres., bd. dirs. Vocat. Adv. Service, 1965-70; bd. dirs. N.Y. Assn. for New Americans, 1967-72; bd. dirs. N.Y. Urban League, 1970—, pres., 1976-78. Served with U.S. Army, 1957-59. Clubs: Century Country (Westchester, N.Y.); Yale, Madison Sq. Garden (N.Y.C.). Office: 55 Water St New York NY 10004

HERRMANN, LACY BUNNELL, investment co. exec.; b. New Haven, May 12, 1929; s. James Joseph and Helen Georgia (Bunnell) H.; A.B., Brown U., 1950; postgrad. London Sch. Econs., 1953-54; M.B.A., Harvard U., 1956; m. Elizabeth Ocumpaugh Beadle, May 23, 1953; children—Diana Parsons, Conrad Beadle. Asst. to purchasing mgr. and buyer Westinghouse Elec. Corp., Metuchen, N.J., 1956-60; asst. v.p. Douglas T. Johnston & Co., Inc., N.Y.C., 1960-66; v.p. Johnston Mut. Fund, Inc., N.Y.C., 1964-66; gen. partner Tamarack Assos., N.Y.C., 1966—; chmn. bd., pres. Family Home Products, Inc., N.Y.C., 1972—, Buxton's Country Shops, Jamesburg, N.J., 1973—; pres., dir. STCM Mgmt. Co., Inc., N.Y.C., 1974—; founder, pres. STCM Corp., N.Y.C., 1974-76; vice chmn. bd. trustees, v.p. Centennial Capital Cash Mgmt. Trust, N.Y.C. successor to STCM Corp., 1976—; founding dir. predecessor to Tower, Perrin, Forster & Crosby; instr. Rutgers U., 1958-59. Organizer, trustee endowed award Internat. div. Grad. Sch. Journalism, Columbia U., 1962—; trustee Meml. and Endowment Trust of St. Paul's Ch., Westfield, N.J., 1968—; mem. capital devel. com. St. Luke's Ch., Darien, Conn., 1978—; mem. coll. scholarship fund com. St. Luke's Ch., Darien, Conn., 1976—. Served to lt. (j.g.) USN, 1951-54; Korea; lt. USNR ret. Mem. N.Y. Soc. Security Analysts, Harvard Bus. Sch. Alumni Assn. N.Y. (dir. and officer 1958-71), Asso. Alumni Brown U. (dir. 1978—, exec. com. 1980—). Republican. Episcopalian. Clubs: Harvard, N.Y. Athletic (N.Y.C.); Brown U. of Fairfield County (pres. 1977—); Univ., Faculty of Brown U. (Providence); Stratton Mountain Country (Vt.). Contbr. articles to profl. jours. Home: 6 Whaling Rd Darien CT 06820 Office: 200 Park Ave New York NY 10017 also Buxton's Country Shops Box 178 Jamesburg NJ 08831

HERRON, GEORGE THOMAS, iron and steel mfg. co. exec.; b. Nashville, Mar. 9, 1936; s. Thomas Spence and Jimmie Irene (Freeman) H.; B.S. in Indsl. Edn., Tenn. State U., 1961; M.S. in Indsl. and Vocat. Edn., Ind. State U., 1968; m. Jemina Jobe, May 21, 1965; children—Victor, Leotta, Bonita, Sonja, Rita. Tchr., coordinator School City, Gary, Ind., 1962-68; asst. regional dir. Ind. Vocat. Tech. Coll., Gary, 1968-70; tng. mgr. automotive div. Budd Co., 1970-75; tng. adminstr. Interlake, Inc., Chgo., 1975—; tchr. continuing edn. Gary Career Center, Prairie State Coll., Chicago Heights, Ill. Served with AUS, 1953-56. Mem. Internat. Registry Orgn. Devel. Profls., Orgn. Devel. Inst., Ill. Tng. and Devel. Assn., Chgo. Orgnl. Devel. Assn. Seventh-Day Adventist. Home: 425 Cleveland St Gary IN 46404 Office: Interlake Inc 135th St and Perry Ave Chicago IL 60627

HERSH, MICHAEL, supermarket exec.; b. Albany, N.Y., Nov. 28, 1937; s. Max H. and Betty Hershkowitz; B.B.A., U. Miami, 1960; children—Kim L., Scott N. Sales promotion mgr., sr. grocery buyer Food Fair Stores, Inc., Miami, 1965-70; head grocery buyer Hills Supermarket, Inc., Brentwood, N.Y., 1970-71; dir. purchasing Staff Supermarket Assos., Jericho, N.Y., 1972-73; packaging mgr. Wakefern Food Corp., 1973—. Served with U.S. Army, 1960-62. Mem. Packaging Inst. Club: B'nai B'rith (v.p. 1980). Home: 157 Howell Ave Fords NJ 08863

HERSHER, KURT BERNARD, bldg. materials exec.; b. Germany, Apr. 4, 1928; s. Bernard and Elsa (Muenzer) H.; came to U.S., 1938, naturalized, 1943; B.S. in Indsl. Engring., Bradley U., 1951; m. Claire Elovitz, Jan. 29, 1956 (div. Mar. 1970); children—Wayne, Terry, Karen; m. 2d, Edith Doby, Nov. 1975. Pres. Stevenson Lumber Co. (Conn.), 1954-68; pres., chief operational officer Stelco Industries, Inc., Stevenson, 1968—; dir. Stelco Indsl. Park, Durham, Conn., Western Conn. Properties, Inc., Bridgeport, Conn., Durham Bldg. Supply Co. (Conn.). Dir., co-founder Builders Supply Credit Bur., Bridgeport, 1960-72. Chmn. Monroe Scholarship Fund, 1960-65; mem. bldg. coms. Trumbull, Fawn Hallow elementary schs., 1960—. Served with Signal Corps, AUS, 1951-53. Mem. Northeastern Retail Lumbermens Assn., Southwestern Conn. Assn. Credit and Financial Mgmt., Fairfield County Builders Assn., Monroe (Conn.) C. of C. Home: Stones Throw Rd Easton CT 06425 Office: Route 111 Stevenson CT 06491

HERSHEWAY, CHARLES EUGENE, mktg. exec.; b. Chgo., Apr. 23, 1933; s. Louis and Jean (Manfre) H.; student U. Ill., 1951-53; B.S., Northwestern U., 1959; m. Priscilla Karas, Dec. 1, 1974; children by a former marriage—Deborah Lynn, Louis Jeffrey. Editorial dir. Nat. Research Bur., Chgo., 1958-62; promotion mgr. Advt. Publs., Inc., Chgo., 1962-64; advt. mgr. Pfaelzer Bros. div. Armour Co., Chgo., 1964-67, mktg. mgr., 1967-70, sales mgr., 1970, v.p. mktg., 1970-74; mktg. cons., 1974-76; pres. Mail Market Makers, Inc., 1976—. Mem. Percy for Gov. Finance Com., 1965. Served with USMCR, 1952-54, USN, 1954-58. Mem. Mail Advt. Club Chgo., Chgo. Federated Advt., Premium Industry Club, Sales Promotion Execs., Mail Advt. Author: NRB Retail Advertising and Sales Promotion Manual, vol. I, 1960, vol. II, 1961, vol. III, 1962; M. P. Brown Collection Letter Manual, 1961; Nat. Research Bur. Discount Store Manual, 1961. Contbr. articles to profl. jours. Home and Office: 125 Eastern Ave Clarendon Hills IL 60514

HERSHEY, COLIN HARRY, mgmt. cons.; b. Everett, Pa., Aug. 31, 1935; s. Harry and Marjorie (Nycum) H.; B.S. in Civil Engring., Lehigh U., 1957; M.B.A., U. Pitts., 1967, postgrad., 1968; m. Jacqueline Anderson, June 14, 1974; children—Barclay Harry, Marjorie Anderson. Various engring. positions, contracting div. Dravo Corp., Pitts., 1957-58, 61-64; field engr. Army Corps Engrs., 1958-61; mgr. mgmt. info. systems, atomic power div. Westinghouse Electric Co., Pitts., 1964-67; controller Planning Dynamics, Inc., Pitts., 1968-70, v.p., 1970-72, pres., 1972—; dir. Bradford Paper, Inc., Ormed Mfg. Inc., J B C Industries. Registered profl. engr., Pa. Mem. N.Am. Soc. Corp. Planners, Planning Execs. Inst., Alpha Tau Omega, Chi Epsilon. Office: Planning Dynamics Inc 850 Ridge Ave Pittsburgh PA 15212

HERSHORIN, RICHARD MARTIN, retail apparel co. exec.; b. Pitts., June 4, 1941; s. Irving and Rose (Rubenstein) H.; B.A., Washington U., St. Louis, 1963; m. Patricia Rae Schiff, Jan. 4, 1964; children—Laura Lynn, William David. With SCDA Industries, Wilmington, Del., 1963-77, buyer Dry Goods div., 1964-69, store mgr., 1969-71, mdse. mgr., 1971-74, 75-77, mdse. comptroller, analyst, 1974-75; owner, pres. Fashion Brands, Inc., Wilmington, 1977—. Club: Rotary. Home: 2608 Majestic Dr Wilmington DE 19810

HERST, JOE, real estate broker; b. Kansas City, Mo., Sept. 19, 1932; s. S. Joseph and Marjorie V. (Allen) H.; student U. So. Calif., 1950-53; m. Marilyn Kay Chastain, Feb. 1, 1969; 1 dau., Leslie Christine. Vice pres. Pizza Hut Inc., Wichita, Kans., 1966-70; real estate broker Tahoe City, Calif., 1971-74; pres. Western Nat. Realtors, Rancho Cordova, Calif., 1975—. Served to maj. USAF, 1954-65. Decorated D.F.C., Air medal (8), Air Force Commendation medal. Mem. Nat. Assn. Realtors, Calif. Assn. Realtors (dir.), Sacramento Bd. Realtors. Address: 2009 Klamah River Dr Rancho Cordova CA 95670

HERSZDORFER, PIERRE JACQUES, banker; b. Marseille, France, Apr. 20, 1939; s. Julius and Paula (Roniger) H.; came to U.S., 1955, naturalized, 1960; B.S. N.Y. U., 1968; m. Doris Buntin, Dec. 24, 1968 (div. 1979). Mem. staff auditing dept. Irving Trust Co., N.Y.C., 1960-68; mem. staff comptrollers div. Citibank, N.Y.C., 1968-71; v.p. internat. div. Hartford Nat. Bank & Trust Co. (Conn.), 1971-79; v.p. Credit Agricole br. Caisse Nationale de Credit Agricole Paris, 1979—; mem. faculty dept. bus careers Manchester (Conn.) Community Coll. Served with U.S. Army Res., 1959-65. Mem. Am. Mgmt. Assn., Council on Internat. Banking (chmn. fraud detection and safeguard com.), Appalachia Mountain Club, Wadsworth Athenaeum Mus. Office: Credit Agricole 55 E Monroe St Chicago IL 60603

HERTEL, PAUL RUDOLPH, JR., ins. co. exec.; b. Rutledge, Pa., Feb. 2, 1928; s. Paul Rudolph and Ruth Marie (Ganss) H.; B.S., U. Pa., 1951; m. Eleanor Thomas, Mar. 7, 1964; children—Paul Rudolph, Mark W. Trainee, Paul Hertel & Co., Inc., Phila., 1954, ins. broker, 1955-65, pres., chief exec. officer, treas., 1965—; chmn. bd. Excelsior Ins. Co., Syracuse, N.Y., 1978—; dir. Windsor Life Ins. Co. of Am., 1970—; underwriting mem. Lloyds of London. Chmn. boys work com. Union League of Phila., 1980-81. Served to lt. (j.g.), USN, 1951-54. Mem. Ins. Soc. Phila., Nat. Assn. Casualty and Surety Agts. Republican. Episcopalian. Clubs: Germantown Cricket; Union League. Home: 267 S 3d St Philadelphia PA 19106 Office: 3d and Chestnut St Philadelphia PA 19106

HERTZBERG, RONALD, cosmetics co. exec.; b. Paterson, N.J., June 6, 1932; s. Harry and Frances (Grabowsky) H.; B.S., Sch. Commerce, N.Y. U., 1955; children—Beverly, Pearce, Taryn. Asst. to v.p. Wella Corp., Englewood, N.J., 1957-60; dir. sales adminstrn. Helene Curtis, Chgo., 1960-63; asst. sales mgr. Zotos Internat., N.Y.C., 1963-68; v.p. mktg., dir. Cleopatra Wigs, N.Y.C., 1969; nat. sales mgr., dir. mktg. Faberge, N.Y.C., 1969-72; nat. sales mgr., mktg. mgr., Revlon, N.Y.C., 1972-73; v.p. mktg., exec. v.p. Turner Hall Corp., Great Neck, N.Y., 1973-78; pres. Pearce Properties, Inc.; exec. dir. United Beauty and Barber Assn.; dir. Mureille Paige Cosmetics Corp. Served to 1st lt. USMC, 1955-57. Mem. Nat. Beauty Barber Mfrs. Assn., Am. Film Inst. Author articles and guide books in field; innovator cosmetics products. Home: 134 Sandpiper Key Harmon Cove Secaucus NJ 07094

HERTZOG, DONALD PAUL, lawyer, oil co. exec.; b. Washington, Apr. 25, 1926; s. Rudolph Paul and Helen (mcGraw) H.; B.A. cum laude, Georgetown U., 1948, LL.B., 1951; LL.M., N.Y. U., 1963; m. Jeanne Gail O'Malley, June 29, 1957; children—Donald (dec.), John, Mary, Matthew. Admitted to D.C. bar, 1951, N.Y. bar, 1958; spl. atty. Office of Chief Counsel, IRS, Washington, 1951-52; spl. asst. to atty. gen. Dept. Justice, Washington, 1952-57; tax atty. Texaco, Inc., N.Y.C., 1957-62, sr. tax atty., 1962-63, gen. tax atty., 1963-71, asso. gen. tax counsel, 1971-72, asso. gen. counsel, 1972-75, dep. tax counsel, 1975-76, gen. tax counsel, 1976—; tax adv. bd. Tax Mgmt., 1971, Tax Found., Inc., 1976—. Served with AUS, 1944-46. Mem. Am. Bar Assn., N.Y. State Bar Assn., N.Y. County Lawyers Assn., C. of C. of U.S. Republican. Roman Catholic. Clubs: Cloud (bd. govs. 1973-77), Pelham Country (bd. govs. 1977, pres. 1979). Office: Texaco 2000 Westchester Ave White Plains NY 10650

HERVEY, LESLIE DAVID, JR., sales and mktg. co. exec.; b. Greenville, Miss., Sept. 12, 1940; s. Leslie David and Sara Anne (Jackson) H.; B.B.A., U. Miss., 1963; cert. Am. Inst. Banking, 1965; m. Kaffie Elizabeth Mallette, July 18, 1964; children—Dawn Douglas, Leslie David III. Asst. v.p. First Nat. Bank, Jackson, Miss., 1964-67; dist. mgr. McGraw-Hill Book Co., N.Y.C., 1967-70; nat. sales mgr. Ednl. Innovations, Inc., Jackson, 1970-75; owner, pres. Hervey & Assos., Jackson, 1976—; v.p. Highland Colony Realty, Inc. Mem. Amway Distbrs. Assn. (Emerald Direct Distbr. 1979), Sunflower Triad Investment Club (pres.). Baptist. Club: River Hills Tennis (Jackson). Home and Office: 4330 Deer Creek Dr Jackson MS 39211

HERVEY, RICHARD PAUL, mgmt. cons.; b. Cleve., July 19, 1941; s. Eugene and Yvonne S. H.; B.A., Coll. of Wooster, 1963; S.B., M.I.T., 1963, S.M., 1964; M.B.A., Rutgers U., 1968; children—Paul, Lee. Research engr. Western Electric Co., Princeton, N.J., 1964-67; v.p. Winters Foundry and Machine Co., Canton, O., 1967-71; pres. Kraftube Fabricators, Roseville, Mich., 1971-74; pres. Sigma Assos., Southfield, Mich., 1974—; chmn. Consol. Metall. Industries, Inc., Farmington, Mich., 1975-80. Am. Soc. Tool and Mfg. Engrs. research fellow, 1964; registered profl. engr., Calif. Mem. ASME, Am. Soc. Metals, Soc. Automotive Engrs., Am. Powdered Metals Inst., Soc. Mfg. Engrs. Office: 4000 Town Center Suite 1301 Southfield MI 48075

HERZFELD, ERNEST HUGH, steel warehouse co. exec.; b. Basel, Switzerland, Oct. 13, 1914; s. Ferdinand and Kaethe (Brunngaesser) H.; came to U.S., 1938, naturalized, 1943; student Swiss Sch. Banking, 1930-33, U. Milano, 1934-35; m. Frances B. Blumenthal, July 14, 1948; children—David H., Stephen P., Julian M. Salesman Ferdinand Herzfeld Co., Basel, 1936-38, Remington-Rand, Balt., 1939-40; jr. sales exec. Dvid L. Wilkoff Co., Pitts. and N.Y.C., 1945-54; founder, pres. Spl. Sections, Inc., Bronx, N.Y., 1954—. Asso. v.p., treas. Chester Heights Civic Assn., 1950-60; pres. Mid-Westchester YMHA, 1962-64; bd. dirs. Steel Service Center Inst., Renaissance Project Inc. Served with AUS, 1941-45; PTO. Democrat. Jewish. Clubs: Sheldrake Yacht, B'nai B'rith. Home: 8 Central Dr Bronxville NY 10708 Office: 2266 Tillotson Ave Bronx NY 10475

HERZOG, RAYMOND HARRY, mfg. co. exec.; b. Merricourt, N.D., Sept. 15, 1915; s. Harry George and Mollie (Klundt) H.; B.A., Lawrence U., 1938, LL.D. (hon.), 1979; m. Jane Cobb, Mar. 25, 1940; children—Mollie, Richard, Raymond Harry. Chemist, W.Va. Coal and Coke Co., 1937-38; coach, sci. tchr., St. Croix Falls, Wis., 1939-41; with Minn. Mining & Mfg. Co., 1941—, gen. mgr. duplicating products div., 1956-59, divisional v.p., 1959-61, corporate v.p., 1961-63, group v.p. graphic systems group, 1963-70, pres., 1970-75, chmn. bd., 1975—, chief exec. officer, 1975-79, also dir.; dir. U.S. Steel Corp., Gen. Motors Corp., NW Airlines, Jim Walter Corp.; trustee Mayo Found. Mem. U.S.-USSR Trade and Econ. Council. Bd. dirs. BEMA, 1967-75, St. Paul Winter Carnival Assn., 1969-72, Goodwill Industries Am., 1968-71; trustee Lawrence U. Mem. Conf. Bd. St. Paul Area C. of C. (dir.). Clubs: Midland Hills Country, White Bear Yacht (Minn.); Pool & Yacht; Minnesota. Home: 23 Shady Woods Rd St Paul MN 55110 Office: 3M Center St Paul MN 51101

HERZOG. RICHARD B., ins. co. exec.; b. Cin., May 21, 1937; s. Arthur E. and Bessie Lois (Berger) H.; cert. Hamilton County (Ohio) Police Acad., 1969; cert. Mktg. Devel. Inst., Purdue U., 1979; m. Sally Annette Bell, Nov. 24, 1956; children—Cindy Sue, Shelly Lynn,

Matthew Barrett. Draftsman, Avco, Cin., 1955-56, Kettcorp., Cin., 1956-57, Trailmobile, Inc., Cin., 1957-62; prin. Allied Film Agy., Cin., 1962-63; enrollment rep. Blue Cross of S.W. Ohio, Cin., 1963-68, mgr. mktg., 1968-72; mgr. regional mktg. Blue Cross Assn., Atlanta, 1972-77, dir. mktg., 1977-78; sr. dir. mktg. S.E. region Blue Cross and Blue Shield Assns., Atlanta, 1978—. Bd. dirs. Jr. Achievement, Cin., 1965-66, Cin. chpt. Cystic Fibrosis Research Found., 1963-64; bd. dirs. Carriage Cluster Civic Assn., 1975-76, pres., 1979-81; minister Dekalb Christian Ch., Atlanta, 1974-78; co-chmn. Aronoff campaign for state senate, 1966-72. Recipient various awards Jaycees. Office: Blue Cross and Blue Shield Assns 4488 N Shallowford Rd Atlanta GA 30338

HESCHEL, MICHAEL SHANE, pharm. co. exec.; b. Fremont, Ohio, June 18, 1941; s. Jerald Herman and Madonna Eudora (Cooper) H.; B.Indsl. Engring., Ohio State U., 1964, M.B.A., 1965, M.S., 1967; Ph.D., Ariz. State U., 1970. m. Judith Ann Franks, 1968; children—Michael Shane, Andrew Dyal. Sr. ops. research analyst Boeing Co., Renton, Wash., 1969-71; sr. system project mgr. FMC Corp., Santa Clara, Calif., 1971-74, mgr. ops. research, Chgo., 1974-76; dir. mgmt. sci. and info. services McGaw Labs., Irvine, Calif., 1976-79; dir. info. systems policies and standards Am. Hosp. Supply Corp., Evanston, Ill., 1980—. NASA fellow, 1967-69. Mem. Operation Research Soc. Am., Am. Mgmt. Assn., Am. Inst. Indsl. Engrs., Inst. Mgmt. Sci. Republican. Roman Catholic. Contbr. articles in field to profl. jours. Address: care Am Hosp Supply Corp One American Plaza FCR 12 Evanston IL 60201

HESELTON, LESLIE RICHMOND, III, projects engr.; b. Asheville, N.C., Jan. 7, 1944; s. Leslie Richmond and Elsie Jane (Thompkins) H.: B.S., U.S. Navel Acad., 1965; M.S. in Computer Systems Mgmt., U.S. Naval Postgrad. Sch., 1971; m. Mary J. DeMarino, June 1, 1968; 1 dau., Lori Renee. Commd. ensign U.S. Navy, advanced through grades to lt. comdr. Res.; sr. software engr. Raytheon Service Co., Washington, 1975-77; sr. systems engr. SEMCOR, Inc., Washington, 1977-78, sr. computer projects engr., Moorestown, N.J., 1978—. Mem. IEEE, Naval Inst. Presbyterian. Home: 5 Wembley Ct Mount Laurel NJ 08054 Office: SEMCOR State Hwy 38 Moorestown NJ 08057

HESLING, DONALD MILLS, cons. engr.; b. Dubuque, Iowa, Nov. 3, 1914; s. Francis J. and Mae L. (Mills) H.; student Muskegon Community Coll., 1934-36, U. Mich., 1936-37; m. Rheata E. Peterson, Apr. 2, 1945; children—Donald, Christine, Mary, Carol, Joanne, Teresa, Judy, David, Debra, Patrice, Daniel, Dennis, Thomas. Master mechanic Sealed Power Corp., Muskegon, Mich., 1946-50, dir. engring., 1950-52, mgr. mfg. and engring., 1952-54, v.p. mfg. and engring., 1954-57, v.p. research and devel., 1957-79; cons. engr. internal combustion engines, 1979—. Mem. IEEE, Soc. Automotive Engrs., Am. Mgmt. Assn., Am. Ordnance Assn., Am. Inst. Mgmt., Internat. Platform Assn. Roman Catholic. Research on bore finishes and their effect on engine performance, 1963, on computer speeds design of piston rings, 1968, on effect of honing on engine life, 1969. Home and Office: 1419 Chapel Rd Muskegon MI 49441

HESS, EDWARD ANTHONY, electromech. and solid state components co. exec.; b. Cin., Sept. 30, 1930; s. Edward August and Clara (Segers) H.; B.S., Xavier U., 1952; postgrad. LaSalle U., 1955-58, Ind. State Tchrs. Coll., 1956, U. Dayton, 1959; M.B.A., U. Calif. at Los Angeles, 1966; m. Virginia Lee Bowen, Oct. 3, 1953 (div. 1968); children—Jennifer, Andrew, Joseph, Matthew, Lynn, Amelia; m. 2d, Shirley Ann Danzeisen, Nov. 13, 1976. Exec. tng. program Pa. R.R. Freight Sales & Service, 1953-57; with Ledex, Inc., Dayton, Ohio, 1960—, product mgr., 1970-71, sales mgr. indsl. markets, 1971-72, comml. markets mgr., 1972-73, gen. sales mgr., 1973-76, mgr. product mgmt., 1976-78, internat. sales mgr., 1978—. Traffic Club Chgo. scholar LaSalle Extension U., Chgo., 1955. Mem. Am. Mktg. Assn., Electronic Industries Assn. (exec. council parts div. 1971-74), Am. Def. Preparedness Assn. Home: 4309 Glenheath Dr Kettering OH 45440 Office: 801 Scholz Dr Vandalia OH 45377

HESS, EMERSON GARFIELD, JR., lawyer, corp. exec.; b. Pitts., Nov. 13, 1914; s. Emerson G. and Nellie (Larson) H.; B.A., Bethany Coll., 1936; J.D., U. Pitts., 1939; m. Ruth Ann Agnew, June 20, 1942; children—Cynthia (Mrs. John Mathe), Suzanne (Mrs. Steven Cole), Richard E., Robert G. Minister, Hazelwood Christian Ch., 1937-44, Shadeland Ave. Christian Ch., 1944-46; admitted to Pa. bar, 1940; practiced in Pitts., 1940-43; chief salary analyst Nat. Tube Co., 1943-46; head orgn. and planning dept. H. J. Heinz Co., 1946-48; sr. partner Hess, Humphreys & Lehman, Pitts., 1948—; pres. Sandy's of Pa., Pitts. 1963-70, sec., dir., 1970—; pres. Winchester North, Inc., 1970-71; sec., dir. Bullinger & Johnson, Inc., 1961-71, pres., 1972—; pres. Carpet Barn Inc., 1976—, All-Star Sports Inc., 1977—; sec., dir. Nat. Organic Corp. Atlanta, 1960-69, Jamaica Organic Fertilizer, Kingston, 1962-69, All-Pak, Inc., 1960-75, Fox Grinders, 1963—, Ganter Roofing, 1961-70, Gateway Hardware, 1962—, Forbes Devel. Co., 1962—, Hurst-Weiss Ins. Co., 1959—, Morite Co., 1959, Ralph J. Meyer Co., 1960—, Pitts. Motor Lodge, 1964—, PMA Corp., 1961-73, Presque Isle Catering Service, 1961—, Triangle Clin. Lab., 1958-77, Try-It Corp., 1964—, Winchester Securities, 1963-71, Electro Nuclear Assos., 1969-76, Wall Street Golf Corp., 1965-67, A & D Furniture, 1960-76, Mossler Industries, 1969-70, Kidztown Furniture, 1970-77, Bldg. Systems, Inc., 1970-77, Geo. Wehn & Co., 1963-76, A.M.F. Inc., 1968—, Allegheny Wholesale Inc., 1967—, Forms C.D.P. Inc., (all Pitts.), Morite of Calif., Los Angeles, Morite of Ohio, Columbus Motor Lodges, Inc. (Ohio), AMF, Inc., Ohio, H.J. Centers, Inc., Calif., Calif. Motor Lodges, Inc., Santa Anita Hotels, Inc. (Calif.), 1978, George Wehn Resilient Floors, Inc., 1970-76, Mediterranean Fund, 1969-71, Boston First Hedge Fund of Boston, 1969-71, Viscount Securities, Inc., Boston, 1969-71, Christie Products, Inc., Pacoma Golf Club, Inc., 1969-76, Pool City, Inc., 1970—, Remnant City, Inc., 1972-76, Immel Bicycle Center, Inc., 1972—, Kenrap, Inc., 1972-77, Fast Food Restaurants, Inc., 1972—, T.S. Danowski, M.D. & Assos., Inc., 1973—, Fast Food Centers, Inc., 1973—, Jacks or Better, Inc. (Calif.), 1973—; partner Triangle Building Assos., Kiness Devel. Instr. pub. speaking Dale Carnegie Inst., 1946-49; lectr. law, psychology Robert Morris Coll., Pitts., 1946-60; developer, condr. exec. tng. programs Bell Telephone Co., Westinghouse Electric Co., Corning Glass Co., Rockwell Mfg. Co., Pepsi-Cola Co. (all Pitts., 1948—). Mem. nat. panel arbitrators; legal counsel jud. com. Pa. Ho. of Reps., 1967-69. Solicitor, Scott Twp. Sch. Bd., 1958-65, Scott Twp., 1968-69, Crafton Borough, 1974-78, Authority for Improvement of Municipalities of Allegheny Twp., 1977-80; sec. Hunter Christian Meml. Trust, 1961—; pres. P.T.A., 1961-62, 63-64; chmn. Pa. Citizens Com. on Penal and Juvenile Instns., 1949-50; pres. Allegheny County Community Councils, 1951-52; bus. adviser Jr. Achievement, 1947-48. Chmn., Scott Twp. Republican Com., 1955-56. Bd. dirs., pres. Med. Research Found., Anesthesia and Rescuscitation Found.; bd. dirs. Golden Triangle YMCA, mem. nat. com.; bd. dirs. WQED, 1958-68, Chartiers Mental Health and Retardation Center, 1972-76, Univ. and City Ministeries, Chatham Assos., Inc., 1970-71; bd. dirs. Civic Light Opera, 1956—, pres., 1967-69; bd. dirs. Amen Corner, 1978. Mem. Pa. Bar Assn., Allegheny County Bar Assn., Pa., Allegheny County municipal solicitors assns., Christian Evang. Soc. Allegheny County (dir., v.p.), Christian Student Aid Assn. (dir., v.p.), Pitts. Jr. C. of C. (pres. 1949-50), World Affairs Council Pitts., Am. Trial Lawyers Assn. Mem. Christian Ch. (trustee, chmn. gen. bd. 1960-61, chmn. congregation 1962). Clubs: Montour Country, Country. Home: 43 Robin Hill Dr McKees Rocks PA 15136 Office: 1000 Lawyers Bldg Pittsburgh PA 15219

HESS, GEORGE WILLIAM, bus. cons.; b. Keytesville, Mo., Mar. 7, 1921; s. Arthur Joseph and Mary Margaret (Clay) H.; B.S., B.A. in Bus. Adminstrn., U. Denver, 1947; m. Ethel Alice Janet McIntyre, June 7, 1947; 1 son, Kevin Clay. Fed. bank examiner, 1949-50; asst. credit mgr. Internat. Harvester Co., 1950-57; data processing mgr. Cal-Farm Ins. Co., Berkeley, Calif., 1957-59; asst. credit mgr. Container Corp Am., San Francisco, 1959-61; registered rep. mem. N.Y. Stock Exchange, 1961-62; controller Creane Supply Co., Brisbane, Calif., 1962-64; bus. cons. George S. May, Internat., San Fraancisco, 1964-67; pvt. practice bus. cons., systems engring., El Cerrito, Calif., 1967—; treas., chief fin. officer, dir. Hawkins-Hawkins Co., Inc., Bayshore Investment Corp., N.L. Hawkins Co.; mem. San Francisco Credit Mgrs. Assn., 1960-64. Merit badge counselor, Mt. Diablo council Boy Scouts Am., Walnut Creek, Calif., 1970-78; guest lectr. econs. El Cerrito High Sch. Served with USAAF, 1940-45. Decorated Air Medal with 9 oak leaf clusters. Mem. Contra Costa Bd. Realtors. Democrat. Baptist. Clubs: Toastmasters Internat. (pres. 1953-55), Masons (Sioux Falls, S.D.). Home: 7505 Rockway Ave El Cerrito CA 94530

HESS, LEON, oil co. exec.; b. 1914; married. With Hess Oil & Chem. Corp. and predecessor, 1946-69, pres., 1962-65, chmn. bd., chief exec. officer, 1965-69, also dir.; chmn. bd., chief exec. officer Amerada Hess Corp. (merger Hess Oil & Chem. Corp. and Amerada Petroleum Corp.), N.Y.C., 1969-71, chmn., chief exec. officer, 1971—, also dir. Served with AUS, 1942-45. Office: Amerada Hess Corp 1185 Ave of the Americas New York NY 10036*

HESS, LINDA GAY, coll. pres.; b. St. Louis, Apr. 2, 1938; d. Warren Sidney and Dollie Mae (Allen) Brooner; children—Diana Evans Blythe, Patricia Evans, Duane B. Norton, Steven A. Norton. Supr. accounting and billing dept. Henderson Sugar Refinery, Mobile, Ala., 1960-62; accountant All Plan Finance & Motors, San Bernardino, Calif., 1962-67; coll. dir. Skadron Coll. Bus. div. Continuing Edn. Corp., San Bernardino, 1967-79, coll. pres., 1979—, corp. v.p., 1977—. Mem. Am. Soc. Women Accts., Exec. Women Internat., Nat., Western, Calif. assns. student fin. aid officers. Home: 256 W 58th St San Bernardino CA 92407 Office: 798 W 4th St San Bernardino CA 92410

HESS, ROBERT, JR., pvt. ambulance service exec.; b. East Cleveland, Ohio, Oct. 22, 1957; s. Robert Hess and Patricia Lou H.; student John Carroll U., 1976—, Cuyahoga Community Coll., 1977-78. With Physician's Ambulance Service, East Cleveland, 1972—, v.p. in charge fin., data processing, med. assurance, 1978—; dir. Hess Enterprises, Inc.; lectr. paramedic tng. Cuyahoga Community Coll. Mem. Ohio Bd. Regents Paramedic Adv. Com., 1980—. Mem. Ohio Ambulance Assn. (trustee), Am. Ambulance Assn. (dir., fin. com.). Republican. Roman Catholic. Club: Rotary (community service com.). Office: 1765 Wymore Ave East Cleveland OH 44112

HESSINGER, CARL JOHN WILLIAM, lawyer; b. Allentown, Pa., Aug. 23, 1915; s. John J. and Mary B. (Notter) H.; Ph.B., Muhlenberg Coll., Allentown, Pa., 1937; LL.B., U. Pa., 1940; m. Marguerite K. Toland, June 10, 1950; children—Nancy K., Patricia A., Mariann, Holly A. Admitted to Pa. bar, 1942, U.S. Supreme Ct. bar, 1972; individual practice law, Allentown, 1942—; v.p., counsel First Federal Savs. & Loan Assn. of Allentown, also dir.; pres. Allen Title Co., Allentown. Trustee, counsel Harry Clay Trexler Found., Allentown. Mem. Am. Bar Assn., Pa. Bar Assn., Lehigh County Bar Assn., Am. Land Title Assn., Pa. Land Title Assn., Humane Soc. Republican. Roman Catholic. Club: Livingston, Lehigh Country, Lehigh Valley, Penquin Figure Skating, Phila. Skating. Home: 1613 Linden St Allentown PA 18102 Office: 522 Hamilton St Allentown PA 18101

HESSON, JAMES MARSH, army officer; b. St. Paul, Nov. 28, 1931; s. Floyd Edward and Hulda Olivia (Jasperson) H.; B.S., St. Benedicts Coll., 1965; M.S., George Washington U., 1973; grad. Indsl. Coll. Armed Forces, 1973; m. Joyce Lorraine Martin, Aug. 1, 1952; children—Leslie Ann, James Marsh, Jeffrey W., Laurie Jo. Commd. 2d lt. U.S. Army, 1952, advanced through grades to brig. gen., 1980; dep. comdg. gen. U.S. Army Troop Support and Aviation Materiel Readiness, St. Louis, 1979—. Served with AUS, 1950-52. Decorated D.F.C., Legion of Merit, Air medal with 2 oak leaf clusters, Commendation medal, Bronze Star, Sec. Army award, 1979. Mem. Assn. U.S. Army, Army Aviation Assn. Home: 505 Richley Dr Ballwin MO 63011 Office: US Army Troop Support and Aviation Materiel Readiness Command 4300 Goodfellow Blvd Saint Louis MO 63120

HESTER, JAMES FRANCIS, JR., fastener mfg. co. exec.; b. Chgo., May 6, 1928; s. James Francis and Marion A. (Meservey) H.; student Marquette U., 1948; B.S. in Commerce, De Paul U., 1951; m. Doris Bauer, Nov. 17, 1951; children—James III, Timothy, Maureen, Stacie, Deidre. Credit mgr. St. Joseph Hosp., Chgo., 1950-53; with Am. Rivet Co., Inc., Franklin Park, Ill., 1953—, v.p., dir., 1960—. Served with U.S. Army, 1946-47. Mem. Franklin Park C. of C. (dir. 1967-70), Ill. Mfg. Assn., Chgo. Assn. Commerce and Industry, Purchasing Mgmt. Assn. Chgo., Nat. Assn. Purchasing Mgmt., Chgo. Midwest Credit Mgmtm. Assn., NAM, N.W. Suburban Mfrs. Assn. (dir. 1967-70, pres. 1976-77). Roman Catholic. Club: River Forest Golf (Elmhurst, Ill.). Office: 11330 W Melrose St Franklin Park IL 60131

HETHCOX, ALBERT HARTSELLE, JR., mortgage co. exec.; b. Talladega, Ala., Oct. 14, 1944; s. Albert Hartselle and Sarah Lillian (Nabors) H.; B.S., Jacksonville State U., 1967; M.B.A., Samford U., 1979; m. Marianna Margaret Fisher, Apr. 15, 1968; children—Albert Hartselle III, Jonathan, Cassidy. Exec. dir. Boy Scouts Am., Birmingham, Ala., 1970-72; asst. v.p. Jackson Co., Birmingham, 1972-76; asst. v.p. Mortgage Corp. of South, Birmingham, 1976; v.p. Engel Mortgage Co., Inc., Birmingham, 1976—; part-time faculty Jefferson State Jr. Coll. Served to capt. U.S. Army, 1967-70, maj. Res. Decorated Bronze Star. Mem. Am. Mgmt. Assn., Nat. Mortgage Bankers Assn., Ala. Mortgage Bankers Assn., Ala. Mortgage Loan Adminstrn. Group. Methodist. Club: Exchange (dir. 1979—). Home: 5072 Juiata Dr Birmingham AL 35210 Office: Engel Mortgage Co Inc 501 John Hand Bldg Birmingham AL 35201

HETHERINGTON, CHARLES RAY, oil co. exec.; b. Norman, Okla., Dec. 12, 1919; s. William Leslie and Helen Rowena (Hudgens) H.; B.S. in Chem. Engring., U. Okla., 1940, M.S., 1941; Sc.D. in Chem. Engring., M.I.T., 1943; m. Rose Cosco Scurlock, June 1967; children—Helen Jane, William Leslie, Childs Pratt, Gail Ann. Research engr. Standard Oil Co. Calif. and Calif. Research Corp., Richmond, 1946-52; cons. engr. Ford, Bacon, Davis, Inc., N.Y.C., after 1946; v.p., mng. dir. Westcoast Transmission Co. Ltd. and Pacific Petroleums Ltd., Vancouver and Calgary, Can., 1959-67; pres., dir. Charles R. Hetherington & Co. Ltd. and Canacrude Oil & Gas Co., Ltd., Calgary, Alta., 1959-67; v.p., dir. West Coast Transmission Co. Ltd., Vancouver, 1967-70; pres., chief exec. officer Panarctic Oils Ltd., Calgary, 1970—; oil and gas cons. Govt. Queensland, Victoria, Australia; dir. Hetherington Ranches Ltd., Panarctic Oils Ltd., Greyhound Lines Can. Ltd. Bd. dirs. Holly Park Condominimum Assn. Registered profl. engr., Alta. Mem. Am. Gas Assn., Calgary Petroleum Club. Clubs: Calgary Golf and Country, Calgary Polo; Eldorado Country, Eldorado Polo. Contbr. articles to profl. jours. Office: Panarctic Oil Ltd 703 6th Ave SW Calgary AB T2P 0T9 Canada*

HETHERINGTON, JAMES RICHARD, ins. co. exec.; b. Indpls., Feb. 3, 1931; s. Frederick Benjamin and Pauline (Suiter) H.; A.B., Ind. U., 1953; m. Susan Esther Bassett, Jan. 31, 1953; children—Robert Bassett, William Frederick, Reporter, Ind. news editor, Daily Mag. editor Louisville Times, 1955-61; asst. city editor Indpls. Times, 1961-63; editorial editor Sta. WFBM, 1963-74; pub. relations dir. Am. United Life Ins. Co., Indpls., 1974—, v.p., 1977—; lectr. broadcast newswriting Butler U., 1970-75. Bd. dirs. Indpls. Family Service Assn., 1969-77, 80—, pres., 1974-76; bd. dirs. Indpls. Public Transp. Corp., 1978—. Served with U.S. Army, 1953-55. Recipient Alfred P. Sloan award, 1966; Peabody award for pub. service, 1969; 5 editorial awards Radio-TV News Dirs. Assn. Mem. Pub. Relations Soc. Am. (pres. Hoosier chpt. 1979), Indpls. Pub. Relations Soc., Life Ins. Advertisers Assn., Sigma Delta Chi (award 1967). Lutheran. Club: Indpls. Press (dir. 1965-68, 75-76, pres. 1967). Home: 7702 Bay Shore Dr Indianapolis IN 46240 Office: 1 W 26th St Indianapolis IN 46206

HETLAND, LARUE E. (LOU), advt. exec.; b. Artesian, S.D., Oct. 21, 1934; s. Elmer Clarence and Edna (Lucid) H.; B.S., U. S.D., 1960; m. Lorma Jane Wittstruck, May 30, 1959; children—James, Nancy, Susan. Corp. dir. advt. Nash-Finch Co., Mpls., 1960-75; regional dir. advt. A & P, Indpls., 1975-77; v.p. McGrath & Co. Advt., Indpls., 1977-78; pres. Image Printing & Typesetting, Inc., 1978—. Pres. Hopkins (Minn.) Little League, 1973. Served to sgt. USMC, 1954-57. Mem. Internat. Platform Assn. Lutheran. Club: Advt. of Indpls. Home: 11 Highland Dr Lamb Lake Trafalgar IN 46181 Office: 611 N Park Ave Indianapolis IN 46204

HETSKO, CYRIL FRANCIS, former lawyer, corp. exec.; b. Scranton, Pa., Oct. 4, 1911; s. John Andrew and Anna (Lesco) H.; A.B., Dickinson Coll., 1933; J.D., U. Mich. 1936; m. Josephine G. Stein, Nov. 12, 1932; children—Jacqueline V. (Mrs. Charles F. Kaufer), Cyril M., Cynthia F. (Mrs. William J. Rainey), Jeffrey F. Admitted to Pa. bar, 1937, N.Y. bar, 1938, U.S. Supreme Ct. bar, 1965; asso. firm Chadbourne, Parke, Whiteside and Wolff, 1936-55, partner 1955-64; gen. counsel Am. Brands Inc. (formerly Am. Tobacco Co.), 1964-77, v.p., 1965-69, dir., 1965-77, sr. v.p., 1969-77; past dir. Am. Brands Export Corp., James B. Beam Distilling Co., James B. Beam Distilling Internat. Co., Andrew Jergens Co., Master Lock Co., Master Lock Export, Inc., Acme Visible Records, Inc., Acushnet Co., Am. Tobacco Internat. Corp., Duffy-Mott Co., Inc., Gallaher Ltd. (Gt. Britain), Swingline, Inc., Swingline Export Corp., Sunshine Bisquits, Inc., Wilson Jones Co. Pres., U.S. Trademark Assn., 1965-66, hon. chmn., 1966-67, dir., 1959-67, 68-72, 73-77, council past pres.'s, 1977—. Mem. Am., Fed., N.Y. State bar assns., Assn. Bar City of N.Y., Order of Coif, Phi Beta Kappa, Phi Delta Theta, Delta Theta Phi. Republican. Presbyn. Clubs: Nat. Lawyers (Washington); Ridgewood (N.J.) Country; Explorers, Williams, Intrepids (N.Y.C.). Home: 714 Waverly Rd Ridgewood NJ 07450

HETT, ROSLIN MARTYN, finance co. exec.; b. Kamloops, B.C., Can., Nov. 22, 1931; s. Roslin Martyn and Phyllis Maude (Slater) H.; came to U.S., 1966; ed. Brentwood Coll., Victoria, B.C., 1950; m. Sophia Penelope Jane Harvey, July 10, 1954; children—Jane, Caroline, John, Jennifer, Mary. Field rep. Niagara Finance Corp., Victoria, 1953; with collections dept. Gen. Motors Acceptance Corp., Vancouver, 1953-55, from field rep. to dist. rep., 1956-60; sales mgr. Morrison Motors, Ltd., Duncan, B.C., 1955-56; with Avco Fin. Services, Inc., and predecessors, Newport Beach, Calif., 1960-79, pres., 1975-79, also dir.; pres., dir. Avco Corp., 1979—; dir. Avco Fin. Services Ins. Group, Avco Everett Research Lab., Paul Revere Life Ins. Co. Episcopalian. Clubs: Balboa Bay, Big Canyon Country, Masons. Home: 2 Strawbridge Ln Greenwich CT 06830 Office: AVCO Corp 1275 King St Greenwich CT 06830

HETZEL, FREDERICK JOSEPH, publishing co. exec.; b. S.I., N.Y., Feb. 27, 1928; s. Frederick Joseph and Anna (Steers) H.; B.B.A., Pace Coll., 1959; m. Sue M. Casper, Sept. 2, 1950; children—Patricia Ann, Frederick John, Michael. With Dow Jones & Co., Inc., Princeton, N.J., 1953—, asst. treas., 1960-70, treas., 1970—, asst. sec., 1965—. Served with U.S. Army, 1948-50, 50-52. Mem. Nat. Assn. Accts., Inst. Newspaper Controllers and Fin. Officers. Roman Catholic. Home: 310 Glenn Ave Trenton NJ 08648 Office: PO Box 300 Princeton NJ 08540

HETZEL, WILLIAM GELAL, mgmt. cons.; b. New Rochelle, N.Y., May 19, 1933; s. William Gelal and Nan Katrinka (Sanes) H.; student Washington Coll., 1949-51; B.B.A., U. Miami, 1953; postgrad. Xavier U., 1957-58; M.B.A., Northwestern U., 1962; m. Clara Etta Clark, May 28, 1975; children—William Gelal, Tara Lynore, John Frederick, Janda Beth. Asso., McKinsey & Co., Inc., Chgo., 1961-64; br. mgr. Xerox Corp., Louisville, 1964-69; dir. mkgt. Maremont Corp., Chgo., 1969-70; pres. Medelco, Inc., Schiller Park, Ill., 1970-72; v.p., div. gen. mgr. ITT Service Industries Corp., Cleve., 1972-74; v.p., Lamalie Assos., Inc., Chgo., 1974-78; sr. v.p. Eastman & Beaudine, Inc., Chgo., 1978—; dir. Cabledata Assos., Palo Alto, Calif. Dir. Republican Workshops of Ill., 1960-64; mem. DuPage County (Ill.) Rep. Central Com., 1970-72; pres. pro tem, bd. local improvements Downers Grove (Ill.), 1970-73; dir. Downers Grove Jr. C. of C., 1959-65. Served to lt. (j.g.) USNR, 1953-56. Mem. Am. Mgmt. Assn. (speaker, recipient cert. of appreciation, 1970). Lutheran. Clubs: Mid-Day Execs. (Chgo.). Office: 111 W Monroe Suite 2150 Chicago IL 60603

HETZER, RICHARD MICHAEL, banker; b. Chgo., Mar. 28, 1941; s. Matthew and June Ann (Koch) H.; grad. certificate in comml. banking Am. Inst. Banking, 1966; student DePaul U., 1976—; m. Patricia Carr; children—Kathryn, Christina, Mary. With Exchange Nat. Bank, Chgo., 1967—, 2d v.p., 1971, asst. v.p., 1972-78, v.p., mgr. customer service dept., 1978—. Pres., mem. exec. com., dir. Chgo. and Northeastern Ill. chpt. Muscular Dystrophy Assn. Named Bus. Man of Day, Sta. WAIT, 1971. Mem. Am. Inst. Banking. Office: Exchange Nat Bank of Chgo 130 S LaSalle St Chicago IL 60603

HEUSSNER, GEORGE JAMES, printing co. exec.; b. Marlette, Mich., Feb. 4, 1935; s. George A. and Ethel H. (Dorn) H.; B.B.A., Mich. State U., 1956; m. Jo Anne Kelly, May 18, 1957; children—Sheila, Julie, Jenny. Auditor, Touche Ross & Co., Detroit, 1956-58; controller, asst. treas. Redman Industries, 1958-63, Nev. Cement Co., 1963-66; asst. treas. Kingsport Press (Tenn.), 1966-69, mktg. mgr., 1969-70; v.p. fin. and adminstrn. Arcata Publs. Group, 1970-71, 73—, v.p., Eastern sales mgr., 1971-73. Mem. budgets and admission com. United Fund, 1967-68. Served to lt. U.S. Army, 1956-57, USAR, 1957-65. Mem. Am. Inst. C.P.A.'s. Presbyterian. Home: 116 Scarlet Oak Drive Wilton CT 06897 Office: 2 Landmark Sq Stamford CT 06901

HEWARD, BRIAN, stock broker; b. Brockville, Ont., Can., July 15, 1900; s. Arthur Richard Graves and Sara Efa (Jones) H.; grad. Lower Can. Coll., 1915; M.A., St. John's Coll., Cambridge (Eng.) U., 1921; m. Anna Barbara Lauderdale Logie, Dec. 28, 1925; children—Barbara, Chilion F. G., Efa (Mrs. Donald Greenwood), Faith (Mrs. William Berghuis). Accountant, P.S. Ross & Sons, 1921-22, Oswald & Drinkwater, 1922-25; partner Jones Heward & Co., 1925-64, sr. partner, 1945-64, co. inc., 1965, pres. Jones Heward & Co. Ltd., 1965, chmn. bd., 1966— (all Montreal, Que., Can.); chmn. bd. Consumers Glass Co., Ltd., Montreal, 1960—. Served as midshipman Royal Canadian Navy, 1918. Home: 11 Anwoth Rd Westmount Montreal PQ H3Y 2E6 Canada Office: 249 St James St Montreal PQ H2Y 1M8 Canada

HEWITT, WILLIAM ALEXANDER, mfg. exec.; b. San Francisco, Aug. 9, 1914; s. Edward Thomas and Jeannette (Brun) H.; A.B., U. Calif., 1937; m. Patricia Deere Wiman, Jan. 3, 1948; children—Anna, Adrienne, Alexander. With John Deere Plow Co., San Francisco, 1948-54, v.p., 1950-54; dir. Deere & Co., Moline, Ill., 1951—, exec. v.p., 1954-55, pres., 1955-64, chmn., 1964—, chief exec. officer, 1955—; dir. Continental Ill. Corp., Continental Ill. Nat. Bank & Trust Co. of Chgo., AT&T, Conoco, Inc., Baxter Travenol Labs., Inc.; mem. internat. adv. com. Chase Manhattan Bank. Founding mem. Bus. Com. for Arts, Emergency Com. for Am. Trade; mem. Pres.'s Commn. for Nat. Agenda for Eighties; trustee Calif. Inst. Tech., Mus. Modern Art, Nat. Safety Council, Carnegie Endowment for Internat. Peace, 1971-75, Council of Americas, St. Katharine's/St. Mark's Sch., 1965-76; bd. govs. Am. Nat. Red Cross, 1967-70; vis. com. Harvard U. Grad. Sch. Bus. Adminstrn., 1962-67, Grad. Sch. Design, 1967-73, vis. com. E. Asian studies, 1977—; incorporator Nat. Corp. for Housing Partnerships, 1968-70; mem. council Stanford Research Inst., 1971-79; mem. hon. nat. bd. Smithsonian Assos.; mem. Nat. Council for Humanities, 1975-80; mem. Wilson council Woodrow Wilson Internat. Center for Scholars, 1977—. Served as lt. comdr. USNR, 1942-46. Mem. Farm Indsl. Equipment Inst., the Conf. Bd., Soc. Automotive Engrs., Internat. C. of C. (trustee U.S. council). UN Assn. (dir. 1970-73), Com. Econ. Devel. (hon. trustee), Advt. Council, Inc., Am. Soc. Agrl. Engrs., AIA (hon.), Bus. Council, Council Fgn. Relations, Ill. Council Econ. Edn. (governing mem. 1970-77), Atlantic Inst. Pub. Affairs, Asia Soc., Nat. Council U.S.-China Trade (vice chmn. 1973-75, chmn. 1975-78, dir. 1973-80), Trilateral Commn., U.S.-USSR Trade and Econ. Council (dir.), Bus. Roundtable, Lincoln Acad. Ill. (laureate), Alpha Delta Phi. Clubs: Pacific-Union (San Francisco); Burlingame (Cal.) Country; Chicago (Chgo.); Bohemian; Pilgrims of U.S. Home: 3800 Blackhawk Rd Rock Island IL 61201 Office: Deere & Co John Deere Rd Moline IL 61265

HEWLETT, WILLIAM (REDINGTON), elec. engr.; b. Ann Arbor, Mich., May 20, 1913; s. Albion Walter and Louise (Redington) H.; A.B., Stanford, 1934, E.E., 1939; M.S., Mass. Inst. Tech., 1936; LL.D., U. Calif. at Berkeley, 1966, Yale, 1976; D.Sc., Kenyon Coll., 1978, Poly. Inst. N.Y., 1978; m. Flora Lamson, Aug. 10, 1939 (dec. 1977); children—Eleanor H. Gimon, Walter B., James S., William A., Mary H. Jaffe; m. 2d, Rosemary Bradford, 1978. Electro-med. research, 1936-39; co-founder, partner Hewlett-Packard Co., Palo Alto, 1939-46, exec. v.p., dir. 1947-64, pres., 1964-77, chief exec. officer, 1969-78, chmn. exec. com., 1977—, also dir.; dir. Chrysler Corp., Utah Internat. Inc. Mem. Pres.'s Gen. Adv. Com. on Fgn. Assistance, 1965-68, Pres.'s Sci. Adv. Com., 1966-69; mem. council Rockefeller U., 1975-78; mem. regional panel commn. on White House Fellows, 1969-70, chm, 1970. Trustee Carnegie Instn. of Washington, 1971—, chmn. bd., 1980—; bd. dirs. San Francisco Bay Area Council; hon. trustee Calif. Acad. Sci. Served with AUS, 1942-45. Fellow IEEE (pres. 1954), Am. Acad. Arts and Scis., Franklin Inst. (life); mem. Nat. Acad. Scis., Nat. Acad. Engring., Instrument Soc. Am. (hon. life). Patentee on electronic devices. Office: 1501 Page Mill Rd Palo Alto CA 94304

HEXTER, RICHARD MARTIN, investment co. exec.; b. Cleve., Nov. 6, 1933; s. Samuel J. and Helen (Apple) H.; B.S. in Chem. Engring., U. Calif., Berkeley, 1954; M.B.A., Harvard, 1956; m. Anne Maren Glasoe, Mar. 7, 1966; children—Douglas O., Elizabeth P., Russell A. Regional sales mgr. TRW, Inc., Los Angeles, 1956-59; exec. v.p. Ovitron Corp., N.Y.C., 1959-61; exec. v.p. Donaldson Lufkin & Jenrette, Inc., N.Y.C., 1961-75; pres., chmn. bd. Ardshiel Assos., Inc., N.Y.C., 1976—; dir. Arcata Corp., Clopay Corp., Burndy Corp., Advanced Micro Devices, Inc., Wavetek Corp.; adj. prof. Grad. Sch. Bus., Columbia, 1976—; disting. faculty fellow Yale U. Sch. Orgn. and Mgmt., 1979-80. Trustee, 1st v.p. Lexington Sch. for Deaf; chmn. bd. dirs. New Sources for Funding, Inc. Kennecott fellow, 1954; Charles Gayley fellow, 1950; Baker scholar, 1956. Chartered fin. analyst. Mem. Wine and Food Soc. N.Y. (dir.), Tau Beta Pi, Phi Eta Sigma. Clubs: Harvard, Harvard Bus. Sch. (dir.) (N.Y.C.); Whippoorwill. Contbr. chpts. to books, articles to profl. jours. Home: 7 Bayberry Rd Armonk NY 10504 Office: 200 Park Ave New York City NY 10017

HEYL, GEORGE RICHARD, econ. geologist; b. Allentown, Pa.; s. Allen Van and Emma (Kleppinger) H.; B.S., Pa. State U., 1932; M.A., Princeton, 1934; Ph.D., 1935; m. Thelma Catherine Tate, Oct. 2, 1936 (div. May 1963); children—Emma Jean (Mrs. T. Rasmussen), Richard A.; m. Carole Ellen Howitt, July 18, 1968; children—Jeremy Samuel, Rebecca Clara Eve. Geologist, Princeton expdns. to Nfld., 1934-35; instr. geology Rutgers U., 1935-37; geologist Geol. Survey Nfld., 1936-37, Standard Oil Co. Calif., 1937-40, U.S. Geol. Survey, 1942-48; chief geologist Creole Petroleum Corp., Caracas, Venezuela, 1948-55; mgr. exploration Standard-Vacuum Oil Co., Melbourne, Australia, 1955-59; prof. geology State U. Coll., State U. of N.Y., New Paltz, 1959—; owner, gen. mgr. Minerals Search & Surveys, Cons., U.S. C.E., State of Conn. Trustee, chmn. Inst. All Nations for Advanced Studies and Research, N.Y. John W. White fellow Pa. State U., 1933; Princeton research fellow 1934; C.E. Procter fellow Princeton, 1935. Fellow Geol. Soc. Am., Mineral. Soc. Am., AAAS, Am. Geog. Soc.; mem. Am. Inst. Mining, Metall. and Petroleum Engrs., Soc. Econ. Geologists, Australian Inst. Mining and Metallurgy, Sociedad Venezolana de Clencas Naturales (Venezuela), Petroleum Exploration Soc. N.Y., Canadian Mineral. Assn., Sigma Xi, Alpha Chi Sigma, Sigma Gamma Epsilon. Clubs: Princeton (N.Y.C.); Faculty of University Calif. (Berkeley); Explorers (N.Y.C.) (London). Author: (with others) Copper in California, 1949. Home: 64 Huguenot St New Paltz NY 12561 Office: POB 582 New Paltz NY 12561

HIAASEN, CARL ANDREAS, lawyer; b. Benson County, N.D., May 26, 1894; s. K.O. and Mary (Flaagen) H.; grad. U. Ill., 1920; J.D., U. N.D., 1922; m. Clara Landmark, June 3, 1924 (dec. Oct. 1930); 1 son, Kermit Odel (dec. Feb. 1976). Admitted to Fla. bar, 1923, U.S. Supreme Ct. bar, 1926, U.S. Ct. of Claims bar, 1964; practice law, Ft. Lauderdale, Fla., 1923—; mem. firm McCune, Hiaasen, Crum, Ferris & Gardner, P.A., 1923—. Mem. com. Chapel of Four Chaplains, Temple U., Phila., 1971—; bd. dirs. Pitts. Theol. Sem., 1973—; mem. pres.'s council U. Fla., 1974—. Served with U.S. Army, World War I. Life fellow Am. Bar Found.; mem. Am. Bar Assn., Bar Assn. City N.Y., Order Coif, Phi Delta Phi, Delta Sigma Rho. Republican. Lutheran. Contbr. articles to legal jours. Home: 2417 NE 27th Ave Fort Lauderdale FL 33305 Office: Century Nat Bank Bldg 25 S Andrews Ave Fort Lauderdale FL 33302

HIATT, ARNOLD SELIG, shoe mfg. co. exec.; b. May 26, 1927; s. Alexander and Dorothy H.; B.A., Harvard U., 1948; m. Anne Wechsler. Pres., Blue Star Shoe Co., Lawrence, Mass., 1952-69; pres., chief exec. officer The Stride Rite Corp., Boston, 1969—; dir., Fiduciary Trust Co., Boston; corporator Charlestown Savs. Bank, Boston, 1971-72, trustee, 1972-77. Bd. dirs. Office of Cultural Affairs, Boston. Mem. Am. Footwear Industries Assn. (chmn.-elect 1980, mem. exec. com., chmn. compensation com., dir.), Young Presidents Orgn. Office: 960 Harrison Ave Boston MA 02118

HIATT, ROBERT NELSON, food co. exec.; b. Maryville, Mo., May 11, 1936; s. Nelson Ricker and Marjorie Madonna (Horton) H.; B.S., Northwestern U., 1957; m. Carroll Curley, Oct. 7, 1977; children—Thomas, David; stepchildren—Nancy Campbell, Patrick Campbell, Kathy Campbell. Product mgr. Procter & Gamble, Cin., 1958-68; asso. Glendinning Assos., Westport, Conn., 1968-69, v.p., 1969-70, exec. v.p., 1970-71; v.p. mktg. Internat. Playtex, N.Y.C., 1971-72, v.p., gen. mgr., 1972-74, group v.p., 1974-77; pres. consumer products div. Swift & Co., Chgo., 1977-78, group v.p. processed foods, 1978-79, pres. processed food div., 1979—. Served with U.S. Army, 1957. Office: 115 W Jackson Blvd Chicago IL 60604

HICKAM, RAY MANUAL, county ofcl.; b. Hiltons, Va., Nov. 22, 1917; s. Moscoe and Cordia Mae (Carter) H.; student Purdue U., 1937-39; m. Billie Jean Cole, Nov. 17, 1944; children—Nancy Jean, Karen Kay. Farmer, Jonesboro, Ind., 1939-66; mem. Ind. Ho. of Reps., 1961-62; clk. Grant County, Marion, Ind., 1967-74, auditor, 1978—; credit dir. Eastern Ind. Prodn., Hartford City, 1956-79; bd. govs. Farm Credit Services, Denver, 1974-77, dir. Eastern Ind., 1956-79, vice chmn., 1958-63, chmn., 1963-79; mem. 4th Farm Credit Dist. Bd., 1971-77, chmn., 1976. Republican. Baptist. Clubs: Lions (pres. 1976—), Moose, Elks, Mason (Shriner). Home: 8379 S Wheeling Pike Jonesboro IN 46938 Office: Office Complex and Security Center S Adams Marion IN 46952

HICKEY, CLARENCE DAREN, bus. exec.; b. Aurora, Ill., Oct. 23, 1925; s. Clarence P. and Marie E. (Challis) H.; B.S. in Accounting, U. Ill., 1950; postgrad. Northwestern U., 1952; m. Alice Gillette, June 7, 1947; children—Patricia Ellen (Mrs. James Zajicek), Laura Marie (Mrs. Robert Osterhoff), Mary Alice, Peter Daren, Maureen Ann, Tracy Lynn, Wendy Ann, Margaret Jo, Timothy Sean. Acting prin. mgr. Hasking & Sells Co., Chgo., 1952-63; controller James B. Beam Distilling Co., Chgo., 1963-67; v.p. and treas. Chevway Corp., Chgo., 1967-68; v.p. and controller Barton Brands, Inc., Chgo., 1968-70; v.p. fin. and adminstrn. Creative Bldg. Systems, Inc., Urbana, Ill., 1970-72; v.p., sec., treas., Nat. Student Mktg. Corp., Chgo., 1972-80; sr. v.p. fin. and adminstrn. Palm Beach, Inc., Cin., 1980—; dir. Nat. Student Mktg. Corp., Sandpaper Inc. Ill. Mem. Wheaton (Ill.) Community Assn.; treas. Wheaton Parent's Club; mem. St. Michael's Sch. Bd., 1969-70. Served With USNR, 1943-46. C.P.A., Ill. Mem. Am. Inst. C.P.A.'s, Ill. Soc. C.P.A.'s, Fin. Execs. Inst., Am. Mgmt. Assn., Tax Execs. Inst. Clubs: Ill. Athletic, Brookwood Country, K.C. Home: 754 WatchPoint Dr Cincinnati OH 45230 Office: 400 Pike St Cincinnati OH 45202

HICKEY, JOHN THOMAS, JR., accountant; b. Worcester, Mass., July 20, 1945; s. John Thomas and Margaret Elizabeth (Cooney) H.; student New Eng. Sch. Accounting, 1963-65, Clark U., 1967-69, Worcester Poly. Inst. Sch. Indsl. Mgmt., 1974-78; m. Gayle Marie Buffone, June 22, 1968; children—Michael John, Steven Patrick, Patricia Marie. With New Eng. High Carbon Wire Corp., Millbury, Mass., 1965—, asst. controller, 1977-78, chief accountant, 1978—, controller, dir., 1979—; tax accountant; small bus. cons. Mem. bus. edn. com. Millbury High Sch., 1975; coach, dir. Little League, Sutton, Mass., 1975—; com. dir. St. Mark's Roman Catholic Ch., Sutton, 1977-79. Recipient award of excellence in accounting Worcester Poly. Inst., 1978. Mem. Nat. Assn. Accountants (chpt. dir. 1973). Clubs: Elks, Singletary Rod and Gun. Editor manuscripts Mgmt. Accounting Mag., 1973. Home: 2 Bashaw Rd Sutton MA 01527 Office: 50 Howe Ave Millbury MA 01527

HICKEY, NORMAN JOSEPH, JR., fin. exec.; b. Evanston, Ill., Nov. 10, 1937; s. Norman Joseph and Margaret Rita (Quick) H.; A.B., Xavier U., 1959; m. Sherren Leigh, Aug. 23, 1969. Trader, E.F. Hutton, Inc., Chgo., 1961-64; v.p. Walston & Co., Inc., Chgo., 1964-74; v.p. Dean Witter Reynolds, Inc., Chgo., 1974—. Bd. dirs. The Geog. Soc. Chgo., 1974—, Cathedral Shelter Chgo., 1974—. Mem. Stockbrokers Assn. Clubs: Bond, Amex, Univ., Cliff Dwellers. Fin. columnist, Chgo. Bus. Rev., 1979—. Home: 571 Blackstone Pl Highland Park IL 60035 Office: 150 S Wacker Dr Chicago IL 60606

HICKEY, THOMAS RICHARD, food co. exec.; b. Northampton, Mass., Jan. 27, 1926; s. Thomas Richard and Alice Margaret (Shea) H.; A.B., Amherst Coll., 1949; m. Mary Ellen Shebek, Aug. 19, 1950; 1 son, Thomas R. Sales and mktg. asso. Gen. Foods Corp., White Plains, N.Y., 1949-67; nat. sales mgr. RJR Foods Inc. div. R.J. Reynolds Industries, N.Y.C., 1967-73; v.p. Schrafft Candy Co. div. Gulf & Western Industries, Boston, 1973-74, Vita Food Products div. Brown & Williamson Tobacco, Greenwich, Conn., 1974-78; v.p. Tille Lewis Foods div. Ogden Corp., Stockton, Calif., 1978—. Chmn., Westport (Conn.) Little League, 1970-73; mem. Select Com. on Recreation, Westport, 1968-75. Served with U.S. Army, 1944-46; ETO. Mem. Am. Mgmt. Assn., Calif. Canners League, Nat. Canners and Packers Assn., Am. Frozen Food Inst., Nat. Fisheries Inst. (bd. dirs. 1960-63), Grocery Mfrs. Assn., Western Grocers Assn., Nat. Food Brokers Assn., VFW, Am. Legion. Club: Sales Exec. (N.Y.). Office: Drawer J Stockton CA 95201

HICKMAN, BRYAN DEVEREUX, mgmt. cons.; b. Rochester, N.Y., Dec. 17, 1945; s. Kenneth Claude Devereux and Eleanor (Whiting) H.; B.A. in Economics, Williams Coll., 1967; M.P.A. (Pub. Affairs fellow, McConnell fellow), Woodrow Wilson Sch. Pub. Internat. Affairs, Princeton, 1969. Staff economist, mgr. social programs research Gen. Electric/Tempo, Washington, 1971-75; cons., rev. of fgn. assistance programs, White House Council Internat. Econ. Policy, Washington, 1973; mgr. bus. environ. analysis, corporate planning group Gulf Oil Corp., Pitts., 1975-78; mgmt. cons., 1978-79; mgr. strategic planning Schlegel Corp., Rochester, 1979—. Contbr. to publs. in field. Home: 113 Westminster Rd Rochester NY 14607 Office: 400 East Ave Rochester NY 14607

HICKMAN, DAVID MICHAEL, paper tableware mfg. co. exec.; b. Salem, Oreg., Dec. 11, 1942; s. Vernon Combs and Margaret Irene (Copley) H.; student public schs.; m. Karen Joyce Cox, Aug. 24, 1968; children—Sean Michael, Shannon Lee. Terr. mgr. Brown & Williamson Tobacco Co., 1964-66, Gibson Greeting Cards, Inc., 1966-69; chain drug specialist Coty, Inc., 1970-73; pres., owner Expressions, Seattle, 1973-75; v.p. sales Paper Art Co., Inc., Indpls., 1975-78, exec. v.p., 1978—; pres., owner Paper Artery Co., Inc., 1979—, Shaniko Mktg. Co., 1978—. Served with USAF, 1960-63. Republican. Presbyterian. Home: 7815 Mohawk Ln Indianapolis IN 46260 Office: 3500 N Arlington Ave Indianapolis IN 46260

HICKMAN, JOHN CALVIN, ins. co. exec.; b. Ark., Feb. 8, 1927; s. Robert Carl and Ruth (Collins) H.; student U. Ark., Fayetteville. 1945-46; m. Patricia Jean Carson, Mar. 5, 1949; children—John Calvin, Julie C., Patrick C. With Union Life Ins. Co., Little Rock, 1947-60, v.p., 1960; home office agy. mgr. 1st Pyramid Life Ins. Co. Am., Little Rock, 1960-62; from supt. agys. to agy. v.p. Piedmont Life Ins. Co., Atlanta, 1961-71; exec. v.p. 1st Nat. Bank, Little Rock, 1971-77; pres., chief exec. officer, dir. Union Life Ins. Co., Little Rock, 1977—, also Nat. Coaches Annuity. Bd. dirs. Salvation Army, 1964-67; bd. dirs. YMCA, 1974-78, chmn. bd., 1979-80; unit chmn. United Way, 1978, trustee, bd. dirs., 1980—. Mem. Little Rock Life Underwriters Assn., Ark. Life Underwriters Assn. (past dir., officer), Little Rock Jaycees (founder, past dir.), Little Rock C. of C. (v.p. 1975, dir. 1975-76), Greater Little Rock C. of C. (dir. 1979-81), Little Rock Gen. Agts. and Mgrs. Assn., Central Ark. Estate Planning Council. Episcopalian. Clubs: Country of Little Rock, Little Rock. Office: PO Box 3101 Little Rock AR 72203

HICKMAN, JOHN HAMPTON, III, industrialist, banker, educator; b. Wilmington, Del., May 19, 1937; s. John Hampton and Martha (Barnett) H.; student Randolph Macon Coll., 1954-56; A.B., Brown U., 1959; certificate in Chinese, Yale, 1960, J.D., 1962; m. Barbara Spurlin; children—Erica Delius, Gretchen Leigh, Rochanya Charlotte, John Hampton IV. Internat. investment banker McDonnell & Co., N.Y.C., 1965-68; mng. partner J.H. Hickman & Co. (now Foster, Hickman & Zaenglein), 1969—; chmn. bd., chief exec. officer Seilon, Inc., N.Y.C., 1968-69, Nev. Nat. Bank, Reno, 1968-69, Thomson Internat., Thibodaux, La., 1968-69; chmn. bd. Lockwood Corp., Gering, Nebr., 1968-69; chmn. bd., pres. First Bancorp., Las Vegas, 1968—; pres., dir. Delanair, Inc. (now Nexus Industries), 1969-70; chmn. finance com. Aberdeen Petroleum Corp. (now Adobe Oil & Gas), Tulsa, 1972—; chmn. C.R. Burr & Co. (now United Nurseries Corp.), Manchester, Conn., 1972—, Peninsula Corp., Melfa, Va.; dir. Video Tape Network, Heany Industries, Scottsville, N.Y., Photog. Scis. Corp., Webster, N.Y., New Democrat Corp.; trustee, treas. Oceanic Soc., San Francisco, 1973—; chmn. Foster, Hickman & Zaeglein Tax Managed Fund (formerly Rochester Fund), 1978—, mem. faculty M.B.A. program U. Conn., U. N.C., Appalachian State U.; prof., chmn. dept. bus. adminstrn. and econs. Tenn. Wesleyan Coll.; chmn. mgmt. studies Rochester Inst. Tech., 1977—. Area rep. Yale Alumni Assembly; trustee, chmn. fin. com. N.Y. State Assn. Human Services, N.Y.C. Bd. dirs. Genesee Valley Arts Found. Mem. Am. Mgmt. Assn. (world council, pres.'s assn., editor publs.), Acad. of Mgmt., Internat. Law Assn., Am. Soc. Internat. Law, Fin. Execs. Inst. Clubs: Denver; Rochester Yacht; Nat. Arts; Cooperstown (N.Y.) Country; Univ.; Yale of Eastern Conn. (pres.). Author articles, booklets. Home: 885 Lake Rd Webster NY 14580 Office: 183 E Main St Rochester NY 14604

HICKMAN, STEPHEN LEE, mfg. co. exec.; b. Adrian, Mich., July 30, 1942; s. Charles E. and Virginia Hickman; B.A., Mich. State U., 1964; married; children—Tracy Lynn, Stephanie Lee. With KVP Sutherland Co., various locations, 1964-68, sales mgr., Chgo., 1966-68; asst. v.p. sales Brazeway, Inc., Adrian, Mich., 1968-76, v.p. mktg., 1976-78, chief exec. officer, 1978—, also chmn. bd. Bd. dirs. YMCA, 1969-75, Goodwill, 1979—; bd. dirs. Jr. Achievement, 1979—, pres., 1980. Served with USAF, 1965. Mem. Young Presidents Orgn. Clubs: Lenawee Country (pres. 1976, dir. 1973-76), Renaissance.

HICKOK, GEORGE ELTON, clin. lab. exec.; b. Los Angeles, Apr. 2, 1929; s. Donald Edward and Helen Alberta (Grover) H.; student Pacific Union Coll., 1954-57; m. Patricia Anne McDowell, Apr. 6, 1966; children—George Edward, Larry William, Darrell Sean, Brian Patrick. Pres. Coll. Ch. Furniture, Angwin, Calif., 1954-61; pres. I.V. Ometer, Inc., Oakland, Calif., 1961-66; exec. sec. Physicians Health Congress, Sacramento, 1966-76; pres., chmn. Med. Modalities Assos. and Miller Pharmacl, Inc., West Chicago, Ill., 1976-78; chief exec. officer, chmn. Drs. Data Inc. and Bio-Med. Data, Inc., West Chicago, 1978—; cons. Med. Modalities Asso., Inc., 1978-80. Libertarian. Home: 430 Carpenter St Lemont IL 60439 Office: PO Box 111 30W101 Roosevelt Rd West Chicago IL 60185

HICKS, EMORY BENJAMIN, petroleum co. exec.; b. Hilton, N.Y., Nov. 29, 1922; s. Roy Emory and Alta Alice (Haight) H.; student Cornell U., 1940-41; m. Ruth Louise Hetzer, Dec. 4, 1943; children—Shirley Ann, Douglas George, Dennis David. Owner, operator Valley View Dairy Farm, Piffard, N.Y., 1942-70; sales rep. Agway Petroleum, Batavia and Rochester, N.Y., 1970-72, petroleum plant mgr., 1973-76, div. sales supr., 1976-79, area sales, service mgr., West Springfield, Mass., 1980—. Mem., v.p. Emergency Squad York Fire Dept. Mem. Fuel Oil Dealers Assn., LP Gas Assn. Methodist. Club: Cape Coral Yacht & Racquet. Home and Office: 77 Winona Dr West Springfield MA 01089

HICKS, IRLE RAYMOND, retail food chain exec.; b. Welch, W.Va., Dec. 21, 1928; s. Irle Raymond and Mary Louise (Day) H.; B.A., U. Va., 1950. Bus. mgr. Hicks Ford, Covington, Ky., 1952-58; accountant Firestone Plantations Co., Harbel, Liberia, 1958-60; auditor Kroger Co., Cin., 1960-66, gen. auditor, 1966-68, asst. treas., 1968-72, treas., 1972—. Bd. dirs. Old Masons Home Ky. Served with AUS, 1950-52. Mem. Fin. Execs. Inst., Bankers Club, Alpha Kappa Psi, Phi Kappa Psi. Episcopalian. Clubs: Cin., Masons, Shriners. Home: 454 Oliver Rd Cincinnati OH 45215 Office: 1014 Vine St Cincinnati OH 45202

HICKS, JOSEPH ROBERT, rubber co. exec.; b. Bloomsburg, Pa., Aug. 27, 1922; s. Joseph Arch and Ada Hartman (Correll) H.; B.A., Pa. State U., 1943; m. Mary Rita Schlitzer, Dec. 12, 1946; children—Robert William, Nancy Jane, Jeffrey Alan, Thomas Joseph, Joanne Elizabeth. Dist. mgr. finance and service operation Gen. Electric Co., Cleve., 1946-62; asst. comptroller The Goodyear Tire & Rubber Co., Akron, Ohio, 1962-64, comptroller, 1964-68, v.p., comptroller, 1968-76, pres., chief exec. officer Goodyear Canada Inc., 1976-78, v.p. fin. Goodyear Tire & Rubber Co., 1978-79, exec. v.p., chief fin. officer, 1979—, also dir. Trustee, Children's Hosp. Med. Center of Akron. Served with AUS, 1943-46. Mem. Fin. Execs. Inst. (dir. 1979—), NAM (dir. 1980—). Clubs: Portage Country, Toftrees Country Club and Lodge. Office: 1144 E Market St Akron OH 44316

HICKS, MELVIN GRAY, ins. co. exec.; b. Winston-Salem, N.C., Jan. 5, 1939; s. Joseph Howard, Sr., and Helen (Hailey) H.; B.S. in Indsl. Relations, U. N.C., 1961; m. Margaret Lavada Weimer, May 12, 1963. Supt., Integon Life Ins. Corp., Winston-Salem, 1961-64; adminstrv. mgr. life Am. Health & Life, Balt., 1964-66; asst. sec. Interstate Life & Accident Ins. Co., Chattanooga, 1966-71; v.p. life adminstrn. Am. Family Life Assurance Co., Columbus, Ga., 1971—. C.L.U. Fellow Life Mgmt. Inst.; mem. Am. Soc. C.L.U.'s, Life Ins. Advertisers Assn. Moravian. Home: 6200 Canterbury Dr Columbus GA 31904 Office: 1932 Wynnton Rd Columbus GA 31999

HICKS, RALPH EDWARD, pharm. co. rep.; b. Barth, Fla., Dec. 26, 1932; s. Frank and Edna (Bush) H.; B.S., Fla. State U., 1954; M.A., Central Mich. U., 1975; m. Elizabeth Huie, Aug. 12, 1955; children—Marcus Wayne, Carin Elizabeth. Profl. rep. Merck Sharp & Dohme, Anderson and Charleston, S.C., 1960-67, sr. profl. rep., 1967-73, exec. profl. rep., 1973—; pres., chmn. bd. Marcus Enterprises, Inc., Charleston, 1977—. Distinguished club pres. Electric City Sertoma Club, Anderson, 1967-68; mem. adminstrv. bd., chmn. edn. dept. Grace United Methodist Ch., Charleston, 1972-73; public mem. Palmetto-Lowcountry Health Systems Agy., 1979—.

Served to capt. USMC, 1954-59. Home: 719 Schaffer Dr Charleston SC 29412

HIDAKA, KENJIRO, elec. engr., trading co. exec.; b. Tokyo, Mar. 15, 1934; s. Rishiro and Masako (Nakata) H.; came to U.S., 1964; B.S., Waseda U., Tokyo, 1958; m. Kuniko Michii, Aug. 15, 1959; children—Misa Hidaka, Miki, Lawrence Kitaro. Import mgr. C. Itoh & Co., Ltd., Tokyo, 1958-64, mktg. mgr. C. Itoh & Co. (Am.) Inc., San Francisco, 1964-70, Los Angeles, 1970-75, v.p. C. Itoh Electronics Inc., Los Angeles, 1975—. Mem. IEEE. Home: 2040 Pelham Ave Los Angeles CA 90025 Office: 5301 Beethoven St Los Angeles CA 90066

HIDDLESTON, RONAL EUGENE, drilling and pump co. exec.; b. Bristow, Okla., Mar. 21, 1939; s. C.L. and Iona D. (Martin) H.; student Idaho State U., 1957-58; m. Marvelene L. Hammond, Apr. 26, 1959; children—Michael Scott, Mark Shawn, Matthew Shane. With Roper's Clothing and Bishop Redi-Mix, Rupert, Idaho, 1960-61; pres., chmn. bd., gen. mgr. Hiddleston Drilling, Rupert, 1961-66, Mountain Home, Idaho, 1966—. Mem. Mountain Home Airport Adv. Bd., 1968—; hon. mem. Idaho Search and Rescue. Cert. driller, Idaho, Utah. Mem. Nat. Water Well Assn. (cert.), Idaho Water Well Assn. (dir., past pres.), Pacific N.W. Water Well Assn. (dir.), N.W. Mining Assn., Nat. Fedn. Ind. Businessmen, Aircraft Owners and Pilots Assn. Clubs: Masons, Shriners, Nat. 210 Owners, Optimist, Ducks Unltd. Designer 3000-foot drilling rig, 1977. Home: 645 E 17th St N Mountain Home ID 83647 Office: Rt 1 Box 610D Mountain Home ID 83647

HIEGEL, JERRY M., mfg. corp. exec.; b. Davenport, Iowa, 1927; B.S., St. Ambrose Coll., 1949; M.B.A., U. Wis., 1950. With Des Moines Register, 1946; with Oscar Mayer & Co., Inc., 1946—, gen. sales mgr., 1963-66, v.p. sales, 1966-70, v.p. mktg., 1970-71, group v.p., 1971-73, exec. v.p., 1973-77, pres., 1977—, chief exec. officer, 1980—, also dir. Served with USN, 1945-46. Office: Oscar Mayer & Co Inc PO Box 7188 Madison WI 53707

HIESERMAN, CLARENCE EDWARD, textile co. exec.; b. Iowa Park, Tex., Jan. 15, 1917; s. Edd and Emma Jane (Weeth) H.; B.S., Tex. Technol. U., 1937; M.S., Mich. State U., 1939; postgrad. Tex. A&M U., 1939-42; m. Margaret Turner, May 24, 1942; children—James E., Robert A., Sylvia Ann. Supt. research Celanese Corp., Cumberland, Md., 1942-52; research sect. head, plant mgr. Monsanto Co., Decatur, Ala., 1952-72, plant mgr., Pensacola, Fla., 1972—. Bd. dirs. United Way of Escambia County, Jr. Achievement, Pensacola, Appeals Rev. Bd., Pensacola. Mem. Asso. Industries Fla. (dir.), Fla. C. of C. (dir.), Pensacola C. of C. (dir.), Am. Chem. Soc. Lutheran. Clubs: Pensacola Country, Pensacola Racquet. Patentee in field. Home: 212 Northcliffe Dr Gulf Breeze FL 32561 Office: PO Box 12830 Pensacola FL 32575

HIGGINS, ALAN MILLS, real estate exec.; b. Cin., Jan. 10, 1945; s. Jack and Agnes (Mills) H.; B.S., Miami U., Oxford, Ohio, 1967; M.B.A., U. Akron, 1979; m. Elaine Marie Benes, May 11, 1968; children—Scott, Jason. Site developer Standard Oil Co. Ohio, 1967-72; corp. real estate rep. Gen. Tire Realty Co., Gen. Tire & Rubber Co., 1972-74, mgr. corp. real estate, v.p., 1974-76, pres., dir., 1976—; chmn. bd., pres. Am. Indsl. Acquisition Cons.'s, 1978—; mem. faculty Sch. Continuing Edn., U. Okla., 1978-80, U. Wis., 1980, U. N.C.-Charlotte, 1981—. Mem. Brecksville (Ohio) Charter Rev. Com., 1973. Served with AUS, 1967-69. Cert. rev. appraiser. Mem. Nat. Assn. Corp. Real Estate Execs. (trustee, dir.), Soc. Indsl. Realtors, Indsl. Devel. Research Council, Soc. Real Estate Appraisers. Home: 495 Bath Hills Blvd Akron OH 44313 Office: 1 General St Akron OH 44329

HIGGINS, BRADLEY CARTER, mfg. co. exec.; b. Worcester, Mass., Nov. 20, 1916; s. John W. and Clara Louise (Carter) H.; grad. Deerfield Acad., 1937; certificate Pratt Inst., 1940; m. Beverly Moore, Feb. 20, 1943 (div. Mar. 1963); children—Lee Cameron Thompson, Clarinda Lutringer, Joanna Reber. Research engr. Aberdeen Proving Grounds, Md., 1941-42, climatic research, 1942-44; plant engr. Worcester Pressed Steel Co., 1944-49, dir., 1964-68; v.p., treas., dir. Livingstone Engring. Co., 1949-51; pres.-treas., dir. Electrosteam Corp., Worcester, 1951—, Bradley C. Higgins Sawmill Inc., Alexandria, N.H., 1978—; v.p., dir. Liggett-Bosworth Co., Inc., Bennington, Vt., 1959-63, Marsh Co., Nashua, N.H., 1960—; pres., treas., dir. Electric Boiler Corp. Am., Worcester, 1962-76; pres., dir. Sapphires, Ltd., 1972—; corporator, John Woodman Higgins Armory, chmn. bd. trustees, 1961-79, trustee emeritus, 1980—; trustee Met. Center Inc., Boston, 1978—, Worcester Art Mus., 1970—; chmn. bd. Central Mass. (and Youth) Symphony Orch., 1979-80; dir., corporator Brooks Pond Water Works, 1951—; pres., treas. Hillside Inn, Inc., 1974—; dir. Internat. Investment Co. Ltd. Mem. phys. edn. com., council YMCA. pres. Worcester Ballet Soc., 1968-71, hon. chmn., 1972—; trustee Joslin Diabetes Found., 1962-79, corporator, 1980—; trustee Craft Center, 1963-68, Worcester Sci. Museums, 1970—, Grahm Jr. Coll., Boston, 1976-77, U.S.S. Constn. Mus., 1977—; bd. dirs. Boston Ballet Co., 1968—; bd. dirs., pres. Boston Ballet Endowment, 1978—; corporator Worcester Art Mus., 1967—; adv. bd. Public Action for Arts, 1979—; patron Worcester County Music Assn., Boys Trade Sch.; clk. Worcester Vocat. Schs., 1963-71, trustee, 1969-71; v.p., dir. Vim Sauna Internat., 1966-68. Notary public. Mem. ASME (elec. boiler code com. 1977—), Worcester Engring. Soc., Worcester Econ. Club, Newcomen Soc., Electric League, Worcester Mechanics Assn., Worcester Pratt Inst. Alumni Club (pres.), Mayflower Soc. (life), Navy League, Am. Ordnance Assn. (life), Boston Ballet Soc., Boston Aquarium, Parents Without Partners (founder, chpt. pres. 1966-67), Citizens Plan E Assn., Worcester Area C. of C. Republican. Episcopalian. Clubs: Rotary, Worcester, Tatnuck Country, Worcester Tennis, Greendale Tennis, Appalachian Mountain. Patent on conductivity control. Home: 30 Westwood Dr Worcester MA 01609 Office: 574 W Boylston St Worcester MA 01606

HIGGINS, BRIAN FRANCIS, graphic arts exec.; b. St. Louis, Oct. 10, 1947; s. Edward Francis and Charlotte Adams (Trent) H.; B.S.A., Bentley Coll., 1971; m. Lola Marie Duke, May 30, 1970; children—Margaret A., Paul B. Asst. treas. Adams & Abbott, Inc., Boston, 1965-69, treas., 1969-73, pre·., 1973-79; owner, mgr. C.H. Wrightson, Inc., Newton, Mass., 1979—; cons. graphic arts tng. programs. Co-pres. Natick West Sch. P.T.O., 1980—. Served with USAR, 1966—. Mem. Printing Industries New Eng., YMCA. Club: Elks. Home: 3 Windsor Ave Natick MA 01760 Office: 90 Bridge St Newton MA 02158

HIGGINS, JAMES HENRY, banker; b. Kansas City, Mo., Feb. 28, 1916; s. Henry Bertram and Helen (Agnew) H.; B.A., Yale U., 1939; m. Elysabeth C. Barbour, Feb. 3, 1945; children—Elysabeth Cochran, James Henry, III, Hilary Barbour. With Bank of Manhattan Co., N.Y.C., 1939-41, 46-50, asst. treas., 1950; asst. v.p. Mellon Bank, N.A., 1951-54, v.p., 1954-65, sr. v.p., 1965-68, exec. v.p., 1968-71, pres., dir., 1971-74, chmn., chief exec. officer, 1974—; chmn., dir. Mellon Nat. Corp., 1974—; dir. White Consol. Industries, Gulf Oil Corp., Joy Mfg. Co. Mem. exec. com., chmn. Allegheny Conf. Community Devel.; bd. dirs. Pitts. Regional Planning Assn., Pa. Economy League, Inc., Regional Indsl. Devel. Corp. of S.W. Pa.; trustee U. Pitts., Presbyn.-Univ. Hosp.; trustee, pres. Penn's S.W. Assn. Served with USNR, 1941-45. Mem. Assn. Res. City Bankers (pres.), Bus. Council Pa. (co-chmn. policy com.). Republican. Presbyn. Clubs: Allegheny Country, Edgeworth (Sewickley); Duquesne, Allegheny (Pitts.); Rolling Rock, Laurel Valley (Ligonier, Pa.); Links (N.Y.C.); Metropolitan (Washington). Home: 608 Maple Ln Sewickley PA 15143 Office: Mellon Bank NA Mellon Sq Pittsburgh PA 15230

HIGGINS, JAY FRANCIS, fin. exec.; b. Gary, Ind., June 25, 1945; s. J. Francis and Veronica (Conroy) H.; A.B., Princeton U., 1967; M.B.A., U. Chgo., 1970; m. Gail Marie Joy, Nov. 23, 1979; 1 dau., by previous marriage, Maura Ellis. With Salomon Bros., N.Y.C., 1970—, v.p., 1976, gen. partner in charge merger and acquisition dept., 1979—. Served with USAR, 1967. Roman Catholic. Home: 333 E 68th St New York NY 10021 Office: 1 New York Plaza New York NY 10004

HIGGINS, JOHN DEBREE, investment banker; b. Bklyn., May 15, 1935; s. John M. and Veronica (Sheehan) H.; B.B.A., Hofstra U., 1960, M.B.A., 1963; m. Lynn King, Aug. 17, 1958; children—John, Gwen, Laurence. Sr. security analyst Bache & Co., Inc., N.Y.C., 1960-64; v.p. corp. fin. Jesup and Lamont, Inc., N.Y.C., 1965-71; prin. corp. fin. Brookville Equity Assos., Inc., N.Y.C., 1971-72; v.p. Morse Capital Corp., N.Y.C., 1973-77; exec. v.p. J. Daren and Sons, Inc., Norwich, Conn., 1977-79; exec. v.p. Vanguard Ventures, Inc., Glen Cove, N.Y., 1979—. Served with AUS, 1953-55. Home: High Farms Rd Glen Head NY 11545 Office: 4 Cedar Swamp Rd Glen Cove NY 11542

HIGGINS, LEO MICHAEL, III, ceramic materials scientist; b. Clinton, Iowa, Dec. 30, 1950; s. Leo Michael and Rosemary Ann (Rieger) H., Jr.; B.S., Rutgers U., 1972, M.S., 1977, Ph.D. (Fed. Mining and Mineral and Mineral Fuel Conservation fellow), 1979. Mgr. research and devel. lab Ceramic div. Joseph Dixon Crucible Co., Jersey City, 1972-73; research fellow, intern dept. ceramic engring. Rutgers U., New Brunswick, N.J., 1973-78; sr. research scientist Kyocera Internat. Inc., San Diego, 1979—; cons. in field. Mem. Am. Ceramic Soc., Nat. Inst. Ceramic Engrs., Soc. Mfg. Engrs., Keramos. Roman Catholic. Home: 10841 Carbet Pl San Diego CA 92122 Office: Kyocera Internat Inc 8611 Balboa Ave San Diego CA 92123

HIGH, JACK LEWIS, JR., data processing exec.; b. Sewanee, Tenn., May 1, 1935; s. Jack Lewis and Elizabeth LaMyrle (King) H.; grad. Phillips Acad., 1954; A.B. cum laude, Tufts U., 1958; postgrad. U. Va., 1958-60; m. Martha Virginia Walton, Feb. 23, 1963; children—Lance Walton, Martha Elizabeth. Programmer/systems analyst Sperry Univac, Washington, 1962-67, data processing cons., 1967-69, proposals mgr., 1969; systems projects mgr. Computer Data Systems, Inc., Washington, 1969; account rep. Sperry Univac, Washington, 1970-72, mgr. product mktg., 1972-76, mgr. congl. liaison, 1976-79, dir. govt. mktg. affairs, 1979—; wine and cheese cons.; pres. LeChai Wine & Cheese, McLean, Va., 1972-75; tchr. Latin, football coach Louisa County (Va.) High Sch., 1960-61. Campaign chmn. Univac United Way, 1975; vestryman St. John's Episcopal Ch., McLean, 1975—, rep. Diocesan Council, 1978. Dartmouth scholar, 1954-55; U. Va. assistantship, 1958-60; United Way Silver award, 1975. Mem. AAU, Armed Forces Communication and Electronics Assn. (arrangements com. 1976—), Va. Alumni Assn., Wolftrap Assos. Clubs: Langley (v.p. 1976—, dir. 1974—), Fairfax Hunt. Author: Contrary to Fact Conditional Statements, 1958. Home: 1000 Abbey Way McLean VA 22101 Office: 2121 Wisconsin Ave NW Washington DC 20007

HILBIG, DAVID MANWARING, health care co. exec.; b. Salt Lake City, Mar. 4, 1947; s. Frederick Walter and Hazel (Manwaring) H.; B.A., U. Utah., 1971, M.S., 1972; m. Barbara Elizabeth Diehl, Aug. 25, 1959; children—Michael, Gregory, Matthew, Elizabeth. Wage and salary analyst U. Utah, Salt Lake City, 1972-73; wage and salary adminstr. Envirotech, Inc., Salt Lake City, 1973-74; personnel adminstr. E-Systems, Inc., Salt Lake City, 1974-76; personnel dir. Snowbird (Utah) Corp., 1976-80; mgr. tng. and devel. Intermountain Health Care, Inc., Salt Lake City, 1980—. Mem. high council Ch. of Jesus Christ of Latter-day Saints, 1979—, exec. sec. Sandy stake. Mem. Am. Soc. Personnel Adminstrs., Am. Hosp. Assn., Am. Soc. Hosp. Personnel Adminstrs., Am. Soc. Tng. and Devel., Kappa Sigma. Home: 554 Howard Dr Sandy UT 84070 Office: 36 S State St Salt Lake City UT

HILBORN, JOHN R., ins. exec.; b. Oak Park, Ill., Dec. 15, 1928; s. John T. and Evelyn N. (Newcomer) H.; B.A., DePauw U., 1951; M.B.A., Northwestern U., 1956; m. Shirley S. Butcher, Dec. 22, 1950; children—James, Janet, John, Jeffrey. Vice pres., treas. Easterling Co., Wheaton, Ill., 1959-63; tax mgr. Cory Corp., Chgo., 1963-68; v.p., treas. Page Engring. Co., Chgo., 1968-74; v.p. finance and personnel Map Internat., Wheaton, Ill., 1974-77; spl. agt. Northwestern Mut. Life Ins. Co., Chgo., 1977—. Pres., LaGrange Highlands Civic Assn., 1957. Served to 1st lt. USMCR, 1951-53. Home and Office: 4446 Gilbert Ave Western Springs IL 60558 Office: 150 S Wacker Dr Chicago IL 60606

HILBRECHT, NORMAN TY, lawyer, state legislator; b. San Diego, Feb. 11, 1933; s. Norman Titus and Elizabeth (Lair) H.; B.A., Northwestern U., 1956; J.D., Yale, 1959; m. Mercedes Mihopulos. Admitted to Nev. bar, 1959, U.S. Supreme Ct., 1963; atty.-asso. firm Jones, Wiener & Jones, Las Vegas, Nev., 1959-62; asso. counsel U.P. R.R., Las Vegas, 1962; pres. Hilbrecht, Jones, Schreck & Bernhard, Chartered and predecessor firm, Las Vegas, 1962—. Pres., Mobil Transport Corp., 1971-72. Asst. lectr. bus. law U. Nev., Las Vegas. Mem. labor mgmt. com. Nat. Conf. Christians and Jews, 1963; mem. Clark County, Nev. Democratic Central Com., 1959—, 1st vice chmn.; mem. Nev. Assembly, 1966-74, minority leader, 1971-72; mem. Nev. Senate, 1974-79, chmn. subcom. profl. liability ins., 1975-77, mem. legis. commn., 1977; del. Western Regional Assembly on Ombudsman, 1972; chmn. Clark County Dem. Conv., 1966; chmn. Nev. Dem. Conv., 1966. Pres., Clark County Legal Aid Soc., 1964, Nev. Legal Aid and Defender Assn., 1965—; trustee Nev. Solar Energy Assn., 1977-79. Served to capt. AUS, 1952-68. Named Outstanding Legislator, Eagleton Inst. Politics, 1969. Mem. Am., Clark County bar assns., Am. Trial Lawyers' Assn., State Bar Nev., Nev. Trial Lawyers (v.p. 1969), Phi Beta Kappa, Delta Phi Epsilon, Theta Chi, Phi Delta Phi. Unitarian. Home: 8601 S Mohawk Las Vegas NV 89118 Office: 600 E Charleston Blvd Las Vegas NV 89104

HILDEBRAND, DAVID JAMES, bus. exec.; b. nr. Omro, Wis., Apr. 17, 1933; s. James Henry and Leone Veronica (Burdick) H.; student U.S. Army Electronics Sch., 1954, Internat. Corr. Sch., 1957, U. Wis., 1962; m. Verna Maliske, Nov. 8, 1952; children—Dennis D., Michele A., Jeffrey G. Farmer, Wis., 1955-57; sales rep. Am. Tobacco Co., Oshkosh, Wis., 1957-60; area field rep. Winnebago Dairy Herd Improvement Assn., Oshkosh, 1960-69; dept. mgr. Chief Equipment Corp., farm equipment, Oshkosh, 1969-71; regional sales mgr. Trojan Seed Co., Pickett, Wis., 1971-76; dist. supr. Blaney Farms, Inc., West Union, Iowa, 1976—, dist. sales mgr., 1978—; owner Hilco Mktg. Fayette, Iowa; owner Imperial Coating Products Co., Fayette; owner, gen. mgr. Hawkeye Enterprises (Iowa). Served with U.S. Army, 1953-55. Recipient Outstanding Sales Achievement award Trojan Seed Co., 1974, Blaney Seed Co., 1977. Home: 308 Volga St Fayette IA 52175 Office: 345 E Main St Hawkeye IA 52147

HILDEBRANDT, FREDERICK DEAN, JR., ins. co. exec.; b. Upper Darby, Pa., Apr. 17, 1933; s. Frederick Dean and Ruth Taylor (Barry) H.; A.B. magna cum laude, Dartmouth, 1954, M.S., Tuck Sch. of Bus. Adminstrn. and Thayer Sch. Engring., 1955; m. Marjorie Louise Smith, July 27, 1968; children—Frederick Dean III, Elizabeth Florence. Engr., Eastman Kodak Co., Rochester, N.Y., 1957-60; systems mgr. J.T. Baker Chem. Co., Phillipsburg, N.J., 1960-63; asso. Booz, Allen & Hamilton Inc., N.Y.C., 1963-72, v.p., 1972-78; sr. v.p. Am. Ins. Assn., N.Y.C., 1978-81; v.p. Travelers Ins. Cos., Hartford, Conn., 1981—; adminstr. All-Industry Research Adv. Council, 1979; adv. bd. Joint Council on Econ. Edn. Served with U.S. Army, 1955-57. Mem. Am. Risk and Ins. Assn., Soc. Ins. Research, Phi Beta Kappa. Home: 21 Outlook Dr Darien CT 06820 Office: One Tower Sq Hartford CT 06115

HILGEMAN, EDWARD HENRY, II, cons. indsl. engr.; b. Bellmont, Ill., Oct. 7, 1911; s. Edward Henry and Maud Monzelle (Scott) H.; B.Sc. in Mech. Engring., Rose-Hulman Inst. Tech., 1933; m. Jane Rambo, June 24, 1933; children—Alyce Sophronia, Kay Marie, Susan Jane, Sallee Ann, Edward Henry III. Labor, prodn. engring. Q.M. div. A&P Tea Co., Terre Haute, Ind., 1933-38, engr. Hdqrs. Operating Dept., N.Y.C., 1938-42; prin. engr. Singmaster & Breyer, N.Y.C., 1942-47, partner, 1947-63; v.p. Fluor-S & B Inc., N.Y.C., 1955-63; pres. Huck Design Corp., N.Y.C., 1963-69; plant mgr. Crown Cork & Seal Corp., Montvale, N.J., 1969-71; pvt. indsl. engring. cons. Cape Coral, Fla., 1971—; dir. Chem. Enterprises, Fluor S & B, Huck Co., Inc., Napex Inc., Execuplane Inc. Regional bd. dirs. Boy Scouts Am., Darien, Conn., 1956-57. Served with USNG, 1932-38. Registered profl. engr., N.Y., N.J. Mem. ASME. Clubs: Cape Coral Golf and Racquet, Sportsman Yacht and Sailing. Address: 2113 Everest Pkwy Cape Coral FL 33904

HILL, ALBERT GORDON, inertial nav., precision instrumentation co. exec.; b. St. Louis, Jan. 11, 1910; s. Glenn Clark and Sarah Alberta (Boogher) H.; B.S., Washington U., St. Louis, 1930, M.S., 1934; Ph.D., U. Rochester, 1937; m. Ruth Harriet Parker, Nov. 23, 1962. Engr., Bell Labs., 1930-32; instr. physics M.I.T., Cambridge, 1937-41, mem. staff, radiation lab., 1941-46, prof. physics, 1946-75, dir. research lab. electronics, 1949-52, dir. Lincoln Lab., 1952-55, v.p. for research, 1970-75, cons. to pres., 1975—; chmn. bd. Charles Stark Draper Lab., Inc., Cambridge, Mass., 1973—; dir. Inst. for Def. Analyses, Washington, 1956-61, v.p., 1956-59; sci. dir. weapons systems Joint Chiefs of Staff, Washington, 1956-58; adviser SHAPE Tech. Center, The Hague; cons. to many industries. Recipient Presdl. cert. of Merit, 1948; Disting. Alumni citation Washington U., St. Louis, 1955; Disting. Civilian Service medal Air Force, 1955, Dept. Def., 1959; Disting. Civilian Service award Am. Ordnance Assn., 1956. Fellow Am. Phys. Soc., IEEE, Am. Acad. Arts and Scis.; Benjamin Franklin fellow Royal Soc. Arts. Club: Cosmos (Washington). Author: (with L.M. Ridenour and Ralph Shaw) Bibliography in Age of Science, 1949. Home: 11171 Oakdale Rd Boynton Beach FL 33437 Office: 555 Technology Sq Cambridge MA 02139

HILL, ARTHUR BURIT, transp. co. exec.; b. N.Y.C., Apr. 2, 1922; s. Alton and Victoria (Ellis) H.; B.S., City U. N.Y., 1966, M. Public Adminstrn., 1973; m. Patricia Ruth Smith, Aug. 5, 1956; children—Arthur Burit, Ernest, Victoria, Joanne. With N.Y. Police Dept., N.Y.C., 1946-73, asst. chief, until 1973; with United Parcel Service, Greenwich, Conn., 1973—, v.p. public affairs, 1977—. Founding dir. Harlem Commonwealth Council; bd. dirs. Manhood Found., 1968—, Better Boys Found., Chgo., 1970—; mem. Fordham U. Council, 1969—; coordinator Sutton for Mayor campaign, 1977; lic. lay reader Episcopal Ch. Served with U.S. Army, 1942-46. Recipient Brotherhood award Nat. Conf. Hispanic Law Enforcement Officers, 1978. Mem. Am. Soc. Public Adminstrn., Acad. Polit. Sci., Am. Acad. Polit. and Social Sci., Am. Acad. for Profl. Law Enforcement, One Hundred Blackmen, NAACP (life), Kappa Alpha Psi (life). Democrat. Clubs: Nat. Democratic, Capitol Hill, Guardsmen, Masons. Home: 187-10 Ilion Ave Hollis NY 11412 Office: United Parcel Service 51 Weaver St GOP 5 Greenwich CT 06830 also 316 Pennsylvania Ave SE Washington DC 20003

HILL, BRIAN RICH, paper mill exec.; b. Buxton, Eng., Oct. 25, 1934; came to U.S., 1967, naturalized, 1976; s. Harold and Enid Mary (Rich) H.; M.S. in Mech. Engring., Imperial Coll. Sci. and Tech.,London U., 1956; m. Bridget M. Bell, June 5, 1959; children—Rosemary J., Meriel S. Design engr. English Electric Co., Rugby, Eng., 1956-62; devel. engr. I.C.I. Fibres, Pontypool, South Wales, 1962-67; devel.supr. Westvaco, Covington, Va., 1967-73; dir. engring. Nicolet Paper Co., subs. Philip Morris, De Pere, Wis., 1973-76, dir. mfg., 1976-77; v.p., gen. mgr. Kerwin Paper div. Amricon Corp., Appleton, Wis., 1977—. Mem. Inst. Mech. Engrs. (London) (chartered mech. engr.), TAPPI, ASME (chmn. N.E. Wis. br.), Republican. Presbyterian. Club: Kiwanis (chmn. club youth services 1979-80) (Appleton). Patentee in field. Home: 1145 N Lake Neenah WI 54956 Office: PO Box 179 Appleton WI 54912

HILL, CHARLES ERVIN, county ofcl.; b. Jacksonville, N.C., Mar. 1, 1936; s. Charles and Ethyl Lillian (Stanford) H.; student City U. N.Y., 1955-57; cert. Cornell U., 1978, Rutgers U., 1978. Cost acct. Pacemaker Corp., Egg Harbor City, N.J., then mgr. customer services Jack Louis Music Centers, Ocean City and Somers Point, N.J., 1970-72; with Atlantic County (N.J.) Opportunity Center for Handicapped, 1972—, workshop supr., 1975—; EEO specialist Atlantic County Div. Manpower; seminar coordinator; cons. in field. Mem. Pleasantville (N.J.) City Council, 1973; N.J. v.p. U.S. Jaycees, 1974, nat. dir., 1975. Served with U.S. Army, 1958-62. Mem. Am. Mgmt. Assn., Assn. EEO and Affirmative Action Specialists, Am. Guild Organists. Home: PO Box 738 Pleasantville NJ 08232 Office: 1601 Atlantic Ave Atlantic City NJ 08401

HILL, CHARLES RICHARD, stock broker; b. Oakdale, Tenn., Nov. 14, 1933; s. Louis Julian and Margret Elizabeth (Colwell) H.; B.S., Ga. Inst. Tech., 1961; m. Bessie Elizabeth Gibbons, Mar. 11, 1955; children—David, Susan, Michael, Scott. Indsl. sales rep. Mead Corp., Balt., 1960-62; account exec. Merrill Lynch Pierce Fenner & Smith, Inc., Macon, Ga., 1962-67, sr. account exec., 1967-71, mgmt. tng., N.Y.C., 1971, on spl. assignment corporate systems long range planning, 1971-72, mgr., Montgomery, Ala., 1972-76, v.p., 1973—, overall coordinator for options, N.Y.C., 1976, mgr. mktg. communications, 1977, mgr., Clearwater, Fla., 1978—; mem. options adv. to N.Y. Stock Exchange, 1977. Served as naval aviator USNR, 1953-58. Mem. Pinellas County Com. of 100. Methodist. Clubs: Rotary, Countryside Country, Harbor View. Home: 1931 Saddle Hill Rd N Dunedin FL 33528 Office: 531 Franklin St Clearwater FL 33516

HILL, DAVID HYDE, internat. trading co. exec.; b. London, Mar. 31, 1927; came to U.S., 1959, naturalized, 1963; s. William and Dorothy Mary (Josey) H.; Higher Nat. Cert. in Mech. Engring., Luton (Eng.) Coll., 1950; M.S. in Mech. Engring., Wayne State U., 1962; m. Joan Virginia Yohannan, June 23, 1951; children—Linda Louise, Sara Lee, Jennifer Ann. Mfg. engr. Ford Motor Co. of Can., 1952-59; mfg.

research engr. Gen. Motors Corp., Detroit, 1959-67, adminstr. systems devel. mfg. staff, 1967-69, dir. Chevrolet systems devel., 1969-70, mgr. Chevrolet info. systems, 1970-73, exec. dir. planning, service parts ops., 1973-74, planning mgr. AC-Delco div., 1974-78, dir. vehicle export programs parent co., 1979, pres. Motors Trading Corp. subs., 1979—. Mem. Instn. Mech. Engrs. (Gt. Britain), Assn. Profl. Engrs. Ont. Inventor mfg. processes. Home: 721 Parkman Dr Bloomfield Hills MI 48013 Office: Room 4-264 Gen Motors Bldg W Grand Blvd Detroit MI 48202

HILL, JAMES EDWARD, ins. co. exec.; b. Chgo., Mar. 3, 1926; s. George and Mary Luella (Hutchens) H.; student Denver U., 1947; M.S. in Fin. Services, Am. Coll., Bryn Mawr, Pa., 1980; m. Jessie Mae Birmingham, Jan. 29, 1949; children—James R., Ellen M. Office mgr., purchasing agt., accountant Steve Tojek Co., Milw., 1948-54; office mgr., accountant Oreg. Athletic Equipment Co., Portland, 1954-56; spl. agt. Prudential Ins. Co., Portland, 1956-58, div. mgr., 1958-70; gen. agt. Great Am. Res. Ins. Co., Portland, 1970—; v.p. Robert A. Amey Co. Inc., mfrs. reps., 1971-75; pres. Diversified Plans, Inc., 1979—. Vice pres. Multnomah County Young Republicans, 1957-58; vice chmn. Washington County Parks Adv. Bd., 1978, chmn., 1979—. Served with U.S. Army, 1944-47. C.L.U.; recipient Edgar M. Kelly award Prudential, 1967. Lic. tax cons., Oreg. Mem. Oreg., Portland (dir. 1978-79, chmn. edn. com. 1978-79, pres. 1980-81) life underwriters assns., Internat. Assn. Fin. Planners, Am. Soc. C.L.U.'s, Assn. Tax Cons. Methodist. Home: 2045 NW Saltzman Rd Portland OR 97229 Office: 1225 NW Murray Rd Suite 106 Portland OR 97229

HILL, JAMES STEWART, cons. elec. engr.; b. Washington, Dec. 2, 1912; s. Hugh Stewart and Isabel (Burch) H.; B.E.E., Case Western Res. U., 1934; m. Elizabeth Barbara Metzger, June 1, 1936; children—Noel E., Hugh S., Gary W., Dawn E. Vice-pres. Smith Electronics, Cleve., 1953-59; project mgr. Jansky & Bailey, Washington, 1959-64; research engr. Genisco Technology Corp., Washington, 1964-69; cons. engr. RCA Corp., Springfield, Va., 1969-78; pres. EMXX Corp., Springfield, Va., 1978—. Registered profl. engr., Ohio. Fellow IEEE; mem. Electromagnetic Compatibility Soc., Soc. Automotive Engrs., Electronic Industries Assn. Clubs: Lincoln Continental Owners, Antique Automobile Club Am., Hudson (Ohio) Tennis, Cleveland, Springfield Golf & Country, The Six Napoleons of Balt., The Red Circle of Washington, Sherlock Holmes Soc. London. Author: Radio Frequency Interference Handbook, 1971; Electromagnetic Compatibility Manual, 1972; EMC Handbook, Vol. 6, 1975. Office: 6706 Deland Dr Springfield VA 22152

HILL, JOHN LUCIUS, ins. co. exec.; b. Terrell County, Ga., Aug. 5, 1921; s. Eli G. and Leila (Matthews) H.; LL.B., U. Ga., 1947; m. Sue Tyler, Mar. 27, 1946; children—Patricia Hill Atwood, R. Tyler, Judy Hill Ankrom. With Hartford Ins. Group (Conn.), 1947—, regional claim mgr., 1964-72, dir., 1972-73, sec., 1974-77, v.p., 1980—. Served with USAAF, 1942-45. Decorated Silver Star, D.F.C. Republican. Baptist. Office: Hartford Ins Group Hartford Plaza Hartford CT 06115

HILL, JOHN ROBERT (BOB), seed co. exec.; b. Enid, Okla., Feb. 15, 1941; s. L. Clifton and Mary Jane (Arnold) H.; B.A., U. Okla., 1963, student U. Okla. Law Sch., 1963-64. Stockbroker, Paine, Webber, Jackson and Curtis, San Francisco, 1965-74; pres. Great Am. Seed Co., Hennessey, Okla., 1974—. Vice pres., bd. dirs. Ballet Okla.; trustee Okla. Mus. Art; com. mem. Phaythopen Charity Soc., 1980. Mem. Am. Seed Trade Assn., Western Seedsmen Assn., Okla. Seed Trade, Beta Theta Pi. Republican. Clubs: Univ., Guardsmen (San Francisco). Home: 1408 Kenilworth Rd Oklahoma City OK 73120 Office: Great Am Seed Co Inc PO Box 725 Hennessey OK 73742

HILL, LLOYD RHEA, ins. co. exec.; b. Memphis, July 25, 1940; s. Thomas Bruce and Pauline (Michie) H.; B.A. in Polit. Sci., Miss. State U., 1962; m. Trudy Cress, Sept. 18, 1976; children—Thomas Alton, Paul Jackson, Margaret Rhea. Public relations dir. Athens (Ala.) Coll., 1963-64, The Birmingham (Ala.) News, 1964-66, Operation New Birmingham, 1966-68; dir. public relations Office of Vice Pres. U.S., Washington, 1968-69; v.p. Statesman- Vulcan Life Ins. Co., Des Moines, 1969—. Bd. dirs. Birmingham Mayor's Council for Youth Opportunities, 1967-68; mem. Urbandale (Iowa) Park and Recreation Commn., 1979—. Democrat. Roman Catholic. Home: 8317 Twana Dr Urbandale IA 50322 Office: 1400 Des Moines Bldg Des Moines IA 50309

HILL, MOZELLE CARLOCK (MRS. HOUSTON ERNEST HILL), gift shop owner, civic worker; b. Oklahoma City, Sept. 11, 1922; d. William Cummings and Laura Mec (Russell) Carlock; student Sullins Coll., 1940-42; B.S., U. Okla., 1944; m. Houston Ernest Hill, Feb. 23, 1947; children—Marilyn, William Franklin, Houston Ernest. Owner, buyer Red Fox, Ltd., splty. gift shop, Oklahoma City, 1963—, now pres. Area chmn. United Fund, Oklahoma City, 1955-58; active membership drives various orgns. including Art Center, 1958-61, Symphony, 1958-61, YWCA, 1958-61; pres. Edgemere Sch. PTA, 1958-59; admission counselor Sullins Coll., 1966-72; rep. Ozark Boys Camp, 1959-68. Mem. Opti-Mrs. (charter pres. 1947), Chi Omega. Democrat, Methodist. Club: Oklahoma City Golf and Country. Home: 1405 Kenilworth Rd Oklahoma City OK 73120 Office: 6433 Avondale Dr Oklahoma City OK 73116

HILL, NATHANIEL MAURICE, JR., mgmt. cons.; b. Kinston, N.C., May 30, 1923; s. Nathaniel M. and Hattie W. (Copeland) H.; B.S. with distinction, U.S. Naval Acad., 1945; m. Mary Lou M. Phillips, Oct. 6, 1962; children—Richard, Christina, Randall, Michael, Katherine, Sara. Commd. ensign U.S. Navy, 1945, advanced through grades to lt.; various assignments on submarines and cruisers, 1945-53; flag lt. U.S. Naval Base, N.Y.C., 1948-51, planning officer, 1950-51, res., 1953; sales engr. Elliott Co., N.Y.C., 1954-56; asst. to chief exec. officer Ohio Injector Co., N.Y.C. and Wadsworth, Ohio, 1956-59; pres. Nathaniel Hill & Assos. Inc., Raleigh, N.C., 1960—, mgmt. cons., 1960—; guest lectr. U. N.C., Chapel Hill and Raleigh. Mem. Inst. of Mgmt. Consultants (founding mem.), Am. Arbitration Assn. (regional bd.), Assn. Mgmt. Consultants (pres. 1979—). Republican. Episcopalian. Clubs: Sphinx, Capital City, Army-Navy, Carolina Country. Home: 2935 Rue Sans Famille Raleigh NC 27607 Office: 4513 Creedmoor Rd Raleigh NC 27612

HILL, RAYMOND JOSEPH, agribus. exec.; b. Chanute, Kans., May 4, 1935; s. Raymond Joseph and Emma Leona (Arthurs) H.; Asso. in Engring., Coffeyville (Kans.) Coll., 1955; M.B.A., U. Denver, 1977; m. Bettie Anne Handshumaker, Mar. 2, 1957; children—David, Dianne, Todd, Scott, Jennifer. Field engr. Phillips Petroleum Co., Bartlesville, Okla., 1957-59; design engr. Thiokol Chem. Corp., Brigham City, Utah, 1959-60; tech. supr. Hercules Chem. Corp., Salt Lake City, 1960-68; project mgr. aerospace div. Ball Corp., Boulder, Colo., 1968-70, plant mgr. and v.p. mfg. metal container div., Findlay, Ohio and Denver, Colo., 1970-78, pres. agrl. systems div., Westminster, Colo., 1978—; dir. Navaho Agrl. Products Industries, United Energy Devel.; mem. policy adv. com. to Office of U.S. Trade Rep., 1980—. Mem. Am. Ordnance Assn., Soc. Tool Engrs., Irrigation Assn. Republican. Episcopalian. Club: Rotary. Home: 2575 Briarwood Boulder CO 80303 Office: 9300 W 108th Circle Westminster CO 80020

HILL, RICHARD DEVEREUX, banker; b. Salem, Mass., Nov. 6, 1919; s. Robert W. and Grace (Dennis) H.; A.B., Dartmouth Coll., 1941; M.C.S., Amos Tuck Sch. Adminstrn. and Finance, 1942; postgrad. Rutgers U. Stonier Grad. Sch. Banking, 1951; LL.D., Babson Coll., Northeastern U.; m. Polly Bergstedt, Sept. 13, 1947; children—Steven D., Johanna Hill Simpson, Richard Devereux. With First Nat. Bank of Boston, 1946—, loan officer, 1948-51, asst. v.p., 1951-55, v.p., 1955-65, exec. v.p., 1965-66, pres., 1966-71, chmn. bd., chief exec., 1971—, also dir.; pres., dir. First Nat. Boston Corp., 1970-71, chmn. bd., chief exec. officer, 1971—; dir. Polaroid Corp., John Hancock Mut. Life Ins. Co., Raytheon Co., New Eng. Tel. & Tel. Co., Boston Edison Co., Fed. Res. Bank Boston, 1978-80. Former chmn. transp. com. New Eng. Council; mem. vis. com. Sloan Sch. Mgmt., M.I.T., 1967-70; mem. Greater Boston adv. bd. Salvation Army; trustee Dartmouth Coll., Boston Urban Found.; overseer Crotched Mountain Found.; former chmn. Bus. Council for Internat. Understanding; vice-chmn. adv. council Japan-U.S. Econ. Relations; mem. corp. Northeastern U. Served to lt. comdr. USNR, 1942-46; PTO. Mem. Internat. Monetary Conf. (dir.), Transp. Assn. Am. (dir., past chmn. investor panel), Assn. Res. City Bankers (past pres.), Am. Inst. Banking (adv. com. Boston chpt.), Dartmouth Alumni Assn. Boston (past v.p.), New Eng. Exeter Alumni Assn. (past pres.), Sigma Nu. Republican. Congregationalist. Mason. Clubs: Algonquin, Commercial, Somerset (Boston); Eastern Yacht (Marblehead); Federal; Economic (N.Y.C.). Home: Sargent Rd Marblehead MA 01945 Office: 100 Federal St Boston MA 02110

HILL, RICHARD FRANK, data processing systems co. exec.; b. Raleigh, N.C., Feb. 8, 1940; s. Richard Frank and Virginia (Ashe) H.; B.S. in Mech. Engring., N.C. State U., 1963; M.S. in Computer Sci., U. Mo., 1971; m. Kathleen Masson, June 3, 1961; children—Christine Marie, Julie Ann, Richard Brian, Dorothy Lynne. Mech. engr. Carolina Power & Light Co., 1963; asst. prof. U. Mo., 1968-71; pres. Hilltop Enterprises, Inc., West Palm Beach, Fla., 1974—. Served with U.S. Army; Vietnam. Decorated Bronze Star with oak leaf cluster, Meritorious Service medal, Joint Service Commendation medal, Army Commendation medal; registered profl. engr., Tex. Mem. Nat. Assn. Home Builders, Home Builders and Contractors Assn. Palm Beach County, Better Bus. Bur. Address: 2636 Forest Hill Blvd West Palm Beach FL 33406

HILL, ROBERT LYNDON, retail chain exec.; b. Houston, Feb. 2, 1930; s. Robert Addington and Manice (Massengale) H.; B.A., Rice U., 1952, M.S.M.E., 1953; M.B.A., Harvard U., 1958; m. Sara Louise Matzner, Aug. 9, 1969; children—Thomas Lyndon, Sara Catharine. Operations research engr. Gen. Dynamics, San Diego, Calif., 1958-63; exec. v.p. Topaz, Inc., San Diego, Calif., 1963-73, now dir.; exec. v.p. Mission Bay Investments, San Diego, 1973-78, pres., 1978—; dir. Organ Exchange, Inc. Served with USNR, 1953-55. Mem. Nat. Assn. Music Mchts., Pres.'s Round Table of San Diego, (exec. com.). Republican. Episcopalian. Home: 1832 Viking Way La Jolla CA 92037 Office: 3636 Camino del Rio Norte San Diego CA 92108

HILL, THOMAS CLARKE, VIII, editor, publisher, cons.; b. Broken Bow, Okla., Mar. 16, 1920; s. James Clifford and Lessie Katherine (Graham) H.; Mech. Engr., U. Okla., 1939; postgrad. Purdue U., 1956-57, So. Meth. U., 1959-60, La. State U., 1963-64; m. Arlene Mae Wertz, Jan. 7, 1967; children—Thomas Clark IX. Owner, Hill Oil Co., Long Beach, Calif., 1946-49; sales mgr. Custom Chem. Co., Redondo Beach, Calif., 1948-52; v.p. Am. Ins. Digest, Deerfield, Ill., 1952-55, editor, publisher, 1955—, pres., 1956—; editor, publisher Ins. Guardian, Deerfield, 1956—; chmn., chief exec. officer Guardian Advisors Corp., Deerfield, 1956—, Hilson Fin. Corp., Rocklin, Calif., Hilson Mgmt. Corp., Rocklin. Dir. ops. United Nat. Life, 1st United Nat. Corp., Springfield, Ill., 1973-76. Chmn. revenue com. Village of Lincolnshire, Ill., fin. dir., treas., 1975-76. Served with USNR, 1942-46: ETO, PTO. Named Man of Year by United Nat. Life, 1973; ambassador State Ariz. Mem. Internat. Platform Assn., Am. Life Underwriters. Mason (32 deg., Shriner); mem. Order Eastern Star. Clubs: Century, 250, Executives, Presidents, Millionaires, Gaslight. Author: The Case for New Life Insurance Companies, 1969; Life Insurance as an Investment, 1970. Contbr. articles to profl. jours. and encys. Home: 64 Berkshire Ln Lincolnshire Sq Lincolnshire IL 60015 Office: 8670 Fair Oaks Blvd Carmichael CA 95608

HILL, THOMAS JOHNATHAN, nuclear research co. exec.; b. Seattle, Jan. 6, 1944; s. Jack Everett and Janet Madeline (Williamson) H.; A.A., Skagit Valley Coll., 1964; B.S. in M.E., Wash. State U., 1967; m. Claire Ann Middel, Aug. 26, 1967; children—Michelle Leigh, Nicole Marie. Engr., Phillips Petroleum Co., Idaho Falls, Idaho, 1967-68; sr. engr. Idaho Nuclear Co., Idaho Falls, 1968-71; engring. supr. Aerojet Nuclear Co., Idaho Falls, 1971-76; mgr. fast breeder reactor programs EG & G Idaho Inc., Idaho Falls, 1976—. Registered profl. engr., Idaho. Mem. ASME, Nat. Soc. Profl. Engrs., Am. Nuclear Soc. Home: 929 12th St Idaho Falls ID 83401 Office: PO Box 1625 Idaho Falls ID 83415

HILL, THOMAS STEWART, mfg. co. exec.; b. Wilmington, Del., Jan. 6, 1936; s. Abraham F. and Mary S. Hill; B.S., U.S. Air Force Acad., 1961; M.B.A., Syracuse U., 1977; m. Elizabeth A. Sitterson, July 8, 1961; children—Douglas A., Stephen M., Thomas F., Bethany J. Sales engr. Pratt & Whitney Aircraft Co., 1965-66; sales engr. Cutler-Hammer, Inc., Hartford, Conn., 1966-74, sales mgr., Syracuse, N.Y., 1975-77, mktg. mgr. Constrn. Apparatus div., Bethlehem, Pa., 1977-79; v.p. sales and mktg. Pillar Corp., West Allis, Wis., 1979-80, v.p., gen. mgr. Melting Systems div., 1980—. Mem. Coventry (Conn.) Bd. Edn., 1970-74; asst. coach high sch. baseball Armijo High Sch., Fairfield, Calif., 1962. Served to capt., USAF, 1961-65. Named Outstanding Sales Engr., Cutler-Hammer Inc., 1970-74. Mem. Assn. M.B.A. Execs., Am. Foundry Soc., Forging Inst. Am., IEEE. Recipient numerous photog. awards. Home: 1385 Hickory Hill Ln Brookfield WI 53005

HILL, W. CLAYTON, mgmt. cons.; b. New Hampton, Mo., Sept. 24, 1916; s. Charles A. and Elva E. (Riggins) H.; B.S. in Bus. Adminstrn., U. Mo., 1937; m. Dorothy L. Crosby, Aug. 24, 1938; children—Charles W., Douglas L. Acct., Gen. Elec. Co., Bridgeport, Conn., 1937-41; sales mgmt. IBM Corp., 1941-50; asst. to pres. Gen. Elec. X-Ray Corp., Milw., 1950-53; v.p. Hotpoint Co. div. Gen. Elec. Co., Chgo., 1953-57; cons., mgr. planning Gen. Elec. Co., N.Y.C., 1957-62; dir. planning Am. Can Co., 1962-64; mgmt. cons. C. Hill Assos., Greenwich, Conn., 1964-80, Prairie Village, Kans., 1980—; instr. Marquette U.; cons. RCA Corp., Sperry Co., Ford Motor Co., Pet, Inc., Gen. Elec. Co., Monsanto Co., others. Rep. Greenwich Rep. Town Meeting; pres. King Merritt Community, Inc.; bd. dirs. Presbyterian Ch., Greenwich. Served with Signal Corps, AUS, 1943-46. Decorated Army Commendation Medal. Mem. Am. Mktg. Assn., Nat. Assn. Accts., Sales Exec. Club N.Y.C. Office: 8713 Catalina Dr Prairie Village KS 66207

HILL, WALTER DONALD, symphony adminstr.; b. Wellington, N.Z., Sept. 26, 1928; s. Walter Ewart and Grace Florence (Penney) H.; B.S. in Phys. Scis., Stanford U., 1950; M.B.A., Harvard U., 1955; m. Geraldine Jamiolkowski, June 7, 1954; children—Eliot Walter, Theodore Gerald, Alexis Donna. Corp. controller GenRad, Inc., Concord, Mass., 1955-77; dir. bus. affairs Boston Symphony Orch., 1977—. Chmn. bd. dirs. Music Serving the Elderly, Inc., Newton, Mass.; treas., bd. dirs., founder Am. Spiritual Healing Assn., Boston; treas. Union Ch., Waban, Mass. Served with Intelligence Corps, U.S. Army, 1951-52. Fellow Planning Execs. Inst. (nat. pres. 1977-78, Neil Denen award 1979); mem. Fin. Dirs., Am. Symphony Orch. League (chmn. fin. dirs.). Author articles on planning and budgeting. Office: Symphony Hall Boston MA 02115

HILL, WARREN JAMES, mfg. co. ofcl.; b. Valparaiso, Ind., Nov. 29, 1936; s. Clarence Orville and Vera Leona (Powell) H.; B.A., Northwestern U., 1964; m. Joyce Edna Woerthwein, Aug. 26, 1956; children—Scott, Todd, Kristin. Acct., Gulf Oil, Hinsdale, Ill., 1956-65; buyer Beeline Fashions, Bensenville, Ill., 1965-67; customer relations mgr. Bagcraft Corp., Chgo., 1967-76; customer relations specialist Universal Packaging Corp. div. Kraft Co., Bow, N.H., 1976—. Mem. Greater Concord (N.H.) Planning Council. Served with U.S. Army, 1956. Mem. Nat. Flexible Packaging Assn., Nat. Assn. Sales Service Mgrs. Republican. Clubs: Lions, Elks. Home: 20 Ridgewood Dr Bow NH 03301 Office: PO Box 918 Concord NH 03301

HILLABRANDT, LARRY LEE, chem. co. exec.; b. Amsterdam, N.Y., Apr. 5, 1947; s. Ronald Edward and Marion Alice (Smith) H.; B.S., Purdue U., 1969, M.S., 1971; m. Beverly Ann Johnson, Jan. 25, 1969; 1 son, Larry Lee. With Mobil Chem. Co., various locations, 1971—, fin. analyst, Jacksonville, Ill., 1973, sr. systems analyst Macedon, N.Y., 1973-74, fin. analyst, 1974, plant controller, Frankfort, Ill., 1974-77, distbn. supt. NE region, Macedon, 1979-80, plant mgr., Belleville, Ont., Can., 1980—. Mem. Purdue Alumni Assn., Krannert Grad. Sch. Alumni Assn., Quinte Dist. Supts. Assn., Zeta Psi Alumni Assn. Clubs: Monroe Golf, Bay of Quinte Country. Home: Rural Route 1 Corbyville ON Canada Office: Mobil-Chem Can Ltd 321 University Ave Belleville ON Canada

HILLBRATH, ARTHUR SPEIR, JR., aluminum and steel culvert co. exec.; b. West Palm Beach, Fla., Aug. 10, 1938; s. Arthur Speir and Helen Francis (Clement) H.; student Palm Beach Jr. Coll., 1958-59; m. Jo Ellen K. Upshaw, Nov. 23, 1980; children—Douglas, Whitney. Estimator Belvedere Constrn. Co., West Palm Beach, Fla., 1961-62; salesman Fla. Steel Corp., Tampa, 1963-64; with Gator Culvert Co., Lantana, Fla., 1965—, pres., 1967—, chmn. bd., 1970—; dir. 1st Am. Bank, North Palm Beach, Fla.; hydraulic gate cons. Gee & Jensen, Walt Disney World East Project, 1968. Mem. Econ. Council of Palm Beach County, Palm Beach Jr. Coll. Found., 1981—. Served with AUS, 1956. Mem. Corrugated Steel Pipe Assn., Better Bus. Bur., Associated Gen. Contractors, Assn. Fla. Engring. Soc. Republican. Clubs: Mayacoo Lakes Country, West Palm Beach Yacht and Country. Home: 17 Spanish River Dr Ocean Ridge FL 33435 Office: PO Box 3318 Lantana FL 33462

HILLE, STANLEY JAMES, coll. dean; b. New London, Minn., Mar. 19, 1937; s. Sigunl Munson and Jennie (Stromme) H.; B.B.A. with distinction, U. Minn., 1959, M.B.A., 1962, Ph.D., 1966; m. Gail Anne Bekowies, Sept. 12, 1964; children—Erik, Peter, Kirsten, Julia. Instr., U. Minn., 1962-65; asst. prof. to prof., chmn. transp., bus. and public policy Coll. Bus. and Mgmt., U. Md., College Park, 1965-74; Chair prof. transp. U. Ala., 1974-78; dean Coll. Bus. Adminstrn., Kent (Ohio) State U., 1978—; cons. U.S. Govt., states of Ala., Tenn. and Md., also pvt. bus. Bd. dirs. Tuscaloosa (Ala.) Tranit Authority Gt. No. Roadway Found. fellow, 1974; Norfolk & Western fellow, 1967. Mem. Am. Soc. Traffic and Transp., C. of C., Delta Nu Alpha (Man of Yr. 1978), Beta Gamma Sigma, Delta Sigma Pi. Contbr. articles to profl. jours. Office: Kent State U Kent OH 44242

HILLENMEYER, HENRY REILING, JR., restaurant co. exec.; b. Temple, Tex., Nov. 13, 1943; s. Henry Reiling and Lucy Carolyn (Taylor) H.; B.A. in Econs., Yale U., 1965; m. Sallie Long Sigler, Oct. 30, 1976; children—Henry Reiling, Edward Ferriday, Taylor Jennings, Morgan Andrew. Trainee, Kanawha Valley Bank, Charleston, W.Va., 1965-67, asst. sec., 1967-68; v.p. CBM, Inc., Cleve., 1968-70, pres., 1970-72, chmn., dir., 1972-74; pres., dir. Ireland's Restaurants, Inc., Nashville, 1974-78; exec. v.p. Womco, Inc., Nashville, 1979—; dir. So. Hospitality Corp., Nashville, Big D Ovens, Inc., Nashville, Hall's Food, Inc., Nashville, So. Fisheries, Inc., Nashville. bd. dirs. Try Angle House, 1979—. Mem. Tenn. Bot. Gardens. Republican. Episcopalian. Clubs: Belle Meade Country, Cumberland, Exchange. Home: 4214 Sneed Rd Nashville TN 37215 Office: 1717 West End Ave Nashville TN 37202

HILLER, EDWARD LOUIS, pharmacist, retail drug exec.; b. Victoria, Tex., May 3, 1931; s. Leonard G. and Julia P. (Fossati) H.; B.S. in Pharmacy, U. Tex., 1953; m. Thoralee Griffin, June 23, 1957; children—Catherine, Patricia, Michael, Terrance, Angela. Staff pharmacist Hardine & Parker Drug Stores, Victoria, 1957-60; pres., chief exec. officer Pharmlease, Inc., Victoria, 1960-72; v.p. MediSave Pharmacy, Victoria, 1972-75; pres. Medi-Save Pharmacies, Inc., Baton Rouge, 1976—. Mem. City Council, Victoria, 1969-71; pres. St. Patrick Parish Council, 1978. Served with USN, 1953-57; Korea. Mem. Am. Soc. Cons. Pharmacists, La. Pharmacy Assn., Tex. Pharmacy Assn. Roman Catholic. Club: Serra (pres. 1970-71). Home: 12403 Lake LaBelle Baton Rouge LA 70816 Office: PO Box 1631 Baton Rouge LA 70821

HILLER, FREDERICK THEODORE, transp. exec.; b. Charleroi, Pa., Oct. 2, 1916; s. Frederick and Tillie (Schmieler) H.; asso. degrees metallurgy and engring. Pa. State U.; m. Wilma Voelker, Oct. 15, 1939; children—Frederick Richard, Barbara Louise. Self employed Food Distbn., Southwestern Pa., 1938-42; metallurgist U.S. Steel, McKeesport, Pa., 1942-45; owner Motor Freight Agy., Pitts., 1945-51; pres. Pitts. & New Eng. Trucking Co., Dravosburg, Pa., 1952—, chmn. bd., 1978—; pres. Hiller Trading Corp., 1954—; owner Hiller Horst Farms, 1950—, Freddy's Restaurant, 1956—; owner, pres. Hiller Pub. Co., 1941—. Chmn. bd. dirs. Pitts. & New Eng. Pension Trust Fund, 1955—; mem. adv. bd. Union Nat. Bank, 1972—. Mem. Pa. Motor Truck Assn. (past pres. Allegheny County, life dir., state pres. 1973, chmn. bd. 1974-76), Am. Trucking Assn. (Pa. v.p. 1974), Am. Turners, Traffic and Transp. Assn. Pitts., Heavy Specialized Carriers Conf. of Am. Trucking Assns. (pres. 1968-69, chmn. bd. 1970, life dir.), Laurel Mountain Traffic Assn., N.Y. Athletic Assn. Lutheran. Mason (32 deg., Shriner). Author: Definite Youth, 1941; Joe Hoak Goes to Hell, 1947; Payload Weight System, 1953; A Trip to Mecca, 1967; Project 70, 1969; The Shrine, 1977. Producer 6 successful long play records, centennial music Syria Temple, 1977. Home: 1528 California Ave McKeesport PA 15131 Office: 211 Washington Ave Dravosburg PA 15034

HILLER, STANLEY, JR., tool co. exec.; b. San Francisco, Nov. 15, 1924; s. Stanley and Opal (Perkins) H.; student U. Calif., 1943; m. Carolyn Balsdon, May 25, 1946; children—Jeffrey, Stephen. Dir. Helicopter div. Kaiser Cargo, Inc., Berkeley, Calif., 1944-45; organized Hiller Aircraft Corp. (formerly United Helicopters, Inc.), Palo Alto, Calif., 1945, pres. and gen. mgr., pres., 1950-64 (co. bought by Fairchild Stratos 1964), became pres. of five operating divs.; resigned as exec. v.p., dir., mem. exec. com. Fairchild Hiller Corp., 1965; chmn. bd., chief exec. officer Reed Tool Co., Houston; chmn. bd., chmn. exec. com. Beking Corp.; chmn. bd. Baker Internat. Corp., 1975; partner Hiller Investment Co.; dir. Lucky Stores, Inc., Pacific Concrete & Rock Co., Ltd., Boeing Co., Crocker Nat. Corp., ELTRA

Corp. Recipient Fawcett award, 1944; Distinguished Service award Nat. Def. Transp. Soc., 1958; named 1 of 10 Outstanding Young Men U.S., 1952. Hon. fellow Am. Helicopter Soc.; mem. AIAA, Am. Soc. Pioneers, Phi Kappa Sigma. Office: 3000 Sand Hill Rd Menlo Park CA 94025*

HILLER, WALTER FREDERICK, business exec.; b. Pitts., Oct. 18, 1933; s. Jesse Anderson and Virginia (McMinn) H.; B.S. in Bus. Adminstrn., Maryville Coll., Tenn., 1955; M.B.A., Emory U., 1956; m. Martha Campbell Dickson, June 28, 1963; children—John Frederick, Scott Anderson. Job analyst RCA Service Co., Cape Canaveral, Fla., 1959-62, adminstr. orgn. devel. tng., Thule, Greenland, 1963-64; personnel asst. Miami Herald Pub. Co. (Fla.), 1964-67; div. personnel mgr. Howard Johnsons, Miami, 1968-72, mgr. corporate employment and tng., Boston, 1972-78; v.p. human resources Sands & Co., Inc., Atlanta, 1978—; seminar leader transactional analysis Boston chpt. Adminstrv. Mgmt. Soc., 1974. Served with Security Agy., U.S. Army, 1957-58. Accredited personnel diplomate in tng. and devel. Mem. Council Hotel Restaurant Trainers (pres. 1977), Personnel Assn. Greater Miami (pres. 1970). Contbr. articles in field to profl. jours. Home: 4333 Revere Circle NE Marietta GA 30062

HILLIARD, JOE ALEXANDER, agrl. co. exec.; b. Lee County, Fla., Jan. 7, 1911; s. William Henry and Carline Margie (Morgan) H.; student public schs., Ft. Myers, Fla.; m. Wilmuth Gabrial Yarbrough, Oct. 20, 1937; 1 son, Joe Marlin. Rancher, farmer, Clewiston, Fla., 1930—; pres. Hilliard Bros. of Fla., Inc., Clewiston, 1973—. Mem. Clewiston C. of C. Republican. Clubs: Clewiston Country, Elks. Home: 524 Osceola Ave Clewiston FL 33440 Office: Hilliard Bros of Fla Inc Hwy 27 Clewiston FL 33440

HILLIARD, ROBERT JOHN, bakery co. exec.; b. Chgo., Nov. 10, 1924; s. Robert John and Agnes (Kelleher) H.; B.S., Northwestern U., 1948, J.D., 1951; postgrad. advanced mgmt. Harvard, 1959; m. 2d, Rita Marie Uchison; children—Janet, Joann, Robert, Richard. Admitted to Ill. bar, U.S. Supreme Ct. bar, 1979; with Am. Bakeries Co., Chgo., 1953—, dir. indsl. relations, 1961-63, v.p. indsl. relations, 1963-68, pres., 1968-70, sr. v.p. indsl. relations, 1970—, dir., 1966—; dir. Gray & Co., Pilgrim Farms, Monarch Egg Co., Westnut Corp., Langendorf United Bakeries, A-Media, Am. Bakeries Domincana. Sec. Wheat and Wheat Foods Found. Trustee Bakery and Confectionery Union and Industry Internat. Pension Fund, Retail, Wholesale and Dept. Store Union Industry Pension Fund; vice chmn. bd. dirs. Am. Inst. Baking; trustee St. Joseph's Hosp. Served with AUS, 1943-46. Decorated Combat Infantryman's Badge. Mem. Am. Bakers Assn. (gov.), Am., Ill. Chgo. bar assns. Home: 19W186 Old Tavern Rd E Oakbrook IL 60521 Office: 10 S Riverside Plaza Chicago IL 60606

HILLIER, FLORENCE BELL, florist shop exec.; b. Hamilton, Ont., Can., Jan. 2, 1916; d. William Wynship and Ethel Gertrude (Stevens) Bell, came to U.S., 1940, naturalized, 1945; B.A. in Modern Langs., U. Toronto, 1937; m. James Hillier, Oct. 24, 1936; children—James Robert, William Wynship. Owner, mgr. The Flower Basket, Princeton, N.J., 1943—; owner The Flower Basket II, Princeton, 1973—; owner, mgr. Applegate Floral Shop, Princeton, 1975—; lectr. in field. Area chmn. Cancer Dr., Princeton, 1958. Mem. Florist Telegraph Delivery Assn., Princeton Art Assn., Garden State Watercolor Assn. Clubs: Princeton Present Day, Women's Investment Princeton. Author: Basic Guide to Flower Arranging, 1974. Home: 22 Arreton Rd Princeton NJ 08540 Office: 110 Nassau St Princeton NJ 08540

HILLIER, J(AMES) ROBERT, architect; b. Toronto, Ont., Can., July 24, 1937; s. James and Florence (Bell) H.; B.A., Princeton U., 1959, M.F.A., 1961; m. Susan Baldwin Smith, June 17, 1961; children—Kimberly, James Baldwin. Project designer J. Labatut, Architect, Princeton, N.J., 1961-62; project mgr. Fulmer & Bowers, Princeton, 1961-66; prin. J. Robert Hillier, Architects/Planners, Princeton, 1966-72; pres. The Hillier Group, Architects, Princeton, 1972—; dir. First Nat. Bank Princeton. Recipient numerous design awards. Fellow AIA (treas. N.J. chpt. 1972-73, chpt. v.p. 1974); mem. Nat. Council Archtl. Registration Bds. Clubs: Princeton Quadrangle, Nassau. Maj. works include Bryant Coll. campus, Smithfield, R.I., Butler Hosp., Providence, Rutgers U. Athletic Center, Piscataway, N.J., N.J. State Justice Complex, Trenton. Home: 87 Ridgeview Circle Princeton NJ 08540 Office: 791 Alexander Rd Princeton NJ 08540

HILLIS, RANDOLPH DALES, mfrs. agent; b. Hobart, N.Y., Jan. 31, 1907; s. Frederick Wager and Lydia (Dales) H.; ed. U. Ill., 1930; m. Virginia Pearl Rankin, Nov. 25, 1932. With load bldg. sales Asso. Gas & Electric, 1928-32; sta. mgr. Mobile Oil, 1932-35; div. sales Am. Seating Co., 1935-39; final assembly mechanic Brewster Aircraft-Bell Aircraft, 1939-41; exptl. technician Curtiss Wright, Columbus, Ohio, 1942-45; record systems Diebold Inc., 1945-47; vending sales NEHI Corp., Columbus, Ga., 1949-55; prodn. engr. div. Sperry Rand, Cobleskill, N.Y., 1957-61; pres. Tinkertown, Inc., Hobart, N.Y., 1966—; chmn. engring. adv. com. N.Y. State U., Delhi, 1968-78. Mem. Bldg. Industries Employees, Gen. Bldg. Contractors, Constrn. Specifications Inst., Am. Def. Preparedness Assn. Episcopalian. Clubs: Elks, Masons, Shriners. Home: W Main St Hobart NY 13788 Office: 1743 Western Ave Albany NY 12203

HILLMAN, ARTHUR DOUGLAS, educator; b. Rockford, Ill., Sept. 16, 1943; s. Arthur Rupert and Elsie Diane (Peterson) H.; A.B., Augustana Coll., 1965; M.S. in Bus. Adminstrn., U. Denver, 1967; Ph.D., U. Mo., Columbia, 1970; m. SueAnn Alice Newton, Aug. 26, 1967. Staff acct. Arthur Andersen & Co., Chgo., 1966-67; asst. prof. acctg. Drake U., Des Moines, 1970-73, asso. prof. acctg., 1973-80, prof. acctg., 1980—, dir. grad. studies in bus., 1973-76; cons. small bus. acctg. systems. Arthur Andersen & Co. Found. dissertation fellow, 1969-70. Mem. Midwest Acctg. Assn., Am. Acctg. Assn. (vice chmn. sect.), Nat. Assn. Accountants, Delta Sigma Pi, Beta Gamma Sigma, Omicron Delta Kappa, Beta Alpha Psi. Clubs: Porsche Am., Central Iowa Sailing Assn., Acanthus Lodge, Masons, Rotary of W. Des Moines (dir. 1977-79, pres. 1979-80). Contbr. articles to profl. publs. Home: 2316 Woodland St West Des Moines IA 50265 Office: Drake University Des Moines IA 50311

HILLMAN, DONALD EARL, engring. constrn. co. exec.; b. Sioux City, Iowa, Feb. 23, 1928; s. John Walter and Ione Ellen (Boggess) H.; student Golden Gate U., 1971-76; m. Lei Lani Gené Shepp, Sept. 12, 1959; children—John Walter, Darci Ann, Lance Randall. Safety engr. Bechtel Corp., Joppa, Ill., 1953-54, safety engr. Pacific Bechtel, Korea, 1954-55, materials supr., Sumatra, 1957-59, purchasing agt. concrete structures, Sioux City, Iowa, 1959-60; purchasing agt. G. W. Galloway Co., Baldwin Park, Calif., 1961; purchasing mgr. Arabian Bechtel Corp., Libya, 1962-67, field procurement mgr. Bechtel Corp., San Francisco, 1968-70, mgr. procurement Internat. Bechtel Inc., S. Africa, 1971, field procurement mgr. Bechtel Overseas Corp., London, 1972-73, mgr. equipment and tools Bechtel Corp., San Francisco, 1974-76, v.p. Internat. Bechtel Inc., mgr. Eastern Equipment Operations, Kuwait, 1977-78. Bd. dirs. Am. Sch., Benghazi, Libya, 1964-66. Served with AUS, 1947-48. Republican. Home and Office: care Internat Bechtel Inc PO Box 20271 Manama Bahrain

HILLMAN, STANLEY ERIC GORDON, corp. exec.; b. London, Eng., Oct. 13, 1911; s. Percy Thomas and Margaret Eleanor Fanny (Lee) H.; ed. Holyrood Sch., also Tonbridge Sch., Eng.; m. May Irene Noon, May 2, 1947; children—Susan, Deborah, Katherine. Came U.S., 1951, naturalized, 1957. With Brit.-Am. Tobacco Co., Ltd., London and Shanghai, 1933-47; dir. Hillman & Co., Ltd., Cosmos Trading Co., FED Inc., U.S.A., Airmotive Supplies Co. Ltd., Hong Kong, 1947-52; v.p. Gen. Dynamics Corp., 1953-61; v.p., group exec. Am. Machine & Foundry Co., 1962-65; v.p., dir. Gen. Am. Transp. Corp., Chgo., 1965-68; exec. v.p. IC Industries, Chgo., 1968-71, pres., 1971-77, vice chmn., 1977-78, also dir., ret., 1978; chmn., chief exec. Ill. Central Gulf R.R., 1976-78; trustee Chgo., Milw., St. Paul & Pacific R.R., 1978-79; dir. Stone Container Corp., Bell & Howell, Avco Corp., Cooper Industries, SFN Cos Inc., Bandag Inc., Bliss Laughlin Industries, Consol. Rail Corp.; trustee Gen. Growth Properties. Mem. Air Force Assn., Navy League, Am. Ordnance Assn., Assn. U.S. Army, Soc. Automotive Engrs. Clubs: Chicago, Mid Am. (Chgo.); Onwentsia (Lake Forest); Royal Poinciana (Naples, Fla.). Home: 1001 Hawthorne Pl Lake Forest IL 60045

HILLMAN, WILLIAM CHERNICK, lawyer; b. Providence, Oct. 15, 1935; s. Harold Samuel and Anne (Chernick) H.; student U. Chgo., 1951-54; J.D. cum laude, Boston U., 1957, LL.M., 1968; m. Edith M. Boren, June 22, 1958; children—Harold Samuel II, Daniel Charles Alexander. Admitted to R.I. bar, 1957; since practiced in Providence and Pawtucket, R.I., also Tel Aviv, Israel; mem. firm Strauss, Factor, Chernick, Hillman, P.C., 1957—; probate judge, Barrington, R.I., 1974—. Commr. on Uniform State Laws, 1969—; mem. disciplinary bd. R.I. Supreme Ct., 1975-80. Mem. Com. on Appropriations, Barrington, R.I., 1963-68; capt. Judge Adv. Gen. Corps, U.S. Army Res., 1958-65. Mem. Internat. (sec. com. on creditors rights 1972-76, vice chmn. 1976—), Am. (antitrust sec. 1958—), R.I., (chmn. antitrust com. 1967-70, chmn. corp. com. 1979—) bar assns. Mason. Clubs: Chester (N.S., Can.) Yacht, Turks Head. Contbr. articles to profl. jours. Home: 54 Rumstick Rd Barrington RI 02806 Office: Dolphin House 403 S Main St Providence RI 02903

HILLS, GEORGE BURKHART, JR., business exec.; b. Jacksonville, Fla., July 17, 1925; s. George Burkhart and Anna Donna (McEnerny) H.; B. Mech. Engring., Ga. Inst. Tech., 1946; B. Indsl. Engring., U. Fla., 1947, M.S. in Engring., 1949; grad. Advanced Mgmt. Program, Harvard, 1972; m. Sarah Anne Davis, Sept. 6, 1947; children—George Burkhart III, Barrett Davis, Sarah Kathryn, Margaret Anne, Harland Andrew. With St. Joe Paper Co., Port St. Joe, Fla., 1949-50, MacMillan Bloedel Ltd., Vancouver, B.C., Can., 1950-61, Stone Container Corp., Chgo., 1961-64, The Continental Group, Inc., N.Y.C., 1964-73; pres., chief exec. officer MacMillan Bloedel (USA) Inc., 1974-77; sr. v.p. Stone Container Corp., Chgo., 1977—. Mem. nat. adv. bd. Ga. Inst. Tech.; mem. bus. adv. council Roosevelt U. Served to lt. (j.g.), USNR, 1943-46. Mem. TAPPI, Am. Paper Inst., Newcomen Soc. N.Am., Phi Delta Theta, Tau Beta Pi, Phi Kappa Phi. Republican. Episcopalian. Club: Exmoor Country (Highland Park, Ill.). Home: 289 E Foster Pl Lake Forest IL 60045 Office: 360 N Michigan Ave Chicago IL 60601

HILLS, LEE, newspaperman; b. Granville, N.D., May 28, 1906; s. Lewis Amos and Lulu Mae (Loomis) H.; student Brigham Young U., 1924-25, U. Mo., 1927-29; LL.B., Oklahoma City U., 1934; Sc.D. in Bus. Adminstrn., Cleary Coll., 1958; L.H.D. (hon.), U. Utah, 1969; LL.D., Eastern Mich. U., 1969; m. Leona Haas, Dec. 25, 1933 (dec.); 1 son, Ronald Lee; m. 2d, Eileen Whitman, June 4, 1948 (dec. 1961); m. 3d, Tina S. Ramos, Oct. 31, 1963. News reporter News-Adv., Price, Utah, 1924-25, editor, 1926; reporter Oklahoma City Times, 1929-32; reporter Okla. News, 1932-35, editor, 1938-39; reporter Cleve. Press, 1935-36, news editor, 1940-42; asso. editor Indpls. Times, 1936-37; asso. editor Memphis Press-Scimitar, 1939-40; mng. editor Miami (Fla.) Herald, 1942-51, exec. editor, 1951-66, asso. pub., 1966-69, pub., 1970-79, editorial chmn., 1979—; exec. editor Detroit Free Press, 1951-69; leave as war corr., Europe, 1945; pub. Detroit Free Press, 1963-79, pres., 1967-73, editorial chmn., 1979—; exec. editor Knight Newspapers, Inc., 1959-66, exec. v.p., 1966-67, pres., 1967-73, chmn. exec. com., 1969-73, chmn. ops. com., 1973-74; chmn. bd., chief exec. officer, Knight-Ridder Newspapers, Inc., 1973-76, editorial chmn., chmn. bd., 1976-79, editorial chmn., 1979—. Admitted to Okla. bar, 1935. Pres., Detroit Arts Commn., 1966-79; trustee Founders Soc., Detroit Inst. Arts. Recipient Maria Moors Cabot Gold medal for distinguished contbn. inter-Am. relations, Columbia, 1946; Pulitzer prize in journalism, 1956. Mem. Internat. Press Inst., Inter-Am. (dir., pres. 1967-68), Mich. press assns., Am. Soc. Newspaper Editors (pres. 1962-63), Am. Newspaper Pubs. Assn., AP Mng. Editors Assn. (past pres.), Fla. AP Assn. (past pres.), United Found. (dir.), Sigma Delta Chi (past pres.). Clubs: National Press; Washington Press; Rennaissance, Detroit, Grosse Pointe (Detroit); Bath (Miami, Fla.); Bankers. Home: 4450 Banyan Lane Miami FL 33137 Office: 1 Herald Plaza Miami Herald Miami FL 33101 also Detroit Free Press 321 W Lafayette Blvd Detroit MI 48231

HILLYER, CRAIG ALLEN, savs. and loan exec.; b. Hendricks, Minn., Dec. 13, 1937; s. Clifford L. and Beatrice R. (Macknikowski) H.; B.S. in Fin., U. Notre Dame, 1959; M.B.A., U. Ariz., 1964; m. Barbara A. Lasiewicz, Aug. 18, 1968; children—Mark C., Audrey A. Exec. v.p. Brookings Internat. Life Ins. Co. (S.D.), 1959-69; analyst Bankers Life & Casualty Co., Chgo., 1969-71; v.p. Montgomery Ward Life Ins. Co., Chgo., 1971-76; pres. DGP, Inc., Brookings, 1976—, dir., 1971—; pres. Home Trust Savs. & Loan Assn., Vermillion, S.D., 1979—, dir., 1978—. Pres., Brookings United Fund, 1965-67. Served to 1st lt., Transp. Corps, AUS, 1962-63. Mem. Am. Contract Bridge League (dir.). Roman Catholic. Clubs: Rotary, Elks (treas. 1967-69), K.C. Office: 700 22d Ave S Brookings SD 57006

HILLYER, IRA B., bus. exec.; b. New London, Conn., July 19, 1932; s. Ira A. and Amy A. (Bartholomy) H.; student U. Md., 1950-52; m. Patricia Baldwin, Feb. 14, 1953; children—David, Michael, Mary, Margaret, Kathryn, Stephen, Joseph, Martha, Dennis, Paula, Ira C., Amy, Anne, Nathaniel, John. Bookkeeper, teller, mortgage officer Savs. Bank, New London, 1952-62; gen. mgr., treas., dir. Submarine Base Credit Union, Inc. (now Community Service Credit Union, Inc.), 1962—; cons. in field. Mem. Credit Union Execs. Soc., Nat. Credit Union Mgmt. Soc., New London County Homebuilders Assn. Republican. Roman Catholic. Clubs: N. Stonington Lions, Holy Name Soc., Navy League. Office: 24 Sailfish Dr Groton CT 06340

HILSINGER, ARTHUR RALPH, JR., eyeglass mfg. co. exec.; b. Orange, N.J., Oct. 8, 1927; s. Arthur Ralph and Alice (McCrea) H.; B.A., Princeton U., 1950; M.B.A., Harvard U., 1952; m. Emmy Lou Davis, Oct. 10, 1953; children—Alice Antonia, Madelyn Metz, Jeanne Louise. Brand mgr. Scott Paper Co., 1952-56; pres. Hilsinger Corp., Plainville, Mass., 1956—; dir. Ourfee Attleboro Bank. Bd. dirs. Better Vision Inst.; trustee, Charles River Sch., 1965-70, Beaver Country Day Sch., 1970-75. Served with U.S. Army, 1946-47. Mem. Optical Mfrs. Assn. (dir.), Asso. Industries Mass. (dir., chmn. bd.), Young Presidents Orgn., Mass. Bus. Roundtable (dir.), Chief Execs. Forum. Club: Dedham (Mass.) Country and Polo. Home: One Common St Dedham MA 02026 Office: The Hilsinger Corp Plainville MA 02762

HILTON, BARRON, hotel exec.; b. 1927; s. Conrad Hilton. Founder, pres. San Diego Chargers, Am. Football League, until 1966; v.p., Hilton Hotels Corp., 1954, pres., chief exec. officer, 1966—, chmn., 1979—, also dir.; mem. gen. adminstrv. bd. Mfrs. Hanover Trust Co., N.Y.C. Address: 9880 Wilshire Blvd Beverly Hills CA 90210*

HILTZHEIMER, CHARLES IRVINE, transp. co. exec.; b. Pulaski, Va., Sept. 17, 1927; s. Charles I. and Mary Senter Hiltzheimer; B.A. in Bus., U. Richmond (Va.), 1950; m. Kathleen Linnea Brandt, Mar. 17, 1973; children—Charles, Sally, John. Asst. personnel mgr. Hercules Powder Co., Radford, Va., 1950-52; mgr. Atlanta dist. Roadway Express Co., Akron, Ohio, 1952-62; with Sealand Services, Inc., 1964—, pres., Menlo Park, N.J., 1975—, chmn. bd., chief exec. officer, 1978—. Trustee Nyack (N.Y.) Coll. Served with USNR, World War II. Named Maritime Man of Yr., Puget Sound Press Assn., Seattle, 1969. Mem. Nat. Def. Transp. Assn. (life) Navy League U.S. (life), Nat. Maritime Council (gov.), Internat. Council Containership Operators, Intercristo (dir.), Newark C. of C. (dir.). Republican. Club: World Trade (San Francisco). Office: PO Box 900 Edison NJ 08814*

HIMELSTEIN, SAUL, communications co. exec.; b. Wülfratshausen, W. Ger., Dec. 1, 1948; came to U.S., 1950, naturalized, 1955; s. Samuel and Ida (Evdokimova) H.; B.S., Lynchburg (Va.) Coll., 1969; M.B.A., U. Va., 1971; m. Joyce Engert. Br. mgr. Avco Fin. Services, Inc., Englewood, N.J., 1969-71; with warehouse ops. dept. Western Electric Co., Inc., Union, N.J., 1970-74; owner Radio Shack store, Short Hills, N.J., 1974-77; cons. J. Limerick & Assos., Atlanta, 1977-78; gen. mgr. Ohio Mobile Telephone, Inc., Columbus, 1978—; dir. Spectrum Group, Inc.; cons. AT&T Systems Group; sponsor Vocat. Indsl. Clubs Am.; adv. N.J. Public Utilities Commn., 1974-76. Served with USAR, 1969-75. Recipient Pres.'s Health and Safety award, 1974, Tandy Achievement award, 1976. Mem. Columbus C. of C., Nat. Assn. Bus. and Ednl. Radio, IEEE, U.S. Golf Assn. Club: Kiwanis. Office: 2899 E Dublin-Granville Rd Columbus OH 43229

HIMES, BILLY LEE, food co. exec.; b. Arkansas City, Kans., Dec. 11, 1930; s. Robert Henry and Ethel Mae (Forshner) H.; student Arkansas City Jr. Coll., 1948-50; B.S. in Chem. Engring., Kans. State U., 1958, M.S., 1960; m. Frances Eva Bender, June 29, 1957; children—Joyce Ann, Billy Lee, Robert Louis, John Wesley. Ops. analyst, ops. research office Johns Hopkins U., Bethesda, Md., 1960-62; mem. tech. staff Research Analysis Corp., McLean, Va., 1962-64; project scientist Booz-Allen Applied Research, Inc., Kansas City, Mo., 1964-65, research dir., 1965-66, research dir., dir. combined arms research office, 1966-67, v.p., mng. officer combined arms research office and inst. for combined arms and support research office, 1967-71; mgr. analytical services Pillsbury Co., Mpls., 1971-74, dir. mktg. research ops., 1974; dir. info services Interstate Brands Corp., Kansas City, Mo., 1975-80, v.p., mgr. info. systems, 1980—. Served with U.S. Army, 1951-54. Recipient Current Affairs award, Time mag., 1948. Mem. Assn. Internal Mgmt. Cons.'s, DAV, Assn. U.S. Army, Sigma Tau, Phi Lambda Upsilon, Phi Kappa Phi, Phi Rho Pi. Contbr. articles to profl. jours. Home: 7947 Webster Ave Kansas City KS 66109 Office: Interstate Brands Corp 12 E Armour Blvd Kansas City MO 64111

HIMES, ROBERT LYNN, candy sales co. exec.; b. Portsmouth, Ohio, Mar. 26, 1945; s. Lowell Rexton and Marylin Louise (King) H.; student Franklin U., Columbus, Ohio, 1963-64; m. Joan Marie Cumberledge, June 21, 1965; children—Scott Michle, Sandy Lynn. Buyer, Gold Circle Stores, Worthington, Ohio, 1968-73; pres. R.L. Himes & Assos., Inc., Columbus, 1973—, Marcus Sales, Inc., 1978—. Mem. Columbus Housewares Club (pres. 1978). Republican. Methodist. Club: Masons. Home: 4245 Maynard Rd Delaware OH 43015 Office: 380 W Olentangy St Powell OH 43065

HIMONAS, JILL, cosmetics co. exec.; b. N.Y.C., July 20, 1944; d. Louis Harold and Isobel (Silleg) Saxon; B.A. in Speech and English Lit., Hunter Coll., 1966; m. James Himonas, Jr., May 9, 1969. Sales rep. to dir. dept. store promotions Lanvin-Charles of the Ritz, 1966-69; brand mgr. Prince Matchabelli div. Chesebrough-Ponds, 1970-71; with Max Factor & Co., Los Angeles, 1972—, v.p., dir. mktg., 1975—; speaker bus. colls. and mgmt. seminars; mem. faculty Town Hall Exec. Seminar Series. Bd. councillors Coll. Continuing Edn., U. So. Calif., also adv. bd. Continuing Edn. for Women. Club: Flintridge Riding. Office: Max Factor & Co 1655 N McCadden Pl Hollywood CA 90028

HIMOTO, TERUO, finance co. exec.; b. Wahiawa, Oahu, Hawaii, Apr. 15, 1923; s. Seizo and Kana (Shigenobu) H.; student Mid-Pacific Inst., 1941; B.A., U. Hawaii, 1950; M.B.A., Northwestern U., 1951; m. Florence Takeko Kametani, Oct. 17, 1952; children—Michael K., Garth K., Grant S. With Hawaiian Pineapple Co., Wahiawa, 1943-47; v.p., controller Am. Savs. & Loan Assn., Honolulu, 1951-67; fin. exec. v.p., dir. Servco Pacific, Inc., Honolulu, 1967-73; exec. v.p., dir. Service Finance Ltd. (now Servo Fin. Corp.), 1967-73; pres., dir. Comml. Finance, Ltd., 1973—; pres., dir. Hawaiiana Advt. Agy., 1969-73, Obun Hawaii, 1970-73; exec. v.p., dir. Rainbow Pacific Travel & Tours, Inc., 1970-73; v.p., dir. Am. Ins. Agy., Inc., 1971-73; tchr. accounting U. Hawaii, 1952-53. Bd. dirs. Kuakini Med. Center, 1964—, treas., 1968-70, v.p., 1971-72; vice chmn., 1972-74, chmn., 1974-76; bd. dirs., treas. Kuakini Research Found., 1965-73. Served with Hawaii Territorial Guard, 1941-42, Hawaii N.G., 1947-50. Recipient Man of Year award Mid-Pacific Inst. Alumni Assn., 1965. Mem. Honolulu (past v.p.), Japanese (past pres.) chambers commerce, Soc. Savs. and Loan Controllers (past pres. Hawaii chpt.), Kalihi Bus. Assn. (past 1st v.p.), Hawaii World Trade Assn. (pres. 1976-77), Hawaii Consumer Finance Assn. (pres. 1977), Hawaii Econ. Study Club (pres. 1976), Mid-Pacific (past pres.), U. Hawaii, Northwestern U. alumni assns., Flora Pacifica (past dir.). Home: 307 Anonia St Honolulu HI 96821 Office: 7 S King St Honolulu HI 96817

HINCKLEY, JOHN, bldg. materials co. exec.; b. Lynn, Mass., Nov. 7, 1922; s. F. Howard and Eunice (Marsh) H.; student Yale U., 1944; m. Bette Ashworth, Oct. 22, 1945; children—Susan, Janice, John David. With John Hinckley & Son Co., Hyannis, Mass., 1946—, pres., 1956—; dir. Barnstable County Nat. Bank. Bd. dirs. Better Bus. Bur., Cape Cod, 1979—; trustee Barnstable County Hosp., 1977—. Served with USMC, 1942-46. Rotary-Paul Harris fellow, 1976. Mem. Mass. Retail Lumbermans Assn. (pres. 1957-58), N.E. Lumbermans Assn. (pres. 1971-72), Nat. Lumbermans Assn. (dir. 1970-74). Episcopalian. Clubs: Rotary, Commiquid Golf, Fraternal Lodge. Home: 83 Kevency Ln Yarmouthport MA 02675 Office: 49 Yarmouth Rd Hyannis MA 02601

HINCKLEY, WALTER JOSEPH, state ofcl.; b. N.Y.C., Apr. 16, 1937; s. George J. and Gertrude V. (McGuire) H.; student Pace U., 1956-60; m. Patricia A. McSherry, Feb. 8, 1964; children—Siobhan Marie, Christopher, Jonathan McSherry, Timothy McGuire. Dir. adminstrn. N.Y.C. Manpower and Career Devel. Agy., 1965-68; insp. gen. N.Y.C. EPA, 1968-70, 1st dep. commr., 1974-75; dep. commr.

N.Y.C. Dept. Consumer Affairs, 1970-71; asst. to mayor, N.Y.C., 1971-73; dep. commr. N.Y.C. Dept. Health, 1973-74; pres., dir. N.Y. State Environ. Facilities Corp., Albany, 1975—; asst. clin. prof. dept. preventive medicine N.Y. Med. Coll., N.Y.C., 1975-78; adj. profl. Lehman Coll., City U. N.Y., 1973-74; mem. N.Y. State Conf. Health Officers and Drug ofcls., 1972-74. Mem. Gov.'s Task Force on Resource Recovery, N.Y. State, 1976-77; Democratic State Committeeman, N.Y., 1964-66; bd. dirs. Environ. Action Coalition, 1977-78. Served with U.S. Army, 1955-57. Recipient Citizen of the Year award N.Y. State Soc. Profl. Engrs., 1977. Mem. Council Pollution Control Financing Agys. (sec. 1978), N.Y.C. Civil Service Ret. Employees Assn. (nat. adv. com. 1970-78). Roman Catholic. Home: 2122 Rosendale Rd Schenectady NY 12309 Office: 50 Wolf Rd Albany NY 12205

HINDS, LINTON BURNHAM, constrn. co. exec.; b. Aberdeen, S.D., Jan. 18, 1930; s. Verne Merle and Vera Louise (Bickel) H.; student No. State Coll., 1950; m. Patricia Ann Berg, June 21, 1952; children—Nancy Lee, William Frederick, Linette Merle, Susan Marie, Mary Alice. Asst. mgr. lumber supply bus., 1952-58; mgr., corporate mem. steel bldg. constrn. co., 1958-66; partner Steel Structures of Aberdeen, 1966—; v.p., dir. Riverview Indsl. Properties, Inc., Aberdeen Fed. Savs. and Loan; pres. Aberdeen Builders Exchange, 1963—, BlueSky, Inc. Chmn., City Planning Commn., 1964; dir. Greater S.D. Devel. Agency, 1978-80. Served with USNR, 1950-52. Recipient C. of C. award, 1963, Jaycees Distinguished Service award, 1964. Mem. Greater S.D. C. of C. (pres. 1968, dir. 1977—), Am. Legion, Flying Farmers. Republican. Lutheran (pres. congregation 1966). Clubs: Masons, Shriners, Elks, Moccassin Creek Country (pres. 1978-79). Home: Prairiewood Village 4136 Greenwood Ln Aberdeen SD 57401 Office: 6 N Dakota St Aberdeen SD 57401

HINDS, RICHARD ELY, utility co. ofcl.; b. Balt., June 29, 1936; s. James Lewis and Lois (Carswell) H.; student Balt. Poly. Inst., 1951-54, Johns Hopkins U., 1954-58; m. Joan Louise Gascoyne, Aug. 24, 1956; children—Margaret, Robert, Nancy, Frederick, Paul. Jr. engr. Potomac Electric Power Co., Washington, 1958-59, asst. engr., 1962-66, asso. engr., 1966-68, project mgr. ins. and loss prevention, 1968-69, mgr. ins. dept., 1969-73; risk mgr. Fla. Power & Light Co., Miami, 1973—; mem. underwriting com. AEGIS Ltd.; chmn. policy forms com. and ins. adv. com. Nuclear Mut. Ltd.; mem. ins. adv. com. and mem. exec. com. Nuclear Electric Ins. Ltd. Active troop com., various positions S. Fla. council Boy Scouts Am. Served to 2d lt. U.S. Army, 1959-62; served to capt. USAR, 1962-68. Mem. Edison Electric Inst. (chmn. 1981; chmn. fire and allied lines ins. subcom. 1977-79, chmn. boiler and machinery ins. subcom. 1973-77, chmn. policy forms subcom. of liability ins. working group 1977), Risk and Ins. Mgmt. Soc. (pres. Fla. chpt. 1978-79, nat. rep. Fla. chpt., dir., 1979-81), Soc. Fire Protection Engrs. (mem. grade 1971—), Nat. Fire Protection Assn. Republican. Presbyterian. Office: PO Box 529100 Miami FL 33152

HINES, ANDREW HAMPTON, JR., utilities exec.; b. Lake City, Fla., Jan. 28, 1923; s. Andrew Hampton and Louise Dixie (Howland) H.; B.S. in Mech. Engring., U. Fla., 1947; m. Margaret Ann Groover, June 28, 1947; children—Andrew Hampton, III, Irene Elizabeth, John Bradford, Daniel Howland. Engr., Gen. Electric Co., Schenectady, 1947-51; asst. prodn. engr., pres., chief exec. officer Fla. Power Corp., St. Petersburg, 1951—, also dir.; chmn. bd., dir. Landmark Union Trust Bank. Trustee, chmn. Nat. Electric Reliability Council; trustee Rollins Coll., Eckerd Coll.; bd. dirs. U. Fla. Found., Fla. Council of 100. Served to 2d lt. USAAF, 1944-45; ETO, maj. Res. ret. Decorated Air medal; recipient Distinguished Alumnus award U. Fla., 1973, Service to Mankind award Sertoma Club, 1971. Registered profl. engr., Fla. Fellow ASME (past chmn. Fla. sect.); mem. Southeastern Electric Exchange (1st v.p., dir.), Phi Kappa Phi, Beta Gamma Sigma, Sigma Tau, Tau Beta Pi. Methodist. Clubs: St. Petersburg Yacht, Lakewood Country (St. Petersburg); Citrus (Orlando). Office: PO Box 14042 Saint Petersburg FL 33733

HINES, HAROLD H., JR., ins. co. exec.; b. Chgo., Nov. 21, 1924; s. Harold H. and Babette (Schnadig) H.; B.A., Yale, 1948; m. Mary Pick, Jan. 23, 1954; children—William H., Anne, David F. Pres., dir. Ryan Ins. Group, Chgo.; dir. Sears Bank & Trust Co.; lectr. profl. ins. groups, assns., 1957—. Bd. dirs. North Shore Country Day Sch., Great Books Found., Adler Planetarium, Local Initiative Support Council; vis. com. Harvard Med. Sch.; trustee Michael Reese Hosp. and Med. Center, Research and Edn. Trust, Newberry Library. Served with U.S. Army, 1943-46. Mem. Am. Soc. Property and Casualty Underwriters, Chgo. Assn. Commerce and Industry (dir.), Assn. Am. Med. Colls. (chmn. nat. citizens council), Chgo. Council on Fgn. Relations (dir.), Pres.'s Council Nat. Coll. of Edn., U. Chgo. Council for Biol. Scis. Clubs: Chicago (exec. com.), Commercial, Standard, Mid-Am., Metropolitan (mem. bd. govs. Chgo.); Lake Shore Country (Glencoe, Ill.). Contbr. articles to ins. jours. Office: 222 N Dearborn St Chicago IL 60601

HINES, JAMES HERMAN, former banker; b. Jackson, Miss., Sept. 18, 1914; s. Hulon Hunter and Ava (Odom) H.; student Jackson Sch. Law, 1935-36, Sch. Banking of South, La. State U., 1950-53; grad. Advanced Mgmt. Program, Harvard Bus. Sch., 1966; LL.D., Millsaps Coll., 1979; m. Martha P. Hamilton, Dec. 25, 1942; children—Martha Hamilton Botts, Linda Hines White, Julie Hines Ditmore. With Deposit Guaranty Nat. Bank, Jackson, 1936—, pres., 1973-74, chmn. bd., chief exec. officer, 1975-79, hon. chmn., 1980—; chmn. bd., chief exec. officer Deposit Guaranty Corp., 1975-79, hon. chmn., 1980—; dir. Mchts. & Planters Bank, Tchula, Miss., Mississippi Valley Title Ins. Co. Founding mem. St. James Episcopal Ch., Jackson, treas. Episc. Diocese, 1954-74; chmn. Miss. Heart Fund, 1980-81; bd. dirs. Miss. affiliate Am. Heart Assn.; treas. bd. trustees Millsaps Coll., 1975—, chmn. devel. council of centennial devel. fund; 1979-81, bd. dirs., mem. exec. com. Miss. Ballet Internat.; pres., bd. dirs. Miss. Higher Edn. Assistance Corp.; chmn., trustee Piney Woods Country Life Sch.; bd. dirs. Jackson State U. Found., YMCA Jackson, Met. YMCA, Miss. Found. Ind. Colls.; mem. adv. bd. St. Dominic Meml. Hosp.; Miss. corp. disaster chmn. ARC; mem. men's com. Miss. U. for Women Found. Served from pvt. to maj. U.S. Army, 1941-46. Mem. Mid-Continent Oil and Gas Assn. (dir.), Newcomen Soc. N.Am. Office: PO Box 1200 Jackson MS 39205

HINES, WILLIAM WALTER, mfg. co. exec.; b. Detroit, Aug. 22, 1935; s. William and Esther Adel (Hines) Fidora; B.S., Calif. Western U., 1976, M.B.A., 1977, Ph.D., 1979; children—Edith Lynne, Mark Andrew, Richard Andrew. Parts analyst Ford Motor Co., Dearborn, Mich., 1972-75; chief tech. writer Eaton Leonard Corp., Santa Ana, Calif., 1976-77; buyer Lockheed Aircraft, Ontario, Calif., 1977—, adv. on handicapped employment, 1977—. Mem. Calif. Gov.'s Com. for Employment of Handicapped, 1979—; attendee Pres.'s Com. for Employment of Handicapped, 1978, 79, 80. Served with USAF, 1954-58. Recipient Gov.'s Trophy, State of Calif., 1979. Mem. Nat. Mgmt. Assn. Republican. Club: Lockheed Mgmt. Contbr. articles to profl. jours. Home: 3830 Valle Vista Dr Chino CA 91710 Office: PO Box 33 Ontario CA 91761

HINKLE, ALLEN OSCAR, JR., oil co. exec.; b. Lockhart, Tex., Aug. 22, 1919; s. Allen Oscar and Rena Kate (Hearne) H.; B.B.A., U. Tex., 1941; postgrad. Northwestern U., Chgo., 1943, Harvard, 1945; m. Margaret Mae Langham, Apr. 12, 1941; children—Margaret Ann Hinkle Cox, Mary Linda (Mrs. C. Joseph Cain), Joan Ellen (Mrs. David M. McClendon). Auditor, State Tex., 1941-42; with Humble Oil & Refining Co. (name now changed to Exxon Co.), Houston, 1946—, gen. auditor, 1959-73, asst. controller, 1974-77, gen. auditor, 1977—, accounting faculty adviser N.Tex. U., 1969-72. Mem. Pres. Council, Houston Bapt. U., 1968-73; active YMCA. Precinct committeeman, del. Democratic party, Harris County, Tex., 1950-52. Served with USNR, 1943-46. Named Distinguished Alumni, U. Tex. Coll. Bus., 1969. C.P.A., Tex. Mem. Am. Inst. C.P.A.'s, Inst. Internal Auditors (mem. research com. 1960-74), Am. Petroleum Inst., Fin. Execs. Inst., Tex. Soc. C.P.A.'s (dir. Houston chpt. 1952-55), Tex. Mid-Continent Oil and Gas Assn., Houston C. of C. Baptist (deacon 1957-74), Beta Alpha Psi. Club: Petroleum, Racquet (Houston); Lakeway Yacht and Country (Austin, Tex.). Home: 439 Brown Saddle Rd Houston TX 77057 Office: 4031 Exxon Bldg Houston TX 77002

HINKLE, DONALD DEAN, acct., fin. cons.; b. Dayton, Ohio, Nov. 29, 1938; s. Herman Earl and Grace Beatrice (Fouts) H.; B.S. (Chrysler Found. scholar), Marquette U., 1967; m. Jacquelyn Mary Vaccaro, June 23, 1962; children—Sheila, Donna. Sr. acct. Price Waterhouse & Co., Milw., 1967-71; v.p. Robert W. Baird & Co., Milw., 1971-78; sr. v.p. Heritage Bank of Milw., 1978-79; partner Ziegert, Smaler, Kaminski & Freyberg, 1979—; mem. advisory bd. Wis. Security Commn., 1974-78, Midwest Stock Exchange Securities Trust Co., 1976-78; chmn. Milw. Bus. Showcase, 1978. Asst. treas. United Performing Arts Fund, 1978—; sect. vol. United Way campaign, 1975-77; treas., dir. Squires Grove Mgmt. Assn. and Water Trust, 1979-81. Mem. Am., Wis. insts. C.P.A.'s, Nat. Assn. Accountants (chpt. v.p. 1976-80, pres. 1981), Beta Gamma Sigma, Beta Alpha Psi. Republican. Clubs: Westmoor Country, Grove (treas. 1980); Kiwanis. Home: 1140 Terrace Dr Elm Grove WI 53122 Office: 200 Bishops Way Suite 200 Brookfield WI 53005

HINMAN, WAYNE ARTHUR, mfg. co. exec.; b. Elizabeth, N.J., Aug. 16, 1946; s. Judson Lester and Elizabeth Francis (Datesman) H.; student Union Coll., Cranford, N.J., 1964-66; B.S. in Math., Belknap Coll., 1968; postgrad. N.C. State U., 1968-69; M.B.A., Va. Inst. Tech., 1974; m. Barbara Ann Bromm, Nov. 1, 1969; children—David T., Stephen A., Mathew S. Grad. teaching asst. N.C. State U., 1968-69; grad. research asst. Va. Inst. Tech., 1973-74; with Air Products & Chems. Co., Allentown, Pa., 1974—, fin. analyst, 1976, mgr. ops. acctg., 1976-78, div. controller, 1978—. Mem. exec. com., mem. council Nativity Luth. Ch., 1978—, chmn. fin. com., chmn. bldg. fund, 1979—. Served to capt. USAF, 1969-73. Mem. Beta Gamma Sigma, Phi Kappa Phi. Republican. Office: Air Products & Chems Co PO Box 538 Allentown PA 18101

HINSHAW, ERNEST THEODORE, JR., investment co. exec.; b. San Rafael, Calif., Aug. 26, 1928; s. Ernest Theodore and Ina (Johnson) H.; A.B., Stanford, 1951, M.B.A., 1957; m. Nell Marie Schildmeyer, June 24, 1952; children—Marc Christopher, Lisa Anne, Jennifer, Amy Lynn. Staff asst. to pres. Capital Research and Mgmt. Co., Los Angeles, 1957-58, dir. planning, 1967-68, also dir.; fin. analyst Capital Research Co., Los Angeles, N.Y.C., 1958-68, v.p., 1962-71, mgr. NY office, 1962-66; dir., exec. v.p. Am. Funds Service Co., Los Angeles, 1968-69, pres., 1970-72, chmn., 1972—; dir., pres. Capital Data Systems, Inc., Los Angeles, 1971-73, chmn., 1973-79; v.p. The Capital Group, Inc., Los Angeles, 1973—; sr. v.p. Growth Fund Am., also Income Fund Am., 1973-74, pres., 1974-76, chmn., 1976—; guest faculty Northwestern U. Transp. Center, 1965-66. Mem. Los Angeles Olympic Organizing Com.; commr. yachting 1984 Olympic Games. Served from pvt. to 1st lt. USMCR, 1951-53. Mem. Soc. Airline Analysts (sec. 1965-66), Fin. Analysts Fedn. (chmn. air transport sub-com. 1966-67), Los Angeles Soc. Fin. Analysts, N.Y. Soc. Security Analysts, Am. Statis. Assn., Nat. Kite Class (pres. 1968-69), Lido 14 Internat. Class Assn. (pres. 1978-79), Assn. Orange Coast Yacht Clubs (commodore 1976), So. Calif. Yachting Assn. (commodore 1979), B.O.A.T., Inc. (dir. 1977—), Pacific Coast Yachting Assn. (dir. 1979-80), U.S. Yacht Racing Union (dir. 1980—), Town Hall of Los Angeles. Democrat. Clubs: Wall St. (N.Y.C.); Univ. (Los Angeles); Lido Isle Yacht (commodore 1973) (Newport Beach, Calif.). Home: 729 Via Lido Soud Newport Beach CA 92663 Office: 333 S Hope St Los Angeles CA 90071

HINSON, LEONARD FRANK, JR., mfg. co. exec.; b. East St. Louis, Ill., Aug. 28, 1948; s. Leonard Frank and Lindell H.; student Parks Air Coll., 1967-68, Washington U., St. Louis, evenings 1974-79; 1 dau., Genice Marie. Pres., owner St. Louis Fgn. Car Ltd., 1971-73; engring. mgr. Indsl. Engring. and Equipment Co., St. Louis, 1974-79; ops. mgr., corp. sec., prin. Nutherm Internat., Mt. Vernon, Ill., 1979—. Mem. Am. Mgmt. Assn., Am. Inst. Indsl. Engrs., Soc. Mfg. Engrs., ASHRAE, Mt. Vernon C. of C. Home: 505 Halia Crest Dr Mount Vernon IL 62864 Office: 501 S 11th St Mount Vernon IL 62864

HINTON, BRUCE VINCENT, constrn. co. exec.; b. New Orleans, Aug. 19, 1944; s. Lavoid and Caudia Nella (Powe) H.; B.S., So. U., Baton Rouge, La., 1967; postgrad. U. Md., 1978; m. Marilyn Farrow, July 31, 1944; children—Tressan Damon, Kelli. Contracts adminstr. G & E Contractos, Inc., Balt., 1973-76; bus. mgr. Robert Clay Inc., Balt., 1976; pres. Carob Contractors, Inc., Balt., 1976—; pres., owner Carob Suppliers, Balt., 1978—; v.p. Mar-Lin Investors, Balt., 1979—. Mem. Md. Minority Contractors Assn., NAACP, Balt. Jaycees. Democrat. African Methodist Episcopal. Club: Mason. Home: 3504 Lynne Haven Dr Baltimore MD 21207 Office: 4033 W Rogers Ave Suites 5 and 6 Baltimore MD 21215

HINTON, BYRON RICHARD, fin. and mgmt. cons.; b. Windsor, Ont., Can., Oct. 15, 1943; s. Byron Fredrick and Thelma H.; B. Eng., Royal Mil. Coll. Can., 1966; children from previous marriage—Jennifer, Todd. Engr., Environment Canada Co., Vancouver, B.C., 1970-74; prin. B.R. Hinton & Assos. Ltd., Environ. Cons., Vancouver, 1972-78; prin. Pilot Mgmt. Corp., Vancouver, 1978—; dir. Synervest Venture Capital Ltd., Victoria, Estate Plan Design Services, others. Served with RCAF 1962-69. Mem. Assn. Profl. Engrs. B.C. Home: 1103-1250 Comox St Vancouver BC V6E 1K8 Canada Office: 1104 Hornby St Vancouver BC V6Z 1V8 Canada

HINTZ, ROBERT LOUIS, holding co. exec.; b. Chgo., May 25, 1930; s. Louis A. and Gertrude V.(Herman) H.; B.S.B.A. magna cum laude, Northwestern U., 1960, M.B.A., 1965; m. Gloria May Safbom, Nov. 12, 1955; children—Cary, Leslie, David, Erin. With Chessie System, 1963—, v.p. corp. services, Cleve., 1974-76, v.p. fin., 1976-78, sr. v.p. fin., 1978—; sr. v.p. CSX Corp., 1980—; dir. Trailer Train Co., Chesapeake & Ohio Ry. Co., Balt. & Ohio R.R. Co., Western Md. R.R. Co., Seaboard Coastline R.R., Louisville & Nashville R.R., Aviation Enterprises. Trustee, Lake Ridge Acad., North Ridgeville, Ohio. Served with USAF, 1950-54; Korea, Japan. Mem. Am. Mgmt. Assn. (fin. council), Fin. Execs. Inst., Delta Mu Delta. Roman Catholic. Clubs: Lakewood Country (fin. com.); Commonwealth of Va. Home: 31038 Manchester Ln Bay Village OH 44140 Office: 3305 Terminal Power PO Box 6419 Cleveland OH 44101

HINZ, DOROTHY ELIZABETH, writer, editor, public relations exec.; b. N.Y.C., Nov. 26, 1926; d. Hans and Anna (Borell) H.; A.B., Hunter Coll., 1948; postgrad. Columbia U. Copy editor Colliers mag., 1948-53; asst. to dir. devel. Columbia U., N.Y.C., 1953-55; mng. editor Grace Log, econs. researcher-analyst, writer speeches, white papers, com. reports Latin Am. affairs, public relations dept. W.R. Grace & Co., N.Y.C., 1955-64; staff writer Oil Progress, fgn. news media, speeches, films, internat. petroleum ops., public relations dept. Caltex Petroleum Corp., N.Y.C., 1964-68; fin. editor Merrill Lynch, Pierce, Fenner & Smith, 1969-74; asst. sec., mgr. speakers bur., mgr. publs., research-writer, editor speeches and reports, corp. communications dept. Mfrs. Hanover Trust Co., N.Y.C., 1974—. Mem. Inter-Am. Round Table, Soc. Am. Med. Writers. Club: Overseas Press. Contbr. articles on multinat. corps., developing nations, trade and fin. to various publs. Home: 600 W 115th St New York NY 10025 Office: Mfrs Hanover Trust Co 350 Park Ave New York NY 10022

HIPP, LOUIS MAYNARD, III, fin. personnel cons.; b. Asheboro, N.C., July 17, 1949; s. Louis Maynard and Dorothy (Jobson) H.; student Duke U., 1967-69, U. Bridgeport, 1970; m. Tracy Chester, June 29, 1974. Personnel cons. Thomas F. Ryan, Inc., Boston, 1969-71; founder, prin. Hipp Waters, Inc., Greenwich, Conn., 1971—. Mem. Greenwich Career Edn. Com.; bd. dirs. Community Answers on Greenwich, 1980-81. Certified personnel cons. Mem. Nat. Assn. Personnel Cons. (chmn. pub. info. com. 1980; 1st v.p. Conn. chpt.), Conn. Assn. Personnel Cons.'s (pres. 1979-81), Ind. Temporary Services Assn. (N.E. regional v.p. 1978-80). Author: Getting Offers: The Guide to Better Interviewing, 1978; contbr. articles to profl. jours. Home: 61 Bluff Ave Rowayton CT 06853 Office: 64 Greenwich Ave Greenwich CT 06830

HIPP, WILLIAM HAYNE, ins. and broadcasting exec.; b. Greenville, S.C., Mar. 11, 1940; s. Francis Moffett and Mary Matilda (Looper) H.; B.A., Washington and Lee U., 1962; M.B.A., U. Pa., 1965; program for mgmt. devel. Harvard Bus. Sch., 1971; m. Anna Kate Reid, June 14, 1963; children—Mary Henigan, Francis Reid, Anna Hayne. With Met. Life Ins. Co., Calif., 1965-69; various positions Liberty Life Ins. Co., Greenville, 1969-79, chmn. bd., 1979—; chmn. exec. com., dir. United Fidelity Life Ins. Co., Dallas., 1979—; vice-chmn., chief exec. officer Liberty Corp., Greenville, 1979—; dir. Cosmos Broadcasting Co., Columbia, S.C., Greater Ariz. S & L Assos., Phoenix, S.C. Nat. Bank, Dan River, Inc., Textile Hall Corp. Trustee, vice-chmn. Nat. Urban League, 1976—; mem. S.C. Devel. Bd., 1980—; trustee Greenville County Found., 1978—; pres. Greenville YMCA, 1979; mem. Leadership S.C., 1979—. Mem. C.L.U. Assn., Am. Council Life Ins. (dir.). Home: One Bonaventure Dr Greenville SC 29615 Office: PO Box 789 Greenville SC 29602

HIRAOKA, WILLIAM TSUGIO, ins. exec.; b. Honolulu, Jan. 28, 1917; s. Kumaichi and Shimo (Sakai) H.; B.A. in Bus. and Econs., U. Hawaii, 1939; m. Ruth Toshiko Nakamoto, Oct. 17, 1946; children—John William, Nancy Ruth. Ins. officer U.S. VA, 1946-49; ins. agt., corp. sec., dir. N. Am. Ins. Agy., Ltd., 1949-53; sales mgr., v.p., exec. v.p., pres., dir. Nat. Mortgage & Fin. Co., Ltd. and Island Ins. Co., Ltd., Honolulu, 1953—; dir. Fed. Home Loan Bank of Seattle, 1979—; chmn., bd. dirs. Hawaii Ins. Rating Bur., 1979-80; bd. dirs. Hawaii Insurers Council. Pres., bd. dirs. Rehab. Hosp. of Pacific; mem. fin. com. Kuakini Med. Center; chmn. personnel appeals bd. Judiciary Dept. State of Hawaii; chmn. Hawaii Commn. for Jud. Qualification, 1970-77. Served to capt. U.S. Army, 1941-46, 50-52; lt. col. Res. ret. Recipient Army Commendation medal; C.P.C.U., Am. Inst. Property and Liability Ins. Mem. Soc. C.P.C.U.'s, Res. Officers Assn. U.S., Ret. Officers Assn. U.S. Democrat. Congregationalist. Clubs: Honolulu Lions, Plaza, Carps. Home: 3212 Woodlawn Dr Honolulu HI 96822 Office: PO Box 1520 1022 Bethel St Honolulu HI 96806

HIROSE, STANLEY KENJI, painting corp. exec.; b. Hilo, Hawaii, May 29, 1937; s. Kazuichi and Momoye H.; B.B.A., U. Hawaii, 1959; M.B.A., Northeastern U., 1963; m. Sharon Kimura, Oct. 22, 1966; 1 dau., Allison. Adminstrv. trainee to div. controller Amfac Inc., 1965-69; v.p., data tech. analyst Fujikawa Painting Co., Inc., Honolulu, 1970-73, controller, 1973-75, pres., 1975—. Served with AUS, 1963-65. Mem. Am. Mgmt. Assn. Club: Elks. Office: Fujikawa Painting Co Inc 2865 Ualena St Honolulu HI 96819

HIRSCH, CARL HERBERT, mfg. co. exec.; b. Pontiac, Mich., Aug. 24, 1934; s. Robert Reynolds and Charlotte (Zeiss) H.; B.S. in Mech. Engring., U. Mich., 1957; M.Indsl. Engring., U. Toledo, 1962, M.B.A., 1967; grad. Advanced Mgmt. Program, Harvard, 1974; m. Anne Louise Dearing, June 27, 1959; children—Jeffrey Todd, Gregory Scott. Product engr. Babcock & Wilcox Co., Barberton, Ohio, 1959-60; product engr. Dana Corp., Toledo, 1960-67, mfg. mgr. Perfect Circle div., 1967-69, pres. C.A. Danaven subs. Dana Corp., Valencia, Venezuela, 1969-72, v.p. Latin Am. Dana Internat. div., Toledo, 1972-73, v.p., gen. mgr. Spicer Clutch div., Ft. Wayne, Ind., 1973-75, Spicer Universal Joint div., Toledo, 1975-76, group v.p. Dana Corp., 1977-78, exec. v.p. vehicular, 1979-80, v.p. corp. planning, 1980—; instr. Earlham Coll., 1967-69, U. Toledo, 1962-65. Bd. dirs. Toledo Area council Boy Scouts Am., NW Ohio Jr. Achievement, Child Abuse Prevention Center, Toledo Zool. Soc. Served to lt. USN, 1957-59. Registered profl. engr., Mich. Mem. Nat. Mgmt. Assn., Sigma Alpha Epsilon. Presbyterian. Home: 4125 Nantucket Toledo OH 43623 Office: PO Box 1000 Toledo OH 43697

HIRSCH, EDWIN PAUL, lawyer, mfg. co. exec.; b. Phila., Oct. 8, 1923; B.S. in Econs., U. Pa., 1947, M.B.A., 1948; LL.B., U. Va., 1951; postgrad. Parker Sch. Fgn. & Comparative Law, Columbia U. m. Dorothy L. Newhook, Aug. 2, 1979; 1 dau., Sharon L. Gonzalez. Admitted to D.C. bar, 1951, Va. bar, 1951; with RCA Corp., Lancaster, Pa., 1952—, sr. counsel picture tube div., 1975-77, staff v.p., sr. counsel picture tube div., 1977—. Served with USAAF, 1943-46. Mem. Am. Bar Assn., Va. Bar Assn., D.C. Bar Assn., Phi Delta Phi. Asso. editor Va. Law Rev., 1951. Office: RCA New Holland Ave Lancaster PA 17604

HIRSCH, GERALD PAUL, investment mgmt. co. exec.; b. Bklyn., Apr. 30, 1938; s. Irving and Celia (Lifshitz) H.; B.S., Cornell U., 1959; D.D.S., U. Pa., 1963; registered options prin. Fleur-Wall Street Tng. Internat., 1976; m. Joyce Davis, Aug. 17, 1961; children—Kenneth, Callie, Gregory, Nancy. Partner, Hirsch-Napach-Storm-Yodowitz, West Haverstraw, N.Y., 1965-77; pres. Pine Assos., West Haverstraw, 1967—, Gerald P. Hirsch Realty (merger into Gerald P. Hirsch Assos. 1975), Suffern, N.Y., 1972—; registered options prin. Churchill Securities, Inc., 1977—; with fin. planning div. Gruntal & Co., N.Y.C., 1978—; partner HNH Precious Metals, 1980—, Nooks & Crannies, Inc.; pres., chmn. bd. Churchill Securities Inc.; pres. Gerald P. Hirsch Realty; dir. Peoples Nat. Bank of Rockland Co., I.G.S. Realty; asso. prof. N.J. Coll. Medicine and Dentistry, 1974—. Committeeman, Town of Ramapo, 1970; chmn. Ramapo Transp. Commn., 1972; pres. Reform Temple, Suffern, 1976; bd. dirs. Ramapo Indsl. Devel. Commn., 1973; chmn. Fusion Party, 1979-80. Served to capt. USAF, 1963-65. USPHS research grantee, 1961-62. Mem. ADA, Internat. Entrepreneurs Assn., Internat. Oceanographic Assn., Alpha Omega. Club: Cornell of Rockland County. Contbr. articles to dental jours.

Home: 29 Campbell Ave Suffern NY 10901 Office: 120 Route 59 Suffern NY 10901

HIRSCH, H. ROBERT, oil co. exec.; b. Sherman, Tex., Dec. 3, 1933; s. Rufus Adolph and Margerie (Cleve) H.; B.S.S., U. Tex., El Paso, 1956; m. Marjorie Smith, June 6, 1959; children—Robert Lesley, Eric Guion. With Mobil Oil Corp., 1956-76, planning asso., N.Y.C., 1968-69, div. exploration mgr., New Orleans, 1969-72, regional exploration mgr., Houston, 1972-75, corp. exploration mgr., N.Y.C., 1975-76, exploration mgr.-tech., 1976—; sr. v.p., dir. Superior Oil Co., Houston, 1976—; dir. Can. Superior Oil Ltd., Falconbridge Nickel Mines. Mem. Soc. Exploration Geophysicists. Republican. Presbyterian. Home: 16150 Parish Hall Spring TX 77373 Office: PO Box 1521 Houston TX 77001

HIRSCH, PHILIP GOODHART, mgmt. cons.; b. Chgo., Dec. 19, 1952; s. Richard Irwin and Nancy (Lesser) H.; A.B., U. Pa., 1975, B.S. in Fin., 1975; M.B.A., Northwestern U., 1976; m. Gail Lee Gibbons, May 10, 1980. Acct., Price Waterhouse & Co., Phoenix, 1976-78; v.p. fin. and adminstrn., corp. sec. Noble Multimedia Communications, Inc., Noble Broadcast Cons.'s, Inc., San Diego, 1978-80; pres. Philip G. Hirsch & Co., mgmt. and fin. cons. specializing in broadcasting, San Diego, 1980-81; v.p. fin. planning Channel Assos., Inc., Santa Barbara, Calif., 1981—. Active Jr. Achievement, United Way, Big Bros. Ariz.; mem. Maricopa County Sheriff's Commn. on White Collar Crime, 1976-77. Recipient cert. of achievement United Way, 1979, Headstart, 1971; C.P.A., Ariz. Mem. Am. Mgmt. Assn., Broadcast Fin. Mgmt. Assn., Am. Inst. C.P.A.'s, Nat. Assn. Accts. Clubs: Univ., San Diego Racquet and Tennis (San Diego). Home: 4592 Newport Ave San Diego CA 92107 Office: PO Box 5487 Santa Barbara CA 93108

HIRSCH, RALPH FRED, equipment mfg. co. exec.; b. Schwinfurt, Germany, May 13, 1931; s. Harry G. and Ruth N. (Hirsch) H.; came to U.S., 1939, naturalized, 1946; B.S. in Bus. Adminstrn., Northwestern U., 1958; m. Shirley A. Abrams, 1969; children—Paula, Steve, Vicki, Teri, Ron, David. Mem. sales mgmt. staff Sears Roebuck & Co., Chgo., 1953-58; dist. sales mgr. Glaser Crandell Co., Chgo., 1958-65; exec. nat. sales mgr. food div. DoAll Co., Des Plaines, Ill., 1965—; instr. Jr. Achievement program Sears, Roebuck & Co. Served with USN, 1949-53. Recipient Teaching award Jr. Achievement, 1956. Jewish. Clubs: B'nai B'rith, T-Bird Hunting Lodge (Wis.). Home: PO Box 82 Barrington IL 60010 Office: 254 N Laurel Ave Des Plaines IL 60016

HIRSCH, ROBERT HENRY, retail co. exec.; b. Kansas City, Mo., May 29, 1925; s. Clarence A. and Ruth (Auerbach) H.; student U. Kans., 1943-44; B.S. in Mech. Engring., U. Calif., Berkeley, 1946; postgrad. Harvard U., 1946-47, N.Y. U., 1948; children—Sydney Suzanne, Leslie Joan, Robert Henry. Trainee, Abraham & Straus, Bklyn., 1948, buyer accessories, coats, suits, 1951-57; founder, owner Brooks Hirsch, Inc., Westport, Trumbull, Fairfield and Stamford, Conn., 1957, pres., 1962—; dir. Conn. Nat. Bank, Westport. Pres., Bd. of Trade, Westport, 1963—, Westport Devel. Commn., 1964-66; trustee Mid-Fairfield County Youth Mus., 1964-76, v.p., 1972-76; chmn. bur. bus. adminstrn. and public relations Fairfield U., 1971—, bd. dirs., 1971—, v.p., 1972, chmn., 1973. Served to lt. (j.g.) USN, 1943-47. Mem. Nat. Retail Mchts. Assn., Westport C. of C. (pres. 1964-65). Republican. Jewish. Clubs: Birchwood Country (gov.), Saints and Sinners Jumbo Tent, Racquet, Sportsman (Westport). Home: 118 Roseville St Westport CT 06880 Office: 403 E State St Westport CT 06880

HIRSCHFIELD, NORMAN, mgmt. and fin. cons.; b. N.Y.C., Jan. 16, 1910; s. Bennet and Minnie (Weissbaum) H.; student Columbia U., 1930; m. Betty Baum, June 22, 1933; children—Alan J., Ellen J. Hirschfield McDonald. With A.M. Lamport & Co., N.Y.C., 1925-37; chmn. bd., pres., Consol. Gas Utilities Corp. (now Ark. La. Gas Co.), Oklahoma City, 1937-54; chmn. bd. Allied Supermarkets, Detroit, 1954-60; pres. Norman Hirschfield & Co., Oklahoma City, 1960—; chmn. bd. Hirschfield Scott Assos., Mgmt. and Fin. Cons., Oklahoma City, Beverly Hills, Calif., Locust, N.J., 1960—; chmn. Okla. Turnpike Authority, 1955-57; bds. dirs. First Nat. Bank and Trust Co. of Oklahoma City, Ark. Western Gas Co. of Fayetteville; cons. N.J. Natural Gas Co., Allen & Co., Fed. Jud. Center, Washington; chmn. bd. Teleregister Corp. (now Bunker Ramo), 1960-62; trustee Four Seasons Nursing Centers, Inc., 1970-71. Pres. St. Anthony Hosp. Found.; trustee St. Anthony Hosp. Office: 2109 First National Center Oklahoma City OK 73102

HIRSCHMAN, JOHN CONRAD, minerals co. exec.; b. Phila., Sept. 25, 1944; s. Conrad John and Anna Elizabeth (Bauer) H.; B.S., Muhlenberg Coll., 1966; M.B.A., Rutgers U., 1971; m. C. Merle Hummel, Oct. 6, 1967; children—Kym, Kristin. Mem. tech. service staff Airco Chem. & Plastics Co., Middlesex, N.J., 1966-68; sales rep. Cincinnati Milacron Chem. Co., New Brunswick, N.J., 1968-71; project mgr. Charles H. Kline & Co., Fairfield, N.J., 1971-76; mgr. bus. research Engelhard Minerals & Chem. Inc., Edison, N.J., 1976—. Mem. Am. Chem. Soc., Chem. Mktg. Research Assn., Chem. Industry Assn., Am. Inst. Mining Engrs. Office: Engelhard Minerals Menlo Park Edison NJ 08817

HIRSHBERG, STEVEN PAUL, import, export, mfg. corp. exec.; b. Lowell, Mass., Feb. 17, 1950; s. Alvan Charles and June Betty (Novick) H.; B.A., Tufts U., 1972; m. Susan Harris, Nov. 6, 1977; 1 son, David A. With Hirshberg & Co., Inc., Andover, Mass., 1972—, v.p., 1975—. Named Eagle Scout, 1964. Mem. Two-Ten Assn., Am. Footwear Industries Assn., Rubber Trade Assn. N.Y., Royal Philatelic Soc. (London). Republican. Jewish. Club: Lanam (Andover). Home: 6 Blueberry Circle Andover MA 01810 Office: Hirshberg & Co Inc 224 Andover St Andover MA 01810

HISAM, HORST GUENTHER, investment co. exec.; b. Berlin, May 2, 1921; came to U.S., 1976, naturalized, 1977; s. Theodor Friedrich Wilhelm and Helene Amalie Rosalie (Meyer) H.; J.D., U. Tuebingen, 1945; m. Ursula M. Domdey, May 25, 1965; children—Thorsten G., Nicole. Bus. cons., Germany, 1946-76; prof. mgmt. U. Bad Harzburg, 1957-73; pres. various investment cos., Germany, 1958-76; bus. cons., U.S.A., 1976—; pres. Swiss and German Investments, Inc., Ft. Lauderdale, Fla., 1976—, Investment and Holding Co. of Fla., Inc., Ft. Lauderdale, 1976—, Gulf Tarra, Inc., Marco Island, Fla., 1976—. Mayor, City of List auf Sylt (Germany), 1969-73. Club: Lions (Lauderdale by the Sea). Author: Die Satzungsgewalt der Gemeinde, 1945; Der Handel in der industriellen Gesellschaft, 1963. Home and Office: 2218 NE 17th Ct Fort Lauderdale FL 33305

HITCH, THOMAS KEMPER, economist; b. Boonville, Mo., Sept. 16, 1912; s. Arthur Martin and Bertha (Johnston) H.; A.B., Stanford, 1934; A.M., Columbia, 1946; Ph.D., London Sch. Econs., 1937; student Nat. U. Mexico, 1932; m. Margaret Barnhart, June 27, 1940 (dec. Nov. 1974); children—Hilary, Leslie, Caroline, Thomas; m. 2d, Mae Okudaira. Mem. faculty Stephens Coll., Columbia, Mo., 1937-42; spl. study commodity markets Commodity Exchange Adminstrn., U.S. Dept. Agr., 1940; acting head current bus. research sect. U.S. Dept. Commerce, 1942-43; labor adviser Vets. Emergency Housing Program, 1946-47; economist labor econs. Pres.'s Council Econ. Advisers, 1947-50; dir. research Hawaii Employers Council, Honolulu, 1950-59; sr. v.p. research div. 1st Hawaiian Bank, 1959—; dir. Hawaiian Telephone Co. Chmn. Gov.'s Financial Adv. Com., 1959-62, Mayor's Adv. Com. on Finance, 1960-68; chmn. com. on taxation and finance Constl. Conv. Hawaii, 1968. Mem. Hawaii Joint Council on Econ. Edn., chmn., 1964-68. Trustee McInerny Found., Tax Found. Hawaii. Served as lt. O.R.C., 1933-38; as lt. USNR, 1943-46. Mem. Nat. Assn. Bus. Economists, Am. Econ. Assn., Indsl. Relations Research Assn., Am. Statis. Assn., Hawaii C. of C. (chmn. 1971), Phi Beta Kappa, Pi Sigma Alpha, Alpha Sigma Phi. Clubs: Pacific (gov. 1963-65); Waialae Country (pres. 1979). Contbr. articles to profl. jours. Home: 257 Portlock Rd Honolulu HI 96825 Office: 1st Hawaiian Bank 165 S King St Honolulu HI 96847

HIX, JAMES GRADY, telephone systems co. exec.; b. Fayetteville, Ark., Oct. 9, 1929; s. John Grady and Myrtis C. (Sealy) H.; student Tex. Tech. Coll., 1956; m. Emma Lou Hix, Jan. 9, 1951; children—Michael C., Clifford W., Terry A., Myrtis M. Pierce. Engr., Univac I, 1956-57, salesman to v.p., Washington, 1960-69; tech. dir. Telurometer, Inc., Phila., 1957-60; v.p. mktg. Comcet (now Comtem), Washington, 1969-70; pres. govt. div. Univ. Computing Co., Washington and Dallas, 1970-72; v.p. sales Harris Corp., Dallas, 1972-74; v.p. mktg. Precision Instrument, Inc., Santa Clara, Calif., 1974-77; dir. western region Mohawk Data Sci., Los Angeles, 1977-79; v.p. sales No. Telecom, Dallas, 1979—. Bd. dirs. Christmas Pageant of Peace, Washington. Served with U.S. Navy, 1948-52. Mem. Armed Services Mgmt. Assn. Democrat. Club: Washington Country. Address: 3001 Laguna Dr Plano TX 75023

HIZER, VILLA SULZBACHER, distbg. co. exec.; b. Rome, Ga., Dec. 16, 1948; d. Joel and Betty (Hanes) Sulzbacher; student Converse Coll., Spartanburg, S.C., 1966-68; B.A. in Math., U. Ga., 1970; postgrad. Ga. Tech. U., 1975; m. L. Courtney Hizer, July 6, 1974. Trainee, Harrell & Miller, C.P.A., Atlanta, 1971; computer analyst, fin. asst. Law Engring. & Testing Co., Atlanta, 1972-73; office mgr. Buckhead Tennis Club, Atlanta, 1973-74; computer programmer, customer tng. Olivetti Corp., Atlanta, 1974-76; word processing rep. Lanier Bus. Products, Atlanta, 1976; v.p., treas. North Ga. Distbg. Co., Rome, Ga., 1976—; dir. Rome Mfg. Co. Treas., Chieftians Mus., Rome, 1980-81. Mem. Rome C. of C. Office: 124 Huffacre Rd Rome GA 30161

HJALMARSON, GORDON ROSS, book pub. co. exec.; b. Dauphin, Man., Can., Apr. 9, 1926; s. John I. and Holmfridur (Johnson) H.; came to U.S., 1942, naturalized, 1951; B.A., Pomona Coll., 1949; M.A., San Francisco State U., 1951; m. Carroll Lorraine Clark, Aug. 9, 1952; children—Gordon R., Melissa A., John C., Eric A. Tchr., Huntington Beach (Calif.) High Sch. Dist., 1952-58; instr., sci. and math., San Francisco State U., 1952; editor Houghton Mifflin Co., Boston, 1958-73, dept. head, 1968-70, v.p., 1970-73, mem. exec. com., 1970-73, dir., 1970-73; pres., dir. Scott Foresman & Co., Glenview, Ill., 1973—, chmn., chief exec. officer, 1976—; chmn. bd., chief exec. officer, pres. SFN Cos., Inc., 1980—, holding co. for William Morrow Co., N.Y.C., Silver Burdette Co., Morristown, N.J., Fleming H. Revell, Tappan, N.J., U. Park Press, South Western Pub. Co., Cin.; dir. Gage Ednl. Pub. (Toronto), GLC Ltd. (Toronto). Mem. Republican Town Com., Wellesley, Mass., 1960-61; asso. pres.'s com. Northwestern U., U. Chgo., Nat. Coll. Edn., Evanston, Ill., U. Ill.; trustee Pomona (Calif.) Coll. Recipient Disting. Alumnus of Yr. award San Francisco State U., 1979; named Top Chief Exec. Officer in Pub. Industry, Wall St. Transcript, 1980. Mem. Am. Assn. Pubs. (dir.). Clubs: Econ., Chgo., Presidents Assn. (N.Y.C.); Chgo.; Sunset Ridge Country. Contbr. articles in field to profl. jours.; lectr. in field. Home: 119 Abingdon Ave Kenilworth IL 60043 Office: 1900 E Lake Ave Glenview IL 60075

HOAG, FRANK STEPHEN, JR., publisher; b. Pueblo, Colo., June 11, 1908; s. Frank S. and Louise (Allebrand) H.; B.A., Princeton, 1931; Litt.D. (hon.), So. Colo. State Coll., 1965; m. LeVert Wiess, June 15, 1935. Pub., Pueblo Star-Jour. and Chieftain, 1943-80, pres. Star-Jour. Pub. Corp., 1980—. Past mem. audit com. Asso. Press. Dir. Minnequa Bank, Pub. Service Co. Colo. Dir., v.p. Colo. Public Expenditures Council. Trustee Colo. Coll., Colorado Springs; bd. dirs. USAF Acad. Found., Colorado Springs; trustee Parkview Episcopal Hosp., Pueblo Devel. Found.; past pres. U. So. Colo. Found. DeMolay Legion of Honor. Mem. Pueblo C. of C. (past pres.), Am. Soc. Newspaper Editors, Colo. Press Assn. (past pres.), Am. Newspaper Pubs. Assn., Colo. Assn. Commerce and Industry (dir.), Sigma Delta Chi. Presbyn. Mason (32 deg.), Rotarian (past pres.), Elk. Home: 305 Argyle St Pueblo CO 81004 Office: 825 W 6th St Pueblo CO 81002

HOAGLAND, HENRY WILLIAMSON, JR., investment cons.; b. Colorado Springs, Colo., Sept. 5, 1912; s. Henry W. and Harriet (Seldomridge) H.; B.A., Stanford, 1934, LL.B., 1937; M.B.A., Harvard, 1939; m. Ray Watkin, June 21, 1961. Exec. asst. to dir. mil. planning div. Office of Q.M. Gen., Washington, 1942-46; dep. dir. Joint Com. on Atomic Energy, 1946-48; sr. v.p. Am. Research and Devel. Co., Boston, 1949-69; with Fidelity Mgmt. and Research Co., Boston, 1969—, cons., 1969-71, pres., dir. FMR Devel. Corp. subsidiary, 1971—; sr. gen. partner Fidelity Ventures Ltd., Boston, 1971-80; vice chmn. bd. Fidelity Ventures Assos., 1974-80, limited partner, 1980—. Republican. Mem. Stanford Assos., Delta Theta Phi. Home: 818 Augusta Dr Houston TX 85704 Office: 82 Devonshire St Boston MA 02109

HOBART, DOROTHY ANN, dance studio owner, instr.; b. Buffalo, Sept. 19, 1938; d. Joseph and Stella (Kosawski) Gay; B.A. Ed., D'Youville Coll., 1960; M.S.Ed., Canisius Coll., 1964; m. Thomas Y. Hobart Jr., Aug. 10, 1963; children—Elizabeth Anne, Catherine Marie, Thomas Y. III. Tchr. English jr. high sch. Lancaster (N.Y.) Bd. Edn., 1960-64; owner, instr. (ballet, modern jazz, ballroom tap) Center for Dance Arts, Buffalo, 1956—. Mem. Dance Master of Am. Inc., Profl. Dance Tchrs. Assn. Democrat. Roman Catholic. Participant charitable dance performances, nursing homes, orphanages. Home: 157 Bassett Rd Williamsville NY 14221

HOBART, THOMAS YALE, JR., profl. union exec.; b. Buffalo, Dec. 26, 1936; s. Thomas Yale Hobart and Anne R. Mulloy; B.S., State U. N.Y., 1960; M.S., Canisius Coll., 1963; m. Dorothy, Aug. 10, 1963; children—Elizabeth, Catherine, Thomas. Pres., Buffalo Tchrs. Fedn., 1969-70, N.Y. State Tchrs. Assn., 1971-72, N.Y. State United Tchrs., 1973—; v.p. Am. Fedn. Tchrs. (AFL-CIO), 1974—; del. World Confedn. of Orgns. of Teaching Professions, 1972-75, Internat. Fedn. Free Tchrs. Unions, 1975, Am. Labor Council for Histradut; del. AFL-CIO, 1973, 75, 77; del. dept. profl. employees AFL-CIO, 1975-77, 79, del. dept. public employees, 1976—; chmn. Pub. Employees for Legis. Actions, 1971; v.p. N.Y. State Tchr. Edn. Conf. Bd., 1973—; mem. Commr.'s Task Force Tchr. Edn. and Certification, 1976, 77; mem. Regent's Adv. Com. on Tchr. Edn. and Certification, 1973-75; mem. N.Y. State Gov.'s Task Force on State Aid to Edn., 1975, task force on Taylor Law, 1974; mem. Regents Com. on Tchr. Edn., Certification and Practice, 1973-75; mem. N.Y. State Advisory Council on Vocat. Edn., 1977; mem. N.Y. State Manpower Services Council (CETA), 1977; mem. Gov.'s Task Force on Equity and Excellence in Edn., 1978—; vice chmn. N.Y. State Employment Tng. Council, 1979. Mem. Cornell Sch. Labor Relations Advisory Com.; del. Jewish Labor Council, 1974-76; exec. bd. Jewish Labor Com., Nat. Trade Union Council on Human Rights, 1978—; mem. St. Joseph's Guild, Buffalo. Served with USAR, 1960-66. Editor: What Price Quotas? 1974; contbg. author: The Governance of Teacher Education by Consortium, 1974. Home: 157 Bassett Rd Williamsville NY 14221 Office: 80 Wolf Rd Albany NY 12205

HOBBS, COLUMBUS ALEXANDER, JR., builder, developer; b. Holmes County, Fla., July 4, 1925; s. Columbus A. and Olga G. (Griffin) H.; student Fla. public schs.; m. Lauryce G. Anderson, Dec. 7, 1946; 1 son, Columbus A. III. Steel connector Bethlehem Steel Co., Atlanta, 1946-48; mechanic A.D. Price Motor Co., Geneva, Ala., 1948-50; supr. automotive machine shop 3d Army Ordinance, Camp Rucker, Ala., 1950-53; owner building supply firm, Westville, Fla., 1953-59, home bldg. bus., Milton, Fla., 1959-60; pres. C.A. Hobbs, Jr., Inc., Pensacola, Fla., 1960—; chmn. bd. Gold Coast Enterprises of Pensacola, Inc.; cons. HUD. Served with USNR, 1942-45. Cert. gen. contractor, Fla.; recipient environ. and energy-efficient constrn. awards. Mem. Nat. Home Builders Assn. (dir.), Fla. Home Builders Assn., Home Builders Assn. West Fla. (dir., past pres.), Nat. Fedn. Ind. Bus., Pensacola Area C. of C., Navy League (life), Nat. Rifle Assn. (life). Club: Shriners. Home: 100 Holmes Dr Pensacola FL 32507 Office: 6900 W Fairfield Dr Pensacola FL 32506

HOBBS, DONALD WILLIAM, JR., mfg. co. mgr.; b. San Mateo, Calif., July 4, 1944; s. Donald William and Polly (Kelly) H.; B.S., San Jose State U., 1967, M.B.A., 1974. Product mgr. corporate staff diagnostics div. Pfizer Inc., N.Y.C., 1975-76, regional sales coordinator, 1976-78; regional sales mgr. Bacharach Instrument div. United Technologies Corp., Santa Clara, Calif., 1978, nat. sales mgr., 1979, mgr. sales and mktg., 1979-80; mktg. mgr. Marin Controls Co., Belmont, Calif., 1980—. Served with U.S. Army, 1969-71. Decorated Bronze Star. Mem. Soc. Advancement Mgmt., San Jose State U. Alumni Assn., Far West Ski Assn. Republican. Roman Catholic. Club: Kiwanis. Home: 1291 Valley Forge Dr Sunnyvale CA 94087 Office: 19 Davis Dr Belmont CA 94002

HOBBS, MARVIN, engring. exec.; b. Jasper, Ind., Nov. 30, 1912; s. Charles and Madge (Ott) H.; B.S. in Elec. Engring., Tri-State Coll., Angola, Ind., 1930; postgrad. U. Chgo., 1932; m. Bernadine E. Weeks, July 4, 1936. Chief engr. Scott Radio Labs., Chgo., 1939-46; cons. engr. RCA, Camden, N.J., 1946-49; v.p. Harvey-Wells Electronics, Southbridge, Mass., 1952-54; asst. to exec. v.p. Gen. Instrument Corp., Newark, N.J., 1958-62; mgr., cons. engr. Design Service Co., N.Y.C., 1963-68; v.p. Gladding Corp., Syracuse, N.Y., 1968-71, cons. corporate devel., 1971-79; mem. adminstrv. group Bell Telephone Labs., Naperville, Ill., 1979—; dir. A.R.F. Products, Inc., Raton, N.M. Mem. Electronics Prodn. Bd., ODM, Washington, 1951-52; operations analyst Far East Air Force, 1945. Recipient Certificate of Appreciation War Dept., 1945, Certificate of Commendation, Navy Dept., 1947. Mem. IEEE (life). Author: Basics of Missile Guidance and Space Techniques, 1959, Fundamentals of Rockets, Missiles and Spacecraft, 1962; Modern Communications Switching Systems, 1974. Inventor low radiation radio receiver. Home: 655 W Irving Park Rd Chicago IL 60613 Office: Bell Telephone Labs Naperville IL 60566

HOBBS, MATTHEWS A., holding co. exec.; b. Fitzgerald, Ga., 1915; married. Pres., Am.-Amicable Life Ins. Co., 1960-74; with Gulf Life Ins. Co., 1969—, now vice chmn., chief exec. officer, dir.; dir. Dealers Service Co., Am.-Amicable Life Ins. Co.; sr. v.p., dir. Gulf Life Holding Co., Fin. Computer Co. Office: Gulf United Corp Gulf Life Tower Jacksonville FL 32207*

HOBBS, MICHAEL EDWIN, broadcasting co. exec.; b. Washington, Nov. 26, 1940; s. Robert Boyd and Barbara Alberta (Davis) H.; A.B., Dartmouth Coll., 1962; J.D., Harvard U., 1965. Admitted to Mass. bar, 1966; staff counsel, asst. to gen. mgr. Sta. WGBH Ednl. Found., Boston, 1966-67; exec. asst. Ednl. Television Stas., Nat. Assn. Ednl. Broadcasters, Washington, 1967-70; sec. Pub. Broadcasting Service, Washington, 1970—, gen. counsel, 1970-71, dir. adminstrn., 1970-73, v.p., 1973, sr. v.p., 1976—. Served with USAF, 1965. Mem. Nat. Assn. Ednl. Broadcasters, Am., Mass. bar assns., Am. Judicature Soc., Nat. Acad. TV Arts and Scis., Phi Beta Kappa. Club: George Town. Home: 419 Cameron St Alexandria VA 22314 Office: 475 L'Enfant Plaza W SW Washington DC 20024

HOBBS, OLIVER KERMIT, agrl. engr., mfg. co. exec.; b. Hobbsville, N.C., Sept. 21, 1918; s. Ephriam J. and Sallie (Brown) H.; student pub. schs.; m. Frances Allsbrook Piland, June 14, 1941; children—Oliver Kermit, Cynthia Russell. Service rep. Sadler Music Co., Suffolk, Va., 1939-42; service mgr. A. E. Sadler Co., Suffolk, 1945-49; gen. mgr. Shotton's Farm Service, Suffolk, 1949-58; dir. research and engring. Benthall Machine Co., Inc., Suffolk, 1958—, also dir.; pres. Hobbs Engring Co., 1963—, Hobbs-Adams Engring. Co., 1970—; chmn. bd. Pioneer Processors, Inc., 1972—; cons. agrl. mech. devices, 1956—. Served with USNR, 1942-45; ETO. Recipient Horace Hayden Meml. trophy, 1954. Mem. Va. Farm Equipment Assn., U.S. C. of C., Sudan-U.S. Bus. Council, Farm Bur., Agribus Council, Suffolk-Nansemond C. of C. (past dir.), Suffolk-Nansemond Hist. Soc., Va. Mfrs. Assn., Internat. Platform Assn., Woodmen of World. Baptist. Clubs: Ruritan, Rotary, (Suffolk), Kings Fork (pres. Suffolk 1959). Patentee automotive, agrl., forest products, material handling fields. Home: 1202 W Point Dr Suffolk VA 23434 Office: PO Box 1833 Suffolk VA 23434

HOBDY, FRANCES LEAP, Realtor; b. Fresno, Calif., Mar. 1, 1920; d. Edward Gerald and Emma (Tittle) Leap; student Coll. William and Mary, 1968, Southwestern Coll., 1972; A.A., Palomar Coll., 1976; m. Morris Matthew Hobdy, May 27, 1972; children by previous marriage—Robert James Rader, Judith Ann Rader. With firm Hatchet and Ford, Hampton, Va., 1962-67; legal sec. Century 21 Denney Realty, 1973-75; real estate broker Mark Realtors, Escondido, Calif., 1975-78; owner, broker Hobody, Realtors, Escondido, 1978—; dir. Robert H. Fowble & Assocs., San Diego. Instr. cardiopulmonary resuscitation, ARC, 1977—; bd. dirs. Unity Ch., Escondido. Mem. Escondido Bd. Realtors, Nat., Calif. assns. realtors, Realtors Nat. Mktg. Inst. Home: 910 Milane Ln Escondido CA 92026 Office: 510 N Escondido Blvd Suite 2A Escondido CA 92025

HOBEN, MICHAEL FRANCIS, oil co. exec.; b. Torrington, Conn., Dec. 8, 1939; s. Francis M. and Theresa M. (Bottazzi) H.; B.A. in Fin., Lehigh U., 1961; M.S. in Econs., Ariz. State U., 1965; postgrad. in econs. N.Y. U., 1964-66; m. Elaine Kathryn Kusako, Jan. 28, 1967; children—Susan, Michael, Bradford. Second v.p. Chase Manhattan Bank, N.Y.C., 1965-73; v.p., sr. pension portfolio mgr., head options dept. T. Rowe Price Assos., investment counseling co., N.Y.C., 1973-78; mgr. equity portfolios Exxon Corp., N.Y.C., 1978—; speaker Chgo. Bd. Options Exchange Instl. Seminar, 1977, Phila. Soc. Security Analysts, 1977; participant program on Fed. Govt. ops. for sr. bus. execs. Brookings Instn., 1980. Active Opera New Eng., 1977. Served to 1st lt. USAF, 1962-65. Fellow Fin. Analysts Fedn.; mem. Investment Counsel Assn. Am. (chartered investment counsellor cert.), Mid-Atlantic Options Soc., N.Y. Soc. Security Analysts, N.Y. Instl. Options Soc. Republican. Home: 1480 Cross Hwy Fairfield CT 06430 Office: 1251 Ave of Americas New York NY 10020

HOBRATSCH, MELVIN JOHN, real estate investment co. exec.; b. Vernon, Tex., Mar. 29, 1936; s. Alvin Walter and Ella Louise H.; B.B.A., N. Tex. State U., 1960; m. Mary Elyse Mook, Feb. 14, 1978; children—Jana Lynn, Jonathan Emerson, Ben Melvin. Various positions land investment cos., Dallas-Ft. Worth area, 1968-79; owner, operator Mel Hobratsch Investment Co., Dallas, 1961-75; pres. E. Tex. Properties Inc., Greenville, Tex., 1975—; also pres. E. Tex. Pork Producers, Inc., Sabine Properties, Inc., comml. investment builders; former dir. Real Estate Advt. Inc., Hobratsch Ranch Inc. Fin. chmn. Republican party Collin County (Tex.), 1972. Served with U.S. Army, 1958-59, 60-61. Mem. Tex. and Southwestern Cattle Raisers Assn., Greenville Bd. Realtors, Hunt County Builders Assn. (1st v.p.). Lutheran. Clubs: Bent Tree Country (Dallas); Hot Springs Village (Ark.) Country. Office: E Texas Properties Inc 6503 Wesley St Greenville TX

HOCH, GARY ALLEN, cert. fin. planner; b. Springville, N.Y., Apr. 5, 1943; s. Henry and Berdena E. (Armstrong) H.; student Bryant and Stratton Bus. Inst., 1961-63, Empire State Coll., 1977-79; m. Rosemary Lee Blakeley, Oct. 12, 1963; children—Kelly, Jeffrey. Underwriter, Exchange Mut. Ins. Co., Buffalo, 1963-67; tax examiner N.Y. State Income Tax Bur., 1967-68; pres. Cushing Capital Corp., Buffalo, 1968-76; individual practice fin. planning, Buffalo, 1976—; ins. cons. Mem. Nat. Assn. Accts., Nat. Assn. Security Dealers, Internat. Assn. Fin. Planners, Profl. Ins. Agts. Presbyterian (elder, trustee). Clubs: Mariners, Ins. of Buffalo. Home and Office: 30 Boyd St Buffalo NY 14213

HOCHBERG, FREDERICK GEORGE, accountant; b. Los Angeles, July 4, 1913; s. Frederick Joseph and Lottie (LeGendre) H.; B.A., U. Calif. at Los Angeles, 1937; children—Frederick George, Ann C. Hochberg May. Chief accountant, auditor Swinerton, McClure & Vinnell, Managua, Nicaragua, 1942-44; pvt. accounting practice, Avalon, Calif., 1946-66; designer, operator Descanso Beach Club, Avalon, 1966; vice pres. Air Catalina, 1967; treas. Catalina Airlines, 1967; pres. Aero Commuter, 1967; v.p., treas., dir. bus. affairs William L. Pereira & Assos., Planners, Architects, Engrs., Los Angeles, 1967-72; v.p., gen. mgr. Mo. Hickory Corp., 1972-74; prin. Fred G. Hochberg Assos., Mgmt. Consultants, 1974—; v.p. Vicalton S.A. Mexico, 1976—; v.p., gen. mgr. Solar Engring. Co., Inc., 1977-79; pres. Solar Assos. Internat., 1979—. Chmn. Avalon Transp. Com., 1952; sec. Santa Catalina Festival of Arts, 1960; pres. Avalon Music Bowl Assn., 1961; chmn. Avalon Harbor Commn., 1960; pres. Catalina Mariachi Assn., 1961-66; treas. City of Avalon, 1954-62, councilman, 1962-66, mayor, 1964-66; sec. Avalon City Planning Commn., 1956-58; chmn. Avalon Airport Com., 1964-66, Harbor Devel. Commn., 1965-66; bd. dirs. Los Angeles Child Guidance Clinic, 1975—, treas., 1978-79, pres., 1979—. Served as ensign USNR, 1944-45. Named Catalina Island Man of Yr., 1956. Mem. Avalon Catalina Island C. of C. (past pres.), Soc. Calif. Accountants, Mensa, Am. Arbitration Assn. (panel), Catalina Island Mus. Soc. (treas. 1964), Los Angeles, El Monte chambers commerce, Town Hall-West (vice chmn). Club: Rotary (pres.). Home: 6760 Hill Park Dr Los Angeles CA 90068 Office: 5900 S Eastern Ave City of Commerce GA 90040

HOCHSCHWENDER, HERMAN KARL, mgmt. cons.; b. Heidelberg, Ger., Mar. 1, 1920; came to U.S., 1930, naturalized, 1935; s. Karl G. and Maria (Recken) H.; B.S., Yale U., 1941; postgrad. Harvard U. Bus. Sch.; m. Jane Elliott (div. 1961); children—Lynn Anne Hochschwender McGowin, Herman Karl, Irene Hochschwender Pate, James E.; m. 2d, Mary Koger, July 3, 1965; 1 son, J. Michael. Asst. indsl. relations mgr. Sargent & Co., New Haven, 1943-45; mgr. corp. planning Firestone Tire & Rubber Co., Akron, Ohio, 1945-56; pres. Mohawk Rubber Co., N.Y.C., 1959, Hochschwender & Assos., Akron, 1959-72, Smithers Sci. Services, Inc., Akron, 1972—. Trustee Akron Gen. Med. Center. Mem. Am. Council Ind. Labs., Ind. Lab. Assn. Am., ASTM, Soc. Automotive Engrs., Am. Assn. Lab. Accreditation, Yale U. Alumni Assn. Clubs: Rotary, Akron City, Portage Country (Akron); Yale (N.Y.C.). Home: 900 Newport Rd Akron OH 44303 Office: 425 W Market St Akron OH 44303

HOCKADAY, GEORGE WARREN, locomotive cons.; b. Anderson, Ind., Feb. 9, 1923; s. Warren Franklin and Bertha May (Fisher) H.; B.S. in Mech. Engring., Purdue U., 1944; m. Biantha Thompson, Feb. 20, 1943; children—Warren F., Bruce D. Product engr. Naval Ordnance Dept., Indpls., 1944-46; engr. of test Monon Ry., Lafayette, Ind., 1946-56; design engr. Alco Products Co., Schenectady, 1956-60, sales service engr., 1960-68; mech. engr., then sr. mech. engr. D&H Ry., Albany, N.Y., 1968-78; locomotivecons., Schenectady, 1978—. Mem. Locomotive Maintenance Officers Assn., Ry. Fuel and Ops. Officers Assn., Soc. Engrs. Eastern N.Y. Methodist. Address: 2029 Careleon Rd Schenectady NY 12303

HOCKENBURY, MYRON DOWNEY, hotel, fund raising exec.; b. Newburgh, N.Y., Jan. 9, 1909; s. Edson J. and Nona (Downey) H.; grad. Mercersburg Acad., 1928; A.B., Princeton, 1932; J.D., Dickinson Sch. Law, 1935; m. Evelyn M. Smith, June 21, 1934; children—Edson Stokes, Nancy Lynn. Admitted to Pa. bar, 1936; sec. The Hockenbury System, Inc., 1935-47, v.p., gen. mgr., 1947-52, pres., 1952—; gen. counsel, dir. Am. Hotels Corp., N.Y.C., 1946-73; sec., dir. Harrisburger Hotel, Harrisburg, Pa., 1951-61; v.p., dir. Grenoble Hotels, Inc., Harrisburg. Mem. Harrisburg Polyclinic Hosp. Council. Served with USNR, 1944-46. Licensed real estate broker, Pa. Mem. Pa., Dauphin County bar assns., Am. C. of C. Execs., Am. Indsl. Devel. Council, Harrisburg Art Assn. Republican. United Methodist (trustee). Clubs: Masons, Shriners, Rotary. Author: Make Yourself a Job, 1936. Composer sacred anthems. Home: 4096 Fawn Dr Harrisburg PA 17112 Office: Payne-Shoemaker Bldg Harrisburg PA 17101

HOCKWITT, MELVYN FRANK, mech. contracting co. exec.; b. Passaic, N.J., Feb. 7, 1943; s. Emil John and Rose Ann (Santangelo) H.; student William Patterson Coll., 1976—; m. Carolyn Hope Becker, Sept. 21, 1968; children—Scott, Laurie. Pres., Group Seven Realty, Cherry Hill, N.J., 1968—; owner Hockwitt Contracting, Clifton, N.J., 1970; partner Brighton Assos., Paterson, N.J., 1976—; owner, mgr. S & L Distributors, Clifton, 1976—; mem. rev. bd. N.J. State Plumbing Code. Cpl., Laurel (M.D.) Rescue, 1969; mem. bd. construction appeals, Clifton, 1978. Served with U.S. Army, 1968-70. Master plumber, N.J. Mem. Passaic Master Plumbers (past pres. and sec.), N.J. League Master Plumbers. Clubs: Nat. Ski Patrol, Barbertown Sportsmen, Am. Legion. Home: 17 Lincoln Ave Clifton NJ 07011 Office: 50 Bergen Ave Clifton NJ 07011

HODDY, GEORGE WARREN, industrialist; b. Columbus, Ohio, Mar. 7, 1905; s. Arthur and Mary E. (Lutz) H.; B.E.E., Ohio State U., 1926, E.E., 1932; Ph.D. in Modern Industry (hon.), Sunshine U., Pinellas County, Fla., 1968; m. Lois L. Mitchell, May 30, 1947; children—John, Peter, Matthew, Elizabeth Hoddy Howe, Rebekeh Hoddy Patton, Melissa. Elec. engr. Day-Fan Electric Co., Dayton, Ohio, 1926-29, Robbins & Myers, Inc., Springfield, Ohio, 1929-31; chief engr. Pioneer div. Master Electric Co., Dayton, 1932-34; v.p., gen. mgr. Redmond Co. Inc., Owosso, Mich., 1934-43; pres., gen. mgr., chief exec. officer Universal Electric Co., Owosso, 1942-71, chmn. bd., 1971-79, vice chmn., 1979—; chmn. bd. Am. Universal Electric (India) Ltd., 1962—, Universal Electric Export, 1973—, Universal Electric Ltd., Gainsborough, Eng., 1974—; vice chmn. Intertherm, Inc., 1972-80, chmn., 1980—; pres. Fiji Marina, Los Angeles, 1968-76; pres., dir. Ventrola Mfg. Co., Owosso, 1968-76. Mem. Owosso Public Sch. Bd., 1957-76, pres., 1975-76; pres. Shiawassee United Way, 1956-59, Shiawassee Found., 1973-77; trustee Meml. Hosp., Owosso, 1948—, pres., 1954-58; trustee Flint (Mich.) Osteo. Hosp., 1958—; bd. dirs. Shiawassee County Mental Health Bd., 1963-67, Owosso Community Concert Assn., 1946-53, United Cerebral Palsy Assn., 1963-65, Mich. State Accident Fund, 1945-61; mem. Owosso Charter Revision Commn., 1956-57, Owosso Citizens Com. Juvenile Deliquency, 1967-67; chmn. Shiawassee County chpt. U.S. Savs. Bonds, 1971-80; trustee, chmn. exec. com. John Wesley Coll., Owosso, Mich., 1980—. Recipient Silver Beaver award Tall Pine council Boy Scouts Am., 1958, Disting. Alumnus award Ohio State U. Coll. Engring., 1970, Alumni Citizenship award Ohio State U., 1975; also other cert. appreciation, service awards. Mem. NAM, U.S. C. of C., Mich. Mfrs. Assn., Owosso-Corunna Area C. of C. (dir. 1948-61, adv. bd. 1961-78), Ohio State U. Alumni Assn., Newcomen Soc., Sigma Xi, Tau Beta Pi, Eta Kappa Nu, Pi Mu Epsilon, Lambda Chi Alpha. Republican. Congregationalist. Clubs: Shriners, Owosso City. Patentee in field. Office: 300 E Main St Owosso MI 48867

HODGE, ARTHUR WILEY, dept. store exec.; b. Morgan County, Ala., Sept. 6, 1931; s. Leonard Wiley and Roberta (King) H.; B.B.A., Miss. Coll., Clinton, 1958; m. Betty Joyce Statum, Nov. 25, 1954; children—Arthur Gregory, Lisa Wilette. Salesman, Brown Shoe Co., 1959-64, Butler Mfg. Co., 1964-69; self-employed, 1969-70; pres., owner McAlpin's Dept. Store, Magee, Miss., 1970—; dir. Bank Simpson Co. Bd. dirs. Andrew Council council Boy Scouts Am.; pres. Vision Found., Inc., 1976—; bd. dirs. Nat. Laymen's Bd., Ch. of God, 1968-76, bd. dir. Nat. Radio and TV Bd., 1976—, chmn. Nat. Laymen's Bd., 1976—; bd. dirs. Miss. Methodist Hour, 1976—. Served with USAF, 1950-54. Mem. Miss. Retail Mchts. Assn. (dir.), Magree C. of C. (dir.). Home: 802 S Main St Magee MS 39111 Office: 102 S Main St Magee MS 39111

HODGE, DAVID CARROLL, economist; b. Morristown, Tenn., July 25, 1921; s. James Ellis and Georgie Cates (Cough) H.; B.S. in Indsl. Edn., U. Tenn., Knoxville, 1949, M.S. in Econs. and Bus. Adminstrn., 1953; postgrad. U. Ga., Athens, 1961-64; m. Alice Arlene Williams, June 14, 1952; children—John David, Alan Andrew. Research asst. Bur. Bus. and Econ. Research, U. Tenn., Knoxville, 1952-59; asso. dir. Bus. Bus. and Econ. Research, U. Ga., Athens, 1959-66; indsl. arts instr. Chattanooga Public Schs., 1949-50; carpenter Hodge Constrn. Co., Morristown, Tenn., 1950-51; research economist Tayloe Murphy Inst., U. Va., Charlottesville, 1966—. Incorporator, Ga. Christian Found., 1966. Served with U.S. Army, 1942-45; ETO. Mem. Am. Statis. Assn., AAUP, So. Econ. Assn., Beta Gamma Sigma. Mem. Ch. of Christ. Author articles in field. Office: 4th Floor 2015 Ivy Rd Charlottesville VA 22903

HODGES, DAVID NELSON, banker; b. Portland, Oreg., Dec. 3, 1948; s. Nelson A. and Virginia J. (James) H.; B.A. with honors, U. Puget Sound, 1972; cert. N.W. Agrl. Credit Sch., 1978; m. Kathryn L. Hatfield, Dec. 18, 1976. Fed. bank examiner Comptroller of Currency, Portland, 1969-76; pres. Mont. Bank of Absarokee, 1976-78; exec. v.p. Mont. Bank of Fairview, 1978; v.p., cashier Mont. Bank of Sidney, N.A., 1978—; tchr. Am. Inst. Banking; mem. adv. bd. Stillwater County Housing Rehab. Mem. Am. Inst. Banking. Episcopalian. Clubs: Absarokee Civic (dir. 1976-78). Lions (dir.). Country. Home: 426 14th Ave SW Sidney MT 59270 Office: PO Box 593 Sidney MT 59270

HODGES, GEORGE ADDISON COOKE, III, banker; b. Howard County, Md., Oct. 15, 1925; s. George Addison Cooke and Marian Champayne (Parlett) H.; B.S., Johns Hopkins, 1958; LL.B., U. Balt., 1967; m. Frances Thompson Skinner, Oct. 13, 1944; children—Frances Hodges Carson, Elizabeth Scott, Kathleen Skinner. With Westinghouse Elec. Corp., 1942-56, Conn. Gen. Life Ins. Co., 1956-60; asst. br. mgr. Penn Mut. Co., Md., 1961-62; asso. gen. agt. Union Trust Co., Balt., 1962-66; trust officer 1st Pa. Bank, Phila., 1967-72, sr. trust officer 1st. Pa. Corp. and 1st. Pa. Internat. Ltd., 1972-75; vice-chmn., mng. dir., chief exec. officer Island Security Bank Ltd., Grand Cayman Island, B.W.I., 1975—; dir. Joseph T. Fewkes Co. Bd. dirs. Child Devel. Corp., Commerce and Industry Combined Health Appeal, Community Arts Center, Walingford, Pa.; v.p. Parents Pub. Sch. Com. Md., 1956-57; mem. Md. Gov.'s Com. Higher Edn., 1962-64. Served with USAAF, 1943-46. Mem. Greater Balt. Com., C. of C. Greater Balt. (life), Practicing Law Inst., Inst. Taxation, Am. Mgmt. Assn., Am. Security Council, Md. Soc. Pa. Republican. Episcopalian. Clubs: Rittenhouse (Phila.); Mchts. (Balt.): Travelers (London). Author fiction and non-fiction under pen-names. Home: Dedication Farm RFD 6016 Emerald Ln Sykesville MD 21784 Office: PO Box 1161 Grand Cayman Island BWI

HODGES, H(ERBERT) ANTHONY, investment mgmt. exec.; b. Manchester, Eng., Jan. 25, 1919; s. Herbert and Annie Agnes (Rankin) H.; came to U.S., 1963, naturalized, 1975; student Manchester Coll. Tech., 1935-37; B.A., Victoria U. Manchester, 1940; m. Mary Press, Sept. 6, 1940 (div. 1970); children—Beverley Anne, Andrea Jane, Thomas Anthony; m. 2d, Joan Bannerot Lappe, Aug. 25, 1973 (div. 1979); m. 3d, Donna Kinneman Hasley, Aug. 5, 1979. Econ. asst. Joint Com. Cotton Trade Orgns., Manchester, 1935-40; asst. treas. Sun Life Can., Montreal, Que., 1946-63; v.p. Mellon Bank, Pitts., 1963-79; v.p., dir. mktg. Fort Hill Investors Mgmt. Corp., 1979—; lectr. finance Sir George Williams U., 1949; dir. Tri-State Kennel Assn.; pres. Gt. Dane Club Western Pa. Served with Royal Navy, 1940-46. Decorated knight comdr. Order St. Lazarus Jerusalem. Mem. Pitts. Soc. Security Analysts. Republican. Roman Catholic. Clubs: Pitts. Bond, Duquesne, Pitts. Athletic Assn.; Gt. Harbour (B.W.I.). Home: 5513 Howe St Pittsburgh PA 15232 Office: 433 Union Trust Bldg Mellon Sq Pittsburgh PA 15219

HODGES, LEO CHARLES, publishing exec.; b. Portland, Tenn., Jan. 31, 1946; s. Cleo Clifton and Leola (Durham) H.; B.A., Purdue U., 1968; J.D., Harvard U., 1971. Admitted to Ind. bar, 1971; asso. firm Ice Miller Donadio & Ryan, Indpls., 1971-73; practice law Savill & Hodges, Indpls., 1973; editor, editorial dept. head R&R Newkirk, Indpls., 1973-79, dir. product devel., 1980—; seminar and inst. speaker. Active Noble Schs. and Industries, Crossroads Rehab. Center, Center for Ind. Living. C.L.U. Mem. Am. Bar Assn., Ind. Bar Assn., Am. Soc. C.L.U.'s. Presbyterian. Editor-in-chief Advanced Underwriting Service, 6 vols., 1973-80; co-author, contbr. Pension Plans Service, 2 vols., 1976—, Charitable Giving Tax Service, 3 vols., 1977—, Estate Planner's Service, 3 vols., 1978—; author, co-author books and monographs including: Retirement Plans After Pension Reform, 1974; Professional Corporations Today, 1976; The Tax Reform Act Manual, 1976; The Tax Companion, 1977, 81; Unified Estate Planning, 1977, 80; One Year of Unified Tax Planning, 1977; The Revenue Act Manual, 1978; Estate Planning Highlights of 1978, 1979, 1980 (1979, 80, 81); Generation-Skipping Transfer Tax, 1979; The Living Legacy: Charitable Gifts of Life Insurance, 1979; Tax Planning for Gifts of Life Insurance, 1979; The Public Life of a Private Annuity, 1980; The Life Insurance Trust Handbook, 1980; contbr. articles to publs. Home: 2026 W 76th St Indianapolis IN 46260 Office: PO Box 1727 Indianapolis IN 46206

HODGES, LUTHER HARTWELL, JR., govt. ofcl.; b. Leaksville (now Eden), N.C., Nov. 19, 1936; s. Luther Hartwell and Martha Elizabeth (Blakeney) H.; A.B. in Econs., U. N.C., Chapel Hill, 1957; M.B.A. (J. Spencer Love fellow), Harvard U., 1961; m. Dorothy Emile Duncan, Feb. 15, 1958; children—Anne Houston, Luther Hartwell III. With N.C. Nat. Bank, Charlotte, 1967-77, vice chmn., 1971-74, chmn. bd., 1974-77; candidate for U.S. Senate, 1977-78; prof. practice mgmt. Duke U., 1978-79; dep. sec. commerce Dept. Commerce, Washington, 1979-80; chmn. bd., chief exec. officer Nat. Bank of Washington, 1980—. Founding chmn. MDC, Inc., Chapel Hill, 1967-77; chmn. N.C. Manpower Council, 1971-73; bd. dirs. Charlotte C. of C., 1971-77, chmn. bd., 1976; bd. govs. U. N.C., 1973-79; chmn. com. univ. governance, trustee, mem. exec. com. Johnson C. Smith U.; mem. central selection com. Morehead Found., Chapel Hill; bd. dirs. Research Triangle Found. N.C. Served to lt. USNR, 1957-59. Recipient award NCCJ, Charlotte, 1975. Mem. Assn. Res. City Bankers (chmn. com. public affairs, 1975-76). Democrat. Episcopalian. Clubs: Met. (Washington); Grandfather Golf and Country, Linville (N.C.) Golf; Charlotte Country. Author: (with Rollie Tillman Jr.) Bank Marketing: Text and Cases; (with Joe S. Floyd Jr.) Financing Industrial Growth, 1962; (with others) Managing Social Performance, 1980. Office: 619 14th St NW Washington DC 20005

HODGES, MILLARD B., accountant; b. Toledo, July 31, 1907; s. William Henry and Sarah Helen (Herrington) H.; student Meadville Bus. Coll., 1927-29, bus. adminstrn. Pace Inst., 1935-37; asso. Nat. Inst. Credit, 1940-41; certificate Cades C.P.A. Sch., 1948; m. Helen Isabel Gaut, Aug. 1, 1931; children—Phyllis Marie (Mrs. John Shipman Osler, Jr.), Carol Elaine (Mrs. Dennis Lee Wilson). Telegrapher, Bessemer & Lake Erie R.R., Greenville, Pa., 1927-30; accountant Am. Viscose Corp., Meadville, Pa., 1930-46, costs and budget supr., 1947-52; asst. treas. Ketchikan Pulp Co., Bellingham, Wash., 1952-62, treas., 1962-76, sec., 1964-68, v.p., 1968-76, dir., 1972-76; partner Metcalf, Hodges & Co., C.P.A.'s, 1972—, mng. partner, 1975-77; treas. Mt. Baker (Ski) Recreation Co., 1968—; dir. Savs. Bank Trust Co. N.W., Seattle; adv. bd. Bellingham br. Seattle-1st Nat. Bank; trustee Mt. Baker Mut. Savs. Bank. Instr. asso. course U.S. Army Command and Gen. Staff Coll., Ft. Leavenworth, Kan., 1959-67. Trustee Western Wash. State Coll., 1969-71, chmn. Found., 1971-77. Served from 2d lt. to maj. AUS, 1942-46; ETO; col. Res. Decorated Bronze Star. Mem. Am. Inst. C.P.A.'s, Bellingham C. of C. (trustee 1968-74). Republican. Methodist. Mason, Rotarian. Club: Rainier (Seattle). Home: 2351 N Shore Rd Bellingham WA 98225 Office: 10 Prospect Mall Bellingham WA 98225

HODGKINS, EARL WARNER, r.r. engring. assn. exec.; b. Woodsville, N.H., June 30, 1919; s. Earl Warner and Elizabeth (Mitchell) H.; B.S. in Civil Engring., U. N.H., 1950; m. Ruth Abbie Davison, Sept. 23, 1939; children—Earl Warner III, Linda Ruth (Mrs. William R. Jacobs), Lorraine Dawn (Mrs. Eddie R. Cunningham). From transferman to messenger to clk. Railway Express Agy., Woodsville, N.H., 1936-50; structural designer B. & M. R.R., 1950-52, student supr., Greenfield, Mass., 1952; asst. supr. bridges and bldgs. Maine Central R.R., Portland, 1953-54, asst. engr. structures, 1954-58; asso. editor Ry. Track and Structures mag., Chgo., 1958-64; asso. engring. editor Ry. Age Weekly, 1958-64; exec. sec. Am. Ry. Engring. Assn., Chgo., 1964-68, exec. mgr., 1968-73, exec. dir., 1974—; exec. vice chmn., engring. div. Assn. Am. Railroads, Chgo., 1964-71, exec. dir. engring. div., 1971—. Active local Boy Scouts Am., 1954-60. Served to 1st lt., C.A.C. and Transp. Corps, AUS, 1942-45; ETO. Mem. Am. Ry. Engring. Assn., Am. Ry. Bridge and Bldg. Assn., Roadmasters and Maintenance of Way Assn. Am., Maintenance of Way Club Chgo., Am. Soc. Assn. Execs., Am. Soc. Engring. Edn., ASCE, Council Engring. and Sci. Soc. Execs., Nat. Geog. Soc. Morman. Office: 238 Marquette St Park Forest IL 60466

HODGKINSON, WILLIAM JAMES, mktg. co. exec.; b. Bklyn., July 31, 1939; s. William James and Augusta Anne (Botka) H.; A.B., Bucknell U., 1961; M.B.A., Columbia U., 1963; m. Virginia Evelyn Humphreys, Sept 7, 1963; 1 dau., Elizabeth Anne. Mktg. research analyst Singer Co., N.Y.C., 1963-66; asst. adminstrn. Writing Paper div. Am. Paper Inst., N.Y.C., 1966-67; market research mgr. Diners Club, N.Y.C., 1967-68; with Dun & Bradstreet Cos., Inc., 1968—, mgmt. cons. William E. Hill Co. div., N.Y.C., 1971-73, mgr. financial seravices group Donnelley Mktg. div., Stamford, Conn., 1973-79. Bd. dirs. Bklyn. Pub. Library br., 1974-79, Enlightenment Together, Inc., 1971-76; research coordinator Presdl. Task Force on Improving Small Bus., 1969-70; v.p., trustee Montessori Sch. Bklyn., 1975-79. Served with U.S. Army, 1963. Grantee Columbia U., 1962-63; recipient Brotherhood award Bucknell U., 1960. Mem. Bank Mktg. Assn., Am. Mktg. Assn., Direct Mail Mktg. Assn., Phi Lambda Theta. Congregationalist. (bd. deacons 1971—, pres. 1977-78). Club: Princeton of N.Y. Contbr. articles to profl. jours. Home: 18 Clover Ln Westport CT 06880 Office: 1515 Summer St Stamford CT 06905

HODIN, JOHN, apparel co. exec.; b. Berlin, July 1, 1929; s. Leo and Ruth (Adam) H.; certificate New Eng. Sch. Accounting, 1956; M.B.A., U. New Haven, 1978; m. Sylvia Zibulsky, Apr. 28, 1951; children—Elizabeth Rose, Fern Helen, Michael Scott. Mgr. data processing and procedures Conn. div. Gen. Time Co., 1960-63; dir. adminstrv. service Seeman Bros. Inc., Carlstadt, N.J., 1963-64; dir. corporate planning and v.p. mgmt. systems. Manhattan Industries Inc., Glen Rock, N.J., 1964-72; v.p. adminstrn. Gant Inc., New Haven, 1972-79; v.p. ops. Exquisite Form Industries Inc., Pelham Manor, N.Y., 1979—; mem. panel arbitrators Am. Arbitration Assn. Served with AUS, 1951-53. Mem. Nat. Assn. Accountants, Data Processing Mgmt. Assn., Am. Apparel Mfrs. Assn. Home: 285 Currier Dr Orange CT 06477 Office: Exquisite Form Industries Inc Pelham Manor NY

HOEFELMEYER, ALBERT BERNARD, cosmetic co. exec.; b. San Antonio, Mar. 27, 1928; s. Albert H. and Anna Theresa (McMonigal) H.; B.S. in Chemistry, St. Mary's U., San Antonio, 1949; M.A. in Chemistry, U. Tex., Austin, 1950; Ph.D. in Chemistry, Tex. A&M U., College Station, 1954. Research chemist Celanese Corp. Am., Clarkwood, Tex., 1953-55; asst. prof. chemistry Tex. A&I Coll., Kingsville, 1955-57; sr. nuclear engr., sr. research scientist Gen. Dynamics, Ft. Worth, 1957-71; v.p. Burkhart Trailer Mfg. Co., Ft. Worth, 1971-74; pres., owner Eagle Labs., Inc., Dallas, 1974—; sci. cons. Bac Stat Systems, Inc., Dallas, 1976—; adj. prof. chemistry evening coll. Tex. Christian U., Ft. Worth, 1958-68. Mem. Soc. Cosmetic Chemists, Am. Chem. Soc., Radiation Research Soc., S.W. Sci. Forum, N.Y. Acad. Scis., Sigma Xi, Phi Lambda Upsilon. Roman Catholic. Home: 7355 Greenacres Dr Fort Worth TX 76112 Office: 3738 W Northwest Hwy Dallas TX 75220

HOEFT, JERALD ROBERT, ins. co. exec.; b. West Bend, Wis., Sept. 3, 1942; s. Robert Herman and Dolores Cecilia (Bales) H.; B.B.A., U. Wis., Whitewater, 1964; m. Sandra Delores Schuster, June 7, 1969; children—Montgomery, Megan Marie. Cost analyst Bendix Corp., 1964-65; audit supr. Ernst & Ernst, Milw., 1965-72; v.p. fin., asst. treas. surg. care Blue Shield, Inc., Milw., 1972-79; v.p. fin., treas.

Wis. Employers Ins. Co., Green Bay, 1980—. C.P.A., Wis.; cert. mgmt. acct. Mem. Fin. Execs. Inst., Am. Inst. C.P.A.'s, Wis. Inst. C.P.A.'s, Nat. Assn. Accts., Inst. Mgmt. Acctg., Ins. and Acctg. Statis. Assn. Republican. Roman Catholic. Home: 4515 Wyandot Trail Green Bay WI 54302 Office: Wis Employers Ins Co 2777 Ridge Rd Green Bay WI 54303

HOEL, EDDIE R., trade assn. exec.; b. Columbia, Tenn., Feb. 18, 1943; s. Roy D. and Vera Christine Hoel; A.A., Beckley Coll., 1965; B.B.A., U. Charleston, 1969, M.A. in Counseling Psychology, 1975; grad. Ann. Seminar Bds. Realtors Adminstrn., 1972. Field rep. W.Va. Workmen's Compensation Fund, 1969-71; adjustor W.Va. Automobile Adjustment, Inc., Charleston, 1971-72; exec. v.p. W.Va. Assn. Realtors, Charleston, 1972-78, Kanawha Valley Bd. Realtors, Kanawha Valley Multiple Listing Service, Charleston, 1972—; cons. W.Va. Inst. Tech., 1979—. Mem. Kanawha County Republican Exec. Com., 1977—; com. chmn. Charleston Neighborhood Housing Services. Served with arty. U.S. Army, 1963-65. Mem. Soc. for Advancement Mgmt., W.Va. Communicators, Am. Soc. Assn. Execs. Clubs: Elks, Kanawha Ski (pres. 1975). Home: 709 Grace Ave Charleston WV 25302 Office: PO Box 6768 109 Pennsylvania Ave Charleston WV 25302

HOEY, JACK BURNS, utility exec.; b. Murrysville, Pa., July 4, 1927; s. Newton Park and Nellie M. (Clements) H.; B.A. in Math., Coll. William and Mary, Williamsburg, Va., 1948; m. Mary Jane Fletcher, July 9, 1955; children—Jack Burns, Susan, David and William (twins), Daniel, Anne. With Peoples Natural Gas Co., Pitts., 1949—, v.p. mktg., then exec. v.p., 1973-77, pres., 1977—, also dir.; dir. Consol. Natural Gas Service Co., Equibank and Equimark Co. Past chmn. bd. Youth Guidance, Pitts.; bd. dirs. United Way Allegheny County; trustee Penn's Southwest Assn.; exec. com. Regional Indsl. Devel. Corp. Southwestern Pa.; mem. exec. com. Western div. Pa. Economy League. Served with AUS, 1950-52. Mem. Am. Gas Assn., Am. Petroleum Inst., Pa. Gas Assn. (dir., chmn. 1980-81), Greater Pitts. C. of C. (dir.). Clubs: Duquesne, Oakmont Country, Allegheny. Office: 2 Gateway Center Pittsburgh PA 15222

HOFER, LAWRENCE JOHN EDWARD, chemist, govt. ofcl.; b. Salt Lake City, June 26, 1915; s. William Mathias and Friederike Wilhelmina (Loder) H.; B.A., U. Utah, 1937, M.A., 1939; Ph.D. (Sherman Clark fellow), U. Rochester, 1941; m. Marguerite Ione Tears, Dec. 25, 1941; 1 son, Richard Lawrence. Research asso. nat. def. research com. Dept. Def., 1941-43; chief phys. and catalytic chem. sect. Office Synthetic Liquid Fuels, Dept. Interior, Washington, 1944-65; head adsorption fellow Mellon Inst., Pitts., 1965-70; chief toxic materials br. div. health tech. Mine Safety and Health Adminstrn., Dept. Labor, Pitts., 1971—; cons. indsl. hygiene, catalysis, synthetic fuels. Fellow AAAS, Am. Inst. Chemists; mem. Am. Chem. Soc., Am. Indsl. Hygiene Assn., Air Pollution Control Assn. Presbyterian. Contbr. numerous monographs and bulls. on carbides of iron, cobalt and nickel, catalysis, automobile exhaust purification, x-ray powder diffraction, adsorption to profl. publs.; patentee in field. Home: 236 Hays Rd Pittsburgh PA 15241 Office: 4800 Forbes Ave Pittsburgh PA 15213

HOFF, PETER L., bus. machines co. exec.; b. Qew Gardens, L.I., N.Y., Oct. 15, 1938; s. Leroy P. and Mary Louise (Taylor) H.; ed. U. Md.; m. Patti Lazarus, Nov. 17, 1967; children—Pamela Louise, Jeffrey, Phillip, Bruce. Prodn. control analyst Burroughs Corp. B.C.D., Plainfield, N.J.; archtl. estimator, design cons. Gumina Constrn. Co., New Brunswick, N.J.; office mgr. Am. Sealcut Corp., West New York, N.J.; advising architect Twp. Planning Bd. Mem. Readington Twp. Planning Bd., 1970-76. Served with Armed Forces. Decorated Purple Heart. Mem. Nat. Rifleman's Assn. Home: 156 Hillcrest Pl North Bergen NJ 07047 Office: 324 55th St West New York NJ 07093

HOFF, RICHARD JOSEPH, pacemaker mfg. co. exec.; b. Buffalo, N.Y., June 7, 1942; s. Joseph Anthony and Marian I. (Schroeder) H.; B.S. in Acctg., SUNY, Buffalo, 1970; m. Michele Sandra Schulman, Aug. 1, 1970. Sr. acct. Ernst & Whinney, Buffalo, 1969-75; acctg. mgr. Band-It/ Houdaille, Denver, 1976-78; controller Telectronics Pty. Ltd., Denver, 1978-79, v.p., controller, 1979—. C.P.A., N.Y. State. Mem. Am. Inst. C.P.A.'s, N.Y. Soc. C.P.A.'s, Am. Prodn. and Inventory Control Soc., Purchasing Mgmt. Assn. Home: 11060 E Linvale St Aurora CO 80014 Office: 8515 E Orchard St Englewood CO 80111

HOFFART, WILBERT WALTER, container mfg. co. exec.; b. Bloomfield, Nebr., Dec. 27, 1943; s. Wilbert E. and Vesta D. (Dudley) H.; student U. Nebr., 1964-67; m. Elaine J. Scott, June 14, 1963; children—Jeffery D., Cindy D. Asst. sec.-treas. Gt. Plains Container Co., Hastings, Nebr., 1967-80, sec.-treas., controller, 1980—; dir. Allied Paper Box Co., Denver. Mem. adv. com. Central Nebr. Tech. Sch. Served with USN, 1962-64. Mem. Data Processing Mgmt. Assn., Hastings Jaycees (pres. 1976-77). Methodist. Club: So. Hills Country (Hastings). Home: 700 Shore Side Cove Hastings NE 68901 Office: 2000 Summit Ave Hastings NE 68901

HOFFARTH, GARRY ROY, utility co. exec., investor; b. Plentywood, Mont., Dec. 10, 1943; s. Roy Paul and Verda Rosella H.; B.S. in Commerce, Mont. State U., 1967; J.D., U. Md., 1968; m. Artha Lee Johansen, Dec. 23, 1961 (div.); children—Lei Arrin, Wade Carl. Admitted to Md. bar, 1968; mem. staff U.S. Sen. Lee Metcalf, Washington, 1961-68; dir. acquisitions, mem. legal dept. Quality Inns, Internat., Silver Spring, Md., 1968-73; dir. corp. devel. Valley Forge Corp. (Pa.), 1973-74; v.p. real estate Gen. Waterworks Corp., Phila., 1974—, also dir. subs.'s; pres., chmn. bd. Phila. Enterprises, Ltd. and Havdeco, Inc., 1977—. Mem. Nat. Assn. Corp. Real Estate Execs., Md. Bar Assn., Phi Alpha Delta. Home: 200 Locust St Philadelphia PA 19106 Office: 1500 Walnut St Philadelphia PA 19102

HOFFMAN, JACK W., ins. exec.; b. San Antonio, Sept. 23, 1930; s. Josh W. and Lillie G. (Cargill) H.; B.S., Baylor U., 1953; m. Joan Frances Mints, Nov. 1, 1952; children—Judy, Jill. Sales rep. Tex. Employers Ins. Assn., San Angelo, Tex., 1957-62, dist. mgr., 1962-64, dist. mgr., Harlingen, Tex., 1964-67, dist. mgr., Austin, Tex., 1967-73; pres. S.W. Ins. Assos. of Austin, Inc., 1973—. Mem. Ethics Commn., City of Austin, 1978-80. Served with USAF, 1952-56. Cert. ins. counselor, Fire Mark Soc. Mem. Ind. Ins. Agts. Austin (pres. 1979), Ind. Ins. Agts. Tex., Ind. Ins. Agts. Am., Ins. Counselors Tex., Profl. Ins. Agts. Am., Soc. Cert. Ins. Counselors. Republican. Baptist. Clubs: Rotary (pres. 1975-76), South Austin Civic (pres. 1979). Home: 7003 Treaty Oak Circle Austin TX 78749 Office: 4405 Pack Saddle Pass Austin TX 78745

HOFFMAN, JAMES WILLIAM, mfg. co. exec.; b. Louisville, Aug. 16, 1943; s. Otto and Freida (Schmitt) H.; B.S. in Mech. Engring., Purdue U., 1965; M.B.A., Ind. U., 1968. Mgr. adminstrv. services div. Arthur Andersen & Co., Chgo., 1968-76; controller AgriProducts Group A.E. Staley Mfg. Co., Decatur, Ill., 1976—. C.P.A., Ill.; Nat. Merit scholar. Mem. Am. Inst. C.P.A.'s, Ill. Soc. C.P.A.'s, Inst. Mgmt. Sci., Tau Beta Pi, Pi Tau Sigma. Home: 2854 Forrest Ln Decatur IL 62521 Office: 2200 Eldorado St Decatur IL 62525

HOFFMAN, JOHN DEAN, ins. broker; b. Lancaster, Pa., Jan. 26, 1945; s. Charles Maurice and Jane Dean (Findley) H.; B.A. in English, Franklin and Marshall Coll., 1966; m. Barbara Ann Williams, June 15, 1962; children—John David, Scott Thomas. Home office rep. Aetna Life and Casualty Co., Hartford, Conn., 1966, Milw., 1967, Buffalo, 1968; with William W. Warren & Assos., Inc. (co. named changed to Warren-Hoffman & Assos. Inc. 1976), Niagara Falls, N.Y., 1969—, v.p., 1970-76, exec. v.p., 1976-78, pres., chief exec. officer, 1978—. Chmn. various coms. United Givers Fund, 1969-71, 73, 75, 76; past pres. bd. assos. Mt. St. Mary's Hosp.; mem. Lewiston-Porter Central Sch. Bd., 1975-79, pres., 1977-78; gen. chmn. Porter Cup, 1980; mem. Youngstown Planning Bd., 1974-77. Recipient Niagara Falls Top Hat award Niagara Frontier Services, Inc., 1978. Mem. Nat. Ind. Ins. Agts. Assn., Nat. Assn. Surety Bond Producers, Constrn. Industry Employers Assn., N.Y. State Ind. Ins. Agts. Assn., Niagara Falls Ind. Ins. Agts. Assn., Niagara Falls C. of C., Niagara Falls Guilders Assn. Republican. Clubs: Niagara Falls, Niagara Falls Country. Office: Warren-Hoffman & Assos Inc 105 Main St Niagara Falls NY 14092

HOFFMAN, JOHN RAYMOND, telephone co. exec.; b. Rochester, N.Y., July 24, 1945; s. Raymond Edward and Ruth Emily H.; student U. Copenhagen, 1966; B.A., Washburn U., 1967; J.D., U. Mo., 1971; m. Linda Lee Moore, Aug. 20, 1970; 1 dau., Heather Anne. Admitted to Mo. bar, 1972, Tenn. bar, 1976, U.S. Supreme Ct. bar, 1975; gen. atty. United Telecommunications Inc., Shawnee Mission, Kans., 1970-75; gen. counsel, corporate sec., asst. treas. United Inter-Mountain Telephone Co. and United Telephone Co. of Carolinas, Bristol, Tenn., 1975-80; v.p., gen. counsel United Telephone System, Inc., Shawnee Mission, Kans., 1980—. Bd. dirs. Ward Park Improvement Assn., 1974-75. Recipient BNA Law Student award, 1971. Mem. Am., Mo., Kansas City, Tenn., Bristol bar assns., Am. Judicature Soc., Kappa Sigma, Phi Delta Phi. Presbyterian. Club: Optimist. Home: 2019 W 70th Terr Mission Hills KS 66208 Office: 2330 Johnson Dr Westwood KS 66205

HOFFMAN, MARION EUREL, fin. co. exec.; b. Matteson, Ill., Jan. 2, 1932; s. Marion Eurel and Christina Irene (Purtee) H.; student Milliken U., 1950; m. Anna Lou Wyatt, Nov. 15, 1953; children—David, Cheryl, Steven, Fianna. Auditor, asst. cashier, asst. v.p. mortgage banking, asst. v.p. installment lending, Ill. Nat. Bank, Springfield, 1950-67; pres. M.E. Hoffman Co., Springfield, 1967—; instr. Ill. Bankers Assn. Sch. Banking, 1961-68, various mortgage banking schs.; mem. Ill. Mortgage Banking Bd., 1980—. Mem. Ill. State C. of C., treas., bd. mem. Springfield C. of C., 1960-67; chmn. Springfield Municipal Band Commn., 1960—; active Springfield Central Area Devel. Assn. Mem. Ill. Home Builders Assn., Ill. Mortgage Bankers Assn. (dir. 1979—), Mortgage Bankers Assn. Am., Ill. State Savs. and Loan League. Republican. Club: Optimist (charter mem, pres. Luncheon Club, 1960). Home: 2234 Warson Rd Springfield IL 62704 Office: 901 S Second St PO Box 1026 Springfield IL 62705

HOFFMANN, RALF LUDWIG, chem. co. exec.; b. Berlin, Oct. 4, 1910; s. Ludwig and Marie (Weisbach) H.; grad. high sch.; m. Ingeborg Seepacher, Nov. 30, 1946; children—Christopher S.L., Michael R. (dec.). Chmn. bd. Hoechst Can., Inc., 1969-80; v.p., dir. Trans-Am. Chems., Ltd., 1958-80; dir. Hoechst Industries, Ltd., Montreal, Que., Can., SKW Electro-Metallurgy Can. Ltd. Mem. Canadian Inst. Internat. Affairs, Chem. Inst. Can., Soc. Chem. Industry. Club: Saint James. Home: 2095 Hanover Rd Montreal PQ Canada Office: 4045 Cote Vertu Saint Laurent PQ Canada

HOFKIN, MARK, heating and air conditioning wholesale co. exec.; b. Lodz, Poland, Aug. 4, 1946; s. Joseph and Wanda (Weiss) H.; came to U.S., 1961, naturalized, 1972; B.A., Temple U., 1970; M.B.A., Pace U., 1977; m. Zina Kopyt, Sept. 12, 1970; children—Monique, Michelle. Instr. Bordentown (N.J.) Mil. Acad., 1970-72; pres. Airmart Co., Phila., 1972-77; pres. Air-Line Corp., Phila., 1977—. Mem. Home Builders Phila., Refrigeration Service Engrs. Soc. Home: 1067 Hillview Turn Huntingdon Valley PA 19006 Office: 2187 E Huntingdon St Philadelphia PA 19125

HOFSTAD, RALPH PARKER, agrl. coop. exec.; b. Phila., Nov. 14, 1923; s. Ottar and Amelia (Davis) H.; student Hamline U., 1942-43, Gustavus Adolphus Coll., 1943-44, Northwestern U., 1944, U. Minn., 1946-47; B.B.A., Northwestern U., 1948; m. Adeline Smedstad, June 14, 1947; children—Diane (Mrs. Roger Dunker), Barbara (Mrs. Dan McClanahan), James, Ron, Tom, Susan. Accountant F S Services, Bloomington, Ill., 1948-51, mgmt. ops., 1953-65; pres. Farmers Regional Coop (Felco), Ft. Dodge, Iowa, 1965-70; sr. v.p. Agrl. Services, Land O'Lakes Inc., Ft. Dodge, 1970—, pres. Land O'Lakes Inc., Mpls., 1974—; dir. Mut. Service Ins. Cos., St. Paul, 1970—, Nat. Milk Producers Fedn., Washington, 1977—, Bd. dirs. Nat. Council Farmer Coops., Washington, 1973—, Goodwill Industries Am., 1977—; chmn. Internat. Energy Coop., Inc., 1979-80, bd. dirs. 1974—. Served with USNR, 1943-46. Methodist. Home: 6608 Field Way Edina MN 55436 Office: Land O'Lakes Inc PO Box 116 Minneapolis MN 55440

HOGAN, DONALD JOHN, JR., mfrs. rep. co. exec.; b. Evergreen Park, Ill., Feb. 23, 1944; s. Donald John and Jane Francis (Rumpf) H.; B.A., U. Notre Dame, 1965, M.A., 1967; m. Carolyn Vivian Smith, June 12, 1965; children—Judy, Molly, Donald III. Asst. football coach U. Notre Dame, 1964-66; mktg. analyst Shell Oil Co., Chgo., 1967; salesman Donald J. Hogan & Co., Chgo., 1967-69, pres., 1969—, chmn. bd., 1980—; pres. Hogan Co., 1980—; pres. Maintenance of Way Supply Group of Chgo., chmn. area com., 1980—. Chmn., St. Barnabas Athletic Bd., 1969—. Mem. Am. R.R. Engring. Assn. (asso.), Chgo., Northwest maintenance of way clubs, St. Ignatius Alumni Assn. (dir.). Democrat. Roman Catholic. Clubs: Monogram (U. Notre Dame). Home: 1943 W 102d St Chicago IL 60643 Office: 327 S LaSalle St Chicago IL 60604

HOGAN, PATRICIA ANNE, data processing service exec.; b. Boston, May 17, 1937; d. John Martin and Doris May (Fitzgerald) H.; B.S., Merrimack Coll., 1958; M.B.A., Loyola U., Balt., 1977. With Harvard Bus. Sch. and The Expt. in Internat. Living, 1958-67, Boston U. and Colby Jr. Coll., 1967-70; dir. fin. aid and student employment Goucher Coll., Balt., 1970-76; account exec. Comml. Credit Corp. of Control Data Corp., Balt., 1976-79; account exec. Sun Info. Services Subs. of Sun Oil Co., Boston, 1979—; cons. HEW. Mem. budget rev. com. United Fund; trustee Cambridge Friends Meeting. Mem. Exec. Women's Network (charter mem. Balt.), Boston Women's Exec. Luncheon Group, NOW. Clubs: Exec. of Boston C. of C., Appalachian Mountain, Balt. Bicycle, League of Am. Wheelmen, Masters Swim. Home: 790 Boylston St 23F Boston MA 02199 Office: Sun Info Services 100 Summer St Boston MA 02110

HOGAN, THOMAS DENNIS, III, oil co. exec.; b. St. Paul, Mar. 13, 1930; d. Thomas Dennis, Jr. and Charlotte (Bork) H.; B.S. in Econs., Yale U., 1953; m. Elizabeth Mansfield Bowen, Apr. 27, 1960; children—Thomas, IV, Kerry, Elizabeth. Gen. mgr. Consol. Industries S.A., Caracas, Venezuela, 1955-61; dir. diversification Singer Sewing Machine Co., N.Y.C., 1962-64; pres. Univest Corp., N.Y.C., 1964-71; dir. Proventa S.A., Mexico City, 1972-75; pres., dir. Oilfunds Investments, Inc., Miami, Fla., 1976—; dir. Griffith Co., HKB Energy Mgmt. Co., Petro Terra Pa. Inc., E.O.R. Tech. Inc. Served to 1st lt. USAF, 1953-55. Mem. Am. Petroleum Inst., Internat. Assn. Fin. Planners, Ky. Oil and Gas Assn., German Am. C. of C. Republican. Roman Catholic. Clubs: Riviera Country, Yale of N.Y. Home: 7135 SW 109th Terr Miami FL 33156 Office: 777 Brickell Ave Miami FL 33131

HOGAN, THOMAS EDWIN, oil drilling co. exec.; b. Shreveport, La., Apr. 14, 1940; s. Arch William and Emily Jane (Oden) H.; B.C.E., Ga. Inst. Tech., 1962; m. Elise Wheless, June 12, 1965; children—Tracey Elise, Mary Emily, William Hobson. Treas., So. Builders, Inc., Shreveport, 1963-73, v.p., 1966-73; asst. to pres. Wheless Drilling Co., Shreveport, 1973—; dir. Tensas Delta Land Co., Monaghan Land Co., Wheless Industries. Div. leader United Fund, 1966, 72; mem. bldg. com. Boy Scouts Am., pres. Norwela council; chmn. bd. trustees Constrn. Industry Advancement Fund, 1969-73, N.W. La. Carpenters Pension Trust, 1972-73; treas., trustee Southfield Sch., 1974-77; regional chmn. Ga. Tech. Ednl. Council, 1972—; bd. dirs. St. Mark's Day Sch., La. Polit. Action Council. Served to 1st lt. USAF, 1962-68. Mem. Associated Gen. Contractors (treas. Shreveport 1970-71, sec. 1971-72), Internat. Assn. Drilling Contractors (nat. dir.). Episcopalian. Home: 948 Trabue St Shreveport LA 71106 Office: 920 Comml Nat Bank Bldg Shreveport LA 71101

HOGAN, THOMAS LEE, sewing machine mfg. co. exec.; b. Detroit, Mar. 9, 1928; s. Thomas Lee and Maybelle Margarite (Wade) H.; B.S. Ind. U., 1954; postgrad. U. Ams., 1954-56; m. Luz Maria, June 9, 1956; children—Luz Maria, Thomas Lee, Brian Robert. Treas., Gen. Electric de Maxico, Mexico City, 1960-68; controller Singer-France, Paris, 1969-70; dir. fin. Singer Sewing Maching Co.-Japan, Tokyo, 1971-72; dir. fin. Singer Mexicana, S.A. de C.V., 1973-77, gen. mgr., v.p., 1978—. Served with U.S. Army, 1946-48, 50-51. Gen. Electric scholar. Mem. U.S. Navy League (treas. Mexico City council 1966-67, pres. 1967-68, pres. emeritus 1976—), Am. C. of C. Mex. Roman Catholic. Office: Singer Mexicana SA Av Nuevo Leon 250-11 Mexico 11 DF Mexico

HOGARTY, MICHAEL W., consumer products industry exec.; b. Chgo., June 10, 1943; s. Thomas P. and Muriel P. (Waterfall) H.; B.S. in Elec. Engring., Yale U., 1965; postgrad. Stevens Inst. Tech., 1965-68; m. Michele L. Reilly, June 24, 1961; children—Dawn, Michael, Cheryl. Devel. engr. Whitney-Blake Co., Hamden, Conn., 1961-65; various mfg. positions Johnson & Johnson Domestic Operating Co., New Brunswick, N.J., 1965-71; v.p. ops. Johnson & Johnson Dental Products Co. East Windsor, N.J., 1971-74; v.p. S.B. Thomas, Inc. unit of CPC Internat. Inc., Totowa, N.J., 1974-78, pres., chief exec. officer, 1978—, also dir. Vice pres. Paterson (N.J.) Regional Devel. Corp.; fund raising chmn. Raritan Valley United Fund, 1971-72, Raritan Valley council Boy Scouts Am., 1967-73. Mem. Am. Bakers Assn. (gov. 1976—), Pres.'s Assn. of Am. Mgmt. Assn. Home: 53 Longridge Rd Montvale NJ 07645 Office: 930 N Riverview Dr Totowa NJ 07512

HOGEMAN, GEORGE L., business exec.; b. Chatham, N.J., Dec. 14, 1916; s. George H. and Gladys (Moore) H.; A.B., Princeton, 1938; m. Mary Danter. With Aetna Life & Casualty Co., Hartford, 1940-69, asso. actuary, 1956-57, asst. v.p., 1957-58, v.p., 1958-69; pres. Paul Revere Life Ins. Co., Worcester, Mass., 1969-74; pres. Avco Corp., Greenwich, Conn., 1974-79, vice chmn. bd., 1979—. Office: 1275 King St Greenwich CT 06830

HOGEMAN, WYLIE BARROW, textile and chem. co. exec.; b. Baton Rouge, Mar. 20, 1931; s. Hubert Henry (dec.) and Mary Louis (West) H.; B.S. in Chemistry, La. State U., 1952, B.S. in Chem. Engring., 1956; postgrad. M.I.T., 1974; m. Lola Elizabeth Fenn, Dec. 28, 1957; children—Mary Laura, Lola Eustis. Chem. engr. Monsanto Textiles Co., Pensacola, Fla., 1956-59, chem. engr., 1959-63, sr. chem. engr., 1963-64, group leader, 1964-67, supr., 1967-68, plant engr., 1968-69, gen. supt. ops., 1969-71, plant mgr. polyester plant, Guntersville, Ala., 1971-74, dir. indsl. fibers bus. group, 1974-76, gen. mgr. mfg. div., St. Louis, 1976-80, gen. mgr. mktg. div., 1980, gen. mgr. rubber chems. div., 1981—; dir. Hale Mfg. Co., Wilmington, Del. Pres., Scenic Hills Improvement Assn., Pensacola, 1960-61. Served with C.E., U.S. Army, 1952-54. Mem. Am. Inst. Chem. Engrs., Am. Textiles Mgmt. Assn. Republican. Episcopalian. Club: Old Warson Country (St. Louis). Patentee in field. Home: 36 Fair Oaks St Saint Louis MO 63124 Office: 800 N Lindbergh St Saint Louis MO 63166

HOGLUND, KENNETH LUDWIG, bus. services co. exec.; b. N.Y.C., Nov. 8, 1946; s. Kaarlo Charles and Viola Ann (Kon) H.; B.A., Hartwick Coll., Oneonta, N.Y., 1968; m. Susan Lee Zaniboni, Sept. 21, 1968; 1 son, Kenneth Tyler. Mgr. catalog store Sears Roebuck & Co., Long Branch, N.J., Hammonton, N.J., Butler, Pa. and Pitts., 1968-73; marketing rep. Purolator Courier Corp., Richmond, Va., 1973-75, dist. mgr., Charleston, W.Va., 1975-76, regional mgr., Phoenix, 1976, Denver, 1977, group sales mgr., 1977—. Mem. Psi Chi. Home: 13318 E Florida St Aurora CO 80012 Office: 4725 Paris St Suite 200 Denver CO 80039

HOGUE, WILLIAM GUY, JR., mfg. co. exec.; b. Benton, Miss., Oct. 26, 1924; s. William Guy and Della Mae (Mize) H.; B.S., Bowling Green Coll. of Commerce, 1949; postgrad. Harvard Bus. Sch., 1970-71; m. Ethel Marie Van Namen, June 27, 1948; children—Sandra Carrol, William Guy, Sharon Lea, Mark Wayne. Pub. acct. John S. Glenn & Assos., Nashville, 1950-53, Arthur Young & Co., Houston, 1953-66; controller CRC Crose Internat., Houston, 1966-70; sec.-treas. Crutcher Resources Corp., Houston, 1970-73, Crutcher-Rolfs-Cummings, Inc., Houston, 1973—; dir. Power Quip Engring., Inc., Prodn. Rentals, Inc., Harvey, La., 1977-79. Deacon, Candlelight Bible Ch., 1964—. Served with USMC, 1943-46. Mem. Am. Inst. C.P.A.'s, Tex. Soc. C.P.A.'s, Miss. Soc. C.P.A.'s, Tenn. Soc. C.P.A.'s, Nat. Assn. Accts., Harvard Alumni Club. Club: Masons. Home: 5035 Candletree Dr Houston TX 77018 Office: PO Box 982 Houston TX 77001

HOGUET, ROBERT LOUIS, investment banker, broker; b. N.Y.C., Dec. 23, 1908; s. Robert Louis and Louise Robbins (Lynch) H.; A.B., Harvard, 1931, M.B.A., 1933; m. Constance M. Roberts, Aug. 3, 1940; children—Robert Louis III, Constance Middleton, George Roberts. With office of sec. U.S. Treasury Dept., Washington, 1933-35; with First Nat. City Bank, 1936-70, v.p., 1947-58, sr. v.p., 1958-62, exec. v.p., vice chmn. trust bd., 1962-70; partner Tucker, Anthony & R.L. Day, Inc., 1970-75, chmn., 1975—; dir. London Guarantee and Accident Co., N.Y.C., Phoenix Assurance Co., N.Y.C. Trustee Hosp. Spl. Surgery, N.Y.C.; bd. dirs. Lincoln Center Performing Arts, 1963-72, chmn., bd. dirs. Repertory Theatre, 1963-72; bd. dirs. French Inst.-Alliance Francaise; vice chmn. bd., trustee Barnard Coll., N.Y.C., trustee Aspen Inst. Humanistic Studies; bd. overseers Harvard Coll., 1965-71. Served from lt. to comdr. USNR, 1942-45. Mem. Council Fgn. Relations. Clubs: Links, Century. Downtown Assn., River (N.Y.C.); Piping Rock; Maidstone. Home: 1 E 66th St New York NY 10021 Office: 120 Broadway New York NY 10005*

HOHM, JOSEPH STEVEN, accountant; b. Los Angeles, Jan. 21, 1947; s. Joseph Edward and Rosina (Byers) H.; B.A. in Bus. magna cum laude, U. So. Calif., 1968, J.D., 1972; m. Theresa Ann D'Alvia, Apr. 30, 1978. TV comml. actor Bernyce Cronin Agency, Los

Angeles, 1964-72; sr. accountant tax dept. Haskins & Sells, Los Angeles, 1968-73; v.p., sec.-treas. GCI Internat., Los Angeles, 1973-75; v.p. fin. Automated Mgmt. Services, Inc., Redondo Beach, Calif., 1975-79; prin. Med. Acctg. Service, tax and fin. cons. to med. profls., also various corps. including Beta Pacific Inc., Hawaii, 1975—. Served with USAR, 1969-75. Recipient various acad. awards from coll.; Arthur Young Accounting scholar, 1967-68. Mem. Calif. Soc. C.P.A.'s, Am. Inst. C.P.A.'s. Republican. Club: Los Angeles Athletic. Office: 21707 Hawthorne Blvd Suite 306 Torrance CA 90503

HOHMAN, J. ALLAN, mfrs. rep.; b. Braddock, Pa., Aug. 1, 1953; s. George M. and Betty N. Hohman; student Clarion State Coll., 1971-73; B.S., U. Houston, 1975; m. Marianne Kufen, Sept. 8, 1979. Plant expeditor Baylor Co., Sugarland, Tex., 1973-74; buyer Keystone Valve Corp., Houston, 1974-76; outside sales/product mgr. Reliance Steel & Aluminum Corp., Houston, 1976, product mgr., 1976-77; v.p. sales Gulf Coast Metal Sales Co., Houston, 1977-80; pres. Tex. Consol. Industries, Inc., Houston, 1980—; dir. Internat. Spring Industries, Houston, 1980—. Youth dir. Central Baptist Ch., Spring Branch, Tex., 1977-78; head football coach, br. dirs. Aliff Sports Assn., Houston, 1977-78; youth dir. basketball Cy Far Sports Assn., Houston, 1979-80; active Inwood Forest Civic Club, Houston, 1978—. Mem. Purchasing Mgmt. Assn. Houston. Clubs: Inwood Forest Country, Houston Ski, Inwood Forest Racquetball. Home: 5942 Arncliffe St Houston TX 77088 Office: Tex Consol Industries 1318 Nance Houston TX 77002

HOILMAN, CHARLES WILLIAM, fin. planner; b. Blacksburg, Va., Mar. 3, 1941; s. Charles W. and Ethlyne (Clark) H.; B.S., USAF Acad., 1964; M.B.A., Babson Coll., Wellesley, Mass., 1972; M.S.T., Bentley Coll., Waltham, Mass., 1976; m. Janet J. McLaughlin, June 20, 1964; children—Charles William, III, Leslie Anne. Registered rep. Westamerica Co., Boston, 1971-73; fin. cons. Trend Assos., Boston, 1973-74; regional mgr., registered prin. Westamerica Fin. Corp., 1974-77; registered fin. prin., v.p. M.H.A. Fin. Corp., Braintree, Mass., 1977-79; pres. MHA Mgmt. Corp., 1979—, MHA Planning Systems, 1979—, MHA Fin. Corp., 1979—; investment adv. Mitchell, Hoilman & Assos., 1977-78; gen. partner MHA Oil & Gas Ltd., 1979—; dir. Fin. Planners Equity Corp., Tex. Gen. Petroleum Corp. Mem. alumni council Babson Coll. Served to capt. USAF, 1964-71; Vietnam. Decorated Silver Star, Purple Heart, D.F.C. (3), Air medal (7); C.L.U., C.F.P. Mem. Internat. Assn. Fin. Planners (pres. 1978, chmn. bd. 1979), Greater Boston Assn. Fin. Planners (pres. 1977), Inst. Cert. Fin. Planners (dir. 1974-75), Boston Life Underwriters Assn., Am. Soc. C.L.U.'s, Boston Bus. and Estate Planning Council. Congregationalist. Club: Middlesex. Home: 4 Pheasant Hill Westwood MA 02090 Office: 150 Wood Rd Suite 403 Braintree MA 02184

HOKANSON, CARL GUSTAF, multinat. corp. exec.; b. Los Angeles, Mar. 9, 1937; s. Carl Gustaf and Blanche Marie (Helton) H.; B.A. in Math. and Liberal Arts, Brown U., 1959; M.B.A. with distinction, Harvard, 1970; m. Mercedes Z. Lasarte-Mogas, June 14, 1969; 1 son, Christer. Vice pres. sales, v.p. market C.G. Hokanson Co., Inc., Los Angeles and Santa Ana, Calif., 1960-66; v.p. marketing Tranps. Support div. Lear Siegle,r Inc., Santa Monica, Calif., 1966-68, v.p. adminstrn. Climate Control Housing Group, 1970-72, dir., 1974-74, pres. internat. div., 1975-77; pres. Carl G. Hokanson, GmbH (Germany); v.p. S.W. Properties, Inc., 1974; dir. Olympic Internat., Inc., 1973, Erma Maschinen Und Waffen Fabrik, GmbH, Germany, 1973-75. Former dir. West Valley Community Hosp. Mem. World Affairs Council, Aerospace Industries Assn., Machinery and Allied Products Inst., West Los Angeles C. of C. (past dir.). Club: Bel Air Country. Inventor latch for aircraft galleys, 1967. Office: 16021 Woodvale Rd Encino CA 91436 also Schloss Strasse 10 5400 Koblenz Federal Republic Germany

HOLAND, PAMELA KRISIDA, investment/stock broker; b. Dallas, Jan. 22, 1940; d. John Lowery and Mary Elizabeth (Matthews) Vines; student Draughon's Bus. Coll., So. Meth. U., Okla. State U., N.D., State U., U. N.D.; children—David, Deborah, DiAnn, Brian, Michael. Service dir. Upjohn Health Care, Mpls., 1977; mgr. shopping center ops. ThorCo, Inc., Mpls., 1977—; investment counselor, broker Bache, Halsey Stuart Shields, Inc. (formerly Bache, Halsey & Stuart, Inc.), Mpls.; mem. N.D. Senate from 21st Dist., 1974-76. Chmn., organizer, founding pres. first hosp. aux. in Pawnee, Okla.; gen. chmn. Heart Fund Drive, Am. Cancer Soc. Fund Drive, 1967-69; chmn., organizer com. founding first public library in W.Fargo, N.D.; math. tutor Unwed Mother Program Luth. Social Services; area dir. N.D. State Com. for Library Devel.; asst. perceptual motor devel. tng. Opportunity Sch. for the Handicapped, Fargo, 1969-72; active LWV, chmn. constl. revision com., 1969-72, bd. dirs. Fargo area, 1972-74; gen. chmn. fund drive, pres. County Am. Cancer Soc., organizer two new chpts.; gen. chmn. com. fundraising com. sta. KFME, ednl. TV, Cass County N.D.; chmn. adv. bd. Fargo Community Day Care Center; bd. dirs. Fargo-Moorhead YWCA; Mpls. YWCA; chmn. legis. com. First Dist. Med. Aux. to Med. Assn.; Leader Red River Valley Campfire Girls program; student adv. bd., counseling center N.D. State U. Fargo; adv. com. N.D. State Social Services Bd.; adv. council to N.D. Mental Health Assn., state bd. dirs., sec. N.D. Med. Aux. to N.D. Med. Assn.; bd. dirs. Community Coordinated Child Care Fargo-Moorhead area; state bd. dirs. N.D. Epilepsy Found.; state chmn. bus. adv. com. to Dakota Assn. Native Americans; mem. Tri-Coll. Women's Bur.; campaign mgr. for candidate for Nat. Committeewoman; precinct chmn. polit. dist. 56A; dist. and state del. to polit. convs.; advisory com. to N.D. Social Services Bd.; mem. N.D. Adv. com. U.S. Commn. on Civil Rights; adv. council N.D. Gov.'s Commn. on Comml. Air Transp.; mem. Nat. Mcpl. League, conv. del., 1972-74. Mem. Profl. Women's Group, Nat. Assn. Female Execs. Club: Women's Rotary of Mpls. Home: 17 S 1st St #1408A Minneapolis MN 55401 Office: Bache Halsey Stuart Shields Inc 1852 IDS Center Minneapolis MN 55402

HOLCOMB, CURTIS ROBERT, computing co. exec.; b. Olive, Okla., Sept. 18, 1930; s. Deward Carter and Capitola (Schoonover) H.; B.S. in Chem. Engring., U. Tulsa, 1959; m. Iva Jean Phillips, Jan. 4, 1951; children—Kenneth Leroy, Robert Gene, William Gary. Process engr. Callery Chem. Co., Muskogee, Okla., 1959, Yuba Heat Transfer Co., Tulsa, 1959-60; sales engr. Indsl. Fabricating Co., Tulsa, 1960-67; partner Chromatic Alloys Co., Sand Springs, Okla., 1967-68; owner Indsl. Computing Co., Tulsa, 1967—. Dir., Educators Preferred Holding Co., 1972-73. Served with AUS, 1950-54. Mem. Am. Inst. Chem. Engrs. Home: 4551 S Columbia St Tulsa OK 74105 Office: 1843 E 15 St Tulsa OK 74104

HOLCOMB, DAVID LEE, petroleum industry research exec.; b. Kermit, Tex., May 16, 1947; s. Clarence Albert and Marjorie Jeanne (Slater) H.; B.S. in Biology and Chemistry, SW Tex. State U., 1970; M.S. in Biochemistry, U. Tex., 1971; m. Mickey Lou Smoot, Feb. 14, 1979. Biochemist, Odessa (Tex.) Water Reclamation Dept., 1972; from research chemist to engring. mgr. Cardinal Chem. Inc., Odessa, 1972-79; dir. research and devel. Smith Energy Services Co., Denver, 1979—. Mem. Soc. Petroleum Engrs., Am. Petroleum Inst. Republican. Methodist. Author papers in field. Home: 18559 W 60th Ave Golden CO 80401 Office: Smith Energy Services Co Junction Hwy 93 and 58 Golden CO 80401

HOLDEN, GEORGE FREDRIC, brewing co. exec.; b. Lander, Wyo., Aug. 29, 1937; s. George Thiel Holden and Rita (Meyer) Zulpo; B.S. in Chem. Engring., U. Colo., 1959, M.B.A. in Mktg., 1974; m. Dorothy Carol Capper, July 5, 1959; children—Lorilyn, Sherilyn, Tamilyn. Adminstr., plastics lab. EDP, prodn., engring. and tool control supervision Hercules Inc., Parlin, N.J., Salt Lake City, Cumberland, Md., 1959-70; by-product sales, new market and new product devel., resource planning and devel. and pub. relations Adolph Coors Co., Golden, Colo., 1971-76, dir. econ. affairs corp. public affairs dept., 1979—; mgr. facilities engring. Coors Container Co., 1976-79; instr. brewing, by-products utilization and waste mgmt. U. Wis., Del., Colo. Republican Conv., 1976, 78, 80. Mem. U.S. Brewers Assn. (chmn. by-products com., Hon. Gavel, 1975), Am. Inst. Indsl. Engrs. (dir. 1974-78). Co-author: Secrets of Job Hunting, 1972; contbr. articles to Chem. Engring. Mag., 1968-76. Home: 6463 Owens St Arvada CO 80004 Office: Adolph Coors Co Dept 733 Golden CO 80401

HOLDEN, JEFFREY BRIAN, computer scientist; b. Marlboro, Mass., Oct. 12, 1946; s. Gordon Leslie and Dorothy (Sargent) H.; B.S. in Engring. Mgmt., Norwich U., Northfield, Vt., 1968; M.S. in Mgmt. Info. Systems, Am. U., 1972; m. Eileen M. Meyer, Sept. 13, 1970; 1 dau., Jessica H. Sales engr. Buffalo Forge Co., 1968-69; With Comten, Inc., 1972-77, sales mgr. Northeast br., 1975-77; dir. mktg. communications products div. Computer Corp. Am., Cambridge, Mass., 1977-78, dir. communications products div., 1978—. Bd. dirs. Advocacy Internat., Washington, 1974-75. Served to capt. USAR, 1969-72. Author papers in field of electronic info. processing. Home: 158 Ministerial Dr Concord MA 01742 Office: 575 Technology Sq Cambridge MA 02139

HOLDEN, RAY LANIER, mgmt. and constrn. cons.; b. Peoria, Ill., Dec. 10, 1927; s. William Grant and Dorothy Louise (Fisk) H.; B.S. in Civil Engring., U. Notre Dame, 1949; m. Mary Susan Smith, June 18, 1960; children—Ray, Mark, Mary, Steven. With Ill. Div. Hwys., Peoria, 1949-51; with The Canonie Cos., Inc., South Haven, Mich., 1954-80, pres., 1972-80; pres. Ray L. Holden, Inc., South Haven, 1980—; dir. Engine & Leasing Co., S.H. Assos., Canonie Cos., Inc., Pullman Bank & Trust Co., All Seasons Marine, Inc., Alpha Engring., Inc. Former vice chmn., head fin. South Haven Community Hosp. Served with Armed Forces, 1952-54. Mem. ASCE, Am. Concrete Inst., Nat., Mich. socs. profl. engrs. Roman Catholic (former pres. parish council). Home: 2 Chestnut St South Haven MI 49090

HOLDER, HAROLD DOUGLAS, citrus and land co. exec.; b. Anniston, Ala., June 25, 1931; s. William Chester and Lucile Marie (Kadle) H.; student Anniston Bus. Coll., 1949, Jacksonville State U., 1954-57; grad. Druitt Sch. Speech, 1962; m. Shirlee Heiden, Apr. 5, 1971; children—Debra Marie Holder Greene, Harold Douglas, Robert Douglas. Dept. mgr. Sears, Roebuck & Co., Anniston, Ala., 1954-57, merchandising mgr., Atlanta, 1957-59, dir. coll. recruiting, 1959-61, dir. exec. devel. program, 1961, asst. personnel dir., 1962-63, store mgr., Cocoa, Fla., 1965-67, Ocala, Fla., 1963-65, asst. zone mgr., Atlanta, 1967-68, asst. gen. mgr. merchandising, 1968-69, sales promotion mgr. Sears in S., 1968; pres. Cunningham Drug Stores, Inc., Detroit, 1969-70, also dir.; v.p. Interstate Stores, N.Y.C., 1971; pres. Rahall Communications Corp., St. Petersburg, Fla., 1971-73, also dir.; chmn. bd., chief exec. officer, dir. Am. Agronomics Corp., 1973—; treas., dir. Bay Capital Corp., Tampa; dir. Sun City Industries, Inc., Key West Harbour Devel. Corp., Miracle Inc.; dir., chmn. exec. com. Coastland Corp. Fla., Cutler-Fed. Inc.; dir., pres. Golden Harvest Inc. Chmn. United Appeal, Ocala, Fla., 1964, Cocoa, 1966; dir. fund-raising dr. Am. Heart Assn., Ocala, 1964; mem. Marion (Fla.) Com. of 100; bd. dirs. So. Coll. Placement Assn., SHARE U. Fla., Marion ARC, Opera Arts Assn.; trustee Eckerd Coll., St. Petersburg, Fla. Served with USMC, 1950-53. Recipient Distinguished Service award Marion County 4-H Club, 1965; named Outstanding Young Man Am., U.S. Jr. C. of C., 1966. Mem. Young Pres.'s Orgn. (past chpt. chmn.), Chief Execs. Forum, Newcomen Soc., DeSoto County C. of C. (bd. dirs.). Episcopalian. Clubs: Detroit Athletic, Detroit Renaissance; Palma Ceia Golf and Country (Tampa); St. Petersburg Yacht; Author: Don't Shoot, I'm Only a Trainee, 1975. Editorial bd. South Mag. Home: 5002 Shore Crest Circle Tampa FL 33609 Office: 4600 W Cypress St Tampa FL 33702

HOLDER, HOWARD RANDOLPH, broadcasting corp. exec.; b. Moline, Ill., Nov. 14, 1916; s. James William and Charlotte (Brega) H.; B.A., Augustana Coll., 1939; m. Clementi Lacey-Baker, Feb. 21, 1942; children—Janice Clementi Holder Collins, Susan Charlotte Holder Mason, Marjory Estelle, Howard Randolph. With radio stas. WHBF, Rock Island, Ill., 1939-41, WOC, Davenport, Iowa, 1945-47, WINN, Louisville, 1947, WRFC, Athens, Ga., 1948-1956, WGAU & WNGC, Athens, 1956—; pres. Clarke Broadcasting Corp., Athens, 1956—, Mid-West Ga. Broadcasting Corp., Griffin, 1965—; dir. Citizens & So. Nat. Bank Athens. Chmn. adv. bd. Salvation Army, 1962-63, mem., 1952—; chmn. Athens Parks and Recreation Bd., 1952-62; chmn. Cherokee dist. Boy Scouts Am., 1966-67, now v.p. bd. N.E. Ga. council; mem. adv. bd. Clarke County Juvenile Ct., 1960-72; chmn. region IV Ga. div. Am. Cancer Soc., 1968; bd. dirs. Athens Crime Prevention Com., 1960-70; mem. Georgians for Safer Hwys., 1970; mem. adv. bd. Athens-Clarke County ARC, 1950-70; trustee Ga. Rotary Student Fund, Inc., 1969—; mem. Model Cities Policy Bd., 1970-71; co-pres. Friends U. Ga. Mus. Art, 1973-75; sec. adv. bd. Henry W. Grady Sch. Journalism, U. Ga., 1973-74, mem., 1972-76; mem. adv. com. Ga. Commn. for Nat. Bicentennial, 1976; bd. dirs. Rec. for the Blind, 1977—. Served with AUS, 1941-46; ETO; maj. USAR ret. Named Boss of Year, Athens Jr. C. of C., 1959; Broadcaster-Citizen of Year, Ga. Assn. Broadcasters, 1962; Employer of Year, Bus. and Profl. Womens Club, 1969; Athens Citizen of Year, Rotary Club, 1971, Athens Womans Club, 1971; Ga. Pioneer Broadcaster of Year award DiGamma Kappa, 1971; Silver Beaver award Boy Scouts Am., 1973; Outstanding Achievement award Augustana Coll. Alumni Assn., 1973; Liberty Bell award Athens Bar Assn., 1977. Robert Stolz medaille, 1973; Paul Harris fellow, 1978. Mem. Res. Officers Assn. (pres. Athens chpt. 1962), Ga. Assn. Broadcasters (pres. 1961), Athens Area C. of C. (pres. 1970), Ga. AP Broadcasters (pres. 1963), Augustana Coll. Alumni Assn. (dir. 1973-76), Internat. Platform Assn., Golden Quill, Gridiron, Sigma Delta Chi, Alpha Psi Omega, Alpha Delta Sigma, DiGamma Kappa, Phi Omega Phi. Clubs: Rotary (pres. Athens club 1957-58, gov. dist. 692, 1969-70); Touchdown (pres. 1963-64) (Athens). Home: 383 Westview Dr Athens GA 30606 Office: 850 Bobbin Mill Rd Athens GA 30604

HOLDER, STUART STROTHARD, aviation cons.; b. Summit, N.J., Oct. 15, 1943; s. Clinton Howard and Kathleen (Strothard) H.; B.A., U. Pitts., 1966; M.A., Kent State U., 1968; m. Sandra Abagail Smith, June 10, 1967; children—Alecia Marjorie, Clinton Charles, James Frederick. City planner City of Oak Ridge, 1967-69; planner Spindletop Research Co., Lexington, Ky., 1969-73; v.p. Landrum & Brown, Inc., aviation cons., Cin., 1973—. Mem. phys. com. bd. M.E. Lyons YMCA, Cin., 1979—; treas. bd. deacons Mt. Washington Presbyterian Ch., 1979-80. Mem. Am. Planning Assn., Gamma Theta Upsilon. Clubs: Coldstream Country, Beechmont Racquet. Home: 638 Bennettwood Ct Cincinnati OH 45230 Office: 290 Central Trust Bldg Cincinnati OH 45202

HOLDING, LAURA ANNE, law librarian, cons.; b. Wilkinsburg, Pa., Sept. 9; d. James Clarke Carlisle and Laura May (Krepps) H.; grad. Baldwin Sch., Bryn Mawr, Pa.; A.B., Mt. Holyoke Coll. Asst. tech. dept. Carnegie Library of Pitts.; librarian Assn. Casualty and Surety Execs., N.Y.C., Air Reduction Co., N.Y.C., 1942-43, Davis Polk & Wardwell, 1943-73, librarian emeritus, 1973—. Active ARC fund drives, 1949-61, Queens div. Am. Cancer Soc., 1957-64; hostess St. Nicholas Club for Servicemen, N.Y.C., 1942-44; vol. Atlantic chpt. Sierra Club, 1976. Recipient award of merit Central Queens chpt. ARC, 1954, 59. Mem. Am. Assn. Law Libraries, Law Library Assn. Greater N.Y. (treas. 1947-48, v.p. 1948-49). Club: Mt. Holyoke (N.Y.C.). Author: Subject Heading Index Guide for Opinions and Memoranda of law, 1976. Editorial bd. Manual of Private Law Library Procedure, 1960-62, also contbr. Home: 69-09 108th St Forest Hills NY 11375

HOLDRIDGE, BARBARA (MRS. LAWRENCE B. HOLDRIDGE), book publishing co. exec.; b. N.Y.C., July 26, 1929; d. Herbert L. and Bertha (Gold) Cohen; A.B., Hunter Coll., 1950; m. Lawrence B. Holdridge, Oct. 9, 1959; 2 children. Asst. editor Liveright Pub. Corp., N.Y.C., 1950-52; co-founder Caedmon Records, Inc., N.Y.C., 1952, partner, 1952-60, pres., 1960-62, treas., 1962-70; pres. Caedmon Records, 1970-75; founder, pres. Stemmer House Pubs., Inc., 1975—. Co-founder v.p. Shakespeare Rec. Soc., Inc., N.Y.C., 1960—, Theatre Rec. Soc., Inc., N.Y.C., 1964—; co-founder History Rec. Soc., Inc., N.Y.C., 1964, pres., 1964-70. Lectr. on Ammi Phillips, 1959—. Recipient Am. Shakespeare Festival award, 1962; named to Hunter Coll. Hall of Fame, 1972. Mem. Phi Beta Kappa Assos. Contbr. articles to Antiques, Art in Am. Home: Stemmer House Caves Rd Owings Mills MD 21117 Office: 2627 Caves Rd Owings Mills MD 21117

HOLDT, ROY HOWARD, mfg. co. exec.; b. Edgewood, Md., Nov. 19, 1920; s. Jacob S. and Francis (Hansen) H.; student Dyke Bus. Coll., 1941, Cleve. State U., 1947; m. Audrie Smith, Oct. 26, 1972; children by previous marriage—Linda D. Holdt Greene, Douglas M. With Lake Erie Chem. Co., Cleve., 1938-40, Apex Elec. Mfg. Co., 1941-56; div. controller White Consol. Industries, Inc., Cleve., 1956-58, controller, 1958-61, v.p., controller, 1961-64, v.p. fin., 1964-67, sr. v.p., 1967-69, exec. v.p., dir., 1969-72, pres., chief operating officer, 1972-76, chmn. bd., chief exec. officer, 1976—; dir. Cleve. Trust Corp., Cleve. Electric Illuminating. Bd. dirs. Greater Cleve. Growth Assn., Fairview Gen. Hosp., Cleve. State U. Devel. Found. Served with U.S. Army, 1942-45. Mem. Nat. Assn. Accountants. Clubs: Pepper Pike (Ohio), Ohio State U. Pres.'s, Westwood Country; Clevelander, Cleve. Athletic, Mid-Day, The 50, Clifton, Union, Treasurers; Duquesne (Pitts.). Home: 174 Plymouth Dr Bay Village OH 44140 Office: 11770 Berea Rd Cleveland OH 44111

HOLIDAY, HARRY, JR., steel co. exec.; b. Pitts., July 2, 1923; s. Harry and Charlotte Poe (Rutherford) H.; B.S. in Metall. Engring. with honors, U. Mich., 1949; m. Kathlyn Collins Watson, Sept. 6, 1947; children—Edith Elizabeth, Harry III, Albert Logan II. Spl. assignment metall. engring. adminstrn. Armco Steel Corp., Middletown, Ohio, 1949-55, asst. to supt. blast furnace, Hamilton, Ohio, 1955-57, supt. blast furnace, 1957-59, asst. gen. supt. steel plant, Middletown, 1959-64, gen. supt. steel plant, 1964-66, dir. raw materials, 1966-67, v.p. steel ops., 1967-69, exec. v.p. steel, 1969-74, pres., 1974-79, now chief exec. officer, also dir.; dir. Cin. Gas & Electric Co., Reserve Mining Co., First Nat. Bank Middletown, Nat. Cash Register. Pres., Middletown YMCA, 1955-58; pres. Moundbuilders Area council Boy Scouts Am., 1963-67. Served to capt. AUS, 1943-46. Mem. AIME (J.E. Johnson, Jr. Blast Furnace award), Am., Internat. iron and steel insts., Tau Beta Pi, Psi Upsilon. Office: Armco Inc 703 Curtis St Middletown OH 45043*

HOLIMAN, CLAUDE EDWARD, JR. (EDDIE), bldg. supply mfg. exec.; b. Canon City, Colo., Nov. 9, 1926; s. C.E. and Lillian J. (Lewis) H.; B.S. in Mktg., U. Colo., 1949; m. Bertha May Johnson, Aug. 25, 1951; children—Cleg Timothy, Shauna Jo. Lumber salesman Henshaw & Ellwanger, Denver, 1949-51, Gene Wright & Dependable Lumber & Supply, Denver, 1952-55; sales mgr., 1956-59; founder, pres. Plateau Supply Co., Denver, 1959—, Backer Rod Mfg. & Supply Co., Denver, 1972—; distbr. adv. com. Certainteed Sales Corp., Valley Forge, Pa., 1975. Served with USNR, 1944-46. Mem. Wood, Inc., Acoustical Soc., Colo. Constrn. League, Hoo Hoo (sec. 1953-54), Sheet Metal and Air Conditioning Assn., Sigma Chi. Clubs: Arrowhead Country (Roxborough Park, Colo.); Los Verdes Golf (Denver). Patentee Denver Foam, open cell polyurethane foam caulking backer-rod. Home: 595 W Lake Ave Littleton CO 80120 Office: 2401 E 40th Ave Denver CO 80205

HOLLAND, CHARLES LEE, mktg. exec.; b. Shelby, N.C., Nov. 17, 1941; B.S. in Nuclear Engring., N.C. State U., 1965; postgrad. U. Va., 1969-70. Asso. engr. Boeing Co., Seattle, 1965-66; mgr. service products Babcock & Wilcox Co., Lynchburg, Va., 1967-74; bus. devel. mgr. Brown & Root, Inc., Houston, 1974-79; v.p. mktg. Blount Internat., Ltd., Montgomery, Ala., 1979—. Active Arrowhead Civic Assn. Mem. Am. Mgmt. Assn., Am. Mktg. Assn., ASME, Newcomen Soc. Republican. Clubs: Arrowhead Golf and Country. Home: 203 Arrowhead Dr Montgomery AL 36117 Office: 4520 Executive Park Dr Montgomery AL 36116

HOLLAND, HAL DERRINGTON, corp. fin. ofcl.; b. Long Beach, Calif., Mar. 22, 1925; s. Charles Philip and Gertrude Marie (Witte) H.; grad. acctg. Long Beach (Calif.) Bus. Coll., 1947; B.S. in Mgmt., U. West Fla., 1971; m. Theresa Margaret Frigo, Sept. 27, 1953: 2 sons, Mark Christian, John Derrington. Chief acct. Buffum's Dept. Store, Long Beach, 1948-50; commd. 2d lt. U.S. Air Force, 1950, advanced through grades to maj., 1964, dir. acctg. and fin., Vietnam, 1968-69, ret. 1969; founder, exec. dir., Am. Tax and Budget, Ft. Walton Beach, Fla., 1969—; acct. Coleman L. Kelly, Kelly Enterprises, C.L. Kelly Trust, Kelly Homes, Inc., Destin, Fla., 1972-73; controller Tolbert Enterprises (Ramada Inn of Ft. Walton) Resort, 1975—. Bd. dirs. United Way Okaloosa County, 1976—. Served with USAAF, 1943-45. Decorated Bronze Star, Air Medal with three oak leaf clusters. Recipient awards, United Way, Good Citizenship, 1975, Exceptional Contribution, 1977. Mem. Nat. Assn. Accts. (Pensacola, Fla., Mktg. Council 1977-78), Ret. Officers Assn., DAV, Internat. Entrepreneurs Assn., Alumni Council U. West Fla. Club: Kiwanis (Ft. Walton Beach, bd. dirs., 1977-80). Developed, established, coordinated exec. devel. program for Air Force plant rep., Republic Aviation Corp., N.Y., 1958-61. Home: 28 Chelsea Dr Fort Walton Beach FL 32548 Office: American Tax and Budget 223 N Eglin Pkwy Fort Walton Beach FL 32548

HOLLAND, HAROLD HERBERT, banker; b. Clifton Forge, Va., Feb. 11, 1932; s. Tristum Shandy and Ida Paxton H.; student Coll. William and Mary, 1952-54; B.A., M.B.A., George Washington U.; m. Nellie M. Thomas, Jan. 15, 1955; children—Richard Long, Michael Wayne. Tech. asst., bank ops. Fed. Res. Bank, Washington, 1959-60; v.p. Falls Church Bank (Va.), 1962-67; exec. v.p. Bank of New River Valley, Radford, Va., 1967-70, First Va. Fin. Plan, Radford, 1967-70; pres. Farmers Nat. Bank, Salem, Va., 1970-74; pres. Am. Nat. Bank, Kalamazoo, 1974-76, chmn. bd., 1976—; chmn. bd., pres. Am. Nat. Holding Co., Kalamazoo; bd. dirs. Assn. Bank Holding Cos. Chmn.

bus.-academia dialogue Kalamazoo Coll. Served with U.S. Army, 1952-54. Recipient Disting. Service award U.S. Jr. C. of C., 1965. Mem. Am. Bankers Assn., Mich. Bankers Assn., Kalamazoo C. of C. Methodist. Clubs: Kalamazoo Country, Park, Rotary. Office: Am Nat Bank 136 E Michigan Ave Kalamazoo MI 49007

HOLLAND, JOHN GORDON, mech. engr.; b. Milw., June 13, 1948; s. William Towne and Doris Jeanette (Berg) H.; B.S.M.E., U. Wis., Madison, 1971, M.B.A., 1975; m. Mary Kay Finley, Nov. 26, 1971. Asst. project engr. Flad & Assos., Inc., Madison, 1971-75; asst. project engr. Broyles & Broyles Inc., Glen Burnie, Md., 1975, project engr., Ft. Worth, 1975-77; v.p. Mech. Economics Co. Am., Inc., Dallas, 1977-81; asst. dir. engring. Jacobs Architects, Pasadena, Calif., 1981—. Recipient Gustav Larson award U. Wis., 1969; registered profl. engr., Wis., Md., Colo., Tex. Mem. Nat., Tex. socs. profl. engrs., ASHRAE. Home: 3124 Dreeben Dr Fort Worth TX 76118

HOLLAND, KENNETH MILTON, mfg. co. exec.; b. Richmond, Calif., Apr. 12, 1923; s. Charles Arthur and Eleanor Catherine (Morse) H.; B.S. in Chemistry, U. Calif., 1943; m. Dorothy Anne Davis, Sept. 24, 1949; 1 son, David Kenneth. Chemist Chevron Research Corp., Richmond, 1945-46, Reinforced Plastics Devel., Richmond, 1946-48; co-founder, v.p., dir. Hexcel Corp., Dublin, Calif., 1948—. Trustee Monterey Inst. Fgn. Studies. Served to lt. AUS, 1943-45; ETO. Mem. Soc. of Plastics Engrs. (founding bd. mem. Golden Gate sect. 1947), Soc. of Plastics Industry (Outstanding Service award, pres. North Calif. chpt. 1955-56). Clubs: Pacheco, Pebble Beach and Tennis, Monterey Peninsula Country. Patentee in field. Home: PO Box 1357 Pebble Beach CA 93953 Office: 11711 Dublin Blvd Dublin CA 94566

HOLLANDER, BETTY RUTH, engring. co. exec.; b. Bayonne, N.J., Jan. 13, 1930; d. Irving David and Gertrude (Friedland) Grodberg; B.A., Douglass Coll., 1951; postgrad. N.Y. U., Harvard U., Stanford U.; m. Milton B. Hollander, June 8, 1952; children—Eva Lynn, Steven, Aaron, Joel. Pres., chmn. bd. Omega Group, Stamford, Conn., 1962—; Conn. rep. White House Conf. on Small Bus., 1980; founding mem. Entrepreneurial Devel. Group of U. Conn.; mem. assos. bd. State Nat. Bank. Active Boy Scouts Am.; mem. small bus. adv. bd. U. Conn. Named Women of Year, Rippowam Bus. and Profl. Women's Club, 1979. Mem. Southwestern Area Assn. Commece and Industry (dir., exec. bd.), Stamford Econ. Assistance Corp. (dir.). Office: 1 Omega Dr Largo Industrial Park Stamford CT 06907

HOLLANDS, JOHN HENRY, electronics co. exec.; b. North Hornell, N.Y., Mar. 14, 1929; s. Henry Ward and Marion Eloise (Stanton) H.; A.B., Cornell U., 1951, M.B.A., 1952; m. Helen Louise Bearer, June 22, 1957; children—Wendy Lynn, Robert John, Kathryn Jean, Christine Elizabeth. Various positions in purchasing Westinghouse Electric Corp., Edison, N.J., 1954-65; gen. mgr. BSR (USA) LTD., Blauvelt, N.Y., 1965-73, pres., 1973-78, chmn., 1978—; dir. BSR (USA) Ltd., BSR (Can.), Ltd., BSR (Japan) Ltd., Audio Dynamics Corp., dbx, Inc. Trustee, St. Thomas Aquinas Coll., 1973-76, Rockland County Center for Arts, 1976. Served to 1st lt. USAF, 1952-54. Mem. Electronics Industry Assn. (gov.). Republican. Methodist. Home: 79 Edgewood Rd Allendale NJ 07401 Office: BSR (USA) Ltd Route 303 Blauvelt NY 10913

HOLLANDSWORTH, KENNETH PETER, consumer products exec.; b. York, Pa., Jan. 18, 1934; s. Dover Daniel and Sarah Kathryn (Meyers) H.; B.A., Gettysburg Coll., 1956; m. Edith D. Butera, Oct. 15, 1960; children—Stephanie, Tracy. Purchasing clk. Certain-Teed Products Corp., York, 1958-59; territorial salesman Todd div. Burrough Corp., Allentown, Pa., 1959-61; dir. presentation and incentive sales then nat. dir. retail sales Hamilton Watch Co., Lancaster, Pa., 1962-69; gen. mgr. Vendome Watch div. Coro Inc., N.Y.C., 1969-71; pres., chief exec. officer Jules Jurgensen Corp. subs. Downe Communications, Inc., N.Y.C., 1972-75; exec. v.p., sec. to corp. Optel Corp. Princeton, N.J., 1975-76, also dir.; pvt. fin. and gen. mgmt. cons., 1976-78; pres., dir. Thomas-Pond Bus. Devel. Group, Inc., 1978-80; v.p. consumer products Commodore Internat. Ltd., 1980—. Served with U.S. Army, 1956-58. Author: The Emerging Watch Industry, 1978. Home: 905 Edgewood Rd Yardley PA 19067

HOLLENBECK, THOMAS MICHAEL, mfg. co. exec.; b. Balt., Apr. 24, 1948; s. Laverne Clarence and Agnes Anne (McNally) H.; student So. Meth. U., 1966-68; m. Kay Elaine Kercheville, Apr. 25, 1970; children—Mark, Melissa. Regional sales mgr. Atlas Match Corp., San Francisco, 1969-74; nat. sales mgr. Open Road Industries, Los Angeles, 1974-76; v.p. sales Nat. Coach Corp., Los Angeles, 1976—. Served with USMCR, 1969. Mem. Recreation Vehicle Industry Assn. Republican. Roman Catholic. Club: Prestonwood Country. Home: 1111 Chautaugua Blvd Pacific Palisades CA 90272 Office: 130 W Victoria St Gardena CA 90248

HOLLENBERG, ROBERT LEE, fin. exec.; b. Arrowwood, Alta., Can., Nov. 7, 1931; s. Quinter Earl and Florence Margaret (Wallace) H. (parents Am. citizens); B.S., Manchester Coll., 1957; m. Helen Ruth Bollinger, Feb. 5, 1955; children—Robert Eugene, Cynthia Ann Hollenberg Cochrane, William Bruce. Accounting trainee Central Soya Co., Inc., Marion, Ohio, 1957-61; jr. accountant Essex Internat., Inc., Ft. Wayne, Ind., 1961-65, sr. accountant, 1965-67, internal auditor, 1967-69, asst. controller, 1969-76; controller Tokheim Corp., Ft. Wayne, 1976—. Chmn. troop com. Boy Scouts Am., Ft. Wayne, 1969-73, com. mem., 1972-74; chmn. Grand Prairie Twp. Zoning Bd. Appeals, Marion, Ohio, 1959-61. Served with USAF, 1951-55. Mem. Nat. Assn. Accountants (chpt. pres. 1976-77), Inst. Internal Auditors (dir. 1968-70), Ft. Wayne C. of C. Republican. Mem. Ch. of the Brethren. Clubs: Ft. Wayne Exec., Mason (Shriner), Order of DeMolay (chmn. adv. council 1975— Hon. Legion of Honor 1978). Home: 3416 Trier Rd Fort Wayne IN 46815 Office: 1600 Wabash Ave Fort Wayne IN 46801

HOLLIDAY, (MARJORIE) RUSSELL, mag. exec.; b. Florence, S.C., July 11, 1949; d. John Monroe Johnson and Marjorie (Russell) Holliday; B.A. in English, Converse Coll., 1971; postgrad. Inst. Fin., 1976. Tchr. English and psychology 1st Bapt. Prep. Sch., Charleston, S.C., 1971-72; mgmt. trainee Sea Pines Corp., Hilton Head, S.C., 1972-73; asst. to v.p. Pee Dee Farms Corp., Galivants Ferry, S.C., 1974; registered rep. Morgan Stanley & Co., N.Y.C., 1974-76; advt. sales account mgr., nat. fashion mgr. Redbook mag., N.Y.C., 1977-80, mktg. mgr., 1981—, advt. dir. Be Beautiful mag., subs. Redbook, 1980-81. Mem. Advt. Women N.Y. Baptist. Home: 175 E 79th St New York NY 10021 Office: 230 Park Ave New York NY 10021

HOLLINGTON, DAVID WILLIAM, banker; b. Cleve., June 9, 1944; s. Richard Rings and Annett Ewing (Kirk) H.; A.B., Univ. Sch., Franklin and Marshall Coll., 1966; postgrad. Western Res. Law Sch., 1966-67, Bus. Sch. Harvard, 1973; m. Deborah Lynn Jones, May 8, 1976; 1 dau., Courtenay L. Asst. v.p. Ohio Bank & Savs. Co., Findlay, 1968-70, sec., 1970-74, v.p., sec., 1974-76, pres., 1976—; dir. various corps. Trustee Hancock Hist. Mus., FANTAM, Hancock County United Way, Arthritis Found. of NW Ohio, 1972—. Mem. Am., Ohio bankers assns., Young Presidents Orgn. Episcopalian. Clubs: Kirtland Country, Findlay Country; Winois Point Shooting. Home: Holly Creek Farm Findlay OH 45840 Office: 236 S Main St Findlay OH 45840

HOLLINS, OREL BROOKS, fabric co. exec.; b. Roanoke, Va., Sept. 25, 1922; s. Oakley Leek and Melissa (Keaton) H.; student Roanoke Coll., 1942; m. Ruby Lee Manning, July 28, 1945; 1 dau., Marcia Elaine. With Burlington Industries, 1943-67, asst. plant mgr., 1967; gen. mgr., Hillsborough Textiles (N.C.) div. Falk Fibers and Fabrics, 1968-77, dir. product planning, 1977-78; pres. Hollins Enterprises, Inc., Hillsborough, 1978-79; v.p. Fairystone Fabrics, Jersey Fabrics, 1980—. Vice pres. Orange County United Way, chmn. campaign drive, 1974; deacon, trustee First Baptist Ch., 1978-80; bd. dirs., chmn. exec. com. Orange County Med. Found., 1978-80. Mem. Am. Assn. Textile Color and Chemist, N.C. Wildlife Fedn. Democrat. Clubs: Exchange (pres. Burlington 1958, pres. Hillsborough 1973), Orange County Fish and Wildlife (pres. 1978), Masons. Home and Office: Route 4 Box 66 Hillsborough NC 27278

HOLLIS, THOMAS, JR., indsl. engr.; b. Cambridge, Mass., Sept. 7, 1918; s. Thomas and Hilda (Smith) H.; B.S. in Indsl. Engring., Northeastern U., 1941; m. Alcester Weare, May 2, 1942; children—Thomas III, Virginia Weare, Marjorie Anne. Machinist, Sanborn Co., Cambridge, 1936-38; tool engr. Gen. Electric Co., Lynn, Mass., 1938-42; sales engr. A.N. Nelson, Inc., Bklyn., 1942-45; v.p. Nelco Tool Co., Inc. (now div. Brown & Sharpe Mfg. Co.), Manchester, Conn., 1945-52, pres., gen. mgr., 1952-63, v.p., gen. mgr. cutting tool div. Brown & Sharpe Mfg. Co., Providence, 1958-63; pres. Brubaker North-eastern, Inc., 1963-64; mgr. cutting tool ops. Pratt & Whitney div. Colt Industries, Inc., 1964-65, v.p., gen. mgr. cutting tool ops., 1965-67, pres. small tool div. Pratt & Whitney, Inc., 1967-75; pres., chief exec. officer, dir. O.K. Tool Co., Inc., Milford, N.H., 1975—; dir. Gammons Investment Co. Mem. corp. Northeastern U., 1978—. Mem. Cutting Tools Mfrs. Assn. (pres. 1980, dir.), Metal Cutting Tool Inst. (dir.). Am. Soc. Tool and Mfg. Engrs., Soc. Carbide Engrs. charter, pres. 1950). Club: Civitan (dir. Manchester 1955). Patentee cutting tools. Home: 50 Pine St Peterborough NH 03458 Office: Elm St Milford NH 03055

HOLLIS, WILLIAM SLATER, univ. dean; b. Little Rock, Feb. 11, 1930; s. William T. and Ida Sue (Johnson) H.; B.S., U. Ark., 1952, J.D., 1969; M.A., Memphis State U., 1962; postgrad. Vanderbilt U., 1964; Ph.D., U. Miss., 1972; m. Nancy Gant, Sept. 4, 1955; children—Laura, John, Leslie, Bruce. Asst. prof. Delta State Coll. Sch. Bus., Cleveland, Miss., 1958-59; asst. prof. dept. bus. The Citadel, Charleston, S.C., 1960-61; producer, presenter Ednl. TV-WKNO, Memphis, 1961-62; admitted to Ark. bar, 1958, Tenn. bar, 1961; individual practice law, West Memphis, Ark., and Memphis, 1958—; prin. advisor to chmn. Shelby County Budget and Fin. Com., Memphis, 1968-72; asst., asso. prof. Coll. Bus., Memphis State U., 1961-73; prof. div. econs. and bus., chmn., dir. undergrad., grad. studies Hardin-Simmons U., Abilene, Tex., 1973-75; dir. task force U.S. Dept. Def., Washington, 1975-76; v.p. fin. and legal Richards Mfg. Co., Inc., Memphis, 1976-78, v.p. adminstrn., asst. to pres., 1978-80; dean Sch. Bus. Adminstrn., Calif. Poly. U., 1980—; cons. faculty U.S. Command and Gen. Staff Coll., 1972—; registered investment adv. U.S. SEC, 1976—. Founder, pres. HELP Corp., 1967-73; chmn. drafting com. New Govt. Structure Commn. Shelby County, 1969-70. Served with inf. AUS, 1952-55; brig. gen. Res. Found. for Econ. Edn. fellow, 1968. Mem. Am. Econ. Assn., Am. Mgmt. Assn., Fin. Mgmt. Assn., Am. Trial Lawyers Assn., Am. Soc. Testing and Materials. Author: The Character of Christ, 1962, Military Compensation—Past, Present and Future, 2 vols., 1976. Contbr. articles to profl. jours. Office: Sch of Business Calif Poly U Pomona CA 91768

HOLLOMON, ICILUS C., banker; b. Delight, Ark., July 2, 1929; d. Edwin E. and Bertha Ann (Lee) Steed; student Gonzalez Bus. Coll., 1960, Am. Inst. Banking, 1965, Banking Sch. South, La. State U., 1973; m. Max Hollomon, Nov. 26, 1951, (dec.). With Bank of Gonzales (La.), 1960—, v.p., cashier, security officer, 1972-80, exec. v.p., cashier, security officer, 1980—. Treas., Gonzales Heart Assn., 1965-70. Mem. Am. Inst. Banking. La. Bankers Assn. (chmn. S.E. group 1975-76), Nat. Assn. Bank Women (past chmn. Baton Rouge group), Bank Adminstrn. Inst. (pres. La. 10 Parish chpt. 1978-79), Jambalaya Assn., Greater Gonzales Area Bus. and Profl. Women's Assn. (pres. 1970-71). Democrat. Universalist. Office: PO Box 1097 Worthy and Burnside Gonzales LA 70737

HOLLOWAY, LAWRENCE MILTON, JR., wholesale exec.; b. Detroit, Jan. 14, 1946; s. Lawrence Milton and Roena Jane (Williams) H.; B.S., Mich. State U., 1968; M.A., Drake U., 1977; m. Charlotte Jane Spiter, June 19, 1970; children—Tiffany Jane, Marque Spiter. Collection supr. Owosso (Mich.) Fin. Co., 1963-66; supr. med. lab. L.M. Holloway Clinic, Flint, Mich., 1966-68; lab. supr. Ferris State U., Big Rapids, Mich., 1968-69; tchr. St. Matthew Sch., Flint, 1969-70; fin. cons. Hamilton Internat. Corp., Farmington, Mich., 1970-71; v.p. Nat. Potential Devel. Co., St. Louis, 1971—; pres. Holloway House, Des Moines, 1971—; instr. Des Moines Area Community Coll., 1978-79. Active, Iowans for L.I.F.E., Inc., 1975—, now mem. exec. com. of bd.; bd. dirs. Des Moines Right to Life, 1978—, polit. chmn., 1979—; bd. dirs. Pro-Life Action Council. Recipient Notable Ams. award Hist. Preservations Am., 1976. Mem. Nat. Assn. Federally Lic. Firearms Dealers, Am. Chem. Soc., Am. Inst. Hypnosis, Iowa Acad. Sci., Iowa Soc. Osteo. Physicians and Surgeons, Am. Soc. Nondestructive Testing, Student Osteopathic Med. Assn. Republican. Mem. Evangelical Ch. Club: Masons (Shriner). Author: Dry Cell Therapy, Its Future, 1964; Biochemical Basis of Learning, 1977. Address: 818 15th St Des Moines IA 50314

HOLLOWELL, DAVID ELWIN, univ. ofcl.; b. Concord, Mass., Mar. 16, 1947; s. Harry M. and Jean B. Hollowell; B.S. in Engring., Boston U., 1969, M. in Mfg. Engring., 1972, M.B.A. with honors, 1974; m. Kathleen A. Prendergast, June 5, 1971. Systems cons. Office of Instl. Research, Boston U., 1970-72, asst. dir. Office of Analytical Studies, 1972-73, dir., 1973-76, asst. to v.p. for adminstrn., 1976-78, asso. v.p. for adminstrn. services, 1978—, lectr. in computer sci., 1979—. Mem. Assn. Computing Machinery, Soc. Coll. and Univ. Planning, Assn. Instl. Research, Boston U. Coll. Engring. Alumni (pres. 1972-73), Tau Beta Pi, Beta Gamma Sigma. Home: 4 Rockridge Rd Natick MA 01760 Office: 881 Commonwealth Ave Boston MA 02215

HOLM, MELVIN CARL, corp. exec.; b. Iron River, Mich., Nov. 9, 1916; s. Charles F. and Edith (Nyquist) Aspholm; student Mich. State Coll., N.Y. U., Syracuse U.; m. Beatrice A. Fritcher, Sept. 28, 1940; children—Melvin E., Joyce Ann. With Carrier Corp., Syracuse, N.Y., 1937—, comptroller, 1950-57, v.p., treas., 1957-60, exec. v.p., dir., 1960-65, pres., dir., 1965-68, chmn., chief exec. officer, 1968—, also dir.; dir. SKF Industries, Inc., United Techs. Corp., N.Y. Telephone Co.; trustee Mut. of N.Y. Mem. Emergency Com. for Am. Trade; mem. adv. com. Nat. 4-H Council; trustee Syracuse U., Suomi Coll. Mem. Machinery and Allied Products Inst. (exec. com., v.p.), Newcomen Soc., Economic Club N.Y. Clubs: Century, Onondaga Golf and Country (Syracuse, N.Y.); India House (N.Y.C.); Naples Yacht (Naples, Fla.); Masons (past master). Home: 4975 East Lake Rd Cazenovia NY 13035 Office: Carrier Tower PO Box 4800 Syracuse NY 13221

HOLMAN, STEELE, bus. and govt. mgmt. cons., property developer; b. Ottawa, Ill., Dec. 31, 1909; s. Harland D. Holman and Esther Lady Jane Lowe Holman Sutherland; B.A. in Polit. Sci., U. Calif. at Berkeley, 1936, postgrad. in Bus. Adminstrn., 1937-41; m. Elizabeth K. Kniveton, Aug. 30, 1941; children—Rodwin William Steele IV, Tamara H. Baren, Soña H. Spl. agt. Sears Roebuck, 1935; probation officer Alameda County (Calif.), 1937; chief supr. So. Calif. Prison, 1941; master shipfitter United Engring. Co., San Francisco, 1941; chief San Francisco Bay Area Shipyard Tng. Staff, 1942; head bus. conf. moderator State of Calif., 1945; pres. Steele Holman & Assos. and Golden Desert Acres, Dayton, Nev., bus. cons., 1945—; cons. Mexican-Am. Hoof and Mouth Commn., Mex., 1948-50, WAPCO, Philippines, 1955; auditor Atlas Constructors, Africa, So. Pacific Co., Pacific Gas & Electric, Merco-Nordstrum Valve Mfg. Co., Pacific Motor Transport, Calgary Cement & Gravel (Can.); econ. devel. officer Trust Ter. Pacific, 1951, 70-72; owner, pres. Million-dollar Golden Desert Acres, 1978-79; co-founder Mgmt. Assistance Council, San Francisco, 1968. Candidate for gov. U.S. Samoa, 1961. Pres., Steele Holman Found.; mem. or past mem. Marin Property Owners Assn., Spanish Speaking Citizens Assn., Samoan Civic Assn. Life mem. San Francisco World Trade Club, U. Calif. Alumni Assn., Philippine Assn. Mgmt. and Indsl. Engrs. (hon.), Mechanics Inst., Nat. Geog. Soc.; mem. Alameda County Employees Credit Union, Truk Coop., Smithsonian Instn., Berkeley Coop., UN Assn., Internat. Platform Assn. Home: 39 N West St Yerington NV 89447 also Box 369 Dayton NV 89403

HOLMAN, WILLIAM GEORGE, business educator; b. Hamilton, Mo., Apr. 28, 1903; s. Willis C. and Bertha Rose (Smith) H.; A.B., Western State Coll., Gunnison, Colo., 1924; M.A., Columbia, 1935; m. Ethel Simmonds, May 17, 1936; children—Susan Alice, Hazel Marie. Head comml. dept. Orlando (Fla.) High Sch., 1925-26; comml. agt. N.Y. Tele- phone Co., 1926-27; auditor Fairchild Aviation Corp., 1927-30; auditor, purchasing agt. Am. Airplane & Engine Corp., 1930-33; with Liberty Aircraft Products Corp., 1933-56, treas., sec., dir., 1939-56; budget adminstr. Fairchild Engine Div., 1957-59; controller, communications and data processing operations Raytheon Co., 1959-61; asst. to pres., controller rep. for subsidiaries Kollsman Instrument Corp., Elmhurst, N.Y., 1963-73; chmn. bus. dept. U. New Haven, 1963—; vis. prof. Campbell Coll., Buies Creek, N.C., Alderson-Broaddus Coll., Phillipi, W.Va., Campbellsville (Ky.) Coll., Benedict Coll., Columbia, S.C. Mem. Nat. Assn. Cost Accountants (past pres., v.p. L.I. chpt.), N.Y. State, Conn. socs. C.P.A.'s., Financial Execs. Inst., Delta Tau Delta. Republican. Episcopalian. Home: 115 Pine St Campbellsville KY 42718

HOLMBERG, RICHARD HJALMAR, electronics co. exec.; b. Wethersfield, Conn., Oct. 19, 1925; s. Hjalmar J. and Glenna A. (Campbell) H.; B.S. in Elec. Engring., M.I.T., 1950; M.S. in Elec. Engring., Stevens Inst. Tech., 1957; m. Barbara G. Wilber, June 2, 1951; children—Richard, Robert, Cheryl. Engr., nuclear program Sandia Labs., 1950; mgr. engring. dept. Lockheed Electronics Co., Plainfield, N.J., 1951-63; mgr. missile div. Lockheed Missiles & Space Co., Sunnyvale, Calif., 1963-73; v.p., gen. mgr., dir. Internat. Signal & Control Co., Lancaster, Pa., 1973—. Served with USN, 1943-46. Mem. Am. Def. Preparedness Assn., Lancaster Assn. Commerce and Industry. Clubs: Red Rose Bridge, Armstrong Bridge; Masons (Plainfield). Patentee transistorized pulse detector. Home: 81 W Elizabeth St Landisville PA 17538 Office: Internat Signal & Control Co 3050 Hempland Rd Lancaster PA 17601

HOLMBERG, ULF TORE, steel mill products agy. exec.; b. Orebro, Sweden, Mar. 30, 1936; came to U.S., 1969, naturalized, 1977; s. Bror Elof and Elvira Josefina (Berggren) Erlandsson; B.S. in Metallurgy, Bergsskolan Filipstad, Sweden, 1962; M.S. in Metallurgy, M.I.T., 1966; m. Lilian Anna Birgitta Frolund, Aug. 11, 1970; children—Mikael, Roger, Henrick. Lab. mgr. AB Akers Styckebruk, Sweden, 1966-69; gen. mgr. Akers Rolls Am., Inc., Pitts., Charlotte, N.C., 1969-75; pres. Ulf Holmberg Co., Inc., Pelham, Ala., 1975—; cons. on rolls Bofors-Akers Am., Inc., Butler, N.J., 1975—. Served with Signal Corps, Swedish Army, 1957-58. Mem. AIME, Am. Soc. Metals, Inst. Roll Design, Assn. Iron and Steel Engrs., Sigma Xi. Republican. Lutheran. Home and office: 932 Ryecroft Rd Pelham AL 35124

HOLMES, CHARLES EVERETT, lawyer, banker; b. Wellington, Kans., Dec. 21, 1931; s. Charles Everett and Elizabeth (Bergin) H.; B.A., Wichita U., 1953; LL.B., Okla. U., 1961; m. Lynn Lacy, Jan. 2, 1954; children—Anne Lacy, Charles Everett III, Rebecca. Trainee Halliburton Oil Well Cementing Co., Great Bend, Kans., 1956-58; admitted to Okla. bar, 1961; practiced in Tulsa, 1961—; mem. firm Rogers, Bell & Robinson, 1969-71; v.p. Nat. Bank of Tulsa, 1971—; lawyer Petro-Lewis Corp.; sec. Sinclair Oil & Gas Co., Sinclair Can. Oil Co., Mesa Pipeline Co., Border Pipe Line Co., Sinclair Transp. Co., Ltd. Del. Okla. Council Cath. Diocese, 1966—; chmn. Cath. Parish Governing Body, 1968—; bd. dirs. Youth Services, Travelers Aid, Com. Fgn. Relations. Served with USAF, 1954-56, 61-62. Mem. Am., Okla., Tulsa County bar assns. Home: 4505 S Yosemite #103 Denver CO 80237

HOLMES, DYER BRAINERD, corp. exec.; b. N.Y.C., May 24, 1921; s. Marcellus B. and Theodora (Pomeroy) H.; B.S. in Elec. Engring. (McMullen scholar), Cornell U., 1943; postgrad. Bowdoin Coll., M.I.T., 1943-44; hon. degrees U. N.Mex., 1963, Worcester Poly. Inst., 1978; m. Dorothy Ann Bonnet, May 22, 1943 (div. 1973); children—Dorothy Kather, Katherine Kobos; m. 2d, Roberta Donohue Plunk, Sept. 17, 1974. Design engr. Western Electric Co., also mem. tech. staff Bell Labs., 1945-53; initiated, developed first precision rec. transmission measuring set, other test equipment; participated devel. long distance coaxial telephone and TV systems, RCA, 1953-61, gen. mgr. maj. def. systems div., 1961; project mgr. Navy Talos land based missile system devel., 1954-57, Air Force Atlas launch control and checkout equipment devel., 1957, USAF ballistic missile early warning system, 1958-61; dep. asso. adminstr. manned space flight NASA, 1961-63; sr. v.p., dir. Raytheon Co., Lexington, Mass., 1963-69, exec. v.p., 1969-75, pres., 1975—, dir., 1969—; dir. Wyman-Gordon Co., Worcester, Mass., First Nat. Boston Corp. and subs. Kaman Corp., Bloomfield, Conn., Beech Aircraft Corp. Mem. corp. Northeastern U. Served with USNR, 1942-45. Recipient Outstanding Leadership medal NASA; Paul T. Johns award Arnold Air Soc. Registered profl. engr., N.J. Fellow mem. Nat. Acad. Engring., AIAA (sr.), Aerospace Assn. U.S. (chmn. bd. govs.), Am. Def. Preparedness Assn. (dir.), Nat. Aero. Assn., Nat. Security Indsl. Assn. (trustee), Navy League, Chi Psi, Tau Beta Pi, Eta Kappa Nu. Clubs: Explorers (N.Y.C.); Nat. Space, Metropolitan (Washington); Algonquin (Boston); New Bedford (Mass.) Yacht. Author articles, papers in field. Office: Raytheon Co 141 Spring St Lexington MA 02173

HOLMES, HAYNON, ins. co. exec.; b. Mansfield, La., Jan. 30, 1936; s. Hersey and Myrtes (Stevenson) H.; student pub. schs., Los Angeles; m. Benita Young, Nov. 12, 1972; children by previous marriage—Haynon, Tyrone W. Newspaper dealer Los Angeles Herald Express Newspaper, 1952-57; sales mgr. Kirby Vacuum Cleaners Co., Los Angeles, 1957-60; store mgr. Fred's Jewelry & Loan Co., Los Angeles, 1960-64; sales mgr. Soundarama Industries, Sherman Oaks, Calif., 1964-67; circulation mgr. Hollywood (Calif.)

Citizen News, 1967-70; agt. Equitable Life Assurance Soc., Los Angeles, 1970-73, dist. mgr., 1973—; guest speaker various bus. and profl. orgns., 1971—. Founder Ever Ready Community Choir, Los Angeles, choir dir., 1955-71; tenor soloist various churches in Los Angeles, 1955-78. Recipient Dist. Mgrs. Nat. Citation award, 1974-78, Mayor's Certificate of Appreciation, Los Angeles, 1975. Mem. Nat. Assn. Life Underwriters, Indsl. Relations Research Assn., Nat. Leaders Corps. Democrat. Baptist. Office: Equitable Life Assurance Co 1900 Ave of Stars Suite 990 Los Angeles CA 90067

HOLMES, NATHAN S., mill co. exec.; b. Hollywood, Calif., Apr. 2, 1946; s. Clifford W. and Rose Holmes; B.A., U.C.L.A., 1969; M.B.A., Pepperdine U., 1971; m. Fritzi R. Smith, Aug. 30, 1968; children—Heather Erie, Galen Raychelle. With Container Corp. Am., 1971—, plant controller, Santa Clara Mill, 1975-77, regional controller combination mills, Phila., 1977-80, mill div. controller, Chgo., 1980—. Republican. Unitarian. Office: One First National Plaza Chicago IL 60603

HOLMES, ROY STEWART, mfr.'s agt., mfg. co. exec.; b. Mt. Vernon, N.Y., Mar. 11, 1929; s. Roy Hills and Violet (Johnson) H.; B.B.A., U. Okla., 1952; m. Dorothy June Sanders; children—Debra Lynn Doufexis, Karen Susan. Salesman, sales mgr., product mgr. Uniroyal Inc., N.Y.C., 1952-67; salesman Shields-Chgo., Dolton, Ill., 1968-69; pres. Specialty Sales, Inc., 1970—, Flo-Couplings Inc., 1975—. Served to lt. (j.g.) USNR, 1952-56. Mem. Nat. Fertilizer Solutions Assn., Mfrs. Agents Nat. Assn. Republican. Baptist. Club: Masons. Home: 421 W 8th Pl Hinsdale IL 60521 Office: 9014 Brookfield Ave Brookfield IL 60513

HOLMES, THOMAS A., machinery mfg. co. exec.; b. Wilmington, Mass., Sept. 12, 1923; s. John Thomas and Marion (Burtt) H.; B.S.M.E., Mo. Sch. Mines, 1950; postgrad. Harvard Bus. Sch., 1969; m. Joan Merritt, March 15, 1952; children—Nanne, Susan, John, Bruce. With Ingersoll-Rand Co., Woodcliff Lake, N.J., 1950—, now chmn. bd., chief exec. officer, dir.; dir. Newmont Mining Corp., N.Y.C. Bd. dirs. Nat. Energy Found., N.Y.C.; trustee Lafayette Coll., Easton, Pa. Served with USNR, 1943-46. Mem. AIME, Mining and Metall. Soc. Am., Am. Mining Congress (dir.). Club: Mining. Home: 445 Round Hill Rd Greenwich CT 06830 Office: 200 Chestnut Ridge Rd Woodcliff Lake NJ 07675

HOLMES, WALTER STEPHEN, JR., corp. exec.; b. South River, N.J., May 23, 1919; s. Walter Stephen and Frances Evans (Heckman) H.; B.S., Lehigh U., 1941, LL.D., 1977; M.B.A., N.Y.U., 1947; m. Elizabeth Jean Pringle, Aug. 20, 1941; children—Walter Stephen III, Richard Alan. With Haskins & Sells, C.P.A.'s, Phila., 1941-42, Franke, Hannon & Withey, N.Y.C., 1946-47; asst. tax dir. RCA, 1947-51, asst. controller, 1951-53, controller, 1954-59; controller CIT Fin. Corp., 1959-62, v.p., 1961-64, exec. v.p. 1965-68, pres., 1968—, also chief exec. officer, 1970-73, chmn., chief exec. officer, 1973—, also dir.; dir. CIT Corp., CIT Fin. Services, RCA Corp., UNC Resources Inc., Tuition Plan, Inc., N.Am. Co. Life & Health Ins., William Iselin & Co., Inc., Meinhard-Comml. Corp. Mem. Presdl. Commn. Fin. Structure and Regulation, 1970-71. Trustee Lehigh U., 1973—; bd. dirs., mem. exec. com. Fin. Aid to Edn. Served as lt. Supply Corps, USNR, 1942-45. Mem. Am. Inst. C.P.A.'s. Clubs: Upper Montclair (N.J.) Country; Seaview Country; Economic (N.Y.). Home: 507 Ridgewood Ave Glen Ridge NJ 07028 Office: 650 Madison Ave New York NY 10022

HOLMES, WILLIAM RONALD, mfg. co. exec.; b. N.Y.C., Jan. 14, 1936; s. William Henry and Valerie (Walenta) H.; B.A., Farmingdale Agrl. and Tech. Coll., 1962; m. Margaret Ann Gabriel, June 29, 1957; children—Brian, Lauren, Melinda, Rachel. Design engr. aerospace related equipment, 1954-65; various mktg./sales positions, aerospace related equipment, 1965—; dir. mktg. Advanced Structures Corp., Deer Park, N.Y., 1977—, v.p., 1980—. Served with USNR, 1952-60. Mem. Am. Soc. Naval Engrs., Soc. Naval Architects and Marine Engrs. Republican. Presbyterian. Club: Setauket Yacht (dir. 1979). Office: Advanced Structures Corp 235 West Industry Ct Deer Park NY 11729

HOLMGREN, THEODORE J., food co. exec.; b. N.Y.C., May 2, 1927; s. Oscar F. and Madeline (Thompson) H.; A.B., Brown U., 1949; M.B.A., Harvard, 1955; m. Miriam Brady, June 3, 1950; children—Miriam Jane, Barbara Lynn, Theodore Douglas. Dir. design services Gen. Foods Corp., White Plains, N.Y., 1960-62, corp. new products mgr., 1962-65, sr. product mgr., 1965-68; sr. cons. marketing Peat Marwick Mitchell & Co., N.Y.C., 1968; v.p. marketing Curtice-Burns, Inc., Rochester, N.Y., 1968—, also dir. Pres. Community Council Chs. Irvington, Ardsley, Dobbs Ferry, Hastings and Hartsdale, N.Y., 1961-63. Trustee Curtice-Burns Charitable Found. Served to lt. (j.g.) USNR, 1951-53. Mem. Alpha Delta Phi. Clubs: Harvard Business School (Rochester. Home: 16 Esternay Ln Pittsford NY 14534 Office: 1 Lincoln First Sq Rochester NY 14602

HOLMQUIST, MERWYN GEORGE, grain and lumber co. exec.; b. Oakland, Nebr., Jan. 28, 1902; s. August C. and Ora Dell (Minier) H.; B.S., U. Nebr., 1923; m. Helen W. Johnson, Sept. 3, 1929; children—Marily Holmquist Keebler, Janet Holmquist Mueller. With Holmquist Grain and Lumber Co., Oakland, 1923—, sec., 1936-57, pres., 1957—. Pres., Oakland Bd. Edn., 1940-52. Mem. Grain and Feed Dealers Assn. (nat. country elevator com.), Oakland C. of C. (pres. 1942), Nebr. Petroleum Industries (dir. 1948-56). Republican. Lutheran. Clubs: Masons, Shriners, Elks. Home: 715 N Thomas St Oakland NE 68045 Office: 200 N Logan St Oakland NE 68045

HOLMQUIST, RICHARD CHARLES, cement co. exec., govt. ofcl.; b. Chgo., Dec. 3, 1915; s. Waldemar T. and Nellie (Holm) H.; B.S., Ind. U., 1937; m. Sarah Eleanor Jennings, Oct. 11, 1941; children—Richard Charles, Robert Jennings. With Gen. Electric Co., Bridgeport, Conn., 1937-41, mgr. employee and community relations, Balt., Fitchburg, Mass., then cons. govt. relations, N.Y.C. and Washington, 1947-61; advt. rep. Meredith Pub. Co., N.Y.C., 1946-47; exec. dir. Va. Industrialization Group, Richmond, Va., 1961-65; regional v.p. Lone Star Industries, Inc., Richmond, also Dallas 1965-71, sr. v.p. parent co., pres. Diversified Industries Group, Greenwich, Conn., 1971—; chmn. Renegotiation Bd., Washington; v.p. Am. Mining Congress. Trustee Intercollegiate Studies Inst., Am. Viewpoint, Inc. Served as lt. USNR, 1942-45. Mem. Navy League, Newcomen Soc. Presbyn. Clubs: Farmington Country (Charlottesville, Va.); Country of Va., Commonwealth (Richmond); University (Washington); Patterson Country (Fairfield, Conn.). Home: Apt 303-S 2111 Jefferson Davis Hwy Arlington VA 22202 Office: 1100 Ring Bldg Washington DC 20036

HOLOUBEK, VERNE RICHARD, designing and mfg. co. exec.; b. Clarkson, Nebr., Nov. 25, 1943; s. Richard W. and Lucille (Jedlicka) H.; B.S., U. Nebr., 1967; m. Terri Terrill, Apr. 9, 1976; children—Courtney Ann, Todd, Sara, Brian. Founder, pres. Holoubek Studios, Inc., Iron-On heat transfer designs, 1962—, Butler, Wis., 1968—, N.Y.C., 1976—; founder, dir. Iron-On Express (U.K.) Ltd., London, 1979—. Chmn. bd. Pinewood Sch. Alternative Edn., 1975. Mem. Wis. Air N.G. Mem. Mktg. Communications Execs. Internat. (pres.), Screen Printing Assn. (pres. heat applied graphics div. 1980), Sigma Delta Chi, Alpha Gamma Rho. Patentee in field. Home: Branch Rd Farm Ixonia WI 53036 Office: 4712 N 125th St Butler WI 53007

HOLSENBECK, WILEY HOWARD, JR., broker, developer; b. Louisville, July 2, 1941; s. Wiley Howard and Mary Alford (Redding) H.; B.S. in Indsl. Relations, U. N.C., 1963; m. Sandra Lee Pullman, Apr. 23, 1966; children—Lee Michael, Lisa Kay. With Owens Ill. Inc., Houston, 1965-68, Laguarta, Gavel & Kirk Co., Houston, 1969-70; owner Holsenbeck Realty Co., Houston, 1971—; chmn. bd. Carolina Corp., 1971—. Trustee Wesley Found. Rice U., 1972-75, vice chmn. bd.; bd. dirs. Houston YMCA; patron Houston Mus. Fine Arts; life fellow U. Houston Library. Served with USMCR, 1963-64. Fellow, Louis Round Wilson Library U. N.C.; mem. Houston C. of C., 100 Club Houston, Houston Bd. Realtors (chmn. admissions 1978, chmn. ethics 1979, vice chmn. civic affairs 1980, chmn. civic affairs 1981), Tex. Assn. Realtors, Nat. Bd. Realtors, U. N.C. Alumni Assn. (pres. Houston chpt. 1973—). Republican. Methodist (chmn. trustees local ch. 1973-75, vice chmn. 1976-77). Clubs: Order Old Well, Houston Realty. Home: 6350 Cambridge Glen Dr Houston TX 77035 Office: 306 3405 Edloe St Houston TX 77027

HOLT, BARBRA BERTANY, mgmt. cons.; b. Bridgeport, Conn., Nov. 4, 1940; d. Stephen Edward and Mary G. Bertany; student Regis Coll., 1958-59; B.A. in English, U. Bridgeport, 1962; m. Robert Holt, Dec. 5, 1971; children—Pamela Maren, Laura Kimbel, Mary Brooke. Instr. speech and theatre U. Bridgeport, 1962-69; gen. mgr. BFL Assos., exec. recruitment, N.Y.C., 1969-72; founder, pres. Barbra Holt & Assos., mgmt. cons., N.Y.C., 1972—; mem. faculty New Sch. Social Research, N.Y.C. Mem. N.Y. Fashion Group, Women in Mgmt. Episcopalian. Club: Atrium (N.Y.C.). Developed and produced videotape career mgmt. series for pub. TV, 1976. Home: Gaybowers Rd Fairfield CT 06430 Office: 527 Madison Ave New York NY 10022 also Box 713 Southport CT 06490

HOLT, JOSEPH WILLIAM, reins. co. exec.; b. Apr. 16, 1930; s. Joseph W. and Helen G. Holt; B.A., Maryville Coll., 1950; M.A., U. Pa., 1954; m. Irina von der Launitz, July 19, 1952; children—Lise Margaret Bradley, Helen Alexandra Lizotte. Mgr. Parker & Co. Internat., Phila., 1952-54, with Price Forbes, London, 1955, Interocean Agy., N.Y.C., 1956-67; co-founder, exec. v.p., dir. Duncanson & Holt, Inc., 1967—; pres. RA Fulton & Co., Inc., 1968—; v.p. Reed & Brown, 1974—; v.p. Aerospace Mgrs., 1974—, D & H Tech. Services, Inc., 1974—; exec. v.p. ERG Mgmt. Corp., 1975—; exec. v.p., dir. Rochdale Ins. Co., 1976—; pres., dir. United Ams. Ins. Co., 1978—; dir. First Manhattan Intermediaries, Inc. Clubs: Union, World Trade. Home: 1100 Rahway Rd Plainfield NJ 07060 also 206 E 61st St New York NY 10021 also Amen Farm Brooklin ME 04616 Office: 99 John St New York NY 10038

HOLT, LEON CONRAD, JR., lawyer, bus. exec.; b. Reading, Pa., June 19, 1925; s. Leon Conrad and Elizabeth (Bright) H.; B.S. cum laude in Metall. Engring., Lehigh U., 1948; LL.B., U. Pa., 1951; m. June M. Weidner, June 30, 1947; children—Deborah L., Richard W. Admitted to N.Y. bar, 1952; with firm Mudge, Stern, Williams & Tucker, N.Y.C., 1951-53; atty. Am. Oil Co., and predecessor, N.Y.C., 1953-57; gen. atty. Air Products & Chems., Inc., Allentown, Pa., 1957-61, v.p., gen. counsel, 1961-76, v.p.-adminstrn., gen. counsel, 1976-77, vice chmn., chief adminstrv. officer, 1977—, also dir.; mem. exec. and pub. policy coms., dir. Catalytic Inc. Vice chmn. Lehigh Centennial Fund, 1964-65; mem. Allentown Sch. Dist. Authority; chmn. Allentown Bd. Ethics, 1970-74; bd. dirs. Allentown YMCA, trustee, 1972-77; bd. dirs. Lehigh County United Way, 1971—, mem. exec. com., 1971-74, gen. chmn., 1971; bd. dirs. Hosp. and Health Council, 1972-78, Indsl. Devel. Corp. Lehigh County, Lehigh Valley Conservancy; trustee, treas. Allentown Art Mus., 1977—; Com. Econ. Devel., trustee Rider-Pool Found. Served to lt. (j.g.) USNR, 1943-46. Mem. Allentown C. of C. (gov. 1965-68), Chem. Mfrs. Assn., Am., N.Y.C. bar assns., Pa. Soc., Tunkhannock Creek Assn., Alpha Tau Omega. Club: Lehigh Country (Allentown). Home: 3003 Parkway Blvd Allentown PA 18104 Office: PO Box 538 Allentown PA 18105

HOLT, THOMAS JUNG, investment adv. firm exec.; b. Hong Kong, May 4, 1928; came to U.S., 1947, naturalized, 1954; s. Ting Jen and Aileen (Chu) H.; B.A., St. John's U., Shanghai, China, 1947; B.S. in Textile Engring., New Bedford Textile Inst., 1950; m. Deborah Ying Wong, Dec. 20, 1951; 1 dau., Evelyn Holt. Security analyst Arnold Bernhard & Co., N.Y.C., 1955-62; dir. corp. fin., Canton, Fitzgerald & Co., N.Y.C., 1962-63; sr. research editor Research Inst. Investors Service, N.Y.C., 1963-67; pres. T.J. Holt & Co., Inc., Westport, Conn., 1967—. Mem. N.Y. Soc. Security Analysts. Episcopalian. Office: 290 Post Rd W Westport CT 06880

HOLTER, JOHN WILLIAM, med. instrument cons.; b. Chgo., Apr. 1, 1916; s. Charles Robert and Favian (Erskine) H.; grad. Spring Garden (Pa.) Inst., 1938; D.Sc. (hon.), U. Sheffield (Eng.), 1976; m. Christiane Dumont, Apr. 14, 1972. Research technician Socony-Vacuum Oil Co., 1946-50, Yale & Towne, 1950-56; founder Holter Co., Bridgeport, Pa., 1956, owner, 1956-67; tech. cons., dir. Extracorporeal Med. Spltys., Inc., King of Prussia, Pa., 1967—; founder Carolina Catamaran Co., 1976; co-founder, v.p., dir. Holter-Hausner Internat. Inc., Bridgeport, Pa., 1977—. Vice pres. Montgomery County chpt. for Retarded Children, 1960-66; pub. relations chmn. Metric Assn. of U.S., 1969. Served with AUS, 1941-45. Recipient A.C.S. award, 1957; named Man of Year, Norristown, Bridgeport (Pa.) V.F.W., 1958. Mem. Soc. for Research into Hydrocephalus and Spina Bifida (hon.), Am. Soc. for Artificial Internal Organs, European Soc. for Paediatric Neurosurgery (hon.), Internat. Soc. Pediatric Neurosurgeons (hon.). Inventor valve for controlling hydrocephalus (original demonstration model now in Smithsonian Instn.), catamaran hull design, small boat ventilating hatch; research on artificial heart; patentee med. devices. Home: 211 Cordova Blvd Saint Petersburg FL 33705 Office: 3d and Mill Sts Bridgeport PA 19405

HOLTKAMP, DORSEY EMIL, med. research scientist; b. New Knoxville, Ohio, May 28, 1919; s. Emil H. and Caroline (Meckstroth) H.; student Ohio State U., 1937-39; A.B., U. Colo., 1945, M.S., 1949, Ph.D., 1951, student Sch. Medicine, 2 1/2 yrs.; m. Marianne Church Johnson, Mar. 20, 1942 (dec. May 1956); 1 son, Kurt Lee; m. 2d, Marie P. Bahm Roberts, Dec. 20, 1957; stepchildren—Charles Timothy, Michael John Roberts. Teaching, research asst. U. Colo., 1945-46, fellow Sch. Medicine, 1946, asst., 1947-48, research fellow in biochemistry, 1948-51; sr. research scientist biochemistry sect. Smith, Kline & French Labs., Phila., 1951-57, endocrine-metabolic group leader, 1957-58; head endocrinology dept. Merrell-Nat. Labs. div. Richardson-Merrell, Inc., 1958-70, group dir. endocrine clin. research, med. research dept., 1970—. Fellow AAAS, Am. Inst. Chemists; mem. Am. Chem. Soc., Am. Soc. Pharmacology and Exptl. Therapeutics, Soc. Exptl. Biology and Medicine, Endocrine Soc., Reticulo-Endothelial Soc., Pacific Coast Fertility Soc., Acad. Med. Cin. (asso.), Am. Inst. Biol. Sci., Am. Soc. Zoologists, N.Y., Ohio acads. scis., Am. Assn. for Lab. Animal Sci., AMA (affiliate), Soc. Study Reprodn., Am. Soc. Clin. Pharmacology and Therapeutics, Am. Fertility Soc., Internat. Family Planning Research Assn., Sigma Xi, Nu Sigma Nu. Republican. Presbyterian. Contbr. articles on endocrinology, pharmacology, tumor metabolism, nutrition, drug research and devel., fertility, sterility, biochemistry, teratology profl. publs. Patentee in field. Home: 9464 Bluewing Terr Cincinnati OH 45241 Office: Merrell-Nat Labs Div Richardson-Merrell Inc 2110 E Galbraith Rd Cincinnati OH 45215

HOLTOM, HAROLD THOMAS, civil engr.; b. Karuizawa, Japan, Sept. 2, 1911; s. Daniel Clarence and Grace (Price) H.; B.A., U. Redlands, 1933; B.S., Calif. Inst. Tech., 1934, M.S., 1935; m. Olive Hume, Nov. 24, 1935; children—Gordon, Katharine, Thomas. With Met. Water Dist. So. Calif., 1935-41; cost engr. Macco Constrn. Co., 1942-45; engr., chief engr. E.S. McKittrick Co. & Normac, Inc., 1946-52; chief engr. Macco-Panpacific, Inc., 1952-54; project engr. Macco Corp. 1955; chief engr. Diversified Builders, Inc. div. Macco Corp., 1956-64; sr. engr. Met. Water Dist. So. Calif., 1964-67, prin. engr., charge sea water desalination div., after 1967; now with Holtom Engring. Corp., Newport Beach, Calif. Mem. Internat. Symposium Sea Water Desalting, Washington, 1965. Fellow Inst. Advancement Engring.; mem. Am. Nuclear Soc., ASCE, Town Hall, Los Angeles, Am. Water-works Assn., Athenaeum (Calif. Inst. Tech.), Los Angeles World Affairs Council. Home: 540 Twin Palms Dr San Gabriel CA 91775 Office: Holtom Engring Corp 230 Newport Center Dr Suite 302 Newport Beach CA 92660

HOLTON, IRA JAMES, meat co. exec.; b. Cedar Rapids, Iowa, Aug. 16, 1919; s. Ed Bacon and Mabel (Donnan) H.; B.A. in Econs., U. Iowa, 1941, J.D., 1947; m. Adelaide Elizabeth Roeder, June 23, 1941; children—Janet, Brooks, Ann. Admitted to Iowa bar, 1947, Minn. bar, 1947; with Geo. A. Hormel & Co., Austin, Minn., 1947—, sec., 1956—, dir., 1961—, exec. v.p., 1968-69, pres., 1969-79, chief exec. officer, 1972—, chmn. bd., 1979—; dir. 1st Bank System, Inc., Mpls. Pres. Austin Community Scholarship Com.; dir. Am. Meat Inst., Hormel Found. Bd. dirs. Mower County chpt. ARC. Served to maj., inf. U.S. Army, 1941-45. Decorated Croix de Guerre (France). Mem. Phi Beta Kappa. Republican. Home: 403 21st SW Austin MN 55912 Office: Box 800 Austin MN 55912

HOLTON, THOMAS LELAND, accountant; b. Prairie Hill, Tex., July 8, 1925; s. Homer and Esther (Rasco) H.; B.B.A., Baylor U., 1949, M.A., 1950; m. Maxine Swearengin, Apr. 7, 1946; children—Dana Ann, Thomas Leland. Staff acct. to mng. partner Eaton & Huddle, San Antonio, 1950-58; with Peat, Marwick, Mitchell & Co., 1958—, mng. partner San Antonio Office, 1958-59, mng. partner Chgo. office and Midwest Area partner, 1959-68, mem. exec. office, N.Y.C., 1968—, chmn. bd., chief exec. officer, 1979—. Served with Supply Corps, USN, 1944-46. Mem. Am. Inst. C.P.A.'s (chmn. com. auditing procedure 1969-72, chmn. com. SEC regulations 1974-77). Clubs: Econ., Links, Pinnacle, Board Room, Skokie (Ill.) Country, Accts. of Am.; Burning Tree (Greenwich, Conn.); Blind Brook (Port Chester, N.Y.). Office: 345 Park Ave New York NY 10022

HOLTZ, GILBERT JOSEPH, steel co. exec.; b. N.Y.C., Jan. 23, 1924; s. Al S. and Carrie (Schindler) H.; student N.Y.U., 1940-42; m. Caria Kahn, July 18, 1948; children—Steven J., Robert A. Vice pres. Hanger Service Co., Yonkers, N.Y., 1946-48; owner Economy Sales Co., Yonkers, 1948-50; v.p. Belvedere Space Saving Products, Inc., 1951-72; pres. Walnut Metal Industries, Inc., Yonkers, 1955-72, Belvedere Home Products Inc. (formerly 411 Walnut St. Corp.), 1962—, Walnut Assn. Inc., 1961—, Belvedere Internat. Ltd., 1970—. Ward leader 2d Ward Republican County Com., Yonkers. Served with AUS, 1943-46. Mem. C. of C. Kiwanian. Patentee in field. Home: 182 Tibbetts Rd Yonkers NY 10705 Office: 1051 Saw Mill River Rd Yonkers NY 10710

HOLTZMAN, ANDRE EDWIN, paper co. exec.; b. Chgo., Sept. 19, 1936; s. Bernard and Juanita (Good) H.; B.S.C., Roosevelt U., 1953-57; student John Marshall Law Sch., 1957-58; M.B.A., Loyola U., 1976; 1 dau., Elizabeth. Mgmt. cons. Booz Allen & Hamilton, 1957-68; v.p., fin., corp. controller Walter E. Heller Industries, 1969-71; pres. Investor Guaranty Corp., 1972-77; v.p. fin., dir. Flint (Mich.) br. Consol. Packaging Corp., Chgo., 1978—. Mem. Fin. Execs. Inst. Republican. Presbyterian. Club: Plaza. Home: 1030 N State St Chicago IL 60610 Office: 111 E Wacker Dr Chicago IL 60601

HOLWAY, JAMES COLIN, steel co. exec.; b. Youngstown, Ohio, Nov. 14, 1927; s. Robert G. and Marie W. (Kane) H.; B.S., Ohio State U., 1950; M.B.A., Pa. State U., 1952; m. Patricia Ann Touscany, Aug. 31, 1957; children—Moira Ann, Colin A., Brent Patrick, Jamesin McAndrew, Jonathan Lynch. Sales trainee U.S. Steel Corp., 1951-55; salesman Republic Steel Corp., Cleve. and Detroit, 1955-58; dist. sales mgr. Tenn. Products & Chem. Corp., Detroit, 1958-60; dist. sales mgr. Nat. Steel Corp., Charlotte, N.C., 1960-72; founder, pres. Southeastern Steel Rolling Mills, Charlotte, 1972-73; co-founder, pres. Decker-Holway Steel Co., 1973-77; founder, pres. Mid-Atlantic Steel Co., Charlotte, 1977—; chmn. bd. Mid-Atlantic Industries, 1979—. Served with USNR, 1945-46. Mem. Am. Inst. Mining, Metall. and Petroleum Engrs. (asso.). Clubs: Country of Detroit (Grosse Pointe, Mich.); Charlotte Athletic, Charlotte City, Charlotte Country. Home: 2312 Pembroke Ave Charlotte NC 28207 Office: PO Box 5603 Charlotte NC 28225

HOLYNSKYJ, NESTOR PETER, mgmt. cons.; b. Mar Del Plata, Argentina, Aug. 7, 1953; came to U.S., 1954, naturalized, 1961; s. Osyp and Irene Maria (Welyczkowsky) H.; B.S. in Elec. Engring., Stevens Inst. Tech., 1975; m. Larissa Maria Paschyn, June 18, 1977; 1 son, Damian Ivan. Customer service rep. MCI Telecommunications, N.Y.C., 1975-76, nat. account sales rep., 1976-77; mgmt. cons. Booz Allen & Hamilton, N.Y.C., 1977-81; asst. treas. communications services dept. Morgan Guaranty Trust Co. of N.Y., 1981—. Mem. Ukrainian Engrs. Soc. Am. Home: 189 Liberty St Bloomfield NJ 07003 Office: 245 Park Ave New York NY 10017

HOM, ANTHONY JAMES, lawyer; b. N.Y.C., Jan. 18, 1949; s. Thomas Gim Wing and May Yuen Yin H.; grad. Hill Sch., 1967; A.B. cum laude, Amherst Coll., 1971; M.B.A., U. Pa., 1975; J.D., 1975. Admitted to Pa. bar, 1977, D.C. bar, 1979, also dist. ct. and ct. appeals bars; asso. firm Hawkins, Delafield and Wood, N.Y.C., 1975-77; asso. firm Duane, Morris and Heckscher, Phila., 1977-79, Reed Smith Shaw & McClay, Phila., 1980—. Bd. dirs., sec. Boys Club of Met. Phila. Mem. Am., Pa., Phila., D.C. bar assns., Nat. Assn. Bond Lawyers (steering com.), Asian M.B.A. Conf. (vice chmn. 1974-76), Asian Mgmt. Bus. Assn. Internat. (dir., sec., counsel bd. 1976—), Delta Kappa Epsilon. Episcopalian. Clubs: Racquet (Phila.); Yale (N.Y.C.), Sharswood Law. Home: 1841 Addison St Philadelphia PA 19146

HOMAN, JOHN ELBURT, publishing co. exec.; b. Whittier, Calif., Sept. 20, 1932; s. Walter Joseph and Marjorie (Carney) H.; A.B., San Francisco State U., 1954, M.Bus. Edn., 1963; m. Barbara Gibson, Mar. 26, 1955; children—Kathleen, Kim. Officer trainee Bank of Am., San Francisco, 1956-57; tchr. bus. Jefferson Union High Sch. Dist., Palo Alto (Calif.) Adult Sch., 1957-59; field rep. South Western Pub. Co., Calif., Hawaii, 1959-69, asst. dist. mgr. for Western U.S., Burlingame, Calif., 1969-76, regional v.p. Western region, Palo Alto, 1976—; mem. Oakland (Calif.) Sch. Vocat. Adv. Com., San Mateo Sch. Dist. Adv. Com., San Francisco Office Occupations Adv. Com.; speaker bus. edn. assn. meetings, Calif., Ariz., Utah, Mont., Hawaii, Tex., Alaska, 1970—; bd. dirs. Calif. Industry Edn. Council. Pres., Marina Inner Circle Townhomes Assn. Served with U.S. Army,

1954-56. Mem. Adminstrv. Mgmt. Soc., Nat. Bus. Edn. Assn., Western Bus. Edn. Assn., Calif. Bus. Edn. Assn. (dir. Fund for Advancement Bus. Edn.), Calif. C. of C., Bus. Edn. Forum (pres. San Francisco area 1978-80), Delta Pi Epsilon (pres. Alpha Kappa chpt. 1964-65, asso. editor Jour. 1963-73), Phi Delta Kappa (pres. Gamma Iota chpt. 1961-62). Republican. Congregationalist. Club: Discovery Bay Yacht and Tennis. Author: Writing Effective Business Letters, 1965; How To Type Term Papers and Reports, 1965; developer typing cartoon posters. Office: 855 California Ave Palo Alto CA 94304

HOME, STEPHEN DUNCAN, ins. exec.; b. San Jose, Calif., July 28, 1940; s. Herbert Duncan and Donna Yvonne H.; B.A., Santa Clara U., 1962, M.B.A., 1966; m. Patricia L. Hendrix, Mar. 26, 1976; children by previous marriage—Stephen, Darren. Sales promotion and advt. exec. Proctor & Gamble, 1966-69; life ins. sales rep. Guardian Life Ins. Co., 1969-74, Jefferson Standard Life Ins. Co., 1974-75; asso. Bankers Life of Nebr., San Jose, Calif, 1975—, also mem. field adv. bd. on product asso. Stephen D. Home & Assos.; tchr. West Valley Coll.; guest lectr. San Jose State U., Santa Clara U., Stanford U.; cons. to bus. on advt. planning and implementation. Bd. dirs. Grad. Sch. Bus., Santa Clara U. Served with inf. U.S. Army, 1962-64. Recipient ins. sales awards. Mem. Nat. Assn. Life Underwriters. Republican. Office: 3031 Tisch Way Suite 1010 San Jose CA 95128

HOMEYER, FRED CARL, banker; b. Austin, Tex., Apr. 7, 1920; s. Fred C. and Mamie (Wilke) H.; B.S., A. and M. Coll. Tex., 1942; postgrad. Savs. and Loan Grad Sch., 1963; m. Betty Sue Tumey, Apr. 3, 1942; children—Fred Charles, William Polk, Janice Sue. Adjuster, asst. office mgr. Comml. Credit Corp., 1946-48; sec. assn. Austin Savs. & Loan Assn., 1948-55; pres. Home Savs. Assn., Odessa, Tex., 1955-66, Northport Fed. Savs. & Loan Assn. (L.I., N.Y.), 1966-69; sr. v.p. First City Nat. Bank, Houston, 1969—. Pres. Odessa Day Nursery Bd., 1959; dir. Odessa Community Chest and United Fund, campaign chmn., 3d v.p., 1959; pres. Go-Dessa orgn., 1959-60; chmn. Black Gold dist. Boy Scouts Am., 1959, mem. exec. com. Buffalo Trail council, 1959-60, recipient Silver Beaver award. Served to maj. AUS, 1942-46; lt. col. Res. Mem. Odessa C. of C. (past dir.), Am. Savs. and Loan Inst. (instr.), Odessa Real Estate Bd., Home Builders Assn., Permian Hist. Soc. (dir.), Soc. Residential Appraisers, U.S. (com. supervision and exams., legis. com.), Nat. (Tex. gov. 1963-65, mem. legis. com.), Tex. (past dir., chmn. edn. com., chmn. by-laws com., mem. league services com., exec. com.) savs. and loan leagues, Chuck Wagon Gang. Presbyterian (deacon). Club: Rotary (pres. Odessa 1962-63). Home: POB 61373 Houston TX 77208 Office: 1000 Main St Houston TX 77002

HONEYBONE, STUART POWELL, indsl. products mktg. exec.; b. Nottingham, Eng., Oct. 10, 1941; came to U.S., 1970; s. Cyril Thomas and Lilian Rita H.; diploma in mktg and mgmt., Ealing Coll., London, 1969; m. Brenda Ann Spencer, Dec. 19, 1970; children—Mark, Andrew, Simon. Market research mgr. Comino Dexion, Eng., 1968-70; mktg. mgr. Dexion, Inc., N.Y.C., 1970-75; internat. mktg. mgr. Gould Indsl. Battery Co., Pa., 1975-79; v.p. mktg. Hinderliter Energy Co., Tulsa, 1979—. Home: 22328 E 67th St Broken Arrow OK 74012 Office: 1240 N Harvard St Tulsa OK 74115

HONG, WILLIAM SUNG WAN, trading co. exec.; b. Seoul, Korea, Jan. 31, 1934; came to U.S., 1956; s. Sung-Pyo and Sook-Ja (Won) H.; B.B.A., U. Oreg., 1960; M.B.A., CCNY, 1965; m. Young Sook Cho, Mar. 2, 1963; children—Gilbert, Patty, Michele. Dir. mktg. Dairylea Coop. Inc., Pearl River, N.Y., 1960-72, C.M.A. Inc., Syracuse, N.Y., 1972-75; pres. W.S. Newco Corp., Hawthorne, N.Y., 1975—. Mem. Am. Dry Milk Industry (adv. com.), Am. Trade Assn. Greater N.Y. Republican. Presbyterian. Home: 57 Butler Rd Scarsdale NY 10583 Office: 140 Broadway Hawthorne NY 10532

HOOD, ANDREW CRAIG, mfg. co. exec.; b. Phila., Nov. 25, 1928; s. Earle Stetson and Edith MacClochlan (Powrie) H.; B.S. in Metallurgy, M.I.T., 1950; m. Loretta A. Swierzynski, Aug. 4, 1951; children—Andrew Craig, Karen Marie, Jennifer Louise. Asst. to chief metallurgist Union Twist Drill Co., Athol, Mass., 1950-52; process metallurgist Midvale Steel Co., Phila., 1952-55; devel. metallurgist Superior Tube Co., Collegeville, Pa., 1955-60; with SPS Technologies, Inc., and predecessor, 1960—, gen. mgr. spl. products div., Ft. Washington, Pa., 1973—; tchr. metallurgy courses, Norristown, Pa. and Phila., 1957-58. Fellow Soc. Metals; mem. Soc. Automotive Engrs., Inst. Dirs., AIME. Club: M.I.T. Del. Valley. Patentee fastener and bolted connections; inventor titanium alloy with maximum ductility using low hardness sponge. Office: Benson East Jenkintown PA 19046

HOOD, FRED H., mgmt. analyst, mayor; b. Granite, Okla., Feb. 23, 1926; s. Fred H. and Gertrude E. (Abel) H.; B.S. in Bus. Mgmt., U. No. Colo., 1974, M. Pub. Adminstrn., 1977; m. Shirley Rose Brenk, July 2, 1964. Served as enlisted man USN, 1944-47, U.S. Air Force, 1956, advanced through grades to tech. sgt., 1972; ret., 1972; indsl. engr. City of Denver, 1972-74; v.p. Community Devel. Co., 1972—; mgmt. analyst USAF, Denver, 1974—; mayor City of Aurora (Colo.), 1975—; guest lectr. U.S. Conf. Mayors, 1978, Colo. Municipal League, 1978. Mem. Denver Regional Council Govt., 1975—, Adams County Council Govt., 1975—, Arapahoe County Council Mayors, 1975—; mem. transp. com. U.S. Conf. Mayors, 1976—; mem. policy bd. Colo. Municipal League, 1976—. Mem. Am. Inst. Indsl. Engrs., Am. Soc. Mil. Comptrollers, Western Govtl. Research Assn., Am. Mgmt. Assn., Air Force Assn., Aurora Hist. Soc., Nat. League Cities. Democrat. Clubs: Lions, Am. Legion (pub. service citation 1976-77), VFW, DAV, Masons. Home: 12255 E Louisiana Ave Aurora CO 80012 Office: 1450 S Havana St Aurora CO 80012

HOOD, MAURICE (MAURY) JOHN, devel. co. exec.; b. Farmington, Wash., Jan. 20, 1935; s. Merle Mohr and Margaret Jo (Pine) H.; B.A. in Archtl. Engring. with honors, Wash. State Coll., 1958; m. Shirley Ann Morris, June 13, 1959; children—Julie Lynn, Paul Michael, Marcus Jon. Plant supr., dist. engr. Shell Oil Co., Seattle, 1958-64, Long Beach, Calif., 1964-65, Colton, Calif., 1965-68; asso. partner Bush Roed & Hutching P.S. Inc., Seattle, 1968-72; v.p., regional mgr. Levitt & Sons of Calif., Nashville, 1972-73; regional mgr. Baker Crow Co., Austin, Tex., 1973-74; v.p. Mayfield Cos., Austin, 1974-79; pres. Jester Devel. Co., 1979—. Mem. exec. bd. Balconies Civic Assn., Austin, 1976-77, NW Austin Civic Assn., 1979-81; pres. Cat Mountain Homeowners Assn., Austin, 1977-79; chmn. environ. bd. City of Austin, 1978-80; mem. Republican Precinct Com., Seattle, 1966-68; bd. dirs. Bellevue (Wash.) Park Bd., 1971-72. Served to 1st lt. U.S. Army, 1958-60. Recipient Shell Oil award Soc. Golden West, 1965; registered profl. engr., Wash. Mem. Community Assns. Inst., Austin Assn. Builders, Nat. Assn. Home Builders, Austin C. of C., Sigma Phi Epsilon, Tau Beta Phi, Phi Kappa Phi, Sigma Tau. Clubs: Courtyard Tennis and Swim, Lions, Toastmasters. Home: 8404 Greenflint Dr Austin TX 78759 Office: PO Box 10061 Austin TX 78766

HOOGESTRAAT, BERNARD LEE, mgmt. cons.; b. Miller, S.D., July 10, 1934; s. Ben and Mabel (Gade) H.; B.S. in Engring., S.D. Sch. of Mines & Tech., 1956; m. Helen Mae Jokela, July 11, 1959; children—James Scott, Debbie Lynn, Jay Richard. Tech. rep. Hercules Powder Co., Butte, Mont., also Spokane, 1956-62; ins. cons., R.W. Grange Assos., Phoenix, 1962-74; pres. The Helmar Corp., Phoenix, 1971-73; owner, Southwest Packaging Co., Phoenix, 1971-74; pres. Exec. Resources, Inc., Phoenix, 1974—; dir. R.W. Grange Tax Benefit Seminars. Chmn. bd. Northeast Phoenix YMCA; bd. dirs. Metro YMCA; vice chmn. bd. govs. All Saints Day Sch.; founder Phoenix Boys League, 1968. Served to 1st lt. AUS, 1956-57. Recipient Frances Moss award YMCA, 1970; named YMCA Layman of the Year, 1971. C.L.U. Mem. Ariz. Estate Planning Council (pres. 1970-71, dir. 1968-72), Central Ariz. CLU, Nat. Manulife C.L.U. Assn. (pres. 1973-75). Lutheran (trustee ch. 1967-70, chmn. personnel com.). Club: Phoenix Execs. Author: A Personal Guide to the Living Trust, 1966. Home: 6112 N 34th St Paradise Valley AZ 85253 Office: 2621 E Camelback Rd Bldg D Suite 145 Phoenix AZ 85016

HOOK, HAROLD SWANSON, ins. co. exec.; b. Kansas City, Mo., Oct. 10, 1931; s. Ralph C. and Ruby (Swanson) H.; B.S. in Bus. Adminstrn., U. Mo., 1953, M.A. in Accounting, 1954; doctoral candidate N.Y. U.; m. Joanne T. Hunt, Feb. 19, 1955; children—Karen Anne, Thomas Wesley, Randall Townsend. With Nat. Fidelity Life Ins. Co., Kansas City, Mo., 1957-66, asst. to pres., 1957-60, bd. dirs., 1959-66, adminstrv. v.p., 1960-61, exec. v.p., 1961-63, pres., 1963-66; sr. v.p. U.S. Life Ins. Co., N.Y.C., 1966-67, exec. v.p., 1967-68, pres., 1968-70, dir., 1967-70; pres., chief exec. officer, dir., mem. exec. com. Calif.-Western States Life Ins. Co., Sacramento, 1970-75, chmn., 1975-79, sr. chmn., 1979—; founder, pres. Main Event Mgmt. Corp., Sacramento, 1970—; pres., dir., mem. exec. com. Am. Gen. Corp. (formerly Am. Gen. Ins. Co.), Houston, 1975-78, chmn., pres., chief exec. officer, 1978—; dir. Panhandle Eastern Pipe Line Co., Houston, Trunkline Gas Co., Houston, Delta-Calif. Industries, Oakland. Trustee Baylor Coll. Medicine, Houston, Am. Coll., Bryn Mawr, Pa.; bd. dirs. Soc. Performing Arts, Houston Symphony Soc., Tex. Research League. Recipient citation of merit U. Mo., 1965, Faculty-Alumni award, 1978; named Man of Year Delta Sigma Pi, 1969, Silver Beaver award Boy Scouts Am., 1974, Distinguished Eagle Scout award, 1976. Served from ensign to lt. (j.g.) USNR, 1954-57. C.L.U. Fellow Life Mgmt. Inst.; mem. Philos. Soc. Tex., Young Pres.'s Orgn., Houston C. of C. (dir., exec. com.), Dirs.' Table, Beta Gamma Sigma. Clubs: Petroleum, Rotary, River Oaks Country, Ramada, Univ. (Houston); Morris County Golf (Morristown, N.J.); Mission Hills Country (Kansas City, Mo.). Home: 2204 Troon Rd Houston TX 77019 Office: 2727 Allen Pkwy Houston TX 77019

HOOKER, ALAN MARTIN, banker; b. Cleve., May 13, 1950; s. Ora L. and Annacetta Hooker; B.A. cum laude, Cleve. State U., 1974; basic cert. Am. Inst. Banking, 1975, standard cert., 1977; postgrad. Essentials of Bank Mktg. Sch., Temple U., 1979; postgrad. in bus. adminstrn. So. Ill. U., 1979—; m. Eileen Marie Szaller, Sept. 17, 1971. With Society Corp., multi-bank holding co., Cleve., 1972-78, asst. mgr., 1974-75, asst. cashier, 1975-76, asst. v.p., mgr., 1976-78; asst. v.p., dir. mktg. McLachlen Nat. Bank, Washington, 1978-80; asst. v.p. Union Trust Co., Balt., 1980—; instr. Am. Inst. Banking, 1977—. Mem. Bank Mktg. Assn., Am. Inst. Banking, Fin. Mktg. Council Greater Washington, D.C. Bankers Assn. Club: Touchdown (Washington). Home: 502 2d St SE Washington DC 20003 Office: Union Trust Co 8630 Fenton St Silver Spring MD 20910

HOOKS, ARTHUR VANCE, railway co. exec.; b. Charlotte, N.C., Mar. 19, 1922; s. Arthur Vance and Leila Ballentine H.; B.C.E., Clemson A&M Coll., 1942; m. Mildred Lee Jones, Aug. 27, 1943; children—Linda L. Hooks Brennan, A. Vance, Mildred Gayle Hooks Greenwood, Henry Townsend. With Atlantic Coast Line R.R., 1946-55, div. engr., 1947-49, engr. maintenance of way, 1951-55; asst. to v.p. Atlanta & Saint Andrews Bay Ry. Co., Dothan, Ala., 1955-64, v.p., 1964-68, pres., 1968-74, chmn., 1972-74, pres., chmn. 1977—; gen. mgr. distbn. and transp. Internat. Paper Co., N.Y.C., 1974-77; dir. Am. Short Line R.R. Assn., Comml. Bank. Pres., Bay County United Way; bd. dirs. Salvation Army, ARC; bd. dirs., v.p. Gulf Coast Community Coll. Found. Served to 1st lt. U.S. Army, 1942-46. Reg. profl. engr., Ala., land surveyor, Fla. Democrat. Methodist. Clubs: St. Andrews Bay Yacht, Panama Country, Panama City Traffic. Office: PO Box 669 Panama City FL 32401

HOON, H. KEITH, retail stores exec.; b. Boston, Oct. 3, 1946; s. Harold D. and Lois I. (Smith) H.; B.A., Eastern Wash. State U., 1968; m. Peggy L. Kaelin, May 26, 1979. Tax acct. Potlatch Inc., Lewiston, Idaho, 1968-69; auditor Ernst & Ernst, C.P.A.'s, Tacoma, 1969-71; controller Elvins Dept. Stores, Puyallup, Wash., 1971—, exec. v.p., 1980—, also dir.; instr. acctg. St. Martins Coll., Lacey, Wash., 1974-76. Mem. acctg. adv. council Eastern Wash. State Coll., 1980—. Mem. Am. Inst. C.P.A.'s, Wash. Soc. C.P.A.'s, Alpha Kappa Psi. Republican. Baptist. Club: Optimist (pres. 1977). Address: 1100 N Meridian St Puyallup WA 98371

HOOPER, CHESTER MORRIS, assn. exec.; b. Detroit, Dec. 7, 1920; s. Chester Allan and Mary Elizabeth (Vivian) H.; cert. Queen's U., 1947; M.B.A., Harvard, 1955; AEP, ASPA Accreditation Inst., 1977; m. Jean A. Kilborn, Aug. 18, 1956; 1 son, Paul. Asst. mgr. indsl. relations Abitibi, Toronto, Ont., Can., 1941-56; mgr. indsl. relations Mannesmann, Sault Ste. Marie, Ont., 1956-61; v.p. indls. relations Seaway Multi Corp Ltd., Toronto, Ont., 1961-76; pres. Health Labour Relations Assn. B.C., Vancouver, 1976—; pres. Hooper Holdings Ltd.; dir. Highgate Realty Ltd. Bd. dirs. ALD Found., Can. Scholarship Found. Am. Mem. Sask. Govt. Royal Commn., 1965. Past mem. bd. dirs. Nat. Multiple Sclerosis Soc. Clubs: Harvard of Toronto, Harvard Bus. Sch. of Toronto. Home: 4651 W 5th Ave Vancouver BC V6R 1S9 Canada Office: 1212 W Broadway Vancouver BC V6H 3V1 Canada

HOOPER, DAVID GEORGE, mktg. exec.; b. Reading, Pa., Sept. 10, 1945; s. George Munn and Ruth (Stevens) H.; B.A., U. Scranton, 1967; M.P.A., U. Kan., 1974; m. Priscilla Hooper, Dec. 27, 1967; 1 son, David G. Asst. to city adminstr. Liberty, Mo., 1973-74; borough mgr. Huntington, Pa., 1974-76; adminstrv. analyst Pa. Dept. Community Affairs, Harrisburg, Pa., 1978-79; with Energy Plus, Huntington, 1976-78; service mgr. Asper Hill, Inc., Mechanicsburg, Pa., 1979—. Served with U.S. Army, 1969-72. Peace Corps selectee, 1966; Ford Found. grantee, 1968. Mem. Am. Soc. Public Adminstrn., Internat. City Mgrs. Assn., South Central Counties Boroughs Assn. (sec. 1975-76), Huntingdon Area Jaycees, Acad. for Profl. Devel. Methodist. Club: Austin-Healey Sports Car and Touring. Home: 741 Collina Dr Lewisberry PA 17339 Office: 6510 Carlisle Pike Mechanicsburg PA 17055

HOOPER, JERE MANN, hotel exec.; b. Brownsville, Tenn., July 6, 1933; s. Carmon Thomas and Annie (Mann) H.; B.A., Vanderbilt U., 1955; m. Alice Anne Caldwell, Feb. 5, 1966; 1 dau., Emily. Exec. trainee Irving Trust Co., N.Y.C., 1958-61; asst. v.p. franchose Holiday Inns, Inc., Memphis, 1961-66; v.p. Chatmar, Inc., San Francisco, 1967-72; v.p. franchise TraveLodge Internat., Inc., El Cajon, Calif., 1972—, also mem. sr. mgmt. group and coordinating council. Served with AUS, 1955-57. Mem. Am. Hotel and Motel Assn., Internat. Franchise Assn., Sigma Alpha Epsilon. Republican. Episcopalian. Club: Cuyamaca. Home: 5141 Marlborough Dr San Diego CA 92116 Office: 250 TraveLodge Dr El Cajon CA 92090

HOOPER, RONALD RAFAEL, finance co. exec.; b. San Mateo, Calif., Dec. 4, 1938; s. Clayton Rafael and Julie (Breemis) H.; student Coll. San Mateo, 1962-65; m. Janet L. Adams, Dec. 27, 1975; 1 dau., Danielle Marie. Salesman, Grow & Doughty, San Mateo, 1963-65, Hancock & Marlin, 1965-68; pres. Champion Mining Co., San Mateo, 1970-74; pres. Monetech Fin. Corp., Burlingame, Calif., 1971—; gen. partner Burlingame Mortgage Investors (Calif.). Served with USN, 1958-62. Republican. Episcopalian. Clubs: Coyote Point Yacht; Commonwealth of Calif. Weekly columnist The Smart Money People, TV Facts Mag., 1974-75. Home: 1231 Avondale Rd Hillsborough CA 94010 Office: PO Box 1661 Burlingame CA 94010

HOOPMAN, HAROLD DEWAINE, oil co. exec.; b. Lucas, Kans., July 22, 1920; s. Ira William and Mary B. (Dorman) H.; B.S. in Mech. Engring., U. Wyo., 1942; student Advanced Mgmt. Program, Harvard, 1964; LL.D. (hon.), Marietta Coll., 1979; m. Eleanor Gessner, July 6, 1946; children—Judith Kristin (Mrs. Fred Hains), David W., Michael J. Exptl. test engr. Wright Aero. Co., Patterson, N.J., 1942-43; with Marathon Oil Co., 1946—, resident mgr., Guatemala, 1957-62, v.p. internat., 1962-67, asst. to pres., 1967-68, v.p. prodn., 1968-69, v.p. mktg. in U.S., Findlay, Ohio, 1969-72, pres., dir., 1972—, chief exec. officer, 1975—; dir. 1st Nat. Bank of Findlay, Owens-Ill., Inc. Served with USNR, 1943-46. Mem. Am. Inst. Mining, Metall. and Petroleum Engrs., Am. Petroleum Inst. (dir.), Findlay City C. of C., Findlay Coll. Assos. Lutheran. Club: Findlay Country. Contbr. articles to profl. jours. Office: 539 S Main St Findlay OH 45840

HOOVER, GARY LYNN, banker; b. Tipton, Ind., Oct. 20, 1937; s. Carmel Wayne and Virginia Ruth (Mitchell) H.; B.S., Purdue U., 1959; div.; children—Devin Page, Melissa Virginia. With First Nat. Bank, Winnetka, Ill., 1961-62; nat. bank examiner-internat. Comptroller of Currency, U.S. Dept. Treasury, Washington, 1962-70; asst. v.p. Lafayette Nat. Bank (Ind.), 1970-71; v.p.-internat. Am. Fletcher Nat. Bank, Indpls., 1971—. Bd. dirs. Indpls. Mus. Art, Indpls. Zool. Soc., Internat. Center of Indpls., Channel 20 TV; mem. Nat. Republican Com. Served with U.S. Army, 1961. Mem. Econs. Club Ind., Purdue Alumni Assn., World Trade Club, Ind. Congregationalist. Clubs: Indpls. Ski, Ambassadair Travel. Home: 225 E North St Apt 1003 Indianapolis IN 46204 Office: 108 N Pennsylvania St Indianapolis IN 46277

HOOVER, L(EWIS) RONALD, mfg. co. exec.; b. Altoona, Pa., July 23, 1940; s. Lewis D. and Doris Evelyn (Nicodemus) H.; B.S., Shippensburg (Pa.) State Coll., 1962; M.A., Washington U., St. Louis, 1963; Ph.D. in Elec. Engring., U. Mo., Rolla, 1972; m. Bonnie Lou Spealman, June 21, 1962; children—Laura, Teena, Ronda. Prof. physics Shippensburg State Coll., 1963-69; research specialist Bell Telephone Labs., Greensboro, N.C., 1972-77; prof. computer sci. Shippensburg State Coll., 1977-79; mgr. engring. and mfg. computer systems AMP Inc., Harrisburg, Pa., 1979—; computer cons. Mem. IEEE (past regional chmn.), Assn. Computing Machinery. Mem. United Brethren Ch. Home: 401 W King St Shippensburg PA 17257 Office: AMP Inc 3705 Paxton St Harrisburg PA 17111

HOOVER, ROBERT B., lumber co. exec.; b. Fresno, Calif., 1916; A.B., Stanford U., 1937, M.B.A., 1939; married. Partner, Al Hoover Co., 1940-63; v.p. sales Pacific Lumber Co., San Francisco, 1963-71, sec., 1965-69, exec. v.p., 1971-73, pres., 1973-80, chief exec. officer, 1973—, chmn. bd., 1980—, also dir.; pres., dir. Sangre de Cristo Timber Co., Yosuba Farm Co.; dir. Pacific Gas & Electric Co., Thermol Dynamics Co. Served to lt. (j.g.) USN, 1944-46. Office: Pacific Lumber Co 1111 Columbus Ave San Francisco CA 94133*

HOOVER, WILLIAM LEICHLITER, educator, fin. cons.; b. Brownsville, Pa., July 29, 1944; s. Aaron Jones and Edith (Leichliter) H.; B.S., Pa. State U., 1966, M.S., 1971; Ph.D., Iowa State U., 1977; m. Peggy Jo Spangler, Aug. 30, 1976; children—Jennifer Mary, Monica Susan. Research asst. Pa. State U., Iowa State U., 1970-74; asst. prof. Purdue U., West Lafayette, Ind., 1974-79, asso. prof. dept. forestry and natural resources, 1980—; sec./treas., dir. econ. and fin. analysis Timber Tech., Inc., W. Lafayette, 1978—. Served to 1st lt., C.E., U.S. Army, 1967-69. Decorated Bronze Star. Mem. Forest Products Research Soc., Am. Econ. Assn., Nat. Assn. Public Accts., Soc. Am. Foresters. Republican. Presbyterian. Asst. editor Timber Tax Jour., 1979—; author: The Timber Owner's Federal Income Tax Guide, 1980. Home: 206 Connolly St West Lafayette IN 47906 Office: Dept Forestry Purdue U West Lafayette IN 47907

HOPE, WILLIAM WAYNE, farm equipment mfg. co. exec.; b. Kansas City, Mo., May 14, 1926; s. David Nicholas and Emma (Shepard) H.; B.S., Rockhurst Coll., Kansas City, Mo., 1951; m. Betty L. Jackson, Aug. 30, 1947; children—Steven D., Mark W., Michael L. Trainee spl. sales, Okla., Mo. and Kans., John Deere Co., Kansas City, Mo., 1951-54, terr. mgr., Kans., 1954-58; sales supr. Massey Ferguson Inc., Kansas City, Mo., 1958-59, sales mgr., Pocatello, Idaho, 1959-60, Stockton, Calif., 1960-63, Kansas City, Mo., 1963-67, regional mgr., Stockton, 1967-75, Hopkins, Minn., 1975—. Served with USAF, 1944-47; PTO. Mem. NW Farm Equipment Assn. (dir. 1975—), Tractor and Equipment Club (pres. No. Calif. 1972-73). Clubs: Interlachen Country, Masons, Shriners. Home: 6801 Telemark Trail Edina MN 55436 Office: 802 St Louis St Hopkins MN 55343

HOPES, JAMES JOHN, bank exec.; b. Moscow, Pa., Mar. 4, 1930; s. James and Jennie (Miller) H.; A.B., U. Pa., 1952; m. Angela Margaret Manno, Feb. 14, 1953; children—Richard J., James R., Deborah L. Mgmt. trainee Nat. Dairies, Phila., 1954-56; computer programming supr. U.S. Mil. Clothing & Textile Supply Agy., Phila., 1956-60; computer programming mgr. RCA Service Corp., Cherry Hill, N.J., 1960-61; dir. systems and programming Bunker Ramo Co., Stamford, Conn., 1961-66; sr. mgr. EDP, mgmt. cons., Price-Waterhouse & Co., N.Y.C., 1966-72; v.p. Chase Manhattan Bank N.Y., 1972—; corp. dir., Payment & Adminstrv. Telecommunication Corp., 1976-77, rep. on N.Y. Clearing House, 1977-80, chmn. systems ops. com., 1979-80. Served with arty. U.S. Army, 1950-52. Certified in data processing, Data Processing Mgmt. Assn. Mem. Assn. Systems Mgmt., Assn. Computing Machinery, Nat. Automated Clearing House Assn. (rep., systems and ops. com. 1978-80). Republican. Methodist. Home: 12 Bonus Hill Dr Scotch Plains NJ 07076 Office: 1 New York Plaza New York NY 10015

HOPKINS, CHARLES IVAN, JR., railroad exec.; b. Chgo., Apr. 27, 1927; s. Charles Ivan and Ethel (Gillow) H.; B.S., U. Ill., 1949, J.D., 1951; m. Elayne M. Ruck, June 21, 1952; 1 son, Randall. Admitted to Ill. bar, 1950, D.C. bar, 1980; atty. Ill. Central R.R., Chgo., 1951-55; partner firm Jacobs, Miller, Hopkins & Rooney, Chgo., 1955-56; atty. N.Y. Central R.R., Chgo., 1956-64; gen. atty. Nat. Ry. Labor Conf., Chgo., 1964-67, chmn., 1977—; asst. v.p. employee relations Am. Airlines, Inc., N.Y.C., 1967-68, v.p. personnel, 1968-72; v.p. personnel relations Flying Tiger Lines, Inc., Los Angeles, 1972-77, also dir. Served with USNR, 1945-46. Mem. Soc. Trial Lawyers, Am. Bar Assn., Am. Judicature Soc., Ill. Bar Assn., Order Coif, Psi Upsilon, Phi Alpha Delta. Office: 1901 L St NW Washington DC 20036

HOPKINS, EDWARD DONALD, paint co. exec.; b. Little Rock, Apr. 16, 1937; s. Edward J. and Mildred (I.) H.; B.S., USAF Acad., 1960; M.B.A., U. So. Calif., 1966; m. Dawn Dee Fritz, May 20, 1965; children—Mark Edward, Scott Edward, Paige Noel. Commd. 2d lt. U.S. Air Force, 1956, advanced through grades to capt., 1964; ret., 1967; unit mgr. Gen. Electric Co., Cin., 1967-70; v.p. mktg. Tri City Builders, Cin., 1971; group v.p. Roch Instrument Systems, Inc., Rochester, N.Y., 1972-74; dir. hermetic motors Gould Inc., St. Louis, 1974-75, v.p. and gen. mgr. powder metal parts div., Salem, Ind., 1976-77, pres. and gen. mgr. indsl. battery div., Langhorne, Pa., 1977-80; pres., gen. mgr. Consumer div. Sherwin-Williams Co., Cleve., 1980—. Office: 1370 Ontario Ave Cleveland OH 44113

HOPKINS, GEORGE MATHEWS MARKS, patent lawyer; b. Houston, June 9, 1923; s. C. Allen and Agnes Cary (Marks) H.; student Ga. Sch. Tech., 1943-44; B.S. in Chem. Engring., Ala. Poly. Inst., 1944; LL.B., U. Ala., 1949; postgrad. George Washington U., 1949-50; m. Betty Miller McLean, Aug. 21, 1954; children—Laura McLean, Edith Cary. Admitted to Ala. bar, 1949, Ga. bar, 1954; instr. math. U. Ala., 1947-49; asso. atty. A. Yates Dowell, 1949-50, Edw. T. Newton, 1950-62; asst. dir. research, legal counsel Auburn Research Found., 1954-55; partner Newton, Hopkins and Jones, 1962-68, Newton, Hopkins and Ormsby, 1968—; sec.-treas. Tufted Patterns, Inc., 1959-62; exec. v.p., sec., treas. Fabulous Fabrics, Inc., 1960-62; chmn. bd. Southeastern Carpet Mills, Inc., Chatsworth, Ga., 1962-78; pres. Entertainment Investments, Inc., 1967-69, GNG Corp., Montgomery, Ala., 1971-72; dir. Xepol Inc., Thomas Daniels & Assos., Inc. Served as lt. submarine service USNR, 1944-46, 50-51. Registered profl. engr., Ga.; registered patent atty., U.S., Can. Mem. Am., Ga. (chmn. patent sect. 1970-71), Atlanta bar assns., Am. Patent Law Assn., Am. Soc. Profl. Engrs., Submarine Vets. of World War II (pres. Ga. chpt. 1977-78, vice comdr. 1976-77, 78-79), Phi Delta Phi, Sigma Alpha Epsilon. Episcopalian. Clubs: Nat. Lawyers (Washington); Cherokee Town and Country; Atlanta City; Univ. Yacht. Home: 1765 Old Post Rd NW Atlanta GA 30328 Office: Equitable Bldg Atlanta Ga 30303

HOPKINS, OREN EDWARD, JR., equipment mfg. co. exec.; b. Norfolk, Va., Feb. 12, 1925; s. Oren E. and Norma B. H.; B.S.I.E., Va. Poly. Inst., 1950; M.S.I.E., Columbia U., 1951; m. Marian Elizabeth Brown, May 2, 1953; children—Jane Chadwick, Oren Edward III, Christian Smith. Mgmt. engring. services E.I. Du Pont de Nemours & Co. Inc., Newark, Del., 1951-55; rental and lease mgr. Watkins Motors Co., Chester, Pa., 1955-56; sales engr. Pennwalt Corp., Phila., 1956-60, dist. mgr., 1961-68, gen. sales mgr., 1969-74; municipal sales mgr. Envirotech, Salt Lake City, 1974-77, v.p. sales and service, 1977—. Pres., Bay Village (Ohio) chpt. Am. Field Service, 1966-68; elder Presbyn. Ch., Salt Lake City, 1960—. Served with U.S. Army, 1943-46. Mem. Alumni Assn. Va. Poly. Inst. (dir. 1968-78), Am. Inst. Chem. Engrs., Am. Inst. Mining, Metall. and Petroleum Engrs., Waste Water Equipment Mfrs. Assn. (bd. dirs. 1980—), Water Pollution Control Fedn., Am. Water Works Assn. Republican. Club: Ft. Douglas Country. Home: 2902 St Marys Way Salt Lake City UT 84108 Office: 669 W 200 S Salt Lake City UT 84110

HOPKINS, ROBERT HOWELL, JR., mortgage banking co. exec.; b. Dallas, June 29, 1931; s. Robert Howell and Anna Pauline (Richardson) H.; B.S. in Commerce, Tex. Christian U., 1952; postgrad. Harvard Grad. Sch. Bus., 1952-53; m. Joanne Schneider, Aug. 16, 1952; children—Robert Howell, Matthew William, Paula. Field rep. Lawyers Title Ins. Corp., Dallas, 1954-58; pres. Gessent Sanders Abstract Co., Roswell, N.Mex., 1958-63, SW Mortgage Co., Roswell, 1963-67, Nat. Mortgage Corp. Am., Dallas, 1967—; chmn. bd. Commodore Life Ins. Co. Chmn., Roswell March of Dimes, 1964; pres. Christian Chs. N.Mex. (Disciples Christ), 1967. Mem. Dallas Mortgage Bankers Assn. (pres. 1977), Tex. Christian U. C. of C. (pres. 1952). Home: 6310 Joyce Way Dallas TX 75225

HOPKINS, WILLARD GEORGE, hosp. adminstr.; b. Balt., Mar. 30, 1940; s. George C. and Laura (Elwell) H.; B.S. in Civil Engring., U. Md., 1963; M.B.A., Cornell U., 1969; M. Hosp. Adminstrn., Sloan Inst. of Hosp. Adminstrn., 1969; m. Valerie Jewell, June 22, 1963; children—Michelle Marie, Tiffany Lynn. Commd. officer USPHS, 1963, project engr. Div. Indian Health, Okla., 1963-65, engr. interstate carrier br. Chgo. Regional Office, 1965-67, hosp. resident Meml. Hosp. for Cancer and Allied Diseases, N.Y.C., 1968; mem. health care cons. staff Arthur Young & Co., San Francisco office, 1969-73, dir. health care practice, 1973-76, dir. Washington health cons. practice, 1976-77; dir. health and med. div. Booz, Allen & Hamilton, Inc., Washington, 1977-79; exec. v.p. Scottsdale (Ariz.) Meml Hosp., 1979—; dir. Comprehensive Health Planning Assn., Contra Costa County, Calif., 1973-77. Fellow Soc. for Advanced Med. Systems, Am. Health Planning Assn.; mem. Am. Coll. Hosp. Adminstrs., Nat. Assn. Mfrs. (mem. employee benefits com. 1976-79), Group Health Assn. Am., Assn. Univ. Programs in Health Adminstrn. (mem. com. on minority group affairs 1976-79). Contbr. articles on health care to profl. publs.; mem. editorial bd. Am. Jour. Health Planning, 1974-79. Home: 4711 E Arroyo Verde Rd Paradise Valley AZ 85253 Office: 7400 E Osborn Rd Scottsdale AZ 85251

HOPPE, ALLEN EARL, fin. analyst; b. Mankato, Minn., Dec. 22, 1953; s. Earl H. and Mary G. (Bisch) H.; B.S. in Fin., St. Cloud U., 1980. Acctg. intern Brown Boveri Turbomachinery, 1979-80; analyst Springsted, Inc., public fin. advisors, St. Paul, 1980—. Served with USMC, 1972-76. Mem. Mcpl. Fin. Officers Assn. (asso.), Delta Sigma Pi (life; corr. Deltasig mag.; alumni chmn.). Roman Catholic. Clubs: Catholic Order Foresters, St. Paul Athletic. Address: 2516 NE Silver Ln Suite 202 Minneapolis MN 55421

HOPPE, WILLIAM EDWARD, realtor; b. Milw., Mar. 30, 1928; s. Edward Clarence and Claire Emily (Ruthe) H.; student U. Wis., 1945-46; m. Audrey L. Stephen, Oct. 22, 1949; children—Craig Allen, Douglas Dean. Owner, operator H&R Foods, Racine, Wis., 1951-55; partner Ed Hoppe Realty, Las Vegas, Nev., 1958-63, v.p., 1963-71; pres. Hoppe Realty, Inc., Las Vegas, 1971—. Committeeman citizen's adv. council Las Vegas Gen. Plan Program, 1973-74; bd. dirs. Center Bus. and Econ. Research U. Nev. Served with USMCR, 1946-48. Recipient Outstanding Service award Multiple Listing Service, 1970; named Realtor of Yr., Las Vegas, 1976. Mem. Nat. (publicity chmn. conv. com. 1972-74, legis. com. 1976-77, polit. action com. 1979, dir. 1981—), Nev. (dir. 1972, 75, treas. 1978, pres. elect 1979, pres. 1980) assns. realtors, Las Vegas Bd. Realtors (1st v.p. 1974, pres. 1975—). Editor: Nev. Realtor, 1972, 74. Home: 716 Starks Dr Las Vegas NV 89107 Office: 708 S 6th St Las Vegas NV 89101

HOPPER, EDMOND LOUIS, assurance co. exec.; b. Newark, June 16, 1933; s. Edmond Louis and Marie Theresa (Murphy) H.; B.S., Seton Hall U., 1955; m. Barbara E. Shinn, Oct. 3, 1959; children—Mark E., J. Douglas, K. Elizabeth. With Allstate Ins. Co., Skokie, Ill., 1961-70, various positions in auditing, audit mgmt.; audit mgmt. Travelers Ins. Co., Hartford, Ct., 1970-71, 2d v.p., 1971-74; dir. internal audit Comml. Union Assurance Co., Boston, 1974—. Served with Mil. Police, U.S. Army, 1955-56. Certified internal auditor. Mem. Inst. Internal Auditors, Ins. Internal Audit Group. Roman Catholic. Home: 26 Crooked Pond Dr Boxford MA 01921 Office: One Beacon St Boston MA 02108

HORAN, JOHN J., pharm. co. exec.; b. S.I., N.Y., July 9, 1920; s. Michael T. and Alice (Kelly) H.; A.B., Manhattan Coll., 1940; LL.B., Columbia, 1946; m. Julie Fitzgerald, Jan. 2, 1945; children—Mary Alice, Thomas, Jack, David. Admitted to N.Y. bar, 1946; with firm Nims, Verdi & Martin, N.Y.C., 1946-52; atty. Merck & Co., Inc., 1952-55, counsel Merck Sharp & Dohme div., 1955-57; dir. pub. relations Merck & Co., 1957-61, exec. dir. research adminstrn., research labs., 1961-62, dir. corp. planning, 1962-63; exec. v.p. mktg. Merck Sharp & Dohme, 1963-67; exec. v.p., gen. mgr., 1967-69, pres., 1969-72, corp. sr. v.p., 1972-74, exec. v.p., 1974-75, pres., chief operating officer, 1975-76, chmn., chief exec. officer, 1976—, also dir.; dir. NCR Corp., Gen. Motors Corp.; bd. mgrs. Beneficial Mut. Savs. Bank, 1971-74. Bd. dirs. Mgmt. Sci. Center of Wharton Sch. of U. Pa., 1971-78; trustee Thomas Jefferson U. and Med. Coll., 1971-74; mem. nat. bd. United Negro Coll. Fund, Am. Found. Pharm. Edn. Served to lt. USNR, 1942-46. Mem. Pharm. Mfrs. Assn. (dir., former chmn.), Bus. Council, Bus. Roundtable, Econ. Club of N.Y., Conf. Bd., Council Fgn. Relations, European Community/U.S. Businessmen's Council, Council for NE Econ. Action (adv. com.). Clubs: Sky, Links; Baltusrol Golf. Office: Merck & Co Inc Rahway NJ 07065

HORDISH, J. ARNOLD, brokerage firm exec.; b. N.Y.C., Nov. 18, 1934; s. Lester and Ann (Steiner) H.; B.B.A., Pace Coll., 1959; m. Carol Wiener, Aug. 15, 1965; children—David Lawrence, Joshua Aaron. With Dean Witter Reynolds Co., Inc., N.Y.C., 1956—, v.p., 1968—. Del., Nat. Council Young Israel, 1970—. Bd. dirs. Am. Jewish Congress, 1970-71, P'Tach, 1979—, Manhattan Day Sch., 1980—; adv. bd. Bellvue Hosp., 1971, Beth Israel Hosp., 1978—; mem. acute health task force Health and Hosps. Corp. N.Y., 1979—. Served with AUS, 1953-56, Recipient Man of Year award Nat. Council Young Israel, 1972, Prime Minister's award State of Israel Bonds, 1973, Community Service award United Jewish Appeal-Fedn. Jewish Philanthropics, 1977. Mem. Nat., Am. (nominating com. bd. govs. 1976—) stock exchanges, N.Y. Merc. Exchange, Young Israel of Fifth Av. (exec. v.p. 1968-71, pres. 1971-74, chmn. bd. nursery sch. 1971-80, Man of Year award 1968). Home: 305 E 24th St New York NY 10010 Office: 130 Liberty St New York NY 10005

HORII, KENNETH JUN, constrn. exec.; b. Honolulu, June 19, 1938; s. Henry Fusao and Masaye (Hashimoto) H.; B.S. in Engring., U. Hawaii, 1962; m. Jacqueline Hirono Miyahara, Feb. 29, 1964; children—Patricia Ann, Christine. With THOHT Constrn., Inc., Honolulu, 1962—, pres., 1971—; trustee Mason's Trust Funds of Hawaii. Mem. UN Day Com. Mem. Constrn. Specifications Inst., Gen. Contractors Assn. Hawaii, Am. Soc. C.E. Office: 636 Laumaka St Honolulu HI 96819

HORIN, MARC BASIL, futures exchange exec.; b. Chgo., Jan. 30, 1953; s. John and Mary Anne (Chlanda) H.; B.A., Shimer Coll., Mt. Carroll, Ill., 1974. Options broker A.G. Becker, Chgo., 1974-76; floor mgr. Pacific Options Exchange, San Francisco, 1976-77; corp. liaison N.Y. Futures Exchange, 1980—, asst. to pres., 1978-80, floor mgr., 1976—. Home: 9100 S Longwood Dr Chicago IL 60620

HORKA, ALFRED EDWARD, plastics co. exec.; b. Passaic, N.J., Feb. 26, 1921; s. Frank Walter and Anna (Haas) H.; B.S. in Chem. Engring., Lehigh U., 1942; m. Jean S. Lawton, Feb. 7, 1945; children—Douglas Lawton, Nancy Jean. Project engr. Bakelite Corp., Bound Brook, N.J., 1945-48; sales engring. various cos., N.Y.C., 1948-56; sales mgr. New Eng. Tape Co., Hudson, Mass., 1956-59; founder, dir. pres. Plastic Extrusion & Engring. Co., Inc., Westborough, 1960—; indsl. panel adviser on modern plastics. Mem. adv. bd. Keene Tech. and Vocat. High Sch.; corp. mem. Goodwill Industries; mem. exec. bd. Algonquin council Boy Scouts Am. Served to capt. USAAF, World War II. Paul Harris fellow Rotary Internat. Mem. Soc. Plastics Engrs. (sr. mem., dir. med. group) Central Mass. Employers Assn. (dir.), Lehigh U. Alumni-Asa Packer Soc., U.S. Power Squadron (editor Rhumb Line). Presbyterian. (elder, trustee). Clubs: Masons, Rotary (charter, past pres., sec. Westboro; past dist. sec., trustee), Hundred of Mass.; Plaza (Worcester, Mass.). Home: Seven Stagg Dr Natick MA 01760 also Ryder Rd North Falmouth MA 02556 Office: 170 Bartlett St Northborough MA 01532

HORMAN, SIDNEY MELVIN, contractor; b. Tooele, Utah, Feb. 21, 1905; s. Thomas De. La. Haye and Sarah Ann (Vowles) H.; student Latter-day Saints Bus. Coll., 1924-25, U. Utah, 1926; m. Veoma L. Holmgren, June 18, 1935; children—Sidney Maurice, Charles H., Vee Drienne (Mrs. Gordon Johnson). Pres., Orem Devel. Corp. (Utah), Colo. Warehouse Corp., Salt Lake City, Cottonwood Mall, Salt Lake City, Horman Warehouse Corp., Salt Lake City, South State Devel. Corp., Salt Lake City, Horman Constrn. Co. Mem. regional bd. Zions First Nat. Bank. Mem. nat. adv. council Coll. Bus. Brigham Young U. Named Citizen of Yr., Utah Assn. Realtors, 1980. Recipient Jesse Knight Indsl. Citizenship award Brigham Young U., 1971, Hon. Alumni award Brigham Young U., 1972, Presdl. medal, 1976; pin Internat. Aero. Hall of Fame. Mem. Internat. Platform Assn., Salt Lake City C. of C. Mem. Ch. of Jesus Christ of Latter-day Saints (devel. com., mem. ch. welfare com. 1959-68). Lion. Club: Knife and Fork (Salt Lake City). Home: 14 Sunwood Ln Pepperwood UT 84070 Office: 1760 S State St Salt Lake City UT 84115

HORMANN, JOHN MATTHEW, aerospace co. exec.; b. N.Y.C., Dec. 7, 1940; s. Hans Matthew and Rose Florence (Roche) H.; B.S., Rider Coll., 1963; m. Elizabeth M. McLeod, Sept. 25, 1965; children—Bruce Matthew, Christopher Michel. With Grumman Aerospace Corp., 1963—, now program fin. control mgr., Islip, N.Y.; guest lectr. Mem. Metall. Soc. Am. Republican. Clubs: Bay Berry Beach and Tennis, Bay Berry Yacht, Point O'Woods. Office: S Oyster Bay Rd Bethpage NY 11714

HORN, CARL, JR., utility exec.; b. Rutherfordton, N.C., Oct. 21, 1921; s. Carl and Freda Wagner (Warden) H.; A.B., Duke, 1942, LL.B., 1947; m. Frances Alice Emmet, Feb. 7, 1948 (dec. 1966); children—Carl III, Claire, Kathrine, Thomas E.; m. 2d, Virginia Grey Johnston, Oct. 27, 1967. Admitted to N.C. bar, 1947, practiced in Charlotte until 1953; asst. gen. counsel Duke Power Co., Charlotte, 1954-59, gen. counsel, 1959-63, v.p., gen. counsel, 1963-66, v.p. finance, gen. counsel, 1966-69, exec. v.p., gen. counsel, 1970-71, pres., 1971—, chmn. and chief exec. officer, 1976—; dir. Integon Corp., J.B. Ivey & Co. Bd. dirs. Charlotte Meml. Hosp.; trustee N.C. Found. Ch. Related Colls., S.C. Found. Ind. Colls., Erskine Coll., Due West, S.C. Served to capt. AUS, 1942-46; PTO; mem. N.C.N.G., 1953-54. Mem. Am., N.C bar assns., Edison Electric Inst. (chmn. legal com. 1967—), Duke Univ. Law Alumni Assn. (pres. 1961), Newcomen Soc. N.Am., Order of Coif. Presbyn. (elder). Office: 422 S Church St Charlotte NC 28202*

HORN, CHRISTIAN FRIEDRICH, business exec.; b. Dresden, Ger., Dec. 23, 1927; came to U.S., 1954, naturalized, 1959; s. Otto and Elsa Horn; diploma Dresden Tech. U., 1951; Ph.D., Aachen Tech. U., 1958; m. Christa Winkler, Feb. 13, 1954; 1 dau., Sabrina. Research scientist German Acad. Scis., E. Berlin, 1951-53; research chemist Farbenwerke Hoechst, W. Ger., 1953-54; research mgr. Union Carbide Corp., Charleston, W.Va. and Brussels, Belgium, 1954-65; pres. Polymer Tech., Inc., N.Y.C., 1965-74; mem. bd. mgmt. H.J. Zimmer A.G., Frankfurt, W. Ger., 1971-73; v.p. W.R. Grace & Co., N.Y.C., 1974—; dir. Davy Powergas, Inc., Lakeland, Fla., 1973-77. Mem. Am. Chem. Soc., German Chem. Soc., German-Am. C. of C. Author, patentee in field. Home: 101 Dingletown Rd Greenwich CT 06830 Office: 1114 Ave Americas New York NY 10036

HORN, ERIC LAURENS, homebuilding co. exec.; b. Huntingdon, Pa., Sept. 23, 1946; s. John Chisolm and Solveig Elizabeth (Wald) H.; B.A., Susquehanna U., 1968; M.B.A., U. So. Calif., 1972; m. Eileen Maria Moninghoff, Aug. 11, 1973; children—Brian Fitzgerald, Dennis Chisolm. Asst. to pres. Watt Industries, Los Angeles, 1972-73, pres. Brookline Co. div., Santa Monica, Calif., 1979—; v.p. Bell Canyon Bldg. Co., Canoga Park, Calif., 1974-76, W & A Builders, Inc., Santa Monica, 1976-79. Pres. Palisades Homeowners Assn., 1975-76; mem. Redondo Beach Superstar Classic com., 1977-79. Served to lt., USN, 1968-70. Mem. Bldg. Industry Assn. (air quality adv. panel 1977-78), Sales and Mktg. Council, So. Calif. U. Commerce Asso., Am. Enterprise Inst., Bldg. Industry Assn. Homebuilders Council. Republican. Lutheran. Club: Victorville Rotary. Home: 18035 Joshua Tree Ln HSR Box 468 Victorville CA 92392 Office: 2716 Ocean Park Blvd Santa Monica CA 90272

HORN, GUENTHER, mfg. co. exec.; b. Giessen, W. Ger., Feb. 14, 1943; came to U.S., 1977; s. Adolf and Emmi (Weber) H.; diploma in physics, Justus Liebig U., Giessen, W. Ger., 1969; m. Ursula Schmeling, May 9, 1969; 1 dau., Susanne. Research asst. Justus Liebig U., Giessen, 1969-70; research physicist Doduco-KG, Pforzheim, Ger., 1971-73; mgr. research and devel. contact labs. Doduco-KG, 1974-77; tech. dir. Art Wire/Doduco, Cedar Knolls, N.J., 1977—; faculty various tech. colls., Ger., 1974-77. Mem. steering com. Holm Confs. on Elec. Contacts. Recipient Cert. of Appreciation for outstanding service Internat. Precious Metal Inst., 1979. Mem. German Phys. Soc., Soc. Mfg. Engrs., Wire Assn., Internat. Precious Metal Inst. Lutheran. Contbr. articles to profl. jours. Home: 11 Peace Rd Randolph NJ 07869 Office: 9 Wing Dr Cedar Knolls NJ 07927

HORN, JOHN CHISOLM, mgmt. cons.; b. N.Y.C., Jan. 16, 1915; s. William M. and Marguerite E. (Jacobs) H.; A.B., Cornell U., 1936, postgrad., 1937; LL.D., Susquehanna U., 1965; m. Solveig E. Wald, June 22, 1938; children—Phyllis Downing, John Chisolm, Stephen Lunde, Eric Laurens, Robert Gregg, Thomas Wald, Dorothy Traill, James Melchior. With John R. Wald Co., 1937-39; sec. Prismo Safety Corp., 1939-45, sec., treas., 1945-49, v.p., 1949-57, exec. v.p., 1957-62, pres., 1962-69; pres. John C. Horn Assos., 1970—; pres. Prismo Universal Corp., 1969-70, vice chmn. bd., 1970—; asst. sec. Wald Industries, Inc., 1950-51, pres., 1951-69; exec. dir. Church Mgmt. Service, Inc., 1971—; dir. Long Siding Corp., Prismo France, Paris, Prismo Universal Ltd., Eng. cooperating cons. Tech. Diversification Services, 1972—. Dir. Huntingdon Bus. and Industry, Inc., 1958—; chmn. Indsl. Devel. Commn., 1959-60, area devel. chmn., 1960-62. Bd. dirs., vice chmn. Wald Found., 1954-63; mem. nat. council Boy Scouts Am., 1950—, nat. com. on cubbing, 1961-68, nat. com. exec. profl. tng., 1971—, exec. com Region III, 1961—, v.p. Juniata Valley council 1951-57, pres., 1957—; pres., bd. dirs. Huntingdon County United Fund, 1959-68; mem. indsl. and profl. council Pa. State U. Bd. dirs. Juniata Valley Schs., St. James Huntington Choir; pres. bd. dirs. Susquehanna U.; mem. bd. publ. Luth. Ch. Am., 1968—. Recipient Silver Beaver, Lamb and Silver Antelope awards Boy Scouts Am., also Outstanding Civic Leader award, 1967. Mem. Army Ordnance Assn., NAM, AIM, Am. Mgmt. Assn., Am. Road Builders Assn., Internat. Bridge Tunnel and Toll Rd. Assn., Inst. Traffic Engrs., C. of C. (dir. 1955), Juniata Mountains Devel. Assn. (pres. 1956). Lutheran (home mission bd. Central Pa. Synod 1948—, com. on music and worship; synodical proposal com. 1957—, exec. bd. 1962-67, higher edn. com. 1967—). Clubs: Huntingdon Music, Huntingdon Country; Indian of Juniata College. Home: Killmarnock Hall Alexandria PA 16611 Office: 301 Penn St Huntingdon PA 16652

HORN, PAUL THOMAS, agribusiness exec.; b. Fargo, N.D., Dec. 5, 1942; s. Paul L. and Margaret E. (McLlarnan) H.; B.S. with honors, Mich. State U., 1964; postgrad. N.D. State U., 1964-65; m. Connie Lee Snider, Aug. 8, 1964; children—Jennifer Lee, Stacey Snider, Jason Paul. Vice pres. Paul Horn Farms Inc., Moorhead, Minn., 1964-74, pres., 1974—; vice chmn. No. Grain Co.; sec. Amcan Investments Co., Inc.; partner BSM; dir. Moorhead State Bank. Bd. dirs. Dakota Med. Found.; treas. Sugarbeet Research and Edn. Bd.; mgr. Buffalo Red River Watershed Dist. Republican. Presbyterian. Office: Paul Horn Farms Inc 2100 5th Ave N Moorhead MN 56560

HORN, ROBERT ERNEST, mfg. co. exec.; b. Galeton, Pa., Nov. 29, 1926; s. Gustav and Myra A. (Smith) H.; B.S. in E.E., Marquette U., 1950; m. Feb. 8, 1947; children—Roberta, Deborah, Charleen, Louise. With Allis Chalmers Co., Milw., 1951-72; exec. v.p. Paragon Electric Co., Inc., Two Rivers, Wis., 1972, pres., 1972—; dir. Metal Ware Corp., Two Rivers. Bd. dirs. Jr. Achievement, Manitowoc County, Wis., 1973-80, Silver Lake Coll., Manitowoc, 1975-80, N.E. Wis. Indsl. Assn., 1973-78. Served with USN, 1944-46. Mem. Wis. Mfrs. and Commerce (dir. 1979—), Manitowoc Two Rivers C. of C. (dir. 1973-79). Clubs: K.C., Elks. Home: 3706 Wildwood Dr Manitowoc WI 54220 Office: 6060 Parkway Blvd Two Rivers WI 54241

HORNADAY, HAROLD PRESTON, textile co. exec.; b. Greensboro, N.C., Mar. 31, 1926; s. Wayne Arrington and Mary Ruth (Dameron) H.; A.B. in Econs., Duke U., 1948; m. Anne Dundas Millikan, June 19, 1948; children—Suzanne Millikan Hornaday Barger, William Harold. Joined Cannon Mills Co., Kannapolis, N.C., 1949, asst. v.p., 1965-66, v.p., 1966-71, dir., 1967—, sr. v.p., asst. to pres., 1971-73, exec. v.p., 1973, pres., chief operating officer, 1973-79, chmn. bd., chief exec. officer, 1975—; dir. NCNB Corp., N.C. Nat. Bank. Bd. dirs. United Way of Cabarrus County, Inc.; adv. bd. Duke Hosp.; first chmn. Gold History Corp. Served with USNR, 1943-46. Mem. Am. Textile Mfrs. Inst. (dir.). Methodist. Club: Goldmine Toastmasters (award 1979). Office: PO Box 107 Kannapolis NC 28081

HORNAY, (THOMAS) RICHARD, clothing mfg. co. exec.; b. Cornwall, Ont., Can., Mar. 31, 1936; s. James William and Simone Alphonse (Drouin) H.; chartered acct., 1962; m. Doreen B. Burkett, July 8, 1961; children—Michael, Jeffrey, Jennifer. With Price Waterhouse & Co., Toronto, Ont., 1957-64; controller Crane Can. Ltd., Montreal, Que., 1964-69; asst. treas., govt. liaison officer Microsystems Internat. Ltd., Montreal, 1969-73; sec. treas. Sovereign Seat Cover Mfg. Co. Ltd., Cornwall, 1973-75; v.p., treas. Warnaco of Can. Ltd., Prescott, Ont., 1975—; dir. Canadays Apparel Ltd., Moose Jaw, Sask. Mem. Inst. Chartered Accts. Ont. Mem. United Ch. Club: Brockville Yacht. Home: 69 Butterfield Pl Brockville ON Canada Office: PO Box 1239 Prescott ON Canada

HORNBRUCH, FREDERICK WILLIAM, JR., corp. cons.; b. Roselle, N.J., July 14, 1913; s. Frederick William and Elsa M. (Becker) H.; M.E., Stevens Inst. Tech., 1934; m. Helen Novak, Apr. 10, 1936; children—Frederick William III, Harlan Richard. Engr., Weston Elec. Instrument Corp., Newark, 1934-40, Falstrom Co., Passaic, N.J., 1940-41; indsl. engr. Bendix Aviation Corp., Phila., 1941-43; prodn. mgr. Columbia Machine Works, Bklyn., 1943-44; chief engr., dir. Rath & Strong, Inc., Boston, 1944-57; v.p. Landers, Frary & Clark, Inc., New Britain, Conn., 1957-59; v.p. Atlas Corp., N.Y.C., 1959-64, dir., 1962-64; pres., dir. Titeflex, Inc., Springfield,

Mass., 1960-64; chmn. bd. Mertronics Corp., Santa Monica, Cal., 1960-64; pres., dir. Internat. Air, Inc., N.Y.C., 1962; v.p. Calumet & Hecla, Inc., Chgo., also gen. mgr. Flexonics div., 1964-68; v.p. Aero-Chatillon Corp., Inc., N.Y.C., 1968-69; v.p. adminstrn. Macrodyne-Chatillon Corp., N.Y.C., 1969; dir. Macrodyne Industries, Inc., 1974-78; pvt. practice corp. cons., Barrington Hills, Ill., 1969—. Mem. Am. Soc. M.E., Soc. Advancement Mgmt., Newcomen Soc., Tau Beta Pi, Pi Delta Epsilon, Phi Sigma Kappa. Presbyn. Clubs: Engineers (N.Y.C.); Barrington Hills Country. Author: (with Bruce and Chadruc) Practical Planning and Scheduling, 1950; Raising Productivity, 1977. Contbr. to Handbook of Bus. Adminstrn., 1967; mem. adv. bd., contbr. Handbook of Modern Mfg. Mgmt., 1967-68. Patentee instrument for synchronizing aircraft engines. Address: Rural Route 2 Three Lakes Rd Barrington Hills IL 60010

HORNBRUCH, HARLAN RICHARD, health industry exec.; b. Bryn Mawr, Pa., Mar. 4, 1947; s. Frederick William and Helen (Novak) H.; B.S.B.A., Northwestern U., 1969, M.B.A., 1970. Product mgr. Gen. Foods Corp., White Plains, N.Y., 1970-72, operation mgr., Washington, 1972-74; distbn. mgr. Wilson Sporting Goods, Chgo., 1974-76, sales div. mgr., Los Angeles, 1977-79; v.p. new bus. ventures Health Industries, Inc., Newport Beach, Calif., 1979-81, v.p. planning and devel., 1981—. Mem. Am. Field Service, Assn. Internat. Students in Scis. of Econs. and Commerce. Office: 610 Newport Center Newport Beach CA 92660

HORNE, JOHN E., mortgage ins. cons., former govt. ofcl.; b. Clayton, Ala., Mar. 4, 1908; s. John Eli and Cornelia (Thomas) H.; Normal certificate Troy State U., 1928; A.B. with honors, U. Ala. 1933, M.A. (fellow in history 1933-35), 1941, LL.D., 1970; m. Ruth F. Kleinman, July 27, 1938; children—Linda (Mrs. Richard Clark), Susan (Mrs. James K. Ewart). Tchr., Pike County, Ala., 1925-26, Columbiana, Ala., 1928-31; rep. Macmillan Pub. Co., 1935-39, Row, Peterson Pub. Co., 1939-42, 46; adminstrv. asst. to Senator John J. Sparkman of Ala., 1947-51, 54-61; adminstr. Small Def. Plants Adminstrn., 1951-53; staff dir. Democratic Senatorial Campaign Com., 1954; asst. campaign mgr. to Adlai E. Stevenson, 1956; exec. dir. Nat. Citizens Com. Kennedy-Johnson, 1960; adminstr. Small Bus. Adminstrn., 1961-63; mem. Fed. Home Loan Bank Bd., 1963-68 chmn., 1965-68; pres. Investors Mortgage Ins. Co., 1969-70, chmn., 1970-78; self-employed cons. Horne Assos., 1979—; cons. to govt.; treas. Mortgage Ins. Cos. Am., 1971-78; dir. Continental Investment Corp., Boston; mem. advisory com. FNMA, 1972-76, AMIRS; Distinguished vis. prof. Troy State U., 1978—; lectr. So. Ala. U., 1979; adv. council Fed. Home Loan Bank Bd., 1978—; dir., chmn. audit com. Midwest Fed. Savs. & Loan Assn., Mpls., 1978—. Pres. Pi Kappa Alpha Meml. Fund, 1967-69; bd. govs. Soc. Fin. Examiners; mem. Bicentennial Commn.; trustee Found. Coop. Housing Internat., 1976—; bd. dirs., treas. Nat. Housing Conf., 1975—. Served from lt. (j.g.) to lt. (s.g.) USNR, 1943-45, capt. Res. Recipient Letter of Commendation for meritorious Navy service, Outstanding D.C. Alumnus award U. Ala., 1965, Outstanding Alumnus award Troy State U., 1968. Mem. Fla. Jr. C. of C., Am. Legion, SCV, VFW, Newcomen Soc., Ret. Officers Assn., Ala. Hist. Soc., Phi Beta Kappa, Omicron Delta Kappa, Phi Delta Kappa, Kappa Delta Pi, Pi Kappa Alpha (chmn. nat. conv. 1958; chmn. distinguished achievement award com. 1961-62; distinguished achievement award 1966; nat. treas. 1966-68). Clubs: Nat. Press, Nat. Capital Democratic (dir.), Internat., Metropolitan (Washington), Elks. Home: 415 Crown View Dr Alexandria VA 22314

HORNE, ROBERT, chem. co. exec.; b. Haslingden, Eng., July 10, 1938; came to U.S., 1967; s. James Nuttall and Hilda Irene (Tattersall) H.; B.A., Cambridge (Eng.) U., 1960; M.B.A., Harvard U., 1968; m. Elizabeth Ann Shaw, July 8, 1967; children—Mark Hirst, Adam James, Hannah Katherine. Product mgr. ICI Am., Stamford, Conn., 1968-72; v.p. Rowland Devel. Corp., Kensington, Conn., 1972-75, Transpo-Safety Inc., New Rochelle, N.Y., 1975-77; gen. mgr. Latin Am. div. Stauffer Chem. Co., Westport, Conn., 1977—. NATO fellow, 1967-68. Mem. Inst. Transp. Engrs. Home: 26 Sterling Dr Westport CT 06880 Office: Stauffer Chem Co Westport CT 06880

HORNER, WILLIAM EDWIN, newspaper pub.; b. Durham, N.C., Nov. 22, 1901; s. Robert Dudley and Sudie (Monk) H.; B.S., U. N.C., Chapel Hill, 1922; Litt.D. (hon.), Meth. Coll., Fayetteville, N.C., 1978; m. Nannie Andrews, Oct. 11, 1924 (dec. Mar. 1978); children—Nancy Horner Hulin, Louise Horner Bowles, William Edwin. With Durham (N.C.) Herald, intermittently, 1918-24; partner R.D. Horner & Son, Contractors, Durham, 1925-30; pub. Sanford (N.C.) Herald, 1930—. Active Sanford chpt. ARC, USO, scrap metal drive, 4th war loan drive; Democratic mem. from Lee County N.C. Ho. of Reps. 1937-45; N.C. state hwy. commr., 1961-65. Blvd. in Sanford named in his honor. Mem. N.C. Press Assn. (pres. 1937-38), Nat. Newspaper Assn., Sanford C. of C. (pres., chmn.). Clubs: Kiwanis (pres.), Masons. Author Good Afternoon column, 1953-81. Home: 549 Summitt Dr Sanford NC 27330 Office: PO Box 100 Sanford NC 27330

HORNSTEIN, MARK, fin. co. exec.; b. N.Y.C., Dec. 7, 1947; s. Joseph and Anne (Fox) H.; B.B.A., Pace U., 1969; postgrad. N.Y. U., 1973. Staff accountant Peat, Marwick, Mitchell & Co., N.Y.C., 1969-70; sr. accountant Robert J. Cofini & Co., N.Y.C., 1972-74; asst. v.p. United Va. Factors Corp., N.Y.C., 1974-77; asst. v.p., adminstrv. head mortgage loan div. James Talcott, Inc., N.Y.C., 1977-78; v.p., dir. Talcott of P.R., Inc. and subs.; loan adminstrn. officer Aetna Bus. Credit, Inc., East Hartford, Conn., 1978-79; asst. v.p. A.J. Armstrong Co. Inc., N.Y.C., 1979—. Served with USNR, 1970-72. Home: 319 E 24th St New York NY 10010 Office: 850 3d Ave New York NY 10022

HORODNICEANU, MICHAEL, transp. exec., educator; b. Bucharest, Rumania, Aug. 4, 1944; s. Philip J. and Clara (Hascalovici) H.; came to U.S., 1970, naturalized, 1977; B.Sc. in Civil Engring., Technion, Haifa, Israel, 1970; M.S. in Mgmt., Columbia U., 1973; Ph.D. in Transp. Planning and Engring., Poly. Inst. N.Y., 1978; m. Bat-Sheva Maltzman, Aug. 22, 1968; children—Oded, Eran. Project mgr. Berger Lehman Assos., White Plains, N.Y., 1970-75; dir. Kreindler & Horodniceanu, Inc., N.Y.C.; asst. prof. transp. planning and engring., asso. dir. Center Internat. Studies, Poly. Inst. N.Y., 1975-80; v.p. Urbitran Assos., Inc., N.Y.C., 1980—; asst. prof. transp. planning, transp. program coordinator Manhattan Coll., N.Y.C., 1980—; bd. dirs. Inst. Safety in Transp.; sec. transp. system safety com. Transp. Research Bd. Registered profl. engr., Calif. Mem. Am. Soc. Planning Ofcls., ASCE, System Safety Soc., Inst. Transp. Engrs., Sigma Xi. Author book, articles, reports. Home: 110-12 69th Ave Forest Hills NY 11375 Office: 15 Park Row New York NY 10038

HOROWITZ, BERNARD HERBERT, distbg. co. exec.; b. N.Y.C., Mar. 29, 1938; s. Joseph and Sylvia H.; student public schs.; m. Barbara Anne May, Oct. 29, 1968; children—Laurie Anne, Teri Leigh, Julie Anne, A. Robert. Vice pres. sales Notions Unltd., Inc., Atlanta, 1961-70; pres., chief exec. officer Nat. Notions, Inc. subs. Montgomery Ward & Co., 1970-75; pres., chief exec. officer B.H. Cattle Co., Dallas, 1975—, Mcht.'s Warehouse, Inc., Dallas, 1976—, M.W.F.W., Inc., Dallas, 1977—, United Linco Corp., Dallas, 1977—. Served with USAR, 1960. Mem. Am. Quarter Horse Assn., Southwestern Cattle Raisers Assn., Tex. Cattle Raisers Assn., Better Bus. Bur. Dallas. Republican. Jewish. Office: 1735 N Stemmons Freeway Dallas TX 75207

HOROWITZ, MICHAEL ROBERT, investment co. exec.; b. Dansing, Poland, May 30, 1946; came to U.S., 1961; s. Usher and Sarah Horowitz; B.B.A., U. Okla., 1974; m. Tina R. Lorance, Jan. 5, 1979. Vice pres. Cyrk & Co., Oklahoma City, 1973—; pres. Intermedia Assos., Oklahoma City, 1977—, MRH Petroleum Corp., Oklahoma City, 1979—. Trustee, bd. dirs. Ballet Okla.; trustee Norman Arts and Humanities Commn. Served with U.S. Army, 1966-67; Vietnam. Republican. Clubs: Redlands Racquet; Colonial Mallet & Ball (a founder) (Oklahoma City). Developer various retail and public spaces. Home: 500 NW 41st St Oklahoma City OK 73118 Office: 50 Penn Pl Suite 340 Oklahoma City OK 73118

HORRIGAN, EDWARD A., JR., tobacco co. exec.; b. N.Y.C., Sept. 23, 1929; s. Edward A. and Margaret V. (Kells) H.; B.S. in Bus. Adminstrn., U. Conn., 1950; A.M.P., Harvard U., 1965; m. Elizabeth Herperger, June 27, 1953; children—Ellen, Christopher, Gordon, Brian. Sales mgr. Procter & Gamble Co., N.Y.C., 1954-58; gen. mgr. Ebonite Co., Boston, 1958-61; div. v.p. T.J. Lipton, Inc., 1961-73; pres., chmn. bd. Buckingham Corp., N.Y.C., 1973-78; chmn. bd., chief exec. officer R.J. Reynolds Tobacco Internat., Inc., Winston-Salem, N.C., 1978-80; chmn., pres., chief exec. officer R.J. Reynolds Tobacco Co., 1980—. Served as officer inf., AUS, 1950-54. Decorated Silver Star, Purple Heart, Mem. Mil. Order World Wars. Clubs: Old Town Country, Windham Mountain. Office: Reynolds Bldg 401 N Main St Winston Salem NC 27102

HORSEY, HARVEY STRICKLER, II, land and cattle co. exec.; b. Easton, Md., Mar. 1, 1928; s. Harvey Strickler and Martha Rebecca (Williams) H.; B.S., U. Md., 1949; m. Nancy Meredith Carroll, July 15, 1951; children—Edythe Rebecca, Harvey Strickler III, Pamela Carroll, Stuart Patrick. Office mgr. Chesapeake Propane Gas Co., Easton, Md., 1949-52; staff accountant Granger Faw & Co., Salisbury, Md., 1952-55, partner, 1955-70; v.p.-fin., treas., chief exec. officer Lincoln County Land & Cattle Co., Georgetown, Md., 1970-77, pres., chief exec. officer, 1977—, dir., 1970—. Dir. budget com. United Fund of Talbot (Md.), 1960-70; treas. bldg. fund dr. YMCA, 1960. C.P.A., Md. Mem. Am. Inst. C.P.A.'s, Md. Soc. C.P.A.'s. Democrat. Methodist. Clubs: Chesapeake Bay Yacht, Talbot Country, Elks. Home: Oaklands Easton MD 21601 Office: PO Box 207 Georgetown MD 21930

HORSEY, JAMES LEROY, data systems cons.; b. Ft. Monmouth, N.J., Oct. 18, 1940; s. Eldridge James and Minerva Grace (Brown) H.; B.S., Tulane U., 1962; M.B.A., Harvard U., 1973; m. Rita Ernestine Reiner, July 4, 1964; children—Helen Rebecca, Katharine Felicity, David Nathaniel. Salesman, outside supt. Washington Plate Glass Co., 1965, 74-76; systems engr. Comml. div. IBM, Washington, 1966-68; engring. group leader Data Systems div. Litton Industries, Van Nuys, Calif., 1968-69; computer specialist U.S. Army Computer Systems Command, Dept. Def., Washington, 1969-71; mgmt. info. services project leader Data Gen. Corp., Westboro, Mass., 1976-77; systems analyst, retail account mgr. NCR Corp., Newton, Mass., 1977-80; ind. data systems cons., Hopedale, Mass., 1980—. Served to 1st lt. USMC, 1962-65. Recipient award for excellence Inst. for Cert. of Computer Profls., 1979; cert. data processor (CDP). Mem. Nat. Rifle Assn. (life). Clubs: Maspenock Rod and Gun (Milford, Mass.); Hopedale Pistol and Rifle. Office: PO Box 137 25 Hopedale St Hopedale MA 01747

HORSFALL, WILLIAM RHODES, JR., corp. exec.; b. Woonsocket, R.I., Nov. 21, 1929; s. William R. and Josephine (Sauner) H.; B.S. in Bus. Adminstrn., Bryant Coll., 1950; M.B.A., Northeastern U., 1960; m. Marion Eleanor Orlup, Aug. 6, 1960; children—William Rhodes III, David Willis, Deborah Josephine. Coiler operator Rice Tube & Channel Co., Inc., Pawtucket, R.I., 1953-56; cost supr. Barry Controls, Inc., Watertown, Mass., 1956-57; budget supr. Tracerlab, Inc., Waltham, Mass., 1957-62, v.p., dir. Tracerlab Employees Fed. Credit Union, 1957-60; chmn. bd. Cascade Engring. Corp., Newton, Mass., 1958-62; plant accountant Polythane Corp., subsidiary Monsanto Co., East Providence, R.I., 1962-66; asst. controller Providence Pile Fabric Corp., Pawtucket, 1966-68; treas. AA Investment Corp., Bedford, Mass., 1966-68; controller Harvard Apparatus Co., Inc., Millis Mass., 1968-73, treas., 1969-73; controller Jayson Co., Portland, Maine, 1973—. Served with inf. AUS, 1953-55. Mem. Nat. Rifle Assn., Nat. Accountants Assn., Antique Car Club Am. Mason. Home: Gore Rd Alfred ME 04002 Office: 73 India St Portland ME 04112

HORSLEY, JACK EVERETT, lawyer; b. Sioux City, Iowa, Dec. 12, 1915; s. Charles E. and Edith V. (Timms) H.; A.B., U. Ill., 1937, LL.B., 1939; m. Sallie Kelley, June 12, 1939 (dec.); children—Pamela, Charles Edward; m. 2d, Bertha J. Newland, Feb. 24, 1950 (dec.); m. 3d, Mary Jane Moran, Jan. 20, 1973; 1 adopted dau., Sharon. Admitted to Ill. bar, 1939, since practiced in Mattoon; admitted to U.S. Supreme Ct. bar, other bars; sr. partner Craig & Craig, attys. for I.C. R.R., Travelers Ins. Co.; specializes defensive trial work; vice chmn. bd., dir. Central Nat. Bank of Mattoon. Rep. del. Jud. Conv., 1951; mem. com. civil jury instrns. Ill. Supreme Ct., 1966-68, chmn. rev. bd. atty.'s registration commn., 1973—; lectr. Ill. Bar Assn. Continuing Ednl. Inst., 1967-69, Practising Law Inst., N.Y.C., 1967—, Ill. Inst. Continuing Legal Edn., 1971; seminar instr. Ct. Practice Inst., Chgo., 1974—; pres. Ill. Def. Counsel, Chgo., 1967—; mem. lawyers adv. council U. Ill. Law Forum, 1960-63, Eastern Ill. U., 1968—; legal cons. Med. Econs. Co. div. Litton Industries, Inc. Mem. speakers service Am. Cancer Soc., 1962; chmn. fund campaign Am. Heart Assn., 1964. Pres. Bd. Edn., Sch. Dist. 100, 1946-48; dir. Young Republicans, 1946-48; hon. bd. dirs. Harlan E. Moore Heart Assn. Served to lt. col. Judge Adv. Gen.'s Dept., USAAF. Recipient Distinguished Alumnus award U. Ill. Law Sch., 1971. Fellow Am. Coll. Trial Lawyers; mem. U. Ill. Law Alumni Assn. (pres. 1961-65), Soc. Trial Lawyers (dir. 1961-62, civil practice com. 1963-64), Am. Judicature Soc., Am., Ill. (exec. com. civil practice 1955-56, exec. council ins. law 1961-62, chmn. profl. publs. com., judge Lincoln Award Profl. Essay contest 1961-62, lectr. Inst. Continuing Legal Edn. 1963-65) bar assns., Ill. Def. Counsel Assn. (dir. 1966-67), Fedn. Ins. Counsel, Internat. Assn. Ins. Counsel (membership com. 1963-64), Am. Arbitration Assn. (nat. panel arbitrators 1963-65), Civil War Roundtable (speakers bur. Midwest), Legal Scribes, Delta Phi (dir. alumni assn. 1960-63, 67-68), Sigma Delta Kappa. Republican. Club: Masons. Author: The Prima Facie Case, 1967; Manual for Illinois Trial Lawyers, 1968; Illinois Civil Practice and Procedure, 1970; Testify: The Medical Expert Witness, 1972; Your Family and the Law, 1976; Your Family and the Law: Business Problems (serialization), 1977-78; also articles in legal publs. Masthead contbr., counsel RN Mag., Oradel, N.J.; contbr. sect. on use of texts in evidence Matthew-Bender Co. Home: 50 Elm Ridge Mattoon IL 61938 Office: 1807 Broadway Ave Mattoon IL 61938

HORSMAN, LARRY RAY, word processing co. exec.; b. Memphis, Nov. 29, 1942; s. Leroy Dewight and Mildred Lucille (Davis) H.; B.S. in Elec. Engring., La. Tech. U., 1966, B.S. in Bus. Adminstrn., 1966; M.S. in Elec. Engring., U. Ill., 1968; m. Joyce Ann Murphree, Aug. 28, 1965; children—Julie Ann, Jennifer Lynn. Design engr. IBM, Poughkeepsie, N.Y., 1968-70; mgr. tape products STC Inc., Louisville, Colo., 1970-75; program mgr. Tex. Instruments, Inc., Austin, Tex., 1975-77; v.p. engring. NBI Inc., Boulder, Colo., 1977-79; mgr. word processing devel. NCR Corp., Columbia, S.C., 1979—. Mem. Eta Kappa Nu, Tau Beta Pi, Omicron Delta Kappa. Republican. Baptist. Patentee in field. Home: 330 White Falls Dr Columbia SC 29120

HORTON, AID MILTON, computer systems co. exec.; b. Malden, Mass., July 31, 1947; s. Aubrey E. and Katherine E. Horton; student indsl. mgmt. Lowell Inst. Tech., 1965-69; student Honeywell Inst. Info. Scis., 1969; Asso. Bus. Adminstrn. and Computer Scis., U. Lowell, 1976; m. Jane R. Houle, Oct. 9, 1971; children—Robert A., Thomas L. With Am. Mut. Ins. Co., Wakefield, Mass., 1969-70, Honeywell Info. Systems Co., various locations in Mass., 1970-72; programmer/analyst ELTRA Corp., Wilmington, Mass., 1972-74, BASF Systems, Bedford, Mass., 1974-76; pres. Pepperell Software Co. (Mass.), 1976—; cons. to Digital Equipment Corp., Raytheon Corp., Qantel, Kollsman Corp., various fin., ins., mfg. and distbg. cos., 1976—; speaker, chmn. various computer convs., 1976—. Mem. Ind. Computer Cons. Assn. (pres. Greater Boston chpt. 1980-81). Office: PO Box 539 East Pepperell MA 01437

HORTON, JACK KING, utilities exec.; b. Stanton, Nebr., June 27, 1916; s. Virgil L. and Edna L. (King) H.; A.B., Stanford U., 1936; LL.B., Oakland Coll. Law, 1941; m. Betty Lou Magee, July 15, 1937; children—Judy, Sally, Harold. Admitted to Calif. bar, 1941; treasury dept. Shell Oil Co., 1937-42; pvt. law practice, San Francisco, 1942-43; atty. Standard Oil Co., 1943-44; sec., legal counsel Coast Counties Gas & Electric Co., 1944-51, pres., 1951-54; v.p. Pacific Gas & Electric Co., San Francisco, 1954-59; pres. So. Calif. Edison Co., Los Angeles, 1959-76, chief exec. officer, 1965-80, chmn. bd., 1968-80, chmn. exec. com., 1980—, also dir.; dir. United Calif. Bank, Pacific Mut. Life Ins., Lockheed Corp., Western Bancorp. Trustee U. So. Calif. Mem. Tax Found., Bus. Council, State Bar Calif. Clubs: Pacific Union, Calif., Los Angeles Country, Bohemian, Cypress Point. Office: 2244 Walnut Grove Ave Rosemead CA 91770

HORTON, JAMES RAY, telephone co. exec.; b. Fayette, Ala., Mar. 17, 1945; s. James Elijah and Nell F. Horton; B.S., U.S. Mil. Acad., 1967; m. Elizabeth V. Bunting, Apr. 2, 1977; 1 son, Todd. Field engr. Gen. Telephone Co., Johnstown, N.Y., 1971-73, installation and maintenance supr., 1973-75, service facilities supr., 1975-78, div. customer service mgr., 1978—. Sec., Johnstown Planning Bd., 1979-80. Served with Signal Corps, U.S. Army, 1965-71. Mem. N.Y. State Ind. Telephone Assn. (comml. practices com.), Fulton County C. of C., Fulton County Indsl. Council. Democrat. Baptist. Home: RD 1 W Fulton Street Extension Gloversville NY 12078 Office: 850 Harrison Street Extension Johnstown NY 12095

HORTON, JOHN THOMAS, real estate co. exec.; b. Washington, May 11, 1918; s. John Calhoun and Mary Elizabeth (Goodwin) H.; certificate Grad. Realtors Inst. U. Va., 1972; m. Lorraine Ellen Knight, July 23, 1941. Commd. major U.S. Army, 1953; ret., 1957; supr., agent Mut. and United of Omaha Ins. Cos., 1957-68; v.p., broker G. Edison Burke & Co., Washington and Arlington, Va., 1967-70; owner, mgr. John T. Horton Real Estate Co., Washington and Fairfax, Va., 1970-71; v.p., broker Town and Country Properties, Inc., Washington and Alexandria, Va., 1971-75; owner, operator Tom Horton Real Estate Co., Arlington, 1975—; cons. in field. Decorated Bronze Star, Purple Heart. Democrat. Episcopalian. Mem. Ret. Officers Assn. Home: PO Box 4119 Arlington VA 22204

HORVATH, DOROTHY M., banker; b. Youngstown, Ohio, Nov. 24, 1946; d. Frank Joseph and Mildred Cecelia (Cover) Bogner; student Oberlin Coll., 1964-65, Youngstown State U., 1966-73; m. Joseph Dean Horvath, June 10, 1967. Loan officer, asst. sec. Peoples Bank of Youngstown, 1969-73; asst. cashier BancOhio/Ohio State Bank, Dayton, 1973-74, asst. v.p., 1974-77, v.p., sr. loan officer, 1977—. Recipient Golden Coin award Bank Mktg. Assn., 1976. Mem. Dayton Assn. Credit Mgmt. (dir. 1975-80, treas., 1978-79, pres. 1980-81), Nat. Assn. Bank Women (sec. Greater Cin. group 1979-80, vice chmn. 1980-81), Robert Morris Assos. (chmn. credit info. exchange Ohio Valley chpt. 1979-80, bd. govs. 1980-81). Office: 111 W 1st St Dayton OH 45402

HORWEDEL, LOWELL CHARLES, lubricant co. exec.; b. Cleve., Nov. 27, 1932; s. Albert C. and Mildred (Hackel) H.; A.A., Los Angeles Jr. Coll., 1957; m. Dorothy A. Deupree, June 21, 1958; children—Mary Lee, Nancy Anne, Lowell Charles. Chemist, Vitaminerals, Inc., 1952-54; chemist Electrofilm, Inc., North Hollywood, Calif., 1956-58, chief chemist, 1958-60, research and devel. mgr., 1960-63, product mgr., 1964-65, gen. mgr. lubricants div., 1966-71, v.p., 1969-71; v.p. operations Microseal Corp., subsidiary Great Lakes Chem. Corp., West Lafayette, Ind., 1971-72, exec. v.p., 1972-73; pres. Microseal Corp., West Lafayette, 1973-74, Everlube Corp., 1973-74, E/M Lubricants, Inc., 1974—; dir. K.N.T.A. and Assos., Phoenix, Ariz. Bd. dirs. Lafayette Art Center. Served with AUS, 1954-56. Mem. Am. Chem. Soc., Am. Soc. Lubrication Engrs. (dir.), Soc. Automotive Engrs. Soc. Aircraft Material and Process Engrs., Ind. Oil Compounders Assn. (dir.). Patentee solid film lubricants. Contbr. articles to profl. jours. Home: PO Box 356 Otterbein IN 47970 Office: Hwy 52 NW West Lafayette IN 47906

HORWICK, STEPHEN HENRY, home services co. exec.; b. Jacksonville, Fla., Sept. 29, 1953; s. Arthur Archie and Billie Rosamond (Manning) H.; student public schs., Atlanta; D.D. (hon.), Ch. Gospel Ministry, Chula Vista, Calif., 1980; m. Katherine Pinckney Campbell, May 3, 1980. Exec. asst. Clover/Commonwealth Co., Chgo., 1971-72; with Weathershield Systems, Inc., Jacksonville, Fla., 1972—, dir. sales, mktg. and public relations, 1980—; pres. Horwick Enterprises, Jacksonville, 1981—; pres. bd. dirs. HMW Novelty Inc., 1980—; co-owner Henry Pinckney Ltd. of Fla., advt. and cons. services. Mem. Steering Com. for Tax Reform, State of Fla., 1979. Recipient cert. of merit Faulkerson Found., 1979; Exterior Designer's award residential bldg. products div. U.S. Steel, 1976. Mem. Nat. Remodelers Assn., Fla. Peace Officers Assn. Office: Weathershield Systems Inc 3102 Beach Blvd Jacksonville FL 32207 also PO Box 17291 Jacksonville FL 32216

HORWITZ, PAOLA, advt. exec.; b. Urbana, Ill., July 22, 1939; d. Cesare and Verna Bertha (Daily) Gianturco; B.A., Stanford, 1961; postgrad. U. So. Calif., 1971; children—Scott Sangster, Howard Horwitz. Pub. relations dir. Joseph Magnin, San Francisco, 1962-67; pub. relations dir., account exec. Hall & Levine Advt. Agy., Los Angeles, 1968-73, v.p., account supr., 1973-76, sr. v.p. ops., 1977—. Bd. dirs. The Country Schs. Mem. Orgn. Women Execs., Women in Communications, Los Angeles Advt. Club, Stanford Profl. Women, Fashion Group, Los Angeles County Museums Art Mus. Council. Home: 3866 Berry Dr Studio City CA 91604 Office: 2029 Century Park E Los Angeles CA 90069

HORWITZ, PHILIP HARVEY, lawyer; b. N.Y.C., Dec. 27, 1938; s. Max Herman and Fay (Miller) H.; B.S., U. Pa., 1960; LL.B., Harvard U., 1963; m. Peggy Dee Soltz, Mar. 19, 1967; 1 son, Josh. Admitted to N.Y. bar, 1963; asso. firm Delson & Gordon, N.Y.C., 1964, partner, 1969-73; partner firm Feldesman & D'Atri, N.Y.C.,

1974-78; co-founder, sr. partner firm Horwitz, Toback & Hyman, N.Y.C., 1978—. Mem. Assn. of Bar of City of N.Y., N.Y. State Bar Assn., Beta Gamma Sigma, Beta Alpha Psi, Omicron Chi Epsilon. Club: Harvard. Office: 1114 Ave of Americas New York NY 10036

HOSKINS, RICHARD IRELAND, III, pump mfg. co. exec.; b. Boston, June 21, 1949; s. Richard Ireland and Alice Josephine (Cleverly) H., Jr.; B.S. in Chem. Engring., U. Dayton, 1972; postgrad. Grad. Sch. Mgmt., U. Rochester, 1976-77; m. Linda Ann Schaedler, Jan. 10, 1970; children—Lisa Ann, Richard Ireland IV. Quality control supr. DAP, Inc., Dayton, Ohio, 1970-71; application engr. Chemineer, Inc., Dayton, 1971-72; application engr., acting product mgr. Fluids Control div. L.F.E., Hamden, Conn., 1972-74; spl. products mgr., sales mgr., mgr. mktg. and sales CUNO-Prevision div. AMF Corp., Meriden, Conn., 1974-75; gen. mgr. PULSAfeeder/INTERPACE Corp., Rochester, N.Y., 1975—; mem. adv. panel Chem. Week, McGraw Hill Co., 1978—. Publicity dir. Mendon (N.Y.) Republican Town Com. Mem. Soc. Plastics Engrs., Am. Inst. Chem. Engrs., Hydraulic Inst. Roman Catholic. Club: Oak Hill Country. Home: 35 Drumlinview Dr Mendon NY 14506 Office: 77 Ridgeland Rd Rochester NY 14623

HOSMER, JOSEPH HOWARD, communication co. exec.; b. Springfield, Vt., Apr. 1, 1949; s. Russell Walker and Billiegene (Boyce) H.; student Mark Hopkins Coll., 1967-68; student Law Sch., U. Maine, 1976-77; m. Aug. 31, 1968 (div. June 1979); children—Megan Walker, Joshua Grant. Lineman, Utilities Constrn. Corp., Springfield, Vt., 1963-68; combination man Union Telephone Co. (Maine), 1968-69; local rep. Continental Telephone Co., Portland, Maine, 1969-71; settlement rep. Continental Telephone Service Corp., Syracuse, N.Y., 1971-73, NE Bell system relations, 1972-73; pres., chmn. bd. Telephone Service Co., Portland, 1973—; v.p., dir. York Spiral Stair, 1978—; owner, operator Mountain, Ltd., 1979—; condr. Buried Cable Sch., Telephone Assn. Maine, 1977-78. Town planner Freeport (Maine) Planning Bd., 1974-79. Mem. Expdn. Research, Inc., Ind. Telephone Pioneers. Republican. Contbr. photographs to Mountain Gazette, Boulder, Colo., 1979, others. Office: 19 Commercial St Portland ME 04101

HOSSMAN, RICHARD JOHN, brick mfg. co. exec.; b. Keene, N.H., June 29, 1947; s. Earl Robert and Laura May (Fitting) H.; student Westminster Coll., 1965-67, Valley Forge Christian Coll., 1967-70; m. Roberta Iris Goodwin, Aug. 3, 1968; 1 dau., Rachel Joan. Owner, pres. Richard J. Hossman Mason Contractor, Gray, Maine, 1973—; owner, pres. Royal River Brick Co., Gray, 1977—; lectr. preservation and restoration. Mem. Gray Fire Dept., 1979—; alt. del. Maine Republican Conv., 1980. Mem. Assn. Preservation Technology, Soc. Preservation New Eng. Antiquities, Early Am. Industries Assn., Nat. Fedn. Ind. Business. Baptist. Exhibited photography in group show Westbrook Coll., Portland, Maine, 1980. Home: Wayne Ave Gray ME 04039 Office: Box 458 Gray ME 04039

HOSTER, DOWNEY D., edit. bookbinding co. exec.; b. Phila., May 30, 1934; s. William Otto and Dolores (McAllen) H.; m. Norma M. Hoster, June 25, 1955; children—Norma J., Kathryn A., Downey D. Printer Phila.-United Life Ins., 1951-57; with prodn. dept. Cuneo Eastern Press, Murphy-Parker Inc., Phila., 1959-78; v.p., gen. mgr. Library Bindery Co. of Pa., Inc., Horsham, Pa., 1978-80; pres. Hoster Bindery, Inc., Hatboro, Pa., 1980—. Active Glenside Youth Athletic Assn., Pa., 1968-74; pres. Abington (Pa.) Football Assn., 1977. Recipient Jr. Execs. Graphic Arts award, 1978. Mem. Graphic Arts Assn. Del. Valley (chmn. bookbinders div. 1975-78), Jr. Execs. Graphic Arts, Phila. Book Clinic (chmn. 1969). Republican. Episcopalian. Club: Masons (past master). Office: Hoster Bindery Inc 244 E County Line Rd Hatboro PA 19040

HOTCHKISS, HENRY WASHINGTON, banker; b. Meshed, Iran, Oct. 31, 1937; s. Henry and Mary Bell (Clark) H.; B.A., Bowdoin Coll., 1958. French tchr. Choate Sch., Wallingford, Conn., 1959-62; v.p. Chem. Bank, N.Y., 1962-80, v.p. Chem. Bank Internat., San Francisco, 1973-80; dir. corp. relations Crédit Suisse, San Francisco, 1980—. Asso. bd. regents L.I. Coll. Hosp., 1969-71, pres., 1971, bd. regents, 1971-73; dir. Indonesia-U.S. Bus. Seminar, Los Angeles, 1979. Served to capt. U.S. Army Res., 1958-59. Mem. Calif. Council Internat. Trade (dir. 1976—, chmn. membership com. 1977-79, treas. 1978-79), New Eng. Soc. in City Bklyn. (v.p., dir. 1968-73). Clubs: Heights Casino (bd. govs. 1971-73) (Bklyn.); St. Francis Yacht, Golden Gate Anglers, Internat. Folkboat Assn. San Francisco (cruise chmn. 1976-77, pres. 1977-79, membership chmn. 1979-80) (San Francisco). Home: 1206 Leavenworth St San Francisco CA 94109 Office: 50 California St San Francisco CA 94111

HOTCHKISS, ROBERT LOUIS, banker; b. Newark, Ohio, May 30, 1946; s. Victor Lee and Mildred Evelyn (Francis) H.; B.A., Bowling Green State U., 1968; m. Joanne A. Marinik, May 22, 1971; children—Jonathon, Justin R. Mgmt. trainee Great Am. Ins. Co., Cin., 1968-69; fed. res. examiner Fed. Res. Bank, Cleve., 1970-72; v.p. Newark Trust Co. (Ohio), 1973-75; v.p., regional br. mgr. Huntington Bank of Wood County, Perrysburg, Ohio, 1975-78; pres., chief exec. officer Genoa Banking Co. (Ohio), 1978—. Mem. Perrysburg Bd. of Edn., 1977-81; mem. Penta County Vocat. Sch. Bd., 1977-81; founding trustee Historic Perrysburg. Mem. Am. Inst. Banking (dir.), Community Bankers (past dir.), Genoa Area C. of C., Alpha Tau Omega. Republican. Mem. United Ch. of Christ. Club: Belmont Country, Falcon. Office: 801 Main Genoa OH 43430

HOUGER, N. WILLIAM, transp. co. exec.; b. Cleve., Dec. 20, 1942; s. Norman William Burdette and Margaret Harriet (Baltes) H.; B.A., Kent State U., 1970, M.A., 1978; m. Adele Kay Friedt, June 6, 1975; 1 dau., Kerri Lyn. Grad. asst. dept. philosophy Kent (Ohio) State U., 1970-71; co-mgr. Kroger Co., Akron, Ohio, 1971-73, store mgr. Akron and Massillon, Ohio, 1973-74; with Miller Transfer & Rigging, Akron, 1974, v.p. spl. commodities div., Youngstown, Ohio, 1974-78, v.p. adminstrn., Akron, 1978-80, v.p. ops. and adminstrn., 1980—. Served with USAR, 1961. Mem. Youngstown Traffic Club, Akron Traffic Club, Delta Nu Alpha. Home: 2144 Yellow Creek Rd Akron OH 44313 Office: PO Box 6077 Akron OH 44312

HOUGH, FREDERICK JOHN, II, chiropractic coll. ofcl.; b. Chgo., Sept. 14, 1936; s. Frederick John and Eleanora Francis (Cyra) H.; A.A., Coll. of DuPage, 1975; B.A., Elmhurst Coll., 1976; m. Lorraine Sacher, July 3, 1957; children—Frederick, Michael, Neil, Linda, Laura. Cost acct. Wilson Sporting Goods Co., 1957-58; office mgr. Howell Tractor and Equipment Co., 1958-60; pres. Great Lakes Sci. Corp., Lombard, Ill., 1960-74; comptroller, mem. faculty Nat. Coll. Chiropractic, Lombard, 1974—; instr. investing, fin., bus. and law, 1974—; lectr., bus. and investment adv., 1974—. Served with USMC, 1954-57. Mem. Adminstrv. Mgmt. Soc., 1st Marine Brigade, Fleet Marine Force, VFW (chpt. treas.), Delta Mu Delta. Republican. Methodist. Club: Ill. Athletic. Author: Investing and Financing, 1980. Home: 326 S Monterey St Villa Park IL 60181 Office: Nat Coll Chiropractic 200 E Roosevelt Rd Lombard IL 60148

HOUGHTON, AMORY, glass mfg. exec.; b. Corning, N.Y., July 27, 1899; s. Alanson Bigelow and Adelaide Louise (Wellington) H.; ed. St. Paul's Sch., Concord, N.H., 1913-17; A.B., Harvard, 1921; LL.D., Hobart and William Smith Colls., Geneva, N.Y., 1947, Alfred (N.Y.) U., 1948, N.Y. U., 1961, Colgate U., 1961, Ohio State U., 1969; D.Eng. (hon.), Rensselaer Poly. Inst., 1949; m. Laura DeKay Richardson, Oct. 19, 1921; children—Elizabeth (Mrs. Sidney J. Weinberg, Jr.), Amory, Alanson Bigelow II, James Richardson, Laura DeKay (Mrs. David W. Beer). With Corning Glass Works, 1921—, asst. to pres., 1926-28, exec. v.p., 1928-30, pres., 1930-41, chmn. bd., 1941-61, chmn. exec. com., 1961-64, hon. chmn., 1964-71, chmn. bd. emeritus, 1971—; dir. emeritus Pitts. Corning Corp., Dow Corning Corp. Asst. dep. dir. materials div. OPM, 1941-42; dep. chief bur. industry brs. WPB, 1942, dir. gen. operations, 1942; dep. chief Mission for Econ. Affairs, 1943-44; mem. bus. adv. council Dept. Commerce, 1943-63, grad. mem., 1963—; ambassador to France, 1957-61; mem. exec. com. U.S. council Internat. C. of C., v.p. internat. council, 1962-64. Hon. v.p., mem. nat. exec. bd. Boy Scouts Am.; mem. adv. council State U. N.Y. Bd. dirs. Atlantic Council of U.S., Fedn. des Alliances Francaises aux Etats-Unit; hon. gov. Am. Hosp. of Paris; chmn. bd., mem. exec. com. France Am. Soc.; bd. overseers Harvard, 1947-53; trustee Houghton Found., Inc., French Inst., Eisenhower Coll., Eisenhower Exchange Fellowships; trustee emeritus Inst. for Advanced Study; trustee, mem. Corning Glass Works Found.; v.p., trustee Corning Mus. of Glass. Decorated Order of Merit Bernardo O'Higgins (Chile); grand croix Legion d'Honneur (France), 1961. Mem. Am. Soc. French Legion Honor (dir.), Nat. Indsl. Conf. Bd. (councillor). Republican. Episcopalian. Clubs: Univ., Harvard, Links (N.Y.C.); Rolling Rock (Ligonier, Pa.); Metropolitan (Washington); Elmire (N.Y.) Country; Corning Country; Eldorado Country. Home: 12 South Rd Corning NY 14830 Office: Corning Glass Works Corning NY 14830

HOUGHTON, JAMES RICHARDSON, glass mfg. co. exec.; b. Corning, N.Y., Apr. 6, 1936; s. Amory and Laura (Richardson) H.; A.B., Harvard U., 1958, M.B.A., 1962; m. May Tuckerman Kinnicutt, June 30, 1962; children—James DeKay, Nina Bayard. With Goldman, Sachs & Co., N.Y.C., 1959-61; with Corning Glass Works, 1962—, v.p., area mgr. Europe, 1964-68, v.p., gen. mgr. consumer products div., 1968-71, vice chmn. bd., 1971—, chmn. exec. com., 1980—, also dir.; dir. Corning Internat. Corp., Corning Glass Internat., Dow Corning Corp., Sperry & Hutchinson Co., Met. Life Ins. Co., CBS, Inc. Trustee, Corning Mus. Glass, Corning Glass Works Found., Inst. Advanced Study, Princeton, N.J., Pierpont Morgan Library, N.Y.C. Mem. Council Fgn. Relations, Internat. C. of C. (trustee), Bus. Com. for the Arts. Republican. Episcopalian. Clubs: River, University, Links, Harvard (N.Y.C.); Brookline (Mass.) Country; Tarratine (Dark Harbor, Maine); Corning Country, Rolling Rock (Ligonier, Pa.), Augusta (Ga.) Nat. Golf; Royal Golf of Belgium. Home: Spencer Hill Rd RD 2 Corning NY 14830 Office: Corning Glass Works Corning NY 14830

HOUGHTON, WILLIAM HENRY, book pub. co. exec.; b. Hartford, Conn., Apr. 13, 1925; s. Henry Ernest and Frances Mary (Plaunt) H.; grad. Exeter Acad., 1943; B.S. magna cum laude, Babson Coll., 1949; m. Marion Jensen, Jan. 28, 1959; children—Robert G., Bradley J. Comml. mgr. Asso. Program Service, Inc., N.Y.C., 1949-52; v.p. marketing Ency. Brit., Inc., Chgo., 1952-62; exec. v.p. Marketways, Inc., Chgo., 1962-63; pres. Collier Services, Inc., Riverside, N.J., 1963-67; pres., dir. Macmillan Book Clubs, Inc., 1967—. Mem. Presidents Assn. Club: Mt. Kisco (N.Y.) Country. Home: 80 Annandale Dr Chappaqua NY 10514 Office: 866 3d Ave New York NY 10022

HOULE, GEORGE JOSEPH, bookseller; b. Troy, N.Y., July 25, 1942; s. Harvey A. and Catherine S. (Chartier) H.; B.A., U. So. Calif., 1965; M.S., Western Mich. U., 1967. Head reference dept. City of Beverly Hills (Calif.) Library, 1968-71; head book dept. Sotheby Parke Bernet, Los Angeles, 1971-75; owner Houle Rare Books and Autographs, Los Angeles, 1975—; lectr. UCLA, 1975—. Mem. Antiquarian Booksellers Assn., Phi Beta Kappa. Club: Book of Calif. Address: 2277 Westwood Blvd Los Angeles CA 90064

HOULIHAN, EDMUND MICHAEL, plastics co. exec.; b. Newport, R.I., Sept. 10, 1939; s. Edmund John and Marion (Boylan) H.; B.S. in Acctg., Providence Coll., 1962; m. Josephine B. Carr, July 9, 1969. With Charles Pfizer Co., 1966-77; internat. controller Continental Diversified Industries, 1977-78, gen. mgr. fin., 1981—; fin. dir. Continental Plastics Industries, N.Y.C., 1978-81. Served as officer USNR, 1963-66; Vietnam; comdr. Res. Mem. Nat. Assn. Accts., Fin. Execs. Inst. Roman Catholic. Home: 212 N Walnut St Ridgewood NJ 07450 Office: 633 3d Ave New York NY 10017

HOULTON, HAROLD GEORGE, phys. chemist, chem. engr.; b. Seattle, Dec. 29, 1908; s. Abner J. and Lilla F. (Smith) H.; B.S., U. Wash., 1930, M.S., 1932, Ph.D., 1936; m. Mildred Ethel Welsh, June 9, 1934; children—Jacqueline Jean, Barbara Sue, Gale Joyce. Teaching fellow U. Wash., 1930-36; process devel. engr. Procter & Gamble, 1936-42; tech. dir. Girdler Corp., 1942-47; asst. dir. research and devel. dept. Colgate-Palmolive-Peet Co., 1947-52; dir. research devel. dept. Ashland Oil Inc. (Ky.), 1952-66, coordinator petrochem. devel. corporate level, 1961-65, exec. asst. to pres., 1965-71; cons. Ashland Oil & Nuclear Engring. Co., 1971-74; financial v.p. Nuclear Engring. Co., Inc., Louisville, 1974-76, exec. v.p., 1976—, cons., 1977—. Registered profl. engr., N.J., Ky. Fellow Am. Inst. Chemists; mem. Am. Inst. Chem. Engrs., Am. Chem. Soc., A.I.M., Soc. Automotive Engrs., Am. Petroleum Inst., Assn. Asphalt Paving Technologists, Am. Inst. Mining, Metall. and Petroleum Engrs., Nat. Assn. Corrosion Engrs., Am. Ordnance Asso., Am. Foundrymen's Soc., AAAS, Am. Mgmt. Assn., Brit. Iron and Steel Inst., N.Y., Ky. acads. sci., Sigma Xi, Phi Lambda Upsilon, Sigma Pi Sigma, Phi Sigma. Rotarian. Home: 1100 Imperial Dr Sarasota FL 33580 Office: 9200 Shelbyville Rd Louisville KY 40222

HOUMES, DALE MAURICE, retail trade co. exec.; b. Stockland, Ill., July 9, 1924; s. John Elsworth and Clarissa Elizabeth (Nolin) H.; B.S., U. Ill., 1950; m. Victoria Taffy, Dec. 28, 1946; children—Dale Maurice, Darrell W. Asst. ins. mgr. Pillsbury Co., Mpls., 1951-56; corp. ins. mgr. Outboard Marine Corp., Waukegan, Ill., 1956-66; dir. corp. risk mgmt. and pension adminstrn. SCOA Industries, Inc., Columbus, Ohio, 1966—, v.p. Interstate Leasing Corp. subs., Columbus, 1968—. Mem. Risk and Ins. Mgmt. Soc. (pres. Wis. chpt. 1960-61, pres. central Ohio chpt. 1975-76), Midwest Pension Conf. Methodist. Elk. Home: 4959 Woodbriar Pl Columbus OH 43229 Office: 155 E Broad St Columbus OH 43215

HOURIGAN, JOHN ALBERT, equipment mfg. co. exec.; b. El Paso, Tex., Dec. 5, 1925; s. John Joseph and Gladys Mary (Tweedy) H.; student Tex. Coll. Mines, 1946-49; m. Evelyn Joyce Aby, May 21, 1949; children—Mary Linda, Eloise Gail, John Albert, Teresa Erin, Kathleen, Patrick. Sales mgr. Capitol Constrn. Co., San Diego, 1949-58; nat. sales mgr. Master Consol., Inc., Dayton, Ohio, 1958-67; v.p. mktg. Va. Internat., Inc., Gainesville, 1967-69; pres. Equipment Assos., Inc., Richardson, Tex., 1969—; dir. Thomas S.W., Inc., Va. Internat., Inc. Served with USAF, 1943-46, 50-52. Decorated Air medal, Bronze Star. Mem. Am. Mgmt. Assn., Pres.'s Assn. Republican. Roman Catholic. Club: K.C. Home: 607 W Arapaho Rd Richardson TX 75080 Office: Suite 412 811 S Central Expressway Richardson TX 75080

HOUSE, EDWARD CHARLES, JR., fin. services co. exec.; b. Victoria, B.C., Can., June 28, 1912; s. Edward Charles and Irene Mathilda (Meyers) H.; B.A., U. Puget Sound, 1934; M.S., N.Y. U., 1935; m. Florence Malone Werts, Oct. 24, 1936; children—Diadre Renee, Diane Benet. With J.C. Penney Co., 1935-56, mgr., Willows, Calif., 1950-56; with Investors Diversified Services, Willows and Sacramento, 1956-67, dist. mgr., 1958-67; div. sales mgr. Waddell & Reed, San Francisco, 1967-73; regional sales mgr., br. mgr. Cornerstone Fin. Services, Willows, 1973—; gen. mgr. Willows Wholesale, 1979—; v.p., treas. Sacramento Valley Newspaper Corp., 1958—; cons. in field; instr. bus. mgmt. Butte Coll., 1974—. Served to lt. USNR, 1943-46; PTO. Republican. Episcopalian. Clubs: Kiwanis (past pres. local chpt., lt. gov. 1976-77); Commonwealth of San Francisco, Marines Meml. (San Francisco). Home: 1 Country Club Estates Willows CA 95988 Office: Route 1 Box 174H Willows CA 95988

HOUSE, MONTE TURNER, banker; b. Lyons, Colo., Apr. 15, 1940; s. William Turner and Lucille Theo (Worrall) H.; B.A. in Acctg. and Bus. Adminstrn., Western State Coll., Gunnison, Colo., 1970; m. Carole Dawn Fink, June 20, 1975; children—Brent Restemayer, Michael House, Mark House, Stephanie Restemayer. Salesman, Farm Bur. Ins. Services, 1961-64; mgr. Hotchkiss Implement & Feed Co., Hotchkiss, Colo., 1964-67; staff auditor Arthur Andersen & Co., C.P.A.'s, Denver, 1970-74; controller First Nat. Bank, Grand Junction, Colo., 1974—; mem. exec. staff First Nat. Banks, 1974—. Served with AUS, 1959-61. C.P.A., Colo. Mem. Am. Inst. C.P.A.'s, Colo. Soc. C.P.A.'s (chpt. dir. 1978-79; Gold Key award 1970), Nat. Assn Accountants, Delta Sigma Pi (Key award 1970). Republican. Club: Masons. Office: PO Box 608 Grand Junction CO 81502

HOUSEHOLDER, ARTHUR WILLIAM, fin. adviser; b. Alva, Okla., June 2, 1948; s. Fred A. and Irene E. H.; B.A., Northwestern Okla. State U., 1970; M.A., U. Okla., 1973; M.A., N.Y. Inst. Fin., 1977; m. Jodie Yorc Piro, Mar. 23, 1978. Wage and salary analyst Cessna Aircraft Co., Wichita, Kans., 1972-73; agt., Lincoln Nat. Sales Corp., Oklahoma City, 1973-75; account exec. Thomson McKinnon Securities, Oklahoma City, 1975-77; account exec. Dean Witter Reynolds, Tulsa, 1977-78; dir. equity ops. NEL Equity Services Corp., Tulsa, 1978-80; exec. asst. to pres. An-Son Corp., 1980—; corp. fin. officer Sterling Pipe & Supply Co., Oklahoma City, 1981—. Pres., Young Republicans, 1975. Mem. Nat. Soc. Registered Reps., Nat. Securities Dealers Assn., Nat. Assn. Life Underwriters, Nat. Soc. Bus. Cons., Internat. Assn. Fin. Planners, Nat. Assn. Accts. Home: 917 24th Ave SW Norman OK 73069 Office: 5707 S Eastern Oklahoma City OK 73143

HOUSEN, CHARLES BERNARD, paper mill exec.; b. Holyoke, Mass., Apr. 21, 1932; s. David and Sadye (Gelb) H.; B.A., Tufts Coll., 1954; m. Marjorie Grodner, Mar. 24, 1957; children—Deborah, Phyllis, Morris. Cons., Work Factor Co., 1955-70; treas. Erving Paper Mills (Mass.), 1970-72, exec. v.p., 1972-74, pres., 1974—; dir. Liberty Mut. Ins. Co., Mass. Electric Co. Served with AUS, 1955-58. Mem. Am. Paper Inst. (dir.), Young Pres.'s Orgn. (dir.), Asso. Industries Mass., Beta Gamma Sigma. Home: Prospect Heights Erving MA 01344 Office: Arch St Erving MA 01344

HOUSER, ROBERT NORMAN, ins. co. exec.; b. Bloomfield, Iowa, Sept. 21, 1919; s. Charles B. and Venna C. (Bartholomew) H.; B.A. summa cum laude, U. Iowa, 1947; m. Doris V. Miller, Dec. 18, 1943; children—Theodore Alan, Judith Eileen, James Robert. With Bankers Life Co., 1936-38, 40-43, 47—, asst. actuary, 1953-60, asso. actuary, 1960-63, 2d v.p., actuary, 1963-68, v.p., actuary, 1968-71, v.p., chief actuary, 1971-72, sr. v.p., chief actuary, 1972-73, pres., 1973—, also chief exec. officer; pres. BLC Growth & Income Funds. Bd. govs. Iowa Coll. Found.; trustee Drake U.; bd. dirs. Greater Des Moines Com., Mercy Hosp., United Way Greater Des Moines; trustee Des Moines Devel. Corp., Civic Center Greater Des Moines. Served to 1st lt. USAAF, 1943-45, USAF, 1951-52. Decorated D.F.C., Air medals. Fellow Soc. Actuaries; mem. Am. Council Life Ins. (dir.), Health Ins. Assn. Am. (dir.), Conf. Bd. Home: 2412 48th St Des Moines IA 50310 Office: 711 High St Des Moines IA 50307

HOUSTON, ALFRED DEARBORN, utilities exec.; b. Quincy, Mass., Aug. 14, 1940; s. Alfred Dearborn and Merriland Curry (Westwood) H.; B.S. in Econs., U. Pa., 1962; m. Patricia Selko, Oct. 23, 1965; children—Melissa, Sherriden. With New Eng. Electric System and subs. New Eng. Power Service Co., New Eng. Power Co., Mass. Electric Co., Westborough, Mass., 1962—, asst. treas., 1973-75, v.p. corporate fin. New Eng. Energy Co., 1975-76, v.p. New Eng. Power Service Co., 1975—, v.p., dist. mgr. Narragansett Electric Co., 1976-77, v.p., treas., 1977—. Active United Way So. New Eng., 1976-79. Mem. U. Pa. Club of Boston (past pres., trustee). Office: Narragansett Electric Co 280 Melrose St Providence RI 02901

HOVDE, RUSSELL JAMES, banker; b. Madison, Wis., Oct. 27, 1927; s. Ingvald and Joseffa O. (Anderson) H.; B.S., U. Wis., 1950; postgrad. Northwestern U., 1955-65; m. Betty Lou Dunn, Feb. 24, 1951; children—David, Martha. Realtor, I. Hovde Realty Co., Madison, 1950-53; asst. to pres. No. Moulding Co., Franklin Park, Ill., 1954-58; Midwest rep., homes div. U.S. Steel Corp., Chgo., 1958-61; with Continental Ill. Nat. Bank & Trust Co., Chgo., 1961—, v.p., 1970—, v.p., mgr. U.S. cash mgmt. div., 1972—; dir. Correct Craft, Inc., Orlando, Fla. Village trustee, fin. chmn., Fontana, Wis., 1975—. Served with USN, 1945-46. Mem. Fin. Mgrs. Assn. Chgo., Bank Adminstrn. Inst. (vice-chmn. 1980, former mem. nat. cash mgmt. council), Phi Kappa Phi, Phi Eta Sigma, Beta Gamma Sigma, Alpha Chi Rho. Republican. Clubs: U. Wis. (Chgo.); Lake Geneva (Wis.) Country. Home: 372 N Lake Shore Dr Fontana WI 53125 Office: 231 S LaSalle St Chicago IL 60693

HOVE, ANDREW CHRISTIAN, SR., banker; b. Minden, Nebr., Oct. 4, 1904; s. Christian and Dorthea (Pedersen) H.; student Minden public schs.; m. Isabel F. Thill, Oct. 30, 1976; children by previous marriage—Andrew Christian, Richard Joseph. With Minden Exchange Bank & Trust Co., 1922—, dir., 1930—, chmn. bd., 1950—; pres. Central Nebr. Public Power & Irrigation; chmn. bd. East View Ct.; dir. Royal Plastics Mfg. Corp. Mem. Minden C. of C. (pres.). Democrat. Methodist. Clubs: Nebr. (Lincoln), Masons, Odd Fellows, Elks, Minden Rotary (pres.). Home: 634 E Hawthorne St Minden NE 68959 Office: 448 N Minden St Minden NE 68959

HOVELL, PETER F., mfg. co. exec.; b. N.Y.C., Dec. 7, 1934; s. Armand C. and Lillian P. Hovell; B.A., Dartmouth Coll., 1956; m. Margaret Mary Tama, Jan. 22, 1970. Engr., Precision Mfg. Co., 1959-62, gen. mgr., 1962-64; mktg. rep. IBM, 1964-67; v.p., gen. subs. Am. Express Co., 1967-68, sr. v.p., gen. mgr. Money Order div., 1969-70; cons. HLC Assos., 1970-73; v.p. mktg. Telepost Co., McLean, Va., 1974, pres., 1975-76; v.p. mktg. Microfilm Enterprises Mktg. Co., Rowayton, Conn., 1976-78; pres. Conn. Micrographics, Inc., Rowayton, 1979—. Rep., Town Meeting of Darien, chmn. data processing com., vice chmn. fin. and budget com. Served to 1st lt. USMC, 1956-59. Mem. Nat. Micrographic Assn. Republican. Episcopalian. Office: 137 Rowayton Ave Rowayton CT 06853

HOVEY, ALAN EDWIN, JR., retail chain store exec.; b. Burlington, Vt., Apr. 23, 1933; s. Alan Edwin and Jessie Miller (Emerson) H.; B.S. in Bus. Adminstrn., U. Fla., 1956; postgrad. Cornell U. Law Sch.; m. Ellen Ann Coffey, Sept. 28, 1956; children—Alison Clair, Kimberly Ann, Christopher Owen, Adam Kimball. Civilian mgmt. anaylst Dept. Army, Orleans, France, 1958-60; with Century Housewares Co., 1961-80, dir. human resources, Buffalo, 1979; dir. personnel Everfast, Inc., Wilmington, Del., 1980—. Mem. E. Aurora (N.Y.) Bd. Edn., 1976-80. Served with AUS, 1956-58. Mem. Wilmington C. of C., Soc. for Preservation and Encouragement of Barbershop Quartet Singing in Am. Republican. Unitarian. Home: 129 W 18th St Wilmington DE 19802 Office: Bancroft Mills Box 670 Wilmington DE 19899

HOVING, JOHN HANNES FORESTER, retail co. exec.; b. N.Y.C., July 18, 1923; s. Hannes and Mary Alma (Gilbert) H.; B.A. in History, U. Chgo., 1947; m. Anne Fisher Spiers, Feb. 1, 1958; children—Christopher, Karen Anne, Katherine Jean. Radio news editor, reporter Milw. Jour., also Capital Times, Madison, Wis., 1947-51; asst. to chmn. Democratic Nat. Com., 1952-54; exec. positions Kefauver, Johnson, Humphrey, Sanford presdl. campaigns; asst. to presdl. asst. for trade policy, 1962; v.p. exec. action Air Transp. Assn. Am., Washington, 1956-64; propr. cons. firm, Washington, 1964-72; sr. v.p. Federated Dept. Stores, Inc., Cin., 1972—; bd. advisers to dean Coll. Bus. Adminstrn., U. Cin., also instr. Chmn. communications com. United Appeal Cin., 1976; bd. dirs. Cin. Council World Affairs, Pub. Affairs Council. Served with AUS, 1943-46. Decorated Purple Heart. Mem. Am. Retail Assn. (dir., exec. com.), Am. Assn. Polit. Cons. Democrat. Episcopalian. Clubs: Metropolitan, Nat. Press, Fed. City, Nat. Capital Dem. (Washington); Queen City (Cin.); Lotos, Sky (N.Y.C.). Home: 947 Paradrome St Cincinnati OH 45202 Office: 7 W 7th St Cincinnati OH 45202

HOVINGA, PETER, office equipment co. exec.; b. Jenison, Mich., July 31, 1930; s. David and Martha (DeKraker) H.; grad. high sch.; m. Hildred Ann Baar, Sept. 6, 1951; children—James Peter, Lynne Marie. Metal finisher Gezon Motors, Grand Rapids, Mich., 1948-50; self-employed carpenter, 1950-52, home contractor, Grand Rapids, 1952-53; service mgr. Ditto Inc., Grand Rapids, 1953-63; material handling engr. Rapistan Inc., Grand Rapids, 1963-65; pres. Hovinga Bus. Equipment Inc. and Hovinga Leasing Co., Inc., Grandville, Mich., 1965—; owner, pres. Mich. Marine Co. Inc., 1975-77; founder Cell-U-Save Mfg. Insulation Co. Inc., 1978-79. Mem. Jenison Bd. Edn., 1958-62, sec., 1960-62; bd. dirs. Mich. Cystic Fibrosis Found., 1956-58; pres. publicity com. Reformed Ch., Grand Rapids, 1972-75; bd. dirs. T.E.L.L. (Evang. Lit. League), 1964-68. Served with U.S. Army, 1949-50. Mem. Mich., Grand Rapids, Grandville chambers of commerce, Mich. Mfrs. Assn. Republican. Mem. Reformed Ch. in Am. Home: 4820 Green Moor Ct Hudsonville MI 49426 Office: 4390 Chicago Dr Grandville MI 49418

HOWARD, ALBERT LAWSON, computer co. exec.; b. Waco, Tex., Jan. 21, 1945; s. Maurice E. and Maggie M. (Mears) H.; B.S. in Aerospace, Tex. A. and M. U., 1967; M.S. in Engring., So. Meth. U., 1969; M.B.A., U. Dallas, 1971; m. Mileen Paroline, Sept. 26, 1969; children—Allison Amanda, Kyle Lawson. Aerodynamics engr. LTV Aerospace, Dallas, 1967-69; applications cons. Tymshare, Dallas, 1969-71; br. mgr. United Computing, Dallas, 1971-74, regional mgr., 1974-77, v.p. sales, 1977-79, sr. v.p. sales, 1980—. Address: 3724 W 119th Terr Leawood KS 66209

HOWARD, BERTIN EDWARD, concrete ready mix processing co. exec.; b. Port Arthur, Tex., July 3, 1938; s. Clarence Eral and Josephine Claire (Bertin) H.; B.B.A. in Econs., Lamar U., 1960, B.B.A. in Acctg., 1969, M.B.A. in Acctg., 1970; m. Frances Green, Feb. 2, 1968; children—Justin Eral, Ellen Claire. Tax acct. Peat, Marwick, Mitchell & Co., Dallas, 1970-71; instr. acctg. Stephen F. Austin U., Nacogdoches, Tex., 1971-73; controller Nacogdoches/Irving Community Hosps., 1973-75; asst. tax mgr. Temple-Eastex, Inc., Diboll, Tex., 1975-78, subs. controller, Austin, Tex., 1978-79; dir. fin. Tex. Med. Liability Trust, Austin, 1979—; controller, sec.-treas., chief fin. officer Contractor's Supplies, Inc., Lufkin, Tex.; mem. faculty Stephen F. Austin U., 1976-78, Austin Community Coll., 1979. Served with USAR, 1961. Cert. Tex. Bd. Public Accountancy. Mem. Nat. Assn. Accts. (past pres. Lufkin/Nacogdoches chpt., nat. com. edn.), Tex. Soc. C.P.A.'s, Am. Inst. C.P.A.'s. Republican. Roman Catholic. Club: Kiwanis. Home: 24 Red Oak Ln Lufkin TX 75901 Office: 303 Webber St Lufkin TX 75901

HOWARD, EDWARD THOMAS, cruise travel co. exec.; b. Riverside, Calif., Mar. 29, 1945; s. John Moss and Helen Joy (Phillips) H.; student Solano Coll., 1967-68, San Francisco State U., 1963-64, 70-72. Owner, Howard Mini-Vacations, Benicia, Calif., San Francisco, 1971-73; travel cons. Royal Viking Line, San Francisco, 1973-74; partner, mgr. World Cruise Assn., San Francisco, 1975-77; now retail and cruise mgr. Ulysses Travel and Tours, Inc.; pvt. cons. cruises, travel agencies and cruise ships, San Francisco, 1977—. Served with Submarine Service, USN, 1964-67. Office: 3247 Sacramento St San Francisco CA 94115

HOWARD, ESTELLE CHARMAINE, personnel co. exec.; b. Atlantic City, May 22, 1952; d. William James and Geraldine Audrey (Vierra) H.; student public schs., Atlantic City; children—Devon Christopher Nanton, Jason Eric Nanton. Personnel cons. Affirmative Actions Assos., N.Y.C., 1977-78; v.p. Rainbow Personnel Cons., N.Y.C., 1978—; guest speaker Temporary Ind. Personnel Soc., 1979. Guest panelist Council of Concerned Black Execs. Job Fair, 1979; coordinator New Yorkers for Charles Bowser, 1979; mem. Coalition of 100 Black Women. Office: 295 Madison Ave New York NY 10017

HOWARD, GRAEME KEITH, JR., fin. cons., editor, lawyer; b. Port Chester, N.Y., Sept. 29, 1932; s. Graeme K. and Margaret (Evans) H.; B.A., Amherst Coll., 1954; LL.B., Yale U., 1960; postgrad. (Fulbright scholar) U. Leiden (Netherlands), 1960-62; children by previous marriage—Elizabeth Lloyd, Graeme Keith III, Cooper Ann, William Reeve. Admitted to Conn. bar, 1960, Pa. bar, 1964; asso. Internat. Tax Service, Internat. Belasting Documentatie Bur., Amsterdam, Netherlands, 1961-62; asso. firm Ballard, Spahr, Andrews and Ingersoll, Phila., 1963-67; asso. corp. fin. dept. Butcher & Sherrerd, Phila., 1967-71, partner, 1971-72; pres. Howard & Co., Phila., 1972-80, sr. partner, 1980—; pub. Business Borrower, Phila., 1975-78, Going Public: The Jour. of Initial Public Offerings, quar., Phila., 1975-79, Going Public: The IPO Reporter, 1980—; lectr. in field, 1970—. Mem. exec. com. Com. of Seventy, Phila., 1975—. Served to capt. USAF, 1954-57. Mem. Nat. Investor Relations Inst. (v.p. Phila. chpt. 1975-77). Republican. Episcopalian. Clubs: Racquet, Yale (Phila.); Dolittle (Norfolk, Conn.). Author: Going Public, 1978; The Risk Capital Market, 1978; editor European Taxation, 1961-62, Taxation of Patent Royalties, Dividends, Interest in Europe, 1963—, Internat. Bus. Law Rev., 1967. Home: 554 Dorset Rd Devon PA 19333 Office: 1528 Walnut St Philadelphia PA 19102

HOWARD, HAROLD NATHANIEL, investment adv.; b. N.Y.C., Sept. 26, 1934; s. Joseph Alexander and Lillian (Goodman) H.; A.B., Union Coll., Schenectady, 1956; postgrad. Sch. Law, Columbia U., 1957, M.B.A., Grad. Sch. Bus. Adminstrn., 1959; m. Alice G. Wigod, Oct. 23, 1960; children—Wendy Elizabeth, Lawrence Eliot. With Hanover Bank (name changed to Mfrs. Hanover Trust Co.), N.Y.C., 1960-64, Brown Bros. Harriman & Co., N.Y.C., 1964-69; v.p. Kuhn, Loeb & Co. (name changed to Lehman, Kuhn Loeb & Co.), N.Y.C., 1969-72; v.p., partner E.M. Warburg, Pincus & Co., N.Y.C., 1972-74; pres. H.N. Howard & Son, Inc., N.Y.C., 1974—. Served with U.S. Army, 1959. Mem. Fin. Analysts Fedn., N.Y. Soc. Security Analysts. Clubs: Wall Street, New Milford Racquet and Swim, Candlewood Yacht. Home: 14 Lake Dr New Milford CT 06776 also 510 E 86th St New York NY 10028 Office: One Rockefeller Plaza New York NY 10020

HOWARD, JAMES WEBB, investment banker, brewery exec., lawyer; b. Evansville, Ind., Sept. 17, 1925; s. Joseph Randolph and Velma Cobb (Johnson) H.; B.S. in Mech. Engring., Purdue U., 1949; M.B.A. in Finance, Western Res. U., 1962; J.D., Western State U., 1976; m. Phyllis Jean Brandt, Dec. 27, 1948; children—Sheila Rae, Sharon Kae. Jr. engr. Firestone Tire & Rubber Co., 1949-50; gen. foreman Cadillac Motor Car div. Gen. Motors Corp., 1950-53; mgmt. cons. M.K. Sheppard & Co., 1953-55; plant mgr. Lewis Welding & Engring., 1956-58; investment banker Ohio Co., 1958-59; chmn. dir. Growth Capital, Inc., Cleve., 1960-68, Chgo., 1968—; pres., dir. JBC, Inc., Santana Rancho, Inc., San Diego, 1975—, Bus. Mart and Home Mart, San Diego, 1976—, Casa del Ranchos, Inc., San Diego; dir. ICE Arena West, Inc., San Diego. Served with 69th Inf. Div., AUS, 1943-46. Registered profl. engr., Ind., Ohio. Mem. Am. Bar Assn., State Bar Calif., ASME, Am. Mgmt. Assn., Nat. Assn. Small Bus. Investment Cos. (past pres.), Beta Gamma Sigma, Pi Tau Sigma, Tau Kappa Epsilon. Presbyterian. Club: Masons. Home: PO Box A-80427 San Diego CA 92138 Office: 2605 Camino del Rio S Suite 300 San Diego CA 92108

HOWARD, JOHN ROBERT, apparel co. ofcl.; b. Boston, July 23, 1942; s. John Arthur and Eva Sarah (Lewis) H.; student public schs., Boston. Clk., Equitable Life Assurance Soc., N.Y.C., 1960-62; asst. to pres. Faultless Strapping & Marking Co., N.Y.C., 1962-63; prodn. mgr. Magic Mix Co., Inc., Englewood, N.J., 1963-67; corp. pres., gen. mgr. Grinch Creations, Inc., N.Y.C., 1968-72; dir. purchasing Wellington Synthetic Fibres, Inc., Paterson, N.J., 1976-80; purchasing mgr. Dynamic Classics, Ltd., Fairfield, N.J., 1980—. Mem. Ridgefield Police Dept., 1968—, recipient Distinguished Expert in Marksmanship award, 1971. Mem. Am. Mgmt. Assn., Am. Law Enforcement Officers Assn., Nat. Rifle Assn. (life), Nat. Travel Club. Republican. Methodist. Club: Palisades Park Game (pres.). Home: 35 Oakwood Ave Bogota NJ 07603 Office: 11 Stewart Pl Fairfield NJ 07603

HOWARD, JOSEPH DESILVA, travel agy. exec.; b. Honolulu, Feb. 8, 1917; s. William and Virginia (Cabral) DeSilva; B.A. in Bus. Adminstrn., U. Hawaii, 1939, postgrad., 1945; postgrad. U. Calif. at Berkeley, 1940, U. Oreg., 1948-49; m. Marguerite E. Barker, June 16, 1952; children—Wendy D., Bradford R. Self-employed, Hawaii, 1946-48; asst. mgr. Coconut Island, resort, 1947-48; with Stokeley Van Camp, 1948-50, sales supr. West Coast div., 1949-50; pres. Howard Tours, Inc., Oakland, Calif., 1950—; mng. dir. Howard Investments; dir. Humphrey Instruments, Inc., Optical Research & Devel. Co.; mng. dir. Inst. Internat. Seminars, 1957—; pres. Energy Dynamics, Inc.; exec. sec. Internat. Dental Seminars. Served with USNR, 1942-46; mem. Res. (ret.). Mem. Oakland C. of C., Oakland Mus. Assn., U. Hawaii, U. Calif. alumni assns., Naval Res. Assn., Ret. Officers Assn., Oakland Symphony Orch. Assn., East Bay Bot. and Zool. Soc. Republican. Presbyterian. Clubs: Rotary of East Oakland (pres. 1979-80); Commonwealth of Calif., Olympic (San Francisco); Oakland Athletic (Oakland). Home: 146 Bell Ave Piedmont CA 94611 Office: 526 Grand Ave Oakland CA 94610

HOWARD, MARGUERITE EVANGELINE BARKER (MRS. JOSEPH D. HOWARD), bus. exec., civic worker; b. Victoria, B.C., Can., July 30, 1921; d. Reuel Harold and Frances Penelope (Garnham) Barker; brought to U.S., 1924, naturalized, 1945; B.A., U. Wash., 1943; m. Joseph D. Howard, June 16, 1952; children—Wendy Doreen Frances, Bradford Reuel. Vice pres., dir. Howard Tours, Inc., Oakland, Calif., 1953—; co-owner, gen. mgr. Howard Travel Service, Oakland, 1956—, mng. dir. Howard Hall, Berkeley, Calif., 1964-74; co-owner, asst. mgr. Howard Investments, Oakland, 1960—; sec./treas. Energy Dynamics, Inc. Bd. dirs. Piedmont council Campfire Girls, 1969-79, pres., 1974-79, mem. nat. council, 1972-76, zone chmn., 1974-76, 77—, nat. bd. dirs., 1976—; bd. dirs. Oakland Symphony Guild, 1969—, pres., 1972-74; mem. exec. bd. Oakland Symphony Orch. Assn., 1972-74, bd. dirs., 1972—; bd. dirs. Piedmont Jr. High Sch. Mothers Club, 1968-69. Mem. Oakland Mus. Assn., Chi Omega Alumni Seattle, Chi Omega East Bay Alumni Berkeley, U. Wash. Alumni, East Bay Bot. and Zool. Soc. Republican. Clubs: Women's Univ. (Seattle); Women's Athletic (Oakland). Home: 146 Bell Ave Piedmont CA 94611 Office: 526 Grand Ave Oakland CA 94610

HOWARD, MELVIN, duplication equipment mfg. co. exec.; b. Boston, Jan. 5, 1935; s. John M. and Molly (Sagar) H.; B.A., U. Mass., 1957; M.B.A., Columbia, 1959; m. Beverly Ruth Kahan, June 9, 1957; children—Brian David, Marjorie Lyn. Fin. exec. Ford Motor Co., Dearborn, Mich., 1959-67; v.p.-adminstrn. Shoe Corps. of Am., Columbus, Ohio, 1967-70; asst. controller Bus. Products group Xerox Corp., Rochester, N.Y., 1970-72, v.p.-fin. bus. devel. group, 1972-74, sr. v.p., sr. staff officer, 1974-75, corp. v.p./controller, 1975-77, corp. v.p./fin., 1977-78, corp. sr. v.p./fin., 1978—; chmn. Xerox Credit Corp.; dir. WVI, Inc., Allendale Ins. Adviser Jr. Achievement, 1959-61. Treas., Boy Scouts of Pittsford (N.Y.), 1971-73; cons. N.Y. Council Arts, 1971. Served to 1st lt. AUS, 1957. Mem. Fn. Execs. Inst., Planning Execs. Inst., Am. Mgmt. Assn., Beta Gamma Sigma. Club: Birchwood Country. Home: 42 Red Coat Rd Westport CT 06880 Office: High Ridge Park Stamford CT 06904

HOWARD, MIKE CURTIS, chain drug store co. exec.; b. Blackwell, Okla., Sept. 19, 1940; s. Louis S. and Theda B. (Curtis) H.; B.S. in Pharmacy, U. Okla., 1962; children—Louis C., Michelle A. Staff pharmacist Meyers & Rosser Pharmacies, Dallas, 1962-64; store mgr. Garland Pharmacies (Tex.), 1964-68; founder, pres. Drug-Mart, Inc., Dallas, 1968—. Mem. Nat. Assn. Chair Drug Stores. Republican. Mem. Christian Ch. (Disciples of Christ). Office: 12561 Perimeter Dallas TX 75228

HOWARD, MURRAY, bus. and mfg. exec., real estate developer, rancher; b. Los Angeles, July 25, 1914; s. George A. J. and Mabel (Murray) H.; B.S., U. Calif. at Los Angeles, 1939. Mgr. budget control dept. Lockheed Aircraft, 1939-45; pres., chmn. bd. Stanley Foundries, Inc., 1945-59, Howard Machine Products, Inc., 1959—, Murray Howard Realty, Inc., 1959—, Murray Howard Investment Corp., 1961—, Howard Oceanography, Inc., 1967—, Ranch Sales, Inc., 1968—, Murray Howard Devel., Inc., 1969—, Murray Howard Cattle Co., Prineville, Oreg.; owner, gen. mgr. Greenhorn Ranch Co., Greenhorn Creek Guest Ranch, Spring Garden, Calif; dir. Airshippers Pub. Corp., Shur-Lok Corp., La Brea Realty & Devel. Co. Served as mem. Gov. Calif. Minority Com. C.P.A., Calif. Mem. Nat. Assn. Cost Accountants (dir., v.p.), NAM. Office: 3450 Wilshire Blvd Suite 510 Los Angeles CA 90010

HOWARD, PHILIP MARTIN, ins. agt.; b. Chgo., Dec. 16, 1939; s. Anthony Gerald and Mary Elizabeth (Smith) H.; student Chgo. parochial schs.; m. Diane R. Miller, Sept. 12, 1964; children—Anne Marie, Philip Martin II, Kevin Vincent. Laborer, tree trimmer Chgo. Bur. Forestry, 1963-66; sales rep. O.H. div. Bell & Howell, Chgo., 1966; sr. account agt. Allstate Ins. Co., Chgo., 1967—. Served with USMCR, 1963-67. Mem. Nat. Assn. Life Underwriters, Marine Corps League, Smithsonian Assos., Am. Film Inst., Inter Am. Soc., Nat. Trust Hist. Preservation, Abraham Lincoln Assn., Ill. State Hist. Soc., Chgo. Council on Fgn. Relations, Am. Diabetes Assn., Meml. Sloan-Kettering Cancer Center, Cousteau Soc., Internat. Platform Assn., Found. Christian Living, Am. Enterprise Inst., U.S. Naval Inst., Inst. of Soc. Ethics and Life Scis., Center Study Presidency, Nat. Audubon Soc., Security and Intelligence Fund, Art Inst. Chgo., Nat. Hist. Soc., Field Mus. Natural History, Acad. Polit. Sci., Am. Life Lobby, Planetary Citizens, Soc. St. Vincent DePaul. Roman Catholic. Club: Mount Greenwood Lions. Home: 11324 S Lawndale Ave Chicago IL 60655 Office: 3401 W 111th St Chicago IL 60655

HOWARD, ROBERT GRAY, brokerage firm exec.; b. Johnson City, N.Y., Nov. 21, 1924; s. Frank Gray and Anna Robertson (Webb) H.; B.A., Hamilton Coll., 1946; m. Janet Wallace Staley, Feb. 7, 1948; children—Susan Howard Bruce, Sarah Platt. Vice pres. A.L. Davis Son Inc., hardware retail, Binghamton, N.Y., 1948-52; partner Reynolds & Co. brokerage, N.Y.C., 1953-71; exec. v.p., sec. Reynolds Securities Inc., N.Y.C., 1971-77, also dir.; exec. v.p., sec., treas., dir. Reynolds Securities Internat. Inc., 1975-77; exec. v.p., dir. Dean Witter Reynolds Inc., 1978—. Campaign chmn. Rye United Fund, 1964, pres., 1965, mem. exec. com., 1966-71; former mem. bd. deacons Rye Presbyn. Ch.; mem. Rye Republican Com., 1962-69, former mem. Rye Zoning Bd. Appeals; former bd. dirs. Rye YMCA; trustee United Hosp. Portchester (N.Y.), 1965-78, Hamilton Coll., Clinton, N.Y., 1975—. Served as pilot USN, 1943-45. Mem. Boston Stock Exchange, N.Y. Cotton Exchange, N.Y. Cocoa Exchange. Republican. Clubs: Apawamis (Rye); Blind Brook (Portchester, N.Y.); Coral Beach and Tennis (Bermuda); Ekwanok Country (Manchester, Vt.); Stock Exchange Luncheon, Univ. (N.Y.C.). Home: 74 Island Dr Rye NY 10580 Office: 130 Liberty St New York NY 10006

HOWARD, RUBY MAE, railroad exec.; b. Anderson, S.C., July 23, 1939; d. Tulie and Olga (Robinson) Griffin; diploma Kennedy-King Jr. Coll., 1973; B.S.B.A., Roosevelt U., 1975, M.B.A., 1977; m. Roland Howard, July 1, 1957; children—Rhonda, Renee, Wendy. Payroll clk. and typist Dept. HEW, Chgo., 1957-59; computer clk. and typist Dept. Treasury, Chgo., 1960-61; sec. C.E. U.S. Army, Chgo., 1961-65; sec. to pres. Burr Oak Cemetery, Chgo., 1965-67; asst. editor, bus. mgr. North Central Assn. Colls. and Secondary Schs., Chgo., 1967-70; adminstrv. asst., bus. mgr. Roosevelt U., 1974-77; fin. analyst Chgo. Rock Island R.R., 1977-79; dir. fin., Controller Hyde Park Fed. Savs. and Loan Assn., Chgo., 1979—. Mem. Women in Mgmt., Phi Gamma Nu (v.p. Alpha Tau chpt. 1974-76), Profl. Panhellenic Assn. Home: 50 W 125th Pl Chicago IL 60628 Office: 5250 S Lake Park Ave Chicago IL 60615

HOWARD, WILLIAM THOMAS, JR., oil co. ins. exec.; b. Hartford, Conn., Oct. 28, 1933; s. William Thomas and Doris C. (Zbikowski) H.; B.A., U. Conn., 1960; student Coll. Ins., N.Y.C., 1963-65; m. Dolores B. LaRose, Aug. 12, 1961; children—Maureen, Kenneth, Steven (twins). Spl. risks underwriter Aetna Casualty & Surety Co., Hartford, 1959-63; home fgn. casualty underwriter Am. Internat. Underwriters, N.Y.C., 1963; asst. ins. supr. Am. Internat. Oil Co., N.Y.C., 1963-67; asst. dir. ins. internat. Continental Oil Co., N.Y.C., 1967-71; dir. corp. ins. Forest Oil Corp., Bradford, Pa., 1971—; trustee Forest Oil Corp. Pension Trust; dir. Oil Ins., Ltd. Bd. dirs. Bradford United Way, 1974-77, Bradford YMCA, 1978—. Served with AUS, 1954-57. Mem. McKean County Indsl. Relations Assn. (v.p.), Risk and Ins. Mgmt. Soc., S.W. Oil Ins. Mgrs. Assn., Assn. Pvt. Pension and Welfare Plans. Clubs: Pennhills Country, Bradford. Home: 119 Jackson Ave Bradford PA 16701 Office: 78 Main St Bradford PA 16701

HOWARTH, HAROLD DONALD, TV exec.; b. Queens, N.Y., Jan. 9, 1950; s. Harold S. and Carmen L. Howarth; B.A., John Jay Coll., 1976; M.A., St. John's U., 1980; m. Barbara Frankel. Cable officer UNICEF, N.Y.C., 1973-75; supply officer UN Devel. Programme, N.Y.C., 1975-79; purchasing and records retention adminstr. United Artists Corp., N.Y.C., 1979-80; mgr. records center ops. CBS Inc., N.Y.C., 1980—. Mem. Republican Nat., Com., 1979—. Served with U.S. Army, 1968-71. Assn. Records Mgrs. and Adminstrs. scholar, 1978. Mem. Center for Study of Presidency, Assn. Records Mgrs. and Adminstrs., Soc. Am. Archivists, Am. Assn. State and Local History, Oral History Assn. Republican. Roman Catholic. Club: U.S. Senatorial. Office: 51 W 52d St New York NY 10019

HOWE, CARROLL LEON, motel and restaurant co. exec.; b. Morgantown, Pa., Dec. 25, 1938; s. Wilkins Brinton and Mary Y. (Yoder) H.; B.S., Bob Jones U., 1961; M.B.A., W.Va. U., 1967; m. Angelyn Karleen Howe, Apr. 27, 1963; children—Kimberly, Kara. Pub. accountant Witschey, Harmon & White, C.P.A.'s, Charleston, W.Va., 1963-67; controller Clayton Industries, Marmora, N.J., 1967-70; controller, treas., dir. Residex Corp. subs. Sun Oil Co., Marmora, N.J., 1970-73; pres., dir. Howe Assos. Inc., Spartanburg, S.C., 1973—; fin. cons., 1973—. Pres., Gideons Internat. N.J., 1975-78. Served with U.S.N.G., 1960-67. Recipient Spl. Manuscript award Nat. Assn. Accountants, 1967; C.P.A. Mem. Am. Inst. C.P.A.'s, W.Va., N.J. socs. C.P.A.'s. Republican. Home and office: Route 2 Box 122E Inman SC 29349

HOWE, CARROLL VICTOR, constrn. equipment co. exec.; b. Kearny, N.J., Dec. 12, 1923; s. Wright and Ada (Hodge) H.; B.A., Princeton, 1947; M.F.A., Yale, 1950; m. Nancy Osborne Stivers, Nov. 24, 1951 (div.); m. 2d, Priscilla Howland Greene, Mar. 1, 1957; children—Gregory Carroll, Christopher David. Writer, producer Pemeho Prodns., N.Y.C., 1950-51; free lance actor, writer, 1952-54; salesman Atlas Rigging Supply Corp., Newark, 1954-56, office mgr., 1956-57, sales mgr., 1957-58, v.p., 1958-62, pres., 1962—; pres. Arsco Industries, Inc., Newark, 1966—. Bd. dirs., pres. 15 Tenant Shareholders, Inc., N.Y.C., 1978—. Served from pvt. to 2d lt. USMCR, 1942-46; served from 1st lt. to capt. USMCR, 1951-52. Mem. West Hudson C. of C., Remsenburg Assn., English-Speaking Union, Am. Mensa Ltd. Episcopalian. Clubs: Quandrangle, Princeton; La Ronde; Westhampton Yacht Squadron (treas. 1970-72, vice commodore 1972-74, commodore 1974-76, dir. 1976—). Author (play): Long Fall, 1950, 1957. Home: 15 W 11th St New York City NY 10011 also Shore Rd Remsenburg NY 11960 Office: 181 Vanderpool St Newark NJ 07114

HOWE, DEBORAH OGLE, telephone co. exec.; b. Benson, Minn., Apr. 29, 1948; d. Howard Daniel and Shirley Marie (Carpenter) Ogle; B.A., Macalester Coll., St. Paul, 1969; m. Thomas Vincent Howe, Apr. 30. Exec. sec. GAC Corp., Miami, 1970-71; communications adviser So. Bell Telephone Co., Miami, 1972-73, supr. area mktg., 1973-74, mgr. bus. services, 1974-77, dir. So. Fla. Communications Center, 1977-79, staff mgr. bus. mktg., 1980—. Recipient Outstanding Service award Vocat. Indsl. Clubs Am., 1976. Mem. Macalester Coll. Alumni Assn. (Ga., Ala., Ky. and S.C. chmn. recruitment activities 1974—), Internat. Platform Assn., Soc. Advancement Mgmt. (pres. Atlanta chpt.). Assn. M.B.A. Execs., Nat. Assn. Female Execs. Baptist. Home: 1079 Redan Trail Ct Stone Mountain GA 30088

HOWE, EDITH L. MILLER (MRS. W. ASQUITH HOWE), real estate exec.; b. Bowling Green, Ohio, Apr. 29, 1913; d. Christie and Alta (Clark) Miller; B.S., Bowling Green State U., 1945; M.A., U. Toledo, 1948; postgrad. Ohio State U., 1949, Temple U., 1965-66; m. W. Asquith Howe, Feb. 2, 1936. Tchr. pub. schs., Wood County, Ohio, 1941-47; tchr. dept. psychology U. Toledo, 1947-48; pres., mgr. Howe Real Estate Investments, Ohio, Pa., Fla. and N.J., 1948—. Mem. Intercontinental Biog. Assn. Home: 218 Crews Ct Port Charlotte FL 33952 also 538 W Shore Dr Brigantine NJ 08203

HOWE, H. PHILIP, banker; b. Manhattan, Kans., July 3, 1932; s. Harold and Ruth Madeline (Riordan) H.; B.S., Kans. State U., 1954; m. Margaret Virginia Griffith, June 1, 1957; children—David, Janet, Evan, Kathleen. Vice-pres., head installment loans Union Nat. Bank, Manhattan, Kans., 1960-68; pres. Kansas State Bank, Manhattan, 1969-73, chmn. bd., 1973—; pres. Griffith Oil Co., Manhattan, 1962-72, chmn. bd., 1972—; v.p. Manhattan Real Properties, Inc., 1963—; v.p. Kans. State Travel Agency, 1968—; pres. Master Med. Corp., 1974—. Bd. trustees Kans. State Endowment Assn., 1976—; bd. trustees St. Mary Hosp., pres., 1975-76; pres. United Way, Manhattan, 1975-76. Served with U.S. Army, 1957-59. Mem. Kans. Bankers Assn., Am. Bankers Assn., Kans. Oilmens Assn., Beta Theta Pi. Roman Catholic. Clubs: Manhattan Country, K.C. Home: 1707 Thomas Circle Manhattan KS 66502 Office: 1010 Westloop Manhattan KS 66502

HOWE, JOHN ALOYSIUS, govt. ofcl.; b. Jersey City, Dec. 30, 1917; s. William Joseph and Mary Margaret (Murphy) H.; B.A., Fordham U., 1940; M.P.A., Fairleigh Dickinson U., 1978; m. Marguerite Nugent, Apr. 3, 1948; children—Gordon, John, Claudia, Cynthia. Pres., Garden State Welding Supply Co., Jersey City, 1947-70; self-employed cons., East Brunswick, N.J., 1970-74; adminstr., purchasing contract officer Old Bridge (N.J.) Twp. Bd. Edn., 1975—. Chmn., East Brunswick Assn. Brain Injured Children, 1963-68, recipient Outstanding Work in Behalf of All Handicapped Children award, 1967; mem. Middlesex County Mental Health Bd., 1966-71; councilman, East Brunswick, 1965-68. Served to capt. USAAF, 1943-46. Cert. public purchasing officer. Mem. Am., N.J. socs. pub. adminstrn., Nat. Inst. Govtl. Purchasing, Govtl. Purchasing Assn. N.J. (sec.), Soil and Health Found., AMVETS, DAV. Democrat. Roman Catholic. Clubs: Piedmont (Lynchburg, Va.); Elks (South River, N.J.). Home: 30 Landsdowne Rd East Brunswick NJ 08816 Office: Adminstrn Bldg Bd Edn Route 516 Matawan NJ 07747

HOWE, JOHN JOSEPH, electronics co. exec.; b. Buffalo, Dec. 1, 1922; s. John William and Angela Theresa (Burkhardt) H.; B.B.A., Canisius Coll., Buffalo, 1943; m. Mary Theresa Mulvey, Oct. 14, 1950; children—Deborah B., Hilary M., Erin M. Sr. staff auditor Graef, Cutting & Coit, C.P.A.'s, Buffalo, 1946-52; chief accountant O-Cel-O div. Gen. Mills, Inc., 1952-56; gen. mgr. distbn. services div. GTE Sylvania, Hartsdale, N.Y., 1956-71; ops. mgr. Gallo Wine Sales Co. N.J., Inc., Elizabeth, 1971-73; v.p. ops., treas. C-Cor Electronics, Inc., State College, Pa., 1973—; cons. data processing. Served to lt. USNR, 1943-46. Mem. Nat. Assn. Accountants (past chpt. v.p., dir.), Soc. Am. Value Engrs. (charter), Soc. Advancement Mgmt. Republican. Roman Catholic. Home: 854 Wheatfield Dr State College PA 16801 Office: 60 Decibel Rd State College PA 16801

HOWE, PATRICIA MARY, investment co. exec.; b. Chgo., Sept. 14, 1927; d. Harry Michael and Helen Mary (Maloeny) H.; student Barat Coll., Lake Forest, Ill., 1944-47; m. Ernest Odin Ellison, Sept. 23, 1977. With mcpl. dept. Blyth & Co., San Francisco, 1952-55; with instl. dept. L.F. Rothschild, Chgo., 1956-65, mgr. br., San Francisco, 1965—, partner firm, 1968—; dir. Lear Siegler. Bd. dirs. Women's Forum West, 1979—, U. San Diego, 1968—, Downtown Assn. San Francisco, 1974—. Named lady Equestrian Order Holy Sepulchre of Jerusalem, 1972. Mem. Securities Industry Assn., Opera Guild, San Francisco Symphony Found., San Francisco Mus. Modern Art, World Affairs Council. Republican. Roman Catholic. Clubs: Bel Air Bay (Los Angeles); San Francisco Bond, World Trade, Metropolitan, Bankers, Villa Taverna, Commonwealth. Office: Suite 3333 L F Rothschild 555 California St San Francisco CA 94104

HOWE, ROBERT MELVIN, mfg. co. exec.; b. Beaumont, Tex., Nov. 27, 1939; s. Robert Melvin and Florence Virginia (MacVeigh) H.; B.S. in Chem. Engring., U. Tex., 1963, M.B.A., 1964; m. Aubyn Stewart Byers, Aug. 26, 1961; children—Blake Christopher, Carol Elizabeth. With Conoco, Houston, 1964-78, exec. asst. to chmn., chief exec. officer, 1977-78; pres., chief exec. officer Continental Carbon Co., Houston, 1979—. Methodist. Clubs: Racquet, Univ. Home: 12206 Cobblestone St Houston TX 77024 Office: 10500 Richmond Ave PO Box 42817 Houston TX 77042

HOWE, ROBERT MICHAEL, ins. co. exec.; b. Phila., Nov. 2, 1946; s. Joseph Bernard and Frances Marie (Wisley) H.; B.S. in Acctg., St. Joseph's U., 1969; m. Clare Anita Mullen, May 8, 1976; children—Erin Clare, Megan Anne. Mgr., Arthur Andersen & Co., Phila., 1969-77; v.p. fin. acctg. Phila. Life Ins. Co., 1977—. C.P.A., Pa. Mem. Nat. Assn. Accts., Am. Inst. C.P.A.'s, Pa. Inst. C.P.A.'s, Soc. Ins. Accts. Roman Catholic. Office: 111 N Broad St Philadelphia PA 19117

HOWE, WESLEY J., med. supplies co. exec.; b. 1921; B.M.E., Stevens Inst. Tech., 1943, M.S., 1953. With Becton, Dickinson and Co., 1949—, dir. product devel. and process engring., 1960-61, chief engr., 1961-63, group dir.-mfg., 1963-64, v.p., 1964-65, v.p. and gen. mgr. Becton-Dickinson div., 1965-68, div. pres., 1968-70, group v.p. parent co., 1968-72, exec. v.p., 1972, pres., 1972—, chief exec. officer, dir., 1974—, chmn. bd., 1980—. Office: Becton Dickinson & Co Mack Centre Dr Paramus NJ 07652

HOWE, WILLIAM A., mfg. co. exec.; b. Rochester, Pa., Dec. 21, 1931; s. William A. and Gertrude (Thomas) H.; A.B., Duke U., 1953; M.B.A. (teaching fellow), U. Pa., 1957; m. Virginia M. Meyers, July 24, 1970; children—Peggy, Linda, Karen. Various sales, mktg., planning and fin. positions IBM, 1957-72; dir. corp. planning Pepsico, Inc., Purchase, N.Y., 1972-76; v.p. bus. and product planning Mosler Safe Co. div. Am. Standard, Hamilton, Ohio, 1976-80; v.p., gen. mgr. WABCO Fluid Power div. Am. Standard, Lexington, Ky., 1980—. Served with USAF, 1954-56. Recipient Lybrand award for excellence in acctg. Wharton Sch., U. Pa., 1957. Club: Stamford (Conn.) Yacht. Office: 1953 Mercer Rd Lexington KY 40505

HOWE, WILLIAM ALFRED, fin. co. exec.; b. Malden, Mass., Apr. 11, 1941; s. George William and Rose Marie (Abbotoni) H.; B.S., U. Maine, 1962; m. Civita Maria Galeno, Dec. 28, 1969; children—Derek, Justin. Asst. store mgr. Kresge, Waterbury, Conn., 1962; cost acct. Litton Industries, Woodland Hills, Calif., 1962-63; with John Hancock Life Ins. Co., Boston, 1963-77; prin. William A. Howe & Assos., Boston, 1978; v.p. fin. Alternative, Inc., Boston, 1979—; acctg. instr. Newbury Jr. Coll., Boston, 1973-77. Active Big Bros. Served with U.S. Army, 1964-65. C.L.U.; cert. internal auditor. Mem. Internat. Bus. Center New Eng., Internat. Assn. Fin. Planners, Internat. Entrepreneurs Assn., Inst. Internal Auditors, Am. Assn. Commodity Traders. Republican. Roman Catholic. Club: Bellevue Golf. Author: The Final Report—A Guide for Financial and Personal Success for the 80's, 1979. Office: 240 Commercial St Boston MA 02109

HOWE-ELLISON, PATRICIA MARY, securities co. exec.; b. Chgo., Sept. 14, 1927; d. Harry Michael and Helen Mary (Maloney) Howe; student Barat Coll., Lake Forest, Ill., 1944-47, Goodman Theatre, Chgo., 1947; m. Ernest O. Ellison. Instl. sales asst. Blyth & Co., 1954-55; with L.F. Rothschild & Co., 1957—, mgr. San Francisco br., 1965—, partner, 1968—; dir. Lear Siegler, Inc. Trustee, U. San Diego; bd. dirs. Women's Forum West, Downtown Assn. Named Lady of Equestrian Order Holy Sepulchre. Mem. Opera Guild, San Francisco Symphony Found., World Affairs Council, Mus. Modern Art. Republican. Roman Catholic. Clubs: Commonwealth, Met., Bankers (dir.), Villa Taverna, Bel Air Bay, World Trade. Home: 1080 Chestnut St San Francisco CA 94109 Office: 555 California St San Francisco CA 94104

HOWELL, DAVID JAMES, corp. exec.; b. Oklahoma City, Dec. 19, 1942; s. Samuel Doy and Mary Elva H.; B.A. in Math., Principia Coll., 1964; M.B.A., Stanford U., 1966; m. Susan Temple Howell; children—Robert James, Amy Elizabeth. Dep. dir. Inst. Geophysics and Planetary Physics, U. Calif., Riverside, 1970-72; treas., controller Pacific Energy Corp., Marina del Rey, Calif., 1972-73; chief fin. officer Rep. Geothermal. Inc., Santa Fe Springs, Calif., also pres. Rep. Drilling Co., Santa Fe Springs, 1973-80; pres., chief exec. officer H & W Drilling, Inc., Los Angeles, 1980—. Trustee, Berkeley Hall Sch. Served to lt. USNR, 1966-70. Cert. data processing Internat. Data Processing Mgmt. Assn. Mem. Geothermal Resources Council.

HOWELL, JAMES BURT, III, tech. sales specialist; b. Bridgeton, N.J., Dec. 11, 1933; s. James Burt and Catharine Stanger (Sparks) H.; B.S. with high honors, Rutgers U., 1956; M.B.A., U. Del., 1980. Agrl. sales rep. Allied Chem. Corp., Phila., 1957-59; sales specialist Asgrow Seed Co. subs. Upjohn Co., Vineland, N.J., 1960—; dir. Advance Weight Systems, Ind., Medina, Ohio. Mem. ofcl. bd. 1st Presbyterian Ch. of Cedarville (N.J.), 1960—; admissions liaison officer U.S. Mil. Acad., West Point, N.Y., 1973—. Served with U.S. Army, 1957. Recipient Burpee Hort. award Rutgers U., 1955. Mem. Am. Def. Preparedness Assn., Vegetable Growers Assn. N.J., Res. Officers Assn. U.S., Phi Beta Kappa, Alpha Gamma Rho, Alpha Zeta. Home: Sayres Neck Cedarville NJ 08311 Office: 930 N Main Rd Vineland NJ 08360

HOWELL, JIMMIE SYLVANUS, oil field service and fabrication co. exec.; b. Forrest County, Miss., July 19, 1940; s. Clayton Eugene and Winnie Eloise (Morgan) H.; B.S. in Accounting, U. So. Miss., 1963; m. Garlane Graham, July 30, 1960; children—Marcus Hunter, Bradley Graham. Masonry contractor, Hattiesburg, Miss., 1959-63; jr. accountant Haskins & Sells, New Orleans, 1963-65, sr. accountant, New Orleans, 1965-68, N.Y.C., 1968-70, prin., New Orleans, 1970-72; asst. to pres., treas., v.p. dir. Laitram Corp., New Orleans, 1972-79; pres., dir. Howell-Loomis, Inc. and A-I Industries, Inc., Harvey, La., 1979—. Vol. worker children's homes, run-away centers. Served with USN, 1959. C.P.A., La., Miss., N.Y. Mem. La. Soc. C.P.A.'s., Am. Inst. C.P.A.'s. Republican. Baptist. Club: Colonial Country. Inventor marble gaming table, chicken eviscerating device. Home: 81 W Imperial Dr Harahan LA 70123 Office: 600 Peters Rd Harvey LA 70059

HOWELL, JOHN ASHBY, JR., oil and coal exploration co. exec.; b. Worland, Wyo., Nov. 6, 1911; s. John Ashby and Helen (Coburn) H.; student U. Wyo., 1931-32; m. Margaret Hellier, Aug. 19, 1947; children—Clare C., Catherine A., Elizabeth C. Owner, v.p. Ashmar Oil Co., Denver, 1959—. Served with U.S. Army, 1943-46. Mem. Am. Assn. Petroleum Landmen, Denver Assn. Petroleum Landmen, English-Speaking Union (v.p., dir. Denver). Republican. Episcopalian. Clubs: Petroleum (life mem.), Denver Chess (pres., dir.); Elks (Sheridan, Wyo.). Home: 244 Colorado Blvd Denver CO 80206 also Story WY 82842 Office: 444 17th St Suite 1003 Denver CO 80202

HOWELL, LARRY ELBERT, moving co. exec.; b. Oklahoma City, Mar. 15, 1946; s. Elbert and Alice T. (Lynch) H.; student Central State U., 1964-66; m. Sherry Rutledge, Aug. 23, 1969; 1 dau., Traci Rae. Sales mgr. Asso. Am. Van Lines, Oklahoma City, 1966-71; pres. Internat. Van & Storage, Inc., Oklahoma City, 1971—. Mem. Motor Carriers Nonpartisan Com. Mem. Asso. Motor Carriers of Okla., S.W. Warehouse and Transfer Assn., Nat. Furniture Warehousemens Assn., Transp. Assn. Am., Nat. Fedn. Ind. Businessmen. Club: Oklahoma City Transp.

HOWELL, MACE DAVID, JR., banker; b. Fayetteville, Ark., June 21, 1948; s. Mace David and Walcie Rhea (Turnbow) H.; B.S., U. Ark., 1971; m. Nov. 26, 1977; children—Mace David, Martin Dane. With 1st State Bank, Springdale, Ark., 1971—, v.p., cashier, 1974-77, pres., 1977—, also dir. Chmn., Pride in Springdale; pres. Springdale United Fund, 1976, chmn. fund drive, 1975; treas. Shiloh Mus. Bd.; active Boy Scouts Am. Served with AUS, 1968. United Methodist (past mem. adminstrv. bd.). Mason (32 deg.), Rotarian. Home: 1507 Camino Real Springdale AR 72764 Office: E Emma Ave PO Box 189 Springdale AR 72764

HOWELL, WARREN RICHARDSON, book dealer, publisher; b. Berkeley, Calif., Nov. 13, 1912; s. John Gilson and Rebecca Ruskin (Richardson) H.; student Stanford, 1930-32; m. Antoinette Oostermayr, Dec. 31, 1953. With John Howell-Books, rare book dealers, pubs., San Francisco, 1932-40, partner firm, 1940-45, mng. partner, 1945-56, owner 1956-71, pres., 1972—. Dir. English Speaking Union, 1956-61; sec., trustee Calif. Hist. Soc., 1956-60; 72-74; dir. Book Club Calif., 1956-71, v.p., 1972, pres., 1973—; dir. Manuscript Soc., 1960-65; founding mem., mem. exec. council Friends of Bancroft Library, 1957— mem. adv. council regions 9 and 10, Nat. Archives, 1972; mem. vis. com. Stanford U. Libraries, 1972. Served to lt. USNR, 1942-45; in U.S.S. Essex; comdr. amphibious forces Pacific fleet, 1943-45. Decorated Bronze Star medal with Combat V. Hon. fellow Morgan Library, N.Y.C. Fellow Calif. Hist. Soc. (Henry R. Wagner Meml. award 1980); mem. Antiquarian Booksellers Assn. Am. (v.p. 1960-62, gov. 1964-67, 1968-72, v.p. 1974-76, pres. 1976-78), Sir Frances Drake Assn. (pres. 1957-59), Lincoln Sesquicentennial Assn. Calif., (v.p. 1959-60). Clubs: Century, Grolier (N.Y.C.); Bohemian, Roxburghe, Chevaliers Du Tastevin (San Francisco); Pacific Union. Contbr. articles on Californians and Western Americana to hist. jours. Home: 1052 Chestnut St San Francisco CA 94109 Office: 434 Post St San Francisco CA 94102

HOWES, ALFRED SPENCER, business and ins. cons.; b. Troy, N.Y., Sept. 10, 1917; s. Alfred G. and Frances (Youngs) H.; student Brown U., 1934-35, U. Ala., 1935-36, Syracuse U. (A.S.T.P.), 1943-44; m. Elizabeth Hoffner, Oct. 10, 1942; children—Wendy, Mary Lee, Constance Ellen. Agt., advanced underwriting cons. for N.Y. and Vt. with Conn. Mut. Life Ins. Co.; organized own Business Cons. Co., 1946; pres. Employee Incentive Plans of Am., Inc., chmn. bd. Utica Duxbak Corp.; pres., dir. Hyden, Inc., Wood Realty Inc., 1970-80; dir. Insulating Shapes, Inc., Emerson Plastics Corp., Century Planning Co., Inc., Hurd Shoe Co., Bering Trading Corp., Mohawk Valley Oil Co., Inc., Scotsmoor Co., Inc., Placid's Parkas, Inc., Utica Bulk Terminals, Inc., Winchester Knitting Mills, Inc., Killip Laundering & Dry Cleaning Co., Inc., Killip Services, Inc., Smiley Bros., Inc., Mech. Tech., Inc., J.A. Firsching & Son, Inc., Broad St. Realty Co.; pub. Gray Letter. Past sec., dir. N.Y.C. Estate Planning Council. Served with Office Gen. Purchasing Agt., ETO, 1943-46. Mem. Nat. (life, pub. relations chmn. Million Dollar Round Table), N.Y. State (chmn. com. to revise laws concerning decedents and their estates, pres. 1966-67), N.Y.C. (dir., pres.) assns. life underwriters, Am. Philatelic Soc., Assn. for Advanced Life Underwriting (pres. 1970-71). Clubs: Collectors, Brown (N.Y.C.); University (Albany); Fort Schuyler (Utica). Author article on taxes. Home: 42 Fenimore Rd Scarsdale NY 10583 Office: 551 Fifth Ave New York NY 10176

HOWICK, BRUCE HENRY, constrn. services and sales co. exec.; b. Thief River Falls, Minn., Dec. 17, 1946; s. Lloyd C. and Elizabeth G. Howick; B.S. in Bus. Adminstrn., U. N.D., 1976; m. Claudette Mae Tisch, Aug. 29, 1974; children—Tamra E., Andrer R. Self-employed aircraft broker, Grand Forks, N.D., 1975-76; dist. mgr. J.I. Case Co., Rapid City, S.D, 1976-78; store mgr. Case Power & Equipment Co., Brookings, S.D., 1978—. Adv., Little I, S.D. State U.; clk. Medary Twp. Bd., Brookings County S.D. Served with USN, 1968-72. Mem. Brookings Area Beef Growers, Brookings C. of C., Retail Farm Equipment Assn. Minn. and S.D. Lutheran. Club: Brookings Optimists. Home: Route 4 Bridle Estates Brookings SD 57006 Office: Case Power & Equipment Co PO Box 459 Brookings SD 57006

HOWLEY, PETER A., telephone co. exec.; b. Phila., Mar. 5, 1940; s. Frank L. and Edith Jenkins (Cadwallader) H.; B. Indsl. Engring., N.Y. U., 1962, M.B.A., 1970; m. M. Mavin Renz, June 25, 1966; children—Tara Noel, Christina Maeve, Sean-Francis Cadwallader. With Long Lines div. AT&T Co., N.Y.C., 1965-73; dir. ops., dir. policy and procedures MCI Telecommunications, Inc., Washington, 1973-76; spl. assignment to Calif., Citizens Utilities Co., Stamford, Conn., 1976-77, gen. mgr. Ariz. Telephone div. Citizens Utilities Co., Kingman, 1977—, Citizens Utilities Rural Co., Kingman, 1977—. Economic devel. com. Kingman C. of C., 1977-81; dist. chmn. Boy Scouts Am., 1978-81; pres. The Kingsmen, 1979-80. Served with USAF, 1962-65, 68-69. Decorated Air Force Commendation medal. Mem. U.S. Ind., Rocky Mountain (dir.), Ariz.-N.Mex. (dir.) telephone assns., Ariz. C. of C. (dir.). Roman Catholic. Clubs: Rotary, Kingman Country, Hualapai Racquet (pres. 1977-78), Elks. Home: 3750 Cantle Dr Kingman AZ 86401 Office: 3405 Northern Ave Kingman AZ 86401

HOXIE, THOMAS MITCHELL, equipment rental co. exec.; b. Electra, Tex., Mar. 19, 1913; s. Thomas Mitchell and Anne (Kennedy) H.; student public schs., Tex.; m. Naomi Evelyn Adams, Nov. 19, 1939; children—Thomas Mitchell, Pamela Sue Hoxie Bowles, Sandra Sheri Hoxie Palmer, Gregory Lance. Contractor, T.M. Hoxie, Los Angeles, 1936-46; owner, mgr. Aero Rental, Tucson, 1947-72, pres., 1972-77, chmn. bd., 1977—; pres., founder Tucson Equipment Assn., 1959. Sec., pres. Catalina (Tucson) Rotary Club, 1957-58. Recipient Disting. Service award Am. Rental Assn., 1968; Rental Man of Yr., Rental Equipment Register, 1964. Mem. Am. Rental Assn. (dir., exec. v.p. 1962), Calif. Rental Assn., Rental Assn. Can., So. Ariz. Rental Assn. Republican. Club: Rotary. Contbr. articles to profl. jours. Office: 3808 E 38th St Tucaon AZ 85713

HOXTER, CURTIS JOSEPH, internat. econ. adviser, pub. relations counselor; b. Marburg, Germany, July 20, 1922; s. Jacob and Hannah (Katzenstein) H.; A.B., N.Y. U., 1948, M.A., 1950; m. Grace Lewis, Feb. 4, 1945 (dec.); children—Ronald Alan, Victoria Ann Finder, Audrey Theresa. Staff contbr. AUFBAU-Reconstn., N.Y.C., 1939-40; feature writer, reporter L.I. Daily Press, 1940-42; editor, writer OWI, 1943-45; public info. officer Dept. State, 1945-47; info. cons. ECA, 1950-55; public relations cons. various cos.; dir. public relations Internat. C. of C., U.S. council Internat. C. of C., 1948-53; free-lance columnist Scripps-Howard Newspapers; exec. v.p. George Peabody and Assos., Inc., 1953-56; pres. Curtis J. Hoxter, Inc., internat. public relations counsels and econ. and fin. advisers, 1956—; dir. China Trade Corp. Adviser, U.S. com. for UN Day; adviser on internat. econ. and fin. problems to govt. agys.; adviser U.S. del. Disarmament Conf., London. Served with AUS, World War II. Mem. Public Relations Soc. Am. Clubs: Atrium, Met., Overseas Press (N.Y.C.); Nat. Press, Internat. (Washington); Royal Auto (London); Bankers (San Juan, P.R.). Author weekly column Scripps-Howard papers, The Foreign Economic Scene. Contbr. nat. mags. Home: 34 Broadfield Rd New Rochelle NY 10804 Office: 745 Fifth Ave New York NY 10022

HOY, MICHAEL LASHA, analyst; b. Salisbury, Md., Feb. 4, 1950; s. Thomas Russell and Mable Catherine (Reid) H.; student Salisbury State Coll., 1972; B.S. in Bus. Adminstrn., U. Md. Eastern Shore, 1972; m. Pamela Elizabeth Scarborough, Nov. 29, 1971; children—Adrienne Michelle, Michael Lasha. Employment coordinator Delmarva Power Co., Salisbury, 1972-79, analyst dist. services dept., 1979-80, sr. analyst regional staff, 1980—. Bd. dirs. Lower Shore Sheltered Workshop; adv. bd. Wicomico County Health Planning Assn., Share up, Inc., Delmar (Del.) Sch. Dist.; occupational/vocat. adv. com. Job Service Improvement Program, Va. Employment Commn.; mem. edn. com. Delmarva Adv. Council. Recipient service award Nat. Alliance Businessmen, United Faith Ch. of Deliverance. Mem. Eastern Shore Personnel Assn., Phi Beta Lambda, Kappa Alpha Psi (achievement award). Democrat. Mem. Holiness Ch. Club: Toastmasters Internat. Home: 804 Ellington St Salisbury MD 21801 Office: Delmarva Power Co Naylor Mill Rd Salisbury MD 21801

HOYT, JOHN CLAXTON, automotive products mfg. co. exec.; b. Boston, Oct. 29, 1930; s. William Fenn and Harriet (Claxton) H.; A.B., Hamilton Coll., 1952; M.B.A., U. Pa., 1954; m. Maryalice Louden, July 26, 1958; children—Judith Ann, Elizabeth Jean, Robert Fenn. Chief statistician Nat. Machine Tool Builders Assn., Cleve., 1955-57; market research analyst Standard Oil Co. Ohio, Cleve., 1957-62; supr. to mgr. to dir. mktg. research Champion Spark Plug Co., Toledo, 1962—; pres., dir. Great Lakes Mktg. Assos., Inc., Toledo. Republican precinct committeeman, 1968—, ward chmn., 1978; exec. bd. Toledo council Boy Scouts Am.; mem. Lucas County Bd. Edn., 1977—, pres., 1980—; trustee Boys Club Toledo, Salvation Army Toledo. Recipient Silver Beaver award Boy Scouts Am., 1968, Vigil Honor award, 1966. Mem. Am. Mktg. Assn., Mktg. Research Assn., Am. Assn. Pub. Opinion Research, Automotive Market Research Council, Automotive Service Industry Assn., Automotive Parts and Accessories Assn., SAR. Congregationalist. Clubs: Laurel Hill Swim and Tennis, Toledo Racquet, Toledo Tennis, Masons. Co-editor: Leading Cases in Marketing Research, 1971. Home: 4140 Northmoor Toledo OH 43606 Office: Champion Spark Plug Co PO Box 910 Toledo OH 43661

HRGA, RICHARD GABRIEL, auto parts mfg. co. exec.; b. Split, Yugoslavia, Mar. 24, 1939; s. Pasko and Mathilda (Snoj) H.; grad. Tech. Trade Sch. Vienna, 1957; student York U., Toronto, 1969, U. Western Ont., 1972; m. Karen Striemer, Mar. 24, 1965; 1 dau., Michelle. Lab. technician Robertshaw Controls Co., Toronto, 1961-65; dir. engring., product mgr. Singer Controls Co., St. Thomas, Ont., 1965-72; pres. Ram Air Mfg. Ltd., Power Motion Mfg., London, Ont., 1972-80; group mgr. 8 divs. Magna Internat., Toronto, 1978-80;

mgmt. cons., London, 1980—; dir. various subs. Magna, Ionetics Calif., Santa Ana. Roman Catholic. Club: Sports. Home: 5 Outer Ct Lambeth ON N0L 1S0 Canada Office: 75 White Oak Rd London ON N6A 4B8 Canada

HRKMAN, NICHOLAS, accountant; b. Johnstown, Pa., Feb. 23, 1945; s. Nicholas and Helen (Tumbas) H.; student U. Miami, Fla., 1965-66; B.S. in Bus. Adminstrn., St. Francis Coll., Loretto, Pa., 1971; m. Karen Ann Russo, May 13, 1972; children—Nicholas, Nathan Peter. Audit sr. Touche Ross and Co., Pitts. and San Francisco, 1972-75; internal audit mgr. Pullman Inc., Pitts., 1975-77, div. controller Pullman Swindell div., Pitts., 1977-79; v.p. fin., engring. and constrn. div. Pa. Engring. Corp., Pitts., 1979—. Served with USNR, 1966-68. C.P.A., Pa. Mem. Am., Pa. insts. C.P.A.'s, Phi Delta Theta. Republican. Serbian Orthodox. Home: 3916 Mimosa Dr Bethel Park PA 15102 Office: 441 Smithfield St Pittsburgh PA 15222

HSIA, SHOU-CHONG ALBERT, computer co. exec.; b. Shanghai, China, Feb. 25, 1940; s. Hsien-Wei William and Jessie (Wang) H.; came to U.S., 1974; B.Sc. with honours, Birkbeck Coll., U. London, 1969; B.A., Open U., Milton Keynes, Eng., 1973; M.Tech. in Computer Sci., Brunel U., London, 1973. Lectr., Poly. of North London, 1970-74; system programmer GTE Info. Systems, N.Y.C., 1974-76, Data Gen. Corp., Westboro, Mass., 1976-77; software engr. Raytheon Data Systems, Norwood, Mass., 1977-78; prin. software engr. Digital Equipment Corp., Tewksbury, Mass., 1978—. Mem. Assn. Computing Machinery, Brit. Computer Soc. Address: 14 Hope Dr Amesbury MA 01913

HSU, FU-TONG, mgmt. cons.; b. Taiwan, May 7, 1936; came to U.S., 1961, naturalized, 1972; s. Teh-Huang and San-Mei (Lo) H.; B.S. in Civil Engring., Nat. Taiwan U., 1959; M.S. in Structural Engring., U. Okla., 1962; M.S. in Ops. Research, Case Inst. Tech., 1968; Ph.D. in Indsl. Engring. and Ops. Research, Kans. State U., 1970; m. Yung-Mei Lin, Dec. 19, 1964; children—Eric Hsu, Jeanette Hsu. Structural engr. Ammann & Whitney, N.Y.C., 1963-66; grad. research asso. Case Inst. Tech., Cleve., 1966-68, Kans. State U., 1968-70; asst. prof. Wayne State U., Detroit, 1970-73; mgmt. cons. Union Carbide Corp., Bound Brook, N.J., 1973—; U.S. del. 7th internat. conf. Internat. Fedn. of Operational Research Socs., Tokyo and Kyoto, Japan, 1975. Founding pres. Formosan Club Fed. Credit Union, 1976-78; dir. Taiwanese Am. Conf., 1976—. Mem. Ops. Research Soc. Am., Inst. Mgmt. Sci., Sigma Xi, Alpha Pi Mu. Contbr. articles to profl. jours. Office: 1 River Rd Bound Brook NJ 08805

HUANG, ROBERT TERTSU, mfg. co. exec.; b. Taiwan, Apr. 24, 1945; came to U.S., 1968, naturalized, 1978; s. Chi-Jung and Sue-yen (Chen) H.; B.S., Kyushu U., 1968; M.A., U. Rochester (N.Y.), 1970, M.S. in Elec. Engring., 1976; M.Mgmt., Sloan Sch., M.I.T., 1978. Mgr. for Far East, Macrodata Corp., Woodland Hills, Calif., 1977; internat. sales mgr. Advanced Micro Devices, Inc., Sunnyvale, Calif., 1979—. Home: 2532 Homestead Rd Santa Clara CA 95051 Office: 901 Thompson Pl Sunnyvale CA 94086

HUBBARD, FREDERICK CONGDON, warehousing exec.; b. St. Louis, Mich., May 25, 1916; s. Benjamin Congdon and Mary Paul (Garrett) H.; A.B., U. Chgo., 1938; m. Millicent McElwee, July 12, 1947; children—Thomas Frederick, Amy Louise. Cost accountant Am. Seating Co., Grand Rapids, Mich., 1939-41; with Elston-Richards Storage Co., Grand Rapids, 1946—, chmn. bd., prin. exec., 1977—; chmn. bd. Mich. Accident Fund, 1979—. Vice pres. Grand Rapids Civic Theatre, 1965-70; pres. Friends of Aquias Coll. Library, Grand Rapids, 1976-77; bd. dirs. Community Health Service, Grand Rapids, 1978—. Served to capt. AUS, 1941-45. Co-recipient Clay award for service to Grand Rapids Civic Theatre, 1970. Mem. Mich. Warehousemen's Assn., Ohio Warehousemen's Assn., Ind. Warehousemen's Assn. (pres. 1976-78), Asso. Warehouses (pres. 1964-65). Republican. Episcopalian. Clubs: Grand Rapids Univ., Masons, U. Chgo. Alumni (pres. Grand Rapids 1940-41). Home: 3211 Lake Dr SE Grand Rapids MI 49506 Office: 3739 Patterson St SE Grand Rapids MI 48508

HUBBARD, WILLIAM NEILL, JR., pharm. exec.; b. Fairmont, N.C., Oct. 15, 1919; s. William Neill and Mary Emma (Fenegan) H.; A.B., Columbia U., 1941; postgrad. U. N.C., 1941-43; M.D., N.Y. U., 1944; Sc.D. (hon.), Hillsdale Coll., 1967, Albany Med. Coll., 1968, Hope Coll., 1979; m. Elizabeth Terleski, Dec. 28, 1945; children—William Neill III, Michael James, Mary Emma, Elizabeth Anne, Susan Ellen. Intern Bellevue Hosp., N.Y.C., 1944-45, mem. house staff 3d med. div., 1944-50; instr. medicine N.Y. U., 1950-53, asst. prof., 1953-59, asst. dean to asso. dean Coll. Medicine, 1951-59; dean U. Mich. Med. Sch., 1959-70, asso. prof. internal medicine, 1959-64, prof., 1964-70, dir. U. Mich. Med. Center, 1969-70; gen. mgr. Pharm. div., v.p. Upjohn Co., Kalamazoo, 1970-72, exec. v.p., 1972-74, pres., 1974—; dir. 1st Am. Bank Corp., Hoover Universal, Inc., Consumers Power, W.K. Kellogg Found.; cons. USPHS. Mem. Nat. Adv. Com. on Libraries, 1966-68, med. adv. com. W.K. Kellogg Found., 1959-67; chmn. Gov.'s Action Com. on Corrections, 1972-73; mem. com. med. edn. Brown U., 1974-77; mem. nat. sci. bd. NSF, 1974-80, cons., 1980—; mem. bd. sci. and tech. for internat. devel. Nat. Acad. Sci., 1978-80; mem. Council on Sci. and Tech. for Devel., 1978—; bd. visitors in East Asian studies U. Mich., 1976—; b. overseers Sch. Medicine, Morehouse Coll., 1976—; bd. dirs. Nat. Med. Fellowships, Inc., 1973-75; mem. Nat. Fund Med. Edn., 1962-75; trustee Kalamazoo Coll., 1973-78, Bronson Meth. Hosp., 1970—; bd. regents Nat. Library Medicine, 1963-67, 72-76, chmn., 1965-67, 74-76, cons., 1976—; mem. Gov.'s Adv. Com. on Edn. Health Care, 1965-69; mem. panel ednl. consultants com. on edn. for health adminstrn., 1973-75; bd. dirs. Am. Near East Refugee Aid, 1977-80; dir. devel. council U. Mich., 1979—; mem. population adv. panel Office of Tech. Assessment, U.S. Congress, 1979—. Fellow A.C.P.; mem. Pharm. Mfrs. Assn. (dir. 1978-80, chmn. bd. dirs. 1980—), Harvey Soc., N.Y. Acad. Medicine, Soc. Alumni Bellevue Hosp., Mich. Med. Soc. (council 1960-62), AMA, Kalamazoo Acad. Medicine, Am. Soc. Clin. Pharmacology and Therapeutics, Assn. Am. Med. Colls. (pres. 1966-67), Sigma Xi, Alpha Omega Alpha. Methodist. Office: 7000 Portage Rd Kalamazoo MI 49001

HUBER, HARRY GEORGE, retail furniture co. exec.; b. Phila., Aug. 4, 1936; s. Oskar Theodore and Marie (Ziegler) H.; student interior design Phila. Mus. Coll. Art, 1957-59; m. Elsie Barbara Munz, Oct. 4, 1959; children—Harry George, Brenda Marie, Barbara Marie, Jeffrey Fred. Vice-pres., mgr. Oskar Huber Inc., Southampton, Pa., 1966—, mgr. drapery div., 1957—; dir. NEFA Corp.; dir., chmn. loan com., mem. audit com., investment com. N.E. Fed. Savs. & Loan. Bd. dirs. Glorie Dei Luth. Corp.; chmn. GDL Plaza Corp. Served with U.S. Army, 1955-57. Mem. Nat. Homefurnishings Assn. Republican. Lutheran. Club: Masons. Home: 2034 Winthrop Rd Huntingdon Valley PA 19006 Office: 606 2d St Pike Southampton PA 18966

HUBER, JANE PRESTON, rubber and chem. mfg. corp. exec.; b. New Haven, July 30, 1943; d. Merrill and Maria (Shaw) Preston; B.A., Willson Coll., 1964; M.B.A. with honors, Case Western Res. U., 1979; m. James F. Huber, Aug. 28, 1965. With BFGoodrich Co., Akron, Ohio, 1968—, asst. to pres., 1972-74, market, bus. projects analyst, 1974-76, mgr. planning internat. div., 1976-78, dir. planning internat. div., 1978-79, dir. internat. econs., 1979-80, dir. personnel and spl. projects, 1980—. Mem. Planning Execs. Inst., AAUW, LWV (dir., officer). Home: 5321 Powder Mill Rd Kent OH 44240 Office: BFGoodrich Co 500 S Main St Akron OH 44318

HUBER, JOAN MACMONNIES, frozen food co. exec.; b. N.Y.C., Dec. 15, 1927; d. Wallace and Marguerite Adele (Searing) MacMonnies; B.S. in Biochemistry, Northwestern U., 1949; postgrad. N.Y. U., CCNY, 1950-57, Northwestern Transp. Inst., 1974; cert. fin. planner Adelphi U., 1979; m. Don Lawrence Huber, June 23, 1951. Research chemist Continental Baking Co., Jamaica, N.Y., 1949-57, research supr., 1953-57; co-owner, asst. mgr. sta. KALE, Richland, Wash., 1957-59; new products mgr., Southland Frozen Foods, Great Neck, N.Y., 1959-62, asst. mktg. mgr., 1962-69, mktg. mgr., 1969-72, v.p. distbn. and corp. planning, 1972—. Mem. Am. Chem. Soc., Am. Mgmt. Assn., Inst. Food Technologists, Am. Frozen Food Inst. (chmn. distbn. council; past chmn. warehousing com.), Internat. Assn. Fin. Planners. Home: 24 Rolling Dr Brookville NY 11545 Office: 1 Linden Pl Great Neck NY 11021

HUBER, JOHN DAVID, banker; b. Bellefontaine, Ohio, May 3, 1946; s. Daniel Russell and Juanita Mae (Engle) H.; B.S., Ohio State U., 1968, M.B.A., 1971; m. Barbara L. Swartz, July 22, 1967; children—David Russell, Wendy Kay. Trust investment adminstr. City Nat. Bank, Columbus, Ohio, 1971-73; investment officer Merc. Trust Co., St. Louis, 1973-78, mgr. personal trust dept., 1978—. Treas., Mt. Zion United Meth. Ch., 1975—. Served with U.S. Army, 1968-70. Mem. Inst. Chartered Fin. Analysts, St. Louis Soc. Fin. Analysts (dir.). Club: Missouri Athletic. Home: 12346 Oak Hollow Dr Creve Coeur MO 63141 Office: Mercantile Trust Co Drawer 387 MPO St Louis MO 63166

HUBER, STAN ANTHONY, hosp. and indsl. cons.; b. Paris, Ark., Sept. 28, 1941; s. George and Sophie Huber; B.S., Ark. Poly. Inst., 1964; postgrad. U. Seattle, Oak Ridge Associated U., U. Mo., Thornton (Ill.) Community Coll.; m. Gerhild Heidi Buschmann, July 3, 1965; children—Sonya Renee, Glenn Anthony, Nicole Alexa. Supr. pharmacy Shaw Pharmacal Co., St. Louis, 1964-65; med. isotope cons., then nuclear biomed. researcher Mallinckrodt/Nuclear Co., St. Louis, 1966-69; hosp. cons., nuclear medicine specialist Huber Services, St. Louis, 1969-73; pres. S.A. Huber Cons., Inc., New Lenox, Ill., 1973—; lectr. in field. Bd. dirs. Provincetown Improvement Assn., County Club Hills, Ill., 1973-74; pres. Dr. Max Thorek Meml. Found., Chgo., 1977-79; bd. dirs., mem. chmn.'s com. U.S. Senatorial Bus. Adv. Bd., Washington, 1980—. Mem. Soc. Nuclear Medicine, Health Physics Soc., Am. Hosp. Assn., U.S. C. of C. Author monographs, booklets, articles in field; editor, pub. Nuclear Medicine Newsletter, 1980—. Address: 235 Essex Ln New Lenox IL 60451

HUCK, JOHN LLOYD, pharm. co. exec.; b. Bklyn., July 17, 1922; s. John Lloyd and Adrienne Byron (Warner) H.; B.S. in Chemistry, Pa. State U., 1946; m. Dorothy B. Foehr, Nov. 20, 1943; children—Lloyd E., Jeanne Huck Miller, Virginia A. With Hoffmann-LaRoche, Nutley, N.J., 1946-58, asst. gen. sales mgr. 1955-58, dir. product devel., 1958; with Merck & Co., Inc., Rahway, N.J., 1958—, pres. Merck Sharp & Pohme div., 1973-75, exec. v.p., 1977-78, pres., chief operating officer, 1978—, also dir. Active numerous civic orgns.; trustee Pa. State U., 1977—; chmn. edn. com. Morristown (N.J.) Meml. Hosp., 1979—. Served with AC, USAAF, 1942-46. Mem. Am. Mgmt. Assn. (trustee 1971-74, Pres.'s Council 1975-77, Gen. Mgmt. Council 1978—), Pa. State U. Alumni Assn. (pres. 1974-76). Clubs: Morris County Golf; Coral Beach and Tennis (Bermuda). Office: PO Box 2000 Rahway NJ 07065

HUCK, LEWIS FRANCIS, lawyer, real estate developer, ret. airline exec.; b. Bklyn., Mar. 19, 1912; s. Frank and Jessie (Green) H.; LL.B., St. John's U., 1938, LL.M., 1939; m. Frances M. Love, Jan. 7, 1950; children—Janet Ahearn, L. Frank, William G., Robert L., James J. Admitted to N.Y. bar, 1939; trust dept. Guaranty Trust Co. N.Y., 1929-41; atty. Gen. Electric Co., Schenectady, 1945-47, chem. counsel, 1947-48, atomic energy counsel, 1948-51, gen. mgr., Richland, Wash., 1951-55; asst. to exec. v.p. Gen. Dynamics Corp., 1955-57; practice law, cons. real estate mgmt. and devel., 1957-68; v.p., dir. real estate devel. Eastern Air Lines, Inc., N.Y.C., 1968—, ret., 1977; lawyer, real estate cons. and developer, Houston, 1977—; pres. Huck Enterprises Co. Inc., 1980—. Served with U.S. Army, 1941-45. Mem. Tex., N.Y., Mass. bar assns. Democrat. Home: 15127 Kimberley Ln Houston TX 77079 Office: Eastern Airlines Miami Internat Airport Miami FL 33148

HUCKLE, JAMES EARL, newspaper exec.; b. Cadillac, Mich., Apr. 3, 1946; s. Earl Thomas and Audrey Ruth H.; B.S., Mich. State U., 1968; postgrad. Wayne State U., 1971; m. Diana Tefft, Dec. 12, 1970; children—Renee, Martha. Mgmt. trainee Gen. Motors, Warren, Mich., 1969-71; personnel specialist City Nat. Bank of Detroit, 1971-72; bus. mgr. Cadillac (Mich.) Evening News, 1972-76; pub. Ionia (Mich.) Sentinel-Standard, 1976—, South Haven (Mich.) Daily Tribune, 1978—, Ionia County News, 1976—, Lake Odessa (Mich.) Wave, 1978—. Pres., United Way of Ionia, 1979-80; chmn. Ionia Revitalization, 1979—. Mem. Mich. League Home Dailies Press Assn. (pres. 1977), Mich. Newspapers Inc. (dir. 1977—), Am. Newspaper Pubs. Assn., Nat. Newspaper Assn., Inland Daily Newspaper Assn., Mich. Press Assn., Internat. Newspaper Advt. Execs., Internat. Newspaper Promotion Assn. Methodist. Clubs: Rotary, Hunt and Fish, Country. Office: 114 N Depot St Ionia MI 48846

HUCKVALE, JOHN FREDERICK, manufactured housing co. exec.; b. Salt Lake City, Jan. 17, 1937; s. Jonathon David and Mary Leona (Wagstaff) H.; student in mgmt. U. Utah, 1955-60; student in advanced mgmt. Calif. State U., 1965-66; LL.B., La Salle Extension U., 1970; m. Helen Carol Dean, Aug. 6, 1956; children—Robert, Richard, Thomas, Donald, Heidi, Christine, Derrick, Sherri. Gen. mgr. FMC Transport Systems div. FMC Corp., Riverside, Calif., 1965-72, Sandpointe Homes, Inc. subs. Fleetwood Enterprises, Inc., Visalia, Calif., 1972-73; v.p. Guerdon Industries, Inc., Louisville, 1973-76; pres. Carolina Internat., Inc., Houston, 1976—. Mem. Manufactured Housing Inst., Nat. Assn. Housing and Redevel. Ofcls., Am. Planning Assn., Delta Sigma Pi (alumni). Republican. Mormon. Home: 8223 Colonial Oaks Ln Spring TX 77379 Office: Carolina Internat Inc 2627 North Loop W Suite 100 Houston TX 77008

HUDAK, THOMAS FRANCIS, retail exec.; b. Donora, Pa., Jan. 29, 1942; s. Thomas Joseph and Ann Marie (Petrus) H.; B.S., St. Vincent Coll., 1963; M.B.A., Ohio State U., 1968; m. Dorothy Ann Palko, July 27, 1963; s. Diana Lynn, Debra Ann, Thomas David. Staff acct. Coopers & Lybrand, Columbus, 1963-65; mgr. dept. data processing Western Electric, Columbus, 1965-66; fin. controls mgr., tax and audit Indsl. Nucleonics Corp., Columbus, 1966-69; sr. v.p. fin., chief fin. officer, chmn. bd. G.C. Murphy Co., McKeesport, Pa., 1981—, also dir.; treas. Mack Realty Co., McKeesport; dir. McKeesport Nat. Bank. Bd. dirs., v.p. G.C. Murphy Co. Found. C.P.A., Ohio. Mem. U.S. C. of C., Fin. Execs. Inst., Assn. Gen. Mdse. Chains, Risk and Ins. Mgmt. Soc., Am. Inst. C.P.A.'s, Nat. Retail Mchts. Assn. (dir. exec. div.). Roman Catholic. Office: 531 5th Ave McKeesport PA 15132

HUDGINS, CATHERINE HARDING (MRS. ROBERT SCOTT HUDGINS IV), business exec.; b. Raleigh, N.C., June 25, 1913; d. William Thomas and Mary Alice (Timberlake) Harding; B.S., N.C. State U., 1929-33; grad. tchr. N.C. Sch. for Deaf, 1933-34; m. Robert Scott Hudgins, IV, Aug. 20, 1938; children—Catherine Harding, Deborah Ghiselin, Robert Scott V. Tchr., N.C. Sch. for Deaf, Morganton, 1934-36; sec. Dr. A.S. Oliver, Raleigh, 1937; tchr. N.J. Sch. for Deaf, Trenton, 1937-39; sec. Robert S. Hudgins Co., Charlotte, N.C., 1949—, v.p., treas., 1960—, also dir. Mem. Jr. Service League, Easton, Pa., 1939; project chmn. ladies aux. Profl. Engrs. N.C., 1954-55, pres., 1956-57; pres. Christian High Sch. P.T.A., 1963; program chmn. Charlotte Opera Assn., 1959-61, sec., 1961-63; sec. bd. Hezekiah Alexander House Restoration, 1949-52, Hezekiah Alexander House Found., 1975—. Mem. N.C. Hist. Assn., English Speaking Union, Internat. Platform Assn., Mint Mus. Drama Guild (pres. 1967-69), Daus. Am. Colonists (state chmn. nat. def. 1973—, corr. sec. Virginia Dare chpt. 1978-79, state insignia chmn. 1979—), D.A.R. (mem. nat. chmn.'s assn., nat. officers club; chpt. regent 1957-59, chpt. chaplain, N.C. program chmn. 1961-63, state chmn. nat. def. 1973-76, state rec. sec. 1977-79, state regent 1979—), Children Am. Revolution (N.C. sr. pres. 1963-66, sr. nat. corr. sec., 1966-68, sr. nat. 1st v.p. 1968-70, sr. nat. pres. 1970-72, hon. sr. nat. pres. life 1972—; 2d v.p. Nat. Officers Club, 1st v.p. 1977-79, pres. 1979-80). Presbyn. (past chmn. home missions, annuities and relief Women of Ch., past pres. Sunday Sch. class). Club: Carmel Country (Charlotte). Home: 1514 Wendover Rd Charlotte NC 28211 Office: PO Box 17217 Charlotte NC 28211

HUDGINS, DUDLEY RODGER, lab. exec.; b. Chgo., Nov. 4, 1937; s. Dudley Wallace and Helen (Sterling) H.; B.A. in Psychology, Kans. U., 1959; m. Pegge Resch, Aug. 8, 1975; children—Brian, Randy; stepchildren—Todd Woods, Mianne Woods. With Marion Labs., Inc., 1961—, tng. mgr., also bids and contracts mgr., 1970-72, dir. sales tng. and devel., Kansas City, Mo., 1972—; cons. in field. Formerly active local Jr. Achievement, Birthright; pres. Zion Lutheran Ch., 1980; hon. dir. Rockhurst Coll., Kansas City, Mo. Served with AUS, 1960. Recipient Builder award Marion Labs., 1979. Mem. Nat. Soc. Pharm. Sales Trainers (past chpt. treas., pres. 1978—, nat. pres. 1979-80), Am. Security Council (nat. adv. bd.). Home: 12817 Sagamore St Leawood KS 66209 Office: 10236 Bunker Ridge Rd Kansas City MO 64137

HUDSON, BOBBY GILEN, ry. service co. exec.; b. Roanoke, Va., Apr. 17, 1930; s. Walter Gilen and Elsie May (Lane) H.; B.S. in Civil Engring., Va. Poly. Inst. and State U., 1952, M.S. in Civil Engring., 1958; m. Eleanor Dean Harrison, Mar. 21, 1952; children—David Alan, Robert Steven, Catherine Lynn. Asst. supr. bridges and bldgs. Norfolk & Western Ry., Roanoke, Va., 1957-59, roadmaster, 1959-64, div. engr., Crewe, Va., 1965-67; div. engr. Akron, Canton & Youngstown Ry., Akron, Ohio, 1964-65; design supr. Newport News Shipbuilding & Dry Dock Co. (Va.), 1967-70; chief engr. Fla. East Coast Ry., St. Augustine, 1970-77; v.p. sales Speno Rail Services, East Syracuse, N.Y., 1977-79, exec. v.p., gen. mgr., 1979—. Mem. Grewe (Va.) Town Council, 1969-70. Served with U.S. Army, 1954-56. Mem. Am. Ry. Engrs. Assn., Roadmaster and Bridge and Bldg. Assn. Democrat. Methodist. Home: 8126 Old Sunridge Dr Manlius NY 13104 Office: PO Box 309 East Syracuse NY 13057

HUDSON, CHARLES DAUGHERTY, ins. agy. exec.; b. LaGrange, Ga., Mar. 17, 1927; s. J.D. and Janie (Hill) H.; student Auburn U., 1945-48; LL.D., LaGrange Coll.; m. Ida Cason Callaway, May 1, 1955; children—Jane Alice Hudson Cauble, Ellen Pinson, Charles Daugherty, Ida Callaway. Partner, Hudson Hardware Co., LaGrange, 1950-57; partner Hammond-Hudson Ins. Agy., LaGrange, 1957-58, owner, 1958-78; pres. Hammond, Hudson & Holder Inc., 1978—; dir., mem. exec. com. Citizens & So. Bank West Ga., LaGrange, 1963—; acting pres. LaGrange Coll., 1979-80; dir., v.p. LaGrange Industries, Inc., 1956—. Mem. exec. com. Camp Viola, LaGrange, 1956—; v.p., trustee Callaway Found., Inc., 1957—, Fuller E. Callaway Found., 1965—; chmn. LaGrange chpt. United Fund, 1964—; mem. LaGrange Bd. Edn., 1967—; chmn. LaGrange Bd. Edn., 1971-74; trustee Ga. Bapt. Found.; chmn. bd. trustees LaGrange Coll., Ga. Baptist Hosp., Atlanta; trustee West Ga. Med. Center, LaGrange, chmn., 1977; trustee, pres. Ocfuskee Hist. Soc., 1975—. Recipient pres.'s award Colonial Life Ins. Co., 1966, 69, 70, 75, 76, 77, 78, 79; Disting. Alumni award Ga. Mil. Acad., 1971; Disting. Service award Ga. Hosp. Assn., 1980; Respect Law award Optimists Assn., 1967; Public Service award Ga. Assn. of AIA, 1977; Leading Producer award Aetna Life & Casualty, 1979. Mem. Ga. Assn. Independent Ins. Agts., Ga. Sch. Bd. Assn. (area dir.), S.A.R., Amicale de Groupe LaFayette (hon.), Chattahoochee Valley Art Assn., Gridiron Secret Soc. (U. Ga.), Sigma Alpha Epsilon, Beta Gamma Sigma. Baptist (deacon 1953—). Mason (Shriner), Elk, Rotarian (pres. club 1964-65). Clubs: Highland Country (LaGrange); Commerce (Atlanta). Home: Country Club Rd LaGrange GA 30240 Office: 106 Church St LaGrange GA 30240

HUDSON, EDWARD VOYLE, linen supply co. exec.; b. Seymour, Mo., Apr. 3, 1915; s. Marion A. and Alma (Vangonten) H.; student Bellingham Normal Coll., 1933-36, also U. Wash.; m. Margaret Carolyn Greely, Dec. 24, 1939; children—Edward G., Carolyn K. Asst. to mgr. Natural Hard Metal Co., Bellingham, Wash., 1935-37; partner Met. Laundry Co., Tacoma, 1938-39; propr., mgr. Peerless Laundry & Linen Supply Co., Tacoma, 1939—; partner Tacoma Electric Co., 1942-44; propr. Independent Laundry & Everett Linen Supply Co., 1946-74, 99 Cleaners and Launderers Co., Tacoma, 1957—; chmn. Tacoma Pub. Utilities, 1959-60; trustee United Mut. Savs. Bank; dir. Tacoma Better Bus. Bur., 1977—. Pres. Wash. Conf. on Unemployment Compensation, 1975-76; v.p. Puget Sound USO, 1972—; pres. Tacoma Boys' Club, 1970; pres., campaign mgr. Tacoma-Pierce County United Way, 1955-62; elder Emmanuel Presbyterian Ch., 1974—. Recipient Distinguished Citizens certificate USAF Mil. Airlift Command, 1977, medal for outstanding pub. service U.S. Dept. Def., 1978. Mem. Tacoma Sales and Mktg. Execs. (pres. 1957-58), Pacific NW Laundry, Dry Cleaning and Linen Supply Assn. (pres. 1959, treas. 1965—), Tacoma C. of C. (pres. 1965), Air Force Assn. (pres. Tacoma chpt. 1976-77), Navy League, Puget Sound Indsl. Devel. Council (chmn. 1967), Internat. Fabricare Inst. (treas., dist. dir.), Tacoma-Ft. Lewis-Olympia Army Assn. (pres. 1970-71). Republican. Clubs: Elks, Shriners, Masons, Rotary (pres. Tacoma 1967-68), Tacoma Country and Golf, Tacoma Knife and Fork (pres. 1964). Home: 3901 N 37th St Tacoma WA 98407 Office: 2902 S 12th St Tacoma WA 98405

HUDSON, FRANKLIN DONALD, diversified co. exec.; b. Asheville, N.C., July 21, 1933; s. Halbert Austin and Lillian Naomi (Cook) H.; B.E.E., Yale U., 1955; M.B.A., N.Y. U., 1962; postgrad. Pace U., 1972-75; m. Rosemary Wheatley, Dec. 1, 1956; children—Lawrence Jamison, Lauren Jean. Sales rep. RCA, N.Y.C., 1959-62; Latin Am. gen. mgr. Fed. Pacific Electric, P.R., 1962-68; dir. mktg. GTE Sylvania, N.Y.C., 1968-71; dir. Home Equipment div. Singer Co., N.Y.C., 1971-75; v.p. internat. Corometrics Med. Systems, Inc., Wallingford, Conn., 1975-78; v.p. planning and devel. Norlin Corp., White Plains, N.Y., 1978—; adj. prof. N.Y. U.; former mem. faculty Yale U., Post Coll. Mem. Yale U. Alumni Bd., 1965-68; mem. Conn. Republican Fin. Com., 1968-74; asst. dir. The Campaign for Yale, 1978. Served to capt., USAF, 1956-58. Mem. Ecuadorean-Am. Assn., Am. Mus. Natural History. Episcopalian.

Clubs: Pine Orchard (Conn.) Yacht and Country, Yale (N.Y.C.); Mory's (New Haven). Contbr. articles to mags. Home: 96 Sunset Hill Dr Branford CT 06405 Office: care Norlin Corp Westchester One White Plains NY 10601

HUDSON, HAROLD JORDAN, JR., ins. co. exec.; b. Kansas City, Mo., Mar. 10, 1924; s. Harold Jordan and Fannie (Jenkins) H.; B.S., U. Mo., 1945, J.D., 1948; m. Patricia Louise Orr, Oct. 1, 1949. Admitted to Mo. bar, 1948; practice law, Kansas City, Mo., 1948-51; atty. Comml. Union Group, 1951-56; with Gen. Reins. Corp., Greenwich, Conn., 1956—, sr. v.p., 1968-70, pres., chief operating officer, 1970-71, pres., chief exec. officer, 1971-73, chmn., chief exec. officer, 1973—; dir. Herbert Clough, Inc., North Star Reinsurance Corp., Gen. Reinsurance Corp. (Europe), Reinsurance Co. Australasia Ltd., Gen. Signal Corp., Putnam Trust Co., U.S. Trust Corp. N.Y.; gov. N.Y. Ins. Exchange. Republican. Episcopalian. Clubs: Brook (N.Y.C.); Indian Harbor Yacht (Greenwich, Conn.). Office: 600 Steamboat Rd Greenwich CT 06830

HUDSON, HUBERT R., lawyer; b. Oklahoma City, July 31, 1928; s. Hubert R. and Dorothy (Hoffman) H.; grad. Culver Mil. Acad., 1945; B.A. with highest honors, Williams Coll., 1949; LL.B., J.D., U. Tex., 1952; m. Sarah Gibbs Pell, June 25, 1949 (div. Sept. 1955); children—William Parke Custis, Sarah Gibbs; m. 2d, Nancy Paxton Moody, Dec. 4, 1959. Admitted to Tex. bar, 1952; pvt. practice law, Brownsville, Tex.; chmn. bd. Cicero-Smith Lumber Cos.; pres. Gt. Nat. Corp., Dallas, 1978-79, dir., 1978—; pres. S. Tex. Acceptance Co.; trustee Hudson Estate; pres., trustee Aspern J. Camille Playhouse, Deco-Unicel, Matamoros, Mexico; dir. Brownsville Savs. & Loan, Brownsville Financial Corp., South Tex. Lumber Co., Seaport Service and Supply, Automatic Insect Control Co., Dalto Electronics (Norwood, N.J.), O.T.C., El Centro Supermarkets, Boca Chica Leasing Co.; dir., mem. exec. com., chmn. trust com., loan and discount com. 1st Nat. Bank, Brownsville; adv. council United Savs. Tex., Houston; dir., mem. exec. compensation com. Southwestern Group Investors, Inc.; dir. Savs. & Loan Holding Co. S.W.; chmn. audit com. Southwestern Group Financial, Inc.; prof. history and constl. law Tex. Southmost Coll., also mem. long-range planning com.; former chmn. State of Tex. Investments Com.; mem. fathers com. Foxcroft Sch., Middleburg, Va.; adv. mem. Tex. Council Crime and Delinquency; chmn. bd. dirs. Greater Brownsville Commn., Episcopal Day Sch. Found.; bd. dirs. Citizens Com., 1955-59; trustee United Fund, Brownsville, 1954-56; chmn. founding of Good Neighbor Settlement House, 1953—; dir. Valley council Boy Scouts Am., 1954-58; pres. Charro Days, Brownsville, 1954, 55; chmn. Rio Grande Valley Festival of Music; trustee, fellow L.S.B. Leakey Found.; mem. governing bd. Tex. Art Alliance; commr. City of Brownsville Water Bd., 1956—; mem. Tex. Senate, 1956-63. Chmn. finance com. Tex. Southmost Coll., 1956-58; sr. trustee Hudson Found., 1956-59; mem. chancellor's com. U. Tex.; bd. dirs. U. Tex. Found. Sch. Bus.; trustee Episcopal Day Sch., U. Tex. Sch. Architecture, Tex. Mil. Inst., Little Theatre Brownsville, Rio Grande Valley Zool. Soc., S. Tex. Heritage Found. Recipient Outstanding Community Award Service medal Nat. Jr. C. of C., 1954, 56. Mem. Am., Tex. bar assns., Rio Grande Valley C. of C. (pres. 1960), Brownsville Hist. Soc. (trustee), San Antonio Symphony Soc. (dir.), Phi Beta Kappa, Phi Alpha Delta. Mem. Church of the Advent. Episcopalian (vestryman 1953-55). Clubs: Austin (Tex.); Piping Rock, Racquet and Tennis (N.Y.C.). Author: The Roosevelt Corollary, 1949. Home: Casa Poinciana Paredes Rd Brownsville TX 78520 Office: PO Box 3229 Brownsville TX 78520

HUDSON, LAWRENCE JOHN, container co. exec.; b. Dunkirk, N.Y., Oct. 20, 1944; s. Robert Charles and Ruth Elenor (Winch) H.; B.A. in History, Pa. Mil. Coll., Chester, 1966; m. Patricia Anne Gullo, June 18, 1966; children—Lawrence J., Melissa A., Amy E., Jennifer L. Sales rep. Procter & Gamble Dist. Co., Rochester, N.Y., 1968-72; sales mgr. Polaroid Corp., Rochester, 1972-75, Xerox Learning Systems, Rochester, 1975-79; sales mgr. Jamestown (N.Y.) Container Corp., 1978—. Coach, Jamestown Little League, 1978-80; active Western N.Y. Multiple Sclerosis Soc., 1978-80. Served to maj. U.S. Army, 1966-68. Decorated Nat. Def. medal, Meritorious Service medal, others. Mem. Am. Mgmt. Assn., Buffalo Sales & Mktg. Execs., Indsl. Mgmt. Council. Republican. Episcopalian. Clubs: Jamestown Rotary, Town, Lakewood Rod & Gun, Moon Brook Country, Elks. Contbr. articles in field to profl. jours. Home: 474 Fairmont Ave Jamestown NY 14701 Office: PO Box 8 Jamestown NY 14701

HUDSON, MARY, petroleum mktg. co. exec.; b. Murchison, Tex., Sept. 30, 1912; d. John Thurmond and Allie (Dewberry) H.; m. Cecil Wayne Driver, Sept. 20, 1930 (dec. 1932); 1 dau., Joyce Ladelle Driver Cady; m. 2d, Frank Bane Vandegrift, June 2, 1945 (dec. 1977). Pres., chief exec. officer Hudson Oil Co., Shawnee Mission, Kans., 1932—. Mem. Soc. Ind. Gasoline Marketers Am. (past pres.), Ind. Gasoline Marketers Council, Nat. Petroleum Council, Am. Petroleum Inst. Mktg., Am. Petroleum Refiners Assn. Clubs: Carriage, Kansas City, Lauderdale Yacht, Saddle and Sirloin, D.A.R., Women's Kansas City Assn. (past pres.). Home: 2900 Verona Rd Mission Hills KS 66208 Office: 4720 Rainbow Blvd Shawnee Mission KS 66205

HUDSON, RAYMOND ARTHUR, engr.; b. Newbury, Mass., Oct. 18, 1905; s. Arthur H. and Almeda B. (Nason) H.; B.S. in Elec. Engring., Mass. Inst. Tech., 1926, M.S., 1928; m. Helen N. Jeffery, Oct. 12, 1928; children—Norma J. (Mrs. Robert B. Feid), Raymond A. Engr., Goodyear Zeppelin Corp., Akron, Ohio, 1930-35; engr., dept. sales mgr. Goodyear Tire & Rubber Co., Akron, 1935-41; plant mgr. Goodyear Aircraft Corp., Ariz. div., 1941-45; resident engr. Detroit, Goodyear Tire & Rubber Co., 1945-50; pres. Paramount Rubber Co., Detroit, 1950-52; sales engr. Nat. Motor Bearing Co., Detroit, 1952-56, Nat. Seal div. Fed. Mogul-Bower Bearings Corp., 1956-57; field engr. Chgo. Rawhide Mfg. Co., 1957-62; v.p., treas., gen. mgr., dir. Mather Fluorotec, Inc., Milan, Mich., 1962-65; gen. mgr. Yale Rubber Mfg. Co., Dawson, Ga., 1965-76; pres. Ray Hudson Assos., Inc., Albany, Ga., 1976-77, Ray Hudson Bus. Counselor, Inc., Missoula, Mont., 1977—; v.p. Ray Hudson Assos., Inc., Missoula, 1977—; chmn. bd. Cuthbert Engring. Mfg. Co., Benevolence, Ga., Indsl. Engring. Supply, Inc., Albany, Ga. Mem. exec. bd. Chehaw council Boy Scouts Am., pres. council, 1967-69, mem. region 6 exec. bd., 1967—; bd. dirs., past pres. S.W. Ga. Art Assn.; bd. dirs. The Anchorage, Albany; trustee Albany Jr. Coll. Found.; mem. SCORE (SBA-Corp. Ret. Execs.); ruling elder, sec. corp. First Presbyterian Ch., Missoula, 1977—; moderator Glacier Presbytery, United Presbyn. Ch. U.S.A., 1980—, chmn. gen. council, 1980—; mem. Commn. Minister and His Works. Mem. Soc. Automotive Engrs. Am. Soc. Bus. and Mgmt. Consultants. Club: Rotary. Home: PO Box 1327 Polson MT 59860

HUDSPETH, WILLIAM ROY, JR., chem. co. exec.; b. Winston-Salem, N.C., Mar. 21, 1923; s. William Roy and Lee (Wilcox) H.; student Wake Forest Coll., 1942, U. Wis., 1943; B.S., U. N.C., 1948, postgrad., 1948; m. Nancy Webber, Dec. 22, 1944; children—William Broughton, Patricia Lee, Nancy Ann. Asst. v.p. mktg. Foote Mineral Co., 1965-67; asst. to pres. McCall Pattern Co., N.Y.C., 1967-68, v.p. mfg., 1968-71; v.p., gen. mgr. chems. div. Chatlem Drug & Chem. Co., Chattanooga, 1971-76; pres., chmn. bd. Hudspeth Corp., Chattanooga, 1976—. Served with USAAF, 1942-44. Mem. Am. Inst. Chem. Engrs. (career guidance bd.), AIME, Am. Ceramic Soc., Am. Chemists Soc., Alpha Chi Sigma, Phi Kappa Sigma. Republican. Lutheran. Clubs: Lions, Rotary. Home and Office: 137 Valleybrook Circle Chattanooga TN 37343

HUEBNER, CHARLES AUGUSTUS, elec. equipment co. exec.; b. Budapest, Hungary, May 17, 1935; s. Andrew N. and Ann (Schmidlechner) H.; came to U.S., 1950, naturalized, 1955; B.S. in Mech. Engring. summa cum laude (Tau Beta Pi fellow), U. Detroit, 1958; M.S. in Astronautics, Mass Inst. Tech., 1960; Ph.D., Am. U., 1967; m. Suzan Lawlor, June 13, 1959; children—Charles J., Christine M., Diane M., Andrea E. Research engr. Ford Motor Co., Dearborn, Mich., 1958; chief earth orbital mission studies Manned Space Flight, NASA, Washington, 1962-68; dir. planning, mgr. new product devel. Am. Can Co., Greenwich, Conn., 1968-71; v.p., dir. planning AMF Inc., White Plains, N.Y., 1971-75; staff exec. strategic planning Gen. Electric Co., Fairfield, Conn., 1975—. Mem. U.S. Govt. Trade Mission to Hungary, 1974; chmn. fin. com. Bridgeport (Conn.) Roman Catholic Synod, 1970-71, St. Luke Ch., Westport, Conn., 1974—. Served as capt. USAF, 1958-62. Recipient Pres.'s award, Engring. Grad. of Year award, Disting. Mil. Grad., U. Detroit, 1958; Am. Rocket Soc. Thiokol award, 1960. Mem. AIAA, IEEE, Sigma Xi, Tau Beta Pi, Blue Key, Pi Tau Sigma, Sigma Gamma Tau, Alpha Sigma Nu. Club: Patterson (Fairfield). Home: 233 Bayberry Ln Westport CT 06880 Office: 3135 Easton Turnpike Fairfield CT 06431

HUEBNER, CHARLES PAUL, investment co. exec.; b. Port Huron, Mich., Aug. 28, 1945; s. Herman Carl and Inez Jean (Ciotti) H.; B.S., Mich. State U., 1968; M.B.A., U. Mich., 1974; m. Laura Jean Marlette, Dec. 21, 1968; children—Jeffrey Charles, Paul John. Salesman securities Goldman, Sachs & Co., Detroit, 1974—. Guest lectr. U. Mich. Grad. Sch. Bus. Served with USN, 1968-72. Mem. Mich. State U. Alumni Assn., U. Mich. Alumni Assn., Fin. Analysts Soc. Detroit, Alpha Kappa Psi. Episcopalian. Clubs: U. Mich. Flying, Detroit Flying, Bond (Detroit). Home: 748 Washington Rd Grosse Pointe MI 48230 Office: 200 Renaissance Center Suite 2966 Detroit MI 48243

HUENEFELD, THOMAS ERNST, banker; b. Cin., July 7, 1937; s. Carl Ernst and Catherine Louise (Messer) H.; B.S. in Bus. Adminstrn., U. Fla., 1961; grad. Nat. Comml. Lending Grad. Sch., U. Okla., 1975; m. Catherine Ann Cogburn, Feb. 5, 1960; children—Richard Ernst, Amy Cogburn. Mgmt. trainee Huenefeld Co., Cin., 1961-62, asst. sec., buyer, 1963-65; credit analyst First Nat. Bank Cin., 1966-68, asst. cashier, 1968-69, asst. v.p., 1969-75, v.p., 1975—; dir. Wolf Machine Co., S. Eastern Materials Corp., Ninth St. Garage, Inc., Logan & Kanawha Coal Co., Inc. Bd. mgrs. Emanuel Community Center, Cin., 1965-70, pres., 1968-70; trustee Huenefeld Meml., Inc., Cin., 1965-72, treas., 1965-69; trustee Funds for Self Enterprise, Cin., 1972-76, pres., 1973-76; trustee Cin. Musical Festival Assn., 1976-79, mem. exec. com., 1977—; trustee Community Ltd. Care Dialysis Center, Cin., 1978—, Merc. Library, 1979—. Cert. comml. lender Am. Bankers Assn. Mem. Am. Fin. Assn. (life), Fin. Mgmt. Assn. (life), Robert Morris Assos., Cin. Assn. Credit and Fin. Mgmt. (dir. 1972-76), Am. Inst. Banking, Newcomen Soc. N.Am., Ohio (life), Cin. (life; trustee 1979—) hist. socs., Cincinnatus Assn., Sigma Chi. Republican. Methodist. Clubs: Cin. Country, Univ., Queen City, Bankers, The Assemblies (chmn. 1972-73), Fanfare (pres. 1979-80). Home: 3440 Principio Ave Cincinnati OH 45226 Office: 111 E 4th St Cincinnati OH 45202

HUEPER, KLAUS WILHELM, real estate appraiser, assn. exec.; b. Chgo., Jan. 14, 1928; s. Wilhelm Carl and Martha Bertha (Sennhenn) H.; A.B., Princeton U., 1950; postgrad. Law Sch., U. Va., 1950-51, 52-53; m. Nancy Louise Lippman, Jan. 11, 1958 (div. July 1980); 1 son, Paul Frederick; m. 2d, Katherine Davis Bernhardt, Sept. 13, 1980. Mortgage underwriter Acacia Mut. Life Ins. Co., 1953-59, sr. appraiser, chief appraiser, 1966-73; comml. loan officer Walker & Dunlop, Inc., 1961-63; v.p. for constrn. and mgmt. B.F. Saul Real Estate Investment Trust, Chevy Chase, Md., 1973-74; mgr. appraisals Fed. Nat. Mortgage Assn., Washington, 1974—. Chmn. subway com. Locust Hill Citizens Assn., Bethesda, Md., 1969-72. Served with U.S. Army, 1946-47. Mem. Am. Inst. Real Estate Appraisers (mem. Appraisal Inst., dir. Washington chpt., chmn. chpt. admissions com.), Soc. Real Estate Appraisers (sr. real property appraiser), Nat. Assn. Realtors. Clubs: Princeton (Washington); Cloister Inn (Princeton). Home: 1613 44 St Washington DC 20007 Office: 3900 Wisconsin Ave NW Washington DC 20016

HUETTNER, RICHARD ALFRED, lawyer; b. N.Y.C., Mar. 25, 1927; s. Alfred F. and Mary (Reilly) H.; Marine Engrs. License, N.Y. State Maritime Acad., 1947; B.S., Sch. Engring., Yale U., 1949; J.D., U. Pa., 1952; children—Jennifer Mary, Barbara Bryan; m. 2d, Eunice Bizzell Dowd, Aug. 22, 1971. Admitted to D.C. bar, 1952, U.S. Ct. Mil. Appeals, 1953, N.Y. bar, 1954, U.S. Ct. Claims, 1961, U.S. Supreme Ct., 1969, U.S. Ct. Customs and Patent Appeals, 1970, other fed. cts.; registered to practice U.S. Patent Office, 1957, Can. Patent Office, 1968; engr. Jones & Laughlin Steel Corp., 1954-55; asso. atty. Kenyon and Kenyon, N.Y.C., 1955-61, mem. firm, 1961—; specialist in patent, trademark and copyright law. Trustee, N.J. Shakespeare Festival, 1972-79, sec., 1977-79; trustee Colonial Symphony Orch., 1972—, mem. exec. com., 1972—, v.p., 1974-76, pres., 1976-79; chmn. bd. overseers N.J. Consortium for Performing Arts, 1972-74; chmn. bd. trustees Center for Addictive Illnesses, Morristown, N.J., 1979—; fellow Silliman Coll., Yale, 1976—; chmn. Yale U. Alumni Schs. Com. of N.Y., 1972-78; trustee Overlook Hosp., Summit, N.J., 1978—, vice-chmn. bd. trustees, 1980—; mem. Yale U. Council, 1978—; bd. dirs. Yale Alumni Fund, 1978—. Served from midshipman to lt. USNR, 1945-47, 52-54; ret. 1967; certified JAG trial counsel, 1953. Mem. Am., N.Y. State bar assns., Assn. Bar City N.Y., N.Y. Patent Law Assn. (chmn. com. meetings 1961-64, chmn. com. econ. matters 1966-69, 72-74), Fed. Bar Council, Assn. Yale Alumni (rep. 1975—, gov. 1976—, chmn. com. undergrad. admissions 1976-78, chmn. bd. govs. 1978—), AAAS, N.Y. Acad. Scis., N.Y. County Lawyers Assn., Am. Judicature Soc., Internat. Patent and Trademark Assn., Yale Sci. and Engring. Assn. (mem. exec. bd. 1972—, v.p. 1973-75, pres. 1975-78). Clubs: Down Town Assn., Yale (N.Y.C.); Morris County Golf (Convent, N.J.); The Graduates (New Haven); Yale of Central N.J. (trustee 1973—, pres. 1975-77). Home: 150 Green Ave Madison NJ 07940 Office: 59 Maiden Ln New York NY 10038

HUEY, ARTHUR SANDMEYER, real estate and investments, ind. petroleum landman; b. Van Buren, Ark., May 18, 1913; s. Richard King and Adele (Sandmeyer) H.; A.B., Amherst Coll., 1935; postgrad. U. Wis., 1939; m. Helen Dorothy Mautz, June 17, 1935; children—Richard King II, Arthur Ticknor, Adele Susan, Sara Louise. Asst. dir. Leelanau Schs., Glen Arbor, Mich., 1935-43, headmaster, owner, 1943-54, pres., owner, 1954-64, pres. emeritus bd. trustees; asst. dir. Camp Leelanau, Glen Arbor, 1935-43, camp dir., 1943-54, pres., owner, 1954-72; mgr. Leelanan Homestead Guest Inn, Glen Arbor, 1935-54, owner, 1943-72, pres., 1954-72; pres. ASH, Inc., 1972-79; ind. petroleum landman. County chmn. Republican Party, 1956-58, finance chmn., 1951-56. Nat. adv. bd. Interlochen Arts Acad.; mem. East Central Regional Bd.-area 2, Boy Scouts Am., Rotary Camps Inc.; bd. dirs. Rotary Charities, Traverse City. Mem. Mich. State C. of C. (past dir.), Traverse City Area C. of C. (Distinguished Service award 1969), U.S. Ski Assn., Mich. Hotel and Motor Hotel Assn. (past pres., past chmn. exec. bd.), Mich. Skeet Assn., Delta Kappa Epsilon. Mason (32 deg., Shriner), Rotarian. Clubs: Traverse City Golf and Country; Detroit Gun. Home: 4962 Overbrook #17 Glen Arbor MI 49636 Office: Overbrook North Glen Arbor MI 49636

HUEY, ROBERT NEFF, govt. agency ofcl.; b. Westhope, N.D., Apr. 29, 1915; s. James Way and Nora (Henderson) H.; student N.D. Sch. Forestry, Bottineau, 1933-34; B.A., Jamestown (N.D.) Coll., 1936; m. Muriel Hildred Ekness, Dec. 2, 1945; children—David, Pamela, Paula, Timothy. Mgr. indsl. dept. Fargo (N.D.) C. of C., 1952-59; asst. dir. econ. devel. commn. State of N.D., Bismarck, 1959-62, exec. dir., 1962-65; officer in charge indsl. devel. div. U.S. Bur. of Indian Affairs, Chgo., 1965—. Bd. dirs. Citizens of Greater Chgo., 1975—. Ruling elder United Presbyterian Ch., 1946—, mem. ministerial relations com. Chgo. Presbytery, 1974—. Served with U.S. Army, 1942-45. Decorated 4 battle stars; recipient certificates of achievement Dept. Commerce, 1950, Dept. Interior, 1976; elected to Gold Club, Am. Indian Athletic Hall of Fame, 1972. Mem. Am. Indsl. Devel. Council. Club: Kiwanis (dir. Chgo. 1969—). Home: 2219 Harrison St Glenview IL 60025 Office: 175 W Jackson Blvd Room A1153 Chicago IL 60604

HUFF, ETHEL FRANCES, packaging mfg. co. exec.; b. St. Louis, Dec. 5, 1947; s. Harold T. and Rose Brown J.; B.S., Northwestern U., 1968; M.B.A., U. Pa., 1975; m. Thomas E. Huff, Sept. 17, 1968. Mem. data processing staff Equitable Life Assurance Soc., N.Y.C., 1968-71, County of Bergen, Hackensack, N.J., 1971-72; mgr. spl. projects Pfizer, Inc., N.Y.C., 1975-78, product mgr., 1978-80; dir. corp. strategy devel. Continental Group, Inc., Stamford, Conn., 1980—. Mem. N.Am. Soc. Corp. Planning, Women in Mgmt. Republican. Presbyterian. Clubs: Cedar Point Yacht, Wharton. Office: Continental Group Inc One Harbor Plaza Stamford CT 06902

HUFF, HARRY REXFORD, textile co. exec.; b. Gilliam, Mo., Aug. 22, 1926; s. Richard Albert and Mary Jewell (Netherton) H.; B.S. in Econs., Central Mo. State U., 1949; children—Cheryl, Susan. Salesman, Procter & Gamble Co., Topeka, 1949-50; sales mgr. Dr. Pepper Co., Pensacola, Fla., 1953-55; cost acct. Chemstrand Corp., Pensacola, 1955-59, 60-64, cost supr., 1964-65, supt. fin., 1966-68, asst. controller, N.Y.C., 1969-71, market planning dir., 1972-73, bus. dir. apparel, 1974-75; dir. comml. adminstrn. Monsanto Textile Co., St. Louis, 1975—; dir. Hale Mfg. Co., Putnam, Conn. Served to 2d lt. U.S. Army, 1944-46; 50-52. Decorated Purple Heart, Silver Star, Bronze Star. Mem. Man Made Fiber Producers Assn. Baptist. Home: 11500 Northbrook Way Saint Louis MO 63141 Office: 800 N Lindbergh Blvd Saint Louis MO 63166

HUGGINS, MARION DIXON, JR., instrument co. exec.; b. Durham, N.C., Apr. 20, 1941; s. Marion Dixon and Edith Slayton H.; B.S. in Applied Math., N.C. State U., 1963; m. Holly S. Egan, Apr. 2, 1980; 1 dau., Pamela C. Mfg. ops. mgr. Sybron-Taylor Instrument Co., Asheville, N.C., 1974-76; v.p. mfg., 1976-78; v.p., plant mgr. Sybron-Med. Products div., Asheville, 1978-80; pres., Erie Mfg. Co., Milw., 1980—. Served with U.S. Army, 1966-72. Mem. Am. Prodn. and Inventory Control Soc. (internat. pres. 1976), Edn. and Research Found. (pres. 1977), Asheville C. of C. (dir. 1978-80), Am. Mgmt. Assn. Republican. Baptist. Clubs: Country, City (Asheville); Milw. Univ. Contbr. articles to profl. jours. Home: 1565 Rolling Meadow Dr Milwaukee WI 53005 Office: 4000 S 13th St Milwaukee WI 53221

HUGHES, ERIC B., furniture mfg. co. exec.; b. Granville, N.Y., Oct. 15, 1918; s. Richard G. and Bessie Lloyd (Thomas) H.; grad. Albany Bus. Coll., 1939; m. Rita Young, Oct. 24, 1942 (dec. Feb. 1973); children—Elizabeth, Eric A., Janice, Diane. With Telescope Folding Furniture Co., Inc., Granville, 1939—, credit mgr., 1947-52, asst. sales mgr., 1953-58, sales mgr., 1958-62, v.p. sales, 1962—. Served to 1st lt. U.S. Army, 1941-46. Decorated Bronze Star medal. Republican. Presbyterian. Home: 17 Potter Ave Granville NY 12832 Office: Telescope Folding Furniture Co Inc Granville NY 12832

HUGHES, GEORGE EDWARD, life ins. co. exec.; b. Charleston, W.Va., Dec. 9, 1949; s. Ellis and Margaret Josephine (Donnally) H.; B.S. in Fin., U. S.C., 1971; m. Lynda C. McElmurray, June 5, 1971; 1 son, David Parker. Brokerage supr. Aetna Life & Casualty Co., Columbia, S.C., 1972-74; with Argus Life Ins. Co., Columbia, 1974—, asst. v.p. sales, 1979, v.p., gen. mgr., 1979—, also dir. Served with USAF, 1971. C.L.U. Mem. Nat. Assn. Life Underwriters, Am. Soc. C.L.U.'s, U. S.C. Alumni Assn. Republican. Club: Palmetto (Columbia). Office: PO Box 1 Columbia SC 29202

HUGHES, IVOR MAYNARD, real estate broker; b. Dawn, Mo., June 6, 1918; s. John Morgan and Persis S. (Hughes) H.; B.A., Calif. State U., Sacramento, 1978; m. Lois Val Smith, Oct. 18, 1944; children—John Philip, Brian Lloyd, Barbara Kay. Partner, Hughes Equipment Co., Dixon, Calif., 1946-51, Hughes Bros. Chevrolet, Dixon, 1949-60; pres. Campus-Chevrolet Buick Inc., Davis, Calif., 1960-73, Four-Way Leasing Inc., Davis and West Sacramento, 1965-73; owner, mgr. Ivor Hughes Co., Sacramento, 1973—; dir. Chevway Corp. Mem. Davis City Housing Authority, 1954-55, Davis City Planning Commn., 1958-59; chmn. Davis Salvation Army, 1966, Davis March of Dimes, 1967; pres. Davis C. of C., 1957. Served with USNR, 1942-45. Mem. Nat. Assn. Realtors, Sacramento Bd. Realtors, Yolo County Bd. Realtors, Sacramento Real Estate Exchange, Cert. Bus. Counselors Assn., Sacramento C. of C. Republican. Clubs: Rotary (past pres. Davis), El Macero Country (charter dir.). Home: 2402 Anza Ave Davis CA 95616 Office: 911 22d St Sacramento CA 95816

HUGHES, IVOR W., tobacco co. exec.; b. Porth, Eng., 1925; ed. Birmingham (Eng.) U., Oxford (Eng.) U. Chmn., chief exec. officer Brown & Williamson Tobacco Corp., Louisville. Office: Brown & Williamson Tobacco Corp 160 W Hill St Louisville KY 40201*

HUGHES, JOHN LAWRENCE, book publishing co. exec.; b. N.Y.C., Mar. 13, 1925; s. John Chambers and Margaret (Kelly) H.; B.A., Yale U., 1948; m. Rose Marie Pitman, Nov. 27, 1947; children—Alexandra, Timothy, Christopher, Ian. Reporter, Nassau Review Star, Rockville Center, L.I., N.Y., 1949; with Pocket Books Inc., N.Y.C., 1949-59, sr. editor, v.p. Washington Square Press., 1956-59; with William Morrow & Co. Inc., N.Y.C., 1960—, pres., chief exec. officer, 1965—, also dir.; dir. SFN Cos. Inc.; trustee Yale U. Press. Trustee Fund for Free Expression, N.Y.C. Served with USMCR, 1943-46, 51. Episcopalian. Office: 105 Madison Ave New York NY 10016

HUGHES, KEITH WILLIAM, banker; b. Cleve., July 1, 1946; s. Delmar V. and Margaret (Smith) H.; B.S., Miami U., Oxford, Ohio, 1968, M.B.A., 1969; m. Cheryl J. Foster, Aug. 30, 1969; 1 dau., Amy. Mktg. mgr. Continental Bank, Chgo., 1970-74; exec. v.p. AFC Securities Corp., South Bend, Ind., 1973-74; v.p., mktg. dir. Northwestern Bank, Mpls., 1974-75; sr. v.p., mgr. retail banking Crocker Bank, San Francisco, 1976—; dir. Western States Bankcard Assn. Mem. Calif. Bankers Assn., Am. Bankers Assn., Western States Bankcard Assn., Bank Mktg. Assn. Office: Crocker Nat Bank 1 Mont St 6th Fl San Francisco CA 94104

HUGHES, PAULA D., govt. ofcl., investment co. exec.; b. N.Y.C., Sept. 25, 1931; student N.Y. Inst. Fin., 1961-62; 1 dau., Catherine Hughes Benton. Sales exec. Brown & Bigelow, N.Y.C., 1953-61; account exec. Shields & Co., N.Y.C., 1961-72; v.p. Halle Stieglitz, N.Y.C., 1972-73; 1st v.p. Thomson McKinnon Securities Inc., N.Y.C., 1973—, also dir.; lectr.-instr. personal investment mgmt. N.Y. U.; bd. govs. U.S. Postal Service, 1980—. Life trustee, mem. fin. and exec. compensation coms. Carnegie-Mellon U. Bd. govs. Greenwich House, Coop. Settlement Soc., City of N.Y., 1961—; bd. dirs. Rye (N.Y.) Art Council, 1969-73, Women's Campaign Fund, Washington, 1978-81; trustee Rye Hist. Soc., 1970-74; panelist N.Y. State Casino Gambling Study Panel, 1979. Named to YWCA Acad. Women Achievers, 1979, One of Wall St.'s Top 10 Brokers, Fin. World, 1976-78, Bus. Woman of Yr., Calif. Bus. Women, 1976; recipient Golden Lady award in fin. AMITA, 1975. Mem. Women's Forum (dir. 1979-81), Sales Execs. Club N.Y. (treas. 1977-79, dir. 1976—), Am. Arbitration Soc., Newcomen Soc., Fin. Women's Assn., Econ. Club N.Y., Internat. Assn. Fin. Planners, Analysts Club N.Y. Republican. Clubs: Duquesne (Pitts.); Shenorock Shore (Rye); Yale N.Y.C. Office: 200 Park Ave New York NY 10166

HUGHES, PHILLIP ROGERS, pub. relations cons.; b. San Francisco, Aug. 27, 1923; s. Wilfred James and Mary Patricia (Glynn) H.; B.S., U. San Francisco, 1947; M.A., Stanford, 1950; postgrad. Georgetown U., 1952-54. Adminstrv. asst. Congressman John F. Shelley, San Francisco, 1960-62; staff asso. Am. Council on Edn., Washington, 1961-62; pub. relations dir. U. San Francisco, 1962-63; asso. dean for pub. information Stanford U. Sch., Stanford-Palo Alto Hosp.; asst. pub. relations adv. VIII Olympic Games Orgn. Com., Squaw Valley, Calif., 1963; pres. Barth, Hughes & Hinckle, San Francisco, 1962-64, Phillip Hughes & Assos., 1965—; now pres. Hughes and Assos. Staff research-writer Republican Policy Com., U.S. Senate, Washington, 1952; adminstrv. mem. Am. For Democratic Action, 1953-54. Pub. relations adv. Spring Opera, San Francisco, 1963, Lincoln U., 1964-67. lectr. Golden Gate U., 1965—. Served with AUS, 1943-46. Mem. San Francisco Press Club. Stanford Assos., Stanford Alumni Assn., Calif. Hist. Soc. Democrat. Roman Catholic. Home: 587 Los Palmos Dr San Francisco CA 94127

HUGHES, ROBERT MERRILL, engr.; b. Glendale, Calif., Sept. 11, 1936; s. Fred P. and Gertrude G. H.; A.A., Pasadena City Coll., 1957; 1 dau., Tammie Lynn Scott. Engr., Aerojet Gen. Corp., Azusa, Calif., 1957-64, 66-74; pres. Automatic Electronics Corp., Sacramento, 1964-66; specialist Perkin Elmer Corp., Pomona, Calif., 1974-75; gen. mgr. Hughes Mining Inc., Covina, Calif., 1975-76; project mgr. LA Water Treatment, City of Industry, Calif., 1976-79; pres. Hughes Devel. Corp., Carson City, Nev., 1979—; chmn. bd. Hughes Mining, Inc., 1979—; dir. Hughes Industries, Inc., Alta Loma, Calif. Registered profl. engr., Calif. Mem. Nat. Soc. Profl. Engrs., Am. Inst. Plant Engrs. Republican. Patentee in field. Home: 10039 Bristol Dr Alta Loma CA 91701 Office: PO Box 723 Alta Loma CA 91701

HUGHES, ROBERT NEAL, risk mgmt. cons.; b. Pecos, Tex., Aug. 11, 1938; s. Alton Parker and Janice (McKellar) H.; B.B.A. cum laude, So. Meth. U., 1960; m. Harriet Hill, June 3, 1960; children—James Alton, Alice. Owner, Hughes Ins. Agy., Pecos, Tex., 1960-72; exec. v.p. Rimco, Inc., Dallas, 1972-78; pres. Robert Hughes Assos., Inc. Dallas, 1978—; dir. Alexander Howden Group, U.S., Inc. Served with U.S. Army N.G., 1960. C.P.C.U. Mem. Soc. C.P.C.U.'s, ASCAP, Phi Gamma Delta. Methodist. Office: 7839 Churchill Way Suite 130 Dallas TX 75251

HUGHES, VESTER THOMAS, JR., lawyer; b. San Angelo, Tex., May 24, 1928; s. Vester Thomas and Mary Ellen (Tisdale) H.; student Baylor U., 1945-46; B.A. with distinction, Rice U., 1949; LL.B. cum laude, Harvard, 1952. Admitted to Tex. State bar, 1952; law clk. U.S. Supreme Ct., 1952; asso. firm Robertson, Jackson, Payne, Lancaster & Walker (name later changed to Jackson, Walker, Winstead, Cantwell & Miller), Dallas, 1955-58, partner, 1958-76; partner firm Hughes and Hill, and predecessor firm, 1976—; dir. Exell Cattle Co. LX Cattle Co., Stewart Systems, Inc., Murphy Oil Corp., Memorex Corp., Austin Industries, Inc., First Nat. Bank Mertzon, Cornell Oil Co. Tax counsel Dallas Community Chest Trust Fund. Bd. dirs. Larry and Jane Harlan Found.; trustee, exec. com. Tex. Scottish Rite Hosp. for Crippled Children; bd. overseers vis. com. Harvard Law Sch., 1969-75. Served to lt. USA, 1952-55. Mem. Am. Bar Assn. (mem. council sect. taxation 1969-72), Am. Law Inst. (mem. council 1966—), Phi Beta Kappa, Sigma Xi. Baptist. Mason (33 deg.); mem. Order Eastern Star. Home: 1222 Commerce St Dallas TX 75202 Office: 1000 Mercantile Dallas Bldg Dallas TX 75201

HUGHS, GARY M., engring. co. exec.; b. Alhambra, Calif., July 10, 1936; s. H. Maxwell and Margaret C. (Dampf) H.; B.S.M.E., Calif. Poly. State U., 1959; m. Grace P. Graham, June 30, 1955; children—Carol, David, Lynne, Wendy. With Carnation Co., 1959-64, asst. to gen. mgr., 1962-64; plant engr. Gilroy Foods, Inc. (Calif.), 1964-67; v.p. Engineered Systems and Processes, Inc., Santa Cruz, Calif., 1967-68; plant engr. Schilling div. McCormich & Co., Salinas, Calif., 1969-72; owner, Systems, Design and Fabrication Co., Capitola, Calif., 1968-75; ops. mgr. Flodin, Inc., Sunnyside, Wash., 1975-76; project mgr. Vitro Engring. Corp., Richland, Wash., 1976—; tchr. Columbia Basin Coll., Richland. Registered profl. engr., Can., Calif.; cert. vocat. instr., Wash.; cert. nat. mfg. engr., Can. Mem. Nat., Wash. socs. profl. engrs., Soc. Mfg. Engrs., Inst. Food Technologists. Republican. Presbyterian. Clubs: Jaycees, Elks. Home: Route 2 Box 2210 Canyon Rd Grandview WA 98930

HUGULEY, JENNIE REBECCA, welding supply co. exec.; b. Tupelo, Miss., Sept. 5, 1941; d. Leonard Forest and Lena Mae (Sheffield) Isbell; student Morton Coll., 1979—; m. Robert C. Huguley, Nov. 1, 1960; children—Rebecca Lynn, Joseph Michael. Keypunch operator Victor Dana Corp., Chgo., 1965-68; tax cons. H & R Block, Berwyn, Ill., 1971-75; sec. Barton Welding Supply Co., Cicero, Ill., 1972—, bookkeeper, 1973—, cost accountant, 1974-75, office personnel dir., 1975—; corp. officer, sec., treas. Cylinders & Equipment Co., Inc., Cicero, Ill., 1977—. Youth dir. Cicero-Berwyn Assembly of God, 1963-68, treas., 1965-71; trustee Morton East High Sch. Music Bd., 1978, 79-80. Mem. Welding Distbr. Assn., Nat. Welding Supply Assn., Cicero Mfrs. Assn., Internat. Platform Assn., Cicero C. of C. Home: 5113 W 29th St Cicero IL 60650 Office: 5919 W Ogden Ave Cicero IL 60650

HUGUS, RICHARD DENNY, water utility exec.; b. Cleve., June 14, 1949; s. Robert Denny and Megan Kieth (Whelan) H.; B.S., Indiana U. of Pa., 1971; postgrad. U. Pitts., 1978-80; m. Susan Patricia Jones, June 19, 1976. Mgmt. asst. Western Pa. Water Co., Pitts., 1972-73, risk mgr., 1973-74, office mgr., 1974-75, budget dir., 1975-79, v.p., 1979—. Project cons. Project Bus. of Jr. Achievement; pres. Wash. Area Indsl. Mgmt. Council, 1975-76. Cert. water works operator, sewerage plant operator, Pa. Mem. Am. Mgmt. Assn., Soc. Advancement Mgmt., Am. Water Works Assn., Pa. Water Works Operators Assn., Nat. Assn. Water Cos., Pa. C. of C. Republican. Roman Catholic. Club: Elks. Home: 735 Thornwick Dr Pittsburgh PA 15243 Office: 250 Mount Lebanon Blvd Pittsburgh PA 15234

HUIZENGA, HARRY WAYNE, waste mgmt. co. exec.; b. Evergreen Park, Ill., Dec. 29, 1937; s. G. Harry and Jean (Riddering) H.; student Calvin Coll., 1957-59; m. Martha Jean Pike, Apr. 1972; children—Harry Wayne, Robert Ray, Harry Scott, Pamela Ann. Owner, Pompano Carting Co., Pompano Beach, Fla., 1960-62; owner, officer, dir. So. Sanitation Service, Pompano Beach, 1962-71; pres., chief operating officer, dir. Waste Mgmt., Inc., Ft. Lauderdale, Fla., 1971—; dir. Barnett Bank of Broward County, 1978—. Bd. dirs. Boys' Clubs of Broward County, Inc., 1979—. Served with USAR, 1959-60. Mem. Nat. Solid Wastes Mgmt. Assn. (Man of Yr. award 1978), Am. Public Works Assn., Young Pres. Orgn. Republican. Mem. Faith Reformed Ch. Clubs: Jockey, Tower, Le Club Internat., Coral Ridge Country, Lauderdale Yacht. Home: 516 Mola Ave Fort Lauderdale FL 33301 Office: 800 NW 62d St Fort Lauderdale FL 33309

HULL, CORDELL WILLIAM, engring.-constrn. and fin. exec.; b. Dayton, Ohio, Sept. 12, 1933; s. Murel George and Julia (Barto) H.; B.E., U. Dayton, 1956; M.S., Mass. Inst. Tech., 1957; J.D., Harvard, 1962; m. Susan G. Ruder, May 10, 1958; children—Bradford W., Pamela H., Andrew R. Admitted to Ohio bar, 1962; asso. firm Taft, Stettinius & Hollister, Cin., 1962-64; atty. C & I Girdler Inc., Cin., 1964-66, gen. counsel, treas., pres., Brussels, 1966-70; v.p. Bechtel Overseas Corp., San Francisco, 1970-73; pres., Worldwide mcht. banks Am. Express, London, 1973-75; pres. Bechtel Financing Services, Inc., San Francisco, 1975—, also v.p. fin. Bechtel group cos., also dir. various affiliates. Trustee, Inst. for Internat. and Fgn. Trade Law. Served with U.S. Army, 1957. Registered profl. engr., Mass. Mem. Am. Bar Assn., Am. Soc. Internat. Law, World Affairs Council No. Calif. (dir.), World Affairs Council San Francisco (trustee, exec. com.). Democrat. Clubs: Bankers, Commonwealth (San Francisco); Harvard, Knickerbocker (N.Y.C.). Contbr. articles to profl. jours. Office: 50 Beale St San Francisco CA 94105

HULL, FRANK JOHN, business exec.; b. Winnipeg, Man., Can., Apr. 18, 1925; s. John H. and Mabel (Moon) H.; student pub. schs., Winnipeg; m. Bethel Louise Smith, Nov. 6, 1959; children—Edward, Sheryll, David, Gayle, Dayle. Prodn. mgr. Hull Printing & Pub., Winnipeg, 1943-52; pres. Liquid Transit Ltd., Winnipeg, 1952-61; asst. dir. maintenance Reimer Express Lines, Ltd., Winnipeg, 1961-71; area maintenance mgr. CP Transport, Calgary, Alta., Can., 1971-75; adminstr. Style Realty Ltd., Calgary, 1975—. Pres., High Point Estates Community Assn., 1979-80; v.p. Alta. Gospel Outreach, 1975-80; bd. dirs. Salem Acres Assn., 1979-80. Recipient mgmt. devel. awards. Evangelical Ch. Home: PO Box 16 Site 11 Rural Route 7 Calgary AB T2P 2G7 Canada Office: 204 4600 Crowchild Trail NW Calgary AB T3A 2L6 Canada

HULL, RICHARD FRANKLIN, ins. brokerage exec.; b. N.Y.C., Nov. 8, 1931; s. Washington and Emily G. (Stevenson) H.; student U. Va., 1949-50, CCNY, 1953-56; m. Dorothy Dale, Dec. 6, 1963; children—Richard Franklin, David Townsend, Christopher Cornelius. Underwriter, Crum & Forster Group, N.Y.C., 1953-56; pres. Hull & Co., Washington, 1956-62, Ft. Lauderdale, Fla., 1962—; dir. Gulfstream Bank & Trust Co., Ft. Lauderdale. Served with USMC, 1950-53. Mem. Am. Assn. Mng. Gen. Agts., Nat. Assn. Profl. Surplus Lines Offices, Fla. Surplus Lines Assn., Calif. Surplus Lines Assn., Ill. Surplus Lines Assn., Ind. Agts. Assn. Republican. Episcopalian. Clubs: Balboa Bay, Drug and Chem., Lauderdale Yacht, Lago Mar Country, Lloyd's Yacht, Ocean Reef, Palm Bay. Home: 201 Fiesta Way Fort Lauderdale FL 33301 Office: 2150 S Andrews Ave Fort Lauderdale FL 33316

HULLIN, TOD ROBERT, real estate exec.; b. Seattle, May 28, 1943; s. Jack Elmer and Floretta Elizabeth (Light) H.; B.A. in Bus. Adminstrn., U. Wash., 1966; m. Susan Lee Kanz, May 6, 1967; Staff asst. domestic council White House, Washington, 1973-74, asso. dir. domestic council for housing and community devel., 1974-76; prin. dep. asst. sec. def. for public affairs, Washington, 1976-77; v.p. Interstate Gen. Corp., St. Charles, Md., 1977—. Served to 1st lt. U.S. Army, 1967-69. Decorated Army Commendation medal; recipient Sec. of Def. award for outstanding public service, 1977. Mem. Nat. Assn. Home Builders, Greater Washington Bd. Trade, U. Wash. Alumni Assn. (trustee, govt. Mid-Eastern region 1979—), Sigma Nu. Republican. Presbyterian. Club: Army Navy Country (Arlington, Va.). Home: 209-A S Union St Alexandria VA 22314 Office: Interstate Gen Corp 336 Post Office Rd Saint Charles MD 20601

HULME, ROBERT DUBOIS, mgmt. cons. co. exec.; b. Phila., June 6, 1928; s. Norman and Elisabeth Randall (DuBois) H.; B.S., U. Va., 1950; M.B.A., Temple U., 1953; Ph.D. exams. completed, U. Pa., 1960; m. Nancy Williams Kenyon, Sept. 11, 1954 (div.); children—Randall Kenyon, Michael Hatheway, Kimberly Dana. Tng. supr. Sun Co., Inc., Phila., 1950-60; div. personnel mgr. Ford Motor Co., Phila., 1960-64; cons. Towers, Perrin, Forster & Crosby, Inc., Phila., 1964-71, v.p., prin., N.Y.C., 1971—; lectr. bus. Temple U., 1953-61. Auditor Swarthmore (Pa.) Bd. Edn., 1958-59. Served as lt U.S. Army Res., 1951-53. Episcopalian. Clubs: Knickerbocker (N.Y.); Racquet (Phila.); Riverton (N.J.) Country; Kennebunk River (Kennebunkport, Maine). Home: 319 Nassau St Princeton NJ 08540 Office: 600 3d Ave New York NY 10016

HULS, BERT WRIGHT, petroleum co. exec.; b. Hanna, Okla., Mar. 1, 1926; s. Leslie G. and Georgia D. (Wright) H.; student U. Okla., 1943; B.S., U. So. Calif., 1945; m. Monica Mae Benedict, Oct. 20, 1945; children—Barbara Ellen, Margaret Ann. Oil and gas leasing exec. Carter Oil Co., Oklahoma City and Tulsa, 1946-56; adminstrv. exec. Standard Oil Co. of N.J., N.Y.C., 1956-57; mktg. exec. Humble Oil & Refining Co., Denver and Los Angeles, 1958-71; mktg. exec. Exxon Co. U.S.A., Los Angeles and Dallas, 1971—. Served to ensign USN, 1943-46, to lt., 1952-53. Mem. Western Oil and Gas Assn. (chmn. So. Calif. community affairs com. 1978), Dallas Bd. Realtors, Dallas Council World Affairs, Kappa Alpha. Republican. Methodist. Clubs: Trojan, Masons. Home: 7715 Mullrany Dr Dallas TX 75248 Office: 3400 Southland Center Dallas TX 75201

HULSEY, BURL B., JR., utility co. exec.; b. Forney, Tex., 1917; B.S. in Elec. Engring., Tex. A and M Coll., 1939. Head transmission dept. Tex. Elec. Service subs. Tex. Utilities Co., Inc., from 1939, v.p., 1962-66, pres., 1966-75, pres. parent co., Dallas, 1975—, also dir.; vice chmn., chief exec. officer Tex. Utilities Fuel Co.; chmn., chief exec. officer Tex. Utilities Generating Co., Tex. Utilities Services Inc. Office: Tex Utilities Co Inc 2001 Bryan Tower Dallas TX 75201

HUMBER, WILLIAM, mfg. co. exec.; b. Schweinfurt, Ger., July 20, 1928; came to Can., 1952, naturalized, 1959; s. Leonhard and Betty (Goldschmidt) Hamburger; B.Sc., U. London; m. Lorraine Muter, July 15, 1954; children—Wendy Ellen, Judy Ruth. Apprentice, C. A. Parsons, Ltd., Newcastle, Eng., 1949-51; with Neosid (Can.) Ltd., Toronto, 1952—, gen. mgr., v.p., treas., chief engring., chmn. bd., 1979—; pres. Etobicoke Indsl. Assn., 1977-79. Pres., Holy Blossom Temple Brotherhood, Toronto, 1977-79, treas. Holy Blossom Temple, 1981; chmn. placement com. Jewish Vocat. Service, Toronto, 1975-77, 80. Mem. Assn. Profl. Engrs. Ont., Can. Ceramic Soc. (chmn. electronics and basic sci. div. 1975), Metal Powder Industries Fedn. (dir. 1980—). Jewish. Contbr. articles to profl. jours. Home: 49 Warlock Crescent Willowdale ON M2K 2H8 Canada Office: 10 Vansco Rd Toronto ON M8Z 5J4 Canada

HUME, HORACE DELBERT, mfg. co. exec.; b. Endeavor, Wis., Aug. 15, 1898; s. James Samuel and Lydia Alberta (Sawyer) H.; student pub. schs.; m. Minnie L. Harlan, June 2, 1926 (dec. May 1972); 1 son, James; m. 2d, Sarah D. Lyles Rood, Apr. 6, 1973. Stockman and farmer, 1917-19; with automobile retail business, Garfield, Wash., 1920-21, partner and asst. mgr., 1921-27; automobile and farm machine retailer, Garfield, partner, mgr., 1928-35, gen. mgr. Hume-Love Co., Garfield, 1931-35, pres., 1935-57; partner, gen. mgr. H.D. Hume Co., Mendota, Ill., 1944-52; pres. H.D. Hume Co., Inc., 1952—; partner Hume and Hume, 1952-72; pres. Hume Products Corp., 1953—; pres., dir. Hume-Fry Co., Garden City, Kans., 1955-73. Mayor, Garfield, Wash., 1938-40. Bd. dirs. Mendota Hosp. Found., 1949-73, pres., 1949-54; bd. dirs. Mendota Swimming Pool Assn.; mem. City Planning Commn., 1953-72, chmn., 1953-69; mem. Regional Planning Commn., LaSalle County, Ill., 1965-73, chmn., 1965-71; mem. Schs. Central Com., 1953—, LaSalle County Zoning Commn., 1966—, LaSalle County Care and Treatment Bd., 1970-73; chmn. Mendota Watershed Com., 1967-73. Mem. Am. Soc. Agrl. Engrs., Mendota C. of C. (pres. 1948-49, dir. 1946-49). Republican. Presbyterian (elder). Clubs: Kiwanis (pres. 1953, dir. 1954), Masons, Shriners, Order Eastern Star, Elks; Lakes (Sun City, Ariz.). Patentee in various fields. Home: 709 Carolyn St Mendota IL 61342 Office: 1701 1st Ave Mendota IL 61342

HUMES, MURRAY FRASER, personnel cons.; b. Chgo., Sept. 18, 1897; s. Wilson Thomas and Maude (Meginnis) H.; student Ill. Inst. Tech., 1919-21; m. Ada Stone, Sept. 29, 1928; 1 son, Stephen Stone. Purchasing agt. Swift & Co., Chgo., 1921-45, statistician fgn. dept., 1915-20, gen. purchasing agt. Swift Internat. Co. (name changed to Internat. Packers Ltd.), 1945-62; dir. personnel Symons Mfg. Co., Des Plaines, Ill., 1963-70; personnel cons., 1970—. Chief cons. petroleum procurement. Office Prodn. Mgmt., WPB, Washington, 1941-45. Methodist (past pres. bd. trustees, mem. ofcl. bd.). Home: 2280 World Pkwy Blvd Apt 36 Clearwater FL 33515

HUMMEL, MARTIN HENRY, JR., advt. exec.; b. Glen Ridge, N.J., May 7, 1927; s. Martin Henry and Florence (Lanken) H.; A.B., Cornell U., 1949; m. Evelyn Mayer, Sept. 19, 1953; children—Martin Henry III, Patricia Katherine. With Vick Chem. Co., 1949-50, J. Walter Thompson, 1950-51, Crowell-Collier Pub. Co., 1952-57; with S.S.C. & B., Inc. (formerly Sullivan, Stauffer, Colwell and Bayles, Inc.), N.Y.C., 1957—, exec. v.p., 1968—, also dir.; vice chmn., mng. dir. SSC & B-Lintas Internat., Ltd.; mem. faculty Am. Mgmt. Assn., 1968. Dir. various N.J. Republican state and county polit. campaigns, 1953-57, 60; mem. Bloomfield (N.J.) Zoning Bd., 1953-55. Served with AUS, World War II. Mem. Am. Assn. Advt. Agys. (chmn. internat. com.), U.S. C. of C. (service industries com.). Clubs: Pinnacle; Glen Ridge Country; Cornell, Overseas Press (N.Y.C.); American (London). Home: 6 Capron Ln Upper Montclair NJ 07043 Office: 1 Dag Hammarskjold Plaza New York NY 10017

HUMPHREY, BINGHAM JOHNSON, chem. co. exec.; b. Proctor, Vt., Feb. 9, 1906; s. Albert Parmlee and Angie T. (Tenney) H.; B.S., U. Vt., 1927, hon. LL.D., 1978; Ph.D., Yale U., 1930; m. Esther R. Stanley, Oct. 25, 1930; children—Eugene B., James R., Sarah. Sr. research chemist Firestone Corp., 1930-42; tech. dir. Conn. Hard Rubber Co., 1942-49; pres. Humphrey-Wilkinson, Inc., 1949-64; pres. Humphrey Chem. Co., Hamden, Conn., 1964-72, chmn. bd., 1972—; dir. Milfoam Corp. Chmn., Hamden Bd. Edn., 1958-66; trustee U. Vt., 1968-74, chmn. trustees, 1973-74. Mem. Am. Chem. Soc., U. Vt. Nat. Alumni Assn. (pres. 1969-70), Sigma Xi. Clubs: N.Y. Chemists, Rotary. Office: Humphrey Chem Co Box 5142 North Haven CT 06473

HUMPHREY, GEORGE MAGOFFIN, II, mining co. exec.; b. Cleve., Mar. 19, 1942; s. Gilbert Watts and Louise (Ireland) H.; B.A., Yale U., 1964; J.D., U. Mich., 1967; m. Marguerite Burton, June 19, 1964; children—Mary O., Sandra. Admitted to Ohio bar, 1967; sales rep. Hanna Mining Co., Cleve., 1970-72, European rep., 1972-77, sales rep., 1977-78, mgr. sales, 1978, v.p. sales, 1978-80, sr. v.p. fin., 1980—. Trustee Hotchkiss Sch., Cleve. Mus. Art, Cleve. Mus. Natual History, Cleve. Scholarship Programs, Inc. Served to capt., USMC, 1967-70. Mem. Am. Iron and Steel Inst., Am. Inst. Mining Engrs. Republican. Episcopalian. Clubs: Union (Cleve.); Duquesne (Pitts.). Home: 480 W Hill Dr Gates Mills OH 44040 Office: 100 Erieview Plaza Cleveland OH 44114

HUMPHREY, PAUL ROBERT, computer co. exec.; b. Greensburg, Ind., Nov. 9, 1922; s. Jesse G. and Maggie M. Humphrey; ed. public schs.; m. Joan Louise Conyers, Dec. 28, 1947; children—John Gregroy, Lynn Ann. Field service engr. IBM Corp., Indpls., 1952-56; with Burroughs Corp., Detroit, 1956-61, Scantlin Electronics, Los Angeles, 1961-64, SCM, Oakland, Calif., 1964-68, Control Data Corp., Los Angeles, 1968-72; v.p. field engring. Braegen Corp., Anaheim, Calif., 1978—. Served with USN, 1945-46. Mem. Assn. Field Service Mgrs. Republican. Presbyterian. Club: Masons. Home: 6508 Abbottswood Rancho Palos Verdes CA 90274 Office: Braegen Corp 3340 E La Palma Anaheim CA 92806

HUMPHREY, ROBERT CHARLES, corp. ofcl.; b. Cleve., Aug. 23, 1948; came to Can., 1961; s. Maxwell Charles and Caroline Mary (Lonero) H.; student Fanshawe Coll., 1972-73; m. Patricia Lynet Pryor, Nov. 8, 1969; children—Gina Lynn, Robert Charles William. With D.H. Howden & Co., London, Ont., 1967, buyer, 1969, mgr. inventory control, 1975-81, systems analyst, 1981—; warehouseman Canadian Tire Corp., London, 1968, supr., 1968; cons.; lectr. Fanshawe Coll., London Sch. Bd. Mem. Can. Assn. Prodn. and Inventory Control, Mensa. Lutheran. Home: 11 Kintail Crescent London ON N6E 1J4 Canada Office: PO Box 2485 London ON N6A 4G8 Canada

HUMPHREY, WILLIAM EDWIN, ins. co. exec.; b. Pauls Valley, Okla., June 19, 1939; s. William Edgar and Mamie Elizabeth (Gooch) H.; A.B., Yale U., 1961; B.S., Okla. State U., 1962; postgrad. Fgn. Service Inst., 1962-63; m. Gay Wells, Mar. 17, 1965; children—Marran Elizabeth, Rebecca Lynn, William Wells. Fgn. service officer U.S. Dept. State, 1962-74, comml. attache, Managua, Nicaragua, 1963-65, vice consul, Istanbul, Turkey, 1965-67, intelligence analyst for Turkey and Cyprus, 1967-69, asst. to U.S. Ambassador to Mex., 1969-72, consul, Florence, Italy, 1973-74; pres., Loftin and Humphrey, Inc., Pauls Valley, Okla., 1974—; dir. Pauls Valley Nat. Bank, Sea Harvest Packing Co.; v.p. Agee and Humphrey, Ltd.; pres. Humphrey Realty; v.p. Better Homes, Inc. Pres. Pauls Valley C. of C., 1977—, Pauls Valley Hist. Soc., mem. Pauls Valley Bicentennial Commn., 1976. Republican. Clubs: Beacon, Whitehall (Oklahoma City), Rotary (Pauls Val dir., officer, 1974-77), Elks (Pauls Valley). Home: 1753 S Walnut Pauls Valley OK 73075 Office: 101 S Willow St Pauls Valley OK 73075

HUMPHREY, WILLIAM ROLAND, aerospace co. exec.; b. Wilcoe, W.Va., Dec. 2, 1917; s. Church Gordon and Clarice (Booth) H.; student Harvard, 1937, Am. Mgmt. Assn., 1962-63; B.S. cum laude, U. Hartford, 1968, M.B.A. magna cum laude, 1978; postgrad. Indsl. Coll. of Armed Forces, 1968-69; m. Alice E. Waters, June 30, 1956; children by previous marriage—Clarice Hilda, Margaret Helena, Stephen William. With N.Y., N.H. & H. R.R., 1937-50, traffic rep., Hartford, Conn., 1944-50; asst. traffic mgr. Billings & Spencer

Co., Hartford, 1950-52; traffic mgr. Mattatuck Mfg. Co., Waterbury, Conn., 1952-56; traffic rep. Clipper Carloading Co., Chgo., 1957; traffic mgr. Kaman Aerospace Corp., Bloomfield, Conn., 1957—. Asst. dir. carrier agy. coordination and liaison Office Emergency Transp., 1964—; mem. Nat. Def. Exec. Res., 1954—; asst. dir. for resource mgmt. U.S. Dept. Transp., 1971—; adj. prof. dept. marketing Austin Dunham Barney Sch. Bus. and Pub. Adminstrn., U. Hartford, 1974—. Trustee East Hartford Inter-Ch. Housing Adminstrn., v.p., 1971—. Served with USCGR, 1940-44. Mem. Aerospace Industries Assn. (nat. vice chmn. traffic com. 1962-63), New Eng. Shipper-Carrier Council, New Eng. Shippers Adv. Bd., Am. Soc. Traffic and Transp., Conn. Internat. Trade Assn., U.S. Naval Inst.. Nat. Def. Transp. Assn., Am. Soc. Internat. Execs., Greater Hartford C. of C., Capitol Region Transp. Assn., Nat. Wildlife Fedn., Am. Mktg. Assn., Nat. Assn. Purchasing Mgmt. (life cert. purchasing mgr.), Charter Oak Shippers Assn., Am. Security Council (com. strikes in transp.), Internat. Platform Assn., Delta Nu Alpha. Methodist (pres. ofcl. bd. 1965—, pres. bd. trustees). Kiwanian. Clubs: Transportation, Conn. Quarter-Century Traffic, City (Hartford). Home: 40 Mountain View Dr East Hartford CT 06108 Office: Old Windsor Rd Bloomfield CT 06002

HUMPHRIES, DEMPSEY MARSHALL, JR., hardware co. exec.; b. Florence, Ala., Nov. 29, 1919; s. Dempsey Marshall and Roberta (Sherer) H.; B.S. in Commerce, U. Ala., 1940; m. Geraldine R. Mitchell, Nov. 14, 1944; children—Lynn, Jane, Joan. In labor relations The Kroger Co., Cin., 1947-50; with Bostwick-Braun Co., Toledo, 1951—, exec. v.p., 1967-72, pres., 1972—, also dir.; dir. First Fed. Savs., Toledo. Bd. dirs. St. Luke's Hosp., Maumee, Ohio. Served with U.S. Navy, 1942-46. Mem. Nat. Wholesale Hardware Assn. (dir.), Eastern Hardware Assn. (dir.). Republican. Episcopalian. Home: 6726 Embassy Ct Maumee OH 43537 Office: PO Box 912 Toledo OH 43692

HUMPHRYS, RICHARD, govt. ofcl.; b. Jasmin, Sask., Can., Mar. 27, 1917; s. William and Olive Mary (Maher) H.; B.A., U. Man., 1937; m. Wilma Kay Grant, Oct. 3, 1942. Actuarial clk. Gt. West Life Assurance Co., Winnipeg, Man., Can., 1939-40; with Dept. Ins. Ottawa (Ont., Can.), 1940-46, chief actuary, 1948-54, asst. supt. ins., 1954-64, supt. ins., 1964—; asst. actuary, asso. actuary Tchrs. Ins. and Annuity Assn. N.Y., 1946-48. Fellow Soc. Actuaries (dir. 1970-73, 74-77, v.p. 1979—), Can. Inst. Actuaries (pres. 1965-66); mem. Internat. Actuarial Assn. (conseil de direction). Club: Ottawa Hunt and Golf. Home: 50 Rothwell Dr Ottawa ON K1J 7G6 Canada Office: 15th Floor East Tower Esplanade Laurier 140 O'Connor St Ottawa ON K1A 0H2 Canada

HUNDERUP, RENE ARUP, pharm. co. exec.; b. Aalborg, Denmark, Nov. 28, 1944; emigrated to Can., 1974, naturalized, 1974; s. Soren Arup and Ruby (Lindholm) H.; diploma in commerce Copenhagen, 1966; M.B.A., Copenhagen Sch. Econs. and Bus. Adminstrn., 1974. Comml. apprentice East Asiatic Co., Copenhagen, 1963-66; export and shipping mgr. Denison Deri Ltd., U.K., 1966-68; asst. export mgr., Novo Industri A/S, Copenhagen, 1969-71; asst. export mgr., Danochemo A/S, Copenhagen, 1971-73; export mgr. Marsing & Co., Copenhagen, 1973-74, sales mgr., Toronto, 1974-78; Canadian mktg. dir. ACIC Ltd., Toronto, 1978—; pres. ScanCorp Mgmt. Ltd., Toronto, 1978—; cons. in field. Mem. Assn. Danish Civil Econs., The Scandinavian Canadian Bus. Assn. (dir. 1980—). Home and Office: 25 Wagon Trailway Willowdale ON M2J 4V4 Canada

HUNDLEY, CHARLES MORGAN, pension adminstr.; b. Champaign, Ill., Feb. 10, 1942; s. Charles E. and June E. H.; student So. Ill. U., 1960-63; degree Life Underwriter Tng. Council, 1970-72; m. Barbara S. Shelton, Sept. 9, 1974. Supr. communications Kentron Hawaii, Ltd., Port Hueneme, Calif., 1966-68, Fed. Elec. Corp., Lompoc, Calif., 1968-69; ins. cons. Met. Life Ins. Co., Decatur, Ill., 1969-74; benefits coordinator U. Ill., Urbana, 1974-80; asso. dir. State Univs. Retirement System Ill., Champaign, 1980—. Treas. local United Way, 1975-76; bd. dirs. Levis Faculty Center, 1976—, also corp. sec.; treas. Developmental Services Center, 1977—, Disabled Citizens Found., 1977—. Served with AUS, 1963-66. Mem. Univ. Risk Mgmt. and Ins. Assn. (editor, pub. newsletter 1975-80), Risk and Ins. Mgmt. Soc., Am. Risk and Ins. Assn., Am. Soc. Personnel Adminstrn., Nat. Assn. Securities Dealers, Internat. Found. Employee Benefit Plans, Mcpl. Fin. Officers Assn., U. Ill. Round Table. Club: Rotary. Home: 2205 Grange Circle Urbana IL 61801 Office: 50 Gerty Dr Champaign IL 61820

HUNSAKER, BARRY, natural gas co. exec.; b. Mesa, Ariz., May 20, 1926; s. Oral H. and Gladys Hunsaker; B.S. in Mech. Engring., U. Ariz., 1950; m. Ruby Merle Tucker, Dec. 22, 1948; children—Barry, Hugh Scott, James Kirk. Vice pres. El Paso Natural Gas Co., 1966-74; exec. v.p. El Paso LNG Co., 1957-78, pres., 1978-80; sr. v.p. So. Natural Gas Co., Houston, 1980—; dir. Am. Bur. Shipping. Bd. dirs. U. St. Thomas, 1975—. Served with USAAF, 1944-45. Mem. ASME, Ind. Natural Gas Assn. Am., Mid-Continent Oil and Gas Producers Assn., Tex. Ind. Royalty Owners Assn., Am. Petroleum Inst., Lloyds Register, Soc. Naval Architects and Marine Engrs., Soc. Internat. Gas Tanker and Terminal Operators (pres.). Presbyterian. Office: So Natural Gas Co PO Box 27710 Houston TX 77027

HUNSAKER, FRED R., savs. and loan exec.; b. Brigham City, Utah, Sept. 7, 1939; s. James T. and Savilla R. Hunsaker; student Weber State Coll., 1957-58; B.S., Utah State U., 1964; postgrad. U. Utah, 1965, 66; grad. Pacific Coast Banking Sch., U. Wash., 1976; m. Sharon Ward, Mar. 15, 1963; children—Brian Ward, Jeff F., Susan. Mgmt. trainee First Security Bank, Ogden, Utah, 1965-66, br. mgr., 1967-70, asst. v.p., asst. mgr., 1970-74, v.p., mgr., 1975-77; exec. v.p., chief exec. officer First Fed. Savs. and Loan Assn. of Logan (Utah), 1977—. Vice pres. bd. dirs. Utah State U. Found.; v.p. exec. com. Cache Valley council Boy Scouts Am., 1977-79; treas., mem. exec. com. Cache Valley Health Care Found., 1977—. Served with USAF, 1978. Mem. U.S. League of Savs. and Loan Assns., Cache Valley C. of C. (pres. 1980). Mormon. Home: 1190 N 1700 E Logan UT 84321 Office: First Fed Savs and Loan Assn of Logan 198 N Main St Logan UT 84321

HUNSSINGER, EDWARD FREDERICK, JR., brokerage co. exec.; b. Chgo., Sept. 20, 1949; s. Edward Frederick and Cleopha F. (Smith) H.; student Loyola U., Chgo., 1967-71; m. Susan M. Malloy, Aug. 21, 1971; children—Michael Malloy, Mary Malloy. Sales rep. Weiss Brokerage Co., Chgo., 1971-74; v.p. sales Bachner Frozen Foods, Chgo., 1974-75; pres. Midland Brokerage Co., Inc., Orland Park, Ill., 1976—; pres., chmn. Silver Lake Farms, Inc., Orland Park, 1979—. Bd. dirs. S.W. Suburban Montessori Schs., 1980—. Home: 8517 W Golfview Dr Orland Park IL 60462 Office: 62 Orland Square Dr Orland Park IL 60462

HUNSUCKER, ROBERT DEAN, pipeline co. exec.; b. Winchester, Kans. Formerly exec. v.p. Panhandle Eastern Pipe Line Co., Houston, now pres., dir.; v.p., dir. Trunkline Gas Co.; dir. Gifford Hill Corp., Anadarko Prodn. Co., Century Refining Co., Dixilyn-Field Drilling Co., Nat. Helium Co. Office: Panhandle Eastern Pipe Line Co 3000 Bissonnet Ave Box 1642 Houston TX 77001*

HUNT, ALBERT B., textile co. exec. Chmn. bd. Fieldcrest Mills Inc., Eden, N.C., 1979—; chmn. bd. Amoskeag Co.; dir. Westville Homes Inc., Fiduciary Trust Co., Suffolk Franklin Savs. Bank. Office: Fieldcrest Mills Inc Stadium Dr Eden NC 27288*

HUNT, EARL THOMAS, home mfg. co. exec.; b. New Albany, Ind., Nov. 2, 1920; s. Everett L. and Pearl E. (Albin) H.; part-time student extension div. Purdue U. and Ind. U., 1941-45; m. Edna Mae Miller, May 16, 1941; children—Paul T., Linda Sue, Daniel E. Mgr. product and tech. service U.S. Steel Homes, New Albany, 1949-54; plant mgr. Empire Homes, Louisville, 1954-56; pres. Tru-Bilt Corp., Louisville, 1956-62, Sterling Custom Homes Corp., Fond du Lac, Wis., 1963—; also dir.; dir. Am. Bank, Fond du Lac. Mem. bd. rev. City of Fond du Lac, 1966-76; bd. dirs. Area Econ. Devel. Corp., Fond du Lac; pres., bd. dirs. Indsl. Safety Council, Fond du Lac. Served with USN, 1943-44; recipient various plaques and citations for community, assn. and industry service. Mem. Nat. Assn. Home Builders (dir.), Nat. Assn. Home Mfrs. (dir. 1980—, treas. 1969-70), Home Builders Assn. (treas., state dir.), Wis. Builders Assn., Forest Products Research Inst., Am. Legion. Independent Democrat. Roman Catholic. Clubs: Rotary, South Hills Country, Elks, K.C. Home: 604 Skyline Ct Fond Du Lac WI 54935 Office: 225 W McWilliams St Fond Du Lac WI 54935

HUNT, FRANK JOHN, mfg. co. exec.; b. Toronto, Ont., Can., Oct. 2, 1937; s. George Ernest and Vera Alice (Ross) H.; student U. Toronto, 1958-59; m. Catherine Jane Stewart, Apr. 14, 1956; children—Blaine, Steven, Brenda, David. With Osler & Hammond, Toronto, 1956-57; pres. Happy Child Nursery Schs., Ltd., Toronto, 1957—; sec.-treas. RDH Custom Metal Fabrication Ltd., Mississauga, Ont., 1973—; pres. F.J. Hunt Ent., Ltd., Mississauga, 1979—. Mem. Profl. Chartered Accts. Assn. Conservative Party. Club: Kiwanis. Home: 23 Hillside Dr Bramalea ON L6S 1A2 Canada Office: 1730 Meyerside Rd Mississauga ON L5T 1A3 Canada

HUNT, FREDERICK TALLEY DRUM, JR., assn. exec.; b. Martinque, French West Indies, Sept. 19, 1947; s. Frederick Talley Drum and Eleanor Conly H.; B.A., Vanderbilt U., 1970; m. Acacia Lynn Graham, Dec. 4, 1976. Counselor to gov. State Tenn., 1968-70; asst. exec. sec. Sigma Nu Nat. Fraternity, Lexington, Ky., 1970-71; White House liaison and spl. projects officer Army Mil. Dist. Washington, 1971-73; dir. program devel. Manufactured Housing Inst., Washington, 1973-74; pres. Hunt Assos., Washington, 1974-77; dir. communications, govt. liaison Am. Acad. Actuaries, Washington, 1977-80; exec. dir. Soc. Profl. Benefit Adminstrs., 1980—. Mem. Council Pres. Actuarial Profession (exec. dir.), Am. Soc. Assn. Execs., U.S. C. of C. Republican. Episcopalian. Clubs: Metropolitan, George Washington U. Home: 5308 Blackistone Rd Westmoreland Hills Washington DC 20016 Office: 1800 K St NW Suite 1030N Washington DC 20036

HUNT, JAMES, banker; b. Rowland, N.C., July 1, 1945; s. James D. and Sallie J. (Locklear) H.; B.S. in Bus. Adminstrn., Pembroke (N.C.) State U., 1974; postgrad. U. N.C.; cert. N.C. Sch. Banking, 1976; cert. Wharton Sch. Bus., U. Pa., 1979. Ops. officer First Union Nat. Bank, Lumberton, N.C., 1974-77; pres., chief exec. officer Lumbee Bank, Inc., Pembroke, 1977—, chmn. exec. bd. dirs., 1978—. Vice chmn. Postal Adv. Com., Lumberton, 1975-77; mem. Robeson County Indsl. Adv. Com.; chmn. Pines of Carolina council Girl Scouts U.S.A. Served with U.S. Army, 1964-70; Vietnam. Decorated D.S.C., Silver Star, Bronze Star with oak leaf cluster, Purple Heart with oak leaf cluster, Air medal; recipient Outstanding Achievement award N.C. Jaycees, 1977, 78, Tarheel of Week award, 1977. Mem. N.C. Bankers Assn. (resolution com.), Internat. Platform Assn., Am. Mgmt. Assn., Pembroke C. of C., VFW, Pembroke State U. Vets. Assn. (v.p.), Pembroke State U. Mgmt. Club (chmn. projects program), Raeford Parachute Club, Pi Beta Chi. Office: PO Box 908 Pembroke NC 28372

HUNT, PATRICK JOHN, univ. adminstr.; b. N.Y.C., May 15, 1935; s. John and Alice (Bradley) H.; B.A., St. Pius Coll., 1957; postgrad. Cath. U. Am., 1962, Fordham U., 1966; m. Therese M. Rolston, Apr. 20, 1968; children—Mary Alice, Robert Barry. Asso. editor LAMP mag., Peekskill, N.Y., 1959-67; staff editor Religious News Service, N.Y.C., 1967-69; dir. public info. SUNY, Stony Brook, 1969-74; dir. public relations Carnegie-Mellon U., 1974-76; dir. univ. relations U. Md., College Park, 1976—. Mem. Public Relations Soc. Am., Internat. Assn. Bus. Communicators, Council Advancement Support Edn., Prince George's County (Md.) C. of C. (dir.). Democrat. Roman Catholic. Home: 6720 W Park Dr Hyattsville MD 20782 Office: U Md Rm 2119 Main Adminstrn Bldg College Park MD 20742

HUNT, ROBERT MAURICE, publishing co. exec.; b. Sault Ste. Marie, Mich., Feb. 7, 1928; s. Maurice and Ruth (Bartlett) H.; student Mich. State U., 1950; m. Janice E. Sutter, Oct. 3, 1953; 3 children. With Chgo. Tribune, 1950—, gen. advt. mgr., 1967, asst. circulation dir., 1967-72, v.p., 1972-74, advt. dir., 1972-74, pres., gen. mgr., 1974-79, chief exec. officer, 1976-79; v.p., div. Tribune Co., 1974-79; pres., pub. N.Y. Daily News, N.Y.C., 1979—. Mem. exec. com., bd. dirs., income devel. com. Chgo. chpt. Am. Cancer Soc., 1976-77, chmn. prevention com. Ill. br., 1977-78; mem. citizens bd. U. Chgo., 1976-77; fund raising chmn. Provident Hosp., 1975-76; chief crusader Crusade of Mercy Dr., 1978; mem. Com. for Stadium Study, 1977-78; bd. trustees Robert McCormick Charitable Trust, 1975—; bd. dirs. Rehab. Inst. Chgo., 1976—; bd. mgrs. Met. YMCA. Fellow Chgo. Inst. Medicine; mem. Met. Sunday Newspapers Inc. (bd. dirs. 1974—, chmn. 1978), Chgo. Assn. Commerce and Industry (bd. dirs. 1976—), Chgo. Opportunities Industrialization Centers Am. (adv. bd. 1977-78), Chgo. Council on Fgn. Relations, Econ. Devel. Commn., Greater North Mich. Ave. Assn. Address: NY Daily News 220 E 42d St New York NY 10017*

HUNT, TORRENCE MILLER, aluminum co. exec.; b. Pitts., Feb. 18, 1921; s. Roy Arthur and Rachel McMasters (Miller) H.; grad. Choate Sch., 1940; B.A., Williams Coll., 1944; m. Joan Kilner, June 17, 1944; children—Torrence Miller, Daniel K., Christopher M., Rachel Hunt Scott. With Aluminum Co. Am., 1947—, sales engr., Pitts., 1947, gen. service engr., Phila., 1947-50, market surveyor, Phila., Pitts., 1950, gen. service engr., Phila., 1951-52, asst. dir. tech. placement, Pitts., 1952-53, mgr. coll. recuiting and dir. tech. placement, Pitts., 1953-55, advt. mgr., 1955-59, gen. mgr. advt. and promotion, Pitts., 1959, mgr. trade relations, 1965-70, v.p. customer devel., 1970—. Bd. mgrs., v.p. Allegheny Cemetery, Pitts.; trustee Acad., Carnegie-Mellon U., Hunt Found.; hon. trustee Eye and Ear Hosp.; trustee, v.p., mem. exec. com. Western Pa. Hosp. Recipient Indsl. Advt. Man of Year award Indsl. Marketing, 1957. Mem. Pitts. Advt. Club (past pres.), Williams Alumni Assn. Western Pa. (past pres.), Pitts. Bibliophiles, Newcomen Soc. Am. Episcopalian (trustee). Clubs: Duquesne, Fox Chapel Golf, Pittsburgh Golf, Harvard-Yale-Princeton (Pitts.); Rolling Rock (Ligonier, Pa.); Williams, Anglers, St. Hubert's Soc., African Safari (N.Y.C.); Game Conservation Internat. (dir.) (San Antonio); Shikar-Safari Internat.; Safari Internat. Home: 5050 Amberson Pl Pittsburgh PA 15232 Office: Aluminum Co Am 1501 Alcoa Bldg Pittsburgh PA 15219

HUNTER, ALAN RICHARD, JR., printing co. exec.; b. Hartford, Conn., July 9, 1949; s. Alan Richard and Elna (Pfau) H.; B.S., Rochester Inst. Tech., 1971; postgrad. U. Hartford, 1972-78; m. Susan Jane Cavalier, May 15, 1971; children—Christopher, Karin. With Guilford Gravure Inc. (Conn.), 1971—, plant mgr., 1975-80, gen. mgr., 1980—. Mem. Clinton Jaycees (treas. 1980—). Republican. Christian Ch. Club: Lions. Home: 12 Bargate Rd Clinton CT 06413 Office: 251 Boston Post Rd Guilford CT 06437

HUNTER, ALLAN OAKLEY, lawyer, mortgage fin. exec.; b. Los Angeles, June 15, 1916; s. Henry Allan and Janet Sarah (Oakley) H.; A.B., Calif. State U., Fresno, 1937; J.D., U. Calif., Berkeley, 1940; m. Loberta Geene Taylor, Jan. 14, 1949; children—Genella Hunter Williamson, Janet Hunter Donini, John Henry, Allan Oakley. Admitted to Calif. bar; spl. agt. FBI, 1940-44; practice law, Calif., 1946-50; mem. U.S. Congress from 12th Calif. Dist., 1951-55; gen. counsel U.S. Housing and Home Fin. Agy., 1955-57; pvt. practice law, 1958-70; chmn. bd., pres. Fed. Nat. Mortgage Assn., Washington, 1970—. Mem. policy adv. bd. M.I.T./Harvard Joint Center for Urban Studies, 1971—; former chmn. Calif. Commn. Housing and Community Devel.; mem. Republican Nat. Com. Served with USNR, OSS, 1944-46; ETO. Mem. Lambda Alpha, Sigma Chi. Office: 3900 Wisconsin Ave NW Washington DC 20016

HUNTER, DANIEL GERARD, banker; b. Chgo., Aug. 3, 1943; s. Leo J. and Frances H.; B.S., No. Ill. U., 1968; M.B.A., U. Colo., 1970; m. Judith Wohoski, Oct. 21, 1967; children—Victoria Lynn, Daniel Brett. With Exchange Nat. Bank of Chgo., 1971-73, asst. v.p., 1973; v.p. United Bank of Denver, 1973-79; chmn. bd., chief exec. officer Dominion Bank of Denver, 1979—. Served with U.S. Army, 1968-70. Office: Dominion Bank of Denver 3251 Syracuse St Denver CO 80207

HUNTER, DEREK REX, ins. exec.; b. Salvage, Nfld., Can., Oct. 27, 1940; s. Thomas S. and Lily M. (Heffern) H.; m. Dorothy Christopher, Oct. 26, 1963; children—Sandra, Derek. Mtmg. trainee The Cooperatives, Toronto, Ont., Can., 1964-65, dist. asst. mgr., 1965-73, dist. mgr., 1973-77, regional mgr., 1977—. F.I.I.C., C.L.U., Can. Mem. Chartered Life Inst., Assn. Life Underwriters, Ins. Inst. Ont. (governing council), Ins. Inst. Can. Mem. Anglican Ch. of Can. Address: 387 Bloor St E Toronto ON M4W 1H8 Canada

HUNTER, E. ALLAN, electric co. exec.; b. Grantsville, Utah, May 27, 1914; s. James Austin and Francis (Fraser) H.; B.E.E., U. Utah, 1937; postgrad. U. Mich., 1955; m. Helen Spindler, July 12, 1941; children—Edward Allan, James Scott. With Utah Power & Light Co., Salt Lake City, 1937—, various positions including asst. to pres., comml. mgr., 1937-62, v.p., 1963-68, asst. gen. mgr., dir., v.p., 1966-68, pres., chief exec. officer, dir., 1969-79, chmn. bd., 1979; v.p. Western Colo. Power Co., 1966-69, pres., dir., 1969-74; dir. 1st Security Corp., ZCMI, Utah Bus. Devel. Corp.; mem. Utah Nuclear Energy Commn., 1970-73; mem. Utah Gov.'s Mineral Lease Fund Adv. Com.; mem. industry adv. com. Def. Electric Power Adminstrn., 1975-77; mem. electric utilities adv. com. FEA, 1975-77, mem. Western regional council, 1977-78. Mem. adv. council Weber State Coll. Bus. and Econs., 1967-71; trustee Utah Found.; mem. Gov.'s Council on Vets.' Issues; mem. adv. council Coll. Bus., Brigham Young U., 1969-71; campaign chmn., bd. dirs. Utah United Funds, 1968-69; mem. campaign adv. com. United Way, 1976; trustee, treas. Utah Blue Cross, 1969-74, High Temperature Reactor Devel. Assn., Inc., 1970-73; bd. advisers U. Utah Coll. Bus., 1975—; bd. dirs. Ballet West, 1969-74, Utah Symphony. Served from 1st lt. to maj. AUS, 1942-46; ETO. Decorated Bronze Star, Purple Heart; recipient citation Nat. Elec. Contractors Assn., 1974; registered profl. engr., Utah. Mem. NAM (past Utah dir.), Nat. Assn. Electric Cos. (dir. 1974-77), Salt Lake Area C. of C. (adv. council 1966-68, 1st v.p. 1970, pres. 1971-72), Nat. Soc. Profl. Engrs. (pres. local chpt. 1963-64, named Utah Outstanding Engr. in Industry 1968), Utah Mfrs. Assn. (dir. 1963-70, Mfr. of Year award 1971), West Assns. (pres. 1970-72), N.W. Electric Light and Power Assn. (dir. 1962-67, chmn. ann. meeting 1968), Edison Electric Inst. (com. on cost of money and taxes, policy com. on research; dir. 1974-77), Utah N.G. Hon. Cols. Assn., U. Utah Alumni Assn. (emeritus club 1978). Mem. Ch. Jesus Christ of Latter-day Saints. Clubs: Rotary, Alta, Timpanogos, Salt Lake Country. Home: 4234 Neptune Dr Salt Lake City UT 84117 Office: 1407 W North Temple St PO Box 899 Salt Lake City UT 84110

HUNTER, ELIZABETH IVES-VALSAM, financial analyst; b. Boston, Sept. 26, 1945; d. Theodore W.J. and Dorothea Alfreda (Sachs) Valsam; B.A. with honors, McGill U., 1967, postgrad., 1967-69; m. Robert Douglas Hunter, Oct. 12, 1968. Adminstrv. asst. to dir. Abbot Meml. Library, Emerson Coll., Boston, 1970-73; asst. examiner Fed. Res. Bank Boston, 1974-76, financial analyst, 1976-79; asst. treas. State St. Bank, Boston, 1979—. Altar Guild Diocese of Mass. Episcopal Ch., chmn. sewing, 1971-73, mem.-at-large, 1973-75; acting treas. Nat. Assn. Diocesan Altar Guilds, 1974-76, treas., 1976—; bd. dirs. charity fund com. Boston City Hosp., 1973-76; bd. dirs. 250 Beacon Condominium Assn., 1977—, pres., 1979—. Summer research fellow McGill U., 1968. Mem. Soc. Financial Examiners, Am. Bankers Assn. Clubs: Women's City (Boston); Norfolk Hunt (Dover, Mass.). Home: 250 Beacon St Boston MA 02116 Office: State St Bank & Trust 225 Franklin St Boston MA 02107

HUNTER, EMMETT MARSHALL, JR., oil co. exec.; b. Denver, Aug. 18, 1913; s. Emmett Marshall and Pearl Jo (Hubby) H.; LL.B., So. Methodist U., 1936; m. Marjorie Louise Roth, Nov. 21, 1941; children—Marsha Louise (Mrs. Leonard Blanchard), Marjorie Maddin, Margaret Anne. Admitted to Tex. bar, 1936; practiced law, Dallas, Longview and Houston, 1936-41; with Exxon Co. USA (formerly Humble Oil & Refining Co.), Tyler, Tex., 1945-78, exploration land supr., 1965-78; pres. Internat. Oil Investments, Tyler, 1978—. Served as lt. USNR, 1942-45. Mem. State Bar Tex., Am. Petroleum Inst., Bus.-Industry Polit. Action Com., E. Tex. C. of C., So. Meth. U. Alumni Assn., Hockaday Dads Club, U.S. Naval Inst., S.A.R. (pres. Tyler chpt., registrar Tex. soc., bd. mgrs.), Tyler Petroleum Club, Tex. Hist. Assn., Lambda Chi Alpha, Pi Upsilon Nu. Author: Adventuring Abroad on a Bicycle and $180, 1938; Marinas: A Boon to Yachting, 1948. Home: 2924 Sunnybrook Dr Tyler TX 75701 Office: PO Box 7402 Tyler TX 75711

HUNTER, FLOYD ROBERT, JR., hotel exec.; b. New Haven, Sept. 21, 1945; s. Floyd Robert and Florence May (Ennis) H.; A.S., Quinnipiac Coll., 1965, B.S., 1970; m. Carolee Martha Locarno, Oct. 7, 1967; children—Russell Miles, Floyd Robert III, Leslie Ann. Bus. mgr. Mountain View House, Whitefield, N.H., 1975-77; asst. mgr. Red Jacket Motor Inn, North Conway, N.H., 1977-78; gen. mgr. Linderhof Resort, Glen, N.H., 1978-79; mgr. Gov. Motor Inns, Plymouth, Mass., 1979-80; dir. sales Viking Hotel Corp., Newport, R.I., 1980—. Mem. N.H. Hospitality Assn., New Eng. Innkeepers Assn., Hotel Sales Mgmt. Assn., Meeting Planners Internat., Nat. Rifle Assn., Whitefield C. of C. (v.p. 1975-76), Alpha Chi Rho. Republican. Roman Catholic. Club: Elks. Home: Kearsarge Rd North Conway NH 03860 Office: 1 Bellevue Ave Newport RI 02840

HUNTER, GORDON COBLE, banker; b. nr. Greensboro, N.C., July 29, 1894; s. Samuel G. and Lalah Vance (Coble) H.; student U. N.C., 1915-17; m. Ethel Gray Wilson, Jan. 26, 1918; children—Rebecca Vance (Mrs. V. Paul Vittur), Rachel Gray (Mrs. George J. Cushwa). With Am. Exchange Nat. Bank, Greensboro, 1919-31; bank examiner

FDIC, 1933; exec. v.p. Peoples Bank, Roxboro, N.C., 1933-57, pres., 1957—, chmn. bd., 1960-69; chmn. bd. emeritus First Union Nat. Bank, Roxboro, 1976—; dir. Radio Sta. WRXO, Morris Telephone Co., Reinforced Plastic Container Corp., Roxboro Devel. Corp. Treas., bd. dirs., treas. Town of Roxboro, 1934-62; Person County chmn. ARC, 1937-38, Polio Fund, 1938—, U.S.O. Drive, 1943-44; N.C. chmn. Nat. Found. 4-H Club, 1955-57; an organizer, bd. dirs. Person County Meml. Hosp.; mem. N.C. Bd. Conservation and Devel.; vol. chmn. war bond sales for 10 counties, 1942-45. Served from pvt. to 2d lt. inf., U.S. Army, 1917-18. Named Citizen of Year, 1956; recipient certificate of appreciation for leadership in war savs. bonds sales from sec. of Treasury, Distinguished Service award U.S. Treasury, Outstanding Service recognition Roxboro Exchange Club, citation for 25 years service March of Dimes. Fellow Internat. Platform Assn.; mem. Am. (nat. research council 1955-57, exec. com. 1946-49, regional v.p. 1958-60, N.C. legislation com. 1960-62), N.C. (pres. 1945-46) bankers assns., Roxboro C. of C. (1st pres. 1935), Am. Legion (past comdr. Lester Blackwell post), 40 and 8, Order of Long Leaf Pine. Methodist (steward). Rotarian (past pres. Roxboro). Home: 115 Academy St Roxboro NC 27573 Office: 203 N Main St Roxboro NC 27573

HUNTER, LEE, automotive equipment mfg. co. exec., inventor; b. St. Louis, Apr. 27, 1913; s. Lee and Ollie (Stark) H.; ed. Westminster Coll., Fulton, Mo., Washington U., St. Louis; m. Jane Franklin Brauer, 1959; stepchildren—Arthur J. Brauer, Stephen F. Brauer. Draftsman, designer Herman Body Co., 1935-36; founder Lee Hunter Jr. Mfg. Co., 1936; pres. Hunter-Hartman Corp., 1937-42; pres. Hunter Engrng. Co., Bridgeton, Mo., 1947-55, chmn. bd., chief exec. officer, 1955—; pres. Hunter Aviation Co., 1955-60; counsul of Belgium, 1977—; adv. dir. St. Louis County Nat. Bank, County Nat. Bancorp. Bd. dirs. Jr. Achievement, YMCA, Webster Coll., Webster Groves, Mo.; trustee Westminster Coll., Fulton, Mo. Served to 1st lt. C.E., AUS, 1942-46. Recipient Alumni Achievement award Westminster Coll., 1972. Mem. Mo. C. of C., Phi Delta Theta. Presbyn. (trustee). Clubs: Le Mirador (Switzerland; Racquet, St. Louis, Bellerive Country, Engrs. (St. Louis). Inventor: 1st rapid battery chargers; dynamic lever theory balancing; 1st on car mech. wheel balancer; 1st discharged battery analyzer; wheel alignment, automotive equipment. Home: Hunter Farms 13501 Ladue Rd Saint Louis County MO 63141 Office: Hunter Engrng Co 11250 Hunter Dr Bridgeton MO 63044

HUNTER, MORGAN VICTOR, paper co. exec.; b. Elk City, Okla., Mar. 18, 1929; s. Victor Earl and Esther (Gunter) H.; B.A. in Journalism, U. Okla., 1953; m. Martha Candell, Oct. 2, 1954; children—David C., Elizabeth G., Susan J. Advt. account supr. Gen. Elec. Co., Schnectady, N.Y., 1953-57; corp. v.p. coffee div. Procter & Gamble, Cin., 1957-75; sr. v.p. Am. Cyanamid Co., Wayne, N.J., 1975-77; pres. R.J. Reynolds Tobacco Co., Winston-Salem, N.C.,1977-79; pres., chief operating officer Scott Paper Co., Phila., 1979—. Served with inf., AUS, 1950-52. Decorated Bronze Star. Office: Scott Plaza I Philadelphia PA 19113

HUNTER, RICHARD WALTER, credit union exec.; b. Chgo., Oct. 21, 1929; s. Howard Walter and Eve Lynn (McKinstry) H.; student pub. schs., Long Beach, Calif.; m. Mary Kathleen Schindorff, Apr. 9, 1955; children—Richard Brent, Frank Clifford. Asst. mgr. Term Plan Fin. Co., Los Angeles, 1955-58; credit mgr. Star Brite Sales Co., Los Angeles, 1958-60; asst. br. mgr. Borg Warner Acceptance Corp., Phoenix, 1960-61; br. mgr. Securities Investment Co., St. Louis and Phoenix, 1961-63; gen. mgr. Motorola Credit Union of Ariz., Phoenix, 1963-73; gen. mgr. Co-op Center Fed. Credit Union, Berkeley, Calif., 1973-75, Salt River Project Fed. Credit Union, Phoenix, 1975—. Mem. Credit Union Execs. Soc. Home: PO Box 431 Mesa AZ 85201 Office: 1511 Project Dr Tempe AZ 85001

HUNTER, TERRY L., human resources systems consulting co. exec.; b. Easton, Md., Oct. 12, 1946; s. Zebulon and Jayne Landon (Parks) H.; children—Greggory Lee, Shannan Michelle. Computer technician Nat. Security Agency, Ft. George G. Meade, Md., 1964-65; systems analyst Alexander & Alexander, Inc., Balt., 1965-67; systems and programming mgr. Benefacts Inc., Balt., 1967-70, cons., 1970-77, v.p., 1977—, dir. ops., 1977-80, div. mgr., 1980—. Served with Army N.G., 1965-71. Mem. Data Processing Mgmt. Assn. Home: 14 Treeway Ct Towson MD 21204 Office: 300 E Joppa Rd Baltimore MD 21204

HUNTER, WILLIAM JAMES, dept. store exec.; b. Phila., Dec. 22, 1940; s. Joseph Gibson and Frances Brooks (Bicking) H.; B.A., Pierce Sch. Bus. Adminstrn., 1961; m. Jan Allison Bocook, Apr. 29, 1978; children—William James, Joseph Gibson. Trainee, Strawbridge & Co., Phila., 1961; buyer Maas Bros., Inc., 1961-73; sales rep. Robert J. Bailey Co., Atlanta, Pinellas County United Way; mem. Republican Exec. Com. Pinellas County; mem. distributive edn. adv. com. Orange County Public Schs. Recipient Sears Roebuck Found. award in distributive edn., 1958. Mem. Clearwater Mall Mchts. Assn. (pres. 1977-79), Winter Park Mall Mchts. Assn. (past treas.), Clearwater C. of C. (mchts. com., govt. affairs com.), Winter Park C. of C. (chmn. retail affairs), Maitland-South Seminole C. of C. (edn. com.), Fla. Conservative Union (dir.). Republican. Lutheran. Clubs: Tides Bath (Redington Beach); Pinellas County Men's Republican (treas.), Gulf Beach-Seminole Republican (founding pres.). Office: PO Box 5705 Clearwater FL 33518

HUNTER, WILMONT LENNINGTON, computer scientist; b. Chgo., July 23, 1927; s. Howard Walter and Eve Lynn (McKinstry) H.; B.S. in Elec. Engring., U. So. Calif., 1959; m. Gloria Catherine Swanson, Feb. 20, 1961; 1 son, Brian John. Elec. engr. Hoffman Labs., Los Angeles, 1953-55, Lockheed MSD, Van Nuys, Calif., 1955-57; engrng. specialist Litton Industries, Van Nuys, 1957-67; electronics engr. Interstate Electronics Corp., Anaheim, Calif., 1967-70; mem. tech. staff Rockwell Internat. Co., Los Angeles, 1971-73; sr. devel. engr. Honeywell, Inc., Seattle and West Covina, Calif., 1973-75; mem. tech. staff Tex. Instruments Inc., Dallas, 1975-78; specialist engr. Boeing Co., Seattle, 1978—. Served with USNR, 1944-46. Decorated Commendation medal. Mem. Assn. Computing Machinery, Mensa, Eta Kappa Nu. Mem. Libertarian Ch. Author, patentee in field. Home: 101 N 46th St Seattle WA 98103 Office: Boeing Co PO Box 3999 Seattle WA 98124

HUNTINGTON, EARL L., natural resources co. exec.; b. Orangeville, Utah, Sept. 2, 1929; s. Llyod S. and Hannah Annette (Cox) H.; grad. U. Utah, 1951, J.D., 1956; LL.M., Georgetown U., 1959; m. Phyllis Ann Reed; children—Jane, Ann, Stephen. Admitted to Utah, N.Y., D.C. bars; trial atty. Dept. Justice, Washington, 1956-63; counsel Texasgulf, Inc., N.Y.C., 1963-74, v.p., gen. counsel, 1974—, also dir. Texasgulf Canada Ltd. Served with U.S. Army, 1951-53. Mem. Am., Utah bar assns., Assn. Bar City N.Y., Order of Coif, Phi Kappa Phi, Beta Gamma Sigma. Home: 1 Maywood Ct Darien CT 06820 Office: High Ridge Park Stamford CT 06904

HUNTZINGER, HOMER G., real estate broker-developer; b. Flagler, Colo., Sept. 9, 1923; s. Sidney V. and Gerda (Brandenburg) H.; master mechanics certificate, Aero Inds. Tech. Inst., 1942; m. Helen J. Harvell, Apr. 8, 1951 (div. 1962); children—Gregory, Ronald, Martin; m. 2d, Rosemary Russell Look, Dec. 15, 1973 (div. 1976). Aircraft mechanic T.W.A., Kansas City, Mo., 1942-44; farmer, rancher, Flagler, Colo., 1944-51; oil operator Oil Ventures, Inc., Denver, 1951-62; purchasing agt., office mgr. Wellington Mine Assn., Breckenridge, Colo., 1962-64 oil operator, Denver, 1964-66; sec., gen. mgr. Pan-Ark Land and Cattle Corp., Denver, 1966—; sec., sales mgr. W-H Land Corp., Denver; developer, real estate broker, owner Pan-Ark Land Co., Denver, 1970—. Elk. Home and office: PO Box 285 Leadville CO 80461

HURABIELL, JOHN PHILIP, ins. co. exec.; b. San Francisco, June 2, 1947; s. Emile John and Anne Beatrice (Blumenauer) H.; student U. San Francisco, 1965-66, 69-71; J.D., San Francisco Law Sch., 1976; postgrad. Golden Gate U., 1978—; m. Judith Marie Worner, June 7, 1969; children—Marie Louise, Michele Anne, Heather Ann. Salesman, Provident Mut. Life Ins. Co., San Francisco, 1968-70; salesman Bankers Life Ins. Co., San Francisco, 1971—; admitted to Calif. bar, 1976, since practiced law, San Francisco; chief fin. officer Direct Mail Mktg. Services, Inc.; v.p., gen. counsel Eu-Mar Corp., Lee-Mil, Inc., Partitions By Design Corp.; estate planning cons., 1976—. Fund raiser for various Republican candidates, 1968-75; bd. dirs. San Francisco SAFE. Served with USN, 1966-68. Mem. Am. (coms.), Calif., San Francisco bar assns., San Francisco Trial Lawyers Assn., San Francisco Life Underwriters Assn. (pres. 1980-81), Nat. (quality awards), Calif. (chmn. ethics com.) assns. life underwriters, Am. Orchid Soc., Nat. Rifle Assn. (endowment mem.), St. Thomas Moore Soc., San Francisco Barristers Club. Republican. Roman Catholic. Club: K.C. (dist. dep.). Editor: State Business Practices Guidelines. Home: 1958 18th Ave San Francisco CA 94116 Office: Suite 1000 505 Sansome St San Francisco CA 94111

HURD, PATRICK JAY, indsl. hygienist; b. Covington, Ky., May 11, 1953; s. Stanley Charles and Willetta Olivia (McEndre) H.; B.S. (Am. Field Service scholar), U. Cin., 1975, postgrad., 1975-76; m. Elizabeth Forton, Aug. 21, 1976; 1 son, Matthew Bryan. Corp. indsl. hygienist The Sherwin-Williams Co., Cleve., 1976-77; indsl. hygienist Nat. Paint and Coatings Assn., Inc., Washington, 1977—; cons. OSHA, 1979—. Mem. Am. Indsl. Hygiene Assn., Am. Coll. Toxicology, Am. Public Health Assn., U.S. Jaycees, Omicron Delta Kappa. Republican. Home: 8943 Rolling Rd Manassas VA 22110 Office: 1500 Rhode Island Ave Washington DC 20005

HURD, RICHARD NELSON, pharm. co. exec.; b. Evanston, Ill., Feb. 25, 1926; s. Charles DeWitt and Mary Ormsby (Nelson) H.; B.S., U. Mich., 1946; Ph.D., U. Minn., 1956; m. Jocelyn Fillmore Martin, Dec. 22, 1950; children—Melanie Gray, Suzanne DeWitt. Chemist, Gen. Electric Co., Schenectady, 1948-49; research and devel. group leader Koppers Co., Pitts., 1956-57; research chemist Mallinckrodt Chem. Works, St. Louis, 1956-63, group leader, 1963-66; group leader Comml. Solvents Corp., Terre Haute, Ind., 1966-68, sect. head, 1968-71; mgr. sci. affairs G. D. Searle Internat. Co., Skokie, Ill., 1972-73, dir. mfg. and tech. affairs, 1973-77, rep. to internat. tech. com. Pharm. Mfrs. Assn., 1973-77; v.p. tech. affairs Elder Pharms., Bryan, Ohio, 1977—. Mem. Ferguson-Florissant (Mo.) Sch. Bd., 1964-66; bd. dirs. United Fund of Wabash Valley (Ind.), 1969-71. Served with USN, 1943-46, 53-55. E. I. DuPont de Nemours & Co., Inc. fellow, 1956. Mem. Am. Acad. Dermatology, Am. Chem. Soc., N.Y. Acad. Sci., AAAS, Sigma Xi. Presbyterian. Clubs: Mich. Shores (Wilmette, Ill.); Pine Valley (Ft. Wayne, Ind.). Patentee in field; contbr. articles to profl. jours. Home: 1537 Ransom Dr Fort Wayne IN 46825 Office: 705 E Mulberry St Bryan OH 43506

HURD, WALTER LEROY, JR., aerospace co. exec.; b. Columbus, Mont., July 8, 1919; s. Walter Leroy and Mary Gibbon H.; B.A., Morningside Coll., 1940; M.A., San Jose State U., 1977; m. Ann Vivian Cornell, Sept. 26, 1941; children—David, Caroline, Drew, Bruce, Kevin. Pilot, v.p., gen. ops. mgr. Philippine Air Lines, Manila, Honolulu, 1946-54; quality control mgr. Nat. Motor Bearing, Inc., Redwood City, Calif., 1954-58; with Lockheed Missile and Space Co., Sunnyvale, Calif., 1958-77, product assurance mgr., 1967-77; corp. dir. product assurance Lockheed Corp., Burbank, Calif., 1977—. Served with USAAF, 1941-46; brig. gen. Res. Decorated D.F.C. with 2 oak leaf clusters, Air medal with 3 oak leaf clusters; registered profl. engr., Calif. Fellow Am. Soc. Quality Control (nat. pres. 1977-78, E.L. Grant award 1971, B.L. Lubelsky award 1971); mem. Philippine Soc. Quality Control (hon.), Australian Orgn. Quality Control (hon.), European Orgn. Quality Control (hon.), Nat. Space Inst. (charter, life), AIAA, Am. Astron. Soc. (sr.), New Zealand Orgn. Quality Control (hon.), Nat. Soc. Profl. Engrs. Office: Lockheed Corp PO Box 551 Burbank CA 91520

HURLBERT, GORDON C., corp. exec.; b. Raymond, S.D., 1924; B.M.E., Marquette U., 1946; M.B.A., Harvard U., 1955; married. With Westinghouse Electric Corp., 1946—, gen. mgr. distbn. transformer div., 1955-62, gen. mgr. power transformation div., 1962-67, v.p. mfg., 1967-69, exec. v.p. power generation, 1969-74, pres. Power Systems Co. subs., Pitts., 1974—. Served to lt. (j.g.), USN, 1944-46. Office: Westinghouse Electric Corp Westinghouse Bldg Gateway Center Pittsburgh PA 15222*

HURLBURT, JOHN BYRON, mfg. co. exec.; b. Ossining, N.Y., June 12, 1943; s. James Parker and Dorothy Lillian (Hosford) H.; student Schenectady County (N.Y.) Community Coll., 1972, U. Md., 1977; m. Apiradee Hurlburt; 1 dau., Catherina Lynsey. Relief man Fisher Body div. Gen. Motors, Tarrytown, N.Y., 1962-68; owner, mgr. Loam Trucking Co., Ossining and Schenectady, N.Y., 1968-73; salesman Syracuse Safety Lites Inc., Mechanicville, N.Y., 1973-76; ter. mgr. sales Champion Parts Rebuilders, Oak Brook, Ill., 1976—. Mem. Va. Automotive Wholesalers Assn., Chesapeake Automotive Wholesalers Assn. (bd. dirs. fed. credit union), Chesapeake Automotive Boosters Club B-17 (organizer, pres.), Automotive Service Industry Assn. Republican. Home: 14377 Berkshire Dr Woodbridge VA 22193

HURLBUT, ROBERT HAROLD, health care services exec.; b. Rochester, N.Y., Mar. 9, 1935; s. Harold Leroy and Martha Irene (Fincher) H.; student Coll. Hotel Adminstrn. Cornell U., 1953-56; m. Barbara Cox, June 14, 1958; children—Robert W., Christine A. Adminstr., dir. Pillars Nursing Home, Rochester, 1956—, Elmcrest Nursing Home, Churchville, N.Y., 1960—, Elm Manor Nursing Home, Canandaigua, N.Y., 1960—, Penfield Nursing Home, Rochester, 1963—, Avon (N.Y.) Nursing Home, 1964—, Newark (N.Y.) Nursing Home, 1965—, Lakeshore Nursing Home, Rochester, 1972—, others; organizer, adminstrv. dir. Rohm Services Corp., hdqrs. Rochester, 1964— organizer, pres. Vari-Care, Inc., hdqrs. Rochester, 1969—. Mem. N.Y. State Assn. Long Term Care Adminstrs., Am. Coll. Nursing Home Adminstrs., Rochester C. of C., Lambda Chi Alpha. Clubs: Oak Hill, Cornell (Rochester). Home: 11 Crestview Dr Pittsford NY 14534 Office: 277 Alexander St Rochester NY 14607

HURLBUT, ROY BROWN, bus. exec.; b. Habana, Cuba, Oct. 23, 1927; s. Roy Cole and Emma Lou (Brown) H. (parents Am. citizens); B.S., Heald Coll., 1962; M.B.A., U. San Francisco, 1968; m. Candis Carol Smyk, July 16, 1967; 1 dau. by previous marriage, Ellayne Margaret. Asst. engr. Pacific Gas & Electric Co., San Francisco, 1949-66, forecast engr., 1970-71; systems planning engr. Lockheed Missile & Space Co., Sunnyvale, Calif., 1966-68; sr. budget analyst U. Calif., Berkeley, 1968-69; utility engr., pub. utility commr. State of Oreg., Salem, 1972-74; sr. coordinator, cost and scheduling Alyeska Pipeline Service Co., Kenmore, Wash., 1975-77; sr. cost engr. Alyeska Pipeline Service Co., Anchorage, 1977-78; sr. ops. analytical engr. Atlantic Richfield Co., Anchorage, 1978-80; commr. Anchorage Mcpl. Light & Power, 1980; N.W. power mgr. Anaconda Industries, Vancouver, Wash., 1980—. Mem. Nat. Assn. Bus. Economists, IEEE. Clubs: Masons (32 deg.), Shriners. Home: 13500 SE 161 Pl Renton WA 98055 Office: PO Box 61493 Vancouver WA 98666

HURLEY, FRANK THOMAS, JR., realtor; b. Washington, Oct. 18, 1924; s. Frank Thomas and Lucille (Trent) H.; A.A., St. Petersburg Jr. Coll., 1948; B.A., U. Fla., 1950. Reporter St. Petersburg (Fla.) Evening Independent, 1948-53; editor Arcadia (Calif.) Tribune, 1956-57; reporter Los Angeles Herald Express, 1957; v.p. Frank T. Hurley Assos., Inc. realtors, 1958-64, pres., 1964—; sec., dir. Beau Monde, Inc., 1977-79. Elected St. Petersburg Beach Bd. Commrs., 1965-69; candidate Fla. Ho. of Reps., 1966; chmn. Pinellas County Traffic Safety Council, 1968-69; pres. Pass-A-Grille Community Assn., 1963, Gulf Beach Bd. Realtors, 1969; mem. St. Petersburg Mus. Fine Arts; bd. govs. Palms of Pasadena Hosp., 1979—. Served with USAAF, 1943-46. Mem. Fla. Assn. Realtors (dir., dist. v.p. 1971), St. Petersburg Beach C. of C. (dir., pres. 1975-76), Vina del Mar Island Assn., Am. Legion, Sigma Delta Chi, Sigma Tau Delta. Author: Surf, Sand and Post Card Sunsets, 1977. Home: 2808 Sunset Way Saint Petersburg Beach FL 33706 Office: 2506 Pass-A-Grille Way Saint Petersburg Beach FL 33706

HURLEY, JAMES WILLIAM, corp. exec.; b. St. Cloud, Minn., July 4, 1939; s. James Warren and Margaret Caroline (Kapphahn) H.; B.S., So. Ill. U., 1967; M.B.A., Northwestern U., 1974; m. Kathleen Ann Krol, Aug. 26, 1978. Sr. auditor Arthur Andersen & Co., Chgo., 1968-72; mgr. taxes Oak Industries, Inc., Crystal Lake, Ill., 1972-74; asst. treas. Trans Union Corp., Lincolnshire, Ill., 1974—. C.P.A., Ill. Mem. Am. Inst. C.P.A.'s, Ill. Soc. C.P.A.'s, Am. Acctg. Assn. Home: 3100 Scotch Ln Riverwood IL 60015 Office: 90 Half Day Rd Lincolnshire IL 60015

HURLEY, JOHN WILLIAM, investment banker; b. Akron, Ohio, June 6, 1925; s. Robert Richard and Veronica A. (Glose) H.; B.S., Lehigh U., 1948; M.B.A., N.Y. U., 1951; m. Joan Marie Young, July 2, 1949; children—Mary, Elizabeth, Kathleen, John, James, Joan. Vice-pres. P.W. Brooks, Inc., N.Y.C., 1961-66; v.p. Blair Co., Inc., N.Y.C., 1966-70; v.p. W.E. Hutton Co., N.Y.C., 1970-74; v.p. Dean Witter Reynolds Securities, N.Y.C., 1974-79; mng. dir. corp. fin. Thomson McKinnon Securities Inc., N.Y.C., 1979—; dir. Foodarama Supermarkets, Inc., Tri-Chem, Inc. Served with U.S. Army, 1943-45. Decorated Purple Heart. Mem. N.Y. Soc. Security Analysts. Club: Downtown Athletic. Office: 1 New York Plaza New York NY 10004

HURLEY, PAUL EDWARD, rubber bur. exec.; b. Boston, Aug. 9, 1928; s. Joseph F. and Pauline M. (Dittler) H.; B.S. in Chemistry, Boston Coll., 1951; m. Rae E. Zoli, Apr. 26, 1958; children—Brian E., Dennis D., Paula J. Developer chem. sales Naugatuck (Conn.) Chem. div. Uniroyal Corp., 1951-61; rubber and chem. salesman Firestone Synthetic Rubber & Latex Co. div. Firestone Tire & Rubber Co., Fall River, Mass., 1961-66; pres., dir. tech. adv. service Malaysian Rubber Bur., Washington, 1966—; speaker on natural rubber and latex, 1966—. Served with U.S. Army, 1954-56. Mem. Am. Chem. Soc. (rubber div.), ASTM, Adhesive and Sealant Council, So. Rubber Group, Boston Rubber Group. R.I. Rubber Group, Conn. Rubber Group, N.Y. Rubber Group, Phila. Rubber Group, Washington Rubber Group, Akron Rubber Group. Roman Catholic. Club: Westwood Country. Contbr. numerous articles on hist., prodn. and tech. aspects of natural rubber and latex to profl. publs. Home: 6815 Melrose Dr McLean VA 22101 Office: 1925 K St NW Washington DC 20006

HURLEY, THOMAS PATRICK, JR., laser beam engraving co. exec.; b. Upper Darby, Pa., July 3, 1934; s. Thomas P. and Louise C. (Culhane) H.; B.S., Villanova U., 1956; student St. Joseph's Coll., 1955; postgrad. N.Y. U., 1968, U. Wis., 1976; m. Lois B. Feldstein, July 16, 1973. Accountant, Bryn Mawr (Pa.) Hosp., 1953-56; in sales Burroughs Corp., Phila., 1956-57, Terry Phone Sales, Pitts., 1959; with Hallmark Cards, Kansas City, Mo., 1960-78; exec. v.p. Lasermation, Phila., 1978-80, exec. v.p., mktg. cons., Englewood Cliffs, N.J., 1980—; cons. Hallmark Cards. Bd. dirs. Advt. Specialty Inst. Served with U.S. Army, 1957-59. Mem. Specialty Advt. Assn., Spl. Advt. Counselors Delaware Valley. Clubs: Premium Mdse. (bd. dirs.); National Premium Sales; Palisades Yacht (trustee 1979—).

HURT, ALLIE TEAGUE, real estate exec.; b. Celina, Tex., 1923; d. Lucious T. and Mary Lee (Whitley) Teague; student El Centro Jr. Coll., 1967-68; B.S., Bishop Coll., 1973; postgrad. N. Tex. State U., 1973-74. Sec., Excelsior Life Ins., Dallas, 1953-56; ins. agt. Universal Life Ins., Dallas, 1957-58; mgr. Pruitt Ins. Agy., Dallas, 1960-65; soc. editor Dallas Express Newspaper, 1973-75; substitute tchr. Dallas Ind. Sch. Dist., 1967-78; real estate sales agt., 1967-72, 75—; owner, mgr., broker Allie T. Hurt Real Estate Co., 1978-79; area mgr. Beeline Fashions Party Plan, Chgo.; pianist various chs., 1959-69; chatelaine, instr. Eta Phi Beta, Dallas, 1978-79. Recipient Cert. of Recognition award Eta Phi Beta, 1978; Cert of Recognition, Iota Phi Lambda, 1979. Mem. Eta Phi Beta, NAACP, Bishop Coll. Alumni Assn. Baptist. Clubs: Rosicrucian Order, P.U.S.H. Home: 5324 Mystic Trail Dallas TX 75241

HURT, HARMON CURVIN, JR., stock broker; b. Dayton, Ohio, Mar. 22, 1949; s. Harmon C. and Evelyn E. (Yaus) H.; B.A., Ohio No. U., 1971; M.B.A., Wright State U., 1973. Financial analyst div. securities Ohio Dept. Commerce, Columbus, 1973-75; account exec. Merrill Lynch, Pierce, Fenner & Smith, Columbus, 1975-77, Oppenheimer & Co., Chgo., 1977-79; stock broker, Chgo., 1979—; lectr. in field. Home: 6010 Oakwood Dr Apt 2B Lisle IL 60532 Office: 7th Floor Three Illinois Center 303 E Wacker Dr Chicago IL 60601

HURT, IKEY WEST, printing co. exec.; b. Mayfield, Ky., Nov. 18, 1928; s. John Bryan and Lula Belle (Harrell) H.; B.S. in Edn. cum laude, Union Coll., 1951; m. Mary Elizabeth French, Nov. 10, 1951; children—Susan, David, John. Statistician, Fawcett-Dearing Printing Co., Louisville, 1953-58, chief estimator, 1958-62, dept. head estimating and billing, 1962-65; asst. gen. mgr. Fawcett-Haynes Printing Co., Louisville, 1965-68; exec. v.p., chief exec. officer, dir. Fawcett Printing Co., Rockville, Md., 1968—. Served with U.S. Army, 1951-53. Mem. Metropolitan Washington Bd. Trade, Am. Inst. Mgmt., U. Md. Terrapin Club, Rockville C. of C., Montgomery County C. of C., Admirals Club, Georgetown Club. Methodist. Club: Congressional Country. Home: 11310 Hounds Way Rockville MD 20852 Office: 1900 Chapman Ave Rockville MD 20852

HURT, ROBERT GLENN, investment banker; b. Pasadena, Calif., Jan. 31, 1919; s. Leslie Milton and Effie Mae (McKim) H.; A.B., U. So. Calif., 1940; postgrad. Harvard, 1941. With sales dept. Calvin Bullock, Ltd., N.Y.C. and Los Angeles, 1946-50, No. Calif. mgr., San Francisco, 1950-65, West Coast mgr., San Francisco, 1965-66, v.p., then sr. v.p. Western U.S., San Francisco, 1967—. Served from pvt. to lt. col., AUS, 1941-46. Mem. San Francisco Stock Exchange Club, Los Angeles Stock Exchange Club, Am. Legion, Mil. Order World Wars (past comdr. San Francisco chpt.). Clubs: Commonwealth (San Francisco); Andreas Canyon (Palm Springs, Calif.). Home: 937

Ashbury St San Francisco CA 94117 Office: 931 The Mills Bldg 220 Montgomery St San Francisco CA 94104

HUSBAND, RICHARD LORIN, SR., bus. exec.; b. Spencer, Iowa, July 28, 1931; s. Ross Twetten and Frances Estelle (Hall) H.; A.A., Rochester State Community Coll., 1953; arts degree U. Minn., 1954; m. Darlene Joyce Granberg, 1954; children—Richard Lorin, Thomas Ross and Mark Thurston (twins), Julia Lynn, Susan Elizabeth. Pres., Orlen Ross Inc., Rochester, Minn., 1962—; partner The Gallery, European antiques, china, gifts, Rochester, 1968—, Millenium III, home furnishings, Rochester, 1975—. Active Episcopal Diocese of Minn., 1951-52, 58—, nat. dept., 1969-73, alt. dept., 1973-75; trustee Seabury Western Theol. Sem., 1975—, exec. com., 1976—; founder Rochester Arts Council, Rochester PTA Community Coll. Scholarship Program, H.D. Mayo Meml. Lecture in Theology, others; pres. Olmsted County (Minn.) Hist. Soc., 1976-77; bd. dirs. Rochester Symphony Orch., Choral, Opera, 1970-78, pres., 1974-75; del. Olmsted County Republican Party, 1974—. Recipient Disting. Service award Rochester Jaycees, 1965, Fifty Mem. award YMCA, 1968, award for Minn. Bicentennial, Gov. Minn., 1976; named 1 of Minn's, 10 Outstanding Young Men, Minn. Jaycees, 1966. Mem. Minn. Home Furnishings Assn. (pres. 1976-79, trustee 1968—), First Dist. Hist. Assembly Minn. (pres. 1969-71), Minn. Retail Fedn. (trustee 1972—), Olmsted County Archeology Soc. (founder), Rochester Civil War Roundtable (founder), Rochester Revolutionary War Roundtable (founder), Rochester Arts Council (founder), Am., Nat. (charter), Minn., Norwegian/Am. hist. socs., Minn. Archeology Soc., Am. Assn. State and Local History, U. Minn. Alumni Assn., U. Minn. Alumni Club (charter) Rochester C. of C., Alpha Delta Phi Alumni Assn., Soc. Mayflower Descs. (trustee Minn.), SAR (Minn. pres.), Descs. Colonial Clergy, Sons Union Vets of Civil War, Minn. Territorial Pioneers (trustee 1978—, 1st v.p. 1979—), Soc. Archtl. Historians. Clubs: Rotary (historian) (Rochester); Sertoma (Austin) (founder). Public speaker. Home: 1820 26th St NW Rochester MN 55901 Office: Orlen Ross Inc 105 N Broadway Rochester MN 55901

HUSKA, PAUL ANTHONY, mineral processing co. exec.; b. Torrington, Conn., Sept. 9, 1935; s. Paul and Irene (Zurick) H.; B.S. in Chem. Engring., Lehigh U., 1958; M.S. in Chem. Engring., 1963, Ph.D. (Esso fellow), 1965; m. Patricia Ann Davco, Feb. 1, 1958; children—Jeffrey, Jennifer. Supr. process studies group Fuller Co., Catasauqua, Pa., 1958-64, mgr. conceptual and project engring. dept., Bethlehem, Pa., 1977—; mem. staff Arthur D. Little, Inc., Cambridge, Mass., 1965-77. Mem. Am. Inst. Chem. Engrs. Home: 1318 Prospect Ave Bethlehem PA 18018 Office: 2040 Ave C Bethlehem PA 18017

HUSS, CHARLES MAURICE, bldg. co. exec.; b. Chgo., Nov. 11, 1946; s. Charles Maurice and June Pierce (Bailey) H.; A.A., Kendall Coll., 1979; m. Winifred Louise Traughber, Dec. 24, 1973; children—Amber Elaine, Ra Ja Lorraine, Micah Alexander, Gabriel Joe, Cameron M. Traffic mgr. The Harwald Co., Evanston, Ill., 1966-67, asst. v.p., 1968-69; traffic mgr. Northwestern U. Press, Evanston, 1969-71; fire chief City of Kotzebue (Alaska), 1971-76, asst. city mgr., 1973-76; dir. maintenance USPHS Hosp., Kotzebue, 1976-79; pres., gen. mgr. Action Builders, Inc., Kotzebue, 1979—. Chmn., Kotzebue Planning Commn., 1978—, Kotzebue Sch. Bd., 1974-79; founding chmn. Kotzebue chpt. ARC; mem. Alaska Criminal Code Revision Commn., 1976-78; mem. Alaska Fire Fighter Tng. Commn. Pullman Found. scholar, 1964-65; Blackburn Coll. scholar, 1964-65; Ill. State scholar, 1964-66. Mem. Constrn. Specifications Inst., Soc. Fire Service Instrs., Alaska Firefighters Assn., Internat. Assn. Fire Chiefs, Home Builders Assn. Alaska, Kotzebue C. of C. Guest essayist: Seven Days and Sunday (Kirkpatrick), 1973. Home and Office: PO Box 277 Kotzebue AK 99752

HUSS, JOHN DAVID, mgmt. co. exec.; b. Covington, Ky., Sept. 1, 1936; s. John Ervin and Viola May (Parker) H.; A.B. in Polit. Sci., Duke U., 1958, A.M. in Polit. Sci. (Univ. fellow), 1960; fellow UCLA, 1959-60; postgrad., George Washington U., 1963-64; m. Janet Patricia Barbour, Dec. 20, 1960. Staff asst. to U.S. Senator Olin D. Johnston, 1956-59; program analyst HEW, Washington, 1961-65; div. dir., sr. mgmt. analyst HUD, Washington, 1965-71; sr. cons. Auerbach Assos., Inc., Arlington, Va. and Phila., 1971-74; Wash. v.p., Ronald Fine & Assos., Inc., Mpls., 1974-75; sec.-treas. D.A. Lewis Assos., Inc., Clinton, Md., 1975-78; pres. Creative Mgmt. Concepts, Inc., Potomac, Md., and New Hope, Pa., 1979—, Fin. Stress & Public Mgmt. Project, Potomac, 1979—. Served with U.S. Army, 1960. Mem. Am. Soc. Public Adminstrn., World Future Soc., Internat. Entrepreneurs Assn. Democrat. Home: 58 W Mechanic St New Hope PA 18938 Office: 205 Semmes Bldg 10220 River Rd Potomac MD 20854

HUSTON, PRESTON DELMAR, advt. exec.; b. Newton, Kans., July 17, 1925; s. Jesse Lester and Ina Vera (Van Huss) H.; B.A., Wichita State U., 1949; m. Barbara Ann Tressler, Oct. 15, 1948; children—Kathryn Delaine, Karen Diane Hubbard, Donna Kay Walker. With Associated Advt. Agy., Inc., Wichita, Kans., 1946-75, prodn. mgr., media buyer, 1948-52, account exec., 1952-53, exec. v.p., 1953-57, pres., 1957-75, chmn., 1977—; v.p. corporate mktg. Hesston Corp., 1975-77. Served with Armed Forces, 1943-46, 51-52; ETO, Korea. Decorated Bronze Star medal. Named Wichita Advt. Man of Year 1958, Advt. Man of Year Am. Advt. Fedn., 1974. Mem. Nat. Fedn. Advt. Agys. (pres. 1963, Mace award), Wichita C. of C. Baptist (deacon, trustee). Rotarian. Clubs: Wichita, Crestview Country. Home: 22 Colonial Ct Wichita KS 67207 Office: Associated Advertising Agency Wichita KS 67218

HUSTON, THOMAS HAL, state ofcl., bank exec.; b. Washington, Iowa, Nov. 9, 1929; s. Harold Lee and Juanita Charlotte (Prizer) H.; B.S. in Farm Ops., Iowa State U., 1951; m. Maryan McDermott, June 16, 1951; m. 2d, Alice Leutner Rowland, Aug. 6, 1966; children—Susan Huston Garman, Mark, John; stepchildren—Dean Rowland, Sarah Rowland Wells. Pvt. practice farming, Columbus Junction, Iowa, 1953-57; mem. faculty Govt. Agr. Sch., Mt. Pleasant, Iowa, 1955-59; with Columbus Junction State Bank, 1958—, pres., 1970—, also dir.; supt. banking State of Iowa, 1975—; dir. SBA, 1970; treas. Iowa State Fair, 1974-75. Pres. Louisa County (Iowa) Comml. Devel. Corp., 1961—; bd. dirs. Louisa County Fair, 1964-75; pres. Louisa County ARC, 1969-70; chmn. Louisa County Cancer Crusade, 1969-71; mem. Columbus (Iowa) Community Sch. Bd., 1973-76. Served with USAF, 1951-53. Mem. Am. Bankers Assn. (econ. adv. com.), Iowa Bankers Assn. (pres. 1972), Ind. Bankers Assn., Sigma Phi Epsilon (pres. alumni bd. 1972-79). Republican. Presbyterian. Club: Cedar Crest Country (pres. 1969-71). Office: Columbus Junction State Bank Columbus Junction IA 52738

HUTCHINS, ROBERT HOWARD, brokerage firm exec.; b. Chehalis, Wash., June 17, 1941; s. Howard Harold and Lelia Margurite (Thompson) H.; student Oreg. State U., 1959-61; B.Th., N.W. Christian Coll., 1965; m. Marilyn Irene Clark, Aug. 24, 1963; children—Robin M., Robert Howard, Heidi M., Richard H. Automotive salesman Edwards Rambler, Portland, Oreg., 1965-68, sales mgr., 1965-66, gen. mgr., 1966-68; stockbroker Blyth & Co., Portland, 1968-73; stock broker Foster & Marshall, Inc., Medford, Oreg., 1973-80, v.p., br. mgr., 1980—, dir., 1981—; dir. Citizens Savs. & Loan Assn. Trustee N.W. Christian Coll., chmn. fin. com., 1976—; chmn. bd. Medford Family YMCA, 1978-80. Recipient Disting. Service award City of Medford-Medford Jaycees, 1971. Mem. N.Y. Stock Exchange, Nat. Assn. Securities Dealers. Republican. Mem. Christian Ch. (Disciples of Christ). Clubs: Rotary, Medford Rogue, Kiwanis (past pres.) (Medford). Office: PO Box 850 Medford OR 97501

HUTCHINS, SUSAN LOUISE, credit union exec.; b. Needham, Mass., Sept. 5, 1953; d. Walter A. and Mary E. (Leonard) H.; B.S. in Math. with honors, Boston State Coll., 1975; postgrad. in Bus. Adminstrn., Babson Coll., 1971—. Coder, John Hancock Life Ins. Co., Boston, 1970-75; comptroller Credit Union League Mass., Inc., Chestnut Hill, 1975—. Pres., St. Mark's Parish Council, Roman Catholic Ch., 1977; del. Democratic Nat. Conv., 1976. Mem. Am. Numis. Assn. Club: Dorchester 350. Office: 850 Boylston St Chestnut Hill MA 02167

HUTCHINSON, CLARENCE HENRY, mgmt. cons.; b. Floodwood, Minn., Apr. 7, 1925; s. Frank W. and Emma C. (Petersen) H.; A.B., Harvard, 1950; M.B.A., 1955; m. Helen J. Dowgialo, Apr. 29, 1951; children—Charles, Sarah, Karen. Accountant, Honeywell, Inc., Mpls., 1955-59, mgr. fin. planning, 1959-60, mgr. data systems, 1960-62; controller Hexcel Corp., Dublin, Calif., 1962-64, finance dir., treas., 1964-68, v.p. finance, sec., 1968-69; internat. fin. dir. Memorex Corp., Santa Clara, Calif., 1970-72; sr. v.p., treas. Courier Terminal Systems, Inc., Phoenix, 1972; v.p. finance, treas. Data Pathing Inc., Sunnyvale, Calif., 1972-74, v.p., sec., treas., 1974-75, sr. vp., 1975-79; exec. v.p. Desa Industries, Balt., 1969-70; dir., treas. Shearmat Structures, Ltd., Winnepeg, Man., Can., 1964-65; dir., pres. Hexcel Structures, Ltd., Winnipeg, 1965-69; treas. Memorex Pacific Corp., Santa Clara, 1971-72; dir., sec. Data Pathing Europa GmbH, Cologne, W.Ger., 1973-79, Data Pathing (U.K.) Ltd., London, 1973-79; asst. sec. Raytek, Inc., Mountain View, Calif., 1979—. Vice pres. Bloomington (Minn.) Civic Theatre, 1961-62; bd. dirs. Jr. Achievement, Oakland, Calif., 1965-66. Served with AUS, 1943-46. Mem. Planning Execs. Inst. (chpt. sec. 1961-62), Nat. Assn. Accountants (chpt. dir. 1960-62), Fin. Execs. Inst., Security Analysts Inst. San Francisco. Republican. Unitarian. Club: Commonwealth of Calif. Home: 22320 Kendle St Cupertino CA 95014 Office: 370 San Aleso Ave Sunnyvale CA 94086

HUTCHINSON, ERIC, alternate energy co. exec.; b. Tacoma, July 21, 1952; s. Harry C. and Yolanda Marie (Espinosa) H.; student bus. adminstrn. (Gibson-Duncan Meml. Trust scholar 1970-73), U. Ark., Little Rock, 1970-73; m. Donna Ruth Gentry, Aug. 15, 1971; children—Amy Carol, Bryan Walter. Mgr., Sears, Roebuck & Co., Little Rock, 1970-75; salesman Dale Carnegie courses, Little Rock, 1975-77; v.p. Lynndale Mfg. Co. Inc., Little Rock, 1977-79; gen. mgr. Lakewood Products, Inc., Little Rock and Toronto, Ont., Can., 1979—; instr. Dale Carnegie courses, speaker seminars and workshops. Mem. Ark. N.G., 1971-78. Mem. Sales and Mktg. Execs. Club Little Rock, Wood Energy Inst. Mem. Christian Ch. (Disciples of Christ). Club: Kiwanis. Office: PO Box 7375 Little Rock AR 72217

HUTCHINSON, HARRIETTE MCCOLM, savs. and loan exec.; b. Washington, Aug. 8, 1944; d. Harry L. and Mary Rose (Cooper) McColm; student Marshall U., 1962-64, W.Va. Career Coll., 1972, Fla. Atlantic U., 1977; hon. diploma U. Tenn., 1978; m. William D. Hutchinson, Apr. 28, 1962; children—Margaret Ann, David. Asst. buyer Anderson/Newcomb, Huntington, W.Va., 1968-69; asst. savs. dept. Huntington Trust & Savs. Bank, 1969-70; adminstrv. asst. Carl F. Arnold, Cons., Lobbyist, Washington, 1971; asst. v.p. mktg. First Fed. Delray, Delray Beach, Fla., 1973—; mem. Fla. League Mktg. Com., 1980. Mem. Inst. Fin. Edn., Savs. Instns. Mktg. Soc. Am., Ad Club Palm Beach. Republican. Baptist. Home: 1601 S Federal Hwy Delray Beach FL 33444 Office: 645 E Atlantic Ave Delray Beach FL 33444

HUTCHINSON, LOREN KELLEY, mfg. co. exec.; b. Buffalo, Oct. 23, 1915; s. William L. and Grace May (Kelley) H.; B.A., Ill. Coll., 1941; postgrad. Harvard, 1954; m. Marjorie Lee Von Tobel, May 14, 1942; children—Loren Kelley, Lynnis Kay, Beth Ellen. Personnel asst. Wilson Packing Co., Chgo., 1941-42; personnel dir. Esquire, Inc., 1945-48; mgr. personnel and labor relations Ill. C. of C., 1948-51; asst. to exec. v.p. Wyman Gordon Co., Worcester, Mass., 1951-54, mgr. indsl. relations, 1954-58, works mgr., 1958-61, mgr. operations Eastern div., 1961-64, dir. orgn. devel., 1964-65; pres., dir. Croname, Inc., Chgo., 1966-69; pres. DSI Corp., Plymouth, Mich., 1969-71; pres., dir. Southworth Inc., Portland, Maine, 1971—; incorporator Maine Savs. Bank; dir. Hussey Mfg. Co., Berwick, Maine. Bd. dirs. Worcester County Musical Assn., 1953-65, Asso. Industries Maine, Portland Symphony Orch., Jr. Achievement So. Maine, Econ. Resources Council Maine; bd. dirs., campaign chmn. United Fund Greater Portland; chmn. bd. Worcester Orchestral Soc., 1951-65; bd. dirs. Worcester Community Chest and Council, 1954-65, Crusade of Mercy, YMCA. Served to lt., 1942-45. Mem. Nat. Assn. Metal Name Plate Mfrs. (dir.), Pulp and Paper Machinery Mfrs. Assn. (dir.), Greater Portland C. of C. (dir.), Newcomen Soc., Republican. Unitarian. Mason. Clubs: Lake Forest; Harvard (Boston); Chicago Press; Detroit Economic; Overseas Yacht (N.Y.C.); Portland Country, Cumberland (Portland). Home: 4 Susan Ln Falmouth ME 04105 Office: 30 Warren Ave Portland ME

HUTCHISON, JOSEPH EUGENE, oil distbr.; b. Elba, Ala., Aug. 16, 1908; s. Ira Augustus and Theodora (Farris) H.; LL.B., Cumberland U., 1931; m. Edna Groedell McGee, Dec. 31, 1930; children—Edward Augustus, Margaret H. Mancuso. Distbr., Mo-Jo Oil Products, 1952-72; pres. High Octane Terminal Co., 1958-72, Pan-handle Towing Co., 1967-72; dir. Crystal Oil Co., Shreveport, La., 1975—; dir. Bay Nat. Bank & Trust Co., 1965-75. Mayor, City of Panama City (Fla.), 1961-65. Recipient Award, Com. of 100, 1967. Named Disting. Alumnus, Ga. Mil. Acad. Mem. Pi Kappa Phi. Democrat. Baptist. Clubs: Panama Country, Rotary, St. Andrews Bay Yacht, Elks. Home: 1405 Bayou Ct Panama City FL 32401

HUTTON, EDWARD LUKE, corporate exec.; b. Bedford, Ind., May 5, 1919; s. Fred and Margaret (Drehoble) H.; B.S. with distinction, Ind. U., 1940, M.S. with distinction, 1941; m. Kathryn Jane Alexander, Dec. 22, 1942; children—Edward Alexander, Thomas Charles, Jane Clarke. Dep. dir. Joint Export-Import Agy., Berlin, 1946-48; v.p., dir. World Commerce Corp., N.Y.C., 1948-51; asst. v.p. W.R. Grace & Co., N.Y.C., 1951-53; cons. internat. trade, finance, 1953-54; v.p., dir. New York & Cuba Mail Steamship Co., N.Y.C., 1954-61, financial v.p., 1958-59; v.p. and group exec. W.R. Grace & Co., 1969-71; exec. v.p., gen. mgr. DuBois Chem. div. W.R. Grace & Co., 1964-68; pres. E.L. Hutton, Assos., Inc., 1960-70; pres., chief exec. officer Chemed Corp., 1971—; dir. Am. States Ins. Co., Am. States Life Ins. Co., Am. Economy, The Veratex Corp. Trustee, Village of Bronxville, 1965-68, Millikin U. Served from pvt. to 1st lt. AUS, 1943-46. Mem. Newcomen Soc. N. Am. Methodist. Clubs: Downtown Assn., University, Economics (N.Y.C.); Queen City, Bankers (Cin.). Home: 6680 Miralake Dr Cincinnati OH 45243 also Harris Rd East Orleans MA 02634 Office: 1200 Du Bois Tower Cincinnati OH 45202 also 1114 Ave of Americas New York NY 10036

HYDE, JOSEPH R., III, business exec.; b. Memphis, 1942; A.B., U. N.C., 1965; married. With Malone & Hyde Inc., Memphis, 1965—, v.p., 1967-68, exec. v.p., 1968-69, pres., chief exec. officer, 1969-72, chmn. bd., 1972—, also dir.; dir. First Tenn. Corp., Wal-Mart, Fed. Express, Browning-Ferris Industries. Bd. dirs. Memphis Univ. Sch. Office: Malone & Hyde Inc 1991 Corporate Ave Memphis TN 39132*

HYMAN, MURRAY, accountant; b. N.Y.C., Nov. 25, 1931; B.S. in Bus. Adminstrn., Temple U., 1952; postgrad. N.Y. U. Sch. Law, 1956; m. Linda Rosen, May 1, 1965; children—David Paul, Jeffrey Michael. With various internat. acctg. firms, 1952-72; individual practice acctg., Hackensack, N.J., 1977—; ind. oil and gas producer, 1980—. Trustee, Englewood Hosp. Assn., 1972—; mem. Bergen County council Boy Scouts Am., 1973—. Served with U.S. Army, 1956-58. C.P.A., N.J., N.Y. Mem. Am. Inst. C.P.A.'s. Republican. Jewish. Club: B'nai B'rith. Home: 1600 Parker Ave Fort Lee NJ 07024 Office: 113 Johnson Ave Hackensack NJ 07602

HYMOFF, EDWARD, research co. exec.; b. Boston, Oct. 12, 1924; s. Gustave and Gertrude Esther (Kravetsky) H.; B.S. in Journalism, Boston U., 1949; M.A. in Public Law and Govt., Columbia U., 1950; divorced; children—Yves K., Jennifer K. Reporter, N.Y. World Telegram and Sun, 1950; bur. chief, war corr. in Korea and Indochina, Internat. News Service, 1951-54; news mgr. NBC News, N.Y.C., 1954-58; dir. news and public affairs Radio Sta. WMGM, N.Y.C., 1959; sci./tech. account rep. Carl Byoir & Assos., 1959-63; editorial dir. Vietnam Mil. Hist. Pubs. Co., Atlantic Highlands, N.J., Vietnam, Hong Kong, 1966-69; asso. editor THINK mag. IBM, 1969-71; exec. editor TV News, NBC News, N.Y.C., 1974; dir. communications and public affairs Corp. Public Broadcasting, Washington, 1977-80; mgr. editorial services Arthur D. Little, Inc., Cambridge, Mass., 1981—; dir. DPL mag.; guest lectr. N.Y. U., Boston U. Sch. Public Communication, Pace Coll.; media/public affairs cons. LWV Voter Edn. Fund for 1980 Presdl. Debates; 1980. Chmn., Atlantic Highlands (N.J.) Citizens Adv. Com., 1964-65. Served with OSS, AUS, 1943-45. Mem. Am. Soc. Journalists and Authors, Internat. Inst. Strategic Studies, Aviation/Space Writers Assn., Authors League, Writers Guild, Co. Mil. Historians, Sigma Delta Chi. Clubs: Overseas Press, Nat. Press, N.Y. Press. Author: The Mission, 1964; the Kennedy Courage, 1965; Internat. Troubleshooter for Peace, 1965; Guidance and Control of Spacecraft, 1966; 1st Marine Division in Vietnam, 1967; the OSS in World War II, 1972, others. Office: Acorn Park Cambridge MA 02140

HYUN, JOHN K. H., lawyer, business exec.; b. Maui, Hawaii, Jan. 10, 1920; s. D.M. and Y.S. (Kim) H.; B.A., Whittier Coll., 1942; J.D., So. Meth. U., 1950; certificate U. Va., 1944, Yale, 1945; m. Elizabeth Y. Kim, Dec. 23, 1963. Commd. 2d lt. U.S. Army, 1943, advanced through grades to col., 1964; ret., 1968; admitted to Okla. bar, 1950, Tex. bar, 1950. Hawaii bar, 1969; dir. facilities and adminstrn. Pacific div. Control Data Corp., 1968-71; sr. partner Hyun, Sandler, Choi Internat., Honolulu, San Francisco, N.Y.C., Seoul, Korea, 1971—, Hyun & Nakagawa, Honlulu, 1971-77; pres. Y.S. Hyun, Ltd., 1968—; dir. Polynesian Fair, Eurasia Travel, Inc., Korea Tourist Bur., Inc., World Promotions, Inc., Maxim's Boutique, The Shopping Center. Pres., Korean Community Assn.; v.p., pres. Korean Community Council, 1977-80; adviser Korean Sr. Citizens League; adv./dir. Assn. Korean Orgns. U.S.; chmn. Asia-Pacific Coalition, Hawaii Democratic party. Decorated Bronze Star medal, Army Commendation medal with 2 oak leaf clusters (U.S.); Chung Mu Mil. medal with gold star, D.S.M. (Korea). Fellow Roscoe Pound Am. Trial Lawyers Found.; mem. Internat. Common Law Exchange Soc., Hawaii Bar Assn., Am. Trial Lawyers Assn., Assn. Immigration and Nationality Lawyers (v.p. Hawaii), Ret. Officers Assn., DAV, Assn. U.S. Army, Internat. Platform Assn. Club: Elks. Office: Suite 990 Pacific Trade Center Honolulu HI 96813

IACOCCA, LIDO ANTHONY (LEE), automotive mfr.; b. Allentown, Pa., Oct. 15, 1924; s. Nicola and Antoinette (Perrotto) I.; B.S., Lehigh U., 1945; M.E., Princeton, 1946; m. Mary McCleary, Sept. 29, 1956; children—Kathryn Lisa, Lia Antoninette. With Ford Motor Co., Dearborn, Mich., 1946-78, successively mem. field sales staff, various merchandising and tng. activities, asst. dirs. sales mgr., Phila., dist. sales mgr., Washington, 1946-56, truck marketing mgr. div. office, 1956-57, car marketing mgr., 1957-60, vehicle market mgr., 1960, v.p. Ford Motor Co., gen. mgr. Ford div., 1960-65, v.p. car and truck group, 1965-67, exec. v.p. of co., 1967-68, pres. of co., 1970-78, pres., chief operating officer Chrysler Corp., Highland Park, Mich., 1978-79, chmn. bd., chief exec. officer, 1979—. Wallace Meml. fellow Princeton. Mem. Tau Beta Pi. Club: Detroit Athletic. Office: care Chrysler Corp 12000 Lynn Townsend Dr Highland Park MI 48231*

IACOE, WILLIAM FRANK, indsl. electronics mfg. co. exec.; b. Milw., Feb. 15, 1939; s. Frank and Jean (Traina) I.; Asso. in Applied Sci., Milw. Inst. Tech., 1964; B.S., No. Mich. U., 1970; M.B.A., Western Mich. U., 1976; m. Corinne N. Lee, July 31, 1966; children—David, Deborah, Lisa. Reliability engr. A.C. Spark Plug div. Gen. Motors Co., Milw., 1958-63; quality assurance engring. mgr. Sunbeam Corp., Racine, Wis. and Ft. Lauderdale, Fla., 1963-66; with Lear Siegler Inc., 1966-77, dir. ops., Zeeland, Mich., 1975-77; v.p. mfg. Marsh Instrument Co., Skokie, Ill., 1977-80; plant mgr. Onan Corp., Fridley, Minn., 1980—; adj. prof. bus. Grand Valley State Coll., Allendale, Mich., 1974-75. Active Boy Scouts Am., Grand Rapids, Mich., 1970-77. Served with USAF, 1957-64. Mem. Soc. Mfg. Engrs. (sr. mem., certified mfg. engr). Republican. Pentacostal. Home: 65 Deer Hills Ct North Oaks MN 55110 Office: 1400 73d Ave Fridley MN 55432

IACONO, DAVID JAMES, govt. ofcl.; b. N.Y.C., Jan. 8, 1948; s. Michael Nicolas and Rose (Sclafani) I.; student N.Y. U., 1966-67; B.A. cum laude, Pa. State U., 1970; postgrad. U. Md. Far East Div., 1971-72; M.S., Elmira Coll., 1976; m. Ann Marie Margaret Loyko, Aug. 26, 1972; children—Jennifer, Christine (dec.). Cons., trainer drug and alcohol U.S. Navy, 1972-74, personnel mgmt. specialist GTE - Sylvania Co., Towanda, Pa., 1974-76, adviser co.'s employee activities assn., 1974; employee relations specialist Social Security Adminstrn., Balt., 1976—; career cons. Balt. area Elmira Coll., 1978—. Chmn., Youth and Industry program Internat. Mgmt. Council, Towanda, 1975-76. Served with USN, 1970-74. NSF grantee, summer 1969. Democrat. Roman Catholic. Home: 2607 John Dr Baltimore MD 21234 Office: Social Security Adminstrn 6401 Security Blvd Baltimore MD 21235

IACOZZI, VINCENT HENRY, JR., data processing co. exec.; b. Lowell, Mass., Jan. 5, 1947; s. Vincent H. and Shirley M. (Willett) I.; student St. Anselms Coll., 1964-65; m. Linda M. Bonarigo, Mar. 18, 1965; children—Lisa, Vincent III, Rachel, Matthew. Foreman, Iacozzi & Sons, Lawrence, Mass., 1966-70; partner V.R.S. Engring. Co., Methuen, Mass., 1970-73; sales and service mgr. Wood Equipment Co., Salem, Mass., 1973-75; dir. constrn. Century Constrn. Co., Derry, N.H., 1975-76; facilities mgr. Centronics Data Computer Corp., Hudson, N.H., 1976-78, dir. facilities, 1978-80; corp. bldgs. engr. Nashua Corp. (N.H.), 1980—. Mem. Nat. Assn. Corp. Real Estate Execs., Nat. Assn. Rev. Appraisers, Nat. Home Builders Assn., Nat. Fire Protection Assn. Democrat. Roman Catholic. Designed mfg. facilities in N.H., W.Va., P.R. and Republic of Ireland. Home: Partridge Ln Derry NH 03038 Office: Nashua Corp Nashua NH

IANNELLA, EGIDIO, banking cons.; b. Buenos Aires, Argentina, May 16, 1921; s. Antonio and Carmen (Barbaro) I.; Pub. Accountant, U. Buenos Aires, 1952; postgrad. in central banking Latinam. Center Monetary Studies, 1953; 1 dau., Maria del Carmen Furey. Gen. accountant Banco Argentino de Commercio, Buenos Aires, 1956-62, asst. gen. mgr., 1962-66, gen. mgr., 1966-67; various positions Banco Central Bank de la Republic Argentina, Buenos Aires, 1939-56, gen. mgr., 1967-69, pres., 1969-70; pres. Banco del Oeste, 1971-72, now dir.; pres., gen. mgr. Banco Federal Argentino, 1971-77; pres. Banco Nacional de Desarrollo, 1978—; pres. A.L.I.D.E.; tchr. banking U. Catolica Argentina, 1970—. Alternate gov. Internat. Bank Reconstrn. and Devel., Internat. Fund of Cooperation, Internat. Devel. Assn., IMF, Interam. Bank of Devel. Tchr. banking, finances U. Buenos Aires, 1960-69. Mem. Argentine Bankers Assn. Home: Santa Fe Ave 3780 1425 Buenos Aires Argentina Office: 611 Via Monte St 1053 Buenos Aires City Argentina

IANNOLI, JOSEPH JOHN, JR., univ. exec.; b. Worcester, Mass., Oct. 28, 1939; s. Joseph John and Alice Bernadette (Moore) I.; A.B., Franklin and Marshall Coll., 1962; M.A., Syracuse U., 1967; m. Gail V. Cummings, Oct. 21, 1972; children—Juliet, Christopher. Devel. officer Franklin & Marshall Coll., Lancaster, Pa., 1965-68; asso. dir. med. devel. U. Miami, 1968-70; asst. dir., cons. Am. Bankers Assn., Washington, 1970-74; cons. Marts & Lundy, Inc., N.Y.C., 1974-78; dir. capital support U. Hartford, Conn., 1978—; sr. cons. J.M. Lord & Assos.; lectr. in field. Recipient Samuel McDonald Humanitarian award, 1958. Mem. Nat. Soc. Fund Raising Execs., Council for Advancement and Support of Edn., Fund Raising Inst., Bushnell Meml. Steering Com. Home: 72 Merline Rd Vernon CT 06066

IBBETSON, EDWIN THORNTON, bus. developer; b. Los Angeles, Apr. 17, 1923; s. Robert Edwin and Ann (Thornton) I.; student Long Beach Jr. Coll., 1941-42, Calif. Inst. Tech., 1942-43; m. Harriett Alice Hudson, Dec. 28, 1947; children—Elizabeth Ann (Mrs. Phillip Hitchcock), Douglas Hudson, Gregory Bruce, Timothy Edwin, Julia Katherine, Erika Alice. With Union Devel. Co., Bellflower, Calif., 1944—, pres., 1961—; partner Paramount Constrn., Bellflower, 1948—; v.p. Valley Properties, Inc., Imperial Valley, 1962—; pres. Union Farms, Inc., Bellflower, 1962—; chmn. bd. dirs. Dutch Village Bowling Center, Inc., Lakewood, 1965—; partner Ibbetson-Marsh Realtors, 1975—; vice chmn. bd. Bellflower Savs. and Loan Assn., 1977—; dir. Garden State Bank, 1974-79, chmn., 1977-79. Bd. dirs. Met. Water Dist. So. Calif., 1959—, sec., 1979—; chmn. Bellflower Water Devel. Com., 1965—; chmn. Los Angeles County Real Estate Adv. Com., 1974—; bd. dirs. armed services YMCA, Long Beach, 1962-72. Trustee St. Mary's Hosp., Long Beach. Served with USNR, 1943-46. Named Young Man of Year, Bellflower Jaycees, 1959. Realtor of Year, Bellflower Dist. Bd. Realtors, 1962, 67, 71. Mem. Am. Soc. Real Estate Counselors (gov., pres. 1977), Calif. Assn. Realtors (treas. 1972-77, dir.; hon. life pres.), Internat. Real Estate Fedn., Nat. Assn. Realtors (dir.), Nat. Inst. Real Estate Brokers (certified comml. investment mem.), Inst. Real Estate Mgmt. (certified property mgr.), Urban Land Inst., Bellflower Dist. Bd. Realtors (pres. 1961), Central Basin Water Assn. (dir.), Calif. Real Estate Polit. Action Com., Internat. Council Shopping Centers. Roman Catholic. Elk, Kiwanian (pres. 1958), Clubs: International Traders, Southern Calif. Tuna (Long Beach, Calif.). Office: 16550 Bloomfield Ave Cerritos CA 90701

IDE, FLOETTA MAE, apparel mfg. co. exec.; b. Portland, Oreg., Sept. 6, 1921; d. Dewane Portland and Mabel Clare (Binder) DeVeny; grad. Northwestern Coll., 1941; m. Lewis Albert Ide, Feb. 13, 1944. With Jantzen Inc., Portland, 1941—, sec. to bd. dirs., exec. sec. to pres., asst. corp. sec., 1961—. Mem. Fifty-Fifty Bus. Women's Club (pres. 1955), Order Eastern Star, Rebekah. Home: 6734 E Burnside St Portland OR 97215 Office: Jantzen Inc PO Box 3001 Portland OR 97208

IGLESIAS, BIENVENIDO AMABLE, constrn. and indsl. export co. exec.; b. Santo Domingo, Dominican Republic, Dec. 21, 1945; s. Salvador Bienvenido and Maria Francisca (Benitez) I.; came to U.S., 1953; B.S., Normal Hostos, 1963; B.A., St. John's U., 1966, M.A., 1968; A.B.D., Case Western Res. U., 1970; m. Bodhild B. Brendryen, Nov. 2, 1969; children—Kristin Desiree, Genevieve Sofie, Lisa Francesca, Janelle Ann. Instr., Fgn. Study League, 1968, program chmn. Western Europe, 1969; teaching fellow Case Western Res. U., Cleve., 1968-70; prof. St. John's U., N.Y.C., 1970-74, 75-76; exec. v.p. Idras Inc., N.Y.C., 1972-75; dir. INDISA Group, Inc., Dominican Republic; dir. U.S. Iglesias Internat. Co., N.Y.C.; radio/TV analyst Latin Am. politics and bus.; guest speaker. Mem. Am. Mgmt. Assn., Am. Polit. Sci. Assn., Latin Am. Studies Assn., Caribbean Studies Assn., Am.-Scandinavian Found., Circulo de Lectores del Museo de Las Casas Reales (Dominican Republic), Sociedad Dominicana de Bibliofilos, Inc. Club: Santo Domingo Tennis. Author: Central American Common Market, 1968. Founder, co-editor Viewpoints: Jour. of Internat. Relations, 1971. Office: 198-60 Pompeii Ave Holliswood NY 11423 also Anacaona No 1 Zona 6 Santo Domingo Dominican Republic

IGLESIAS, MANUEL, fin. exec.; b. Havana, Cuba, Jan. 4, 1944; came to U.S., 1962, naturalized, 1980; s. Jose Antonio and Alicia I.; cert. in computer scis., Pace U., 1975, A.A.S. in Acctg. and EDP, 1976; m. Isabel Santana, Oct. 3, 1970; children—Alejandro. Comptroller, Commerce Service Inc., West New York, N.J., 1977-78; fiscal officer Hoboken (N.J.) Family Planning, Inc., 1978—. Mem. Smithsonian Instn., Am. Mus. Natural History, Nat. Rifle Assn., Am. Mgmt. Assn., AF Assn., N.J. Rifle and Pistols Clubs, Inc. Office: Hoboken Family Planning Inc 124 30 Grand St Hoboken NJ 07030

IGNAT, JOSEPH NORD, bus. services co. exec.; b. Oberlin, Ohio, Sept. 28, 1943; s. Joseph Allen and Mary Elizabeth (Nord) I.; B.S., Otterbein Coll., 1965; M.B.A., U. Colo., 1971; m. Pamela Kay Williams, Dec. 14, 1971; children—Brian, Todd. Indsl. engr. Martin-Marietta Co., Denver, 1969-72; systems analyst, mgmt. cons. Peat Marwick Mitchell & Co., Denver, 1973-77; pres. Supervision Inc., bus. services, Denver, 1978—. Chmn. bd. Mackintosh Acad. Served to lt. (j.g.) USNR, 1966-69; Vietnam. Office: Suite 1375 410 17th St Denver CO 80202

IGOE, PHILIP ANDREW, lawyer, corp. cons. co. exec.; b. Muskegon, Mich., Dec. 12, 1950; s. Philip Andrew and Lilliam Ann (Bomher) I.; B.S., U. Ill., 1972; M.S., Roosevelt U., 1977; J.D., Chgo.-Kent Coll., 1977. Admitted to Ill. bar, 1977; asst. dir. engring. div. Perma-Line Corp. of Am., Chgo., 1970-74; pres. Igoe Assos., Oak Lawn, Ill., 1975—; in-house legal cons. to Ill. Sec. of State, 1978—; asst. to Ill. State Senator John Merlo, 1979-80; design cons. J.P. Constrn. Co. Strawn fellow, 1975; recipient Patrick Henry award, 1970. Mem. ASTM, Am. Chem. Soc., Decalogue Soc., Am., Ill. State, Chgo. bar assns. Nichiren Shoshu Buddhist. Club: Lincoln Turners. Home: 645 W Barry Ave Chicago IL 60657 Office: 134 N LaSalle St Suite 818 Chicago IL 60602

IHENACHO, HERBERT UCHENDU, fin. and mgmt. cons. co. exec.; b. Imo State Nigeria, Dec. 15, 1946; came to U.S., 1966; s. Ihenacho Ogbuoge and Onyekwere Aduku (Anushiem) Nnoshiri; B.S. in Bus. Adminstrn., Morgan State U., 1970, M.B.A., 1972; certs. Am. Inst. Banking, 1979; m. Naomi Elizabeth Peete, Nov. 25, 1972; children—Uchendu, Nnoshiri, Adaku. Acct., King & Brooks, Balt., 1970-72; controller Md. Inst. Art, 1972-73; with Neighborhood Parents Club, Inc., Balt., 1973—, asst. dir. fin., 1977-79. Sec., v.p. Nat. Bus. League, Balt. Mem. Am. Bankers Assn., Am. Mgmt. Assn. Club: Masons. Home: Ezeogba Emekuku Owerri Imo State Nigeria Office: 1400 Orleans St Baltimore MD 21231

IHLE, HERBERT DUANE, fast food co. exec.; b. Ames, Iowa, July 8, 1939; s. Joe and Martha Marie (Larson) I.; A.A., Waldorf Jr. Coll., 1957-59; B.A., Concordia Coll., 1961; M.S., U. Minn., 1963; m. Catherine Eileen Klein, Dec. 27, 1959; children—Brena Kristen, Valerie Anne, Michael David. With Pillsbury Co., Mpls., 1967-79, 80—, dir. control fin. consumer group, 1976-78, v. p. fin. consumer group, 1978-79, 80—; sr. v.p. fin. Burger King Corp., Miami, Fla., 1979-80. Mem. Fin. Execs. Inst., Planning Execs. Inst., Nat. Assn. Accts. Republican. Lutheran. Office: MS 1219 608 2d Ave S Minneapolis MN 55402

IHLE, JOSEPH ALFRED, food processing co. exec.; b. Bristow, Okla., Aug. 7, 1922; s. Joseph Alfred and Iva May (LeCrone) I.; student U. Okla., 1940-42; m. Dorotha Faye Vail, Sept. 17, 1972; children by previous marriage—Joseph Alfred, Mary, Bill, Ruth Ann. Pres., S.W. Pecan Co., Bristow, 1946—; pres. Pecan & Agrl. Equipment, Inc., Bristow, 1969—; dir., v.p. Ag No 1 No., Bristow, 1973—. Pres., Bristow Meml. Hosp. Found., 1957-60, dir., 1954—. Served USMCR, 1942-46. Mem. Nat. Pecan Shellers Assn. (pres. 1967-70, dir. 1955—), Democrat. Methodist. Elk. Clubs: Oak Tree Golf (Edmond, Okla.); Bristow Country. Home: Country Club Dr Bristow OK 74010 Office: 200 Industrial Rd S Bristow OK 74010

IIDA, DAVID TAKASHIGE, toy mfr.; b. Vancouver, Wash., Mar. 20, 1923; s. Kametaro and Koma (Inoue) I.; B.A., U. Yokohama, 1943; M.B.A., U. Chgo., 1956; m. Kazu Suzuki, Apr. 10, 1958; children—Elizabeth and Margaret (twins). With Louis Marx & Co., Inc., 1956-73, gen. mgr. Far East, Tokyo, Hong Kong, Far East coordinator, Stamford, Conn., 1973-76; pres. Tomy Corp., Carson, Calif., 1976—. Mem. Toy Mfrs. Am. (dir.), Am. Toy Inst. (trustee), Am. Mtmg. Assn., Los Angeles Area C. of C. Club: Rolling Hills Country, Japan (pres.), Mesa Verde Country. Home: 26742 Nokomis Rd Rancho Palos Verdes CA 90274 Office: 901 E 233d St Carson CA 90745

IKEDA, TAKESHI, banker; b. Osaka, Japan, Dec. 21, 1931; s. Hajime and Hisano Ikeda; B.A. in Econs. and Bus., Osaka City U., 1954; m. Sadako Higashino, Oct. 17, 1957; 1 dau., Masami. With Dai-Ichi Kangyo Bank, Tokyo, 1954-79, dep. gen. mgr., N.Y.C., 1968-71, dep. gen. mgr. Kandaekimae br., Tokyo, 1971-73, chief supr. domestic bus. devel. div., 1973-74, dep. gen. mgr. bus. div., 1974-77, dep. gen. mgr. Internat. Bus. Adminstrn. div., 1977-79; pres. First Pacific Bank of Chgo., 1979—. Mem. Japanese Am. Council, Japanese C. of C. and Industry of Chgo. (exec. com.), Japan Am. Soc. (v.p., dir.). Clubs: Met., Chgo. Athletic Assn. Office: 1st Pacific Bank of Chicago 111 S Wabash Ave Chicago IL 60603

ILACQUA, ROSARIO S., securities analyst; b. Albany, N.Y., Aug. 12, 1927; s. Anthony and Carmela (Gerasia) I.; B.S., Siena Coll., 1950; M.S., Columbia, 1955. With L.F. Rothschild, Unterberg, Towbin, N.Y.C., 1957—, partner, 1972—. Served with USNR, 1945-46. Mem. Nat. Assn. Petroleum Investment Analysts (pres. 1977), N.Y. Soc. Security Analysts, Oil Analysts Group N.Y. (pres. 1972). Club: N.Y. Athletic. Home: 2 Horatio St New York NY 10014 Office: 55 Water St New York NY 10041

ILETT, WILLIAM KENT, truck sales co. exec.; b. Boise, Idaho, Aug. 12, 1944; s. Frank Kent and Lela Alice I.; A.A., Boise State Coll., 1965, B.A., 1967; m. Christina L. Totorica, June 26, 1976. Staff acct. Ernst & Ernst, C.P.A., Boise, 1967-68; sec.-treas. Transport Holding Corp., Boise, 1968-72; pres. Interstate Mack, Inc., Boise, 1972—; chmn. Mack Trucks Regional Distbr. Council, 1973-80. Bd. dirs. Bronco Athletic Assn., Boise, 1971-73. Served as sgt. Air N.G., 1963. Mem. Nat. Assn. Accountants, Am. Inst. C.P.A.'s, Sales and Mktg. Execs., Idaho Motor Transport Assn. (dir. 1976—), Boise State U. Alumni Assn. (pres. 1970), Euzkaldunak Basque Assn., SAR, Alpha Kappa Psi. Home: 747 Charie Rd Boise ID 83705 Office: 3939 Transport St Boise ID 83705

ILLICK, CHRISTOPHER DAVID, investment banker; b. Bethlehem, Pa., Mar. 21, 1939; s. Joseph Edward and Margaret Catherine (Flexer) I.; B.A., Trinity Coll., 1961; LL.B., U. Va., 1964; m. Susan Selden Dunbar, June 9, 1962; children—Hilary Selden, Christopher David. Admitted to N.Y. bar, 1965; mem. firm Brown, Wood, Fuller, Caldwell & Ivey, N.Y.C., 1964-67; with Investment Banking div. Paine, Webber, Jackson & Curtis, N.Y.C., 1967-69; pres., dir. Robert Fleming, Inc., N.Y.C., 1969—; dir. Dorset Corp., Intersil, Inc., Investment Annuity, Inc., Merc. & Gen. Reins. Co. of Am., Pegasus Internat. S.A., Loehmann's, Inc. Mem. Brit.-Am. C. of C. (dir.). Episcopalian. Clubs: Links, Racquet and Tennis (N.Y.C.); Pretty Brook Tennis (Princeton). Home: Cherry Valley Rd Princeton NJ 08540 Office: 630 Fifth Ave New York NY 10020

ILSON, BERNARD, public relations firm exec.; b. N.Y.C., Dec. 26, 1924; s. Abraham and Goldie (Zeff) I.; student Coll. City N.Y., 1942; B.A., Bklyn. Coll., 1946; M.A., Columbia, 1949; m. Carol Ruth Geller, May 10, 1955; children—David Drew, James Joseph. TV writer NBC, N.Y.C., 1955-56; dir. TV publicity David O. Alber Assocs., N.Y.C., 1956-58; v.p., dir. TV publicity Rogers & Cowan, N.Y.C., 1958-63; founder, pres. Bernie Ilson, Inc., N.Y.C., 1963—; lectr. Baruch Coll. Mem. Pub. Relations Soc. Am., Writers Guild Am. East, Explorers Club. Home: 82-14 192d St Jamaica NY 11423 Office: 65 W 55th St New York City NY 10019

IMBROGNO, EUGENE FRANCIS, real estate exec.; b. Montgomery, W.Va., Oct. 26, 1922; s. Eugene and Marguerite (Gay) I.; B.S., W.Va. Inst. Tech., 1942; m. Alice J. Winkiewicz, Sept. 6, 1943; children—Catherine, Eugene Francis, III, Ellen, Mark, Mary Eve. Mgr., Home Outfitting Co., Montgomery, 1946-50; pres. Hillside Realty Co., Montgomery, 1948—, Realmark Devels., Inc., Montgomery, 1962—; real estate coordinator BBF Restaurants, Columbus, Ohio, 1962-69; real estate mgr. BBF div. Borden Inc., 1969-72; sec.-treas. Wendys W.Va., Wendys S. Fla., Sea Food Ohio, Inc., Sea Food Fla., Inc., Front IV, Inc., Churchick, Inc., 1972-78; sec.-treas. Rax of Tidewater, Inc., 1979—, Front IV, Inc., 1972—; chmn. Citizens Nat. Bank, Follansbee, W.Va., 1969-79; v.p. Montgomery Nat. Bank, 1957-80, dir. emeritus, 1980—; pres. Diversifoods, Inc., 1980—. Mem. vis. com. W.Va. U. Coll. Bus., 1978—. Served with USNR, 1942-46. Decorated Navy Commendation medal. Named Hon. Citizen of Korea, 1966, Hon. Gov. Ohio, 1975, Hon. Adm. Kanawha River Navy, 1972. Mem. Montgomery C. of C. (pres. 1950), Upper Kanawha Valley Devel. Assn. (pres. 1959-64). Republican. Roman Catholic. Clubs: Charleston Yacht, Berry Hills Country (Charleston); Naples (Fla.) Bath and Tennis Bears Paw Country; K.C., Elks. Home: 3 Dreamview Ln Charleston WV 25314 also 1200 Cherrystone Ct Naples FL 33942 Office: Suite 1 Wendy Bldg Summers and Lee Sts Charleston WV 25301

IMMASCHE, FRANCIS WILLIAM, econ. adviser, farmer; b. Saffordville, Kans., Oct. 21, 1907; s. William George and Margaret (Lyles) ImM.; B.S., Kans. State U., 1929; M.A., U. Chgo., 1933. Livestock economist Armour & Co., Chgo., 1930-31, Fed. Farm Bd., Washington, 1931-33; asst. chief, econ. and credit research div., FCA, Washington, 1933-42; dep. dir. livestock and dairy div. U.S. Dept. Agr., Washington, 1947-65; pres. Goldpoint Mining Co. (Nev.), 1941—; pres. Meml. Lawn Cemeteries Assn., Emporia, Kan., 1959-70; adviser on livestock and wool situation Australia and New Zealand, 1971—; farmer, Chase County, Kans. Served from 1st lt. to col., USAF, 1942-47; now col. USAF ret. Mem. Sigma Alpha Epsilon, Alpha Zeta, Alpha Kappa Psi. Clubs: Congressional Country, Capitol Hill (Washington); Indian Wells (Calif.) Country. Home: 3133 Connecticut Ave Washington DC 20008 also Strong City KS 66869

IMPARATO, EDWARD THOMAS, securities co. exec.; b. Flushing, N.Y., Jan. 6, 1917; s. Charles and Romilda (DelliBovi) I.; B.S. in Bus., U. Tampa (Fla.), 1963; grad. Inst. Investment Banking, U. Pa., 1972; m. Jean Catherine deGarmo, Aug. 19, 1947; 1 son, Edward Thomas. Flying instr., comml. pilot, 1937-39; commd. 2d lt. USAAF, 1939, advanced through grades to col., 1944; test pilot, co. marshall; chief staff Carribean Air Command, 1958-61; ret., 1961; instr. course portfolio mgmt. St. Petersburg (Fla.) Jr. Coll., 1964; mem. bd., founding dir. Med. Sci. Internat. Corp., Clearwater, Fla., 1968-71, Vikintactin Instrument Co., Clearwater, 1968-71, Snibbe Publns., Inc., Clearwater, 1969-71; account exec. Goodbody & Co., 1963-69, mgr., 1969-71; with Merrill Lynch, Pierce, Fenner & Smith, Inc., Clearwater, 1971—, v.p., 1973—. Treas. Clearwater chpt. A.R.C., 1963; founding pres., now chmn. bd., pres. Morton F. Plant Hosp. Found. Inc.; mem. Com. 100 Pinellas County, Fla., 1973—. Trustee St. Petersburg Mus. Fine Arts, 1970-72; pres. Fla. Gulf Coast Art Center, 1967-69; bd. dirs. Clearwater Concert Assn., 1969-77. Decorated Legion of Merit, D.F.C., Air medal with 2 oak leaf clusters, Berlin Airlift medal. Mem. Mil. Order World Wars, Am. Security Council, Internat. Platform Assn., Ret. Officers Assn., Delta Sigma Phi. Episcopalian. Club: Sword and Shield (U. Tampa). Author: How to Manage Your Money, 4th edit., 1967. Home: 155 Bayview Dr Belleair FL 33516 Office: 531 Franklin St Clearwater FL 33516

INATOME, RICK, computer co. exec.; b. Detroit, July 27, 1953; s. Joseph T. and Atsuko Nan (Kumagai) I.; B.A. in Econs., Mich. State U., 1976; m. Joyce Helen Kitchen, Aug. 18, 1979. Vice pres., gen. mgr., founder Computer Mart, Inc., Clawson, Mich., 1976—; lectr., cons. computers; instr. Marygrove Coll., Macomb Community Coll. Mem. Engring. Soc. Detroit, Am. Mgmt. Assn., Assn. Computer Machinery, Phi Delta Theta. Home: 2932 Roundtree St Troy MI 48084 Office: 560 W 14 Mile Rd Clawson MI 48017

INCAPRERA, FRANK PHILIP, internist, indsl. physician; b. New Orleans, Aug. 24, 1928; s. Charles and Mamie (Bellipanni) I.; B.S., Loyola U. of South, 1946; M.D., La. State U., 1950; m. Ruth Mary Duhon, Sept. 13, 1952; children—Charles, Cynthia, James, Christopher, Catherine. Intern, Charity Hosp., New Orleans, 1950-51, resident, 1951-52; resident VA Hosp., New Orleans, 1952-54; practice medicine specializing in internal medicine, New Orleans, 1957—; adminstrv. mgr. Internal Medicine Group, New Orleans, 1973—; med. dir. Owens-Ill. Glass Co., New Orleans, 1961—, Kaiser Aluminum Co., Chalmette, La., 1975—, Tenneco Oil Co., Chalmette, 1978—; co-founder Med. Center E. New Orleans, 1975; clin. asso. prof. medicine Tulane U. Sch. Medicine, 1971—; mem. New Orleans Bd. Health, 1966-70. Bd. dirs. Methodist Hosp., 1971—, Lutheran Home New Orleans, 1976-80, Chateau de Notre Dame, 1977—; mem. New Orleans Human Relation Com., 1968-70; bd. dirs. Emergency Med. Services Council, 1977— pres. La. southeastern region, 1979-81; bd. dirs. New Orleans Opera Assn., 1975—. Served to capt. USAF, 1955-57. Named Man of Yr., St. Gabriel Holy Name Soc., 1964; recipient Order of St. Louis medal, 1980. Diplomate Am. Bd. Internal Medicine. Fellow A.C.P., Am. Occupational Medicine Assn., Am. Geriatrics Soc.; mem. La. (v.p. 1975-76), Orleans Parish (sec. 1972-74) med. socs., New Orleans Acad. Internal Medicine (pres. 1969), La. Occupational Medicine Assn. (pres. 1971-72), La. Soc. Internal Medicine, Am. Group Practice Assn. (del.), Blue Key, Delta Epsilon Sigma. Home: 2218 Lake Oaks Pkwy New Orleans LA 70122 Office: 5640 Read Blvd New Orleans LA 70127

INCE, PETER CHARLES, real estate developer; b. Washington, Dec. 27, 1944; s. Richard William and Martha Heddons (Good) I.; B.S. in Mktg., Miami U., Oxford, Ohio, 1967. Sales mgr. Procter & Gamble, N.Y.C., 1967-77; account exec. The Marshalk Co., N.Y.C., 1977-79; pres. Ibis Coastal Co., Delray Beach, Fla., 1979—. Republican. Clubs: Univ., (N.Y.C.), Gypsy Trail of Carmel (dir. 1978-79). Home: 2929 S Ocean Blvd Boca Raton FL 33432 Office: 1018 Del Haven Dr Delray Beach FL 33444

INDERMUEHLE, NORMAN DWIGHT, automotive after market exec.; b. Springfield, Mo., Apr. 20, 1927; s. Leslie Floyd and Melvina A. (Tucker) I.; ed. pub. schs.; m. Geneva Agness Ball, Oct. 13, 1951; children—Cynthia Lynn, Cheryl Ann. Sales, Stenger Auto Supply, North Little Rock, Ark., 1949-55, mgr., 1956; mgr. A-1 Auto Supply, Joplin, Mo., 1957; owner Norman Auto Supply, Jefferson City, Mo., 1958-68, Mexico, Mo., 1962-68; pres. Normans of Jefferson City, 1968—, Normans of Mexico, 1968—; owner NDI Warehouse, Jefferson City, 1968—. Served with U.S. Navy, 1945-46; PTO. Address: 314 Mulberry St Jefferson City MO 65101

INGALLS, ROSCOE CUNNINGHAM, JR., stock broker; b. N.Y.C., Dec. 10, 1920; s. Roscoe Cunningham and Marjorie (Riegel) I.; B.S., Bowdoin Coll., 1943; m. Marjorie G. Davis, Oct. 4, 1947 (dec. June 1978); children—Lynn Knight, Roscoe Cunningham III, Andrew Riegel. Partner Ingalls & Snyder, N.Y.C., 1949-69, sr. partner, 1969—; dir. Rexham Corp., Barclays Bank N.Y., Eastern Savs. Bank. Trustee Bowdoin Coll., 1973—; mem. bd. govs. Lawrence Hosp., Bronxville, N.Y., 1959-66; mem. Nat. Recreation and Park Assn., 1950-77; v.p. Nat. Recreation Found., 1950—; mem. Zoning Bd. Appeals, Bronxville, N.Y., 1970-74. Served to lt. USNR, 1943-46. Mem. Securities Industry Assn., N.Y.C. C. of C. Republican. Mem. Reformed Ch. Clubs: Downtown Assn., Siwanoy Country, Am. Yacht. Home: 27 Locust Ln Bronxville NY 10708 Office: 61 Broadway New York NY 10006

INGEBRITSON, JACK GORDON, real estate developer and financier; b. Berwyn, Ill., Mar. 22, 1946; s. Gordon L. and Hazel J. (Ulberg) I.; B.S. in Bus. Adminstrn., Northwestern U., 1968; postgrad. Northwestern U., 1969, Ariz. State U., 1971. With advt. dept. Chgo. Tribune, 1970; pres. Wellington Investment Co., Inc., 1971-73, Ingebritson Investment Co., Inc., Phoenix, 1973—; gen. partner J.I. Assos., Ltd., La Espanada, Ltd.; partner Residential Mktg. Systems; dir. Spear S Land & Cattle Co., Inc.; cons. to corps. Lic. real estate broker, Ariz. Mem. Home Builders Assn. Central Ariz., Sales and Mktg. Council, Phoenix C. of C., Scottsdale C. of C., Phi Delta Theta. Republican. Club: Jockey. Adv. panel Housing Mag., 1980-81. Home:

1905 E Medlock St Phoenix AZ 85016 Office: Suite 103 5301 N 7th St Phoenix AZ 85014

INGERMAN, MICHAEL LEIGH, hosp. cons.; b. N.Y.C., Nov. 30, 1937; s. Charles Stryker and Ernestine (Leigh) I.; B.S., George Washington U., 1963; m. Marie Ann Cosner, Apr. 19, 1962; children—Shawn Marie, Jenifer Lyn. Health planner Marin County, Calif., 1969-70, 70-72; regional cons. Bay Area Comprehensive Health Council, San Francisco, 1972-73; hosp. cons. Booz, Allen & Hamilton, San Francisco, 1974; health planning coordinator Peralta Hosp., Oakland, Calif., 1975-76; hosp. cons., Nicasio, Calif., 1976—. Treas. No. Calif. regional office Am. Friends Service Com., 1974-79, exec. com., 1969—, mem. nat. bd., 1969-75, 80—; treas. Coll. Park Friends Edn. Assn., 1974-79; mem. Marin County Civil Grand Jury, 1977-78; asst. chief Nicasio Vol. Fire Dept., 1976—. Mem. Am., Calif. hosp. assns. Address: 2101 Nicasio Valley Rd Nicasio CA 94946

INGERSLEW, NEILL DENNIS, printing co. exec.; b. Kirksville, Mo., Oct. 6, 1934; s. John P. and Lissa (Madsen) I.; B.S. in Edn., U. Mo., 1958; m. Shirley Ann Bareis, Oct. 8, 1954; children—John, Susan, Cheryl, Nancy. With Western Pub. Co., Hannibal, Mo., 1956—, mgr. Data Page div., St. Charles, Mo., 1969-77, sr. v.p., mgr. Metomail ops., 1977—. Republican. Lutheran. Club: Masons (32 deg.). Home: 404 Lincoln St Seward NE 68434 Office: 901 W Bond St Lincoln NE 68521

INGERSOLL, WILLIAM COWLES, accounting firm exec.; b. New Castle, Ind., Aug. 8, 1927; s. Harold G. and Florence (Shephard) I.; B.A., Knox Coll., 1951; M.B.A., Harvard, 1953; m. Marilyn H. Jones, Aug. 12, 1951. With Arthur Andersen & Co., Boston, 1952-53, Chgo., 1953-59, 70-78, Geneva, 1978—, N.Y.C., 1959-69, partner, 1962—. Mem. finance com. Chgo. council Girl Scouts U.S.A., 1974-75; bd. trustees Knox Coll., 1970—; bd. dirs. Harvard Bus. Sch. Chgo., 1971-74. Served with U.S. Army, 1946-47. Mem. Phi Gamma Delta. Republican. Presbyterian. Clubs: Rotary, Mid Am.; Racquet (Chgo.). Home: 9B Plateau De Frontenex 1208 Geneva Switzerland Office: 18 Quai General-Guisan 1211 Geneva Switzerland

INGOLD, PETER JOHN, bus. machines co. exec.; b. Bern, Switzerland, June 2, 1928; came to U.S., 1977; s. Werner F. and Margret I.; M.B.A. in Econs., U. Bern, 1953; m. Carmen Marmillod, 1975. Mng. dir. Chalet Cheese Co. Ltd., Switzerland, 1960-66; dir. mktg. Myerson Tooth Corp., Cambridge, Mass., 1966-73; v.p. internat. div. Hermes Precisa Internat., Yverdon, Switzerland, 1973-77; corporate v.p. Hermes Products Inc., Linden, N.J., 1977—. Served with Swiss Armed Forces, 1947-60. Office: 1900 Lower Rd Linden NJ 07036

INGRAHAM, JOHN WRIGHT, banker; b. Evanston, Ill., Nov. 10, 1930; s. Harold Gillette and Mildred Gail (Wright) I.; A.B., Harvard, 1952, M.B.A., 1957; postgrad. N.Y. Grad. Sch. Bus., 1963-68; m. Barbara Gaye Barker, Nov. 18, 1967. With Citibank, N.Y.C., 1957—, sr. v.p., sr. credit officer, 1970—; dir., vice chmn. bd. Penn Central Corp., 1978—; dir. Robertson Distbn. Systems, Houston, 1972—; chmn. ofcl. creditors com. W.T. Grant Co., 1975-76; mem. task force on conceptual framework for acctg. and fin. reporting Fin. Acctg. Standards Bd., 1974—. Served with USNR, 1952-55. Mem. Robert Morris Assos. (dir. 1972-75), Am. Bankers Assn. Republican. Christian Scientist. Clubs: Sleepy Hollow Country, Rockaway Hunting, Harvard Bus. Sch., Union (N.Y.C.). Home: 950 Park Ave New York NY 10028 Office: Citibank 399 Park Ave New York NY 10028

INGRAM, CLARENCE COWAN, savs. and loan assn. exec.; b. Statesville, N.C., Apr. 17, 1920; s. James Preston and Mary Ethel (Cowan) I.; B.S., Appalachian State U., 1941; m. Mary Jane Kelly, Nov. 4, 1950; 1 dau., Charlotte Jane. Mgr. loans Comml. Credit Corp., Hickory, N.C., 1946-47, Winston-Salem, N.C., 1947, office mgr., Fayetteville, N.C., 1948-52, dist. rep., 1952-56; mgr. loans Cross Creek Savs. & Loan Assn., Fayetteville, 1956, sec.-treas., 1957-62, exec. v.p., 1963-70, pres., 1970—. Dir., Fayetteville Indsl. Devel. Corp., Cape Fear Wood Preserving Corp. Pres. Methodist Coll. Found., 1972-73, treas., 1973-74. Bd. dirs. Fayetteville United Fund, 1973-74, Southeastern Speech and Hearing Services, Fayetteville, 1973—. Served with USNR, 1942-45. Mem. Downtown Fayetteville Assn. (dir., treas.), Am. Legion. Presbyterian (elder). Mason (Shriner, dir. Center), Lion. Club: Highland Country (Fayetteville). Home: 2000 Winterlochen Rd Fayetteville NC 28305 Office: 230 Green St Fayetteville NC 28305

IQBAL, JAWAID KHAWAJA, bus. exec.; b. New Delhi, India, Apr. 4, 1944; s. Khawaja Mohammed and Amina Iqbal (Bano) I.; B.B.A., Govt. Commerce Coll., U. Karachi, 1964; m. July 22, 1966; children—Nabila J., Humaira J. Factory asst. Zeba Textile Co., 1965-69; mgr. Karachi (Pakistan) Towels Ltd., export dir. Eastern Agencies Ltd., Karachi, 1969-77; partner, dir. Al Najah Constrn. Co., Karachi, 1977; exec. v.p. Am. Internat. Med. Inc., Bensenville, Ill., 1977-78; pres. Merc Internat. Inc., Woodlands, Tex., 1978—; internat. rep. Pacifica Mortgage, Newport Beach, Calif., 1978—; Tex. rep. Persepolis Holding Co. of Geneva. Mem. Inst. Mgmt. Moslem. Clubs: Lincoln Park Rowing (Chgo.); Karachi Boat, Karachi Yacht; Sir Frank Worrell Cricket (Evanston, Ill.); Internat. Sporting, London Rowing (London). Home: 7310 Brou Ln Houston TX 77074 Office: 4590 MacArthur Blvd Newport Beach CA 92660 also PO Box 7098 Woodlands TX 77380

IQBAL, MUZAFFAR, biochemist; b. Gurdaspur, India, Apr. 24, 1936; came to U.S., 1977; s. Tassudduq Hussain and Iqbal Begum Qureshi; B.Sc., Punjab U., Lahore, Pakistan, 1962, M.Sc., 1964; diploma in gen. biochemistry London U., 1968, diploma in biochemistry, 1970, Ph.D., 1975; m. Nasreen, Apr. 6, 1969; children—Syma, Umer, Usman. Research biochemist Seravac Labs. (Pty) Ltd., Maidenhead, Berkshire, Eng., 1964-69; Union Internat. Co., Ltd., London, 1969-70; researcher, instr., in charge enzyme prep. lab. Oxford Enzyme Group, U. Oxford, 1970-75; head enzyme unit Wessex Biochems., Bournemouth, Eng., 1975-77; mgr. quality control Coulter Diagnostics, Hialeah, Fla., 1977-78; dir. enzyme div. JBL Chem. Co., San Luis Obispo, Calif., 1978—. Mem. Royal Inst. Chemistry (Eng.), Inst. Biology (London), Biochem. Soc., Am. Assn. Clin. Chemistry, Am. Assn. Quality Control. Islam. Home: 81 Encanto Ln San Luis Obispo CA 93401 Office: JBL Chem Co Inc 825 Capitolio Way San Luis Obispo CA 93401

IRACI, JOHN JOSEPH, publishing co. exec.; b. N.Y.C., Apr. 5, 1921; s. John and Giustina (Badala) I.; student Georgetown U., 1939-42; m. Antoinette Caldiero, June 24, 1945; children—Donna Maria Iraci DeBlasis, Juidth Ellen Iraci Manni. Dist. mgr. Codell Publs., N.Y.C., 1945-48; pubs. rep. Donnell Co., N.Y.C., 1948-50; adv. mgr. Bryan Davis Publs., N.Y.C., 1950-55; dist. sales and eastern regional sales mgr. Sutton Pub. Co., White Plains, N.Y., 1955-72, v.p., advt. sale coordinator, 1972—. Mem. Transp. Com., Boro of Paramus (N.J.), 1956-58. Served with U.S. Army, 1942-45. Decorated Purple Heart. Mem. Am. Bus. Press Assn., Bus. Profl. Adv. Assn., 88th Inf. Div. Assn., Holy Name Soc. Roman Catholic (pres. parish council 1978-79). Home: 179 Arundel Pl Paramus NJ 07652 Office: 707 Westchester Ave White Plains NY 10604

IRANI, RIYAD RIDA, chem. co. exec.; b. Beirut, Jan. 15, 1935; s. Rida A. and Naz (Kiani) I.; came to U.S., 1953, naturalized, 1959; B.A. summa cum laude, Am. U. Beirut, 1953; Ph.D., U. So. Calif., 1957; m. Joan D. French, Jan. 8, 1956; children—Glenn, Lillian, Martin. Research chemist Monsanto Chem. Co., St. Louis, 1957-60, research group leader, 1960-63, sr. research group leader, 1963-67; asso. dir. research T.R. Evans Research Center, Diamond Shamrock Corp., Painesville, Ohio, 1967-69, dir. research, 1969-73; v.p. chem research and devel. Olin Corp., Stamford, Conn., 1973-74, sr. v.p. chems., 1974-76, exec. v.p., 1976—, chief operating officer chems., 1978, pres. chems., 1978—, corp. pres., 1980—. Mem. Research Soc. Am. (pres. 1962-63), Am. Chem. Soc., Sigma Xi, Phi Beta Kappa, Phi Lambda Upsilon. Author: Particle Size, 1963. Home: 250 Lost District Dr New Canaan CT 06840 Office: 120 Long Ridge Rd Stamford CT 06904

IREIFEJ, JIRIES YOUSEF, constrn. co. exec.; b. Ajlun, Jordan, May 6, 1948; came to U.S., 1975, naturalized, 1981; s. Yousef Salameh and Farideh Shihadeh (Sayegh) I.; B.S., Manhattan Coll., 1978, M.B.A., 1981; m. Singwala S., Aug. 5, 1979; 1 son, Shadi. Tchr. French, Jerusalem and Lebanon, 1967-71; office mgr. Planum Co., Amman, Jordan, 1971-74, 78—; pres. Ireifej Inc., Giant Hero Restaurant, Yonkers, N.Y., 1978—; fin. aid counselor Manhattan Coll., 1981. Address: 12 Bell Pl Yonkers NY 10701

IRETON, JOHN FRANCIS, food processing co. exec.; b. Balt., May 15, 1939; s. J. Francis and Mary (O'Neill) I.; B.A., Loyola Coll., 1961; m. Dorothy Anne Minakowsky, Nov. 23, 1962; children—Mary Catherine, Megan, Amy, Allison, Elizabeth. Acct., Main Hurdman & Cranston, Balt., 1957-62; exec. v.p., chief fin. officer Gino's, Inc., King of Prussia, Pa., 1962-72; pres., chief exec. officer Am. FoodService Corp., King of Prussia, 1972—. Mem. Phila. Crime Commn. Mem. Fin. Execs. Inst. Home: 339 Beaumont Rd Devon PA 19333 Office: 400 Drew Ct King of Prussia PA 19406

IRISH, GARY DON, securities firm exec.; b. Topeka, Kans., Nov. 10, 1933; s. Roland C. and Martha L. (Stachelback) I.; B.S. in Fin., U. Kans., 1955; m. Barbara Ley, Oct. 21, 1961; children—Michael Shawn, Kelly Ann, Megan Lee. Securities analyst Bankers Life Co., Des Moines, 1958-59; instl. security sales E.F. Hutton & Co. Inc., Kansas City, Mo., 1959—, asst. v.p., 1968-69, asso. br. mgr., 1969-71, v.p., 1971-80, 1st v.p., 1980—; dir. Blakemore Bros. Bldg. Co., Inc., House of Commons, Inc.; ann. guest prof. bus. U. Kans. Bd. dirs. Kansas City (Mo.) Red Bridge YMCA, 1975—, Sigma Nu House Corp. Served with USN, 1955-58. Recipient Wall St. Jour. Excellence in Finance award, 1955. Republican. Presbyterian. Clubs: Kansas City, Indian Hills Country. Home: 2108 Arno Rd Shawnee Mission KS 66208 Office: 920 Baltimore St Kansas City MO 64105

IRISH, PATTY WILLIAMS, employment service adminstr.; b. San Marcos, Tex., Sept. 5, 1936; d. Walter Lee and Pawnee (Gracey) Williams; B.S., Cornell U., 1958; m. Jerry A. Irish, June 21, 1958; 1 son, Jeffrey Scott. Vocat. counselor Bayshore Employment Center, 1971-72; co-dir. New Ways to Work, Palo Alto, Calif., 1973-75; founder, dir. Work Options, YWCA, Wichita, Kans., 1976-79; dir. Work Options for Women, Inc., Wichita, 1979—; mem. Nat. Task on Women and Non-Traditional Jobs, Wichita Task Force Career Edn. in Pub. Schs. Bd. dirs. Planned Parenthood Kans. Mem. Wichita League Women Voters (chmn. human resources com.), Women's Coalition, Women's Polit. Caucus. Democrat. Home: 311 Whitfield Pl Wichita KS 67206 Office: 231 N Market St Wichita KS 67202

IRVINE, R(AYMOND) GERALD, JR., elec. engr.; b. N.Y.C., Mar. 31, 1937; s. Raymond Gerald and Jane T. (Schenck) I.; B.S. with honors in Elec. Engring. (Gen. Motors Scholar), Norwich U., 1959; postgrad. U. Vt., 1959-60, Union U., 1971-73; m. Elizabeth Ann Williams Bazemore, Nov. 23, 1966; children—Juanita Leigh, Edward Bruce, Terri Sue, Wendy Lynn. Asso. design engr. Y-12 plant Nuclear div. Union Carbide Corp., Oak Ridge, 1963-64; engr. electric div. Stone & Webster Engring. Corp., Boston, 1964-68; elec. engr. Fed. Power Commn., Washington, 1968-70; staff engr. N.Y. State Dept. Pub. Service, Albany, 1970-74; project engr. Dubin-Mindell-Bloome Engrs., N.Y.C., 1974; staff elec. engr. IBM, Sterling Forest, N.Y., 1974-78; sr. engr. Western Electric Co., N.Y.C., 1978—; cons. electric power engr., 1968—; cons. Vols. in Internat. Tech. Assistance. Served to 1st lt. Signal Corps, U.S. Army, 1960-63. Registered profl. engr., Mass., N.Y., D.C.; cert. airplane pilot, 1st class radiotelephone and radar operator. Mem. IEEE, Nat. (mem. energy com. 1978), N.Y. State (pres. capital dist. 1974) socs. profl. engrs., Assn. of Energy Engrs., ASHRAE, Illuminating Engring. Soc., Norwich Engrs. Soc., Nat. Fire Protection Assn., Internat. Assn. Elec. Inspectors, Tau Beta Phi. Democrat. Club: Masons. Contbr. articles on elec. power engring. to profl. jours. Home: 77 Mile Rd Suffern NY 10901 Office: Western Electric Co 222 Broadway New York NY 10038

IRVINE, THOMAS LYNN, tng. cons. co. exec.; b. Schenectady, Oct. 31, 1940; s. George Lynn and Genevieve (Jones) I.; A.A., Menlo Coll., 1960; B.S., U. Denver, 1964; M.B.A., C.B.A. Inst., Chgo., 1976; m. Patricia Friedlander, Feb. 7, 1962. Field rep. Adolph Coors Co., Golden, Colo., 1964-66; field sales rep. G. D. Searle & Co., Chgo., 1966-69, dist. sales mgr., 1969-72, mgr. sales tng., 1972-74; gastrointestinal products mgr., 1974-76; dir. med. mktg. Systema Corp. Chgo., 1976-77, v.p., 1977—. Served with Security Agy., U.S. Army, 1961-64. Mem. Assn. Mgmt. Consultants, Nat. Soc. Performance and Instrn. Republican. Presbyterian. Club: Northbrook (Ill.) Sports. Contbr. articles to profl. jours. Home: Route 1 Box 31A Grayslake IL 60030 Office: 150 N Wacker Dr Chicago IL 60606

IRVING, ROBERT CHURCHILL, mfg. co. exec.; b. Waltham, Mass., Sept. 15, 1928; s. Frederick Charles and Emily Alvina (Churchill) I.; A.S., Franklin Inst. of Boston, 1965; certificate of profl. achievement Northeastern U., 1975; children—Robert F., John W. Sr. draftsman Mason-Neilan, Boston, 1948-54; mgr. design services Kinney Vacuum Co., Gen. Signal Corp., Boston, 1955-69; mgr. engring. services Sturtevant div. Westinghouse Electric Corp., Hyde Park, Mass., 1978—. Served with U.S. Army, 1946-48. Mem. Am. Def. Preparedness Assn., Am. Soc. for Quality Control (sr.), Nat. Mgmt. Assn. Republican. Home: 11 Linda Ave Brockton MA 02401 Office: 25 Damon St Hyde Park MA 02136

IRWIN, GEORGE ROBERT, govt. agy. adminstr.; b. Hoboken, N.J., Nov. 3, 1935; s. George McClave and Anna Frances (Tansey) I.; B.S. in Bus. Adminstrn., St. Peter's Coll., Jersey City, 1959; M.B.A., N.Y. U., 1963; m. Mary J. Hojnacki, Oct. 1, 1960; children—George John, Stephen Andrew. Bank examiner Mfrs. Hanover Trust Co., N.Y.C., 1954-59, 61-62; asst. office mgr. H.A. Caeser Co., N.Y.C., 1962-68; asst. v.p. First Union-Caesar Corp., N.Y.C., 1968-71, v.p., controller, 1971-73, v.p., account exec., 1973-75; mgr. postal accounts U.S. Postal Data Center, N.Y.C., 1975-77, gen. mgr. systems and programming div., 1977—. Served with U.S. Army, 1959-61. Mem. N.Y. U. Alumni Assn., Am. Mgmt. Assn., Factors Controllers Assn. Home: 4 Ginda Ave Carteret NJ 07008 Office: Main PO Bldg 33d St and 8th Ave New York NY 10099

IRWIN, NANCY BARBARA, internat. chem. co. exec.; b. Cleve., Apr. 16, 1944; d. L. M. and Barbara L. (Boer) I.; A.B., Miami U., 1965; M.B.A., Cleve. State U., 1977. With Scientific Products, Edison, N.J., 1970-71; chief advt. and pub. relations U.S. Army Recruiting Main Sta., Edison, 1972; product mgr. Harshaw Chem. Co., Cleve., 1975-77, mktg. mgr., 1977-79; regional sales mgr. Armak, 1980—. Served to capt. U.S. Army, 1965-69. Mem. Sales and Mktg. Execs.-Internat., Chem. Market Research Assn., Beta Gamma Sigma, Sigma Kappa (auditor Cleve. W. Shore Alumnae). Episcopalian. Club: Women's City (Cleve.). Home and Office: 1925 Lakeview Ave Rocky River OH 44116

IRWIN, RICHARD DUCKWORTH, photog. co. exec.; b. Cin., May 31, 1935; s. Harry Whetstone and Helen Elise Anna (Duckworth) I.; B.A. in Math., U. Maine, 1958; m. Virginia Jefferson Davis, Apr. 29, 1966; children—Katherine Seward, Christopher Jefferson. With Chase Manhattan Bank, N.Y.C., 1957-58, 60-62, Suburban Trust Co., Westfield, N.J., 1962-65, Hayden Stone, Inc., 1965-70; with Fotomat Corp., Stamford, Conn., 1970—, now chmn. bd., pres., chief exec. officer. Served in U.S. Army, 1958-60. Episcopalian. Office: 64 Danbury Rd Wilton CT 06897*

ISAAC, WILLIAM MULLER, community devel. co. exec.; b. India, Dec. 29, 1922; came to U.S., 1965, naturalized, 1973; s. Vedanayagam Thangiah and Packiam Lakshimi Illangudi; A.A., Spicer Meml. Coll., India, 1944; B.S., Columbus Union Coll., 1967; m. Annammal Ponniah, Aug. 30, 1944; children—Starlet, Catherine, Marjorie, Sophia. Contract auditor United Planning Orgn., Washington, 1967-69, gen. ledger acct., 1969-74, chief acct., 1974-76, dir. fin., 1977—. Elder Seventh-day Adventist Ch., Takoma Park, Md. Mem. Smithsonian Instn., So. Asia Adventist Assn. Democrat. Editor: Tamil Messenger, 1957-60. Home: 422 Lincoln Ave Takoma Park MD 20012 Office: 1021 14th St NW Washington DC 20005

ISAACSON, BARRY JOEL, owner legal assistance co.; b. Chgo., Apr. 16, 1948; s. William M. Dorothy (Schlinsky) I.; B.A. in Histroy, U. Ill., Chgo. Circle Campus, 1970, M.A.T., Urbana, 1977. Founder, pres. Atty. Aid Assocs., Inc., Chgo., 1972—; instr. legal assts. Chgo. City Coll., 1975-76; cons. Mass. Mut. Life Ins. Co. Arbitrator, Chgo. chpt. Better Bus. Bur., 1973—. Jewish. Home: 2216 N Sedgwick St Chicago IL 60614 Office: 109 N Dearborn Chicago IL 60602

ISAACSON, HENRY CARL, JR., steel co. exec.; b. Seattle, Mar. 24, 1927; s. Henry Carl and Martha Evelyn (Lindberg) I.; B.S., U.S. Mcht. Marine Acad., 1948; B.A., U. Wash., Seattle, 1951; m. Carol Francis Turner, Feb. 9, 1952; children—Susan N., Jody L., Henry Carl, III, Thomas G., John H. Served as 3d mate U.S. Lines, 1948; with Isaacson Corp., and predecessor, Seattle, 1952-57, 59—, sales mgr., v.p., 1959-65, pres., 1967—, chmn., 1975—; founder, exec. v.p. Pacific Am. Comml. Co., 1957-59; chmn. Young Corp., 1967—; dir. Rainier Nat. Bank, Rainier Ban Corp. Bd. dirs. Swedish Hosp., Seattle, 1971—. Served as officer USNR, 1945-57. Mem. Soc. Naval Architects and Marine Engrs. Clubs: Bohemian, Pacific Union (San Francisco); Rainier, Seattle Yacht, University (Seattle). Home: Cedar Grove Olympic Dr The Highlands Seattle WA 98177 Office: 8620 E Marginal Way S PO Box 3625 Seattle WA 98124

ISACK, FILIP IACOV, stock broker; b. Jerusalem, May 28, 1949; s. Haim and Josephine (Kaner) I.; came to U.S., 1971, naturalized, 1976; student Poly. Inst. Bucharest, 1969; B.S., U. Ill., 1972. Wine cons. Pieroth Wines, River Grove, Ill., 1972-74; stockbroker Bache Halsey Stuart, San Francisco, 1974-77, Blyth, Eastman, Dillon, San Francisco, 1977-80; v.p. Paine Webber-Blyth, Eastman, San Francisco, 1980—. Republican. Jewish. Home: 2357 Jackson St San Francisco CA 94115 Office: 55 California St San Francisco CA 94111

ISAUTIER, BERNARD FRANÇOIS, oil co. exec.; b. St. Symphorien, Indre et Loire, France, Sept. 10, 1942; immigrated to Can.; s. François and Genevieve (Roy) I.; grad. Ecole des Mines, Paris, 1966; grad. Institut d'Etudes Politiques, Paris, 1968; m. Charlotte Roche, July 22, 1968; children—Anne-Caroline, Armelle, Francois. Adv. to Pres., Republic of Niger (Africa), 1968-70; head mining exploration dept. Ministry of Industry, Paris, 1970-73, adv. for energy and raw materials, 1973-75; gen. mgr. SEREPT, 1976-78; now pres. Aquitaine Co. of Can. Ltd., Calgary, Albt.; dir. Al-Aquitaine Exploration Ltd., Aquitaine Pa. Inc., Cansulex Ltd., Rainbow Pipe Line Co. Ltd., The Sulphur Inst., Universal Gas Co., Served with French Army. Decorated Chevalier de l'Ordre du Merite. Mem. Canadian Petroleum Assn, Calgary C. of C. Clubs: Calgary Petroleum, U. Calgary Chancellors, La Chambre de Commerce Française au Can., L'Alliance Française de Calgary, Ranchmen's. Office: 555 4th Ave SW Calgary AB T2P 0J6 Canada

ISBELL, HAROLD M., banker; b. Maquoketa, Iowa, Sept. 20, 1936; s. H. Max and Marcella E. I.; B.A. cum laude (scholar), Loras Coll., 1959; M.A. (fellow), U. Notre Dame, 1962; m. Mary Carolyn Cosgriff, June 15, 1963; children—Walter Harold, Susan Elizabeth, David Harold, Alice Kathleen. Instr. U. Notre Dame, South Bend, Ind., 1963-64, asso. prof. St. Mary's Coll., 1969-72; asst. prof. San Francisco Coll. for Women, 1964-69; with Continental Bank & Trust Co., Salt Lake City, 1972—, v.p., 1977—, comml. credit officer, 1978—, also dir. Trustee, Judge Meml. Cath. High Sch. Salt Lake City; mem. Utah Gov.'s Council for Handicapped and Developmentally Disabled Persons; active ACLU, Common Cause. Mem. MLA, Mediaeval Acad. Am., Robert Morris Assos. Democrat. Roman Catholic. Club: Alta. Editor and translator: The Last Poets of Imperial Rome, 1971; contbr. to publs. in field of Latin and contemporary Am. Lit. Office: PO Box 30177 200 S Main St Salt Lake City UT 84125

ISBELL, MARION WILLIAM, restaurant and hotel exec.; b. nr. Memphis, Aug. 12, 1905; s. Howard James and Mary (Mayfield) I.; student pub. schs.; m. Ingrid Lucida Helsing, Oct. 2, 1927; children—Marion William, Mary Elaine, Robert James. Owner, pres., dir. Isbell's, chain of restaurants, Chgo., 1943-46; pres. Ramada Inns, Inc., 1962-70, chmn. bd., 1962-79, hon. chmn. bd., 1979—. Chief instl. users br. OPA, 1943-45, dir. Chgo. Met. Area, 1943-45; active ARC, Chgo. Community Fund. Mem. Nat. (past pres., dir.), Chgo. (past pres., dir.) restaurant assns. Clubs: Arizona (Phoenix); Paradise Valley Country (Scottsdale, Ariz.). Office: Ramada Inns 3838 E Van Buren St Phoenix AZ 85008

ISELI, ANDRÉ WERNER, investment banker; b. La Chaux-de-Fonds, Switzerland, Dec. 22, 1932; s. Werner W. and Germaine (Banderet) I.; came to U.S., 1940, naturalized, 1955; B.A., Linfield Coll., 1955; postgrad. Sorbonne U., 1955-56, La Salle U., 1965; m. Gail A. Radke, Apr. 8, 1956; children—Tracy Kay, Elliette Gail, Werner Andre. Asst. mgr. Iris Theatre, Los Angeles, 1958-59; asst. floor mgr. Pacific Coast Stock Exchange, 1960-61; trainee Morgan & Co., 1961-64; br. mgr. Morgan, Olmstead & Allen, 1964-65, mgr. fgn. instns. dept., 1965-66; v.p. Morgan, Olmstead, Kennedy & Gardner, Inc., Los Angeles, 1966-68, sr. v.p., 1968—, also chmn. investment com.; pres. Brookmere Assn., Inc., also vice chmn. bd.; pres. Iseli & Iseli Assos., Iseli Nursery, Inc.; partner ICM Corp.; dir. LaTerre Corp., Double Eagle Exploration, Project 5 Drilling Co. Mem. Americanism Ednl. League, 1967—. Pres. Iseli Found., Iseli Nursery; chmn. bd. trustees, mem. exec. com., mem. alumni council Linfield Coll., McMinnville, Oreg., Los Angeles World Affairs Council; trustee Am. Hort. Soc. Served with AUS, 1956-58. Recipient Service award Am. Heart Assn., 1965. Mem. Internat. Comml.

Exchange Inc., Town Hall, Los Angeles World Affairs Council, Produce Exchange, Los Angeles C. of C. Clubs: Los Angeles Athletic; Santa Monica Racquet; Baur au Lac (Zurich). Home: 10297 SE Eastmont Gresham OR 97030 Office: Governor's Palace 123 E Powell Blvd Gresham OR 97030

ISERI, THOMAS TADAMITU, produce co. exec.; b. Sumner, Wash., Nov. 26, 1907; s. Mat Matahichi and Kisa (Okuna) I.; student Wilsons Modern Bus. Coll., Seattle, 1929-30; m. Winona Eilene Behrbaum, Feb. 25, 1937; children—Margie Iseri Anderson, Elizabeth Iseri Simpson, Janet Iseri Palmer, Timothy Matthew. Foreman, Rainier Packing Co., Thomas, Wash., 1929, Puget Sound Vegetable Growers Assn., Sumner, 1930-32; foreman, bookkeeper Wash. Pea Growers Assn., 1933-34; partner Western Producers Exchange, Auburn, Wash., 1935-42; foreman Jaekel & Rogers, Weiser, Idaho, 1942, partner, Ontario, Oreg., 1943-62; pres., mgr. Thomas Iseri Produce Co., Ontario, 1962—; pres., dir. Just Rite Farms, Inc., Thomas T. Iseri, Inc., Thomas Iseri Produce Co. of Wash.; mem. Idaho Eastern Oreg. Onion Control Com., 1956-75. Pres., sec. Valley Civic League, 1933-37; chmn. N.W. Dist. council Japanese-Am. Citizens League, 1935-36, 41-42, pres. Snake River Valley chpt., 1947, also mem. One Thousand Club; mem. City Budget Bd., 1955-57; mem. Malheur County Budget Bd., 1967-70, chmn., 1970. Bd. dirs. Holy Rosary Hosp., Ontario, 1974-77. Mem. Idaho-Oreg. Fruit and Vegetable Assn. (dir. 1965-74, pres. 1967), Nat. Onion Assn. (trustee 1970-79), Idaho Eastern Oreg. Onion Promotion Com. Kiwanian. Home: 762 SW 12th St Ontario OR 97914 Office: PO Box 250 Ontario OR 97914

ISERN, EDWARD HENRY, real estate broker; b. Kansas City, Mo., Sept. 28, 1942; s. Edward Henry and Marian Isbell (Moses) I.; student U. Kans., 1960-61; B.A., Western N.Mex. U., 1964; postgrad. U. Stockholm, 1964-65, U. Colo., 1965-67; m. Margaret Ann Carter, Jan. 25, 1973; children—Edward, Gretchen Mattox, Jill Mattox, Kristine. Staff researcher Colo. Legis. Council, Denver, 1967-69; salesman Jim Reich Realty, Boulder, Colo., 1969-71; partner Reynolds & Co., Boulder, 1971—; pres. Diagonal Indsl. Center, Inc., Boulder, 1972—; dir. Platte Enterprises, Inc., Boulder. Bd. dirs. Grace Luth. Found., 1968-72; Republican precinct chmn., 1976-78; gen. operating partner ACE Investment Co., Boulder, 1978—. Am. Swedish Found. grantee U. Stockholm, 1964-65. Mem. Boulder Bd. Realtors. Republican. Lutheran (v.p. 1967-68). Clubs: Colo. Ducks Unltd. (asst. state chmn. 1976-78); Ducks Unltd. (chmn. 1971-76) (Boulder). Home: 503 Kalmia Ave Boulder CO 80302 Office: 3216 Arapahoe St Boulder CO 80302

ISERT, JOSEPH WILLIAM, JR., real estate exec.; b. Louisville, Apr. 11, 1924; s. Joseph William and Sara Frances (Martine) I.; student U. Ky., 1980—; m. Jannette Lee Reynolds, Dec. 20, 1962; children—Stephen Michael, Joseph William. Owner, Isert Appraisal Co., Lexington, 1947—; mortgage banker Realty Mortgage Co., Lexington, 1954-61, The Kissell Co., Lexington, 1961-62, United Mortgage Service, Lexington, 1963-66, Lincoln Mortgage Co., Lexington, 1966-68, James H. Pence Co., Lexington, 1968-70; dist. rev. appraise Ky. Dept. Hwys., Lexington, 1970-72; chairholder in real estate Lexington Tech. Inst., U. Ky., 1976-80, asst. prof. real estate studies, 1976—. Served with USN, 1941-46, 50-51. Mem. Internat. Soc. Real Estate Appraisers, Nat. Assn. Corp. Real Estate Execs., Nat. Real Estate Educators Assn., Am. Assn. Cert. Appraisers, Nat. Assn. Rev. Appraisers, Am. Soc. Fine Arts Appraisers, AAUP, Assn. Community and Jr. Colls., Am. Real Estate and Urban Econs. Assn. Republican. Roman Catholic. Club: K.C. Home: 4074 Solberg Ln Lexington KY 40503 Office: Lexington Tech Inst U Ky Oswald Bldg Cooper Dr Lexington KY 40506

ISRAEL, ADRIAN CREMIEUX, banker, mcht.; b. N.Y.C., Nov. 6, 1915; s. Adolph Cremieux and Babette (Bloch) I.; grad. Phillips Acad., Andover, Mass., 1932; B.S., Yale, 1936; m. Joy Whitmore, June 25, 1971; children by previous marriage—Ellen I. Rosen, Andrew C. (dec.), Thomas C., Nancy Israel. With A.C. Israel Enterprises, Inc., N.Y.C., 1936—, pres., 1945-65, chmn. bd., 1965—; ltd. partner Bache & Co., N.Y.C., 1945-64, gen. partner, chmn. exec. com., 1964-65, pres., dir., 1965-66; chmn. bd. Havenfield Corp., N.Y.C., 1967-73; pres., chief exec. officer, dir. ACLI Internat., Inc., 1971—, Adrian & James, Inc., Stamford, Conn., 1936—; chmn. bd., dir. Lane Drug Corp., Inc., Toledo, 1956-76, A.C. Israel Woodhouse Co., Ltd., London, Eng., 1970—, Peoples Drug Stores, Washington, 1976—; mem. N.Y. Cocoa Exchange, N.Y. Coffee and Sugar Exchange, Commodity Exchange, N.Y. Futures Exchange, Chgo. Bd. Trade. Cons. WPB, also War Food Adminstrn., 1942-46. Bd. dirs., pres. A. Cremieux Israel Found., 1946—; bd. dirs. Yale Devel. Bd., 1964—; trustee Montefiore Hosp., N.Y.C.; bd. incorporators Stamford (Conn.) Hosp. Clubs: Governor's, Wall Street, Bond (N.Y.C.); Yale (Stamford and N.Y.C.); Century Country (Purchase, N.Y.); Landmark (Stamford); Stanwich (Greenwich, Conn.); Metropolitan (Washington); Bermuda Dunes (Calif.) Country; Mid-Ocean (Bermuda). Home: 247 Ingleside Rd Stamford CT 06903 Office: 717 Westchester Ave White Plains NY 10604

ISRAEL, DENNIS ROBERT, communications exec.; b. Detroit, Dec. 15, 1942; s. Charles and Bernice Joy (Nemer) I.; B.A., U. Detroit, 1965; M.A., U. Ill., 1971; children—Dawn, Marcus. Vice pres. Westinghouse Broadcasting Co., 1968-71, RCA Corp. and NBC, 1971-76; exec. v.p. Straus Communications, N.Y.C., 1976-78; pres., chief exec. officer Greater L.I. Communications, Inc., Babylon, N.Y., also pres. Dennis R. Israel & Assos., N.Y.C., 1978—; adj. prof. N.Y. U. Mem. Nat. Assn. Broadcasters, L.I. Radio Broadcasters Assn. Republican. Jewish. Club: Friars (N.Y.C.). Contbr. articles to broadcast publs. Home: 34 Princess Gate Oakdale Long Island NY 11769 Office: 1290 Peconic Ave Babylon Long Island NY 11734 also 60 E 42d St Suite 822 New York NY 10017

ISRAEL, LEONARD, consumer electronics exec.; b. N.Y.C., May 25, 1940; s. Jack and Clara (Rautenberg) I.; B.B.A., CCNY, 1962; M.B.A., L.I. U., 1972; m. Sandria Slawson, Sept. 13, 1968; children—Jason, Tyler. Sr. acct. Eisner & Lubin, C.P.A.'s, 1962-66; mgr. internal audits F & M Schaefer Brewing Co., 1968-75; controller Sony Video Co., N.Y.C., 1976—; adj. prof. CUNY. Served with USAR, 1963. Mem. Am. Inst. C.P.A.'s, N.Y. State Soc. C.P.A.'s. Contbr. articles on fin. and acctg. to Nat. Assn. Accts. Home: 25 Gallaway Ln Valhalla NY 10595 Office: 9 W 57th St New York NY 11019

ITIN, ROBERT BRUCE, JR., oil co. exec.; b. Batavia, Ohio, Sept. 15, 1931; s. Robert B. and Carrie I.; B.S.C., Ohio U., 1953; m. June C. Rucker, Sept. 5, 1953; children—Robin, Janel. Mem. sales staff Shell Oil Co., 1955-61; various sales mgmt. positions Texaco, Inc., 1961-69; pres. Itin Oil Co., Dearborn Heights, Mich., 1969—, Dearborn Wheels Inc., 1974—. Pres. Dearborn Inter Service Club Council, 1981. Served to 1st lt. U.S. Army, 1953-55. Mem. Delta Sigma Pi, Sigma Nu. Republican. Presbyterian. Clubs: Kiwanis (pres. 1979, lt. gov. Div. 4 Mich. Dist. 1981) (Dearborn, Mich.); Masons, Shriners. Home: 646 Mohawk St Dearborn MI 48124 Office: Itin Oil Co 6425 N Telegraph St Dearborn Heights MI 48127

ITIN, THOMAS WILLIAM, internat. fin. cons.; b. Mt. Holly, O., Sept. 14, 1934; s. Robert Bruce and Carrie (Crouch) I.; B.S., Cornell U., 1957; M.B.A., N.Y. U., 1959, postgrad., 1959-60; m. Shirley Besemer, Jan. 28, 1955; children—Dawn Elizabeth, Timothy Sean. Mem. employee relations dept. Mobil Oil Co., N.Y.C., 1957-60; employee relations adviser Mobil Internat., Libya, Europe, Africa, 1960-62; instr. U. Md., Libya, 1960-62; self-employed ins. broker, Elmhurst, Ill., 1962-63; pres., chmn. bd. Acrodyne Corp., investment bankers, Detroit, 1963—, TWI Internat., Inc., Consultants Corp. Devel., 1968—; chmn. bd. TimberLee Hills Inc., 1968-76, Aseco, Inc., 1969-70, Steel Tree Group Inc., 1971—; chmn. bd., pres. Lilliendahl Corp.; chmn. bd. Colo. Ridge Corp., Itin Oil, Inc., Dearborn Wheels, Inc. Mem. Personnel Mgmt. Council Libya (past pres.), Racing Patrons Inc. of Mich. (co-founder, pres.). Republican. Contbr. articles to trade newspapers, mags. Home: 4831 Old Orchard Trail Orchard Lake MI 48033 Office: 29621 Northwestern Hwy Southfield MI 48034 also POB 252 Tripoli Libya

ITO, MORIO, trading co. exec.; b. N.Y.C., Oct. 14, 1924; s. Takeo and Tsuneko (Komuro) I.; student Tokyo U. Commerce, 1942-44, B.A., 1948; m. Atsuko Asahara, Apr. 27, 1961; children—Yukiko, Mikiko, Rieko, Kaeko. With Toshoku Ltd., Tokyo, 1948-52, N.Y.C., 1952-56, San Francisco, 1956-59, Tokyo, 1959-63, London, 1963-65; mgr. Toshoku GmbH, Hamburg, Ger., 1965-69, Toshoku Ltd., San Francisco, 1969-72; gen. mgr. Tokyo Machinery Dept., Tokyo, 1972-77, dir., 1977—; pres. Toshoku Am., Inc., N.Y.C., 1977—, Toshoku Can., Ltd., 1977—; mng. dir. Toshoku Ltd., 1979—. Trustee, Japanese Ednl. Inst. of N.Y. Mem. Japanese C. of C. of N.Y. (dir. and chmn. gen. mdse. div. 1977—), Chgo. Bd. Trade, Bd. Trade of Kansas City, Mpls. Grain Exchange, Coffee, Sugar and Cocoa Exchange, Japan Soc. Club: The Nippon. Office: 551 Fifth Ave New York NY 10017

ITOH, SEIICHI, banker; b. Tokyo, Japan, June 24, 1933: s. Doki and Mie (Sugimori) I.; M.B.A., Tokyo U., 1956; m. Michiko Kato, Nov. 26, 1961. Sr. v.p., br. mgr. Bank of Tokyo Trust Co., N.Y.C., 1974-76; sr. regional mgr. Bank of Tokyo, Tokyo, 1976-78; chmn. bd., pres. Chgo.-Tokyo Bank, Chgo., 1979—. Clubs: Econ., Exec., University (Chgo.). Office: 40 N Dearborn St Chicago IL 60602

IVERSEN, PHILLIP GORDON, computer leasing co. exec.; b. Chgo., Mar. 4, 1933; s. Norman Samuel and Marion Cornelia (Gordon) I.; B.S., U. Ariz., 1955; M.B.A., U. Chgo., 1969; m. Karen Hayes, Sept. 30, 1966; children—Gordon Christopher, Derek Robert. Systems rep. IBM Corp., Evanston, Ill., 1957-59; regional systems mgr., nat. accounts mgr. Honeywell Inc., Chgo., 1959-67; dir., chmn. bd. Indecon, Inc., Chgo., 1968-72; dir. ins. mktg. Univ. Computer, Dallas, 1972-74; dir. market planning Greyhound Computer, Phoenix, 1974—. Served with U.S. Army, 1955-57. Certified in data processing. Mem. Data Processing Mgmt. Assn. Episcopalian. Home: 5211 E Orchid St Paradise Valley AZ 85253 Office: Greyhound Tower Phoenix AZ 85077

IVERSON, ALVIN ARNOLD, instrument engr.; b. Venice, Fla., Feb. 21, 1944; s. Alvin Glen and Mildred (Steiro) I.; A.A., Ranger Jr. Coll., 1964; B.A. in Physics, North Tex. State U., 1968, postgrad. in physics and chemistry, 1969-72. Instrument maintenance engr. dept. chemistry North Tex. State U., Denton, 1968-69; project engr. Tex. Instruments, Dallas, 1972-74; maintenance engr. Celanese Chem. Co., Bishop, Tex., 1974-76; project mgr. The Bendix Corp., Lewisburg, W.Va., 1976-79; sr. instrument engr. Arco Chem. Co., Channelview, Tex., 1979—; speaker Internat. Symposium on Molecular Spectroscopy, 1970, 71; optical cons., 1970-72. Vice pres. Greenbrier Valley Theatre, Lewisburg, 1978-79; capt. Fairlea (W.Va.) Vol. Fire Dept., 1979; trustee Channelview Vol. Fire Dept., 1980—. Mem. Am. Mgmt. Assn., Instrument Soc. Am. (sr.), Am. Inst. Chem. Engrs., TAPPI, Tex. Fire Marshall and Firefighters Assn., Harris County Firefighters Assn., Sports Car Club Am., Sigma Pi Sigma (charter), Phi Theta Kappa. Episcopalian. Club: Elks. Contbr. articles on quantum chemistry and molecular spectroscopy to profl. jours. Office: PO Box 777 Channelview TX 77530

IVERSON, IVAN NED, investment analyst; b. Provo, Utah, Mar. 3, 1943; s. Ivan Charles and Nihla Marie (Hiatt) I.; student Weber State Coll., Ogden, Utah, 1961-62, 65; B.S. in Bus. Mgmt. and Finance, Brigham Young U., 1968; M.B.A., Northwestern U., 1969; m. Linda Whitesides, Sept. 6, 1968; children—Andrea, Paul Ned, Kathryn, Kara, Daniel Evan. Family security analyst Met. Life Ins. Co., Denver, 1969-70; instr. bus. adminstrn. Weber State Coll., 1970-73; investment analyst Ch. of Jesus Christ of Latter-day Saints, Salt Lake City, 1973—; fin. cons.; asst. treas. Desert Mut. Benefit Assn.; lectr. finance and ins. Alvin Barrett scholar, First Security Corp. scholar. Mem. Fin. Analysts Fedn., Fin. Mgmt. Assn., Profl. Bus. Assn. Mem. Ch. of Jesus Christ of Latter-day Saints (missionary N.E. Eng. 1962-64). Contbr. articles to profl. publs. Home: 434 W Gentile St Layton UT 84041 Office: 50 E N Temple Salt Lake City UT 84150

IVERSON, STEVEN MARTIN, univ. lab. adminstr.; b. Bklyn., Oct. 29, 1944; s. Louis G. and Gloria (Alpert) I.; B.S. in Indsl. Relations, N.Y. U., 1966; m. Annette M. Rosa, Dec. 1, 1968; children—Paul, Lisa. Supr., selection and compensation Standard Plastic Products Inc., S. Plainfield, N.J., 1968-69; mgr. employment Personal Products Co., Milltown, N.J., 1970-72; dir. selection and benefits Ortho Pharm. Corp., Raritan, N.J., 1972-74; dir. personnel Johnson & Johnson Dental Products Co., E. Windsor, N.J., 1974-78; dir. personnel Plasma Physics Lab., Princeton, U., 1978—. Mem. Am. Soc. Personnel Adminstrn. (founding pres. Central N.J. chpt.). Home: 18 Sutton Pl East Windsor NJ 08520 Office: Plasma Physics Lab PO Box 451 Forrestal Campus Princeton U Princeton NJ 08544

IVES, CHARLES CROMWELL, banker; b. Montclair, N.J., Oct. 26, 1935; s. Gordon F. and Helen H. Ives; B.A., Franklin and Marshall Coll., 1961; m. Marianne G. Robinson, Sept. 5, 1969; children—Carolyn, Nicholas, Elizabeth. With New Eng. Mchts. Nat. Bank, Boston, 1961—, sr. trust officer, 1979—. Bd. dirs., mem. exec. com. North Shore Children's Hosp., Salem, Mass., 1977—. Served with USMC, 1954-56. Mem. Boston Estate and Bus. Planning Council (exec. com. 1972-75, 1st v.p.). Republican. Episcopalian. Club: Eastern Yacht (Marblehead, Mass.). Home: 2 Gallison Ave Marblehead MA 01945 Office: 28 State St Boston MA 02109

IVEY, WILLIAM HAMILTON, audio visual cons. co. exec.; b. Newport News, Va., July 11, 1951; s. Henry Reese and Margaret Vaughan (Farmer) I.; B.A. in Communications, U. Central Fla., 1973; m. Frances Katrina Parks, May 14, 1977. Lab. technician Colorcraft, Inc., Orlando, Fla., 1973-74; prodn. mgr. Internal Communications Systems, Atlanta, 1974-77, v.p., 1977-79; pres. Bill Ivey & Co., Atlanta, 1979—. Mem. adv. bd. Atlanta Area council Boy Scouts Am., 1975—. Mem. Assn. for Multi-Image. Presbyn. Home and Office: 3120 Ann Rd Smyrna GA 30080

IVY, CONWAY GAYLE, corp. exec.; b. Houston, July 8, 1941; s. John Smith and Caro (Gayle) I.; student U. Chgo., 1959-62; B.S. in Natural Scis., Shimer Coll., 1964; postgrad. U. Tex., 1964-65; M.B.A., U. Chgo., 1968, M.A. in Econs., 1972, postgrad. 1972-74; m. Diane Ellen Cole, May 25, 1973; 1 son, Brice McPherson. Geol. asst. John S. Ivy, Houston, 1965-72; securities analyst Halsey Stuart & Co. and successor Bache & Co., Chgo., 1973-74, Winmill Securities Inc., Chgo., 1974; econ. and fin. cons., Chgo., 1974-75; dir. of corporate planning Gould Inc., Rolling Meadows, Ill., 1975-79; pres. Ivy Minerals, Inc., Boise, Idaho, 1978—; v.p. corp. planning and devel. Sherwin-Williams Co., Cleve., 1979—. Mem. Am. Econs. Assn., N.Y. Acad. Scis., Phi Gamma Delta. Republican. Author of numerous analytical reports for brokerage industry. Office: 101 Prospect Ave NW Cleveland OH 44115

IX, ROBERT EDWARD, corp. exec.; b. Woodcliffe, N.J., Oct. 15, 1929; s. William Edward and Helen (Gorman) I.; B.A., Princeton, 1951; M.B.A., U. Pa., 1956; m. Mildred Saxton Gilmore, June 27, 1959; children—Helen Adele, Alesia Gilmore, Robert Owens Gilmore, Julia Ryan, Christopher Prouty. Securities analyst Merrill Lynch, Pierce, Fenner & Beane, N.Y.C., 1951; mgmt. cons. Arthur D. Little, Inc., Cambridge, Mass., 1956-63; dir. mktg. Browne-Vintners Co., N.Y.C., 1963-66; v.p. mktg. Schweppes (U.S.A.) Ltd., 1966-68; pres., chief exec. officer Cadbury Schweppes U.S.A., Inc., Stamford, Conn., 1971; chmn., chief exec. officer Am. region Cadbury Schweppes Ltd., 1976—; dir. Cadbury Schweppes Ltd., London, Hendrie's Inc., Boston, Northeast Bancorp Inc., Union Trust Co. Conn., Loctite Corp. Trustee Greenwich Acad.; mem. adv. bd. Wharton Sch., U. Pa. Served to lt. comdr. USNR; ETO. Decorated master Knight Mil. Order Malta (U.S.A.). Mem. Chief Execs. Forum, Navy League (pres. Conn. council). Roman Catholic. Clubs: Belle Haven (Greenwich, Conn.); University (N.Y.C.); Wardroom (Boston); Landmark (Stamford). Home: Walsh Ln Greenwich CT 06830 Office: Cadbury Schweppes USA Inc 1200 High Ridge Rd Stamford CT 06905

IYER, MANI, civil engr.; b. Karachi, Pakistan, Oct. 16, 1936; s. V. Krishnan and Saraswathi K. Iyer; came to U.S., 1965, naturalized, 1974; B.C.E., Gujarat U., India, 1959; M.C.E., Villanova (Pa.) U., 1966; M.B.A., N.Y. U., 1974; m. S. Lakshmi Bhanumathi, Sept. 4, 1968; children—Krishnan, Manohar. Asst. engr. Heavy Elec. (India) Ltd., Bhopal, 1959-62; asst. exec. engr. Border Rds. Devel. Bd., Ministry Transport and Communications, Govt. of India, New Delhi, 1962-64; fabrication engr. Testeels Ltd., Ahmedabad, India, 1964; engr. Bechtel Corp., N.Y.C., 1966-67, Parsons-Jurden Corp., N.Y.C., 1967-69; asst. engr., then engr. Gibbs & Hill Inc., N.Y.C., 1969-78, sr. engr. computer applications, 1978—. Registered profl. engr., N.Y. Mem. ASCE, Beta Gamma Sigma. Hindu. Home: 139-32 250th St Rosedale NY 11422 Office: 393 7th Ave New York NY 10001

IZQUIERDO, LUIS RAMOS, JR., real estate broker; b. Havana, Cuba, Oct. 20, 1934; s. Luis A. and Mirtha (Guerra) Ramos-Izquierdo; came to U.S., 1961, naturalized, 1965; LL.B., Villanova U., 1957; m. Helena Novoa, Aug. 31, 1958; children—Helena, Luis. Admitted to Cuban bar, 1957; pvt. practice law, Havana, Cuba, 1957-61; research co. exec., 1961-65; with real estate div. Trust Mortgage Corp., San Juan, P.R., 1965-71; pres. Luis Ramos-Izquierdo and Assos., San Juan, 1971—. Named Realtor of Year, P.R. Assn. Realtors, 1976. Mem. San Juan Bd. Realtors, Mortage Bankers Assn., Home Builders Assn., P.R. Assn. Realtors (dir. 1976—). Home: 29 Fresa St Milaville Rio Piedras PR 00657 Office: Suite 1103 Housing Inv Bldg Hato Rey PR 00918

JACK, JAMES NICHOL, engring. cons.; b. Hamilton, Scotland, Nov. 14, 1937; came to U.S., 1973, naturalized, 1978; s. Charles Robertson and Agnes Craig (Nichol) J.; B.S.E.E., Met. Coll. London, 1965; M.S. in Engring., Calif. Western U., 1974; m. Christina Arutunoff, Dec. 2, 1973; children—Anya Margaret, Charles Magregor. Engr. BICC Co. Ltd., Eng. and B.W.I., 1963-68; gen. mgr. Island Pubs. Ltd., B.V.I., 1968-72; project engr. C. H. Guernsey, Cons. Engr., Oklahoma City, 1973-75; sr. engr. Williams Bros. Engring., Tulsa, 1976-78; pres. Britannia Inc., Tulsa, 1978—; pres. ESD Internat. Tech. Services Inc.; dir. Francis Drake Ltd. (BVI). Served with Brit. Coldstream Guards, 1957-60. Mem. IEEE, Engrs. Soc. Tulsa, Ind. Cons. Am. Republican. Clubs: Tulsa Country, Elks (Tulsa). Home: 2128 E 25th Pl Tulsa OK 74114 Office: Suite 214 The Harvard Center Tulsa OK 74114

JACKEL, SIMON SAMUEL, food products co. exec., tech. cons.; b. N.Y.C., Nov. 11, 1917; s. Victor and Sadie (Ungar) J.; A.M., Columbia, 1947, Ph.D., 1950; B.S., Coll. City N.Y., 1938; postgrad. U. Ill., 1941-42; m. Betty Carlson, Jan. 22, 1954; children—Phyliss Marcia, Glenn Edward. Head fermentation div. Fleischmann Lab., Stamford, Conn., 1944-59; v.p. research and devel. Vico Products Co., Chgo., 1959-61; dir. lab., research and devel.v.p., dir. lab. and tech. research Quality Bakers of Am. div. Sunbeam Baked Foods, N.Y.C., 1961—; dir. research and devel., mem. operating com. Bakers Research Devel. Service, N.Y.C., 1969—; pres. Plymouth Tech. Services, N.Y.C., 1951—; dir. hearing and audiology Jewish Home and Hosp. for Aged, N.Y.C., 1951-76. Mem. sci. adv. com. Am. Inst. Baking, 1970—, mem. sanitation edn. adv. com., 1978—. Mem. industry adv. com. N.D. State U., 1971—; chmn. Am. Bakers Assn. tech. liaison com. to U.S. Dept. Agr., 1975—. Recipient USAAF Exceptional Civilian Service award, 1943; USPHS research grantee, 1947-50. Fellow Am. Inst. Chemists, AAAS; mem. Am. Chem. Soc., Am. Assn. Cereal Chemists (chmn. milling and baking div. 1973-74, chmn. N.Y. sect. 1973-74) Am. Soc. Bakery Engrs. (chmn. engrs. information service 1970—), ASTM, Am. Bakers Assn. (nutrition com. 1971—, tech. liaison com. to U.S. Dept. Agr. 1965—, food tech. regulatory affairs com. 1977—), Assn. for Environ. Protection, Ind. Bakers Assn. (cons., food safety com. 1977—, labeling com. 1978—, tech. affairs com. 1978—), Inst. Food Technologists, Am. Mgmt. Assn., Nutrition Today Soc., Soc. Nutrition Edn., Environ. Mgmt. Assn., N.Y. Acad. Sci., N.Y.C. Chemists Club, Sigma Xi, Phi Lambda Upsilon. Jewish. Author tech. articles; tech. editor Bakery Prodn. and Marketing Mag., 1968—; contbr. articles to tech. jours. Patentee in field. Home: 46 Kings Hwy N Westport CT 06880 Office: 70 Riverdale Ave Greenwich CT 06830

JACKLICH, GAIL GRUNDMANN, ednl. adminstr., dental products co. exec.; b. Oak Park, Ill., July 1, 1941; d. Charles Richard and Emeline Pamela (Allers) Grundmann; B.S. in Chemistry, Mundelein Coll., 1963; postgrad. No. Ill. U., 1967; C.D.A., Loyola U. Dental Sch., Chgo., 1973; M.B.A., Pepperdine U., 1980; m. John Jacklich, Apr. 19, 1964; children—John III, Christina, Steven Shore. Research asst. Campbell Soup Co., 1963-65; tchr. chemistry public schs., Joliet, Ill., 1965-66; pres. Quality Porcelain Studio, 1967-72; v.p. Computer Letter Service, Joliet, 1974-76; owner, operator Continuing Edn. Cons., Joliet, 1975; v.p. Continuing Edn. Centers Am., Santa Cruz, Calif., 1976—; pres. Spl. Products Inc., Santa Cruz, 1978—; cons. direct mail, seminars. Office: 102 Western Ct Santa Cruz CA 95060

JACKSON, CHARLES EDWARD, machine and tool mfg. exec.; b. Stouffville, Ont., Can., May 23, 1937; s. Frederick Charles and Minnie Alberta (Taylor) J.; student Shaw Bus. Sch., 1956-58; cert. course for credit union and coop. personnel Wilfred Laurier U., 1978; m. Carol Jeanette Hoover, Oct. 31, 1959; children—Christopher, Timothy, Anna, Douglas. Clk., Stouffville Post Office, 1954-56; dep. clk.-treas. Village of Stouffville, 1956-66; v.p., sec.-treas. Stouffville Machine & Tool Works Ltd., 1966—; dir. Stouffville Dist. Credit Union Ltd., 1966-69, pres., 1968-69; treas., mgr. (part-time) York Ednl. and Aurora Community Credit Union Ltd., 1973-80. Vol. fireman

Stouffville Fire Brigade, 1958—, sec.-treas., 1963-77; sec.-treas. (part-time) Stouffville Dist. High Sch. Bd., 1962-69. Recipient Outstanding Service award Stouffville Fire Brigade, 1971. Mem. Soc. Mgmt. Accts. Ont., Guild Indsl., Comml. and Instl. Accts., Met. Toronto Bd. Trade, Can. Payroll Assn., Can. Mfrs. Assn. Club: Masons (sec. Richardson lodge Stouffville 1965-68, treas. 1974-80). Home: 191 Main St W Stouffville ON L0H 1L0 Canada Office: 40 Freel Ln Stouffville ON L0H 1L0 Canada

JACKSON, DON MERRILL, electronics co. exec.; b. Kansas City, Mo., July 31, 1934; s. Don M. and Henryette J. (Boese) J.; A.B. in Physics, William Jewell Coll., 1956; M.S. in Physics, Iowa State U., 1959; Ph.D. in Elec. Engring., Ariz. State U., 1974; m. Barbara Petre, Aug. 28, 1954; children—Susan, Paul, Kevin. Mng. dir. ASM/America, Phoenix, 1976—. Served with USNR, 1952-60. Motorola Don Noble fellow, 1972-76. Mem. Am. Electronics Assn., Assn. Corp. Growth, IEEE, Electrochem. Soc., Sigma Xi. Republican. Patentee semicondr. electronics. Home: 6208 E Desert Cove Scottsdale AZ 85254 Office: ASM/America 4302 E Broadway Phoenix AZ 85040

JACKSON, DONALD FRANK, orgn. devel. cons., mgmt. trainer; b. Dallas, Aug. 2, 1941; s. Carter Vaden and Eloise Carol (Lovelady) J.; A.A. with highest distinction, Phoenix Coll., 1966; B.S. in Mgmt. with high distinction, Ariz. State U., 1969; m. Susanne L. Cater, 1979; children—Shawna, Eric. Research mgr. Phoenix Newspapers, Inc., 1959-69; exec. dir. Community Orgn. for Drug Abuse Control, Phoenix, 1970-72; pres. Don Jackson Co., Inc., Phoenix, 1972—; partner Community Orgn. Inst., 1972—; instr. dept. mass communication Ariz. State U., Phoenix Coll.; cons. numerous govt. agys., public utilities, electronic firms. Del., White House Conf. on Children, 1970; chmn. Distbv. Edn. Adv. Council, 1969; mem. Charter Govt. Selection Com., 1973; mem. Phoenix Men's Art Council, Phoenix Art Mus. Bd. dirs. Citizens Crime Commn., 1971-72, Am. Sch. Bd. Assns., 1971-75, Maricopa County Comprenhensive Health Planning Council, 1971-74, N.E. YMCA, 1973-75, Maricopa County ARC, Wesley Community Center, 1974-75; trustee Phoenix Union High Sch. System, 1969-74, Verde Valley High Sch., 1975—. Recipient Distinguished Service award Maricopa County Med. Soc., 1970, Liberty Bell award Maricopa County Bar Assn., 1971; named Outstanding Young Man of Ariz., Ariz. Jaycees, 1971. Mem. Am. Mktg. Assn. (sec. 1969), Nat. Speakers Assn. (charter mem.), Phoenix C. of C., Ariz. State U. Alumni Assn., Ariz. Acad., Sigma Delta Chi, Beta Gamma Sigma, Sigma Iota Epsilon, Phi Kappa Phi, Phi Theta Kappa. Republican. Mason, Kiwanian. Clubs: Phoenix Executives (dir. 1971-73), Phoenix Press, Kiva, Jockey. Office: PO Box 7554 Phoenix AZ 85011

JACKSON, DONALD RAYMOND, real estate co. exec.; b. Bethesda, Md., May 14, 1928; s. Raymond Clark and Pauline (Hiett) J.; B.S., U. Md., 1951, M.B.A., 1952; m. Betty Carol Corbett, Feb. 28, 1964; children—Donald Clark, Linda Marian. Sr. v.p. fin. and adminstrn. Heublein Inc., Hartford, Conn., 1968-73; exec. v.p. Citizens Fidelity Corp., Louisville, 1974-75; pres., dir. Internat. Rubber Industries, Inc., Louisville, 1975-78; pres., vice-chmn., dir. Barlow Corp., Washington, 1974—; dir. Stearns Co., Frankfort, Ky. Served with U.S. Army, 1946-47. C.P.A., Md. Mem. Nat. Assn. Corporate Dirs., Presidents Assn., Fin. Execs. Inst., Am. Inst. C.P.A.'s, Sigma Phi Epsilon. Presbyterian (elder). Club: Chevy Chase Athletic. Home: 5003 Broadway Bethesda MD 20016 Office: 5454 Wisconsin Ave Chevy Chase MD 20015

JACKSON, EUGENE WESLEY, publisher; b. Tulsa, Feb. 23, 1928; s. George Wesley and Ora (Cook) J.; B.A. in Scis., Okla. State U., 1950; postgrad. U. Tulsa, 1952-55; m. Marie-Louise Vermeiren, Jan. 17, 1961; children—Susan Lynne, Geoffrey William. Lab. technician, tech. writer Carter Oil Co., Tulsa, 1952-55; mng. editor Consultant, Smith Kline & French Labs., Phila., 1955-65, editor, 1966-69; chmn. bd. Intermed Communicications, Inc., Horsham, Pa., 1970—; chmn. bd. Nurses Service Corp.; chmn. bd. Realites U.S.A. Publs., Inc.; editorial dir. Realites Mag.; partner Skillbook Co.; dir. Ravenswood Publs., Ltd. (U.K.). Served with M.C., U.S. Army, 1950-52. Contbr. articles to profl. jours. Office: 132 Welsh Rd Horsham PA 19044

JACKSON, JAMES ALBERT, constrn. co. exec.; b. Madison, Wis., Aug. 19, 1917; s. James Albert and Lillian Claire (Doster) J.; B.S., U. Wis., Madison, 1939; m. Aileen Francis (O'Connor), July 24, 1968; children by previous marriage—James A., Gary, Patte Kay, Steve; stepchildren—Rosemarie, James, Marianne. Prin., Spa Products Co., Inc., Hot Springs, Ark., 1945-52; engr. asphalt maintenance Alaska Road Commn., Anchorage, 1952-55; prin. Jim Jackson, Contractor, Little Rock, 1955—; pres. Asphalt Planers, Inc., Little Rock, 1955—. Served with U.S. Army, 1942-45. Mem. Am. Inst. Contractors (pres. 1977), Am. Road Builders Assn. (dir. 1976), Associated Gen. Contractors, Am. Council Constrn. Edn., Assn. Asphalt Paving Technologists, Nat. Asphalt Pavement Assn., Am. Pub. Works Assn. Republican. Episcopalian. Clubs: Little Rock, Capital. Patentee asphalt planing, scarifying equipment. Home: 8330 Cantrell Rd Little Rock AR 72207 Office: PO Box 988 Little Rock AR 72203

JACKSON, JOHN TILLSON, corp. exec.; b. Milw., May 13, 1921; s. John F. and Elizabeth (Tillson) J.; B.S. in Adminstrv. Engring., Cornell U., 1942; m. Suzanne Bartley, Apr. 1953; children—Suzanne, Jennifer, John Tillson, Jr. engr. George S. Armstrong & Co., Inc., 1946-48, sr. engr., 1948-49, v.p., 1949, dir., 1951; asst. to pres. Fed. Telecommunication Labs., 1953-55; asst. to pres. ITT, N.Y.C., 1956-57, asst. v.p., 1957-58, v.p., 1959-60; v.p. Remington Office Equipment div. Sperry Rand Corp., 1960-66; v.p. Gen. Waterworks Corp., 1966-68; v.p. IU Internat., 1968-69, sr. v.p., 1969-72, exec. v.p., chmn. exec. com., 1973—, chmn. C. Brewer & Co., Ltd. subs., 1975—; dir. Explorer Fund, Gemini Fund, Trustees Equity Fund, Windsor Fund, others. Trustee Acad. Natural Scis.; bd. dirs. Bus. Council for Internat. Understanding, Greater Phila. Partnership, Internat. Bus. Forum. Served from 2d lt. to maj. AUS, 1942-46. Mem. ASME, Zeta Psi. Clubs: Union League, University (N.Y.C.); Gulph Mills Golf, Merion Cricket, Merion Golf, Phila., Racquet (Phila.); Milw. Athletic. Home: 155 Rose Ln Haverford PA 19041 Office: 1500 Walnut St Philadelphia PA 19102

JACKSON, NED COLEMAN, chem. co. exec.; b. Sioux City, Iowa, June 19, 1935; s. Robert McUen and Verda Ellen (Henry) J.; B.S.I.E., Iowa State U., 1961; m. Nan Spotswood Lucas, Dec. 7, 1963; children—Robert, Benjamin, Daniel, John, Ned. With E.I. DuPont De Nemours & Co., Wilmington, Del., 1961—, planning asst., 1965-67, area supr., 1968-71, product supt., 1972-74, asst. plant mgr., 1975, product mgr. mktg., 1975-78, prodn. mgr., 1978—. Served with U.S. Army, 1956-59. Home: 730 Foxdale Rd Wilmington DE 19803 Office: Dupont Bldg 12015 Wilmington DE 19899

JACKSON, PAZEL G., JR., bank exec.; b. Bklyn., Feb. 21, 1932; s. Pazel G. and Adalite M. (Morton) J.; B.C.E., CCNY, 1954, M.C.E., 1959; M.S. in Bus. Adminstrn., Columbia, 1972; m. Catherine M. Faulkner, Aug. 4, 1962; children—Karen, Pazel, Peter, Allyson. Civil engr., N.Y.C., 1956-62; chief of design Worlds Fair Corp., N.Y.C., 1962-66; dep. gen. mgr. N.Y.C. Dept. Pub. Works, 1966-67, asst. commr. N.Y.C. Dept. Bldgs., 1967-69; sr. v.p. Bowery Savs. Bank, N.Y.C., 1969—; chmn. Mutual Real Estate Investment Trust, 1975—; dir. Nat. Housing Partnership Corp., N.Y. State Urban Devel. Corp., N.Y.C. Housing Devel. Corp., Bedford Stuyvesant Restoration Corp. Bd. dirs. Community Service Soc., Citizens Housing and Planning Council. Served to lt. C.E., U.S. Army, 1954-56. Named Man of Yr. Bklyn. Civic Assn., 1967; recipient spl. award for bldg. design Paragon Fed. Credit Union, 1968. Mem. N.Y. Profl. Engrs. Soc., ASCE, N.Y. Bldg. Congress, City Coll. Alumni Assn., Lambda Alpha. Episcopalian. Club: Columbia Bus. Home: 135 Rutland Rd Brooklyn NY 11225 Office: 110 E 42d St New York NY 10017

JACKSON, RALPH ELLIOT, III, life ins. co. ofcl.; b. Quincy, Mass., Apr. 7, 1950; s. Ralph Elliot, Jr. and Franziska J.; cert. Quincy Jr. Coll., 1971, A.S. with honors, 1975; cert. Am. Inst. Banking, Boston, 1974, Harvard U., 1976. Acctg. analyst 1st Nat. Bank Boston, 1971-73, Investment Cos. Service Corp., Boston, 1973-77; ins. commns. analyst Keystone Provident Life Ins. Co., Boston, 1977—; symposium speaker, 1976—. Recipient Charles Palmer Davis award Am. Edn. Publs., 1965. Roman Catholic. Office: 99 High St Boston MA 02110

JACKSON, RANDALL C(ALVIN), lawyer; b. Baird, Tex., Mar. 21, 1919; s. J. Rupert and Anna (Faust) J.; D.J., U. Tex., 1946, B.B.A., 1941; m. Betty S. Johnson, June 18, 1955; 1 son, Randall Calvin. Admitted to Tex. bar, 1946, also U.S. Supreme Ct.; practiced in Baird, 1946-62, Abilene, Tex., 1962—; partner Jackson & Jackson, 1949—; dir. T.S. Langford & Sons Co.; dir., gen. counsel Bank of Commerce, Abilene; partner Jackson Bros. & Son Ranch. Charter mem. Tex. Bar Found.; mem. Tex. Securities Bd., 1966-69; former chmn. bd. regents Tex. Woman's U.; past chmn. Sears Meml. Meth. Home for Ret., N.W. Tex. Meth. Conf.; chmn. trustees Abilene Meth. Dist.; bd. dirs. Abilene Boys Ranch; mem. Tex. Democratic Exec. Com., 1960-64. Enlisted USAC, 1942, disch. capt., 1946, assigned Exec. Office Statis. Control Unit, Guam. Cert. probate and estate planning specialist, Tex. Mem. Am., Tex. (chmn. bd. legal specialization), Abilene (past pres.) bar assns., Am. Coll. Probate Counsel, S.W. Legal Found., Am. Legion (past comdr.), Abilene C. of C., Southwestern Legal Found., W. Tex. (pres.), Tex. (dir.), Concho and Sweetwater (dir.) Hereford assns. Methodist (chmn. dist. trustees). Clubs: Abilene Country, Headliners (Austin), Masons, Shriners. Home: Rt 2 Box 703 Abilene TX 79601 Office: Bank of Commerce Bldg Abilene TX 79605

JACKSON, REGINALD SHERMAN, pub. relations counselor; b. Newport, R.I., Dec. 25, 1910; s. Sherman Clinton and Gertrude (Miller) J.; student U. Toledo, 1929-34; m. Frances Holland, Jan. 20, 1941; 1 son, Reginald Sherman, Jr. Northwestern Ohio, Pub. relations dir. Works Progress Adminstrn., 1935-36; reporter Toledo News-Bee, 1937; pub. relations dir. Ohio N.G., 1939-40; account exec. Flournoy & Gibbs, Inc., Toledo, 1945-51, 53-63, v.p., 1963-76, treas., 1967-76; pub. relations dir. Atlas Tours & Travel Service, Inc., Toledo, 1976-78. Trustee Boys Club of Toledo, 1959-78, Toledo-Lucas County Pub. Library, 1968-78; bd. dirs. Friends of Toledo-Lucas County Library. Served from 1st lt. to lt. col. AUS, 1940-46; lt. col. U.S. Army Res., 1951-60. Decorated Bronze Star medal with two oak leaf clusters. Mem. Res. Officers Assn. (pres. Toledo 1949), Am. Legion (Toledo comdr. 1949), Heather Downs PTA (pres. 1954), Pub. Relations Soc. Am. (pres. Toledo chpt. 1963, nat. treas. 1972), Toledo C. of C., Beta Gamma Sigma (hon.). Clubs: Toledo Press, Toledo, Rotary, Masons. Home: 3707 Richlawn Dr Toledo OH 43614

JACKSON, ROBERT L., fin. exec.; b. Jefferson, Ia., Apr. 8, 1945; s. Robert G. and Mildred L. (Lind) J.; B.S., Ariz. State U., 1973; grad. Am. Inst. Banking, 1975; children—Robert W., Jeffrey S., Nicolle L. Vice pres., mgr. Pinal County area Ariz. Bank, Phoenix, 1970-80; v.p., sec.-treas. Concord Cos., Inc., Phoenix, 1980—; cons. Concord Constrn., Inc., Concord Investments, others. Chmn., Greater Casa Grande Econ. Devel. Com., 1978-80; bd. dirs. Tempe United Way, 1974-76, Casa Grande Town Hall, 1978-80. Recipient Public Service award City of Casa Grande, 1977, 78, 79. Mem. Casa Grande C. of C. (v.p. 1978—, dir.), Am. Inst. Banking, Robert Morris Assos., Casa Grande Bd. Realtors, Mesa-Tempe Chandler Bd. Realtors. Republican. Methodist. Clubs: Rotary, Elks. Home: 1214 Delano St Casa Grande AZ 85222 Office: 777 W Southern St Suite 211 Mesa AZ 85202

JACKSON, ROBERT WILLIAM, utility co. exec.; b. Beaumont, Tex., June 22, 1930; s. Robert and Elizabeth Louise (Watler) J.; B.B.A., U. Tex., Austin, 1953; m. Theta Ann Watt, Aug. 14, 1959; 1 son, Robert William. With Gulf States Utilities Co., Beaumont, Tex., 1955-79, sec., 1972-74, sec.-treas., 1974-75, v.p. fin., chief fin. officer, 1975-79; v.p. fin., corp. sec. Central Ill. Public Service Co., Springfield, 1979-80, sr. v.p. fin., corp. sec., 1980—; dir. First Nat. Bank Springfield. Served with AUS, 1953-55. Mem. Am. Soc. Corp. Secs., Fin. Execs. Inst., Edison Electric Inst. (exec. fin. com.). Methodist. Office: 607 E Adams St Springfield IL 62701

JACKSON, WALTER EDWARD, corp. fin. exec.; b. Milw., Oct. 31, 1929; s. Walter and Helen (Rhode) J.; student Spencerian Bus. Coll., 1947-48, Marquette U., 1952-55, 1966; m. Irene F. Lorenz, Feb. 16, 1952; children—David M., Kathleen A., Thomas A. With AC Spark Plug div. AC Electronics Corp., Milw., 1950-67; asst. resident controller Allison div. Gen. Motors Corp., Cleve., 1967-68; div. controller Joy Mfg. Co., Franklin, Pa., 1968-71, dep. corporate controller, Pitts., 1971-75; mgr. corporate planning and devel. Nat. Mine Service Co., Pitts., 1976-77, corporate controller and sec., 1977—. Bd. dirs. Franklin (Pa.) chpt. ARC, 1968-71; bd. dirs. Franklin Gen. Authority, 1969-71; gen. chmn. United Fund, Franklin; mem. mayor's budget com., Franklin, 1970-71. Mem. Fin. Exec. Inst., Nat. Assn. Accountants. Republican. Club: Downtown (pres. 1980) (Pitts.). Home: 183 Boxfield Rd Pittsburgh PA 15241 Office: 4900/600 Grant St Pittsburgh PA 15219

JACKSON, WILLIAM CALHOUN (DECKER), JR., investment banker; b. Celeste, Tex., Mar. 20, 1907; Registered pharmacist, Danforth Sch. Pharmacy, 1928; m. Sally Carolyn Harrington, May 28, 1928. Mem. comml. banking dept. First Nat. Bank, Plano, Tex., 1929-30; dir., chmn. bd. First Southwest Co., Dallas, 1946—; pres., dir. Antelope Oil Corp., 1950—, Provident Oil Co., 1954—. Chmn. bd. Municipal Adv. Council, Tex., 1956-57. Served as lt. comdr. USNR, 1945. Mem. Investment Bankers Assn. Am. (gov. 1954-55, v.p. 1955-57, pres. 1957-58). Clubs: Dallas, Dallas Country, Northwood, City, Chaparral (Dallas). Home: 5122 Shadywood Ln Dallas TX 75209 Office: Mercantile Bank Bldg Dallas TX 75201

JACKSON, WILLIAM HARRISON, steam generation equipment exec.; b. Carlisle, Pa., Jan. 23, 1915; s. William Lewis and Grovene Mayfield (Snook) J.; B.S., Lafayette Coll., 1936, M.E., 1953; m. Natalie Hale, Jan. 2, 1942; children—William Lewis II, Patricia H. With Babcock & Wilcox Co., N.Y.C., 1936-59, 72-79, v.p. mktg., Barberton, Ohio, 1972-79; v.p. Diamond Power Splty. Corp., Lancaster, Ohio, 1959-64, pres., 1964-72; dir. Frog, Switch & Mfg. Co., Carlisle, Pa., Babcock & Wilcox Can. Ltd., Cambridge, Ont., Can.; mktg. and gen. bus. cons., Fla., 1980—; part-time faculty Ohio U. Chmn., Fairfield County (Ohio) Health Planning Commn., 1970-72. Served with USNR, 1943-46. Fellow ASME; mem. Nat. Soc. Profl. Engrs., Symposiarchs, U.S. Power Squadrons, Delta Kappa Epsilon. Clubs: Lancaster Country (pres. 1968-70); Usseppa Island (Fla.); Great Lakes Cruising; Akron City; Yale (asso.), Cloud (N.Y.C.). Home: PO Box 145 Sanibel FL 33957

JACKSON, WILLIAM JOHN, grain storage co. exec.; b. Pomeroy, Iowa, June 8, 1917; s. John Corbus and Olive Viola (Holmes) J.; student pub. schs.; m. Dorothy Neita Yost, Oct. 12, 1940; children—Larenne (Mrs. Joseph Haas), Donna Sutton Jackson Brown. Erection contractor Ill. Concrete Crib Co., Mendota, Ill., 1938-57; pres., Agrl. Bldg. Co., Mendota, Ill., 1958—. Lutheran. Clubs: Antique Automobile Model A Ford; Kissel Kar. Patentee in field. Home: Rural Route 2 Mendota IL 61342 Office: Box 266 Mendota IL 61342

JACO, CHARLES MAPLES, JR., bus. and indsl. cons. exec.; b. Montgomery County, Miss., Jan. 28, 1924; s. Charles Maples and Ada Marie (Dorris) J.; B.S., U.S. Mil. Acad., 1946; M.Chem. Engring., U. Del., 1957; m. Jennie Erle Cox, June 12, 1946; 1 son, Charles Erle. Commd. 2d lt. U.S. Army, 1946, advanced through grades to lt. col., 1966; served in Redstone Arsenal, Huntsville, Ala., 1951-54, Gorgas Labs., 1953-54, Marshall Islands, 1954-55; mem. engring. Faculty U.S. Mil. Acad., West Point, N.Y., 1956-59; army attache Am. embassy, Berne, Switzerland, 1962-65; bn. comdr. 1st Armored Div., 1965-66, ret., 1966; mgr. corp. devel. Dravo Corp., Pitts., 1966-72; dir. ops. Marks Equipment Co., Cleve., 1973; pres., plant mgr., gen. mgr. Georgetown Ferreduction Corp. (S.C.), 1973-74; pres. Midrex Corp., Charlotte, N.C., 1974-76; partner N. Hill & Assos., Inc., Charlotte, 1976—; speaker U.S. and Can. Bd. dirs. English Speaking Sch., Berne, Switzerland, 1963-64, River Hills Community Assn., 1978-79; exec. bd. Allegeheny Trails council Boy Scouts Am., 1971-72. Mem. Am. Mgmt. Assns., Am. Inst. Chem. Engrs., Am. Def. Preparedness Assn., Iron and Steel Engrs. Democrat. Methodist. Clubs: Charlotte City, River Hills Country; Propeller (Georgetown, pres. 1973). Author: (with others) West Point Ordnance Engineering Textbooks. Contbr. articles to profl. jours. Patentee iron ore reduction and other processes. Home: River Hills Plantation Clover SC 29710 Office: N Hill & Assos Inc 500 E Morehead St Charlotte NC 28202

JACOB, HARRY MYLES, mining co. exec.; b. Bloomfield, N.J., Mar. 19, 1913; s. Henry Martin and Edith Marguerite (Myles) J.; B.C.S., N.Y. U.; m. Elsie Mary Medlicott, June 12, 1938; children—Reid M., Jere V. With Pogson, Peloubet & Co., C.P.A.'s, 1930-36; with Inspiration Consol. Copper Co., N.Y.C., 1936—, beginning as asst. sec.-treas., successively sec., treas., v.p. and sec., exec. v.p., pres., 1936-73, chmn., chief exec. officer, 1973-78, dir., 1953—; dir. 1st Fed. Savs & Loan Assn. N.Y., Sperry Corp., Callahan Mining Corp. C.P.A., N.Y. Mem. Am. Inst. Mining, Metall. and Petroleum Engrs. (William Lawrence Saunders gold medal 1974), Mining and Metall. Soc. Am. Clubs: Mining, Copper, Met. (N.Y.C.), Spring Brook Country (Morristown, N.J.), Clove Valley Rod and Gun. Home: Box 140 RD 5 Flemington NJ 08822

JACOBINI, LOIS ALBERGO, indsl. cons., author, public speaker; b. N.Y.C., Dec. 12, 1947; d. William Joseph and E. Frances Albergo; student Texarkana Jr. Coll., 1965; grad. McGrane Inst. Psycholinguistics, Cin., 1978; postgrad. Cath. U. Am., 1979. Asst. mgr. polit. div. for N.Y. and Pa., Com. to Re-elect the Pres., Washington, 1972; dir. paralegal div. Baker & Botts, Washington, 1972-76, pub. and editor Daily Report, 1973-76; chief exec. officer Washington Experts, Ltd., energy and polit. cons., 1976—, pub. and editor Energy Briefing newsletter, 1976-79, Monday Morning Outlook newsletter, 1976-79; founder Washington Polit. Sci. Internship Program, 1976—; human resources cons. Gen. Electric Co., Aircraft Engine Group, Evendale, Ohio, 1979—; indsl. cons. to higher edn. Coll. of Mt. St. Joseph, Cin.; lectr. career devel. to univ. students, 1976—. Mem. Nat. Speakers Assn. Club: Toastmasters. Author: (with Dottie Walters) The Pearl of Potentiality, 1980. Home: 200 Magnolia Ave Glendale OH 45246 Office: Washington Experts Ltd 1211 Connecticut Ave NW Washington DC 20036

JACOBS, DENHOLM MUIR, investment cons.; b. Ardmore, Pa., Dec. 31, 1922; s. Reginald R. and Sophia (Yarnall) J.; B.A., Yale U., 1945; student Haverford Coll., 1946, Harvard, 1947-48; m. 2d, Margaret Weed Sanne, May 4, 1974; children by previous marriage—Mary Muir, Robert Bottomly, Denholm Muir, Margaret Yarnall. Pvt. financial cons., 1964-73; exec. v.p. Leathem, Lowell & Jacobs, Inc., investment counsel and pvt. financial advisers, Boston, 1973-76; now v.p. Morrison, Jenkins & Jacobs, Inc.; acting dep. commr. Mass. Dept. Commerce, 1953-55. Recipient Carnegie medal. Mem. Soc. Colonial Wars. Republican. Episcopalian. Clubs: Boston Yale; Norfolk Hunt; Harvard (Boston). Home: 5 W Cedar St Boston MA 02108 Office: 55 Kilby St Boston MA 02109

JACOBS, DONALD P., educator; b. Chgo., June 22, 1927; s. David and Bertha (Nevod) J.; B.A., Roosevelt Coll., 1949; M.A., Columbia U., 1951, Ph.D., 1956; children—Elizabeth, Ann, David; m. 2d, Dinah Nemeroff, May 28, 1978. Mem. research staff Nat. Bur. Econ. Research, 1952-57; instr. CCNY, 1955-57; mem. faculty to Morrison prof. fin. Northwestern U. Grad. Sch. Mgmt., 1970-78, chmn. dept., 1957—, dean, 1975—, Gaylord Freeman Disting. prof. banking, 1978—; faculty Inst. Mgmt., Inst. Internat. Mgmt., Burgenstock, Switzerland; formerly chmn. bd. dirs. Amtrak; dir. Benefit Trust Life Ins. Co., Commonwealth Edison, Union Oil Co., Hart, Schaffner & Marx, Galaxy Carpet Mills, Inc.; co-dir. fin. studies Presdl. Commn. Fin. Structure and Regulation, 1970-71; sr. economist banking and currency com. U.S. Ho. of Reps., 1963-64; dir. Conf. Savs. and Residential Fin., 1967—. Served with USNR, 1945-46. Ford Found. fellow, 1959-60, 63-64. Mem. Am. Econ. Assn., Am. Statis. Assn., Am. Fin. Assn., Econometrics Soc., Inst. Mgmt. Sci. Editor Proc. Conf. Savs. and Residential Fin., 1967, 68, 69; contbr. articles to profl. jours. Office: JL Kellogg Graduate School of Management Northwestern University 2001 Sheridan Rd Evanston IL 60201

JACOBS, HARRY ALLAN, JR., investment firm exec.; b. N.Y.C., June 28, 1921; s. Harry Allan and Elsie (Wolf) J.; B.A., Dartmouth Coll., 1942; m. Marie Stevens, Dec. 31, 1942; children—Nancy Jacobs Haneman, Harry Allan III. With Bache Group Inc. subs. Bache Halsey Stuart Shields Inc., N.Y.C., 1946—, partner, 1956—, dir., 1966—, pres., 1968—, chief exec. officer, 1976—, chmn. bd., 1978—; trustee, chmn. finance com. Greenburgh Savs. Bank, Hawthorne, N.Y.; mem. N.Y. adv. com. Chase Manhattan Bank; bd. govs. N.Y. Stock Exchange, 1969-72. Bd. dirs. Bache Corp. Found., Clear Pool Camp of Madison Sq. Boys Club, 1968-70; bd. dirs., bd. mgrs. Madison Sq. Boys Club, 1968-70; trustee Trudeau Inst., Lake Placid, N.Y., Paul Smith's Coll. Served to 1st lt. USAAF, 1942-45. Mem. Bond Club N.Y. (past gov., sec.), Assn. Stock Exchange Firms (past com. chmn., mem. exec. com.), Investment Bankers Assn. (past gov., chmn. pub. relations com.), Investment Assn. N.Y. (past pres.). Clubs: Wall Street, N.Y. Stock Exchange Luncheon (N.Y.C.); Ardsley (N.Y.) Country; Lake Placid (N.Y.). Office: 100 Gold St New York NY 10038

JACOBS, HERMAN SOLOMON, mgmt. cons. co. exec.; b. Amsterdam, Holland, Oct. 9, 1933; s. Joost Karel and Juliemarth (Konijn) J.; came to U.S., 1940, naturalized, 1946; S.B., Mass. Inst. Tech., 1955, S.M., 1957; m. Carolyn Dayton White, Oct. 23, 1960; children—Bettina Marion, Bruce James. Fin. analyst CBS-TV, N.Y.C., 1959-61; cons. Dasol Corp., N.Y.C., 1962-63; dir. mgmt.

services Touche, Ross, Phila., 1963-64; founder Software Scis. Corp., N.Y.C., 1968-74; cons. Boeing Aircraft Corp., N.Y.C., 1974-77; pres. Exec. Controls, Inc., N.Y.C., 1964—; dir. N.V. Linmij, Amsterdam, Nassau Combine Inc., Software Scis. Corp.; cons. to UN, Young Presidents Orgn., Citicorp. Active Boy Scouts Am., United Fund. Served with U.S. Army, 1957-59. Mem. Am. Mgmt. Assn., Assn. for Computing Machinery, Am. Bankers Assn., Am. Soc. for Tng. and Devel. Democrat. Jewish. Author: Executive Productivity, 1975; More Than Words, 1977; Interactive Communication, 1978. Home and Office: 49 Roger Dr Port Washington NY 11050

JACOBS, HOWARD ALFRED, accountant; b. San Francisco, Aug. 12, 1923; s. Reuben and Labelle (Fisher) J.; student San Francisco Jr. Coll., 1941; B.C.S., Golden Gate Coll., 1948; certificate indsl. mgmt. Coll. San Mateo, 1969; m. Margot Kahn, June 8, 1945; children—Michael, Stephen, Robert, Donald, Sheryl, Susan, Debra, Denise, David, Richard, Thomas, Michelle. Pub. accountant, San Francisco, 1944-49; asst. to financial v.p. Lenkurt Elec. Co., San Carlos, Calif., 1949-59; internal auditor Lockheed Aircraft Corp., Sunnyvale, Calif., 1959-66, mgmt. systems specialist, 1966-73, also staff asst. to mgr.; head govt. accounting Watkins-Johnson Co., Palo Alto, Calif., 1973—. Served with AUS, 1943. C.P.A., Calif. Mem. Am. Inst. C.P.A.'s, Calif. Soc. C.P.A.'s, AAU. Clubs: Commonwealth, Press (San Francisco). Home: 1900 Willow Rd Hillsborough CA 94010 Office: 3333 Hillview Ave Palo Alto CA 94304

JACOBS, NORMAN ALLAN, mfg. co. exec.; b. Providence, Aug. 17, 1937; s. Daniel and Bertha (Fain) J.; B.E., Yale, 1958; M.S. (NSF fellow), Mass. Inst. Tech., 1959; M.B.A. (Baker Scholar), Harvard, 1961; m. Elaine Marcia Kritz, Aug. 16, 1959; children—Marjorie Ilene, Alan Jeffrey. With spl. products dept. market devel. Rohm & Haas Co., Phila., 1961-62; treas., dir., v.p. Amicon Corp., Lexington, Mass., 1962-71, pres., dir., also dir. Amicon subs.'s in U.S., Europe, Japan, 1971—; dir. Romicon, Inc. (joint venture of Amicon and Rohm and Haas Co.), 1972—; lectr. Harvard Bus. Sch. Mem. Licensing Execs. Soc. (pres.-elect 1974-75, pres. 1975-76, treas. 1970-74), Am. Chem. Soc., Research Mgmt. Assn. (bd. govs. 1973-76), Internat. Center New Eng. (dir. 1980—), Health Industry Mfrs. Assn., Mass. High Tech. Council, Sigma Xi, Tau Beta Pi. Contbr. articles to profl. jours. Home: 141 Worthen Rd Lexington MA 02173 Office: 25 Hartwell Ave Lexington MA 02173

JACOBS, RANDALL SCOTT DAVID, lawyer; b. Manhattan, N.Y., Sept. 6, 1944; s. Irving and Sylvia J.; B.S., N.Y. U., 1967, LL.M., 1971; J.D., Temple U., 1970. Admitted to N.Y. State bar, 1977, U.S. Dist. Ct. bar, 1979, U.S. Circuit Ct. Appeals bar, 1980; asso. firm Coudert Bros., N.Y.C., 1968; atty. Comml. Coverage Corp., N.Y.C., 1971-78; mem. firm C. M. Sohn, N.Y.C., 1979—. Mem. Am. Bar Assn., N.Y. State Bar Assn., Assn. Bar City N.Y. Contbr. articles to profl. jours. Office: 529 Fifth Ave New York NY 10017

JACOBS, RICHARD ALAN, advt. exec.; b. N.Y.C., Apr. 16, 1923; s. Joseph and Millicent (Krancef) J.; B.S. in Econs., U. Pa., 1943; m. Patricia Breschel, Dec. 17, 1945; children—Diane, Suzanne Jacobs Schwartz. With Joseph Jacobs Orgn., Inc., 1945-57; advt. dept. sales rep. Washington Times-Herald, 1947-48; with Joseph Jacobs Orgn., Inc., N.Y.C., 1947—, v.p., 1955-67, pres., 1967—. Trustee, pres. Congregation Emanu-El of Westchester, 1964-72; trustee Ednl. Alliance, 1970-74, Fedn. Jewish Philanthropies of N.Y., 1974—. Served with USNR, 1943-46. Mem. Sales Exec. Club N.Y., Produce Mktg. Assn.. Republican. Clubs: Century Country (Purchase, N.Y.), B'nai B'rith. Contbr. articles to trade publs. Office: 60 E 42d St New York NY 10165

JACOBS, RICHARD DEARBORN, machinery mfg. co. exec.; b. Detroit, July 6, 1920; s. Richard Dearborn and Mattie Phoebe (Cobleigh) J.; B.S., U. Mich., 1944; m. Mary Lou Hammel, Sept. 16, 1971; children—Richard, Margaret, Paul, Linden, Susan. Engr., Detroit Diesel Engine div. Gen. Motors, 1946-51; mgr. indsl. and marine engine div. Reo Motors, Inc., Lansing, Mich., 1951-54; chief engr. Kennedy Marine Engine Co., Biloxi, Miss., 1955-59; marine sales engr. Nordberg Mfg. Co., Milw., 1959-69; marine sales mgr. Fairbanks Morse Engine div. Colt Industries, Beloit, Wis., 1969—. Served with AUS, 1944-46. Registered profl. engr., Mich., Miss. Mem. Soc. Naval Architects and Marine Engrs. (chmn. sect. 1979-80), Soc. Automotive Engrs., Am. Soc. Naval Engrs., Soc. Am. Mil. Engrs., ASTM, Navy League U.S., Assn. U.S. Army, Propeller Club U.S. Unitarian. Clubs: Country (Beloit); Rockford Polo, Masons. Home: 7887 Louella Dr Roscoe IL 61073 Office: 701 Lawton St Beloit WI 53511

JACOBS, RICHARD OLIVER, lawyer; b. Superior, Wis., May 7, 1931; s. Saul and Olive H. (Olson) J.; B.B.A., U. Wis., 1954; J.D. magna cum laude, Stetson U., 1967; m. Joanne Marie Swanson, Aug. 29, 1953; children—Julie, John. Life ins. sales rep. and mgr., 1956-66; admitted to Fla. bar, 1967; partner firm Jacobs, Robbins & Gaynor and predecessor firms, St. Petersburg, Fla., 1967—; dir. Park Bank of Fla.; former lectr. ins. law Stetson U.; chmn. exec. com. tax sect. Fla. Bar, 1977-78. Trustee Bayfront Med. Center, 1971-78, chmn., 1976-77; trustee Eckerd Coll., 1976—. Served to 1st lt. U.S. Army, 1954-56. C.L.U. Mem. Am., Fla., St. Petersburg bar assns., Phi Beta Kappa, Phi Kappa Phi, Beta Gamma Sigma. Republican. Methodist. Contbr. articles on estate planning to trade jours. Home: 1742 Serpentine Dr S Saint Petersburg FL 33712 Office: 445 31st St N Saint Petersburg FL 33713

JACOBS, WILLIAM I, fin. co. exec.; b. N.J., Sept. 26, 1941; s. Daniel Leo and Rose Lynn (Schweid) J.; B.S., Am. U., 1963; J.D., Washington Coll. Law, 1966; m. June 6, 1970; children—Wendy Sue, Richard I. Asst. v.p. Mfrs. Hanover Trust Co., N.Y.C., 1967-72; v.p. Citibank, N.Y.C., 1972-75; treas., chief fin. officer Mut. Tennis Inc., Westport, Conn., 1975-77; exec. v.p., chief exec. officer, dir. S & B Brokerage Service Corp., White Plains, N.Y., 1977—; lectr. Practicing Law Inst., N.Y.C., Am. Stock Exchange. Bd. govs. Am. U., 1968-71. Mem. Phi Epsilon Pi (dir. 1969). Home: 507 Croton Ave Peekskill NY 10566 Office: 34 S Broadway White Plains NY 10601

JACOBSEN, BERNARD MARTIN, broadcasting exec.; b. Clinton, Iowa, Sept. 14, 1917; s. William Sebastian and Mae (Madsen) J.; student Am. U., 1937-40; m. Ruth Irons, Oct. 28, 1953; children—Susan L. Jacobsen Williams, Samuel K. Lane, Rebecca L. Jacobsen Nutter, Martha Ann. Asst. producer Double or Nothing radio show WOL, Washington, 1940-41; asst. publicity and pub. relations dir. WLW, Cin., 1946-47; organizer builder WSKI, Montpelier, Vt., 1947; pres., 1947-51; gen. mgr. KROS, Clinton, 1951-73, pres., 1955-73; pres. Jacobsen Co., real estate, 1959—; pres. Iowa Radio Network, 1965-66, Clinton Cable TV Co.; mng. dir. Clinton Area Devel. Corp., 1975-80. Mem. Clinton Plan Commn., 1960-79, chmn., 1971-73; mem. Iowa Small Bus. Adv. Council, 1967-68. Served to lt. comdr. USNR, 1942-46. Office: PO Box 3 Clinton IA 52732

JACOBSEN, PARLEY PARKER, accountant; b. Hou, Denmark, July 21, 1924; s. Andrew and Anna (Sorenson) J.; came to U.S., 1929, naturalized, 1938; student U. Wis., 1942-43, Henager's Bus. Coll., 1946-47, accounting U. Utah, 1947-51; m. Alice White, Mar. 15, 1946; children—Karen Ann, Steven Craig, Kelli, Kathleen Alice, Kimberli. Staff accountant Ernst & Ernst, C.P.A.'s, 1952-54; owner, sec.-treas. Abajo Petroleum Co., also Kmoco Oil Co., 1957-59; partner Hansen, Jacobsen & Barnett, C.P.A.'s, Salt Lake City and predecessor firm, 1954—; partner H & J Investment Co., real estate, Salt Lake City, 1963-77; v.p. fin. Harman-Mgmt. Corp. 1964—, corp. cons., 1977—; treas., dir. Harman Assos. Cos.; dir. Harman-Saratoga, Inc., San Jose, Calif., Harman Mgmt. Corp. and asso. cos.; mem. Estates, Inc., also treas. 225 Harman affiliated cos. Served with USNR, 1942-46. C.P.A.; cert. internal auditor, data processing auditor. Mem. Am. Inst. C.P.A.'s, Utah Soc. C.P.A.'s (com. on auditing procs. 1955-56), Salt Lake C. of C., Nat. Restaurant Assn., Data Processing Mgmt. Assn., Inst. Internal Auditors, EDP Auditors Assn., V.F.W. Club: Fort Douglas. Home: 2820 Commonwealth Ave Salt Lake City UT 84109 Office: 1270 East 2100 South Salt Lake City UT 84106

JACOBSON, CALVIN LAVERN, mfg. co. exec.; b. Ottosen, Iowa, July 28, 1925; s. Edgar and Lylus Pearl (Firkins) J.; B.A., Iowa State Tchrs. Coll., 1949; m. Audrey Marie Ferkin, Mar. 3, 1946. Math., sci. tchr. Irwin (Iowa) High Sch., 1949-57; partner Cabin Sporting Goods, Atlantic, Iowa, 1957; with Harlan Mfg. Co., Inc. (Iowa), 1958—, v.p., prodn. mgr., 1959—. Commr., Harlan Airport Commn., 1965-74; mem. City of Harlan Bd. of Adjustment, 1979—; mem. vocat. edn. adv. bd. Harlan Community Schs.; mem. adv. bd. Center for Indsl. Research, Iowa State U., 1979-81. Mem. Harlan C. of C. (pres. 1973), Kappa Mu Epsilon. Republican. Methodist. Clubs: Masons, Shriners, Order Eastern Star (past worthy patron), Harlan Country, Gun, 8-Ball Aviation (Harlan). Home: 1421 Onyx Dr Harlan IA 51537 Office: 1000 Industrial Ave Harlan IA 51537

JACOBSON, DENNIS LEONARD, business exec.; b. Stoughton, Wis., May 19, 1945; s. Leonard Harold and Elaine Marie (Folbrecht) J.; B.S. in Bus. Adminstrn. and Econs., U. Wis., 1967; m. Jane Marie McGill, June 3, 1967; children—Timothy Dennis, Darren Todd. Price analyst Caterpillar, Geneva, 1967-71, pricing supr., Peoria, Ill., 1971-73; mgr. pricing Overseas div. Internat. Harvester Co., Chgo., 1973-76, asst. to mng. dir. Internat. Harvester Germany, Neuss/Rhine, W. Ger., 1976-78, mgr. distbr. mktg. Internat. Harvestor Agrl. Equipment Europe, Paris, 1978—. Pres., parent faculty assn. Am. Internat. Sch., 1977-78. Club: Am. Men's. Home: 152 Blvd de Gen de Gaulle 92380 Garches France Office: 87 Ave de la Grande Armee 75782 Paris Cedex 16 France

JACOBSON, GERALD M., dairy products co. exec.; b. Bklyn., July 17, 1938; s. Samuel and Rose (Nussbaum) J.; B.B.A., Baruch Sch., CCNY, 1960; m. Selma Richstone, Dec. 12, 1964; children—Marc, Laurence, David, Lesley. Acct., Weinicke & Sanders, C.P.A.'s, N.Y.C., 1961-62; tax acct. Asiel & Co., stock brokers, N.Y.C., 1962-65; mgr. Jason Dairy Products Co., Bklyn., 1965—, pres., 1972—. Mem. Associated Industries of N.Y., Greater N.Y. Met. Food Council, Baruch Sch. Alumni Assn. Office: Brooklyn NY 11236

JACOBSON, JACOB LEON, electronics co. exec.; b. Johannesburg, South Africa, Nov. 2, 1939; s. Simon and Gertrude (Sulski) J.; came to U.S., 1965, naturalized, 1976; B.Sc. with honors, U. Witwatersrand (South Africa), 1961; M.B.A. with distinction, Harvard, 1970; Ph.D., U. London, 1965; m. Sylvia Greta Serebro, Feb. 26, 1961; children—Russel, Andrew, Rachel. Research fellow U. Pa., Phila., 1965-66; research scientist Am. Cyanamid, Stamford, Conn., 1966-68; mgmt. cons. McKinsey & Co., N.Y.C., 1970; div. ops. mgr. ICD div. Teradyne Inc., Boston, 1970—. Asso. chmn. Combined Jewish Philanthropies of Met. Boston, 1975-76, asso. chmn., 1977-78. Council for Sci. and Indsl. Research grantee, 1959, 60, 61. Mem. Am. Phys. Soc., Am. Chem. Soc. (chmn. edn. com. S.W. Conn. 1967), IEEE, Harvard Bus. Sch. Assn. Club: Harvard of Boston. Contbr. articles to profl. jours. Home: 206 Windsor Rd Newton MA 02168 Office: 183 Essex St Boston MA 02111

JACOBSON, JOEL ROSS, state ofcl.; b. Newark, July 30, 1918; s. Herman Morton and Gussie (Ross) J.; B.S., N.Y. U., 1941; Litt.D. (hon.), Montclair State Coll., 1959; LL.D. (hon.), Rutgers U., 1974; m. Lucie Pressburg, Aug. 7, 1964; children—Monica, Howard. Pres., N.J. CIO Council, 1960-61; exec. v.p. for N.J., AFL-CIO, 1961-64; pres. N.J. Indsl. Union Council, AFL-CIO, Newark, 1964-68; dir. community relations Region 9 United Auto Workers, Cranford, N.J., 1968-74; mem. N.J. Public Utility Commn., Newark, 1974-77, pres., 1976-77; commr. N.J. Dept. Energy, Newark, 1977—. Served with U.S. Army, 1942-46. Decorated Bronze Arrowhead. Democrat. Jewish. Office: 1100 Raymond Blvd Newark NJ 07102

JACOBSON, LEE DALE, feed mfg. co. exec.; b. Lexington, Nebr., Apr. 14, 1928; s. Guy Kenneth and Bernice Olive (France) J.; B.S. in Mech. Engring., Ill. Inst. Tech., 1951; m. Betty Jane McKee, June 20, 1949; children—Kenneth, Janis, JoAnn. Trainee, Westinghouse Electric Co., Pitts., 1951-52, prodn. engr., 1952-53, prodn. supr., 1953-57, asst. plant mgr., 1957-58; v.p. Lexington Mill & Elevator Co., 1958-60, pres., 1960—. Pres., Lexington Sch. Bd., 1973-78. Mem. Am. Feed Mfrs. Assn. (chmn. sales council 1976—), Nebr. Grain and Feed Dealers Assn. (pres. 1977), Nebr. Assn. Commerce and Industry (v.p. 1976-79). Republican. Presbyterian. Home: 1710 N Cleveland St Lexington NE 68850 Office: Box 719 Lexington NE 68850

JACOBSON, ROBERT VAUGHAN, computer security cons.; b. Portland, Maine, Oct. 24, 1925; s. Arthur Olaf and Bertha Lucy (Smith) J.; B.Engring., Yale U., 1946, M.S. in Elec. Engring., 1948; m. Carolyn Underwood MacBrayne, Sept. 1, 1972; children by previous marriage—Christine Jacobson Kimball, Jeanette Jacobson MacInnes. Radar engr. Raytheon Co., Bedford, Mass., 1950-52, mgr. air force mktg., 1959-67; v.p. Arthur Jacobson Co., Boston, 1952-59; sr. scientist Bolt, Beranek & Newman, Cambridge, Mass., 1967-69; pres. Bradford Security Systems, N.Y.C., 1969-72; v.p., cons. Sr. Security Group, N.Y.C., 1972-74; asst. v.p. info. systems security Chem. Bank, N.Y.C., 1974-78; staff dir. N.Y. Contingency Facility, N.Y.C., 1978—; founder, pres. Internat. Security Tech., Inc., N.Y.C., 1978—; dir. Identifax, Ltd.; instr. Yale U., 1949-50, New Haven Jr. Coll., 1950. Served with USMCR, 1943-46. Mem. Nat. Fire Protection Assn., Assn. Computing Machinery, Am. Soc. Indsl. Security (certified protection profl.). Episcopalian. Clubs: Union, Church, Yale (N.Y.C.). Contbr. articles on computer security to profl. jours.; developer technique for quantitative analysis of computer security risk exposures, 1978. Home: 201 E 66th St New York NY 10021 Office: 51 E 42d St New York NY 10017

JACOBSON, WILLIAM RALPH, finance co. exec.; b. Johannesburg, South Africa, Nov. 29, 1936; s. Morris Jacob and Sylvia (Margolius) J.; B. Commerce, U. Cape Town, 1956, LL.B., 1958; M.B.A. (Asso. Students Stanford scholar), Stanford U., 1960; m. Yvonne Elsie Olson, Oct. 28, 1962; children—Michelle Ann, Mark Zachary, Laura Ruth. Came to U.S., 1963, naturalized, 1969. Dir. market research Consol. Glassworks Ltd., Wadeville, South Africa, 1960-63; admitted Supreme Ct., South Africa, 1961; systems engr. IBM Corp., San Francisco, 1963-65; staff specialist corporate planning office of pres. Bechtel Corp., San Francisco, 1966-69; exec. v.p. Geometrics, Inc., Palo Alto, Calif., 1969-73; pres. Microfab Systems Corp., Palo Alto, 1973-75; chmn., pres. CALAF Holdings, Inc., finance and trading co., Palo Alto, 1975—, also dir. Home: 26715 Birch Hill Way Los Altos Hills CA 94022 Office: Two Palo Alto Sq Suite 120 Palo Alto CA 94304

JACOBUS, DAVID PENMAN, pharm. co. exec.; b. Boston, Feb. 26, 1927; s. David Dinkel and Margaret Elizabeth (Penman) J.; B.A., Harvard, 1949; M.D., U. Pa., 1953; m. Claire Robinson, Oct. 6, 1956; children—Marget H., Claire H., William P., Laura R., John L. Intern, Hosp. of U. Pa., 1953-54, resident, 1954-57; asst. chief dept. nuclear medicine Walter Reed Army Inst. of Research, D.C., 1957-59, chief dept. radiology, 1959-63, chief dept. medicinal chemistry, 1963-65, dir., 1965-69; v.p. inflammation and Arthritis Research Merck Sharp & Dohme Research Labs., div. Merck & Co., 1969—; owner Jacobus Pharm. Co. Past trustee Cold Spring Harbor Lab., N.Y.; cons. exptl. medicine St. Luke's Hosp. Center, N.Y.; mem. U.S. Pharmacopeial Com. on Revision; chmn. com. systems mgmt. Nat. Cancer Inst. Served to capt. U.S. Army, 1957-59. Decorated Meritorious Civilian Service, 1969; recipient certificate of Achievement Walter Reed Army Inst. Research, 1969. Fellow Royal Soc. Medicine, London; mem. AAAS, Am. Soc. for Info. Sci., N.Y. Acad. Scis., Internat. Inflammation Research Soc. Episcopalian. Clubs: Harvard, N.Y. Patentee in field; contbr. articles in field to profl. jours. Home: 37 Cleveland Ln Princeton NJ 08540

JACOBY, HENRY J., heavy constrn. co. exec.; b. Lorain, Ohio, Feb. 23, 1917; s. Sol and Jennie (Cohen) J.; B.Chem. Engring., Ohio State U., 1940, M.S., 1941; m. Doris Goodman, Mar. 23, 1941; children—Ruth E., Karen, Jean. Engr. corp. engring. dept. Am. Viscose Corp., Marcus Hook, Pa., 1941-43; engr. Wagner Co., N.Y.C., 1943-45; v.p., treas. Grow Constrn. Co., Inc., N.Y.C., 1945-69, now dir.; pres. Grow Tunneling Corp. div. Alpha Portland Industries, N.Y.C., 1969-77, chmn. bd., 1978—. Trustee, treas., pres. Walden Sch., N.Y.C., 1956-69. Registered profl. engr., N.Y. State, N.J. Fellow ASCE (past chmn. com. on tunneling and underground constrn., mem. awards com. constrn. div.); mem. Brit. Tunneling Soc., Am. Underground Space Assn., Rapid Excavation and Tunneling Conf. (exec. com.), AAAS, Moles (trustee), Beavers, Sigma Xi, Tau Beta Pi. Jewish. Club: Tupper Lake Country. Contbr. articles on tunneling to profl. jours. Patentee in U.S. and Eng. Home: 305 Riverside Dr New York NY 10025 Office: 1775 Broadway New York NY 10019

JACOBY, ROBERT EAKIN, JR., advt. exec.; b. Union City, N.J., Mar. 26, 1928; s. Robert E. and Anna M. (Bach) J.; A.B. cum laude in Econs., Princeton U., 1951; m. Monica Ann Flynn, Oct. 23, 1954; children—Debra Jean, Cynthia Marie, Patricia Ann, Laura Jayne. Econ. analyst Shell Oil Co., N.Y.C., 1951-52; v.p., account supr. Compton Advt. Agy., N.Y.C., 1952-62; sr. v.p., dir. Needham, Harper & Steers Advt., N.Y.C., 1963-65; v.p., account group head Ted Bates & Co., N.Y.C., 1962-63, pres., 1965—, also chief exec. officer, chmn. Served with AUS, 1946-47; Japan. Mem. Sales Execs. Club N.Y., Assn. Am. Advt. Agys., Phi Beta Kappa. Office: Ted Bates & Co 1515 Broadway New York NY 10036

JACOTTET, CARL MAURICE, chem. and pharm. co. exec.; b. Neuchatel, Switzerland, Feb. 7, 1904; s. Maurice and Jeanne (Fitz) J.; ed. Philipps U., Marburg, Germany; Dr. h.c. Polit. Sci., U. Basle, 1962; m. Charlotte Jacottet, Sept. 1, 1928; children—Eleonore Charlotte, Ursula Irene. With Behring-Werke, Marburg, Germany, 1922-29; with Sandoz Ltd., Basle, Switzerland, 1929—, procurist, 1933-39, sub-mgr., 1939-44, dep. mgr., 1944-48, mgr., 1949-56, mem. exec. com., 1956-67, mng. dir., 1960-63, vice chmn. bd., 1964-67, chmn. exec. com., 1967-73, chmn. bd., 1968-76, hon. chmn. bd., 1976—. Fellow Royal Soc. for Encouragement Arts, Mfrs. and Commerce; mem. Swiss-Am. Soc. (vice chmn.), Académie Suisse des Sciences Médicales (hon.). Contbr. articles to profl. jours. Home: 34 Therwilerstrasse CH-4153 Reinach Switzerland Office: Sandoz Ltd CH-4002 Basel Switzerland

JACOX, JOHN WILLIAM, engring. and consulting co. exec.; b. Pitts., Dec. 12, 1938; s. John Sherman and Grace Edna (Herbster) J.; B.S. in Mech. Engring., Carnegie Mellon U., 1962, B.S. in Indsl. Mgmt., 1962; 1 son, Brian Erik. Mfg. engr. Nuclear Fuel div. Westinghouse Elec. Co., Pitts., 1962-65; data processing salesman IBM, Pitts., 1965-68; mktg. mgr. nuclear products MSA Internat., Pitts., 1966-72; v.p. Nuclear Consulting Services, Inc., Columbus, Ohio, 1973—; dir. NUCON Europe Ltd.; cons./lectr. Nat. Center for Research in Vocat. Edn., 1978—. Coop. edn. adv. com. Otterbein Coll. Mem. ASME (chmn. various coms.), Am. Nuclear Soc., Nat. Rifle Assn. Club: The Sun Bunch (pres. 1980-81). Office: PO Box 29151 Columbus OH 43229

JADEL, JOHN CHARLES, chem. co. exec.; b. Toledo, Mar. 21, 1930; s. Frank Andrew and Iva Marie (Robb) J.; A.B., Bowling Green State U., 1952; M.B.A., Ind. U., 1955; m. Miriam Elsa Baade, Aug. 30, 1952; children—Pamela Ann, Jeffrey William. Mem. sales staff Dow Chem. Co., St. Louis, 1955-60; sales staff Celanese Chem. Co., 1960-67, dist. sales mgr., Boston, 1960-63, product dir., N.Y.C., 1963-67; asst. gen. mgr. Staley Chem. Co., Kearny, N.J., 1967-70; pres. Noury Chem. Co., Burt, N.Y., 1970—; v.p. Armak Co., Chgo., 1973—. Dist. chmn. Niagara Falls dist. Boy Scouts Am., 1971-75, bd. dirs., v.p. fin. N.E. Ill. council, 1976-79, pres., 1980—. Served to 1st lt. Arty., AUS, 1952-54; Korea. Mem. Soc. Plastics Engrs., Delta Upsilon. Congregationalist. Club: Kenilworth. Home: 1401 Ashland Ln Wilmette IL 60091 Office: 300 S Wacker Dr Chicago IL 60606

JAECKLE, ANDRE GEORGE, import co. exec.; b. Flushing, N.Y., June 30, 1953; s. Karl B. and Rita R. J.; B.A., Cornell U., 1974; M.B.A., Stanford U., 1978. With Eli Lilly & Co., Springfield, Ill., 1974-75; with Otto Roth & Co., Inc., Moonachie, N.J., 1975—, exec. v.p., 1975—. Office: 14 Empire Blvd Moonachie NJ 07074

JAFFE, DAVID BRUCE, bus. exec.; b. Great Neck, N.Y., Dec. 23, 1941; s. Herman and Hannah Louise (Blum) J.; B.A., Lafayette Coll., 1963; student Fordham U. Sch. Law, 1963-65, Bernard Baruch Sch. Bus. Adminstrn., 1964-66; m. Georganne Klee Vogel, Dec. 14, 1969; children—Pamela Klee, David Bruce. Sr. mgmt. cons. Ernst & Ernst, N.Y.C., 1965-67, 1969-70; project dir. Cadence Industries, Inc., N.Y.C., 1970-73; ind. cons., N.Y.C., 1973; exec. v.p., chief exec. officer, dir. Peerless Plastics div. Faber, Coe & Gregg, Inc., N.Y.C., 1974-76; pres., dir. Quinn Sheet Metal Corp., Ft. Worth, 1977—, Jaffe-Klee Corp., Ft. Worth, 1977—; instr. U.S. Army Logistics Mgmt. Sch., Va.; lectr. in field. Served to capt. U.S. Army, 1967-69; Vietnam. Recipient Bronze Star. Mem. Assn. Corp. Growth (exec. v.p.), Assn. Mgmt. Cons., Delta Kappa Epsilon. Clubs: Shady Oaks Country (Ft. Worth); Yale (N.Y.C.). Home: 4545 S Lindhurst Dallas TX also 19 E 88th St New York NY 10003 Office: 3313 May St Fort Worth TX 76110

JAFFE, JEFF HUGH, candy co. exec.; b. Washington, Dec. 25, 1920; s. Henry A. and Mildred (Loewenberg) J.; B.S., Va. Poly. Inst., 1942; m. Natalie Rubin, Dec. 30, 1945; children—Bonnie, Holly. Pres., The Chunky Corp., N.Y.C., 1950-67, Ward Candy Co., N.Y.C., 1967-71, Ward Foods Co., N.Y.C., 1971-72, pres. Schrafft Candy Co., Boston, 1974-78; guest lectr. Harvard Bus. Sch., 1962-78. Mem. Assn. Mfrs. Confectionery and Chocolate (chmn., pres.), Young Pres. Orgn. (nat. treas., nat. dir.). Home: 180 Beacon St Apt 2E Boston MA 02116 Office: 739 Boylston St Boston MA 02116

JAFFE, MELVIN, stockbroker; b. N.Y.C., May 20, 1919; s. Benjamin and Zelda (Karp) J.; B.S. in Edn., Bucknell U., 1940; m. Muriel Hauptman, June 8, 1941; children—Meredith, Marcy Jaffe Goot. Football mgr., student dir. athletics Bucknell U., 1940; pres. Banjamin Jaffe & Son Inc., Bklyn., 1945-68; stockbroker Blair & Co., N.Y.C., 1969-70; sr. stockbroker Dean Witter & Co., Garden City, N.Y., 1970—, now v.p. investments Eastern region. Served in U.S. Army, 1942-45. Licensed stockbroker 21 states. Jewish. Clubs: Lions Internat. (pres. 1964), Bucknell U. Bison, Masons. Home: 289 Exeter St Brooklyn NY 11235 Office: 1075 Franklin Ave Garden City NY 11530

JAFFE, RICHARD ROBERT, cons. firm exec.; b. N.Y.C., Oct. 23, 1937; s. Herman and Hannah B.; B.S. in Indsl. Engring., Trinity Coll., 1959; M.B.A., N.Y. U., 1965; postgrad. U. Va. Sch. Law, 1961-62; m. Miriam Margolin, July 1, 1965; children—Marisa Lyn, Sara Patricia. Mgmt. cons. Touche Ross & Co., 1963-65; pilot Pan Am. Airways, 1965-68; exec. v.p. Tioga Textile Industries, N.Y.C., 1968-72; pres. Sci.-Tex. N.Am. Corp., Stamford, Conn., 1972-74; v.p., gen. mgr. Camsco, Inc., Dallas, 1975-77; chmn., pres. Trans-Modal Corp., Dallas, 1977-80; pres. Richard R. Jaffe & Co., Dallas, 1980—; dir. Fleet Truck Equipment Co., 1977—, Transport Equipment Co., 1977—. Bd. dirs., trustee Dallas Symphony Assn., 1977-81. Served to Maj. USAF, 1962-65. Decorated Air medal. Fellow Am. Inst. Indsl. Engrs.; mem. Am. Mgmt. Assn., Am. Soc. Knitting Technologists, Am. Assn. Textile Technologists, Am. Soc. Mfg. Engrs., Clubs: Columbia Country; Princeton of N.Y. Contbr. articles in field to profl. jours. Home: 7318 Royal Circle Dallas TX 75230 Office: Richard R Jaffe & Co 11551 Forest Central Dr Dallas TX 75243

JAFFE, ROBERT HENRY, lawyer; b. Jamaica, Queens, N.Y., June 25, 1936; s. Charles Saul and Rachel (Goldman) J.; A.B., Harvard U., 1957; M.B.A., Columbia U., 1961; J.D., Seton Hall U., 1969; m. Birgitte Holst, June 18, 1960; children—Barron Lars, Erik Meyer, Peter Samson, Charlotte Elizabeth. Admitted to N.J. bar; staff acct. Price Waterhouse & Co., N.Y.C., 1960-61; staff acct. J.H. Cohn & Co., Newark, 1962-64; exec. v.p. Middle Atlantic Utilities Co., Westfield, N.J., 1964-70; partner Reisdorf & Jaffe, Esqs., Springfield, N.J., 1971-74; prin. officer Robert H. Jaffe, P.A., Springfield, 1974—; dir. Randy Internat., Ltd. (London). Democratic committeeman Union County, 1968-78. Served with USAR, 1961-62, 58. C.P.A., N.J. Mem. Am. Bar Assn., N.J. Bar Assn., Union County Bar Assn., N.J. Soc. C.P.A.'s, Fed. Bar Assn. Jewish. Clubs: Harvard (N.J.C.); Oz (San Francisco). Office: 8 Mountain Ave Springfield NJ 07081

JAFFE, WILLIAM WARREN, transp. co. exec.; b. Bklyn., Aug. 23, 1949; s. Edward B. and Lucille (Nussbaum) J.; B.S. cum laude in Fgn. Service, Georgetown U., 1970; M.B.A. with honors, Dartmouth Coll., Hanover, N.H., 1972; m. Anne F. Merritt, Mar. 17, 1968; children—William Sydney, Karen Frances. Statistician, Nat. Life of Vt., Montpelier, 1973-75; sr. analyst Amtrak Computer Systems, Washington, 1975-76, chief payroll systems, fin. dept., 1976-78, mgr. engring. NE Corridor Improvement Program, Phila., 1978-79, dir., 1979—. Republican. Jewish. Club: Am. Contract Bridge League. Home: 132 Drakes Drum Dr Bryn Mawr PA 19010 Office: 1617 JFK Blvd Room 1583 Philadelphia PA 19103

JAGOW, CHARLES HERMAN, lawyer, corp. fin. cons.; b. Winona, Minn., Jan. 23, 1910; s. Walter Paul and Anna Marie (Thode) J.; student LaCrosse (Wis.) State Tchrs. Coll., 1928-30; A.B. cum laude, U. Wis., 1932, LL.B. cum laude, 1934; LL.M., Columbia, 1936; m. Alice MacFarlane, Aug. 3, 1940 (dec. 1967); children—Paul M., Richard C. Admitted to N.Y. bar, 1937; asso. firm Cravath, Swaine & Moore, N.Y.C., 1936-52; atty. Met. Life Ins. Co., N.Y.C., 1952-75, asso. gen. counsel, 1957-75, v.p., 1967-75; dir. corp. debt. financing project Am. Bar Found., Chgo., 1975—; cons. in corp. fin., 1975—; cons. N.Y. State Law Revision Commn., 1979—. Mem. Assn. Life Ins. Counsel, Am. Bar Assn., Assn. Bar City N.Y. (securities regulation com. 1962-65, investments of funds com. 1969-74), Order of Coif, Phi Kappa Phi, Delta Sigma Rho, Gamma Eta Gamma. Presbyn. (elder). Home: Smalley Corners Rd Carmel NY 10512 Office: 510 E 23d St New York City NY 10010

JAHNKE, ERROL ROSS, real estate co. staff; b. American Falls, Idaho, July 2, 1950; s. Curtis Ross and Tillie Manda (Friesen) J.; student U. Calif., Santa Barbara, 1968-72, Santa Barbara (Calif.) City Coll., 1973-74; m. Eloise Carolyn Ellis, Aug. 19, 1972; 1 dau., Alexis Carolyn; m. 2d, Barbara Ann Willis, Aug. 23, 1980; 1 dau., Theresa Lea. Vice pres., treas. Curtis Investment Co., Santa Barbara, 1972—; v.p., treas. Foothill Investment Co., Inc., Santa Barbara, 1972—; asso. Sunset Co., Santa Barbara, 1975—; lectr. in field. Mem. Nat., Calif. bds. realtors. Republican. Club: Univ. Santa Barbara. Home: 1720 Calle Boca Del Canon Santa Barbara CA 93101

JAICKS, FREDERICK G., steel co. exec.; b. Chgo., 1918; ed. Cornell U., 1940. Pres., dir. Inland Steel Co., 1966-72, chmn. bd., chief exec. officer, 1972—; dir. Inland Steel Container Co., Champion Internat. Corp., R.R. Donnelley & Sons Co., 1st Nat. Bank Chgo., Carson Pirie Scott & Co. Served with USN, 1942-45. Office: Inland Steel Co 30 W Monroe St Chicago IL 60603

JAIRAM, RAJU, structural engr.; b. Madras, India, Aug. 29, 1948; s. Ramachandra and Nagalakshmi (Gopalakrishna) J.; came to U.S., 1970; B.Tech., Indian Inst. Tech., 1970; M.S. (scholar), Colo. State U., 1971; m. Hemalatha Subramanian, Mar. 22, 1973; 1 dau., Maya D. Trainee, Reid Burton Constrn. Co., Ft. Collins, Colo., 1971, field engr., 1972, structural engr. and estimator, 1973, project engr., 1974, chief estimator, 1975, project engr., Rapid City, S.D., 1976-77, chief engr. and chief estimator, 1978-79; project mgr. Charles Pankow Assos., Honolulu, 1979—. Active Hunger Project, Colo. Asso. Gen. Contractors Com. on Energy and Environ., Green Peace Found. Registered profl. engr., Colo., S.D., Wyo. Mem. ASCE. Clubs: Toastmasters, Masons. Home: 633 Ululani St Kailua HI 96734 Office: 567 S King St Honolulu HI

JAKACKI, BERNARD CARL, food co. exec.; b. Phila., Jan. 28, 1934; s. Benhard and Violet (Wagner) J.; A.B., U. Pa., 1955, M.B.A., 1960; m. Barbara J. Logie, June 29, 1963; children—Diane, Robert, Lynne. Dir. product mgmt. Thomas J. Lipton, Inc., Englewood, N.J., 1962-73; v.p. Continental Grain Co., N.Y.C., 1973-77; pres. Quality Bakers of Am., N.Y.C., 1977—; lectr. in field. Served with U.S. Navy, 1955-57. Mem. Am. Mktg. Assn., Am. Bakers Assn. (mem. exec. com.), Ind. Bakers Assn. (mem. exec. com.), Am. Inst. Baking (trustee), Newcomen Soc. N.Am., The Pres.'s Assn. Republican. Congregationalist. Office: 70 Riverdale Ave Greenwich CT 06830

JAKES, BRIAN PETER, savs. and loan exec.; b. Syracuse, N.Y., Sept. 27, 1939; s. William Ewart and Edna (Strong) J.; B.F.A., Ohio U., 1963; postgrad. U. Buffalo, 1968; children—Brian Peter, B. Patrick, Kelli Rae. Vice pres. Mfrs. & Traders Trust Co., Buffalo, 1966-75; sr. v.p. Am. Fed. Savs. & Loan Assn., Southfield, Mich., 1975—, dir. service corp., 1975—. Pres., Mental Health Corp. IV, Buffalo, 1972-73; treas. Services for Mentally Retarded, Buffalo, 1971-72; trustee WNED-TV, Buffalo, 1972-75. Served to capt. U.S. Army, 1963-65. Mem. Savs. Inst. Mktg. Soc., Southfield C. of C. (dir. 1976—, pres. 1980—), Delta Tau Delta. Republican. Office: Am Fed Savs & Loan Assn 24700 Northwestern Hwy Southfield MI 48075

JAKOBSSON, KJELL, lumber exporting co. exec.; b. Gothenburg, Sweden, July 30, 1924; came to U.S., 1979; s. John Emanuel and Ingrid Ebba (Stromwall) J.; grad. Gothenburg Comml. Coll., 1944. Exec. v.p. Varmlands Travaruexport AB, Saffle, Sweden, 1954-71; chief comml. mgr. Twico, Dar-es-Salaam, Tanzania, 1972-74; div. mgr. Skaneskog AB, Hassleholm, Sweden, 1974-79; exec. v.p. Iggesund-USA, Inc., Atlanta, 1979—. Mem. Varmland State Council, 1962-70. Served with Swedish Army, 1944-45. Contbr. articles on internat. lumber industry to Swedish trade papers. Home: 1674 Johnson Rd NE Atlanta GA 30306 Office: 1001 International Blvd Suite 1040 Atlanta GA 30354

JALLOW, RAYMOND, economist; b. Najaf, Iraq, Oct. 10, 1930; came to U.S., 1953; s. Jawad M. and Naima (Hussain) J.; B.A., U. Bagdad, 1951; M.A., U. So. Calif., 1956; Ph.D., UCLA, 1966. Auditor, Robert Young, C.P.A., Pasadena, Calif., 1956-57; with United Calif. Bank, Los Angeles, 1959—, fin. economist, 1960, dir. econ. research and planning, 1961-64, asst. v.p., dir. research, 1964-66, v.p., chief economist, dir. research and planning div., 1966-70, sr. v.p., chief economist, dir. research and planning div., 1970—; faculty mem. U. Calif. Extension, Los Angeles, 1962-68; speaker ann. forecasting seminars. Mem. fin. com. Seaver's Inst.; mem. New Dimensions, Calif. Luth. Coll.; bd. dirs. U.S. Arab C. of C. (Pacific), Inc. Mem. Nat. Assn. Bus. Economists (founder, 1st pres. So. Calif. chpt.), Am. Bankers Assn. (econ. adv. com. 1972-75), Am., Western econ. assns., Am. Mgmt. Assn., Los Angeles Area C. of C. (exec. research com.), Town Hall Los Angeles, Blue Key, Beta Gamma Sigma. Contbr. articles to profl. jours.; author ann. econ. and monetary forecast. Home: 2530 Park Oak Ct Los Angeles CA 90068 Office: 707 Wilshire Blvd Los Angeles CA 90017

JAMES, ALEXANDER, JR., banker; b. Branchville, S.C., Nov. 2, 1933; s. Alexander and Rever (Myers) J.; B.E.E. cum laude, CCNY, 1961; M.E.E., N.Y. U., 1963; m. Dorothy L. Jones, Oct. 17, 1954; children—Audrey D., Gregory A., Kevin E.S. Mem. tech. staff Bell Telephone Labs., Holmdel, N.J., 1961-68; mgr. Market Monitor Data, Inc., 1968-69; sr. v.p. E.F. Shelley & Co., 1969-75; v.p. Citibank, N.A., N.Y.C., 1975—; vis. prof. Nat. Urban League Black Exec. Exchange Program. Mem. Middletown Twp. (N.J.) Human Rights Commn., 1975—; trustee Pilgrim Baptist Ch., Red Bank, N.J.; mem. Democratic County Exec. Com. Monmouth County. Served with AUS, 1953-55. Recipient Community Achievement award Nat. Assn. Negro Bus. and Profl. Women's Clubs, 1978. Mem. Am. Mgmt. Assn., IEEE, Eta Kappa Nu, Tau Beta Pi. Club: The Enterprisers. Home: 10 Pineridge Ave Middletown NJ 07748 Office: Citbank NA 399 Park Ave New York NY 10043

JAMES, DANIEL JOSEPH, ednl. adminstr.; b. Vincennes, Ind., July 14, 1936; s. Lyle L. and Goldie (Richardson) J.; B.S., Eastern Ill. U., 1962, M.S., 1963; Ed.D., Ind. U., 1972; m. Sharon M. Wyeth, June 3, 1956; children—Daniel Joseph, II, Cathleen Renae. Grad. asst. Eastern Ill. U., 1961-63, Ind. U., 1971-72; tchr. Lincoln-Way High Sch., New Lenox, Ill., 1963-67; mem. faculty Ill. State U., Normal, 1967-69; bus. mgr. Libertyville (Ill.) Public Schs., 1969-72; asst. supt.-bus. Rockwood Sch. Dist., Eureka, Mo., 1972—. Served with U.S. Army, 1958-60. Mem. Ill. Sch. Bus. Ofcls., Mo. Sch. Bus. Ofcls., Assn. Sch. Bus. Ofcls., Ind. U. Alumni Assn., Assn. Sch. Adminstrs., Phi Delta Kappa. Clubs: Rotary, Lions. Home: 362 Cerny Ave Eureka MO 63025 Office: 111 E North St Eureka MO 63025

JAMES, DAVID DWIGHT, investment co. exec.; b. Russellville, Ala., July 7, 1954; s. Hazel Norris and Doris Marie (Holden) J.; grad. high sch., Russellville; m. Tamra Lynne Gilley, June 2, 1974; children—Christopher Michael, David Brandon. With V.J. Elmores, Birmingham, Ala., 1973-75; mgr. P.N. Hirsch & Co., Savannah, Tenn., 1975-79; mgr. Kents, Inc., Red Bay, Ala., 1979—; pres. Diversified Investment Corp., Red Bay, 1978—, Stateside Oil & Gas Corp.; dir. Delta Internat. Corp., Savannah. Deacon, Sunday sch. tchr. Freedom Hills Holy Ch. of Christ; treas. Russellville chpt. Future Farmers Am., 1972-73, recipient Pub. Speaking award. Democrat. Baptist. Home: PO Box 597 Red Bay AL 35582 Office: 4th Ave S Red Bay AL 35582

JAMES, DAVID LLOYD, data service co. exec.; b. Scranton, Pa., Apr. 12, 1941; s. David L. and Lillian (Reese) J.; student U. Md., 1959-63, Fenn Coll., Cleve., 1963-65; m. Judith Anne McMillen, Nov. 7, 1964; children—David, Christina, Lisabeth, Jason. Programmer, Suburban Trust Co., Hyattsville, Md., 1960-63; system analyst, corp. services rep. Nat. City Bank, Cleve., 1963-66; sales dir. Midwest div. Computer Tech., Inc., Sterling Forest, N.Y., 1966-67; v.p., dir. P.G. Data Center, Inc., Garrettsville, Ohio, 1967—, pres., 1976—; chief exec. officer D.L. James & Assos., Inc., 1974—; v.p., gen. mgr. Citicorp Remote Computing Services Inc., 1980—; instr. Hiram Coll., 1970-71. Cubmaster Western Res. council Boy Scouts Am., Garrettsville, 1975-76. Mem. Nat. Assn. Bank Servicers (pres. 1979-80, past dir.), Penn-Ohio Bank Servicers, C. of C., Data Processing Mgmt. Assn. Mem. United Ch. Christ. Club: Kiwanis (pres. Garrettsville 1974). Home: 7800 State Route 82 Garrettsville OH 44231 Office: Memory Ln Garrettsville OH 44231

JAMES, EARL MOSES, mech. designer; b. Bronx, N.Y., Mar. 18, 1949; s. Harris and Claire (Johnson) J.; 1 son, Earl James. Draftsman, Sci. and Phys. Edn. Bldg., CCNY, 1970-73; mech. designer Consentini Assos., N.Y.C., 1973—. Home: 630 Lenox Ave New York NY 10037 Office: Cosentini Assos Two Penn Plaza New York NY 10001

JAMES, EDWIN HUGH, editor, publishing co. exec.; b. Great Falls, Mont., Mar. 26, 1917; s. Edwin Hugh and Lois Maude (Kelly) J.; student U. So. Calif., 1935-38; m. Arabella Huntington Watkins, Sept. 5, 1972; children by previous marriage—Patricia Louise Eaton, Michael Ward, Edwin Hugh III. Reporter, asst. city editor City News Service Los Angeles, 1938-42; with Broadcasting Publs., Inc., Washington, 1945—, mng. editor, 1954-61, v.p., 1961—, exec. editor, 1961—. Served to maj. AUS, 1942-45. Decorated Bronze Star medal; recipient Jesse H. Neal awards Am. Bus. Press Inc., 1956, 59, 63. Mem. Sigma Delta Chi. Democrat. Contbr. articles to publs. including Fortune, Reader's Digest, Financial Times London. Home: 3133 Connecticut Ave NW Washington DC 20008 Office: 1735 DeSales St NW Washington DC 20036

JAMES, FRANCIS EDWARD, JR., investment co. exec.; b. Woodville, Miss., Jan. 5, 1931; s. Francis Edwin and Ruth (Phillips) J.; B.S., La. State U., 1951; M.S., Rensselaer Poly. Inst., 1966, Ph.D., 1967; m. Iris Senn, Nov. 3, 1952; children—Francis, Barry, David. Commd. 2d lt. U.S. Air Force, 1950, advanced through grades to col., 1972; prof. mgmt. and stats. Air Force Inst. Tech., Wright Paterson AFB, Ohio, 1967-77, chmn. dept. quantitative studies, 1967-71, dir. mgmt. programs Grad. Edn. div., 1972-74; pres. James Investment Research, Inc., Alpha, Ohio, 1973—. Decorated Legion of Merit, D.F.C.; recipient Outstanding Acad. Achievement award Rensselaer Poly. Inst., 1965; Eckles award Soc. Logistics Engrs.; NSF Study grantee, 1970. Mem. Am. Statis. Assn., Am. Fin. Assn., Mil. Ops. Research, Am. Inst. Decision Scis., Investment Counsel Assn. Am., Market Tech. Assn., Epsilon Delta Sigma, Sigma Iota Epsilon. Clubs: Rotary, Masons. Author 2 textbooks; contbr. articles to profl. jours. Home: 2604 Lantz Rd Xenia OH 45385 Office: PO Box 8 Alpha OH 45301

JAMES, GARY MICHAEL, mortgage banker; b. Tulsa, Dec. 9, 1945; s. J.T. and Helen Marie (Housley) J.; student U. Tulsa, 1964-66; A.A., Okla. Sch. Accountancy, 1968, B.Comml. Sci., 1971; grad. Sch. Mortgage Banking Northwestern U., Chgo., 1972; m. Mary; children—Jody, Julie, Jeanne. Insp., N. Am. Aviation (now Rockwell Internat.), Tulsa, 1964-67; price and audit clk. Skelly Oil Co., Tulsa, 1967-68; tchr. Okla. Sch. Accountancy, 1977—; instr. Tulsa Jr. Coll.; v.p. Lomas & Nettleton Co., Tulsa, 1968—; pres., owner Mike James Properties, Walker Motel, Lucky Motel, James Apts. and Rental Houses, Maple Leaf Laundry and Dry Cleaners, Al's Laundry and Dry Cleaners; owner Pine Sq. Laundry and Dry Cleaners, The Electronic Silver Mint. Mem. adv. com. Tulsa Jr. Coll., 1977-80. Mem. Tulsa Met. Bd. Realtors, Tulsa Met. Homebuilders Assn. (chmn. fin. com. 1975), Rogers County Homebuilders Assn., Okla. (dir. 1976—), Tulsa (pres. 1974) mortgage bankers assns., Tulsa Milti-list Service. Democrat. Christian. Home: 7230 S Richmond Tulsa OK 74136 Office: 3105 E Skelly Dr Tulsa OK 74105

JAMES, GEORGE BARKER, II, printing and pub. co. exec.; b. Haverhill, Mass., May 25, 1937; s. Paul Withington and Ruth Arlene (Burns) J.; A.B., Harvard, 1959; M.B.A., Stanford, 1962; m. Beverly A. Burch, Sept. 22, 1962; children—Alexander North, Christopher Burch, Geoffrey Abbott, Matthew Bradstreet. Fiscal dir. EG&G, Inc., Bedford, Mass., 1963-67; asst. to treas. Am. Brands, Inc., N.Y.C., 1967-69; v.p. Pepsico Leasing Corp., N.Y.C., 1969-72; sr. v.p. Arcata Nat. Corp., Menlo Park, Calif., 1972—; dir. Pacific States Industries, Morgan Hill, Calif. Mem. Andover (Mass.) Town Com., 1965-67. Chmn., Towle Trust; v.p., trustee San Francisco Ballet Assn.; trustee Nat. Corp. Fund for Dance, N.Y.C. Served with AUS, 1960-61. Mem. Newcomen Soc. N.Am., Fin. Execs. Inst. Clubs: Harvard (N.Y.C.); Menlo Circus (Atherton, Calif.); Commonwealth of Calif., Stock Exchange (San Francisco); Harvard Varsity (Cambridge, Mass.). Author: Industrial Development in the Ohio Valley. Home: 215 Coleridge Ave Palo Alto CA 94301 Office: 2750 Sandhill Rd Menlo Park CA 94025

JAMES, HOWARD P., hotel chain exec.; b. Estes Park. Colo.. July 9, 1923; s. Howard P. and Edna (Cobb) J.; student Cornell U., 1941, 46; B.S. in Hotel Mgmt., U. Denver, 1948. Food and beverage dir. Hilton Hotel Corp., 1958-60; exec. v.p. Del E. Webb Hotel Corp., 1960-65; pres. Sahara-Nev. Corp., 1965-70; chmn., pres., chief exec. officer Sheraton Corp., Boston, 1970—. Past pres. Boulder Dam (Colo.) council Boy Scouts Am., mem. exec. bd. Boston council, 1970-71, 74—, pres., 1971-72, chmn., 1972-73, treas. Scout Forward Fund, 1973-74. Served with Armed Forces, World War II. Decorated D.F.C., Air Medal with oak leaf cluster. Mem. Am. Hotel and Motel Assn. (dir., adv. council). Office: Sheraton Corp 60 State St Boston MA 02209

JAMES, JOHN ALAN, mgmt. cons.; b. Pocahontas, Iowa, Apr. 11, 1927; s. Clarence Grant and Blanche (Westholm) J.; S.B., Northwestern U., 1950; M.B.A., U. Chgo., 1957, postgrad., 1958-59; m. Diane Margot Thomas, Dec. 26, 1955; children—Carolyn, Cynthia, Alison. Partner, Hewitt Assos., Chgo., 1950-57, McKinsey & Co., N.Y.C., 1960-61; exec. counsellor CPC Internat., N.Y.C., 1961-67; pres. Mgmt. Counsellors Internat., Brussels, 1967—; vis. lectr. Northwestern U., European Sch. Bus. Adminstrn., Fontainebleau, Centre d'Etude Industrielle, Geneva. Served with USAAF, 1944-46. Mem. Internat. Mgmt. Assn., Beta Gamma Sigma, Delta Phi Epsilon. Republican. Episcopalian. Club: Met. (N.Y.C.). Author: Industrial Democracy in Europe, 1975; Termination of Employment Laws in Europe, 1976; also articles; editor, publisher publs. on European labor law, collective bargaining. Address: 12 Contentment Island Rd Darien CT 06820

JAMES, JOHN V., corp. exec.; b. Plains Twp., Pa., July 24, 1918; s. Stanley S. and Catherine N. (Jones) J.; B.S. in Econs., U. Pa., 1941, certificate in mgmt., 1948; m. Helen L. June 25, 1949; 1 dau., Barbara Ann. Office mgr., controller Carr Consol. Biscuit Co., Wilkes Barre, Pa., 1941-42; div. controller Corning Glass Works, 1948-56, mgr. budgets and procs., 1956-57; asst. controller Dresser Industries, Inc., Dallas, 1957-58, v.p. finance subsidiary Clark Bros. Co., Olean, N.Y., 1958-60, controller parent co., 1960-65, v.p., 1962-65, group v.p. machinery, 1965-68, exec. v.p., 1968-69, pres., chief exec. officer, 1970—, chmn. bd., 1976—, also dir. Served to capt. AUS, 1943-46. Mem. Fin. Execs. Inst., Nat. Assn. Accountants (dir. 1960-62), Beta Gamma Sigma. Conglist. Mason, Rotarian (pres. Corning 1957). Home: 7222 Azalea Ln Dallas TX 75230 Office: Dresser Bldg 1505 Elm St PO Box 718 Dallas TX 75221

JAMES, MICHAEL JONATHAN, leasing and fin. co. exec.; b. Bridgeport, Conn., Feb. 3, 1943; s. John and Elvira (Vaszauskas) J.; ed. Toswon State U., Loyola Coll., Mt. Vernon Law Sch.; music degree Peabody Coll. Music; m. Mary Meredith, Mar. 3, 1964; 2 children. Exec. sales broker, mktg. cons., fin. adv., 1970-78; chmn. bd. James & James Motor Car Co. and gen. agt. James & James Ins. Agy., Balt., 1970-74; chmn. bd., chief exec. officer Internat. Mktg. & Mfg. Services, Inc., Winter Park, Fla., 1978—; pres. Monroe Heavy Equipment Rentals, Inc., Winter Park, 1978—, Internat. Leasing Co., 1978—, Deltona-DeLand Trolley Lines, 1980—; chmn. bd. Toonerville Transit Corp., 1981—, Internat. Leasing Co., 1978—, Am. Paper Corp., 1981—. Chmn., Balt. chpt. Am. Cancer Soc., 1976; mem. Va. Democratic Com. Served with USAF, 1964-66. Mem. C. of C. (sec. 1979), Am. Legion. Roman Catholic. Club: Lions. Home: 1651 Bamboo Ct Deltona FL 32725 Office: 1 Purlieu Pl Suite 154 Winter Park FL 32792 also PO Box 22 DeBary FL 32713

JAMES, MILDRED HANNAH, hypnotist; b. Hopewell, Va., Oct. 18, 1918; d. Charles and Fannie (Enoch) Feldman; student Sch. Tech. Hypnosis, Ethical Hypnosis Tng. Center, Am. Inst. Hypnosis; m. Albert W. James, Dec. 31, 1965; children by previous marriage—Shiela, Leslie, Andrea, David, Valerie, Kelly. Apprentice in hypnosis, 1959-60; practicing hypnotist, 1961—; pres., chmn. bd. Mildred H. James, Inc., Kent, Wash., 1976—; lectr., condr. seminars. Mem. Am. Inst. Hypnosis. Author weight reduction methods and smoking control methods; producer cassette tapes. Address: PO Box 422 Hwy 66 Zolfo Springs FL 33890

JAMES, ROBERT LEIGH, banker, lawyer, author; b. Worthington, Ohio, July 29, 1918; s. Frank and Jessie (Brummitt) J.; student Ind. U., 1937-39, U. Calif. at Los Angeles, 1938; A.B., U. Chgo., 1941, J.D., 1947; m. Genevieve Palmer Capouch, Oct. 4, 1943; 1 dau., Alexandra Mary. U.S. Fgn. Service officer, 1947-50; admitted to Ill. bar, 1947; atty. Bank of Am., 1951-52; land and legal rep. Western Hemisphere, Calif. Exploration Co., 1952-58; v.p. Moa Bay Mining Co., Nicaro Nickel Co., Island Exploration Co., 1958-60; v.p., Washington rep. Bank of Am. Nat. Trust and Savs. San Francisco, 1960—. Served to lt. comdr. USNR, 1941-46. Mem. State Bar Calif., D.C., Ill. bar assns., Washington Inst. Fgn. Affairs, Theta Chi. Clubs: The Nineteen Twenty-five F Street, The City Tavern Assn., Internat. of Washington; Metropolitan; Chevy Chase (Md.). Author: The Chameleon File; The Capitol Hill Affair; The Pushbutton Spy; Penelope's Zoo; Janus; Triple Mirror; The Caliph Intrigue. Home:

4301 Bradley Ln Chevy Chase MD 20015 Office: 1800 K St NW Washington DC 20005

JAMES, ROBERT LEO, advt. exec.; b. N.Y.C., Sept. 23, 1936; s. Leo Francis and Mildred Virginia (Schaffa) J.; A.B., Colgate U., 1958; M.B.A., Columbia, 1961; m. Anne Krapp, Feb. 2, 1968; children—Robert Leo, Victoria, Jeffrey. Field researcher Farm Jour., Inc., Cleve., 1956-57; salesman, sales mgr. Procter & Gamble Co., Schenectady, 1958-60; product mgr. Colgate Palmolive Co., N.Y.C., 1961-64; account exec. Ogilvy & Mather, Inc., N.Y.C., 1964-65, v.p., account supr., 1965-68; sr. v.p., mgmt. service dir. Marschalk Co., Inc., N.Y.C., 1968, dir., 1969, exec. v.p., 1970, gen. mgr., 1971, pres., 1974, chmn. bd., chief exec. officer, 1975—; vice chmn. Interpublic Group of Cos., 1980—, also dir.; adj. asso. prof. mktg. Fordham U., 1968-69. Trustee Fordham Prep. Sch., 1977. Mem. Am. Mgmt. Assn., Am. Mktg. Assn., Young Pres.'s Orgn., Greenwich Power Squadron, Colgate U. Nat. Service Council, Delta Kappa Epsilon. Clubs: Millbrook; Indian Harbor Yacht; N.Y. Yacht; Colgate U. Pres.'s; NY40 Assn. Home: 68 W Brother Dr Greenwich CT 06830 Office: 1345 Ave of Americas New York NY 10019

JAMES, WILLIAM W., banker; b. Springfield, Mo., Oct. 12, 1931; s. Will and Clyde (Cowdrey) J.; A.B., Harvard U., 1953; m. Carol Ann Muenter, June 17, 1967; children—Sarah Elizabeth, David William. Asst. to dir. overseas div. Becton Dickinson & Co., Rutherford, N.J., 1956-59; stockbroker Merrill Lynch, Pierce, Fenner & Smith, Inc., St. Louis, 1959-62; with trust div. Boatmen's Nat. Bank of St. Louis, 1962—, v.p. in charge of estate planning, 1972—; dir. Heer-Andres Investment Co., Springfield. Mem. gift. and bequest council Barnes Hosp., St. Louis, 1963-67, St. Louis U., 1972-78. Served with U.S. Army, 1953-55. Mem. Estate Planning Council St. Louis, Mo. Bankers Assn., Bank Mktg. Assn., Am. Inst. Banking. Republican. Clubs: Harvard (pres. 1972-73), Noonday (St. Louis). Office: Boatmen's Nat Bank St Louis PO Box 7365 Saint Louis MO 63166

JAMESON, PAUL ELMER, wholesaler; b. Granite City, Ill., Sept. 5, 1930; s. Paul Elmer and Ruth Arlene (Kenney) J.; B.S. in M.E., Washington U., St. Louis, 1959, M.B.A., 1971; postgrad. So. Ill. U., 1961-64; m. Nelda Crabtree, Dec. 13, 1950; children—Ruth Ann, Michael Lawrence, Carolyn Irene, Mathew Tyler. Laborer to combustion engr. Granite City Steel Co., 1950-72; partner Cycle Products Distbg. Co., Granite City, 1970-74, pres., 1974—; pres. Cycle Products Co., Inc. Served with USAAF, 1948-49. Baptist. Home: 1611 Primrose Ave Granite City IL 62040 Office: 1908 State St Granite City IL 62040

JAMIESON, JOHN KENNETH, mfg. co. exec.; b. Medicine Hat, Alta., Can., Aug. 28, 1910; came to U.S., 1959, naturalized, 1964; s. John Locke and Kate Alberta (Herron) J.; B.S. in C.E., M.I.T., 1931; m. Ethel May Burns, Dec. 23, 1937; children—John Burns, Anne Frances. With Brit. Am. Oil Co., Calgary, Alta., 1934-38; v.p. Imperial Oil Co. Ltd., Toronto, Ont., Can., 1948-58; pres. Internat. Petroleum Co. Ltd., Coral Gables, Fla., 1959-61; v.p. Exxon Co., Houston, 1961-62, exec. v.p., 1962-63, pres., 1963-64; exec. v.p. Exxon Corp., N.Y.C., 1964-65, pres., 1965-69, chmn. bd., 1969-75, dir., 1964-81; chmn. bd. Crutcher Resources Corp., Houston, 1977—; dir. Equitable Life Assurance Soc., Raychem Corp. Chmn., Nat. Fgn. Trade Council, 1979—; vice chmn. Center for Internat. Bus., 1976—; co-chmn. labor-mgmt. com. Nat. Council on Alcoholism, 1978—. Mem. Houston C. of C. (dir.), Bus. Council, Am. Council on Ger., Council on Fgn. Relations, Am. Petroleum Inst., Midcontinent Oil and Gas Assn. Episcopalian. Clubs: Houston Country, Augusta Nat. Golf, Ramada. Office: 1100 Milam Bldg Suite 4601 Houston TX 77002

JAMISON, M. HENRY, petroleum co. exec.; b. Somerville, Mass., Oct. 28, 1921; s. Harry and Sarah (Serabian) J.; B.S. in Chem. Engring., U. Ala., 1946, M.S., 1947; M.B.A. in Marketing, U. Chgo., 1949; m. Anna Jo Byrd, Dec. 26, 1948; children—Nancy Ellen, Carol Lee. With Swift & Co., 1947-50, W.R. Grace Co., 1950-52; chem. sales mgmt. Celanese Chem. Co., 1952-60; market devel. mgmt. Sun Oil Co., Phila., 1960-62; mgr. mktg. research, mgr. mktg. research and devel., mgr. corp. mktg. studies, corporate planning and bus. devel. Phillips Petroleum Co., Bartlesville, Okla., 1962—; J.A. Burrows lectr. Okla. State U., 1967. Served with USNR, 1942-46. Mem. Comml. Devel. Assn., Chem. Market Research Assn., Am. Chem. Soc. Home: 3408 Willowood Dr Bartlesville OK 74003 Office: Phillips Petroleum Co Phillips Bldg Bartlesville OK 74003

JAMISON, RICHARD GATES, mfg. co. exec.; b. York, Pa., Aug. 11, 1930; s. Earnest Gates and Evelyn (Pritz) J.; B.S., Drexel U., 1953; m. Mary E. von Glahn, July 12, 1952; children-Robert B., Douglas G., Karen L., Pamela L. Asst. personnel mgr. Vick Mfg. div. Richardson Merrell Inc., 1953-56, personnel mgr. Nat. Drug div., Phila., 1956-64; dir. compensation Gen. Mills, Inc., Mpls., 1964-74; dir. compensation Rockwell Internat., Pitts., 1974—. Chmn. bd. Inds. Sch. Dist. #287 Minnetonka, Minn., 1973-74; mem. Sch. Bd., 1968-74. Mem. Am. Soc. Personnel Adminstrn. (nat. v.p. 1973-75, nat. treas. 1971-73, dir. 1969—), Am. Compensation Assn., Personnel Accreditation Inst. (treas., dir.), Pitts. Personnel Assn. (v.p., dir.), Conf. Bd. (exec. com. council on compensation). Clubs: Valleybrook Country, Lakeview Country. Home: 344 Oaklawn Dr Pittsburgh PA 15241 Office: 600 Grant St Pittsburgh PA 15219

JAMISON, ROLLAND WILLIAM, bus. exec.; b. Winterset, Iowa, Apr. 19, 1925; s. Paul Finley and Edith May J.; student Iowa State U., 1946-47; Drake U., 1957-62; Augustana Coll., 1965-67; m. Carolyn Marjorie Wilson, May 5, 1946; children—David Allen, Brenda Sue. Secy., John Deere, Des Moines, 1947-48; foreman, 1948-49, parts mgr., 1949-53, indsl. engr., 1953-58, div. engr., 1958-62, chief indsl. engr. Moline, Ill., 1962-67, mgr. mfg. engr., 1967-70, mgr. value analysis, Dubuque, Iowa, 1970—; lectr. in field; mem. Citizens advisory com. Iowa Dept. of Trans. Served with U.S. Army, 1943-45. Mem. Soc. of Am. Value Engrs. (certified), Am. Inst. of Indsl. Engrs., Iowa Honey Producers Assn., 520 First Asso. Republican. Methodist. Club: Rotary Internat., Thunder Hills Country, John Deere Dubuque Works Suprs. Author: Gallery of Ideas Spurs Suppliers V.A. Help, 1974; Buyers Move to Strengthen Vendor Relations, 1975; Value Consciousness, A Plan For Survival, 1976. Home: Rural Route #2 Bellevue IA 52031 Office: John Deere Rd Dubuque IA 52001

JANCAUSKAS, DON, ins. co. exec.; b. Hanau, Germany, July 16, 1946; s. Paul and Stase J.; came to U.S., 1949, naturalized, 1973; student Bentley Coll., 1964-65, U. Maine, 1965-66, Boston U., 1966, Northeastern U., 1966-67. With John Hancock Ins. Co., 1970—, sales mgr., Boston and Jacksonville, Fla., 1974-76, ednl. cons. to mktg. dept., Boston, 1976-78, asst. field v.p., Dallas, 1978-79, gen. agt. S. Tex., Corpus Christi, 1979—; regional dir. Profesco Corp., 1979—. Served with U.S. Army, 1967-70. Mem. Gen. Agts. and Mgrs. Assn., Nat. Assn. Life Underwriters, VFW, Nat. Rifle Assn. (life). Office: 4949 Everhart Corpus Christi TX 78411

JANCOWSKI, RICHARD WILLIAM, logging and constrn. co. exec.; b. Nanaimo, B.C., Can., Sept. 18, 1915; s. Frederick Richard Jancowski and Gladys Barrett-Lennard; ed. Victoria High Sch.; m. Kathleen Mary Lange, Aug. 29, 1946; children—Richard, John, David. New equipment demonstrator Rendell Tractor, Vancouver, B.C., 1930-40; partner Delaney & Jancowski Logging Co., Hope, B.C., 1940-47; mgr. E.W. Lansdowne Logging Co., Alert Bay, B.C., 1947-53; owner, mgr. Jancowski Logging and Constrn. Co., Vancouver, 1954—. Alderman, Village of Alert Bay, 1956-60. Served with RCAF, 1942-45. Home: Rural Route 3 Budington Rd Courtenay BC V9N 5M8 Canada Office: care Davis & Co 14th Floor 1030 W Georgia St Vancouver BC V6E 3C2 Canada

JANECEK, LENORE ELAINE, chamber of commerce exec.; b. Chgo., May 2, 1944; d. Morris and Florence (Bear) Picker; M.A.J. in Speech Communications (talent scholar), Northeastern Ill. U., 1972; postgrad. (Ill. Assn. C. of C. Execs. scholar) Inst. for Organizational Mgmt., U. Notre Dame, 1979-80; m. John Janecek, Sept. 12, 1964; children—Frank, Michael. Adminstrv. asst., exec. dir. Ill. Mcpl. Retirement Fund, Chgo., 1963-65; personnel mgr. Profile Personnel, Chgo., 1965-68; personnel rep. Marsh Instrument Co., Skokie, Ill., 1971-73; restaurant mgt. Gold Mine Restaurant and What's Cooking Restaurant, Chgo., 1974-76; pres., owner Secretarial Office Services, Chgo., 1976-78; founder, exec. dir. Lincolnwood (Ill.) C. of C. and Industry, 1978—; rep. 10th dist. U.S. C. of C., 1978—. Mem. mktg. bd. Niles Twp. Sheltered Workshop; pres. Lincolnwood Sch. Dist. 74 Sch. Bd. Caucus; bd. mem., officer, founder Ill. Fraternal Order Police Ladies Aux.; bd. mem., officer Lincolnwood Girl's Softball League, PTA; mem. sch. curriculum com. Lincolnwood Bd. Edn. Mem. Am. C. of C. Execs., Ill. Assn. C. of C. Execs., Women in Mgmt., Nat. Assn. Female Execs., Am. Notary Soc., Ill. LWV, Nat. Council Jewish Women, Hadassah, City of Hope. Jewish. Home: 6707 N Monticello St Lincolnwood IL 60645 Office: 6731 N Lincoln Ave Lincolnwood IL 60645

JANELLE, ANDREW HENRY, mfg. co. exec.; b. Manchester, N.H., Nov. 23, 1939; s. Alphee Edgar and Lucille Yvette (Poulin) J.; B.S. in Indsl. Engring., Gen. Motors Inst., 1960; m. Louise Boivin, Nov. 24, 1960; children—Michael, Denise, Christopher. Mgr. prodn. and inventory control Foster Grant Co., Inc., Leominster, Mass., 1964-68; successively div. mgr., corporate mgr., dir. engring. and personnel Ilco Corp., Fitchburg, Mass., 1968-73; v.p., gen. mgr. Unican Security Systems Corp., Rocky Mount, N.C., 1973—. Mem. Nash County (N.C.) Indsl. Park Commn.; v.p. Rocky Mount United Fund. Mem. Am. Inst. Indsl. Engrs. (sr.), Am. Prodn. and Inventory Control Soc., Soc. Automotive Engrs., Am. Soc. Metals, New Eng. Time Standards Group, Rocky Mount Indsl. Orgn. (pres.). Roman Catholic. Clubs: Optimists, Lions, Kiwanis, Elks, K.C. Home: 1108 Westminster Ln Rocky Mount NC 27801 Office: 400 Fawn Dr Rocky Mount NC 27801

JANES, CHARLES MARTIN, fin. exec.; b. Greenfield, Mass., Mar. 6, 1937; s. Eben Benjamin and Evangeline Victoria (Solacz) J.; student U. Md., 1976, U. Miami, 1976, George Washington U., 1977, U. Pa., 1977; m. Leslie Sharon Ruse, Dec. 31, 1965; children—Wendy Lee, Stacey Lynn, Michael Grant. With Riverside (Conn.) Yacht Club, 1960-64, Woodway Country Club, Darien, Conn., 1964-69, First Restaurant Corp., White Plains, N.Y., 1969-71; v.p. adminstrn. Steed Mortgage Co., Wheaton, Md., 1971-73, exec. v.p., 1973-79; exec. v.p. Washington Fin. Service Corp., 1979—. Served with USAF, 1955-60. Lic. real estate salesman, life and casualty ins. salesman. Mem. Mortgage Bankers Assn. Am., Nat. Assn. Rev. Appraisers, Metro. Washington Mortgage Bankers Assn. Club: Optimist (treas. 1975). Office: 5101 Wisconsin Ave Washington DC 20016

JANES, JOHN MICHAEL, electronics co. exec.; b. Chgo., Nov. 7, 1931; s. Michael and Tacia B. (Chaltis) J.; B.S., U. Ill., 1954; M.S., Ill. Inst. Tech., 1956; LL.B., LaSalle U., 1975; m. Deloris McCarthy, Aug. 22, 1952; children—Pamela, Lawrence, John M., Lynda, Christopher, Nicole. Mgr. mfg. engring. ITT-Telecommunications, Chgo., N.Y.C., N.J., 1956-62; mfg. mgr. Raytheon Co., Mass., Calif., 1962-69; v.p., div. mgr. Rucker Co., Oakland, Calif., 1969-72; gen. mgr. Marantz div. Superscope Inc., Sun Valley, Calif., 1973-75; dir. mfg. ops. Vivitar Corp., Santa Monica, Calif., 1975-79; v.p., gen. mgr. Marantz Div., Chatsworth, Calif., 1980—; dir. ops. Superscope, Inc., 1979-80; cons. Conejo Valley Bd. Realtors, 1977-78; faculty U. Calif. Extension, Santa Barbara. Served with U.S. Army, 1949-52. Mem. Am. Mgmt. Assn., Am. Inst. Indsl. Engrs., Sigma Iota Epsilon, Tau Beta Pi. Author: Developing Creativity, 1965; Theory and Practice of Improvement Curves, 1963; Production Line Balancing and Model Mix Optimization, 1969; Productivity Improvement, 1970. Home: 5801 Valley Circle Woodland Hills CA 91367 Office: 20525 Nordhoff Chatsworth CA 91311

JANIN, JACQUES, indsl. machining co. exec.; b. Montreal, Que., Can., Feb. 10, 1921; s. Alban and Alexia (Gregoire) J.; B.A., Montreal Coll., 1941; postgrad. in commerce U. Montreal, 1945; m. Jeannine Vidal, June 21, 1945; children—Alban, Nicole, Francois. Estimator, A. Janin & Co. Ltd., 1945-49; pres. Nova-Drug Ltd., Montreal, Indsl. Machining Ltd., Montreal; dir. A. Janin & Co. Ltd., gen. contractors, Montreal. Mem. C. of C. Dist. Montreal, C. of C. Province Que. Roman Catholic. Clubs: St-Denis (Montreal); Mont Bruno Country, Inc., Kanada Fish and Game, Inc. Office: 3650 St-Joseph Blvd Montreal PQ H1X 1W6 Canada

JANIS, JAY, savs. and loan exec.; b. Los Angeles, Dec. 22, 1932; s. Ernest and Diana (Friedman) J.; A.B. with high honors, Yale U., 1954; m. Juel Mendelsohn, 1954; children—Laura, Jeffrey. Partner, community developer Janis Corp. (named changed to MGIC-Janis Properties 1970) and related cos. in pvt. bldg. industry, South Fla., 1956-64, 69-75; with Dept. Commerce, Washington, 1964-66, exec. dir. nat. citizens' com., community relations service, 1964-65, dir. OEO, spl. asst. to under sec. Commerce, 1965-66; exec. asst. to sec. HUD, Washington, 1966-69, under sec., 1977-79; chmn. Fed. Home Loan Bank Bd., Washington, 1979-80; pres. Calif. Fed. Savs. & Loan Assn., Los Angeles, 1981—; sr. v.p. for mgmt. and bus. affairs U. Mass., 1976-77; former prin. housing adviser to gov. Fla.; former bd. dirs. Nat. Assn. Home Builders, Nat. Com. against Discrimination in Housing; former mediator labor disputes in constrn. industry. Past pres. bd. trustees Fla. Internat. Univ. Found., Miami. Served with Intelligence Corps, U.S. Army, 1954-56. Office: Office of Pres Calif Fed Savings & Loan Assn 5670 Wilshire Blvd Los Angeles CA 90036

JANKOWSKI, WALTER FRANCIS, mktg. exec.; b. Perth Amboy, N.J., Apr. 28, 1936; s. Walter Joseph and Mary M. Jankowski; B.S., St. Peter's Coll., 1957; M.B.A., Seton Hall U., 1966; 1 son, Alan W. Research chemist Merck Sharpe & Dohme Research Labs., 1957-64; market research engr. GAF Corp., N.Y.C., 1964-66; mktg. mgr. M&T Chems., Rahway, N.J., 1966-70; mktg. mgr. Engelhard Industries, Inc., East Newark, N.J., 1970—. Home: 609 Hazelwood Ave Middlesex NJ 08846 Office: Engelhard Inc 1 W Central Ave East Newark NJ 07029

JANKOWSKI, WALTER JOSEPH, bus. exec.; b. Bayonne, N.J., Dec. 15, 1920; s. Michael J. and Cecelia M. (Ludwiecheski) J.; student N.Y. U., 1940-42; B.B.A., Rutgers U., 1950; m. Sylvia D. Keller, May 8, 1948; children—W. Jan, Deborah A. Asst. treas. Chipman Chem. Co., Inc., Bound Brook, N.J., 1956-64; mgr. credit So. Nitrogen Co., 1964-69; v.p. Arboreal Assos., Inc., Harriman, N.Y., 1971, exec. v.p., 1971, pres., chief exec. officer, 1972-76; chmn. bd. World Wall Systems, Inc., 1973-75; chmn. bd., pres. Winslow Farms, Inc., 1973-76; chmn. bd. Arboreal Environ. Botanists, Inc., Harriman, 1976—; chmn. bd. Engage' Fragrances, Harriman, 1979—; sec., treas., dir. Humsey Chem. Co. Inc., Bklyn., 1977—. Fin. chmn. St. Francis Cabrini Ch., Savannah, Ga., 1970; charter mem. Exchange Club Met. Savannah, 1967-69; sec., committeeman Boy Scouts Am., Bayonne, 1931-41. Served with USAAF, 1941-45. Recipient Community Leader and Noteworthy Americans award, 1975-76. Fellow Internat. Biog. Soc.; mem. Alumni Assn. Grad. Sch. Credit and Fin. Mgmt. Dartmouth, DAV (life). Club: La Vida Country (Savannah). Author: Changing Patterns in Agricultural Marketing, 1967. Home: 208 Holly St Cranford NY 07016 Office: Box 7 Main St Harriman NY 10926

JANNEN, ROBERT LAWRENCE, business exec.; b. N.Y.C., May 3, 1927; s. John and Emma (Wilson) J.; B.S. in Chem. Engring., Tri-State U., 1950, LL.D., 1975; M.B.A., U. Calif. at Los Angeles, 1961; m. Dolores Shegelski, Dec. 22, 1945; children—Robert, Judith Jannen Perry. Engr., C.F. Braun Co., Los Angeles, 1950-52; sales mgr. Fansteel Metall. Corp., Chgo., 1952-55, AMF Corp., Los Angeles, 1955—; pres. Leach Corp., Los Angeles, 1959-75, also dir.; pres. John Blue Co., Huntsville, Ala., 1975—; pres., dir. Subscription TV Inc., N.Y.C., 1975—, Burnley Corp., Huntsville; lectr. numerous univs.; dir. LRE Inc., Munich, Germany, Leach Corp., Los Angeles, Lockwood Mfg. Co., Cin. Pres., West Covina (Calif.) Little League, South Hills Homeowners Assn.; exec. council Boy Scouts Am.; bd. dirs. Huntsville Boys Club, 1978—; trustee Tri-State U., Multiple Sclerosis Soc. Served with AUS, 1943-46. Certified profl. mgr. Mem. Farm Equipment Mfrs. Assn., Nat. Fertilizer Inst., Nat. Fertilizer Solutions Assn., Electronic Engrs. Assn., Internat. Rocket Soc., Am. Mktg. Assn., Sales Execs. Club, C. of C. of Los Angeles, Newcomen Soc., U. Calif., Tri-State U. alumni assns., Skull and Bones, Tau Sigma Psi. Republican. Clubs: Huntsville Country, Los Angeles Athletic, Masons, Elks, Moose. Contbr. numerous articles to trade publs.; patentee in field. Home: 6775 Grandola Dr Las Vegas NV 89103 Office: PO Box 1607 Huntsville AL 35807

JANNETT, IRA ROGER, furniture co. exec.; b. Detroit, Feb. 5, 1947; s. Samuel S. and Marian (Mandell) J.; B.S., Lawrence Inst. Tech., 1970, B.S. in Acctg., 1971; m. Yolande Barouch, Aug. 24, 1969; children—Jacques, Jason. Controller, Corey Dinette Furniture, Detroit, 1970-75, v.p., 1975—; dir. Rogers Creative Advt., Detroit, 1979—. Mem. Profl. Furniture Mchts. Panel of Experts. Jewish. Club: B'nai B'rith. Office: 26400 Plymouth Rd Redford MI 48239

JANOWIAK, ROBERT MICHAEL, electronics co. exec.; b. Chgo., July 7, 1935; s. Michael and Jane J.; B.S.E.E., U. Ill., 1957; M.S.E.E., Ill. Inst. Tech., 1961; M.B.A., U. Chgo., 1963; m. Patricia Marie Lane, Sept. 1, 1956; children—James, Lauretta, Judith, John, Michael, Mary Patricia. Dir. computer scis. Ill. Inst. Tech. Research Inst., Chgo., 1958-71; v.p., gen. mgr. info. products div. Rockwell Internat., 1971-73, v.p. mktg. M.G.D. Graphics div., 1973-75; pres. Signal div. Fed. Signal Corp., Blue Island, Ill., 1975—. Mem. Chgo. Crime Commn. Mem. Nat. Engring. Consortium (dir.), IEEE, Am. Mgmt. Assn., Mid Am. Arab C. of C. (dir.), U. Ill. Elec. Engring. Alumni (pres., dir.), Ill. Inst. Tech. Alumni Assn. (v.p., dir.), Eta Kappa Nu, Tau Beta Pi. Clubs: Economic, Metropolitan, Presidents, Internat. Trade. Home: 810 Taft Rd Hinsdale IL 60521 Office: 136th and Western Ave Blue Island IL 60406

JANSEN, WOLFGANG LUDWIG, steel co. exec.; b. BergischOGladbach, W. Ger., Aug. 22, 1940; s. Armand and Maria (Scheben) J.; student Coll. of Langs., Cologne, W. Germany, 1957-60; m. Hannelore Wurr, Jan. 11, 1964; children—Stefan, Michael, Silvia, Alexander. Mgmt. trainee Otto-Wolff, 1957-60; comml. mgr. steel dept. Otto Wolff, Lagos, Nigeria, 1962-64; dept. gen. mgr. W. African Steel & Wire Ltd., Ikeja-Lagos, Nigeria, 1964-67; pres. Georgetown Steel Corp. (S.C.), 1967-74; pres. Korf Industries, Inc., Charlotte, N.C., 1974-77; pres., chmn., chief exec. officer Intercontinental Metals Corp., Charlotte, 1977—; dir. Exposaic Industries, Inc., Berg Steel Pipe Corp., Ohio River Steel Corp., N.C. Nat. Bank. Bd. dirs. Mercy Hosp., Jr. Achievement, Charlotte Opera Assn.; trustee Arts and Sci. Council; bd. visitors Belmont Abbey Coll. Mem. Am. Iron and Steel Inst., Am. Mgmt. Assn. Roman Catholic. Clubs: Quail Hollow Country, Kiawah Island. Home: Route 3 Box 123 B Waxhaw NC 28173 Office: 6525 Morrison Blvd Charlotte NC 28211

JANSON, JOHN ROBERT, hwy. engring. technician; b. Yreka, Calif., Sept. 15, 1928; s. John Kegg and Gladys J.; A.A., Sacramento City Coll., 1949; student U. Calif., 1949-79; m. Bernice C. Krpan, Apr. 7, 1961; 1 dau., Catherine A. With Calif. Div. Hwys., Sacramento, 1960—, hwy. engring. technician geology unit, 1967—; dir. Janson-Soldane-Davis Corp. Served to capt. USAF, 1953-59. Mem. Calif. State Employees Assn. (pres. chpt. 55 1975-78), Air Force Assn. Roman Catholic. Home: 4062 Fotos Ct Sacramento CA 95820 Office: 5900 Folsom Blvd Sacramento CA 95819

JANSSEN, TERRANCE ERNEST, real estate developer; b. Yankton, S.D., Oct. 18, 1942; s. Ernest A. and Kathryn S. (Markeson) J.; student public schs.; m. Glenna J. Milander, Apr. 29, 1961; children—Terasa, Ross, Joel. Automobile salesman, then ins. salesman, mortgage banker, 1960-72; pres. Golden West Corp., South Sioux City, Nebr., 1972-74, Janssen/Dak. Corp., Beresford, S.D., 1974-79, Janssen Cos., Beresford, 1979-80, Hudson, Wis., 1980—; charter pres. S. Sioux City Home Builders Assn., 1972-74. Past pres., bd. dirs. Beresford Bus. and Indsl. Devel. Corp. Mem. Nat. Assn. Home Builders (various awards), Am. Soc. Planning Ofcls., Rural Am. Republican. Presbyterian. Clubs: Hudson Country, Southview Country. Home: Riverview Acres Rt 2 Box 116 Hudson WI 54016

JANSSON, JOHN PHILLIP, architect, assn. exec.; b. Phila., Nov. 27, 1918; s. John A. and Isabelle (Ericson) J.; B.Arch., Pratt Inst., 1947; postgrad. State U. N.Y., 1949; m. Ann C. Winter, Apr. 8, 1944 (div. Oct. 1970); children—Linda Ann, Lora Joan; m. 2d, Elizabeth Clow Peer, Jan. 21, 1978. Architect for various firms, 1949-54; pvt. practice architecture, N.Y.C., 1949—; cons. marketing of products, materials and services to bldg. and constrn. industry, 1949—; exec. v.p. Archtl. Aluminum Mfrs. Assn., N.Y.C., 1954-58; mgr. market devel. Olin-Metals Div., N.Y.C., 1958-62; dir. Pope, Evans & Robbins, cons. engrs.; partner Morris Ketchum, Jr. and Assos., Architects, 1964-68; exec. dir. N.Y. State Council on Architecture, 1968-73, cons., 1973-74; dir. Gruzen and Partners, Architects Planners, Engineers, 1972-74; pres. Bldg. Constrn. Tech., 1975-78; v.p. The Ehrenkrantz Group, Architects and Planners, 1974—. Cons. N.Y. State Pure Waters Authority, 1968-69; chmn. N.Y. State Architecture-Constrn. Interagy. Com., 1968-74; sec. N.Y. State Gov.'s Adv. Com. for State Constrn. Programs, 1970-71. Mem. N.Y. State Citizens Com. Pub. Schs., 1952-55; v.p. citizens adv. com. Housing Authority, Town Oyster Bay, N.Y., 1966-68; bd. dirs. Bldg. Industry Data Adv. Council, 1976-78. Served to capt. USMCR, 1943-46. Registered architect, N.Y. Mem. AIA (architects in govt. com. 1971-77), Am. Arbitration Assn., Constrn. Specification Inst., Nat. Inst. Archtl. Edn., BRAB Bldg. Research Inst., Archtl. League N.Y., N.Y. Bldg. Congress, N.Y. State Assn. Architects (dir.), Soc. Archtl. Historians, Nat. Trust for Historic Preservation, Mus. Modern Art, Victorian Soc. Am., Asso. Council Arts, Am. Mgmt. Assn., Soc. Mil. Engrs., Soc. Value Engrs., Municipal Art Soc. N.Y.C. Clubs: University, Orient Yacht, East Hampton Yacht. Home: 10 W 66th St New York NY 10023 also 1200 S Ocean Blvd Boca Raton FL 33432 Office: 19 W 44th St New York NY 10036

JANTZEN, WILLIAM J., banker; b. N.Y.C., 1909. Vice chmn. bd. dirs. Sterling Nat. Bank & Trust Co. N.Y.; hon. pres., dir. N.Y. Credit and Financial Mgmt. Assn., Inc.,; vice chmn. bd. govs. Credit Men's Frat., Inc.; hon. chmn. bd. trustees N.Y. Inst. Credit, Inc. Mem. exec. bd. Boy Scouts Am.; trustee Nat. Asthma Center, Denver. Recipient Humanitarian awards Anti Defamation League, 1963, Children's Asthma Research Inst. and Hosp., 1970; Leadership award in credit edn. N.Y. Inst. Credit, 1974; Top Hat award Toppers Credit Club, 1972. Mem. West Side Assn. Commerce (dir.), Am. Arbitration Assn. (nat. panel). Home: 1241 E 26th St Brooklyn NY 11210 Office: 1410 Broadway New York NY 10018

JANURA, JAN AROL, apparel retail exec.; b. Chgo., May 12, 1949; d. Harold Charles and Violet (Mary) (Trinner) J.; B.S. in Psychology, Colo. State U., 1971; M.A. in Theology, Fuller Grad. Sch., Pasadena, Calif., 1973. Area dir. Young Life, Seattle, 1973-76; chief exec. officer Carol Anderson, Inc., Los Angeles, 1977—; pres. Los Angeles Electric Motor Car Works; cons. apparel industry. Regional bd. dirs. So. Calif. Young Life, 1978—. Mem. Calif. Fashion Creators. Club: Los Angeles Athletic. Home: 1711 Grismer Townhouse 70 Burbank CA 91504 Office: 719 S Los Angeles Suite 910 Los Angeles CA 90014

JAQUITH, PETER C., lawyer, investment banker; b. N.Y.C., June 27, 1936; s. Morton and Margaret Jaquith; A.B., Dartmouth Coll., 1960; LL.B. cum laude, U. Minn., 1964; m. Sharon Lesk, Nov. 8, 1979. Admitted to N.Y. bar, practiced in N.Y.C.; atty. firm Shearman & Sterling, 1964-70; gen. partner Lazard Freres & Co., N.Y.C., 1973—. Home: 405 E 56th St New York NY 10022 Office: Lazard Freres & Co 1 Rockefeller Plaza New York NY 10020

JARETT, IRWIN M., acct., educator; b. Lubbock, Tex., Apr. 28, 1930; s. Jerry and Nellie (Bloomberg) J.; B.A., Tex. Tech. Coll., 1958, M.B.A.; Ph.D. in Acctg., La. State U., 1964; m. Rhoda Goldman, May 28, 1952; children—Andrew Robert, Debra Hope, Alex Scott. Instr., Tex. Tech. Coll., 1957-58; mgr. adminstrv. services div. Arthur Andersen & Co., St. Louis, 1962-68; chmn. acctg. So. Ill. U., Edwardsville, 1968-71, asso. dean health care planning Med. Sch., Springfield, 1971-75, prof. med. econs., 1975—; founder, pres. Irwin M. Jarett C.P.A. Ltd., 1979—; adj. prof. Tulane U. Sch. Public Health, New Orleans, 1974-80. C.P.A., Mo., Ill., La., Tex. Mem. Am. Inst. C.P.A.'s, Ill. Soc. C.P.A.'s (chmn. state of the art), Continuing Profl. Edn. Found. Mem. editorial bd. Computer Graphics for Mgmt., 1981—; contbr. articles to profl. jours. Office: 960 Clock Tower Dr Springfield IL 62704

JARMAN, DAVID BRUCE, comml. banking co. exec.; b. East Orange, N.J., Feb. 19, 1943; s. John Francis and Margaret Keen (Woodland) J.; B.A. in Econs., Trinity Coll., Hartford, Conn., 1965; M.B.A. in Fin., U. Pa., 1967; m. Audrey Mary Christine Fowler, Feb. 4, 1978. With Bankers Trust Co., N.Y.C., 1967—, v.p., 1976—, dep. div. head, 1978—. Served with U.S. Army, 1967-69. Decorated Bronze Star. Mem. Robert Morris Assos. (gov. 1978—). Club: Lake Forest Yacht. Home: 52 Woodlawn Terr Lake Hopatcong NJ 07849 Office: Bankers Trust Co 280 Park Ave New York NY 10017

JARNUTOWSKI, ROBERT JOHN, instrument co. exec.; b. Chgo., Mar. 11, 1938; s. John K. and Evelyn M. (Borowinski) J.; Ph.B., Northwestern U., 1967; m. Joei E. Boquist, Sept. 12, 1964; children—Paul, Wendi, Daniel. With Beckman Instruments, Fullerton, Calif., 1961—, beginning as product line specialist, successively applications chemist, regional applications chemist, applications mgr., sales tng. mgr., 1961-78, mgr. profl. devel., 1978—. Vol. ARC, Salvation Army. Mem. Am. Chem. Soc., AAAS, Coblentz Soc., Am. Assn. Clin. Chemists, Nat. Soc. Sales Tng. Execs. Roman Catholic. Home: 332 Cienaga Dr Fullerton CA 92635 Office: 2500 Harbor Blvd Fullerton CA 92634

JAROSKI, EDWARD LEONARD, ins. co. exec.; b. Camden, N.J., Dec. 16, 1946; s. Edward Leonard and Rose Dorothy Jaroski; B.B.A., Temple U., 1969, also postgrad. Investment mgr. Phila. Life Ins. Co., 1969-76, asst. v.p. investments, 1976, 2d v.p. investments, 1977, v.p. fin., 1978—; pres. Phila. Life Asset Planning Co., 1979—, also dir.; Asst. chmn. major contbns. Phila. United Fund, 1974; treas. Haddonfield (N.J.) Rep. Club, 1979-80. Served with U.S. Army, 1969-76. C.L.U. Fellow Life Ins. Mgmt. Assn.; mem. Phila. Fin. Analyst Soc., Phila. Securities Assn. Club: Phila. Racquet. Home: 400 Haddon Ave 16 Haddonfield NJ 08033 Office: 111 N Broad St Philadelphia PA 19107

JARRARD, JERALD OSBORNE, food and hotel services exec.; b. Mt. Washington, Mo., Oct. 12, 1917; s. Frank Lewis and Mary Minerva (Osborne) J.; student Kansas City (Mo.) Jr. Coll., 1935-36, 38-39; J.D., magna cum laude, U. Mo., 1947; m. Blondeen Morgan, Sept. 29, 1978; children—Sharon Louise Jarrard Lloyd, Jerry Michael, Janeece Rene. Admitted to Mo. bar, 1947; with Trans World Airlines, 1942-60, dir. labor relations, 1957-60; v.p. indsl. relations Eastern Airlines, 1960-63; v.p. personnel Am. Airlines, Inc., 1963, regional v.p. sales and services, N.Y., 1964-66, system v.p. sales and services, 1966-68; pres. In-Flite Services div. Marriott Corp., Washington, 1968-78, sr. corp. v.p., 1978—. Mem. Mo. Integrated Bar, Inst. Radio Engrs., Am. Soc. Travel Agts., Newcomen Soc. N. Am., Nat. Restaurant Assn., Nat. Rifle Assn., Sales Execs. Club, Phi Delta Phi. Methodist. Clubs: Pinnacle, Wings (N.Y.C.); Congressional (Washington); River Bend (Great Falls, Va.). Editor U. Mo. Law Rev., 1944-46. Home: 9629 Weathered Oak Ct Bethesda MD 20034 Office: Marriott Corp Marriott Dr Washington DC 20058

JARRELL, JAMES HENRY, fin. cons.; b. Athens, Ga., Oct. 17, 1938; s. James Ernest and Annie Bob (Johnson) J.; B.S., Ga. Inst. Tech., 1961; postgrad. Sch. Banking of South, La. State U., 1973; m. Laura Gay Branda, Apr. 23, 1961; children—James Ernest, Laura Anne. With Trust Co. Ga., Atlanta, 1961-76, v.p. electronic funds transfer system research and planning, 1974-76; sr. v.p. Payment Systems, Inc., Atlanta, 1976—; bd. dirs. Nat. Automated Clearing House Assn., 1974-76, chmn. systems/ops. com., 1974-75, pres., 1975-76. Chmn. Atlanta COPE Com., 1973-74. Served with USCG, 1958-59. Mem. Ga. Tech. Alumni Assn., Phi Delta Theta. Methodist. Clubs: Capital City, Leadership Atlanta Alumni. Contbr. articles to profl. jours. Home: 2996 Margaret Mitchell Ct Atlanta GA 30327 Office: 100 Peachtree St Suite 2735 Atlanta GA 30303

JARRETT, CHARLES EDWARD, acct.; b. Terre Haute, Ind., July 29, 1924; s. Isaac Edward and Eliza May (France) J.; B.S. in Acctg., Ind. U., 1948; cert. exec. devel. program U. Mich., 1959; M.B.A. in Procurement and Contracting (Office Sec. Def. fellow), George Washington U., 1971; m. Mary Frances Seiler, Apr. 8, 1944; children—Susan Elizabeth, Barbara Jane, Charles Edward. Public acct. Dieterle and Thompson, C.P.A.'s, Bloomington, Ind., 1948-49; auditor U.S. Air Force, various locations, 1949-65; br. chief Hdqrs. Def. Contract Audit Agy., Washington, 1965-67; procurement specialist Office Sec. Def., Washington, 1967-76; owner, mgr. Charles Edward Jarrett, C.P.A., Tallahassee, 1976—; cons. on pricing and preparing proposals for govt. contracts, 1976—. Served with U.S. Army, 1943-44. C.P.A., Ind., Ohio, Va., Fla. Mem. Am. Inst. C.P.A.'s, Fla. Inst. C.P.A.'s, Inst. Internal Auditors, Nat. Contract Mgmt. Assn., Assn. Govt. Accts. Prin. editor: Armed Services Pricing Manual, 1975. Home and office: 3204 Beaumont Dr Tallahassee FL 32308

JARRETT, JAMES WARREN, semiconductor co. exec.; b. Cleve., June 25, 1944; s. Andrew E. and Regina (Snyder) J.; B.A., Kenyon Coll., 1966; m. Laurie Thornton Thompson, July 12, 1968; children—Tracey, Alison, Lindsay. Trainee, Ruder & Finn, Inc., N.Y.C., 1966-67, account exec., 1969-70; account exec. T.J. Ross & Assos., Inc., N.Y.C., 1970-73, v.p., San Francisco, 1974-79; mgr. corp. communications Intel Corp., Santa Clara, Calif., 1980—. Bd. govs. San Francisco Public Relations Roundtable, 1978—; chmn. Santa Clara County Adv. Commn. on Developmentally Disabled, 1978-80. Served with U.S. Army, 1967-69. Mem. Pub. Relations Soc. Am., Nat. Assn. Retarded Citizens, Am. Assn. on Mental Deficiency. Republican. Episcopalian. Home: 1844 Hamilton St Palo Alto CA 94303 Office: 3065 Bowers St Santa Clara CA 95051

JARRETT, JERRY V., banker; b. Abilene, Tex., Oct. 31, 1931; s. Walter E. and Myrtle (Allen) J.; B.B.A., U. Okla., 1957; M.B.A., Harvard, 1963; m. Martha Ann McCabe, June 13, 1953; children—Cynthia, Charles, Christopher, John. Sales mgr. Tex. Coca-Cola Bottling Co., Abilene, 1957-61; with Marine Midland Bank-N.Y., N.Y.C., 1963-74, asst. treas., 1965-67, asst. v.p., 1967-68, v.p., 1968-70, sr. v.p., 1970-72, exec. v.p., 1972-74; exec. v.p. AmeriTrust Co., 1974-76, vice chmn., dir., 1976—, pres., 1978—; vice chmn., dir. AmeriTrust Corp., 1976—, pres., 1978—; vice chmn., dir. Bank Leumi (U.K.); dir. Cook United, Inc. Chmn. tchrs. salary com. Westfield (N.J.) Parent Tchrs. Council, 1969-70; chmn. Joint Civic Com., Westfield, 1970-71; trustee Cleve. Clinic, St. Luke's Hosp., Cleve.; bd. dirs. Up With People. Served with USAF, 1950-54. Mem. Delta Sigma Pi, Phi Gamma Delta. Clubs: Union, Canterbury Golf (Cleve.); Board Room (N.Y.C.); Mid America (Chgo.). Author: (with Henderson, Hintz, Marbot, White) Creative Collective Bargaining, 1964. Home: 2751 Chesterton Rd Shaker Heights OH 44122 Office: 900 Euclid Ave Cleveland OH 44101

JARVIS, PAUL SAMUEL, leisure services exec.; b. Schenectady, Jan. 5, 1937; s. Samuel Frank and Mary Jane (Moraski) J.; B.A. in Econs., Union Coll., 1959; M.B.A. in Mktg., U. Pa., 1961; m. Jacquelyn T. Buksa, Feb. 9, 1963; children—Jeffrey Paul, Todd Edward. Mgr. advt. and sales promotion Gen. Electric Co., N.Y.C., 1962-68; dir. mktg. Mohawk Airlines, N.Y.C., 1968-70; mgr. leisure mktg. Eastern Airlines, N.Y.C., 1970-71; v.p. leisure mktg. and sales Hertz Corp., N.Y.C., 1972-75; v.p. mktg. and sales Bekins Co., Los Angeles, 1975-79; v.p., gen. mgr. sales Vivitar Corp., Santa Monica, Calif., 1979-80; v.p. mktg. and sales Del Webb Hotels, Las Vegas, 1980—. Served with U.S. Army, 1961-67. Mem. Sales and Mktg. Execs., Union Coll. Alumni Assn. Democrat. Roman Catholic. Home: 3361 S Westwind Rd Las Vegas NV 89201 Office: PO Box 7548 Las Vegas NV 89101

JASKOLL, IRA LESLIE, coll. adminstr.; b. Bronx, Feb. 5, 1949; s. Saul Jacob and Edith Alva (Presberg) J.; B.A., Yeshiva U., 1971; M.B.A., L.I. U., 1973; m. Hannah Topel, June 24, 1974; children—Shabtai, Chaim. Asst. to dean L.I. U., Bklyn., 1973-76; fin. systems cons. Rapidata, Fairfield, N.J., 1976-77; dir. Bramson ORT Tech. Inst., N.Y.C., 1977-79; adj. prof. Fairleigh Dickinson U., Teaneck, N.J., 1976—, Kean Coll. of N.J., 1975-76. Recipient Norman Palefsky award Yeshiva U., 1971; Fedn. Jewish Women's Orgns. award, 1980. Mem. Soc. Advancement of Mgmt., Am. Mgmt. Assn., Assn. Computer Machinery, Nat. Bus. Edn. Assn., Assn. M.B.A. Execs., Am. Assn. Univ. Adminstrs., Am. Soc. Pub. Adminstrn., Am. Vocat. Assn., Yeshiva Coll. Alumni Assn., Pi Mu Epsilon. Jewish. Home: 616 Rutland Ave Teaneck NJ 07666 Office: 44 E 23d St New York NY 10010

JASON, IHOR CHANDRYCKI, computer systems designer; b. Jasina, Ukraine, July 24, 1939; came to U.S., 1968, naturalized, 1974; s. Ivan and Eudokia (Andrejczuk) Chandrycki; engring. degree in econs. Prague Sch. Econs., 1967; Ph.D. in Math., Charles U., Prague, 1963; m. Hana Hyncik, Jan. 8, 1966; children—Katherina, Margareta. Systems analyst Orgn. Service, Prague, 1965-68, Med. Mut., Cleve., 1969-71; ops. research mgr. Progressive Data Mgmt., Cleve., 1971-73; owner, pres., chief systems designer Prim Systems Inc., Redmond, Wash., 1973—. Mem. Ops. Research Soc. Am., Am. Def. Preparedness Assn. Home: 2211 W Lake Sammamish Pkwy NE Redmond WA 98052

JASPER, JIMMY ALBERT, ins. co. exec.; b. Torrance, Calif., Dec. 14, 1943; s. Thomas Burks and Wonona Leona (Foster) J.; student U. N.Mex., 1961-63; m. Patricia Ellen Geer, Nov. 12, 1961; children—Todd Thomas, Jennifer Lynn, David Paul. Trainee, T-B-L Adjusters, Alamogordo, N.Mex., 1963-64; adjuster, Las Cruces, N.Mex., 1964-66; adjuster Safeco Ins. Co., Alamogordo, Roswell, N.Mex. and Denver, 1966-70; adjuster Trans America Ins. Group, Denver and Phila., 1970-74, property claims mgr. Can. Surety Co. subs., Toronto, 1974-77, v.p. claims, 1978-80; v.p. Fireman's Fund Ins. Co., 1980—; mem. claims com. Ins. Bur. Can. Small bus. chmn. United Way, 1968; chmn. Highland Youth Center, 1976-77. Mem. Can. Ins. Claims Mgrs. Assn., Bd. Trade Met. Toronto. Republican. Home: 49 Roslin Ave Toronto ON M4N 1Z1 Canada Office: 350 Bloor St E Toronto ON M5W 1L9 Canada

JASTREM, JOHN FRANK, accountant; b. Plains, Pa., May 28, 1955; s. Frank J. and Bernadine J.; B.S. cum laude in Commerce and Fin., Wilkes Coll., 1977. Jr. acct. Andrew Kovalchek, C.P.A., Wilkes-Barre, Pa., 1976; internal auditor Ingersoll-Rand Co., Woodcliff Lake, N.J., 1976; experienced sr. acct. Arthur Andersen & Co., Los Angeles, 1977—. Mem. Am. Mgmt. Assn., Nat. Assn. Accts., Los Angeles Jaycees. Roman Catholic. Club: K.C. Home: 87 S Main St Plains PA 18705 Office: Arthur Andersen & Co 911 Wilshire Blvd Los Angeles CA 90017

JAUCH, JAMES A., safety and security exec.; b. Ft. Wayne, Ind., Sept. 1, 1927; s. Robert J. and Sarah M. (Boyles) J.; student Ind. U., 1947-49; B.S., Findlay U., 1955; m. Janet L. Winje, Sept. 27, 1958; children—Laura, Robert, Michael. Dir. safety and security N. Am. Van Lines, Inc., Ft. Wayne, 1958—; instr. defensive driving Nat. Safety Council, 1974—. Served with USN, 1949-53; Korea. Mem. Nat. Safety Council, Am. Trucking Assn., Ind. Motor Truck Assn. Am. Movers Conf., Kappa Sigma. Republican. Unitarian. Club: Elks. Contbr. articles to profl. jours. Address: NAm Van Lines Inc PO Box 988 Fort Wayne IN 46801

JAUNZEMS, IMANTS, jewelry co. exec.; b. Riga, Latvia, Oct. 18, 1931; came to U.S., 1948, naturalized, 1955; s. Max and Elza (Dembrovsky) J.; grad. UN Lang. Sch., 1948; student Lewis Hotel Sch., Washington, 1960-61, U. Puget Sound, 1960; m. Rita Pezkins, Dec. 5, 1969. Investigator, translator Wash. State Liquor Control Bd., Seattle, 1948-50; mgr. Winthrop Hotel, Tacoma, 1956-58; owner Tiki Club, Tacoma, 1958-60; mgr. Fleur de Les, Honolulu, 1960-62; mfr.'s rep., Honolulu, 1962-70; mgr. Rainbow Products, Zamco Jewelry and Alpha Jewelry, Honolulu, 1962—. Mem. Republican Nat. Com. Served with U.S. Army, 1950-56. Decorated Combat Inf. badge. Mem. DAV, VFW. Lutheran. Clubs: Tacoma Sportsmen's, Eagles. Home and Office: 2825 A Waialae Honolulu HI 96826

JAVAHERIAN, SARA LUCINDA, lawyer; b. Carbondale, Ill., July 12, 1943; d. William Douglas and Lucile Rae O'Neil; B.A., So. Ill. U., 1965; J.D., U. Ill., 1972. Admitted to Ill. bar, 1972; atty. Internat. Harvester Co., Chgo., 1972-79; asst. counsel Ryder System, Inc., Miami, Fla., 1979-80; regional counsel Citicorp, Person to Person, Inc., St. Louis, 1980—. Mem. Am. Bar Assn., Ill. State Bar Assn., Am. Judicature Soc., Internat. Fedn. Women Lawyers. Baptist. Speaker internat. profl. conf., Iran, 1969. Home: 10345C Corbeil Creve Coeur MO 63141 Office: 11475 Olde Cabin Rd Saint Louis MO 63141

JAY, BARRY, wholesale rubber co. exec.; b. N.Y.C., Oct. 16, 1938; s. Sam and Rose Jay; B.S. in Econs., Babson Coll., 1961; LL.D. (hon.), U. London, 1972; m. Ronnay Harrison, Apr. 11, 1965; children—Toni, Kimberly, Cindy. With Salco Rubber Co. Inc., Bronx, N.Y., 1961—, v.p., 1965-68, pres., 1968—, chief exec. officer, 1975—, also dir.; partner Jay Assos., Scarsdale, N.Y., 1975—; v.p. S & B Tire Co., Bronx, 1965—, also dir.; pres. S.R.C. Trading Corp., Bronx, 1977—, also dir.; dir. Holon Tire Co Inc. Hon. dep. sheriff Westchester County, N.Y. Mem. Am. Mgmt. Assn., Nat. Tire Dealers and Retread Assn. Republican. Office: 1150 Webster Ave Bronx NY 10456

JAY, FRANCIS, realtor; b. Syracuse, N.Y., May 13, 1919; s. Nicholas and Angeline (Lodico) J.; student pub. schs.; m. Alice M. McGowan, Sept. 9, 1946; children—Jean Ann Jay Cicaarelli, Linda Jay Robinson. Pres., United Realty, Syracuse, 1952—. Bd. dirs. Syracuse Youth Center. Republican. Roman Catholic. Moose. Home: 310 Bear St Syracuse NY 13208 Office: 238 Charles Ave Solvay NY 13209

JAY, JAMES ALBERT, ins. co. exec.; b. Superior, Wis., Aug. 24, 1916; s. Clarence William and Louie (Davies) J.; student pub. schs., Mpls.; m. Margie Hoffpauir, Dec. 23, 1941; 1 son, James A. Franchisee with The Stauffer System of Calif., 1946-49; Ala. dist. mgr. Guaranty Savs. Life Ins. Co., Montgomery, 1949-51, state mgr. La., Baton Rouge, 1951—, dir., 1952—, gen. agt., 1964—; La. gen. agt., mem. adv. bd. dirs. Gen. United Life Ins. Co. Des Moines, 1969-80; gen. agt. Lincoln Liberty Life Ins. Co. of Des Moines, mem. U.S. Life Group, 1980—. Commr. Attakappas council Boy Scouts Am., 1961-62, Manchau dist., 1967. Served with USMC, 1942-45; PTO. Decorated Purple Heart. Mem. Baton Rouge C. of C., Nat. Assn. Life Underwriters, Gen. Agts. and Mgrs. Conf., Baton Rouge Life Underwriters Assn., Internat. Platform Assn. Methodist. Elk. Home: 5919 Clematis Dr Baton Rouge LA 70808 Office: 3404 Convention St Baton Rouge LA 70806

JAY, ROBERT RAYMOND, electronics exec.; b. Detroit, May 10, 1930; s. Leonard A. and Tracy Doris (Harris) J.; B.S. cum laudi, U. Notre Dame, 1952; M.B.A. with distinction, Harvard U., 1957; m. Tay Ann Timm, July 20, 1957; children—Jeffrey Robert, Tracy Ann, Thomas Christopher, Andrew Timothy. With Semiconductor div. Gen. Electric Co., 1957-58, Syracuse, N.Y., 1958, dist. sales mgr., N.J., 1959, L.I., 1960-61; product mktg. mgr. Sprague Electric Semiconductors, Concord, N.H., 1962-65, asst. mktg. mgr., 1966-67, mktg. mgr. Semiconductor div., 1968; founder Micro Networks, Worcester, Mass., 1969, pres., treas., 1969—. Treas., Worcester Heritage Soc., 1973-76, bd. dirs., 1973-78; bd. dirs. Salisbury Mansion Assn., 1979—, Worcester Bus. Devel. Commn., 1979—. Served with USN, 1952-55. Mem. Worcester Hist. Mus., Worcester Hort. Soc., Mechanics Assn., IEEE. Roman Catholic. Clubs: Worcester Country, Eastman Golf, Harvard Bus. Sch., Rotary, Higgins Armory, Chief Executives. Home: E Lake Dr Grantham NH 03753 Office: 324 Clark St Worcester MA 01606

JAYARAM, GRAMA KASTURI, systems planning cons.; b. Bhadravati, India, Sept. 18, 1941; s. Grama K. and Grama K. (Sheshamma) Rangachar; came to U.S., 1968; B.Sc., Mysore U., India, 1959; B.Engring., Bangalore U., India, 1965; M.B.A., Indian Inst. Mgmt., 1968; Ph.D. in Mgmt., U. Calif., Los Angeles, 1976; m. Mrinalini Vudayagiri, Sept. 28, 1979. Organizational cons., Los Angeles, 1968-74; instr. U. Calif. Grad. Sch. Edn. and Grad. Sch. Mgmt., Los Angeles, 1969-74; sr. cons. G.D. Searle & Co., Chgo., 1974-75; vis. asso. prof. Inst. Social and Econ. Change, India, 1973; research cons. on projects with Govt. of India, 1976; sr. cons. Arthur D. Little, Inc., Cambridge, Mass., 1977-79; pres. G. K. Jayaram Assos., Inc., Lexington, Mass., 1980—. Ford Found. fellow, 1968-69. Mem. Orgn. Devel. Network, Beta Gamma Sigma. Contbr. articles on systems planning to profl. publs. Home and Office: 87 Fifer Ln Lexington MA 02173

JAYME, DEMETRIO SOMOSA, shipping co. exec.; b. Dumaguete City, Philippines, Aug. 13, 1916; s. Felix and Fortunata (Somosa) J.; B.B.A., U. of the East, 1947, M.B.A., 1949; m. Justina Reyes, Jan 18, 1944; children—Josephine Victoria, Ernesto Jose, Demetrio R., Ramon Alberto, Antonio Eugenio, Alfredo Miguel, Banjamin Gemelo, Lidia Theresa. Asst. chief accountant, br. mgr. Compania Maritima, Manila, Philippines, 1935-59; owners rep. Maritime Co. of the Philippines, San Francisco, 1959—; dir. Philippine Bank of Calif. Mem. Filipino Businessmen and Profls. Assn. San Francisco (founder, past pres.), Filipino Am. C. of C. of San Francisco (founder). Served with Philippine Army, 1939-41. Democrat. Roman Catholic. Clubs: Commonwealth, World Trade (San Francisco). Office: 100 California St Suite 1060 San Francisco CA 94111

JEANFREAU, ALVEY JOSEPH, economist; b. Norco, La., Feb. 6, 1939; s. Alvey J. and Odalie Marie (Cambre) J.; B.S. in Indsl. Tech., La. State U., 1962; diploma N.Y. Inst. Fin., 1969; m. Suzanne Nystrom, Apr. 14, 1961; children—Michael Paul, Winthrop Edward, Heidi Nell, Hilda Catherine, Matthew David, Andrew Joseph. Registered rep. Goodbody & Co., Colorado Springs, Colo., 1969-70; prin. Alvey J. Jeanfreau, III, economist and cert. fin. planner, Portland, Oreg., 1976—; instr. econs. and fin. (part-time) Portland State U., 1976—; guest speaker fin. planning seminars and confs., 1976—. Served to capt. USAF, 1963-69. Mem. Am. Inst. Econ. Research, Internat. Assn. Fin. Planners (nat. dir.), Inst. Cert. Fin. Planners, Am. Econ. Assn. Republican. Mormon. Contbr. articles to profl. jours. Office: Suite 821 200 Market Bldg Portland OR 97201

JECK, ROBERT VAN HOUTEN, mfg. co. exec.; b. Atlantic, Iowa, Oct. 8, 1931; s. George Van Houten and Gladys (Thomson) J.; student Dartmouth Coll., 1948-50; B.S., Iowa State Coll., 1952; postgrad. London Sch. Econs., 1955-57; M.B.A., U. Pa., 1958; A.M.P., Harvard U., 1973; m. Beverly Jean Braniff, July 9, 1955; children—Thomas V., Tamara Lynn, Cynthia Denise. With DuPont Co., 1958-68, with Amerace Co., 1968-79, v.p., 1972-76, group v.p., 1976-79; pres., chief exec. officer Worthington Pump Inc., Mountainside, N.J., 1979-80; pres. Worthington Group, 1980—; dir. subs.; bd. dirs. Truck Safety Equipment Inst., 1970-79, pres., 1970-72. Served with U.S. Navy, 1953-57. Mem. Soc. Plastics Engrs., Soc. Automotive Engrs., Motor Equipment Mfrs. Assn. (chmn. 1979-80), Beta Gamma Sigma, Sigma Delta Chi. Clubs: Rockaway River, Inverness, Seaview, Baltusrol. Office: 233 Mount Airy Rd Basking Ridge NJ 07920

JEDD, JOSEPH, univ. adminstr.; b. Tarnow, Poland, Aug. 21, 1919; s. Thomas and Josephine (Tadler) Jedrzykiewicz; came to U.S., 1948, naturalized, 1953; B.A. in Econs., U. Fribourg (Switzerland), 1944; postgrad. London U., U. Rome, Northwestern U.; m. Maria Alina

Karpinski, Dec. 26, 1946; children—Maya Veronica, Gregory J. Auditor, Sears, Roebuck & Co., Chgo., 1948-51; asst. controller Magnecord, Inc., Chgo., 1951-55; food and beverage controller Oceanic S.S. Co., San Francisco, 1956-59; self-employed cons., 1959-60; bursar Stanford U., 1960—; treas., dir. Profit Mgmt. Inc., Michael's Restaurant, Sunnyvale, Calif. Served with Polish Army, 1939, French Army, 1940, Free French Forces, 1944, Brit. Intelligence, 1944-48. Clubs: Palo Alto Rotary, Stanford U. Faculty (dir.). Home: 636 Palm Ave Los Altos CA 94022 Office: 104 Old Union Bldg Stanford Univ Stanford CA 94305

JEDEL, PETER HAROLD, mfg. co. exec.; b. Bklyn., May 19, 1939; s. Joseph L. and Marjory (Zucker) J.; B.A., Cornell U., 1960; M.B.A., N.Y. U., 1962; m. Elaine T. Binder, July 1, 1962; children—Marc, Lynn. Credit analyst Chem. Bank, 1960-63; fin. analyst Gen. Foods Co., 1963-65; sr. fin. analyst Xerox Co., Rochester, N.Y., 1965-68; mgr. strategic planning TWA, N.Y.C., 1968-69; investment banker Alan-Maged, N.Y.C., 1969-70; chief economist Cities Service Co., Tulsa, 1970—, dir. Fed. Credit Union; chmn. adv. com. Tulsa Sch. Econs. Mem. Northeastern Okla. Econs. Adv. Com.; mem. Mayor's Budget Rev.; dir. Arts and Humanities Council. Served with U.S. Army, 1962-63. Mem. UN Assn., Nat. Assn. Bus. Economists (council), Tulsa Econs. Club (chmn., founder), Am. Econ. Assn. Republican. Jewish. Club: Tulsa So. Racquet. Author: Economic Impact of the Arts; Use of Cycle Analysis; public speaker. Home: 7308 E 68th Pl Tulsa OK 74133 Office: PO Box 300 Tulsa OK 74102

JEFFCOAT, GAINES RAY, cotton mill exec.; b. Covington County, Ala., Feb. 14, 1922; s. Julius Claude and Ruth Hightower (Breedlove) J.; student Perkinston Jr. Coll., 1941-42, Auburn U., 1941-42; B.S., Duke, 1944; m. Audrey Wilson, Sept. 12, 1946; children—David, Everett. Master mechanic Opp Cotton Mill (Ala.), 1946-48, engr., 1948-55, supt., 1959-62; asst. supt. Opp & Micolas, 1955-59, gen. mgr., 1962-74, v.p., 1965-74, pres., 1974—; dir. Ala. Electric Co.; v.p. Dixie Investment Co.; dir. Johnston Industries, 1st Nat. Bank of Opp. Chmn., Ala. Adv. Bd. Vocation Edn.; mem. MacArthur Tech. Coll. Com.; past pres. P.T.A., Ala.-Fla. council Boy Scouts Am., Opp United Fund, Ala. Textile Mfrs. Assn., Ala. Textile Edn. Found.; former mem. Opp City Council; bd. dirs. Opp & Micolas Scholarship Fund, Goodwill Industries Central Ala., Mizell Meml. Hosp., City of Opp Sch. Bd. Served with USMCR, 1944-46. Hon. mem. staff gov. Ala.; recipient Silver Beaver award Boy Scouts Am. Mem. Am. Textile Mfrs. Inst. (dir.), Nat. Cotton Council (dir.), Phi Psi. Methodist (lay speaker, Sunday sch. tchr., mem. world service and finance com. Ala.-W. Fla. conf., past chmn. program council; del. gen. conf.). Lion (past pres.), Toastmaster (past pres.). Home: Forest Park Opp AL 36467 Office: PO Drawer 70 Opp AL 36467

JEFFERDS, JOSEPH CROSBY, JR., distbn. co. exec.; b. Charleston, W.Va., June 24, 1919; s. Joseph Crosby and Agnes Atkinson (Arbuckle) J.; B.S. in M.E., M.I.T., 1940; Sc.D. (hon.), W.Va. Inst. Tech., 1970; m. Olivia Polk Evans, May 15, 1943; children—Joseph Crosby, Marion Evans, Olivia Polk, Robert Grosvenor. Trainee, Bethelhem Steel Corp. (Pa.), 1940; staff Kanawha Drug Co., Charleston, 1946-47, v.p., dir., 1947—; pres. Jefferds Corp., St. Albans, W.Va., 1947—; pres. Mech. Equip. Service Co., Inc., Charleston, 1952—; dir. C & P Telephone Co. of W.Va., Kanawha Banking & Trust Co. N.A. Mem., pres. W.Va. Bd. Edn., 1957-65. Served to lt. col. Ordnance Corps, U.S. Army, 1941-46. Mem. Charleston Area C. of C. (dir., pres. 1972), ASME (pres. W.Va. sect. 1952-53), Am. Inst. Indsl. Engrs., Def. Preparedness Assn., Res. Officers Assn., Sigma Chi, Tau Beta Pi. Republican. Episcopalian. Clubs: Rotary (pres. 1957), Edgewood Country (pres. 1957), Berry Hills Country. Author: A History of St. John's Episcopal Ch., 1975; Captain Matthew Arbuckle, A Documentary Biography, 1980. Home: 3 Scott Rd Charleston WV 25314 Office: Winfield Rd Saint Albans WV 25177

JEFFERS, DONALD E., ins. co. exec.; b. Louisville, Ill., Aug. 21, 1925; s. Byron and Alice (Burgess) J.; B.S., U. Ill., 1948; m. Marion D. Benna, Aug. 14, 1948 (dec.); 1 son, Derek B.; m. Janice C. Smith, Apr. 21, 1979. Sr. acct. Coopers & Lybrand, N.Y.C., Chgo., 1948-56; asst. v.p. Continental Casualty Co., Chgo., 1956-64; dep. comptroller 1st Nat. Bank, Boston, 1965-67; exec. v.p., treas. Interstate Nat. Corp., Chgo., 1967-74, pres., chief exec. officer, dir. 1974—; chmn., dir. Interstate Fire and Casualty Co., Chgo. Ins. Co., Interstate Indemnity Co., Geo. F. Brown & Sons, Inc. Served with U.S. Army, 1943-45. Decorated Purple Heart. Mem. Am. Inst. C.P.A.'s, Ill. Soc. C.P.A.'s, Clubs: Mid-America, Attic, Econ., Carlton, Westmoreland Country. Home: 860 Lake Shore Dr Chicago IL 60611 Office: 55 E Monroe St Chicago IL 60603

JEFFERS, JOHN TERRY, publishing co. exec.; b. Balt., Feb. 16, 1941; s. John C. and Anna Marie (Terry) J.; B.A. in Econs., Brigham Young U., 1967; M.B.A. in Internat. Econs., U. Calif., Berkeley, 1969; m. Deanna Mae Shirley, June 13, 1969; children—Tracy Anne, Lindsay Marie. Mktg. rep., data processing div. IBM, Palo Alto, Calif., 1969-72, regional rep., NW region, data processing div., San Francisco, 1973-75; pres. Target, Inc., San Ramon, Calif., 1975—; pres. Target Travel Internat.; chmn. bd. Fin. Planning Services. Vice pres. Free-the-Eagle lobbying group; chmn. Ruff Found. Mem. Newsletter Assn. Am. (dir.). Republican. Mormon. Clubs: Round Hill Country, Riverside Country. Author: How to Organize Your Life and Plan For an Uncertain Future, 1978. Office: Target Inc 2411 Old Crow Canyon Rd San Ramon CA 94583

JEFFERY, ALEXANDER HALEY, ins. co. exec., lawyer; b. London, Ont., Can., Jan. 29, 1909; s. James Edgar and Gertrude (Dumaresq) J.; student London South Collegiate Inst., 1922-27; grad. U. Western Ont., 1931, Osgoode Hall, Toronto, 1934; m. Eulalie E. Murray, June 29, 1934; children—Alexander M., Judith E. Admitted to Ont. bar, 1934; pvt. practice law, London, Ont., 1934—; named Queen's counsel; gen. counsel, pres. London Life Ins. Co.; pres., dir. Forest City Investments Ltd.; dep. chmn. bd. Thames Valley Investments Ltd., London Realty Mgmt. & Rentals Ltd., London Winery, Ltd., Can. Trust Huron & Erie. M.P. for Constituency City of London, 1949-53. Anglican. Clubs: London Hunt and Country, London; Royal Can. Yacht, Univ. (Toronto); Windsor Yacht; Sarnia Yacht; Port Stanley Sailing Squadron; Gt. Lakes Crusing; Masons. Home: 104 Commissioners Rd E London N6C 2T1 ON Canada Office: PO Box 2095 174 King St London ON N6A 4E1 Canada

JEFFERY, IVAN LEE, foundry exec.; b. Coldwater, Mich., May 13, 1946; s. George W. and Mary C. (Rendell) J.; B. degree in bus. adminstrn., Mich. State U., 1969; m. Wilhelmina Stunz, Jan. 8, 1977; children by previous marriage—Trinka Kathleen, Clifford Thomas. Owner, founder, Navi Industries, Bronson, Mich., 1969-73; plant supt. Aluminum Alloys, Inc., Sinking Spring, Pa., 1973-74, gen. mgr., 1977-79; gen. mgr. Crescent Brass Mfg. Corp., Reading, Pa., 1974-77, v.p., gen. mgr., 1979-81, pres., 1981—, also dir.; dir. Aluminum Alloys, Inc.; mem. industry sector adv. com. on nonferrous ores and metals U.S. Dept. Commerce. Trustee, Bronson Bd. Edn.; pres. Bronson Devel. Corp., 1972-73. Mem. Am. Foundrymen's Assn., Non-Ferrous Foundrymen's Soc. (alternate dir., pres. Eastern Pa. mgmt. group). Home: RD 1 Box 166-C Birdsboro PA 19508 Office: Crescent Brass Mfg Co 7th and Spruce Sts Reading PA 19603

JEFFREDO, JOHN VICTOR, mfg. co. exec.; b. Los Angeles, Nov. 5, 1927; s. John Edward and Pauline Matilda (Whitten) J.; grad. in aero. engring. Cal-Aero Tech. Inst., 1948; A.A., Pasadena City Coll., 1951, Palomar Coll., 1978; student U. So. Calif., 1955-58; M.B.A. candidate La Jolla U., 1980—; m. Elma Jean Nesmith, July 1953 (div. 1958); children—Joyce Jean, Michael John; m. 2d, Doris Louise Hinz, Feb. 18, 1958; children—John Victor, Louise Victoria; m. 3d, Gerda Aldeheid Pillich, Nov. 29, 1980 (div. 1980). Design engr. Douglas Aircraft Co., Long Beach and Santa Monica, Calif., 1955-58; devel. engr. Honeywell Ordnance Corp., Duarte, Calif., 1958-62; cons. Honeywell devel. labs., Seattle, 1962-65; supr. mech. engr. dept aerospace div. Control Data Corp., Pasadena, Calif., 1965-68; project engr. Cubic Corp., San Diego, 1968-70; supr. mech. engring. dept. Babcock Electronics Co., Costa Mesa, Calif., 1970-72; owner, operator Jeffredo Gunsight Co., Fallbrook, Calif., 1971—; chief engr., exec. dir. Western Designs, Fallbrook, 1972—; engring. cons. Energy Sci. Corp., Seattle, Gen. Dynamics, San Diego; exec. dir., bd. dirs. India World Corp. Mem. San Diego County Border Task Force, 1980. Served with U.S. Army, 1951-53. Mem. Nat. Hist. Soc., Nat. Rifle Assn. (life), San Diego Zool. Soc., Sierra Club. Patentee: agrl. frost control system, deep sea pressure hull, internal combustion engine emission control, vehicle off-road drive system, recoil absorbing system for firearms, telescope sight mount system for firearms, breech mech. sporting firearm, elec. switch activating system, others. Home: 938 N Knoll Park Ln Fallbrook CA 92028 Office: 120 N Pacific St San Marcos CA 92069

JEFFREY, JACQUELINE ELAINE LANDER, health and beauty care co. exec.; b. Mpls., Aug. 18, 1943; d. Eugene Nels and Helen Lucy (Vanek) Lander; B.S. in Math., U. Minn., 1965; M.B.A., Harvard, 1972. Asst. product mgr. L'eggs, Winston-Salem, N.C., 1972-73; product mgr. Crown Zellerbach, San Francisco, 1974-75; mktg. mgr. United Vintners, San Francisco, 1976-78, Carter-Wallace, N.Y.C., 1978-79, Lever Bros., N.Y.C., 1979—. Mem. Am. Mktg. Assn. Club: Harvard (N.Y.C.). Home: 12 Beekman Pl Apt 7D New York NY 10022 Office: Lever House 390 Park Ave New York NY 10022

JEFFREYS, ELYSTAN GEOFFREY, geologist, oil co. exec.; b. N.Y.C., Apr. 26, 1926; s. Geoffrey and Georgene Frances Theodora (Littell) J.; Geol. Engr., Colo. Sch. Mines, 1951, grad. Econ. Evaluation and Investment Decision Methods, 1972; m. Pat Rumage, May 1, 1946; children—Jeri Lynn, David Powell; m. 2d, Peggi Villar, Feb. 28, 1975. Partner, G. Jeffreys & Son, 1951-53, Jeffreys and Launius, 1953-55; instr. structural geology U. So. Miss., 1955; pvt. practice petroleum exploration, 1954-77; exploration mgr. Arrowhead Exploration Co., Mobile and Brewton, Ala., 1977—; cons. geologist, 1964—; pres., chmn. Major Oil Co., Jackson, Miss., 1961—. Mem. Mobile Historic Devel. Commn. Served with 281st Combat Engrs., U.S. Army, 1944-46; ETO. Registered profl. engr., Miss.; registered land surveyor, Miss. Mem. Am. Assn. Petroleum Geologists, Gulf Coast Assn. Geol. Socs. (treas. 1960, cert. of service 1971), Soc. Petroleum Engrs. AIME, Am. Assn. Petroleum Landmen, Miss. Geol. Soc., Ind. Petroleum Assn. Am., Okla. Ind. Petroleum Assn., English Speaking Union, Historic Mobile Preservation Soc., Pi Kappa Alpha. Clubs: Athlestan, Shriners (Mobile); Capital City Petroleum (Jackson, Miss.); Masons (Jackson); Curzon (London). Home: 1810 Old Government St Mobile AL 36606 Office: 1509 Government St Suite 100 Mobile AL 36604

JEFFRIES, EDWIN CLIFFORD, ret. land devel. co. exec., lawyer; b. Elgin, Ill., July 9, 1913; s. James G. and Veda (Jones) J.; B.S. in Bus., Kan. U., 1934, LL.B., J.D., 1937; m. Catherine Huey, Feb. 1, 1941; children—Edwin J., Catherine E., Jennifer L., Mary V. Admitted to Kans. bar, 1937, Calif. bar, 1948; with Harris Trust & Savs. Bank, Chgo., 1937-39, Lansing B. Warner, Inc., Chgo., 1939-41; pvt. practice, San Diego, from 1948; U.S. atty., San Diego, 1953-54; mng. dir. Manchester Twenty-One Hundred-Land Devel. Co. Del. Calif. Bar Conv., 1952. Mem. Calif. Republican Central Com., 1952-53; chmn. Sight Conservation Fund. Served as lt. USNR, 1942-46; PTO. Mem. Am. Judicature Soc., Am., San Diego (sec. 1941-52) bar assns., No. San Diego County Asso. (past pres.), Cardiff-by-the-Sea (past pres.) chambers commerce. Episcopalian (sr. warden). Home: 2535 Navarra Dr Rancho La Costa Carlsbad CA 92008 Office: Box 123 Cardiff-by-the-Sea CA 92007

JEFFRIES, ROBERT SEMPLE, JR., mgmt. cons.; b. Chattanooga, Mar. 29, 1928; s. Robert Semple and Marion Bruce (Daniel) J.; B.S. Va. Mil. Inst., 1949; m. Barbara Ann Warden, May 12, 1962; children—Robert Semple, III, Christopher Warden, Andrew Hill. Engr., E.I. DuPont de Nemours & Co., Inc., Martinsville, Va., 1952-58; asso. McKinsey & Co., N.Y.C., 1958-63; mgr. Gen. Foods Corp., White Plains, N.Y., 1963-68; asso. Cresap, McCormick & Paget, Inc., N.Y.C., 1968-71; pres. R.S. Jeffries, Jr., Mgmt. Cons., New Canaan, Conn., 1971—; dir. Knowlton Bros., Inc., Chattanooga, 1977-80. Served as 1st lt., arty. U.S. Army, 1949-50, 50-52. Mem. Inst. Mgmt. Consultants (certified mgmt. cons.), Nat. Council Phys. Distbn. Mgmt. Club: New Canaan Field. Home: 207 Sleepy Hollow Rd New Canaan CT 06840 Office: 72 Park St New Canaan CT 06840

JEGLIC, JOHN MARY, cons. co. exec.; b. Yugoslavia, June 11, 1931; s. Milko and Cirila (Kleindienst) J.; came to U.S., 1950, naturalized, 1955; B.S.C.E., U. Notre Dame du Lac, 1957; M.S.C.E., So. Meth. U., 1961; m. Ann Catherine Alexander, 1980; children by previous marriage—Nancy Diane, Julie Irene. Structural engr. Gen. Dynamics Co., Ft. Worth, 1957-61; supervising engr. re-entry systems Gen. Electric Co., King of Prussia, Pa., 1961-69; mgr. systems applications Keystone Computer Assos., Fort Washington, Pa., 1969-71; chmn. bd., pres. Decision Research Scis., Inc., Ambler, Pa., 1971—; partner Computer Composition Assos., 1980—; dir. Mktg. Cons., Inc. Served with U.S. Army, 1951-53. World Student Service Fund scholar, 1950-51. Republican. Roman Catholic. Contbr. articles to profl. jours. Home: 912 Woodbridge Rd Spring House PA 19477 Office: 300 Axewood E Butler & Skippack Pikes Ambler PA 19002

JEHLE, JOHN LOUIS, mech. contractor; b. Alton, Ill., June 27, 1917; s. John J. and Louise (Degenhardt) J.; B.S.M.E., U. Notre Dame, 1938; married; children—Antionette, Caroline, John, Jane, Theresa, Mark, Mary, Margaret. Design engr. Carbon & Carbide Chm. Co., Charleston, W.Va., 1941-42; piping engr. M.W. Kellog Co., Wood River, Ill., 1942-44; asst. plant engr. Chevrolet div. Gen. Motors Co., St. Louis, 1944-48; sch. dist. engr. Alton public schs., 1948-51; pres. Alton Plumbing & Heating Corp., 1951—. Mem. Nat. Assn. Plumbing-Heating-Cooling Contractors, Ill. Assn. Plumbing-Heating-Cooling Contractors, Ill. Mech. Specialty Contractors Assn. (pres. 1980). Republican. Roman Catholic. Club: Rotary (pres. club 1964). Home: Fairmount Addition Alton IL 62002 Office: 217 William St Alton IL 62002

JELINEK, WILLIAM ROBERT, farm machinery mfg. co. exec.; b. Cary, Ill., Dec. 7, 1932; s. Frank Louis and Elizabeth Ann (Holan) J.; student Marquette U., 1951-52, U. Ill., 1955-58; m. Barbara Jean Gilzow, June 16, 1962; children—Jamie, Donna, Kathy. With Buehler & Kautt, C.P.A.'s, Elgin, Ill., 1959, James G. Condon & Assos., Woodstock, Ill., 1960-61; with Mathews Co., Crystal Lake, Ill., 1961—, v.p., 1965-76, asst. treas., 1967-76, pres., 1976—, also dir. Served with U.S. Army, 1951-53. Mem. Crystal Lake C. of C. (pres. 1968, dir. 1967-69). Roman Catholic. Club: Kiwanis. Home: 6417 Walkup Ln Crystal Lake IL 60014 Office: 500 Industrial Ave Crystal Lake IL 60014

JELLIFFE, CHARLES GORDON, banker; b. Mansfield, Ohio, Nov. 28, 1914; s. Charles Mitchell and Florence (Findley) J.; B.Sc., Ohio State U., 1937; m. Carolyn V. Wolf, Oct. 3, 1942; children—Charles Martin, Joyce Findley, John Bour, Janell W. Salesman, Hawley Huller & Co., investment securities, Cleve., 1937-40; with Columbus Coated Fabrics Corp. (Ohio), 1940-64, pres., chmn. bd., 1961-64; former vice chmn. bd., pres. City Nat. Bank & Trust Co., Columbus, 1964-74, also dir.; chmn., chief exec. officer, dir. 1st Nat. Bank of N.J., Totowa, 1974—; sec.-treas., dir. 1st Bank Group of Ohio Inc., 1968-74; dir. Lumbermans Mut. Ins. Co., Mansfield, O. Bd. dirs. Columbus Downtown Area Commn., 1966-74, Devel. Com. Greater Columbus, 1962-74. Pres., trustee Gladden Community House, Columbus, 1955-63; trustee Columbus United Community Council, 1964-74, Columbus Gallery Fine Arts, 1963-74, Defiance (Ohio) Coll., 1961-74. Served to maj. AUS, 1941-46. Congregationalist (chmn. trustees). Clubs: Scioto Country (Columbus); University, Pinnacle (N.Y.C.); Royal Poinciana Golf (Naples, Fla.); Arcola Country (N.J.); Indian Trail (Franklin Lakes, N.J.). Home: 920 Cherokee Ln Franklin Lakes NJ 07417 Office: 515 Union Blvd Totowa NJ 07512

JELSMA, EDWARD RICHARD, transp. cons.; b. Enid, Okla., Mar. 15, 1915; s. Edward Darwin and Orilla (Hackathorn) J.; B.S., Okla. State U., 1937, M.S., 1938; postgrad. Stanford, 1939-40; diploma internat. law U.S. Naval War Coll.; diploma Mind Control Inst.; Ph.D. (hon.), Colo. Christian Coll., 1973; m. Marjorie Marie Crain, Feb. 12, 1948; children—Schuyler, Richard, Lisa. Asst. to tax counsel Standard Oil Co. Calif., San Francisco, 1940-41; dep. fiscal dir. Bur. Ordnance, U.S. Dept. Navy, Washington, 1946-48, asst. fiscal dir. dept., 1948-49; engaged in citrus industry, 1949—; profl. mem. Interstate and Fgn. Commerce Com., U.S. Senate, 1949-55; dir. bur. transport econs. and statistics ICC, 1955-58; admitted to ICC bar, 1958; pres. E.R. Jelsma & Assos., transp. cons., 1958—; pres. Skyland Farms; grad. asst. Okla. State U., 1937-38; instr. Northwestern State Coll., 1938-39, Am. U., 1946-49; guest lectr. U. Louisville, 1942-43. Pres., Sylvan Shores Assn., Mt. Dora, 1973-78. Served from ensign to lt. comdr., USNR, 1941-52. Mason (32 deg.). Author: Minimum Wage Legislation, 1938. Office: 1811 Morningside Dr Mount Dora FL 32757

JENEFSKY, JACK, marketing exec.; b. Dayton, Ohio, Oct. 27, 1919; s. David and Anna (Saeks) J.; B.S. in Bus. Adminstrn., Ohio State U., 1941; postgrad. Harvard Bus. Sch., 1943; M.A. in Econs., U. Dayton, 1948; m. Beverly Jean; children—Anna Elizabeth, Kathryn Jean Mueller. Surplus broker, Dayton, 1946-48; sales rep. Remington Rand-Univac, Dayton, 1949-56, mgr. AF account, 1957-59, br. mgr., Dayton, 1960-61, regional mktg. cons. Midwest region, Dayton, 1962-63; pres. Bowman Supply Co., Dayton, 1963—. Mem. 3d dist. selection adv. bd. Air Force Acad., chmn., 1974—. Served from pvt. to capt. USAAF, 1942-46; CBI. Served as maj. USAF, 1951-53; col. USAFR. Mem. Air Force Assn. (comdr. Ohio wing 1957-58, 58-59), Res. Officers Assn. (pres. Ohio dept. 1956-57, nat. council 1957-58, chmn. research and devel. com. 1961-62), Res. Officers Assn. (air force affairs com., research and devel. com.), Dayton Area C. of C. (chmn. spl. events com. 1970-73), Ohio State U. Alumni Assn. (pres. Montgomery County, Ohio 1959-60), Civil Air Patrol (Gt. Lakes region res. assistance coordinator 1970-73), Nat. Sojourners (pres. Dayton 1961-62). Jewish. Lion. Club: Harvard Business Sch. (pres. 1961-62) (Dayton). Home: 136 Briar Heath Circle Dayton OH 45415 Office: 225 N Irwin St Dayton OH 45403

JENETT, ERIC, engring. exec.; b. N.Y.C., Aug. 11, 1923; s. Henry and Maria Carolina Louisa J.; B.S. in Chem. Engring., Columbia, 1948, M.S. in Chem. Engring., 1949; m. Dorothy Virginia Williams, Sept. 22, 1944; children—Bruce Williams, Jon Eric. Research engr. Tenn. Eastman Corp., Kingsport, 1949-51; process engr. Brown & Root, Inc., Houston, 1951-57, project engr., 1957-60, chief process engr., 1960-75, v.p. engring. design, 1975-76, v.p. indsl.-civil div., 1977-79, v.p. MAPI Group, PGM div., 1980—, project gen. mgmt.; leader seminars and short courses schs. and profl. socs. Pres., chmn. bd. Project Mgmt. Inst., 1969-72. Served to 1st lt. USAAF, World War II; ETO. Registered profl. engr., Tex. Mem. Am. Inst. Chem. Engrs., Houston Engring. and Sci. Soc., Sigma Xi, Phi Lambda Upsilon. Contbg. editor Perry's Chem. Engrs. Handbook, 1977; contbr. articles to profl. jours. Home: 2421 Westcreek St 116H Houston TX 77027 Office: PO Box 3 Houston TX 77001

JENKINS, CHARLES SNEDEKER, ins. agy. exec.; b. Mineola, N.Y., Oct. 27, 1939; s. John B. and Jane (Snedeker) J.; B.A., Dickinson Coll., 1961; M.A., L.I. U., 1967; m. Barbara Elaine Giles, July 27, 1963; children—Susan, Charles. With Snedeker-Jenkins Ins. Agy., Inc., Manhasset, N.Y., 1961—, v.p., 1965-71, pres., 1971—. Mem. nat. council U.S.O., 1970-72; commr. Manhasset Park Dist., 1970—; chmn. disaster com. ARC, Manhasset. C.P.C.U. Mem. Nassau County Independent Ins. Agts. Assn., Profl. Ins. Agts., Alpha Chi Rho, Pi Gamma Mu. Mason, Rotarian. Mem. Reformed Ch. in Am. (deacon). Club: Port Washington (N.Y.) Yacht. Home: 6 Willow Ct Plandome Heights Manhasset NY 11030 Office: 21 George St Manhasset NY 11030

JENKINS, DALE AUBREY, investment co. exec.; b. Pottsville, Pa., June 14, 1938; s. Joseph Aubrey and Elfey Othalia (Carlsen) J.; A.B., Harvard U., 1960; M.B.A., Columbia U., 1966; m. Amanda Bowman, Mar. 18, 1976; 1 son, David A. With Smith Barney, Harris Upham & Co., 1966-70, Paine Webber Jackson & Curtis, N.Y.C., 1970-72, Hill Samuel & Co., Ltd., London and N.Y.C., 1972-77; pres. Hill Samuel Securities Corp., 1974-77, Hanover Gen. Corp., N.Y.C., 1977—. Served from ensign to lt. (j.g.) USN, 1960-63. Clubs: Racquet and Tennis (N.Y.C.); Tuxedo. Home: 940 Park Ave New York NY 10021 also Tower Hill Rd Tuxedo Park NY 10987 Office: Hanover Gen Corp 230 Park Ave New York NY 10017

JENKINS, GEORGE POLLOCK, fin. cons.; b. Clarksburg, W.Va., Feb. 24, 1915; s. Roy N. and Gertrude S. (Pollock) J.; grad. Blair Acad., 1932; A.B., Princeton U., 1936; M.B.A., Harvard U., 1938; m. Marian E. O'Brien, Apr. 10, 1945; children—James P., Robert N., Richard G. With Met. Life Ins. Co., N.Y.C., 1938-80, v.p., 1956-62, fin. v.p., 1962-65, chmn. fin. com., 1965-80, vice chmn., 1969-73; chmn. bd., 1973-80; fin. cons. W.R. Grace & Co., 1980—; dir. St. Regis Paper Co., Am. Broadcasting Cos., Inc., Bethlehem Steel Corp., W.R. Grace Co. Trustee Blair Acad., Blairstown, N.J., U. So. Calif. Served to capt. U.S. Army, 1942-46. Mem. Phi Beta Kappa. Clubs: Links (N.Y.C.); Baltusrol Golf (Springfield, N.J.). Office: WR Grace & Co 1114 Ave of Americas New York NY 10036

JENKINS, JOHN JOSEPH, mfg. co. exec.; b. Trenton, N.J., May 2, 1936; s. John B. and Kathleen C. (Kennedy) J.; B.S., Rider Coll., 1958; postgrad. Pace Coll., 1960-61; m. Alice Keefe, Nov. 19, 1960; children—John, James, Jason. Controller, Petry Storage Co., Trenton, 1960-61; acct. Gen. Motors, Detroit, 1961-67; acct. Xerox Corp., Rochester, N.Y., 1969; mgr. inventory acctg., 1969-72, sr. acct., 1968-69, mgr. disbursements, 1969, bus. analyst, 1972, audit mgr., 1972-73, bus. cons. 1973-75, mgr. planning and analysis, 1975-79, fin.

tech. specialist, Webster, N.Y., 1979-80, chmn. productivity task force, product cost engring., 1980—. Mem. pres.'s council St. Joseph's Coll., 1973-80; adj. faculty Rochester Inst. Tech., 1975-77; faculty Empire State Coll., 1976. Club: McQuaid Booster. Office: 800 Phillips Rd Bldg 207C Webster NY 14580

JENKINS, RICHARD LEE, mfg. co. exec.; b. Lynchburg, Va., July 20, 1931; s. Robert Julian and Beulah Vivian (Crews) J.; B.A. cum laude, Lynchburg Coll., 1957; M.B.A., U. Mass., 1970; m. Doris E. Rucker, Dec. 24, 1958; children—Terena M., Richard C. Successively fin. trainee, mem. audit staff, various fin. mgmt. positions Gen. Elec. Co., 1957-72; controller Overhead Distbn. Transformer div. Allis-Chalmers, Pitts., 1972-74, mgr. mfg. ops., 1974-75, plant mgr., Cin., 1975, mgr. mfg. ops. Indsl. Pump div., 1975-76, gen. mgr., 1976—; sr. v.p. Lynchburg (Va.) Foundry div. Mead Corp., 1979—; treas., dir. Micah Corp. of Berkshire County, Va. Nat. Bank, Lynchburg. Dir. comml. and indsl. div. Loan Execs. Program, United Community Services, 1970; auditor Berkshire chpt. ARC, 1966; campaign chmn. Piedmont Heart Assn. Served with USN, 1950-54. Mem. Nat. Assn. Accountants, Mfg. Exec. Luncheon Group of Cin. Club: Kenwood Country (Cin.). Home: 1216 Norvell House Ct Lynchburg VA 24503 Office: Drawer 411 Lynchburg VA 24505

JENKINS, ROBERT DAVID, beverage co. exec.; b. N.Y.C., Jan. 26, 1952; s. David Gordon and Dorothy C. (Scobie) J.; B.S., U. Ariz., 1973; M.B.A., U. Tenn., 1975; m. Susan J. Schneller, Oct. 1, 1978; 1 son, Michael Edward. Staff acct. Philip Morris Internat., N.Y.C., 1974; staff accountant, internat. div. Can. Dry Corp., N.Y.C., 1975-77, fin. analyst, internat. div., 1977-78, internat. fin. mgr., 1978-80, internat. controller, 1980—. Mem. Nat. Assn. Accts., Inst. Mgmt. Acctg. Home: 2 Spireview Rd Ridgefield CT 06877 Office: Can Dry Corp 100 Park Ave New York NY 10017

JENKINS, ROBERT SPURGEON, mgmt. cons.; b. Wellston, Ohio, Oct. 24, 1921; s. Isaac Spurgeon and Carolyn (Burns) J.; A.A., Rio Grande Coll., 1943; A.B., Denison U., 1946; M.A., Ohio State U., 1948, Ph.D., 1951; m. Margaret Gene Kennard, Sept. 1, 1946; children—Deborah Gene and Priscilla Ann (twins), Roberta Kennard, Cynthia Carolyn. Capital investment analysis supr. Ford div. Ford Motor Co., 1952-55, asst. to exec. v.p., 1956-57, asst. orgn. and systems mgr. L-M div., 1958-60, mktg. adminstrn. mgr., 1960-63, sales and marketing mgmt. mgr., 1964-65; sr. dir. personnel Trans World Airlines, 1965-69; pres. R.S. Jenkins & Co., Mgmt. Cons. and Exec. Search, 1970-71; sr. v.p., mng. partner Eastman & Beaudine, Inc., Internat. Mgmt. Cons., 1971—, also dir. Asst. dir. research Ohio Tax and Revenue Study Commn., 1951; prof. indsl. mgmt. Henry Ford Coll., 1958-63; lectr. Am. Mgmt. Assn., 1968-69; personnel cons. Peace Corps, Washington, 1970. Mem. Livonia (Mich.) Sch. Bd., 1957, Plymouth (Mich.) Sch. Bd., 1965; pres. Plymouth Symphony Soc., 1960-62. Mem. personnel bd. N.Y. Light House Assn., N.Y.C., 1968-70. Served with USAAF, 1943-46. Mem. Am. Econ. Assn., Am. Mgmt. Assn., Sigma Chi. Presbyn. (elder 1969-71). Clubs: University, Board Room, Wings (N.Y.C.); Landmark (Stamford, Conn.); Wee Burn Country (Darien, Conn.). Home: 21 Stephanie Ln Darien CT 06820 Office: 437 Madison Ave New York NY 10022

JENKINS, RUBEN LEE, lawyer, pharm. and cosmetics mfg. co. exec.; b. Beggs, Okla., Nov. 27, 1929; s. William Arnold and Myrtle (Kimble) J.; B.A., U. Okla., 1952, LL.B., 1956; LL.M. in Internat. Law (Ford Found. scholar, Fulbright scholar), N.Y. U., 1959; m. Sylvia Griffin, July 17, 1956; children—Amy, Kimble Lee, William Griffin. Admitted to Okla. bar, 1956; practiced in Argentina, 1959-60; exec. v.p. White Eagle Internat. Inc., Midland, Tex., 1960-65; v.p. corp. devel. Plough, Inc., Memphis, 1965-70, sr. v.p., 1970-73, exec. v.p., 1973-75, pres., 1975—, also dir.; dir. Schering-Plough Corp., Memphis, 1971—, sr. v.p., 1976—. Served to capt. USMC, 1952-54. Mem. Am. Bar Assn., Okla. Bar Assn., Proprietary Assn. (dir.), Grocery Mfrs. Assn. Presbyterian. Club: Union League (N.Y.C.). Office: 3030 Jackson Ave Memphis TN 38151

JENKINS, THOMAS ALAN, packaging co. exec.; b. Columbus, Ohio, Feb. 1, 1927; s. John O. and Elsie (Palmer) J.; B.S., Ohio State U., 1950; m. Mary Ashwell, Sept. 26, 1953; children—Nancy, Martha, Megyn. With Owens-Illinois, Inc., Toledo, 1950—, v.p. glass container div., 1973—. Served with U.S. Mcht. Marine, 1945, USAAF, 1945-46. Mem. Glass Packaging Inst., Packaging Edn. Found., Toledo C. of C., U.S. C. of C., Sigma Alpha Epsilon. Office: PO Box 1035 Toledo OH 43666

JENKINS, THOMAS NELSON, fin. planner; b. Balt., Mar. 15, 1933; s. Glenn Llewellyn and Serena Elizabeth (Forberg) J.; B.S., Purdue U., 1957; m. Carol Louise Snelling, June 6, 1954; children—David Glenn, Stephen Ralph. Br. mgr. Francis I. DuPont & Co., Cleve., 1959-63; pres. Thermox Corp., Lakewood, Ohio, 1969—; pres. Conceptual Fin. Planning, Inc., Cleve., 1975—; v.p. Loeb Rhoades, Hornblower & Co., Cleve., 1963-80; chmn. bd. Resource Properties, Inc., 1978—; mng. gen. partner Enersource Ltd. Served with U.S. Army, 1953-55. Mem. Internat. Assn. Fin. Planners (pres. N.E. Ohio chpt. 1976-77, chmn. 1977-78), Inst. Certified Fin. Planners, Ohio Soc. Fin. Counselors (chmn. 1978). Clubs: Rotary, Cheshire Cheese, Toastmaster Internat. Home: 1544 St Charles Ave Lakewood OH 44107 Office: 14706 Detroit Ave Cleveland OH 44107

JENKINS, WILLIAM MAXWELL, banker; b. Sultan, Wash., Apr. 19, 1919; s. Warren M. and Louise (Black) J.; B.A., U. Wash., 1941; M.B.A., Harvard, 1943; m. Elisabeth Taber, Oct. 12, 1945 (div. 1976); children—Elisabeth Cordua, Ann Hathaway, William Morris, Karen Louise, Peter Taber, David M., Barbara Fessenden. Asst. cashier, asst. v.p., asst. mgr. Met. Br. Seattle First Nat. Bank, 1945-53, became exec. v.p. Everett br., 1961, also chmn., dir., 1962—; v.p. First Nat. Bank, Everett, Wash., 1953-54, exec. v.p., 1954-57, pres., 1956-61; chmn. Everett Trust & Savs. Bank, 1956-61; chmn. Seattle-First Nat. Bank, 1962—, also dir.; chmn. Seafirst Corp., 1974—, also dir.; dir. Scott Paper Co., Western Gear Corp., Pacific N.W. Bell, UAL, Inc., United Airlines, Safeco Co. Adv. com. Sch. Bus. Adminstrn., U. Wash.; bd. dirs. Harvard U. Grad. Sch. Bus., Econ. Devel. Council Puget Sound; trustee Downtown Seattle Devel. Assn.; chmn. men's adv. bd. Children's Orthopedic Hosp., Seattle; incorporator, mem. exec. com. Fifth Ave Theater Assn.; bd. assos. Harvard Bus. Sch. Served to lt. (j.g.) USNR, 1943-45. Decorated Navy Cross, Croix de Guerre with palme. Mem. Assn. Res. City Bankers (pres. 1973-74), Internat. Monetary Conf. (dir. 1978—). Republican Presbyn. Clubs: Cascade, Seattle Tennis, Harbor, Rainier, University, Golf (Seattle). Office: Seattle-First Nat Bank Box 3586 Seattle WA 98124

JENKS, DOWNING BLAND, railroad exec.; b. Portland, Oreg., Aug. 16, 1915; s. Charles O. and Della (Downing) J.; B.S., Yale, 1937; m. Louise Sweeney, Nov. 30, 1940; children—Downing B., Nancy Randolph. Chainman, Spokane Portland & Seattle Ry., Portland, 1934-35; asst., engr. corps Pa. R.R., N.Y. div., 1937-38; successively roadmaster, div. engr., trainmaster various divs. G.N. Ry., 1938-47, div. supt., Spokane, Wash., 1947-48; gen. mgr. C. & E.I. R.R., 1949-50; asst. v.p. ops. Rock Island Lines, Chgo., 1950-51, v.p. ops., 1951-53, exec. v.p., dir., 1953-55, pres., 1956-61; pres. M.P.R.R., 1961-71, chmn., 1972—, also dir.; chmn., chief exec. officer, dir. Mo. Pacific Corp., 1971—; dir. 1st Nat. Bank, St. Louis, Bankers Life Co., 1st Union Bancorp. Life trustee Northwestern U.; nat. pres. Boy Scouts Am., 1977-80. Served from 1st lt. to lt. col. 704th Ry. Grand Div., AUS, 1942-45; ETO, MTO. Mem. Tau Beta Pi. Home: 8 Greenbriar Saint Louis MO 63124 Office: Mo Pacific Bldg Saint Louis MO 63103

JENKS, JOHN BERNARD, fiberglas co. exec.; b. Chgo., Feb. 4, 1937; s. John Bernard and Margaret Clara (Koll) J.; B.B.A., U. Mich., 1960, M.B.A., 1961; m. Patsy Lee Borgstadt, Sept. 6, 1958; children—Jeffrey A., Julie A., Jason A. Various mktg. mgmt. positions Dow Chem. Co., Midland, Mich., 1961-68; mktg. mgr. resins and coatings div. Owens-Corning Fiberglas Corp., Toledo, 1968-76, v.p. sales, textile and indsl. operating div., 1976-79, v.p. fiberglas composites and equipment mktg. div., 1979—. Mem. Soc. Plastics Industry. Methodist. Home: 5443 Brixton Dr Sylvania OH 43560 Office: Owens-Corning Fiberglas Corp Fiberglas Tower Toledo OH 43659

JENKS, MARLOWE DRYDEN, hatchery exec.; b. Tangent, Oreg., Mar. 3, 1917; s. Enoch M. and Elizabeth (Moser) J.; B.B.A., U. Oreg., 1941; m. Edna Elizabeth Bowles, Feb. 14, 1939; children—Sharon, Gregory, Gary, Larry. Pres., Jenks Hatchery, Inc., Tangent, 1941—, Shore Pines Inc., mobile home devel., Tangent, 1958—; sec.-treas. Jenks-Smith Corp., 1968—, United Poultry Inc., Aurora, Oreg., 1975—; dir. Pederson's Inc., Tacoma. Mem. Linn County Planning Commn., 1970. Bd. dirs. Albany (Oreg.) Boys Club, 1964—. Mem. Poultry and Egg Inst. Am. (dir. for Oreg. 1964-73), Oreg. Poultry Hatchery Assn. (dir. 1955—, past pres., Meritorious award 1965), Willamette River Power Squadron (dir. 1973, 76). Methodist (chmn. bd. trustees 1972). Mason (Shriner, K.T.), Rotarian (treas. Albany); mem. Order Eastern Star. Address: 32521 Hwy 99E Tangent OR 97389

JENKS, ROY JEROME, ins. exec.; b. Roy E. and Esther (Lumphrey) J.; A.A., U. Minn., 1955, B.S., 1958; grad. U.S. Army Command and Gen. Staff Coll., 1976; m. Darlene, Oct. 12, 1979; children—Brian K., Roxanne M., Shelly R., Brenda K. Tchr. phys. edn. and coach, pub. schs., Mpls., 1959-67; underwriter Bankers Life Ins. Co., Mpls., 1967—. Gen. mgr. Jr. Hockey Team, Mpl. Athletic Club; pres. Kennedy Hockey Club; v.p. Bloomington Amateur Hockey Assn. Served with USAR, 1960-79. Recipient nat. quality awards Million Dollar Round Table(6). Mem. Minn. Assn. Life Underwriters, Bankers Life Premier Club, Res. Officers Assn., U.S. Hockey League (v.p.). Roman Catholic. Clubs: Mpls. Athletic, Fort Snelling Officers. Home: 8145 Oakland St S Bloomington MN 55420 Office: 1120 Builders Exchange Minneapolis MN 55402

JENNE, JENNIFER SELFRIDGE, mgmt. cons.; b. Lawrence, Mass., July 30, 1947; d. Walter Robert and Audrey Helen (Nowell) Selfridge; B.A., U. Mass., Boston, 1970; student No. Essex Community Coll., 1971-73; m. Paul Cleveland Jenne, Dec. 20, 1969; children—Jeremiah Greenleaf, Abigail Packard. Counselor, Arrington & Brown Co., Boston, 1970-71; asst. to pres. Keezer Mfg. Co., Plaistow, N.H., 1971-72; lectr. Weight Watchers of N.H., Inc., Nashua, 1974-77; exec. asst. The Network, Andover, Mass., 1976-79; dir. Adminstrv. Mgmt. Services, Inc., Plaistow, 1979—. Vol., Greater Haverhill Campaign for Relief to Cambodia, So. N.H. Ecumenical Community Program; tchr. sch. Unitarian Ch., 1978-80. Mem. Greater Haverhill Bus. and Profl. Women (chmn. fin. 1977-79, newsletter editor 1979-80). Democrat. Address: 113 Main St Plaistow NH 03865

JENNINGS, DANIEL FREDERICK, mfg. co. exec.; b. Covington, Tenn., Apr. 21, 1937; s. Daniel Frederick Barfield and Mary Thomas (Lindsey) J.; B.S., U. Tenn., 1961; M.B.A., N.E. La. U., 1972; m. Evelyn Kay Cothran, Jan. 1, 1956; children—Courtney, Christopher. Indsl. engr. Armstrong Cork Co., 1961-64, Kaiser Aluminum and Chem. Co., Baton Rouge, 1964-66; with OlinKraft Inc. div. Johns Mansville, 1966-77, plant mgr., 1975-77; ops. mgr. Boise Cascade Corp., 1977-79; plant mgr. Certain Teed Corp., Waco, Tex., 1979—. Mem. Am. Inst. Indsl. Engrs., La. Engring. Soc., Tex. Engring. Soc., TAPPI, Soc. Advancement Mgmt. Democrat. Baptist. Clubs: Jaycees, Sertoma. Home: 702 Woodland W Waco TX 76710 Office: 2400 Franklin Ave Waco TX 76703

JENNINGS, FRANK WILKINS, III, real estate exec.; b. Eufaula, Ala., May 19, 1949; s. Frank Wilkins, Jr. and Ruth (Aurin) J.; B.S., U. Ill., 1971; postgrad. in real estate UCLA, 1975; m. Gloria Harriet Fisher, Aug. 11, 1974; 1 son, Jay Robert. Asso. producer Chuck Barris Prodns., Hollywood, Calif., 1971-73; comml. talent agt. William Schuller Agy., Hollywood, 1973-74; comml. and investment real estate asso. George Elkins Co., Beverly Hills, Calif., 1974-75; oer, pres. Frank Jennings & Assos., Beverly Hills, 1976—; real estate rep. Tuneup Masters, Woodland Hills, Calif.; West Coast rep. Jacobs/Kahan & Co., Chgo.; western region real estate mgr. Midas, Internat., Fullerton, Calif.; cons. real estate developers, nat. chains; arbitration panel mem. Beverly Hills Bar Assn. Mem. Nat. Assn. Realtors, Calif. Assn. Realtors, Beverly Hills Bd. Realtors (co-chmn. income/investment div.), Internat. Council Shopping Centers (affiliate), Aircraft Owners and Pilots Assn., Beverly Hills C. of C., Beverly Hills Civic Assn., Beverly Hills Bus. and Profl. Men's Assn., Phi Delta Theta, Pi Epsilon Delta. Clubs: Beverly Hills Kiwanis (v.p.), Beverly Hills Men's (dir.); Town Hall of Calif. Home: 144 N Wetherly Dr Beverly Hills CA 90211 Office: 9701 Wilshire Blvd Beverly Hills CA 90212

JENNINGS, JOHN BAKER, airline exec.; b. N.Y.C., Nov. 26, 1943; s. Milton Smith and Ruth May (Baker) J.; B.S. in E.E., Yale U., 1965; M.S. in E.E., M.I.T., 1968, Ph.D. in Ops. Research, 1970; m. Rosemary Ralph, July 24, 1977; 1 dau., Aubrey Megan. Dir. criminal justice research The Rand Corp., N.Y.C., 1968-73; dir. mgmt. services N.Y.C. Office of Ct. Adminstrn., 1973-77; sr. cons. M.A.S., Deloitte Haskins & Sells, N.Y.C., 1977-78; dir. ops. research Am. Airlines, N.Y.C. and Dallas, 1978—. Chmn., Manhattan Borough Council, 1975-78, N.Y.C. Comprehensive Health Planning Agy. and Health Systems Agy., 1975-78. Mem. Ops. Research Soc. Am., Inst. Mgmt. Sci. Home: 1731 Spring Lake Dr Arlington TX 76012 Office: PO Box 61616 DFW Airport TX 75261

JENNINGS, JOSEPH ASHBY, banker; b. Richmond, Va., Aug. 12, 1920; s. Joseph Ashby and Leone J.; B.S., U. Richmond, 1949; m. Anne Barrow Hatcher, Oct. 29, 1960; children—Joseph Ashby, Ashby Anne. With United Va. Bank/State Planters Bank (name changed to United Va. Bank 1971), 1946—, pres., chief exec. officer, chmn., 1972—; dir. Life Ins. Co. Va., United Va. Bankshares, Universal Leaf, Commonwealth Natural Resources. Trustee, U. Richmond, Union Theol. Sem., Va. Found. for Ind. Colls.; dir. Capital Funds United Way. Served with USAAF, 1942-46. Mem. Fin. Analysts Fedn. (past v.p., dir.), Richmond Soc. Fin. Analysts (past pres.), Assn. Res. City Bankers, Va. Bus. Council, Va. State C. of C. (trustee), Phi Beta Kappa, Omicron Delta Kappa, Beta Gamma Sigma. Presbyterian. Clubs: Country, Commonwealth; Union League (N.Y.C). Office: 900 E Main St Richmond VA 23219

JENNINGS, ROBERT MARTIN, ednl. co. exec., educator; b. Jeffersonville, Ind., July 3, 1924; s. Thomas L. and Mary C. (Ryan) J.; student Colo. Sch. Mines, 1943-44; B.S., U. Louisville, 1949, M.B.A., 1952; M.S. in Edn., Ind. U., 1955, D.B.A., 1959; m. Mary Rose Julius, June 4, 1946; children—Patricia, Rebecca (dec.), Robert Martin, Laura, Pamela. With GMAC, Louisville, 1947-53; instr. Ind. U., Jeffersonville, 1955-59, chmn. div. bus. and econs., New Albany, 1967-70, prof., 1967—; asst. prof. Duquesne U., Pitts., 1959-60; asst. prof. Colo. State U., Ft. Collins, 1960-62, asso. prof., 1964-66, prof., 1966-67; asso. prof. Parsons Coll., Fairfield, Iowa, 1962-64; dir. edn. Monroe Shine & Co., New Albany, 1977—. Bd. dirs. United Fund, Jeffersonville, 1969-71. Served with U.S. Army, 1943-46. C.P.A., Ind.; Ford Found. postdoctoral fellow, 1964. Mem. Am. Inst. C.P.A.'s, Am. Econ. Assn., Am. Accounting Assn., Acad. Accounting Historians, Sci. Fiction Research Assn. Author: Cost Accounting, 1973; contbr. articles to profl. jours. Home: 303 Rosewood Dr Jeffersonville IN 47130 Office: Ind U SE 4201 Grant Line Rd New Albany IN 47150

JENNINGS, THOMAS HAROLD, metal fabrication mfg. co. exec.; b. Chattanooga, Tenn., Dec. 26, 1932; s. James (stepfather) and Ruby (Williams) Sivley; student Ga. Inst. Tech., 1957-59; B.S. in Indsl. Engring., U. Tenn., Chattanooga, 1965; postgrad. Ga. State U., 1971; m. Bettie Ellen Sutton, June 2, 1956; children—Deborah Sue, Jeanne Sue. Plant mgr. Alloway Stamping & Mfg. Co., Chattanooga, 1960-63; asst. maintenance supt. Wheland Foundry, Chattanooga, 1963-65; chief engr. Chattanooga Royal, 1965-67; v.p. ops. and mfg. Bramo Products, Canton, Ga., 1967-74; v.p. mfg. Pneumafil Corp., Charlotte, N.C., 1974-77; v.p. mfg. Lummus Industries, Columbus, Ga., 1978—. Served with USAF, 1953-57. Mem. Soc. Mfg. Engrs., Am. Inst. Indsl. Engrs., Am. Prodn. and Inventory Control Soc., Columbus C. of C. Nazarene. Office: 712 10th Ave Columbus GA 31904

JENRETTE, RICHARD HAMPTON, investment banker; b. Raleigh, N.C., Apr. 5, 1929; s. Joseph M. and Emma (Love) J.; A.B., U. N.C., 1951; M.B.A., Harvard U., 1957. With Brown Bros., Harriman & Co., N.Y.C., 1957-59; chmn. Donaldson, Lufkin & Jenrette, Inc., N.Y.C., 1959—; dir. Roses Stores, Inc. News & Observer Co. Chmn., Pres.'s Adv. Council on Historic Preservation; mem. vis. com. U. N.C. Mem. N.Y. Soc. Security Analysts, U. N.C. Soc. (bd. govs., bd. dirs.). Clubs: Harvard, City Midday, Brook (N.Y.C.); Carolina Yacht (Charleston, S.C.). Home: Edgewater Barrytown NY 12507 also 9 E Battery St Charleston SC Office: 140 Broadway New York NY 10005

JENSCH, W. RUSSELL, ins. co. exec.; b. Milw., May 30, 1919; s. William J. and Theresa D. (Herzog) J.; B.A., U. Wis., 1942; m. Evelyn E. Bump, Jan. 30, 1943; children—Theresa, Mary, William, Richard, David, Thomas, Robert, Margaret. Agt., Lincoln Nat. Ins. Co., 1946; adjuster, then dist. mgr. Farmers Mut. Ins. Co., Madison, Wis., 1946-54; ind. gen. ins. agt., 1954-59; dir., then exec. dir. Nat. Family Ins. Co., St. Paul, 1959-69, chmn. bd., chief exec. officer, 1969—. Served with USNR, 1942-45. Decorated Silver Star, Bronze Star (10). Mem. Minn. Profl. Ins. Agts., Arabian Horse Club Am., Am. Shorthorn Assn. Republican. Roman Catholic. Club: K.C. Office: 2147 University Ave St Paul MN 55114

JENSEN, BRYANT I., ret. diversified fin. corp. exec.; b. Mason City, Iowa, May 2, 1927; s. I.C. and Norma (Bryant) J.; B.S., U. Iowa, 1950, M.A., 1951; m. Lucy Johnson, June 10, 1955; children—Natalie M., Phebe C. Mem. audit staff Arthur Andersen & Co., N.Y.C., from 1951, audit mgr., to 1966; v.p. Wheelabrator-Frye Inc. and subsidiaries, 1966-71; v.p. subsidiary U.S. Gypsum Co., 1971-74; v.p., chief accounting officer The Chubb Corp., N.Y.C., 1974-80. Served with AUS, 1945-47. C.P.A., N.Y. Mem. N.Y., Ia. Socs. C.P.A.'s, Am. Inst. C.P.A.'s, Financial Execs. Inst. Home: 2 Peter Cooper Rd New York NY 10010

JENSEN, CHESTER ALLEN, ins. agy. exec.; b. McIntosh, Minn., Dec. 28, 1917; s. Arthur Colby and Mabel (Alrick) J.; B.S., N.D. State U., 1948; m. Frances Evelyn Wee, June 11, 1948; children—Richard A., Jerry A. Asst. mgr. Oklee Farmers Elevator (Minn.), 1938-39; baker Solberg Bakery, McIntosh, 1939-41; farmer, McIntosh, 1939-41; sales trainee Standard Oil Co., 1948; ins. agt. Mut. Service Ins. Cos., Moorhead, Minn., 1949-62; owner, mgr. C.A. Jensen Ins. Agy., Moorhead, 1962—. Served to 1st lt. U.S. Army, 1941-46; ETO. Decorated Bronze Star. Mem. Profl. Ins. Agts. Minn. (pres. region 3, 1977-78), N.D. Farm Bur., Am. Legion. Lutheran. Clubs: Elks, Eagle, Masons, Shriners. Home: 64 16th Ave N Fargo ND 58102 Office: 200 5th St S Moorhead MN 56560

JENSEN, EDMUND PAUL, bank holding co. exec.; b. Oakland, Calif., Apr. 13, 1937; s. Edmund and Olive E. (Kessell) J.; B.A., U. Wash., 1959; m. Marilyn Norris, Nov. 14, 1959; children—Juliana L., Annika M. Mgr. fin. analysis, mktg. production coordinator Dole/Castle & Cooke, Honolulu and San Jose, Calif., 1960-67; mgr. fin. planning & evaluation Technicolor, Inc., Los Angeles, 1967-69; group v.p. Nat. Industries Louisville, 1969-72; v.p. fin. Wedgewood Homes, Beaverton, Oreg., 1972-74; exec. v.p. U.S. Bancorp., Portland, Oreg., 1974—. Active Multnomah County Healty Care Commn., 1978—, Found. Oreg. Research & Edn., 1975-77. Served to capt. USAR, 1959-67. Mem. Portland C. of C. (dir.). Club: Portland Downtown Rotary. Office: 309 SW 6th St Portland OR 97204

JENSEN, GRADY EDMONDS, apparel co. exec.; b. Pitts., Nov. 8, 1922; s. Claude Henry and Margaret (Edmonds) J.; B.A., Hobart Coll., 1943; M.B.A., U. Pa., 1949; certificate Stonier Sch. Banking, Rutgers U., 1967; m. Mary Margaret Wilber, July 5, 1952; children—Timothy Sage, Margaret Eliza, Caroline Grosvenor. Asst. to asst. treas. U. Pa., Phila., 1949-50; staff engr. Cresap, McCormick & Paget, mgmt. consultants, N.Y.C., 1950-55; bus. mgr. Sta. WABC-TV, N.Y.C., 1955-56; asso. bus. mgr. N.Y. U., N.Y.C., 1956-61; asst. budget dir. Eastern Air Lines, Inc., N.Y.C., 1961-62; asst. to v.p. bus. and fin. Columbia U., N.Y.C., 1962-63; 2d v.p. internat. dept. Chase Manhattan Bank, 1963-70; dir. orgn. and mgmt. devel. Am. Express Co., N.Y.C., 1970-74; v.p. adminstrn. Harwood Cos., Inc., N.Y.C., 1974—. Mem. Scarsdale (N.Y.) Village Bd. Trustees, 1975-79, mayor, 1979-81. Served with USNR, 1943-45. Mem. Guild of Book Workers (dir.), Am. Revolution Round Table of N.Y., Naval Aviation Commandery, Mensa, Westchester County Hist. Soc., S.A.R., Soc. Mayflower Descs., Pilgrim Soc. Soc., N.Y. Geneal. and Biog. Soc., Am. Soc. Corp. Secs. Clubs: Town (past pres.) (Scarsdale); Hobart (N.Y.) (past pres.); University, Grolier (N.Y.C.). Home: 16 Ridgecrest W Scarsdale NY 10583 Office: 666 Fifth Ave New York NY 10019

JENSEN, HAROLD WILLIAM, office furniture designer; b. Iowa City, Iowa, Dec. 10, 1929; s. John Christian and Esther Fredericka (Stock) J.; student Santa Rosa Jr. Coll., 1953-58, Sonoma State Coll., 1968-70; m. Jean Elsie Tam, Jan. 7, 1951; children—Jeanne, Joan, Judith. Heavy equipment operator, 1953; owner, operator paving and grading co., 1953-64; accountant Cloverdale Kiln Co. (Calif.), 1965-68; gen. mgr. Gates Acousinet Co., Rohnert Park, Calif., 1968-73; owner, pres., gen. mgr. Jensen Engring., Inc., Santa Rosa, Calif., 1973—. Served with USAF, 1948-52. Mem. Internat. Word Processing Soc., Nat. Fedn. Ind. Bus., Calif. Horseman's Assn., Santa Rosa C. of C., Internat. Platform Assn., Better Bus. Bur. Democrat. Lutheran. Clubs: Exchange (Santa Rosa); Odd Fellows. Home: 2275 Hearn Ave Santa Rosa CA 95401 Office: 1589 Hampton Way Santa Rosa CA 95401

JENSEN, HARRY ARTHUR, mfg. co. exec.; b. Council Bluffs, Iowa, July 17, 1918; s. Arthur J. and Bess (Crowl) J.; A.B., Grinnell Coll., 1940; m. Lydia Cole, July 30, 1941 (dec. 1979); children—Stephen, Kristie, Eric; m. 2d, Abby C. Koehler, May 10, 1980. With Armstrong Cork Co., Lancaster, Pa., 1940—, successively floor div. salesman, Chgo., asst. dist. mgr., dist. mgr., Lancaster, mktg. mgr., 1940-61, gen. sales mgr. floor div., 1961-62, v.p., gen. mgr. floor and indsl. ops., 1962-68, exec. v.p., 1968-78, pres., chief exec. officer, 1978—, also dir.; dir. Pa. Power & Light Co., Fed. Res. Bank Phila. Served as lt. (j.g.) USNR, 1943-46. Presbyn. Clubs: Lancaster Country, Hamilton (Lancaster). Home: 620 Millcross Rd Lancaster PA 17601 Office: Armstrong Cork Co Lancaster PA 17604

JENSEN, JERRY KIRTLAND, food co. exec.; b. Chgo., Sept. 27, 1947; s. Harry Dybdahl and Violet May (Nowak) J.; B.S. (John McMullen scholar 1965-69), Cornell U., 1969, M.Indsl. Engring., 1971. Pres., Jensen's Cinema 16, Western Springs, Ill., 1970—; indsl. engr. Gen. Foods, Chgo., 1970-72, sr. indsl. engr., 1972-73, prodn. scheduling supr., 1973-74, prodn. control mgr., 1974-76; mgmt. systems specialist Beatrice Foods Co., Chgo., 1976-77, operating services project mgr., 1977-79, mgr. indsl. engring., 1980—; v.p., sec. Country Residential, Inc., Western Springs and Crystal Lake, Ill. Film festivals chmn. Western Springs Recreation Commn., 1969-70, 73-81. Mem. Am. Prodn. and Inventory Control Soc., Great Lakes English Springer Spaniel Breeders Assn. (pres. 1979-81), Alpha Phi Omega, Beta Theta Pi. Clubs: Cornell, Variety. Author: (with Dr. Joel Ross) Improving Productivity in Your Organization, 1981. Home: 4524 Howard Ave Western Springs IL 60558 Office: 2 N LaSalle St Chicago IL 60602

JENSEN, LOUIS JOHN, systems analyst; b. Manhattan, N.Y., July 16, 1949; s. Louis Stanley Jensen and Ann W. Milkowski; student Wright State U., 1969-72, Fairleigh Dickinson U., 1977-81. Programmer, systems analyst, designer, group leader, redesigner drug distbn. data system Cambridge Computer Corp./IMS Am. Ltd., Ambler, Pa., 1972-76; sr. systems analyst performance mgmt., systems integration, library mgmt., installation standards Pan Am. Airways, Rockleigh, N.J., 1976—. Served in USAF, 1968-72. Home: 579 N Central Ave Ramsey NJ 07446 Office: Pan Am Airways Rockleigh Indsl Park Rockleigh NJ 07647

JENSEN, ROBERT P., electronics co. exec.; b. Chgo., Dec. 29, 1925; s. Louis P. and Ellen (Goede) J.; B.S. in Mech. Engring., Iowa State Coll. at Ames, 1947; postgrad. U. Mich., 1953-54; grad. advanced mgmt. program Harvard, 1965; m. Anne F. Burke, June 15, 1980; children—Erik P., Curtis R. Salesman, br. and dist. mgr., gen. sales mgr., operations mgr. Kaiser Aluminum & Chem. Sales, Inc., 1954-61, gen. mgr. building products div., 1963-66, dir. bus. planning aluminum div., 1967; exec. v.p., gen. mgr. Olin Foil Packaging Corp. subsidiary Olin Mathieson Chem. Corp., 1961-63; v.p. aluminum group Howmet Corp., N.Y.C., 1967-68, exec. v.p. Howmet Corp., 1968-70, chief operating officer, dir., 1970, pres., chief exec. officer, 1971-72; pres., chief exec. officer, dir. GK Technologies, Inc., Greenwich, Conn., 1973—, chmn. bd., 1978—; chmn. Automation Industries, Inc.; dir. Conoco, Inc., Irving Bank Corp., Irving Trust Co., Jostens, Inc., Singer Co. Sprague Electric Co. Trustee Council of Ams., Stamford Hosp., Hartman Theatre Co., Stamford; mem. corp. Greenwich Hosp. Assn.; bd. dirs. Nat. Multiple Sclerosis Soc., Greenwich Boys Club Assn. Served to lt. (j.g.) USN, 1944-46. Mem. Aluminum Assn. (chmn.'s adv. council), U.S. Power Squadron. Clubs: Westchester Country (Rye, N.Y.); Union League, Economic, Board Room (N.Y.C.); Capitol Hill (Washington); Greenwich Country, Indian Harbor Yacht (Greenwich); Landmark (Stamford). Home: PO Box 956 Greenwich CT 06840 Office: 500 W Putnam Ave Greenwich CT 06830

JENSON, ART CLIFFORD, pub. co. exec.; b. Newman Grove, Nebr., Dec. 30, 1931; s. Arvid Fritz and Esther (Thompson) J.; B.E.A., Wayne State Tchrs. Coll., 1953; M.M., U. Wyo., 1959; m. Donna Bess Walstead, Mar. 10, 1955; children—Scott, Lauri. Tchr. public schs., Iowa, Nebr., 1955-63; v.p. Hal Leonard Pub. Co., Milw., 1964-70; pres. Jenson Publs., Inc., New Berlin, Wis., 1977—. Served with U.S. Army, 1953-55. Mem. Music Pubs. Assn., Retail Sheet Music Dealers Assn., Am. Sch. Bd. Dirs. Assn. Author books in field of music instruction. Office: 2880 S 171st St New Berlin WI 53122

JENSON, SHERMAN MILTON, ins. co. exec.; b. Berthold, N.D., Jan. 15, 1920; s. Canute T. and Emma (Rohne) J.; B.A., Luther Coll., 1941; diploma bus. adminstr. LaSalle U., 1948; m. Mary G. Blaul, Oct. 14, 1948; 1 dau., Jennifer Ann. Chemist, Solvay Process Co., Hopewell, Va., 1941-43; pharm. salesman Lakeside Labs., St. Paul, 1946-47; regional group mgr. Minn. Mut. Life Ins. Co., Chgo., 1947-55; v.p. group Am. United Life Ins. Co., Indpls., 1955-69; gen. mgr. group div. Bankers Life & Casualty Co., Chgo., 1969-73; pres., chief exec. officer, chmn. exec. com. Nat. Investors Life Ins. Co., Little Rock, 1973—; v.p. Baldwin-United Corp., Cin.; chmn. bd., pres. NOR Securities Co., Little Rock; chmn. bd., pres., chmn. exec. com. Investors Pension Ins. Co., Little Rock. Served with USNR, 1943-46. Clubs: Little Rock, Capital, Pleasant Valley Country. Home: 11900 Fairway Dr Little Rock AR 72212 Office: 2d and Broadway Little Rock AR 72201

JEPPSON, MORRIS RICHARD, energy cons.; b. Logan, Utah, June 23, 1922; s. Robert Baird and Elsie (Smith) J.; B.S., U. Nev., 1946; postgrad. U. Calif., Berkeley, 1946-50; m. Molly Ann Hussey, July 10, 1960; children—Nancy, Carol, Richard, Sally. Research scientist N. Am. Aviation Co., at U. Calif. at Berkeley, 1949-52; pres., founder Applied Radiation Corp., Walnut Creek, Calif., 1954-62, Cryodry Corp., San Ramon, Calif., 1962-67; founder MPH Systems, Carmel, Calif., 1976—. Served with USAAF, 1943-46. Decorated Silver Star; U.S. Dept. Energy grantee, 1977-78. Mem. Inst. Food Technologists. Republican. Patentee in field. Address: PO Box 221489 Carmel CA 93922

JEPSON, ROBERT SCOTT, JR., internat. banking specialist; b. Richmond, Va., July 20, 1942; s. Robert Scott and Inda (Hodges) J.; B.S., U. Richmond, 1964, M.Commerce, 1975; m. Alice Finch Andrews, Dec. 28, 1964; children—Robert Scott III, John Steven. With Va. Commonwealth Bankshares, Richmond, 1966-68; v.p. corp. fin. Birr Wilson & Co., Inc., San Francisco, 1968-69; with Calif. Capital Mgmt. Corp., Irvine, 1970-73; pres. Calcap Securities Corp., Los Angeles, 1970-73; v.p., dir. corp. fin. Cantor Fitzgerald & Co., Beverly Hills, Calif., 1973-75; dir. corp. planning and devel. Campbell Industries, San Diego, 1975-77; v.p., mgr. merger and acquisition div. Continental Ill. Bank, Chgo., 1977—; asst. prof. finance Nat. U., 1976. Served to 1st lt. Mil. Police Corps, AUS, 1964-66. Mem. Omicron Delta Kappa, Alpha Kappa Psi. Republican. Clubs: Mid-Am., Chicago. Home: 85 Hills and Dales Rd Barrington Hills IL 60010 Office: 231 LaSalle St Chicago IL 60693

JERDING, BERNARD PAUL, mfg. co. exec.; b. Chgo., Dec. 18, 1925; s. Barney M. and Mary Ellen (Lillis) J.; student U. Ill., 1946-47, George Williams Coll., 1947-49; m. Mary Joan Cassidy, Sept. 3, 1949; children—Bernard Paul, Patrick M., G. Timothy, Karen M., Kevin J., Michael W., Eileen S., Sean D. Dist. scout exec. Boy Scouts Am., Mich., Ill., Ind., 1949-60; salary analyst Brunswick Corp., Skokie, Ill., 1961, corp. salary adminstr., 1961-63, orgn. planning asso., 1963-65, indsl. relations rep., 1965-67, div. personnel mgr., 1967-71, dir. edn. and tng., 1971-77, dir. mgmt. placement, 1977—; conf. leader, instr. Am. Mgmt. Assn., 1972—; lectr. U. Wis., Western Ill. U., 1978—. Pres., St. John Chrysostrom Sch. Bd., Bellwood, Ill., 1968-70, Cath. Youth Orgn., Bellwood, 1966-70; treas. Proviso Twp. Mental Health Commn., 1965-66; dir. Bellwood Boys Baseball, 1962-70. Served with U.S. Army, 1944-46. Decorated Bronze Star with valor, Purple Heart with two oak leaf clusters. Recipient St. George award Diocese of Evansville, 1957; cert. mgr. Mem. Meeting Planners Internat. (pres. Chgo. area 1979-80), Am. Soc. Tng. and Devel., Am. Mgmt. Assn., So. Coll. Placement Assn. Home: 437 53d Ave Bellwood IL 60104 Office: 1 Brunswick Plaza Skokie IL 60077

JEROME, JAMES LEONARD, mfg. co. exec.; b. Winchendon, Mass., Jan. 15, 1937; s. Leonard John and Esther Elizabeth (Labarge) J.; B.S. in Edn., Fitchburg (Mass.) State Coll., 1974; A.S. in Mgmt., Northeastern U., 1972; Advanced Mgmt. Program, M.I.T., 1970; Advanced Computer Sci. Program, Boston U., 1973; m. Joanne Theresa Buja; 1 dau., Robin. Supr. computer ops. M.I.T., Lincoln Lab., 1969-72; supr. computer ops. Raytheon Co., Waltham, Mass., 1972-77, configuration mgmt., 1977—; pres., chief exec. officer Marinere Corp., 1979-80, chmn. bd., 1980—. Served with USN, 1955-60. Home: 7-9 Mechanic St Foxboro MA 02035 Office: Raytheon Inc Wayland MA 01778

JERREMS, ALEXANDER STAPLER, electronics exec.; b. Kansas City, Mo., May 9, 1919; s. William George and Anna (Stapler) J.; B.E.E., Calif. Inst. Tech., 1942; postgrad. Mass. Inst. Tech., 1946-48; m. Eva Lion, Aug. 22, 1954; 1 son, Brian David. Mem. tech. staff radiation labs. Mass. Inst. Tech., 1942-45; sr. staff scientist Los Alamos Sci. Lab., 1945-46; research asso. physics dept. Mass. Inst. Tech., 1946-48; dir. tech., aerospace group Hughes Aircraft Co., Los Angeles, 1948-70, dir. tech., 1970—. Cons., Air Force, Washington, 1962—, Def. Sci. Bd., 1974—. Mem. I.E.E.E., Am. Inst. Aeros. and Astronautics, A.A.A.S., Sci. Research Soc. Am., Sigma Xi, Tau Beta Phi. Contbr. articles to sci. jours. Home: 141 North Anita Ave Los Angeles CA 90049 Office: Hughes Aircraft Co Centinela and Teale Sts Culver City CA 90230

JERRITTS, STEPHEN G., computer co. exec.; b. New Brunswick, N.J., Sept. 14, 1925; s. Steve and Anna (Kovacs) J.; student Union Coll., 1943-44; B.M.E., Rensselaer Poly. Inst., 1947, M.S., 1948; m. Audrey Virginia Smith, June 1948; children—Marsha Carol, Robert Stephen, Linda Ann; m. 2d, Ewa Elizabet Rydell-Vejlans, Nov. 5, 1966; 1 son, Carl Stephen. With IBM, various locations, 1949-58, IBM World Trade N.Y.C., 1958-67; with Bull Gen. Electric div. Gen. Electric, France, 1967-70, merged int. Honeywell Bull, 1970-74; v.p. and mng. dir. Honeywell Info. Systems Ltd., London, 1974-76, group v.p. U.S. Info. Systems, Boston, 1977-80, pres., dir. Honeywell Info. Systems, Mpls. 1980—. Mem. Mass. Employment and Tng. Council, 1978-79, Mass. Bus. Roundtable, 1978-79; bd. dirs. Guthrie Theatre, 1980, Charles Babbage Inst., 1980; mem. adv. bd. Rensselaer Poly. Inst., 1980. Served with USNR, 1943-46. Mem. Computer Bus. Equip. Mfrs. (dir. 1979-80), Asso. Industries Mass. (dir. 1978-80). Club: Wellesley (Mass.) Country. Home: 2480 Lafayette Rd Wayzata MN 55391 Office: Honeywell Plaza Minneapolis MN 55408

JESELNICK, JOHN ANTHONY, accountant; co. exec.; b. St. Mary's, Pa., Mar. 9, 1949; s. Edward Stanley and Yoland Rose (Boland) J.; B.S., Pa. State U., 1971; M.S. I.A., Purdue, 1972; Staff cons. Arthur Andersen & Co., Pitts., 1972-76, mgr., 1976—. Advisor local Boy Scouts Am. Mem. Nat. Assn. Accountants, Hosp. Fin. Mgmt. Assn., Pa. State U., Purdue U. alumni assns., Tau Beta Phi. Office: 69 W Washington St Chicago IL 60602

JESSEE, MICHAEL ALAN, bank exec.; b. Richmond, Va., Oct. 10, 1946; s. Ralph S. and Clara (Higdon) J.; B.A., Randolph-Macon Coll., 1968; M.B.A., U. Pa., 1972, M.A., 1973, Ph.D., 1976; 1 dau., Deborah. Corp. planning analyst Bank of Va. Co., Richmond, 1966-70; economist Fed. Res. Bank N.Y., N.Y.C., 1973-77; sr. v.p., chief economist Fed. Home Loan Bank of San Francisco, 1977—. Bd. dirs. real estate research council No. Calif.; mem. policy adv. bd. U. Calif., Berkeley. Served with U.S. Army Res. Mem. Am. Fin. Assn., Am. Econ. Assn., Am. Real Estate and Urban Econs. Assn., Nat. Assn. Bus. Economists, Phi Beta Kappa, Omicron Delta Kappa. Author: Bank Holding Companies and the Public Interest, 1978. Methodist. Contbr. articles to profl. jours. Home: 48 Las Cascadas Orinda CA 94563 Office: Fed Home Loan Bank of San Francisco 600 California St San Francisco CA 94120

JESSEL, JOSEPH BRAND, retail exec.; b. Houston, Dec. 26, 1922; s. Maurice K. and Esther (Brand) J.; student U. Tex.; m. Dorothy Marian Lieberman, Nov. 5, 1944; children—Barbara Jessel Lack, Susan Jessel Martin, Jack L. Stockboy, Battelsteins Co., Houston, 1937-39; with Liebermans, Robstown, Tex., 1946—, v.p., 1960-70, pres., 1970—; dir. State Nat. Bank, Robstown. Pres. Coastal Bend Youth City, 1968-69, life mem. bd. dirs., 1964—; bd. dirs. Driscoll Found. Children's Hosp., 1976—; v.p. S.W. region Union Am. Hebrew Congregations, 1973—; pres. Temple Beth El, 1967-69; bd. dirs. NCCJ, 1955—. Served with USNR, 1942-46. Decorated Air medal. Named Outstanding Jewish citizen B'nai B'rith, 1974. Mem. Tex. Retailers Assn., Navy League. Club: Rotary. Office: PO Box 1106 Robstown TX 78380

JESSUP, JOE LEE, educator, mgmt. cons.; b. Cordele, Ga., June 23, 1913; s. Horace Andrew and Elizabeth (Wilson) J.; B.S., U. Ala., 1936; M.B.A., Harvard U., 1941; LL.D., Chung-Ang U., Seoul, Korea, 1964; m. Genevieve Quirk Galloway, Aug. 29, 1946; 1 dau., Gail Elizabeth. Sales rep. Procter & Gamble, 1937-40; liaison officer bur. pub. relations U.S. War Dept., 1941; spl. asst. and exec. asst. Far Eastern div. and office exports Bd. Econ. Warfare, 1942-43; exec. officer office deptl. adminstrn. Dept. State, 1946; exec. sec. adminstr.'s adv. council War Assets Adminstrn., 1946-48; v.p. sales Airkem Capitol & Service Co., 1948-49; asso. prof. bus. adminstrn. George Washington U., 1949-52, prof., 1952-77, prof. emeritus, 1977—, asst. dean Sch. Govt., 1951-60; pres. Joe L. Jessup & Co., Ft. Lauderdale, Fla., 1957—; dir. Hunter Assos. Labs., Inc., Fairfax, Va., 1964-69, exec. com., 1966-69, exec. v.p., gen. mgr., 1967-69; coordinator air force resources mgmt. program, 1951-57; mem. 4-man team surveying fgn. market devel. program for soybeans and soybean products U.S. sec. Agr., 1964; dir. Giant Foods, Inc., Washington, 1971-75, mem. audit com., 1974-75; mem. Md. Econ. Devel. Adv. Commn., 1973-75, Nat. Adv. Council Center for Study Presidency, 1974—; del. in edn. 10th Internat. Mgmt. Conf., Sao Paulo, Brazil, 1954, 11th Conf., Paris, 1957, 12th Conf., Sidney, Melbourne, Australia, 1960, 13th Conf., N.Y.C., 1963, 14th Conf., Rotterdam, Netherlands, 1966, 15th Conf., Tokyo, 1969, 16th Conf., Munich, Germany, 1972. Mem. Arlington County (Va.) CSC, 1951-54; trustee Tng. Within Industry, Summit, N.J., 1954-58. Served from 2d lt. to lt. col. AUS, 1941-46. Decorated Bronze Star; recipient Certificate of Appreciation, Sec. Air Force, 1957. Mem. Am. Mktg. Assn., Acad. Mgmt. Clubs: Coral Ridge Yacht (Fort Lauderdale); Harvard (N.Y.C.). Home: 2801 NE 57th St Fort Lauderdale FL 33308 also PO Box 11063 Fort Lauderdale FL 33339

JESTER, ROBERTS CHARLES, JR., engring. services co. exec.; b. Atlanta, July 12, 1917; s. Roberts Charles and Lynwood (Waters) J.; B.S., U. Ga., 1940; grad. Advanced Mgmt. Program, Harvard, 1957; m. Ann Nell Padgett, Dec. 31, 1936; children—Rita (Mrs. Charles B. Jones, Jr.), Carol (Mrs. John M. Sisk, Jr.), Janelle (Mrs. Michael C. Patty). Chief clk. Ga. R.R., 1936-40; project mgr. Mich. Design & Engring. Co., 1941-42; partner Allstate Engring. Co., Dayton, Ohio, 1943-45, pres., 1945—; pres., chief exec. officer Allstates Design & Devel. Co. Inc., Trenton, N.J., 1954—; dir. N.J. Nat. Bank. Bd. dirs., hon. vice chmn. Greater Trenton Symphony Assn.; bd. dirs. George Washington council Boy Scouts Am.; bd. govs. Hamilton Hosp.; trustee YMCA, Trenton; mem. lay adv. bd. St. Francis Hosp. Mem. Greater Trenton C. of C. (dir.), Trenton Coalition, Metro 49'ers. Republican. Presbyn. Mason (Shriner, Jester). Clubs: Engineers, Trenton Country (past pres.); Key Biscayne (Fla.) Yacht; Metropolitan (N.Y.C.); Pittsburgh Athletic; Little Egg Harbor Yacht (N.J.). Home: 367 Pennington Ave Trenton NJ 08607 Office: 367 Pennington Ave POB 1693 Trenton NJ 08607

JESTRAB, FRANK F., lawyer, govt. ofcl.; b. Havre, Mont., Jan. 28, 1914, s. Frank F. and Anna U. (Larson) J.; LL.B. cum laude, Mont. State U., 1938, B.A., 1946; spl. student Harvard Law Sch., 1946-47; m. Elvira Waidt Evensen, Jan. 18, 1952; children—Laural Ann, James David. Admitted to Mont. bar, 1938; mem. legal dept. Anaconda Copper Mining Co., Butte, Mont., 1938-42; practice law, N.Y.C., 1946-48, Houston, 1948-49; lectr. labor law U. Houston, 1948; div. atty. Amerada Petroleum Corp., Casper, Wyo., 1949-51; mem. firm Bjella & Jestrab, Williston, N.D., 1952—; dir. N.W. Fed. Savs. & Loan Assn., Insured Titles, Inc., Wichita. Mem. Nat. Conf. of Commrs. on Uniform State Laws, 1956—; commr. Fed. Mine Safety and Health Rev. Commn., 1978—. Served as capt. inf., AUS, 1942-46. Mem. Am., Mont., Wyo., Tex., N.D. (pres. 1966-67) bar assns., Am. Law Inst., Bar Assn. City N.Y. Clubs: Williston Petroleum, Rotary (Williston, dist. gov. 1959-60); Univ. (Washington). Home: The Plaza Apt 603 800 25th St NW Washington DC 20037 Office: 111 E Broadway Williston ND 58801 also 1730 K St NW Washington DC 20006

JETTON, GIRARD REUEL, JR., lawyer; b. Washington, Feb. 19, 1924; s. Girard Reuel and Hallie (Grimes) J.; B.S. in Engring., George Washington U., 1945, B.A., 1947; J.D., Harvard Law Sch., 1950; postgrad. Benjamin Franklin U., 1952-56; m. Mera Riddell, Sept. 4, 1948; children—Mara Elizabeth, Robert Girard, James Thomas. Elec. engr. Taylor Model Basin, Dept. Navy, Carderock, Md., 1944-45; admitted to D.C. bar, 1951, Ohio bar, 1960, Md. bar, 1960; patent atty., Washington, 1950-51; atty. IRS, Washington, 1951-54; trial atty. Dept. Justice, Washington, 1954-55; asso. firm McClure & McClure, Washington, 1955-58, partner, 1958-60; tax atty. Marathon Oil Co., Findlay, Ohio, 1960-64, gen. mgr. tax orgn., 1964-69, asst. to pres., 1969-72, asst. to chmn., 1972-73, corp. sec., 1973—. Served with USN, 1945-46. Mem. Am. Bar Assn., Bar Assn. D.C., Ohio State Bar Assn., Fed. Bar Assn., Findlay Hancock County Bar Assn., Tax Execs. Inst., Am. Soc. Corp. Secs., Am. Petroleum Inst. Episcopalian. Club: Metropolitan (Washington). Office: 539 S Main St Findlay OH 45840

JEWELL, ROBERT DON, coll. pres.; b. Muskegon, Mich., Aug. 1, 1930; s. Gaylord Alexander and Wilma Elizabeth (Barger) J.; B.A., Alma Coll., 1952; m. Marianne Geerlings, Aug. 29, 1953; children—Susan, Thomas. Vice pres. Muskegon (Mich.) Bus. Coll., 1953-65, pres., 1966—; pres. Baker Jr. Coll., Flint, Mich., 1965—; pres. RDJ Corp., ednl. cons. Mem. Mich. Bus. Schs. Assn., Mich. Bus. Edn. Assn., Assn. Ind. Colls. and Univs. Mich. (dir. 1977-79), Muskegon C. of C. (dir. 1976—). Republican. Club: Am. Bus. Home: 100 Bear Lake Rd Muskegon MI 49445 Office: Muskegon Bus Coll 141 Hartford St Muskegon MI 49442

JHA, CHANDRA KANT, constrn. co. exec.; b. Bihar State, India, July 2, 1928; s. Lakshmi Kant and Yogmaya Debi J.; came to U.S., 1953, naturalized, 1967; B.S. in Civil Engring., Bihar Coll. Engring., Patna, India, 1950; M.S. in Structural Engring., Ill. Inst. Tech., 1957; M.B.A., U. Chgo., 1962; m. Hekmat Elkhanialy, Dec. 20, 1969; 1 dau., Lakshmi. Design engr. Harza Engring. Co., Ranchi, India, 1950-53; with Harza Engring. Co., Chgo., 1953-55; sr. design engr. McDonald Engring. Co., Chgo., 1955-57; with John Moore & Sons, Chgo., 1957-64, staff engr., 1962-64; mgr. sci. mgmt. services Lester B. Knight Assos., Chgo., 1964-67; v.p. Tishman Realty & Constrn. Co., Chgo., 1967-77; pres. PSM Internat. Corp., Chgo., 1977—. Active mem. Campaign Chgo., U. Chgo., 1976-77. Recipient civic award Detroit Indian Community, 1976. Mem. Ops. Research Soc. Am., Inst. Mgmt. Sci., Project Mgmt. Inst., ASCE, Am. Mgmt. Assn., India League Am. (founder, pres. 1972-76, dir. 1977—). Club: Met. (Chgo.). Author: (with Goldhaber and Macedo) Construction Management: Principles and Practices, 1977. Office: 200 W Monroe St Chicago IL 60606

JOAQUIM, RICHARD RALPH, hotel exec.; b. Cambridge, Mass., July 28, 1936; s. Manuel and Mary (Marrano) J.; B.F.A., Boston U., 1955, Mus. B., 1959; m. Nancy Phyllis Reis, Oct. 22, 1960; 1 dau., Vanessa Reis. Social dir., coordinator summer resort, Wolfeboro, N.H., 1957-59; concert soloist N.H. Symphony Orch., Vt. Choral Soc., Choral Arts Soc., Schenectady Chamber Orch., 1957-60; coordinator performance functions, mgr. theatre Boston U., 1959-60, asst. program dir., 1963-64, dir. univ. programs, 1964-70; gen. mgr. Harrison House of Glen Cove; dir. Conf. Service Corp., Glen Cove, N.Y., 1970-74, sr. v.p., dir. design and devel.; v.p. Arltec, also mng. dir. Sheraton Internat. Conf. Center, 1975-76; v.p., mng. dir. Scottsdale (Ariz.) Conf. Center and Resort Hotel, 1976—; pres. Internat. Conf. Resorts, Inc., 1977, chmn. bd., 1977-78; pres. Western Conf. Resorts; concert solist U.S. Army Field Band, Washington, 1960-62. Creative arts cons., editorial cons., concert mgr. Commr. recreation Watertown, Mass., 1967—; mem. Spl. Study Com. Watertown, 1967—; mem. Glen Cove Mayor's Urban Renewal Com. Bd. dirs. Nat. Entertainment Conf. Served with AUS, 1960-62. Mem. Assn. Coll. and Univ. Concert Mgrs., Am. Symphonic League, Am. Fedn. Film Socs., Assn. Am. Artists, Am. Personnel and Guidance Assn., Nat. Alumni Council Boston U. Office: 7700 McCormick Pkwy Scottsdale AZ 85258

JOCHUM, ROBERT DENNIS, telephone co. exec.; b. Wheeling, W.Va., July 25, 1942; s. Joseph G. and Helen M. (Antrobious) J.; B.S.E.E., U. Notre Dame, 1964; M.S.I.A., Purdue U., 1965; m. Janet Clarke, Feb. 5, 1966; children—Lisa Kristine, Patricia Ann, Michelle Lynn, Joseph Brian. Mgmt. asst. Ind. Bell Telephone Co., Indpls., 1964-69, dist. plant mgr., Crawfordsville and South Bend, 1969-73, gen. equipment engr., Indpls., 1973-77, gen. mgr. distbn., 1977—. Bd. dirs. Better Bus. Bur., 1978—, Asso. Patient Services, 1978—. Registered profl. engr., Ind. Club: Indpls. Athletic. Office: 220 N Meridian St Indianapolis IN 46204

JOCKERS, JANE AHLERS, hearing center adminstr.; b. Newburgh, N.Y., Sept. 5, 1924; d. William George and Mae Mathilda Ahlers; m. Gustave John Jockers, Dec. 27, 1942; children—Patricia Ann, Sandra, Gustave, Susan. With display advt. dept. Walden (N.Y.) Citizen Herald, 1955-58; owner, operator Hearing Center Orange County, Newburgh, 1958—. Pres. Wallkill (N.Y.) Parents Club, 1954, 55-56; mem. election bd. Newburgh Republican party, 1955-65. Certified hearing aid audiologist. Mem. Upstate (treas. 1959-61), N.Y. State hearing aid dealers assns., Nat. Assn. Hearing Aid Audiologists, Central Dist. Dealers Assn. Republican. Methodist. Club: Order

Eastern Star (trustee 1965-66, 77). Home: 279 Lakeside Rd Newburgh NY 12550 Office: 1025 Union Ave PO Box 615 Newburgh NY 12550

JODOIN, MAURICE ALAIN, business exec.; b. Montreal, Que., Can., Mar. 30, 1939; s. Lucien and Donalda (Cormier) J.; B.A., U. Montreal, 1959, L.Sc.Com., 1962; m. Louise Marchand, June 29, 1963; children—Nathalie, Valerie. Economist Bank of Can., 1962-65; portfolio mgr., v.p., dir. Bolton, Tremblay Inc., 1965-74; v.p., gen. mgr. Sodarcan, Montreal, 1974—, also dir., mem. exec. com.; dir. Gerard Parizeau Limitee, J.E. Poitras, Inc., Dale-Ross Holdings Ltd., La Nationale Compagnie de Reassurance du Canada, Hebert, LeHouillier & Assos., J.B.M. Murray Ltd., LeBlanc, Eldridge, Parizeau, Inc., P.H. Plourde Inc., Canadian Internat. Reins. Brokers Ltd., Gestas Inc., Westpar Ins. Mgrs. Ltd., Intermediaries of Am., Inc., Société Européenne de Gestion de Réassurance, S.A., Caisse Populaire Place Desjardins. Mem. Chartered Fin. Analysts. Address: 2 Complexe Desjardins PO Box 183 Desjardins Sta Montreal PQ H5B 1B3 Canada

JOHANSEN, ROBERT JOSEPH, ins. co. exec.; b. N.Y.C., May 2, 1922; s. Irving Joseph and Margaret (McKee) J.; B.A., Manhattan Coll., 1943; M.A., Columbia U., 1974; m. Mary Carroll Hayes, June 27, 1964; children—Mary Carroll, Robert Hayes, David McKee. With Met. Life Ins. Co., N.Y.C., 1947—, 3d v.p., 1964-68, 2d v.p., 1968-69, v.p. personal ins. adminstrn., 1969-70, v.p., 1970-72, v.p., actuary, 1972—. Trustee, Dominican Coll., Blauvelt, N.Y., 1970—; pres. Van Cortlandt Ter. Assn., 1979-81; mem. Mayor's Com. for Community Relations, Yonkers, N.Y., 1978—. Served with USAAF, 1943-46. Fellow Soc. Actuaries (treas. 1980—, chmn. com. on govt. stats. 1980—, chmn. com. to recommend a new mortality basis for individual annuity valuation 1980—); mem. Am. Acad. Actuaries, Am. Statis. Assn., N.Y. Acad. Sci., Internat. Actuarial Assn., N.Y. Actuaries Club (treas. 1978—), Actuarial Studies in Non-Life Ins., Council Profl. Assns. on Fed. Stats. (sec. 1980—). Roman Catholic. Office: 1 Madison Ave New York NY 10010

JOHANSON, NORMAN ERIC, mfg. co. exec.; b. Glen Ridge, N.J., Feb. 14, 1940; s. John E. and Edna L. Johanson; B.S. in Indsl. Engring., N.J. Inst. Tech., 1965; m. Donna Kerner, Aug. 25, 1979. Pres. Johanson Mfg. Corp., Boonton, N.J., 1970-78, Johanson Dielectrics, Inc., Boonton and Burbank, Calif., 1978—. Trustee Riverside Hosp., Boonton, 1980—. Mem. Internat. Soc. for Hybrid Microelectronics, Morristown (N.J.) C. of C. (chmn. govt. affairs com. 1979-80), Boonton C. of C. (pres. 1978-79), Com. 1000. Club: Morris County 200. Home: 276 Kingsland Rd Boonton NJ 07005 Office: Rockaway Valley Rd PO Box 10 Boonton NJ 07005

JOHANSSON, DONALD RODNEY (ANDRÉ), ins. co. exec.; b. Newton, Mass., Apr. 26, 1931; s. Carl Wilhelm and Elsa Ingaborg (Lundvall) J.; A.A., Glendale Coll., 1954; B.S., U. Calif. at Los Angeles, 1958; M.B.A., U. So. Calif., 1963; m. Gladys Lucille Gunnell, Apr. 20, 1956; children—Andrea Gean, Carl Bradley, Greta Kristen. Mgr. agy. Travelers Ins. Co., San Fernando Valley, Calif., 1958-63; mgr. Safeco Ins. Co. Orange County, Orange, Calif., 1963-67; asst. v.p. Bayly, Martin & Fay, Inc. ins. brokers, Los Angeles, 1967-73; v.p. Kindler & Laucci, Inc., Los Angeles, 1973-78, sr. v.p., Newport Beach, Calif., 1978-81, also dir.; partner Amberwood Ins. Brokers, Inc., Santa Ana, Calif., 1981—. Vice chmn. Los Angeles Open Golf Tournament, 1960-65; chmn. 1st Internat. Music Festival Los Angeles, 1962. Bd. dirs. Community Pride, Inc., 1971, Young People of Watts, 1972. Served with U.S. Army, 1952-54. Area speech winner Toastmasters Internat., 1966. Mem. Ins. Brokers Soc. of So. Calif. (pres. 1980), Calif. Joint Producers Council (chmn. 1979-80), Orange County Fieldmen's Assn. (pres. 1963), Alpha Kappa Psi (nat. v.p. 1972—). Clubs: Marrakesh Country (Palm Desert, Calif.); Irvine Coast Country (Newport Beach); Town Hall, World Affairs Council, Los Angeles Squires, Stockyard Athletic (Los Angeles). Home: 1501 Lincoln Ln Newport Beach CA 92660 also 47220 Amir Dr Palm Desert CA Office: 4500 Campus Dr Newport Beach CA 92660

JOHN, DEBORAH IRENE, wholesale electric distbr. exec.; b. Erie, Pa., Oct. 1, 1952; d. Paul Edward and Ruth Irene (Kessler) J.; A. in Acctg., Pa. State U., 1975. Kardex operator WESCO Co., Erie, 1970-72, sec., 1972-73, inside salesperson, 1974, br. adminstrv. mgr., 1974—. Vol. Drs. Osteo. Hosp., Erie. Mem. Adminstrv. Mgmt. Soc. (pres. Erie chpt. 1980-81). Democrat. Lutheran. Home: 2424 Taggert St Erie PA 16510 Office: 1107 Hess Ave Erie PA 16503

JOHN, JOSEPH, corp. exec.; b. Madura, India, Mar. 14, 1938; came to U.S., 1964, naturalized, 1976; s. Thomas and Kunjamma J.; B.Sc., Madras Christian Coll., 1958; M.A. (AEC fellow), U. Madras, 1960; Ph.D. (grad fellow), Fla. State U., 1968; M.B.A., Pepperdine U., 1980; m. Urmila Vishnu Dabholkar, Apr. 22, 1967; 1 child, Melind. Sci. officer, then jr. research officer Atomic Energy Establishment, Bombay, 1959-64; sr. scientist, then staff scientist Gulf Gen. Atomic Co., San Diego, 1968-72; program mgr. tech. application dept. Gulf Radiation Tech. Co., San Diego, 1972-73; with IRT Corp., San Diego, 1973—, v.p., 1977—, mgr. nuclear systems div., 1978—; mgr. Califronium-252 Demonstration Center, San Diego, 1972-78; lectr. Union Christian Coll., Alwaye, India, 1958; cons in field. Mem. exec. com. India Village Project, San Diego, 1966-69. Recipient Cooke Meml. prize, 1953, Hensman Meml. award, 1950, Sanders Meml. prize, 1951, Bicknell Meml. prize, 1952; IAEA fellow, 1964-66. Mem. Am. Phys. Soc., Am. Nuclear Soc., Am. Soc. Nondestructive Testing, ASTM, Am. Mgmt. Assn., Soc. Advancement Mgmt., San Diego Bd. Realtors, Calif. Assn. Realtors, Nat. Assn. Realtors, Am. Def. Preparedness Assn., Assn. U.S. Army. Democrat. Author, patentee in field. Home: 2707 Curie Pl San Diego CA 92122 Office: PO Box 80817 San Diego CA 92111

JOHN, MILLARD KENNETH, artist, designer; b. Rolla, Mo., Apr. 1, 1942; s. Millard Raymond and Mayme Aleen (Curtis) J.; student pub. schs., Rolla, Mo., 1948-60; student pvt. art tchrs.; m. Patty Marie Cockshoot; 1 son, Von Eric. With U.S. Geol. Survey, U.S. Dept. Interior, Rolla, Mo., 1962-69; with Stanley Cons., Inc., Muscatine, Iowa, 1969—, head graphic arts dept., 1978—; custom paint and design cons. Bandag Tire & Rubber Internat. Served with USNG, 1962-69. Recipient numerous awards in airbrush-custom painting. Certified engring. technicians grade Inst. Certification of Engrs. Technicians; certificate of achievement in engring. data tng. Eastman Kodak Mktg. Edn. Center. Mem. Art Dirs. Assn. Iowa, Indsl. Graphics Internat., Internat. Soc. Artists, Internat. Show Car Assn. Am. Home: 409 W 5th St Muscatine IA 52761 Office: Stanley Bldg Muscatine IA 52761

JOHN, WILLIAM WYNN, plant physiologist; b. Malad City, Idaho, Sept. 15, 1946; s. Ellis Wynn and Ila Mae (Williams) J.; B.S., Utah State U., 1970; M.S., Purdue U., 1972, Ph.D., 1975; m. Pamela Robison, Aug. 29, 1968; children—Wynn, Brett, Colette, Melissa, Brannon. Research asst. Utah State U., Logan, 1969-70, Purdue U., West Lafayette, Ind., 1970-75; post-doctoral research asso. U. Calif., Davis, 1975-76; research biologist Mobil Chem. Co., Edison, N.J., 1976-79, sr. research biologist, 1979-80; plant physiologist Shell Devel. Co., Modesto, Calif., 1980—. Served with U.S. Army, 1972. Mem. Am. Soc. Plant Physiologists, Plant Growth Regulator Working Group, Weed Soc. Am., Alpha Zeta, Gamma Sigma Delta, Phi Kappa Phi. Republican. Mormon. Contbr. articles to sci. jours. Home: 3808 Atwood Dr Modesto CA 95355 Office: Shell Devel Co PO Box 4248 Modesto CA 95352

JOHNS, DONALD LIGHTHALL, ins. exec.; b. Plainfield, N.J., May 12, 1925; s. Kenneth Major and Ina Julia (Lighthall) J.; student U. Ala., 1942-43; m. Shirley A. Figlow, July 26, 1972; children—Sandra L. Keith, Patricia A. Johns Fountain, David L., Robert A. Adjuster, Johns & Co., Sarasota and Miami, Fla., 1946, br. mgr., 1947-53, partner, 1954-66; pres. Johns & Co., Ins. Adjusters, Inc., Sarasota, 1966-70; pres. Johns Eastern Co., Inc., Sarasota, 1971—; chmn. bd. S.E. Bank of Siesta Key, Sarasota, 1976-78; dir. S.E. First Nat. Bank of Sarasota, 1979—. Mem. Sarasota County Bd. Public Instrn. for Sarasota County, 1954-58; founder, pres. Jefferson Center, Inc., Sarasota, 1962-70. Served to cpl., U.S. Army, 1943-46; ETO. Mem. Nat. Assn. Ind. Ins. Adjusters (sec.-treas. 1979-80, pres.-elect 1980-81, pres. 1981-82), Internat. Inst. Loss Adjusters (regional v.p. 1975-77), Can. Ind. Adjusters Conf., Atlanta Claims Assn., West Coast Claims Assn., Pinellas County Claims Assn., Sarasota-Bradenton Claims Assn. Republican. Unitarian. Clubs: Field, University. Home: 501 Sandy Cove 4 4900 Ocean Blvd Sarasota FL 33581 Office: PO Box 4175 2238 Gulf Gate Dr Sarasota FL 33578

JOHNS, HERBERT KIMBROUGH, shoe co. exec.; b. Corpus Christi, Dec. 6, 1940; s. Herbert T. and Mary Ruth (Ayers) J.; B.B.A. in Acctg., Tex. A. and M. U., 1963; m. Karla Frances Ehrman; children—Darin Kimbrough, Eric Brannan. Auditor, Coopers & Lybrand, Dallas, 1967-69; v.p., controller Graham-Brown Shoe Co., Dallas, 1969-76, v.p., chief fin. officer, 1979—; v.p. fin. and adminstrn. Slaughter Industries, Inc., Dallas, 1976-79; dir., mem. exec. com. Graham-Brown Shoe Co. Bd. dirs., treas. Fathers for Equal Rights, 1979—. Served with USAF, 1963-67. C.P.A., Tex. Mem. Am. Inst. C.P.A.'s, Tex. Soc. C.P.A.'s, Fin. Execs. Inst., Retail Fin. Execs. Assn. Republican. Mem. Ch. of Christ. Home: Fort Worth TX Office: Graham-Brown Shoe Co PO Box 10020 1715 N Industrial Blvd Dallas TX 75207

JOHNS, ROY CLINTON (BUD), JR., apparel mfg. co. exec., writer; b. Detroit, July 9, 1929; s. Roy Clinton and Isabel (Horton) J.; B.A., Albion Coll., 1951; m. Judith Spector Clancy, Mar. 28, 1971. Reporter, Flint (Mich.) Jour., 1947-51, 1953-56, San Diego Union, 1956-60; bur. chief Fairchild Publs., San Diego, 1960-61, San Francisco, 1961-69; pres. Synergistic Press, Inc., San Francisco, 1968—; dir. public relations Levi Strauss & Co., San Francisco, 1969-71, dir. corp. communications, 1971-79, v.p. corp. communications, 1979—; author: The Ombibulous Mr. Mencken, 1968; contbr. numerous articles to various mags.; author film script: What Is This Madness?, 1976. Bd. dirs. Stern Grove Festival Assn., San Francisco, 1970—, Documentary Research, Inc., Buffalo, 1978—; mem. Nat. Council for Museum Am. Indian, 1980—. Served with USMC, 1951-53. Co-editor: Bastard in the Ragged Suit, 1977; originator ann. ride and tie race, 1971—. Office: 2 Embarcadero Center San Francisco CA 94106

JOHNS, STEPHEN MARTIN, banker; b. Mpls., Nov. 30, 1942; s. Dale Martin and Ruth (Dobson) J.; student Syracuse U., 1960-61, 62-63; B.S., U. Iowa, 1965, J.D., 1968; m. Mary Lou Haskett, Aug. 15, 1964; 1 son, Eric Herbert. Registered rep. White & Co., Chgo., 1968-69; mcpl. bond underwriter Continental Ill. Nat. Bank and Trust Co. of Chgo., Inc., 1969-72; v.p. Continental Bank, N.Y.C., 1972—. Active Cub Scouts, 1977-80. Mem. Iowa State Bar Assn., Mcpl. Forum of N.Y. Clubs: Mcpl. Bond (N.Y.C.); Downtown Athletic, Amazing Feet Running. Home: 611 Mountain Ave Berkeley Heights NJ 07922 Office: Continental Bank 91 Liberty St New York NY 10006

JOHNSEN, ERIC MATHIAS, JR., dentist; b. Riverside, N.J., May 13, 1943; s. Eric Mathias and Lois Joyce (Randall) J.; B.S., Southwest Tex. State U., 1970; D.M.D., Fairleigh Dickinson U., 1974; m. Joan Eileen Marsan, Dec. 16, 1967; children—Jennifer Lyn, Eric Mathias. Gen. practice dentistry, Franklin, Pa., 1974—; cons. in field. Dir. Health Systems Inc. of Northwestern Pa., 1975—, sec., 1975-76; dir. Statewide Health Coordinating Council, 1976—; dir. Venango Forest Unit Am. Cancer Soc., 1975—, v.p., 1976-78, pres., 1978—. Served with USAF, 1961-67. N.J. State Health Professions fellow. Mem. Am., Pa., Pa. 9th Dist. (pres. 1979), Venango County dental socs., Acad. Gen. Dentistry. Lutheran. Office: 1263 Elk St Franklin PA 16323

JOHNSEY, WALTER FRANK, utility exec.; b. Jasper, Ala., Aug. 22, 1924; s. Floyd G. and Bertha (Herring) J.; B.S. in Elec. Engring., Auburn U., 1949; LL.B., Birmingham Sch. Law, 1964, J.D., 1968; m. Doris V. Slocumb, Dec. 21, 1946; children—Ronald Grant, Sharon Lynn. Admitted to Ala. bar, 1964; with Ala. Power Co., various locations, 1951—, v.p. adminstrn., finance, Birmingham, 1972-75, exec. v.p., chief fin. officer, 1975-79, also dir., until 1979; pres., owner Summit Super Markets, Birmingham; co-owner, chief exec. officer Perry Supply, Inc., Birmingham Bd. dirs. Diabetes Trust Fund, U. Ala., Birmingham. Served with Signal Corps, U.S. Army, 1943-45. Registered profl. engr., Ala. Mem. Ala., Nat. socs. profl. engrs., IEEE, Ala., Birmingham, Am. bar assns., Nat. Assn. Accountants, Am. Foundryman's Soc., Nat. Mgmt. Assn., Fin. Execs. Inst., Newcomen Soc. Methodist. Home: 3809 Dunbarton Dr Mountain Brook AL 35223 Office: 831 1st Ave N Birmingham AL 35201

JOHNSON, ALAN STACEY, lawyer; b. Brookline, Mass., Apr. 12, 1945; s. Melvyn and Charlotte (Glashow) J.; B.A., Brown U., 1967; M.A., Rutgers U., 1968; J.D., Northeastern U., 1972. Admitted to Mass. bar, 1972, U.S. Dist. Ct. Mass. bar, 1978; staff dir. Spl. Commn. on Govtl. Ops., 1968-69; mem. staff Office Mgmt. and Budget, Washington, 1970; staff atty. Mass. Law Reform Inst., Boston, 1971-73; dir. field orgn. Dukakis for Gov. Campaign, Boston, 1973-75; dir. Gov.'s Legis. Office, Boston, 1975-76; asst. chief sec. to Gov. Mass., 1976-77; gen. counsel Mass. Energy Office, Boston, 1977—; cons. in field; del. New Eng. Energy Congress on Energy. Mem. Boston Brookline Health Resources Orgn., Brookline Council for Planning and Renewal, Nat. Govs. Assn. (state rep. task force on energy and conservation). Club: Mass. Brown. Home: 34 Carruth St Dorchester MA 02124

JOHNSON, ALBERT WESLEY, broadcasting exec.; b. Insinger, Sask., Can., Oct. 18, 1923; s. Thomas William and Louise Lillian (Croft) J.; B.A., U. Sask., 1942; M.A., U. Toronto (Ont., Can.), 1945; M.P.A. (Littauer fellow), Harvard U., 1950, Ph.D. (Littauer fellow), 1963; LL.D. (hon.), U. Regina, 1977, U. Sask., 1978; m. Ruth Elinor Hardy, June 27, 1946; children—Andrew, Frances, Jane, Geoffrey. Dep. provincial treas. Govt. of Sask., Regina, 1952-64; asst. dep. minister fin. Govt. of Can., Ottawa, Ont., 1964-68, econ. adviser to prime minister on constn., 1968-70, sec. treasury bd., 1970-73, dep. minister nat. welfare, 1973-75; pres. CBC, Ottawa, 1975—. Bd. dirs. Nat. Film Bd., 1970—, U. Sask. Hosp., 1957-64; mem. Nat. Arts Centre, 1975—; bd. govs. U. Sask., Saskatoon, 1952-63. Decorated Order of Can.; recipient Gold medal Profl. Inst. of Pub. Service of Can., 1975. Mem. Commonwealth Broadcasting Assn. (standing com.), Ottawa Polit. Economy Assn. (pres. 1969-70), Inst. Public Adminstrn. Can. (pres. 1962-63, Vanier medal 1976; nat. council 1951-69), Can. Polit. Sci. Assn. (exec. council 1963-64). Mem. United Ch. of Can. Contbr. articles to profl. publs.; editorial bd. Can. Public Policy, 1974-75. Office: CBC 1500 Bronson Ave Ottawa ON K1G 3J5 Canada*

JOHNSON, ANDREW HAL, air freight co. exec.; b. Cuthbert, Ga., Aug. 26, 1947; s. Andy Hall and Crockette (Warner) J.; student Morehead (Ky.) State U., 1970-72, U. Hawaii, 1972; m. Marjorie Lou Bohn, Feb. 14, 1970; children—Zachary Needham, Helen Martha, Alice Hope. With Motors Imports, Honolulu, 1972; mgr. Inter-Island, DHL Hawaii Inc., 1972-73; v.p. DHL Corp., Chgo., 1974, San Francisco, 1974; v.p. D.H.L. Internat. Express Ltd., Vancouver, B.C., Can., 1976-77, pres., 1977—; dir. DHL Cumstoms Brokerage. Served with USN, 1966-70. Mem. Can. Internat. Freight Forwarders Assn. (pres.), Internat. Fedn. Freight Forwarders Assn., Vancouver Bd. Trade. Home: 3280 Ullsmore Dr Richmond BC V6X 1S1 Canada

JOHNSON, ARNOLD HEMMING, ins. co. exec.; b. Bridgeport, Conn., Apr. 29, 1917; s. Alfred and Agda (Anderson) J.; grad. high sch.; m. Mary Louise Walter, Feb. 14, 1948 (div. Aug. 1973); children—Jeffrey Walter, Nancy Fee, Jill Anders; m. 2d, Helene Brown Whalen, Sept. 26, 1976. With spl. risks dept. Aetna Casualty & Surety Co., Hartford, Conn., 1935-43; with U.S. Aviation Underwriters, Inc., N.Y.C. and Washington, 1945-49; with Am. Mercury Ins. Co., Washington, 1949-60; v.p. Avemco Ins. Co., 1960, dir., 1963, pres., 1965-75; v.p., dir. Avemco Corp., Bethesda, Md., 1964-71, sr. v.p., 1971-73, chmn. bd., 1973—, also chmn. 7 subsidiaries. Mem. Citizens Com., North Chevy Chase, Md., 1954-56. Served as pilot USAAF, 1943-45; ETO. Decorated Air medal with 3 oak leaf clusters. Mem. Aircraft Owners and Pilots Assn., Quiet Birdmen, Air Force Assn. Clubs: International (Washington); Nat. Aviation, Manor Country, Sea Pines, Hilton Head Island, S.C. Home: 4601 North Park Ave 817 Chevy Chase MD 20015 also 15 Turtle Lane Club Hilton Head Island SC Office: 7315 Wisconsin Ave Bethesda MD 20014

JOHNSON, ARTHUR WALTER, corp. exec.; b. Mpls., May 1, 1942; s. Raymond Edmond and Burnetta Elizabeth J.; student Dept. Def. Info. Sch., New Rochelle, N.Y., 1965; m. Sharon L. Godbey, Apr. 14, 1978; children—Kerri, Tani, Kristen, Lance, Trina. Sales promotion & public relations specialist Hyster Co., Portland, Oreg., 1968-76; dir. mktg. mgr. Tektronix, Inc., Beaverton, Oreg., 1976-79, sales promotion mgr., 1979—; owner Bus. Promotions, 1976—; chmn. Indsl. Direct Mktg. Forum, 1979-81. Served with USMC, 1960-68. Mem. Direct Mail Mktg. Assn. Republican. Baptist. Clubs: Christian Adult Singles Group (co-founder). Lectr. in field. Home: 2030 SW 185th Aloha OR 97006 Office: 2035 SW 58th Suite 211 Portland OR 97221

JOHNSON, BARBARA ANNE, airline sales exec.; b. Portsmouth, Va., Nov. 23, 1946; d. A.W. and Anne (Eller) J.; B.A., Coll. William and Mary, 1969; postgrad. U. Madrid, 1969-70. Sales rep. LAN-Chile Airlines, Boston, 1970-74, comml. sales rep., N.Y.C., 1974-75; sr. sales exec. Aero-Peru, N.Y.C., 1975-77; accounts exec. Gulf Air, N.Y.C., 1977-79, sales mgr., 1979—. Bd. dirs. Mass. Partners of Americas, 1972-74. Mem. Nat. Passenger Traffic Assn., Airline Sales Mgrs. Assn., Am. Soc. Travel Agts., Pacific Area Travel Assn., Arab Am. Women's Friendship League, Kappa Kappa Gamma. Clubs: Chilean of Mass.; Boston Women's City. Home: 435 E 65th St New York NY 10021 Office: 245 Park Ave New York NY 10017

JOHNSON, BENJAMIN F., VI, cons. economist; b. Kingston, N.Y., Sept. 17, 1952; s. Benjamin F. and Alice (Terry) J.; B.A. in Econs., U. South Fla., 1974; M.S. in Econs., Fla. State U., 1977, postgrad., 1978; m. Eileen Brown Parramore, Jan. 5, 1980. Sr. utility analyst Office of Public Counsel, State of Fla., 1974-77; pres., cons. economist Ben Johnson Assos., Inc., Tallahassee, Fla., 1977—; expert witness govtl. agys. Mem. Am. Econ. Assn., Am. Statis. Assn., Internat. Assn. Energy Economists, Nat. Assn. Bus. Economists, So. Econ. Assn., Western Econ. Assn. Contbr. articles to Public Utilities Fortnightly. Office: Suite 115 1311 Executive Center Dr Tallahassee FL 32301

JOHNSON, BILL JAY, feed mfg. co. exec.; b. Okla., Sept. 2, 1930; s. Willie and Buelah Edith (Curl) J.; B.S., Ariz. State U., 1955; widower; children—Ron, Brenda. With Farnam Co., Phoenix, 1953—, v.p. sales and mktg., 1968—; pres. Silver State Silver, Reno; sec.-treas. RJ Enterprises, Prescott, Ariz., Big Sky Enterprises, Prescott. Served with USNR, 1948-49. Mem. Western and English Mfrs. Assn. (pres. 1975-77), Nat. Feed Ingredients Assn. Republican. Home: 301 W Maryland St Phoenix AZ 85013 Office: 2230 E Magnolia St Phoenix AZ 85036

JOHNSON, BIRGITTA WILHELMINA, banker; b. Goteborg, Sweden, June 22, 1937; came to U.S., 1958, naturalized, 1966; d. Sture V. and Rut I. (Andersson) Johansson; B.S. in Bus. Adminstrn. (pres.'s scholar), Quinnipiac Coll., 1976; m. Roy A. Johnson, Apr. 29, 1967; 1 dau., Soli Ruth. Fgn. exchange clk. Skandinaviska Banken, Goteborg, 1957-58; clk., sec. 2d Nat. Bank of New Haven and successor bank 2d New Haven Bank, 1958-69, asst. mgr. Whitney Ave. br., 1969-75, br. officer, 1971-75, mgr. Whitney Ave. office, 1975-76, asst. v.p., 1976, mgr. main office, 1976-77, v.p., 1977, merged with Colonial Bank, 1978, mgr. retail sales & support, 1978—; seminar leader Nat. Assn. Bus. Women Career Mgmt., mng. exec. priorities seminars, 1976-79. Bd. dirs. Internat. Center, New Haven, 1972—, pres., 1979—; bd. dirs. Heritage Hall Devel. Corp., 1979—. Mem. Nat. Assn. Bank Women (chmn. Conn. group 1977-78, regional v.p. New Eng. 1980-81), Am. Inst. Banking, Network Inc. of Conn., Delta Mu Delta. Office: 135 Church St New Haven CT 06510

JOHNSON, BRUCE WILLIAM, nuclear systems co. exec.; b. N.D., Oct. 21, 1925; s. Corwin L. and Elizabeth (Macgillvary) J.; B. Econs., U. Wash., 1951, M.B.A., 1952; m. Avonelle Bailey, Jan. 10, 1945; children—Lynnette Johnson Hoerler, Leslie Jean, Scott E. Dir. public relations Rayonier, Inc., Hoquiam, Wash., 1952-59; dir. public affairs Boeing Co., Seattle, 1959-71; pres. Chem-Nuclear Systems, Inc., Bellevue, Wash., 1971—; dir. Uniflite, Inc., Bellingham, Wash. Chmn. bd. Found. for Pvt. Enterprise Edn., Olympia, Wash., 1979—; pres. Assn. Wash. Bus., 1965-67, mem. exec. com., 1956—; bd. dirs. Jr. Achievement Greater Puget Sound. Served with U.S. Army, World War II. Republican. Clubs: Wash. Athletic, Rainier (Seattle); Bellevue (Wash.) Athletic. Office: 10602 NE 38th Pl Kirkland WA 98033

JOHNSON, CECIL A(UGUST), lawyer; b. Stratford, Iowa, June 9, 1905; s. Franklin A. and Louise (Erickson) J.; student Iowa State Coll., 1922-23, LL.B., Southeastern U., 1936, M.P.L., 1938, B.C.S., 1939; LL.M., Columbus U., Washington, 1937; m. Esther M. Nelson, June 30, 1926 (dec. Aug. 1959); children—Newell D., M. Nadyne, Franklin C., Richard A.; m. 2d, Harriet L. Page, Sept. 1, 1960. Pvt. bus., Ames, Iowa, 1926-33; exec. asst. A.A.A., U.S. Dept. Agr., 1933-35, dir. commodity loans, 1935-38; sec. and asst. mgr. Fed. Crop Ins. Corp., Washington, 1938-42; directed reorgn. Office Civilian Def., Washington, 1942, asst. to gov. U.S. Farm Credit Adminstrn., Kansas City, Mo., 1942-44; admitted to Iowa bar, 1936, D.C. bar, 1937, Ill. bar, 1945, Nebr. bar, 1950; partner law firm Ekern, Meyers & Matthias, Chgo., 1944-51; gen. counsel C.A. Swanson & Sons, Omaha, 1951-55, Paxton & Gallagher Co. (name changed to Butler-Nut Foods Co.), Omaha, 1959-63, Swanson Enterprises,

Omaha, 1951—; dir. Yellow Freight Systems, Kansas City, Mo. Dir., adviser indsl. alcohol prodn., govt. alcohol plant, 1944-49; lay mem. Nat. Adv. Council for Neurol. Diseases and Blindness, USPHS, 1950-51; chmn. devel. Immanuel Med. Center, Omaha; former chmn. bd. trustees Midland Luth. Coll., Luth. Ch. in Am. Found., N.Y.C.; bd. dirs. Omaha Pub. Power Dist. Mem. Am., Iowa, Ill., Nebr., Chgo. bar assns., Am. Judicature Soc., Theta Chi. Democrat. Lutheran (mem. Bd. Am. Missions). Mason. Co-author Fed. Crop Ins. act and Nat. All Risk Crop Ins. program. Home: 8717 Capitol Ave Omaha NE 68114 Office: 8717 Capitol Ave Omaha NE 68114

JOHNSON, CHARLES NEAL, banker, lawyer; b. Hobbs, N.Mex., Nov. 5, 1942; s. Charles K. and Frances Neal J.; B.A., U. Colo., 1964; J.D., U. N.Mex., 1967; M.P.A., U. Okla., 1976; m. Sue WagnerJohnson, Aug. 25, 1979. Admitted to N.Mex. bar, 1964, Colo. bar, 1964, U.S. Supreme Ct. bar; lt. (j.g.), Judge Adv. Corps, U.S. Navy, 1964, advanced through grades to lt. comdr., 1973; resigned, 1976; asso. firm Civerolo, Hanson & Wolf, Albuquerque, 1972; asso. firm McCormick, Paine & Forbes, Carlsbad, N.Mex., 1976; exec. v.p., dir. 1st Nat. Bank of Artesia, N.Mex., 1976—. Bd. dirs. Council for Human Services, 1977-79; mem. Artesia City Library Bd., 1977—, chmn., 1979; pres. North Eddy County United Fund, 1977—; vice chmn. Democratic Party precinct, 1977; mem. Arts Council Bd., 1977—. Mem. N.Mex. Bankers Assn. (bd. dirs.), Am. Bankers Assn., C. of C. Democrat. Clubs: Elks, Moose. Home: 2503 Sierra Vista Rd Artesia NM 88210 Office: Drawer AA Artesia NM 88210

JOHNSON, CHARLES SILAS, banker; b. Muscatine, Iowa, Mar. 1, 1909; s. Raymond E. and Edna I. (Ryan) J.; student Drake U., 1926-29; m. Orpha B. Christian, July 28, 1928; children—Sally Ann (Mrs. Gerald Schomers), Raymond C., Nancy K. (Mrs. Harry Mooney). With Des Moines Nat. Bank, 1924-29; bank examiner State of Iowa, 1929-40; pres. First Nat. Bank of Perry (Iowa), 1940-58; exec. v.p. Brenton Banks, Inc., Des Moines, 1958-74, cons., dir., 1974—; chmn. exec. com., dir. South Des Moines Nat. Bank, 1962—, First Nat. Bank of Perry, 1962—; vice chmn. various Brenton banks in Iowa; chmn., pres. Iowa Bus. Devel. Credit Corp., Des Moines, 1973-79. Chmn. Herman L. Rowley Meml. Masonic Home; pres. Perry Ind. Sch. Dist., 1948-51; chmn. Republican Central Com., Dallas County, 1952-58; chmn. Dallas County Hosp. Bd., 1952-58. Recipient Outstanding citizen award Kiwanis, 1953, Legion of Honor award Iowa DeMolay, 1969. Mem. Perry C. of C. (pres. 1946, 47). Lutheran. Mason (grand treas. 1978-79), Moose, Rotarian (pres. 1950), Elk. Clubs: Des Moines, Embassy, Bohemian. Home: 7004 Bellaire Ave Des Moines IA 50311 Office: 555 39th St PO Box 961 Des Moines IA 50306

JOHNSON, CHARLES WINTHROP, ins. co. exec.; b. Stamford, Conn., Apr. 19, 1939; s. Carl Arthur and Anne Frances (Pearce) J.; B.S. in Bus., Miami U., Oxford, Ohio, 1965; postgrad. Oklahoma City U., 1973-74; m. Nancy Belle Chase, July 7, 1962; children—Lisa Hardon, Kristin Lee. Mgr. office adminstrn. Hartford Ins. Group, Manchester, N.H., 1972-73, Oklahoma City, 1973-74, Omaha, 1974-78, San Antonio, 1978—; dir. Wonder Land, Inc. Vice pres. Riverside Lakes Coop. Assn., 1977, pres., 1978—; sec. Green Spring Valley Homeowners Assn., 1980—. Served with U.S. Army, 1960-64, USAF, 1965-66, to capt. U.S. Army, 1966-72. Decorated Bronze Star medal, Air medal. Mem. Adminstrv. Mgmt. Soc. (dir. Omaha chpt., Good Mem. award 1976, Outstanding Service award, Harry H. Knapp award 1977), Am. Soc. Personnel Adminstrn., Alpha Kappa Psi. Democrat. Episcopalian. Home: Green Spring Valley 15411 River Bend Dr San Antonio TX 78247 Office: Hartford Ins Group 4803 NW Loop 410 San Antonio TX 78229

JOHNSON, CLAYTON ERROLD, poultry co. exec.; b. DeSota, Wis., Apr. 20, 1921; s. James and Louella (Goodin) J.; student U. Wis., 1940-41, Tex. A. and M. Coll., 1946; m. Betty J. Higenbotham, May 23, 1943; children—Roderick and Ronald (twins), Richard. Gen. bldg. contractor, Walnut Creek, 1948-51; now chmn. bd. Flavor Fresh Brand, ACO, Inc., Green Valley Farms. Served with USAAF, 1942-45. Home: 3111 Bel Air Dr 9G Las Vegas NV 89109

JOHNSON, CRAIG THEODORE, paper co. exec.; b. New Orleans, Sept. 6, 1941; s. Theodore Joseph and Melba (McKnight) J.; B.A., Fla. State U., 1963; M.A., Central Mich. U., 1980; m. Barbara Sue Bohannon, Feb. 14, 1969. Account exec. Coca Cola Co., Los Angeles, 1965-68; with Champion Papers, 1968—, nat. sales mgr. bus. and uncoated printing papers, 1980—. Served with USNR, 1963-65. Mem. Sigma Chi. Home: 146 Mill Rd Stamford CT 06903 Office: One Champion Plaza Stamford CT 06921

JOHNSON, CRAWFORD TOY, III, soft drink co. exec.; b. Mpls., Jan. 4, 1925; s. Crawford Toy and Mary Stuart (Snyder) J.; student Stevens Inst. Tech., Hoboken, N.J., 1943-44; B.S., U. Va., 1945; m. Virginia Jemison Goodall, Nov. 11, 1950; children—Virginia Walker Johnson Jones, Mary Stuart Johnson Young, Katherine Johnson Nielsen, Irene Johnson Botsford. With Crawford Johnson & Co., 1946-72, mgr. westside plant, 1954-56, sec., 1956-61, v.p., 1961-65, pres., chief fin. officer, 1965-72, chief exec. officer, 1972—; pres. Coca-Cola Bottling Co. United, Inc., Birmingham, Ala., 1974—; dir. Ala. Power Co., Protective Life Ins. Co., 1st Nat. Bank Birmingham, Russell Corp., Alexander City, Ala. Trustee So. Research Inst.; bd. dirs. U. Ala. Health Services Found., Birmingham; chmn. United Fund Dr., Birmingham, 1960; pres. Jefferson County (Ala.) Community Chest, 1969; chmn. Nat. Alliance Businessmen, Birmingham, 1969. Served to ensign U.S. Navy, 1945-46. Mem. Coca Cola Bottlers Assn. (bd. govs.). Episcopalian. Clubs: Rotary, The Club, Downtown, Mountain Brook, Birmingham Country. Home: 3829 Forest Glen St Birmingham AL 35213 Office: PO Box 2006 Birmingham AL 35201

JOHNSON, DAVE TOBIN, SR., ins. co. exec.; b. Pensacola, Fla., May 2, 1909; s. Joseph I. and Annie (Tobin) J.; grad. parochial schs.; m. Mary Catherine Comforter, Dec. 16, 1937; children—Mary Catherine (Mrs. James R. Thompson), Patricia Ann (Mrs. Gregory Deal), David Tobin. With Fisher-Brown, Inc., Pensacola, 1923—, asst. sec., 1932-39, v.p., 1939-50, exec. v.p., 1950-55, pres., 1955—, chmn. bd., 1975—; dir. Citizens & Peoples Nat. Bank. Past chmn., mem. U. West Fla. Found., Inc.; mem. adv. bd. Bapt. Hosp. Served with USMCR, 1943-45. Named Boss of Year, Bus. Man of Year, 1963; recipient Kiwanis Cup for Outstanding Civic Achievement, 1963. Mem. Pensacola Fire and Casualty Agts. (past pres.), Fla. Assn. Ins. Agts. (past pres.), Nat. (past chmn. nat. advt. com., fidelity, surety com., past mem. exec. com., past v.p.), Fla. (past pres.) assns. ins. agts., So. Agts. Assn. (past chmn.). Democrat. Roman Catholic. Rotarian, Elk, K.C. (4 deg.). Clubs: Pensacola Country, Yacht. Home: 1517 N 19th Ave Pensacola FL 32503 Office: Box 711 Pensacola FL 32593

JOHNSON, DAVID L(IVINGSTONE), engring. ednl. adminstr.; b. Gustavus, Ohio, Feb. 17, 1915; s. David Charles and Margaret (Delaney) J.; A.B., Berea Coll., 1936; M.A., State U. Iowa, 1938, B.S. in Elec. Engring., 1942; M.S., Okla. State U., 1950, Ph.D., 1957; m. Eugenia Gibson McQuarie, Jan. 23, 1954. Instr., U.S. Naval Tng. Sch., Okla. State U., 1942-44; field engr. Airborne Coordinating Group, 1944-45; instr. Spartan Sch. Aeros., Tulsa, 1945-48; asst. prof. Okla. State U., 1948-55; prof. elec. engring. La. Tech. U., Ruston, 1955—; cons. automatic controls. Registered profl. engr., La., Okla. Mem. AAAS, Am. Soc. Engring. Edn., Assn. Computing Machinery, IEEE, Nat. Soc. Profl. Engrs., Soc. Indsl. and Applied Math., Sigma Xi, Eta Kappa Nu, Phi Kappa Phi, Pi Mu Epsilon, Omicron Delta Kappa, Upsilon Pi Epsilon, Tau Beta Pi. Home: 1604 Valley Dr Ruston LA 71270

JOHNSON, DAVID OWEN, supply co. exec.; b. Portland, Oreg., July 16, 1918; s. Leonard Eric and Margaret Garwood (Pfeuffer) J.; student U. Calif., Berkeley, 1940, U. Oreg., 1960; m. Murel Olive Kelsey, Dec. 6, 1943; children—Mignon Johnson Ervin, Cynthia Kelsey. Mgr. accounts payable dept. Pacific Nat. Fire Ins. Co., San Francisco, 1936-42; with constrn. dept. Johns-Manville Corp., Los Angeles, 1946-48; founder, pres. Johnson Acoustical & Supply Co., Portland, 1948—; mem. nat. adv. bd. Armstrong Cork Co., 1968-74; chmn. adv. bd. U. Oreg. Grad. Sch. Bus. Conf., 1971. Chmn. bd. local Jr. Achievement, 1969, chmn. bd. govs., 1975-76; pres. Portland Chamber Orch., 1958; bd. dirs. Campfire Girls, 1965-67, Builders Exchange Coop., 1964-65, Portland Opera Assn., 1977; mem. exec. bd. Columbia-Pacific council Boy Scouts Am. Served to master sgt. C.E., U.S. Army, 1943-46. Recipient Contractor of Yr. award, 1967, Disting. Eagle award Boy Scouts Am., 1980. Mem. Am. Inst. Constructors, Ceilings and Interior Systems Contractors Assn. (nat. pres. 1966-67), Asso. Interior Contractors Oreg. (pres. 1976-77), Oreg. Club. (pres. 1964), Oreg. Execs. (pres. 1958), Portland Rose Festival Assn. (dir. 1973-76), Nat. Eagle Scout Assn., Multnomah Athletic Club, Lang Syne Soc., Philalethes Soc. Republican. Mem. Christian Ch. Clubs: Univ., Arlington, Multnomah Rotary (treas. 1978-79), City, Masons (grand insp. gen. Oreg.), Shriners. Home: 3434 SW Lakeview Blvd Lake Oswego OR 97034 Office: 6140 S W Macadam Ave Portland OR 97201

JOHNSON, DEAN EVAN, ins. exec.; b. Kiester, Minn., Aug. 16, 1931; s. Ingvard M. and Annette A. (Kapplinger) J.; B.S., Ill. Inst. Tech., 1953; m. Margaret M. Mentink, Mar. 24, 1951; children—Stephanie, Kevin. Insp., engr., asst. mgr. Iowa Inspection Bur., 1953-66; with Protection Mut. Ins. Co., Park Ridge, Ill., 1966—, v.p., dir. underwriting, 1970—, v.p., dir. ops., 1973-76, exec. v.p., 1976-78, pres., chief exec. officer, 1978—, also dir.; pres. Park PM Corp., Park Ridge, 1978—; dir. Factory Mut. Internat., London, Eng., Factory Service Corp., Norwood, Mass., Factory Mut. Service Bur., Factory Mut. Engring. Assn., Factory Mut. Engring. Corp., Factory Mut. Research Corp. (all Norwood). Mem. Nat. Fire Protection Assn., Soc. Fire Protection Engrs., Soc. Chartered Property and Casualty Underwriters, Salamander Hon. Fire Protection Engring. Soc., Mental Health Assn. Greater Chgo. (award), Newcomen Soc. N.Am., Theta Xi. Clubs: Chgo. Athletic Assn., Park Ridge Country. Home: 15 Nottingham Dr Deerfield IL 60015 Office: 300 S Northwest Hwy Park Ridge IL 60068

JOHNSON, DON BAKER, maintenance services co. exec.; b. Provo, Utah, Aug. 26, 1943; s. Don LaRell and Grace Yvonne (Baker) J.; student Brigham Young U., 1961-65, N.Mex. State U., 1968; B.S., Pittsburg State U., 1977, M.S., 1978; m. Kathy Diane Mueller, Jan. 18, 1974; children—William LaRell, Pauline Mary, Don Baker II. Dispatcher, Aero Mayflower Transit Co., Indpls., 1969-70, Atlas Van Lines, Evansville, Ind., 1970-73; propr., decorating contractor Johnson's Painting Service, Evansville, 1973-74; field service rep. United Mine Workers Health and Retirement Funds, Pittsburg, Kans., 1975-76; pres., gen. mgr. Pittsburg Custom Service, Inc., 1977—. Mem. Neighborhood Rehab. Com., Pittsburg, 1978-79; counselor to bishop Ch. Jesus Christ of Latterday Saints, 1978—. Mem. Am. Personnel and Guidance Assn., N. Am. Soc. Adlerian Psychologists, Phi Delta Kappa, Psi Chi. Address: 418 E 11th St Pittsburg KS 66762

JOHNSON, DONALD ELWOOD, owner home bldg. co.; b. Sutherland, Nebr., July 3, 1933; s. Willis Windom and Theda Lorena (Whisler) J.; B.S. in Mech. Engring., U. Wyo., 1960; m. Mary Jane Patton, Sept. 2, 1956; children—Timothy D., Jacklyn M. Job engr. Standard Oil of Calif., El Segundo, 1960-62; engr. Hercules Powder Co., Bacchus, Utah, 1962-64; partner Ratton & Johnson Builders, Laramie, Wyo., 1964-73, owner, 1973—; sec. Quad Devel., Inc., Laramie, 1979—. Mem. Albany County Sch. Bd., 1969-72. Served with U.S. Army, 1954-56. Mem. Nat. Home Builders Assn., Laramie C. of C., U.S. C. of C. Republican. Clubs: Kiwanis, Rotary (Laramie, Wyo.). Home and Office: 1160 Escalera Rd Laramie WY 82070

JOHNSON, DWIGHT LEONARD, bus. cons.; b. Denver, Mar. 4, 1938; s. Ralph Edgar and Edith Jane (Sturgeon) J.; B.S. in Elec. Engring. and Bus. Mgmt., U. Colo., 1961; m. Elizabeth Jane Camp, Aug. 5, 1961; children—Dwight Leonard, Eric S., Stephen D. Sales engr. Sturgeon Electric Co., Denver, 1962-65, v.p., sales mgr., 1965-70, chmn. bd., pres., gen. mgr., 1970-76; chmn. bd. dirs. Estimatic Corp.; fin., estate and bus. cons., 1978—. Bd. dirs. Goodwill Industries, U. Colo. Sch. Engring.; v.p. Met. Denver YMCA; trustee Children's Asthma Research Inst. and Hosp.; bd. dirs., exec. com. Nat. Jewish Hosp./Nat. Asthma Center; chmn. adv. council U. Colo. Sch. Bus.; elder Wellshire Presbyn. Ch. Served with USNR, 1956-62. Mem. Illuminating Engring. Soc. (past dir., chmn.), Fellowship of Christian Athletes (past chmn. bd., nat. trustee), Downtown Denver Improvement Assn. (dir.), Young Pres.'s Orgn., Sigma Alpha Epsilon. Presbyn. (bd. dirs. ch.). Rotarian (dir. Denver). Home: 3 Sunset Dr Englewood CO 80110 Office: 789 Sherman Suite 600 Denver CO 80203

JOHNSON, EARL ALFRED, mfg. co. exec.; b. Trinidad, Colo., June 7, 1918; s. Nils A. and Elsie (Eakins) J.; student Colo. State U., 1935-37, Omaha U., 1944-45, Creighton U., 1950-51: m. Jean Jenkins, Oct. 24, 1942; children—Kim Ellen, Kirk Alan, Kay Ann. Gen. accountant Colo. Interstate Gas Co., Colorado Springs, 1939-41; camp dir., sec. Nat. council Boy Scouts Am., Cimarron, N.Mex., 1941-42; controller Farm Crops Processing, Omaha, 1943-50; gen. mgr., sec. Kimball Bros. Co., Omaha, 1951-54; ind. systems analyst, Omaha, 1955-58; mfg. plant controller Vickers div. Sperry Rand, Omaha, 1958-68, mgr. mgmt. information systems, mobile div., 1968—; cons. bus. and systems techniques. Active local Boy Scouts Am. Mem. Nat. Accountants Assn. (charter mem. Omaha chpt.), Systems and Procedures Assn. (charter mem., dir. memberships), Budget Execs. Inst. (charter mem., pres. Omaha chpt.), Am. Mensa Soc. (dir. pub. relations Nebr.-W. Iowa chpt.). Mason (32 deg.), Elk. Contbr. articles to profl. jours. Home: 512 S 8th St Council Bluffs IA 51501 Office: 6600 N 72d St Omaha NE 68122

JOHNSON, EARL DALLAM, aviation and fin. cons.; b. Hamilton, Ohio, Dec. 14, 1905; s. Sidney Cornelius and Marion Esley (Felton) J.; B.A., U. Wis., 1928; grad. Randolph and Kelley Fields, 1931; m. Mytle O. Vietmeyer, Nov. 3, 1932; children—Raud Earl, Susan Lynne, Cynthia Lee. Vice pres., dir. Loomis Sayles & Co., Boston, 1933-41; asst. sec. army Dept. Army, Washington, 1950-51, undersec. army, 1952-54, also chmn. bd. Panama Canal, 1952-54, pres. Air Transport Assn. and Air Cargo Inc., Washington, 1954-55; sr. v.p., exec. v.p., pres., vice chmn. bd. Gen. Dynamics Co., N.Y.C., 1955-63; exec. v.p. Delta Airlines, Atlanta, 1963-64; cons. aviation, Greenwich, Conn., 1964—; dir. numerous corps., including Gen. Dynamics, Damson Oil, Menasco Mfg. Co. Ltd.; lectr. in field; Def. Dept. sr. ofcl. on Japanese Peace Treaty. Trustee Air Acad. Found., Colorado Springs, Bataan Meml. Hosp., Albuquerque, Lovelace Med. Found., Albuquerque. Served to col. AC, U.S. Army, 1931-33, 1941-45. Mem. Navy League (life), Nat. Security Indsl. Assn., Nat. Transp. Assn., Air Force Assn., Phi Beta Kappa, Pi Kappa Alpha. Clubs: Greenwich Country; Rolling Rock (Ligonier, Pa.); Explorers (N.Y.C.). Home: 36 W Brother Dr Greenwich CT 06830

JOHNSON, EARLE BERTRAND, ins. exec.; b. Otter Lake, Mich., May 3, 1914; s. Bert Monroe and Blanche (Sherman) J.; B.S. in Bus. Adminstrn., U. Fla., 1937, J.D., 1940; m. Frances Pierce, 1940 (dec.); children—Earle Bertrand, Victoria, Julia, Sheryl; m. 2d, Peggy Minch, 1972. Admitted to Fla. bar, 1940; spl. agt. FBI, 1942-44; gen. practice law, Jacksonville, Fla., 1944-52; with State Farm Ins. Cos., Fla., 1940—, claim dept., 1940-42, dist. mgr., Fla., 1947-58, regional agy. dir., Bloomington, Ill., 1958-60, regional v.p., 1960-65, v.p., sec., dir., mem. exec. com. State Farm Mut. Automobile Ins. Co., Bloomington, Ill., 1965—; treas. State Farm County Mut. Ins. Co. Tex., 1963-80, sr. v.p., 1965-80; chmn. bd., mem. exec. com., dir. State Farm Life Ins. Co., 1970—; v.p., dir. State Farm Gen. Co. and State Farm Fire & Casualty Co., 1966—, dir. State Farm Investment Mgmt. Corp., 1968—. Mem. Am., Fla. bar assns., Soc. Former FBI Agts., Agy. Officers Round Table (exec. com. 1970—), Gen. Agy. Mgmt. Assn., Life Ins. Mktg. Assn. (dir. 1975-78), Life Underwriters Tng. Council (trustee), Pedlars, Phi Alpha Delta, Phi Kappa Tau. Home: 215 Imperial Dr Bloomington IL 61701 Office: One State Farm Plaza Bloomington IL 61701

JOHNSON, EARLE WALTER, tool co. exec.; b. Harvard, Ill., Mar. 20, 1915; s. Walter Nels and Alice May (Bowen) J.; student Beloit Coll., 1933-34, U. Ill., 1940-41, Purdue U., 1953; m. Helene Janet Grady, May 27, 1939; children—Stephen E., Michael B., Janet A., Jeffrey L., Susan B. With Rockford Machine Tool (Ill.), 1937-56, chief engr., 1950-56; founder, pres., gen. mgr. Jonco Tool Supply, Inc., Rockford, 1956—. Sponsor, Boy Scouts Am., Rockford, 1950-65, Boys Club, Rockford, 1968-80, YMCA, 1950-80, Rosecrance Home, Rockford, 1970-80. Mem. Rockford Engring. Soc. (pres. 1964), Soc. Mfg. Engrs. (past chmn.), Greater Rockford Indsl. Distbrs. (past pres.), Rockford and Loves Park C. of C. Republican. Methodist. Clubs: Elks, Mauh-Nah-Tee-See, Svithiod. Patentee on hydraulic and machine mechanisms, 1950-55; contbr. articles to profl. jours. Home: 1126 Arden Ave Rockford IL 61107 Office: 6010 Forest Hills Rd Rockford IL 61130

JOHNSON, EDWARD ALDEN, coll. dean; b. Palmerton, Pa., May 11, 1937; s. John Alden and Mary Amelia (Ronemus) J.; B.A. in Psychology, Antioch Coll., 1960; M.Indsl. and Labor Relations, Cornell U., 1962; Ph.D. in Mgmt., Mich. State U., 1968; m. Beryl Ann Benschop, June 26, 1965; 1 son, Edward Blaine. Research asso. Cornell U., Ithaca, N.Y., 1960-62; asst. prof., asso. prof. mgmt. W.Va. U. Morgantown, 1966-72, dir. grad. programs in bus., 1968-70; dean Coll. Bus. Rochester (N.Y.) Inst. Tech., 1972-79; dean M.J. Neeley Sch. Bus., Tex. Christian U., Ft. Worth, 1979—; chmn. bd. dirs. Blue Cross of Rochester. Mem. social goals com. United Community Chest, Rochester, 1976-77; mem. council Urbanarium, Rochester, 1973-74. Mem. Acad. Mgmt., Indsl. Relations Research Assn., Am. Inst. Decision Scis., Beta Gamma Sigma, Phi Kappa Phi. Contbr. articles to profl. jours. Home: 3901 Arlan Ln Fort Worth TX 76109 Office: MJ Neeley Sch Bus Tex Christian U Fort Worth TX

JOHNSON, EDWARD FULLER, investment banker, cons.; b. Princeton, N.J., Sept. 14, 1921; s. Rankin and Kate Gilbert (Fuller) J.; M.E., Cornell U., 1946; m. Joan Van Alstyne, Apr. 1, 1950; children—Susan, Keats, Kate, Kimball, David, Edward. With J.G. White Constrn. Co., Venezuela, 1947-48, George S. Armstrong, Mgmt. Cons. Engrs., N.Y.C., 1948-50; partner Van Alstyne Noel Co., N.Y.C., 1952-61; dir. Johnson Redbook Service, Vanden Broeck Lieber, Brokers, N.Y.C., 1962-70; sr. v.p., dir. Johnson Redbook Service, Prescott, Ball & Turben, N.Y.C., 1970—; cons. to diversified industries. Councilman, Englewood, N.J., 1967-70; chmn. bd. dirs. Englewood Community Chest, 1976-78. Served to capt. USAF, World War II and Korea. Decorated Air medal with 2 oak leaf clusters. Mem. N.Y. Analysts Soc., Apparel and Textile Analysts Group, Chem. Analysts Group, Retail Analysts Group, Home Furnishing Analysts Group. Republican. Presbyterian. Clubs: Englewood Field; Bayhead (N.J.) Yacht; Bond, Cornell, India House (N.Y.C.). Home: 821 East Ave Bayhead NJ 07631 Office: One Battery Park Plaza New York NY 10004

JOHNSON, EDWARD WILLIAM, cons. mech. engr.; ret. govt. ofcl.; b. Chgo., May 3, 1909; s. Axel Edward and Hilda (Johansson) J.; B.S., Ill. Inst. Tech., 1934, B.S. in Mech. Engring., 1935, postgrad. Carnegie Inst. Tech., 1936-40, Mass. Inst. Tech., 1943, McGill U., 1950, George Washington U., 1953-57; m. Irmgard Maria Zeisberg, Mar. 15, 1957; 1 son, Robert David. Jr. mech. engr. Internat. Harvester Co., Chgo., 1934-39; asst. insp. naval material U.S. Navy Dept., Pitts., 1939-40; asso. mech. engr. U.S. Army Ordnance, Balt., 1940-42; mech. engr., asst. chief vehicle devel. U.S. Army Corps Engrs., Ft. Belvoir, Va., 1946-47, chief engring. sect. climatic research, 1947-48; environ. engr. Bur. Yards and Docks, Washington, 1948-52, head research programming, 1953-57; mech. engr. U.S. Naval Weapons Lab., Dahlgren, Va., 1957-59; head engring. specifications U.S. Naval Weapons Plant, Washington, 1959-60; sr. engr., asst. chief procurement U.S. Bur. Pub. Rds., 1960-62; asst. chief postal lab. office research engring. U.S. Post Office Dept., Washington, 1962-66, sr. engr., 1966-71; mech. engr. Williams Enterprises, Inc., Merrifield, Va., 1970-71; engring. mgr. Basic Testing Labs., Inc., Centreville, Va., 1971-72; sr. engr. Value Engring. Co., Alexandria, Va., 1972-74; cons. mech. engr., Springfield, Va., 1974—; sr. staff engr. Ciccone Assos., Inc., Woodbridge, Va., 1979—. Served with USNR, 1943-46, lt. comdr. CEC, USNR, ret. Registered profl. engr., D.C. Mem. ASME, Am. Inst. Aeros. and Astronautics, Nat., Va. socs. profl. engrs., Am. Ordnance Assn., Soc. Automotive Engrs., Am. Polar Soc., Swedish Pioneer Hist. Soc., Soc. Automotive Historians. Clubs: Masons, Shriners, Explorers. Author profl. articles. Home: 6944 Essex Ave Springfield VA 22150

JOHNSON, EVERETT EUGENE, steel warehouse exec.; b. Manistique, Mich., Sept. 11, 1917; s. Erick G. and Frieda M. (Hagberg) J.; student Aero. U., 1938-39; m. Evelyn L. Mueller, July 19, 1941; children—Stephen E., Richard K. With A.C. McClurg Co., Chgo., 1936-40; insp. U.S. Navy, 1941-45; with Chgo. Tube & Iron Co., Milan, Ill., 1945—, gen. mgr. br., 1975-79, asst. to gen. mgr., 1979—. Bd. dirs. Awana Youth Assn., Rolling Meadows, Ill. Mem. Am. Mgmt. Assn., Milan C. of C. Republican. Baptist. Home: 11727 6th St Milan IL 61264 Office: 1040 11th St Milan IL 61264

JOHNSON, FRANCIS RUSS MARION, investor, ret. banker; b. Durant, Miss., Sept. 11, 1909; s. Edwin Rembert and Margaret Lauda (Comfort) J.; student Millsaps Coll., 1926-27, Rutgers U. Grad. Sch., 1937-41; grad. Am. Inst. Banking; m. Rosalind Gwin Hutton, Apr. 14, 1943; 1 dau., Martha Ryburn (Mrs. Robert Lafayette Stainton). With Mchts. Bank & Trust Co., Jackson, Miss., 1927-33; with Deposit Guaranty Nat. Bank, Jackson, Miss., 1933—, v.p. investments, 1946-53, exec. v.p., dir., 1953-80, chmn. exec. com., 1958-69, chmn. bd., chief exec. officer, 1969-75, also dir.; with Deposit Guaranty Corp., Jackson, 1968-80, chmn. bd., chief exec. officer, 1969-75, also dir.; dir. Carthage Bank (Miss.). Staff mem. gov. of Miss., 1964-68, 72-76. Past pres. Andrew Jackson council Boy Scouts Am., past mem. exec. com. Region V, mem. exec. bd. Andrew Jackson council, mem-at-large Nat. council; active fund raising for United Givers, various civic, religious and cultural orgns., hosps., ch.-related schs., liberal arts colls.; past mem. Miss. Agrl. and Indsl. Bd.; former mem. Miss. Gov.'s Emergency Council; commr. Gen. Assembly, Presbyn. Ch. U.S.A., mem. Bd. Annuities and Relief, chmn. finance com.; pres. Bd. dirs. Miss. Econ. Council; 1958. Served from pvt. to capt., AUS, 1942-46; ETO. Mem. Am. Bankers Assn. (past Miss. rep. exec. council, past mem. exec. com. state bank div., mem. govt. borrowing com.), Newcomen Soc., Am. Legion, Chi Psi (Distinguished Service award 1976). Presbyn (elder). Lion. Clubs: Jackson Country; Boston (New Orleans). Home: 4323 Brook Dr Jackson MS 39206

JOHNSON, FRANK H., hotel co. exec.; b. El Paso Tex., July 27, 1929; s. Albin Carl and Bertha H. J.; student U. Nev., 1946-52; m. Joyce Elizabeth McElwain, June 12, 1949; children—Frank, Judy Lynn Johnson Lockwood, Susan Joy. Photographer Nev. State Jour., Reno, 1952-53, reporter, 1953-55, city editor, 1955-58, capitol bur. mgr., 1958-61, asst. mng. editor, 1961-67; chmn. Nev. Gaming Control Bd., 1967-71; v.p. Hilton Hotels Corp., Las Vegas, 1971—, exec. v.p. Hilton Systems, Inc., 1976—, also dir.; dir. Hilton Casinos, Inc., Benco, Inc., Lebanco, Inc. Mem. U.S. Dept. Commerce Def. Exec. Res., So. Nev. United Way; bd. dirs. Nev. Taxpayers Assn.; adv. bd. U. Nev. Sch. Med. Scis. Mem. C. of C. Greater Las Vegas (pres.), Sigma Delta Chi, Kappa Tau Alpha. Republican. Episcopalian. Clubs: Press (Reno), Prospectors. Home: 2770 Palma Vista Ave Las Vegas NV 89121 Office: 3000 Paradise Rd Las Vegas NV 89109

JOHNSON, FRANK LEE, retail bus. machines co. exec.; b. Powell, Wyo., Feb. 23, 1918; s. Archie D. and Lida Lee (Birney) J.; B.S. in Bus. Adminstrn., U. Nebr., 1939; m. Evelyn Mae Stevenson, May 31, 1947. Trainee for store mgr. Montgomery Ward Co., Grand Rapids, Iowa, 1940-41; salesman Burroughs, Omaha, 1941-42; partner Kennedy Bus. Machines, Inc., San Jose, Calif., 1946—, v.p., 1968-72, pres., 1972—, chmn. bd., 1972—. Active Better Bus. Bur. Served to lt. USN, 1942-46; PTO. Mem. Nat. Office Machines Assn., Western Office Machines Assn., No. Calif. Office Machines Assn., San Jose C. of C. Republican. Clubs: Lions, Elks. Home: 1258 Chateau Dr San Jose CA 95120 Office: 170 S 2d St San Jose CA 95113

JOHNSON, FRANKLIN RIDGWAY, lawyer, fin. exec.; b. Boston, Mar. 23, 1912; s. Howard Franklin and Mary Helena (Morse) J.; LL.B., Northeastern U., 1939; postgrad. Harvard, 1941-42; m. Sarah Q. Shaw, Aug. 16, 1962; children by previous marriage—Nathaniel, Samuel, Anne, Rebecca. Admitted to Mass. bar, 1939; partner Choate, Hall & Stewart, Boston, 1950-56; sr. officer, legal counsel Colonial Mgmt. Assos., 1956-63, Eaton & Howard, Inc., 1963-65; sr. v.p., gen. counsel Keystone Custodian Funds, Inc., 1965-77; pres., dir. Keystone OTC Fund, Inc., Boston, 1974-77; of counsel firm Choate, Hall & Stewart, Boston, 1978-80; individual practice law, Boston, 1980—; pres., trustee Middlesex Instn. for Savs.; dir., mem. audit com. Pioneer Fund, Pioneer II, Pioneer Bond Fund. Mem. Concord (Mass.) bd. selectmen, 1951-55, chmn. bd., 1953-55; mem. adv. com. Harvard Law Sch. Study of State Securities Regulation, 1954-56. Mem. Am. Bar Assn., Nat. Assn. Securities Dealers (gov. 1971-73), Investment Co. Inst. (gov. 1959-62, 68-71). Republican. Episcopalian. Clubs: Harvard (Boston); Concord Country. Home: 91 Carleton Rd Carlisle MA 01741 Office: 294 Washington St Boston MA 02108

JOHNSON, FRED EUGENE (GENE), photog. co. exec.; b. Kansas City, Mo., Feb. 27, 1922; s. Tade E. and Ruth (Sloan) J.; B.S., U. Okla., 1944. With Eastman Kodak Co., Rochester, N.Y., 1944—, successively photographer, tchr., writer, editor, lectr., 1944-57, specialist, 1957—, supervising specialist, 1969-70, sr. specialist, 1970—. Mem. Profl. Photographer Am., Photog. Soc. Am., Soc. Photog. Scientists and Engrs., Soc. Tech. Writers and Pubs., Internat. Platform Assn. Contbr. articles to profl. jours. Home: Pittsford Manor 3654B Monroe Ave Pittsford NY 14534 Office: 343 State St Rochester NY 14650

JOHNSON, FREDERICK ROSS, food products co. exec.; b. Winnipeg, Man., Can., Dec. 31, 1931; s. Frederick Hamilton and Caroline (Green) J.; B.Comm., U. Man., 1952; M.Comm., U. Toronto (Ont., Can.), 1956; LL.D. (hon.), St. Francis Xavier U., 1978; m. Laurie A. Graumann; children—Bruce, Neil. Pres. Standard Brands Inc., 1975, pres., chief exec. officer, 1976, chmn., chief exec. officer, 1977—. Bd. dirs. Multiple Sclerosis Soc. Mem. Grocery Mfrs. Assn. (dir.), Phi Delta Theta. Clubs: Economic (trustee), Brook, The Links, Blind Brook. Home: 30 Coley Dr Weston CT 06883 Office: 625 Madison Ave New York NY 10022

JOHNSON, GARY REID, ednl. adminstr.; b. Ingram Branch, W.Va., Feb. 23, 1934; s. Ernest Reid and Sophrona Edyth (Tredway) J.; Mus.B., U. Mich., 1954, M.B.A., 1956, M.A., 1958; Ph.D., U. Calif., 1980. Asst. bus. mgr. for sponsored research U. Mich., Ann Arbor, 1958-66; spl. asst. to dean U. Calif., Davis, 1966-69; asst. to vice chancellor U. Calif., San Diego, 1969-74; exec. dir. bus. and fin. Health Scis. Centers, Tex. Tech. U., Lubbock, 1974-79; pres. SERGJCO, Ltd., Santa Barbara, Calif., 1979—; cons. legis. com. on Higher Edn., Hawaii, 1968-72. Fellow Am. Acad. Med. Adminstrs.; mem. Am. Soc. Pub. Adminstrn., Acad. Mgmt., Acad. Polit. Sci., Am. Hosp. Assn., Am. Acad. Polit. and Social Scis., Am. Assn. Sch. Adminstrs., Assn. Supervision and Curriculum Devel., Nat. Assn. Coll. and Univ. Bus. Officers, Assn. Am. Med. Colls. Group on Bus. Affairs, Internat. Soc. for Philos. Enquiry, Intertel, Mensa, SAR, SCV, Soc. Colonial Wars, Tau Kappa Epsilon, Alpha Kappa Psi, Phi Mu Alpha, Kappa Kappa Psi. Contbr. articles to profl. jours. Home: PO Box 6545 Santa Barbara CA 93111

JOHNSON, GEORGE CHRISTIAN, mgmt. cons.; b. Bklyn., Apr. 30, 1943; s. George Christian and Helen Alice (Murphy) J.; B.S., Fordham U., 1964; M.S., Poly. Inst. N.Y., 1966; M.B.A., N.Y. U., 1973; m. Carol Ann Brunner, June 26, 1965; children—Christine Carol, George Christian, Eric Charles. Purchasing agt. Pfizer, N.Y.C., 1965-66; prodn. mgr. Johnson & Johnson, New Brunswick, N.J., 1966-69; mgmt. cons. Touche Ross & Co., N.Y.C., 1969-71; fin. mgr., adminstrv. dir. research and devel. lab. Schlumberger Ltd., Houston, Paris, 1971-78; mng. partner John Stork & Partners, Greenwich, Conn., 1978—; dir. John Stork & Partners, Internat., Ltd., London, 1978—; faculty Fordham U., 1979-80. Active, Boy Scouts Am., Little League; bd. dirs. N.Y. U. Grad. Sch. Bus. Adminstrn. M.D.L. program, 1979-80. NSF grantee, 1963-64. Mem. Nat. Assn. Corp. and Profl. Recruiters, Am. Mgmt. Assn., Am. C. of C., French Chess Fedn. Roman Catholic. Clubs: The Champions Golf, Princeton, Wolfpit Running, Kiwanis. Home: 145 Saint Johns Rd Ridgefield CT 06877 Office: 35 Mason St Greenwich CT 06830

JOHNSON, GEORGE ELLIS, industrialist; b. Richton, Miss., June 16, 1927; s. Charles D. and Priscilla D. (Howard) J.; hon. degrees: D.B.A., Xavier U., 1973; H.H.D., Clark Coll., 1974; D. Comml. Sci., Coll. Holy Cross, 1975; LL.D., Babson Coll., 1976, Fisk U., 1977, Tuskegee Inst., 1978, Lake Forest Coll., 1979; L.H.D., Chgo. State U., 1977; Lemoyne-Owen Coll., 1979; m. Joan Betty Henderson; children—Eric, John, George Ellis, Joan Marie. Pres., chmn. bd. Johnson Products Co., Inc., Chgo., 1954—; chmn. bd. Independence Bank of Chgo.; dir. Commonwealth Edison Co., Met. Life Ins. Co. Pres. George E. Johnson Ednl. Fund, George E. Johnson Found.; mem. corp. Babson Coll.; exec. bd. Chgo. Area council Boy Scouts Am.; governing mem. Chgo. Orchestral Assn.; bd. dirs. Chgo. Urban League, Dearborn Park Corp., Internat. African C. of C., Lyric Opera of Chgo., Nat. Asthma Center, Northwestern Meml. Hosp., Operation PUSH, Protestant Found. Greater Chgo.; trustee Chgo. Sunday Evening Club, Northwestern U., Ravinia Festival Assn.; mem. nat. adv. com. Interracial Council Bus. Opportunity; v.p. Jr. Achievement of Chgo.; sponsoring com. NAACP Legal Def. Fund. Recipient Abraham Lincoln Center Humanitarian Service award, 1972, Am. Black Achievement award Ebony Mag., 1978, Public Service award Harvard Club Chgo., 1979. Mem. Econ. Club Chgo., Cosmetic, Toiletry and Fragrance Assn. (dir.). Congregationalist; Clubs: Burnham Yacht, Chgo. Yacht, Comml. of Chgo., Met., Carlton, Hundred of Cook County, Mid-Am. (gov.), PIPS Internat., Runaway Bay Country (Jamaica), Tres Vidas en la Playa (Acapulco), Jockey (Miami), Le Mirador (Switzerland). Office: 8522 S Lafayette St Chicago IL 60620

JOHNSON, GLENN ROBERT, mail order co. exec.; b. Chgo., Mar. 14, 1950; s. Edwin C. and Viola M. (Toigo) J.; student Prairie State Coll., Chicago Heights, Ill., 1967-69, U. Ill., 1973—; m. Arlene Ann Sheffhold, Oct. 30, 1971. Programmer, U. Ill., Urbana, 1972-73; mgr. custom software services The Colwell Co., Champaign, Ill., 1973, mgr. data processing, 1974—, systems engr., 1978—; cons. in field. Pres. Village of Bondville (Ill.), 1977—. Mem. Gen. Automation Users Group Exchange (pres.), Assn. Computer Programmers and Analysts, Am. Inst. Indsl. Engrs. Home: 103 S Market St Bondville IL 61815 Office: 201 Kenyon Rd Champaign IL 61820

JOHNSON, GUY CHARLES, elec. engr.; b. N.Y.C., Dec. 24, 1946; s. Leon Everod and Marjorie Clarene (Watts) J.; B.S.E.E., Columbia U., 1968, M.S.E.E., 1972; m. Janet Smith, Mar. 30, 1968; children—Tracey Renee, Eric Ahmed. Devel. engr. Western Electric Co., Whippany, N.J., 1968-73, info. systems staff, N.Y.C., 1973-76, sr. planning engr., N.Y.C., 1978-79, dept. chief, N.Y.C., 1979—; staff specialist AT&T Co., Basking Ridge, N.J., 1976-78. Co-founder Co-Op City Black Caucus, sec., 1971; active Nat. Urban League Black Exec. Exchange Program. Mem. Tau Beta Pi. Club: Nat. Jogging Assn. Office: 222 Broadway New York NY 10038

JOHNSON, HARRY CLARENCE, investment banker, stock broker; b. Ashby, Minn., Oct. 15, 1913; s. H. Severin and Caroline (Jansen) J.; B.B.A., U. Minn., 1946; m. Elizabeth Ellen Phelps, Sept. 16, 1939 (dec. Dec. 1973); children—Karen Johnson Mauer, Stephen Phelps. Accountant, Glacier Park Co. Resort Hotel, East Glacier, Mont., 1937; cost accountant Synder Drug Co., Mpls., 1938; auditor Mpls. Star Tribune, 1938-43; controller St. Paul Foundry & Mfg. Co., 1943-49; comptroller Otter Tail Power Co., Fergus Falls, Minn., 1949-70, v.p., chief financial officer, 1970-78, treas., 1959-78, sr. v.p., 1978; asst. commr. Dept. Econ. Devel., State of Minn., 1979-80; in investment banking and stock brokerage, 1980—; dir. Northwestern Nat. Bank, Fergus Falls, Acton Constrn. Co. Pres., dir. Otter Tail Mgmt. Corp., 1969—. Bd. dirs. Lake Region Hosp., Fergus Falls, 1959-77; trustee, pres. First Luth. Ch. Found. Mem. Financial Execs. Inst., N. Central Electric Assn. (treas. 1968-77), Financial Mgmt. Assn., Edison Electric, Thomas Alva Edison Found. Clubs: Rotary, Elks. Home: Route 5 Box 210 Fergus Falls MN 56537

JOHNSON, HENRY CLYDE, mfr., engr., lawyer, fin. exec.; b. Niagara Falls, N.Y., June 18, 1914; s. Willis Oscar and Della R. (Hagerty) J.; S.B., S.M., Mass. Inst. Tech., 1936; J.D., Harvard, 1940; m. Dorothy Diedre Montagu, Feb. 11, 1955; 1 stepdau., Martha Browning (Mrs. Robert T. Mast). Admitted to Mass. bar, 1940, N.Y. bar, 1940, U.S. Supreme Ct. bar, 1944; asso. firm Phipps, Durgin & Cook, Boston, 1940-41; div. purchasing agt., mgr. planning dept. on staff pres. Philco Corp., Phila., 1946-50; mem. central finance staff, engring. bd., controller engring. div. Ford Motor Co., Dearborn, Mich., 1950-58; chmn. bd., pres., owner Phil Wood Industries Ltd. (formerly Gar Wood Industries of Can. Ltd.), Windsor, Ont., Can., 1958-69, hon. chmn., 1969—. Mem. Windsor Econ. Com.; benefactor Detroit Inst. Arts; patron mem. Detroit Symphony Orch.; maj. donor Meadowbrook Festival; mem. pres.'s club Oakland U.; life mem. Cranbrook Inst. Sci.; mem. Archives Am. Art. Trustee, chmn. ednl. policy com., mem. exec. com. Detroit Inst. Tech., 1972-78. Served from lt. to col. Signal Corps, AUS, 1941-46. Decorated Army, Navy commendation medals, registered profl. engr., Pa. Sr. mem. IEEE (life); mem. Am. Bar Assn., Am. Mgmt. Assn. (Personal plaque 1960), AAAS (life), Aircraft Owners and Pilots Assn., Am. Radio Relay League (life), Cranbrook Inst. Sci. (life), English Speaking Union, Quarter Century Wireless Assn. (life), Sigma Alpha Epsilon, (founder mem.). Episcopalian. Clubs: Economic, M.I.T., Detroit Athletic (Detroit); Otsego (Mich.) Ski; Circumnavigators (life) (N.Y.C.); Harvard (Mich.); Cranbrook Tennis (Bloomfield Hills, Mich.). Patentee automatic tripping snow plow. Home: 3000 Quarton Rd Bloomfield Hills MI 48013

JOHNSON, HOWARD B., restaurant and motel co. exec.; b. Boston, Aug. 23, 1932; s. Howard D. and Bernice (Manley) J.; grad. Andover Acad., 1950; B.A., Yale U., 1954; student Harvard Bus. Sch.; m. Patricia A. Bates, Jan. 17, 1958; children—Howard Bates, Marissa Turull, Patricia Bates. Pres., dir., chmn. bd. Howard Johnson Co. Office: Howard Johnson Co 50 Rockefeller Plaza New York NY 10020

JOHNSON, J. WAYNE, truck leasing co. exec.; b. Greensboro, N.C., Jan. 24, 1941; s. J.P. and Bertha A. (May) J.; B.B.A. in Accounting, Pace U.; m. Shirley Anderson, Oct. 9, 1965; 1 dau., Jennifer Marie. With Price Waterhouse & Co., N.Y.C., 1969-72; mgr. NBC Div. RCA, N.Y.C., 1972-74; dir. Ryder Truck Rental, Inc., div. Ryder System, Inc., Miami, Fla., 1974-77; asst. treas. Ryder System, Inc., 1977-80; v.p., controller Ryder Truck Rental, Inc., 1980—; instr. bus., colls. C.P.A. Office: Ryder Truck Rental Inc 3600 NW 82d Ave PO Box 520816 Miami FL 33152

JOHNSON, JACK AUSTIN, JR., assn. exec.; b. Ottawa, Ill., Aug. 18, 1947; s. Jack Austin and Shirley Irene (Gaddis) J.; B.S., Ill. State U., 1970; m. Barbara C. Burns, Nov. 8, 1969; children—Kirk A., Eric E. Elem. tchr. Oak Knoll Grade Sch., Cary, Ill., 1970-71; exec. Boy Scouts Am., 1971—, dist. exec. Two Rivers Council, St. Charles, Ill., 1971-75, dist. exec. M/M, 1976-77, field dir. Illowa Council, Davenport, Iowa, 1977—. Recipient Spencer award Boy Scouts Am., 1972, 73, 74, 75. Presbyterian. Clubs: Jaycee (sec., dir. 1972-76), Kiwanis. Home: 2590 New Lexington Dr Bettendorf IA 52722 Office: 2804 Eastern Ave Davenport IA 52803

JOHNSON, JAMES ARNOLD, bus. cons.; b. Detroit, June 15, 1939; s. Waylon Z. and Elsie Jean (Peuser) J.; B.A., Stanford, 1961; M.B.A., U. Chgo., 1968; m. Glenda Lin Chow; 1 dau., Stephanie Louise. Asst. cashier, internat. banking First Nat. Bank of Chgo., 1965-68; partner in charge mgmt. cons. Peat, Marwick, Mitchell & Co., Honolulu, 1968-79, partner in charge small bus. services, 1977-80; co-mng. partner Asia/Pacific Initiatives, Ltd., Honolulu, 1980—; pres. Johnson Internat., Inc., Honolulu, 1980—. Bd. dirs. Honolulu Symphony Soc. Served to lt. USNR, 1962-65. C.P.A., Hawaii, Calif. Mem. Am. Inst. C.P.A.'s, Hawaii Soc. C.P.A.'s (past chmn. mgmt. adv. com.). Clubs: Waikiki Yacht, Honolulu, Sales and Mktg. Execs. of Honolulu. Home: 1221 Victoria Apt 2705 Honolulu HI 96814 Office: 733 Bishop Suite 2777 Honolulu HI 96813

JOHNSON, JAMES CASEY, aerospace co. exec.; b. Kinston, N.C., Mar. 24, 1936; s. Talmadge Casey and Rachel (Murr) J.; B.S., N.C. State U., 1958; m. Barbara Marie Clark, Dec. 25, 1955; s. Kenneth James, Amy Lynn. Tchr. math. high sch., Fla., 1960-62; contract price analyst USAF, NASA, 1962-65; mgr. pricing, mgr. contracts E-Systems, Inc., Greenville, Tex., 1965-75, program dir., 1975-77, controller Greenville div., 1978—, v.p., 1979—; v.p. fin. Air Asia Co. Ltd., Tainan, Taiwan, 1979—. Served with AUS, 1958-60. Mem. Greenville C. of C. (dir.). Republican. Methodist. Home: Rt 2 Box 79 Greenville TX 75401 Office: Major's Field Greenville TX 75401

JOHNSON, JAMES GORDON, ins. cons.; b. Ft. Worth, Apr. 13, 1927; s. Gilbert Arthur and Volina J.; student Tex. Coll. Mines, 1942-43, Tex. Tech. U., 1943; B.B.A., U. Tex., Austin, 1948, M.Profl. Accounting, 1949; m. Faye Anderson, July 22, 1949; 1 son, Gerald Wayne. Sec.-treas. Whyburn & Co., El Paso, Tex., 1950-68; pres. Whyburn Services, Inc., El Paso, 1962-70; exec. v.p. Pannational Group Inc., El Paso, 1970-76; mng. partner DeWitt, Rearick, Dycus & Johnson, El Paso, 1977—; chmn. bd. Computer Services, Inc.; dir. State Nat. Bank, El Paso, Citizens Nat. Bank, Austin. Bd. dirs. Rio Grande council Girl Scouts U.S. Served with USNR, 1944-46. Decorated Purple Heart. Recipient pub. service award El Paso. Jr. C. of C., 1958, El Paso C. of C., 1964. Mem. Nat. Assn. Accountants, El Paso Bd. Realtors, El Paso Assn. Ins. Agts. (trustee), Beta Alpha Psi Sigma Phi Epsilon. Methodist. Club: Sertoma (pres. El Paso 1962-63, Outstanding Club Pres. award 1965). Home: 4251 Ridgecrest El Paso TX 79902 Office: 6024 Gateway E El Paso TX 79905

JOHNSON, JAMES PETER, food service distbn. co. exec.; b. Milw., Aug. 15, 1941; s. Donald Kenneth and Evelyn (Miller) J.; B.S., U. Wis., 1964, postgrad., 1 1965-68; m. Phyllis McGeough, Aug. 5, 1972; children—Christopher, Alison. Sr. adminstrv. services Arthur Andersen & Co., Chgo., 1968-72; mgr. planning and fin. systems Booth Fisheries div. Consol. Foods, Chgo., 1972-77, sr. fin. analyst corp. staff, 1977-79, dir. fin. and adminstrv. planning frozen foods group, 1979-80; v.p., controller PYA/Monarch, Inc., Greenville, S.C., 1980—. Home: 404 Piney Grove Rd Greenville SC 29607 Office: PO Box 1569 Greenville SC 29602

JOHNSON, JAMES WARREN, communications co. exec. le Falls, N.Y., June 10, 1927; s. Emil Newton and Mary (Schuetz) J.; B.S., Fordham U., 1949, P.G., 1950, M.B.A., 1977; m. Florence Riccobono, Sept. 12, 1953; n—James, Marla, Michael, Margaret, Robert, Hillary, Victoria. Teaching fellow Syracuse U., 1950; TV technician CBS, 1950-64; prodn. coordinator Reeves Co., N.Y.C., 1964- engr., technician Videotape Center, N.Y.C., 1965-68; sales mgr. Technicolor Inc., N.Y.C., 1968-69; dir. mktg., prodn. services med. TV, TNT Communications Inc., N.Y.C., 1969-72; v.p. radio and TV, dir. med. edn. TV Wesson & Warhaftig Advt. Co., N.Y.C., 1972-73; v.p. Mgmt. TV Systems, N.Y.C., 1973-74; pres. TeleConcepts in Communications, N.Y.C., 1974—; panelist, speaker in field; cons. TV communications, imaging, networking. Vice chmn. bd. dirs. Georgian Ct. Coll.; active community youth and ch. activities. Served with USNR, 1945-46; PTO, China. Mem. Soc. Motion Picture, TV Engrs., Nat. Acad. TV Arts and Scis., World Future Soc., Health Sci. Communications Assn. (pres.-elect, dir.), Health Edn. Media Assn., Pharm. Advt. Club, Internat. Indsl. TV Assn., AAAS. Republican. Roman Catholic. Club: Vets of 7th Regt. Contbr. articles to trade publs. and newsletters. Home: 113 E 81st St New York NY 10028 Office: 145 E 49th St New York NY 10017

JOHNSON, JEH VINCENT, architect; b. Nashville, July 8, 1931; s. Charles Spurgeon and Marie Burguette J.; A.B., Columbia Coll., 1953; M. Arch., Columbia U., 1958; m. Norma E. Edelin, Dec. 28, 1956; children—Jeh Charles, Marguerite Marie. Designer, Paul R. Williams, Architect, Los Angeles, 1956, Adams & Woodbridge, Architects, N.Y.C., 1958-62; asso. William E. Gindele, Architect, Poughkeepsie, N.Y., 1962-71; pres. Gindele & Johnson, Architects, Poughkeepsie, 1971—; lectr. Vassar Coll., 1964—; trustee Poughkeepsie Savs. Bank, 1977—; chmn. N.Y. State Bd. for Architecture, 1979—. Served with U.S. Army, 1953-55. William Kinne Fellows traveling fellow, 1958. Fellow AIA; AAUP, Nat. Assn. Minority Architects, Sigma Pi Phi. Mason. Designer Newburgh Houses on Lake, 1971, Whitney M. Young Health Center, Albany, N.Y., 1974, St. Simeon Homes, Poughkeepsie, N.Y., 1972, Dutchess County (N.Y.) Mental Health Center, 1970, Lagrange (N.Y.) Town Hall, 1970. Office: 14 Edgehill Rd Wappingers Falls NY 12590

JOHNSON, JERRY LEE, banker; b. Kankakee, Ill., June 22, 1939; s. Kenneth C. and G. Irma (Palmer) J.; B.S., MacMurray Coll., 1961; grad. Pacific Coast Banking Sch., U. Wash., 1979; m. Linda L. Moody, July 21, 1977. Asst. mgr. Assos. Discount Corp., Springfield, Ill., Seattle, 1961-66; with Rainier Nat. Bank, Seattle, 1966—, asst. v.p., 1974—, credit examiner, 1978-81, asst. mgr. Mt. Vernon br., 1980—. Office: 420 1st St Mount Vernon WA 98273

JOHNSON, JOHN ALLEN, bus. exec.; b. Kansas City, Mo., Mar. 7, 1933; s. Thomas Eldon and Geraldine (Taylor) J.; student Harvard, 1951-53; B.B.A., U. Mo., 1958; m. Beverly Ann Williams, Aug. 22, 1953; children—Vicki (Mrs. Lee Reiswig), Sharon Ann, Jackie Jo. Staff asst. to asst. controller Farmland Industries, Kansas City, 1958-62; asst. controller, pump div. Colt Industries, Kansas City, 1962-64; controller BROS Inc., Mpls., 1964-67; v.p. mfg. Behavioral Research Labs., Palo Alto, Calif., 1967-73; sec.-treas. finance Berglund, Inc., Napa, Calif., 1973-76; owner Johnson's Fin. Services, Napa, 1976—; gen. mgr. Bay Valve Service, Martinez, Calif., 1977-78, Am. Elevator Co., 1978-79; v.p. fin. The Learning Line, Palo Alto, 1980—. Home: 2063 W Park Napa CA 94558

JOHNSON, JOHN H., editor, publisher; b. Arkansas City, Ark., Jan. 19, 1918; student U. Chgo., Northwestern U.; LL.D., Central State Coll., Shaw U., N.C. Coll., Benedict Coll., Carnegie-Mellon Inst., Morehouse Coll., N.C. A. and T. State U., Syracuse U., Eastern Mich. U., Hamilton Coll., Lincoln U., Malcolm X Coll., Upper Iowa Coll., Wayne State U., Pratt Inst.; m. Eunice Johnson; children—John Harold, Linda. Pres., pub. Johnson Pub. Co., Inc., Chgo. N.Y.C., Los Angeles, Washington, 1942—; pub., editor Ebony, Black Stars, Jet, Ebony Jr. mags.; pres. Sta. WJPC, Chgo., Fashion Fair Cosmetics, Chgo.; chmn., chief exec. officer Supreme Life Ins. Co., Chgo.; dir. Marina Bank, Chgo., Bell & Howell Co., Greyhound Corp., 20th Century-Fox Film Corp., Zenith Radio Corp. Mem. adv. council Harvard Grad. Sch. Bus.; trustee Boston U., Art Inst. Chgo. Named Outstanding Young Man U.S. Jaycees, 1951; recipient Horatio Alger award, 1966; John Russwurm award Nat. Newspaper Pubs. Assn., 1966, Spingarn medal NAACP, 1966, Henry Johnson Fisher award Mag. Pubs. Assn., 1971, Communicator of Year award U. Chgo. Alumni Assn., 1974, Columbia Journalism award, 1974; named to Acad. Disting. Entrepreneurs, Babson Coll., 1979. Fellow Sigma Delta Chi; mem. Mag. Pubs. Assn. Office: 820 S Michigan Ave Chicago IL 60605 also 1270 Ave of Americas New York NY 10020 also 1750 Pennsylvania Ave NW Washington DC 20006 also 3600 Wilshire Blvd Los Angeles CA 90005*

JOHNSON, JOHN LENEAL, investment banker; b. Seoul, Republic of S. Korea, Mar. 5, 1953; s. Robert Miles and Nan Yon (O), J.; A.B., Harvard, 1972; M.B.A., U. Pa., 1974; m. Kinda Kay McGaha,

Nov. 2, 1975; 1 son, Yale R. L. Mgmt. trainee, economist Atlantic Richfield Co., Phila., 1974; investment analyst Mellon Bank N.A., Pitts., 1975; asst. controller Macy's Co., San Francisco, 1975; pres., mng. partner John L. Johnson & Co., San Francisco, 1976—; exec. dir. U.S. Black C. of C., San Francisco, 1979-80; instr. bus. adminstrn. Chabot Coll.; dir. S. Bklyn. Manpower Corp. Woodrow Wilson fellow, 1972. Mem. Am. Mgmt. Assn., Nat. Urban League, NAACP, Golden State Bus. League, Assn. Former Intelligence Officers, San Francisco Black Bus. C. of C., Phi Beta Kappa. Roman Catholic. Clubs: San Francisco Tennis, Wharton Sch. (San Francisco); Harvard (N.Y.C.). Home: 1221 Kirkham St San Francisco CA 94122 Office: 414 Gough St Suite 3 San Francisco CA 94102

JOHNSON, JOSEPH ERNEST, educator; b. Raleigh, N.C., Jan. 24, 1942; s. Ernest Johnson; B.A., U. N.C., Chapel Hill, 1964; M.B.A., Ga. State U., 1966, D.B.A., 1969; m. Jane Young Woodbury, May 1963; children—Joseph Ernest, Jane, Cornelia, Llewellyn. Asst. prof. Ga. State U., 1968-69; asst. prof. bus. adminstrn. U. N.C., Greensboro, 1969-73, asso. prof., 1973-78, prof., 1978—, head dept. bus. adminstrn., 1975—, dir. continuing edn., dir. summer session, 1973-75, acting head dept. acctg., 1977-79; cons.; pres. N.C. Ins. Edn. Found., 1970—, bd. dirs., 1971—; bd. dirs., trustee Southeastern Ins. Inst., 1974—; bd. dirs. Ins. Inst. of Piedmont. Mem. adv. bd. St. Mary's Episcopal Student Center, 1972-74; bd. dirs. Better Bus. Bur. Central N.C., 1976-79; chmn. Central N.C. chpt. Nat. Multiple Sclerosis Soc., 1972-73; chmn. precinct 12 Guilford County Democratic Party. Mem. Am. Risk and Ins. Assn., So. Risk and Ins. Assn. (dir. 1979—), Risk and Ins. Mgmt. Soc., Ins. Co. Edn. Dirs. Soc., Ins. Soc. N.Y., Acad. Mgmt., Fin. Mgmt. Assn., Soc. Ins. Research, Greensboro C. of C., Beta Gamma Sigma, Delta Sigma Pi. Clubs: Rotary, Greensboro City. Author: Georgia Insurance Fact Book, 1969; Insurance Instruction in North Carolina Institutions of Higher Education, 1972; Insurance Rating Systems: An Analysis (with J. Finley Lee), 1974; (with Steven R. Strader) North Carolina Insurance Fact Book, 1976, rev. edit. (with Mary Elizabeth McSwain), 1978; Insurance Instruction in North Carolina Institutions of Higher Education, 1977-1978 (with Rosalie McGrane), 1979; contbr. articles to profl. jours. Home: 1128 Gridland Rd Greensboro NC 27408 Office: 366 Bus and Econs Bldg U NC Greensboro NC 27412

JOHNSON, JOSEPHINE A., ins. co. exec.; b. N.Y.C., May 26, 1938; s. Salvatore and Anna Ilardi; B.S. in Chemistry/Math. summa cum laude, St. John's U., 1958; M.B.A. with distinction, N.Y. U., 1975; m. James W. Johnson, Oct. 21, 1972; 1 dau., Leslie Ann. Various positions Shell Chem. Co., 1958-70; project mgr. analyst Equitable Life Ins. Co., N.Y.C., 1970-78, asst. v.p., 1978-80, v.p., dept. head, 1980—. Recipient awards Equitable Co., 1978. Club: Fortune 500 Women's. Office: 1285 6th Ave New York NY 10021*

JOHNSON, JOYCE MARIE BETTS, stockbroker, columnist; b. East Chicago, Ind., Jan. 18, 1938; d. Hobart and Mattie (Upshaw) Betts; B.S. magna cum laude, U. Md., 1976; m. Emmitt Johnson, July 6, 1959; children—Roderick, Terence. Tchr. shorthand Univ. Lang. Center, Taipei, Taiwan, 1963; adminstrv. asst. exec. sec. U.S. Army Intelligence, Munich, Germany, 1969-73; tchr. McArthur Jr. High Sch., Ft. Meade, Md., 1974-75; bus. mgr. The Reading Center, Gary, Ind., 1976-77; stockbroker A. G. Edwards Co., Merrillville, Ind., 1977—; columnist Info Newspaper, Gary, also Dollars & Sense mag. Bd. dirs. Women's Assn. NW Ind. Symphony Soc., 1978, Friends Lake County Library, 1978, N.W. Ind. Opera Theater; mem. adv. bd. Businesswomen's Ednl. Programs. Mem. Nat. Council Negro Women, AAUW (dir. Gary-Merrillville br. 1977—), Am. Soc. Women Accts., Nat. Soc. Registered Reps., League Black Women, Phi Kappa Phi, Alpha Sigma Lambda, Delta Sigma Theta. Club: Civitan. Office: 8300 Mississippi St Merrillville IN 46410

JOHNSON, KEITH LIDDELL, food products co. exec.; b. Darlington, U.K., July 22, 1939; s. Arthur Henry and Beatrice (Liddell) J.; came to U.S., 1948, naturalized, 1958; B.A., U. Mich., 1960; m. Margaret Elaine Meston, Aug. 29, 1959; children—Leslie Margaret, Kevin Liddell, Gregory Norman, Kathleen Elaine. Chem. technician Ajem Labs., Livonia, Mich., 1956-60; research chemist Swift & Co. Labs., Chgo., 1960-63, project mgr., 1963-67, group leader research and devel. center, Oak Brook, Ill., 1967-71, adminstrv. asst. to exec. v.p., Chgo., 1971-72, quality assurance mgr., refinery div. Swift Edible Oil Co., Chgo., 1972-73, corporate quality assurance mgr., 1973-74, quality assurance dir., 1974-77, group mgr. plant quality assurance Swift & Co., 1977-79, group mgr. processed food quality assurance, 1979—; mem. Chgo. Manpower Area Planning Com., 1971. Mem. Chgo. Chemists Club, Chem. Arts Forum Chgo. (v.p. 1980), Am. Chem. Soc., Am. Oil Chemists Soc., Am. Soc. Quality Control, Chgo. Jr. Assn. Commerce and Industry (dir. 1968, v.p. 1969, exec. v.p. 1970, pres. 1971), U.S. (dir. 1972), Ill. (v.p. 1972) jr. chambers commerce. Episcopalian. Contbr. articles in field to profl. jours. Holder 17 U.S. and 25 Fgn. patents. Home: Route 1 Box 68 Matteson IL 60443 Office: 115 W Jackson Blvd Chicago IL 60604

JOHNSON, KENNETH OSCAR, oil co. exec.; b. Center City, Minn., Apr. 11, 1920; s. Oscar W. and Sigrid M. (Hollsten) J.; B.S. in Chem. Engring., U. Minn., 1942; m. Apr. 18, 1945; 1 son, Eric W. With Exxon Corp., 1942—, refining engr., supr., 1942-55, mgr. supply planning, dir., pres. subs. Tuscarora Pipeline Co., 1955-61, mgr. supply purchase and exchange, 1961-69, heavy fuel mgr., 1969-71, wholesale fuels mktg. mgr., 1971-74, pres., chief exec. officer, Belcher Oil Co., Miami, 1974—; dir. S. E. 1st Nat. Bank, Miami, Petroleum Industry Research Found. Inc. Mem. Fla. State C. of C., Clubs: Miami, Bankers, Port Royal (Naples, Fla.). Patentee in field. Home: 845 Admiralty Parade Naples FL 33940 Office: 2050 Coral Way Miami FL 33145

JOHNSON, LARRY GLENN, banker; b. Tulsa, Oct. 14, 1945; s. GlennMarion and Muriel Louise Johnson; B.S., U. Tulsa, 1967; M.B.A., 1970; m. Sherryl Diann Kramer, June 17, 1972; children—Philip Glenn, Curtis Dean. Vice pres. Broken Arrow Fed. Savs. & Loan Assn. (Okla.), 1971-75, pres., 1976—, also dir. Supt., Sunday Sch., Owasso Assembly of God, 1976—; bd. dirs. Gatesway Found., Inc., 1980-81. Served with AUS, 1967-69. Conoco Oil scholar, 1965. Mem. Broken Arrow C. of C. (dir., treas. 1979, 80, 81, Citizen of Yr. award 1980), Savs. and Loan Assns. Okla. (sec., dir. 1979, dir., pres. 1981). Clubs: Mensa, Gideons Internat., Rotary. Office: 311 S Main St PO Box 637 Broken Arrow OK 74012

JOHNSON, LAWRENCE WALDMAN, utility co. exec.; b. Los Angeles, Sept. 1, 1942; s. Mark Meehan and Joyce Sallie (Waldman) J.; student USAF Air U., 1960-62; m. Patricia Ann LaFace, Apr. 20, 1969; children—Shane Christopher, Joshue Alan, Bret Joseph, Jodie-Marie, Lawrence Waldman, Jr. Archtl. draftsman Lundean & Assos., Los Angeles, 1958-59; sales engr. Fibco Plaxtics, Buena Park, Calif., 1962; analyst So. Calif. Edison, Los Angeles, 1962—. Scoutmaster Walter Knott council Boy Scouts Am., Cypress, Calif., 1970-74, explorer post adv. Ventura (Calif.) council, 1979-81. Served with USAF, 1959-62. Mem. Pacific Coast Electric Assn., Nat. Rifle Assn., Republican. Mormon (leader). Home: 1876 Pelican St Ventura CA 93003 Office: 10060 Telegraph Ventura CA 93003

JOHNSON, LLOYD PETER, banker; b. Mpls., May 1, 1930; s. Lloyd Percy and Edna (Schlampp) J.; B.A., Carleton Coll., Northfield, Minn., 1952; M.B.A., Stanford U., 1954; m. Rosalind Gesner, July 3, 1954; children—Marcia, Russell, Paul. With Security Trust & Savs. Bank, San Diego, 1954-57; with Security Pacific Nat. Bank, Los Angeles, 1957—, sr. v.p. Northwestern div. adminstrn., 1970-72, exec. v.p., head No. Calif. adminstrn., 1972-76, exec. v.p. charge corp. banking, 1976-78, vice chmn., mem. office chief exec., 1978—; mem. faculty Pacific Coast Banking Sch., 1969-72; instr. acctg. Am. Inst. Bankers, 1959. Trustee, Harvey Mudd Coll., Carleton Coll.; regent emeritus U. San Francisco; adv. bd. U. Wash. Grad. Sch. Bus. Served with U.S. Army, 1955-56. Mem. Calif. Bankers Assn. (pres. 1977-78), Assn. Res. City Bankers. Republican. Episcopalian. Clubs: Family, Calif., Pacific Union, San Francisco Golf, Los Angeles Golf. Home: 206 Inverness Dr Flintridge CA 91011 Office: 333 S Hope St Los Angeles CA 90071

JOHNSON, LOY YATES, JR., textile broker; b. Spartanburg County, S.C., Jan. 12, 1937; s. Loy Yates and Fannie Aline (Eden) J.; B.A., Furman U., 1959; m. Anna Margaret Dean, Aug. 6, 1966; children—Loy Yates III, Margaret Eden, John Edward, Wesley Miller Camp. Sales rep. Milliken Yarn, 1960-62; with Stowe Spinning Co., Belmont, N.C., 1962-63; founder, broker Yates Johnson & Co., Inc., Spartanburg, S.C., 1963—, pres., 1980—. Chmn. Explorer Scouts, Palmetto council Boy Scouts Am., 1970; maj. div. United Way, Spartanburg, 1980. Mem. Am. Textile Mfrs. Inst., Carolina Yarn Assn. Republican. Episcopalian. Clubs: Rotary, Alston Wilkes Soc., Piedmont, Country of Spartanburg, SAR. Home: 120 Hillbrook Dr Spartanburg SC 29302 Office: PO Box 2482 300 Hillcrest Offices Spartanburg SC 29304

JOHNSON, MALCOLM CLOUD, utilities co. exec.; b. Columbia, S.C., Mar. 27, 1919; s. Malcolm Cloud and Vineta (Ackerman) J.; B.E.E., Clemson U., 1939; m. Velva Jo Coyle, Oct. 15, 1943; children—Susan, Malcolm, Robert. With S.C. Electric & Gas Co., Columbia, 1939—, v.p. electric system ops., transmission, distbn., 1968-70, v.p., group exec. spl. services and purchasing, 1977—. Served to capt. Signal Corps, AUS, 1941-46. Registered profl. engr., S.C. Mem. IEEE (sr.; past chmn. S.C. chpt.), Edison Electric Inst. (chmn. elec. system and equipment com. 1977-78), Electric Power Research Inst. (chmn. rotating elec. machinery task force 1975-78, mem. system adv. bd. 1975-78), S.C., Columbia chambers commerce. Methodist. Clubs: Columbia Country, Palmetto, Kiwanis. Home: 4700 Wrenwood Ln Columbia SC 29206 Office: 328 Main St Columbia SC 29218

JOHNSON, MAXINE CHAMPAGNE, economist, educator; b. Oketo, Kans., Mar. 30, 1925; d. Cedric Boyd and Victoria A. (Keck) Champagne; B.A., Washington State U., 1948; M.A., U. Mont., 1952; m. Manford E. Johnson, Dec. 27, 1947; 1 son, Kurt Boyd. Research asst. Bur. of Econ. and Bus. Research, Washington State U., Pullman, 1948-49; research asso. U. Mont., Missoula, 1950-72, dir. Bur. of Bus. and Econ. Research, 1972—, prof. of mgmt., 1975—; dir. Mont. Power Co., Butte, 1975—, 1st Bank Western Mont., Missoula, 1973—; chmn. Bd. of Investments, State of Mont., 1974-77. Mem. Gov.'s Commn. on the Status of Women, State of Mont., 1969-71; mem. Sec. of Agr. Advisory Com. on Multiple Use of Nat. Forests, 1967-68. Mem. AAUW, Assn. for U. Bus. and Econ. Research (pres. 1972), Phi Beta Kappa. Contbr. numerous articles on econs. to profl. publs. Home: 3717 Creekwood Rd Missoula MT 59801 Office: Univ of Montana Missoula MT

JOHNSON, MORRIS ARTHUR, chem. co. exec.; b. Wellington, Kans., May 26, 1938; s. Richard William and Doris Loretta (Palmer) J.; B.S. in Chemistry, U. Kans., 1960; M.A. in Organic Chemistry, U. Calif., Santa Barbara, 1967; m. Marion Monika Schaefer, June 18, 1965; children—Mark Alexander, Stephanie Alice. Mem. research and devel. staff Continental Oil Co., Ponca City, Okla., 1968-77; with consumer products research div. Am. Cyanamid Co., Clifton, N.J., 1977—, group leader household products devel., 1977—. Adviser Okla. Teenage Republicans Fedn., 1973-76; vice chmn. Okla. Young Reps. Fedn., 1976-77; v.p. Ramsey (N.J.) Rep. Club, 1978-79. Served with U.S. Army, 1960-64. Mem. Chem. Specialties Mfrs. Assn. (sci. com.), ASTM. Republican. Methodist. Contbr. articles to profl. jours.; patentee in field of electrochemistry. Home: 101 Summit Ave Ramsey NJ 07446 Office: Am Cyanamid Co 697 Route 46 Clifton NJ 07015

JOHNSON, PAUL H., banker; b. New Haven, Oct. 26, 1936; s. Harold R. and Esther L. J.; B.A., Brown U., 1958; J.D., U. Conn., 1966; postgrad. Harvard, 1971; m. Gwendolyn Davies, Aug. 4, 1962; children—Kirsten, Philip, Peter. Admitted to Conn. bar, 1966; pres., chief exec. officer Conn. Savs. Bank, New Haven, 1971—; v.p., sec. 1st. Bank, New Haven, 1961-71; dir. Cooper Thermometer Co., Middlesex Assurance Co., New Haven Water Co., So. Conn. Gas Co., Long Wharf Theatre. Chmn. Campaign for Yale, Emergency Med. Services, State of Conn., 1976—; dir. Mut. Investment Fund Conn. Bd. dirs. Brown U. Served with USNR, 1958-61. Named outstanding young man of yr., New Haven and Conn. jr. chambers commerce, 1971. Mem. Am., Conn. bar assns. Clubs: Mory's Assn., New Haven Lawn, Quinnipiack, Landmark. Home: Andrews Rd/Leete's Island Guilford CT 06437 Office: Conn Savs Bank 47 Church St New Haven CT 06510

JOHNSON, PHILIP EDWARD, health ins. co. exec.; b. Jersey City, Dec. 2, 1918; s. Robert J. and Katherine (Davis) J.; B.S. in Bus. Adminstrn., Duquesne U., 1941; m. Ann Marie Ely, Apr. 15, 1944; children—Kathleen Marie, Philip Edward, Richard Joseph, Edward George, Anna Marie, James Michael, David Michael. Sr. accountant Scovill Wellington & Co., Phila., 1946-48; sr. accountant Price, Waterhouse & Co., Pitts., 1948-53; with Blue Cross of Western Pa., Pitts., 1954—, now sr. v.p., treas.; v.p., treas., dir. Standard Property Corp., Madison Realty Corp., Jacsan Inc. Mem. accounting com. Gov.'s Hosp. Study Commn., Commonwealth of Pa., 1963-71. Bd. dirs., chmn. Central Blood Bank, Pitts., 1964—. Served to capt. Ordnance Corps., AUS, 1941-46. C.P.A. Mem. Hosp. Financial Mgmt. Assn., Am. Mmgt. Assn., Duquesne U. Alumni Assn., Financial Execs. Inst. Republican. Roman Catholic. K.C. Home: 716 Pinetree Rd Pittsburgh PA 15243 Office: 1 Smithfield St Pittsburgh PA 15222

JOHNSON, RAY ARVIN, constrn. co. exec.; b. Long Prairie, Minn., May 2, 1920; s. Walter David and Rosalind (Hesser) J.; student Iowa State U., 1942, U. Minn., 1948-51; spl. courses Coll. William and Mary, 1969; m. Kay Meredith Durbahn, May 14, 1960; children—Sherry Kay, Diane Rosalind, Laura Faye. Partner, Johnson Constrn. Co., Litchfield, Minn., 1941—, project mgr. hwy. constrcts, 1951-58, contracts, estimator, claims negotiations, 1955-73, mgr. planning and devel., 1957-59; co-founder, dir. Johnson Bros. Corp. (formerly Johnson Bros. Hwy. & Heavy Constructors, Inc.), Litchfield, 1959—, v.p., 1959-67, sr. v.p., 1968-72, chmn. bd., 1973—, mgr. bridge div., 1960-63, mgr. underground utilities div., 1961-67, 69-72, Western div. mgr., 1967-69, mgr. labor relations, 1970-77; instr. equipment mgmt. Mankato State Coll., 1975-76. Mem. nat. joint task force Asso. Gen. Contractors Am. and U.S. Bur. Reclamation, 1969-78; mem. joint task force com. Asso. Gen. Contractors Minn. and Minn. Hwy. Dept., 1971—; mgmt. trustee Joint Trusteed Funds for mgmt. health, welfare and pension funds Asso. Gen. Contractors Minn. and Minn. Teamsters Constrn. Unions, 1970—; mem. Asso. Gen. Contractors Minn. for Statewide Labor Negotiations for Hwy. and Heavy Constrn. Industry, 1970-78. Commr., City of Minnetonka Park Bd., 1973-75. Served with USNR, 1942-45. Mem. Soc. for Preservation and Encourgement of Barbershop Quartet Singing in Am., Caballeros del Norte, East Africa Wild Life Soc., Asso. Gen. Contractors Minn. (chmn. hwy. force account com. 1970—, chmn. equipment value recovery rate schedule com. 1971—, hwy. dir. 1973-74, v.p. hwy. div. 1974), Regional Congress Constrn. Employers Minn. (dir. 1973-75), Asso. Gen. Contractors Am. (nat. heavy dir. 1973-74, nat. municipal-utilities dir. 1973—, equipment expense com. 1974—). Lutheran. Mason (32 deg., Shriner). Home: 2227 Platwood Rd Minnetonka MN 55343 Office: PO Box Box 1002 Litchfield MN 55355

JOHNSON, RICHARD CAMPBELL, mfg. co. exec.; b. Boise, Idaho, July 25, 1946; s. Richard Mercer and Jeanette (Campbell) J.; B.A., Franklin and Marshall Coll., Lancaster, Pa., 1968; M.B.A. with high honors, Notre Dame U., 1970; m. Elizabeth Jayne Roth, Mar. 29, 1969; children—Vaughan, Brinlea. Dir. fin. aid and admissions Lenoir Rhyne Coll., also Woodrow Wilson adminstrv. intern, 1970-71; sr. cons. Touche Ross & Co., C.P.A.'s, Phila., 1971-75; dir. fin. plans and presentations Rockwell Internat. Co., Pitts., 1976-78, dir. strategic planning, gen. industries ops., 1978—; dir. K.J. Lesker Co., Pitts. Mem. audit com. Fox Chapel (Pa.) Episcopal Ch. C.P.A., Pa. Mem. Am. Inst. C.P.A.'s, Pa. Inst. C.P.A.'s. Republican. Club: Fox Chapel Racquet. Home: 80 Quail Hill Ln Pittsburgh PA 15238 Office: 400 N Lexington Ave Pittsburgh PA 15208

JOHNSON, RICHARD EDWIN, employee benefits brokerage co. exec.; b. Tacoma, Aug. 29, 1945; s. Edwin Richard and Paula Irene (Gebo) J.; B.A. in History, Pacific Lutheran U., Tacoma, 1970; m. Kendall Dawn Yeagle, Apr. 19, 1974; children—Dawn Elaine, Kathryn June. Owner, Health Au Naturel, health foods, Tacoma, 1972-73; account rep. Pacific N.W. Bell Telephone Co., 1974-75; dir. mktg. Wash. Physicians Service, Seattle, 1976-78; account exec. William M. Mercer Co., Seattle, 1978—; lectr. nutrition, 1972-76; chmn. Western Conf. Prepaid Med. Service Plans, 1977; condr. seminars. Mem. Sales and Mktg. Execs. Internat. (membership chmn. Seattle 1977-78), Anchorage C. of C., Seattle C. of C., Internat. Found. Employee Benefit Plans, N.W. Health-Welfare-Pension Adminstrs., Employee Benefits Planning Assn., U.S. Handball Assn., Smithsonian Assos. Republican. Lutheran. Clubs: Wash. Athletic (Seattle), Elks. Home: 5011 91st Ave SE Mercer Island WA 98040 Office: Norton Bldg Seattle WA 98104

JOHNSON, ROBERT ALBERT, communications systems engr.; b. Phila., Dec. 10, 1946; s. Burton Kendall and Doris Radcliff (Neely) J.; B.S., Pa. State U., 1968; M.E., Widener U., 1978; m. Suzanne Ella Kemberling, July 26, 1969; children—Graham Robert, Tamara Lynn. Simulation engr. Boeing Vertol Co., Ridley Twp., Pa., 1968-72, flying qualities engr., 1973-74; systems project engr. Scott Paper Co., Chester, Pa., 1974-79, sr. systems engr., 1979—; cons. Pres. bd. trustees Hancock United Meth. Ch., 1977-79. Republican. Home: 100 Ashbrook Ln Aston PA 19014 Office: Front and Ave of the States Chester PA 19013

JOHNSON, ROBERT ARTHUR, mfg. co. exec.; b. Avalon, Pa., Jan. 29, 1917; s. Edward A. and Maude Elsie (Kipp) J.; B.S., U. Pitts., 1938; m. Mary Catherine Foley, Apr. 26, 1943; children—Carol Smith, Robert Arthur, Richard, Mary Kipp Delbyck, Donald, Susanne. With Rockwell Mfg. Co., Pitts., 1939-73, pres. Valve div., 1969-73; corp. v.p., gen. mgr. Carter Carburetor div. ACF Industries, St. Louis, 1973—; chmn. bd. dirs. Carter Weber Inc., 1980—, Carter Precision Inc., 1978-80. Bd. dirs. St. Louis Commerce and Growth Assn., 1979—. Served with USN, 1944-46. Mem. Motor and Equipment Mfrs. Assn. (dir. 1979—), Automotive Pres. Council (chmn. 1980—). Clubs: Old Warson Country, Red Run Golf, Saint Louis, Innesbrook Resort. Address: 9666 Olive St Rd Saint Louis MO 63132

JOHNSON, ROBERT EDWARD, transp. and agrl. equipment co. exec.; b. Austin, Tex., July 26, 1935; s. Robert Edward and Irene Laura (Neese) J.; B.B.A., Southwestern U., Georgetown, Tex., 1957; postgrad. U. Houston; m. Dianne Davenport, Apr. 18, 1959; children—Lisa Carol, Robert Scott. Pres., Internat. Harvester of P.R., Inc., San Juan, 1973-75; mgr. export sales Internat. Harvester Co. Gt. Britain Ltd., London, 1975-77; regional mgr. for Asia Pacific, Internat. Harvester Co., Singapore, 1977-78; pres., mng. dir. Internat. Harvester Macleod, Inc., Manila, 1978—. Pres., Internat. Little League Assn. Manila, Inc., 1979-80; vestry Holy Trinity Ch., 1979-80. Served with USAR, 1958. Mem. Truck Mfrs. Assn. Philippines (v.p.), Am. Assn. of Philippines, Am. C. of C. Philippines. Republican. Clubs: Manila Polo, Nichols Golf; Rotary (Manila). Home: 1606 Dasmarinas Village Makati Metro Manila Philippines Office: Internat Harvester Macleod Inc 744 Romualdez Ermita Manila Philippines*

JOHNSON, ROBERT EDWARD, lawyer, communications co. exec.; b. Louisville, Aug. 15, 1927; s. Arthur M. and Maybelle A. Johnson; J.D., U. Louisville, 1952; m. Mary Lou Schickli, Apr. 11, 1953; children—Michael, Douglas, Stephan. Admitted to Ky. bar; practiced in Louisville, 1953-57; pres.Central Ky. Broadcasters Corp., Georgetown, 1957—, Georgetown Cable TV Corp., 1973—. Served with USCG, 1945-48. Mem. Ky. Bar Assn., Ky. Cable TV Assn. (pres. 1980). Office: Iron Works Rd Georgetown KY 40324

JOHNSON, ROBERT MONTAGUE, direct mktg. exec.; b. Wytheville, Va., Apr. 22, 1946; s. Robert Eley and Jane Buffin (Powell) J.; B.A., Davidson Coll., 1968; M.B.A., U. Va., 1970; m. Sherry Lynn Bledsoe, Aug. 5, 1977; 1 son, Bramley Powell. Mktg. rep. Data Processing div. IBM, Denver, 1970-72; v.p. Independence Investment Co., Denver, 1972-74; nat. mktg. mgr. Dusco, Inc., Dallas, 1974-77; exec. v.p. Nat. Demographics Ltd., Denver, 1977—, also dir. Co-dir. WCT United Bank Tennis Classic, 1973; fundraiser Colo. Heritage Center, 1976. Lic. real estate broker, Colo. Mem. Direct Mail Mktg. Assn., Denver Hist. Soc., Denver Art Mus. Episcopalian. Clubs: Denver Tennis, Arapahoe Tennis, Denver, The Hundred (Denver); Princeton (N.Y.C.). Office: 1624 Market St Denver CO 80202

JOHNSON, RODERICK GERARD, pharm. co. exec.; b. Aruba, Netherlands Antilles, May 30, 1949; came to U.S., 1956, naturalized, 1967; s. Arthur Chester and Anna Burnadena (Sloteridijk) J.; B.S. in Elec. Engring., U. Houston, 1971; M.B.A. (fellowship, research asst. 1971-73), Tulane U., 1973; m. Pamela Ann Szymski, Sept. 8, 1979. With Baxter Travenol Labs., Inc., 1974—, mgr. domestic treasury ops., Deerfield, Ill., 1978-79, asst. treas.-internat., 1979—. Served as 1st lt. USAR, 1974. C.P.A., Ill. Mem. Inst. Mgmt. Acctg., Eta Kappa Nu, Beta Alpha Psi. Roman Catholic. Home: 1532 Walters Ave Northbrook IL 60062 Office: 1 Baxter Pkwy Deerfield IL 60015

JOHNSON, ROGER WAYNE, computer co. exec.; b. Hartford, Conn., June 24, 1934; s. Reinhold P. and Evelyn W. (Webster) J.; B.B.A., Clarkson Coll. Tech., 1956; M.B.A., U. Mass., 1962; Litt.D. (hon.), Peralta Coll., 1973; m. Janice Mary Rowlands, Aug. 11, 1956; children—Mary L., Eric R., Daniel W. With Gen. Electric Co., 1956-69; v.p. ops. Singer Co., San Leandro, Calif., 1969-74; v.p., gen.

mgr. Memorex Inc., Santa Clara, Calif., 1974-78; pres. Products Group, System Devel. Corp., Santa Monica, Calif., 1978-80; v.p., group exec. Office Systems Group, Burroughs Corp., Danbury, Conn., 1980—. Gen. mgmt. cons. project bus. tchr. Jr. Achievement, 1979; chmn. Lanesboro (Mass.) Sch. Com., 1962-64. Republican. Home: 325 Arno Way Pacific Palisades CA 90272 Office: 30 Main St Danbury CT

JOHNSON, ROGERS BRUCE, chem. co. exec.; b. Boston, Apr. 8, 1928; s. Rogers Bruce and Dorothy Squires (Aiken) J.; B.A., Harvard U., 1949, M.B.A., 1955; m. Margery Ruth Howe, June 25, 1951; children—Wynn, Carol, Stephen, Herrick. With Dow Chem. Co., 1957—, U.S. area styrenic bus. mgr., Midland, Mich., 1965-70, corp. product dir. splty. products, 1970-76, v.p. U.S. area supply, distbn., planning, 1976-80, group v.p. U.S. area, 1980—, dir. Dow Can., 1973-76, Dow Pacific, 1973-76. Mem. operating bd. Midland Community Tennis Center, 1974—, pres., 1976, 77. Served with USAF, 1951-53. Decorated Bronze Star medal. Republican. Office: Dow Chem Co 2020 Dow Center Midland MI 48640

JOHNSON, ROLLAND CHARLES, mortgage banking co. exec.; b. Omaha, May 22, 1942; s. Carl Otto and Doris Matilda (Anderson) J.; B.S., U. Nebr., 1965; m. Lynn Virgie Pacey, Aug. 21, 1964; children—Tami Lynn, Mark Charles. With Western Securities Co., Omaha, 1963-79, asst. v.p., 1968-72, v.p., 1972-77, exec. v.p., 1977-79; dir. Multiple Listing Service, 1973-75, v.p., 1975; pres., chief exec. officer BI Mortgage Co., 1979—. Mem. Nebr. Mortgage Assn. (pres. 1975), Mortgage Bankers Assn. Am., Am. Mgmt. Assn., Am. Assn. Mortgage Underwriters, Omaha Assn. Independent Ins. Agents, Nat. Assn. Review Appraisers, Nebr. Realtors Assn., Sales and Mktg. Execs. of the Midlands, Omaha C. of C., Fontenelle Forest Assn. Republican. Lutheran. Clubs: Omaha Field, Omaha, Ak-Sar-Ben. Home: Box 180 Rural Route 5 Omaha NE 68112

JOHNSON, STANLEY ROBERT, contract adminstr.; b. Lancaster, Pa., Oct. 20, 1942; s. Robert Edward and Louise Jane (Pierce) J.; A.S., Harrisburg Area Community Coll., 1966; B.S. cum laude, Jacksonville U., 1967; M.B.A., Shippensburg State Coll., 1980; m. Mary Ann Hartman, Dec. 16, 1967. Systems analyst Sperry-Univac, Harrisburg, Pa., 1967-68, sales rep., 1968-74; contract analyst AMP, Inc., Harrisburg, 1974-75, mgr. group adminstrv. services, 1975-78, div. pricing adminstr., 1978-80, corp. contract adminstr., 1980-81, mgr. corp. contracts and pricing, 1981—. Served with USNR, 1961-65. Mem. Am. Legion. Democrat. Presbyterian. Office: PO Box 3608 Harrisburg PA 17105

JOHNSON, STEVEN GREG, educator; b. Lafayette, La., Sept. 7, 1950; s. William Chester and Anna Louise (Ahrens); J.; B.S. in Bus. Econs., Northwestern State U. La., 1973; Ph.D. in Econs., La. Tech. U., 1981; m. Connie Jane Sanders, May 24, 1975. Part-time instr. La. Tech. U., Ruston, 1974-76; mem. faculty Cameron U., Lawton, Okla., 1977—, asst. prof. fin., 1977—; pvt. practice investment counseling, 1978—; fin. cons. to various businessess, 1978—; pres. S.W. Bus. Consultants, Inc., 1981—. Mem. Fin. Mgmt. Assn., Southwestern Fin. Assn., Omicron Delta Epsilon. Republican. Baptist. Home: 4905 Dover Dr Lawton OK 73501 Office: 2800 W Gore Blvd Lawton OK 73505

JOHNSON, THOMAS FRANK, economist; b. Lynchburg, Va., Sept. 27, 1920; s. Thomas Frank and Inez (McDaniel) J.; student Lynchburg Coll., 1939-41; B.A., U. Va., 1943, M.A., 1947, Ph.D., 1949; m. Margaret Ann Emhardt, Dec. 29, 1951; children—Thomas Emhardt, Sarah Lee, William Harrison Johnson. Economist, U. S. Dept. Agr., Washington, 1949-51, U.S. C. of C., 1951-54; asst. commr. FHA, 1954-58; dir. legislative analysis Am. Enterprise Inst. for Pub. Policy Research, Washington, 1958-59, dir. research, 1960-76, dir. econ. policy studies, 1976—; mem. faculty Continuing Edn. Center, U. Va. and George Mason U. Sec.-treas. The Inst. for Social Sci. Research, Washington. Bd. dirs. Alexandria Hosp., 1965-71; adv. com. Va. Urban Assistance Incentive Fund. Served to lt. USNR, 1943-45, PTO; lt. comdr. Res. Mem. Am., Western, So., Royal econ. assns., Nat. Tax Assn., Am. Finance Assn., Nat. Assn. Bus. Economists. Episcopalian. Club: Cosmos. Contbr. articles to profl. publs. Home: 1113 N Gaillard St Alexandria VA 22304 Office: 1150 17th St NW Washington DC 20036

JOHNSON, THOMAS NELSON PAGE, JR., investment banker; b. Farmville, Va., Mar. 2, 1918; s. Thomas Page and Elizabgth Rebecca (Robertson) J.; grad. Woodberry Forest Sch., 1937; B.A., U. Va., 1946; m. Helen Elizabeth Smith, July 7, 1942; children—Mary Parke, Thomas Nelson Page III, Elizabeth Anne, Helen, James. Asst. supt. leaf dept. Export Leaf Tobacco, Richmond, Va., 1944-47; mgr. Eastern Bldg. Supply Co., Norfolk, Va., 1947-50; pres. North Linkhorn Devel. Corp., 1950-58; account exec. Anderson & Strudwick, 1958-60; sales mgr. Scott and Stringfellow, Richmond, Va., 1960-62; br. mgr. Anderson & Strudwick, Virginia Beach, Va., 1962-63; v.p. Investment Corp. Va., Norfolk, 1963-76; sr. v.p., dir. Davenport Co. Va., 1976—; former gen. partner Coriva Assos.; dir. Wythe Corp. Va. Ventures, Inc. Trustee, past mem. exec. com. Student Aid Found. U. Va., past chmn. athletic adv. com. Served as pilot, 1st lt. USAAF, 1941-43. Mem. Raven Soc., Financial Analyst Soc., Soc. Descs. of Signer Declaration of Independence, Jamestowne Soc., Bond Club Va. (past pres., gov.), Phi Gamma Delta. Clubs: Princess Anne Country (past dir.) (Virginia Beach, Va.); Country of Va., Bull and Bear (Richmond); Farmington Country (Charlottesville); Harbor, Virginia (Norfolk). Home: 400 51st St Virginia Beach VA 23451 Office: 311 Ross Bldg Richmond VA 23219

JOHNSON, THOMAS STEPHEN, banker; b. Racine, Wis., Nov. 19, 1940; s. H. Norman and Jane Agnes (McAvoy) J.; A.B. in Econs., Trinity Coll., 1962; M.B.A. with distinction, Harvard U., 1964; m. Margaret Ann Werner, Apr. 18, 1970; children—Thomas P., Scott M., Margaret A. Coordinator, instr. Master of Bus. Program, Ateneo de Manila U., 1964-66; spl. asst. to controller U.S. Dept. of Def., Washington, 1966-69; exec. v.p. Treasury div. Chem. Bank, N.Y.C., 1969—. Bd. dirs. Union Theol. Sem., Trinity Coll. Club N.Y., Yard Sch. of Art, N.J. Theatre Found. Mem. Fin. Execs. Inst. Clubs: Wall St., Trinity Coll. (N.Y.C.); Montclair (N.J.) Golf. Author: (with others) Condominium—Housing of the Future, 1964. Office: 20 Pine St New York NY 10005

JOHNSON, VERNON ARTHUR, ret. aircraft mfg. co. exec.; b. Heavener, Okla., Dec. 15, 1914; s. Arthur and Lillian Bell (Bradley) J.; A.B., U. Calif., 1936; grad. Advanced Mgmt. Program, Harvard, 1963; m. Dorothy Lee Thompson, June 18, 1939; children—Brian A., Curtis B., Shirley L. (Mrs. Joseph E. Henderson). Asst. mgr. San Bernardino (Calif.) C. of C., 1937-38, mgr., Redlands, Calif., 1939-40, Bakersfield, 1941-42; staff assembly div. Lockheed Aircraft Corp., 1943, asst. pub. relations mgr., 1944-47, staff Washington office, asst. to pres., 1948-54, Washington mgr., 1954-58, v.p. Eastern region, 1958-72, sr. v.p. Eastern region, 1972-74, sr. adviser, 1974-79. Trustee Palm Beach-Martin County Med. Center. Clubs: Aero (pres. 1953), Congressional Country (v.p. 1957-58), Burning Tree (pres. 1970-71) (Washington); Turtle Creek (pres. 1977-78) (Tequesta, Fla.). Home: 14 Turtle Creek Dr Tequesta FL 33458

JOHNSON, WALLACE DEVON, investment banker; b. Etna Green, Ind., July 15, 1926; s. Devoe Ward and Pauline Magdalene (Burgh) J.; B.A., Lake Forest Coll., 1950; m. Barbara Mary Smail, June 6, 1950 (div.); children—Anne J. (Mrs. James W. East, Jr.), Mary S. (Mrs. Robert Salzarulo), Joseph S. With Baker, Walsh & Co., Chgo., 1950-52, Farwell Chapman & Co., Chgo., 1952-60; partner David A. Noyes & Co., Chgo., 1960-64; pres. Howe, Barnes & Johnson, Inc., Chgo., from 1965, now chmn. emeritus. Bd. commrs. Chgo. Transit Authority, 1970-76; mem. adv. bd. high speed ground transp. Fed. R.R. Commn., U.S. Dept. Transp., 1973-77. Del., Republican Nat. Conv., 1964. Bd. dirs., pres., mem. finance com. Home for Destitute Crippled Children, 1966-78; trustee, mem. exec., athletic and student affairs com. Lake Forest Coll.; bd. dirs., treas., fin. cons. Scottish Rite Cathedral Assn., Chgo. Valley; bd. dirs., chmn. investment com. Presbyn. Home, Evanston, Ill.; trustee, chmn. bd. Indiana Soc. Chgo. mem. exec. com. of adv. bd. Salvation Army; mem. citizens bd., council of Salvation Army's Booth Meml. Hosp.; mem. citizens bd., finance com. Ill. Masonic Med. Center; mem. trustees com. on hosps. and clinics U. Chgo. Served with USNR, 1944-46. Recipient Disting. Service citation Lake Forest Coll., 1975. Mem. Chgo. Assn. Stock Exchange Firms (chmn. 1970-71), Securities Industry Assn. (chmn. exec. com. Mid-Continental dist. 1977). Mason (Shriner, 33 deg.), Rotarian (pres. Rotary One 1976). Clubs: Bond (sec., dir. 1969-70), University, Attic, Quadrangle (Chgo.). Author articles on transp. Home: 111 E Chestnut St 56-D Chicago IL 60611 Office: 135 S LaSalle St Chicago IL 60603

JOHNSON, WALTER HENRY, bus. cons.; b. Norwalk, Conn., Aug. 17, 1920; s. Henry Louis and Edith Andrietta (Young) J.; B.Aero. Engring., N.Y. U., 1942, M.S. in Meteorology, 1943; postgrad. Johns Hopkins U., 1946-48; m. Edith Elizabeth Havey, July 7, 1945; children—David Manning, Thomas Perry. Instr. synoptic meteorology N.Y. U., N.Y.C., 1943; aero. engr., ballistics research lab. U.S. Army, Aberdeen, Md., 1946-48; various positions IBM, N.Y.C., and White Plains, N.Y., 1948-61, mgr. govt., edn. and med. mktg., N.Y.C. and Washington, 1961-70, asst. to v.p. fed. mktg. and cons. fed. bus. relations, Washington, 1971-79; cons. govt. relations, Washington, 1979—; dir. Comml. and Savs. Bank, Winchester, Va. Bd. dirs. Grafton Sch.; pres., chmn. bd. Grafton Corp., 1977, 78, 79. Served to capt. USAAF, 1941-46. Methodist. Clubs: Univ. (N.Y.C.); Winter Harbor Yacht. Home: Stubblefield Farm Berryville VA 22611 Office: 1801 K St NW 12th Floor Washington DC 20006

JOHNSON, WALTER J., publisher; b. July 29, 1912; ed. U. Heidelberg, U. Paris à la Sorbonne, U. Coll., London; Sc.D. (hon.), Albany Med. Coll., 1978; m. Thekla E. Johnson; 3 children. Founder, pres. Walter J. Johnson, Inc., N.Y.C. and London, Eng., 1942—; founder, pres. Acad. Press (merged with Harcourt Brace Jovanovich 1969), N.Y.C. and London, 1942-72, Johnson Reprint Corp. (became subsidiary Acad. Press 1967), 1946-72; dir. Harcourt Brace Jovanovich, 1979—. Trustee Albany (N.Y.) Med. Coll. Served with NG, 1941-44. Fellow Pierpont Morgan Library; mem. ALA, Am. Med. Library Assn., Friends Columbia U. Club: Grolier (N.Y.C.). Home: 19 Hewitt Ave Bronxville NY 10708 Office: 355 Chestnut St Norwood NJ 07648

JOHNSON, WAYNE CARL, municipal govt. ofcl., real estate cons.; b. Iron Mountain, Mich., June 3, 1937; s. Emil S. and Elna M. (Anderson) J.; B.S., Eastern Mich. U., 1966; m. Janet A. Lindquist, June 29, 1957; 1 son, Douglas W. Real property appraiser City of Ann Arbor (Mich.), 1960-63, dep. property tax assessor, 1963-68, city property tax assessor, 1968—; pvt. practice real estate cons., Ann Arbor, 1970—; guest lectr. U. Mich., Washtenaw Community Coll. Designated CRA (certified rev. appraiser), Nat. Assn. Rev. Appraisers; Level IV Assessor, State Assessors' Bd. Mem. Mich., Southeastern Mich. assessors' assns., Internat. Assn. Assessing Officers (pres., past exec. bd., designated CAE—certified assessment evaluator, recipient citation by exec. bd. 1977), Soc. Real Estate Appraisers (past pres. Washtenaw chpt., designated SRA—sr. residential appraiser). Lutheran. Home: 1815 Ivywood Ann Arbor MI 48103 Office: 100 N 5th Ave Ann Arbor MI 48104

JOHNSON, WILLIAM ARTHUR, II, civil engr.; b. Columbia, S.C., Dec. 31, 1952; s. William Henry and Peggy Otis (Mims) J.; B.S. in Civil Engring., Calif. State U., Los Angeles, 1975; M.S. in Civil and Structural Engring., Stanford U., 1976, Degree of Engr., 1981; postgrad. Harvard U., 1981—; m. Vanessa Nicholson, Aug. 16, 1980. Engr. aid Los Angeles County Flood Control Dist., 1973-74; civil and structural engr. Bechtel Inc., San Francisco, 1976; geotech. engr. Pacific Soil Engring. Inc., Los Angeles, 1977; civil and structural design engr. Bechtel Inc., 1978-79; v.p., dir. Kercheval & Assos., Inc., Stanford, Calif., 1980; owner B/J Engring. Assos.; mem. com. minorities in engring. NRC; mem. post earthquake insp. program Calif. Office Emergency Services. Registered profl. engr., Calif., Kans., Mo., Nev. Mem. ASCE, Nat. Soc. Black Engrs. (a founder, 1st nat. chmn. 1976; Leadership award 1977), San Francisco Engrs. Socs., AAUP, Am. Soc. Engring. Edn., Calif. Soc. Profl. Engrs., Nat. Soc. Profl. Engrs., Structural Engrs. Assn. Calif., Prestressed Concrete Inst. Author papers in field. Office: PO Box 2022 Stanford CA 94305

JOHNSON, WILLIAM BENJAMIN, business exec.; b. Salisbury, Md., Dec. 28, 1918; s. Benjamin A. and Ethel (Holloway) J.; A.B. maxima cum laude, Washington Coll., 1940, LL.D., 1975; LL.B. cum laude, U. Pa., 1943; m. Mary Barb, Dec. 19, 1942; children—Benjamin H., Kirk B., John P., Kathleen M. Editor-in-chief U. Pa. Law Rev.; admitted to Md. bar, 1943, Pa. bar, 1947; atty. U.S. Tax Ct., 1945-47; asst. solicitor Pa. R.R., 1947-48, asst. gen. solicitor, 1948-51, asst. to gen. counsel, 1951-52, asst. gen. counsel, 1952-59; pres., dir. Ry. Express Agy., Inc. (name changed to REA Express, 1964), N.Y.C., 1959-66, chmn. bd., 1966; pres., chief exec. officer, dir. Ill. Central R.R., Ill. Central Industries, 1966-68; chmn. bd., chief exec. officer I.C. R.R., 1969-72, chmn. exec. com., 1972-76; chmn. bd., pres., chief exec. officer Ill. Central Industries, Inc., 1968-72, chmn., chief exec. officer, 1972—; dir. Conill Corp., Continental Ill. Nat. Bank & Trust Co. Chgo., Esmark, Midas-Internat., Abex Corp., Ill. Central Gulf R.R. Pepsi-Cola Gen. Bottlers, Inc., Pet Inc., Trans-Union Corp. Mem. Chgo. Central Area Com. Trustee Mus. Sci. and Industry, Com. for Econ. Devel., U. Chgo.; mem. Northwestern U. Assos.; bd. visitors Tulane U. Served as spl. agt., Security Intelligence Corps, AUS, 1943-45. Mem. Am., Phila. bar assns., ICC Practitoners Assn., Transp. Assn. Am., Assn. Am. Railroads, Nat. Def. Transp. Assn. (life mem., past chmn. bd. dirs.), Conf. Bd., Md. Soc. of Pa., Newcomen Soc. N.Am., S.A.R., Order of Coif, Omicron Delta Kappa, Kappa Alpha. Clubs: Sky, Links (N.Y.C.); Western Ry., Execs., Econ., Comml., Chicago, Room 100, Metropolitan, Mid-America (Chgo.); Onwentsia (Lake Forest, Ill.); Old Elm (Highland Park, Ill.). Home: 971 N Hawthorne Pl Lake Forest IL 60045 Office: IC Industries 111 E Wacker Dr Chicago IL 60601

JOHNSON, WILLIAM BERNARD, constrn. co. exec.; b. Youngstown, Ohio, Oct. 10, 1929; s. Andrew R. and Ida I. (Norgren) J.; student public schs., Boardman, Ohio; m. Alice Mae Lewis, May 26, 1951; children—Deborah, Rochelle, Robin. With A.R. Johnson & Sons, Youngstown, 1948-71, Albee Homes, Niles, Ohio, 1971-72; with Ryan Homes, Inc., Pitts., 1973—, now prodn. mgr. Republican. Methodist. Club: Swedish Lodge. Home: 4835 Spring Valley Dr Allison Park PA 15101 Office: 6000 Babcock Blvd Pittsburgh PA 15237

JOHNSON, WILLIAM FRANK, electronics cons. co. exec.; b. Chgo., Feb. 11, 1934; s. Orville Adelbert and Libbie (Bishop) J.; E.E., Ga. Inst. Tech., 1958; postgrad. U. South Ala., 1978; m. Rita Nell Hall, Sept. 16, 1967; children—Rhonda Mechelle, Kevin Daniel. With Potter Co., Wesson, Miss., 1962-73, dir. engring., 1962-66, mktg. mgr., 1966-73; sr. engring. specialist Data Systems div. Litton, Pascagoula, Miss., 1973-79; gen. mgr. Electromagnetic Tech., San Diego, 1979—; cons. electromagnetic compatibility; mem. various industry/govt. coms. on writing specifications and standards, 1967—. Sec., Pascagoula Civitan Club, 1979. Mem. Electronic Industries Assn., Soc. Automotive Engrs. (vice-chmn. electromagnetic compatibility com.), IEEE. Republican. Methodist. Home: 10321 Empress San Diego CA 92126 Office: 4410 Glacier San Diego CA 92120

JOHNSON, WILLIAM HARRY, home bldg. and developing co. exec.; b. Nashville, Sept. 24, 1954; s. Aubrey Herman and Malvin (Fuller) J.; B.S. in Bus. Mgmt., David Lipscomb Coll., 1976. Vice pres. A.H. Johnson Co., comml., indsl., residential builders and developers, Belinda City, New Town, Mt. Juliet, Tenn., 1976—; pres. Harding Homes, Inc., Mt. Juliet, 1976—. Mem. Nashville-Middle Tenn. Home Builders Assn. (local dir.), Alpha Kappa Psi. Mem. Ch. of Christ. Home: 344 S Mt Juliet Rd Mount Juliet TN 37122 Office: Belinda Pkwy Mount Juliet TN 37122

JOHNSON, WILLIAM POTTER, publisher; b. Peoria, Ill., May 4, 1935; s. William Zweigle and Helen Marr (Potter) J.; A.B., U. Mich., 1957; m. Pauline Ruth Rowe, May 18, 1968; children—Darragh Elizabeth, William Potter. Gen. mgr. Bureau County Republican Inc., Princeton, Ill., 1962-71; pres. Johnson Newspapers Inc. (Calif.), 1972-75; pres. Johnson Newspapers Inc., Evergreen, Colo., 1974—; dir. 1st Nat. Bank Evergreen. Alt. del. Republican Nat. Conf., 1968. Served to lt. USNR, 1958-61. Mem. Beta Theta Pi, Sigma Delta Chi. Roman Catholic. Clubs: San Francisco Press; Denver Press; Hiwan Country (Evergreen); Oro Valley Country (Tucson). Home: 445 W Rapa Pl Tucson AZ 85704 Office: 4009 S Colorado Hwy 74 Evergreen CO 80439

JOHNSON, WILLIAM RAY, ins. co. exec.; b. West Union, Ohio, Feb. 12, 1930; s. A. Earl and Helen (Walker) J.; B.S. in Edn., Wilmington Coll., 1951; m. Anne Abrams, Mar. 27, 1954; children—Elizabeth Anne, William Randall. Tchr., theater dept. Miami U., Oxford, Ohio, 1951; div. mgr. Prudential Ins. Co. of Am., Waco, Tex., 1956-57; nat. training cons. Paul Revere Life Ins. Co., Dallas, 1960; health and accident ins. cons., Dallas, 1965-68; pres. MSP Service Corp., Dallas, 1974—; partner Wiedeman & Johnson, Dallas, 1967—, treas.-sec., 1967—. Pres. bd. dirs. Suicide Prevention of Dallas, 1975-76; bd. dirs. Sr. Citizens of Greater Dallas, Inc., 1977—, Dallas Child Guidance Clinic, 1977—; mem. Bishops Adv. Com. on Planning and Devel., Episcopal Diocese of Dallas, 1976—; sr. warden St. Michaels Episcopal Ch., 1979—; trustee Episcopal Theol. Sem. of SW, Austin, Tex., 1981—. Served to 1st lt. USAF, 1951-55. Clubs: Dallas City, Dallas Country. Office: 3615 Hall St Dallas TX 75219

JOHNSON, WYATT THOMAS, JR., publisher; b. Macon, Ga., Sept. 30, 1941; s. Wyatt Thomas and Josephine Victoria (Brown) J.; A.B. in Journalism, U. Ga., 1963; M.B.A., Harvard, 1965. Reporter, mgmt. trainee Macon Telegraph and News, 1957-65; White House fellow, 1965-66; asst. press sec. to Pres. U.S., 1966, dep. press sec., 1967, spl. asst. to Pres., 1968, exec. asst., 1969-70; exec. v.p., dir. Tex. Broadcasting Corp., Sta. KTBC-AM-FM-TV, Austin, 1970-73; exec. editor, v.p., dir. Dallas Times Herald, 1973-75, publisher, 1975-77; pres. Los Angeles Times, 1977-80, pub., 1980—. Mem. Pres.'s Commn. on White House Fellows, 1968, 77, Bd. Fgn. Scholarships, 1969-72, Pres.'s Com. on Youth Opportunity, 1968-69, Peace Corps Advisory Council, 1969, Neiman Fellows Selection Com., Harvard U., 1977; chmn. Austin March of Dimes/Nat. Found., 1972. Pres. advisory bd. Henry W. Grady Sch. Journalism, 1974-75. Bd. dirs. U. Ga. Sch. Journalism, U. Tex. Sch. Communications, U. Tex. Coll. of Bus., Goals for Dallas, Salvation Army, Goodwill Industries, Baylor Coll. Dentistry, Peabody Awards; mem. exec. com. Lyndon B. Johnson Found. Named Nat. Man of Year, Sigma Nu, 1962, Outstanding Young Man of Ga., Jr. C. of C., 1967, One of Five Outstanding Young Texans, Tex. Jaycees, 1969, One of 10 Outstanding Men of U.S., 1975. Mem. Council on Fgn. Relations New York, Sphinx Soc., Dallas C. of C. (dir.), Young Pres. Orgn., Dallas Assembly, Gridiron Soc. (Ga.), Harvard Bus. Sch. Alumni, Sigma Delta Chi. Phi Kappa Phi, Phi Eta Sigma. Methodist. Co-author: Automating Newspaper Composition, 1965. Office: Los Angeles Times Times Mirror Sq Los Angeles CA 90053

JOHNSON, ZANE QUENTIN, oil co. exec.; b. Bristow, Okla., Mar. 5, 1924; s. Sylvester B. and Meta B. (Biggs) J.; B.S. in Chem. Engring., U. Okla., 1947; m. Nila Jean Caylor, June 4, 1949; children—Zane Quentin, Mark Caylor, Janis Lyn. With Gulf Oil Corp. and subsidiaries, 1947—, with Port Arthur (Tex.) refinery, 1947-58, dir. planning and mfg. dept., Pitts., 1958-60, Corpus Christi, Tex., 1960-61; gen. mgr. Gulf Oil Raffinaderij NV, Netherlands, 1962-64, mgr. refining Gulf Eastern Co., London, 1964-67, exec. v.p., Houston, 1968-69, pres., chief operating officer Gen. Atomics, Inc., San Diego, Calif., 1969-70, exec. v.p., Pitts., 1970-75, pres. Gulf Sci. and Tech. Co., Pitts., 1975—. Bd. dirs. Boy Scouts Am., Duquesne U., Sch. Chem. Engring. U. Okla.; trustee Shadyside Hosp.; mayor City of Port Arthur, 1957-58; bd. dirs. United Community Services of San Diego County, 1969-70. Served to 1st lt. USAAF, World War II; PTO. Decorated Air Medal with 3 oak leaf clusters; named to Hall of Fame, U. Okla. Coll. Engring. Mem. Am. Inst. Chem. Engrs., Am. Petroleum Inst., NAM (dir.), Petroleum Club Houston. Republican. Presbyterian. Clubs: Duquesne, Fox Chapel Golf, Laurel Valley Golf, Rolling Rock. Office: 439 7th Ave Pittsburgh PA 15219

JOHNSON, ZENOBA ORARHEA, property mgmt. co. exec.; b. Seminole, Okla., May 27, 1929; d. Jessie Daniel and Eliza Belle (Mangis) O'Keefe; student Central Bus. Coll., 1956-57, Oklahoma City South West Coll., 1969-70; m. Hobert Levert Johnson, Aug. 27, 1946; 1 dau., Levertta Kay. Office bookkeeper Humpty Dumpty Grocery, Oklahoma City, 1951-56; officer mgr., bookkeeper, sec. Scrivner Boogaart Co., Oklahoma City, 1957-70; sec. Midland Property Mgmt. Corp., Oklahoma City, 1970-76; area mgr. PRC Mgmt. Co., Oklahoma City, from 1976; now v.p., treas. Property Mgmt. Cons., Inc. Mem. Am. Bus. Women's Assn. (nat. nominating chmn. 1974, nat. v.p. dist. III). Democrat. Baptist. Home: 4305 NW 11th St Oklahoma City OK 73107

JOHNSTON, CARL WILLIAM, lumber and kitchen home center co. exec.; b. Chgo., Apr. 4, 1926; s. John Henry and Clarissa Christine (Dillman) J.; B.S., Syracuse U., 1949; m. Margaret Reynolds Caves, June 19, 1948; children—Jilaine Jo, Joel Caves, John Stuart, Judith Ann. With Stuart S. Caves, Inc., Henrietta, N.Y., 1950—, v.p. retail sales, 1954, exec. v.p., 1957, pres., 1962—; exec. v.p. Better Living Homes Corp., Canandaigua, N.Y., 1960—; pres. W. Lake Rd. Estates Corp., Canandaigua, 1965—; pres. Genesse Res. Supply, Inc., 1963, chmn. bd., 1965-66. Chmn., Canandaigua Town Planning Bd.,

1968-72. Served with USAAF, 1944-46. Recipient Bus. Ethics award Rotary, 1964; Pres.'s award C. of C., 1972. Mem. Greater Canandaigua C. of C. (pres. 1976), Am. Inst. Kitchen Dealers. Episcopalian. Clubs: M-B of Am., Masons. Office: 3081 E Henrietta Rd Henrietta NY 14467

JOHNSTON, DAVID WHITE, JR., textile co. exec.; b. Atlanta, Ga., Mar. 31, 1921; s. David White and Annie Kate (Johnson) J.; B.S. in Indsl. Mgmt., Ga. Inst. Tech., 1942; postgrad. U. Western Ont., 1958; exec. tng. program U. N.C., 1962-63; m. Sally Onie Ingram, July 30, 1949; children—Elizabeth, David. Plant mgr. Dominion Textile Co., Drummondville, Que., Can., 1952-60, v.p. mfg., 1964-68; div. v.p. Deering Milliken, Gainesville, Ga., 1960-64; v.p. mfg. Bibb Mfg. Co., Macon, Ga., 1968-70; pres. Dan River, Inc., Danville, Va., 1977—, also dir.; dir. Dibrell Bros., Bank of Va. Trustee, Averett Coll.; bd. dirs. Danville Meml. Hosp., Roman Eagle Nursing Home, Danville; mem. adv. bd. Duke U. Hosp., Durham, N.C., Served to lt. USN, 1942-46. Mem. Danville C. of C. (dir.). Presbyterian. Club: Danville Golf. Home: 134 Acorn Ln Danville VA 24541 Office: 2291 Memorial Dr Danville VA 24541

JOHNSTON, DENNIS ROY, corp. interior design co. exec.; b. Wahoo, Nebr., June 29, 1937; s. Roy Alfred and Wilma Jean (Weidensall) J.; Student U. Nebr., 1955-56, 57-58, U. Colo., 1961-64; m. Dorothy McLay Carr, June 19, 1965; children—Kristin Anne, Ami Carr. City planner Denver Urban Renewal Authority, 1965-69; dir. graphics Haines, Lundberg & Waehler, N.Y.C., 1969-72; v.p., sr. project mgr. LCP Assos., Inc., N.Y.C., 1972—. Co-chmn. Family Life Council. Mem. Adminstrv. Mgmt. Soc. (cert. of merit), Am. Mgmt. Assn. Republican. Methodist. Home: 3 Sussex Ave Chatham NJ 07928 Office: LCP Assos Inc 25 Tudor City Pl New York NY 10017

JOHNSTON, DON, advt. exec.; b. Elmira, N.Y., 1927; grad. Mich. State U., 1950. With J. Walter Thompson Co., N.Y.C., 1951—, chief exec. officer, dir., 1978—. Office: 420 Lexington Ave New York NY 10017*

JOHNSTON, FRANKLIN ELMO, constrn. co. exec.; b. Manhattan, Kans., Nov. 7, 1944; s. Elmo F. and Florence R. (Nanninga) J.; B.S.E.E., Kans. State U., 1967; postgrad. Tex. A. and M. U., 1967-68, St. Marys U., 1968-71, U. Kans., 1971-72; m. Barbara L. Goss, Aug. 6, 1971; children—Jennifer Medora, Amanda Beth. Design engr. Robertson, Peters & Williams, Lawrence, Kans., 1971-72, Black & Veatch Cons. Engrs., Kansas City, Mo., 1972-73; mng. partner Goss-Johnston Bldg. Constrn., Kerrville, Tex., 1973—; cons. elec. engr.; researcher solar energy. Served to capt., design engr., USAF, 1967-71. Registered profl. engr., Tex., Kans. Methodist. Office: Goss Johnston Bldg Construction Co PO Box 1562 Kerrville TX 78028

JOHNSTON, FREDERICK THOMAS, food distbn. co. exec.; b. Alpena, Mich., Feb. 11, 1918; s. John R. and Nellie May (Plowman) J.; student Alma (Mich.) Coll., 1936-38; B.S. in Bus. Adminstrn., Cleary Coll., Ypsilanti, Mich., 1940; m. Jan. 31, 1941; children—Janis Lou, Josephine Ann, Julie Douville, Jere Douville, James Erickson, John Frederick. Mem. dept. accts. receivable Besser Co., Alpena, Mich., 1942-45; pres. Johnston Motor Sales, Inc., Alpena, 1945-55, Douville Bakery Co., Alpena, 1946-57, Douville-Johnston Corp., Alpena, 1958—, Alpena Wholesale Grocer Co., 1946—, pres. Sta. WBKB-TV, Alpena, pres. The Mole Hole of Claremont, Calif., Inc.; dir. Peoples Bank & Trust, Alpena. Chmn. dept. public works County of Alpena, 1972—; pres., trustee Besser Found., 1968—. Republican. Presbyterian. Clubs: Lost Lake Woods, Alpena Country, Alpena Yacht, Doctors Hunting, Masons, Elks. Home: 100 E Dunbar St Alpena MI 49707 Office: 170 N Industrial Hwy Alpena MI 49707

JOHNSTON, GLENN W., drug co. exec.; b. 1920; B.S.E., Wharton Sch. Fin., U. Pa., 1941. Sales mgr. McKesson & Robbins, Inc., 1942-53; owner, mgr. Johnston Buick Co., 1953-56; product mgr. J.B. Williams Co., 1957; market specialist and product mgmt. Sterling Drug Inc., N.Y.C., 1957-61, v.p. Glenbrook Labs. div., 1961-66, exec. v.p. Lehn & Fink Products div., 1966-67, pres., 1967-70, v.p., dir. parent co., 1968—, v.p. Domestic Consumer Products div., 1970-71, exec. v.p., 1971-74, pres., chief operating officer, 1974—. Served to capt. USAAF, 1942-45. Office: Sterling Drug Inc 90 Park Ave New York NY 10016

JOHNSTON, HARRY JOSEPH, banker; b. Rochester, Pa., Aug. 20; s. Harry I. and Elsa M. J.; B.A., Grove City Coll., 1954; m. Marie LeGoullon, July 20, 1963. Teller, Nat. Bank of Beaver County, Monaca, Pa., 1955-58, asst. cashier, 1958-73, asst. v.p., 1973-75, v.p., 1975-77, exec. v.p., 1977-79, pres., 1979—. Treas. Boro of Monaca, also Monaca Sch. Dist. Served with USN, 1955-57. Mem. Am. Inst. Banking. Presbyterian. Club: Beaver Valley Country. Home: 47 Darlington Rd Beaver Falls PA 15010 Office: Nat Bank of Beaver County 1001 Pennsylvania Ave Monaca PA 15064

JOHNSTON, JAMES CRAIG, mktg. exec.; b. Buffalo, Nov. 24, 1937; s. James and Sylvia Bell J.; B.A., Western Res. U., 1960; postgrad. Grad Sch. Bus., U. Calif., 1964; m. Arline P. Barker, Aug. 22, 1970; children—Corey, Craig. Gen. mgr. mfg. and sales Magnus Corp., Los Angeles, 1966-71; nat. mktg. mgr. Sues, Young & Brown, Commerce, Calif., 1971-75; nat. market devel. specialist Zenith Radio Corp., Chgo., 1975-77; v.p. sales and mktg. Altec Lansing Corp., Anaheim, Calif., 1977-78; v.p., gen. mgr. Jensen Sound Labs. div. Esmark, Chgo., 1978—. Served with USMCR, 1956-58. Home: 1597 Clendenin Ln Riverwood IL 60015

JOHNSTON, JAMES WAYNE, constrn. co. exec.; b. Sheboygan, Wis., Feb. 28, 1948; s. Lester D. and Marcella (Kerchak) J.; B.S. in Zoology, Mich. State U., 1974, postgrad., 1975; m. Shari Gross, June 19, 1976. Constrn. mgr. Music Stop Inc., Madison Heights, Mich., 1976-77; pres. JIMSHA Constrn. Inc., Ypsilanti, Mich., 1977—. Served with USMCR, 1968-70. Mem. Washtenaw County Contractors Assn. Roman Catholic. Club: Mid-Mich. Community Coll. Veterans (pres.). Home: 2314 Ellsworth Rd Apt 202 Ypsilanti MI 48197 Office: PO Box 392 Ypsilanti MI 48197

JOHNSTON, JOHN PHILLIPS LITTLE, lawyer, furniture mfg. co. exec.; b. Memphis, Aug. 19, 1939; s. William Rodgers and Louise (Little) J.; A.B., Duke U., 1960; LL.B., U. N.C., 1963; m. Dorothy Ann James, Dec. 20, 1970; children—John Phillips Little, Dorothy James. Ofcl. asst. Citicorp., N.Y.C., 1963-65; founder, pres., chief exec. officer Currier Piano Co., Marion, N.C., 1965-79; admitted to N.C. bar, 1963; pres., chief exec. officer Erwin-Lambeth, Inc., Thomasville, N.C., 1979—; pres. Norman Perry, High Point, N.C., Chantry Lamp and Accessory Co., High Point; dir. N.C. Nat. Bank, Marion, Marion Mfg. Co., So. Film Extruders, High Point, N.C., R.L. James & Son, Marion. Chmn., McDowell County United Fund, 1973-74, Marion Gen. Hosp., 1974-79. Mem. N.C. Bar Assn., Kappa Alpha. Republican. Episcopalian. Clubs: Biltmore Country (Asheville, N.C.); Emerywood Country (High Point). Author: Success in Small Business Is a Laughing Matter, 1979. Office: 201 E Holly Hill Rd Thomasville NC 27360

JOHNSTON, LARRY K., foundry exec.; b. Decatur, Ill., Jan. 14, 1942; s. Huber K. and Mabel E. (Glick) J.; B.A. in Bus. Economics, Murray (Ky.) State U., 1964; m. Linda F. Lancaster, Mar. 3, 1968; children—Larry K., Tia, Michael. With Westinghouse Elec. Corp., Peoria, Ill., 1964-67, Artze Constrn., Decatur, 1967-68; maintenence supr. CFD div. Gen. Motors Corp., Danville, Ill., 1968-72; maintenence supt. Hayes-Albion Corp., Tiffin, Ohio, 1973-79; mgr. plant engring. and maintenance Grede Foundries, Iron Mountain, Mich., 1979—. Roman Catholic. Home: Star Route 2 Box 10 F Pine Ridge Estates Iron Mountain MI 49801

JOHNSTON, LOWELL PRESTON, engring. co. exec.; b. Farmersville, Tex., Jan. 6, 1926; s. Claude and Opal (Biggerstaff) J.; B.S., Tex. A. & M. U., 1950; M.S., Tex. U., 1952; LL. B., South Tex. Coll. Law, 1963; m. Margie Sue Thomas, Nov. 12, 1950; 1 dau., Judy. With Shell Oil Co., 1952-73; sr. staff engr., pres. C.E. Crest Offshore, Tulsa, 1973-77; pres. Lowell Johnston & Assos.; adviser Technip Geoprodn., France; dir. Redpath Offshore Design Assn. (Eng.). Chmn. vis. com. Tex. U. Served with AUS, 1944-47. Mem. Am. Petroleum Inst., ASCE. Republican. Mem. Ch. of Christ. Contbr. articles to profl. jours. Home: 6412 S Hudson Tulsa OK 74136 Office: 5800 E Skelly Dr Suite 500 Tulsa OK 74135

JOHNSTON, LYNN HENRY, ins. exec.; b. Woodstock, Ga., Mar. 15, 1931; s. Hugh Lee and Sara (Carnes) J.; B.B.A. cum laude, Emory U., 1952; m. Doris Lacy, Dec. 22, 1950; children—Sharon, Ronnie, Carolyn. With Life Ins. Co. Ga., Atlanta, 1954—, gen. acct., supr. mortgage loans, asst. mgr. gen. acctg., asst. treas., asst. v.p. acctg., v.p. acctg., 1954-78, pres., 1978—, dir., 1975—, exec. com., 1976—; pres. Ga. U.S. Corp.; dir., exec. com. Ins. Systems Am.; dir. Ga. U.S. Data Services, Inc. Chmn. bus. unit United Way Met. Atlanta; trustee Reinhardt Coll.; bd. visitors Emory U.; adv. council Coll. Bus. Adminstrn., Ga. State U.; chmn. bldg. com. 1st Methodist Ch. of Chamblee. Served with AUS; Korea. Fellow Life Mgmt. Inst.; mem. Am. Council Life Ins. (state v.p.), Ga. Life Insurers Conf. (exec. com.). Clubs: Capital City, Kiwanis (Atlanta). Office: 600 W Peachtree St Atlanta GA 30308

JOHNSTON, RALPH KENNEDY (KEN), aerospace engr.; b. Ft. Sam Houston, Tex., Oct. 2, 1942; s. Abraham R. and Janace R. (White) J.; B.S. in Aerospace Engring., Oklahoma City U., 1962; B.S. in Bus. Mgmt., Union Exptl. Colls. and Univs., 1974, B.S. in Aviation Mgmt., 1974; m. Florence Ann Sheehy, Oct. 29, 1963; children—Theresa Ann, Ralph Kennedy, Michael Andrew. Test pilot Grumman Aerospace Corp., 1966-69, human factors engr. lunar module spacecraft, 1966-69; supr. lunar sample data control dept. Northrop Services Inc., Houston, 1969-72; cost engr. Fluor Engring. & Constrn., Houston, 1974-77; aerospace engr. space div. Rockwell Internat., Houston, 1977—; chief flight instr. Four-K Enterprises, Houston, 1977—. Served with USMC, 1962-66. Named Outstanding Young Man Am., 1971, Disting. Alumni, Oklahoma City U., 1978; cert. flight instr. Mem. AIAA, Am. Assn. Cost Engrs., Nat. Mgrs. Assn., SCV, SAR. Home: 4211 Lucian Ln Frendswood TX 77546 Office: ILC Industries Johnson Space Center Code EC-5 Houston TX 77098

JOHNSTON, RAYMOND G., banker; b. Lake City, Ark., Oct. 23, 1928; s. John Wesley and Yula Vera (Pounds) J.; student, Drake U., 1948-56; grad. Stonier Grad. Sch. Banking, 1966; m. Mary Lou Brown, Oct. 26, 1948; children—Pamela, Rebecca, Timothy. Vice pres. Central Nat. Bank & Trust Co., Des Moines, 1965-71, sr. v.p., 1971-74, pres., dir., 1974-76, pres., chief exec. officer, 1976—; dir. Quality Control Equipment Co., Iowa Bus. Devel. Corp., Iowa Transfer Systems Inc. Chmn., Greater Des Moines United Way, 1970-71; mem. Nat. Export Expansion Council, U.S. Dept. Commerce, 1968-71; chmn. Iowa Small Bus. Adv. Council, 1962, Iowa Regional Export Expansion Council, 1968-70; mem. small bus. adv. council SBA, 1962-64; bd. dirs. Jr. Achievement Des Moines, 1976—. Mem. Assn. Res. City Bankers, Am. Bankers Assn., Iowa Bankers Assn., Greater Des Moines C. of C. Clubs: Des Moines, Wakonda, Rotary. Office: 6th and Locust Sts Central Nat Bank Des Moines IA 50304

JOHNSTON, ROGER DOUGLAS, banker; b. San Francisco, July 13, 1941; s. Douglas Robert and Margaret Ann (Taylor) J.; B.A. in History, Stanford U., 1963; B.A. in Fgn. Trade, Am. Inst. Fgn. Trade, 1966; M.B.A., N.Y. U., 1972; m. Susan Leslie Taylor, June 25, 1966; children—Jennifer Taylor, Samantha Hunter, Ashley Taylor. Vol. in urban community devel. Peace Corps, Santiago, Dominican Republic, 1963-65; Mexican rep. Mfrs. Hanover Trust Co., 1969-74, officer in charge Eastern European activities, 1974-76; v.p. loan syndications, spl. financing Bancomer, S.A., Mexico City, 1976, sr. v.p. internat. promotion div., Mexico City, 1976-79, sr. v.p. internat. ops. div., 1979—; alt. dir. Libra Bank, London, Arrendadora Bancomer, S.A. Mem. Mexican Bankers Assn. Clubs: Univ., Mexican Banker's (Mexico City). Contbr. articles to profl. jours. Home: Lazcano # 44 Mexico 20 DF Mexico Office: Apartado Postal 9 Bis Mexico 1 DF Mexico

JOHONG, JOONDU, Korean trade center exec.; b. Namhai, Korea, Dec. 14, 1926; s. Jongwon and Somak Johong; grad., Pusan Nat. Fisheries Coll., 1950; m. Uyeon Ju, Nov. 19, 1960; children—Seung-A, Lasan. Sales mgr. Barclays & Co., Seoul, Korea, 1950-55; dir. Korea Trade Centers, Los Angeles, Bangkok, London, Brussels, 1962-79; econ. adv. to Govt. of Ghana, 1978; resident v.p. in U.S. and exec. dir. Korea Trade Promotion Center, N.Y.C., 1979—; v.p., dir. Korea Promotion Corp., Seoul. Recipient Suktap Indsl. medal Korean Govt., 1979. Mem. Korea Trade Research Assn., Market Research Assn. of Britain. Clubs: Yeoju Country, Felix Tennis (Seoul). Author numerous articles on export promotion. Home: 21 Beechwood Rd Cresskill NJ 07626 Office: 460 Park Ave New York NY 10022

JOINES, JAMES EMORY, JR., mgmt. cons.; b. Mountain City, Tenn., Jan. 14, 1946; s. James Emory and Josephine (Banner) J.; student U. Tenn., 1964-66; B.S., Appalachian State U., 1968, postgrad., 1969-70; m. Mary Christine Hill, May 28, 1970; children—Stephanie Denise, James Emory. Office mgr. Computer Bus. Service, Greensboro, N.C., 1969-70, regional mgr., 1970; prof. econs. Croft Coll., Greensboro, 1970; with Profl. Cons., Inc., Greensboro and Lynchburg, Va., 1971—, area mgr., 1971-78, pres., Lynchburg, 1978—, also dir.; dir. Applied Radiant Energy Corp.; vis. prof. U. Va., Charlottesville, 1975—. Mem. vestry Grace Meml. Episcopal Ch., 1975-79, sr. warden, 1977-78. Mem. Soc. Profl. Bus. Cons.'s (nat. public relations dir. 1978-80), Inst. Cert. Profl. Bus. Cons.'s, Am. Inst. Profl. Cons.'s. Clubs: Boonsboro Country, Lions (pres. 1980). Contbr. editor Physicians Mgmt. Jour., 1974—. Home: 2103 Link Rd Lynchburg VA 24505 Office: 1928 Thomson Dr Lynchburg VA 24501

JOLLY, BRUCE DWIGHT, steel products mfg. co. exec.; b. Wheeling, W.Va., Aug. 27, 1943; s. Edward B. and Martha Elizabeth (Glass) J.; A.B. in Math. and Econs., Dartmouth Coll., 1965; M.B.A., U. Va., 1967; m. Alice O'Beirne, May 25, 1974; children—Mara, Brock. Systems engr. IBM, Richmond, Va., 1967-68; fin. analyst Keystone Consol. Industries, Peoria, Ill., 1970-73; controller Hon Industries, Inc., Muscatine, Iowa, 1973-76, sec.-treas., 1976-79; v.p. fin. Hawkeye Steel Products Inc., Waterloo, Iowa, 1979—. Served with U.S. Army, 1968-70. Decorated Bronze Star. Republican. Home: Rural Route 1 Box 86 B Denver IA 50622 Office: 324 Duryea Waterloo IA 50701

JOLLY, RAYMOND ALONZO, JR., lawyer, power co. exec.; b. Anderson, S.C., Feb. 23, 1936; s. Raymond Alonzo and Quinton Elizabeth (Lassiter) J.; B.A. in English, U. N.C., 1958, J.D., 1961; m. Elizabeth Kimm Howard, Aug. 21, 1960; children—Carole Lynn, Christopher Howard, David Lassiter. Admitted to N.C. bar, 1961; asso. firm Ruff, Perry, Bond, Cobb & Wade, Charlotte, N.C., 1964-67, partner, 1968-70; partner firm Hedrick, McKnight, Parham, Helms, Warley & Jolly, Charlotte, 1971-72; asst. gen. counsel Duke Power Co., Charlotte, 1971-74, asso. gen. counsel, 1974—. Served to capt. USAF, 1961-64. Mem. Am., N.C. bar assns., 26th Judicial Dist Bar (past sec.), Phi Beta Kappa. Club: Olde Providence Racquet and Swim. Home: 1509 Scotland Ave Charlotte NC 28207 Office: 422 S Church St PO Box 33189 Charlotte NC 28242

JONAS, GARY FRED, cons. co. exec.; b. N.Y.C., Apr. 26, 1945; s. Otto and Hilde (Levy) J.; B.S., Columbia U., 1966; M.B.A., Harvard U., 1968; m. Rosalyn Ethel Levy, July 29, 1973. Mgmt. cons. FRY Consultants, Washington, 1968-69; mgmt. cons. Univ. Research Corp., Washington, 1969-72, exec. v.p., 1972-75, pres., 1975—; pres. Center for Human Services, Washington, 1978—; dir. Human Services Group, Inc., 1977—; adj. professorial lectr. Grad. Sch. Bus. Adminstrn., Am. U., 1975—. Bd. dirs. Nat. Council Profl. Services Firms, 1975—, chmn. com. on fed. contracting practices, 1979—. Recipient Charles Kandel medal Columbia U., 1966; cert. mgmt. cons. Mem. Young Presidents Orgn., Am. Public Health Assn., Nat. Contract Mgmt. Assn., Council for Applied Social Research. Democrat. Clubs: Harvard (N.Y.C.); Potomac Tennis, Harvard Bus. Sch. of Washington. Contbr. articles to The New Republic, Jour. Negro Edn., MBA Mag., others. Home: 5370 28th St NW Washington DC 20015 Office: 5530 Wisconsin Ave NW Washington DC 20015

JONAS, GLENN FRANKLIN, mgmt. cons. co. exec.; b. Door County, Wis., May 29, 1934; s. Fred Karl and Esther Cora (Honold) J.; B.S.M.E., U. Wis., Madison, 1961; B.B.A., U. Wis., Milw., 1963; m. Rita Marie Koss, June 8, 1963; children—Jory Lynn, Jamey Lee, Glenda Sue, Fredric. Prodn. mgr. Square D Co., Milw., 1963-68; mfg. mgr. switchgear div. Allis Chalmers Corp., Milw., 1968-71; planning & control mgr. Johnson Controls Co., Milw., 1971-72; gen. mgr. Jonas & Assos., Inc., Milw., 1972—; guest lectr. U. Wis., Whitewater, 1975-79, Milw., 1977—. Bd. dirs. Brown Deer Sch. Bd., 1975-79. Served with U.S. Army, 1953-55. Mem. Wauwatosa C. of C., Met. Assn. Commerce, Sales & Mktg. Execs. of Milw. (dir.). Lutheran. Club: Kiwanis. Home: 9173 N Alpine Ln Brown Deer WI 53223 Office: 3333 N Mayfair Rd Milwaukee WI 53222

JONAS, HARRY, JR., real estate co. exec.; b. Richmond, Va., Oct. 6, 1943; s. Harry and Ruth Ethel (Kruger) J.; B.A. in Econs., U. So. Calif., 1966; m. Jane Elizabeth Manus, May 2, 1976; 1 dau., Ann Rachel. Exec. asst. to pres. Kruger Pulp & Paper Co., Montreal, Que., Can., 1969-71; founder, pres. Hank Jonas Realty Corp., N.Y.C., 1971—; pres. dir. Group Lakeshore Inc., Detroit. Served with USN, 1966-69. Mem. Nat. Assn. Realtors. Clubs: City Athletic, Shelter Island Yacht (N.Y.C.); Palm Beach (Fla.) Sailing.

JONAS, JOSEPH PAUL, tanning co. exec.; b. Chgo., Feb. 22, 1905; s. Coloman and Esther (Balogh) J.; student U. Denver, 1925; m. Mary Elizabeth Harcourt, Apr. 7, 1928 (dec.); children—Joseph Paul, John Harcourt. Pres., Colo. Tanning & Fur Dressing Co., Denver, 1962—, Jonas Bros., Inc., Denver, 1962—. Mem. Denver C. of C., Master Furriers Guild (regional v.p. 1958), Shikar-Safari Club. Republican. Clubs: Rotary, Denver Country, Pinehurst Country. Home: 7170 E Princeton Ave Denver CO 80237 Office: 1037 Broadway Denver CO 80203

JONES, ALAN PORTER, JR., meat packing co. exec.; b. Milw., Feb. 27, 1925; s. Alan Porter and Eleanor Pratt (Bright) J.; B.A., Harvard U., 1948, M.B.A., 1950; m. Jean E. Drummond, Sept. 12, 1953; children—Richard, Susan, Cynthia, Alexandra. With Jones Dairy Farm, Ft. Atkinson, Wis., 1950—, asst. treas., 1953-61, treas., 1961-74, v.p. and treas., 1974—, also dir.; pres. Uncle Josh Bait Co., 1978—; dir. Bank Ft. Atkinson, PDQ Corp. Bd. dirs. Dwight Foster Pub. Library; mem. Fort Atkinson Sch. Bd., 1968-69; trustee Ripon (Wis.) Coll., 1974-77; mem. Wis. Citizens Environ. Council. Served with inf. U.S. Army, 1943-45. Decorated Bronze Star, Combat Inf. badge. Mem. Newcomen Soc. Nat. Audubon Soc., Sierra Club, Nature Conservancy. Republican. Congregationalist. Home: 433 Adams St Fort Atkinson WI 53538 Office: Jones Dairy Farm Fort Atkinson WI 53538

JONES, BARRY LEE, mgmt. cons.; b. Richmond, Va., Apr. 11, 1945; s. Albert H. and Thelma Irene Jones; B.S., Va. Commonwealth U., 1969; B.A., Ga. State U., 1973; M.S., Boston U. (Alcoa Found. scholar), 1975; m. Margaret Roberts. Dir. pub. relations Lowery Group, Atlanta, 1969-73; corp. v.p. Pub. Relations Inst., Inc., Richmond, Va., 1974-78; v.p., partner Howard Chase Enterprises, Inc., Stamford, Conn., 1978-80; prin. Jones Goldman & Co., Stamford, 1980—; asso. U. Conn. Inst. Public Issue Mgmt., 1978—; adj. prof. U. Conn. Grad. Sch. Bus. Recipient Merit award Advt. Club Richmond, 1977. Mem. Pub. Relations Soc. Am., Am. Acad. Polit. and Social Sci., Acad. Polit. Sci., Soc. Profl. Journalists, World Future Soc., Publicity Club N.Y., Sigma Delta Chi. Home: 28 1/2 Tomac Ave Old Greenwich CT 06870

JONES, BENJAMIN E., found. exec.; b. N.Y.C., Sept. 8, 1935; s. Ashton and Evelyn (Beaumann) J.; B.A., Bklyn. Coll., 1971; M.B.A., Pace U., 1974; m. Delcenia R. Boyd, Apr. 21, 1962; children—Leslie, Delcenia. Adminstr. Radio Recepter Co., 1959-60; accountant ECS div. Paal Corp., 1962-66; sr. contract adminstr., negotiator Singer-Gen. Precision Inc., Little Falls, N.J., 1966-71; program dir. Interracial Council for Bus. Opportunity, N.Y.C., 1971; pres. Capital Formation, Inc., Econ. Devel. Found., N.Y.C., 1971—; dir. MBA Mgmt. Cons. Inc. Columbia U., 1973—; mem. minority bus. opportunity com. Fed. Exec. Bd., 1972—. Bd. dirs. Upper Park Ave Community Assn. Day Care Center, 1974—. Served with USAF, 1955-58. Mem. Am. Mgmt. Assn., Nat. Bus. League, Council Concerned Black Execs. (past sec., dir. 1973-75), Nat. Assn. Black Mfrs. (dir. 1978—), Assn. M.B.A. Execs., NAACP, One Hundred Black Men, Inc., Uptown C. of C., N.Y. Urban League, Bklyn. Coll. Alumni, Am. Assn. Mesbics. Home: 45 W 132d St New York NY 10037 Office: 2112 Broadway New York NY 10023

JONES, BILLIE BURK, packaging co. exec.; b. Hillsboro, Tex., Jan. 23, 1926; s. Roy William and Mamie (Burk) J.; B.A., U. Tex., 1950; postgrad. Syracuse U., 1957-58; m. Patricia Valerie Monk, Dec. 2, 1950; 1 son, Jeffrey David. With Owens-Ill., Inc., Toledo, 1950—, gen. mgr. forest products div., 1972-75, gen. mgr. glass container div., 1975-78, group v.p., gen. mgr. consumer and tech. products group, 1978—. Served with A.C., U.S. Navy, 1943-45. Mem. Grocery Mfrs. Am. Episcopalian. Clubs: Muirfield Village Golf, Belmont Country. Office: PO Box 1035 Toledo OH 43666

JONES, BRIAN HERBERT, research and devel. co. exec.; b. Chester, Eng., Apr. 23, 1937; came to U.S., 1966, naturalized, 1971; s. Herbert and Christine Josephine (Williams) J.; B.Engring. with 1st class honors, U. Liverpool (Eng.), 1961, Ph.D., 1965; m. Deborah Ganz, Sept. 7, 1974. Lectr., U. Liverpool, 1963-65; group leader McDonnell Douglas Aircraft, Long Beach, Calif., 1966-69; cons. Aero Research Assos., Princeton, N.J., 1969-71; v.p. engring. Goldsworthy Engring. Corp., Torrance, Calif., 1971-75; pres., gen. mgr. Compositek Engring. Corp. subs. Kelsey-Hayes Co., Buena Park, Calif., 1975—; owner Replex Internat., San Gabriel, Calif., 1977—; cons. Luxfer USA, Commonwealth Indsl. Gases/Australia, 1978-80. James Clayton fellow, Inst. Mech. Engrs., 1961-63; Edward Busk scholar Royal Aero. Soc., 1961-62; Inst. Mech. Engrs. (London) prizes, 1957, 58; Whitworth Soc. prize, 1956; Tech. State scholar (U.K.), 1956. Mem. ASME, Soc. Plastics Industry, Soc. Automotive Engrs. Contbr. articles to profl. jours.; patentee in field. Home: 407 Country Club Dr San Gabriel CA 91775 Office: 6925-1 Aragon Circle Buena Park CA 90620

JONES, CHARLES DAVID, personnel cons. co. exec.; b. Mpls., Apr. 15, 1939; s. Charles T. and Beatrice S. Jones; B.S. in Bus., U. Minn., 1961; M.B.A., 1970; M. Mary J. Jensen, July 20, 1961; children—Christopher, Julie, Jennifer. Store mgr. The Kroger Co., Cin., 1961-64, grocery buyer, 1964-65, grocery field rep., 1965-66, advt. and sales promotion mgr., 1966-70; pres. Roth Young Personnel Service, Mpls., 1970—. Mem. gen. council Presbytery of Twin Cities Area. Mem. Nat. Assn. Personnel Consultants (dist. dir. 1976-77, treas. 1978, 1st v.p. 1979, pres. 1980), Minn. Assn. Personnel Consultants (officer, dir. 1973—, Disting. Service award 1977). Club: Decathlon Athletic (v.p., treas.). Home: 4110 Pebblebrook Dr Bloomington MN 55437 Office: 7600 Parklawn Ave Edina MN 55435

JONES, CHARLES DAVIS, disability cons.; b. Abraham, W. Va., Jan. 6, 1917; s. Benjamin Franklin and Mary Catherine (Smith) J.; A.B., Marshall U., 1947; M.A., N.Y. U., 1956; postgrad. Am. U., 1957; m. Letha Arbell Plumley; children—Charles Davis, Irvin Howard; m.2d, Margaret Lee Greene, Aug. 4, 1951. With Social Security Adminstrn., 1951-77, field rep., Charleston, W. Va., 1951-54, policy examiner, sect. chief, state ops. officer, Balt., 1954-66, area chief field ops. Bur. Disability Ins., Balt., 1966-71, dir. gen. policy coordination and liaison, 1971-75, chief eligibility policy to Office of Policy and Regulations, 1975-77; partner in visual arts prodn. firm, 1976—; disability cons., 1977—; mem. staff sec's. task force on medicaid and related programs HEW, 1969; mem. Social Security Adminstrn. Task Force on Social Security Adminstrn. Regional Orgns. and Functions, 1970. Active Roland Park Civic League, Balt., Balt. Mus. Art. Served to 1st lt., pilot USAF, 1942-45. Decorated 4 Air medals. Mem. Nat. Assn. of Disability Examiners, Mensa, VFW, Nat. Trust for Historic Preservation, Nat. Hist. Soc. Home: 903 W University Pkwy Baltimore MD 21210

JONES, CHARLES HILL, JR., banker; b. N.Y.C., July 14, 1933; s. Charles Hill and Susan Roy (Johnston) J.; grad. Groton (Mass.) Sch., 1952; B.A. in Econs., U. Va., 1956; m. Hope Haskell, Jan. 28, 1961; children—Hope H., Charles Hill III, Henry M.T. With Wood, Struthers & Winthrop, Inc., N.Y.C., 1956-73, gen. partner, 1968-69, v.p., dir. research, 1969-73; sr. v.p., chief investment officer Midlantic Nat. Bank, Newark, 1974—; pres., dir. McBee Jones Corp., 1964—. Treas. N.Y. chpt. R.E. Lee Meml. Found., 1964-69; trustee, chmn. fin. co. Monmouth Med. Center; trustee Rumson (N.J.) Country Day Sch., Assn. for Children of N.J. Served with AUS, 1956-57. Chartered fin. analyst. Mem. Inst. Chartered Fin. Analysts, N.Y. Soc. Security Anaylsts, Met. Squash Racquets Assn. (bd. govs. 1964-69). Clubs: Bond, City Midday (trustee, treas. 1965— v.p. 1972-74) (N.Y.C.). Author: (with Joseph D. Davis) Toll Road Bonds, 1959; Growth Rates, 1967. Home: 90 Ridge Rd Rumson NJ 07760 Office: 744 Broad St Newark NJ 07101

JONES, CHARLES MEREDITH, mcht.; b. Plummerville, Ark., Dec. 1, 1921; s. Slater C. and Ernestine (Griswood) J.; grad. high sch., Dermott, Ark.; m. Ethelyn E. Brown, Apr. 16, 1945; children—Wayne Theodore, Judy Charlyn, Lynn Audean. With J.T. Browns Store, Craig, Alaska, 1946—, owner, 1963—. Mem. Alaska Ho. of Reps., 1960-61; former mayor, councilman, sch. bd. mem., Craig. Served with USCG, 1941-45. Democrat. Club: Moose. Home: Box 40 Craig AK 99921 Office: JT Browns Store Box 40 Craig AK 99921

JONES, CHARLES ROSCOE, petroleum co. exec.; b. New Castle, Ind., Feb. 18, 1921; s. G. Herman and Bernice E. (Hiatt) J.; B.A., Wabash Coll., 1942; m. Barbara J. Westfall, Aug. 3, 1941; children—Philip K., Sherry L. Jones Ryan. With aviation div. Studebaker Corp., 1941-45, Socony Vacuum Oil Co., Chgo., 1946-57; div. sales mgr. Socony Mobil Oil Co., Albany, N.Y., 1958-63; aviation mgr. Mobil Oil Corp., N.Y.C., 1964-68, U.S. pricing mgr., 1969-73, mgr. transp. sales, 1974—; v.p. mktg., dir. Mobil Oil Can., Ltd. Mem. Am. Petroleum Inst., Soc. Automotive Engrs., Am. Inst. Aeros. and Astronautics, Sigma Chi, Sigma Xi. Republican. Clubs: Kiwanis; Sky; Wings; Univ. Home: 6626 Madison-McLean Dr McLean VA 22101 Office: 3225 Gallows Rd Fairfax VA 22037

JONES, CHARLES RUDOLPH, water heater mfr.; b. Los Angeles, Jan. 9, 1917; B.S. in Bus. Adminstrn., U. So. Calif., 1942; m. Genevieve Rae Harshman, Dec. 19, 1941; children—Charles Rudolph, Randy, Craig. With Rheem Mfg. Co., 1942—, v.p., Atlanta, 1960—. Office: Rheem Mfg Co 5780 Peachtree Dunwoody Rd N Atlanta GA 30342

JONES, CHARLOTTE SCHIFF, cable TV exec.; b. N.Y.C., Jan. 21, 1933; d. Maurice and Selma (Goldberg) Grad; B.A., Bklyn. Coll., 1953; M.B.S., Columbia U., 1977; children—David, Richard, Paul. Prodn. coordinator, Screen Gems Internat., N.Y.C., 1966-68; producer various off-Broadway shows, N.Y.C. area, 1968; v.p., exec. producer Drew Lawrence Prodns., N.Y.C., 1968-71; nat. dir. community devel. Teleprompter Corp., N.Y.C., 1971-74; exec. v.p. Manhattan Cable TV, Inc. subs. Time, Inc., N.Y.C., 1974-77; asst. pub. PEOPLE mag., subs. Time Inc., N.Y.C., from 1977; now v.p. mktg. CBS Cable div., N.Y.C.; guest lectr. in field. Active mem. Women's Polit. Caucus, NOW, Women Against Rape, also Democratic Party activities; appointee N.Y. State Manpower Services Council, 1977. Recipient achievement award YWCA, N.Y.C., 1976, program award Nat. Cable TV Assn., 1973, citation Bus. Week Mag., 1976. Mem. Nat. Acad. TV Arts and Sci., Mag. Pubs. Assn., Women in Cable, Cable TV Advt. Bur., Nat. Cable TV Assn. Home: 215 E 68th St New York City NY 10021 Office: CBS 51 W 52d St New York NY 10019

JONES, CLARENCE ROLLINS, mech. engr.; b. Ashton, S.C., Nov. 7, 1923; s. Clarence Rollins and Susan (Black) J.; B.S. in Mech. Engring., Clemson A. and M. Coll., 1947, M.S., 1949; m. Eunice Varn Polk, July 26, 1944; children—Susan Varn, Mary Deborah. Instr., Clemson (S.C.) Coll., 1947-49; project engr. Patchen & Zimmerman Engrs., Augusta, Ga., 1949-51; owner, cons. engr., Jones Engring. Co. engring., archtl. firm, Augusta,; chmn. bd., pres. Jones & Fellers, architects, engrs. and planners, Mid-South Corp., 1951-75; chmn. bd. HDR Energy Devel. Corp., Augusta. Past chmn. Greater Augusta Arts Council. Served from pvt. to 1st lt. AUS, 1942-47; PTO. Registered profl. engr. Ga., S.C., N.C., Idaho, Ohio., Ala., Ky., Miss., W.Va., Tex., La., Fla., Va., N.Y., Md., N.J., Tenn., Ill., Ind., Hawaii, Ariz. Mem. Nat. Soc. Profl. Engrs. (past v.p., past vice chmn. profl. engrs. in pvt. practice), Am. Soc. Heating Refrigerating and Air Conditioning Engrs., ASME, Soc. Am. Mil. Engrs., Assn. U.S. Army, Ga. Soc. Profl. Engrs. (pres., dir. 1962—), Augusta Com. of 100, Augusta C. of C. (past chmn. red carpet com.). Mason, Lion (dir. Augusta 1960—), Elk. Methodist. Clubs: Augusta Country, Augusta Sailing. Prin. works include design of various comml., indsl. and instnl. facilities throughout U.S., and abroad. Home: 3445 Walton Way Augusta GA 30909 Office: Clarence R Jones Cons Ltd PO Box 1508 1508 Augusta GA 30903

JONES, CURTIS EDISON, ret. banker; b. Bellevue, Pa., Oct. 21, 1918; s. Chester D. and Jane (Green) J.; B.S., U. Pitts., 1950; m. Margaret R. McFarland, Apr. 21, 1943; children—Craig W., R. Scott. With Union Trust Co., Pitts., 1936-46; with Mellon Bank, N.A. (merger Union Trust Co. and Mellon Bank), Pitts., 1946—, asst. cashier, 1950-53, asst. v.p., 1953-56, v.p., 1956-70, sr. v.p. charge nat. dept., 1970-73, exec. v.p., 1973-74, pres., 1974-79; dir. Koppers Co., Inc., Martin Marietta Corp. Served from pvt. to lt. col. AUS, 1941-46. Mason. Office: Mellon Sq Pittsburgh PA 15230

JONES, DAVID B., lawyer, investment co. exec.; b. Jamestown, N.Y., Oct. 12, 1943; s. Gustav E. and Jeane Louise (Nord) J.; A.B., Dartmouth, 1965; M.B.A., U. So. Calif., 1967, J.D., 1970; m. Cornelia Corson Morris, Sept. 3, 1966; children—Caroline, David Kristofer. Admitted to Calif. bar, 1971; atty. firm Agnew, Miller & Carlson, Los Angeles, 1970-72; investment analyst Union Venture Corp., Los Angeles, 1972-73, sec., investment officer, 1973-74, v.p., sec., 1974-78; v.p. fin. and adminstrn. Am. Tech., Inc., Northridge, Calif., 1978, Tannery West Corp., San Francisco, 1978-79; pres. Western Bancorp Venture Capital Co., Los Angeles, 1979—. Mem. Am., Los Angeles County bar assns., State Bar Calif., Western Assn. Venture Capitalists (v.p., dir.), Dartmouth Club So. Calif. (v.p., dir.), Commerce Assos., Zeta Psi, Phi Delta Phi. Home: 1215 Wynn Rd Pasadena CA 91107 Office: 707 Wilshire Blvd Los Angeles CA 90017

JONES, DAVID C., corp. exec.; b. Rochester, N.Y., July 14, 1946; s. Carl Albert and Jacqueline Elizabeth (Oerth) J.; B.A., U. Conn., 1968; M.Div., Crozer Theol. Sem., 1971; M.B.A., Western New Eng. Coll., 1976; m. Sara Ramsey Davis, Aug. 26, 1967; children—Paul, Christopher, Steven. Customer service agt. Eastern Airlines, Windsor Locks, Conn., 1972-75; sr. cons. W.E. Donoghue & Co., Holliston, Mass., 1976-77; v.p. ops., treas. Automated Parts Removers, Springfield, Mass., 1977-78; coordinator advanced research and devel. Coleco Industries, Hartford, Conn., 1979—. Mem. Nat. Assn. Accts., Assn. M.B.A. Execs., Cash Mgmt. Assn. New Eng. Congregationalist. Author: Commercial Banking, rev. edit., 1979; also articles. Home: 44 Robinson Dr Westfield MA 01085 Office: 945 Asylum Ave Hartford CT 06105

JONES, E(BEN) BRADLEY, steel co. exec.; b. Cleve., Nov. 8, 1927; s. Eben Hoyt and Alfreda Sarah (Bradley) J.; B.A., Yale U., 1950; m. Ann Louise Jones, July 24, 1954; children—Susan Robb, Elizabeth Hoyt, Bradley Hoyt, Ann Campbell. With Republic Steel Corp., Cleve., 1954—, asst. dist. sales mgr., Chgo., 1964-65, asst. mgr. sales flat rolled div., 1965-67, sr. asst. mgr. sales flat rolled div., Cleve., 1967, mgr., 1967-71, v.p. mktg., Cleve., 1971-74, v.p. comml., 1974-76, exec. v.p., 1976-79, pres., 1979—, also chief operating officer, dir.; vice chmn., dir. Republic Supply Co.; v.p., dir. Union Drawn Steel Co. Ltd.; dir. Mooney Aircraft Corp., Republic Bldgs. Corp., Nat. City Bank Cleve., Nat. City Corp.; pres., dir. Ga. Tubing Corp.; dir. Republic Hibbing Corp., Republic Builders Products Corp., Res. Mining Co. Mem. exec. bd. Greater Cleve. council boy Scouts Am.; trustee, v.p., mem. exec. com. Cleve. Clinic Found.; trustee, exec. com. Univ. Sch., Cleve.; bd. dirs. INROADS/Cleve., Inc.; adv. bd. Case Inst. Tech., Cleve. Served with U.S. Army, 1950-53. Mem. Am. Iron and Steel Inst, Delta Kappa Epsilon. Office: PO Box 6778 Cleveland OH 44101*

JONES, EDWARD THOMAS, accountant; b. Mechanicville, N.Y., Nov. 12, 1933; s. Jesse and Loula (Whitfield) J.; B.B.A., Siena Coll., 1961; M.B.A., Pace U., 1979—; m. Rachel Manley, Aug. 22, 1970; children—Mark, Kimberly. Ins. examiner N.Y. State Ins. Dept., N.Y.C., 1961-65; asst. sec. treas. dept. Crum & Forster Ins. Co., N.Y.C., 1965-71; chief accountant N.Y. Fair Plan, N.Y.C., 1971-72; controller, chief fiscal officer United Negro College Fund, Inc., N.Y.C., 1972—. Served with U.S. Army, 1952-55. Mem. Nat. Assn. Black Accountants (past nat. sec.). Democrat. Baptist. Home: 47 E 56th St Brooklyn NY 11203 Office: 500 E 62d St New York NY 10021

JONES, EDWIN LEE, JR., constrn. co. exec.; b. Charlotte, May 6, 1921; s. Edwin Lee and Annabel Lambeth J.; B.S. in Civil Engring., Duke U., 1948; m. Lucille Finch, Oct. 16, 1943; children—Edwin, Annabel, Sam, John, David. With J.A. Jones Constrn. Co., Charlotte, 1948—, sec., 1953-57, v.p., 1957-60, pres., 1960—, also chmn.; dir. First Union Nat. Bank. Pres. YMCA, Charlotte, Mint Mus. Art; bd. dirs. Heineman Med. Research Center, Charlotte; trustee Duke U. Served with USMC, 1942-45. Mem. Soc. Am. Mil. Engrs., Phi Mu Epsilon, Chi Epsilon. Clubs: Quail Hollow Country, Charlotte City, Grandfather Golf and Country. Office: 6060 St Albans St Charlotte NC 28287

JONES, EMMETT WILLIAM, JR., beer and wine distbr.; b. Glasgow, Mont., Oct. 17, 1920; s. Emmett William and Della Caroline (Detchman) J.; B.Mortuary Sci., San Francisco Coll. Mortuary Sci., 1947; student U. Idaho, 1947-48; m. Joyce McCrum, Mar. 29, 1952; children—Candace, Emmett William III, Jerry R., Kevin M. Warehouseman, Morrison-Knudsen, Hanford, Wash., 1948-49; salesman Colyear Motor Sales, Spokane, Wash., 1949-51; partner beer distributorship, Sandpoint, Idaho, 1951-66, pres. Bill Jones Distbrs., Inc., 1979—. Served with U.S. Army, 1940-45. Mem. Idaho Wholesales (dir.), Sandpoint C. of C., Priest Lake and Priest River C. of C., Rocky Mountain Beverages Assn., Am. Legion, VFW. Democrat. Clubs: Masons, Shrine (pres. Panhandle club 1968-70), Lions, Elks, Eagles. Home and Office: Box 97 US 95 S and Lignite Rd Sandpoint ID 83864

JONES, EUNECE RITA BOEHLER, constrn. machinery co. exec.; b. Springfield, Ill., Oct. 8, 1946; d. Lawrence John and Alma Elizabeth (House) Boehler; A.A. in Bus. Adminstrn., Central YMCA Community Coll., 1976; B.A. in Human Resources Mgmt., Sangamon State U., 1978; m. Richard Earl Jones, June 26, 1965. With Fiat-Allis Constrn. Machinery Inc., Springfield, Ill., 1966—, personnel and salary adminstr., 1979—. Mem. cert. profl. sec. adv. com., mem. resource and referral adv. com. Lincoln Land Community Coll.; mem. Right to Read adv. council Ill. Office of Edn.; mem. adult edn. adv. council Springfield Public Schs. Recipient Sec. of Yr. award Nat. Secs. Assn., 1972; cert. of appreciation Ill. Welfare Assn., 1978; cert of merit Sangamon State U., 1979; cert. of recognition Springfield Mental Health Assn., 1979; cert. profl. sec. Mem. Am. Mgmt. Assn., Am. Personnel Assn., C. of C. Home: 112 N Wilson St Girard IL 62640 Office: Fiat-Allis Constrn Machinery Inc 3000 S 6th St Springfield IL 62710

JONES, EVAN VOORHEES, parking co. exec.; b. San Diego, Apr. 3, 1919; s. Albert J. and May (Voorhees) J.; B.A., Stanford, 1939; m. Sally Stevens, May 4, 1946; children—Steven, Scott, Wendy. Partner, mgr. Albert J. Jones & Son, real estate and ins. brokers, San Diego, 1939-50; owner, pres. Ace AutoParks, Inc., 1950—; dir. San Diego Fed. Savings and Loan Assn. Pres. San Diegans, Inc., 1967-69, chmn., 1969-71. Past pres. bd. dirs. Francis W. Parker Sch.; past dir. Bishops Sch.; past mem. Stanford Athletic Bd., Stanford Camp Assn.; bd. dirs. Donald M. Sharp Community Hosp., 1970—, Children's Hosp. Health Center, 1968-72; mem. San Diego Regional Coastal Commn., 1973-75. Served to lt. USNR, 1942-45. Mem. Nat. Parking Assn. (dir. 1960—, pres. 1966-68, chmn., 1968-70), San Diego Fine Arts Soc. (pres. 1966-67), San Diego C. of C. (dir. 1971-78, treas. 1974-75, pres. 1976), San Diego Symphony Assn. (dir. 1971-74), San Diego Downtown Assn. (v.p. 1971-73), Theta Delta Chi. Republican. Rotarian. Clubs: Stanford University Buck (pres. 1964-65), San Diego Yacht, University. Home: 530 San Fernando St San Diego CA 92106 Office: 770 B St San Diego CA 92101

JONES, GARY JAMES, respiratory therapist; b. Easton, Md., Aug. 8, 1947; s. James Orval and Ella Jane (Marshall) J.; A.A., Chesapeake Coll., Wye Mills, Md., 1975; B.A. in Health Care and Adminstrn., Ottawa U., Kansas City, Mo., 1980; m. Ruth Ann Williams, June 19, 1976. Electronics technician Harper's TV Service, St. Michaels, Md., 1966; mem. staff Meml. Hosp., Easton, 1969—, asst. dir. respiratory therapy, 1976—; instr. in field. Active Little League Football. Mem. Am. Lung Assn., Md. Eastern Shore Heart Assn. (chmn. CPR com. 1976-78), Md. Thoracic Soc., Am. Assn. Physicians Assts. Democrat. Episcopalian. Home: Route 1 Box 54 Easton MD 21601 Office: Memorial Hosp S Washington St Easton MD 21601

JONES, GERRE LYLE, mktg. and pub. relations cons.; b. Kansas City, Mo., June 22, 1926; s. Eugene Riley and Carolyn (Newell) J.; B.J., U. Mo., 1948, postgrad., 1953-54; m. Charlotte Mae Reinhold, Oct. 30, 1948; children—Beverly Anne Jones Putnam, Wendy Sue. Exec. sec. C. of C., Ill., 1948-50; field rep. Nat. Found. for Infantile Paralysis, N.Y., 1950-57; dir. pub. relations Inst. Logopedics, Wichita, Kans., 1957-58; owner Gerre Jones & Assos., Pub. Relations, Kansas City, Mo., 1958-63; info. officer Radio Free Europe, Munich, Germany, 1963-65, spl. asst. to dir. pub. relations, 1965-66; exec. asst. pub. affairs Edward Durell Stone, architect, 1967-68; dir. mktg. and communications Vincent C. Kling & Partners, Phila., 1969-71; mktg. cons. Ellerbe Architects, Washington, 1972; exec. v.p. Gaio Assos., Ltd., Washington, 1972-76; pres. Gerre Jones Assos., Inc., Washington, 1976—; sr. v.p. Barlow Assos., Inc., Washington, 1977-78; editor, pub. Profl. Mktg. Report, newsletter, 1976—; vis. lectr. mktg. various colls. and univs. Served with USAAF, 1944-45; maj. USAFR ret. Mem. Internat. Radio and Television Soc., Nat. Assn. Sci. Writers, Public Relations Soc. Am., Newsletter Assn. Am., Internat. Assn. Chiefs Police, Sigma Delta Chi, Alpha Delta Sigma, Phi Delta Phi. Republican. Mem. Christian Ch. Mason. Author: How To Market Professional Design Services, 1973; How To Prepare Professional Design Brochures, 1976; Public Relations for the Design Professional, 1980; contbr. articles to profl. jours. Clubs: Kansas City Press; Overseas Press; Deadline (N.Y.C.). Home: 2123 Tunlaw Rd NW Washington DC 20007 Office: PO Box 32387 Washington DC 20007

JONES, GILBERT TIMMONS, transp. co. exec.; b. Chamblee, Ga., Jan. 19, 1937; grad. Woodrow Wilson Sch. of Law, 1961; m. Jane Dyer, June 15, 1957; children—Gilbert Timmons, Patti Ann. With Allied Van Lines, 1957-64; with Home Transp. Co., Inc., Marietta, Ga., 1965—, v.p. sales and commerce, 1973-75, pres., chmn. bd., 1975—. Mem. Am. Mgmt. Assn., Nat. Assn. Specialized Carriers (sec.), Ga. Motor Trucking Assn. (dir.). Office: Home Transportation Co Inc PO Box 6426 Sta A Marietta GA 30065

JONES, GORDON BURR, ins. co. exec.; b. Peabody, Mass., Sept. 10, 1918; s. Burr Frank and Helen (Robinson) J.; A.B., Colby Coll., 1950; M.B.A., Harvard U., 1942; m. Geraldine A. Stefko, Sept. 12, 1942; children—Carol L., Gordon Burr, David R., Valerie G. Jones Roy, Allison G., Randall B. Investment analyst Providence Mut. Life Ins. Co. of Phila., 1945-48; with John Hancock Mut. Life Ins. Co., Boston, 1948—, v.p., 1966, sr. v.p., 1966-68, exec. v.p., 1968—, mem. exec. com., 1968—; dir. John Hancock Advs., Inc., John Hancock Growth Fund, Inc., John Hancock Bond Fund, John Hancock Investors, Inc., John Hancock Income Securities Corp., John Hancock Realty Devel. Corp., John Hancock Case Mgmt. Trust, John Hancock Tax-Exempt Income Trust, Raytheon Co., Jeffrey Co., Seiler Corp.; corporator, trustee Eliot Savs. Bank, Boston. Mem. corp. Mus. Sci., Boston; trustee, chmn. investment com. Colby Coll.; bd. dirs. Mass. Soc. Prevention Cruelty to Animals. Clubs: Boston Economic, Boston Security Analysts, Union, Brae Burn Country, Boston Madison Sq. Garden. Office: PO Box 111 Boston MA 02117

JONES, GRANT, state senator; b. Abilene, Tex., Nov. 11, 1922; s. Morgan and Jessie Kenan (Wilder) J.; B.B.A., So. Methodist U., 1947; M.B.A., Wharton Sch., U. Pa., 1948; m. Anne Smith, Aug. 21, 1948; children—Morgan Andrew, Janet Elizabeth. Engaged in ins. bus., 1948-72; admitted to Tex. bar, 1974; mem. Tex. Ho. of Reps. from 61st and 62d Dist., 1965-72; mem. Tex. Senate from 24th Dist., 1972—, chmn. fin. com., 1979—; vice chmn. bd. First Security Savs. Assn. Abilene, 1976—. Served to 1st lt. USAAF, World War II. C.P.C.U. Mem. Assn. C.P.C.U., State Bar Tex., Tex. Assn. Ins. Agts. (past pres.). Democrat. Methodist. Club: Kiwanis. Office: PO Box 5138 Abilene TX 79605

JONES, GREGORY BUDD, ins. agy. exec.; b. Woodbury, N.J., May 31, 1952; s. Joseph Warren and Lois (Budd) J.; B.S. in Bus. Adminstrn., Elizabethtown Coll., 1974; m. Marilyn Floy Bakes, Dec. 22, 1973. Ins. agent Storrie & Budd & Jones Agy., Inc., Woodbury, N.J., 1974—, broker, 1975—, sales mgr., 1977, mktg. mgr., corporate sec., 1978—. Mem. Woodbury Old-City Restoration Com. Mem. Profl. Ins. Agts., N.J., Woodbury (dir. 1975-77, pres. 1980-81) Jaycees, Woodbury C. of C. Home: 615 Lake Ave Woodbury Heights NJ 08097 Office: 35 Cooper St Woodbury NJ 08096

JONES, HARRY MCCOY, cons. engr., investor; b. Stillwater, N.Y., Oct. 19, 1896; s. Louis Benson and Isabelle (Gray McCoy) J.; B.S., U.S. Naval Acad., 1918; postgrad. in finance N.Y. U., 1927-28; m. Caroline A. Murray-Browne May 10, 1969. Financial work Wall Street, 1927-28; engring. work Walker Signal Equipment Co., 1928-30; distbn. mgr. Dry-Ice Corp. of Am., 1930-34; pvt. practice cons. engring., 1934-37; partner Weaver Assos., 1937-39; sr. partner Dunn & Jones, cons. engrs., 1940-48, sole partner, 1949-65; pres., dir. H-H Inc., real estate, investments and ranching, 1940—. Founder U.S. Naval Acad. Found., 1946, chmn., 1946-64, trustee, 1946—; trustee Textile Mus., Washington, 1967-72. Served as midshipman USN, 1915-18, ensign to lt., 1918-26, lt. to lt. comdr. USNR, 1926-43. Recipient Meritorious Pub. Service citation Dept. Navy; Scroll of Honor, Navy League U.S., 1963; Ann. Man of Year award U.S. Naval Acad. Assn. N.Y., 1961; named Hon. Adm., Brigade of Midshipmen, U.S. Naval Acad. Mem. Mil. Order World Wars, Soc. Am. Mil. Engrs., Am. Ordnance Assn., Am. Soc. Naval Engrs., Soc. Naval Architects and Marine Engrs., Am. Inst. Iranian Studies, Brit. Inst. Persian Studies, Assn. Interstate Commerce Practitioners, U.S. Naval Acad. Athletic Assn., Friends of Winterthur, U.S. Naval Acad.

Alumni Assn., Navy League U.S. (life), Naval Inst. (life), Rug Soc. Washington (pres.), Internat. Hajji Baba Soc. (pres.). Episcopalian. Clubs: Army and Navy Country, Cosmos, Arts (Washington); Hajji Baba, Army and Navy (N.Y.); Family, Marines' Memorial (San Francisco); Prospectors (Reno); Oriental Rug (Toronto, Can.); Las Cruses (Baja California, Mexico). Lectr., writer and collector antique Oriental rugs and Am. antiques. Home: 2280 Idlewild Dr Reno NV 89502 also 6122 Massachusetts Ave Washington DC 20016

JONES, JAMES DANIEL, liquor retailer; b. Hagerstown, Md., Aug. 8, 1931; s. Harvey Talmadge and Anna Virginia (Wilson) J.; m. Mary M. Gilmore, Feb. 14, 1953; children—Lamont, Lawanda. Mem. prodn. staff U.S. Steel Co., Morrisville, Pa., 1954, Gen. Motors Corp., Trenton, 1954-56; with U.S. Postal Service, 1956-70; pres. Viking Liquors, Inc., Kendall Park, N.J., 1970—. Mem. Middlesex County Welfare Bd., 1972; vice chmn. Middlesex County Bd., 1973-74; mem. South Brunswick Juvenile Conf., 1969-75; dist. fire commr., South Brunswick, 1980—. Served with USAF, 1949-53. Mem. Central Jersey Liquor Store Assn. (pres. 1980), South County C. of C. Democrat. Lutheran. Club: Rotary. Home: RD 4 Box 776 Princeton NJ 08540 Office: 3126 Lincoln Hey Kendall Park NJ 08824

JONES, JOHN GEORGE, retail games co. exec.; b. Paterson, N.J., Sept. 22, 1945; s. John J. and Anne T. Jones; B.S., Fairleigh Dicksnson U., 1974; m. Kimberley A. Cook, June 4, 1966; children—John M., Eric D. Sectional mgr. Two Guys, Totowa, N.J., 1968-74; contractor home improvements, Pompton Plains, N.J., 1974-77; owner Game Room, Fairfield, N.J., 1977—, sec./treas. Jones & Masters Games, Inc. Fairfield, 1977—. Served with USNR, 1966-68. Mem. Am. Legion. Home: 16 Bissell Rd Tewksbury NJ 08822 Office: Game Room 461 Route 46 Fairfield NJ 07006

JONES, JOHN GRANDEL, financial exec.; b. Mpls., 1920; ed. U. Minn., 1941, Harvard Bus. Sch. Formerly served as controller GM Container Machinery and other exec. positions; with Bostitch div. Textron, Inc., East Greenwich, R.I., Gen. Electric Co., Bridgeport, Conn.; chief fin. officer, dir., mem. exec. com. Chesebrough-Pond's Inc., N.Y.C.; sr. v.p. fin., chmn. finance com., dir. Econs. Lab., Inc., St. Paul; v.p. CBS, Inc., N.Y.C.; now sr. v.p., dir. corp. fin. Ross Stebbens, Inc., N.Y.C. Served with supply corps USNR, World War II. Home: 30 Sunswyck Rd Darien CT 06820 Office: 120 Broadway New York NY 10022

JONES, KENNETH CALLOW, III, mgmt. cons.; b. Evanston, Ill., Sept. 27, 1945; s. Kenneth Callow Jr. and Phyllis Rae (Wheelock) J.; B.A., Denison U., 1967; M.Govtl. Adminstrn., U. Pa., 1968; m. Ann Baker Mahone, Nov. 30, 1968; 1 son, Aaron McKennon. Budget analyst positions, dir. crime control program City of Rochester (N.Y.), 1968-71, dir. fed. program rev., 1972, dep. budget dir., 1973; budget officer City of Portland (Oreg.), 1973-78, dir. Office of Mgmt. Services, 1978-80; pres. Performance Mgmt. Assos., 1980—; adj. asst. prof. Portland State U., 1976—; instr. Inst. for Tng. in Municipal Adminstrn., Internat. City Mgmt. Assn., 1976—. Served to 1st lt. USAR, 1968-74. Samuel S. Fels scholar, 1967-68, fellow, 1968. Mem. Internat. City Mgmt. Assn., Am. Soc. Pub. Adminstrn., Municipal Finance Officers Assn., Am. Mgmt. Assn., Alpha Kappa Delta, Pi Sigma Alpha, Psi Chi. Office: 9530 SW Washington St Portland OR 97225

JONES, KENNETH EDWIN, JR., fin. exec.; b. Richmond, Va., May 13, 1948; s. Kenneth E. and Phyllis Ruth (McCoy) J.; B.S. in Nuclear Engring., U. Va., 1970, M.B.A., 1972; m. Donna Therese Hilburger, Feb. 3, 1973. Systems engr. AccuRay Corp., Columbus, Ohio, 1972-73, account mgr., 1973-76, mgr. credit and collections, 1976-77, mgr. fin. services, 1977-79, ops. mgr.-Japan, Tokyo, 1979—. Mem. Mensa, Phi Sigma Kappa. Home: 1009 Azadu Towers 1-3 Azabudai 2-chome Minato-ku Tokyo 106 Japan

JONES, KIRBY, trade and public affairs cons.; b. Bryn Mawr, Pa., Oct. 23, 1941; s. Maitland and Irma (Tillmanns) J.; B.A. in Polit. Sci., U. N.C., 1963; m. Linda Gail Jennings; children—Eliza Brandon, Kirby Maitland. Vol., Peace Corps, 1963-65, program officer, 1965-67; asst. to v.p. public affairs Columbia U., 1968-69; public affairs cons. Ted Van Dyk Assos., 1969-71, press sec. to George McGovern, 1971-72; exec. dir. Nat. Exec. Conf., 1972-75; pres. Alamar Assos., Inc., Washington, 1975—; spl. corr. CBS News, 1974; lectr., speaker profl. orgns. Campaign staff Sen. Robert Kennedy, 1968; campaign mgr. Allard Lowenstein for Congress, 1968; state field coordinator Richard Ottinger for U.S. Senate, N.Y., 1970. Recipient Claude M. Feuss award for disting. contbn. to public service Phillips Acad., Andover, Mass., 1967, citation of excellence for best TV interpretation of fgn. affairs Overseas Press Club, 1974. Author: (with others) With Fidel: A Portrait of Castro and Cuba, 1975; contbr. articles to New Rep., Politics Today, Fla. Commentary, Oui Mag. Office: 1511 K St NW Suite 830 Washington DC 20005

JONES, LOREN FARQUHAR, ednl. services co. exec.; b. St. Louis, July 4, 1905; s. E. F. B. and Cecil (Hough) J.; B.S. in Elec. Engring., Washington U., 1926; student Grad. Sch. Bus. Stanford, 1928-29; m. Mary Anna Larzelere, Sept. 30, 1950; children—Dayton L., Douglas H. Devel. engr. Gen. Electric Co., Schenectady, 1926-28; devel engr. RCA, Camden, N.J., 1929-37, fgn. rep., 1930, 37-38, mgr. research and devel. marketing, 1939-49, mgr. new product div., 1950-54, mgr. indsl. electronics planning, def. advanced tech. mktg., 1954-64, mgr. new bus. engring., 1964-68, dir. ednl. devel., 1968-70, cons. in electronics and edn., 1970-76; pres. Tech. and Ednl. Services, Inc., 1977—. With OSRD, 1941-45; mem. sci. adv. bd. USAF, 1947-48. Decorated Presdl. Certificate of Merit (U.S.). Fellow Inst. Areo. Scis. (asso.), I.E.E.E., Franklin Inst.; mem. Sigma Xi. Episcopalian. Pantentee in electronics. Home: 503 W Mermaid Lane Philadelphia PA 19118

JONES, LUCIUS SANDERFORD, savs. and loan exec.; b. Elizabeth City, N.C., Sept. 24, 1942; s. Thomas Graham and Mildred (Privette) J.; accounting student Hardbarger's Bus. Coll., 1961-62; bus. student N.C. State U., 1962-63; m. Carolyn Barnes, Mar. 1, 1964; 1 son, Lucius Sanderford. Auditor, Farmers Coop. Exchange, Raleigh, N.C., 1962-66; pres., mgr. Wendell Fed. Savs. & Loan Assn., Wendell, N.C., 1966—; dir. First Citizens Bank & Trust Co., Wendell. Vice chmn. Wake County (N.C.) Land Use Com., 1973-74; mem. Triangle J. Council Govts., 1973; mem. Wendell Town Bd., 1971—; officer Democrat precinct, 1969-74, Wendell Planning Bd., 1970-72. Mem. Wendell (pres. 1971), N.C. (v.p. 1972, presdl. adviser 1974), U.S. (adminstrv. nat. dir. 1973) jr. chambers commerce, Wake County Homebuilders Assn., Wake County Fireman's Assn. Home: Selma Rd Wendell NC 27591 Office: Box 10 Wendell NC 27591

JONES, MICHAEL ALLAN, mgmt. and ins. agy. exec.; b. N.Y.C., Jan. 18, 1940; s. Theodore Butler and Dorothy Hazel (Kingsland) J.; B.A. (NSF fellow), Colgate U., 1960; postgrad. U. So. Calif. Grad. Bus. Sch., 1969-71; m. Edna Elizabeth DesVerney, Aug. 1, 1964; children—Stephen Allan, Tanya Elizabeth. Personnel supr. Avon Products Co., Pasadena, Calif., 1967-70, sales service mgr., 1970-73, personnel mgr., 1973-76; v.p. mgmt. div. Christensen & Jones, Mgmt. & Ins. Services, Inc., Los Angeles, 1976—. Bd. dirs. Watts Tng. Center, Pasadena Urban Coalition; mem. industry adv. council Los Angeles Opportunities Industrialization Center; bd. dirs. Alhambra Am. Little League. Served with USN, 1960-67; Vietnam. Mem. Am. Soc. Pension Actuaries, Personnel and Indsl. Relations Assn., Am. Soc. Personnel Mgmt. Office: 1015 Wilshire Blvd Los Angeles CA 91754

JONES, MILDRED JOSEPHINE, realtor; b. Anniston, Ala., Jan. 29; d. Howard McFadden and Gladys Eulala (Carr) J.; student Howard Coll., Birmingham, Ala., 1947. Retail and secretarial positions, 1948-65; area, then dist. mgr. in Montgomery, Ala. for Field Enterprises Ednl. Corp., 1965-71; engaged in real estate sales, 1971—; founder, owner Southland Realty Co., Montgomery, 1974—. Mem. Nat. Assn. Realtors, Farm and Land Inst., Montgomery Bd. Realtors. Presbyterian. Club: Point Aquarius Country. Home: 3024 Biltmore Ave Montgomery AL 36109 Office: 2006 Mulberry Montgomery AL 36106

JONES, PAUL EUGENE, JR., computer service co. exec.; b. Oberlin, Ohio, Aug. 2, 1932; s. Paul Eugene and Dorothy (Landis) J.; A.B., Harvard U., 1954, S.B., 1959; m. Janet F. Wright, Dec. 28, 1957; children—Peter Cunningham, David Blandford. Research asso. Harvard Computation Lab., 1958-60; profl. staff mem. Arthur D. Little, Inc., Cambridge, Mass., 1960-69, sr. staff mem., 1975-79; v.p., dir. Corp.-Tech Planning, Inc., Waltham, Mass., 1969-75; pres. Gaylord Library Systems, Liverpool, N.Y., 1979—; cons. in large scale data base design, 1968—. Mem. exec. com., bd. dirs. Brooks Sch. Concord, Inc., 1966-69, pres., 1968-69; pres. Point Meadows Assn., 1978—. Served to lt. (j.g.) USN, 1954-57; Korea. Mem. Assn. for Computing Machinery, Sigma Xi. Clubs: Harvard Varsity, Speakers (pres. 1954). Co-author: Automatic Language Processing, 1969; author: Framework for Logical Data Base Design, 1976; contbr. articles to profl. jours.; patentee apparatus for optical character recognition. Home: Hoffman Ln Cazenovia NY 13035 Office: 7272 Morgan Rd Liverpool NY

JONES, RALPH LLOYD, credit union exec.; b. Gainesville, Fla., Oct. 5, 1946; s. Richard Palmer and Alice Ruth (Adams) J., Jr.; B.S. in Applied Math., Ga. Inst. Tech., 1968; m. Gloria Faye Huckaby, June 24, 1978; children—Shanna Celeste, Michael Shane, Eric Quincy. Asst. mgr. HEW Atlanta Fed. Credit Union, 1969-78, mgr., 1978—; pres. Ga. Central Credit Union, Atlanta, 1980—; pres., treas. Bond Community Fed. Credit Union, 1975-78. Pres., performing mem. Gypsy Rainbow Dance Theatre, 1974-78. Mem. Credit Union Execs. Soc., Ga. Credit Union League (dir.), Nat. Assn. Fed. Credit Unions, Ga. Credit Union Mgrs. Assn. (organizer), Greater Atlanta Credit Union Chpt. (dir.), Atlanta C. of C., Triple Nine Soc. Home: PO Box 54818 Atlanta GA 30308 also 763 Dixie Ave NE Atlanta GA 30307 Office: PO Box 1710 Atlanta GA 30301 also 101 Marietta Tower Suite 812 Atlanta GA 30303

JONES, REGINALD HAROLD, elec. mfg. co. exec.; b. Stoke-on-Trent, Staffordshire, Eng., July 11, 1917; s. Alfred John and Gertrude (Cartlidge) J.; B.S. in Econs., U. Pa., 1939; m. Grace Butterfield Cole, Mar. 2, 1940; children—Keith Edwin, Grace Seymour Jones Vineyard. With Gen. Electric Co., 1939—, bus. trainee and traveling auditor, 1939-50, asst. to comptroller, apparatus dept. assignments, 1950-56, gen. mgr. Air Conditioning div., 1956-58, gen. mgr. Gen. Electric Supply Co. div., 1958-61, v.p. parent co., 1961—, gen. mgr. constrn. industries div., 1964-67, group exec., 1967-68, v.p. finance, 1968-70, sr. v.p., 1970-72, vice chmn., 1972, pres., 1972-73, chmn. bd., chief exec. officer, 1973—; dir. Federated Dept. Stores, Inc. Office: 3135 Easton Turnpike Fairfield CT 06431*

JONES, ROBERT JAMES, mech. engr.; b. Tennille, Ga., July 24, 1943; s. Willie James and Ola (Jordan) J.; B.S. in Mech. Engring. (Engring. Graphics award 1968), Tuskegee (Ala.) Inst., 1972; m. Shirley Roberson, Aug. 24, 1968. Process, then project engr. E.I. duPont Co., Newark, Del. and Parlin, N.J., 1972-76, shift supr., Aiken, S.C., 1976-79; project mgr. Philip Morris, U.S.A., Richmond, Va., 1979—; dir. Jones and Geer Enterprises, Inc., Richmond, 1980—. Served with USAF, 1962-66. Mem. ASME, Am. Mgmt. Assn. Baptist. Office: 6301 Midlothian Turnpike Richmond VA 23225

JONES, ROBERT LEE, petroleum co. exec.; b. Hutchinson, Kans., Apr. 13, 1927; s. Ralph Wilson and Bertha Christina (Peterson) J.; A.B., M.A., U. Kans., 1949; children—Mary Christina, Michael Allen. Founder, pres. Amco Petroleum Co., Chgo., 1954—, Apco Records, Chgo., 1958—; pres. Amco Stores Corp., Chgo., 1962—; founder, pres., chmn. bd. Amco Tire Corp., Chgo., 1966—; founder Am. Nat. Opera Co., Chgo., 1962; owner, operator Consultants Internat., Inc., Chgo., Washington, Bellevue, Nebr. Served with AUS, 1945-46. Mem. Retail Store Assn., Tire Mktg. Assn., Petroleum Mktg. Inst. Republican. Methodist. Author: The Jew and the Gentile, 1960; The Man Who Played God, 1962. Home: 1902 Gregg Rd Bellevue NE 68005 Office: PO Box 126 Bellevue NE 68005 also PO Box 8329 Chicago IL 60680

JONES, ROBERT LETTS, ret. publishing co. exec.; b. Oakland, Cal., Nov. 9, 1913; s. Madison Ralph and Carolyn (Oliver) J.; student U. Ariz., 1935; A.B., Stanford, 1936; m. Darlene M. Zahalka, stepchildren—Michelle Zahalka, Christina Zahalka. Editor, bus. mgr. Stanford (U.) Daily, 1935-36; war corr. Spanish Civil War, U.P.I., 1936; free lance League of Nations Session, Geneva, 1936; editorial side Chronicle, San Francisco, 1937-39; editor, pub. Vallejo (Calif.) Evening-News, 1939-42; asst. bus. mgr. Los Angeles Examiner, 1946-47; asst. pub. Salem (Oreg.) Capital Jour., 1947-53; asst. gen. mgr. Detroit News, 1953-57; dir. Inst. Newspaper Ops., 1955-56; dir. personnel Copley Press, Inc., La Jolla, Calif., 1957-59, v.p., dir., 1959-65, pres., 1965-75, mem. exec. com., 1963-75; hon. chmn. Copley Internat. Corp., 1968-74; dir. So. Calif., Asso. Newspapers. Mem. U.S. State Dept. Joint Com. on U.S.-Japan Cultural and Ednl. Cooperation, 1971-74; dir. Audit Bur. Circulations, 1963-65; mem. advisory com. Stanford Profl. Journalism Fellowships Program. Pres. Calif. Newspaperboy Found., 1963-64, 1st v.p., 1962-63, chmn. bd., 1964-65; bd. dirs. Anita Oliver Lunn Found., 1961—; trustee Scripps Clinic & Research Found., 1964-79. Served with USMCR, 1942-46. Decorated Bronze Star, Purple Heart; recipient First prize for editorial writing in Oreg., 1948; Honor certificate Freedoms Found., 1965. Mem. Internat. Press Inst., U.S. C. of C. (taxation com. 1959-63), Am. Council on Edn. for Journalism, Am. Newspaper Pub. Assn. (taxation com. 1959-72, labor relations com. 1969-74), Stanford Assos., Stanford Alumni Assn., Marine Corps Res. Officers Assn., 5th Marine Div. Assn., Soc. Calif. Pioneers, Wine and Food Soc. London, Confreries de la Chaine des Rotisseurs, Co. Mil. Historians, Navy League, Internat. Fedn. Newspapers Pubs., Delta Upsilon, Sigma Delta Chi. Republican. Congregationalist. Clubs: Circumnavigators; La Jolla Beach and Tennis; Adcraft (Detroit); Nat. Press (Washington); Explorers, Overseas Press (N.Y.C.); Bohemian, San Francisco. Home: 17520 Rancho de Oro Ramona CA 92065

JONES, ROBERT STUART, publisher; b. Pasadena, Calif., Apr. 1, 1942; s. Edward Winslow and Jean Eileen (Wolfe) J.; A.A., DeAnza Coll., 1972; B.A., Calif. State U., Fullerton, 1976; m. Nancy Anne Spindle, Jan. 11, 1964; children—Carolyn Jean, Robert Stuart. Mil. acct. exec. Nat. Semi-condr. Corp., Santa Clara, Calif., 1971-73; sr. sales engr. Intel Corp., Santa Clara, 1973-75; pres., editor-in-chief pub. Interface Age Mag., Cerritos, Calif., 1975—; pres., editor-in-chief, pub. Interface Age Mag. Verlag GmbH Ger., Haar b. Munich, W. Ger., 1981—; dir. Tech-Ser, Inc., rep. orgn. Served with U.S. Army, 1962-65. Mem. Soc. Bus. Press Editors (charter), Western Pubs. Assn. (Maggie award 1978, 79). Author booklets: A Tutor on Small Business Computing, 1977; Starting Your Own Computer Business: Aspects of Promotion, Sales, and Marketing, 1978. Office: 16704 Marquardt St Cerritos CA 90701

JONES, RODDIS STEWART, constrn. and land devel. co. exec.; b. Marshfiled, Wis., Jan. 11, 1930; s. Henry Stewart and Sara Roddis J.; B.A.M.E., Auburn U., 1952; P.M.D., Harvard U., 1960; postgrad. U. Wis., Madison, 1959; m. Anne Crook Orum, Jan. 7, 1955; children—Patricia, Jeffrey, Jennifer. Project engr. Marathon Corp., Rothschild, Wis., 1955-57; prodn. supt. indsl. engring., mgr. cost acctg. Roddis Plywood Corp., Marshfield, Wis., 1957-60; br. mgr. Weyerhaeuser Co., Hancock, Vt., Oakland, Calif. and Federal Way, Wash., 1960-78; pres., gen. mgr. Roddis Jones Cos., Solarcrete N.W., Investment Bldg. & Devel. Co., Paneling Place, Seattle, 1978—. Served as officer USN, 1952-55. Mem. Seattle Master Builders. Republican. Episcopalian. Clubs: Rotary, Elks, Masons. Home: 104 Cascade Key Bellevue WA 98006 Office: 915 Industry Dr Seattle WA 98188

JONES, ROY STEVEN, bus. forms mfg. co. mgr.; b. Weston, W.Va., Dec. 22, 1944; s. Lloyd Hall and Ethel Marie (Flinn) J.; student W.Va. Wesleyan Coll., 1962-63, Glenville (W.Va.) State Coll., 1963; A.A., Santa Barbara City Coll., 1967; B.A., U. Calif. at Santa Barbara, 1973; m. Rebecca Susan Piercy, Mar. 26, 1964; children—Stephanie Lynne, Allyson Elise. Hwy. insp. W.Va. Rd. Commn., Weston, 1964-66; shipping clx. Automated Bus. Forms Inc., 1966-68, collator, pressman, 1968-72, asst. plant mgr. prodn., 1972-79, co-owner, plant mgr., corp. sec., 1979—. Active Citizens for Good Water, 1978—; chmn. bd. dirs. Vocat. Instrn. Pub. Schs.; exec. dir. Com. for Goleta Valley, 1979—; mem. Santa Barbara County Democratic Central Com., 1979—; v.p. Goleta Valley Dem. Club, 1979—. Mem. Goleta C. of C. (v.p.), Tri-Counties Graphic Industries Assn., Nat. Bus. Forms Assn. (corporate). Democrat. Baptist. Clubs: Santa Barbara Men's Golf, Los Paisanos Latinos. Home: 6171 Verdura Ave Goleta CA 93017 Office: 137 Aero Camino Goleta CA 93017

JONES, RUTHANNE M., mgmt. cons.; b. Warrensburg, Mo., Oct. 19, 1935; d. J. Kenneth and Ruth A. (Noble) Marr; B.A., U. So. Calif., 1956, B.S., 1958; postgrad. London Sch. Econs., 1956-57; M.A., Central Mo. State U., 1962; m. Keith D. Jones, Jan. 31, 1964; children—Brian, Stephen. Dir., Cerebral Palsey Nursery Sch., UCLA, 1959; pres., dir. Jones and Assos., Warrensburg, Mo., 1970—; owner, adminstr. Mid-Am. Rehab., Rehab. Equipment, Inc. Mem. Nat. Assn. Rehab. Agys. (pres.-elect 1980), Am. Phys. Therapy Assn. Presbyterian. Club: Warrensburg Country. Home: 711 S Holden St Warrensburg MO 64093 Office: 122 E Market St Warrensburg MO 64093

JONES, T. EMBURY, JR., comml. mortgage and bus. fin. co. exec.; b. Warren, Ohio, Apr. 11, 1931; s. T. Embury and Leah Albertine (Pettit) J.; A.B., Columbia U., 1953; m. Marilyn Aileen Shay, Aug. 8, 1953; children—Gordon Embury, Aileen Leah. Ops. supr. Gt. Lakes Steel Corp., Detroit, 1958-60; research and devel. engr. central staff Ford Motor Co., Dearborn, Mich., 1960-62; salesman IBM Corp., East Orange, N.J., 1962-64, Honeywell Corp., N.Y.C., 1964-65; mgmt. cons. Ernst & Ernst, Hartford, Conn., 1965-66; gen. mgr. Buckingham Data Center, Southport, Conn., 1966-67; systems mgr. Travelers Ins. Co., Hartford, 1967-72; adminstr. Aetna Life & Casualty Co., Hartford, 1972-75; chief exec. officer Mart Internat., Inc., West Hartford, Conn., 1975—; vis. tchr. Hartford Inst. Accounting, 1978—. Served with USN, 1953-58; capt. Res. Mem. Nat. Mortgage Exchange, Am. Credit Exchange, Greater Hartford C. of C., 43d Flying Club, Flying Comdrs. (pres.). Republican. Episcopalian. Home: 1909 Blvd West Hartford CT 06107 Office: 179 Allyn St Suite 310 Hartford CT 06103

JONES, THOMAS ARGOLUS, fin. co. exec.; b. Ocala, Fla., June 19, 1926; s. Thomas Argolus and Lillian Elizabeth (Baskin) J.; student U. Fla., Massey Bus. Coll., Jacksonville, Fla., Gen. Electric Co. Mgmt. Inst.; m. Myrtle Juanita Evers, June 4, 1948; 1 dau., Debra Ann Jones Mordaunt. With dist. acctg. office Firestone Tire & Rubber Co., Jacksonville, 1942-44, 46-48; With Gen. Electric Credit Corp., 1948—, v.p., gen. mgr. indsl. equipment fin. dept., Stamford, Conn., 1971—; dir. Genelcan, Toronto, Ont., Can. Deacon, Greenwich (Conn.) Baptist Ch., 1976—; mem. Mayor Stamford Downtown Middle Income Housing Council, 1978—. Served with USNR, 1944-46. Mem. Southwestern Area Commerce and Industry Assn. Republican. Club: Winged Foot Golf (Mamaroneck, N.Y.). Home: 2042 High Ridge Rd Stamford CT 06903 Office: 260 Long Ridge Rd Stamford CT 06904

JONES, THOMAS LANE, accountant; b. Jayton, Tex., June 8, 1927; s. Thomas Lemarcus and Itha (Lane) J.; B.S., Tex. A&M U., 1950; B.B.A., Lamar State Coll., 1956; m. Katherine Olivia Harris, Aug. 6, 1978; children—Thomas Lemarcus, Richard Hamilton. Mgr. plant systems Eastex, Inc., Beaumont, Tex., 1960-67; chief accountant Star Engraving Co., Houston, 1966-67; mgr. plant systems Rockwell Internat. Corp., 1967-71; v.p., dept. mgr. Cameron-Brown Co., Raleigh, N.C., 1977—. Served with USN, 1945-47. C.P.A., N.C., 1962. Mem. Am. Inst. C.P.A.'s, Tex. Soc. C.P.A.'s. Democrat. Methodist. Home: 7001 Pleasant Dr Charlotte NC 28211 Office: 1st Union Plaza Charlotte NC 28288

JONES, THOMAS VICTOR, aero. exec.; b. Pomona, Calif., July 21, 1920; s. Victor March and Elizabeth (Brettelle) J.; student Pomona Jr. Coll., 1938-40; B.A. with great distinction, Stanford, 1942; LL.D., George Washington U.; m. Ruth Nagel, Aug. 10, 1946; children—Ruth Marilyn, Peter Thomas. Engr., El Segundo div. Douglas Aircraft Co., 1941-47; tech. adviser Brazilian Air Ministry, 1947-51; prof., head dept. Brazilian Inst. Tech., 1947-51; staff Rand Corp., 1951-53; asst. to chief engr. Northrop Corp., 1953, dep. chief engr., 1954-56, dir. devel. planning, 1956-57, corp. v.p., 1957, sr. v.p., 1958-59, pres., 1959-75, chief exec. officer, 1960—, chmn. bd., 1963—. Trustee Harvard Sch., Los Angeles. Fellow Am. Inst. Aeros. and Astronautics; mem. Nat. Security Indsl. Assn., Los Angeles World Affairs Council. Clubs: Sunset; The California; The Beach (Santa Monica). Author: Capabilities and Operating Costs of Possible Future Transport Airplanes, 1953. Home: 1050 Moraga Dr Los Angeles CA 90049 Office: 1800 Century Park E Century City Los Angeles CA 90067

JONES, W(ILLIAM) KENTLEY, investment banker; b. Wyoming, Pa., May 18, 1943; s. Kentley Rollin and Ruth May (Semmens) J.; B.S. in Math., USAF Acad., 1965; M.B.A. in Fin., Harvard U., 1972; m. Nelda Jeanette Brents, Mar. 28, 1970. Commd. 2d lt. USAF, 1965, advanced through grades to capt., 1968, resigned, 1970; procurement officer, 1965-67; chief Incentive Contracting Program Office, Dept. Def., 1967-70; with Smith Barney, Harris Upham & Co., N.Y.C., 1972—, v.p. pub. fin. div., 1977-79, 1st v.p., 1979—. Decorated Meritorious Service medal. Office: 1345 Ave of the Americas New York NY 10105

JONES, W. RICHARD, business exec.; b. Glenwood Springs, Colo., Aug. 27, 1927; s. Shattuc and Laura (Mills) J.; B.S. in Bus. Adminstrn., U. Denver, 1955, postgrad., 1955-56; postgrad. San Fernando Valley State Coll., 1960, U. Cal. at Los Angeles, 1960; m. Shirley Ann Nyhus, June 4, 1955; children—Craig Nyhus, Dana Ann, Kelly Shattuc. Partner, Jones & Shinkle, C.P.A.'s, Denver, 1954-60; with Rexall Chem. Co., Los Angeles, 1961; mgmt. cons. Ernst & Ernst, Los Angeles, St. Louis, 1962-64; sec.-controller, dir. Von Hoffmann Co., Crestwood, Mo., 1965-68; dir. internat. finance, automotive internat. div. TRW, Inc., Cleve., 1968-72; dir. bus. mgmt. finance, systems communications div. Motorola, Inc., Schaumburg, Ill., 1972-73; v.p., chief fin. officer Clow Corp., Oak Brook, Ill., 1973-75; pres. Mercury Metal Products, Schaumburg, 1975—. Instr., U. Denver, 1955-56. Bd. dirs., chmn. Found. for Human Ecology; bd. dirs. Luth. Inst. Human Ecology, Parkside Found., Parkside Human Services, 1980—; treas. Arapahoe County Young Republicans, 1956. Served with USN, 1943-47, 50-51. C.P.A., Colo., Calif., Mo. Mem. Am. Inst. C.P.A.'s, Nat. Assn. Accountants, Sales and Mktg. Execs., Fin. Execs. Inst., Am. Mgmt. Assn., Beta Alpha Psi. Republican. Lutheran. Kiwanian. Home: 470 Duck Pond Ln Barrington IL 60010 Office: 1201 S Mercury Dr Schaumburg IL 60193

JONES, WAYNE PAUL, restaurant chain exec.; b. Louisville, Aug. 3, 1942; s. James Paul and Dorothey Smiles (Pace) J.; B.S., U. Ky., 1964; M.B.A., U. Louisville, 1970; m. Linda Allen, Dec. 16, 1966; children—Andrea Lynn, Rebecca Allison. With Standard Oil of N.J., 1964-66, H.J. Heinz Co., 1966-70; with Heublein, 1970-78, pres. Heublein (Can.), 1976-78; v.p. corp. devel. Arby's Inc. div. Royal Crown Cos., Inc., Atlanta, 1979—. Mem. Nat. Restuarant Assn., Am. Mgmt. Assn. Republican. Methodist. Club: Brookfield West Country. Office: Arby's Inc One Piedmont Center 3565 Piedmont Rd NE Atlanta GA 30505

JONES, WILLIAM STANLEY, psychol. cons.; b. Rochester, Pa., Feb. 1, 1934; s. William Stanley and Philippa Alice (Stokes) J.; B.A., Carson Newman Coll., 1955; M.A., U. N.C., 1960, Ph.D., 1961; A.A., Mars Hill Coll., 1953; m. Dotty Lou Phillips, Jan. 22, 1955; children—James David, Linda Diane, Donna Lynn. Staff psychologist Mead Corp., Chillicothe, Ohio, 1960-61; dir. research S.C. State Hosp., 1961-62; supr. assessment Standards Oil Co. Ohio, Cleve., 1962-65; partner William Lynde and Williams, Inc., Painesville, Ohio, 1965-79; pres.William S. Jones, Inc., Cleve., 1979—; dir. Profl. Devel., Inc., 1974—; adj. prof. U. S.C., 1961-62, Kent State U., 1963-66. Mem. task force Aurora City Schs., 1972, 74. USPHS fellow, 1958-60; lic. psychologist, Ohio. Mem. Am. Psychol. Assn., Ohio Psychol. Assn., Ohio Acad. Cons. Psychologists, Nat. Psychol. Cons.'s to Mgmt. Republican. Baptist. Author: (with Robert Finkle) Assessing Corporate Talent, 1970; (with Guyon) Managerial Game Plan, Appraisals in Action, 1974, 2d edit. 1976, You The Supervisor, 1971, Performance Reviews That Build Commitment, 1970. Home: 311 Fox Run Trail Aurora OH 44202 Office: 2915 Terminal Tower Cleveland OH 44113

JONSON, CHAD REID, assn. exec.; b. St. Paul, Aug. 14, 1943; s. Reid Geddis and Arlene Jannis (Larson) J.; B.A. in Bus. Adminstrn., Eastern Wash. State Coll.; M.A., Kinman Bus. U.; m. Sharon Kay Storkson, Sept. 7, 1968; children—Gavin Marc, Shelby Dawn, Jennifer Kay. With Pacific Fruit & Produce Co., Seattle, 1965-66; traffic mgr. N.W. Steel Rolling Mills, Seattle, 1966-67; supr. inventory control Crane Supply Co., Seattle, 1967-68; gen. mgr. Reid G. Jonson Co., gen. contractors, Spokane, 1968-76; nat. membership chmn., enrollment and program growth mgr. U.S. Jaycees, Tulsa, 1976-77, S.W. regional rep., Phoenix, 1977—, bd. dirs., 1974—; pres. V. King Engring. and Constrn. Co. Inc.; now v.p. Double AA Constructors, Inc., Phoenix. Pres., Jaycees, Lynnwood, Wash., 1967, bd. dirs. Spokane, 1970, v.p. Wash., 1973-74, bd. dirs., 1972—, internat. senator; bd. dirs. Jaycee Youth Center, Spokane. Home: 6306 N 34th Dr Phoenix AZ 85017

JORDAN, CHUCK, publishing co. exec.; b. N.Y.C., Apr. 5, 1937; s. James Lawrence and Maria Rosa (Zema) Giordano; B.S. in Bus. Adminstrn., Rutgers U., 1958. Reporter, city editor various newspapers, 1959-68; news dir. sta. KWSL, Grand Junction, Colo., 1965-68, Sta. KDGO, Sta. KIUP, Durango, Colo., 1968-70; stringer UPI, AP, 1965-70; owner, mgr. Aries Pub. Co., Phoenix, 1974—; dir. advanced underwriting Met. Life Ins. Co., Phoenix, 1975—. Served with USCG, 1952-58. Mem. Nat. Assn. Securities Dealers, Million Dollar Round Table, Met. Life President's Conf. (officer). Author: Promises to Keep, 1974, Once More Love, 1979, Survival Kit for The New Life Insurance Agent, 1980. Office: Met Life Ins Co 3118 N 7th Ave Phoenix AZ 85013

JORDAN, DUPREE, JR., editor, pub., educator, mgmt. cons., bus. exec.; b. Decatur, Ga., May 14, 1929; s. DuPree and Roslyn (Moncrief) J.; A.B., Mercer U., 1947; M.Ed., Emory U., 1954; LL.B., Atlanta Law Sch., 1951, LL.D., 1963, D. Litt., 1971; postgrad. Crozer Theol. Sem., 1948-49, Nat. Inst. Pub. Affairs, summer 1967, Inst. Life-Long Learning, Harvard U., 1979; m. Margaret Virginia Malone, Dec. 28, 1948; children—Peggy (Mrs. Vernon Lee DeSear, Jr.), Duke, Lyn (Mrs. William Danny Whitworth), Terri Lee (Mrs. Michael David Chesser). Ordained to ministry Bapt. Ch., 1945; pastor Eden Bapt. Ch., Savannah, Ga., 1946-47, Duluth (Ga.) Bapt. Ch., 1954-55; reporter Chester (Pa.) Times, 1948-49; news dir. radio sta. WVCH, Chester, Pa., 1948-49; asso. dir. Radio and Television Commn. So. Bapt. Conv., Atlanta, 1949-52, acting dir., 1952-53; tchr. history, speech U. Ga., Atlanta, 1952-55, Bible, English, Westminster Schs., Atlanta, 1954-55; editor, pub., owner West End Star, Atlanta, 1955-66, N. DeKalb Record, Chamblee, Ga., 1956-64, TriCounty Graphic, Atlanta, 1962-64, Piedmont Satellite, 1967-68; pres. Jordan Enterprises, Inc., 1957—, Jordan & Jordan, Advt. and Pub. Relations, 1954—, Fun Products, Inc., 1968-69, Success Publs., Inc., 1969—; pub. Success Orientation, 1969—; partner WE Inc., convenience food stores, 1968-69; dir. pub. affairs So. region Office Econ. Opportunity, Atlanta, 1965-69. News reporter, panelist television stas., Atlanta, 1955-76; exec. dir. Assn. Pvt. Colls. and Univs. in Ga., 1970—; dir. Successful Selling seminars; pres. Ga. Coll. for Leadership Devel., 1969—. Mem. Gov.'s Rapid Transit Com., 1963-64. Gov.'s Com. for World's Fair in Atlanta, 1962-64; nat. religious liaison officer OEO, Washington, summer 1968; pres. Christian Council Met. Atlanta, 1973. Bd. dirs. Atlanta Girls Club, YMCA, Boy Scouts Am. Named Man of Year radio stas., Atlanta, 1962, 63, West End Jr. C. of C., 1962; recipient Quill award Sigma Delta Chi, 1962, 63, named Ky. col., 1967; mem. hon. staff Gov. Ga., 1962-66, 70-74, 74-78; honored with Rev. Dr. DuPree Jordan, Jr. Day in State of Ga., 1973. Mem. Ga. Press Assn. (bd. mgrs. 1964-65), Nat. Editorial Assn., Nat. Press Club Washington, West End Bus. Men's Assn. (pres. 1962-63), Chamblee-Doraville Bus. Men's Assn. (pres. 1963-64), Fulton County Grand Jurors Assn. (dir. 1961), Atlanta, DeKalb County (dir. 1961) chambers commerce, World Future Soc., Pub. Relations Soc. Am., Adminstrv. Mgmt. Soc., Am. Soc. for Pub. Adminstrn., Sales and Mktg. Execs. Internat., Soc. for Advancement Mgmt., Am. Mgmt. Assn., A.I.M., Am. Marketing Assn., Am. Soc. for Tng. and Devel., Am., Ga. Socs. assn. execs., Soc. Assn. Mgrs., Am. Assn. Coll. and Univ. Execs., So. Assn. Colls. (State Execs. Council coordinating chmn. 1980), State Assn. Execs. Council, Ga., Internat. assns. bus. communicators, Internat. Soc. Ednl. Planners, Am. Acad. Polit. and Social Sci., Meeting Planners Internat., Nat. Speakers Assn. (profl. awards com.), Assn. Mgmt. Consultants, Internat. Mgmt. Council, Inst. Mgmt. Consultants, Sigma Delta Chi (dir. 1963), Blue Key, Phi Delta, Alpha Chi Omega, Alpha Psi Omega, Kappa Sigma. Home: 1204 Warren Hall Ln NE Atlanta GA 30319 Office: 3121 Maple Dr NE Suite One Atlanta GA 30305

JORDAN, EDWARD GEORGE, railroad exec.; b. Oakland, Calif., Nov. 13, 1929; s. Edward A. and Alice J.; B.A. in Econs. with honors, U. Calif., Berkeley, 1951; M.B.A., Stanford U., 1953; m. Nancy Phyllis Schmidt, June 20, 1954; children—Susan Gail, Kathryn Claire, Jonathan Edward, Christopher Austin. With Avery Products Corp., Los Angeles, 1961-68, v.p., gen. mgr., 1964-68; group v.p. Computing and Software, Inc., Los Angeles, 1968-73; pres. Pinehurst Corp., Los Angeles, 1973-74; chmn., chief exec. officer Consol. Rail Corp., Phila., 1975—; pres. U.S. Ry. Assn., Washington, 1974-75; bd. mgrs. Western Savs. Bank; dir. ARA Services, Inc., Shearson Loeb Rhodes, Inc.; mem. panel Carnegie Endowment Internat. Peace, U.S. Security and Future Arms Control, 1980; mem. policy com. Bus. Council Pa. Bd. govs. Franklin Inst.; bd. dirs. Greater Phila. Partnership (dir.). Clubs: Univ., Merion Golf, Phila. Office: 6 Penn Center Plaza Philadelphia PA 19104

JORDAN, FRANK J., lawyer; b. New Canaan, Conn., June 13, 1929; s. Michael and Anna (Markva) J.; B.S., U.S. Mcht. Marine Acad., 1953; J.D., N.Y. Law Sch., 1961; m. Sheila Filene, June 19, 1960. Admitted to N.Y. bar, 1961, U.S. Supreme Ct. bar, 1967, U.S. Ct. Customs and Patent Appeals bar, 1968; patent atty. Am. Standard, Inc., N.Y.C., 1963-65; asso. firm Brown & Seward, N.Y.C., 1965-66; atty. Am. Can Co., Greenwich, Conn., 1966-68; individual practice law, N.Y.C., 1969-78; partner firm Jordan & Hamburg, N.Y.C., 1979—. Served as lt. USN, 1953-55; Korea. Mem. N.Y. Patent Law Assn., Am. Bar Assn., Assn. Bar City N.Y., N.Y. Law Sch., U.S. Mcht. Marine Acad. alumni assns. Club: Capri Yacht. Contbr. articles in field to profl. jours. Home: 205 3d Ave New York NY 10003 Office: 122 E 42d St New York NY 10017

JORDAN, JAMES M., bank exec.; b. Monticello, Ark., July 23, 1935; s. Horace and Vera Mae J.; B.S., Northwestern State U., 1957; m. Dorothy E. Hudson, Aug. 23, 1957; children—Lisa, Laurel, James. Prodn. planner Internat. Paper Co., Bastrop, La., 1957-58, Litchfield, Ill., 1959-62, prodn. supt., 1962-66; prodn. mgr. Gt. Plains Bag Co., Des Moines, 1966-68; div. mgr. Gilman Paper Co., St. Marys, Ga., 1968-76, v.p., mgr., 1976-80; chmn. bd. Peoples Bank, St. Marys, 1978—. Mem. Packaging Inst. (profl. mem.), Paper Bag Inst., Paper Shipping Sack Mfrs. Assn., St. Marys C. of C. (pres. 1978). Democrat. Home: 111 Nancy Dr Saint Marys GA 31558 Office: PO Box 386 Saint Marys GA 31558

JORDAN, LUCIUS DONALD, JR., investor; b. Kosciusko, Miss., Sept. 12, 1929; s. Lucius Donald and Elva (Allen) J.; B.S., Miss. Coll., 1951; M.B.A., Harvard U., 1953; m. Marlene Drury, June 28, 1958; children—Cynthia, Jennifer, Lucius Donald III. Unit mgr. Procter & Gamble, Tex., Ga., 1955-59; dir. mktg. First Miss. Corp., Jackson, 1959-61; western regional mgr. Mead Johnson & Co., Tex. and Calif., 1961-68; v.p. nat. accounts Drackett Products Co., Cin., 1969; v.p. sales Internat. Distbrs. div. Plough Inc., Memphis, 1970-72; exec. v.p. Selective Mktg. Inc., Memphis, 1972-75; mng. partner Jor-Lo Co., Memphis, 1975—. Served with U.S. Army, 1953-55. Mem. SAR. Republican. Presbyterian. Clubs: Harvard Alumni, Racquet (Memphis). Home: 2276 Wickerwood Cove Memphis TN 38138 Office: PO Box 17143 Memphis TN 38117

JORDAN, MICHAEL J., bus. exec.; b. New Haven, May 14, 1949; s. Harold M. and Rita M. J.; B.S., Boston Coll., 1971. Self employed real estate broker, Boston, 1971-72; life ins. agent Conn. Gen. Life, Boston, 1972-75; pres. Jordan & Co., Boston, 1975—. Mem. Estate Planning Council of Boston Coll., Nat. Assn. Life Underwriters, Boston Assn. of Life Underwriters, Internat. Assn. Fin. Planners. Roman Catholic. Clubs: Beacon Soc., Algonquin (Boston), Brae Burn Country Club (Newton). Office: 223 Commonwealth Ave Boston MA 02116

JORDAN, STEVEN JEFFREY, indsl. mktg. exec.; b. N.Y.C., June 17, 1945; s. Willy and Ellen Jordan; student N.Y.C. Community Coll., 1964-66; m. Renae Rabinowitz, Feb. 17, 1968; children—Stacie, Jenniffer. Indsl. salesman Milo Electronics, N.Y.C., 1966-69; indsl. salesman Federated Purchaser Inc., Springfield, N.J., 1969—, sales mgr., 1971-76, v.p. indsl. mktg., 1976—. Served with AUS, 1966-72. Mem. Nat. Electronics Distbrs. Assn., Electronic Distbrs. Research Inst., Am. Mgmt. Assn., N.J. C. of C., U.S. Jaycees, U.S. Tennis Assn. Office: 155 US Route 22 Springfield NJ 07081

JORDAN, THOMAS JOSEPH, JR., hosp. fin. exec.; b. Donora, Pa., July 21, 1944; s. Thomas Joseph and Helen Louise (Zelenak) J.; diploma in bus. adminstrn. Duff's Bus. Inst., 1964; student Waynesburg Coll., 1979—; m. Cheryl Louise Sullivan, June 28, 1975; children—Heather Ann, Amy Elizabeth. Jr. accountant Fisher Sci. Co., Pitts., 1964-65, 67-68; accountant Montefiore Hosp., Pitts., 1968-70, asst. controller, 1970-74, controller, 1974-76; controller, chief fin. officer Butler County Meml. Hosp., Butler, Pa., 1976-79; asst. adminstr. fiscal services, chief fin. officer Greene County Meml. Hosp., Waynesburg, Pa., 1979—. Served with U.S. Army, 1965-67. Fellow Hosp. Fin. Mgmt. Assn. (cert. mgr. patient accounts), Nat. Assn. Accts. Democrat. Roman Catholic. Clubs: Eagles (pres. 1973-74) (Donora); Elks (Etna, Pa.). Home: 165 Colonial Dr Waynesburg PA 15370 Office: Greene County Meml Hosp 7th St and Bonar Ave Waynesburg PA 15370

JORDING, KEITH NORMAN, mfg. co. exec.; b. Moline, Ill., July 20, 1945; s. Gilbert H. and Nina M. (Dawson) J.; B.B.A., U. Cin., 1968; m. Deborah M. Jording. With Kelsey Hayes Corp., Springfield, Ohio, 1965-69, process engr., 1968-69; cons. staff mem. Ritchie & Assocs., Los Angeles, 1971; sales trainee Robbins & Myers, Inc., Springfield, 1971, marketing research analyst, 1972-75, customer service mgr., Cheshire, Conn., 1975-76, asst. sales mgr., 1975-77, product mgr., 1977-79; product mgr. Robbins & Myers, Springfield, Ohio, 1979—. Adv., Jr. Achievement, Springfield, 1972-73. Served with U.S. Army, 1969-71. Decorated Army Commendation medal. Mem. Phi Delta Theta. Republican. Lutheran. Home: 1934 N Fountain Blvd Springfield OH 45504 Office: 1345 Lagonda Ave Springfield OH 45501

JORGENSEN, DEREK GILROY, constrn. co. exec.; b. North Vancouver, B.C., Can., Apr. 3, 1939; s. Ralph Hoffard and Ruth Eileen (Bower) J.; student public schs., B.C.; children—Sandra Lee, Guy Ralph. Heavy equipment operator, Western Can., 1957-64; labor rep. Internat. Union of Operating Engrs., Prince George, B.C., 1964-70, fin. sec. local 115, 1965-69; pres. Prince George & Dist. Bldg. Trades Council, Prince George, 1965-69; mgr., shareholder Interior Crane Co., Ltd., Kamloops, 1969-75; owner, pres. Western Shotcrete Systems, Inc., Ft. McMurray, Alta., Can., 1975—; dir., shareholder Mammoth Crushing Ltd., 1980—. Mem. Am. Concrete Inst., Am. Soc. Concrete Constrn., Mt. McMurray Businessmen's Assn., Ft. McMurray C. of C. Progressive Conservative. Mem. Ch. of Eng. Club: Opimian Soc. Home: 204 Grey Crescent Fort McMurray AB T9H 2N6 Canada Office: 245 MacDonald Crescent Fort McMurray AB T9H 4B5 Canada

JORGENSEN, GORDON DAVID, engring. co. exec.; b. Chgo., Apr. 29, 1921; s. Jacob and Marie (Jensen) J.; B.S. in Elec. Engring., U. Wash., 1948, postgrad. in bus. and mgmt., 1956-59; m. Nadina Anita Peters, Dec. 17, 1948 (div. Aug. 1971); children—Karen Ann, David William, Susan Marie; m. 2d, Barbara Noel, Feb. 10, 1972 (div. July 1976). With R.W. Beck & Assos., Cons. Engrs., Phoenix, 1948—, partner, 1954—; pres. Beck Internat., Phoenix, 1971—. Served to lt. (j.g.) U.S. Maritime Service, 1942-45. Recipient Outstanding Service award Phoenix Tennis Assn., 1967; Commendation, Govt. Honduras, 1970. Registered profl. engr., Alaska, Ariz., Calif., Colo., Nev., N.Mex., N.D., Utah, Wash., Wyo. Mem. IEEE (chmn. Wash.-Alaska sect. 1959-60), Nat. Soc. Profl. Engrs., Am. Soc. Appraisers (sr. mem.), Ariz. Cons. Engrs. Assn., Ariz. Soc. Profl. Engrs., Internat. Assn. Assessing Officers, Southwestern Tennis Assn. (past pres.), U.S. Lawn Tennis Assn. (2d v.p.). Presbyterian (elder). Project mgr. for mgmt., operation studies and reorgn. study Honduras power system, 1969-70. Home: 5329 N 25th St Phoenix AZ 85020 Office: 3003 N Central St Phoenix AZ 85012

JORGENSEN, ROBERT WESTENGAARD, electronics exec.; b. Chgo.; s. Jens W. and Ida T. (Raarup), J.; M.E., Cornell U., 1929; student Central Station Inst., Chgo., 1930, Northwestern U., (night sch.), 1934-35; m. Dorothy O. Meade; children—Brian W., Jill Mary, Deirdre Sue, and Meade Robert. Asst. treas. Central & S.W. Utilities Corp., Dallas, 1930-33; sales planning mgr. Peoples Gas Light & Coke Co., Chgo., 1933-41; asst. to exec. v.p. and sales mgr. Chgo. Metal Hose Corp., 1941-47; mgmt. engr. Booz, Allen & Hamilton, Chgo., 1947-50, 60; dir., mng. partner Linton, Maupin & Linton, Chgo., 1950-52; gen. mgr. spl. gear div. Foote Bros. Gear & Machine Co., 1950-52; v.p., gen. mgr. plastic products div. The Richardson Co., 1952-60; v.p. marketing and corp. planning, gen. mgr. comml. div. The Hallicrafters Co., 1960-64; prin. Tice & Assos., also v.p. Peifer & Assos., mgmt. consultants, 1964-73; pres. Jorgensen Assos., mgmt. consultants, Northfield, Ill., 1973—; pres. Techny Plastics Corp., 1976—. Mem. Cornell Soc. Engrs., Soc. Plastics Engrs., Soc Archtl. Historians (treas.). Home: 555 Walnut St Winnetka IL 60093 Office: 540 Frontage Rd Northfield IL 60093

JOSEPH, DONALD LOUIS, med. assn. exec.; b. Chgo., Dec. 29, 1942; s. Herbert H. and Florence (Gaertner) J.; B.S. in Engring. Sci., Washington U., 1964; M.B.A., Harvard U., 1966; m. Bonnie M. Suckow, Aug. 23, 1975. Systems Engr. Teletype Corp., Skokie, Ill., 1966-68; sr. asso. Brandon Applied Systems, Inc., Chgo., 1968-71; sr. cons. Daniel D. Howard Assos., Inc., Chgo., 1971-72; dir. mgmt. systems Opelika Mfg. Corp., Chgo., 1972-77; dep. exec. dir. Am. Soc. Clin. Pathologists, Chgo., 1978-80, v.p. fin. and adminstrn., 1980—. Bd. dirs. Horizon House, Chgo. Mem. Am. Assn. Med. Soc. Execs., Harvard Bus. Sch. Assn. Chgo., Am. Soc. Assn. Execs., Chgo. Soc. Assn. Execs., Assn. M.B.A. Execs., Better Govt. Assn., Assn. Systems Mgt., Tau Beta Pi, Omicron Delta Kappa. Home: 5733 N Sheridan Rd Chicago IL 60660 Office: 2100 W Harrison St Chicago IL 60612

JOSEPH, EARL CLARK, computer co. exec.; b. St. Paul, Nov. 1, 1926; s. Clark Herbert and Ida Bertha (Schultz) J.; A.A., U. Minn., 1947, B.A., 1951; m. Alma Caroline Bennett, Nov. 19, 1955; children—Alma (Mrs. Richard Chadner), Earl, Vincent, René. Mathematician/programmer Remington Rand Univac, Arlington, Va., 1951-55, supr., St. Paul, 1955-60, systems mgr. Sperry Univac, St. Paul, 1960-63, staff scientist-futurist, 1963—; pres. Anticipatory Scis.; chmn. bd. Future Systems. Vis. lectr. U. Minn., Mpls., 1971—; mem. Sci. and Mgmt. Adv. Com., U.S. Army, 1972-74. Futurist in residence Sci. Mus. of Minn., 1973—; chmn. bd. Future Systems. Chmn., Met. Young Adult Ministry, 1967-69; mem. Gov.'s Planning Commn. for City Center Learning, 1968. Served with USNR, 1944-46. Distinguished lectr. I.E.E.E. Computer Soc., 1971-72, 76-78, Assn. Computer Machinery, 1976-78. Mem. I.E.E.E. (sr.), Minn. Futurists (founder, dir., past pres.), World Future Soc., Soc. for Gen. Systems Research, Assn. Computer Machinery (gen. chmn. 1975, pres. chpt. 1976-77), AAAS, Data Processing Mgmt. Assn., Beta Phi Beta. Patents, publs. in field; co-author 30 books; founding editor jour. Futurics; editor Future Trends Newsletter, Systems Trends Newsletter. Home: 365 Summit Ave St Paul MN 55102 Office: Univac Park PO Box 3525 St Paul MN 55165

JOSEPH, GERALDINE E., ins. exec., health service orgn. adminstr.; b. Oak Park, Ill., Oct. 28, 1929; d. Harold Wallace and Estelle Dorothea (Johnson) Shurtleff; B.A. in Edn., Nat. Coll. Edn., 1973; certificate Keller Grad. Sch. of Mgmt., 1976; m. Harold John Joseph, June 11, 1949; 1 dau., Jennifer Ann. Personnel supr. Nat. Easter Seal Soc. for Crippled Children and Adults, Inc., Chgo., 1955-65, 1972—; field coordinator Internat. Assn. Rehab. Facilities, Bethesda, Md., 1965-68; asst. to project dir. Chgo. Heart Assn., 1968-72; in-home services coordinator Proviso Council on Aging, 1978—. Vice pres. ch. council Transfiguration Luth. Ch., Berkley, Ill., 1976-78; bd. dirs. Proviso Twp. Family Services and Mental Health Center, Westchester, 1974—, sec., 1977-78, chmn. personnel com., 1978—. Mem. Adminstrv. Mgmt. Soc. Home: 629 Morris Ave Bellwood IL 60104 Office: 1006 Bellwood Ave Bellwood IL 60104

JOSEPH, JEFFREY CRAIG, travel agy. exec.; b. Los Angeles, Mar. 8, 1949; s. Ben and Gloria (Guzik) J.; B.A., Hebrew U., Jerusalem, 1971. Rate desk supr. Air France, Los Angeles, 1973-74, sr. tariff analyst, N.Y.C., 1974-77; exec. v.p. Cosmos of London, Forest Hills, N.Y., 1977—. Mem. Am. Soc. Travel Agts. Democrat. Jewish. Home: 90 Lexington Ave New York NY 10016 Office: Cosmos of London 69-15 Austin St Forest Hills NY 11375

JOSEPH, RONALD ANTHONY, mktg. exec.; b. Providence Jan. 12, 1939; s. John Maroon and Amelia Marie (Pepin) J.; student U. R.I., 1957-58; B.A., U. Miami, 1961; grad. Dale Carnegie Inst., 1972; children—Cheryl, Ronald, Michael. Pres., New Imports, Inc., Seekonk, Mass., 1963-70, New Eng. Toyota Distbrs., Inc., Woburn, Mass., 1971-78, Butler Industries, Inc., Boston, 1978—, Econo-Car Internat., Inc., Boston, 1980—. Mem. Boston Com. for Neighborhood Improvement, 1978-79, Gibran Sq. Dedication Com., 1979. Served with U.S. Army, 1961-63. Recipient Cert. of Achievement, Gen. Motors Inst., 1962. Mem. Nat. Automobile Dealers Assn., Am. Imported Automobile Dealers Assn. Democrat. Roman Catholic. Office: 60 State St Boston MA 02109

JOSEPHS, EILEEN SHERLE, fin. cons.; b. Johnstown, Pa.; d. David and Freda (Beerman) Venetsky; B.S. cum laude, U. Pitts., 1956, M.A., 1969; m. Gerald Lisowitz, 1953; children—Mara, Carlyn; m. 2d, Marvin Josephs, 1969. Tchr., Pitts. Public Schs., 1958-59, U.S. Army, Fort Lee, Va., 1965; bus. and fin. cons. real estate devel., 1968—; sales person Equity Real Estate, Pitts., 1977-79; women's div. buyer Coach House Stores, Pitts., 1980—. Founding bd. dirs. Group Against Smog Pollution, 1969-70; publicity co-chmn. 3 Rivers Arts Festival, 1965; ednl. staff Carnegie Inst., Pitts., 1971-77. Mem. Pitts. Plan for Art. Home: 134 W Lyndhurst Dr Pittsburgh PA 15206

JOSEPHSON, MORRIS RAGNOR, copper co. exec.; b. Ironwood, Mich., Oct. 9, 1919; s. Axel Arvid and Olive (Backman) J.; B.S. in Mech. Engring., Mich. Techno. U., 1949; m. Elizabeth Jean Tremain, Aug. 16, 1947; children—Donna Jean, Dennis Gerald. Mech. supt. Anglo-Lautaro Nitrate Corp., Antofagasta, Chile, 1949-61; with So. Peru Copper Corp., Tacna, 1961—, now v.p., gen. mgr. ops. Served with U.S. Army, 1942-45. Mem. Am. C. of C. Peru. Club: Bankers Peru. Home and Office: Casilla 303 Tacna Peru

JOSIAH, WALTER JAMES, JR., lawyer; b. N.Y.C., Nov. 9, 1933; s. Walter James and Marion (Godfrey) J.; B.S., Fordham U., 1955; LL.B., Harvard U., 1962; m. Joan Dunseath, Aug. 1, 1959; children—Walter Robert, Terence James, Lawrence Kenneth. Admitted to N.Y. bar, 1963; asso. firm Simpson Thacher & Bartlett, N.Y.C., 1962-67; legal staff Paramount Pictures Corp., N.Y.C., 1967-69, asst. resident counsel, 1969, resident counsel, 1970, v.p. 1971, v.p., chief resident counsel, 1971—; adj. prof. Benjamin F. Cardozo Sch. of Law, fall, 1979; lectr. N.Y. Inst. Tech., 1980. Served with USAF, 1955-58. Mem. Am. Bar Assn., Assn. Bar City N.Y., N.Y. State Bar Assn. Office: 1 Gulf and Western Plaza New York NY 10023

JOSKOW, JULES, econ. research co. exec.; b. N.Y.C., July 19, 1922; s. Abraham and Mollie (Neuberg) J.; B.S., Coll. City N.Y., 1941; M.A., Columbia, 1942, Ph.D., 1953; m. Charlotte Epstein, June 24, 1945; children—Paul, Margaret, Andrew. Faculty, econs. dept. Coll. City N.Y., 1941-60; research dir. Boni, Watkins, Jason & Co., N.Y.C., 1952-61; v.p. Nat. Econ. Research Assos., N.Y.C., 1961-70, sr. v.p., 1970-75, exec. v.p., 1976—; pres. Nera Systems Corp., 1969-77. Mem. nat. governing bd. Am. Jewish Congress, 1968-71. Mem. Am. Econ. Assn., Am. Statis. Assn., Nat. Assn. Bus. Economists. Clubs: Harbor View, Glen Head Country. Home: 127 Station Rd Kings Point NY 11023 Office: 80 Broad St New York NY 10004

JOSLEN, ROBERT ANDREW, automobile dealer; b. Altadena, Calif., June 28, 1929; s. Fred L. and Elsie A. (Westlake) J.; B.S. in Bus. Adminstrn., Anderson (Ind.) Coll. and Theol. Sem., 1952; M.B.A., George Washington U., 1966; m. Eldine Frazee, Dec. 18, 1949; children—Robert, Lisa, Nancy. Adminstrv. asst., adminstrv. resident Washington Hosp., Washington, 1965-67; asst. dir. U. Mo. Med. Center, Columbia, 1967-69, also mem. faculty dept. community health and med. practice U. Mo. Med. Sch.; adminstr. St. Bernard Hosp., Chgo., 1969-73; pres. Saginaw (Mich.) Osteo. Hosp., 1973-78; preceptor adminstrv. residents in hosp. adminstrn. George Washington U., 1975—, Trinity U., San Antonio, 1971—. Bd. dirs. Englewood Sr. Citizens Centers, 1969-73, chmn., 1970-71; bd. dirs., treas. Dr. Mary Fisher Med. Center, Pagosa Springs, Colo., 1980—; mem. regional council Western Colo. Health Systems Agy., 1981—; bd. dirs. Comprehensive Research and Devel., 1971-73, Englewood Manor Apts., 1969-73, Group Health Service Mich., 1975-78, Community Hosp. Services, 1973-78; now owner, operator Joslen Chevrolet, Pagosa Springs, Colo. Served with AUS, 1946-48. Fellow Am. Coll. Hosp. Adminstrs., Mich. Hosp. Assn. (trustee 1977-78; chmn. unemployment compensation com. 1975-77); mem. Mich. Osteo. Hosp. Assn. (v.p. 1977-78 dir. 1974-78), Am. Hosp. Assn., Am. Pub. Health Assn., Acad. Health Care Cons.'s, Pagosa Springs C. of C. (dir. 1979—). Clubs: Elks, Rotary. Home: PO Box 961 Pagosa Springs CO 81147 Office: Joslen Chevrolet 5th & San Juan Pagosa Springs CO 81147

JOSLIN, PERRY EDWIN, mfg. co. tech. exec.; b. Milford, Mass., Jan. 27, 1932; s. Perry Edward and Louise Viola (Mason) J.; B.S., Worcester (Mass.) Poly. Inst., 1958, M.S., 1960; M.B.A., U. Conn., 1968; m. Linda Jane Swenson, June 13, 1959; children—Perry Edward, Kimberly Ruth. Devel. engr. Electric Boat Co., Groton, Conn., 1959-62; research engr. Pratt & Whitney Co., West Hartford, Conn., 1962-65; project engr. Hamilton Standard Co., Windsor Locks, Conn., 1965-73; owner, gen. mgr. Joslin Dodge, Inc., Pittsfield, Mass., 1973-80; v.p., tech. dir. Milford Rivet & Machine Co. (Conn.), 1980—; past mem. faculty U. Hartford. Mem. Bolton (Conn.) Republican Town Com., 1968-72; bd. dirs. Bolton Congl. Ch., 1971-72. Served with AUS, 1953-54. Recipient commendation award NASA, 1969. Registered profl. engr., Conn. Mem. Sigma Xi. Clubs: Hebron Sportsman's, Masons. Home: 2 Pinecrest Dr Lenox MA 01240 Office: 1000 Seamons Ln Milford CT 06460

JOTCHAM, THOMAS DENIS, advt. exec.; b. Lladudno, Wales, Feb. 21, 1918; s. George James and Marion (Brand) J.; student Lower Can. Coll., 1929-36, McGill U., 1937-39; m. Margaret Jean Thirlwell, Aug. 10, 1940; children—Patricia, Douglas, Joy, Candace. Sales rep. Montreal Lithographing Co., Ltd., Montreal, 1945-47; sales mgr. Wesco Waterpaints Can., Ltd., Montreal, 1947-48; advt. mgr. Pepsi-Cola Co. Can., Ltd., 1948-52, mgr., Montreal, 1952-54; asst. advt. mgr. Reader's Digest Assn., Ltd., Montreal, 1954-56; mgr., v.p. Foster Advt. Ltd., Montreal, 1956-73, exec. v.p., 1973-75, pres., 1976—; pres. Sherwood Communications Group Ltd.; mem. council Montreal Bd. Trade, 1973-75, v.p., 1977-78, pres., 1979, hon. chmn., 1980-81. Bd. dirs. Grace Dart Hosp., 1973—, pres., 1979—; bd. dirs. Can. Council Christians and Jews, 1978—, Les Grands Ballets Canadien, 1976-77. Served from lt. to maj. Army, 1940-45. Fellow Inst. Can. Advt. (pres. 1976-77); mem. Can. Advt. and Sales Assn. (pres. 1960-61), Advt. and Sales Execs. Club (pres. 1956-58), Advt. and Sales Assn. Montreal (pres. 1948-49, now hon. pres.), Advt. Agy. Council Que. (pres. 1975-76), Can.-S. African Soc. (dir. 1980—), Psi Upsilon. Clubs: Mount Stephen (pres. 1967-68), St. James's (com. mem. 1979—), Thistle Curling (pres. 1977-78). Home: 1509 Sherbrooke St W Apt 21 Montreal PQ H3G 1L7 Canada Office: Suite 915 L'Edifice Provinces-Unics 2021 Union Ave Montreal PQ H3A 2S9 Canada

JOVANOVICH, WILLIAM, publisher; b. Louisville, Colo., Feb. 6, 1920; s. Iliva M. and Hedviga (Garbatz) J.; A.B., U. Colo., 1941; postgrad. Harvard U., 1941-42, Columbia U., 1946-47; Litt.D., Colo. Coll., 1966, U. Colo., 1971, Adelphi Coll., 1971, Middlebury Coll., 1971, Ohio State U., 1971; LL.D., U. Alaska, 1971; m. Martha Evelyn Davis, Aug. 21, 1943. With Harcourt Brace Jovanovich, Inc. (formerly Harcourt, Brace & Co.), N.Y.C., 1947—, asso. editor, 1947-53, v.p., dir., 1953-54, pres., dir., 1955-70, chmn., 1970—; Regent prof. U. Calif. at Berkeley, 1967; lectr. Adelphi U., 1973. Regent, State of N.Y., 1974—. Recipient Norlin award distinguished achievement U. Colo., 1963. Fellow Morgan Library, N.Y.C. William Jovanovich lectrs. in pub. affairs named in honor, Colo. Coll., 1976-79. Mem. Phi Beta Kappa. Author: Now Barabbas, 1964; Madmen Must, 1978; also essays. Office: 757 3d Ave New York NY 10017

JOY, LUCINDA JEAN, advt. exec.; b. Berea, Ohio, July 4, 1952; d. John W. and Elsie (Fuller) Joy; student public schs., Kent, Ohio; children—Michael S., Jennifer Joy. Sec., Kent Vis. Nurses, 1969-71; printing clk. HUD, Washington, 1973-74; housing clk. Dept. Def., Ft. Belvoir, Va., 1974-75; adminstrv. asst. public relations dept. Am. Meat Inst., Arlington, Va., 1975-78; adminstrv. asst. to pub. Builder mag., coordinator merchandising services, advt. mgr. Nat. Assn. Home Builders, Washington, 1978—. Bd. dirs. United Methodist Ch., Kent, 1968-69. Mem. D.C. Police Wives Assn. (v.p. 1976-78). Home: 1933 Leonard Rd Falls Church VA 22043 Office: Nat Assn Home Builders 15th and M Sts NW Washington DC 20005

JOY, PAUL WILLIAM, diversified mining and mfg. co. exec.; b. Niagara Falls, N.Y., Feb. 2, 1924; s. William Thomas and Amy J. (Dunn) J.; B.S. in Elec. Engring., U. Toronto (Ont., Can.), 1951; grad. advanced mgmt. program Harvard U., 1965; m. Helen Joan Todd, Sept. 3, 1949; children—Paula Margaret Joy Reinhold, Marsha Ann Joy Sullivan, Stephen Todd. With Carborundum Co., Niagara Falls, 1951-79, v.p. Resistant Materials Group, 1973-74, sr. v.p., 1974-78, pres., 1978-80; exec. v.p. Kennecott Copper Corp., Stamford, Conn., 1979-80; exec. v.p. Kennecott Corp., Stamford, 1980—; dir. CPC Internat., Inc., Englewood Cliffs, N.J. Served with RCAF, 1943-47. Mem. IEEE. Club: Niagara Falls Country. Office: Ten Stamford Forum Stamford CT 06904

JOYCE, HARRY ALEXIS JONES, ins. exec.; b. Columbia, Tenn., Mar. 7, 1924; s. John Clarence and Watha Bess (Jones) J.; B.S., U.S. Naval Acad., 1946; m. Margaret Sinclair Henry, Sept. 22, 1951; children—Alexis Jones, Douglas Henry. Commd. ensign USN, 1946, advanced through grades to lt., 1949; with 1st Am. Nat. Bank, Nashville, 1949-51, 53-54; with Nat. Life & Accident Ins. Co., Nashville, 1954—, v.p., treas., 1973—; treas. NLT Computer Services Corp., 1970—, NLT Corp., 1971—; treas. Nat. Property Owners Ins. Co., 1973—; treas. WSM, Inc., 1974—, NLT Mktg. Services Corp., 1978—. Active YMCA, United Fund, Cheekwood, Salvation Army, Nashville Symphony. Episcopalian. Clubs: Exchange, Belle Meade Country, Cumberland, Linville (N.C.) Golf. Home: 422 Sunnyside Dr Nashville TN 37205 Office: National Life Center Nashville TN 37250

JOYCE, JOSEPH FRANCIS, sports arena exec.; b. N.Y.C., Apr. 8, 1929; s. Joseph F. and Dorothy (Devere) J.; A.B., Coll. Holy Cross, 1951; LL.B., Fordham U., 1957; m. Elizabeth Trotter, Sept. 11, 1954; children—Elizabeth Ann, Mary, Joseph, Eugene Jane, Ellen John, Teresa, Paul, Maura, Timothy, Patrick, Michael. Admitted to N.Y. State bar, 1957; counsel Precision Components div. Norden Ketay Corp., Commack, N.Y., 1957-59; partner firm Steinbugler, Joyce & Scully, N.Y.C., 1959-61, Joyce & Malloy, Smithtown, N.Y., 1964-71; individual practice law, Commack, N.Y., 1961-64; exec. v.p. N.Y.C. Off-Track Betting Corp., N.Y.C., 1971-74; sr. v.p., dir. Madison Square Garden Corp., N.Y.C., 1974—; chmn. bd., dir. Roosevelt Raceway, Inc., Westbury, L.I., N.Y.; chmn. bd., pres. Arlington Park-Washington Park Rack Tracks Corp.; pres. Amsterdam Fund, Inc., 1959-61. Served to capt. USMC, 1951-53. Recipient Man of Year award Chgo. div. Horseman's Benevolent Protective Assn., 1976. Mem. N.Y. Trial Lawyers' Assn., N.Y. State, Suffolk County bar assns. Home: 400 Forest Ave Oak Park IL 60302 Office: Arlington Park Race Track Corp PO Box 7 Arlington Heights IL 60006

JUBIE, JERRY JOHN, banker; b. Cloquet, Minn., Apr. 28, 1936; s. Robert Marion and Marie Helen (Jerina) J.; m. Irene M. Haller, Nov. 21, 1959; children—Timothy J., Thomas A., Janine I., Todd M., Nanette M., Kimberly A., Jerry J., Jennifer A. Teller, 1st Nat. Bank, Cloquet, Minn., 1958-60; field examiner 1st Bank Corp., Mpls., 1960-62; field bank examiner U.S. Treasury Dept., 1962-66; chmn. bd. dirs., pres. 1st State Bank of Floodwood (Minn.), 1966—, Miller Hill State Bank of Duluth (Minn.), 1978—; pres. Floodwood Agy., Inc., Windjammer Computer Service; v.p. Ponderosa Realty & Investment Co. Chmn., Arrowhead Regional Devel. Commn., Duluth, Minn., 1974-78, Nat. Assn. Devel. Orgns., Washington, 1976-78, Econ. Devel. Assn. St. Louis County, 1973-78. Served with USMCR, 1955-58. Mem. Ind. Bankers Minn., Ind. Bankers Am., Minn. Bankers Assn., Am. Bankers Assn. Democrat. Roman Catholic. Club: Kitchi Gammi (Duluth). Office: 4929 Decker Rd Duluth MN 55811

JUCKETT, JACOB WALTER, paper mill machinery co. exec.; b. West Springfield, Mass., May 26, 1908; s. Frank A. and Laura P. (Fassett) J.; B.S. in Elec. Engring., Norwich U., 1930, D.Sc. (hon.), 1962; m. M. Elizabeth Brown, Aug. 24, 1940; children—David Warren, Nancy Juckett Brown. Chmn. bd., chief exec. officer Sandy Hill Corp., Hudson Falls, N.Y., 1957—; trustee Sandy Hill Found., Hudson Falls; pres. Richmor Aviation Inc.; dir. Kamyr Inc. Vice pres. Mohican council Boy Scouts Am., mem.-at-large Nat. council; mem. Hudson Falls Bd. Edn., 1946-74, pres., 1958-74; trustee Adirondack Community Coll., Glen Falls, Citizens Public Expenditures Survey Inc., N.Y. State; vice chmn. bd. trustees Norwich U.; chmn. Lake Champlain Cancer Research Orgn.; mem. area adv. com. N.Y. Bus. Devel. Corp.; mem. adv. bd. N.Y. Bus. Devel. Corp.; elder First Presbyterian Ch., Hudson Falls; past pres. Nat. Council United Presbyn. Men. Served to capt. U.S. Army, 1942-45. Mem. Sigma Alpha Epsilon, Tau Beta Pi. Republican. Home: 31 Pearl St Hudson Falls NY 12839 Office: Sandy Hill Corp 27 Allen St Hudson Falls NY 12839

JUDD, JOSEPH LAWRENCE, mfrs.' rep.; b. Williamsport, Pa., Sept. 29, 1936; s. Nelson Thomas and Sara (Martin) J.; student Pa. State U., 1954-57; m. Alice Artley, Aug. 15, 1954; children—Stephen L., Anna S., Tamara M., Jessica A., Joshua N. With wholesale auto parts co., 1957; field geologist, 1958; with Redisco, Inc., Harrisburg, Pa., 1959-62; mfrs.' rep. R.A. Johnson & Co., Harrisburg, 1963-67, Joseph Soraghan Assos., Washington, 1967-68, Sid Dubinsky Assos., Balt., 1968-70; pres. Joe Judd, Ltd., Columbia, Md., 1970—. Bd. dirs. 1st Lutheran Ch., Ellicott City, Md., 1970-73, YMCA, 1973-78; chmn. bd. dirs. West Balt. Luth. Parish, 1973. Named Salesman of Year Paul Mueller Co., 1977. Mem. Mfrs.' Agts. Nat. Assn. (dir. 1978), Instrument Soc. Am., Am. Soc. Heating and Refrigerating Engrs., Elec. Mfrs. Reps. Assn. (sec. 1966), Air Pollution Control Soc. Home: 4806 Hale Haven Dr Ellicott City MD 21043 Office: Suite 232 Joseph's Sq Harper's Farm Rd Columbia MD 21044

JUDD, WILLIAM FLOYD, oil co. exec.; b. Nashville, July 18, 1932; s. Edgar Floyd and Floribel (Kline) J.; B.S. in B.A., U. Ark., 1954; m. Lisa Meadows, Apr. 21, 1956; children—Elise, David, Claude. Vice pres., dir. Seay, Sharp & Co., Dallas, 1962-68; sr. accountant Peat, Marwick, Mitchell & Co., Dallas, 1957-62; pres. Tex. Am. Oil Corp. Midland, 1968—. Served with USAF, 1954-57. C.P.A., Tex. Mem. Permian Basin Soc. C.P.A.'s, Sigma Chi. Presbyterian. Home: 2100 Oaklawn St Midland TX 79701 Office: 300 W Wall St Suite 1012 Midland TX 79701

JUDELSON, DAVID N., corp. exec.; b. 1928; B.S. in Mech. Engring., N.Y.U., 1949; married. With Oscar I. Judelson, Inc., mgrs. indsl. equipment, Jersey City, from 1949, last position as chmn. bd.; with Gulf & Western Industries Inc., N.Y.C., 1958—, v.p., dir., 1959-61, mem. exec. com., 1961-65, chmn. exec. com., 1965-66, exec. v.p., 1967-72, pres., 1972—, also dir.; dir. A.P.S., Inc. Office: Gulf & Western Industries Inc 1 Gulf and Western Plaza New York NY 10023*

JUDGE, JAMES HOWARD, mfg. co. exec.; b. Olean, N.Y., Mar. 3, 1923; s. John L. and Nora L. (McCarthy) J.; B.S. in Sci., St. Bonaventure U., 1944, postgrad. in chemistry and edn., 1945-46; m. Anne Belle Weatherell, Apr. 16, 1949; children—Molly Lorraine, Jill Dianne, Jacqueline Dana. Analytical chemist Vanderhorst Co., Olean, N.Y., 1944-45; tchr. sci. N.Y. State high schs., 1945-50; application engr. Clark Bros./Dresser Co., Olean, N.Y., 1950-56, application engr./mgr., Bradford, Pa., 1956-59; mgr. product mktg. for Ajax products Cooper Energy Services, Corry, Pa., 1959—. Pioneered devel. of standard compressor packages for oilfield applications. Home: RD 2 Corry PA 16407 Office: 19 N Center St Corry PA 16407

JUDGE, JOHN EMMET, marketing cons.; b. Grafton, N.D., May 5, 1912; s. Charles C. and Lillian (Johnson) J.; B.S., U. N.D.; m. Clarita Garcia, Apr. 18, 1940; children—Carolyn (Mrs. Samuel Stanley), J. Emmet, Maureen, Eileen, Susan. Asst. to adminstr. Fed. Works Agy., Washington 1939-42; staff mem. Wallace Clark & Co., mgmt. cons., 1942-46; v.p. Morgan Furniture Co., Asheville, N.C., 1946-48; mgr. financial analysis Lincoln Mercury div. Ford Motor Co., 1949-53, asst. gen. purchasing agt., 1953-55, merchandising mgr., 1955-58, mgr. Mercury marketing, 1958-60, mgr. product planning office, 1960-62; v.p. marketing services Westinghouse Electric Corp., Pitts., 1963-67; v.p. marketing Indian Head Inc., 1967-68; marketing cons., Birmingham, Mich., 1968—; dir. Instem Ltd., Cambridge Instrument Co., Kratos Inc., Cashiers Plastic Inc. Mem. nat. adv. com. marketing to sec. Dept. Commerce. Chmn. library study com., Birmingham, Mich., 1957; dir Boysville of Mich., 1957; pres. Emmet County Lakeshore Assn. Mem. Am. Ordnance Assn., Soc. Advancement Mgmt., Engring. Soc. Detroit, ASME, Nat. Assn. Accts., Soc. Automotive Engrs., U.S. C. of C. (consumer com.), N.A.M. (marketing com.), Newcomen Soc. N.Am., Sigma Tau, Alpha Tau Omega. Roman Catholic. Clubs: Detroit Athletic, Economic (Detroit); Orchard Lake County (dir.). Office: Shore Dr Harbor Springs MI 49740

JUDSON, ARTHUR, II, investment banker; b. Phila., Sept. 6, 1930; s. Francis Edward and Henrietta (Chapman) J.; A.B., Dartmouth, 1952; M.B.A., Harvard, 1956; m. Bright Miller, Nov. 30, 1957; children—Arthur III, Virginia Wallis, Henrietta Chapman, Christopher Bright. Asst. area sales mgr. Procter & Gamble, Phila., 1956-57; registered rep. C.C. Collings & Co., Phila., 1957-60, corporate syndicate mgr., 1960—, v.p., 1964-76, mem. exec. com., 1972—, exec. v.p., 1977—; pres., dir. Arthur Judson, Inc. Chmn. bd. govs., mem. fin. com., mem. exec. com., trustee Phila. Stock Exchange, Inc., 1968—. Active various community drives; bd. dirs., pres. Settlement Music Sch., 1976—; chmn. Armed Services YMCA Phila., 1978—. Served with USNR, 1952-54; ETO. Mem. Investment Assos. Phila. (treas. 1962), Phila. Securities Assn., Investment Bankers Assn. Am. (edn. com. 1969-70). Pa. Soc., Mil. Order Fgn. Wars of U.S. (vice comdr. 1975—), Bond Club Phila., Navy League U.S. (dir. 1975—, pres. 1980—), Theta Delta Chi. Republican. Episcopalian. Clubs: Phila. Rotary (chmn. internat. com.), Harvard Business School (treas. Phila. 1961, 66), Dartmouth (exec. com. Phila. 1962-64), Athenaum of Phila. Home: 149 Northwestern Ave Philadelphia PA 19118 Office: Fidelity Bldg Philadelphia PA 19109

JUDSON, FRANKLYN SYLVANUS, lawyer; b. Cleve., May 13, 1915; s. Calvin Albert and Beatrice (Harding) J.; A.B., Case Western Res. U., 1938, J.D., 1940; m. Nancy Elizabeth Nevin, July 29, 1939; children—Franklyn N., William W., Ann Louise, Kenneth G., Carolyn. Admitted to Ohio bar, 1940, Pa. bar, 1954; law librarian Western Res. U., Cleve., 1940-41; jr. atty., prin. trial atty., asst. regional adminstr. SEC, Cleve., 1942-53; atty., asst. sec. I-T-E Circuit Breaker Co., Phila., 1953-55, sec., 1955-68, gen. counsel, 1967-68; sec., gen. counsel I-T-E Imperial Corp. (merger I-T-E Circuit Breaker Co. and Imperial Eastman), 1968-69, v.p., sec., gen. counsel, 1969-72, v.p., 1967-75, gen. counsel, 1967—, sr. v.p., gen. counsel, 1975-77; cons. on establishing and evaluating corporate law depts., 1977—. Past pres. bd. trustees Friends Central Sch. Mem. Internat., Am., Cleve., Phila. bar assns., Am. Soc. Corp. Secs., Am. Arbitration Assn., World Assn. Lawyers (com. edn. in bus. ethics). Mem. Soc. of Friends (dir.). Club: Union League (Phila.). Home: 820 Colony Rd Bryn Mawr PA 19010 Office: One Radnor Sta King of Prussia Rd Radnor PA 19087

JUDY, PAUL RAY, investment banker; b. Portland, Ind., Feb. 18, 1931; s. Paul R. and Mary E. (Hanlin) J.; A.B., Harvard U., 1953, M.B.A., 1957; m. Mary Ann Dorsey, Nov. 27, 1954; children—Carol Ann, Mary Hannah, John Hanlin, Beth Ellen. With The Becker Warburg Paribas Group Inc. (formerly A.G. Becker & Co. Inc.), Chgo., 1958—, v.p. corp. fin., 1961-65, chmn. exec. com., 1965—, pres., chief exec. officer, 1968-78; co-chmn. Warburg Paribas Becker Inc., Chgo., 1978—; bd. govs. N.Y. Stock Exchange, 1968-71. Trustee, pres. Chgo. Orch. Assn.; bd. dirs. United Way of Met. Chgo.; trustee Fin. Acctg. Found., Northwestern U., Carnegie Hall Soc., Field Found. Ill. Served to 1st lt. USMCR, 1953-55. Clubs: Harvard, Econ. (dir.), Chgo., Mid-Am., Comml. (Chgo.); Old Elm; Links (N.Y.C.); Sankaty Head (Siasconset, Mass.). Home: 14 Country Ln Northfield IL 60093 Office: 2 First Nat Plaza Chicago IL 60603

JUELL, BRUCE C., amusement park operator; B.S. in M.E., U. So. Calif., 1955, M.B.A., 1963; m. Jean Juell. Successively mgmt. cons. McKinsey & Co., Inc.; mgr. info. systems mktg. Spacor Info. Systems div. N. Am. Aviation; v.p., treas., acting pres., mgr. Builders Resources Corp.; exec. Property Research Corp.; partner Victor Palmieri/Bruce Juell & Co., 1970-72; pres. Great S.W. Corp., Los Angeles, 1971—; pres., chief exec. officer 6 Flags, Inc., GSC Devel. Corp., Coto de Caza Devel. Corp. Nat. corps. com., bd. dirs. United Negro Coll. Fund; chmn. So. Calif.-Nev. Corps. Campaign Com., 1976; bd. trustees City of Hope; dean's council U. Calif. Los Angeles Sch. Architecture and Urban Planning. Served with USNR, 1955-58. Mem. Young Pres.'s Orgn., M.B.A. Assos., M.B.A. Alumni Assn (bd. dirs.), Urban Land Inst., Theta Xi, Beta Gamma Sigma. Club: Calif. Address: 530 W 6th St Los Angeles CA 90014*

JULIANO, JOE VICTOR, physician, automobile co. exec.; b. Ft. Bragg, N.C., Dec. 6, 1949; s. Amore Victor and JoAnn (Davison) J.; B.S., Baylor U., 1973; M.D., Ph.D., U. Tex., 1976; postgrad. U. Calif. at San Diego, 1976-77; m.Mary Lynn Briesemeister, Aug. 24, 1973. Instr. chemistry U. Tex., Baylor, 1973; research scientist biochem. pharmacology, Houston, 1974-76; researcher brain hormones U. Calif. at San Diego, 1976-77; cons. practice medicine, specializing in diabetes, San Diego, 1976—; sales mgr. Ferrari of San Diego, 1976—; lectr. in field. Mem. Am. Chem. Soc., Am. Diabetes Assn. (profl.), Neuropsychiat. Research Orgn. Researcher morphine, estrogen drug receptors, adolescent diabetes.

JUMAN, MARTIN, ins. agy. exec.; b. N.Y.C., Sept. 4, 1938; s. Benjamin and Lillian J.; student CCNY; grad. Am. Coll.; m. Phyllis S. Field, Sept. 21, 1958; children—Michael, Marla. Rep., Cohen, Simonson & Rea, 1960-67; with Weis, Voisin, Inc., 1967-73, exec. v.p. sales, 1970-73; owner, agt. Martin Juman Agy., Garden City, N.Y., 1979—. Mem. Am. Soc. C.L.U.'s, Nat. Assn. Life Underwriters, Million Dollar Roundtable (life). Home: 3011 Holiday Park Dr Merrick NY 11566 Office: 100 Ring Rd W Garden City NY 11530

JUNCHEN, DAVID LAWRENCE, pipe organ mfg. co. exec.; b. Rock Island, Ill., Feb. 23, 1946; s. Lawrence Ernest and Lucy Mae (Ditto) J.; B.S. in Elec. Engring. with highest honors, U. Ill., 1968. Founder, owner Junchen Pipe Organ Service, Sherrard, Ill., 1968—; co-owner Junchen-Collins Organ Corp., Woodstock, Ill., 1975-80; mng. dir. Baranger Studios, South Pasadena, Calif., 1980—. Named Outstanding Freshman in Engring. U. Ill., 1963-64. Mem. Am. Inst. Organbuilders, Am. Theatre Organ Soc., Mus. Box Soc., Automatic Mus. Instrument Collectors Assn., Theatre Organ Soc. Australia, Cinema Organ Soc. London, Tau Beta Pi, Sigma Tau, Eta Kappa Nu. Contbr. to Ency. Automatic Mus. Instruments; composer, arranger over 60 music rolls for self-playing mus. instruments. Office: 729 Mission St South Pasadena CA 91030

JUNE, CHARLES ALLAN, business cons.; b. Hartford, Conn., Apr. 16, 1930; s. Charles Knapp and Lorna Elizabeth (Lyle) J.; B.A.B.A., Allegheny Coll., 1951; postgrad. in aerological engring. U.S. Naval Postgrad. Sch., 1954. With Gen. Electric Co., 1951-70, supr. gen.

accounts and accounts payable, Chicago Heights, Ill., 1963-66; mgr. gen. accounts, Oklahoma City, 1966-70; mgr. gen. accounts, mgr. sales and inventory acctg. Honeywell Infos. Systems Inc., Oklahoma City, 1970-73; pres. Small Bus. Mgmt. Brevard Inc. doing bus. as Gen. Bus. Services, Titusville, Fla., 1973—; Mem. North Brevard County (Fla.) Devel. Commn., 1973—, treas., 1974-78. Recipient numerous awards in bus. counseling Gen. Bus. Services, Inc., Washington, 1973—. Mem. Am. Mgmt. Assn., U.S. Naval Inst. Republican. Methodist. Home: 2750 Mangrum Pl Titusville FL 32780 Office: PO Box 402 Titusville FL 32780

JUNES, RUBE GENE, public acct.; b. Menagha, Minn., Aug. 19, 1944; s. Ferdinand W. and Elma H. (Lein) J.; B.S. in Bus. magna cum laude (Alpha Kappa scholar), U. Idaho, 1967; m. Fay Marie Bunting, Sept. 21, 1963; children—Eric A., Amie A. Acct., Price Waterhouse & Co., Seattle, 1967-69; partner pub. acctg. firm, Lewiston, Idaho, 1969-73, Junes, DePew & Co., C.P.A.'s, Lewiston, 1973-78, Morris, Lee & Co., Lewiston, 1978—. Treas. Idaho Jaycees, 1973-74; Bd. dirs. North Idaho Children's Home, 1975—, exec. com., asst. treas., 1976—, v.p., 1977, pres., 1978—; bd. dirs., exec. com. Twin County United Way, 1976—. Recipient Wall St. Jour. student award U. Idaho, 1967, Distinguished Service award Lewiston Jaycees, 1977. C.P.A., Idaho. Mem. Am. Inst. C.P.A.'s, Idaho, Wash. socs. C.P.A.'s, Greater Lewiston C. of C. (dir. 1978—), Phi Kappa Phi, Alpha Kappa Psi. (scholarship 1967). Elk. Home: 2804 Country Club Dr Lewiston ID 83501 Office: PO Box 499 Lewiston ID 83501

JUNK, SHALON JEAN, personnel adminstr.; b. Ft. Wayne, Ind., Sept. 27, 1945; d. Edwin C. and Jean Opal Ezzelle; m. Richard Ellis Junk, Aug. 22, 1964; children—Richard Edwin, Scott Michael. Sec., Gen. Telephone Co., 1966-72; with Super Market Service, Ft. Wayne, 1974—, personnel mgr., 1975-76, human resource mgr., 1976—. Mem. Am. Soc. Personnel Adminstrn., Ind. Personnel Assn., Personnel Assn. Ft. Wayne, Delta Sigma Kappa. Baptist. Home: 2109 Kentucky Ave Fort Wayne IN 46805

JURENKO, DAVID MICHAEL, communications electronics co. exec.; b. Rankin, Pa., Oct. 18, 1938; s. John and Olga Irene (Kalley) J.; B.S. in Elec. Engring., U. Pitts., 1960; m. Beverly Elish, May 14, 1960; 1 dau., Beverly B. Electronics engr. to mgr. mktg. and communications security programs Ford Aerospace & Electronics, Willow Grove, Pa., 1960-77; dir. Phila. ops. Fairchild Weston Systems Inc., Horsham, Pa., 1977—. Judge figure skating U.S. Figure Skating Assn.; active March of Dimes and J. Wood Platt Caddie Scholarship Fund. Recipient cert. IEEE, 1970. Mem. Acoustical Soc. Am., AFCEA, Assn. U.S. Army, Phila. Area Assn. Figure Skating Clubs (past pres.). Clubs: Sandy Run Country (bd. govs.), Old York Rd. Skating (past pres.), Wissahickon Skating. Home: 1666 Cavan Dr Dresher PA 19025 Office: Fairchild Weston Systems Inc 219 Witmer Rd Horsham PA 19044

JURGENS, WILFRED REINHART, oil and propane jobber; b. Wymore, Nebr., June 12, 1922; s. Thee Henry and Tena (Parde) J.; student pub. schs.; m. Lydia Rosetta Schuster, May 9, 1947; children—Melody, Teresa. Owner, Jurgens Oil & Propane, Filley, Nebr., 1945—; mem. adv. council Omaha dist. Mobil Oil Corp., 1975—; pres. J & P Corp., Jurgens-Vrooman Corp.; pilot. Mem. Filley Town Council, 1952-66, mayor, 1953-66; mem. Consol. Sch. Bd., 1969—; treas. Lutheran Ch., 1955-58, mem. ch. council, 1975—; vol. fireman; asst. fire chief; spl. dep. Sheriff; mem. rebldg. com. Gage County Courthouse, Blue Valley Flood and Gage County Tornado Disaster; chmn. adv. council Boy Scouts Am.; bd. dirs. Luth. Hosp. Soc., Foot Printers; mem. legis. Alert Network. Served with USNR, 1942-45. Mem. Nebr. Petroleum Marketers (dir.), LP Gas Assn Nebr., Nat. LP Gas Assn., Nat. Fedn. Ind. Bus., Am. Legion, VFW. Democrat. Clubs: Elks, Eagles. Home and office: PO Box 86 Filley NE 68357

JUSSAWALLA, MEHEROO FRAMJI, economist; b. Secunderabad, India, July 15, 1923; came to U.S., 1977; d. Sohrab J. and Pootli B. (Chinoy) Dalal; B.A. (Sturge scholar), Madras U., 1943, M.A. in Econs., 1945; postgrad. Wharton Sch., U. Pa., 1957; Ph.D. in Econs., Osmania U., 1963; m. Framji J. Jussawalla, Nov. 30, 1945 (dec. 1971); children—Sohrab, Feroza. Lectr. econs. Nizam Coll. India, 1945-57, reader in econs., 1957-68; prof., pres. Univ. Coll. for Women, Hyderabad, India, 1968-70, 72-73; vis. prof. Hood Coll., Frederick, Md., 1970; prof., dean Faculty of Social Scis., Osmania U., Hyderabad, 1973-75; prof. econs. St. Mary's Coll., St. Mary's City, Md., 1975-77; research economist East-West Center Communication Inst., Honolulu, 1978—; affiliate prof. econs. U. Hawaii. Recipient award Bus. and Profl. Women's Club, Placid Harbor, Md., 1977. Mem. Am. Econ. Assn., Western Am. Econ. Assn., Internat. Communication Assn., World Future Soc., AAUW, Indian Econ. Assn. (life), Indian Inst. Econs. (life). Zoroastrian. Author: Economic Theory, 1960; Cost-Benefit Analysis of Nizamsagar Irrigation Project, 1968; Economics of Development, 1974; Dynamics of Economic Development, 1980; contbr. articles to profl. jours. Office: East-West Center Communication Inst 1777 East-West Rd Honolulu HI 96848

KABAK, MARTIN, housewares co. exec.; b. N.Y.C., Oct. 26, 1922; s. David and Anna (Weinstein) K.; B.S., N.Y. U., 1944; m. Vivian Witkowsky, Nov. 3, 1945 (dec. 1977); children—Anne, Wayne. Asso. exec. Loring Fabrics, Inc., N.Y.C., 1945-51; sales mgr. Heller Hostess Ware, Inc., N.Y.C., 1951-56; gen. sales mgr. Salton, Inc., N.Y.C., 1956-67, v.p. sales, 1967-77, vice chmn., 1977—. Republican. Home: 1 Redwood Rd White Plains NY 10605 Office: 1260 Zerega Ave Bronx NY 10462

KABAKOW, EDWIN, mag. exec.; b. N.Y.C., Nov. 17, 1935; s. Joseph and Sara (Leff) K.; B.A., Hunter Coll., 1957; m. Margaret Ingrid Weil, Nov. 19, 1961; children—James A., Robert J. Sales mgr. Cosmopolitan Advt. Co., N.Y.C., 1958-60; with Hearst Mags., N.Y.C., 1960-66; v.p. advt. sales Campbell-Reynolds, Inc., N.Y.C., 1966-68, pres., 1968-76; pres. Media People, Inc., N.Y.C., 1976—; lectr., cons. profl. orgns., colls. Mem. Direct Mail Mktg. Assn. Am. Home: 111 Orchard Rd Demarest NJ 07627 Office: 2 W 45th St New York NY 10036

KABAYAMA, MICHIOMI ABRAHAM, chemist; b. Kanazawa, Japan, Apr. 18, 1926; naturalized U.S. citizen, 1965; s. Jun and Maki (Tomegawa) K.; student U. Man., 1944-46, U. Toronto, 1948-50; B.Sc., Sir George Williams U., 1952; M.Sc., U. Montreal, 1956, Ph.D., 1958; m. Joan Eleanor Mount, Aug. 25, 1951 (div. Oct. 1979); children—Maki Eleanor, Noreen Migiwa, Lawrence Makoto, Allison Keiko, Allen Kichiji. Research chemist E.I. DuPont de Nemours, Buffalo, 1958-65; group leader Ethicon, Somerville, N.J., 1965-67; research mgr. Bell-No. Research, Ottawa, Ont., Can., 1967-76; tech. dir. Soc. Plastics Industry, Toronto, Ont., 1976—. Vice pres. CORE, Buffalo, 1960-62; pres. North Lucerne Residents Assn., 1974-75. Fellow Chem. Inst. Can.; mem. Assn. of Chem. Profession of Ont. (pres. 1977-79), Soc. Plastics Engrs. Home: 4 Conway Ave Toronto ON M6E 1H2 Canada Office: 1262 Don Mills Rd Suite 104 Don Mills ON M3B 2W7 Canada

KACHMAR, JOHN JOSEPH, JR., assn. exec.; b. Bethlehem, Pa., Feb. 26, 1948; s. John Joseph and Irene M. (Ehasz) K.; B.A. in History, Moravian Coll., 1972; m. Christine Mesko, July 5, 1969; children—Timothy, Elizabeth. Dir. govt. programs Counties of Northampton and Lehigh (Pa.), 1972-73; adminstr. govt. programs Lehigh Valley Public Employment Program, 1973-74; exec. dir. Lehigh Valley Manpower Program, Allentown, 1974-80; dir. employment and tng. council U.S. Conf. Mayors, 1979—; v.p. tng. and tech. systems Nat. Alliance Bus., Washington, 1980—; mem. Pa. State Adv. Council Vocat. Edn., 1980. Mem. exec. bd. Minsi Trails council Boy Scouts Am.; mem. community relations com. Sta. WLVT-TV, Bethlehem. Served with USMC, 1966-68. Decorated Purple Heart with oak leaf cluster; Vietnamese Cross Gallantry. Mem. Nat. Assn. Counties, Nat. Assn. Pvt. Industry Councils, Mid-Atlantic Manpower Profls. (pres.), Bethlehem Jaycees. Republican. Roman Catholic. Office: Nat Alliance Bus 1015 15th St NW Washington DC 20005

KADIN, FRED MARTIN, banker; b. N.Y.C., July 4, 1942; s. Sidney Stanley and Adelaide (Harris) K.; student U. Geneva, 1962-63; B.S. (N.Y. State Regents scholar), Columbia U., 1971; m. Christine Kadin-Stadler, June 29, 1972; children—Katherine-Anne, Karen Lee. Retail bank tng./ops. officer Bankers Trust Co., 1969-72; asst. v.p. Bank of Am., Internat., Paris, 1972-74, mgr., London, 1974-75; asst. v.p. corp. fin. Crocker Nat. Bank, London, 1975-76, regional rep. Amsterdam, Netherlands, 1976-77; v.p. Europe, Middle-East, Africa, N.Y.C., Crocker Bank, Internat., N.Y.C., 1977—; civilian staff Center Naval Analysis, Arlington, Va., 1963-64. Mem. N.Y. Inst. Credit, N.Y. Credit and Fin. Mgmt. Assn. Roman Catholic. Clubs: Hilversumse (Netherlands) Golf; Hilversumse Lawn Tennis (Melkhuisje). Office: 299 Park Ave New York NY 10017

KADOLA, KARNIL SINGH, trucking co. exec.; b. Bunpar, India, 1916; s. Somma S. and Pritiam K. Kadola; m. Amur Mann, Oct. 30, 1934; 3 children. Owner, Fairview Sawmills Ltd., A.M. Sawmills Ltd., Vancouver, B.C., Can., 1960-63; owner Karnil Fuels Ltd., Vancouver, 1980—; dir. Kadola's Sales & Transport Ltd. Mem. Forest Indsl. Relations.

KADOMOTO, THOMAS S., acct.; b. Phoenix, Aug. 24, 1917; m. Thomas Shosaku and Kio (Fujino) K.; student acctg. Lamson Bus. Coll., 1946-48; m. Kiyomi Kay Matsumori, Mar. 24, 1942; children—Eileen, Nancy, Dan, Larry. Acct., Stewart Concrete Co., 1948-52; owner, mgr. acctg. co., Glendale, Ariz., 1952-60, ins. and real estate co., Glendale, 1960-73; comptroller Ariz. Automotive Inst., Glendale, 1973-75, Phoenix Inst. Tech., 1976—; instr. Japanese, Phoenix Coll., 1975—; hon. consul of Japan for Ariz., 1977—. Bd. dirs. NCCJ; treas., bd. dirs. Ariz. Buddhist Ch., 1975-78; pres. Glendale Elem. Sch. Bd., 1969-70, Glendale Unit IV Sch. PTA, 1965, Japanese Am. Citizens League, 1946—, Glendale Toastmasters, 1964. Served to 2d lt. U.S. Army, 1941-46. Decorated Bronze Star medal; recipient Civic Service award Glendale C. of C., 1963, Top Worker award Glendale United Fund, 1963, award Govt. of Japan, 1960. Mem. Nat. Assn. Public Accts., Glendale Bd. Realtors (pres. 1963, Realtor of Yr. 1964). Republican. Home: 7635 N 46th Ave Glendale AZ 85301 Office: 2555 E University Dr Phoenix AZ 85034

KADRMAS, EDWIN E., publishing co. exec.; b. Dickinson, N.D., Feb. 18, 1934; s. William J. and Emilie A. Kadrmas; B.S., N.D. State U., 1956; postgrad. Mont. State U.; m. Melda Pfenning, Aug. 16, 1955; children—Ronald L., Robert R., Russell W., Roger J. Instr. bus. Rosebud (Mont.) High Sch., 1956-58, Dawson County (Mont.) High Sch., 1958-59, Dawson County Jr. Coll., Glendive, Mont., 1958-59; coll. and gen. rep. South-Western Pub. Co., 1959-67, asst. regional mgr., West Chicago, Ill., 1967-78, regional v.p., 1979—. Chmn., West Chicago Crusade of Mercy, 1974-75; pres. United Way of West Chicago, 1975-77; pres. Suburban Mgmt. Assn., 1974, top mgmt. adv. com., 1975—; div. v.p. Internat. Mgmt. Council, 1974-76. Cert. profl. mgr. Mem. Ill. State C. of C., Ill. Bus. Edn. Assn., Am. Vocat. Assn., Nat. Bus. Edn. Assn., Chgo. Bus. Edn. Assn. Republican. Club: Rotary (gov.'s rep. 1977—, dist. gov.-elect). Home: 25 W 360 Plamondon Wheaton IL 60187 Office: 355 Conde St West Chicago IL 60185

KADUNC, RICHARD JOHN, mech. engr.; b. Cleve., Aug. 5, 1947; s. Albert Joseph and Barbara Sophia (Stempien) K.; B.S. in Mech. Engring., Ohio State U., 1969; M.S. in Systems Mgmt., U. So. Calif., 1974. Field engr. Pan Am. Petroleum Corp., High Island, Tex., 1969; research and devel. test engr. Towmotor Corp., Mentor, Ohio, 1970; program acquisition mgr. Naval Air System Command, Washington, 1972-79; dist. mgr. U.S. C. of C., Dallas, 1979-81; prodn. engr. Def. Contract Adminstrn. Services, Tex. Instruments, Dallas, 1981—. Mem. Internat. Platform Assn., Ohio Soc. Washington. Club: Cleveland (Washington). Home: 5008 Hatherly Dr Plano TX 75023 Office: Def Contract Adminstrn Services Texas Instruments PO Box 226015 M/S 256 Dallas TX 75266

KAEGEL, RAY MARTIN, real estate and ins. broker; b. St. Louis, Dec. 7, 1925; s. Ray E. and Loyola (Mooney) K.; B.S. in Secondary Edn., Washington U., St. Louis, 1948, M.B.A., 1955; m. Daniel Marilyn Dugger, July 2, 1943. Mgr., St. Louis Amusement Co., Inc., 1941-43, 46-52; gen. mgr. Md. Real Estate & Ins. Agy., Inc., Granite City, Ill., 1953-60; pres., gen. mgr., dir. Kaegel Real Estate & Ins. Agy., Inc., Granite City, 1961—. Sec., Granite City Bd. Realtors, 1959-63, 66-77, pres, 1964-65, 79—. Vice chmn. Tri-Cities Area Red Cross, 1972. Served to lt. (j.g.) USNR, 1943-46. Mem. Nat. (exec. officer's council 1959-77), Ill. assns. real estate bds., Tri-Cities Ind. Ins. Agts. Assn. (pres. 1971-73), Ind. Ins. Agts. Ill., Tri-Cities C. of C., Granite City Multiple Listing Service (sec.-treas. 1971—). Optimist. Home: 11255 Ladue Rd St Louis MO 63141 Office: 2721 Madison Ave Granite City IL 62040

KAESER, CLIFFORD RICHARD, leisure products mfg. exec.; b. Boise, Idaho, Feb. 17, 1936; s. Clifford M. and Bertha (Minton) K.; B.A., Coll. Idaho, 1959; D.J., Yale, 1962; m. Carol R. Roach, May 11, 1979; children—Richard Lynn, Cindy Marie, Kenneth Ray. Admitted to Calif. bar, 1962; asso. firm Lawler, Felix & Hall, Los Angeles, 1962-63; asst. div. counsel Lockheed Missile & Space Div., Sunnyvale, Calif., 1963-64; group counsel, then acquisition counsel Litton Industries, Inc., Beverly Hills, Calif., 1963-68; adminstrv. v.p., gen. counsel Hitco, Los Angeles, 1969—; v.p., gen. counsel then adminstrv. v.p. Hitco, Los Angeles, 1969-73, chief exec. officer Leisure Products Group; pres. Chaparral Industries, 1969—; v.p., dir. Parsons Corp., Wickes Industries, Inc., Conn. Hard Rubber Co.; mem. gen. mgmt. com. ARMCO Steel Corp., 1969-73; v.p., gen. counsel Conroy, Inc., also Sno-Jet, Inc., Nauta-Line, Inc., San Antonio, Tex., 1973—, Dobbs Houses, Inc., 1980—; chmn. bd. dirs. Vancom, Inc. Mem. Am. Bar Assn., State Bar Calif., Am. Mgmt. Assn., Mchts. and Mfrs. Assn., Seratoma, Am. Inst. Mgmt. Office: 5100 Poplar Ave Memphis TN 38137

KAFARSKI, MITCHELL I., chem. processing exec.; b. Detroit, Dec. 15, 1917; s. Ignacy A. and Anastasia (Drzazgowski) K.; student U. Detroit, 1941, Shrivenham Am. U., Eng., 1946; m. Zofia Drozdowska, July 11, 1967; children—Erik Michael, Konrad Christian. Process engr. Packard Motor Car Co., 1941-44; founder, dir. Artist and Craftsman Sch., Esslingen, Germany, 1945-46; with Nat. Bank of Detroit, 1946-50; founder, pres., dir. Chem. Processing Inc., 1950-65; treas., dir. Detroit Magnetic Insp., 1960-65, Packard Plating, Inc., 1962-67; v.p., dir. KMH, Inc., 1960-64; chmn. bd., pres., treas. Aactron, Inc., 1965—. Commr., Mich. State Fair, 1965-72, also exec. officer; mem. devel. and planning com. to build Municipal Stadium, 1965-69; patron, mem. founders soc. Detroit Inst. Arts; chmn. Am.-Polish Action Council; mem. dist. adv. council U.S. Small Bus. Adminstrn., 1971-73; trustee Straith Meml. Hosp., Detroit, 1971—; v.p., treas. Straith Meml. Hosp., Southfield, Mich., 1972—, chmn. bd., 1977—; bd. dirs. Bloomfield Arts Assn., U.S. Govt. Corp., Pa. Ave. Devel. Corp., Washington, 1973—, Friends of Kresege Library, Oakland U., 1975—; trustee Detroit Sci. Center; del. White House Conf. on Aging, 1971; vice-chmn. Republican State Nationalities Council Mich., 1969-73 mem. Gov.'s Council, State of Mich., 1975—; bd. dirs. Pa. Ave. Devel. Corp., Washington, 1976—. Served with AUS, 1944-46: ETO; Recipient Nat. award for war prodn. invention, 1943; Knight's Cross Order Poland's Rebirth. Mem. N.A.M. (nat. resources com.), Cranbrook Acad. Arts, Nat., Mich. (dir. 1966—, pres. 1976—), assns. metal finishers, Am. Electroplaters' Soc., Clubs: Otsego Ski; Capitol Hill (Washington); Detroit Athletic; La Coquille (Palm Beach, Fla.). Home: 240 Chesterfield Rd Bloomfield Hills MI 48013 Office: Aactron Inc 29306 Stephenson Hwy Madison Heights MI 48071

KAGAN, IRVING, footwear co. exec.; b. Lynn, Mass., Dec. 19, 1928; s. Max and Nettie (Kagan) K.; B.S., Mass. Inst. Tech., 1948; m. Paula Helene Gelb, Oct. 7, 1950; children—Candace, Leslie Jarige, Nikki, Daniel. With Penobscot Shoe Co., Old Town, Me., 1948—, exec. v.p., 1964, pres., 1968—, chmn. bd., chief exec. officer, 1973—; dir. Merrill Trust Co., 1971—. Corporator, Eastern Maine Med. Center, 1971—; bd. dirs. Sugarloaf Ednl. Ski Found., 1974—; trustee Jewish Community Endowment Assos., 1963—, Max Kagan Family Found., 1953—, Maine Maritime Acad., 1978—. Republican. Jewish. Office: 450 N Main St Old Town ME 04468*

KAHLENBECK, HOWARD, JR., lawyer; b. Fort Wayne, Ind., Dec. 7, 1929; s. Howard and Clara Elizabeth (Wegman) K.; B.S. with distinction, Ind. U., 1952; LL.B., U. Mich., 1957; m. Sally A. Horrell, Aug. 14, 1954; children—Kathryn Sue, Douglas H. Admitted to Ind. bar, 1957; partner firm Krieg DeVault Alexander & Capehart, Indpls., 1957—. Sec., dir. Maul Technology Corp. (formerly The Buehler Corp.), Indpls., 1971—, Am. Monitor Corp., Indpls., 1971—, Am. Interstate Ins. Corp. of Wis., Milw., 1973—, Am. Interstate Ins. Co. Ga., Atlanta, 1973—, Am. Underwriters, Inc., Indpls., 1973—. Served with USAF, 1952-54. Mem. Am., Ind., Indpls., bar assns., Delta Upsilon (sec., dir. 1971—), Beta Gamma Sigma, Alpha Kappa Psi, Delta Theta Phi. Lutheran. Home: 6320 Old Orchard Rd Indianapolis IN 46226 Office: 2860 Indiana Nat Bank Tower Indianapolis IN 46204

KAHLER, ROBERT GEORGE, printing co. exec.; b. Baltimore County, Md., Oct. 25, 1931; s. Robert Daniel and Doris Catherine (Winterstein) K.; B.S. in Bus. Mgmt., U. Balt., 1964, postgrad. Law Sch.; m. Zedith T. Barrenger, Oct. 28, 1951; children—Karen Kahler Adler, Allison Leslie. Successively apprentice meat cutter, meat cutter, mgr. meat dept. Acme Markets Inc., Balt., 1948-59, mem. corp. indsl. relations staff, 1963-70; pres. and bus. rep. local 162, Amalgamated Meat Cutters Union, 1959-61, sec.-treas. and bus. rep. local 117, 1961-63; labor and mgmt. cons. Pension Planners Balt., 1970-71; regional personnel mgr. mfg. Frito-Lay Inc., 1971-73; regional mgr. indsl. relations and personnel graphic arts group Am. Standard Inc., 1973-80, dir. indsl. relations and personnel bank check group hdqrs., Hunt Valley, Md., 1980—; dir. Penny Lane Flowers Inc. Area dir. Springlake Community Assn.; trustee Towson (Md.) Presbyn. Ch. Served with USMCR, 1952-54. Mem. Am. Soc. Personnel Adminstrn., Indsl. Relations Research Assn., Printing Industries Am. Club: Masons. Author booklets. Home: 2311 Foxley Rd Timonium MD 21093 Office: 11350 McCormick Rd Hunt Valley MD 21031

KAHLIG, BERNARD WALTER, farmer, grain dealer, cotton ginner, ins. agt.; b. Westphalia, Tex., July 18, 1922; s. Joseph Frank and Clothilde (Hentschel) K.; student Tex. A. and M. U.; m. Zita Cecelia Fuchs, June 12, 1945; children—Kenneth Bernard, Nancy Jeanette, Linda Marie, Curtis Raymond. Salesman fraternal ins. Farm Mut. Ins. Co., Brenham, Tex., 1952-76; owner Cen-Tex Fertilizer & Grain Co., Temple, Tex., 1968—; dir. Germania Farm Mut., Brenham; owner, dir. Temple Compress Warehouse Co. (Tex.). Mem. Tex. Cotton Ginners Assn., Tex. Grain and Feed Assn. Roman Catholic. Address: Central Texas Fertilizer Grain Rt 3 Ratibor Temple TX 76501

KAHN, ALLEN EARL, electronics and communications mfg. co. exec.; b. Milw., Oct. 19, 1936; s. Earl Andrew and Fae (Brown) K.; B.A., U. Tex., El Paso, 1962; postgrad. Long Beach State Coll., 1964-65; m. Kathleen Teresa Logan, 1977. Systems engr., IBM, Long Beach, 1963-65; data processing mgr. Reeves Rubber Co., San Clemente, Calif., 1965-67; regional systems mgr. Recognition Equipment Co., Los Angeles, 1967-69; br. mgr. Boothe Resources Internat., Los Angeles, 1969-70, Eastern regional mgr., N.Y.C., 1970-71; account mgr. Memorex Corp., Los Angeles, 1971-72; nat. account mgr. Data 100, Los Angeles, 1972-75; nat. account mgr. Harris Corp., Los Angeles, 1975-77, dist. mgr., 1977—. Dir. bus. div. United Way, 1963; chmn. data processing com. Republican Central Com., 1966. Served with USAF, 1954-58. Recipient Citizenship commendation Gov. Ronald Reagan, 1967. Republican. Lutheran. Home: 14006 Palawan Way Marina del Rey CA 90291 Office: 5839 Green Valley Circle Culver City CA 90230

KAHN, BERNARD DAVID, bus. cons.; b. N.Y.C., 1922; s. Herman L. and Pauline S. K.; B.A., Rutgers U., 1942; m. Helen Penrose, Jan. 27, 1960; children—Geoffry, David, Antonia. Creative supr. Ted Bates Co., N.Y.C., 1952-54; exec. v.p. creative services Grey Advt. Co., N.Y.C., 1954-68; pres. Kahn Assos. Inc., growth cons., N.Y.C., 1968-80; lectr. profl. assns., Harvard U., Yale U., N.Y. U. Served to capt. AC, U.S. Army, 1942-45. Decorated Silver Star, D.F.C., Air medal with oak leaf cluster, Purple Heart. Mem. Assn. Corp. Growth, Am. Mgmt. Assn. Died July 22, 1980. Office: 78 E 56th St 8th Floor New York NY 10022

KAHN, EDWARD, custom-built homes co. exec.; b. Phila., May 22, 1933; s. Bernard and Fannie (Mitchell) K.; B.S., Temple U., 1955; M.B.A., U. Detroit, 1958; postgrad. Grad. Sch. Bus. Adminstrn., N.Y. U., 1960-61; m. Shirley Osterneck, Dec. 19, 1959; children—Jeffrey David, Andrew Mitchell. Instr. mktg. Temple U., Phila., 1958-68, asst. to dean Sch. Bus. Adminstrn., 1961-64, Grad. Sch., 1965-68; mktg. cons., 1961-68; dir. mktg., v.p. mktg. Ridge Homes, Evans Products Co., Blue Bell, Pa., 1968-72, gen. mgr., 1973-74, exec. v.p. Homes Group, 1974-78, pres. Homes Group, 1978—, exec. v.p. parent co., 1978—, also dir. Co-editor: (with Lazo, Corbin and Kelley) Marketing Managemian Annotated Bibliography, 1963. Office: 1777 Walton Rd Blue Bell PA 19422

KAHN, EDWIN WALTER, constrn. co. exec.; b. Pitts., June 3, 1922; s. Theodore and Helen Henrietta (Meyers) K.; B.S., U. Calif. at Berkeley, 1948; m. Arleen Barbara Rudolph, Dec. 23, 1951; children—Greg, Julie, David. Chief structural designer Gen. Engring. Service Co., Los Angeles, 1948-54; partner Pollack-Kahn & Assos., Engrs., Los Angeles, 1954-56, Mogil-Kahn Constrn. Co., Los Angeles, 1956-60; pres. Kahn Constrn. Co., Los Angeles, 1960—. Cons. civil engr. Served with USAAF, 1942-45. Registered profl. engr., Calif.; lic. comml. pilot. Mem. ASCE, Am. Concrete Inst.,

Archimedes Circle, Town Hall of Calif., Natural History Mus. Alliance, Aircraft Owners and Pilots Assn., Air Force Assn., Smithsonian Assos., Cousteau Soc., Los Angeles World Affairs Council, Inter-Am. Soc. Mason (32 deg. Shriner). Club: Varsity (U. Calif. at Los Angeles). Home: 13029 Mindanao Way Marina DelRey CA 90291 Office: 1535 6th St Santa Monica CA 90401

KAHN, JOSEPH JEROME, business exec.; b. Washington, Mar. 11, 1920; s. Isadore Lewis and Elizabeth L. (Bergazin) K.; student U. Md., 1937; B.S., U. Va., 1942; postgrad. Cambridge (Eng.) U., 1944, Southeastern U., 1947; m. Florence Jayne Kaufman, Sept. 8, 1947; children—Cathryn Dee, Patricia Lynn. Pres. Budco, Inc., Chevy Chase, Md., 1960—; energy cons. J.J. Kahn Consultancy, Chevy Chase, 1979—; dir. energy conservation dept. Shannon & Luchs Cos., Washington, 1974-78; exec. v.p. Hydrocontrol Corp., 1979; cons. real estate sales, leasing, constrn., energy conservation. Pres. Chevy Chase Citizens Assn., 1953—. Served to capt., USAAF, 1942-45. Cert. property mgr. Mem. Nat. Assn. Homebuilders, Washington Assn. Homebuilders, Nat. Bd. Realtors, Washington Bd. Realtors, Inst. Real Estate Mgmt., Property Mgrs. Assn., Res. Officers Assn., Nat. Gymnastica. Democrat. Jewish. Contbr. articles to publs. Home and Office: 3312 Shepherd St Chevy Chase MD 20015

KAHN, RICHARD STEWART, leasing corp., truck rental exec.; b. Denver, July 14, 1951; s. Joseph A and Florence S (Stark) K.; student pub. schs., Denver. Vice pres. Westguard Leasing Corp. subs. F.K.A. S.H.W. Capital Corp., Sausalito, Calif., 1973-79; sr. credit officer, mgr. ops., v.p. Intercoastal Leasing Corp.; pres., chief exec. officer Marin Truck Rentals Inc., San Rafael, Calif., 1977-79; chmn. bd., chief exec. officer Garden Tubberies Ltd. Mem. Western, Am. assns. equipment lessors, Am., Calif. rental assns. Democrat. Jewish. Home: 1107 Sir Francis Drake Blvd Kentfield CA 94904 Office: 1299 4th St Suite 304 San Rafael CA 94901

KAHN, ROBERT IRVING, business counselor; b. Oakland, Calif., May 17, 1918; s. Irving Herman and Francesca (Lowenthal) K.; A.B. with honors, Stanford, 1938; M.B.A. (Baker scholar), Harvard, 1940; LL.D. (hon.), Franklin Pierce Coll., 1977; m. Patricia Elizabeth Glenn, Feb. 14, 1946; children—Christopher Glenn Kahn, Roberta Anne Kahn. Researcher exec. R.H. Macy's, N.Y.C., 1940-41; controller Smiths and Moneyback Smiths, Inc., Oakland, 1946-51; dir., v.p., treas. Sherwood Swan & Co., Oakland, 1953-56; now pres. Robert Kahn & Assos., bus. counsellors, Lafayette, Calif.; pres. Kahn & Harris, fin. counselors, San Francisco; v.p. Hambrecht & Quist, investment bankers, 1977-80; v.p., dir. Marc Paul, Inc., Coast Med. Corp.; dir. Menlo Trading Co., Burlingame, Calif., Lipps, Inc., Santa Monica, Calif., Simon Hardware Co., Walnut Creek, Piedmont Grocery Co., Oakland, Wal-Mart Stores, Inc., Bentonville, Ark., Components Corp. Am., Dallas; pub. Retailing Today. Mem. exec. com., gov., treas. United Bay Area Crusade, 1955-66, mem. finance com., trustee, 1966-69, mem. gen. budget com., 1971-76, chmn. membership com., 1976-79; past mem. Nat. Budget and Consultation Com.; past v.p. Alameda County United Fund; bd. dirs. Bay Area Council for Social Planning, Downtown Property Owners Assn., Oakland; past dir. Oakland chpt. A.R.C., East Bay Fedn. Chests; bd. dirs., past v.p. San Francisco Bay council Girl Scouts; past mem., past vice chmn. Jewish Community Relations Commn. Alameda-Contra Costa Counties. Former mem. adv. council on fed. reports Retail Industry Com. Served from 2d lt. to lt. col. USAF, 1941-46, 51-52; lt. col. Res. (ret.). Mem. Nat. Retail Mchts. Assn. (past dir. San Francisco Bay cities controllers group), Stanford Alumni Assn., Harvard Bus. Sch. Alumni Assn., Res. Officers Assn., Air Force Assn., Nat. Rifle Assn., Assn. Mgmt. Consultants (past trustee, past pres.), Inst. Mgmt. Consultants (a founder), Newsletter Assn. Am., Phi Beta Kappa. Home: 3684 Happy Valley Rd Lafayette CA 94549 Office: PO Box 249 Lafayette CA 94549

KAHN, ROBERT SAMUEL, non-ferrous metal mfg. co. exec.; b. Chgo., Feb. 14, 1918; s. Lee and Mildred (Arnheim) K.; B.S. in Chem. Engring., Rose-Hulman Inst. Tech., 1939, D.Engring. (hon.), 1981; m. Louise Franck Schock, Apr. 5, 1942. Div. mgr. R. Lavin & Sons, Chgo., 1945-51; v.p. Tube City Iron & Metal Co., Glassport, Pa., 1952-59, Luria Bros. & Co., Pitts., 1960-68; pres., chmn. Keystone Resources, Pitts., 1969—. Served with USN, 1941-45. Decorated Bronze Star. Mem. Nat. Assn. Recycling Industries (pres.), Bur. Internacional de la Recuperacion (v.p.). Republican. Lutheran. Clubs: Duquesne, St. Clair Country (Pitts.); Mining, Chemists (N.Y.C.); Ill. Athletic (Chgo.). Office: Frick Bldg Pittsburgh PA 15219

KAHN, SANDERS ARTHUR, realty cons.; b. N.Y.C., Jan. 20, 1919; s. Robert and Hattie (Grossman) K.; B.B.A., CCNY, 1947; M.B.A., N.Y. U., 1949, Ph.D., 1962; m. Miriam Lefkowitz, Mar. 19, 1948; children—Leslie Arlene, Susan Betty, Richard Steven. With Adams & Co., Real Estate, Inc., 1938-42; v.p. Walter Oertly Assos., Inc., 1946-48; with Dwight-Helmsley, 1948-49; asst. prof. real estate U. Fla., 1949-50; mgr. real estate planning div. Port of N.Y. Authority, 1951-53; pres. Sanders A. Kahn Assos., Inc., N.Y.C. and Clifton, N.J., also affiliated offices in London, Edinburgh and Cairo, 1953—; supr. real estate edn., adj. prof. Baruch Coll., City U. N.Y., 1953—; pres. Transp. Realty Devel. Corp. Bd. dirs. Citizens Housing and Planning Council N.Y.; former pres. adv. bd. Mercy Coll.; former bd. dirs. YMCA, Clifton, Passaic and Garfield, N.J. Served with USAAF, 1942-45; ETO. Recipient George L. Schmutz award Am. Inst. Real Estate Appraisers, 1979; Sanders A. Kahn Realty Edn. Scholarship Fund established Bernard Baruch Coll., 1980. Fellow Valuers and Auctioneers Soc. (Gt. Britain), Am. Soc. Appraisers (past internat. gov. and internat. edn. chmn.; pres., dir. Greater N.Y. chpt.); mem. Am. Soc. Planning Ofcls., North Jersey Planning Assn. (dir.), Am. Soc. Real Estate Counsellors, Soc. Bus. Adv. Professions, So. Econ. Assn., Urban Land Inst., Am. Right-of-Way Assn. (pres. N.Y. chpt. 1966, past chmn. valuation com., past nat. dir.), Soc. Real Estate Appraisers (N.Y. Man of Year 1980), N.Y. U. Alumni Club, Nat. Realty Club, Columbia Soc. Real Estate Appraisers, Lambda Alpha, Alpha Epsilon Pi. Author: (with others) Real Estate Appraisal and Investment; Principles of Right of Way Acquisition; columnist Down to Earth. Home: 428 Green Hill Rd Smoke Rise Kinnelon NJ 07405 Office: 341 Madison Ave New York City NY 10017 also Styertowne Shopping Center 1051 Bloomfield Ave Clifton NJ 07012

KAHN, STEVEN MARK, real estate and investment broker; b. Columbus, Ohio, Apr. 14, 1946; s. Harry and Nancy (VanGrow) K.; grad. Ohio Real Estate Inst., Ohio State U., 1970; certified property mgr. Inst. Real Estate Mgmt., 1975; m. Maryellen McGath, Sept. 9, 1973; 1 dau., Lori. Trainee, Sears Roebuck & Co., Columbus, 1967-68; salesman Brad Salt Realtors, Columbus, 1968-70; property mgmt., brokerage Lee Wears & Co., Columbus, 1970-75; partner firm Wears, Kahn, McMenamy & Co., Columbus, 1976—; partner Great N.W. Co., Hexagon Equity Co. Mem. Nat., Ohio assns. realtors, Columbus Bd. Realtors, Columbus Area C. of C., Columbus Mortgage Bankers Assn., Inst. Real Estate Mgmt. Jewish. Clubs: Athletic of Columbus, Columbus Maennerchor, German Village Soc. Home: 165 E Deshler Ave Columbus OH 43206 Office: 81 S 5th St Columbus OH 43215

KAILAS, LEO GEORGE, lawyer; b. N.Y.C., May 28, 1949; s. George and Evanthia (Skoulikas) K.; A.B., Columbia U., 1970, J.D., 1973. Admitted to N.Y. bar, 1974; asso. firm Olwine, Connelly, Chase, O'Donnell and Weyler, N.Y.C., 1973-77; partner specializing in admiralty litigaton, firm Milgrim Thomajan Jacobs & Lee, P.C., N.Y.C., 1977—. Active St. John's Greek Orthodox Ch., Tenafly, N.J. Mem. Am. Bar Assn., Assn. Bar City N.Y. Home: 1040 Park Ave New York NY 10028 Office: 405 Lexington Ave New York NY 10017

KAILING, ALEXANDER MICHAEL, II, investment advisor; b. Milw., Jan. 21, 1939; s. Richard Reed and Mary Elizabeth (Malone) K.; B.A., Georgetown U., 1962; M.B.A., Northwestern U., 1965; m. Marieluise Baur, Sept. 2, 1972; children—Alexander Michael, Karl Joseph, Katherine Marie. Jr. accountant Ernst & Ernst, Milw., 1965-66; investment officer Prudential Ins. Co. Am., Newark, 1966-72; sr. analyst Lord, Abbett & Co., N.Y.C., 1972-74; v.p. State Nat. Bank, Evanston, Ill., 1974-79; prin. A. M. Kailing & Assos., Ltd., Chgo., 1979—. Mem. Investment Analysts Soc. Roman Catholic. Clubs: Wis., Milw. Athletic, Union League. Office: Three First Nat Plaza Chicago IL 60603

KAINDL, JAMES ERIC, engr.; b. Dallas, Oct. 8, 1940; s. Harry and Mary (Goggans) K.; B.B.A., So. Meth. U., 1964; B.S.E.S., U. Tex., 1972; m. Barbara Ann Brock, May 24, 1980. Stockbroker, Rauscher Pierce Securities, Dallas, 1966-70; project engr. ICA, Berkeley, Calif., 1973-75; environ. engr. Pacific Steel Corp., Berkeley, 1975-77; gen. mgr. Hy-Bon Engring. Co., Midland, Tex., 1977—; tchr. U. Kans., U. Okla., Permian Basin Grad. Center. Served in USMC, 1964-66. Mem. Air Pollution Control Assn., Marine Corps League, Alpha Tau Omega. Republican. Methodist. Clubs: Masons (32 deg.), Shriners. Office: 2121 W Florida St Midland TX 79701

KAINRAD, ALAN, mfg. co. exec.; b. Ravenna, Ohio, Sept. 16, 1951; s. John and Elsie (Nussbaumer) K.; student U. Akron, 1969-70; B.S. in Mktg. Ohio State U., 1973. Sales rep. Folger's Coffee, Milw., 1973-74; owner A-J Leathercraft, Milw., 1974-75; pres., controller Koleaco, Inc., Garland, Tex., 1975—. Mem. Garland C. of C. Roman Catholic. Club: Rotary. Home: 1610 Hastings St Garland TX 75042 Office: 203 N Kirby St Garland TX 75042

KAISER, E(DGAR) F(OSBURGH), industrialist; b. Spokane, Wash., July 29, 1908; s. Henry J. and Bessie (Fosburgh) K.; student U. Calif., 1927-30; L.H.D. (hon.), U. Calif. at Berkeley; LL.D. (hon.), U. Portland, Pepperdine Coll., Mills Coll., Golden Gate U., U. Pacific; m. Sue Mead, Aug. 24, 1932 (dec. June 1974); children—Carlyn, Becky, Gretchen, Edgar Fosburgh, Henry Mead, Kim John; m. 2d, Nina McCormick, Feb. 1, 1975. Constrn. supt. natural gas line Kans. to Okla., 1930-32; shift supt. Boulder Dam, Nev., 1932-33; adminstrn. mgr. Columbia Constrn. Co., Bonneville (Oreg.) Dam, 1934-38; project mgr. Grand Coulee Dam, Wash., 1938-41; v.p., gen. mgr. Oreg. Shipbldg. Corp. and Kaiser Co., Inc., Portland, Oreg., Vancouver, Wash., 1941-45; pres., dir. Kaiser Motors Corp., 1945-56; pres. Kaiser Industries Corp., 1956-67; chmn. emeritus Kaiser Found. Hosps., Kaiser Found. Health Plan, Inc.; chmn. emeritus, hon. dir. Kaiser Steel Corp., Kaiser Aluminum & Chem. Corp., Kaiser Cement Corp., Kaiser Resources Ltd.; past chmn. incorporators Nat. Corp. for Housing Partnership. Former mem. Pres.'s Adv. Com. on Labor-Mgmt. Policy; former mem. President's Adv. Com. on Refugees; hon. mem. The Bus. Council; former mem. President's Adv. Com. on Nat. Health Ins. Issues; former mem. bus. leadership adv. council OEO; former mem. bd. incorporators Communications Satellite Corp., nat. chmn. UN Day, 1966; past v.p., hon. dir. Oakland-Alameda County Coliseum; hon. chmn. bd. dirs. Oakland Symphony Orch. Assn.; vice chmn. bd. trustees The Henry J. Kaiser Family Found.; trustee, past chmn. Bay Area Council; dir. San Francisco Opera Assn. Decorated comdr. Nat. Order So. Cross, Republic of Brazil, grand officer Republic Ivory Coast; recipient Moles award for outstanding achievement in constrn. industry, 1962; Hoover medal, 1969; named Industrialist of Yr., Calif. Mus. Sci. and Industry, 1966; named Constrn.'s Man of Yr., Engring. News-Record, 1968; Alumnus of Yr., U. Calif., 1969; Medal of Freedom, Pres. U.S., 1969; Bus. Statesman of Yr., Harvard Bus. Sch. of No. Calif., 1971; Golden Beaver award for mgmt. The Beavers, 1975; Internat. Achievement award World Trade Club San Francisco, 1975; New Oakland Com. award for Nat. Achievement, 1976; Mfr. of Yr. award Calif. Mfrs. Assn., 1976; Humanitarian of Yr. award Easter Seal Soc. Alameda County, 1978. Fellow Am. Acad. Arts and Scis.; mem. ASCE, Soc. Naval Architects and Marine Engrs., Pan Am. Soc., U.S. (life), Nat. Com. U.S.-China Relations (life). Office: 300 Lakeside Dr Oakland CA 94643

KAISER, EDGAR F(OSBURGH), JR., steel co. exec.; b. Portland, Oreg., 1942; A.B., Stanford U., 1965; M.B.A., Harvard U., 1967. With econ. div. AID, Vietnam, 1968; White House fellow, Washington, 1968; with Kaiser Steel Corp., Oakland, Calif., 1970-71, 79—, pres., chief exec. officer, 1979-80, chmn. exec. com., 1979—, chmn. bd., 1980—; with Kaiser Resources Ltd., Vancouver, B.C., Can., 1969—, pres., chief exec. officer, 1973-78, chmn. bd., chief exec. officer, 1978-80; dir. Toronto (Ont., Can.) Dominion Bank, B.C. Resources Investment Corp., Daon Devel. Corp. Trustee, Henry J. Kaiser Family Found., Calif. Inst. Tech.; mem. Trilateral Commn., Can.-Am. Com.; mem. Can.-Japan Bus. Coop. Com.; also active other govt., civic, orgns. Office: 300 Lakeside Dr PO Box 58 Oakland CA 94604

KAISERMAN, STUART WARREN, real estate exec.; b. Chgo., Nov. 14, 1937; s. Sol Jack and Frances (Weber) K.; B.S. in Bus. Adminstrn., Roosevelt U., Chgo., 1960; m. Geraldine M. Solar, May 30, 1960; children—Jami, Stephanie, Mindy, David, Laurel. Vice pres., dir. Real Estate Capitol Corp., Chgo., 1970; v.p. regional dir. Arlen Realty & Devel. Corp., Chgo., 1972; real estate investments, Chgo., 1980—; real estate mgr., adviser Chancery div. Circuit Ct. Chgo.; real estate adviser Prudential Life Ins. Co., Equitable Life Ins. Co., U. Chgo., others. Bd. dirs. Ill. Housing and Devel. Authority. Recipient Real Estate Man of Year award Ill. State of Israel Bonds, 1977. Licensed certified property mgr. Mem. Inst. Real Estate Mgmt., Chgo. Real Estate Bd., Apt. Bldg. Mgrs. Assn., Bldg. Owners and Mgrs. Assn., Prime Ministers Club State of Israel (bd. govs.). Jewish. Home: 224 Park Ave Highland Park IL 60035 Office: 109 N Dearborn Chicago IL 60602

KALAHER, RICHARD ALAN, lawyer, mining co. exec.; b. Milw., Apr. 4, 1940; s. Willard Michael and Mildred May (Koch) K.; A.B., Union Coll., Schenectady, 1962; J.D., Northwestern U., 1965; m. Ann Hoogland, Aug. 8, 1970; children—Richard Alan, Kathleen Marie, Kimberly Ann, Alison Helene. Admitted to N.Y. bar, 1965; asso. firm Shearman & Sterling, N.Y.C., 1965-74; sr. atty. AMAX Inc., N.Y.C., 1974-75; v.p., gen. counsel AMAX Coal Co., Indpls., 1975-77; asso. gen. counsel AMAX Inc., Greenwich, Conn., 1977—. Home: 280 Chestnut Hill Rd Wilton CT 06897 Office: AMAX Inc AMAX Center Greenwich CT 06830

KALB, CLIFFORD CLARK, pharm. co. exec; b. Newark, June 15, 1949; s. Daniel and Lorraine (Halpern) K.; B.A., Rutgers U., 1973; M.B.A., Fairleigh Dickinson U., 1976; m. Barbara Sadowsky, May 27, 1973; 1 dau., Laurie Dyan. Research technician Cin. Milacron Chem., New Brunswick, N.J., 1970-72, Nat. Starch & Chem. Co., Plainfield, N.J., 1973-74; sales rep. Marion Labs., Kansas City, Mo., 1974-75; sales rep. Pfizer Inc., N.Y.C., 1975-78, mktg. research analyst, 1978-79; asso. mgr. public policy Hoffmann LaRoche, Inc., Nutley, N.J., 1979—; pharm. adv. bd. Fairleigh Dickinson U., 1977—. N.J. State scholar, 1968-71; N.J. State Golf Assn. Caddy scholar, 1968-71; S.Orange (N.J.) Businessman's Assn. scholar, 1968-71. Mem. Pharm. Mfrs. Assn., Nat. Pharm. Council. Club: Order of Arrow. Contbr. articles to profl. jours. Home: 47 Gettysburg Dr Manalapan NJ 07726 Office: Hoffmann LaRoche Inc 340 Kingsland St Nutley NJ 07110

KALB, ROLAND JAY, mgmt. cons.; b. Vienna, Austria, June 6, 1916; s. Oskar and Helen K.; Elec. Engr., Tech. Lehranstalt, Vienna, 1938; postgrad. Ecole Radio Technique Paris, 1938-39; m. Lore Weil, Feb. 3, 1953; children—Linda Susan, Richard Oskar. Mgr. quality control Minerva Radio, Vienna, 1937-38, chief engr., Paris, 1938-39; plant mgr. Air King Products, N.Y.C., 1941-47; gen. mgr. Teletone Radio, N.Y.C., 1947-50; chmn. bd. Herold Radio and Electronics, Yonkers, N.Y., 1950-61; pres. Roland Radio Corp., 1950-61; group v.p. Fairbanks Morse & Co., Yonkers, 1961-63; chief exec. Pilot Radio Corp., 1963-65; group v.p. Harmon Kardon & Jerrold Corp., 1963-65; pres. Roland Electronics Corp., N.Y.C., 1965—, Roland J. Kalb Asso., Inc., mgmt. cons., Scarsdale, N.Y., 1965—. Vice chmn. bd. trustees Center for Preventive Psychiatry, 1968-72, chmn., 1973-78; pres. Oskar Kalb Meml. Found., 1964—. Recipient numerous appreciation and leadership awards. Mem. Internat. Cons. Assn., Am. Mgmt. Assn., Am. Hosp. Assn., Am. Public Health Assn., Weitzman Inst. Sci. Home: 2 Eaton Ln Scarsdale NY 10583 Office: 60 E 42d St New York NY 10017

KALEN, RICHARD TRAVIS, exec. personnel co. exec.; b. Kansas City, Mo., Oct. 12, 1942; s. Richard Travis and Dorothy Maybell Kalen; B.S., U. Kans., 1965; postgrad. U. Tulsa, 1975-76; m. Susan M. Hughes, Dec. 5, 1976; 1 son, Richard Travis. Salesman, Hallmark Cards, Inc., Kansas City, Mo., 1965-67, sr. account mgr., 1967-68, sales employment counselor, Atlanta, 1968-70, sales employment mgr., Kansas City, 1970-73; employment mgr. Waddell & Reed, Inc., Kansas City, 1972-73, mgr. manpower devel., 1973-74; exec. staffing mgr. Williams Cos., Tulsa, 1974-75, mgr. manpower, planning and staffing, 1975, dir. human resources, 1975-77; v.p. Spencer Stuart and Assos., Dallas, 1978—. Served to capt. USMC, 1965-66. Decorated Purple Heart, Bronze Star, Silver Star. Mem. Am. Mgmt. Assn. Republican. Presbyterian. Office: 2626 Republic National Bank Tower Dallas TX 75201

KALEN, THOMAS HARRY, banker; b. Balt., Mar. 14, 1938; s. Harry Lawrence and Angela Carolyn (Nockels) K.; B.S., UCLA, 1960; m. Judith L. Cochran, Aug. 29, 1959; children—John Merrill, Bonnie Jean. Account exec. Dean Witter & Co., San Bernardino, Calif., 1966-69; v.p. Chase Investment Mgmt. Co., N.Y.C., 1969-71, Transamerica Corp., Los Angeles, 1971-77, No. Trust Co., Chgo., 1977—. Vice pres., chmn. public relations Calif. Jaycees, 1968; dist. chmn. UCLA Scholarship Soc., 1974-77; chmn. public relations com. Mass Transit for Los Angeles, 1976. Served with USAF, 1960-66; Vietnam. Named Calif. Outstanding Jaycees, 1968. Mem. Nat. Assn. Security Dealers, Western Pension Conf., Instl. Investor Conf., Pension and Investment Conf. Club: Union League (Chgo.). Office: 50 S LaSalle St Chicago IL 60675

KALES, ROBERT GRAY, mgmt., finance, mfg., real estate exec.; b. Detroit, Mar. 14, 1904; s. William R. and Alice (Gray) K.; grad. Phillips Exeter Acad., 1923; B.Sc., Mass. Inst. Tech., 1928; M.B.A., Harvard, 1933; m. Jane Webster, Nov. 27, 1932; children—Jane (Mrs. William H. Ryan), Robert Gray, William R., Anne W. (Mrs. Jeffrey M. Howson); m. 2d, Miriam Wallin, Jan. 6, 1945; 1 son, David Wallin; m. 3d, Herma Lou Boyd, Mar. 6, 1951; m. 4th, Shirley L. McBride, Feb. 14, 1961; children—John Gray, Nancy Davis. With Whitehead & Kales Co., Detroit, 1928-31, 43-76, v.p., 1943-76, also dir., chmn. bd.; with Union Guardian Trust Co., Detroit, 1933-34; analyst, sec.-treas. Investment Counsel, Inc., Detroit, 1934-35; organizer Kales Kramer Investment Co., Detroit, 1935, pres., dir., 1935—; pres., dir. Indsl. Resources, Inc., 1955-71, Automotive Bin Service Co., Inc., 1955-71, Kales Bldg. Co., 1944-67, Kales Realty Co., 1935-74, Midwest Underwriters, Inc., 1938—, Modern Constrn., Inc., 1938-60 (all Detroit); v.p., dir. Basin Oil Co., Metamora, Mich., 1947-74; dir. Ind. Liberty Life Ins. Co., Grand Rapids, Mich., Atlas Energy, Inc., Dallas. Chmn. vets. com. Detroit Armed Forces Week, adv. bd. Patriotic Edn., Deland, Fla.; chmn. trustees, pres. Kales Found. Served to lt. comdr. USNR, 1942-45; capt. Res. Mem. Am. Legion, Navy League U.S. (past pres. Southeastern Mich. council), Mil. Order World Wars (past nat. comdr.-in-chief), Nat. Sojourners, Naval Order U.S., S.A.R., U.S. Naval Inst., Sigma Chi. Episcopalian. Mason (K.T., Shriner). Clubs: Army and Navy, Capitol Hill, University (Washington); Bayview Yacht, Detroit Country, Detroit Athletic, Detroit, Curling, Detroit Power Squadron, The Players, St. Clair Yacht, Scarab, University (Detroit); Black River Ranch (Onaway, Mich.); Longwood Cricket, Union Boat (Boston); Stone Horse Yacht (Harwich, Mass.); La Coquille (Palm Beach, Fla.); Triton Fish and Game (Quebec, Can.); Grosse Pointe (Mich.) Hunt, Grosse Pointe Yacht; Ocean Reef (Key Largo, Fla.). Home: 87 Cloverly Rd Grosse Pointe Farms MI 48236 Office: 1900 E Jefferson Ave Detroit MI 48207

KALES, SHIRLEY MCBRIDE (MRS. ROBERT GRAY KALES), investment co. exec.; b. Detroit, Feb. 18, 1927; d. George L. and Elsie J. (Storey) McBride; student Wayne State U., 1946-48, Detroit Conservatory Music, 1948-50; m. Robert Gray Kales, Feb. 14, 1961; children—John Gray, Nancy Davis. Mem. advt. staff Detroit Evening News Assn., 1949-55; mem. advt. and publicity staff Bielfield Agy., Detroit, 1955-59; mem. advt. and sales dept. Mich. Bell Telephone Co., Detroit, 1959-60; mem. sales promotion and advt. staff Mich. Consol. Gas Co., Detroit, 1960-61; asst. personnel dir. Kales Kramer Investment Co., Detroit; dir. Automotive Bin Service Co., Inc., Detroit. Mem. Detroit Mus. Art Founders Soc., Navy League U.S., Fine Arts Soc. Detroit. Clubs: Women's City, Detroit Review, Country (Detroit); Grosse Pointe (Mich.) Yacht. Home: 87 Cloverly Rd Grosse Pointe Farms MI 48236 Office: Kales Bldg Detroit MI 48226

KALI, ROBERT JAMES, fin. cons.; b. Rockville Center, N.Y., Dec. 5, 1954; s. Anthony J. and Lydia K.; B.A., Colgate U., 1977; M.B.A., N.Y. U., 1979. Fin. applications cons. Nat. CSS Inc. subs. Dun & Bradstreet, Chgo., 1979-80, CompuServe subs. H.R. Block, Chgo., 1980—. Mem. Planning Execs. Inst., Midwest Planning Assn., Fin. Mgmt. Assn. Home: 722 W Roscoe Ave Chicago IL 60657 Office: 200 W Monroe St Chicago IL 60606

KALIL, DAVID THOMAS, steel co. exec.; b. Detroit, Sept. 22, 1926; s. David A. and Rose (Gannon) K.; B.S. in Chem. Engring., U. Mich., 1948; LL.B., Detroit Coll. Law, 1951, LL.M., N.Y. U., 1962; m. Helga Amelia Hersacher, Nov. 1, 1958; children—David Eugene, John Thomas. Admitted to Mich. bar, 1951, N.Y. bar, 1961; with U.S. Patent Office, Washington, 1951-52; practice law, Detroit, 1953-59; with Inco, N.Y.C., 1959-63, Kaynar Mfg. Co., Inc., Fullerton, Calif., 1963-64, AMAX, Inc., N.Y.C. and Greenwich, Conn., 1964-77; with Jones & Laughlin Steel Corp., Pitts., 1977—, v.p., gen. counsel; dir. subs. corps. Served with USAAF, 1944-46. Mem. Am. Iron and Steel Inst., Am. Soc. Metals, AAAS, Am. Bar Assn., Am. Welding Soc., C. of C. Greater Pitts. (dir.). Roman Catholic. Clubs: Duquesne, Oakmont Golf. Home: 111 Shannon Dr Pittsburgh PA 15238 Office: 3 Gateway Center Pittsburgh PA 15263

KALINOWICZ, HENRY RICHARD, real estate co. exec.; b. Poland, June 3, 1914; emigrated to Can., 1949, naturalized, 1954; s. Stanislas and Gustawa K.; M. Law, U Warsaw, 1936; LL.D., U. Vilno, 1938; m. Irene Nagel, May 23, 1946; children—Carol-Joy, Robert S. Public prosecutor, Poland, 1939-46; mng. dir. Triad Group Cos., Ville Sainte Laurent, Que., 1968—. Trustee Weston Sch. Corp., Montreal, Que., 1979-80. Served with Polish Armed Forces, 1944-46. Home: 19 Cressy St Hampstead PQ H3X 1R3 Canada Office: 3767 Thimens Ville Sainte Laurent PQ H4R 1W4 Canada

KALJIAN, THOMAS EDWARD, automobile dealer, real estate broker, rancher; b. Los Banos, Calif., Mar. 5, 1942; s. Charles Thomas and Zita B. (Thomas) K.; B.S., U. Calif. at Davis, 1964; m. Mary Grace Soares, Aug. 1, 1970; children—Charles Thomas, Suzanne Marie. With Kaljian Motor Co., Los Banos, 1965—, partner, 1967—; mgr. C T Kaljian Ranches, Los Banos, 1970—; broker T. Kaljian Real Estate, Los Banos, 1976—; dir. Tri Cast Inc., Los Banos. Mem. adv. bd. San Luis Water Dist., 1970-76. Mem. Los Banos C. of C. (v.p. 1973-75, dir.), Merced County Bd. Realtors, Nat. Automobile Dealers Assn., Calif. Farm Bur. Republican. Club: Rotary. Home: 1508 7th St Los Banos CA 93635 Office: PO Box 1408 Los Banos CA 93635

KALKIN, EUGENE W., retail corp. exec.; b. Forest Hills, N.Y., May 6, 1929; s. Murray and Rose (Blum) K.; B.A., U. Vt., 1950; postgrad. Bernard Baruch Sch. Bus., 1951; m. Joan Lazarus, June 4, 1961; 2 children. Buyer, div. merchandise mgr. Allied Stores Corp., N.Y.C., 1952-58; founder pres. Great Eastern Linens, Inc., Totowa, N.J., 1958-72; v.p. Daylin, Inc., 1972-75; founder, pres. E.W. Kalkin, Inc., West Orange, N.J., 1975—; bd. dirs. Merchandise Alliance Corp. Bd. trustees Temple B'nai Jeshurun, Short Hills, N.J., 1978—. Office: Essex Green Shopping Center Prospect Ave West Orange NJ 07052

KALLAY, MICHAEL ALAN, bus. editor; b. Louisville, Nov. 26, 1946; s. Edwin A. and Mary Jane (Cottom) K.; B.A., Bellarmine Coll., Louisville, 1969; m. Sandra Lee Pollard, May 16, 1970; children—Kathryn Lee, Andrew Michael, Alison Curran. Writer editor Louisville Times, 1965-69, 71-72; community affairs dir. Nat. Industries, Inc., Louisville, 1972-73, corporate dir. communications, 1973-77; bus. editor Louisville Times, 1977—, chmn., 1978-80. Sec., bd. dirs. SE Family YMCA, Louisville, 1976; bd. dirs. Met. YMCA, 1978—, Boys Clubs of Louisville, 1978—, Ky. Opera Assn., 1980—. Served with U.S. Army, 1969-71. Decorated Bronze Star. Democrat. Roman Catholic. Office: Courier-Jour and Louisville Times Co 525 W Broadway Louisville KY 40202

KALLMAN, THEODORE WILLIAM, ins. co. exec.; b. Shirley, Mass., Feb. 28, 1952; s. James T. and Mildred E. K.; student Alma Coll., 1970, Spring Arbor Coll., 1972-74; B.A. with honors, Mich. State U., 1976; m. Claudia A. Sherwood, July 28, 1974; children—Benjamin B., James S. Salesman, Buxton Paper Co., East Lansing, Mich., 1976-77, John Hancock Mut. Life Ins. Co., Lansing, Mich., 1977-78; dist. sales mgr. and asso. G.A. James Civille and Assos., Okemos, Mich., 1978-79; agy. mgr. Farm Family Ins. Cos. Eastern Mass., Bridgewater, 1979—; v.p. Kallman, Inc. Youth retreat speaker and musician, 1970—; area capt. Capital Area United Way Dr., 1976; bd. dirs. Trinity Sch. of Cape Cod, 1981; Sunday Sch. Supt. Osterville Bapt. Ch., 1981. Mem. Nat. Assn. Life Underwriters, Gen. Agts. and Mgrs. Assn., Cape Cod Farm Bur., Cape Cod Christian Men's Fellowship Group. Republican. Baptist. Club: Brockton Kiwanis. Home: 22 Frost Ave West Yarmouth MA 02673 Office: Farm Family Ins Cos 9 N Main St West Bridgewater MA 02379

KALLMYER, CHARLES GREGORY, banking exec.; b. Cumberland, Md., May 26, 1950; s. Charles Franklin and Mary Teresa (Shertzer) K.; B.S. cum laude, Mount St. Mary's Coll., Md., 1972; J.D., U. Balt., 1977; m. Elizabeth Ann Hughes, Nov. 24, 1973. With Union Trust Co. Md., Balt., 1972—, asst. v.p., 1978—. Coach, Youth Football Team, Towson, Md., 1973—; lector St. Joseph's Ch., Cockeysville, Md. Democrat. Roman Catholic. Home: 31 Daria Ct Lutherville MD 21093 Office: Baltimore and St Paul Sts Baltimore MD 21203

KALLSTROM, DAVID H., real estate co. exec.; b. Akron, Ohio, Mar. 6, 1928; s. Gust R. and Norma P. (Peterson) K.; student Case Inst. Tech., 1945-47; B.S., Ohio State U., 1949; m. Jacqueline V. Kallstrom; children—James D., Neil G. Vice pres. Gust Kallstrom, Inc., builders and developers, Akron, 1949-60; pres. Kallstrom Realtors, Akron, Kallstrom Ins. Agy., Inc., Kallstrom's Comml. & Investment Real Estate, Inc., 1961—, Kallstrom Tele-Video Prodns., Inc.; guest lectr. Kent State U., 1963-68; cons. Cleve. Trust Co., 1970—. Chmn., Cuyahoga Falls YMCA Bldg. drive, 1960; mem. exec. com. Tri County Regional Planning Commn., 1963-65; mem. Com. of 100, Goals for Greater Akron Area, 1973; mem. adv. commn. to Summit County Govt., 1973; trustee Kallstrom Trust. Mem. Appraisal Inst., Soc. Real Estate Appraiser's (pres.), C. of C., Akron Area Bd. Realtors, Internat. Platform Assn. Home: 316 W Streetsboro Rd Hudson OH 44236 Office: 141 Broad Blvd Cuyahoga Falls OH 44221

KALM, MAX JOHN, pharm. co. exec.; b. Munich, Germany, Nov. 27, 1928; came to U.S., 1938, naturalized, 1944; s. Emil and Emmy (Berliner) K.; B.S., U. Calif., Berkeley, 1952, Ph.D., 1954; m. Lila Jane Dayhoff, Aug. 2, 1969; children—Denise Patricia, Deborah Ann. Research asso., research fellow U. Mich., 1954-55; research asso. G.D. Searle & Co., Skokie, Ill., 1955-65; with Cutter Labs., Inc., Berkeley, 1965—, dir. quality assurance, 1974-79, div. v.p. quality assurance, 1979—. Mem. Am. Chem. Soc., Am. Inst. Chemists, Am. Pharm. Assn., AAAS, Pharm. Mfrs. Assn., Sigma Xi. Republican. Club: Commonwealth of Calif. Contbr. articles to profl. jours.; patentee in field. Home: 120 Hacienda Dr Tiburon CA 94920 Office: Cutter Lab Inc 4th and Parker Sts Berkeley CA 94710

KALMAN, ANDREW, mfg. co. exec.; b. Hungary, Aug. 14, 1919; came to U.S., 1922, naturalized, 1938; s. Louis R. and Julia M. (Bognar) K.; m. Violet Margaret Kish, June 11, 1949; children—Andrew Joseph, Richard Louis, Laurie Ann. Exec. v.p., gen. mgr. Detroit Engring. & Machine Co., 1947-66; exec. v.p., dir. Indian Head, Inc., N.Y.C., 1966-75; dir. Acme Precision Products, 1960-80, Reef Energy Corp., 1980—; officer and dir. various privately held cos. Trustee, Alma (Mich.) Coll.; bd. dirs. Am.-Hungarian Found., New Brunswick, N.J. Home: 11 Shady Hollow Dr Dearborn MI 48124 Office: 2616 Detroit Bank & Trust Bldg Detroit MI 48226

KALSEM, MILLIE E., investment co. exec.; b. Huxley, Iowa, Dec. 12, 1896; d. Ole J. and Anna (Nelson) K.; B.S., Iowa State Coll., 1921; dietetic study Michael Reese Hosp., Chgo., 1922-23; postgrad. U. Ill. Med. Sch., 1935-36. Tchr. home econs. and physiology Monticello (Iowa) High Sch., 1921-22; hosp. dietitian Beaver Valley Gen. Hosp., New Brighton, Pa., 1923, Ia. Meth. Hosp., Des Moines, 1923-27, Ill. Tng. Sch. for Nurses and Cook County Sch. of Nursing, 1927-38; chief exec. dietitian Cook County Hosp., 1938-62; v.p., dir., registered rep. All Am. Mgmt. Corp., investment broker, Chgo. Bd. govs. Iowa State U. Found., 1977. Selected by Carrie Chapman Catt as one of 100 Women, Women's Centennial Congress, 1940; recipient Alumni merit award, Ia. State Coll., 1946, alumni medal, 1956. Mem. Am. (v.p. 1946-47), Ill. (organizer and 1st pres.), Chgo. dietetic assns., Women's Finance Forum Am. (research chmn. 1954-57, regional dir. 1960—), Art Inst. Chgo. (life), Order of Knoll, Omicron Nu, Phi Kappa Phi, Chi Omega. Club: Altrusa (pres. Chgo. 1959-61). Home: 111 Lynn Ave Ames IA 50010 Office: Suite 224 2250 Devon Ave Des Plaines IL 60018

KALT, SAMUEL RICHARD, broadcasting co. exec.; b. Detroit, Oct. 2, 1945; s. Charles Allen and Pearl (Sperber) K.; student Eastern Mich. U., 1963-69; m. Sandra Lynn Sulkin, Aug. 6, 1964; children—Stephanie, Mya Charlette. Acct. exec. Koch Broadcasting Corp., Ypsilanti, Mich., 1968-70, Kops Monahan Communications, New Haven, 1970-71; sta. mgr., sales mgr., account exec. Metro Conn. Media, 1971-76; v.p., gen. mgr. Gen. Communicorp., New Haven, 1976-78, sr. v.p., gen. mgr., 1978-80; pres. Conn. Radio Network, 1981—; lectr. Yale U., 1980, U. New Haven, 1976-79, Boston Coll., 1978-79. Bd. dirs. Combined Health Appeal, 1979-80; Media Council New Haven, 1979-80, Leukemia Soc. Am., 1979-80; mem. media council Greater New Haven United Way, 1975-80; pres. New Haven Roadrace, Inc. Found., 1978-80. Cert. radio mktg. cons. Mem. Greater New Haven C. of C. (dir.), S. Central Conn. Amateur Radio Assn., Nat. Radio Broadcasters Assn., ARRL. Jewish. Mem. disaster com. ARC, New Haven. Author: Playgirl, 1974. Office: 1294 Chapel St New Haven CT 06511

KALTENBACH, HUBERT L., newspaper pub. co. exec. Pres., Copley Press, Inc., La Jolla, Calif. Office: Copley Press Inc PO Box 1530 La Jolla CA 92038*

KALTINICK, PAUL R., retail exec.; b. N.Y.C., Dec. 1, 1932; s. Morris and Vera (Halpern) K.; B.B.A. in Accounting, Pace U., N.Y.C., 1954; m. Alice Levy, Dec. 26, 1954; children—Vera, Marjorie, Pamela. Accountant, mgmt. cons. Peat, Marwick, Mitchell & Co., N.Y.C., 1959-63; exec. v.p. Flowerized Presentations, N.Y.C., 1963-64; staff asst. to treas. J.C. Penney Co., Inc., N.Y.C., 1964-65, asst. treas., 1965-69, treas., 1969-74, v.p., 1974—, dir. financial mgmt., 1976-78, v.p., dir. tech. support ops., 1978—; dir. J.C. Penney Financial Corp. Served to 1st lt., USMC, 1954-56. Mem. Am. Inst. C.P.A.'s, N.Y. State Soc. C.P.A.'s, Financial Execs. Inst. Club: Treasurers. Home: 352 I U Willets Rd Roslyn Heights NY 11577 Office: 1301 Ave of the Americas New York NY 10019

KALTMAN, JACK, plastics co. exec.; b. N.Y.C., July 1, 1925; s. Harry and Rose K.; student CCNY, 1943-47; m. Selma Berger, June 16, 1946; children—Hannah, Ilya, Naomi, Alice. Sales mgr. Union Carbide Corp., 1948-60; gen. mgr. Equitable Bag Co., 1961-67; pres. Continental Extrusion Corp., Garden City, N.Y., 1967—. Bd. dirs. North Shore div. Am. Jewish Congress. Served to lt. USNR, 1945-52. Mem. Flexible Packaging Assn. Office: 2 Endo Blvd Garden City NY 11530

KALWEIT, GORDON GEORGE, ins. co. exec.; b. New Salem, N.D., Aug. 3, 1927; s. Max Kalweit and Gladys (Kleir) Kalweit Baughman; B.S. in Accounting, U. Denver, 1950; C.L.U., U. Colo., 1966; m. Shirley Carolyn Smith, June 29, 1967; children—Leslie Susan, Gary Edison, Christopher Sheldon, Bradford J., Whitney G., Terri Gayle, Bradley Jay. Mgr, accountant N.Y. Furniture House, Inc., Denver, 1950-57; asst. br. mgr. Occidental Life Ins. Co. Calif., Denver, 1957-61, gen. agt., Boulder, 1961—. Served with USN, 1945-46. C.P.A., Colo.; recipient Nat. Sales Achievement award, 1965-76, Nat. Quality award Occidental Life Ins. Co. Calif., 1961-76. Mem. Nat., Boulder assns. life underwriters, Boulder Estate Planning Council, Million Dollar Round Table (life, qualifying), Am. soc. C.L.U.'s, U.S. Volleyball Assn., YMCA, Am. Legion. Club: Elks. Home: 4020 Caddo Pkwy Boulder CO 80303 Office: 75 Manhattan Dr suite 105 Boulder CO 80303

KAMDAR, KIRIT SHANTILAL, conveyor co. exec.; b. Piplia, India, Jan. 30, 1942; came to U.S., 1965, naturalized, 1975; s. Shantilal R. and Jayaben C. Kamdar; B.S. in Mech. Engring., U. Bombay (India), 1963; M.S. in Indsl. Engring. and Mgmt., Okla. State U., 1966; m. Urmila Mehta, Nov. 18, 1972; 1 dau., Neha. Head indsl. engring. Cameron Iron Works, Houston, 1966-71; gen. mgr. Mallard Mfg. Corp., Sterling, Ill., 1971-74; pres. Kamflex Corp., Addison, Ill., 1974—. Mem. Am. Soc. Quality Control, Alpha Pi Mu. Patentee san. conveyor. Home: 220 King Arthur Ct Elgin IL 60120 Office: Kamflex Corp 904 S Westgate St Addison IL 60101

KAMEESE, JOSEPH HAROLD, fin. adv. co. exec.; b. Columbia, Mo., May 24, 1949; s. William Samuel and Marylin Ann (Miller) K.; A.B.A., Massasoit Community Coll., Brockton, Mass., 1974; postgrad. Stonehill Coll., Easton, Mass., 1981—; m. Lucinda Ann Gerrek, Sept. 2, 1973; children—Joseph Richard, Erin Maria. Transp. acct. United Brands Co., Boston, 1975-79; fin. analyst Air New Eng., Inc., Boston, 1979-80; comptroller Depari Corp., Dedham, Mass., 1980; pres. KBC Enterprise, West Bridgewater, Mass., 1980—; cons. in field. Served with U.S. Navy, 1968-72. Mem. Am. Ind. Cons. (bd. govs. 1980-82), Jaycees. Home: 38 Brewster Rd West Bridgewater MA 02379 Office: PO Box 61 West Bridgewater MA 02379

KAMERSCHEN, ROBERT JEROME, consumer industry exec.; b. Laurium, Mich., Feb. 16, 1936; s. Robert Raymond and Elsie (Barsanti) K.; B.S., Miami U., Oxford, Ohio, 1957, M.B.A., 1958; m. Judith A. Campbell, July 26, 1958; children—Kathryn, Carol, Jean. With Nat. Cash Register, 1958-59, Foote, Cone & Belding, Chgo., 1959-60; dir. consumer mktg. Scott Paper Co., Phila., 1960-71; v.p. mktg. Revlon Inc., N.Y.C., 1971-73; sr. v.p. mktg. ops. Dunkin' Donuts Inc., Randolph, Mass., 1973-76; pres. Chanel Inc., N.Y.C., 1976-78, Christian Dior Perfumes Inc., N.Y.C., 1976-78; sr. v.p., sector exec., office of chmn. Norton Simon, Inc., N.Y.C., 1979—; pres., chief exec. officer Max Factor & Co., Hollywood, Calif., 1979—; Disting. practitioner/lectr. Coll. Bus. Adminstrn., U. Ga., 1978—; guest lectr. univs. and trade assns. Mem. bus. adv. council Miam U., 1980—. Mem. Order of Artus, Beta Gamma Sigma, Sigma Alpha Epsilon, Delta Sigma Pi. Clubs: N.Y. Athletic, Metropolitan, Canadian of N.Y. Home: 204 Parade Hill Rd New Canaan CT 06840 Office: Norton Simon Inc 277 Park Ave New York NY 10017 also Max Factor & Co 1655 N McCadden Pl Hollywood CA 90028

KAMIN, ARTHUR ZAVEL, publishing exec.; b. South River, N.J., Nov. 25, 1930; s. Isadore and Elsie (Kaminsky) K.; B.A., Rutgers U., 1954; m. Virginia Palew, Jan. 30, 1955; children—Blair, Brooke. Reporter, The Daily Register, Red Bank, N.J., 1956-61, copy editor, 1961-62, asso. editor, 1962-65, editor, 1965—, pres., 1971—; mem. adv. bd. First Nat. Bank. Mem. Monmouth County Transp. Coordinating Com.; mem. Monmouth County Criminal Justice Coordinating Council. Chmn. publs. com. Rutgers Alumni Mag.; former pres. N.J. AP; chmn. Rutgers Fund Council, mem. exec. com. Rutgers U. Found. Bd. Overseers; mem. N.J. Energy Crisis Study Commn.; mem. pres.'s advisory council Brookdale Coll., Monmouth Coll. Bd. dirs. Monmouth Arts Found., Monmouth council Boy Scouts Am., Red Bank YMCA. Fair Haven Community Appeal, Monmouth County Heart Assn., NCCJ, Multiple Sclerosis Soc.; bd. dirs. v.p. Monmouth County Mental Health Assn.; trustee Rutgers U.; past pres. Monmouth County Community Services Council; active Monmouth County United Fund. Served to lt. AUS, 1954-56. Mem. Rutgers Alumni Assn., Am. Soc. Newspaper Editors, Am. Newspaper Publishers Assn., N.J. Press Assn. (news-editorial com.). Jewish (trustee congregation). Club: Monmouth County Rutgers (past pres.). Home: 15 Grange Walk Fair Haven NJ 07701 Office: 1 Register Plaza Shrewsbury NJ 07701

KAMIN, ROBERT YALE, mgmt. cons. exec.; b. Lima, Ohio, Oct. 28, 1928; s. Samuel and Elizabeth (Bloom) K.; student Purdue U., 1946-49; B.S. in Econs., U. Pa., 1951; m. Arlene Lonker, May 25, 1951; children—Harriet Ann, Rena Esther, Edward Barry, Pamela Joy. With Neon Products, Inc., Lima, 1951-69, time and motion study engr., 1951-53, prodn. mgr., 1953-55, v.p. mfg., 1955-62, sec.-treas., 1962—; pres. B-K Office Equipment, Inc., 1962—; pres. Robert Y. Kamin Assos.; v.p. Corp. Finance Assos., Phila., 1972-73; exec. v.p. Kardon Industries Inc., Phila., 1973-79, pres., chief operating officer, 1979—. Pres. Jr. Achievement, Lima, 1958-59. Mem. Am. Soc. for Personnel Adminstrn., Assn. Commerce. Mason. Author: Supervisory Training in Small Industry, 1962; Modern Shop Management, 1969. Home: 648 Broad Acres Rd Narberth PA 19072 Office: 1201 Chestnut St Philadelphia PA 19103

KAMIN, ROGER DALE, acct., savs. and loan exec.; b. Milw., Jan. 19, 1948; s. Edwin F. and Virginia (Appenzeller) K.; B.B.A. in Acctg. (Wis. Inst. C.P.A.'s scholar), U. Wis., 1969; m. Ruth Elaine Conradt, May 10, 1969; children—Jeffrey, Gregory, Douglas. Supervising sr. tax specialist Peat, Marwick, Mitchell & Co., Milw., 1969-73; self-employed acct., Milw., 1975—; v.p. Security Savs. & Loan Assn., Milw., 1975—; mem. nat. steering com. Internal Audit div. Fin. Mgrs., 1978—. Bd. regents Wis. Luth. Coll.; sec. CSC, City of Greenfield (Wis.), 1973-76, mem. bldg. needs com., 1972; treas., acct. Woodlawn Luth. Ch., 1973—; treas. Concerned Officers and Employees Polit. Action Com., 1976—. Recipient commendation City of Greenfield, 1976, Wis. Luth. Coll. Bd. Regents, 1978. C.P.A., Wis. Mem. Am. Inst. C.P.A.'s, Wis. Inst. C.P.A.'s, Fin. Mgrs. Soc. for Savs. Instns., Inst. Fin. Edn., Savs. League Wis. (audit and examination com.). Republican. Office: 184 W Wisconsin Ave Milwaukee WI 53203

KAMINSKI, WILLIAM ARTHUR, hair stylist; b. Brainerd, Minn., May 30, 1944; s. Steve Stanley and Mildred K.; student St. Paul Barber Coll., 1965, Minn. Sch. Real Estate, 1975, Sassoon Sch. Hair Styling, 1977; m. Susan Marie Ellstrom, June 1, 1966; children—Stacey, Steve. Hair stylist, barber The Modern Barbershop, Mpls., 1967; hair stylist The Barbers, Mpls., 1968, owner, stylist, Rochester, Minn., 1972, Madison, Wis., 1977—; pres. Split Hair Ltd., Square Hair Ltd., Wet Hair Ltd. Recipient 28 trophies, awards for hairstyling, Midwest, S.D., Iowa, Wis. Mem. Internat. Hairstyling Assn., Assn. Barbers and Beauticians Am., Minn. Barbers Union (chmn. state conv.), C. of C., Nat. Hairdressers, Cosmetologist Assn. Roman Catholic. Clubs: Sertoma, Jaycees, Toastmasters, Elks. Home: 3805 Valley Ridge Rd Middleton WI 53562 Office: 324 Westgate Mall Madison WI 53711

KAMM, CARL JACOB, greenhouse co. exec.; b. Rocky River, Ohio, Dec. 18, 1914; s. Jacob and Minnie (Christensen) K.; A.B., Baldwin Wallace Coll., 1937; m. Jean Roth, Sept. 14, 1944; children—Carl II, Lauren, Karen. Pres., Rocky River Greenhouse Co., 1948-64; sec-treas. Am. Growers, Inc., Huron, Ohio, 1950—; treas. Lorain Ave. Greenhouse Co., Cleve. 1950-72; dir. Cleve. Quarries Co., 1956-61, treas., 1960-61; dir. Silica Chems., Inc., Amherst, Ohio, 1956-61; Cleve. Stone Co., 1958-61. Trustee Berlin-Milan Library Bd. Mem. Ohio Grange, Alpha Sigma Phi. Mem. Soc. of Friends. Mason (Shriner). Club: University of Cleveland. Home: Route 1 Huron OH 44839 Office: Route 1 Huron OH 44839

KAMM, JACOB OSWALD, economist; b. Cleve., Nov. 29, 1918; s. Jacob and Minnie K. (Christensen) K.; A.B. summa cum laude, Baldwin-Wallace Coll., 1940; LL.D., 1963; LL.D., Erskine Coll., 1971; A.M., Brown U., 1942; Ph.D., Ohio State U., 1948; m. Judith Steinbrenner, Apr. 28, 1966; children—Jacob Oswald Kamm II, Christian Philip. Asst. in econs. Brown U., 1942; instr. Ohio State U., 1945, Baldwin-Wallace Coll., 1945-46, asst. prof., 1947-48, asso. prof., 1948, prof., dir. Sch. Commerce, 1948-53, vis. distinguished prof., 1977; exec. v.p. Cleve. Quarries Co., 1953-55, pres., dir., 1955-67, chmn., chief exec. officer, dir., 1967—; dir., exec. com. United Screw & Bolt Corp.; exec. v.p., treas., dir., then pres. Am. Shipbldg. Co., 1967-69, pres., 1973-74; dir. Bibb Co., MTD Products Inc., Electric Furnace Co., Fairmont Foods Co.; vice chmn., dir. Cardinal Fed. Savs. & Loan Assn. Cleve., Nordson Corp., Oatey Co. Columnist, 1953—. Trustee, mem. exec. com., chmn. investment com. Baldwin-Wallace Coll., 1953-78, hon. trustee, 1978—; mem. com. grad. edn. and research Brown U.; bd. regents State of Ohio; mem. bd. counselors Erskine Coll.; life fellow Cleve. Zool. Soc., St. Lukes Hosp. Assn.; mem. pres.'s club Ohio State U. Recipient Wisdom award Honor, 1970; Pro Mundi Beneficio medal Acad. Humanities, Sao Paulo, Brazil; Jacob O. Kamm Hall at Baldwin Wallace Coll. named in his honor. Fellow World-Wide Acad. Scholars (life); mem. Am. Econ. Assn., Am. Fin. Assn., Ohio Mfrs. Assn. (chmn., trustee), Royal Econ. Soc., AAUP, Indsl. Assn. North Central Ohio (pres. 1960), Assn. Ohio Comdrs., Ohio Soc. of N.Y., Nat. Alumni Assn. Baldwin-Wallace Coll. (pres. 1961-63), John Baldwin Soc., Newcomen Soc. N.Am., Phi Beta Kappa, Beta Gamma Sigma, Delta Phi Alpha, Delta Mu Delta, Phi Alpha Kappa. Methodist. Clubs: Brown Univ. (N.Y.C.); Clifton (Lakewood, Ohio); Union (Cleve.); Duquesne (Pitts.); Masons (33 deg.), Shriners, Scottish Rite Valley of Cleve. (treas., trustee). Author: Economics of Investments, 1951; Making Profits in the Stock Market, 1952, rev., 1959, 61, 66; Investor's Handbook, 1954; contbg. editor Webster's New World Dictionary; also articles profl. publs. Home: Rt 1 Huron OH 44839 Office: PO Box 261 Amherst OH 44001

KAMME, WALTER RICHARD, computer programmer, analyst; b. N.Y.C., Nov. 29, 1955; s. Walter Francis and Mary Elizabeth (Crawford) K.; student Queens Coll., 1973-75, Honeywell Edn. Center, 1975; diploma Tandem Computer Edn. Center, 1980; m. AnneMarie Reiprecht, Mar. 19, 1977; 1 dau., Michelle Marie. Computer programming mgr., ops. supr. Dubovsky & Sons, Inc., Glendale, N.Y., 1974—. Republican. Roman Catholic. Home: 6112 Palmetto St Ridgewood NY 11385 Office: 66-35 Otto Rd Glendale NY 11385

KAMON, ROBERT BURTON, petroleum engr.; b. Casper, Wyo., Sept. 6, 1927; s. Rudolph and Isabel (Burton) K.; B.S., U. Tex. at Austin; m. Effie Laverne Hart, Dec. 25, 1957; children—Ken, Kaye. Ind. petroleum engr., geologist specializing in fgn. oil and gas leasing; officer, dir. Golden Triangle Royalty & Oil, Inc., Black Giant Oil Co., Internat. Drilling Corp., Australian Grazing & Pastoral Co. Pty. Ltd., Internat. Oil Lease Service, Internat. Australian Energy Corp.; v.p. Internat. Royalty & Oil Co. Registered profl. engr., Tex. Mem. Am. Inst. M.E., Australian Geol. Soc. Presbyterian (elder, life mem.). Home: 1304 Ave L Cisco TX 76437 Office: PO Box 1629 Cisco TX 76437

KAMP, THEO, advt. corp. exec.; b. Amsterdam, Netherlands, Mar. 18, 1936; s. Theo and Margarete (Klaussner) K.; came to U.S., 1948; student Fordham U., Columbia U., 1954-58; m. Adele Edelman, Dec. 17, 1967; children—Ariane Rose, Teddy Alex. Formerly account supr. Grant Advt. Internat.; pres. KPH & B, Inc., White Plains, N.Y., 1968; dir. subs. Westchester Design Group; vis. prof. mktg. Coll. New Rochelle; frequent speaker before bus. and civic groups. Pres. Westchester-Hudson Valley chpt. Leukemia Soc. Am. Served with

AUS, 1959-61. Mem. Advt. Club Westchester (pres.), Dirs. Guild Am., Writers Guild Am., Westchester Advt. Assn. Clubs: Sports Car of Am. (N.Y.C.). Contbr. articles to bus. jours. Office: KPH & B Inc 2 Westchester Plaza Cross Westchester Exec Park Elmsford NY 10523

KAMPF, HENNING ERNST, food co. exec.; b. Athens, Greece, July 6, 1933; s. Erich Carl and Ilse (Hercksen) K.; student West London Coll. Commerce, 1959; m. Madeleine Lina Albiez, Mar. 26, 1959; children—Markus H.H., Melanie M. Asst. to gen. mgr. Elektroholmen A.B., Stockholm, Sweden, 1959; sales mgr. No. Europe, Gordon Johnson-Stephens, Ltd., Gloucester, Eng., 1959-63; mng. dir. McCormick GmbH, Frankfurt, Germany, 1963—; dep. chmn. supervisory bd. Black & Decker GmbH., 1974—. Hon. comml. judge State Ct. Frankfurt, 1973. Recipient Merit award West London Coll. Commerce, 1959. Mem. Mktg. Execs. Club Germany, Internat. Mgmt. Assn., Am. C. of C. Germany, Frankfurt C. of C. (wholesale com.), German Spice Industry Assn. (chmn. packer div.). Club: Union Internat. (Frankfurt). Home: 2 Friedrich-Bender-Str 624 Koenigstein West Germany Office: 10-12 Frankfurter Allee 6236 Eschborn Ts West Germany

KAMPF, PAUL BERNARD, life ins. exec.; b. N.Y.C., Aug. 19, 1920; s. Murray S. and Lillian G. Kampf; B.S., Davis and Elkins (W.Va.) Coll., 1942; M.S., Ind. U., 1948; postgrad. U. Mich.; m. Nan H. Haight, Aug. 26, 1951; children—Pamela Diane, Martha Nan, Paula Jo, Ward A. Football coach Kans. State U., Bradley U., Peoria, Ill., U. N.D., also Winnipeg (Can.) Blue Bombers profl. team, 1950-51; engaged in life ins. bus., 1951—; propr. Kampf Agy., Oklahoma City, 1961—, also pres. Bd. dirs. Oklahoma City Libraries, 1965; vestryman All Souls Episcopal Ch., Oklahoma City, 1975; pres. Brotherhood St. Andrews, 1977. Served with USMCR, 1942-45; PTO Charter mem. Soc. Underwriting Brokers Am. (past pres.), Risk Appraisal Forum; mem. Nat. Assn. Life Underwriters, Oklahoma City Life Underwriters Assn. (past dir.), Gen. Agts. and Mgrs. Club Oklahoma City. Republican. Clubs: Quail Creek Golf and Country, Petroleum, Beacon (Oklahoma City). Author articles. Editor-pub. newsletter The Vital Margin, 1973—; contbr. articles to ins. jours. Address: Kampf Agy 601 Cravens Bldg Oklahoma City OK 73102

KAMY, EUGENE MITCHELL, mgmt. cons.; b. Chgo., May 9, 1927; s. Matthew and Marie (Polanski) K.; B.S., U. Ill., 1951; M.S., Loyola U., Chgo., 1957; postgrad. Ill. Inst. Tech., 1954-55, DePaul U., 1956-57; m. Margaret Elizabeth Ocsai, May 20, 1976; children—Deborah Ann, Elizabeth. Vice pres. Chgo. Hardware Foundry, North Chicago, Ill., 1960-67; pres. Eugene M. Kamy & Assos., Inc., McHenry, Ill., 1962—; founder, pres. Tolerance Mfg. Co., Waukegan, Ill., 1966-67, Profl. Growth Counselors Inc., McHenry, 1973—. Lectr. Sch. Bus. Northwestern U., Evanston, Ill., 1958-70; professorial lectr. Walter Heller Sch. Bus. Roosevelt U., Chgo., 1970—. Rep., Community Fund Lake County, 1965-66. Registered profl. engr., Calif., Can.; certified mfg. engr., U.S.A., Can. Mem. Am. Mktg. Assn., Am. Inst. Indsl. Engrs., Am. Prodn. and Inventory Control Soc., Nat., Ill. socs. profl. engrs., Soc. Mfg. Engrs., Indsl. Mgmt. Soc., Ill. Alumni Assn. (life), Waukegan C. of C., Delta Sigma Pi, Phi Chi Theta, Psi Chi. Club: Chicago Farmers. Home: 5524 Brittany Dr McHenry IL 60050 Office: 4723 W Elm St McHenry IL 60050

KAMZAN, JACK, motivational mktg. and travel co. exec.; b. N.Y.C., Mar. 18, 1924; s. Nathan and Rose K.; B.S., N.Y. U., 1947; m. Lucille Nachman, June 23, 1945; children—Stephen L., Marni J. Accountant, Klein, Hinds and Finke, N.Y.C., 1946-47; sales mgr. Leslie Home Sales, 1947-57; exec. v.p. Leslie Enterprises, Inc., Long Island City, N.Y., 1957-70, pres., chief exec. officer, 1970—; pres. Leslie Travel Co., 1973—. Served with USNR, 1942-45. Recipient Humanitarian award United Jewish Appeal. Mem. Premium Advt. Assn. Am., L.I. Advt. Club. Democrat. Jewish. Home: 49-18 Horatio Pkwy Bayside NY 11364 also 1107 Glengarry Ln Walnut Creek CA 94596 Office: 46-14 B Q E West Long Island City NY 11103 also 55 New Montgomery St San Francisco CA

KANAI, MELVYN TADAO, elec. contracting co. exec.; b. Honolulu, June 18, 1944; s. Takao and Jane Mitsue (Kotsubo) K.; B.E.E., Northrop U., 1970; m. Helen Hisako Yamaguchi, July 26, 1969; children—Laury, Jeffrey. Asst. elec. engr. H.K. Porter Co., Belmont, Calif., 1968-69; estimater Hygrade Electric Co., Honolulu, 1971-74, v.p., 1974-79, pres., 1979—, also dir.; cons. in field. Served with U.S. Army, 1962-65. Mem. IEEE, Gen. Contractors Assn. (legis. com. 1979—), Pacific Elec. Contractors Assn. (dir. 1976—, pres. 1979—). Democrat. Episcopalian. Home: 1248 Kina St Kailua HI 96734 Office: 2718 S King St Honolulu HI 96826

KANARKOWSKI, EDWARD JOSEPH, advt./public relations exec.; b. Jersey City, N.J., May 5, 1947; s. Joseph Anthony and Lillian Dorothy (Pietrowicz) K.; B.A., St. Peter Coll., 1969; m. Carol Ann Miller, Sept. 14, 1969; children—Edward, Kelly, Paul, Karen. Corporate communications cons., N.J., 1973-75; staff writer Daily and Sunday Register, Shrewsbury, N.J., 1975-77; with ADP, Clifton, N.J., 1977—, mgr. corp. mktg. services, 1978—. Served with U.S. Army, 1969-73, to capt., N.J. Army N.G., 1979—. Decorated Army Commendation medal. Mem. Internat. Assn. Bus. Communicators, Assn. U.S. Army, U.S. Army N.G. Assn., 3d U.S. Inf. Div. Assn. Roman Catholic. Club: Ft. Monmouth Officers Golf and Tennis. Home: 132 Yellowbank Rd Toms River NJ 08753 Office: 205 Main Ave Clifton NJ 07015

KANDEL, HERBERT, profl. placement exec.; b. Rockaway Beach, N.Y.; s. Louis and Dora Kandel; B.B.A., Am. Internat. Coll., 1959; M.A. in Edn., Westfield State Coll., 1965; m. Anita Louise Masingill, Dec. 21, 1975; children—William, Victoria, Lisa. Mgr., Winfield Hat Co., Holyoke, Mass., 1950-65; gen. mgr. Blessings Corp., N.Y.C., 1965-74; pres. Exec. Enterprises, Inc., New Orleans, 1974—. Mem. Nat. Assn. Personnel Cons., Nat. Assn. Temporary Services, Intercity Personnel Assos., La. Assn. Personnel Cons. (chmn. ethics com.; chmn. New Orleans chpt.), La. Cert. Personnel Cons. Soc. (dir.). Clubs: Sertoma, Masons. Home: 149 Pinewood Dr Slidell LA 70458 Office: Exec Enterprises Inc One Shell Sq Suite 1111 New Orleans LA 70139

KANDELL, KARL ALFRED, real estate developer; b. Jackson, Mich., May 2, 1936; s. Alfred F. and Helen E. (Nichol) K.; student Mich. State U.; m. Anne E. Ekern, Aug. 8, 1964; children—Tami, Julie, Tracy, Karl; stepchildren—Steven, William, Richard. Engr., A. C. Spark div. Gen. Motors Corp., Milw., 1957-60, Sparton Electronics Corp., Jackson, Mich., 1961-62, RCA, Cambridge, Ohio, 1962-64, Daniels & Assos., Denver; tech. rep. Teleprompter Corp., N.Y.C., 1966-67; gen. contractor, real estate developer Universal Profile, Inc., Atlanta, 1967—, also pres., dir.; dir. Martin County Little Club, Inc. Served in USMC, 1954-57. Recipient certificate of Excellence, Nat. Assn. Architects. Mem. Nat. Assn. Real Estate Brokers, Nat. Assn. Home Builders. Republican. Lutheran. Clubs: Frenchmen's Creek (N. Palm Beach); Lake Toxaway (N.C.); Atlanta Country. Home: 2535 Johnson Ferry Rd Marietta GA 30062 Office: 380 Interstate N Atlanta GA 30339*

KANE, DAVID SHERIDAN, ins. co. exec.; b. Deadwood, S.D., July 12, 1940; s. Arthur Sheridan and Grace Marie K.; Ph.B., U. N.D., 1964. Agt., Fidelity Union Life Ins. Co., Grand Forks, N.D., 1963-65, gen. agt., 1965; pres., founder D.S. Kane & Assos., Inc., Fargo, N.D., 1968—; pres. Coll. Agy. Mgmt., Inc., Fargo, 1971-80; pres., founder, dir. Midwest Internat. Life Ins. Co., Fargo, 1976—; nat. sales dir. ITT Life Ins. Co., 1981—; dir. Target Energies. Mem. Nat. Assn. Life Underwriters, Nat. Assn. Employee Stock Ownership Trust Planners (dir. 1976-78), Fargo-Moorhead Life Underwriters Assn. (pres.), Am. Soc. C.L.U. Lutheran. Office: D S Kane & Associates Inc PO Box 5676 University Station Fargo ND 58105

KANE, DONNE FRANK, economist, realtor, bus. cons.; b. Cleve., Mar. 19, 1930; s. Bernard Martin and Selma Jean (Greenbaum) K.; B.S. in Bus. Adminstrn., Ohio State U., 1951; M.A. in Managerial Econs., Case Western Res. U., 1977; m. Judith Evelyn Lesnick, Sept. 19, 1954; children—David, Todd, Brian, Jon. Vice pres. sales Kane Co., Cleve., 1955-59; founder, pres. Kane Supply Co., Cleve., 1960-70; founder, parther Kane-Petrovic & Assos., Cleve., 1971-78; mem. faculty Cuyahoga Community Coll., Cleve., 1974-78; comml. realtor Land & Homes Real Estate Investment Co., Orlando, Fla., 1978—; pvt., corporate bus., econ. cons., to various firms, 1971—. Trustee Orange Community Athletic Assn., 1970-78; bd. dirs. Jane Adams Vocat. Sch., 1968-70; adv. bd. Cuyahoga Community Coll., 1974-78, Winter Park Art Festival, 1979—; founder, trustee Orange Sch. Dist. Athletic Assn., 1966-78; active United Appeal, others. Served as officer USMC, 1951-54; Korea. Mem. Nat. Assn. Bus. Economists, Nat. Assn. Realtors, Orlando-Winter Park Bd. Realtors, Nat. Assn. Life Underwriters. Club: Rotary. Contbr. articles to profl. jours. Home: 1300 Venetian Way Winter Park FL 32789 Office: 1408 Gay Dr Winter Park FL 32789

KANE, EDWARD RYNEX, chem. co. exec.; b. Schenectady, N.Y., Sept. 13, 1918; s. Edward Marion and Elva (Rynex) K.; B.S. in Chemistry, Union Coll., 1940; Ph.D., in Phys. Chemistry, Mass. Inst. Tech., 1943; m. Doris Norma Peterson, Apr. 3, 1948; children—Christine, Susan. With E.I. duPont de Nemours & Co., Inc., Wilmington, Del., 1943—, gen. mgr. indsl. and biochem. dept., 1967-69, v.p., mem. exec. com., 1969-73, pres., chief operating officer, vice chmn. exec. com., 1973-79, dir., 1969—; dir. J.P. Morgan & Co. Inc., Morgan Guaranty Trust Co., Mead Corp.; gen. dir. Tex. Instruments, Inc. Past chmn. Nat. Adv. Council on Minorities in Engring. Past trustee Com. for Econ. Devel.; past dir. Council Financial Aid to Edn.; trustee Union Coll., 1972-77; mem. corp. M.I.T. Mem. Am. Chem. Soc., Soc. Chem. Industry (chmn. Am. sect. 1974, pres. soc. 1979-80), Societe de Chimie Industrielle (Internat. Palladium medal Am. sect.), Nat. Acad. Engring., Am. Inst. Chem. Engrs., Chemists Mfg. Assn. (chmn. 1975), Sigma Xi. Clubs: Wilmington Country (Wilmington); Greenville (Del.) Country; Links (N.Y.C.). Home: Greenville DE 19807 Office: duPont Bldg Wilmington DE 19898

KANE, GARY PAUL, lawyer; b. San Francisco, Feb. 4, 1943; s. Philip John and Elynor Ruth Kane; A.B., U. Calif., Berkeley, 1963, J.D., 1966. Admitted to Calif. bar, 1966, D.C. bar, 1974; tax counsel Calif. Franchise Tax Bd., 1966-70; atty. Sacramento Redevel. Agy., 1970-72; dir. state housing fin. agy. programs HUD, Washington, 1972-75; v.p., gen. counsel Calif. Housing Fin. Agy., Sacramento, 1975-76; individual practice law, Sacramento, 1976-78; asso. legis. counsel Nat. Assn. Home Builders, Washington, 1978-81; exec. dir. N.C. Housing Fin. Agy., Raleigh, 1981—; instr. housing and community devel. Golden Gate U., Sacramento, 1972-73; cons. hist. preservation law. Cert. real estate broker, Calif. Mem. Am. Bar Assn., Calif. Bar Assn., D.C. Bar Assn. Contbr. articles to profl. publs. Office: 512 N Salisbury St Raleigh NC 27611

KANE, GEORGE MITCHELL, agr. credit co. exec.; b. Mundelien, Ill., May 14, 1922; s. Earl H. and Luella (Mitchell) K.; B.S., U. Ill., 1939; m. Florence Kmet, Oct. 10, 1943; children—Nancy Kane Hall, George Mitchell, Lawrence, Kathryn. Farmer, McHenry County, Ill., 1945-56; gen. mgr. NE Ill. Prodn. Credit Assn., Woodstock, 1956-67; v.p. AgriStor Credit Corp., Milw., 1967—; dir. Gehl Co., West Bend, Wis. Chmn., McHenry County Planning Commn., 1966-67; mem. Mequon (Wis.) Planning Commn., 1969-74, 79-80; pres. Milw. Farmers Inc., 1976-77. Methodist. Editor: Farm Fin. Rev., 1975—. Home: 12340 N Granville Rd Mequon WI 53092 Office: PO Box 2000 Elm Grove WI 53122

KANE, JAY BRASSLER, banker; b. Bklyn., June 4, 1931; s. Arthur Ferris and Margaret (Brassler) K.; grad. Poly. Prep. Sch., 1949; A.B., Columbia, 1953, postgrad. Sch. Bus., 1954; M.B.A., N.Y. U., 1961; m. Marian Albertson, Oct. 15, 1960; children—Lisa Ferris, James Brassler. With Met. Life Ins. Co., N.Y.C., 1954-55; with Bankers Trust Co., N.Y.C., 1955—, asst. v.p., 1965-68, v.p., 1968—, also mgr. corporate pension funds. Speaker Am. Bankers Assn. Mem. Am. Pension Conf., N.Y. Soc. Security Analysts, Financial Analysts Fedn. Clubs: Riverside (Conn.) Yacht. Contbr. articles to profl. jours. Home: Hilton Heath Cos Cob CT 06807 Office: 280 Park Ave New York NY 10017

KANE, RALPH EDGAR, savings and loan exec.; b. Akron, Ohio, July 16, 1921; s. Albert Anton and Ida Martha (Golz) K.; student U. Akron, 1940-42, 46-47, S.D. State Coll., 1943-44; achievement certificate Am. Savings & Loan Inst., 1953; m. Alice Mabel Zantow, July 2, 1945; children—Paul Anton, Elisabeth Ann. With B.F. Goodrich Co., Akron, 1940-42, 46; with First Fed. Savs. and Loan Assn., Wooster, Ohio, 1947—, treas., 1950-79, v.p. fin., 1979—, advt. mgr., 1960—. Chmn., Citizens Com. for Study Local Taxation, Wooster, 1965, Citizens Com. Reapportionment of Wooster, 1968, 71; chmn. bldg. com. Wooster Municipal Bldg., 1960-61; unit treas. Am. Cancer Soc., 1948-52. Councilman-at-large, Wooster, 1958-61. Trustee, Wooster Cemetery Assn., 1960-73. Served with AUS, 1943-46. Named man of the year 20-30 Club Wooster, 1961; recipient award Clipper Graphic Arts, 1973, 74. Mem. Fin. Mgrs. Soc. for Savs. Instns. (br. operations com. 1963-65), Savs. Instns. Mktg. Soc. (mktg. research com. 1968-71), Ohio Savs. and Loan League, Wayne County Builders Exchange, Wooster C. of C., Wayne County Hist. Soc. (treas. 1965-70), Internat. Platform Assn. Republican. Lutheran (endowment treas. 1948—), Kiwanian (pres. 1969). Clubs: 20-30 (pres. 1950), Century (pres. 1971-72) (Wooster). Author: 25 Years of Christmas Poems, 1965; Your Meter is Running (poems), 1980; (plays) A Modern Version of the Christmas Story, 1967, T.H.E.A.T.R.E., 1975, T.H.E.R.A.P.Y., 1980. Home: 315 Oakley Rd Wooster OH 44691 Office: PO Box 385 135 E Liberty St Wooster OH 44691

KANE, RICHARD CHARLES, banker; b. N.Y.C., Feb. 8, 1940; s. Nathaniel S. and Estelle R. (Grollman) K.; B.Ch.E., N.Y. U., 1960; M.S., U. Mass., 1967; M.B.A., Harvard U., 1968; m. Pearl Rock, June 18, 1961; children—Bradley Jay, Laura Beth, Leslie Jill, Lisa Dale. With Monsanto Chem. Corp., Springfield, Mass., Trenton, Mich., 1960-66, Inmont Corp., N.Y.C., 1968-72; with Citicorp N.Y.C., 1972—, pres. Citicorp Credit Services, Inc., also dir. Mem. Am. Bankers Assn. (mem. exec. com. bank card div.). Clubs: Harvard, Harvard Bus. Sch. (N.Y.C.). Office: 575 Lexington Ave New York NY 10043*

KANE, SAM, meat co. exec.; b. Spisske Podhradie, Czechoslovakia, June 23, 1919; s. Leopold and Bertha (Narcisenfeld) Kannengiesser; grad. Rabbinical Coll. Galanta, 1939; m. Aranka Feldbrand, Jan. 15, 1946; children—Jerry, Harold Ira, Esther Barbara. Came to U.S., 1948, naturalized, 1953. Pres., Sam Kane Wholesale Meat, Inc., Corpus Christi, Tex., 1956—, Sam Kane Meat, Inc., Corpus Christi, 1956—, Sam Kane Packing Co., Corpus Christi, 1962—, Kane Enterprises, Inc., Corpus Christi, 1956—; pres., chmn. bd. Sam Kane Beef Processors, Inc., 1975—; dir. Corpus Christi Bank and Trust. Pres., Jewish Welfare Appeal, 1962—; pres. Combined Jewish Appeal, 1968, chmn. bd., 1962-64; mem. nat. cabinet United Jewish Appeal. Recipient award chmn. bd. edn. B'nai Israel Synagogue, 1965; Israel Service award, 1966; Koach award State of Israel, 1976; named Outstanding Jewish Citizen of Corpus Christi, 1969. Jewish (pres. synagogue 1964-65). Mem. B'nai B'rith. Home: 27 Hewit Dr Corpus Christi TX 78404 Office: 9001 Leopard St Corpus Christi TX 78410

KANIA, ALAN JAMES, pub. relations and comml. photography exec.; b. Lawrence, Mass., Nov. 30, 1949; s. Frank J. and Genievieve (Martin) K.; B.S., Emerson Coll., 1971; student Boston U., 1967-69. Dir. membership and pub. relations Grand Junction (Colo.) C. of C., 1976; sports info. dir., athletic dept. Mesa Coll., 1976-77; author, creator Clean Break 19, Grand Junction, 1976—; day care coordinator Grand Junction Day Care Task Force, 1978—; prin. The Concept Group (formerly Alan Kania & Assos.) Denver, 1976—; news cameraman KOA-TV, KBTV, Denver, 1976—. Asst. coordinator Colo. Nat. Monument Bicentennial Activities, 1976; pub. relations coordinator Colo. Assn. Pub. Employees, 1978-79; pub. relations advisor Hilltop House Speech and Hearing Clinic, Grand Junction, 1977-78; pub. relations advisor Western Colo. Hist. Mus. and Inst., Grand Junction, 1976-78. Mem. Colo. Assn. Broadcast Communicators, Mesa County Hist. Soc. (publicity and publs. chmn. 1975-78). Christian Scientist. Club: Sertoma. Pub., editor Copperlite Mag., 1975; wild horse researcher, investigator, lectr. Internat. Soc. Protection Mustangs and Burros, 1971—. Office: Concept Group 7830 S Platte Canyon Rd Littleton CO 80123

KANIA, ARTHUR JOHN, lawyer; b. Moosic, Pa., Feb. 11, 1932; s. Stanley J. and Constance (Jerry) K.; B.S., U. Scranton, 1953; LL.B., Villanova U., 1956; m. Angela Volpe, Apr. 24, 1954; children—Arthur, Sandra, Kenneth, Karen, James, Linda, Stephen. Admitted to Pa. bar, 1956; accountant Peat, Warwick, Mitchell & Co., Phila., 1954-55; asso. Davis, Marshall & Crumlish, Phila., 1956-58, partner, 1958-61; sr. partner Kania & Garbarino and predecessor firm, Phila., 1961—; gen. partner Tunbridge Leasing Co.; exec. v.p., dir. Greater Bay Hotel Corp. and affiliated cos.; ltd. partner Walters Assos., Summit Leasing Co., Crest Leasing Co.; chmn., dir. Center City Assos., Inc.; dir. Piasecki Aircraft Corp., Jordan Chem. Co., Consol. Mortgage Co., Internat. Consol. Investment Co., Opt-Scis. Corp., Continental Bank, Capitol Exchange Corp. Bd. dirs. Piasecki Found.; trustee Villanova U.; past chmn. bd. trustees Hahnemann Med. Coll.; mem. chmn.'s adv. com. Dept. Health Adminstrn., Temple U. Mem. Fed., Am., Pa., Phila. bar assns., Com. of 70. Clubs: Pine Valley Golf (Clementon, N.J.); Overbrook (Bryn Mawr, Pa.); Los Angeles, Los Angeles Athletic, Squires Golf (Phila.); Boca Raton (Fla.). Home: 21 Righters Mill Rd Gladwyne PA 19035 Office: Two Bala Cynwyd Plaza Bala Cynwyd PA 19004

KANN, FRED S., holding co. exec.; b. Bad Kreuznach, Germany, June 1, 1926; s. Karl and Johanna (Rapp) K.; B.S., City U. N.Y., 1948; M.S. in Engring., Columbia U., 1952; m. Margot Katz, June 12, 1949; children—Robert Lawrence, Barry Steven, Michael Howard. Civilian exec. U.S. Army, Joliet, Ill., 1951-55; mktg. mgr. Gruen Watch Co., Cin., 1955-57; v.p. dir. REDM Corp., Wayne, N.J., 1957-73, chmn., pres., 1974-79; chmn., pres. REDM Industries, Inc., Wayne, 1979—. Served with U.S. Army, 1944-46. Mem. Am. Def. Preparedness Assn. (dir.). Office: REDM Industries Inc 70 Old Turnpike Rd Wayne NJ 07470

KANOVSKY, GERALD, packaging co. exec.; b. Winnipeg, Man., Can., Sept. 20, 1935; s. Manuel and Annie (Lifshitz) K.; B.A., U. Man., 1957; M.B.A., Baruch Coll., City U. N.Y., 1962; m. Marlene S. Friedman, Aug. 23, 1959; children—Andrea Jan, Lisa Jill. Research dir. Boni, Watkins, Jason Assos., econ. and mgmt. cons., N.Y.C., 1959-63; sr. mgmt. cons. Joel Dean Assos., N.Y.C., 1964-65; with Am. Can. Co., Greenwich, Conn., 1965-80, chief fin. officer Internat. div., 1971-75, mng. dir. mktg. and bus. devel., 1975-77, spl. asst. to v.p., gen. mgr. food packaging, 1977, mng. dir. dairy, bakery and frozen food packaging, 1977-79, mng. dir. Mktg. Paperboard Packaging div., 1979-80; v.p., gen. mgr. Packaging div. Packaging Systems Corp., Orangeburg, N.Y., 1980—; dir. Dixie-Union Verpakungen GmbH, Kempten, W.Ger., Goossens, S.A., Maroq-en-Baroeul, France, Trentesaux-Toulemonde, S.A., Tourcoing, France, Envases Antillanos, C. por A., Santiago, Dominican Republic, Nueva Modelo, S.A., Mexico City, U.S. San. de Mex., Mexico City, Envases Venezolanos, S.A., Caracas, Am. Can Export Corp., Greenwich. Capt., United Way, Stamford, Conn., 1977-78. Recipient gold award United Way, Stamford, 1978. Mem. N.Am. Soc. for Corp. Planning (chmn. speakers bur. 1967-68, mem. program com. 1967-69), Am. Mktg. Assn., Paperboard Packaging Council, Carded Packaging Inst. Club: Twin Lakes Tennis (Stamford). Home: 72 Millbrook Rd Stamford CT 06902 Office: 400 Route 303 Orangeburg NY 10962

KANTER, SELMA ROSLYN, publisher; b. N.Y.C., Apr. 4, 1925; d. Jack S. and Francese I. (Jacobson) Lapin; student Hofstra U., 1942-44; m. William Ehrenreich, Feb. 4, 1946; children—Andrew David, John Daniel, James Matthew, Peter Adam. Fashion coordinator Bonwit Teller Co., N.Y.C., 1944-47; account exec. Lester Harrison Inc., N.Y.C., 1947-53; cons. Bestsellers Ltd., London, 1963-69; pres. Printing Press Inc., 1972—; pres., pub. Gilberton Co. Inc., Stamford, Conn., 1973—, Penny Press, Inc., Stamford, 1973—. Home: 355 Rockrimmon Rd Stamford CT 06903

KANTOR, NATHAN, telecommunications co. exec.; b. N.Y.C., Aug. 22, 1942; s. Harry and Bertha (Levey) K.; B.S., U.S. Mil. Acad., 1965; M.S., Fla. State U., 1968; m. Etta S. Rosenbach, June 13, 1965; children—Kenneth, Karen, Jennifer. Subcontract mgr. systems Mgmt. div. Sperry Rand Corp., Great Neck, N.Y., 1969-72; v.p. adminstrn. MCI Telecommunications Corp., N.Y.C., 1972-76, v.p. opns., 1976—. Served to capt. USAF, 1965-69. Mem. Am. Mgmt. Assn. Home: 4 Pilgrim Trail Westport CT 06880 Office: MCI Telecommunications Corp 1301 Ave of Americas New York NY 10019

KAPADIA, DARIUS, hotel and restaurant exec.; b. Nagpur, India, May 13, 1950; came to U.S., 1977; s. Dhunjishaw and Freny (Dastur) K.; grad. hotel mgmt. Inst. of Hotel Mgmt. and Catering Tech., Bombay, India, 1970; m. Manpreet Duggal, Oct. 28, 1979. Camp supr. Albert Abela Co., Abu Dhabi, 1970-71; gen. mgr. Indo-Arab Enterprises, Beirut, Lebanon, 1971-73; owner restaurant, Nicosia, Cyprus, 1974-76; partner restaurant, Beirut, 1974-77; gen. mgr. Indian Resorts and Restaurants Inc., N.Y.C., 1977-78, v.p., 1978—; partner Shelkap Assos., Trenton, N.J.; pres. Capitol Plaza Inc., Trenton. Mem. Better Bus. Bur., Indian C. of C., N.Y. Conv. and Visitors Bur. Clubs: Lions, Manhattan Squash. Home: 240 W State St Trenton NJ

08608 Office: Indian Resorts and Restaurants Inc 57 W 48th St New York NY 10020

KAPLAN, EDWARD BURTON, mfg. co. exec.; b. Worcester, Mass., Sept. 5, 1940; s. Irving Abraham and Yetta (Bretholtz) K.; B.S. in Plastics Tech., Lowell (Mass.) Tech. Inst., 1963; M.S. in Plastics Engring. (fellow Plastics Inst. Am.), Stevens Inst. Tech., Hoboken, N.J., 1965; m. Renee Marsh, June 5, 1966; children—Allison, Jennifer. Engr., Enjay Polymer labs. Exxon Corp., Linden, N.J., 1965-67; gen. mgr. Leslynn Products Corp., also tech. dir. Sterling Last Corp., Long Island City, N.Y., 1967-73; asst. to pres. Dynamic Plastics Corp., Flushing, N.Y., 1974-75; gen. mgr. Polyversion Inc., Tulsa, 1975-77; v.p. parent co. Armin Corp., Tulsa, 1977-78; pres. Coating Labs., Tulsa, 1979—, Kaplan Cons., 1978—. Mem. Soc. Plastics Engrs. Jewish. Club: Tulsa Kiwanis. Patentee in field. Home: 7324 S Canton St Tulsa OK 74136 Office: 3133 E Admiral Pl Tulsa OK 74110

KAPLAN, JEFFREY JAY, info. systems cons.; b. Milw., Dec. 1, 1946; s. Victor Samuel and Florence Betty (Stein) K.; A.A.S., Milw. Area Tech. Coll., 1967; B.B.A., U. Wis.-Whitewater, 1970; m. Laura Beth, Feb. 14, 1971. Programmer analyst Mobil Oil Corp., Milw., 1970-74; data base adminstr. Blue Cross of Wis., Milw., 1974-77, supr. software specialist tech. support, Milw., 1977—. Mem. Milw. Area IMS Users Group (pres.), Midwest DB/DC Users Conf. (planning com.). Jewish. Office: 501 W Michigan Ave Milwaukee WI 53201

KAPLAN, JUDITH HELENE, philatelic co. exec.; b. N.Y.C., July 20, 1938; d. Abraham and Ruth (Kiffel) Letich; B.A., Hunter Coll., 1955; postgrad. New Sch. for Social Research, 1955-56; m. Warren Kaplan, Dec. 31, 1958; children—Ronald Scott, Elissa Aynn. Registered rep. Herzfeld & Stern, N.Y.C., 1963; agt. New York Life Ins. Co., N.Y.C., 1964-69; registered rep. Scheinman, Hochstin & Trotta, 1969-70; v.p. Alpha Capital Corp., N.Y.C., 1970-74; pres. Tipex, Inc., N.Y.C., 1966—; v.p. Alpha Pub. Relations, N.Y.C., 1970-73; pres. Utopia Recreations Corp., 1971-73, Howard Beach Recreation Corp., 1972-73; chmn. bd. Alpha Exec. Planning Corp., 1970-72; field underwriter N.Y. Life Ins. Co., 1974-75; participant White House Conf. on Small Bus., 1979; Wyo. adv. on woman suffrage. Named Outstanding Young Citizen, Manhattan Jaycees. Mem. NOW (ins. coordinator nat. task force on taxes, v.p. N.Y. chpt.), Nat. Women's Polit. Caucus, Women Leaders Round Table, Nat. Assn. Life Underwriters, Assn. Stamp Dealers Am., Am. First Day Cover Soc. (life), Am. Philat. Soc. (life). Author: Woman Suffrage, 1977; contbg. editor Stamp Show News, M & H Philatelic Report; also articles in profl. jours.; creator, producer Women's History series of First Day Covers, 1976—. Home: 577 Silver Course Circle Ocala FL 32672 Office: 484-C Cypress Rd Ocala FL 32672

KAPLAN, MELVIN JORDAN, investment banker; b. Boston, June 29, 1937; s. Samuel and Anne (Singer) K.; B.S., U. Calif., Berkeley, 1962; m. Margaret A. Bohannon, Feb. 2, 1961; children—Mark Geoffrey, Craig Andrew, Stephen Joseph, David Benjamin, Jonathan Michael. Propr., Melvin J. Kaplan Assos., San Francisco, 1962; gen. partner Wellington Realty Investments, San Francisco, 1977; pres., chief exec. officer Wellington Fin. Group, San Francisco, 1976—; lectr. Sch. Bus. Adminstrn., U. Calif., Berkeley, 1974—. Mem. Delta Phi Epsilon. Club: Commonwealth. Office: 155 Montgomery St San Francisco CA 94104

KAPLAN, MICHAEL DAVID, health mgmt. cons.; b. N.Y.C., Nov. 4, 1940; s. Harry J. and Rose K. Kaplan; B.A., Syracuse U., 1962, postgrad., 1963; postgrad. N.Y. U., 1964; m. Barbara Oberstein, Aug. 30, 1964; children—Jeremy Scott, Abigail Sarah. Polit. reporter AP, N.Y.C., 1965-69; v.p. mktg. First Healthcare Corp., Chgo., 1969-74; pres. Resource Dynamics, Inc., Chgo., 1974-79, also dir.; pres. Randmark Corp., Louisville, 1979—, also dir.; lectr. Acad. Gerontol. Edn. and Devel. Bd. dirs. Louisville Jewish Community Fedn., Kenesth Israel Synagogue, Louisville, Bur. Jewish Edn., Louisville. Club: Standard (Louisville). Author: Comprehensive Guide to Health Care Marketing, 1974; contbr. articles to profl. jours.; contbg. editor Nursing Homes mag., 1978—. Home: 1801 Tyler Ln Louisville KY 40205 Office: Watterson City W Louisville KY 40218

KAPLAN, RONALD V., investment co. exec.; b. N.Y.C., Oct. 23, 1930; s. Morris and Ethel (Glass) K.; B.B.A., N.Y. U., 1951; M.B.A. in Accounting, Columbia, City U. N.Y., 1956; m. Bette Wise, June 27, 1954; children—Bruce, Jerry, Michael. Supervising sr. accountant Ernst & Whinney, C.P.A.'s, N.Y.C., 1954-66; treas., chief fin. officer Gen. Hose & Coupline Co., Caldwell, N.J., 1966-68; v.p., treas., chief fin. officer Midland Capital Corp., N.Y.C., 1968—; chmn. bd., pres. Flight Service, Inc.; chmn. bd. Sunstream Jet Center, Inc.; dir. 1st Fulton Corp., Nat. Nursing Home Devel. Corp. C.P.A., N.Y. Mem. Am. Inst. C.P.A.'s., N.Y. State Soc. C.P.A.'s, Beta Gamma Sigma. Club: K.P. Home: 21 Tammy Terr Wayne NJ 07470 Office: 110 William St New York NY 10038

KAPLAN, SHELDON Z., internat. lawyer; b. Boston, Nov. 15, 1911; s. Jacob and Lizzie (Strogoff) K.; grad. Boston Latin Sch., 1928; A.B. with honors, Yale, 1933; postgrad. Harvard Law Sch., 1933-34; B.A. in Jurisprudence, Brasenose Coll., Oxford (Eng.) U., 1937, M.A., 1945; doctorate in internat. law student U. Paris and L'Ecole Libre des Sciences Politiques, 1945; Doctor (Hon. Causa), Inca Garcilaso de la Vega U., Peru, 1970, San Martin de Porres U., 1979; m. Megan Vondersmith, May 8, 1947; children—Eldon, Deborah, Daniel, Philip, Rebecca, Abigail. Research asso. Elder Whitman and Weyburn, Boston, 1937-40; admitted to Mass. bar, 1940, also D.C. bar, U.S. Supreme Ct. bar; pvt. law practice, 1940-42; asst. to legal adviser Dept. State, Washington, 1947-49; staff cons. House Fgn. Affairs Com., 1949-57; counsel law firm Wilkinson, Cragun & Barker, 1962-67; gen. counsel Central Am. Sugar Council, 1963-65; counsel Central Bank of Honduras, 1962-64, SAHSA Airlines (Honduras), 1964-78; spl. internat. counsel Morrison-Knudsen Co., 1971-74; partner Bechhoefer, Sharlitt & Lyman, Washington, 1976—. Mem. U.S. Spl. Mission to Costa Rica, 1949, El Salvador, 1950, Europe, 1951, 53, Pakistan, India, Thailand, Indochina, 1953, Latin Am., 1954, Uruguay, 1955, C.A., 1955; congl. adviser and mem. U.S. delegation to 10th Gen. Assembly of UN, 1955; counsel to Govt. Guatemala, 1960-62, 77-78; spl. cons. on internat. econ. affairs Am. Assn. for UN, 1958; del. Govt. Nicaragua to 18th-19th sessions Internat. Sugar Council, London, Eng., 1964, 65. Mem. adv. bd. Campion Hall, Oxford (Eng.) U., 1974—. Served as capt. AUS, 1942-46; ETO. Decorated La Medaille de la Reconnaissance Francaise (France); Bronze Star medal (U.S.); Orden Del Quetzal (Guatemala); Orden Al Merito (Peru). Mem. Harvard Law Sch. Assn., Brasenose (Oxford, Eng.) Soc., A.S.C.A.P., Nat. Steeplechase and Hunt. Jewish. Clubs: Yale, British Schools and Universities (N.Y.C.); Cosmos, Army and Navy, Capitol Hill (Washington). Co-author: Panama-Canal Issues and Treaty Talks, 1967. Author numerous govt. pub. documents, reports on fgn. affairs. Contbr. to profl. jours. Composer popular songs. Home: 7810 Moorland Ln Bethesda MD 20014 Office: 1747 Pennsylvania Ave NW Washington DC 20006

KAPLAN, WILLIAM MEYER, lawyer; b. N.Y.C., Dec. 10, 1920; s. Morris and Lena (Hammer) K.; B.S.S., CCNY, 1940; LL.B., Fordham U., 1947; J.S.D., N.Y. U., 1951; m. Ann Auerbach, Sept. 21, 1947; children—Cathy Melissa, Darlene Melinda. Admitted to N.Y. bar, 1947; asso. Linder & Mayer, N.Y.C., 1947-49, Pindyck & Bernstein, N.Y.C., 1950, Paul, Weiss, Rifkind, Wharton & Garrison, N.Y.C., 1951; partner firm Aranow, Brodsky, Bohlinger, Benetar & Einhorn, N.Y.C., 1951-79, firm Miller, Singer, Michaelson & Raives, N.Y.C., 1979—; dir. Triangle Pacific Corp. Bd. govs. N.Y. Young Republican Club, N.Y.C., 1947-48; pres. Bronx Young Rep. Club, 1946-47. Served with AUS, 1942-46. Mem. Am. Bar Assn. (sect. econ. law 1975—), N.Y. County Lawyers Assn. (sec. com. profl. ethics 1956-58, mem. com. 1976—), Phi Beta Kappa. Contbr. articles to profl. jours. Home: 4455 Douglas Ave Riverdale NY 10471 Office: 555 Madison Ave New York NY 10022

KAPLANGES, JAMES, chem. mfg. co. exec.; b. Balt., Feb. 23, 1938; s. Konstantinos and Katina (Anagnostou) K.; ed. U. Balt., 1957, U. Md., 1962; m. Iona Pantaloukas, Feb. 22, 1959; children—Konstantinos, Andrew. Founder, G.P. 66 Chems., Balt., 1966, since pres.; mem. Region III Small Bus. Adv. Council, Balt. City Adv. Council on Small Bus. Pres. Apollo Civic Club, Balt., 1974—, Roosevelt Democratic Club, 1968; chmn. Greek-Am. Legis. Liaison Com. Md., 1975, Senatoral Advisory Bd. Cyprus-Turkey Issue, 1975—. Recipient Dominic Mimi Di Pietro award Balt. City Council, 1978, Pres.'s citation Balt. City Council, 1978, U.S. Senatorial commendation, 1978, other citations, commendations. Mem. Am. Chem. Soc., N.Y. Hist. Soc., ASTM, Smithsonian Instn., United Dem. Assn., Ahepa (v.p. Lord Balt. chpt. 1980). Greek Orthodox. Devel. indsl. chem. cleaners. Office: 1636 E Lombard St Baltimore MD 21231

KAPLIN, THOMAS ALAN, proposal cons.; b. Jackson, Mich., July 11, 1937; s. John William and Harriet (Eggelston) K.; student public schs., Detroit. Free-lance engring. aide, technician, tech. writer, 1959-65; subcontract proposal cons., 1965-74; co-owner, v.p. Proposal Mgmt., Inc., Phila., 1974-75; co-owner, chief cons., exec. v.p. Techmedia Corp., proposal mgrs., cons., pubs., Phila., 1975—. Served with USAF, 1955-59. Home: 1804 La Cima San Clemente CA 92672 Office: Techmedia Corp 121 N Orianna St Philadelphia PA 19106

KAPPER, WILLIAM CLEMENT, TV tuner mfg. co. exec.; b. Olney, Ill., July 17, 1935; s. Cornelius Joseph and Johanna Helen (Dumstorff) K.; grad. electronics technician Bailey Tech. Trades Sch., 1962; m. Anne Montgomery, July 9, 1960; 1 dau., Lisa Anne. Electronics technician Sarkes Tarzian Inc., Bloomington, Ind., 1962-70, prodn. foreman, 1970-73, elec. test maintenance foreman, 1974-76, process mgr., 1977-78, supr. indsl. engring. dept., 1979—. Served with USMC, 1953-57. Clubs: K.C., Moose. Home: 3131 Market Pl Bloomington IN 47401 Office: 1600 E Hillside Dr Bloomington IN 47401

KAPPES, GEORGE, JR., ins. exec.; b. Milw., May 2, 1928; s. George William and Ann G. (von Nimitz) K.; B.A., U. Wis., 1950; m. Grace Roberta Baldwin, May 29, 1957; children—George, Margaret Ann. Underwriter, Continental Casualty Co., Milw., 1950-53; underwriting supr. Marketmen's Mut., Milw., 1953-56, Ohio Casualty Co., Hamilton, Ohio, 1956-64; regional underwriting mgr., asst. sec. Utica Mut. Ins. Co., Alhambra, Calif., and Waltham, Mass., 1964-72; v.p. Medallion Ins. Group, Kansas City, Mo., 1972-73; pres. MGA Ins. Mktg., Torrance, Calif., 1973-77; pres., chmn. Kappes-Coombe Ins. Services, San Diego, 1977—; instr. Ins. Inst. Am., 1968-70, Boston U., 1968-70, Northeastern U., Boston, 1970-72. Founder, Greater Hamilton Civic Theatre, 1958; bd. dirs. Hamilton Civic Music Assn., 1958; bd. dirs. Arcadia Civic Theatre, 1965; chmn. Winter Carnival, Hopkinton, Mass., 1971; trustee Religious Sci. Ch. Center, San Diego, 1980—. Asso. in mgmt., Ins. Inst. Am., 1968. Mem. Milw. Ins. Underwriters Assn. (pres. 1950-53), Am. Mgmt. Assn., Ind. Ins. Agts. Assn., Ins. Inst. Am., Am. Security Council (nat. adv. bd. 1978-80), Nat. Assn. Profl. Surplus Lines Offices, U.S. Naval Inst., Profl. Ins. Agts. Assn. Republican. Club: King Harbor Yacht. Home: 5509 Paseo de Pablo Torrance CA 90505 Office: 12200 Sylvan St Suite 200 North Hollywood CA 91606

KAPPES, PHILIP SPANGLER, lawyer, lab. equipment co. exec.; b. Detroit, Dec. 24, 1925; s. Philip Alexander and Wilma Fern (Spangler) K.; B.A. cum laude, Butler U., 1945; J.D., U. Mich., 1948; m. Glendora Galena Miles, Nov. 27, 1948; children—Susan Lea, Philip Miles, Mark William. Admitted to Ind. bar, 1948, U.S. Supreme Ct. bar, 1970; practiced in Indpls., 1948—; asso. firm Armstrong and Gause, 1948-49; asso. law offices C.B. Dutton, 1950-52; partner Dutton, Kappes & Overman, 1952—; chmn. bd., sec., dir. Lab. Equipment Co., Mooresville, Ind.; dir., asst. sec. Wellman Dynamics Corp., Creston, Iowa; dir., sec. Creston Corp., Mid-West Food Center, Inc., SW Inc., Indpls.; instr. bus. law Butler U., 1948-49, chmn. bd. govs., 1965-66. Bd. dirs., v.p. adminstrn. and fin., exec. com., legal com. Crossroads Am. council Boy Scouts Am., 1968—, pres., 1977-78; trustee Children's Mus., Indpls. Mem. Am. Judicature Soc., Am., Ind. (ho. dels. 1959—, mem. chmn. pub. relations exec. com. 1966-69, sec. 1973-74, bd. mgrs. 1975-77), Indpls. (treas., 1st v.p. 1965, pres. 1970, bd. mgrs. 1959-70, 76-77) bar assns., Indpls. Legal Aid Soc., Indpls. Jr. C. of C. (past 1st v.p.), Butler U. (past pres.), Mich. alumni assns., Phi Delta Theta, Tau Kappa Alpha. Republican. Presbyterian (deacon, elder, past pres. bd. trustees). Clubs: Meridian Hills Country, Lawyers, Gyro (pres. 1966) (Indpls.), Masons (past master), Shriners, Scottish Rite. Home: 7450 North Park Ave Indianapolis IN 46240 Office: Guaranty Bldg Indianapolis IN 46204

KAPSCH, FRANCIS EDWARD, JR., govt. agy. ofcl.; b. Chgo., Mar. 4, 1943; s. Francis Edward and Dorothy Catherine (Hedges) K.; B.A., U. Minn., 1969, postgrad., 1969-71; m. Sharon Gail Hillestad, Aug. 22, 1970. Grad. research staff asst. U. Minn., 1969-71; labor mgmt. relations specialist NLRB, Mpls., 1971-74, sr. labor mgmt. relations specialist, 1974—. Chairperson, Mpls. Police Precinct Citizens Adv. Council; mem. CRV adv. com. Mpls. Public Schs.; vol. instr. Minn. Youth Firearm Safety Program. Served with U.S. Army, 1963-66; officer USCG Aux., 1979—. Mem. NLRB Union (pres. region 18 1977-78), United Sportsmen Minn., Iota Rho Chi (v.p. 1970-71). Roman Catholic. Home: 5137 Knox Ave S Minneapolis MN 55419 Office: 110 S 4th St Minneapolis MN 55401

KAPUSTIN, RAFAEL, real estate developer; b. Havana, Cuba, Dec. 29, 1939; came to U.S., 1960, naturalized, 1970; s. Jacobo and Cila (Berenthal) K.; B.S. in Mech. Engring., Stevens Inst. Tech., Hoboken, N.J., 1963; m. Sara Rabinovich, June 23, 1968; children—Andrew Jay, Gina Eve. Self-employed cons., San Juan, P.R., 1970-72; real estate broker, investor, developer, Miami, Fla., 1972—; gen. partner Miamiland Ltd., 1972—, Miamiland Ltd. II, 1973—, Biscayne Properties Ltd., 1978—; pres. Love 'n Flowers Internat., 1978—, Splty. Groves I, II and III, Inc., 1978-80; founder, dir., sec. Internat. Savs. & Loan Assn., Miami. Mem. Downtown Miami Bus. Assn. (dir.). Office: 25 SE 2d Ave Miami FL 33131

KARASH, RICHARD IVAN, computer co. exec.; b. Cleve., Feb. 20, 1946; s. Walter John and Vivian H. K.; S.B., Mass. Inst. Tech., 1969, S.M., 1974; m. Karla Hurst, June 1, 1968; 1 dau., Ann. Founder, MSC Assos., Boston, 1967-70; asst. to v.p. Digital Equipment Corp., Boston, 1969-70; cons. Mgmt. Decision Systems, Boston, 1970—, v.p., 1974—, gen. mgr., 1976—. Mem. Am. Mktg. Assn., Beacon Hill Civic Assn. Clubs: Bus. Assos., Wellesley Racquetball. Home: 47 Chestnut St Boston MA 02108 Office: 300 3d Ave Waltham MA 02154

KARASIK, MYRON SOLOMON, mgmt. cons.; b. N.Y.C., June 3, 1950; s. Jack and Bertha Clara (Shapiro) K.; M.S.E.E., Purdue U., 1972; M. Mgmt. with distinction (Austin scholar), Northwestern U., 1975; m. Sara Louise Lieber, Aug. 29, 1976. Mem. tech. staff, acting supr. Bell Telephone Labs., Piscataway, N.J., 1972-73; cons. Deloitte Haskins & Sells, Chgo., 1975-78; v.p. adminstrn. J.P. Walsh, Inc., Chgo., 1979; prin. cons., mgr. info. services MWS Cons., Inc., Chgo., 1980; dir. mgmt. adv. services Veatch, Rich & Nadler, Chartered, 1980—. Chmn. Project 200 com. Congregation Emanuel, 1980, v.p. Brotherhood, 1980. C.P.A., Ill. Mem. IEEE, Ill. Soc. C.P.A.'s, Am. Mgmt. Assn. Republican. Jewish. Designer expenditure control system for maj. fgn. govt. Office: 13 Northbrook Center 425 Huehl Rd Northbrook IL 60062

KARCH, ROBERT E., diversified co. exec.; b. Bklyn., May 30, 1933; s. Charles H. and Etta R. (Becker) K.; A.B., Syracuse U., 1953, M.B.A., 1958; student in Russian, Army Lang. Sch., Monterey, Calif., 1953-54; m. Brenda Schechter, Sept. 7, 1958; children—Barry S., Karen D., Brian D. With Karch Beauty Supply Co. Inc., Syracuse, N.Y., 1956—, pres., 1966-74, chmn., 1974—, also dir.; sales mgr. Helen of Troy Corp., El Paso, Tex., 1974-76, v.p. sales and mktg., 1976-79, also dir.; v.p., dir. Bormex Constrn. Inc., 1980—; real estate agt. Bonded Realty, 1979—. Pres. Syracuse Hebrew Day Sch., 1972-73. Served with U.S. Army, 1953-56. Lic. comml. pilot. Mem. Beauty and Barber Supply Inst., Direct Mail/Mktg. Assn., Aircraft Owners and Pilots Assn., Jewish War Vets., El Paso Aviation Assn. Club: Coronado Country. Author: Data Processing for Beauty/Barber Dealers, 1968. Home: 6016 Torrey Pines El Paso TX 79912 Office: 11012 Pebble Hills Blvd El Paso TX 79936 also 2600 Erie Blvd E Syracuse NY 13224

KARCHER, JOHN DRAKE, textile co. exec.; b. Washington, Sept. 10, 1939; s. Raymond Edward and Mary Frances (Drake) K.; B.B.A., Wake Forest U., 1961; M.B.A., Wharton Sch., U. Pa., 1964; m. Lois Allison Lynch, Apr. 3, 1965; children—Kimberly Price, John Drake, II, Christopher Brett. Exec. v.p., dir. Spectrum Textured Fibers, Inc., N.Y.C., 1971-72; pres. Wamsutta Decorative Fabrics, N.Y.C., 1972-77, Baxter/Kelly, Inc., N.Y.C., 1977—; dir. Scorpio Equestrian Ventures, Inc., 1976—. Co-chmn. Ox Ridge Sch. PTA, Darien, Conn., 1977-78; mem. bldg. fund drive Darian YMCA, 1977; head coach Darien Youth Hockey, 1977-79, Darien Little League, 1977-79; active fund raising Wake Forest U., New Canaan Country Sch. Named Darien Little League Coach of Yr., 1977. Mem. Nat. Assn. Furniture Mfrs., So. Furniture Mfrs. Assn. Presbyterian. Clubs: Wee Burn Country, Ox Ridge Hunt (bd. stewards, chmn. show com. 1979—). Home: 2 Dew Ln Darien CT 06820 Office: 205 Lexington Ave New York NY 10016

KARCZMAR, MIECZYSLAW, economist, banker; b. Lodz, Poland, Jan. 22, 1923; s. Henryk and Franciszka (Lubicz) K.; came to U.S., 1973; M.S. in Econs. Commerce, Acad. Commerce, Poznan, Poland, 1945-48; Ph.D. in Econ., Main Sch. Planning Statistics, Warsaw, Poland, 1949-51, 60; postgrad. banking seminar London Sch. Econs., 1958; m. Gabriela Bogucka, Dec. 22, 1947; children—Thomas, Peter. With Nat. Bank Poland, Warsaw, 1949-62, dep. dir. planning dept., 1955-58, dep. dir. internat. dept., 1958-62; dir. fin. dept. Polish Ministry Fgn. Trade, Warsaw, 1962-69, trade commr., comml. counsellor to Can., Montreal, 1969-73; head econs. dept. European Am. Bank & Trust Co., European Am. Banking Corp., N.Y.C., 1974—, chief economist, 1977—; dir. Bank Handlowy, Warsaw, 1962-69; mem. supervisory bd. Warta—Ins. Reins. Co., Warsaw, 1962-69; lectr., asst. prof. Main Sch. Planning Statistics, Warsaw, 1951-68; lectr. vocat. courses in fin. planning and credit system, 1950-56. Author: (with W. Pruss) Credit in Trade, 1956; (with others) Accountant's Guidebook, 1956; (with others) Money and Credit, 1960; contbr. articles to profl. jours.; researcher money, credit theory, internat. monetary system, banking. Office: European American Bank 10 Hanover Sq New York NY 10005

KARDON, LEROY, packaging co. exec.; b. Phila., June 25, 1951; s. Robert J. and Janet Doris (Stolker) K.; B.S. in Bus. Adminstrn., Boston U., 1973; M.B.A., Temple U., 1975; m. Gail Helene Friedman, May 25, 1975. Dir. indsl. relations United Container Co., Phila., 1975-76; sales rep. Kardon Composite Can & Tube, St. Paris, Ohio, 1977-78; mgr. mfg. Kardon Industries, Inc., Phila., 1978-81, v.p., dir., 1981—. Mem. Am. Soc. Personnel Adminstrn., Am. Soc. for Tng. and Devel., Phila. Family Bus. Council (v.p., Golden Slipper award). Home: 226 W Rittenhouse Sq Philadelphia PA 19103 Office: 1201 Chestnut St Philadelphia PA 19107

KARGOL, MICHELE, bank exec.; b. Highland Park, Mich., Dec. 30, 1948; d. Michael and Virginia B. (Narozny) K.; B.B.A. in Accounting, U. Detroit, 1975; 1 son, Daniel F. Kotwicki. Data processing technician Bauer Ordnance Co., Warren, Mich., 1966-67; cost accountant Allen Industries, Troy, Mich., 1967-69; fin. analyst Bank of the Commonwealth, Detroit, 1969—, asst. v.p., 1976—. Mem. Am. Mgmt. Assn., Econ. Club Detroit, Am. Inst. Banking, Women's Econ. Club. Roman Catholic. Home: 1883 Farmbrook Dr Troy MI 48098 Office: 719 Griswold St Detroit MI 48226

KARL, ALAN GEORGE, orgn. exec.; b. Chgo., Sept. 16, 1949; s. Francis George and Josephine Rose (Spiotto) K.; student U. Ill., Champaign; B.S., Northwestern U. Systems analyst Ill. Bell Telephone Co., Chgo., 1970-73; sr. cons. Applied Info. Devel. Co., Oakbrook, 1974—. Recipient City of Chgo. citation for public service, 1977, 79, Applied Info. Devel. Achievement award, 1975, 80. Mem. Mensa. Author Sorcery computer source library and maintenance system. Home: 260 E Chestnut St Chicago IL 60611 Office: 823 Commerce Dr Oakbrook IL 60521

KARL, GREGORY PAUL, acct.; b. Saginaw, Mich., Feb. 7, 1950; s. Harry F. and Mary E. (Knox) K.; B.S. in Acctg. magna cum laude, U. Detroit, 1971; m. Mary Rose Capizzo, July 15, 1972; children—Sheri Lynn, Matthew John, Joseph Harry. Sr. tax acct. Ernst & Whinney, Saginaw, 1971-74; asst. controller J.P. Burroughs & Son, Inc., Saginaw, 1974-75, controller, 1975-79; corporate staff Gen. Motors Corp., 1979-80; controller Wickes Engineered Materials div. Wickes Cos., Inc., Saginaw, 1980—; soccer coach Dwight D. Eisenhower High Sch., Saginaw. C.P.A., Mich. Mem. Am. Inst. C.P.A.'s, Mich. Assn. C.P.A.'s, Mich. Assn. Professions, Am. Acctg. Assn., Am. Mgmt. Assn., Am. Inst. Corp. Controllers, U.S. Yacht Racing Union. Home: 315 Holbrook Saginaw MI 48603

KARLAN, FRANCES ROSS, dentist, educator; b. Boston, Apr. 15, 1921; d. Robert and Etty (Feitelberg) Ross; B.S., Mass. Inst. Tech., 1942; D.D.S., Columbia U., 1949; M.B.A., Fordham U., 1972; m. Jac H. Karlan, Sept. 24, 1942; children—Debora Karlan Block, Daniel M. Lab. technician Lederle Labs., Orangeburg, N.Y., 1942; research technician Babies Hosp., N.Y.C., 1942-44, Columbia U. Dental Sch., 1944-45; dentist Rockland State Hosp., Orangeburg, N.Y., 1952-53; asst. v.p. Met. Life Ins. Co., N.Y.C., 1953-79, dental claims cons., 1979—; asso. prof. dept. stomatology Sch. Dental Oral Surgery Columbia. Mem. ADA, Assn. Indsl. Dentists (pres.), Assn. Dental

Alumni Columbia U. (past pres.). Home: 37A Haddon Rd Cranbury NJ 08512 Office: Sch Dental and Oral Surgery 630 W 168th St New York NY 10032

KARLSON, BEN EMIL, kitchen design co. exec.; b. Hedemora, Sweden, Aug. 27, 1934; s. Emil W.J. and Ester Linnea (Hellman) Karlsson; came to U.S., 1954, naturalized, 1960; grad. bus. mktg. Alexander Hamilton Inst., N.Y.C., 1967, Am. Inst. Kitchen Designers, 1972; grad. Dale Carnegie Inst., 1972; m. Susan Jo Kaupert, Feb. 7, 1958; children—David, Kristine, Thomas. Salesman, Edward Hines Lumber Co., Chgo., 1954-63; v.p., gen. mgr. Lake Forest Lumber Co. (Ill.), 1963-67; pres. Karlson Home Center, Inc., Evanston, Ill., 1967—, Bank Ln. Investors, Lake Forest, 1971-72, Poggenpohl-Midwest/USA, Inc., Evanston, 1979—; founder chmn. Evanston Home Show, 1973, 74; judge, Nat. Design Contest, 1974; showroom design cons., Ill., Poggenpohl Kitchens Germany. Mem. steering com. Covenant Methodist Ch., Evanston, 1968-69; bd. dirs. Evanston Family Counseling Service, 1973-75, Evanston United Community Services, 1974-75, mid-Am. chpt. No. region ARC, 1974; chmn. bus. div. Evanston United Fund, 1974, gen. campaign chmn., 1975. Recipient awards for community service. Certified kitchen designer. Mem. Am. Inst. Kitchen Designers (pres. 1975-76), Evanston C. of C. (dir. 1973-74, v.p. 1975, pres. 1976), Nat. Fed. Ind. Bus., Mid-Am. Swedish Trade Assn. Club: Evanston Rotary. Contbr. kitchen designs to nat. mags. Home: 2311 Central Park Ave Evanston IL 60201 Office: 1815 Central St Evanston IL 60201

KARLSRUD, GARY MICHAEL, dental tech. co. exec.; b. Gary, Ind., Oct. 31, 1946; s. Gilbert and Jessica Mae (Rutherford) K.; A.A.S., Milw. Area Tech. Coll., 1968; B.S., U. State N.Y., 1978; M.A. in Health Care Edn., Central Mich. U., 1979; m. Patricia Lynn Matheus, Apr. 12, 1975. Dental tech. trainee Kramer Dental Studio, Mpls., 1968-69; dept. supv. Larry Glaze Dental Lab., Inc., Waukesha, Wis., 1972-74; v.p. research and edn. Sanford Dental Lab, Inc., Milw., 1974—; pres. Saber Dental Studio Inc., Mpls., 1979—; instr. Milw. Area Tech. Coll., 1975—. Served with USN, 1969-72. Mem. Dental Tech. Assn. Wis. (membership chmn. 1976), Dental Ceramist Soc. Mid Am., Chgo. Dental Techs. Study Group, Nat. Jogging Assn., South Shore Striders (pres.), Tau Theta Epsilon. Democrat. Lutheran. Author: Inservice Training in the Dental Lab, 1978; contbr. articles in field to profl. jours. Home: 2910 S Ellen Milwaukee WI 53207 Office: 6800 Shingle Creek Pkwy Brooklyn Center MN 55430

KARMAZIN, JOSEPHINE ROSE, Realtor; b. N.Y.C., Feb. 9, 1922; d. John and Rose Marie (Mares) K.; grad. Bradford Jr. Coll., 1941. Personnel mgr. Kline's Store, Detroit, 1945-53; asst. buyer and advt. Hutzel Store, Ann Arbor, Mich., 1953-55; v.p. personnel and labor relations Karmazin Products Corp., 1955-69; now sales asso. Lee H. Clark, realtor, Grosse Ile, Mich. Chmn. bd. mgmt. Downriver YWCA, 1970-73; chmn. Camp Cavell com. YWCA Met. Detroit, 1974, chmn. expansion com., 1975-78, 2d v.p., 1978—, mem. planning and devel. com., 1980—; sec. Wyandotte Community Theatre Relocation Com., 1980; mem. bd. mgmt. Family Neighborhood Services, 1958-68; del. Mich. Republican Conv., 1978. Presbyterian (deacon). Clubs: Women's Econ. (Detroit); Grosse Ile Yacht; Soroptimist (pres. 1961, 63) (Wyndotte, Mich.). Home: 22085 Thorofare Grosse Ile MI 48138 Office: 8600 Macomb St Grosse Ile MI 48138

KARMEL, ROBERTA SARAH, lawyer; b. Chgo., May 4, 1937; d. Jacob Herzl and Eva (Elin) Segal; B.A., Radcliffe Coll., 1959; LL.B., N.Y. U., 1962; m. Paul Richard Karmel, June 9, 1957; children—Philip, Solomon, Jonathan, Miriam. Admitted to bar; successively atty., br. chief, asst. regional adminstr. SEC, 1962-68; asso. firm Willkie, Farr & Gallagher, 1969-72; partner firm Rogers & Wells, Washington, 1972-77, 80—; commr. SEC, Washington, 1977-80; adj. prof. Bklyn. Law Sch., 1973-77. Mem. vis. com. U. Chgo. Law Sch., 1978—. Recipient Woman of Year award New Bus. Leadership, The Ladies Home Jour., 1978. Mem. Am. Bar Assn., Assn. Bar City N.Y., Fed. Bar Assn. Democrat. Jewish. Contbr. articles to profl. jours. Home: 26 Hopke Ave Hastings-on-Hudson NY 10706 Office: 200 Park Ave New York NY 10017

KARNAS, GEORGE JAMES, airline exec.; b. Duluth, Minn., Mar. 5, 1930; s. James George and Mary (Rozinka) K.; student Ariz. State U., Tempe, 1948; m. Lois Picconatto, Apr. 10, 1951; children—Kathryn, James, Michael, Darcy Ann. Insp., Coolerator, Duluth, 1947-52; agt. N. Central Airlines, Duluth, 1952-54, sr. agt., 1954-59, mgr. fleet service, 1959-73, v.p. inflight service, 1973—; sr. v.p. inflight service Republic Airlines, 1979—; officer Airline Agts. Union, 1956-59, chmn., 1958-59; dir. Richfield Bank & Trust Co. (Minn.). Treas. Richfield Sch. Bd., 1972, vice chmn., 1973-75, chmn., 1976-77; coach Am. Legion Baseball, 1969-78. Served with AUS, 1947-48, 50-51. Mem. Richfield Am. Legion, Nat. Restaurant Assn., Inflight Food Service Assn. (pres. 1977-78, dir.), Twin City Aviation Mgmt. Assn., Richfield C. of C. (dir.), Airline Catering Assn. (chmn. 1962-63, dir. 1973-80). Roman Catholic. Clubs: Decathlon Athletic, Minn. Valley Country. Home: 2921 Washburn Circle Richfield MN 55423 Office: 7500 Airline Dr Minneapolis MN 55450

KARP, DONALD MATHEW, lawyer, banker; b. Newark, Jan. 15, 1937; s. Michael N. and Beatrice (Laufer) K.; B.S., U. Vt., 1958; LL.D., Cornell U., 1961; m. Margery Lesnik, June 28, 1962; 2 children. Admitted to N.J. bar, 1961; practice law, Newark, 1964—; regional counsel SBA N.J., 1966; vice chmn., counsel, dir. Broad Nat. Bank, Newark. Served as 1st lt. U.S. Army, 1962-64. Mem. Am., N.J., Fed., Essex County bar assns., Comml. Law League Am. Club: Mountain Ridge County (West Caldwell, N.J.). Office: 905 Broad St Newark NJ 07102

KARP, STEPHEN ROBERT, real estate developer; b. Boston, Mar. 15, 1940; s. Harold and Beatrice G. K.; student Johns Hopkins U., 1958-60; A.B., Boston U., 1962; m. Jill Ellen Feinstein, Apr. 14, 1973; children—Douglass Evan, Jana Michelle. With Thomas Diab & Sons Real Estate, 1963-65; with State Properties of New Eng., Boston, 1965—, partner, treas., 1970—. Bd. trustees Horizons for Youth. Served with USAFR, 1960-66. Mem. Greater Boston Real Estate Bd., Urban Land Inst., Internat. Council Shopping Centers (v.p.). Office: 1 Wells Ave Newton MA 02159

KARPEN, MARIAN JOAN, fin. exec.; b. Detroit, June 16, 1944; d. Cass John and Mary Jay K.; A.B., Vassar Coll., 1966; postgrad. Sorbonne, Paris, N.Y. U. Grad. Sch. Bus., 1974-77. New Eng. corr. Women's Wear Daily Fairchild Publs.-Capital Cities Communications, 1966-68, Paris fashion editor, TV and radio commentator Capital Cities Network, 1968-69; fashion editor Boston Herald Traveler, 1969-71; nat. syndicated newspaper columnist and photojournalist Queen Features Syndicate, N.Y.C., 1971-73; account exec. Blyth Eastman Dillon, N.Y.C., 1973-75, Oppenheimer, N.Y.C., 1975-76; v.p., municipal bond coordinator Faulkner Dawkins & Sullivan (merged Shearson Hayden Stone), N.Y.C., 1976-77; mgr. retail mcpl. bond dept. A.G. Becker Warburg, Paribas, Becker Group), N.Y.C., 1977-79, v.p. and prin., 1977—. Mem. Nat. Assn. Securities Dealers, N.Y. Stock Exchange, English Speaking Union. Vassar, Skating (N.Y.C. and Boston). Home: 233 E 69th St New York City NY 10021 Office: 55 Water St New York City NY 10041

KARPOUZIS, PAUL DIMITRIOS, watch mfg. co. exec.; b. Island of Kos, Dodecanese, Greece, Apr. 21, 1934; s. Dimitrios Andrew and Ekaterini Peter (Flaskos) K.; came to U.S., 1955, naturalized, 1966; B.S., Franklin and Marshall Coll., 1959; M.Ed., Temple U., 1963; M.S.Ed., U. Pa., 1964; m. Kyvele Parikas, June 16, 1963; children—Tina Elaine, Pamela Kay, Katerina Paula. Tchr. math. Lancaster (Pa.) Country Day Sch., 1960-62, The Tatnall Sch., Wilmington, Del., 1964-66; prof. math. York Coll., 1967-68; gauge analyst Hamilton Watch Co., Lancaster, 1959-60, quality control engr., 1966-69, dir. purchasing, 1969-74, dir. materials mgmt., 1974-76, v.p. materials mgmt., 1976-80, v.p. ops., 1980—. Mem. Am. Soc. Quality Control (chmn. edn. and program coms. Harrisburg sect. 1967-68, auditing com. 1969-70), Am. Prodn. and Inventory Control Soc., Nat. Assn. Purchasing Mgrs., Am. Hellenic Ednl. Progressive Assn. Republican. Greek Orthodox. Club: Lancaster N.E. Rotary. Home: 163 Hamilton Rd Lancaster PA 17603 Office: 901 Wheatland Ave Lancaster PA 17603

KARSATOS, JAMES GUST, food co. exec.; b. Phoenix, Aug. 17, 1931; s. Gust and Doris (Wildman) K.; B.S., Ariz. State U., 1959; M.B.A., U. So. Calif., 1968; m. Valerie L. Kovach, Jan. 25, 1958; children—James Joseph, Kelly Ann. Accounting supr. Shell Oil Co., Los Angeles and San Francisco, 1959-62; accounting mgr. Norton Simon, Inc., Fullerton, Calif., 1962-68; controller Howmet Corp., Pomona, Calif., 1968-71; v.p. fin. Van de Kamps, Los Angeles, 1971-73; sr. v.p., chief adminstrn. officer, treas. Kern Foods, Inc., Industry, Calif., 1973—; dir. Fruit Nectars, Inc., Carolina Foods, Inc., West Indies Can, Kern Ranch, Inc.; cons. in field. Past dir. United Way, Los Angeles, mem. Western Region Adv. Bd., Town Hall Calif.; trustee N. Orange County Mus. Served in U.S. Army, 1954-56. Mem. Nat. Assn. Accountants, Fin. Execs. Inst., Commerce Assos., Los Angeles World Affairs Council, Old Guard Soc., Delta Sigma Pi. Clubs: Sunny Hills Racquet, Rotary Internat. Office: 13000 E Temple Ave Industry CA 91749

KARSTAEDT, ARTHUR RAY, tool and die mfg. co. exec.; b. Beloit, Wis., Jan. 12, 1927; s. Arthur R. and Marion E. (Conklin) K.; B.A., U. Wis., 1949; m. Virginia L. Sorensen, Sept. 20, 1947; children—Arthur R. III, Sarah A. Asst. to labor relations mgr. Ray-O-Vac Co., Madison, Wis., 1949-53, customer relations mgr., 1953-60; sales promotion mgr. Willson Products, Reading, Pa., 1960-63; mktg. mgr. Richard Bros. Punch, Detroit, 1964-69, v.p. mktg. 1977—; mktg. mgr. Pioneer Engring. & Mfg. Co., Warren, Mich., 1969-72; v.p. sales automotive products Irvin Industries, Inc., Madison Heights, Mich., 1973-77. Served with U.S. Army, 1945-46. Mem. Soc. Am. Value Engrs. (v.p. Detroit chpt., 1972-73), Engring. Soc. Detroit, Am. Soc. Safety Engrs., Sales-Mktg. Execs. Internat., Am. Mgmt. Assn., NAM, Common Cause (chmn. legis. contact 1976-77), U. Wis. Union (life), U. Wis. Alumni Assn. (life). Unitarian. Club: Masons. Home: 4135 Sandy Ln Birmingham MI 48010 Office: Richard Bros Punch Co 26400 Capitol Detroit MI 48239

KARSTEN, JOHN ALAN, electronics co. exec.; b. Oak Forest, Ill., Mar. 23, 1932; s. Ernst William and Elva Marie (Hueneke) K.; B.S. in Engring., UCLA, 1954; postgrad. U. So. Calif., 1958-62; m. Patricia Holley, Aug. 1, 1954; children—Steven, Holley. Sr. design engr. Burroughs Corp., Pasadena, Calif., 1957-62; program mgr. Consol. Systems Corp., Pomona, Calif., 1962-67; co-founder, dir., v.p. adminstrn. MSI Data Corp., Costa Mesa, Calif., 1967-73; pres. Karsten/Kastle Industries, Anaheim, Calif., 1973-75; co-founder, dir., exec. v.p., chief fin. officer Wespercorp, Tustin, Calif., 1975—. Served with U.S. Navy, 1954-57. Lic. pvt. pilot with multi-engine ratings. Mem. Am. Electronics Assn., Aerostar Owners Assn., Airplane Owners and Pilots Assn., Nat. Bus. Aircraft Assn. Lutheran. Office: 14321 Myford Rd Tustin CA 92680

KARTALIA, MITCHELL P., elec. equipment mfg. co. exec.; b. Yukon, Pa., Mar. 31, 1913; s. Peter and Julia (Juras) K.; E.E., U. Cin., 1940; m. Rebecca Dunham, Oct. 7, 1939; children—David E., Janet E., Diane S., Peter J., Mitchell J. With Am. Rolling Mill Co., Butler, Pa., 1939-40; with Square D Co., Park Ridge, Ill., 1940—, v.p., 1958-65, exec. v.p., 1965-68, pres. 1968-78, chief exec. officer, 1968—, chmn. bd., 1976—, also dir.; dir. Hobart Corp., Household Fin. Corp., Rexnord Inc. Recipient Golden Plate award Am. Acad. Achievement, 1972; Distinguished Alumnus award U. Cin. Coll. Engring., 1969; Merit award Nat. Assn. Elec. Distbrs., 1974. Mem. Nat. Elec. Mfrs. Assn. (bd. govs.), Ill. Mfrs. Assn. (dir.), Eta Kappa Nu. Clubs: Masons, Shriners. Home: 212 Biltmore Dr Barrington IL 60010 Office: Square D Co Executive Plaza Palatine IL 60067

KARVELIS, LEON J., JR., mcpl. fin. analyst; b. Bklyn., Dec. 10, 1942; s. Leon and Jennie K.; A.B. (scholar), Bklyn. Coll., 1964; M.B.A., Pace U., N.Y.C., 1974; m. Marie D'Ambrosia, June 6, 1964; 1 dau., Andria. Public fin. asso. White, Weld & Co., Inc., N.Y.C., 1969-73; asst. treas. public fin. Morgan Guaranty Trust Co., N.Y.C., 1973-75; v.p., founder, mgr. mcpl. research dept. Citbank N.A., N.Y.C., 1976-78; mgr., v.p., specialist mcpl. research dept. Merrill Lynch Pierce Fenner & Smith, Inc., N.Y.C., 1978—; tchr. gen. obligation mcpl. analysis Mcpl. Bond Club Bond Sch., N.Y.C., 1980; speaker; specialist in state and local govt. fin. and econs.; adv. to state and local govts. Former vice chmn. Community Dist. Planning Bd. 18, N.Y.C. Mem. N.Y. Mcpl. Analysts Group, Public Securities Assn., Mcpl. Fin. Officers Assn. (asso.). Roman Catholic. Club: Elks. Contbr. articles to profl. jours. and newspapers. Office: One Liberty Plaza New York NY 10080

KASCHAK, LILLIAN ANNE, fin. fund exec.; b. Plymouth, Pa.; d. Stanley and Mary Christine (Sinkiewicz) Javer; student Wyo. Sem., Dean Sch. Bus., 1946-47, Wilkes Coll., 1952-53; m. Joseph V. Kaschak; 1 son, Thomas J. Sr. clk. Prudential Ins. Co., Kingston, Pa., 1953-58; with advt. dept. Wyoming Valley Distbg. Co., Wilkes-Barre, Pa., 1968-69; adminstrv. mgr. Keystone Welfare & Pension Funds, Wilkes-Barre, 1969—; partner Kaschak & Slesinski, 1977—. Mem. Eastern Pa. Adminstrs. Assn. (sec.-treas. 1975-79), Tri-County Personnel Assn. (publicity chmn. 1976-78), Madam Curie Soc. Roman Catholic. Clubs: Quota (membership chmn. 1972-79), Wyoming Valley Ski. Home: 306 Stephanie Dr Plymouth PA 18651 Office: Keystone Welfare & Pension Funds 9 E Market St Wilkes-Barre PA 18701

KASCHUBE, GUNTHER A(UGUST), mech. engring. supr.; b. Grueneberg, Germany, Dec. 20, 1920; s. Max Ewald and Wanda Emma (Muennich) K.; came to U.S., 1957, naturalized, 1962; Mech. Engr., Ingenieurschule Berlin, 1954; m. Christel E. Trube, Oct. 16, 1948; 1 dau., Doris. Toolmaker apprentice prodn. plant, Germany, 1935-39, technician, 1939-41; pvt. trucker, Grueneberg, 1947-51; mech. design engr. E. Ger. Energy Bur., Berlin, 1951-55; draftsman, designer, mech. engr. B.D. Bohna, cons. engrs., Vancouver, B.C., Can., 1956-57, San Francisco, 1957-61; project design sect. supr. Pacific Gas & Electric Co., San Francisco, 1962—; cons. in field. Mem. nat. adv. bd. Am. Security Council, 1962—, founder Center for Internat. Security Studies; mem. Calif. Tax Reduction Movement; sustaining mem. Republican Nat. Com. Served with German Armed Forces, 1941-43, POW, 1943-47. Mem. ASME, Pacific Coast Elec. Assn., Project Mgmt. Inst., Orinda Assn. Lutheran. Clubs: U.S. Senatorial, Mercedes-Benz Am. (sec. pres. 1974-76). Home: 202 Overhill Rd Orinda CA 94563 Office: 77 Beale St San Francisco CA 94106

KASDORF, JOHN COLIN, investment cons.; b. Milw., Mar. 12, 1943; s. Clifford Carl and Jane Elizabeth (Henderson) K.; B.S., Northwestern U., 1965; M.B.A., U. Wis., 1971; m. Cheryl J. Nicks, June 21, 1969; children—Kurt Paul, David John. Investment analyst, counselor Heritage Investment Advisors, Milw., 1971-74; cons. Hewitt Assos., Milw., 1975-79; pres. Kaztex Financial, Wauwatosa, Wis., 1979—. Served to lt. comdr. USNR, 1965-69. Chartered fin. analyst. Mem. Soc. Chartered Fin. Analysts, Wis. Retirement Plan Profls., Milw. Fin. Analysts Soc., Northwestern Alumni Assn. (v.p. Milw. 1974). Home: 1738 Alta Vista Ave Wauwatosa WI 53213 Office: 7332 W State St Suite 4 Wauwatosa WI 53213

KASHUBARA, PETE ZACHARY, automobile co. exec.; b. Youngstown, Ohio, May 14, 1947; s. Pete and Virginia (Gagliano) K.; B.S. in Bus. Adminstrn., Youngstown State U., 1969; M.B.A., U. Detroit, 1979; m. Janet Irene Blum, July 8, 1978; 1 dau., Krystin; children by previous marriage—Pete, Laura, Kenneth. Pre-prodn. control programmer Ford Tractor ops. Ford Motor Co., Troy, Mich., 1970, analyst scheduling and parts control, 1970, engring. change coordinator, 1972, buyer tractor ops., Romeo, Mich., 1973-79, purchase analyst, Troy, 1979—. Served with U.S. Army, 1970-72; Vietnam. Democrat. Roman Catholic. Home: 112 Longford St Rochester MI 48063 Office: 2500 E Maple Rd Troy MI 48084

KASMAN, LOUIS PERRY, transp. co. exec.; b. Bklyn., Apr. 13, 1943; s. Elias and Florence (Dodes) K.; B.A., William Coll., 1964; m. Deborah Jean Kehl, Dec. 2, 1972. Dir. adminstrn. and mktg. Air Express Internat., N.Y.C., 1968-72; corp. dir. mktg. Shulman Transport Enterprises, Inc., Cherry Hill, N.J., 1972-75, also gen. mgr. Skycab Div.; v.p., mng. dir. Air Freight div. Allied Van Lines, Chgo., 1976-78; pres. U.S. Air Freight, Inc., Jamaica, N.Y., 1978—; cons. in field. Served with U.S. Army, 1966-68. Mem. Internat. Air Freight Agts. Assn. (dir.), Execs. Club Chgo., Nat. Def. Transp. Assn., Delta Nu Alpha. Jewish. Club: Wings (N.Y.C.). Author: The Small Package Air Freight Market, 1972; Helping the Customer Understand Total Cost of Distribution Economics, 1977; Professionalism in Air Freight Forwarding, 1978. Home: 85 Westwood Dr Westbury NY 11590 Office: 147-48 182d St Jamaica NY 11413

KASPER, THOMAS ALLEN, investment banker; b. Phila., Apr. 17, 1953; s. Thomas J. and Esther W. Kasper; B.A. magna cum laude, St. Lawrence U., 1975; M.B.A. in Fin. and Stats., U. Chgo., 1977. Asso., Shearson Loeb Rhoades Inc., N.Y.C., 1977-79; asso. Salomon Bros., N.Y.C., 1979-80, v.p., 1980—. Mem. Am. Econ. Assn., Am. Fin. Assn., Phi Beta Kappa. Republican. Home: 178 E 80th St New York NY 10021 Office: One New York Plaza New York NY 10004

KASPRICK, LYLE CLINTON, beverage co. exec.; b. Angus, Minn., Aug. 23, 1932; s. Max Peter and Mary (Taus) K.; B.S. in Bus. Adminstrn. magna cum laude, U. N.D., 1959; m. Harriet Susan Lydick, July 14, 1953; children—Susan, Michael, John; m. 2d, Kathleen M. Westby, June 4, 1977; 1 stepdau., Kristin Westby. Tax mgr. Arthur Andersen & Co., Mpls., 1959-69; v.p. Search Investments Corp., Mpls., 1969-77; financial v.p., treas. Tropicana Hotel and Country Club, Las Vegas, 1970-72; chief operating officer Key Pharms., Inc., Miami, Fla., 1972-76, dir., 1976—; dir. Search Investments Corp., 1973-77, Mo Am Co Corp., 1975-76; v.p. MEI Corp., Mpls., 1977—. Speaker before profl. and civic groups. Del. Republican Party dist. and city convs., 1964, 66, 68, 70. Served with USN, 1951-55. C.P.A., Minn. Mem. Am. Inst. C.P.A.'s, Minn. Soc. C.P.A.'s, Nat. Assn. Accountants, Am. Legion. Republican. Roman Catholic, K.C. Home: 7105 Heatherton Trail Minneapolis MN 55435 Office: 710 Marquette Ave Minneapolis MN 55402

KASS, FREDERICK (FRITZ) JOHN, JR., electronics co. exec.; b. Albany, N.Y., Nov. 5, 1942; s. Frederick J. and Audrey B. K.; B.S. in Mktg. and Accounting, Lehigh U., 1964; M.B.A. in Mktg., State U. N.Y. at Albany, 1970; student U.S. Naval War Coll., 1968, Armed Forces War Coll., 1979; m. Susan Wescott, June 19, 1971; children—Sam, Fred. Pres., Lehigh Valley Travel, Inc., 1962-64; pres. Aguna Areo, charter/flight sch., 1964-67; treas., controller Seiden Sound Co., Albany, 1968-70; founder, pres. Action Audio, Inc., Newburgh, N.Y., 1970—; treas., dir. Intercollegiate Broadcasting System, Inc.; instr., mem. adv. bd. Mt. St. Mary's Coll., 1978—; congl. info. officer and adv. Naval Acad., 1977—. Served to lt. comdr. USNR, 1964-67; Vietnam. Mem. U.S. Navy League (pres. Orand and Rockland council), Res. Officers Assn. (life), Navy Res. Assn. (life), West Point Officers Club, New Windsor C. of C. (treas., dir. 1974—), VFW, Alpha Kappa Psi, Iota Bega Sigma. Republican. Methodist. Clubs: Rotary (dir. local club), Middletown (N.Y.) Rifle and Pistol Club and Lodge. Pub. Jour. Coll. Radio, 1963-72. Home: 23 Sheldon Dr Cornwall NY 12518 Office: 339 Windsor Hwy Newburgh NY 12550

KASSAB, JOHN LOUIS, securities, fin. and ins. exec.; b. Syria, May 28, 1923; came to U.S., 1937, naturalized, 1943; S. Saíd A. and Estella H. (Hannah) K.; B.S., N.Y. U., 1949; m. Elizabeth D. Farmer, Jan. 13, 1951; children—Bruce R., Lori Jean. Ins. agt., mgr. Met. Life, N.Y.C., 1951-59; regional mgr. Conn. and Pa., Union Central Life, 1960-65; mgr. Prudential Ins. Co., San Francisco, 1966-78; regional v.p. Putnam Fin. Services, San Francisco, 1972-78; owner, operator G.B.A. Fin. Programs & Ins. Mktg. Co., San Francisco and Walnut Creek, Calif., 1978—; regional dir. Univ. Securities Corp., San Francisco and Walnut Creek, 1978—. Served with U.S. Army, 1943-46. Decorated Bronze Star; named Man of Yr., W.R.Y.T., Pitts., 1965; recipient Howard Cox award Union Central Life, 1965, Nat. Trophy award Prudential Ins. Co., 1970. C.L.U.; cert. fin. planner. Mem. San Francisco Gen. Agts and Mgrs. Com., Assn. C.L.U.'s, Internat. Assn. Fin. Planners, Am. Coll. C.L.U.'s (instr., pres. chpt. 1977-78). Republican. Clubs: N.Y. U.; Racquetball (Walnut Creek). Home: 707 Wimbledon Rd Walnut Creek CA 94598 Office: 1243 Alpine Rd Suite 111 Walnut Creek CA 94598

KASSABAUM, GEORGE EDWARD, architect; b. Atchison, Kans., Dec. 5, 1920; s. George A. and Dorothy (Gaston) K.; B. Arch., Washington U., 1947; m. Marjory J. Verser, Jan. 22, 1949; children—Douglas, Ann, Karen. Faculty, Washington U., St. Louis, 1947-50; asso. firm Hellmuth, Yamasaki & Leinweber, St. Louis, 1950-55, prin. Hellmuth, Obata & Kassabaum, 1955—. Dir. Tower Grove Bank. Bd. dirs. YMCA, St. Louis, 1970—, Downtown St. Louis Inc., St. Louis Symphony; trustee Washington U., St. Louis. Served with USAAF, 1944-45. Named Mo. Architect of Yr., 1978; registered profl. architect, Mo., Kans., Pa., Ohio, Fla., D.C., Mass., N.Y., Alaska, Wis., Calif., Md., Colo., N.C., Tex., N.J. Fellow AIA (pres. St. Louis chpt. 1964, nat. pres. 1968-69, chancellor 1978); mem. Sociedad Colombiana de Arquitectos (hon.), La Sociedad de Arquitectos Mexicanos, Royal Archtl. Inst. Can. (hon.), Sigma Chi. Clubs: Noonday, Racquet, Media, Old Warson, St. Louis Country, Bogey Country (St. Louis). Prin. archtl. works include: Terminal, Dallas-Ft. Worth Airport, Equitable Bldg., St. Louis, Smithsonian Air-Space Mus., Washington, Squibb Hdqrs., Lawrenceville, N.J., Duke Hosp., Durham, N.C., McAuto Computer Center, St. Louis, Conv. Center, San Francisco, U. Riyad, Riyadh, Saudi Arabia, Riyadh Airport, Saudi Arabia, Exxon Research and Engring. Facilities, Clinton, N.J. Contbr.

articles to profl. jours. Home: 761 Kent Rd Saint Louis MO 63124 Office: 100 N Broadway Saint Louis MO 63102

KASSER, IVAN MICHAEL, forest products cons.; b. Budapest, Hungary, Dec. 9, 1940; came to U.S., 1950, naturalized, 1956; s. Alexander Sandor and Elisabeth (Aranyi) K.; B.S., M.I.T., 1960, M.S., 1961; Dr.Engring., U. Grenoble, France, 1964; M.B.A., Harvard U., 1968; m. Lynn Von Kersting, Feb. 2, 1974. Project engr. Technopulp de Ingeneria, Madrid, 1964-66; sr. fin. analyst W. R. Grace & Co., N.Y.C., 1968-69, dir. mgmt. info. systems chem. group, 1969-70, mgr. fin. planning and evaluation Indsl. Chem. Group, 1970-71; pres. Technopulp, Inc., Montclair, N.J., 1971, Imaco, Inc., Montclair Forest Products Invesment Co., 1972; chmn. bd. Booher Lumber Co., Lafayette, N.Y., 1972—, N.E. Forest Products, Inc., Bernards Bay, N.Y., 1979—, Sundowneer Mgmt. Co., Montclair, 1975—; forest products cons. in fin., gen. mgmt., tech., N.Y.C., 1971—. Bd. dirs. Am. Hungarian Found., 1972; trustee Actors' Studio, 1977. Registered profl. engr., N.J. Mem. Empire State Forest Products Assn. (dir. 1979, v.p. 1979), TAPPI, Am. Chem. Soc., Technique de l'Industrie Papetiere, Nat. Hardwood Lumber Assn. Contbr. articles to profl. jours.; patentee in field. Home: 812 Fifth Ave New York NY 10021 Office: 26 Park St Montclair NJ 07042

KASSIN, HAROLD HOWARD, lawyer, corp. exec.; b. Bklyn., Dec. 2, 1927; s. Louis and Anna (Gorelick) K.; student Columbia, 1948; J.D., U. Miami, 1951 m. Delores Jean Robey, Nov. 27, 1971; children—Kimberly Ann, Dawn Elizabeth. Admitted to Fla. bar, 1951, U.S. Supreme Ct. bar, 1955, other fed. bars; pvt. practice law, Miami; sec. Kassin Investment Corp., Miami, Flagler Ponce Realty Corp., Miami; partner Kensington Assos., Miami. Served with AUS, 1946-47. Mem. Am., Dade County bar assns., Fla. Bar, Fla. Real Estate Broker, Nu Beta Epsilon. Democrat. Home: 1921 NE 188th St North Miami Beach FL 33179

KASTLER, BERNARD ZANE, natural gas co. exc.; b. Billings, Mont., Oct. 30, 1920; s. B.Z. and Elsie (Grossman) K.; student U. Colo., 1940-41; LL.B. with high honors, U. Utah, 1949; m. Donna Irene Endicott, July 24, 1948; children—Lynn, Kerry Sue. Admitted to Utah bar, 1949, Mont. bar, 1948; pvt. practice law, Salt Lake City, 1949-52; counsel Salt Lake City Civil Service Commn., 1949-50; with Mountain Fuel Supply Co., Salt Lake City, 1952-58, sec., asst. treas., gen. counsel, 1958-68, v.p. finance, treas., 1968-72, pres., 1972-74, 76—, chief exec. officer, 1974—, chmn. bd., 1976—; chmn. bd. Entrada Industries, Inc., Mountain Fuel Resources, Inc., Wexpro Co.; dir. Albertson's, Inc., Bonneville Internat. Corp., Intermountain Health Care, Inc., 1st Security Corp.; mem. Utah Ho. of Reps., 1963-64. Bd. dirs. Mountain States Legal Found. Served with USNR, World War II. Mem. Salt Lake City C. of C. (bd. govs. 1967—, v.p. govt. and pub. affairs council 1968—, pres. 1977-78), U. Utah Alumni Assn., Am., Utah, Salt Lake County, Mont., Fed. Power bar assns., Ind. Natural Gas Assn., Pacific Coast Gas Assn. (chmn. 1980), Rocky Mountain Oil and Gas Assn., Order of Coif, Phi Kappa Phi, Phi Delta Phi. Conglist. Mason, Kiwanian (pres. 1967-68). Contbr. articles to profl. jours. Office: Mountain Fuel Supply Co 180 E 1st South St Salt Lake City UT 84139 Mailing address: PO Box 11368 Salt Lake City UT 84139

KATO, TAIKI, bank exec.; b. Tokyo, June 10, 1931; s. Yasunobu and Hata K.; Master of Law, Tokyo U. Sch. Law, 1960; 1 son, Hiroo. With The Bank of Tokyo, Ltd., 1953—, mgr. loans and discounts dept., 1970-71, with N.Y. agy., 1971-76, dep. gen. mgr., 1972-76, acting gen. mgr. funds and forex div., Tokyo, 1976-78, gen. mgr. Asia and Oceania div., Tokyo, 1978-80, pres., dir. Bank of Tokyo Trust Co., 1980—; dir. Shimano Corp., Tohlease Corp., Bank of Tokyo Trust Co. (Cayman), Ltd. Clubs: Nippon (dir.), Wall St. Office: 100 Broadway New York NY 10005

KATZ, ALEX JOSEPH, mfg. co. exec.; b. Trenton, N.J., Mar. 24, 1920; s. Moritz and Gizella K.; student N.J. State U., Hillwood Lakes, 1938-39; m. Muriel Bank, Aug. 22, 1943; children—Merrill, Karen, James E. Salesman, Super Sagless Corp., Tupelo, Miss., 1946-48, plant mgr., 1948-51, exec. v.p., 1951-56, pres., 1956—; dir. B.H. Bunn Co., Alsip, Ill., Cornwell Industries, South Park, Maine. Served with USAF, 1940-45. Decorated Air medal, D.F.C. Mem. Am. Mgmt. Assn. Patentee in field. Home: 5375 Piping Rock Dr Boynton Beach FL 33437 Office: PO Box 197 Tupelo MS 38801

KATZ, DAVID EVANS, exec. search mgmt. cons.; b. Malden, Mass., Apr. 22, 1952; s. Hyman and Ruth Diane (Weiner) K.; B.A., Northeastern U., 1975, M.Ed., 1976. Staff asso. Northeastern U., Boston, 1974-76; dir. coop. edn. C. W. Post Center, L.I. U., 1976-78; asst. dir. profl. recruiting Touche Ross & Co., Boston, 1978-79; sr. cons. Bartholdi & Co., Wellesley Hills, Mass, 1979-81, Peat, Marwick, Mitchell & Co., Boston, 1981—. Mem. Gamma Phi Kappa Alumni Assn. (dir.). Republican. Author: (with P. B. Farnsworth) A Report of Northeastern University Faculty Attitudes on Collective Bargaining, 1975. Home: 53 Gordon St Malden MA 02148 Office: One Boston Pl Boston MA 02108

KATZ, JOSEPH MORRIS, diversified mfg. exec.; b. Iampole, Russia, July 7, 1913; s. Samuel and Sarah (Averbach) K.; brought to U.S., 1914; student U. Pitts., 1931-34; m. Agnes Roman, 1937; children—Marshall, Andrea Katz Plesset. Founder, chmn. bd. Papercraft Corp., Pitts., 1945—; chmn. bd. Knomark, Inc., Knomark Can. Ltd., Kim Color Corp., LePage's, Inc., Gloucester, Mass., Am. Universal Inc., Modern Ortho Corp. Mem. Pa. Gov.'s Bus. Adv. Council, 1972-74; mem. State Planning Bd., Pa., 1973—. Bd. dirs., v.p. Allegheny Trails Council Boy Scouts Am., Pitts., Civic Light Opera, Pitts.; trustee U. Pitts., also chmn. visitors Faculty Arts and Scis., Grad. Bus. Sch.; trustee Katz Found., Montefiore Hosp., Pitts. Symphony Soc., Nat. Found. Ileitis and Colitis., Am. Jewish Com. Named Businessman of Year, Pitts., 1965; Salesman of Year, 1969; recipient Herbert Lehman Israel award, 1970, Human Relations award Am.-Jewish Com. Pitts., 1972; Brotherhood award NCCJ, 1975; Emanuel Spector award United Jewish Fedn. Greater Pitts., 1977. Clubs: Westmoreland Country, Concordia, Standard (Pitts.); Harmonie (N.Y.C.). Home: Gateway Towers Pittsburgh PA 15222 Office: Papercraft Corp Papercraft Park Pittsburgh PA 15238

KATZ, MARTIN, mktg. researcher; b. N.Y.C., June 22, 1939; s. Alfred L. and Johanna (Bauer) K.; B.S., N.Y. U., 1961; M.B.A., CUNY, 1969; m. Eleana Master, Jan. 2, 1962; children—David C., Gary A. Sr. research analyst Singer Corp., N.Y.C., 1966-68; group research asso. Gen. Foods Corp., White Plains, N.Y., 1968-72; mgr. market research and analysis Xerox Corp., Rochester, N.Y., 1972-75; v.p., mgr. mktg. research Chase Manhattan Bank, N.Y.C., 1975—; guest lectr. Rutgers U., 1977. Served with U.S. Army, 1962-63. Mem. Am. Mktg. Assn., Bank Mktg. Assn. Home: 6 Byron Ln Larchmont NY 10538 Office: 1211 Ave of Americas New York NY 10036

KATZ, MATTHEW, chemist, chem. research exec.; b. N.Y.C., Mar. 20, 1929; s. Benjamin and Frieda (Hausman) K.; B.A. cum laude, Yeshiva U., N.Y.C., 1949; M.A., Columbia U., N.Y.C., 1950; Ph.D. (fellow) in Polymer Chemistry, Poly. Inst. Bklyn., 1964; m. Bernice Fay Weisberg, Oct. 24, 1954; children—Henni, Pynchas. Chief chemist research and devel. Harte & Co., Bklyn., 1955-57; exec. v.p. Minitronics Corp., N.Y.C., 1957-58; mgr. tantalum capacitor dept. Astron Corp., East Newark, N.J., 1958-61, dir. research and devel., 1961-62; mgr. chem. sect. Central Materials Lab., Gen. Precision, Inc., Kearfott div., Little Falls, N.J., 1962-64; tech. dir. electro-tech. products div. Sun Chem. Corp., Nutley, N.J., 1964-66; pilot plant mgr. Genset div. Tenneco Chemicals, Inc., Carlstadt, N.J., 1966-67, tech. dir. gen. foam div., 1967-69; tech. dir. Herculite Protective Fabrics Corp., N.Y.C., 1969-72; sr. scientist Plastics Inst., Centre for Industrial Research, Technion City, Haifa, Israel, 1972-77; gen. mgr. and dir. Chomerics Israel Ltd., Technion City, 1978—; mng. dir., dir. research Internat. Polymer Corp. Ltd., Technion City, 1976—; lectr. Rupin Acad., Emek Hefer, Israel, 1975—; dir. Nat. Med. Implant Co., Haifa. Trustee, Crown Heights Yeshiva Sch., 1968-77. Recipient Meritorious Service award Crown Heights Yeshiva Sch., 1969. Mem. Am. Chem. Soc., Soc. Plastics Engrs., Israel Plastics Soc., Israel Energy Assn., ASTM, Sigma Xi, Phi Lambda Upsilon. Contbr. articles on polymer chemistry to tech. jours.; patentee in field. Home: 23 Einstein St Haifa Israel Office: Internat Polymer Corp Technion City Haifa Israel

KATZ, NORMAN, apparel mfg. co. exec.; b. Zwickau, Germany, Apr. 10, 1925; s. Paul and Dora (Ungar) K.; came to U.S., 1940, naturalized, 1944; B.A. in Econs., Columbia U., 1943; children—Ira and Stephen (twins). Exec. v.p. John Weitz Jrs., Inc., N.Y.C., 1947-52; pres. Norman Katz, Inc., N.Y.C., 1952-58; pres. At Home Wear, Inc., N.Y.C., 1959-75; pres. I. Appel Corp., N.Y.C., 1976—; instr. econs. CCNY, 1947-51. Trade chmn. Fedn. Jewish Philanthropies, 1957-71. Served with AUS, 1943-46. Clubs: Saugatuck Harbor Yacht (Westport, Conn.); Harrow U.S.A. (N.Y.C.). Home: 10 Waterside Plaza New York NY 10010 Office: 99 Madison Ave New York NY 10016

KATZMAN, MAURICE, fin., mktg., tech. exec.; b. Detroit, Dec. 24, 1934; s. Samuel and Sofie K.; B.S. in Mech. Engring., Lawrence Inst. Tech., Southfield, Mich., 1956; B.S. in Elec. Engring., 1960; M.B.A. in Fin. and Mktg., U. Mich., 1961; m. Barbara A. Halprin, Aug. 15, 1961; children—Sheri, Steve, Alyssa. Cons. engring. supr. Migdel & Layne Cons. Engrs., 1954-57; project mgr. missile and space vehicles div. Chrysler Def. Co., 1957-60; Western regional field mgr. Inland Steel Corp., 1960-62; sr. sales engr. Consol. Electrodynamic Corp., 1962-64; Eastern regional mgr. Cook Electric Co., 1964-65; sr. mktg. rep. Ampex Corp., Redwood City, Calif., 1965-68; nat. automotive industry mgr. Univac div. Sperry Rand, 1968-71, Digital Equipment Corp., 1971-73; Eastern and central regional mgr. Bendix Corp. Advanced Tech. div., 1973-75; Midwest regional mgr. Sykes Datatronics, Inc., Southfield, Mich., 1975-79, sr. mgr. systems engring. labs., 1979—. Served with USAF, 1957-58, USAFR, 1958-63. Mem. Engring. Soc. Detroit, Jewish Community Center. Jewish. Clubs: Southfield Athletic, B'nai B'rith, Investment, Masons. Home: 30200 Northgate Dr Southfield MI 48076

KAU, FRED, computer corp. exec.; b. Honolulu, Feb. 6, 1948; s. George Sung Pui and Dorothy (Fujii) K.; A.S.E.T., Honolulu Community Coll., 1970; student U. Hawaii, 1979—. Computer mechanic Lockheed Missiles & Space Co.; Honolulu, 1969-73; computer programmer East-West Population Inst., Honolulu, 1973-75; computer field engr. Formation, Inc., Honolulu, 1975-78; pres. Internat. Hawaii, Inc., Honolulu, 1978—. Active YMCA. Democrat. Lutheran. Home: 1810 University Ave Honolulu HI 96822 Office: PO Box 8446 Honolulu HI 96815

KAUFFMAN, DEAN, data processing cons.; b. Stuttgart, Ark., Mar. 8, 1947; s. Earnest D. and Marguerite (Cobb) K.; B.Mus., U. Ark., 1969; Woodrow Wilson fellow, N.Y. U. fellow, N.Y. U., 1969-72. Computer programmer and analyst Automatech Graphics Corp., N.Y.C., 1972-75; telecommunications systems programmer Dean Witter & Co., N.Y.C., 1975-76, Chem. Bank, N.Y.C., 1976-79; systems cons. wholesale money transfer Freyberg Systems Assos., Inc., N.Y.C., 1979—. Mem. Assn. Computing Machinery, Phi Beta Kappa. Republican. Episcopalian. Office: Freyberg Systems Assos Inc 20 Exchange Pl New York NY 10005

KAUFFMANN, HOWARD C., oil co. exec.; b. Tulsa, Feb. 25, 1923; s. Howard C. and Polly Ethyl (Myers) K.; B.M.E., U. Okla., 1943; m. Suzanne McMurray, Nov. 5, 1944; children—Craig, Robert Lane, Kristine, Douglas, Scott. Petroleum engr., prodn. mgr. Carter Oil Co., 1946-57; ops. mgr. Internat. Petroleum Co., Ltd., Peru and Colombia, 1958-62; asst. regional coordinator Latin Am., Exxon Corp., 1962-64; dir., v.p., then exec. v.p., pres. Internat. Petroleum Co. Ltd., Coral Gables, Fla., 1964-66; pres., dir. Esso Inter-Am., Inc., Coral Gables, 1966-68; exec. v.p., dir., then pres. Esso Europe, Inc., London, 1968-73; sr. v.p., dir. Exxon Corp., N.Y.C., 1974-75, pres., dir., 1975—; dir. Chase Manhattan Corp., United Technologies Corp., Chase Manhattan Bank, N.A.; bd. dirs. Am. Petroleum Inst. Bd. dirs. United Fund Greater N.Y., Econ. Devel. Council N.Y.C., N.Y. C. of C. and Industry; mem. adv. com. on bus. programs The Brookings Instn.; chmn. Nat. Adv. Council on Minorities in Engring.; trustee Nat. Fund for Minority Engring. Students, Inst. Advanced Study, Princeton; vice-chmn. bd. govs. corp. fund for performing arts Kennedy Center; mem. council Internat. Exec. Service Corps. Served to lt. (j.g.) USNR, World War II. Mem. Nat. Planning Assn. (co vice-chmn. exec. com. changing internat. realities), Pi Gamma Delta, Tau Beta Pi, Sigma Tau, Pi Tau Sigma, Tau Omega. Baptist. Office: Exxon Corp 1251 Ave of Americas New York NY 10020

KAUFMAN, A(LBERT) N(ICK), mfg. exec.; b. Warsaw, Ind., May 16, 1924; s. Emanuel Kaufman; student Ind. U., 1948; m. Gwendolyn Ione, May 1, 1943; children—Victoria Joyce, Timothy N. With Arnolt Corp., Indpls., 1942-62, v.p. mfg., dir., 1953-62; pres. K-T Corp., Shelbyville, Ind., 1962—, Kaufman Enterprises, Inc., Mo. Metal Shaping Co., St. Louis; group v.p. splty. products Alco Standard Corp.; sec.-treas. Kaufman Energy Devel. Corp., Indpls. Bd. pensions, v.p., mem. investment com. Ch. of God, Anderson, Ind. Served with USN, World War II. Mason (Shriner). Home: 6220 N Chester Ave Indianapolis IN 46220 Office: 850 Elston St Shelbyville IN 46176

KAUFMAN, ALEX, plastics and chem. co. exec.; b. Lemburg, Poland, Sept. 9, 1924; s. Isadore and Bronislava (Halpern) K.; Degree in Chemistry, Stuttgart Poly Inst. (Germany); m. Amalia Fuss, Sept. 6, 1951; children—Bernice, Mark, Irene. Came to U.S., 1950, naturalized, 1955. With Hatco Chem. div. W.R. Grace & Co., Fords, N.J., v.p., 1961-62, pres., 1962-69, 78—, v.p. parent co., 1967, exec. v.p., 1968-78, also dir., pres. Grace Petrochems. Inc., P.R., 1969-78; pres. Kalex Chem. Products Inc., 1978—, Hatco Chem. Corp., 1978—. Bd. dirs. Raritan Bay Health Services Corp., 1979—. Mem. Soc. Chem. Industry, Soc. Plastics Industry, Chem. Mfrs. Assn., Newcomen Soc., Woodbridge (N.J.) C. of C. Home: 57 Century Ln Watchung NJ 07060 Office: King George Post Rd Fords NJ 08863

KAUFMAN, BARRY MORTON, elec. engr., mfg. co. exec.; b. San Francisco, Aug. 19, 1934; s. Edward and Florence Gladys (Blue) K.; B.E.E., U. Calif., Berkeley, 1958; m. Audrey Herson, Jan. 11, 1962; children—Debra, Steven. Pres., MuWestern, Electronics Co., San Carlos, Calif., 1963-67; dir. engring. Vega Electronics Co., Santa Clara, Calif., 1968-71, ITT Mobile Communications Co., Clark, N.J., 1972-73; v.p. engring., corp. dir. RFL Industries, Inc., Boonton, N.J., 1973—. Mem. IEEE (sr.), Radio Club Am., Audio Engring. Soc. Republican. Jewish. Contbr. articles to tech. jours.; patentee telecommunications field. Home: 30 Cheryl Rd Pinebrook NJ 07058 Office: RFL Industries Inc Powerville Rd Boonton NJ 07005

KAUFMAN, GERALD RAY, fin. cons.; b. Louisville, Ky., Mar. 5, 1946; s. Garland Washington and Elizabeth Ferguson K.; B.S.C., U. Louisville, 1976; m. Lillian Bland, Sept. 24, 1976; 1 dau., Tracye Kaufman. With Dun & Bradstreet, Louisville, 1966-69; city revision analyst Humana, Inc., Louisville, 1969-72; accounts mgr. Vt. Am. Corp., Louisville, 1972-78; pres. Kaufman Enterprises, Inc., Louisville, 1978—. Pres., Louisville-Jefferson County Health and Welfare Council, 1972; bd. dirs. Op. Push, 1979-80, Center for Youth Alternatives, 1979-80. Mem. Ky. Minority Bus. Assn. (treas. 1979-82), Nat. Assn. Accts., Inst. Internal Auditors, Am. Mgmt. Assn. Democrat. Methodist. Home: PO Box 281 Russell Ln LaGrange KY 40031 Office: 2318 Maple St Louisville KY 40211

KAUFMAN, HARVEY, telecommunications equipment co. exec.; b. Boston, Nov. 10, 1931; s. Hyman M. and Sophie (Spear) K.; A.B., Harvard U., 1953. Product mgr. Gen. Electric Co., Auburn, N.Y., 1964-69, mgr. overseas bus. devel., Syracuse, N.Y., 1969-72; eastern regional mgr. NEC Telephones, Inc., Glen Cove, N.Y., 1972-77, dir. large systems mktg., Melville, N.Y., 1977-79; v.p. applications engring. Telecom Equipment Corp., Long Island City, N.Y., 1979—. Served with Signal Corps, U.S. Army, 1953-55. Mem. IEEE, Petroleum Electric Supply Assn. Club: Harvard of L.I. Home: 14 Sycamore Rd Glen Cove NY 11542 Office: 48-40 34th St Long Island City NY 11101

KAUFMAN, IRVING, engring. co. exec.; b. N.Y.C., Jan. 21, 1924; s. Samuel and Mary (Jagorda) K.; B.E.E., Coll. City N.Y., 1950; postgrad. Bklyn. Poly. Inst., 1953; m. Ruth Lillian Soicher, Sept. 12, 1949; children—Richard Brian, Joan Ellen, John Stephen. Vice pres. Color Sales Co., Lynbrook, N.Y., 1951; div. dir. Airborne Instruments Lab., Deer Park, N.Y., 1964-66; v.p., gen. mgr. Gen. Instrument Corp., Hicksville, N.Y., 1966-71, group v.p. def. and engring. products, 1972; pres., chief exec. officer Northrop Page, Vienna, Va., 1972—; pres., chief exec. officer Communications Corp. Am., Washington; sr. v.p. Loral Electronic Systems, Yonkers, N.Y. Trustee, United Fund L.I. Mem. IEEE, Air Force Assn., Assn. Old Crows, Am. Mgmt. Assn., Am. Ordnance Assn. Home: 11 Woody Ln Westport CT 06880 Office: 999 Central Park Ave Yonkers NY 10704

KAUFMAN, JOHN GILBERT, JR., aluminum co. exec.; b. Balt., Oct. 14, 1931; s. John Gilbert and Emma Louise (Langville) K.; B.S. in Civil Engring., Carnegie Inst. Tech., 1953, M.S., 1954; M.S. in Mech. Metallurgy, Carnegie Mellon U., 1975; m. Ruth Carson Hobbs, June 13, 1953; children—John Gilbert III, Ruth Ann, Keith Carlin. With Aluminum Co. of Am., Pitts., 1954-80, mgr. engring. properties, 1971-75, mgr. tech. devel., 1976-79, mgr. fabricating metallurgy, 1979-80; dir. research Anaconda Aluminum Co., Louisville, 1980—. Bd. dirs. Allegheny Valley Concert Assn., 1965-80, pres., 1973-75; treas. Peoples Library, Pitts., 1973-80. Fellow Am. Soc. Metals, ASTM (award of Merit); mem. Sigma Xi, Tau Beta Pi. Contbr. 80 articles on metallurgy and properties of aluminum alloys to profl. jours. Home: 5117 Shadow Wood Ln Prospect KY 40059 Office: Anaconda Aluminum Tower Bldg Main St Louisville KY 40232

KAUFMAN, MICHAEL DAVID, duplication machinery mfg. co. exec.; b. Bklyn., Apr. 7, 1941; s. Abraham and Shirley (Blank) K.; B.M.E., Poly. Inst. Bklyn., 1962, M.S. in Indsl. Mgmt., 1967; m. Susan G. Zipkis, June 30, 1962; children—Robert Jay, Craig Douglas. Mgr. advance mfg. planning Grumman Aircraft Engring. Corp., Bethpage, N.Y., 1963-67; with Xerox Corp., Stamford, Conn., 1967—, edn. div. controller N.Y. ops., 1967-68, dir. corp. product and strategy analysis, 1978-80; pres. Centronics Data Computer Corp., 1980—; lectr. M.B.A. program U. Conn. Mem. Am. Inst. Indsl. Engrs. (sr.), ASME, Nat. Soc. Profl. Engrs. (affiliate), Poly. Inst. N.Y. Alumni Assn. (asso. dir.). Home: 120 Echo Hill Dr Stamford CT 06903 Office: Stamford CT 06904

KAUFMAN, SIDNEY LOUIS, uniform mfg. corp. exec.; b. Little Rock, Jan. 30, 1927; s. Meyer and Fannie (Bennett) K.; student U.S. Maritime Acad., 1945-46, Washington U., 1948; m. Eileen S. Schwartz, Nov. 23, 1947; children—Lorin Stephanie, Wendy Arlin. Eastern sales mgr. Schwartz Tailoring Co., Cin., 1949-51; nat. sales mgr. Schwartz-Robert Corp., Cin., 1951-55; nat. sales mgr., Pettibone Bros. Mfg. Corp., Cin., 1955-73, pres., 1973—; pres. Midwest Mktg. Assos., 1963—, Proven Premium Products Co., 1965—; hon. vice consul of Spain for Ohio; sec. Cin. Consular Corps. Bd. dirs. Big Bros. Assn., Cin.; staff Congressman Thomas Luken, Hamilton County, 1977-78; fin. chmn. Richard Celeste, Lt. Gov. Ohio, 1978. Mem. Nat. Assn. Uniform Mfrs., Council on World Affairs, Cin. Mktg. Council, Internat. Consular Acad., Cin. Consular Corps, Zeta Beta Tau. Democrat. Jewish. Clubs: Losantville Country, Camargo Racquet, World Trade, Rockdale Temple, Masons. Home: 8635 Arborcrest Dr Cincinnati OH 45236 Office: 23 E 77th St Cincinnati OH 45216

KAUFMAN, SUSAN JANE, broadcast, advt. exec.; b. Hubbell, Mich., Feb. 13, 1944; d. Joseph R. and Marie (LaChance) K.; student Marquette U., 1965; B.A., Mich. Technol. U., 1976; M.S., Ind. State U., 1981. AP intern Green Bay (Wis.) Press-Gazette, 1963; reporter Milw. Sentinel, 1965-66, Rockford (Ill.) Morning Star, 1966-68, Green Bay Register, 1968-71; sports info. dir. U. Wis., Green Bay, 1975, WMPL-AM/FM, 1976-77; ops. coordinator WGGL-FM, Houghton, Mich., 1977—, also founding partner UP Media, 1976; asst. gen. mgr. WAAC Radio 13, Terre Haute, Ind.; instr. journalism Ojibway Indian Tribe. Asso. Women's Inst. for Freedom of the Press; v.p. Hubbell Sch. Bd. Recipient award for outstanding feature of year Ill. Med. Soc.; 10 awards Women's Press Assn. Wis., 1970, AP awards, 1966. Mem. Mich. Assn. Sch. Bds., NOW (media reform com.). Clubs: Milw. Press, Wabash Valley Press, Bus. and Profl. Women's. Editor: Battered Women, 1976; Women in Labor, 1976. Home: 201 Crawford 207 Terre Haute IN 47807 Office: WAAC Radio 13 643 Ohio St Terre Haute IN 47807

KAUFMANN, ARTHUR, business exec.; b. Denver, 1913; married. With Redeker-Stanley, Ahlberg & Wilch, Denver, to 1941: controller Gilbane Bldg. Co., 1941-45; with Arthur Andersen & Co., 1945-56; with Kuhlman Corp., Birmingham, Mich., 1956—, treas., 1965-75, exec. v.p., 1965-70, exec. v.p. fin., 1970-72, pres., 1972-75, pres., 1975-79, chief exec. officer, 1975—, chmn. bd., 1979—, also dir. C.P.A. Office: Kuhlman Corp Box 288 Birmingham MI 48012

KAUFMANN, DWIGHT WINSTON, steel co. exec.; b. Pitts., Jan. 4, 1919; s. Frank Joseph and Doris Francis (Standley) K.; B.S. in Metallurgy, Pa. State U., 1940; m. Mildred Joyce Bach, Aug. 3, 1946; children—John, Patricia. Metallurgist, Crucible Steel Co., Syracuse, N.Y., 1940-50, Pitts., 1950-52; sales mgr. Rem-Cru Titanium Inc., Midland, Pa., 1952-57; asst. v.p. sales Crucible Steel Co., Pitts., 1958-68, v.p. marketing, 1969; Washington rep. Crucible Stainless Steel div. Colt Industries, Inc., 1970, v.p. mktg. Midland, 1970-77, pres., 1977—; instr. metallurgy Syracuse U., 1946-47. Republican. Presbyn. Club: Duquesne (Pitts.). Home: 1616 Tier Dr Pittsburgh PA 15241 Office: Midland Ave Midland PA 15059

KAUFMANN, HANS ALEX, gen. agt.; b. Hannover, Germany, Nov. 12, 1923; came to U.S., 1938, naturalized, 1943; s. Julius and Irma L. (Levy) K.; B.S. in Elec. Engring., La. State U., 1948; m. Betty Waldman, Sept. 5, 1948; children—Donald, Janet Kaufmann Black. Gen. agt. Franklin Life Ins. Co., 1950-58; v.p. La. Cos., 1958-63; gen. agt. Occidental Life Ins. Co. of Calif., Baton Rouge, 1963—; owner Kaufmann & Co. Ins. Agy. Chmn. Israel Bond Drive, 1970-71; bd. dirs. Jewish Welfare Fedn., 1973. Served with U.S. Army, 1943-46. Decorated Purple Heart. Recipient nat. quality award, 1955-58, nat. sales achievement award, 1965-80. Mem. Million Dollar Round Table (life), Baton Rouge Assn. Life Underwriters (pres., 1970, Man of Yr. 1978), Am. Contract Bridge League (life master), Baton Rouge Bus. and Estate Planning Council (treas.), Pres.'s Council, Leading Producers Club of Occidental Life. Club: City of Baton Rouge. Home: 3720 S Lakeshore Dr Baton Rouge LA 70808

KAUFMANN, MARK STEINER, banker; b. N.Y.C., Dec. 3, 1932; s. Milton L. and Elsa S. (Steiner) K.; B.S. cum laude in Bus. Adminstrn., Lehigh U., 1953; m. Carole Richard, June 16, 1957; children—Jon Richard, Susan Helen. Vice pres., dir. mktg. Standard Fin. Corp., N.Y.C., 1958-64; sr. v.p., dir. Milberg Factors, Inc., N.Y.C., 1964-73; v.p., dir. corp. devel. Chase Manhattan Bank, N.Y.C., 1973—; dir. Chase Manhattan Capital Corp., Chase Nat. Corp. Services, Chase Comml. Corp. Co-chmn. banking div. Fedn. Jewish Philanthropies; past treas. bd. trustees Calhoun Sch., N.Y.C.; co-chmn. banking div. Anti-Defamation League; trustee Temple Israel, N.Y.C. Served as 1st lt. USAF, 1953-55. Recipient Human Relations award Anti-Defamation League, 1973. Mem. Am. Arbitration Assn., Beta Gamma Sigma, Lambda Mu Sigma, Pi Gamma Mu, Omicron Delta Kappa. Democrat. Clubs: Old Oaks Country, Lehigh (dir.) (N.Y.C.). Home: 124 W 79th St New York NY 10024 Office: 1 Chase Manhattan Plaza New York NY 10081

KAUSHIK, SURENDRA KUMAR, economist; b. Malsisar, Jhunjhunu, India, June 21, 1944; came to U.S., 1970, naturalized, 1980; s. Laxminarain Sharma and Ratni Chaturvedy; B.Com., U. Rajashan (India), 1965, M.A. in Econs., 1967; Ph.D. in Econs., Boston U., 1976; m. Helena Pokornicki, Sept. 12, 1973. Research asst., instr. Inst. Econ. Growth, Delhi, India, 1968-70; teaching fellow, research asst., sr. teaching fellow., lectr., Boston U., 1971-75; instr. Northeastern U., Boston, 1972-73; lectr. Boston State Coll., Lowell Technol. Inst., 1973-74; asst. prof. Babson Coll., Wellesley, Mass., 1976-81; asso. prof. Westchester campus Pace U., White Plains, N.Y., 1981—; cons. UN, 1976-77. Mem. Am. Econ. Assn., Am. Fin. Assn., AAUP, Western Econ. Assn., Eastern Econ. Assn., Atlantic Econ. Soc. Condr. research internat. banking and fin.; editor: Banking, Money Markets and Monetary Policy, 1980. Office: Pace U Lubin Grad Sch Bus 55 Church St White Plains NY 10601

KAVANAGH, KEVIN PATRICK, ins. co. exec.; b. Brandon, Man., Can., Sept. 27, 1932; s. Martin and Katherine (Power) K.; B.Comm., U. Man., 1953; m. Elizabeth Mesman, July 1963; children—Sean K., Jennifer T. With Great-West Life Assurance Co., Winnipeg, Man., 1953—, v.p. U.S. ops., Denver, 1973-76, v.p. group ops., Winnipeg, 1976-78, sr. v.p. group ops., 1978, pres., chief exec. officer, 1978—, also dir. Bd. govs. Man. Mus. Man and Nature; bd. dirs. St. Boniface Gen. Hosp. Research Found., Inc., Winnipeg Symphony Orch. Mem. Canadian Life and Health Ins. Assn. Inc. (dir.). Clubs: Men's Can. of Winnipeg (exec. com.); Manitoba; Winnipeg Winter. Office: 60 Osborne St N Winnipeg MB R3C 3A5 Canada

KAVANAGH, ROGER PIERCE, JR., home builder; b. Greenwich, Conn., Aug. 27, 1917; s. Roger Pierce and Eleanor (Geffem) K.; student Princeton, 1936-38; m. Jeanette Rusovich, June 5, 1943; children—Basil John, Roger Pierce III. Mgr., N.M. Timber Co., 1938-40; salesman Am. Houses, Inc., N.Y.C., 1945-53; pres. Kavanagh, Smith & Co., Greensboro, N.C., 1953-66, Westminster Co., 1966—; dir. N.C. Nat. Bank. Mem. N.C. Conservation and Devel. Bd., 1960-64; state chmn. Radio Free Europe, 1966; mem. N.C. Sediment Control Commn., 1974—. Served with Ordnance Dept., AUS, 1941-45. Decorated Bronze Star medal. Mem. Nat. Assn. Home Builders, Greensboro C. of C. (dir.). Home: 605 Sunset Dr Greensboro NC 27408 Office: 405 Parkway Dr Greensboro NC 27405

KAVAZANJIAN, JOHN DANIEL, computer mfg. co. exec.; b. Long Beach, N.Y., Jan. 22, 1951; s. Edward and Amelia Bertha (Dryer) K.; S.B. in Chem. Engring., M.I.T., 1972, S.M. in Mgmt., 1974. Prodn. control mgr. original equipment mfg. Digital Equipment Corp., Westminster, Mass., 1974-77; bus. mfg. mgr. PDP8 mfg., 1977-79, bus. mfg. mgr. internal equipment, 1979, product group bus. mgr. comml. original equipment mfg. products, Merrimack, N.H., 1979—. Loaned exec. Montachusett United Fund, 1978. Mem. Fitchburg C. of C. (dir. 1979), Delta Upsilon (dir. tech. chpt. 1975—). Armenian Orthodox.

KAVEE, ROBERT CHARLES, brokerage co. exec.; b. N.Y.C., Aug. 9, 1934; s. Julius and Kate K.; A.B. in Math., U. Rochester, 1956; M.S. in E.E., Columbia U., 1959; postgrad. U. Pa., 1974; m. Donna Helene Auld, Jan. 31, 1959; children—Andrew L., Patti M., Stacie R. Def. space electronics and systems engr. ITT Labs. and Sperry Rand Systems Group, Nutley, N.J. and Great Neck, N.Y., 1959-66; NSF sr. research fellow Poly. Inst. Bklyn., 1966-68; sr. systems specialist ITT Data Services, Paramus, N.J., 1968-70; mgr. ops. research ITT World Hdqrs., N.Y.C., 1970-75; mgr. instnl. applications devel. Merrill Lynch Pierce Fenner & Smith, N.Y.C., 1975—. Mem. Rep. Town Meeting, Greenwich, Conn. Mem. Inst. Quantitative Research in Fin., Bond Quantitative Group, Am. Fin. Assn., IEEE. Club: Old Greenwich Yacht. Designer early cardiac ballisto-cardiogram, early cardiac pacemaker, 1959. Home: 51 Mary Ln Riverside CT 06878 Office: Merrill Lynch Pierce Fenner & Smith 1 Liberty Plaza New York NY 10080

KAVELMAN, DOUGLAS ALAN, physician, pharm. co. exec.; b. Iroquois Falls, Ont., Can., Apr. 5, 1932; came to U.S., 1976; s. John Henry and Florence May (Lautenschlager) K.; M.D., U. Toronto, 1956; m. Anne Grieves Ward, Dec. 29, 1956; children—Carol Lynn, Robert D., Diane B. Intern, Hamilton (Ont.) Gen. Hosp., 1956-57, resident, 1957-62; resident also resident Westminster Hosp., London, Ont.; asst. med. dir. Confedn. Life Assn., Toronto, 1964-65; med. dir. Ames Co. Can., Ltd., Toronto, 1965-67; med. dir. Miles Labs., Ltd., Toronto, 1967-76, U.S. Ames div., Elkhart, Ind., 1976-78, v.p. med. affairs, 1978—. Bd. dirs. Ont. Assn. Mentally Retarded, 1970-76, v.p., 1975-76. Fellow Royal Coll. Physicians and Surgeons Can.; mem. Pharm. Mfrs. Assn. Can. (chmn. med. sect. 1973-74), Proprietary Assn. Can. (dir. 1975-76), Canadian Med. Assn., N.Y. Acad. Scis., Am. Diabetes Assn., Am. Soc. Clin. Pathologists (asso.). Home: 3021 Crabtree Ln Elkhart IN 46514 Office: Ames Div Miles Labs Inc PO Box 70 1127 Myrtle St Elkhart IN 46515

KAVENEY, CHARLES ALTON, bldg. material distbn. co. exec.; b. Erie, Pa., Feb. 20, 1921; s. Charles Albert and Georgia Eleanor (Owen) K.; B.A., Pa. State U., 1943; m. Mary Elizabeth Werts, Aug. 1, 1944; children—Cynthia Alice, Deborah Ruth. With Remington Rand Co., 1946-48, Clary Multiplier Co., 1948-50; with Nat. Gypsum Co., 1950-62, sales mgr., 1960-62; sales devel. gypsum products Johns Manville Corp., 1962-65; founder, 1965, thereafter pres. Stanton Supply Co., Malvern, Pa.; pres. Camco Supply Co., 1967—, R.J. Hanson Supply Co., 1979—; cons. constrn. systems fireproofing, sound and insulation. Chmn. East Whiteland (Pa.) Twp. Planning Commn., 1956-63; mem. East Whiteland Twp. Bd. Adjustments, 1966-75. Served with U.S. Army, 1942-46. Decorated Purple Heart. Mem. Phila. Bldg. Materials Dealers Assn. (past pres.). Republican. Presbyterian. Home: 109 Ashton Way West Chester PA 19380 Office: 56 Sproul Rd Malvern PA 19355

KAWAI, ZENJIRO, pub. co. exec.; b. Hiroshima, Japan, May 20, 1929; s. Hisataro and Shizuko (Nagatomi) K.; student Keio U., Tokyo, 1948-53; m. Haruko Fujita, Nov. 2, 1957; children—Yasuhide, Yoshio. With Kajima Corp., 1953-64; pres. Kajima Inst. Pub. Co. Ltd., Tokyo, 1980—; pres. Yaesu Book Center Co., Ltd., 1977—; dir. Chutetu Bus Co. Ltd., Hiruzen Kanko Co. Ltd., Chugoku Kotu Co. Ltd., Goei Kogyo Co. Ltd., Chutetu Syoji Co. Ltd., Hiruzen Co. Ltd., KK Trading Co. Ltd., Fukuyama-kai. Trustee Japan Book Pub. Assn., Seishi-Sha; chmn. Jyohoku High Sch. PTA. Served with Japanese Navy, 1945. Clubs: Mita-kai (Keio U.); Fukuyama-kai, Rotary (Tokyo); Keio. Home: 402-22-11 5-chome Roppongi Minato-ku Tokyo Japan Office: 5-13 6-chome Akasaka Minato-ku Tokyo Japan

KAWAKITA, NAGAMASA, film co. exec.; b. Tokyo, Japan, Apr. 30, 1903; s. Daijiro and Koko (Ito) K.; student U. Peking, 1921-23; m. Kashiko Takeuchi, Oct. 10, 1929; 1 dau., Kazuko. Founder, pres. Towa Co. Ltd., 1928—, dir., 1938—; pres. Toho Internat. Co. Ltd., 1969—; dir. Osawa Co. Ltd., Toho Co. Ltd. (all Tokyo). Film export com. Ministry of Internat. Trade and Industry, Japan. Decorated Legion of Honor (France); Order of Commendatore (Italy); medal of Honor with Blue Ribbon, Order Sacred Treasure (Japan). Mem. Fgn. Film Importers and Distbrs. Assn. Japan (pres. 1958—). Clubs: Tokyo, American. Home: 2-2 Yukinoshita Kamakura Japan Office: 2-2 Ginza Tokyo Japan

KAWALKOWSKI, FRANK JOHN, JR., real estate exec.; b. San Francisco, May 12, 1930; s. Frank J. and Lillian (Gianotti) K.; A.B., Stanford U., 1952. Co-founder, pres. Damon Raike & Co., San Francisco, 1959—. Served to lt. (j.g.), USCG, 1952-54. Mem. San Francisco C. of C., Bankers Club, World Trade Club. Clubs: St. Francis Yacht, N.Y. Yacht. Olympic. Office: 120 Montgomery St San Francisco CA 94104

KAY, DONALD JOHN, engring. and service co. exec.; b. Chgo., June 19, 1928; s. John Lawrence and Mary (Dzubinski) Kwiatkowski; student Allied Inst. Tool Design; M.E., Chgo. Tech. Coll.; m. Marion Zivan, Sept. 4, 1954; children—Gregory, Kathleen, Bradley. Tool designer Falcon Tool & Engring., Chgo., 1951-52; project mgr. Tammen & Dennison, Chgo., 1952, then field mgr., salesman, to 1960; pres., dir. Kay & Assos., Inc., Mt. Prospect, Ill., 1960—. Served with U.S. Army, 1946-47. Club: Rolling Green Country. Office: 800 E Northwest Hwy Mount Prospect IL 60056

KAY, HERBERT JACK, redevel. agy. exec.; b. N.Y.C., Aug. 16, 1919; s. Harry and Rose (Weiner) K.; A.A., U. Fla., 1938, B.S., 1940; postgrad. Emory U., 1940-41, Manhattan Coll., 1941-42, N.Y. U., 1946-47; M.A., Ohio State U., 1959; postgrad. Boston U., 1969-70; m. Jeanne Sandra Young, Jan. 1, 1943; children—Carol (Mrs. Allan Monosoff), Robin (Mrs. Terry Covel), Dennis Michael. Engring. draftsman Gibbs & Hill, cons. engrs., N.Y.C., 1941-42, M.W. Kellog Co., N.Y.C., 1942, 46; mgr. H.J. Kay Gen. Contractor, Miami Beach, Fla., 1947-51; commd. 2d lt. U.S. Army, 1940, advanced through grades to col., 1967; chmn. rev. bd., dep. comdr. U.S. Army Phys. Disability Agy., Washington, 1967-68; chief ind. tng. div., dep. chief of staff, personnel Dept. Army, Pentagon, 1966-67; dir. research and oral communications Info. Sch., Dept. Def., Ft. Benjamin Harrison, Ind., 1964-66; comdr. 2d Arty. Bn., 2d F.A., Ft. Sill, Okla., 1963-64; ret., 1968; mgr. employment and employee devel. Quincy Shipbldg. div. Gen. Dynamics (Mass.), 1968-73, corp. mgr. Equal Opportunity Program, St. Louis, 1973-75; corp. mgr. Mgmt. Devel. and Communications, 1975-77; pres. Acupuncture Treatment Centers, Inc., Miami, Fla., 1977-78; exec. adminstr. Miami Beach Redevel. Agy., 1979—; instr. speech U. Md. at Heidelberg, Germany, 1961-63. Commr. Boy Scouts, Ft. Sill, Okla., 1963-64; commr. Ft. Sill Little League Football, 1963-64; mem. adv. bd. Positive Program for Boston, NAACP, 1969-73; mem. Gov.'s South Shore Adv. Bd. to Mass. Commn. Against Discrimination, 1971-73; bd. dirs. Work, Inc. sheltered workshop for handicapped, Quincy, 1971-73; mem. Amigos de Ser Jobs for Progress, 1973-75; mem. bd. St. Louis Am. Jewish Com., 1976-77, mem. adv. bd. Miami, 1980—. Served with AUS, 1942-46. Decorated Legion of Merit, Bronze Star with oak leaf cluster; Joint Services Commendation medal; Army Occupation medal (Germany). Mem. Ohio State Alumni Club (chpt. treas. 1971-73), Am. Soc. Tng. and Devel., Am. Bus. Communications Assn., Internat. Platform Assn., Nat. Assn. Uniformed Services, Assn. U.S. Army (chpt. pres. 1980—), Ret. Officers Assn., Nat. Assn. Housing and Redevel. Ofcls., Speech Communications Assn., DAV, Phi Beta Delta. Home: 330 N Hibiscus Dr Miami Beach FL 33139 Office: 335 Alton Rd North Miami Beach FL 33139

KAYE, ALEX ROBERT (SANDY), mfg. and mktg. co. exec.; b. N.Y.C., Dec. 24, 1936; s. Saul and Vilma K.; B.B.S., Coll. City N.Y., 1958; m. Farida Karoon, June 27, 1954; 1 dau., Lorie. Div. mgr. Sears Roebuck & Co., 1956-58; v.p., br. mgr. Field Enterprises Edn. Corp., San Mateo, Calif., 1958-76; pres., chmn. bd. Energy Assos., Latham, N.Y., 1966-67, Land N'Sea Craft Inc., San Jose, Calif., 1969-74, Porta-Bote Internat., Menlo Park, Calif., 1974—; cons. mktg. to industry; chmn. bd. San Francisco Better Bus. Bur. Sales Ethics Com., 1968-69; mem. Am. Boat and Yacht Council, 1969-71; bd. dirs. San Mateo Better Bus. Bur., 1971-72. Mem. Concerned Citizen Com., Menlo Park. Recipient Fisher Body Craftsman's Guild award Gen. Motors, 1951, Soc. Automotive Engrs. award Coll. City N.Y., 1955, Mahareshi award City of Palo Alto (Calif.), 1978. Mem. Big. Bro. Orgn. Club: Commonwealth.

KAYE, BARRY, ins. co. exec.; b. N.Y.C., May 20, 1928; s. Herbert and Blanche (Sabin) K.; C.L.U., Am. Coll. Life Underwriters, 1966; m. Carol Golison, Mar. 16, 1962; children—Fern L., Alan L., Howard S. Pres., Barry Kaye, Inc., 1968—, Profl. Corp. Programs, Inc., 1969—, Profl. Exec. Programs, Inc., 1970—; owner Barry Kaye Assos., Beverly Hills, Calif., 1970—. Mem. faculty Practicing Law Inst., 1969—; lectr. U. Calif., Los Angeles, 1970—. Mem. adv. bd. Eddie Cantor Charitable Found., 1973—. Bd. govs. Diamond Circle of Hope; bd. trustees City of Hope. Fellow, Ben Gurion Soc., Ben Gurion U. of the Negev. Recipient Founders award Diamond Circle City of Hope, 1972; Man of Year award Gen. Agts. and Mgrs. Conf., 1965, 66, 67. Mem. Western Pension Conf., Beverly Hills C. of C., Am. Soc. Pension Actuaries, Am. Soc. C.L.U.'s, NCCJ (trustee). Mem. B'nai B'rith. Clubs: Presidents of the Thailians, Uncles of Vista del Mar. Author: How to Save a Fortune on Your Life Insurance. Office: One Century Plaza 2d Floor 2029 Century Park E Los Angeles CA 90067

KAYE, HAROLD, mfg. co. exec.; b. N.Y.C., Aug. 20, 1945; s. Joseph and Fanny (Feldberg) K.; B.A., CCNY, 1973; cert. Nat. Credit Office Sch., 1966; cert. merchandising technique, 1973; m. Tina Korotzer, Aug. 25, 1968; children—Shari, Adam, Michael. Credit mgr. Ingersoll Rand, N.Y.C., 1967; asst. credit mgr. Bulova, Flushing, N.Y., 1968-70; credit mgr. Remington Aluminum, Hicksville, N.Y., 1970, fin. mgr., 1971, adminstrv. mgr., 1972, dir. mktg., 1974-78, asst. to pres., 1978, v.p., 1979—. Active in wetlands preservation. Served with N.Y. N.G., 1965-70. Recipient drummer awards Bldg. Supply News, 1975, 78. Republican. Jewish. Club: K.P. Home: 939 Gerry Ave Lido Beach NY 11561 Office: 100 Andrews Rd Hicksville NY 11801

KAYE, NORMAN, entertainer, business exec.; b. Detroit, Sept. 22, 1922; s. John and Maude (Oakdale) Kaaihue; A.A., Albion Coll., 1943; doctorate in arts and letters, U. China, Hong Kong; m. Patricia Allen, 1946; children—John, Spencer, Tracy Burton; m. 2d, Cheryle Jeanne Thompson, Sept. 27, 1964; children—Richard Warren Karl, Donald Norman, Alexander James. Appeared in movies including Cha Cha Cha Boom, 1956, Bop Girl, 1957, various night clubs and TV shows as Perry Como, Colgate, Red Skelton Show, Dinah Shore Show, Red Buttons Show, Budweiser and Texaco Star Theatre; with Mary Kaye Trio, 1946-64; pres. Norman Kaye Real Estate Co., Las Vegas, Nev., 1957—, MKT Music Pub. Co., 1961—, Lanson Rec. Co., 1962—, K.B. Mining Co., 1963-64, House of Zog Music, 1963—, Vic Vegas Music Pub. Co., Western Empire Petroleum Co., I.C.D.C. Realty, Inc.; officer Chanem Travel, Hilton Hotel, Mosden Travel.; dir. Am. Bank of Commerce. Condr., Las Vegas Ambassador-Young People's Community Sing-Out; chmn. emeritus Las Vegas Community Theatre; pres. Combined Health Agencies, State of Nev., 1978; chmn. Underprivileged Children's Soc., 1978; chmn. Orem Grayson's Valley Hosp., Las Vegas, 1978; nat. rep. Nev. Multiple Sclerosis Soc., Retinitis Pigmentosa Soc.; bd. dirs. Drug Abuse Council, Heart Assn., Nev. Bicentennial Bd. U. Nev. at Las Vegas, Rosa de Loma Hosp. Served with USAAF, 1942-46. Decorated Bronze Star. Named Poet Laureate, State Nev. Mem. ASCAP (awards 1962-65, 67, 71), Screen Actors Guild, AFTRA, Nat. Assn. Security Dealers. Club: Jockey (chmn. bd.) (Las Vegas). Composer songs including: Let's Love, Why Did You Leave Me, I'm in Love, Losing You, Toreador, Throw a Dime My Way (ofcl. 1965 March of Dimes campaign song), Have a Heart, Lend a Hand (internat. theme song Variety Clubs World), many others. Office: 4813 Paradise Rd Las Vegas NV 89109

KAYE, ROBERT MARTIN, Realtor; b. Long Branch, N.J., Mar. 12, 1937; s. Irving and Jean (Weisman) K.; student U. Conn., 1954-58, Boston Coll., 1958-59; m. Nancy Roberts; children—Jonathan Steven, Steven Andrew, Kimberly Jean. Pres., Planned Residential Communities, Inc., West Long Branch, N.J.; mem. advisory bd. N.J. Nat. Bank. Mem. N.J. Shore Builders Assn. (past dir.), Inst. Real Estate Mgmt. (dir. N.J. chpt.), Young Pres. Orgn. Home: 21 Sheraton Ln Rumson NJ 07760 Office: 60 Monmouth Park Hwy West Long Branch NJ 07764

KEAN, ROBERT W., III, real estate developer; b. N.Y.C., Jan. 30, 1948; s. Robert Winthrop and Luz M. K.; student U. Calif., Santa Barbara, 1966-70; m. Patricia Patterson, Sept. 12, 1970; 1 son, Robert Winthrop IV. Exec. v.p. Caleb Devel. Corp. subs. Realty Transfer Co., Elizabeth, N.J., 1977—. Home: Upper Kennels Farm Gladstone NJ 07934 Office: Caleb Devel Corp One Elizabethtown Plaza Elizabeth NJ 07207

KEANE, ROGER J., fin. co. exec. Pres., chief exec. officer First Texas Fin. Corp. Office: PO Box 64889 Dallas TX 75206*

KEANEY, JOSEPH CHARLES, JR., mfrs.'s rep.; b. Pitts., May 15, 1929; s. Joseph Charles and Mary Elizabeth (Cummings) K.; B.A., Denison U., 1951; m. Sally Elizabeth Coutts, Apr. 16, 1955; children—Kathleen Elizabeth, Mary Claudia, Patricia Eileen, Joseph Charles III. Partner, J.C. Keaney & Sons, Pitts., 1951-63, v.p., treas. J.C. Keaney & Sons, Inc., 1963-69, pres., 1969—; vice chmn. Glass Industry Award Com., 1978, chmn., 1979. Mem. Upper St. Clair (Pa.) Bd. Sch. Dirs., 1974—, v.p., 1978-79, pres., 1979. Mem. Am. Ceramic Soc., Soc. Glass Tech. (U.K.). Republican. Presbyterian. Clubs: Duquesne, St. Clair Country, Masons (32 deg.), Shriners. Home: 222 Trotwood Dr Upper St Clair PA 15241 Office: 101 Pennsylvania Blvd Pittsburgh PA 15228

KEARNEY, RICHARD JAMES, chem. co. exec.; b. Kansas City, Mo., Aug. 25, 1927; s. Emmett Leo and Irene Elizabeth (Ruddock) K.; B.S. in Chem. Engring., U. Mich., 1951; m. Caroline Hamilton Archer, Sept. 19, 1953; children—Caroline Hamilton, Richard James. Chem. purchasing agt. Hercules, Inc., Wilmington, Del., 1954-62; chmn. bd., pres., sr. v.p. Kearney Chems. Inc., Tampa, Fla., 1962—. Served with USNR, 1945-46, AUS, 1951-53; Korea. Mem. Am. Chem. Soc., Sigma Chi. Episcopalian. Clubs: U. Mich. Pres.'s, Tampa Yacht and Country. Office: 5201 W Kennedy Tampa FL 33609

KEARNS, DAVID TODD, mfg. co. exec.; b. Rochester, N.Y., Aug. 11, 1930; s. Wilfred M. and Margaret May (Todd) K.; B.A., U. Rochester, 1952; m. Shirley Virginia Cox, June 1954; children—Katherine, Elizabeth, Anne, Susan, David Todd, Andrew. With IBM Corp., 1954-71, v.p. market ops., data processing div., to 1971; with Xerox Corp., 1971—, group v.p. info. systems, 1972-75, group v.p. in charge Rank Xerox and Fuji Xerox, 1975-77, exec. v.p. in charge internat. ops., 1977, pres., chief operating officer, 1977—, also dir.; dir. Rank Xerox Ltd., Fuji Xerox, Ltd., Time, Inc. Mem. Pres.'s Commn. on Exec. Exchange; bd. visitors Duke U. Grad. Sch. Bus.; chmn. bd. trustees U. Rochester; trustee Stamford (Conn.) Hosp., Inst. Aerobics Research; chmn. nat. bd. dirs. Jr. Achievement; bd. dirs. Nat. Urban League, Nat. Action Council for Minority Engrs.; adv. council Grad. Sch. Bus. Stanford U.; chmn. U.S. council Internat. Yr. of Disabled Persons. Served with USNR, 1952-54. Address: Xerox Corp Stamford CT 06904

KEARNS, FREDERICK RONALD, aircraft mfg. co. exec.; b. Quyon, Que., Can., Mar. 11, 1924; s. Thomas J. and Inex Mary (Whelan) K.; student St. Patrick Coll., Ottawa U., 1945-46, McGill U. Sch. Commerce, 1949; m. Elizabeth Black, July 3, 1948; children—Sandra, Michael, John, Stephen, Jane. With Canadair Ltd., Montreal, 1949—, exec. v.p. 1960-65, pres., chief exec. officer, 1965—, also dir.; dir. Asbestos Corp. Ltd. Served with RCAF, 1942-45. Mem. Fin. Execs. Inst., Can. German C. of C. (dir.), Can. Assn. Latin Am. (bd. govs.), Air Industries Assn. Can. (dir.), Can. China Trade Council (dir.). Clubs: Mount Bruno Country, Royal Ottawa Golf, Mount Royal; Wings (N.Y.); Mid-Ocean (Bermuda). Office: PO Box 6087 Montreal PQ H3C 3G9 Canada

KEARNS, WILLIAM MICHAEL, JR., investment banker; b. Orange, N.J., June 26, 1935; s. William Michael and Doris Mae (Hodgkinson) K.; A.B., U. Maine, 1957; postgrad. Boston Coll. Law Sch., 1957-58; A.M., N.Y. U., 1960, postgrad., 1960-64; m. Patricia Ann Wright, Aug. 17, 1957; children—William Michael III, Susan Elizabeth, Kathleen Anne, Michael Patrick, Elizabeth Anne. With Chase Manhattan Bank, N.Y.C., 1958-59; security analyst Hayden Stone & Co. Inc., N.Y.C., 1960-62; assso. institutional sales and syndicate dept. Kuhn, Loeb & Co., Inc., N.Y.C., 1962-64, asst. v.p., 1964-66, v.p., 1966-68, sales mgr., 1968-69, gen. partner, 1970-77; mng. dir. Lehman Bros. Kuhn Loeb Inc., 1977—; dir. N.J. Realty Co., Morristown; dir., chmn. fin. com. SRI Corp., Branchville, N.J. Mem. faculty Coll. Bus. Adminstrn. Fairleigh Dickinson U., 1959-68; instr. security analysis N.Y. Inst. Finance, 1961-67; adj. prof. Grad. Sch. Bus. Adminstrn., N.Y. U., 1971-72. Trustee, Morris Mus. Arts and

Scis.; mem. N.J. Republican Fin. Com. Served with USMCR, 1955-61. Mem. Securities Industry Assn. (minority capital com. 1978—, exec. com. N.Y. dist. 1970—, vice chmn. 1973-74, chmn. 1974), Nat. Assn. Security Dealers (corp. fin. com. 1976-80), New Eng. Soc., Investment Assn. N.Y. (v.p. 1970), Beta Theta Pi, Kappa Phi Kappa. Clubs: Univ. (asst. treas., council), Bond, Econ., Down Town Assn. (N.Y.C.); Morris County Golf (gov. 1976—, treas. 1978—) (Convent, N.J.); Monday (Morristown); Skytop (Pa.). Home: Village Rd New Vernon NJ 07976 Office: 55 Water St New York NY 10041

KEATING, CORNELIUS FRANCIS, broadcasting exec.; b. Boston, Aug. 3, 1925; s. Cornelius Francis and Mary (Grey) K.; A.B., Harvard, 1947, LL.B., 1950; children—Cecily, Gregory, David, Christopher, Elisabeth. Admitted to N.Y. bar, 1951; atty. Thayer & Gilbert, N.Y., 1951-53, Life Ins. Assn. Am., 1953-55, Columbia Records, 1955-57, gen. atty., 1957-58; gen. mgr. Columbia Record Club, 1958-60, v.p., gen. mgr., 1960-67; pres. CBS Direct Mktg. Services (div. CBS) (now Columbia House), N.Y.C., 1967-79; pres. CBS Columbia Group, 1979—; dir. Nat. Bus. Lists, Inc. Trustee Rheedlen Found. Served to ensign USNR, 1943-46. Mem. Direct Mail Mktg. Assn., Asso. 3d Class Mail Users (dir.), Harvard Law Sch. Assn. N.Y., Confrerie des Chevaliers du Tastevin, Commanderie de Bordeaux. Club: Harvard of New Canaan. Home: 1161 Ponus Ridge New Canaan CT 06840 Office: 51 W 52d St New York NY 10019

KEATING, FRANK J., paper co. exec.; b. Phila., Jan. 2, 1928; s. Joseph Gerald and Alice (Quinn) K.; student Londonderry Coll., No. Ireland; children—Carolyn M., Mary E., Frank J. With Daring Paper Co. div. Kardon Industries, Inc. Phila., 1946-71, successively truck loader, shipping clk., asst. shipper, shipper, prodn. scheduler, prodn. mgr., asst. to gen. mgr. United Container Co., 1957-58, asst. to pres. Daring Paper Co., 1958-60, v.p., gen. mgr., 1960-71, exec. v.p., also v.p. parent co., exec. v.p. Morris Sales Service Corp., KFC Fibre, Inc.; now pres. Keating Fibre Inc., Keating Fibre Internat., Inc., Converters Internat. Inc. Mem. Chester County Conservation Com. Served with USNR, 1944-46. Mem. Am. Mgmt. Assn., Downingtown C. of C., Pa. Water Pollution Control Assn., Am. Paper Inst., Fibre Box Assn., TAPPI, Nat. Council Stream Improvement, Montgomery County C. of C., Internat. Platform Assn. Clubs: Whitemarsh Valley Country; Phila. Aviation Country. Home: 614 Meadow Rd Abington Twp Huntingdon Valley PA 19006 Office: Whitemarsh Plaza 15 Ridge Pike Conshohocken PA 19428

KEATING, STEPHEN FLAHERTY, ret. corp. exec.; b. Graceville, Minn., May 6, 1918; s. Luke J. and Blanche (Flaherty) K.; B.S., U. Minn., 1940, J.D., 1942; m. Mary E. Davis, Dec. 14, 1945; children—Stephen, Elizabeth, Thomas, Mary. Admitted to Minn. bar, 1942; spl. agt. FBI, Norfolk, Va., Detroit, 1942-43; asso. Otis. Faricy & Burger, St. Paul, 1946-48; mgr. mil. contracts, aero div. Mpls. Honeywell Regulator Co., 1948-54, divisional v.p., 1954-56, v.p., 1956-61, exec. v.p., 1961-65; pres. Honeywell Inc., 1965-74, chmn., 1974-78, vice-chmn., 1978-80; dir. Gen. Mills, Inc., Honeywell, Inc., Toro Co., PPG Industries, Donaldson Co., Econs. Lab., Inc., INCO Ltd.; dir., chmn. Fed. Res. Bank Mpls. Chmn. bd. trustees Mayo Found.; chmn. Minn. State Arts Bd.; pres. Minn. Bus. Partnership. Served as air combat intelligence officer USNR, 1943-46. Mem. Order of Coif. Clubs: Minneapolis, Woodhill. Home: 688 Hillside Dr Wayzata MN 55391 Office: 1930 Midwest Plaza Bldg Minneapolis MN 55402

KEATINGE, RICHARD HARTE, lawyer; b. San Francisco, Dec. 4, 1919; A.B. with honors, U. Calif. at Berkeley, 1939; M.A., Harvard, 1941; J.D., Georgetown U., 1944. Sr. economist, sr. indsl. specialist WPB, Washington, 1941-44; admitted to D.C. bar, 1944, N.Y. bar, 1945, Calif. bar, 1947; sr. partner Keatinge, Pastor & Mintz and predecessor firms, 1948-79, Reavis & McGrath, Los Angeles, 1979—; spl. asst. atty. gen. State of Calif., 1964-68; mem. Calif. Law Revision Commn., 1961-68, chmn., 1965-67; public mem. Adminstrv. Conf. U.S., 1968-74. Trustee Coro Found., 1965-73; trustee, mem. exec. com. U. Calif. Berkeley Found., 1973—, v.p., 1978—. Fellow Am. Bar Found. (life); mem. Am. Law Inst., Am. Bar Assn. (nat. sec. jr. bar conf. 1949-50, mem. ho. of dels. 1974—, standing com. resolutions 1973-74, council adminstrv. law sect. 1961-64, 65-69, 74-78, chmn. sect. 1967-68, mem. commn. on law and economy 1976-78, vice chmn. 1977-78, council mem. econs. of law practice sect. 1974-75, mem. spl. com. housing and urban devel. law 1968-73, vice chmn. adv. commn. on housing and urban growth 1974-77, gov. 1978-79), Inter-Am. Bar Assn., Internat. Bar Assn., State Bar Calif. (del. conf. dels. 1966-67, 77—, mem. exec. com. public law sect. 1976—), Los Angeles County Bar Assn. (chmn. taxation sect. 1966-67, mem. housing and urban devel. law com. 1971—, arbitration com. 1974—, fair jud. election practices com. 1978—, new quarters com. 1979—, exec. com. law office mgmt. sect. 1977—), Am. Judicature Soc., Assn. Bus. Trial Lawyers (gov. 1974-79, pres. 1978-79), Lawyers Club Los Angeles, Am. Arbitration Assn. (nat. panel arbitrators 1950—, com. to maintain diversity jurisdiction 1978—), Phi Beta Kappa. Episcopalian. Home: 1141 S Orange Grove Pasadena CA 91105 Office: 6th Floor 700 S Flower St Los Angeles CA 90017

KEAY, JAMES WILLIAM, banker; b. Manley, Iowa, Nov. 16, 1921; s. William J. and Valborg (Biorn) K.; B.A. in Econs., U. Colo., 1947; M.B.A., Northwestern U., 1948; grad. Rutgers U. Grad. Sch. Banking, 1956, Harvard Advanced Mgmt. Program, 1964; m. Frances Lee Oglesby, Mar. 20, 1954; children—Martha Evelyn, James William, Stuart Enslie. With Republic Nat. Bank, Dallas, 1949—, asst. cashier, 1953, asst. v.p., 1953-56, v.p., 1956-61, sr. v.p., 1961-63, mem. exec. com., 1962—, exec. v.p. loans, 1963-65, exec. v.p. adminstrn., 1965, pres., 1965-74, chmn., chief exec. officer, 1974—; vice chmn. bd., dir. Republic of Tex. Corp., 1974—; dir. United Fidelity Life Ins. Co., Austin Industries, Inc., Dallas Power & Light Co., Gen. Am. Oil Co. Tex., Gen. Automotive Parts Corp. Bd. dirs. State Fair of Tex. Served with U.S. Army, World War II; ETO, MTO. Mem. Pi Gamma Mu. Lutheran (elder). Clubs: Augusta Nat. Golf, Idlewild, Brook Hollow Golf, City, Dallas, Terpsichorean, Preston Trail Golf, Petroleum, Dallas Country (Dallas). Office: PO Box 225961 Dallas TX 75265

KEBO, COLLIN K., moving and storage co. exec.; b. Denson, Ark., May 5, 1943; s. Frank and Opal K.; B.B.A., Gustavus Adolphus Coll., 1965; M.A., U. Minn., 1971; children—Collin B., Mark Andrew. Supr. personnel Control Data Corp., Mpls., 1966-71; dir. indsl. relations Schult Homes Corp., Middlebury, Ind., 1971-77; dir. employee relations Eltra Corp., Toledo, 1977-78; v.p. personnel Mayflower Corp., Indpls., 1978—. Project bus. cons. Jr. Achievement. Mem. Am. Mgmt. Assn., Indpls. Personnel Assn., Am. Soc. Personnel Adminstrn. Office: PO Box 107B Indianapolis IN 46206

KECK, MARY JANE, banker; b. Bklyn., May 4, 1939; d. Frederick Albert and Marion (Flaherty) K.; B.A., Manhattanville Coll., 1961; M.A., Fordham U., 1969; postgrad. N.Y. U. Tchr., adminstr. Soc. of the Sacred Heart, 1961-71; office mgr. Stone/Clark Prodns., 1971-74; with Mfrs. Hanover Trust Co., N.Y.C., 1974—, asst. v.p., 1978-79, tng. and devel. officer internat. div., 1980—. Mem. Am. Banking Assn. (internat. personnel com.). Republican. Roman Catholic. Club: Apawamis (Rye, N.Y.). Home: 33 E 38th St New York NY 10016 Office: 350 Park Ave New York NY 10016

KECK, ROBERT CLIFTON, lawyer; b. Sioux City, Iowa, May 20, 1914; s. Herbert A. and Harriet (McCutchen) K.; A.B., Ind. U., 1936; J.D., U. Mich., 1939; L.H.D., Nat. Coll. Edn., 1973; m. Ruth P. Edwards, Nov. 2, 1940; children—Robert Clifton, Laura E. (Mrs. John A. Simpson), Gloria E. (Mrs. Paul Sauser). Admitted to Ill. bar, 1939; practiced in Chgo., 1939—; mem. firm Keck, Mahin & Cate, 1939—, partner, 1946—; dir. Signode Corp., First Ill. Corp., Schwinn Bicycle Co., 1st Nat. Bank & Trust Co. Evanston, Union Spl. Corp., Rust-Oleum Corp., Methode Electronics, Inc. Trustee, chmn. Nat. Coll. Edn.; trustee Sears-Roebuck Found., 1977-79. Served with USNR, 1943-45. Fellow Am. Coll. Trial Lawyers; mem. Fed., Am., Ill., Chgo. bar assns., Bar Assn. 7th Fed. Circuit (pres. 1976-77), Phi Gamma Delta. Republican. Mason. Clubs: Biltmore Forest Country (Asheville, N.C.); Westmoreland Country (Wilmette, Ill.); Glen View (Golf, Ill.); Chgo., Met. (Chgo.). Home: 1043 Seneca Rd Wilmette IL 60091 Office: 233 S Wacker Dr Chicago IL 60606

KEEFE, HARRY VICTOR, JR., investment banker; b. Boston, Apr. 9, 1922; s. Harry V. and Catherine T. (Dennis) K.; B.A., Amherst Coll., 1943; postgrad. Boston U., 1945-46; m. Jean Marie Mulcahy, Sept. 25, 1943; children—Kathleen K. Raffel, Harry Victor III. Analyst, R.L. Day & Co., Boston, 1946-52, partner, 1952-56; partner Tucker Anthony & R.L. Day, N.Y.C., 1956-62; founder, chmn., chief exec. officer, dir. Keefe, Bruyette & Woods, Inc., N.Y.C., 1962—; chmn. Keefe Mgmt. Services Inc., N.Y.C., 1973—. Trustee Brunswick Sch., Greenwich, Conn., Lafayette Coll. Served with USNR, 1942-46. Mem. Pacific Coast, N.Y., Boston stock exchanges, Conn. Investment Bankers Assn. (dir. 1952-53), Conn. Amherst Alumni Assn. (pres. 1955-56). Roman Catholic. Clubs: Bond Hartford (pres. 1954—), Wall St., Greenwich Country, Fairfield County Hounds, John's Island. Author: Banking, A Vital and Stable Industry. Contbr. articles banking to fin. publs. Home: Aiken Rd Greenwich CT 06830 Office: 91 Liberty St New York City NY 10006

KEEFE, ROGER MANTON, banker; b. New London, Conn., Feb. 26, 1919; s. Arthur T. and Mabel F. K.; B.A., Yale U., 1941; m. Ann Hunter, June 4, 1949; children—Christopher, Matthew Foran, Michael Devereux, Susan, Robin Mary, Victoria Morrill. Sr. v.p. Chase Manhattan Bank, 1945-71; exec. v.p. Conn. Bank & Trust Co., 1971-76, vice chmn., 1976—; vice chmn. CBT Corp., 1976—; dir. Callahan Mining Corp. Bd. dirs. St. Joseph Hosp., 1978—; trustee Green Farms Acad., 1978—, Am. Shakespeare Theatre/CCPA, 1974—, St. Thomas More Corp., 1962—. Served with U.S. Army, 1941-46. Decorated Bronze Star with cluster, Purple Heart, Silver Star. Mem. Assn. Res. City Bankers, Southwestern Area Commerce and Industry Assn. (vice chmn. 1978—). Clubs: Wee Burn Country (Darien); Internat. (Washington); Yale (N.Y.C.); Norwalk Yacht; Landmark (Stamford); Seal Harbor. Office: CBT Plaza Darien CT 06820

KEELE, LYNDON ALAN, electronics co. exec.; b. Clyde, Tex., Nov. 3, 1928; s. Theadore Fannin and Zada (Sikes) K.; B.B.A., U. Tex., 1951; m. Muriel Alice Murphy, June 1, 1968; children—Carolyn Chase, Tiffany Ames. With York div. Borg-Warner Co., York, Pa., 1953-58, asst. gen. plant mgr., 1956-58; program mgr. Sylvania Elec. System div. Gen. Telephone & Electronics Co., Needham, Mass., 1958-62; program mgr. ITT Fed. Labs., Nutley, N.J., 1962-68; exec. v.p. TeleSciences, Inc., Moorestown, N.J., 1968-73; pres. Science Dynamics Corp., Cherry Hill, N.J., 1973—. Served with AUS, 1946-47, USAAF, 1951-53. Mem. IEEE. Club: Ocean Reef. Office: 13 Forage Ln Cherry Hill NJ 08003

KEENAN, ROBERT JOSEPH, assn. exec.; b. San Francisco, May 25, 1946; s. Lawrence Alexander and Elma Patricia (Frenor) K.; B.S. in Pub. Relations, Armstrong Coll., 1971; postgrad. U. Santa Clara, 1972-75; m. Hildegard Irmtradd Gerlitz, Aug. 22, 1969; children—Michael Alexander, Patrick Sean. Asst. mgr. Redwood City (Calif.) C. of C., 1971-73; exec. v.p., gen. mgr. Lancaster (Calif.) C. of C., 1973-76; exec. v.p. Montclair (Calif.) C. of C., 1976-79; adminstrv. dir. Calif. Electric Sign Assn., also Sign Users Council Calif., Los Angeles, 1979—. Bd. dirs. Friends of Ontario (Calif.) Airport. Served with AUS, 1966-69. Named one of outstanding young men Am., 1974-77. Mem. Armed Forces Benefit and Aid Assn. (hon. life). Rotarian (sgt.-at-arms Lancaster 1974). Home: 878 W Bonita Claremont CA 91711 Office: 747 E Green St Pasadena CA 91101

KEENAN, ROBERT WAGER, metalworking co. exec.; b. Cleve., Jan. 13, 1928; s. William Carroll and Herma V. (Wager) K.; S.B. in Indsl. Adminstrn., Yale, 1949; M.B.A., Harvard, 1951; m. Nancy Jane Schmuck, Sept. 8, 1951 (dec.); children—Sara M. Keenan Hunt, Scot B., Jeffrey J.; m. 2d, Margaret Weaver Walker, July 8, 1961 (div.); 1 son, Bradford W. Salesman, Congoleum-Nairn, Kearney, N.J., 1951-52; supr. Westinghouse Electric Corp., Sharon, Pa., 1952-56; mgr. Sharon Steel Corp. (Pa.), 1956-67; exec. v.p. Satec Corp., Grove City, Pa., 1967-68, pres., chief exec. officer, dir., 1968-73; group v.p., steel Bliss & Laughlin Industries, Oak Brook, Ill., 1973-79; pres., chief exec. officer, dir. BLK Steel, Inc., Batavia, Ill., 1976-79; pres. Astor Assos., Chgo., 1979—; chmn. Cold Finished Steel Bar Inst., 1976-78. Episcopalian. Home and Office: 45 E Division St Chicago IL 60610

KEENE, THOMAS VICTOR, aerospace co. exec.; b. Indpls., July 15, 1923; s. Thomas Victor and Marion (Craig) K.; B.S., Harvard U., 1945, M.B.A., 1947; m. Doris Dennis, June 16, 1950; children—Thomas Victor, III, Dennis M. With Eli Lilly Co., 1945-46, Ford Motor Co., 1947-48, Hughes Aircraft Co., 1949-54, Litton Industries, 1954-68, Shareholders Mgmt. Corp., 1968; self-employed, 1969-71; with Hughes Aircraft Co., 1971—, v.p. fin., Culver City, Calif., 1974—. Served with AUS, 1943. Mem. Fin. Execs. Inst. Office: Hughes Aircraft Co Centinela and Teale Sts Culver City CA 90230

KEENER, JEAN SMITH, savs. and loan exec.; b. Morristown, Tenn., Apr. 4, 1918; d. George F. and Rose (Rice) Smith; ed. Sullins Coll., Bristol, Va.; m. Frank T. McGuffin, Dec. 28, 1939; children—George B., Jan. M. McGuffin Jessee, Dorothy McGuffin Schwalb; m. 2d, George G. Keener, Nov. 25, 1965. With Morristown Fed. Savs. & Loan Assn., pres., 1964—. Mem. U.S. Savs. and Loan League, Tenn. Savs. and Loan League (v.p.), Morristown C. of C. (dir.). Democrat. Methodist. Office: 622 W 1st North St Morristown TN 37814

KEENER, WILLIAM HENRY, bank exec.; b. Herington, Kans., Dec. 1, 1945; s. William Henry and Shirley Anne (Driscoll) K.; B.A., U. Miss., 1967; children—Joseph Bragg, William Henry. Banking officer Wachovia Bank & Trust, N.A., Charlotte, N.C., 1971-74; v.p. First Nat. Bank of Commerce, New Orleans, 1974-77; pres. First City Bank, New Orleans, 1977—. Bd. dirs. New Orleans United Way; Jr. Achievement; Vis. Nurses Assn. Served with USAF, 1967-71. Mem. Am. Bankers Assn., La. Bankers Assn., Robert Morris Assn. Republican. Roman Catholic. Clubs: Pendennis, Petroleum, Metairie Country.

KEENEY, WILLIAM EDWIN, JR., space systems co. exec.; b. Clarinda, Iowa, Aug. 22, 1930; s. William Edwin and Dorothy LaVerne (Enerson) K.; B.B.A., U. Nebr., 1952, B.E.E., 1958; m. L. Eileen Faull, Oct. 3, 1980. With AC Electronics div. Gen. Motors, Milw., 1959-67, successively as systems engr., engring. supr., systems engring. group head; with Perkin-Elmer Corp., Wilton, Ct., 1967-77, successively as spacecraft cabin analyzer program mgr., test equipment sect. mgr., systems integration sect. mgr., systems engring. dept. mgr., solid state sensor camera program mgr.; dir. govt. orbital payloads Harris Corp., Melbourne, Fla., 1977—; asst. prof. U. Notre Dame, South Bend, Ind., 1954-56. Mem. Danbury (Conn.) City Council, 1973-77; bd. dir. Assn. Religious Communities, Danbury; chmn. com. Conn. council Boy Scouts Am. Served to lt. USN, 1952-56. Mem. IEEE, Smithsonian Inst., Air Force Assn., Internat. Platform Assn. Democrat. Presbyterian. Book reviewer Jour. Astronatical Scis., 1976—. Home: 305 Hwy A1A Satellite Beach FL 32937 Office: PO Box 37 Melbourne FL 32901

KEGELMAN, WILLIAM, optical instrument co. exec.; b. Bridgeport, Pa., Nov. 27, 1907; s. Jacob and Bertha (Graf) K.; B.S.E.E., Drexel U., 1930; m. Lisa Ihle, Oct. 19, 1934; children (adopted)—Michael (dec.), Thomas. With AT&T, Phila., 1930-32, Philco Co., Phila., 1934-36, Pa. R.R., Phila., 1937-59; with Phila. Electric Co., 1937-59; owner, operator Kegelman Bros., Huntingdon Valley, Pa., 1959—, pres., chief exec. officer, 1980—. Registered profl. engr., Pa. Fellow Nat. Contract Mgmt. Assn.; mem. IEEE, Nat. Soc. Profl. Engrs., Optical Soc. Am., Soc. Indsl. Math., Soc. Mfg. Engrs., Phi Kappa Phi, Tau Beta Pi. Republican. Lutheran. Home and Office: 393 County Line Rd Huntingdon Valley PA 19006

KEHLE, ANTHONY GEORGE, III, ins. agy. exec.; b. Toledo, Jan. 18, 1941; s. Anthony George and Jeanne Esther (Kurts) K.; B.B.A., U. Toledo, 1960; postgrad. U. Stetson Law Sch., 1961-62; children—Kelly McGhee, Kory Sean. State mgr. Alaska Combined Ins. Co. Am., Anchorage, Alaska, 1964-72; owner, pres. Schweitzer Ins. Agy. Inc., Sandpoint, Idaho, 1973—; pres. Idaho Coach Corp., Sandpoint, 1977—, Mountain States Distbg. Co. Inc., Sandpoint, 1977—; owner Ponderay Ranch Inc., 1972—. Mem. fin. com. Republican Nat. Com., 1969-70. Served with USMCR, 1956-60. Named C.I.C.A. Internat. Man of Yr., 1964. Mem. Life Underwriters Assn., Idaho State Draft Horse Assn. (mgr./founder Internat. 1977-79, cert. appreciation 1979), North Idaho Draft Horse Assn. (dir. 1977, 78), U. Toledo Alumni Assn. (life), Pi Kappa Alpha Alumni (life). Roman Catholic. Clubs: Spokane Polo, Spokane Athletic, Round Table. Author: poetry Girdwood, 1972. Home: Drawer D Sandpoint ID 83864 Office: Schweitzer Ins Agy Inc PO Box D Sandpoint Idaho 83864

KEHOE, JOHN PATRICK, shareholder relations/fin. services mktg. cons.; b. N.Y.C., Aug. 5, 1938; s. John Michael and Mary (Denning) K.; B.S., Fordham U., 1960; cert. N.Y. Inst. Fin., 1961; M.S. in Bus. Policy, Columbia U., 1979; m. Patricia Alden White, May 4, 1973; children—Sandra Smith, Kimberly Smith, Maura, John, Teryl Smith, Kevin, Brendan. Asso., Baker Weeks & Co., N.Y.C., 1957-58, 59-61; asst. to pres. McDonnell & Co., Inc., N.Y.C., 1961-63; asst. v.p., 1963-64, v.p., dir. investment mgmt. services div., 1964-65; pres., dir., chmn. investment policy com. McDonnell Fund, N.Y.C., 1965-67; exec. v.p., dir. C.M. Kelly & Assos., N.Y.C., 1967-69; founder, mng. dir. Kehoe, White, Towey & Savage, Inc., N.Y.C., Boston and Los Angeles, 1969—; lectr. profl. orgns. Served with USMC, 1957-58. Mem. Nat. Investor Relations Inst. (charter), Beta Gamma Sigma. Clubs: Princeton, Racquet and Tennis (N.Y.C.); Eastern Yacht, Gut 'n Feathers (Marblehead, Mass.). Author articles in field; contbg. editor Merger and Acquisitions Negotiating Strategy, 1970. Home: One Ballast Ln Marblehead MA 01945 Office: 551 Fifth Ave New York NY 10017 also One Boston Pl Boston MA 02108

KEHRL, HOWARD HARMON, automobile co. exec.; b. Detroit, Feb. 2, 1923; s. Howard and Martha Sophy (Horlacher) K.; student Wayne State U., 1940-43; B.S., Ill. Inst. Tech., 1944; M.S. in Engring. Mechanics, U. Notre Dame, 1948; S.M. (Sloan fellow), M.I.T., 1960; m. Mary Katherine Maloney, June 29, 1946; children—John Howard, Howard Richard, David James, Kathleen Mary. Grad. in tng. Gen. Motors Corp. Research Labs., 1948. research engr., 1949-51, sr. project engr., asst. staff engr. Cadillac Motor Car div. tank plant, Cleve., 1951-54, devel. engr., dir. engring. labs. Chevrolet Central Office, Detroit, 1954-61, mgr. quality control, 1961-64, asst. chief engr. Oldsmobile, 1964-69, chief engr., 1969-72, gen. mgr., 1972-74, v.p., mem. adminstrn. com. Gen. Motors Corp., 1972-73, group exec. charge Car and Truck Group, 1973-74, exec. v.p., 1974-78, exec. v.p. overseas ops. and design, engring., mfg. and research staffs, dir., 1978—; dir. Dayton-Hudson Corp. Mem. exec. bd. Detroit Area council Boy Scouts Am.; mem. exec. com. Mich. United Fund; bd. dirs. Harper-Grace Hosp., U.S.-Korea Econ. Council. Served with USNR, 1943-46. Mem. Soc. Automotive Engrs. Club: Bloomfield Hills Country. Patentee in field. Office: 767 Fifth Ave New York NY 10022*

KEIL, CHARLES E., publisher; b. N.Y.C., Aug. 27, 1936; s. E. William and Marie Katherine (Diebold) K.; A.B., Bklyn. Coll., 1964, postgrad., 1964-65; m. Patricia Ann O'Toole, Dec. 21, 1970; 1 son, Brett. Sales mgr. Columbian Bronze Corp., Freeport, N.Y., 1960-66; sr. v.p., pub., mng. dir. Marine Engring.-Log Group, Simmons Boardman Pub. Co., N.Y.C., 1966-78; sr. v.p. Thomas Internat. Pub. Co., N.Y.C., 1978—. Served with USNR, USMCR, 1956-58. Mem. Marine Tech. Soc., Soc. Naval Architects and Marine Engrs., Am. Bus. Press, Walter Badehot Soc., Mensa, Internat. Soc. Philos. Enquiry, Propeller Club of U.S. Office: 1 Penn Plaza New York NY 10001

KEISER, DAVID PAUL, electric mfg. co. exec.; b. Dover, Ohio, Jan. 12, 1926; s. Henry Patrick and Edith Anne (Herzig) K.; B.E.E., Marquette U., 1946; M.A., Western Mich. U., 1959, M.B.A., 1963; m. Mary Elizabeth Pate, June 30, 1951; children—David Paul, Lisa Anne. Sales engr. Westinghouse Electric Corp., Detroit, 1947-51, sales engr., Kalamazoo, Mich., 1953-65, supr. personnel devel. programs, Pitts., 1965-66, mgr. mktg. personnel devel., 1965-68, mktg. mgr. small power transformers, South Boston, Va., 1968-76, group mktg. mgr. transmission and distbn., Pitts., 1976-79, Midwest regional sales mgr., 1979—. Served with USNR, 1943-46, 51-53. Mem. Am. Mktg. Assn., Sales and Mgmt. Execs. Internat., Res. Officers Assn. Roman Catholic. Clubs: Inverness Golf, Elks, Kiwanis, K.C. Home: 155 Kimberly Ln Palatine IL 60667 Office: 10 S Riverside Plaza Chicago IL 60606

KEISER, HENRY BRUCE, lawyer, publisher; b. N.Y.C., Oct. 26, 1927; s. Leo and Jessie (Liebeskind) K.; B.A., U. Mich., 1947; J.D. cum laude, Harvard, 1950; m. Jessie E. Weeks, July 12, 1953; children—Betsy Cordelia, Matthew Roderick. Admitted to N.Y. bar, 1950, D.C. bar, 1955, Fla. bar, 1956, U.S. Supreme Ct bar, 1954; trial atty. CAB, Washington, 1950-51; head counsel alcoholic beverages sect. OPS, 1951-52; legal asst. to Judge Eugene Black, Tax Ct. U.S., 1953-56; practice in Washington, 1956—; pres., chmn. bd. Fed. Pubs., Inc., 1959—; chmn. bd. Gene Galasso Assos., Inc., Washington, 1963—; chmn. Crown Eagle Communications Ltd., London, 1977-78. Mem. adv. cabinet Southeastern U., 1965—; cons. AEC, 1965-74; profl. lectr. Dept. Agr., 1960-77, George Washington U., 1961-79, U. San Francisco, 1965—, Coll. William and Mary, 1966-75, Calif. Inst. Tech., 1967-72, U. So. Calif., 1973-74, U. Denver, 1975—, Air Force Inst. Tech., 1975-76, U. Santa Clara, 1975—. Trustee Touro Coll., 1979—. Served to 1st lt. Judge Adv. Gen. Corps, USAF, 1951-52; maj. Res. (ret.). Fellow Nat. Contract Mgmt. Assn.; mem. Am. (council pub. contract law sect. 1972-75), N.Y., Fla., D.C. (dir. 1965-66, chmn.

adminstrv. law sect. 1964-65) bar assns. Jewish. Home: 6009 Plainview Rd Bethesda MD 20034 Office: One Lafayette Centre Washington DC 20036

KEISTER, DENNIS RICHARD, realtor, acct.; b. Lewisburg, Pa., June 25, 1949; s. Merle Charles and Charlotte Edith (Richard) K.; Asso. in Bus. Adminstrn., Williamsport Area Community Coll., 1969; m. Diane Louise Sprenkel, Dec. 31, 1967; children—Jeffrey A., Timothy C., Julia A. Public acct. J.A. Bailey, Lake Wales, Fla., 1969-71, Fisher, Clark, Lauer, C.P.A.'s, Selinsgrove, Pa., 1972-73; cost acct. ACF Industries, Milton, Pa., 1973-74; comptroller Nat. Limestone Quarry, Inc., Middleburg, Pa., 1974-76; pvt. practice acctg., Hummels Wharf, Pa., 1972-80; public acct. Lynd A. Gemberling, real estate, Hummels Wharf, 1977—; realtor Villager Realty Inc., Hummels Wharf, 1979-80. Mem. Pa. Soc. Public Accts., Pa. Realtors Assn., Nat. Realtors Assn., Nat. Soc. Public Accts., Nat. Fedn. Ind. Bus., U.S. C. of C. Clubs: Kreamer Sportsmen's, Freeburg Fire Co. Home: 108 Helen St Shamokin Dam PA 17876 Office: Box 70 Route 11415 Hummels Wharf PA 17831

KEITER, WILLIAM EDWARD, ins. co. exec.; b. Orange, N.J., Dec. 7, 1929; s. Ernest R. and Florence H. (Reineke) K.; B.A., Muhlenberg Coll., 1951; M.B.A., Wharton Sch., U. Pa., 1952; m. Jeanne D. Flauss, May 16, 1953; children—Nancy, John, Susan. With N.Y. Life Ins. Co., 1954—, sr. v.p. in charge investment dept., N.Y.C., 1974-79, exec. v.p., 1979—. Trustee Diocesan Trust of Episcopal Diocese Newark, Muhlenberg Coll., United Student Aid Funds, N.Y.C. Served with Fin. Corps, U.S. Army, 1952-54. Office: 51 Madison Ave New York NY 10010

KEITH, BILLY RAY, mfg. engr.; b. Breckenridge, Tex., June 14, 1929; s. James Elgin and Frances Palestine (Vail) K.; diploma bus. adminstrn., Draughon's Bus. Coll., Abilene, Tex., 1949; grad. in acctg. Arlington (Tex.) State Coll., 1962; m. Galya LaFaye Stephen, Feb. 12, 1969; children—James, Cheri, David, Kathy, Stephen. Machinest, L.T.V. Co., Dallas, 1959-64; mfg. engr. Gen. Dynamics Co., Ft. Worth, 1964-67, Vought Corp., Dallas, 1967-72, Bell Helicopter Textron Co., Ft. Worth, 1972—; owner Data Unltd., cons., 1979—. Mem. Numerical Control Soc. (publns. chmn. North Tex. chpt. 1978). Democrat. Mem. Ch. of Christ. Home: 4024 Eldridge St Fort Worth TX 76107 Office: Machining Center Bell Helicopter Textron Co PO Box 482 Fort Worth TX 76101

KEITH, DAVID STEPHEN, govt. ofcl.; b. Great Bend, Kans., July 18, 1944; s. William Glen and Maxine R. (LaSure) Shafer; B.A., Fla. State U.; B.S. magna cum laude in Hotel and Restaurant Mgmt., Fla. Internat. U.; m. Pamela Ann Swope, Feb. 25, 1967; 1 dau., Stephanie Lauren. Commd. 2d lt. U.S. Army, 1966, advanced through grades to capt., 1968, discharged, 1975; served to maj. Res.; restaurant and catering mgr.-multiunit Stouffer's Corp.-Hotel Div., Cleve., 1977-78; restaurant mgr. Piccadilly Properties, Cleve., 1978-79; mgmt. analyst, clubs and restaurants Club Mgmt. Directorate, Dept. Army, Washington, 1979—; cons. restaurant mgmt. Decorated Bronze Star, Air medal, Joint Service Commendation medal, Purple Heart, Army Commendation medal, Cross of Gallantry. Mem. Nat. Restaurant Assn., Internat. Mil. Club Execs. Assn., Mil. Intelligence Assn., VFW, Am. Legion. Home: 12720 Rolling Brook Dr Woodbridge VA 22191 Office: DAAG-CMO 1000 Independence Ave Washington DC 20314

KEITH, HOWARD EDWIN, JR., retail automobile co. exec.; b. Wolfeboro, N.H., Mar. 11, 1932; s. Howard Edwin and Josephine L. (Pinkham) K.; student U. N.H., 1959-61. Pres., Deep Six Inc., Wolfeboro, 1961-68; salesman various auto dealerships, 1968-72; pres. Spring Branch Motors Inc., Houston, 1972—; adv. Garrison Metal Products Inc., 1979—. Served with USAF, 1952-56. Winner 1st place 1980 Acad. Model Aeronautics Championships, Wilmington, Ohio, Mem. Tex. Ind. Auto Dealers Assn., Houston Ind. Auto Dealers Assn., Houston Area Radio Kontrol Soc. Mem. Christian Ch. Clubs: Jetero Radio Control, Manned Space Center Radio Control. Home: 596 Van Molan St Houston TX 77022 Office: Spring Br Motors Inc 597 E Crosstimbers St Houston TX 77022

KEKST, GERSHON, pub. relations cons.; b. Peabody, Mass., Oct. 12, 1934; B.S., U. Md., 1956; children—Ilana, Michele, David. Founder, pres. Kekst & Co., corporate and fin. pub. relations counsel, N.Y.C., 1970—; dir. Loral Corp. Bd. dirs. Lexington Sch. for Blind, Am. Friends Weizmann Inst. Sci. Served with U.S. Army. Mem. Pub. Relations Soc. Am. (counsellors sect.), Am. Acad. Polit. and Social Sci. Clubs: N.Y. Economic, Harmonie (N.Y.C.). Office: 430 Park Ave New York NY 10022

KELLAM, HAROLD BLANTON, ins. agency exec.; b. Princess Anne County, Va., Nov. 7, 1912; s. Abel E. and Clara O. (Eaton) K.; student Atlantic U., Coll. William and Mary, 1931-32; m. Frances Marian Arthur, June 26, 1937; children—Harold Blanton, Elizabeth Hardy Kellam Mowry. Cashier, Reliance Life Ins. Co., Norfolk, Va. and Jacksonville, Fla., 1934-44; partner Kellam-Eaton Ins. Co., gen. ins. and real estate, Virginia Beach, Va., 1944—; pres. K&E Corp.; v.p. VAB Fin. Corp.; dir. Beach Motel Corp., Sta. WVAB. Pres., ARC, Virginia Beach; dist. lay leader Norfolk dist. United Methodist Ch.; trustee Va. Ann. conf. United Meth. Ch.; chmn. pres.'s adv. council Va. Wesleyan Coll.; chmn. bd. trustees Virginia Beach United Meth. Ch. Mem. Va. Ind. Ins. Agts., Virginia Beach Ind. Agts., Nat. Ind. Agts. Assn., Virginia Beach C. of C. (pres. 1956-57). Democrat. Clubs: Rotary (pres. Virginia Beach 1952-53; dist. gov. 1960-61); Princess Anne Country. Home: 214 71st St Virginia Beach VA 23451 Office: 3111 Pacific Ave Virginia Beach VA 23451

KELLER, GARY LEE, automotive rental co. exec.; b. Ong, Nebr., Dec. 15, 1944; s. Ralph Edward and Betty Jean (Coverdale) K.; ed. high sch.; m. Catherine Swett, Aug. 30, 1968; children—Shaunett, Bridget. Sec.-treas. Custom Inc., also gen. mgr. Thrifty Rent-a-Car, Thrifty Rent-a-Truck, and Quality Leasing Co., Salt Lake City, 1967-78, mem. nat. advt. com., 1974-78; pres. Utah Car and Truck Rentals Inc. dba Am. Internat. Rent-a-car, Salt Lake City and Park City, Utah and Idaho Falls, 1978—. Served with USAF, 1963-67. Mem. Car and Truck Renting and Leasing Assn. (sr. v.p. Utah chpt. 1976-78), Am. Car Renting Assn., Salt Lake Area C. of C., Utah Ski Assn. Office: Utah Car and Truck Rentals Inc 1355 W North Temple St Salt Lake City UT 84116

KELLER, GEORGE MATTHEW, oil co. exec.; b. Kansas City, Mo., Dec. 3, 1923; s. George Matthew and Edna Louise (Mathews) K.; B.S. in Chem. Engring., M.I.T., 1948; m. Adelaide McCague, Dec. 27, 1946; children—William G., Robert A., Barry R. Mem. engring. dept. Standard Oil Calif., San Francisco, 1948-63, fgn. ops. staff, 1963-67, asst. v.p., asst. to pres., 1967-69, v.p., 1969-74, dir., 1970—, vice-chmn., 1974—; dir. Caltex Petroleum Corp., Arabian Am. Oil Co., Bahrain Petroleum Co., Western Bancorp., United Calif. Bank. Served to 1st lt. USAAF, 1943-46. Mem. M.I.T. Club No. Calif. (dir. 1972—), Council Fgn. Relations, World Affairs Council No. Calif. (trustee 1972—). Clubs: Peninsula Golf and Country (San Mateo, Calif.); San Francisco Golf, World Trade, Bankers, Stock Exchange (San Francisco). Office: Standard Oil Co 225 Bush St San Francisco CA 94104*

KELLER, HENRY FREDERICK, mfg. co. exec.; b. Bklyn.; s. Henry and Helen Agnes (Mannix) K.; B.S. in Mech. Engring., Hartford (Conn.) U., 1965; postgrad. N.Y. U., 1965-67; m. May 25, 1952; 2 children. Salesman, Nat. Cash Register Co., 1952-53, Stratos div. Fairchild Engine & Aircraft Corp., 1953-58; product line mgr. Hamilton Standard div. United Tech. Co., 1958-65; prodn. mgr. Harris Intertype Co., 1965-67; dir. worldwide indsl. engring. ITT Co., 1967-71; pres. orthopedic div. Howmedica Co., 1971-75; corp. officer, v.p. mfg. Becton Dickinson & Co., 1975-78; group v.p. diagnostic equipment Picker Corp., subs. RCA, Cleve., 1978—, also dir.; mem. faculty Bergen (N.J.) Community Coll., 1976. Asst. to pres. Windsor (Conn.) Civic Assn., 1964. N.Y. State scholar, 1951; Cornell U. scholar, 1951; Engring. scholar Stratos div., 1954. Congregationalist. Office: 595 Miner Rd Cleveland OH 44143

KELLER, J. ADREON, bus. exec.; b. Balt., Oct. 3, 1918; s. J. Adreon and Teresa (Latchford) K.; student Balt. Poly. Inst., 1936; B.S. in Mech. Engring., Ga. Inst. Tech., 1939; M.S., Lehigh U., 1941; m. Patricia Powers, June 10, 1944; children—Blanid T., Joseph A., James W., Sarah L., Suzanne L., Paul P., Kathryn A., Christian C. Spl. engr. Carnegie-Ill. Steel Corp., Chgo., 1941-45; v.p. George Fry & Assos., Chgo., 1947-54; v.p. ops. Mergenthaler Linotype Co., Bklyn., 1955-57, exec. v.p., 1957-58, pres., chief exec. officer, 1958-63; pres., chief exec. officer Eltra Corp., N.Y.C., 1963-74, chmn. bd., chief exec. officer, 1974—. Mem. nat. adv. bd. Ga. Inst. Tech. Served to ensign C.E.C., USNR, 1945-46. Mem. Am. Mgmt. Assn., Am. Ordnance Assn., Econ. Club, Beta Theta Phi. Clubs: Univ. (Chgo.); Univ. (N.Y.C.); Bald Peak Colony. Office: 2 Pennsylvania Plaza New York NY 10001*

KELLER, JOHN PAUL, steel co. exec.; b. Cleve., July 26, 1939; s. Paul and Jane (Beeson) K.; B.S., Yale U., 1961; M.B.A., Harvard U., 1963; m. Judith Anne Klein, Aug. 8, 1960; children—Lizabeth, Susan, John Robert. Product planner Ford Motor Co., Detroit, 1963-64; asst. to pub., bus. mgr. Time mag. Time, Inc., N.Y.C., 1964-69, pres. Pioneer Press, Wilmette, Ill., 1970-72; pres. Keller Steel Co., Northfield, Ill., 1972-80; dir. A.M. Castle Co. Bd. advs. Salvation Army, Chgo. Mem. Young Presidents Assn. (chmn. Chgo. chpt. 1978-79). Clubs: Racquet (Chgo.); Union (Cleve.); Glen View, Kirtland. Home: 1095 Pine St Winnetka IL 60093 Office: One Northfield Plaza Northfield IL 60093

KELLER, PATRICK ERLE, property analyst; b. Los Angeles, June 5, 1947; s. Olin Thomas and Helen Elizabeth (Sell) K.; B.S. in Fin., Calif. State U., Long Beach, 1971, M.B.A., Pacific Northwestern U., 1973; m. Maud May Kahalolani Napoleon, May 10, 1975; children—Amy Patricia, Katie Kahololani, Erle Teminihi, Hilarie Kulamanukaekaeluni. Engaged in real estate appraising, 1964—; owner, chief appraiser Patrick E. Keller & Assos., Hawthorne, Calif., 1976—; dir., fin. officer Southbay Credit Union. Res. police officer, Hawthorne, 1975—; fin. officer local Mormon Ch., 1977-80; treas. Flag. of the Free Com., 1978-81, Republican Central Com. of Los Angeles County, 1978—; active local YMCA, Boy Scouts Am. Sr. mem. Nat. Assn. Rev. Appraisers, Am. Assn. Cert. Appraisers, Nat. Assn. Ind. Fee Appraisers; mem. Am. Soc. Appraisers; asso. Soc. Real Estate Appraisers, Nat. Soc. Real Estate Appraisers, Hawthorne C. of C. (dir. 1978-80). Republican. Club: We-Tip. Address: 4734 W Broadway Hawthorne CA 90250

KELLER, RANDALL CHRISTOPHER, med. products co. exec.; b. Elmhurst, N.Y., Feb. 26, 1946; s. Frank J. and Ruby C. Keller; student Georgetown U., 1964-67; B.B.A., Adelphi U., 1969; M.B.A. cum laude, 1975; m. Kristina Zinn, Oct. 4, 1969; children—Christopher Rahland, Erik Randall. Ins. mgr. Binney & Smith, Inc., N.Y.C., 1969-71, asst. corp. sec., 1971-75, corp. mgr. compensation and benefits, Easton, Pa., 1975-78; corp. mgr. compensation and benefits C.R. Bard, Inc., Murray Hill, N.J., 1979—; v.p. Frank J. Keller Found. Mem. Am. Soc. Personnel Adminstrn., Am. Compensation Assn. Office: 731 Central Ave Murray Hill NJ 07974

KELLER, RICHARD LEE, mfg. co. exec.; b. Williamsport, Pa., Aug. 26, 1952; s. Joseph Dennis and Mary Albertine Keller; B.S. in Bus. Adminstrn., U. Central Fla., 1974; M.S. in Mgmt., U. LaVerne (Calif.), 1980; m. Christine Louise Behrens, Feb. 14, 1977; children—Katherine Marie, Nicholas Anthony. Mgmt. trainee, Martin Marietta Aerospace Co., Orlando, Fla., 1974-75; store mgr. Standard Sales Co., Orlando, 1975-76; base activation master scheduler, mgmt. visibility group leader Rockewell Internat. Co., 1976-77; sr. prodn. control specialist, supr. fabrication prodn. control Hughes Aircraft Co., Irvine, Calif., 1977—; v.p. Keller Engring. Assos., 1975—; condr. seminars, lectr., cons. in field. Mem. Am. Assn. M.B.A. Grads., Am. Prodn. and Inventory Control Assn., Hughes Aircraft Mgmt. Club, Tau Kappa Epsilon. Roman Catholic. Author articles in field. Home: 14442 Poplar Tustin CA 92680 Office: 17150 Van Karman Ave Irvine CA 92714

KELLER, ROBERT WILLIAM, lawyer; b. Chgo., Feb. 8, 1940; s. Joseph H. and Irene C. (Annis) K.; B.S. in Elec. Engring., Ill. Inst. Tech., 1961, M.S. in Elec. Engring., 1963; J.D. with honors, De Paul U., 1968; m. Judith M. Barnes, Mar. 8, 1969; 1 son, Thomas. Teaching asst. Ill. Inst. Tech., Chgo., 1961-63, research engr. IIT Research Inst., 1963-67; admitted to Ill. bar, 1968, Calif. bar, 1970; asso. firm Hofgren and Wegner, Chgo., 1967-69; patent lawyer IBM, San Jose, Calif., 1969-73, Schatzel and Hamrick, Santa Clara, Calif., 1973-77; patent counsel TRW Def. and Space Systems Group, Redondo Beach, Calif., 1977—. Bd. dirs. Legal Aid Soc. Santa Clara County, 1970-77. Mem. Calif. Bar Assn., Ill. Bar Assn., Am. Patent Law Assn., Calif. Patent Law Assn., Los Angeles Patent Law Assn., Nat. Security Indsl. Assn., Ill. Soc. Profl. Engrs., Tau Beta Pi. Home: 30170 Matisse Dr Rancho Palos Verdes CA 90274 Office: One Space Park Redondo Beach CA 90278

KELLER, RONALD CHARLES, mfg. co. exec.; b. Jersey City, Nov. 24, 1932; s. Charles and Anna (Senn) K.; M.E., Stevens Inst. Tech., 1955; M.M.S., 1980; m. Evelyn Joan Walderman, June 30, 1956; children—Lynda Ann, Eric Ronald, Roy Christopher. Project engr. Foster Wheeler Corp., N.Y.C., 1955-57; sales engr. N.J. Machine Corp., Hoboken, 1957-60; gen. mgr. PMC Industries, Hackensack, N.J., 1960-71; pres. Zimmer Machinery Systems, Gladstone, N.J., 1971-72; project dir. Automation & Product Devel. Corp., Darien, Conn., 1972-73; mgr. mfg. engring. Bristol-Myers, Hillside, N.J., 1973-80; mgr. sales and mktg. Solbern Corp., Fairfield, N.J., 1980—. Registered profl. engr., N.J., Conn. Mem. Nat. Soc. Profl. Engrs., Passaic County Soc. Profl. Engrs., Packaging Inst., Am. Mgmt. Assn., Beta Theta Pi. Lutheran. Contbg. author: Guide to Labeling Equipment and Practices, 1967; mem. editorial bd. Packaging Tech., 1980-81. Home: 31 Corvair Pl Wayne NJ 07470 Office: 8 Kulick Rd Fairfield NJ 07006

KELLER, SANDRA ANN, travel industry exec.; b. N.Y.C., July 17, 1946; d. Matthew John and Evelyn Theresa (Zaranko) Dost; grad. Katherine Gibbs Sch., 1965; cert. of completion Dale Carnegie Course, 1978; m. Charles Edward Keller, Oct. 14, 1967. Sec., CBS, N.Y.C., 1967; exec. sec., pres./v.p. Gumina Bldg. & Constrn., New Brunswick, N.J., 1970-72; med. staff sec. Hamilton Hosp., Hamilton Square, N.J., 1973; office mgr. Trenton (N.J.) Urologic Group, 1974; advt. adminstrv. asst. Six Flags Great Adventure, 1975-77, advt. and promotions coordinator, 1977-78, sales promotion account supr., Jackson, N.J., 1978—. Mem. Citizens Com. Egg Harbor Twp. (N.J.), 1980—. Recipient awards, Dale Carnegie, 1979. Mem. Nat. Assn. Female Execs. (dir. 1980—). Office: Caesar's Boardwalk Regency Casino Hotel Atlantic City NJ

KELLER, STEPHEN J., cons. firm exec.; b. Perth Amboy, N.J., Feb. 10, 1938; s. Stephen Keller and Mary Keller Homer; B.S. in Fgn. Service, Georgetown U., 1958; 1 dau., Lisa. Grad. trainee Ford Werke AG subs. Ford Motor Co., Cologne, W. Ger., 1962-63; personnel specialist Internat. Latex Corp., Dover, Del., 1963-64, tech. employment supr., 1964-66; exec. recruiting supr. Borden, Inc., N.Y.C., 1966-69; sr. cons. Peat, Marwick, Mitchell & Co., Frankfurt, W. Ger., 1969-71; prin. Stephen J. Keller, Mgmt. and Exec. Selection Cons., Hofheim am Taunus, W. Ger., 1971—; guest lectr. career planning European Bus. Sch., Oestrich-Winkel (Rheingau), W. Ger., Mem. for Germany, Democratic Party in Europe Com. Served with U.S. Army, 1959-62. Mem. Rhein-Main Mktg. Club. Democrat. Roman Catholic. Contbr. articles on exec. selection in internat. envirn. to mgmt. mags. Home: Falkensteiner Weg 2a 6238 Hofheim am Taunus Federal Republic Germany Office: PO Box 1420 Hofheim am Taunus Federal Republic Germany

KELLER, THOMAS WHITNEY, city ofcl., bldg. supply co. exec.; b. Hinsdale, Ill., July 26, 1921; s. Raymond L. and Mildred (Whitney) K.; B.A., Duke, 1946; m. Marcia E. Marland, Sept. 6, 1951; children—Peter J., Mark T., Marcia E, II, Scott R. With E.A. Keller Co., La Grange, Ill., 1946-71, sec., 1949-71; pres. TriCounty Land Corp., Lemont, Ill.; owner Keller Plantations, Holland, Mich., 1971—; dir. emeritus La Grange State Bank, adv. bd., 1979—. Commr., Village of La Grange (Ill.) Parking Commn., 1957-77. Former mem. asso. bd. La Grange Community Meml. Gen. Hosp.; former bd. dirs. West Suburban YMCA. Served with AUS, 1942-45. Mem. Am. Legion, Sigma Chi. Methodist. Mason, Kiwanian. Clubs: La Grange Country. Home: 15346 Leonard Rd Spring Lake MI 49456 Office: 306 New Ave Lemont IL 60439

KELLER, WILLIAM HALL, JR., cable TV co. exec.; b. Greenville, Ga., June 16, 1924; s. William Hall and Martha Nettie (Turner) K.; student Ga. Inst. Tech., 1944, 47-48, U. Ill., 1945; m. Dorothy Moore, Apr. 17, 1948; children—William Hall, III, Richard, Scott. Pres., gen. mgr. Dee Rivers Broadcast Group, Atlanta, 1951-55; broadcast equipment salesman RCA, Atlanta, 1955-56; owner, mgr. sta. WGOV, Valdosta, Ga., also WCRY, Macon, Ga., 1956-64; with Clearview Cable TV Co., Dublin, Ga., 1964—, exec. v.p., 1970-74, pres., 1974—. Mem. Valdosta City Council, 1964-72; pres. Valdosta Civic Roundtable, 1961, Sallas-Mahone PTA, Valdosta, 1959; chmn. bd. Salvation Army, Valdosta, 1959-62; bd. dirs., sec. Valdosta Boys Club, 1957-72; bd. stewards, Sunday sch. pres., tchr. First United Methodist Ch., Valdosta, 1972-80. Mem. Ga. Assn. Broadcasters (past dir.), Ga. Cable TV Assn. (pres. 1978-79), Ga. Inst. Tech. Soc. Democrat. Clubs: Valdosta Country, Kiwanis (past pres. Valdosta). Home: 905 Pineridge Dr Valdosta GA 31601 Office: Box 340 Dublin GA 31021

KELLERMAN, ROBERT EUGENE, petroleum engr.; b. Beggs, Okla., Dec. 20, 1927; s. John Austin and Mary (Bungard) K.; B.S. in Petroleum Engring., U. Tex., 1949; m. Shirley Pulley, Sept. 3, 1949; children—Robert Scott, Shelby Kay. Dist. engr. Republic Natural Gas Co., 1949-52; dist. engr., chief engr., gen. mgr., partner Tex. Crude Oil Co., Ft. Worth, 1952-69; pres. Weiner Industries, N. Am. Internat., Inc., Petroleum Leaseholds, Inc., Tex. Crude Oil Co., Inc., 1965-71; pres. Oppenheimer Oil & Gas Inc., Ft. Worth, 1971—; dir. Gateway Nat. Bank Ft. Worth. Past mem. Ft. Worth Art Commn., chmn. Central area Oil Information Com., 1958-60. Recipient silver certificate for service. Registered profl. engr., Tex. Mem. Tex. Mid-Continent Oil and Gas Assn., Am. Petroleum Inst., Am. Inst. Mining, Metall. and Petroleum Engrs., Friars, Tau Beta Pi, Sigma Gamma Epsilon. Democrat. Mem. Disciples of Christ (deacon, elder). Home: 4833 Lafayette St Fort Worth TX 76107 Office: 207 Ridglea Theatre Bldg Fort Worth TX 76116

KELLEY, DUANE NEIL, real estate exec.; b. Cody, Wyo., Aug. 13, 1953; s. Billy Gene and Maxine Jane (Hill) K.; B.B.A. Morehead State U.; m. Debra Lynne Keeton, May 10, 1975; children—Jalayna Lynne, Shane Neil. Central office adminstr. Ky. Drilling and Operating Corp., Lexington, 1974-78; v.p. fin., comptroller Correll Ent., Somerset, Ky., 1978—, also dir.; dir. Correll Properties, C & N Real Estate, G & C Devel., A-1 Builders. Mem. U.S. C. of C., Ky. C. of C., Somerset Pulaski County C. of C., Am. Mgmt. Assn., Nat. Fedn. Ind. Bus. Democrat. Baptist. Home: 3700 Hickory Hill Dr Somerset KY 42501 Office: Suite 205 Correll Bldg Somerset KY 42501

KELLEY, ESTEL WOOD, foods co. exec.; b. Sharpsville, Ind., Mar. 24, 1917; s. Floyd and Maude (Wood) K.; B.A., Ind. U., 1939, LL.D., 1971; postgrad. Northwestern U., 1940; m. Wilma E. Lippert, June 17, 1939; children—E. Wood, Wayne L., Karen. Controller, treas., dir., mem. exec. com. R.H. Macy & Co., Kansas City, Mo., 1951-56; successively gen. mgr. distbn.-sales, treas., gen. mgr. Birds Eye div., corp. v.p. Gen. Foods Corp., White Plains, N.Y., 1956-64; exec. v.p., dir., mem. exec. com. Heublein, Inc., Hartford, 1964-68; corp. v.p. Gulf and Western Industries, Inc., pres. Consumer Products group, chmn. subs. Consol. Cigar Corp., Polly Bergen Co., 1968-74; pres., chief exec. officer, dir. Fairmont Foods Co., N.Y.C., 1974—; pres. Kelley & Partners, Ltd., Kelley, Inc., Prairie, Inc.; instr. mktg., mfg. cost Columbia. Co-founder Prickett Chair, founder E.W. Kelley Mktg., Fin. and Accounting Fund, Ind. U. Mayor, Leawood, Kans., 1955-56; bd. dirs. Ind. U. Found.; dean's adv. council Ind. U. Sch. Bus., mem. pres.'s priorities coordinating com.; chmn. internat. div. YMCA, mem. fin. com. bd. trustees nat. bd.; bd. dirs. Houston Symphony. Recipient Silver Beaver award Boy Scouts Am.; C.P.A., Ind. Mem. Nat. Assn. Accountants, Fin. Execs. Inst. (dir.), Acad. Alumni Fellows, Am. Mgmt. Assn., Beta Gamma Sigma (dir. table). Clubs: Metropolitan (N.Y.C.); Kokomo Country; Lake Region Yacht and Country, Fla. Citrus (Winter Haven); Kokomo (Ind.) Country; Masons (32 deg.). Quaker. Home: 131 Woden Way SE Winter Haven FL 33880 Office: 333 W Loop North Houston TX 77024 also 1 Gulf and Western Plaza New York NY 10023

KELLEY, GAREN NILE, steel co. exec.; b. Moundsville, W.Va., Mar. 2, 1923; s. Roy and Elisabeth (Ruckman) K.; grad. high sch.; m. Naomi L. Hudkins, Oct. 10, 1948; children—Sue Ann, Michael John. Steel supt. Hunkin-Conkey Constrn. Co., Cleve., 1949-58; pres., gen. mgr. Kelley Steel Erectors, Inc., Bedford, Ohio, 1958—; dir. Twinsburg Banking Co. (Ohio), N.E.A., Washington. Served with USMCR, 1943-45. Decorated Purple Heart, Gold Star. Clubs: Shaker Heights (Ohio); Cleve. Athletic, Cleve. Racquet, Union (Cleve.); Lost Tree (North Palm Beach, Fla.). Home: 2978 Courtland Blvd Shaker Heights OH 44122 Office: 7220 Division St Bedford OH 44146

KELLEY, JOHN FRANCIS, mfg. co. exec.; b. Rockford, Ill., Feb. 21, 1917; s. John Francis and Mary (Carey) K.; B.B.A., Northwestern U., 1943; m. Mary Jean Fairbairn, Nov. 27, 1948; children—Maureen L., John Francis, Paul A., Nancy J., James C., Brian J. With Pullman Inc., Chgo., 1952—, treas. Pullman Standard div., 1953-71, treas. Pullman Inc., 1955-71, v.p., treas., 1971—; dir. Pullman Leasing Co., Trailmobile Fin. Co.; chmn., dir. Canadian Trailmobile Fin. Ltd.

Served with USN, 1943-46. Decorated Purple Heart. Clubs: Chicago Athletic Assn., Westmoreland Country. Office: 200 S Michigan Ave Chicago IL 60604

KELLEY, MICHAEL TIMOTHY, gas corp. exec.; b. Bennington, Vt., Aug. 21, 1943; s. John Michael and Margaret (Butler) K.; A.B., Fairfield U., 1965; postgrad. Georgetown U., 1969; m. Susan J., May 25, 1974; 1 dau., Mary Kathleen. Staff asst. U.S. Ho. of Reps., 1965-66; asst. govt. affairs mgr. Babcock & Wilcox Co., Washington, 1968-76; mgr. govt. affairs Union Camp Corp., Washington, 1976-79; asst. to chmn. govt. affairs Houston Natural Gas Corp., Arlington, Va., 1979—. Mem. Nat. Coal Assn., Am. Gas Assn., Am. Waterways Operators. Roman Catholic. Home: 7800 Foxhound Rd McLean VA 22102 Office: Houston Natural Gas Corp Suite 919 1700 N Moore St Arlington VA 22209

KELLEY, NELLIE JANE, printing co. exec.; b. Altoona, Pa., Feb. 11, 1942; d. Earle Henry and Nancy Clemmens (Brady) Brumbaugh; B.B.A., LaSalle Coll., 1975. Mgr., Indsl. Tng. Systems, Inc., Willow Grove, Pa., 1969-72; practice acctg., 1972-74; supr. gen. acctg. Diversified Printing Corp., Atglen, Pa., 1979—; cons. in field. Mem. Nat. Assn. Accountants, Pa., Del. Valley assns. sch. bus. ofcls., LaSalle Coll. Alumni Assn. Home: 629 Overlook Dr Downingtown PA 19335 Office: Route 372 Atglen PA 19310

KELLEY, RICHARD EVERETT, mgmt. cons.; b. El Paso, Tex., Sept. 9, 1927; s. Lawrence E. and Sue (Spanton) K.; A.B., Harvard, 1948. Sales mgr. Goodyear Co., Brazil, 1956; mgmt. cons. Robert Heller & Assos. Inc., Cleve., 1956-61; v.p. Bell Intercontinental Corp., N.Y.C., 1961-64; dep. group exec. internat. group AMF Inc., London, Eng., 1964-66; pres. Pacific div. W.R. Grace & Co., 1967-69; mgmt. cons., 1970—. Office: Connecticut Office Bldg 21 Charles St Westport CT 06880

KELLEY, ROBERT BRUCE, TV prodn., electronics mgmt. exec.; b. Portland, Oreg., Sept. 19, 1936; s. Bruce Fred and Stella Josephine (Bakke) K.; B.A. in Social Sci., Calif. State Coll., Hayward, 1968; m. Vita Ann Ferrara, July 9, 1961; children—Jason Bruce, Glenn Anthony; m. 2d, Sharlene Jean Tank, Dec. 14, 1979. Ship's purser Matson Navigation Co., 1958-61; customer relations rep. Shell Oil Co., San Francisco, 1961-62, GTE-Sylvania, Mountain View, Calif., 1980—; tchr. Atascadero (Calif.) Sch. Dist., 1968-70; owner-operator Kelleys Distbg. Co., Coulterville, Calif., 1970-80; in TV prodn., 1980—. Served with USCG, 1956-58. Mem. Calif. Tchrs. Assn., Mariposa County Bus. Assn. (past pres.). Republican. Mem. Unity Ch. Address: 5098 McCoy Ave San Jose CA 95130

KELLEY, THOMAS WALDEGRAVE, pub.; b. S.I., N.Y., Apr. 15, 1931; s. Edward Thomas and Alethea (Mulligan) K.; B.A., Dartmouth Coll., 1953; postgrad. Syracuse U. Law Sch., 1957-58; m. Katherine Joseph Kelley, Feb. 8, 1955; children—Katherine Alethea, Thomas W., Timothy J., Elise. Regional mgr. coll. div. The Macmillan Co.; mgr. paperback dept., then pub. coll. dept. McGraw-Hill Book Co., N.Y.C.; pres. Butterworth Pubs., Inc., Woburn, Mass.; dir. Butterworth & Co. Ltd., London. Served to capt. USAF, 1953-57. Republican. Office: 10 Tower Office Park Woburn MA 01801

KELLIHER, ROBERT F., mfg. co. exec.; b. Taunton, Mass., Oct. 26, 1934; s. Matthew T. and Anna (Brady) K.; B.S., Stonehill Coll., 1959; M.B.A., Boston Coll., 1965; m. Muriel J. Garey, June 13, 1959; children—Robert, Stephen, Brian. Mgr. corp. fin. Kollmorgen Corp., Hartford, Conn., 1965-70; v.p., treas. Diano Corp., Woburn, Mass., 1970-77; v.p. fin. Victor Electric Wire & Cable Corp., West Warwick, R.I., 1977—; lectr. fin. Providence Coll., 1978—. Served with U.S. Army, 1953-55; Korea. Mem. Nat. Assn. Accts. Club: Taunton Bridge. Home: 34 Power St Taunton MA 02780 Office: 618 Main St West Warwick RI 02893

KELLMANSON, JOEL S., bldg. demolition contractor; b. Rochester, N.Y., Sept. 3, 1938; s. Charles L. and Hazel M. Kellmanson; B.S., Syracuse U., 1960; M.B.A., U. Pa., 1964; m. Elaine Golfe, Dec. 19, 1965; children—Jeffrey, Lynn. With Rochester Atlas Wrecking Co. Inc., 1964—, v.p., 1968-72, pres., treas., 1972—; v.p. Atkell Services Co., Rochester, 1966-72, pres., 1972—. Adv. bd. Rochester Salvation Army, 1978—. Served with USAR, 1961. Mem. Nat. Assn. Demolition Contractors (sec., dir. 1977—), Bldg. Service Contractors Assn. Club: Rotary. Home: 38 Framingham Ln Pittsford NY 14534 Office: 245 Mt Read Blvd Rochester NY 14611

KELLOGG, ALEXANDER SANFORD, fin. services corp. exec.; b. N.Y.C., Jan. 17, 1911; s. Frank Leonard and Emilie Humphreys (Baker) K.; A.B., Princeton U., 1935; m. Wilhelmina Van Neyhoff, Nov. 7, 1969; children—Emilie L., Neal Becker. With Wood Struthers and Co., N.Y.C., 1935-38, N.Y. Dock Co., N.Y.C., 1938-41, 45-56; pres., dir. Richland Peet Mines, Maine, 1956-59; with Investors Overseas Services, Lausanne, Switzerland, 1959-61; prin. ASK Fin. Services, Greenwich, Conn., 1961—; v.p., sec., dir. Chronogram Corp., Greenwich, 1973—. Dir., v.p. Mt. Desert Island Hosp., 1952-64; chmn. town council Bar Harbor, Maine, 1956-59. Served with C.E. U.S. Army, 1941-45. Certified port engr., Phila. Cargo Port of Embarkation, 1942-46. Republican. Episcopalian. Clubs: N.Y. Yacht, Indian Harbor, Bar Harbor Yacht, Harbor (Seal Harbor, Maine), Pot and Kettle, Cruising Club Am., Storm Trysail, Masons. Copyrighter fin. forms and systems. Home: Guinea Rd Cos Cob CT 06807 also Loom Point Route 1 Box 98B Bar Harbor ME 04609

KELLOGG, BERTRAM CECIL, ins. exec., cons. engr.; b. Port Angeles, Wash., Sept. 16, 1924; s. Bertram Fredrick and Loretta Louise (Woods) K.; student various univs.; div.; children—Mary Alice, Debora JoEllen Kellogg Douglas, Bertram Scott, Dennis Bertram. Mgr. engring. Firemen's Fund Am., Seattle, 1965-69; dir. indsl. relations Feather River Lumber Co., Loyalton, Calif., 1960-62; v.p. Kalor Corp, Anchorage, Alaska, 1969-76; mgr. tech. services Aetna Cravens Dargan & Cos., Sacramento, 1978—; fire and safety cons. City of Pasadena (Calif.), U.S. Power Squadron. Sect. chmn. Los Angeles Safety Council, 1960-65; dir. safety services ARC, Pasadena, 1957-60. Mem. Assn. Gen. Contractors, Am. Soc. Safety Engrs. (past pres.), Bd. Cert. Safety Profls. of Ams., Nat. Fire Protection Assn., Engring. Council Sacramento Valley, Vets. of Safety. Republican. Episcopalian. Clubs: Toastmasters, Lions, Elks. Author programs in life safety for use by industry. Home: 161 Magnolia Ave Sacramento CA 95828 Office: 2255 Watt Ave Suite 280 Sacramento CA 95825

KELLOGG, JOSEPH CHRISTOPHER, corp. exec.; b. St. Paul, Apr. 24, 1926; s. Joseph M. and Serine (Christopher) K.; student Southeastern La. Coll., 1947-48, Southwestern La. U., 1948-49; B.S. in Civil Engring.-Bus. Adminstrn., U. Minn., 1951; children—Virginia, Christine, Janet, Karen. Field engr. Al Johnson Constrn. Co., Mpls., 1951-53, project engr., project mgr., 1953-58, chief engr., 1958-64, v.p., chief engr., 1964-67, asst. sec. bd. dirs., 1964-70, v.p., mgr. Western div., 1967-70; pres. Kellogg Corp., Littleton, Colo., 1970—; guest lectr. Stanford U., U. Calif. at Berkeley, U. Minn., U. Colo., Cornell U., Colo. State U., 1965—; U.S. del. OECD Conf. on Tunneling. Campaign sect. chmn. United Fund Hennepin County, Mpls., 1961-63, campaign vice chmn., 1964-66, campaign chmn., 1967; mem. admission and allocation com., 1968; mem. Citizens League Mpls., 1967-68; mem. Mayor's Commn. on Urban Planning, 1971-72. Served with USNR, 1944-46. Recipient Outstanding Citizenship award United Fund Hennepin County, 1967. Mem. ASCE (chmn. nat. research council underground excavation, mem. task com. inspection, constrn. edn. and mgmt.; Outstanding Constrn. Engr. award, Constrn. Mgmt. award 1974), Engring. Found. (chmn. constrn. engring. and mgmt. research conf.), Asso. Gen. Contractors Am. (mem. nat. constrn. edn. com., Bur. Reclamation task com., joint corp. coms. with A.S.E.E., ASCE, A.G.C.), Am. Inst. Constrn., C. of C., Beavers, Moles, Toastmasters' Internat. Republican. Presbyterian. Author publs. on contract mgmt., cost control systems, systematic problem solving, prodn. planning, environmental design technology assessment and constrn. research. Home: 3675 S Cherokee St Englewood CO 80110 Office: 5601 S Broadway Littleton CO 80121

KELLOGG, STEPHEN RICHARD, environ. engr.; b. Northampton, Mass., Feb. 6, 1951; s. Richard Vernon and Doris Lillian (Hastey) K.; B.S. magna cum laude in Civil Engring., U. Mass., 1972; M.S. summa cum laude in Environ. Engring., Cornell U., 1973; m. Susan Ada Roetter, Aug. 23, 1969; children—Amy Elizabeth, Stephen Richard. Trainee, EPA, 1972-73; with Roy F. Weston, Inc., West Chester, Pa., 1973-78, sr. project engr., 1975-76, project mgr., 1976-77, govt. services cons., 1977-78; mgr. engring. York Research Corp., Stamford, Conn., 1978-79; v.p., gen. mgr. York Wastewater Consultants, Inc., Stamford, 1979-80, pres., 1980—. Mem. Delaware River Basin Water Resources Commn. Recipient Charles M. Anderson ednl. award Mass. Land Surveyors and Civil Engrs., 1971; Pa. Engring. Excellence award Am. Cons. Engring. Council, 1977; registered profl. engr., Conn., Pa., N.J.; cert. wastewater treatment facility operator, Pa. Mem. Water Pollution Control Fedn., ASCE (pres. 1972), Nat. Soc. Profl. Engrs., New Eng. Water Pollution Control Assn., N.Y. Water Pollution Control Assn., Conn. Soc. Profl. Engrs., Phi Kappa Phi, Tau Beta Pi. Democrat. Home: 1172 Melville Ave Fairfield CT 06430 Office: York Wastewater Consultants Inc One Research Dr Stamford CT 06906

KELLOW, MARK DENNIS STUDLEIGH, paper co. exec.; b. Cardiff, Wales, Jan. 20, 1924; s. William Henry and Elsie May (Spriggs) K.; came to Can., 1929, citizen, 1973; B.A. in History (hon.), U. Toronto (Ont., Can.), 1951; m. Imelda Louise Ketterer, May 1974; children—Vanessa, Nicole, Owen. Asst. naval sec. for warfare Canadian Dept. Nat. Def., Ottawa, Ont., 1951-57; mgr. personnel and corporate affairs Quaker Oats Co. Can. Ltd., Peterboro, Ont., 1957-72; v.p. personnel and pub. relations Abitibi Paper Co. Ltd., Toronto, 1972—. Tchr., cons., arbitrator in field; mem. adv. com. on orgn. behavior Faculty Mgmt. Studies, U. Toronto, 1973—. Pres. Ont. Indsl. Edn. Council, 1961-62. Served with Royal Canadian Navy Vol. Res., 1943-45; commd. Royal Canadian Arty. Militia, 1951. Mem. Personnel Assn. Toronto, Canadian Mfrs. Assn., Royal Canadian Mil. Inst., Royal Canadian Arty. Assn., Can. (dir. 1974-76), Ont. (pres. 1970-71), Peterborough (pres. 1967) chambers commerce. Home: 101 Snowshoe Crescent Thornhill ON L3T 4M8 Canada Office: Toronto Dominion Centre Toronto ON M5K 1B3 Canada

KELLY, ARTHUR F., aviation exec.; b. Tombstone, Ariz., Feb. 22, 1913; s. J.J. and Grace (Angelus) K.; A.B., U. Utah, 1933; m. Sally Payne, Jan. 31, 1942; children—James J. III, Arthur Francis II. Exec. sec. Airport Commn., Salt Lake City, 1933-35; with United Air Lines, 1935-37; with Western Air Lines, Inc., Los Angeles, 1937—, v.p. sales, 1949-68, sr. v.p., 1968-73, sr. v.p. mktg., 1970-73, pres., chief exec. officer, 1973-76, chmn., chief exec. officer, 1976—, also dir. Served to col. USAAF, World War II. Decorated Bronze Star medal. Mem. Air Force Assn. (pres. 1952—), Sigma Chi. Office: 6060 Avion Dr Los Angeles CA 90009

KELLY, DONALD PHILIP, holding co. exec.; b. Chgo., Feb. 24, 1922; s. Thomas Nicholas and Ethel M. (Healy) K.; student Loyola U., Chgo., 1953-54, De Paul U., 1954-55, Harvard U., 1965. Mgr. tabulating United Ins. Co. Am., 1946-51; mgr. data processing A.B. Wrisley Co., 1951-53; mgr. data processing Swift & Co., 1953-65, asst. controller, 1965-67, controller, 1967-68, v.p. corporate devel., controller, 1968-70, fin. v.p., dir., 1970-73; fin. v.p., dir. Esmark, Inc., Chgo., 1973, pres., chief operating officer, 1973-77, pres., chief exec. officer, 1977—, also dir.; dir. Harris Bankcorp., Inc., Harris Trust & Savs. Bank, Inland Steel Co., G.D. Searle & Co., McGraw-Edison Co. Bd. dirs. Lyric Opera, Chgo.; trustee Michael Reese Hosp. and Med. Center, Chgo., St. Norbert Coll., De Pere, Wis., Ill. Inst. Tech. and IIT Research Inst., Chgo., Com. for Econ. Devel., Washington, Mus. Sci. and Industry, Chgo.; mem. citizens bd. U. Chgo.; mem. exec. com. adv. council Coll. Bus. Adminstrn., U. Notre Dame. Served in USNR, 1942-46. Mem. Fin. Execs. Inst., Chgo. Council Fgn. Relations (dir.), Chgo. Assn. Commerce and Industry (dir.). Clubs: Comml., Chgo., Econ. (Chgo.). Office: 55 E Monroe St Chicago IL 60603

KELLY, GALEN GREGORY, security and law enforcement cons.; b. Englewood, N.J., Jan. 13, 1947; s. Michael J. and Marie (Knapp) K.; B.A., Bloomfield Coll., 1970; student Backster Polygraph Sch., 1971, Kodak Sch. Law Enforcement Photography, 1974; m. Elizabeth Thoma, Apr. 20, 1974; children—Dillon, Meghan, Christopher, Michael. With Mgmt. Safeguards, Inc., N.Y.C., 1971-74, asst. dir. investigations, 1973-74; prin. G. Kelly Assocs., Kingston, N.Y., 1974—; lectr. in field. Licensed investigative cons., N.Y., N.J. Mem. Am. Polygraph Assn. (U.S. rep. 1977), Am. Soc. Indsl. Security. Republican. Mem. Reformed Ch. Am. Club: Masons. Address: 293 Wall St Kingston NY 12401

KELLY, JAMES PATRICK, JR., natural resources co. exec.; b. Bklyn., July 19, 1933; s. James Patrick and Marion Rita (Gleason) K.; B.S. in Engring., U.S. Naval Acad., 1955; postgrad. U. Houston, 1968-69; m. Nancy Karen Sather, June 10, 1967; children—Kathryn, Mark, Lisa Angelique, Trevor, Lisa, James. Asst. site mgr. Pathfinder Reactor, Allis Chalmers Mfg. Co., Sioux Falls, S.D., 1963-67; nuclear project mgr. Brown & Root Co., Houston, 1967-69; mgr. constrn. project, asst. v.p. Gibbs & Hill subs. Dravo Corp., Omaha, 1969-73, N.Y.C., 1973-75, pres. Dravo Lime subs., Pitts., 1975-77, group v.p. natural resources parent co., 1976—; dir. So. Industries, Inc. Mem. Sioux Falls Bd. Edn., 1965-66, Assn. for Retarded Citizens, 1970—; bd. dirs. S.D. Mental Health Assn., 1966-67, Western Pa. Sch. for Blind Children, 1978—. Served with USN, 1955-63. Registered profl. engr., Calif. Mem. Nat. Soc. Profl. Engrs., Am. Nuclear Soc., Am. Iron and Steel Inst., Western Pa. Engrs. Soc., Mensa, Sierra Club. Club: Duquesne (Pitts.). Contbr. articles on nuclear reactors to profl. jours. Home: 2778 Beechwood Blvd Pittsburgh PA 15217 Office: One Oliver Plaza Pittsburgh PA 15222

KELLY, JOAN ELEANOR BRAND (MRS. PHILIP JOHN KELLY), banker; b. N.Y.C., Aug. 17, 1938; d. William Herman and Rosa (Werne) Brand; B.B.A., St. John's U., 1967; certificate basic banking Am. Inst. Banking, 1971; M.B.A., So. Meth. U., 1972; postgrad. Southwestern Grad. Sch. Banking (Nat. Assn. Bank Women scholar), 1974-76; m. Philip John Kelly, Nov. 19, 1960. Research asst. to trust officer Fed. Bank and Trust Co., N.Y.C., 1958-67; research officer econ. research div. Republic Nat. Bank of Dallas, 1967-76, mgr. bus. devel., 1977—. Mem. LWV, Am. Mktg. Assn., Am. Statis. Assn., Southwestern Social Sci. Orgn., Dallas Council on World Affairs, Nat. Assn. Bank Women, AAUW, Bus. and Profl. Women's Club of Dallas, So. Meth. U., Alumni Assn., St. John's Alumni Assn., Alpha Beta Chi, Omicron Delta Epsilon. Roman Catholic. Club: Altrusa. Home: 2808 Sherwood Ln Colleyville TX 76034

KELLY, JOHN WILLIAM, engring. and constrn. co. exec.; b. Roselle Park, N.J., May 11, 1924; s. John Patrick and Katherine C. (Von Ohlen) K.; B.S., Swarthmore Coll., 1945; M.S., Stevens Inst. Tech., 1951; postgrad. M.I.T., 1976, Northeastern U., 1977; m. Suzanne C. DeSchaepdryver, Aug. 6, 1953; children—Patricia, Kathleen, Anthony, John, Anne, Christopher. Mech. equipment engr., resident engr. Exxon Research and Engring. Co., Florham Park, N.J., 1946-60, group head gen. engring. dept., 1960; project mgr. The Badger Co., Inc., Cambridge, Mass., 1961-72; with Badger America, Inc., Cambridge, 1973—, v.p. ops., 1975-81, sr. v.p. ops., 1981—. Served to lt. (j.g.) U.S. Navy, 1945-46. Registered profl. engr., Mass., N.J., Fla., Mem. Nat. Constructors Assn. (bd. dirs., 1977—), Am. Inst. Chem. Engrs. (engring. and constrn. exec. com. 1974—), ASME, Nat. Soc. Profl. Engrs. Roman Catholic. Office: 1 Broadway Cambridge MA 02112

KELLY, JOSEPH FRANCIS, JR., broadcasting exec.; b. Bklyn., July 24, 1941; s. Joseph Francis and Mary Genevive (Griffin) K.; B.S., Fordham U., 1965; M.B.A., N.Y. U., 1969; m. Sharon Parke, Dec. 26, 1965; children—Steven, Deborah, Michael, David. Bus. mgr. various divs. ABC Radio Network, N.Y.C., 1962-72, account exec., Detroit, 1972-74, Chgo., 1974-75, sales mgr., Detroit, 1975-77, v.p., regional sales mgr., Southfield, Mich., 1977—. Mem. Detroit Radio Advt. Group (treas., 1975, sec., dir., 1979—, v.p. 1980), Am. Mktg. Assn. (membership chmn. Detroit chpt., dir. 1979—). Republican. Roman Catholic. Clubs: K.C., Lions, Recess, Bloomfield Open Hunt. Home: 5766 Bingham Troy MI 48098 Office: ABC Broadcasting 20777 W Ten Mile Rd Southfield MI 48075

KELLY, MARVIN CECIL, mgmt. cons.; b. N.Y.C., May 25, 1932; s. Alfred G. and Beatrice L. (Crowell) K.; B.S. in Chem. Engring., Bucknell U., 1954; M.B.A., U. Mich., 1958; m. Virginia V. Martin, May 16, 1959; children—Marvin J., Pamela S., Mark C. Analyst, Union Carbide Corp., N.Y.C., 1957; indsl. engr. Colgate Palmolive, N.Y.C., 1958-64; cons. mgmt. adv. services Deloitte Haskins & Sella, N.Y.C., 1964-67, mgr., 1967-70, dir., 1970—; instr. fin. modeling, prodn. planning, mgmt. info. continuing edn. program. Treas., Oak Knoll Environ. Assn., 1976; chmn. Mendham (N.J.) Rd. Edn., 1975-78; chmn. audit com. Mendham Presbyterian Ch., 1979. Served with Signal Corps, AUS, 1954-56. Cert. mgmt. cons. Mem. Inst. Mgmt. Consultants, Am. Inst. Chem. Engrs., Inst. Mgmt. Sci., Sigma Alpha Epsilon. Clubs: Williams, Roxiticus Golf. Office: 1114 Ave of Americas New York NY 10036

KELLY, MICHAEL LEWIS, electronic distbn. sales exec.; b. San Francisco, June 23, 1952; s. William L. and June S. (Chopnik) K.; student Canada (Calif.) Coll., 19—, Coll. of Redwoods, Calif., 1971-72, L'Abri, Switzerland, 1973, Trinity Coll., Chgo., 1973-76; m. Susan A. Becker, Nov. 29, 1977. Tennis profl., Highland Park, Ill., 1973-76; distbr., sales mgr. James Heaton Co., Redwood City, Calif., 1976-78; gen. mgr., sales mgr. Shelley Electronics, Inc., Mountain View, Calif., 1978—; tchr. seminar passive components Dale Electronics. Republican. Presbyterian. Home: 270 Enriquez Ct Milpitas CA 95035 Office: 2660 Marine Way Mountain View CA 94043

KELLY, NORMAN MICHAEL, electronics distbn. co. exec.; b. Newark, Jan. 13, 1937; s. Gregory Paul and Virginia Lee (Patten) K.; B.Ch.E., Rensselaer Poly. Inst., 1959; M.B.A., Harvard U., 1962; postgrad. U. Pa., 1963-65; div.; 1 son, John Hamilton. Mgr. spl. studies Atlantic Richfield Co., N.Y.C., 1962-69; treas., controller Oxirane Corp., Princeton, N.J., 1969-72; corp. controller Arrow Electronics, Inc., Greenwich, Conn., 1973-79, pres. consumer products div., 1975-77, corp. v.p., 1975—, exec. v.p. electronics distbn. div., 1979—; dir. Serios, Inc. Served to 2d lt. U.S. Army, 1960-61. Mem. Fin. Execs. Inst. Unitarian. Club: Ardsley (N.Y.). Curling. Home: 351 E 84th St Apt 32A New York NY 10028 Office: 900 Broad Hollow Rd Farmingdale NY 11735

KELLY, PAUL RICHARD, pacemaker co. exec.; b. Williamsport, Pa., Mar. 20, 1928; s. John Collins and Nelle Marie (Dutton) K.; B.A., U. Mo., 1950, B.S. in E.E., 1956; m. Gloria Jean Maniscalco, June 4, 1955; children—Kevin Joseph, Theresa Marie, James Gerard, Patrick Collins, Timothy Paul. Design engr. Gen. Electric Co., Hanford Operation, Richland, Wash., 1956-62, Advanced Biomed. Systems, Milw., 1962-69, mgr. product planning, biomed. sect., 1969-70, mgr. pacemaker engring., 1970-75, mgr. pacemaker product assurance, 1975-77; exec. v.p., chief operating officer, dir. Telectronics, Ltd., Milw., 1977—. Served with U.S. Army, 1950-53. Patentee in field. Home: 6201 S 116 St Hales Corners WI 53130 Office: 301 W Vogel St Milwaukee WI 53207

KELLY, ROBERT DUFF, investment counsellor; b. N.Y.C., Mar. 13, 1931; s. Joseph Duff and Mary (Coleman) K.; B.S. in Econs., U. Pa., 1954; m. Christy Hatch, Apr. 21, 1972; children—Robert Duff, Michael. Vice pres. A Morgan Maree Jr. & Assos. Inc., Los Angeles, 1962-71; v.p., investment counsel Jess S. Morgan & Co., Inc., Los Angeles, 1976—. Served with U.S. Army, 1954-56. Mem. Bond Club Los Angeles, Sigma Chi. Club: Marina City (gov.). Office: 6420 Wilshire Blvd Los Angeles CA 90048

KELLY, THOMAS JOSEPH, librarian service exec.; b. N.Y.C., Sept. 23, 1938; s. Daniel Paul and Margaret Catherine (Kelly) K.; B.A., Manhattan Coll., 1961; M.B.A., Columbia U., 1964. Dir. client relations Quantum Sci. Corp., N.Y.C., 1964-67; library cons. Callaghan & Co., Wilmette, Ill., 1968-70; pres. Associated Library Service, Inc., N.Y.C., 1971—. N.Y. State Coll. scholar, 1956. Mem. ALA. Democrat. Roman Catholic. Office: 80 Broad St New York NY 10004

KELLY, WILLIAM BRET, ins. exec.; b. Rocky Ford, Colo., Sept. 28, 1922; s. William Andrew and Florence Gail (Yant) K.; B.A. cum laude, U. Colo., 1947; m. Patricia Ruth Ducy, Mar. 25, 1944; children—Eric Damian, Kathryn Gail Kelly Schweitzer. With Steel City Agencies, Inc., and predecessor, Pueblo, Colo., 1946—, pres., 1961-76, chmn. bd., 1977—; dir. United Bank Pueblo, 1963—, Pub. Expenditure Council, 1967—. Mem. Pueblo Area Council Govts., 1971-73; trustee Pueblo Bd. Water Works, 1966-80, pres., 1970-71; pres. Pueblo Single Fund Plan, 1960-61, Pueblo Heart Council, 1962, Family Service Soc. Pueblo, 1963; mem. 10th Jud. Dist. Nominating Com., 1967-71; trustee U. So. Colo. Found., 1967—, Jackson Found., 1972—, Farley Found., 1979—. Served with inf. AUS, 1943-45. Decorated Silver Star, Bronze Star with oak leaf cluster, Purple Heart with oak leaf cluster; C.P.C.U. Mem. Soc. C.P.C.U., Colo. Ins. Edn. Found., Pueblo C. of C. (past pres.), Phi Beta Kappa. Democrat. Clubs: Pueblo Kiwanis (past pres.), Pueblo Country (treas. 1964-66). Home: 700 W 17th St Pueblo CO 81003 Office: 1414 W 4th St Pueblo CO 81004

KELMENSON, LEO ARTHUR, advt. exec.; b. N.Y.C., Jan. 3, 1927; s. Joseph A. and Ruth (Rothberg) K.; B.S., Columbia, 1951, postgrad. Grad. Sch. Bus., 1952; children—Todd-Arthur, Joel Adam; m. 2d, Barbara Dauphin, Feb. 20, 1973. From TV prodn. to sr. v.p., asst. to pres. Lennen & Newell, 1951-65; exec. v.p., mem. exec. com. Norman

Craig & Kummel, 1965-66; sr. v.p., dir., mem. exec. com. Kenyon & Eckhardt, 1967-68; pres. Kenyon & Eckhardt Advt. Inc., 1968—; pres., chief exec. officer, chmn. exec. com. Kenyon & Eckhardt Inc., C.P.V., 1970—; pres. Kelmerson Funds Ltd.; dir. Locations Unltd.; lectr. New Sch. Social Research. Adviser communications office U.S. Atty. Gen., 1960-63; spl. project officer Dept. State, 1952-64; v.p., dir. African Med. and Research Found., 1957—; mem. pub. relations com. Nat. Cancer Found., 1958—; adv. com. Nat. Cultural Center, 1962; pres. Shoes for Little Souls, 1960, Remsenburg Assn., 1968; bd. dirs. ASPCA; mem. pres.'s adv. com. Am. Diabetes Assn. Served with USMCR, World War II. Recipient Theodore Roosevelt Man of Year award, 1955; Silver Quill Poetry award 1955; Res. Officers Assn. award, 1965; Guggenheim World Peace award, 1951. Mem. U.S. Olympic Com., N.Y. Advt. Club, Soc. Am. Businessmen Club, Sigma Phi Epsilon. Clubs: Sands Point (N.Y.) Yacht; L.I. Polo; Mission Hills Country (Palm Springs, Calif.). Author: (poetry) Epilogue, 1964; also short stories. Home: LI NY also Palm Springs CA Office: 200 Park Ave New York NY 10166

KELSEY, GREGORY LYNN, computer co. exec.; b. Logan, Utah, Nov. 8, 1947; s. Daniel B. and Vera (Griffin) K.; B.S., Brigham Young U., 1969; M.B.A., U. Santa Clara, 1972. Mem. investment div. Wells Fargo Bank, San Francisco, 1969-71; with FMC Fin. Co., San Jose, Calif., 1971-72; with Arcata Nat. Corp., Menlo Park, Calif., 1972-76, fin. mgr., 1975-76; asst. treas., dir. public relations Amdahl Corp., Sunnyvale, Calif., 1976—. Home: 765 San Antonio Rd Palo Alto CA 94303 Office: 1250 E Arques Ave Sunnyvale CA 94086

KELSEY, JAREL ROBERT, health care industry exec.; b. Cherry Grove, W.Va., Sept. 11, 1937; s. Charles T. and Nola E. (Bennett) K.; B.S. in Chemistry and Biology, No. Ill. U., 1963; postgrad. Loyola U., Chgo. Tech. rep. Dade div. Am. Hosp. Supply Corp., 1964-67, nat. sales mgr., 1967-69, v.p., Miami, Fla., 1975-76; exec. v.p. Internat. Reagent COrp., Kobe, Japan, 1970-74; v.p. BioQuest div. Becton-Dickenson Corp., Cockeysville, Md., 1977-78; pres. Analytab Products div. Ayerst Labs. div. Am. Home Products, L.I., N.Y., 1978-79, J.T. Baker Diagnostics div. Richardson-Merrill, Inc., Bethlehem, Pa., 1979—. Served with AUS, 1955-58. Mem. Health Industry Mfrs. Assn., Am. Soc. Med. Technologists, Am. Soc. Clin. Pathologists (affiliate), BioMed. Mktg. Assn. Office: 2266 Ave A Bethlehem PA 18017

KELSEY, ROLAND JACK, mfg. co. exec.; b. Barrington, Ill., Dec. 10, 1920; s. Harold D. and Theresa K.; B.S., U. Ill., 1942; m. Maxine M. Kelley, June 16, 1945; children—Robert J., James A., Susam M. Mem. fin. staff, Bendix Co., 1943-46, Drake Mfg. Co., 1947-50, Ford Motor Co., 1951-52, Aeroquip Co., 1953-58, Unistrut, 1959—; sr. partner McGladrey Hendrickson & Co., Barrington, 1960-79; pres. Kelco Industries, Inc., Woodstock, Ill., 1980—, C.P.A., Ill. Mem. Ill. C.P.A. Soc. (dir. 1973-74; chpt. pres. 1972), Barrington C. of C. (pres. 1962, dir. 1969-79), Econ. Club Chgo., Am. Inst. C.P.A.'s, Chgo. Estate Planning Council. Republican. Clubs: Barrington Hills Country, Elks. Home: 666 Park Dr Barrington IL 60010 Office: 9210 Country Club Rd Woodstock IL 60098

KELSO, JAMES, JR., mfg. co. exec.; b. Portsmouth, Ohio, Dec. 26, 1919; s. James and Mabel E. (Ely) K.; grad. Ohio State U., 1943, postgrad., 1950-51; m. Mary Ruth Gayer, Jan. 7, 1944; children—Daniel J., Cristin Lee. Salesman, Drumstick Co., Ft. Worth, 1948-50, WRFD Radio, Worthington, Ohio, 1951-53; v.p., account exec., Byer & Bowman Advt. Agy., Columbus, Ohio, 1953-60; v.p. mktg. Big Drum, Inc. subs., Columbus, 1960-78; pres. Drumstick Co. div. Big Drum, Inc., Columbus, 1978—, also dir. Served with U.S. Army, 1943-46. Mem. Dairy and Food Industries Supply Assn., Sales Exec. Club (past pres.). Clubs: Masons, Shriners.

KELSO, LOUIS ORTH, investment banker, lawyer, economist; b. Denver, Dec. 4, 1913; s. Oren S. and Nettie I. (Wolfe) K.; B.S. cum laude, U. Colo., 1937, LL.B., 1938; D.Sc., Araneta U. (Philippines), 1962; children—Martha Jennifer Brookman, Katherine Elizabeth Von Stein; m. 2d, Patricia Hetter. Admitted to Colo. bar, 1938, Calif. bar, 1946; practiced in Denver, 1938-42, San Francisco, 1946-75; asso. firm Pershing, Bosworth, Dick & Dawson, 1938-42; asso. prof. law U. Colo., 1945-46; partner Brobeck, Phleger & Harrison, 1946-58; sr. partner Kelso, Cotton, Seligman & Ray, 1958-70; mng. dir. Louis O. Kelso, Inc., P.C., 1970-75; chmn. bd. Kelso & Co., Inc., investment bankers, 1975—; sec., dir. Precision Data Corp., Palo Alto, Calif.; pres., dir. Prometheus Press, San Francisco; dir. Kelso & Co., Inc., San Francisco, Statesman Group, Inc., Des Moines, Aetna Variable Fund Inc., Aetna Variable Encore Fund, Inc., Aetna Income Shares, Hartford, Conn. Bd. dirs. Inst. for Study Econ. Systems, San Francisco; founding trustee Crystal Springs Sch. for Girls; trustee Inst. Philos. Research, Chgo. Served from ensign to lt. USNR, 1942-45. Mem. Am., Calif., San Francisco bar assns. Clubs: Bohemian, Pacific Union, Bankers, Villa Taverna (San Francisco); Chicago (Chgo.). Author: (with Mortimer J. Adler) The Capitalist Manifesto, 1958, The New Capitalists, 1961; (with Patricia Hetter) Two-Factor Theory: The Economics of Reality, 1968, Finishing the Unfinished Capitalist Revolution, 1981. Contbr. articles to profl. polit. and intellectual jours. Office: 111 Pine St San Francisco CA 94111

KELSON, IRWIN STUART, ins. data processing cons.; b. Perth Amboy, N.J., Feb. 28, 1932; B.S. in Indsl. Engring., Johns Hopkins U., 1954; M.Indsl. Engring., U. So. Calif., 1961. With IBM, 1962-78, sr. program mgr. data processing div., 1976-78; pres., chief operating officer Ins. Inst. for Research, White Plains, N.Y., 1978-81; computer cons. to ins. agts. and cos., Purchase, N.Y., 1981—. Mem. Soc. Ins. Research, Assn. Computing Machinery, Am. Inst. Indsl. Engrs., Am. Soc. Assn. Execs., Am. Mgmt. Assn. Home: 4 Dorado Dr Purchase NY 10577 Office: 4 Dorado Dr Purchase NY 10577

KELTON, JOHN T(REMAIN), lawyer; b. Bay City, Mich., Mar. 12, 1909; s. Frank P. S. and Jessie (Eleanor Tremain) K.; student Culver (Ind.) Mil. Acad., 1925-28; S.B. in Chem. Engring., Mass. Inst. Tech., 1932; LL.B., Harvard, 1935; m. Carol E. Copeland, July 9, 1935; children—Carol E. M., Joy T. Admitted to N.Y. bar, 1935; asso. Watson, Bristol, Johnson & Leavenworth, N.Y.C., 1935-40, 46-49; mem. Watson Johnson Leavenworth & Blair, 1950-53, Watson Leavenworth Kelton & Taggart, 1954—. Served from 2d lt. to lt. col. AUS, 1940-46. Mem. Am. (bd. mgrs. 1964-67, pres. 1974), N.Y. (pres. 1967) patent law assns. Conglist. Home: Nutmeg Ln Westport CT 06880 Office: 100 Park Ave New York NY 10017

KELVIN, ALLAN E., psychologist; b. N.Y.C., Apr. 8, 1932; s. Arthur J. and Hilda (Garber) K.; B.S. in Psychology, Purdue U., 1955; M.B.A. in Indsl. Psychology, CCNY, 1968; postgrad. Center for Modern Psychoanalytic Studies, 1977—, Adelphi U., 1977—; m. Edith Legumsky, Dec. 21, 1958; children—Lisa, Marjorie, Debra. Tng. analyst research and advanced devel. div. AVCO, Wilmington, Mass., 1956-60; human factors group leader Am. Machine & Foundry, Stamford, Conn., 1960-62; operational and program requirement group leader System Devel. Corp., Paramus, N.J., 1962-63; sr. staff psychologist, life scis. Grumman Aerospace Corp., Bethpage, N.Y., 1963—; instr. abnormal psychology SUNY, Farmingdale, 1979. Vol. psychologist Narcotics Guidance Council, Huntington, N.Y., 1972-73, Pederson-Krag Mental Health Clinic, Huntington, 1977-79. Served with U.S. Army, 1957. Mem. Am. Psychol. Assn., Nat. Assn. for Advancement of Psychoanalysis, Human Factors Soc. (v.p. Met. Chpt., 1974). Home: 23 Maxwell Ct Huntington NY 11743 Office: Mail Stop B-16 Plant 25 Grumman Aerospace Corp Bethpage NY 11714

KEM, LAWRENCE R., profl. services co. exec.; b. Sikeston, Mo., Apr. 22, 1935; s. Louis R. and Rosa M. (Bohannon) K.; B.S. summa cum laude in Accounting, SE Mo. State U., 1956; m. Barbara Hope Kem, Sept. 1, 1956; children—Elizabeth, Laura. Mem. staff mfg. and distbn. Procter & Gamble, S.I., N.Y., St. Louis, 1958-64; partner mgmt. cons. McKinsey & Co., Cleve., London, 1964-72; group v.p., gen. mgr. spl. products operation Gen. Cable Corp., Greenwich, Conn., 1972-74; chmn., dir., chief exec. officer Am. Appraisal Assos., Inc., Milw., 1974—, dir. Sta-Rite Industries, Inc., Milw., Marine Nat. Exchange Bank, Milw. Trustee, Univ. Sch., Milw.; bd. dirs. Greater Milw. Com., Met. Milw. Assn. Commerce. Mem. Young Pres.'s Orgn. Clubs: Univ., Milw., Town (Milw.); Union League (N.Y.C.). Office: American Appraisal Associates Inc 525 E Michigan St Milwaukee WI 53201

KEMP, ROBERT BOWERS, JR., bank exec.; b. Balt., July 25, 1941; s. Robert Bowers and Edwina Reid (Rose) K.; B.S., U. Md., 1963; M.B.A., U. Houston, 1968; m. Suzanne Marie Durham, Dec. 18, 1976; 1 dau., Amy Nicole. Market mgr. Kimberley Clark Corp., Neenah, Wis., 1968-70; dir. research, sr. portfolio mgr. Provident Mgmt. Co., Phila., 1970-73; trust investment officer First Tenn. Nat. Bank, Chattanooga, 1973-77; v.p. investment strategy Mchts. Nat. Bank, Indpls., 1977—; prin. R. B. Kemp & Assos., investment advisor; adj. prof. U. Tenn., Chattanooga, 1976. Mem. exec. and ch. councils, fin. sec. King of Glory Lutheran Ch., Carmel, Ind. Mem. Indpls. Soc. Fin. Analysts, Chartered Fin. Analysts Assn., Nat. Assn. Bus. Economists. Club: Econs. Indpls. Home: 11 Hamp Ct Carmel IN 46032 Office: Merchants Nat Bank One Merchants Plaza Indianapolis IN 46255

KEMPE, ROBERT ARON, sci. instrument mfg. co. exec.; b. Mpls., Mar. 6, 1922; s. Walter A. and Madge (Stoker) K.; B.Chem. Engring., U. Minn., 1943; postgrad. metallurgy, bus. adminstrn. Case Western Res. U., 1946-49; m. Virginia Lou Wiseman, June 21, 1946; children—Mark A., Katherine A. Various positions TRW, Inc., Cleve., 1943-53, div. sales mgr., 1953; v.p. Metalphoto Corp., Cleve., 1954-63, pres., 1963-71, pres. Allied Decals, Inc., affiliate, Cleve., 1963-68; v.p., treas. Horizons Research Inc., 1970-71; pres. Reuter-Stokes, Inc., Cleve., 1971—; v.p. Miles Ahead, Inc. Served to lt. (j.g.) USNR, 1944-46; PTO. Mem. Inst. Dirs. (London), Am. Nuclear Soc. (vice-chmn. No. Ohio sect.), Sigma Chi. Club: Chemists (N.Y.C.); Country of Hudson (Ohio). Contbr. articles to profl. jours. Patentee in field. Home: 242 Streetsboro St Hudson OH 44236 Office: 18530 S Miles Pkwy Cleveland OH 44128

KEMPER, DORLA DEAN (EATON), real estate broker; b. Calhoun, Mo., Sept. 10, 1929; d. Paul McVey and Jesse Lee (McCombs) Eaton; student William Woods Coll., 1947-48; B.S. in Edn., Central Mo. State U., 1952; m. Charles K. Kemper, Mar. 1, 1951; children—Kevin Keil, Kara Lee. Tchr. pub. schs., Twin Falls, Idaho, 1950-51, Mission, Kans., 1952-53, Burbank, Calif., 1953-57; real estate saleswoman Minn., 1967-68, Calif., 1971-73; Deanie Kemper, Realtor (name changed to Deanie Kemper, Inc. Real Estate Brokerage 1976), Loomis, Calif., 1974-76, pres., 1976—, also dir. Pres. Battle Creek Park Elementary Sch. PTA, St. Paul, 1966-67; mem. Placer County (Calif.) Bicentennial Commn., 1976. Named to Million Dollar Club (lifetime) Sacramento and Placer County bds. realtors, 1978; designated Grad. Realtors Inst., Cert. Residential Specialist. Mem. Nat., Calif. assns. realtors, Sacramento, Placer County (mem. profl. standards com.) bds. realtors. Republican. Mem. Christian Ch. Clubs: DAR (chpt. regent 1971-73, organizing chpt. regent 1977—, dist. dir. 1978-80, state registrar Calif. 1980—), Hidden Valley Women's (pres. Loomis club 1970-71). Home: 8165 Morningside Dr Loomis CA 95650

KEMPER, JAMES SCOTT, JR., ins. co. exec.; b. Chgo., Apr. 8, 1914; s. James Scott and Mildred (Hooper) K.; A.B., Yale, 1935; LL.B., Harvard, 1938; m. Joan Hoff, Dec. 27, 1960; children—James Scott III, Linda Kemper White, Stephen H., Judith (Mrs. Harrie Lewis), Robert C. Admitted to N.Y. bar, Ill. bar, Calif. bar; with Antitrust div. Justice Dept.; pvt. practice law, N.Y.C., Chgo., Los Angeles; now chmn. Lumbermens Mut. Casualty Co. and Kemper Corp., Long Grove, Ill. Dir., Am. Mut. Ins. Alliance; trustee The Conf. Bd., Inc. Bd. dirs. Nat. Council on Alcoholism, Boys Clubs of Am., Chgo. Boys Club, Lyric Opera of Chgo.; pres., trustee J.S. Kemper Found.; trustee Kemper Ednl. and Charitable Fund, Northwestern Meml. Hosp., Chgo., Ill. Inst. Tech.; mem. adv. com. Drug Abuse and Alcoholism Program of Citizens Conf. on State Legislatures; mem. adv. bd. Chgo. Met. Council on Alcoholism, Inc. Served to lt. comdr. USNR, World War II. Recipient award Freedoms Found. at Valley Forge, 1968, Alpha Kappa Psi Found. award for distinguished service to higher edn., 1973, William H. Spurgeon award Nat. Exploring Div., Boy Scouts Am., 1973, Coll. of Humanities award, 1973, Gold Key award Nat. Council on Alcoholism, 1974; ALMACA award Assn. Labor Mgmt. Adminstrs. and Consultants on Alcoholism, 1977. Mem. Econ. Club of Chgo., Alpha Sigma Phi. Clubs: Chicago; Glen View; Bohemian (San Francisco); Pauma Valley Country; Ironwood Country (Palm Desert, Calif.). Office: Lumbermen's Mut Casualty Co Long Grove IL 60049*

KEMPER, YVES JEAN, automotive engr., research exec.; b. Paris, Feb. 29, 1936; came to U.S., 1976; s. Frederic and Jacqueline (Rigaut) K.; grad. Ecole Poly., Lausanne, Switzerland, 1964; m. Anne Brigitte Marie Petry, June 19, 1965; children—Frederic, Stanislas, Helene Kemper Guillaume. Cons. engr. Battelle Inst., Geneva, 1965-66; project engr. SNECMA, Villaroche, France, 1966-68; dir. research and devel. Sambron Sarl, Ponchateau, France, 1968-71; chief exec. officer DEMECA, Maisons Lafitte, France, 1971-76; pres. Vadetec Corp., Troy, Mich., 1976—; asst. instr. Inst. de Thermodynamique and Ecole Poly. Federale, Lausanne, 1964-68. Mem. ASME (com. on traction drives), Engring. Soc. Detroit. Patentee automotive engines and machine parts. Home: 841 Glengarry Birmingham MI 48010 Office: 2681 Industrial Row Troy MI 48084

KEMPF, KARLTON, instrument mfg. co. exec.; b. Ill., Mar. 1949; s. Paul S. and Dorothea R. Kempf; B.S. in Biology, San Diego State U., 1972, M.S. in Radiol. Physics, 1975. Gen. mgr. Metron Marker Co., Solana Beach, Calif., 1972-73; lectr. physics San Diego State U., 1975-77; v.p. ops. Metron Optics, Inc., Solana Beach, 1977-79, exec. v.p., 1979—; pres. Metron Concepts Inc., 1978—, also dir.; dir. Widescope, Inc. Boy Scouts Am. Mem. Health Physics Soc., Sigma Pi Sigma. Christian. Home: Escondito CA 92027 Office: 813 Academy Dr PO Box 690 Solana Beach CA 92075

KEMPF, LLOYD C., bank exec.; b. Ashley, N.D., Mar. 6, 1928; s. Michael J. and Lydia (Weisz) K.; grad. Bismarck Jr. Coll., 1949; student U. Denver, 1950, Inter Agy. Bank Examiners Sch., Washington, 1953; m. Janice I. Marquis, July 2, 1950; children—Mark, James, Lori, Lesa. Clk., N.D. State Tax Commn., Bismarck, N.D., 1949-50; mem. staff acctg. dept. Swift and Co., Denver, 1950-52; asst. dep. examiner N.D. Banking Commn., Bismarck, 1952-55, dep. examiner, 1955-58, chief dep. examiner, 1958-61; asst. securities commr. N.D. Securities Commn., Bismarck, 1958-61; pres., chief exec. officer Grant County State Bank and partner Grant County Ins. Agy., Carson, N.D., 1961-72, also dir. bank; pres., chmn. bd., chief exec. officer Goose River Bank, Mayville, N.D., 1972—, also dir.; pres., dir. Goose River Ins. Agy., Mayville, Goose River Holding Co., Mayville; partner Mayville Bldg. Co.; chmn. bd. Oakley Nat. Bank, Buffalo, Minn.; v.p., dir. Oakley Investors Group, Inc., Buffalo. Pres. Mayville Improvement Assn.; 1976—; v.p. Mayville Mut. Aid Corp., 1975—; mem. internship adv. com. Mayville State Coll., 1975—; chmn. Traill county (N.D.) U.S. Savs. Bonds.; bd. dirs. Mayville State Coll. Found., 1978—. Served with Paratroops, U.S. Army, 1946-47. Mem. Am. Bankers Assn. (cert. comml. lender), N.D. Bankers Assn. (pres. S.W. group 1966). Republican. Lutheran. Clubs: Elks, Masons, VFW, Am. Legion, Eagles. Home: 21 Westwood Dr Mayville ND 58257 Office: 44 W Main St Mayville ND 58257

KEMPTHORNE, RICHARD LEWIS, constrn. industry exec.; b. Orange, N.J., Jan. 7, 1927; s. James Lewis and Eleanor (McKelvey) K.; Asso. Bus. Adminstrn., Nichols Coll., 1949; B.S., Syracuse U., 1951; m. Alice Clair Prost, Feb. 26, 1949; children—James Lewis III, Ann. Vice pres. Sprayed Insulation Inc., Newark, 1951-53; head Columbia Acoustics & Fireproofing Co., Stanhope, N.J., 1954-56; chief exec., sec.-treas. Fla. Insulation & Fireproofing Co., Miami, Fla., 1957-65; pres., dir. Sprayed Fibers, Inc., Miami, 1963-71, Spraydon Overseas Corp., Miami, 1966-71, Midwest Sprayon Corp., 1966-71, Western Sprayon, Inc., 1970-71; v.p. Tex. Fireproofing Co., Houston, 1960-63; pres., dir. Sprayon Research Corp., Fort Lauderdale, Fla., 1964—; pres., dir. Sprayon Internat., Inc., Bklyn., 1971-73, SprayDon Corp., Ft. Lauderdale, 1975—, SprayDon Corp. Ltd., Curacao, Netherlands Antilles, 1975—; pres. Am. Energy Products Corp., Edison, N.J.; acoustical cons. Pres., Miami Shores Prep. Sch., 1968-72. Mem. bd. elections Young Republicans. Miami, 1958—. Served with USNR, 1944-46. Mem. Am. Soc. Testing and Materials, Nat. Fireprotection Assn., Assn. Walls and Ceiling Contractors Internat., AAU. Clubs: Palm-Aire Country (Pompano Beach, Fla.); Marina Bay. Patentee in field. Office: 5701 Bayview Dr Fort Lauderdale FL 33308

KEMSLEY, WILLIAM GEORGE, JR., publisher; b. Detroit, Apr. 11, 1928; s. William G., and Verna (Smith) K.; student Columbia, 1948-49, Wayne State U., 1949-52; m. Marcella Bennis Myers, Sept. 10, 1966; children—Diane Amelia (from previous marriage), Molly O., Katie, William George III, Andrew, Maggie. Adminstrv. dir. Archives of Am. Art, Detroit, 1958-60; free lance writer, cons., 1961-64; asst. to pres. Detroit Bolt & Nut Co., 1960-61; exec. v.p. Corp. Ann. Reports, Inc., N.Y.C., 1964-68; propr. WKA Corp. Graphics, N.Y.C., 1968-79; exec. editor, pub. Backpacker mag., 1972-80; propr. Foot Trails Publs., Inc., Greenwich, Conn., 1980—. Served with USNR, 1945-46. Mem. Sierra Club, Nat. Audubon Soc., Wilderness Soc., Friends of the Earth, Nat. Wildlife Fedn., Am. Hiking Soc. (founder), Nat. Parks and Conservation Assn. Episcopalian. Clubs: Explorers, Appalachian Mountain, Adirondak Mountain, Colo. Mountain, Swiss Alpine. Contbr. articles on travel and sports to mags. and newspapers. Home and Office: Bedford Rd Greenwich CT 06830

KENDALL, DONALD MCINTOSH, consumer goods and services co. exec.; b. Sequim, Wash., Mar. 16, 1921; s. Carroll C. and Charlotte (McIntosh) K.; student Western Ky. State Coll., 1941-42; LL.D., Stetson U., 1971; m. Sigrid Ruedt von Collenberg, Dec. 22, 1965; children—Donna Lee Kendall Warren, Edward McDonnell, Donald McIntosh, Kent Collenberg. Spl. field rep. Pepsi-Cola Co., 1947-48, mgr. fountain sales, 1948-49, br. plant mgr. fountain sales, 1949-50, spl. rep., 1950-52, asst. sales mgr., 1952, asst. v.p., 1952—, v.p. nat. accounts fountain sales, 1952-57, pres. Pepsi Cola Internat., 1953-63, pres. Pepsi-Cola Co., 1963-65 (merger with Frito-Lay 1965), PepsiCo, Inc., 1965—, chmn. bd., chief exec. officer, 1971—, also dir.; dir. Pan Am. Airways, Atlantic Richfield, Investors Diversified Services Mut. Fund Group. Chmn., Nat. Alliance Businessmen, 1969-70, dir., 1970-78. Chmn., Nat. Center for Resource Recovery, Inc. 1970-76, dir., 1976—; chmn. Emergency Com. for Am. Trade, 1969-76, mem., 1976—; dir. U.S.-USSR Trade and Econ. Council. Chmn., Am. Ballet Theatre Found., 1973-77, chmn. exec. com., 1977—; trustee Manhattanville Coll. Served to lt. AC, USNR, 1942-47. Mem. Internat. C. of C. (trustee council), C. of C. U.S. (vice-chmn. 1980—). Clubs: Blind Brook, Links, Lyford Cay, River, Round Hill. Home: Porchuck Rd Greenwich CT 06830 Office: Pepsico Inc Purchase NY 10577

KENDALL, RICHARD HALE, food co. exec.; b. Indpls., Mar. 24, 1930; s. Max L. and Elberta (Hodson) K.; A.B., Earlham Coll., 1952; M.B.A., Ind. U., 1953; m. Ann Woolley, Sept. 6, 1953; children—Michael F., Thomas H. Bus. mgr. Friends United Meeting, Richmond, Ind., 1953-59; v.p., treas. Honeggers & Co., Inc., Fairbury, Ill., 1959-68; v.p. Heath Tecna Corp., Kent, Wash., 1968-71; chmn. bd., treas., dir. Maplehurst Farms, Inc., Indpls., 1971—; pres., chief exec. officer, treas., dir. Advanced Mktg. Systems Corp., Indpls., 1971—; sec., dir. Sr. Trust Corp., Indpls., 1971—; past pres., dir. Master Dairies, Inc.; pres., dir. Master Dairies, Inc.; chmn. bd., chief exec. officer, treas., dir. Maplehurst Deli-Bake, Inc., 1971—; chmn. bd., chief exec. officer, dir. Maplehurst Deli-Bake/South, Inc., Carrollton, Ga., 1977—. Mem. nat. export expansion council U.S. Dept. Commerce, 1969-71; mem. spl. levy tax com. State Wash., 1970-71; bd. dirs. Greater Indpls. Progress Com., 1977; chmn. adminstrn. and orgn. Highline Coll., 1970-71; trustee Earlham Coll., 1977—, also mem. exec. com.; trustee Friends United Meeting, 1974—; advisory council Conner Prairie Pioneer Settlement, 1977-78, dir. Friends World Com. for Consultation, 1977—. Mem. Milk Found. Indpls. (dir. 1971—), Midwest Dairy Products Assn. (dir., v.p. 1973—). Clubs: Rotary, Indpls. (v.p., dir.), Meridian Hills Country. Athletic Home: 7505 N Central Ave Meridian Hills Indianapolis IN 46240 Office: 8929 W Washington St Indianapolis IN 46241

KENDRICK, JAMES EARL, orgnl. communications cons.; b. Indpls., Sept. 12, 1940; s. John William and Mable E. (Colman) K.; B.A., Butler U., 1963; m. Carrie L. Fair, July 19, 1969. Exec. dir. Knox County Econ. Opportunity Council, Barbourville, Ky., 1965-66; research scientist N.Y. U., 1967-68; mgr. Volt Info. Scis., Washington, 1968-71, Nat. Urban Coalition, 1972-74; pres. Kendrick & Co., Washington, 1974—. Recipient Rural Service award OEO, 1968; citation Washington chpt. Am. Soc. Tng. and Devel., 1971. Mem. Internat. Assn. Bus. Communicators, Soc. Profl. Mgmt. Cons., Met. Washington Bd. Trade, Sigma Delta Chi. Author: Community Energy Workbook, 1974; National Urban Agenda Survey, 1974; also articles. Home: 1412 Dale Dr Silver Spring MD 20910 Office: 733 15th St NW Washington DC 20005

KENDRICK, JAMES RICHARD, moving co. exec.; b. La Belle, Mo., Aug. 8, 1929; s. William Howard and Oneta Jane (Cooter) K.; B.S., NE Mo. State U., 1961; m. Katherine Kendrick, Feb. 14, 1965; children—Debra Kay, Mark McRae. Acct., Peat, Marwick, Mitchell & Co., 1961-65; controller Bi-State Devel. Agy., 1965-78; v.p. fin. United Van Lines, Inc., Fenton, Mo., 1978—. Served with U.S. Army, 1951-52. C.P.A., Mo. Mem. Am. Inst. C.P.A.'s. Office: United Van Lines Inc 1 United Dr Fenton MO 63026

KENIG, NOE, electronics co. exec.; b. Warsaw, Poland, June 5, 1923; came to U.S., 1974; naturalized, 1980; s. Lazaro Hersz and Felisa (Elenbogen) K.; diploma mech. and elec. engring., Nat. U. La Plata, Buenos Aires, Argentina, 1951; mech. technologist diploma, Nat. Indsl. Sch. Luis M. Huergo, Buenos Aires, 1951; m. Ida Melnik, Apr. 17, 1948; children—Jorge Alberto, Carlos Eduardo. Licensee, Westinghouse Electric Corp., Argentina, 1941-49, Bendix Home Appliance Corp., Argentina, 1949-67; dir. Philco Argentina Corp., 1959-62; asst. pres., group gen. mgr. subs. Nat. Distillers and Chem. Corp., Argentina, 1958-72; with Motorola Inc., 1972—, v.p. multinat. ops., regional dir. Americas, Schaumburg, Ill., 1980—, also dir. subs. Office: 1303 E Algonquin Rd Schaumburg IL 60196

KENLY, F(RANKLIN) CORNING, JR., fin. cons.; b. Lake Forest, Ill., Feb. 21, 1915; s. F. Corning and Ruth (Farwell) K.; B.S., Harvard U., 1937, Advanced Mgmt. Program, 1964; m. Miriam Little, May 21, 1941; children—M.B. Kenly Earle, David F., F. Corning III. Loan adminstr. Harris Trust & Savs. Bank, Chgo., 1938-39; fin. exec. Household Fin. Corp., Chgo., 1940-41; sr. v.p. fin. ops. New Eng. Mut. Life Ins. Co., Boston, 1948-80; pres., dir. NEL Income Fund, Inc., Boston, 1973-80, NEL Tax Exempt Bond Fund, Inc., 1975-80, NEL Cash Mgmt. Account, Inc., 1977-80; v.p., dir. NEL Equity Fund, Inc., 1972-80, NEL Growth Fund, Inc., 1972-80, NEL Retirement Equity Fund, Inc., 1972-80; mem. real estate adv. bd. Citibank, N.A., N.Y.C., 1979—; dir. Nat. Mine Service Co., Pitts., 1980—; mem. adv. bd. Boston Bay Capital Co., 1980—; bd. assos. R.T. Madden Co., Inc., N.Y.C., 1980—. Chmn. capital plans adv. com. Town of Manchester (Mass.), 1978—, mem. fin. com., 1976—; mem. corp. Boston Mus. Sci., 1976; bd. dirs. Better Bus. Bur. Eastern Mass., 1970-80; trustee Harvard Adv., Cambridge, Mass., 1948—; mem. alumni exec. com. Thacher Sch., Ojai, Calif., 1948; trustee, fin. com. Cardigan Mountain Sch., Canaan, N.H., 1970. Served to lt. comdr. USNR, 1941-46. Mem. Boston Security Analysts Soc. Clubs: Econ., Union, Somerset (Boston); Manchester Yacht, Essex County (Manchester).

KENLY, GRANGER FARWELL, holding co. exec.; b. Portland, Oreg., Feb. 15, 1919; s. F. Corning and Ruth (Farwell) K.; A.B. cum laude, Harvard, 1941; m. Suzanne Warner, Feb. 7, 1948 (div. Nov. 1977); children—Margaret Farwell, Granger Farwell; m. 2d, Stella Brown Angevin, Oct. 8, 1978. Adminstrv. asst. to v.p. Poole Bros., Inc., Chgo., 1941-42; asst. advt. mgr. Sunset Mag., San Francisco, 1946-47; pub. relations, sales promotion mgr. Pabco Products, Inc., San Francisco, 1947-51; v.p., mgmt. supr. Needham, Louis & Brorby, Inc., Chgo., 1951-60; mgr. marketing plans dept. Pure Oil Co., Palatine, Ill., 1961-62, v.p. pub. relations, personnel, 1962-66; v.p. pub. affairs Abbott Labs., North Chicago, Ill., 1966-71; v.p. corp. and investor relations IC Industries, Inc., Chgo., 1972—. Bd. dirs. Evanston Hosp.; trustee Lawson YMCA, Chgo.; former mem. Zoning Bd. Appeals, Northfield, Ill.; mem. 22d ann. global strategy conf. U.S. Naval War Coll., 1970; mem. public affairs com. Am. Productivity Center. Served to maj. USAAF, 1942-46; ETO. Mem. Pub. Relations Soc. Am, Pub. Relations Seminar, New Eng. Soc. in City N.Y., Chgo. Assn. Commerce, Newcomen Soc. N.Am. Republican. Episcopalian. Clubs: Chicago, Econ., Univ., Execs. (Chgo.); Glen View Golf (Ill.); Onwentsia (Lake Forest, Ill.); Lagunitas Country (Ross, Calif.); Harvard (N.Y.C.). Home: 1160 N Sheridan Rd Lake Forest IL 60045 Office: 111 E Wacker Dr Room 2700 Chicago IL 60601

KENNA, EDGAR DOUGLAS, JR., bus. exec.; b. Summit, Miss., June 11, 1924; s. Edgar Douglas and Norma Catchings (Carruth) K.; B.S., U.S. Mil. Acad., 1945; m. Jean Cruise, June 12, 1945; children—Edgar Douglas III, Marilyn, Susan, Michael Earl. Asst. to gen. mgr. Crosley div. Avco Corp., Cin., 1952-54, exec. v.p. Avco Corp., N.Y.C., 1959-68; mgr. product div. Westinghouse Electric Corp., Mansfield and Columbus, Ohio, 1954-59; pres. Fuqua Industries, Atlanta, 1968-70; pres. Robert B. Anderson, Ltd., N.Y.C., 1970-73; pres. NAM, Washington, 1973-77, dir., 1977—; exec. v.p. Carrier Corp., Syracuse, N.Y., 1977-78, pres., chief operating officer, 1978—; dir. Carlisle Corp., Cin., Phillips Petroleum Corp. Trustee, U.S. Mil. Acad., 1975—; pres., bd. dirs. Upstate Med. Found., Syracuse, 1979—; bd. dirs. Nat. Football Found. and Hall of Fame, 1979—. Served with U.S. Army, 1945-49. Recipient Freedoms Found. medal, 1975, Gold Knight award Nat. Mgmt. Assn., 1975. Mem. Mfrs. Assn. Central N.Y. (dir. 1977—), Syracuse C. of C. (dir. 1980—). Clubs: Congressional (Washington); Onondaga Country (Syracuse). Developer reentry systems for Apollo, Atlas, Titan and Minuteman missile systems. Office: 120 Madison St Syracuse NY 13221

KENNEDY, CORNELIUS BRYANT, lawyer; b. Evanston, Ill., Apr. 13, 1921; s. Millard Bryant and Myrna (Anderson) K.; A.B., Yale, 1943; J.D., Harvard, 1948; m. Anne Martha Reynolds, June 20, 1959; children—Anne Talbot, Lauren Asher. Admitted to Ill. bar, 1949, D.C. bar, 1965; practiced in Chgo., 1949-54, 55-59, Washington, 1965—; sr. mem. firm Kennedy & Webster, and predecessors, Washington, 1965—; asst. U.S. atty. Dept. Justice, Chgo., 1954-55; counsel to minority leader U.S. Senate, Washington, 1959-65; public mem. Adminstrv. Conf. U.S., 1972—, chmn. com. on rulemaking, 1973—. Trustee, St. John's Child Devel. Center, Washington. Served to 1st lt. USAAF, 1943-46. Fellow Am. Bar Found.; mem. Am. Law Inst., Am. Bar Assn. (council sect. adminstrv. law 1967-70, chmn. sect. 1976-77), Fed. (chmn. com. adminstrv. law 1963-64), D.C., Chgo. bar assns. Clubs: Gibson Island (Md.); Chevy Chase, Met., Capitol Hill (Washington); Adventurers (Chgo.); Explorers (N.Y.C.). Contbr. articles to legal jours. Home: 7720 Old Georgetown Pike McLean VA 22102 Office: 888 17th St NW Washington DC 20006

KENNEDY, DONALD PARKER, title ins. co. exec.; b. San Jacinto, Calif., Oct. 16, 1918; s. Louis Rex and Elsie (Parker) K.; A.B., Stanford U., 1940; LL.B., U. So. Calif., 1948; m. Dorothy Alice Suppiger, Dec. 20, 1946; children—Parker Steven, Elizabeth Ann, Amy Frances. Admitted to Calif. bar; asso. council Orange County Title Co., 1948-58; exec. v.p. 1st Am. Title Ins. Co., Santa Ana, Calif., 1958-63, pres., 1963—, also dir.; pres. 1st Am. Fin. Corp., Santa Ana, 1963—, also dir.; founder, dir. Pacific View Meml. Park, Newport Beach, Calif., Premier Savs. & Loan Assn., Orange, Calif.; dir. Western Pacific Fin. Corp., Newport Beach, Christiana Oil Corp., Huntington Harbour, Calif., Mission Bank, El Toro, Calif., Mission Savs. & Loan Assn., Santa Ana, Los Alamitos (Calif.) Race Course, 1st Am. Title Ins. Co. Ariz., Phoenix, 1st Am. Title Ins. Co. N.Y., Garden City, 1st Am. Title Ins. Co. Oreg., Portland, Mass. Title Ins. Co., Boston, Title Guaranty Co. Wyo., Casper, Butler Housing Corp., Irvine, Calif., Western Fed. Savs. & Loan Assn.; adv. bd. 1st Western Bank, Santa Ana. Chmn. pres.'s council Chapman Coll.; pres. Santa Ana-Tustin Community Chest; mem. Santa Ana Bd. Edn., 1953; Orange County chmn. U.S. Savs. Bond Program; bd. dirs. Santa Ana YMCA, World Affairs Council Orange County, Emphysema Found. Am., 1980—, So. Calif. Bldg. Funds, 1974—; trustee St. Joseph's Found., 1970—. Served to lt. Office Intelligence, USNR, 1942-46. Mem. Calif. Land Title Assn. (pres. 1960), Am. Land Title Assn. (chmn. fin. com.), Calif. Bar Assn., Orange County Bar Assn., Phi Delta Phi, Calif. C. of C. (So. Calif. council, exec. com.), So. Calif. Golf Assn. Club: Orange County Press (Headliner of Yr. in Bus. 1969). Republican. Clubs: Santa Ana Country; LaQuinta (Calif.) Country. Office: First Am Title Ins Co 114 E 5th St Santa Ana CA 92701

KENNEDY, DOUGLAS PATERSON, cement mfg. co. exec.; b. Lake Forest, Ill., Jan. 8, 1913; s. Ernest Burt and Frances Gildersleeve (Paterson) K.; grad. Stanford U., 1936; m. Adele O'Meara Cardoso, Apr. 28, 1927; children—Scott, Robert, Kay, John. Chief chemist Cia Uruguay de Cemento Portland, Montevideo, 1940-46, later pres. bd.; chief chemist Cia Narioua de Cemento Portland, Rio, Brazil, 1946-48; asst. supt. Lone Star Cement Co., Greencastle, Ind., 1948-50; asst. mgr. Cia Aregniua de Cemento Portland. Chmn. Council of Am. in Uruguay, 1974. Mem. Academica Nacional de Economia Uruguay, Causejo Ineteramericano de Canorcioy Producida (Uruguayan del.), Am. Assn. Uruguay (pres. 1976-77), Am. C. of C. in Uruguay (pres. 1975). Republican. Roman Catholic. Club: Rotary (pres. local club 1969). Office: Casilla Correa 112 Montevideo Uruguay

KENNEDY, EVELYN SIEFERT, investment co. exec.; b. Pitts., Nov. 11, 1927; d. Carmine and Assunta (Iacobucci) Rocci; B.S. magna cum laude, U. R.I., 1969, M.S. in Textiles and Clothing, 1970; m. George J. Siefert, May 30, 1953 (div. 1974); children—Paul, Carl, Ann Marie; m. 2d, Lyle H. Kennedy, Oct. 12, 1974. Tchr., Pitts. Pub. Schs., 1945-50; with Goodyear Aircraft Corp., Akron, Ohio, 1950-54; clothing instr., dept. adult edn., Groton, Conn., 1958-68; v.p. Kennedy Capital Advisers, Groton, 1973-78, Kennedy Mgmt. Corp., Groton, 1974, Kennedy Inter Vest, Inc., Groton, 1975; pres. Sewtique, Groton, 1970—. Pres. bd. dirs. PRIDE Found., Inc., 1978, exec. dir., 1978—; mem. nat. adv. council SBA, 1976—, also regional adv. council; adv. council U. R.I., 1978—; clothing cons. U. Conn. Extension, 1975—; founder Conn. Home Economists in Bus., 1977—; adj. faculty U. Conn., 1976—, also Eastern Conn. State U.; mem. faculty St. Joseph Coll., 1979—. Bd. dirs. Child Guidance Clinic of S.E. Conn., League Women Voters. Recipient Bus. and Profl. Woman of Year award, 1977, award of distinction U. R.I., 1969. Mem. Am., Conn. home econs. assns., Nat. Bedding Inst. (dir. Better Sleep Council), Coll. and Univ. Bus. Instrs. Conn. (dir.), Groton Bus. and Profl. Women, Omicron Nu, Phi Kappa Phi. Democrat. Roman Catholic. Club: Zonta (New London). Author: Dressing with Pride, 1980. Home: 7 Mulberry Dr Gales Ferry CT 06335 Office: 1159 Poquonnock Rd Groton CT 06340

KENNEDY, GEORGE D., chem. co. exec.; b. Pitts., May 30, 1926; s. Thomas Reed and Lois (Smith) K.; B.A., Williams Coll., 1947; m. Valerie Putis; children—Charles Reed, George Danner, Jamey Kathleen, Susan Patton, Timothy Christian. With Scott Paper Co., 1947-52, Champion Paper Co., 1952-65; pres. Brown Co., 1965-71, also dir.; exec. v.p. Internat. Minerals & Chem. Corp., Northbrook, Ill., 1971-78, pres., 1978—, dir., 1975—; dir., mem. exec. com. SCM Corp.; dir. Brunswick Corp., Riegel Textile Corp. Mem. exec. bd. N.E. Ill. council Boy Scouts Am.; bd. dirs. Chgo. Assn. Commerce and Industry, Children's Meml. Hosp., Chgo.; bd. govs. Orchestral Soc., Chgo. Symphony. Clubs: Board Room, N.Y. Athletic (N.Y.C.); Larchmont (N.Y.) Yacht; Sleepy Hollow Country (Scarborough, N.Y.); Skokie Country (Glencoe, Ill.). Home: Winnetka IL Office: 2315 Sanders Rd Northbrook IL 60062

KENNEDY, JAMES HARRINGTON, editor, publisher; b. Lawrence, Mass., Feb. 20, 1924; s. James H. and Margaret Helen (Hyde) K.; B.S., Lowell Textile Inst., 1948; M.S., Mass. Inst. Tech., 1950; m. Sheila Conway, July 1, 1950; children—Kathleen, Brian, Kevin, Gail, Patricia, Maureen, Constance. Mgmt. trainee Chicopee Mfg. Corp., Manchester, N.H., 1950-51; mng. editor Textile World McGraw Hill Pub. Co., Greenville, S.C., 1951-54; dir. communications Bruce Payne & Assos., Westport, Conn., 1954-57; pres. James H. Kennedy & Co., Westport, 1957-70; editor, pub. Consultants News, Fitzwilliam, N.H., 1970—. Founder, Fitzwilliam Conservation Corp., pres., 1970-72; chmn. Fitzwilliam Sq. Dances, 1970—; mem. Fitzwilliam Planning Bd., 1970-72; trustee Am. Liquid Trust, Greenwich, Conn., 1975-78. Served to capt., inf. AUS, 1942-46. Mem. Fitzwilliam Hist. Soc., Acad. Mgmt., Phi Psi. Republican. Roman Catholic. Clubs: Fitzwilliam Swimming (pres.), Chemists. Address: Templeton Turnpike Fitzwilliam NH 03447

KENNEDY, JOHN RAYMOND, paper co. exec.; b. N.Y.C., Sept. 21, 1930; s. John R. and Ethel R. (Leavy) K.; B.S., Georgetown U., 1952; m. Elizabeth Calagerakis, Oct. 24, 1974; children—John Raymond III, James, Nicholas, Andrew, Paula. With Fed. Paper Bd. Co., Inc., Montvale, N.J., 1952—, v.p., 1960-66, pres., 1966—; dir. Am. Mut. Ins. Co., Am. Mut. Policyholder Ins., Chgo. Pneumatic Tool Co., 1st Nat. State Bank N.J. Pres., Assn. Retarded Children, Bergen/Passaic (N.J.) Unit, 1972; bd. regents Georgetown U.; bd. dirs. N.Y. Sch. for Deaf, White Plains, N.Y.; trustee Davis and Elkins Coll. Mem. Am. Paper Inst. Clubs: Woodway Country, Nat. Golf Links Am., Maidstone, Devon Yacht, Univ. Office: 75 Chestnut Ridge Rd Montvale NJ 07645

KENNEDY, JOSEPH HOWARD, banker; b. Terra Ceia, Fla., Jan. 19, 1929; s. Joseph Howard and Mildred (Perry) K.; B.S. in Bus. Adminstrn., The Citadel, Charleston, S.C., 1952; m. Joyce A. Hamilton, June 21, 1952; children—Joseph Howard, Karen. With Palmetto Bank and Trust Co. (Fla.), 1960—; v.p., cashier, then exec. v.p., 1964-69, pres., 1969—; past vice chmn., dir. First Comml. Bank Manatee County, Bradenton, Fla., 1979; mem. Econs. Devel. Com. Manatee County; past pres. Palmetto Jr. C. of C. Served to capt. USAF, 1951-56. Decorated Air medal. Mem. Am. Bankers Assn., Manatee Bankers Assn., Palmetto Mchts. Assn. (past pres.), Manatee County C. of C. (past pres.). Clubs: Palmetto Kiwanis (past pres.), Conquistadores, Bradenton Country, Bradenton Yacht. Address: Palmetto Bank and Trust Co 700 8th Ave W Palmetto FL 33561

KENNEDY, LYLE H., investment cons.; b. N.Y.C., Mar. 29, 1933; s. Michael M. and Margaret E. (Kennedy) Kuhn; student Columbia, 1949-50, Grinnell Coll., 1952-53, N.Y. U., 1953; LL.B., Blackstone Sch. Law, 1970; m. Hertha G. Baird, July 29, 1961 (div. July 1974); children—Peter W., Lyle H., Lyla H.; m. 2d, Evelyn R. Siefert, Oct. 12, 1974; children—Paul K., Carl J., Ann M. Vice pres. Devon Plans Fidelity Funds, Boston, 1960-61; cons. to pres. Investors Planning Corp. Am., N.Y.C., 1961-62; dir. Inst. Financial Independence, Seattle, 1962-63; v.p. DuPont Capital Corp., San Francisco, 1963-65; cons. to pres. Value Line Securities, N.Y.C., 1965-66; pres., chmn., dir. Kennedy Capital Advisors, Inc., Groton, Conn., 1966—; pres., dir. Kennedy Mgmt. Corp., Groton, 1972—; gen. partner Kennedy InterVest Fund, Ltd., 1976—; pres., dir. Kennedy InterVest, Inc., Kennedy InterVest Ins., Inc., Kennedy InterVest Realty, Inc., Kennedy InterVest Securities, Inc.; adj. prof. N.Y. U., 1976. Bd. dirs. Eastern Conn. Symphony, Groton, Blue Curtain Youth Found., N.Y.C.; chmn., bd. dirs. PRIDE Found., Inc., 1978—; bd. regents Internat. Coll. Financial Counselling; also pvt. trusts. Served with AUS, 1953-55. Mem. Photographers Soc. Am. Republican. Unitarian. Clubs: Lawyers, Lambs (N.Y.C.); Shennecosset Yacht. Asso. editor Stock Market Mag., 1969. Home: 7 Mulberry Dr Gales Ferry CT 06335 Office: 1159 Poquonnock Rd Groton CT 06340

KENNEDY, MARK BRUCE, holding co. exec.; b. Phila., May 5, 1948; s. John Rainey and Julia (Hogan) K.; B.S. in Finance, U. Pa., 1970; M.B.A. magna cum laude, U. Mich., 1973; m. Heath Mirick, Sept. 20, 1975. Pvt. cons. to several small businesses, Detroit, 1971-73; employee office of chmn. Consol. Foods Corp., 1973-74; asst. to chmn. Safeguard Industries, 1974-78; pres. The Cutting Edge Inc., 1974—, Capra Gem Co., Inc., 1979—, Aviatex Corp., 1980—, Gen. Hardware Co., Inc., 1980—; treas. Safety Med. Corp., 1980—; speaker fin. mgmt. Class fund raiser The Episcopal Acad. Republican. Clubs: Racquet, Rittenhouse, Merion Cricket. Home: 101 Cherry Ln Ardmore PA 19003 Office: 390 W Lancaster Ave Haverford PA 19041

KENNEDY, ROBERT PHELPS, JR., mfrs. rep.; b. Buffalo, July 25, 1922; s. Robert Phelps and Rebecca (Showalter) K.; student Swarthmore Coll., 1940-42; B.S.E.E., U. Rochester, 1949; m. Helen Anne Dubosky, Oct. 26, 1943; children—William Morehouse, Kathryn Anne. Sales mgr. Holliday-Hathaway Co., Inc., Boston, 1949-54; pres. R.P. Kennedy Co., Inc., Rochester, N.Y., 1954—; cons. ROKENCO. Served to capt. Signal Corps, AUS, 1943-45. Named Salesman of Year, Fenwal Electronics, 1974, 79. Mem. IEEE, Am. Radio Relay League, Nat. Geog. Soc., Internat. Wine and Food Soc. (London). Episcopalian. Clubs: Masons, Jesters, Shriners. Contbr. articles to tech. jours. and mags. Home and Office: 1570 Westfall Rd Rochester NY 14618

KENNEDY, THOMAS PATRICK, broadcasting exec.; b. N.Y.C., Oct. 13, 1932; s. Andrew Francis and Marie P. (Scullen) K.; B.S., St. Peter's Coll., 1958; postgrad. Seton Hall U., 1959; m. Mary P. Drennan, Jan. 14, 1956; children—Thomas Patrick, Kevin M., Michael J., Mary P., Deborah A. Accountant, Haskins & Sells, C.P.A.'s, N.Y.C., 1953-54, 55-57; staff Emerson Radio & TV, N.Y.C., 1957-58; various exec. positions CBS, N.Y.C., 1958-67; with Ford Found., N.Y.C., 1967; dir. fin. Pub. Broadcasting Lab., N.Y.C., 1967-69; with Children's TV Workshop, N.Y.C., 1969—, v.p. fin. and adminstrn., 1969—; treas. 1969—, sr. v.p., 1978—; pres. Tomken Mgmt., Ltd., 1980—; cons. in field. Bd. advisers Franciscan Communication Center; bd. dirs., exec. dir. Center for Non-Broadcast TV. Served with C.E., U.S. Army, 1954-55. Mem. Fin. Exec. Inst., Internat. Radio and TV Soc., Inst. Broadcast Fin. Mgmt., Nat. Assn. Accountants, Internat. Broadcast Inst., Internat. Inst. Communication, Internat. Assn. Fin. Execs. Roman Catholic. Home: 133 E 64th St New York NY 10021 Office: 1 Lincoln Plaza New York NY 10019

KENNEDY, THOMAS WILLIAM, JR., state ports authority engring. exec.; b. Charleston, S.C., June 24, 1942; s. Thomas William and Gertrude Lillith (Von Glahn) K.; B.S.C.E., The Citadel, 1964, M.B.A., 1979; M.S.C.E., W.Va. U., 1966; m. Lorena Jeanette Maher, June 18, 1966; children—Thomas William, Tamara Leigh. Structural engr. U.S. Navy, 1964-66; soils and founds. engr. Law Engring. Testing Co., Jacksonville, Fla., 1969-70; sales engr. Sloan Constrn. Co. Inc., Columbia, S.C., 1970-72; project engr. Ballenger Corp., Republic of Panama, 1972-74; v.p., treas. Palmetto Engring. Co. Inc., Columbia, 1974-76; project engr. Epting Ballenger Corp., Charleston, S.C., 1976-78; corp. cost and scheduling engr. Ballenger Corp., Greenville, S.C., 1979; chief design engring. S.C. State Ports Authority, Charleston, 1980—. Mem. council Boy Scouts Am. Served in USAF, 1966-69, maj. Res. Decorated Air Force Commendation medal with oak leaf cluster; registered profl. engr., S.C., Ga., N.C., Fla., C.Z.; registered land surveyer, S.C.; lic. gen. contractor, S.C. Mem. Assn. Citadel Men (life), Nat. Soc. Profl. Engrs., S.C. Soc. Registered Land Surveyors, ASCE, Res. Officers Assn. Roman Catholic. Clubs: Propeller, Port of Charleston, Civil Engrs. of Charleston; Brigadier, Elks. Office: PO Box 1111 Mount Pleasant SC 29464

KENNEDY, VIRGINIA RAYE, real estate broker; b. Elkton, Md., Nov. 28, 1944; d. Raymond Bernard and Mildred Anne (Warrington) Weed; student Harford Community Coll., 1964-66, Towson State Coll., 1968. Real estate agt. A.C. Litzenberg & Sons, Realtors, 1975-77; partner, mgr. R.D. McDaniel Real Estate, Elkton, Md., 1977-79; asso. broker '80 Century 21, Ulrich & Co., Elkton, 1980—. Mem. Nat. Assn. Realtors, Cecil County Bd. Realtors, New Castle County Bd. Realtors. Democrat. Home: 334 Old Chestnut Rd Elkton MD 21921 Office: 251 Bridge St Elkton MD 21921

KENNEDY, WILLIAM JESSE, III, ins. co. exec.; b. Durham, N.C., Oct. 24, 1922; s. William Jesse, Jr. and Margaret Lillian (Spaulding) K.; B.S. in Bus. Adminstrn., Va. State Coll., 1942; M.B.A., U. Pa., 1946; M.B.A. in Finance and Investments, N.Y. U., 1950; m. Alice Charlene Copeland, Jan. 29, 1949; 1 son, William Jesse IV. With N.C. Mut. Life Ins. Co., Durham, 1950—, fin. v.p., 1966-69, sr. v.p., 1969-72, pres., 1972—, chmn. bd., chief exec. officer, 1979—; dir. Mechanics & Farmers Bank, Durham, Urban Nat. Corp., Boston, Mobil Oil Corp., Pfizer, Inc., N.Y.C., J.A. Jones Constrn. Co., Charlotte, N.C. Mem. Durham Com. on Affairs of Black People, NAACP, Durham Bus. and Profl. Chain, N.C. Central U. Found. Served with AUS 1943-45. Charles E. Merrill Found. fellow Stanford Exec. Program, 1971. Mem. The Conf. Bd. (sr.), N.C. Soc. Fin. Analysts, Omega Psi Phi. Baptist (trustee 1950—). Kiwanian. Home: 102 E Masondale Ave Durham NC 27707 Office: Mutual Plaza Durham NC 27701

KENNELLEY, JAMES ANDREW, indsl. chemist; b. Rochester, N.Y., Aug. 23, 1928; s. James Andrew and Florence Bessie (Marsh) K.; B.A. in Chemistry, Coll. of Wooster (Ohio), 1949; Ph.D. in Chemistry, Mich. State U., 1955; m. Sarah T. Wade, Aug. 27, 1955; children—Kevin James, Mark William, Judith Ann. Tech. dir. uranium div. Mallinckrodt, Inc., St. Louis, 1955-65; group v.p. Quebec Iron and Titanium Corp. (Can.), Sorel, 1965-78; pres. Direct Reduction Corp., N.Y.C., 1978—. Mem. AIME, Am. Chem. Soc., Am. Soc. Metals, Sigma Xi, Pi Mu Epsilon, Kappa Mu Epsilon. Club: Larchmont (N.Y.) Yacht. Home: 17 Huguenot Dr Larchmont NY 10538 Office: 230 Park Ave New York NY 10017

KENNEWAY, ERNEST KEATING, JR., valve mfg. co. exec.; b. Worcester, Mass., May 12, 1938; s. Ernest Keating and Pauline J. (Menzenski) K.; B.S. in Bus. Adminstrn., Clark U., 1961; postgrad. Sch. Indsl. Mgmt., Worcester Poly. Inst., 1969; m. Marlene Toloczko, Sept. 11, 1966; children—Melissa, Matthew. Asst. purchasing agt. Hobbs Mfg. Co., Worcester, 1963-65, prodn. control supr., 1965-66; inventory mgr. George Meyer Mfg. Co., Worcester, 1966; materials mgr. Leland-Gifford Co., Worcester, 1966-69, controller, 1969-71; v.p. fin. Americold Compressor Co., Cullman, Ala., 1971-74; pres., gen. mgr. R-P&C Valve, Inc., Fairview, Pa., 1974—. Served with U.S. Army, 1962. Mem. Valve Mfrs. Assn., Fluid Controls Inst., U.S. C. of C., Erie Mfrs. Assn. Office: 8150 W Ridge Rd Fairview PA 16415

KENNEY, F. DONALD, investment banker; b. Olean, N.Y., Mar. 9, 1918; s. John P. and Winifred (Shortell) K.; B.A., Coll. of Holy Cross, 1939; M.A., Harvard, 1941, M.B.A., 1951; postgrad. Oxford (Eng.) U., 1948. Teaching fellow English, Harvard, 1947-51; with Harriman Ripley & Co., Inc., 1951-70 asst. v.p., 1958-61, v.p., dir., 1961-70; pres., dir. Harriman Ripley (Can.) Ltd., Toronto, Ont., 1960-70; chmn. Harriman Ripley Internat. S.A-R.L., Luxembourg, 1964-70; vice chmn. Merrill Lynch, Pierce, Fenner & Smith Securities Underwriter Ltd., 1970-74, chmn., 1974-76; co-chmn. bd. Goldman Sachs Internat. Corp., 1976—; treas., dir. 785 Park Ave. Corp., 1969—; dir. United Reins. Corp. of N.Y., 1977—. Trustee, Suomi Coll., 1974—; bd. dirs. Internat. Council Museums Found., 1977—. Served from ensign to lt. commdr. USNR, 1942-46. Decorated comdr. Order of Lion, Finland, 1963; comdr. Order Merit, Luxembourg, 1971; knight comdr. Royal Norwegian Order of St. Olaf. Mem.

Finnish Am. (dir. 1967—, v.p. 1968-70, pres. 1970), Norweigian Am. chambers commerce, Securities Industry Assn. (internat. fin. com. 1965—), Council Fgn. Relations, Pilgrims, Ireland U.S. Council. Clubs: Harvard (N.Y.C., Boston); Knickerbocker, Downtown Assn. (N.Y.C.). Home: 785 Park Ave New York NY 10021 Office: 55 Broad St New York NY 10004

KENNON, JOHN DAVID, ins. corp. exec.; b. Pitts., June 11, 1917; s. James Henry and Acsa (Ellis) K.; B.A., Pa. State U., 1938; m. Catherine Bechtold, July 8, 1950; children—Karen, John David, Betsy, Jacquelynn. Pres. Crusader Life Ins. Co., Phila., 1964-66; pres. Kennon Ins. Cons., Inc., Pitts., 1966—; dir. Damco Inc. Served to lt. USNR, 1943-46. Named one of Pittsburgh's Men of Tomorrow, Time mag., 1953. Mem. Million Dollar Round Table (life), Nat. Life Underwriters Assn., Alpha Delta Assn. (dir., pres., 1969-70), Kappa Sigma. Republican. Presbyterian. Clubs: Duquesne, University (dir., pres., 1978-79), Fellows (dir., pres., 1974), Royal Order of Jesters, Shrine. Home: 2120 Greentree Rd Apt 410E Pittsburgh PA 15220 Office: 250 Manor Oake One Pittsburgh PA 15220

KENNY, THOMAS HENRY, JR., land and mine developer, broker, builder, author, artist; b. Bridgeport, Conn., Jan. 12, 1918; s. Thomas Henry and Marie (Sorgi) K.; student pub. schs., Stamford, Conn.; m. Stella Wasylkoski, Aug. 9, 1941; children—Thomas Henry III, Michael A., Lisa A., Lee Ann. Real estate broker, Roslyn, N.Y., 1962—; pres., dir. Kenny Realty Corp.; pres. Samaratan Oil Corp.; dir. Kenny Devel. Corp., Rainy Lake Mining Ltd., Kenny Constrn. Corp., K-P Records Inc., K.-P Music Inc. Exhibited paintings in museums in 14 countries, 1976 mus. shows; represented in permanent collections Stedlijk, Amsterdam, Met. Mus. Art, N.Y.C., Phila. Mus., Nat. Gallery Greece, Athens, Albertina, Vienna, Helsingfors Stads Mus. Finland, Mus. Tel Aviv (Israel), Museo de Arte Moderno, Mexico, Gallery Modern Art, N.Y.C., Bibliotheque Nationale, Paris, Mus. Modern Art, Miami, Boston Athenaeum, Library of Congress, Washington; works in permanent collections of 367 museums in 27 countries. Past bd. govs. LaSalle Mil. Acad. Served with Signal Corps, USAAF, 1942-46, ETO. Fellow Royal Soc. Art London; mem. Coll. Art Assn., Inst. Contemporary Art, London, Assn. Internat. Artists. Author: Retail Values of Mechanical and Semi-Mechanical Banks, 1952; Jesus Christ Speaks, 1972; Confucius Speaks, 1973; Soul Travel-There Is No Death, 1975; Garlic, the Modern Miracle, 1976; Arthritis-Its Causes and Cure, 1977; How to Live to 100, 1977; The Evil Eye Through the Ages, 1978; Researching Hypoglycemia, 1978; Fasting-Good and Bad, 1978. Home: 5063 Chaparral Way San Diego CA 92115 Office: Kenny Realty Corp Box 3337 La Jolla CA 92037

KENT, FREDERICK HEBER, lawyer; b. Fitzgerald, Ga., Apr. 26, 1905; s. Heber and Juanita (McDuffie) K.; J.D., U. Ga., 1926; m. Norma C. Futch, Apr. 25, 1929; children—Frederick Heber, Norma Futch K. Lockwood, John Bradford, James Cleveland. Admitted to Ga., Fla. bars, 1926, since practiced in Jacksonville, Fla.; sr. partner firm Kent, Watts, Durden, Kent & Mickler; chmn. bd. Kent Theatres, Inc.; pres. Kent Enterprises, Inc.; dir. Fla. 1st Nat. Bank of Jacksonville, Nat. Banks of Fla., Inc. Chmn. local ARC, 1934, 1950; pres. Jacksonville's 50 Years of Progress Assn., 1951; bd. dirs. YMCA, pres., 1946-50; bd. dirs. Jacksonville Community Chest-United Fund, 1955-59, pres., 1958-59; chmn. Fla. State Plant Bd., 1955-56; bd. regents (control) Fla. Instns. of Higher Learning, 1953-58, chmn., 1955-56; bd. dirs. Riverside Hosp. Assn., 1956-76, pres., 1964-65; chmn. State Jr. Coll. Council, 1962-72; mem. adv. com. Fla. Higher Edn. Facilities Act, 1963, 64; chmn. bd. trustees Fla. Jr. Coll., Jacksonville, 1965-71; mem. Select Council on Post High Sch. Edn. in Fla., 1967, Fla. Gov.'s Commn. for Quality Edn., 1967; trustee Bolles Sch., Jacksonville, 1954-65, Theatre Jacksonville, 1966-78; chmn. Fla. Quadricentennial Commn., 1962-65; mem. Jacksonville City Council, 1933-37; chmn. Fla. Democratic Exec. Com., 1938-40. Served as lt. USNR, 1942-45. Recipient Disting. Service award U.S. Jr. C. of C., 1933, Ted Arnold award Jacksonville C. of C., 1961; Fred H. Kent campus Fla. Jr. Coll. at Jacksonville named in his honor, 1974. Mem. Internat., Am., Fla., Jacksonville bar assns., Jacksonville C. of C., Am. Judicature Soc., Newcomen Soc. N.Am., Am. Legion, Sigma Alpha Epsilon, Delta Sigma Pi. Republican. Clubs: Rotary (pres. 1958-59), Timuquana Country, Florida Yacht, Seminole, Friars, Ye Mystic Revellers, Ponte Vedra, River, Sawgrass Country; Highlands (N.C.) Country; Blowing Rock (N.C.) Country. Home: 2970 St Johns Ave Apt 12-A Jacksonville FL 32205 Office: 850 Edward Ball Bldg Jacksonville FL 32202

KENT, JOHN BRADFORD, lawyer; b. Jacksonville, Fla., Sept. 5, 1939; s. Frederick Heber and Norma (Futch) K.; grad. Phillips Exeter Acad., 1957; B.A., Yale, 1961; J.D., U. Fla., 1964; LL.M. in Taxation, N.Y. Grad. Sch. Law, 1965; m. Monett Powers, Dec. 18, 1969; children—Katherine Lane, Monett Bradford, Susan Whitfield Powers, Sally Marshall McLeod. Admitted to Fla. bar, 1964; asso. atty. firm Ulmer, Murchison, Kent, Ashby & Ball, Jacksonville, 1965-67; partner firm Kent, Watts, Durden, Kent & Mickler and predecessor firms, Jacksonville, 1967—; pres. Kent Theatres, Inc., Jacksonville, 1967-70, v.p., gen. counsel, 1970—, also dir.; v.p. Kent Enterprises, Inc., Kent Properties, Inc., Melbourne Theatres, Inc., Blanding Theatres, Inc., Kent Amusements, Inc., 1965—, also dir.; pres., dir. Kent Investments, Inc., Jacksonville, 1977—; v.p., dir. Merritt Twin Cinemas, Inc., 1980—. Treas., trustee St. Mark's Episcopal Day Sch., Jacksonville, 1971-74, 80—; dir. Children's Home Soc. Fla., 1974—, v.p., 1976-77, asst. counselor, 1974—, asst. sec., 1977—, dir. N.E. div., 1966—, pres., 1976-77; bd. dirs. Jacksonville Legal Aid Soc., 1973-75; bd. govs. Fla. Jr. Coll. at Jacksonville Found., 1973—, pres., 1976-77. Mem. Am., Fla., Jacksonville, bar assns., Am. Judicature Soc., Nat. Assn. Theatre Owners (dir. 1972, 78—), Nat. Assn. Theatre Owners Fla. (v.p. 1968-72, dir. 1973—), Gov. Wm. Bradford Compact (Plymouth, Mass.), Delta Kappa Epsilon, Phi Delta Phi, Manuscript Sr. Hon. Soc. (Yale). Rotarian (treas. 1976-77). Episcopalian (vestry 1970-73). Clubs: Ponte Vedra (Ponte Vedra Beach, Fla.); Friars, Ye Mystic Revellers, Timuquana, River, YMCA; Mory's Assn. (New Haven). Home: 4948 Morven Rd Jacksonville FL 32210 Office: 850 Edward Ball Bldg PO Box 4700 Jacksonville FL 32201

KENT, PAULA (MRS. STANLEY J. LLOYD), pub. relations, mgmt. and mktg. cons., lectr.; b. Bklyn., Oct. 19; d. John and Estelle (Frye) Smith; B.S., State Tchrs. Coll., Worcester, Mass., 1939; M.S., Grad. Sch. Bus. Adminstrn., Boston U., 1941; m. Stanley J. Lloyd, Jan. 23, 1943; children—Diane Adrienne Noel, Robin Michele Cheri, Kevin Christopher Kent, Gisele Nicolette Jolie. Methods engr. IBM, 1941-42; personnel dir. Daily Jour., San Diego, also cons. also radio sta. KSDJ, 1946-48; fashion editor San Diego Union, 1949; promotion dir. San Diego Union and Evening Tribune, 1950-70; extension div. faculty U. Calif. at San Diego, 1961-63; pub. relations and marketing cons., San Diego, 1970—; v.p. La Jolla Clin. Labs., Inc., 1970—; lectr. mktg. workshop seminars, Brussels, Paris, Madrid. Pub. relations adviser nat. Mrs. Am. Pageant, 1966-67, nat. Unlimited Hydroplanes, Races, Bowl-Down Cancer; producer ann. Holiday for Housewives, San Diego, 1955-60; exec. dir. San Diego Ann. Golden Gloves Boxing Tournament, San Diego Ann. Metrotennis Championships, Ann. Jr. Golf Championships, Ann. Model Yacht Regatta, Ann. Investment Clinic, Ann. Hole-in-One Tournament, Ann. Soap Box Derby, 1951-59; del. Nat. Fedn. Press Women touring Russia, 1973. Recipient 158 awards, 1950—, including 39 nat., 18 western states, 100 Calif. state awards, 1 local award, resulting from ann. competitions sponsored by Los Angeles Advt. Women's Club, Nat. Newspaper Assn. Mgrs., N.Y. Stock Exchange, Calif. Newspaper Publs. Assn., Calif. Press Women, Los Angeles Sales Promotion Execs. Assn., Nat. Fedn. Press Women, Editor and Pub., also numerous community recognition awards, including Woman of Year, San Diego, 1965; Man of Year, Los Angeles, 1965; Woman of Achievement, San Diego, 1958, 59, 64; named woman of achievement Nat. Fedn. Bus. and Profl. Women, 1966; named San Diego Advt. Man of Distinction, 1972, Distinguished Service award Investment Edn. Inst. Detroit, 1969, Golden Spear award Twin Cities, Sales Promotion Execs. award Mpls., 1965; Outstanding Service award San Diego council Boy Scouts Am., 1962, 65; honored spl. luncheon London Press Club, 1970; many other honors. Mem. Advt. and Sales Club San Diego (dir.), Sales and Marketing Execs. Club San Diego (v.p., past pres., former dir. and bull. editor), Personnel Mgmt. Assn. (hon., past bull. editor), Nat. Newspaper Promotion Assn. (past pres. Western region), Internat. Newspaper Promotion Assn. (dir. 1969-72), Am. Advt. Fedn. (edn. chmn. Western States 1970-71), Calif. Assn. Press Women, Nat. Fedn. Press Women, Sales and Marketing Execs. Internat. (dir.-at-large), Sales Promotion Execs. Assn. Los Angeles, Am. Mgmt. Assn. Roman Catholic. Club: Kona Kai. Former editor Monthly Bull. Personnel Mgt. Assn., 1955-59; editor SME Sales Tales, 1964-66. Chmn. San Diego's Ann. Giant Sales Rally, 1953, 54, 65, 71; Advt. Recognition Week Campaign. San Diego, 1953-54, San Diego Cancer Cruise-Aid, 1964. Commd. ensign, Women's Reserve, USNR, 1942, transferred USCG, served from ensign to lt. (s.g.), 1943-46. Home: 515 Bon Air St La Jolla CA 92037 Office: PO Box 2243 La Jolla CA 92038

KENT, WILLIAM HORACE, mcht. banker; b. Phila., Sept. 7, 1935; s. Horace Leesor and Evelyn Louise (Huber) K.; B.A., Cornell U., 1958; postgrad. N.Y. U., 1964; m. Susannah Strickland Simpson, June 21, 1958; children—Elizabeth Patterson, Harlan McBriar. Sr. research analyst, mgr. corporate cons. dept. R. W. Pressprich & Co., N.Y.C., 1961-65; chmn. Berger-Kent Adv. Corp., pres., dir. Berger-Kent Spl. Fund, Wilmington, Del., 1965-72; chmn. William Kent & Co., Inc., Greenwich, Conn., 1965—; chmn. Interiors Internat. Inc.; dir. Internat. Fin. Advisers, Kuwait; lectr., cons. to firms doing bus. in Middle East. Trustee Internat. Coll., Beirut, Lebanon. Served to lt. USN, 1958-61. Mem. Middle East Inst., Arab-Am. Assn., China Inst., Newcomen Soc., Certified Fin. Analysts Fedn., N.Y. Soc. Security Analysts. Clubs: Turf (London); Round Hill (Greenwich); Verbank (Millbrook, N.Y.); Explorers (N.Y.C.). Home: 1005 Lake Ave N Greenwich CT 06830 Office: 1 E Putnam Ave Greenwich CT 06830

KEOGH, FRANCES TROXLER, communications and mfg. ofcl.; b. Rockingham County, N.C., Jan. 28, 1926; d. James Harrison and Pearl Lee (Simpson) Troxler; bus. adminstrn. cert. Elon Coll., 1958; m. John Milton Keogh, Dec. 23, 1948; 1 son, James Robert. With Western Electric Co., 1951-66, 72—, profl. adminstrv. employee, methods devel., Greensboro, N.C., 1972-77, profl. adminstrv. employee, corp. benefits, 1977-80, chief corp. records sect., 1980—; sales service asst. So. Bell Telephone Co., Cocoa Beach, Fla., 1966-67. Adv. Secretarial Explorer Post, Nat. Greene council Girl Scouts U.S.A.; sec. Greensboro Inter Club Council, 1974-75. Recipient PPP award Western Electric Co., 1975. Mem. Am. Bus. Women's Assn. (pres. local chpt. 1959, 73, 75, Woman of Yr. 1975), SCORE (chmn. Greensboro chpt. 1981), Am. Mgmt. Assn., Telephone Pioneers Am., Internat. Platform Assn. (hospitality com. 1979, red carpet com. 1980), Beta Sigma Phi (treas. 1972-73). Democrat. Methodist. Originator, pub. govt. systems secretarial manual. Home: 1 Hastings Circle Greensboro NC 27406 Office: I-85 Guilford Center Greensboro NC 27420

KEPHART, RONALD DEAN, lumber and bldg. products distbn. co. exec.; b. Belpre, Kans., Oct. 17, 1936; s. Virgil Eugene and Alta Marie (Whitley) K.; B.S., Carthage Coll., Kenosha, Wis., 1966; m. Patricia Josephine Liegler, Oct. 27, 1957; children—Kerri Teresa, Kathy Anne, Kristine Robin, Kimberly Marie. Controller, chief fin. officer DC Internat., Denver, 1966-69; v.p. planning Time-DC Inc., Lubbock, Tex., 1969-73; exec. v.p., chief fin. officer Drawing Board, Inc., Dallas, 1972-79; v.p. fin., treas. Slaughter Bros., Inc., Dallas, 1979—; lectr. U. Tex., Dallas, 1976—. Bd. dirs. Jr. Achievement, Dallas, 1976—. Served with USAF, 1955-59. C.P.A., Tex. Mem. Tex. Soc. C.P.A.'s. Republican. Club: Canyon Creek Country. Home: 1106 Chapel Creek Ct Richardson TX 75080 Office: 11050 Plano Rd Dallas TX 75238

KEPHART, SAMUEL ROBINSON, security systems co. exec.; b. Phila., Nov. 20, 1950; s. Alvin Evans and Marie Elizabeth (Kenny) K.; B.B.A., Nat. U., San Diego, 1976; student U. Calif., San Diego, 1969-70, Free Enterprise Inst., 1975—. Owner, mgr. Exec. Service Systems, LaJolla, Calif., 1970-71; dir. mktg. Westinghouse Security Systems, Phila., 1971-73, sr. security cons., San Diego, 1973—; pres. Global Factors, Inc., San Diego, 1976—. Mem. World Affairs Council San Diego, World Trade Assn. San Diego (charter mem.), Am. Soc. Indsl. Security, Mcht. Brokers Exchange of London. Episcopalian. Clubs: Phila. Country, Univ. of San Diego, Toastmasters Internat. Home: 3790 Riviera Dr San Diego CA 92109 Office: 8485 Commerce Ave San Diego CA 92121

KEPLER, CHARLES WILLIAM, exec. personnel corp. exec.; b. Detroit, Dec. 29, 1930; s. Murry John and Alice G. Kepler; B.B.A., U. Mich., 1953, M.B.A., 1953; m. Alice Anne Sichler, Sept. 8, 1952; children—Peter, Karin, Susanne, Daniel, Jennifer. Mgr. mktg. consumer electronics Gen. Electric Co., Utica, N.Y., 1955-68; dir. product devel. consumer products Motorola Corp., Chgo., 1968-73; v.p. new bus. div., mem. operating com. Gould Inc., Chgo., 1973-76; v.p. mktg. Callaghan & Co., Chgo., 1976-78; sr. v.p. Russell Reynolds Assn. Inc., Chgo., 1978—. Served with AUS, 1953-55. Clubs: Univ., Met. (Chgo.); Leland (Mich.) Country. Home: 428 Cedar St Winnetka IL 60093 Office: Russell Reynolds Assn Inc 230 W Monroe St Chicago IL 60606

KEPLEY, THOMAS HOWARD, securities co. exec.; b. Salisbury, N.C., Jan. 31, 1933; s. Thomas Oscar and Helen Gould (Gantt) K.; B.S., U. N.C., 1955; certificate of honor in investment banking Northwestern U., 1959; certificate of achievement N.Y. Inst. Finance, 1969; m. Elizabeth Ann Doscher, Nov. 25, 1961; children—Thomas Howard, Elizabeth Anne Gilmore. With McCarley & Co., Inc., mems. N.Y. Stock Exchange, Am. Stock Exchange, Asheville, N.C., 1956-58, Columbia, S.C., 1958—, mgr. S.C. bond dept., 1958-64, v.p., 1964-72, exec. v.p., 1972-79, merged with Interstate Securities Corp., 1979, v.p., 1979—, dir., 1965—; chmn. bd. dirs., pres. H.W. Bischoff Transp. Co., Columbia, Charleston, S.C., 1968-74; dir. Computerecords, Inc., Columbia, Happy Folks, Inc., 1971—. Chmn., Sports-A-Rama, 1969; mem. U. N.C. Edn. Found., Columbia Com. of 100, 1965—. Trustee, Incarnation Devel. Found., Columbia, 1973—, sec., 1974, treas., 1975, v.p., 1976; bd. govs., chmn. investment and comml. coms. S.C. Reins. Facility, 1974—; adv. bd. Lutheran So. Sem.; bd. dirs., v.p. Kidney Found. S.C., 1975—; chmn. United Fund Com., 1974, 75; founding mem. S.C. Debutante Ball, Inc., pres., bd. dirs., 1981—. Served with AUS, 1956-58. Recipient George Washington Honor medal Freedom Found., Valley Forge, Pa., 1969, Key to City of Seoul (Korea), 1958. Mem. N.Y. Stock Exchange (allied), Am. Stock Exchange (allied), Nat. Security Traders Assn. (conduct and ethics com. 1973-75), Securities Dealers of Carolinas (sec. 1964-65, v.p. 1971-72, pres. 1972-73, chmn. bd. dirs. 1974—, permanent chmn. conv. chmn. 1975—, permanent chmn. edn. com. 1975—), Columbia C. of C., Hibernian Soc., Smithsonian Assos., Kappa Alpha Order. Lutheran (chmn. worship and music com. 1971-72, vice chmn. finance com. 1972, chmn. ch. council 1973-74, pulpit com. 1973-75; audit com. Calif. Synod 1973—). Mason. Clubs: Forest Lake Country (Columbia); Sertoma (charter life mem., exec.); Walnut Hill Hunt. Pioneer indsl. devel. bond underwriting. Home: 4765 Heath Hill Rd Columbia SC 29206 Office: 1st Nat Bank Bldg Suite 650 PO Box 1730 Columbia SC 29202

KEPLINGER, LORRAINE JOYCE MILLER (MRS. RICHARD ALAN KEPLINGER), book and music co. exec.; b. Lena, Ill., Apr. 9, 1931; d. Arthur Leroy and Elizabeth Maude (Baker) Miller; student Ill. Wesleyan Sch. Music, 1949-50, Kent State U., 1963-67; A.A. in Gen. Edn., 1979; m. Richard Alan Keplinger, Aug. 20, 1950; children—Karen (Mrs. Thomas R. Kaufman), Marilyn (Mrs. Roger P. Yekisa), Joy (Mrs. Curtis Elifritz), Sales clk. Gantt's Grocery, Lena, Ill., 1947-52; gen. operator Gospel Book Store, New Philadelphia, Ohio, 1962-68; owner, operator Gospel Book & Music Co., New Philadelphia, 1969—. Tchr. Peniel Holiness Christian Day Sch., Beach City, Ohio, 1968-71. Council pres. P.T.A., 1966-68; active Tusarawas County Philharmonic Orch. Mem. Am. Legion Aux. (unit treas. 1971, pres. Tuscarawas County 1976-78), Music Study Club (sec. 1978, pres. 1980). Lutheran (asst. organist 1971—, chmn. worship com. 1974—, mem. ch. council 1974-78, council sec. 1975-78, Sunday sch. supt. 1978-80, chmn. Christian edn. com. 1979—). Home and Office: 144 3d St SW New Philadelphia OH 44663

KERESEY, THOMAS MORTIMER, banker; b. N.Y.C., Feb. 22, 1931; s. Thomas Mortimer and Frances Kelley K.; B.A., Yale U., 1953; m. Anne L. Sory, Apr. 24, 1954; children—Katharine Keresey Ault, Mary T., Thomas Kelley, Caroline F. Mem. mktg. and internat. sales staff Owens Corning Fiberglas Corp., N.Y.C., 1953-61; partner Model, Roland & Co., mems. N.Y. Stock Exchange, N.Y.C., 1961-68; exec. v.p., dir. Clark, Dodge & Co., N.Y.C., 1969-74; v.p., dir. Kidder, Peabody & Co., N.Y.C., 1974-76; pres. First Nat. Bank in Palm Beach (Fla.), 1978—, also dir. Trustee Palm Beach Day Sch.; bd. dirs. Palm Beach Civic Assn., Good Samaritan Hosp.; treas. Palm Beach Round Table. Served with USNR, 1949-56. Office: First Nat Bank in Palm Beach 255 S County Rd Palm Beach FL 33480

KERIN, EDWARD LAWRENCE, mfg. exec.; b. Wichita, Kans., Mar. 28, 1942; s. Edward Lawrence and Marguerite Katherine (Conroy) K.; B.A., U. Ariz., 1964; M.I.M., Am. Grad. Sch. Internat. Mgmt., 1971; m. Michelle Louis Morris, June 14, 1974; 1 son, David Michael. Latin Am. area mgr. Hallmark Cards, Inc., Kansas City, Mo., and Republic of Panama, 1965-69; regional mgr. for Europe, Africa and Middle East, Libby McNeil & Libby, Chgo., 1971-73; internat. mktg. mgr. Hunt Wesson Foods, Fullerton, Calif., 1973-78; v.p. internat. ops. Binney & Smith, Inc., Easton, Pa., 1978—. Active United Way. Office: Binney & Smith Inc 1100 Church Ln Easton PA 18042

KERIN, KENNETH JOSEPH, assn. exec.; b. New Britain, Conn., Dec. 15, 1938; s. Harry Dennis and Anna (Trembley) K.; B.A., U. Conn., 1962, M.A., 1964, postgrad., 1964-66; m. Evelyn Brown, Sept. 2, 1961; children—Susan, Christopher, Stephanie. Asst. prof. econs. U.S. Naval Acad., Annapolis, Md., 1966-69; research economist ITT Research Inst., Washington, 1969-71; asst. dir. research Nat. Assn. Realtors, Washington, 1971-74, dir., 1974-79, v.p., 1979—. Adv. com. 1980 Census; bldg. research advisory bd. Nat. Acad. Scis. NDEA fellow, 1964-66. Mem. Nat. Assn. Bus. Economists, Am. Real Estate and Urban Econs. Assn., Nat. Tax Assn., Fed. Statistics Users Conf., Lambda Alpha. Home: 2619 Mountain Laurel Pl Reston VA 22091 Office: Nat Assn Realtors 925 15th St NW Washington DC 20005

KERN, GERTRUDE, apparel mfg. co. exec.; b. Bklyn., July 29, 1931; d. Julius David and Sylvia (Eiler) Seide; m. Arthur Kern, Sept. 2, 1950; children—Stephen, Leslie, Robert. Asst. controller Ballet Makers, Inc., Fairlawn, N.J., 1969-72; account supr., credit mgr. Gentry Internat., Fairlawn, 1972-75; sr. credit mgr. Gen. Sportcraft Co. Ltd., Bergenfield, N.J., 1975-79; credit mgr. Donmoor, Inc., N.Y.C., 1979-81, Murjani, Internat., Secaucus, N.J., 1981—. Organizer, Glen Rock (N.J.) Girl Scouts U.S.A., 1969-70. Mem. Am. Soc. Profl. and Exec. Women, N.Y. Credit and Fin. Mgmt. Assn., N.Y. Credit Women's Group, Nat. Apparel Credit Assn. (dir.)

KERNAN, JOHN TERENCE, info. systems co. exec.; b. Balt., Feb. 17, 1946; s. Anthony Eugene and Mildred Mary (Farson) K.; B.S., Loyola Coll., Balt., 1969; m. Dianne Mary Ruminski, May 11, 1973; 1 dau., Amy Beth. Project mgr. G.W. Stephens & Assos., Towson, Md., 1962-69; systems analyst McCormick & Co., Balt., 1969-73, mgr. info. services, 1973-75, dir. systems services, 1976-77; dir. info. systems Borden Foods div. Borden, Inc., Columbus, Ohio, 1977-79; v.p. product devel. Deltak, Inc., Oak Brook, Ill., 1979—. Served to 1st lt. Md. NG, 1965-72. Mem. Assn. Systems Mgmt., Am. Mktg. Assn., Am. Prodn. and Inventory Control Soc. Home: 6463 Cape Cod Ct Lisle IL 60532 Office: 1220 Kensington Rd Oak Brook IL 60521

KERNAN, SCOTT VINCENT, publisher; b. Corpus Christi, Tex., Nov. 3, 1950; s. William Henry and Mary Barbara (Conn) K.; B.S. in Indsl. Adminstrn., Iowa State U., 1974; m. Judith Jean Lausten, July 8, 1972; 1 dau., Ann Meridith. Personnel mgr. Dakota North Plains Corp., Aberdeen, S.D., 1974-76; bus. mgr. Homemaker Mag., Aberdeen, 1976—, North Plains Press, 1979—; owner, pub. The Comet, 1979—; curriculum advisor State Sch. Sci., Wahpeton, N.D. Mem. Nat. Alliance Businessmen (exec. bd. 1975-76), Nat. Assn. Circulation and List Mgrs. Republican. Club: Elks. Home: 601 Willow Dr Aberdeen SD 57401 Office: Box 910 Aberdeen SD 57401

KERNER, FRED, publisher; b. Montreal, Que., Can., Feb. 15, 1921; s. Sam and Vera (Goldman) K.; B.A., Sir George Williams U., Montreal, 1942; m. Jean Elizabeth Somerville, July 17, 1945 (div. Apr. 1951); 1 son, Jon Fredrik; m. 2d, Sally Dee Stouten, May 18, 1959; children—David Lassen, Diane Gail. Asst. sports editor Montreal Gazette, 1942-44; news editor Canadian Press, Montreal, Toronto, N.Y., 1944-50; asst. night city editor AP, N.Y.C. 1950-57; editor Hawthorn Books, N.Y.C., 1957-58; exec. editor Crest-Premier Books, N.Y.C., 1958-62, editor-in-chief, 1963-64; pres., editor-in-chief Hawthorn Books, Inc., N.Y.C., 1965-67, Centaur House, Inc., 1965—; pres. Paramount Security Corp., N.Y.C., 1965-67; mng. dir. Fred Kerner/Pub. Projects, N.Y.C., 1968—; pub. dir., book and edn. divs. Readers Digest (Can.) Ltd., 1969-75; v.p., dir. pub. Harlequin Enterprises, Ltd., 1975—; pres. Athabaska House, 1975-77; v.p. Publitex Internat. Corp., 1968—; dir. Peter Kent, Inc., Personalized Systems, Inc., Nat. Mint Inc., Pennorama Crafts, Inc., Disque Designs, Inc.; faculty SW Writers Conf., Breadloaf Writers Conf., others. Chmn. book pub. com. and promotion com. Edward R. Murrow Meml. Fund; mem. Protestant Sch. Bd. Greater Montreal Parents Com., 1970—, chmn., 1971-72; mem. Local 4 Sch. Bd., N.Y.C. Bd. govs. Concordia U., Montreal; bd. dirs. Canadian Book Pub. Council, Canadian Copyright Inst.; trustee Gibson Lit. Awards, Benson & Hedges Lit. Awards, CAA Lit. Awards. Can. Authors Assn. Lit awards; founding chmn. Toronto Lit. Luncheon. Recipient award for lit. Montreal YMCA, Crusade for Freedom award Am. Heritage Found., Air Can. award, Queen's Silver Jubilee medal. Mem. Canadian Soc. N.Y., Canadian Assn. for Restoration Lost Positives (pres.), Sir George Williams U. Alumni Assn. (pres. N.Y. chpt. 1961-69, pres. 1971-73), Canadian Authors Assn. (nat. v.p., past pres. Montreal br.), Mystery Writers Am., Authors Guild, Authors League Am., Internat. Platform Assn., Am. Acad. Polit. and Social Sci., Canadian Soc. Profl. Journalists, Am. Mgmt. Assn., Sigma Delta Chi. Clubs: Advertising, Overseas Press (chmn. elections com., pres.'s com., book pub. com.) (N.Y.C.); Toronto Men's Press; Authors' (London, Eng.). Author 12 books including: (with Leonid Kotkin) Eat, Think and be Slender, 1954; (with Walter M. Germain) The Magic Power of Your Mind, 1956; A Treasury of Lincoln Quotations, 1965. Home: 25 Farmview Crescent Willowdale ON M2J 1G5 Canada Office: 51 E 42d St New York NY 10017 also 225 Duncan Mill Rd Don Mills ON H3B 3K9 Canada

KERNS, MARTIN LANE, pension cons., ins. mgmt.; b. Great Bend, Kans., Mar. 3, 1941; s. Harold and Fern V. K.; student Wichita State U., 1959-62; C.L.U., Am. Coll. Life Underwriters, 1969; m. Billie Jean Kennedy, Nov. 17, 1962; children—Martin Lane II, Michelle LeAnn. Agt., supr. Penn Mut. Life Ins. Co., Wichita, Kans., 1962-67; gen. agt. Central Life of Iowa, Wichita, 1967-69; agt. New Eng. Mut. Life Ins. Co., Great Bend, 1970-77, gen. agt., 1978-80, Houston, 1981—; pres. The Kerns Orgn., Inc., 1981—, Compensation Planning, Inc., Great Bend, 1971-80; chmn. research com. Million Dollar Round Table, to 1980; mem. advisory bd. Top of the Table, 1979-81; speaker ins. and pension field; traveling faculty Am. Coll. Life Underwriters. Former pres. Barton County chpt. Am. Cancer Soc. Mem. Golden Belt Estate Planning Council (past pres.), Central Kans. Life Underwriters Assn. (past pres.), Am. Soc. C.L.U.'s (pres. Wichita chpt. 1979), Assn. Advanced Life Underwriting, Am. Soc. Pension Actuaries, Nat. Assn. Pension Consultants. Republican. Episcopalian. Home: 3801 McKinney St Great Bend KS 67530 Office: PO Box J Great Bend KS 67530

KERPELMAN, HOWARD EUGENE, banker; b. Suffolk, Va., Feb. 26, 1936; s. Arthur Z. and Rose A. (Laderberg) K.; B.S., Va. Commonwealth U., 1960; M.B.A., U. New Haven, 1976; m. Anne Virginia Wigg, Sept. 14, 1960; 1 son, Keith David. With Central Nat. Bank, Richmond, Va., 1963-64; asst. v.p. Hartford Nat. Bank, Stamford, Conn., 1964-66; asst. v.p., br. mgr. Cititrust, 1966-73; asst. v.p., br. adminstr. The Banking Center, Waterbury, Conn., 1973-74; pres., chief exec. officer Litchfield Savs. Bank (Conn.), 1974—. Mem. Litchfield Sewer Commn. Served with USAF, 1961-62. Mem. Am. Inst. Banking, C. of C. Northwestern Conn., Litchfield Area Bus. Assn. Clubs: Lions, Masons. Office: West St Litchfield CT 06759

KERR, BYRON THOMAS, mgmt. cons. co. exec.; b. Campbellton, N.B., Can., Dec. 28, 1924; s. Thomas F. and Isobel (Arseneault) K.; Engring. cert. Colchester Coll. Mount Alison U., Sackville, N.B., 1945; B. Engring., N.S. Tech., 1947; m. Shirley Bulmer, Dec. 27, 1947; children—Peter Thomas, Patricia Ann, Susan Winifred. Field engr. Shawinigan Engring. Co., 1947-49, resident engr., 1949-51; mng. dir. The Purdy & Henderson Co., Montreal, Que., 1950-51, pres., 1953; pres. The Charles Warnock Co. Ltd., La Salle, Que., 1954-56; exec. v.p. The Warnock Hersey Co., LaSalle, 1956-63, pres., chief exec. officer, 1963—; pres., chief exec. officer Warnock Hersey Profl. Services Ltd., 1978—. Mayor City of Saint Lambert (Que.), 1961-64. Fellow Engring. Inst. Can.; mem. Order Engrs. of Que., Profl. Engrs. Ont., Profl. Engrs. Geologists and Geophysicists of Alta., Profl. Engr. of N.B., Profl. Engrs. of Nfld., Profl. Engrs. N.S. Clubs: Mount Stephen, Reform, Cerc le Universitair, Montreal Country. Home and Office: 240 1st St Saint Lambert PQ J4R 1B5 Canada

KERR, JAMES ROBERT, mfg. exec.; b. Las Vegas, N.Mex., Sept. 23, 1917; s. Louis Alexander and Mary Louise (Lynch) K.; student Pasadena City Coll., 2 yrs.; m. Colleen Warrick, Sept. 18, 1943; children—Mary Lou, Cathy S., James Robert, William Lawrence. Dir. West Coast office Avco Corp., 1954-56, v.p. def. planning N.Y. office, 1956-57, pres. Lycoming div., 1957-60, pres. research and advanced devel. div., 1958-60, exec. v.p., 1960-61, pres., 1961-74, chief exec. officer, 1969—, chmn. bd., 1974—, also dir.; dir. Avco Financial Services, Republic Steel Corp., Paul Revere Corp., Avco Community Developers, Inc. Bd. govs. United Way Am., 1970-77; bd. dirs. Nat. Multiple Sclerosis Soc., 1978—; trustee Sacred Heart U. Conn., Nat. Safety Council. Served with USAF, 1942-54; col. Res. Decorated knight St. Gregory, Holy Sepulchre; recipient Outstanding Service award USO. Clubs: N.Y. Yacht, Jockey (N.Y.C.); Blind Brook (Port Chester N.Y.); La Jolla (Calif.) Country (Washington). Home: 1175 Muirlands Dr La Jolla CA 92037 Office: 1275 King St Greenwich CT 06830

KERR, WILLIAM AGNEW, publishing co. exec.; b. New Castle, Pa., Mar. 24, 1934; s. Harold Agnew and Rita (Patton) K.; B.S., Cornell U., 1957; postgrad. Northwestern U. Grad. Sch. Bus. Adminstrn., 1960-65, Fla. Technol. U., 1975-77. With employee relations dept. Pullman Inc., Chgo., 1957-67; cons. M-I-A Services, Evanston, Ill., 1967-69; adminstr. Computer Data Processing Co., Detroit, 1969-70; asso. Kudjus & Assos., Highland Park, Mich., 1970-72; with Dzus Fastener Co. Inc., West Islip, N.Y., 1972-74; treas., dir. Anna Pub. Inc., Winter Park, Fla., 1975-77; pub., gen. mgr. Oakland Press, Winter Park, 1977-80, mng. dir., 1980—; chmn. bd. Jarvis-Kerr Inc., Orlando, Fla., 1977-80; adminstr. Fla. Dept. Revenue, 1978-80; v.p., gen. mgr., dir. M-I-A Communications Corp., 1980—. Bd. dirs. Detroit Sparks Wheelchair Athletic Assn., 1970-72. Served with U.S. Army, 1957-59. Recipient Reeves Meml. Writing award George Reeves Meml. Found., 1959; Klepser Found. prize for photography, 1975; Chew-Buzek grantee and fellow, 1975-77. Mem. Soc. Mfrs. Agts. (dir. 1971-72), Indsl. Relations Research Assn., Cornell Soc. Engrs., U.S. Robotics Soc. Republican. Presbyterian. Club: Cornell U. Author: (with L. Till) Personnel Classification Inventory, 1964; author, photographer: Shadow of the El, 1966; North on Woodward, 1968; I-75 South, 1971; Princess of Blue-Green Aura, 1975; author: Interactive MicroOperating Systems, 1977.

KERSEY, DALLAS MANYETTE, credit and fin. co. exec.; b. Washington, Mar. 14, 1942; s. Aaron Austin and Evelyn N. (Burke) K.; B.A., U. Va., 1964; m. Mary Irons, Apr. 6, 1974; children—Debra, Melissa, Tristram. Mgr. news bur. Richmond (Va.) Times Dispatch, 1964; mgr. subs. relations Philip Morris Inc., 1967; dir. communications Philip Morris Indsl. Co., 1971; v.p. public affairs and communications Am. Express Co., 1978—. Mem. Public Relations Soc. Am. Club: Overseas Press (N.Y.C.). Office: 125 Broad St New York NY 10004

KERSHAW, THOMAS ABBOTT, restaurant corp. exec.; b. Phila., Dec. 1, 1938; s. Melville Gartside and Florence Frieda (Yackle) K.; B.S. in Mech. Engring., Swarthmore Coll., 1960; M.B.A., Harvard U., 1962. Mem. market devel. staff E.I. duPont de Nemours, Wilmington, Del., 1962-64; production mgr. Data Packaging Corp., Cambridge, Mass., 1964-65; owner Primus Assos., Warren, Vt., 1965-66; market devel. mgr. Bolt Beramek & Newman, Cambridge, 1966-69; pres. Exec. Townhouse Corp., Boston, 1969—, Hampshire House Corp., 1969—. Pres., Beacon Hill Bus. Assn.; bd. dirs. Beacon Hill Civic Assn. Republican. Presbyterian. Clubs: Harvard (Boston, N.Y.C.); Union Boat, Corinthian Yacht. Home: 84 Beacon St Boston MA 02108

KERSTING, ROBERT EDWARD, lawyer; b. Clinton, Iowa, Aug. 26, 1916; s. Augustus Henry and Eva (Schaub) K.; student pub. and pvt. schs.; B.S. in Econs., Northwestern U., 1938, J.D., 1941; m. Dolores Shoup, Dec. 19, 1978; children—Judith, Sheryl, Lynn, Laura, Linda. Admitted to Ill. bar, 1941, Ariz. bar, 1946; pvt. law practice, Chgo., 1941-42, Phoenix, 1946—; pres. Red Rock Ranches and Ariz. Aviation Co., 1945-50; spl. asst. atty. gen. Ariz., 1954—; test pilot, exec. Howard Aircraft, Chgo., 1942-43; sec., treas., dir. Savage Industries, Inc., 1947—, Ariz. Welding Equipment Co., 1947—, Savage Mfg. Co., 1948—, Phoenix Irrigation Service, Inc., 1957—, Trust Investment Enterprises, 1959—, Sun States Land and Devel. Co.; chmn. bd., counsel Sunshine Land & Cattle Corp.; pres., dir., gen. counsel Yauapai Hotels Corp., Western Growth Capital Corp.; dir., gen. counsel Ins. Corp. Am., Queen Creek Land & Cattle Corp.; dir., mem. exec. com. Financial Corp. Ariz.; field counsel Fed. Nat. Mortgage Assn.; pres. Integrity Escrows of Ariz., 1st Western Funding Corp., 1st Tex. Holding Corp.; gen. counsel, mem. exec. com., dir. Investors United Life Ins. Co., Western Nat. Mortgage Corp. Active A.R.C.; sec., dir. Phoenix Symphony Assn.; treas. Phoenix charter govt. com., 1950; chmn. Phoenix Athletic Commn., 1952. Mem. Ariz. State Democratic Central Com., 1951—, alt. del. nat. conv., 1952, 56; pres. Phoenix Young Dems. Club, 1948, nat. com. Young Dems. Ariz., 1950; pres. Ariz. Dem. Assn., 1955; del., mem. rules com. Dem. Nat. Conv., 1960; treas. Maricopa County Dem. Central Com. Bd. dirs. McCune Found. Served as chief flight instr. USAAF, also with flight tng. program USN, 1941-45. Mem. Am., Ariz. bar assns., Navy League of U.S., N.U. Alumni Club (pres. 1947), C. of C., Teen-Age C. of C. (dir. 1947), Am. Detective Assn. (pres. 1957—), Phi Gamma Delta, Phi Delta Phi. Episcopalian. Moose. Clubs: 20-30, Phoenix Press, Phoenix Country, Paradise Valley Racquet, Racquet (Palm Springs, Calif.); Executive, Fraternal Order of Police. Home: 7510 N 14th Ave Phoenix AZ 85021 Office: Del Webb Bldg Phoenix AZ 85012

KESNER, RICHARD LOUIS, pension cons.; b. E. Orange, N.J., Nov. 6, 1945; s. Irving J. and Lucile B. Kesner; B.S. in Journalism, Bradley U., Peoria, Ill., 1967; m. Jean Susan Crum, June 18, 1970; children—Kelly Lynn, Adam Douglas. Regional pension mgr. N.Am. Life Ins. Co., Chgo., 1972-74; v.p. mktg. NBF Corp., Chgo., 1974-77; pres. Benefit Programs Inc., Deerfield Beach, Fla., 1977-80, Benefit Cons., Inc., Boca Raton, Fla., 1980—. Mem. Nat. Assn. Life Underwriters, Gen. Agts. and Mgrs. Assn., Internat. Assn. Fin. Planners (chpt. sec. 1980). Office: 299 W Camino Gardens Blvd Suite 301 Boca Raton FL 33432

KESSLER, JOHN WHITAKER, real estate cons. exec.; b. Cin., Mar. 7, 1936; s. Charles Wilmont and Elizabeth (Whitaker) K.; B.S., Coll. Bus. Adminstrn., Ohio State U., 1958; m. Charlotte Hamilton Power, Aug. 8, 1964; children—Catherine, Elizabeth, Jane. Mem. sales dept. Armstrong Cork Co., Lancaster, Pa., 1958-59; mgr. spl. products div. M & R Dietetics Labs., Columbus, Ohio, 1959-62; co-founder, mng. partner Multicon, Columbus, 1962-70, pres. Multicon Communities div. Multicon Properties, Inc., 1970-72; prin. John W. Kessler Co., Columbus, 1972—; pres. Marsh & McLennan Real Estate Advs., Inc., Columbus, 1980—; mem. Fed. Res. Bd., Cleve.; dir. Ohio State Life Ins. Co., Southwide (N.Y.), Limited Stores, Inc., Columbus. Vice pres. Children's Hosp., Columbus, pres. Children's Hosp. Research Found.; trustee Battelle Meml. Inst. Found., Columbus Mus. Art, Columbus Sch. Girls; bd. dirs. Spoleto, U.S.A., Charleston, S.C.; pres. Pres.'s Club Ohio State U. Mem. Columbus C. of C. (past chmn.). Office: John W Kessler Co 100 E Broad St Suite 1501 Columbus OH 43215

KESSLER, LAURENCE, food service co. exec.; b. N.Y.C., Oct. 25, 1942; s. David and Mollie (Havio) K.; B.A., Adelphi U., 1965; m. Judith Lesk, Dec. 25, 1966; children—Reeca L., Jonathan P. Vice pres. Walston & Co., N.Y.C., 1968-72; v.p. Thomson Securities Co., N.Y.C., 1972-75; pres. No. Trinity Enterprises Inc., owners chain Burger King Restaurants, Fairport, N.Y., 1975—; mem. N.Y. State Gov.'s Task Force on Fast Foods, 1980—. Mem. N.Y. State council Burger King Franchisees. Mem. N.Y. Restaurant Assn., Nat. Restaurant Assn. Jewish. Office: 464 Perinton Hills Office Park Fairport NY 14450

KESSLER, RICHARD LEE, auto mfg. co. exec.; b. Jackson, Minn., Oct. 27, 1926; s. Charles John and Alice May (Kruger) K.; B.S. in Mech. Engring., Mich. Tech. U., 1949; M. Automotive Engring., Chrysler Inst. Engring., 1951; m. Patricia A. McCann, Feb. 23, 1952; children—Lee, Chris, Craig, Pamela. With Chrysler, various locations, 1949—, mgr. quality control, assembly div., Detroit, 1967-73, plant mgr. assembly plant, St. Louis, 1973-77, plant mgr. assembly plant, Newark, Del., 1977-80; dir. mfg. Chrysler de Mexico, 1981—. Served with USAAF, 1944. Republican. Episcopalian. Club: Club de Golf La Hacienda. Home: Bosque de Ahuehuetes 1262 Bosque de Las Lomas Mexico DF Mexico Office: Chrysler de Mexico Lago Alberto 320 Mexico DF Mexico

KESSLER, RONY ITZCHAK, public accountant; b. Tel Aviv, Mar. 30, 1942; came to U.S., 1959, naturalized, 1965; s. Leo and Bertha (Helfer) K.; A.A.S. in Chemistry, N.Y.C. Community Coll., 1962; B.S. in Acctg., Queens Coll., 1966; M.B.A. in Acctg., L.I.U., 1973; m. Ellen Zang, Mar. 30, 1971; children—Robin, Debbie, David, Jason. With Price Waterhouse & Co., 1966-71; dir. mgmt. follow-up Capital Formation Co., N.Y.C., 1971-72, pres., 1973—; pres. Blum, Blake, Lowery & Kessler, P.C., public accts., Queens Village, N.Y., 1971—; mem. faculty York Coll., 1972-73, Hunter Coll., 1974-75, Queens Community Coll., 1975-76. Mem. budget and fin. com. West Hempstead Jewish Center, 1979-80. Served with U.S. Army, 1967-69. Mem. Am. Inst. C.P.A.'s, N.Y. State Soc. C.P.A.'s, Accts. Club Am. Club: Rotary (dir.; community service chmn. 1979—, Queens Village). Home: 756 Cornwell Ave West Hempstead NY 11552 Office: 221-10 Jamaica Ave Queens Village NY 11428

KESTENBAUM, LOUIS, polyethylene mfg. co. exec.; b. Muncachevo, Czechoslovakia, Aug. 21, 1922; s. Manuel and Hermina (Spiegel) K.; came to U.S., 1947, naturalized, 1952; student bus. adminstrn. U. Brno (Czechoslovakia); m. Gertrude Kallus, Aug. 1, 1945; children—Serena Carol, Lynda Gay. Comptroller, Buhl Jewelry, Pitts., 1950-55; gen. mgr. Linland Corp., Pitts., 1955-58; pres. Kest Constrn. Co., Pitts., 1958-62, Eden Gardens Devel. Corp., Los Angeles, 1962-68, Elkay Plastics Co. Inc., Los Angeles, 1968—. Treas., Shelters for Israel, 1964-68, fin. sec., 1968-74, asso. pres., 1974-81, pres., 1981; bd. dirs. Sha'arei Tefila Israel Temple, Los Angeles, 1972—. Prisoner in concentration camp, World War II. Mem. Calif. Film Extruders and Converters Assn. (dir. treas. 1979, pres. 1980). Democrat. Inventor serv-view screen. Home: 2224 Hercules Dr Los Angeles CA 90046 Office: 2320 E 49th St Los Angeles CA 90058

KESTLER, BERNIE A., energy and tech. services co. exec.; b. Chgo., Oct. 26, 1932; s. Nicholas J. and Katherine (Keller) K.; B.S., U.S. Naval Acad., 1953; m. Beverly Carol Lawson, Apr. 16, 1955; children—Paul, Mark. Field engr. IBM, Chgo., 1955-58; project mgmt. Sperry, Phoenix, 1958-66; field sales mgr. Gen. Electric Co., Tampa, 1966-74; dir. Honeywell, Phoenix. 1974—. Mem. Honeywell Polit. Action Com., 1976—. Served with USNR, 1953-55. Mem. Phoenix C. of C. Republican. Methodist. Home: 501 W Gleneagles Dr Phoenix AZ 85023 Office: 16404 N Black Canyon Hwy Phoenix AZ 85023

KETCHUM, ALTON HARRINGTON, advt. exec.; b. Cleve., Oct. 8, 1904; s. Wesley H. and Velma M. (Davis) K.; B.A., Western Res. U., 1926; m. Robyna Neilson, Apr. 27, 1940; 1 dau., Deborah (Mrs. Harvey Lambert). Spl. corr. United Press, 1926-27; editorial, advt. work Penton Pub. Co., Powers-House Co., Nesbitt Service Co., 1927-33; with McCann-Erickson, Inc., 1934-62, beginning as copy writer, successively copy group head, v.p., creative supr. internat. div., 1948-62, v.p. Infoplan, 1963-64; mem. corporate staff Interpublic Group of Cos., 1964-69; mng. dir. Harrington's (Hist. Resources), 1969—. Spl. asst. Petroleum Adminstrn. for War, 1943-44; supr. nat. campaign to explain Am. econ. system sponsored by Advt. Council, 1948-51; bd. dirs. Fed. World Govt., Inc., 1945-48, World Govt. News, 1948-51; spl. rep. USIA, India, 1954, cons., 1956—, mem. exec. res., 1957-70; designed People's Capitalism exhibit for USIA, 1956, Golden Key Exhibit for Dept. Commerce, 1956. Organizer Westchester-Fairfield (Conn.) com. Am. Assn. for UN, 1946; gave original designs for baton and badge of marshals of France to French people, 1953. Mem. Greenwich (Conn.) Aux. Police. Recipient award Freedoms Found., 1949; chosen one of 100 top copywriters, 1954; award of merit USIA, 1956; Ohio Gov.'s Achievement award, 1965. Mem. Nat. Planning Assn., Assn. Am. Geographers, Am. Acad. Polit. and Social Sci., Am., Greenwich hist. socs., India-Am. League (founder, 1st pres. 1960), Hist. Assn. Gt. Britain. Author: Follow the Sun, 1930; The Miracle of America, 1948; The March of Freedom, 1951; Let Freedom Ring, 1952; Our Hopes March Side by Side, 1955; Your Great Future in a Growing America, 1958; Uncle Sam, the Man and the Legend, 1959. Editor: Principles and Practices of Marketing Communications, 1966; Inst. Marketing Communications Bull. Contbr. to Doubleday Ency. of Careers. Home: 333 Cognewaug Rd Cos Cob CT 06807

KETCHUM, GEORGE HENRY, petroleum exec., cons.; b. Albuquerque, July 31, 1910; s. James Hampton and Irene (Troutman) K.; student Compton Coll., 1929-30, UCLA, 1936-40; m. Beryle Josephine Healy, Sept. 9, 1933. With Mobil Oil Corp., 1936-74, West Coast regional land advisor, Los Angeles, asst. sec., 1966-74; asst. sec. No. Natural Gas Producing Co., N.Y.C., 1966-74; petroleum cons., 1974—; v.p. Minoco So. Corp., 1980—; pres. Phoenix Energy Services, Inc., 1980—. Mem. adv. bd. Internat. Oil & Gas Ednl. Center of Southwestern Legal Found. Served with AUS, 1943-45. Mem. Am. (treas. 1966-67), Los Angeles (pres. 1958-59) assns. petroleum landmen, Am. Petroleum Inst., Rocky Mountain, Western (chmn. pub. lands com. Los Angeles 1963-64) oil and gas assns., Los Angeles C. of C., Petroleum Club Los Angeles. Author: Business Beneath the Seas, 1973; also profl. articles. Home: 16742 Octavia Pl Encino CA 91436

KETELSEN, JAMES LEE, diversified industry exec.; b. Davenport, Iowa, Nov. 14, 1930; s. Ernest Henry and Helen (Schumann) K.; B.S., Northwestern U., 1952; m. Joan Velde, Feb. 22, 1953; children—James V., Lee. Accountant, Price Waterhouse & Co., C.P.A.'s, Chgo., 1955-59; v.p. fin., treas. J.I. Case Co., Racine, Wis., 1962-68, pres., chief exec. officer, 1968-72; exec. v.p. Tenneco Inc., Houston, 1972-77, pres., 1977—, chmn. bd., chief exec. officer, 1978—; dir. Morgan Guaranty Trust Co. Bd. dirs. Nat. Jr. Achievement; trustee Northwestern U., Houston Symphony Soc., Houston Ballet, Com. for Econ. Devel. Served to lt. USNR, 1952-55. C.P.A., Tex., Ill. Mem. Am. Petroleum Inst. (dir.), Chi Psi. Clubs: River Oaks Country, Petroleum (Houston). Home: 5608 Briar Dr Houston TX 77027 Office: 1010 Milam St Houston TX 77001

KETT, ROBERT HENRY, contracting co. exec.; b. Phila., Jan. 26, 1943; s. Russell C. and Harriet (Peltz) K.; B.S., Temple U., 1964; M.B.A., U. Pa., 1969; diploma Calvary Bible Inst., 1975; m. Lynn Kosmahl, Aug. 7, 1964; children—Joanna, Nathan, Daniel. Various positions with Rohm and Haas, Phila., 1964-74; v.p., treas. Rulon Co., Souderton, Pa., 1975-79; pres., chief exec. officer BBW Group, Inc., Lansdale, Pa., 1979—. Head basketball coach Calvary Baptist High Sch., 1973—. Served with U.S. Army, 1966-68. Republican. Home: 2145 Kriebel Rd Lansdale PA 19446 Office: Box 5 Lansdale PA 19446

KETTEL, EDWARD JOSEPH, oil co. ofcl.; b. N.Y.C., Sept. 13, 1925; s. Harold J. and Evelyn M. (Melbourne) K.; student St. John's U., 1943; B.A., St. Francis Coll., 1949; M.A., Columbia U., 1953; m. Janet M. Johnson, Nov. 27, 1952; children—Dorothy A., David A. Ins. mgr. Arabian Am. Oil Co., 1950-56, Ethyl Corp., 1956-65; asst. treas. Atlantic Richfield Co., Los Angeles, 1965—; chmn. bd. Oil Ins., Ltd.; pres. Greater Pacific, Ltd.; dir. Am. S.S. Owners Mut. Protection and Indemnity Assn., Inc., Internat. Tanker Indemnity Assn., Ltd. Served with inf. AUS, 1943-46. Decorated Bronze Star, Purple Heart with oak leaf cluster. Mem. Am. Petroleum Inst., Mfrs. Chem. Assn., Nat. Fire Protection Assn., Risk and Ins. Mgmt. Soc. Clubs: N.Y. Athletic, Los Angeles Athletic, Palos Verdes Country. Office: 515 S Flower St Los Angeles CA 90071

KEULER, ASTRID LINNEA, constrn. co. exec.; b. N.Y.C., Oct. 24, 1929; d. Tage Ragnwald and Victoria Hulda (Gustafson) Flyborg; student East Stroudsburg State Coll., 1966-68; m. Jacob H. Keuler, Nov. 14, 1947; children—Daniel, Marc. Estimator, prodn. liaison Ind. Offset-Lithographers, N.Y.C., 1953-56; dir., owner The Art Gallery, Strathmore, N.J., 1960-63; treas., tchr. The Sch. at Kirkridge, Bangor, Pa., 1968-69; pres., Jacob-Clark Constrn. Co., Inc., Buck Hill Falls, Pa., 1971—; partner The Hamlet, residential community, Canadensis, Pa., 1972—; dir. Jacob-Stroud Corp. Treas., Monroe County Indsl. Devel. Authority, Stroudsburg, Pa., 1975—; founder, pres. Phoenix Players, 1965—. Mem. Nat. Assn. Home Builders (nat. dir. 1977—), Barrett Bus. Assn. (dir. 1979—), Pocono Builders Assn. (dir. 1974—), Pocono Mountains C. of C. (pres. 1980-81, Dir. of Yr. award 1978), Alpha Psi Omega. Democrat. Home: Box 15 Buck Hill Falls PA 18323 Office: Route 940E Paradise Valley Cresco PA 18326

KEVY, LAWRENCE WILLIAM, accountant; b. N.Y.C., Feb. 12, 1943; s. Jack and Ruth (Rosenblatt) K.; B.B.A., CCNY, 1963; m. Marlene Beth Trager, May 27, 1972. From staff acct. to mgr. tax dept. Eisner & Lubin, C.P.A.'s, N.Y.C., 1963-78; partner Ferber & Trager, C.P.A.'s, N.Y.C., 1978—. Mem. Army N.G., 1964-70. C.P.A., N.Y. Mem. Am. Inst. C.P.A.'s, N.Y. State Soc. C.P.A.'s, Tau Epsilon Phi (life), Beta Alpha Psi. Office: 370 Lexington Ave New York NY 10017

KEY, WILLIAM KENNETH, investment banker; b. Columbus, Ga., Sept. 23, 1949; s. William B. and Vera Elanor (Cochrane) K.; student Columbus Coll., 1967-69, Miami Inst. Fin., 1974, N.Y. Inst. Fin., 1975. Asst. to corp. credit mgr. Rhodes, Inc., Atlanta, 1969-72; comptroller Nat. Can Corp., N.Y.C., 1972-73; investment banker Hibbard O'Connor & Weeks, Fort Lauderdale, Fla., 1973-74; account exec. Thomson & McKinnon, Fort Lauderdale, 1974-75; v.p. Legal, Ashcraft & Winston, 1976; investment banker E.S.M. Group, Inc., Fort Lauderdale, 1977-79; pres. Spa Performance, Inc., Fort Lauderdale, 1979—; pres. Spa Encounters, Inc., 1979—; sec.-treas. Spa Installation and Design, Inc., 1979—. Clubs: One Hundred of

Broward County, Tower, LeClub Internat. Author: (with others) The New Challenge - Asset Management, 1977. Home: 2929 NE 40th St Fort Lauderdale FL 33308 Office: 4431 NE 11th Ave Fort Lauderdale FL 33334

KEYES, EDWARD LAWRENCE, JR., electric co. exec.; b. N.Y.C., Apr. 19, 1929; s. Edward Lawrence and Emily (Shepley) K.; B.A. cum laude, Princeton, 1951; m. Mary Ann Elliott, June 27, 1959; 1 dau., Elisabeth Elliott. Asst. to pres. Emerson Electric Co., St. Louis, 1961-64, asst. v.p. adminstrn., 1964-66, v.p. adminstrn. Emerson Motor div., 1966-67, exec. v.p., dir. Day-Brite Lighting div., 1967-70, pres. Builder Products div., 1970, pres. Chromalox Comfort Conditioning div., 1970-71, pres. Day-Brite Lighting div., 1971-73, dir. div., group v.p. corporate, 1973-74, exec. v.p. ops., 1974-77, pres. co., 1977—, chief operating officer, 1978—, corp. dir., 1973—, also dir.; dir. 1st Nat. Bank Clayton, Sterling Everest, Clayton, Beaird-Poulan div., Harris Calorific div., Ridge Tool div., Spl. Products div., AB Chance Co., Skil Corp. Served to 1st lt. USAF, 1951-56. Republican. Roman Catholic. Clubs: Cottage (Princeton); Saint Louis Country, Racquet (St. Louis); Log Cabin, Univ., Mo. Athletic. Home: 60 Briarcliff Saint Louis MO 63124 Office: 8100 W Florissant Ave Saint Louis MO 63136

KEYKO, GEORGE JOHN, watch and electronics co. exec.; b. New Britain, Conn., May 6, 1924; s. John Simonovich and Nellie Ivanovna (Gretcha) K.; B.S., Yale, 1949; m. Anne Romanchuk, Jan. 31, 1948; children—David, Mark. Spl. rep. Lederle Labs., Conn. and N.Y., 1949-52; pres. Teacher Toys, Inc., Conn., 1952-56; sales mgr. Washington Forge, N.J., 1956-60; sales mgr. shaver div. Ronson Corp., Woodbridge, N.J., 1960-63; sales mgr. Caravelle and BEP div. Bulova Watch Co., N.Y.C., 1963-66; v.p. mktg. Technipoqer div. Benrus Watch Co., Ridgefield, Conn., 1966-68; exec. v.p. Heuer Time & Electronics Corp., Springfield, N.J., 1969, pres., 1970-75; now pres. George Keyko Internat., Inc.; dir. Electrodata Concepts, Inc., Conn., Mintex Corp., Minn. Field solicitor United Fund, Westfield, 1965-67, 69, 70; chief timer internat. Ski Racers Assn., 1970—. Recipient Spl. award from INTREPID 22 - 12 Meter Yacht America's Cup, 1970. Mem. Am. Watch Mfg. Assn., Sports Car Club Am., N.Y. Sales Exec. Club. Republican. Episcopalian. Club: Echo Lake Country (Westfield, N.J.). Home: 931 Kimball Ave Westfield NJ 07090

KHADEM, RIAZ, mgmt. and computer cons.; b. Tehran, Iran, Nov. 21, 1939; came to U.S., 1958; s. Zikrullah and Malektaj (Javidi) K.; B.S., U. Ill., 1962; M.S., Harvard U., 1963; Ph.D., Balliol Coll., Oxford U., 1967; m. Linda Joan Scott, Aug. 3, 1968; children—Nasr, Tina. Lectr. dept. math. U. Southampton, 1967-69; asso. prof. dept. math. Laval U., Que., Can., 1970-72; systems cons. Bell Can., Montreal, 1972; chmn. dept. computer sci. Sch. Planning and Computer Applications, Tehran, 1972-75; pres. Info. Systems Mgmt., Tehran, 1975-79; cons. Peat Marwick Mitchell & Co., Chgo., 1979, Tarkenton & Co., Atlanta, 1979; systems cons. Baha'i World Center, Haifa, Israel, 1978-80; pres. Tarkenton Info. Systems, 1980—. Recipient Lisle Abott Rose award U. Ill., 1962; Eleemosary grantee Oxford U., 1965; Can. Council grantee Laval U., 1972. Contbr. articles to Jour. Info. Retrieval, Quar. Applied Math., Internat. Jour. Engring. Sci. Home: 600 River Valley Rd Atlanta GA 30328 Office: 3340 Peachtree Rd Suite 444 Atlanta GA 30326

KHALIFA, IBRAHIM MARZOUK, internat. bus. and tech. cons.; b. Cairo, Egypt, June 19, 1926; s. Mahmoud I. and Aleya (El Chawarby) K.; B.Sc. in Elec. Engring., Cairo U., 1949; m. Claire Courtney, May 12, 1951; children—Amin, Omar, Karim, Aly. With Phelps Dodge Internat. Corp. and subsidiaries, N.Y.C., 1966—, v.p. Eastern hemisphere, 1966-70, group v.p., dir., 1970-73, sr. v.p., 1975—, also dir.; exec. v.p. Phelps Dodge Communications Co., 1973-75; pres. Phelps Dodge Oversees Mktg. Corp., 1975-78; pres. Epic Internat. Consultants, Inc., Riverside, Conn., 1978—; cons. Phelps Dodge Industries, Inc., N.Y.C., Overseas Bechtel Inc., San Francisco; dir. UBAF Arab Am. Bank, UBAF Fin. Services Ltd. Recipient Robert G. Page award Phelps Dodge Industries, Inc., 1972. Mem. IEEE (sr. mem.), Am. Mgmt. Assn., Wire Assn., Internat. Council of the Conf. Bd. Club: Siwanoy Country. Home: 81 Hendrie Ave Riverside CT 06878 Office: Suite 933 60 E 42d St New York NY 10165

KHOYLIAN, ROUZAS RUSSELL, engring. exec.; b. Iran, May 8, 1926; Rafael and Vartandosh (Vartanian) K.; came to U.S., 1963, naturalized, 1975; B.S. in M.E., Worcester Poly. Inst., 1950; m. Janet Babajanian, Sept. 28, 1955; children—Razmik, Rima, Roubina, Armen. Chief engr. Electricity and Agr. Devel. Co., Iran, 1952-60; pres. Still Engring., Iran, 1960-63, Design and Process Engring., Inc., Burlington, Mass., 1965—; cons. thermodynamics, 1955-63. Dir. Youth Fedn., 1945-46; trustee Armenian Schs., Iran, 1951-56. Mem. Iranian and European Profl. Assn., Council Armenian Execs., Friends of Armenian Culture Soc. (dir.). Mem. Apostolic Ch. Patentee in field. Home: 34 Lincoln St Belmont MA 02178 Office: 29 31 B St Burlington MA 01803

KIBLER, JOHN CORNELIUS, mfg. co. exec.; b. Buffalo, Mar. 15, 1949; s. Cornelius John and Jacqueline Margarette (Faller) K.; B.A., Canisius Coll., Buffalo, 1970; postgrad. U. Buffalo, 1977-79; m. Marilyn Jean Spohr, May 2, 1975; children—John Cornelius, Laura. Personnel mgr. Mallory Timers Co., Warsaw, N.Y., 1974-76, mgr. prodn. and material control, 1976—. Pres. Warsaw United Funds, 1978. Served as officer USAR, 1970-73. Mem. Warsaw C. of C. Democrat. Roman Catholic. Home: 141 W Court St Warsaw NY 14569 Office: 200 Allen St Warsaw NY 14569

KICE, JACK WILBUR, inventor, mfg. co. exec.; b. Wichita, Kans., Jan. 10, 1915; s. James Wilbur and Minnie M. (Winzer) K.; student Armour Inst. Tech.; grad. Chgo. Tech. Coll., 1935; m. Anna Ruth Jones, Jan. 1, 1937; children—Richard Lee, Mary Ann (Mrs. Richard L. Grant), John Edward. Asst. chief engr. Lennox Furnace Co., Marshalltown, Iowa, 1937-40; engr. Stratosphere Lab., Boeing Airplane Co., Wichita, 1940-45; asst. to pres. Coleman Co., Inc., Wichita, 1945-56; v.p. engring. Kice Metal Products Co., Inc., Wichita, 1956—, now chmn. bd.; v.p. CFM Corp., Blackwell, Okla. Registered profl. engr. Mem. ASHRAE (life mem.), Nat. Soc. Profl. Engrs., C. of C. Republican. Presbyterian. Contbr. articles to profl. jours. Holder more than 30 patents in field of air pollution control, other indsl. air systems, energy conservation and prodn. Home: 8701 Brookhollow Ave Wichita KS 67211 Office: 2040 S Mead Ave Wichita KS 67211

KIDD, DAVID THOMAS, transp. and natural resources co. legal exec.; b. Laramie, Wyo., Feb. 1, 1934; s. David T. and Sarah Lucille (Love) K.; student Dartmouth, 1952-55; B.A., U. Wyo., 1957, J.D., 1960; m. Sally Louise Noble, Sept. 1, 1956; children—Lynden Louise, David Thomas II. Admitted to Wyo. bar, 1960, U.S. Supreme Ct. bar; asso. firm Brown Healy Drew Apostolos & Barton, Casper, Wyo., 1960-62, Schwartz, McCrary, Bon & Kidd, Casper, 1962-74; gen. officer, Western natural resources counsel Union Pacific Corp., Casper, 1974—; sec.-treas., dir. Capital Corp. Wyo., Inc., Wyo. Indsl. Devel. Corp.; pres. Jewett/Kidd Ranches, Big Piney, Wyo., Jewett Land & Livestock Co., Big Piney; atty., chief legis. counsel Wyo. Ho. of Reps., 1961-63, mem. Ho. of Reps., 1963-67; mcpl. judge Casper, 1963-68, mayor, 1971; mem. bd. litigation Mountain States Legal Found.; trustee Wyo. Heritage Found. Mem. Rocky Mountain Oil and Gas Assn. (dir., mem. exec. com.), Natrona County, Wyo., Am. bar assns., Wyo. Trial Lawyers Assn., Petroleum Assn. Wyo. (v.p.), Wyo. Mining Assn., Wyo. Taxpayers Assn. (v.p., dir.), Petroleum Club Casper. Club: Casper Country. Home: 2076 Willow Creek Rd Casper WY 82601 Office: 600 1st National Bank Bldg Casper WY 82601

KIDDE, JOHN EDGAR, restaurant exec.; b. Kansas City, Mo., May 4, 1946; s. Gustave Edgar and Mary Sloan (Orear) K.; B.A., Stanford U., 1968; M.B.A., Northwestern U., 1971; m. Donna Carolyn Peterson, Aug. 4, 1973; 1 dau., Kari Lauren. Corp. banking officer United Calif. Bank, Los Angeles, 1971-73; asst. to pres. Colony Foods, Inc., Newport Beach, Calif., 1973-75; v.p. ops., 1975-78; pres. Western Host Food Services, Inc., Irvine, Calif., 1978—. Mem. alumni admissions com. Phillips Acad. Served to 1st lt. AUS, 1969-70. Mem. Nat., Calif., So. Calif. restaurant assns., Stanford Univ. Alumni Assn. Republican. Episcopalian. Club: Racquet. Mem. adv. bd. Restaurant Bus. Mag. Home: 3907 Inlet Isle Dr Corona del Mar CA 92625 Office: 2102 Business Center Dr Irvine CA 92715

KIDDE, JOHN LYON, diversified industry exec.; b. Montclair, N.J., June 5, 1934; s. John Frederick and Katharine Lyon K.; grad. Hotchkiss Sch., 1952; A.B., Princeton U., 1956; postgrad. Columbia Law Sch., 1956-57; m. Ruth Mandeville, Mar. 14, 1970; children—Jonathan Lawrence, Jeremy Adam; children by previous marriage—Wilson Hand, Andrew Davis, Geoffrey Carter. Fin. dir. Walter Kidde S.A. Brazil, Rio de Janeiro, 1959-61; European mgr. Walter Kidde & Co., Inc., Paris, 1961-66, v.p., dir. internat. ops., Clifton, N.J., 1967—; dir. The Futures Group, Glastonbury, Conn., Fire Fighting Enterprises, Sydney, Australia, Mahler & Emerson, Inc., N.Y.C., Drukker Communications, Passaic, N.J., Baldwin United Co., Inc., Cin., W.S. Kirkpatrick Co. Inc., Fairfield, N.J., Solar-en Corp., Denville, N.J.; mem. adv. bd. N.J. Bank N.A., Pasaic, 1971—; mem. exec. com. Constrn. Specialties, Cranford, N.J. Bd. dirs. Nat. Council Crime and Delinquency; pres. Econ. Council Pakistan, N.Y.C.; trustee, mem. exec. com. Pace U., N.Y.C.; trustee Internat. Coll. Cayman Islands, Grand Cayman, Clara Maass Meml. Hosp., Belleville, N.J., Montclair (N.J.) Art Mus. Served with AUS, 1956-58. Clubs: Quantuck Beach (Westhampton, N.Y.); Pennington (Passaic); Princeton of N.Y. (N.Y.C.); Fellsbrook (Essex Falls, N.J.). Home: 154 Oldchester Rd Essex Fells NJ 07021 Office: 9 Brighton Rd Clifton NJ 07012

KIEFER, WILLIAM LEE, computer co. exec.; b. St. Louis, Aug. 19, 1946; s. Nellie Emma Lindsey; A.A. with honors in Bus. Adminstrn., St. Louis Community Coll., 1972; B.S. in Bus. Adminstrn., U. Mo., St. Louis, 1975; m. Joyce Ann Cwiklowski, Aug. 15, 1970; 1 son, Jason Lee. Computer operator Wetterau, Inc., 1969-73, Life & Casualty Ins. Cos., St. Louis, 1973-75, GAF Corp., St. Louis, 1975-79; computer account mgr. Computer Central Corp., St. Charles, Mo., 1979-81; with Microdata Corp., St. Louis, 1981—. Mem. St. Louis Ambassadors, 1976-79; chmn. North Park Neighborhood Assn.; Democratic committeeman 27th Ward, City of St. Louis, 1976-79. Served to staff mgr. USMC, 1965-69; Vietnam. Decorated Joint Service Commendation medal; recipient cert. of appreciation Mo. Senate, 1977. Mem. Data Processing Mgmt. Assn., Am. Inst. Design Drafting, Ind. Computer Cons. Assn., St. Louis Jaycees, U. Mo. St. Louis Bus. Alumni Assn. (pres.), VFW, Am. Legion, MVETS. Democrat. Roman Catholic. Club: Sgts. Home: 1656 Grape St Saint Louis MO 63147 Office: Microdata Corp 1864 Craig Rd Saint Louis MO 63141

KIEFFER, WILLIAM TOLBERT, JR., ins. co. exec.; b. St. Louis, Apr. 18, 1928; s. William Tolbert and Rosemary Catherine (Morgan) K.; B.A., Yale, 1950; m. Ann Murray Feeley, Dec. 28, 1974; children by previous marriage-Sarah A., William Tolbert III, Peter S., Anthony R., Mary D. (dec.); stepchildren—Taintor Davis, Jonathan E. Davis, Oliver E. Davis. With sales dept. group div. Aetna Life & Casualty Co., Nashville, N.Y.C., and Hartford, Conn., 1950-58, with mgmt. dept., 1959-68, asst. v.p., mkt. mgr., Hartford, 1968—; v.p. Aetna Capital Mgmt., Inc.; mem. adv. bd. dirs. Nat. Found. Employee Benefits, 1966-69; mem. research com. Internat. Found. Employee Benefits, 1973. Campaign dir. Republican candidate for Conn. Gov., 1962; bd. dirs. Hartford Symphony Soc., 1963-69, founding pres. Condr.'s Council, 1964; bd. dirs. Yale Alumni Fund, 1966; trustee Leukemia Soc. Am., Combined Health Appeal of Hartford, Central Conn. Civic, Cultural and Charitable Corp.; chmn. Mountain Chapel, Inc., Stowe, Vt. Served with U.S. Army, 1946-47; to lt. USAR, 1950-54. Democrat. Episcopalian. Club: Harvard of Boston. Home: 149 Westland Ave West Hartford CT 06107 Office: 151 Farmington Ave Hartford CT 06115

KIERNAN, CATHERINE HILL, oil co. exec.; b. Hillsboro, Ill., Nov. 30, 1910; d. Lou Vene and Josephine (Williams) Hill; cert. Juilliard Sch. Music, 1933; Mus.B. cum laude, N.Y. U., 1943, M.A. in Elementary Edn., 1948; m. George Henry Kiernan, May 9, 1962. Tchr. music Walden Sch., N.Y.C., 1948-63; tchr. lang. arts, Haverhill, Mass., 1964-76; v.p., treas. Oil Service Corp., Schenectady, 1974—. Mem. Am. Mgmt. Assn., NEA, DAR. Republican. Episcopalian. Home: 4 Division St Glens Falls NY 12801 Office: PO Box 708 Glens Falls NY 12801

KIESCHNICK, WILLIAM FREDERICK, oil co. exec.; b. Dallas, Jan. 5, 1923; s. William Frederick and Effie Elizabeth (Meador) K.; B.S., Rice U., 1947; m. 2d, Keithann Chapman Allen, Apr. 21, 1979; children from previous marriage—Michael Frank, Meredith Jane. Research engr. Atlantic Richfield Co., Dallas, 1947-59, asst. to gen. mgr. exploration, 1959-61, dist. mgr. prodn. and exploration Eastern region, Lafayette, La., 1961-63, regional mgr. dists. exploration and prodn. N. Am. producing div., Dallas, 1963-67, v.p. synthetic fuel and mineral ops., 1967-69, v.p. ARCO Chem. Co., Phila., 1970-72, v.p. corp. planning, Los Angeles, 1972-73, exec. v.p., 1973-75, group exec. v.p. chem., fuels and transp. divs., 1975-78, vice-chmn. bd. in charge of ops., 1979-81, pres., 1981—, also dir.; dir. Coldwell Banker Co., Los Angeles, Elderhostel, Inc., Elderworks. Mem. World Affairs Council Los Angeles, 1973—, Town Hall Calif., Los Angeles, 1973—; trustee adv. bd. Energy Productivity Center, Mellon Inst., Washington; mem. Rice U. Fund, 1971-74. Served to capt. USAAF, 1943-46. Decorated Bronze Star. Mem. Am. Inst. Chem. Engrs., Am. Petroleum Inst., Soc. Petroleum Engrs., Am. Assn. Petroleum Geologists, Cousteau Soc., Los Angeles Area C. of C. (dir. 1979—). Contbr. articles to profl. jours. Office: 515 S Flower St Los Angeles CA 90071

KIESER, JOHN FREDERICK, aluminum co. exec.; b. Frankfurt, Germany, July 8, 1937; s. Frederick Christian and Mary Olga (DeLoutsky) K.; came to U.S., 1949, naturalized, 1955; grad. certificate Am. Grad. Sch. Internat. Mgmt., 1960; m. Valerie Jean Tognazzini, Apr. 8, 1961. Mem. internat. ops. and credit adminstrn. staff Bank of Am., San Francisco, 1960-67; internat. officer Bank of Calif., San Francisco, 1967-68; with Kaiser Aluminum and Chem. Corp., Oakland, Calif., 1968—, internat. fin. rep., 1969-70, mgr. internat. banking, 1970-72, asst. treas. internat. ops., 1972-77, asst. treas., 1977—; instr. Golden Gate U., San Francisco. Served with U.S. Army, 1956-59. Home: 3437 Crane Way Oakland CA 94602 Office: 300 Lakeside Dr Oakland CA 94643

KIESEWETTER, THEODORE CAMBIER, internat. trade co. exec.; b. Seattle, May 21, 1937; s. E.C. and Wilhelmina L. (Cambier) K.; B.A., San Francisco State U., 1961; M.A., U. Lausanne (Switzerland), 1962; postgrad. N.Y. U., Leiden, Holland, 1962-63; m. Barbara L. Souza, Dec. 21, 1958; children—Jacqueline, Anita. Regional sales mgr. for Europe, Omark Internat., Portland, Oreg., 1962-67; pres. Fischer of Am., Inc. (named Internat. Playthings, Inc. 1977), Montclair, N.J., 1967—; internat. trade cons. with European mktg. orgns., 1968—. Served with USN, 1955-57. Home: 551 Park St Upper Montclair NJ 07043 Office: 151 Forest St Montclair NJ 07042

KIESSLING, GERD, sales rep.; b. Durrenberg, Germany, May 8, 1942; s. Alfred Ernst and Helene Paula (Wiese) K.; came to U.S., 1966, naturalized, 1976; student Interpreter Sch., Cologne, Germany, 1961-63, Acad. Bus. and Econs., Cologne, 1961-66, U. Evansville, 1966-67; m. Carole Judy Cook, Jan. 25, 1969. Export sales specialist heavy steel forgings Wuppermann, Ltd., Leverkusen, Germany, 1961-63; prodn. control ofcl. Ford Motor Co. of Germany, Cologne, 1963-66; auditor Fruehauf Corp., Detroit, 1967-68, material contoller, 1968-70; material cost analyst Ford Motor Co. of Europe, Cologne, 1971-74; purchasing agt. Telemation, Inc., Salt Lake City, 1974-75; realtor asso. Ken Mayne, Inc., Salt Lake City, 1975-78; sales rep. Cline's Mazda & Peugeot, Salt Lake City, 1978—. Mem. Nat. Right to Work Com.; nat. adv. bd. Am. Security Council. Mem. Salt Lake Bd. Realtors. Republican. Mormon. Club: Bonneville Kiwanis (Salt Lake City). Research on ops. cost control. Home: 258 W Benson Way Sandy UT 84070 Office: 4528 S State St Salt Lake City UT 84107

KIKKERT, ELIZABETH, city ofcl.; b. Paterson, N.J., Oct. 18, 1931; d. Joseph Paul and Elfriede Becker; student Fairleigh Dickinson U., 1970-75, Rutgers U., 1973-74, Cornell U., 1975, N.Y. Inst. Fin., 1979, Profl. Sch. of Bus., 1980; children—Martin Joseph, Pamela, Sandra, Betty Ann, Bonnie Lee. Prodn. supr. Pinlites, Inc., Fairfield, N.J., 1965-70; office mgr. Van Houten Realty Co., Inc., Paterson, N.J., 1970-71; dir. div. of treasury City of Paterson (N.J.), 1971—. Mem. Assn. Govt. Accts., Am. Mgmt. Assn., Nat. Assn. Female Execs. Home: 98 Main St Bloomingdale NJ 07403 Office: City of Paterson 155 Market St Paterson NJ 07505

KILBORNE, GEORGE BRIGGS, investment co. exec.; b. N.Y.C., Oct. 7, 1930; s. Robert Stewart and Barbara Briggs K.; B.A., Yale U., 1952; m. Lucie Wheeler Peck, Nov. 12, 1960 (div. 1978); children—George Briggs, Kim McNeil, Sarah Skinner. Vice pres. William Skinner & Sons, N.Y.C., 1955-60; pres. Bus. Research Co., Birmingham, Mich., 1961-74, Creative Capital of Mich., Inc., Birmingham, 1962-70; partner Comac Co., 1968-70; chmn., pres. First Citizen Bank, Troy, Mich., 1970-74; engaged in real estate investing and cons., Palm Beach, Fla., 1975-79; mng. dir. corp. acquisitions Bessemer Securities Corp., N.Y.C., 1980—; chmn. State Bank of Mich., Coopersville, 1966-67, Muskegon (Mich.) Bank & Trust, 1967-68, Bank of Lansing (Mich.), 1968-69; vice chmn. Creative Capital Corp., N.Y.C., 1968-70, Hockey Club of Pitts., 1968-70. Bd. dirs. Oakland (Mich.) unit. Am. Cancer Soc., 1973-74; mem. Republican Com., Dist. 13, Palm Beach County, Fla., 1976-80; mem. Palm Beach County Rep. Exec. Com., 1976-80; bd. dirs. Palm Beach Rep. Club, 1977-80. Served to lt. (j.g.) USN, 1953-55. Recipient Disting. Service award First Citizen Bank, Troy, 1974, Midwest Assn. Small Bus. Investment Cos., 1970. Mem. Nat. Assn. Small Bus. Investment Cos. (gov. 1967-70, mem. exec. com. 1967, pres. Midwest assn. 1970). Clubs: Yale of the Palm Beaches (pres. 1979-80), Bath and Tennis (Palm Beach, Fla.); Wianno (Mass.) Yacht. Office: Bessemer Securities Corp 245 Park Ave New York NY 10017

KILBOURN, GARY LYNN, advt. and mktg. cons.; b. Indio, Calif., Dec. 24, 1948; s. Charles Edward and Ruby Blair (Harrell) K.; B.S., Am. U., 1968; m. Marilyn Ruth Davis, Aug. 24, 1969; children—Gary Lynn, Charles Edward, Sean Paul, Ryan Taylor, Adam Matthew. Gen. sales mgr. On-Cue Prodns., Long Beach, Calif., 1971; sales mgr. public relations Teleprompter Cable TV, San Bernardino, Calif., 1972-74; regional mgr. Gen. Telephone Yellow Pages, 1974; public relations exec. Armed Services Press, 1974-75; regional sales cons. Calif. Direct Mail Shoppers, 1974-78; pres. Advt. Devel. Systems, Rialto, Calif., 1978—. Served with U.S. Army, 1966-68. Republican. Baptist. Clubs: Jaycees (past lt. gov.), Lions. Address: 5782 Magnolia Ave Rialto CA 92376

KILBURN, HENRY THOMAS, JR., investment banker; b. N.Y.C., Aug. 1, 1931; s. Henry Thomas and Florence (Cross) K.; A.B., Princeton U., 1953; J.D., Columbia U., 1959. Exec. trainee Bankers Trust Co., N.Y.C., 1953-54; admitted to N.Y. State bar, 1959; asso. firm Kelley Drye Newhall & Maginnes, N.Y.C., 1959-66; v.p. finance, gen. counsel W.E. Parfitt & Assos. Inc., N.Y.C., 1967-71; asso., 1st. v.p., sr. v.p., dir. utility fin., dir. Blyth Eastman Dillon & Co., Inc., N.Y.C., 1972-78, exec. v.p., mem. exec. com., 1978-80; mng. dir., mem. commitment com. Blyth Eastman Paine Webber, Inc., N.Y.C., 1980—; pres., dir. Wyodak Constrn. Co., 1975-77; dir. Bedco Leasing Corp. Served to 1st lt., F.A., U.S. Army, 1954-56. Mem. Securities Industry Assn. (chmn. regulated industries com. 1980), N.Y. Bar Assn. Republican. Episcopalian. Home: 1160 5th Ave New York NY 10029 Office: Blyth Eastman 1221 Ave of Americas New York NY 10020

KILGORE, JAMES WILLIAM, data systems exec.; b. Auschafenburg, Germany, Aug. 28, 1953; came to U.S., 1960, naturalized, 1960; s. William Dawson and Therese Oswine (Larem) K.; student Seattle Community Coll., 1971, 72, 76; m. Patricia Lynne Russell, Aug. 22, 1980. Co-founder, Installation Mgmt. Systems, Inc., N.Y.C., 1973-75, established Seattle br., 1975-77; founder, pres. Progressive Data Systems, Inc., Seattle, 1977—; lectr. users of small to medium size computers. Mem. Soc. Am. Inventors (hon.). Republican. Patentee occupational safety product. Office: PO Box 98416 Tacoma WA 98499

KILGORE, ROBERT MARTIN, lawyer; b. Beckley, W.Va., Jan. 3, 1924; s. Harley Martin and Lois (Lilly) K.; B.S. in Physics, Georgetown U., 1947; postgrad. Columbia, 1947-49; J.D., George Washington U., 1952; m. Helen Hogan, Dec. 14, 1974. Admitted to D.C. bar, 1952, W.Va. bar, 1953; patent examiner U.S. Patent Office, Washington 1951-55, 68—; counsel Com. on Judiciary, U.S. Senate, 1955-58; asso. firm Powell, Dorsey & Blum, Washington, 1959-61; pvt. practice, Washington, 1961—; legal cons. Bd. Vet. Appeals, VA, 1966-67. Civil Def. dir. Forest Heights, Md., 1956-58; instr. first aid A.R.C., 1955-76, first aid chmn. D.C. chpt., 1971-75, instr. sailing, 1972-76; pres. 2d Homeowners Assn., 1973-76, P.T.O. Credit Union, 1980. Served from pvt. to lt. AUS, 1943-46. Registered parliamentarian. Mem. Am., Fed., W.Va., D.C. bar assns., DAV, W.Va. State Soc. (v.p. 1956-58), S.A.R., Patent Office Soc. (exec. com. 1972-80, pres. 1975-77, chmn. bd. govs. jour. 1977—), Am. Camillia Soc., Nat. Assn. Parliamentarians (unit pres. 1976-78), Am. Inst. Parliamentarians (nat. dir. 1974-75, pres. D.C. chpt. 1974-76), Washington Area Intergroup Assn. (chmn. 1971). Democrat. Clubs: George Washington U.; Toastmaster (dist. lt. gov. 1971-73). Home: 14827 N Anderson Ct Woodbridge VA 22193 Office: Box 2038 Arlington VA 22202

KILLIAN, JOHN MICHAEL, banker; b. Bloomington, Ill., May 17, 1946; s. John Joseph and Helen Marie (O'Brien) K.; grad. Joliet Jr. Coll., 1966; B.S., So. Ill. U., 1968; m. Mary Pat Powers, Aug. 21, 1976; children—David Michael, Colleen Michelle. With First Nat. Bank & Trust Co., Clinton, Ill., 1969—, trust officer, 1974—, pres., 1977—. Served with Ill. N.G., 1968-73. Roman Catholic. Clubs: Elks, Eagles. Office: First Nat Bank & Trust Co 400 S Side of Sq Clinton IL 61727

KILLIAN, WILLIAM PAUL, mfg. co. exec.; b. Sidney, Ohio, Apr. 26, 1935; s. Ray and Erie Killian; B.Chem. Engring. with honors, Ga. Inst. Tech., 1957; M.Engring. Adminstrn. with honors, U. Utah, 1968; m. Beverly Ann Buchanan, Sept. 7, 1957; children—William, Katherine, Michael. Chem. engr. Esso Standard Oil Co., Baton Rouge, 1957-58; mgr. research and devel., engring., later project engring. Thiokol Corp., Brigham City, Utah, 1958-68; mgr. corp. project mgmt. Masonite Corp., Chgo., 1968-70, mgr. new bus. ventures, 1970-73; mgr. strategic planning, chem. and metall. group Gen. Electric Co., Columbus, Ohio, 1973-77; dir. corp. planning and devel. Hoover Universal Inc., Ann Arbor, Mich., 1977—. Mem. Assn. for Corp. Growth, N. Am. Soc. Corp. Planners, Am. Mgmt. Assn., Mensa, Tau Beta Pi, Omicron Delta Kappa, Phi Kappa Phi, Pi Delta Epsilon, Phi Eta Sigma. Clubs: Travis Pointe Country; Ann Arbor Court; Liberty Racquet. Home: 3153 Parkridge Dr Ann Arbor MI 48103 Office: Hoover Universal Inc Box 1003 Ann Arbor MI 48106

KILPATRICK, ROBERT DONALD, life ins. co. exec.; b. Fairbanks, La., Feb. 5, 1924; s. Thomas David and Lula Mae (Crowell) K.; B.A., U. Richmond (Va.), 1948; postgrad. Harvard U. Grad. Sch. Bus., 1973; m. Faye Hines, May 29, 1948; children—Robert Donald, Kathleen Spencer, Lauren Douglas, Tracy Crowell, Thomas David. With Conn. Gen. Life Ins. Co., Hartford, 1954—, sr. v.p., 1973-76, pres., chief exec. officer, 1976—; dir. Fed. Res. Bank Boston, Scovill Mfg. Co., Waterbury, Conn. Mem. Pres. Carter's Nat. Ridesharing Task Force; bd. dirs. United Way; trustee Conn. Pub. Expenditure Council, U. Richmond, S.S. Huebner Found. for Ins. Edn., Wharton Sch. of U. Pa.; corporator Hartford Hosp., Inst. Living, Hartford; bd. regents U. Hartford. Served with USNR, 1942-46, 50-54. Mem. Am. Council Life Ins. (dir.), Conn. Bus. Industry Assn. (dir., mem. exec. com.), Bus. Round Table, Health Ins. Assn. Am. (adminstrv. com.), Greater Hartford C. of C. (dir.). Clubs: Hartford; Economic (N.Y.C.). Office: Conn Gen Life Ins Co Hartford CT 06152*

KIM, KEITH, freight forwarding co. exec.; b. Seoul, Korea, Oct. 11, 1935; s. Rinsuk and S.E. (Chu) K.; came to U.S., 1953, naturalized, 1969; A.A., Los Angeles City Coll., 1955; B.A., Los Angeles State Coll., 1957; m. Theresa Lee, Sept. 5, 1968; children—Dominick, Glenn. Import mgr. Judson Sheldon Internat. Corp., Los Angeles, 1965-69; import mgr. P.I.E. Transport, Inc., Inglewood, Calif., 1969-70; v.p. Shiloh Internat., Inc., Los Angeles, 1970-76, pres., 1976—; corporate v.p., cons. Dunbar Customs Services, Inglewood, 1973-77; pres. Alpha Cargo Service, 1978—. Licensed customshouse broker U.S. Treasury Dept. Home: 28523 Rothrock Dr Rancho Palos Verdes CA 90274 Office: 1222 E Imperial Ave El Segundo CA 90245

KIMBREL, MONROE, banker; b. Miller County, Ga., Aug. 4, 1916; s. Charlie C. and Effie (Folds) K.; B.S., U. Ga., 1936; grad. Stonier Grad. Sch. Banking, Rutgers U., 1949; m. Nita Matlock, Apr. 17, 1941; children—Jenny Wood (Mrs. James Bunn III), Charles Daniel. With Farm Credit Adminstrn., Columbia, S.C., 1936-46; with First Nat. Bank, Thomson, Ga., 1946-65, chmn. bd., 1961-65; chmn. bd. Bank of Fort Valley (Ga.), 1963-65; dir. Fed. Res. Bank Atlanta, 1960-65, sr. v.p., 1965, 1st v.p., 1965-68, pres., 1968-80; vice-chmn., dir. First R.R. & Banking Co. Ga., 1980—; pres., owner Thomson Oak Flooring Co., Inc. (Ga.), 1979—; dir. Ga. R.R. Bank & Trust Co., Augusta, Ga., John H. Harland Co., Gwinnett Industries, Inc., Decatur, Ga., First Fin. Mgmt. Corp. Mem. Am. (pres. 1962-63), Ga. (pres. 1956-57) bankers assns., U. Ga. Alumni Assn. (pres. 1970-71, 72-73). Rotarian (past dist. gov.). Home: Rt 1 Box 6 Thomson GA 30824

KIMEN, THOMAS W., JR., bank exec.; b. Highland Park, Mich., Aug. 23, 1936; s. Thomas W. and Aira K.; B.A., Mich. State U., 1958; M.B.A., U. Mich., 1959; m. Gail Carmichael, Oct. 6, 1962; children—Thomas W., Amy McLean. With No. Trust Co., Chgo., 1959-73, 2d v.p., 1966-68, v.p., 1968-70, exec. div., trust dept., 1970-73; v.p. Security Trust Co., Miami, 1973, pres., dir., 1973—; chmn. bd. Security Trust Co., Naples, Palm Beach and Sarasota, Fla.; dir. Security Trust Co., Miami. Trustee, Mercy Hosp. Served with AUS, 1960. Presbyterian. Clubs: 200 of Miami, Miami, Key Biscayne Yacht, Riviera Country. Home: 1000 Mariner Dr Key Biscayne FL 33149 Office: 700 Brickell Ave Miami FL 33131

KIMMEL, MARK, venture capital co. exec.; b. Denver, Feb. 15, 1940; s. Earl Henry and Gerry Claire K.; B.S. in Elec. Engring., U. Colo., 1963, B.S. in Mktg., 1963; M.B.A. in Fin., U. So. Calif., 1966; m. Gloria J. Danielewicz, Jan. 29, 1966; 1 son, Kristopher. Market research analyst 3M Co., Calif. and Minn., 1963-70; mktg. mgr. Am. Computer and Communications, Calif., 1970-71; mgr. new bus. devel. Motorola, Inc., Schaumburg, Ill., 1971-76; v.p. corp. devel. Nat. City Lines, Denver, 1976-77; pres. Enervest, Inc., Denver, 1977—; dir. Vac-Tec Systems Inc., BSL Tech., Corsicana Petroleum Corp., Exidyne, Inc., Teletek, Inc., Petrol Fin, Inc. Mem. Colo. Small Bus. Council, Nat. Assn. Small Bus. Investment Cos., Denver C. of C., Rocky Mountain Inventors Assn. (dir.), S.W. Small Bus. Investment Cos. Assn. (v.p.), Creative Initiative Found., Colo. Assn. Commerce and Industry. Republican. Home: 4815 S Joplin St Aurora CO 80015 Office: 7000 E Belleview Ave Englewood CO 80111

KIMMEL, ROBERT O., sales engring. exec.; b. Bklyn., Aug. 31, 1928; s. Philip Murray and Katherine (Mittleman) K.; B.S.E.E. cum laude, Bklyn. Poly. Inst., 1951; children by previous marriage—Kenneth, Jeanne; m. Barbara Gajdik, Oct. 12, 1969; children—Katherine Nicole, Todd Philip. Field engr. Gen. Electric Co., 1951-53; sales engr. Raytheon Co., Los Angeles, 1953-60; regional mktg. mgr. Hughes Aircraft Co., Torrance, Calif., 1960-69; v.p. ABC Electronic Sales, Inc., Williston Park, N.Y., 1969—; dir. Acroamatics, Inc., Danbury, Conn. Mem. IEEE, Tau Beta Pi, Eta Kappa Nu. Home: 2 Willard Ave Tarrytown NY 10591 Office: 99 Hillside Ave Williston Park NY 11596

KIMMICH, JERE RAE, transp. exec.; b. Lancaster County, Pa., Mar. 30, 1940; s. Richard Albert and Iona Gertrude (DeVerter) K.; student U.S. Armed Force Inst., 1957-59; m. Ada C. Cauler, Jan. 24, 1959; children—Lori Ann, Jere Rae, Kelly Lynn. With Motor Freight Express, York, Pa., 1977—, terminal mgr., 1965-70, regional mgr., 1970-79, dir. transp., 1979—. Active Little League, high sch. athletics. Served with USMC, 1957-60. Mem. Equipment Interchange Assn. (dir. 1979-81, chmn. nets com.), Nat. Equipment Transaction Settlement Com. (nat. chmn. 1980-81). Republican. Lutheran. Club: Pa. Interscholastic Athletic Assn. Home: 1315 Fieldstead Ln Lancaster PA 17603 Office: PO Box 1029 York PA 17405

KIMSEY, JAMES VERLIN, investment banker; b. Washington, Sept. 15, 1939; s. Verlin and Dorothy Lee (Yates) K.; student Georgetown U., 1957-58; B.S., U.S. Mil. Acad., 1962; m. Bronwen Diane Krummeck, June 13, 1964; children—Michael P., Mark J., Raymond C. Commd. 2d lt. U.S. Army, 1962, advanced through grades to maj., 1968; ret., 1970; v.p. Aarsand & Co., Washington, 1970-71; chmn. bd. Exchange Ltd. restaurant chain, Washington, 1970—; pres. Bronwen Corp., Washington, 1971-75, Cousteau Corp., Washington, 1976—, Kim King Corp., 1979—. Bd. dirs. World Mercy, Inc., Washington. Decorated Bronze Star medal with oak leaf cluster, Joint Service Commendation medal, Army Commendation medal with 2 oak leaf clusters, Combat Inf. badge. Mem. Nat. Assn. Securities Dealers, Independent Broker Dealer Trade Assn. (bd. govs.). Clubs: University (Washington); Army Navy Country (Arlington, Va.). Home: 7411 Dulany Dr McLean VA 22101 Office: 1801 K St NW Washington DC 20006

KIMURA, MICHIO, chem. co. exec.; b. London, Sept. 9, 1924; s. Seizo and Chiyo (Nose) K.; came to U.S., 1959; B.A., Keio U. (Japan), 1949; m. Haruko Wada, Feb. 22, 1954; children—Yukiko, Kathryn Mari. With Nichimen Co. Ltd., Osaka, Japan, 1949-59, N.Y.C., 1959-67, sec., 1966-67; mgr. N.Y. office Nippon Shokubai Kagaku Koygo Co. Ltd., Osaka, Japan, 1967—; founder, pres., treas. Japan Catalytic Internat., Inc., N.Y.C., 1973—. Served with Japanese Navy, 1945. Mem. U.S. C. of C., Japanese C. of C., Japan Soc. Buddhist. Home: 241 Walnut Rd Glen Cove NY 11542 Office: 1221 Ave of the Americas New York NY 10020

KING, ALFRED MEEHAN, appraisal co. exec.; b. Boston, Oct. 31, 1933; s. Lester S. and Marjorie C. (Meehan) K.; A.B. magna cum laude, Harvard Coll., 1954, M.B.A., 1959; m. Mary Jane Oliver, Dec. 19, 1976; 1 son, Thomas A. Acctg. supr. Gen. Motors Co., LaGrange, Ill., 1959-64; asst. controller J.I. Case Co., Racine, Wis., 1964-69; v.p. fin. Am. Appraisal Co., Milw., 1969-77; sr. v.p. fin. Valuation Research Corp., Milw., 1978—; adj. asst. prof. U. Wis.-Parkside, Kenosha, 1978—. Treas., Village of North Bay, Wis., 1972-76, Racine Symphony Orch., 1979—. Mem. Nat. Assn. Accountants (nat. dir.), Fin. Execs. Inst. Republican. Congregationalist. Club: Country (Racine). Author: Increasing the Productivity of Company Cash, 1969. Home: 2327 River Shore Dr Racine WI 53405 Office: 250 E Wisconsin St Milwaukee WI 53202

KING, CAMPBELL STIRLING, assn. ofcl.; b. Rouleau, Sask., Can., Apr. 21, 1939; s. William Campbell and Helen June (Dunton) K.; student Sask. Tchrs. Coll., 1957-58; B.B.A., Red River Community Coll., 1973; m. Myrna Lynne Christina, Aug. 21, 1965; children—John William Stirling, Tannis-Lynne Christina. Tchr., St. James, Man., Can., 1963-64; asst. phys. dir. St. James YMCA, 1964-65; dir. water safety service Man. div. Can. Red Cross Soc., 1965-74, asst. commr., 1974-77, commr., 1977—. Chmn., Man. Leadership Prayer Breakfast, 1978-80; pres. Man. Safety Council, 1975; bd. dirs. Nativity Celebrations, 1975—, Transcona Alliance Ch., 1969—. Mem. Adminstrv. Mgmt. Soc. (pres. Winnipeg chpt. 1978-79), Royal Life Saving Soc. (hon. asso.). Author articles on water safety. Home: 130 Laurentia Bay Winnipeg MB R2C 0H1 Canada Office: 226 Osborne St N Winnipeg MB R3C 1V4 Canada

KING, DAVID MERVIN, securities co. exec.; b. nr. Ottawa, Kans., July 3, 1927; s. Alvin Jesse and Gertrude Beatrice (Jones) K.; B.S., Emporia (Kans.) State U., 1950; m. Bernice Arlene Owen, June 11, 1950; 1 dau., Elizabeth A. Salesman, Mut. Life of New York, Wichita, Kans., 1950; mgr. Colby (Kans.) C. of C., 1952-54; self employed, 1954-56; dist. mgr. King Merritt & Co. Investments, Colby, Kans., 1956-60; v.p., regional mgr. Westamerica Securities, Inc., Hays, Kans., 1960-78; v.p. Investment Mgmt. and Research Co., 1978—; pres. Home Security Services of Am., Inc., David M. King and Assos., King Fin. Services Corp.; partner Berdeak Assos. Served with USMCR, 1945-46, 50-52. Mem. Internat. Assn. Fin. Planners, Inst. Cert. Fin. Planners (pres. 1978), Hays C. of C. Republican. Presbyn. Mason (Shriner), Rotarian. Home: 3007 Tam O'Shanter St Hays KS 67601 Office: Box 707 Hays KS 67601

KING, EDWARD BEVERLY, JR., publishing co. exec.; b. Roanoke, Va., Aug. 17, 1939; s. Edward Beverly and Gladys Ruth Mae (Johnson) K.; B.S. in Edn., Wilberforce U., 1963; postgrad. U. Dayton, 1968, Hofstra U., 1969-70; Ed.D., Mt. Sinai U., 1971. Tchr. pub. high sch., Charlotte, N.C., 1963-64, Gary, Ind., 1964-66; exec. dir., jour. editor Office Alumni Affairs, Wilberforce U., 1966-68; presdl. asst. Hofstra U., 1968-70; staff dir. Assn. Am. Pubs., N.Y.C., 1970-75; sales rep./ednl. specialist eastern region Steck-Vaughn publisher, Norfolk, Va., 1975—; instr. Purdue U., summer 1966; vis. prof. coll. relations Chase Manhattan Bank, N.Y.C., 1968; guest speaker Voice of Am., 1968. Named Dist. Alumnus of Year, Wilberforce U., 1968; Among co-founders, dir. Student Nonviolent Coordinating Com., Atlanta, 1960-61; sponsor, Pearl S. Buck Found., 1979. Recipient New Career Opportunities award Tallodega Coll., 1971, Nat. Alliance Businessmen, 1973; highlighted in numerous books and articles on Black Americans. Mem. NEA, Nat. Hist. Soc., Am. Negro Commemorative Soc., Wilburforce U. Alumni Assn., Alpha Psi Omega. Democrat. Baptist. Actor, TV production Walk In My Shoes, 1961. Home: 8128 Jerry Lee Dr Norfolk VA 23518

KING, EMMETT ALONZO, ins. brokerage exec.; b. Norfolk, Va., June 9, 1942; s. Emmett and Mary Lee (Sutton) K.; student Mary-Hardin-Baylor Coll., 1967, Coll. of Ins., 1971; m. Yvonne L.; children—Andre, Jacqueline, Ricky, Roland. Benefits rep. EBS Mgmt. Consultants, Inc., N.Y.C., 1968; sr. group adminstr., group ins. sales office Conn. Gen. Life Ins. Co., N.Y.C., 1968-70; successively group adminstr., account exec., asst. v.p., v.p., mgr. employee benefits dept. Bayly, Martin & Fay, Inc., N.Y.C., 1971—. Charter mem. Tri-W Black Families, Inc., 1979—. Served with U.S. Army, 1961-67. Mem. Nat. Ins. Industry Assn., 100 Black Men Inc., Am. Spl. Risks Assn., Group Ins. Assn. Greater N.Y., N.Y.C. C. of C. Home: Westport CT 06880 Office: 110 Maiden Ln New York NY 10005

KING, FRANKLIN MARVIN, JR., real estate appraiser; b. Lakeland, Fla., Oct. 15, 1942; s. Franklin M. and Myriam H. K.; student U. Ga., U. Alaska; grad. Alaska State Realtors Inst., 1973; m. Mary Linda Beall, July 2, 1962; 1 son, Glenn. Appraiser, negotiator Alaska Dept. Hwys., Fairbanks, 1964-67; mortgage loan officer 1st Nat. Bank Fairbanks, 1967-69; ind. fee appraiser, Fairbanks, 1969-73; pres. Real Estate Services Corp., Anchorage, 1973—. Mem. Alaska Bd. Edn., 1971-73, Anchorage Bd. Equalization, 1975—. Served with USAF, 1960-64. Mem. Am. Inst. Real Estate Appraisers (past pres. Alaska chpt.), Am. Right of Way Assn.; affiliate mem. Nat. Assn. Realtors, Alaska Assn. Realtors, Anchorage Bd. Realtors. Republican. Home: 3720 Westminster Way Anchorage AK 99504 Office: Real Estate Services Corp 507 W Northern Lights Blvd Anchorage AK 99503

KING, GEORGE JOSEPH, med. and health care exec.; b. Rochester, N.Y., Feb. 18, 1922; s. Harold Hunt and Anna Mae (Schnitzer) K.; student Niagara U., 1940-41, Rochester Inst. Tech., 1948-50, Cornell U., 1957; m. Marian Katherine Sullivan, Sept. 18, 1943; children—Thomas, (dec. 1967), Kathryn Ann. Prodn. mgr. Burroughs Corp., Rochester, 1942-66; fin. cons., Penfield, N.Y., 1966-70; v.p. Med. Scis., Internat., Inc., Orange, Conn. and Stoneham, Mass., 1970-73; pres. George King Bio-Med., Inc., Salem, N.H., 1973—; treas. GMK Enterprises, Inc., Salem, 1974-78. Pres., Nat. Hemophilia Found., N.Y.C., 1974—, recipient vol. of year award, 1973, mem. exec. com., 1967—; vol. Rochester Community Chest, 1949-66; mem. Rochester council Boy Scouts Am., 1956-64. Recipient spl. commendation Argentina Acad. Medicine, 1972. Roman Catholic. Club: K.C. Established nat. program to provide hepatitis antibody plasma and source for coagulation deficient plasma for diagnostic and therapeutic uses. Office: 36 Corporate Woods Suite 3610 Overland Park KS 66210

KING, GUNDAR JULIAN, fin. exec., bus. educator; b. Riga, Latvia, Apr. 19, 1926; s. Attis K. and Austra K. (Dale) Kenins; came to U.S., 1950, naturalized, 1953; B.B.A., U. Oreg., 1956; M.B.A., Stanford U., 1958, Ph.D., 1964; m. Valda K. Andersons, Sept. 18, 1955; children—John T., Marita A. Exec., Internat. Refugee Orgn., Germany, 1948-50; br. office mgr. Williams Form Engring. Corp., Portland, Oreg., 1952-58; cons., 1958—; v.p., dir. Amber Land & Investment Co., Mercer Island, Wash., 1966—; prof., dean Sch. Bus. Adminstrn., Pacific Lutheran U., Tacoma, Wash., 1960—. Mem. Council Reorgn. of Wash. State Govt., 1965; mem. Wash. State Supply Mgmt. Adv. Bd., 1976—; staff cons. Commn. on Govt. Procurement, 1971-72. Served with AUS, 1950-52; Korea. Certified purchasing mgr. Nat. Assn. Purchasing Mgmt.; certified profl. contract mgr. Nat. Contract Mgmt. Assn. Mem. Assn. Advancement Baltic Studies (pres.), Am. Mktg. Assn. (chpt. pres. 1968-69), Fin. Execs. Assn. (chpt. dir. 1976-78). Republican. Lutheran. Author: Economic Policies in Occupied Latvia, 1965; Teaching Trends in Business, 1966; also articles on indsl. mgmt., fin. and materials mgmt., Baltic studies, econs. Home: PO Box 44401 Parkland WA 98444 Office: School of Business Administration Pacific Lutheran University Tacoma WA 98447

KING, HENRY LAWRENCE, lawyer; b. N.Y.C., Apr. 29, 1928; s. H. Abraham and Henrietta (Prentky) K.; A.B., Columbia Coll., 1948; LL.B., Yale U., 1951; m. Barbara Hope, 1949 (dec. May 1962); children—Elizabeth Hope, Patricia Jane King Cantlay, Matthew Harrison; m. 2d, Alice Mary Sturges, Aug. 1, 1963 (div. Dec. 1979); children—Katherine Masury, Andrew Lawrence, Eleanor Sturges. Admitted to N.Y. State bar, 1952; mem. firm Davis Polk & Wardwell, N.Y.C., 1951—, partner, 1961—. Trustee, Legal Aid Soc., Columbia U. Press, Chapin Sch., Fed. Bar Council, Yale Law Sch. Fund, Yale Law Sch. Assn.; mem. exec. com. Pres.'s Lawyers Com. Civil Rights Under Law; bd. dirs. Berkshire Farm Center and Services for Youth; chmn. Columbia Coll. Fund, 1972-73; pres. Columbia U. Alumni Fedn., 1973-75, Columbia Coll. Alumni Assn. Recipient Columbia Alumni medal. Fellow Am. Coll. Trial Lawyers; mem. Am. Law Inst., Am., N.Y. State (chmn. antitrust law sect. 1979-80; exec. com.; ho. of dels.) bar assns., Assn. Bar City N.Y., N.Y. County Lawyers Assn., Am. Judicature Soc. Clubs: Fishers Island Country, Hay Harbor, Century, River, Anglers, Wall St., Pilgrims; Met. (Washington). Home: New York NY 10021 also Fishers Island NY 06390 Office: 1 Chase Manhattan Plaza Davis Polk & Wardwell New York NY 10005

KING, JERRY LARUE, econ. and indsl. developer; b. Kings Mountain, N.C., Dec. 1, 1934; s. Denver Olan and Louise Ola (Bobbitt) K.; B.S., Western Carolina U., 1957; postgrad. N.Y. U., Gaston Coll., U. N.C., U. Okla., Cleve. County Tech. Inst.; children—Karen, Michael, Todd, Susan and Finley (twins). Sec.-treas. Sedgefield Realty Co., Gastonia, N.C., 1963-64; area coordinator S.C. for credit card ops. First Union Nat. Bank, Charlotte, 1964-69; asst. v.p. S.C. Nat. Bank, Columbia, 1969-74; accountant, partner King's Acctg., Kings Mountain, 1974-78; owner Jerry L. King Real Estate, Kings Mountain, 1975-80, King Enterprises, Kings Mountain, 1980—; exec. dir. Kings Mountain C. of C. and Mchts. Assn., 1976-77; mgr., accountant Kings Mountain Country Club, 1976-78; dir. Country Club Estates; sec. Community Devel. Corp.; adv. council Bella-Hess Dept. Stores; instr. Cleve. County Tech. Inst. Treas., First Presbyn. Ch., Kings Mountain, 1976; mem. Kings Mountain Centennial Commn. Served to lt. USNR, 1957-63. Mem. Am. Indsl. Devel. Council, So. Indsl. Developers Council, N.C. Indsl. Developers Assn., Am. Legion. Democrat. Clubs: Rotary, Sertoma, Masons. Home: 213 Fulton St Kings Mountain NC 28086 Office: 101-103 W Gold St Kings Mountain NC 28086

KING, JOHN F., former oil co. exec.; b. Holbrook, Mass., Jan. 7, 1904; s. John and Anne (Coffey) K.; A.B. cum laude, Harvard, 1925, LL.B., 1931; m. Catherine Arnold Brown, Sept. 2, 1932; children—Anne Frances (Mrs. Thomas Franges), John Scott. With prodn., purchasing depts. Nash Motors Co., Milw., 1924-28; admitted to N.Y. bar; asso. Root, Clark, Buckner & Ballantine, 1931-37; with Mut. of N.Y., N.Y.C., becoming 2d v.p. for securities investment, 1937-69; v.p., dir. Forest Oil Corp., Denver, 1969-77, dir. emeritus, 1977—. Mem Am. Petroleum Inst., Ind. Petroleum Assn. Am., Newcomen Soc. N.Am., Phi Beta Kappa. Clubs: Harvard of N.Y.C.; York Golf and Tennis, Broad Street. Home: Robin Hill Shore Rd Cape Neddick ME 03902

KING, MICHAEL JOE, accountant; b. Berkeley, Calif., Oct. 10, 1952; s. Edmund Joe and Betty (Young) K.; B.S. in Bus. Adminstrn., U. Calif. at Berkeley, 1973, M.B.A., 1977; m. Stephanie Arleen Chow, Sept. 7, 1975; 1 dau., Jennifer Stephanie. Trainee accounting Bank of Am., San Francisco, 1974-75, head real and personal property accounting, 1975-76, head domestic consolidation accounting and external reporting, 1976-77, domestic profit and loss control officer, 1977-78; with audit dept. Deloitte Haskins & Sells, 1978—. Home: 313 Fairway Dr San Francisco CA 94080 Office: 44 Montgomery St San Francisco CA 94104

KING, RICHARD HARDING, food co. exec.; b. Louisville, Oct. 19, 1925; s. Harvey M. and Margaret (Farley) K.; B.B.A., Tulane U., 1946; M.B.A., Northwestern U., 1948; m. Marjorie R. Jones, Feb. 19, 1959; children—Ronald Craig, David Malcolm. Asst. sales office mgr. elec. div. Olin-Mathieson, New Haven, 1947-53; chief analyst product planning dept. Ford div. Ford Motor Co., Dearborn, Mich., 1953-59; mgr. profit analysis and control Chrysler Internat., S.A., Geneva, Switzerland, 1959-61; financial analyst and cons. controller's dept. Raytheon Co., Lexington, Mass., 1961-62, sr. adminstrv. analyst, controller's office, 1962-64; v.p. corporate planning The Glidden Co., Cleve., 1964-67; v.p. corporate devel. staff, dir. long range planning SCM Corp., N.Y.C., 1967-68; corporate controller Internat. Multifoods Corp., Mpls., 1968-70, v.p. finance, 1970—. Instr. New Haven Jr. Coll., 1948-53. Mem. steering com. Minn. Gov.'s Loaned Exec. Action Program, 1972. Bd. dirs. Goodwill Industries Mpls., 1970-76, vice chmn., 1976; bd. govs. Meth. Hosp., Mpls., 1974—; trustee Laymen's Ministerial Endowment Fund. Mem. Am. Mgmt. Assn. (co-chmn. speaker long range planning courses 1965—), Financial Execs. Inst., Nat. Indsl. Conf. Bd., World Future Soc., Beta Gamma Sigma, Omicron Delta Kappa. Clubs: Minneapolis, Interlachen Country, Tower, Six O'Clock. Speaker and writer on planning concepts and methods. Home: 4705 Annaway Dr Edina MN 55436 Office: Multifoods Bldg Minneapolis MN 55402

KING, ROBERT E(UGENE), gas industry exec.; b. Glamorgan, Va., Sept. 21, 1930; s. Thomas O. and Flo Tilla K.; B.S. in Chem. Engring., Okla. U., 1958; m. Jean Taylor, Aug. 19, 1952; 1 son, Robert Irl. Engr., El Paso Natural Gas Co., Jal, N.Mex 1958-62; with Fla. Hydrocarbons Co., Brooker, 1962—, supt. ops., 1969-75, gen. mgr., 1975-80, v.p., 1980—. Served with USAF, 1948-52. Republican. Methodist. Home: Route 3 Box 1768 Keystone Heights FL 32656 Office: Route 1 Box 83 Brooker FL 32622

KING, ROBERT HOWARD, publisher; b. Excelsior Springs, Mo., June 28, 1921; s. Howard and Nancy Eaton (Henry) K.; student Kenyon Coll., Gambier, Ohio, 1942; m. Marjorie Kerr, Feb. 26, 1966; children—John McFeeley, Mary Nan, Sarah Ann. Vice pres. sales Ency. Brit., Chgo., 1946-61; pres. Spencer Internat. Press, Chgo., 1961-66; v.p. Dill Clitherow & Co., Palatine, Ill., 1966-68; pres. Time-Life Libraries, Palatine, 1968-79; chmn. bd., chief exec. officer World Book-Childcraft Internat., Inc., Chgo., 1979—. Chmn. bd. Direct Selling Ednl. Found. Served to capt. AUS, 1942-46. Mem. Direct Selling Assn. (past chmn. bd., chmn. nominating com.), World Fedn. Direct Selling Assns. (chmn. bd.), Sales and Mktg. Execs. Internat., Internat. Trade Club. Clubs: Meadow; Chgo. (Chgo.); Lighthouse Point Yacht (Fla.); Ocean Reef (Key Largo, Fla.). Home: 155 Harbor Point Chicago IL 60603 Office: 510 Merchandise Mart Plaza Chicago IL 60654

KING, SANDRA THERESA, mgmt. cons.; b. Kingston, Jamaica, Sept. 16, 1951; came to U.S., 1971; d. Ronald George and Pearl (Saunders) K.; B.A. in Econs. and Bus. Adminstrn., Elmira Coll., 1974; M.B.A., Northeastern U., 1977; m. Robert Thomas Tunis, Nov. 25, 1978. Mfg. planning analyst Corning Glass Works (N.Y.), 1974-75; mktg. adminstr. Port Authority Kingston, 1975-76; instr. mktg. and market research Northeastern U., 1975-77; mgmt. cons. Arthur D. Little Inc., Cambridge, Mass., 1977-80; mktg. mgr. New Eng. Bus. Services Inc., Groton, Mass., 1980—; mem. faculty Babson Coll. Concert adv. Concerts in Black and White, symphony group, Boston, 1977—; founder Bus. Women's Forum, Cambridge, 1980. Mem. Am. Mktg. Assn., M.B.A. Assn. (v.p.), Northeastern U. M.B.A. Assn. Roman Catholic. Office: 500 N Main St Groton MA 01450

KING, SEMMES WALMSLEY, investment co. exec.; b. New Orleans, Nov. 6, 1943; s. Frederick Jenks and Augusta (Walmsley) K.; A.B., Francisco Coll., 1967, LL.B., 1971. Pres., King Petroleum Co., Bains, La., 1971-79; pres. Semmes, Inc., Bains, 1979-81, Bains Investment Corp., Houston, 1981—. Home: Cedars Plantation Bains LA 70713 Office: 1669 S Voss Suite 538 Houston TX 77057

KING, SUSAN BENNETT, chairperson U.S. Consumer Product Safety Commn.; b. Sioux City, Iowa, Apr. 29, 1940; d. Francis Moffatt and Marjorie (Rittenhouse) Bennett; B.A., Duke U., 1962; postgrad. Cath. U. Am. Law Sch., 1975-77. Washington dir. Nat. Com. for an Effective Congress, 1967-73; exec. dir. Center for Public Financing of Elections, Washington, 1973-75; exec. asst. to chmn. Fed. Election Commn., Washington, 1975-77; chairperson U.S. Consumer Product safety Commn., Washington, 1978—; vice-chairperson U.S. Regulatory Council, Washington, 1980; mem. campaign fin. study group Inst. Politics, Harvard U. Bd. dirs., co-founder Women's Campaign Fund, 1975-78; bd. dirs. Nat. Assn. for So. Poor, 1970—. Mem. Phi Beta Kappa, Pi Sigma Alpha. Democrat. Office: Consumer Product Safety Commn 1111 18th St NW Washington DC 20207

KING, TERRY DEBBS, mech. contractor; b. Goose Creek, Tex., Dec. 19, 1928; s. Jesse Lee and Virginia Agnes (Young) K.; B.B.A., U. Tex., 1952; m. Vera Louise Buck, Oct. 8, 1955; children—Kathleen Buck, Terry Debbs. Sales engr., sales supr. Mpls. Honeywell, Houston, 1955-64; mfrs. rep. Barber Colman Co. and H.D Grant Co., Houston, 1964-66; sales engr. Atlas Air Conditioning Co., Houston, 1966-71, sales mgr., 1971-76, gen. mgr., 1976-79; founder King Envirco, Inc., mech. constrn. co., 1979—. Mem. bd. regents Autry House, 1971-78. Served to lt. USNR, 1952-55. Mem. ASHRAE, Mech. Contractors Assn., Am. Subcontractors Assn., Am. Soc. Energy Engrs., Sigma Phi Epsilon. Republican. Episcopalian. Home: 10031 Valley Forge Houston TX 77042 Office: PO Box 42999-177 Houston TX 77042

KING, WILLIAM DOUGLAS, hazardous waste mgmt. co. exec.; b. Balt., Nov. 21, 1941; s. James and Mary Jane (Molloy) K.; B.S., U. N.C., 1964; M.B.A., Harvard U., 1969; m. Maribeth Ann McDermott, July 22, 1977; 1 son, William Douglas; stepsons—Douglas John McDonald, Collin John McDonald. Sr. asso. McKinsey & Co., Inc., Los Angeles, 1969-73; pres. Davis Pacific Corp., Beverly Hills, Calif., 1974-76, Leeds Travelwear, Clayton, Del., 1976-79; pres., dir. IT Corp., Wilmington, Calif., 1979—. Served as capt. USMCR, 1964-67. Mem. Young Pres.'s Orgn. Republican. Episcopalian. Clubs: Calif., Los Angeles Country; Links, Harvard of N.Y.C. Home: 92 Crest Rd E Rolling Hills CA 90274 Office: IT Corp 336 W Anaheim St Wilmington CA 90744

KING, WILLIAM MICHAEL, elec. systems tech. advisor, investor; b. San Diego, Nov. 13, 1941; s. Billy Woodruff and Maria Seraphina Rosario (Vaca-Calderon) K.; student Capitol Radio Engring. Inst., 1962; m. Jo Ann Franchetto, July 2, 1960; children—Shannon (dec.), Stephanie, Christopher. Retail audio store mgr., 1959; elec. lab. supr. Cornell-Dubilier Electronics, Los Angeles, 1960-63; engring. mgr. West Coast systems Filtron Co., Culver City, Calif., 1963-66; sr. tech. specialist Garrett Airesearch Co., Torrance, Calif., 1966-67; asst. chief engr., lab. mgr. radar relay div. Teledyne Corp., Santa Monica, 1967; mgr. EMI/EMC ops. Cornell-Dubilier Electronics, Venice, Calif., 1967-77; mgr. pvt. investments, 1977—; tech. advisor in electromagnetic compatibility to computer industry and mil. contractors; free-lance sound rec. engr., ind. record producer, 1959-63. Pres., Exceptional Children's Found., 1978-80, bd. dirs., bd. dirs. Calif. Assn. for Retarded, 1978-79. Mem. Soc. Automotive Engrs. (group AE-4). Researcher in fields of data processing equipment, cardiac pacemakers. Patentee enhanced safety method of interference suppression in hand-held elec. devices, others. Home and Office: 510 17th St Santa Monica CA 90402

KING, WILLIAM PATRICK, plastics co. exec.; b. Cin., Mar. 10, 1947; s. John Thomas and Ann Marie (Mullaney) K.; B.B.A., U. Cin., 1971, M.B.A., 1972; m. Mary Lynn Carrigan, Aug. 17, 1974; children—Michael, Beth. Auditor, Arthur Young & Co., Cin., 1968-71; asst. controller Chemed Corp., Cin., 1972-75; controller Dare Pafco, Inc., Cin., 1977-78, chief operating officer, 1978-79; controller Xtek Inc., 1980—. Mem. Cin. C. of C., Ohio Soc. C.P.A.'s, Am. Inst. C.P.A.'s, Assn. M.B.A.'s Execs., Fin. Execs. Inst. Home: 1963 Finsburg Ct Cincinnati OH 45230 Office: 211 Township Ave Cincinnati OH 45241

KINGSBERY, WALTON WAITS, JR., accountant; b. Evergreen, Ala., June 25, 1928; s. Walton Waits and Alpha Lee (Eaton) K.; B.S. with honors, U. Ala., 1950; m. Helen Elizabeth Clayton, Mar. 21, 1953; children—Walton Waits, III, J. Clayton, Peter C. With Price Waterhouse & Co., C.P.A.'s, 1950—, partner, 1965—, mng. partner, Cleve., 1977—, mem. policy bd., 1979—. Chmn. Shrewsbury (N.J.) Planning Bd., 1972; bd. dirs. Greater Cleve. Growth Assn., 1978-80; trustee Beech Brook, 1979-80, Cleve. Play House, 1980; clk. Village of Hunting Valley. Served with AUS, 1950-53. C.P.A., Ohio, N.J., N.Y. Mem. Am. Inst. C.P.A.'s, Nat. Assn. Accts., Ohio Soc. C.P.A.'s, N.J. Soc. C.P.A.'s, N.Y. State Soc. C.P.A.'s, Bluecoats, Newcomen Soc. N.Am. Clubs: Cleve. Country, Union, Racquet (Cleve.); Duquesne (Pitts.). Author articles in field. Office: 1900 Central Nat Bank Blvd Cleveland OH 44114

KINGSLEY, DANIEL (THAIN), public relations co. exec.; b. Portland, Oreg., Oct. 1, 1932; s. George Archibald and Jane (Powers) K.; A.B., Princeton U., 1954; m. Nancy Cassedy, Dec. 2, 1979; children—Daniel T., Clay P., Blake M., Chris W., Elizabeth L., Reed B. Pres., Kingsley Lumber Co., Portland, 1962-70; commr. GSA, Washington, 1969-71; spl. asst. to Pres. of U.S., Washington, 1971-74; asso. adminstr. Small Bus. Adminstrn., Washington, 1974-76; pres. Milwaukie Lumber Co. (Oreg.), 1976—, Ed Kingsley Lumber Co., Portland, 1976—; exec. v.p. Deaver and Hannaford Inc., Washington, 1977—. Served with U.S. Army, 1954-56. Republican. Episcopalian. Clubs: Multinomah Athletic, Racquet (Portland); Congl. Country (Potomac, Md.); Georgetown (Washington). Home: 10705 Stanmore Dr Potomac MD 20854 Office: 1225 19th St NW Washington DC 20036

KINKLEY, MARK WAYNE, electronic controls and servo drives mfg. co. exec.; b. Celina, Ohio, July 7, 1923; s. Brice and Gertrude (Wille) K.; B.S. cum laude, Ohio State U., 1948; m. Janet MacDonald, Sept. 14, 1946; children—Gary, Tom, David. With Potter & Brumfield div. AMF Inc., Princeton, Ind., 1957-68, v.p. mktg., 1964-66, pres., 1966-68; v.p. fin. Allen Bradley Co., Milw., 1968-70, v.p. ops., 1970-75; group v.p. Crouse Hinds Co., Syracuse, 1976-79; pres. Unico Inc., Franksville, Wis., 1979—, also dir. Bd. dirs. St. Lukes Hosp., Milw., 1970-75. Served with USAF, 1943-46. C.P.A., Ill. Mem. Fin. Execs. Inst., Nat. Assn. Accountants. Presbyterian. Clubs: Milw. Athletic, Masons. Home: 4400 Kings Cove Rd Racine WI 53406 Office: 3725 Nicholson Rd Franksville WI 53126

KINNEY, ABBOTT FORD, radio broadcasting exec.; b. Los Angeles, Nov. 11, 1909; s. Gilbert Earle and Mabel (Ford) K.; student Ark. Coll., 1923, 26, 27; m. Dorothy Lucille Jeffers, Sept. 19, 1943; children—Colleen, Joyce, Rosemary. Editor Dermott News, 1934-39; partner Delta Drug Co., 1940-49; pres., gen. mgr. S.E. Ark. Broadcasters, Inc., Dermott and McGehee, 1951—; corr. Comml. Appeal, Memphis, Ark. Gazette, Little Rock, 1935-53; research early aeros. Inst. Aero. Scis., 1941, castor bean prodn., 1941-42. Mem. Ark. Geol. and Conservation Commn., 1959-63; chmn. Ark. Planning Commn.; mem. Mississippi River Pkwy. Commn., Park Commn. Past pres., mem. exec. bd. DeSoto Area council Boy Scouts Am.; chmn. County Library Bd.; mem. past pres. Hosp. Adv. Bd.; mem. bd. McGehee-Dermott Indsl. Devel. Corp., Chicot Fair Assn., Christian Rural Overseas Program. Recipient Silver Beaver award Boy Scouts Am.; honored with Abbott Kinney Day by civic orgns. and schs. S.E. Ark., 1955; named one of Ark.'s 10 Outstanding Community Leaders, 1969. Mem. AIM, Nat. Assn. Radio and TV Broadcasters, Ark. Broadcasters Assn., Ark., S.E. Ark. chambers commerce, Internat. Broadcasters Soc. (editorial adv. bd.), Ark. Hist. Assn., Am. Numis. Assn. Club: Rotary. Home: Dermott AR 71638 Office: Southeast Ark Broadcasters Inc Dermott AR 71638

KINNEY, EARL ROBERT, food co. exec.; b. Burnham, Maine, Apr. 12, 1917; s. Harry E. and Ethel (Vose) K.; A.B., Bates Coll., 1939; postgrad. Harvard U., 1940; children—Jeanie Elizabeth, Earl Robert, Isabella Alice. Founder, North Atlantic Pack Co., Bar Harbor, Maine, 1941, pres., 1941-42, treas., dir., 1941-64; with Gorton Corp. (became subs. Gen. Mills, Inc. 1968), 1954-68, pres., 1958-68; v.p. Gen. Mills, Inc., 1968-69, exec. v.p., 1969-73, chief fin. officer, 1970-73, pres., chief operating officer, 1973—, now chmn., chief exec. officer; dir. Nashua Corp., Sun Co., Honeywell, Inc., Jackson Lab., Bar Harbor. Trustee, Bates Coll., also chmn. alumni drives, 1960-64; bd. dirs., mem. exec. com. Mpls. YMCA; bd. dirs. Minn. Orch. Office: PO Box 1113 Minneapolis MN 55440

KINNEY, JAMES JOSEPH, JR., fin. corp. exec.; b. East Stroudsburg, Pa., Feb. 16, 1942; s. James Joseph and Ann Marie (O'Malley) K.; B.A., U. Scranton, 1964; M.A., U. Mo., 1966; M.B.A. (Senatorial scholar), U. Pa., 1970; m. Martina Clement, Jan. 6, 1968; children—Martin, Shane, Devin. Asso. product mgr. H. J. Heinz Co., Pitts., 1970-73; product mgr. Borden Co., Columbus, Ohio, 1973-75; new services product mgr. U.S. Postal Service, Washington, 1975-78; sr. officer, v.p., mktg. dir. Signal Fin. Corp., Pitts., 1978—; dir. Elec. Funds Transfer Assn., Washington, 1978—. Served with USMCR, 1966-72. Mem. Nat. Consumer Fin. Assn. (communications com.), Pitts. Advt. Club, Wharton Alumni Assn. Roman Catholic. Home: 409 Marney Dr Coraopolis PA 15108 Office: Robinson Plaza 3 PO Box 2944 Pittsburgh PA 15230

KINNEY, MARJORIE SHARON, savs. and loan exec.; b. Gary, Ind., Jan. 11, 1940; d. David H. and Florence C. Dunning; student El Camino Coll., 1957, 58, UCLA Extension; m. Daniel D. Kinney, Dec. 31, 1958 (div. 1973); children—Steven Daniel, Michael Alan, Gregory Lincoln, Bradford David. Partner, Kinney Advt. Inc., Inglewood, Calif., 1958-68; pres. Greeters of Am., 1967-69; chmn. Person to Person Inc., Cleve., 1969-72; pres. Kinney Mktg. Corp., Encino, Calif., 1972-80; sr. v.p. Beverly Hills Savs. & Loan Assn. (Calif.), 1980—; dir. Safeway Stores, Inc., Chubb/Pacific Indemnity Co.; lectr. Bd. dirs. ARC, 1976—, United Way, 1979—. Mem. Women of Wall St. West (dir.), Calif. Savs. and Loan League, Savs. Instns. Mktg. Soc. Am. Republican. Presbyterian. Office: 9401 Wilshire Blvd Beverly Hills CA 90212

KINNUCAN, ROBERT CARROLL, tree care co. exec.; b. Harrodsburg, Ky., Mar. 9, 1948; s. Paul Frederick and Anita Hillary (Waters) K.; student Kendall Coll., 1968-69; B.S. in Econs., U. Ky., 1972; m. Dec. 24, 1974; children—Judson, Christine. Pres., chmn. bd., dir. R. Kinnucan Tree Experts, Lake Forest, Ill., 1972—. Mem. Nat. Arborist Assn., Internat. Soc. Arboriculture, Lake Forest C. of C. Club: Lake Forest-Lake Bluff Lions. Office: R Kinnucan Tree Experts 884 S Waukegan Rd Lake Forest IL 60045

KINOSHITA, YASUHIRO DAVID, airline exec.; b. Kobe, Japan, Jan. 16, 1942; s. Kazuo and Nariko K.; came to U.S., 1961; B.S., Calif. State U., Los Angeles, 1969; m. Tazuko Ando, Aug. 6, 1967; 1 son, Kotaro John. Sales rep. Toho Internat. Inc., Los Angeles, 1962-69; Western area Orient sales mgr. Varig Brazilian Airlines, Los Angeles, 1969—. Mem. Japan Trader's Club, Japan Travel Agy. Assn. Buddhist. Club: Lions. Home: 3312 Beethoven St Los Angeles CA 90066 Office: 606 S Olive St Los Angeles CA 90014

KINSELLA, JAMES JOSEPH, holding co. exec.; b. Peoria, Ill., Sept. 14, 1921. Prin., James J. Kinsella Enterprise Inc., holding co., Peoria, 1977—; founder, mgr. Key Resort Club Am., Peoria, 1977—; founder, owner B.V. Corp., Peoria, 1977—, also dir.; owner U.S. Enterprises Corp.; notary public. Mem. Republican Nat. Com. Mem. Common Cause, Nat. Resources Def. Council. Republican. Clubs: Eagles, Playboy, Loom, Sea World Dolphin, Enterprise, Inc., U.S. Senatorial. Home and Office: PO Box 37 Peoria IL 61650

KINSELLA, JOHN JAMES, advt. exec.; b. Joliet, Ill., Jan. 1, 1929; s. John Jules and Eileen (Baskerville) K.; B.A. in Polit. Sci., Notre Dame U., 1950; M.B.A., DePaul U., 1952; m. Jeanette Cullinane, June 15, 1963; children—Jeanette, Mary Catherine, Eileen, Margaret, John. With McCann-Erickson, Chgo., 1954-59, account supr., 1955-59; with Leo Burnett Co., Inc., Chgo., 1959—, pres., 1972—, also dir. Bd. dirs. Sacred Heart Acad., Chgo., Santa for the Very Poor, Chgo. Roman Catholic. Clubs: Westchester Country (Rye, N.Y.); Saddle and Cycle, Racquet (Chgo.); Shore Acres Country (Lake Forest, Ill.). Home: 166 Sheridan Rd Winnetka IL 60093 Office: Prudential Plaza Chicago IL 60601

KINSER, RICHARD EDWARD, mgmt. cons.; b. Los Angeles, May 14, 1936; s. Edward Lee and M. Yvonne (Withes) K.; B.A. in Econs., Stanford U., 1958; m. Suzanne Carol Logan, Mar. 22, 1958. Mgr., U.S. Steel Corp., San Francisco, 1958-65; v.p. Booz-Allen & Hamilton, Inc., San Francisco, 1965-78, Washington, 1971-73; sr. v.p., dir. William H. Clark Assos., Inc., San Francisco, 1979—; dir. Measurmatic, Inc., San Francisco. Bd. dirs. San Francisco Bicentenial Com., 1976. Mem. World Affairs Council. Republican. Clubs: Bankers; Orinda Country, Commonwealth. Office: 517 Washington St San Francisco CA 94111

KINTZ, GEORGE JEROME, lawyer, textile mfg. co. exec.; b. Kingston, Pa., Dec. 30, 1931; s. George Jacob and Ann Maxine (Lewis) K.; A.B. in Acctg., Duke U., 1953, LL.B., 1958; m. Lila Sue Tyson, Aug. 25, 1956; children—Charles Douglas, Gregory Jerome, Bruce Stephen, Lois Jean. Admitted to N.C. bar, 1959; tax acct. Arthur Andersen & Co., N.Y.C., 1958-64; tax mgr. Prince Waterhouse & Co., N.Y.C., 1964-65, Atlanta, 1965-68; tax mgr. Colonial Stores Inc., Atlanta, 1968-73; asst. treas. for taxes Dan River Inc., Greenville, S.C., 1974—. Scoutmaster, Boy Scouts Am., Atlanta, 1971-74, bd. dirs. Blue Ridge council, 1979—. Served with U.S. Army, 1953-55. C.P.A., N.C. Mem. Am. Inst. C.P.A.'s, N.C. Soc. C.P.A.'s, Nat. Assn. Accts., N.C. State Bar. Republican. Presbyterian. Clubs: Greenville Gun, Poinsett (Greenville). Home: 5 Timber Ln Route 12 Greenville SC 29609 Office: PO Box 6126 Station B Greenville SC 29606

KIORPES, CHARLES ANTHONY, constrn. machinery mfg. co. exec.; b. Yonkers, N.Y., Aug. 27, 1923; s. Anthony and Georgia Kiorpes; B.S., Columbia U., 1948; m. Ferne Wilkins, Dec. 2, 1945; children—Anthony Lloyd, Timothy Charles, Lynn. With Ford Motor Co., 1948-71, plant mgr., San Jose, Calif., 1967, Mahwan, N.J., 1968-71; group v.p. White Motor Corp., Cleve., 1972-77; v.p., gen. mgr. Constrn. Machinery div. Clark Equipment Co., Benton Harbor, Mich., 1977—; chmn. Clark Equipment Can. Ltd., 1979—. Served with USAAF, 1943-46. Registered profl. engr., Mich. Mem. Soc. Automotive Engrs., Am. Mgmt. Assn., Tau Beta Pi. Home: 4376 Tanglewood Trail Saint Joseph MI 49085 Office: Clark Equipment Co Box 547 Benton Harbor MI 49022

KIRBY, CALVIN JON, aircraft co. exec.; b. Bklyn., Sept. 1, 1940; s. Major Henry and Helen Eleanor (Sorell) K.; B.S. in Physics, Long Beach State U., 1969; M.Engring., UCLA, 1979; m. Ann White, Oct. 26, 1963. Tech. supr. Teledyne Semiconductor Co., Hawthorne, Calif., 1970-71; research and devel. engr. TRW Semiconductor, Hawthorne, 1971-72; mem. tech. staff Hughes Aircraft Co., El Segundo, Calif., 1972—, engring. supr., 1973-75, sr. staff engr., 1975-76, head engring. dept., 1976-78, engring. mgr., 1978—; cons. in metallic attachment techniques with indsl. applications, 1975—. Mem. Soc. Mfg. Engring., Am. Def. Preparedness Assn., Hughes Mgmt. Assn. Mem. Christian Ch. Author tech. articles. Home: 16165 Mount Gustin Fountain Valley CA 92708 Office: 2060 E Imperial Hwy El Segundo CA 90245

KIRBY, FRED MORGAN II, investment co. exec.; b. Wilkes Barre, Pa., Nov. 23, 1919; s. Allan P. and Marian G. (Sutherland) K.; grad. Lawrenceville Sch., 1938, A.B., Lafayette Coll., Easton, Pa., 1942; postgrad. Harvard Grad. Sch. Bus. Adminstrn., 1946; m. A. Walker Dillard, Apr. 30, 1949; children—Alice Kirby Horton, Fred Morgan III, S. Dillard, Jefferson W. Vice pres., then pres., dir. Allan Corp., 1953-74; pres., chmn. Filtration Engrs.; Inc., 1951-56; exec. v.p., then chmn., pres. Alleghany Corp., 1961-68, chmn., 1967—, pres., 1968-77; dir., mem. exec. com. Pittston Co., U.S. Industries, Inc.; dir. F.W. Woolworth Co., Hotel Waldorf Astoria Corp. Trustee, Fred M. and Jessie A. Kirby Episcopal House, Inc.; pres. bd. dirs. F.M. Kirby Found. Inc. Served to lt. (s.g.) USNR, 1942-46. Mem. Zeta Psi. Clubs: Westmoreland (Wilkes Barre, Pa); Morris County (N.J.) Golf; Racquet and Tennis, The Club at World Trade Center (N.Y.C.); Spring Valley Hounds (N.J.); Tower (Mpls.). Office: 17 DeHart St Morristown NJ 07960

KIRBY, FREDERICK CASPER, economist; b. Modena, Mo., Sept. 24, 1936; s. Chesnut Warren and Wilma Ruth (Butcher) K.; B.S., Washington U., 1959; Ph.D. in Econs., Wayne State U., 1969; m. Sarah Beck Kirby, May 24, 1973; 1 son, Frederick C.; 1 son from previous marriage, Patrick Ian. Asst. prof. econs. and fin. U. Tenn., Knoxville, 1967-69; sr. economist City Devel. dept. City of Kansas City, Mo., 1970-73; pres. Kirby Research, Inc., Overland Park, Kans., 1973—. Served with U.S. Army, 1959-62. Mem. Am. Econ. Assn., Regional Sci. Assn., So. Econ. Assn. Methodist. Contbr. articles to profl. jours. Address: 10220 Granada Ln Overland Park KS 66207

KIRBY, GEORGE FRANCIS, petroleum co. exec.; b. Cheneyville, La., Dec. 7, 1916; s. George Francis and Vesta (Mason) K.; A.B., La. Coll., 1936; M.S., La. State U., 1938, Ph.D., 1940; postgrad. Harvard, 1952; m. Nannette Dutsch, Dec. 12, 1941; children—Michael E., John M. With Ethyl Corp., N.Y.C., 1940-69, v.p. research and devel., 1955-62, exec. v.p., 1963-64, pres., 1964-69, also dir.; dir., mem. exec. com. Tex. Eastern Corp., Houston, 1969—, exec. v.p., 1970-71, pres., 1971—, chief exec. officer, 1973—, also chmn.; dir. La. Nat. Bank, First City Bancorp., Houston. Bd. dirs. La. State U. Found. Mem. Am. Chem. Soc., Am. Inst. Chem. Engrs., AAAS, Am. Petroleum Inst. (dir.), Inst. Gas Tech. (dir.), Gulf Research Inst. (trustee), Soc. Automotive Engrs., Gulf Univs. Research Consortium (trustee). Clubs: Pinnacle (N.Y.C.); Baton Rouge Country, Camelot (Baton Rouge); Houston, Petroleum, Ramada (Houston). Office: PO Box 2521 Houston TX 77001 also 277 Park Ave New York NY 10017

KIRBY, ROBERT EMORY, mfg. co. exec.; b. Ames, Iowa, Nov. 8, 1918; s. Robert Stearns and Ora (Walker) K.; B.S., Pa. State U., 1939; M.B.A., Harvard U., 1956; m. Barbara Anne McClintock, July 11, 1942; children—Mary Linda Kirby Mewshaw, Donna Susan (dec.). With W.Va. Pulp & Paper Co., 1939-43; with Westinghouse Elec. Corp., 1946—, gen. mgr. electronics div., 1958-63, v.p. engring., 1963-64, group v.p. indsl. group, 1964-66, exec. v.p., dir., 1966-69, pres. Industry and Def. Co., 1969-74, vice chmn. ops., 1974-75, chmn., chief exec. officer, 1975—; chmn. Cleve. br. Fed. Res. Bank. Bd. dirs. Pitts. Symphony; trustee U. Pitts., chmn. vis. com. Grad. Sch. Bus. Adminstrn.; mem. bus. adv. council Grad. Sch. Indsl. Adminstrn., Carnegie-Mellon U.; mem. nat. adv. com. Profl. Golfers Assn. Am.; chmn. Pres.'s Commn. on Exec. Exchange. Served with USNR, 1943-46. Mem. Pitts. C. of C., IEEE, Am. Soc. Naval Engrs., Am. Def. Preparedness Assn., Engrs. Soc. Western Pa., Kappa Gamma Psi, Beta Theta Pi. Clubs: Chartiers Country, Duquesne (dir.) (Pitts.); Bay Hill; Rolling Rock; Laurel Valley (Ligonier, Pa.); Sky (N.Y.C.). Home: 250 Tech Rd Pittsburgh PA 15205 Office: Westinghouse Bldg Pittsburgh PA 15222

KIRCHDORFER, HELLMUT FRITZ, packaging systems and material co. exec.; b. Munich, Germany, Mar. 26, 1939; came to U.S., 1977; s. Rudolf E. and Heinrike Elise (Roger) K.; B.A. U. Heidelberg (Germany), 1962; M.B.A., U. Kiel (Germany), 1965; m. Kerstin I. Moncke, Apr. 21, 1962; children—Ulf F., Bjorn O. Export mgr. Felix AB Sweden, Eslov, 1965-68, Tetra Pak, Rigello, Lund, Sweden, 1969-70; pres., chief exec. officer Tetra Pak S, Vienna, 1971-76; pres., chief exec. officer Brik Pak, Inc., Dallas, 1977—, also dir. Served with German Army, 1959. Mem. Presidents Assn., Sweden Economists

Assn., Am. Mgmt. Assn. Club: City Club Dallas. Office: 2775 Villa Creek Dr 165-D Dallas TX 75234

KIRCHER, JOHN EDWIN, petroleum co. exec.; b. Wayland, Mo., Dec. 7, 1917; s. Henry Frederick and Anna Dee (Porter) K.; B.A. in Chemistry, Culver Stockton Coll., 1939; Ph.D. in Organic Chemistry, U. Mo., 1942; m. Dorothy June Eaton, Jan. 19, 1946; children—Mark Henry, Gary John, Elizabeth Jessica. Research chemist Sharples Chem. Co., Wyandotte, Mich., 1942-50; dir. devel. Stepan Chem. Co. Chgo., 1950-51; with Continental Oil Co., 1951—, dir., 1966—, pres. Eastern Hemisphere Petroleum div., N.Y.C., Stamford, Conn., 1969-74, corp. pres., Stamford, 1974-75, dep. chmn., 1975—; dir. GK Techs., Turner Constrn. Co. Nat. dir. Boys Clubs Am., Jr. Achievement. Mem. Am. Petroleum Inst. (dir. exec. council on fgn. diplomats), Am. Chem. Soc. Clubs: University; Economic; Greenwich Country. Office: Continental Oil Co High Ridge Park Stamford CT 06904*

KIRCHHOFF, DONALD JOSEPH, bus. exec.; b. Richmond Heights, Mo., June 29, 1925; s. Joseph V. and Freida (Kruger) K.; B.S., Miami U., Oxford, Ohio, 1946; M.B.A., Harvard, 1949; m. Bluette Hartman, May 24, 1947; children—Susan Lee, Barbara Ann, Karen Mari. Accountant, Kroger Co., 1949-51; controller Nat. Food Stores Mich., 1953-56; with Standard Fruit & S.S. Co., 1956-59, v.p., 1961-62, exec. v.p., 1962-64, pres., dir., 1964-69; exec. v.p., dir. Castle & Cooke, Inc., 1970-73, pres., chief exec. officer, 1975—. Served to lt. USNR, 1943-48, 51-53. Mem. Honolulu C. of C. Club: Pacific (Honolulu). Home: 3635 Diamond Head Rd Honolulu HI 96816 Office: Financial Plaza of Pacific Honolulu HI 96813

KIRCHHOLTES, WERNER KARL, electronics import co. exec.; b. Frankfurt am Main, Germany, Aug. 9, 1919; came to U.S., 1946, naturalized, 1950; s. Heinrich and Gertrud (Sulzbach) K.; A.A., Kaiser Wilhelms Gymnasium, Frankfurt am Main, 1937; m. Leona Thursack, Dec. 23, 1950; 1 dau., Maureen. Vice pres. Transmares Corp., N.Y.C., 1946-50; gen. mgr. export-import H. Gafney Co., N.Y.C., 1950-53; ind. exporter-importer, 1954-56; dir. fgn. sales nuclear div. Daystrom, Inc., Murray Hill, N.J., 1957; gen. mgr. Daystrom GMBH, Frankfurt am Main, 1958-63; pres., owner Indsl. Electronics GmbH, Frankfurt am Main, 1963—; dir. Kitronic AG. Served with German Army, 1939-41. Mem. Frankfurt C. of C., Am. C. of C. Frankfurt am Main, Steuben-Schurz Soc. of Frankfurt. Lutheran. Club: Union Internat. (Frankfurt am Main) (hon. pres.). Home: 16 Flughafenstrasse 6 Frankfurt am Main Federal Republic Germany Office: 14 Klüberstrasse 6 Frankfurt am Main Federal Republic Germany

KIRK, JOHN EDMUND, printing and pub. co. exec.; b. Kansas City, Kans., Apr. 21, 1919; s. John Elmer and Ellen Eugenia (Hynes) K.; student Los Angeles Jr. Coll., 1939-41; m. Vivienne Frances Taylor, May 17, 1946; children—John Michael, Dennis Brian. Mgr. advt., public relations Mid Continent Airlines, Kansas City, Mo., 1946-50; v.p. Kansas City Poster and Printing Co., 1950—; pres. K.C. Colony, Inc., 1950—; pres. Mid Continent Aviation, Inc., Flight and Mechanics Sch., 1962-68; chmn. ITA Internat., Inc., multi-lingual communications co., Kansas City, Mo., 1973—; cons. bus. and real estate. Com. chmn. Area council Boy Scouts Am., 1960-67. Served with Royal Air Force, 1941-43. Mem. Nat. Fedn. Ind. Bus., Third Order St. Francis. Republican. Roman Catholic. Club: Advt. and Sales Exec. Author: How to Build a Fortune Investing in Land, 1973. Home: 5500 W 69th Terr Prairie Village KS 66208 Office: 4010 Washington St Kansas City MO 64111

KIRK, ROBERT CHARLES, lawyer; b. Jersey City, N.J., Nov. 18, 1944; s. Charles E. and Ruth A. (Hartzel) K.; A.B., Lafayette Coll., 1966; J.D., Cornell U., 1969; m. JoAnn M. Devine, Aug. 21, 1971; children—Brendan C., Laura L. Admitted to Pa. bar, 1969, U.S. Supreme Ct. bar, 1973; atty. U.S. Steel Corp., Pitts., 1969-73; atty. Jones & Laughlin Steel Corp., Pitts., 1973-78; asso. counsel Remington Arms Co., Inc., Bridgeport, Conn., 1978—. Mem. Am. Bar Assn., Westchester Fairfield Corp. Counsel Com. Republican. Office: 939 Barnum Ave Bridgeport CT 06602

KIRKLAND, BERTHA THERESA (MRS. THORNTON CROWNS KIRKLAND, JR.), constrn. co. exec.; b. San Francisco, May 16, 1916; d. Lawrence and Theresa (Kanzler) Schmelzer; m. Thornton Crowns Kirkland, Jr., Dec. 27, 1937 (dec. July 1971); children—Kathryn Elizabeth, Francis Charles. Engaged as supr. hospital operations Am. Potash & Chem. Corp., Trona, Calif., 1953-54; office mgr., T.C. Kirkland, elec. contractor, 1954-56; sec.-treas., dir. T.C. Kirkland, Inc., San Bernardino, Calif., 1958-74; design-install estimator Add-M Electric, Inc., 1972—, v.p., 1974—. Episcopalian. Club: Arrowhead Country (San Bernardino). Home: 526 E Sonora St San Bernardino CA 92404 Office: 387 S Arrowhead Ave San Bernardino CA 92408

KIRKLAND, WALLACE TALMAGE, real estate appraiser, cons.; b. Guntersville, Ala., July 15, 1931; s. Grover and Ona (McClendon) K.; B.S., Auburn U., 1953; postgrad. U. Fla., 1955-56; m. Martha Alma Cotter, June 2, 1962; children—Lorraine Phyllis, Dawn Ellen. Pres., Kirkland Builders, Guntersville, Ala., 1958-59; asso. regional appraiser Gen. Services Adminstrn., Atlanta, 1959-65; pres. Kirkland & Co., Atlanta, 1965—. Served with USAF, 1953-55. Mem. Am. Inst. Real Estate Appraisers, Soc. Real Estate Appraisers, Inst. Real Estate Mgmt., Pi Kappa Phi, Delta Sigma Pi. Home: 1656 Merton Rd NE Atlanta GA 30306 Office: 400 Colony Sq Atlanta GA 30361

KIRKPATRICK, CLAYTON, newspaper editor; b. Waterman, Ill., Jan. 8, 1915; s. Clayton Matteson and Mable Rose (Swift) K.; A.B., U. Ill., 1937; m. Thelma Marie De Mott, Feb. 13, 1943; children—Pamela Marie Kirkpatrick Foy, Bruce, Eileen Bea Kirkpatrick Sipos, James Walter. Reporter, City News Bur., Chgo., 1938; mem. staff Chgo. Tribune, 1938—, day city editor, 1958-61, city editor, 1961-63, asst. mng. editor, 1963-65, mng. editor, 1965-67, exec. editor, 1967-69, editor, 1969-79; v.p. Chgo. Tribune Co., 1967-77, exec. v.p., 1977-79, pres., 1979-81, chmn., 1981—. Served with USAAF, 1942-45. Decorated Bronze Star medal; recipient Elijah Parish Lovejoy award Colby Coll., 1978; William Allen White award U. Kans., 1977; Fourth Estate award Nat. Press Club, 1979. Mem. Phi Beta Kappa, Sigma Delta Chi. Republican. Methodist. Clubs: Chicago, Tavern, Chicago Press, Commercial, Glen Oak Country, Butler Nat. Golf. Office: 435 N Michigan Ave Chicago IL 60611

KIRKPATRICK, DAVID MELVIN, engring. co. exec.; b. Nevada, Mo., Dec. 1, 1935; s. Dale Melvin and Parma Dixon (Leinbach) K.; B.M.E., U. Houston, 1963; m. Barbara Nevon Wyant, Sept. 3, 1957; children—Amy Elizabeth, Marshall Lane, Neil McKinnon. Design engr. Todd Shipyards, Houston, 1964-65, Dow Chem. Co., Freeport, Tex., 1965-66; project engr. Celanese Polymer Co., Deer Park, Tex., 1966-67; chief mech. engr. Spinoza Inc., Houston, 1967-68; sr. project engr. Bechtel Corp., Houston, 1968-69; project engr. Gulf Interstate Engring. Co., Houston, 1969-72; sr. project engr. Litwin Corp., Wichita, Kans., 1972-76, tech. devel. rep., 1976-79, dir. mktg. electric tech., 1979-80; prin. process engr. Hallanger Engrs., Bellevue, Wash., 1980—. Vice pres. Harris (Tex.) Young Republican Club, 1966; pres. Greater Houston Young Rep. Club, 1968. Registered profl. engr., Tex. Mem. Electrochem. Soc. Mem. Christian Ch. Club: Toastmasters. Author articles in field. Home: 514 Forrest Park Dr Tacoma WA 98466 Office: 1621 114th Ave SE Bellevue WA 98004

KIRKPATRICK, FORREST HUNTER, mgmt. cons.; b. Galion, Ohio, Sept. 4, 1905; s. Arch M. and Mildred (Hunter) K.; student U. Dijon, 1926; A.B., Bethany (W.Va.) Coll., 1927, LL.D., 1949; A.M., Columbia U., 1931, profl. diploma, 1934, 36; postgrad. U. Pitts., U. London, U. Pa., U. Cambridge; LL.D., Coll. Steubenville, 1958, Drury Coll., 1968. Dean, prof. Bethany Coll., 1927-40, 46-52; vis. prof. or lectr. N.Y. U., Columbia U., U. Akron, U. Pitts., Cornell U., U. Wis., 1940-63; gen. mgr., personnel adminstrn. RCA, 1941-46, ednl. cons., 1946-53; asst. to chmn. Wheeling-Pitts. Steel Corp., 1952-64, v.p., 1964-70; vis. prof. W.Va. U., 1970-80; adj. prof. Bethany Coll., 1970—; dir. Blue Cross of No. W.Va., Inc., 1955—, chmn., 1970-78; dir. Sharon Tube Co. (Pa.), Banner Fibreboard Co., RCA Inst., Inc., First Steuben Bancorp, Inc., Consumers Mining Co., Carryore, Ltd., Hansand Steamship Co., Shelby Bus. Forms, Inc., First Nat. Bank & Trust Co., Steubenville, Ohio; met. chmn. Nat. Alliance Businessmen, 1971-72; cons. War Manpower Commn., 1942-44, U.S. Civil Service, 1945, State Dept., 1944, Post Office Dept., 1953; mem. mission to Sweden, Dept. Labor, 1962, manpower adv. com. Dept. Labor, 1963-68, USAF ednl. program com., 1948-51; cons. Am. Council on Edn., 1938-45, Ednl. Testing Service, 1946-52. Bd. dirs. Wheeling Symphony Soc., Inc., 1950-80, Wheeling Coll., 1972—; trustee Ohio Valley Med. Center, Inc., Wheeling, 1954—; bd. govs. W.Va. U., 1957-69, W.Va. Commn. on Higher Edn., 1964-70, W.Va. Com. for Humanities and Pub. Policy, 1972-77, Edn. Commn. of States, 1973-78, W.Va. Water Resources Bd., 1975—; mem. No. Panhandle Mental Health Center, Inc., 1974-80. Mem. Acad. Polit. Sci. (life), Indsl. Relations Research Assn. (life), Am. Econs. Assn., Am. Personnel and Guidance Assn. (life), NEA (life), Internat. Assn. Applied Psychology (Brussels), Am. Mgmt. Assn., AAUP (emeritus), Beta Theta Pi, Phi Delta Kappa, Kappa Delta Pi, Alpha Kappa Psi, Beta Gamma Sigma. Clubs: University (N.Y.C. and Pitts.); Duquesne (Pitts.); Wheeling Country; Ft. Henry (Wheeling); Soc. Friends of St. George (Windsor); Lake View Country (Morgantown, W.Va.). Author research reports and articles on mgmt. and labor econs. Home: Tally-Ho Apts 931 National Rd Wheeling WV 26003 Office: PO Box 268 Wheeling WV 26003

KIRKPATRICK, FRED EDWIN, corp. exec.; b. Bingham County, Blackfoot, Idaho, June 29, 1953; s. Glen E. and Oral (Felsted) K.; student Idaho State U., 1979; m. Sally L. Montgomery; children—Angela, Jamie. Welder, Scott Mfg. Co., Blackfoot, 1971; bridge welder Union Pacific R.R., 1971, various positions welder to insp., 1971-76; exec. v.p. Hurricane Inc., Blackfoot, 1978—, also chmn. bd. Vol. tchr. community edn. Served with USNG, 1972-74. Corp. mem. Wood Energy Inst. Co-inventor solid fuel room heater, 1976. Office: PO Box 327 Blackfoot ID 83221

KIRKPATRICK, JOSEPH GRAHAM, mktg., engring. and fin. cons.; b. Pitts., Aug. 11, 1926; s. Theodore Wilson and Elizabeth (Lloyd) K.; B.S. in Indsl. Engring., B.S. in Bus. Adminstrn., Lehigh U., 1949; M.B.A., U. Pitts., 1950; m. Jean Lude, June 9, 1948; children—Joseph Graham, David P., J. Theodore, Douglas M., James R. Treas., dir. Monessen Southwestern Ry., 1954-55; mgr. sales office Pitts. Steel Co., 1955-56; dist. rep. Johnson Steel & Wire Co., 1956-68, dir. sales, Western region, 1968-74, dir. corp. sales, 1974-76, v.p. sales, 1976-78; cons. Bay State Cons., Sterling, Mass., 1978-79, pres., 1979—; dir. Pa. Investment Corp., Consol. I.A. Inc., Closeburn Corp. Served with U.S. Army, 1942-46. Mem. Splty. Wire Assn. (pres. 1973), New Eng. Lehigh Alumni Assn. (dir.), Army Officers Assn., SAR. Republican. Episcopalian. Clubs: Plaza, Masons. Author: How To Lobby in Washington, 1979; A Marketing Plan for the 80's, 1979. Office: Bay State Cons 22 Griffin Rd Sterling MA 01565

KIRKWOOD, MAURICE RICHARD, banker; b. Tipton, Ind., Dec. 24, 1920; s. Walter Bryan and Lettie (Cooper) K.; B.S. with distinction, Ind. U., 1942, M.S., 1943; m. Anne Elizabeth Smith, Aug. 30, 1942; children—Candace Lynn, Susan Kay. Instr., Ind. U., Bloomington, 1942-43; gen. mgr. Stars and Stripes, Darmstadt, Ger., 1946-52; v.p. Fidelity Bank & Trust Co., Indpls., 1952-59; v.p., cashier, sec. to bd. Am. Fletcher Nat. Bank & Trust Co., Indpls., 1952-59; v.p., cashier, sec. to bd. Am. Fletcher Nat. Bank & Trust Co., Indpls., 1959—; sec., dir. 101 Monument Corp., 1996-70; v.p., sec. Am. Fletcher Corp., 1975—. Bd. dirs. Am. Fletcher Found., 1972—, Ind. Dept. Fin. Insts., 1965—; treas. Muscular Dystrophy, 1959-64; bd. dirs. Meth. Home for Aged, 1964-72; dist. chmn. United Fund, 1957-59; mem. Indpls. Traffice Safety Found., 1954-59, Ind. Credit Men's Assn., 1958-68, Indpls. Civic Progress Assn., 1957-59. Served with U.S. Army, 1942-46. Recipient Meritorious Civilian Service award Dept. Army, 1952; Award of Appreciation, Office of Comptroller of the Currency, 1962; Robert Morris Assos. Disting. Service award, 1974. Mem. Robert Morris Assos., Nat. Assn. Accountants, Indpls. C. of C., Sigma Nu, Beta Gamma Sigma, Phi Eta Sigma, Delta Sigma Pi. Methodist. Clubs: Hillcrest Country, Columbia, Ind. U. Men's. Author: National Banks and the Future, 1962. Home: 5214 Nob Ln Indianapolis IN 46226 Office: 101 Monument Circle Indianapolis IN 46277

KIRMSE, WILLIAM ANDREWS, hotel exec.; b. N.Y.C., June 16, 1942; s. William Albert and Jane (Andrews) K.; B.S., Cornell U., 1967; m. Mary Goh, Oct. 9, 1971; children—David, Christopher. With Inter-Continental Hotels Corp., various locations, 1967—, mgr. Pakistan, 1974-77, dir. ops. and planning, N.Y.C., 1977, mgr. Hotel Inter-Continental, Miami, 1978—; mem. Fla. Gov.'s Council on Tourism, Dade County Tourism Devel. Task Force. Served with USAF, 1963-67. Mem. Greater Miami Hotel and Motel Assn. (dir.), Greater Miami C. of C. (dir.), Coral Gables C. of C., Cornell Soc. Hotelmen. Republican. Episcopalian. Clubs: Rotary, Coral Gables Country. Home and Office: 801 S Bayshore Dr Suite 1828 Miami FL 33131

KIRSCHBAUM, JAMES LOUIS, ins. co. exec.; b. San Francisco, July 5, 1926; s. John David and Sarah (McLennan) K.; B.S., U. Calif., Berkeley, 1949; M.B.A., Golden Gate U., 1951; m. Beverly Hardman, Mar. 28, 1947; children—Larry, Carol, John, Scott, Jean. With Fireman's Fund Ins. Cos., 1949—, ops. exec. western states, San Francisco, 1978-80; pres., chief exec. officer Fireman's Fund Ins. Co. of Can., Toronto, Ont., 1980—. Served with U.S. Navy, 1943-46. C.P.C.U. Mem. Soc. Chartered Property and Casualty Underwriters. Republican. Mormon (pres. Toronto stake). Home: 5 Edenbrook Hill Islington ON M9A 3Z5 Canada Office: Fireman's Fund Ins Co of Can 350 Bloor St E Toronto ON Canada

KIRSNER, STUART BERNARD, ins. exec.; b. Bklyn., Sept. 27, 1946; s. George and Frances (Feltenstein) K.; student Hunter Coll., N.Y.C., 1965-67; m. Ellin Kay Schwartz, Dec. 26, 1970; children—Craig, Russell. Asst. art dir. Mines Press, N.Y.C., 1967-68; art dir. Marshalk Co., N.Y.C., 1969-70; creative coordinator Dick Barnett Advt. Assos., N.Y.C., 1971-72; salesman N.Y. Life Ins. Co., N.Y.C., 1972—; propr. Stuart Kirsner & Co., Inc., ins. brokerage, N.Y.C., 1976—, Stuart Fin. Group, pension adminstrn. and design services. Served with AUS, 1966. Mem. Million Dollar Round Table, 1974-80. Mem. Nat. Assn. Life Underwriters, Life Underwriters Assn. N.Y.C., Internat. Assn. Fin. Planners. Author mag. articles. Address: Sunnyside Ln Westport CT 06880

KIRST, WILLIAM JAMES, JR., geophysicist; b. Kenmore, N.Y., June 3, 1923; s. William James and Barbara Louise (Wagner) K.; B.S., Yale U., 1947; postgrad. Casper (Wyo.) Jr. Coll., 1954, Santa Barbara Jr. Coll., 1955, U. Alta., 1960, 67, U. Calgary, 1966, So. Alta. Inst. Tech., 1977, Mt. Royal Coll., Calgary, 1979; m. Frances Patricia Borders, Nov. 19, 1948; children—Dubhe, Heidi, William James, Joshua, Forest, Tracy, Alexander, Whitehorn. Party mgr., party chief, computer Western Geophys. Co., Wyo., Utah, Colo., N.D., Mont., Calif., 1948-55, Alta., B.C., N.W.T., Can., Arctic, 1955-66; No. dist. physicist Canadian Pacific Oil and Gas Co. Ltd., Calgary, Alta., Can., 1966-67; geophys. cons. Kirst Exploration, Calgary, 1967—; dir. cable TV show; photographer, owner Kirst Photographers studio; photographer Calgary Real Estate Bd.; dir. Take 5 Graphic Arts Ltd. Vol. resource person, bd. dirs. Calgary Drug Info. Centre; pres. Southwood Community Assn., 1962, 63; pres. Calgary Boys and Girls Band and Baton Corps, 1966-67; chmn. bd. dirs. Calgary Distress Centre/Drug Centre, 1980-81. Served with USMC, 1943-46. Registered profl. engr., Alta.; profl. geophysicist, Alta.; geophysicist, Calif.; pvt. pilot. Mem. Canadian Soc. Exploration Geophysicists, Yale Football Y Assn., Yale Sci. and Engring. Assn., St. Elmo Soc., Soc. Exploration Geophysicists. Attempted circumnavigation of Banks Island, Arctic Ocean, in kayak with son, 1971. Home: 3809 Elbow Dr SW Calgary AB T2S 2J9 Canada Office: 2406 - 505 - 6th St SW Calgary AB T2P 1X5 Canada

KIRTLAND, CLIFFORD M., JR., broadcasting exec.; b. Buffalo, Jan. 15, 1924; s. Clifford M. and Honor (Fowler) K.; B.A., Mich. State U., 1945; M.B.A., Harvard U., 1947; m. Jane McCullough, Aug. 31, 1951; children—Kim, Jimmy, Tommy, John. Sr. accountant Price Waterhouse & Co., 1947-51; v.p., treas., controller Abstract & Title Corp., 1951-54, Transcontinent TV Corp., 1955-63; with Cox Broadcasting Corp., Atlanta, 1963—, sec.-treas., 1964, v.p., 1967, exec. v.p., 1969-74, pres., chief exec. officer, 1974—; chmn. bd. Fed. Res. Bank Atlanta, 1980—; dir. Sci. Atlanta, Inc., Cox Cable Communications, Inc., Hawick Fund. Inc. Mem. bd. mgmt. Northside br. Atlanta YMCA; bd. dirs. Met. Atlanta A.R.C.; trustee Lovett Sch.; mem. bd. visitors Emory U. Served with USNR, World War II; PTO. Mem. N.Y., Ga. socs. C.P.A.'s, Financial Execs. Inst., Nat. Assn. Broadcasters, Inst. Broadcasting Financial Mgmt. (dir.), Advt. Council (dir.), Harvard Bus. Sch. Atlanta (1st v.p.). Presbyn. Rotarian (dir.). Clubs: Harvard (Atlanta and N.Y.C.); Peachtree Golf (Atlanta) Office: 1601 W Peachtree St NE Atlanta GA 30309*

KISELIK, PAUL HOWARD, folding carton co. exec.; b. Newark, Nov. 29, 1937; s. Jerome W. and Rose (Ramo) K.; B.S. with honors, Lehigh U., 1960; M.S., Newark Coll. Engring., 1965; m. Teri Nimaroff, Sept. 6, 1959; children—Daniel, Jonathan. Vice-pres. Nimrow Carton Co., Elizabeth, N.J., 1961-71; pres., chief exec. officer, Sebro Packaging Corp., South Hackensack, N.J., 1971—, Rayart Folding Box Co., South Hackensack, 1971—. Served with ordnance U.S. Army, 1960-61. Registered profl. engr. N.J., Pa. Mem. TAPPI, Newtonian Soc., Tau Beta Pi, Alpha Pi Mu. Author: Equity Financing of a Small Business, 1965. Office: 262 Green St South Hackensack NJ 07606

KISHPAUGH, ALLAN RICHARD, mech. engr.; b. Dover, N.J., Aug. 31, 1937; B.S. in Mech. Engring., N.J. Inst. Tech., 1967; m. Maryann H. Bizub, July 31, 1965. Engring. technician Stapling Machines Co., Rockaway, N.J., 1956-65; design engr. Airoyal Engring. Co., Livingston, N.J., 1965-66; project engr. Simautics Co., Fairfield, N.J., 1966-67; design engr. Pyrofilm Resistor Mfg. Co., Cedar Knolls, N.J., 1967-68; sr. engr., project mgr. packaging systems div. Standard Packaging Corp., Clifton, N.J., 1968-77; sr. machine design engr. Travenol Labs., Round Lake, Ill., 1977-79; dir. engring. TEC, Inc., Alsip, Ill., 1979-80; mgmt. cons., machine developer, Palos Heights, Ill., 1980—; expert Expertise Adv. Service, Inc., 1980—. Councilman, Borough of Victory Gardens (N.J.), 1969-71, council pres., 1971, police commnr., 1970-70, chmn. fin. com., 1970; pres. Pompton River Assn., Wayne, N.J., 1976-77; mem. Wayne Flood Control Commn., 1976-77; past deacon, elder, Sunday sch. tchr. and supt. local Presbyn. chs. Served with Air N.G., 1960-61, 62-65, with USAF, 1961-62. Registered profl. engr., N.J., Ill. Mem. ASME (vice chmn. N.J. sect. 1973-74, numerous other regional offices), Nat. Soc. Profl. Engrs. Patentee mechanism for feeding binding wire, wirebound box-making machine, method packaging granular materials, others in field. Address: 6118 W 123d St Palos Heights IL 60463

KISLIK, RICHARD WILLIAM, business exec.; b. N.Y.C., Oct. 31, 1927; s. Louis K. and Isabelle Kislik; A.B. magna cum laude, Harvard U., 1948, Baker scholar, 1949; m. Audrey Gerber, June 19, 1949; children—Nancy Kislik Eisner, Andrew, Laurie, Wendy. Research asst. Harvard Bus. Sch., Boston, 1949-50; asst. controller Maidenform Brassiere Co., Bayonne, N.J., and N.Y.C., 1950-54; controller Doubleday & Co., Inc., N.Y.C., 1954-60; treas., dir. Ziff-Davis Pub. Co., N.Y.C., 1960-61; v.p. fin., dir. Random House, Inc., N.Y.C., 1961-68, cons., 1968; pres. Intext Ednl. Pubs., Inc., N.Y.C., 1968-69; exec. v.p. Intext, Inc., Scranton, Pa., 1970-71, pres., 1971-79, chmn. bd., chief exec. officer, 1973-79; bus. cons., Darien, Conn., 1979-80; exec. v.p., dir. W.H. Smith Publs., N.Y.C., 1981—; dir. Lin Broadcasting. Mem. Assn. Am. Pubs., Pubs. Lunch Club. Clubs: Players, Harvard (N.Y.C.); Waccabuc. Home: The Hook Waccabuc NY 10597 also 940 Park Ave New York NY 10028

KISSINGER, WALTER BERNHARD, automotive parts and service equipment mfg. co. exec.; b. Furth, Germany, June 21, 1924; s. Louis and Paula (Stern) K.; came to U.S., 1938, naturalized, 1939; B.E., Princeton, 1951; M.B.A., Harvard, 1953; m. Eugenie Van Drooge, July 4, 1958; children—William, Thomas, Dana Marie, John Frans. Asst. to v.p. fgn. ops. Gen. Tire & Rubber Co., Akron, Ohio, 1953-56; pres. Advanced Vacuum Products Co., Stamford, Conn., 1957-62; exec. v.p. Glass-tite Industries, Providence, 1960-62; asst. to pres. Jerrold Corp., 1963-64; exec. v.p., dir., chmn. exec. com. Jervis Corp., Hicksville, N.Y., 1964-68; chmn., pres., chief exec. officer Allen Electric & Equipment Co. (name changed to Allen Group, Inc.), Melville, N.Y., 1969—; mem. adv. bd. Mfrs. Hanover Trust Co. Served to capt. AUS, 1943-46, 50. Decorated Commendation medal. Club: Princeton on New York. Home: Lower Dr Huntington Bay NY 11743 Office: 534 Broad Hollow Rd Melville NY 11746

KISSLING, FRED RALPH, JR., ins. agy. exec.; b. Nashville, Feb. 10, 1930; s. Fred Ralph and Sarah Elizabeth (FitzGerald) K.; B.A., Vanderbilt U., 1952, M.A., 1958; m. Ruth McAllister; children—Sarah FitzGerald, Jane Kirkpatrick. Spl. agt. Northwestern Mut. Life Ins. Co., Nashville, 1953-58, gen. agt., Lexington, Ky., 1962-80; gen. agt. New Eng. Mut. Life Ins. Co., 1981—; mgr. life dept. Bennett & Edwards, Kingsport, Tenn., 1958-62; pres. Employee Benefit Cons., Inc., Lexington, 1961—; partner Kennington Assos., 1967—; pub. Leader's mag., 1973—; dir. Bank of Lexington. Adv. bd. Salvation Army, Lexington, 1971—; gen. chmn. United Way of Blue Grass, 1975, bd. dirs., 1975-78; trustee, chmn. bd. Lexington Children's Theatre, 1979-81. Mem. Am. Soc. C.L.U.'s (chpt. pres. 1969-70, 80-81, regional v.p. 1972-73), Ky. Gen. Agts. and Mgrs. Assn. (pres. 1965-66), Million Dollar Round Table (life mem., v.p. program 1976), Assn. for Advanced Underwriting (dir. 1976—, sec.-treas. 1979-80, v.p. 1980-81), Am. Soc. Pension Acutaries (dir. 1971—, pres. 1974), Sigma Chi. Mason (Shriner). Clubs: Nashville City; Lexington, Lexington Polo; Lafayette. Author: Sell and Grow

Rich, 1966. Editor: Questionaire in Pension Planning, 1971, Questionnaire in Estate Planning, 1971. Home: 2091 Norborne Dr Lexington KY 40502 Office: 98 Dennis Dr Lexington KY 40503

KISTNER, DONALD OWEN, fin. exec.; b. Austin, Tex., Jan. 18, 1930; s. Owen Edward and Lorena Marie (Ford) K.; student Cornell U., 1956-57; B.A., Tex. Tech. Coll., 1956; m. Danna Junge, Dec. 28, 1968; children—Dain, Gavin, Chandra, Baird. Regional dir. sales Grubin Horth & Lawless, San Francisco, 1971-74; pres. Am. Real Estate Investment Trust, San Francisco, 1974-77, Amereit, Inc., San Francisco, 1974-77; exec. v.p. Evans-Pitcairn Corp., Phila., 1980—, dir., 1979—. Served with USAF, 1948-52. Mem. Urban Land Inst. Republican. Mem. New Ch. of Jerusalem. Clubs: Huntingdon Valley Country, Independence Hall Assn. Home: Cairnwood Farm Box 486 Bryn Athyn PA 19009 Office: Jenkintown Plaza Jenkintown PA 19046

KITCHEN, LAWRENCE OSCAR, aircraft co. exec.; b. Ft. Mill, S.C., June 8, 1923; s. Samuel Sumpter and Ruby Azalee (Grigg) K.; ed. Foothill Coll.; m. Brenda Lenhart, Nov. 25, 1978; children by previous marriage—Brenda, Alan, Janet. Served as enlisted man U.S. Marine Corps, 1942-46; aero. engr. U.S. Navy Bur. Aeronautics, Washington, 1946-58, staff asst. to asst. chief bur., 1958; with Lockheed Missiles & Space Co., Sunnyvale, Calif., 1958-70, mgr. product support logistics, 1964-68, dir. fin. controls, 1968-70; v.p.-fin. Lockheed-Ga. Co., Marietta, 1970-71, pres., 1971-75; pres. Lockheed Aircraft Corp., Burbank, Calif., 1975—, chief operating officer, 1976—. Mem. bd. visitors Emory Inst.; mem. founders bd. Hollywood Presbyn. Hosp.; mem. nominating com. Aviation Hall of Fame. Served with USMC, 1942-46. Mem. Nat. Def. Transp. Assn., AIAA, Nat. Assn. Accountants, Navy League, Am. Def. Preparedness Assn., Soc. Logistics Engrs., Air Force Assn., Assn. U.S. Army. Clubs: Lakeside Golf, Capital City, Wings, Cherokee Town and Country. Office: PO Box 551 Burbank CA 91520

KITCHENMASTER, ROBERT WESLEY, acct., mgmt. co. exec.; b. Luverne, Minn., Jan. 8, 1948; s. Wesley Emil Albert and Alma Margarite (Funck) K.; B.S., Mankato State U., 1969; m. Karen Kristine Aklestad, June 5, 1976; 1 son, Karl Robert. Mem. staff Touche Ross & Co., Denver, 1969-70; pres. Clapper Kitchenmaster & Co., Mankato, Minn., 1972—; co-founder, pres. Diversified Systems, Inc., Mankato, 1974—; co-founder, dir. Profl. Mgmt. Systems, Inc., Madison, Wis., 1974—; speaker, presenter numerous seminars, 1972—. Treas., pres. Messiah Luth. Ch., 1978-79; chmn. Luth. Council Chs. of Greater Mankato area. Served with USN, 1970-72. C.P.A., Minn. Mem. Am. Inst. C.P.A.'s, Minn. Soc. C.P.A.'s (1st v.p. So. Minn. chpt. 1979-80, pres. 1980-81), Internat. Assn. Fin. Planners, Nat. Assn. Accts., Mankato Area C. of C. (legis. com. 1979—). Republican. Club: Key City Sertoma (charter pres. 1975-76, Sertoman of Yr. award 1976). Home: 1620 Sherwood Ct North Mankato MN 56001 Office: 209 S 2d St Mankato MN 56001

KITTERMAN, STEPHEN LEE, holding co. exec.; b. Indpls., Nov. 16, 1941; s. John Spenser and Eloise (Osborne) K.; B.S.I.E., Gen. Motors Inst., 1964; M.B.A., Harvard U., 1966; m. Catherine Francis Stein, Mar. 7, 1968; 1 son, Stephen Spencer. Mfg. mgr. Cameron Iron Works, Inc., Houston, 1966-70; pres., gen. mgr. Wayne Valve div. Fluidic Industries, Houston, 1970-72; ind. cons., Houston, 1972; asst. v.p. ops. Alaska Interstate Co., Houston, 1973—; chmn. bd. Stardust Cruiser Mfg. Co., Chattanooga, 1978—, Hales Bar Resort & Marina Inc., Chattanooga, 1979—, Interstate Resources, Inc., 1980—, Hilburn Custom Marine, Inc.; adv. dir. Pyramid Prodns.; sec. RAR Mgmt., Inc., RAR Investment, Inc., Mo.-Kans. Selectune, Inc., Houston; partner Ross, Kitterman & Cantey, investment banking. Mem. AAAS, Houston C. of C. (indsl. devel. com.). Contbr. articles to profl. jours. Home: 210 Paul Revere Houston TX 77024 Office: 50 Briar Hollow Houston TX 77027

KITTINGER, EDWARD PARRISH, telephone co. exec.; b. Rocky Mount, Va., Aug. 27, 1922; s. Oscar Tyree and Irene King K.; B.S., Va. Poly. Inst., 1943; m. Rose Leggette, Mar. 31, 1948; children—Constance Raye Whiteside, Edward P. With Carolina Telephone & Telegraph Co., 1948-70, gen. plant mgr., Tarboro, N.C., 1961-70; v.p. ops. United Telephone Co. of Fla., Fort Myers, 1970-72; pres., 1972-77, pres. United Telephone System-Fla. Group, Altamonte Springs, 1977-79, chmn., chief exec. officer, 1979—; dir. Atlantic Bank of Orlando (Fla.). Mem. Indsl. Commn. Mid-Fla., Inc., 1979—. Served with U.S. Army, 1943-46. Decorated Bronze Star. Mem. Fla. Telephone Assn. (past pres.), Fla. Ind. Telephone Pioneers Assn. (past pres.), Fla. State C. of C. (dir.). Democrat. Presbyterian. Office: PO Box 5000 Altamonte Springs FL 32701

KITTNER, EDWIN HENRY, gypsum indsl. products mfg. co. exec.; b. Utica, N.Y., Mar. 7, 1925; s. Emanuel Joseph and Genevieve Victoria (Rybicki) K.; B.S., Kans. State U., 1950; m. Mary Elizabeth Totten, Oct. 20, 1950; children—Jane Elizabeth, Katherine Ann, Joseph Andrew, John David. Plant engr. Certain-Teed Products Co., Blue Rapids, Kans., 1950-57; chief project engr. Bestwall Gypsum Co., Blue Rapids, Kans., 1957-61, project engr. central engring. dept., Paoli, Pa., 1961-63; with Georgia-Pacific Corp., Blue Rapids, Kans., 1963—, maintenance and engring. supt., 1963—; condr. seminars. Mem. Blue Rapids (Kans.) Bd. of Edn., 1963-72; mem. Jayhawk Council Exec. Bd., Boy Scouts Am., 1963-80; mayor and councilman City of Blue Rapids, 1954-61, 74-80. Served with U.S. Army, 1943-46; ETO. Decorated Purple Heart. Recipient Silver Beaver award Boy Scouts Am., 1969; registered profl. engr., Kans. Mem. Nat. Soc. Profl. Engrs., Kans. Engring. Soc., Tri-Valley Engring. Soc. (pres. 1980), Am. Legion, VFW. Republican. Roman Catholic. Club: Lion (pres., zone chmn. 1955-65). Contbr. articles in field to profl., jours., also profl. handbooks. Home: 604 East Ave Blue Rapids KS 66411 Office: Box 187 Blue Rapids KS 66411

KJELDSEN, CHRISTIAN CURTIS, mfg. co. exec.; b. Elizabeth, N.J., Aug. 23, 1944; s. Curtis A. and Caroline (Sam) K.; B.S. in Commerce, Rider Coll., 1966; m. Marcia Gordon, May 17, 1969. Supr. order services Permacel, New Brunswick, N.J., 1968-70, supr. distbn., 1970, supr. customer service, 1970-72, buyer, 1972, mgr. sales and distbn. services, 1972-73, mgr. prodn., 1973-74, mgr. distbn., 1974-75, mgr. wage relations, 1975-77, dir. personnel, 1977—, also dir. Mem. adv. bd. Raritan Valley Workshop for Handicapped, 1977-80; exec. bd. Thomas A. Edison council Boy Scouts Am., 1977—; trustee United Way of Central N.J., 1981. Served with U.S. Army, 1966-68. Decorated Bronze Star, others. Republican. Office: Permacel US Route 1 New Brunswick NJ 08903

KLAGSBRUNN, HANS A(LEXANDER), lawyer; b. Vienna, Austria, Apr. 28, 1909; came to U.S., 1912; s. Hugo and Lili (Brandt) K.; student Vienna Gymnasium, 1922-25; B.A., Yale, 1929, LL.B., 1932; student Harvard Law Sch., 1932-33; m. Elizabeth Mapelsden Ramsey, Jan. 27, 1934. Admitted to D.C. bar, 1935, U.S. Supreme Ct. bar; asso. with RFC and affiliates, 1933-45; exec. v.p., gen. counsel, dir., mem. exec. com. Def. Plant Corp.; surplus property dir., asst. gen., counsel RFC; RFC mem. Hancock Contract Settlement Bd. and Clayton Surplus Property Bd. in Office War Mblzn.; dep. dir. Office War Mblzn. and Reconversion, White House, 1945-46; pvt. practice law, 1946—; mem. com. on admissions and grievances U.S. Ct. Appeals, 1967-74, chmn., 1972-74; mem. Jud. Conf. D.C. Circuit, 1964-66, chmn. com. criminal indigents; mem. reorgn. com. Army Chem. Corps, 1955-56. Mem. budget steering com. Health and Welfare Council, 1956-61, chmn., 1958-61, dir., 1958-73, pres., 1961-63; mem. exec., campaign coms. United Givers Fund, 1961-63; mem. task force on U.S. energy policy Twentieth Century Fund, 1976-77; mem. Piedmont Environ. Council, 1975-76; bd. dirs. Columbia Hosp. for Women, 1964-74; bd. dirs. Friendship House, 1957-68, pres., 1959-68. Recipient Community Service awards Health and Welfare Council, 1961, 63. Mem. Nat. Planning Assn., Am. Arbitration Assn. (nat. panel), Am. Bar Found., AIM, D.C., Fed., Am. (past chmn. and mem. several coms.) bar assns., Am. Judicature Soc., Newcomen Soc., Phi Beta Kappa, Order of Coif, Phi Beta Kappa Assos., Nat. Symphony Orch. Assn. Clubs: Metropolitan, Yale, Nat. Press, City Tavern. Home: 3420 Q St NW Washington DC 20007 also Salem Farm RFD 1 Purcellville VA 22132 Office: Ring Bldg Washington DC 20036

KLASHNA, MICHAEL JOSEPH, JR., marine transp. cons.; b. East Chicago, Ind., Feb. 21, 1941; s. Michael Joseph and Agnes Marie (Lambert) K.; B.S. in Bus. Adminstrn., So. Ill. U., 1968; M.B.A., Washington U., St. Louis, 1975; m. Carolyn Sue Gueldner, June 3, 1972. With Monsanto Co., St. Louis, 1968-79, distbrn. analyst, 1970-74, tanker ops. mgr., 1974-77, mgr. barge ops., 1977-79; marine transp. cons., St. Louis, 1979—; partner Brentwood Marine Investments. Served with USAF, 1958-62. Named Man of Yr., Meadowbrook Farm Assn., 1976. Mem. St. Louis Port and Harbor Assn. (dir.), Nat. Council Phys. Mgmt., St.Louis Milling and Grain Club, St. Louis Coal Club., Propeller Club St. Louis. Republican. Roman Catholic. Club: Yacht (St Louis). Home: 16452 Horseshoe Ridge Rd Chesterfield MO 63017 Office: 2510 S Brentwood Blvd St Louis MO 63144

KLATT, WILLIAM ALFRED, communications co. exec.; b. Bronx, N.Y., Jan. 29, 1940; s. Carl and Kathryn (Vignali) De Marco; B.S. in Indsl. Mgmt., Fairleigh Dickinson U., Teaneck, N.J., 1968; M.B.A., U. Guam, 1975; m. Patricia Ann Roberts, Feb. 7, 1965; children—William Robert, Debra Ann. With AT&T, N.Y.C., 1960-69; project mgr. Brooks Internat. Corp., Westwood, N.J., 1969-71; with RCA Global Communications, Inc., 1971—, mgr. telephone ops., Guam, 1973-75, gen. mgr. Guam and Micronesia, 1975-77, mgr. telephone services, Wayne, N.J., 1977-79, dir. telephone service and planning, 1979—. Mem. Armed Forces Communications and Electronics Assn. (exec. v.p. 1976—), Am. Inst. Indsl. Engrs., IEEE, Fairleigh Dickinson U., U. Guam Alumni Assn. Address: 27 Morgan Ct Wayne NJ 07470

KLAUS, GEORGE LEONARD, corporate exec.; b. Chgo., Aug. 17, 1924; s. George Michael and Marie (Schaaf) K.; B.S. with honors, U. Ill., 1949; m. Joan Ruthy, June 6, 1949; children—Cynthia, Susan, Jill. Staff accountant W. H. Stout, 1949-50; accountant Darling & Co., 1950-52; sr. auditor Arthur Andersen & Co., Chgo., 1952-58; corporate budget mgr. Brunswick Corp., Chgo., 1958-63, dir. internal auditing, 1963-68; audit mgr. Internat. Telephone & Telegraph Co., N.Y.C., 1968-72, dir. spl. projects, 1972-79, dir. mfg. cost controls, 1979—. Village treas. Glen Ellyn, Ill., 1959-62; mem. police pension bd., Glen Ellyn, 1959-62. Served to 1st lt. USAAF, 1942-45. Decorated Air Medal. C.P.A., Ill.; certified internal auditor. Mem. Am. Inst. C.P.A.'s, Budget Execs. Inst., Inst. Internal Auditors, Fourth Fighter Group, Schwaben-Verein, Beta Alpha Psi, Chi Gamma Iota (national pres. 1949). Presbyn. (deacon). Home: 33 Glenwood Rd Weston CT 06883 Office: ITT 320 Park Ave New York NY 10022

KLAUSER, ARTHUR EBBERT, gen. trading co. exec.; b. Toledo, Apr. 26, 1923; s. Arthur O. and Georgia (Grosvenor) K.; student DePauw U., 1941-43; certificate in Japanese, U. Chgo., 1944; A.B., U. Mich., 1945, M.A., 1948; J.D., Yale U., 1958; grad. Advanced Mgmt. Program, Harvard U., 1974, Sr. Mgrs. in Govt., 1977; m. Dec. 28, 1960 (dec.). Admitted to N.Y. State bar, 1959, also D.C. bar; atty. Vicks Chem. Co., N.Y.C., 1957-59, Richardson Found., N.Y.C., 1959-60; v.p. Royal Crown Internat., Coral Gables, Fla., 1960-62; dir. licensing/planning AMF Internat., Geneva and London, 1962-65; gen. mgr. consumer products Pfizer Internat., Tokyo, 1965-67; with Dow Corning Corp., 1967-79, dir. corp. communications, Midland, Mich., 1973-76, dir. govt. relations and pub. affairs, Washington, 1976-78, asst. sec. corp., 1978-79, v.p. govt. relations and pub. affairs, 1978-79; sr. v.p., exec. asst. to pres. Mitsui & Co. (U.S.A.), Inc., Washington, 1979—; adv. U. Mich. Sch. Bus.; lectr. on Japanese bus. to univs., profl. groups. Mem. steering com. Japan-U.S. Friendship Com. Served to lt. U.S. Army, 1943-47. Mem. Am., N.Y. State bar assns., Assn. Bar City N.Y., Am. C. of C., Tokyo Arbitration Assn., Asiatic Soc., Am.-Japan Soc. (trustee), Washington Export Council, Washington Internat. Bus. Council, Midland Symphony Orch. Soc., Pub. Affairs Council. Episcopalian. Clubs: Yale of N.Y.; Internat., Univ., Harvard, Nat. Democratic, Capitol Hill (Washington); Congl. Country. Contbr. articles on bus. in Japan to profl., trade jours.; translator (into Japanese): The Young Lions (Irwin Shaw), 1951. Home: 4200 Massachusetts Ave NW Washington DC 20016 Office: 1800 M St NW Washington DC 20036

KLEEMAN, ROBERT EARLE, JR., acctg. co. exec.; b. Hinsdale, Ill., Nov. 4, 1948; s. Robert Earle and Renaulda (Kolodziejski) K.; A.A., Coll. of DuPage, 1967; B.S., No. Ill. U., 1969; m. Judith K. McAvoy, Aug. 29, 1970; children—Robert Earle III, Tricia Kay, Timothy Keith, Karin Marie. Staff acct. Arthur Andersen & Co., Chgo., 1969-72; internat. tax mgr. Barbor Greene Co., Aurora, Ill., 1972-74; self-employed acct., St. Charles, Ill., 1974-78; partner Kleeman, Brooks & Co., St. Charles, 1978-79, Mueller, Sieracki, Kaun, Miller & Co., Elgin, St. Charles, Crystal Lake, Ill., 1979—; instr. taxation Aurora Coll., 1974-77; dir. Landmark Pub. Co., Blue Goose Supermarkets, Inc. Bd. dirs. St. Charles Community Chest, 1976—, Delnor Men's Found., 1976. Named Outstanding Young Man of Am., U.S. Jaycees, 1977; C.P.A., Ill. Mem. Am. Inst. C.P.A.'s, Ill. Soc. C.P.A.'s, Fox Valley Estate Planning Council, McHenry County Estate Planning Council (dir.), McHenry County Life Underwriters Assn., Delta Sigma Pi. Methodist. Club: St. Charles Kiwanis (dir. 1978-80). Office: 1750 Grandstand Pl Elgin IL 60120

KLEIMAN, JOSEPH, materials co. exec.; b. Grand Rapids, Mich., Oct. 1, 1919; s. Jacob and Bessie (Targowitch) K.; B.S. in Engring., U. Mich., 1941, M.S., 1942; m. Shirley Ruth Present, Aug. 30, 1942; children—Richard Neil, Robert, William. Engr., Reeves Instrument Corp., N.Y.C., 1946-51; v.p., gen. mgr. Belock Instrument Corp., College Point, N.Y., 1951-58; v.p., gen. mgr. Whittaker Gyro div. Telecomputing Corp., Los Angeles, 1958-59, exec. v.p. corp., 1959-64; v.p. corporate devel. Whittaker Corp., 1964-67, sr. v.p., 1967—, also dir.; dir. Yardney Electric Corp. Vice chmn. Union Am. Hebrew Congregations, 1975-79; v.p. Am. Soc. for Technion-Israeli Inst. Tech. Mem. Nat., Calif. socs. profl. engrs., Sigma Xi, Phi Lambda Upsilon, Iota Alpha. Jewish. Home: 11240 Chalon Rd Los Angeles CA 90049 Office: 10880 Wilshire Blvd Los Angeles CA 90024

KLEIN, BERNARD, publisher, author; b. N.Y.C., Sept. 20, 1921; s. Joseph J. and Anna (Wolfe) K.; B.A., Coll. City N.Y., 1942; m. Betty Stecher, Feb. 17, 1946; children—Cheryl Rona, Barry Todd, Cindy Ann. Founder, pres. U.S. List Co., N.Y.C., 1946-70; founder, pres., chief editor B. Klein Publs., Inc., Coral Springs, Fla., 1953—; cons. on direct mail advt. and reference book pub. to pubs. and industry, 1950—. Served with AUS, 1942-45; ETO. Mem. Direct Mail Advt. Assn. Mason. Author: Guide to American Directories, Guide to American Educational Directories, Mail Order Business Directory, Directory of College Media, Directory of Coll. Stores, Ency. of Am. Indian, all pub. biennially, 1954—. Home: 7309 Corkwood Terr Tamarac FL 33321 Office: POB 8503 Coral Springs FL 33065

KLEIN, BRUCE PETER, fin. exec.; b. N.Y.C., Nov. 2, 1933; s. Jacob and Rhoda (Schraeger) K.; B.S. in B.A., Lehigh U., 1954; m. Terry Berger, May 21, 1962; children—Scott Michael, Peter Andrew. With Peat, Marwick & Mitchell, N.Y.C., 1954-56, Klein, Katcher & Co., N.Y.C., 1956-63; pvt. practice pub. accounting, N.Y.C., 1964; sec.-treas., dir., stockholder Preload Concrete Structures, Inc., Garden City, N.Y., 1965—, Preload Co., Inc., 1965—, Preload Tech., Inc., 1969—. C.P.A., N.Y. Mem. N.Y. Soc. C.P.A.'s. Democrat. Home: 197-4OH Peck Ave Fresh Meadows NY 11365 Office: 839 Stewart Ave Garden City NY 11530

KLEIN, CHARLES HENLE, lithographing co. exec.; b. Cin., Oct. 5, 1908; s. Benjamin Franklin and Flora (Henle) K.; student Purdue U., 1926-27, U. Cin., 1927-28; m. Ruth Becker, Sept. 23, 1938; children—Betsy (Mrs. Marvin H. Schwartz), Charles H., Carla (Mrs. George Fee III). Pres., Progress Lithographing Co., Cin., 1934-59, Novelart Mfg. Co., Cin., 1960—; dir. R.A. Taylor Corp. Founding mem. Chief Execs. Forum. Clubs: Losantiville Country, Queen City, Bankers (Cin.). Home: 6754 Fairoaks Dr Amberley Village Cincinnati OH 45237 Office: Section Rd and P-C RR Cincinnati OH 45237

KLEIN, DAVID ALAN, limousine service exec.; b. N.Y.C., Aug. 4, 1945; s. George Henry and Norma (Swinger) K.; B.S. in Bus. Adminstrn., N.Y. U., 1967. Owner, pres. Dav-El Services, Inc., N.Y.C., 1966—; pres. Dav-El West, Inc., Los Angeles, 1976—. Bd. dirs. Endymion Ensemble, 1978—; mem. Landmarks Preservation Com. West Side, N.Y.C., 1980. Jewish. Office: 219 W 77th St New York NY 10024

KLEIN, DAVID HARRY, ins. co. exec.; b. Albany, N.Y., Oct. 22, 1948; s. Joseph and Sarah Raskin K.; B.S., Rensselaer Poly. Inst., 1970; M.B.A., U. Chgo., 1972; m. Nancy Sabesan, Aug. 17, 1969; 1 son, Randall. With Blue Cross and Blue Shield Assns., Chgo., 1972—, sr. v.p. mktg. support services and research; v.p. ops. Health Services Found., Chgo., 1977—; mem. faculty Gov.'s State U., Park Forest South, Ill., 1975-77. Mem. Am. Coll. Hosp. Adminstrs., Hosp. Mgmt. Systems Soc., Am. Public Health Assn. Home: 2031 N Clifton Chicago IL 60614 Office: 676 N St Clair Chicago IL 60611

KLEIN, JAY WILLIAM, direct mail advt. exec.; b. Yonkers, N.Y., Apr. 1, 1926; s. Morris and Marion (Berger) K.; B.A., U. Bridgeport, 1950; M.B.A., Columbia, 1960; m. Renee (Cohen), June 29, 1952; children—Bruce D., Leslie J. Analytical reporter Dun & Bradstreet, N.Y.C., 1952-62; sales mgr. Am. Credit Indemnity, N.Y.C., 1962-65; exec. v.p. Ed Burnett, Inc., N.Y.C., 1965-72; dir. sales Action Markets, N.Y.C., 1972-73; mktg. mgr. Consumers Mktg. Research, Hackensack, N.J., 1973-74; v.p. Bus. Mailers, Inc., Ridgefield Park, N.J., 1974—; v.p. Ace Parker Inc., Miami, Fla., 1977—. Mem. Republican State Com., 1965-71; Rep. town chmn., 1972-78. Served with U.S. Army, 1943-46. Decorated Bronze Star, Purple Heart, Combat Infantry Badge. Mem. Pharm. Advt. Council, Direct Mail Advt. Assn., Mail Advt. Services Assn. Jewish (mem. bd. dirs. Monsey Jewish Center). Clubs: 100 Million (N.Y.C.); Mason. Home: 9 Pearl Dr Monsey NY 10952 Office: 245 Main St Ridgefield Park NJ 07660

KLEIN, JEROME EUGENE, banker; b. Phila., June 20, 1917; s. Louis and Jessie (Resnick) K.; A.B., Oberlin Coll., 1939; postgrad. U. Wis., 1940, Bristol U., 1944; m. Jean Elise Loewy, Oct. 5, 1940; children—Robert M., Judith A. Various positions with Earl Newsom Assos., 1941-43; corporate promotion and pub. relations dir. Lane Bryant, Inc., N.Y.C., 1946-73; asst. v.p. mktg., adminstrv. mgr. European-Am. Bank, N.Y.C., 1973—. Served with AUS, 1943-45; ETO. Decorated Bronze Stars (3). Recipient Oscar of Industry awards Lane Bryant, Inc., 1963-68, Silver Anvils Am. Pub. Relations Soc., 1956, 62. Certificate of Achievement Pub. Relations News, 1965. Mem. Nat. Retail Mchts. Assn. (trustee sales promotion div. 1966-72), Overseas Press Club, Soc. Am. Travel Writers, Pub. Relations Soc. Am., Publicity Club N.Y., Sales Promotion Execs. Assn. Author: Great Views to Dine By Around the World, 1961; Great Shops of Europe, 1969; Great Hotels and Resorts of Europe, 1969; Travelogs-Europe and Israel, Canada, U.S.A., 1968; Traveldex on London, Rome, Paris, 1966; We Occupy, 1944; Great Tennis Resorts of the World, 1972; First International Directory of Condominiums, Retirement and Vacation Homes, 1972. Home: 127 Andover Rd Roslyn Heights NY 11577 Office: 651 New Bridge Rd East Meadow NY 11554 also 10 Hanover Sq New York NY 10005

KLEIN, JOHN ELLIOTT, mfg. co. exec.; b. N.Y.C., June 25, 1941; s. August P. and Muriel A. (Binzen) K.; B.S., U.S. Mcht. Marine Acad., 1963; M.B.A., N.Y. U., 1967; m. Charlotte E. deWilde, Aug. 17, 1968; children—John E., Kara E., Timothy B. Mktg. rep. IBM Corp., N.Y.C., 1967-71, dist. mktg. rep., 1971-72, mktg. mgr., 1972-74, adminstrv. asst. White Plains, N.Y., 1974, br. mgr., Cin., 1974-78, corp. exec. devel., 1978-80, gen. bus. group orgn., 1980—. Vice pres. Downtown Council of Greater Cin., 1975-77, pres., 1977-78; bd. dirs. Cin. Urban League, 1977. Mem. Greater Cin. C. of C. Republican. Roman Catholic. Clubs: Queen City, Camargo Racquet, Indian Hill. Home: 80 Hemmelskamp Rd Wilton CT 06897 Office: care IBM Armonk NY

KLEIN, KENTON MAGILL, food broker; b. Des Moines, Jan. 20, 1928; s. Randall Thomas and Mary Esther (Magill) K.; B.S., U. Iowa, 1952; m. Lois Marjorie Martin, Aug. 12, 1950; children—Kenton Magill, Jr., Ward Martin. Clk, Bankers Trust Co., Des Moines, 1945-46; with Seavey & Flarsheim Brokerage Co., Inc., Des Moines, 1952—, div. pres., 1963—; dir. Sales Force Co's., Inc., Schiller Park, Ill., chmn. profit sharing com., 1978-80, mem. investment adv. com., 1975-80. Capt., United Campaign, Des Moines, 1959. Served with U.S. Navy, 1946-48. Mem. Des Moines Food Brokers Assn. (pres. 1957), Iowa Food Distbrs. Assn. (dir. 1970), Iowa Retail Grocers Assn., Nat. Food Brokers Assn., Grocers Mfrs. Assn. Iowa, Des Moines C. of C., Nat. Alcohol Beverage Control Assn. Republican. Episcopalian. Clubs: Des Moines; Wakonda Country; New Pioneer Gun. Office: 2122 Grand Ave Des Moines IA 50312

KLEIN, LOUIS SAMUEL, accountant; b. Chgo., Sept. 13, 1908; s. Joseph and Lena (Groveman) K.; C.P.A., U. N.Y., 1946; m. Syd Bass, June 2, 1934; children—Letty Sandra, Adele Phyllis, Walter Jay. Accountant, auditor Federated Purchaser, Inc., N.Y.C., 1932-35; comptroller accountant Ala. Braid & Ribbon Co., C.M. Offray & Son, Gadsden, 1935-37; practicing C.P.A., 1937—; partner Louis S. Klein & Co. Gadsden, 1937-69, Klein, Lambert & Evans, Gadsden, 1969-73; spl. partner Cherry, Bekaert & Holland, Gadsden, 1973—; mng. partner Comml. & Financial Co., Ltd., 1972—; pres. Klein & Assos., P.A. Mem. Jewish Welfare Bd., Etowah County; auditor Gadsden Concert Assn., 1961-72, 75—. Mem. C. of C., N.Y., Ala. (past v.p., chmn. Gadsden-Anniston chpt.), socs. C.P.A.'s, Am. So. insts. mgmt. Am. Accounting Assn., Am. Inst. C.P.A.'s. Jewish (past pres.). Mem. B'nai B'rith (past pres.). Club: Civitan (past pres., past lt. gov.). Home: 9541 Sunrise Lakes Blvd Sunrise FL 33322 Office: 228 S 6th St Gadsden AL 35901

KLEIN, MELVYN NORMAN, lawyer, bus. exec.; b. Chgo., Dec. 27, 1941; s. Harry H. and Bertha M. (Gleicher) K.; A.B. (Gen. Motors Nat. scholar 1960-63), Colgate U., 1963; J.D. (Internat. fellow 1963-65), Columbia U., 1966; postgrad. Johns Hopkins U., 1966-67; m. Annette L. Grossman, Mar. 13, 1976; 1 dau., Jacqueline Anne. Cons., McKinsey & Co., Washington, 1967-68; admitted to D.C. bar, 1968; treas. Nat. Businessmen's Com. for Humphrey-Muskie, Washington, 1968; sr. v.p., dir. Donaldson, Lufkin & Jenrette, N.Y.C., 1969-77; pres., chief exec. officer Altamil Corp., Corpus Christi, Tex., 1977—; sr. investment advisor Sprout Capital Group, N.Y.C., 1976—; chmn. fin. com., dir. Playboy Enterprises, Inc., 1977—; dir. Damson Oil Corp., N.Y.C., Victorio Co., Phoenix, Corpus Christi Bank & Trust, RSR Corp., Donaldson, Lufkin & Jenrette Capital Corp. Mem. Corpus Christi Indsl. Commn.; bd. govs. Art Mus. S. Tex. Mem. Am., D.C. bar assns., Young Pres.'s Orgn. Clubs: Corpus Christi Country, Corpus Christi Yacht; Standard (Chgo.); City Midday (N.Y.C.). Home: 4270 Ocean Dr Corpus Christi TX 78411 Office: 1940 Bank and Trust Tower Corpus Christi TX 78477

KLEIN, PETER MARTIN, lawyer, transp. co. exec.; b. N.Y.C., June 2, 1934; s. Saul and Esther (Goldstein) K.; A.B., Columbia, 1956, J.D., 1962; m. Ellen Judith Matlick, June 18, 1961; children—Amy Lynn, Steven Ezra. Admitted to D.C. bar, 1964, N.Y. State bar, 1962, U.S. Supreme Ct. bar, 1966; asst. counsel mil. sea transp. service Office Gen. Counsel, Dept. Navy, Washington, 1962-65; trial atty. civil div. Dept. Justice, N.Y.C., 1966-69; gen. atty. Sea-Land Service Inc., Menlo Park, N.J., 1969-76, v.p. law, gen. counsel, sec., 1976-79, dir., 1976-78; v.p., gen. counsel, sec. Sea-Land Industries, Inc., Menlo Park, N.J., 1979—; asso. gen. counsel R.J. Reynolds Industries, Inc., Winston-Salem, N.C., 1978—; mem. shipping coordinating com., adv. com. on pvt. and internat. law State Dept., 1974—. Trustee Temple B'nai Abraham, Essex County, N.J., 1973—, v.p., 1976—; trustee Jewish Edn. Assn. Met. N.J., 1973-76. Served as officer with USN, 1956-59. Mem. Am. Polar Soc., Am., Fed., N.Y. State, D.C., Internat. bar assns., Maritime Law Assn. U.S., Am. Maritime Assn. (dir. 1974-78, chmn. com. on law and legislation 1974-79). Home: 42 Billingsley Dr Livingston NJ 07039 Office: Sea Land Industries Inc PO Box 900 Edison NJ 08817

KLEIN, ROBERT NICHOLAS, real estate investment and devel. co. exec.; b. Cin., Apr. 24, 1916; s. Sultan S. and Ida (Siverston) K.; A.B., U. Calif. at Los Angeles, 1938; M.S., U. So. Calif., 1940; m. Helen Smades, Sept. 26, 1963; children—Robert Nicholas II, Jeff, Kathi, Debbie, Patti, Cindy. Asst. city mgr., San Jose, Calif., 1948-50; city mgr., Monterey Park, 1950-52, Santa Cruz, 1952-58; chief adminstrv. officer City of Fresno (Calif.), 1958-63; pres. Robert Klein & Assos., also "K" Devel. Co., Fresno, 1963—. Mem. adv. com. Calif. Hwy. Commn., 1969-78. Pres., bd. dirs. Fresno Downtown Assn., 1969—. Served to lt. comdr. USNR, 1942-45; now lt. comdr. Res. ret. Mem. Internat. City Mgrs. Assn., Soc. Indsl. Realtors, Zeta Psi. Clubs: Rotary, Downtown (pres. 1977), University Sequoia Sunnyside. Home: 1440 W Robinwood Ln Fresno CA 93711 Office: 108 W Shaw Fresno CA 93704

KLEIN, WILLIAM ALLEN, comml. broker; b. Bklyn., Aug. 2, 1935; s. Abe and Belle (Fein) K.; B.S. in B.A., Temple U., 1956; postgrad., 1962; m. Nora Good, Mar. 15, 1959; children—Joyce, Amy, Jeffrey. Asst. personnel officer Phila. Fire Dept., 1957-60; personnel dir. Goodwill Industries Phila., 1960-62; employment rep. RCA Service Co., Riverton, N.J., 1962-64; asst. personnel mgr. Monsanto Co., Addyston, Ohio, 1964-67; with Foster Grant Co., Inc., Leominster, Mass., 1967—, mgr. employment and affirmative action, 1973-75, mgr. affirmative action and personnel, 1975-78 (merged with parent co. 1978), mgr. corporate affirmative action Am. Hoechst, Corp., Somerville, N.J., 1978-79; corp. personnel mgr. Tropicana Products, Inc., Bradenton, Fla., 1979-80; sec.-treas. Main Bus. Brokers, Inc., Sarasota, Fla., 1980—; instr. Mt. Wachusett Community Coll. Mem. Alcoholism Commn.; bd. dirs. Community Center, YMCA. Served with USAR, 1957-63. Rotary Found. grantee, Philippines, 1960. Mem. Indsl. Devel. Com., C. of C. (past dir.), Employment Mgmt. Assn., Leominster Personnel Mgrs. Council (past pres.). Club: Rotary. Home: 6208 9th Ave W Bradenton FL 33529 Office: 1900 Main St Sarasota FL 33577

KLEINMAN, DOROTHY SCHWARTZ, personnel cons. co. exec.; b. Queens, N.Y., Aug. 31; d. Herman L. and Rose (Mintz) Schwartz; student N.Y. U.; children—Scott Leon, Jay Leon; 1 stepson, David Kleinman. Successively head teen dept. H.L. Schwartz Sportswear Co., N.Y.C.; sales mgr. Vanity Blouse Co., N.Y.C.; entertainer, producer, dir. amateur prodns.; personnel cons. S.H.S. Internat. (name later N.F.I. Agy. Inc. of Melville), Melville, N.Y., 1968-72, pres., 1972—; public speaker bus. assns., high schs., colls., scouting orgns., 1970—. Mem. L.I. Employment Agy. Council (dir.), Assn. Personnel Cons. N.Y., NEA, L.I. Assn. Commerce and Industry. Office: NFI Agy Inc of Melville 900 Route 110 Melville NY 11747

KLEINMAN, IRA JEFFREY, ins. co. exec.; b. N.Y.C., Apr. 11, 1947; s. Arthur and Lenore S. (Schwartz) K.; B.A. in Econs., Queens Coll., 1969; m. Jean Merulla, Dec. 29, 1974; 1 dau., Lindsay Ann. Spl. agt. Prudential Ins. Co., N.Y.C., 1969-71, tng. specialist, Newark, 1971, asst. mgr., Washington, 1972, regional field cons., Chgo., 1973-74, mgr. ordinary agy., Oak Brook, Ill., 1975-77, dir. agencies Central Atlantic home office, Ft. Washington, Pa., 1978, v.p. regional mktg., 1978—; guest speaker mgmt. confs. Bd. govs. Community Meml. Hosp., La Grange, Ill., 1976—. Served with N.Y. Army N.G., 1969-72, Va. Res., 1972-75. C.L.U. Mem. Nat. Assn. Life Underwriters, Gen. Agts. and Mgrs. Assn. (Nat. Mgmt. award 1977), Am. Coll. C.L.U.'s (Golden Key sponsor). Home: 522 Edann Rd Glenside PA 19038 Office: care Prudential Ins Co PO Box 388 Fort Washington PA 19034

KLEINSMITH, JAMES JOSEPH, data processor; b. Murdo, S.D., Oct. 23, 1934; s. Frederick John and Monica Rose (Herber) K.; student George Washington U., 1953-55; B.S. in Physics, Spring Hill Coll., 1962; M.A. in Philosophy, 1963; M.B.A., St. Mary's Coll., 1981; m. Nicole Michelle Bridelle, Aug. 15, 1966; children—David, Nicole, Niela. Systems designer, analyst Systems Devel. Corp., Santa Monica, Calif., 1965; tchr. various primary, secondary schs., colls., U.S.A. and fgn. countries, 1963, 65-67; research technician U.S. Bur. Standards, 1957-58; communication systems program mgr., European announcement mgr. IBM, Paris, 1972-75; distributed processing systems specialist for comml. banks and savs. and loan assns., San Francisco, 1976—. Active in city planning and devel., Clayton, Calif., 1976—. Served with U.S. Army, 1955-57. Mem. Data Processing Mgmt. Assn., Sigma Pi Sigma. Republican. Roman Catholic. Club: Toastmasters. Home: 8 London Ct Clayton CA 94517 Office: 425 Market St San Francisco CA 94105

KLEMENS, EBERHARD RUDOLF, computer software co. exec.; b. Hannover, Germany, Mar. 11, 1950; came to U.S., 1956, naturalized, 1969; s. Rudolf and Kaethe Erna (Fuchs) K.; B.S. in Engring., U. Ill., 1974; m. Cynthia Lee Woelfer, Apr. 12, 1975. Systems analyst U. Ill., Chgo., 1971-77; v.p. Schrager Klemens and Krueger, Inc., Rosemont, Ill., 1977—, also dir. Office: 10400 W Higgins Rd Rosemont IL 60018

KLEVANA, LEIGHTON QUENTIN JOSEPH, lawyer, corp. exec.; b. Czechoslovakia, Oct. 7, 1934 (born Am. citizen); s. Joseph V. and Bellina N. (Karlovsky) K.; B.A., Cornell U., 1957; postgrad. U. Paris, The Sorbonne, 1958; J.D., U. Va., 1961; m. Wanda Minge-Kalman, Dec. 8, 1978. Admitted to N.Y. bar, 1963, Vt. bar, 1971; asso. atty. Meyer, Kissell, Matz & Seward, N.Y.C., 1961-63, Olwine, Connelly, Chase, O'Donnell & Weyher, 1963-67; sec. Helme Products, Inc., N.Y.C., 1967, sec., gen. counsel, 1967-70; v.p., sec., dir. Transit Air Freight, Inc., 1966-75; partner law firm Mahady & Klevana, 1973-76, Klevana & Rounds, P.C., 1977-79; pres., dir. Windsor County Properties, Inc., 1974-76, Practicing Real Estate Inst., Inc., 1974—, Connecticut River Valley Properties, Inc., 1976—. Asst. atty. gen., 1970-73. Home: 221 Mt Auburn St Cambridge MA 02138 Office: 62 Main St Windsor VT 05089

KLIEWER, WILLIAM PHILLIP, ins. agy. exec.; b. Weatherford, Okla., Feb. 13, 1950; s. William Gerald and Ollie Fern (De Cou) K.; B.S., Nicholls State U., 1972; M.S., Am. Technol. U., 1979; m. Mary Helen Bigham, Dec. 23, 1976; 1 son, John William. Partner, Bigham Ins. & Real Estate Co., Killeen, Tex., 1978—; instr. ins. Central Tex. Coll., since 1979—. Past pres. Killeen Downtown Inc. Served with U.S. Army, 1972-77. Mem. Ind. Ins. Agts. Am., Ind. Ins. Agts. Tex., Ind. Ins. Agts. Central Tex. (pres.), Nat. Assn. Life Underwriters, Tex. Assn. Life Underwriters, Greater Killeen Assn. Life Underwriters, Greater Killeen C. of C. (com. chmn. 1979-80), Assn. U.S. Army (v.p. Central Tex. Ft. Hood chpt. 1979-80). Club: Cen-Texans Kiwanis (dir. 1979-80). Home: 708 Illinois St Killeen TX 76541 Office: PO Box 996 807 N 8th St Killeen TX 76541

KLINE, ALAN HERBERT, assn. exec.; b. Boston, Oct. 14, 1941; s. George and Barbara Doris (Gorshel) K.; student Lawrence U., 1960-62; B.S., N.Y. U., 1965; student Seton Hall U. Law Sch., 1966; postgrad. Rutgers U., 1967-68; m. Harriet Sawyer Dennis, 1964; children—Rebecca Bartlett, David Townsend, Benjamin Gordon; m. 2d, Joyce Ann Ondrako Wilson, Apr. 15, 1978; stepchildren—Michael Scott Wilson, Dione Lee Wilson. Purchasing mgr. Coated Products, Inc., Middlesex, N.J., 1965, asst. to pres., 1966-70; gen. mgr. Com-Tech Inc., Middlesex, 1969, pres., 1970-71; pres. Kleentype, Inc., Keene Valley, N.Y., 1971-75; owner Kline & Sons, Keene Valley, 1971-75; mgr. purchases and staff tng. Am. Mgmt. Assn., Saranac Lake, N.Y., 1974—. Mem. Keene Valley Vol. Fire Dept., 1970-71; pres. Hunterdon Reclamation Center, 1968-69. Mem. Nat. Assn. Purchasing Mgmt., Am. Mgmt. Assn., Soc. Preservation and Encouragement Barbershop Quartet Singing in Am. Home: 34 River St Lake Placid NY 12946 Office: PO Box 319 Saranac Lake NY 12983

KLINE, EUGENE R., steel co. exec.; b. Lewistown, Pa., Apr. 26, 1931; s. Russell E. and C. Pauline (Knepp) K.; B.A., Gettysburg Coll., 1953; M.B.A., U. Pa., 1957; P.M.D., Harvard Bus. Sch., 1973; m. Anne R. Rogan, Aug. 20, 1955; children—Timothy Russell, Betsy Anne. With Bethlehem (Pa.) Steel Corp., 1957—, asst. to v.p. public affairs dept., 1970-77, asst. v.p., 1977-79, v.p. public affairs dept., 1979—. Trustee, St. Luke's Hosp., Bethlehem, 1977, Allentown Coll. of St. Francis de Sales, 1979, Gettysburg Coll., 1980. Served to lt., U.S. Army, 1953-55. Mem. Am. Iron and Steel Inst. (chmn. com. public relations, NAM (public relations council 1979—), Machinery and Allied Products Public Affairs Council, The Conf. Bd. (public affairs research council 1979—). Club: Saucon Valley Country. Office: Bethlehem Steel Corp Bethlehem PA 18016

KLINE, FRANK ROBERT, JR., computer exec.; b. Mahanoy City, Pa., Sept. 5, 1950; s. Frank Robert and Agnes (Hawkes) K.; B.S. in Commerce, Rider Coll., 1972; M.S. in Bus. Adminstrn., U. Mass., 1974; m. Shelly G. Lipkin, Aug. 27, 1972; Corp. market analyst Echlin Mfg. Co., 1974-75; market research analyst Internat. Data Corp., 1975-76, spl. research analyst, 1976, sr. research analyst, 1976-78, sr. mgr., 1979-80; v.p. research specializing in computer industry Drexel Burnham Lambert, Inc., N.Y.C., 1980—; litigation cons. Mem. Am. Mktg. Assn., Assn. Computing Machinery, Inc. Home: 180 Old Huckleberry Rd Wilton CT 06897 Office: 60 Broad St New York NY 10004

KLINE, L. PATTON, ins. co. exec.; b. Kansas City, Mo., Nov. 6, 1928; s. Leonard Charles and Ruth Carr (Patton) K.; grad. Middlesex Sch., 1946; B.S. in Applied Econs., Yale U., 1950; m. Jean Caruthers Lysle, Dec. 29, 1950; children—Leonard Patton Jr., Charles L., Laura F. With Mann-Kline, Inc., Kansas City, Mo., 1950-69, co. merged with Marsh & McLennan Inc., 1969; sr. v.p. Marsh & McLennan Inc., 1969-74, exec. v.p., 1974-75, pres., 1975-78, chmn. bd., chief exec. officer, 1978-81; dir. Marsh & McLennan Cos. Inc., 1975—, sr. v.p., 1977-81, pres., chief operating officer, 1981—; dir. Kline Bros. Land Devel. Co., Beech Aircraft Corp., First Nat. Charter Corp. Mem. nat. council Met. Opera Assn.; trustee The Coll. of Ins., Middlesex Sch.; bd. dirs. N.Y. Heart Assn. Served with USAF, 1951-53. Mem. SAR. Clubs: Kansas City Country, River (Kansas City); River, India House, Sky, Economic (N.Y.C.); Baltusrol Golf; Blind Brook, Watch Hill Yacht, Misquamicut. Home: 840 Park Ave New York NY 10021 Office: 1221 Ave of Americas New York NY 10020

KLINE, PAUL V., export co. exec.; b. Toronto, Ont., Can., June 12, 1923; s. William Arthur and Genevieve (Shelman) K.; student Pace Coll., 1948-49, Acad. Advanced Traffic, 1950-51; m. Mary Desposati, May 10, 1953; children—Donna J., John A. Asst. traffic mgr. U.S. Gypsum Co., N.Y.C., 1951-53, Freeport Sulphur Co., 1953-58; dir. transp. Sulphur Export Corp., 1958-66; asst. v.p., mgr. transp. Freeport Export Corp., 1966—; instr. Acad. Advanced Traffic. Mem. exec. com. Civic Assn. of the Bellmores, Inc.; mem. No. Bellmore Bd. Edn., 1965-73, pres., 1967-68; mem. bd. edn. Central High Sch. Dist. No. 3, 1966-72, pres., 1971-72; vestryman Ch. of the Redeemer, Merrick, L.I., 1963-66, clk. of vestry, 1964-66, treas., 1975. Served in U.S. Army, 1943-46. Recipient Am. Legion Citation of Appreciation award, 1974; Citizen of Year award Bellmore K.C., 1976. Mem. Am. Soc. Traffic and Transp. (bd. govs. N.Y. State chpt. 1972-75, v.p. 1974), Traffic Club (N.Y.), Assn. ICC Practitioners. Episcopalian. Office: 200 Park Ave New York NY 10166

KLINE, ROBERT PARKS, banker; b. Lincoln, Nebr., Nov. 17, 1923; s. Leonard Wilson and Daisy Irene (Parks) K.; B.S. in Bus. Adminstrn., U. Nebr., 1947; M.B.A., Harvard, 1949; postgrad. Stonier Grad. Sch. Banking, 1960; m. Marcia Virginia Seely, Apr. 25, 1953; children—Stephen Parks, Karen Sue. Credit analyst No. Trust Co., Chgo., 1949-53, loan officer comml. banking dept., 1953-60, v.p., 1960-67, v.p., div. head, 1967-69; exec. v.p. Ill. Nat. Bank & Trust Co., Rockford, 1969-71, pres., 1971-74, also dir.; chmn., pres., chief exec. officer, dir. Lake View Trust & Savs. Bank, Chgo., 1974-76; pres., chief exec. officer, trustee Peoples Savs. Bank, Providence, 1977—; pres., chief exec. officer, dir. Peoples Corp., 1977—, Peoples Trust Co., 1977—, 667 Corp., Providence, 1977—. Bd. dirs. R.I. Pub. Expenditure Council, Bus. Devel. Co. R.I.; corporator Kent County Meml. Hosp., 1979—; div. chmn. campaign Rockford United Fund, 1971, campaign chmn., 1972; mem. exec. bd. Blackhawk Area council Boy Scouts Am., 1970-74, treas., 1971-74, exec. bd. N.W. Suburban council, 1974-76; chmn. Rockford Econ. Expansion Task Force, 1971-73; pres. Rockford Area Econ. Devel. Commn., 1973-74; chmn. Leadership Greater Providence, 1980—; bd. dirs. Rock River Valley chpt. Jr. Achievement, 1970-73, Jr. Achievement of R.I., 1979—. Served to 2d lt., USAAF, 1943-45. Mem. Harvard Bus. Sch. Alumni Assn., Robert Morris Assos., Sigma Nu. Clubs: Hope, Turk's Head (Providence); Warwick (R.I.) Country. Home: 1255 Waterford Dr East Greenwich RI 02818 Office: 145 Westminster St Providence RI 02903

KLINE, STEPHEN JOSEPH, pvt. sch. ofcl.; b. Phila., Nov. 7, 1925; s. Emanuel and Hettie (Salkowe) K.; B.S., Pa. State U., 1950; postgrad. Wharton Sch., U. Pa., Temple U.; m. Arlene Rubin, June 24, 1956; children—Mitchell, Marsha. Self-employed in real estate, life and health ins., property ins., as stock broker, 1951-58; founder, co-owner Electronic Instrument Co., 1966-69; controller Penn Airborne Products Co., Southampton, Pa., 1966-70, Kuljian Corp., Phila., 1970-74; bus. mgr. Germantown Friends Sch., Phila., 1974—; dir., officer Polymetric Devices Co., 1st Central Corp., Standard Toch Industries. Mem. exec. bd. Eastern Montgomery County div. Jewish Community Relations Council. Served with USN, 1943-46. Lic. real estate salesman. Mem. Pa. Area Ind. Schs. Bus. Officers (past pres.), Bus. Officers Assn Delaware Valley (past pres.). Home: 1875 Bertram Rd Huntingdon Valley PA 19006 Office: Germantown Friends School 31 W Coulter St Philadelphia PA 19144

KLING, STEPHEN LEE, banker, ins. exec.; b. St. Louis, Dec. 22, 1928; s. Fred and Rose (Bothman) K.; B.S. in Bus. Adminstrn., Washington U., 1950; m. Rosalyn Marie Hauss, May 4, 1962; children—Stephen, Frank, Lee, Allan. Ins. broker Gen. Insurors Inc., St. Louis, 1952-58, v.p., 1958-65; chmn. bd. Ins. Cons. Inc. (now Reed Shaw Stenhouse Inc.) St. Louis, 1965-75; chmn. bd., pres., chief exec. officer Landmark Bancshares Corp., 1975-79, also dir.; vice chmn. bd. Reed Shaw Stenhouse Inc., ins. brokers, 1975-78; asst. spl. counselor for inflation, White House and dep. to ambassador Robert S. Strauss, 1979—; group v.p. Wylain Corp., Dallas, 1969-73, now dir.; chmn. bd., pres., chief exec. officer Landmark Bancshares Corp.; vice-chmn. bd. Shaw Stenhouse, Inc.; dir. E-Systems, Inc., N.W. Energy Co., Falcon Products Co., Amtrak. Finance chmn. Democratic Nat. Com., 1973-76, chmn. Dem. Ho. and Senate Council, 1977—; nat. treas. Carter-Mondale Com., 1980; bd. dirs. Jewish Hosp., St. Louis, Lindenwood Coll., St. Charles, Mo., YMCA, St. Louis Regional Commerce and Growth Assn., St. Louis Symphony Soc. Served to 1st lt. AUS, 1950-52. Mem. Young Pres.'s Orgn., Million Dollar Round Table. Clubs: St. Louis, Westwood Country (St. Louis); Standard (Chgo.); F St., Univ. (Washington). Home: 802 Blue Springs Rd Saint Louis MO 63131 Office: 10 S Brentwood Blvd Clayton MO 63105

KLINGENSMITH, RITCHEL GEORGE, computer scientist; b. Armstrong County, Pa., Jan. 4, 1942; s. Ritchel George and Cecile Ida (Bowser) K.; student Montgomery Jr. Coll., 1965, in bus. adminstrn. Ind. U., 1965-67, State U. N.Y., 1978—; m. Arlene Ruth Mauthe, Aug. 3, 1963; children—Debra Kristine, Kenneth Floyd. Staff asst. Virto Lab., Silver Spring, Md., 1962-65; sr. staff specialist Automation Industries, Silver Spring, 1967-76; computer analyst HEW, Washington, 1976—; computer analyst/cons. Leader Lutheran Youth Activities, Woodbine, Md., 1974-76; v.p. Mt. Airy (Md.) PTA, 1975-76, treas., 1976-78, v.p., 1978-79. Served with USN, 1959-62. Mem. Washington Mark IV Users Exchange, Airplane Owners and Pilots Assn. Republican. Lutheran. Club: Seneca. Home: 4828 Ridge Rd Mount Airy MD 21771 Office: HEW 7th and D St SW Washington DC 20202

KLINGENSTEIN, FREDERICK ADLER, investment co. exec.; b. N.Y.C., Apr. 13, 1931; s. Joseph and Esther (Adler) K.; grad. Deerfield Acad., 1949; B.A., Yale, 1953; postgrad. Harvard Bus. Sch., 1954; m. Sharon M. Lowe, June 12, 1953; children—Kathy Ann, Susan Jane, Amy Jo, Lucy Lowe. With Wertheim & Co., Inc., N.Y.C., 1956-60, partner, 1960-70, mng. partner, 1970-72, pres., chmn. bd., from 1972, now chmn.; chmn. Barber Oil Co. Chmn. YM-YWHA Mid-Westchester Scarsdale, N.Y. Past mem. N.Y. State Bd. Social Welfare; trustee Mt. Sinai Hosp. and Med. Center, N.Y.C., Am. Mus. Natural History, N.Y.C., St. Lawrence U., Fedn. Jewish Philanthropies, N.Y.C., Rye (N.Y.) Country Day Sch.; past trustee Jewish Communal Fund N.Y.C. Served to 1st lt., arty. AUS. Office: 200 Park Ave New York NY 10017

KLION, STANLEY RING, accounting co. exec.; b. N.Y.C., May 9, 1923; s. Samuel M. and Henrietta (Ring) K.; A.B., Rutgers U., 1942; m. Janet Tucker, Dec. 16, 1951; children—Catherine B., Emily J., Jenny T. With Peat, Marwick, Mitchell & Co., N.Y.C., 1955—, partner, Phila., 1958-66, Boston, 1968-69, N.Y.C., 1969-75, vice chmn. mgmt. cons. dept., 1975—, also dir.; exec. v.p., dir. IRC, Inc., Phila., 1967-68; dir. Nash Engring. Co., 1967-68; adj. prof. Grad. Sch. Bus., N.Y. U.; mem. U.S. Navy Audit Advisory Bd., 1972-75. Pres. Citizens Council City Planning, Phila., 1964-66. Served to maj. US. Army, 1942-46. C.P.A., N.Y., Pa., Mass., D.C. Mem. AAAS, Am. Inst. C.P.A.'s (chmn. MAS exec. com. 1975-78, mem. council 1979-80), Phi Beta Kappa. Republican. Jewish. Clubs: Economic of N.Y., Sunningdale Country, Board Room, Harmonie. Home: 25 Bailiwick Rd Greenwich CT 06830 Office: 345 Park Ave New York NY 10154

KLIPPER, IONEL JOHN, mfg. co. exec.; b. Czernowitz, Romania, Nov. 16, 1938; s. Nathan and Lucie (Bronstein) K.; B.S. in Elec. Engring., U. Vienna, 1962; M.S. in E.E., N.Y. U., 1966; M.B.A., 1969; m. Miriam Zeldner, Aug. 25, 1963; children—Nathaniel, Alexander. Mgr. import dept. Compagnie Generale d'Electricité, N.Y.C., 1962-68; v.p., group exec. electronics group Walter Kidde & Co., Huntington Valley, Pa., 1968—. Mem. IEEE, Am. Mgmt. Assn. Home: 878 Lowrenceville Rd Princeton NJ 08540 Office: 3063 Philmont Ave Huntingdon Valley PA 19006

KLITZBERG, RICHARD, investment co. exec.; b. Bklyn., Dec. 9, 1941; s. Samuel and Lillian R. (Gruber) K.; B.A., Western Md. Coll., 1963; J.D., U. Balt., 1966; m. Judith N. Callahan, Apr. 9, 1965; children—Robert, Dana, James. Admitted to Md. bar, 1967; account exec. Bache Halsey Stuart Shields, Inc., N.Y.C., 1969-74, regional coordinator investment mgmt., 1974-75, nat. mgr. investment mgmt. services, 1975—, asst. v.p., 1976, 2d v.p., 1977, v.p., 1977-80; pres. First Investors Asset Mgmt. Co., N.Y.C., 1980—. Mem. Temple Neve Shalom, 1946—; mem. adv. bd. Metuchen (N.J.) Pool Commn.; pres. MMP Parents' Assn. Served to capt. U.S. Army, 1967-69. Mem. Am., Md. bar assns., Common Cause, Sierra Club, Am. Pension Conf., Assn. Pvt. Pension and Welfare Plans, Internat. Found. Employee Benefit Plans. Clubs: Woodbridge Racquet, Inman Racquet. Home: 9 Whitman Ave Metuchen NJ 08840 Office: 120 Wall St New York NY 10005

KLOCKER, THOMAS DORSEY, fin. co. exec.; b. Davas, Okla., Oct. 16, 1941; s. Sylvester J. and Vina (Smith) K.; A.A., Pasadena City Coll., 1961; B.S., UCLA, 1963; M.B.A., Pacific Western U., 1977, Ph.D., 1979; children—Thomas, Timothy, Todd. Vice pres. Life of Va., Los Angeles, 1961-69; sr. v.p. Fin. Industries Corp., Los Angeles, 1969-75; chmn., pres. Western Fin. Specialist Corp., Los Angeles, 1975—; dir. Calif. Pacific Bank, 1977. Mem. Am. Soc. Pension Actuaries, Kappa Phi Delta (pres. 1960-63). Originator Futur-ity

Program, 1977. Home: 6086 Gabbert Rd Moor Park CA 93021 Office: 20969 Ventura Blvd Suite 18 Woodland Hills CA 91364

KLOETSTRA, CHARLES TSJALLING, customs broker; b. Noord Bergum, Netherlands, Nov. 24, 1942; immigrated to Can., 1950, naturalized, 1963; s. Dirk and Jacoba (Feenstra) K.; customs broker lic. London Coll. Bible and Missions, 1967; m. Barbara Marie Hewer, Jan. 27, 1968; children—David Thomas, Darryl Jeffery. Sales clk. Rossman's Clothing, Ft. Erie, Ont., 1962-63; customs broker clk. J. MacD Thomson Ltd., Ft. Erie and Toronto, Ont., 1962-64; clk. to sales rep. Border Brokers, Ltd., Niagara Falls, Sarnia, Toronto, London, Ont., 1964-74; gen. mgr., pres. Link Customs Services, Ltd., London, 1975—; guest lectr. U. Western London, 1976-78. Mem. Dominion Chartered Customs House Brokers Assn. (dir. 1978—), Purchasing Mgmt. Assn. Baptist. Club: London Dist. Transp. Home: 481 Oak Park Dr London ON N6H 3N6 Canada Office: PO Box 580 Lambeth ON N0L 1S0 Canada

KLOPFENSTEIN, PEYTON, real estate exec.; b. Elk City, Okla., Oct. 14, 1928; s. Ivan Otis and Jewell Mina (King) K.; student Oklahoma City U., 1948-49, Am. U., Washington, 1962-63; m. Vanda Lee Sherbourne, July 22, 1945; children—Linda Jane, Terrie Lynne, Frank Allen. Partner, Peyton-Amana Co., Oklahoma City, 1956-57; regional sales mgr. Amana Refrigeration, Inc., Amana, Iowa, 1957-60; mgr. comml. sales Routh Robbins Real Estate Corp., Alexandria, Va., 1961-63; prin. Peyton Klopfenstein, Realtor (merged into Real Estate Assos. Va., Inc., 1970), McLean, 1963-69, chmn. bd., 1971-76; chmn. Va. Real Estate Commn., 1975—; trustee Profl. Real Estate Trust, Va.; instr. Realtors Inst., Sch. Gen. Studies, Realtors Inst., U. Va., U. Del. Mem. Planning Commn. City of Falls Church (Va.), 1972-75; pres. George Mason U. Found., 1977-78. Office: 5203 Leesburg Pike Suite 500 Bailey's Crossroads VA 22041

KLOPMAN, WILLIAM ALLEN, mfg. corp. exec.; b. 1921; grad. Williams Coll., 1943; married. With Burlington Industries, Inc., 1946—, pres. Klopman Mills div., 1963-71, group v.p. parent co., Greensboro, N.C., 1971-72, exec. v.p., 1972-74, pres., mem. exec. fin. com. and mgmt. policy com., 1974-76, pres., 1976-78, chmn. bd., chief exec. officer, 1976—, also dir. Served with USNR, 1943-45. Office: Burlington Industries Inc 3300 W Friendly Ave Greensboro NC 27420

KLOPPENBORG, GERALD JOHN, data processing co. exec.; b. State Center, Iowa, Feb. 8, 1940; s. John Harlan and Clara (Celestina) K.; student Iowa State U., 1958. Draftsman, Fisher Governor Co., Marshalltown, Iowa, 1959-63, programmer, 1963-67; mgr. systems and programming Lennox Industries, Inc., Marshalltown, 1967-73; mgr. system software J.I. Case Co., Racine, Wis., 1973-74; sr. asso. PRC Pub. Mgmt. Services, Inc., San Francisco, 1974; sr. systems analyst, mgr. data processing Lockwood Corp., Gering, Nebr., 1974—; cons. in field. Democrat. Roman Catholic. Club: Eagles. Home: PO Box 222 Gering NE 69341 Office: PO Box 160 Gering NE 69341

KLOS, ALAN RICHARD, heating and air conditioning mfg. co. exec.; b. Montclair, N.J., Nov. 10, 1940; s. Gustave John and Lucille Emily (Kloss) K.; B.S. in Engring., U.S. Naval Acad., 1962; postgrad. in mech. engring. U. Wichita, 1963-64; postgrad. in mktg. and fin. U. Wis., La Crosse, 1966-69; m. Eleanor Burrell Townsend Hills, June 7, 1962; children—Eric, Wendra, Lisa, David. Mgr. mil./govt. projects team The Trane Co., 1966-69; product mgr., mgt. product devel. comml. market sales mgr. Environ. Products div. ITT, Phila., 1969-72; regional mgr., field sales mgr. Climate Control div. Singer Co., Carteret, N.J., 1972-76; v.p. sales and mktg. Weil-McLain div. Wylain, Inc., Michigan City, Ind., 1976—. Fund raising chmn. Boy Scouts Am., Cherry Hill, N.J.; dir. acolytes Christ Ch., Episcopal, LaCrosse. Served with USAF, 1962-66. Mem. Am. Mgmt. Assn., Gas Appliance Mfg. Assn., Hydronics Inst., Naval Inst. Republican. Clubs: Long Beach Country, Masons, Shriners. Office: Weil-McLain A Marley Co Blaine St Michigan City IN 46360

KLOSSON, KRAIG, banker; b. Ft. Sill, Okla., Oct. 6, 1939; s. Kenneth Alan and Alis (Bowman) K.; B.A. with honors, Tulane U., 1961; M.A., U. Va., 1962; m. Michele Jean Ference, Oct. 14, 1972; children—Michael B., Kenneth A., Richard D., James S. From trainee to v.p. 1st Nat. City Bank (now Citibank), N.Y.C. and various fgn. locations, 1962-73; v.p. charge Western Hemisphere asset based financing Chem. Bank, 1973-76; exec. v.p., chief exec. for N. Am., London & Continental Bankers Ltd., N.Y.C., 1976-79; exec. v.p., chief operating officer, dir. U.S. Concord, Inc., N.Y.C., 1979—. Served with U.S. Army, 1962-63. Proctor & Gamble scholar, 1957-61; Woodrow Wilson fellow, 1961-62; NDEA fellow, 1961-62. Mem. Overseas Bankers Assn., Fgn. Policy Assn., Bankers Assn. Fgn. Trade, Am. Assn. Equipment Lessors, Smithsonian Assos., Phi Beta Kappa, Pi Sigma Alpha, Phi Eta Sigma. Clubs: Stanwich, Singapore Am. (past sec.), Manila Polo, Royal Selangor Golf, La Confrerie Saint-Etienne d'Alsace. Home: 52 Ridgeview Ave Greenwich CT 06830 Office: 1890 Palmer Ave Larchmont NY 10538

KLOTHEY, M(ICHAEL) E(DWARD), electronic mfg. co. exec.; b. Detroit, Feb. 14, 1946; s. Jackson Seymour and Marianne Patrica (Ambriose) K.; B.B.A., Columbia U., 1968; M.B.A., U. Mich., 1971. Asst. comptroller Dow Chem. Co., Midland, Mich., 1971-75; v.p. fin. Edcon Industries, Midland, 1975—; asso. prof. bus. adminstrn. Saginaw Valley State Coll., 1974—; dir. 1st Midland Bank & Trust Co. Pres., Central Mich. Arts Council, 1972—. Guggenheim fellow, 1969-70; A.P. Sloan fellow, 1970-71. Mem. Am. Mgmt. Assn., Am. Inst. Fin. Republican. Methodist. Clubs: Midland City, Masons, Kiwanis. Author: Capital and The Small Corporation, 1975. Home: 31 Drawer Midland MI 48640 Office: PO Box 82 Midland MI 48640

KLOTSCHE, CHARLES MARTIN, real estate devel. co. exec.; b. Milw., Jan. 30, 1941; s. J.M. and Roberta; B.A. in Econs., Babson Coll., 1962; M.B.A. in Fin., U. Wis.-Milw., 1968; m. Christine, Feb. 13, 1972; children—Lyna, Kelly. Pres., Sante Fe Equities, Inc., 1978—. Bd. dirs. N.Mex. Spl. Olympics for Mentally Retarded. Served with USMC, 1964-67. Mem. U.S. Mortgage Brokers Assn., Nat. Assn. Realtors, Urban Land Inst., N.Mex. Gen. Contractors Assn. Republican. Lutheran. Author: The Encumbered, Perceptive and the Intrepid, 1978; Real Estate Investing: A Practical Guide to Wealth Building Secrets, 1980. Home: 854 Camino Ranchitos Santa Fe NM 87501 Office: 809 St Michaels Dr Santa Fe NM 87501

KLOTT, DAVID LEE, lawyer; b. Vicksburg, Miss., Dec. 10, 1941; s. Isadore and Dorothy (Lipson) K.; B.S.B.A. summa cum laude, Northwestern U., 1963; J.D. cum laude, Harvard U., 1966; m. Maren J. Randrup, May 25, 1975. Admitted to Calif. bar, 1966, U.S. Ct. of Claims bar, 1968, U.S. Supreme Ct. bar, 1971, U.S. Tax Ct. bar, 1973; partner firm Pillsbury, Madison & Sutro, San Francisco, 1966—; mem. tax adv. group to subchpt. C, J and K, Am. Law Inst.; tchr. Calif. Continuing Edn. of Bar, Practising Law Inst., Hastings Law Sch.; commentator new Calif. non-profit corp. law. Served with USAR, 1967. Mem. Am., Calif., San Francisco (exec. com. tax sect.) bar assns., Beta Gamma Sigma, Beta Alpha Psi (pres. local chpt.). Clubs: Stock Exchange, Olympic, San Francisco Harvard, Commonwealth of San Francisco, Northwestern U. of San Francisco. Office: 225 Bush St San Francisco CA 94104

KLOTZ, HERBERT WERNER, corp. exec.; b. Berlin, Germany, Feb. 24, 1917; s. Herbert and Gertrud (Koppel) Klotz; B.A., Zuoz (Switzerland) Coll., 1935; student U. Zurich (Switzerland), 1935-36; m. Patricia Radford Hopkins, Apr. 3, 1954; children—Radford Werner, Leslie Ritchie, James Taylor. Came to U.S., 1937, naturalized, 1944. With Smith, Barney & Co., and predecessor, N.Y.C., 1937-42, W.E. Hutton & Co., N.Y.C., 1946-48; engaged in mgmt. personal investments, 1949-52; with Winslow, Douglas & McEvoy, N.Y.C., 1953-54; pres., treas. Tex. Securities Corp., N.Y.C., 1954-57, Southwest Adv. Services, Inc., N.Y.C., 1954-57; with Alex Brown & Sons, Washington, 1957-60; spl. asst. to sec. Dept. Commerce, 1961, dep. to sec., 1961-62, asst. sec. for adminstrn., 1962-65; exec. v.p. Am. Growth Investment Co., 1966-67; dir. Govt. Systems Center, Kurt Salmon Assos., Inc., mgmt. cons., 1968-69; pres., chmn. bd. Quest Research Corp., McLean, Va., 1970—; chmn. bd. Dynamic Engring. Inc., Newport News, Va., 1976—; chmn. bd. DHR, Inc., Washington, 1978—; dir. Washington Internat. Horse Show, Inc., 1970—. Asso. dir. Nat. Com Bus. and Profl. Men and Women for Kennedy-Johnson, 1960. Served to 1st lt. AUS, 1942-45; maj. Res., ret. Democrat. Episcopalian. Clubs: 1925 F Street, Metropolitan, Federal City (Washington); Fauquier, Warrenton (Va.) Hunt. Home: 1401 Langley Pl McLean VA 22101 Office: 6858 Old Dominion Dr McLean VA 22101

KLOTZ, PAUL NORMAN, business exec.; b. N.Y.C., June 15, 1936; s. Joseph and Sylvia (Gidden) K.; B.A., Williams Coll., 1958; LL.B., Yale U., 1961; m. Nancy Leah Slosberg, Feb. 6, 1961; children—Julie Lisbeth, Meredyth Anne, Abbey Susan, Hilary Beth. Vice pres., dir. Oppenheimer Industries, Inc., Kansas City, Mo., 1961-62; admitted to N.Y. bar, 1962, R.I. bar, 1964; partner firm Greene & Klotz, N.Y.C., 1968-71; pres., dir. Butler Bros. Oil Co., Inc., Westerly, R.I., 1963—, Downes-Patterson Corp., Westerly, 1963—; officer, dir. United Builders Supply Co., Westerly, 1963—, Am. Propane Co., Waterford, Conn., 1965—, Castle Realty Co., Westerly, 1963—; treas., dir. Pegasus Petroleum Corp., Oklahoma City; partner Pawaget Devel. Co., Westerly, 1973—. Mem. Westerly Citizens Adv. Com., 1968-69, Westerly Republican Town Com., 1967-68; vice chmn. Westerly Waterways Study Commn., 1974-75; mem. advisory com. SENE study New Eng. River Basins Commn., 1975; incorporator, bd. dirs. Westerly Hosp.; incorporator Westerly Public Library. Mem. R.I., Washington County bar assns., Assn. Bar City N.Y. Clubs: Watch Hill Yacht, Yale of N.Y., Williams of N.Y., Univ. (Providence). Home: Misquamicut Hills Westerly RI 02891 Office: 30 Oak St Westerly RI 02891

KLOTZ, WILLIAM HENRY, JR., office products mfg. co. exec.; b. Chgo., Dec. 18, 1919; s. William Henry and Lillian Ann (Attwood) K.; B.S. in Commerce, Northwestern U., 1952; m. Dorothy Evelyn Oberto, June 6, 1953; children—William Henry III, Evelyn Ann, Laura Jean. Controller, Cook Electric Co., 1948-52; controller Cummins-Aliison Corp., Chgo., 1952-55, from salesman to sales tng. mgr., 1956-59; from sales mgr. to v.p. mktg., 1959-75, exec. v.p., gen. mgr., 1976-78, pres. Office Products div., 1979—, also dir.; dir. Cummins-Am. Corp. Served with inf. U.S. Army, 1941-45. Mem. Am. Mgmt. Assn. Republican. Roman Catholic. Club: Elks. Home: 515 Providence Rd Palatine IL 60067 Office: 4740 N Ravenswood Ave Chicago IL 60640

KLOTZSCH, HELMUT R., health care industry exec.; b. Dresden, Germany, Feb. 15, 1929; s. Rudolf Louis and Olga Milda (Brueckner) K.; came to U.S., 1964; B.S. in Chem. Engring., Chemistry Sch. Berlin, 1949; postgrad. U. Berlin, 1950-52; grad. Exec. Mgmt. Program, N.Y. U., 1970; m. Sigrid G. Zeye, Apr. 10, 1952; children—Isabel, Helmut Werner. Teaching asst. dept. agr. U. Berlin, 1950-52; research biochemist Max Planck Inst. for Cell Physiology, Berlin, 1952-59; dept. head biochem. div. Boehringer Mannheim, Tutzing, Germany, 1959-64, corporate v.p., N.Y.C., 1965-75; pres. Biomed. Data Co., N.Y.C., 1976—; guest lectr., cons. Nat. Health Inst. Served with German Army, 1945. Registered nuclear chemist, Berlin, AEC. Mem. Am. Chem. Soc., Am. Assn. Clin. Chemistry, Sales Execs. Club N.Y., N.Y. Acad. Sci., Biomed. Mktg. Assn., Nat. Com. Clin. Lab. Standards, Health Industry Mfg. Assn. Contbr. chpts. to books, articles to profl. jours.; developer assessment of mood and motivation for field sales personnel; patentee in field. Home: 10 Cayuga Ln Irvington NY 10533 Office: 60 E 42d St New York NY 10017

KLUCINA, JOHN LOUIS, editor; b. New Orleans, Nov. 14, 1935; s. John J. and Emma Betty (Manzie) K.; student Bradley U., Peoria, Ill., 1951-52, So. Ill. U., Carbondale, 1952-53, Boston U., 1955, LaSalle Inst., Chgo., 1970, Cornell U., 1975-76, Wharton Sch., U. Pa., 1976, 77, 80; m. Marie Elizabeth Schrider, Oct. 24, 1970; children—John Jaie, Mathew Michael, MariBeth. Account exec. Gottschaldt & Assos. Advt., Miami, Fla., 1960-61, Keyes, Maddon & Jones, Chgo., 1961-63; with Martin E. Janis & Co., Chgo., 1963; owner, gen. mgr. Klucina Assos., Toledo, 1963-65; account exec., account supr. Talifarro Assos., Tampa, Fla., 1965-66; sports editor Perry Newspapers, Inc., West Palm Beach, Fla., 1966-68; asst. city editor Knickerbocker News, Capital Newspaper Group div. Hearst Corp., Albany, N.Y., 1970-72, state editor, 1972-73, city editor, 1973-74, regional editor, 1974-75, bus./econs./fin./automotive editor, 1975—. Active United Fund; pres. parish council St. Helen's Parish, Niskayuna, N.Y.; trustee Capital Newspapers Employee Pension Fund. Served with AC, USN, 1955-59. Mem. Pub. Relations Soc. Am., Indsl. Relations Research Assn., Newspaper Guild (past pres., mem. exec. bd., council v.p., chief negiotiator, grievance chmn.), Sigma Delta Chi (chpt. pres., mem. exec. bd., dep. nat. regional dir.). Roman Catholic. Club: K.C. Home: 439 Consaul Rd Schenectady NY 12304 Office: Box 15-627 Albany NY 12212

KLUCKMAN, REVONE W., television and radio co. exec.; b. 1929; B.S., U. S.D., 1952; married. Partner, Arthur Andersen & Co., 1952-67; controller Zenith Radio Corp., Glenview, Ill., 1967-68, v.p., controller, 1968-71, sr. v.p. mfg. and material, 1971-77, pres., chief operating officer, 1977—, also dir. Office: Zenith Radio Corp 1000 N Milwaukee Ave Glenview IL 60025*

KLUG, RICHARD PAUL, banker; b. Milw., Sept. 13, 1934; s. Aaron Emil and Theodora Maria (Wendt) K.; B.A., Elmhurst Coll., 1956; grad. U. Wis. Grad. Sch. Banking, 1966; grad. Comml. Lending Sch., U. Okla., 1971; m. Arleen Joann Wittig, Apr. 23, 1958; children—Jeffrey Richard, Jennifer Jo Anne. Mgr. Household Finance Corp., Milw., 1956-60; exec. v.p., sec. to bd., chief operating officer Farmers & Mchts. Bank, Menomonee Falls, Wis., 1960—, dir., 1974—; treas., dir. Ranch, Inc. dir. Leasenu Inc. Gen. chmn. Menomonee Falls Diamond Jubilee, 1967; area chmn. United Fund, 1968-71; past chmn. Menomonee Falls Youth Center, 1963-65. Chmn. Menomonee Falls Police and Fire Commn., 1962—. Chmn. bd. mgrs. Tri-County YMCA, 1970-73, now bd. dirs.; mem. corp. bd. Met. Milw. YMCA, 1970—; bd. dirs. Waukesha County Mental Health Assn., 1967-68. Served with AUS, 1951-53. Named Man of Year, Menomonee Falls C. of C., 1970. Mem. Wis. Installment Bankers Assn. (pres. 1972), Wis. Bankers Assn. (mem. coms., chmn. Forms and Procedures com.). Mem. United Ch. Christ. Clubs: North Hills Country, Masons, Rotary. Home: N87 W15796 Kenwood Blvd Menomonee Falls WI 53051 Office: N88 W16554 Main St Menomonee Falls WI 53051

KLUTTZ, ROBERT HAIRSTON, employee benefits and fin. cons.; b. Winston-Salem, N.C., Aug. 3, 1948; s. William Clarence and Sara (Whittle) L.; B.A., U. N.C., 1970; M.B.A. in Fin., Emory U., 1975; m. Bess Acra Adams, May 1, 1971; children—Robert Hairston, Sara Whittle. Investment officer First Union Nat. Bank, Charlotte, N.C., 1970-73; v.p. Booke and Co., Winston-Salem, 1975—. Bd. dirs. Voluntary Action Center, 1979—. Democrat. Episcopalian. Home: 622 Oaklawn Ave Winston-Salem NC 27104 Office: 610 Coliseum Winston-Salem NC 27102

KLUTZNICK, THOMAS JOSEPH, real estate co. exec.; b. Omaha, Apr. 19, 1939; s. Philip Morris and Ethel K.; B.A., Oberlin Coll., 1961; m. Ellen Diengott, Aug. 3, 1960; children—Karen, John, Daniel, Katherine. With Draper & Kramer, 1961-63, Klutznick Enterprises/KLC Ventures, 1963-68; exec. v.p. Urban Investment & Devel. Co., Chgo., 1968-72, pres., chief exec. officer, 1972-78, chmn. bd., chief exec. officer, 1978—; dir. Datapoint Corp. Bd. dirs. Jewish Fedn. Met. Chgo.; mem. Chgo. exec. com. Anti-Defamation League; bd. mgrs. YMCA Met. Chgo.; trustee Oberlin Coll., Nat. Jewish Hosp., Denver, Rush-Presbyn.-St. Luke's Med. Center, Chgo.; bd. overseers Grad. Sch. Fine Arts, U. Pa., Phila.; mem. U. Chgo. Citizens Bd. Mem. Chgo. Assn. Commerce and Industry (officer), Econ. Club Chgo., Execs., Club Chgo., Nat. Realty Com., Internat. Council Shopping Centers, Met. Housing and Planning Council, Urban Land Inst., Northwestern U. Assos., Lambda Alpha. Clubs: Carlton, Met., Whitehall, Standard. Office: 845 N Michigan Ave Chicago IL 60611

KNAEBEL, JOHN BALLANTINE, mining cons.; b. Denver, Jan. 1, 1906; s. Ernest and Cornelia (Park) K.; student Cornell U., 1924-28, Northwestern U., summer 1928; B.S. in Engring., Stanford, 1929, E.M., 1930; m. Joy James, June 23, 1931 (div. May 1956); children—Jeffrey James, Stephen Park; m. 2d, Nelle M. McNulty, Mar. 14, 1958; 1 stepson, Terrence Patrick McNulty. Mining engr. Cananea Consol. Copper Co., Mexico, 1929; engr. U.S. Bur. Mines, 1931-33; supt., mgr. East Mindanao Mining Co., Tinabingan, Mindanao, P.I., 1934-37; cons. geologist, engr., Western U.S., Mex., Can., Latin Am., 1937-39; mng. dir. Amparo Mining Co., Ltd., Vancouver, B.C., Can., 1939-40; successively supt., asst. mgr., asst. to v.p., asst. mgr. Western Mines, U.S. Smelting, Refining & Mining Co., N.M., Utah, Western U.S., 1940-46; engr. in charge Anaconda Brit. Guiana Mines, Ltd., Georgetown, also mng. dir. Mineracao Gurupi, S.A., Belem, Brazil (Anacona Copper Mining Co. subsidiaries), 1946-50, mgr. N.M. operations Anaconda Co., Grants, 1951-56, asst. to v.p. in charge mining operations, N.Y.C., 1956-58, cons., 1958, gen. mgr. new mines, 1962-71, dir., v.p. subsidiary cos., Toronto, Ont., Can. and Vancouver, 1958-71, v.p. Anaconda Co., 1964-71, cons., 1971-72; v.p. Western Expln. div. Anaconda Am. Brass Ltd., 1963-71, pres., mng. dir. Anaconda Iron Ore Ltd., Port Arthur, Ont., 1958-71; v.p. western div. Anaconda Co., Ltd., Vancouver, 1962-71; dir. Chaleur Bay Mines, Ltd., Can., 1958-71; pvt. practice as cons. to mining cos. and financial instns., 1971—. Bd. dirs. N.M. chpt. Arthritis and Rheumatism Found., 1955-56. Named Mining Man of Year, Mining World Mag., 1957; recipient William Lawrence Saunders gold medal for distinguished achievement in mining Am. Inst. Mining, Metall. and Petroleum Engrs., 1959; Daniel C. Jackling award Soc. Mining Engrs., 1972; named Distinguished mem. AIME, 1975. Mem. Ariz. Acad. Pub. Affairs, Am. Mining Congress, Geol. and Mining Soc., Am. Inst. Mining, Metall. and Petroleum Engrs., Soc. Econ. Geologists,, Canadian Inst. Mining and Metallurgy, Assn. Profl. Engrs. Ont., Assn. Profl. Engrs. B.C., Ariz. Mining Assn. (dir. 1965-69), N.W. Mining Assn., Tucson C. of C. (dir. 1966-69), Aircraft Owners and Pilots Assn., Am. Forestry Assn., Nat. Rifle Assn., Quiet Birdmen, Sigma Xi, Sigma Gamma Epsilon. Author articles, tech. papers on mining. Home and Office: PO Box L Winston OR 97496

KNAPKE, EDWARD BERNARD, savs. and loan assn. exec.; b. Coldwater, Ohio, May 27, 1938; s. Edward H. and Helen (Dues) K.; A.S., Miami-Jacobs Coll., 1958; B.A., U. Cin., 1966; m. Toni Ann Clark, May 9, 1964; children—Betsy, Josef. Examiner, Ohio Div. Bldg. and Loan, Columbus, 1960-66; asst. sec. Citizens Savs. & Loan, Tiffin, Ohio, 1966-67; v.p. Hancock Savs. & Loan, Findlay, Ohio, 1967-71; pres. Central Savs. Assn., Lima, Ohio, 1972—; dir. Port Clinton Savs. & Loan, Athens County Savs. & Loan, G. O. Service Corp., C.S.A. Service Corp. Trustee Lima Downtown Bus. Assn., Lima Area Devel. Corp.; trustee, mem. exec. com. Community Urban Redevel. Com. of Lima and Allen County; mem. Lima Mayor's Commn. on Fair Housing. Served with AUS. Mem. Ohio Savs. and Loan League (mem. legis. com., trustee), U.S. League Savs. Assn. (investment and mortgage lending com.), Savs. and Loan Polit. Action Com., Young Pres.'s Orgn. Roman Catholic. Clubs: Shawnee Country, Elks. Office: 215 W Market St Lima OH 45802

KNAPP, GEORGE FRANCIS, communications co. exec.; b. N.Y.C., Sept. 6, 1931; s. George F. and Annette R. (McCabe) K.; B.E.E., Manhattan Coll., 1953; M.B.A., N.Y. U., 1964; grad. Advanced Mgmt. Program, Harvard, 1974; m. Ann Eileen Stanley, Jan. 9, 1954; children—Eileen, Kathleen, George, Margaret, Richard. Engr., Westinghouse Elec. Corp., Pitts., 1953; div. engr. N.Y. Telephone Co., 1956-58, various mgmt. positions, 1961-65; engr. Bell Telephone Labs., 1959-60; dir. ops. Chilean Telephone Co., Santaiago, 1966-68; pres. P.R. Telephone Co., San Juan, 1969-74; pres. ITT Worldcom Inc., N.Y.C., 1975—, ITT Am. Cable & Radio Corp., N.Y.C., 1975—; v.p. ITT Corp., 1976—; chmn. bd. and/or pres., dir. ITT telecommunications subs. Bd. dirs. Greater N.Y. council Boy Scouts Am. Served with AUS, 1954-56. Registered profl. engr., N.Y. Mem. Armed Forces Communications and Electronics Assn., IEEE. Republican. Roman Cath. Clubs: Metropolitan (N.Y.C.): Hackensack (N.J.) Golf. Office: ITT 67 Broad St New York NY 10004*

KNAPP, PAUL RAYMOND, ins. co. exec.; b. Long Beach, Calif., Sept. 8, 1945; s. Franklin L. and Ella Jo (Andrews) K.; B.S., Calif. State U., 1970; M.B.A., U. Chgo., 1977; m. Shirley Kay Wheeler, July 14, 1967; children—Michele, Erica, Matthew. Fire protection engr. Factory Ins. Assn., San Francisco, 1967-69; with Kemper Group, 1969-77; asst. to pres. Kemper Fin. Services, Inc., Chgo., 1977-79, 1st v.p., treas., chief fin. and adminstrn. officer, 1979—; exec. v.p. Kemper Investors Life Ins. Co., Chgo., 1978—. Mem. Soc. Chartered Property and Casualty Underwriters, Planning Execs. Inst., Beta Gamma Sigma. Republican. Clubs: Monroe, Itasca Country. Office: 120 S LaSalle St Chicago IL 60603

KNAPP, WILLIAM VESTRUS, banker; b. Bloomington, Ind., Mar. 6, 1935; s. William R. and Mildred P. (Day) K.; m. Elizabeth A. Hyde, Feb. 22, 1957; children—Timothy W., Thomas H., Tricia S. Asst. cashier First Nat. Bank, Bloomington, 1955-69; pres., dir. First State Bank, Saginaw, Mich., 1969—. Trustee, Saginaw Vol. Action Center. Mem. Ind. (v.p., dir. Region 6, 1967-69), Mich. (chmn. Group V) bankers assns., Bank Adminstrn. Inst. (pres. S. Central Ind. Conf. 1966). Elk. Clubs: Germania of Saginaw, Saginaw Country (bd. govs.), Saginaw Optimist (treas.). Home: 1190 River Forest Dr Saginaw MI 48603 Office: 101 S Washington St Saginaw MI 48607

KNAPPEN, THEODORE COMPTON, bus. co. exec.; b. N.Y.C., Jan. 19, 1944; s. Theodore Temple and Betty (Compton) K.; B.A., U. Va., 1965, LL.B., 1968; m. Maribel Chandeck, Jan. 15, 1972; children—Carmen, Lisa. Admitted to Va. bar, 1969, U.S. Supreme Ct. bar, 1972; trial atty. Office of Gen. Counsel, ICC, 1971-75; asso. gen.

counsel, 1975-76; v.p., gen. counsel Trailways, Inc., Dallas, 1976-77, div. sr. v.p., Washington, 1977-79, sr. v.p., 1979—; dir. 8 Trailways, Inc., Tex., N.Mex. and Okla. Coach Lines, KG Lines. Served to lt. U.S. Navy, 1968-71. Mem. Am. Bus. Assn. (dir., exec. com.), Nat. Trailways Bus System (dir., exec. com.), Nat. Bus. Traffic Assn. (dir.), Motor Carrier Lawyers Assn., Phi Delta Theta, Phi Alpha Delta. Office: Trailways Inc 1200 Eye St NW Washington DC 20005

KNAUB, RICHARD ALLEN, mfg. co. exec.; b. Scottsbluff, Nebr., Aug. 27, 1936; s. Jake N. and Freida Knaub; B.A., UCLA, 1958; m. Suzzanne M. Maier, Feb. 22, 1958; 1 son, Steven Richard. Mfg. engring. mgr. Bunker Ramo Corp., Canoga Park, Calif., 1962-66; ops. mgr. TRW Semicondrs. Co., Lawndale, Calif., 1967-75; pres. Roy J. Maier Products Corp., Sun Valley, Calif., 1975—, chmn. bd., 1976—; chmn. bd. La Voz Corp., North Hollywood, Calif., 1976—. Mem. Town Hall, Los Angeles, 1980—; bd. dirs. Am. Music Conf. Served with USN, 1958-60. Mem. UCLA Alumni Assn. Republican. Club: Bruin Beach.

KNEDLIK, WILL, fin. exec.; b. Snoqualmie, Wash., May 20, 1946; s. Virgil M. and Anna M. (Saville) K.; B.A., U. Wash., 1967, Ph.D., 1977; J.D., Harvard U., 1972; m. Janet Leslie Blumberg, Mar. 15, 1967. Exec. dir. Am. Alpine Club, N.Y.C., 1973; partner law firm Knedlik & Goddard, Kirkland, Wash., 1974-78; admitted to Wash. bar, 1974; pres. Marathon/Knedlik Investment Group, Kirkland, 1978—; adj. prof. Lincoln Inst. Land Policy, Cambridge, Mass., 1979—. Mem. Wash. State Ho. of Reps., 1977-79. Charles Bullard postdoctoral forest research fellow Harvard U., 1978-79. Mem. Wash. Bar Assn., Am. Soc. Assn. Execs., Phi Beta Kappa. Club: Northwest. Office: 26 Trowbridge St Cambridge MA 02138

KNEECE, JAMES FRANK, JR., mfg. co. exec.; b. Charleston, S.C., May 26, 1927; s. James Frank and Mary Alma (Thompson) K.; B.S., U.S. Naval Acad., 1951; m. Alice Susan Crafts, Sept. 16, 1961; children—Frank III, Mark, Richard. With Westinghouse Electric Corp., Pitts., 1955-63, dir. planning and budget, lamp div., 1959-63; with Olin Corp., 1963—, corp. v.p., 1972—, gen. mgr. indsl. products div., 1972-74, Winchester group v.p., 1974—. Bd. dirs. YMCA, Wilton, Conn., 1971—. Served with USN, 1951-55. Mem. U.S. Naval Acad. Alumni Assn. Congregationalist. Club: Quinnipiack (New Haven). Home: 33 Old Wagon Rd Wilton CT 06897 Office: 275 Winchester St New Haven CT 06504

KNEELAND, GEORGE J., bus. exec.; b. N.Y.C., 1916; married. With St. Regis Paper Corp., N.Y.C., 1939—, asst. v.p., 1957-63, v.p., 1963-69, exec. v.p. adminstrn., 1969-71, vice chmn. bd. fin. and adminstrn., 1971-72, chmn. bd., chief exec. officer, 1972—, chmn. exec. com., 1975-79, also dir.; mem. exec. com., dir. Aluminum Press Vessel Holdings Ltd.; dir. Orange & Rockland Utilities Inc., Employers Ins. of Wausau, Hackensack Water Co. Office: St Regis Paper Co 150 E 42d St New York NY 10017

KNEEN, RUSSELL PACKARD, accountant; b. Fall River, Mass., July 30, 1923; s. Russell Packard and Lucy Sanford (Smith) K.; B.S., Boston U., 1949; m. Joyce Elaine Knapper, Aug. 4, 1951; children—John, James, Andrew, Robert. Mem. profl. staff Touche Ross & Co., Boston and Detroit, 1949-52; pvt. practice pub. accounting, Kalamazoo, 1952-55; partner Lawrence Scudder & Co., Kalamazoo, 1955-68, Alexander Grant & Co., Kalamazoo, 1968—; extension service instr. Western Mich. U., 1954-56; spl. lectr. econs. Kalamazoo Coll., 1962-66. Pres., Kalamazoo County United Way, 1970-71, Southwestern Mich. Area Health Edn. Corp., 1974-76; pres. planning commn. Kalamazoo Hosp., 1975—; campaign treas. Congressman Garry Brown, 1966—; pres. Kalamazoo Child Guidance Clinic, 1957-58; accounting adv. com. Ferris State Coll., 1962—, Western Mich. U., 1978—. chmn. bd. trustees Bronson Meth. Hosp., 1975—; trustee Kalamazoo Inst. Arts, 1975—. Served with AUS, 1943-45. Mem. Mich. Hosp. Assn. (com. on governance 1979—), Kalamazoo County C. of C. (pres. 1964-66), Mich. C. of C. (vice chmn. 1968-70), Am. Inst. C.P.A.'s, Mich. Assn. C.P.A.'s, Nat. Assn. Accountants. Republican. Methodist. Clubs: Kalamazoo Country, Park. Home: 1209 Edgemoor St Kalamazoo MI 49008 Office: 1300 American Nat Bldg Kalamazoo MI 49006

KNEPPER, EUGENE ARTHUR, Realtor; b. Sioux Falls, S.D., Oct. 8, 1926; s. Arlie John and May (Crone) K.; B.S.C., Drake U., Des Moines, 1951; m. LaNel Strong, May 7, 1948; children—Kenton Todd, Kristin Rene. Accountant, G.L. Yager, pub. accountant, Estherville, Iowa, 1951-52; auditor R.L. Meriwether, C.P.A., Des Moines, 1952-53; accountant govt. renegotiation dept. Collins Radio Co., Cedar Rapids, Iowa, 1953-54; head accounting dept. Hawkeye Rubber Mfg. Co., Cedar Rapids, 1954-56; asst. controller United Fire & Casualty Ins. Co., Cedar Rapids, 1956-58; sales asso. Equitable Life Assurance Soc. U.S., Cedar Rapids, 1958-59; controller Gaddis Enterprises, Inc., Cedar Rapids, 1959-61; owner Estherville Laundry Co., 1959-64; sales asso., comml. investment div. mgr. Tommy Tucker Realty Co., Cedar Rapids, 1961-74; owner Real Estate Investment Planning Assos., Cedar Rapids, 1974—; controlling partner numerous real estate syndicates; cons. in field; also fin. speaker; fin. guest lectr. Kirkwood Community Coll., Cedar Rapids, Mt. Mercy Coll., Cedar Rapids, Cornell Coll., Mt. Vernon. Active YMCA; patron Cedar Rapids Symphony; bd. dirs. Oak Hill-Jackson Outreach Fund, 1970—, pres., 1973-74; bd. dirs. Consumer Credit Counseling Service Cedar Rapids-Marion Area, 1974—, pres., 1974—. Served with USNR, 1945-46. Recipient Storm Manuscript award, 1976. Mem. Nat., Iowa (pres. comml. investment div., mem. legis. com.) assns. realtors, Nat. Assn. Accountants, Nat. Inst. Real Estate Brokers (membership chmn. Iowa 1972-73), Real Estate Securities and Syndication Inst., Cedar Rapids Bd. Realtors, Eastern Iowa Execs. Club (dir.), Internat. Platform Assn. Methodist. Club: Cedar Rapids Optimist (chmn. boys work com.). Contbr. articles to profl. jours. Home: 283 Tomahawk Trail SE Cedar Rapids IA 52403 Office: 1602 IE Tower Cedar Rapids IA 52401

KNEPPER, HAROLD CHESTER, printing co. exec.; b. Hartville, Ohio, Dec. 31, 1933; s. Harold M. and Viola G. (Parks) K.; student pub. schs., Massilon, Ohio; m. Betty Edwards, Oct. 1, 1955; 1 dau., Pamela Lynn. Pressman, Holsing Litho, Canton, Ohio, 1951-55; plant foreman Shandling Litho, Tucson, 1955-61; owner, pres. Glenbar Lithographers, San Diego, Calif., 1961—; owner, breeder thoroughbred race horses. Adv. com. San Diego Community Colls.; bd. dirs. Redevel. Agy. City of San Diego Dells Project. Recipient Letterhead Contest prize Gilbert Paper Co., 1962; Graphic Design Merit award Whiting-Plover Paper Co., 1971; Certificate of Craftsmanship award Weyerhaeuser, Oct. 1974, Dec. 1974, Jan. 1975, Oct. 1975; Sportsman award Simpson Paper Co., 1977. Mem. Printing Industries Assn. of San Diego (dir. 1965—, v.p.), Nat. Fedn. of Ind. Businessmen, Master Printers of Am., San Diego Wholesale Credit Men's Assn. Patentee printing products. Home: 6120 La Port St La Mesa CA 92041 Office: 3240 F St San Diego CA 92102

KNICELY, HOWARD VINCENT, gen. industry exec.; b. Parkersburg, W.Va., Mar. 2, 1936; s. Howard V. and Edith H. (White) K.; B.A., Marietta Coll., 1959; M.S. (Inst. Indsl. Relations fellow), W.Va. U., 1960; m. Peggy Ann Thorne, Aug. 31, 1958; children—Cynthia, Michael. Mgr. indsl. relations chem. div., FMC Corp., Charleston, W.Va., 1961-68; regional employee relations mgr. chem. div. Mobil Oil Corp., Edison, N.J., 1969, dir. employee and labor relations, N.Y.C., 1970-74; v.p. personnel Admiral Group, Rockwell Internat., Chgo., 1974-75, v.p. personnel Consumer Ops., 1975-77; v.p. human resources Hart, Schaffner & Marx, Chgo., 1977-79; v.p. human relations TRW, Inc., Cleve., 1980—; instr. personnel and mgmt. scis. Morris Harvey Coll., Charleston, W.Va., 1964-66. Mem. Am. Soc. Personnel Adminstrn., Bus. Roundtable (labor-mgmt. com.), Conf. Bd. (personnel adv. com.), Labor Policy Assn., Am. Mgmt. Assn., Indsl. Relations Assn. Chgo. (past pres.). Home: 32131 Meadowlark Way Pepper Pike OH Office: 23555 Euclid Ave Cleveland OH 44117

KNIERIEM, JAMES HENRY, service mgmt. co. exec.; b. Nyack, N.Y., Nov. 15, 1934; s. Matthew A. and Ethel Catherine (Kelly) K.; B.S., Fordham U., 1957; M.B.A., N.Y. U., 1968; postgrad. Temple U., 1973-75; m. Joanna M. Knieriem, Nov. 26, 1966; children—Kevin J., Robert M. Regional sales mgr. Olivetti Underwood Corp., 1957-67; exec. v.p. AGS Services, 1967-71; sr. v.p. operations services ARA Services, Inc., Phila., 1971—. Served with AUS, 1957. Mem. Am. Mktg. Assn., Am. Hosp. Assn., Nat. Restaurant Assn., Am. Mgmt. Assn., Nat. Automatic Merchandising Assn. Roman Catholic. Clubs: Ramblewood Country, Downtown. Home: 303 St David Dr Mount Laurel NJ 08054 Office: Independence Sq W Philadelphia PA 19106

KNIGHT, FREDERICK, chems. and plastics co. exec.; b. N.Y.C., Aug. 20, 1929; s. John Jacob and Rose Knight; B.S., Cornell U., 1951; m. Elizabeth Ann Shinn, Aug. 29, 1953; children—Thomas Frederick, Bruce James, Susan. Purchasing agt. Darling & Co., Chgo., 1954-59; chem. buyer Borg Warner Chems. Co., Parkersburg, W.Va., 1959-62, purchasing agt., 1962-65, dir. purchases, 1965-68, dir. petrochems. and materials, v.p. petrochems., 1976—. Served from pvt. to capt. C.E., U.S. Army, 1953-55; Korea. Mem. Nat. Petroleum Refiners Assn. (dir., petrochem. com.), Chem. Mfrs. Assn., Nat. Assn. Purchasing Mgrs., Petrochem. Energy Group, Drug, Chem. and Allied Trades Assn. Home: 103 Wildwood Dr Marietta OH 45750 Office: PO Box 1868 Parkersburg WV 26101

KNIGHT, HERBERT BORWELL, corp. exec.; b. Oak Park, Ill., July 4, 1928; s. Herbert Alfred and Bessie Carne (Borwell) K.; A.B., Dartmouth Coll., 1951, M.B.A., 1952; m. Nancy Gordon, June 29, 1963; children—Sharon, Tom. Vice-pres. mktg. B.K. Johl, Montreal, Que., Can., 1968-69; asst. to pres. Bliss & Laughlin Industries, Oak Brook, Ill., 1969-71; pres. Newport News Indsl. Corp. (Va.), 1975-80, Torroco Inc., 1980—; dir. Oak Park Trust & Savs. Bank. Mem. Atomic Indsl. Forum. Episcopalian. Clubs: Metropolitan, Economic (Chgo.). Office: PO Box 2511 Houston TX 77001

KNIGHT, JAMES L., newspaperman; b. Akron, Ohio, 1909. Dir. Knight-Ridder Newspapers, Inc., Knight Pub. Co., Charlotte, N.C.; chmn. bd. Miami (Fla.) Herald Pub. Co.; v.p., dir. Beacon Jour. Pub. Co.; dir. Tallahasse Democrat, Macon Telegraph Pub. Co., So. Prodn. Program, Inc., Boca Raton News, Inc., Bradenton Herald, Inc., Broward Times, Inc., Detroit Free Press, Inc., Ridder Publs., Inc., Twin Coast Newspapers, Inc., N.W. Publs., Inc., Knight-Ridder Broadcasting, Inc., Viewdata Corp. Am., Inc., Lexington Herald-Leader Co., Phila. Newspapers, Inc. Treas. bd. govs. United Way Am., 1971—. Mem. So. Newspaper Pubs. Assn. (pres. 1957; chmn. bd. 1958), Am. Newspapers Pubs. Assn. (dir.). Clubs: Portage Country (Akron); Bath, LaGorce, Indian Creek, Surf (Miami); Detroit; Chicago; Key Largo Anglers, Chub Cay, Hatteras Marlin, National Press; Lyford Cay (New Providence, Bahamas). Office: care Miami Herald 1 Herald Plaza Miami FL 33101

KNIGHT, JOHN FRANCIS, ins. co. exec.; b. N.Y.C., Sept. 30, 1919; s. Samuel F. and Abigail (Sullivan) K.; B.B.A., cum laude, St. John's U., 1952; m. Marilyn Rockefeller, Oct. 30, 1948; children—Jeffrey J., Melanie J., John Mark, Jane M., James M. With Republic Financial Services, Inc., Republic Ins. Group, Dallas, 1939—, agy. supr., 1950-56, asst. v.p., 1956-60, v.p., 1960-67, sr. v.p., 1967-69, exec. v.p., 1969-71, sr. exec. v.p., 1971-72, pres., 1972—, also dir.; pres. Vanguard Ins. Co., Blue Ridge Ins. Co.; dir. Dollar Fed. Savs. & Loan Assn., Malverne, N.Y. Served to maj. AUS, 1942-46. Decorated Bronze Star. Mem. Ins. Club Dallas. Home: 5569 Wenonah Dr Dallas TX 75209 Office: 2727 Turtle Creek Blvd Dallas TX 75219

KNIGHT, KENNETH SHERRELL, mcht.; b. Belleville, Ill., June 15, 1950; s. Harold Eugene and Rosemary (Guthrie) K.; B.B.A., Baylor U., 1972. Accounts payable supr. Trinity Valley Foods, Inc., Dallas, 1972; internal auditor Coit Internat., Inc., Dallas, 1973; sales promoter Houston div. Baker Knapp & Tubbs, 1974; exec. buyer Bloomingdale's, Inc., N.Y.C., 1975-77; founder, pres., chief exec. officer Under Arrest, Inc., Dallas, 1977—; cons. to retail stores Under Arrest Concepts div. UA, Inc., 1979—; rep. Mus. Modern Art publs. in Southwest, 1980—. Mem. Dallas C. of C. Home and office: PO Box 58666 Dallas TX 75258

KNIGHT, KIRK LAY, investment mgr. and mgmt. cons. co. exec.; b. Winnetka, Ill., Apr. 17, 1939; s. Harry William and Agnes Louise (Berger) K.; B.A., Amherst Coll., 1961; M.B.A., Harvard U., 1963; J.D., Stanford U., 1966; m. Virginia Harrison, Feb. 24, 1973. Research asso., mem. teaching staff Grad. Sch. Bus., Stanford U., 1966-69; founder, chmn. bd. dirs. Kirk Knight & Co., Menlo Park, Calif., 1969—; pres., chmn. bd. dirs. Menlo Fin. Corp., Menlo Park, 1974—; pres. Calif. N.W. Fund, Inc., 1976—; dir. System Industries, Inc., Manpower, Inc./Calif. Peninsula; bd. govs., mem. exec. com. NASBIC. Mem. Western Electronics Mfrs. Assn. Clubs: Menlo Country, University. Home: Two Coalmine View Portola Valley CA 94025 Office: 3000 Sand Hill Rd Menlo Park CA 94025

KNIGHT, PAUL FORD, pharm. co. exec.; b. Washington, Aug. 8, 1947; s. Herbert Paul and Eleanor Kent (Hall) K.; B.A., U. Minn., 1969, M.S., 1971; m. Yvonne M. Adams, Aug. 6, 1977. Planning analyst Royal Globe Ins. Co., N.Y.C., 1971-72, sr. planning analyst, 1972-74; fin. analyst Pfizer, Inc., N.Y.C., 1974, fin. mgr., 1974, div. controller, 1975, asst. group controller, 1976, group product mgr., 1976-78, dir. mktg., 1978—. Mem. Am. Mktg. Assn., Pharm. Advt. Club. Republican. Methodist. Club: Jaycees. Home: 401 E 74th St New York NY 10021 Office: 235 E 42d St New York NY 10017

KNIGHT, ROBERT EDWARD, banker; b. Alliance, Nebr., Nov. 27, 1941; s. Edward McKean and Ruth (McDuffee) K.; B.A., Yale U., 1963; M.A., Harvard U., 1965, Ph.D., 1968; m. Eva Sophia Youngstrom, Aug. 12, 1966; Asst. prof. U.S. Naval Acad., Annapolis, Md., 1966-68; lectr. U. Md., 1967-68; fin. economist Fed. Res. Bank of Kansas City (Mo.), 1968-70, research officer, economist, 1971-76, asst. v.p., sec., 1977, v.p., sec., 1978-79; pres. Alliance Nat. Bank (Nebr.), 1979—; pres. Robert Knight Assos., banking and econ. cons., Alliance, 1979—; mem. faculty Colo. Grad. Sch. Banking, Am. Inst. Banking, U. Mo., Kansas City, 1971-79; thesis adv. Stonier Grad. Sch. Banking. Bd. regents Nat. Comml. Lending Sch., 1980—; trustee Knox Presbyn. Ch., Overland Park, Kans., 1965-69. Woodrow Wilson fellow, 1963-64. Mem. Am. Econ. Assn., Am. Fin. Assn., So. Econ. Assn., Western Econ. Assn., Econometric Soc., Am. Bankers Assn. (econ. adv. com. 1980—), Nebr. Bankers Assn. (com. state legis. 1980—), Am. Inst. Banking (state com. Nebr. 1980—). Republican. Clubs: Rotary, Masons. Contbr. articles to profl. jours. Home: Drawer E Alliance NE 69301 Office: Alliance Nat Bank Alliance NE 69301

KNIGHT, ROBERT HUNTINGTON, lawyer; b. New Haven, Feb. 27, 1919; s. Earl Wall and Frances Pierpont (Whitney) K.; B.A., Yale U., 1940; LL.B., U. Va., 1947; m. Rosemary C. Gibson, Apr. 19, 1975; children—Robert Huntington, Jessie Valle, Patricia Whitney, Alice Isabel, Eli Whitney. With John Orr Young, Inc., advt. agy., 1940-41; asst. prof. U. Va. Law Sch., 1947-49; admitted to N.Y. bar, 1950; asso. firm Shearman & Sterling & Wright, N.Y.C., 1949-55, partner, 1955-58; dep. asst. sec. for internat. security affairs Dept. Def., 1958-61, gen. counsel Treasury Dept., 1961-62; partner firm Shearman & Sterling, N.Y.C., 1962—; dep. chmn. Fed. Res. Bank N.Y., 1976-77, chmn., 1978—; counsel to bd. United Technologies Corp.; dir. Owens-Corning Fiberglas Corp., Brit. Steel Corp., Inc., Pechiney Ugine Kuhlmann Corp.; chmn. Howmet Corp., Howmet Turbine Corp. Mem. Intelsat Arbitration Panel, 1971—. Bd. dirs. Internat. Vol. Services; chmn. bd. dirs. U. Va. Law Sch. Found.; bd. dirs. Asia Found. Served to lt. col. USAAF, 1941-45. Mem. Am., Fed., Internat., Inter-Am. bar assns., Bar Assn. City N.Y., N.Y. County Lawyers Assn., Internat. Law Assn., Washington Inst. Fgn. Affairs, Council Fgn. Relations. Clubs: Down Town Assn., Pilgrims, India House, Links (N.Y.C.); Army and Navy, Met., City, Tavern (Washington); Round Hill (Greenwich, Conn.). Office: Shearman & Sterling 53 Wall St New York NY 10005*

KNOEBEL, DANIEL MCCLELLAN, manufactured housing co. exec.; b. Sunbury, Pa., Jan. 16, 1928; s. Edward Lott and Mary Susan (James) K.; student pub. schs., Northumberland, Pa.; m. Dorothy Wilson, July 9, 1948; children—Norwood B., Sandra M., Steven M., Deborah. Propr., D.M. Knoebel, Builder and Developer, Vero Beach, Fla., 1950-61, D.M. Knoebel, distbrs. U.S. Steel Homes, Vero Beach and Winter Park, Fla., 1962-65; pres., treas., chmn. bd. D.M. Knoebel Corp., Orlando, Fla., 1965-74, Nobel Homes Corp., Orlando, 1975—; propr. Dan Knoebel Corp., 1980—. Mem. Am. Arbitration Assn. (panel arbitrators 1979). Author: Applied Theory of Prerequisites of Manufactured Housing, 1972; Code Compliance Manual, 1972-80. Home: 911 Osceola Ave Winter Park FL 32789 Office: 3748 Bengert St Orlando FL 32808

KNOELL, W.H., business exec.; b. Pitts., Aug. 1, 1924; s. William F. and Hazel (Holverstott) K.; student Cornell U., 1942; B.S. in Mech. Engring., Carnegie-Mellon U., 1947; J.D., U. Pitts., 1950; m. E. Anne Kirkland, Jan. 26, 1952; children—Kristin Anne, Susan Elizabeth, Amy Lynn, Gretchen. Practice law with firm Shoemaker-Knoell, 1949-50; asst. to exec. v.p. Pitts. Corning Corp., 1950-55; asst. sec. Crucible Steel Co. Am., 1955-57, sec., 1957-63, v.p., 1963-67; v.p., asst. to pres. Cyclops Corp., Pitts., 1967-68, exec. v.p., 1968-72, pres., 1972—, chief exec. officer, 1973—, also dir; dir. Duquesne Light Co., Am. Sterilizer Co., Pitts. br. Fed. Res. Bank Cleve. Bd. visitors U. Pitts. Law Sch.; trustee, mem. exec. com., mech. engring. vis. com. Carnegie-Mellon U.; bd. dirs. St. Clair Meml. Hosp., Com. for Corp. Support of Pvt. Univs., Inc., United Way Allegheny Country, Mid-Atlantic Legal Found.; chmn. adv. council Jr. Achievement of SW Pa. Served with USAAF, 1943-45. Mem. Am. Iron and Steel Inst. (dir.), Am. Bar Assn., Pi Tau Sigma, Theta Tau, Beta Theta Pi, Phi Alpha Delta. Clubs: Univ., Duquesne (dir.), St. Clair Country (Pitts.); Laurel Valley Golf; Rolling Rock Golf. Home: 1802 Murdstone Rd Pittsburgh PA 15241 Office: 650 Washington Rd Pittsburgh PA 15228

KNOLL, KENNETH ROBERT, export mgmt. co. exec.; b. Bklyn., Jan. 26, 1922; s. Max and Frieda (Oltmann) K.; B.S. in Bus. Adminstrn., Lehigh U., 1946; m. Karin Berglund, Nov. 25, 1950; children—Robert, Lynn, Richard. With Bristol-Myers Co., N.Y.C., 1947—, asst. controller, 1966-73, asst. treas., 1973-76; controller Martin Bros. Tobacco Co., Inc., N.Y.C., 1976—. Active Little League; dist. commr. Boy Scouts Am., 1966-67. Lectr. Am. Mgmt. Assn. Served to 1st lt. AUS, 1943-46. Decorated Combat Infantry Badge, Purple Heart. Mem. Inst. Internal Auditors, Financial Execs. Inst., Theta Xi, Alpha Kappa Psi. Lutheran (mem. ch. council and treas. 1967-72). Mason (master 1959, treas. 1960-80). Club: St. Andrew's Curling. Home: 60 Buena Vista Dr White Plains NY 10603 Office: 60 E 42d St New York NY 10017

KNOPF, ALFRED A., publisher; b. N.Y.C., Sept. 12, 1892; s. Samuel and Ida (Japhe) K.; A.B., Columbia U., i912; L.H.D., Yale U., 1958, Columbia U., 1959, Bucknell U., 1959, Lehigh U., 1960, Coll. William and Mary, 1969, U. Mich., 1969, Bates Coll., 1971; LL.D., Brandeis U., 1963; D.Litt., Adelphi U., 1966, U. Chattanooga, 1966, C.W. Post Center, L.I. U., 1973; m. Blanche Wolf, 1916 (dec.); 1 son, Alfred; m. 2d, Helen Norcross Hedrick, 1967. Founded pub. firm, 1915, pres. Alfred A. Knopf Inc., N.Y.C., 1918-57, chmn. bd., 1957-72, chmn. bd. emeritus, 1972—. Decorated comendador Ordem Nacional do Cruzeiro do Sul (Brazil); recipient Cornelius Amory Pugsley gold medal for conservation and preservation, 1960; Alexander Hamilton medal Assn. Alumni Columbia U., 1966; Outstanding Service award Nat. Parks Centennial Commn., 1972; Francis Parkman Silver medal Soc. Am. Historians, 1974; Distinguished Service award Assn. Am. Univ. Presses, 1975; Distinguished Achievement award Drexel U. Library Sch. Alumni Assn., 1975. Mem. Am. Acad. Arts and Scis. Clubs: Cosmos (Washington); Century Country (Harrison, N.Y.); Lotos (N.Y.C.). Home: 63 Purchase St Purchase NY 10577 Office: 201 E 50th St New York NY 10022

KNORPS, GEORGE FRANK, data processing exec.; b. Chgo., Feb. 26, 1946; s. Leo Casmir and Adeline (Stodolny) K.; B.S., U. Ill., 1968; m. Christine Dolores Perry, Oct. 25, 1969; children—Brooke Vanessa, Marc Christopher, Lindsay Allison. Systems engr. Control Data Corp., Mpls. and Los Angeles, 1968-70; corp. software devel. supr. Standard Oil (Ind.), Chgo., 1973-78; corp. mgr. support systems GATX Corp., Chgo., 1978—; pres. G.F. Knorps Cons., Winnetka, Ill., 1978—. Served with USN, 1970-73. Mem. Assn. Computing Machinery, Data Processing Mgmt. Assn., Chgo. Indsl. Communications Assn., U. Ill. Alumni Assn., Chi Psi. Roman Catholic. Contbr. articles to profl. jours. Home: 1174 Ash St Winnetka IL 60093 Office: GATX Corp 120 S Riverside Plaza Chicago IL 60606

KNORR, GERALD ROGER, utility exec.; b. Jamaica, N.Y., Sept. 21, 1943; s. Julius Frank and Madelyn G. (Knutsen) K.; B.B.A., Hofstra U., 1965; m. Elizabeth Howell, Aug. 17, 1968; children—Timothy R., Matthew S., Susan E. Sr. staff accountant Price Waterhouse & Co., Mineola, N.Y., 1965-71; asst. treas. Am. Electric Power Service Corp., N.Y.C., from 1971, now Columbus, Ohio. C.P.A. Mem. Am. Inst. C.P.A.'s, N.Y. State Soc. C.P.A.'s. United Methodist.

KNORR, ROBERT OTTO, JR., fin. exec.; b. N.Y.C., July 15, 1940; s. Robert O. and Mary (Novhard) K.; B.S. in B.A., Rutgers U., 1962; m. Madeline Nicholes, July 29, 1967; 1 dau., Madeline Lee. Vice pres. fin. Bowmar Ali, Acton, Mass., 1973-75; v.p. fin. Fram Corp., Providence, 1975-79, v.p. mfg., 1980; v.p. fin. Auto group Bendix Corp., Southfield, Mich., 1980—. Mem. Fin. Execs. Inst. Office: Bendix Corp Exec Offices Southfield MI 48037

KNORTZ, HERBERT CHARLES, communications co. exec.; b. Bklyn., Mar. 31, 1921; s. John Walter and Elizabeth (Grotyohann) K.; B.B.A., St. Johns U., 1946, D.C.S. (hon.), 1977; M.B.A., N.Y. U., 1949; m. Lorraine Marion Kraut, Aug. 12, 1949; children—Steven

Holbrook, Elizabeth Alyn, David Cartwright. Supervising clk. Bklyn. Trust Co., 1938-43; with Price Waterhouse & Co., C.P.A.'s, N.Y.C., 1945-51; supr. standard costs Lever Bros. Co., 1951-55; mgr. cost dept. Crown Cork & Seal Co., 1955-56; asst. comptroller Royal McBee Corp., 1956-60; controller Mack Trucks, Inc., Plainfield, N.J., 1960-61; dep. comptroller IT&T, 1961-63, v.p., controller, 1963-66, sr. v.p., comptroller, 1966-73, exec. v.p., controller, 1973—, also dir.; dir., officer several subsidiaries; dir. Hartford Fire Ins. Co.; partner Cortina Shops, 1957-60, Lewisboro Tennis Club, 1971-72; dir. Peerage Properties Inc., 1971-73; trustee Corporate Property Investors, 1973—. Lectr. profl. meetings. Trustee Vincent Ross Research Found; mem. adv. bd. St. John's U. Served with USAAF, 1943-45. C.P.A., N.Y. Mem. Fin. Execs. Inst. (v.p. research found, mem. internat. com.), Am. Mgmt. Assn. (gen. mgmt. council), Am. Contract Bridge League, Am. Inst. C.P.A.'s, Nat. Assn. Accountants, Inst. Mgmt. Accounting (bd. regents), Internat. Assn. Fin. Exec. Insts., Delta Mu Delta, Beta Gamma Sigma. Clubs: Economics, Board Room, Armonk Tennis, Internat. Golf, Flint River Forests, Accountants. Contbr. to Handbook of International Management, Financial Executives Handbook, also profl. jours. Editor: Food for Thought. Home: 14 Manor Rd Ridgefield CT 06877 Office: IT&T 320 Park Ave New York NY 10022

KNOTT, JOHN EDWARD, leasing co. exec.; b. Mobridge, S.D., Aug. 25, 1941; s. Lawrence Patrick and Pearl Delila (Hedblom) K.; student S.D. Sch. Mines and Tech., 1959-61; B.S., U. S.D., 1963; m. Monica Breitkopf, July 31, 1965; children—Tanja Kaye, John Edward. Data analyst Tex. Instruments, Dallas, 1963-64; Southwestern sales supr. AMF/Paragon Electric Co., Two Rivers, Wis., 1964-67; mktg. rep. Honeywell EDP div., St. Louis, 1967-69; mktg. rep., br. mgr. Duplex Products, St. Louis, 1969-71; sales rep. Mgmt. Assistance, Inc., St. Louis, 1971-73; leasing cons. Todd Equipment Leasing Co., St. Louis, 1973-74; owner, pres. Universal Equipment Leasing Co., St. Louis, 1974—. Mem. Data Processing Mgmt. Assn., Am. Contract Bridge League, Westport C. of C., Hub Club St. Louis. Lutheran. Home: 141 Renoir Ct Lake Saint Louis MO 63367 Office: 75 Worthington Dr Maryland Heights MO 63043

KNOWLES, GREGG KERN, publisher; b. Oelwein, Iowa, July 31, 1953; s. Richard Radbourne and Deloris Arlene (Kern) K.; student public schs., Denison, Iowa; m. Susan Jane Germeroth, May 26, 1972; children—Mindee Elizabeth, Lucas Oliver. Chief photographer Oelwein Daily Register, 1971; advt. mgr. Denison Bull. and Rev., 1972-78; editor, pub. weekly newspapers Sun Pub. Co., Sac City, Iowa, 1978—; pres. Eleventh Hour Devel. Corp., Sac City; dir. Sac Devel. Corp. Active Sac City Community Chest, Sac County Republican Com. Recipient Blue Ribbon Newspaper award Nat. Newspaper Found., 1979, 80; named Optimist of Year, Denison Optimist Club, 1977-78. Mem. Nat. Newspaper Assn., Iowa Press Assn., C. of C., Jr. C. of C. Methodist. Clubs: Masons, Shriners. Home: 111 N 7th St Sac City IA 50583 Office: Sun Pub Co 1405 W Main St Sac City IA 50583

KNOWLES, JEROME, JR., ret. real estate exec.; b. Northeast Harbor, Mt. Desert, Maine, May 24, 1906; s. Jerome and Lilla Belle (Smallidge) K.; student U. Maine, 1924-28, Radio Inst. Am., 1928; student radio engring. N.Y. U., 1928; m. Evelyn Ada Farris, Aug. 16, 1930; 1 dau., Kathryn Frances. Radio engr. RCA, 1929-30; real estate broker and ins. agt., 1931-73; real estate appraiser and property mgr., 1937-72; appraiser of municipalities for taxation purposes, 1949-72; counselor The Knowles Co. Trustee Nat. Home and Property Owners Found., 1946-47. Mem. Am. Inst. Real Estate Appraisers (governing council 1958-62, v.p. 1957-58, mem. exec. com. 1962, edn. com. 1963-64, appraisal legislation com. 1963-64, admissions com. 1964-65, instr. univ. courses 1958-68, editorial bd. The Appraiser 1959-65, editor in chief, chmn. editorial bd. Appraisal Jour. 1966-70, recipient honorarium for service 1980), Soc. Residential Appraisers (sr. mem., bd. govs., admissions com., chmn. edni. com. 1957-58, recipient citation for outstanding contbns. 1960), Am. Soc. Real Estate Counselors (edn. com. 1962-69), Nat. Inst. Real Estate Brokers (bd. govs. 1950-52; v.p. 1952), Nat. Assn. Real Estate Bds. (v.p., dir.), Brokers Inst. (v.p. 1952-54), Maine Real Estate Assn. (pres. 1946-47), Bangor Bd. Realtors (treas. 1946-47), Mt. Desert C. of C., Alpha Tau Omega. Lectr. on real estate appraising and allied subjects. Republican. Episcopalian. Mason, Lion. Author and publisher: Residential Cost Manual, 1953; Real Estate Appraisal Manual, 1957, rev. 1965; Appraisal Manual for Vermont Listers and Assessor's Real Estate Manual, 1964, author Single-Family Residential Appraisal Manual, 1967. Contbr. real estate articles to newspapers and trade bulls. Home: 207 SW 14th Ave Boynton Beach FL 33435 also Sinclair Rd Northeast Harbor ME 04662

KNOWLES, JOSEPH ROBERT, planning cons.; b. Ann Arbor, Mich., Jan. 10, 1930; s. Michael Thomas and Marion Thelma (Voorheis) K.; student Eastern Mich. U., 1948-51; m. Marilyn Bernidete Givin, Nov. 29, 1951; children—Kristi Lee, Kurtis Lawrence. Urban renewal dir., Lincoln Park, Mich., 1960-63; dir. advance planning City of Chattanooga, 1963-64; community devel. dir. City of Muskegon (Mich.), 1964-72; pres. Genesee Twp. Econ. Devel. Corp., 1976-78; dir. econ. and energy devel. mgmt. THY & Assos., Inc., Flint, Mich., 1978—; sec.-treas. Environ. Resources Mgmt.; v.p. United Synergistic Systems, 1972, dir. Energy Indsl. Mall Corp., River Village Devel. Corp., Genesee Real Estate Corp. Councilman, City of Lincoln Park, 1957-60. Mem. Nat. Assn. Housing and Redevel. Ofcls., Tech. Mktg. Soc. Am., Am. Soc. Small Research Firms, Mich. Soc. Planning Cons. Democrat. Episcopalian. Home: 910 Glenbrook Circle Flint MI 48503 Office: 705 Kelso St Flint MI 48506

KNOWLTON, RICHARD L., meat packing co. exec.; b. 1932; B.A., U. Colo., 1954; married. With George A. Hormel & Co., Austin, Minn., 1948—, mgr. meat products div. and route car sales, 1967-69, asst. mgr. Austin plant, gen. mgr. Austin plant, 1969-74, v.p. ops., 1974, group v.p. ops., 1975-79, pres., chief operating officer, 1979—, also dir.; dir. First Nat. Bank of Austin. Trustee U. Minn. Office: George A Hormel & Co 501 16th Ave NE Austin MN 55912

KNOWLTON, WINTHROP, publishing co. exec.; b. N.Y.C., Sept. 1, 1930; s. Hugh and Christine (Stanley) K.; B.A., Harvard U., 1953, M.B.A., 1955; m. Mina Elizabeth Minnerly, June 23, 1951 (div. 1960); children—Winthrop, Christopher, Oliver; m. 2d, Grace Daniels Farrar, July 8, 1960 (separated 1980); children—Eliza Courtney, Samantha Farrar. With White, Weld & Co., Inc., N.Y.C., 1955—, v.p., 1961, gen. partner, 1962-65, ltd. partner, 1965—; with Office Edn., Washington, 1965; dep. asst. sec. treasury for internat. affairs, 1965-66, asst. sec., 1966-68; exec. v.p., dir. Harper & Row 1968-70, pres., 1970-79, chmn., 1979—, also chief exec. officer, dir.; dir. Mpls. Star & Tribune Co., Equitable Life Assurance Soc. U.S., Govt. Research Corp. Trustee, Tchrs. Coll.; bd. dirs. N.Y.C. Ballet, pres. and chief exec. officer, 1979—. Mem. Council Fgn. Relations. Clubs: Century, Harvard, Univ. Co-author: A Killing in the Market, 1958; author: Growth Opportunities in Common Stocks, 1965; Shaking the Money Tree, 1972. Home: 24 W 55th St New York NY 10019 Office: Harper & Row 10 E 53d St New York NY 10022

KNOX, JAMES ENOCH, acct.; b. Pitts., Jan. 16, 1948; s. Enoch L. and Marian S. (Hoffman) K.; B.S., Shippensburg State Coll., 1971; 1 son, James E. Owner, operator H&R Block, Greencastle, Pa., 1971-72; controller intern Dept. Army Letterkenny Army Depot, 1972-73; asst. controller Loewengart & Co., Inc., Mercersburg, Pa., 1973-78; controller Martins Famous Pastry Shoppe, Inc., Chambersburg, Pa., 1978—. Republican. Home: 1012 Stoneybridge Dr Chambersburg PA 17201 Office: 1048 Lincoln Way E Chambersburg PA 17201

KNOX, LANCE LETHBRIDGE, venture capital exec.; b. Hartford, Conn., Sept. 25, 1944; s. Robert Chester and Leonice Price (Merrels) K.; B.A., Williams Coll., 1966; M.B.A., N.Y. U., 1970; children—Michele Merrels, Elizabeth McVarish. Asst. cashier Citibank, N.A., N.Y.C., 1968-70, asst. v.p., 1970-72, v.p., 1972-74, sr. credit officer, 1973-74; v.p. fin. GATX Corp., Chgo., 1974-77; pvt. investor venture capital, 1978—; pres., dir. Plimpton Knox & Co., Chgo.; chmn., dir. NTC, Inc., Nat. Trailer Convoy, Inc., Tulsa. Mem. Assos. Rush-Presbyn.-St. Lukes Med. Center, Chgo.; trustee Kingswood-Oxford Sch. Inc., West Hartford, Conn.; treas., bd. dirs. Better Govt. Assn., 1978—. Mem. Chgo. Forum. Republican. Presbyterian. Home: 195 Ridge Ave Winnetka IL 60093

KNOX, NANCY THERESE, fashion exec.; b. Hollywood, Calif., Apr. 16, 1923; d. John Joseph and Anne Veronica (Taughran) Holland; student Regis Coll., 1941-42, Bryant Coll., 1943. Asst. fashion dir. I. Miller Shoes, N.Y.C., 1953-55; partner fashion cons. firm Clark-Knox, N.Y.C., 1956-59; co-founder, sec. Jags Unltd. Inc., N.Y.C., 1959-63; co-founder, v.p. Renegade Corp., N.Y.C., 1963-71, designer Renegade line, 1963—, pres., 1971—; pres. The Very Best of Nancy Knox, Ltd., N.Y.C. Recipient Caswell Massey design award Renegades, 1968, Creative Menswear design ann. mention, 1969, Coty award, 1971, 75. Mem. Council of Fashion Designers of Am., Show Women's Execs. (v.p. 1967-68), Fashion Group, Internat. Platform Assn. Home: 2 Beekman Pl New York City NY 10022 Office: 40 W 55th St New York City NY 10019

KNUDSEN, CONRAD CALVERT, bus. exec.; b. Tacoma, Oct. 3, 1923; s. Conrad and Annabelle (Callison) K.; LL.B., U. Wash., 1950; Univ. fellow in law, Columbia U., 1951; m. Nov. 22, 1950; children—Conrad Calvert, Elizabeth Page, Colin Roderick, David Callison. Admitted to Wash. bar, 1950; asso. firm Bogle, Bogle & Gates, Seattle, 1951-61; exec. v.p., dir. Aberdeen Plywood & Veneer Co. (Wash.) 1961-63; exec. v.p., pres., chief adminstrv. officer, vice chmn. Evans Products Co., Portland, Oreg., 1963-68; sr. v.p. Weyerhaeuser Co., Tacoma, 1969-76; chmn., chief exec. officer, dir. MacMillan Bloedel, Ltd., Vancouver, B. C., Can., 1976—; dir. Rainier Bancorp., Rainer Nat. Bank, Castle & Cooke, Inc., Cascade Corp., Termicold Corp., Koninklijke Nederlandse Papierfabrieken N. V., Safeco Corp., Celupal S. A., Can. Imperial Bank Commerce, West Fraser Timber Co. Ltd. Served with U. S. Army, 1942-46. Mem. Am. Bar Assn., Wash. Bar Assn. Clubs: Vancouver, Vancouver Badminton and Lawn Tennis; Terminal City; Rainier, Univ., Seattle Tennis (Seattle); Multnomah Athletic (Portland); Arlington. Office: MacMillan Bloedel Ltd 1075 W Georgia St Vancouver BC V6E 3R9 Canada

KNUDSEN, SEMON EMIL, mfg. co. exec.; b. Buffalo, Oct. 2, 1912; s. William S. and Clara Elizabeth (Euler) K.; student Dartmouth, 1931-32; B.S. in Engring., Mass. Inst. Tech., 1936; m. Florence Anne McConnell, June 16, 1938. With Gen. Motors Corp., 1939-68, exec. v.p., 1966-68, also dir.; pres. Ford Co., 1968-69, also dir.; chmn. Rectrans, Inc., 1970-71; chmn. bd., chief exec. officer White Motor Corp., Cleve., 1971-80, pres., 1972-75, also dir.; dir. United Airlines, Mich. Nat. Bank, UAL, Inc., 1st Nat. Bank, Palm Beach, Fla., Ohio Bell Telephone Co., Cowles Communications Co., Mich. Bank. Bd. dirs., past pres. Boys' Clubs of Detroit; bd. dirs. Boys Clubs Am., Greater Cleve. Growth Assn., Nat. Multiple Sclerosis Soc.; mem. corp. Mass. Inst. Tech.; trustee Oakland (Mich.) U. Found., Cleve. Clinic Found.; mem. nat. commn. NASCAR, 1978—. Recipient Brotherhood award Detroit Round Table, NCCJ, 1961; Man of Yr. award Sales and Mktg. Execs. of Cleve., 1974; Mktg. Salesman of Yr. award Sales and Mktg. Execs. Internat., 1974. Mem. Motor Vehicle Mfrs. Assn. (sec. 1972-73, treas. 1973-74, vice chmn. 1974-76, chmn. 1977-78, sec. 1978-79), Soc. Automotive Engrs., Am. Soc. Tool Engrs., Delta Upsilon. Clubs: Detroit, Detroit Athletic; Bloomfield Hills Country; Union, Pepper Pike (Cleve.); Augusta (Ga.) Nat. Golf; Everglades; Seminole. Office: 1700 N Woodward Suite E Bloomfield Hills MI 48013

KNUDSON, GENE D., lumber and paper co. exec.; b. 1916; B.S., Oreg. State U., 1939; married. Chief forester Bur. Land Mgmt., U.S. Dept. Interior, 1940-46; cons. Mason, Bruce & Girard, Cons. Foresters, 1947-49; chief forester, mgr. logging Wilamette Industries Inc., Portland, Oreg., 1949-56, v.p., 1956-64, exec. v.p., 1964-70, pres., chief operating officer, 1970—, also chief exec. officer, now chmn. bd. Served to maj. U.S. Army, 1942-46. Office: Willamette Industries Inc 1300 SW 5th Ave Portland OR 97201*

KNUDTEN, RICHARD DAVID, corp. exec.; b. Yokohama, Japan, June 19, 1932; s. Arthur C. and Ruth (Crum) K.; A.B., Wittenberg U., 1954; M.A., Pacific Sch. of Religion, 1957; M.Div., Pacific Luth. Theol. Sem., 1957; M.A., U. Calif., Berkeley, 1959; M.A., Case Western Res. U., 1959, Ph.D., 1964; postdoctoral U. Chgo., 1969-71; m. Mary Swedlund, July 6, 1958; children—Stephen, David, Thomas, Susan. Pres., Evaluation/Policy Research Assos. Ltd., Milw., 1975—, Socio-Environ. Research Center, Ltd., Milw., 1975—; treas. Center for Applied Social Sci., Inc., 1980—; prof. sociology Marquette U., Milw., 1971—. Pres., Nat. Orgn. Victim Assistance, 1978-79, bd. dirs., 1976-80, exec. com., 1978-80; bd. dirs. Bel Canto Chorus, Milw.; mem. Milw. Symphony Orch. Chorus. Luther fellow, 1955-59; Synodical scholar, 1950-54. Mem. Am. Sociol. Assn., Religious Research Assn., Am. Soc. Criminology, Internat. Soc. Victimology, Soc. for Study of Social Problems, World Soc. Victimology. Lutheran. Author 12 books, numerous articles. Home: 4107 N Lake Dr Shorewood WI 53211 Office: Suite 300 1200 E Capitol Dr Shorewood WI 53211

KNUTH, MELVIN (PAT) R., electronic telephone equipment mfg. co. exec.; b. Cleve., Mar. 19, 1929; s. Edward Albert and Irene (Smith) K.; B.S. in Bus. Adminstrn., Miami U., Oxford, Ohio, 1952; m. Nancy Ann Bee, June 17, 1952; children—Sussette, Sandra, Patricia Ann. Asst. br. mgr. Bus. Extension Bur., San Diego, 1954-56; supr. site ops. Gen. Dynamics Corp., San Diego, 1956-65; plant mgr. RCA, Huntsville, Ala., 1965-70; v.p. ops. Xenotech Inc., Irvine, Calif., 1970-72; program mgr. ops. Norden div. United Air Craft (now United Tech.), Norwalk, Conn., 1972-75; v.p. mfg. Tele/Resources Inc., Ballston Lake, N.Y., 1975—. Mem. Huntsville Indsl. Expansion Com., 1966. Served to lt. (j.g.), USN, 1952-54; Korea. Mem. Am. Mgmt. Assn., Soc. Logistics Engrs. Home: 12 Lonesome Pine Trail Gansevoort NY 12831 Office: Northway 10-Exec Park Ushers Rd Ballston Lake NY 12019

KOCH, DONALD LEIGH, economist; b. N.Y.C., Sept. 17, 1946; s. David and Ruby (Leigh) K.; B.A., Principia Coll., 1968; M.A., Trinity Coll., Hartford, Conn., 1971; postgrad. Harvard U., 1966-67, M.I.T., 1979; m. Christina Kirkman, Sept. 7, 1968; 1 son, Christian Gad. Sr. security analyst Conn. Bank & Trust, Hartford, 1971-73; corp. economist, exec. officer Barnett Banks of Fla., Inc., Jacksonville, 1973-80; sr. v.p., dir. research Fed. Res. Bank Atlanta, 1980—; advisor FOMC; lectr. U. North Fla. Past mem. Lt. Gov.'s Energy Element Policy Adv. Com.; mem. Gov.'s Econ. Adv. Council. Mem. Econ. Adv. Council, Am. Bankers Assn., Am. Econs. Assn., Nat. Assn. Bus. Economists (pres. local chpt.). Asso. editor Bus. Econs., 1979. Office: 104 Marietta St Atlanta GA 30303

KOCH, ROBERT ALLEN, mfg. co. exec.; b. Stanley, Wis., Mar. 22, 1947; s. Harvey Lawrence and Dorothy Lillian (Schara) K.; B.S. in B.A., U. Wis., 1969; m. Joann Stoker, Oct. 5, 1974; children—Mark, Dean, Pam. With Conrath Co-op. Cheese Factory (Wis.), 1971-72; with County Line Cheese Co. div. Beatrice Foods Co., Auburn, Ind., 1972—, ops. mgr., 1980—. Served with USMC, 1969-71. Mem. Nat. Bus. Edn. Assn., Phi Beta Lambda. Club: Tri-State Dairy Tech. (v.p. 1979-80). Address: 6813 Windham Ct Fort Wayne IN 46815

KOCH, ROBERT LOUIS, II, coating machinery and drying ovens co. exec.; b. Evansville, Ind., Jan. 6, 1939; s. Robert Louis and Mary Loretta (Bray) K.; B.S., U. Notre Dame, 1960; M.B.A., U. Pitts., 1962; m. Cynthia Marian Ross, Oct. 17, 1964; children—David, Kevin, Kristen, Jennifer. Engr. George Koch Sons, Inc., Metalcraft Div., Evansville, Ind., 1958-60, Thermal Products div., 1960-62, mgr. Ashdee Div., 1962-64, pres., 1964—; pres. Fesk, Inc., Evansville, 1964—, chmn. bd., 1980—; v.p., dir. Gibbs Aluminum Die Casting, Inc., Henderson, Ky., 1972—; dir., sec., v.p. George Koch Sons, Inc., Evansville, 1973—; pres. Koch Indsl. Equipment, Inc.; gen. partner Univ. Leasing, 1979—, Century Leasing, 1979—; dir., sec. Santa Claus Land, Inc. (Ind.), 1972—. Mem. Sch. Bd. Screening Com., Evansville, 1971-73; dep. mayor Evansville, 1976-80, controller, 1976-80; mem. Ind. Tax and Fin. Commn., 1977—. Bd. dirs. Jr. Achievement Southwestern Ind., 1969-78, ARC, Evansville, 1970-77, YMCA, 1973-80, Holy Rosary Sch., 1975-77; bd. dirs., treas. Cath. Edn. Found., 1973-78, v.p., 1978-80, pres., 1980—. Served to 1st lt. AUS, 1960-61. Registered profl. engr., Ind. Named Boss of Year, Nat. Secs. Assn., 1980. Mem. Am. Plywood Assn., Screen Printing Assn., Forest Products Research Assn., TAPPI, Soc. Mfr. Engrs. (cert.), Am. Waterworks Assn., Nat. Soc. Profl. Engrs., Ind. Controllers Assn. (dir.), Young Pres.'s Orgn., Woodworking Machinery Mfrs. Am., Soc. Paint Tech., Nat. Kitchen Cabinet Assn., Ind. Soc. of Chgo., Tau Beta Pi. Roman Catholic. Clubs: Evansville (Ind.) Country, Kennel, Central Turners, Evansville Petroleum, K.C., Tri-State Racquet, Christmas Lake Golf and Country (Santa Claus, Ind.). Patentee in field. Contbr. articles to profl. jours. Home: 525 Martins Ln Evansville IN 47715 Office: PO Box 325 10 S 10th Ave Evansville IN 47702

KOCH, RODERIC MALCOLM, business exec.; b. Evansville, Ind., Sept. 29, 1904; s. Louis J. and Clarice (Ashburn) K.; student U. Wis., 1922-23; A.B., Evansville Coll., 1945; m. Loretta M. Kaltenbacher, Jan. 8, 1925; 1 dau., Constance. Machine shop foreman George Koch Sons, Inc., 1924-30; asst. shop supt., 1930-34, supt. 1934-38, asst. gen. mgr., 1938-41, gen. mgr., 1941-52, v.p. 1951-55, exec. v.p. 1955—; pres. McMasters, 1955—, R. Malcolm and Assos., Inc., 1956—, Standard Indsl. Products, Inc., Evansville, George Koch Realty Corp., Evansville, Comml. Office Services, Evansville, St. Nicholas Corp., Santa Claus, Ind., v.p. Modern Products, Inc., Santa Claus Land, Santa Claus Samaritans, Carter-Clay Corp. (both Santa Claus, Ind.), Ashdee Corp., Evansville; dir. Gibbs Die Casting Aluminum Corp., Henderson, Ky. Treas. Evansville Pub. Schs., 1943-46. Pres. Evansville Mus. Arts and Sci., 1951-56, bd. dirs.; pres. Ind. Found. for Arts and Scis. Mem. A.A.A.S. (life), Am. Numis. Assn. (life). Evansville Coll. Alumni Assn. (dir.). Home: 2200 Lincoln Ave Evansville IN 47714 Office: 10 S 11th Ave Evansville IN 47712

KOCH, WILLIAM PAULSON, fin. exec.; b. Detroit, Nov. 16, 1945; s. William and Doris K.; B.S. in Engring., U.S. Mil. Acad., West Point, 1967; m. Bernadette Watson, May 30, 1970. Account exec. Compton Advt., N.Y.C., 1971-72; v.p., corporate bond trader R.W. Pressprich, N.Y.C., 1972-77, Josephthal & Co., Inc., N.Y.C., 1977—. Served as officer with F.A., U.S. Army, 1967-71. Decorated D.F.C., Bronze Star (2), Air medal (9). Mem. West Point Soc. N.Y. Clubs: Downtown Athletic, Richmond Country. Home: 66 Royal Oak Rd Staten Island NY 10314 Office: 120 Broadway 22d Floor New York NY 10271

KOCHER, BRYAN STANLEY, data processing co. exec.; b. Easton, Pa., July 3, 1948; s. Stanley C. and Virginia May (Paulson) K.; A.B. cum laude, Moravian Coll., 1970; M.S., U. Mass., 1975; m. Sandra Lee Wagner, Jan. 3, 1971; 1 dau., Ellen. Systems analyst Gen. Dynamics Eastern Data Systems Center, Groton, Conn., 1975-76; data base project leader Comml. Union Assurance Co., Boston, 1976-77; mgr. bus. systems design Raytheon Data Systems Co., Norwood, lMass., 1977-80; analyst Cullinane Corp., Wellesley, Mass., 1980—; adj. prof. computer sci. Boston U., 1979—. Served with U.S. Army, 1970-73. Mem. Inst. Certification Computer Profls. (certified data processor), Assn. Computing Machinery (chmn. Boston chpt.), Data Processing Mgmt. Assn., Ops. Research Soc. Am., Alpha Pi Mu, Phi Alpha Theta. Home: 250 Edge Hill Rd Sharon MA 02067 Office: 1415 Boston-Providence Turnpike Norwood MA 02062

KOCOUR, MAX GREGORY, mgmt. cons.; b. Andale, Kans., Feb. 14, 1921; s. John E. and Emma (Falk) K.; B.A., Wichita U., 1943, Minn. U., 1948; m. R. Heloise Hillbrand, Nov. 21, 1945; children—Ruth Anne, Mary Camille, Colette, Michel, Stephen, Michael. With Harold E. Wood & Co., 1946-48, Pillsbury Co., 1949-56, Needham Louis & Brorby, 1957-60; sr. v.p. Simoniz Co., Chgo., 1961-69; exec. v.p. Milprint Inc., Milw., 1969-73; v.p., gen. mgr. Nat. Can Corp., Chgo., from 1973; now mgmt. cons. Sustaining mem. Boy Scouts Am. Bd. dirs. St. Elizabeth's Hosp. Served with AUS, 1943-46. Decorated Silver Star, Bronze Star, Purple Heart Normandy Beachhead Arrow (U.S.); Croix de Guerre (France). Mem. Am. Mgmt. Assn. Club: North Shore Country. Home: 515 Warwick Rd Kenilworth IL 60043 Office: 20 N Wacker Dr Chicago IL 60606

KOEBEL, THOMAS ROY, investment co. exec.; b. nr. St. Louis, June 10, 1951; s. Roy Jacob and Celeste Elizabeth (Deutschmann) K.; B.A., U. Mo., 1973; M.B.A., U. Oreg., 1977. Real estate broker Ira E. Berry, Inc., St. Louis, 1974, 78; pres., chmn. bd. dirs. Koebel International Ltd., Clayton, Mo., 1978—; pres., chmn. bd. dirs. Koebel Investment Co., Inc., Clayton, Mo., 1978—. Mem. World Future Soc., U. Mo. Columbia Alumni Assn., U. Oreg. Alumni Assn. Roman Catholic. Home: Route 3 Box 16 Hermann MO 65041 Office: Box 11786 Clayton MO 63105

KOEHLER, WALTER HERMAN, JR., bakery exec.; b. North Little Rock, Jan. 13, 1924; s. Walter Herman and Eva M. (Siepiela) K.; B.S.C., St. Louis U., 1947; postgrad. Harvard U., 1945; m. Mary Evelyn Troillett, June 8, 1948; children—Daniel W., Robert M., Ralph E. With Koehler Bakery Co., North Little Rock, 1947—, pres., 1955—; pres. Kitty Koehler's Kitchens, Inc., North Little Rock, 1965—; sec.-treas. Compko, Inc., North Little Rock, 1977—; dir. First Am. Nat. Bank, North Little Rock. Mem. exec. com. ARC, 1977-80, v.p., 1977-80. Served to lt. (j.g.) USNR, 1943-46. Mem. Am. Soc. Bakery Engrs., Retail Bakers Am. Clubs: Rotary (dist. gov. 1972-73); K.C.; The Little Rock; North Hills Country; Elks. Home: 32 Heritage Park Circle North Little Rock AR 72116 Office: 5902 Warden Rd North Little Rock AR 72116

KOENEN, AUSTIN VOORHEES, investment banker; b. Morristown, N.J., Oct. 15, 1941; s. William and Elsie (Voorhees) K.; student Stevens Inst. Tech., 1959-60; B.S., U.S. Naval Acad., 1964; M.B.A., Harvard U., 1972; m. Kathleen Ann Chase, June 19, 1966; children—Karestan Chase, Erin Kathleen, Austin Voorhees. With Nuclear Energy Liability & Property Ins. Co., N.Y.C., 1969-71; asso. Kuhn Loeb & Co., N.Y.C., 1972-76; v.p. Salomon Bros., N.Y.C., 1976-77; sr. v.p., mgr. public fin. div. Lehman Bros. Kuhn Loeb Inc., N.Y.C., 1977—. Mem. Pequannock Twp. (N.J.) Planning Bd., 1972-74, Pequannock Twp. Council, 1974-75; mem. Pequannock Twp. Bd. Edn., 1975—, pres., 1977-78. Served with USN, 1964-68; Vietnam. Mem. Mcpl. Analysts Group N.Y. Democrat. Club: Harvard. Office: Lehman Bros Kuhn Loeb Inc 55 Water St New York NY 10041

KOENIG, STEPHAN MICHAEL, electronics co. exec.; b. N.Y.C., Dec. 29, 1941; s. Ira and Fay K.; A.A.S., N.Y. Inst. Tech., 1961, B.S., 1963; M.B.A., Adelphi U., 1967; m. Lynn Prince, Feb. 22, 1964; children—Robert Lawrence, David Scott. Engr. digital systems Grumman Aircraft Corp., Bethpage, N.Y., 1963-66; design engr., program mgr., mgr. systems engring., mgr. program adminstrn., mgr. contract adminstrn. Info. Displays Inc., Mt. Kisco, N.Y., 1966-74; group mgr. contracts, corp. mgr. contracts Digital Equipment Corp., Maynard, Mass., 1974—; pres. Info. Systems Co., Spring Valley, N.Y., 1968-74. Mem. adv. commn. Ramapo Sch. Bd., 1972-74; active youth sports; adv. commn. reorgn. govt. Town of Ramapo (N.Y.), 1974; bd. dirs. Rapid Reading Inst., 1971-74. Mem. Nat. Contract Mgmt. Assn., Am. Mgmt. Assn. Home: 14 Ledgewood Rd Framingham MA 01701 Office: 129 Parker St Maynard MA 01754

KOERS, FRANK HAROLD, clothing co. exec.; b. Ft. Smith, Ark., Mar. 9, 1932; s. Frank Herman and Ida Marie (Kremer) K.; B.S. in Bus. Adminstrn. (Watts-Payne Advt. scholar), U. Tulsa, 1954; postgrad. Ind. U., summer 1957, U. Okla., 1957-58; m. Rachel Brown, Oct. 21, 1959; children—Emilie M., Julie M. With Gardner-Denver Co., 1958; with Thermo Jac Sportswear, 1958-70, v.p. sales, 1969-70; mfrs. rep., 1970; v.p. sales Bressler Industries, Atlanta, 1970-75; with Ship n Shore div. Gen. Mills Co., 1975—, v.p. sales, southeast, 1979—. Served to 1st lt. USAF, 1955-57. Mem. Sales and Mktg. Execs. Atlanta. Republican. Club: Woodland Tennis and Swim (pres. 1979-80). Home: 545 Spender Trace Dunwoody GA 30338 Office: Ship n Shore Suite 3-S-340 Atlanta Apparel Mart 250 Spring St Atlanta GA 30303

KOGA, RUTH KAMURI, retail store exec.; b. Honolulu, July 19, 1929; d. Nenichi and Mino (Ozama) K.; B.A., Smith Coll., 1951; m. George M. Koga, Nov. 22, 1958; 1 dau., Suzanne. Pres., Ritz Dept. Stores, Honolulu, 1975—. Bd. dirs. Am. Cancer Soc.; trustee Hawaii Newspaper Agy. Founds., 1980, St. Louis High Sch., 1980. Mem. Nat. Retail Mchts. (past dir.), Sales and Mktg. Execs. Home: 1254 Center St Honolulu HI 96816 Office: 1143 Fort St Honolulu HI 96816

KOHL, MICHAEL PAUL, mgmt. cons.; b. Lebanon, Pa., Oct. 12, 1951; s. Warren P. and Dorothy P. K.; B.S.M.E., U. Pitts., 1973, postgrad. in bus., 1976-78; postgrad. in bus. adminstrn. U. No. Colo., 1974-76; m. Evelyn Helen Matro, Mar. 2, 1974. Engr., Buell Envirotech, Lebanon, Pa., 1973-74; project mgr. U.S. Steel Co., Pitts., 1976-79; cons. asso. Mgmt. Analysis Co., San Diego, 1979—; asso. prof. bus. LaRoche Coll., 1978-79; vis. lectr. in project mgmt. M.I.T., 1979—. Served with USAF, 1974-76. Registered profl. engr., Tex. Mem. Am. Mgmt. Assn., ASME, Project Mgmt. Inst. Home and Office: 4737 Shenandoah Dr Louisville KY 40222

KOHLENBERG, STANLEY, cosmetics co. exec.; b. Bklyn., Aug. 19, 1932; s. Max and MininMinnie (Roth) K.; B.S., Columbia, 1953; postgrad. N.Y. U., 1956-58; m. Ruth Barbara Itkin, Dec. 11, 1955; children—Robin Sue, Mark Stuart, Howard Scott. Account supr. L.W. Frohlich, N.Y.C., 1959-62; advt. mgr. Pfizer Lab., N.Y.C., 1962-63; marketing dir. Tussy Cosmetics, N.Y.C., 1964; sr. v.p., dir. client service Sudler & Hennessey, N.Y.C., 1964-66; publisher Cosmetics Fair mag., N.Y.C., 1966-68; exec. v.p. Spectrum Cosmetics, 1968-70; pres. Coty Inc., 1970-72; exec. v.p. Revlon Inc., N.Y.C., 1972-76; pres. Calvin Klein Cosmetics, Inc., N.Y.C., 1977—; cons., advt. and sales promotion. Served with M.D., AUS, 1953-55. Home: 30 Lincoln Plaza New York NY 10023 Office: 205 W 39th St New York NY 10018

KOHLER, FRED CHRISTOPHER, financial analyst; b. Cleve., Oct. 21, 1946; s. Fred Russell and Ruth Mary (Harris) K.; B.S. (Austin scholar), Northwestern U., 1968; M.B.A. (Faville fellow), Stanford, 1970. Sr. analyst adminstrv. services div. Arthur Andersen & Co., San Francisco, 1970-75, financial systems analyst, sr. cost accountant Hewlett Packard Co., Palo Alto, Calif., 1975-77, internat. mktg. systems adminstr., 1977-80, sr. planning and reporting analyst corp. hdqrs., 1980—. Mem. World Affairs Council No. Calif., Internt. Forum (steering com.), Northwestern U. Alumni Club No. Calif. (dir.), Stanford Alumni Assn., Beta Gamma Sigma. Home: 1736 Oak Creek Dr Palo Alto CA 94304 Office: 1501 Page Mill Rd Palo Alto CA 94304

KOHLER, GEORGE BARRY, banker; b. Attleboro, Mass., Oct. 12, 1945; s. George Lewis and Rosanna (Perry) K.; B.Sc., B.A., Bryant Coll., 1968; M.B.A., U. Notre Dame, 1970; postgrad. transp. mgmt. program Harvard U., 1979; m. Sylvia Silberstein, Sept. 21, 1975. Nat. accts. officer Marine Midland Bank, N.Y.C., 1970-75; asst. v.p., world banking div. Bank of Am. NT & SA, N.Y.C., 1975-79, v.p., product mgr. World Banking div., 1980—. Mem. Am. Trucking Assn. (fin. relations com. 1975—), Bryant Coll. Alumni Assn., Notre Dame Alumni Assn. (dir.), Nat. Acctg. and Fin. Council, Transp. Assn. Am. (policy devel. com.). Roman Catholic. Author: Financial Analysis of the Motor Carrier Industry, 1978; The For-Hire Tank Truck Industry, 1980. Office: 299 Park Ave New York NY 10017

KOHLER, LINDA LEE, plastics co. exec.; b. Allentown, Pa., Sept. 16, 1947; d. Ernest E. and Anna A. Kohler; student U. Fla., 1965-66, South Fla. Jr. Coll., 1966-67, Polk Jr. Coll., 1967-68; 1 son, David Wayne. Vice pres. Fla. Containers, Inc., Sebring, 1969-75, pres., 1975—; pres. Sebring Air Terminal Operators, 1978—; mem. task force White House Conf. on Small Bus. Women, 1979-80; mem. Sebring Indsl. Devel. Bd. Named Fla. Small Bus. Person of Yr., SBA, 1979. Mem. Soc. Plastics Engrs. (govt. affairs com.), Single Service Inst. (dir.), Sebring C. of C., Fla. Small Bus. Assn. (dir.). Democrat. Home: Sebring FL Office: PO Box 1149 Sebring FL 33870

KOHLHEPP, EDWARD JOHN, educator, cons.; b. Phila., Aug. 11, 1943; s. Edward H. and Helen Kathleen (Egan) K.; B.S. in Acctg., LaSalle Coll., 1967; M.B.A. in Mgmt., Temple U., 1969; m. Elizabeth A. Bretschneider, June 21, 1969; children—Edward Joseph, Karen Ann, Mary Beth. Instr., Bucks County Community Coll., Newtown, Pa., 1969-72, asst. prof., 1976-79, asso. prof., 1979—; sec./treas. Lincoln Investment Planning, Inc., Jenkintown, Pa., 1972-75; cons. Neil G. Kyde, Inc., Yardley, Pa., 1975-79; v.p. William L. Marshall Assos., Inc., Doylestown, Pa., 1979-80; pvt. practice cons., 1980—. Cert. pension cons.; C.L.U.; enrolled actuary, registered prin. N.A.S.D. Mem. Internat. Assn. Fin. Planners, Am. Soc. Pension Actuaries, Nat. Assn. Life Underwriters, Bucks County Estate Planning Council, Beta Gamma Sigma, Beta Alpha. Home: 29 Woods End Dr Doylestown PA 18901 Office: 121 S State St Newtown PA 18940

KOHLMANN, PAUL ALEXANDER, metals and minerals co. exec.; b. Gruenstadt, Germany, Sept. 19, 1923; s. Henry and Martha (Loeb) K.; came to U.S., 1938, naturalized, 1944; student Coll. City N.Y., 1941-43; m. Ursula Pollak, Mar. 26, 1950; children—Peter Stephen, Susan Joan. With A.E. Nydegger & Co. Inc., freight forwarders, 1941-43; pres. Uno Shipping Co. Inc., N.Y.C., 1946-53; v.p. Dutch Am. Raw Materials Corp., N.Y.C., 1953-59; v.p. Philipp Bros. div. Engelhard Minerals & Chems. Corp., N.Y.C., 1959—. Vice-pres., trustee Hebrew Tabernacle, N.Y.C., 1973—. Served to sgt., U.S. Army, 1943-46; PTO. Mem. Am. Ceramic Soc., Self Help Community Services Inc. (dir. N.Y.C. 1974—). Democrat. Club: Lake-Over Country and Golf (Bedford Hills, N.Y.). Home: 2465 Palisade Ave Riverdale NY 10463 also Indian Ln South Salem NY 10590 Office: Philipp Bros div Engelhard Minerals & Chems Corp 1221 Ave of Americas New York NY 10020

KOHN, ROBERT SAMUEL, JR., real estate cons.; b. Denver, Jan. 7, 1949; s. Robert Samuel and Marian Lackner (Neusteter) K.; B.S., U. Ariz., 1971; 1 son, Randall Stanton. Asst. buyer Robinson's Dept. Store, Los Angeles, 1971; agt. Neusteter Realty Co., Denver, 1972-73, exec. v.p., 1973-76; pres. Project Devel. Services, Denver, 1976-78, pres., chief exec. officer, 1978—; pres. Kohn and Assos., Inc., 1979—. Mem. Bldg. Owners and Mgrs. Assn. (pres. 1977-78, dir. 1972-78, dir. SW Conf. Bd. 1977-78), Denver Art Mus., Denver U. Library Assn., Central City Opera House Assn., Denver Assn. Bldg. Owners and Mgrs., Inst. Real Estate Mgmt. Republican. Jewish. Club: Denver Athletic. Home: 1740 Marguerite Ave Corona del Mar CA 92625

KOHNEN, MICHAEL PHILLIP, ins., loans, real estate exec.; b. Eau Claire, Wis., Jan. 16, 1942; s. Albert Rae and Virginia M. Kohnen; Asso. Tech., N.W. Mo. State U., 1974; m. Vicki Lee Melland, Feb. 7, 1980; children by previous marriage—Deloris L.E., Michael Phillip, John F., William P. Ins. agt., Eau Claire, 1967—; real estate broker, loan broker, Eau Claire, 1977—; real estate investor, ind. distbr. Wilderness Log Homes, Eau Claire, 1973—; sole owner, pres. Michael P. Kohnen, Rhu & Assos., Inc., Eau Claire, 1969—. Membership com. Eau Claire YMCA; mem. Republican Nat. Com. Served with USAF, 1962-66. Recipient Am. Spirit Hon. medal DAV, 1973; registered profl. disability and health ins. underwriter. Mem. Nat. Assn. Health Ins. Underwriters (state pres., 1976-77), Wis. Assn. Health Underwriters (dir.), Nat. Assn. Realtors, Nat. Taxpayers Union. Lutheran. Club: Swim and Run for Your Life. Home: 1814 Vine St Eau Claire WI 54701 Office: 405 S Farwell St Suites 35-36 Eau Claire WI 54701

KOHNEN, ROBERT EUGENE, ins. co. exec.; b. Chgo., May 13, 1933; s. Arthur and Eugenia (Knecht) K.; B.S. in Mech. Engring., Ill. Inst. Tech., 1959; M.B.A., Mich. State U., 1962; m. Sharon Ann Klingaman, Sept. 17, 1960; children—Michelle Ann, Susan Renae, Brett Eugene. Quality control engr. Bendix Corp., Mishawaka, Ind., 1959-62; v.p. security analysis Growth Research, Inc., Chgo., 1962-67; treas., asso. portfolio mgr. Growth Industry Shares, Inc., Chgo., 1967-73; v.p. and investment mgr. Protection Mut. Ins. Co., Park Ridge, Ill., 1973—. Served with AUS, 1953-55. Chartered fin. analyst; C.P.C.U. Mem. Inst. Chartered Fin. Analysts, Inst. C.P. and C.U.'s, Chgo. Soc. Security Analysts, Fin. Analysts Fedn., Ill. Inst. Tech. Alumni Assn. (sec. treas. 1968-69), Indian Boundary Y's Men's Assn. (pres. 1973-74). Presbyterian. Home: 5733 Fairmount St Downers Grove IL 60515 Office: 300 S Northwest Hwy Park Ridge IL 60068

KOHNSTAMM, PAUL LOTHAIR, corp. exec.; b. N.Y.C., Nov. 14, 1922; s. Lothair S. and Madeline (Peck) K.; B.A., Williams Coll., 1944; m. Mary Loeb, May 7, 1944; children—Paul Kenneth, Peter L., Daniel Frank, Katherine, Joshua G., Emily. With H. Kohnstamm & Co., N.Y.C., 1945—, chmn. bd., chief exec. officer; pres. Gen. Color Co., Newark; chmn. exec. com. Internat. Banknote Co.; dir. Horace Gory & Co., Ltd., Oswald McCardell & Co., Ltd.; chmn. bd. H. Kohnstamm Co. (U.K.), Ltd. (all Eng.); pres. Kohnstamm Co., Ltd., Montreal; dir. Globe Ticket Co., Horsham, Pa. Chmn. bd. trustees Hosp. Joint Diseases Orthopedic Inst., 1980; asst. treas. Fedn. Jewish Philanthropies, 1978; mem. Pound Ridge Devel. Town Com.; nat. committeeman Am. Jewish Com.; hon. trustee Horace Mann-Barnard Sch.; pres. elect Hosp. Joint Diseases and Med. Center, N.Y.C., 1962-78; trustee Jewish Home and Hosp. for Aged, 1951—, N.Y. Soc. for Deaf, 1975—; co-chmn. chems., plastics and paints div. United Jewish Appeal-Fedn. Jewish Philanthropies, 1975—; committeeman United Negro Coll. Fund. Served with AUS, 1943-45. Fellow Am. Inst. Chemists; mem. Am. Chem. Soc., Synthetic Organic Chem. Mfrs. Assn., Chemists Club, Gargoyle Soc. Democrat. Clubs: Century Country (White Plains, N.Y.); Williams (N.Y.C.); B'nai B'rith. Office: 161 Ave of Americas New York NY 10013

KOHR, THOMAS JOSEPH, JR., mech. contractor; b. Hanover, Pa., Oct. 10, 1928; s. Thomas Joseph and Evelyn Louise (Coppersmith) K.; student public schs.; m. Nancy A.M. Easter, June 19, 1954; children—Thomas Joseph III, Mark, Kimberly, Stephen, Danny. Interior decorator Hutzler Bros., 1948-49; driver Nat. Plastics, 1949-51, 1952-53; clk. U.S. Post Office, 1953-54; estimator Heer Bros., 1954-55; owner, v.p. So. Mech., Inc., Balt., 1955—; musician, orch. leader. Leader, Cub Scouts, Boy Scouts Am., 1963-68; active Reisterstown Civic Assn., P.T.A.; mem. council Luth. Ch. Served with Q.M.C., U.S. Army, 1951. Registered master plumber, stationary engr. Mem. ASHRAE, Assn. Builders and Contractors, Bldg. Congress and Exchange, U.S. Jaycees (former v.p., internat. dir.), Antique Motor Club Am. Republican. Clubs: Elks, Masons, Tall Cedars of Lebanon. Home: 1230 Greenspring Valley Rd Lutherville MD 21093 Office: 2607 Annapolis Rd Baltimore MD 21230

KOK, HANS GEBHARD, engring. co. exec.; b. Potshausen, Germany, Apr. 5, 1923; s. George J. and Antina K. (Janssen) K.; student Suderburg (Germany) Engring. Coll., 1940-42, Hamburg Engring. Coll., 1945-46; Dipl. Ing., Technische Hochschule, Aachen, 1950; m. Roselle V. Venier, June 22, 1960; children—George H., Karen R. Came to U.S., 1951, naturalized, 1959. Design engr. Lummus Co., N.Y.C., 1951-53; structural engr. M. H. Treadwell Co., N.Y.C., 1953-56, head structural engring. sect., 1956-62, chief structural engr., 1962-63; mgr. plant design div. Treadwell Corp., N.Y.C., 1963-69, asst. v.p. engring., 1969-73, v.p. engring., 1973—; pres. Treadwell Corp. Mich. Inc., 1974—; dir. Basset Miller Treadwell Pty. Ltd. Chmn. exec. com. Council Engring. Laws, 1976. Recipient 1st award James F. Lincoln Arc Welding Found., 1966. Registered profl. engr., N.Y., Pa., Ill., Mich., Mo., Minn., Ohio, W. Va., Utah, Tex., La., N.M., Ariz., Md., Mass., Tenn. Fellow Am. Soc. C.E.; mem. Nat., N.Y. State socs. profl. engrs., Am. Inst. Mining, Metall. and Petroleum Engrs. (chmn. materials handling com.), Am. Mining Congress, Mining Club N.Y., Am. Mgmt. Assn. Contbr. to profl. jours. Home: 28 W 95th St New York NY 10025 Office: 1700 Broadway New York NY 10019

KOKJER, JORDAN NUTZMAN, securities co. exec.; b. Blair, Nebr., Feb. 3, 1915; s. Jordan Madsen and Julia Catherine (Nutzman) K.; A.B., Doane Coll., Crete, Nebr., 1939; postgrad. math. U. Nebr., U. So. Calif.; diploma Coll. Financial Planning, Denver, 1973; m. Helen Allis, July 18, 1937 (dec. Dec. 9, 1965); children—Kenneth J., Nancy, W. Dean; m. 2d, La Vonne Loveless, Feb. 11, 1967. Tchr., coach pub. schs., Nebr., 1936-46; agt. Met. Life Ins. Co., 1946-55; owner furniture store, also finance bus., North Platte, Nebr., 1955-61; gen. agt. Surety Life Ins. Co. Nebr., 1961-67; broker, v.p., dir. Sur Equity, Inc., Salt Lake City, 1968-70; broker ManEquity, Inc., Denver, 1970—, pres., dir., 1972—; v.p., treas., dir. Manequity Mgmt. Co., 1975—; pres., dir. Western Credit Corp., 1960-63. Bd. regents Coll. Fin. Planning, 1973—. Recipient spl. recognition Tri-Trials council Boy Scouts Am., 1963. Mem. Inst. Certified Fin. Planners (nat. pres. 1976—). Presbyterian (mem. session 1950-75, exec. rep. Presbytery 1958-59). Home: 9717 S Deer Creek Canyon Rd Littleton CO 80127 Office: 5889 S Syracuse Circle Englewood CO 80111

KOLBER, E. LEO, real estate devel. co. exec.; b. Montreal, Que., Can., 1929; grad. McGill U., 1949. Formerly pres. Cemp Investments Ltd.; now vice chmn. Cadillac Fairview Corp. Ltd., Willowdale, Ont., Can.; pres., dir. Toronto-Dominion Centre Ltd., Claridge Investments Ltd.; dir. Supersol Ltd., Seagram Co., Ltd., Pacific Centre Ltd., Toronto-Dominion Bank, Multiple Access Ltd., Kruger Pulp & Paper Co. Office: Cadillac Fairview Corp Ltd 1200 Sheppart Ave E Willowdale ON M2K 2R8 Canada*

KOLESAR, STEPHEN MERO, ins. and investment cons.; b. Ft. Bragg, Calif., June 8, 1948; s. Stephen and Joan Mary (Shafsky) K.; student Ariz. State U., 1966-70; m. Linda Sue Price, Oct. 30, 1971; children—Kathryn Marie, Christina Elizabeth. With New Eng. Life Ins. Co., 1980—; gen. partner real estate devel. co.; pres. Asbestolit N. Am., Ltd., Meroux Ltd. Internat. Import & Export Cons.; dir. Tri-City Life Underwriters; sec.-treas. Ariz. Life Underwriters Polit. Action Com., 1975-78, state chmn., 1979—; cons. life ins. mktg.; tchr. ins., investments to high schs., chs., civic groups. Mem. Ariz. Republican Campaign Com., 1978; mem. alumni com. Brophy Coll. Prep. Sch., Phoenix. Recipient Eagle Scout award Boy Scouts Am., 1965, Nat. Quality award Nat. Assn. Life Underwriters, 1978; named to Million Dollar Round Table, 1977-79. Mem. Am. Soc. C.L.U.'s, Nat. Assn. Life Underwriters, Internat. Assn. Fin. Planners (pres. Ariz. chpt. 1976-77), Tri-City Estate Planning Council, Tri-City Life Underwriter's Assn. Roman Catholic. Office: 3900 E Camelback Rd Suite 200-S Phoenix AZ 85018

KOLIN, MICHAEL JOHN, automobile co. exec.; b. Ipswich, Eng., Feb. 4, 1946; s. LeRoy Charles and Vera Ellen (Cranmer) K.; came to U.S., 1946, naturalized, 1946; B.B.A., Eastern Mich. U., 1969; m. Denise M. Delarosa, Sept. 29, 1972. Analyst, Ford Motor Co., Dearborn, Mich., 1969-71, zone service mgr., 1971-73, owner relations rep., 1973-74, service mgmt. specialist, 1974-75, supr. spl. liaison unit owner relations dept., 1975-76, supr. correspondence unit, 1976-77, mgr. owner relations dept. Washington dist., 1977-78, mgr. parts and service devel. dept. Washington dist., 1978, gen. field mgr. Seattle dist., 1978—; v.p. Northwest Cycle, Inc., Seattle. Mem. Mich. Bicycle Fedn. (consumer bd.), Ferrari Club Am. Club: Rainbow Cycling (coach). Co-author: The Ten Speed Bicycle; The Custom Bicycle; contbg. editor Bicycling Mag. Home: 14642 NE 174th St Woodinville WA 98072 Office: 10604 NE 38th Pl Suite 123 Kirkland WA 98033

KOLIOS, THEODORE ANDREAS, steamship co. exec.; b. Greece, Sept. 8, 1933; came to U.S., 1956, naturalized, 1962; s. Andreas John and Efthalia A. (Pappas) K.; grad. U. Athens, 1956; postgrad. Columbia U., 1958, Bernard Baruch Sch. Bus. Adminstrn., 1959-63; m. Aphrodite Dalianis, July 2, 1961; children—Efthalia, Arthur. Asst. chief acct. Triton Shipping, Inc., N.Y.C., 1958-62; asst. treas. Star Line, Inc., N.Y.C., 1962-64; v.p. Dynamic Shipping, Inc., N.Y.C., 1964-66; treas. C Ventures, Inc., Ram Broadcasting Corp., Off-Shore Services Corp., N.Y.C.; dir. 7 W 54th St. Realty Corp. Mem. Am. Mgmt. Assn., Assn. Water Transp. Acctg. Officers. Clubs: N.Y. Athletic, Masons, Knights of Malta. Office: C Ventures Inc 7 W 54th St New York NY 10019

KOLMAN, LAURENCE STEVEN, filtration co. exec.; b. Bklyn., Nov. 24, 1940; s. Sol S. and Sylvia Kolman; B.A., Hofstra Coll., 1962; M.A., State U. N.Y., 1976; m. Elaine Susan Siegel, Apr. 7, 1963; children—Michele Blaine, Geoffrey Scott. Registered rep. E.F. Hutton & Co., Inc., Garden City, N.Y., 1967-70; account mgr. Burroughs Corp., Hempstead, N.Y., 1970-74; sr. account mgr. Xerox Data Systems div. Xerox Corp., N.Y.C., 1974-75; prin., exec. Rich Plan Food Corp., Vestal, N.Y., 1975-78; prin., exec. LEEM Filtration Products, Inc., Mahwah, N.J., 1978—. Chmn. Youth Services, Suffolk, 1972-73; mem. Friends of the Library Com., N.Y., 1972-74; bd. dirs. Harborfields-Elwood Youth Devel. Assn., pres., 1972-74. Served to capt. USAF, 1962-67; Vietnam. Decorated Air Force Commendation medal; recipient George M. Estabrook Distinguished Service award, 1966. Mem. Am. Assn. Meat Processors, N.Y. State Council Retail Mchts., Hornell Area, Albany Area chambers commerce, Hofstra Alumni Assn., Pi Delta Epsilon. Jewish. Club: Kiwanis (pres. 1970-73). Home: 3 Lodi Ln Monsey NY 10952 Office: 124 Christie Ave Mahwah NJ 07430

KOLNER, EDWARD ALOYSIUS, engring. services co. exec.; b. Dixonville, Pa., June 21, 1915; s. Francis Joseph and Suzanne Mary (Parana) K.; B.S., Lock Haven State Coll., 1940; m. Mary Kathryn Lais, Sept. 27, 1943. Tchr., Western Pa., 1940-45; mem. personnel staff Arth McKee & Co., Cleve., E.F. Hauserman Co., Cleve., Aluminum Co. Am., Cleve., 1945-57; personnel mgr. Chemplant Designs, Inc. div. Devenco Inc., N.Y.C., 1957-70, v.p., 1970—, pres., 1972—, also dir. div. and parent co. Recipient Distinguished Service award Lock Haven State Coll. Alumni Assn., 1972. Democrat. Roman Catholic. Clubs: Water Gap Country, Delaware Water Gap; Emerson (N.J.) Country. Home: 101 Prospect Ave Hackensack NJ 07601 Office: 140 Cedar St New York NY 10006

KOLS, DAVID MICHAEL, tour operator; b. Balt., Sept. 13, 1950; s. Henry S. and Irene Louise (Simons) K.; B.S. in Bus. and Econs., Lehigh U., Bethlehem, Pa., 1972. Founder, pres. Am. Student Travel Center, 1972—; pres. Breakaway Tours (USA) Inc., 1975-79; pres., dir. Value Vacations, Inc., Winsted, Conn., 1975—. Bd. dirs. Am. Student Travel Center. Mem. Assn. Charter Tour Operators Am., Assn. Internat. Etudiant Scientifique et Commerciale, Sigma Alpha Mu. Office: 151 Main St Winsted CT 06098

KOLTERER, FRANZ, photochem. co. exec.; b. Ljubljana, Yugoslavia, May 21, 1931; came to U.S., 1956, naturalized, 1961; s. Franz and Anna (Ritovsek) K.; student Ljubljana U., 1952-54, U. Vienna, 1954-56; B.S. in Bus. Adminstrn., Graphic Arts Sch., Vienna, 1956; m. Julie Muller, Apr. 20, 1963; children—Peter F., John F., Franz M., Richard F., Tanya J. Founder, Micro Sci. Assos., Mountain View, Calif., 1962—; founder, pres., Koltron Corp., Sunnyvale, Calif., 1974—, gen. mgr., 1980—, chmn. bd., 1980—, also dir. Mem. Am. Electronics Assn., Electronic Assn. Calif., Semicondr. Equipment Mfg. Assn., Aircraft Owners and Pilots Assn., Photochem. Milling Inst., Calif. Circuits Assn. Inventor in photochem. field. Home: 23828 Ravensbury Ave Los Altos Hills CA 94022 Office: Koltron Corp 1380 Bordeaux Dr Sunnyvale CA 94086

KOLTON, BARRETT DAVID, bus. exec.; b. Newark, Jan. 17, 1933; s. Heyman and Celia (Markowitz) K.; B.M.E., Cornell U., 1955; m. Barbara Sherman, Sept. 5, 1954; children—Lynne, Jeffrey, Wendy. Engring. mgr. Kolton Elec. Mfg. Co., Newark, 1957-61; pres. B-K Elec. Products Inc., West Orange, N.J., 1961-74, Sun Elec. Products, Parsippany, N.J., 1973-74; pres., dir. Biksun Mfg. Co., Inc., Parsippany, 1974-76; pres. BD Kolton & Assos., 1977-78; pres. B-K Industries, East Hanover, N.J., 1978—. Essex County (N.J.) committeeman, 1962-63; chmn. citizens adv. com. West Orange Bd. Edn., 1972-75; mem. N.J. Bd. Mediation, 1975-78. Served to 1st lt. Signal Corps, U.S. Army, 1955-57. Mem. N.J. Mfrs. Assn., Young Pres.'s Orgn., Cornell Soc. Engrs., Alpha Epsilon Pi. Home: 16 Steven Terr West Orange NJ 07052 Office: 265 Route 10 East Hanover NJ 07936

KOLTVEIT, JAMES MITCHELL, accountant; b. Pontiac, Ill., Jan. 17, 1941; s. Oscar John and Marie Elizabeth K.; student Ill. State U., 1959-60; B.S. in Accountancy, U. Ill., 1963; m. Ruth Ann Beaumont, Apr. 30, 1966; children—Lisa Ann, Jeffrey Allen. Staff acct. Mc Gladrey Hendrickson & Co., Davenport, Iowa, 1963-67, supr., 1967-68, charge Muscatine (Iowa) office, 1968-69, partner, 1969—, charge Keokuk (Iowa) office, 1969-72, Rock Island (Ill.) office, 1972—, also coordinator services to banks, 1977—; speaker confs.; instr. banking seminar Asso. Acctg. Firms Internat.; chmn. Ann. Update Banking Conf. of Ill. C.P.A. Soc. Treas. Railsback for Congress Com., 1980; treas., bd. dirs. Rock Island Family YMCA, 1976-80; bd. dirs. Friendship Manor, 1976-80. Served with Army NG, 1963-69. Mem. Am. Inst. C.P.A.'s, Ill. C.P.A. Soc., Iowa Soc. C.P.A.'s, Nat. Assn. Accts., Rock Island C. of C. (treas., dir. 1979-80). Republican. Mem. Evangelical Free Ch. Club: Rotary. Office: 525 17th St Rock Island IL 61201

KOMEN, RICHARD BEN, restaurateur; b. Bellingham, Wash., Mar. 18, 1933; s. Benedict and Opal May (Roaney) K.; B.A. in Accounting, U. Wash., 1955; m. Joan Rae Romstead, Feb. 14, 1959; children—Mark, Gregory, Bradley. Founder, mgr. Volume Service Co., food concessions and catering, Seattle, 1962-72; founder, owner Restaurants Unlimited, Inc., operating restaurants in Wash., Oreg., Calif., Alaska and Hawaii, 1972—; dir. Canlis restaurants; cons. Interstate United Corp. Served to 1st lt. arty. U.S. Army, 1956-58. Mem. Nat. Restaurant Assn., Restaurant Assn. State Wash. (dir.). Clubs: Inglewood Country (past pres.), Washington Athletic, 101, Chaine des Rotisseurs. Home: 16305 Inglewood Rd Bothell WA 98011 Office: 1331 N Northlake Way Seattle WA 98103

KOMULAINEN, WILLIAM PETER, optical co. exec.; b. Indpls., June 11, 1949; s. William Peter and Betty June (Summa) K.; B.A., Salem State Coll., 1971; m. Beverly Langford Burgess, May 14, 1977; 1 son, William; 1 son by previous marriage, Jason. Sales rep. Am. Optical Corp., Southbridge, Mass., 1970-73, instrument sales mgr., 1973-74, field sales trainer, 1974-75, tng. editor, 1975, trainer in-house, 1975-76, sales tng. mgr., 1976-78, mgr. product promotion, 1978-79, mgr. sales tng. and mgmt. devel., 1979-80, mgr. mgmt. tng. and orgn. devel., 1980—; v.p. Alternative Systems & Designs, Inc., Sturbridge, Mass., 1978—; asso. Orgn./Mgmt. Cons.'s Co., Charlton, Mass., 1980—; faculty optics Worcester (Mass.) Poly., 1975. Town selectman, Hempstead, N.H., 1974-75. Mem. Am. Mgmt. Assn., Am. Soc. Tng. and Devel., Nat. Soc. Profl. Instrs., Nat. Rifle Assn., Orgn. Devel. Network, Newburyport (Mass.) Art Assn. Contbr. articles to tng. publs. Home: Box 755 J Davis Rd Charlton City MA 01508 Office: 12 Mechanic St Southbridge MA 01550

KONCHAR, FRANK HERMAN, utility exec.; b. Carbondale, Pa., July 18, 1935; s. Frank C. and Sophie K.; B.S., Pa. State U., 1957; M.S., Lehigh U., 1962; m. Janet Elaine Hobbes, July 2, 1960; children—Frank M., Sonya J., Mark D., Katie M. Trainee engring. mgmt. Pitts. Des Moines Steel Co., Pitts., 1962-65, project mgr. test facilities, 1965-66, project mgr.-nuclear, 1966-71; dir. project constrn. services dept. Consumers Power Co., Jackson, Mich., 1971-79, project mgr. wood demonstration power plant, 1979-80, mgr. constrn. and testing, 1980—. Served with U.S. Army, 1958. Mem. ASCE, Project Mgmt. Inst., Nat., Mich. socs. profl. engrs., Phi Kappa Theta. Mem. Cursillos Christianity. Home: 5933 Salabelle Jackson MI 49201 Office: 1945 W Parnall Rd Jackson MI 49201

KONDI, ANDREW GORDON, oil co. exec.; b. Niagara Falls, Ont., Can., Apr. 14, 1933; s. Andi and Elizabeth K.; B.Sc., McMaster U., 1956; m. Ruth Marie Scott, Sept. 22, 1956; children—Karen L., Kathy L., Andrew B., Scott C. Staff geologist Imperial Oil Ltd., 1956-59; chief geologist, exploration mgr. Williamson Oil & Gas, Ltd., Calgary, 1959-64; cons., Calgary, 1964-68; sr. geologist Scurry Rainbow Oil Ltd., Calgary, Alta., 1968-75, chief geologist, 1975-77, exploration mgr., 1977-80; mgr. fgn. exploration Home Oil Co., Calgary, 1980; exec. v.p. Precision Resources Ltd., Calgary, 1980—; Mem. Am. Assn. Petroleum Geologists, Can. Soc. Petroleum Geologists, Calgary Petroleum Club. Home: 40 Moorgate Pl SW Calgary AB T2U 2H1 Canada Office: 1020-500 4th Ave SW Calgary AB T2P 2U6 Canada

KONECKY, NATHAN, computer services co. exec.; b. Bklyn., Apr. 9, 1943; s. Paul and Bertha (Yellan) K.; B.S. in Math., Clarkson Coll., 1963; m. Judith Lee Green, Dec. 30, 1975; children—Deborah, Aaron, Erika. Programmer, Univac Co., Phila., 1963-66, Keystone Computer Assos., Fort Washington, Pa., 1966-68; chmn. bd., pres., sec., treas. NSA, Inc., Cherry Hill, N.J. and officer, dir. subs. cos. Nat. System Analysts, Inc., MGA, Inc., Arms, Inc., 1968—. Home: 531 Maple Ave Collingswood NJ 08108 Office: One Cherry Hill Cherry Hill NJ 08002

KONHEIM, HARVEY, mgmt. cons.; b. N.Y.C., July 2, 1902; s. Gustave A. and Ida (Leavy) K.; student Coll. City N.Y., 1920-23; m. Beatrice S. Goldstein, Nov. 29, 1933; children—Susan (Mrs. Burton Sobel), Jon. Product and mfg. engr. Viscosity Devices Corp., N.Y.C., 1928-34, Gen. Electric Co., Bridgeport, Conn., 1942-44, Western Electric Co., Kearny, N.J., 1944-49, W.L. Maxson Corp., N.Y.C., 1950-54; exec. staff Remington Rand Univac div. Sperry Rand Corp., N.Y.C., 1956-60, mgr. mfg. Univac, Phila., 1960-67; mgmt. cons., N.Y.C., 1968—; mem. Exec. Vol. Corps, N.Y.C. Econ. Devel. Adminstrn., 1968-75. Active in conservation as mem. Adirondack Mountain Club, Sierra Club. Mem. Am. Soc. M.E., Am. Soc. Tool Engrs. Office: 500 E 77th St New York NY 10021

KONIE, ROBERT B., real estate and ins. co. exec.; b. Chgo., May 14, 1936; s. Joseph and Sophie (Malkiewicz) Konieczny; B.S., Loyola U., Chgo., 1958, postgrad., 1961. Owner, R.B. Konie & Co., Evergreen Park, Ill., 1966—. Served with AUS, 1959-61. Mem. Nat., Ill. assns. realtors, S.W. Suburban Bd. Realtors, Chgo. Bd. Underwriters. Roman Catholic. Club: Elks. Office: 3100 W 95th St Evergreen Park IL 60642

KONOWITZ, HERBERT HENRY, mfg. co. exec.; b. Brookline, Mass., Feb. 13, 1937; s. Robert Isaac and Sarah (Freedman) K.; B.S. in Bus. Adminstrn., Babson Coll., 1958; m. Linda Phyllis Swartzman, Dec. 20, 1958; children—Cindy Lee, Jeffrey Scott. Vice pres. Vita Rest Sales Co., N.Y.C., 1958-63, Lady Linda Covers Inc., N.Y.C., 1963—; pres. Milford Stitching Co. (Del.), 1968—; v.p. Comml. Drapery Contractors, Inc., Silver Springs, Md., 1976—; dir. Greater Del. Corp., Dover, Del. Nat. Life, Yankee Land, Inc., Reclamation Center, Inc., 1972-75, G.L.K., Inc. Mem. Gov. Del. Council Consumer Affairs, 1971-76; commr. State Lottery Commn., 1978—; bd. dirs. Job for Del. Grads., Inc., 1979. Chmn. Local Republican Dist. Com., 1971-75; mem. Del. Rep. Central Com., 1971—; vice chmn. Kent County Rep. Com., 1975-79, chmn., 1979-81; v.p. Kent County chpt. Am. Heart Assn., 1974-75, pres., 1975-76; trustee Broadmeadow Sch., 1980—, Congregation Beth Sholom, 1980—. Clubs: Masons, Elks. Home: 55 Beloit Ave Dover DE 19901 Office: Milford Stitching Co S Marshall St Milford DE 19963

KONSKI, JAMES LOUIS, civil engr.; b. N.Y.C., Nov. 4, 1917; s. Herbert D. and Ruby (Louis) K.; B.S. in Civil Engring., U. Mo., 1950, M.S. in C.E., 1951; children—Alexander, Christina, Marguerite. Engr. Bur. Yards and Docks, Washington, 1951; structural engr. Sanderson & Porter, N.Y.C., 1951-52; field engr. Ebasco Services, Inc., Owensboro, Ky., 1952-53; chief structural engr. Berger Assos., Syracuse, N.Y., 1953-54, Endman, Anthony & Hosley (formerly Berger Assos.), Syracuse, N.Y., 1954-57; sr. partner Konski Engrs., P.C., Syracuse, 1957—. U.S. cons. engr. Trade Mission to Africa, 1965, to Far East, 1970; mem. State Govt. Adv. Group for Emergency Constrn. Served with USMC, 1939-46, maj. Res. ret. Registered profl. engr., N.Y., Ky., R.I. Fellow Am. Soc. C.E. (v.p. 1972-73, nat. dir. 1966-70); mem. Internat. Assn. Bridge and Structural Engrs., N.Y. Assn. Cons. Engrs. (past chpt. pres.), Nat. Soc. Profl. Engrs. (past chpt. pres.), Am. Concrete Inst., Prestressed Concrete Inst., Cons. Engrs. Council (past chpt. pres.), Am. Inst. Cons. Engrs., Am. Congress Surveying and Mapping, Am. Mil. Engrs., Am. Water Works Assn., Am. Road Builders Assn., Am. Soc. Photogrammetry, League Am. Wheelmen (regional dir.), Amateur Bicycle League Am., Sigma Xi, Tau Beta Pi, Chi Epsilon, Pi Mu Epsilon. Club: Onondaga Cycling (pres.). Contbr. articles to profl. jours. Home: 514 Mt View Ave Syracuse NY 13224 Office: 113 E Onondaga St Syracuse NY 13202

KOOCHER, RONALD LAURENCE, Realtor; b. Boston, Sept. 27, 1934; s. Jacob and Ida (Adler) K.; B.A., Boston U., 1956; m. Barbara Ruth Davis, Jan. 5, 1955; children—Bonnie Lyn, Ilisa Beth. Exec., Morton's Inc., Boston, 1958-67, Lane Bryant, N.Y.C., 1967-70; pres. Koocher & Co., Newton, Mass., 1970—; dir. Shoppers' Wrold, Framingham, Mass., South Shore Plaza, Braintree, Mass. Mem. Nat., Mass. assns. Realtors, Greater Boston, Newton real estate bds., Rental Housing Assn. Author: Techniques and Applications, 1975. Home: 19 Bothfeld Rd Newton Centre MA 02159 Office: 850 Boylston St Chestnut Hill MA 02167

KOOGLER, DAVID MANGUS, mining co. exec.; b. Spottswood, Va., Oct. 28, 1928; s. William Mangus and Leslie Anna (Lamb) K.; B.S. in Indsl. Engring., Va. Poly. Inst., 1950; M.B.A., Drexel Inst. Tech., 1955; m. Margery Crougey, Mar. 10, 1951; children—David Mark, Dana Rene. Smelter supt., supt. concentrator ops., dir. indsl. engring., mgr. ops. Braden Copper Co., El Teniente, Chile, 1956-67; asst. to v.p., gen. mgr. reduction and metals divs. Kaiser Aluminum, Oakland, Calif., 1967-69; asst. v.p. Newmont Mining Corp., N.Y.C., 1969-74; exec. v.p., dir. natural resources div. G&W, Bethlehem, Pa., 1974-76; pres., dir. Va. Met. Coal Co., Wise, 1976, Jersey-Ky. Coal Co. and Jersey-W.Va. Coal Co., 1976; pres., dir. Mark-Dana Corp., 1976—, Penn Pocahontas Coal Co., 1976—, Gary Coal Co., 1977-79, D & M Investment Co., 1977—, Bethlehem Resources, 1977—, Dana Mark Mgmt. Services Corp., 1977—; partner Koogler Devel. & Constrn. Co., 1976—; pres., dir. Mullins Coal Co., 1978-79; dir. Thai Zinc Ltd., N.J. Zinc Exploration Co., Va. Met. Coal Co., Jersey-Ky. Coal Co., Jersey-W.Va. Coal Co.; v.p., dir. Carlin Gold Mining Co., Idarado Mining Co., Granduc Operating Co., Similkameen Copper Minind Co., Newmont Service Co. Ltd. Served with U.S. Army, 1950-52. Recipient Bausch and Lomb Sci. Award 1946; registered profl. engr., Calif. Mem. Am. Inst. Indsl. Engrs., AIME, Am. Mining Congress. Clubs: Mining of N.Y., Bethlehem, Pa. Soc., Elks. Home: Route 4 Bingen Rd Bethlehem PA 18015

KOOGLER, RUSSELL LEWIS, pvt. investigator; b. Zanesville, Ohio, Sept. 12, 1938; s. Emerson L. and Betty J. (DeSantel) King; student Sacramento Jr. Coll., 1972-74; B.Police Sci. and Bus., Fullerton Coll., 1975; m. Jacolyn Rae Karpus, June 28, 1968; children—Patricia Louise. Fed. police officer U.S. Postal Inspectors, Los Angeles, 1967-77; head security K-Mart Corp., Peoria, Ariz., 1977—; owner Koogler & Asso., Pvt. Investigators, Glendale, Ariz., 1979—; spl. agt. Internat. Police Congress, Washington; head security K-Mart Corp., Phoenix. Tchr., instr. CPR and first aid and disaster courses ARC, Santa Ana, Calif., 1971-78, disaster chmn., 1976-78. Served with Signal Corps, U.S. Army, 1961-64. Recipient awards, ARC 1973, 74, 75, Freedom Train award, 1976. Mem. Internat. Assn. Credit Card Investigators, Ariz. Retail Investigators Assn., Credit Data of Am., Internat. Consumer Credit Assn., Cole's Directory Service Greater Phoenix, Alpha Gamma Sigma, Calif. State Assn. EMT's. Contbr. articles in field to profl. jours. Home: 7045 N 7th St Phoenix AZ 85020 Office: PO Box 35384 Phoenix AZ 85069

KOONCE, JOHN PETER, investment co. exec.; b. Coronado, Calif., Jan. 8, 1932; s. Allen Clark and Elizabeth (Webb) K.; B.S., U.S. Naval Acad., 1954; postgrad. U. So. Calif., 1957, U. Alaska, 1961, U. Ill., 1968-69; M.S. in Ops. Research, Fla. Inst. Tech., 1970; postgrad. Claremont Grad. Sch., 1970; m. Marilyn Rose Campbell, Sept. 21, 1952; children—Stephen Allen, William Clark, Peter Marshall. Indsl. engr. Aluminum Co. Am. Lafayette, Ind., 1954-56; electronic research engr. Autonetics Div. N.Am. Aviation, Downey, Calif., 1956-57; systems field engr. Remington Rand Univac, Fayetteville, N.C., 1957-59; project engr. RCA Service Co., Cheyenne, Wyo., 1959-60, project supr., Clear, Alaska, 1960-62, project supr., Yorkshire, Eng., 1962-64, re-entry signature analyst, Patrick AFB, Fla., 1964-66; mem. tech. staff TRW Systems Group, Washington, 1966-68; mgr. ops research systems analysis Magnavox Co., Urbana, Ill., 1968-69; tech. advisor, EDP, to USAF, Aerojet Electro Systems Co., Azusa, Calif., Woomera, Australia, 1969-72; investment exec. Shearson Hammill, Los Angeles, 1972-74; investment exec. Reynolds Securities, Los Angeles, 1974-75; v.p. investments Shearson Hayden Stone, Glendale, Calif., 1975-77; v.p. accounts Paine, Webber, Jackson & Curtis Inc., Los Angeles, 1977—; tchr. investments Citrus Coll., Azusa, Calif., Claremont (Calif.) Evening Sch. Vice pres. Claremont Republican Club, 1973, pres., 1974. Chmn., Verdugo Hosp. Assos., 1979. Recipient Merit certificate RCA, 1966. Mem. Nat. Assn. Security Dealers, Naval Acad. Alumni Assn. Clubs: Masons. Kiwanis. Contbr. articles to bus. jours. Home: 3718 Chevy Chase Dr Flintridge CA 91011 Office: 700 S Flower St Los Angeles CA 90017

KOONCE, SAMUEL DAVID, chem. co. exec.; b. Titusville, Fla., Nov. 26, 1915; s. Martin Egbert and Sara Elizabeth (Thompson) K.; A.B., Oberlin Coll., 1936; M.S., Ohio State U., 1940, Ph.D., 1943; m. Helen Mathews, Dec. 28, 1940; children—Kathryn, Samuel, Richard. Mgr. market devel. Jefferson Chem. Co., N.Y.C., 1952-55; mgr. market research dept. comml. devel. div. Am. Cyanamid Co., N.Y.C., 1955-61; mgr. comml. devel. Lummus Co., N.Y.C., 1961-68; mgr. mktg. Ugine Industries, Inc., N.Y.C., 1968-73; dir. tech. div. Ugine Kuhlmann of Am., Englewood Cliffs, N.J., 1973-75, v.p., 1975—; v.p. Pechiney Ugine Kuhlmann Devel. Corp., 1977—. Fellow AAAS; mem. Chem. Mktg. Research Assn. (pres. 1954-55), Comml. Devel. Assn., Am. Chem. Soc., Sigma Xi. Club: Chemists. Contbr. to Chemical Market Research in Practice, 1954; Chemical Marketing Research, 1967. Home: 240 Hempstead Rd Ridgewood NJ 07450 Office: 13 Sunflower Ave Paramus NJ 07652

KOONTS, ROBERT HENRY, lawyer; b. Greensboro, N.C., May 8, 1927; s. Henry Valentine and Margaret (Andrew) K.; B.S. in Commerce, U. N.C., 1949, LL.B., 1952, grad. exec. program, 1967; m. Edna Mildred Matthes, Mar. 8, 1952; children—Linda Suzanne, Barbara Jane. Admitted to N.C. bar, 1952, U.S. Supreme Ct. bar; gen. practice, High Point, N.C., 1952-57; now v.p., asso. gen. counsel Jefferson Standard Life Ins. Co., Greensboro; sec., dir. Enterprise Co., Beaumont, Tex., Clearwater (Fla.) Newspapers, Inc., Laredo (Tex.) Newspapers, Inc., Texas City (Tex.) Newspapers, Inc., Altus (Okla.) Newspapers, Inc. Plant City (Fla.) Newspapers, Inc.; sec., dir. Jefferson-Pilot Publs., Inc., Greensboro; v.p., asso. gen. counsel Jefferson-Pilot Corp. Served with USNR, 1945-46. Mem. Assn. Life Ins. Counsel, Am., N.C., Greensboro bar assns. Phi Delta Theta, Phi Delta Phi. Presbyterian. Clubs: Greensboro City, Greensboro Country. Home: 3600 Starmount Dr Greensboro NC 27403 Office: Jefferson Standard Life Ins Co Greensboro NC 27420

KOONTZ, HAROLD, educator, mgmt. cons.; b. Findlay, Ohio; May 19, 1908; s. Joseph Darius and Harriett (Dellinger) K.; A.B., Oberlin Coll., 1930; M.B.A., Northwestern U., 1931; Ph.D., Yale, 1935; m. Mary Learey, June 16, 1935; children—Karen Kathryn (Mrs. Gene Dickinson), Jeanne Carol (Mrs. Erling Gullixson). Instr. bus. adminstrn. Duke, 1933-34, accounting and transp. U. Toledo, 1934-35; asst. prof. econs. Colgate U., 1935-42; chief traffic br. WPB, Washington, 1942-44; asst. to v.p. Assn. Am. R.R.'s, 1944-45; asst. to pres., dir. planning Trans-World Airlines, 1945-48; dir. comml. sales Consol. Vultee Aircraft Corp., 1948-50; prof. bus. policy and transp. Grad. Sch. Bus. Adminstrn., UCLA, 1950-62, Grad. Sch. Mgmt., 1973—, Mead Johnson prof. mgmt., 1962-76, emeritus, 1976—; chmn. bd. Genistron, Inc., 1958-63; dir. Genisco Tech. Corp., 1951-63, chmn. bd., 1963-72; dir., cons. Farr Co., 1954-79, Dust Control, Inc., 1956-70, Roberts Consol. Industries, Planning Dynamics Inc., 1956-71; dir. Found. Adminstrv. Research, 1965—; chancellor Internat. Acad. Mgmt., 1975—. Lectr. mgmt., Japan, Australia, Indonesia, S.Am., Egypt, USSR, other countries, 1960—; cons. on mgmt. and mgmt. devel. to various cos. including Lockheed Aircraft Co., Hughes Tool Co., Hughes Aircraft Co., KLM, Nippon Mgmt. Assn., Purex Corp., S.F. Ry. Co., Occidental Petroleum Corp., Gen. Telephone Corp. Mem., v.p. Los Angeles Bd. Airport Commrs., 1961-65. Recipient Mead Johnson Mgmt. award, 1962, U.S. Air U. award, 1971, Taylor Key award Soc. Advancement Mgmt., 1974, Fort Findlay award, 1975, Conley award, 1977. Fellow Am. Acad. Mgmt. (pres. 1963), Internat. Acad. Mgmt. (past vice chancellor); mem. Am. Mgmt. Assn., Found. Adminstrv. Research (pres. 1965-71), Am. Soc. Traffic and Transp., Soc Advancement Mgmt., Nat. Indsl. Conf. Bd., Beta Gamma Sigma, Alpha Kappa Psi. Author: Goverment Control of Business, 1941; (with Cyril O'Donnell) Principles of Management, 1955, 5th edit., 1972, 6th edit., 1976; (with Heinz Weihrich) Readings in Management, 1959, 7th edit., 1980; Management: A Book of Readings, 1964, 5th edit., 1980; (with R. W. Gable) Public Control of Private Enterprise, pub. 1956; Toward a Unified Theory of Management, 1964; The Board of Directors and Effective Management, 1967; Appraising Managers as Managers, 1971; (with Cyril O'Donnell) Essentials of Management, 1974, 2d edit., 1978; (with R.M. Fulmer) Practical Introduction to Business, 1975, 3d edit., 1981. Contbr. numerous articles to profl. jours. Home: 4838 Gloria Ave Encino CA 91436 Office: UCLA Los Angeles CA 90024

KOONTZ, LESLIE LESTER, coal sales co. exec.; b. Charleston, W.Va., Apr. 25, 1928; s. Leslie Lester and Mary Martha (Otey) K.; B.S., W.Va. U., 1950; postgrad. U. Toledo, 1951; m. Brenda Copley Koontz, Dec. 24, 1968; children—Kelly, Michael Ann; 1 son from previous marriage, Mark Timothy. With Island Creek Coal Co., Huntington, W.Va., 1951-58, asst. div. mgr., 1956-58; asst. v.p. N. Am. Coal Corp., Cleve., 1958-60; asst. to pres. Sovereign Pocahontas Co., Cleve., 1960-66; mgr. sales Pickands, Mather & Co., Cleve., 1966-67; with Osborne Mining Co., Bluefield, W.Va., 1967-69; pres. Osborne-Koontz Coal Sales Co., 1969—; pres. B&C Oil Co.; pres. Koontz Coal Sales Co., Matewan, W.Va.; pres. Kelly Oil Co.; dir. Allegheny Coal and Land Co., Sandy Delta Coal & Dock Co., K&M Realty Co. Served with USNR, 1944-46. Mem. Tug Valley C. of C. (dir.), W.Va. Gasoline Dealers Assn., Nat. Oil Dealers Assn. Democrat. Episcopalian. Clubs: Tug Valley Country, Guyan Golf and Country, Duck Woods Golf, Elks, Moose. Home: 250 Ridgewood Rd Huntington WV 25701 Office: Mate St Matewan WV 25678

KOPELCHECK, PAUL, ins. co. exec.; b. Pitts., Nov. 28, 1937; s. Paul and Helen (Volenick) K.; B.B.A., U. Pitts., 1958; m. Edith Mae Schlag, Dec. 26, 1958; 1 son, David. Agency controller Aetna Life & Casualty Ins. Co., Richmond, Va., 1963-65, field rep., Hartford, Conn., 1966-68, mgr. regional service centers, Hartford, 1970-71, dir. regional service centers, Hartford, 1972-73, nat. dir. field adminstrn., Hartford, 1973-77, div. planning and control, 1977-79; v.p. bus. systems Colonial Penn Ins. Co., Phila., 1979—; cons. McKinsey & Co., N.Y.C., 1969; ins. cons. pension and profit sharing plans. Town chmn. Heart Fund, 1975. Served with USN, 1958-63. Fellow with distinction Life Office Mgmt. Assn., Life Office Mgmt. Inst. (sec. office and personnel com.); mem. Ins. Accounting and Statis. Assn. (program chmn.). Presbyterian. Home: 293 Upper Gulph Rd Radnor PA 19087 Office: 5 Penn Center Philadelphia PA

KOPLOW, HAROLD STANLEY, office products mfg. co. exec.; b. Boston, Nov. 21, 1940; s. Leo and Gertrude (Doctorman) K.; B.S., Mass. Coll. Pharmacy, 1962; M.S., Tufts U., 1968; m. Eleanor Lee Rosenthal, Aug. 26, 1962; children—Bonnie, Laurence, David, Heather. With Wang Labs., 1962—. v.p. research and devel. office products, Lowell, Mass., 1968—. NDEA fellow, 1964. Patentee in field. Home: 16 Willowby Way Lynnfield MA 01940 Office: 1 Industrial Ave Lowell MA 01851

KOPP, CARL ROBERT, advt. agy. exec.; b. Detroit, Apr. 8, 1921; s. Andrew Russell and Bertha (Hecke) K.; student Ill. Inst. Tech., Advanced Mgmt. Program, Harvard U.; div.; children—Deborah Ann, Jeffrey. Various sales and advt. positions Marathon Corp., 1947-54; account exec. Needham, Louis & Brorby, 1954-55; successively account exec., account supr., mgmt. dir., exec. v.p., pres. Leo Burnett U.S.A., Chgo., 1955-75; pres. Leo Burnett Co., Inc., Chgo., 1975-80, chmn. bd., chief exec. officer, 1978—. Mem. Chgo. Crime Commn. Served with U.S. Army, World War II; Korea. Decorated Purple Heart, Bronze Star with V. Office: Prudential Plaza Chicago IL 60601*

KOPP, RAINER, air force officer; b. Furth, W. Ger., Apr. 13, 1948; stepson Hans Fred and Ilse (Knorr) Strebel; came to U.S., 1951, naturalized, 1967; B.A. in Bus. Econs., Sacred Heart Coll., 1973; M.B.A., Rensselaer Poly. Inst., 1979; m. Lyn A. Fennelly, Dec. 23, 1967; children—JoAnn Elizabeth, Eric William. Enlisted U.S. Air Force, 1967, advanced through grades to capt., 1979; budget analyst McConnell AFB, Wichita, Kans., 1971-74; cost analyst U.S. Air Force Acad., Colorado Springs, Colo., 1974-75; adminstr. materiel and services mgmt. U.S. Air Force Hosp., Kincheloe AFB, Mich., 1975-77, Plattsburgh AFB, N.Y., 1977-80, Ehrling Bergquist Regional Hosp., Offutt AFB, Nebr., 1980—. Decorated Air Force

Commendation medal with 2 oak leaf clusters, Air Force Outstanding Unit award with valor device and 2 oak leaf clusters, Nat. Def. Service medal, Vietnam Service medal with 3 Bronze stars, Air Force Longevity Ribbon with 2 oak leaf clusters, Republic of Vietnam Gallantry Cross with Palm, Republic of Vietnam Campaign medal. Mem. Am. Purchasing Soc., Soc. Logistics Engrs., Am. Mgmt. Assn. Protestant. Office: USAF Hosp/SGL Offutt AFB NE 68113

KOPPERL, PAUL BURGER, investment banker; b. Orange, N.J., May 19, 1933; s. M. O. and Lorna (Delano) K.; B.S. in Engring., Princeton, 1954; M.B.A., Harvard, 1959; children—Hendrik D., Andrew D., Brian M. O. Asso., Goldman, Sachs & Co., N.Y.C., 1959-67; v.p., prin. Kidder, Peabody & Co. Inc., N.Y.C., 1967-75; pres. Delano & Kopperl, Inc, and predecessor firm, Stamford, Conn. and N.Y.C., 1976—; adj. prof. Pace U., N.Y.C., 1973, 75-76. Bd. dirs., chmn. fin. com. Meet the Composer, Inc., N.Y.C., 1978—; bd. dirs., treas., mem. exec. com. Manhattan Theatre Club, Inc., N.Y.C., 1978—. Served with U.S. Army, 1954-56. Club: The Recess (N.Y.C.). Home: 108 Valley Rd PO Box 109 Cos Cob CT 06807 Office: Delano & Kopperl Inc 477 Madison Ave New York NY 10022

KOPPERL, SIDNEY HOWARD, banker; b. N.Y.C., May 6, 1947; s. Harold and Miriam C. (Lederer) K.; B.A., L.I. U., 1969; M.P.A., U. Hartford, 1977; postgrad. Grad. Sch. Credit and Fin., Williams Coll., 1980; m. Mary Jane Keef, Feb. 14, 1976; children—Robin Lee, Adam Sloan. Asst. mgr. Trade Bank & Trust Co., N.Y.C., 1966-69; mgr. credit dept. Nat. Bank N. Am., N.Y.C., 1969-72, Bank of Leumi, N.Y.C., 1973-74; comml. loan officer New Britain (Conn.) Bank & Trust Co., 1975-77; v.p., comml. loan officer Citytrust, Bridgeport, Conn., 1977—. Treas., Upson for Congress campaign, 6th Conn. Dist., 1978; fund raiser St. Mary's Hosp. of Waterbury (Conn.). Served with USMC 1966. Mem. Am. Soc. Public Adminstrn., Central Conn. Devel. Corp., Waterbury C. of C. Republican. Jewish. Club: Diplomat. Address: Jacqueline Dr Southbury CT 06488

KOPPERUD, ROY MILTON, farmer; b. Lake Preston, S.D., Apr. 18, 1914; s. Arthur and Nellie (Knutson) K.; grad. high sch. Engaged in farming, Lake Preston, 1933—; dir. Farmers Union Oil Co., Lake Preston, 1958—, pres., 1960—; asst. sec., treas., dir. CENEX, wholesale farm supplies, South St. Paul, 1974—; partner Kopperud Bros. Farms. Served with AUS, 1941-45. Democrat. Lutheran. Address: RFD 1 Lake Preston SD 57249

KOPPIUS, WIBRANDUS JOHANNES, internat. business cons.; b. Groningen, Netherlands, May 27, 1928; came to U.S. 1956, naturalized, 1961. s. Wybrandus Johannes and Rigtje Grietje (van Eldik) K.; Ir., WE, Delft U., 1948-56; M.Sc. in Engring., Swiss Fed. Inst. Tech., 1954; postgrad. Advanced Mgmt. Program, Harvard U., 1976; m. Jennie Townsend Pond, Mar. 15, 1958; children—Clarissa, Julia. Sr. project engr. Chrysler Corp., Detroit, 1956-59; dir. engring. Gits Bros. Mfg. Co., Chgo., 1959-61; mgr. internat. mfg. staff Parker Pen Co., Janesville, Wis., 1961-65; pres., chief exec. officer Monroe Auto Equipment Internat., Brussels, 1965-77; internat. bus. cons., North Palm Beach, Fla., 1977—; pres. European Shock Absorber Mfrs. Assn., 1975-77; sec. European Automotive Parts Mfrs. Assn., 1976-77. Trustee, Limburg (Belgium) Econ. U., 1971-77. Recipient citation for exemplary performance during flood disaster Dutch Govt., 1953. Mem. Royal Inst. Engrs. (Netherlands), Soc. Automotive Engrs., Am. and Common Market Club (Belgium). Clubs: Harvard (N.Y.C); Old Port Yacht (North Palm Beach); Cruising Assn. (London); Chateau Ste Anne (Brussels). Patentee in field. Home and office: 108 Lakeshore Dr Apt 1239 North Palm Beach FL 33408

KORANDA, JOHN TIMOTHY, financial writer; b. Fort Wayne, Ind., July 26, 1950; s. Leroy Frederick and Jean Esther (Weil) K.; B.A., Colgate U., 1971; B.S., M.S., Mass. Inst. Tech., 1973; M.B.A., N.Y. U., 1976; m. Iris Violeta Hernandez, July 22, 1973. Staff writer N.W. Ayer & Son, N.Y.C., 1973-75; broker, investment counselor Bache & Co., N.Y.C., 1975-76; free lance financial writer, N.Y.C., 1976-78; financial relations cons. GRM Communications, Inc. div. Carly Ally, also Doremus Inc., N.Y.C., 1976—; speech writer Citibank, N.A., 1978—; asso. mem. Commodity Futures Trading Commn.; registered mem. Chgo. Bd. Trade. Mem. Nat. Democratic Club; sustaining mem. Nat. Multiple Sclerosis Soc. Recipient Saturday Rev./World Corporate Communications award, 1973, Esquire Corporate Responsibility Advt. award, 1973. Mem. Assn. for Symbolic Logic, Econ. History Assn., Phi Beta Kappa. Democrat. Clubs: Copy of N.Y., Advt. of N.Y. Home: 135-10 Grand Central Pkwy Jamaica NY 11435 Office: 399 Park Ave New York NY

KORCHUN, PAULA, fin. exec.; b. Long Branch, N.J., June 14, 1953; d. Walter and Sophia (Stabak) K.; B.A., U. Mass., 1974; M.P.A., George Washington U., 1979; postgrad. N.Y. U., 1980—. Summer youth program coordinator Bergen County Community Action Program, Hackensack, N.J., 1974-77; program analyst HUD, Washington, 1978; program devel. specialist N.J. Dept. Civil Service, Trenton, 1978-79; mcpl. bond analyst Oppenheimer & Co., N.Y.C., 1979-80; public fin. asso. Bache Halsey Stuart Shields Inc., N.Y.C., 1980—. Fund raiser Multiple Sclerosis and N.J. Easter Seals Soc. Am. Soc. Public Adminstrn. fellow, 1977-78; Maithas Fund fellow, 1977-79; Wolcott Found. scholar, 1977-79; Kappa Kappa Gamma fellow, 1977-79. Mem. Am. Soc. Public Adminstrn., Pi Alpha Alpha. Address: 425 W 57 St Apt 5A New York NY 10019

KORESSIS, LUCAS, transl. services exec.; b. Athens, Greece, Feb. 8, 1928; emigrated to Can., 1956, naturalized, 1961; s. Timoleon Spyros and Paraskevi (Arakas) K.; student Grad. Sch. Indsl./Comml. Studies, Athens, 1949-55, U. Mich., 1973; m. Elizabeth Dowell, June 25, 1961; children—Christine, Timoleon. Instr. modern Greek, Berlitz Sch. Langs., Toronto, 1961-67; founder, mgr. Greek Transl. & Interpreters Service, Toronto, 1967-80; founder, pres. Global Transl. & Interpreters Services, Toronto, 1972—. Served with Greek Air Force, 1949. Mem. Bd. Trade Toronto, Assn. Translators and Interpreters Am., Order of Ahepa. Greek Orthodox. Office: 88 University Ave Suite 601 Toronto ON M5J 1T6 Canada

KORFF, WALTER HENRY, automotive research and devel. co. exec.; b. Evansville, Ind., May 29, 1909; s. Henry W. and Lenora (Schwiersch) K.; student Evansville Coll., 1927-29, Tri-State Coll., Angola, Ind., 1929-30; m. Mary C. Nicholas, Apr. 30, 1954; children by previous marriage—Barbara Ann, Rebecca Naomi. Body engr. Chrysler Corp., Detroit, 1930-36; v.p., gen. mgr. Cummins Diesel Sales and Service of Ind., Indpls., 1936-39; with Lockheed Aircraft Corp., Burbank, Calif., 1940-68, design specialist, sr. engring., 1964-68; pres., gen. mgr. Korff Corp., Burbank, Calif., 1969—; tchr. aircraft design Wartime Night Sch. U. Calif., 1942-43. Fellow Am. Inst. Aero. and Astronautics (asso.); mem. Soc. Automotive Engrs. Conservative Republican. Mem. Ch. Divine Sci. Patentee tailess aircraft, single blade propeller, 3 wheel automobile, auto body designs. Home and Office: 449 N Lamer St Burbank CA 91506

KORINS, LEOPOLD, fin. services co. exec.; b. Boston, July 8, 1933; s. Charles and Hilda (Feltquate) K.; A.A., Boston U., 1952; B.S. in Econs., U. Pa., 1954; 1 son, Jeffrey M. Account exec. Merrill Lynch, Boston, 1957-65, floor broker, N.Y.C., 1966-75; asst. div. dir. ops. Merrill Lynch Pierce Fenner & Smith, N.Y.C., 1976-77, dir. equity trading, 1978-79, dir. sales support group, 1979, dir. instl. sales, 1980—; mem. N.Y. Stock Exchange, 1966-75; mem. Pickard Com. Brokerage Industry, 1978-79. Chmn. fin. com. Scarsdale Town Club, 1969-70, United Way campaign, 1978. Served with AUS, 1955-57. Mem. Investment Assn. N.Y., Security Traders Assn. N.Y., Security Industry Assn. Inst. Republican. Jewish. Clubs: N.Y. Stock Exchange Luncheon, Wharton (N.Y.C.). Office: 165 Broadway New York NY 10080

KORMAN, BERNARD JOSEPH, med. services co. exec.; b. Phila., Oct. 13, 1931; s. Samuel and Fanny (Smolen) K.; B.S. in Econs., U. Pa., 1952, LL.B., 1955; m. Vivienne Melnick, Dec. 19, 1954; children—Charles H., Paula, Martin W. Admitted to Pa. bar, 1955; partner firm Gold, Bowman & Korman, Phila., 1961-68; founder Am. Medicorp Inc., Phila., 1968, pres., chief operating officer, chief exec. officer, chmn. bd., 1968-76, also dir.; pres., dir. R H Med. Services Inc., Elkins Park, Pa., 1976—; dir. Lincoln Nat. Corp., Crothall Internat. Ltd., Security Capital Corp., Hosp. Mortgage Group, Safeguard Bus. Systems. Bd. dirs. Grad. Hosp., Phila., 1977—. Mem. Am. Bar Assn., Phila. Bar Assn., Am. Hosp. Assn., Soc. Hosp. Attys. Office: 60 E Township Line Elkins Park PA 19117

KORN, BARRY PAUL, equipment leasing co. exec.; b. N.Y.C., May 27, 1944; s. Nat and Judith (Safro) K.; B.B.A. in Accounting, CCNY, 1966; M.B.A. in Fin., City U. N.Y., 1969; m. Judith Ann Kron, Aug. 2, 1969; children—Lisa Michele, Suzanne Leslie, Amy Beth. Asso. E.M. Warburg, Pincus & Co., Inc., N.Y.C., 1964-70; treas., sec. DPF Inc., Hartsdale, N.Y., 1970-75; pres. Barrett Capital & Leasing Corp., White Plains, N.Y., 1975—. Mem. Supt. Schs. Adv. Council, White Plains, 1975-78. Mem. Am. Mgmt. Assn., Am. Assn. Equipment Lessors (dir. 1974-77), Fin. Execs. Instr. (pres. Westchester chpt. 1976-77), Computer Lessors Assn. (treas. 1971-72), Computer Dealers Assn. (dir. 1979—). Office: 707 Westchester Ave White Plains NY 10604

KORN, LESTER BERNARD, business exec.; b. N.Y.C., Jan. 11, 1936; s. Raymond H. and Jetta (Spieler) K.; B.S., U. Calif. at Los Angeles, 1957, M.B.A., 1959; postgrad. Harvard, 1960; m. Carolbeth Goldman, June 30, 1961; children—Jodi Lynn, Jessica Susan. With Bank of Am., Los Angeles, 1960-61; mgmt. cons. Peat, Marwick, Mitchell & Co., Los Angeles, 1961-66, partner, 1966-69; pres. Korn/Ferry Internat., Los Angeles, 1969—; dir. Daylin, Inc., Continental Am. Properties, Leisure Tech. Corp. Bd. dirs. NCCJ, Reiss-Davis Child Care Center, City of Hope Med. Center, So. Calif. Bus. Research Council, Cedars Sinai Med. Center; trustee UCLA Found.; mem. Commn. of the Califs.; bd. councilors Grad. Sch. Bus. Adminstrn. and Sch. Bus., U. So. Calif. Mem. Calif. Soc. C.P.A.'s, Am. Inst. C.P.A.'s, Century City C. of C. (dir.), Am. Bus. Conf. Clubs: Harvard Business, Los Angeles Athletic, Hillcrest Country (Los Angeles); Board Room (N.Y.C.). Office: 277 Park Ave New York NY 10017

KORN, RALPH ANTHONY, winery exec.; b. Chgo., July 9, 1938; s. Stanley Andrew and Louise Caroline (Wunsch) K.; student Iowa State Coll., 1956; B.S.C., Loyola U., Chgo., 1961; m. Mary Ennes, June 2, 1962; children—Michael, Patricia, Linda, Steven. Dir. ins. Duplan Corp., Winston-Salem, N.C., 1969-74; dir. ins. E & J Gallo Winery, Modesto, Calif., 1974—. Served with U.S. Army, 1961. Mem. Am. Soc. Ins. Mgmt., Risk Ins. Mgmt. Soc. (pres. Piedmont chpt. 1972-73). Home: 3108 Guinevere Ln Modesto CA 95350 Office: 600 Yosemite Blvd Modesto CA 95353

KORNBLAU, SEYMOUR, pharm. co. exec.; b. N.Y.C., Oct. 1, 1920; s. Harry and Anna Kornblau; B.S., CCNY, 1941; M.B.A., U. Chgo., 1960; m. Monica Regina Robbins, Dec. 31, 1960; children—Ann, Michael. With Chemway Corp., Chgo., 1947-60, now v.p.; plant mgr. Sterling Drug Inc., Brazil, 1961-69, v.p. tech. services, N.Y.C., 1969-72, sr. v.p. plants and prodn. Sterling Internat. Group, 1972—. Served with AUS, 1945-46. Mem. Pharm. Mfg. Assn. (internat. tech. sect.). Home: 1 Sunhaven Ct Tarrytown NY 10591 Office: Sterling Internat Group 90 Park Ave New York NY 10016

KORNEY, JOHN JOSEPH, banker; b. Grand Rapids, Mich., Apr. 24, 1908; s. Onufrey and Anna (Dodyk) K.; A.B., Mich. State U., 1931; LL.B., U. Detroit, 1943, J.D., 1968; m. Margaret E. Ruggles, Feb. 20, 1943; children—J. Douglas, Margaret Anne, Mary Kathleen. Trust officer Bankers Trust Co., Detroit, 1931, v.p., trust officer, 1948-50; trust officer, Bankers-Equitable Trust Co., Detroit, 1950-51; asst. cashier, Bank of the Commonwealth, Detroit, 1951, v.p. 1955—. Mem. Detroit Com. Econ. Devel.; v.p. Ukranian Am. Cultural Com.; mem. Mich. State U. Devel. Fund; budget com. United Community Services of Met. Detroit; mem. Wayne County Bd. Suprs., Mich. Bd. Escheats; chmn. Detroit Bd. Canvassers. Recipient Outstanding Young Man of Year award, Mich. Jr. C. of C.; Major S Key award Mich. State U., Distinguished Alumni award, 1966. Mem. Am. Hist. Assn., Am. Ordnance Assn., Soc. Genealogists, Am. Acad. Polit. and Social Sci., Am. Finance Assn., Acad. Polit. Sci., Mich. Bankers Assn. (chmn. trust com. 1950), Am. Inst. Banking (pres. Detroit chpt. 1949, nat. vice chmn. conv. 1967), Detroit Life Ins. (v.p. trust council 1949), Detroit Bd. Commerce, Detroit Internat. Inst., Detroit Sportsmens Congress, Mich. State U. Alumni Assn. (exec. bd.), Am. Econ. Assn., Mich. C. of C., Financial Pub. Relations Assn., U. Detroit Law Alumni Assn., Ukranian Profl. Soc. (v.p.), Mich. State Alumni Assn. (dir.), Nat. Assn. Counties (welfare Com.), Mich. United Conservation Clubs (dir.), Mich. Municipal League (trustee), Mich. Assn. Suprs., Mich. Amateur Hockey Assn. (dir.), Am. Bankers Assn. (govt. relations council), Detroit Hist. Soc. (dir.), Delta Theta Phi. Democrat. Clubs: University (Detroit); Redwood Golf (Houghton Lake, Mich.); Economic, Detroit Bankers, Ukrainian Graduates. Author: Suggested Aids for Drawing Wills and Trusts, 1947. Contbr. articles to profl. jours. Home: 16771 Patton St Detroit MI 48219 Office: Bank of the Commonwealth Dime Bldg Detroit MI 48233

KORNFELD, LEONARD ROBERT, fin. cons.; b. Bklyn., Dec. 27, 1939; s. Louis and Bertie (Fleisig) K.; ed. City Coll. of N.Y.; m. Marilynn S. Kaye, Dec. 17, 1966; children—Michelle Robyn, Sean Michael. Analyst, Eastern Precision Resistor Co., Bklyn., 1957-58; prodn. mgr. U.S. Box Crafts Inc., Bklyn., 1961-62, sales mgr., 1962-65, exec. v.p., dir., 1965-78; exec. v.p., dir. U.S. Box Corp., Newark, 1965-78; pres. Acorn Box Corp., Amityville, N.Y., 1978-80, City Devel. Corp., Huntington Station, N.Y., 1978—, Hi Groman Assos., East Meadow, 1980—, Propesco of Met. N.Y., East Meadow, 1981—; packing cons. to many firms. Served with U.S. Army, 1958-60. Recipient many packaging design awards. Mem. Internat. Assn. Fin. Advisors, L.I. C. of C., Am. Mensa Ltd., Mfg. Jewelers and Silversmiths Am., Nat. Rare Blood Assn., Am. Def. Preparedness Assn., DAV, Nat. Rifle Assn. (life). Jewish. Clubs: Clearmeadow, Masons. Patentee and trademark holder for displays and package designs. Home: 457 Wolf Hill Rd Dix Hills NY 11746 Office: Suite 206 1900 Hempstead Turnpike East Meadow NY 11554

KORNREICH, MORTON ALAN, ins. brokerage co. exec.; b. N.Y.C., Dec. 4, 1924; s. Saul and Gertrude Kornreich; B.A. cum laude, U. Pa., 1949; m. Jo Anne Colnes, Nov. 26, 1950; children—James, Thomas, Nancy. Asst. to v.p. sales promotion Allied Stores, N.Y., 1949; with S. Kornreich & Sons, Inc., N.Y.C., 1950—, v.p., 1960, chmn. bd., 1973—; pres. Kornreich Life Assos., N.Y.C., 1972—, Kornreich Internat., N.Y.C., 1974—. N.Y. State fin. chmn. Udall for Pres. Campaign, 1975; v.p. Westchester Jewish Community Council; Westchester chmn. United Jewish Appeal-Fedn. Joint Campaign, steering com. Greater N.Y., 1980; pres. Congregation Emanu El, Westchester, 1981. Served with USAAF, 1943-46; C.L.U.; registered health underwriter. Mem. Top of Table-Million Dollar Round Table (life). Democrat. Clubs: Brae Burn Country (past pres.) (Purchase, N.Y.); Harmonie (N.Y.C.). Home: Franklin Ln Harrison NY 10528 Office: 522 Fifth Ave New York NY 10036

KOROLNEK, HARRY, bottle co. exec.; b. Toronto, Ont., Can., Aug. 10, 1913; s. Max and Ann (Goldkin) K.; student public schs., Toronto; m. Mary Davis, Aug. 11, 1939; children—Mark, Joy. With Consol. Bottle Co., Ltd., Toronto, 1931—, pres., 1971—. Mem. Packaging Assn. Can., Cosmetic, Toiletry and Fragrance Assn., Packaging Inst., Drug Chem. and Allied Trades. Office: PO Box 369 Sta D Toronto ON M6P 3J9 Canada

KORSCHOT, BENJAMIN CALVIN, mut. fund exec.; b. Lafayette, Ind., Mar. 22, 1921; s. Benjamin Garrett and Myrtle Pearl (Goodman) K.; B.S., Purdue U., 1942; M.B.A., U. Chgo., 1947; m. Marian Marie Schelle, Oct. 31, 1941; children—Barbara (Mrs. L. Craig Carver), Lynne (Mrs. Stephen Gooding), John Calvin. Vice pres. The No. Trust Co., Chgo., 1947-64; sr. v.p. St. Louis Union Trust Co., 1964-73, asso. dir., 1968-73; treas. First Union Inc., St. Louis, 1969-73; exec. v.p., dir. Waddell & Reed, Kansas City, Mo., 1973-74, pres., 1974-79, vice chmn. and chief investment officer, 1979—; pres. Research Mgmt. Assos., 1974—, United Funds, Inc., 1975—; dir. Roosevelt Fed. Savs. & Loan Assn., St. Louis, United Investors Life Ins. Co. Chmn. bd. govs. Investment Co. Inst., 1980—; bd. dirs. Coll. for Fin. Planning, 1975-77. Chmn. trust investments Southwestern Grad. Sch. Banking, 1963-73. Served to lt. comdr., USNR, 1943-46, 50-52. Chartered fin. analyst. Fellow Fin. Analysts Fedn. (chmn. 1978-79, dir. 1972-74, 76-80); mem. Kansas City Soc. Fin. Analysts, St. Louis Soc. Fin. Analysts (pres. 1968), Fin. Execs. Inst. Republican. Methodist. Clubs: Bellerive Country (St. Louis); Kansas City, Indian Hills Country. Contbr. articles in field to profl. jours. Home: 101 Hackberry Lee's Summit MO 64063 Office: One Crown Center Kansas City MO 64108

KORST, KATHLEEN MARY, secretarial agy. exec.; b. St. Paul, Aug. 26, 1941; d. Leo George and Margaret Rose (Gegan) K.; student pub. schs., Park Rapids, Minn. Legal sec., adminstrv. asst. to various attys., Mpls., 1959-75; owner, mgr. Korst & Assos. secretarial service, tel. answering, Mpls., 1975—. Cons. Hennepin County Vo-Tech Sch. Chmn. jud. campaign Hubbard County, 1966; staff sec. jud. election, 1970. Mem. Mpls. Legal Secs. Assn. (pres. 1969-70), Mpls. C. of C. Office: 987 Northwestern Bank Bldg Minneapolis MN 55402

KORSTS, VOLDEMARS, wholesale trade co. exec.; b. Sloka, Latvia, Oct. 4, 1909; s. August and Anna (Rup) K.; student State U. Lativia, 1936; postgrad. U. Berlin, 1941-42; m. Milda Bone, Aug. 29, 1932; children—Liga Streips, Anda Korsts-Zaleman, Gunda Korsts-Claus. Came to U.S., 1950, naturalized, 1955. Orderly Cape Cod Hosp., Hyannis, Mass., 1951-53; auditor Howard Mann Co., Boston, 1953-55; bus. mgr. Osteopathic Hosp., Chgo., 1959-60; asst. comptroller Transistor Corp., Boston, 1955-58; treas. Carman Conley, Inc., wholesale trade, Chgo., 1962—; cons. accounting and fin. affairs T.L.C. (Extel) Corp., 1977—. Tchr. U. Liepaja, 1936-38. Spl. adv. on pub. opinions Sec. State, U.S., 1970—. chmn. Latvian Am. Republican Nat. Com., 1968; chmn. resolutions and foreign affairs coms. Republican Nat. Nationalities Council, 1970—. Mem. Latvian Central Council (v.p. 1945-49), Am. Latvian Assn. Editor: Heritage-Nationalities News. Home: 2932 W Eastwood Ave Chicago IL 60625

KORTEN, THEODORE (TED) FREDERICK, retail exec.; b. Chgo., Apr. 9, 1910; s. Charles A. and Lydia B. (Boehl) K.; student Wash. State U., 1928-29; m. Margaret R. Heltzel, June 20, 1934; children—David Craig, Robert Philip. With Kortens, Inc., Longview, Wash., 1977—, chmn. bd., chief exec. officer, 1978—; v.p., dir. First Fed. Savs. and Loan of Longview, 1962—; pres., dir., Longview Meml. Park, 1971—; v.p., dir. Cascade Music Co., Portland, Oreg., 1962—; dir. Brudi Equipment Co., Kelso, Wash., Wayron Corp., Longview. Pres., ARC, Longview, 1950-51; bd. dirs. Monticel Med. Center, 1967-78; mem. Wash. Retail Council, 1960—, pres., 1970-72; active Boy Scouts Am., 1944-45. Mem. Longview C. of C. (pres. 1953), Nat. Assn. Music Mchts. (dir. 1948-63, pres. 1961-63), Am. Music Conf. (pres. 1970-72), Assn. Wash. Bus. (dir. 1962—), Nat. Assn. Retail Dealers, Phi Mu Alpha. Republican. Methodist. Clubs: Kiwanis (lt. gov. 1946), Longview Country, Elks. Home: 2327 Cascade Way Longview WA 98632 Office: 1400 Commerce Ave Longview WA 98632

KOSCHELLA, EUGENE JOHN, trade assn. exec.; b. Detroit, Oct. 18, 1930; s. John Joseph and Eleanor (Zontini) K.; B.B.A., U. Tex., 1957; M.B.A., Case Western Res. U., 1960; m. Shirley Ann Cocreham, June 11, 1955; children—LeeAnn, Lara Lynn. With Warner & Swasey Co., Cleve., 1957-60; adminstr. Nat. Machine Tool Show, Inc., Washington, 1962-68; dir. tech. services Nat. Machine Tool Builders' Assn., Washington, 1960-68; asst. to staff v.p. Consumer Electronics Group, Electronics Industries Assn., Washington, 1968-74, dir. industry devel., 1974-79, dir. industry devel., consumer electronics shows, 1976-79, dir. edn., 1980—. Served with USAAF, 1951-59. Mem. Soc. Mfg. Engrs. (chmn. Washington chpt. 1970), Numerical Control Soc. (founding mem.), Am. Personnel and Guidance Assn., NEA, Am. Vocat. Assn., Nat. Assn. Exhibit Mgrs., Am. Def. Preparedness Assn., Nat. Assn. Execs. Club: Washington. Home: 10507 Streamview Ct Potomac MD 20854 Office: 2001 Eye St Washington DC 20006

KOSHUBA, WALTER JOSEPH, engring. exec.; b. St. Paul, Aug. 22, 1917; s. John and Pauline (Rychley) K.; B.Metall. Engring., U. Minn., 1940; m. Renella J. Waaland, Sept. 8, 1945; children—Walter Joseph, Mykola J. Supt. research engring. Allis Chalmers Mfg. Co., Milw., 1940-46; gen. supt. Solar Aircraft Co., Des Moines, 1946-47; head materials sect. NEPA div. Fairchild Engine & Airplane Corp., Oak Ridge, 1947-51; head metall., ceramic engring. aircraft nuclear propulsion div. Gen. Electric Co., Cin., 1951-56, mgr. tech. prodn., 1956-61; div. mgr. Nuclear div. Kawecki-Berylco Industries Inc., Hazelton, Pa., 1961-64, gen. mgr., 1964-65, mgr. alloy div., 1965-70, mgr. mfg. tech., 1970-72; engring. mgr. United Nuclear Corp., New Haven, 1972-74; v.p. engring. and constrn. Uranium Recovery Corp. subs. United Nuclear Corp., Mulberry, Fla., 1974-78, v.p. spl. projects, 1979—. Fellow Am. Inst. Chemists; mem. Am. Soc. Metals (past chmn. Cin.), AIME, Am. Ceramic Soc., Inst. Ceramic Engrs., Am. Nuclear Soc., Hazleton C. of C. (indsl. council), Mfrs. Assn. (civic and govt. affairs com.). Office: PO Box 765 Mulberry FL 33860

KOSINAR, PATRICIA TAIT, mgmt. cons.; b. Birmingham, Ala., Nov. 9, 1940; d. Albert Lewis and Martha Claire (Walker) T.; B.A. in Polit. Sci., U. Okla., 1962; M.B.A., Harvard U., 1973; m. William J. Kosinar, July 1, 1966. Tchr. polit. sci., Norman, Okla., 1962-65; research asso. Charles River Assos., Boston, 1965-66; asst. dir. arithmetic project U. Ill., 1966-68; editor math. Harcourt Brace Jovanovich, Inc., N.Y.C., 1968-70; ind. mgmt. cons., Boston, 1970-71; sr. cons. Hennig Jardim Assos., Inc., Weston, Mass., 1973-78, dir., 1974—; dir. middle mgmt. program Simmons Coll.,

Boston, 1977-78; pres. Kosinar Assos. Inc., Newton, Mass., 1978—; trustee Charlestown Savs. Bank, Boston; instr., speaker, adviser in field. Trustee, Campus Free Coll., Washington; mem. corp. Babson Coll., Wellesley, Mass. Mem. Harvard U. Bus. Sch. Assn., Phi Beta Kappa, Kappa Kappa Gamma. Club: Harvard (Boston). Author articles.

KOSKINEN, SULO MATIAS, electronics exec.; b. Vassa, Finland, Sept. 15, 1922; s. William and Emma (Ollus) K.; student Kansan Valistus Seura Inst., 1941-45, Cleve. Inst. Radio Electronics, 1949-51; m. Anna Miriam Liunakallio, Aug. 4, 1946; children—Jarmo, Pirjo, Ellen. Came to Can., 1951, naturalized, 1956. Product mgr. Chisholm Industries, 1952-56; dir. engring. Anaconda Electronics Ltd. (formerly Tele Signal Electronics), Vancouver, B.C., Can., 1956-75, also dir.; pres. Koskinen Electronic Lab., Ltd. Pres., Finnish Canadian Rest Home Assn., 1964—, Finnish Kalevava Bros., Vancouver, 1964—; treas. Loyal Finns in Can., 1962-75. Served with Finnish Air Force, 1941-44. Mem. IEEE, Soc. Cable TV Engrs., Internat. Soc. Hybrid Microelectronics. Club: Finlandia (pres. 1978-79) (Vancouver). Contbr. articles to tech. jours. Home: 5390 Frances St Burnaby BC Canada

KOSLO, WILLIAM J., bus. exec.; b. Mt. Carmel, Pa., Mar. 6, 1930; s. Joseph J. and Mary M. K.; B.S., Fordham U., 1951; m. Margaret M. Walsh, June 10, 1953; children—Karen, William, Mark, Patrick. With U.S. Printing Co., after 1951, sales mgr., after 1956; v.p., gen. mgr. Diamond Nat. Corp., after 1959; group v.p. Diamond Internat. Corp., N.Y.C., 1970-74, exec. v.p., 1974-77, pres., chief exec. officer, 1977-80, chmn. bd., 1980—. Bd. dirs. U. Maine Pulp and Paper Found. Served with USMC, 1952-55. Mem. Am. Paper Inst. (dir.), Conf. Bd. Republican. Clubs: Cherry Valley Golf, Sky (N.Y.C.); K.C. Office: Diamond Internat Corp 733 Third Ave New York NY 10017*

KOSLOW, WALTER, graphic engr., printing and lithographic co. exec.; b. N.Y.C., Aug. 21, 1917; s. Arthur M. and Lena M. (Goldstein) K.; grad. graphics engring. Mechanics Inst., 1937; student graphics, public relations, mgmt., indsl. relations N.Y. U., Cornell U., 1949-69; m. Shirley Rodnon, Sept. 7, 1940; children—Mitchell Karl, Lane Mark, Karen Sue. Prodn. mgr. various printing cos., 1937-41; specification writer, expediter U.S. Govt. Printing Office, 1941-42; gen. mgr. Correct Printing Co., 1947-49; gen. mgr. Proper Press, Inc., N.Y.C., 1950-77, v.p., 1949-50, pres., 1954—; pres. M.D. Danon Printing Co., N.Y.C., 1960—; pres., dir. Met. Savs. & Loan, N.Y.C., 1949—; cons. to printing industry. Hon. chief N.Y.C. Fire Dept. Served as warrant officer Submarine Forces, USN, 1942-46; PTO. Recipient Meritorious Service citation N.Y. Fire Officers Assn., 1957, citation Mayor City N.Y., 1978, FBI, 1969. Mem. Am. Mktg. Assn., Club Printing House Craftsmen N.Y., Printing Industries Met. N.Y., Young Printing Execs. Club, Navy League, U.S. Power Squadron, U.S. Coast Guard Aux. (comdr., div. service officer). Republican. Clubs: Engelwood Yacht, Masons, Shriners, Elks. Home: 79-28 215th St Bayside NY 11364 Office: 155 Ave of Americas New York NY 10013

KOSSOFF, RICHARD MORSE, chem. and plastics cons.; b. N.Y.C., Dec. 12, 1935; s. Joseph Edward and Shirley Ruth (Bookbinder) K.; B.S., Cornell U., 1957, M.B.A., 1959; m. Arlene Edith Plitt, June 14, 1964; children—Andrew, Laura. With Am. Cyanamid, Pearl River, N.Y., 1957-59, Allied Chem. Co., N.Y.C., 1960-63, Celanese Plastics Co., Newark, 1963-65; pres. R. M. Kossoff & Assos., Inc., Internat. Cons., N.Y.C., 1965—; dir. Precision Polymer; cons. UN Indsl. Devel. Orgn., 1968—; lectr. N.Y. Poly. Inst. Pres., Younger Democrats of N.Y., 1961-62. Served with U.S. Army, 1959-60. Mem. Am. Chem. Soc., Comml. Devel. Assn., Licensing Execs. Soc., Japan Soc. Clubs: Chemists, Cornell, Masons. Author: Studies in Plastic Fabrication and Application, 1970; Guidelines for Acrylic Sheet Production in Developing Countries, 1971. Home: 375 West End Ave New York NY 10024 Office: 680 Fifth Ave New York NY 10019

KOSTELANETZ, BORIS, lawyer; b. Leningrad, Russia, June 16, 1911; s. Nachman and Rosalie (Dimshetz) K.; brought to U.S. 1920, naturalized, 1925; B.C.S. N.Y. U., 1933; B.S., 1936; J.D., magna cum laude, St. John's U., 1936; m. Ethel Cory, Dec. 18, 1938; children—Richard Cory, Lucy Cory. C.P.A., Price, Waterhouse Co., 1934-37; admitted to N.Y. bar, 1936; asst. U.S. atty. for S. Dist. N.Y., and confidential asst. to U.S. atty. for S. Dist. N.Y., 1937-45; instr. accounting, N.Y. U., 1937-47; adj. prof. taxation, 1947-69; spl. asst. to atty. gen. of U.S., 1943-46; chief war frauds, Dept. of Justice, 1945-46; gen. practice of law with firm of Kostelanetz & Ritholz and predecessors, 1946—. Spl. counsel. U.S. Senate Com. to Investigate Crime in Interstate Commerce, 1950-51; chmn. Kefauver for Pres. Com. of N.Y. State, 1952; mem. com. on character and fitness N.Y. State Supreme Ct., 1974—. Recipient N.Y. U. Meritorious Service award, 1954, St. John's U. Pietas medal, 1961; N.Y. U. Madden Meml. award, 1969. C.P.A., N.Y. Fellow Am. Coll. Trial Lawyers, Am. Bar Found.; mem. Internat., Fed., Am. (mem. council sect. on taxation 1978—, chmn. spl. com. standards tax practice 1964-66, com. on appointments to tax ct. 1959—, spl. com. on adminstrn. criminal justice 1957—), N.Y. State bar assns., N.Y. U. Finance Club (pres. 1953-54), N.Y. County Lawyers Assn. (dir. 1958-64, 71-74, chmn. com. on judiciary 1965-69, v.p. 1966-69, pres. 1969-71), Assn. Bar City N.Y., N.Y. State Soc. C.P.A.'s, N.Y. U. Sch. Commerce Alumni Assn. (pres. 1951-52), St. John's Law Sch. Alumni Assn. (pres. 1955-57. Democrat. Clubs: India House, Nat. Lawyers (Washington); N.Y. U., N.Y. U. Faculty. Author: (with Louis Bender) Criminal Aspects of Tax Fraud Cases, 1957, 68, 80. Contbr. legal, accounting and tax jours. Home: 37 Washington Sq W New York NY 10011 Office: 80 Pine St New York NY 10005

KOSTEVA, EDWIN T., ins. co. exec.; b. Kingston, Pa., Feb. 20, 1949; s. Andrew Charles and Anna Thresa (Grutko) K.; B.S., Cornell U., 1971, M.B.A., 1973; m. Jane E. Hollister, Sept. 24, 1977; children—Angela, Kenneth. With Columbia Life Ins. Co., 1973—, v.p. pensions, 1979—. Mem. Am. Soc. C.L.U.'s (v.p. chpt.), Nat. Assn. Life Underwriters, Pa. Assn. Life Underwriters, Nat. Assn. Health Underwriters. Republican. Roman Catholic. Clubs: Berwick Golf, YMCA Co-ed Volleyball and Softball. Home: RD 2 Berwick PA 18603 Office: Columbia Life Ins Co RD 5 Bloomsburg PA 17815

KOSTNER, JOSEPH OTTOKAR, lawyer; b. Chgo., Nov. 15, 1923; s. Joseph Ottokar and Florence (Custy) K.; B.A. in Polit. Sci., Yale, 1947; postgrad. Northwestern U. Law Sch., 1947-49; J.D., Chgo.-Kent Coll., 1954; m. Mary Fredericka Pigott, Aug. 3, 1956; children—Fredericka Mary, Florence Delia, Jan Virginia. Admitted to Ill. bar, 1954, U.S. Supreme Ct. bar, 1963; mem. firm Quinn, Jacobs, Barry & Latchford, Chgo., 1955-66; practice law, Chgo., 1966-67; sr. partner firm Frankel, McKay, Orlikoff, Denten & Kostner, Chgo., 1967-79; individual practice law, Chgo., 1979—; mem. securities adv. com. to sec. state Ill., 1973—. Bd. dirs. Lawson YMCA, 1978—. Served to maj. AUS, 1943-46. Decorated Bronze Star, Purple Heart with two oak leaf clusters. Mem. Internat., Am. (com. fed. regulation securities, award of merit com.), Fed. (com. on fed. regulation of securities 1972—), Ill. (assembly del. 1972—, chmn. fin. com. 1972-74, council corp. and securities law com.), Chgo. (securities law com., fin. instns. com.) bar assns., Ill. Trial Lawyers Assn., Nat. Assn. Security Dealers (arbitration panel). Roman Catholic. Clubs: Chgo. Athletic, Met. (Chgo.); Yale, Lotos (N.Y.C.); Nat. Lawyers (Washington). Home: 49 E Cedar St Chicago IL 60611 Office: 230 W Monroe St Chicago IL 60606

KOTCHOUBEY, ANDREW, data processing and photocomposition co. exec.; b. Florence, Italy, Mar. 31, 1938; s. Serge M. and Irene (Gabritchevsky) K.; came to U.S., 1953, naturalized, 1958; M.E., Stevens Inst. Tech., 1959; M.A. (Watson fellow 1959-60), Columbia U., 1961, Ph.D., 1966; m. Daria Gortchacow, Nov. 25, 1968; children—Alexander, Helen, Tatiana, Nicholas. Supr. computing installation Watson Lab., IBM, N.Y.C., 1960-62, research asst. applied math., 1962-66, mem. staff applied math. and computing, 1966-69; dir. info. systems Interway Corp., N.Y.C., 1969-71, pres. subs. I/W Data Systems, Inc., N.Y.C., 1971-73; v.p. Automatech Graphics Corp., N.Y.C., 1973—; asso. grad. faculty dept. math. Columbia U., 1967-68, adj. asst. prof., 1968-69. Bd. dirs. Tolstoy Found. Mem. Assn. Computing Machinery, AAAS, Soc. Indsl. and Applied Math., Sigma Xi. Russian Orthodox. Office: 114 Fifth Ave New York NY 10011

KOTEEN, ANNE THELMA GEFFIN, human resources cons.; b. Brookline, Mass., June 27, 1949; d. Philip P. and Eileen M. (Sawyer) Geffin; B.S. in Bus. Adminstrn., U. R.I., 1971; M.B.A., Suffolk U., 1976. Bus. mgr., computer research center for econs. and mgmt. sci. Nat. Bur. Econ. Research, Cambridge, Mass., 1971-73; employee relations cons. Evans Products Co., Braintree, Mass., 1973-75; owner, pres. Koteen Assos., Inc., exec. search and placement for computer industry, Boston, 1975—; instr. dept. mktg. Coll. of Bus. and Profl. Studies, U. Mass., 1980—. Mem. Am. Mgmt. Assn., Assn. Systems Mgrs., Data Processing Mgmt. Assn., Nat. Assn. Personnel Consultants, Boston C. of C., Boston Jr. C. of C., U. R.I. Alumni Assn. (v.p. Boston chpt.). Club: Execs. Home: 50 Commonwealth Ave Boston MA 02116 Office: 10 Post Office Sq Boston MA 02109 also 97 4th Ave Waltham MA 02154

KOTLARCHUK, EUGENE MICHAEL, banker, lawyer; b. N.Y.C., Mar. 9, 1947; s. Emil and Lidia Nadia (Maceluch) K.; B.A., Fordham U., 1970; B.S., Columbia U., 1970, J.D., 1973, M.B.A., 1978; LL.M., N.Y. U., 1979; m. Marie I. Chiminec, June 19, 1976; 1 dau., Daria. Admitted to N.Y. State bar, 1974, D.C. bar, 1980; mem. firm Fish & Neave, N.Y.C., 1974-76, Sage, Gray, Todd & Sims, N.Y.C., 1976-77; cons., lawyer Booz Allen Acquisition Services subs. Booz, Allen & Hamilton, Inc., N.Y.C., 1977-80; policy specialist N.Y. Stock Exchange, 1980; sr. corp. fin. officer Girard Bank, Phila., 1980—; lectr. Fulbright-Hayes fellow, 1967. Mem. Am. Bar Assn., N.Y. State Bar Assn., D.C. Bar Assn., Am. Soc. Internat. Law, Am. Arbitration Assn., Am. Soc. Corp. Growth, Alpha Pi Mu. Home: 13-03 Pheasant Hollow Dr Princeton Meadows Plainsboro NJ 08536 Office: 4 Girard Plaza 15th Floor Girard Bank Philadelphia PA 19101

KOTLARCHUK, IHOR O. E., lawyer; b. Ukraine, July 31, 1943; brought to U.S., 1946, naturalized, 1957; s. Emil and Lidia N. (Maceluch) K.; B.S. in Fin., Fordham U. Sch. Bus., 1965; J.D., Fordham U. Sch Law, 1968; LL.M., Georgetown U., 1974. Admitted to N.Y. State bar, 1969; trial atty. criminal sect. tax div. U.S. Dept. Justice, Washington, 1973-78, civil sect. tax div., 1978-80, fraud sect. criminal div., 1980—; mem. U.S. Dept. Justice's Fgn. Corrupt Practices Act Rev. Com., 1980—. Served with JAG, U.S. Army, 1969-73. Decorated Bronze Star. Mem. U.S. Supreme Ct., U.S. Tax Ct., U.S. Ct. Mil. Appeals, N.Y. State Bar, D.C. Bar, Am. Bar Assn., N.Y. State Bar Assn., Phi Alpha Delta, Res. Officers Assn. Ukrainian Catholic.

KOTZIAN, GENE R., JR., fin. exec.; b. Oct. 13, 1943; s. Eugene R. and Helen (Keller) K.; B.A., San Francisco State U., 1965, M.B.A., 1968; m. Carol Ann Pool, Nov. 5, 1966; With First Calif. Co., San Francisco, 1969-73, Wulff Hansen Co., San Francisco, 1973-75; with Emmett A. Larkin Co., Inc., San Francisco, 1975—, chmn. bd., chief exec. officer, 1979—; dir. A.R. Assos., 1974-75. Chmn. fund dr. Am. Cancer Soc., San Mateo, Calif., 1964; pres. Foster City Homeowners Assn., 1971-72, Foster City Taxpayers League, 1973-74. Served with USNG, 1980. Mem. Pacific Stock Exchange, Nat. Assn. Securities Dealers, Securities Industry Assn., Phila. Stock Exchange. Republican. Roman Catholic. Clubs: Bond, Comml., Bombay, Bayside Tennis, Toastmasters (pres. 1973). Contbr. articles to profl. jours. Home: 348 Mullet Ct Foster City CA 94404 Office: 235 Montgomery St Suite 1430 San Francisco CA 94104

KOUTSOUBOS, TED ALEXANDER, restaurant exec.; b. Kansas City, Mo., Mar. 2, 1943; s. Alex Elias and Demetra K.; B.A., U. Ariz., 1967. Owner, operator Paragon Enterprises, Inc., Aspen, Colo., 1973—. Mem. Nat. Restaurant Assn. Republican. Greek Orthodox. Clubs: Elks, Eagles. Home: PO Box 3291 Aspen CO 81611 Office: Paragon Enterprises Inc PO Box 9064 Aspen CO 81611

KOVACIK, VICTOR PAUL, indsl. control systems mfg. co. exec.; b. St. Louis, Aug. 2, 1927; s. Paul and Anna (Matusovic) K.; B.S.M.E., Washington U., St. Louis, 1948; M.S. in Aero. Engring., Purdue U., 1949; diploma Oak Ridge Sch. Reactor Tech., 1951; M.B.A., Harvard U., 1957; m. Winifred Ann Hartzell, July 9, 1955; 1 dau., Ellissa. Project engr. Wright Air Devel. Center, Dayton, Ohio, 1949-55; engring. supr. Pratt & Whitney div. United Techs. Corp., Boston, 1956-57; mgr. dept. elec. products TRW Inc., Cleve., 1957-69; dir. new tech. ventures Studebaker-Worthington Corp., N.Y.C., 1969-70; pres. Frolic Friends, Inc., Mentor, Ohio, 1971—, also dir.; chmn. bd. Cyberex Inc., Mentor, 1968-77, dir., 1968-80; pres. Mead Dijit Inc., subs. Mead Corp., Dayton, 1973-75; pres. Micromenex Corp., Willoughby, Ohio, 1975—, also dir.; pres. Orttech, Inc., Willoughby, 1980—. Served with USN, 1945-46, to 1st lt. USAF, 1953-55. Recipient IR-100 award Mead Corp., 1973. Mem. IEEE, Soc. Mfg. Engrs., Greater Cleve. Growth Assn., Council Small Bus. Enterprises. Author: Impact of High Temperature Technology, 1957; patentee torpedo propulsion system, stored thermal energy; developer ink jet printing system. Home: 522 Saddleback Ln Gates Mills OH 44040 Office: 4760 Beidler Rd Willoughby OH 44094

KOVELESKI, ANTHONY MICHAEL, car equipment and model exec.; b. Moosic, Pa., Nov. 29, 1932; s. Anthony John and Ann (Chisdock) K.; grad. tech. high sch.; m. Elaine Helen Ivanik, Nov. 8, 1952; children—Robert, Sharon, Lee Ann, Christopher. Mgr. hobby shop, 1952-55; founder mail order bus. Auto World, Inc., 1958, now pres., corporate dir.; co-founder Car Model mag., 1962; cons. toy and hobby industry. Served with AUS, 1952-55. Mem. Polish Race Drivers Am. (pres.), Sports Car Club Am. (past dir.), Hobby Industry Assn. Am. (chmn. model car racing div.), Motor Racing Safety Soc. (past dir.), Internat. Motorsports Assn., Aircraft Owners and Pilots Assn., Pilots Internat. Assn., Exptl. Aircraft Assn., Air Force Assn. Contbr. articles on auto hobby market to profl. and consumer publs.; author handbooks and guidebooks. Home: 1130 W Grove St Clarks Summit PA 18411 Office: 701 N Keyser Ave Scranton PA 19508

KOVNER, SPENCER RONALD, newspaper publisher; b. Los Angeles, Dec. 1, 1940; s. Joseph Eli and Shirley Kovner; student Los Angeles Trade Tech. Coll., 1975; 1 son, Jeffrey Howard. Photographer, Jr. Advt. Club Los Angeles, 1974; apprentice Aldeen Printing Co., Los Angeles, 1961; account exec. Eastern Group Publs., Los Angeles, 1979—; propr. Kovner Publs. Inc., Los Angeles, 1979; freelance photographer, 1960—; owner, mgr. Budget Graphics, Los Angeles, 1969—; sales rep. Jose Mass Martinez Dynamic Communications Industries, Los Angeles, 1975; photographer SEK Photography, Los Angeles, 1977—. Adv. bd. Roosevelt Adult Sch., 1977—; bd. dirs., publicity chmn. Hollenbeck Police and Bus. Council, 1977; Boyle Heights rep. Los Angeles Bicentennial Commn., 1980. Recipient various service awards. Mem. Advt. Prodn. Mgrs. Club, Boyle Heights C. of C. (bd. dirs. Christmas parade 1980, past dir., publicity chmn.). Democrat. Jewish. Office: 317 N Soto St Los Angeles CA 90033

KOWALEWSKI, EDWARD STANLEY, mgmt. cons.; b. Scranton, Pa., Feb. 8, 1947; s. Edward Stanley and Sophie Dolores (Mysko) K.; B.S. in Communications, Temple U., 1969; M.S.A. in Organizational Behavior, George Washington U., 1979; m. Sheila Anne Zgavec, Oct. 14, 1972. Asst. dir. emergency employment program Lackawana County (Pa.), 1971-72; zone mgr. Mark IV Homes, Inc., Scranton, Pa., 1972-74; market and mgmt. analyst First U.S. Army, Ft. George G. Meade, Md., 1974-80; asst. exec. officer Office of Chief Army Res., Pentagon, Washington, 1980—; lectr. U. Balt. Grad. Sch. Mgmt.; prof. Columbia Coll., Hyattsville, Md. Served to maj. U.S. Army. Decorated Army Commendation medal; named Outstanding Young Man Am., U.S. Jr. C. of C., 1976. Mem. Am. Mgmt. Assn., Am. Soc. Tng. and Devel., Res. Officers Assn., Public Relations Soc. Am., Am. Mktg. Assn., Temple U. Alumni Assn., George Washington Alumni Assn., Severn Civic Assn., Torchbearers of Bishop Haffey. Clubs: Am. Legion, K.C. Author in-house publs. on mgmt., mktg. Home: 540 Epping Forest Rd Annapolis MD 21401 Office: Hdqrs First US Army Fort Meade MD 20155

KOZIOL, JOSEPH DENNIS, commodity broker; b. Phila., Oct. 3, 1950; s. Alfred Reynold and Jessie (Jajko) K.; B.S., Villanova U., 1971; M.B.A., N.Y. U., 1973; postgrad. in fin. Columbia U., 1973-74; m. Marjorie Anne Tyler, June 26, 1976; children—Peter, Christine, Kathryn. Research and grad. asst. N.Y. U., 1971-73, Columbia U., 1973-74; economist commodity dept. Shearson Hayden Stone, N.Y.C., 1974-78; managed accounts adv. commodity div. Merrill Lynch, Pierce Fenner and Smith, N.Y.C., 1978—. Mem. Am. Econ. Assn., Am. Fin. Assn., Am. Agrl. Assn., Am. Statis. Assn., So. Agrl. Econs. Assn., Mensa, Omicron Delta Epsilon, Gamma Phi, Beta Gamma Sigma. Roman Catholic. Research on commodity portfolio theory and applications, market price behavior. Office: Merrill Lynch 1 Liberty Plaza New York NY 10080

KOZLOWICZ, THOMAS JOSEPH, credit union exec.; b. Milw., Apr. 23, 1945; s. Frank J. and Esther A. (Colwell) K.; B.A., St. Marys Coll., 1967; postgrad. U. Utah, 1967; m. Lynda J. McCook, May 30, 1969; 1 son, Frank J. Vista vol. Fort Duchesne, Utah, 1967-69; salesman K-D Mailing Service, Franklin Park, Ill., 1969-70; loan officer Paysaver Credit Union, Melrose Park, Ill., 1970-77, pres., treas., 1977—; dir., sec.-treas. Ill. Credit Union League; v.p. Internat. Harvester Assn. of Credit Unions. Com. chmn. Cub Scouts, Boy Scouts Am., 1976—. Mem. Credit Union Execs. Soc. Republican. Roman Catholic. Home: 250 Oaklawn Elmhurst IL 60126 Office: 4419 W North Ave Melrose Park IL 60160

KOZLOWSKI, LEO DENNIS, mfg. co. exec.; b. Irvington, N.J., Nov. 16, 1946; s. Leo Kelly and Agnes (Kozell) K.; B.S., Seton Hall U., 1968; M.B.A., Rivier Coll., 1976; m. Angeles Suarez, Mar. 13, 1971; children—Cheryl Marie, Sandra Lisa. Internal auditor SCM Corp., N.Y.C., 1968-71; supr. internat. audit Cabot Corp., Boston, 1971-74; mgr. finance, adminstrn. Nashua Corp. (N.H.), 1974-75; dir. audit, asst. controller Tyco Labs. Inc., Waltham, Mass., 1975-76, v.p. fin. Grinnell Fire Protection Systems div., Providence, R.I., 1976—. Mem. Essex County (N.J.) Vocat. Sch. Bd., 1968-70; cons. Nashua Bd. Edn., 1975-76. Certified internal auditor, N.Y. Mass. Mem. Inst. Internal Auditors (v.p. New Eng. chpt., chmn. 1976 internat. conf., seminar leader), Fin. Execs. Inst. Home: 4 Johnson Dr Cumberland RI 02864 Office: 10 Dorrance St Providence RI 02903

KOZLOWSKI, TADEUSZ, ins. co. exec.; b. Warsaw, Poland, Aug. 3, 1926; came to U.S., 1956, naturalized, 1964; s. Jozef and Czeslawa (Miketta) K.; B. Commerce, U. London, 1953; m. Danuta Ewa Grajski, Feb. 12, 1955; children—Jan Mariusz, Maria Teresa, Anna Monika. Securities analyst Grumbar & See, London, 1953-56; with Moody's Investors Service, N.Y.C., 1956-57; sr. security analyst, asst. dir. research A.M. Kidder & Co., Inc., N.Y.C., 1957-63; sr. security analyst, dir. research, mem. investment policy com. Abraham & Co., N.Y.C., 1963-74; v.p. fin. Unity Fire and Gen. Ins. Co., Gen. Assurance Corp. of N.Y., Urbaine Life Reins. Co., chief investment officer, cons. to parent co. L'Union des Assurances de Paris. Trustee, treas. Polish Assistance, Inc., N.Y.C., 1970—; trustee Polish Scouting Orgn., Inc., N.Y.C., 1979-80. Served with Polish Underground, 1942-44; prisoner of war, Germany, 1944-45; served with 1st Polish Armored Div., 1945-47. Mem. Inst. Chartered Fin. Analysts, N.Y. Soc. Security Analysts. Home: 117 Maplewood Ave Maplewood NJ 07040 Office: 127 John St New York NY 10038

KRAEMER, PHILIPP, mfg. co. exec., inventor; b. Hahn, Ger., Jan. 17, 1931; s. George Heinrich and Anna Erna K.; student vocat. sch., Darmstadt, Ger.; m. Rosemarie Sandner, June 2, 1956; children—Lynda, Irene, Sandra. Tool and die maker, 1956-61; tool maker Quality Tool & Massey Ferguson, 1961-64; founder Kraemer Tool & Mfg. Co., Ltd., Weston, Ont., Can., 1964, since pres., gen. mgr. Mem. Pollution Control Assn., Can. Mfg. Assn. Lutheran. Club: German Can. Harmony (Toronto, Ont.). Patentee oil-sand separator, others (8). Home: 34 Kendleton Dr Rexdale ON M9V 1V4 Canada Office: 190 Milvan Dr Weston ON M9L 1Z9 Canada

KRAEN, DONALD PATRICK, banker; b. Buffalo, Wyo., Oct. 16, 1929; s. Louis and Mary Elizabeth Kraen; diploma U. San Francisco, 1949; m. Vyonne Irene Joubert, Oct. 19, 1954; children—Vernita, Gary, Shelley, Teresa, Lisa. Clk., treas. City of Buffalo, 1954-57; with Wyo. Bank & Trust Co., Buffalo, 1957—, teller, 1958-60, loan officer, 1960-62, cashier, 1962-75, pres., 1975—, also dir. Pres., Johnson County Library Bd., 1961-64; treas. Johnson County Sch. Bd., 1968-71; mem. Buffalo City Council, 1954-57, Buffalo Hwy. Com., 1961-62; fin. chmn. Meml. Hosp. Served with arty. U.S. Army, 1951-53. Mem. N.E. Bankers Assn., Wyo. Bankers Assn. (award of merit 1975), Buffalo C. of C. Roman Catholic. Clubs: K.C., Elks, Buffalo Kiwanis (pres. 1961, lt. gov. Rocky Mountain dist. 1966, Man of Yr. award 1962, Outstanding Lt. Gov. award 1966). Office: 99 S Main St Buffalo WY 82834

KRAFT, ANTHONY T., food services co. exec.; b. Hempstead, N.Y., June 27, 1937; B.B.A., Adelphi U. Audit mgr. Arthur Andersen & Co., N.Y.C., Beirut, Barcelona and Madrid, 1959-73; v.p. fin. ARA-Europe div. ARA Services Inc., London, 1973—; dir. ARA Food Services Ltd., ARA Services GmbH, Adibu Sa Vending Industries NV. C.P.A., N.Y. State. Mem. Brit. Mensa Soc., Am. Inst. C.P.A.'s, Brit. Inst. Mgmt. Clubs: Kennel (UK), Anglo Spanish Soc. Home: 48 Staveley Rd London W 4 England Office: Rex House Hampton Rd W Feltham Middlesex England

KRAFT, CHARLES WILLIAM, JR., homebuilder; b. Kansas City, Kans., Oct. 7, 1950; s. Charles William and Helen Virginia (Herrington) K.; B.A., Mid-Am. Nazarene Coll., 1973; postgrad.

Baker U., Baldwin City, Kans., 1978-79; m. Brenda Joyce, July 31, 1976. Pres., Kraft III, Inc., Olathe, Kans., 1979—. Mem. Home Builders Assn. Kansas City, Olathe C. of C. Address: 14512 Summer Tree Olathe KS 66061

KRAFT, DONALD EUGENE, product design engr.; b. Rochester, N.Y., Aug. 10, 1929; s. Nicholas Raymond and Rosella Theresa (Miller) K.; student U. Rochester, 1948-51; B.S. in Engring., Bus. Adminstrn. and Econs., Empire State Coll., 1977; m. Rosemarie Ursula Kraus, Apr. 24, 1965; children—Eva Maria, Christian Martin, Donald Alexander Nicholas. Sales rep. C.A. Brewer Co., Rochester, 1952-56; civil and san. engr. design Lozier Engrs., Inc., and Morrison & Morrison, 1956-61; v.p., gen. mgr. Profl. Chem. Corp., 1962-65; project engr. new product devel. Caldwell Mfg. Co., Inc., 1965-71; applications engr. Schlegel Corp., 1971-72; pres. Don Kraft Co., Rochester, 1973—; cons. to industry. Served with USNR, 1947-48. Registered profl. engr., N.Y. Mem. Rochester C. of C., Civic Music Assn., Meml. Art Gallery. Republican. Roman Catholic. Club: Rochester Yacht. Patentee in hydraulics, pneumatics, dental equipment, window hardware and weather seals. Home: 928 Winona Blvd Rochester NY 14617

KRAFT, GARY, athletic products co. exec.; b. Hamilton, Ohio, Apr. 24, 1949; s. Gordon Lee and Jean (Hegler) K.; student Miami U., Oxford, Ohio, 1971. Nat. sales mgr. Gen. Athletic Products Co., Greenville, Ohio. Bd. dirs. Hamilton YMCA, 1977-80, Jr. Achievement, 1978-79, Hamilton United Way, 1978-79; mem. Community Forum Com., 1978-80. Mem. Hamilton Jaycees (youth, sport dir. 1976, v.p. 1977, pres. 1978-79, state dir. 1980-81), Hamilton C. of C., Fairfield C. of C. Roman Catholic. Home: 607 Harrison Ave Hamilton OH 45013 Office: 607 Riffle Ave Hamilton OH 45331

KRAFT, GERALD, economist; b. Detroit, July 1, 1935; s. Jule and Shirley (Schwartz) K.; student U. Chgo., 1951-52; B.A., Wayne U., 1955; M.A., Harvard U., 1957; m. Sandra Doris Johnson, Aug. 7, 1955; children—Michael Stanton, Lynn Barbara. Mng. dir. Harvard U. Statis. Lab., Cambridge, Mass., 1957-58; prin. United Research Inc., Cambridge, 1958-61; sr. research asso. Systems Analysis and Research Corp., Boston, 1961-64, Regional and Urban Planning Implementation, Inc., Cambridge, 1964-65; pres., dir. Charles River Assos. Inc., Boston, 1965—; lectr. M.I.T., Harvard U., U. Pa.; mem. planning com., dir. Maritime Transp. Research Bd., NRC, 1976-79, mem. Group I Council, mem. coms. Transp. Research Bd., 1977-80; pres. Transp. Research Forum, 1977, v.p. program, 1976. Trustee, mem. fin. com. Beth Israel Hosp. Mem. Am. Econ. Assn., Econometric Soc., Am. Statis. Assn., Inst. Mgmt. Scis., Ops. Research Soc. Am., Inst. Math. Stats., Phi Beta Kappa. Clubs: Beefeater, Internat. Wine and Food Soc., Wine and Food Soc. Boston (treas.), Le Premier Club du Vin. Author: (with others) The Role of Transportation in Regional Economic Development, 1971; co-author Report of Task Force on Transp. and Sci. Adv. panel to Com. on Pub. Works, U.S. Ho. of Reps., 1974; contbr. articles to profl. publs. Home: 60 Scotch Pine Rd Weston MA 02193 Office: 200 Clarendon St Boston MA 02116

KRAKAR, MARCUS JACOB, mfg. co. exec.; b. Chgo., Apr. 9, 1937; s. Marcus Jacob and Bernice Dorothy (Felbinger) K.; student Joliet Jr. Coll., 1954-55, Lewis Coll., 1956; m. Patricia Louise Vogen, Mar. 15, 1978; children—Amy, Patrick. Shop supt. Appogee Electronics, Chgo., 1961-62; pres. Krakar Mfg. Co., Joliet, Ill., 1962—. Trustee, Joliet Artist League, 1967-68; treas. Joliet Spanish Center, 1969-70; bd. dirs. Joliet Drama Guild, 1975-76; chmn. Will-Grundy County Pvt. Industry Council, 1980—. Served with USMC, 1956-58. Mem. Joliet Region C. of C. Lutheran. Home: 808 Barber Ln Joliet IL 60435 Office: 251 N Republic Ave Joliet IL 60435

KRAKAUER, JOHN LYLE, computer co. exec.; b. Buffalo, June 26, 1941; s. Hans S. and Elizabeth (Gottschalk) K.; B.A. in Econs., Cornell U., 1962; m. Carol M. Johnson, Nov. 27, 1969; children—Keith L., Laura L. Actuarial trainee John Hancock Ins. Co., 1962-63; with IBM Corp., 1965-67; bus. systems mgr. FMC Corp., 1967-69; founder, 1969, since v.p., gen. mgr. health care systems div. Optimum Systems Co. (now Bradford Nat. Co.), Santa Clara, Calif., dir. health services div., 1980—. Served with USAR, 1963-65. Decorated Army Commendation medal. Republican. Congregationalist. Home: PO Box 132 Saratoga CA 95070 Office: 1095 E Duane Ave Sunnyvale CA 94086

KRAKOFF, ROBERT LEONARD, exposition mgmt. exec.; b. Pitts., May 4, 1935; s. Frank and Della (Zionts) K.; B.S. with honors, Pa. State U., 1957; M.B.A., Harvard, 1959; m. Sandra Gusky, June 22, 1958; children—Roger, Hope, Reed. Staff v.p. mktg. planning TransWorld Airlines, N.Y.C., 1963-70; v.p., controller, consumer product div. Singer, N.Y.C., 1970-71; staff v.p. strategic planning RCA, N.Y.C., 1971-72; pres. Am. Internat. Travel Service, Boston, 1972-73; pres. Cahners Travel Group, N.Y.C., 1973-74; pres. Cahners Exposition Group; v.p. Cahners Pub. Co., 1974—; trustee Centennial Cash Mgmt. Trust. Served with USAR, 1957-63. Mem. Nat. Assn. Exposition Mgrs., Beta Gamma Sigma. Home: 29 Sachem Rd Weston CT 06883 Office: 331 Madison Ave New York NY 10017

KRAKOWER, BERNARD HYMAN, mgmt. cons.; b. N.Y.C., May 11, 1935; s. David and Bertha (Glassman) K.; B.A. in Advt., U. Calif., Los Angeles, 1959, certificate in real estate, 1966, certificate in indsl. relations, 1972; M.B.A., Pepperdine U., 1979; m. Sondra Joan Fishbein, Apr. 14, 1968; children—Lorna, Victoria, Ariel Shauna. Loan officer Lytton Fin. Corp., Los Angeles, 1961-65; mgmt. cons. James R. Colvin & Assos., Los Angeles, 1965-67; sr. indsl. relations rep. Sci. Data Systems, 1967-68; dir. ops. Tratec, Inc., Los Angeles, 1968-70; pres. Krakower/Brucker Internat., Inc., Los Angeles, 1970—. Mem. citizens liaison com. Los Angeles Dept. Recreation and Parks, 1973; pres., bd. dirs. Western Los Angeles Chamber Found. Recipient certificates of appreciation City of Los Angeles, 1974, 77, 78, 79, certificates of merit Western Los Angeles Regional C. of C., 1976, 77. Mem. Western Los Angeles Regional C. of C. (dir., ex-officio mem. exec. com.). U. Calif. Los Angeles Alumni Assn. Club: Sierra (exec. com. West Los Angeles 1971-72). Office: 10960 Wilshire Blvd Suite 1406 Los Angeles CA 90024

KRAL, MICHAEL, steel co. exec.; b. Prague, Czechoslovakia, July 26, 1920; s. Dominic and Marie (Triner) K.; came to U.S., 1946, naturalized, 1948; B.S., U. Prague, 1937, M.S., 1939; m. Audrey Howland, Nov. 8, 1973. Vice pres. Overseas Raw Materials Corp., N.Y.C., 1950-54; pres. U.S. Ore Corp., N.Y.C., 1954-70, Michael Kral Co., N.Y.C., 1960—, Michael Kral Industries, N.Y.C., 1970—; chmn. bd. Electralloy Corp., Oil City, Pa., 1967—; dir. Venango Metall. Products, 1970—, Kokomo (Ind.) Tube Co., 1975—. Mem. Am. Iron and Steel Inst. (dir. 1975—), Assn. Iron and Steel Engrs., Am. Soc. for Metals, ASTM, Am. Def. Preparedness Assn. Clubs: Cornell U., Wanango Country, Rand, RSA. Contbr. articles in field to profl. jours. Home: 200 Central Park S New York NY 10019 Office: 1290 Ave of Americas New York NY 10104

KRALL, GEORGE FERGUSON, JR., info. mgmt. cons.; b. Phila., May 1, 1936; s. George Ferguson and Edna Mae (Young) K.; B.S. in Mech. Engring., Drexel U., 1958; M.B.A., U. Pa., 1962; m. Lois Jane Williamson, Dec. 31, 1959; children—George W., Cynthia L., Elizabeth O. Account mgr. IBM Corp., Phila., 1962-68; pres. Krall Mgmt. Inc., Radnor, Pa., 1969—; instr. Drexel U., 1967-69. Rectors warden, acctg. warden St. David's Ch. Vestry, 1973-79; pres. Main Line Young Republicans, 1968; bd. dirs. Main Line chpt. ARC, 1969-71. Served to 1st lt. AUS, 1959-61. Mem. Assn. Cons. Mgmt. Engrs. (dir. 1975-79, v.p. 1978-79). Episcopalian. Clubs: Union League, Merion Cricket (Phila.); Army and Navy (Washington). Home: Tunbridge Rd Haverford PA 19041 Office: Two Radnor Corporate Center Radnor PA 19087

KRAMER, CHARLES EUGENE, mfg. co. exec.; b. Hamilton, Ohio, Mar. 10, 1919; s. George M. and Deborah (Begley) K.; B.M.E., Purdue U., 1940; m. Nelda M. Wood, Aug. 12, 1942; children—Janet Lynn Kramer Allen, Robert M. With Fairfield Mfg. Co., Lafayette, Ind., 1940—, chief indsl. engr., 1951-58, factory mgr., 1958-63, v.p. mfg., 1963-73, pres., 1973—; dir. Lafayette Nat. Bank, Schwab Safe Co., Lafayette. Trustee Lafayette YMCA; mem. lay adv. bd. St. Elizabeth Hosp., Lafayette; dir. Capital Fund Fedn., Lafayette; mem. Purdue Research Found.; trustee Ind. Vocat. and Tech. Coll., 1976—. Served with U.S. Army, 1944-46. Mem. Pres. Assn., Am. Mgmt. Assn., ASME, Am. Inst. Indsl. Engrs., C. of C. (dir.). Republican. Methodist. Clubs: Lafayette Country, Elks. Home: 3918 Gate Rd Lafayette IN 47905

KRAMER, DONOVAN MERSHON, editor, publisher; b. Galesburg, Ill., Oct. 24, 1925; s. Verle V. and Sybil (Mershon) K.; B.A. in Journalism, U. Ill., 1948; m. Ruth A. Heins, Apr. 3, 1949; children—Donovan M., Eric, Diana, Kara. Editor, pub. Fairbury (Ill.) Blade and Forrest News, 1948-63; pub. Casa Grade (Ariz.) Dispatch, 1962—, also Coolidge Examiner, 1971—, Florence Reminder, 1970—, Blade-Tribune, 1971—, Eloy Enterprise, 1967—, Gila Bend Herald, 1973—; pres. Casa Grande Valley Newspapers, Inc., 1963—. Chmn., Pinal County Devel. Bd.; past chmn. Ariz. Econ. Planning and Devel. Bd.; pres. Casa Grande Indsl. Authority; bd. freeholders City of Casa Grande; mem. Ariz. Gov.'s Land Use Task Force. Served with USAAF, 1944-46. Recipient many nat. and state newspaper awards. Mem. Community Newspapers Ariz. (past pres.), Ariz. Newspapers Assn. (pres.; named 1976 Master Editor-Pub.), Casa Grande C. of C. (presdl. award 1964), Ariz. Acad., Internat. Newspaper Promotion Assn., Nat. Newspapers Assn., Inst. Newspaper Controllers and Finance Officers, Am. Newspaper Pubs. Assn., Greater Casa Grande Devel. Assn. (dir.), Central Ariz. Project Assn. (dir.). Independent Democrat. Lutheran. Clubs: Rotary (Casa Grande); Elks, Mason. Home and office: PO Box 639 Casa Grande AZ 85222

KRAMER, FERDINAND, real estate exec.; b. Chgo., Aug. 10, 1901; s. Adolph Ferdinand and Ray (Friedberg) K.; Ph.B., U. Chgo., 1922; m. Julia Wood McDermott; children—Anthony, Douglas, Barbara Bailey. Engaged in real estate and mortgage banking, 1972—; chmn. bd. Draper & Kramer Inc., Chgo., 1972—. Bd. govs. Met. Housing and Planning Council, 1934; exec. com. Dearborn Park Corp., 1980; life trustee U. Chgo.; past chmn. U. Chgo. Alumni Fund, Pres.'s Club; past trustee Urban Am., Inc.; past pres., life bd. dirs. Michael Reese Hosp., Chgo.; bd. dirs. Reading Is Fundamental, 1975—; program supr. div. def. housing Nat. Housing Agy., 1941-42. Recipient public service citation U. Chgo., 1947, Nat. Assn. Housing and Redevel. Ofcls., 1952; award Chgo. Commn. Human Relations, 1962; Joint Negro Appeal award, 1965; Citizen fellowship Inst. Medicine Chgo., 1970. Mem. Chgo. Mortgage Bankers Assn. (past pres.); Mortgage Bankers Assn. Am., Nat. Assn. Housing Ofcls., Chgo. Assn. Commerce and Industry (past v.p.), Fed. Nat. Mortgage Assn. (past dir.). Clubs: Quadrangle, Chgo., Comml., Standard, Tavern, Mid-Town Tennis, Ridge and Valley Tennis (Chgo.). Home: 1115 S Plymouth Ct Chicago IL 60605 Office: 30 W Monroe St Chicago IL 60603

KRAMER, IRWIN HAMILTON, investment co. exec.; b. N.Y.C., Aug. 19, 1921; s. Nathan and Lillian (Green) K.; B.A., Yale, 1944; m. Terry Allen, Aug. 3, 1958; children—Toni Allen, Nathaniel Charles Allen, Angela Frances Allen. Vice pres., owner, gen. mgr. Hotel Edison, N.Y.C., 1954-69; with Allen & Co. Inc., N.Y.C., 1969—, exec. v.p., 1975—; dir. Columbia Pictures Industries, Inc. Bd. dirs. YM-YWHA of Greater N.Y. Served to 1st lt. AUS, 1942-45. Home: 730 Park Ave New York NY 10021 Office: 711 Fifth Ave New York NY 10022

KRAMER, JOHN RICHARD, mortgage banker; b. Pitts., May 11, 1939; s. Orran H. and Helen A. (Ahern) K.; B.S., Lehigh U., 1961; m. Sally S. Kramer, June 1, 1968; children—J. Douglas, Matthew A., Mark A. Indsl. engr. U.S. Steel Corp., 1962-66; asst. v.p., mgr. James W. Rouse & Co., Pitts., 1966-71, v.p., dir. new bus. devel., Columbia, Md., 1971-73, v.p., mgr. Washington, 1973-75, sr. v.p., Columbia, 1976; pres. Century Real Estate Fin., Inc., Pitts., 1976—; pres. Carey, Kramer, Crouse & Assos., Inc., Pitts. Sec.-treas., bd. dirs. Kay and Shadyside Boys Clubs. Served with USCG, 1961-62. Republican. Office: 730 Grant Bldg Pittsburgh PA 15219

KRAMER, PHILIP, petroleum refining exec.; b. N.Y.C., Jan. 27, 1921; s. Saul and Malvina (Kuttner) K.; B.B.A., Coll. City N.Y., 1940; M.B.A., Harvard U., 1942; m. Sarah Greenberg, Dec. 27, 1942; children—Noell M., Marilyn B., Glenn M. Mem. research staff Harvard Grad. Sch. Bus., 1942, 46; v.p. Paragon Oil Co., 1947-60; v.p. Pittston Co., 1960-69; pres. div. Met. Petroleum Co., 1960-69; exec. v.p. Amerada Hess Corp., 1969-72, pres., 1972—, also dir. Served to lt. USNR, World War II. Home: 870 UN Plaza New York NY 10017 Office: 1185 Ave of Americas New York NY 10019

KRAMER, RUTH, accountant; b. N.Y.C., June 20, 1925; d. Isidore and Sarah (Heller) Kleiner; B.A., Bklyn. Coll., 1946; m. Paul Kramer, Oct. 27, 1946; children—Stephen David, Lynne Adair. Tchr. elementary sch. N.Y.C. Bd. Edn., 1946-50; accountant Lichtenstein & Kramer, N.Y.C., Lynbrook, N.Y., 1954; jr. partner Paul Kramer & Co., Lynbrook, 1954-56, partner, 1956-65, mng. partner, 1965—; cons. Nassau County (N.Y.) Dist. Attys. Office, 1956-65; expert witness accounting matters Nassau County Grand Juries, 1956-65; mem. IRS liaison com. Bklyn. Dist., 1965-76; dir. Flinch & Bruns Funeral Home, Inc. Troop leader Girl Scouts U.S.A., 1947-48; chmn. Tri Town sect. Anti Defamation League, 1952-53; active Heart Fund; pres. Lynbrook Womens Republican Club, 1956-58; treas. Assembly Candidates Campaign Com., 1964; mem. Nassau County Fedn. Rep. Women, Syosset Woodbury Rep. Club. Named Woman in Accounting, local TV channel, 1974. Registered pub. accountant, N.Y. Mem. Nat. Soc. Pub. Accountants (del.), Empire State Assn. Pub. Accountants (Meritorious Service award, 2d v.p., 1975-76, 1st v.p. 1977-78, pres. 1978-79, past pres. exec. bd., 1979—, pres. Nassau County chpt. 1962, 63, 75, 76), Tax Inst. C.W. Post Coll., Accounting Inst. C.W. Post Coll. Jewish. Clubs: Sisterhood North Shore Synagogue; Am. Jewish Congress, Lynbrook Pythian Sisters. (past chief). Home: 23 Hilltop Dr Syosset NY 11791 Office: 23 Hilltop Dr Syosset NY 11791

KRAMM, SAMUEL EVERETT, furniture mfg. co. exec.; b. Mexico, Mo., Jan. 24, 1926; s. Hartzell Wolfe and Maurine Lucille (McDonald) K.; B.S. in Edn., Western Ill. U., 1952; m. Sarah Clark, July 12, 1975; children—Kelli, Karrie, Kathy, Kim. Tchr. indsl. arts Western Ill. U., Macomb, 1952-62; pres., treas., designer The Wood Shop, Inc., Washington, 1964—. Trustee 4th Presbyterian Ch., Bethesda, Md., 1972-76; sec. Internat. Inst. Devel., Inc., 1976-78; treas. Bibles for World, Washington, 1977-78. Served with U.S. Navy, 1943-46. Mem. Direct Mktg. Club Washington, Aircraft Owners and Pilots Assn., Am. Bonanzo Assn. Republican. Home: Oak Manor Farm 3904 Mill Creek Rd Hay Market VA 22069 Office: 3100 M St NW Washington DC 20715

KRANICK, CYRIL ROBERT, mineral beneficiation cons.; b. Scranton, Pa., Dec. 9, 1910; s. Andrew Paul and Susan Margaret (Gasper) K.; B.A., U. Pa., 1932; m. Vivian M. Flynn, Feb. 22, 1936; children—Cyril, Robert, Richard, Joanne. Salesman, Jacob Dold Packing Co., Buffalo, 1932-38; supt., asst. to pres. Valley View and Belleview Coal Co., Scranton, 1938-51; sales mgr.-coal Wemco div. Envirotech Corp., Clarks Summit, Pa., 1951-76, cons. Envirotech Corp., 1976—. Registered profl. metall. engr., Pa. Mem. Am. Inst. Mining, Metall. and Petroleum Engrs., Am. Mining Congress. Democrat. Roman Catholic. Clubs: Scranton Elks, Lakeview Country. Home: 316 Tulip Circle Clarks Summit PA 18411

KRANIK, FRANK MICHAEL, environ. cons. co. exec.; b. Braddock, Pa., Jan. 22, 1953; s. John and Mary Post K.; B.S., Davis and Elkins Coll., 1974; M.S., U. Pitts., 1976. Research asst. Pa. Gov.'s Energy Council, Harrisburg, 1976; regional mgr. Ecology and Environment, Inc., Denver, 1980—. Recipient Disting. Service award Concerned Parents of Gen. Braddock, 1976. Mem. Nat. Assn. Environ. Profls. (registered), Rocky Mountain Oil and Gas Assn., AAAS. Home: 9002 E Amherst Dr Denver CO 80231 Office: 243 E 19 Ave Suite 300 Denver CO 80203

KRANTZ, FREDERICK HAROLD, mgmt. cons.; b. Kansas City, Mo., June 15, 1926; s. Harold F. and Elizabeth L. (Crispin) K.; B.S., Drexel Inst., 1949; M.S., U. Pa., 1956; postgrad. Harvard, 1970; m. Patricia M. Jorgensen, Sept. 3, 1949 (div. Nov. 1975); children—Steven, Laurel; m. 2d, Vicki L. Brumagin, Dec. 19, 1975. Research technologist Leeds & Northrup, Phila., 1950-55; program mgr. for radar and beacon video processing Burroughs Labs., Paoli, Pa., 1955-61; program mgr. for communications and tactical systems IBM, Gaithersberg, Md., 1961-68; mgr. command and controls programs RCA, Burlington, Mass., 1969, chief engr., 1969-70, v.p. electromagnetic and aviation systems div., gen. mgr., Van Nuys, Calif., 1971-75; v.p., gen. mgr. Gen. Dynamics Electronics Div., San Diego, 1975-78; mgmt. cons., Solana Beach, Calif., 1978—. Served with USAAF, 1944-46. Registered profl. engr., Mass. Mem. IEEE, Sigma Xi, Eta Kappa Nu, Tau Beta Pi. Home: 940 Santa Queta Solana Beach CA 92075 Office: 215 S Hwy 101 Solana Beach CA 92075

KRAUCH, WILLIAM KARL, shopping center devel. co. exec.; b. Pasadena, Calif., Apr. 1, 1943; s. William Henry and Velma Ann (McDonald) K.; B.S. in Bus. Adminstrn., UCLA, 1966; m. Christine Lorey, Apr. 8, 1977. Sales cons. Coldwell Banker Comml. Brokerage Co., Los Angeles, also Portland, Oreg., 1969-77; v.p. Hahn Devcorp. subs. Ernest W. Hahn, Inc., Portland and Los Angeles, 1977—. Served to capt. AUS, 1966-68; Vietnam. Decorated Bronze Star. Mem. Internat. Council Shopping Centers, Portland Com. Fgn. Relations. Club: Portland City. Home: 4941 Rolling Meadows Rd Rolling Hills Estates CA 90274 Office: PO Box 92936 Los Angeles CA 90009

KRAUS, HARRY ARNOLD, mktg. communications co. exec.; b. N.Y.C., Aug. 11, 1936; s. Harry A. and Rosalie K.; student Pace Coll., 1954-58, N.Y. U., 1963-65, New Sch., 1966-69; m. Diana Izzi, Apr. 18, 1971; 1 dau., Juliana Margaret; children by previous marriage—Ellen Beth, David Joseph. Vice pres. LHO Inc., N.Y.C., 1969-72; dir. market services Nat. Union Electric Corp., Stamford, Conn., 1962-69; dir. advt. and sales promotion Fedders Corp., Edison, N.J., 1958-62; pres. Modular Mktg. Inc., N.Y.C., 1972—; lectr. and writer in field. Mem. Queens County Republican Com., 1963-65. Recipient Boli awards 1975, 76, 77, 79, Andy awards 1976, 77, 78, 79. Mem. Direct Mail Mktg. Assn. Clubs: Atrium, Nat. Sales Exec. Home: 125 W 76th St New York NY 10023 Office: 1841 Broadway New York NY 10023

KRAUS, JOHN FRANK, cons., former communications co. exec.; b. Elizabeth, N.J., Oct. 18, 1909; s. Leo J. and Katherine (Volar) K.; B.S. in Elec. Engring., Cooper Union, 1931; postgrad. N.Y. U., CCNY; m. Virginia E. Smith, Aug. 26, 1934; children—Elizabeth Ann, John Minard. With N.Y. Telephone Co., 1928-43, 45-73, plant, engring. and engring. staff; mem. tech. staff Bell Telephone Labs., 1943-45. Past pres. North Plainfield Citizens Assn.; past v.p. North Plainfield Bd. Health; past chmn. North Plainfield Assessment Commn., Parking Authority and Planning Bd.; past dist. chmn. A.R.C. and Community Chest; past commr., sec. N.J. Met. Rapid Transit Commn. and Bi-state (N.J. & N.Y.) Met. Rapid Transit Commn.; past chmn. Inter-Municipal Group for Better Rail Service, Inter-Municipal Group for Solid Waste Disposal. Mem. I.E.E.E., Raritan Valley Commuters Assn. (past pres.). Presbyn. (elder). Mason (past master). Club: Plainfield Engineers. Home and office: 4 Edgewood Ct North Plainfield NJ 07060

KRAUS, PANSY DAEGLING, editor; b. Santa Paula, Calif., Sept. 21, 1916; d. Arthur David and Elsie (Pardee) Daegling; A.A., San Bernardino Valley Jr. Coll., 1938; student Longmeyer's Bus. Coll., 1940; grad. gemologist diploma Gemological Inst. Am., 1966; m. Charles Frederick Kraus, Mar. 1, 1941 (div. Nov. 1961). Clk., Convair, San Diego, 1943-48, San Diego County Schs. Publs., 1948-57; mgr. Rogers and Boblet-Art Craft, San Diego, 1958-64; part-time editorial asst. Lapidary Jour., San Diego, 1963-64, asso. editor, 1964-69, editor, 1970—; lectr. gems. gemology local gem, mineral groups; gem and mineral club bull. editor groups. Recipient fellowship diploma Gemmol. Assn. Gt. Britain, 1960. Mem. San Diego Mineral and Gem Soc., Gemol. Soc. San Diego, Gemol. Assn. Great Britain, Mineral. Soc. Am., Epsilon Sigma Alpha. Editor, layout dir.; Gem Cutting Shop Helps, 1964; The Fundamentals of Gemstone Carving, 1967; Appalachian Mineral and Gem Trails, 1968; Practical Gem Knowlege for the Amateur, 1969; Southwest Mineral and Gem Trails, 1972. Home: 6127 Mohler St San Diego CA 92120 Office: 3564 Kettner Blvd San Diego CA 92101

KRAUS, PHILLIP, mfg. co. exec.; b. N.Y.C., Sept. 11, 1914; s. Joseph and Clara (Kuhn) K.; A.B., UCLA, 1936, M.A., 1938; J.D., U. So. Calif., 1940; m. Annette Meyer, Dec. 12, 1948; children—Kathy Jo, Laurie Jan. Admitted to Calif. bar, 1941; spl. asst. to atty. gen. anti-trust div. U.S. Dept. Justice, 1948-51; chief counsel OPS, Calif., 1951-53; pres. Calif. Custom Accessories Co., Los Angeles, 1953-74; v.p., counsel Orion Industries Inc., Los Angeles, 1969—. Vice pres. Peninsula Symphony Assn.; pres. Palos Verdes B'nai B'rith; campaign chmn. United Jewish Welfare Fund. Served with U.S. Army, 1942-46. Decorated Army Commendation award. Mem. Calif. State Bar, U. So. Calif. Alumni Assn. (life), UCLA Alumni Assn. (life), Legion Lex, Order of Coif, Pi Sigma Alpha, Pi Gamma Mu, Phi Kappa Phi. Democrat. Author articles legal jours.; bd. editor U. So. Calif. Law Rev., 1939-40. Home: 7088 Crest Rd Palos Verdes CA 90274 Office: 19914 S Via Baron St Compton CA 90220

KRAUS, VIRGIL KELLY, geologist, oil co. exec.; b. Pecos, Tex., Mar. 13, 1928; s. Kirk Kelly and Jessie Mae (Shaum) K.; student U. Tex., 1946-49; B.S. in Geology, U. Houston, 1956; m. Jane Lee Muir, Aug. 8, 1951; children—Kenneth W., Linda Gayle. Geologist, Dow Chem. Co., Houston, 1956-72, chief geologist, 1972-73; chief geologist Buttes Gas & Oil Co., Houston, 1973-76; geologist, partner Chapman Oil Co., Houston, 1976—; pres. Chapman Internat. Oil Co., Tex-Lou Co.; dir. Lou-Tex Trust Co., Allied Oil Co., Transgas Co.; v.p. Chapman Oil Co. Israel. Mem. Am. Assn. Petroleum Geologists, Houston Geol. Soc. Republican. Methodist. Clubs: Houston Met. Racquet, Houston. Home: 10803 Pine Bayou Houston TX 77024 Office: 808 Travis Houston TX 77002

KRAUSE, AL R., mfg. co. exec.; b. Raeville, Nebr., May 4, 1932; s. Aloysius August and Della Fredricka (Meyers) K.; B.Sc. in Elec. Engring., U. Nebr., 1960; m. Janet Thelma Hunter, Feb. 4, 1952; children—Deborah, Douglas, Dawne, Daniel, Deanna, David, Denice, Dirk, Derek, Dorinda. Mgr. research and devel. TRW Inc., Boone, Inc., 1963-65, project mgr., 1965-67, plant mgr., 1967-69, ops. mgr., 1969-75, div. mgr., 1975—. Mem. president's com. Appalachian State U., 1972—, bd. dirs. nat. bus. adv. council, 1974—. Served with USAF, 1952-56. Registered profl. engr., Nebr. Mem. Am. Mgmt. Assn., Am. Mktg. Assn., Nat. Alliance Businessmen, VFW. Democrat. Roman Catholic. Club: Moose. Home: Route 4 Boone NC 28607 Office: TRW Inc Box 1860 Boone NC 28607

KRAUSE, ARTHUR WALTER, mfg. co. exec.; b. Milw., Jan. 2, 1919; s. Arthur R. and Selma (Kruse) K.; student U. Wis., evening div., 1947-56; m. Margaret E. Keller, June 21, 1941; 1 dau., Lynn Margaret. Asst. gen. mgr. Delta Mfg. Co., Milw., 1950-54; works mgr. Rockwell Mfg. Co., Pitts., 1954-55; chief methods engr. Controls Co. Am., 1955-59; gen. mgr. Hydraulic Machinery Co., Waukesha, Wis., 1959-62, v.p. fabricated metal products, 1962-64; pres. Hydraulic Power Equipment Corp., Milw., 1964-71; dir. br. ops. Pettibone Corp., Chgo., 1971-80, dir. corp. communications, 1980—; pres. Pettibone Wis. Corp., Milw., 1971—. Served with USMC, 1944-46. Republican. Lutheran. Home: 4532 W Fountain Ave Brown Deer WI 53223 Office: 9501 W Devon Ave Rosemont IL 60018

KRAUSE, LEONARD L., computer systems co. exec.; b. Cleve., June 21, 1922; s. Edward L. and Julia Krause; student U. San Francisco, 1942-43; B.B.A., Baldwin-Wallace Coll., 1947; postgrad. Western Res. U.; m. Mildred M. Tarnovsky, Sept. 27, 1947; children—Karen, Leonard E., Connie L., Kenneth J., Raymond J., Candia S., Kristin V. Staff acct. Scovell Wellington & Co., C.P.A.'s, 1948-50; supr. controller's office Ford Motor Co., Cleve., 1951-58; controller Bellows-Valvair div. IBEC, Akron, Ohio, 1958—, treas., 1959-61, v.p. fin., 1962-69, v.p. internat. ops., 1970-72; pres. Computer/Dynamics Inc., Cleve., 1974—. Clk.-treas. Village of Fairlawn, 1962-69, mem. village council, 1978—, pres. village council, 1980—. Served with U.S. Army, 1942-46; ETO. Mem. Am. Prodn. and Inventory Control Soc. Roman Catholic. Clubs: Fairlawn Country, K.C. Office: Computer/Dynamics Inc Commerce Park Dr Cleveland OH 44142

KRAUSS, JEFFREY DAVID, ins. agy. exec.; b. N.Y.C., Feb. 11, 1946; s. Milton and Eve (Silverberg) K.; B.S., N.Y. U., 1967; postgrad. N.Y. Law Sch., 1967-68; m. Laura Bernstein, Mar. 29, 1969; children—Michael, Lea. Stockbroker, Pressman, Frohlich & Frost, N.Y.C., 1968-70; ins. agt. Mut. Benefit Life Ins. Co., N.Y.C., 1970-71; v.p. White House Agy., Inc., N.Y.C., 1971-75; pres. Dascit/White & Winston, Inc., N.Y.C., 1975—; estate planning/pension cons.; dir. Group Plan Adminstrs., Inc., Unltd. Service Agy. Guest speaker First Estate Planning Seminar of Boys Town of Jerusalem, 1979, Nat. Found. for Ileitis and Colitis, Inc., 1977. C.L.U.; registered health underwriter. Mem. N.Y.C. Estate PLanners Council, Am. Soc. C.L.U.'s, Nat. Assn. Life Underwriters, Nat. Assn. Health Underwriters, Internat. Assn. Fin. Planners. Contbr. articles to profl. jours. Office: 1140 Ave of the Americas New York NY 10036

KRAUTER, CHARLES FREDERICK, diversified industries exec.; b. Hackensack, N.J., June 26, 1929; s. Charles Frederick and Helen Marie (Faughnan) K.; student Lafayette Coll., 1947-48, Rutgers U., 1948-49, Coll. of Ins., 1954-57; m. Suzanne Clark Grove, Jan. 26, 1952; children—Neil C., Lynn G. Ins. supr. Arabian Am. Oil Co., N.Y.C., 1949-57; asst. ins. mgr. St. Regis Paper Co., N.Y.C., 1957-60; asst. treas. W.R. Grace & Co., N.Y.C., 1960—. Lectr. Coll. of Ins. Trustee, Rumson Improvement Assn. Served with USCGR, 1950-53. Mem. Risk and Ins. Mgmt. Soc. (asst. treas., chmn. financial operations com.), Assn. Ex-Mems. Squadron A, Delta Kappa Epsilon. Roman Catholic. Clubs: New York Yacht; Seabright Beach (bd. govs.) (Seabright, N.J.); Shrewsbury Sailing and Yacht (Oceanport, N.J.). Home: Orchard Ln Rumson NJ 07760 Office: 1114 Ave of Americas New York NY 10036

KRAUTHAMER, GARY LEWIS, exec. search and mgmt. cons. co. exec.; b. N.Y.C., Nov. 19, 1948; s. Morris Krauthamer; B.S. in Fin. and Bus. Adminstrn., Am. U., 1970; m. Nancy Kadian, June 2, 1970; children—Adam, Coby. Mgr. fin. dept. Mgmt. Recruiters Internat., Washington, 1968-70; founder, pres. Profl. Recruiters Inc., Washington, Balt., Fairfax, Va. and San Francisco, 1970-77, Krauthamer Assos., internat. exec. search co., Washington and New Delhi, 1972—; com. rep. ILO, 1976; pres. Washington Personnel Assn., 1977; lectr. various univs. U.S., 1970—. Home: 24315 Old Hundred Rd Dickerson MD 20753 Office: 5530 Wisconsin Ave Washington DC 20015

KREBILL, DOUGLAS DWIGHT, feed and fertilizer products co. exec.; b. Keokuk, Iowa, July 21, 1948; s. Dwight Hubert and Mildred Edith Krebill; B.S. in Agrl. Bus. (C.H. Chasescholar 1969), Iowa State U., 1970; m. Lorrie Ann Leabo, Nov. 28, 1970; children—Kelli Ann, Darin Douglas. Office mgr. Agrifax, Eastern Iowa Prodn. Credit Assn., DeWitt, 1970-72; distbn. mgr. ConAgra, Inc., Omaha, 1972-75; div. mgr. feed products CF Industries, Long Grove, Ill., 1975-79, div. mgr. feed and fertilizer products, 1979—; dir. Fresh Egg Farms, 1973—. Bd. dirs. CF Credit Union, 1979, pres., 1980. Mem. Am. Feed Mfrs. Assn., Nat. Feed Ingredients Assn., Canadian Feed Industry Assn., Fertilizer Inst., Canadian Fertilizer Inst. Republican. Lutheran. Clubs: Lions, Moose. Home: 6915 Hillcrest Dr Crystal Lake IL 60014 Office: CF Industries Salem Lake Dr Long Grove IL 60047

KREBS, THOMAS MCGRATH, steel co. exec.; b. Clearfield, Pa., July 1, 1925; s. Henry Louis and Delia (Beahan) K.; B.S. in Metallurgy, Pa. State U., 1949; m. Eleanor Rüth Wilson, June 6, 1947; children—Ann, James, Mary Ellen, Amy, Jane, Catherine, Joseph. Metallurgist, Babcock and Wilcox Tubular Products Div., Beaver Falls, Pa., 1949-53, metallurgist supr., 1954-59, plant metallurgist, 1960-65, asst. mgr. tubing ops., 1966-67, mgr. tubing ops., 1967-69, plant mgr. Beaver Falls and Elkhart, 1970-72, asst. div. gen. mgr., 1973-76, div. v.p., gen. mgr., 1977—. Pres. Beaver campus adv. bd. Pa. State U., 1972—; pres. United Way of Beaver County, 1979—; past pres. Beaver Valley Community Concert Assn. Served in USN, 1943-46. Recipient Distinguished Service award Beaver campus Pa. State U. Mem. Am. Soc. Metals, Am. Mgmt. Assn., Am. Petroleum Inst., Am. Iron and Steel Inst., Mfrs. Assn. Beaver County (past pres.). Club: Beaver Valley Country. Contbr. articles in field to prfl. jours. Home: 1920 7th Ave Beaver Falls PA 15010 Office: Box 401 Beaver Falls PA 15010

KRECH, EDWARD M., JR., engring. co. exec.; b. Paterson, N.J., June 28, 1932; s. Edward M. and Virginia (Pardee) K.; B.M.E., Cornell U., 1955, M.B.A., 1958; m. Joan Gras, Nov. 1, 1953; children—Susan Carol, Edward M., Kathleen Joan. With Procter & Gamble Co., 1958—, engring. and group head P & G Internat. Engring. Dept., Cin., 1958-66, mech. sect. head P & G European Tech. Center, Brussels, Belgium, 1966-70, mfg. capacity coordinator P & G GmbH, Frankfurt, Germany, 1970-71, mgr. design & constrn. P & G Ltd., Newcastle-upon-Tyne, Eng., 1971-75, internat. engring. dept. head Asia and Latin Am., Cin., 1975-76, asso. dir. P & G Internat. Engring., Asia & Latin Am., Cin., 1976-79, asso. dir. for internat. projects and constrn., Cin., 1979—. Served with USNR, 1955-57. Mem. ASME, Cornell Soc. Engrs. Club: Royal Yachting Assn. (Eng.). Climbing expdn. to Mt. Everest, Nepal, 1978; diving expdn. to Truk Lagoon, Micronesia, 1979. Office: 6060 Center Hill Rd Cincinnati OH 45224

KREDER, JAMES GRAY, planning corp. exec.; b. Kingston, Pa., Nov. 13, 1937; s. Karl Holt and Hazel James (Gray) K.; A.B., Princeton, 1960; M.B.A., U. Pa., 1962; m. Nancy Anne Hilton, June 1, 1963; children—Karl Holt, Peter Hilton. Salesman, Met. Life Ins. Co., Atlanta, 1962-64, sales mgr., Atlanta and Charlotte, N.C., 1964-70, pension cons., N.Y.C., 1970-71; pres. Pacific Cons. Corp., Newport Beach, Calif., 1971-74, also dir.; dir. employee benefit plans Pacific Mut. Life Ins. Co., Newport Beach, 1974-79; founder, pres. Synergistic Planning Corp., 1979—; lectr. and speaker seminars and meetings on life ins. and pensions. Vice pres. North Laguna Community Assn., 1976, pres., 1978. Mem. Western Pension Conf., Am. Soc. C.L.U.'s, Nat. Assn. Life Underwriters, Am. Soc. Pension Actuaries, Internat. Assn. Fin. Planners. Republican. Home: 374 Pinecrest Dr Laguna Beach CA 92651 Office: 305 N Coast Hwy Suite L Laguna Beach CA 92651

KREEDMAN, S. JON, banker; b. Detroit, Feb. 10, 1921; m. Marlene Gurian; children—Barbara T., Dale R. With Am. City Bank, Los Angeles, 1964—, now chmn., chief exec. officer, pres.; chmn. S. Jon Kreedman & Co.; lectr. Harvard Bus. Sch., U. So. Calif., UCLA. Bd. dirs. City of Hope, Cedars-Sinai Hosp., Guardian Jewish Home for Aged. Office: American City Bank 1 Wilshire Blvd Los Angeles CA 90017*

KREER, HENRY BLACKSTONE, mktg. and assn. exec.; b. Pitts., Sept. 2, 1923; s. George William and Fay Palmer K.; student Princeton U., 1941-42, Northwestern U., 1946; m. Irene Overman, Dec. 22, 1946; children—Laurene, Linda (Mrs. Thomas Witt). Copy writer Batten, Barton, Durstine & Osborn, Chgo., 1947-51; account supr. Campbell-Mithun Inc., Chgo., 1951-55; owner Henry B. Kreer & Co., Chgo., 1955-68; partner, pres., dir. Stevens Kirkland, Kreer Inc., Chgo., 1968-78; chmn. McKinney/Mid Am., 1978—; pres. Nat. Accounts Mktg., Inc., 1975—; exec. dir. REACT Internat., Inc., 1962—. Chmn. radio subcom. Nat. Industry Adv. Com. FCC, 1967-73. Served to capt. USMCR, 1942-45. Decorated D.F.C., Air medal with 4 clusters. Home: 1904 Glen Oak Dr Glenview IL 60025 Office: 111 E Wacker Dr Chicago IL 60601

KREGG, DAVID HENRY, cons. engr.; b. N.Y.C., Oct. 31, 1921; s. Gus John and Anna (Ludwig) K.; B.S. in Mech. Engring., Purdue U., 1946; m. Rosemary Block, Oct. 12, 1945; children—Geoffrey David, Pamela Joy. Equipment engr. Standard Oil Devel. Co., Linden, N.J., 1946-51; mech. engr. Burns and Roe Inc., Los Angeles, 1951-54, project mgr., 1954-70, v.p., 1970—; chmn. Burmot Australia Pty Ltd.; dir. Fegles Power Services, Burns and Roe Pacific, Inc. Served with U.S. Army, 1943-46. Decorated Bronze Star, Purple Heart. Fellow Instn. Engrs. Australia; mem. Nat. Soc. Profl. Engrs., ASME. Home: 17855 Bernardo Trails Pl San Diego CA 92128 Office: Burns and Roe Inc 550 Kinderkamack Rd Oradell NJ 07649

KREHBIEL, ADOLF JACOB, banker, lawyer; b. Geary, Okla., Dec. 6, 1898; s. Jacob Samuel and Kathrine (Ringelman) K.; A.B., Bethel Coll., 1923; LL.B., U. Kans., 1929, J.D., 1968; m. Frances Morgan, May 27, 1943; children—Marcia, Jay, Phil, Ann. Admitted to N.Mex. bar, 1929; city atty. Clayton, N.Mex., 1931-53; chief counsel N.Mex. Tax Commn., 1961-63; atty. N.Mex. Bur. of Revenue, Santa Fe, 1968-69; dir., house counsel 1st Nat. Bank, Clayton, 1976—. Pres., Clayton Rotary, 1952-53, dist. gov., 1976-77. Recipient Silver Beaver award Boy Scouts Am., 1948. Mem. Green Inn, Am., N.Mex. bar assns., Phi Delta Phi. Home: 402 Oak St Clayton NM 88415 Office: 1st Nat Bank Annex Clayton NM 88415

KREHBIEL, WILLIAM RHODES, mfg. co. exec.; b. Norton, Kans., Aug. 20, 1932; s. Marion R. and Lela A. (Rhodes) K.; B.S. in Chem. Engring., U. Kans., 1954; postgrad. U. Wash., 1957-61; m. Nancy VanCura, Apr. 3, 1954; children—Karen, Kevin. Mgr., Gen. Electric Co., Richland, Wash., Mt. Vernon, Ind. and San Jose, Calif., 1957-69; v.p. Mgmt. Sci. Am., Inc., Palo Alto, Calif., 1969-73; exec. v.p. Bactomatic, Inc., Palo Alto, 1973-74; pres. Audio/Electronics div. Dictaphone Co., Mountain View, Calif., 1974-79; chmn. Advanced Energy Tech., Inc., Los Gatos, Calif., 1979—; chmn. Datacognition, Inc., Los Altos, Calif., 1974—; dir. Polygon Concepts, Inc., Cupertino, Calif., 1970-73, Tech. Service Corp., Santa Monica, Calif., 1977-78, ADPAC Corp., San Francisco, 1980—. Served with USNR, 1955-57. Mem. Solar Energies Industries Assn., Scabbard and Blade, Sigma Tau. Home: 324 Monterey Dunes Way Castroville CA 95012 Office: PO Box 949 Los Altos CA 94022

KREISER, FRANK DAVID, real estate exec.; b. Mpls., Sept. 20, 1930; s. Harry D. and Olive W. (Quist) K.; student U. Minn., 1950-51; m. Patricia Williams, Aug. 23, 1973; children—Sally, Frank David, Susan, Paul, Mark, Patti, Richard. Founder, owner Frank Kreiser Real Estate, Inc., Mpls., 1966—, pres., 1979—; partner, founder B & K Properties Co., Mpls., 1976—; chmn. bd., founder Transfer Location Corp., Atlanta, 1979—. Served with U.S. Army, 1948-50, Korea. Certified resdl. specialist and resdl. broker. Mem. Nat. Assn. Realtors, Mpls. Bd. Realtors (dir. 1972), St. Paul Bd. Realtors, Dakota County Bd. Realtors, Minn. Assn. Realtors, Realtors Nat. Mktg. Inst., Employers Relocation Council. Lutheran. Club: Decathlon Athletic. Address: 5036 France Ave S Minneapolis MN 55410

KREITLER, HOBART, office equipment mfg. co. exec.; b. Newark, May 14, 1930; s. Herman L. and Ethel M. (Cornelius) K.; B.A., Princeton U., 1952; M.B.A., Harvard U., 1956; m. Sally Stowell, June 23, 1956; children—Thomas S., Katherine T., Karen R., James S., John M. From staff asst., v.p. purchases to purchasing agt. Westinghouse Electric Corp., 1957-62; dir. purchasing Dictaphone Corp., Rye, N.Y., 1962-64, dir. materials, 1964-65, dir. corp. devel., 1965-66, corp. v.p., 1966-69, group v.p. dictaphone products and systems, 1969-74, group pres. dictaphone products and systems, 1974-77, pres. corp., 1977—, chief exec. officer, 1980—; dir. Pitney Bowes Co., 1979—, corp. v.p., 1980—. Bd. dirs. YMCA, Bridgeport, Conn., 1972-74. Served from 2d lt. to 1st lt., F.A., AUS, 1952-54. Congregationalist. Clubs: Fairfield Beach, Country of Fairfield (gov.). Office: Dictaphone Corp Walter Wheeler Dr Stamford CT 06904*

KRENSKY, HAROLD, dept. store exec.; b. Boston, Apr. 7, 1912; s. Philip and Katherine (Bladd) K.; LL.B., Boston U., 1935; m. Adele Falk, July 5, 1936; 1 dau., Jane Paula. Admitted to Mass. bar, 1937; with Hearst Publs., 1935-42; mdse. mgr. R.H. White's, Boston, 1942-47; sr. v.p. charge merchandising and publicity Bloomingdale's, N.Y.C., 1947-59, chmn. bd., mng. dir., 1967-69; exec. v.p. William Filene's Sons Co., Boston, 1960-63, pres., 1963-65, chmn. bd., chief exec. officer, 1965-66; v.p. Federated Dept. Stores, Inc., 1965-69, group pres., 1969-71, dir., 1969—, vice chmn., 1971-73, pres., 1973-80, chmn. exec. com., 1980—; dir. Liberty Mut. Ins. Co., Boston, Liberty Mut. Fire Ins. Co., Boston, Asso. Merchandising Corp., Norlin Corp., Bache Group Inc. Trustee, City of Hope, Nat. Jewish Hosp.; adv. council Tobe Coburn Sch., also 1969 Tobe awardee; adv. bd. N.Y. Fashion Designers, Inc., also 1970 awardee; exec. com. Fashion Inst. Tech. Home: 860 UN Plaza New York NY 10017 Office: Federated Dept Stores 104 W 40th St New York NY 10018

KREPS, JUANITA MORRIS, economist; b. Lynch, Ky., Jan. 11, 1921; d. Elmer M. and Cenia (Blair) Morris; A.B., Berea Coll., 1942, M.A., Duke U., 1944, Ph.D., 1948; hon. degrees: Bryant Coll., 1972, U. N.C., 1973, Denison U., 1973, Cornell Coll., 1973, U. Ky., 1975, Queens Coll., 1975, Berea Coll., 1979, Claremont Grad. Sch., 1979, Colgate U., 1980; m. Clifton H. Kreps, Jr., Aug. 11, 1944; children—Sarah, Laura, Clifton. Instr. econs. Denison U., 1945-46, asst. prof., 1948-50; mem. faculty Duke, 1955-77, asso. prof., 1962-68, prof. econs., 1968-77, James B. Duke prof., 1972-77, asst. provost, 1969-72, v.p., 1973-77; sec. U.S. Dept. Commerce, Washington, 1977-79; dir. ARMCO, J.C. Penney Co., Citicorp, AT&T, UAL, Inc., United Airlines, Eastman Kodak, R.J. Reynolds Inc.; trustee Duke Endowment; former bd. dirs. N.Y. Stock Exchange. Trustee, Tchrs. Ins. and Annuity Assn., 1968-72, Coll. Retirement Equities Fund, 1972-77, Nat. Merit Scholarship Corp., Ednl. Testing Service; mem. Nat. Commn. Manpower Policy, Nat. Manpower Policy Task Force; mem. N.C. Manpower Commn., vice chmn. bd., 1972-74. Fellow Gerontol. Soc. (v.p. 1971-72); mem. Am. Econ. Assn., So. Econ. Assn. (pres. elect 1975-76), Am. Assn. Higher Edn., AAUP, AAUW, Indsl. Relations Research Assn. (exec. com.). Author: (with C.E. Ferguson) Principles of Economics, 2d edit., 1965; Lifetime Allocation of Work and Income, 1971; Sex in the Marketplace: American Women at Work, 1971; Sex, Age and Work, 1975; Women and the American Economy, 1976; co-author: Contemporary Labor Economics, 1973. Editor: Employment, Income and Retirement Problems of the Aged, 1963; Technology, Manpower and Retirement Policy, 1966. Address: 115 East Duke Bldg Duke U Durham NC 27708

KRESKY, EDWARD MORDECAI, investment banker; b. N.Y.C., Aug. 15, 1924; s. Henry and Celia (Oltarsh) K.; B.A., Cornell U., 1948; M.P.A., N.Y. U., 1950, Ph.D., 1960; m. Mary J. McAniff, Nov. 1972; children from previous marriage—Ann Cecilia, Susan Elizabeth. Pub. adminstrn. intern State N.Y., 1950-51; personnel dir. N.Y. State Rent Commn., 1951-54; asst. personnel dir. City N.Y., 1954-57; asso. dir. N.Y. State Constl. Revision Commn., 1957-61; program asso. Office of Gov. Nelson A. Rockefeller, N.Y., 1961-65; sec. Met. Transp. Authority, N.Y.C., 1965-71; gen. partner Wertheim & Co., N.Y.C., 1971—; dir., sec. Mut. Life Ins. Co. N.Y., 1976—. Mem. N.Y. Council on Arts, 1971—; mem. Regents Commn. on Doctoral Edn. in N.Y. State, 1971-72; mem. Gov.'s Task Force on Financing Higher Edn., 1972-73; regional v.p. Nat. Municipal League; wice chmn. bd. dirs. Municipal Assistance Corp., N.Y.C., 1975—; chmn. adv. council Grad. Sch. Public Adminstrn., N.Y. U., 1976—; bd. dirs. N.Y.C. Ballet, 1976—. Served with AUS, 1943-46. Mem. Am. Polit. Sci. Assn., Regional Plan Assn. Club: Wall Street (N.Y.C.). Home: 10 W 66th St New York NY 10023 also Brushy Hill Rd Newtown CT 06470 Office: Wertheim & Co 200 Park Ave New York NY 10017

KREUTZ, OSCAR R., savs. and loan assn. exec.; b. Sioux City, Iowa; s. John and Jennie (Pehrson) K.; student schs., Sioux City, Cambridge, Mass.; m. Marion Benton, 1926 (dec. Apr. 1972); m. 2d, Virginia F. Skelton, Oct. 20, 1973; children—Mary Ann Kreutz Dodson, Barbara Jane Kreutz Barrett. Organizer, 1st Fed. Savs. & Loan Assn., Sioux City, 1923, mgr. officer, 1923-33; sec. Iowa Bldg. and Loan League, 1925-33; v.p. Fed. Home Loan Bank Chgo., 1934; chmn. rev. com. Fed. Home Loan Bank Bd., 1934-41; gen. mgr. Fed. Savs. and Loan Ins. Corp., Washington, 1941-44; exec. mgr. Nat. League Insured Savs. Assn., Washington, 1944-53, exec. cons., 1953-54, mem. exec. com., 1953-54; exec. v.p. Fla. Fed. Savs. and Loan Assn. (formerly First Fed. Savs. and Loan Assn.), St. Petersburg, 1953-54, pres., chmn. bd., 1954-68, chmn. bd., 1968-75, chmn. emeritus and cons., 1975—; hon. v.p. Internat. Union Bldg. Socs. and Savs. Assn. Pres. bd. dirs. United Fund, St. Petersburg, 1956-57; pres. Com. 100, St. Petersburg, 1958-59; pres. St. Petersburg Improvement Found., 1961-62; mem. adv. bd. Abilities Inc. Fla.; hon. bd. dirs. Sci. Center, St. Petersburg, St. Petersburg Symphony Soc.; trustee Eckerd Coll. Named Mr. Sun, Producers of Sunshine Festival of States, 1962. Mem. Fla. Savs. and Loan League (pres. 1961), Nat. Savs. and Loan League (pres. 1960), Suncoasters of St. Petersburg, Inc. (pres.), Navy League U.S., Am. Legion. Clubs: Masons, Rotary, St. Petersburg Yacht, Golden Triangle Civic. Presbyterian. Author: The Way It Happened, 1972. Home: One Beach Dr SE Apt 1106 Saint Petersburg FL 33701 Office: Fla Fed Bldg Suite 902 Saint Petersburg FL 33701

KREWSON, CHARLES NORMAN, diversified industries exec.; b. Williamsport, Pa., Nov. 22, 1927; s. George Norman and Harriet DeHart (Cawley) K.; B.S., U. Pa., 1951; m. Pamela Lee Hudson, June 6, 1953; children—Charles Norman, Patricia, Robert, Katherine, Douglas. With Gen. Electric Co., various locations, 1951-71; v.p. mktg. and internat. devel. Talley Industries, Inc., Mesa, Ariz., 1971-79; pres. Comml. Products Group, 1976-79; group v.p. Gen. Time Corp. subs. Talley Industries, Mesa, 1972, pres., 1973-79, also dir.; chmn., dir. Eastern Time Ltd., Hong Kong, Westclox Can. Ltd., GT Investment Ltd., Can.; chmn., pres. Antilles Industries, Inc., C. N. Krewson Assos., Inc., 1979—; pres., dir. Talley Internat. Sales Corp.; dir. Industria Relojera Mexicana S.A. Adv. bd. Fiesta Bowl, 1977—. Served with USN, 1943-44. Mem. U.S. C. of C., Nat. Security Indsl. Assn., Am. Def. Preparedness Assn., Phi Gamma Delta, Beta Alpha Psi. Mason (Shriner). Clubs: Arizona (Phoenix); Mountain Shadows Country, Paradise Valley Country, Rotary (Scottsdale, Ariz.). Home: 4138 E Lakeside Ln Scottsdale AZ 85253

KRIEG, ADRIAN HENRY, mfg. wholesale, import, export, internat. real estate exec.; b. St. Gallen, Switzerland, Oct. 23, 1938; came to U.S., 1952, naturalized, 1957; s. Victor J. and Gertrude (Altheer) K.; student U. Mexico at San Miguel de Allende, also Elmhurst Coll., 1957-58; m. Audrey Ann Jones, Oct. 23, 1968; children—Ivan Victor, Alistair William. Sec. to exec. v.p. V.J. Krieg Inc., N.Y.C., 1960-62; founder Widder Corp. (merged with Victor J. Krieg Inc. 1962), pres., chief exec. officer, 1962—, chmn., 1977—; sec., treas., gen. mgr. Mamaroneck Depot Plaza Corp.; sec. Rovic Mfg. Co., Inc., Mamaroneck, 1976—; sec., gen. mgr. Nugget Realty Co., Inc., 1977—; adv. bd. Colonial Bank and Trust Co., 1979-81. Served with USAF; Germany. Recipient Advt. Efficiency award Thomas Pub. Co., 1975; notary public. Mem. Soc. Mfg. Engrs. (cert.; founder chpt. 216, vice chmn. 1976 Sci. in Engring. award 1975), Fabricating Machinery Assn. (plate sect. data book 1979), Am. Welding Soc., Ohio Hardware Assn., Am. Supply and Machine Mfg. Assn., Swiss Soc. N.Y., Nat. Jewlers and Silversmiths Assn., Am. Importers Assn. (meeting com. 1975), Machine Tool Importers Group (internat. fin. adv. council 1976-79), Nat. Rifle Assn. (life). Clubs: Masons (32 deg.), K.T. Author sect. in American Machinist Reference Book; contbr. Contbr.

numerous articles to profl. jours. Patentee in field of metal-working machinery, metal forming and fastening. Home: 119 Maple Vale Woodbridge CT 06525 Office: Great Hill Rd Naugatuck CT 06770

KRIEG, DONALD LAWRENCE, ins. co. exec.; b. Oelwein, Iowa, Dec. 8, 1928; s. Lawrence D. and Gladys (Godden) K.; B.A., U. Iowa, 1951; m. Janet E. Shacklett, July 15, 1949; children—Lance L., Wade C. With Bankers Life Co., Des Moines, 1954—, v.p., 1971—; pres., BLC Ins. Co., 1974—, also dir. Trustee Des Moines Police and Fire Retirement Systems, 1971—. Served with USMCR, 1946-48, 51-53. C.L.U., C.P.C.U. Fellow Life Mgmt. Inst.; mem. Des Moines C. of C., Phi Beta Kappa, Order Artus. Republican. Unitarian. Club: Des Moines. Home: 1917 Willowmara Dr Des Moines IA 50315 Office: 711 High St Des Moines IA 50307

KRIEG, LOWELL EDWIN, industrialist; b. Marion, Ind., June 25, 1916; s. Charles M. and Ethel C. (Wolfe) K.; A.B. in Econs., U. Mich., 1937, student Grad. Sch. Bus. Adminstrn., 1938; m. Roberta J. Cole, Jan. 21, 1938; children—Peter, Stephanie, Michael, Melissa, Meredith, Christopher. Indsl. engr. King-Seeley Corp., 1939-40, Murray Corp. Am., 1941-45; mgmt. cons. Ernst & Ernst, 1945-46; with Ford Motor Co., 1946-61, gen. operations mgr. automotive electronic equipment operations, 1960-61; v.p. Olin Mathieson Chem. Corp., gen. mgr. Winchester-Western div., 1961-64, exec. v.p., dir., 1964-65; chmn. bd. Winchester-Western (Can.) Ltd., 1961—; vice chmn. bd. FRIA, Compagnie International pour la Production de L'Alumine; pres. Standard Packaging Corp., 1965—, chief exec., 1966-71, also dir.; pres. Lowell E. Krieg Assos., 1971—. dir. Fonda Container Co., Quality Park Envelope Co., Mexican Restaurant Assos., Inc., Lone Star Industries, Inc. Served with USNR, 1944-45. Mem. Am. Ordnance Assn., Am. Mgmt. Assn., Newcomen Soc. N. Am. Clubs: Quinnipiac (New Haven); Saugatuck Harbor Yacht (Westport); Union League (N.Y.C.); Beverly Hills (Calif.). Office: 2080 Century Park E Suite 201 Los Angeles CA 90067

KRIEG, WILLIAM LLOYD, electronics mfg. co. exec.; b. St. Louis, Jan. 28, 1946; s. Lester P. and Maxine J. Krieg; B.S. in Elec. Engring., U. Mo., 1968; postgrad. N. Tex. State U., 1970; m. Phyllis Carol Adams, Jan. 25, 1969 (div.); children—Kristen Lea, William Jason. Asst. engr. Chevrolet div. Gen. Motors Corp., St. Louis, 1965-68; process engr. mfg. Tex. Instruments, Inc., Dallas, 1969-70; diode div. operation mgr. Transitron Electronics Corp., Laredo, Tex., 1970-73; exec. v.p. Meridian Industries, Inc., Laredo, 1973—, also dir.; v.p., dir. Industrias Ensambladoras S.A. de C.V., Nuevo Laredo, Mex., 1973—, Chill Air, Inc., Laredo. Named Small Bus. Person of Yr., State of Tex., 1979. Home: 311 Belair Dr Laredo TX 78041 Office: 4602 Modern Ln Laredo TX 78041

KRIEGER, BENJAMIN WILLIAM, paper co. exec.; b. Cin., July 7, 1937; s. William Anthony and Catherine Regina (McDevitt) K.; A.A., U. Cin., 1965; m. Rosemary George, Apr. 12, 1958; children—Gregory, Kenneth, Catherine. With Union Paper & Twine Co. div. Mead Corp., Cleve., 1967-78, v.p., 1969-75, gen. mgr. and pres., 1975-78, pres., Mich. area mgr. Beecher Peck & Lewis Co. div., 1978—; with Chatfield Paper Corp., Cin., 1956-57, asst. sales mgr., 1965-67; pres. Cleve. Graphic Arts Council, 1975; nat. adv. bd. Mead Papers, 1971-73; chmn. nat. adv. bd. Gilbert Paper Co., 1973-75; mem. Reynolds Metal Distbr. Adv. Council, 3M Distbr. Adv. Council. Trustee No. Hills Assn., 1973-75, pres., 1974-75; active United Appeal Fund drive, Jr. Achievement, Greater Cleve. Growth Assn. Mem. Newcomen Soc., Buckeye Paper Trade Assn., Craftsman Internat., Sales and Mktg. Execs. Cleve., Cleve. Advt. Club, Cleve. Graphic Arts Assn., Advt. Prodn. Club, Hon. Order Ky. Cols., Assn. Ohio Commodores. Republican. Roman Catholic. Clubs: Pine Lake Country, Renaissance, Fairlane. Home: 75 Quarton Ln Bloomfield Hills MI 48013 Office: 14451 W Chicago Ave Detroit MI 48228

KRIEGER, GEORGE M., commodity mcht. co. exec.; b. Vienna, Austria, Feb. 18, 1929; s. Henry and Anna K.; came to U.S., 1940, naturalized, 1945; student Hartwick Coll., 1946-47; B.S., U. Colo., 1950; M.A., Grad. Sch. Bus., Columbia U., 1951; m. Susan L. Prochaska, Sept. 29, 1973. Tchr., Henry Krieger & Co., N.Y.C., 1953-54; v.p. J. Aron & Co., N.Y.C., 1954-65; pres. A.C. Israel Coffee Co., N.Y.C., 1965-71, pres. Internat. Trade Devel. Co. div. ACLI Internat. Inc., also v.p. parent firm, N.Y.C., 1972—. Bd. mgrs. Coffee, Cocoa and Sugar Exchange; bd. dirs. Nat. Council U.S.-China Trade; mem. East-West Trade Council. Served to 1st lt., USAF, 1952-53. Mem. Am. Importers Assn. (v.p., dir. 1977—), Aircraft Owners and Pilots Assn., U.S. Parachute Assn. (v.p. 1973-75, U.S. team leader 1976), Alpha Kappa Psi. Clubs: Wings, India House, Stamford Yacht. Office: Internat Trade Devel Co div ACLI Internat 717 Westchester Ave White Plains NY 10604

KRIEGER, PHILIP SHERIDAN, ins. broker, lawyer; b. N.Y.C., May 29, 1947; s. Lawrence Weston Krieger; B.S., U.S. Mil. Acad., 1970; M.B.A., Adelphi U., Garden City, N.Y., 1976; J.D., Fordham U., 1980; m. Juliet A. McGhie. Underwriter, fin. analyst Am. Internat. Group, N.Y.C., 1977-79; account exec., atty. Johnson & Higgins, N.Y.C., 1979—; admitted to N.Y. bar, 1980. Served to capt. U.S. Army, 1970-76. Decorated Army Commendation medal. Mem. Am. Bar Assn., N.Y. State Bar Assn. Home: 175 W 12th St New York NY 10011 Office: 95 Wall St New York NY 10005

KRIEGER, RONALD ARTHUR, economist; b. Greeley, Colo., Oct. 22, 1937, s. Benjamin S. and Anne L. Krieger; B.A., U. Colo., Boulder, 1960; M.S., U. Wis., Madison, 1961, Ph.D., 1965. Staff writer Denver Post, 1961-63; economist World Bank, Washington, 1965-67; asst. prof. internat. econs. U. Denver, 1967-69; sr. economist Citibank, N.Y.C., 1969-72; econs. editor Bus. Week mag., N.Y.C., 1972-73; prof. econs., chmn. dept. Goucher Coll., Towson, Md., 1973-78; v.p., dir. econ. publns. Chase Manhattan Bank, N.Y.C., 1978—; adj. prof. Johns Hopkins, 1975-78, Columbia U., 1979—; bd. advisers Patterson Sch. Diplomacy and Internat. Commerce, U. Ky., 1973—. Served with USAR, 1961. Recipient Disting. Teaching award Goucher Coll., 1978; Woodrow Wilson fellow, 1960-61; Fgn. Area fellow, 1963-64; Wis.-Ford Found. fellow, 1964-65. Mem. Am. Econ. Assn., Nat. Assn. Bus. Economists, N.Y. Assn. Bus. Economists. Author: Brazil: An Economic Survey, 1971, Mexico: An Economic Survey, 1971; also articles. Office: 1 Chase Manhattan Plaza New York NY 10081

KRISHER, PATTERSON HOWARD, acctg. exec.; b. Oklahoma City, Sept. 14, 1933; s. Sherman and Gladys (Patterson) K.; B.S. in Indsl. Engring., Okla. State U., 1956; A.M.P., Harvard U., 1971; m. Mary Anne Howard, Nov. 21, 1973; children—Sherman H., Bryan P. Plant indsl. engr. Procter & Gamble Mfg. Co., Dallas, 1959-60; mktg. rep. IBM, Dallas, 1960-61; mgmt. cons., nat. dir. mgmt. services Arthur Young & Co., N.Y.C., 1961—; guest instr. U. Tex., Ohio State U. Chmn. Arthur Young Polit. Action Com., 1978—; bd. dirs. Homeowners Assn. Served with USAF, 1956-59. Cert. mgmt. cons. Congregationalist. Clubs: Marco Polo, Sky (N.Y.C.); Burning Tree Country (Greenwich, Conn.). Contbg. author: Handbook of Business Problem Solving, 1980. Office: 277 Park Ave New York NY 10017

KRIST, DONALD EUGENE, ins. assn. exec.; b. Topeka, June 26, 1926; s. George M. and Florence (McInerny) K.; B.A., Drake U., 1951; m. Marilyn McClurkin, May 29, 1948; children—Lisa Ann, James Eric. Public relations dir. U.S. Jr. C. of C., 1953-55, Meredith Co., 1955-60; exec. v.p. Iowa Consumer Fin. Assn., 1960-66, Profl. Ins. Agts. Iowa, West Des Moines, 1973—; owner, mgr. Donald Krist & Assos., Inc., public relations consultants, Des Moines, 1966-73; instr., lectr. public relations Drake U., Des Moines, 1957-70. Served with USN, 1943-46. Cert. assn. exec. Recipient Outstanding Achievement award Iowa 1752 Club, 1980. Mem. Am. Soc. Assn. Execs. (Mgmt. Achievement award 1976), Iowa Soc. Assn. Execs., Smithsonian Instn. Assos. Clubs: Statesman's, Bohemian, Des Moines Press (Pres. 1959) (Des Moines). Editor Iowa Ins. Interpreter mag., 1973—. Home: 800 52d Ct West Des Moines IA 50265 Office: Valley Plaza Bldg West Des Moines IA 50265

KRISTY, JAMES E(UGENE), fin. mgmt. cons.; b. Kenosha, Wis., Sept. 3, 1929; s. Eugene H. and Ann T. Kristy; B.S. in Econs., U. Wis., 1951; M.B.A. in Fin., U. So. Calif., 1964; postgrad. Claremont (Calif.) Grad. Sch.; Ph.D. in Mgmt. and Edn., Columbia-Pacific U., 1981; m. Edith L. Reid, Feb. 19, 1955; children—James R., Ann E., Robert E. Gen. credit mgr. Technicolor, Inc., Los Angeles, 1967-69; v.p. Lloyds Bank Calif., Los Angeles, 1969-71; chief treasury officer Computer Machinery Corp., Los Angeles, 1971-75; sr. v.p., chief fin. officer Century Bank, Los Angeles, 1979; self-employed cons., writer, Buena Park, Calif., 1975-78, 80—. sr. instr. U. San Francisco, 1977; mem. faculty Redlands (Calif.) U., 1978, Golden Gate U., San Francisco, 1978; seminar leader Am. Mgmt. Assn., at U. Calif., Berkeley, Santa Cruz, Irvine and Riverside; past dir. Grycner Motors Corp., Madera Mfg. Co. Served as 1st lt. U.S. Army, 1951-53; Korea. Recipient Public Service award SBA, 1971. Author: Analyzing Financial Statements: Quick and Clean, 3d edit., 1980; Guide to Financial Planning, 1977; Handbook of Budgeting, 1981. Address: 5482 Burlingame Ave Buena Park CA 90621

KRIT, ROBERT LEE, devel. exec.; b. Chgo., Apr. 6, 1920; s. Jacob and Tania (Etzkowitz) K.; B.S. in Commerce, DePaul U., 1946; A.B.A., N. Park Coll., 1939; children—Melissa, Margaret, Justin. Dir. Chgo. Herald Am. Mercy Fleet charity drives, 1940-41; asst. exec. dir. cancer research found. U. Chgo., 1947-48; state campaign dir. Am. Cancer Soc., Inc., Chgo., 1948-63; dir. med. devel. U. Chgo., 1963-67; v.p. devel. Chgo. Med. Sch., 1967—. Moderator, TV series Tension in Modern Living, Drug Abuse, Aging and Retirement, Health and Devel. Children, Cancer, Healthy Life Style, NBC-TV; host producer TV series Med. Looking Glass, Relevant Issues in Health and Medicine, Coping; mem. adv. bd. Central States Inst. for Addiction Services; v.p. Drug Abuse Council of Ill.; mem. adv. council Campfire Girls Met. Chgo.; bd. dirs. Lawson YMCA. Served from pvt. to 1st lt., USAAF, 1942-46. Fellow Inst. Medicine Chgo. (co-chmn. com. on public info., mem. editorial bd. Proceedings); mem. Chgo. Soc. Fund Raising Execs. (pres. 1964-65), Chgo. Assn. Commerce and Industry (mem. health-in-industry com.), Nat. Acad. TV Arts and Scis. Home: 1139 Deerfield Rd Apt 1-B Deerfield IL 60015 Office: 200 E Randolph Dr Suite 7026 Chicago IL 60601

KRITICOS, NICKOLAS, publishing co. exec.; b. N.Y.C., Sept. 9, 1950; s. Nickolas and Marcela K.; A.A.S. with honors in Mktg. Mgmt. and Sales, N.Y.C. Tech. Coll., 1971; B.A. cum laude in Polit. Sci., Baruch Coll., 1975. Asso. buyer Korvette Dept. Stores, N.Y.C., 1975-76; sales rep. Holt, Rinehart & Winston, C.B.S., Inc., N.Y.C., 1976—. Mem. legis. adv. com. 21st dist. N.Y. State; participant alumni career adv. program Baruch Coll. Recipient Dime Savs. Bank award, N.Y. Tech. Coll., 1971. Mem. N.Y.C. Ednl. Sales Assn., Am. Mgmt. Assn., Tau Phi Sigma. Club: Sales Exec. of N.Y. Home: 9524 Ft Hamilton Pkwy Bay Ridge NY 11209

KRIVSKY, WILLIAM ANTHONY, bus. exec.; b. Stafford Springs, Conn., Mar. 26, 1927; s. Anton Martin and Katherine Alice K.; S.B., M.I.T., 1951, D.Sc., 1954; m. B. Susan Benson; children—Wayne Alan, Wendy Ann, Cynthia Susan, Holly Lee. Group v.p. Gen. Cable Corp. (now GK Tech), N.Y.C., 1968-71; pres. crucible splty. metals div. Colt Industries, Inc., N.Y.C., 1971-74; sr. v.p. CertainTeed Corp., Valley Forge, Pa., 1974-80; pres., chief operating officer Compo Industries, Inc., Waltham, Mass., 1980—, also dir.; dir. Krauss Maffei Corp. Served in USAAF, 1945-47, 48. Mem. Franklin Inst. (life; Clamer Gold medal 1977), AIME (Gold Medal award 1969; dir. 1969-72), Am. Soc. Metals. Patentee Linde Argon-oxygen stainless steel process. Home: 155 Beacon St Boston MA 02116 Office: 125 Roberts Rd Waltham MA 02154

KRIZ, EDWARD STAVRUM, banker; b. Washington, Jan. 21, 1946; s. Edward Matthew and Marjory Emma (Stavrum) K.; B.S., U. Pa., 1968; M.B.A., U. Mich., 1972; m. Nancy Riley, July 21, 1973; children—Elizabeth, Carolyn. Mem. Citibank Mgmt. Tng. Program, 1972; account officer chems. dept. Citicorp (U.S.A.), Inc., Miami, Fla., 1973-75, asst. v.p. extractive industries dept., 1975-78, v.p., officer in charge, 1978—. Active Jr. Achievement-Project Bus. Served to 1st lt. AUS, 1968-70. Decorated Army Commendation medal. Mem. Miami Fin. Group, Bankers Club Miami. Democrat. Roman Catholic. Office: 1 SE 3d Ave Miami FL 33101

KROBOTH, RICHARD, electric utility exec.; b. N.Y.C., Apr. 15, 1933; s. Royal Albert and Anna (Onderdonk) K.; B.S.E.E., Rensselaer Poly. Inst., 1955; M.B.A., Syracuse U., 1959; m. Lynda S. Manchester, Aug. 20, 1955; children—Melanie, Melissa, Scarlett. Asst. sec.-treas. N.Y. State Electric and Gas Corp., Binghamton, 1966-70, asst. to pres., 1970-75, asst. to chmn., 1975—. Trustee, Vestal (N.Y.) Public Library, 1975—. Served to 2d lt. U.S. Army, 1957. Mem. Am. Gas Assn. (fin. com.). Clubs: Binghamton Endicott Toastmasters. Home: 405 Denal Way Vestal NY 13850 Office: 4500 Vestal Pkwy E Binghamton NY 13902

KROC, RAY A., restaurant co., baseball club exec.; b. Chgo., Oct. 5, 1902; ed. Oak Park (Ill.) Public Schs.; m. Jane Dobbins. With Lily Tulip Cup Co., 1923-41, sales mgr., until 1941; with Mult-A-Mixer Co., 1941-55; pres. McDonald's Corp., Chgo., 1955-68, chmn. bd., 1968-77, sr. chmn., 1977—; chmn. San Diego Padres Baseball Team, 1974—, treas., 1974-78, pres., 1979—. Served in Ambulance Corps, World War I. Author: Grinding It Out: The Making of McDonalds, 1977. Office: McDonald's Corp McDonald's Plaza Oak Brook IL 60521*

KROCH, CARL ADOLPH, retail book bus. exec.; b. Chgo., June 21, 1914; s. Adolph Alfred and Gertrude Marie (Horn) K.; B.A., Cornell U., 1935; m. Jeanette Kennelly, Aug. 12, 1939. With Kroch's Bookstore, Inc., Chgo., 1935-54, pres., 1950-54, also dir.; pres., chief exec. officer Kroch's & Brentano's, Inc., Chgo., 1954—, also dir.; pres., chief exec. officer Booksellers Catalog Service, Inc., Chgo., 1954—; dir. Nat. Blvd. Bank Chgo. Bd. dirs. Northwestern Meml. Hosp., Chgo., Better Bus. Assn. Chgo., Ill. Humane Soc., USO, Chgo., Center for Book, Library of Congress, Washington. Served to lt. USNR, 1942-45. Mem. Ill. Retail Mchts. Assn. (dir.), Am. Booksellers Assn. Clubs: Tavern, Univ. Chgo., Chgo. Yacht, Mid-Am., North Shore Country, Pauma Valley Country. Author: So Red The Nose, 1935. Office: 29 S Wabash Ave Chicago IL 60603

KROEGER, CARROLL VINCENT, mgmt. cons., educator; b. Trenton, Mo., Jan. 3, 1926; s. August Carl and Sarabel (Newman) K.; student Rice U., 1945-46; B.A., Vanderbilt U., 1949, M.B.A., 1973; m. Grace Lee Bolton, Oct. 20, 1946; children—Carroll Vincent, Sheryl Lynn. Engr., Blackstone Valley Gas & Electric Co., 1949-50, Central Ind. Gas Co., 1952-56, Washington Natural Gas Co., 1956-59; cons. Stone & Webster Mgmt. Cons., N.Y.C., 1959-64; sr. adv. Exxon, The Hague, Netherlands, 1964-66; adv. Esso Europe Inc., London, 1966-69; pres., founder Kroeger & Smith, S.A., Zug, Switzerland, 1969-71; project cons. Vanderbilt U., 1973-74; dir. Tenn. Energy Office, Nashville, 1974-75; mgmt. cons., Nashville, 1975—; asso. prof. mgmt. Belmont Coll., 1978—; energy adv. of Gov. Tenn., 1973-74. Lic. layreader, chalice bearer St. George's Episcopal Ch., Nashville. Served with USNR, 1943-46, 50-52. Fellow Inst. Energy, Inst. Dirs., Instn. Gas Engrs.; mem. Assn. Technique L'Industrie du Gaz (France), ASME, Am. Gas Assn. Contbr. numerous articles to profl. jours.; internat. editor Gas mag., 1970-72, Energy mag., 1973-74. Home and Office: 1617 17th Ave S Nashville TN 37212

KROEHLE, THOMAS PIERCE, mining machinery mfg. co. exec.; b. Cleve., Sept. 25, 1931; s. Vernon and Kathryn Ellen K.; B.S. in M.E., Purdue, 1953; m. Barbara L. Dorsam, Nov. 6, 1954; children—Thomas Pierce, Jeffrey William. Vice pres. mktg. Brown Fintube Co., Elyria, Ohio, 1962-67, v.p., gen. mgr., 1967-69; v.p. opns. Jeffrey Mining Machinery Co., Columbus, Ohio, 1969-73, pres., 1973-74, pres. Jeffrey Mining Machinery div. Dresser Industries, 1974-77, acting pres. Marion Power Shovel div., 1977-79; pres. Lee Norse Co., subs. Ingersol-Rand Co., 1979—; dir., vice chmn. Mfrs. div. Am. Mining Congress, 1973-79; dir. Bituminous Coal Research Inc., Served with AUS, 1954-56. Bd. dirs. United Way Franklin County, 1975-78. Mem. Am. Mining Congress, Nat. Coal Assn., Am. Soc. Mining Engrs., Am. Soc. Mech. Engrs. Republican. Episcopalian. Clubs: Golf, Rotary. Patentee in field of heat transfers. Office: PO Box 2863 Pittsburgh PA 15230

KROEKER, WALTER EDWIN, agrl. and broadcasting co. exec.; b. Winkler, Man., Can., Sept. 2, 1915; s. Abram Arthur and Elizabeth (Nickel) K.; student agr. U. Man., 1936-37, 40, U. Minn., 1938; m. Madeline Ruth Epp, May 30, 1940; children—Marlyce (Mrs. Peter Swinnerton), Walter Edwin, Allan Arthur, Randolph Harold. Vice pres. A.A. Kroeker & Sons Ltd., Winnipeg, Man., 1955-74, pres., 1974-79; v.p. Kroeker Seeds Ltd., Winkler, Man., 1956-74, pres., 1974-79; pres. So. Manitoba Broadcasting Co., Ltd., 1958-78, Golden West Broadcasting, Ltd., 1977—, Community Communications Inc., 1977—, Kroeker Farms Ltd., 1979—, Kroeker Sales Ltd., 1979—; dir. Frontier City Broadcasting Ltd., Palliser Broadcasting Ltd. Pres., Can. Hort. Council, 1967-68; sec. Man. Vegetable Mktg. Bd., 1973-76. Mem. Com. Man.'s Econ. Future, 1965-66; chmn. Pembina Valley Devel. Assn., 1953; trustee Kroeker Found; Recipient Man. Golden Boy award, 1966. Home: 875 Wellington Crescent Winnipeg MB R3M 0A7 Canada

KROGER, MARLIN GLENN, cons. co. exec.; b. Hampton, Nebr., Jan. 22, 1926; s. Adolph Thomas and Minnie (Harders) K.; B.S. in Elec. Engring., U. Nebr., 1949; m. Delores C. Holmes, June 7, 1949; 1 son, Stephen Glenn. Research engr. RCA Labs., 1949-52; sr. project engr. Motorola, Inc., 1952-56; chief engr., 1956-60, asso. dir. research and devel., 1960-63; asst. to pres. autonetics div. N.Am. Rockwell, Anaheim, Calif., 1963-66, v.p. information systems div., 1966-69, asst. to v.p., research and engring. group, 1969-73; pres. M.G. Kroger Assos., Palos Verdes Estates, 1973—. Cons. Office Sec. Defense, U.S. Navy Electronics Systems Command, 1966—. Served with Signal Corps, AUS, 1944-46. Recipient Research award RCA, 1951. Mem. I.E.E.E., Sigma Xi, Sigma Tau, Eta Kappa Nu, Pi Mu Epsilon. Patentee in field. Address: 1117 Via Goleta Palos Verdes Estates CA 90274

KROGIUS, TRISTAN ERNST GUNNAR, food co. exec.; b. Tammerfors, Finland, Apr. 13, 1933; s. Helge Lorenz and Valborg (Antell) K.; B.A., U. N.Mex., 1954; M.A., Calif. State U., Los Angeles, 1962; postgrad. Advanced Mgmt. Program, Harvard U., 1980; m. Barbara Brophy, Aug. 29, 1952; children—Ferril, Lars, Karin, Eric, Marian, Rebecca. With Scott Paper Co., Phila., 1960-65, new products mgr., 1965; with Hunt Wesson Foods, Fullerton, Calif., 1965-75, pres. Hunt Wesson Foods of Can. Ltd., Toronto, 1970-71, Hunt Wesson Frozen and Refrigerated Foods, Fullerton, Calif., 1971-75; pres., chief exec. officer Dalgety Foods, Inc., Salinas, Calif., 1975-78; v.p., gen. mgr. processed foods div. Tenneco West, Inc., Bakersfield, Calif., 1978—; mem. Almond Bd. Calif., 1979—. Bd. dirs. South Coast Community Hosp., Laguna Beach, 1969-70, 72-74, pres., chief exec., 1974. Served to capt. USMC, 1954-60. Mem. Am. Frozen Food Inst. (dir. 1977-78), Calif. Frozen Vegetable Council (chmn. 1977-78). Republican. Episcopalian. Office: PO Box 9380 Bakersfield CA 93309

KROHA, BRADFORD KING, electronics co. exec.; b. Rochester, N.Y., Dec. 16, 1926; s. George Frederic and Neva Alice (Smy) K.; B.E.E., Yale U., 1947, B.S. in Indsl. Adminstrn., 1948; postgrad. Harvard U. Grad. Sch. Bus. Adminstrn., 1952; m. Nona Jane Hobbs, June 15, 1979; children—Nancy, Judy, Sally, Jane, Robert. Gen. mgr. Can. Motorola Ltd., 1969-72; dir. internat. subsidiaries, then asst. gen. mgr. communications internat. div. Motorola Inc., Schaumburg, Ill., 1977-79, v.p. European communications div., 1979—. Served with USNR, 1944-46. Republican. Presbyterian. Clubs: Barrington Hills (Ill.) Country; Frankfurter Golf (Frankfurt, W.Ger.).

KROLL, ARNOLD HOWARD, investment banker; b. N.Y.C., Jan. 20, 1935; s. Henry and Jean (Brecker) K.; B.A., Dartmouth, 1956; LL.B., Harvard, 1959; m. Lois Ann Montana, Aug. 11, 1965; children—Alison Cordelia, Luisa Clayton, Heather Todd. Admitted to N.Y. bar, 1959; asso. Lehman Bros., N.Y.C., 1960-70; 1st v.p. Dean Witter & Co., Inc., N.Y.C., 1970-72; partner C.E. Unterberg, Towbin Co., N.Y.C., 1972-77, L.F. Rothschild, Unterberg, Towbin, 1977—. Trustee Lexington Sch. for Deaf, N.Y.C., 1972—, Hewitt Sch., N.Y.C., 1980—. Served to 1st lt., arty. U.S. Army, 1959-60. Clubs: Century Country (Purchase, N.Y.); India House, University (N.Y.C.). Home: 4 E 72d St New York City NY 10021 Office: 55 Water St New York City NY 10041

KROLL, EVELYN BRENNAN, athletic equipment mfg. co. exec.; b. Staten Island, N.Y., Oct. 5, 1927; d. John Cornelius and Evelyn May (Sanford) Maher; student Hunter Coll., 1949-57; m. John L. Kroll, Dec. 29, 1966; children by previous marriage—John and James Brennan; 1 stepdau., Sharon Kroll. Tchr. public schs., N.J., 1952-53; advt. rep. The N.Y. Times, 1954-60, asst. dir. sch. and camp advt. dept., 1960-65; prin. Sanmarev Advt. Agy., Stamford, Conn., 1965-67; dir. advt. and public relations Jayfro Corp., Waterford, Conn., 1968-72, v.p. mktg. and public relations, 1972-79, pres., 1979—; co-founder, dir. Nat. Catalog Distbn. Corp., Harbor City, Calif., 1973; co-founder, mng. editor Nat. Trade Newsletter, 1973—; founder Kroll Press, Pub. and Advt. Co., Waterford, Conn., 1978. Trustee, Eugene O'Neill Theater Center, Waterford, Conn. and N.Y.C. Mem. Nat. Sporting Goods Assn. (sustaining), Sporting Goods Mfrs. Assn. (steering com. bd. annual internat. expn. and conv. 1976-79, com. phys. edn. and recreation 1979—), Nat. Sch. Supply and Equipment Assn. (com. equipment for handicapped 1977), Am. Sports Edn. Inst. (public relations com.), Mitchell Coll. (New London, Conn.) fundraising orgn. Clubs: La Coquille (Palm Beach); Delray Beach (Fla.); 2001 (Dallas). Author: (with John L. Kroll and Frank Smith) It Doesn't Pay to Work Too Hard, 1977; editor: Blueprint for Safety in Sports and Recreation, 1978; regular mktg. and salemanship columnist The Sporting Goods Dealer mag., 1974—, contbr. articles to other publs. in field. Home: 4201 South Ocean Blvd Highland Beach FL 33431 also 535 Pequot Ave New London CT 06320 Office: Jayfro Corp PO Box 400 Hartford Turnpike Waterford CT 06385

KROLL, JOHN LEON, athletic equipment mfg. co. exec.; b. Buffalo, Sept. 5, 1925; s. Hammond and Sylvia (Heimberger) K.; B.S. in Phys. Edn. and Recreation, N.Y. U., 1948, M.A. in Health Edn., 1948; postgrad. U. Conn., 1953-55; m. Evelyn Maher, Dec. 29, 1966; 1 dau., Sharon Ann; stepchildren—John Brennan, James Brennan. Phys. edn. tchr. N.Y.C. Bd. Edn., 1948-49; dir. phys. edn. Waterford (Conn.) Pub. Schs., 1949-51; founder Jayfro Corp., mfr. athletic equipment, Waterford, Conn., 1953, also chmn. bd.; co-founder Nat. Athletic Mfrs. Catalog Distbg. Corp., Harbor City, Calif., 1973-77, owner, 1975—; dir. N.Am. Recreation, Convertibles, div. Gamecraft, Westport, Conn., 1967-79, Snitz Mfg. Corp., East Troy, Wis., 1968, Arrow Systems, Inc., Lawrence, Mass., 1972-77; co-founder Kroll Press, Pub. & Advt. Co.; co-pub. Jayfro Periscope Nat. Newsletter, 1973—; bd. advisers, cons. Gymnastic Supply Co., Inc., San Pedro, Calif., 1975—; dir. adv. bd. Southeastern Conn. area Conn. Bank & Trust Co., 1980. Chmn. promotional programs com. U.S. com. Sports for Israel, Inc., N.Y.C., 1975-78; bd. dirs. Tennis Found. N.Am., 1973-78, Boca Raton (Fla.) YMCA, 1977-80; mem. membership com. Ice Skating Inst. Am., 1975-80; hon. bd. dirs. Flatbush Boys Club, Bklyn., 1975-79 mem. adv. bd. Nat. Sports Mgmt. Studies Found., 1980. Served with USN, 1943-46, U.S. Army, 1951-53. Recipient Honor award Pres.'s Council Phys. Fitness and Sports, 1977; Distinguished Service award City and County Adminstrs. of Health and Phys. Edn., AAHPER, 1978; honored at 25th ann. industry testimonial dinner, 1977. Mem. Athletic Inst. (dir. 1975-76), Am. Council Internat. Sports (dir. 1977—), Edn. Industries Assn. (dir. 1972-76), Exhibitors Assn. AAHPER (exec. bd. dirs. 1970-76, pres., 1973-74), Nat. Intramural-Recreational Sports Assn. (exhibitors com. 1974—, hon., life), Nat. Sporting Goods Assn., Sporting Goods Mfrs. Assn. (phys. edn. and sports com. nat. hdqrs. North Palm Beach, Fla. chpt. 1969, chmn. 1973-76, mem. racket sports com. 1972—, mem. internat. sporting goods show steering com. 1973—, chmn. membership com. 1975-78), Nat. Sch. Supply and Equipment Assn. (dir., exec. com. 1973-75, chmn. conv. and exbhns. com. 1975-78), U.S. Tennis Ct. and Track Builders Assn., Booster Club Assn. Am. (co-founder 1978). Clubs: Jockey (Las Vegas); Lambs (N.Y.C.); Delray Beach; La Coquille (Palm Beach, Fla.); Rotary (Waterford, Conn.). Author: (with Frank Smith) It Doesn't Pay To Work Too Hard; contbr. articles on mktg., merchandising and salesmanship to profl. and trade jours. Patentee in field. Home: 535 Pequot Ave New London CT 06320 also 4201 S Ocean Blvd Highland Beach FL 33431 Office: PO Box 400 Waterford CT 06385

KRONE, FRANK WILLIAM, dairy coop. exec.; b. Billings, Mont., Dec. 19, 1928; s. Henry C. and Karen E. (Nymen) K.; B.A., U. Colo., 1950; posgrad. U. Denver; m. Shirley Ann Maser, Aug. 29, 1950; children—Frank William, Linda Susan, Sharen Elizabeth. Sales mgr. Meadow Gold Dairies, Denver, 1953-64; v.p. ops. King Food Host USA, Lincoln, Nebr., 1964-71; sales mgr. Home Dairies, Nampa, Idaho, 1971-72; asst. sec., gen. mgr. Dairymen's Creamery Assn., Caldwell, Idaho, 1972—; exec. com. Western Dairymen's Coop. Inc.; past bd. dirs. Idaho Coop. Council; chmn. Idaho Dairy Adv. Council, 1978. Served with USN, 1950-53. Mem. Nat. Milk Producers Fedn. (dir.), Asso. Dairies (chmn. 1974—), Sales and Mktg. Execs., Idaho Milk Processors Assn. (past pres.), Consol. Dairy Products Assn. (past dir.), Coop. Dairy Farmers (treas.), Ret. Officers Assn. Methodist. Club: Crane Creek Country. Home: 525 E Braemere Rd Boise ID 83702 Office: 520 Albany St Caldwell ID 83605

KRONENWETTER, DONALD ROBERT, electronic components mfg. co. exec.; b. St. Mary's Pa., Oct. 20, 1933; s. Harold G. and Cecelia (Yaeger) K.; B.B.A., St. Bonaventure U., 1955; student Fairleigh Dickinson U., 1960-62, Am. U., 1963, Syracuse U., 1965, Harvard U., 1972; m. Ruth Ilene Wykoff, Feb. 25, 1956; children—David, Deborah, John, James. With Electronic Component Group, GTE Sylvania, 1955—, v.p., gen. mgr. distbr. and spl. markets div., Waltham, Mass., 1976—. Pres., Seneca Falls (N.Y.) Little League, 1965-74; mem. Seneca Falls Bd. Edn., 1972-76. Served with USNR, 1955-57. Mem. Young Presidents' Orgn., Sales Exec. Club N.Y. Clubs: Andover Country, Red Jacket Yacht (Seneca Falls). Office: GTE Sylvania 100 1st Ave Waltham MA 02154

KROON, DEBRA LYNETTE, hospitality co. exec.; b. San Luis Obispo, Calif., Sept. 13, 1956; d. Thomas Stephen and Eva Anita (Spurlock) K.; student Calif. public schs. Vol. part time Nat. Park Service Mus., Yosemite, Calif., 1974; sec. Yosemite Park & Curry Co., 1974-76, asst. mgr. public relations, 1978-79, public affairs adminstr., 1980—; treas., dir. Yosemite West Chapel Broadcasts, Inc. Recipient sci. medal Bausch and Lomb, 1974. Mem. Nat. Assn. Female Execs., Public Relations Soc. Am., Calif. Hist. Soc., Mariposa County Hist. Soc., Santa Paula Hist. Soc., Nat. Sheet Music Soc., Oakland Mus. Assn., Press Club of San Francisco, Sierra Club, Native Daus. of the Golden West, Yosemite Natural History Assn., Soc. Am. Travel Writers, Calif. Scholarship Fedn. (life). Republican. Club: Yosemite Winter. Contbg. editor Yosemite Sentinel, 1975-76, editor, 1976—. Office: Yosemite Park & Curry Co Yosemite Nat Park CA 95389

KROOT, JOHN B(ERNARD), electronic mfg. co. exec.; b. Chgo., Sept. 20, 1928; s. John M. and Anna (DeVaan) K.; student evenings Northwestern U., 1946-49, B.S. in Acctg., 1954; m. Ann M. LoMonaco, Feb. 26, 1957; 1 son, John Philip. Chief acct. A. Brandwein & Co., 1946-51, controller, 1953-57; treas. Standard Transformer Co., Warren, Ohio, 1957-61, v.p., gen. mgr., 1961-64; treas., v.p. Sterling Salem Corp., Salem, Ohio, 1959-64; v.p. Cree Coaches, Marcellus, Mich., 1962-64; pres. Improved Laminated Metals Co., Providence, 1964-71, Hodgman Mfg. Co., Taunton, Mass., 1968-71; v.p. fin. Internat. Metals & Machines, Chgo., 1971-76; pres. Ludlow Typograph Co., Chgo., 1972-76; chief exec. officer Paramount Wedding Ring Co., Chgo., 1977-78; v.p. Am. Antenna Co., Elgin, Ill., 1979—; pres. JBK & Assos., cons. Vice pres. indsl. services Providence C. of C., 1970-72. Served with U.S. Army, 1951-53; Korea, Japan. Roman Catholic. Clubs: Biltmore Country (Barrington, Ill.); Chgo. Athletic; Quidnessett Country (East Greenwich R.I.). Home: 445 Red Barn Ln Barrington IL 60010 Office: 1500 Executive Dr Elgin IL 60120

KROPF, FRANCES MAY SCOTT TURNER (MRS. ARNOLD K. KROPF), ret. publisher; b. Franklin, Ill., July 13, 1913; d. Edward D. and Anna (Bollar) Scott; student Ill. State U., 1930-32; B.S., U. Ill., 1935; certificate phys. therapy Northwestern U. Med. Sch., 1938; m. Carl L. Turner, Jan. 9, 1942 (dec. June 1962); children—Mark C., Scott B.; m. 2d, Arnold K. Kropf, Jan. 29, 1965 (dec. Oct. 1969). Tchr. phys. edn. Washburn, Ill., 1935-36, Lawrenceville, Ill., 1936-37; phys. therapist Crippled Children's Sch., Columbus, Ohio, 1938-40, Dr. Harlan Wilson, Columbus, 1940-44; pub. Waupaca County Post, Picture Post, Wis. State Farmer, Waupaca, Wis., 1962-80; pres. Waupaca County Pub. Co., 1948-80. Active Cub Scouts Am. Named Outstanding Bus. Women of Yr., Bus. and Profl. Woman's Orgn., 1967; Person of Year, Waupaca C. of C., 1975. Mem. Waupaca C. of C. (citation 1966), Nat. Editorial Assn., Wis. (Golden Mem. award 1976), Central Wis. (chmn. 1965) press assns., N.E. (Wis. sec. 1959-61), Waupaca (pres.) women's golf assns., AAUW. Republican. Methodist (pres. Women's Soc. Christian Service 1957-59). Clubs: Waupaca Curling, Waupaca Country. Home: 118 N Blvd of Presidents Sarasota FL 33577

KROPILAK, STEVE JOSEPH, ins. co. exec.; b. Whitney, Pa., July 22, 1928; s. Stephen Joseph and Mary (Maletz) K.; student parochial and public schs., Whitney and Republic, Pa.; m. Eleanor A. Pasta, May 29, 1965; children—Robert, John, Lloyd, Stephen. With U.S. Steel Co., Gary, Ind., 1946; joined U.S. Coast Guard, 1947, advanced through grades to chief petty officer, 1959, ret., 1967; safety engr. Continental Ins. Co., various locations, 1967—, mgr. loss control dept., Cleve., 1977—. Mem. Am. Soc. Safety Engrs., Soc. Fire Protection Engrs., Am. Welding Soc., Mich. Boiler Inspectors Assn., Ohio Boiler and Machinery Assn., Vets. of Safety, Chief Petty Officers Assn., Am. Legion (adj. post 315 1970-74). Roman Catholic. Home: 10748 Waterfall Rd Strongsville OH 44136 Office: Continental Ins Co 6111 Oaktree Blvd Independence OH 44131

KROPLICK, HOWARD ALAN, pharm. co. exec.; b. N.Y.C., May 9, 1949; s. Philip and Eva (Steuerman) K.; B.E. SUNY at Stony Brook, 1971; M.B.A., U. Pa., 1973; m. Rosalind Mandel, May 29, 1971. Mktg. cons. Uniwave, Inc., N.Y.C., 1972; product analyst Pfizer Pharms., N.Y.C., 1973; asst. product mgr. Roerig Pfizer, N.Y.C., 1974-75, product mgr., 1976-77, group product mgr., 1978—. Hosp. vol.; sr coordinator United Fund. Mem. Tau Beta Pi. Home: 201 E 17th St Apt 17H New York NY 10003 Office: 235 E 42d St New York NY 10017

KROUNER, LEONARD WILLIAM, investment adv., lawyer; b. Albany, N.Y., Aug. 24, 1947; s. Isidore and Helen (Markusfeld) K.; B.S., Cornell U., 1969; J.D., N.Y. U., 1972. Adtted to N.Y. State bar, 1972, Fla. bar, 1973, D.C. bar, 1973; confidential law asst. appellate div. N.Y. Supreme Ct., Albany, 1972-73, sr. law clk. to N.Y. Supreme Ct. Justice 1977-78; sr. law clk. to judge Hugh R. Jones, N.Y. Ct. Appeals, Utica, 1973-74; practiced in N.Y.C., Albany and Fla., 1974—; founder Securities Investor Protective Corp. Fund. Founder Capital Dist. Youth Team Tennis. Mem. Am., N.Y. State, Fla., D.C. bar assns., Pine Investment Club. Contbr. articles to legal and fin. jours. Office: 79 Euclid Ave Albany NY 12203 also 645 Madison Ave New York NY 10022 also 5151 Collins Ave Miami Beach FL 33140 also 20 Parkwood St Albany NY

KRUCKS, WILLIAM, electronics mfg. co. exec.; b. Chgo., Dec. 26, 1918; s. William and Florence (Olson) K.; B.S., Northwestern U., 1940; postgrad. Loyola U., Chgo., 1941-42; m. Lorraine C. Rauland, Oct. 23, 1947; children—William Norman, Kenneth Rauland. Auditor, Benefit Trust Life Ins. Co., Chgo., 1940-42; chief tax accountant, asst. to comptroller C., M., St.P. & P. R.R., Chgo., 1942-56; asst. comptroller, dir. taxation, asst. treas. Chgo. & Northwestern Ry. Co., 1956-58, treas., 1968-72; treas. Chgo. & Northwestern Transp. Co., 1972-75; pres., chmn., chief exec. officer Rauland-Borg Corp., 1975—, also dir.; asst. treas. N.W. Industries, Inc., 1968-70; treas., dir. Des Moines and Central Iowa Ry. Co., Ft. Dodge, Des Moines & So. Ry. Co.; dir. Norbic, Chgo. Chmn. Western R.R.'s Income Tax Accounting Conf. Bd. dirs. Civic Fedn. Chgo. Mem. Ry. Systems Mgmt. Assn., Nat. Tax Assn., Tax Execs. Inst., Nat. Assn. Ry. Tax Commn., Assn. Am. R.R.'s, Ill. C. of C. Republican. Mem. United Methodist Ch. Clubs: Tower; Executive's, Union League (Chgo.). Home: 21 Indian Hill Rd Winnetka IL 60093 Office: 3335 W Addison St Chicago IL 60618

KRUEGER, ANNE OSBORN, economist, educator; b. Endicott, N.Y., 1934; d. Leslie A. and Dora Emma (Wright) Osborn; B.A. in Econs., Oberlin Coll., 1953; M.S. in Econs., U. Wis., 1956, Ph.D. (fellow), 1958. Instr. dept. econs. U. Wis., Madison, 1958-59; asst. prof. econs. U. Minn., Mpls., 1959-63, asso. prof., 1963-66, prof., 1966—, research asso. Upper Midwest Econ. Study, 1962-64; cons. AID, 1963-72, Upper Midwest Research and Devel. Council, 1966, USIA, 1972-73, U.S. Treasury, 1972-76, Harvard Inst. Internat. Devel., 1974-76; sr. research asso. Nat. Bur. Econ. Research, 1969—; mem. econs. panel NSF, 1971-73; vis. prof. Mass. Inst. Tech., Cambridge, 1973-74, Monash U., Melbourne, Australia, 1973, 76, 77; vis. fellow Australian Nat. U., 1977; mem. adv. bd. Econs. Inst., Boulder, Colo., 1976-79; mem. research adv. council NSF, 1974-78; mem. research adv. bd. Com. for Econ. Devel., 1978—; mem. Minn. Investment Adv. Council, 1978—. Mem. Am. (v.p. 1977), Minn. (pres. 1971-72), Midwest (pres. 1974-75), Internat. (council 1980—) econ. assns. Author: (with James M. Henderson) National Growth and Economic Change in the Upper Midwest, 1965; Economic Growth and Adjustment in the Upper Midwest, 1967; Foreign Trade Regimes and Economic Development: Turkey, 1974; The Benefits and Costs of Import Substitution in India, 1975; Foreign Trade Regimes and Economic Development Liberalization Attempts and Consequences, 1978; The Republic of Korea 1945-1975: The Developmental Role of the Foreign Sector and Aid, 1979. Editor: Trade and Development in Korea, 1975; contbr. book revs. and articles to profl. jours.; editorial bd. Jour. Econ. Lit., 1973-76, Econs. Letters, 1978—, Am. Econ. Rev., 1980—; book rev. editor Jour. Internat. Econs., 1974-77; cons. editor Portfolio publ. USICA. Home: 6401 Willow Wood Rd Edina MN 55436 Office: Dept Econs Univ Minn Minneapolis MN 55455

KRUEGER, ARTHUR FORD, JR., banker; b. Newport News, Va., Aug. 16, 1950; s. Arthur Ford and Margaret Burden (Pleasants) K.; student Erskine Coll., 1968-69, Clayton Jr. Coll., 1969, Auburn U., Montgomery, 1979—, Ala. Banking Sch., 1980; m. Phyllis Ramsey, Aug. 26, 1972; 1 son, Todd Winthrop. Collection mgr. Bank of Fulton County, East Point, Ga., 1970-73; systems officer Central Bank and Trust Co., Jonesboro, Ga., 1973-75; asst. v.p., data processing mgr. Bank of Huntsville (Ala.), 1975-78; asst. v.p. Bank of Tallassee (Ala.), 1978—. Troop leader Boy Scouts Am., Tallassee; treas. Tallassee chpt. ARC. Mem. Bank Adminstrn. Inst., Ala. Young Bankers. Republican. Methodist. Club: Masons. Home: 505 James St Tallassee AL 36078 Office: 304 Barnett Blvd Tallassee AL 36078

KRUEGER, ARTUR W. G., mgmt. cons. co. exec.; b. Neuendorf, Ger., Jan. 16, 1940; came to U.S., 1975; s. Werner Georg and Charlotte (Klein) K.; Betriebswirt, Wirtschafts-Akademie, Bremen, Ger., 1968; M.B. in Bus. Policy, Columbia U., 1978. Mktg. mgr. Rosenthal Espana S.A., Madrid, 1970-71; dir. Rosenthal Skandinavien AB, Stockholm, 1971-74; v.p. tech. ceramics div. Rosenthal U.S.A. Ltd., N.Y.C., 1975-79; partner Am. European Cons., Co., N.Y.C., 1980—; lectr. in field. Mem. Am. Mgmt. Assn., Semiconductor Equipment and Materials Inst., Columbia Bus. Assos. Office: 300 E 40th St New York NY 10016

KRUEGER, DAN KIRBY, govt. ofcl.; b. Taylor, Tex., Oct. 30, 1950; s. Edward Hugo and Minnie Pauline (Ganzert) K.; A.A., Blinn Coll., 1971; student U. Tex., 1971-77; m. Becky Lynn Rinderknecht, Aug. 25, 1973; 1 dau., Audrey Meredith. With H.E.B. Food Stores, Taylor, 1968-71; equipment specialist Tex. Dept. Mental Health and Mental Retardation, Austin, 1971—; pvt. kitchen cons. Mem. adv. com. Sta. KRLN/KRLU ednl. TV. Recipient cert. of Appreciation, Tex. Dept. Mental Health and Mental Retardation, Tex. Restaurant Assn., Tex. Public Employees Assn., March of Dimes. Mem. Tex. Public Employees Assn. (pres. 1978-79, chmn. bd. 1980—), Soc. Foodservice Systems, State Employee Golf Assn. Republican. Episcopalian. Home: 2405 N Shields Dr Austin TX 78758 Office: 909 W 45th St Austin TX 78756

KRUEGER, DONALD P., mfg. co. exec.; b. Cleve., Nov. 3, 1926; s. Louis F. and Viola B. (Triska) K.; m. Mary Ann Anton, Apr. 10, 1948; children—Donna, Joe, Mike, Mary Ann, Alice, Don. With Krueger Millwright Service, Strongsville, Ohio, 1946—, pres., chief exec. officer, 1959—. Roman Catholic. Home: 3412 Park Dr Parma OH 44134 Office: 19706 Progress Dr Strongsville OH 44136

KRUEGER, RICHARD GUSTAVE, sci. instrument co. exec.; b. Phila., June 24, 1928; s. Fred Emil and Edna Elizabeth (Effinger) K.; student Drexel U., 1947, B.S. in Chem. Engring., 1956; student Temple U., 1947-50; children—David Allen, Paul Stewart, Mark James, Ruth Ann. Profl. musician, 1947-65; indsl. hygienist Electric Storage Battery, Phila., 1951-54; sales engr. Foxboro Co., Bala Cynwyd, Pa., 1954-58; sales engr. Am. Instrument Co., Phila., 1958-65, regional sales mgr., Collingswood, N.J., 1971-75; market mgr. chem. process industries Leeds & Northrup Co., North Wales, Pa., 1965-69; market mgr. process control Barber Colman Co., Rockford, Ill., 1969-71; market mgr., mgr. spl. products div. Flexitallic Gasket Co., Inc., Camden, N.J., 1975—. Publicity mgr. Lansdale (Pa.) Pop Warner Midget Football, 1966-70; active Boy Scouts Am., 1966-71; mem. Ambler Symphony Orch., 1952-60, Willow Grove Am. Legion Concert Band, 1952-60. Mem. Am. Chem. Soc. (sr.), Instrument Soc. Am. (sr., v.p. Phila. sect. 1971), Am. Inst. Chem. Engrs. (sr.), Am. Petroleum Inst. (subcom. on instrumentation 1967-72). Lutheran (asst. supt. Sunday Sch. 1956-60, asst. chmn. Christian edn. 1963-65). Asso. editor Analysis Instrument Div.-ISA Ann. Procs., 1968-69. Home: Forest Creek Apts 3813 Clubhouse Dr West Deptford NJ 08066 Office: 5 Linden St Camden NJ 08002

KRUGER, ALBERT JOHN, fin. exec.; b. Buffalo, Aug. 16, 1949; s. Paul A. and Patricia J. (Schoenhart) K.; B.B.A., St. Bonaventure U., 1973; M.A., Empire State Coll., 1975; m. Susan E. Rice, Apr. 27, 1973. With Century Housewares, Inc., Orchard Park, N.Y., 1974—, dir. facilities, 1980—; guest lectr. SUNY, Buffalo, 1975-80. Mem. Blasdell Jaycees (sgt.-at-arms 1979—). Democrat. Roman Catholic. Home: 3635 Howard Rd Hamburg NY 14075 Office: 3095 Union Rd Orchard Park NY 14127

KRUMSKE, WILLIAM FREDERICK, JR., savs. and loan exec.; b. Chgo., Dec. 17k 1952; s. William Frederick and Harriet Marie (Piwowarczyk) K.; B.S., Ill. Inst. Tech., 1974; M.S. in Bus. Adminstrn., No. Ill. U., 1978. Salesman, warehouse mgr. Lus-Ter-Oil Beauty Products, Palos Heights, Ill., 1972-74; pub. relations dir. Crouching Lion Motor Inn, Alsip, Ill., 1974; mgr. food and beverage Inn Devel. & Mgmt., Chicago Heights, Ill., 1974-75; v.p., dir. mktg. DeKalb Savings and Loan Assn., DeKalb, Ill., 1975—; instr. Coll. Bus., No. Ill. U., 1978—; mktg. mgr. Jordan Gallagher for State's Atty. campaign, 1976; mem. Republican Nat. Com., 1978—. Recipient Wm. J. Hendrickson award No. Ill. U. Alumni, 1980. Mem. Ill. Inst. Tech. Alumni Admission Corps, Am. Mktg. Assn., Savs. Instn. Mktg. Soc. Am., Ill. Savs. and Loan League (mktg. com. 1977-78, chmn. 1979-80), Beta Gamma Sigma. Lutheran. Contbr. articles to profl. jours. Home: 118 Augusta Ave DeKalb IL 60115 Office: 3d St and Locust St DeKalb IL 60115

KRUPER, JOHN GERALD, sales and mktg. mgr.; b. Carbondale, Pa., Feb. 10, 1949; s. John Joseph and Evelyn (Bernosky) K.; B.S. in Bus. Adminstrn. and Accounting, U. Scranton, 1970; postgrad. State U. N.Y., 1974; m. Renee Jane Shugg, Aug. 4, 1973; children—Melissa, Kevin John. Store mgr. Endicott Johnson Corp., Schenectady, 1970-71, retail mdse. distbr., Endicott, N.Y., 1971-72, asst. mdse. buyer, 1972-74, full line mdse. buyer, 1974-76, dir. advt. and sales, 1976-80, gen. mgr. Ranger Safety div., 1980—. Served with U.S. Army, 1970. Home: 3601 Matthews Dr Endwell NY 13760 Office: 1100 E Main St Endicott NY 13760

KRUPKA, FRANK JOSEPH, data processing adminstr.; b. Cleve., Sept. 18, 1949; s. Frank Joseph and Elsie Anna (Bagaria) K.; student Cleve. State U., 1967-68, Thomas Edison Coll., Trenton, N.J., 1978-80; m. Linda Rolene Raftery, Oct. 2, 1971; children—Frank, James, Elizabeth, Kathryn. Computer operator Cleve. Trust Co., 1968-69; computer programmer/analyst Computer Service Centers, Inc., Cleve., 1970; sr. systems analyst Nixdorf Computer, Cleve., 1970-78; with Sperry Univac, Cleve., 1978—, central ops. implementation mgr., 1979—. Mem. Data Entry Mgmt. Assn. Democrat. Roman Catholic. Home: 2250 Green Rd Cleveland OH 44121 Office: 4500 Rockside Rd Independence OH 44131

KRUPNICK, JEROLD BARRY, food mfg. co. exec.; b. N.Y.C., Sept. 22, 1943; s. Harry and Ethel K.; student Boston U., 1961-63; B.S. in Accounting, N.Y. U., 1965; J.D., Bklyn. Law Sch., 1968; m. Sherrie Becker, June 20, 1970; children—Marc, Sarah. Mgr., Man-Vana Sales Corp., N.Y.C., 1968-69; sec., dir. Amigo Foods Corp., N.Y.C., 1969-71; founder, pres., dir. Kineret Foods Corp., N.Y.C., 1971—. Sec. and trustee Brandeis Hebrew Day Sch.; bd. dirs. YM-YWHA, 1980-81. Recipient Nat. Kashruth award Union of Orthodox Jewish Congregations Am.; Shofar award Nat. Council of Young Israel, 1980. Mem. Eastern Frosted Food Assn. Club: B'nai B'rith. Contbr. articles to Quick Frozen Foods mag.; pioneer in frozen kosher foods, U.S., Can.; developer new items, including frozen ready-to-bake challah dough. Office: 434 Row D New York Terminal Market Bronx NY 10474

KRUSSMAN, LOUIS FREDERICK, jewelry mfg. co. exec.; b. East Orange, N.J., Aug. 25, 1915; s. Leo Frederick and Henriette (de Percin) K.; A.B., Fordham U., 1937; m. Alyce Garcin, Feb. 23, 1952; children—Marie Therese Barbara, Denise Marie Louise. With Trifari, Krussman & Fishel, Inc., N.Y.C., 1937—, v.p., 1952-64, treas., 1952-73, pres., 1964-78, cons., 1979-80, also dir. Mem. Cardinal's Com. of Laity of Catholic Charities, 1964—; mem. Cath. Youth Orgn., 1957—, bd. dirs., 1973—. Bd. dirs. Jewelry Industry Council, 1957-80, Jewelers Vigilance Com., 1967-80; bd. govs. N.Y. chpt. Arthritis Found., 1953—, v.p., 1960—; bd. dirs. Fashion Inst. Tech., N.Y.C., 1973—. Served to capt. USAAC, 1941-45. Recipient Floyd B. Odlum award Arthritis Found., 1970; Brotherhood award NCCJ, 1973; hon. dep. sheriff Westchester County, 1974—. Mem. Internat. Platform Assn., Vets. 7th Regt., N.Y.C., Assos. Engr. Corps 7th Regt., N.Y. Srs. Golf Assn. Republican. Roman Catholic. Knight of Malta. Clubs: Westchester Country (gov. 1964—, pres. 1973-74) (Rye, N.Y.); Union League, Twenty-Four Karat (pres. 1964, dir. 1963-73, 75-78, chmn. banquet com. 1975-78) (N.Y.C.); Seaview (N.J.) Country. Home: Justin Rd Harrison NY 10528 Office: 16 E 40th St New York NY 10016

KRYVICKY, JEFFREY STEPHEN, indsl. rubber and plastic distbn. and engring. co. exec.; b. Detroit, Sept. 23, 1940; s. Steven and Sophie K.; B.S.E.E., Wayne State U., 1961; children—Anthony, Shannon, Robert, Kristi, Patrick. Chief exec. officer, F.B. Wright Co., Cleve., 1961—, 1965—, also dir.; dir. Reinforced Tubing Corp., Moldex Corp., Landmark Industries, Inc., RPD Industries. Republican. Clubs: Trout, Chagrin Valley Country, Cleve. Athletic, Mid-Day, Tower. Author: Distribution Today, 1974; Changing Business of Distribution, 1976; Small Business in Today's World, 1977. Home: Cedar Rd Gates Mills OH 44040 Office: 624 Alpha Dr Cleveland OH 44143

KUBIAS, FRANK OWEN, coatings co. exec.; b. Cedar Rapids, Iowa, Feb. 27, 1927; s. Frank J. and Ruth L. Kubias; B.S. in Chem. Engring., Iowa State U., 1950; m. Beverly Jean Aschinger, Dec. 28, 1950; children—Craig O., Kirk E. Process engr. Mallinckrodt Inc., St. Louis, 1950-55, mfg. supt., 1955-64, mgr. health and safety, 1964-73; mgr. safety SCM/Glidden-Durkee, Cleve., 1973-77; mgr. loss prevention SCM/Glidden Coatings & Resins, Cleve., 1977—; gen. chmn. chem. sect. Nat. Safety Council, 1976-77. Served with USNR, 1945-46. Recipient Disting. Service to Safety award Nat. Safety Council, 1979; registered profl. engr., Calif.; cert. safety profl. Mem. Am. Inst. Chem. Engrs. (mem. founding com. and charter dir. safety and health div.), Am. Soc. Safety Engrs. (pres. St. Louis chpt. 1970-71), Nat. Fire Protection Assn., Ohio Soc. Safety Engrs., Am. Radio Relay League, U.S. Power Squadron. Presbyterian (elder). Club: Masons. Office: SCM/Glidden Coatings & Resins 900 Union Commerce Bldg Cleveland OH 44115

KUBICKA, RICHARD JOSEPH, telecommunications co. exec.; b. Newark, June 1, 1936; s. Joseph Charles and Yolande (Behul) K.; B.E.E., Newark Coll. Engring., 1958; m. Christa Horn, Oct. 19, 1964; children—Richard Joseph, Eric. Area mgr. North Electric Co., Wiesbaden, Ger., 1962-65; program mgr. Computer Scis. Corp., Paramus, N.J., 1965-69; mgr. installation and test, N.Y.C., then mgr. program mgmt., Brussels, ITT, 1969-75; dir. technology and standardization GTE, Stamford, Conn., 1975—. Mem. Sigma Pi. Contbr. articles to profl. jours.; co-editor reference works in field. Home: 11 Surrey Rd New Canaan CT 06840 Office: One Stamford Forum Stamford CT 05904

KUCHARAVY, ROBERT M., public relations exec.; b. Syracuse, N.Y., Nov. 25, 1946; s. Milton and M. Margaret (Lutz) K.; B.A. in Sociology, Le Moyne Coll., Syracuse, 1969. With Rath Orgn., Syracuse, 1969-75, account exec., 1972-75; pres. R.M.K. Assos., Syracuse, 1975—. Bd. dirs. Syracuse Jaycees, 1971-72, Priority One of Greater Syracuse, 1970-74; exec. com., bd. dirs. Consortium for Children's Services, 1973-77; bd. dirs. Central N.Y. Home Aides, 1976—. Mem. Onondaga County Republic Citizens Com. Mem. Le Moyne Coll. Alumni Assn. (bd. govs. 1970—), Public Relations Soc. Am. Republican. Home: 457 Ridgewood Dr Syracuse NY 13206 Office: PO Box 6207 Teall Ave Sta Syracuse NY 13217

KUCHENBECKER, RUTH HELEN, constrn., carpet co. exec.; b. Neenah, Wis., Mar. 4, 1937; d. August Herman and Rose E. (Buss) Peapenburg; student pub. schs., Neenah, Wis.; m. Alfred Paul Kuchenbecker, Nov. 16, 1957; children—Ann Marie, Mary Kay, Amy Lynn. Sec., bookkeeper Wis. Paper Group, Menasha, 1955-65, Towne, Inc. Mech. Contractors, Appleton, Wis., 1967-69; partner, sec.-treas. Kuchenbecker Builders, Neenah, Wis., 1968—; owner, pres. Kuchenbecker Carpets Inc., Neenah, 1975—; co-owner, sec. Wholesale Builders Supply, Inc., Neenah, 1979—. Mem. Nat. Right to Work Com. Mem. Nat. Assn. Women in Constrn. (past pres., bd. dirs. Fox Valley chpt.), Nat. Assn. Home Builders Women's Auxiliary. Republican. Lutheran. Home: 2689 Oakridge Rd Neenah WI 54956 Office: 1001 S Lake St Neenah WI 54956 also 1573 Deerwood Dr Neenah WI 54956

KUCHINKA, THOMAS JOSEPH, univ. adminstr.; b. Bellaire, Ohio, Apr. 1, 1939; s. Joseph Aloysius and Stella Eleanor K.; B.S. in Bus. Adminstrn., Youngstown (Ohio) State U., 1968, M.B.A., 1973; m. Clara Marie DiTommaso, May 5, 1962; 1 dau., Shari Renee. Mgr., Kobacker Shoe Co., Youngstown, 1963-64; partner Kuchinka-Caldwell Tax Service, Youngstown, 1964-67; budget officer Youngstown State U., 1967-70, dir. audits and systems, 1970—, instr. accounting Sch. Bus. Adminstrn., 1974—; partner Sheetz-Kuchinka Tax Service; v.p., treas. Uinu Corp. Pres., St. Anthony Booster Orgn., Youngstown, 1976-78. Served with AUS, 1957-59. Lic. public acct.; cert. internal auditor. Mem. Inst. Internal Auditors, Nat. Assn. Accountants, Assn. M.B.A.'s. Address: 410 Wick Ave Youngstown OH 44555

KUDO, FRANKLIN TY, automotive dealership exec.; b. Honolulu, Oct. 3, 1950; s. Charles T. and Fujie (Hayakawa) K.; B.S., U. Colo., 1972; M.B.A., U. Wash., 1974; cert. mgmt. systems analysis Inst. Advanced Tech., Control Data Corp., 1977; m. Lei Yukie Hirano, Aug. 6, 1978; 1 child, Lindsey. Sr. acct. Peat, Marwick, Mitchell & Co., C.P.A.'s, Honolulu, 1974-78; v.p., controller Aloha Motors, Inc., Honolulu, 1978—. Budget dir. Hawaii campaign Carter/Mondale, 1976; fin. chmn. Democratic State Conv. Hawaii, 1977-78, 79-80. C.P.A., Hawaii. Mem. Hawaii Soc. C.P.A.'s, Am. Soc. C.P.A.'s. Democrat. Home: 4126-3 Keanu St Honolulu HI 96816 Office: 1743 Kapiolani Blvd Honolulu HI 96814

KUEHNEN, HARALD, banker; b. Rheydt, Germany, Aug. 6, 1912; s. August and Emma (Rolshoven) K.; Dr. jur. honoris causa, U. Cologne (Germany); m. Gertrud Funke, Sept. 15, 1943. With Dresdner Bank, 1931-45; partner Bank Kirchholtes & Co., 1946-51; partner Bank Sal. Oppenheim Jr. & Cie., Koln, Germany, 1951—; chmn. bd. Klöckner-Humboldt-Deutz AG, Rheinisch-Westfallsche Boden-Credit-Bank, also various other banking and indsl. corps. Bd. dirs. Thyssen Found. Named Hon. Senator, U. Cologne, 1960. Mem. German Bankers Assn. (pres. 1979—). Home: 67 Goethestrasse Koln-Marienburg Federal Republic of Germany Office: 4 Unter Sachsenhausen Koln Federal Republic of Germany

KUENDIG, WILLIAM NORMAN, mfg. exec.; b. Canton, Ohio, Nov. 6, 1924; s. E. O. and Corinne (McKee) K.; student Miami U., Oxford, Ohio, 1942-43, Mt. Union Coll., 1946-47; B.S. in Bus. Adminstrn., Kent State U., 1949; m. Betsy Cox, Sept. 23, 1944; children—William Norman, David E., John T., Herbert M., Richard C., Elizabeth A. Asst. sales mgr. E.W. Bliss Co., Canton, 1949-55; asst. to pres. Lake Erie Engring. Co., Buffalo, 1956-58; mgmt. cons. Rath & Strong, Inc., Boston, 1959-62; v.p. mfg. and operations Merriman, Inc., Boston, 1963-64, v.p., gen. mgr., 1964-67, pres., gen. mgr., 1967-68, also dir.; asst. exec. v.p. Chgo. Pneumatic Tool Co., 1968-70; pres. Androck Corp., Worcester, Mass., also Rockford, Ill. and Watford, Ont., Can., 1969-72, also dir.; v.p. Roblin-Hope Industries, Buffalo, 1969-71; v.p., gen. mgr. Watts Regulator Co., Lawrence, Mass., Webster Valve Co., Franklin, N.H., 1972—, Watts Fluid Power, Kittery, Maine 1972—, New Eng. Foundry, Cleve. Casting Co., Kinsman, Ohio, Webster Foundry Co.; incorporator Franklin Savs. Bank; adviser N.H. Tech. Inst. Mem. Hingham Town Adv. Bd.; trustee Franklin Regional Hosp. Registered profl. engr., Mass. Mem. New Eng. Council, Bus. and Industry Assn. N.H. (chmn.), Sigma Nu. Republican. Episcopalian (past sr. warden, vestryman). Mason, Rotarian. Clubs: Chemists (N.Y.C.); Hingham Yacht; Cohasset Golf; Mojalaki Country. Home: 64 Prospect St Franklin NH 03235 Office: Route 3A S Main St Franklin NH 03235

KUERBITZ, GARY RAYMOND, battery distbn. center exec.; b. Bay City, Mich., Mar. 15, 1947; s. Elmer Otto and Blanche (Bolduc) K.; B.S. in Math., Saginaw Valley State Coll., 1971, cert. in secondary edn., 1971; m. Kathleen Sullivan, Jan. 28, 1978. Loan mgr. Comml. Credit Corp., Buchanan, Mich., 1974-75, br., mgr., 1975-76; owner, pres. Interstate Battery System, Bay City, 1976—. Served with U.S. N.G., 1971-72. Club: Elks (Bay City). Home: 2108 Essex St Essexville MI 48732 Office: 1408 Marquette Bay City MI 48706

KUERST, ALFRED ERTEL, ret. retail exec.; b. Indpls., July 1, 1915; s. Alfred William and Elsie Mae (Ertel) K.; B.S., Lake Forest Coll., 1937; M.B.A., Harvard, 1939; m. Sara Kiningham, Apr. 28, 1940; 1 dau., Joann Kuerst Huntington. Salesman, Marshall Field & Co., Chgo., 1933-37; with L. S. Ayres & Co., Indpls., 1939-80, v.p. adminstrn., 1965-70, v.p. adminstrn. and control, 1970-80. Pres., Community Service Council, 1963-64, council Boy Scouts Am., 1966-67; v.p. Central Ind. Health Planning Council, 1973-74, Central Ind. Council on Aging, 1974—; bd. dirs. Greater Indpls. Civic Progress Com., 1973-76, Indpls. Symphony Orch., 1976—; bd. dirs. Indpls. Day Nursery Found., 1972—, pres., 1978—. Served as lt. USN, 1944-46. Recipient Silver Beaver award Boy Scouts Am.; Sagamore of Wabash award Gov. of Ind.; Distinguished Service award Lake Forest Coll. Mem. Indpls. C. of C. (chmn. research com. 1976—), Better Bus. Bur. (pres. 1961-62), Soc. Ret. Execs., Ind. Econ. Forum, Harvard Club N.Y.C., Hoosier Power Squadron. Republican. Presbyterian (elder). Clubs: Indpls. Sailing (comdr. 1968), Kiwanis (Disting. Career award). Home: 5515 N Capitol Ave Indianapolis IN 46208

KUGELMAN, L(AWRENCE) RICHARD, assn. exec.; b. Montreal, Que., Can., Nov. 1, 1936 (parents Am. citizens); s. Lawrence J. and Hilda (Blockman) K.; A.B., Dartmouth Coll., 1959; M.B.A., Northwestern U., 1961; grad. (inst. scholar) Inst. for Not for Profit Mgmt., Columbia U., 1977; m. Lynn C. Wilson, June 20, 1959; children—Lawrence Richard, Kristen Greeley. Mem. staff spl. devel. program Chase Manhattan Bank, N.Y.C., 1961-64; budget coordinator network ops. CBS, N.Y.C., 1964-66; mgr. spl. studies internat. group Singer Co., N.Y.C., 1966-69; dir. fin. and adminstr. div. prodn. services Reeves Telecom. Corp., N.Y.C., 1969-70; v.p., treas. Camp Affiliates, Inc., N.Y.C., 1970-74, also dir.; exec. dir. Planned Parenthood of N.Y.C., Inc., 1974—; cons. Family Planning Advs., Albany, N.Y., 1977-78. Served with U.S. Army, 1960-62; mem. Res., 1962-65. Episcopalian. Home: 60 Cowdin Circle Chappaqua NY 10514 Office: Planned Parenthood NYC 380 Second Ave New York NY 10010

KUGLER, ALFRED ERNEST, mfg. co. exec.; b. Wyndotte, Mich., Mar. 13, 1931; s. Gottlieb Fredrich and Ernestine Gerta (Pfaff) K.; B.S. in M.E., Gen. Motors Inst., 1956; M.S. (Sloan fellow), M.I.T., 1963; m. Elenore Kerscher, Feb. 2, 1952; children—Linda, Laura, Heidi, Lisa, Kurt. Master mechanic Fisher Body div. Gen. Motors Corp., Marion, Ind., 1950-67; mfg. mgr. crane hoist & tower div. Dresser Industries, 1967-69; v.p. plant ops. gen. products div. Teledyne Continental Motors, 1969-79; v.p. ops. E.W. Bliss div. Gulf & Western Inc., Southfield, Mich., 1979—. Mem. Am. Inst. Indsl. Engrs. Lutheran. Address: 18520 Shawnee Dr Spring Lake MI 49456

KUGLER, E(RNEST) RICHARD, mgmt. cons.; b. Providence, June 25, 1932; s. Edward Herman and Aimee Louise (Paquette) K.; A.B. in Philosophy (NROTC scholar), Brown U., 1956; m. Elaine Clara Rattey, June 9, 1956; children—Ernest Richard, David Rattey, Gail Anne, Cheryl Gertrude, Eric Edward. Pres., founder Kugler Konstruction, Johnston, R.I., 1960-66; sr. asso. program analyst IBM, Kingston, N.Y., 1966-70; chief of installations Alexander Proudfoot Co., Chgo., 1970-71; founder, pres. Kfoury, Kugler & Assos., Inc., Kingston, 1971-73, E. Richard Kugler Mgmt. Counsel, Inc., Woodstock, N.Y., 1973—, I/O Systems, Inc., Woodstock, Rochester, N.Y., 1977—; cons. on computer systems and organizational structures to industry, assns., 1970—. Founder, pres. Johnston (R.I.) Citizens Com. for Better Edn., 1965; founder, treas. Onteora Sch. Dist. Citizen's Com., 1976—. Served to capt. USMC, 1956-60. Mem. Am. Prodn. and Inventory Control Soc., Assn. Computing Machinery, Bricklayer's, Mason's and Plasterer's Internat. Union. Home: Byrdcliffe Woodstock NY 12498 Office: Byrdcliffe Woodstock NY 12498

KUHL, MARGARET HELEN CLAYTON (MRS. ALEXIUS M. KUHL), banker; b. Louisville; d. Joseph Leonard and Maude (Mitzler) Clayton; student Loyola U. Home Study Div., Chgo., 1955—, Buena Vista Coll., Storm Lake, Iowa, summer 1964-65, 66; m. Alexius M. Kuhl, Apr. 21, 1936; children—Carol Lynn Kuhl Wassmuth, James Michael (adopted). Sales lady, buyer Silverberg, Akron, Iowa, 1924-34; owner dress shop, Fonda, Iowa, 1934-40; librarian, Fonda, 1940-43; bookkeeper, teller First Nat. Bank, Fonda, 1943-44; tchr. speech and drama, librarian asst. Our Lady Good Counsel Sch., Fonda, 1963-69; pres., chmn. bd. Pomeroy State Bank, 1975—, also dir. Recipient Adult Leadership award Catholic Youth Orgn., 1967, Pro Deo Juventute award, 1969. Mem. Cath. Daus. Am. (dist. dep. 1964-70, state chmn. ecumenism 1970-72, state treas. 1970-72), Diocesan Council Cath. Women (chmn. orgn. and devel. 1964-65), Nat. Council Cath. Women (diocesan pres. 1968-70, diocesan sec. 1966-67; chmn. Women in Community Service Sioux City Diocesan Bd. 1971-72), Internat. Platform Assn., Nat. Assn. Bank Women, Women in Community Service (pres. Iowa bd. 1972-73), Legion of Mary (pres. curia 1964-66, 67-70), Marquis Library Assn., Intercontinental Biog. Assn. Club: Fonda Country.

KUHN, CHARLES, indsl. exec.; b. Cin., Nov. 29, 1919; s. Leo and Vivian (Van Hallenger) K.; student Purdue U., 1938-39; m. Elna Jane Smith, Nov. 17, 1944 (div. 1975); children—James Roland, Karen Jo Ann; m. 2d, Patricia L. McVicar, Nov. 27, 1976 (div. 1980). Vice pres. Fansteel Metall. Corp., 1950-55, Hills McCanna Co., 1955-58; v.p. Dresser Mfg. div. Dresser Industries, Inc., 1958-60, pres., 1960-64, group v.p., dir. parent co., 1964-65; exec. v.p., 1965-68, pres., 1968-70, also chief operations officer, dir. subsidiary cos.; pres., dir. Wylain Inc., Dallas, now chmn. bd., chief exec. officer; dir. Gen. Portland Corp., Valley View State Bank, (all Dallas), Falcon Products, Inc., St. Louis. Bd. dirs. So. Meth. U. Found. for Sci. and Engring. Served with USNR, 1940-42. Mem. Am. Gas Assn., Newcomen Soc. N.Am., Am. Water Works Assn., Pa. Soc., Canadian Gas Assn., Tex. Mid-Continent Oil & Gas Assn., Home: 10820 Netherland Dr Dallas TX 75229 Office: 17250 Dallas Pkwy Dallas TX 75248

KUHN, LOUIS, apparel co. exec.; b. Bklyn., May 18, 1912; s. Jacob and Malvina (Futtersack) K.; student Bklyn. Coll. evenings 1929-33; m. Lee Kahn, Dec. 15, 1940; children—Robert L., Karen J. Salesman, Neptune Raincoat Co., N.Y.C., 1936-43, 45-46; founder Lou Kuhn, Inc., 1947 (name changed to Chief Apparel, Inc. 1947), N.Y.C., chmn., 1956—. Mem. adv. bd. Marine Midland Bank-N.Y., N.Y.C. Mem. Philanthropic 50, N.Y., 1949—, Fedn. Jewish Charities, N.Y., 1949—; vice chmn. United Jewish Appeal, 1970; founder Albert Einstein Sch. Medicine, 1967; pres. Lee and Lou Kuhn Found., 1965—. Served with AUS, 1943-45. Decorated Combat Inf. badge. Office: 10 W 33d St New York NY 10001

KUHNS, WILLIAM GEORGE, pub. utility holding co. exec.; b. Milw., Apr. 26, 1922; s. Harold Eugene and Edna (Paulus) K.; B.A., U. Wis., 1946, J.D., 1949; m. Joan P. Beutell, July 9, 1948; children—Nancy, Janet, Linda, Pamela, Elizabeth Kuhns. Admitted to Wis. bar, 1949; with operating research bur. Wis. Electric Power Co., Milw., 1949-55; with Gen. Pub. Utilities Corp., N.Y.C., 1955—, sec., 1955, treas. 1957-61, v.p., 1961-67, pres., chief exec. officer, 1967-74, chmn., chief exec. officer, 1974—; chmn. bd., chief exec. officer, mem. exec. com., dir. Met. Edison Co., Jersey Central Power & Light Co., Pa. Electric Co.; chmn. bd., chief exec. officer GPU Service Corp.; dir. Marine Midland Banks Inc., Home Life Ins. Co., Hammermill Paper Co.; dir., mem. project rev. com. Breeder Reactor Corp. Bd. dirs. Atomic Indsl. Forum, Edison Electric Inst. Mem. N.J. Utilities Assn. (dir.), State Bar Wis., Delta Tau Delta, Phi Eta Sigma, Beta Gamma Sigma. Clubs: Econ., Univ., Recess (N.Y.C.); Englewood Field; Knickerbocker Country (N.J.). Office: 100 Interpace Pkwy Parsippany NJ 07054

KUKIN, IRA, chem. co. exec.; b. N.Y.C., Apr. 4, 1924; s. William and Clara (Wachtel) K.; B.S. in Chemistry, CCNY, 1945; M.A., Harvard U., 1949, Ph.D., 1951; m. Doris Liener, June 14, 1954; children—Marrick Lee, Lori Sue, Jonathan L. Mgr. additives research Gulf Research and Devel. Co., Pitts., 1951-57; dir. research Sonnenborn Chem. and Refining Corp. (div. Witco Corp.), N.Y.C., 1958-63; pres., chief exec. officer Apollo Technologies, Inc., Whippany, N.J., 1963—; cons. air pollution control systems. Founder, pres. Congregation Bnai David, West Orange, N.J., 1963-64; bd. dirs. Congregation Ahawas Achim. Served with U.S. Army, 1946-48. Recipient Product Advancement award, 1977. Mem. Nat. Assn. Corrosion Engrs., Nat. Petroleum Refiners Assn., Am. Chem. Soc., Soc. Automotive Engrs., ASME. Author chpt. Pollution: Engineering and Scientific Solutions, 1973; contbr. articles to profl. pubs.

KULCH, CHARLES CHESTER, electronic games mfg. co. exec.; b. Montague, Mass., Sept. 6, 1950; s. Chester Alexander and Henrietta Mary (Sokoloski) K.; A.A., Greenfield Community Coll., 1970; B.S. in Mgmt., U. Mass., 1972; M.B.A. in Acctg., Western New Eng. Coll., 1977; m. Cathy Theresa Puffer, June 9, 1973; 1 dau., Kerri Ann. Acctg. supr. Millers Falls Tool Co., Greenfield, Mass., 1972-74; staff acct. Roy B. Chapin & Co., C.P.A.'s, Greenfield, 1974-75; acting divisional controller Varian Assos., Florham Park, N.H., 1975-78; corp. acctg. mgr. Centronics Data Computer Corp., Hudson, N.H., 1978-79; corp. controller Gamex Industries Inc., Hudson, 1979—. Roman Catholic. Club: Rotary. Home: 25 Heritage Circle Hudson NH 03051 Office: 21 Park Ave Hudson NH 03051

KULESH, WILLIAM ADAM, ins. co. exec.; b. Bronx, N.Y., Sept. 13, 1929; s. William Adam and Sophia Annastatia (Kurtz) K.; student pub. schs., Bklyn.; m. Catherine Marie Bechler, May 25, 1957; children—Claudia Elizabeth, Christopher John, Terence William. Field underwriter Mchts. Fire Assurance Corp. N.Y., N.Y.C., 46-57; dist. mgr. Kemper Ins. Group, Garden City, N.Y., 1957-59; mgr. Frank E. Wright & Sons Agy., Inc., West Hempstead, N.Y., 1959-64; founder, pres., chief exec. officer Nat. Coverage Corp., Jericho, N.Y., 1964—. Served with U.S. Army, 1951-53. Mem. Nat. Small Bus. Assn., L.I. Assn., Ind. Ins. Agts. Assn. Russian Orthodox. Clubs: Cherry Valley Country, New Hyde Park Elks. Home: 62 1st St Garden City NY 11530 Office: Nat Coverage Corp 333 N Broadway Jericho NY 11753

KULLBERG, DUANE R., business exec.; B.B.A. with honors, U. Minn., 1954. Partner, Arthur Andersen & Co., 1967—, mng. partner, Mpls., 1970-75, dep. mng. partner, Chgo., 1975-78, vice chmn. acctg. and audit practice, 1978-80, mng. partner, chief exec. officer, 1980—. Chmn. devel. com. Sch. of Art Inst. Chgo.; trustee Northwestern U.; bd. dirs. Chgo. Council on Fgn. Relations, Arthritis Found., North Shore Country Day Sch.; Mem. U.S. C. of C. (adv. council on Japan-U.S. econ. relations), Chgo. Council on Fgn. Relations (dir.), Beta Gamma Sigma (Dirs. Table), Beta Alpha Psi. Clubs: Chgo., Attic, Mid.-Am., Monroe, Econ., Execs. (Chgo.); Minneapolis. Office: 69 W Washington St Chicago IL 60602 also 18 quai General-Guisan 1211 Geneva 3 Switzerland

KULOK, WILLIAM ALLAN, exec. tng. co. exec.; b. Mt. Vernon, N.Y., July 24, 1940; s. Sidney Alexander and Bertha (Lembeck) K.; B.S. in Econs., Wharton Sch., U. Pa., 1962; m. Susan B. Glick, June 26, 1965; children—Jonathan, Brian, Stephanie. Acct., David Kulok Co., N.Y.C., 1962-67; asst. to pres. Syndicate Mags., N.Y.C., 1967-70; founder, 1970, since pres. N.Y. Mgmt. Center, Inc., N.Y.C.; dir. Listcomp Corp., Mail Mgmt. Corp.; lectr. Wharton Sch., U. Chgo., N.Y. U. Pres. N.Y. Soc. Ethical Culture, 1978-80; vice chmn. bd. Ethical Culture Schs., 1979. C.P.A., N.Y. Mem. Am. Inst. C.P.A.'s. Clubs: Rockaway River Country, Pinnacle. Home: 40 E 84th St New York NY 10028 Office: 360 Lexington Ave New York NY 10017

KUMAGAI, YOSHITARO, indsl. sewing machine mfg. co. exec.; b. Sendai, Japan, June 23, 1947; came to U.S., 1970; s. Rikizo and Tomiko (Bunya) K.; B.S., Hosei U., Tokyo, 1970, Ga. State U., Atlanta, 1973; m. Yoko Hirayama, Mar. 24, 1973. Engr., Mitsubishi Mining and Cement Co., Tokyo, 1970; with Sunbrand div. Willcox & Gibbs, Atlanta, 1973—, market research mgr., 1980—. Mem. ASME. Club: Horseshoe Bend Country. Home: 4308 Smithsonia Dr Tucker GA 30084 Office: Sunbrand Div Willcox & Gibbs 3900 Green Industrial Way Atlanta GA 30341

KUMM, WILLIAM HOWARD, energy products co. exec.; b. Bahia, Brazil, Feb. 6, 1931; s. Henry William and A. Joyce (Beale) K.; brought to U.S., 1938, naturalized, 1949; B.A., Amherst Coll., 1952; certificate bus. adminstrn., McCoy Coll., Johns Hopkins, 1959; m. Anne K. Gibson, July 11, 1953; children—John H., Elizabeth A., Katharine L. With Westinghouse Electric Corp., 1952-78, student, Pitts., 1952-53, jr. engr. AirArm div., Balt., 1953-54, sr. engr., 1955-60, supervisory engr. Westinghouse Surface div., Balt., 1961-62, supervisory engr. Systems Ops. div., 1962-65, mgr. advanced concept engring. sect. Westinghouse Ocean Research & Engring. Center, Annapolis, Md., 1965-69, subdiv. mgr., 1969-71; presdl. interchange exec. Pres.'s Commn. on Personnel Interchange, assigned NOAA, 1971-72; staff Nat. Adv. Com. on Oceans and Atmosphere, Washington, 1972; program mgr. submarine transp. project U.S. Maritime Adminstrn., 1972-73; mgr. marine programs Westinghouse Oceanic Div., 1973-78; pres., chief exec. officer Arctic Enterprises, Inc., 1978—, Trans Polar Shipping Co., Ltd., Calgary, Alta., Can., 1981—; participant joint Nat. Acad. Scis.-Nat. Acad. Engring. planning effort on Internat. Decade Ocean Exploration for Nat. Council on Marine Resources and Engring., 1968-69. Mem. Rural Area Devel. Bd., Carroll County, N.H., 1964-65; mem. Citizens Adv. Council on Edn., 1970-72; del. County Council PTA's, 1970, 71, treas. Cub Scout pack 332, Boy Scouts Am., Catonsville, Md., 1963-65. Registered profl. engr., Md. Mem. U.S. Naval Inst., Marine Tech. Soc., Presdl. Interchange Exec. Assn. Patentee in field. Contbr. chpt. to Man Beneath the Sea, 1972. Home: 511 Heavitree Ln Severna Park MD 21146 Office: 1220 L Gemini Dr Annapolis MD 21403

KUMMEL, EUGENE H., advt. exec. Chmn. bd., past chief exec. officer McCann-Erickson, Inc., N.Y.C Office: McCann-Erickson Inc 485 Lexington Ave New York NY 10017*

KUNA, SAMUEL, biologist, pharm co. exec.; b. Velke Levare, Czechoslovakia, May 7, 1912; s. Samuel and Anna (Jurka) K.; came to U.S., 1913, naturalized, 1925; student Union Jr. Coll., 1935-37; B.A., N.Y.U., 1943, Ph.D., 1957, postgrad. Rutgers U., 1944-45, U. Pa. 1946; M.A., Temple U. 1950, m. Olga Lehman, Dec. 26, 1936; children—Robert Alan, Samuel Thomas. Technician, Merck Inst. for Therapeutic Research, Merck & Co., Rahway, N.J., 1934-43, head gen. pharmacology dept., 1943-50, head dept. research pharamacology, 1950-53, research asso. head depts. biocontrol and spl. problems in pharmacology, 1953-57; head pharmacology dept.

Bristol-Myers Co., Hillside, N.J., 1957-60, head biol. research, 1960-61, asst. dir. biol. and chem. research, 1961-62, asst. dir. research and devel., 1962-67; dir. toxicology Calgon Consumer Products Research Labs. div. Merck & Co., Rahway, N.J., 1967-74, dir. biol. research, 1974-77; cons. in toxicology Beecham Research Labs., 1977—; prof. toxicology, dir. toxicology program Rutgers U. Grad. Sch., 1980—; chmn. bd., pres., chief exec. officer 1st Bank of Colonia. Woodbridge, N.J., 1963—; lectr. pharmacology Temple U., 1947-50; lectr. grad. biochemistry N.Y.U., 1962-63. Bd. dirs., treas. Middlesex Coll. Found. Fellow Acad. Medicine N.J., N.Y. Acad. Scis.; mem. Am. Soc. for Pharmacology and Exptl. Therapeutics, Toxicological Soc., Am. Pharm. Assn., AAAS, Woodbridge C. of C. (dir.), Sigma Xi. Contbr. articles to profl. jours. Patentee in field. Club: Colonia Country. Home: 746 Hyslip Ave Westfield NJ 07090 Office: 1st Bank of Colonia 505 Inman Ave Colonia NJ 07067

KUNG, EDWARD YEN-CHUNG, ins. co. exec.; b. Shanghai, China, Jan. 15, 1934; s. Shien-Woo and Wei-Ven (Yao) Kung; B.S., N. Central Coll., Naperville, Ill., 1954; B.S., U. Ill., 1954; Ph.D., Carnegie Mellon U., 1959; m. Marcia Smiley, July 29, 1967; children—Peter, Tana. Research engr. to supr., systems research Jones & Laughlin Steel Corp., Pitts., 1959-68; dir. ops. research Ins. Co. N.Am., Phila., 1968-70, asst. v.p., then v.p. computer div., 1970-73, sr. v.p., fin. adminstrn. INA Reins. Co., 1973-75, v.p. comml. casualty dept. Ins. Co. N.Am., 1975-76, sr. v.p., mgmt. services, 1976-77, sr. v.p. loss control, 1977-79, exec. v.p. INA Diversified Services, Inc., 1979—. Chmn. bd. trustees Penn Center Acad., 1976—. Mem. Am. Mgmt. Assn., Sigma Xi, Pi Mu Epsilon. Author tech. papers on computer simulation, ops. research, info. systems. Home: 418 S Van Pelt St Philadelphia PA 19146 Office: 1600 Arch St Philadelphia PA 19101

KUNKEL, GEORGE MYHRE, electronic software and hardware co. exec.; b. Los Angeles, Nov. 26, 1929; s. Hugo Carl and Letty Jean (Myhre) K.; A.A., Los Angeles City Coll., 1959; B.S., U. Calif. at Los Angeles, 1962, M.S., 1968; m. Eulalia Dolores Niewinska, July 24, 1964; children—Bonnie Ann, Michael Andrew, Wendy Anne. Engr., Applied Research Lab., 1962-63, Sprague Electric Co., 1963-64; sect. mgr. Electronic Specialty Co., 1964-67; engr. Jet Propulsion Lab., 1967-68; product mgr. Scanbe Mfg. Co., 1968-69; self-employed as engring. cons., Los Angeles, 1969-72; owner Electro-Data Tech., Burbank, Calif., 1972—; instr. Don White Cons., 1977—; pres. Spira Mfg. Corp., Burbank, 1978—; mem. teaching staff U. Calif. at Los Angeles Extension, 1968-76. Chmn. fin. com. Verdugo br. YMCA, 1978—; precinct chmn. Republican party, Montrose, Calif., 1962. Served with AUS, 1955-58. Mem. IEEE. (chmn. specialist working group on grounding and bonding 1968-75, chmn. tech. com. on interference control 1975—, adv. com. 1976—), Soc. Automotive Engrs. (chmn. bonding and grounding subcom. 1966—), Triangle. Patentee in field. Home: 8402 McGroarty St Sunland CA 91040 Office: 2808 Naomi St Burbank CA 91504

KUNSTADT, HERBERT, cons. engr.; b. Austria, July 28, 1931; s. Lipman and Rosalie (Merling) K.; came to U.S., 1962, naturalized, 1967; M.S.M.E., U. Bucharest (Rumania), 1954; Ph.D., Tech. U. Vienna, 1972; m. Dorothy Kunstadt, Oct. 20, 1967. Project engr. Sulzer Bros., Vienna, 1955-61; project mgr. Cosentini Co., N.Y.C., 1961-67; asso. Syska & Hennessy, N.Y.C., 1967-73; chmn. bd., chief exec. officer Falotico Inc., N.Y.C., 1973-75, Kunstadt Assos., P.C., N.Y.C., 1975—; pres. Marina Properties, Inc., Calif., 1978—; asso. prof. life support systems Pratt Inst., 1974—. Served in Mil., 1951-53. Registered profl. engr., N.Y., N.J., Conn., D.C., Tex., Calif., Fla., Mass., Pa. Mem. Nat. Soc. Profl. Engrs., Am. Soc. Heating, Refrigeration and Air Conditioning Engrs., Assn. Energy Engrs. (chmn. Energy Conservation Cons. Council, pres. N.Y. chpt.). Club: Harvard (N.Y.C.). Contbr. articles to profl. jours. Home: 870 Fifth Ave New York NY 10021 Office: 415 Lexington Ave New York NY 10017

KUNTZ, HAL GOGGAN, petroleum exploration corp. exec.; b. San Antonio, Dec. 29, 1937; s. Peter A. and Jean M. (Goggan) K.; B.S.E., Princeton U., 1960; M.B.A., Oklahoma City U., 1972; children—Hal Goggan, Peter A. V, Michael B. Line, staff positions Mobil Oil Corp., Dallas, Oklahoma City, New Orleans, 1963-74; co-founder, pres. CLK Corp., New Orleans, Houston, 1974—, IPEK Co., New Orleans, 1975—; pres. Gulf Coast Exploration Co., New Orleans, 1979—, CLK Investments I, 1979—, CLK Producting, 1980—. Mem. Mus. Fine Arts, Houston, 1978—, Houston Opera Soc., 1978—. Served with AUS, 1960-63. Mem. Am. Mgmt. Assn., Nat. Small Bus. Assn., Inter-Am. Soc., Soc. Exploration Geophysics, Am. Assn. Petroleum Geologists, Aircrafts Owners and Pilots Assn. Republican. Roman Catholic. Clubs: Presidents Council, University of Houston, Order of Alamo (San Antonio). Office: Suite 510 5373 W Alabama Ave Houston TX 77056

KUNTZ, LOUIS HENRY, retail corp. exec.; b. New Orleans, Mar. 20, 1930; s. Louis Henry and Agnes Annie (Scheffer) K.; B.B.A., So. Meth. U., 1951; m. Barbara Ann Mitchell, Feb. 8, 1957; children—Karen, Louis, John, Christopher. With Western Auto Supply Co., City of Industry, Calif., 1948—, regional v.p. retail, 1967-80, v.p. field ops., 1980—, mem. exec. com., 1980—. Mem. Delta Chi, Alpha Kappa Psi. Home: 851 Arbolado Dr Fullerton CA 92635 Office: 500 S 7th St City of Industry CA 91744

KUNZ, SHARON ELIZABETH, utility co. exec.; b. Bklyn., May 25, 1945; d. Albert Valentine and Dorothy Lee (Jacobs) Kunz; student S.I. Coll., 1978. Student in bus. adminstrn./mgmt. St. John's U., 1978—. With Consolidated Edison Co., 1963—, dist. office teller, 1967-69, accounting clk., customer service area, 1967-72, asst. supr. Manhattan customer service, 1972-78, gen. supr. Dist. Ill-Westside, Manhattan customer service, from 1978, now unit mgr. Dist III. Lic. pvt. pilot. Mem. Con. Edison Engring. Soc., Nat. Rifle Assn., Nat. Airplane Owners and Pilots Assn. Democrat. Office: 4 Irving Pl New York NY 10003

KUNZE, RALPH CARL, savs. and loan exec.; b. Buffalo, Oct. 31, 1925; s. Bruno E. and Esther (Graubman) K.; B.B.A., U. Cin., 1950; postgrad. Ind., U. 1954-56, U. Cin., 1962-63, U. So. Calif., 1973; m. Helen Hites Sutton, Apr. 29, 1978; children by previous marriage—Bradley, Diane, James. With Mt. Lookout Savs. & Loan Co., Cin., 1951-63; v.p. Buckeye Fed. Savs. & Loan Assn. Columbus, Ohio, 1963, v.p., sec., 1964-67, exec. v.p., 1967-70, pres., sec., 1970-77, vice chmn. bd., 1970-77; exec. v.p. Gate City Savs. and Loan Assn., Fargo, N.D., 1977, pres., chief operating officer, bd. dirs., 1978—. Trustee, Wesley Glen Meth. Retirement Center, 1974-77; pres. United Way of Franklin C, Ohio, 1977; past pres. Ohio. Soc. Prevention Blindness; bd. dirs. Arthritis Found., N.D. and S.D. Served with USNR, 1944-45. Mem. U.S. League of Savs. Assns. and Service Corps., N.D. League of Savs. Assns., Nat. Assn. Home Builders. Lambda Chi Alpha. Clubs: Fargo Country, Rotary, Masons (32 deg.), Shriners. Home: 1246 Elm St N Fargo ND 58102 Office: 500 2d Ave N Fargo ND 58102

KUOLT, MILTON GERMANN, II, resort camping exec.; b. Madras, India, June 16, 1927; came to U.S., 1940, naturalized, 1951; s. Milton Germann and Martha (Daeumler) K.; diploma Bartlett Sch. Tree Surgery, Stanford, Conn., 1945; B.A. in Econs., Central Wash. Coll., Ellensburg, 1951; children—Milton, Randolph, Ronald, Suzanne, Sandra, Maria. Successively storekeeper, facilities planner, mem. fin. dept. Boeing Co., Seattle, 1946-70; founder Pacific Rim Group, 1969; chief exec. officer, chmn. bd. Thousand Trails, Inc., Seattle, 1969—. Served with USNR, 1945-46. Republican. Lutheran. Office: 4800 S 188th Way Seattle WA 98188

KUPANOFF, TRIFON MINO, JR., mktg. and mgmt. co. exec.; b. Springfield, Ohio, Jan. 1, 1949; s. Trifon Mino and Martha Dean (Martin) K.; B.S. in Bus. Adminstrn., Xavier U., 1971, M.B.A., 1973. Zone mgr. ind. and dealer channels Cin. Dist. Office, Ford Motor Co. Mktg. Corp., 1973-78; mgmt. cons. Klekamp, Wallace & Co., mgmt. cons., Cin., 1978-79; gen. mgr. Paul Watts Inc., Cin., 1979-80; v.p., chief exec. officer Kupanoff & Assos. Inc., Springfield, 1980—; prof. bus. Coll. Mt. St. Joseph, Cin., 1978-79; cons., speaker at seminars, 1979—. Roman Catholic. Home: 1839 N Fountain Blvd Springfield OH 45504 Office: 2215 Olympic Dr Springfield OH 45503

KUPCHIK, PHILIP, pharm. co. exec.; b. Bklyn., Dec. 2, 1917; s. Abraham and Fannie (Silvergleid) K.; B.A. in Chemistry, Bklyn. Coll., 1937, postgrad., 1937-40; postgrad. in elec. engring. U. Cin., 1943-44, Ohio State U., 1944; m. Jeanne Genevieve Herson, Mar. 13, 1943; children—Michael Alan, Diane Maureen, Francine Rhonda. Purchasing agt. Schenley Industries, Larchmont, N.Y., 1945-50; dir. purchasing, dir. prodn. Organon, Inc., West Orange, N.J., 1950-68, asst. v.p. prodn. and purchasing, 1968-71, v.p. adminstrn., 1971—, also v.p., dir. sub. cos.; mem. Nat. Council Joint Distbn. Com., 1964—. Bd. dirs. Edn. Found. Human Sexuality, Montclair State Coll., 1967—, chmn., 1976—; chmn. United Way Cedar Grove (N.J.), 1966, chmn. spl. gifts com., 1978—, trustee North Essex (N.J.) chpt., 1979—, v.p., 1980—; bd. dirs., mem. exec. com. chmn. mems. and funds com. Essex (N.J.) chpt. ARC, 1968—; chmn. United Jewish Appeal, Cedar Grove, 1961-77, chmn. Israel Bonds, 1963-73; v.p. Cedar Grove Sr. Citizens Housing Assn., 1975—; pres. Temple Sholom of West Essex, 1964-65, chmn. bd. trustees, 1966-69, treas., 1959-62, trustee, 1974—; trustee Sr. Service Corp., 1980—. Served with AUS, 1941-45. Named to Scroll of Honor, State of Israel Bonds, 1969; named Man of Yr., Temple Sholom, 1975. Mem. Am. Mgmt. Assn., N.J. Pharm. Purchasing Agts. Assn. Club: B'nai B'rith (trustee local club). Home: 123 Harper Terr Cedar Grove NJ 07009 Office: 375 Mount Pleasant Ave West Orange NJ 07052

KUPERSMITH, AARON HARRY, lawyer, fin. exec., real estate exec.; b. Newark, June 13, 1925; s. David and Bessie (Rubinstein) K.; student chem. engring, Newark Tech. Sch., 1941-43; diploma Drury Coll., 1943; B.S. cum laude, N.Y.U., 1948; LL.B., Bklyn. Law Sch., 1954, J.S.D., 1956, J.D., 1968; m. Cynthia Skolnick, Dec. 24, 1947; children—Farrell Preston, Mark Jeffrey, Linda Ellen. Accountant A.H. Kupersmith & Co., N.Y.C., 1948; admitted to N.Y. bar, 1954; practice as atty., tax, bus., financial cons., N.Y.C., 1954—; partner Ramapo Manor Nursing Center, Suffern, N.Y., 1957-75, McQuire Holiday Motel, N.J., 1962-70, various real estate, instns. and housing devels., 1956—; pres., chmn. Verson Prodns., Inc., N.Y.C., 1962-68; Exec. Financial Planning Corp., N.Y.C., 1956-75; exec. v.p., sec.-treas., dir., mem. exec. com. Del Labs. Inc., and subsidiaries, N.Y.C., 1962-65; pres., chmn. Am. Inst. Econ. Growth, 1965—; dir. RAM Group, Inc., 1974; gen. counsel Hyfin Credit Union, Council Jewish Orgns. in Civil Service, Inc., Council Civil Service Orgns., Civil Service-Independent's Party, 1971—. Lectr., Columbia U., 1966-67; spl. counsel, cons., lectr groups and assns. on law, taxes, corporate finance, mergers and acquisitions, housing, real estate, tax shelters, 1958—; mem. Columbia U. adv. com. to N.Y. State on rates for nursing home care, 1966. Trustee Martin Revson trusts, also various pvt., charitable founds. Served with USAAF, 1943-45. Recipient Wisdom Honor award, 1969. Mem. Am. Bar Assn., Bar Assn. City N.Y., Lawyer to Lawyer Consultation Panel, Alpha Epsilon Pi, Psi Chi Omega, Beta Gamma Sigma. Author: An Economic Study of the American System, 1956; Tax Havens, 1959; Corporate Finance and Taxes, 1959; Tax Treaties of United States, 1960; United States Industry and Executives Abroad, 1960; Executive Compensation Constructive Receipt, 1961; Corporate Finance and Taxes Defined, 1963; Considerations in Mergers and Acquisitions, 1965; Break Even Techniques, 1965; Men and Their Money, 1966; Is Nursing Home Business for You, 1968; Nursing Home Industry Review, 1968; Major Health Crisis, 1968; Private Placements, 1970; Equity and Venture Capital, 1970; Tax and Investment Shelters, 1971; Capital Growth, 1971; Investments-Rental Housing vs. Condominiums, 1972, Purchase and Sale of Businesses-Checklist, 1972; Real Estate Partnerships-Government and the Private Investor, 1973; Tax Sheltered Investments, 1973; also articles. Fin., legal columnist Drug and Trade News and Drug News Weekly, 1965-68. Home: 45 Woodland Ave West Orange NJ 07052 Office: 275 Madison Ave New York City NY 10016 also 4130 NW 88th Ave Coral Springs FL 33065 also 45 Woodland Ave West Orange NJ 07052

KUPERSMITH, FARRELL PRESTON, mgmt. cons.; b. N.Y.C., Apr. 5, 1949; s. A. Harry and Cynthia (Skolnick) K.; B.S., N.Y. U., 1972, M.B.A., 1974; m. Barbara S. Kocolatos, May 27, 1972. Dir. sales and bus. devel. Health Resorts and Spas Corp., Lakewood, N.J., 1970-71, gen. mgr., chief operating exec., 1971-72; mgr. ops. analysis and fin. planning Revlon Internt. Corp. subs. Revlon, Inc., N.Y.C., 1972-73, dir. fin. planning and bus. devel., 1973-74; cons. partner Touche Ross & Co., Detroit, 1974-76, Cleve., 1976-79, N.Y.C., 1979—, mem. bus. policy com., fgn. policy com., 1979—; partner C & F Realty, N.Y.C., 1974—, B & F Realty, Pearl Plaza (Ohio), 1977—; fin. counsel various charitable orgns. and pvt. trusts, 1974—; guest lectr. various instns. and orgns. Clubs: N.Y. U. (N.Y.C.); Kenilworth (Bal Harbor, Fla.); Burning Tree (Greenwich, Conn.). Author: Avoiding the Commercial Pitfalls of Detente, 1973. Home: 53 Londonderry Dr Greenwich CT 06830 Office: 1633 Broadway New York NY 10019

KURFEHS, HAROLD CHARLES, JR., book distbn. and pub. co. exec.; b. Jersey City, Dec. 10, 1939; s. Harold Charles and Matilda Gertrude (Ruschman) K.; B.S. (Oaklawn Found. scholar), St. Peter's Coll., 1962; M.B.A., Wharton Sch., U. Pa., 1964; m. Linda Roberta Lepis, Aug. 1, 1964; children—Harold Charles III, Diane E. Product mgr. Am. Brands, Inc., N.Y.C., 1958-62, 64-66; account exec. Benton & Bowles, N.Y.C., 1966-68; account mgr. Wells, Rich, Greene, Inc., N.Y.C., 1968-69; v.p., dir. marketing Meta-Language Products, Inc., N.Y.C., 1969-70; sr. account exec. McCaffrey & McCall, Inc., N.Y.C., 1970-71; dir. advt. Ethan Allen, Inc., N.Y.C., 1972-75; v.p., gen. mgr. retail/franchise div. N.Am. ops. Reed Ltd., Toronto, Ont., Can., 1975-76, also v.p., gen. mgr. fabric div. Reed Nat. Drapery Co., Sanderson, Can., 1975-76; pres. Fairfield Book Co. Inc., Brookfield, Conn., 1977—. Trustee N.E. Leonia (N.J.) Civic Assn., 1970-71, chmn., 1971-72. Mem. Co. Mil. Historians, Wharton Grad. Club N.Y., U.S. Naval Inst., Nat. Def. Preparedness Assn., Nat. Rifle Assn. (life), Pi Sigma Phi. Home: 42 Obtuse Rd N Brookfield Center CT 06805 Office: Fairfield Book Co Inc PO Box 289 Brookfield Center CT 06805

KURPIS, LOUIS W., chem. co. exec.; b. Bronx, N.Y., Sept. 29, 1947; s. Charles and Anita (Forella) K.; M.S. in Acctg., L.I. U., 1969; m. May 2, 1971; 2 children. Mgr. audit staff Main LaFrance & Co., C.P.A., N.Y.C., 1970-73; asst. mgr. published reports ITT, N.Y.C., 1973-77; asst. treas. Clabir Corp., Old Greenwich, Conn., 1977-78; v.p., treas. Publicker Industries Inc., Greenwich, Conn., 1978—. C.P.A. Mem. Am. Inst. C.P.A.'s, N.Y. State Soc. C.P.A.'s. Home: 51 Fowler St Yonkers NY 10701 Office: Publicker Industries Inc 777 W Putnam Ave Greenwich CT 06830*

KURSEWICZ, LEE Z., mktg. cons.; b. Chgo., Oct. 26, 1916; s. Antoni and Henryka (Sulkowska) K.; ed. Chgo. and Bata ind. schs.; m. Ruth Elizabeth Venzke, Jan. 31, 1940; 1 son, Dennis. With Bata Shoe Co., Inc., 1936-78, plant mgr., Salem, Ind., 1963-65, v.p., mng. dir., Batawa, Ont., Can., 1965-71; v.p., dir. Bata Industries, Batawa, 1965-71, plant mgr., Salem, 1971-76; pres. Bata Shoe Co., Inc., Belcamp, Md., 1976-77, sr. v.p., dir., 1977-79. City mgr. City of Batawa, 1965-71; vice chmn. Trenton (Ont.) Meml. Hosp., 1970-71; pres. Priestford Hills Community Assn., 1979-80; chmn. adv. bd. Phoenix Festival Theatre, Hartford County Community Coll., 1980-81. Mem. Am. Mgmt. Assn. Clubs: Rotary, Bush River Yacht (commodore 1956), Bush River Power Squadron (comdr. 1957), Western Hills Country of Salem (pres. 1975), Trenton Country (pres. 1968-69), Md. Country. Home and Office: 211 Goucher Way Churchville MD 21028

KURTH, WALTER RICHARD, assn. exec.; b. Normal, Ill., Jan. 21, 1932; s. Walter H. and Irene (Freitag) K.; B.S., U. Ill., 1954; m. Mary Elisabeth Taylor, Aug. 23, 1958; children—Mary Helen, Sarah Jane, Elisabeth Irene. Publ. dir. Asso. Credit Burs. of Am., Inc., St. Louis, 1954-57, marketing dir., 1957-62, asst. gen. mgr., 1962-66, asst. gen. mgr., treas., Houston, 1966-68, adminstrv. v.p., treas., 1968-69; exec. v.p., treas. Asso. Credit Burs., Inc., 1969-75; sec.-treas. Credit Bur. Automation, Inc., Houston, 1966-75; vice chmn. bd. Credit Services Internat., 1970-75; pres., sec.-treas., vice chmn. bd. ACB Services, Inc., 1970-75; sr. v.p. Nat. Consumer Finance Assn., Washington, 1976-77, exec. v.p., 1977-80, pres., 1980—. Mem. Houston dist. council SBA, 1971-75; adv. council Credit Research Center, 1977—. Chmn. Republican Dist. Fund Drive; Rep. precinct chmn., 1969-75. Bd. dirs. Econ. Edn. Found. for Clergy, 1976—; bd. mgrs. Thompson Retreat Center, St. Louis, 1963-64. Mem. Am., Tex., Washington, St. Louis (pres. 1962), Houston (pres. 1974) socs. assn. execs., U.S. C. of C. (assn. com.), Cert. Assn. Execs. Star and Scroll (pres. 1953), C. of C., Am. Mgmt. Assn., Alpha Kappa Lambda (pres. 1953). Republican. Presbyn. (elder). Mason (32 deg., Shriner). Home: 9205 White Chimney Ln Great Falls VA 22066 Office: 1000 16th St NW Suite 601 Washington DC 20036

KURTZ, LAWRENCE WILLARD, fin. co. mgr.; b. St. Louis, Dec. 19, 1950; s. Willard Lawrence and Violet Olive (Schoenberg) K.; student U.S. Mil. Acad., 1968-69; A.B. in Econs., Princeton U., 1972; M.A. in Journalism, Mo. U., 1975; m. Melissa Adams Leeds, May 12, 1979. Overseas credit analyst Chase Bank, N.Y.C. and Frankfurt, Germany, 1973-74; account exec. Burson-Marsteller, N.Y.C., 1975-77, sr. account exec., Chgo., 1977-78; treas., dir. corporate communications Southwestern Group Fin., Inc., Houston, 1978-80; account supr. Burson-Marsteller, Houston, 1980, client services mgr., 1981—. Mem. Nat. Investor Relations Inst., Public Relations Soc. Am. Club: Sunrisers. Home: 2555 Bering St Apt 9 Houston TX 77057 Office: 6363 Richmond St Suite 300 Houston TX 77057

KURUCZ, JOHN, lawyer; b. Yonkers, N.Y., Sept. 19, 1930; s. John J. and Anna (Timan) K.; B.C.E., Rensselaer Poly. Inst., 1952; J.D., Georgetown U., 1957; postgrad. U. Conn., 1965-66; m. June Reynolds, Feb. 20, 1960 (div. Oct. 1967); children—Debra Jeanne, Jonna Stiles; m. 2d, Mary K. Semon, May 26, 1973; children—Mary Anne, John Joseph R. Patent searcher Pennie, Edmonds, Morton, Barrows & Taylor, 1954; patent examiner U.S. Patent Office, 1955-56; patent adviser Dept. Army, 1956-57; admitted to Va. bar, 1957, N.Y. bar, 1959; practiced in N.Y.C., 1957—; asso. Kane, Dalsimer, Kane & Smith, 1957-69; partner Kane, Dalsimer, Kane, Sullivan & Kurucz, N.Y.C., 1969—; former dir. Diversified Investors Planning Corp., N.Y.C., Cartafax Corp., N.Y.C.; dir. LK Mfg. Corp., L.I., Hydrostack Corp., Huntington, N.Y.; former sec., dir. Impetus Industries, N.Y.C.; former v.p., dir. Breed Corp.; sec., dir. Spraysol, Inc., Ft. Lee, N.J.; dir. Spraysol GmbH, W.Ger. Served to 1st lt. C.E., AUS, 1952-54. Mem. Fed., Am., Va., N.Y. State, Westchester County, N.Y. County, N.Y.C. bar assns., Am., N.Y. patent law assns., Am., N.Y. State, Westchester County profl. engrs. socs., Chi Epsilon, Alpha Tau Omega. Clubs: University (N.Y.C.); Scarsdale (N.Y.) Golf; Ponte Vedra (Fla.) Golf. Home: 604 Colony St Hartsdale NY 10530 Office: 420 Lexington Ave New York NY 10017

KURZ, GERHARD EUGEN, oil co. exec.; b. Stuttgart, Germany, Aug. 25, 1939; s. Eugen and Martha (Fried) K.; came to U.S., 1965, naturalized, 1973; B.A. with honors, U. Wales, 1964; M.B.A., N.Y. U., 1971; m. Emma Margaretha E. Olving, Oct. 2, 1964; children—Thomas, Christopher, Annika, Christina. With Mobil Shipping Co., 1964—, mgr. industry studies, N.Y.C., 1972-75, mgr. joint ventures, 1976-79, mgr. fin. planning, analysis, and controls, 1980—. Mem. N.Am. Soc. for Corporate Planning, Westfield Jr. C. of C. (treas., dir. 1973-74), Am. Mgmt. Assn., Transp. Research Forum. Presbyterian. Club: Echo Lake Country (Westfield, N.J.). Home: 320 Woodland Ave Westfield NJ 07090 Office: 150 E 42d St New York NY 10017

KUSAR, DANIEL DUSAN, automotive and aluminum mfg. co. exec.; b. Ljubljana, Yugoslavia, May 9, 1928; came to U.S., 1950, naturalized, 1953; s. Savo A. and Angelica Setina K.; M.B.A., U. Chgo., 1957; m. Rosanne M. Egelske, Sept. 24, 1960; children—Angelica, Jennifer. Asst. to pres. Calumet Steel div. Borg Warner Corp., 1957-61; pres. Kusar Investment Corp., 1961-67; corp. fin. asso. Hornblower-Weeks, Hemphill, Noyes, 1967-71; chmn., pres. Darfield Industries, Inc., Chgo., 1971—; chmn. All Products Co., Sun Valley Products, Inc. Served with U.S. Army, 1951-53. Republican. Roman Catholic. Clubs: Univ., Econs. Office: Darfield Industries Inc 208 S LaSalle St Chicago IL 60604

KUSHNER, ARTHUR S., water treatment co. exec.; b. N.Y.C., May 9, 1940; s. Joseph B. and Dora C. Kushner; B.A., U. Evansville, 1962; Ph.D., Pa. State U., 1966; M.B.A., Cleve. State U., 1978; m. Roberta Groden, Aug. 2, 1964; children—Jeremy, Michael. Postdoctoral fellow U. Chgo., 1966-68; asst. prof. Cleve. State U., 1968-74; mgr. tech. support services, group leader Horizons Research, Inc., Cleve., 1974-75; research asso. Internat. Paper Co., Tuxedo Park, N.Y., 1975-76; sr. chemist, group leader, product mgr. Mogul div. Dexter Corp., Chagrin Falls, Ohio, 1976-79, regional sales mgr., 1979-80, tech. mgr. central div., 1980—. Cub scout leader Boy Scouts Am. NSF fellow, 1963-66. Mem. Am. Chem. Soc., Am. Electroplaters Soc., ASTM, Am. Soc. for Metals, Sigma Xi, Beta Gamma Sigma. Contbr. articles to profl. jours. Office: PO Box 200 Chagrin Falls OH 44022

KUSHNER, HARVEY DAVID, research exec.; b. N.Y.C., Dec. 28, 1930; s. Morris and Hilda (Zwiebel) K.; B. Engring., Johns Hopkins, 1951; m. Rose Rehert, Jan. 14, 1951; children—Gantt A., Todd R., Lesley K. Gas turbine lab. research USN Engring. Expt. Sta., 1951; asso. engr. USN Bur. Ships, 1951-53; mem. tech. staff Fluid Mechanics Group, Central Research Lab., math. services group, flight simulation div. Melpar, Inc., 1952-55; with ORI, Inc. (formerly Ops. Research Inc. subs. Reliance Group, Inc.), Silver Spring, Md., 1955—, tech. dir. govt. and indsl. systems div., 1962-67, corp. dir., 1958-68, exec. v.p., 1962-68, dir. corp. programs, 1967-68, chmn. bd., pres.,

1969—; v.p. Reliance Group, Inc., 1971-77; pres. Disclosure, Inc., subsidiary, 1972-77; tech. dir. Analysis Task Group of Project T, cons. to com. on undersea warfare Nat. Acad. Sci., 1963. Mem. econ. adv. council Montgomery County (Md.). Fellow N.Y. Acad. Scis.; mem. AAAS, Nat. Security Indsl. Assn. (v.p. 1973-74, trustee 1975—), Ops. Research Soc. Am., Nat. Space Club (bd. govs. 1979—), Inst. Mgmt. Scis., IEEE (sr.), ASME, Nat. Council Profl. Services Firms (dir. 1975—). Club: Cosmos (Washington). Ops. research, systems analysis, mgmt. cons. Home: 9607 Kingston Rd Kensington MD 20795 Office: 1400 Spring St Silver Spring MD 20910

KUSHNER, JEFFREY A., ins. co. exec.; b. Bronx, N.Y., Mar. 25, 1939; s. Bernard M. and Claire E. Kushner; B.S., N.Y. U., 1961. With Nat. Preferred Risks, Inc., Great Neck, N.Y., 1961-75, underwriting mgr., 1969-75, asst. v.p., 1970-75; pres. Realco Agy. Ltd., Great Neck, 1975—. Mem. Ind. Ins. Agts. Nassau County (dir.), U.S. Coast Guard Aux. (treas. flotilla 12-2), Great Neck C. of C. (v.p. 1981—). Clubs: Great Neck Lions (sec. 1980-81, pres. 1969-71), Masons (past master, sec.), B'nai B'rith (v.p., treas. Great Neck lodge 1981—). Home: 19 Hutchinson Ct Box 145 Great Neck NY 11022 Office: 107 Northern Blvd Great Neck NY 11021

KUSHNER, ROBERT A., mfg. co. exec.; b. N.Y.C., 1935; B.S., N.Y.U., 1957, J.D., 1960. Admitted to N.Y. bar, 1960; atty. Fed. Trade Commn., 1960-61, firm Parker, Chapin, Flattau & Klimpl, 1961-67; with Ward Foods, Inc., 1967-72, v.p., legal sec., corp. counsel, 1969-72; asst. gen. counsel Pan Am. World Airways, Inc., N.Y.C., 1972-76; v.p., sec., gen. counsel Cyclops Corp., 1976—. Home: 30 Vernon Dr Pittsburgh PA 15228 Office: 650 Washington Rd Pittsburgh PA 15228

KUSINITZ, MICHAEL JEFFREY, mgmt. cons.; b. Bronx, N.Y., Aug. 16, 1950; s. Martin Norman and Jean (Linzner) K.; B.A., Coll. City N.Y., 1972; M.B.A. in Exec. Mgmt., St. John's U., N.Y.C., 1978; m. Sandra Adler, June 30, 1974; 1 son, Adam. With Greenleigh Assos., Inc., N.Y.C., 1972-80, program dir. employee consultation service, 1977-78, dir. spl. programs, manpower cons., 1978-80; sr. mgmt. devel. specialist Blue Cross/Blue Shield of Greater N.Y., Yonkers, 1980—; expert witness N.Y. Human Rights Commn. Exec. v.p. Beacon Hill Estates Coop., Inc. Mem. Am. Mgmt. Assn., Assn. Labor-Mgmt. Adminstrs. and Cons.'s on Alcoholism. Research on exec. perceptions of indsl. alcoholism. Home: 389 Concord Rd Yonkers NY 10710

KUTAK, JEROME FRANK, lawyer; b. Prague, Czechoslovakia, Oct. 3, 1903; s. Frank Joseph and Mary (Stok) K.; came to U.S., 1909, naturalized, 1917; student U. Omaha, 1922-24; LL.B., U. Chgo., 1928; m. Jessamine Mary Geagan, June 23, 1928; children—Carolyn, Robert, Anne, Mary Louise. Admitted to Ill. bar, 1928, Ind. bar, 1941; atty. Fed. Life Ins. Co., 1928-38; sec., gen. counsel Sterling Ins. Co., 1938-40; v.p., counsel Guarantee Res. Life Ins. Co., Hammond, Ind., 1940-56, pres., 1956-71, chmn. bd., gen. counsel, 1971-77; individual practice law, Munster, Ind., 1977—; dir. S.E. Nat. Bank, Chgo. Mem. Hammond Bd. Zone Appeals, 1963-67; adv. bd. St. Margaret Hosp.; bd. dirs. Hammond Downtown Council; pres. bd. trustees YMCA, 1972. Recipient Good Citizenship award Com. of 100, Chgo., 1963. Mem. Am. Ind., Chgo., Hammond bar assns., Am. Judicature Soc., Hammond C. of C. (pres. 1967-69), Phi Sigma Phi. Republican. Presbyterian. Clubs: Mason (32 deg.), Kiwanis (pres. Hammond 1972,) Woodmar Country (Hammond); South Shore Country (Chgo.). Author: Principles of Claim Adjusting, 1951. Home: 18 Glendale Park Hammond IN 46320 Office: 8230 Calument Ave Munster IN

KUTCHER, FRANK EDWARD, JR., printing co. exec.; b. Teaneck, N.J., Dec. 20, 1927; s. Frank Edward and Helen Marie (Crowley) K.; B.S. cum laude, Fairleigh Dickinson U., 1953; m. Elizabeth Vespaziani, Jan. 19, 1952; children—Kenneth, Karen, Kristin. Mgmt. cons. Peat, Marwick, Mitchell & Co., 1961-63; controller Celanese Plastics Co., 1963-65; controller Pfister Chem. Co., Ridgefield, N.J., 1965-67; v.p. fin. Litton Industries, N.Y.C., 1967-70; v.p., controller, dir. McCall Pub. Co. (subs. Norton Simon, Inc.), N.Y.C., 1970-73; pres., dir. Foote and Davies Printing Co. (subs. J.P. Stevens & Co., Inc.), Atlanta, 1973—, Foote and Davies Transport Co., Atlanta, 1973—, also Mid-Am. Webpress, Inc., Lincoln, Nebr. 1978—; pres. Conf. Bd. Major Printers; dir. Printing Industries of Am., Inc., Graphic Arts Tech. Found. Served with USN, 1945-46. Mem. Fin. Execs. Inst., Nat. Assn. Accountants, Mensa. Clubs: Athletic, Commerce (Atlanta); Atrium (N.Y.C.). Home: 3827 Rosebud Rd Loganville GA 30249 Office: 3101 McCall Dr Atlanta GA 30340

KUTRIEB, RONALD EARL, investment exec.; b. Canton, Ohio, May 13, 1942; s. Howard Earl and Mae A. (Ahlquist) K.; B.A. in Econs., Colgate U., 1962; M.B.A., Harvard U., 1969; m. Wendy M. Morgan, Sept. 11, 1965; children—Joshua, Benson. Pres., chief exec. officer Tramsar Mgmt. Corp., Providence, 1981—; treas., trustee Realty Income Trust, Providence, 1969—; pres. Providence Advisors, fin. cons., 1979—; dir. Sunergy Communities, Inc., Denver; corporator Citizens Bank, Providence. Incorporator, Kent County Hosp., Warwick, R.I.; founding dir. Providence Indsl. Devel. Corp.; founding pres., bd. dirs. Providence Preservation Soc. Revolving Fund, Inc. Mem. Nat. Assn. Real Estate Investment Trusts (gov.), Providence Preservation Soc. (dir.). Clubs: Univ. (gov.) (Providence); Dunes (gov.) (Narragansett, R.I.). Office: 321 S Main St Providence RI 02903

KUTZ, KENNETH JOHN, mining exec.; b. Rosetown, Sask., Can., Nov. 16, 1926; came to U.S., 1957, naturalized, 1962; s. John and Leah (Lefevre) K.; B.S. summa cum laude in Geol. Engring., U. Sask., 1948; m. Nora M. Marchand, Nov. 10, 1948; children—Shirley Mae Kase, Gerald John. Miner, surveyor Howe Sound Co., Britannia Beach, B.C., 1947-48, research engr., 1950-51, asst. chief engr., 1951-54, chief engr., maintenance supt., Snow Lake, Man., 1954-55, mine supt., Cobalt, Idaho, 1956-57; mine supt. Lakeview Mining Co. (Oreg.), 1958-59, Sunshine Mining Co., Kellogg, Idaho, 1960-61; mining engr. Texasgulf Inc., Moab, Utah, 1961-62, mine supt., 1963-65, tech. asst. to gen. mgr., 1965-66, tech. asst. to v.p. Potash div., Salt Lake City, 1966-68, adminstrv. asst., 1968-69, asst. to pres., mgr. Australian iron ore projects, 1969-73, v.p. Internat. div., 1973—; pres. Texasgulf Australia, Texasgulf Panama; mng. dir. Pandora Mining (Pty.) Ltd.; Ltd.; dir. Cliffs Western Australia Mining Co. Ltd., Cerro Colorado, S.A. Registered Profl. engr., B.C., Oreg. Mem. Mining and Metall. Soc. Am. (past pres.), AIME, Can. Inst. Mining and Metallurgy, Australian Inst. Mining and Metallurgy, Australian Mining Industry Council, Mining Club N.Y. (pres., bd. govs., program chmn.). Republican. Roman Catholic. Clubs: Innis Arden Golf, Marco Polo, Sky, Landmark. Patentee in field. Home: 7 Whaling Rd Darien CT 06820 Office: Texasgulf Inc High Ridge Park Stamford CT 06904

KUYKENDALL, GREGORY LEWIS, food co. exec.; b. Long Beach, Calif., June 28, 1947; s. Ben F. and Neva J. (Eitel) K.; B.S. in Chemistry, U. Tex., Austin, 1970; Ph.D. in Chemistry (Robert A. Welch fellow), Tex. Tech U., 1976; m. Sharon L. Andersen, Apr. 3, 1980; children by previous marriage—Wendy Lorraine, Daniel Matthew. Quality assurance engr. Anderson Clayton Co., Dallas, 1976-77, quality control mgr, Fresno, Calif., 1977—; cons. in field. Mem. Am. Chem. Soc. (Outstanding Speaker award 1975), Am. Soc. for Quality Control, Inst. of Food Tech. Democrat. Baptist. Contbr. articles to profl. jours. Home: 3486 E Saginaw Way Fresno CA 93726 Office: PO Box 10051 Fresno CA 93745

KUZARA, STANLEY ANDREW, real estate exec.; b. Dietz, Wyo., Oct. 15, 1906; s. George and Sophia (Mendrick) K.; B.A., U. Wyo., 1929; m. Pauline E. Caywood, June 8, 1935; children—Janet Kuzara Kilpatrick, Richard, Robert. Area dir. Nat. Youth Adminstrn., 1935-42; field dir. ARC, 1942-45; dir. Vets. Info. Center, Colorado Springs, Colo., 1945-49; engaged in real estate, 1950—; propr. Kuzara Agy., Sheridan, Wyo., 1954—; pres. Wymo Oil, Inc., 1958-69; dir. Capital Savs. & Loan Assn., Sheridan. Mem. Sheridan City Planning Commn., 1969-76; hon. dir. N. Am. Indian Found.; hon. chmn. Cedars Home for Children, Lincoln, Nebr. Named Wyo. Realtor of Year, Wyo. Assn. Realtors, 1969; Wyo. Citizen of Year, Wyo. State Elks Assn., 1972. Mem. Wyo. Realtors Assn. (pres. 1964), Nat. Assn. Realtors (regional v.p. 1976), Internat. Assn. Turtles (pres. 1960—). Clubs: Elks (past exalted ruler, hon. life mem. (dist. dep., grand exalted ruler Wyo. N. 1975-76, mem. grand lodge com. credentials 1976-77), Masons, Shriners. Author, pub.: Black Diamonds of Sheridan—A Facet of Wyoming History, 1977. Home: 372 W Loucks St Sheridan WY 82801 Office: 21 S Jefferson St Sheridan WY 82801

KUZNIK, ROBERT WILLIAM, disposal co. exec.; b. Springfield, Ill., Sept. 5, 1947; s. Robert W. and Margaret E. Kuznik; A.A., Solano Coll., 1967; B.S., Calif. State U., 1969; m. Carolyn S. Winnett, Feb. 1, 1969; 1 son, Brian. Prodn. mgr. FMC Corp., Mech. Foundries, Los Angeles, 1969-71; asst. dir. public works City of Palm Springs (Calif.), 1971-72, asst. dir. transp. and ops., 1972-76, asst. dir. community devel., 1976-77; exec. mgr./corp. officer Jaycox Disposal Co., Inc., Anaheim, Calif., 1977—; corp. officer Waste Disposal Services, Inc., Palm Springs, 1978—; planning commr. City of Placentia (Calif.), 1980—. Mem. Orange County citizen's energy com., 1978—; bd. dirs. Solar Energy Devel. Inst. of Palm Springs, 1976-77. Served with Calif. N.G., 1969-75. Mem. Anaheim C. of C. (dir. 1979—, exec. com. 1979—, chmn. legis. com. 1978-80), Soc. Advancement Mgmt., Am. Mgmt. Assn., Am. Public Works Assn. Office: 1016 E Katella Ave Anaheim CA 92805

KVINGEDAL, PAULINE ELVA LORENSEN (MRS. EARL JOHN KVINGEDAL), coop. exec.; b. Cambridge, Mass., June 19, 1931; d. Joseph Nectar and Helga Pontoria (Helstrom) Lorensen; student Academie Moderne, 1957, Harvard U., 1965, Emerson Coll., 1967; m. Earl John Kvingedal, Oct. 14, 1950; children—Donna Lee, DeAnne Leslie. With Promotions, Inc., Boston, 1955-66; display dir., designer William Filenes, Boston, 1963-65; buyer jr. and women's dept. Harvard Coop. Soc., Cambridge, 1966—. Pub. speaker to various schs., chs., clubs, bus. and social orgns. Vol. tchr., worker Salvation Army, 1950-68. Past mem. Evangelical Free Ch. (pres. ladies guild 1954-58, v.p. women's club 1969-71); active Park St. Congl. Ch., 1969—. Home: 41 Shade St Lexington MA 02173 Office: 1400 Massachusetts Ave Cambridge MA 02138

KWARCIAK, THADEUS RAYMOND, fin. service group exec.; b. Rockville, Conn., June 18, 1921; s. Benjamin and Veronica K.; student public schs., Mass.; m. Gladys Hood, Jan. 13, 1945; 1 dau., Diane. Pres., Sturbridge Fin. Service Group (Mass.); dir., gen. partner various cos. Mem. community com. local ch., also mem. ch. fin. com. Served with C.E., U.S. Army, 1942-46. Mem. Assn. Advanced Life Underwriters, Am. Coll. Life Underwriters, Million Dollar Round Table, Internat. Assn. Fin. Planners. Contbr. articles on ins. and fin. planning to profl. jours. Office: Sturbridge Office Center Sturbridge MA 01566

KWASHA, H. CHARLES, cons. actuary; b. Providence, Dec. 2, 1906; s. Barned and Lena (Lisker) K.; A.B., Brown U., 1928; m. Sylvia I. Herman, Aug. 20, 1939; children—Linda Dianne, Bruce Charles, Robert Dexter. Mem. faculty Brown U., 1929, actuary Travelers Ins. Co., 1929-37; head pension dept. Marsh and McLennan, Inc., 1937-44; organized firm, cons. actuarial work H. Charles Kwasha, cons. actuary, 1944; partner Kwasha & Lipton, 1947—. Mem. Soc. Actuaries, Sigma Xi, Phi Beta Kappa. Author articles on employee retirement, employee benefit programs. Home: Westchester Country Club Apt 615 Rye NY 10580 Office: 429 Sylvan Ave Englewood Cliffs NJ 07632

KWIT, KENNETH JEREMY, lawyer, consumer products co. exec.; b. N.Y.C., Apr. 18, 1935; s. Morris Troy and Audrey Mabel (Baxter) K.; B.A. in Econs. with distinction, Cornell U., 1956; LL.B., Columbia U., 1959; children—Keith Ethan, Jeffrey Daniel, Alexander Baxter. Admitted to N.Y. State bar, 1959, since practiced in N.Y.C.; asso. firm Simpson, Thacher & Bartlett, N.Y.C., 1960-64; founder, partner firm Roth, Carlson, Kwit & Spengler, N.Y.C., 1964-72; v.p. corp. affairs and legal, gen. counsel, sec. Norton Simon, Inc., N.Y.C., 1972-75; chmn. bd., pres., chief exec. officer Sonoma Vineyards, Inc., Windsor, Calif., 1975—; dir. Jamesway Corp. Mem. Am., N.Y. State bar assns., Assn. Bar City N.Y. Editor: Columbia Law Rev., 1959. Contbr. articles to profl. jours. Home: 1950 W Dry Creek Rd Healdsburg CA 95448 Office: Sonoma Vineyards Windsor CA 95492

KWON, JOON TAEK, chemist; b. Kimpo, Korea, Mar. 10, 1935; came to U.S., 1955, naturalized, 1975; s. Young Tae and Byoung Soon (Kim) K.; student Seoul Nat. U., 1953-55; B.S., U. Ill., 1957; M.S., Cornell U., 1959, Ph.D., 1962; m. Moon Ja You, Aug. 15, 1964; children—Howard Albert, Daphne Elsa. Postdoctoral teaching fellow U. B.C. (Can.), Vancouver, 1962-64, instr. II, 1964-65; asso. research chemist Chemcell Ltd., Edmonton, Alta., Can., 1965-66, research chemist, 1966-67; sr. research chemist Celanese Corp., Summit, N.J., 1967-70; sr. research chemist Lummus Co., Bloomfield, N.J., 1970-78, prin. research chemist, 1978—. NRC Can. grantee, 1964-65; grantee-in-aid, 1965-67. Mem. Am. Chem. Soc., Korean Chem. Soc., Chem. Soc. London, Catalysis Soc. N.Y., N. Am. Thermal Analysis Soc., Illini Alumni Assn., Cornell U. Alumni Assn. Contbr. articles to profl. jours.; patentee in field. Home: 142 Derby Dr Freehold Township NJ 07728 Office: 1515 Broad St Bloomfield NJ 07003

KYLE, ANDREW CROCKETT, III, instrument co. exec.; b. Eagle Mountain Lake, Tex., Nov. 3, 1945; s. Andrew Crockett, Jr., and Betty K.; B.S.E.E. cum laude (H.A. Lott scholar), U. Tex., Austin, 1968; engring. fellow, U. Tex., Houston, 1968-69; m. Regina Anne Walker, Apr. 26, 1975; children—Andrew Crockett IV, Tricia Anne. Design engr. Paragon Systems, 1969; electronics design engr. Baylor U. Coll. Medicine, 1969-74; chief engr. Life-Tech Instruments, Houston, 1974—, v.p., 1977—, also dir. Mem. Urodynamics Soc. Am., Tau Beta Pi, Eta Kappa Nu, Phi Eta Sigma. Designer electronic med. instruments. Office: PO Box 36221 Houston TX 77036

KYLE, CORINNE SILVERMAN, mgmt. cons.; b. N.Y.C., Jan. 4, 1930; d. Nathan and Janno (Harra) Silverman; B.A., Bennington Coll., 1950; M.A., Harvard U., 1953; m. Alec Kyle, Aug. 29, 1959 (div. Feb. 1969); children—Joshua, Perry (dec.), Julia. Asso. editor Inter-Univ. Case Program, N.Y.C., 1956-60; co-founder, chief editor Financial Index, N.Y.C., 1960-63; research analyst McKinsey & Co., N.Y.C., 1963-64; sr. research asso. Mktg. Sci. Inst., Phila., 1964-67; founding partner Phila. Group, 1967-70; sr. asso. Govt. Studies and Systems, Phila., 1970-72, cons. program planning and control, Phila., 1972—, sr. asso. Periodical Studies Service, 1978—; dir. Verbena Corp., N.Y.C. Mem. adv. council to 8th Dist. city councilman, Phila., 1971—; mem. 22d Ward Democratic Exec. Com., 1971-78, State Dem. Com., 1974-76; mem. Pa. Gov.'s Council on Nutrition, 1974-76; v.p. Miquon Upper Sch. Bd., Phila., 1977—. Mem. Am. Polit. Sci. Assn. Contbr. numerous articles to profl. publs. Home: 14 Hamilton Ave Princeton NJ 08540

KYLE, DUDLEY NORMAN, elec. engr.; b. Richmond, Ind., Dec. 7, 1926; s. William Jennings and Fayetta (Stevens) K.; B.S. Ind. Inst. Tech., 1949; M.S. in Elec. Engring., U.S. Naval Postgrad. Sch., 1959; diploma Indsl. Coll. Armed Forces, 1966; m. Helen Richardson, June 18, 1952; children—John, William, Michael. Engr., Lockheed Aircraft Co., Mariette, Ga., 1954-55; radar engr. Emerson Electric Co., St. Louis, 1955; sect. mgr. Cumpter Scis. Corp., Arlington, Va., 1977; sr. scientist Calculon Inc., Arlington, Va., 1979—. Pres. bd. dirs. Stockbridge Community Assn. Served to lt. col. USMC, 1945-46, 50-53, 55-72. Decorated Bronze Star with combat V, Meritorious Service medal (2), Navy Achievement medal. Mem. Armed Forces Communications and Electronics Assn., Marine Corps Assn., U.S. Naval Inst., Am. Def. Assn. Club: Army-Navy Country. Home: 9334 Tovito Dr Fairfax VA 22031 Office: 1501 Wilsen Blvd Arlington VA 22209

KYLE, EARLE FLEETWOOD, JR., pub. co. exec.; b. Mpls., Nov. 17, 1938; s. Earle Fleetwood and Mary Edith (James) K.; B.S., U. Minn., 1961; children—Earle F. (dec.), Kimberly Marie, Earle F., Lance William. Electronic design cons., 1961-63; sr. electronic design engr. Honeywell Aerospace div. Apollo Flight Systems, Mpls., 1963-67; mgr. advanced program devel. Litton Systems, Inc., Mpls., 1967-71; producer ednl. video prodns. Sta. KTCA-TV, Inc., St. Paul, 1968-71; electro-optics cons. North Star Research and Devel. Inst., Mpls., 1970-71; corp. advanced planning cons. new bus. ventures div. 3M Co., St. Paul, 1971-73; co-founder Minds for Progress, Inc., Mpls., 1972, bd. dirs., 1972—, pres., 1974; program mgr., sr. physicist Central Research div. 3M Co., St. Paul, 1973-77; v.p. Minn. Sentinel Pub. Co., Twin Cities Courier, Mpls., 1975—; dir. applied systems div. Carnegie-Mellon Inst. Research, Pitts., 1977-80; mgr. advanced systems devel. Xerox Corp., Rochester, 1980—; bd. dirs. Datamart, Inc., Atlanta, 1978—. Mem. AAAS, Am. Inst. Physics, Am. Ordnance Assn., Bioelectromagnetics Assn., IEEE, Minn. Newspaper Assn., Optical Soc. Am., Soc. Info. Display. Clubs: Mpls. Monitors, Harvard Efficacy Assos., Minn. Press. Author: To Shape the Future, 1975; contbr. articles to profl. jours. Office: Minn Sentinel Pub Co 84 S 6th St Suite 501 Minneapolis MN 55402 and Xerox Corp Joseph C Wilson Center of Technology Bldg 129 Webster NY 14580

KYLE, ROBERT TOURVILLE, bus. cons.; b. Deadwood, S.D., Jan. 15, 1910; s. Robert Doughty and Mellanie Irene (DeTourville) K.; B.E, Johns Hopkins U., 1931; M.B.A., Northeastern U., 1965; m. Colette Hart, May 29, 1937; 1 son, Robert Hart. Gas engr. Iroquois Gas Corp., Buffalo, 1934-46; br. mgr. Gen. Controls Co., Cleve., 1946-48; v.p., gen. mgr. Gas Machinery Co., Cleve., 1948-59; sr. cons. Commonwealth Services Co., N.Y.C., 1959-61; v.p. Bay State Gas Co., Boston, 1961-74; pres. Kyle Assos. Inc., San Diego, 1974—; tchr. energy; dir. Gas Machinery Co. Pres., Bernardo Home Owners Corp., San Diego, 1978; bd. dirs., v.p. Center Continuing Edn., San Diego, 1979-80; mem. town council, chmn. public services commn. Town of Rancho Bernardo, 1980. Recipient Disting. Community Service award Rancho Bernardo Town Council, 1975; named to Hall of Fame of Rancho Bernardo, 1980. Mem. Am. Gas Assn. (Service award 1968), Nat. Soc. Profl. Engrs., Am. Inst. Plant Engrs., Am. Econ. Assn. Home and Office: 18024 Sencillo Dr San Diego CA 92128

KYLER, ORVILLE ROSS, engring. co. exec.; b. Shawville, Pa., Mar. 11, 1930; s. Orville Britton and Maude Ellen (Records) K.; B.S. in Elec. Engring., Ind. Inst. Tech., 1955, B.S. in Civil Engring., 1955; m. Joyce Isabel Dots, Apr. 8, 1951; children—Daniel Ross, Jennie Beth. Student instr. physics dept. Ind. Inst. Tech., Ft. Wayne, 1953-55, instr., 1955-56; sr. engr. Melpar, Inc., Falls Church, Va., 1956-58; sr. engr., design specialist Martin-Marrieta Corp., Orlando, Fla., 1958-66; project engr. Northrop Corp., Ventura (Calif.) div., 1967—, div. program mgr., 1974—, also mgr. engring. design. Served with USN, 1948-52. Mem. Am. Def. Preparedness Assn. - Anti-Submarine Warfare Div. Home: 2166 Foster Ave Ventura CA 93001 Office: 1515 Rancho Conejo Blvd Newbury Park CA 91320

KYPRIOS, EMANUEL ANTHONY, banker; b. Summit, N.J., Dec. 12, 1942; s. Anthony James and Anna (Stamation) K.; B.S. in Econs., U. Pa., 1965, M.B.A., 1968. Asst. v.p. Bankers Trust Co., N.Y.C., 1958-74, Mfrs. Hanover Trust Co., N.Y.C., Athens, 1974-79; v.p. Marine Midland Bank, N.Y., 1980—. Mem. Hellenic Am. C. of C. (dir. 1974-80, sec., chmn. program com. 1977-80). Club: Wharton (N.Y.C.). Home: 1675 York Ave New York NY 10028 Office: 140 Broadway New York NY 10015

LA BARBERA, FRANK THOMAS, retail exec.; b. Lakeland, Fla., Mar. 13, 1944; s. Frank Thomas and Florence (Patrinostro) LaB.; A.A., St. Leo Coll., 1962, B.A., 1964; m. Joyce Marie Chenel, Aug. 8, 1964; children—Frank Thomas III, Paul Andrew. Displayman, Sears, Roebuck & Co., Lakeland, 1964-69; display mgr. Montgomery Ward & Co., Lakeland, 1969-75; interior designer, sales rep. Badcock Furniture Corp., Lakeland, 1975—; fleet and leasing salesman Lakeland Ford Co.; pres. Success Technologies Ltd. Mem. Polk County Bicentennial Steering Com., 1972-76. Named Outstanding Jaycee of Yr., Plant City Jaycees, 1967, 69. Mem. Fla. (state v.p. 1973-74, regional dir. 1974-75, external v.p. 1976-77), Plant City (pres. 1972-73) Jaycees, C. of C. Clubs: Lions (3d v.p. 1976-77) (Mulberry, Fla.); Sertoma (Lakeland); Italian-American, Seminole Gun. Home: PO Box 1395 Plant City FL 33566 Office: Badcock Furniture 4955 S Florida Ave Lakeland FL 33803

LA BARGE, PAUL WILLSON, data communications wiring co. exec.; b. Pittsfield, Mass., Aug. 18, 1928; s. Henry J. and Margaret (Willson) LaB.; m. Nanette M. Passier, Nov. 12, 1949; children—Marie, Christopher, Ralph, Paul, Michelle, Renee. With tech. service NCR Corp., Dayton, Ohio, 1952-59, mgr. tech. service, 1959-68; mgmt. cons. Alexander Proudfoot Co., Chgo., 1968-69; nat. service mgr. Credit Systems Inc., Colmar, Pa., 1969-72; pres. Data Line Corp., Englewood, N.J., 1972-75; pres. Control Cable Inc., Wilmington, Del., 1975—. Served with U.S. Navy, 1946-48, 51-52. Roman Catholic. Home and office: 2106 Weatherton Dr Wilmington DE 19810

LABAT, JORGE, chem. co. exec.; b. Buenos Aires, Argentina, Jan. 10, 1926; came to U.S., 1967, naturalized, 1973; s. Emilio Antonio and Paule Louise (Vignaux) L.; Ph.D. in Chemistry, Buenos Aires U., 1952; M.B.A., Northwestern U., 1972; m. Rose Marie Roche, Dec. 2, 1953; children—Jorge P., Maria Martha, Rose Marie, Marie Giselle, Marie Yvonne. Research chemist E.R. Squibb, Argentina, 1952-56; chief chemist Lederle Co., Argentina, 1957-60; plant mgr. Searle Argentina, 1960-67; dir. sci. affairs Searle Internat., 1967-73; pres. Searle de Mex., 1974-75; v.p. mktg. Searle Chems. Inc., Chgo., 1976—. Mem. Am. Chem. Assn. Home: 2550 Walters Ave Northbrook IL 60062 Office: 4901 Searle Pkwy Skokie IL 60077

LABATE, CHARLES RAYMOND, pub. co. exec.; b. Koppel, Pa., July 4, 1938; s. Raymond Richard and Elda Marie (Nardone) L.; B.S. in Bus., Bradley U., 1960; m. Adolphine Gryzlo, Nov. 20, 1965;

children—Constance, Amanda, Lauren. Asst. plant accountant Blaw-Knox Co., East Chicago, Ind., 1961-66; corp. systems mgr. Vulcan Materials Co., Chgo., 1966-69, Bekins Van Lines Co., Hillside, Ill., 1969-70; co-founder, pres. CAL Systems & Forms, Inc., LaGrange, Ill., 1970-79; v.p. sales Allen Press, Inc., 1979-80. Bd. dirs. Jr. Achievement, East Chicago, 1963-64; treas. East Chicago council Boy Scouts Am., 1964-65. Mem. Data Processing Mgmt. Assn. (dir. Chgo. 1974-80, pres. 1978), Bus. Forms Mgmt. Assn. (treas. Chgo. 1973-74, 80-81), Nat. Bus. Forms Assn. (membership com.), Bradley U. Alumni Club, Tau Kappa Epsilon. Roman Catholic. Home: 327 Forest Rd Hinsdale IL 60521 Office: 140 N LaGrange Rd LaGrange IL 60525

LA BATTE, JEROME JOHN, power equipment co. exec.; b. St. Paul, Feb. 22, 1924; s. Jerome and Naomi (French) LaB.; B.E.E., U. Minn., 1948; postgrad. in Mgmt., Case Western Res. U., 1974; m. Frances Kronick, June 1, 1946; children—Susan, Michael, Stephanie, Vincent, Jerry, Mary, Jean, Annette. With Ideal Electric & Mfg. Co., Mansfield, Ohio, 1949-54; design engr. G-M Labs., Chgo., 1954-55; with Lear Siegler Inc., Cleve., 1955—, chief project engr., elec. machines, 1967-68, chief engr. elec. power system, 1968-71, dir. then v.p. engring., 1971, v.p. ops., 1972-79, dir. planning, 1979—. Served with U.S. Army, 1943-46. Mem. Am. Mgmt. Assn., Aerospace Council Automotive Engrs. Soc. Roman Catholic. Home: 387 Apple Hill Dr Sagamore Hills OH 44067 Office: 17600 Broadway Maple Heights OH 44137

LABER, MARIAN ROBERTA OPPENHEIM (MRS. LAWRENCE E. LABER), real estate broker; b. Hanford, Calif., Jan. 18, 1918; d. Leon and Isabelle (Estrada) Oppenheim; student San Francisco City Coll., 1966, Golden Gate Coll., 1969; m. Lawrence E. Laber, Feb. 22, 1941; children—Lawrence E., Pamela, Deborah (Mrs. Thomas McDermott), James Harrison. Telephone operator Pacific Tel. & Tel. Co., 1936-39, instr., 1940-42; mgr. office Press Wireless, Washington, 1942-43; owner Marian Lawrence, children's shop, San Francisco, 1945-48; owner, mgr. San Bruno 5-10, San Francisco, 1947-50; girl Friday, Lampley Realty, San Francisco, 1968-72, owner, real estate broker, 1972—. Active Boy Scouts Am., Girl Scouts U.S.A., Campfire Girls; pres. local PTA, 1954-55. Trustee Drew Coll. Prep. Sch. Mem. ARC, Am. Cancer Soc., San Francisco Real Estate Bd., Calif. Real Estate Assn. Roman Catholic (pres. ch. group 1950-51). Home: 2235 Laguna San Francisco CA 94122 Office: 2101 Pine St San Francisco CA 94115

LA BLANC, CHARLES WESLEY, JR., corp. exec.; b. Bayshore, L.I., N.Y., June 4, 1925; s. Charles Wesley and Anne (Dobson) LaB.; B.S., Tufts Coll., 1949; M.B.A., N.Y.U., 1962; m. Marie Dolan, Oct. 26, 1963; children—Charles Wesley III, Gregory, Suzanne. Security analyst Merrill, Lynch, Pierce, Fenner & Beane, N.Y.C., 1950-52; securities portfolio mgr. Manhattan Life Ins. Co., N.Y.C., 1952-57; asst. to pres. Magnavox Co., Ft. Wayne, Ind., 1957-60; financial relations cons. C.W. LaBlanc & Assos., N.Y.C., 1960-62; treas. Macke Co., Cheverly, Md., 1962-72, chmn. fin. com., dir., 1975—; exec. v.p., v.p. finance, sec., treas., dir. After Six Inc., Phila., 1973—, also pres. After Six subs. Bert Paley Ltd., Inc. Pres. Queens County Young Reps., 1955-57. Served with AC, USNR, 1943-46. Mem. Washington Soc. Investment Analysts, N.Y. Soc. Security Analysts, Am. Accounting Assn., Am. Soc. Ins. Mgmt., Pub. Relations Soc. Am., Nat. Assn. Bus. Economists, Nat. Investor Relations Inst., Financial Analysts Phila., Financial Execs. Inst., Financial Mgmt. Assn., Nat. Assn. Corp. Dirs. Clubs: New York University, Nat. Economists, Union League, Peale (Pa. Acad. Fine Arts). Home: 370 Aubrey Rd Wynnewood PA 19096 also 111 N Pompano Beach Blvd Pompano Beach FL 33062 Office: 2137 Market St Philadelphia PA 19103

LA BLANC, ROBERT EDMUND, utility co. exec.; b. N.Y.C., Mar. 21, 1934; s. Charles Wesley and Anne Rosilie (Dobson) La B.; B.E.E., Manhattan Coll., 1956; M.B.A., N.Y. U., 1962; OETP, Bell Telephone Labs., 1962; m. Elizabeth Anne Lammers, Dec. 29, 1962; children—Beth, Robert Edmund, Jeanne, Paul, Michelle. In various tech. and mgmt. positions with Bell System, 1956, 59-69, mktg. mgr. A.T. & T., 1967-68, long range planning engr., 1968-69; mgr. Salomon Bros., N.Y.C., 1969-73, v.p., 1973-75, partner, 1975-79; vice chmn. bd. Continental Telephone Corp., N.Y.C., 1979—; dir. M/A-Com, Storage Tech., European Am. Bank; mem. space applications bd. Nat. Engring. Council, Nat. Acad. Scis. Served to 1st lt. USAF, 1956-59. Named Wall Sts.' Leading Telecommunications Analyst, Instl. Investor Mag., 1973, 74, 75, 76, 77, 78. Fellow Fin. Analysts Fedn.; mem. Assn. Computing Machinery, Soc. Rate of Return Analysts, N.Y. Soc. Security Analysts (sr.). Republican. Roman Catholic. Club: Univ. Office: 405 Park Ave New York NY 10022

LA BONTÉ, C(LARENCE) JOSEPH, entertainment industry exec.; b. Salem, Mass., Sept. 23, 1939; s. Arthur and Alice Belle (Lecombe) LaB.; A.S. in Mech. Engring. and B.S. in Indsl. Tech., Northeastern U., 1966; M.B.A. with distinction (Baker scholar), Harvard, 1969; m. Donna Marie Chiaradonna, Aug. 2, 1959; children—Linda Jean, Joseph Michael. With H.P. Hood & Son, Boston, 1958-63; project engr., mktg. coordinator Market Forge Co., Everett, Mass., 1963-67; with ARA Services Inc., various locations, 1969—, v.p., Phila., 1971-72, pres. Western Co., Los Angeles, 1972-76, exec. v.p., Phila., 1976-79; pres. Twentieth Century Fox Film Corp., 1979—. Nat. bd. dirs. Big Bros. Am., 1970-74; vis. bd. dirs. Northeastern U.; bd. dirs. Los Angeles Philharm. Assn.; mem. Harvard Bus. Sch. Fund. Recipient Brown award Harvard Bus. Sch. Mem. Harvard Bus. Sch. Assn. (dir. So. Calif. chpt.), Husky Assos. Northeastern U. Clubs: Bankers (San Francisco); Vesper, Down Town, Phila. Country, Harvard Bus. Sch. (Phila.). Home: 1696 Rico Pl Palos Verdes Estates CA 90274 Office: PO Box 900 Beverly Hills CA 90213

LABRECQUE, RICHARD JOSEPH, compressor mfg. co. exec.; b. Lawrence, Mass., Dec. 19, 1938; s. Eugene N. and Ludivine (Roy) L.; B.S. in Elec. Engring., Tufts U., 1962; M.S. in Indsl. Adminstrn., Union Coll., Schenectady, 1970; m. Janet M. Michaud, July 16, 1960; children—David, Lisa, Susan. Vice pres., gen. mgr. Central Moloney Transformer div. Colt Industries, Inc., St. Louis, 1971-73, pres. Fairbanks Morse Pump div., Kansas City, Kans., 1974-79, pres. Quincy Compressor div. (Ill.), 1980—. Mem. Hydraulic Inst. (pres. 1979), Am. Mgmt. Assn., Compressed Air and Gas Inst. (exec. bd.). Home: Rural Route 5 Quincy IL 62301 Office: 217 Maine St Quincy IL 62301

LABRECQUE, THOMAS GOULET, banker; b. Long Branch, N.J., Sept. 17, 1938; s. Theodore Joseph and Marjorie (Uprichard) L.; B.A., Villanova U., 1960; postgrad. Am. U., 1962-64, N.Y. U., 1965; m. Sheila English Cardone, June 16, 1962; children—Thomas, Douglas, Karen, Barbara. Asst. treas. corporate adviser Chase Manhattan Bank, N.A., N.Y.C., 1966, 2d v.p., 1967, v.p., mgr. corr. bank adv. dept., 1969, mgr. customer adv. div., 1970, asso. planning sec. to corporate exec. office, 1970, sr. v.p. bank portfolio group, 1971-74, exec. v.p. portfolio and investment banking dept., also treas. Chase Manhattan Bank, 1974—, also dir.; exec. v.p., mem. mgmt. com. Chase Manhattan Corp., 1976-81, vice-chmn., chief operating officer, 1981—, also dir.; lectr. Stonier Grad. Sch. Banking, Rutgers U., 1968—, others. Mem. Twp. Bd. Elections, 1964-66; mem. transp. and commutation com. N.J. Bayshore Area, 1970—. Mem. endowment fund investment com. Villanova U., 1972—; mem. investment com. Nat. Council Chs. of Christ U.S. Served to lt. USNR, 1960-64. Roman Catholic (financial adviser 1964—). Office: 1 Chase Manhattan Plaza New York NY 10015*

LACHANCE, KEITH EDGAR, paper box co. exec.; b. Ottawa, Ont., Can., Aug. 10, 1926; s. Edgar and Winifred Marie (Fitzpatrick) L.; B.S. with honors in Chem. Engring., Queen's U., Kingston, Ont., 1947; m. Verna May McClure, Sept. 18, 1948 (dec.); m. 2d, Patricia Cleone Mercer Crawford, May 10, 1975; children—Karen Louise, Robert Keith, Kimberley Anne, David Kevin, Kenneth Neil. Various positions E.B. Eddy Co., Ottawa and Hull, Que., 1947-60; MacMillan Bloedel Ltd., Vancouver, B.C., 1960-79; gen. mgr. Nat. Paper Box div. Somerville-Belkin Industries, Vancouver, 1979—. Mem. Printing House Craftsmen (past pres. Ottawa and Vancouver, past gov. 10th dist.), TAPPI (past chmn. prodn. com. corrugated containers div.), Canadian Pulp and Paper Assn. (past chmn. fine papers com.), Assn. Profl. Engrs. Ont., Queen's U. Alumni Assn. (past pres. Vancouver br.). Progressive Conservative. Anglican. Home: 735 W 54th Ave Vancouver BC V6P 1M3 Canada Office: Box 2067 Vancouver BC V6B 3S3 Canada

LACHERMEIER, JOSEPH LEO, ins. co. exec.; b. Watertown, Minn., June 28, 1936; s. Joseph C. and Catherine (Rogers) L.; m. Hermine Heister, Feb. 20, 1960; children—Judith, Pamela, Joseph, Thomas, Patricia, Timothy. Various sales positions Washington Nat. Ins. Co., Evanston, Ill., Gt. West Life Assurance Co. Can., other ins. firms, 1959-73; state sr. gen. agt. Grange Mut. Life Nampa (Idaho), Denver, 1973—. Bd. dirs. Met. Child Dental Care Denver, 1971—; active Democratic party. Mem. Adams County (Colo.) Chamber, Adams County Com. 100, Adams County Ambassador Club, Nat., Denver assns. life underwriters, Gen. Agts. and Mgrs. Assn. Roman Catholic. Club: Rotary (pres. 1969-70) (Northglenn, Colo.). Home: 11164 Cherokee St Denver CO 80234 Office: 51 W 84 Ave Suite 330 Grange Mut Life Ins Co Denver CO 80221

LACKEY, HOLLIS RAY, JR., med. co. exec.; b. Oklahoma City, Dec. 3, 1943; s. Hollis Ray and Dorothy Ann (Thomas) L.; B.S., Central State U., 1966; m. Virginia Anderson, Mar. 22, 1941; children—Scott, Barrett. Salesman, William A. Webster Co., Oklahoma City, 1966-69, sales mgr., 1969-78; parenteral specialist Travenol Labs., Deerfield, Ill., 1978-80; dist. sales mgr. Alcon Labs., Edmond, Okla., 1972—. Mem. Am. Mgmt. Assn., Soc. Advancement Mgmt. Democrat. Methodist. Home: 2309 Brookside Dr Arlington TX 76012

LACOVARA, PASQUALE PHILIP, lawyer, editor; b. N.Y.C., Mar. 25, 1914; s. Philip and Theodora (Perillo) L.; A.B., Coll. City N.Y., 1933; J.D., Columbia, 1936; m. Elvira Mangieri, Jan. 9, 1938; children—Carole (Mrs. Robert M. Ciano), Philip A., Doreen (Mrs. Jonathan J. Rusch). Admitted to N.Y. bar, 1937; various editorial positions Trusts and Estates Mag., N.Y.C., 1936-65; sr. v.p., gen. counsel Fiduciary Trust Co. N.Y., N.Y.C., 1965-78; editor Real Property, Probate and Trust Jour., 1966-76, The Probate Lawyer, 1974—; lectr. N.Y. U. Law Sch., 1945-46, Columbia U. Law Sch., 1977. Mem. com. on trust and estate gift plans Rockefeller U. trustee Marymount Manhattan Coll., Phi Kappa Theta Found. Mem. Am. Bankers Assn. (mem. trust counsel com. 1975-76), N.Y. State Bankers Assn. (com. on estate and gift taxes 1967-78), Am. Bar Assn., Corporate Fiduciaries Assn. (sec.-treas. 1971-78, Phi Kappa Theta. Author: (with Bush and Schlesinger) The Best of Trusts and Estates, 1965; (with Joseph Trachtman) Estate Planning, 1945. Contbr. articles to profl. jours. Home: 68-61 Yellowstone Blvd Forest Hills NY 11375 Office: 2 World Trade Center New York NY 10048

LACROIX, EUGENE THOMAS, restaurant chain exec.; b. Midland, Mich., Dec. 20, 1923; s. Eugene Joseph and Emma B. (DesJardins) LaC.; B.A., Mich. State U., 1950; m. Betty Lou Saur, May 6, 1972; children by previous marriage—Gene, David, Holly, Steven, Donald, Suzanne, Mark. Salesman, Sun Life of Can., 1947-52, unit mgr., 1952-59, br. mgr., Grand Rapids, Mich., 1959-78; pres. Onion Crock, Inc., Grand Rapids, 1977—. Pres. Western Mich. br. Nat. Multiple Sclerosis Soc., 1960-66, pres. Mich. chpt., 1968, 70, trustee, 1958—. Served with U.S. Navy, 1943-45. Mem. Nat. Assn. Life Underwriters, Nat. Restaurant Assn., Mich. State U. Alumni Assn. Roman Catholic. Club: Elks. Home: 30 College St SE Apt 72 Grand Rapids MI 49503 Office: 252 Michigan St NE Grand Rapids MI 49503

LADAU, ROBERT FRANCIS, architect, planner; b. N.Y.C., Jan. 31, 1940; s. A. Ralph and Marguerite Louise (de Valois-Vignand) L.; A.B., Columbia U., 1961, B.Arch., M.Arch., 1965; m. Anne Horton, May 30, 1970. Chmn. bd. dirs., chief exec. officer Environers Inc., N.Y.C., 1964-66, dir., 1966-73; asso. Rogers, Butler & Burgun, Architects, N.Y.C., 1966-69; prin. Robert F. Ladau, AIA Architect/Planner, N.Y.C., 1969-70, pres., 1973—; partner Metcalf & Assos. Architects & Engrs., Washington and N.Y.C., also founder and partner Sir Robert Matthew, Metcalf & Partners, London and Edinburgh, 1970-73; v.p. architecture A.M. Kinney Affiliation Architects & Engrs., Cin., N.Y.C., Chgo., Denver, Los Angeles, San Juan and Basel, Switzerland, 1975-80; sr. v.p. Welton Becket Assos., Architects, N.Y.C., 1980—; lectr. on planning, design health facilities; mem. N.Y.C. Mayor's Panel Architects; mem. nat. panel Am. Arbitration Assn. Bd. fellows Frick Collection; chmn. long range planning com. bd. govs. Columbia U. Club N.Y.; mem. Bedford (N.Y.) Conservation Bd., 1975-78. Recipient Group Exhibit award Rockefeller Found., 1964; design awards Rockefeller Found., 1962, N.Y. Soc. Architects, 1966, Internat. Conf. Med. Primatology, 1974; William Kinne Fellows travelling fellow, 1965; registered architect, N.Y., N.J., Del., D.C. Mem. AIA, N.Y. Soc. Architects, N.Y. State Assn. Architects, Am. Hosp. Assn., Nat. Council Archtl. Registration Bds. (certified). Clubs: Princeton, Mashomack, Gunners. Contbr. articles to profl. jours. designer numerous office and comml., health, ednl., urban, recreational, residential and indsl. facilities. Home: Mooney Hill Rd Patterson NY 12563 Office: 321 E 44 St New York NY 10017

LADD, CONRAD MERVYN, mech. engr.; b. Lakewood, Ohio, Dec. 16, 1926; s. Warren Cheney and Mae Melissa (Deslippe) L.; B.S.M.E., U. Mich., 1949; postgrad. U. Pitts.; m. Bonnie Lou Hinrichs, June 27, 1976; children by previous marriage—Craig, Sue Ann, Patricia, Deborah. Design engr. Duquesne Light Co., Pitts., 1949-51; nuclear engr. Westinghouse Atomic Power Div., Pitts., 1951-52; cons. design, devel. Commonwealth Assos. Inc., Jackson, Mich., Consumers Power Co., Jackson, Atomic Power Devel. Assos., Detroit, 1952-59; mktg. product devel. mgr. Brush Beryllium Co., Cleve., 1959-63; utility mktg. mgr. Atomics Internat. div. Rockwell Internat., Canoga Park, Calif., 1963-74; dir. v.p. Stone & Webster, Mich., Inc., Boston, asst. mgr. mktg., Boston and Denver, 1974-76; dir., v.p., engring. sales exec. Stearns-Roger Mich. Inc., Glendale, Colo., 1976—. Bd. dirs., v.p. Aspen Townhouse Assn., 1978, Dillon Valley East (Condominium Assn., 1978—, Triskellion Inc., 1973. Served with USNR, 1945-46. Registered profl. engr. Mem. ASME (power div. exec. com.), Atomic Indsl. Forum, Pacific Coast Elec. Assn. Republican. Presbyterian. Clubs: Jonathan, Santa Monica Yacht. Patentee in field. Home: 7077 S Madison Way Littleton CO 80122 Office: Stearns-Roger Inc 4500 Cherry Creek Dr Glendale CO 80217

LADEHOFF, LEO WILLIAM, metal castings mfg. co. exec.; b. Gladbrook, Iowa, May 4, 1932; s. Wendell Leo and Lillian A. L.; B.S., U. Iowa, 1957; m. Beverly Joan Dreessen, Aug. 1, 1951; children—Debra K., Lance A. Supt. assembly ops. Square D Co., 1957-61; mfg. mgr. Federal Pacific Electric Co., 1961; v.p. ops. Avis Indsl. Corp., Detroit, 1961-67; pres. energy products group Gulf & Western Industries, Inc., Oakbrook, Ill., 1967-78; pres., chief exec. officer Dayton Malleable Inc. (Ohio), 1978—, also dir. Served with USAF, 1951-54. Mem. Soc. Automotive Engrs., Am. Foundrymen's Soc., Iron Castings Soc., Metals Research and Devel. Found., Newcomen Soc., U. Iowa Alumni Assn., Alpha Kappa Psi. Republican. Clubs: Moraine Country, Dayton Racquet. Office: 3931 S Dixie Ave Dayton OH 45439

LADEN, BEN ELLIS, economist; b. Savannah, Ga., Mar. 4, 1942; s. Bernard and Fannie Rachel (Cooper) L.; A.B. in Math., Princeton U., 1963; Ph.D. in Econs., Johns Hopkins U., 1969; m. Susan Sherman, Aug. 16, 1964; children—Francine, Jonathan, Paul. Asst. prof. econs. Ohio State U., Columbus, 1967-71; economist Fed. Res. Bd., Washington, 1971-74; v.p., chief economist T. Rowe Price Assos., Inc., Balt., 1974—; mem. research com. Investment Co. Inst. Mem. dean's profl. adv. council U. Md. Bus. Sch. Mem. Nat. Assn. Bus. Economists, Am. Econs. Assn., Balt. Econ. Soc. (chmn. bd.), Am. Fin. Assn. Contbr. articles to bus. and econ. jours.; author letter on econ. devels. Home: 3111 Rittenhouse St NW Washington DC 20015 Office: 100 E Pratt St Baltimore MD 21202

LADEN, STEVEN, investment banking exec.; b. Chgo., Apr. 28, 1935; s. Harold S. and Florence R. L.; B.S. in Mech. Engring., Cornell U., 1958; m. Lee Voigt, Jan. 27, 1963; children—Scott, Drew. Account exec. Paine Webber Jackson & Curtis, Phila., 1966-69; br. mgr. Blair & Co., Phila., 1969-70; resident br. mgr. and 1st v.p., instl. sales Drexel Burnham Lambert Inc., Phila., 1970—. Mem. council bd. trustees, mem. secondary schs. com. Cornell U. Served with USAF, 1958-59. Mem. Phila. Securities Assn., Jr. C. of C. (v.p., dir. 1961-64, named outstanding bd. mem. 1964). Clubs: Cornell (dir. 1964-67), Cornell Tower, Racquet. Home: 108 Windsor Ave Philadelphia PA 19126

LADENDORFF, EDMUND, JR., food co. exec.; b. Butte, Mont., May 29, 1925; s. Edmund and Isabel Elizabeth (Blewett) L.; B.S., U. Oreg., 1949; M.B.A., Harvard, 1951; m. Zoe Ann Windham, Sept. 1, 1956; children—Daryl Ann, Mark Edmund, Dana Lynne, David Scott, Alyson Paige. Asst. to mktg. v.p., product mgr. Congoleum Nairn, Kearny, N.J., 1951-56; cons., asso. Booz, Allen & Hamilton, mgmt. consultants, N.Y.C., 1956-63; new products coordinator, dir. coordination and diversification Thomas J. Lipton, Inc., Englewood Cliffs, N.J., 1963—, dir. corp. devel., until 1972, v.p. corp. devel., 1972-80, v.p. mktg. support and devel., 1980—. Pres. bd. trustees Mountainside Hosp. Served with USAAF, 1943-45; ETO. Mem. Am. Mgmt. Assn. (lectr. 1964—, seminar leader 1964—), Inst. Food Technologists, Assn. for Corporate Growth, Nat. Soc. Corporate Planning. Conglist. (trustee). Clubs: Harvard Business School of N.Y., Univ. (N.Y.C.); Montclair (N.J.) Golf. Home: 102 Clinton Ave Montclair NJ 07042 Office: 800 Sylvan Ave Englewood Cliffs NJ 07632

LADOULIS, CHARLES THEODORE, pathologist; b. Boston, May 29, 1938; s. Theodore and Etta L.; A.B., Harvard U., 1960; M.D., SUNY at Buffalo, 1964; m. Barbara L. Sickles, Sept. 10, 1966; children—Julia, Niki, Chris, Kathryn. Intern Buffalo Gen. Hosp., 1964-65; resident Peter Bent Brigham Hosp., Boston, 1965-70; instr. Harvard Med. Sch., Boston, 1970-71; asst. prof. U. Pitts., 1971-77, dir. photography lab., 1972-77, dir. grad. program exptl. pathology, 1972-77; asso. prof. pathology and biochemistry U. Tex. Med. Br., Galveston, 1977—, dir. pathology photography lab., 1977-78, dir. immunochemistry lab., 1977-80, dir. clin. immunopathology, 1980—; dir. New Eng. Med. Lab., Waltham, Mass., 1970. Chmn. Powers Run Civic Assn., Pitts., 1976-77. NIH spl. fellow, 1970; diplomate Am. Bd. Pathology. Mem. AAAS, Am. Assn. Pathologists, Am. Assn. Immunologists, Am. Soc. Cell Biologists, Reticuloendothelial Soc., N.Y. Acad. Scis., Houston Soc. Clin. Pathologists, Am. Soc. Clin. Pathologists. Club: Harvard. Contbr. numerous articles on membrane biochemistry, immunology to profl. publs. Office: U Tex Med Br Dept Pathology Galveston TX 77550

LADY, JACK HENRY, tile mfg. co. exec.; b. Knoxville, Tenn., Oct. 20, 1913; s. Henry F. and Harriett P. L.; student pub. schs., Knoxville; m. Geraldine Beretta, Jan. 19, 1939; children—Saundra, John, Gary. Coordinator traffic dept. Aluminum Co. Am., Alcoa, Tenn., 1941-43; with transp. dept. So. Ry. Co., Knoxville, 1935-40; purchaser-expediter Turner Constrn. Co., Oak Ridge, 1943-45; sales mgr., designer Mon-Bolt Mfg. Co., Knoxville, 1945-47; with John Beretta Tile Co., Knoxville, 1948—, sales mgr., 1950—, designer, 1976—. Served to capt. USCG Aux., 1970-72. Named Comdr. of Year, USCG Aux., 1969, 71. Mem. Am. Inst. Kitchen Dealers (certified designer). Presbyterian. Clubs: Deane Hill Country (Knoxville); Elks. Home: 817 Roderick Rd Knoxville TN 37923 Office: 2706 Sutherland Ave Knoxville TN 37919

LA FAVE, EDWARD J., JR., banker; b. Starbuck, Minn., Mar. 16, 1924; s. E. J. and Helena LaF.; B.S. in Bus. Econs., U. Minn., 1947; grad. Sr. Bank Officer's Mgmt. Seminar, Harvard U., 1966, Midwest Banking Inst., U. Minn., 1973; m. Patricia Paul, Sept. 3, 1947; children—Carol, Edward Joseph, Julie, Cathy, Paul. Pres. Citizens Bank, Morris, Minn., 1970—, Citizens Realty & Bus. Devel. Co., Inc., 1970—; pres., owner Citizens Ins. Agy., 1970—; sec., treas. LaFave Bldg. Co., Holidell, Inc., Wisconsin Dells, Wis., 1978—. Founder, past dir. Midwest Banking Inst., 1970—; dir., organizer Barnes Aastad Soil and Water Conservation Assn. founder, dir. Villa of St. Francise Nursing Home, Morris, Minn. Served with USN, 1943-45. Recipient Morris Disting. Services award U. Minn., 1978, Disting. Services award Soil Conservation Soc. Am., 1980. Mem. Am. Banker's Assn. (community banker's com. 1980—), West Central Ednl. Devel. Assn., 7th Dist. Minn. Banking Assn. Office: 600 Atlantic Ave Morris MN 56267

LAFAVE, RODNEY JAY, computer service co. exec.; b. Duluth, Minn., July 5, 1935; s. Wesley Peter and Irene Marion (Round) L.; student U. Minn., Duluth, 1954; m. Kathleen Robison, Dec. 18, 1971; children—Jeffrey, Douglas, Debra, Julie. Computer operator St. Louis County, Duluth, 1958-60, data processing mgr., 1960-66; owner, mgr. Compudata Corp., Duluth, 1966—, Compudata Computer Store, Duluth, 1979—. Dir. Duluth Portorama, 1964; founder, pres. Duluth Fight Inefficient Govt. Hiking Taxes (FIGHT) Orgn., 1976; ch. fin. chmn., 1976-77. Mem. Data Processing Mgmt. Assn. (pres. Head of Lakes 1962, 71, internat. dir. 1977—, outstanding performance awards), Duluth Jaycees (hon. life mem., v.p. 1965, 66, various awards), Duluth C. of C., Duluth Conv. and Visitors Bur. Republican. Methodist. Club: Kiwanis (pres. 1972) (Duluth). Home: 202 Hawthorne St Duluth MN 55812 Office: Compudata Corp 104 W Superior St Duluth MN 55802

LAFFERRE, BRUCE ALLEN, utility co. exec.; b. Louisville, Dec. 17, 1949; s. James Allen and Mary Juanita (Thompson) L.; B.A., U. Louisville, 1971; student U. Detroit, 1976-79; M.B.A., Mich. State U., 1981; m. Nancy Jean Ganz, June 15, 1974. Fin. and estate planner

Conn. Gen. Ins. Co., Louisville, 1971; engring. systems product rep. Bruning div. AM Internat., Louisville, 1971-73, Detroit, 1973-76; microsystems product rep. Xerox Corp., Detroit, 1976-78; micrographics systems analyst Detroit Edison Co., 1978-79, residential market planner, 1979—. Recipient Olsten award excellence in records mgmt. programs. Mem. Engring. Soc. Detroit, Nat. Micrographics Assn., Assn. M.B.A. Execs., Soc. Preservation and Encouragement of Barbershop Quartet Singing in Am. (internat. chorus champion 1969), Detroit C. of C. Republican. Clubs: Detroit Athletic, Shriners, Econ. Detroit. Home: 1867 Derby St Birmingham MI 48008 Office: Detroit Edison Co 2000 2d Ave Room 383 WCB Detroit MI 48226

LAFFERTY, CHARLES DOUGLAS JOSEPH, advt. sales co. exec.; b. Rochester, Pa., Mar. 27, 1930; s. William Charles and Kathryn (Devine) L.; B.A., U. Pitts., 1956; m. Inger A. Sorum, Nov. 20, 1967. Vice pres., mgr. sales devel. Moloney, Regan & Schmitt, N.Y.C., 1956-69; exec. v.p., dir. mktg., corp. treas. Branham Corp., N.Y.C., 1969—; sec., treas., dir. Cinema Mktg., Inc., 1979—. Served with USMC, 1948-52. Mem. Internat. Newspaper Promotion Assn. (dir.), Newspaper Research Council (founder, dir.), Internat. Newspaper Advt. Execs., So. Newspaper Pubs. Assn. Republican. Clubs: Aspetuck Valley Country (Weston, Conn.); Marco Polo (N.Y.C.). Home: 58 Redcoat Rd Westport CT 06880 Office: 733 3d Ave New York NY 10017

LAFFIN, JOHN (JACK) CHARLES, diversified mfg. co. exec.; b. Los Angeles, June 12, 1931; s. William Price and Marguerite Elsbeth (Oetting) L.; B.S., U. So. Calif., 1956; m. Rachel S. Lane, June 18, 1955; children—Suzanne, Linda, Jennifer, William. Advt. mgr. Northrop Corp., Hawthorne, Calif., 1956-60; various internat. mktg. positions N.Am. Aviation, Anaheim, Calif., 1960-68; with N.Am Rockwell and Rockwell Internat., Anaheim, 1968-70, Pitts., 1970—, dir. internat. communications, 1978—. Served with USAF, 1951-52. Guest of honor at 78th Ann. Nobel Found. Banquet, Stockholm, 1979. Mem. Internat. Advt. Assn. (sustaining bd. mem.), Assn. Nat. Advertisers, Public Relations Soc. Am., Bus. Publs. Audit Circulation (dir. 1976-78), Pitts. Advt. Club (dir. 1975-77). Republican. Club: St. Clair Country. Office: 600 Grant St Pittsburgh PA 15219

LA FLEUR, DAVID JEROME, meat packing co. exec.; b. Jefferson, S.D., July 9, 1931; s. J.C. and Marion (Bernard) LaF.; student So. State Tchrs. Coll., Brookings, S.D., 1949; m. Ruth Eilene Orr, Apr. 15, 1950; children—Colette, Kevin, Pamela, Mary, Joseph, David. Tchr. pub. schs., Jefferson, 1949-50; supt. prodn. and purchasing Armour Co., Sioux City, Iowa, 1950-63; salesman, maintenance adminstr. H.D. Laughlin Co., Ft. Worth, Tex., 1963-64; plant mgr. Iowa Beef Processors, Dakota City, Nebr., 1964-68; v.p. ops. Mo. Beef Packers, Inc., Friona, Tex., 1968-70, exec. v.p., Amarillo, Tex., 1970, pres., from 1971; pres. MBPXL Corp., 1974—; dir. Kans. Beef Industries Phila., Inc., 1974, Jay Lines, Inc., Circle E Ranch, Inc., Aspen Internat., Inc., Santa Fe Foods, Inc. Mem. Nat. Ind. Meat Packers Assn. (dir.). Roman Catholic. Office: PO Box 2519 Wichita KS 67201*

LA FLEUR, JAMES KEMBLE, mech. engr., mfg. co. exec.; b. Los Angeles, Apr. 23, 1930; s. Herbert L. and Janet (Read) L.; B.S.M.E., Calif. Inst. Tech., 1952; M.B.A., Pepperdine U., 1980; m. Helene de Crais, May 4, 1964; children—Lynn Kathleen, Michele Janet, Juliet Elizabeth. Design engr. Boeing Airplane Co., Seattle, 1952; devel. engr. AiResearch Garrett Corp., Los Angeles, 1952-56; pres. Dynamic Research Inc., Los Angeles, 1957-59; chmn. bd. LaFleur Corp., Torrance, Calif., 1960-65, Indsl. Cryogenics, Inc., Los Angeles, 1966-71, chmn. bd., chief exec. officer GTI Corp., San Diego, 1975—; cons. in field. Registered profl. engr., Calif. Mem. ASME (chmn. 1973-75, nuclear cycles com. gas turbine div. 1973-75). Clubs: Duquesne, Univ. (Pitts.); N.Y. Yacht, Soaring of Am., Ferrari; Navy League (Beverly Hills). Patentee turbomachinery and cryogenics; contbr. articles to profl. jours. Home: 4337 Talofa Ave Toluca Lake CA 91602 Office: GTI Corp 10060 Willow Creek Rd San Diego CA 92131

LA FORGE, PAUL EDWARD, constrn. co. exec.; b. Davenport, Iowa, Nov. 18, 1947; s. Paul Francis and Ellen Berniece (Treiber) LaF.; student Labette Community Coll., 1965-67; B.S. in Civil Engring., U. Kans. at Lawrence, 1970, B.S. in Bus. Adminstrn., 1970, m. Linda Joyce Miller, Aug. 24, 1968; children—Natalie Jeanette, Valerie Lynn, Paul Jason. Foreman, LaForge & Budd Constrn. Co., Inc., Parsons, Kans., 1962-67, project supt., 1970-72, corp. exec., 1972—; individual practice, Kansas City and Lawrence, Kans., 1968-70. Mem. Nat. Soc. Profl. Engrs., U. Kans. Alumni Assn. Roman Catholic. Home: PO Box 484 Parsons KS 67357 Office: 3101 Main St Parsons KS 67357

LAGER, RICHARD WILLARD, health care exec.; b. Chgo., Apr. 1, 1948; s. Eric Willard and Marilyn (Nicholson) L.; B.S., No. Ill. U., 1970; m. Wanda Louise Dickie, July 13, 1974; children—Mary Amoret, Brian Richard. Inventory specialist Modern Drop Forge Co., Blue Island, Ill., 1968-69; with savs. dept. Drovers Nat. Bank, Chgo., 1969-70; with Baxter Travenol Labs., Deerfield, Ill., 1974—, operation planning mgr., prodn. scheduling, 1976—. Served with USAF, 1970-74. Republican. Presbyterian. Home: 1512 Silver Strand St Palatine IL 60067 Office: One Baxter Pkwy Deerfield IL 60015

LAGIN, MARTIN HARRY, finance co. exec.; b. N.Y.C., Jan. 12, 1925; s. Aaron Harry and Sophie (Malamud) L.; B.A., Washington Sq. Coll., N.Y. U., 1948; m. Rhoda Serklew, Jan. 21, 1950; children—Eric Lee, Steven Robert. Owner, Sunset Mobile Homes, Paramount and Harbor City, Calif., 1956—; pres. Mobilehome Investment Co., Inc., Paramount, 1958—; registered fin. investment adviser, 1975—. Mem. Los Angeles County Art Mus., Palm Springs Art Mus., Phoenix Art Mus., Glenbow Mus., Calgary, Alta., Can. Served with inf. U.S. Army, 1943-45. Decorated Purple Heart. Mem. Mobile Home Dealers Assn. (dir.). Home: 1108 Laurel Way Beverly Hills CA 90210 Office: 15100 Paramount Blvd Paramount CA 90723

LA HOWCHIC, NICHOLAS JOHN, food co. ofcl.; b. N.Y.C., Apr. 11, 1947; s. Nicholas and Mary Ellen (Dunne) La H.; student Marquette U., 1964-66; B.S. in Acctg., Fairleigh Dickinson U., 1970; M.B.A., Pace U., 1980. Acct. Okonite Cable Corp., Passaic, N.J., 1966-68; cost analyst Philips Broadcast Equip. Corp., Paramus, N.J., 1968-69; corporate acct. Thomas J. Lipton, Inc., Englewood Cliffs, N.J., 1969-70, fin. systems analyst, 1970-72, mgr. cash mgmt., 1972-73, mgr. hdqrs. distbn. services, 1974-76, mgr. distbn. and sales services, 1976-77, mgr. ops. planning, 1977-79; gen. mgr. McGraw Hill Book Co., N.Y.C., 1979-81; dir. inventory mgmt. Standard Brands Inc., N.Y.C., 1981—; cons. in field. Mem. Nat. Assn. Accts., Am. Mgmt. Assn., Am. Prodn. and Inventory Control Soc. (dir. 1979-80), Nat. Council Phys. Distbn. Mgmt., Internat. Materials Mgmt. Soc. Home: 131 E 29 St New York NY 10016 Office: 625 Madison Ave New York NY 10022

LAIDLAW, DOUGLAS MCNEILL, printing co. exec.; b. Santa Monica, Calif., Feb. 19, 1922; s. Harold Beverly and Helen Roltair (McNeill) L.; B.S., U. Calif., Los Angeles, 1947; m. Jean Metcalf Monroe, Jan. 27, 1952; children—Susan Elizabeth Laidlaw Denniston, Douglas McNeill, Bruce William. With H.B. Laidlaw Co., Los Angeles, 1947-50; sec.-treas. Los Angeles Lithograph Co., Inc., 1950-67, pres., 1967-71; pres. Interweb, Los Angeles, 1971-80, also dir.; chmn., pres. Creative Web Systems, Inglewood, Calif., 1980—; dir. Metroweb, Erlanger, Ky. Served with AUS, 1943-46. Decorated Bronze Star. Mem. Graphic Arts Tech. Found. (dir.), Nat. Edn. Council Graphic Arts (dir.), Soc. Tech. Writers and Pubs. (pres. 1962), Nat. Assn. Printers and Lithographers (dir.), Printing Industry Am. (dir., pres. web-offset sect. 1973), Printing Industries Assn. So. Calif. (pres., Man of Year award 1975), Soderstrom Soc., Delta Kappa Epsilon. Republican. Episcopalian. Home: 868 Norman Pl Los Angeles CA 90049 Office: 371 N Oak St Inglewood CA 90302

LAIN, CECIL, fin. services co. exec.; b. Johannesburg, S. Africa, Apr. 18, 1939; s. Jack and Minnie (Neifeld) L.; B.Commerce, U. Witwatersrand, 1960; m. Leone Hilary Meyers, Mar. 7, 1968; children—Jacqueline Frances, Trevor Norman, Edward Lewis. Past dir. FPS Ltd., Johannesburg; mng. exec. Integrated Resources Equity Corp., Dallas, 1978—. Mem. Dallas Life Underwriters Assn. Club: Brookhaven Country (Dallas). Home: 7024 Townbluff Dr Dallas TX 75248 Office: Suite 840 Hartford Bldg Dallas TX 75201

LAINO, KENNETH F., personnel and mgmt. cons.; b. Trenton, N.J., Feb. 3, 1936; s. Daniel and Elizabeth Turner (Gable) L.; B.S. in Bus. Adminstrn., N.J. Sch. Bus., 1969; m. Betty Ann Ricci, Nov. 23, 1968; children—Kenneth Paul, Kathleen Ann. Supt. aircraft maintenance U.S. Dept. Def., Atlantic City, 1955-67; mgr. mfg. Teledyne Electronics div. Teledyne, Inc., Burlington, N.J., 1967-70; installation mgr. Alexander Proudfoot Co., Chgo., 1970-73; systems dir., v.p. Retention Systems, Aniston, Ala. and Egg Harbor, N.J., 1973-75, pres., 1975—. Served with USAF, 1968. Mem. Am. Mgmt. Assn., Southeastern Poultry and Egg Assn. Home: RFD 1 Egg Harbor NJ 08215 Office: 2500 White Horse Pike PO Box 107 Egg Harbor NJ 08215

LAIRD, STEWART WILSON, med. center ofcl.; b. Anoka, Minn., May 6, 1937; s. Harry Cecil and Clementine Marie (Donais) L.; B.A., St. John's U., 1959; M.H.A., U. Minn., 1965; m. Kathleen Mary Sullivan, Nov. 25, 1961; children—Michael, Mary, Peter, Christopher, Thomas, Ann. Asst. adminstr. St. Mary's Hosp., Wausau, Wis., 1965-68, asso. adminstr., 1968-70; adminstr. Wausau (Wis.) Hosp. South, 1970-71, adminstr. Wausau Hosp., 1971-74; pres., chief exec. officer St. Francis Med. Center, LaCrosse, Wis., 1974—; dir. Blue Cross-Blue Shield United of Wis. Preceptor, U. Minn. and Xavier U.; bd. dirs. Chileda Inst. for Multi-Handicapped, Western Wis. Health Systems Agy., Shared Health Services; chmn. Wis. Health Facilities Authority. Served to capt. U.S. Army, 1959-63. Fellow Am. Coll. Hosp. Adminstrs.; mem. Cath. Health Assn. of U.S. (dir.), Cath. Hosp. Assn. Wis. (past pres.), Western Wis. Hosp. Dist. Assn. (past pres.), Wis. Public Health Assn. Republican. Roman Catholic. Clubs: Rotary, Elks, Sierra. Home: 600 S 28th St LaCrosse WI 54601 Office: 700 S West Ave LaCrosse WI 54601

LAIRD, WALTER JONES, JR., brokerage exec.; b. Phila., June 15, 1926; s. Walter Jones and Rebecca Anne (Sedberry) L.; B.S., Princeton, 1948; M.S., Mass. Inst. Tech., 1950; m. Antonia Valerie Bissell, Nov. 24, 1951; children—David E., W. Ian, Philip L., Walter Jones III, Emily B., Stephen P. Marketing mgr. E.I. duPont de Nemours & Co., Inc., Wilmington, Del., 1950-68; exec. v.p., dir. Laird, Bissell & Meeds, Inc., brokerage, Wilmington, 1968-73; v.p. Dean Witter Reynolds, Inc., Wilmington, 1973—; dir. Del. Trust Co. Treas., Tower Hill Sch.; v.p., exec. com. Henry Francis duPont Winterthur Mus.; chmn. investment com. Catholic Diocese Del.; trustee, exec. com. St. Andrews Sch. Served with USNR, 1944-46. Mem. Financial Analysts Soc., Soc. Colonial Wars, Friends of Winterthur (treas.), Chevaliers du Tastevin. Episcopalian. Clubs: Princeton of N.Y., Wilmington, Wilmington Country, Vicmead Hunt. Home: 1103 Barley Mill Rd Wilmington DE 19807 Office: PO Box 749 Wilmington DE 19899

LAISERIN, JERRY ALBERT, devel. cons.; b. Atlanta, Oct. 19, 1944; s. Maurice and Dorothy (Kaufman) L.; B.A., Brandeis U., 1966; M.Arch., Princeton U., 1971; M.B.A., N.Y. U., 1974; children—Rachel Beth, Aaron Jacob. Pres., Exponential Systems Corp., Princeton Junction, N.J., 1973—.

LAJOIE, JAMES FRANCIS, II, ins. co. exec.; b. Pittsfield, Mass., Oct. 30, 1945; s. James Francis and Geraldine Annette (Spring) LaJ.; student Berkshire Community Coll., 1963-64, Fairleigh Dickenson U., 1967, Mgmt. Sch., Life Ins. Mgmt. Assn., 1968; m. Sara Jean Nickum, Aug. 20, 1977; children—Christine Frances, Michelle Jane, Corrine Jean. Mgr. new agt. devel. Berkshire Life Ins. Co., Pittsfield, 1967-73, benefit plans cons., 1973-75; dir. spl. markets Am. Amicable Life Ins. Co., Waco, Tex., 1975-77; dir. pensions, domestic and internat. pension plans Am. Internat. Group, N.Y.C., 1977—; instr. Life Underwriters Tng. Council, 1971—. Bd. dirs. Pittsfield YMCA, 1967-74, Camp Fire Girls, 1968-74, Nat. council YMCA, 1973-74; lector St. John's Ch.; pres. Men's Club, YMCA, 1967-71. Mem. Life Office Mgmt. Assn. (group pension adminstrn. com. II, ops. and systems council), Indsl. Mgmt. Club (dir. 1969-73), Nat. Ski Patrol. Democrat. Clubs: Alford Brock (sec.-treas. 1971-75), Lions (pres. Pittsfield 1966-74, zone chmn. 1973). Home: 21 Treat Ave Stamford CT 06906 Office: 70 Pine St New York NY 10005

LAJOIE, RICHARD JOHN, JR., controller; b. Kansas City, Mo., Apr. 10, 1947; s. Richard John and Julia Hortense (Bush) L.; B.B.A. in Fin., U. Notre Dame, 1969; M.B.A. in Accounting, Xavier U., 1972; m. Mary Alice Herod, Aug. 21, 1971; children—Richard John, Mary Eleanor. Staff accountant Peat, Marwick, Mitchell & Co., Washington, 1972-75, sr. accountant, Cin., 1975-77; mgr. internal audit Clopay Corp., Cin., 1977-80, controller plastic products div., 1980—. Bd. dirs. Clopay Employees Fed. Credit Union, 1979—, pres., 1980. vol. United Appeal, Kindervelt. Served with inf. AUS, 1969-71. Decorated Bronze Star with 3 oak leaf clusters, Army Commendation medal with oak leaf cluster, Purple Heart, Air medal; C.P.A., Ohio. Mem. Am. Inst. C.P.A.'s, Ohio Soc. C.P.A.'s, Inst. Internal Auditors (bd. govs. 1980—). Roman Catholic. Clubs: Notre Dame, Queen City Racquet. Editor Cin. Internal Auditor. Home: 2122 Winchester Pl Fairfield OH 45014 Office: Clopay Sq Cincinnati OH 45214

LAKE, CHARLES WILLIAM, JR., printing co. exec.; b. LaPorte, Ind., June 21, 1918; s. Charles William and Jessie Mae (Lyon) L.; student U. Wis., 1936-37; B.S., Cornell U., 1941; M.B.A., U. Chgo., 1949; m. Louise Safford Sprague, July 4, 1946; children—Charles William III, Elizabeth Sprague. With R.R. Donnelley & Sons Co., Chgo., 1946—, successively asst. to treas., mgr. mgmt. studies, dir. indsl. engring., 1947-56, dir. engring. research and devel., 1956-58, dir. operating, 1958-59, dir. Chgo. mfg. div., 1959-63, dir. sales div., 1963-64, v.p. co., 1953-63, sr. v.p., 1963-64, pres., 1964—, chmn. bd., 1975—, also dir.; dir. No. Trust Co., Inland Steel Co., Am. Hosp. Supply Corp., C.B.I. Industries. Mem. Adv. Com. for Arthritis in Industry; sr. mem. The Conf. Bd.; mem. Chgo. Com. Mem. vis. com. Div. Sch., Grad. Sch. Bus. and Div. Phys. Scis., also citizens bd. U. Chgo.; trustee emeritus, mem. emeritus engring. council Cornell U.; trustee Mus. Sci. and Industry; bd. dirs. Protestant Found. Greater Chgo., John Crerar Library; mem. Northwestern U. Assos. Served from 2d lt. to capt., ordnance, AUS, 1941-46. Mem. Am. Inst. Indsl. Engrs., Tau Beta Pi, Beta Gamma Sigma. Conglist. Mason. Clubs: University, Economic, Chicago Sunday Evening (trustee), Comml., Chicago, Cornell (Chgo.); Hinsdale Golf; Old Elm Golf, Sky, Hemisphere (N.Y.C.); Coleman Lake (Wis.); Blind Brook (N.Y.) Golf; Royal Poinciana Golf, Hole in the Wall Golf (Naples, Fla.). Home: 222 E 4th St Hinsdale IL 60521 Office: 2223 Dr Martin Luther King Jr Dr Chicago IL 60616

LAKE, DOUGLAS EDWARD, educator; b. Vermontville, Mich., Mar. 1, 1916; s. Glenn Alfred and Beulah Edna (Smith) L.; B.S. in Chem. Engring., Mich. State U., 1938, M.S., 1939; m. Gladys Ione Spotts, Aug. 8, 1940; children—Norman E., Kenneth R., Marjorie E. Prodn. engr. Dow Chem. Co., Midland, Mich., 1939-63, mgr. fin. and bus. service, 1972-79, mgr. planning services, 1979-80; pres., gen. mgr. Ethyl-Dow Chem. Co., 1965-70; tchr. mgmt. systems Northwood Inst., Midland, 1974, adj. prof. bus. and mktg., 1980—. Chmn., Zoning Bd. Appeals, Midland, 1976-79. Registered profl. engr., Mich. Mem. Am. Chem. Soc., Am. Inst. Chem. Engrs. Republican. Methodist. Clubs: Masons; Kiwanis. Patentee in field. Home: 3802 Devonshire St Midland MI 48640

LAKE, MENO TRUMAN, ins. co. exec.; b. Esterhazy, Sask., Can., Aug. 19, 1919; s. Truman Thomas and Marguerite Elizabeth (White) L.; B.Comm., U. Man., 1940; m. Jean Ivy Hancock, Sept. 6, 1940; children—Bruce Meno, William Truman, Ralph Robert, Rex, Nora. With Occidental Life Ins. Co. Calif., Los Angeles, 1940-42, 46—, actuarial student, underwriter, controller's dept., supr. research actuarial dept., asst. actuary, asso. actuary, chief actuary, 1954—, pres., chief adminstrv. officer, 1971-77, pres., chief exec. officer, 1977—, also dir.; prin. cost accountant Basic Magnesium Co., Las Vegas, 1942-44; dir. Am. Life Ins. Co. N.Y., Transam. Ins. Co., Transam. Investment Mgmt. Co., Countrywide Life Ins. Co., Transam. Ins. Corp., Occidental Life Ins. Co. Cal., Transamerica Life Ins. & Annuity Co. Served with USNR, 1944-46. Fellow Soc. Actuaries; mem. Actuarial Club Pacific States (past pres.), Los Angeles Actuarial Club (past pres.). Methodist. Club: California. Office: Occidental Center Los Angeles CA 90015*

LAKE, RICHARD HARRINGTON, internat. trade and pub. affairs cons.; b. Carlisle, Pa., Oct. 15, 1919; s. William Harrington and Diana C. (Strube) L.; grad. Strategic Intelligence Sch., 1951, Command and Gen. Staff Coll., 1954; B.S. in Commerce, Roosevelt U., 1958, M.A. in Econs. and Bus., 1961; Fgn. Service Inst., 1965, Indsl. Coll. Armed Forces, 1972; m. Blair Moody, July 17, 1954; children—Richard Moody, Mary Anne (dec.), William Moody, Sara Blair. Free-lance writer, 1937-38; underwriter's asst. Guardian Life Ins. Co., 1938-40; cons. for mktg. fgn. motion pictures in U.S., 1940; commd. 2d lt. U.S. Army, 1940, lt. col., 1956; comdr. inf. and mil. police units in U.S. and overseas, 1941-46; chief agt. Criminal Investigations Div., Europe, 1947; chief liaison to USSR forces, Berlin, Germany, 1947-48; pub. relations and protocol officer Mil. Gov., High Commr. for Germany, 1948-50; staff officer 2d Army Hdqrs., Ft. Meade, Md., 5th Army Hdqrs., Chgo., 1951-53; sr. adviser to Royal Thai Army, Bangkok, Thailand, 1954-56; dir. indsl. security, enforcement, criminal investigations U.S. Army, 1957-61; faculty Roosevelt U. Coll. Bus. Adminstrn., Chgo. 1958-60; cons. internat. affairs Dept. Commerce, Washington, 1961, alternate for sec. commerce to 1st White House Food for Peace Conf., 1961, exec. sec. Fgn.-Trade Zones Bd. of U.S., 1961-69, dir. fgn.-trade zones staff Bur. Internat. Bus. Operations, 1961-62, Bur. Internat. Commerce, 1963-69; owner Richard H. Lake Assos., 1970—; mem. Bangkok-Sattahip Port Study Group, Thailand, 1972; chief econ. devel. mission UN Indsl. Devel. Orgn., Belize, Brit. Honduras, 1973, Port-of-Spain, Trinidad and Tobago, 1974; asso. Buckley Engring., Inc., Port-au-Prince, Haiti, 1980—. Mem. Res. Officers Assn., Ret. Officers Assn., D.A.V., Ill. Assn. Chiefs of Police, Marquis Biog. Library Soc., Policia Secreta Nacional de Panama (hon.). Episcopalian. Contbr. articles to govt. and bus. publs. Address: PO Box 385 Annandale VA 22003

LAKE, VICTOR HUGO, mfg. co. exec.; b. Quincy, Mass., Nov. 11, 1919; s. Victor Hugo and Edna Beatrice (Blott) L.; student Lawrence Inst. Tech., 1939-42, U. Maine, 1943; m. Jeannette Elzena Stewart, Apr. 26, 1942; children—Victor Stewart, Valerie Jean; m. 2d, Jacqueline Rose Davis, July 4, 1975. Asst. supt. Taylor Winfield Corp., Detroit, 1938-43; prodn. control mgr. Fed. Machine & Welder Co., Warren, Ohio, 1944-49; with Am. Welding & Mfg. Co., Warren, 1949—, mgr. materials, 1969—. Served with AUS, 1943-44. Mem. Am. Soc. Metals, Trumbull County Indsl. Mgmt. Assn. (pres. 1972-73). Republican. Methodist. Home: 1675 Parkman Rd NW Warren OH 44485 Office: American Welding and Mfg Co 190 Dietz Rd Warren OH 44482

LAKE, YVONNE ELAINE, mgmt. cons.; b. Kingston, Jamaica, W.I., Jan. 10, 1940; came to U.S., 1978; d. James MacDonald and Ethel Eunice (Beecher) L.; B.A. with honors, U. London, 1962; diploma in edn. U. W.I., 1963, diploma in mgmt., 1973. With Ont. Med. Services, Toronto, Can., 1965-66; adminstrv. officer Ministry Labor and Nat. Ins., Kingston, Jamaica, 1966-67; mgmt. analyst O & M Div., Govt. Jamaica, 1967-70, Peat, Marwick, Mitchell & Co., Kingston, 1970-72; asso. Lambie & Co., Kingston, 1973-76; prin. Yvonne Lake & Asso., Kingston, 1976-78; staff exec. mgmt. services George S. May Internat. Co., Park Ridge, Ill., 1978—, mgmt. cons., staff exec. mgmt. services, 1978—; asso. Lambie & Co., Mgmt. Cons., Kingston, 19—; prin. Yvonne Lake & Assos., Kingston, 1976-78. Jamaica Centenary scholar for girls, 1958. Mem. Am. Soc. Profl. and Exec. Women, Nat. Assn. Female Execs. Club: Playboy.

LAKES, DAVID VERNON, banker; b. Brookville, Ind., Apr. 15, 1939; s. Harold and Hattie Mae (Price) L.; B.S., Ball State U., 1969; M.B.A., Xavier U., 1976; m. Carolyn Sue Thompson, June 1, 1968; children—Stephanie Ann, Todd Wayne. Asst. mgr. Franklin Fin. Co., 1962-63; agt. Met. Life Ins. Co., 1963-64; asst. cashier Franklin County Nat. Bank, Brookville, Ind., 1964-67; v.p. Fifth Third Bank, Cin., 1969-78; v.p. BancOhio Nat. Bank, 1978-79, pres. Northeastern region, Akron, 1979—. Mem. fund raising com. WCET TV, Cin.; corp. fund drive U. Cin. Served with USMC, 1958-62. Mem. Am. Inst. Banking, Am. Bankers Assn., Ohio Bankers Assn., Newcomen Soc., Cin. C. of C. (chmn. membership com.), Bankers Club Cin. Methodist. Club: Cascade. Office: 1 Cascade Plaza Akron OH 44308

LALONDE, WILLIAM SALEM, III, natural gas distbn. co. exec.; b. East Orange, N.J., Dec. 24, 1932; s. William Salem and Marion (Howard) LaL.; B.S. in Chem. Engring., Cornell U., 1955, M.B.A., 1956; m. Susanne R. Stewart, June 25, 1960; children—Bruce G., Scott W., Todd J. With Public Service Electric and Gas Co., N.J., 1956-68, dist. supt. until 1968; chief engr., asst. v.p. ops. Elizabethtown Gas Co., 1968-74, v.p. rates, gas supply and planning, 1974-76, v.p. ops. and engring. services, 1976-78; pres., chief exec. officer The Gas Service Co., Kansas City, Mo., 1978—, also dir. Bd. dirs. Greater Kansas City United Way, Heart of America council Boy Scouts Am.; bd. regents Rockhurst Coll. Fellow ASCE; mem. Nat. Soc. Profl. Engrs., Kans. Soc. Engrs., Cornell Soc. Engring. (past pres. N.J. sect.), Am. Gas Assn., Kans. Assn. Commerce and Industry (dir.). Episcopalian. Club: Kansas City. Office: 2460 Pershing Rd Kansas City MO 64108

LAM, DAVID KITPING, semicondr. equipment co. exec.; b. Kwangtung, China, Feb. 10, 1943; came to U.S., 1967; s. I-Pin and Heng-Kwan (Yim) L.; B.A.Sc., U. Toronto, 1967; M.S., M.I.T., 1970, Sc.D. (Halcon Internat. fellow), 1973; m. Eppie Cheuk-Fong Chung, Aug. 1, 1967; children—David Jekit, Brian Jesun. Mem. tech. staff semicondr. research and devel. lab. Tex. Instruments, Inc., Dallas, 1974; asso. scientist Joseph C. Wilson Center Tech., Xerox Corp., Webster, N.Y., 1975-76; sr. mem. tech. staff labs. Hewlett-Packard Co., Palo Alto, Calif., 1976-79; pres. Lam Research Corp., Santa Clara, Calif., 1979—; cons. semicondr. processing tech. Mem. AAAS, IEEE, Am. Chem. Soc., Am. Inst. Chem. Engrs., Electrochem. Soc., Am. Vacuum Soc., N.Y. Acad. Sci., Sigma Xi. Contbr. articles to sci. and tech. jours.

LA MARCA, ANTHONY JOSEPH, bank exec.; b. S.I., N.Y., Feb. 6, 1934; s. Anthony G. and Carrie (Scaramuzzo) La M.; B.S. in Accounting, S.I. Community Coll., 1965; m. Barbara Helen Alexander, Dec. 10, 1955; children—Kevin, Robert, Anthony, Darren. Asst. cashier, ops. and lending officer Bank of Am., N.Y.C., 1952-68; asst. v.p., head ops. and bus. dev. City Nat. Bank, Detroit, 1968-70; head ops. and personnel Harris Bank Internat. Corp., N.Y.C., 1970-72; v.p., head internat. ops. Franklin Nat. Bank, N.Y.C., 1972-74; head adminstrn. ops. and personnel Rainier Internat. Bank, N.Y.C., 1974-75, exec. v.p., mgr. 1976-78, also dir.; sr. v.p. Global Union Bank, N.Y.C., 1978—. Treas. Kinnelon County com.; trustee-treas. Kinnelon Library Bd.; councilman, Kinnelon Borough, 1977—, fin. chmn., 1978; pres. Kinnelon Republican Club, 1975. Served in USNG, 1952-60. Mem. Com. on Internat. Banking (chmn. 1976-77), Nat. Council Com. Internat. Banks (chmn. 1978), Nat. Council on Internat. Trade Documentation, Bankers Assn. on Fgn. Trade, Am. Inst. Banking. Roman Catholic. Clubs: Downtown Athletic, World Trade, N.J. Library Trustee Assn., Elks. Home: 264 Long Meadow Rd Smoke Rise Kinnelon NJ 07405 Office: Global Union Bank Wall St Plaza New York NY 10005

LAMARRE, BERNARD, cons. engr.; b. Chicoutimi, Que., Can., Aug. 6, 1931; s. Emile and Blanche (Gagnon) L.; student Mont-St. Louis Coll., Montreal, Que., 1944-48; B.Sc., Ecole Polytechnique, Montreal, 1952; M.Sc., U. London (Eng.), 1955; diploma Imperial Coll., London, 1955; D. honoris causa, St. Francis Xavier U., Can.; m. Louise Lalonde, Aug. 30, 1952; children—Jean, Christine, Lucie, Monique, Michele, Philippe, Mireille. Engr., Lalonde-Valois Co., cons. engrs., Montreal, 1955-58, chief engr., 1958-62; partner Lalonde, Valois, Lamarre, Valois & Assos., cons. engrs., Montreal, 1962-72; pres., chief exec. officer Lavalin Group, Montreal, 1972—. Fellow Engring. Inst. Can.; mem. Roads and Transp. Assn. Can. (pres. Que. chpt. 1970—). Clubs: Mount Royal, St-James, St-Denis, Laval-sur-le-lac (Montreal). Prin. designer, planner East-West Expressway Montreal, 1964-74. Home: 4850 Cedar Crescent Montreal PQ H3W 2H9 Canada Office: Lavalin Inc 1130 Sherbrooke St W Montreal PQ H3A 2R5 Canada

LAMB, RAYMOND AUGUSTUS, bank exec., lawyer; b. Grand Forks, N.D., June 13, 1940; s. Raymond Franics and Frances Emeline (Cox) L.; B.S. in Bus. Adminstrn., U. N.D., 1962; postgrad. U. Minn., 1963; LL.B., George Washington U., 1964; m. Nancy Vogel, Aug. 26, 1967; children—Elizabeth Ince, Raymond Patrick, Philip Augustus. Admitted to N.D. bar, 1965, Minn. bar, 1965, U.S. Dist. Ct. bar, 1965, 74, U.S. Supreme Ct. bar, 1970, U.S. Circuit Ct. of Appeals bar, 1971; law clk. to Hon. Edward J. Devitt, Chief Judge of U.S. Dist. Ct. Minn., 1964-65; pres. firm Lamb, Schaefer, McNair & Larson, Ltd., Fargo, N.D., 1966—; pres., gen. counsel Dakota Bankshares, Inc., Fargo, 1979—; vice chmn., gen. counsel Dakota Bank and Trust Co., Fargo; dir., v.p. Goose River Bank, Mayville, N.D., State Bank of Marion (N.D.), 1st Bank of Drake (N.D.); dir., sec. Elec.-Lighting Mgmt. Co., Tucson; dir. 1st 1st State Bank of Buffalo (N.D.), Billings Lighting Supply Co., Tuscon; county atty. Clay County, Minn., 1967-70. Mem. N.D. Bar Assn., Minn. Bar Assn., Sigma Chi. Roman Catholic. Clubs: Oxbow Country, Detroit Lakes Country, Eagles, K.C., Elks. Home: 15 Briarwood Pl Fargo ND 58103 Office: 52 Broadway Fargo ND 58102

LAMBERT, ALBERT SAMUEL, diving sch. exec.; b. Orillia, Ont., Can., Nov. 20, 1935; s. Albert Ernest and Edith Mary Jane L. With Can. Post Office, Toronto, Ont., 1960-67; pres. Sterling Catering, Toronto, 1967-73; founder Can. Scuba Schs. Ltd., Toronto, 1973, pres., tng. dir., 1973—. Served with RCAF, 1955-60. Mem. Profl. Assn. Diving Instrs., Nat. Assn. Underwater Instrs. Roman Catholic. Author column for Canadian Diving News, 1973-75. Office: PO Box 157 Sta H Toronto ON M4C 5H7 Canada

LAMBERT, BERNARD LEONARD, engring. co. exec.; b. Winona, Minn., Nov. 10, 1931; s. Leonard and Katherine Marie (Neeck) L.; student Marquette U., 1953-55; m. Mary Joan McGraw, July 27, 1968; children—Julie Ann, John J., Thomas J., Joan M. Configuration mgmt. A.C. Electronics div. Gen. Motors Corp., Milw., 1956-68; sub-contract adminstr. Fed. Cartridge Corp., Mpls., 1968-69; contracts mgr. Gulf & Western Advanced Devel. and Engring. Center, Swarthmore, Pa., 1969-79, Dataproducts New Eng., Inc., Wallingford, Conn., 1979—. Served with USN, 1949-53. Mem. Nat. Contracts Mgmt. Assn., Am. Legion, VFW.

LAMBERT, HARVEY RICHARD, ry. and indsl. supply co. exec.; b. Bronxville, N.Y., June 10, 1935; s. Edward H. and Grace M. L.; B.A. in Econs., U. N.C., Chapel Hill, 1961; m. Deborah Kristine Ketchum, Nov. 23, 1963; children—Harvey Richard, Eric Harrington. With Efcon div. Gen. Instrument Corp., Garden City, N.Y., 1961-63; sales and mktg. exec. ACF Industries, Inc., N.Y.C., 1963-65, Ellcon Nat., Inc., Totowa, N.J., 1965-72; owner, pres. McLean Indsl. Supply Co., McLean, Va., 1973—. Mem. ASME, N.Y. R.R. Club, So. Ry. Club. Congregationalist. Club: Univ. (Jacksonville, Fla.). Home: 1945 Lorraine Ave McLean VA 22101 Office: 1340 Old Chainbridge Rd McLean VA 22101

LAMBERT, ROBERT DAVID, lawyer; b. Davenport, Iowa, Oct. 3, 1951; s. Robert Lansing and Margaret Irene (Philhour) L.; B.A., U. Ill., 1974; J.D., Drake U., 1977. Admitted to Iowa bar, 1977; mem. firm Betty, Neuman, McMahon, Hellstrom and Bittner, Davenport, Iowa, 1977—. Mem. Am. Bar Assn., Scott County Bar Assn., Iowa State Bar Assn., Greater Davenport C. of C. Home: 3410 Heatherton Dr Davenport IA 52804 Office: 600 Union Arcade Davenport IA 52801

LAMBERT, SHIRLEY ANN, newspaper exec.; b. Greensburg, Pa., Nov. 18, 1933; d. John H. and Genevieve M. (Grube) Myers; student public schs., Greensburg; m. Karl W. Lambert, Sept. 11, 1971. Advt. account exec. Tribune Rev. Pub. Co., Greensburg, 1956-70; office mgr. Program Service Inc., pub. Mil. Newspapers Va., Norfolk, Va., 1975-76, exec. dir., 1977—. Home: 930 Englewood Dr Chesapeake VA 23320 Office: 4 Koger Executive Center Suite 145 Norfolk VA 23502

LAMBKIN, CLAIRE ALICE, librarian; b. Bklyn., Nov. 16, 1925; d. Clarence Vincent and Pauline Eliza (Rooney) L.; B.A., Bklyn. Coll., 1953; M.L.S., St. John's U., Jamaica, N.Y., 1957. Tchr. of library N.Y.C. Bd. Edn., 1953-57; adminstrv. librarian U.S. Army Europe-W. Ger., 1959-61; librarian Am. Mgmt. Assn., N.Y.C., 1961-69, chief librarian, 1969—. Mem. Spl. Libraries Assn. (chmn. info. tech. group N.Y. chpt. 1980-81), Am. Soc. Info. Sci., L.I. Hist. Soc. (counselor 1980-82), Bklyn. Coll. Alumni Assn. (dir.). Roman Catholic. Office: 135 W 50th St New York NY 10020

LAMELA, MARK CHARLES, steel industry exec.; b. Paterson, N.J., Sept. 12, 1954; s. Charles William and Daphne Iris (Vidale) L.; B.Adminstrn. cum laude, Rider Coll., Trenton, N.J., 1976. Eastern credit mgr. V. Mueller div. Am. Hosp. Supply Corp., Linden, N.J., 1976-78; asst. treas., corp. credit mgr. Thyssen Inc., N.Y.C., 1978—; founder Cambridge Investment Group, 1981; instr. evening sch. N.Y. Inst. Credit; cons. in field. Treas., Colonial Estates Civic Assn., 1979. Mem. Nat. Assn. Credit Mgmt., N.Y. Credit and Fin. Mgmt. Assn., N.Y. Credit Group, Am. Mgmt. Assn., Phi Sigma Epsilon. Republican. Roman Catholic. Clubs: Manhattan Squash (N.Y.C.); Outrigger (Miami, Fla.); Platform Tennis Assn. (E. Brunswick, N.J.). Contbr. articles to profl. jours. Office: 1114 Ave Americas New York NY 10036

LAMLE, HUGH ROY, investment co. exec.; b. Yonkers, N.Y., July 20, 1945; s. Paul and Lee (Wolf) L.; B.A., City U. N.Y., 1967, M.B.A., 1970; m. Elizabeth Bowman, Jan. 12, 1969. Founder, pres., portfolio mgr. Investment Research Assos., N.Y.C., 1967-75; asst. to exec. v.p. Douglas T. Johnson & Co., N.Y.C., 1969-70; v.p., portfolio mgr. Lenox Capital Mgmt. Co., and predecessors, N.Y.C., 1970-74; exec. v.p., dir., investment mgr. M.D.Sass Investors Service, Inc., N.Y.C., 1974—; dir. CCC Advisors, Corp. Capital Cons.; prin. CCC Resources, Inc.; lectr. and writer in field. N.Y. State Regents scholar. Fellow Fin. Analysts Fedn.; mem. N.Y. Soc. Security Analysts, N.Y. Instl. Options Soc. (charter), Internat. Assn. Fin. Planners, Internat. Found. Employee Benefit Plans. Address: 5 Oak St Woodmere NY 11598

LAMMERS, LOWELL, architect, civil engr.; b. Chgo., Oct. 29, 1908; s. Herman C. and Antoinette (Belitz) L.; student M.I.T., 1930-33; B.S. in Architecture, Armour Inst. Tech., 1936; m. Jean C. Wegener, Oct. 17, 1936; children—John William, Carol Lee, Leslie Jean. Archtl. draftsman E.W. Bridges, 1931-34, Holsman & Holsman, 1934-39; chief draftsman J.C. Christensen, 1939-41; constrn. engr., archtl. practice, sr. partner Lammers Partnership, Baytown, Tex., 1941—; pres., dir. 201 Corp., 1960—; pres. Tex. State Bldg. Co.; owner Real Estate Co. Tex.; chmn. bd., treas. L & R Devel. Co., Inc., L & R Mgmt. Co., Inc., Tex. State Constrn. Co., Inc.; gen. partner Bicentennial Sq. Co., Watauga Co. Commr. City of Baytown Adv. Bd., 1958-62; mem. Tex. Water Commn., 1962; CD disaster engr., 1960-70; mem. disaster relief com. ARC, 1961; chmn. Baytown Civic Forum, 1955-57; bd. dirs. Health Bd. Recipient citation for sch. design and contrn. Am. Assn. Sch. Adminstrs., 1957, citation for hosp. and clinic design Am. Hosp. Assn., 1959. Registered profl. engr., Ill.; registered architect, Ill., Tex., Ariz., Tenn.; cert. Nat. Council Archtl. Registration Bds. Mem. Constrn. Specifications Inst, AIA, Tex. Soc. Architects, Am. Soc. Profl. Engrs., Soc. Mil. Engrs., Baytown C. of C. (dir.), Houston Engring. Club. Clubs: Rotary (pres.), Knife and Fork (dir.), Goose Creek Country, Newport Country. Writer, producer, actor radio program Your Home, 1948-60; moderator TV program Architecturally Speaking, 1962-64. Office: Box 600 Baytown TX 77520

LAMON, HARRY VINCENT, JR., lawyer; b. Macon, Ga., Sept. 29, 1932; s. Harry Vincent and Helen (Bewley) L.; B.S. cum laude, Davidson Coll., 1954; J.D. magna cum laude, Emory U., 1958; m. Ada Healey Morris, June 17, 1954; children—Hollis Morris, Helen Kathryn. Admitted to Ga. bar, 1958; practiced in Atlanta, 1958—; mem. firm Crenshaw, Hansell, Ware & Brandon, 1958-62, Hansell, Post, Brandon & Dorsey, 1962-73, Henkel & Lamon, 1973—. Adj. prof. law Emory U., 1960—; dir. Sockwell Enterprises, Inc., Leaselite, Inc., Fulton Bros. Electric Co. (all Atlanta), Meidinger & Assos., Inc., Louisville. Mem. adv. bd. Met. Atlanta Salvation Army, 1963—, chmn., 1975-79, mem. nat. adv. council, 1976—; mem. adv. council employee welfare and pension benefit plans to Sec. Labor; cons. Office of Mgmt. and Budget. Trustee, past pres. So. Fed. Tax Inst.; bd. visitors Davidson Coll., 1975—. Served to 1st lt. AUS, 1954-56. Decorated companion Order of Cross of Nails; recipient Others award Salvation Army, 1979. Fellow Am. Coll. Probate Counsel, Internat. Acad. Estate and Trust Law; mem. Am., Atlanta, Fed., Internat. bar assns., Am. Law Inst., Am. Pension Conf., So. Pension Conf. (founder, pres. 1972), Atlanta Tax Forum, State Bar Ga. (chmn. sect. taxation 1969-70, chmn. Southeastern regional liaison tax com. with IRS 1969-74, 79—), Am. Judicature Soc., Lawyers Club Atlanta, Nat. Emory U. Law Sch. Alumni Assn. (pres. 1967), Am. Law Inst., ALI-ABA Inst., C.L.U.'s Inst., Phi Beta Kappa, Omicron Delta Kappa, Phi Delta Phi, Phi Delta Theta (community day service chmn. 1969-72, legal commr. 1973-75). Episcopalian (vestryman cathedral, del. gen. conv. 1979). Mason (Shriner), Kiwanian (pres. 1973-74, Atlanta). Clubs: Peachtree Racquet, Breakfast, Capital City, Commerce, Cherokee Town and Country; University (Washington). Author: Fiduciary Responsibility Under New Pension Reform Law. Home: 3375 Valley Rd NW Atlanta GA 30305 Office: 2500 Peachtree Center-Cain Tower 229 Peachtree St NE Atlanta GA 30303 also Suite 300 1527 18th St NW Washington DC 20036

LAMONT, EDWARD MINER, banker; b. N.Y.C., Dec. 10, 1926; s. Thomas Stilwell and Elinor B. (Miner) L.; B.A., Harvard, 1948, M.B.A., 1951; m. Camille Haines Buzby, June 23, 1951; children—Edward Miner, Helen B., Camille H. Staff, ECA, Washington, 1951-52; economist secretariat NATO, Paris, 1952-53; loan officer IBRD, Washington, 1953-56; investment officer Internat. Finance Corp., Washington, 1956-61; v.p. Morgan Guaranty Trust Co. N.Y., N.Y.C., 1961-71, 1974-80; dep. adminstr. New Communities Adminstrn., Washington, 1971-74; pres. Morgan Community Devel. Corp. subs. J.P. Morgan & Co., Inc., 1974-80, cons., 1980—; vice chmn., fin. dir. duPont Aerospace Co., Inc., 1980—. Vice pres. Children's Aid Soc.; bd. dirs. Regional Plan Assn., CORO Found.; vestryman St. John's Ch., Cold Spring Harbor, N.Y. Served with USNR, 1945-46. Home: Moores Hill Rd Syosset NY 11791 Office: 30 Rockefeller Plaza Room 5432 New York NY 10012

LA MONTAGNE, ARTHUR LEROY, alarm service co. exec.; b. Moose Jaw, Sask., Can., Sept. 16, 1928; s. Arthur Delphus and Jean Ruth (MacDonald) LaM.; student Regina and Moose Jaw, Notre Dame Coll., Wilcox, Sask.; specialized courses in electricity and electronics; m. Marlene Velma Shea, Dec. 16, 1953; children—Darle Marlene, Curtis Arthur. Sask. area supr. Amplitrol Electronics Ltd., 1963-65, regional mgr., Ont., 1966-67; pres., gen. mgr. All-Comm Alarm Services Ltd., Regina, 1968—; elec. adv. to German Air Force, 1958-60. Elder, mem. ofcl. bd. Lakeview United Ch., Regina, 1970—; dir. Regina Buffalo Days Com., 1976—. Served with Royal Can. Horse Arty., 1950-52, RCAF, 1954-62. Decorated Korean medal, UN medal. Mem. Regina C. of C. Mem. Liberal Party. Mem. United Ch. of Can. Clubs: Regina Rotary (sgt.-at-arms 1980-81), Regina Kennel and Obedience (v.p. 1974-75). Home: 2930 Rae St Regina SK S4S 1R5 Canada Office: 401 Smith St Regina SK S4R 2L3 Canada

LAMOTHE, WILLIAM EDWARD, food co. exec.; b. Bklyn., Oct. 23, 1926; s. William John and Gertrude (Ryan) LaM.; A.B., Fordham U., 1950; m. Patricia Alexander, June 24, 1950. With Kellogg Sales Co., 1950-60, product devel. coordinator, 1958-60; asst. to pres. Kellogg Co., Battle Creek, Mich., 1960-62, v.p., 1962-65, v.p., corporate devel., 1965-70, sr. v.p. corporate devel., 1970-73, pres., chief operating officer, 1973-79, pres., chief exec. officer, chief operating officer, 1979-80, chmn. bd., chief exec. officer, 1980—, also dir. Office: 235 Porter St Battle Creek MI 49016*

LAMOTTE, WILLIAM MITCHELL, ins. brokerage co. exec.; b. Phila., Sept. 3, 1938; s. Ferdinand and June (Mitchell) LaM.; B.A., Princeton U., 1961; m. Elizabeth Ewing, Sept. 16, 1961; children—William Mitchell, Anne Hilliard, Nicole. Underwriter, Chubb & Son, N.Y.C., 1961-62; various assignments Johnson & Higgins Pa., Inc., Phila., 1962-69, pres. Johnson & Higgins Wilmington, Del., 1969-75, pres. Johnson & Higgins Mo. Inc., St. Louis, 1975-77, Johnson & Higgins Ill. Inc., Chgo., 1977—, dir. parent firm. Vice-pres. Boys Clubs Wilmington, 1974-75; bd. dirs. St. Louis Zoo Friends Assn., 1976-77. Clubs: Corinthian Yacht (Phila.); Chicago, Chgo. Yacht. Home: 109 Greenbay Rd Hubbard Woods IL 60093 Office: Johnson & Higgins Ill Inc 101 S Wacker Dr Chicago IL 60606

LAMOUREUX, GERARD WILLIAM, container mfg. co. exec.; b. Chgo., July 27, 1946; s. Donald Benjamin and Anna Rita (Williamson) L.; B.S. in Mech. Engring. Tech., Purdue U., 1970; m. Gloria Jean Kempa, Feb. 13, 1971; children—Gerard Joseph, Jennifer Ann, Brian Gerard. Design draftsman Whiting Corp., Harvey, Ill., 1967-69; plant engr. DeSoto, Inc., Chicago Heights, Ill., 1970-74; maintenance mgr. Panduit Corp., Tinley Park, Ill., 1974-75; plant engr., plant supt. Container Corp. Am., Dolton, Ill., 1975-79, plant engr., Anderson, Ind., 1979—. Mem. mech. adv. bd. Thornton Community Coll., South Holland, Ill., 1975-79. Mem. South Holland United Fund-Crusade of Mercy Com., 1976-78; bd. dirs. Madison County Jr. Achievement, 1980—. Mem. Am. Inst. Plant Engrs., Christian Fellowship Businessmen, Purdue U. Alumni Assn., South Holland Jaycees (pres. 1978-79, state dir. 1976-77), Madison County Mgmt. Club. Roman Catholic. Home: 815 Northwood Dr Anderson IN 46011 Office: 3N Sherman St Anderson IN 46011

LAMPARIELLO, VINCENT CASTELLO, importer; b. N.Y.C., Oct. 11, 1943; s. Dominick and Phyllis (Castello) L.; B.S. in Commerce and Fin., N.Y. U., 1965, M.B.A., 1968; 1 dau., Rosanne. Pres., D. Lampariello & Son, Inc., N.Y.C., 1963—, also v.p. Marco Polo Mktg., Ltd., 1976—; dir. N.Y.C. Bd. Trade, 1977. Bd. dirs. Little Italy Restoration Assn., 1974-77; state dir. Jaycees, 1977-78, pres. N.Y.C., 1976-77, named Jaycee of Year, 1974, outstanding local pres., 1977. Mem. Nat. Fedn. Ind. Bus. (action council 1978—), Italy-Am. C. of C., Packaging Inst. Office: 210 Grand St New York NY 10013

LAMPARTER, WILLIAM C., trade assn. exec.; b. Bklyn., July 13, 1929; s. William C. and Nadine (Lesch) L.; B.S., Springfield (Mass.) Coll., 1951; M.S., Boston U., 1952; m. Ann E. Martyn; children—Ellen, Susan, David. Vice pres., gen. mgr. Mead Digital Systems, 1975-78; pres. Nat. Assn. Painters & Lithographers, 1978—. Served with U.S. Army. Cert. profl. printing inst. of Printing, London. Mem. Internat. Assn. Printing House Craftsmen, Nat. Printing Equipment Assn. (past dir.), Graphic Arts Tech. Found., Research & Engring. Council of Graphic Arts. Author: Forecast of Long-Term Business & Technological Trends in The Graphic Arts, 1968, transl. into Polish, Russian, 1973; lectr. in field. Office: 780 Palisade Ave Teaneck NJ 07666

LAMPERT, ELEANOR VERNA, employment devel. specialist; b. Porterville, Calif., Mar. 23; d. Ernest Samuel and Violet Edna (Watkins) Wilson; student in bus., fin. Porterville Jr. Coll., 1977-78; grad. Anthony Real Estate Sch., 1971; m. Robert Mathew Lampert, Aug. 21, 1935; children—Sally Lu Winton, Lary Lampert, Carol R. John. Bookkeeper, Porterville (Calif.) Hosp., 1956-71; real estate sales staff Ray Realty, Porterville, 1973; sec. Employment Devel. Dept., State of Calif., Porterville, 1973—, orientation and tng. specialist CETA employees, 1978—. Sec., Employer Adv. Group, 1973-80; mem. U.S. Senatorial Bus. Adv. Bd., 1981. Recipient Merit Cert., Gov. Pat Brown, State of Calif., 1968. Mem. Lindsay Olive Growers, Sunkist Orange Growers, Am. Kennel Club, Internat. Assn. Personnel in Employment Security, Nat. Wildlife Fedn. Club: Internat. Sporting and Lgisure.

LANAHAN, JOHN STEVENSON, hotel exec.; b. Pitts., June 13, 1922; s. James S. and Katharine. L. (Lauck) L.; B.A., Duke, 1947; M.B.A., Harvard, 1949; m. Rosemary Lourdes Ford, Feb. 20, 1954; children—Margaret Kayne, Brian James, Ellen Ford. Sales mgr. mid-Atlantic region Allen B. Dumont Labs., East Paterson, N.J., 1950-53; sr. asso. Booz, Allen & Hamilton, Inc., N.Y.C., 1954-59; pres. Richmond Hotels, Inc. (Va.), 1959-69, Flagler System, Inc., Palm Beach, Fla., 1969-71, Carlton House Resort Inns, Inc., Richmond, 1971-73; exec. v.p. Braniff Internat. Hotels, Dallas, 1973-74; pres. The Greenbrier, White Sulphur Springs, W.Va., 1975—; sr. v.p. Chessie System, Inc., 1979—; dir. White Sulphur Springs Co. Mem. adv. bd. W.Va. Found. Ind. Colls.; mem. adv. com. W.Va. U. Sch. Bus.; chmn. bd. Richmond Forward, 1968. Served to lt. (j.g.) USNR, World War II. Mem. Am. Hotel and Motel Assn. (dir., exec. com.), W.Va. Hotel and Motel Assn. (dir.), Va. Hotel Assn. (pres. 1965), So. Innkeepers Assn. (v.p.), Beta Theta Pi, Omicron Delta Kappa. Republican. Roman Catholic. Clubs: Commonwealth of Richmond, Rotary. Office: The Greenbrier White Sulphur Springs WV 24986

LANCASTER, LIONEL GLOVER, constrn. co. exec.; b. Grosse Pointe Shores, Mich., May 12, 1920; s. William John and Edith (Allor) L.; student U. Detroit, 1939-41; B.C.E., U. N.Mex., 1950; m. Lois Jean Wherle, Feb. 29, 1967; children—Lionel G., Jeffery B., Patrick, Daniel, Cathy, Tara, Gary. Constrn. mgr. Trans Mountain Canadian Pipeline, Vancouver, B.C., Can., 1964-67; project mgr. constrn. Apollo V Launch Facilities, NASA, Cape Kennedy, Fla., 1955-58; pres. L.G. Lancaster & Assos., Tucson, 1962-68; exec. v.p. ops., dir., Simpson Industries, Allied Engring. Co., South Gate, Ga., 1968-70; cons. engr. Leslie C. Gates & Assos., Bechley, W.Va., 1970-72; v.p. design and constrn. Big Sky Montana Inc., Big Sky, 1972—; owner Lancaster Cos., Phoenix; dir. Beacon Steel; mgmt. cons. to constrn. industry. Served with USAF, 1941-45. Decorated Silver Star, D.F.C., Air medal with four oak leaf clusters; recipient Merit award Intercontinental Ballistic Missile Site Devel. USAF, 1964; registered profl. engr. Ariz., N.Mex., W.Va., Alta, Can. Mem. Nat. Soc. Profl. Engrs., Soc. Am. Mil. Engrs., Chi Epsilon. Republican. Roman Catholic. Home: 6816 E North Ln Scottsdale AZ 85253 Office: 10210 N 32d St Phoenix AZ 85028

LANCE, JAMES WINSLOW, lawyer, fin. corp. exec.; b. Little Rock, July 26, 1943; s. Lawrence Winslow and Kathryn Joyce (Haggard) L.; B.S.B.A., U. Ark., Fayetteville, 1965, J.D., 1972; m. Frances Virginia Shepherd, June 11, 1966; 1 dau., Paige Virginia. Admitted to Ark. bar, 1973; sr. mgmt. analyst, dir. corp. planning First Pyramid Life Ins. Co. of Am., Little Rock, 1969-70; exec. dir. Little Rock Unlimited Progress, Inc., 1970-72, dir., 1973—; exec. v.p. Ark. Fin. Services, Inc., Little Rock, 1972-73, pres., chief exec. officer, 1973—; dir. Nat. Savs. and Loan League, Washington, 1978—; chmn. service corp. com. U.S. League of Savs. Assns., Chgo., 1979—; chmn. Multiply-Owned Service Corps. Group, 1977-78. Served to 1st lt. U.S. Army, 1967-69. Recipient Outstanding Law Student award E.L.

Cullam Found., 1966. Mem. Ark. State C. of C. (dir. 1978—), Little Rock C. of C., Ark. Bar Assn. (chmn. savs. and loan assns. sect. 1980—), Am. Bar Assn., Pulaski County Bar Assn., Mortgage Bankers Assn. Am., Ark. Mortgage Bankers Assn., Savs. Instns. Mktg. Soc. of Am. Methodist. Clubs: Little Rock, Capital, North Hills Country, Rotary. Home: 10 Heritage Park Circle North Little Rock AR 72116 Office: Suite 800 Three Hundred Spring Bldg Little Rock AR 72201

LANCE, THOMAS BERTRAM, bank exec., former state ofcl.; b. Gainesville, Ga., June 3, 1931; s. Thomas Jackson and Annie Rose (Erwin) L.; student Emory U., 1948-50, U. Ga., 1951; Grad. Sch. Banking of South, La. State U., 1956; grad. Grad. Sch. Banking Rutgers U., 1963; m. Lethia Belle David, Sept. 9, 1950; children—Thomas Bertram, David Jackson, Stuart Austin, Claude Beverly. Exec. v.p. Calhoun (Ga.) 1st Nat. Bank, 1958-63, pres., chief exec. officer, 1963-74, chmn. bd., 1974—, dir., 1958—; pres. CNB Investments Inc., Calhoun, 1958—; pres. Nat. Bank Ga., Atlanta, 1975-76, pres., chief exec. officer, 1976—; hwy. dir. State of Ga., 1970-73; dir. Office of Mgmt. and Budget, Exec. Office of Pres., Washington, 1977; dir. Astro Dye Works, Inc., Edward Lacy Mills, Crown Crafts, Inc., Atlantic Am. Corp., Astro Carpet Finishing Co.; dir. adv. bd. Central of Ga. R.R. Former mem. regional adv. com. to comptroller currency; chmn. 7th Dist. Savs. Bond Drive; active various community drives; mem. exec. com. Central Ga. Progress, Atlanta; mem. steering com. Ga. Agrirama, Tifton; adv. council Coll. Indsl. Mgmt., Ga. Inst. Tech., Atlanta; mem. pres.'s adv. council Agnes Scott Coll., Atlanta; bd. sponsors Alliance Theatre, Atlanta Arts Alliance; chmn. chair pvt. enterprise Ga. State U., Atlanta; trustee Ga. Found. for Ind. Colls., Cherokee Boys Estate; chmn. bd. trustees Reinhardt Coll.; bd. counselors Oxford Coll. of Emory U.; adv. council Ga. State U.; mem. com. of 100, Emory U. Mem. AIM (pres. council 1965), Ga. Bankers Assn., Gridiron Secret Soc., Atlanta C. of C. (dir.), Ga. Bus. and Industry Assn. (gov.), Sigma Chi. Methodist (dist. lay leader). Home: 409 E Line St Calhoun GA 30701 Office: PO Box 637 Calhoun GA 30701

LANCEY, RODERIC CHARLES, pharm. co. exec.; b. Gardner, Mass., July 17, 1927; s. Clifford S. and Leila E. (Timpany) L.; B.S., Worcester Poly. Inst., 1951, M.S. (Research Corp. grantee), 1952; M.B.A., Harvard, 1957; m. Susan Eustis, Nov. 27, 1954 (div. Feb. 1973); children—Elizabeth E., Kenneth G.; m. 2d, Mary Stevenson Goodall, Nov. 27, 1976. Project mgr. new product market devel. and mktg. research Monsanto Co., St. Louis, 1957-64; long range planning fin. analyst Internat. Minerals and Chem. Corp., Skokie, Ill., 1964-67, fin. mgr., 1967-68; dir. long range planning G.D. Searle & Co., Skokie, Ill., 1968-78, dir. planning and acquisitions Searle Med. Products Group, 1978—. Served with USNR, 1945-46. Mem. Midwest Planning Assn. (dir. 1972-75, nat. sec.-treas. 1977-78), Planning Execs. Inst., N.Am. Soc. Corporate Planning, Internat. Affiliation of Planning Socs. (v.p. 1973-75, pres. 1975-77), Am. Chem. Soc., Thistle Sailing Assn. Clubs: Harvard Bus. Sch. of Chgo., Chgo. Curling. Home: 952 Spruce St Winnetka IL 60093 Office: PO Box 1045 4711 Golf Rd Skokie IL 60076

LANDALE, THOMAS DAVID, mfg. and constrn. exec.; b. Omaha, Nebr., Jan. 2, 1927; s. Edwin Munderloh and Olive Margaret (Williams) L.; B.C.E., Cornell U., 1948; S.M. in C.E., Mass. Inst. Tech., 1954; m. Suzanne Therese Chevalier, Dec. 23, 1950; children—Edwin Thomas, David Paul, Carol Jeanne, Nora Margaret, Raymond Daniel (dec.), Louis Arthur, James Benjamin, Marjorie Suzanne, Katherine Lucille, Stephen Andrew. Project engr. Brown-Roberts & Assos., Marion, Ohio, 1955-56; v.p., treas., chmn. Nalews, Inc., Meredith, N.H., 1960-62; with Pullman Kellogg div. Pullman Inc. and predecessor and affiliated cos., 1954-77, office and field positions, 1954-55, 56-60, dir. constrn. Kellogg Internat. Corp., London, Eng., 1962-68, gen. mgr. Chimney div., Williamsport, 1968-72, v.p., gen. mgr. Power Piping and Chimney, Williamsport, 1972-77, pres. Pullman Power Products div., 1977—; dir. K.U.B. Co. of Can., Ltd., St. Johns, Nfld., Williamsport Nat. Bank; chmn., dir. Schweizer-Dipple, Inc., Cleve. Mem. exec. bd. Susquehanna council Boy Scouts Am. Served with USNR, 1945-46. Registered profl. engr., Ohio, N.Y., N.H. Mem. Nat. Soc. Profl. Engrs., Cornell Soc. Engrs., Sigma Xi. Club: Williamsport Country. Home: 90 Selkirk Rd Williamsport PA 17701 Office: PO Box 1007 Williamsport PA 17701

LANDAU, ABRAHAM, publisher's rep., sales and pub. cons.; b. N.Y.C., Aug. 20, 1920; s. Harry and Fannie (Lev) Lipkowitz; B.S. in Social Sci., City Coll. N.Y., 1942, M.B.A., Baruch Sch. Bus. Adminstrn., 1963; m. Josephine Seaman, Aug. 21, 1949; children—Lynn, Pauline. Media dir. Byrde Richard and Pound Advt. Agency, N.Y.C., 1946-52; v.p. Playbill Mag., N.Y.C., 1952-71; pres. A.J. Landau, Inc., N.Y.C., 1971—; adj. asso. prof. mktg. Sch. Continuing Edn., N.Y. U. Mem. Am. Mktg. Assn., N.Y. Sales Execs. Club. Office: 310 Madison Ave New York NY 10017

LANDAU, HERMAN H., importer; b. Fuerth, Ger., Sept. 9, 1907; came to Can., 1951, naturalized, 1956; s. Joshua and Natalie (Rothenberg) L.; student Ecole Talmudique, Montreux, Switzerland, 1943-48; m. Helen Bombach, May 24, 1942; children—Esther, Samuel-Moise, Natalie (dec.). With Ruco Metallwarenfabrik, Fuerth, 1923-25; procurist S.D. Zimmer, Fuerth, 1925-38; owner, pres. Swissrose Co., Toronto, Ont., 1951—. Mem. world exec. Agudath Israel World Orgn., 1980—; mem. exec. Agudath Israel, Toronto, 1952—; bd. dirs. Eitz Chaim Schs., Toronto, 1953—; mem. nat. exec. Canadian Jewish Congress, 1980—, mem. regional council, 1978—; bd. dirs. Agudath Israel of Am., 1976—, Beth Jacob High Sch. and Sem., Toronto, 1955—; treas. Canadian Friends of Torah Schs. for Israel, Toronto, 1955, Canadian Friends of Telshe Yeshiva, 1960, Canadian Friends of Bikur Cholim Hosp. on Jerusalem, 1979, Canadian Friends of Bene Berak Hosp., 1979, Canadian Friends of Sde Chemed, 1978; bd. dirs. Ner Israel Yeshivah Coll. of Toronto, 1974—. Recipient Community Service award, Agudath Israel of Am., 1978. Mem. Canadian Importers Assn. Jewish. Home: 579 Old Orchard Grove Toronto ON M5M 2H2 Canada

LANDE, DAVID STEVEN, lawyer; b. N.Y.C., Aug. 1, 1944; s. Jerome J. and Selma S. L.; B.S., Cornell U., 1966; J.D., N.Y. U., 1969; m. Fern Margolis; children—Jill M., Jeffrey B., Jerome J. Admitted to N.Y. bar, U.S. Supreme Ct. bar; legal asst. indsl. chems. group W. R. Grace & Co., N.Y.C., 1969; asso. firm Javits & Javits, N.Y.C., 1970-71, Kreindler Relkin Olick & Goldberg, N.Y.C., 1971-74; individual practice law and labor arbitration, N.Y.C., 1974—; mem. panel arbitrators Am. Arbitration Assn.; mem. panel of arbitrators Fed. Mediation and Conciliation Service, N.Y., N.J. state mediation bds., N.J. Pub. Employee Relations Commn., N.Y.C. Office Collective Bargaining. Mem. U.S. SSS Bd. 14, N.Y.C., 1971-76; dist. leader Republican Party 69th Assembly Dist. North Part, N.Y.C., 1974—; mem. N.Y. Republican State Com., 1976—. Mem. Am., N.Y. State bar assns., Assn. Bar City N.Y., New York County Lawyers Assn. (sec. com. on Supreme Ct.). Home: 315 Riverside Dr New York NY 10025 Office: 1290 Ave of Americas New York NY 10019

LANDEAU, RALPH, chem. engr.; b. Phila., May 19, 1916; s. Stanley and Deanna L.; B.S., U. Pa., 1937; Sc.D., Mass. Inst. Tech., 1941; m. Claire, July 14, 1940; 1 dau. Research asst. in chem. engring. Mass. Inst. Tech., 1939-41; devel. engr. M.W. Kellogg Co., 1939, 1941-43, 1946; head chems. dept. Kellex Corp., 1943-45; exec. v.p., dir. Sci. Design Co., Inc., N.Y.C., 1946-63; pres. Halcon Internat., Inc., 1963-75, chmn., 1975—. Life mem. corp. Mass. Inst. Tech. Recipient Chem. Industry medal, Perkin medal. Mem. Nat. Acad. Engring., Sigma Xi, Tau Beta Pi. Clubs: Sky, Princeton, Chemists (N.Y.C.); Tryall (Jamaica). Author papers, chpts.; patentee in field. Office: 2 Park Ave New York NY 10016

LANDEFELD, CHESTER WILLIAM, savs. and loan exec.; b. Canton, Ohio, Oct. 5, 1939; s. Chester Warren and Rose Ann (Riegler) L.; B.B.A., Ohio State U., 1963; M.B.A., Xavier U.; m. Renate Karola Welcher, Mar. 19, 1977; children—C. Richard, Michael, Timothy. Asst. mgr. sales order clearance dept. Diebold, Inc., Canton, 1963-69; real estate salesman Denoff Agy., North Canton, Ohio, 1969-71; asst. v.p. Akron Savs. & Loan Assn. (Ohio), 1971-77; pres., mng. officer Cin. Savs. Assn., 1977—, also dir. Served with AUS, 1963-65. Mem. Greater Cin. C. of C., Cin. Bd. Realtors, Greater Cin. Home Builders Assn., U.S. League Savs. Assns., Savs. and Loan League Southwestern Ohio. Republican. Presbyterian. Clubs: Bankers, Eastern Hills Exchange. Office: 7373 Beechmont Ave Cincinnati OH 45230

LANDER, DONALD H., automobile mfg. co. exec.; b. Aug. 2, 1925; ed. U. B.C.; m. Dorothy M. Lander. With GM Can., 15 yrs.; passenger car sales mgr. Chrysler Can., 1959, Ont. zone mgr., 1960-67, v.p., 1967-69, exec. v.p., from 1969, now pres. Office: Chrysler Centre PO Box 1621 Windsor ON N9A 4H6 Canada*

LANDER, RICHARD ERNEST, machinery mfg. co. exec.; b. Forest Hills, N.Y., Feb. 20, 1926; s. William P.S. and Lotta (Edwards) L.; student U. Notre Dame, 1944-46; B.S. in Civil Engring., Tufts U., 1948; m. Patricia Ball Riter, Feb. 5, 1949; children—Richard Bankson, Nina Holloway, Frederick Alan. Engr. Harris-Dechant Assos., Phila., 1948-59, asso., 1954-59; plant mgr. Certain-Teed Corp., Valley Forge, Pa., 1959-67, v.p. mfg., 1967-71; v.p. Edge Wallboard Machinery Co. Downingtown, Pa., 1972—. Mem. Tredyffrin Twp. (Pa.) Municipal Authority, 1960-62, treas., 1962. Served with USNR, 1944-46, 52-54. Registered profl. engr., Pa., N.H., Del. Mem. Paper Industry Mgmt. Assn., TAPPI. Republican. Episcopalian. Home: 6 Forest Rd Wayne PA 19087 Office: 930 Bondsville RD Downingtown PA 19335

LANDERKIN, JAMES CANBY, mfg. co. exec.; b. Balt., Aug. 7, 1946; s. James Canby and Lillian Edith (Winn) L.; B.S. in Mktg., U. Balt., 1977; m. Nancy Lee Schupp, Feb. 24, 1968; children—Gregory, Jeffrey, Brandon. With IBM, Balt., 1968-74, Western Union Telegraph Co., Balt., 1974-77, Honeywell Info. Systems. Columbia, Md., 1977-78; nat. account mgr. Intel Corp., Silver Spring, Md., 1978—. Served with USAF, 1964-68. Contbr. articles to computer jours. Home: 5705B Harpers Farm Rd Columbia MD 21044 Office: 1620 Elton Rd Silver Spring MD 20903

LANDERMAN, RICHARD CRAIG, lawyer; b. Corpus Christi, Tex., Sept. 11, 1942; s. Robert Emmett and Ritta Jeanette (Robertson) L.; J.D., U. Utah, 1969; m. Janet Louise Henderson, June 17, 1964; children—Amy, Heather, Mark Ryan, Kristen, Erin. Instr. bus. and govt. U. Guam, 1969-71; admitted to Utah bar, 1971; asso. firm Beaslin, Nygaard, Coke & Vincent, Salt Lake City, 1971-72; hearing examiner Public Service Commn. Utah, Salt Lake City, 1972; partner firm Landerman & Rodgers, Salt Lake City, 1972—; owner, mgr. Bankers Bur., cons. to banking, thrift and fin. industry, 1978—; organizer, dir., corp. sec. Brighton Bank, Salt Lake City, 1976-78, Western Home Bank, Salt Lake City, 1978-79; organizer Community Bank & Trust, Salt Lake City, 1973, Rocky Mountain State Bank, Salt Lake City, 1975, Security Savs. & Loan Assn., Pleasant Grove, Utah, 1978; pres. Diversified Energy Corp., 1980—. Served with USNR, 1969-71. Mem. Am. Bar Assn., Utah Bar Assn. Democrat. Mormon. Office: 2290 East 4500 South Suite 200 Salt Lake City UT 84117

LANDERS, NEWLIN JEWEL, contractor; b. North Salem, Ind., July 10, 1906; s. DeLoy and Pearl (Paige) L.; student Skadron Contractor's Sch., 1963; m. Vernette Trosper, May 2, 1959; children—Lawrence, Marlin. Owner, mgr. Landers Machine Shop, Bell Gardens, Calif., 1940-41; partner Selwyn-Landers Co., Los Angeles, 1942-54; owner Havasu Landing, Needles, Calif., 1955, Navajo Tract, Apple Valley, Calif., 1957—; owner, mgr. Landers Water Co. (Calif.), 1958—. Mem. Landers Vol. Fire Dept., 1963—. Recipient Plaque Sheriff Rangers' Search and Rescue, 1972. Moose. Home: 905 Landers Ln Landers CA 92284 Office: 1105 Landers Ln Landers CA 92284

LANDIS, CHARLES, night club exec.; b. Mpls., July 21, 1917; s. Morris and Mollie (Landau) L.; B.A., U. Minn., 1940; m. Florence Regina Alsobrook, Aug. 1, 1950; children—Steven, Todd, Jan, Tim. Pres., Largo, Inc., Los Angeles, also Sacramento, 1957—, Chas. Landis Enterprises, Los Angeles, 1967—, Lanvan Artists Prodns., Ltd., Los Angeles, Mission Road Enterprises, Inc., 1968—, Clan Record Co., Monterey Park, Calif., 1970—, Franklin Plaza Industries, Las Vegas, 1974—; sec.-treas. Roxy Theater Corp., Hollywood, Calif., 1971—; owner Starlite Motel Co., Los Angeles, 1969—; pres. Monterey Park Devel. Co., 1975—, C.L. Record Corp., Monterey Park, 1975—, Chuck Landis' Country Club, Inc., Reseda, Calif., 1977—; owner Wilshire-Westlake Bldg., Los Angeles, 1975—, W-W-B Interior Designs, Los Angeles, 1973—. Hon. mayor West Hollywood, Calif., Sunset Strip, Hollywood, 1968—. Home: 7509 March Ave Canoga Park CA 91304 Office: 18415 Sherman Way Reseda CA 91335

LANDIS, LEWIS, accountant; b. Mpls., Mar. 11, 1920; s. Morris and Mollie (Landau) L.; B.B.A., U. Minn., 1942; postgrad. Law Sch. U. So. Calif., 1950-51; m. Anita Gisela Hering, Aug. 27, 1957; children—Jeffrey Michael. Sr. acct. Homes & Davis, C.P.A.'s, 1946-50; individual practice acctg., Los Angeles, 1951-55; sr. systems acct. U.S. Air Force, Weisbaden, Ger., 1955-57; individual practice acctg., Los Angeles, 1957—. Served to 1st lt. AUS, 1942-46. C.P.A., Calif. Mem. Calif. Soc. C.P.A.'s, Beta Alpha Psi. Home: 3721 Holden Circle Los Alamitos CA 90720

LANDIS, RICHARD G., food products co. exec.; b. Davenport, Okla., Apr. 5, 1920; s. John W. and Venna (Perrin) L.; B. Social Sci., Laverne Coll.; postgrad. in social scis. Claremont Grad. Sch.; m. Leota Beth Throne, Nov. 6, 1943; children—Gary P., Dennis M., Kay E. With Del Monte Corp., San Francisco, 1942—, mgr. Eastern ops., San Francisco, 1964-65, v.p. Pacific Coast ops., 1966-68, v.p. U.S. prodn., 1968-69, group exec. v.p., 1969-71, dir., 1970—, pres., chief operating officer, 1971—, chief exec. officer, 1977—, chmn. bd., 1978—; dir. Crocker Nat. Corp., Crocker Nat. Bank. Bd. regents U. of Pacific; trustee, mem. pres.'s adv. council U. La Verne; bd. visitors U. Calif. at Los Angeles; bd. dirs. Stanford Research Inst.; mem. adv. council Sch. Bus. Adminstrn., U. Calif. Office: PO Box 3575 San Francisco CA 94119

LANDMESSER, ROBERT WILLIAM, environ. cons. co. exec.; b. Montclair, N.J., Mar. 31, 1949; s. Charles F. and Cecilia F. Landmesser; B.A. in Econs., Fairfield U., 1971; m. Susan Walter, June 4, 1977. Project coordinator Sunrise Services Corp., Fairfield, N.J., 1971-73; salesman Proctor & Gamble Co., Cranford, N.J., 1973-74; N. Jersey sales rep. Sci. Inc./Gaess Environ. Tech. Services Co., Scotch Plains and Passaic, N.J., 1974-76; pres. Advanced Environ. Tech., Morris Plains, N.J., 1976—. Home: 41 Misty Mountain Rd Randolph NJ 07869 Office: Dayton Bldg 520 Speedwell Ave Morris Plains NJ 07950

LANDY, PHILIP FRANCIS, real estate broker and appraiser; b. Cleve., Apr. 19, 1946; s. Thomas Matthew and Agatha (Horrigan) L.; student John Carroll U., Cuyahoga Community Coll.; m. Dorothy I. DuHaime, Sept. 15, 1975; children—Jenny, Lucy. Real estate sales and mgmt. exec. A.H. Landy & Sons, Cleve., 1967-72; owner, mgr. Market Info. Systems, 1973; appraiser J.M. Cleminshaw Co., Ohio and Conn., 1973-75; appraiser Sabre Systems, Cleve., 1975-76; owner, mgr. Philco Realty Co., Cleveland Heights, Ohio, 1976—. Notary pub., Ohio. Asso. mem. Am. Soc. Appraisers. Home and Office: 2647 Berkshire Rd Cleveland Heights OH 44106

LANE, DONALD MARSTON, telecommunications exec.; b. Bklyn., Sept. 10, 1946; s. Gilbert Hurd and Elizabeth (Dean) L.; B.S.E.E., Norwich U., 1969; M.S.E.E., U. Va., 1971; postgrad. Babson Coll., 1973—. Electronics engr. Naval Air Test Center, Potuxent River, Md., summers 1969-70; microwave system design engr. New Eng. Telephone, Framingham, Mass., 1972-75, constrn. budget engr. toll equip., 1975-78, mgr. large accounts engring., 1978—. Jr. Achievement advisor, 1973-75. Served to capt., USAR, 1971-76. Mem. Tau Beta Pi, Eta Kappa Mu. Club: Innitou Ski Runners. Contbr. articles to profl. jours. Home: 383 Main St Ashland MA 01721 Office: 350 Cochituate Rd Framingham MA 01701

LANE, GARY, lawyer, public affairs consulting co. exec.; b. N.Y.C., Jan. 2, 1946; s. J. Roger and Ruth (Lehrer) L.; B.A. in Govt., City U. N.Y., 1966; J.D., U. San Diego, 1969; LL.M. in Legislation, George Washington U., 1970; M.A. in Policy Processes, U. So. Calif., 1973; LL.M. in Constitutional & Adminstrv. Law, N.Y. U., 1974; postgrad Harvard U., 1976. Admitted to N.Y. State bar, 1977, D.C. bar, 1974, Calif. bar, 1972, U.S. Ct. Mil. Appeals bar, 1973, U.S. Supreme Ct. bar, 1975; individual practice law and public affairs consulting, N.Y.C., Washington and Los Angeles, 1972—; bd. counselors Citizens Legal Def. Alliance. San Diego County chmn. Rafferty for U.S. Senate; gen. counsel Fisher for Congress, Los Angeles. Recipient San Diego City Council Disting. Service award, 1969, San Diego Bd. Edn. Disting. Service award, 1969, U.S. Congress Disting. Service Letter, 1974. Mem. Am. Bar Assn., Los Angeles County Bar Assn., Fed. Bar Assn. Republican. Author: Congress and Subversion, 1970; The UN in the Congo, 1971; The President vs. the Congress, 1971; Compensatory Education and the Law School, 1972; Why Congress?, 1972; Absentee Voting Laws in the U.S., 1974; Law School Joint Degree Programs, 1975; The Screening of Judicial Candidates in New York, 1974. Home: 11578 Wyoming Ave Apt 203 West Los Angeles CA 90025 Office: 707 Wilshire Blvd Suite 3627 Los Angeles CA 90017

LANE, J. FRANK, real estate investor; b. Belmont, Mass., Apr. 2, 1923; s. John F. and Agnes G. (Maher) L.; B.S.E.E., Tufts U., 1949; m. Kathleen F. Young, June 30, 1951; 1 dau., Patricia. Engr., Raytheon, 1949-56, engring. mgr., 1956-61; pres. Applied Microwave Lab., Inc., 1961-66; engring. mgr. RCA Corp., 1966-69; owner Lane Management, Lincoln, Mass., 1969—. Home: Lincoln MA Office: PO Box 666 Lincoln MA 01773

LANE, RICHARD JOSEPH HODGSON, accountant; b. Man., Can., Nov. 30, 1912; came to U.S., 1922, naturalized, 1927; s. Joseph B. and Violet (Hodgson) L.; student public schs., Santa Cruz, Calif.; 1 son, Stephen Edward. With Lane's Frozen Custard, Santa Cruz, Calif., 1936-53, owner, 1949-53; pvt. practice acctg., Santa Cruz, 1964—. Served with USCG, 1943-45. Republican. Presbyterian. Club: Watsonville Band. Patentee in field. Address: 721 Bay St Santa Cruz CA 95060

LANE, WILLIAM NOBLE, III, holding co. exec.; b. Evanston, Ill., Aug. 2, 1943; s. William Noble and Marjorie Elizabeth (Hamilton) L.; A.B., Princeton U., 1965; m. Wendy C. Henry, Dec. 31, 1977; children by previous marriage—Campbell, Heather, Carl. Mem. sales staff Wallace Press, Inc., 1965-66; mgr. corp. planning Gen. Binding Corp., Northbrook, Ill., 1966-72, vice chmn., 1978—; pres. Northwestco, Inc., Chgo., 1972-78; chmn., pres. Lane Industries, Inc., Northbrook, 1978—; chmn. Lake View Trust & Savs. Bank, Northwest Nat. Bank of Chgo., Pioneer Bank & Trust Co., Northbrook Trust & Savs. Bank; dir. Hydraulic Component Services, Inc., Otis Assos., Schwaab, Inc. Trustee, Rush Presbyn. St. Luke's Med. Center, Lake Forest Acad., Chgo. Zool. Soc.; bd govts. United Republican Fund of Ill.; mem. econ. adv. council Princeton U.; bd. dirs. Irving Park YMCA. Republican. Episcopalian. Clubs: Winter, Onwentsia (Lake Forest, Ill.); Princeton, Explorers (N.Y.C.); Port Royal Beach (Naples Fla.); Univ., Econs. (Chgo.); Adventurers. Office: Gen Binding Corp One GBC Plaza Northbrook IL 60062

LANFORD, OSCAR ERASMUS, JR., univ. adminstr.; b. Louisa County, Va., Dec. 19, 1914; s. Oscar Erasmus and Ruth Evelyn Miller L.; B.S., Va. Mil. Inst., 1934; M.A., Columbia U., 1937, Ph.D., 1939; m. Caroline Capp Sherman, Aug. 24, 1937; children—Oscar Erasmus III, Caroline Aldrich Eastman, Henry Sherman, William Armistead, Virginia Bowen Lanford Hemani. Research chemist Golddust Corp., 1934-36; mem. faculty, chemistry dept. Columbia U., N.Y.C., 1936-40; prof. chemistry SUNY, Albany, 1940-52, dean of coll., 1952-61, dir. Atmospheric Scis. Research Center, 1961; pres. Fredonia Coll., SUNY, 1961-71; dir. Commn. Univ. Purposes and Goals, 1970-71; vice chancellor SUNY, Albany, 1971—, chief exec. officer SUNY Constrn. Fund, 1972—. Mem. Am. Mgmt. Assn., Am. Angus Assn. (life), N.Y. State Farm Bur., Sigma Xi, Phi Lambda Upsilon. Club: Univ. (Albany). Home: 2567 Brookview Rd Castleton-on-Hudson NY 12033 Office: SUNY Constrn Fund State Univ Plaza Albany NY 12201

LANG, FRANCIS H., lawyer; b. Manchester, Ohio, June 4, 1907; s. James Walter and Mary (Harover) L.; A.B., Ohio Wesleyan U., 1929; J.D., Ohio State U., 1932; m. Rachel Boyce, Oct. 20, 1934; children—Mary Sue, Charles B., James R. Admitted to Ohio bar, 1932; practice law, East Liverpool, Ohio, 1932—; chmn. bd., dir. First Fed. Savs. & Loan Assn. East Liverpool, 1948—; mem. trust and exec. coms., dir. 1st Nat. Bank East Liverpool, 1952—; dir. emeritus 1st Nat. Bank of Chester (W.Va.), Sayre Electric Cos.; pres. Walter Lang Co., Lang Gas Co. Mem. regional com. nat. council Boy Scouts Am., 1956-78. Recipient Silver Beaver award Boy Scouts Am., 1955, Silver Antelope, 1960; Distinguished Service award East Liverpool Jr. C. of C., 1940, named Citizen of Year, 1955. Mem. East Liverpool C. of C. (past pres.), Ohio C. of C. (past dir.), Ohio, Columbiana County (past pres.) bar assns. Methodist (mem. bd. missions 1968-72, bd. global ministries 1972-76). Rotarian (past dist. gov.), Mason (33 deg.). Home: Highland Colony East Liverpool OH 43920 Office: 517 Broadway East Liverpool OH 43920

LANG, JAMES DEVORE, JR., investment exec.; b. Ft. Lewis, Wash., Apr. 29, 1941; s. James DeVore and Margaret (Van Oosbree) L.; B.S. in Engring., U.S. Air Force Acad., 1963; postgrad. U. Dayton, 1965; M.B.A., Pepperdine U., 1978; m. Barbara Jo Drury, July 3, 1965; children—Kathrena Louise, Teresa Lea, Christina Noble, Angela Lynn. Registered rep. Lorraine L. Blair, Inc., San Francisco,

1969-70, West Coast regional v.p., San Rafael, Calif., 1970-71; with Capital Planning Securities Co., Novato, Calif., 1972-74, pres., 1972—, chmn., 1973-74; exec. v.p., dir. Capital Planning Assos., Inc., 1971-74; pres. Delger Fin. Corp.; chmn. bd., pres., dir. Delger Corp.; v.p. C/P Realty Advisers, Inc., 1973-74; sec., trustee C/P Realty Trust, 1973-74; chmn. bd. Delger Fin. Corp.; pres., dir. Alt. Energy Systems, Inc., 1977-79; pres. Shiloh Resources, Inc., 1979—. Trustee, Coll. Fin. Planning, 1975-76; bd. dirs. Pro Athletes Outreach, 1979—. Served to capt. USAF, 1963-68. Decorated Air medal (6); Paul Harris fellow; certified fin. planner. Mem. Internat. Assn. Fin. Planners (pres. 1973-74, chmn. bd. 1974-75), Finance Forum Am. (regional dir. 1968-70), Air Force Assn., Air Force Acad. Alumni Assn., Internat. Platform Assn., Inst. Certified Fin. Planners. Republican. Presbyterian. Club: Rotary. Home: PO Box 1521 Novato CA 94947 Office: PO Box 871 Novato CA 94947

LANG, JAMES RICHARD, computer co. exec.; b. Cleve., Feb. 7, 1945; s. Francis H. and Rachel L. (Boyce) L.; B.A., Mt. Union Coll., 1967; m. Marilyn F. Hosken, July 1, 1967; children—Christopher Charles, James Walter. Salesman, Stas. WOHI-AM/WRTS-FM, East Liverpool, Ohio, 1967-68; gen. mgr. Sta.-WEIR-AM, Weirton, W.Va., 1969-76; v.p. sales Paperwork Systems Inc., Bellingham, Wash., 1976-78; v.p. market devel. Sta. Bus. Systems div. Control Data Corp., Greenwich, Conn., 1978—. Served with USN, 1968-69. Recipient Outstanding Service to Community award Italian Sons and Daus. Am., 1970. Mem. Nat. Assn. Broadcasters, Nat. Cable TV Assn., Jaycees (Community Service award 1975), Internat. Fellowship Magicians. Methodist. Club: Rotary (Man of Year 1975). Home: 24 Primrose Dr Trumbull CT 06611 Office: 600 W Putnam St Greenwich CT 06830

LANG, PAUL JOSEPH, ins. co. exec.; b. Amityville, N.Y., Jan. 13, 1947; s. Jerome and Hannah (Hauft) L.; B.S., Rider Coll., 1968; postgrad. U. So. Calif., 1972; m. Stephanie Laudenbach, July 1, 1977. Staff auditor Prudential Ins. Co., Chgo., 1973-74, asst. auditor, Newark, 1974-76, mgr. auditing Prudential Reins. Co., Newark, 1976-79, mgr. and asst. treas., 1979-80; asst. treas. Gibraltar Casualty Co., Dryden & Co.; mgr. gen. acctg. Prudential Ins. Co., Iselin, N.J., 1980—; treas. Pruco Syndicate, Inc., Pruco Mgrs., Inc. Served to capt. USAF, 1968-73. Cert. internal auditor. Fellow Life Mgmt. Inst. Home: 4 Snowdrift Dr Piscataway NJ 08854 Office: 200 Wood Ave S Iselin NJ 08830

LANG, VICTOR JOHN, JR., bus. exec.; b. Galveston, Tex., June 28, 1936; s. Victor John and Katherine Loretta (Burkett) L.; B.A., U. Tex., 1960, postgrad. Sch. Law, 1960-61, Grad. Sch. Bus., 1961-62. Asst. exec. sec. to Gov. Price Daniel, Austin, Tex., 1957-61; adminstrv. asst. state Sen. Aaron R. Schwartz, Austin and Galveston, 1961-63; adminstrv. asst. Congressman Clark W. Thompson, Washington, 1963-66; congressional liaison officer HUD, 1966-67; prof. staff mem. Subcom. on Intergovtl. Relations, U.S. Senate, 1967; v.p. govt. affairs IU Internat. Corp., Phila., 1968—; mem. Pa. State Planning Bd.; lectr. contemporary politics New Studies Center, Phila. Coll. Performing Arts. Bd. dirs. Athenaeum of Phila., 1977—, Phila. Opera Co., 1978. Served with U.S. Army, 1960-62. Mem. Nat. Water Co. Conf. (govt. relations com.). Clubs: Confrerie des Chevaliers du Tastevin; Galveston Arty.; George Town; Penn; Racquet, Rittenhouse, Union League (Phila.); Savile (London). Home: Apt 2602 Hopkinson House Washington Sq S Philadelphia PA 19106 Office: 1500 Walnut St Philadelphia PA 19102

LANGDON, RICHARD COLLINS, mfg. co. exec.; b. New London, Conn., Nov. 8, 1919; s. Frederick S. and Ruth R. (Rogers) L.; M.E., Norwich U., 1941; m. Kathleen Geraghty, Feb. 7, 1942; children—Richard, James. Asst. supt. P & W Aircraft, East Hartford, Conn., 1941-46; asst. plant mgr. Foote Bros. Gear & Machine, Chgo., 1946-48; quality control mgr. Merrow Machine Co., Hartford, Conn., 1948-55, New Britain Tools (Conn.), 1955-62, asst. plant mgr., 1962, plant mgr., 1966, quality control dir., 1970, dir. quality assurance, Newington, Conn., 1980—. Leader, Boy Scouts Am., 1952-68; bd. dirs. Handicapped Workshop, New Britain, 1969—. Served with U.S. Army, 1944-46. Decorated Purple Heart; recipient Service award Am. Nat. Standards Inst., 1944; Citizen's Service award, Indsl. Mgmt. Assn., 1969; Boy Scout Am. Scouters Key, 1959. Mem. Am. Nat. Standards Inst., Hand Tool Inst. Republican. Home: 3 Briarwood Rd West Hartford CT 06107 Office: 492 Cedar St Newington CT 06111

LANGDON, ROBERT BRAYTON, systems analyst; b. Utica, N.Y., Mar. 14, 1945; s. Robert Brayton and Kathryn Marie (Cromie) L.; B.A. in Math., Utica Coll., Syracuse U., 1967; postgrad. Catholic U. Am., 1967-68; M.B.A., Syracuse U., 1979; m. Deborah Jean Ireland, Aug. 8, 1970; children—Robert Brayton, David Raymond, Michael Jon. Tchr., Harrisville (N.Y.) Public Schs., 1968-70; asso. engr. quality control Remington Arms Co., Ilion, N.Y., 1970-73, systems analyst programmer, 1973-74, supv. systems planning, 1974-78, systems analyst Powder Metal Products div., 1978-79, material requirements planning, 1979-80; systems analyst Gen. Electric Co., Utica, 1980—. Active Boy Scouts Am., 1969—. Mem. Data Processing Mgmt. Assn., Am. Production and Inventory Control Soc., Assn. M.B.A. Execs. Democrat. Roman Catholic. Clubs: K.C., Elks. Home: 513 Steuben Rd Herkimer NY 13350 Office: Gen Electric Co French Rd Utica NY 13502

LANGE, HANS WILLIAM, mfg. co. exec.; b. Pitts., Mar. 13, 1930; s. Ewald and Elizabeth (Engle) L.; B.S., Carnegie Mellon U., 1952; M.B.A., Harvard U., 1956; m. Melissa McMurry, Dec. 19, 1953; children—Leslie, Allison, Hans William. Project mgr. Babcock & Wilcox Co., Lynchburg, Va., 1956-59; gen. mgr. Va. Indsl. Metals, Lynchburg, Va., 1959-65; plant mgr. Brenco, Inc., Petersburg, Va., 1965-67; v.p., gen. mgr. AMF, Inc., Richmond, Va., 1967-70; pres. Seamco, Inc., Stamford, Conn., 1970-72; with AMF, Inc., White Plains, N.Y., 1972—, exec. v.p. ops., 1977—. Bd. dirs. New Cannan Inn, Inc. Served with U.S. Army, 1952-54. Presbyterian. Office: AMF Inc 777 Westchester Ave White Plains NY 10604

LANGE, MILTON DAVID, oil co. exec.; s. Frederick George and Olive Mae (Beiber) L.; B.S., U. Pitts., 1951; m. Jean, June 16, 1951; children—David, Mary. With B.F. Goodrich Co., 1950-55, asst. purchasing agt., 1951-55; with Cities Service Co., Akron, Ohio, 1956—, mktg. coordinator columbian carbon div., 1970-72, customer service mgr., 1972-77, adminstrv. mgr., 1977—. Pres. Bridal Paths Estates Civic Improvement Assn., 1975-78. Served with USAF, 1942-46. Mem. So. Group Rubber Group (chmn. 1968-69), Am. Chem. Soc. (chmn. exhibits policy rubber div. 1976-77). Republican. Home: Rt 1 Box 427 Claremore OK 74017 Office: Box 37 Tulsa OK 74102

LANGENBERG, FREDERICK CHARLES, steel inst. exec.; b. N.Y.C., July 1, 1927, s. Frederick Charles and Margaret (McLaughlin) L.; B.S., Lehigh U., 1950, M.S., 1951; Ph.D., Pa. State U., 1955; postdoctoral Mass. Inst. Tech., 1955-56; m. Jane Bartholomew, May 16, 1953; children—Frederick C., Susan Jane. Technologist, U.S. Steel Corp., Pitts., 1951-53; supr. pyrometallurgy Crucible Steel Co., Pitts., 1956-58, material and process engr., 1958-59, chief devel. metallurgist, 1959, mgr. process research, asst. dir. process research and devel., 1959-64, dir. process research and devel., 1964-65, dir. technology, 1965-67, v.p. research and engring., 1967-68, also mem. exec. policy, operating and appropriations coms.; pres. Trent Tube Co. subsidiary Colt Industries, 1968-70; exec. v.p. Jessop Steel Co., Washington, Pa., 1970, pres., 1970-75, also dir.; pres. Am. Iron and Steel Inst., 1975-79, Interlake, Inc., 1979—; dir. Millcraft Industries, Inc. Served with USNR, 1945-46. Fellow Am. Soc. Metals (trustee); mem. Am. Inst. M.E. (chmn. phys. chemistry of steelmaking com. iron and steel div.), Am. Chem. Soc., Am. Ordnance Assn. (pres., dir. Pitts. chpt.), Am. (dir.), Brit. iron and steel insts., Am. Iron and Steel Engrs., Phi Beta Kappa, Tau Beta Pi, Sigma Xi, Phi Lambda Upsilon, Phi Kappa Phi. Clubs: Duquesne, University (Washington); St. Clair Country, Chgo. Golf, Congressional, Carlton, Butler Nat. Golf, Burning Tree. Contbr. articles to profl. jours. Patentee in field. Home: 22 Bradford Ln Oakbrook IL 60521 Office: Interlake Inc 2015 Spring Rd Oak Brook IL 60521

LANGENHEIM, ROGER ALLEN, oilfield products co. exec., lawyer; b. Seward, Neb., Feb. 21, 1935; s. Elmer L. and Esther L. (Gerkensmeyer) L.; B.S., U. Nebr., 1957, LL.B., 1960; m. Susan C. McMichael, Aug. 31, 1963; children—Ann Elizabeth, Mark Allen, Sara Ann. Admitted to Nebr. bar, 1960, Mo. bar, 1960; asso. firm Stinson, Mag, Thomson, McEvers & Fizzell, Kansas City, Mo., 1960-66; v.p., gen. counsel Black, Sivalls & Bryson, Inc., Kansas City, Mo., 1966-70; internat. atty. Dresser Industries, Inc., Dallas, 1970-71; group counsel Petroleum & Mineral Group, Houston, 1971-75; v.p., gen. counsel Oilfield Products Group, Houston, 1975—; v.p., gen. counsel Magcobar Group, Houston, 1980—. Mem. Am., Nebr., Mo. Houston bar assns., Order of Coif. Republican. Roman Catholic. Clubs: Houston Petroleum, Elks. Editor U. Neb. Law Rev., 1958-59. Home: 14911 Carolcrest Houston TX 77079 Office: 601 Jefferson Houston TX 77002

LANGFORD, BARRY EUGENE, ins. co. exec.; b. Greenville, Miss., Nov. 14, 1947; s. William Levi and Bonnie Jean L.; B.S. in Bus. Adminstrn., U. So. Miss., 1969; m. Janyne Pierce, Dec. 13, 1976; 1 dau., Angela Rhea; 1 stepdau., Tracy L. Florand. Mktg. rep. Aetna Ins., 1969-72; agy. underwriter Harlan Ins., 1972-73; mktg. mgr. Reliance Ins. Co., Chgo., Atlanta and Birmingham, Ala., 1973-77; pres. Salem Underwriters Inc., v.p. Integon Corp., Winston-Salem, N.C., 1977-80; pres. Centralia Ins. Group, Inc., Memphis, 1980-81, Lanford-Fitzsimmons, Inc., Hattiesburg, Miss., 1981—. Founder, Lafayette (La.) Better Bus. Bur., 1972, Willow Run Recreation Assn., Winston-Salem, 1979. Served with USNR, 1967-70. Mem. Am. Assn. Mng. Gen. Agts., Nat. Assn. Profl. Surplus Lines Offices, Sigma Nu (co-founder Theta Gamma chpt. U. So. Miss. 1967). Republican. Baptist. Home: Rt 2 Box 193-A Jayess MS 39641 Office: PO Box 1721 Hattiesburg MS 39401

LANGFORD, GERALD TALMADGE, exploration co. exec.; b. Kilgore, Tex., Jan. 13, 1935; s. DeWitt and Lillian (Easterling) L.; B.S. in Geology, U. Tex., 1957; m. Ora Kay Hess, June 11, 1955; children—Cheryl Kay, Randall, Robin Leigh, David Larkin, Matthew Talmadge, Mary Camille. Pres., Tex-L Exploration Corp., Longview, Tex., 1960-64, Cal-L Exploration Corp., Santa Barbara, Calif., 1964-68, Sabre Exploration Corp., Dallas, 1968—. Mem. Dallas Geol. Soc. Baptist. Clubs: Brookhaven Country, Bent Tree Country. Home: 13900 Hillcrest St Dallas TX 75240 Office: 4925 Greenville Ave Suite 1340 Dallas TX 75206

LANGHOUT, HENRY JOHN, forest products co. exec.; b. Norwood, Ohio, July 11, 1923; s. Theodore John and Eunice (Herdtner) L.; B.A. in Bus., Miami U., Oxford, Ohio, 1947; m. Mary Virginia Schlientz, June 16, 1945; children—Bruce John, Michael Floyd, William Thomas. Salesman, Internat. Paper Co., Dallas and Cin., 1947-54, sales mgr. paperboard grades, Chgo., 1954-60; Eastern sales mgr., nat. sales mgr. Crossett div. Ga.-Pacific Corp., N.Y.C. and Chgo., 1961-65; Eastern sales mgr., nat. sales mgr. paperboard/linerboard grades Weyerhaeuser Co., Chgo., 1965-67, secondary fibre mgr., Tacoma, 1968-70, gen. mgr. shipping container div., Manitowoc, Wis., 1970-79; gen. mgr. Champion Internat. Corp., Joliet and Naperville, Ill., 1979—. Bd. dirs. Manitowoc-Two Rivers YMCA, pres., 1977-78; bd. dirs. Manitowoc County Taxpayers Assn., 1974-77, Jr. Achievement, 1973—, pres., 1974-75. Served with USNR, 1943-45. Recipient Layman of Year award YMCA, 1975. Mem. Fibre Box Assn. (zone 13 chmn. 1975-76), N.E. Wis. Indsl. Assn. (dir., chmn. 1977-78), Manitowoc-Two Rivers C. of C. (dir.), Delta Sigma Pi. Presbyterian (elder 1974). Club: Branch River Country of Branc (Wis.) (sec., dir.). Home: 8 Fernilee Ct Prestbury Aurora IL 60504 Office: PO Box 151 Joliet IL 60434

LANGRALL, CLARKE, ins. broker; b. Balt., Dec. 1, 1924; s. H. Morton and Hazel (Clarke) L.; B.S., U.S. Mcht. Marine Acad., 1945; postgrad. Johns Hopkins, 1947-49; m. Bettie Carolyn Davis, May 2, 1964. Sales engr. Pilbrico Co., Balt., 1946-50; ins. broker, solicitor Thompson & Jones, Balt., 1950-55; pvt. ins. broker, Balt., 1955—; pres. Clarke Langrall, Inc.; mem. advisory bd. Chesapeake Nat. Bank, Cockeysville, Md., pub. speaker; moderator radio program Religion Today, 1970-72. Pres. Loch Raven Sch. PTA, 1956, Loch Raven Inter-Community Council, 1958. Coordinator Vice Pres. Agnew's Inaugural Com., 1969. Served with USNR, 1943-46; MTO, PTO. C.L.U. Mem. Am. Soc. C.L.U.'s, Nat. Assn. Security Dealers, Soc. St. George, Eastern Shore Soc. Md., Advt. Club Balt., Nat. Assn. Ins. Agts., Nat. Assn. Life Underwriters, Million Dollar Roundtable, Alumni Assn. U.S. Mcht. Marine Acad., Towson. Mem. Baha'i Faith. Club: Loch Raven Kiwanis (pres. 1959). Contbr. articles to trade jours. Office: 606 Providence Rd Towson MD 21204

LANGSTON, A. VINCENT, acctg. service co. exec.; b. Fort Wayne, Ind., Mar. 4, 1918; s. Robert E. and Ethel R. (Roby) L.; B.S., Butler U., 1939; m. Evelyn I. Woodruff, Aug. 30, 1940; children—Robert C., Janis D. Asst. mgr. zone office Firestone Tire & Rubber, Indpls., 1939-41; supr. inventory control dept. Allison div. Gen. Motor Corp., Indpls., 1941-46; mgr. internal audit dept. Pierson-Hollowell Co., Inc., Indpls., 1946-51; asst. sec., treas. Howard W. Sams & Co., Inc., Indpls., 1951-77; owner, mgr. Central States Acctg. Service, Carmel, Ind., 1977—; dir. The Bobbs-Merrill Co., Inc. Mem. Nat. Assn. Accts. (pres. Indpls. chpt. 1959-60, nat. dir. 1961-62, 75-76) Electronic Data Processing Assn. (treas. 1966). Republican. Methodist. Home: 5850 E 79th St Indianapolis IN 46250 Office: 1089 3d Ave SW Carmel IN 46032

LANGVARDT, LARRY WILLIS, mfg. co. fin. exec.; b. Lansing, Mich., Mar. 12, 1929; s. Lawrence Cris and Gertrude Margaret (Mass) L.; student U. Calif., 1951; grad. in accounting and bus. adminstrn., Lansing Bus. U., 1955; m. Mary Frances Davis, July 26, 1952; children—Guy David, Tod Kevin. Chief accountant Hardrives Co., Fort Lauderdale, Fla., 1955-56; project cost analyst Standard-Vacuum Oil Co., Philippines and Australia, 1956-61; mgr. dept. treasury Goodyear Tire & Rubber Co. Gt. Britain, Wolverhampton, U.K., 1962-65, asst. treas., Manila, 1966-67, dir.-treas., 1968-78, asst. mng. dir. and sec. Goodyear Orient Co., Singapore, 1978—; dir., sec. Goodyear Singapore Pte. Ltd., 1978—; dir. G Y Real Estate Inc., Port Motors, Inc. Trustee Jr. Achievement of Philippines, 1969-75, v.p., 1971-73, pres., 1974-75. Served with USAF, 1948-52; Japan. Recipient resolution of commendation Jr. Achievement of Philippines, 1975, cert. of appreciation Philippine Cancer Soc., 1978. Mem. Fin. Execs. Inst. of Philippines (treas., dir.), Mgmt. Assn. of Philippines (sec./treas., gov.), Am. Assn.-Philippines (treas., dir.), Navy League U.S. (v.p. local chpt.), Center for Research and Communication., Am. Bus. Council Singapore. Clubs: Manila Polo, American; Club Singapore, Brit. Philippine, Am. Assn. Singapore. Office: 1211 Upper Boon Keng Rd Singapore 1438 Republic of Singapore

LANHAM, FRED B., III, bakery co. exec.; b. Tampa, Fla., Dec. 7, 1938; s. Fred B. and Thelma Lynn L.; A.B. in Econs., Guilford Coll., 1964; m. Linda Morgan, Aug. 24, 1964; children—Drew Taylor, Dana Lynn. With Pepperidge Farm Bakery, Miami, Fla., 1965-70, August Bros. Bakery, Miami, 1970-74; with Coosa Bakery - Merico, Inc., Rome, Ga., 1974—, v.p., gen. mgr. Bd. dirs. Boy's Club, Rome. Served with USAF, 1957-60. Mem. Am. Soc. Bakery Engrs., So. Bakers Assn., C. of C. Methodist. Club: Exchange (Rome). Home: Route 10 Huntington Rd Rome GA 30161 Office: Coosa Bakery - Merico Inc Darlington Dr Rome GA 30161

LANIER, JOSEPH LAMAR, JR., mfg. co. exec.; b. Lanett, Ala., Feb. 9, 1932; s. Joseph Lamar and Lura Brown (Fowlkes) L.; B.S., Washington and Lee U., 1954; student Harvard Grad. Sch. Bus., 1954-55; m. Ann Morgan, Aug. 21, 1954; children—Joseph Lamar III, Ann M. Asst. mgr. Fairfax mill West Point-Pepperell, Inc., 1958-62, corp. v.p., 1962-68, pres. indsl. fabrics div., dir., 1968-70, corporate exec. v.p., 1970-74, now chmn., chief exec. officer; dir. Textile Hall Corp., Trust Co. Ga., Flowers Industries, Inc., Liberty Nat. Ins. Co.; dir. So. regional bd. Arkwright-Boston Ins. Co. Bd. dirs. Am. Textile Mfrs. Inst. Trustee LaGrange Coll.; bd. visitors Berry Coll. Mem. Ala. C. of C. (dir.), Ga. Textile Mfrs. Assn. (dir.). Home: 1703 Spring Rd Lanett AL 36863 Office: West Point Pepperell Inc PO Box 71 West Point GA 31833

LANIER, SIDNEY EDWARD, mfg. co. exec.; b. Knox City, Tex., Aug. 1, 1945; s. S. E. and Ella (Wilson) L.; B.S. in Aerospace Engring., U. Tex., 1968, postgrad, 1969—; m. Bonnie Joy Root, July 31, 1971. Mng. partner L & L Investment Co., 1973—, pres., 1976—; Project test engr., sect. head, project engr., program mgr., dir. Chaff Products, Tracor, Inc., 1968-75, v.p., gen. mgr., pres. Tracor Radcon, Inc., Austin, Tex., 1975—; pres. AIM Enterprises Unltd., 1976—; instr. math. U. Tex., 1970-73. Chmn., counselor, advisor Tex. Atty. Gen. Youth Conf., 1963-65; precinct chmn. Republican. Party, Austin, 1970-73; pres. bd. trustees I Am School, Inc., 1976—. Mem. Tex. Soc. Profl. Engrs., Aircraft Owners and Pilots Assn., Assn. Am. Prepardness, Assn. Old Crows. Home: 5510 Shoalwood Ave Austin TX 78756 Office: 6500 Tracor Ln Austin TX 78721

LANIGAN, ROBERT JOSEPH, mfg. exec.; b. Bklyn., Apr. 26, 1928; s. John F. and Kathryn (Sheehy) L.; A.B. in Econs., St. Francis Coll., N.Y., 1950; m. Mary E. McCormick, Dec. 30, 1950; children—J. Kenneth, Betty Jane Lanigan Reed, Kathryn Ann Lanigan Armstrong, Jeanne Marie, Suzanne Marie. With Owens-Ill., Toledo, 1950—, beginning as mgmt. trainee, successively mgr. orgn. planning Glass Container div., v.p. adminstrn. and control Forest Products div., gen. mgr. primary operations Forest Products div., v.p., dir. corp. planning, asst. gen. mgr. Lily Tulip div., gen. mgr. Lily Tulip div., gen. mgr. Glass Container div., exec. v.p., gen. mgr. packaging group, and dir., pres., chief operating officer domestic ops. and dir., 1950-79, pres., chief operating officer internat. ops., dir., 1979—; dir. Nat. Petrochems Corp., Dun & Bradstreet Cos., Barry-Wehmiller Co., United Glass Ltd. (Eng.). Trustee Cath. U. Am., Toledo Symphony Orch.; b. dirs. Greater Toledo Community Chest; mem. Pres.'s Council of Toledo Mus. Art. Mem. U.S. Brewers Assn. (asso. dir.). Republican. Roman Catholic. Clubs: Toledo Country, Toledo, Inverness, Belmont Country (Toledo); Imperial Golf (Naples, Fla.); Muirfield Village Golf (Dublin, Ohio); Burning Tree (Bethesda, Md.); Blind Brook (Purchase, N.Y.). Office: PO Box 1035 Toledo OH 43666*

LANKFORD, ROBERT J., ins. co. exec.; b. Edwardsville, Ill., Apr. 18, 1929; s. James M. and Wilma I. L.; student U. Ill., 1948; B.B.A., So. Meth. U., 1950; cert. in Estate Planning, Am. Coll. Life Underwriters, 1966, postgrad. cert. in accounting and bus. evaluation, 1977, cert. in advanced pension planning, 1978, in bus. tax planning, 1979, in employee benefit planning, 1980; m. LaVern Olney, Dec. 29, 1959; children—Bruce, Craig, Leigh, Stuart. Sales rep., Haughton Pub. Co., Dallas, 1950; agent New Eng. Mut. Life Ins. Co., Dallas, 1950; instr. personal fin. Bishop Coll., Dallas, 1970-71; mem. spl. task force com. investigating problems in sale of ins. in Tex., 1976-77. Bd. dirs. So. Meth. U., YMCA, 1956-66, Downtown Br. YMCA, 1958-60; chmn. Dallas County Blood Security Program, 1968. Recipient Vanguard award New Eng. Life, 1975; C.L.U. Mem. Nat. Assn. Life Underwriters and C.L.U.'s, Dallas Assn. Life Underwriters (dir. 1968-76), Dallas Estate Planning Council (gov. 1966-68, 79—), Million Dollar Round Table (life and qualifying), New Eng. Life's Leaders Assn. (compensation com.), New Eng. Life's Hall of Fame. Republican. Presbyterian. Club: Willow Bend Polo and Hunt. Contbr. articles in field to The Pilots Log, Flitcraft Mag., 1966. Home: 4228 Caruth Blvd Dallas TX 75225 Office: 3131 Turtle Creek Blvd Suite 1015 Dallas TX 75219

LANNA, ROBERT ARTHUR, ins. agy. exec.; b. Yonkers, N.Y., Sept. 22, 1934; s. Ettore and Clelia F. (Fornells) L.; B.S., Hartwick Coll., 1958; postgrad. Sacred Heart U., 1979—; m. Catherine F. Russo, June 15, 1957; children—Christopher Joseph, Susan Mary, John Anthony. With Glens Falls Ins. Co. (N.Y.), 1958-65, agy. supt., 1961-62, mgr., 1962-65; v.p. Dowler Agy. Inc., Hempstead and Rockville Centre, N.Y., 1965-74, pres., 1974-77; v.p. Rollins, Burdick, Hunter of N.Y., Inc., Rockville Centre, 1977-79, sr. v.p., 1979-80, sr. v.p., Sr. account adv., N.Y.C., 1980—, dir., 1979—. Commr., City-wide Little League Baseball, Nashville, 1963; pres. Hempstead (N.Y.) Community Chest, 1971; bd. dirs. N.E. Nassau Psychiat. Hosp., 1974; founder, pres. Concerned Citizens Party of Rockville Centre, 1972-74; chmn. bd. Coalition of Voluntary Community Mental Health Agys. Nassau County Inc., 1975; pres. Mental Health Assn. Nassau County, Inc., 1976-80; nat. chmn. ann. alumni fund Hartwick Coll., Oneonta, N.Y., 1979-80. Served with U.S. Army, 1952-54; Korea. Recipient Community Service award Nashville Jr. C. of C., 1963; Brotherhood award Hempstead service clubs, 1971; Man of Yr. award Mental Health Assn. Nassau County, 1980. Republican. Roman Catholic. Club: Lake (New Canaan, Conn.). Home: 737 Carter St New Canaan CT 06840 Office: Rollins Burdick Hunter of NY Inc 605 Third Ave New York NY 10158

LANNAMANN, RICHARD STUART, exec. recruiting cons.; b. Cin., Sept. 4, 1947; s. Frank E. and Grace I. (Tomlinson) L.; A.B. in Econs., Yale U., 1969; M.B.A., Harvard U., 1973; m. Margaret Appleton Payne, June 21, 1969; children—Thomas Cleveland, Edward Payne, John Stewart. Investment analyst U.S. Trust Co. N.Y., N.Y.C., 1969-71; research analyst Smith, Barney & Co., N.Y.C., 1973-75, 2d v.p., 1975-77, v.p. successor firm research div. Smith Barney Harris Upham & Co., 1977-78; v.p. Russell Reynolds Assos., Inc., N.Y.C., 1978—. Vice-chmn., Campaign for Yale, Greenwich, 1976-79. Mem. Assn. Exec. Recruiting Cons.'s, N.Y. Soc. Security Analysts, Fin. Analysts Fedn., Inst. Chartered Fin. Analysts, Yale Alumni Assn. (dir. Greenwich 1978—, sec. 1980—). Clubs: Riverside (Conn.) Yacht; Links, Yale (N.Y.C.). Home: 22 Spruce St Riverside CT 06878 Office: 245 Park Ave New York NY 10167

LANNERS, FRED THOMAS, JR., chem. mfg. co. exec.; b. St. Paul, Nov. 14, 1917; s. Fred T. and Aurelia M. L. B.Chem.E., U. Minn., 1948; m. Leonette Wurm, Feb. 18, 1946; children—Michael J., Aurelia Lanners Peschken, Shirley Jean, Cynthia L., Fred Thomas III, John J., Carol Lanners Nelson, Alan J., Robert J., Kathleen Ann. With Econs. Lab., Inc., 1948—, pres. internat. ops., N.Y.C., 1967-78, chmn. bd., pres., chief exec. officer, St. Paul, 1978—, also dir.; dir. Am. Hoist & Derrick, St. Paul, 1st Bank St. Paul, Profl. Econs. Bur. Bd. dirs. St. Paul Greater United Way. Served with C.E., U.S. Army, 1942-45. Mem. Minn. Bus. Partnership, Nat. Assn. Mfrs. (dir.), Am. Mgmt. Assn., Minn. Assn. Commerce and Industry, St. Paul C. of C. (dir., 1st v.p. 1979-80, pres. 1980), Upper Midwest Council, Conf. Bd., Chem. Specialties Mfg. Assn., Bus. Internat. Clubs: St. Paul Athletic, Town and Country.

LANO, CHARLES JACK, mfg. co. exec.; b. Port Clinton, Ohio, Apr. 17, 1922; s. Charles Herbin and Antoinette (Schmitt) L.; B.S. summa cum laude, Ohio State U., 1949; m. Beatrice Irene Spees, June 16, 1946; children—Douglas Cloyd, Charles Lewis. Pub. accountant Arthur Young & Co., Toledo and Tulsa, 1949-51; div. controller Ex-Cell-O Corp., Lima, Ohio, 1951-59, Avco Corp., Cin., 1959-61; controller, asst. sec. Servomation Corp., N.Y.C., 1961; asst. controller Scovill Mfg. Co., Waterbury, Conn., 1961-62, comptroller, 1962-67; controller C F & I Steel Corp., Denver, 1967-69, v.p. adminstrn., controller, 1969-70; controller Pacific Lighting Corp., Los Angeles, 1970-76; exec. v.p. Arts-Way Mfg. Co., Armstrong, Iowa, 1976—. Served with USMCR, 1942-45. C.P.A., Okla. Mem. Am. Inst. C.P.A.'s, Calif. Soc. C.P.A.'s, Iowa Soc. C.P.A.'s, Fin. Execs. Inst., Nat. Assn. Accountants. Home: Box 198 Armstrong IA 50514 Office: Arts-Way Mfg Co Armstrong IA 50514

LANSFORD, JAMES ROBERT, marine electronics co. exec.; b. Corpus Christi, Tex., Sept. 8, 1931; s. Claude Keeran and Geneva Ardel (Bomer) L.; LL.B., Western State U. at San Diego, 1973; student Abilene Christian U., 1949-50, U. Wis., 1951-52, U. Tenn., Memphis, 1957-59, Cerritos Coll., 1965-67; m. Patricia Ethel Wilkes McFarland, May 31, 1969; children—Steven Doyle. Field engr. N. Electric Co., Galion, Ohio, 1960-61; dist. mgr. Allied Electronics Corp., Chgo., 1961-65; field engr. Consol. Vacuum Corp. Rochester (N.Y.), 1965-66; field sales engr. Winters & Co., Los Angeles, 1966-68; gen. mgr. Electronic Supply Co., Las Vegas, 1968-69; owner, mgr. Sea Tronics, San Diego, 1969—; instr. marine electronics and elec. systems. Asst. scoutmaster Boy Scouts Am. Served with USN, 1950-60. Mem. Nat. Assn. Corrosion Engrs., Am. Boat and Yacht Council, Nat. Marine Electronics Assn., Southern Calif. Marine Radio Council, Mensa. Republican. Home: 6305 Raydel Ct San Diego CA 92120 Office: 2826 Canon St San Diego CA 92106

LANSFORD, RAYMOND WILLIAM, ednl. adminstr.; b. Linn, Mo., Sept. 25, 1920; s. Frank A. and Annie L. (Miller) L.; B.S., S.W. Mo. State U., 1947; M.A., Northwestern U., 1948; Ed.D., N.Y. U., 1954; m. Beuna Alma Ridenhour, May 25, 1945. Mem. faculty Joplin (Mo.) Jr. Coll., 1946-47, S.W. Mo. State Coll., Springfield, 1947, Central Mo. State Coll., 1947-52, 54-57, N.Y. U., N.Y.C., 1952-54; prof. finance U. Mo., Columbia, 1957-60, asst. dean, 1960-68, 72-75, placement dir., 1968-72, dir. ednl. services, 1972—; pres. Broadway Inn, Inc., 1968-72, Stewart Rd. Apts., 1966-71; sec. Boles Land Ltd., Columbia, 1972—. Mem. Higher Edn. Com. for Christian Ch. Schs., 1955-58. Served with USAAF, 1943-45. Mem. Nat., Mo. realtors assns., Mo. Real Estate Assn. (dir. edn. 1972-76), Phi Delta Kappa, Delta Pi Epsilon, Pi Omega Pi, Kappa Sigma Kappa, Alpha Kappa Psi. Mason, Kiwanian (dist. gov. 1974-75, chmn. internat. com. 1976-77, internat. trustee 1979—). Home: 115 W Ridgeley Rd Columbia MO 65201 Office: 11 Middlebush U Mo Columbia MO 65201

LANSHE, JAMES CLEMENT, JR., lawyer; b. Allentown, Pa., May 9, 1946; s. James Clement and Alice Mary (McDermott) L.; A.B., Georgetown U., 1964; J.D., Cornell U., 1971; M.B.A., U. Hawaii, 1975; doctoral candidate Union Grad. Sch.; m. Jane Parcells, July 8, 1972; children—Neila Hunter, James C. Admitted to Pa. bar, 1971, U.S. Ct. Mil. Appeals, 1972, U.S. Supreme Ct. bar, 1978; adminstrv. asst. Sen. Hugh Scott, Washington, 1971; partner Lanshe Lanshe & Lanshe, Allentown, Pa., 1975—; mem. faculty Cedar Crest Coll.; U.S. trial observer Cts. of Japan, 1973. Mem. City Planning Commn., Allentown, 1980—; pres. bd. assos. Muhlenberg Coll., 1980; bd. dirs. Lehigh County Soc. Crippled Children and Adults, 1980—; mem. pres.'s council Allentown Coll. of St. Francis DeSales, 1980—; v.p. bd. dirs. YMCA Allentown. Served to capt. USMC, 1972-74. Mem. Am. Bar Assn., Pa. Bar Assn., D.C. Bar Assn., Am. Arbitration Assn., Beta Gamma Sigma. Republican. Roman Catholic. Club: Kiwanis (pres. found. 1979). Office: 123 N Broad St Allentown PA 18104

LANSING, SHERRY LEE, motion picture studio exec.; b. Chgo., July 31, 1944; d. Norton and Margot L.; B.S. summa cum laude, Northwestern U., 1966. Exec. story editor Wagner Internat., 1970-73; v.p. charge prodn. Heyday Prodns., 1973-75; v.p. creative affairs MGM Studios, 1975-77; sr. v.p. prodn. Columbia Pictures, 1977-79; pres. Twentieth Century-Fox Prodns., Beverly Hills, Calif., 1980—. Office: Twentieth Century Fox PO Box 900 Beverly Hills CA 90213

LANSTROM, SIGVARD WILLHELM, steel co. exec.; b. Youngstown, Ohio, Sept. 24, 1934; s. Carl Thure and Harriett S. (Swanson) L.; B.S. in Elec. Engring., Carnegie-Mellon U., 1956; m. Mary Edith Winegeart, May 29, 1958; children—Elizabeth Louise, Kendall Thure. With U.S. Steel, Pittsburg Works (Calif.), 1956—, gen. foreman tin finishing maintenance, 1967-75, asst. supt. maintenance, engring. and utilities, 1975-76, asst. supt. cold reduction, 1976-78, works maintenance engr., 1978-80, supt. maintenance and utilities, 1980—. Mem. adult com. Am. Field Service, Antioch, Calif., 1969-71, chmn. home selection com., 1970-71; mem. Carnegie-Mellon Admissions Council San Francisco Bay Area, 1970—. Served to 1st lt. Signal Corps, AUS, 1956-58. Mem. I.E.E.E. (program com. Bay area sect. 1968), Assn. Iron and Steel Engrs. (chmn. San Francisco sect. 1972-73, nat. dir. 1974, chmn. western conf. 1974, 76, 78, 80), Antioch C. of C. (dir., pres.). Methodist (chmn. adminstrv. bd. 1977—, trustee 1974-76). Clubs: Chamber Ambassadors, Delta Kiwanis (dir.) (Antioch). Home: 3223 View Dr Antioch CA 94509 Office: US Steel Pittsburg Works PO Box 471 Pittsburg CA 94565

LANTINBERG, SHELDON, horticulturist; b. N.Y.C., Jan. 2, 1937; s. Louis and Anne (Finkelstein) L.; B.S., SUNY, 1959; m. Marcia Carp, July 3, 1963; children—Lisa, Richard, Karin. Pres., Sheldon Lantinburg, Inc., N.Y.C., 1964-72, Enviro-Gro, Inc., N.Y.C., 1972-78; pres., chief exec. officer United Brands Floriculture, Perrine, Fla., 1978—. Served with U.S. Army, 1964-66. Jewish. Home: 12230 SW 68 Ave Miami FL 33183 Office: 17455 SW 157th Ave Perrine FL 33157

LANTZSCH, GUENTHER CHRISTIAN, banker; b. Krogis, Germany, Feb. 12, 1925; s. R. Edwin and Louise (Ettmeier) L.; B.A., Antioch Coll., 1951; M.B.A., U. Detroit, 1954; m. Margarette Joyce Kennedy, June 25, 1949; children—Barbara Ann, Geoffrey Christian. With Ford Motor Co., 1951-61, supr. budgets and profit analysis, 1957-61; planning mgr. Ford Motor Credit Co., 1961-62, mgr. mktg. and planning, 1962-65; forward ops. mgr. Ford Internat., 1965-69; v.p., comptroller Mellon Bank & Trust Co., Pitts., 1969-72; sr. v.p., comptroller Mellon Bank, N.A., Pitts., 1972—; v.p., treas. Mellon Nat. Corp., 1972-80, vice-chmn., treas., dir., 1980—; treas., dir. Mellon Nat. Mortgage Corp.; sr. v.p., dir. Mellon Internat. Fin. Corp.; sr. v.p., chief financial officer Mellon Bank, N.A., 1974-78, exec. v.p., chief fin. officer, 1978-80; dir. Duquesne Light Co., Pitts. Bd. dirs., treas. Pitts. Symphony Soc., Heinz Hall Performing Arts; bd. dirs. Am. Symphony Orch. League. Served to 1st lt., inf., AUS, 1943-47. Mem. Financial Execs. Inst., Am. Bankers Assn. Clubs: Sewickley Hunt; Duquesne (Pitts).; Allegheny Country; Rolling Rock; Flyfishers (London). Office: PO Box 15629 Pittsburgh PA 15244*

LANZ, ROBERT FRANCIS, utilities exec.; b. Greenwich, Conn., Oct. 30, 1942; s. John Edwin and Katheryn Loretta (Jerman) L.; B.A., LaSalle Coll., 1964; M.B.A., U. Conn., 1975; m. Elizabeth Kienlen; children—Christopher Robert, Jennifer Elizabeth. Corporate trust officer Chase Manhattan Bank, N.Y.C., 1966-70; cons. Stone & Webster Mgmt. Cons., N.Y.C., 1971; sr. cons. Ebasco Services Inc., N.Y.C., 1971-73; asst. v.p. finance Pacific Power & Light, Portland, Oreg., 1973-79, asst. v.p. fin. controls, head controller's dept., 1979-80, v.p. corp. fin., 1980—; guest lectr., securities regulation and utility financing U. Oreg., Portland State U.; cost of money witness in utility rate cases. Office: 1400 Public Service Bldg Portland OR 97204

LANZ, ROBERT L., laminated metal mfg. co. exec.; b. N.Y.C., Feb. 27, 1947; s. Herman and Lillian (Lee) L.; B.S. in Indsl. Engring., Northeastern U., 1970; M.B.A., Rutgers U., 1973; m. Doris B. Hamilton, July 19, 1969. Project engr. Western Electric Co., Kearny, N.J., 1970-72; gen. mgr. Foster & Allen, Inc., Somerville, N.J., 1972-75; controller Krementz & Co., Newark, 1975; pres. Improved Laminated Metals Co., Providence, 1976—. Bd. dirs. Manhattan Career Devel. Center, 1977—. Mem. Mfg. Jewelers and Silversmiths of Am., Providence Jewelers Club, Phi Sigma Kappa. Home: 95 Briarbrook Dr North Kingstown RI 02852 Office: 775 Eddy St Providence RI 02905

LANZISERA, ANGELO DANIEL, cons. civil and environ. engr.; b. Valley Stream, N.Y., July 30, 1930; s. Giuseppe and Angela Maria (Masiello) L.; B.C.E., Tri-State U., 1955; m. Elizabeth M. Duggan, Jan. 3, 1953 (div. 1964); children—Kathleen, Elizabeth, Eileen, Mary. Asst. post engr., chief bldgs. and grounds C.E., U.S. Army, Bklyn. and W. Ger., 1964-66; asso. Teas & Barrett, Malverne, N.Y., 1966-74; prin. A.D. Lanzisera, Valley Stream, N.Y., 1974-76; partner Teas & Barrett, Malverne, N.Y., 1976-79, Teas, Barrett, Lanzisera & Frink, 1979—; village engr. Village of Malverne, 1976—, Village of Laurel Hollow (N.Y.), 1976—. Dir. engring. CD Butler County, Ohio, 1960-64. Served with USMCR, 1947-48, U.S. Army, 1948-52; ETO. Registered profl. engr., Ohio, N.Y. State; registered land surveyor Ohio; diplomate with splty. in water supply and wastewater engring. Am. Acad. Environ. Engrs. Mem. Soc. Am. Mil. Engrs., Nat. Soc. Profl. Engrs., Am. Congress Surveying and Mapping. Republican. Roman Catholic. Home: 87 S Corona Ave Valley Stream NY 11580 Office: 125 Church St Malverne NY 11565

LAPIDUS, NORMAN ISRAEL, food broker; b. N.Y.C., July 20, 1930; s. Rueben and Laurette (Goldsmith) L.; B.B.A., CCNY, 1952, candidate M.Internat. Relations, 1956; postgrad. N.Y. U., 1957-60; m. Myrna Sue Cohen, Nov. 20, 1960; children—Robin Anne, Jody Beth. Salesman, Rueben Lapidus Co., N.Y.C., 1954-56, pres., 1960—; sales trainee Cohn-Hall-Marx, N.Y.C., 1955; salesman to v.p. Julius Levy Co., Millburn, N.J., 1964-66, pres., 1966—; salesman Harry W. Freeman Co., 1975-76, v.p., treas., 1976—. Mem. Maplewood (N.J.) Bd. Adjustment; chmn. Maplewood Citizens Budget Adv. Com., Maplewood United Jewish Appeal Drive; exec. com. Citizens for Charter Change in Essex County (N.J.); founder, chmn. Music Theatre of Maplewood; v.p. Maplewood Civic Assn. Served with U.S. Army, 1952-54; Korea. Mem. Nat. Food Brokers Assn. (regional dir., recipient cert. exceptionally meritorious service), Met. Food Brokers Assn. (dir., v.p.), Assn. Food Distbrs., Am. Legion, LWV. Republican. Jewish. Clubs: Lions, B'nai B'rith. Active local theatricals. Home: 21 Lewis Dr Maplewood NJ 07040 Office: 183 Millburn Ave Millburn NJ 07041

LAPIN, ROBERT CHARLES, investment banker; b. Bronx, N.Y., Oct. 30, 1930; s. Morris and Ruth Miriam Lapin; B.S., N.Y. U., 1952; m. Helene Ann Golub, Oct. 24, 1953; children—Karen, Joyce, Debra, David, Lissa. Pres., chmn. bd. Laurriet Printing Co., Inc., N.Y.C., 1953-77; partner, dir. Radix Orgn. Investment Bankers, N.Y.C., 1977—; chmn. bd. Templepan Inc. Holding Co., N.Y.C., 1977—; dir. Mahrco Industries, Inc., Styro Sales, Inc., Freedman & Slater Transport Co., Inc., Freedman & Slater Air Cargo, Inc., Tex. Bldg. Centers, Inc. Served with USAF, 1952. Jewish. Club: Haworth Country. Home: 166 Millbrook Circle Norwood NJ 07648 Office: 230 Park Ave New York NY 10017

LAPLACA, PETER JOHN, mgmt. cons.; b. N.Y.C., Dec. 9, 1946; s. Damiano John and Lillian Mary (Celauro) LaP.; B.S., Rensselaer Poly. Inst., 1968, M.S., 1969, Ph.D. in Mgmt., 1973; m. Sherry Cutler, Sept. 2, 1967; children—Michelle, Matthew. Instr., SUNY, Albany, 1970-72; asst. prof. U. Hartford, 1972-74; asso. prof. mktg. U. Conn., 1974—; mgmt. cons., 1968—. Treas., Vernon Elem. Sch. P.T.O., 1979—; coach Vernon Youth Soccer, Vernon Little League; leader Cub Scouts; mem. Vernon Econ. Devel. Commn. Recipient Research Design award Am. Mktg. Assn., 1971-72. Mem. Am. Mktg. Assn. (v.p. NE 1979-81, pres. Conn. chpt. 1976-77), Acad. Mktg. Sci. (v.p. fin. 1977-79), Am. Inst. Decision Scis. (v.p. NE 1973-74, 75-78), World Future Soc., Assn. Consumer Research. Editor: Strategic Planning in a Changing Economy, 1975; Strategic Planning in a Period of Transition, 1976; The New Role of the Marketing Professional, 1977; Marketing Strategies for a Tough Environment, 1979; Strategic Planning for Uncertain Environments, 1980; asso. editor Indsl. Mktg. Mgmt., 1976—; editorial rev. bd. Jour. Acad. Mktg. Sci., 1976—; editor Conn. Marketer, 1978-80. Republican. Roman Catholic. Home: 24 Quarry Dr Vernon CT 06066 Office: U41M U Conn Storrs CT 06268

LA POE, WAYNE GILPIN, business exec.; b. Waynesburg, Pa., July 13, 1924; s. James Lindsay and Mary (Gilpin) LaP.; B.A., Pa. State U., 1947; m. Margaret Louise Clark, Feb. 21, 1953; children—Deborah Jean, Marqui Lynne. Personnel, sales Armstrong Cork Co., Lancaster, Pa., Chgo., San Francisco, 1947-53; personnel dir. Safeco Ins. Group, 1953-63, v.p., 1963—; v.p. Safeco Corp., 1976-80, sr. v.p., 1980—; v.p. Gen. Ins. Co. of Am., 1963—, Safeco Ins. Co. of Am., 1963—, Safeco Life Ins. Co., 1963—, First Nat. Ins. Co. of Am., Seattle, 1963—, Safeco Nat. Ins. Co., St. Louis, 1972—. Mem. White House Conf. Children and Youth, 1960; Bd. dirs. Ind. Colls. Washington. Served to capt. USAF, 1943-46, and 1951-52. Decorated D.F.C., Air Medal with three oak leaf clusters. Mem. Acad. Polit. Sci., Am. Polit. Items Collectors (past pres.), Am. Aviation Hist. Soc., Soc. Archtl. Historians, Nat. Trust for Historic Preservation, Phi Kappa Tau. Republican. Home: 11986 Lakeside Pl NE Seattle WA 98125 Office: Safeco Plaza Seattle WA 98185

LAPORTE, WILLIAM FREDERIC, chem. mfg. exec.; b. N.Y.C., Sept. 3, 1913; s. William Frederic and Florence M. (Kahn) L.; A.B., Princeton, 1936; M.B.A., Harvard, 1938; m. Ruth W. Hillard, June 15, 1946; children—Suzanne H., Lynn E., William Frederic III. With Am. Home Products Corp., N.Y.C., 1938—, asst. to pres. subs. Anacin Co., 1939-42, asst. to pres. corp., 1943-44, v.p. gen. mgr. Anacin Co., 1944, v.p. gen. mgr. subs. Whitehall Pharmacal Co., 1944-48, pres. co., 1949-57, v.p., dir. corp., 1957-60, pres. dir., 1960-65, chmn. bd., pres., chief exec. officer, 1965-73, chmn. bd., chief exec. officer, 1973—; pres. dir. Buck Hill Falls Co.; dir. Mfrs. Hanover Trust Co., Am. Standard, Inc., B.F. Goodrich Co.; trustee Dime Savs. Bank of N.Y. Nat. chmn. Heart Fund campaigns, 1968, 69; trustee Columbia-Presbyn. Hosp. Mem. Proprietary Assn., Bus. Council, Bus. Roundtable. Clubs: Elm (Princeton); River, Pinnacle (N.Y.C.). Home: 435 E 52d St New York NY 10022 Office: 685 3d Ave New York NY 10017

LAPPIN, W. ROBERT, soft drink co. exec.; b. Boston, Feb. 23, 1935; s. Albert A. and Emma G. Lappin; B.F.A., Ithaca Coll., 1957; m. Dorothy M. Liftig, June 2, 1967; children—Lawrence B., James H., Jennifer, Lisa A., Jonathan E. Exec. v.p. Goodyear Rubber Co., Middletown, Conn., 1959-62; with Pepsi-Cola Bottling Co. of Hartford-Springfield, Inc., Windsor, Conn., 1962—, pres., chmn., 1977—; with Pepsi-Cola Bottling Co. of New Haven, Inc., Branford, Conn., 1962—, pres., chmn., 1977—; chmn. bd. Lappin Communications, Inc., Springfield, Mass., 1978—; chmn. bd. Bubble Up Internat. Ltd., Bubble Up, Inc., Los Angeles, 1972. Vice chmn. United Fund, Middletown, 1961, Greater Hartford Arts and Council Fund Drive, 1977; bd. dirs. Symphony Soc. Greater Hartford; trustee Wilbraham and Monson Acad., 1970-72. Named One of Outstanding Young Men in Am., U.S. Jaycees, 1970. Mem. Young Presidents Orgn., Nat. Soft Drink Assn., Hartford, Windsor, Springfield chambers commerce, Nat. Broadcasters Assn., Conn. Mfrs. Carbonated Beverages (past v.p., dir.), Assn. Pepsi-Cola Bottlers of Conn. (pres. 1969-70), New Eng. Pepsi-Cola Bottlers Assn. (v.p. 1970-71, dir. 1968-71). Clubs: Masons, 100 Club Conn. (dir. 1973—, v.p. 1977-80, 1st v.p. 1980, pres. 1981—). Office: 1050 Kennedy Rd Windsor CT 06095

LARD, CHARLES WALTER, diversified mfg. co. exec.; b. La Mesa, Calif., Feb. 13, 1946; s. Walter Coleman and Lydia Agnes (Johnson) L.; B.S., La. State U., 1968; M.B.A., Harvard U., 1971; m. Jackie Lyn Hoffmeier, Sept. 14, 1974; children—Benjamin Charles, Holly Elizabeth. Pres., C. Lard Assos., N.Y.C., 1971-72; partner Hamershlag, Borg, N.Y.C., 1973-75; asst. treas.-pension investment mgmt. United Technologies Corp., Hartford, Conn., 1975—. Mem. Hatford Soc. Fin. Analysts, Pension Group East (v.p.). Presbyterian. Author: Bonds II, 1970; Convertible Cookbook, 1976; also articles. Home: 35 Ridgewood Rd West Hartford CT 06107 Office: United Technologies Bldg Hartford CT 06101

LAREAU, GERARD ARTHUR, fin. counselor; b. N.Y.C., Sept. 8, 1939; s. Gerard A. and Gladys L. Lareau; B.A., Syracuse U., 1961; m. Marybeth Bass, June 6, 1970. Asst. sec. Mfrs. Hanover Trust Co., N.Y.C., 1967-73; founder, pres. Consumer Credit Counseling Service, N.Y.C., 1974—. Served to capt. USAF, 1962-67; Germany. Home: 140 West End Ave New York NY 10023 Office: 450 7th Ave New York NY 10001

LARGENT, JACK LACY, constrn. co. exec.; b. Adrian, Mo., Mar. 14, 1932; s. Arlie Everett and Ruby Lacy (Grossmart) L.; student Oreg. State Coll., 1954-58; m. Apr. 12, 1954 (div.); children—Mark, Dean. With Roofing and Lathing Contracting Co., Salem, Oreg., 1958—; founder, pres. Jack Largent Co. Inc., Salem, 1967—. Served with USAF, 1951-55. Mem. Nat. Home Builders Assn., Nat. Roofing Contractors Assn., Salem C. of C. Club: Jockey, Tiffany's. Home: 4378 Alderbrook Ave Salem OR 97302 Office: 2315 Pringle Rd Salem OR 97302

LARIMER, MILO CHARLES, mfg. co. exec.; b. Geneseo, Ill., Oct. 1, 1938; s. Paul Justin and Florence Elizabeth (Carlson) L.; student U. Iowa, 1956-58; B.S. in Bus. Adminstrn., U. Fla., 1961; m. Frances Diane Keck, May 10, 1975; 1 son, Aaron Todd. Mgr. sales Armstrong Cork Co., Boston, 1963-67; gen. mgr. Allied Personnel of Am. Internat., Denver, 1967-70; Western regional sales mgr. The Leisure Group Inc., Denver and Kansas City, Mo., 1970-78; sales mgr. High Standard, Inc., 1978—. Mem. Republican Com., Kansas City, Kans. Served to 1st lt. U.S. Army, 1961-63. Mem. U.S. Lawn Tennis Assn. (hon. life), Nat. Rifleman Assn. Republican. Methodist. Club: Kansas City Tennis. Home: 10009 70th St W Merriam KS 66203 Office: 114 Rainbow Circle Unit 129 Raymore MO 64083

LARKIN, FELIX EDWARD, corp. exec.; b. N.Y.C., Aug. 3, 1909; s. John A. and Maria C. (Henry) L.; A.B., Fordham U., 1931, LL.D. (hon.), 1978; M.B.A., N.Y. U., 1933; J.D., St. John's U., 1942; m. Evelyn Wallace, Dec. 28, 1937; children—Nancy Larkin Carr, John, James. Engaged security bus., 1933-37; lectr. Fordham U. Sch. Bus., 1937-42; law sec. Judge James Garrett Wallace, Ct. Gen. Sessions, N.Y.C., 1939-47; asst. gen. counsel Dept. Def., 1949, gen. counsel, 1949-51; v.p. charge indsl. relations W.R. Grace & Co., N.Y.C., 1951-58, exec. v.p. adminstrn., 1958-69, exec. v.p., sr. mem. office of pres., 1969-71, pres., 1971-74, chmn. corp., 1974—. Trustee Fordham U., 1969-78, emeritus, 1978—, chmn. bd., 1970-77; trustee Gregorian Found.; bd. govs. New Rochelle (N.Y.) Hosp. Med. Center Assn. Recipient highest civilian award Dept. Def., 1951; Nat. Brotherhood award NCCJ, 1980; named Man of Yr., N.Y. U. Grad. Sch. Bus., 1963; named to Fordham U. Sports Hall of Fame, 1979. Mem. Friendly Sons St. Patrick, Am. Arbitration Assn. (dir. 1975—). Clubs: Winged Foot Golf (v.p., gov. 1967-72, 74-76) (Mamaroneck); Larchmont (N.Y.) Yacht; N.Y. Univ., Pinnacle (gov.) (N.Y.C.); Knights of Malta; Pine Tree Golf (Boynton Beach, Fla.). Home: 1030 Old White Plains Rd Mamaroneck NY 10543 Office: 1114 Ave of Americas New York NY 10036

LARRANCE, WILLIAM HARRY, former steel foundry exec.; b. Rock Island, Ill., Mar. 20, 1910; s. Harry Omer and Elsie Elizabeth (Ferguson) L.; student Knox Coll., Galesburg, Ill., 1928; m. Vivian Estelle Nicholson, Aug. 9, 1941; children—Robert William, Stephen Michael. Clk., Ill. Wholesale Grocery, Rock Island, 1929-31; sta. operator Standard Oil Co., Rock Island, 1931-36; routine chemist to melting foreman Northwestern Steel & Wire Co., Sterling, Ill., 1936-41; melting foreman, cleaning room supt. Ordnance Steel Foundry Co., Bettendorf, Iowa, 1941-45; plant mgr. Campbell, Wyant & Cannon, Muskegon, Mich., 1945-46; plant supt. Riverside Foundry, Bettendorf, 1946-61, co. became div. Sivyer Steel Casting Co., Milw., 1961, now dir.; plant supt., works mgr. Riverside div. Sivyer Steel Casting Co., 1961-70, v.p. mfg. Riverside and Milw. divs., 1970-73, v.p. mfg. and corporate planning, also corporate dir., 1973-76, dir., v.p. Riverside Products Co., Bettendorf, 1968—; exec. v.p. Sivyer Steel Corp., Bettendorf, 1976-78, 80—, dir. emeritus, 1978—; dir. Russeloy Foundry, Durant, Iowa, Quality Aluminum Casting Co., Waukesha, Wis. Mem. Mayor's Indsl. Devel. Group, 1967, Quad City Air Pollution Control Bd., 1970; dir. Scott County Jr. Achievement, 1969. Mem. Bettendorf C. of C. (dir. 1974-76), Am. Foundrymen's Soc. (chmn. Quad City chpt. 1959-60, dir. 1956-60), Steel Founders Soc., Asso. Industries Quad Cities (pres. 1967, dir. 1964-67). Presbyterian. Clubs: Masons, Rotary (dir. 1970). Home: 3127 Crestline Dr Davenport IA 52803 Office: 255 S 33d St Bettendorf IA 52722

LARSEN, CURTIS LEROY, paint co. exec.; b. Escanaba, Mich., May 13, 1934; s. Willmer Oden and Pearl (Lorenson) L.; B.A., Mich. State U., 1958; m. Mary Louise Goetze, Sept. 8, 1956;

children—Karen Louise, Gregory Lee. Supr. gen. accounting Commonwealth Assos., Inc., Jackson, Mich., 1958-61; mgr. gen. accounting and credit Aircraft div. Aeroquip Corp., Jackson, Mich., 1961-65, controller Barco div., Barrington, Ill., 1965-70, asst. sec. corp., 1965-70; v.p. adminstrn. Kysor of Byron div. Kysor Indsl. Corp., Byron, Ill., 1970-74; v.p. finance and adminstrn. Ill. Bronze Paint Co., Lake Zurich, 1974-79; v.p. finance Fendall Co., Arlington Heights, Ill., 1979-81; dir. M.I.S. Kelco Industries Inc., Woodstock, Ill. Pres., dir. Barrington area United Dr., 1967-68; co. rep. Met. Crusade Mercy, 1966-69; mem. personnel and budget com. Countryside YMCA; mem. devel. com. Good Sheperd Hosp.; mem. Barrington Planning Commn.; mem. econ. com. Barrington Area Council Govts.; pres. Barrington Meadows Homeowners Assn. Mem. Nat. Assn. Accountants, Barrington C. of C. (pres. 1968-69). Republican. Lutheran. Mason, Rotarian. Home: 357 Beverly Rd Barrington IL 60010 Office: 300 E Main St Lake Zurich IL 60047

LARSEN, LOUIS ROYTER, electronics co. exec.; b. Phila., July 4, 1916; s. Lauritz and Anna (Royter) L.; student Pa. Mil. Coll., 1946; B.S., U. Pa., 1949, M.B.A., 1956; m. Eugenia Riddell Jacobs, Oct. 20, 1944; children—Louis Royter, Eric Risor, Peter Christian, Geoffrey Stang. Instr., U. Pa. Phila., 1949-51; factory accountant Sprague Electric Co., North Adams, Mass., 1951-65, dir. analysis and controls, 1965-67, controller, 1967—. Served with USAAF, 1942-45. Mem. Nat. Assn. Accountants. Home: Valley Rd Wellfleet MA 02667 Office: 87 Marshall St North Adams MA 02147

LARSON, CHARLES FRED, JR., indsl. assn. exec.; b. Gary, Ind., Nov. 27, 1936; s. Charles F. and Margaret Jane (Taylor) L.; B.M.E., Purdue U., 1958; M.B.A., Fairleigh Dickinson U., 1973; m. Joan Ruth Grupe, Aug. 22, 1959; children—Gregory Paul, Laura Ann. Project engr. Combustion Engring., Inc., E. Chgo., 1958-60; sec. Welding Research Council, N.Y.C., 1960-70, asst. dir., 1970-75; exec. dir. Indsl. Research Inst., Inc., N.Y.C., 1975—; sec. Indsl. Research Inst. Research Corp., N.Y.C., 1975—. Mem. Wyckoff (N.J.) Bd. Edn., 1973-78, pres., 1976-77. Registered profl. engr., N.J. Mem. AAAS, ASME, Soc. Research Adminstrs., Assn. Research Dirs., Am. Soc. Assn. Execs. Clubs: 60 E. (N.Y.C.); Masons; High Mountain Golf (Franklin Lakes, N.J.). Asso. editor Jour. Pressure Vessel Tech., 1973-75; contbr. articles in field to profl. jours.; editor mech. engring. articles. Office: Industrial Research Institute 100 Park Ave New York NY 10017

LARSON, CHARLES LARRY, investment co. exec.; b. Chgo., June 10, 1936; s. E. Larry and Bernice E.; B.A., DePauw U., 1957; postgrad. Coll. Life Ins., 1974, Coll. Fin. Planning, 1978; m. Catherine M., June 12, 1960; children—Mary, Ann, Christopher. Regional v.p. investment mgmt. Am. Express, San Francisco, 1968-71, Supervised Investment Service, Chgo., 1971-74, Dreyfus Sales Corp., N.Y.C., 1974-77; v.p. nat. sales, dir. Union Service Distbr., N.Y.C., 1977—. Pres., DePauw Alumni Assn., N.Y. Mem. Investment Co. Inst., Certified Fin. Planners, Levere Meml. Trust, Exec. Assn., Internat. Assn. Fin. Planners (dir.), Nat. Assn. Security Dealers (prin.), N.Y. Stock Exchange, PBW Stock Exchange (prin.), Pacific Coast Stock Exchange (prin.), Greenwich Art Assn., Sigma Alpha Epsilon. Home: 7 Wyndover Ln Cos Cob CT 06807 Office: Bankers Trust Plaza New York City NY 10006

LARSON, JOHN LOUIS, pharm. co. exec.; b. Grand Rapids, Mich., July 7, 1933; s. George Russell and Faye (McMillan) L.; B.S. in Mech. Engring., Mich. State U., 1955; m. Joanne E. Mapes, May 5, 1956; children—Susan, Sandra, Steven. With Eli Lilly & Co., various locations, 1955—, mng. dir. corp. facilities planning, 1967-79, dir. facilities planning and engring., 1979-80, dir. corp. materials planning, 1980—. Bd. dirs. Pleasant Run Childrens Home, 1968—, pres., 1974-76; mem. Washington Twp. Sch. Found. Mem. Indpls. C. of C., Compensation Execs. Assn., Indsl. Engring. Group. Home: 6364 N Ewing St Indianapolis IN 46220 Office: 307 E McCarty Indianapolis IN 46206

LARSON, RAY ORLANDO, specialty steel mfg. co. exec.; b. Denver, July 17, 1942; s. Reynold O. and Irene E. (Schmidt) L.; B.B.A., Pacific Lutheran U., 1965; postgrad. U. Calif., Los Angeles, 1965-66; 1 son, Christian O. With Kaiser Aluminum & Chem. Corp., Oakland, Calif., 1965-75, sales rep., 1970-71, gen. mgr., 1972-75; gen. mgr. western ops. Teledyne Rodney Metals Co., Pico Rivera, Calif., 1975-78, gen. sales mgr., New Bedford, Mass., from 1978; now sales mgr. Edgcomb Metals Co., Memphis, Tenn. Mem. Am. Soc. Metals. Republican. Lutheran. Home: 6204 Village Grove Dr Memphis TN 38115 Office: 1 Auction Ave Memphis TN 38101

LARSON, ROBERT ALTON, cutting die mfg. co. exec.; b. Quincy, Mass., Mar. 30, 1937; s. Alton John and Esther Hedvik (Olson) L.; B.Bus. Mgmt., Northeastern U., 1960; m. Letitia Jane Bernard, Jan. 23, 1960; children—Christa Ann, Erik Christian, Mark Robert. Exec. v.p., treas. Boston Cutting Die Co., 1974-77, exec. v.p., treas., 1977—; pres. Novelty Die Corp., Kingston Forge. Chmn. personnel bd. Town of Norwell, Mass., 1976-78; asst. scoutmaster Boy Scouts Am., 1977—, explorer adv. post 66, 1980—. Served to capt. Signal Corps, U.S. Army, 1960-63. Mem. Internat. Assn. Clothing Designers (pres. Indsl. chpt. 1976-77), Nat. Diemakers and Diecutters Assn. (dir. 1979—). Mem. United Ch. of Christ. Contbg. editor to Diemaking and Diecutting Mag., 1964-72. Patentee in field. Office: 50 Freeport St Boston MA 02122

LARSON, STANLEY EARL, aircraft parts sales co. exec.; b. Americus, Kans., Sept. 17, 1931; s. Walter Hilding and Velma Mildred (Getchell) L.; B.A., U. Wichita, 1957; m. Nancy Ann Felker, July 14, 1955; children—Larry Dean, Donald Everett, Deborah Nanette. Sheet metal assembler Boeing Airplane Co., Wichita, Kans., 1952-53; with Cessna Aircraft Co., Wichita, 1956-74, inventory systems and control mgr., 1964-74, data processing coordinator, 1974; mgr. spares and logistics support Mitsubishi Aircraft Internat., Inc., San Angelo, Tex., 1974—. Served with USN, 1948-52; Korea. Mem. Internat. Materials Mgmt. Soc. Clubs: Confederate Air Force, Masons, Optimists (dir. local chpt. 1975-77, 77-78). Author: Inventory Systems and Control Handbook, 1976. Office: PO Box 3848 San Angelo TX 76901

LARSON, WALTER RAMEY, electronic co. exec.; b. Los Angeles, Mar. 14, 1918; s. Walter Alexander and Jessie Ramey (McCune) L.; B.S. in Elec. Engring., Calif. Inst. Tech., 1940; m. Harriet A. Stover, Feb. 24, 1951; 1 dau. by previous marriage—Linda Anne Larson Stover. Instrumentation engr. N.Am. Aviation, 1946-47; mgr. instrumentation and test equipment design Northrop Aircraft Co., Hawthorne, Calif., 1948-63; design specialist McDonnell Douglas, Long Beach, Calif., 1963-69; cons., 1969-70; v.p. 3R Vinyl Co., Inc., Garden Grove, Calif., 1971-73, pres., 1973-77; pres. L.Z. Enterprises, Inc., 1977—. Radio amateur Sta. W6WL; chmn. North Orange County Alumni fund dr. Calif. Inst. Tech., 1973-77. Served to capt. USAAF, 1941-46, to lt. col. USAFR, 1946-68. Mem. Caltech Alumni Assn., Combat Pilots Assn., Res. Officers Assn. Republican. Congregationalist. Home: Stage Rd Hampstead NH 03841 Office: PO Box 5891 Orange CA 92667

LA SARDO, CAMILLE GABRIELLA, mfg. co. exec.; b. Jersey City, Aug. 5, 1945; s. James Frances and Ida Angela (Gagliano) LaS.; grad. Montclair State Coll., 1980. Personnel mgr. Luft-Tangee, Inc., Carlstadt, N.J., 1972-75, Channel Cos., Inc., Whippany, N.J., 1975-76, J.L. Prescott Co., Passaic, N.J., 1976—. Mem. Am. Soc. Personnel Adminstrn. (v.p. North Jersey chpt. 1980-81), Personnel Mgrs. Assn., Meadowlands C. of C. Home: 483 Liberty Ave Jersey City NJ 07307 Office: 27 8th St Passaic NJ 07055

LASATER, DONALD E., banker; b. St. Louis, Dec. 8, 1925; s. Jacques and Kathryne (Haessel) L.; student S.E. Mo. State Coll., 1942-43, U. Iowa, 1943; LL.B., U. So. Calif., 1948; grad. Nat. Trust Sch., 1960; m. Mary E. McGinnis, Apr. 4, 1951; children—Kevin Michael, Timothy Patrick, Thomas Brady, Laura Clark, John Robert. Admitted to Mo. bar; individual practice law, St. Louis, 1949-54; asst. pros. atty. St. Louis County, 1955-56; counselor, 1957-58; with Merc. Trust Co., St. Louis, 1959—, asst. v.p., 1960-63, v.p. trust adminstrn., 1963-65, v.p. charge trust dept., 1965-67, pres., dir., 1967-70, chmn. bd., chief exec. officer, 1970—; dir. Gen. Am. Life Ins. Co., Interco, Inc. Exec. com. St. Louis area council Boy Scouts Am.; bd. dirs. Barnes Hosp., Jr. Achievement, United Way Greater St. Louis, Inc.; trustee Washington U. Served with USNR, 1943-45. Recipient Levee Stone award Downtown St. Louis, Inc., 1979. Mem. St. Louis Bar Assn., Mo. Bar Assn., Assn. Res. City Bankers, Am. Bankers Assn. Republican. Roman Catholic. Clubs: Noonday, St. Louis, Bogey, Old Warson Country. Office: 1 Mercantile Center Saint Louis MO 63101

LASER, CHARLES, JR., cons. firm exec.; b. Redford Twp., Mich., July 8, 1933; s. J.C. and Gertrude L.; student Mich. Tech. U., 1952-54, Central Mich. U., 1959-60; m. Glenda Johnson, Sept. 30, 1972; 1 dau., Susan Faye. With Retail Credit Co., 1958-60; exec. dir. Saginaw County Republican Party, 1960-65; exec. dir. Republican Party of D.C., 1967; fin. dir. San Joaquin Republican Party, Stockton, Calif., 1968; owner Laser Advt., Bay City, Mich., 1969-75; exec. v.p. Vindell Petroleum, Inc., Midland, Mich., 1972-75, Geo Spectra Corp., Ann Arbor, Mich., 1977—; pres. Laser Exploration Inc., Grand Blanc, Mich., Am. Tech. Explorations, Grand Blanc. Served with U.S. Army, 1954-58. Clubs: Kiwanis, Elks. Office: 320 N Main Suite 301 Ann Arbor MI 48104

LASHMAN, FRANK A., answering service exec.; b. Washington, Aug. 28, 1920; s. Morris and Betty L.; student U. Miami, 1948; 1 son, Michael A. Owner, operator cosmetic co., 1955; promotion dir., publicity man for Jane Mansfield, 1959; photographer, 1958-60; owner, operator Toll Free America Inc., Ft. Lauderdale, Fla., 1978—. Troop chmn. Boy Scouts Am., 1975-79. Served with U.S. Army, 1944-46. Mem. Asso. Telephone Answering Exchange, Ft. Lauderdale C. of C. Democrat. Clubs: Moose, Elks, Broward Dolphin Booster (dir.). Office: 5460 N State Rd Seven Suite 215 Fort Lauderdale FL 33319

LASKEY, WALTER JOHN, investment co. exec.; b. Plymouth, Mich., Oct. 3, 1941; s. Edward Charles Laskey and Alice (Sehmer) Laskey Russell; B.A., Whittier Coll., 1965; m. Shirley Chisako Fujisaki, Aug. 14, 1965; children—Ryan, Jonathan, Jason. Account exec. Merrill, Lynch, Pierce, Fenner & Smith, Inc., Honolulu, 1971-74, instl. fixed income specialist, 1974-75, mgr. instl. dept., 1975-77, sales mgr., 1977-80, asst. v.p., 1980—; public speaker investment field. Served with AC, USNR, 1966-71. Decorated Air medal. Mem. Honolulu Investment Soc. Home: 762 Kalanipuu St Honolulu HI 96825 Office: PO Box 1720 Honolulu HI 96806

LASKIN, HAROLD, stockbroker; b. Phila., Aug. 5, 1918; s. Nathaniel and Celia L.; B.S. in Econs., Villanova Coll., 1939; postgrad. U. Pa., 1939-41; m. Lynn Bailer, Feb. 19, 1949; 1 son, Mark J. Pres., Nu-Eve, Inc., Phila., 1947-65; v.p. The Villager, Inc., Phila., 1966-68; registered rep. Auchincloss, Parker & Redpath, Phila., 1969-71; investment exec. Shearson, Hammill & Co., Phila., 1972-74; resident mgr. Herzfeld & Stern, Phila., 1974—; tchr. Main Line Adult Sch., 1975—. Mem. Internat. Assn. Fin. Planners, Phila. Securities Assn. Clubs: Radnor Valley Country (Ithan, Pa.); Urban (Phila.). Home: 56 Parkridge Dr Bryn Mawr PA 19010 Office: 1760 Market St Philadelphia PA 19103

LASKY, PAUL H., corporate exec.; b. San Francisco, Nov. 6, 1937; s. Philip G. and Pearl S. (Spillman) L.; Sc.B., Mass. Inst. Tech., 1959; Ph.D., U. Wash., 1965; m. Barbara Schurr, Sept. 16, 1962. Mem. corporate staff Sandia Corp., 1965-68; sr. mgmt. cons. Stanford Research Inst., 1968-72; dir. fin. and corporate devel. Fluor Corp., Los Angeles, 1972-76; mgr. fin. planning LTV Corp., Dallas, 1976-78; v.p. corporate devel. Baker Industries, Beverly Hills, Calif., 1978—. Mem. Fin. Execs. Inst., Assn. Corp. Growth, AAU. Office: 360 S Carmelina Ave Los Angeles CA 90049

LASNICK, JULIUS, business exec.; b. Paterson, N.J., Aug. 15, 1929; s. Herman and Badana L.; B.S. in Textiles, N.C. State U., 1951; m. Ann Kaplan, July 20, 1958; children—David, Laurie. With Milliken & Co., N.Y.C., 1951-78, gen. mgr., until 1978; exec. v.p. mktg. M. Lowenstein Corp., N.Y.C., 1978—; pres. Apparel Fabrics. Served with U.S. Army, 1951-55. Office: M Lowenstein Corp 1430 Broadway New York NY 10018

LASSETTER, JAMES GREEN, Realtor; b. Villa Rica, Ga., Sept. 13, 1916; s. John G. W. and Addie (Green) L.; student W. Ga. Jr., Coll., 1935-36; B.S., U. Ga., 1940; m. Maggie Samples, Apr. 7, 1939; children—Margaret Ann (Mrs. Charles W. Rushing), Mary Lynn (Mrs. Earl Maxwell), James W. Asst. supr. Farm Security Adminstrn., Carrollton, Ga., 1940; soil conservationist U.S. Dept. Agr., Soil Conservation Service, Marianna, Fla., 1941-43, Chipley, Fla., 1943-52, DeFuniak Springs, Fla., 1952-54; real estate broker James G. Lassetter, DeFuniak Springs, 1954-56, Tallahassee, 1956-58; pres. Tallahassee Realty Co., 1958—, Lassetters of Fla., 1959—, Palm Cove Estates, Inc., 1959—. Mem. Tallahassee Bd. Realtors (pres. 1964), Fla. Assn. Realtors (dist. v.p. 1962, 65), Nat., Fla. assns. farm and land brokers, Nat. Assn. Realtors, Nat. Inst. Real Estate Brokers, Nat. Soc. Rev. Appraisers, Nat. Assn. Ind. Fee Appraisers, Phi Kappa Phi. Baptist. Home: PO Box 1333 Tallahassee FL 32303 Office: 1020 E Lafayette St PO Box 1333 Tallahassee FL 32302

LASSIG, KENNETH H., communications co. exec.; b. Jamaica, N.Y., Nov. 20, 1934; s. Herman and Luise (Guldi) L.; B.B.A. cum laude, Hofstra U., 1956; m. Ann Errett, June 17, 1956; children—Richard K., Robert A., Virginia A. Accountant, Arthur Young & Co., N.Y.C., 1956-60; controller Dorne & Margolin Inc. mfg., Westbury, N.Y., 1960-65; financial analyst Celanese Corp., N.Y.C., 1966; with Western Union, various locations, 1967-77, asst. comptroller, Mahwah, N.J., 1972-73, comptroller, 1973-77; v.p. Oxbow Constrn. Corp., Port Washington, N.Y., 1977-79; controller RCA Global Communications, Inc., N.Y.C., 1979—. Served to 1st lt. AUS, 1957. C.P.A., N.Y. Mem. Am. Inst. C.P.A.'s, N.Y. State Soc. C.P.A.'s, Financial Execs. Inst. Mason. Home: 212 Wayfair Ln Franklin Lakes NJ 07417 Office: 60 Broad St New York NY 10004

LASSITER, JOE FRANK, JR., corp. exec.; b. Montgomery, Ala., May 1, 1943; s. Joe F. and Rose (Tatum) L.; B.S. in Bus. Adminstrn., U. Ala., 1965, J.D., Cumberland Sch. Law, 1968; m. Clare Cleere, June 6, 1966; children—Christine Clare, Joe Frank. Admitted to Ala. bar, 1968; law clk. Deramus and Johnston, Birmingham, Ala., 1967-68; asso. firm Miller and Hoffman, Montgomery, 197-73; asst. gen. counsel, v.p., dir. procurement Daniel Constrn. Co. div. Daniel Internat. Corp., Greenville, S.C., 1973-79, corp. v.p., mktg. counsel, 1979—; v.p.-law, sec.-treas. Seige Corp., Greenville, 1979—. Served as capt. U.S. Army, 1968-70. Decorated Bronze Star with cluster. Mem. Nat. Assn. Purchasing Mgmt., Am., Ala., S.C. bar assns. Presbyterian. Club: Kiwanis. Home: 186 Chapman Rd Greenville SC 29605 Office: Daniel Internat Corp Daniel Bldg Greenville SC 29602

LASTER, OLIVER, wholesale lumber co. exec.; b. Vienna, Austria, Aug. 4, 1921; s. Alan and Caroline (Harband) L.; came to U.S., 1940, naturalized, 1946; student U. London, 1938-39; B.Sc. in Mech. Engring. magna cum laude, U. Wash., 1943; m. Elizabeth Aschner, Sept. 4, 1949; children—Andrew J., Geraldine D., Steven B. Project engr. Standard Oil Co. Calif., San Francisco, 1943-47; sales mgr. Woodex Lumber Corp., N.Y.C., 1947-51, v.p., 1951-65, pres., Valley Stream, N.Y., 1965—. Mem. Sigma Xi, Tau Beta Pi, Zeta Mu Tau. Office: 99 W Hawthorne Ave Valley Stream NY 11582

LASTRA, BARRY NORMAN, petroleum co. exec.; b. Santa Monica, Calif., Nov. 18, 1938; s. Joseph B. and Dorothy J. (Miller) L.; A.A., Diablo Valley Coll., 1975; m. Nancy L. Lastra, Dec. 15, 1956; children—David, Dian, Dennis. Salesman, Standard Stas., Inc. (Standard Oil Co. of Calif.), Santa Barbara, 1957-58, asst. mgr., 1958-60, mgr., 1960-64; retail rep. Standard Oil Co. of Calif., San Jose, 1964-65, automotive service rep., Los Angeles, 1965-68, retail sales specialist, San Francisco, 1968-70, mktg. tng. coordinator, 1970-76; sr. adv. personnel devel. Chevron USA, Inc., San Francisco, 1977—; mem. com. on tng. and devel. for refining Am. Petroleum Inst., 1980—. Mem. adv. bd. United Way of Bay Area, 1977-78. Mem. Nat. Soc. Sales Tng. Execs. (honor award 1978, dir. 1979—), Am. Soc. Personnel Adminstrn. (diplomate tng. and devel.). Republican. Office: Chevron USA Inc 575 Market St San Francisco CA 94105

LATELLA, ROBERT MATTHEW, retail furniture co. exec.; b. London, Ont., Can., Apr. 5, 1932; s. Joseph M. and Rose L.; diploma De La Salle Boys Coll., London, Ont., 1952; m. Jeanne Lynn Britton, Sept. 10, 1955; children—David, Paul, Jackie, Matthew. Gen. mgr. Channer's Ltd., 1952-56, owner, pres., 1956-72; owner Latella's Decorator's Boutique, London, 1974-76; pres., gen. mgr., Latella's Ethan Allen Gallery, Hyde Park, Ont., 1976—; pres., dir. Furniture Row Ltd. Pres. Downtown London Assn., 1966-72. Mem. Nat. Home Furnishings Assn., London Ad and Sales Club (pres. 1972-73), London C. of C. Liberal. Roman Catholic. Club: Rotary. Office: PO Box 8022 London ON N6G 2B0 Canada also 474 Victoria St London ON N5Y 4B3 Canada

LATENDRESSE, JAMES JOSEPH, pharm. co. exec.; b. St. Paul, Aug. 17, 1927; s. James Joseph and Vina Marie (Maranda) L.; B.S., Ind. U., 1955; M.B.A., Rutgers U., 1962; m. Irene Clara Goodspeed, May 5, 1951; children—James Joseph III, Candace Ann, Mark Jeffery, Lisa Marie. With indsl. relations P.R. Mallory Co., Indpls., 1955-57; dir. personnel Haag Drug Co., Indpls., 1957-58; with research div. personnel and adminstrn. with Merck & Co., Inc., Rahway, N.J., 1958-73, corporate dir. orgn. devel., 1966-73; v.p. ops. in Far East and Middle East, Warner-Lambert Co., 1974, pres. Warner-Lambert Europe, 1974; v.p. internat. pharms., diagnostics, chems. and capsules, Morris Plains, N.J., 1976-77; pres. Rorer Internat., Fort Washington, Pa., 1977—. Served to capt. USAF, 1949-53. Mem. Am. Mgmt. Assn., Soc. for Advancement Mgmt., Ind. U., Rutgers U. alumni assns., Beta Gamma Sigma. Republican. Roman Catholic. Club: Am. (Sydney, Tokyo and London); K.C. Home: 32 Oak Knoll Rd Mendham NJ 07945 Office: 500 Virginia Dr Fort Washington PA 19034

LATER, MONTE QUINN, retail store exec.; b. Pocatello, Idaho, Sept. 26, 1931; s. Steven Call and Lillian (Quinn) L.; student Idaho State U., 1948-51; m. Beverly June Barnard, Sept. 28, 1950; children—Michael, Jeffrey, Chad Steven. Salesman, Standard Oil Co., 1949-51; clk. Later's Market, St. Anthony, Idaho, 1951-68; owner, pres. Later's Inc., St. Anthony, 1968—; partner, pres. Aspen Square, St. Anthony, 1978—. Chmn., Yellowstone Park Adv. Bd.; mem. St. Anthony City Planning and Zoning Commn.; mem. exec. com., chmn. profl. standards com. Fremont Gen. Hosp. Bd.; mem. adv. bd Fremont Sr. Citizens; bd. dirs. Idaho Parks Found. Mem. Nat. Assn. Retail Grocers, Internat. Council Shopping Centers, Idaho Retailers Assn., Idaho Food Dealers (past dir.). Clubs: Lions, Elks. Co-author: Where the Wind Blows Bittersweet, 1976. Home: 140 N 7th St E Saint Anthony ID 83445 Office: Aspen Square Saint Anthony ID 83445

LATHAM, BERNARD GERALD, apparel retail exec.; b. Kenosha, Wis., Aug. 15, 1939; s. Bernard C. and Geraldine F. (Deignan) L.; student U. Wis., Whitewater, 1958-61; m. Joann F. Mentus, Jan. 21, 1967. Mdse. trainee Carson Pirie Scott, Chgo., 1962-63, asst., 1963-65, buyer, 1965-69; pres. Latham Ltd., Chgo., 1969—; mem. retail adv. bd. Apparel Center, Chgo. Club: Chgo. Athletic.

LATHAM, FRANK WINFORD, JR., retail store exec.; b. Fort Worth, Jan. 30, 1945; s. Frank Winford and Mary Lucylle (Cox) L.; ed. Baylor U.; m. Jeannie Brown, Feb. 5, 1966; children—Frank, Robert Emery, John Harwell. With R.E. Cox Co., Waco, Tex., 1970—, merchandise mgr., 1972-76, v.p., 1976—, also dir. Chmn. bus. adv. com. Retail Inst. McLennan Community Coll.; bd. dirs. Historic Waco Found., 1978-79; pres. Heart of Tex. Goodwill Industries, 1979—; mem. adminstrv. bd. Austin Ave. United Meth. Ch., 1977—; trustee Scottish Rite Found. of Tex., 1979—; advisory bd. Tex. Ranger Found., 1979; bd. dirs. Am. Soc. Prevention Cruelty to Children, 1980; exec. bd. Heart of Tex. Council Boy Scouts Am. Served with USAF, 1963-67. Recipient Silver Good Citizenship medal S.A.R., 1978, DeMolay Legion of Honor, 1979, Order of Red Cross of Constantine, 1980. Mem. Am. Soc. Indsl. Security, Assn. Former Intelligence Officers, Tex. Assn. Bus., Nat. Retail Mchts. Assn., Tex. State Hist. Assn. Clubs: S.A.R. (v.p. chpt.), Masons, Shriners, S.C.V. Office: 501 Westview Village Waco TX 76710

LATHAM, GERALD TALIAFERRO, former newspaper exec.; b. Latham, Mo., Sept. 7, 1912; s. Peter Conway and Ethel (Smith) L.; student So. Oreg. Normal Coll., 1932-34, Medford Bus. Coll., 1934; m. Lois Lindsey, July 3, 1937; children—Lynn Ann (Mrs. Bradley B. Lane), Julie Lee (Mrs. Dennis Vincent). Carrier, Medford (Oreg.) Mail Tribune, 1924-28, circulation collector, 1928-31, part time circulation mgr., 1931-33, circulation mgr., 1933-53, bus. mgr., 1954-67, exec. v.p., gen. mgr., 1967-77; dir. Medford Printing Co., Medford Mail Tribune Co., Mt. Ashland Corp. Active United Medford Crusade drive, Rogue Vally hosp. drive; chmn. Jackson County (Oreg.) Water Resource Bd., 1956; mem. Jackson County Rural Sch. Bd., 1958-60; mem. Jackson County Planning Commn., 1958-66, chmn., 1964-66; adv. com. travel info. div. Oreg. Hwy. Dept., 1965—; mem. Medford Water Commn. Bd., 1962-66. Mem. Young Reps., 1947-51, Rep. Central Commn., 1952-56; bd. dirs. Rogue Basin Flood Control and Water Resources, 1962—, vice-chmn., 1980, chmn., 1981; adv. bd. Sacred Heart Hosp., 1962-66, vice chmn., 1967-68, chmn., 1969-70; mem. adv. bd. Providence Hosp., 1966—; bd. dirs. Providence Community Health Found., 1978—, pres., 1980. Recipient Community Service award U.S. Jr. C. of C., 1971; Amos Voorhies Oreg. Newspaper Roll of Honor award,

1978. Mem. Pacific N.W. Internat. Circulation Mgrs. Assn. (pres. 1945), Oreg. Newspaper Pubs. Assn. (dir. 1960-66, pres. 1965), Medford and Jackson County C. of C. (dir. 1958-60, 67-70, 72—, pres. 1960, chmn. bd. 1961), Pacific N.W. Newspaper Assn. (dir.), Asso. Oreg. Industries (dir. 1971-77), Civic Music Assn., Jackson County Health Assn. Mem. Christian Ch. Elk. Club: Medford Knife and Fork. Home: 815 Park Ave Medford OR 97501

LATHAM, JAMES ARTHUR, oil co. exec.; b. El Dorado, Ark., Feb. 24, 1926; s. James Emmett White, Jr. and Emily (Ross) Latham; B.S., U.S. Naval Acad., 1951; B.S. in Petroleum Engring., U. Okla., 1955, M.S. in Petroleum Engring., 1956; m. Marian Willson Malone, Oct. 25, 1958; children—Laura, Anna, Madeleine, James Arthur. Sr. reservoir engr. Ark. Fuel Oil Corp., 1956-60; cons. petroleum engr., Shreveport, La., 1961-63; pres., chief exec. officer Latham Oil Co., Inc., Shreveport, 1962-68; pres. chief exec., dir. Transcontinental Oil Corp., Shreveport, 1968-80, Latham Resources Corp., Shreveport, 1980—; instr. math. night sch. Centenary Coll., 1958-60. Bd. dirs. adv. bd. Vols. of Am.; bd. visitors Air U., Maxwell AFB. Served with USAAF, 1944-45; to 1st lt. USAF, 1951-54. Mem. Soc. Petroleum Engrs. (past chmn. and dir. Shreveport), Am. Assn. Petroleum Geologists, Am. Mgmt. Assn., Pres.'s Assn., U.S., Shreveport chambers commerce, Tau Beta Pi, Sigma Gamma Epsilon, Pi Epsilon Tau. Methodist (past chmn. ofcl. bd., mem. adv. and budget coms.). Clubs: Shreveport, Shreveport Country, Shreveport Petroleum; Univ.; Pierremont Oaks Tennis. Home: 6936 Gilbert Dr Shreveport LA 71106 Office: 700 American Tower Shreveport LA 71101

LATHROP, JAMES DUANE, real estate broker; b. Midland, S.D., Jan. 26, 1930; s. Linnley Duane and Lucille Ellenor (Henn) L.; B.A., Alaska Meth. U., 1966; m. Ione Helena Engen, June 21, 1965; children—James David, Cynthia Helen. With Action Realty Inc., Anchorage, 1967-68, Totem Realty, Anchorage, 1968-70, 76—; pres., owner, operator Sun Realty, Inc., Anchorage, 1970—; owner Golden North Motel, Fairbanks, Alaska, Central Spenard Enterprises, Terrace On The Lake; part owner Lucky Co. Served with USN, 1948-52. Lutheran (elder). Address: 4009 Kingston Dr Anchorage AK 99504

LATHROP, MITCHELL LEE, lawyer; b. Los Angeles, Dec. 15, 1937; s. Alfred Lee and Barbara (Mitchell) L.; B.Sc., U.S. Naval Acad., 1959; J.D., U. So. Calif., 1966; children—Christin Lorraine, Alexander Mitchell, Timothy Trewin Mitchell. Admitted to D.C., Calif. bars, 1966, U.S. Supreme Ct. bar, 1969; dep. counsel Los Angeles County, Calif., 1966-68; mem. firm Brill, Hunt, DeBuys and Burby, Los Angeles, 1968-71; partner Macdonald, Halsted & Laybourne, Los Angeles, 1971—. Spl. advisor Los Angeles County Delinquency and Crime Commn., 1969-73; lectr. in law Advanced Mgmt. Research, Inc., N.Y.C., Am. Bar Assn.-Am. Law Inst., Practising Law Inst., N.Y.C., State Bar Calif. Bd. dirs., Western regional co-chmn. Met. Opera Nat. Council, N.Y.C.; trustee Thatcher Sch., 1972-76; trustee Honnold Library at Claremont Colls., v.p., 1971-72. Served with USN, 1959-63; comdr. Res. Mem. Am. Bar Assn. (com. officers and dirs. and profl. liability law), State Bar Calif. (disciplinary bd. 1976—), Am. Bd. Trial Advs., Los Angeles County, San Diego County bar assns., Internat. Assn. Ins. Counsel, Los Angeles Opera Assos. (pres. 1970-72), Friends of Claremont Colls. (dir. 1975—, pres. 1978—), Friends of Huntington Library, Soc. Colonial Wars (gov. Calif. 1970-72), Phi Delta Phi. Clubs: California, Brit. United Services (sec. 1974-75) (Los Angeles); Valley Hunt (Pasadena, Calif.); Met. (N.Y.C.). Contbr. articles to profl. jours. Home: 706 Stafford Pl San Diego CA 92107 Office: 1200 Wilshire Blvd Los Angeles CA 90017 also 110 W A St San Diego CA 92101

LATIMER, HUGH ALFRED, found. investment adv.; b. Holyoke, Mass., Apr. 11, 1926; s. Claude Alfred and Ethel Marion (Schwetje) L.; B.S.E.E., Va. Poly. Inst., 1948; LL.D., W.Va. Wesleyan Coll., 1979; m. Alice Marye Finke, Nov. 14, 1953; children—Hugh Scot, Paul Louis. Adminstrv. asst. engring. dept. Chesapeake & Potomac Telephone Co. Va., Richmond, 1948-49, staff asst. 1949, engr., 1949-52, staff engr. Washington, 1953, plant extensions engr. Richmond, 1954-57, div. traffic mgr., 1957-60, gen. traffic supr., equipment and bldg. engr., 1960-62, chief engr., gen. engring. mgr., v.p., gen. mgr., dir. Charleston, W.Va., 1962-69; asst. v.p. A.T.&T., N.Y.C., 1969-71; v.p. Ill. Bell Telephone Co., Chgo., 1971-80, treas., 1972-78; investment adv. MacArthur Found., Chgo., 1980—. Trustee, W.Va. Wesleyan Coll., 1969—, chmn., 1973-80; mem. gen. bd. pensions United Methodist Church, 1978, mem. investment com., 1976—, chmn., 1980—. Served with U.S. Army, 1944-45. Mem. Omicron Delta Kappa (hon.), Tau Beta Pi (hon.), Eta Kappa Nu (hon.), Pi Delta Epsilon (hon.). Methodist. Clubs: Univ., Mid-Day. Office: 140 S Dearborn St Chicago IL 60603

LATIN, JOHN SYLVESTER, engr.; b. Yonkers, N.Y., Sept. 9, 1939; s. John Chester and Sophie Marie (Oscar) L.; B.E.E., Manhattan Coll., 1961; B.A. in Math., Calif. State U., 1971. Research engr. Republic Aviation Corp., Farmingdale, N.Y., 1961-64; space shuttle test engr. and program speaker Apollo Command and Service Module program Rockwell Internat., Downey, Calif., 1964—. Coordinator, Downey-Norwalk, Joint Action in Community Service U.S. Dept. Labor, 1971-76. Recipient Vol. award U.S. Dept. Labor, 1973; Service to Youth award, Downey, 1975. Mem. Nat. Mgmt. Assn. (Leadership award 1974), Nat. Space Inst., IEEE, Nat. Speakers Assn. Democrat. Roman Catholic. Club: Toastmasters (dir. 1977-79). Home: 1010 Calle Ortega San Dimas CA 91773 Office: 12214 Lakewood Blvd Downey CA 90241

LATORTUE, GERARD RENE, economist, educator; b. Haiti, June 19, 1934; s. Rene A. and Francoise A. (Dupuy) L.; LL.B., U. Haiti, 1955, LL.M., 1956; Degree in Econ. Devel., U. Paris (France), 1960; m. Marlene Zephirin, Sept. 3, 1966; children—Gaielle, Stephanie, Alexia. Economist, Labor Dept., Port-au-Prince, Haiti, 1960-62; prof. econs. U. Haiti, Port-au-Prince, 1961-63; co-founder, co-dir. Institut de Hautes Etudes Commerciales et Economiques, Port-au-Prince, 1961-63; prof. econs. Inter-Am. U. of P.R., San German, 1963—, chmn. dept. econs. and bus. adminstrn., 1968-72; project mgr. assistance to small-scale industries in Togo, UN Indsl. Devel. Orgn., 1972-74, chief adviser, 1974-77 UNIDO Chief adviser, Ivory Coast, 1977—. Decorated officer Nat. Labor Order (Haiti). Mem. Am. Econ. Assn., Soc. for Internatl. Devel., Am. Marketing Assn., Nat. Planning Assn. Club: Lions. Contbr. chpts. to books. Home: 01 BP 1318 Abidjan 01 Ivory Coast West Africa Office: UNDP Office PO Box 1747 Abidjan Ivory Coast West Africa

LA TOUR, JOSEPH LYNNE, hotel exec.; b. Malone, N.Y., Dec. 15, 1942; s. Joseph Eugene and Margaret Theresa (Laroche) La T.; B.S. in Hotel Adminstrn., U. Nev., 1971; m. Peggy Ann O'Brien, Aug. 21, 1971; 1 son, Michael Joseph. Supr., Sky Chefs Internat., Chgo. and N.Y.C., 1971-72; asst. mgr. Dobbs House, Phila., 1972-73, Denny's Restaurant, Las Vegas, 1973-74; banquet mgr. MGM Grand Hotel, Las Vegas, 1974—; lectr. in field. Served with USNR, 1962-66. Mem. Capts. and Maitre d's Assn., U. Nev. Alumni Assn., U. Nev. Rebel Boosters Assn. Roman Catholic. Club: K.C. Home: 1670 Westwind Rd Las Vegas NV 89102 Office: MGM Grand Hotel Las Vegas NV 89109

LA TOURNERIE, GERARD JEAN CLOVIS, internat. banker, cons.; b. N.Y.C., June 21, 1950; s. Jean Clovis and Helen L. Bastier (Dempsey) LaT.; B.A. in Economics/Govt., Austin Coll., 1972; M.P.A. in Internat. Mgmt., N.Y. U., 1974; Research grantee, intern N.Y.C. Commn. for UN and Consular Corps, N.Y.C., 1974; asst. dir. Univ. Yr. for Action, Mayor's Office N.Y.C., 1974; with Polytechnique Systems, Dix Hills, N.Y., 1974-76; internal mgmt. cons. Mfrs. Hanover Trust Co., N.Y.C., 1976-78; internat. compliance officer and asst. to Sr. ops. officer Chem. Bank-Internat., N.Y.C., 1978—. Mem. Assn. Public Adminstrs., Assn. M.B.A. Execs., N.Y. U. Alumni Assn., Austin Coll. Alumni Assn. Home: 160 Front St Apt 4-F New York NY 10038 Office: 20 Pine St New York NY 10005

LATZER, RICHARD NEAL, investment co. exec.; b. N.Y.C., Jan. 6, 1937; s. Paul John and Alyce A. Latzer; B.A., U. Pa., 1959, M.A., 1961; m. Ellen Weston, Sept. 5, 1965; children—Steven, David. Security analyst Mut. Benefit Life Ins. Co., Newark, 1963-66; portfolio mgr. Equitable Life Ins., Washington, 1966-68; securities analyst Investors Diversified Services, Mpls., 1968-69, dir. cert. and ins. investments, 1969-77, v.p. cert. and ins. investments, 1977—; asst. treas. Investors Syndicate Life Ins. & Annuity Co., Mpls., 1969-72; v.p. IDS Life Ins. Co., Mpls., 1973-80, v.p. investments, 1980—; v.p. Investors Syndicate of Am., 1973-77, v.p. investments, 1977—; v.p. Investors Syndicate Title & Guaranty Co., 1977—; investment officer IDS Life Ins. Co. of N.Y., 1977—; dir. Investors Syndicate Devel. Corp., Mpls., 1970—, Nuveen Realty Corp., Mpls., 1976—. Served to lt., USN, 1960-63. Chartered fin. analyst. Mem. Twin City Soc. Security Analysts, Inst. Chartered Fin. Analysts, Am. Council of Life Ins. Home: 6835 Harold Ave Golden Valley MN 55427 Office: 3000 IDS Tower Minneapolis MN 55402

LAU, JOHN TZE, investment co. exec.; b. China, Aug. 19, 1948; came to U.S., 1963, naturalized, 1969; s. Hon Hing and Kaok Yu (Leung) L.; B.S. in Physics, SUNY, Stony Brook, 1970, M.A., 1973; m. Betty Seto, Aug. 28, 1976. Mgr. data processing Dah Chong Hong Trading Corp., N.Y.C., 1973-76; mgr. data communications Citibank, N.A., N.Y.C., 1976-80; mgr. data communications, ops. and planning Shearson, Loeb, Rhoades Inc., N.Y.C., 1980—. Bd. dirs. Chinatown Planning Council Inc., N.Y.C., 1974—. Recipient Outstanding Vol. award Citicorp, 1976. Mem. Am. Mgmt. Assn. Home: 1 Megan Ct Edison NJ 08820 Office: 1 WVI Plaza New York NY 10004

LAUBACH, GERALD DAVID, chem. co. exec.; b. Bethlehem, Pa., Jan. 21, 1926; s. Steward Lovine and Bertha (Rader) L.; student Mt. St. Mary's Coll., 1944-45; A.B. in Chemistry, U. Pa., 1947; Ph.D., M.I.T., 1950; D.Sc. (hon.), Hofstra U., 1979; m. Winifred Isabel Taylor, Oct. 3, 1953 (dec. Oct. 1979); children—Stephen, Andrea, Hilary. With Chas. Pfizer & Co., Inc., Groton, Conn., 1950—, mgr. medicinal products research, 1958-61, dir. dept. medicinal chemistry, 1961-63, group dir. medicinal research, 1963-64, v.p. medicinal products research and devel., 1964-68, dir., 1968—; mem. exec. com. Pfizer Pharms., 1969—, pres., 1969-72; exec. v.p. Pfizer Inc., 1971-72, pres., 1972—; dir. Loctite Corp., PMA, Conn. Gen. Ins. Corp., Hartford, Millipore Corp. Chmn. bd. trustees Conn. Coll.; mem. council Rockefeller U.; mem. corp. Poly. Inst. N.Y. Served with USNR, 1944-46. Mem. Am. Chem. Soc., AAAS, Soc. Chem. Industry, Am. Mgmt. Assn., N.A.M., N.Y. Acad. Scis., Chemists Club N.Y. (dir. 1968—, exec. com. 1969—). Contbr. articles to tech jours. Patentee in field. Home: Blood St Lyme CT 06371 Office: 235 E 42d St New York NY 10017

LAUBE, ROGER GUSTAV, banker; b. Chgo., Aug. 11, 1921; s. William C. and Elsie (Drews) L.; ed. Roosevelt U., 1938-42, John Marshall Law Sch., 1942, 48-50, Northwestern U. Nat. Trust Sch., 1960, Pacific Coast Grad. Trust div. U. Wash., 1962-64; m. Irene Mary Chadbourne, Mar. 30, 1946; children—David Roger, Philip Russell, Steven Richard. With Chgo. Title & Trust Co., 1938-42, 48-50; with Nat. Bank Alaska, Anchorage, 1950-72, mgr. mortgage dept., 1950-56, v.p., trust officer, mgr. trust dept., 1956-72; v.p., trust officer, chmn. marketing div. Bishop Trust Co. Ltd., Honolulu, 1972—. Mem. exec. com. 47th Western Trust Conf., Honolulu; charter mem. Anchorage Estate Planning Council, 1960-72, pres., 1960-63; mem. Hawaii Estate Planning Council, 1972—, mem. exec. com., 1978—, pres., 1980; mem. Anchorage Community Chorus, 1946-70; Gideons Internat., Anchorage, 1947-72, Honolulu, 1972—; mem. adv. bd. Faith Hosp., Glennallen, Alaska, 1960—; sec.-treas. Alaska Baptist Found.; mem. bd. Alaska Festival Music; mem. bd. advisers Salvation Army, Anchorage, 1961-72, chmn., Anchorage, 1969, bd. advisers, Honolulu, 1972—, chmn. bd. dirs., Honolulu, 1976-78. Bd. dirs. Anchorage Symphony; mem. exec. com. capital fund drive Hawaii Bapt. Acad. Served with AUS, 1942-48, asst. staff Judge Adv., Alaskan Command, 1946-48. Mem. Am. Inst. Banking (instr. trust div. 1961—), Am. Bankers Assn. (mem. legislative council trust div. 1961-72), Nat. Assn. Life Underwriters (asso.), Internat. Assn. Financial Planners. Baptist (exec. com. conv. 1959-61, dir. music Chgo. 1938-50, Anchorage 1950-72, Hawaii 1972—; chmn. trustees Anchorage 1970-72, Hawaii 1972—), Am. Assn. Handbell Ringers. Home: 1879 Halekoa Dr Honolulu HI 96821 Office: Bishop Trust Co Ltd 140 S King St Box 2390 Honolulu HI 96804

LAUBER, EVELYN GREMLI, real estate broker; b. Sarasota, Fla., July 8, 1917; d. Erwin and Mamie (Rewiss) Gremli; student Juilliard Sch. Music, 1940-42; m. Merritt Russell Lauber, July 28, 1940; children—Merritt Erwin, Douglas Ross. Owner, Erwin Gremli Real Estate, Inc., Sarasota, 1970—. Named Realtor of Year Women's Council of Sarasota, 1977; cert. residential specialist. Mem. Sarasota Bd. Realtors, Women's Council Realtors (pres. 1976), Multiple Listing Service Sarasota (sec.-treas.), Realtors Nat. Mktg. Inst., Fla. Assn. Realtors, Sarasota C. of C. Presbyterian. Club: Order Eastern Star. Home: 230 Scott St Sarasota FL 33580 Office: 1535 2d St Sarasota FL 33577

LAUER, PETER H., cons. co. exec.; b. Hamburg, Germany, May 25, 1918; s. Paul and Mathilde Lauer; came to U.S., 1938, naturalized, 1941; M.B.A., U. Chgo., 1956; m. Therese A. Paleczny, Feb. 26, 1974; children—Steven K., Linda A. Controller Ill. Inst. Tech. Research Inst., Chgo., 1946-56; controller, treas. Flexonics Corp., Chgo., 1956-60; v.p. fin. Interstate United Corp., Chgo., 1960-65; v.p. fin., dir. Eugene Dietzgen Co., Chgo., 1965-69; partner Cousins & Preble, Inc., Chgo., 1969-70; pres. Lauer, Sbarbaro Assos., Inc., Chgo., 1970—; instr. Univ. Chgo. Grad. Sch. Bus., 1957-59, DePaul Grad. Sch. Bus., 1968-72. Mem. Ill. Soc. C.P.A.'s, Am. Inst. C.P.A.'s, Fin. Execs. Inst. Club: Union League (Chgo.). Home: 505 N Lake Shore Dr Chicago IL 60611 Office: 1 N La Salle St Chicago IL 60602

LAUER, RICHARD KEITH, computer co. exec.; b. San Fernando, Calif., Apr. 29, 1945; s. Joseph P. and Rita L. (Miller) L.; B.A. in Bus. Adminstrn., Calif. State U., 1969; M.B.A., Pepperdine U., 1979; m. Mary McGann, Jan. 30, 1978. Zone mgr. Burrougas Corp., Santa Ana, Calif., 1969-72; account mgr. Basic/Four Corp., Irvine, Calif., 1972-79; exec. v.p. So. Calif. Data Co., Los Angeles, 1974-79; exec. v.p. MRP, Inc., Santa Ana, 1979—; pres. Govt. Systems Group, Inc., Santa Ana, 1980—; instr. Santa Ana Coll. Republican. Presbyterian. Home: 6731 La Cumbre Dr Orange CA 92669 Office: 1420 S Village Way Santa Ana CA 92705

LAUER, ROBERT LOUIS, appraisal co. exec.; b. Payette, Idaho, July 1, 1922; s. Edwin M. and Eva L. (Gish) L.; student U. Idaho, 1941-42, Idaho State Coll., 1942-43, U. Wash., 1943-44; m. Dorothy Sorensen, Feb. 8, 1946; children—David, Barbara, John. With Gen. Appraisal Co., Seattle, 1944-61, Los Angeles, 1962-80, treas., 1955-69, dir., 1956-69, sec., treas., 1963-69, sr. v.p., 1969, exec. v.p., 1970-71, pres., 1971-80; sr. v.p. Am. Appraisal Assos., Inc., 1980—, mng. dir. internat. ops., 1981—, also dir. Registered profl. engr., Wash. Fellow Am. Soc. Appraisers; mem. Pasadena Tournament of Roses, Am. Soc. Tech. Appraisers (internat. pres. 1951-52). Rotarian (dir. Pasadena club 1970-74, pres. 1972-73, Paul Harris fellow 1972, dist. gov. So. Calif.-Nev. 1979-80). Club: Pasadena University. Home: 1000 Fairview Ave Apt 5 Arcadia CA 91006 Office: 150 E Colorado Blvd Suite 301 Pasadena CA 91105

LAUER, WILLIAM LEONARD, food mfg. ofcl.; b. Union City, N.J., Mar. 21, 1927; s. William Charles and Henrietta Rose (Potter) L.; student Am. Sch., Chgo., 1958-61, Dale Carnegie Inst., 1966, Syracuse U., 1971-72; m. Grace Irene Hasbrouck, Nov. 27, 1948; children—Pamela C., Carol Ann, William Edward. With Nabisco, Inc., 1951—, beginning as sales rep., Jersey City, successively sales supr., Jersey City, br. mgr., Jersey City, then Dunellen, divisional sales mgr., Belleville, N.J., dir. sales ops., N.Y.C., 1973-74, dir. personnel services, N.Y.C. and East Hanover, N.J., 1974-79, sr. dir. personnel services, 1979—; instr. Dale Carnegie Inst. Pres. Ft. Lee Fire Dept., also hon. life mem.; trustee Syracuse U. Grad. Sch. Sales, Mgmt. and Mktg. Served. with USNR, 1945-46. Mem. Sales Mgmt. Execs. Internat. Methodist. Clubs: Masons, DeMolay (knight). Home: 1 Kipling Ln Scotch Plains NJ 07076 Office: River Rd East Hanover NJ 07936

LAUFFER, ANDRE MARC, electronics mfg. co. exec.; b. Antwerp, Belgium, Apr. 10, 1933; s. Jacques and Freda (Spira) L.; came to U.S., 1939, naturalized, 1945; B.S., N.Y. U., 1953, M.B.A., 1956, J.D., 1960; m. Marcia Tobin, Nov. 13, 1954; children—Jason, Robin. Admitted to N.Y. State bar, 1961; supr. Stern Porter Kingston and Coleman, N.Y.C., 1955-58; mgr. acctg. policy CBS, N.Y.C., 1959-61; individual practice law, N.Y.C., 1961-63; gen. counsel Profit Research, Inc., Mineola, N.Y., 1963-66; dir. corp. devel., tax counsel Walworth Co., Inc., N.Y.C., 1966-68; chmn. of office of pres., chief fin. officer Central Foundry Co., N.Y.C. and Tuscaloosa, Ala., 1968-72; v.p., controller Servo Corp. Am., Hicksville, N.Y., 1972-74; exec. v.p. finance Marine Electric Corp., Bklyn., 1974—; dir. Marine Electric Ry. Products Div., Inc., Microcom Internat.; chmn. bd. Wayne Transformer Corp.; instr. Bell and Howell Schs. Regular Republican candidate N.Y.C. City Council, 1968; Rep. county committeeman, 1968-72; bd. dirs. 39th A.D. Rep. Club, 1968-73, Mill Island Civic Assn., 1964-70; mayor mem. State Community Mayors, 1975—; Cub Scout pack chmn., Bklyn. council Boy Scouts Am., 1969-71. Served with U.S. Army, 1953-55. C.P.A., N.Y. Mem. N.Y. State Bar Assn., N.Y. State Soc. C.P.A.'s, Police Conf. N.Y., Stuyvesant High Sch. Alumni Assn. (v.p., counsel 1974-77, pres. 1977). Clubs: Forsgate Country, Downtown Athletic, Masons. Author Bell and Howell Schs. fed. income tax textbook, 1975. Home: 2226 National Dr Brooklyn NY 11234 Office: 600 Fourth Ave Brooklyn NY 11215

LAUGHLIN, LOUIS GENE, banker; b. Santa Barbara, Calif., Sept. 20, 1937; s. Eston A. and Cornelia Helen (Snively) L.; student Pomona Coll., 1955-58; B.A., U. Calif., Santa Barbara, 1960; postgrad. Claremont Grad. Sch., 1966-70, Sch. Bank Mktg., U. Colo., 1974-75. Mgr., Wheeldex-Los Angeles Co., 1961-62; v.p. Warner/Walker Assos., Inc., Los Angeles, 1962; cons. Spectra-Sound Corp., Los Angeles, 1964-65; rep. A.C. Nielsen Co., Chgo., 1962-64; research analyst Security Pacific Nat. Bank, Los Angeles, 1964-67, asst. research mgr., 1967-68, asst. v.p., 1968-72, v.p., mgr. market information and research div., 1972-76, v.p. research adminstrn. public affairs-research dept., 1976—; mem. policy council Nat. Conf. Competition in Banking, 1978-79. Sec. econs. Town Hall of Calif., 1966. Mem. Am., Western econ. assns., Nat. Assn. Bus. Economists, Bank Mktg. Assn., Am. Mktg. Assn., Am. Mgmt. Assn. Home: 277 Sycamore Glen Pasadena CA 91105 Office: Security Pacific Plaza 333 S Hope St Los Angeles CA 90071

LAUGHNER, WILLIAM CLIFFORD, JR., corrugated fibreboard mfg. co. exec.; b. Brownsville, Pa., Nov. 10, 1949; s. William Clifford and Euphemia (Murray) L.; student Bethlehem-Center public schs., Fredericktown, Pa.; m. Sharon Marie Peduti, Feb. 20, 1971; children—Shannon Daye, Shawndel Raye, Shalynn Kaye, William Clifford. With Greif Bros. Corp., Washington, Pa., 1967— asst. prodn. mgr., 1970-74, prodn. mgr., 1974—, plant dir. safety and indsl. relations, 1971-77; pres. local 815, United Papermakers and Paperworkers, 1969-70. Head coach softball team Richeyville (Pa.) Community Ch., 1976-78. Mem. Fibre Box Assn., Greater Lakes Area Prodn. Mgrs., Ind. Converters Council, Nat. Registry Emergency Med. Technicians. Presbyterian. Club: Lakeview Inn and Country (Morgantown, W.Va.). Home: 227 Locust St Richeyville PA 15358 Office: 5 Grable Rd Washington PA 15301

LAUMEISTER, BRUCE ROBERT, bus. exec.; b. Watertown, N.Y., Mar. 16, 1935; s. Frank H. and Edith M. (Spieler) L.; B.M.E., Rensselaer Poly. Inst., 1956; M.B.A., Rutgers U., 1962; m. Virginia Scott Marsh, June 22, 1957; children—Brett, Glenn, Cody. Maj. accounts mgr., market devel. specialist, sales engr., devel. engr. Union Carbide Corp., 1956-62; product mgr. insulating materials dept. Gen. Elec. Co., 1962-65, nat. sales mgr., 1965-67, mgr. advanced products ops., corp. new bus. devel. ops., 1967-69, gen. mgr. outdoor power equipment ops., 1969-73; exec. v.p. J.T. Baker Chem. Co., 1973-77, also dir.; v.p. Lens & Labs. Bus. Group, Am. Optical Co., 1977-79; pres., chief exec. officer Primex Plastics Corp., 1979-80; chmn. bd. Starson Corp. and pres. CTC Corp., 1980—. Mem. nat. governing bd. Common Cause, 1974-80, nat. membership chmn., 1975-77; pres. Better Neighborhoods, Inc., 1968-72, chmn., 1972-74; chmn. Greater Easton (Pa.) Housing Devel. Corp., 1975-78; bd. dirs. Environ. Clearinghouse, 1972-74; active Nat. Trust Hist. Preservation, Save the Children Fedn. Named Young Man of Yr., Schenectady, 1969, Outstanding Young Men Am., 1970; recipient distinguished service awards Jaycees, 1968, 69, 70; recipient G.L. Phillippe award Gen. Electric Co., 1970. Mem. Sigma Xi, Tau Beta Pi. Clubs: Elfun Soc., Appalachian Trail Conf. (life). Inventor battery electric tractor. Office: 254 Benmont Ave Bennington VT 05201

LAUREYSSENS, FRANCIS, banker; b. Brasschaat, Belgium, Jan. 2, 1946; s. Francois Felix and Maria Mathilda (De Vries) L.; came to U.S., 1974; degree in Econs. and Fin., St. Ignatius Coll., Antwerp, Belgium, 1968, Comml. Engr., 1969. With Continental Bank S.A., Brussels, 1970-74; internat. banking officer Continental Ill. Nat. Bank and Trust Co. Chgo., 1974—, 2d v.p., 1976-78, with Amsterdam br., 1978—, v.p., 1980—. Served with Belgian Army, 1969-70. Home: 205 Ridge Rd Wilmette IL 60091 Office: 231 S La Salle St Chicago IL 60693

LAURIDSEN, NEAL ARTHUR, athletic footwear co. exec.; b. Hillsboro, Oreg., June 15, 1948; s. Morten J. and Evelyn B. (Brookhart) L.; B.S., U. Mo., St. Louis, 1973. Retail mgr. BRS, Inc., Garden Grove, Calif., 1973, Los Angeles, 1974, ops. mgr., Beaverton, Oreg., 1975-77, Eastern sales mgr., Raymond, N.H., 1977-78, mng.

dir. Far East ops., Taiwan, 1979—. Served with USAF, 1966-70. Mem. Am. Prodn. and Inventory Control Soc. Address: Sunset View Towers Suite 1601 2230 Roxas Blvd Pasay City Metro Manila Philippines

LAUTERBACH, HENRY SEBASTIAN, mfg. co. exec.; b. Bronxville, N.Y., Apr. 19, 1915; s. Henry and Kathryn (Hyde) L.; B.A., Rollins Coll., 1937; m. Shirley Mae Kroll, Mar. 27, 1964; children—Henry William, Kathryn Hyde, Craig Alan, Paul Henry, Lynn Marie. With Sta Rite Industries, Inc., 1939—, chmn. bd., pres., Delavan, Wis., 1973-75, chmn. bd., 1976-78; pres., chief exec. officer Superior Stainless, Inc., Delavan, 1977—; dir. Citizens Bank of Delavan, Wagner Electric Corp., Parsippany, N.J. Mem. Sinnissippi council Boy Scouts Am., 1972-78; met. vice chmn. for Walworth County, Tri-County Alliance of Businessmen, 1974—, met. dir. for Kenosha, Racine and Walworth Counties, 1979. Bd. dirs. Wis. Assn. for Mental Health, 1969-74; trustee Whitewater State U. Found., Whitewater, Wis., 1970-74, Walworth County (Wis.) Nursing Home and Farm, 1977-80; mem. Polish-U.S. Econ. Council, 1975-78; past dir., pres. Water System Council. mem. pres.'s exec. senate Marquette U., 1978—. Recipient Am. Inst. Mgmt. Marquis award, ann. award Supplier and Man of Year Sears Plumbing and Heating div., 1965. Mem. Wis. Mfrs. Assn. (past dir.), Navy League (life), Army Ordnance Assn. Clubs: Milw.; Big Foot Country (Fontana, Wis.). Home: PO Box 157 Route 2 Hwy 11 Delavan WI 53115 Office: 211 Sugar Creek Rd Delavan WI 53115

LAVELLE, ROBERT E., finance co. exec.; b. Ames, Iowa, Oct. 10, 1922; s. Thomas Emmett and Lillian E. (Daugherty) LaV.; B.S., Iowa State U., 1947; postgrad. U. Chgo., 1959, Harvard, 1970; m. Anne M. Bosnak, Apr. 24, 1949; children—David, Richard, Annette, Lisa. With Internat. Harvester Co., Chgo., 1947—, v.p. fin. services, 1974—; v.p. Internat. Harvester Credit Corp., Chgo., 1962-69, pres., 1969—; chmn. bd. dirs. Harco Leasing Co. subs. Internat. Harvester Co. and Harco Holdings, Inc., Chgo., 1975—; pres. Monarch Agy., Inc. subs. Internat. Harvester Credit Corp., Chgo., 1969—. Served to 1st lt., AUS, 1943-46. Office: 401 N Michigan Ave Chicago IL 60601*

LAVERTY, CHARLES ALPHONSUS, editor, pub.; b. Moy, Ireland, Oct. 11, 1930; s. Bernard and Margaret (Carlin) L.; came to U.S., 1948, naturalized, 1953; B.S., Fordham U. Sch. Edn., 1965; m. Mary T. O'Connor, Apr. 20, 1968; children—Brian, Conor, Maeve. Editor, Rubber World mag. Bill Publs., N.Y.C., 1969-70, Akron, Ohio, 1970-71; mng. editor Home & Auto mag. Harcourt Brace Jovanovich Publs. Co., N.Y.C., 1972-75; editor, pub. Automotive Week newsletter Automotive Buyer Pub. Co., Wayne, N.J., 1975—; cons. to industry assns. Chmn. various Irish-Am. hist. coms., 1956-72. Served with Army, 1951-53, Spl. Forces, 1956-70. Home and Office: 28 Jacobus Ave Wayne NJ 07470

LAVEY, FREDERICK ADOLPH, lawyer, pub. co. exec.; b. Manchester, Conn., Sept. 15, 1916; s. Frederick Henry and Hilma (Anderson) L.; B.S., Harvard, 1938, postgrad. bus. adminstrn., 1938-39; postgrad. U. Va. Law Sch., 1940-42, J.D., 1946; m. Evelyn Heatwole, Jan. 16, 1943; 1 son, Frederick Painter. Admitted to Conn. bar, 1946, D.C. bar, 1947; asso. firm Hewes and Awalt, Hartford, Conn., 1946-47, Awalt Clark and Sparks, Washington, 1947-51; with Public Utilities Reports, Inc., Arlington, Va., 1951—, exec. v.p., 1956-61, gen. mgr., 1959-61, pres., gen. mgr., 1961—, dir., 1968—; pres. 2d Class Mail Publs., Inc., N.Y.C., 1966-70, dir., 1966—; exec. sec. Utilities Publ. Com., Arlington, 1961—; dir. Lebhar-Friedman, Inc., N.Y.C., 1976—; mem. pub. mgmt. com. Am. Bus. Press, Inc., 1963-68, dir., 1968-70. Mem. adv. com. to U.S. Postmaster Gen., 1966-68, 70-73. Pres., chmn. bd. dirs. Shenandoah Retreat Civic Assn., 1958-62, 69-71. Chmn. local troop com. Boy Scouts Am., 1961-63. Served to lt. USNR, 1942-46. Mem. Am. (chmn. publ. com. pub. utility law sect. 1974—, council mem. 1978-80, sec. 1980—), D.C. bar assns., Raven Soc., Delta Theta Phi. Lutheran. Clubs: Retreat Golf and Country, Harvard, Harvard Bus. Sch., U. Va., Internat. (Washington); Farmington Country. Home: 4204 Thornapple St Chevy Chase MD 20015 Office: 1700 N Moore St Suite 2100 Arlington VA 22209

LAVEY, THOMAS CAMERON, computer services co. exec.; b. Elizabeth, N.J., June 12, 1944; s. John Cameron and Mary Jarvis (Cleveland) L.; B.S. in Math., Pa. State U., 1966; M.B.A., U. So. Calif., 1971; m. Judith Wright, Sept. 12, 1967; 1 son, Cameron Wright. Cons., Xerox Computer Services, Los Angeles, 1971-73, Hackensack, N.J., 1973-74; v.p. mfg. Fulton Mfg. Co., Berwick, Pa., 1974-76; mgr. product devel. div. bus. systems ITEL Corp., White Plains, N.Y., 1976-78; v.p. mktg. ASK Computer Services, Los Altos, Calif., 1978—; lectr. on mfg. data systems. Served with C.E. U.S. Army, 1966-69; Vietnam. Decorated Bronze Star; recipient award of merit Am. Soc. Mil. Engrs., 1967. Fellow Am. Prodn. and Inventory Control Soc., New Fairfield (Com.) Jaycees (state dir. 1977-78), Pi Mu Epsilon, Beta Gamma Sigma. Club: Brookside Tennis (Saratoga, Calif.). Contbr. articles to profl. jours. Home: 19467 Dorchester Dr Saratoga CA 95070 Office: 730 Distel Dr Los Altos CA 94022

LAVORGNA, DENISE APRIL, govt. adminstr.; b. Phila., Apr. 26, 1952; d. Emanuel and Mafalda (Gentile) L.; B.S. with high honors, Drexel U., 1973. Computer programmer Drexel U., Phila., part-time 1972-73; computer programmer Def. Personnel Support Center, Phila., 1973-78, computer systems analyst, 1978—. Tutor, Phila. Sch. System, Project Give, 1975-77, 80-81. Recipient Beneficial Suggestion award Def. Personnel Support Center, 1974, named Employee of Month, 1975. Mem. Nat. Wildlife Fedn., Phila. Zool. Soc., Phi Kappa Phi, Beta Gamma Sigma, Pi Nu Epsilon. Baptist. Club: Def. Personnel Support Center Management. Office: Def Personnel Support Center 2800 S 20th St Philadelphia PA 19101

LAW, SALLY ELIZABETH, financial cons. exec.; b. Reading, Pa., Mar. 29, 1943; D. Richard Ellwood and Mary (Ludwig) L.; A.A., Columbia (Mo.) Coll., 1963; postgrad. Albright Coll., 1963, Mo. State U., 1964, Am. U., 1972. Asst. to Senator Wayne L. Morse, 1964; acting dir. research Democratic Nat. Com., 1967-69; polit. researcher for Hubert H. Humphrey and Edmund Muskie, 1968; asst. dir. Kendall Sch. for Deaf, Gallaudet Coll., Washington, 1969; pub. service officer Gallaudet Coll., 1971-73; with Investor Financial Services, Inc., Chevy Chase, Md., 1973; co-founder, Am. Financial Cons., Inc., Silver Spring, Md., 1974, prin., v.p., 1974-80; pres. Law & Assos., 1980—. Named Outstanding Collegiate Journalist, U. Mo., 1964. Mem. Internat. Assn. Financial Planners (v.p. planning D.C. chpt. 1975-76), Assn. Women Businessowners, Federally Employed Women, Registry Interpreters for the Deaf. Mem. Ch. of Christ. Author: Financial Attitudes for Women, 1974. Home: 5300 Mohican Rd Bethesda MD 20016

LAWING, ALVIN LEON, JR., real estate exec.; b. Maiden, N.C., Nov. 25, 1933; s. Alvin Leonard and Mary Alva (Hicks) L.; B.B.A., Wake Forest U., 1956; m. Elizabeth Ann Rascoe, Oct. 6, 1956; children—Angela Loraine, Alvin Lee. Acct., A.M. Pullen & Co., Greensboro, N.C., 1956-61; controller Kirman & Koury, Inc., Greensboro, 1961-64; fin. v.p., treas. Hardee's Food Systems, Inc., Rocky Mount, N.C., 1964-69; fin. v.p., treas., dir. Carolando Corp., Orlando, Fla., 1969-73; fin. v.p. Maj. Realty Corp., Orlando, 1973-76; pres., dir., 1976—. Served with AUS, 1956. Mem. N.C. Assn. C.P.A.'s, Am. Inst. C.P.A.'s, Fla. Inst. C.P.A.'s, Orlando C. of C. Republican. Baptist. Clubs: Bay Hill Country (Orlando); Benvenue Country (Rocky Mount). Home: 5141 Cypress Creek Dr Orlando FL 32805 Office: 5750 Major Blvd Suite 500 Orlando FL 32805

LAWLER, EDWARD J., lawyer; b. Chgo., Sept. 15, 1908; s. Edward James and Sarah (Gahan) L.; Ph.B., U. Chgo., 1930; LL.B., Harvard, 1933; m. Elizabeth Falls Dunscomb, Dec. 16, 1939. Admitted to Ill. bar, 1933, Tenn. bar, 1941; atty., auditor income tax sect. Office Collector Internal Revenue, Chgo., 1933-34; spl. atty. Bur. Internal Revenue, 1935-36, practicing lawyer, 1937-38; atty., SEC, 1939-40; practicing lawyer, Memphis, 1941—. Dir. Chromasco Ltd., Mid-South Title Co. Served as lt. comdr. USN, 1942-45. Decorated Bronze Star. Fellow Am. Bar Found. (sec. 1965-66, chmn. 1966-67); mem. Am., Tenn., Memphis, Shelby County, Chgo., Internat. bar assns., Am. Law Inst., Phi Beta Kappa. Home: 644 S Belvedere Blvd Memphis TN 38104 Office: 1st Nat Bank Bldg Memphis TN 38103

LAWLER, LAWRENCE THOMAS, JR., fin. co. exec.; b. Denver, Aug. 21, 1949; s. Lawrence Thomas and Jean Eleanore (Jasonek) L.; B.A. cum laude, Boston Coll., 1971; M.B.A., U. Pa., 1975; m. Maureen Mallon, Sept. 9, 1972. Loss control analyst Hartford Ins. Group, Newark, 1972-73; dir. middle market comml. bus. planning Chem. N.Y., N.Y.C., 1975-77; asst. v.p. corp. lending Chem. Bank, N.Y.C., 1978-79; v.p., treas. Alanthus Corp., Westport, Conn., 1979—; project cons. Phila. 76ers. Mem. Am. Fin. Assn., Fin. Mgmt. Assn., Wharton Grad. Club N.Y.C. Clubs: Downtown Athletic, Shenorock Shore. Home: 69 Hillcrest Ave Larchmont NY 10538 Office: 315 Post Rd W Westport CT 06880

LAWLER, ROBERT EUGENE, radiologist; b. Munfordville, Ky., Sept. 14, 1939; s. William Roscoe and Bonnie Katherine (Crouch) L.; B.S., Western Ky. U., 1960; M.D., Vanderbilt U., 1964; m. Lavona Sue Munden, Dec. 17, 1966; children—Robert Eugene, David Michael, Richard Edward. Intern, Butterworth Hosp., Grand Rapids, Mich., 1964-65; resident Vanderbilt Hosp., Nashville, 1965-68; practice medicine, specializing in radiology, Wuesthoff Hosp., Rockledge, Fla., 1970—; pres. So. Viedo Systems, Inc., Tampa and Orlando, Fla., 1977-79. Served with USAF, 1968-70. Mem. Am., Fla. med. assns., Broward Med. Soc., Am. Coll. Radiology, Fla. Radiol. Soc., Soc. Nuclear Medicine. Republican. Mem. Ch. of Christ. Inventor of radiol. technique caliper, 1970. Home: 875 N Indian River Dr Cocoa FL 32922 Office: 145 Orange Ave Rockledge FL 32955

LAWLESS, KIRBY GORDON, JR., mfg. co. exec.; b. Birmingham, Ala., Aug. 12, 1924; s. Kirby Gordon and Ethel May (Black) L.; B.A., Auburn U., 1948; LL.B., Emory U., 1951; m. Dora May Busbee, Mar. 13, 1951; children—Kirby, Madelene, Marc. Admitted to Ga. bar, 1950; gen. counsel CAA, Washington, 1951-53; credit officer, purchasing mgr. Southeastern Tool & Die Co., Birmingham, 1953-55; pres. Phifer Wire Products, Inc., Tuscaloosa, Ala., 1956-72, v.p., 1972-75, sr. v.p., 1975—, also dir.; sr. v.p. Phifer Internat. Sales, Inc., Tuscaloosa, 1975—. Chmn. tax study com. Tuscaloosa County and City, 1971, 72; chmn. Tuscaloosa Zoning Bd. Adjustment, 1968—; mem. Ala. Republican State Com., 1962—, vice chmn., 1973—; chmn. Ala.-Miss. dist. export council U.S. Dept. Commerce, 1974—; mem. Dept. Commerce Exec. Res., 1974—; adv. mem. Nat. Maritime Council, 1975—. Served with USNR, World War II. Mem. Tuscaloosa C. of C. (dir. 1968-72), Navy League, Wire Weavers Assn. (vice chmn. 1972-73), Aluminum Assn. (chmn. bar, rod and wire com. 1970-72), Archtl. Aluminum Mfrs. Assn. (dir. 1970-72), Ala. Export Council (vice chmn. 1972—), Asso. Industries Ala. (dir. 1976—). Methodist. Clubs: Kiwanis (v.p. Tuscaloosa 1957—), Ala. World Trade (dir. 1976—, named Ala. World Trade Man of Yr. 1976); North River Yacht (Tuscaloosa). Home: 1228 Claymont Dr Tuscaloosa AL 35401 Office: Box 1700 Tuscaloosa AL 35401

LAWRENCE, ALBERT WEAVER, ins. exec.; b. Newburgh, N.Y., Aug. 4, 1928; s. Claude D. and Janet W. Lawrence; B.S.A.E., Cornell U., 1950; postgrad. Rensselaer Poly. Inst., 1975; m. Barbara Corell, June 28, 1950; children—David, Janet, Elizabeth. Engaged in ins. business, 1953—; pres. A.W. Lawrence & Co., Inc., Schenectady, 1968—, Senate Ins. Co., Ariz., 1979—, Senate Ins. Co. Ltd., Bermuda, 1980—; dir. Mohawk Nat. Bank, Schenectady. Bd. dirs., sec. Schenectady Indsl. Devel. Corp.; bd. dirs. Nat. Alliance Businessmen, Albany, N.Y.; pres. Jr. Achievement Capital Dist.; past pres. Schenectady Girls Club, Family and Child Service Schenectady; past chmn. Schenectady United Fund drive. Served with AUS, 1946-47. Recipient Sca-Nec-Ta-De Civic award, 1967. Mem. Schenectady Hist. Soc. (trustee), Schenectady C. of C. (past pres.). Republican. Mem. Dutch Reformed Ch. Clubs: Mohawk, Mohawk Golf, Curling, Rotary (past pres.) (Niskayuna); Univ. (Albany); Cornell, N.Y. Athletic (N.Y.C.); No. Lake George Yacht (commodore). Address: 1601 Baker Ave Schenectady NY 12309

LAWRENCE, ALLEN M., ins. brokerage exec.; b. Los Angeles, Apr. 23, 1941; s. Maurice and Eva L.; student U. So. Calif., 1961-63; m. Suzanne Krieger. Pres., Allen Lawrence & Assos., Inc., Van Nuys, Calif., 1972—; dir. W. Valley Bank, Tarzana, Calif. Mem. Calif. State Democratic Central Com., 1979-81; trustee Sherman Oaks Community Hosp. Office: 15213 Burbank Blvd Van Nuys CA 91411

LAWRENCE, DEAN WEBSTER, date processing co. exec.; b. Kansas City, Mo., Sept. 1, 1936; s. Charles Webster and Goldie Bess (Finney) L.; B.S. in Math., Baker U., 1958; certificate in numerical analysis U. Calif. at Los Angeles, 1962; M.A. in Math., U. Kans., 1964. Mathematician, U.S. Naval Ordnance Test Sta., Pasadena, Calif., 1959-62; analyst Midwest Research Inst., Kansas City, 1962-65, mgr. computer scis. br., 1965-68; v.p., co-founder Trans Tech Inc., Kansas City, 1968-70; v.p. L & A Computer Industries, Overland Park, Kans., 1970-76; pres. Unimark, Inc., Overland Park, 1976—; lectr. in computer sci. U. Mo. at Kansas City, 1964-66. Pres. Apollo Gardens Homes Assn., Mission, Kans., 1971-73, also dir. Mem. Assn. For Computing Machinery (pres. 1970-71), U.S. Ski Assn. (pres. 1980—), Rocky Mountain Ski Assn. (dir. 1976—), Alpha Delta Sigma, Pi Mu Upsilon. Club: Kansas City Ski (pres. 1975-76). Contbr. articles to trade jours. Home: 7 Wycklow Shawnee Mission KS 66207 Office: 10520 Barkley St Overland Park KS 66207

LAWRENCE, GEORGE H., assn. exec.; b. Bartlesville, Okla., Nov. 1, 1925; s. Chester Allen and Pearl (Nation) L.; B.S. in Indsl. Engring., Okla. State U., 1949; LL.B., S. Tex. Coll. Law, 1957; m. Shirley Jo Thompson, Sept. 4, 1948; children—Michael, Linda, George H., Amy Jo. Petroleum engr. Humble Oil & Refining Co., Houston, 1949-59, atty., 1959-62, asst. mgr. natural gas div., 1962-63; admitted to Tex. bar, 1957; practice law and petroleum engring. cons., Houston, 1963; natural gas coordinator Am. Petroleum Inst., Washington, 1964-68; mgr. Washington office Am. Gas Assn., 1968-70, v.p., sr. v.p., Arlington, Va., 1970-76, exec. v.p., pres., 1976—; vice chmn., dir. Nat. Energy Found., N.Y.C.; bd. dirs. Council for Energy Studies, Tulsa. Bd. dirs., treas. Center for Urban Studies, Washington; trustee Ford Theatre Found., Washington. Served with USMC, 1943-46. Recipient Ann. award Center of Urban Environ. Studies, 1979; Disting. Service award Nat. Energy Resources Orgn., 1980. Mem. Am. Bar Assn., Tex. Bar Assn., Soc. Profl. Engrs., Am. Soc. Assn. Execs., Sigma Chi. Democrat. Methodist. Clubs: Capitol Hill, Kiwanis, Univ. (Washington); Burning Tree Congl. Country (Bethesda, Md.). Home: 8707 Eaglebrook Ct Alexandria VA 22308 Office: Am Gas Assn 1515 Wilson Blvd Arlington VA 22209

LAWRENCE, GEORGE HUBBARD CLAPP, investment co. exec.; b. Bronxville, N.Y., Aug. 9, 1937; s. Christopher and George-Anne (Collin) L.; student Columbia Coll., N.Y.C., 1956-58; B.Profl. Studies, Pace U., 1975; m. Suzanne Spear, June 4, 1966; children—Christopher C., Arthur W. Asso., R. W. Pressprich & Co., N.Y.C., 1964-67, G.H. Walker & Co., N.Y.C., 1967-70; pres., chief exec. officer Lawrence Investing Co., Inc., Bronxville, 1970—; dir. Cotton Petroleum Corp. subs. United Energy Resources, Scarsdale Nat. Bank. Pres., Charles Edison Meml. Youth Fund, 1971-75; exec. bd. Westchester Putnam council Boy Scouts Am.; chmn. Westchester Heart Fund, 1977-78; bd. govs. Lawrence Hosp.; chmn. Westchester County Tricentennial Commn., 1981—; mem. nat. adv. council SBA, 1971-77; bd. dirs. Westchester Heart Assn., Kensico Cemetery, Legal Aid Soc. Westchester; mem. Republican State Com.; mem. staff Richard M. Nixon, 1968-69; dir., officer Westchester County Assn., 1973—. Mem. Nat., N.Y. State assns. realtors, Westchester County Real Estate Bd. Episcopalian. Clubs: Mill Reef Ltd., Adirondack League, Bedford Golf and Tennis, Links. Home: Charles Rd RFD 2 Mount Kisco NY 10549 Office: 4 Valley Rd Bronxville NY 10708

LAWRENCE, GERALD GRAHAM, mgmt. cons.; b. U.K., June 21, 1947; came to U.S., 1972, naturalized, 1977; s. Raymond Joseph and Barbara Virginia L.; B.A. in Math., Northeastern U., 1970, M.A. in Econs. (fellow), 1973; M.B.A. (adminstrv. fellow), U. Pa., 1975; m. Isabelle M. McDade, July 11, 1970; 1 son, Ian Andrew. Intern, Corning Glass Works, Inc. (N.Y.), 1974; asst. brand mgr. Procter & Gamble, Cin., 1975-76; asso. Theodore Barry & Assos., N.Y.C., 1976-79; mgr. performance improvement systems Stone & Webster Mgmt. Consultants, N.Y.C., 1979—; dir. Olympus, Inc., Social and Environ. Assessment, Inc. Active Jaycees, named Outstanding Man of Year, 1979. Mem. Fin. Analysts, Transp. Research Forum. Reviewer Procs. Transp. Research Forum, 1973; Contbr. to Elec. World. Home: Thistle Ln RD 1 Flemington NJ 08822 Office: 90 Broad St New York NY 10004

LAWRENCE, MARGERY H(ULINGS), utilities exec.; b. Harmarville, Pa., June 17, 1934; d. Richard Nuttall and Alva (Burns) Hulings; student Bethany Coll., 1951-52; B.S. in Home Econs., Carnegie-Mellon U., 1955. Asst. mdse. buyer Joseph Horne Co., Pitts., 1955-57; home econs. editor Pitts. Group Cos. Columbia Gas System, Pitts., 1957-64, dir. home econs., 1968-72; home economist Columbia Gas Pa., Jeannette, 1964-68, dist. marketing mgr., 1972-73, mgr. dist. gas utilization, 1973—. Pub. relations chmn. Pitts. Home Economists in Bus., 1970-71, chmn. ways and means, 1972—. Mem. Am. Gas Assn. (Home Service Achievement award 1964), Assn. Iron and Steel Engrs. (asso.; mem. papers com.), Sales Mktg. Execs. Pitts., Sales Mktg. Execs. Internat., Exec. Women's Council Pitts. Presbyterian. Republican. Office: Columbia Gas Pa Inc 1405 McFarland Rd Pittsburgh PA 15216

LAWRENCE, MARY WELLS BERG, advt. exec.; b. Youngstown, O., May 25, 1928; d. Waldemar and Violet (Meltz) Berg; ed. Carnegie Inst. Tech., 1949; LL.D., Babson Coll., 1970; m. Harding Lawrence, Nov. 25, 1967; children—James, State, Deborah, Kathryn, Pamela. Copywriter McKelvey's Dept. Store, Youngstown, 1951-52, fashion advt. mgr. Macy's, N.Y.C., 1952-53; copy group head McCann-Erickson, N.Y.C., 1953-56; v.p., asso. copy chief Doyle, Dane, Bernbach, N.Y.C., 1957-64; sr. partner, creative dir. Jack Tinker & Partners, N.Y.C., 1964-66; pres. Wells, Rich, Greene, Inc., N.Y.C., 1966-71, chmn. bd., chief exec. officer, 1971—; Named to Copywriters Hall of Fame, Copy Club, 1969; named Marketing Saleswoman of Year, Sales Exec. Club N.Y., 1970, Advt. Woman of Year, Am. Advt. Fedn., 1971. Mem. Dallas Advt. Club. Office: 767 Fifth Ave New York NY 10022

LAWSON, DANIEL WEBSTER, airline pilot; b. Oklahoma City, Oct. 18, 1933; s. Fred and Hazel (McCoury) L.; student Murray Jr. Coll., Tishomingo, Okla., 1952-54; B.S. in Geology, Okla. State U., 1960; m. Helen McKelvey, Jan. 2, 1956; children—M. Perry, M. Patrick. Geologist, U.S. Dept. Agr., Phoenix, 1960-62; pilot United Airlines, Los Angeles, 1962-63; pilot Western Airlines, San Francisco, 1963—, capt., 1969—; dir. Seven-Keys, Inc., Air Nevada Inc.; pres., chmn. bd. Basin Canyon Mining Co., Inc. Served with USMC, 1954-58. Certified flight instr. Mem. Air Lines Pilots Assn. Club: Elks. Home: 33 Kenwood St Napa CA 94558 Office: 33 Kenwood St Napa CA 94558

LAWSON, FRED RAULSTON, banker; b. Sevierville, Tenn., Mar. 26, 1936; s. Arville Raulston and Ila Mary (Lowe) L.; student U. Tenn. at Knoxville, 1953-59, La. State U., 1965-68, Harvard, 1968; children—Terry Lee, Laura Ann. With Blount Nat. Bank, Maryville, Tenn., 1958—, pres., 1968—; pres. Tenn. Nat. Bancshares, Inc., 1971—; past dir. Fed. Res. Bank, Nashville; dir. Bank of Pensacola, Bank of Cannon County, Mchts. & Farmers Bank, Citizens State Bank, Tenn. Nat. Bancshares, Inc., Blount Nat. Bank, Southeastern Life Ins. Co., EMT Corp. Vice chmn. Tenn. Banking Bd., 1973-77; mem. adv. com., select financial com. Maryville Coll., 1970-71; mem. chancellors assos. U. Tenn. at Knoxville, 1972-78; mem. Tenn. Indsl. Devel. Authority, 1972—. Bd. dirs., pres. Blount County Indsl. Bd., 1969-80, bd. dirs. Tenn. Bapt. Children's Home, 1972—; pres. United Fund, 1973. Served with USNR, 1956-57. Mem. Tenn. Bankers Assn. (chmn. state legis. com. 1980), Assn. Bank Holding Cos. (dir.), Am. Bankers Assn. (govt. relations com.), Knoxville C. of C. (dir. 1979—). Republican. Baptist. Mason (32 deg.). Home: PO Box 333 Maryville TN 37801 Office: PO Box 608 Maryville TN 37801

LAWSON, MATHEW S., data processing industry exec.; b. New Fairfield, Conn., Aug. 8, 1946; s. Charles Sherman and Rosalie June (Scholnicoff) L.; A.B., Hamilton Coll., 1968; m. Mary Coryn, Jan. 2, 1978. Account exec. Foote, Cone & Belding Advt., Inc., Los Angeles, 1969-71, account dir., 1971-72; corp. pub. affairs mgr. Mazda Motors of Am., Inc., Los Angeles, 1972-74; v.p., account supr. Eisaman, Johns and Laws Advt. Inc., Los Angeles, 1974-76; dep. news sec. to Gov. Ronald Reagan Presdl. Campaign, 1976, 80; dir. corporate communications Computer Scis. Corp., El Segundo, Calif., 1976—. Mem. Calif. Republican State Central Com., 1969-71; dir. Calif. Rep. Assembly, 1969-73; communications dir. Lt. Gov. John Harmer, 1974. Mem. Public Affairs Council, Nat. Investor Relations Inst., Soc. Automotive Engrs. Club: Capitol Hill (Washington). Home: 14811 Mulholland Dr Los Angeles CA 90024 Office: 650 N Sepulveda Blvd El Segundo CA 90245

LAWSON, RICHARD LEON, oil co. exec.; b. San Bernardino, Calif., July 24, 1944; s. Shirley Harvey and Alta L. (Johnson) L.; m. June 10, 1965; children—Jennifer, Victoria, Staci. Pricing clk. Apco Oil Corp., Oklahoma City, 1964-65, asst. mgr. supply, 1965-70; asst. mgr. supply Champlin Petroleum, Enid, Okla., 1970-75; mgr. supply Ecol Corp., Houston, 1975-76; mgr. supply N.E. Petroleum Corp., Houston, 1976-77, v.p. crude supply, 1977-80; exec. v.p. Fedco Oil Co., Houston, 1980—. Served with Okla. Air N.G., 1963-69. Mem. Nat. Petroleum Refiners Assn., Am. Petroleum Refiners Assn. Clubs: Plaza, Raveneaux Country. Office: 1800 One Houston Center Houston TX 77002

LAWSON, THOMAS ELSWORTH, advt. agy. exec.; b. Taunton, Mass., May 30, 1937; s. Wilbur Lougheed and Margaret Mary (Walsh) L.; B.A., Harvard, 1959; 1 son, Patric. Media trainee, media supr., account exec., v.p. account supr., sr. v.p. mgmt. supr. Ogilvy & Mather Inc., advt. agy., N.Y.C., 1961-70; co-founder, pres. Rosenfeld, Sirowitz & Lawson Inc., N.Y.C., 1971—. Served to 1st. lt. Inf., Paratroops, AUS. Mem. Am. Assn. Advt. Agys. (dir.), Young Pres.'s Orgn. Club: Harvard (N.Y.C.). Home: 157 E 61st St New York NY 10021 Office: 1370 Ave of Americas New York NY 10019

LAWSON, WILLIAM HOGAN, III, mfg. co. exec.; b. Lexington, Ky., Feb. 3, 1937; s. Otto Kirksy and Gladys (McWhorter) L.; B.S. in Mech. Engring., Purdue U., 1959; M.B.A., Harvard U., 1961; m. Martha Ann Grubb, Aug. 24, 1963; children—Elizabeth E., Cynthia M. From computer systems analyst to dir. prodn. Toledo Scale Co., 1963-68; with Skyline Corp., Elkhart, Ind., 1968—, v.p. ops., 1973-75, exec. v.p., chief ops. officer, dir., 1975—; dir. JSJ Corp.; instr. Western New Eng. Coll., U. Toledo. Served with USAR, 1961-63. Decorated Meritorious Service award, 1963. Mem. Manufactured Housing Inst. (chmn. state legis. com. 1975), Harvard U. Bus. Alumni Assn. Republican. Presbyterian. Author papers in field. Home: 5 Holly Ln Elkhart IN 46514 Office: 2520 By-Pass Rd Elkhart IN 46514

LAY, B. ALLEN, computer systems co. exec.; b. Archie, Mo., Oct. 7, 1934; s. Robert Marvin and Florence Catherine (Rittman) L.; B.S. in Bus. Adminstrn. and Indsl. Mgmt., U. Kans., 1956; m. Dorothy Valeria Rossel, June 6, 1956; children—John Robert, Katherine Marie. Mfg. mgr. Computer Products div. Ampex, 1959-66; material mgr. Computer Measurements Corp., 1966-67; v.p., ops. mgr. Pertec Computer Corp., 1967-74, sr. v.p., group officer Data Systems Group, 1975-79; pres., chief operating officer, dir. Cado Systems Corp., Torrance, Calif., 1979—; dir. PerSci Inc. Active YMCA, Boy Scouts Am. Served to maj. USMC, 1956-59. Mem. Am. Mgmt. Assn., Am. Electronics Assn., Beta Gamma Sigma. Republican. Methodist. Office: 2771 Toledo St Torrance CA 90503

LAY, JOE LAFAYETTE, food packing co. exec.; b. Knoxville, Tenn., Jan. 17, 1925; s. Ira Vivian and Ava Edna (Parrott) L.; B.S. in Bus. Adminstrn., U. Tenn., 1948; m. Sarah Randolph Lowry, Oct. 15, 1948; children—Sally, Joe Lafayette, Tillman L. With Lay Packing Co., Knoxville, 1948—, sales mgr., 1958-69, v.p. sales, 1969-70, exec. v.p., 1970—. Bd. dirs. Better Bus. Bur. Served with AUS, 1943-45. Mem. Knoxville C. of C., Knoxville Tourist Bur., Am. Meat Inst., Nat. Ind. Meat Packers Assn., Tenn. Ind. Meat Packers Assn. (dir. 1961-75, v.p. 1975-77, pres. 1977—) Sigma Nu, Phi Kappa Phi, Omicron Delta Kappa. Rotarian. Home: 4003 Avon Park Circle Knoxville TN 37918 Office: 400 E Jackson Ave Knoxville TN 37915

LAYFIELD, MAURICE HUBERT, retail co. exec.; b. Winchester, Ky., Mar. 28, 1933; s. Ira Hubert and Pearl Mary (Ford) L.; B.A., Kent State U., 1966; m. Ann Marie Miles, Dec. 17, 1955. Police officer Cuyahoga Falls, Ohio, 1955-66; chief of police, Chesterland, Ohio, 1966-69; security supr. Kroger Co., Cleve., 1969-70, security dir., 1970-73, risk mgr. Erie mktg. area, 1973-80, dir. risk mgmt. SuperX Drug div., 1980—; guest lectr. Case Western Res. U. Served in USMC, 1950-55; Korea. Decorated Air medal with two clusters. Mem. Internat. Assn. Chiefs of Police, NAM, Nat. Assn. Safety Mgrs., Ohio Self Insurers Assn., Ohio Retail Security Assn., Aircraft Owners and Pilots Assn. Home: 7846 Westwind Ln Cincinnati OH 45242 Office: 175 Tri County Pkwy Cincinnati OH 45240

LAYFIELD, PHILIP BANES, govt. ofcl.; b. Balt., Oct. 30, 1942; s. Samuel Banes and Mary Virginia (Banes) L.; B.B.A., George Washington U., 1964, M.B.A., 1971; m. Nancy Lynn Abbott, Mar. 22, 1974; children—Lauren Banes, Lisa Hollis, Todd Gracen. With Potomac Electric Power Co., Washington, 1964-75, staff asst., 1974-75; mgr. utility sector Systems Control Inc., Washington, 1975-76; mgmt. cons. United Research Co., 1976-77; cons. Ernst & Whinney, energy cons., Washington, 1977-80; dep. dir. div. power supply and reliability Dept. Energy, 1980—; instr. prins. of mgmt. personnel mgmt. and fundamentals of data processing Prince George's Community Coll., 1971-74, Ben Franklin U., 1971-73. Mem. U.S. (met. chmn. Mid-Atlantic region 1973-74), Downtown (pres. 1972-73) Jaycees. Club: Masons. Home: 11204 Tack House Ct Saddleridge Potomac MD 20854 Office: 2000 M St NW Washington DC 20006

LAYMAN, LESTER CHARLES, ins. cons.; b. Covina, Calif., Mar. 23, 1904; s. Charles Henry and Grace Grazella (Mueller) L.; B.A. U. Redlands, 1927; m. 2d, Alice Elida Bedell Connolly, Oct. 31, 1959; children—Lester Charles, Barbara Layman Landreth. Spl. agt. Maryland Casualty Co., Los Angeles, 1928-31; v.p. Gibraltar Casualty Assn., Los Angeles, 1931-35; examiner ins. dept. State of Calif., 1935-37; with Aetna Ins. Group, 1937-51, chmn. multiple line study com., Hartford, Conn., 1950, sec., sr. officer, 1951; exec. v.p. Balboa Ins. Co., Los Angeles, 1952-53, pres., chief exec. officer, 1953-56; exec. v.p. Security Ins. Group of New Haven, 1956, pres., chief exec. officer, 1957-59; v.p. Beneficial Fire & Casualty Ins. Co. subs. Beneficial Standard Life Ins. Co., Los Angeles, 1959-64; exec. v.p., 1964-68; exec. v.p. Pacific region Transit Casualty Co. and Selective Ins. cos. subs. Beneficial Standard Life Ins. Co., 1964-68; pres., chief exec. officer Leatherby Ins. Co. New York, subs. Leatherby Cos. of Fullerton, Calif., 1968-71, subs. Richmond Corp., 1970-77, Continental (Can) Group Inc. (merger Richmond Corp. and Continental Can Group Inc. 1977), 1968-78; ins. cons., Rancho Mirage, Calif., 1979—. Recipient various awards. Mem. Am. Arbitration Soc., Underwriters Club Hartford, Western Info. Service (dir.), Nat. Bur. Casualty Underwriters, Nat. Automobile Underwriters Assn. Republican. Clubs: Masons, Shriners; Desert Island Country (Rancho Mirage). Contbr. articles on ins., co. orgn. and other ins. subjects to profl. jours. Home and Office: 899 Island Dr E Suite 405 Rancho Mirage CA 92270

LAYMON, JAMES ROGER, TV exec.; b. Fort Wayne, Ind., Aug. 24, 1931; s. John L. and Estella Mable (Sprunger) L.; B.S. in Bus. with distinction, Ind. U., 1968; children—Ann Michelle, Elizabeth Carol. Mgr. contract adminstrn., product mgr. Magnavox Co., Fort Wayne, 1959-69; v.p., treas. O & U Securities, Cedar Rapids, Iowa, 1969-70; treas., controller Bonsib, Inc., Fort Wayne, 1970-72; dir. fin. services Jasper County Hosp., Rensselaer, Ind., 1972-73; prvt. practice fin. cons., Fort Wayne, 1973-74; mgr. market planning Collins Avionics div. Rockwell Internat., Cedar Rapids, 1974-76; bus. mgr., asst. treas. Cedar Rapids TV Co., 1976—, also dir.; cons. in field. Served with U.S. Army, 1951-54. Mem. Nat. Assn. Accountants, Broadcast Fin. Mgmt. Assn., Broadcast Credit Assn., Am. Mgmt. Assn., Beta Gamma Sigma, Phi Eta Sigma. Home: 6504 Medford Ln NE Cedar Rapids IA 52402 Office: 2d Ave at 5th St SE Cedar Rapids IA 52401

LAZAR, MAX SEYMOUR, pharm. corp. ofcl.; b. N.Y.C., Dec. 6, 1943; s. Harry and Bessie L.; A.B. in Chemistry, Bklyn. Coll., 1966; postgrad. Baruch Sch. Bus., City U. N.Y., 1967-68; m. Sherry Dorf, Sept. 5, 1965; children—Lawrence, Lisa. With Hoffmann-LaRoche, Inc., Nutley, N.J., 1966-68, Belvidere, N.J., 1969—, analyst quality control, 1966, asst. chemist, 1967, supr., 1968, head quality control, 1969-73, mgr. quality control, 1973-78, dir. quality control, 1978—. Bd. dirs. Parkette Nat. Gymnastic Team. Mem. Am. Chem. Soc., AAAS, N.J. Pharm. Quality Control Assn., ASTM (chmn. D-19.05.04), Pharm. Mfrs. Assn. (chmn. environ. quality assurance com., chmn. standing com. pharm. chems.), N.Y. Acad. Scis., Sigma Xi. Office: PO Box 238 Belvidere NJ 07823

LAZARE, JOHN NICHOLAS, printing co. exec.; b. Chgo., May 24, 1925; s. Nicholas J. and Elizabeth M. (Stapf) L.; ed. Printing Industry Sch. Estimating, Chgo., 1948-49; m. Martha Helfrich, Jan. 8, 1946; 1 son, John Nicholas. Apprentice pressman McCord Printing Co., Chgo., 1946-48, pressman, 1948-52, foreman, 1952-64; partner McCord-Lazare Printing Co. (now John Lazare Printing Co.), Chgo., 1964-75, owner, 1975—. Mem. MidAm. Commodity Exchange, Chgo. Served with USNR, 1943-46; PTO. Mem. Lincoln Park C. of C., V.F.W., Printing Industry Ill. Inc., Master Printers Am., North Side Printers Guild Chgo. (dir. 1975-76), Royal Arcanum. Club: Board of Trade Fellowship (dir. 1963-69, 75—, v.p. 1970-71, pres. 1972-74). Home: 15332 Harbor Dr Madeira Beach FL 33708 Office: 709 W Wrightwood Ave Chicago IL 60614

LAZARUS, ARLIE GARY, corp. exec.; b. N.Y.C., Jan. 29, 1938; s. Leon and Celia L.; B.S., Hunter Coll., 1959; m. Gloria Hindman, Mar. 29, 1959; children—Mark, Lee, Lisa. Accountant, Eisner & Lubin, C.P.A.'s, N.Y.C., 1959-64; controller Miracle Mart, Inc., N.Y.C., 1964-68; fin. v.p. Jamesway Corp., Secaucus, N.J., 1968-73, exec. v.p., 1973-76, pres., 1977—. Mem. Young Pres.'s Assn., Nat. Mass Retailing Inst. Jewish. Office: 40 Hartz Way Secaucus NJ 07094

LAZARUS, HARRY JOSEPH, banker; b. Chgo., Nov. 12, 1912; s. Joseph and Sarah Lazarus; B.A., U. Chgo., 1934; mgmt. cert. Harvard Grad. Sch. Bus., 1969; m. Hildene Abrams, Jan. 1, 1936; children—Robert Frederick, Daryl Jane, Alan Arthur. Vice pres., sr. account exec. Bozell & Jacobs, Inc., Chgo., 1944-50; v.p., treas. Dancer, Fitzgerald, Sample, Inc., Chgo., 1950-62; v.p., dir. Geyer, Morey, Ballard, Inc., Chgo., 1962-64; chmn., chief exec. officer Bank of Highland Park (Ill.), 1955-80, Bank of Paradise Valley, Phoenix, 1978—. Served as capt. U.S. Army, 1941-44. Recipient award Chgo. Advt. Club, 1956. Mem. Ill. Bankers Assn. (pres. public relations div. 1975-77). Clubs: Chgo. Press, Highland Park Country. Contbr. articles to banking jours. Home: 7475 E Royal Palm Scottsdale AZ 85258 Office: Bank of Paradise Valley Tatum and Cactus Sts Phoenix AZ 85046

LAZARUS, RALPH, mcht.; b. Jan. 30, 1914; s. Fred and Meta (Marx) L.; grad. Dartmouth Coll., 1935, LL.D., 1965; LL.D., U. Miami (Fla.), 1961, Xavier U., 1965; D.C.S. (hon.), Suffolk U., 1962; m. Gladys Kleeman, June 24, 1939; children—Mary (dec.), Richard, John, James. With F. & R. Lazarus & Co., 1935-51, v.p., 1947-51; exec. v.p. Federated Dept. Stores, Inc., Cin. 1951-57, pres., 1957-67, chief exec. officer, 1966—, chmn. bd., 1967—; dir. Scott Paper Co., Chase Manhattan Bank, Gen. Electric Co. Mem. Bus. Com. for Arts, Nat. Com. on U.S.-China Relations, Bus. Council, Council Fgn. Relations, Bus. Roundtable, Corp. Fund for Performing Arts at Kennedy Center, Nat. Urban League; mem. Pres.'s Adv. Com. on Trade Negotiations; trustee Com. for Econ. Devel., Eisenhower Exchange Fellowships, Inc., Dartmouth Coll., Cin. Council World Affairs; mem. council Rockefeller U. Clubs: Athletic, Winding Hollow Country, Univ. (Columbus); Queen City, Losantiville Country, Camargo Country, Dartmouth, Comml., Commonwealth (Cin.); Harmonie, Sky (N.Y.C.); Blind Brook Country (White Plains, N.Y.); La Quinta (Calif.). Country. Home: 1009 Catawba Valley Dr Cincinnati OH 45226 Office: 7 W 7th St Cincinnati OH 45202

LAZRUS, SHERMAN, health co. exec.; b. Worcester, Mass., June 26, 1933; s. Abe S. and Minnie (Granofsky) L.; B.A., George Washington U., 1961, M.B.A., 1963; m. Charlotte D. Dunyer, Mar. 21, 1954; children—Jay Neal, Abbe Sue. With U.S. Dept. HEW, Washington, 1958-73; dep. asst. sec. Dept. Def., Washington, 1973-76; v.p. Am. Med. Internat. Inc., Washington, 1976-77; pres. Am. Health Assos., Inc., Rockville, Md., 1977—; cons. U.S. Dept. Labor; lectr. Montgomery Coll. Pres., Greater Colesville Civic Assn., 1968-70. Served with USAF, 1952-56. Mem. Am. Soc. Pub. Adminstrn., Nat. Rehab. Assn. Home: 13208 Banbury Pl Silver Spring MD 20904 Office: 4701 Randolph Rd Rockville MD 20852

LEA, ALBERT ROBERT, mfg. exec.; b. Melrose, Mass., May 27, 1921; s. Robert Wentworth and Lillian (Ryan) L.; A.B., Amherst Coll., 1943; student Harvard Grad. Sch. Bus. Adminstrn., 1943; m. Joyce Winona Padgett, May 17, 1943 (div.); children—Patricia, Jennifer, Anne, Melissa; m. 2d, Helen Clay Jones, May 12, 1961; children—Albert Robert, Robert Wentworth II. With Ashcraft, Inc., Kansas City, 1951—, now pres., dir.; pres., dir. Process Plate Co., Continental Service Industries Inc., Trade-Plant Inc. Served as lt. supply corps, USNR, 1943-46. Clubs: Mission Hills Country; University, Kansas City (Kansas City); Metropolitan (N.Y.C.); Surf (Surfside, Fla.). Home: 625 W Meyer Blvd Kansas City MO 64113 Office: 816 Locust St Kansas City MO 64106

LEA, PAUL MILWARD, III, mech. engr.; b. Chgo., Sept. 19, 1942; s. Paul M. and Elda M. (Hendrickson) L.; B.S.M.E., Bradley U., 1965; m. Geri Lou Guede, Nov. 25, 1965; children—Paula Marie, Paul M. IV. Maintenance supr. U.S. Steel Co., Gary, Ind., 1965-68; project engr. Amsted Research Lab., Bensenville, Ill., 1968-71, research engr., 1971-73; chief engr. vacuum process div. John Mohr & Sons, Chgo., 1973—. Chmn. lay council United Ch. Christ, 1973-75; chmn. pack com. Calumet council Boy Scouts Am., 1977-78, cubmaster, 1978-80. Mem. ASME, Soc. Automotive Engrs., Am. Soc. Metals. Club: Internat. Order Foresters. Inventor continuous method of and apparatus for making bars from powdered metal. Home: 679 E 152d St Dolton IL 60419 Office: 3200 E 96th St Chicago IL 60617

LEACH, EDWARD RUFFNER, publisher; b. Schenectady, Nov. 1, 1941; s. Edward Alfred and Louise Lenore (Ruffner) L.; B.A., U. Tulsa, 1964, student U. Tulsa Coll. Law, 1965-66; m. Carol Ann Czarowitz, July 31, 1969; children—Edward Philip, Mary Lenore. Adminstrv. asst. Gov. Dewey F. Bartlett of Okla., 1966-67; asst. pub. relations dir. Williams Bros. Co., Tulsa, 1967-69; exec. editor Pipeline & Gas Jour., Dallas, 1969-71; dir. corporate communications Resource Scis. Corp., Tulsa, 1971-78; pres. Cimarron Industries, Tulsa, 1978-80; pub. The Monadnock Ledger, Peterborough, N.H., 1980—. Adv. council Salvation Army, Tulsa, 1976—. Mem. Am. Petroleum Inst., Sigma Delta Chi. Republican. Episcopalian. Home: 7 Keenan Dr Peterborough NH 03458

LEACH, RONALD LEE, automotive mfg. co. exec.; b. Athens, Ohio, Aug. 22, 1934; s. Ralph and Lelia Celesta (Woodruff) L.; B.S., Ohio U., 1958; m. Marilyn Rose Dreger, Sept. 3, 1956; children—Cynthia Diane, Mark Ronald, Douglas Ralph. With Ernst & Ernst, Cleve., 1960-70, mgr., 1967-70; asst. to v.p. and controller Eaton Corp., Cleve., 1970-72; asst. controller fin. acctg., 1972-77, corp. controller, 1977-78, v.p., controller, 1979—, dir., officer several subs. Bd. visitors Coll. Bus. Adminstrn., Ohio U., 1978—. Served with USAF, 1958-60. Mem. Fin. Execs. Inst. (dir. N.E. Ohio chpt. 1979-80, v.p. 1980-81, pres. elect 1981—, mem. com. on corp. reporting 1979-80), Greater Cleve. Growth Assn., Am. Mgmt. Assn., Am. Inst. C.P.A.'s, Ohio Soc. C.P.A.'s, Am. Acctg. Assn., Nat. Assn. Accts., Beta Alpha Psi, Pi Gamma Mu, Beta Gamma Sigma. Republican. Mem. Ch. of God (treas. 1968—, trustee 1969—). Club: Clevelander. Office: 100 Erieview Plaza Cleveland OH 44114

LEADER, SUSAN JOSLIN, financial journalist; b. Providence, R.I., Apr. 5, 1946; d. Alfred Hahn and Roberta Grant Joslin; B.A., Wellesley Coll., 1968; M.B.A., N.Y. U., 1975; m. Jonathan Leader, Aug. 30, 1970; children—Jessica, Amanda. Methods analyst N.Y.C. Housing and Devel. Adminstrn., 1968-72; project asso. Donaldson, Lufkin & Jenrette, N.Y.C., 1972-74; conf. programming dir., contbg. editor Institutional Investor, N.Y.C., 1975—. Home: 40 E 62d St New York NY 10021 Office: 488 Madison Ave New York NY 10022

LEAFBLAD, RONALD STEWART, mfg. co. exec.; b. Waukegan, Ill., June 7, 1942; s. Harold Lawrence and Elveria (Nelson) L.; B.S., U. Wis., 1965; postgrad. Northwestern U., 1966-67; m. Diane E. O'Melia, Aug. 28, 1965; children—Erica, Kristen, Andrew. Sales order mgr. Oliver Corp., Chgo., Columbus, Ohio, 1967-68; mktg. mgr. Equipment div. White Constrn. Co., Celve., 1968-70, pres., 1970-72; v.p., group dir. mktg. and sales farm equipment White Farm Equipment Co., Oak Brook, Ill., 1972-74; group v.p. The Toro Co., Bloomington, Minn., 1974-77; pres., gen. mgr. Ag-Chem Equipment Co., Inc., Mpls., 1977—. Pres. bd. dirs. Meth. Hosp. Found.; bd. dirs. Scholarship Found.; bd. dirs. U. Wis., 1964-66. Served with USAF, 1966-67. Mem. Am. Mining Congress (dir.), Nat. Fertilizer Solutions Assn., Fertilizer Inst., Young Presidents Orgn. Baptist. Clubs: U. Wis. Alumni, Nat. W (dir. Mpls. chpt., pres. Chgo. chpt.), Decathelon, Edina Country. Home: 4700 Sunnyside Rd Edina MN 55424 Office: 4900 Viking Dr Minneapolis MN 55435

LEAHEY, RAYMOND, army officer; b. Erie, Pa., July 14, 1939; s. Harry William and Marie Rose (Mensing) L.; student Gannon Coll., 1957; B.S., Pa. State U., 1961; M.B.A., Mich. State U., 1970; m. Roberta Lee Fenwick, Dec. 29, 1964; 1 son, Patrick Sean. Commd. 2d lt. U.S. Army, 1961, advanced through grades to col., 1981; exec. asst. to surgeon gen., Washington, 1974-75; chief health manpower requirements Office of Army Surgeon Gen., Washington, 1975-78; comdr. 1st Med. Bn., Ft. Riley, Kans., 1978-80; student Army War Coll., 1980-81; dir. tng. devel. Acad. Health Scis., U.S. Army, Fort Sam Houston, Tex., 1981—; asst. prof. bus. mgmt. U. Md., Far East, 1971-72; mem. exec. com. Dept. Def. Health Care Productivity Planning, 1976-78, mem. exec. com. Health Care Regionalization Planning Group, 1975-78. Decorated Bronze Star, Meritorious Service medal with 2 oak leaf clusters, Commendation medal with oak leaf cluster. Mem. Assn. Mil. Surgeons, Assn. M.B.A. Execs., Am. Coll. Hosp. Adminstrs., Pa. State U. Drummer Soc., Sigma Pi Eta, Beta Gamma Sigma. Address: Acad Health Scis Fort Sam Houston TX 78234

LEAHY, MAURICE LEWIS, indsl. sales exec.; b. Fresno, Calif., Oct. 16, 1920; s. Guy H. and Estella (Lewis) L.; student Fresno State Coll., 1938-40; m. Vivian Grace Wilkinson, July 27, 1941; children—Pamela Maureen Leahy Bottomley, Stanley Richard, Jeryl Ann Leahy Techman, Michael Maurice. Regional mgr. Premier Indsl. Corp., Cleve., 1950-59; v.p., dir. sales Western region Lawson Products, Inc., Des Plaines, Ill., 1959—; mktg. cons. Talk, Inc., Las Vegas, Nev. Served with USNR, 1941-46. Republican. Clubs: Prudhoe Bay Arctic Ocean Golf and Country, Shriners. Home: 5879 E Clubview Dr Fresno CA 93727 Office: 1666 E Touhy Des Plaines IL 60018 also 1237 W Walnut St Compton CA 90220

LEAHY, THOMAS FRANCIS, broadcast co. exec.; b. N.Y.C., June 30, 1937; s. Thomas Donald and Mary Ann (McCarthy) L.; B.E.E., Manhattan Coll., 1959; m. Patricia B. Flanagan, May 5, 1962; children—Patricia Ann, Allison, Thomas Francis, Kirsten. With ABC-TV Sales Service, N.Y.C., 1960-61; account exec. WGN, N.Y.C., 1961-62, WCBS-TV, N.Y.C., 1962-64, CIN, CBS-TV Network, Chgo., 1964-66, N.Y., 1966-69; dir. daytime sales CBS-TV, N.Y.C., 1969-71; v.p. sales CBS TV Stas. div., CBS, Inc., N.Y.C., 1971-73, v.p., gen. mgr., 1973-77, pres., 1977—; gen. mgr., v.p. Sta. WCBS-TV, 1973-77. Trustee, Fordham Prep. Sch., Coll. Mt. St. Vincent; former bd. dirs. ARC of Greater N.Y.; former trustee Big Bros. of N.Y. Served with U.S. Army. Mem. Internat. Radio and TV Soc. (dir.), Nat. Acad. TV Arts and Scis. (pres. internat. council), N.Y. State Broadcasters Assn. (past dir.). Office: 51 W 52d St New York NY 10019

LEAHY, WILLIAM F., lawyer, ret. ins. co. exec.; b. N.Y.C., July 28, 1913; s. William F. and Anna (Murphy) L.; pre-law cert. CCNY, 1936; LL.B. cum laude, Bklyn. Law Sch., 1939, LL.M., 1940; m. Catherine Patricia Carlin, Oct. 19, 1940; children—William C., Michael J. Admitted to N.Y. bar, 1940; with Met. Life Ins. Co., N.Y.C., 1932—, asso. gen. counsel, 1962-65, v.p. real estate financing, 1965-76, sr. v.p., 1976-78; sr. real estate cons. Goldman Sachs Realty; dir. City Title Ins. Co., Dollar Fed. Savs. & Loan Assn., Malverne, N.Y., Pulte Home Corp.; mem. adv. bd. N.Y. State Tchrs. Retirement Fund. Served to lt. col. USAAF, 1941-46. Mem. Am. Bar Assn., Real Estate Bd. N.Y. (gov.), N.Y. State Title Assn. Home: 34 Roosevelt Ave Lynbrook NY 11563

LEANEAGH, JERRY DEL, publisher; b. Algona, Iowa, Nov. 11, 1932; s. Del and Arlouine (Palmer) L.; B.S., Iowa State U., 1954; student U. Heidelberg, Germany, 1956, Drake U., 1958-60; m. Helen Schmidt, Mar. 21, 1951; children—David, Alan, Joan, John, Beth Ann; m. 2d, Sandra Johnson, Mar. 11, 1972; children—Randy, Tamera. Sales engr. Westinghouse Elec. Corp., Des Moines, 1957-60; operator L. & L. Constrn. Co., Algona, 1961-63; gen. mgr., pres. Directory Service Co., Algona, 1961-80, Boulder, Colo., 1980—. Served with AUS, 1955-57. Recipient Distinguished Services award, Algona, 1963. Mem. Aircraft Owners and Pilots Assn., Young Pres.'s Orgn. Home: 264 Pine Brook Hills Boulder CO 80302 Office: PO Box 9200 Boulder CO 80301

LEAR, JAMES RICHARD, savs. and loan exec.; b. Terre Haute, Ind., July 16, 1927; s. Charles and Nettie Bell (All) L.; B.S., Ind. State U., 1950; m. Wanda Louise McDonald, Oct. 17, 1956; children—Jill Sizanne, James Richard II. With Mut. Fed. Savs. & Loan, Terre Haute, 1950—, pres., dir. Pres., Bethesda Corp., non-profit corp. for promotion elderly and low income housing, Terre Haute. Served with USN, 1945-47. Mem. Savs. and Loan League Ind. (past dir.), Savs. and Assns Polit. Acting Com., U.S. League Savs. Assns., Am. Legion. Presbyterian. Clubs: Terre Haute Country, Elks. Office: 498 Ohio St Terre Haute IN 47807

LEARNED, CHARLES ALDEN, securities exec.; b. Stafford, Kans., Sept. 14, 1933; s. Wilmer Harrison and Vivian Edith (Hendershot) L.; B.S., Sterling Coll., 1955; m. Jean Starbuck, June 13, 1954; 1 son, Rodney David. Cashier municipal bond dept. Small-Milburn Investment, Inc., Wichita, Kans., 1956-58; mgr. municipal bond dept. Stockyards Nat. Bank, Wichita, 1958-64; exec. v.p., mgr. municipal bond dept. Mid-Continent Securities Corp., Wichita, 1964-68; v.p., mgr. municipal bond dept. Columbian Securities Corp., Wichita, 1968—; pres., dir. Learned Investments, Inc., Wichita, 1970—. Recipient Merit award Adminstr. Mgmt. Soc., 1971, Diamond Merit award, 1974. Mem. Adminstrv. Mgmt. Soc. (chpt. pres. 1970-72, dir. edn. div. on internat. bd. dirs. 1972-74), Wichita Ind. Bus. Assn., C. of C. Mem. Evangelical Free Ch. Mason (Shriner), Moose (life), Kiwanian. Clubs: Wichita Racquet, Wichita Shocker, Knife and Fork. Home: 6705 Magill St Wichita KS 67206 Office: 321 E William St Wichita KS 67202

LEARNER, DAVID BIMBERG, bus. services co. exec.; b. N.Y.C., Sept. 19, 1930; s. Benjamin and Carolyn (Bimberg) L.; B.A., Ohio State U., 1951, M.A., 1952, Ph.D., 1956; m. Vicky Eigenmacht, May 31, 1953; children—Leslie Diane, Douglas Alan. Asso. Dunlap & Assos., Stamford, Conn., 1956-57; dept. mgr. Gen. Motors Corp. Research Labs., Detroit, 1958-60; v.p. Batten, Barton, Durstine & Osborn, N.Y.C., 1960-68; chmn., pres. Applied Devices Corp., N.Y.C., 1968-73; pres., chief exec. officer Market Research Corp. Am., Stamford, Conn., 1973—; adj. prof. bus. adminstrn., Carnegie Mellon U., 1966-68; lectr. in field; dir. Federated Devel. Co., Federated Reins. Corp. Served with USN, 1953-55. Recipient McKinsey Found. award, 1968. Mem. Inst. Mgmt. Sci., Ops. Research Soc., Am. Psychol. Assn., Market Research Council. Contbr. articles to tech., sci. and bus. jours. Home: 519 Haviland Rd Stamford CT 06903 Office: 4 Landmark Sq Stamford CT 06901

LEARY, ROBERT MICHAEL, investment counselor; b. Omaha, Oct. 9, 1913; s. Henry Shellington and Nell (Swift) L.; B.S.C., Creighton U., 1934; M.B.A., Northwestern U., 1936; children—Sharon Leary Reichert, Sheila Leary Daly, Michele (Mrs. Dale Alexander), Kathleen (Mrs. Jeffrey Lee), Suzanne (Mrs. William Mason). With 7 Up Bottling Co., 1939-52, pres., Hastings, Nebr., 1946-52; dir., zone mgr. Investors Diversified Services, Inc., Hays, Kans., 1953-55; div. mgr. King Merritt & Co., Hays, 1956-60; exec. v.p. Westamerica Securities Inc., Denver, 1960-68; pres. R.M. Leary & Co., Inc., 1968—; pres., dir. Meridian Capital Corp., 1969-70; v.p., dir. Mountain Haus Devel. Co., 1970-75; chmn. Refinery Corp., 1970-72; pres., dir. Excalibur Ltd., 1970-72; sec., trustee First Gen. Resources Co., 1970-73; v.p. Petro Silver, Inc., 1971—; v.p., dir. Carr Mason & Leary, 1972-78. Served to lt. (j.g.) USNR, 1944-45. Mem. Soc. Fin. Counselling Ethics (trustee 1969-71), Internat. Assn. Fin. Planners (trustee 1969-73), Am. Legion, V.F.W., 40 and 8, Delta Sigma Pi. Democrat. Roman Catholic. Elk. K.C. Clubs: Optimist Internat. (past pres.) (St. Joseph, Mo.); Mt. Vernon Country, 26; La Costa Country (Calif.). Home: 3131 E Alameda St Denver CO 80209 Office: 2800 1st Nat Bank Bldg Denver CO 90212

LEASENDALE, FRANK OTTO, non-profit orgn. exec.; b. Jersey City, May 15, 1921; s. F. Otto and Lydia (Klix) L.; student Clemson Coll., 1942-43; B.Sc., N.Y. U., 1950, M.B.A., 1955; m. Mildred E. Schlenger, June 12, 1949; children—Nancy, Jeffrey. Chief accountant Gen. Aniline & Film Corp., N.Y.C., 1939-64; mgr. corporate accounting Prentice-Hall, Inc., Englewood Cliffs, N.J., 1964-66; treas. Volkswagen N. Central Distbr., Inc., Deerfield, Ill., 1966-69; v.p. finance, treas. Burnham Van Service, Inc., Columbus, Ga., 1969-75; v.p. fin. and adminstrn. Kinnett Dairies Inc., Columbus, Ga., 1975-78; partner Va. Bus. Consultants, Richmond, 1978-80; bus. adminstr. Am. Assn. Occupational Health Nurses, Inc., N.Y.C., 1980—; instr. budgets and forecasting CCNY, 1955-57; dir. Burnham Enterprises, Inc., 1973-75, Bi-City Truck Sales & Service, Inc., Complete Truck Paint and Body Shop Inc. Mgr., Little League; coach Pop Warner Football League; rev. bd. United Funds Appeal; mem. Citizens Com. for Better Edn. Served with AUS, 1942-45. Mem. Nat. Assn. Accountants, Inf. Mus. Assn. (life), Am. Trucking Assn. (dir. 1975-76, nat. acctg. and fin. council), N.Y. U. Alumni Assn. Presbyterian (elder). Clubs: N.Y. U., Masons, Kiwanis. Home: 75 Barrows Ave Rutherford NJ 07070 Office: 575 Lexington Ave New York NY 10022

LEASK, SAMUEL, III, dept. store exec.; b. Santa Cruz, Calif., Mar. 5, 1920; s. Samuel Johnson and Marjorie (Drullard) L.; student U. Santa Clara, 1938-40; B.S. in Retailing, U. So. Calif., 1947; m. Mary Irene McKenna, June 25, 1949; children—Samuel IV, Katherine Ann. Exec. trainee Broadway Dept. Stores, Los Angeles, 1947-49; with Samuel Leask & Sons, Santa Cruz, Calif., 1949—, mng. partner, 1966; dir. County Bank Santa Cruz. Bd. dirs. Blue Cross of No. Calif., 1976-78, chmn., 1976-78. Mem. Calif. Library Adv. Bd., 1968-75; pres. Santa Cruz Community Chest, 1953-54, hon. life bd. mem.; pres. Santa Cruz City-County Conv. Center Authority, 1968-74. Mem. Santa Cruz City Council, 1964-69, mayor, 1967-68. Served with U.S. Army, 1941-45. Named Outstanding Young Man of Year, Santa Cruz Jr. C. of C., 1953, Outstanding Man of Year, Santa Cruz Area C. of C., 1969, Outstanding Mcht. of Year, Downtown Assn. Santa Cruz, 1975. Mem. Calif. Retailers Assn. (pres. 1981—, dir.), Am. Legion. Clubs: Santa Cruz Yacht (commodore 1952), Saint Francis (Calif.) Yacht, Dry Gulch Gun (pres. 1958—), Rotary. Home: 120 Green St Santa Cruz CA 95060 Office: 1405 Pacific Ave Santa Cruz CA 95060

LEATHAM, JOHN TONKIN, ins. exec.; b. Chgo., July 4, 1936; s. Chester and Betty (Collins) L.; B.A., Lawrence U., 1958; m. Sheila K. Andersen, Sept. 13, 1958; children—Lisa M., John A., Bronwen Gay, Douglas Q. Asst. cashier, lending officer Continental Ill. Nat. Bank & Trust Co., Chgo., 1962-68; with Reliance Group, Inc. (formerly Leasco Corp.), N.Y.C., 1968-79, treas., 1968-69, v.p., 1969-71, sr. v.p., 1971-72, chief fin. officer, 1971-79, exec. v.p., chief operating officer, 1972-79, also dir., mem. exec. com.; dir., chmn. exec. com., chief exec. officer MEDSERCO Inc., St. Louis, 1980—; dir., sec.-treas. Energy Clinic Corp.; dir. Internat. Capital Equipment Ltd., Wilcam Food Products, Inc. Mem. nat. bd. dirs., exec. com. Reading Is Fundamental; trustee St. Luke's Sch., Lawrence U. Served to 1st lt. USAF, 1958-62. Mem. Lawrence U. Alumni Assn. (dir. 1965-71, 2d v.p. 1966-68, v.p. 1968-70). Clubs: Union League (Chgo.); Country (Darien, Conn.). Home: 6 Hummingbird Ln Darien CT 06820 Office: 1034 S Brentwood Blvd Suite 1400 Saint Louis MO 63117

LEATHAM, LOUIS SALISBURY, bank exec.; b. Salt Lake City, Nov. 16, 1902; s. Wm. and Martha Ann (Salisbury) L.; student U. Utah, 1923-24; m. Grace Carn, Sept. 24, 1930; children—William Wallace, Janet Leatham Penman, Jon Paul. Served as missionary Ch. Jesus Christ of Latter-day Saints, Scotland and Eng., 1927-29, high councilor East Riverside Stake, 1951-57, Kearns Stake, 1958-61, Riverside Stake, 1962-63, patriarch Ensign Stake, 1966-73, Salt Lake Stake, 1975—; cashier, sec. Nat. Savs. & Loan Assn. of Am., 1929-33; sec., dir. Park Fairfield Mining Co., 1931-35; chief cashier, auditor U.L.C.C., 1935-40; bank examiner State of Utah, 1950-51, chief bldg. and loan examiner, 1950-51, bank commr., 1951-56; pres. Bank of Kearns, Salt Lake County, 1956-59; exec. v.p., chief exec. officer, dir. Beehive State Bank, Salt Lake City, 1959-68; exec. v.p. Comml. Security Bank, 1968-70; pres. United Investors Corp., 1970—; sec.-treas. Gold Internat. Corp., 1971-75. Hon. consul Republic of Senegal, 1969—. Pres., State Depository Bd. of Utah, 1951-56, Salt Lake Clearing House Assn., 1965-66; pub. rep. Utah State Employees Assn., 1960-72; treas., v.p. World Trade Assn. of Utah, 1962-71, pres., 1972-73. Treas., Salt Lake County Am. Cancer Fund Crusade, 1962-64. Chmn. Pine Dale dist. Boy Scouts Am., fin. chmn. Red Butte dist., 1962-65; treas. Salt Lake Area United Fund, 1965-67; bd. chancellors Consular Corps Coll. and Internat. Consular Acad.; bd. dirs., treas. United Health Found., 1966-73; hon. trustee Nitecaps Internat. Assn., 1965-75. Served 1st lt. to lt. col. U.S. Army, 1940-50; chief fin. instns. br. Office Mil. Govt. for Hesse, Weisbaden, Germany, 1947-48; staff officer on Gen. Lucius Clay's European Command, logistics div., 1948-49. Mem. Nat. Assn. Suprs. of State Banks (chmn. Fifth Dist.), Nat. Assn. State Savs. and Loan Suprs., Assn. Small Loan Adminstrs., Am., Utah (mem. exec. com. 1963-64) bankers assns., Utah Mfrs. Assn., Salt Lake City C. of C., Utah Hist. Soc., Newcomen Soc. N.Am. Republican. Mormon. Clubs: University, Kiwanis. Author: The Leatham Family Book of Remembrance, 1955; The Joshua Salisbury Family-Book of Remembrance, 1961; Karl S. Little, Utah's Mr. Credit Union, 1963; The Louis Salisbury Leatham Book of Remembrance, 1977; also ch. articles for mags. Home: 532 12th Ave Salt Lake City UT 84103 Office: 546 De Soto St Salt Lake City UT 84103 also PO Box 1627 Salt Lake City UT 84110

LEATON, EDWARD K., actuarial and cons. co. exec.; b. Mt. Vernon, N.Y., Oct. 2, 1928; s. Lionel M. and Henrietta (Kline) L.; B.S. in Mech. Engring., Lehigh U., 1949; M.B.A., Yale, 1950; m. Janet Kemp; children—Edward M., Kenneth (dec. Mar. 1974), William (dec. Aug. 1972), Robert, Thomas, James, Richard. Grad. instr. Yale, 1949-50; from trainee to asst. supt. Gen. Motors Corp., 1950-54; asst. to exec. v.p. Rowe Mfg. Corp., Whippany, N.J., 1955-56, v.p., dir. mfg., 1956-57; cons. Lambert M. Huppeler Co., Inc., N.Y.C., 1957-69, exec. v.p., 1969-74, pres., chief exec. officer, 1974—, chmn., 1978—, also dir.; pres. Leaton & Huppeler Co., Inc., N.Y.C., 1967-78, vice chmn., 1978—, also dir.; gen. agt. Edward K. Leaton Agy., N.Y.C.; pres. Exec. Programs, Inc. and Analytical Estate Planning Services, Inc. (both N.Y.C.); dir. G.A.M.C.; mem. 2 pension industry coms. on implementation Employee Retirement Security Act of 1974. Chmn. coordinating com. ERISA; sr. warden, lay reader St. Paul's Ch.; mem. leadership com. Community Fund. Trustee Barrington (R.I.) Coll. Mem. Am. Ordnance Assn. (pres. Lehigh Valley post 1948-49), Life Mgrs. Assn. N.Y. (pres., dir.), Life Underwriters Assn. N.Y.C. (chmn. bd.), Am. Soc. Pension Actuaries (v.p., dir.), Assn. Advanced Life Underwriters, Am. Soc. C.L.U.'s, Am. Mgmt. Assn., Am. Pension Conf., Nat. Assn. Pension Cons.'s and Adminstrs. (v.p., dir.), Small Bus. Council Am. (dir.). Clubs: Union League, Yale (N.Y.C.); Country of Darien (gov., trustee), Nutmeg Curling (Darien, Conn.); Mid-Ocean (Tucker's Town, Bermuda). Contbr. articles to profl. jours.; speaker before numerous internat., nat. and regional orgns. Office: 430 Park Ave New York NY 10022

LEAVITT, DANA GIBSON, corp. exec.; b. Framingham, Mass., Dec. 4, 1925; s. Luther C. and Margaret (Gibson) L.; B.A., Brown U., 1948, student Harvard Bus. Sch., 1954-55; m. Frances Smith, Apr. 12, 1952; children—Margaret Gibson, Jonathan. Home office rep. Aetna Life Ins. Co., Boston also Long Beach, Calif., 1949-54; v.p., sec.-treas., exec. v.p. North Am. Title Ins. Co., Oakland, Calif., 1955-64; pres. Transam. Title Ins. Co., Oakland, 1964-72, now dir.; v.p. Transam. Corp., 1969-71, group v.p., 1971-77, exec. v.p., 1977—; chmn. bd. Transam. Fin. Corp., Transam. Ins. Co., Occidental Life Ins. Co. of Calif.; dir. Transam. Title Ins. Co., Lyon Moving and Storage Co., Transam Interway, United Artists Corp., Trans Internat. Airlines, DeLaval Turbine, Inc., Regional chmn. Brown U. Fund, 1969-72. Bd. dirs. Children's Hosp. Med. Center, 1969-72, Children's Hosp. Med. Center Found., 1969-72; trustee Lewis and Clark Coll., Portland, Oreg., 1972-75; trustee Brown U., Providence, R.I., 1973-78, emeritus, 1978—. Served with USMCR, World War II. Mem. Delta Kappa Epsilon. Republican. Clubs: Brown U. Club No. Calif., Harvard Bus. Sch. of No. Calif., Orinda Country, Bohemian, Napa Valley Country. Home: 600 Montgomery St San Francisco CA 94111 Office: 600 Montgomery St San Francisco CA 94111

LEAVITT, DAVID S., indsl. co. exec.; b. 1925; B.S.E.E., Purdue U., 1946; married. Vice pres. Nikoh Tube div. Internat. Rolling Mill Products Corp., 1946-56; pres. Leavitt Tube Inc., 1956-70; sr. v.p., mem. exec. com., chief operating officer Unarco Industries Inc., 1970-71, exec. v.p., 1971-72, pres., chief operating officer, 1972-80, pres., chief exec. officer, 1980—, also dir. Served with U.S. Army, 1943-45. Office: Unarco Industries Inc 332 S Michigan Ave Chicago IL 60604*

LEAVITT, GLADYS G., banker; b. Chgo., Oct. 2, 1920; s. d. Benjamin B. and Dora (Ziff) Levinson; m. Alex E. Leavitt, July 24, 1939; children—Stanley S., Adrienne R. Stevens. Supr., Devon Bank, Chgo., 1950-56; supr. bookkeeping and proof, Bank of Lincolnwood (Will.), 1956-61; asst. cashier 1st Nat. Bank of Lincolnwood, 1962-67; asst. v.p. South Central Bank, Chgo., 1968-69, v.p., 1970-73; v.p. Nat. Republic Bank, Chgo., 1973—. Chairperson adv. bd. Ill. Hosp. Sch. for Crippled Children, 1978—; mem. Near West Side Community Council; mem. M & M Found. for Retarded Children, Cabrini Hosp. Guild, 12th Dist. Beat Rep. Police Dept. Program, Gail Ann Ditore Hotchkins Meml. Orgn. Mem. Ill. Bank Assn. for Women, Nat. Womens Bank Assn., Ill. Safe Deposit Assn. Club: Exec. of Chgo. Home: 1454 W Flournoy Chicago IL 60607 Office: 500 S Racine Ave Chicago IL 60607

LEAVOY, NORMAN PHILIP, excavating co. mgr.; b. Noranda, Que., Can., May 7, 1950; s. William Ernest and Jean (Daugherty) L.; B.A. with honors, Principia Coll., 1972. Adminstrn. officer Pacific div. Toronto-Dominion Bank, 1972; supr. Leavoy Excavating Ltd., North Vancouver, B.C., 1973—, also office mgr. Christian Scientist. Club: North Shore Winter.

LEBECK, WARREN WELLS, cons.; b. Chgo., Mar. 13, 1921; s. Emil and Hazel Alma (Wells) L.; A.B., North Central Coll., Naperville, Ill., 1942; m. Dorothy Mae Lester, Feb. 1, 1943; children—Sara Beth, Kenneth, Clayton, Ricky. Asst. to sec. to chmn. bd. Montgomery Ward & Co., Chgo., 1946-47, sec. to chmn. bd., 1947-54; asst. to sec. Chgo. Bd. Trade, 1954-57, sec., 1957-65, exec. v.p., sec., 1965-73, pres., 1973-77, sr. exec. v.p., 1977-79, cons., 1979—; cons. First Nat. Bank Chgo., 1979—; dir. Gen. Grain, Inc., Early & Daniel Co., Inc., Tidewater Grain Co.; mem. agrl. policy adv. com. for U.S. spl. trade rep. to Multinat. Trade Negotiations. Christmas Seal chmn. for Chgo. and Cook County, 1966-67; chmn., pres. South Loop Improvement Project, Chgo., 1968-71; trustee Downers Grove (Ill.) Community High Sch., 1955-58. Served to lt. USNR, 1943-46; PTO. Clubs: Union League, Met., Midday, Commodity (Chgo.). Home: 432 Minneola St Hinsdale IL 60521 Office: 141 W Jackson Blvd Chicago IL 60604

LEBEDEFF, NICHOLAS BORIS, fin. cons. co. exec.; b. Hollywood, Calif., Apr. 16, 1944; s. Boris Paul and Alexandra E. (Koshell) L.; B.B.A., Loyola U., Los Angeles, 1967; M.B.A., U. So. Calif., 1970; m. Judith Leah Moffett, Nov. 22, 1969; 1 dau., Christina. Budget and adminstrv. analyst City of Los Angeles, 1967-73; mgr. budget and fiscal ops. Van De Kamp's Holland Dutch Bakers div. Gen. Host Corp., Los Angeles, 1973-74; mgr. fin. planning and analysis dept. U.S. Borax and Chem. Corp., Los Angeles, 1974-75; corporate planning and fin. analysis cons. NBL Assos., Los Angeles, 1976—; pres. Micro-Software, Inc., 1977—, The Planning Systems Group, Inc., 1980—. Bd. dirs. Friends of Ft. Ross in So. Calif., Am. Med. and Ednl. Services in Africa; mem. Ft. Ross Citizens Adv. Com. Mem. Am. Mgmt. Assn., Planning Execs. Inst., So. Calif. Corporate Planners, U. So. Calif. Alumni Assn., Commerce Assos., Brit. Interplanetary Soc., Los Angeles World Affairs Council. Republican. Mem. Orthodox Ch. Am. Home and Office: 123 S Arden Blvd Los Angeles CA 90004

LEBENSON, JAY, ins. exec.; b. N.Y.C., Dec. 18, 1938; s. Herbert and Charlotte (Springer) L.; B.B.A., Hofstra U., 1960; m. Susan Karp, Dec. 12, 1976; children—Beth, Jonathan. Trainee to co-owner Hess Agy., Inc., 1959-68; sec., v.p. Hess Morris Lebenson, Inc., Manhasset, N.Y., 1968—; pres. Hess Morris Lebenson of Conn., Inc., Washington Depot, Conn., 1978—; v.p., treas. Hess, Lebenson, Hunt, Inc., Coral Gables, Fla., 1980—; dir. Jonathan Trumbull Assos. (Hartford, Conn.). Mem. Profl. Ins. Agts. Assn., Nassau County Ind. Ins. Agts. Assn. (dir.), Greater N.Y. Ins. Brokers Assn., Conn. Ind. Ins. Agts. Assn., Fla. Ind. Ins. Agts. Assn. Club: K.P. Designer ins. program, Great Adventure, Inc. Home: Barnes Rd Washington CT 06793 Office: 1615 Northern Blvd Manhasset NY 11030

LEBL, GIORA M., cons. co. exec.; b. Subotica, Yugoslavia, July 31, 1931; s. Marcell S. and Clara J. (Frenkel) L.; B.S., Columbia U., 1960; M.B.A., U. Pa., 1963; children—Marc J., John A. Account dir. McCann Erickson Advt. Co., N.Y.C., 1962-67; mktg. mgr. for Latin Am., Revlon Inc., N.Y.C., 1967-70; dir. for Europe, Helene Curtis Industries, Chgo., 1970-71; pres. Spalding Internat. div. Questor Co., Chicopee, Mass., 1972-74; pres. J. Linmar Internat. Ltd., Longmeadow, Mass., 1975—. Club: U. Pa. Alumni. Office: 813 Williams St Longmeadow MA 01106

LE BLANC, MORELAND PAUL, JR., public accountant; b. Baton Rouge, Aug. 9, 1921; s. Moreland Paul and Carmen Marie (Haydel) LeB.; B.S., La. State U., 1948, M.B.A., 1949; m. Lillian Frances Lanford, Sept. 16, 1946; children—Sharon Frances, Julie Ann, Paul Lanford, Mary Martha. With Arthur Andersen & Co., C.P.A.'s, 1949—, partner charge New Orleans office, 1958-66, mng. partner N.Y. office, 1966-78, vice chmn., 1972-75, co-chmn., 1975-80, chmn., 1980—. Adv. council Tulane U. Sch. Bus.; bd. dirs. Nat. Jr. Achievement. Served to lt. (j.g.) USN, 1943-46. C.P.A., N.Y. Mem. Am. Inst. C.P.A.'s, N.Y. State Soc. C.P.A.'s. Clubs: University, Union League, Recess, Racquet and Tennis; Wee Burn Country, Landmark (Conn.); Chicago; Blind Brook. Home: 6 Cloudy Ln Darien CT 06820 Office: 1345 Ave Americas New York NY 10105

LEBLANC, RICHARD STEVEN, med. products and hosp. supplies distbg. co. exec.; b. Honolulu, May 11, 1948; s. Leslie Gerard and Cloia Virginia LeB.; B.B.A., Campbell U., 1975; M.B.A. U. Central Fla., 1976. Sales rep. IBM Corp., Orlando, Fla., 1976-77; regional ops. mgr. Baxter Travenol Labs., Inc., Atlanta, 1977-80, regional mgr. home patient services, Garden Grove, Calif., 1980—. Served with USMC, 1969-73. Mem. Atlanta Drug Assn. Republican. Presbyterian. Home: 2845-F Fairview Rd Santa Ana CA 92704 Office: 12131 Western Ave Garden Grove CA 92641

LEBOR, JOHN F(RANCIS), corporate exec.; b. Portland, Oreg., Mar. 22, 1906; s. John G. and Jettie P. (Cook) L.; B.B.A., U. Oreg., 1928; M.B.A. with distinction, Harvard, 1930; m. Violette Steinmetz, Oct. 7, 1931; children—Andrew Scott, John Cook. Investment analyst Scudder, Stevens & Clark, N.Y.C., 1930-33; financial staff Radio-Keith-Orpheum Corp., 1933-40; sec.-treas. York (Pa.) Corp., 1940-46; treas. Federated Dept. Stores, Inc., Cin., 1946-51, v.p., treas., dir., 1951-57, v.p., dir., 1958-60, exec. v.p., dir., 1960-65; dir. Bobbie Brooks, Inc., Cleve., Carlisle Retailers, Inc., Ashtabula, Ohio, Gateway Option Income Fund, Cin., U.S. Shoe Corp., Cin., others. Recipient Disting. Alumnus award U. Oreg. Sch. Bus. Area chmn. United Appeal; mem. Hamilton County (Ohio) Republican fin. com. Mem. Phi Beta Kappa, Beta Gamma Sigma, Beta Alpha Psi, Alpha Kappa Psi. Episcopalian. Clubs: Queen City, Bankers (Cin.); Chgo. Home: 222 Oliver Rd Cincinnati OH 45215 Office: 511 Walnut St Cincinnati OH 45202

LEBOUTILLIER, MARTIN, securities co. exec.; b. Phoenix, Dec. 7, 1921; s. Martin and Cornelia Throop (Geer) LeB.; A.B., Yale U., 1943; m. Clelia Delafield, Sept. 11, 1948 (div.); m. 2d, Polly Kinnear, Sept. 28, 1957; children—Clelia, Cynthia (dec.), Martin III, John. Sales trainee Firestone Tire & Rubber Co., 1946; asso. Fred Eldean Orgn., Inc., 1947; gen. partner Delafield & Delafield, N.Y.C., 1950-54; with dept. new bus. Dean Witter & Co., Investment bankers, San Francisco, 1955-61, gen. partner, 1961-68; with Paine, Webber, Jackson & Curtis, Inc., N.Y.C., 1968—, gen. partner, 1968-70, exec. v.p., chief operating officer, 1970-71, pres., mem. exec. com., 1971-74, chmn. exec. com., 1974-78, dir. div. fixed income securities, 1975-78, chmn. fin. com., 1979—, also dir.; dir. various subs.; dir. Abacus Fund Security Corp. Bd. dirs. Francis Ward Paine Found., Inc., Sheltering Arms Children's Service, N.Y.C.; gov. Am. Stock Exchange, Inc., 1953-54, ofcl., 1974-78, com. mem., 1974-78. Served to lt. jr. grade USN, 1943-46. Mem. Investment Bankers Assn. (N.Y. Group edn. com. 1970), Securities Industry Assn. (mem. com. firm relationships 1972, chmn. 1974), Pilgrims U.S., St. Nicholas Soc., Delta Kappa Epsilon. Republican. Episcopalian. Clubs: Down town Assn., N.Y. Yacht; Clove Valley Rod and Gun (LaGrangeville, N.Y.); Bohemian (San Francisco). Office: 140 Broadway New York NY 10005

LEBOWITZ, MORTIMER CHARLES, retail co. exec.; b. N.Y.C., Mar. 18, 1912; s. Henry I. and Esther (Roth) L.; A.B., U. Pa., 1932; student N.Y. U. Law Sch., 1933-35; m. Adele Gusack, June 4, 1940; children—John William, Emily (Mrs. Richard Olbrich), Caroline (Mrs. Richard Simon), Petrina (Mrs. Sam Huston). Buyer, The Mart, Paterson, N.J., 1933-35; founder, pres. Morton's, Washington, 1935—. Bd. dirs. Washington Urban League, 1956—, pres., 1960-61; chmn. Washington Commn. Human Resources, 1962-71; chmn. inner city com. Nat. Capital area council Boy Scouts Am., 1967-74, mem. Nat. council, 1970—, mem. interim bicentennial com., 1971-72. Trustee Va. Coll.; bd. overseers Coll. V.I.; bd. dirs. Center Met. Studies, 1961-71. Recipient Human Relations award Capitol Press Club, 1961; Merit award D.C. C. of C., 1962; Equal Opportunity Day award, 1963, 67; Silver Beaver award Boy Scouts Am., 1968; Whitney Young award, 1973; spl. citation Pigskin Club, Washington, 1980. Mem. D.C. Bd. Trade, D.C. Retail Bur., D.C. C. of C. (dir. 1977—), Am. Jewish Com., Alpha Phi Omega, Tau Epsilon Phi. Mem. B'nai B'rith. Home: 6319 Georgetown Pike McLean VA 22101 Office: 310 6th St S Arlington VA 22202

LE BRETON, ALVIN FRANCIS, communication co. exec.; b. New Orleans, Apr. 13, 1922; s. Joseph Francis and Louisette Marie (Guerin) Le B.; B.C.S., Tulane U., 1964; diploma Loyola U., New Orleans, 1953, Soule Bus. Coll., New Orleans, 1948; m. Ethel Norma Daigle, Sept. 5, 1942; children—David Michael, Kathryn Elyse, Geary Robert, Mark Stephen. With Western Union, 1940—, spl. asst. to v.p., N.Y.C., 1970-72, dir., Moorestown, N.J., 1972-77, dir. fin. and adminstrn., 1977—. Vice pres. Burlington County council Boy Scouts Am., 1972-77; mem. Mt. Laurel (N.J.) Sch. Bd., 1974-75. Served with USNR, 1942-45, 50-52. Recipient Meritorious Service medal; Silver Beaver award Boy Scouts Am., 1976; Scholarship and Leadership award Alpha Sigma Lambda, 1964; Paul Harris fellow, 1978. Mem. Res. Officers Assn., Naval Res. Assn., Washington C. of C., VFW. Republican. Roman Catholic. Club: Rotary. Home: 146 Knotty Oak Dr Mount Laurel NJ 08054 Office: #1 Lake St Upper Saddle River NJ 07446

LEBRO, THEODORE PETER, property tax service exec.; b. Fulton, N.Y., Feb. 12, 1910; s. Peter and Mary (Karpala) L.; B.S., Syracuse U., 1954; m. Wanda Saffranski, Oct. 16, 1932. Farmer nr. Fulton, 1935-76; various positions restaurants, grocery, Fulton, 1929-54; owner, operator Lebro Real Estate and Ins. Agency, Fulton, 1951—; dir. Real Estate Property Tax Service Agy., Fulton, 1972—. Mem. Fulton Parking Authority, 1960—; bd. dirs. Lee Meml. Hosp.; pres. Catholic Youth Orgn. Fulton, 1976—. Served with 35th inf. U.S. Army, 1942-46; PTO. Certified property mgr. Mem. Soc. Real Estate Appraisers, Oswego County Bd. Realtors, N.Y. State Soc. Appraisers, Assn. County Dirs., V.F.W., Am. Legion, St. Michael's Soc. (pres. 1960—). Republican. Roman Catholic. Clubs: Beaver Meadow, K.C.,

Elks, Pathfinders Game and Fish (life). Home: RFD 1 Box 111 Rt 48S Phoenix NY 13135 Office: 316 W 1st St Fulton NY 13069

LECHT, DANIEL, mfg. co. exec.; b. Providence, Apr. 1, 1929; s. Morris and Lillian (Goldman) L.; student bus. adminstrn. Bryant Coll., 1948; student machine design R.I., Sch. Design, 1950; B.S. in Graphic Arts, U. R.I., 1954; m. Eileen Smith, Dec. 28, 1964; children—Michael, Richard, Lisa. Founder, pres. R.I. Lithograph (acquired by Advanced Computer Techniques 1970-79), Pawtucket, 1957—, also dir. Chmn. R.I. State Council Arts; mem. Presdl. adv. bd. for performing arts John F. Kennedy Center. Served with U.S. Army, 1946-48. Mem. Graphic Arts Tech. Found., R.I. State C. of C. Clubs: To-Kalon, Providence Art, Masons, Shriners; Quatuor Coronati (London). Home: 33 Rockler Dr Warwick RI 02818 Office: 35 Monticello Pl Pawtucket RI 02862

LEDBETTER, JOHN COLEMAN, petroleum co. exec.; b. Obion, Tenn., Dec. 15, 1935; s. Paul Rudolph and Gertrude (Anderson) L.; B.S., U.S. Mil. Acad., 1957. Commd. 2d lt. U.S. Army, 1957, advanced through grades to 1st lt., 1958; resigned, 1960; with McDonnell & Co., N.Y.C., 1960-62, Morris & Co., N.Y.C., 1962-63, Childs & Co., N.Y.C., 1963-65, Van Alstyne, Noel & Co., N.Y.C., 1965-67; pres., chief exec. officer Nyvatex Oil Corp., Billings, Mont., 1968—, Nyvatex Mktg. Corp.; dir. Whole Earth Corp. Mem. Soc. Petroleum Engrs. Office: 3021 6th Ave N Box 1835 Billings MT 59103

LEDBETTER, STEWART MANEE, govt. ofcl., real estate exec.; b. N.Y.C., Nov. 9, 1932; s. John Nelson and Gladys Stewart (Manée) L.; B.A., Rollins Coll., 1955; M.B.A., Stanford, 1957; postgrad. Columbia, 1960-61; grad. Realtors Inst., Concord, N.H., 1974; m. Sheila Barbara Tynan, June 18, 1959; children—Stewart Manee, John Patton. Vice pres. 1st Nat. City Bank, N.Y.C., 1961-71; pres. Real Estate Assos. Vt., Manchester, 1971—; pres. Ledbetter Properties, Inc., Dorset, Vt., 1972-76; pres. Investment Assos. So. Vt., Manchester, 1971—; commr. banking and ins. State of Vt.; commr. Vt. Housing Fin. Agy.; chmn. Vt. Home Mortgage Guaranty Bd.; mem. Gov.'s Council Econ. Advisors; pres. S. Central Vt. Bd. Realtors, 1975. Chmn., Republican Town Com., Dorset; bd. dirs. adv. bd. Vt. Job Start; trustee Vt. State Tchrs. Retirement Fund. Served to 1st lt., Fin. Corps, U.S. Army, 1957-60. Mem. Vt. Assn. Realtors (dir.), Nat. Assn. Realtors, Nat. Assn. Ins. Commrs. (chmn. zone 1), Conf. State Bank Suprs. (vice-chmn. dist. 1), Nat. Inst. Real Estate Brokers. Clubs: Stanwich (Greenwich, Conn.); Stowe Country; Dorset Field. Home: 25 Hubbard Park Dr Montpelier VT 05602 Office: 120 State St Montpelier VT 05602

LEDERMAN, MICHAEL WAINWRIGHT, automobile restoration exec.; b. N.Y.C., Jan. 9, 1948; s. Rocky H. and Jeanette (Wainwright) L.; B.S., Cornell U., 1969, M.S., 1970; Ph.D., U. Bologna (Italy) 1976. Founding partner Lederman Service, restoration and racing preparation of Porsche automobiles, Bronx, N.Y., Bologna and Parma (Italy), 1976—, sr. operating officer, 1978—; racer of Porsche in Europe, 1976—. Mem. Emergency Service, Parma. Registered engr., Parma. Mem. Porsche Club Am., Porsche Club Gt. Britain, U.S. Polo Assn. Club: Cornell (N.Y.C.). Home: Murmuring Hollow Farms Accord NY 12404 Office: Strada-9 Quart Negrona 3 Parma Italy 43100 also 100-15 Asch Loop Bronx NY 10475

LEDNEY, GEORGE, mining co. exec.; b. Jerome, Pa., Apr. 26, 1922; s. Charles and Susan (Stredney) L.; extension student Pa. State U.; m. Margaret Mihalacki, July 15, 1950; children—Gerald G., George M., Douglas A. With Berwind-White Coal Mining Co., Windber, Pa., 1941-62, supt., 1961-62; mgr. Sta. WWBR, Windber, 1964-65; ins. agt., 1962-64; supt. Reitz Coal Co., Windber, 1965-69; pres., dir. Longwall Mining Co., Windber, 1969—, C C & L Trucking, Inc., 1976—; v.p., dir. Lunar Mining, Inc., 1975—; v.p. Colonial Coal Co., 1978—; partner Colech Enterprises, 1975—. Pres., Windber Public Library, 1974-75, 79-80, 1st v.p., 1976, bd. dirs., 1972—; pres. Somerset County Library System, 1980; mem. Windber Fire Co., 1979-80; bd. dirs. Windber Redevel. Assn., 1970-76, Windber Recreation Assn., 1967-70; mem. adv. bd. Admiral Peary Vocat. Tech. Sch., 1975—; v.p. Windber Borough Council, 1974-78; mem. Somerset County Devel. Council, 1977—; mem. Somerset County Library Bd., 1978—, Windber Area Recreation and Park Bd., 1978—. Served with USNR, 1943-45. Mem. Am. Legion, VFW. Republican. Byzantine Catholic. Clubs: Windber Rotary (past dir.), Windber Country. Home: 1705 Hillside Ave Windber PA 15963 Office: 900 Mine 42 Windber PA 15963

LEE, CHARLES ROBERT, holding co. exec.; b. Pitts., Feb. 15, 1940; s. John Anthony and Margaret V. (English) L.; B. Metall. Engring., Cornell, 1962; M.B.A. with distinction, Harvard, 1964; m. Ilda Gerhardt, Dec. 31, 1958; children—Douglas, Dana, Debra, Dawn, Daryn. Mgr. bus. research U.S. Steel Corp., Pitts., 1964-70; asst. treas. corporate investments Penn Central Transp. Co., Phila., 1970-71; v.p. fin., sec. Pa. Co., Arlington, Va., 1971-79; sr. v.p.-fin. The Penn Central Corp., 1978-79; sr. v.p., chief fin. officer Columbia Pictures Industries, Inc., 1980—. Home: 9609 Persimmon Tree Rd Potomac MD 20854

LEE, CHEW HOY, property devel. exec.; b. Honolulu, Mar. 26, 1933; s. Moon Sung and Lum She L.; student St. Louis Coll., 1951; B.S.C.E., U. Hawaii, 1955; m. Suzanne Tran, Mar. 31, 1963; children—Marvin, Ross. With Moses Akiona, Ltd., 1949-55; engr., estimator, constrn. and engring. exec. Morrison-Knudsen Co., 1955-69; project mgr. to v.p. Amfac Properties, Honolulu, 1969—; projects include St. Lawrence Seaway, Karadj Dam (Iran), Wishon and Courtright Dams. Mem. State of Hawaii Dept. Planning and Econ. Devel.; mem. State of Hawaii Council Housing and Constrn. Industry, City and County of Honolulu Council Housing Industry, Pearl City Neighborhood Bd. Mem. Devel. Assn. Hawaii (treas.), Land Use Found. Hawaii (dir.), People for Sensible Growth (pres.). Democrat. Buddhist. Home: 2247 Amokemoke St Pearl City HI 96782 Office: PO Box 3140 Honolulu HI 96802

LEE, CHI-WEN JEVONS, educator; b. Yun-nan, China, Sept. 28, 1944; s. Kai-Chang and Fei-Zen (Chen) L.; Ph.D., U. Rochester, 1977; came to U.S., 1970; m. Chin-Shya, Aug. 14, 1971; 1 son, Spencer. Asst. prof. Wesleyan U., Middletown, Conn., 1977-78, Knox Coll., Galesburg, Ill., 1978-80; asst. prof. Grad. Sch. Bus., U. Chgo., 1980—; cons. Liberty Fund fellow, 1977; Gen. Electric Found. fellow, 1978; Univ. House fellow, 1979; NSF grantee, 1979; A.W. Mellon Found. grantee, 1980. Mem. Am. Econ. Assn., So. Econ. Assn., Atlantic Econ. Assn. Contbr. articles to econ. jours. Home: 5107 S Blackstone St Apt 1206 Chicago IL 60615 Office: Grad Sch Bus U Chgo 1101 E 58th St Chicago IL 60637

LEE, CURTIS HOWARD, cons. engr.; b. San Francisco, June 7, 1928; s. Quong and Kum Ho (Lee) Lum; B.S. with honors, Calif. State Poly. U., 1952; postgrad. McGeorge Coll. Law, 1964-67; children—Roberta, Sabrina, Kristina. Mech. engr. Buonaccorsi & Assos., Cons. Engrs., San Francisco, 1953-57; mech. engr. Eagleson Engrs., San Francisco, 1957-59, 60-63; chief engr. C.S. Hardeman, San Francisco, 1959-60; spl. project engr. A.E. D'Ambly, Cons. Engrs., Phila., 1963-64; cons. engr., Sacramento, 1964-67; chief engr. G.W. Dunn & Assos., Cons. Engrs., San Diego, 1967-69; prin. Dunn-Lee-Smith-Klein & Assos., Cons. Engrs., San Diego, 1969—. Adv. panel Calif. State Bldg. Commn., 1971-76; mem. San Diego City Bd. Appeals, 1974-79, Chula Vista (Calif.) City Bd. Appeals, 1980—; regional adv. council Am. Arbitration Assn., 1977—. Served with U.S. Army, 1947-49. Registerd profl. engr., Ariz., Calif., Colo., Fla., Ga., Nev., N.Mex., Ohio, Oreg., Pa., Tex., Wash. Mem. Am. Cons. Engrs. Council, Am. Soc. Quality Control, Am. Soc. Heating, Refrigerating and Air-Conditioning Engrs., ASME, Am. Soc. Plumbing Engrs., Am. Soc. Prof. Estimators, Constrn. Specifications Inst., Instrument Soc. Am., Internat. Assn. Plumbing and Mech. Ofcls., Internat. Solar Energy Soc., Nat. Soc. Profl. Engrs., Nat. Fire Protection Assn. Office: 1003 Plaza Blvd Suite 206 National City CA 92050

LEE, DAE SOO, import-export co. exec.; came to U.S., 1961, naturalized, 1976; b. Seoul, Feb. 17, 1937; s. Chong Yun and Mae Soon (Shin) L.; B.A., Yonsei U., 1960; postgrad. U. Wis., 1961, Wharton Sch., U. Pa., 1971; B.S., Westcoast U., 1968; m. Chung Sun, Apr. 6, 1967; children—Eunice, Yvette, David. Vice pres. Aic, Inc., Los Angeles, 1967-74; pres. D.S. Lee and Assos., Inc., Los Angeles, 1974-76; v.p. Daewoo Internat. (Am.) Corp., Los Angeles, 1976-79, pres., Carlstadt, N.J., 1979—. Presbyterian. Home: 269 Lotte Rd Ridgewood NJ 07450 Office: Daewoo Internat (America) Corp 100 Daewoo Pl Carlstadt NJ 07072

LEE, FRANK AYRE, chem. engring. co. exec.; b. Greenville, Pa., May 19, 1924; s. Raymond C. and Nora (Ayre) L.; B.S. in Chem. Engring., Carnegie Inst. Tech., 1949; m. Bettye J. Easley, July 3, 1948; children—Gary H., Linda M., Janet E., Raymond C. With Humble Oil & Refining Co., Baytown, Tex., 1949-50, Petro-Chem. Devel. Co., N.Y.C., 1950-56, Howe-Baker Engrs., Inc., Westwood, N.J., 1957-59; with Foster-Wheeler Corp., Livingston, N.J., 1959—, v.p., 1965-69, sr. v.p., 1969-72, pres., chief exec. officer, 1972—, dir., 1975—; chmn. bd., mng. dir. Foster-Wheeler Ltd., London, 1967—; dir. Fidelity Union Trust Co., Fidelity Union Bancorp., Internat. Gen. Industries. Served with U.S. Army, 1943-46. Mem. Theta Xi. Club: Queen's (London). Patentee tubular process furnaces held. Office: 110 S Orange Ave Livingston NJ 07039

LEE, FRANK HOWELL, JR., homebuilder, real estate developer; b. Jackson, Ala., Dec. 3, 1949; s. Frank Lee and Hazel Clair (Daugherty) L.; student U. Ala., 1968-71. Plant mgr. Central Ala. Builders Supply Corp., Camden, 1971-72; v.p. Gt. Am. Homes Corp., Camden, 1972-74, pres., chmn. bd., chief exec. officer, 1974—; dir. Wilcox County Devel. Corp.; mem. Wilcox County Rural Devel. Exec. Com. Mem. Wilcox County Democratic Exec. Com., 1978—, chmn., 1980. Mem. Home Builders Assn. Ala., Pres.'s Assn. Ala., Nat. Assn. Homebuilders, Camden C. of C. (dir. 1974), Phi Delta Theta. Methodist. Club: Camden Exchange. Office: Route 2 Box 44G Camden AL 36724

LEE, J. RICHARD, advt. exec., clergyman; b. Indpls., Jan. 11, 1925; s. Edgar L. and Laura (Hamm) Meischke; B.A., Anderson Coll. and Theol. Sem., 1946; Ph.D. in Communications, D.D., P.E. Univ., London, Eng., 1965; m. Dorothy Katherine Dyer, Apr. 10, 1960; 1 dau., Jane Allison. Announcer, Sta. WIRE, Indpls., 1944-45; nat. radio-TV dir. Ch. of God, Anderson, Ind., 1946-52; TV newscaster, religious dir. KKTV, prodn. mgr. KVOR, Colorado Springs, Colo., 1953-54; pres., chief exec. officer J. Richard Lee, Inc., Advt., Los Angeles, Calif., 1954—; pres. Continental Radio Network, Hollywood, Calif., 1962—, Exxel Co., Los Angeles and Oceanside, Calif., 1977—. Ordained to ministry Ch. of God, 1946; minister Country Ch. of Hollywood, 1956-60, Christ's Ch., Los Angeles, 1961—. Fellow Royal Geog. Soc. London (Eng.). Home: 127 N Highland Ave Los Angeles CA 90036 Office: 5670 Wilshire Blvd Los Angeles CA 90036

LEE, JAMES EDWARD, petroleum co. exec.; b. Kiln, Miss., Dec. 13, 1921; s. Fitzhugh and Bonnie Mae (Lenoir) L.; B.S., La. Tech. U., 1942; m. Kathleen Ruth Edwards, Apr. 18, 1943; children—Kay, Janet, Douglas B., James Stephen. Chem. engr. Gulf Oil Corp., Port Arthur, Tex., 1942-47, asst. foreman, Phila., 1947-52, supt., 1953-59, area rep., coordinator, Manila, 1959-63, Tokyo, 1963-66, mng. dir. Kuwait Oil Co., 1966-69, pres. Gulf Oil Co.-Eastern Hemisphere, London, 1969-72, corp. exec. v.p., 1972-73, pres., 1973—, also dir.; dir. Gulf Can. Ltd., Joy Mfg. Co., Pitts. Nat. Bank. Bd. dirs. Carnegie-Mellon U., Hwy. Users Fedn., La. Tech. Engring. Found., West Penn Hosp., Pitts. Theol. Sem., Shady Side Acad. Mem. C. of C. Greater Pitts., YMCA. Clubs: Pitts. Field, Rolling Rock, Duquesne. Office: 439 7th Ave Pittsburgh PA 15230

LEE, JAMES HENRY, JR., geologist, geophysicist; b. Jacksonville, Fla., Dec. 27, 1950; s. James Henry and Rose Elinor (DeVaughn) L.; B.S. (NSF fellow), Purdue U., 1974, postgrad., 1974; postgrad. Mich. State U., 1975, 77. Seismologist trainee Seismography Services Corp., 1975; geologist, geophysicist, scout The Wiser Oil Co., Metamora, Mich., 1975, 76; ind. cons., Lansing, Mich., 1976; founder Exploration Cons. Assos., Inc., East Lansing, Mich., 1976, Houston, 1978—; founder U.S.X., Inc., 1980. Mem. Am. Geophys. Union, Soc. Exploration Geophysicists, European Assn. Exploration Geophysicists, Am. Assn. Petroleum Geologists, Mich. Basin Geol. Soc., Geophys. Soc. Houston, Mich. Soc. Exploration Geophysicists (pres. 1977-78). Republican. Presbyterian. Home: 1601 S Shepherd St Apt 264 Houston TX 77019 Office: Exploration Cons Assos Inc 3801 Kirby Dr Suite 307 Houston TX 77098

LEE, JOE RAIFORD, food industry exec.; b. Blackshear, Ga., Dec. 18, 1940; s. John Pope and Audice L. Lee; student Valdosta (Ga.) State Coll., 1966-67; m. Carolyn Dale, Sept. 5, 1961; children—Michael Frederick, Keena Rene. Engaged in farming, Blackshear, 1963-66; restaurant mgr. Ramada Inn, Valdosta, Ga., 1966-67, Darden Enterprises, Waycross, Ga., 1967-68; restaurant mgr., then dir. ops. Red Lobster Restaurants, Orlando, Fla., 1968-72, v.p. ops., then pres., 1972-76; v.p. Gen. Mills, Inc., Orlando, 1975—, v.p. restaurant group; dir. Sun First Nat. Bank, Orlando; mem. marine and fisheries adv. com. NOAA. Mem. Nat. Restaurant Assn. Republican. Baptist. Club: Citrus. Office: PO Box 1431 Orlando FL 32802

LEE, JOHN CHEE MOU, physician; b. Amoy, China, July 21, 1937; s. Ching-Ming and Hua-Ling (Koo) L.; came to U.S., 1967, naturalized, 1974; M.D., Chekiang Med. Coll., China, 1960; M.B.A., Fairleigh Dickinson U., 1977; m. Theresa T. Lau, Mar. 5, 1966; children—Jack Hong, Terry May. Physician, Hangchow, China, 1960-61, Hong Kong Free Clinic, 1962-63; med. rep. Beecham Research Lab., Hong Kong, 1963-64, Upjohn Internat., Hong Kong, 1964-67; research pharmacologist U. Calif., Los Angeles, 1967-68; NIMH fellow psychiatry, 1968-70; NIH fellow psychiatry Duke U., Durham, N.C., 1971-72; asst. dir. Schering Corp., Bloomfield, N.J., 1973-76; group dir. CNS Clin. Pharmacology, Lederle Lab., Pearl River, N.Y., 1976—. Fellow Acad. Psychosomatic Medicine; mem. AAAS, Assn. for Psychophysiol. Study of Sleep, Am. Electroencephalographic Soc., Am. Med. EEG Assn., N.Y. Acad. Scis., Soc. Biol. Psychiatry. Contbr. articles in field to profl. jours. Home: 38 Heritage Ct Woodcliff Lake NJ 07675 Office: Lederle Labs N Middletown Rd Pearl River NY 10965

LEE, JOHN JEROME, business cons.; b. Estherville, Iowa, July 8, 1947; s. John Julian and Ruth Maxine (Lenz) L.; student Santa Barbara (Calif.) City Coll., 1965-67; grad. Bus. Systems Sch., Santa Barbara, 1968; m. Darylann Nielson, Dec. 3, 1967; children—Gretchen, Jason, Corinne, Robin, Benjamine, Sarah. Bus. systems mgr.-sales NCR Corp., Santa Barbara, 1968-70, Las Vegas, Nev. and San Diego, 1972-75; bus. fin. cons. Dan Kim & Assos., Los Angeles, 1970-71; controller Argon Internat., Boulder, Colo., 1971-72; chmn. bd., controller Sullins Electronics Corp., San Marcos, Calif., 1975-78; pres. The Bountiful West Corp., San Marcos, 1976-79; pres. Silvercrest, Inc. and gen. partner Silvercrest Films, 1979—; bus. cons. motion picture distbn. Mem. Freeman Inst.; founder San Diego Repertory Theatre. Mem. Am. Film Inst. Mormon. Column editor Applause Mag., 1974; author screenplay The Wildman, 1976; exec. producer feature film Where's Willie, 1976. Home: 403 Deer Springs Rd San Marcos CA 92069 Office: PO Box 757 San Marcos CA 92069

LEE, JOHN JOSEPH, JR., energy-natural resources co. exec.; b. N.Y.C., Sept. 26, 1936; s. John Joseph and Ernestine Frieda (Hegenberger) L.; B.S., Yale U., 1958, M.S., 1959; m. Gayle D. King, Feb. 25, 1961; children—Jocelyn, Lauren, John Joseph III, Roger. Project mgr. constrn. and operating overseas chem. plants W.R. Grace Co., 1959-64; founder, pres. Purvin & Lee, Inc. (acquired by Barber Oil Corp. 1975), N.Y.C., 1964-75; exec. v.p., chief ops. officer Barber Oil Corp., N.Y.C., 1975-78, pres., chief exec. officer, 1978-80, also dir.; pres. Trinidad Corp., Phila., 1975-77; chmn. Am. Gilsonite Co., Salt Lake City, 1978-80, also dir.; group exec. energy and natural resources Engelhard Minerals & Chems. Corp., N.Y.C., 1980—. Past chmn. alumni fund Engring. Sch., Yale U. Recipient Disting. Alumni award Sch. Engring., Yale U., 1977. Mem. Am. Inst. Chem. Engrs., Am. Chem. Soc., Am. Petroleum Inst. (dir.), Yale Sci. and Engring. Assn., Mid-Continent Oil and Gas Assn., Young President's Orgn., Berzelius Soc., Aurelian Honor Soc., Tau Beta Pi, Chi Phi. Episcopalian. Clubs: Sky, Yale (N.Y.C.); Larchmont (N.Y.) Yacht, Univ. Contbr. chpt. to Pipeline Shipment, 1979. Home: 18 Walnut Ave Larchmont NY 10538 Office: Engelhard Minerals Corp 1221 Ave of Americas New York NY 10021

LEE, NANCY RANCK, mgmt. and mktg. cons.; b. Yonkers, N.Y., Oct. 31, 1932; d. William Edward and Marion Edna (Steigerwalt) Ranck; B.S. with distinction, Cornell U., 1953; postgrad. Boston U., 1977—; m. John G. Lee, Aug. 7, 1963; children—J. Gregory, Paul Edward. Fashion publicist Macy's, N.Y.C., 1956-59; mgr. advt. and pub. relations Josiah Wedgwood & Sons, N.Y.C., 1960-65; dir. communications Gregory Fossella Assos., Boston, 1969-71; dir. mktg. Kuras & Co., Boston, 1971-73; internat. sales mgr. Laser Focus mag., Newton, Mass., 1973-74; prin., pres. Lee Assos., mgmt. and mktg. cons., West Newton, Mass., 1973—; lectr. bus. policy, planning and procedure Simmons Coll.; lectr. Keedick Lecture Bur.; cons. Nat. Assn. Bank Women. Mem. Am. Mgmt. Assn., Am. Mktg. Assn., Bank Mktg. Assn., Assn. Women Cons.'s, Phi Kappa Phi. Episcopalian. Club: Boston Lucheon. Author: Targeting the Top: Everything a Woman Needs to Know to Develop a Successful Career in Business, Year After Year, 1980. Office: Lee Assos PO Box 13 West Newton MA 02165

LEE, PAUL PO LO, travel agt.; b. China, Apr. 18, 1919; came to U.S., 1975, naturalized, 1980; m. Kuo Yuen and Mei Lan (Wu) L.; grad. Nanking U., 1936; m. Nancy Chan Wang, Dec. 21, 1945; children—Spencer B., Landa W.C., Bih Ching, Landna W.C. Gen. mgr. C.C.L.G. Tours Inc., N.Y.C., 1978-79; pres. Golden Horse Tours Inc., N.Y.C., 1979—; Shing Wah Daily News rep., N.Y., Can. Served to col. Chinese Army, 1946-49. Decorated Victory medal Chinese Army; recipient award Am. Overseas Chinese Import-Export Assn., 1978. Mem. N.Y. Lees Family Assn. (dir.). Home: 25 Woodruff Ave Apt C2 Brooklyn NY 11226 Office: 40 Bowery New York NY 10013

LEE, TERRY GLEN, sporting goods mfg. co. exec.; b. Salt Lake City, Feb. 28, 1949; s. Glen E. and Lavern L.; student U. Utah, 1971-72, Weber State Coll., 1972-74; m. Karen Freer, Aug. 30, 1967; children—Richard Glen, Stephanie, Bryan Grant. Sales rep. Mobil Oil Co., Salt Lake City, 1968; with Wilson Sporting Goods Co., 1970—, nat. customer service mgr., 1975, regional distribution mgr. East Coast, 1976, S.E., 1977, South central, 1978, v.p. distbn. planning, River Grove, Ill., 1980—. Office: 2233 West St River Grove IL 60171

LEE, TONG HOON, trading co. exec.; b. Pusan, Korea, Apr. 28, 1948; s. Hu Rak and Yun Hee (Chung) L.; came to U.S., 1968, naturalized, 1972; B.S., Rollins Coll., Winter Park, Fla., 1972; m. Young Hai Kim, Dec. 21, 1971; children—Jay Hwan, Suck Hwan, Jun Hwan. Dir., gen. mgr. investment dept. First Marine & Fire Ins. Co., Seoul, Korea, 1972—; dir. Golden-Bell Trading Co., Korea, also mktg. gen. mgr., gen. mgr. Los Angeles office, 1973—; founder, pres. Koex Trading Co., Inc. and Koen Corp., Los Angeles, 1974—; pres. R. C. Allen Co., Inc., Grand Rapids, Mich., 1978—; rep. Korea explosives group in U.S. Served with Korean Army, 1966. Named Hon. Citizen Winter Park, 1971. Club: Korean Army Vets. Home: 1445 Club View Dr Los Angeles CA 90024 Office: 2001 S Acacia Ave Compton CA 90220

LEE, WALLACE WILLIAMS, JR., ret. hotel exec.; b. Nacogdoches, Tex., June 28, 1915; s. Wallace Williams and Caryl (Ames) L.; B.S. in Hotel Adminstrn., Cornell U., 1936; Exec. Program in Advanced Bus. Mgmt., Columbia U., 1954; m. Doris Card, Sept. 19, 1942; children—Doris, Frederic Williams. Asst. mgr. Broadmoor Hotel, Colorado Springs, Colo., 1938-42; resident mgr. Hotel Thayer, West Point, N.Y., 1945-47; mgr. Hotel Anderson (Ind.), 1947-48; resident mgr. Hotel Roosevelt, N.Y.C., 1951-53, gen. mgr., 1954; asst. mgr. Waldorf-Astoria, N.Y.C., 1948-51, mgr., 1954-59, v.p., resident mgr., 1959-61; gen. mgr. The Barclay and Park Lane Hotels, N.Y.C., 1961-63; group v.p. accommodations Howard Johnson Co., 1963-80. Vice chmn. adv. com. to Statler Found., 1966-72; mem. exec. bd. Greater N.Y. councils Boy Scouts Am., 1960-71, bd. dirs. Boston council, 1971-79, chmn. camping Northeast region, 1972-73; v.p. bd. dirs. YMCA of Greater N.Y., 1965-71; bd. dirs. Travelers Aid Soc., N.Y.C., 1959-66; trustee Am. Hotel Found., 1973-78; bd. dirs., pres. Hospitality, Travel and Research Found., 1976-80. Served to capt. U.S. Army, 1942-45. Recipient Silver Beaver award Boy Scouts Am., 1964. Mem. Am., Hotel/Motel Assn. (mem. industry adv. council 1973-80), Discover Am. Travel Orgn., Cornell Soc. Hotelmen (pres. 1953-54), Hotel Sales Mgrs. Assn., Nat. Restaurant Assn. Congregationalist. Club: Timber Trails. Home: Box 265 Sherman CT 06784

LEE, WILLIAM CHANG, trading co. exec.; b. China, May 28, 1944; s. Wen In and Whei Jen (Chang) L.; came to U.S., 1968, naturalized, 1977; M.S. in Chemistry, Princeton U., 1974; m. Elsie C. Lee, Dec. 1, 1972; 1 dau., Eva C. Sales engr. Elephant Trading Co., Taipei, Taiwan, 1964-67; sr. sales engr. United Export Co., Taipei, 1967-68; mgr. dir. Pioneer Enterprises Ltd., Taipei, 1972—, Penta Shipping & Trading Co., Taipei, 1972—, Princeton Internat. Industries Corp. (N.J.), 1974—, Taiwan Valve & Fitting Co., Taipei, 1974—, Cosmos Engring. Corp., Taipei, 1974—; dir. Superior Engring. Corp., Taipei. Mem. Import/Export Assn. Taipei, N.Y. Chinese Engrs. Home: 32 Bear Brook Rd Princeton Junction NJ 08550 Office: 20 Nassau St Suite 229-230 Princeton NJ 08540

LEE, WILLIAM CRAIG, mfg. co. exec.; b. Duluth, Minn., Jan. 27, 1920; s. Irving Willard and Helen (Forsyth) L.; Ph.B., U. Wis., 1943; s. Beverly Jane Rupp, Mar. 5, 1944; 1 dau., Claudia Joan (Mrs. Patrick Weir). With Gen. Motors, various locations, 1946—, gen. sales mgr. replacement sales AC Spark Plug div., Flint, Mich., 1970-74, exec. dir. sales Service Parts Ops. Group, Detroit, 1974—, gen. mgr. AC-Delco div., 1974—. Bd. regents Gen. Motors Inst. Served with USNR, 1943-45; PTO. Named Man of Yr., Sales and Mktg. Execs. Flint, 1973; Automotive Man of Yr., 1979. Mem. Motor and Equipment Mfrs. Assn. (dir.). Presbyterian (elder). Home: 2175 Bordeaux Ct S West Bloomfield MI 48033 Office: 400 Renaissance Center Detroit MI 48243

LEE, WILLIAM MARSHALL, lawyer; b. N.Y.C., Feb. 23, 1922; s. Marshall McLean and Marguerite (Letts) L.; ed. U. Wis., 1939-40; B.S. in Aero. Engring., U. Chgo., 1942; postgrad. U. Calif., Los Angeles, 1946-48; J.D., Loyola U., Chgo., 1952; m. Lois Kathryn Plain, Oct. 10, 1942; children—Marsha (Mrs. Thomas J. Johnson), William Marshall, Victoria C. (Mrs. Larry Nelson). With thermodynamics group Northrop Aircraft Co., Hawthorne, Calif., 1947-49; with Hill, Sherman, Meroni, Gross & Simpson, Chgo., 1949-51, Borg-Warner Corp., Chgo., 1951-53; admitted to Ill. bar, 1953; partner Hume, Clement, Hume & Lee, Chgo., 1953-72; pvt. practice law, Chgo., 1973-74; partner Lee & Smith, Chgo., 1974—; v.p., dir. Power Packaging Inc.; dir. Strenger Assos. Inc. Pres., Glenview (Ill.) Citizens Sch. Com., 1953-57; v.p. Glenbrook High Sch. Bd., 1957-63. Served as lt. USNR, 1942-46; CBI. Recipient Pub. Service award Glenbrook High Sch. Bd., 1963. Mem. Am. (sec. sect. patent, trademark and copyright law 1977-80, mem. council 1980—), Ill., Chgo., 7th Fed. Circuit bar assns., Internat., Am., Chgo. patent law assns., Licensing Execs. Soc. (treas. 1977-80, pres.-elect 1980—), Phi Delta Theta, Phi Alpha Delta. Republican. Clubs: Law, Tower, Univ., Snow Chase (pres. 1963-64) (Chgo.). Contbr. articles to legal jours. Home: 84 Otis Rd Barrington IL 60010 Office: 10 S Riverside Plaza Chicago IL 60606

LEEDOM, JOHN NESBETT, distbn. co. exec.; b. Dallas, July 27, 1921; s. Floyd H. and Gladys Lorraine (Nesbett) L.; B.S. in Elec. Engring., Rice U., 1943; m. Betty Lee Harvey, Mar. 17, 1956; children—Jo Ann, Judy, Eddie Kennedy, Danny Kennedy, Linda, John Nesbett. Engr. Naval Research Lab., Washington, 1943-45; asst. sales mgr. Sprague Products Co., North Adams, Mass., 1945-50; founder, pres. Wholesale Electronic Supply, Inc., Dallas, 1950—; sec., treas., dir. Ginger Patch, Inc., 1973—; dir. Promade Nat. Bank. Chmn. Republican Party of Dallas County, 1962-66, mem. state exec. com., 1966-68; mem. Dallas City Council, 1975-80, Tex. State Senate, 1980—. Served to lt. (j.g.) USNR, 1943-45. Mem. Nat. Electronic Distbrs. Assn. (pres. 1971-72), Nat. Assn. Wholesale Distbrs. (pres. 1972-73), IEEE, Mil. Order of World Wars, Navy League, Tau Beta Pi. Home: 11012 Westmere Circle Dallas TX 75230 Office: 2809 Ross Ave Dallas TX 75201

LEEDS, RONALD P. E., corp. exec.; b. N.Y.C., Nov. 14, 1939; s. George J. and Virginia (Jantzen) L.; B.Sc., Wharton Sch., U. Pa., 1962; 1 dau., Natalie. Commd. ensign U.S. Navy, 1962, advanced through grades to lt., 1966; naval attache, Lebanon, Jordan, Syria, Cyprus, 1966-68; ret., 1968; exec. dir. Exec. Services Internat. SARL, Beirut, 1969-73; pres. Exerv Corp. S.A., Switzerland, 1973—; chmn. Jesup & LaMont Holding Co., Inc., Hendrich Bldg. Systems, Inc.; dir. Aiand Internat. Corp. Mem. campaign com. Am. Cancer Soc., N.Y.C. div., 1978-79; mem. nat. com. Republican Party. Mem. Naval Res. Assn. Roman Catholic. Clubs: Golf de St. Cloud (Paris); St. Georges (Beirut); Zuoz (Switzerland). Office: care Jesup & Lamont 100 Park Ave New York NY 10017 also EXERV Corp PO Box 11-7284 Beirut Lebanon

LEEGARD, ARLIE LONGSWORTH, mfg. co. exec.; b. Webster, S.D., Dec. 31, 1919; s. Albert and Ida Olivia (Engebretson) L.; m. Bernice Loretta Chessey, Aug. 16, 1941; children—Bruce Michael, Mark Jeffrey, Bonnie Jean, Nancy Jean. Dist. mgr. Colgate Palmolive Co., Mpls., 1939-48; v.p., gen. mgr. Nesbitt Fruit Products, Inc., Los Angeles, 1948-66; pres. Instl. Marketeers, San Jose, Calif. and Memphis, 1966—; adviser to instl. grocery trade. Served to lt. (j.g.) U.S. Maritime Service, 1944-45. Recipient Nugget award Nugget Distbrs. Inc., 1969, Nifda award, 1972; Pitts. Corning award, 1974-80. Mem. Am. Mktg. Assn., Pitts. Corn Producers Club. Republican. Baptist. Clubs: Masons, Shriners. Developer various food improvements in restaurant operation. Office: 1880 Dobbin Dr San Jose CA 95133

LEEK, JAMES MICHEAL, elec. contracting co. exec.; b. Bowling Green, Ky., Nov. 1, 1949; s. James F. and Doris Jean (Meeks) L.; A.A., U. Fla., 1969; B.S., Western Ky. U., 1971; B.A., U. Denver Law Sch. Masters Inst., 1979; m. Penelope Susan Corey, Aug. 26, 1972; children—Tamra Chantel, Natasha Nicole, Dawn Michele, Troy Joseph. Gen. mgr. Village Elec. Inc., Pompano, Fla., 1971-72, Delta Elec. & Mech. Co., Orlando, Fla., 1973-75; v.p. Broyles & Broyles, Inc., Lawrence, Kans., 1975-78; exec. v.p. Industrotech Constructors, Inc., 1978—. Mem. Am. Mgmt. Assn., Elec. Council, Fla. Assn. Elec. Contractors, Am. Soc. Profl. Estimators, Constrn. Specifications Inst. (bus. adv. bd.), Orlando C. of C., Cosmopolitan Internat., Orlando Jaycees. Republican. Roman Catholic. Clubs: Young Reps., Home: 3551 Cedar Corners Pl Norcross GA 30092 Office: PO Box 175 Fort Campbell KY 42223

LEENAARTS, JACK PAUL, sales exec.; b. Drunen, N.B., Netherlands, Sept. 2, 1950; came to U.S., 1953; s. Jack John and Irene Paula (Wolfstein) L.; B.B.A., Campbell U., 1972. With The Cooper Group, 1972—, regional sales mgr., Denver, 1977—. Mem. Jaycees. Club: Pot and Kettle. Developer new products, methods and mktg. strategies to suit Rocky Mountain industry. Home: 7255 202 E Quincy St Denver CO 80237 Office: 3535 Glenwood Ave Raleigh NC 27622

LEETZOW, LEONARD ERMOND, JR., investment co. exec.; b. Elgin, Ill., Mar. 29, 1938; s. Leonard Herman and Alvina Elizabeth (Meinke) L.; B.S., U.S. Naval Acad., 1962; m. Cherie Lee Cuthbert, Nov. 27, 1959; children—Joni Lynn, Michael Leonard, Mark Winston. Design engr. Electro-Mech. Research Inc., Sarasota, Fla., 1959-64; with Shearson Loeb Rhoades, Inc., Sarasota, 1964—, sr. v.p. investments, 1976—. Little League coach, 1972-76; bd. dirs. Girls Club Sarasota County, 1975—, treas., 1975-79; bd. dirs. Sarasota County 4-H Found., 1975—; bd. dirs. Saratoga County div. Am. Cancer Soc., also chmn. youth adv. com., 1979-81; bd. deacons Presbyterian Ch. of the Palms, Sarasota, 1965-68, trustee, 1968-71, mem. bd. elders, 1972-75; trustee Sarasota County YMCA Found., 1980—. Served with USN, 1956-59. Mem. Sarasota C. of C. (dir. 1975-79). Clubs: Univ., Field, Gator Creek Golf, Masons, Shriners. Home: 7007 Clark Rd Sarasota FL 33583 Office: 2045 Siesta Dr Sarasota FL 33579

LEFEVRE, HARVARD STANLEY, engring. co. exec.; b. Stephenson, Mich., Oct. 3, 1920; s. Louis and Delia (Gardner) L.; grad. USAAF Tech. Sch., 1943, San Angelo Army Air Field Bombardier Sch., 1943; student Sch. Bus. Administrn., U. Mich., 1952; exec. tng. Alexander Hamilton Inst., 1955; m. Mary Lee Moore, Apr. 10, 1943; children—Linda, Terese, Stephen. With King Engring. Corp., Ann Arbor, Mich., 1941—, exec. v.p., 1956-67, pres., 1967—, acting chmn. bd., 1970-76, chmn. bd., 1976—, treas., 1970—, also dir. Served with USAAF, 1942-46. Mem. Engring. Soc. Detroit, Soc. Mfg. Engrs., Am. Mgmt. Assn., Ann Arbor Mfrs. Assn., Ann Arbor C. of C. (dir. 1976—), Ann Arbor Personnel Assn. Roman Catholic. Patentee gas dispersoid separator. Home: 801 Mt Pleasant St Ann Arbor MI 48103 Office: 3201 S State St Ann Arbor MI 48106

LEFEVRE, THOMAS VERNON, utility co. exec., lawyer; b. Dallas, Dec. 5, 1918; s. Eugene H. and Callie (Powell) L.; B.A., U. Fla., 1939, LL.B., 1942; LL.M., Harvard U., 1946; m. Lillian Herndon Bourne, Oct. 12, 1946; children—Eugene, Nicholas, Sharon, Margot. Admitted to Fla. bar, 1945, N.Y. State bar, 1947, D.C. bar, 1951, Pa. bar, 1955, U.S. Supreme Ct. bar, 1953; asso. firm Morgan, Lewis & Bockius, Phila., 1955, partner, 1956-79; pres., chief exec. officer, dir. UGI Corp., Valley Forge, Pa., 1979—; dir. AVC Corp. Mem. adv. group to commnr. IRS, 1976-77; adv. bd. N.Y. U. Tax Inst., 1962-67, U. Pa. Tax Conf., 1970-79; bd. dirs. Greater Phila. Found., 1965-79, Fox Chase Center, Center Phila. Area Devel., World Affairs Council Phila., Am. Lung Assn. Phila. and Montgomery County; v.p., mem. exec. com., bd. dirs. Delaware Valley Housing Assn., 1959-66; chmn. bd. trustees Agnes Irwin Sch., 1968-74; mem. health affairs com., asso. trustee U. Pa., 1976-78; mem. long range planning com. U. Pa. Med. Sch., 1975-79; trustee, Inst. Cancer Research; trustee, past chmn. Steering com. Community Leadership Seminar; bd. mgrs. Franklin Inst. Served with USMC, 1942-46; PTO. Fellow Am. Bar Assn. (past v.p. govt. relation taxation sect.); mem. Pa. Bar Assn., Phila. Bar Assn., Fla. Bar Assn., Am. Law Inst., Greater Phila. C. of C. (bd. dirs., past mem. exec. com., gen. counsel). Republican. Episcopalian. Clubs: The Sunday Breakfast, Union League, Phila. (Phila.); Merion Cricket (Haverford, Pa.); SanKaty Head Golf (Nantucket, Mass.). Office: PO Box 858 Valley Forge PA 19482

LE FEVRE, WILLIAM MATHIAS, JR., brokerage co. exec.; b. Muskegon, Mich., Dec. 22, 1927; s. William Mathias and Crystal (Atkinson) LeF.; student U. Mich., 1946-48; m. Ada Marie Cannon, Sept. 10, 1949 (div. Feb. 1973); children—Marie L. Keidel, Jeanne L. Van Vlandren, William Mathias III, Suzanne C.; m. 2d, Mathilda Bock Maguire, July 31, 1976. Floor partner Arthur Wiesenberger & Co., N.Y.C., 1956-60; asso. oddlot broker DeCoppet & Doremus, N.Y.C., 1961-64; v.p. Carter, Walker & Co. Inc., N.Y.C., 1964-68, Bruns, Nordeman & Co., N.Y.C., 1969-71; dir. research Sade & Co., Washington, 1972-73, Mack Bushnell & Edelman, N.Y.C., 1973-74; v.p. investment strategy Granger & Co., N.Y.C., 1974-80, Purcell, Graham & Co., N.Y.C., 1980—; mem. N.Y. Stock Exchange, 1958-64; asso. mem. Am. Stock Exchange, 1960-62. Mem. Fin. Analysts Fedn. (profl. conduct com. 1977—), N.Y. Soc. Security Analysts (investment strategy and portfolio mgmt. com. 1977-80), Fin. Analysts Phila., Western Mich. Soc. Fin. Analysts, Market Technicians Assn. N.Y., Nat. Assn. Bus. Economists, N.Y. Assn. Bus. Economists, Wall St. Forum, Fin. Symposium, Thursday Lunch Group. Club: Stock Exchange Luncheon. Editor: Monday Morning Market Memo, 1973—. Home: 132 E 35th St New York NY 10016 also 78 Grassy Hill Rd Old Lyme CT 06371 Office: Purcell Graham & Co 61 Broadway New York NY 10006

LEFF, JOEL BASIL, investment advisor; b. N.Y.C., Apr. 4, 1935; s. Morris and Zena (Kahn) L.; B.S., U. Pa., 1957; M.B.A., Harvard U., 1961; 1 son, Adam Bodfish. Faculty, Harvard U., Cambridge, Mass., 1961-62; partner Hawkes & Co., N.Y.C., 1963-64, Forstmann-Leff Assoc., N.Y.C., 1968—; exec. v.p. FLA Asset Mgmt. Inc., N.Y.C., 1977—; dir. Research Frontiers, Inc., N.Y.C., 1963-70; guest lectr. Columbia U., N.Y.C.; pres. Master Art Sales; speaker, mem. Internat. Fedn. Employee Benefit Plans; speaker instl. investor confs.; mem. investment adv. bd. Honeywell Inc. Mem. Bur. Nat Affairs Pension Reporter Adv. Bd., Securities Inst. Assn., Internat. Found. Employee Benefits, Soc. for Investigation of Recurring Events, N.Y.C. Soc. Security Analysts. Clubs: Harvard, Atrium, Buckingham Hunt. Home: 120 E 61st St New York NY 10021 Office: 767 Fifth Ave New York NY 10022

LEFFEL, CHARLES POAGUE, appliance mfg. co. exec.; b. Evanston, Ill., May 30, 1928; s. Philip Clark and Catherine Smith (Poague) L.; A.B., Amherst Coll., 1950; m. Grace Ann (Hartnett) L.; June 2, 1962; 1 dau., Kay. Sales work Goodbody & Co., Chgo., 1950-51, Internat. Paper Co., Cleve., 1951-54; with No. Electric Co., Chgo., 1957-72, exec. v.p., 1972-74, pres., 1974-76; group v.p. Sunbeam Corp., Chgo., 1974-76, exec. v.p., 1976-77, pres., 1977—, also dir. bd. mgrs. Robert E. Wood Boys Club, Chgo.; bd. dirs. summer camp Chgo. Boys Club. Served with AUS, 1954-56. Presbyn. Clubs: Deke (N.Y.C.); Met., Racquet, Chgo., Carlton (Chgo.); Glen View Golf, (Ill.). Home: 30 E Scott St Chicago IL 60610 Office: Sunbeam Corp 2001 S York Rd Oak Brook IL 60521

LEFFLER, ALBERT LOT, JR., material handling and fluid power co. exec.; b. Pitts., Jan. 18, 1936; s. Albert Lot and Helen Patricia (Purcell) L.; student U. Pitts., 1954-55, Pa. State U., 1955-58; m. Gloria Jean Mitchell, Aug. 26, 1960; children—Albert Lot III, Elizabeth Evans. Advt. mgr. Carnegie (Pa.) Signal-Item, 1958-60; account exec. Batten, Barton, Durstine & Osborn, Pitts., 1960-62; advt. mgr. Duff-Norton Co., Charlotte, N.C., 1962-67; mktg. and planning mgr. Duff-Norton Co. subs. Amstar Corp., Charlotte, 1967-79, dir. mktg., 1979—. Bd. dirs. Jr. Achievement, 1965, 66; mem. founding com. Charlotte Invitational Tennis Tournament. Mem. Material Handling Inst. (dir. 1975—), Bus. and Profl. Advt. Assn. (founder and charter pres. Carolinas chpt. 1968-70, internat. dir. 1968-69), Zeta Psi (past chpt. alumni pres.), Alpha Delta Sigma. Republican. Presbyterian. Home: 2016 Beverly Dr Charlotte NC 28207 Office: 100 Pioneer Rd Charlotte NC 28232

LEFFLER, MARVIN, mktg. exec., author; b. N.Y.C., July 29, 1922; s. Saul S. and Bertha (Cohen) L.; B.S., N.Y. U., 1942, M.B.A., 1951; m. Shirley D. Schleicher, Sept. 3, 1944; children—Bruce, Nancy. Exec. v.p. Continuous Sales Corp., Long Island City, N.Y., 1946—; pres. Flexible Fabricators, Inc., Port Jervis, N.Y., 1962—; pres. Nat. Council Salesmen's Orgn., Inc., N.Y.C., 1960-64, chmn. bd., 1964—. Mem. adv. council N.Y. State SBA, 1964—; pres. Town Hall Found., 1979—. Served with USAAF, 1942-46. Mem. Sales Reps. Assn. (chmn. bd.), Am. Arbitration Assn. (nat. panelist), N.Y. U. Alumni Fedn. (pres. 1980—), N.Y. U. Sch. Commerce Alumni Assn. (v.p., dir. 1951-60), N.Y. U. Grad. Sch. Bus. Adminstrn. Alumni Assn. (dir. 1966—, pres. 1968-69). Clubs: Glen Hollow Country (pres. 1973-76), New York University (pres. 1973). Author: How To Become a Successful Manufacturer's Representative, 1951; How To Increase Your Sales Volume As A Manufacturer's Agent, 1958. Editor Voice of Salesman, 1961—. Home: 76-30 174th St Flushing NY 11366 Office: 35-18 37th St Long Island City NY 11101

LEFKOWITZ, ALAN ZOEL, lawyer; b. Pitts., Dec. 1, 1932; s. Curtis and Lily Rose (Selznick) L.; A.B., U. Pitts., 1953; J.D., U. Mich., 1955; m. Francine Marcia Kaplan, Feb. 5, 1956; children—Curtis Robert, Gail Ann, David Edward. Admitted to Pa. bar, 1956, U.S. Supreme Ct. bar, 1959; with firm Kaplan, Finkel & Roth (now Kaplan, Finkel, Lefkowitz & Ostrow), Pitts., 1955—, mng. partner, 1972—; sec., dir. TPC Communications, Inc.; sec. Computer Research, Inc.; lectr. in field. Trustee, United Jewish Fedn., Pitts., 1962-64; trustee Rodef Shalom Congregation; v.p. Jewish Family and Children's Service, Pitts., 1967-68; bd. dirs. Pitts. Arts and Crafts Center; 22d dist. committeeman Democratic Party, Pitts., 1964-68. Served with CIC, 1956-59. Mem. Am., Pa., Allegheny County bar assns., Am. Assn. Jewish Edn., Am. Soc. Arts and Scis. (photog. sect.). Clubs: Photoimagers Guild, Pitts. Council for Internat. Visitors. Home: 5514 Woodmont St Pittsburgh PA 15217 Office: 1612 Frick Bldg Pittsburgh PA 15219

LEGROS, EMILE ARTHUR, JR., investment banking co. exec.; b. Cleve., Mar. 12, 1935; s. Emile Arthur and Lucile (Dieters) L.; B.A. in Bus., Hiram Coll., 1957; m. Barbara Ann Greene, Sept. 5, 1959; children—Lucille Alease, Emile Arthur. With Prescott Ball & Turben, Cleve., 1957-77, 80—, sr. v.p. sales, to 1977, sr. v.p., 1980—; v.p. corp. fin. Butcher & Singer, Inc., 1977-80; dir., mem. audit com. Cedar Point Inc. Vice pres., trustee Lake County (Ohio) Blue Coats, 1973—. Home: 9751 Metcalf Rd Willoughby OH 44094

LEGUM, JEFFREY ALFRED, automobile co. exec.; b. Balt., Dec. 16, 1941; s. Leslie and Naomi (Hendler) L.; B.S. in Econs., U. Pa., 1963; grad. Chevrolet Sch. Merchandising and Mgmt., 1966; m. Harriet Cohn, Nov. 10, 1968; children—Laurie Hope, Michael Neil. With Park Circle Motor Co. doing bus. as Legum Chevrolet, Balt., 1963—, exec. v.p., 1966-77, pres., 1977—, also dir.; partner Pkwy. Indsl. Center, Dorsey, Md., 1965—; v.p., dir. P.C. Parts Co., 1967—; v.p. Westminster Motor Co. (Md.), 1967-72, pres., dir., 1972—; pres. One Forty Corp., Westminster, 1972—; dir., exec. com. United Consol. Industries, 1970-73; dist. chmn. Chevrolet Dealer Council, 1975-77. Chmn. auto div. Asso. Jewish Charities, Balt., 1966-69; trustee, mem. exec. com. The Park Sch., Balt., 1979—; bd. dirs. Asso. Placement Bur., Balt., v.p., 1972-76; adv. bd. The Competitive Edge, Albuquerque, 1977—. Recipient award of honor Asso. Jewish Charities of Balt., 1967, 68. Mem. Md. Auto Trade Assn., Young Pres.'s Orgn., Greater Balt. Com., Carroll County C. of C., Balt. County C. of C. Clubs: Suburban (Baltimore County); University of Pa. (Balt.). Home: 10 Stone Hollow Ct Baltimore MD 21208 Office: 7900 Eastern Ave Baltimore MD 21224

LEHNERT, PETER KARL, wholesale co. exec.; b. Rumburku, Czechoslovakia, May 13, 1938 (came to U.S., 1962); s. Franz and Erna (Hentschel) L.; ed. Gymnasium, Cologne, West Germany; m. Heidrun Lingen, May 26, 1969 (div. May 1976); children—Natasha, Norman. Mgr. br. Pan Am. Trade Devel. Corp., N.Y.C., 1962-65; founder, pres. Lensteel, Inc., Houston, 1966—; pres. Alliance Iron & Steel Inc., 1974—; v.p. mcht. and structural steel dept. Crispin Co., 1969-74. Mem. Tex. Assn. Steel Importers (v.p.). Home: 510 W Forest St Houston TX 77079 Office: 7700 San Felipe Suite 444 Houston TX 77063

LEHR, FRANK HENRY, engring. co. exec.; b. Easton, Pa., Apr. 2, 1925; s. Francis H. and Sadie (Fulse) L.; B.S. in Engring., Pa. State U., 1950; M.S., Newark Coll. Engring., 1956; m. Veronica Shevock, June 24, 1950; children—Diane C., Frank F., Janice S. Field engr. C.R.R. of N.J., Jersey City, 1950-51; structural designer Arthur G. McKee & Co., Union, N.J., 1951, 53-54; constrn. engr. Jersey Testing Lab. Inc., Newark, 1954-57; pres. Frank H. Lehr Assos., cons. civil engrs., East Orange, N.J., 1957—. Chmn. Joint Meeting Sewer Commn. Union and Essex Counties (N.J.), 1969-75; mem. Summit (N.J.) Bd. Sch. Estimate, 1964-69, Summit Bd. Appeals, 1958-70. Mem. City Council Summit, 1962—, pres., 1970-75, mayor, 1976-80; county commr. Union County, 1981—. Served to capt. USMCR, 1943-47, 51-53; lt. col. Res. Registered profl. engr., N.J., N.Y., Pa., Mass., Conn., Ohio. Fellow ASCE, Cons. Engrs. Council; mem. Union County Soc. Profl. Engrs. (past pres.), Execs. Assn. N.J. (pres. 1981-82), Marine Corps. Res. Officers Assn., ASTM, Bldg. Ofcls. N.J. Club: Kiwanis (dir. East Orange). Home: 16 Myrtle Ave Summit NJ 07901 Office: 15 Freeman Ave East Orange NJ 07018

LEHR, HARVEY GLENN, constrn. co. exec.; b. Menno, S.D., Sept. 25, 1937; s. Herbert and Elsie Katherine (Handel) L.; B.C.E., S.D. State U., 1960; m. Janis Kaye Gullickson, June 19, 1960 (dec.); children—Michael, David. Field engr. Fegles Power Service Corp., Mpls., 1960-65, project mgr., 1965-71, gen. supt., 1971-76; pres., dir. NCI of Minn., Inc., Mpls., 1977—. Served to 2d lt. F.A., AUS, 1962. Mem. Assn. Gen. Contractors Am., ASCE, Am. Arbitration Assn. Republican. Club: Elks. Home: 6020 Walnut Dr Edina MN 55436 Office: 10000 Hwy 55 W Minneapolis MN 55441

LEHR, LEWIS WYLIE, diversified mfg. corp. exec.; b. Elgin, Nebr., Feb. 21, 1921; s. Lewis H. and Nancy (Wylie) L.; B.S. in Chem. Engring., U. Nebr., 1947, Sc.D. (hon.), 1977; m. Doris Stauder, Oct. 13, 1944; children—Mary A. Lehr Makin, William L., Donald D., John M. With 3M Co., St. Paul, 1947—, v.p. med. products div., 1960-72, health care products group, 1972-74, tape and allied products group, 1974-75, pres. U.S. ops., 1975-79, vice chmn., chief exec. officer, 1979-80, chmn., chief exec. officer, 1980—; dir. 1st Bank Systems, Inc., Mpls., Gen. Mills, Inc., Mpls. Trustee Hamline U., St. Paul, 1978—; bd. overseers Harvard Coll. Vis. Com. Med. and Dental Schs., 1977-79; bd. dirs. United Way of St. Paul Area, 1977-80, Guthrie Theater Found., 1977—. Served with AUS, 1943-46; ETO. Recipient Alumni Achievement award U. Nebr. Alumni Assn., 1976. Mem. Am. Chem. Soc., Am. Mgmt. Assn. Clubs: North Oaks Golf, St. Paul Athletic, White Bear Yacht, Minnesota. Office: Minn Mining & Mfg Co 3M Center Saint Paul MN 55144

LEIBER, CATHY LEE, mfg. co. exec.; b. Santa Maria, Calif., Sept. 22, 1950; d. William Henry and Patricia Lee (Myers) Horne; B.A. in Internat. Relations, U. Calif., Davis, 1972; M.B.A. with highest honors, Pace U., 1978; m. Scott Leiber, Nov. 5, 1972. Bilingual editorial asst. UN, N.Y.C., 1972-74; dir. public relations N.Y. Infirmary Hosp., N.Y.C., 1974-78; mgr. promotion programs devel. Philip Morris, Inc., N.Y.C., 1978—. Mem. Am. Mgmt. Assn., N.Y. State Fedn. Bus. and Profl. Women (vice chmn. public relations, Young Career Woman of Yr. 1978), N.Y. League Bus. and Profl. Women (dir.), Jr. League of Westchester-on-Hudson. Home: 13 Captain Honeywell's Rd Ardsley NY 10502 Office: 100 Park Ave New York NY 10017

LEIBOWITT, SOL DAVID, lawyer; b. Bklyn., Feb. 12, 1912; s. Morris and Bella (Small) L.; B.A., Lehigh U., 1933; LL.B., Harvard, 1936; m. Ethel Leibowitt, June 18, 1950. Admitted to N.Y. bar, 1937, Conn. bar, 1970; pvt. practice, N.Y.C., 1937—, Milford, Conn., 1970—; gen. counsel New Haven Clock and Watch Co., 1955-59, pres., 1958-59; pres. Mid-Atlantic Fund, Inc., 1964-72, Apco Capitol Corp., 1975—; dir. Data Card Internat. Corp., Hevany, Eng., 1977—. Recipient Human Relations award, 1969, Meml. award Anti-Defamation League, 1971. Mem. Assn. Bar N.Y.C., Am., Conn., N.Y. State bar assns., Anti-Defamation League, Am. Soc. for Technion U. (mem. bd., nat. pres.). Clubs: Lotos, Harvard (N.Y.C.); Rolling Hills Country. Home: 2 Fanton Hill Rd Weston CT 06880 Office: 63 Broad St Milford CT

LEIDER, GERALD J., motion picture/TV producer; b. Camden, N.J., May 28, 1931; s. Myer and Minnie L.; B.A., Syracuse U., 1953; m. Susan Trustman, Dec. 21, 1968; children—Matthew Trustman, Kenneth Harold. Theater producer in N.Y.C., London, 1956-59, producer Gielgud's Ages of Man, 1958-59; dir. spl. programs CBS-TV, 1960-61, dir. program sales, 1961-62; v.p. TV ops. Ashley Famous

Agy., Inc., N.Y.C., 1962-69; pres. Warner Bros. TV, Burbank, Calif., 1969-74; exec. v.p. fgn. prodn. Warner Bros. Pictures in Rome (Italy), 1975-76; ind. producer motion pictures and TV GJL Prodns., Inc., Los Angeles, 1977—; feature motion pictures include The Jazz Singer with Neil Diamond, 1980; TV films include: And I Alone Survived, 1978, Willa, 1979, The Hostage Tower, 1980. Recipient Arents Alumni medal Syracuse U., 1977. Fulbright fellow U. Bristol (Eng.), 1954. Mem. Acad. TV Arts and Scis., Am. Film Inst., Hollywood Radio and TV Soc. (pres. 1975-76), Second Decade Council. Office: Samuel Goldwyn Studio 1041 N Formosa Ave Los Angeles CA 90046

LEIFERMAN, IRWIN HAMILTON, corp. exec.; b. Chgo., Jan. 8, 1907; s. Beril and Ida (Rosenbaum) L.; student Crane Jr. Coll., 1923, Northwestern U., 1924-29; m. Silva Weiner, Apr. 20, 1947. Purchasing agt. Hamilton-Ross Corp., Chgo., 1924-30; pres. Hamilton Industries Co., 1931-64, chmn. bd., 1964—; pres. Winston Lamp and Shade, 1948-55, Ill. Wire Goods Co., Beaumont Electric Supply Co., 1940-46; pres. Leiferman Investment Co., 1964—; v.p. Bet-R-Lite Co., 1940-46, Comet Prodns., Inc. (TV), 1964-66. Mem. industry com. Dept. Labor, 1940. Mem. advisory com. Brandeis U., 1961-62; asso. U. Chgo. Cancer Research Found., 1958; pres., co-founder Silva and Irwin H. Leiferman Found.; mem. com. Miami Beach Opera Guild; mem. nat. bd. govs., Chgo. bd. govs. Bonds for Israel; a founder Mt. Sinai Hosp. Greater Miami, Fla., 1969, Greater Technion Israel Inst. Tech., 1972; patron numerous cultural socs. and instns. Recipient citation Community Leaders Am. Jewish religion, citation Mt. Sinai Hosp., others. Mem. Chgo. Assn. Commerce and Industry, Ill. Mfrs. Assn., Ill. C. of C., Internat. Platform Assn., Art Inst. Chgo. (life), Miami Mus. Modern Art (life), Greater Miami Cultural Art Center, Friends of Lowes Mus. Clubs: B'nai B'rith; Standard, Exec., Bryn Mawr Country (Chgo.); Westview Country (Miami Beach, Fla.); Jockey, Brickell Bay (Miami, Fla.); Bayshore Service. Home: 10155 Collins Ave Bal Harbour FL 33154 Office: Standard Club 320 S Plymouth Ct Chicago IL 60604

LEIFERMAN, SILVIA WEINER (MRS. IRWIN HAMILTON LEIFERMAN), sculptress, civic worker, bus. exec., philanthropist; b. Chgo.; d. Morris H. and Anna (Caplan) Weiner; student U. Chgo., 1960-61; studied design and painting Chgo., Mexico, Rome, Madrid, Provincetown, Mass.; m. Irwin Hamilton Leiferman, Apr. 20, 1947. One woman shows include: D'Arcy Galleries, N.Y.C., 1964, Stevens Annex Bldg., Chgo., 1965, Hollywood (Fla.) Mus. Art, Schram Galleries, Ft. Lauderdale, Fla., 1966, 67, Miami Mus. Modern Art, 1966, 72, Contemporary Gallery, Palm Beach, Fla., 1966, Westview Country Club, 1968, Gallery 99, Miami Beach, Fla., 1969, Hall Gallery, Miami Beach; group shows include: Bryn Mawr Country Club, 1961, 62, Riccardo Restaurant Gallery, Chgo., 1961, 62, Covenant Club, 1963, D'Arcy Galleries, N.Y.C., 1965, 66, 67, Miami Mus. Modern Art, 1967, Baccardi Gallery, Miami, 1967, Internat. Platform Assn., 1967, Barry Coll., 1968, Gallery 99, Miami Beach, 1968, Hollywood Mus. Art, 1968, Lowe Art Mus., Beau Art Gallery Lowe Mus. at U. Miami; work represented in numerous pvt. collections; v.p., sec. Leiferman Investment Co., 1969-78, chmn. bd., 1978—; pres. Active Accessories by Silvia; v.p., sec. Silvia and Irwin H. Leiferman Found. Founder, Mt. Sinai Hosp., Miami Beach, 1969, Greater Technion Inst. Tech., Israel, 1972, Silvia and Irwin H. Leiferman Found.; organizer, met. chmn., charter mem. womens div. Hebrew U., Chgo., 1947; originator, met. Chgo. chmn. Ambassador's Ball, State of Israel, 1956, Presentation Ball, 1963, 64, 65; organizer women's div. Edgewater Hosp., 1954; chmn. salute to med. research met. campaign City of Hope, 1959; met. Chgo. chmn. Dior Israel Fashion Show, 1962; originator, chmn. presentation com. Ambassador's Ball, Bonds for Israel, 1963, 64, 65; originator, met. chmn. Paris in the Spring fashion show Nat. Council Jewish Women, also Alice in Fashion Land; originator met. chmn. Hawaii Holiday, Nathan Goldblatt Soc. Cancer Research; chmn. spl. sales and events Greater Chgo. Com. for State of Israel; met. chmn. opening gala luncheon, mem. bd. North Shore women's aux. Mary Lawrence Jewish Children's Bur.; internat. chmn. Bal Masque, Miami Ballet Soc., 1971, 72; patron Royal Ballet Soc. Miami, Lowe's Mus. Art, Greater Art Center Miami, Philharmonic Soc. Miami, Greater Miami Opera Guild; patron Greater Miami Cultural Arts Center, mem. hon. com. for gala, 1972; donor St. Joseph Hosp., Michael Reese Hosp., Chgo., 1978; Sponsor Miami Heart Inst., 1980; trustee, life mem. Nathan Goldblatt Soc. Cancer Research; trustee Jewish Fedn. Greater Miami; bd. dirs. North Shore aux. Jewish Fedn. Chgo., Mary Lawrence chpt. Jewish Children's Bur., Nat. Council Jewish Women, Fox River Sanitorium, Temple Sholom, Edgewater Hosp., Orgn. Rehab. and Tng., women's guild Greater Miami Philharmonic Soc., numerous others; mem. nat. bd. govs. Bonds for Israel; hon. chmn. Miami Art Center. Named Woman of Valor, State of Israel, 1963; 73; recipient Achievement award State of Israel, 1963; keys to all 5 met. dists. Miami and surrounding counties, 1972; Pro Mundo Beneficio gold medal and diploma Brazilian Acad. Humanities, 1976; Donor award Miami Heart Inst., 1976; numerous plaques and citations. Fellow Royal Soc. Arts and Scis. (life); mem. Internat. Platform Assn. (The Club), Internat. Council Museums, Am. Fedn. Arts, Miami Beach Opera Guild, Artists Equity Assn., Miami Art Center, Greater Miami Cultural Art Center, Sculptors of Fla., Inc., Lowe Art Mus. (life), Friends of Lowe's Mus., Am. Contract Bridge League, Am. Friends of Hebrew U., Friends of Haifa U., Ft. Lauderdale Mus. Arts, Miami Mus. Modern Art (life), Art Inst. Chgo. (life), numerous others. Clubs: Internat., Whitehall, Key, Covenant, Standard, Bryn Mawr Country (Chgo.); Westview Country, Brickell (Miami); Greenacres Country (Northbrook, Ill.): Runaway. Address: 10155 Collins Ave Apt 1404 Bal Harbour FL 33154 also Standard Club 320 S Plymouth Ct Chicago IL 60604

LEIGH, LYNN LAVERNE, engring. co. exec.; b. Burley, Idaho, 1925; B.S. in Engring., U. Kans., 1948. Export sales mgr., nat. supply div. Armco Steel Corp., N.Y. and Houston, 1948-63; v.p., gen. mgr. Cardwell Mfg. Co., 1963-66, with Gardner-Denver Co., Dallas, 1967—, mem. exec. and operating coms., 1972-73, pres., chief exec. officer, 1973-79, merger with Cooper Industries, 1979, now vice-chmn. dir. Served to lt. j.g. USN, 1943-46. Mem. AIME, Compressed Air and Gas Inst. (dir.), Am. Mining Congress (bd. govs. mfg. div.), NAM (dir. S.W. region), Sigma Chi. Methodist (adv. bd.). Clubs: Dallas Petroleum, Northwood (Dallas). Office: 8585 Stemmons Freeway Suite 500 Box 47114 Dallas TX 75247

LEIGH, RUTH R. SOKOLSKI (MRS. MURRAY STUART LEIGH), realtor; b. N.Y.C., Feb. 19; d. A. Lawrence and Anne (Frieder) Sokolski; student Hunter Coll., 1934-36, U. Pa. Wharton Sch., 1942; m. Murray Stuart Leigh, June 13, 1943; 1 dau., Leslie Susan. Sales dept. mgr., buyer Saks 34th St., N.Y.C., 1935-37; radio comms. WMCA, N.Y.C., 1936-39; interior decorator Roxberg, Inc., N.Y.C., 1937-40; broker Harold N. Sloane Co., ins. brokers, N.Y.C., 1940-43; br. mgr. Manpower Inc., N.Y.C., 1952-53; interior designer Storr & Co., N.Y.C., 1949—; builder-broker Ruth S. Leigh, N.Y.C., 1965—. Dist. dir. Girl Scouts U.S.A., 1952-54; fund raiser N.Y. Heart Assn., 1955—, Salvation Army, 1960—; mem. chmn.'s com. U.S. Senatorial Bus. Adv. Bd., 1980—; dir. Interfaith Neighbors, 1964-66; dist. liaison officer Black & White Assos. supporting Odyssey House Drug Addicts, 1969-70; trustee Bloomingdale Ho. of Music. Mem. Real Estate Bd. N.Y., Unitarian-Universalist Women's Fedn. (dist. pres. 1966-70), Am. Unitarian Assn. (asst. non-govtl. org. rep. UN, nat. chmn. UN seminars 1958-62). Republican. Unitarian (v.p. bd. trustees 1972, deacon 1974, chmn. commn. ch. community 1977-80). Home: 1010 Fifth Ave New York NY 10028 Office: 1220 Lexington Ave New York NY 10028

LEIGH, SHERREN (MRS. NORMAN J. HICKEY, JR.), advt. agy. exec.; b. Cleve., Dec. 22, 1942; d. Walter Carl and Treva (Everstine) Maurushat; B.S. in Journalism, Ohio, U., 1965; m. Norman J. Hickey, Jr., Aug. 23, 1969. Pub. relations dir. Metal Lath Assn., Cleve., 1965-68; pres. Your Write Arm, Chgo., 1969-71; v.p., creative dir. Robert L. Cohn, Inc., Chgo., 1971-78, sr. v.p.; pres. Leigh Communications, Inc., Chgo., 1978—; founder, dir. Women's Career Conv. Mem. Am. Women in Communications, NOW, Zeta Tau Alpha. Home: 571 Blackstone Pl Highland Park IL 60035 Office: 676 Saint Clair Chicago IL 60611

LEIGHTON, CHARLES MILTON, leisure time firm exec.; b. Portland, Maine, June 4, 1935; s. Wilbur F. and Elizabeth (Loveland) L.; A.B., Bowdoin Coll., 1957; M.B.A., Harvard, 1960; m. Deborah Throop Smith, Aug. 30, 1958; children—Julia Loveland, Anne Throop. Produce line mgr. Mine Safety Appliances Co., Pitts., 1960-64; instr. Harvard Bus. Sch., 1964-65; group v.p. Bangor Punta Corp., Boston, 1965-69; chmn., chief exec. officer CML Group, Inc., Boston, 1969—; dir. New Eng. Mut. Life Ins. Co., Boston. Area fin. chmn. campaign for Senator Edward Brooke, 1966. Republican. Episcopalian. Clubs: New York Yacht; Chatham (Mass.) Yacht (vice commodore 1957); Harvard of New York City and Boston, Harvard Bus. Sch. (dir.) (Boston); Somerset. Home: 33 Liberty St Concord MA 01742 Office: 80 Thoreau St Concord MA 01742

LEIMER, MYRT, pub. co. exec.; b. LaHabra, Calif.; d. Oscar J. and Wilhelmine (Kleine) Leimer; B.A. cum laude, U. Calif. at Los Angeles, 1946; postgrad. Inst. Design Chgo., 1947-48, Chouinard Art Inst., Los Angeles, 1952, U. Calif. at Los Angeles, 1967-69. Advt. dir. group dept. Pacific Mut. Life Ins. Co., Los Angeles, 1952-53; prodn. mgr. dir. mdse. design, asst. dir. publs. Regal Books, Glendale, Calif., 1953-67; circulation mgr. World Vision Mag., Monrovia, Calif., 1967-69; advt. mgr. Am. Bibliog. Center-Clio Press, Santa Barbara, Cal., 1969-76, v.p. mktg. services, 1976-80, v.p. ops., 1980—. Designer corporate graphics. Mem. U. Calif. at Los Angeles Alumni Assn. Lutheran. Office: Riviera Campus 2040 APS Santa Barbara CA 93103

LEIMKUHLER, GERARD JOSEPH, JR., fin. holding co. exec.; b. Phila., June 13, 1948; s. Gerard Joseph and Dorothy Joan (Gaffney) L.; B.B.A., Temple U., 1970; m. Karen Roberta Hall, Oct. 13, 1973; 1 dau., Courtney Hall. Mem. Phila. Stock Exchange, 1971-75; v.p., Oxford 1st Corp., Phila., 1975—; v.p., Hilt n Head Co., Phila., 1975—; pres. Gen. Acquisitions Corp., Phila., 1977—, also dir.; dir. Lakeside Properties, Inc., First Mountain Properties, Inc., Indian Lake Maintenance, Inc., First Resorts, Inc. Mem. Newtown Twp. (Delaware County, Pa.) Planning Commn., 1976-77, 81—. Served with U.S. Army, 1970-71. Registered investment adviser SEC. Mem. Nat. Assn. Securities Dealers, Am. Mgmt. Assn. Republican. Roman Catholic. Clubs: Malta Boat, Temple U. Varsity. Home: 306 French Rd Newtown Square PA 19073 Office: Oxford 1st Corp 6701 N Broad St Philadelphia PA 19126

LEIPOLD, LEE DAVID, fin. analyst; b. Norfolk, Va., July 18, 1953; s. Bob Lee and Iris D. (Mueller) L.; B.S. in Adminstrn. of Justice, U. Mo., 1976, B.S. in B.A., 1977; M.B.A., S.E. Mo. State U., 1978; m. Mary M. Dziuba, Oct. 20, 1979; 1 son, David Micheal Thomas. Grad. asst. to dean of continuing edn. S.E. Mo. State U., Cape Girardeau, 1977-78, grad. asst. staff asso. to pres., 1977-78, grad. asst. in acctg., 1978; corporate cash adminstr. Gen. Dynamics, St. Louis, 1979-80, asst. treas., voluntary polit. contbn. plan, 1979-80, mgmt. group steering com. treas., 1979-80; fin. analyst Mallinckrodt, Inc., St. Louis, 1980—. Planning council mem. United Way of Greater St. Louis, 1979—. Mem. Assn. M.B.A. Execs., Nat. Assn. Accts. Club: Lion (3d v.p. 1979—). Home: 1424 Windward Ridge Saint Louis MO 63127 Office: 675 McDonnell Blvd PO Box 5840 Saint Louis MO 63134

LEIS, UNO, optics co. ofcl.; b. Kassel, Germany, Nov. 13, 1946; came to Can., 1948, naturalized, 1956; s. Johannes and Salme (Otto) L.; B.S., Carleton U., Ottawa, Ont., Can., 1969. Ops. mgr. Strato Geol. Ltd., Vancouver, B.C., Can., 1969-72, gen. mgr., 1972-75; western sales mgr. Union Optics Corp. Can. Ltd., Vancouver, B.C., 1975-79, nat. sales mgr., Toronto, Ont., 1979—; dir. Vat Petroleum Ltd., Dorado Resources Ltd. Home: 103-709 Dunsmuir St Vancouver BC V6C 1M9 Canada Office: 2 Principal Rd Scarborough ON M1R 4Z3 Canada

LEISER, DEAN, health care exec.; b. Akron, Ohio, Oct. 2, 1934; s. Charles Henry and Frances Elizabeth (Bruch) L.; B.S. cum laude, Kent (Ohio) State U., 1957; M.B.A., U. Chgo., 1959; m. Joanne Elizabeth Turrin, June 10, 1956; children—Gary Edward, Pamela Anne, Karen Alyce. Asst. adminstr. Ohio State U. Hosps., Columbus, 1960-61, Cin. Children's Hosp., 1961-66; asso. adminstr. Akron Children's Hosp., 1966-71; adminstr. Kadlec Hosp., Richland, Wash., 1971-72; asst. dir. Huron Road Hosp., Cleve., 1972-73; dir. hosp. services Damm and Assos., Cleveland Heights, Ohio, 1974-75; pres., chmn. bd. Health Care Analysis, Inc., Willoughby, Ohio, 1975—; dir. Advance Inc., Akron. Mem. Am. Coll. Hosp. Adminstrs., Health Care Adminstrs. Assn. N.E. Ohio. Republican. Presbyterian. Home: 38750 Johnnycake Ridge Rd Willoughby OH 44094 Office: 4135 Erie St Willoughby OH 44094

LEISEY, ALVIN LEWIS, JR., photog. and office equipment co. exec.; b. Birdsboro, Pa., May 10, 1923; s. Alvin Lewis and E. Marie (Leidenberger) L.; student U. Pa., Cornell U.; B.A., Pa. State U., 1948; m. Mary Helen Abbott, Feb. 24, 1945; children—Laloni, Randall, Mary Ellen, Ronald, Kimberly, Kathryn. Systems analyst Lukens Steel Co., Coatesville, Pa., 1948-51; with New Holland Machine Co. (Pa.), 1951-56; asst. controller Internat. Latex Corp., Dover, Del., 1956-63; v.p. adminstrn., controller Morse Twist Drill & Machine Co., New Bedford, Mass., 1963-66; dir. mgmt. info. Universal Am. Corp., 1966-68; v.p. adminstrn. Itek Bus. Products, Rochester, N.Y., 1968-73; corporate controller, chief fin. officer Minolta Corp., Ramsey, N.J., 1973—; corporator Fairhaven Instn. for Savs., Five Cents Savs.; dir. Mohawk Mktg. Corp., Virginia Beach, Va. Twp. supr. West Whiteland, Pa., 1953-56; mem. Dover Bd. Edn., 1961-63; chmn. Planning and Zoning Commn., Dover, 1958-63; mem. N.J. State Commn. Economy and Efficiency in State Govt. Bd. dirs. YMCA, United Fund, New Bedford; pres. Lakeland Regional High Sch. Bd. Edn., 1977-81. Served with USMCR, 1941-45. Decorated Purple Heart. Named Systems Man of Year, Delaware Valley, 1962; recipient Merit award Adminstrv. Mgmt. Assn., 1963. Mem. Fin. Execs. Inst., Am. Mgmt. Assn., Systems and Procedures Assn. (past pres. Keystone chpt.), Nat. Office Mgmt. Assn. (past pres. Lancaster), Internat. Systems and Procedures Assn. (sec., dir.), No. N.J. Chamber Commerce and Industry, Conf. Bd., Am. Soc. Personnel Adminstrs., Planning Execs. Inst. Republican. Presbyterian. Mason (Shriner). Club: National Holiday Rambler Travel Trailer (past pres.). Lion. Contbr. articles to profl. jours.; speaker on mgmt. topics. Home: 5 Birch Pl Ringwood NJ 07456 Office: 101 Williams Dr Ramsey NJ 07446

LEISHER, GEORGE LOY, JR., pharm. co. exec.; b. St. Louis, Feb. 11, 1945; s. George Loy and Wilma (Schrumm) L.; A.Bus., St. Louis Jr. Coll., 1966; B.S.B.A., U. Mo., 1967, postgrad. Law Sch., 1968; m. Rebecca Callaham, May 29, 1970. Asst. personnel dir. Edwin Guth Co., St. Louis, 1967-70; dir. indsl. relations Falstaff Brewing Co., St. Louis, 1970-73; dir. personnel and tng. St. Louis County Dept. Police, St. Louis, 1973-76; corp. v.p. personnel and indsl. relations, dir. K-V Pharm. Co., St. Louis, 1976—. Treas., Mo. Young Republicans, 1966; bd. dirs. Goodwill Industries, Galveston, 1971-72. Served in U.S. Army, 1969. Mem. Am. Soc. Personnel Adminstrn., Phi Alpha Delta, Indsl. Relations Club St. Louis. Roman Catholic. Club: Optimists. Home: 10 Colonial Hills Pkwy Creve Coeur MO 63141 Office: 2503 S Hanley Rd Saint Louis County MO 63144

LEISY, JAMES FRANKLIN, publisher; b. Normal, Ill., Mar. 21, 1927; s. Ernest Erwin and Elva (Krehbiel) L.; B.B.A., So. Meth U., 1949; m. Emily Ruth McQueen, June 8, 1949; children—James Franklin, Scot, Rebecca. Field rep. Prentice-Hall, Inc., N.Y.C., 1949-52, asso. editor, 1952-54; editor Allyn & Bacon, Inc., Boston, 1954-56; exec. editor Wadsworth Pub. Co., Inc., San Francisco, 1956-59, v.p., 1959-60, pres., 1960-77, chmn., chief exec. officer, 1977-80, chmn., 1980—, dir., 1962—; chmn. Prindle, Weber & Schmidt, Inc.; chmn., dir. CBI Pub. Co., Inc.; dir. Baron Data Systems, Inc., Internat. Thomson Orgn., Inc., San Francisco Mag. Inc.; cons. Vols. for Internat. Tech. Assistance; trombonist, mus. dir. T. Ford and the Model A's Dixieland Band, 1967—. Bd. dirs. Bethel Coll., 1969-77; bd. dirs., mem. exec. com. Calif. Council for Econ. Edn., 1968-71; deans council Sch. Bus. Calif. State U., San Jose; mem. UN Day Com., 1978. Served with USNR, 1945-46. Mem. Young Pres.'s Orgn. (dir. 1970-73), Chief Execs. Forum, World Bus. Council, ASCAP, So. Meth. U. Alumni Assn. (dir. 1965-70), Phi Eta Sigma, Alpha Phi Omega, Alpha Kappa Psi (nat. chmn. song com. 1963-71), Kappa Alpha. Named Career Hall of Fame, So. Meth. U., 1968. Author: Abingdon Song Kit, 1957; Let's All Sing, 1958; Songs for Swinging Housemothers, 1960; Songs for Singin', 1961; Songs for Pickin' and Singin', 1962; Beer Bust Song Book, 1963; Hootenanny Tonight, 1964; Folk Song Fest, 1964; The Folk Song Abecedary, 1966: Alpha Kappa Psi Sings, 1967; The Folk Song Omnibus, 1973; The Good Times Songbook, 1974; Scrooge, The Christmas Musical Play, 1978; The Fitness and Weight Control Diary, 1980; Calories In and Calories Out, 1980. Composer several popular songs including Keep a Little Christmas in Your Heart, An Old Beer Bottle, Please Tell Me Why, A Personal Friend of Mine, A Little Old Lady in Tennis Shoes, Clemen Who?, Isn't This a Lovely Christmas?, What Does Christmas Mean to You?, The Girl in the Freudian Slip. Office: 10 Davis Dr Belmont CA 94002

LEITER, STEVEN DAVID, ins. co. exec.; b. Phila., Sept. 26, 1946; s. Samuel S. and Beverly A. L.; B.S. in Edn., Temple U., 1968; m. Eileen Mary Sudall, June 6, 1970; children—Jennifer A., Richard M., Melanie. Automobile underwriter State Farm Ins., Springfield, Pa., 1968-70, sr. automobile underwriter, 1970-71, automobile underwriting specialist, 1971-72, agy. tng. staff asst., 1972-74, dir. edn. and tng., 1974-76, mgr., policy service rep., 1976-78, field mgmt. rep., 1978—, agy. mgr., 1980—; ins. industry career rep. Bucks County Community Coll., Newtown, Pa., 1979-80. Mem. Am. Soc. Tng. and Devel., Am. Mgmt. Assn. Editor: State Farm Ins. Co. Keystone Mag., 1974-76, Leader Mag., 1974-76 (both Pa.). Home: 95 Brook Dr Holland PA 18966 Office: 13020 Bustleton Ave Philadelphia PA 19116

LEITES, IRVING, tanning co. exec.; b. N.Y.C., Oct. 31, 1922; s. Julius and Molly (Romm) L.; B.A. in Commerce and Fin., Pa. State U., 1948; m. Rose Rosenberg, Mar. 11, 1944; children—Jeffrey Lee, Debra Sue. Controller, Loree Footwear Co., Big Run, Pa., 1969-71, Sun Cal Footwear Co., Los Angeles, 1971-73; v.p., treas. Sonoma Internat., San Francisco, 1973-76; pres., gen. mgr. Los Angeles Tanning Co., 1976—. Served with Signal Corps, U.S. Army, 1943-46; ETO, PTO. Mem. Tanners Council Am. (dir.).

LEITNER, STANLEY ALLEN, solid waste co. exec.; b. St. Louis, Sept. 11, 1938; s. Perry O. and Ruth A. Leitner; student U. Bordeaux, France; m. Janet Sue Sherman, Aug. 1, 1964; 1 dau., Stacy. Vice pres. United Disposal, Inc., St. Louis, 1968-71; regional dir. SCA Services, St. Louis, 1971-72, corp. v.p., Boston, 1972-76; pres. Futura Energy Resources Corp., St. Louis, 1977—; chmn. bd. CS Mfg. Co. Inc., St. Louis, Weapons Corp. Am., 1979-80; pres. Leitner & Assos., 1979-81. Served with AUS, 1955-58. Recipient Most Humorous Businessman of Year award Humor Socs. U.S., 1976. Author: Last Chance to Live, 1978; (with Jan Leitner) Ultimate Woman, 1981. Home: 1593 Foxham St Chesterfield MO 63017 Office: 1415 Eldridge Payne Rd Suite 260 Chesterfield MO 63017

LEKER, JAMES EDWARD, mfg. co. exec.; b. Kansas City, Mo., Mar. 6, 1922; s. Edward Henry and Mildred Howard (Woodcock) L.; B.S. in Agr., Kans. State U., 1947; postgrad. Mich. State U., 1948; grad. program environ. policy and mgmt. Harvard U., 1979; m. Mary Eleanor Pearson, Nov. 19, 1943; children—Karen Elizabeth, James Grant, Stephen Rives. Prodn. supt. Staley Milling Co., Kansas City, Mo., 1948-50, gen. prodn. mgr., 1950-63; coordinator Wendland's Farm Products, Temple, Tex., 1963-65; by-products mgr. Masonite Corp., Laurel, Miss., 1965-71, corp. environ. adminstr., Chgo., 1971-79, corp. environ. mgr., 1979—; chmn. Timber Products Effluent Guidelines Litigation Com., Nat. Forest Products Assn.; mem. point source action com., chmn. timber products subcom. Am. Paper Inst.; instr. Infantry Sch., Ft. Benning, Ga.; cons. Livestock Feed Mfrs., Belgium and Venezuela; mem. planning, tech. com's. Feed Prodn. Sch., Econ. Impact Action Com., Am. Paper Inst., Non-Point Action Com. Served in U.S. Army, 1943-47. Decorated Purple Heart, Bronze Star. Mem. Forest Products Research Soc., Am. Hardboard Assn. (chmn. environ. affairs com.), Nat. Forest Products Assn. (air, water com.), Calif. Forest Products Assn., Miss. Mfrs. Assn. (environ. com.), U.S. C. of C. (environ. affairs com.). Club: Rotary Internat. (dir.) (Laurel, Miss.). Contbg. author: Am. Feed Prod. Handbook; inventor sugar coating process livestock pellets. Home: 214 Biltmore Dr Barrington IL 60010 Office: 29 N Wacker Dr Chicago IL 60606

LE LACHEUR, RAE EDMOND, electronics mfg. co. exec.; b. Boston, Jan. 22, 1936; s. Ernest Thomas and Rita Caroline (Cirigliano) LeL.; student Northeastern U., 1956-61; m. Arline Rita Oxner, Aug. 19, 1961; children—Deborah Lynn, Edmond Ray. Asso. engr. Raytheon Co., Waltham, Mass., 1957-58, quality engr., 1958-61, quality assurance specialist, 1961-63; quality control mgr. Space Scis. Inc., Waltham, 1963-65; quality assurance mgr. Ikor Inc., Burlington, Mass., 1965-71, mfg. mgr., 1971-74; mfg. mgr. Datametrics div. Gould Inc., Wilmington, Mass., 1974-77; mfg. ops. mgr. Internat. Teletron Inc., Bedford, Mass., 1977-78; mfg. mgr. power supply div. Stevens-Arnold Inc., Boston, 1978—; pres. RMQ Inc., cons. reliability, mfg., quality assurance. Served with USMC, 1953-56. Mem. Am. Soc. Quality Control, Am. Mgmt. Assn. Home: 16 Fairview Ave Natick MA 01760 Office: 7 Elkins St South Boston MA 02127

LEMASTERS, KENNETH GRANT, lubrication co. exec.; b. Middletown, Mo., Oct. 9, 1926; s. William Elsia and Oma Lee (Chandler) L.; student pub. schs.; m. Fern May Schuler, Feb. 15, 1964;

children—Jean, Janet, Jannine, Jo Ann, Joy Judy. Farmer, 1943-53; with constrn. firm, 1953-63: sales magr. Schaeffer Mfg. Co., Fulton, Mo., 1963-78; owner Pow'R Oil & Chem. Inc., Kingdom City, Mo., 1978—. Mem. Montgomery City Council, 1956-60. Mem. Mo. Dump Truckers Assn., Mo. Land Improvement Assn. Presbyterian. Clubs: Masons, Shriners. Home: 1407 Marbrook St Fulton MO 65251 Office: PO Box 51 Kingdom City MO 63362

LEMATTY, ROGER S., apparel co. exec.; b. 1907; married. Office mgr. Globe Superior Corp., to 1936; with Blue Bell Inc., Greensboro, N.C., 1936—, treas., 1943-48, v.p., 1948-62, exec. v.p., 1962-66, pres., mem. exec. com., 1966-73, vice chmn., 1973—, also dir. Office: 335 Church Ct Greensboro NC 27401*

LEMAY, ALICE MAY HENDERSON, spectator seating mfg. co. exec.; b. Portsmouth, N.H., Sept. 28, 1944; d. Hugh K. and May Alice (Dooley) Henderson; A.A. in Bus., U. Maine, 1976; m. Cleo A. Lemay, July 3, 1964; 1 dau., Sabrina. Office mgr. Hussey Mfg. Co., Inc., North Berwick, Maine, 1970-72, asst. controller, 1972-76, asst. treas., 1976—, also acctg. mgr. Mem. Town Meeting, Sanford, Maine, 1975. Mem. Nat. Assn. Accountants. Home: RFD 1 Box 112 Springvale ME 04083 Office: Hussey Mfg Co Inc Dyer St North Berwick ME 03906

LEMBECK, RICHARD SANFORD, textile co. exec.; b. Bklyn., Apr. 7, 1928; s. Irving and Hannah (Reisner) L.; student N.Y. U., 1948; diploma in textile engring. Phila. Coll. Textiles and Sci., 1952; m. Rhoda Apfelbaum, Mar. 18, 1956; children—Anthony Jon, Liza Ruth. Asst. stylist Bachmann-Uxbridge Worsted Corp., N.Y.C., 1952-54; head stylist Fabrex Corp., N.Y.C., 1954-56; exec. v.p., prin., dir. Republic Comml. Corp., N.Y.C., 1956-71; v.p. Burlington Industries, N.Y.C., 1972-74; pres. Rodik Textiles, Ltd., N.Y.C., 1975—; cons. Active United Fund, co-chmn. 5 towns clubs div., 1979, chmn., 1980; cons. Fedn./United Jewish Appeal; mem. Philanthropic Fifty, 1956—, pres., 1973-75, now treas.; patron Smithsonian Instn., Inst. for Arts, Washington, Met. Opera, N.Y.C. Served with USN, 1946-48. Mem. Phila. Coll. Textiles and Sci. Alumni Assn. (past mem. bd. govs.), Am. Assn. Textile Tech., Young Men's Assn. Apparel Trades. Republican. Clubs: Middlebay Country (past bd. govs.) (Oceanside, N.Y.); B'nai B'rith (past vp., treas.). Editor: Textile Dictionary (G. Linton), 1954. Home: 22 Beechwood Dr Lawrence NY 11559 Office: 1290 Ave of Americas New York NY 10019

LEMCKE, NORMAN ROHDE, lawyer; b. N.Y.C., Dec. 3, 1894; s. Albert William and Dora (Rohde) L.; B.S., Amherst Coll., 1917; LL.B., N.Y. Law Sch., 1924, J.D., 1969; m. Elizabeth Bouteiller, Sept. 3, 1918; 1 son, Norman Rohde. Admitted to N.J. bar, 1924; practiced with Smith & Slingerland, Newark, 1924-27; joined Prudential Ins. Co. Am., 1927, br. office atty., Montreal, 1927-28, regional appraiser and supr. at Newark, home office, 1928-34, mgr. regional office, Phila., 1934-35, N.Y.C., 1935-37, supr. West Coast, 1937-44, East Coast, 1944, asst. sec., Newark, 1944-46, gen. mgr., 1946-47, 2d v.p., 1947-61, v.p., 1961-63; mem. firm Eisner & Lemcke, Newark, 1963-68; dir. Leeds & Lippincott Co., Atlantic City. Dir. govt. sponsored Housing Enterprises of Can., 1945-47. Former trustee Essex County Youth House, Child Guidance Clinic the Oranges, Maplewood, Millburn. Served as ensign USN, 1917-19. Mem. Am., N.J. bar assns., Phi Beta Kappa, Alpha Delta Phi, Delta Theta Phi. Methodist. Intercollegiate 50 yd. swimming champion, 1916. Home: 5 W Main St Brookside NJ 07926

LEMIEUX, JANET A., process control instrumentation co. exec.; b. Woonsocket, R.I., Apr. 16, 1947; d. Gertrude Lemieux; B.S. in Bus. Adminstrn. summa cum laude, Bryant Coll., 1970, M.B.A. with honors, 1978. Sr. acct. Laventhol & Horwath, Providence, 1972-74; sr. plant acct. Foxboro Co. (Mass.), 1974-76, internal auditor, 1976-78, asst. to corp. controller, 1978-79, mgr. acctg., 1979—. C.P.A., R.I. Mem. Am. Inst. C.P.A.'s, R.I. Soc. C.P.A.'s. Club: Quota (sec.-treas. dist. 15 1974-76) (Woonsocket). Office: Foxboro Co Neponset St Foxboro MA 02035

LEMIRE, ANDRE, investment co. exec.; b. Quebec City, Can., Mar. 15, 1943; s. Adrien and Gabrielle (Martel) L.; B.Sc., U. Ottawa, 1967; m. Ann C. Chisholm, Sept. 6, 1969. Tax analyst Bell Can., Montreal, 1968-69; investment analyst Jones Heward Co., Ltd., Montreal, 1969-72; asst. dir. research Levesque, Beaubien Inc., Montreal, 1972-74, dir. investment research, 1974-78, v.p. investment research, 1978, v.p. internat. and chmn. investment com., 1978—; mem. Montreal Stock Exchange Listing Com., 1976—, asst. program chmn. Mem. Montreal Soc. Fin. Analysts (seminar chmn.), Cercle Finance et Placement, Montreal Mus. Arts. Roman Catholic. Clubs: St. James, Montreal Badmington and Squash. Home: 174 Edge Hill Rd Westmount PQ H3Y 1E9 Canada Office: 360 Saint James St Montreal PQ H2Y 1P7 Canada

LEMKE, RICHARD LOUIS, elec. engr.; b. San Mateo, Calif., Apr. 4, 1939; s. Joseph Bernhart and Frances Margaret (Becker) L.; B.A., Dartmouth, 1961; B.S., U. Calif. at Berkeley, 1965, M.S., 1966; m. Martha Gaile McCall, Mar. 10, 1962; children—David Louis. Sr. engr. EG & G, Santa Barbara, Calif., 1966-69, Aerojet Gen., Azusa, Calif., 1970-71; lectr. computer sci. Bendigo (Australia) Inst. Tech., 1971-73; semiconductor test systems engring. mgr. Tektronix, Inc., Beaverton, Oreg., 1976-79, logic and data communication analyzers engring. mgr., 1979—; staff E-H Research Labs., Oakland, Calif., 1973-74. Tchrs. for E. Africa fellow, Columbia U., 1961. Mem. IEEE, Phi Beta Kappa. Democrat. Club: Mazamas. Home: 1270 NW Summit Ave Portland OR 97210 Office: PO Box 500 Beaverton OR 97077

LEMMERMAN, CHARLES HENRY, sales exec.; b. Ridgewood, N.Y.C., Sept. 13, 1920; s. Charles H. and Elizabeth Estelle (Schramm) L.; student Bucknell U., 1939-42; m. Gloralie Lores Collier, Mar. 16, 1946; children—Carl Henry, Gloralie Lores. Tool designer Glenn L. Martin Co., Balt., 1945; salesman, broker Real Estate & Bus. Brokerage, N.Y.C., 1946-48; salesman Wood-Metal Industries, Inc., Kreamer, Pa., 1948—, became nat. sales mgr., 1959, v.p., dir. marketing, 1964—. Served with USAAF and OWI, 1942-44. Mem. Forest Products Research Soc., A.I.M. (fellow pres.' council 1970), Sales and Marketing Execs. Internat., Am. Inst. Kitchen Dealers (cert. kitchen designer), Am. Mgmt. Assn., Nat. Assn. Home Builders, Color Mktg. Group (chairholder), Mfrs. Agts. Nat. Assn., Kreamer Snyder County Sportsman's Assn., Am. Legion (jr. vice comdr. 1954, sr. comdr. 1955-56, comdr. 1957-58), Sigma Alpha Epsilon. Lutheran. Elk, Moose. Club: Susquehanna Valley Country. Home: 82 Fairmount Dr Lewisburg PA 17837 Office: Wood-Metal Industries Inc Kreamer PA 17833

LEMMEX, RONALD MILLARD, clergyman; b. Spokane, Wash., July 5, 1914; s. Charles Harris and Mabel Constance (Cole) L.; A.B., Phillips U., Enid, Okla., 1938; Ph.D., Sussex (Eng.) Coll., 1977; D.D. (hon.), Am. U. Found., 1974; m. Jewel Josephine Holliday, June 7, 1939; children—Sandra, Lorelle, Larry, Connie, Kent, Ronee, Robert, Diana, James. Ordained to ministry Disciples of Christ Ch., 1939; pastor Christian Chs. (Disciples of Christ) in Wash., Calif., 1937-57, Congl. Chs. in Calif., 1958-65; profl. counselor in religion, 1966-78; pres., exec. officer J.F. Rowny Found., Santa Barbara, Calif., 1978—; pres. Listen-Books Pubs., Santa Barbara, 1979—; dir. campus ministries So. Calif. Christian Ch., 1949-54. Mem. Assn. Ind. Pubs., Com. of Small Mag. Editors and Pubs. Republican. Author: (audio-cassette book) Walking Jesus, 1979; (audio-cassette albums) The Oracle of Wise Behavior, 1980, Perapetetic Education, 1980. Address: 1500 Mission Canyon Rd Santa Barbara CA 93105

LEMP, JOHN, JR., telecommunications engr.; b. Trenton, N.J., Dec. 10, 1936; s. John and Helena M. (Braddock) L.; B.S. in Elec. Engring., Princeton U., 1959; M.S. in Elec. Engring., Poly. Inst. Bklyn., 1968; M.B.A., Colo. State U., 1973; m. Susan N. Rose, 1955; children—John, Thomas K., Carl A., Adam F.H. Project engr. Gen. Devices, Inc., Princeton, N.J., 1959-60; with Bell Telephone Labs., N.J. and Colo., 1962-74; mgr. bus. planning Aeronutronic Ford Corp., Willow Grove, Pa., 1974-76; mgr. research and devel. ITT, Corinth, Miss., 1976-78; lectr. Sch. Bus., Temple U., Phila., 1976; project leader Nat. Telecommunication and Info. Adminstrn., U.S. Dept. Commerce, Boulder, Colo., 1978—. Mem. Civil Air Patrol, 1970—; pres. Carolyn Heights Civic Assn., 1972-73; treas. Frazier Woods Civic Assn., 1975-76. Served with USAF, 1960-63, 1973-74. Decorated Air Force Commendation medal; named Outstanding Elec. Engr., Armed Forces Communications & Electronics Assn., 1959; cert. instrument flight instr., FAA. Mem. IEEE, Armed Forces Communications and Electronics Assn., Air Force Assn. Patentee in field; contbr. articles to profl. jours. Home: 3745 23d St Boulder CO 80302 Office: NTIA/ITS-4 325 Broadway Boulder CO 80303

LEMPERT, PHILIP, design and mktg. exec.; b. East Orange, N.J., Apr. 17, 1953; s. Sol and Lillian E. L.; B.S. in Mktg., Drexel U., 1974; M.S. in Package Design, Pratt Inst., 1978; m. Susan W. Tobias, June 26, 1977. Account exec. The Lempert Co., Belleville, N.J., 1974-76, art dir., 1977, creative dir., 1978, v.p., 1978—; adj. prof. Fairleigh Dickinson U., Seton Hall U. Co-chmn. new leadership com. United Jewish Appeal, 1978-80; Drexel U. Alumni ambassador, 1976—; v.p. Sons of Bosses, 1975-77. Recipient 1st prize in graphic Printing Industries N.Y., 1979, 80, 1st prize in packaging Nat. Office Products Assn., 1976, 77, 2d prize, 1978, Art Dirs. award, 1980. Mem. Packaging Inst., Graphic Artists Guild, Nat. Food Brokers Assn. (chmn. food services com.), Am. Mktg. Assn. Republican. Jewish. Clubs: Greenbrook Country, B'nai B'rith, Rotary. Home: 5 Collamore Terr West Orange NJ 07052 Office: 202 Belleville Ave Belleville NJ 07109

LENAHAN, EDWARD PATRICK, pub. co. exec.; b. 1925; B.A., Harvard U., 1950; married. With Time Inc., N.Y.C., 1955—, ad sales rep., bus. mgr., gen. mgr., advt. dir. Fortune, to 1970, gen. mgr. Life, 1970-73, pub. Fortune, 1973-74, v.p. Time Inc., 1973, treas., 1975, corp. v.p., pub. Fortune, 1979—. Served with USN, World War II. Office: Time and Life Bldg New York NY 10020

LENCER, WILLIAM THOMAS, trade co. exec.; b. Troy, N.Y., Aug. 26, 1936; s. Jacob and Thelma Rose (Cummins) L.; B.A., U. Wash., 1960; m. Karen Kay Klawitter, Mar. 14, 1956; children—William Thomas, Corrine Kay. Acct., Alaska King Crab Co. div. San Juan Fishing & Packing Co., Kodiak, Alaska, 1960-64, New Eng. Fish Co., Seattle, 1965-66, Austin Co., Seattle, 1966-67; treas. Tradewell Stores, Inc., Kent, Wash., 1967—; sec.-treas. Abigail's, Inc., Kent, 1976—; lectr. in field. Mem. bus. and office adv. com. Kent Public Schs., 1977; mem. Kent Valley Studies Task Force, 1979; active Seattle-King County Mcpl. League, 1977—; trustee Tradewell Employees Retirement Fund. Mem. Greater Kent Area C. of C. (pres. 1975). Republican. Clubs: Rotary (pres. Kent 1977-78), Elks. Home: 21404 35th Ave S Seattle WA 98188 Office: Tradewell Stores Inc 7890 S 188th St Kent WA 98031

LENGEFELD, FRANCIS ROLAND, utility co. exec.; b. Gatesville, Tex., Jan. 29, 1928; s. Charles Ernest and Elsie May L.; B.S.E.E., Tex. A. and M. U., 1949; postgrad. in bus. adminstrn. St. Louis U., 1960-63; m. Julia Ann Sheridan, July 1, 1949; children—Lynn Frances, James Charles, Leigh Ann. With Union Electric Co., St. Louis, 1949-76, mgr. transmission and distbn. operating, 1966-69, mgr. dept. elec. engring., 1969-76; exec. v.p. Mo. Utilities Co., Cape Girardeau, 1976-77, pres., chief exec. officer, chmn. bd., 1977—; dir. First Nat. Bank Chmn. bd. dirs. Mo. Bd. Architects, Profl. Engrs. and Land Surveyors, 1974-78; bd. dirs. United Way of Cape Girardeau, 1977—, campaign dir., 1977-78, pres., 1978-79; bd. dirs. S.E. Mo. Hosp., Cape Girardeau, 1978—, mem. exec. com., 1979—; bd. deacons First Presbyterian Ch., Cape Girardeau, 1978—, chmn. bd. deacons, 1980; active Boy Scouts Am., 1961—, mem. exec. com. Southeast Mo. council, 1979—. Served to 1st lt. Signal Corps, U.S. Army, 1951-52. Mem. Edison Electric Inst., Nat. Soc. Profl. Engrs., Mo. Soc. Profl. Engrs., IEEE, S.W. Power Pool, Midwest Gas Assn., Mo. C. of C. (bd. dirs. 1976—), Cape Girardeau C. of C. (bd. dir. 1976—, pres. 1980). Clubs: Rotary, Cape Girardeau Country, Tower. Office: 400 Broadway Cape Girardeau MO 63701

LENNARTSON, JAMES ROGER, mktg. exec.; b. Jamestown, N.Y., June 6, 1933; s. Anders Leo and Elna Signey (Bloomberg) L.; B.S., U. Buffalo, 1956; m. Barbara Ann Wilson, Jan. 25, 1958; children—Jennifer Lynn, James Roger. Asst. account exec. power systems Westinghouse Nuclear Center, Pitts., 1962-63, sr. account exec. nuclear communications, 1963-66, asst. mgr. power systems mktg. communications, 1966-68, mgr. power systems mktg. communications, 1968-72, staff mgr. mktg. communications, 1972—. Mem. Atomic Indsl. Forum, Pitts. Conv. and Visitors Bur., Assn. Nat. Advertisers. Republican. Presbyterian. Club: Rotary. Office: Westinghouse Nuclear Center Box 355 Pittsburgh PA 15230

LENNON, TIMOTHY FRANCIS, aerospace co. exec.; b. Greensburg, Pa., Mar. 17, 1942; s. Francis Joseph and Jean Anastasia (Waters) L.; B.S. in Bus. and Finance, St. Vincent Coll., 1964; m. Nina B. Martin, Mar. 12, 1970; children—Sean P., Kevin M. Jr. cost acct. Kennemetal, Inc., 1962-64, cost acct. 1964-66; cost analyst Birdseye div. Gen. Foods Corp., 1966-68; stockbroker Singer, Deanne & Scribner, Pitts., 1968-69; chief cost acct. Midland Frame div. Midland Ross Corp., 1969-70; plant controller nat. aluminum div. Nat. Steel Corp., Hawesville (Ky.) Rolling Mill, 1970-72; ops. controller nat. accounts div. Maremont Corp., Chgo., 1973-74, controller brake systems div., 1972-74, controller worldparts div., 1975-76, controller worldparts, Gabriel sales and distbn. divs., 1976-77, v.p., controller, 1977-79; controller E. W. Bliss and Ferrous Foundry divs. Gulf & Western Industries, Inc., Southfield, Mich., 1974-75; v.p. fin., asst. corporate sec.-treas. Avco Aerostructures Div., Nashville, 1979—. Mem. Nat. Mgmt. Assn., Nashville Area C. of C. Roman Catholic. Home: 3891 Priest Lake Dr Nashville TN 37217 Office: PO Box 210 Nashville TN 37202

LENNOX, EDWARD NEWMAN, holding co. exec.; b. New Orleans, July 27, 1925; s. Joseph Andrew and May Alice (Newman) L.; B.B.A., Tulane U., 1949; m. Joan Marie Landry, Sept. 3, 1949; children—Katherine Sarah, Anne Victoria, Mary Elizabeth, Laura Joan. Mktg. service clk. Shell Oil Co., New Orleans, 1949; with W.M. Chambers Truck Line, Inc., 1950-60, exec. v.p., 1954-60; v.p., gen. mgr. Radcliff Materials, Inc., New Orleans, 1961-71; v.p. Office Pub. Affairs, So. Industries Corp., 1971—; dir. Home Savs. & Loan Assn. Pres., La. Tank Truck Carriers, 1954-55; mem. La. Bd. Hwys., 1965-67; chmn. New Orleans Aviation Bd., 1960-67; bd. dirs. Travelers Aid Soc., 1966-68, Met. Area Com., 1967-80, Constrn. Industry Legis. Council, 1968—, Miss. Valley Assn., 1969-72; pres. bd. levee commrs. Orleans Levee Dist., 1969-72. Pres. Met. New Orleans Safety Council, 1969-70; bus. and fin. adviser Congregation Sisters of Immaculate Conception; vice chmn. transp. task force Goals for La., 1969-72; mem. New Orleans Bd. Trade, 1971—; mem. Ala. Gov.'s Adv. Council on Econs., 1971-72, Gov.'s Adv. Com. River Area Transp. and Planning Study, 1971-72; area v.p. Public Affairs Research Council La., 1971-72; mem. exec. com. La. Good Roads Assn., 1972-74; mem. career advisement com. Tulane Grad. Sch. Bus. Adminstrn., 1972—; industry del. La. Constl. Conv., 1973; mem. exec. com. Miss. Valley World Trade Council, 1973-74. Bd. dirs., exec. com. Meth. Hosp., 1963—; bd. dirs. Boys' Clubs Greater New Orleans, 1973-79; bd. dirs., mem. exec. bd. Goodwill Industries Greater New Orleans, Inc., 1975-79; bd. dirs. Americanism Forum, 1975—, Tragedy Fund, Inc., 1976—; bd. govs. La. Civil Service League, 1974—, pres., 1977-78; dir. bd. trustees La. Ind. Coll. Fund, 1980—. Served to capt. AUS, 1943-46. Recipient Industry Service award Asso. Gen. Contractors Am., 1967; Certificate of Appreciation, Constrn. Industry Assn. New Orleans, 1972; New Orleans Jr. C. of C. award, 1960; certificate Merit, City New Orleans, 1964, 67; Monte M. Lemann award La. Civil Service League, 1976; named hon. citizen and ambassador at large City of Jacksonville, 1966. Mem. NAM (public affairs steering com. So. div. 1979—), La. Motor Transport Assn. (pres. 1963-64), Ala. Trucking Assn. (v.p. 1956-60), So. Concrete Masonry Assn. (pres. 1963-68), Greater New Orleans Ready Mixed Concrete Assn. (pres. 1966-68), La. Shell Producers Assn. (pres. 1966-68), C. of C. New Orleans Area (dir. 1968-73, 75-77, pres. elect 1973), Internat. House (dir. 1977-79), Traffic Club New Orleans, Lakeshore Property Owners Assn. (dir. 1974, pres. 1976-80), Tulane Alumni Assn., Mobile Area C. of C. Club: Metairie Country (bd. govs. 1976-80, pres. 1980). Home: 862 Topaz St New Orleans LA 70124 Office: 1010 Common St New Orleans LA 70112

LENNOX, VINCENT JOSEPH, JR., bldg. service co. exec.; b. Bronx, N.Y., Dec. 4, 1947; s. Vincent Joseph and Helen T. (Luedke) L.; student Iona Coll., 1968-69, U. Nebr., 1971-73. Account exec. Owners Maintenance Corp. div. Helmsley Spear, N.Y.C., 1972-76; v.p. Colin Service Systems, Inc., Yonkers, N.Y., 1976—; speaker building service contractor seminars. Served with USAF, 1969-72. Recipient Dir.'s award Colin Service Systems, Inc., 1976. Mem. Adminstrv. Mgmt. Assn., Bldg. Service Contractors Assn. Clubs: Sales Execs. of Westchester County, Soc. Friendly Sons of St. Patrick. Home: Peekskill Hollow Rd Kent Cliffs NY 10512 Office: South Kensico Ave White Plains NY

LENON, RICHARD ALLEN, corp. exec.; b. Lansing, Mich., Aug. 4, 1920; s. Theo and Elizabeth (Amon) L.; B.A., Western Mich. Coll., 1941; postgrad. Northwestern U., 1941-42; m. Helen Johnson, Sept. 13, 1941; children—Richard Allen, Pamela A., Lisa A. Mgr. finance div. Montgomery Ward & Co., Chgo., 1947-56; v.p. finance Westinghouse Air Brake Co., 1963-67, treas., 1965-67; v.p., treas. Internat. Minerals & Chem. Corp., Skokie, Ill., 1956-63, group v.p. finance and adminstrn., 1967-68, exec. v.p., 1968-70, pres., 1970-78, chmn., 1977—; dir. Am. Standard Co., Bankers Trust Co., Fed. Paper Bd. Co., The Signal Cos., Inc. Served to lt. comdr. USNR, 1942-47. Clubs: University, Glen View (Chgo.); Economic (N.Y.C.). Home: 803 Solar Ln Glenview IL 60025 Office: Internat Minerals & Chemical Corp 2315 Sanders Rd Northbrook IL 60062

LENS, KARL GEORGE, plastic mfr.; b. N.Y.C., June 29, 1927; s. Jack and Anna (Lipner) L.; B.Ch.E., Coll. City N.Y., 1950; m. Shirley Savodik, Sept. 11, 1948; children—Jack Ira, Robin Laurie. Prodn. supr. Aerenol Chem. Co., Long Island City, N.Y., 1950-51; partner, v.p. Jadelle Corp., N.Y.C., 1951-53; pres. Crest-Chem Indsl. Corp., N.Y.C., 1954-69; chmn. bd., sec.-treas. Crest-Foam Corp., Moonachie, N.J., 1955—. Trustee Fair Lawn Jewish Center. Mem. Am. Inst. Chem. Engrs., Am. Mgmt. Assn., Soc. Plastics Engrs. (sr.), Soc. Plastics Industry, AAAS, Coll. City N.Y. Alumni Assn., Am. Philatelic Soc., N.J. Acad. Sci. Club: Edgewood Country. Mem. reader adv. bd. Chem. Engring., 1974—, Chem. Week, 1974—. Developed 1st comml. process for chemically expanded vinyl foam in U.S. Office: 100 Carol Pl Moonachie NJ 07075

LENTZ, DAVID BRUCE, ins. co. exec.; b. Woburn, Mass., May 9, 1950; s. David Joel and Phyllis Lorraine (Hetzel) L.; B.A., Bates Coll., 1972. Editor, Prudential Ins. Co., Boston, 1974-76; specialist advt., sales promotion New Eng. Life Ins. Co., Boston, 1976-78; mgr. advt. and sales promotion U.S. Mktg. Pan-Am. Life Ins. Co., New Orleans, 1978—; cons. in field Recipient 2 ADDY awards. Mem. New Orleans C. of C., Life Advertisers Assn. (advt. research com., 1st pl. award of Excellence coop. advt. 1978, other awards), Greater New Orleans Advt. Club, New Orleans Track Club, New Orleans Bus. Communicators, Coll. Club Bates Coll. Office: Pan-Am Life Ins Co Pan-Am Life Center New Orleans LA 70130

LENTZ, THOMAS WILLIAM, office furniture and supplies co. exec.; b. Ashland, Ohio, Apr. 5, 1941; s. Harold H. and Mary Eleanor (Selby) L.; B.A., Wittenberg U., 1963; M.Div., Hamma Sch. Theology, 1966; S.T.M., Yale U., 1967; m. Martha Sue Kantonen, Sept. 4, 1965; children—Thomas Jeffrey, Laura Elizabeth. Ordained to ministry, 1967; asso. pastor St. Luke Luth. Ch., Lima, Ohio, 1967-69; pres. C.S.S. Pub. Co., Lima, 1970-75; advt. exec. The Daily News, St. Thomas, V.I., 1975-76; pres. The Noonan Co., Lima, 1976—. Stewardship dir., bd. dirs., asst. pastor St. Luke's Luth. Ch.; bd. dirs. Lima Better Bus. Bur., Lima Symphony Orch., Lima Area Devel. Corp., Lima YWCA, Lima Downtown Bus. Assn. Mem. Young Execs. Forum, Nat. Office Products Assn. Republican. Clubs: Shawnee Country, Kiwanis, Elks. Author: Keeping Faith in the Seventies, 1970; Genesis: A Study in Beginnings, 1971. Home: 1510 W Market St Lima OH 45805 Office: 220 W Market St Lima OH 45802

LENZ, HENRY PAUL, ins. co. exec.; b. N.Y.C., Nov. 24, 1925; s. Ernest and Margaret (Schick) L.; A.B., U. N.C., 1946; M.B.A., Coll. of Ins., 1974; m. Norma M. Kull, Jan. 25, 1958; children—Susan, Scott, Theresa. Underwriter, U.S. Casualty Co., N.Y.C., 1948-55; underwriting mgr. Mass. Bonding & Ins. Co., N.Y.C., 1955-60; with Home Ins. Co., N.Y.C., 1960—, sr. v.p., 1972-75, exec. v.p., 1975—, also dir.; chmn. bd., pres. City Ins. Co. U.K. Ltd., 1980—; pres., dir. Home Indemnity Co., 1978—, City Ins. Co., 1978—, Home Ins. Co. Ill., 1978—, Home Ins. Co. Ind., 1978—; chmn. bd. Home Reins. Co., Seaboard Surety Co.; pres., dir. Home Group Risk Mgmt. Inc.; dir. Thico Plan Inc., Thico Fin. Inc., Scott Wetzel Services, Inc. Served with USNR, 1944-47, 52-53. Decorated Army Commendation medal. Mem. Soc. C.P.C.U.'s, Sigma Nu, Phi Beta Kappa. Home: 21 Audubon Ct Short Hills NJ 07078 Office: 59 Maiden Ln New York NY 10038

LENZ, LAWRENCE RICHARD, food co. exec.; b. Bklyn., Dec. 4, 1946; s. Harold and Rosalind Emilie (Baist) L.; B.A., Va. Mil. Inst., 1969; M.B.A., L.I. U., 1971; m. Linda Maria Zimmermann, June 5, 1971. Export/import lending officer Franklin Nat. Bank, N.Y.C., 1971-73; export lending officer Europe, Export Credit Corp., N.Y.C., 1973-74; fin. asso., corporate controllers staff Gen. Foods Corp., White Plains, N.Y., 1974-76, product analyst Kool Aid, 1976-77, supr. ann./5 yr. plans for powdered beverages, product coordinator, 1977-78, acctg. and asset mgmt. supr. beverage and breakfast food div., 1978—. Mem. M.B.A. Assn., Am. Mgmt. Assn., Smithsonian Assos., Naval Inst., Animal Protection Inst., First Empire Hist. Assn. Lutheran. Address: 107 Stadley Rough Rd Danbury CT 06810

LEOGRANDE, LOUIS, JR., investment exec.; b. Uitca, N.Y., Jan. 1, 1939; s. Louis P. and Mary (Nichol) L.; B.A., Utica Coll., 1962; grad. Public Adminstrn. Grad. Course, N.Y. U., 1966; m. Linda LaPone, June 25, 1975. Mgr. L Truck Stop & Service, Inc., Yorkville, N.Y., 1963-70; asst. mgr. McDonalds Restaurant, Whitesboro, N.Y., 1970-71; asst. v.p., investment exec. Shearson Loeb Rhoades, Inc., Utica, N.Y., 1971—; guest speaker. Sustaining mem. Republican Nat. Com.; former co-chmn. Greater Utica United Fund Retail Div.; active Civil Affairs Assn., Utica Coll. Alumni Assn. Served to maj. USAR, 1962—. Registered rep. N.Y. Inst. Fin. Mem. Nat. Assn. Security Dealers, Commodity Futures Trading Commn., Res. Officers Assn. (past v.p. local chpt.), N.Y. Life Ins. Agts., N.Y. State Notary Publics, New Hartford Hist. Soc. Clubs: U.S. Senatorial; Tyrolean Ski. Home: 16 Gary Ave New Hartford NY 13413 Office: 185 Genesee St Utica NY 13501

LEONARD, BYRON HERBERT, JR., cons. engr ; b. Sedalia, Mo., Aug. 19, 1924; s. Byron Herbert and Eula (Schuchmann) L.; B.S., U.S. Mcht. Marine Acad., 1946; B.M.E., Cornell U., 1948; m. Martha Titterington Reid, Mar. 29, 1960; children—Cheryl, Sally, Byron Herbert III; step-children—Christie, Lois, Carter. With Leonard Welding and Mfg. Co., St. Louis, 1948-49, 1951-55, design engr., 1948-49, chief engr., plant mgr., 1951-53, pres., 1954-55; pres. Nat. X-Ray Corp., 1951-55; design engr. U.S. Bur. Mines, Louisiana, Mo., 1949-51; gen. mgr. mfg. Webrib Steel Corp., St. Louis, 1955-56; chief mech. engr. Internuclear Co., div. Petrolite Corp., St. Louis, 1956-62; chief mech. engr. sci. devel. div. Bechtel Corp., San Francisco, 1962-68, project engr. power and indsl. div., 1968-72, prin. engr. Bechtel Power Corp., 1973-76; cons. engr., 1976—. Served to lt. (j.g.) USNR, World War II. Registered profl. engr., Calif., Mo., Tex., Wash. Mem. Am. Soc. M.E., Am. Nuclear Soc., A.A.A.S., Nat. Soc. Profl. Engrs., Cornell Engrs., Sigma Chi. Club: Missouri Athletic. Contbr. articles tech. jours. Patentee mech. and nuclear fields. Home: 62 Linda Vista Ave Atherton CA 94025

LEONARD, EDWARD CHARLES, chem. co. exec.; b. Burlington, N.C., Aug. 21, 1927; s. Edward Charles and Murlie (Hinds) L.; B.S. in Chemistry, U. N.C., 1947, Ph.D. in Chemistry, 1951; M.B.A., U. Chgo., 1974; m. Evelyn Ruspini, Aug. 2, 1952; 1 son, Edward Charles III (dec.). Chemist, research supr. Union Carbide Corp., 1951-64; research exec. Borden Chem. Co., 1964-67; research exec., v.p. Humko Chem. div. Witco Chem. Corp., 1967—; dir., v.p. Enenco, Inc., Memphis. Mem. Am. Chem. Soc. Methodist. Editor: Vinyl and Diene Monomers, 3 vols., 1969-71; The Dimer Acids, 1975. Home: 409 Twelve Oaks Circle Memphis TN 38117 Office: Humko Sheffield Chem Co Box 398 White Station Tower Memphis TN 38101

LEONARD, FRANK EDWARD, II, resort exec.; b. Rexburg, Idaho, Dec. 29, 1949; s. Edward Cyrus and Lois (Sherrard) L.; B.A. in Journalism, Drake U., 1972; degree in Advt./Research, Mich. State U., 1974; m. Georgia Louise Leonard, Aug. 31, 1976; 1 child. Dir. devel. United Cerebral Palsy Nat. Assn., Des Moines, 1974-75; exec. dir. United Cerebral Palsy of Ill., Peoria, 1975-76; v.p., gen. mgr., owner Glen Eden Inc. Four Season Resort, Clark, Colo., 1976—; cons. in field. Treas., N. Routt Fire Bd. Dist. Mem. Steamboat Springs C. of C. (dir.). Democrat. Roman Catholic. Home: 1160 Boulevard Steamboat Springs CO 80477 Office: PO Box 812 Clark CO 80428

LEONARD, GENE FRANCIS, computer software co. exec.; b. Easton, Md., May 3, 1935; s. William J. and Marjorie (Frampton) L.; B.S. in Elec. Engring. with honors, Princeton, 1957; m. Ann M. Howard, Apr. 6, 1956; children—Lynn A., William H.; m. 2d, Theda M. Jack, Oct. 1, 1960; children—Melissa S., Matthew H.; m. 3d, Patricia I.W. Turner, Mar. 17, 1973. Computing analyst Douglas Aircraft Co., Inc., Santa Monica, Calif., 1957-58; mathematician Tech. Ops., Inc., Washington, 1958-60, Burlington, Mass., 1960-61; dir., sr. staff mem. Mass. Computer Assos., Inc., Wakefield, 1961-62, dir., v.p., treas., 1962-66;, dir., exec. v.p., 1966-67, trustee profit sharing plan and trust 1962-67; dir. new products ITT Data Services div. ITT, Parmaus, N.J., 1967-68, gen. mgr., 1968, v.p., gen. mgr. Computer Services, 1968-70; v.p. Citicorp Leasing Internat., London, Eng., 1970-72; v.p. First Nat. City Bank, also gen. mgr.-Europe, Internat. Computer Services, 1972-73; chmn. Computer Projects Ltd., London, Eng., 1972-73; mng. dir. Citicorp Data Services, Geneva, Switzerland, 1971-73; v.p., gen. mgr. Softech, Inc., Waltham, Mass., 1973-74; pres. Gene F. Leonard & Assos., San Francisco, 1974-76; mgr. computer and software systems Space div. Gen. Electric Co., 1976—. Reviewer, Computing Revs. 1965-70. Mem. Assn. for Computing Machinery, AAAS, Sigma Xi. Contbr. articles to profl. jours. Researcher in programming system design, 1961-70. Home: 179 Midfield Rd Ardmore PA 19003 Office: PO Box 8555 Philadelphia PA 19101

LEONARD, GEOFFREY CURTIS, pharm. co. exec.; b. Cootamundra, New South Wales, Australia, July 7, 1935; s. Geoffrey Gleeson and Phyllis Rhuane (Curtis) L.; student Royal Mil. Coll., Duntroon, Australia, 1953-54; m. Lynette P. Edwards, Apr. 8, 1960; children—Susan Michelle, Anthony Charles. Export mgr. Nicholas Pty. Ltd., Melbourne, Australia, 1959-64; nat. sales mgr. Elanco Products Co., Sydney, Australia, 1964-65; gen. mgr. Menley & James Labs., Sydney, 1965-69; gen. mgr. Richardson-Merrell Ltd., Auckland, N.Z., 1970-72, market dir., Sydney, 1972-78; mng. dir. Richardson-Merrell (Can.) Ltd., Toronto, Ont., 1978-81, pres. Richardson-Vicks Ltd., Toronto, 1981—. Fellow Australian Inst. Mgmt.; mem. Proprietary Assn. Can. (dir. 1978—), Australian Inst. Advt., N.Z. Inst. Mgmt. Home: 1867 Will Scarlett Dr Mississauga ON L5K 1J6 Canada Office: 2 Norelco Dr Weston ON M9L 1R9 Canada

LEONARD, GEORGE EDMUND, JR., savs. and loan exec.; b. Phoenix, Nov. 20, 1940; s. George Edmund and Marion Elizabeth (Fink) L.; student Ariz. State U., 1958-60; B.S., U.S. Naval Acad., 1964; postgrad. Pa. State U., 1969-70; M.B.A., U. Chgo., 1973; m. Gloria Jean Henry, Mar. 26, 1965; children—Tracy, Amy, Kristin. Commd. ensign U.S. Navy, 1964, advanced through grades to lt. comdr., 1975, resigned, 1975; v.p. First Nat. Bank Chgo., 1970-75; exec. v.p. fin. First Fed. Savs. & Loan Assn. of Phoenix, 1975—, also dir.; dir. First Service Mortgage Corp., First Service Corp., First Service Mgmt. Corp. Mem. Phoenix Thunderbirds, 1980, St. Joseph's Devel. Com., 1978-80; adv. dir. Roosevelt council Boy Scouts Am., 1979-80. Mem. Savs. and Loan League Ariz. (dir., v.p. 1978-79, pres. 1979-80), Fin. Mgrs. Soc., Inst. Fin. Edn. (1st v.p. chpt. 1977-78, pres. 1978-79, chmn. edn. com. 1976-78), Fin. Execs. Inst., Phoenix C. of C., (bd. dirs., v.p. urban affairs com. 1977-80). Republican. Clubs: Kiwanis (dir., program chmn.), Paradise Valley Country, Met. Athletic, Kiva. Home: 4617 E Calle del Norte Phoenix AZ 85018 Office: 3003 N Central Ave Suite 2400 Phoenix AZ 85011

LEONARD, GEORGE PERRY, ret. contracting engr.; b. Stillwater, Minn., Dec. 19, 1904; s. William Henry and Orlindia Elizabeth (Gilmore) L.; A.B., Macalester Coll., 1927, LL.D., 1975; m. Wilma Fox, Dec. 24, 1931; children—Barbara (Mrs. Franklin Robben), Thomas George (dec.), Mark George. Gen. supt. Martin Wunderlich Co., Jefferson City, Mo., 1928-44; exec. v.p. Wunderlich Contracting Co., Omaha, 1944-66; pres. Bakers Beach Apts., San Francisco, 1952-64, Stinson Beach Water Co. (Calif.), 1955-74; v.p. Consol. Lands, San Bruno, Calif., 1955-67; dir. Wunderlich Contracting Co., Bakers Beach Apts., Stinson Beach Water Co., Consol. Lands; dir. Wherry Housing Assn., pres., 1963-65. Chmn. constrn. div. United Crusade, San Mateo County, Calif., 1958; mem. Marin County (Calif.) Planning Commn., 1971-73; v.p. Inverness Music Festival, 1974—, Marin Symphony Assn., 1973-77; trustee Macalester Coll., 1960—; bd. dirs. Marin County Sr. Coordinating Council, 1975-78; bd. regents St. Mary's Coll., Moraga, Calif., 1976—. Recipient Golden Beaver award Nat. Assn. Heavy Constrn. Contractors, 1963; Outstanding Citizen award Macalester Coll. Alumni Assn., 1965; Service award Marin Sr. Coordinating Council, 1974; Centennial medal Macalester Coll., 1974, 1st Pace Setter award, 1976. Fellow ASCE (life). Home: PO Box 576 Stinson Beach CA 94970

LEONARD, JOHN DUANE, banker; b. Iowa City, Iowa, Nov. 17, 1930; s. John S. and Margaret (Maher) L.; B.S.C., U. Notre Dame, 1952; M.B.A., U. Denver, 1955; m. Sue Ihinger, Apr. 4, 1964; children—Matthew David, Nancy Elizabeth. With Bank of Am., various locations, 1955—, asst. mgr., Red Bluff, Calif., 1965-68, asst. mgr., asst. v.p., Hanford, Calif., 1968-70, mgr., Shafter, Calif., 1970-79, v.p., credit adminstr., Fresno, 1979—; instr. Am. Inst. Banking. Chmn., ARC; active Jr. Achievement, Cub Scouts. Served with U.S. Army, 1952-54. Mem. Shafter C. of C. and Agr. (dir.; pres. 1974), Calif. Bankers Assn. Republican. Roman Catholic. Club: Rotary (pres. 1972, 76). Office: 1560 E Shaw Fresno CA 93710

LEONARD, PAUL JAMES, diversified mfg. co. exec.; b. Bristol, Va., Sept. 6, 1913; s. Isaac G. and Nancy (Davis) L.; student DeForests Sch. Radio, 1931-32, Bryant and Stratton Sch. Bus., 1939-40; m. Jane Angeline McKee, Oct. 13, 1938; children—Angeline, Nancy Sue, Paul Andrew, Cynthia, Mark. Announcer, operator radio sta. WOPI, Bristol, Tenn., 1932-36; with radio and operations dept. Am. Airlines, Boston, 1936-40; dispatcher All Am. Aviation, Pitts., 1940-41; exec. sec. Egg Driers, Inc., Cedarburg, Wis., 1941-43; partner Absogood Packing Co., Jackson, Mo., 1943-47; pres. Wagner Mfg. Co. (now Lenco, Inc.), Jackson, 1948—, Redarco, Inc., Jackson, 1968—; dir. Lenco Welding Accessories, Windsor, Ont., Lenco de Mex., Monterrey. Commr. Shawnee council Boy Scouts Am., Jackson, 1952—; mem. Nat. Assn. Mental Deficiency, 1958—; mayor of Jackson, 1971-73; non-partisan candidate for Gov. Mo., 1972; bd. dirs. Nat. Mongoloid Council, Chgo. Served with AUS, 1944-45. Mem. Am. Welding Soc., Jackson Kimbeland C. of C., Internat. Platform Assn. (gov. 1968—). Club: Rotary (pres. Jackson 1946-47). Home: 823 E Washington St Jackson MO 63755 Office: 319 W Main St Jackson MO 63755

LEONARD, SUE ANN, data processing exec.; b. Evansville, Ind., Nov. 3, 1946; d. William and Helen Leona (Hierstein) Johnson; student Ind. State U., 1964-66; B.S., Ind. U., 1972; m. David J. Leonard, Sept. 10, 1966. With Standard Oil Co. (Ind.), Chgo., 1967-78, programmer analyst, 1973-75, sr. instr., 1975-78, 80—; sr. cons. SRZ Software Services, Inc., Chgo., 1978-79; sr. staff instr. Sears, Roebuck Co., Chgo., 1979-80. Mem. Chgo. Zool. Soc., Anti-Cruelty Soc., Smithsonian Instn., Midwest Mark IV Users Group (pres. 1976-77, dir. 1977-78), Nat. Mark IV Users Group (dir. IV League 1977-78, pres. 1978-79, winner best speaker contest 1978), GUIDE. Club: Toastmasters (ednl. v.p. 1980; Toastmaster of Year 1979). Home: 1732 76th Ct N Elmwood Park IL 60635 Office: 200 E Randolph Dr Chicago IL

LEONARD, TALBERT ARMLON, JR., trucking co. exec.; b. Walthourville, Ga., Nov. 4, 1916; s. Talbert Armlon and Leila Helen (Quarterman) L.; student U. Miami, 1937; m. Lucy Elizabeth Setzler, May 19, 1940; children—Thomas Armlon, Raymond Louis, John Sterling, Catherine Louise. With L. & L. Freight Lines, Inc., Atlanta, 1935-39; mgr. Leonard Bros. Trucking Co., Inc., Miami, Fla., 1940-45, v.p., 1945-50, pres., 1950-66, chmn. bd., 1966-78; dir. Pan Am. Bank of Miami, N.A., S.L.O. Realty Corp., Pensacola, Fla.; chmn. bd. Talbert Trailer Mfg. and Sales of Fla., Inc. Mem. Nat. Hwy. Safety Adv. Com., U.S. Dept. Transp., 1969-71; pres. Leonard Bros. Trucking Found., Inc.; trustee Columbia Theol. Sem., 1965-75; mem. citizens bd. U. Miami, 1968—; bd. govs. Mus. of Sci. and Space Planetarium, 1970—; chmn. bd. pres. Dade County Citizens Safety Council, 2 yrs. Mem. Am. Trucking Assn. (exec. com.), Heavy Specialized Carriers Conf. (pres., chmn. bd.), Nat. Assn. Specialized Carriers (dir.), Miami-Dade County C. of C., Fla. Trucking Assn. (treas., dir.). Presbyterian (elder). Clubs: Rotary, Tiger Bay Luncheon. Patentee in field. Home: 6945 Sunrise Terr Coral Gables FL 33133 Office: 2515 NW 20th St Miami FL 33152

LEONARD, THOMAS M., diversified mfg. co. exec.; b. Chgo., Mar. 22, 1920; s. Thomas M. and Lyda Pearl (Heck) L.; ed. Johns Hopkins U., N.Y. U., Columbia U.; m. Ethel Andrews, Mar. 15, 1946; children—Susan Jane, Janet Carol. With Continental Can Co., Balt., Chgo. and N.Y.C., 1947-50, 51-62, corporate control officer; with Chase Brass & Copper Co., Waterbury, Conn., 1950-51; group v.p. Textron, Inc., Providence, 1962-68; group v.p., dir. Keene Corp., 1968-69; pres. SW Industries, Inc. (acquired by BTR Ltd. 1976), 1970-71, chmn. bd., chief exec. officer, 1971-76; chief exec. officer, dir. BTR Inc., 1976—; dir. BTR Ltd., London. Served with USAAF, 1942-46. Decorated D.F.C., Air medal with 4 oak leaf clusters. Home: 611 Indian Harbor Rd Vero Beach FL 32960 Office: PO Box 8126 Vero Beach FL 32960

LEONARD, WARREN RAMSDELL, banker; b. Washington, Sept. 23, 1937; s. William Ramsdell and Elizabeth (Warren) L.; A.B., Amherst Coll., 1959; M.A., Johns Hopkins U. Sch. Advanced Internat. Studies, 1961; m. Mary Aylward, Nov. 6, 1965; children—Catherine, Laura. Exec. trainee Chase Manhattan Bank, N.Y.C., 1963-66; investment officer Chase Internat. Investment Corp., N.Y.C., 1967-70, 2d v.p., 1970-71, v.p., 1971-77; pres. Chase Manhattan Overseas Banking Corp., Newark, Del., 1978—; dir. Latin Am. Agribus. Devel. Corp. S.A. Chmn. Rose Valley (Pa.) Zoning Hearing Bd. Served with U.S. Army, 1961-63. Office: Chase Manhattan Overseas Banking Corp Commonwealth Bldg University Plaza Newark DE 19702

LEONE, RICHARD JOSEPH, hosp. adminstr.; b. Jersey City, Mar. 30, 1940; s. John F. and Marie T. (Campanile) L.; B.S., Seton Hall U., 1962. Sr. accountant Haskins & Sells, C.P.A.'s, N.Y.C., 1962-63, 65-67; asst. to fin. v.p., Columbia-Presbyn. Med. Center, N.Y.C., 1967-68; asst. dir., controller Point Pleasant Hosp. (N.J.), 1968-70, dir., 1970-79, pres., 1980—; mem. adv. council nursing Ocean County Coll.; bd. dirs. Central N.J. Comprehensive Health Planning Council, 1973-76. Chmn., Ocean County (N.J.) Cancer Crusade. Served to 1st lt. U.S. Army, 1963-65. C.P.A., N.J. Mem. Am. Coll. Hosp. Adminstrs., Am. Inst. C.P.A.'s, N.J. Soc. C.P.A.'s, N.J. Hosp. Assn. (council govt. relations, council hosp. reimbursement, trustee 1979—). Home: 33 Locust Way Spring Lake Heights NJ 07762 Office: Point Pleasant Hospital Point Pleasant NJ 08742

LEONG, LINCOLN, fin. co. exec.; b. Los Angeles, Apr. 18, 1929; s. Kwai Ngam Leong and Kwan Ngan Ying; student Golden Gate U., 1954, U. Calif., Berkeley, 1973. Dist. mgr. Putnam Fin. Services div. Putnam Fund Distbrs., Inc. San Francisco, 1957—; salesman Mut. Fund Assos., San Francisco, 1956-57; notary pub., San Francisco, 1964—; gen. ins. broker Lincoln Leong Ins. Agy., 1976—; real estate broker, San Francisco; owner A-Aabe Advt. Agency, 1978—; income tax and bookkeeping service. Co-chmn., Miss Chinatown, U.S.A. Pageant, 1964. Served with Intelligence Corps, U.S. Army, 1950-52. Cert. bus. counselor. Mem. Golden Gate Council Stockbrokers Soc. Home: 751-B Clay St San Francisco CA 94108 Office: 751-B Clay St San Francisco CA 94108

LEONHART, WILLIAM HAROLD, corp. exec.; b. Parkersburg, W.Va., May 2, 1906; s. William Henry and Dorah Catherine (Chancellor) L.; student pub. schs. and Marshall Coll. Model Sch., Huntington, W.Va., 1917-18, Parkersburg, W.Va. high sch., Balt. City Coll. night sch., 1921-26; m. Martha Elizabeth Curtis, 1935; children—William Harold, James Chancellor, John Lawrence, Martha Jean (Mrs. Gerard V. Anfossi), Mery Curtis, Valerie Ann. Vice pres. J. Ramsay Barry & Co., Inc., Balt., 1921-41; propr. W. Harold Leonhart, Balt., 1941-43; pres. Leonhart & Co., Inc., reins., brokers, Balt., N.Y.C., 1943—; Chmn. CARE and MEDICO (Md.), 1963-71; chmn. adv. bd. Frederick (Md.) Acad. Visitation, 1966—, Boys Town Homes Md., 1969-72. Mem. S.A.R. Democrat. Roman Catholic. Club: Eaglehead (Frederick). Home: 215 E Church St Frederick MD 21701 also Essex House 550 4th Ave S Naples FL 33940 Office: 330 N Charles St Baltimore MD 21201

LEPAGE, ALBERT REGIS, bakery exec.; b. Lewiston, Maine, Feb. 5, 1947; s. Regis Adien and Corinne O. (Croteau) L.; A.B., Villanova U., 1969; M.B.A., Tulane U., 1971. Treas., Lepage Bakeries, Auburn, Maine, 1971-77, exec. v.p., 1977-78, pres., 1978—; pres. Siger Corp.; corporator Mechanics Savs. Bank. Bd. dirs. United Way, 1975—, LPL and APL Arts Council, 1977-78, Goodwill of Maine, 1978; trustee Bates Summer Theater, 1976-77, chmn., 1978; mem. Maine Commn. Arts and Humanities, 1979—, Maine Gov.'s Mgmt. Task Force, 1979—; trustee Portland (Maine) Symphony Orch., 1978. Mem. Am. Bakers Assn. (pub. relations com. 1974—, nat. affairs com. 1972—, gov. 1972—). Democrat. Roman Catholic. Clubs: Cumberland, Martindale Country. Home: 789 Hotel Rd Auburn ME 04210 Office: 60 2d St Auburn ME 04210

LEPERA, LEONARD J., real estate corr.; b. Gilroy, Calif., Feb. 16, 1941; s. Louis and Louisa (Carpignano) L.; B.S., U. Calif., Berkeley, 1966, M.B.A. (fellow), 1967; m. Meriel Mura, Feb. 3, 1973. Rep. Pacific Mut. Life Ins. Co., Los Angeles, 1969-70, supr., 1970-71, mgr., 1971-73, dir., 1973-74, asst. v.p., 1974-76, 2d. v.p., 1976-77, v.p., 1977-80; partner Property Corrs., Newport Beach, Calif., 1980—; pres., dir. Pacific Lake Park Devel. Co. Mem. Alpha Kappa Psi (life). Home: 3592 South Mall Irvine CA 92714 Office: 160 Newport Center Dr Suite 135 Newport Beach CA 92660

LE PREVOST, THOMAS FREDERICK, retirement facility exec.; b. Princeton Junction, N.J., July 31, 1934; s. Reginald Thomas and Florence LePrevost; A.A., Rider Coll., 1964, B.S., 1965; Masters candidate N. Tex. State U.; m. Ruth Lee Conover, June 18, 1955; children—Thomas J., Allen K., Timothy A., Trevor J. Accountant, Pharmacraft Corp. div. Joseph Seagrams Corp., Cranbury, N.J., 1960-61; accounting mgr. Fifth Dimension, Inc., Princeton, 1961-67; v.p. Presbyn. Homes of N.J., Princeton, 1967—. Trustee, Presbytery of New Brunswick (N.J.), 1976—, treas., 1960-61, 76—; treas. Stony Brook dist. Boy Scouts Am., 1966-67, W. Windsor Twp. PTA, 1963-64; pres. bd. trustees Lewis Clinic for Ednl. Therapy, 1979—. Served with USN, 1952-56. Mem. Hosp. Fin. Mgmt. Assn., United Presbyn. Health, Edn. and Welfare Assn., Am. Coll. Nursing Home Adminstrs., Soc. Licensed Nursing Home Adminstrs., Nat. Assn. Housing and Redevel. Ofcls., N.J. Assn. Non-profit Homes for Aging, Am. Assn. Homes for Aging. Republican. Home: PO Box 222 Rural Route 4 Trenton NJ 08691 Office: PO Box 2184 Princeton NJ 08540

LERMAN, ROBERT ALLAN, investment, mineral and mfg. exec.; b. N.Y.C., Jan. 23, 1935; s. Nathan and Eva (Nichomoff) L.; B.M.E., Coll. City N.Y., 1957; M.S., Adelphi Coll., 1961, U. Conn., 1964; postgrad. Rensselaer Poly. Inst., 1964-68; m. Ellen Finkelstein, Nov. 28, 1957; children—Joanne, Kenneth, Beth, Carla, Andrea. Engr., Kollsman Instrument Corp., Elmhurst, N.Y., 1957-59, Adler Electronics, New Rochelle, 1959-61, United Aircraft Corp., Windsor Locks, Conn., 1961-68; pres., dir. Predictor Mgmt. Corp., Windsor, Conn. 1966-78; v.p., treas., dir. Spectrum, Inc., New Britain, Conn., 1968—; pres., dir. Predictor, Inc., Windsor, 1966-78; v.p. fin. Stampede Internat. Resources, Ltd., Toronto, Ont., Can., 1978—; pres., dir., treas. Spiral Tubing Corp., New Britain, 1978—; pres., dir., treas., chief operating officer Turbotec Products, Inc., New Britain, 1978—; pres., dir. Xtec Inc., New Britain, 1979—, GaSaver Corp., New Britain, 1979—; tchr. grad. course elec. engring. U. Conn., 1961-62. Contbr. to Handbook of Wealth Management, 1977; contbr. articles to profl. jours. Home: 29 Soby Dr West Hartford CT 06107 Office: 533 John Downey Dr New Britain CT 06051

LERNER, ALFRED, real estate investor; b. N.Y.C., May 8, 1933; s. Abraham and Clara (Abrahamson) L.; B.A., Columbia U., 1955; m. Norma Wolkoff, Aug. 7, 1955; children—Randolph David, Nancy Faith. Chmn., Realty Refund Trust, Cleve., 1971—, Multi-Amp. Corp., Dallas, 1970—; pres. Reafund Advisers, Cleve., 1971—, Mid-Am. Mgmt., Cleve., 1965—; dir. Bancohio Nat. Bank, Cleve. Served to 1st lt. USMC, 1955-57. Mem. Young Pres.'s Orgn. Clubs: Harmonie, Commerce. Office: 1101 Euclid Ave Cleveland OH 44120

LERNER, WILLIAM, lawyer; b. Phila., July 17, 1933; s. Al and Tillie (Goodman) L.; B.A., Cornell U., 1955; LL.B., N.Y. U., 1960; m. G. Billie Campbell, Aug. 15, 1957; children—Bonnie, Edwina. Admitted to N.Y. bar, 1961; atty. SEC, 1960-64; asst. v.p. Am. Stock Exchange, 1965-68; sr. v.p., sec. Shearson-Hayden Stone, Inc. (formerly Cogan, Berlind, Weill & Levitt, Inc.), N.Y.C., 1968-70, Berg & Cornell, Buffalo, 1970-71, Kavinoky, Cook, Sandler, Gardner & Wisbaum, Buffalo, 1971-72; v.p., counsel Utilities and Industries Corp., 1973, Saperston, Day & Radler, Buffalo, 1973-78; sr. v.p. law, counsel Sportsystems Corp., Buffalo, 1978-79; sr. partner firm Robshaw & Lerner, P.C., Buffalo, 1979—; dir. Unimax Group, Inc., N.Y.C. Mem. Cornell U. Arts Coll. Council, 1977—, Erie County Sportsboard, 1978—; chmn. Erie County Pub. Utilities Task Force, 1974-75. Served to 1st lt. Q.M.C., U.S. Army, 1955-57. Mem. Am., N.Y. State (regulation of securities com. 1968—) bar assns. Club: Buffalo. Contbg. editor The Stock Market Handbook, 1969. Home: 150 Rollingwood Williamsville NY 14221 Office: 875 Hopkins Rd Buffalo NY 14221

LE SCHACK, LEONARD ALBERT, research and devel. co. exec.; b. N.Y.C., Mar. 6, 1935; s. David B. and Selma (Kaminsky) LeS.; B.S., Rensselaer Poly. Inst., 1957; diploma in oceanography U.S. Dept. Agr. Grad. Sch., 1962; postgrad. Ecole Pratique, Alliance Francaise, Paris, 1963, U. Wis., 1963-64; m. Lorraine Marlene Levy, Mar. 3, 1962; children—Christopher Erik, Adam Alexander. Geophys. trainee Shell Oil Co., Houston, 1957; asst. seismologist U.S. IGY, Antarctic Expdn., 1957-59, Polar regions project officer, EXPO-67, Montreal, Que., Can., 1965-66; pres., chmn. bd. Le Schack Assos., Ltd. (formerly Devel. and Resources Transp. Co.), Silver Spring, Md. and San Ramon, Calif., 1966—; pres. Trident Exploration Ltd., Silver Spring, 1978—, Trident Arctic Exploration Ltd., Montreal, 1979—; U.S. ofcl. rep. Argentine Antarctic expdn., 1962-63; participant 2d

Internat. Conf. on Permafrost, Yakutsk, Siberia, USSR, 1973. Served to lt. (j.g.), USNR, 1959-63; comdr. Res. Decorated Legion of Merit; recipient Antarctic Service medal Nat. Acad. Scis., NRC, 1966; Arctic Inst. N.Am. grantee Expeditions Polaires Francaises, Paris, 1963. Mem. Soc. Exploration Geophysicists, Am. Geophys. Union, Am. Soc. Photogrammetry, AAAS, Arctic Inst. N.Am. Oceanographic and geophys. research in Polar Regions; transp. studies in jungle and Arctic areas for econ devel., exploration for geothermal energy; contbr. chpt.: Photographic Techniques in Scientific Research, 1978; contbr. articles to profl. jours. Home: Silver Spring MD also Long Key FL Office: 1111 University Blvd W Silver Spring MD 20902

LESHER, DEAN STANLEY, newspaper pub.; b. Williamsport, Md., Aug. 7, 1902; s. David Thomas and Margaret Eliot (Prosser) L.; B.A. magna cum laude, U. Md., 1924; J.D., Harvard U., 1926; m. Kathryn C. Lesher, Nov. 2, 1929 (dec. Mar. 1971); children—Carolyn Lee (dec.), Dean Stanley, Melinda Kay, Cynthia Lesher Rice; m. 2d, Margaret Louise Lisco, Apr. 2, 1973. Admitted to Mo. bar, 1926; practiced corp., ins., newspaper and trial law, Kansas City, Mo., 1926-41; gen. counsel Postal Life & Casualty Ins. Co., Kansas City, Mo., 1936-41; newspaper owner, 1938—; pres. 5 newspaper and radio owning corps., including pres., pub. East Bay Newspapers Inc., Walnut Creek, Calif., 1960—. Trustee, Calif. State Univs. and Colls., 1973—; regent St. Mary's Coll.; mem. Calif. Post-Secondary Edn. Commn., 1979—. Named News Pub. of Calif., 1977, Best Bus. Leader Walnut Creek Area, 1978. Mem. Am. Newspaper Pubs. Assn., Suburban Newspapers Am. (dir.), Calif. Newspaper Pubs. Assn. (dir.), C. of C. (pres.), Phi Kappa Phi, Phi Delta Theta, Theta Sigma Phi, Sigma Delta Chi. Republican. Clubs: Rotary (past dist. gov.), Masons, Round Hill Coutry, Concord Century, Harvard. Contbr. articles to trade publs. Home: Seven Oaks Circle Orinda CA 94563 Office: East Bay Newspaper Inc 2640 Shadelands Dr Walnut Creek CA 94598

LESHER, EUGENE ALBERT, former household chem. co. exec.; b. Sunman, Ind., Sept. 3, 1914; s. Walter E. and Bertha (Miller) L.; student U. Cin., 1932-34; m. Ella M. Brinegar, May 16, 1936; children—Charles E., Thomas A., Katherine J. Clk., A.S. Boyle Co., Cin., 1930-36, salesman, 1936-40; with Boyle Midway div. Am. Home Products Corp., 1944-77, v.p. nat. sales, N.Y.C., 1957-66, v.p. So. region, Atlanta, 1967-77; ret., 1977. Pres. Berkeley Lake Property Owners Assn. Mem. Sales and Mktg. Execs. Internat. (dir., past pres.), Pi Sigma Epsilon. Methodist. Club: Cherokee Town and Country (Atlanta). Home: 150 Bayway Circle Berkeley Lake Duluth GA 30136 Office: 4111 Pleasant Dale Rd Atlanta GA 30340

LESHER, JOHN LEE, JR., mgmt. cons. co. exec.; b. Harrisburg, Pa., Feb. 7, 1934; s. John Lee and Mary Alice (Watkeys) L.; B.A. cum laude, Williams Coll., 1956; M.B.A., Harvard U., 1958; m. Nancy Smith, July 11, 1970; children by previous marriage—John David, James Elam, Andrew Gwynne. Budget dir., asst. sec. The Barden Corp., Danbury, Conn., 1958-61; cons. Booz, Allen & Hamilton Inc., N.Y.C., 1962-64, asso., 1964-66, v.p., 1966-76, pres., 1976—. Vice chmn. fund raising com. Am. Mus. Natural History; mem. fund raising com. Phillips Exeter Acad., United Way N.Y.C. Clubs: Harvard Bus. Sch., Williams, Bedens Brook Country, Watch Hill Yacht, Misquamicut (Watch Hill, R.I.); Round Hill (Greenwich, Conn.); River. Office: Booz Allen & Hamilton 245 Park Ave New York NY 10167

LESKE, REINHOLD HERMAN, mining co. ofcl.; b. Sheboygan, Wis., Mar. 28, 1929; s. George William and Martha (Killig) L.; B.S. in Mining Engring., U. Wis., 1957; m. Dolores K. Kunstman, Sept. 6, 1952; children—Randall Lee, Sandra Jean. Corp. safety engr. Bethlehem (Pa.) Steel Co., 1968-73; indsl. relations mgr. Hecla Mining Co., Casa Grande, Ariz., 1974-77; safety dir. N. Am. Coal Co., Cleve., 1977; safety dir. Exxon Minerals Co., Casper, Wyo., 1977-80; mgr. safety Amoco Minerals Co., Denver, 1980—. Served with USN, 1948-52. Mem. AIME, Am. Soc. Safety Engrs. Republican. Lutheran. Home: 7931 S Adams Way Littleton CO 80122

LESLIE, HENRY ARTHUR, banker; b. Troy, Ala., Oct. 15, 1921; s. James B. and Alice (Minchener) L.; B.S., U. Ala., 1942, LL.B., 1948; J.S.D., Yale, 1959; grad. Sch. Banking, Rutgers U., 1964; m. Anita Doyle, Apr. 5, 1943; children—Anita Lucinda (Mrs. David Miller), Henry Arthur. Asst. prof. bus. law U. Ala., 1948-50, 52-54, prof. law, asst. dean Sch. Law, 1954-59; v.p., trust officer Birmingham Trust Nat. Bank (Ala.), 1959-64; v.p., sr. trust officer Union Bank & Trust Co., Montgomery, Ala., 1964-73, sr. v.p., dir., 1973-76, exec. v.p., dir., 1976-78, pres., chief exec. officer, 1978—; admitted to Ala. bar, 1948. Pres., Children's Center, Montgomery, 1971; chmn. bd. Ala. Bankers Ednl. Found., 1974-76; state chmn. Radio Free Europe Fund, 1973. Served to capt. AUS, 1942-46; to lt. col. Judge Adv. Gen.'s Corps, Res. Decorated Bronze Star. Mem. Am., Fed., Ala., Montgomery bar assns., Ala. Bankers Assn. (pres. trust div. 1963-65), Montgomery C. of C. (dir. 1978—), Farrah Order Jurisprudence (pres. 1973-75), Newcomen Soc. in N.Am., Delta Sigma Pi, Phi Delta Phi, Omicron Delta Kappa, Pi Kappa Phi. Episcopalian (vestry, sr. warden). Clubs: Maxwell Gunter Officers, Montgomery Country; Capital City. Contbr. articles to profl. jours. Home: 3332 Boxwood Dr Montgomery AL 36111 Office: Union Bank & Trust Co Montgomery AL 36104

LESLIE, JAMES ALLEN, JR., county sch. dist. ofcl.; b. Hinton, W.Va., June 28, 1945; s. James Allen and Beulah Frances (Hank) L.; B.S. in Bus. Adminstrn., Concord Coll.; M.A. in Bus. Adminstrn., W.Va. Coll. Grad. Studies; m. Patricia Ann Edwards, Apr. 22, 1966; 1 son, James Derrick. Bus. mgr. Summers County Bd. Edn., Hinton, 1969-74, Hancock County Bd. Edn., Weirton, W.Va., 1972; treas. Mercer County Bd. Edn., Princeton, W.Va., 1974—. Councilman, City of Hinton, 1973-75. Mem. Internat., W.Va. (pres. 1974-75) assns. sch. bus. ofcls., Am. Assn. Sch. Adminstrs. Home: 2805 Grandview Ave Bluefield WV 24701 Office: 1420 Honaker Ave Princeton WV 24740

LESLIE, JOHN, paper co. exec.; b. Coral Gables, Fla., Nov. 10, 1933; s. John C. and Marion Jean (Savage) L.; B.S., Princeton, 1956; M.B.A., Columbia, 1961; m. Susan Lee Wallin, July 20, 1963; children—Michael, John, William. With Hercules Corp., 1956-60, Standard Oil Co. (N.J.), 1961-69; chmn. bd., pres., dir. Penntech Papers, Inc., N.Y.C., 1969—. Served to capt. AUS, 1957-58. Mem. Beta Gamma Sigma. Home: 48 Taunton Rd Scarsdale NY 10583 Office: 600 3d Ave New York NY 10016

LESLIE, JOHN ETHELBERT, investment banker; b. Vienna, Austria, Oct. 13, 1910; s. Julius and Valerie (Lawetzky) L.; Dr. Jur., U. Vienna, 1932; diploma Consular Acad. Polit. Sci. and Econs., Vienna, 1934; M.S., Columbia, 1942; m. Evelyn Ottinger Goetz, Mar. 28, 1940. Came to U.S., 1938, naturalized, 1944. Sec. to judges Fed. Law Cts. Austria, 1934-36; pvt. practice, Vienna, 1936-38; sr. auditor Arthur Andersen & Co., C.P.A.'s, N.Y.C., 1941-46; prin. R.G. Rankin & Co., tax cons., N.Y.C., 1946-55; with Bache Halsey Stuart Shields Inc., N.Y.C., 1955—, chmn. bd., 1969-77, chmn. exec. com., 1968-69, chief exec. officer, 1970-76, chmn. emeritus, 1980—; chmn. bd. Bache Group Inc., 1970-78, chmn. policy com., 1977-79; pres., dir. 920 Fifth Ave. Corp. Mem. N.Y. Stock Exchange Adv. Com. on Internat. Capital Markets, chmn., 1973-75; chmn. Nat. Market Adv. Bd., 1975-76. Hon. consul gen. Austria in N.Y.C., 1965—; trustee Inst. Internat. Edn.; bd. dirs. H.L. Bache Found., N.Y. Infirmary-Beekman Downtown Hosp.; mem. adv. bd. Leeds Castle Found.; mem. adv. council internat. affairs Sch. Internat. Affairs, Columbia U.; bd. dirs. N.Y.C. Partnership, Inc.; trustee German Sch. N.Y. Decorated Cruz Vermelha de Dedicacao (Portugal); comdr. Golden Order Merit, Great Badge Honor Great Gold Cross of Honor with star (Austria); officer Nat. Order Merit (France); officer's cross Order of Merit of Fed. Republic of Germany; Golden Star Merit City of Vienna; recipient certificate appreciation City N.Y. Mem. Soc. Fgn. Consuls in N.Y.C., chambers commerce in N.Y.C. of Austria (chmn. bd. dirs.), Belgium, France, Germany, Gt. Britain, Italy, The Netherlands, Spain, N.Y. Chamber Commerce and Industry (dir.), France-Am. Soc. (bd. dirs.), Alumni Assn. Sch. Bus. Columbia, Am. Fgn. Service Assn., Am. Soc. Internat. Law, Securities Industry Assn. (internat. com.), Fgn. Policy Assn. (bd. dirs.), UN-U.S.A. (vice chmn., bd. govs.), Econ. Devel. Council N.Y. (dir.), Council Fgn. Relations, Belgian Am. Ednl. Found., N.Y. Zool. Soc. (bd. advisers), Pilgrims U.S. Clubs: Union, 25 Ltd. Luncheon, Bond, Economic, Paris-American, Wall St. Doubles (N.Y.C.); Piping Rock. Home: 920 Fifth Ave New York NY 10021 Office: Bache Plaza 100 Gold St New York NY 10038

LESLIE, JOHN HAMPTON, mfg. exec.; b. Evanston, Ill., June 28, 1914; s. John W. and Alma (Bertles) L.; B.S., Harvard, 1937; m. Virginia Andersen, Aug. 5, 1950; children—James Woodworth, Victoria Hall. Design engr. Signode Corp., Chgo., 1937-41, v.p. engring. and research, 1946-49, pres., 1949-62, chmn., 1962—, chief exec. officer, 1949-75; dir. Detroit & Can. Tunnel Corp., Union Spl. Corp. (Chgo.), Ill. Power Co. (Decatur); chief engr. South-Wind div. Stewart Warner Corp., 1941-46. Trustee Village of Winnetka, 1955-59; mem. Winnetka Bd. Edn., 1963-69; trustee Signode Found. Inc., Northwestern U.; bd. dirs. Hosp. Planning Council Met. Chgo., 1957-70, Evanston Hosp. Clubs: Univ., Mid-Am., Comml. (Chgo.); Indian Hill (Winnetka, Ill.). Home: 909 Sheridan Rd Winnetka IL 60093 Office: 3600 W Lake Ave Glenview IL 60025

LESLY, PHILIP, pub. relations counsel; b. Chgo., May 29, 1918; B.S. magna cum laude, Northwestern U., 1940; m. Ruth Edwards, Oct. 17, 1940 (div. 1971); 1 son, Craig. Asst. news editor Chgo. Herald & Examiner, 1935-37; copywriter advt. dept. Sears, Roebuck & Co., Chgo., 1940-41; asst. dir. publicity Northwestern, 1941-42; account exec. Theodore R. Sills & Co., pub. relations, Chgo., 1942, v.p., 1943, exec. v.p., 1945; dir. pub. relations Ziff-Davis Pub. Co., 1945-46; exec. v.p. Harry Coleman & Co., pub. relations, 1946-49; pres. Philip Lesly Co., pub. relations, Chgo., 1949—; lectr. pub. relations, pub. opinion to bus. and sch. groups. Chmn. advt. pub. relations com. Nat. Fund Med. Edn., 1958-59. Bd. dirs. Nat. Safety Council, 1967-70. Recipient Award of Merit, Am. Pub. Relations Assn., 1946; Silver Anvil, Pub. Relations Soc. Am., 1963, 65. Mem. Pub. Relations Soc. Am. (charter; Gold Anvil 1979), Internat. Pub. Relations Assn., Phi Beta Kappa. Club: Mid-America (Chgo.). Co-author: Public Relations: Principles and Procedures, 1945. Author: Everything and The Kitchen Sink, 1955; The People Factor, 1974; How We Discommunicate, 1979; Selections from Managing the Human Climate, 1979; (bimonthly) Managing the Human Climate; also articles in U.S., Can., Brit. mags. and trade publs. Editor: Public Relations in Action, 1947; Public Relations Handbook, 1950, 62, 67; Lesly's Public Relations Handbook, 1971, rev. edit., 1978. Home: 155 Harbor Dr Chicago IL 60601 Office: 130 E Randolph St Chicago IL 60601

LESPERANCE, SUDRE, banker; b. Haiti, Feb. 2, 1925; s. Alexandre and Pascaline (Jean) L.; came to U.S., 1965, naturalized, 1978; grad. U. Haiti, 1949; diploma Ecole de Commerce et de Comptabilite, U. Haiti, 1962; m. Antoinette Beaudouin, Mar. 26, 1961; children—Joubert, Herve. Tchr., Anse-a-Veau and Port-au-Prince, Haiti, 1950-62; banker in Port-au-Prince, 1962-65; with Bank of Tokyo, N.Y.C., 1965-78; asst. v.p., mgr. documentary credit Banque de L'Union Europeenne, N.Y.C., 1978—. Office: 1 Citicorp Centre 153 E 53d St New York NY 10022

LESS, JERARD LEONARD, apparel co. exec.; b. Houston, May 6, 1941; s. Jack and Corrine S. L.; B.S., N.Y. U., 1963. Buyer, Foley's Houston, 1963-65; asst. to pres. Alfred of N.Y., 1965-66; pres. Jerard Less, Inc., N.Y.C., 1967-69; merchandise mgr. Excello, 1969-70; div. head men's wear Concord Fabrics, N.Y.C., 1971-72; v.p. mktg. and sales Garan, Inc., N.Y.C., 1973-75; exec. v.p., gen. mgr. Fishman & Tobin, N.Y.C., 1976—. Active Big Bros., Inc., N.Y.C. Mem. Boys' and Young Men's Apparel Mfrs. Assn. (dir. 1979—). Home: 256 W 10 St New York NY 10014 Office: 112 W 34th St New York NY 10001

LESSALL, KENNETH CHARLES, bus. exec.; b. N.Y.C., Apr. 20, 1938; s. George and Frances (Schlanger) L.; B.A., Trinity Coll., 1959; J.S.D., Cornell U., 1962; m. Lenore Fellner, Oct. 1, 1967; children—Matthew Adam, Julia Beth. Various positions Glemby Internat. N.Y.C., 1962-70, v.p., U.K., 1970-75, sr. v.p., N.Y.C., 1975—, dir. Glemby Internat. S. Africa. Served with U.S. Army, 1959-62. Mem. Inst. of Dirs. (London), Pi Gamma Mu, Phi Alpha Delta. Clubs: City Athletic (N.Y.C.), Dyrham Park Country (London); Metropolis Country (White Plains, N.Y.). Home: 32 Valley View Chappaqua NY 10514 Office: 120 E 16th St New York City NY 10003

LESSARD, ARNOLD FRED, internat. bus. exec.; b. Newburyport, Mass., Oct. 9, 1923; s. Fred Soloman and Azilda Mary (Goodreau) L.; diploma in acctg. Burdett Coll., 1943: B.S. with honors, Boston U., 1949; M.A. with honors, Columbia U., 1951; postgrad. Georgetown U., 1953-56, George Washington U., 1953-56; m. Francine Colette Treutenaere, June 30, 1975; 1 son, Arnaud Alfred. Head personnel devel. div. Nat. Security Agy., 1951-56; cons. Booz, Allen & Hamilton, Inc., N.Y.C., 1956-59, asso., 1959-61, v.p., 1961-69, regional v.p., 1969-71; chmn. bd. Resources Engring. & Mgmt. Internat., London and Denver, 1971-78; v.p., dir. Chase World Info. Corp. (Chase Manhattan Bank), N.Y.C., 1978-79, v.p., dir. strategic and market planning Trade Bank (Chase Manhattan Bank), N.Y.C., 1979—; founding chmn. Internat. Coal Exploration Symposium, London, 1975. Served with USAAF, 1943-46; served to capt. USAF, 1951-53. Mem. Inst. Mgmt. Consultants (founding mem., cert. mgmt. cons., regional v.p. Europe 1971-78), Soc. for Personnel Adminstrn., Acad. Mgmt., Phi Delta Kappa, Pi Gamma Mu, Kappa Delta Pi. Club: Reform (London). Home: 7002 Blvd E Guttenberg NJ 07093 Office: 1 World Trade Center 78th Floor New York NY 10048

LESSENBERRY, ROBERT ADAMS, retail exec.; b. Barren County, Ky., May 7, 1926; s. Robert Long and Hugh Barret (Adams) L.; A.B., Centre Coll. Ky., 1950; m. Mary Lloyd Howard, Dec. 26, 1946; children—Robert Howard, Hugh Barret, Leigh Langford. With Glasgow Ry. Co. (Ky.), 1946—, pres., 1965—; owner Lessenberry Realty, 1954—; pres. Lessenberry Bldg. Centre, Inc., Glasgow, 1953—, Lessenberry Devel. Co., Inc., 1969—, Lessenberry Electric & Plumbing Centre, Inc., 1973—; partner Parkview Devel. Co., Inc., 1959—, Lessenberry Enterprises, 1968—; v.p. Modern Manor Park, Inc., 1973-76; pres., v.p., sec., treas., dir. Hardware Wholesalers, Inc., 1973-79; real estate broker, 1972—. Vice chmn. exec. council Louisville Presbytery, Presbyn. Ch., 1962-66; financial chmn., Glasgow, 1962-66, mayor, 1966-68, chmn. water commn., 1966-68, mem. elec. plant bd., 1978—; trustee Ind. Coll. Found., 1972-80; pres. bd. trustees Westminister Terrace Presbyn. Home for Sr. Citizens, 1968-79; bd. dirs. Barren River Area Devel. Council, 1969-72. Served to 2d lt. AUS, 1944-46, to capt., 1950-53. Decorated Bronze Star with cluster. Mem. Nat. Retail Lumber Dealers Assn. (dir. 1978-79), Ky. Retail Lumber Dealers Assn. (pres. 1968-74), Ind.-Ky. Hardware Assn. (sec., v.p., dir. 1975—), Glasgow C. of C. (dir. 1972), Glasgow Concert Assn. (pres. 1953-58). Presbyn. (elder 1952). Rotarian, Mason (32 deg., Shriner). Home: 913 S Green St Glasgow KY 42141 Office: 1010 W Main St Glasgow KY 42141

LESSIN, ARLEN RICHARD, cons. co. exec.; b. Chgo., Oct. 11, 1936; s. Maurice and Beatrice Ethel L.; B.A., U. Calif., 1956; student Harvard U., 1953-54; postgrad. U. Calif. Sch. Law, 1956-57, Columbia U., 1977-78; m. Carol Barbara Schultz, May 4, 1958; m. 2d, Sandra Harrison, June 24, 1975; children—Victoria, Alice-Anne. Exec. adminstr. Gt. Books div. Ency. Brit., Inc., Chgo., 1958-60; asso. dir. mktg. McCann-Erickson, Inc., Chgo., 1960-61; founder, exec. v.p. Golden Book Ednl. Services, Inc., N.Y.C., 1961-68; a founder, v.p. Arcata Nat. Communications, Inc., N.Y.C., 1968-73; chmn. bd., pres. Communications Cons. Corp., N.Y.C., 1973—; adv. in communications to Office of Pres. U.S., Office Mgmt. and Budget, 1978—. Mem. alumni bd. dirs. Aspen Inst. Humanistic Studies, 1959-62; chmn. bd. dirs. Soc. for Advancement Early Childhood Edn., 1970-78, Am. Theatre Alliance, N.Y.C., 1980—. Served with USAR, 1953-58. Recipient Man of Yr. award Gt. Books, 1959, Presdl. citation Vice-Pres. U.S. Hubert H. Humphrey, 1966, Nat. Pres.'s award Arcata Nat. Communications, Inc., 1972. Mem. Internat. Communications Assn., Am. Mgmt. Assn., Am. Bus. Assn., Am. Inst. Mgmt., Pvt. Communications Assn. (pres.), Nat. Communications Assn. (pres.), Internat. Platform Assn., ASCAP, Phi Alpha Delta. Club: Tower. Author: The Crisis in Communications, 1977; Telecommunications Technology Advances, 1979; Communications Concepts, 1980; The History of Communications Competition in America, 1981; others. Home: 7 Park Ave New York NY 10016 Office: 485 Fifth Ave New York NY 10017

LESSLER, RICHARD SIGMUND, advt. agy. exec.; b. Lynbrook, N.Y., Aug. 26, 1924; s. William S. and Minnie (Gold) L.; B.A. in Exptl. Psychology, U. N.C., 1943; M.B.A., Columbia, 1948; postgrad. N.Y. U., 1948-52; m. Evelyn Sobotka, Aug. 31, 1952; children—Michael Jay, Jonathan Peter, Daniel Stephen. Research asso. CBS, 1948-49; with Dancer-Fitzgerald-Sample, Inc., 1949-55; with Grey Advt., Inc., 1955-72, chmn. bd., 1967-72, also dir., mem. exec. com., chmn. mgmt. com.; vice chmn. bd., chief operating officer U.S., chmn. exec. com. McCann-Erickson, Inc., N.Y.C., 1972-79; vice chmn. bd. chmn. ops. com. The Interpublic Group Cos., Inc., N.Y.C., 1979-80, exec. cons., 1980—; gen. mgr. Western region Canter, Achenbaum, Heekin, Inc., mktg. cons., N.Y.C., 1980—; adj. prof. advt. and mktg. U. Ariz., Tucson, 1980—. Served to lt. USNR, World War II. Mem. Phi Beta Kappa, Beta Gamma Sigma. Author: (with Brown and Weilbacher) Advertising Media, 1957; (with Nugent Wedding) Advertising Management, 1962. Home: RL Ranch PO Box 181 Patagonia AZ 85624 Office: PO Box 768 Patagonia AZ 85624

LESTER, NICK C., telephone co. and cable TV exec.; b. Madison, Wis., Apr. 10, 1943; s. Inice Heintz; A.S. in Elec. Engring., Wis. Sch. Electronics, Madison, 1966; B.S. in Elec. Engring., U. Wis., 1971; m. Kathryn C. Mallon, June 15, 1963; children—Craig N., Karen K. Technician, Bell Telephone Labs., Naperville, Ill., 1967; engr. Gen. Telephone Co. Wis., 1971; acting mgr. Platteville, Dickeyville, Belmont, Cuba City Telephone and Platteville Cable TV Co. (Wis.), 1972—; telemetry cons. wildlife ecology dept. U. Wis., 1970. Bd. dirs., treas. House of Peace, Platteville, 1979; pres. Luth. Ch. of Peace, Platteville, 1977-78. Served with U.S. Army, 1961-62. Mem. IEEE. Republican. Club: Platteville Optimist (2d v.p.). Research on miniatrue wildlife telemetry equipment design. Home: 610 Linden St Platteville WI 53818 Office: 135 N Bonson St Platteville WI 53818

LESTER, ROBERT WILLIAM, mfg. co. exec.; b. N.Y.C., Apr. 26, 1921; s. Julius Walter and Lillian Augusta (Johnson) L.; M.E.E., U. So. Calif., 1946; m. Ursula Fascher, Feb. 26, 1956; children—Kirsten, Ingrid, Carl, Eric. Elec. engr. C.E., U.S. Army, Okinawa, Japan, 1947-49; power plant engr. Ford Motor Co., Germany, 1950-54; pres. Transolite Corp., N.Y.C., 1955-60, Thermotronics Corp., N.Y.C., 1960-64, Lester Controls Corp., N.Y.C., 1965-70, Intersonics Corp., N.Y.C., 1971—; chmn. bd. Static-Systems Corp., 1978—; dir. Intersonics Corp.; cons. in field. Served with USAF, 1943-45. Recipient Lighting award Gen. Elec. Corp. Mem. IEEE, Illuminating Engring. Soc., Info. Display Soc. Clubs: Netherlands, Sportsman (N.Y.C.). Patentee in field. Home: 46 Abbey Rd Manhasset NY 11030 Office: 30 Rockefeller Plaza New York NY 10020

LESTER, WILLIAM DALE, architect, engring. co. exec.; b. Graves County, Ky., Oct. 29, 1922; s. Paul and Lottie Pearl (Hawes) L.; student Murray State U., 1946-47; B.S. in Civil Engring., U. Ky., 1949; m. Carolyn Ray, Mar. 26, 1948; children—Dale, Paul. Supt. constrn. Ky. Dept. Hwys., Paducah, 1949-51; area engr. F.H. McGraw & Co., Paducah, 1951-53; structural supr. Geffels & Vallet, Portsmouth, Ohio, 1953-55; structural designer Rust Engrs., Birmingham, Ala., 1955-56; v.p., prodn. mgr. Watson & Co., Tampa, Fla., 1956-76, pres., 1976-78, vice chmn., 1978—, also dir. Active United Fund, 1961; cubscout master Boy Scouts Am., 1959. Served with USAAF, 1943-45. Registered profl. engr., Fla., Ky. Fellow Fla. Soc. Profl. Engrs.; mem. ASCE, Nat. Soc. Profl. Engrs., Fla. Engring. Soc. Democrat. Baptist. Club: Palma Ceia Golf and Country. Home: 3208 Morrison Ave Tampa FL 33609 Office: PO Box 18405 3010 Azeele St Tampa FL 33679

LETENDRE, GERALD JOSEPH, metalworking co. exec.; b. Manchester, N.H., Dec. 9, 1941; s. Ulysses Joseph and Eva (Boisvert) L.; B.S.M.E., U. N.H., 1963; M.S.M.E., Rensselaer Poly. Inst., 1966; m. Evelyn S. Poirier, Sept. 8, 1962; children—Christine, Gerald, Jon. Sr. analytical engr. Pratt & Whitney Aircraft, East Hartford, Conn., 1963-66; project mfg. engr. Hitchiner Mfg. Co., Milford, N.H., 1966-69; gen. mgr. Diamond Casting and Machine Co., Inc., Hollis, N.H., 1969-72; pres., 1972—. Registered profl. engr., N.H. Mem. Nat. Soc. Profl. Engrs., Am. Soc. Metals, Bus. and Industry Assn. N.H. (dir. 1980). Home: 340 Wallace Rd Bedford NH 03102 Office: RTE 130 Hollis NH 03049

LETICA, HELEN, co. exec.; b. Belgrade, Yugoslavia, July 21, 1923; d. Charles and Renee Santich; came to U.S., 1941, naturalized, 1945; B.A., N.Y. U., 1945, postgrad., 1945-47; postgrad. New Sch., 1947-48; m. Jack W. Fine, Aug. 3, 1968; children—Gregory, Nicholas Letica. Exec. v.p. Zeller & Letica Inc., mailing list compilers, N.Y.C., 1954-71, pres., 1971—; lectr. in field. Mem. Women's Direct Response Group, Direct Mail Mktg. Assn., Mail Advt. Service Assn. Club: Mill River Country (Brookville, N.Y.). Office: Zeller & Letica Inc 15 E 26th St New York NY 10010

LETOURNEAU, GERARD NORMAN, consumer products mfg. co. exec.; b. Orleans, Vt., Sept. 11, 1935; s. George and Margaret (James) L.; B.Indsl. Engring., Ga. Inst. Tech., 1962; M.B.A., Ga. State U., 1964; m. Jean A. Parker, Feb. 14, 1964; children—Kim, Gerard, Melissa. With Scientific Atlanta, Inc., 1956-68; v.p. Fuqua Industries, Atlanta, 1968-71; owner, pres. Santa Anita Mobile Homes,

Cucamonga, Calif., 1971-75; pres. Insley Mfg. Co., Indpls., 1975-76; v.p. ops. Varco Pruden, Memphis, 1976-79; exec. v.p. Airstream div. Beatrice Foods Co., Jackson Center, Ohio, 1979—. Served with U.S. Army, 1953-56. Republican. Methodist. Home: 1730 Port Sheffield Pl Newport Beach CA 92660 Office: Airstream Div Beatrice Foods Co 419 W Pike St Jackson Center OH 45334

LEUBERT, ALFRED OTTO PAUL, internat. business cons.; b. N.Y.C., Dec. 7, 1922; s. Paul T. and Josephine (Haaga) L.; B.S., Fordham U., 1946; student Dartmouth Coll., 1943; M.B.A., N.Y. U., 1950; m. Celestine Capka, July 22, 1944 (div. 1977); children—Eloise Ann Leubert Cronin, Susan Beth Leubert Melvin; m. 2d, Hope Sherman Drapkin, June 1978; 1 stepson, Richard J. Drapkino. Account mgr. J.K. Lasser & Co., N.Y.C., 1948-52; controller Vision, Inc., N.Y.C., 1952-53; with Old Town Corp., 1953-58, controller, 1953-54, sec., controller, 1954-56, sec., treas., 1956-57, v.p., treas., 1957-58, dir. subsidiaries Old Town Internat. Corp., Old Town Ribbon and Carbon Co., Inc. (Mass., also Calif.), 1955-58; v.p., controller Willcox & Gibbs, Inc., N.Y.C., 1958-59, v.p., treas., 1959-65, pres., dir., chief exec. officer, 1966-76; founder, pub., pres. Leubert's Compendium of Bus., Fin. and Econ. Barometers, 1978—; dir. N.Y.C., Chyron Corp., Inc., S.R.C. Labs., Inc., Oh Dawn!, Inc.; instr. accountancy Pace Coll., 1955-57. Bd. dirs. United Fund of Manhasset, 1963-69, pres., 1964-65; adv. bd. St. Anthony's Guidance Clinic, 1967-69. Served from pvt. to 1st lt., Inf. platoon leader, USMCR, 1943-46. Decorated Bronze Star; recipient Humanitarian award Hebrew Acad., 1971. Mem. Nat. Assn. Accountants, Catholic Accountants Guild, Am. Inst. C.P.A.'s, N.Y. State Soc. C.P.A.'s, Financial Execs. Inst., Fordham U. Alumni Assn., Am. Arbitration Assn. (nat. panel arbitrators), Newcomen Soc. N.Am. Clubs: N.Y. U., N.Y. Athletic (N.Y.C.). Home: One Lincoln Sq New York NY 10023 Office: One Lincoln Plaza New York NY 10023

LEUNG, JOHN K. C., recruiting co. exec.; b. China, Oct. 30, 1940; s. Ying Kwai and Tak Fun (Hui) L.; came to U.S., 1969, naturalized, 1975; M.B.A., U. Chgo., 1973; m. Shirley Leung, June 1, 1969; children—Elaine, Andrea. Auditor, Hong Kong Govt., 1967-69; adminstrv. asst. Am. Nat. Bank & Trust, Chgo., 1969-71, asst. comptroller, 1971-73, 2d v.p., 1973-80; pres. First Fin. Consultants and Recruiters, 1980—. C.P.A., Ill. Mem. Ill. Soc. C.P.A.'s (mem. acctg. principles com.), Am. Inst. C.P.A.'s, Nat. Assn. Accountants, Chgo. Tax Club. Home: 806 S Elmhurst Rd Mount Prospect IL 60056

LEUPOLD, GEORGE FRED, JR., ins. co. exec.; b. Phila., Aug. 7, 1942; s. George Fred and Sophronia (Hamersley) L.; B.S., Ursinus Coll., 1964; postgrad. Am. Coll., 1973; m. Carol Gilbert, July 24, 1965; children—Eric Jonathan, Todd Gilbert. Salesman Am. Foresight Inc., Phila., 1964-65, asst. to pres., 1965-66, sales mgr., 1966-67, v.p. sales, 1967-70; individual practice ins. agt. and registered rep., also agt. Columbus Mut. Life Ins. Co., 1970-74; prin. Leupold Assos., Cherry Hill, N.J., 1974—. Active Camden County Red Cross. C.L.U., certified Adv. Estate Planning. Mem. Estate Planning Council So. N.J., Sales Mktg. Execs. (pres. Phila. 1975), Life Underwriters Assn. Greater Camden, C.L.U. Assn. (S. Jersey chpt.), Cherry Hill C. of C. (treas.). Clubs: Camden Lions; Garden State Rotary (Cherry Hill). Office: Leupold Assos 103 E Gate Dr Cherry Hill NJ 08034

L'EUROPA, STEVEN DENNIS, advt. exec.; b. Providence, Feb. 8, 1947; s. Rocco and Josephine C. (Priete) L'E.; A.A., Roger Williams Coll., 1965; postgrad. Art Inst. Boston, 1966-68; m. Cheryl Ann Blanchard; children—Kristin Steven, Julie Ann. Art dir. Halladay Advt., Inc., East Providence, R.I., 1968-71, account exec., 1971—. Home: 25 Cider Ln Greenville RI 02828 Office: PO Box 4294 East Providence RI 02914

LEUTNER, ROBERT DOUGLAS, steel co. exec.; b. Racine, Wis., June 16, 1920; s. William and Olga (Klingbeil) L.; B.S. in Bus. Adminstrn., Marquette U., Milw., 1942; M.B.A., U. Wis., Madison, 1957; m. Virginia E. Anderson, Sept. 21, 1942; 1 dau., Carole Gene. With Racine Steel Castings Co. (name changed from Belle City Malleable Iron Co. 1971), Racine, 1947—, treas., asst. sec., 1961-74, v.p. adminstrn., 1974-78, sr. v.p. fin. and adminstrn., 1978—. Vice pres. St. Luke's Hosp., Racine, 1973-74, chmn. bd. dirs., 1975-79. Served as officer USAAF, 1942-46. Mem. Nat. Assn. Accts. (past pres.), Fin. Execs. Inst., Racine C. of C. (dir. 1980—). Home: 4927 King's Cove Rd Racine WI 53406 Office: 1442 N Memorial Dr Racine WI 53404

LE VAN, DANIEL HAYDEN, business exec.; b. Savannah, Ga., Mar. 29, 1924; s. Daniel Hayden and Ruth (Harner) LeV.; grad. Middlesex Sch., 1943; B.A., Harvard, 1950; student Babson Inst., 1950-51. With underwriter's dept. Zurich Ins. Co., N.Y.C., 1951-52; co-owner, dir. Overseas Properties, Ltd., N.Y.C.; dir. Lowell Gas Co., Cape Cod Gas Co., Lowell Factors, Mass. Assos., Gas Appliances; trustee Colonial Gas Energy System. Served with AUS, 1943-46. Clubs: Harvard (N.Y.C.); Harvard (Boston). Home: Box 158 DeLeon Springs FL 32028 Office: Colonial Gas Energy System 73 E Merrimack St Lowell MA 01853

LEVANGIE, JOSEPH EDWARD, energy co. exec.; b. Cambridge, Mass., Aug. 15, 1945; s. Joseph and Marion Theresa (Finnegan) L.; S.B., Mass. Inst. Tech., 1967; M.B.A., Harvard, 1969; m. Pamela Andrea Kurtz, Aug. 28, 1971; children—Joel Jeremy, Ann-Michelle. Sr. bus. analyst Avco Systems Div., Wilmington, Mass., 1969-71, mgr. planning and venture analysis, 1973-74, dir. planning and communications, 1974-77; div. mgr. Indsl. Devel. div. No. Energy Corp., Cambridge, 1977—; mgr. new bus. ventures Sperry Rand Corp., Sudbury, Mass., 1971-73; mem. faculty Northeastern U., 1968—. Mem. Am. Mgmt. Assn., Am. Mktg. Assn., Small Bus. Assn., Harvard Bus. Sch. Assn. of Boston, Planning Execs. Inst., Mass. Inst. Tech. Alumni Assn. Home: 9 Cot Hill Rd Bedford MA 01730 Office: 470 Atlantic Ave Boston MA 02110

LEVAVY, ZVI, accountant; b. Jerusalem, Palestine, Oct. 1, 1910; s. Zeev and Esther (Shapiro) Leibowitz; B.C.S., N.Y. U., 1934; m. Berenice Bardin, Nov. 27, 1935; 1 son, Bardin. Came to U.S., 1929, naturalized, 1944. Sec. Palestine Trust Co., Tel Aviv, 1934-36; sec., chief accountant Palestine Brewery Richon LeZion, 1936-38; comptroller Zionist Orgn. Am., 1940-43; now practicing as C.P.A., N.Y.C. Pres., Perth Amboy Zionist Orgn., 1949-50; mem.-at-large Jewish Community Council, Perth Amboy, pres., 1963-66; pres. Morris J. and Betty Kaplun Found.; v.p. Perth Amboy Bd. Edn., 1966-74; mem. Perth Amboy Bd. Sch. Estimate, 1966-74; mem. Middlesex County Coll. Found.; trustee Am. Friends Hebrew U., Am. Assn. Jewish Edn.; v.p. bd. govs. Dropsie U., 1976—. Served as sgt. AUS, World War II; ETO. Mem. Am. Inst. C.P.A.'s, N.Y., N.J. socs. C.P.A.'s. Home: 148 Kearny Ave Perth Amboy NJ 07522 Office: 21 E 40th St New York NY 10016

LEVENSON, ALAN MARK, greeting card mfg. co. exec.; b. Los Angeles, Dec. 14, 1947; s. Sol and Ethel (Zweig) L.; student UCLA, 1968; m. Elizabeth Jeannette Sutton, June 21, 1948; children—Jennifer Anne, Zachary Aaron. Pres., Small World Greetings, Inc., El Segundo, Calif., 1969—; pres. Creative Imports-Exports, Los Angeles, 1979—; cons., lectr. UCLA, U. So. Calif. Grad. Sch. Bus. and Fin.; U. Loma Linda. Mem. Los Angeles County Mus. Art, Huntington Library. Contbr. articles to bus. jours. Office: 4955 W 145th St Hawthorne CA 90250

LEVENSON, WILLIAM ISRAEL, retail mcht.; b. Balt., Sept. 10, 1920; s. Reuben Hyman and Miriam (Klein) L.; B.S. in Bus. and Public Adminstrn., U. Md., 1943; m. Gloria Waldman, June 12, 1949; children—Judith, Jerrold, Emily. With Md. Drydock & Shipbldg. Co., 1941-42; with Levenson & Klein, Inc., Balt., 1946—, mdse. mgr., 1952-60, v.p., sec., 1960-72, pres., 1972—; retail rep., bd. dirs. United Furniture Action Com., 1976-78; mem. adv. council furniture mktg. curriculum High Point Coll., 1979-80; chmn. Furniture Industry Liaison Com., 1980. Served to lt. USN, 1942-46. Mem. Nat. Home Furnishing Assn. (chmn. govt. affairs com. 1976-78, pres. 1979-80, chmn. exec. com. 1980-81), Nat. Retail Mchts. Assn. (home furnishings bd. dirs. 1972-73), Furniture Retailers Md. (v.p. 1970-79), VFW, Sigma Alpha Mu. Jewish. Office: Levenson & Klein Inc Monument and Chester Sts Baltimore MD 21205

LEVERNIER, THOMAS JOHN, personnel exec.; b. Glencoe, Ill., July 19, 1930; s. Loren Carl and Laura Marie (Fehd) L.; B.A., Calif. State U. at Fresno, 1953; postgrad. U. Santa Clara, 1962-63. Personnel asst. McClatchy Newspapers and Broadcasting Co., Sacramento, 1949-61; mgr. site indsl. relations Western Devel. Lab. div. Philco-Ford Corp., Palo Alto, Calif., 1961-70; dir. personnel Bancroft Whitney Co., San Francisco, 1970—; dir. Bancroft-Whitney Co. Served with AUS, 1953-55. Mem. Am. Soc. Personnel Adminstrn., Am. Compensation Assn., No. Calif. Indsl. Relations Council. Home: 1922 Jackson St San Francisco CA 94109 Office: Bancroft-Whitney Co 301 Brannan St San Francisco CA 94107

LEVESQUE, PASCAL, mfg. exec.; b. St. Pascal, Que., Can., May 16, 1923; s. P. Wilfrid and Rose (Marier) L.; B.A. cum laude, Ste. Ann Coll., 1943; M.A., Laval U., 1947, B. Applied Sci., 1947; postgrad. Ohio State U., 1947, U. Wis., 1947-48; Ph.D., Ill. Inst. Tech., 1953; M.B.A., Northeastern U., 1961; m. Cecile Dube, Sept. 6, 1947; children—Claude, Louise. Came to U.S., 1947, naturalized, 1954. Chemist, Nat. Aluminate Corp., Chgo., 1948-50; engr. Sylvania Electric Products, Boston, 1952-53; mem. research staff Raytheon Co., Waltham, Mass., 1953-58, mgr. materials, mfg. engring., Newton, Mass., 1959-60; pres. Electronic Metals and Alloys, Inc., Attleboro, Mass., 1960-64; gen. mgr. Electronized Chems. Corp., 1964-65, exec. v.p., 1966, pres., 1967-73, vice chmn., 1973-79, also dir.; pres., chief exec. officer, dir. High Voltage Engring. Corp., Burlington, Mass., 1970—. Mem. Sigma Xi. Home: Elm St Medfield MA 02052 Office: S Bedford St Burlington MA 01803

LEVIANT, JACQUES, chem. co. exec.; b. Russia, Oct. 22, 1921; s. Kalman and Riva Leviant; student Lycee Claude Bernard, Paris, Toulouse (France) U.; B.S.B.A., Columbia U., 1944; m. Dolores Smithies, June 8, 1976; 1 son, Alexandre Jacques. Pres., Alloychem, Inc., N.Y.C., ICD Group, Inc., N.Y.C. Mem. Drug, Chem. and Allied Trades Assn., N.E. Petrochem. Assn., others. Club: City Athletic of N.Y. Home: 895 Park Ave New York NY 10021 Office: 641 Lexington Ave New York NY 10022

LEVIN, HERMAN L., hotel owner; b. Phila., Dec. 4, 1917; s. Samuel and Esther Levin; grad. high sch.; m. Isabel Lavin, Oct. 29, 1939; children—Stephen, Lynda Levin Rybinski, David. Engaged in bus., Phila.; pres. Springlake Ranch, Ritz Lodge, Manatee River Hotel, New Fla. Hotel, Palm Beach Hotel, Sunset Hotel, Ritz Hotel (all Fla.). Served with USN, 1941-46. Recipient recognition from Pres. Roosevelt. Jewish. Club: B'nai B'rith. Office: 130 S Massachusetts Ave Lakeland FL 33801

LEVIN, JERRY WAYNE, food industry exec.; b. San Antonio, Apr. 18, 1944; s. Bernard H. and Marion B. Levin; B.S. in Math., U. Mich., 1966, B.S. in Elec. Engring., 1968; M.B.A. in Fin., U. Chgo., 1968; m. Carol Lee, Dec. 18, 1966; 1 son, Joshua. Mgr. fin. dept. Tex. Instruments Co., 1968-72; v.p. Marsh & McLennan, 1972-74; dir. aquisitions, then v.p. mergers and acquisitions Pillsbury Co., Mpls., 1974-79, v.p. corp. strategy and acquisitions, 1980—. Mem. Assn. Corp. Growth (dir.). Jewish. Clubs: Mpls., Oak Ridge Country. Office: 1356 Pillsbury Bldg 608 2d Ave S Minneapolis MN 55402

LEVIN, MARTIN PAUL, pub. co. exec.; b. Phila., Dec. 20, 1918; s. Harry and Sarah (Haimon) L.; B.S., Temple U., 1950, postgrad. (Personnel Council fellow), 1950. Adminstrv. officer U.S. War Dept., 1940-44, VA, 1945-50; sr. v.p. Grosset & Dunlap, Inc., N.Y.C., 1950-66; pres. book pub. div. Times Mirror Co., N.Y.C., 1966—; chmn. bd. New Am. Library, Inc.; dir. New English Library, Ltd., C.V. Mosby Co., Year Book Med. Pubs., Harry N. Abrams, Inc., New Australian Library. Cons. Ford Found., India, 1957-58. Served with AUS, 1944-45. Recipient Benjamin Gomez award as Book Pub. of Yr., 1980. Mem. Assn. Am. Pubs. (dir., vice-chmn. mem. del. to USSR 1976, People's Republic of China 1979), Book Industry Study Group (dir.). Clubs: Pubs. Lunch (pres.), Friars. Office: 280 Park Ave New York NY 10017

LEVIN, ROBERT BARRY, advt. agy. exec.; b. Chgo., May 31, 1943; s. Albert Harold and Sally Ethel (Bloom) L.; B.S. in Journalism, U. Ill., 1965; m. Bonnie Lee Aaron, Feb. 6, 1965; children—Jordan, Leigh. Catalog copywriter Sears, Roebuck & Co., 1965; public relations specialist Natural Gas Pipeline Co. Am., 1965-68; account exec. Rink Wells & Assos., Chgo., 1968-70; account supr. Hurvis Binzer & Churchill, Chgo., 1970-71; pres. Bob, Pete & Howard, Inc., Chgo., 1972-75; v.p., mgmt. supr. McCann-Erickson, Inc., Chgo., 1975-79, sr. v.p., dir. account services, 1979; exec. v.p. Leibson, Lightle & Assos., Chgo., 1979—. Bd. dirs. Nat. Father's Day Council; co-chmn. Chgo. Father of Year award, 1977-78. Mem. Am. Assn. Advt. Agys., Chgo. Advt. Club, Am. Mgmt. Assn., Am. Mktg. Assn., Men's Fashion Assn. Office: One Illinois Center Chicago IL 60601

LEVIN, RUBEN, editor, mgr.; b. Warsaw, Poland. Aug. 2, 1902; s. Benjamin D. and Ida (Gochlik) L.; brought to U.S., 1904, naturalized, 1917; B.A., U. Wis., 1930; m. Bertha Greenberg, June 7, 1931; children—Hilda Levin Tanenholtz (dec.), David A., Jonathan H. Reporter, copyreader various dailies, 1924-38; writer Labor Newspaper, 1938—, mgr., 1953—. Recipient Distinguished Service awards Sidney Hillman Found., U. Wis., Internat. Labor Press Assn., Eugene V. Debs Found. Mem. Am. Newspaper Guild, Indsl. Relations Research Assn., Nat. Press Club, Assn. R.R. Editors (pres., 1978-79), Nat. Consumers League, ACLU. Democrat. Jewish. Contbr. articles to profl. jours.; contbr. Grolier-Americana Ency. Yearbooks. Home: 2712 Blaine Dr Chevy Chase MD 20015 Office: 400 First St NW Washington DC 20001

LEVINE, ALAN MICHAEL, mgmt./mktg. cons.; b. Bklyn., Mar. 7, 1936; s. Carl and Sylvia (Godlis) L.; B.A. cum laude, Ithaca Coll., 1957; m. Margo Berkman, Apr. 12, 1964; children—Seth, Aron. With Jos. E. Seagram & Sons, N.Y.C., 1959-64; nat. merchandising mgr. P. Ballantine & Sons Co., Newark, 1964-66; sr. mktg. exec. Doyle Dane Bernbach Inc., advt., N.Y.C., 1966-70; sr. brand mktg. mgr. Tobacco Products, Philph Morris, U.S.A., N.Y.C., 1970-75, v.p. mktg. Am. Safety Razor div., 1975-77; v.p., dir. mktg. Fleischmann Distilling Co. div. Standard Brands Inc., 1977-80; pres. Alan M. Levine Mktg. Assos., mgmt. and mktg. cons., N.Y.C., 1980—. Mem. Mktg. Communications Execs. Internat. (pres. 1975-77, chmn. bd. 1978-79). Jewish. Home: 610 West End Ave New York NY 10024

LEVINE, ALFRED DAVID, film producer; b. Cleve.; s. Manuel and Jessie (Bialosky) LeV.; grad. Western Res. U., 1937; postgrad. Ohio State U. Law Sch., 1938; m. Frances Elaine Leberman, Jan. 16, 1948. Advt. and sales promotion staff Cleve. News, 1939-42; advt. dir. Cunningham Drug Stores, Detroit, 1946; mdse. mgr. Goldblatt Bros., Chgo., 1947; Midwest mgr. Chen Yu Cosmetics, Chgo., 1948; dir. advt. Cunningham's, Detroit, 1949; account exec. Snader Telescriptions, Chgo., 1950-51; sales mgr. Consol. Television, Chgo., 1952-54; gen. mgr. Sportlite Films, Chgo., 1955—, also head film producer; partner Sandford-Alfred Assos.; co-chmn. Resources Program Chgo., Case Western U., 1979—; nat. distbr. maj. league baseball video cassettes, 1979; chief judge Indsl. Film Festival, 1971—. Head law enforcement com. Lakeview Citizens Council, Chgo., 1958; vice chmn. cleanup com. N.E. Neighbors, 1961; mem. Com. 100, Jewish Fedn. Chgo., 1962; vice chmn. communications div. Combined Jewish Appeal, 1960—; mem. com. Woodlawn Assn., 1966; active Ill. 9th dist. campaign Decker for Congress, 1964; bd. mgrs. Old Town Boys Club, 1976—, citation, 1976. Served to capt. USAAF, 1942-45; ETO. Decorated Bronze Star medal, Presdl. citation with cluster, 12 maj. battlestars. Mem. Western Res. U. Alumni Assn. (alumni steering com. 1975—, mem. fund raising com. Millis Sch. Bldg. 1964), Wyo. Hunters Protective Assn., Info. Film Producers Assn. (chmn. Midwest chpt. 1971-74), Chgo. Film Council (dir. 1980—), Chgo. Council Fgn. Relations, Antique Car Club Am. (charter), Chgo. Hist. Auto Mus. Clubs: Indpls. Athletic; Chgo. Press. Producer, mktg. and mail order distbr. sports ednl. films for libraries, instns., systems and bus. including Am. Film Festival nominee Second to None, 1961, Big 10 Football for TV, 1960-62, Indpls. 500, 1963, Drivers Choice, 1964, Womens World of Golf, 1971, U.S. Open, 1971, 72, 73. Home: 2970 Lake Shore Dr Chicago IL 60657 Office: 20 N Wacker Dr Chicago IL 60606

LEVINE, ARTHUR ALVIN, stockbroker; b. Brookline, Mass., May 20, 1948; s. Manuel and Minnie (Butter) L.; B.A. in Polit. Sci. and Acctg., U. Denver, 1970; M.B.A. in Fin., Boston Coll., 1972; m. Laurie Ruth Miller, Aug. 7, 1969; children—Joanna Leslie, Michele Hope, Dana Lynn. Investment counselor Profl. Econs., Boston, 1972-73; stockbroker Blyth Eastman Dillon, N.Y.C., 1973-74; v.p. Oppenheimer & Co., Inc., N.Y.C., 1974-78; v.p. L. F. Rothschild, Unterberg, Towbin, N.Y.C., 1978-81, 1st v.p., sr. portfolio mgr., 1981—; cons. Saddle River Group Inc.; cons., lectr. Treas., Temple Beth Shalom, Ramsey, N.J., 1978-79. Recipient various performance awards. Mem. Nat. Bus. Execs. Home: 50 Grist Mill Ln Upper Saddle River NJ 07458 Office: 666 Fifth Ave New York NY 10103

LEVINE, HYMAN JOSEPH, chem. co. exec.; b. Bklyn., Aug. 11, 1909; s. Joseph and Dora (Alpert) L.; student Columbia U. Sch. Pharmacy, 1931; m. Gertrude Sendrowitz, Mar. 25, 1944; 1 son, Theodore. Owner, mgr. Adams & Nassau Pharmacy, Bklyn., 1931-46, Chelsea Pharmacy, N.Y.C., 1946-49; pres., founder Ruger Chem. Co. Inc., N.Y.C., 1949—; pres. Amend Drug & Chem. Co. Inc., Irvington, N.J., 1965—, GLS Realty Co., 1971—, A & R Sales Corp., 1974—, 500 Chancellor Ave., 1976—. Served with USAAF, 1941. Mem. Drug, Chem., Allied Trades. Jewish. Club: B'nai B'rith. Home: 300 Winston Dr Cliffside Park NJ 07010 Office: 83 Cordier St Irvington NJ 07111

LEVINE, JULIUS, retail store exec.; b. Bklyn., Nov. 22, 1927; s. Samuel David and Rachael (Balberg) L.; B.S., Rutgers U., 1949; m. Frances Tobias, Mar. 28, 1954; children—Ruth, Naomi, David. Mdse. controller Interstate Dept. Stores, 1952-67, Kings Dept. Stores, Newton, Mass., 1968-69; systems exec. Cornwall Equities Ltd. and Franklin Stores, Bronx, N.Y., 1969-80, dir. systems, 1980—. Served with U.S. Army, 1950-51. Mem. Controllers Congress. Club: B'nai B'rith (past pres.). Home: 17 Williamson Rd Bergenfield NJ 07621 Office: 815 Hutchinson River Parkway Bronx NY 10465

LEVINE, LAURENCE E., fin. cons.; b. N.Y.C., Dec. 17, 1941; s. Martin and Beulah (Brandt) L.; B.A. (Francis Biddle prize 1961), Princeton U., 1964; LL.B., Stanford U., 1967. Admitted to N.Y. State bar, 1968, Pa. bar, 1975; v.p., voting shareholder Drexel Burnham Lambert, N.Y.C., 1968-71; corp. planning officer Office of Chmn., Ogden Corp., N.Y.C., 1971-73; pres. Investment Research Assos., fin. cons., West Chester, Pa. and Pompano Beach, Fla., 1973—; pres. Sales Imports, Inc., nat. distbr., importer and exporter, Pompano Beach, Fla., 1978—. Bd. visitors Stanford U. Law Sch., 1968-71, exec. com., 1970. Served with USMCR, 1961-65. Mem. N.Y. State Bar Assn., Pa. Bar Assn. Clubs: City Athletic, Princeton (N.Y.C.); Kennett Sq. (Pa.) Golf and Country; Palm Beach (Fla.) Country. Office: 447 S Cypress Rd Pompano Beach FL 33060

LEVINE, MATTHEW, accountant; b. Bayonne, N.J., Jan. 20, 1929; s. Bernard and Sarah (Katchen) L.; B.A., Temple U., 1969; m. Naomi Millstein, Jan. 23, 1955; children—Barry, Terry, Steven. Mgr. cost acctg. and property acctg. Thiokol Chem. Corp., Trenton, N.J., 1956-71; fin. analyst N.J. Hosp. Assn., Princeton, 1971-75; acctg. mgr. St. Francis Med. Center, Trenton, N.J., 1975—. Served with U.S. Army, 1951-53. Decorated Bronze Star, Purple Heart, Combat Infantryman's badge. Mem. Nat. Assn. Accountants. Democrat. Jewish. Club: K.P. Home: 15 Vitaloak Ln Levittown PA 19054

LEVINE, PAUL HENRY, electronics co. exec.; b. N.Y.C., Nov. 2, 1940; s. Philip M. and Beatrice L.; B.S. in Accounting, U. Conn., 1962; m. June 26, 1969; children—Robert, Mark. Accountant, Alfred R. Bachrach & Co., N.Y.C., 1963-65; sr. accountant Arthur Young & Co., N.Y.C., 1965-67; treas., dir. Magnetic Analysis Corp., Mt. Vernon, N.Y., 1967—; instr. Pace U.; speaker on careers in accounting and bus. at local high schs., colls. Served with USAR, 1962. C.P.A., N.Y. Mem. Am. Inst. C.P.A.'s, N.Y. State Soc. C.P.A.'s, Nat. Assn. Accountants (nat. com. on research 1978-81, pres. Westchester chpt. 1977-78, Banner award 1978). Republican. Jewish. Home: 2 Pinecrest Rd Riverside CT 06878 Office: Magnetic Analysis Corp 535 S Fourth Ave Mount Vernon NY 10550

LEVINE, STANLEY WALTER, chem. co. exec.; b. Boston, Dec. 13, 1929; s. Bernard T. and Sonia (Spector) L.; B.S. in Journalism, Butler U., 1952; postgrad. Boston Coll., 1967; children—Robert, Douglas, Elizabeth. Nat. mktg. dir. Bates Mfg. Co., N.Y.C., 1965-68; mgmt. cons. Frederick Chusid Co., N.Y.C., 1971-76, Fashioncade, N.Y.C., 1968-71; pres. Internat. Coating & Chem. Co. Inc., Westport, Conn., 1976—. Mem. Republican Com. Fairfield County (Conn.). Served to capt. USAF, 1952-55. Decorated Korean Honor medal. Mem. Am. Mgmt. Assn. Chem. Week Contbrs., Pres.'s Club N.Y., Nat. Chem. Club, Sigma Delta Chi. Club: Harmonie N.Y. Contbr. articles to Nat. Chem. Weekly, Harpers. Home: 33 Hermit Ln Westport CT 06880 also 1801-1 E Frier Dr Phoenix AZ 85020 Office: 25 Sylvan Rd S Westport CT 06880

LEVINGSTON, ERNEST LEE, engring. co. exec.; b. Pineville, La., Nov. 7, 1921; s. Vernon Lee and Adele (Miller) L.; B.M.E., La. State U., 1960; m. Kathleen Bernice Bordelon, June 23, 1944; children—David Lewis, Jeanne Evelyn (Mrs. James Woltz), James Lee. Gen. foreman T. Miller & Sons, Lake Charles, La., 1939-42; sr. engr., sect. head Cities Service Refining Corp., Lake Charles, 1946-57;

group leader Bovay Engrs., Baton Rouge, 1957-59; chief engr. Augenstein Constrn. Co., Lake Charles, 1959-60; pres. Levingston Engrs., Inc., Lake Charles, 1961—. Mem. Lake Charles Planning and Zoning Commn., 1965-70; mem. adv. bd. Sowela Tech. Inst., 1969—; mem. Regional Export Expansion Council, 1969-70, chmn. code com., 1966—; mem. La. Bd. Commerce and Industry, 1978—; bd. dirs. Lake Charles Meml. Hosp. Served with USNR, 1942-46. Named Jaycee Boss of Year, 1972. Registered profl. engr., La., Tex., Miss., Ark., Tenn., Pa., Md., Del., N.J., D.C., Okla., Colo. Mem. La. Engring. Soc. (pres. 1967-68, state dir. 1967-68), Lake Charles C. of C. (dir. 1969-73). Baptist (deacon 1955—). Clubs: Lake Charles Quarter Horse (pres. 1966—), Rotary. Home: Levinwood Rd Lake Charles LA Office: PO Box 1865 Lake Charles LA 70601

LEVINS, FRANK JOSEPH, acct.; b. Los Angeles, Jan. 28, 1919; s. Francis Joseph and Amelia Bertha (Fischer) L.; student U. Colo., 1940-42, U. Calif., Irvine, 1972-75; m. Margaret Joan Hergert, July 31, 1962; 1 son, Frank J. Chmn. bd. Levins-Aikman, Inc., Long Beach, Calif., 1957—, Reward Ceramic Color Mfrs., Inc., Glen Burnie, Md., 1957-73; partner Dumont Aviation Assos., Long Beach, 1946-55; dir. Tempco Radiation Corp., Lee Deane Products, Inc., Cal Neva Corp. Mem. adv. council SBA, 1953-55. Served with U.S. Army, 1936-39, 43. Republican. Roman Catholic. Clubs: Masons, Shriners. Home: 3027 Via de Caballo Encinitos CA 92024 Office: 2689 St Louis Ave Long Beach CA 90806

LEVIS, THOMAS DENNIS, investment banker; b. N.Y.C., Aug. 19, 1937; s. William Lawrence and Mary Ann (Callahan) L.; student Coll. City N.Y., 1957-58; m. Angela Rice Healy, June 18, 1960; children—Mary Ann, Helen Kathlen, Patricia Marie, Christine Therese, Eileen Frances. Registered rep. First Investors Corp., N.Y.C., 1958-59; fin. prin. Investors Co., N.Y.C., 1959—; cons. Thermo Mold Med. Products subs. Hooker Chem. Co., 1974-76, S.R.C. Labs., Inc., 1975—, Automated Tech. Corp., 1969—, A.J. Sipin, Inc., 1976-77. Pres., St. Sebastians Home Sch. Assn., 1978—. Recipient Spl. Recognition award, Queens Children's Hosp., N.Y.C., 1976. Mem. Nat. Assn. Securities Dealers (dist. com. 12, 1977-79), Vets. 7th Regiment. Republican. Roman Catholic. Author: Your Money at Work - The Mutual Fund Story, 1962 (booklet). Home: 41-15 51 St Woodside NY 11377 Office: care Dominick & Dominick 90 Broad St New York NY 10004

LEVIT, VICTOR BERT, lawyer, fgn. govt. ofcl.; b. Singapore, Apr. 21, 1930 (parents Am. citizens); s. Bert W. and Thelma (Clumeck) L.; A.B. in Polit. Sci. with great distinction, Stanford, 1950, LL.B., 1952; m. Sherry Lynn Chamove, Feb. 25, 1962;, children—Carson Victor, Victoria Lynn. Admitted to Calif. bar, 1953; mng. partner firm Long & Levit, San Francisco, also Los Angeles, 1953-55, partner, 1955—; asso. and gen. legal counsel U.S. Jaycees, 1959-60, 59-61; guest lectr. Stanford Law Sch., 1958—; lectr. Haile Selassie I Law Sch. (Ethiopia), 1972-74; grader Calif. Bar Exam., 1956-61; hon. consul of Ethiopia, 1971-76, hon. vice dean San Francisco Consular Corps, 1975—. Del., San Francisco Municipal Conf., 1955-64, vice chmn., 1960, chmn., 1961-64; pres. San Francisco Young Republicans, 1955; mem. San Francisco Rep. County Central Com., 1956-63; asso. mem. Calif. Rep. Central Com., 1956-63, 71-73; bd. visitors Stanford Law Sch., 1969-75; bd. dirs. San Franciso Planning and Urban Renewal Assn., 1959-60, Medico, 1961-62, Nat. Found. Infantile Paralysis, 1958, Red Shield Youth Assn., Salvation Army, San Francisco, 1960-74; bd. dirs. San Francisco chpt. NCCJ, 1959—, chmn. No. Calif., 1962-64, 68-70, trustee nat. bd., 1964-76; bd. dirs., treas. San Francisco Assn. Mental Health, 1964-73, pres., 1968-71; adv. com. Jr. League San Francisco, 1971-74; bd. dirs. San Francisco Tb and Health Assn., 1962-70, treas., 1964, pres., 1965-67; trustee United Bay Area Crusade, 1966-73, chmn. communities div., 1967; trustee Ins. Forum San Francisco, 1971-74. Named Outstanding Young Man San Francisco by mng. editors San Francisco newspapers, 1960; one of Five Outstanding Young Men, Calif., 1961. Fellow Internat. Consular Acad.; mem. World Assn. Lawyers (chmn. com. rules of parliamentary procedure 1976—), Am. Bar Assn. (taxation com.; chmn. profl. liability com. of gen. practice sect.), San Francisco Bar Assn. (chmn. ins. com. 1962, 73-74, chmn. charter flight com. 1962-66, mem. grievance com.), Am. Bar Found., Am. Arbitration Assn. (arbitrator), San Francisco and Los Angeles Consular Corps, Consular Law Soc., San Francisco Jaycees (pres. 1958), U.S. Jaycees (exec. com. 1959-61), Jr. Chamber Internat. (life, senator), Calif. Scholarship Fedn., San Francisco C. of C. (dir.), Order of Coif, Phi Beta Kappa, Pi Sigma Alpha. Clubs: San Francisco Comml. (dir. 1967-69); Calif. Tennis; Concordia; Tiburon Peninsula; Commonwealth of Calif. (quar. chmn.). Author: Legal Malpractice, 1977. Note editor Stanford Law Rev., 1952-53. Contbr. articles legal jours. Home: 45 Beach Rd Belvedere CA 94920 Office: 465 California St San Francisco CA 94104

LEVITCH, HARRY HERMAN, retail exec.; b. Memphis, Dec. 24, 1918; s. Samuel Arthur and Lena (Feingold) L.; LL.B. cum laude, So. Law U. (now Memphis State U.), 1941; m. Frances Wagner, May 31, 1940; 1 son, Ronald Wagner. Mdse. mgr. Perel & Lowenstein, Inc., 18 yrs.; pres. Harry Levitch Jewelers, Inc., Memphis, 1955—, also treas.; lectr. on diamonds Memphis State U., Shelby State U. Pres., mem. exec. bd. Leo N. Levi Nat. Arthritis Hosp., Hot Springs Nat. Park, Ark.; del. Conf. on Am.'s Cities, Washington, Regional Conf. U.S. Fgn. Policy, Louisville, Conf. of U.S. Dept. State and So. Center for Internat. Studies; bd. dirs. B'nai B'rith Home and Hosp. for Aged, Memphis; adv. bd. dirs. Libertyland and Mid-South Fair Assn.; be. dirs. W. Tenn. chpt. March of Dimes, NCCJ; lt., spl. dept. sheriff Shelby County (Tenn.). Served with Judge Adv. Gen. Corps, USAAF, 19—. Recipient Outstanding Civic Service award City of Memphis; Outstanding Leadership award Christian Bros. Coll.; col. a.d.c. Gov. Tenn.; named Hon. citizen Tex., Ala., Ark., New Orleans. Mem. Memphis Area C. of C., Retail Jewelers of Am., Jewelers Vigilance Com., Jewelry Industry Council. Jewish. Clubs: B'nai B'rith (internat. v.p.), Rotary, Summit, Masons, Shriners. Home: 4972 Peg Ln Memphis TN 38117 Office: Harry Levitch Jewelers Inc 400 Perkins St Extended Memphis TN 38117

LEVITT, ARTHUR, JR., banker; b. Bklyn., Feb. 3, 1931; s. Arthur and Dorothy (Wolff) L.; B.A., Williams Coll., 1952; m. Marylin Blauner, June 12, 1955; children—Arthur III, Lauri. Asst. promotion dir. Time, Inc., N.Y.C., 1954-59; v.p., dir. Oppenheimer Industries, Inc., Kansas City, Mo., 1959-61; pres. Shearson Hayden Stone Inc., N.Y.C., 1961-77; trustee East N.Y. Savs. Bank, N.Y.C.; gov. Am. Stock Exchange, chmn., chief exec. officer, 1978—. Spl. cons. for edn. to Mayor of N.Y.C., 1963-64. Trustee Community Service Soc., Bklyn. Hosp., Poly Prep County Day Sch.; vice chmn. trustees Albany Coll. Served with USAF, 1952-54; maj. Res. Mem. Investment Bankers Assn., N.Y. Real Estate Bd., Sierra Club, Phi Beta Kappa, Phi Sigma Kappa. Clubs: Adirondack Mountain, Century Country, India House, Bond, Economic. Office: 86 Trinity Pl New York NY 10006*

LEVITT, EDWARD HURLEY, real estate exec.; b. Budapest, Hungary, June 8, 1906; s. Louis and Rosza (Pascovits) L.; came to U.S., 1916, naturalized, 1926; student W.Va. U., 1925-26; LL.B. cum laude, N.J. Sch. Law, 1929; m. Edna Mae Lankin, May 17, 1959; children—Rita E. Zeleny, Lois Monaco, Albert M. Pres., Sub-Div. Sales Corp., New Orleans, 1955-60; mng. dir. Crown Indsl. Co. Ltd., Brit. Colony Hong Kong, 1960-71; community mgr. Raldon Housing Corp., Lewisville, Tex., 1972-75; v.p. mktg. and sales Goldsmith Devel. Corp., Canyon Creek Ridge, Richardson, Tex., 1975; pres. Town Gate, Inc., Dallas, 1975-77; exec. dir. mktg. The Landing, Ft. Worth, 1977—; dir. sales and The Knolls Diman Fin. Corp., D.M. Venture II, Waterfall Crossing Condos, Richardson; v.p. Dondi Mktg. & Sales. Served with USNR, World War II. Mem. Mktg. Dirs. Dallas, Lewisville C. of C. Clubs: Masons (32 deg.), Shriners, Optimists; Royal, Hong Kong Jockey, Canyon Creek Country. Contbr. articles to profl. jours. Home: 10732 Sandpiper Ln Dallas TX 75230 Office: 7995 LBJ Freeway #118 Dallas TX 75251

LEVITT, MICHAEL HENRY, sewing machine co. exec.; b. Long Beach, N.Y., Dec. 14, 1943; s. Benjamin and Ruth (Zand) L.; B.A., Lehigh U., 1965; M.B.A., Columbia, 1971; m. Carole Pestronk, Sept. 10, 1967; children—Jason, Amy. With Kwasha Lipton Co., 1965-69, Gen. Electric Co., 1969-70; with Singer Co., 1971—, dir. planning, Syosset, N.Y., 1974-75, controller U.S. mktg., 1975-77, fin. v.p. U.S. sewing div., 1977-78, corp. staff dir. profit planning and fin. analysis, 1978—. Mem. Larchmont (N.Y.) Vol. Ambulance Corp., 1972-76, treas., dir., 1972-73; Republican county committeeman, 1974. Mem. Am. Mgmt. Assn., Nat. Assn. Accountants. Home: 3 Pheasant Run Larchmont NY 10538 Office: 8 Stamford Forum Stamford CT

LEVITZ, WILLIAM LAWRENCE, food service exec.; b. Albany, N.Y., June 8, 1943; s. Ira and Doris (Berger) L.; B.S. in Chem. Engring., Clarkson Coll., 1965; M.B.A. in Mktg., Columbia U., 1967; m. Susan Levitz; children—Jason Drew, Lee Jared. Supr. comml. intelligence center Allied Chem. Corp., Morristown, N.J., 1967-69; v.p. ops. Hobi, Inc. div. Bevis Industries, Lake Success, N.Y., 1969-70; co-founder, exec. v.p. Med. Analytics, N.Y.C., 1970-73; sr. v.p., gen. mgr. Horn & Hardart, N.Y.C., 1973—. Mem. Assn. Food Service Mgmt., Assn. M.B.A. Execs. Home: 160 E 38 St New York NY 10016 Office: 1163 Ave of Americas New York NY 10036

LEVY, ALAN DAVID, real estate exec.; b. St. Louis, July 19, 1938; s. I. Jack and Natalie (Yawitz) L.; grad. Sch. Real Estate, Washington U., 1960; m. Abby Jane Markowitz, May 12, 1968; children—Jennifer Lynn, Jacqueline Claire. Property mgr. Solon Gershman Inc., Realtors, Clayton, Mo., 1958-61; gen. mgr. Kodner Constrn. Co., St. Louis, 1961-63; regional mgr. Tishman Realty & Constrn. Co., Inc., N.Y.C., 1963-69, v.p., Los Angeles, 1969-77; exec. v.p., dir. Tishman West Mgmt. Corp., 1977—; dir. Metro-Plex Airline, Dallas; guest lectr. on real estate mgmt. to various forums. Mem. bldg. owners and mgrs. assns. Los Angeles (dir.), N.J. (co-founder, hon. dir.), Inst. Real Estate Mgmt. (certified property mgr.), Urban Land Inst., Internat. Council Shopping Centers. Contbr. articles on property mgmt. to trade jours. Home: 541 Loring Ave Los Angeles CA 90024 also 10960 Wilshire Blvd Los Angeles CA 90024

LEVY, CHARLES, JR., business exec.; b. Chgo., Apr. 27, 1913; s. Charles and Bertha (Friend) L.; student Wharton Sch., U. Pa., 1931-35; m. Ruth Doctoroff, Oct. 15, 1939; 1 dau., Barbara. Chmn. bd. dirs. Charles Levy Circulating Co., Chgo., 1961—. Bd. dirs. Jewish Fedn. Chgo., Michael Reese Hosp., Chgo., Park View Home, Temple Sholom, Mt. Sinai Med. Research, Lincoln Park Zool. Soc. Served with AUS, 1942-46. Decorated Bronze Star. Mem. Periodical Inst., Mid-Am. Periodical Assn., Council Periodical Distbrs. Clubs: Standard, Bryn Mawr Country, Carleton, Mid-Am. Office: Charles Levy Co 1200 N Branch St Chicago IL 60622

LEVY, CHARLES ROGER, financial adviser; b. Bklyn., May 23, 1951; s. Benjamin and Lilyan Rhoda (Meyerson) L.; stepson Bernard Belkin; B.S. in Econs., U. Pa., 1973; M.B.A. in Fin. with distinction, N.Y. U., 1974; m. Margaret A. Seider, Aug. 2, 1980. Fin. analyst NL Industries, Inc., N.Y.C., 1974-75, mgr. mro material control, Highstown, N.J., 1975-76, mgr. investment recovery, 1976-78; v.p. fin. and mktg. Hobe Cie Ltd., N.Y.C., 1978-80; asst. to mng. partner Cowen & Co., N.Y.C., 1980—; fin. cons. to various asset mgrs. Coordinator, South Phila. Tutorial Service, 1970-73; mgr. Urban Bus. Assistance Corp., N.Y.C., 1973-74. Mem. Assn. M.B.A.'s, Nat. Honor Soc., Beta Gamma Sigma. Jewish. Home: 500-213 High Point Dr Hartsdale NY 10530 Office: care Cowen & Co 1 Battery Park Plaza New York NY 10004

LEVY, EDWIN M., banker; b. Bklyn., July 17, 1925; student Columbia U., 1947-51; m. Mavis Yoss. With Clinton Trust Co., N.Y.C., 1946-54; trust officer Fedn. Bank & Trust Co., N.Y.C., 1959-63; mgr. investments L. F. Rothschild & Co., N.Y.C., 1963-65; sr. v.p. Sterling Nat. Bank, N.Y.C., 1965-74, Security Nat. Bank, Melville, N.Y., 1974; v.p. Fidelity Union Trust Co., Newark, 1975-76; pres., chief exec. officer, dir. Central State Bank, N.Y.C., 1976—. Home: 254 E 68th St New York NY 10021 Office: 24 W 48th St New York NY 10036

LEVY, HAROLD P., public relations cons.; b. Trinidad, Colo., Mar. 8, 1907; s. Phan and Fannie (Akerman) L.; A.B., U. Wash., 1929; m. Alice Klund, Sept. 8, 1938. Reporter, Seattle Union Record and Seattle Post-Intelligencer, 1926-29; reporter, editor Seattle Times, 1929-34; resident writer Henry St. Settlement, N.Y.C., 1934-35; dir. publicity Nat. Conf. Social Work, Columbus, Ohio, 1935-39; research asso. Russell Sage Found., N.Y.C., 1939-45; nat. dir. public relations Commn. Community Interrelations, N.Y.C., 1945-47; founder, pres. Harold P. Levy Public Relations, Los Angeles, 1947—; faculty U. Calif. Extension, 1947-49. Bd. dirs. tb and Health Assn. Los Angeles County, 1958-64, pres., 1962-63; bd. dirs. Calif. Orgn. Public Health Nursing, 1949-52. Mem. Public Relations Soc. Am. (nat. dir. 1954, chpt. dir. 1950-54), Sigma Delta Chi. Clubs: Chevy Chase Country, Athenaeum. Author: Public Relations for Social Agencies, 1956; Building a Popular Movement, 1944; A Study in Public Relations, 1943; contbr. articles to profl. jours. Address: 2980 Edgewick Rd Glendale CA 91206

LEVY, ROBERT I., packaging co. exec.; b. Chgo., July 21, 1912; s. Charles I. and Celia (Weinshenker) L.; student U. Ill., 1929-30; B.S. in Optometry, No. Ill. Coll., also O.D., 1933; m. Florence Greenblatt, Dec. 17, 1939; children—Maurice Lewis, Burt Samuel. Pres. optical co., 1933-46; with Milprint, 1947-53, Traver Corp., 1953, Container Corp. Am., 1953-56; pres. Allpak Co., Chgo., 1956—; spl. cons. Allied Paper Co., 1960—. Mem. City of Chgo. Welfare Council, 1963—; adv. council SBA; past v.p. Chgo. Met. Council on Alcoholism. Past trustee Packaging Found., Mich. State U., Lawrence Hall, Chgo.; bd. dirs. Chgo. Met. Council Alcoholism; bd. govs. Psychiat. Inst., Northwestern U.; bd. dirs. Cathedral Shelter; past trustee North Shore Congregation Israel; bd. dirs. Congregation Kol Ami. Recipient Man of Year award Bonds for Israel, 1973. Mem. A.I.M. (pres.'s council 1967-70). Mem. B'nai B'rith (local pres.). Home: 2800 Lake Shore Dr Chicago IL 60657 Office: 209 W Jackson Blvd Chicago IL 60606

LEVY, RONALD TRESTON, distbg. co. exec.; b. St. Louis, June 9, 1932; s. Isadore J. and Natalie (Yawitz) L.; B.J., U. Ill., 1954; m. Joyce Anne Hamburg, Aug. 15, 1954; children—Sharon Cay, Robert Jay, Mark Andrew. Research asst. Gardner Advt. Co., St. Louis, 1956-57, media research supr., 1957-59, dir. of media research, 1959-60; salesman Hamburg Distbg. Co., Champaign, Ill., 1960-62, asst. v.p., 1960-64, v.p., sec., 1964-66, pres., dir., 1966—; dir. Comml. Bank, Metropolex Helicopter Airways, Inc.; adviser Champaign-Urbana Liquor Commr., 1970-74, 79-80, Ill. Liquor Control Commn., 1972—; wine cons. U. Ill., 1966-76. Pres., PTA, Champaign, 1964-66; spl. bus. chmn. United Way, Champaign, 1970-71; v.p. B'nai B'rith, Champaign, 1966-68; bd. dirs. Playmakers, Founder, 1967, Nat. Acad. Arts, 1976; pres. Ill. liquor div. City of Hope, 1979—. Served to 1st lt. USAF, 1954-56; Korea. Recipient Spl. Commendation, United Way, 1970, Confraternita del Monferrato, Italian govt., 1973. Mem. Wholesale Liquor Distbrs. of Ill. (dir. 1970—, sec. 1975-76, pres. 1979—), Champaign-Urbana Beer Distbrs. Assn. (pres. 1968—), Wine and Spirits Wholesalers of Am. (dir. 1980—), Champaign C. of C., Nat. Beer Wholesalers of Am., Asso. Beer Distbrs. of Ill., Champaign-Urbana Advt. Club, U. Ill. Alumni Assn., Inter-Fraternity Alumni Assn. (pres. 1971), Zeta Beta Tau (trustee 1960-72, Nat. Service award 1972), Alpha Delta Sigma. Jewish. Clubs: Moose, Masons (32 deg.), Shriners, Elk, Champaign Country. Home: 5 O'Connor Court Champaign IL 61820 Office: 3104 Farber Dr Champaign IL 61820

LEVY, WILLARD LINZ, vocational apparel co. exec.; b. St. Louis, June 8, 1914; s. Mont M. and Elma (Linz) L.; ed. U. Pa., 1936; m. Alice Rudolph, Aug. 7, 1964; children—Elma Levy Sachar, Jill Levy Petzall. With Angelica Corp. (formerly Angelica Uniform Co.), St. Louis, 1934—, pres., 1946-73, 76—, chmn. bd., chief exec. officer, 1973—, also dir.; dir. First Nat. Bank St. Louis. Mem. St. Louis Joint Bd. Health and Hosps.; mem. president's council St. Louis U., gen. chmn. for 1978 Danforth Challenge campaign; nat. exec. bd., past nat. v.p. Am. Jewish Com. Bd. dirs. Jewish Hosp. St. Louis, St. Louis Symphony; trustee St. Louis Art Mus.; life dir., past pres. Jewish Fedn. St. Louis; bd. dirs. United Fund Greater St. Louis; adv. bd. St. Louis Minority Econ. Devel. Agy. Recipient Human Relations award Am. Jewish Com., 1968; named hon. col. Mo. Mem. Eliot Soc. of Washington U., Washington U. Faculty Center. Clubs: Westwood Country, Stadium, St. Louis, Press, Noonday (St. Louis); Cat Cay (Bahamas); Palm Bay (Miami, Fla.); Ocean Reef (Key Largo, Fla.). Office: Angelica Corp Suite 100 10176 Corporate Sq Saint Louis MO 63132*

LEWALSKI, THEODORE F., leather finishing co. exec.; b. Peabody, Mass., May 11, 1917; s. John and Veronica (Swiderski) L.; student North Shore Community Coll.; m. Lydia Michelazzo, Apr. 16, 1944; children—Wayne, Carolyn, Paul, Steven. Owner, operator Ted's Service Stations, Peabody, 1947-59; with Comet Leather Finishing Co., Inc., Peabody, 1959—, pres., treas., 1969—; with A&J Embossing Co., Peabody, 1959—, pres., treas., 1969—; corporator Warren Five Cents Savs. Bank, Peabody, 1974—. Mem. sign review bd. City of Peabody, 1975—. Served with AUS, 1942-46. Mem. Peabody C. of C. (dir., 1951—, pres., 1971-73), Amvets (founder), Am. Legion. K.C. Club: Italian American Citizens. Home: 45 Lynnfield St Peabody MA 01960 Office: 5th St Peabody Industrial Park Peabody MA 01960

LEWANDOWSKI, HENRY AUGUST, financial exec.; b. Staten Island, N.Y.; s. John Francis and Olga Martha (Dey) L.; student pub. schs., Staten Island, N.Y., Am. Inst. Banking, 1969-70. Asst. agt. Am. Express Internat. Banking Corp., 1969; foreign exchange and Euro currency dealer Allied Bank Internat., N.Y.C., 1971-74; asst. v.p., internat. money broker Savage Lane Ltd., N.Y.C., 1974-75; v.p., internat. money broker Tullett Riley Greenshields, Inc., N.Y.C., 1975-78; v.p. domestic and internat. money broker Garvin Guybutler, N.Y.C., 1978-80; sr. v.p. internat. and domestic money broker R. P. Martin, N.Y.C., 1980; partner Custom Furniture Co., 1969-71. Mem. Forex Assn. N. Am. Home: 36 Overlook Ave Staten Island NY 10304

LEWELLYN, JESS WILLIAM, mfg. co. exec.; b. Cedar Hill, Tex., Sept. 1, 1933; s. J.R. and Earlene (Burns) L.; student Arlington State Coll., 1958, Tex. Wesleyan Coll., 1953; B.S. in Mech. Engring., U. Tex. at Austin, 1960; m. Ann Truitt, Aug. 5, 1955; children—Debbie Jane, Jess William. Project engr. Tex. Instruments, Dallas, 1959-64; mgr. mfg. Beta Corp. subs. Koppers, Dallas, 1964-67; dir. mfg. Gulf Aerospace Corp., Houston, 1967-69; dir. mfg. Volkswagen Products Corp., Ft. Worth, 1969-76; gen. mgr. Royal Mfg. Co., Inc., Grand Prairie, Tex., 1976-77; pres. Metroplex Metal Products, Inc., Hurst, Tex., 1977—, Glass Center of Hurst, Inc., 1977—, Metroplex Glass Center, Inc., 1979—, Northridge Constrn., Inc., Arlington, Tex., 1980—. Fund raiser Abilene Christian Coll., 1967-68; elder Randol Mill Ch. of Christ. Served with AUS, 1953-55. Mem. Tex. Soc. Profl. Engrs., ASME. Republican. Club: Lions. Home: 1608 Northridge Dr Arlington TX 76012 Office: 3524 Bell Dr Hurst TX 76053

LEWIN, DEREK JOHN, internat. relocation mgmt. exec.; b. Stamford, Conn., Jan. 19, 1943; s. Helmut Louis and Elizabeth (Broder) L.; B.A., U. Colo., 1964; postgrad. Wharton Sch., U. Pa., 1976; children—Nancy, Daniel. Mgr., Hertz Corp., Denver, 1964-67; dir. corp. mktg. Homequity, Inc., Wilton, Conn., 1967-72; pres. Van Relco, Inc., Denver, 1973—. Mem. Employee Relocation Council. Home: Sugarloaf Mountain Boulder CO 80302 Office: 1515 Arapahoe Denver CO 80202

LEWIN, HENRI, hotel exec.; b. Potsdam, Germany, Feb. 20, 1923; s. David and Edith (Bernheim) L.; student pub. schs., Hotel and Restaurant Sch., 1937; m. Brigitta Oppenheimer, Feb. 25, 1951; children—Larry, Jerry, Barry. Banquet mgr. Fairmont Hotel, San Francisco, 1947-51, catering and banquet mgr., 1951-56, dir. catering and sales, 1956-64; asst. to gen. mgr., dir. catering San Francisco Hilton, 1964-66, gen. mgr., 1966-80; sr. v.p. Hilton Hotels Corp.; exec. v.p. Hilton Nev. div., exec. v.p. hotel/casino ops., gaming div., 1980—; owner El Mirando Hotel, Sacramento, 1963—. Program chmn. City of Hope-Man of Year, 1966; bd. dirs. Nat. Jewish Hosp., Better Bus. Bur. Decorated Knight grand cross Sovereign Order of Hospitallers of St. John Jerusalem, Knights of Malta; named Man of Year, Nat. Jewish Hosp. and Research Center, 1974; Man of Year, Am. Jewish Com., 1976. Mem. San Francisco Conv. and Visitors Bur. (pres.), Hotel Employers Assn. (dir.), San Francisco C. of C. (dir.), No. Calif. Hotel and Motel Assn. (dir.), Calif. Hotel and Motel Assn. (dir.), Downtown Assn. Mem. B'nai B'rith. Mem. editorial adv. bd. Hotel and Motel Mgmt. Home and Office: Las Vegas Hilton 3000 Paradise Rd Las Vegas NV 89109

LE WINE, JEROME MARTIN, lawyer; b. Phila., Feb. 9, 1940; s. Irwin and Rose (Baram) LeW.; B.Chem. Engring., Yale U., 1961; LL.B., Harvard U., 1964; children—David Winslow, Sarah Elizabeth. Admitted to N.Y. State bar, 1965; asso. firm Wickes, Riddell, Bloomer, Jacobi & McGuire, N.Y.C., 1964-68; mem. firm Spengler, Carlson, Gubar, Churchill & Brodsky, N.Y.C., 1968-76, Christy & Viener, N.Y.C., 1977—; dir., mem. exec. com. Sensormatic Electronics Corp., Deerfield Beach, Fla., 1974—. Bd. mgrs. Inwood House, N.Y.C., 1970—. Mem. Am. (Ross essay contest winner 1965), N.Y. State (civil rights com. 1967-70) bar assns., Assn. Bar City N.Y. (com. on fed. legis. 1966-69, corp. law 1974-77, children's rights 1974-77), Tau Beta Pi. Home: 1140 Fifth Ave New York City NY 10028 Office: 620 Fifth Ave New York City NY 10020

LEWINS, STEVEN, securities analyst, investment advisor; b. N.Y.C., Jan. 22, 1943; s. Bruno and Kaethe L.; B.A., Queens Coll., City U. N.Y., 1964, M.A., 1966, postgrad. in Bus. Adminstrn., 1969-72; cert. in Public Adminstrn., N.Y. CSC, N.Y. State U., 1967; m. Rayna Lee Kornreich, July 4, 1968; children—Shani Nicole, Scott Asher. Park ranger-historian Nat. Park Service, Statue of Liberty, N.Y.C., 1964-66; traffic asst. AT&T, White Plains, N.Y., 1966;

adminstrv. intern N.Y. State, Albany, 1966-67; sr. adminstrv. asst. to commr. N.Y. State Narcotics Addiction Control Commn., N.Y.C., 1967-69; analyst A.B. & Co., Value Line Investment Survey, Value Line Data Services, N.Y.C., 1969-71, asso. research dir., 1971-74, research dir., 1974, research dir., directing editor, 1974-80, v.p. Value Line Data Services, 1975-80; v.p. Arnold Bernhard & Co., 1975-80, dir., 1976-80, mem. exec. com., 1977-80; dir. Value Line Mut. Funds, 1976-80; pres. RayLux Assos., 1980-81, dir., 1980—; founder RayLux Fin. Service, 1980; v.p. Salomon Bros., 1981—, asso. research dir., mem. investment com., 1981—; partner Ray-Lux Products, 1978-80; advisor corp. disclosure com. SEC; registered investment advisor, 1980—; speaker securities analysis, econs., corp. disclosure. Mem. Croton Narcotics Guidance Council, Cortland Indsl. Com. Fellow Fin. Analyst Fedn.; mem. N.Y. Soc. Security Analysts (sr. security analyst, mem. membership com., mem. computer applications symposium), N.Y. Bus. Economists Council, Assn. Computer Users, Tau Delta Phi. Democrat. Club: Shattemuc. Author: Knowing Your Common Stocks. Home: 2 Charles W Briggs Rd Croton-on-Hudson NY 10520 Office: One New York Plaza New York NY 10004

LEWIS, CRAIG GRAHAM DAVID, pub. relations exec.; b. Dearborn, Mich., Jan. 25, 1930; s. Floyd B. and Elizabeth (Hickey) L.; A.B., UCLA, 1951; m. Karen Kerns, Oct. 23, 1954; children—Mark, Kern, Arden, Robin. Corr., McGraw-Hill, Inc., Washington, 1952-56; bur. mgr. Aviation Week mag., Dallas, 1957-59, Washington news editor, 1959-61; dep. dir. pub. affairs FAA, Washington, 1961-63; v.p. pub. relations Air Transport Assn., Washington, 1963-64; dir. pub. relations Martin Marietta Corp., N.Y.C., 1964-67; asso. Earl Newsom & Co., N.Y.C., 1967—, dir., 1968—, pres., 1975—. Mem. Nat. Press Club, Aviation/Space Writers Assn., Pub. Relations Soc. Am. Club: Univ. (N.Y.C.). Home: 6 Avon Rd New Rochelle NY 10804 Office: 10 E 53d St New York NY 10022

LEWIS, DALE PAUL, aerospace co. exec.; b. Detroit, Aug. 20, 1932; s. Floyd Berchard and Elizabeth Ann (Hickey) L.; A.A., Glendale Coll., 1958; postgrad. U.S. Coast Guard Acad., 1959; m. Ann Moody, Feb. 12, 1960; children—Leonard Jonathan, Kimberly Ann, Amanda Eliz, Christian Floyd. Regional dir. adminstrn. C-E-I-R, Beverly Hills, Calif., 1962-65; dir. EAI Applied Research and Computation Center, El Segundo, Calif., 1965-68; pres., chmn. ICX Group, 1968—; pres., chmn. bd. ICX Aviation, Inc., Washington, 1971—; pres., chief exec. officer, chmn. bd. Lewis Aircraft Corp., Washington, 1979—; cons. in field. Co-chmn. Fairfax County Budget and Econs. Group, McLean, Va. Served to lt. (j.g.) USCG, 1958-60. Recipient Pub. Service citation U.S. Dept. Commerce, 1977. Roman Catholic. Author: (with S. Schram) Dynamic Simulation of Distillation Column, 1968. Home: 6124 Ramshorn Dr McLean VA 22101 Office: 1101 Connecticut Ave NW Suite 800 Washington DC 20036

LEWIS, DAVID SLOAN, JR., corp. exec., engr.; b. North Augusta, S.C., July 6, 1917; s. David S. and Reuben (Walton) L.; student U. S.C.; B.S., Ga. Inst. Tech.; D.Sc. (hon.), Clarkson Coll. Tech., 1971; m. Dorothy Sharpe, Dec. 20, 1941; children—Susan, David Sloan III, Robert, Andrew. Aerodynamicist, Glenn L. Martin Co. Balt., 1939-46; chief aerodynamics McDonnell Douglas Corp., St. Louis, 1946-52, chief preliminary design, 1952-55, sales mgr., 1955-57, v.p., project mgr., 1957-60, sr. v.p. operations, 1960-61, exec. v.p., 1961-62, pres., 1962-70, also chmn. Douglas Aircraft Co. div.; chmn. bd., chief exec. officer Gen. Dynamics Corp., St. Louis, 1970—; dir. BankAm. Corp., Ralston Purina Co., Mead Corp. Alderman, Ferguson, Mo., 1951-54; trustee Washington U., St. Louis. Recipient Robert J. Collier trophy, 1975. Fellow AIAA; mem. Aerospace Industries Assn. (exec. com., bd. govs.), Nat. Acad. Engring. Episcopalian. Home: 10045 Litzsinger Rd Saint Louis MO 63124 Office: Gen Dynamics Corp Pierre Laclede Center Saint Louis MO 63105

LEWIS, DON, broadcasting, real estate, airline and resort exec.; b. Joliet, Ill., Feb. 10, 1938; s. I.H. and S. (Steinberg) L.; A.B., U. Ill. Pres. Sta. WHBI, N.Y.C., 1962—, Riverside Tower, N.Y.C., 1968—, Sta. WRNW, N.Y.C., 1969—, SST Airlines, N.Y.C., 1972—, Golden Rock Resort, N.A., 1976—. Office: 80 Riverside Dr New York NY 10024

LEWIS, ELLIOT L., real estate exec.; B.S., Boston U.; M.A. (Meville Jacoby fellow), Stanford U. Vice pres. econ. research orgn.; now exec. v.p. Sanford R. Goodkin Research Corp., Del Mar, Calif., Ft. Lauderdale, Fla., Los Angeles and Tucson, also pres. Leisure Systems, Inc. Dir. tourism seminars Econ. Devel. Adminstr., Dept. Commerce. Address: 2190 Carmel Valley Rd Del Mar CA 92014

LEWIS, ERNEST WILLIAM BELLEW, ret. investment corp. exec.; b. London, Eng., Nov. 15, 1909; s. Ernest and Daisy Frances (Brunker) L.; articled pupil, 1926-31; student Princeton, 1944-45; m. Lilian Patricia Rice, Aug. 25, 1932; children—Glenna Frederica Patricia (Mrs. Gerald H. Kean), Lorna Christina Roberta (Mrs. Michael R. Millbourn). Accountant, Imperial Airways Ltd., London, 1933-37; treasury rep. Westinghouse Electric Internat. Co., London, 1938-46, treas., N.Y.C., 1947-63, v.p. fin., 1963-70; v.p. fin. Westinghouse World Investment Corp., London, 1970-74, also Westinghouse Electric Europe N.V., Brussels; v.p., treas. overseas financing Eastern hemisphere Westinghouse Electric Corp., Pitts., 1970-74. Served with RAF, 1940-46. Decorated officer Order Brit. Empire. Fellow Inst. Chartered Accountants, Inst. Dirs. Club: Royal Automobile (London). Home: 22 Coleytown Rd Westport CT 06880 also 21 Eaton Mews S London SW 1 England

LEWIS, FLOYD WALLACE, electric utility exec.; b. Lincoln County, Miss., Sept. 23, 1925; s. Thomas Cassidy and Lizzie (Lofton) L.; B.B.A., Tulane U., 1945, LL.B., 1949; m. Jimmie Etoile Slawson, Dec. 27, 1949; children—Floyd Wallace, Gail, Julie, Ann, Carol, Michael Paul. Admitted to La. bar, 1949; with New Orleans Pub. Service, Inc., 1949-62, v.p., chief fin. officer, 1960-62; v.p. Ark. Power & Light Co., Little Rock, 1962-63, sr. v.p., 1963-67; exec. v.p., dir. La. Power & Light Co., New Orleans, 1967-68, pres., 1968-70, chief exec. officer, 1968-71, chmn. bd., 1970-72; pres. Middle South Utilities, Inc., 1970-79, chmn. bd., 1979—, also dir., chief exec. officer, 1972—; pres., dir. Middle South Services, Inc., New Orleans, 1970-75, chmn., chief exec. officer, 1975-76, 79—, chmn., 1976-79; pres., dir. Middle South Energy, Inc., 1974—; chmn. bd. System Fuels, Inc., 1972—; chmn. electric utility industry's Three Mile Island ad hoc nuclear oversight com., 1979—; dir. New Orleans br. Fed. Res. Bank, 1974-75, chmn., 1975; dir. Fed. Res. Bank of Atlanta, Breeder Reactor Corp., New Orleans Pub. Service, Inc., Ark. Power & Light Co., Ark.-Mo. Power Co., La. Power & Light Co., Miss. Power & Light Co.; mem. adv. com. Elec. Cos. Advt. Program, 1969-72, chmn., 1970-71; mem. electric utility adv. com. to Fed. Energy Adminstrn., 1975-77; chmn. Edison Electric Inst., 1976-77, exec. com., 1974-77, chmn. policy com. on nuclear power, 1974-75; mem. exec. com. Assn. Edison Illuminating Cos., 1973—; mem. coal advisory com. Dept. Interior, 1976-77. Deacon, Baptist Ch., 1950—; commr., mem. exec. com. Quapaw Area council Boy Scouts Am., 1964-66, v.p. Quapaw Area council, chmn. Pioneer dist., 1967, mem. exec. bd. New Orleans Area council, 1967—, v.p., 1970-74, 77—, pres., 1975-76, mem. bd. South Central region, 1976—; vice chmn. campaign United Fund, New Orleans, 1970, chmn., 1971; bd. dirs. New Orleans Symphony Soc., 1974, Pub. Affairs Research Council of La.; trustee New Orleans Bapt. Sem. Found., 1969—, pres., 1974-76; trustee New Orleans Bapt. Theol. Sem., 1954-62, 68-78, v.p., 1970-78; trustee Com. Econ. Devel., 1973—; bd. adminstrs. Tulane U., 1973—, bd. visitors, 1968-71, gov. Med. Center, 1969-73, vice chmn., 1969-71, chmn. alumni adv. council Grad. Sch. Bus., 1970-73; v.p. Internat. House, 1970; trustee Gulf South Research Inst.; trustee Com. Better La., 1975-76, sr. v.p., 1976-77, pres., 1977-78; bd. dirs. Electric Power Research Inst., 1977—, chmn., 1979—; chmn. parents council Furman U., 1978-79; mem. parents council Wake Forest U., 1979—. Served to ensign USNR, 1945-46. Recipient Outstanding Alumni award Tulane U., 1970; Silver Beaver, Silver Antelope awards Boy Scouts Am. Mem. Am., La. bar assns., Tulane Alumni Assn. (exec. com., treas. 1970), New Orleans Area C. of C. (v.p. 1970, dir. 1970-73, 78), Order of Coif, Beta Gamma Sigma, Omicron Delta Kappa, Beta Theta Pi, Phi Delta Phi. Home: 5557 Berkley Dr New Orleans LA 70114 Office: 225 Baronne St New Orleans LA 70161

LEWIS, GEORGE MCKOY, banker; b. Valley Mills, Tex., Aug. 3, 1902; s. Samuel Knight and Mary Rebecca (Barrett) L.; B.S., Tex. A. and M. U., 1924; M.B.A., Harvard U., 1927; Inst. Meat Packing fellow U. Chgo., 1929-30; m. Mary Gregory Bunting, Feb. 10, 1940. Mem. staff Dept. Agr., 1924-25; asst. dir. Bur. Bus. Research, U. Tex., 1927-29; dir. dept. mktg. Am. Meat Inst., Chgo., 1939-57, v.p., 1950-63; v.p. Am. Meat Inst. Found., 1957-63; vice chmn. bd. Jefferson State Bank, San Antonio, 1963—. Mem. S.A.R., Sons Republic Tex. Mason (Shriner). Clubs: Quadrangle, Union League, University, South Shore Country (Chgo.); Argyle (San Antonio). Home: 715 Wiltshire Ave San Antonio TX 78209 Office: Jefferson State Bank PO Box 5190 San Antonio TX 78284

LEWIS, GEORGE STEPHEN, architect; b. Boston, Dec. 7, 1908; s. William Joseph and Florence Ann (Whitehead) L.; evening student Lowell Inst., 1925-26, 40-41; grad. Boston Archtl. Center School (Harvard scholar in architecture), 1931, Sch. Architecture, Harvard, 1932; Rotch Traveling Fellow in Architecture, 1933-35; bus. courses Boston U., 1938-39, 42-43; cert. in city planning M.I.T., 1942; cert. in post war and regional planning Harvard U., 1942; cert. engr. sch. courses U.S. Army, 1957, 63; grad. Indsl. Coll. Armed Forces, 1954, 63, Command and Gen. Staff Coll., 1956; U.S. Dept. Def. certificate USN mgmt. course, 1964. Asso. firm Maginnis & Walsh, architects, 1925-31; architect Works Projects Bd. City of Boston, 1935-36; asso. firm John A. McPherson, Boston, 1936; architect Desmond & Lord, Boston, 1936-37, E.B. Badger & Sons Co., 1937-41, J.R. Worcester Co., 1941; mem. firm George Stephen Lewis & Assos., 1947—; architect-engr. Met. Dist. Commn., San. Bldg., Nahant, Mass., 1948-49; supervising architect State House renovations, Boston, 1948-51; pvt. practice, 1928-43; chief architect USN, Charlestown, Mass., 1953-65. Mem. planning com. traffic com., off-street parking, 1947-48; pres. Roslindale Bd. Trade, 1949-50, dir., 1948, 51-52, also chmn. civic awards com., 1957; chmn. judge, design, seal and slogan contest USN, 1957; chmn. Army Affiliation Program for Architects, Mass., 1949-51; chmn. architects group United Fund campaign, 1961-62; chmn. employees coop. com. for U.S. Navy, Boston Naval Shipyard, 1969-70; mem. nat. adv. com. Guidelines Program for Constrn. Materials, 1970, 71; mem. Archtl. Engring. Firms Contract Bd., 1971-73; rep. Nat. Archtl. Engring. Pub Affairs Conf., Washington, 1972-76. Served with AUS, 1943-46. Decorated Franco-Britain medal, Paris, 1960; chevalier de Merite, Paris, 1961, grand knight, 1962; Gt. Silver Medal of Paris, 1962; Armed Forces Res. medal U.S. Army, 1953, Hour Glass insignia, 1965; recipient award sustained outstanding service, certificate U.S. Navy Dept., 1968; Presdl. citation for service promoting Nat. Found. Arts and Humanities; Honor award, named to Hall of Fame, 1970; other awards and citations. Registered profl. architect, Mass., N.H., Minn., Vt., Maine, Conn., R.I., N.Y. Mem. AIA (Mass. chpt. del. to nat. convs. 1946, 48, 50, 51, 57-63, 65-80, mem. nat. com. on fed. agys. 1969, nat. legis. minuteman 1968-80, mem. New Eng. regional council 1942-80), Mass. Assn. Architects (chmn. publicity com. 1950-51, vice chmn. archtl., govtl. relations com. 1947-53, chmn. com. on Architects Research Center 1952), Boston Soc. Architects (profl. practice com. 1974-80, urban design com. 1980), Constrn. Specifications Inst. (nat. del. 1958, 73, tech. documents com. 1980, mem. nominating com. 1962, com. on documents 1965-66, alt. del. 1966, chmn. adv. com. for nat. chpt. affairs 1967, mem. competition evaluation panel Boston chpt. 1966-67, del. Tri-Regional Conf. 1967, 68, 69, 71, program com. Boston chpt. 1973-74, chmn. publicity com. Boston chpt. 1974-75, chpt. dir. 1978-80, 20 yr. pin. 1978; cert. of appreciation 1980), Boston Archtl. Center (dir. 1941-43, 48-50, chmn. library com. 1950-51, chmn. nominating. com. 1959-60), Inst. Contemporary Art, Greater Boston C. of C. (regional planning com. 1956, 57), Fed. Profl. Assn., Order of Lafayette (dir., nat. v.p., historian 1958-80), Mil. Order World Wars (marshal 1956, 57, chmn. com. on mem. listing 1958, treas. 1958-60, mem. award com. 1969, 70, mem. exec. com. 1972-80; sr. mem. award), Res. Officers Assn. (pres., nat. del.; del., mem. resolution com. Mass. Dept. conv. 1963, mem. nominating com. and army council 1974-77, dept. del. 1979, 80), Am. Legion, Archtl. Assn. Eng., Internat. Friendship League, UN (charter), Friend of Symphony Orch. (Boston). Clubs: Harvard (Boston); Mass. Republican. Contbr. articles to newspapers, profl. jours. Home: 1376 Commonwealth Ave Suite 21 Boston MA 02134 Office: George Stephen Lewis & Assos 294 Washington St Room 816 Boston MA 02108

LEWIS, GEORGE WITHROW, automobile distbg. co. exec.; b. Berwyn, Ill., May 13, 1929; s. George Edward and Katherine (Withrow) L.; A.B., Princeton U., 1951; M.B.A., Harvard U., 1955; m. Ellen Freer Baker, Sept. 14, 1963; children—George Baker, Martha Freer. With Ford Motor Co., 1955-62; cons. McKinsey & Co., N.Y.C., 1962-64; mng. dir. Rolls-Royce Motors Internat., Lyndhurst, N.J.; chmn. bd. Park Ward Motors, N.Y.C.; dir. Rolls-Royce Motors Ltd., Eng. Served to 1st lt. arty. U.S. Army, 1951-53. Mem. Automobile Importers of Am., Brit-Am. C. of C. (dir.). Clubs: Met., Princeton (N.Y.C.); Reform (London); Plainfield Country. Home: 50 Century Ln Watchung NJ 07060 Office: Lyndhurst Corp Center Lyndhurst NJ 07071

LEWIS, GORDON LEE, automobile service co. exec.; b. West Chester, Pa., Dec. 19, 1936; s. Harvey H. and Carrie Mae (Miller) L.; student Gen. Motors Tech. Schs., 1955-60; m. Dorothy E. Frisby, Oct. 6, 1956; children—Brenda Lee, Glenn Allan and Gail Alane (twins), Gordon Lee. Auto mechanic, parts mgr. Mostellers Chevrolet Co., West Chester, 1953-64; owner, operator, pres. Gordies Auto Service, Inc., West Chester, 1964—. Com. chmn. Pack 52, Cub Scouts, Chester County council Boy Scouts Am., 1972-74. Mem. adv. bd. Certified Automotive Repairman's Soc. Auto Mechanic Certification Program. Recipient awards Gen. Motors Parts Div., 1961-63. Mem. Automotive Service Councils Assn. (past state pres., state legis. chmn., nat. chmn. industry liaison com., local pres., Man of Year awards, nat. v.p.). Home: 1320 Sherwood Dr West Chester PA 19380 Office: 633 S Bolmar St West Chester PA 19380

LEWIS, GRADY WILLIAM, sporting goods co. exec.; b. Boyd, Tex., Mar. 25, 1917; s. William Edward and Martha Carol (Hamilton) L.; student Southwestern State U., Okla., 1935-37; B.S., U. Okla., 1940; m. Eleanor Maxine Steele, July 5, 1941; children—Rodney Steele, Ginger Lu. Statistician, Phillips Petroleum Co., Bartlesville, Okla., 1939-42, sales coordinator, 1946-47; profl. basketball player-coach, Detroit, Balt., St. Louis, 1947-50; with Converse Rubber Co. (became div. Eltra 1971), Chgo., 1950—, asst. sales mgr., 1952-56, gen. sales mgr., 1956-66, v.p., 1966-75, sr. v.p. Converse div., 1975—. Trustee, Naismith Basketball Hall of Fame; mem. honors com., chmn. nominating com. Basketball Hall of Fame. Served to lt. (j.g.) USNR, 1942-46. Elected to Helms Found. Hall of Fame, 1965; Nat. Assn. Intercollegiate Athletics Hall of Fame, 1975. Mem. Sporting Goods Mfg. Assn. (pres. 1967-69), Athletic Inst. (dir.), Fellowship of Christian Athletes, Athletic Goods Mfg. Assn. (dir.). Republican. Baptist. Home: 13062 N 80th Pl Scottsdale AZ 85260

LEWIS, HUNTER, fin. cons.; b. Dayton, Ohio, Oct. 13, 1947; s. Welbourne Walker and Emily (Spivey) L.; A.B. magna cum laude, Harvard U., 1969. Asst. to office of pres. Boston Co., 1970, v.p., 1972-73; pres. Boston Co. Fin. Strategies, Inc., 1971-72; founding partner Lewis, Bailey Assos., Inc., Washington, 1973—. Trustee Groton Sch., Am. Sch. Classical Studies in Athens. Served with USMC, 1969-70. Clubs: University, Knickerbocker (N.Y.C.); Union Boat (Boston). Contbr. articles to Atlantic Monthly, Washington Post, other mags. and newspapers; author monographs on specialized fin. subjects. Office: 600 New Hampshire Ave NW Washington DC 20037

LEWIS, JAMES LUTHER, savs. and loan exec.; b. Bridgeport, Ohio, Sept. 29, 1912; s. William Luther and Gwen (Evans) L.; grad. Mercersburg Acad., 1931; B.A., Yale, 1935; m. Mary Anne Glen, Oct. 26, 1943; children—William Luther II, Gwendolyn. Salesman, asst. sales dist. mgr. Chgo. Pneumatic Tool Co., 1935-43, asst. to pres., 1946-55; v.p., adminstrn. and sales, dir. Van Norman Industries, Inc., 1956; pres. Insuline Corp., 1956-58; v.p. corporate devel. Norris Thermador Corp., Los Angeles, 1959-65; pres., dir. Am. Savs. & Loan Assn., Reno, 1965—, Sierra Financial Corp., 1968—. Served to lt. USNR, 1943-46. Decorated Purple Heart, Presdl. Unit citation. Presbyn. Home: 7755 Lakeside Dr Reno NV 89511 Office: 67 W Liberty St Reno NV 89501

LEWIS, JAMES W., newspaper pub.; b. Hammond, Ind., Nov. 30, 1933; s. Jay P. and Lucille (Miller) L.; B.A., Purdue U., 1956; m. Emily Slaby, June 13, 1953; children—James Bruce, Brian Jay, Brent Allen. Gen. mgr. Hammond Pubs., The Times, 1956-75; pub. Auburn Pub. C., The Citizen, Auburn, N.Y., 1975-76; pub. Freeport (Ill.) Jour. Standard, Inc., 1977—. Bd. dirs. N.W. YMCA, Greater Downton Freeport. Mem. Am. Newspaper Pubs. Assn., Ill. Press Assn., Inland Daily Press Assn., Nat. Newspaper Assn., Freeport C. of C. (bd. dirs.). Office: 27 S State Freeport IL 61032

LEWIS, JOHN CALVIN, retirement community exec.; b. Monterey Park, Calif., May 10, 1932; s. Charles Simmons and Ruth Dickinson (Weed) L.; B.S. in Mktg., U. So. Calif., 1953; postgrad. in econs., U. N.Mex., 1956; m. Ann Taylor Rohlffs, Aug. 27, 1977; children—Jill P., John Calvin, Melissa B., Peter D., Carolyn B., Joy E. Founder, pres., chief exec. officer Western Propane, Inc., Portland, Oreg., 1960-76, now cons. engr.; pres., chief exec. officer, dir., chmn. exec. com. Panorama Corp. of Wash., Lacey, 1977—; gen. mgr. Panorama Partnership; pres. Lease-Line Ltd., Calvin Co. Adminstrv. and fin. bd. United 1st Methodist Chs.; active United for Wash., Young Ams. for Freedom; bd. trustees Oreg. Mus. Sci. and Industry. Served to lt. col., USAF, 1954-60. Mem. Nat. Liquified Petroleum Gas Assn. (Ancient Gasser award, H. Emerson Thomas Safety award 1970), Assn. of Wash. Bus., Res. Officers Assn. (life), Smithsonian Fellows (charter), Air Force Assn. (life), U. So. Calif. Alumni (life), Nat. Rifle Assn. (life), Aircraft Owners and Pilots Assn. (dir.), Olympia C. of C. (chmn. bus. and indsl. devel. com.), Lacey C. of C., Internat. Comanche Soc., Commanche 400 Assn. (chief), Nat. Search and Rescue Assn., Internat. Bush Pilots Assn., Wash. Pilots Assn., Oreg. Pilots Assn. (dir.), Seattle Aircraft Owners and Pilots Assn. (dir.), Izaak Walton League, Pierce Arrow Soc. Republican. Methodist. Clubs: Olympia Country and Golf, Tumwater Valley Athletic, Multnomah Athletic, Ranier, Baja Bush Pilots, Knife and Fork, Fort Lewis Officers, McChord AFB Officers, Panorama Supper, Order of Daedalians, Ducks Unltd. Home: 5047 Cooper Point Rd NW Olympia WA 98502 Office: 150 Circle Dr Lacey WA 98503

LEWIS, JOHN HARTLEY, distbg. co. exec.; b. Newton, Mass., July 5, 1918; s. Arthur Leon and Eva Caroline (Hilton) L.; A.B., Harvard U., 1940; postgrad. Chrysler Inst. Engring., 1941; m. Joan Harding, Mar. 28, 1967; children—Florence H., Duncan H., Fay E., Ann L., Arthur Leon II. With Lewis Shepard Co., Watertown, Mass., 1946-68, pres., 1965-68; with Lewis Shepard div. Hyster Co., Watertown and Waltham, Mass., 1968-71; partner, owner Lewis/Boyle Inc., Waltham, 1971-80, exec. v.p., 1978—; pres. Fidipisa, Inc., Boston, L/B Leasing, Waltham; treas. New Eng. Engines, Inc. Served with Ordnance Dept., U.S. Army, 1941-46. Mem. ASME, Material Handling Equipment Distbrs. Assn., Nat. Council Phys. Distbn. Mgmt. Congregationalist. Clubs: Harvard, Sakonnet Golf, Dedham Country and Polo, Mashantum Tennis, Waltham Tennis and Racquet, Norfolk Hunt, Kakonnet Golf. Home: 314 North St Medfield MA 01052 Office: Box 632 Waltham MA 02154

LEWIS, JOHN MILTON, cable TV co. exec.; b. nr. Slocomb, Ala., Mar. 29, 1931; s. Phil Truman and Vermell Beatrice (Avery) L.; grad. high sch.; m. Mary Lee Robledo, June 9, 1951; children—Janet Lee, Lee Michael. With Gulf Power Co., Panama City, Fla., 1949-56; self employed vehicle service co., Panama City, 1956-58; v.p., dir., Burnup & Sims, Inc., West Palm Beach, Fla., 1958-70; pres., dir. Wometco Cable TV, Inc., Miami, Fla., 1970—, Middlesex Cablevision, East Brunswick, N.J., 1971-80, Allstate Cablevision, Plainfield, N.J., 1971—, Plainfield Cablevision, 1971-80, LaFourche-Communications, Inc., Thibodaux, La., 1972—, St. Landry Cable TV, Inc., Opelousas, La., 1973—, Ausable Communications, Inc., Plattsburg, N.Y., 1972—, Alert Cable TV Okla., Paior, Alert Cable TV, Inc., Fort Benning, Ga., Alert Cable TV N.C., Garner, Miami Communications, Inc.; pres. Wometer Home Theatre Inc., N.Y.C., 1977-80; cons. in field. Democrat. Mason. Home: 8385 SW 143d St Miami FL 33158 Office: 316 N Miami Ave Miami FL 33128

LEWIS, KENNETH, shipping exec.; b. N.Y.C., Aug. 23, 1934; b. Nathaniel and Hana Evelyn (Kotler) L.; A.B., Princeton, 1955; J.D., Harvard, 1958; m. Carol Ann Schnitzer, Aug. 3, 1958; children—Scott, Laurence, Kathleen. Admitted to N.Y., Oreg. bars, 1959; law clk. to judge U.S. Dist. Ct., N.Y.C., 1958-59; asso. King, Miller, Anderson, Nash & Yerke, Portland, Oreg., 1959-61; gen. counsel Indsl. Air Products Co., Portland, 1961-63; v.p. to exec. v.p. Lasco Shipping Co., Portland, 1963-79, pres., 1979—. Mem. Port of Portland Commn., 1974—, treas., 1977, v.p., 1978, pres., 1979; trustee Lewis and Clark Coll., 1974—; mem. Portland Met. Area Boundary Commn., 1974-74, Portland Met. Mass. Transit Dist. Bd., 1973-74; pres. Portland Zool. Soc., 1970, World Affairs Council of Oreg., 1969. Mem. Am., Oreg. bar assns., Propeller Club U.S., Portland Steamship Operators Assn. Democrat. Jewish. Clubs: Multnomah Athletic, Univ., West Hills Racquet, Masons, City (Portland). Office: 3200 NW Yeon Ave Portland OR 97210

LEWIS, LARRY DWIGHT, steel co. exec.; b. Springfield, Mass., June 8, 1929; s. Richmond Lewis and Laura (Dwight) L.; B.A. in Geology, U. Ariz., 1952; m. Cynthia Hoye, Oct. 3, 1967; children by previous marriag—Lorinda, Charles C. II, Richmond Dwight. With

Charles C. Lewis Co., Springfield, 1952—, pres. 1971—; dir. Newspapers of New Eng. Inc., Am. Mut. Liability Ins. Co.; steel warehouse cons. U.S. Dept. Commerce, 1969-77. Served to lt. USAF, 1952-54. Mem. Am. Iron and Steel Inst., Steel Service Center Inst. Clubs: Met. (N.Y.C.); Algonquin (Boston); Jonathan (Los Angeles); Duquesne (Pitts.). Home: 69 Tunxis Village Farmington CT 06032 Office: POB 1810 Springfield MA 01101

LEWIS, LEONARD J., lawyer; b. Rexburg, Idaho, Jan. 10, 1923; s. Jack and Hannah (Beesley) L.; B.S., U. Utah, 1947; J.D., Stanford U., 1950; m. Lois Ann Cannon, Oct. 12, 1947; children—Leslie Ann, John, James C., Janet. Admitted to Utah bar, 1950; mem. firm Van Cott, Bagley, Cornwall & McCarthy, Salt Lake City, 1950—, pres., 1975—, now chmn.; dir. Fed. Resources Corp., S.W. Energy Corp., Temple St. Investment Co., Am. Ins. and Investment Corp., Centennial Devel. Co. Mem. bd. visitors Stanford U. Law Sch., 1979-80. Served with U.S. Army, 1941-43. Mem. Am. Bar Assn., Am. Trial Lawyers Assn., Salt Lake County Bar Assn., Internat. Bar Assn., Utah Bar. Assn. (past chmn. ct. adminstrv. com.). Clubs: Salt Lake Country, Alta, University, Hamilton Racquet. Home: 910 Donner Way Apt 701 Salt Lake City UT 84108 Office: 50 S Main St Suite 1600 Salt Lake City UT 84101

LEWIS, MALCOLM, engring. exec.; b. Glendale, Calif., Feb. 6, 1946; s. Patton and Claire (Pauli) L.; B.S. in Engring., Harvey Mudd Coll., Claremont, Calif., 1967; D.Engring., Dartmouth Coll., 1971; m. Virginia Anne Sheerin, Aug. 21, 1977. Mgr. product engring. Levitt Bldg. Systems, Inc., Battle Creek, Mich., 1971-72; asst. to pres. Levitt Constrn. Systems, Inc., Fountain Valley, Calif., 1972-74, pres., 1974-76; prin. Malcolm Lewis Assos., cons. engrs., Laguna Beach, Calif., 1976—, also pres. Design Computing Group, Inc., Laguna Beach, 1978—; cons. on energy and economics Calif. State Architect, 1976-78. Trustee, Harvey Mudd Coll., 1974—; bd. overseers Thayer Sch. Engring. of Dartmouth Coll., 1972-75. NDEA grad. fellow, 1967-71; registered profl. engr., Calif. Mem. AAAS, ASHRAE, Assn. Energy Engrs. Episcopalian. Office: 220 Park Ave Laguna Beach CA 92651

LEWIS, ORME, lawyer; b. Phoenix, Jan. 7, 1903; s. Ernest W. and Ethel (Orme) L.; LL.B., George Washington U., 1926; m. Barbara C. Smith; 1 son, Orme. Admitted to Ariz. bar, 1926, Calif. bar, 1931, U.S. Supreme Ct., 1955, D.C. bar, 1969; practice in Phoenix, 1926—; mem. firm Lewis and Roca; asst. sec. Dept. Interior, 1953-55. Mem. 9th Ariz. Legis. Fellow Am. Bar Assn.; mem. Ariz., Calif., Fed. bar assns. Clubs: Arizona, Paradise Valley Country (Phoenix); Metropolitan, Capitol Hill (Washington). Home: 97 Mountain Shadows W Scottsdale AZ 85253 Office: First Nat Bank Plaza Phoenix AZ 85003

LEWIS, PATRICIA ANN, legal intern; b. Miami Beach, Fla., Sept. 21, 1945; d. William Byron and Thelma Marie (Dauber) L.; B.A. with distinction in English, San Diego State U., 1975; J.D., Western State U., 1980. Paralegal asst. to William T. Tyson, Esq., San Diego, 1967-75, legal intern, office mgr., 1979—; owner, operator Ramona (Calif.) Lighting, Ltd., 1976-79. Mem. Save Our Heritage Orgn., John Paul Stevens Senate, Smithsonian Assos., Delta Theta Phi. Home: 1842 Clove St San Diego CA 92106 Office: 1660 Hotel Circle N Suite 222 San Diego CA 92108

LEWIS, PHILLIP MASON, JR., food wholesaler; b. Brunswick, County, Va., Aug. 8, 1943; s. Phillip Mason and Dora (Thompson) L.; B.S. in Bldg. Constrn., Va. Poly. Inst., Blacksburg, 1966; m. Cynthia Louise DeLoach, Dec. 25, 1965; children—Phillip Shawn, Leigh DeLoach. With Kroger Co., 1968-80, mgr. faculty engring., spl. assignment, Cin., 1974, mgr. facility engring. Mich., Livonia, 1974-80; dir. store engring. Hudson-Thompson, Montgomery, Ala., 1980; mgr. bldg. and office renovations Kroger Co., Cin., 1980—; guest lectr. Sch. Mktg., U. Ark., Little Rock. Adviser local Jr. Achievement, 1969-71; mem. Republican Nat. Com., 1974—. Served with C.E., AUS, 1966-68. Mem. Am. Mgmt. Assn., ASHRAE, Bus. Utility Users Rate Intervention Com., Mich. Mchts. Council and Assos., Am. Legion. Republican. Methodist. Home: 7225 Camargo Woods Dr Cincinnati OH 45243 Office: 1014 Vine St Cincinnati OH 45201

LEWIS, ROBERT WALTON, modeling agy. exec.; b. Albany, Ga., Oct. 22, 1952; s. John Earle and Mildred R. Lewis; student Gardner Webb Coll., 1971-72, U. S.C., 1972-73; m. Sadie Diane Pedersen. With Sears, Roebuck & Co., 1970-73; terr. mgr. Colonial Life and Accident Ins. Co., 1973-78; sales rep. Royal Bus. Machines Co., Kansas City, Mo., 1978-79; gen. mgr., founder Mille Lewis Sch. of Fashion Careers, Columbia, S.C., 1979—. Bd. dirs. local Explorer program Boy Scouts Am. Mem. Modeling Assn. Am., East Columbia Jaycees, Columbia C. of C. Democrat. Episcopalian. Clubs: Olde Grey Rugby (pres. 1979), Toastmasters (Columbia). Office: 3022 Millwood St Columbia SC 29205

LEWIS, ROY ROGERS, fast food service co. exec.; b. Dayton, Ohio, Jan. 13, 1944; s. Harold Harrell Hedges and Helen Louise (Mees); student Wilmington Coll., 1962-63, Central State U., 1965, Wittenburg U., 1970; m. Margo Ann Andersen, July 3, 1978; children by previous marriage—Roy Rogers, Andrew Cary, Jeffrey Paul, Brandi Eileen; 1 stepdau., Jennifer Marie Hansen. Various sales positions, 1963-65; mgr. Red Barn Systems, Inc., Washington, 1966-68; dept. mgr. Montgomery Ward & Co., Xenia, Ohio, 1968-69; assembly line worker Morris Bean & Co., Yellow Springs, Ohio, 1969; restaurant mgr. McDonalds Systems, Inc., Dayton, 1970-71, mktg. tng. coordinator, 1971, field cons., Ohio, 1972-73, prof. Hamburger U., Elk Grove, Ill., 1973, nat. audio-visual prodn. tech. advisor, 1973-74, sr. prof., 1974, asst. dean, 1975—, corp. tng. materials devel. mgr., 1979—. Dept. advisor Sinclair Community Coll., Dayton, 1971-72; advisor Patterson Coop. High Sch., Dayton, 1971-72; v.p. Young Reps., 1971-72; mem. Zoning Bd. Appeals, Xenia, 1971-72; pres. Homeowner Assn., 1978-80. Served with USNG, 1963-69. Republican. Quaker. Home: 1623 Cornell Pl Hoffman Estates IL 60194 Office: McDonald's Plaza Oak Brook IL 60154

LEWIS, SHERMAN RICHARD, JR., investment banker; b. Ottawa, Ill., Dec. 11, 1936; s. Sherman Richard and Audrey Julia (Rusteen) L.; A.B., Northwestern U., 1958; M.B.A., U. Chgo., 1964; m. Dorothy Marie Downie, Sept. 9, 1967; children—Thomas, Catherine, Elizabeth, Michael. With investment dept. Am. Nat. Bank and Trust Co., Chgo., 1961-64; v.p. Halsey, Stuart & Co., N.Y.C., 1964-70, v.p. in charge N.Y. corp. fin. dept., 1970-73; partner Loeb, Rhoades & Co., N.Y.C., 1974-76, partner in charge corp. fin. dept., 1975-76, exec. v.p., dir., 1976-77, pres., chief exec. officer, 1977, vice chmn., office of chief exec. Loeb Rhoades, Hornblower & Co., 1978-79; pres. Shearson Loeb Rhoades Inc., N.Y.C., 1979—. Served as commd. officer USMC, 1958-61. Mem. N.Y. Soc. Security Analysts. Clubs: Bond, India House, Ridgewood Country, Univ. Home: 623 Belmont Rd Ridgewood NJ 07450 Office: 14 Wall St New York NY 10005

LEWIS, WILLIAM EMIL, mgmt. cons., engr.; b. Omaha, June 29, 1927; s. Emil W. and Kathryn M. (Babic) L.; B.S.M.E., U. Nebr., 1944; postgrad. U. Wyo., 1945, Am. Inst. Banking, 1947; m. Dorothy Elizabeth Forsythe, June 29, 1963. Asst. controller Live Stock Nat. Bank, Omaha, 1942-43; spl. agt. U.S. Treasury Dept., Kansas City, Mo., 1947-48; accountant, auditor R.F. Hassman, C.P.A.'s, Omaha, 1948-49; West coast gen. mgr. Kelsey-Hayes Co., Los Angeles, 1949-62; prodn. mgr. Norris-Thermador Corp., Los Angeles, 1962-63; gen. mgr. Star div. Divco-Wayne Industries, Inc., Santa Fe Springs, Calif., 1963-65; sr. v.p., corporate gen. mgr. Kit Mfg. Co., Long Beach, Calif., 1965-72, exec. v.p., 1972-73, also dir.; pres. Viking Homes div. Ludlow Corp., Anaheim, Calif., 1974-76; sr. v.p. RTL, Inc., Paramount, Calif., 1976; asst. pres. Advance Engring., Gardena, Calif., 1977—; self-employed profl. cons. engr., 1978; v.p. mfg. Divajex, Inc., Tustin, Calif., 1979—. Served with AUS, 1944-46. Registered profl. engr., Calif., Can.; certified mfg. engr. Mem. Nat., Calif. socs. profl. engrs., Soc. Mfg. Engrs. Republican. Mem. Christian Ch. Home: 2275 W 25th St SP 209 San Pedro CA 90732

LEYDECKER, BYRON W., banker; b. Oakland, Calif., Aug. 28, 1927; s. Theo O. and Ruby (Forderer) L.; B.A. in Econs., Stanford, 1950; m. Mary Elizabeth Kraft, Sept. 16, 1951 (div. Mar. 1969); children—Caroline, John, David; m. 2d, Patricia Lombard, Apr. 2, 1969. Securities salesman Brush Slocomb & Co., San Francisco, 1952-53; v.p. Crocker Citizen's Nat. Bank, San Francisco, 1953-62; pres., chief exec. officer Redwood Bank, San Rafael, Calif., 1962-74, chmn. bd., chief exec. officer, San Francisco, 1974—; pres. Redwood Bancorp, 1973—. Mem. Marin County (Calif.) Bd. Suprs., 1963-66, chmn., 1966; mem. bd. United Bay Area Crusade, 1968-70, Bay Area Social Planning Council, 1967-73. Served with USNR, 1945-46, AUS, 1950-52. Mem. Am. Mgmt. Assn., Pres. Assn., Internat. Motor Sports Assn., Sports Car Club Am. (prodn. class champion San Francisco region 1977). Democrat. Home: 50 Mt Tiburon Tiburon CA 94920 Office: 735 Montgomery St San Francisco CA 94111

LI, LYMAN GOON, architect; b. China, Aug. 17, 1925; s. Wah Sing Lee and Fong Shee; came to U.S., 1939, naturalized, 1963; B.S. in Architecture, Heald Coll., 1948; postgrad. U. Calif. at San Francisco, 1948-52, U. Va., 1953-54, George Washington U., 1956; m. Betty L. Ng, Aug. 4, 1956; children—Berdine, Gary, Carl. Draftsman, Ryan & Lee, San Francisco, 1948-52; asst. job capt. Faulkner, Kinsbury & Stenhouse, Washington, 1952-56; asst. designer Vincent G. Kling, Phila., 1956-57; with Meyer & Evers, San Francisco, 1957, Wurster, Bernardi & Emmons. San Francisco, 1958; asso. architect with Paul A. Ryan, San Francisco, 1958-68; project architect Robert B. Liles, Inc., architects and engrs., Marin County, Calif., 1968—. Mem. Chinatown tech. adv. com. San Francisco Planning Commn., 1964-65. Served with AUS, 1943-45. Decorated Bronze Star, Purple Heart. Registered architect, D.C., Calif. Mem. AIA, Internat. Platform Assn. Prin. works include Convent of Sacred Heart Sch., San Francisco and Menlo Park, Calif., St. Finn Barr Sch., San Francisco, Carmelite Monastery, San Jose, Calif., St. Mary's Cathedral, San Francisco, Country Club Plaza, Sacramento, Country Club Shopping Center, Sacramento, Montgomery Ward stores, Sacramento and Sunnyvale. Home: 501 Park Way Mill Valley CA 94941 Office: 200 Tamal Vista Suite 525 Corte Madera CA 94925

LIAKOS, DENNIS F., lawyer, cons.; b. Boston, Oct. 14, 1940; s. E. Frederic and Anne T. Liakos; J.D., Suffolk U., 1968; m. Brenda Walkenstein, Mar. 8, 1965; children—Victoria Alexandra, D. Christian. Project mgr. E Street Assos., Boston, 1963-65, project dir. Boston, 1965-68; admitted to Mass. bar; partner firm Yanakakis-Kindregan, Maleson & Liakos, Boston, 1968-72, Kirk, Liakos, Burkinshaw & Richardson, Boston, 1972-78; pres. Advanced Consulting, Norwood, Mass., 1977—. Trustee, Farr Acad.; mem. airport com. Town of Concord (Mass.); mem. adv. bd. SBA. Served with USMC. Mem. Mass. Bar Assn., Middlesex Bar Assn., Ancient and Honorable Arty. Co. Republican. Roman Catholic. Home: 70 Philip Farm Concord MA 01742 Office: Advanced Consulting 51 Morgan Dr Norwood MA 02620

LIAO, HSIANG PENG, chemist; b. Nanping, China, May 4, 1924; s. Samuel and Chung (Chang) L.; B.S., Fukien Christian U., 1945; Ph.D., Northwestern U., 1952; m. Chen Hansing, Jan. 6, 1950; children—Jacob, Wesla Mildred, Michael Lawrence. Came to U.S., 1948, naturalized, 1953. Chemist, Standard Oil Co., Ind., 1952-60; research chemist FMC Corp., Balt., 1960—; lectr. Fukien Christian U., 1945-47; grad. seminar lectr. Johns Hopkins, W.Va. U., 1961. Mem. AAAS, Am. Chem. Soc. Sigma Xi, Alpha Chi Sigma, Phi Lamda Upsilon. Methodist. Patentee in field. Home: 260 Fisher Pl Princeton NJ 08540 Office: FMC Corp PO Box 8 Princeton NJ 08540

LIBERMAN, MICHAEL IRA, flag mfg. co. exec.; N.Y.C., Sept. 16, 1944; s. Abraham and Esther Norma (Tabb) L.; B.S. in Econs., U. Pa., 1966, M.S., 1967; m. Eleanor Toby Levine, Mar. 27, 1976; 1 son, Alexander Jean. children by previous marriage—Debra Sue, Scott Evan. Mem. audit staff, mgmt. cons. Touche, Ross & Co., accountants, N.Y.C., 1967-69; treas. Valley Forge Flag Co. Inc., N.Y.C., 1969-75, pres., chmn. bd., 1975—; chmn. bd. Anderson Assos., N.Y.C., 1979—; chmn. bd. Valley Forge Fabrics Inc., N.Y.C., 1977—. Mem. Am. Inst. C.P.A.'s N.Y. State Soc. C.P.A.'s, Beta Alpha Psi. Jewish. Home: Office: Valley Forge Flag Co Inc One Rockefeller Plaza New York NY 10020

LICALZI, ROBERT JOHN, banker; b. N.Y.C., Oct. 10, 1952; s. Santo Peter and Anne (Cafaro) L.; B.A. in Econs., Queens Coll., 1974; M.B.A. in Fin., Baruch Coll., CUNY, 1976. Contract specialist Dept. Def., Garden City, N.Y., 1974-76; fin. analyst internat. banking group Citibank, N.Y.C., 1976-79; asst. v.p., controller Capital Markets Inc., 1979—. Active Vol. Services for Children, Inc. Mem. Nat. Assn. Accts. Home: 47 Bell St Valley Stream NY 11580 Office: 5 Hanover Sq New York NY 10043

LICARI, PETER JOSEPH, health care co. exec.; b. Phila., Oct. 13, 1948; s. Joseph Salvatore and Jean (Rotella) L.; student Community Coll. Phila., 1966-68; B.S. in Bus. Adminstrn., Pa. State U., 1968-70; m. Susan Ference, Aug. 14, 1971; 1 son, Peter George. Trainee, Acme Markets, 1970; unit mgr. St. Christophers Childrens Hosp., Phila., 1970-72; nursing home adminstr. Geriatrics Inc., Phila., 1972-73; regional dir. Am. Med. Affiliates Inc., St. Petersburg, Fla., 1973—, Montgomery, Ala., 1977—, asst. v.p. ops., 1974—; nursing homes lobbyist Fla. Legislature, 1974-75. Mem. Fla. Ombudsman Com., 1980—. Mem. Am. Coll. Nursing Home Adminstrs., Fla. Nursing Home Assn. (sec.-treas. polit. action com., mem. govt. relations com. 1975-77, chmn. legis. com. 1974-75), Ala. Nursing Home Assn., Suncoast C. of C. Clubs: Lake Seminole Tennis and Country; Photography. Home: 9287 119th Ave N Largo FL 33543 Office: 3420 21st Ave S Saint Petersburg FL 33711

LICARI, SAM JOSEPH, retail cons.; b. Ilion, N.Y., Apr. 9, 1947; s. Louis Charles and Lucy Ann L.; A.A., SUNY, Cobleskill; B.S., SUNY, Albany, M.B.A., 1975; m. Ann Marie Markwardt, Apr. 16, 1977. Mktg. specialist Dairy ICA Coop., Utica, N.Y., 1971-73; grad. asst. SUNY at Albany, 1973-75; retail grocery mgr. Louis Clicari Foodland Inc., Fort Plain/Dodgeville, N.Y., 1975-78, treas., retail cons., 1978—; treas. Developmental Estates, Inc. Serves as officer USAR N.G., 1970—. Mem. Am. Mgmt. Assn., Assn. M.B.A. Execs., Militia Assn. N.Y. Address: 7 Gibson St Dodgeville NY 13329

LICHOK, STEPHEN JOSEPH, former insulation co. exec.; b. Natrona Heights, Pa., Oct. 20, 1927; s. Stephen J. and Amelia M. (Treskon) L.; student Chgo. Tech. Coll., 1949; m. Patricia L. Ross, Nov. 15, 1951; children—Susan Lichok Ambrosino, Stephen A., Michael R. Dir. purchasing Kettler Bros., Inc., Washington, 1962-68; sales and credit mgr. Takoma Insulators, Inc., Silver Spring, Md., 1968-72; mgr. Asbestos Covering and Roofing Co., Inc., Frederick, Md., 1972-74; pres. Frederick Insulation Co., Inc., 1974-80; ret., 1980. Served with U.S. Army, 1946-47. Mem. Nat. Assn. Home Builders, Republican. Roman Catholic. Clubs: Holly Hills Country, Moose. Home: 8114 E Wood Dr Scottsdale AZ 85260

LICHTENSTEIN, GAYLE WEST, banker; b. Lexington, Ky., July 7, 1926; s. Philip F. and Grace (Ashworth) L.; B.S. in Commerce, St. Louis U., 1949. Asst. nat. bank examiner, 1949-52; asst. v.p. Am. Nat. Bank, St. Louis, 1952-53, chmn., 1974—; v.p. Brentwood Bank, St. Louis, 1953-57, pres., 1957-75, chmn., 1975-77; chmn. City Bank, St. Louis, 1974—; dir. LLC Corp. Served with inf. U.S. Army, 1946-47. Mem. Mo. Bankers Assn., St. Louis Bankers, Robert Morris Assos. (life). Republican. Baptist. Clubs: Mo. Athletic, Racquet, Woodland Yacht. Home: 4954 Lindell Blvd Saint Louis MO 63108 Office: Am Nat Bank 4625 Lindell Blvd Saint Louis MO 63108

LICHTENSTEIN, MORRIS SPITZ, retail exec.; b. Milw., Sept. 8, 1917; s. Emil Alexander and Freda (Spitz) L.; B.A., U. Wash., 1937, M.A., 1940; postgrad. U. Chgo., 1938-39; m. Margaret Evelyn Clarke, Apr. 11, 1948; 1 stepson, James Clarke Roddey. With Lichtenstein's, Inc., Corpus Christi, 1942-77, sec.-treas., controller, 1952-75, exec. v.p., 1972-77; v.p. fin. Battelstein's, Inc., subs. Lichtenstein's, Houston, 1977-78; v.p. fin. planning Frost Bros., Inc., San Antonio, 1978—; v.p., dir. World Wide Travel of Tex., Inc., Corpus Christi, 1963—. Bd. dirs. United Way of Coastal Bend, Corpus Christi, 1970-77, treas., 1974-75; bd. dirs. Corpus Christi Symphony Soc., 1970-78. Jewish. Club: Rotary (San Antonio). Home: 3724 Morning Mist San Antonio TX 78230 Office: 217 E Houston St San Antonio TX 78205

LICHTIGMAN, CHARLES STEPHEN, real estate devel. co. exec.; b. N.Y.C., Oct. 9, 1941; s. Isidore Morris and Jean (Rubin) L.; LL.B., Yale, 1966; A.B., U. Mich., 1962; m. Anne Lambert, Jan. 27, 1968; children—Edward Douglas, Becky Anne. Admitted to N.Y. State bar, 1967; mem. acquisitions and planning staff Continental Can Corp., N.Y.C., 1966-69; asst. to pres. Sun Chem. Co., N.Y.C., 1969-72; v.p. comml. indsl. devel. and sales, also housing and new ventures ITT Community Devel. Corp., Palm Coast, Fla., N.Y.C. and Miami, 1972-78; pres. Republic Funding Corp. Fla., Orlando, 1979—; officer, dir. Republic Funding Corp. (N.Y.), Charles Wayne Co., Riverwood Partners, Republic Funding Corp. (Del.), Birch Hill Water Co., Edward Douglas Realty Holdings Ltd. Served with USAR, 1967. Mem. Urban Land Inst., Internt. Council Shopping Center. Club: Yale of N.Y. Home: 22 Riverridge Trail Ormond Beach FL 32074 Office: 201 E Pine St Orlando FL 32801

LICKISS, EDWIN EMMETT, fin. planner; b. Oakland, Calif., Sept. 19, 1947; s. Edwin E. and Norma A. (Hayden) L.; B.A., Calif. State U., 1970, M.A., 1972; Cert. in Fin. Planner, Coll. for Fin. Planning, 1979; m. Marilyn L. Whelton, Sept. 13, 1969; children—Jennifer, Michael, Thomas. Tchr. for deaf Concord, Calif., 1971-74; prin., gen. agt. life and disability ins. Orinda (Calif.) Fin. Group, 1974—; registered securities rep., 1976—. Bd. dirs. San Ramon (Calif.) Home Owners Assn., 1976-77; mem. Parish Council, St. Joan of Arc Ch., San Ramon, 1980—; vol. interpretor for deaf, 1971—. Mem. Nat. Assn. Securities Dealers, Internat. Assn. Fin. Planners, Inst. Cert. Fin. Planners. Christian Ch. Club: Commonwealth. Office: 43 Avenida de Orinda Orinda CA 94563

LICKSON, CHARLES PETER, lawyer; b. N.Y.C., May 16, 1939; s. Leonard L. and Maxine (Pritzker) L.; B.A., Johns Hopkins, 1961; J.D., Georgetown U., 1964; m. Judith M. Epstein, Sept. 3, 1961; children—Laura, Karen. Admitted to Conn. bar, 1968, since practiced in Stamford; law clk. to Alexander Holtzoff, U.S. Dist. Judge, Washington, 1964-65; atty., asst. sec. Bunker-Ramo Corp., 1967-68; sec., gen. counsel Tymponics Corp., Energy Systems, Inc., Patent Am. Corp. PAC European, Ltd., Convair Investments Ltd., Cottell Ultrasonic Combustion Corp., Triton Energy & Devel. Corp., Ultra Internat. S.A., Sterifilter Corp. Mem. Com. for Performing Arts, Inc., Stamford, 1968—, State Opera, Inc., 1970—; dir. West Main St. Community Center, Stamford, 1970-72, QUEST, 1971-72; chief Aux. Police Corps, Stamford, 1970-73; dep. dir. Stamford Emergency Service, 1971-75; dep. dir. Darien CD, 1975-77. Served to capt. AUS, 1965-67. Mem. Am. Bar Assn., Conn. Bar Assn., World Peace Through Law Center, Stamford Bar Assn., Empowerment Orgn. Stamford, Conn. Jr. C. of C. (gen. counsel 1969), Alpha Psi Omega, Pi Delta Epsilon, Phi Sigma Alpha, Phi Epsilon Pi. Clubs: Landmark (Stamford); Curzon House (London, Eng.). Contbr. articles to profl. jours. Office: 520 West Ave Norwalk CT 06850

LIDDLE, GORDON MCALLISTER, diamond tool mfg. co. exec.; b. Provo, Utah, Dec. 12, 1940; s. Parley H. and Clara Irene (McAllister) L.; student So. Utah State U., 1959-60; B.S., Utah State U., 1966; M.B.A., U. Utah, 1967; m. Linda Gayle Kirk, Dec. 18, 1964; children—Deborah Ann, Jennifer Irene, David Gordon. Asst. mgr. Christensen Diamond Services, 1967-68, gen. mgr., 1968-69; dir. finance, treas. Christensen Diamond Products Co., Salt Lake City, 1969—; v.p. fin., dir. Christensen Inc., 1974-79, sr. v.p., 1979—; pres. Christensen Diamond Tools, Inc., 1979—; partner Liddle Farms; v.p., dir. Trustco, Inc.; dir. Boyco Inc. Investment Co. Bd. dirs. Utah Safety Council. Republican. Mem. Ch. of Jesus Christ of Latter-day Saints. Club: University (Salt Lake City). Office: 4446 W 1730 S Salt Lake City UT 84118

LIDDY, RICHARD ANGIER, ins. co. exec.; b. Fairfield, Iowa, Sept. 3, 1935; s. Lucius B. and Ruth A. (Angier) L.; B.S., Iowa State U., 1957; postgrad. U. Conn., 1958-59; m. Joanne Sjostrom, July 3, 1957; children—Jeanne, Robert, James. With Conn. Gen. Ins. Corp., Bloomfield, Conn., 1957—, pension cons., 1957-65, reins. sales mgr., 1965-71, pres. broker/dealer securities, 1971-74, regional v.p., 1974-77, v.p. charge brokerage, 1977-80, v.p. mktg., 1980—; dir. CG Equity Sales Co., Investment Co. Inst., Washington. Corporator, Hartford Sem. Found. Served with AUS, 1958. C.L.U. Mem. Life Ins. Mgmt. and Research Assn. (chmn. equity products com. 1972, 73, mem. brokerage com. 1979). Republican. Universalist. Club: Hartford Golf. Home: 423 Mountain Rd West Hartford CT 06107 Office: Conn Gen Ins Corp Hartford CT 06152

LIEBENOW, LARRY ALBERT, fiber and textile co. exec.; b. Hillsboro, Oreg., Dec. 7, 1943; s. John Albert and Esther Christine L.; B.A., Willamette U., 1966; M.B.A., Cornell U., 1968; m. Kathleen Mae Bendix, May 28, 1966; children—Danika, Anna Petra, Valeska. Dir. fin. Dalmine Siderca, Buenos Aires, Argentina, 1968-71; exec. v.p. Grupo Pliana, S.A., Industrias Polifil, S.A., Mexico City, 1971—, also dir., mem. exec. com.; pres. Texel S.A. de C.V.; vice chmn. bd. Formfit Rogers, Inc., N.Y.C. Chmn. Oreg. Republican Coll. League, 1965-66; vice chmn. internat. bd. dirs. Internat. Walther League, 1966-68. Mem. Am. C. of C. Mexico City. Republican. Lutheran. Clubs: Univ., Industriales (Mexico City). Office: Palmas 555-9 Mexico 10 DF Mexico

LIEBERMAN, CALVIN, mfg. co. exec.; b. Toledo, Apr. 3, 1912; s. Jacob E. and Jennie Rose (Berman) L.; B.B.A. cum laude, U. Toledo, 1934; m. Sadie, June 16, 1935; children—Karen Jean, Bruce Irwin.

Vice-pres. Kasle Iron and Metal Co., 1937-47; pres. Ace Steel Baling, Toledo, 1947-76; v.p. Ace Steel div. Magnimet Corp., Toledo, 1977—. Sec., v.p. Temple Bnai Israel, 1954-58; bd. dirs. Toledo Hearing and Speech Center, 1974-80. Mem. ASTM, Inst. Scrap Iron and Steel (v.p.), Ohio C. of C., Am. Public Works Assn. Homee 2818 Meadowwood Dr Toledo OH 43606 Office: Box 7329 RC Station Toledo OH 43615

LIEBERMAN, LEONARD, supermarket exec.; b. Elizabeth, N.J., Jan. 23, 1929; s. Joseph Harry and Bessie (Bernstein) L.; B.A., Yale, 1950; LL.B., Columbia, 1953; grad. Advanced Mgmt. Program, Harvard, 1970; children—Elizabeth Susan, Nancy Ellen, Anne Judith. Admitted to N.J. bar, 1954; asso. firm Greene and Hellring, Newark, 1954-56, Bernard Hellring, Newark, 1956-60; mem. firm Hellring, Linderman and Lieberman, Newark, 1960-63, Ehrenkranz and Lieberman, Orange, N.J., 1963-65; v.p., gen. counsel Supermarkets Operating Co., Union, N.J., 1963-66; v.p., gen. counsel Supermarkets Gen. Corp., 1966-69, sr. v.p., 1969—, exec. asst. to pres., 1979-80, chmn. Pathmark div., 1977-79, chief adminstrv. and fin. officer, 1980—, also dir.; dir. Supermarkets Operating Co., 1963-66, Quantronix Corp., 1969-79; instr. Am. Inst. Banking, 1954-55. Bd. dirs. Jewish Counseling and Service Agy., Essex County, N.J., 1968-73, Coalition Venture Corp., 1969, Better Bus. Bur. Greater Newark; treas. Newark Beth Israel Med. Center, 1972-73, pres., 1973-78, trustee, 1972—; trustee Jewish Community Fedn. Met. N.J., 1974-77. Mem. Am., Essex County bar assns., Am. Arbitration Assn. (bd. arbitrators). Jewish. Home: 1025 Harmon Cove Towers Secaucus NJ 07094 Office: 301 Blair Rd Woodbridge NJ 07095

LIEBMAN, EMMANUEL, lawyer; b. Phila., Mar. 26, 1925; s. Morris and Pearl (Zucker) L.; B.S. in Econs., U. Pa., 1950; J.D., Rutgers U., 1954; m. Anita Forman, Dec. 24, 1953; children—Judith H. Winslow, Lawrence H. Admitted to N.J. bar, 1954, U.S. Supreme Ct. bar, 1960; practice law specializing in fed. taxation, Cherry Hill, N.J., 1954—; mem. firm Liebman & Flaster, P.C.; lectr. Inst. Continuing Legal Edn. Pres. Kiwanis Club Cherry Hill Found., 1964-73; pres., trustee N.J. State Bar Found. Served with USNR, 1943-46. Mem. Cherry Hill C. of C., Am. Arbitration Assn., Am., N.J. (mem. exec. council taxation sect., chmn. com. bus. taxes 1967-69, 71-73, chmn. state capitol com. 1974-77, chmn. ad hoc com. on financing legal fees 1976-79), Camden County (chmn. com. fed. taxation, 1964, 68-70) bar assns. Clubs: Penn Alumni of Southern N.J. (pres. 1959), Haddon Field, Woodcrest Country. Developer N.J. State Bar Found. legal fee fin. plan. Home: 46 Dublin Ln Cherry Hill NJ 08003 Office: 409 E Marlton Pike Cherry Hill NJ 08034

LIEBMANN, FELIX G., lawyer; b. Dec. 25, 1923; B.S. cum laude, Coll. City N.Y., 1948; J.D. with distinction, Cornell U., 1951; m. Betty Virginia Osterholm, Sept. 9, 1950 (dec.); children—Joanne, Karen, Susan, Geoffrey Edward. Admitted to N.Y. bar, 1951, also U.S. Supreme Ct. bar; fin. investigator U.S. Treasury Dept., 1945-46; asso. Davis, Polk, Wardwell, Sunderland & Kiendl, N.Y.C., 1951-56; tax supr. Arabian Am. Oil Co., N.Y.C., 1956-58; tax counsel Carrier Corp., Syracuse, N.Y., 1958-61; with firm Harris, Beach, Wilcox, Rubin & Levey, and predecessor, Rochester, N.Y., 1961—, partner, 1963—; dir. Caldwell Mfg. Co., Rochester. Trustee, former pres., bd. dirs. Hillside Children's Center, Rochester. Served with AUS, 1943-45. Mem. N.Y. State, Monroe County bar assns., Am. Judicature Soc., Nat. Hist. Soc., Acad. Polit. Sci., Am. Acad. Polit. and Social Sci., Smithsonian Assos., N.Y. State Conservation Council, Nat. Wildlife Fedn., Rochester Com. on Fgn. Relations, Order of Coif, Phi Beta Kappa, Phi Kappa Phi. Lutheran. Editor-in-chief Cornell Law Quar., 1950-51. Home: 130 Rowland Pkwy Rochester NY 14610 Office: 2 State St Rochester NY 14614

LIEBSON, LAURENCE S., computer co. exec.; b. N.Y.C., May 11, 1945; s. Jerry S. and Lucille B. Liebson; B.S. in Engring., Northeastern U., 1971; M.S. in Mgmt. Sci. (Sloan fellow), M.I.T., 1979. Pres., Xylogic Systems, Inc., Natick, Mass., 1970-76; chmn. bd. Xylogics, Inc., Burlington, Mass., 1976—, also dir.; pres. Harbor Assos., Inc., Fair Oaks, Calif., 1976—, also dir.; dir. Prime Devel. Corp. Mem. Assn. for Computing Machinery, IEEE, Am. Inst. Indsl. Engrs. Home: 4361 Winding Woods Way Fair Oaks CA 95628 Office: 5710 Garfield Ave Sacramento CA 95841 also 42 3d Ave Burlington MA 01803

LIECHTY, G(EORGE) FREDERICK, health service exec.; b. Monroe, Ind., Jan. 1, 1914; s. Menno Simon and Rosina (Wittwer) L.; A.B., Eastern Mich. U., 1938; M.B.A., U. Mich., 1940; m. Helen Holly Van Sickle, June 23, 1945; children—Susan, John, Thomas, Jane. Bus. mgr. U. Mich. Hosp., Ann Arbor, 1941-45; br. mgr. Blue Cross-Blue Shield, Chgo., 1945-47, asst. dir. 1947-63, v.p. mktg., 1963-67, sr. v.p., 1967-79; ret.; with Cyrus Realtors, Evanston, Ill., 1979—; lectr., Sch. Hosp. Adminstrn. Northwestern U., Evanston, 1946-50; mem. Corp. Responsibility Group Greater Chgo. Mem. Bd. Edn., Evanston Twp. High Sch., 1965-72; com. on pub. policy Welfare Council Met. Chgo. Trustee Meth. Student Found., Northwestern U., 1952-58, Northwestern Meml. Hosp., 1970-80; lay mem. Ill. Conf. United Meth. Ch., Chgo., 1965-79; bd. dirs. Minority Info. Referral Center, Chgo., 1976-79; bd. dirs., mem. exec. com. Chgo. Lung Assn., 1975—. Mem. Chgo. Assn. Commerce and Industry, Field Mus. Natural History (asso.), Ill. C. of C., Am. Mgmt. Assn., Am. Pub. Health Assn., Pub. Affairs Council U.S., Consumer Fedn. Ill., C. of C. U.S., Ill. Hist. Soc. United Methodist (chmn. bd. trustees 1973-77). Rotarian (pres. 1962-63). Clubs: Chicago Athletic Assn., Executives (Chgo.). Home: 2436 Central Park Ave Evanston IL 60201 Office: 233 N Michigan Ave Chicago IL 60601

LIECHTY, JOHN DANIEL, ins. co. exec.; b. Aibonito, P.R., Mar. 21, 1948; s. Simon P. and Lea J. (Delagrange) L.; B.A. in Edn., Inter-Am. U. P.R., 1970; M.S., St. Francis Coll., Ft. Wayne, Ind., 1979; postgrad. Century U., Beverly Hills, Calif.; m. Carmen A. Colon, June 6, 1970; children—Jonatha, Janelle, Janett. Tchr., asst. prin. various public and pvt. schs., P.R., 1968-74; tchr., program coordinator St. Vincent Treatment Center, Ft. Wayne, Ind., 1974-76; social service dir. Benito Juarez Cultural Center, Ft. Wayne, 1976; counselor Occupational Devel. Center, Bluffton, Ind., 1977; human resource devel. specialist Mut. Security Life Ins. Co., Ft. Wayne, 1978—. Mem. Am. Soc. for Tng. and Devel., Am. Soc. for Personnel Adminstrn., Am. Personnel and Guidance Assn., Nat. Vocat. Guidance Assn., Nat. Employment Counselor Assn. Home: 2204 Cass St Fort Wayne IN 46808

LIEDING, ROBERT KENNETH, JR., mfg. co. exec.; b. Madison, Wis., Feb. 25, 1938; s. Robert and Joann L.; B.S., U. Wis., 1960; postgrad Harvard Bus. Sch., 1977; m. Constance, Aug. 25, 1962; children—Heather, Suzanne, Cynthia. Dist. head salesman Proctor & Gamble Co., Mpls., 1961-64; asst. regional sales mgr. Hunt Wesson Foods Co., Chgo., 1964-68; v.p. mktg., sales Questor Juvenile Furniture Co., Ravenna, Ohio, 1969-74; v.p. mktg. sales Lee L. Woodard Sons Inc., Owosso, Mich., 1975-79; partner H. Barkow, Inc., Milw., 1979—. Del., County and State Republican presdl. convs., 1976; treas. Shiawasse County Rep. Com., 1977-78. Served to capt. AUS, 1960-61. Mem. Am. Mgmt. Assn., Nat. Assn. Furniture Mfrs., Owosso C. of C., Mich. Antique Arms Collectors, Wis. Alumni Assn. Congregationalist (deacon). Clubs: Owosso Lions (charter); Renaissance (Detroit) (charter). Co-holder patent steel frame baby carrier. Home: 611 Alta Loma Thiensville WI 53092 Office: 8501 W Tower Ave Milwaukee WI 53224

LIEDTKE, JOHN HUGH, petroleum exec.; b. Tulsa, Feb. 10, 1922; B.A., Amherst Coll., 1942; postgrad. Harvard Grad. Sch. Bus. Adminstrn., 1943; LL.B., U. Tex., 1947; m. Betty Lyn; children—Karen, Kristin, John Hugh, Blake, Kathryn. Chmn., chief exec. officer Pennzoil Co., Houston; Pennzoil United, Inc. (formerly United Gas Corp.); dir. Elk Refining Co., Penn Grade Assn., 1st Nat. Bank Midland (Tex.), Capital Nat. Bank, Houston. Trustee Houston United Fund, Kincaid Sch., Houston, Rice U., Baylor Coll. Medicine, U.S. Naval Acad. Found.; bd. dirs. Meth. Hosp., Houston. Mem. Tex. Mid-Continent Oil and Gas Assn. (dir.), Nat. Petroleum Refiners Assn. (dir.), Am. Petroleum Inst. (dir.), Nat. Petroleum Council (dir.), Independent Petroleum Assn. Am. (dir.); Beta Theta Pi, Phi Alpha Delta. Clubs: Houston Country, Ramada; Pennhills, Bradford Country (Bradford, Pa.); Rolling Rock (Ligonier, Pa.); Racquet (Midland, Tex.); Calgary (Alta., Can.) Petroleum. Office: PO Box 2967 Houston TX 77001

LIEMANDT, GREGORY JOSEPH, mfg. co. exec.; b. Mpls., Mar. 30, 1943; s. Clarence Gregory and Marie Gertrude (Jeub) L.; B.S., St. Johns U., 1965; M.B.A., U. Minn., 1967; m. Diane R. Ennen, Aug. 22, 1964; children—Chiara, Joseph, Melissa. Mktg. analyst Minn. Mining & Mfg. Co., St. Paul, 1967-69; mgmt. cons. Booz, Allen & Hamilton, Chgo., 1969-72; ops. staff exec. ITT, N.Y.C., 1972-74; mgr. strategic planning Gen. Electric Co., Pittsfield, Mass., 1974-77; gen. mgr. Gen. Electric Co., Gainesville, Fla., 1978—. Home: 420 SW 80th Dr Gainesville FL 32601 Office: Box 114 Gainesville FL 32602

LIEN, ANDREW CLYDE, figure salon exec.; b. N.Y.C., Jan. 19, 1943; s. Julius Martin and Sylvia Z. (Schotter) L.; B.A., CCNY, 1964; M.B.A., N.Y. U., 1966; student Cornell U., 1965; m. Claire Abby Levine, June 3, 1965; children—Christopher Adam, Rebecca Anne. Mktg. exec. Procter & Gamble Co., Cin., 1966-72, Manila, Philippines, 1973-75; dir. new bus. devel. Gillette Co., Boston, 1975-77; pres., chief exec. officer Elaine Powers Figure Salons, Inc., also Elaine Powers Nutrition Co., Inc., Gym Equipment Research & Devel. Co., Inc., Milw., 1977—. N.Y. Regents scholar, 1960-64. Mem. Am. Mgmt. Assn. Clubs: Manila Polo, Lakeshore, Eastlake Golf and Country. Home: 9736 N Lake Dr Milwaukee WI 53217 Office: 105 W Michigan Milwaukee WI 53203

LIFSCHULTZ, PHILLIP, tax cons.; b. Oak Park, Ill., Mar. 5, 1927; s. Abraham Albert and Frances (Siegel) L.; B.S. in Accounting with honors, U. Ill., 1949; J.D., John Marshall Law Sch., 1956; m. Edith Louise Leavitt, June 27, 1948; children—Gregory Ross, Bonnie Gail, Jodie Ann. Admitted to Ill. bar, 1956; tax mgr. Arthur Andersen & Co., Chgo., 1957-63; with Montgomery Ward & Co., Inc., Chgo., 1963-78, asst. controller taxes and ins., 1963-67, divisional v.p. taxes, 1967-69, v.p. taxes, 1969-78; fin. v.p. and controller Henry Crown & Co., Chgo., 1978-80; lectr. accounting and taxation DePaul U., Chgo., 1957-61; mem. adv. bd. to Ill. auditor gen., 1965-73, chmn., 1972-73; chmn. transition task force Ill. Dept. Revenue, 1972-73; chmn. property tax reform com. Civic Fedn., dir., 1975, pres., 1980—; mem. adv. council Coll. Commerce and Bus. Adminstrn. U. Ill., Urbana-Champaign, 1977-78; coordinator Exec. Service Corps Cons. Project to chief fin. officer Chgo. Bd. Edn. Served with AUS, 1945-46. C.P.A., Ill., 1950. Mem. Ill. Soc. C.P.A.'s, Nat. Retail Mchts. Assn. (chmn. tax com. 1975-78), Am. Retail Fedn. (chmn. taxation com. 1971), Am. Inst. C.P.A.'s, Ill. Bar Assn., Nat. Assn. Tax Adminstrs., Tax Execs. Inst. (v.p. Chgo. chpt. 1978), Internat. Assn. Assessing Officers, Nat. Tax Assn.-Tax Inst. Am., Internat. Fiscal Assn., Execs. Club Chgo., Tau Delta Phi, Beta Alpha Psi. Club: Standard (Chgo.). Home: 976 Oak Dr Glencoe IL 60022 Office: 300 W Washington St Chicago IL 60606

LIGGETT, DENNIS BRADLEY, constrn. co. exec.; b. Indpls., Aug. 2, 1946; s. Donald Glamour and Lena Belle (Hollenbaugh) L.; B.S., Brigham Young U., 1970; M.P.A., U. Alaska, 1977; m. Muriel Ann Rollins, Dec. 20, 1968; children—Annette Dionne, Jennifer Dawn, Matthew Donald, Valerie Denae, Natalie Darlene. Police officer American Fork City, Utah, 1970; instr. El Paso Community Coll., 1973; gen. mgr., treas. O. Kay Constrn. Inc., Roy, Utah, 1977-80; v.p., gen. mgr. Ins. Claim Services, Salt Lake City, 1980-81; partner, registered agt. Ad-Vantage, Roy, 1978—; pres. Am. Vista Inc., Roy, 1979—, Laund Enterprises, Roy, 1981—. Troop com. chmn. Boy Scouts Am., Ft. Richardson, Alaska, 1974, 76-77; Bishop's counselor Anchorage, 1976-77; vol. sports ofcl., 1976—. Served with U.S. Army, 1970-77. Lic. real estate agt., Utah; lic. life and health agt., Utah; lic. ind. and public adjuster, Utah; notary public, Utah. Mem. Ogden Bd. Realtors, Non-Commd. Officers Assn., Res. Officers Assn., Utah Council Small Businesses, Nat. Guard Assn. Mormon. Home: 3820 W 5850 S Roy UT 84067 Office: PO Box 51 Roy UT 84067

LIGHT, JOHN RICHARD, investment cons.; b. Kalamazoo, Oct. 11, 1940; s. Richard Light and Rachel Mary (Upjohn) L.; B.A., Yale U., 1962; m. Frances Mary Hesser, June 21, 1969; 1 dau., Aimee Upjohn. Asst. advt. mgr. Verson Allsteel Press Co., Chgo., 1967-68; pub. relations copywriter Barton Brands, Chgo., 1970-71; investment cons., Chgo., 1972—. Bd. dirs. Juvenile Protective Assn., Chgo., 1975—, Kalamazoo Child Guidance Clinic, 1969—. Recipient Distinguished Service award Publicity Club Chgo., 1972. Roman Catholic. Clubs: Gull Lake Country (Richland, Mich.); Publicity (Chgo.) (dir. 1975-77, mgr. club publs. 1972-73, chmn. seminar com. 1976-77). Editor: Impact Machining, 1968. Home: 3270 N Lakeshore Dr Apt 2A Chicago IL 60657 Office: 3270 N Lakeshore Dr Chicago IL 60657

LIGHT, VIRGINIA ELAINE, pub. co. exec., solar energy co. exec.; b. Mpls., Oct. 10, 1929; d. Charles and Clara Josephine (Fox) Flanagan; B.A., U. Minn., 1956; m. Theodore B. Light, Mar. 12, 1960; children—Steven Thomas, Gregory James, Bradley David. Sec., Richard N. Olofson Co., Mpls., 1950-54; exec. dir. Cannon Falls (Minn.) council Girl Scouts U.S.A., 1956-59; pres. Summit Publs., Inc., Oakton, Va., 1975—, founder, pres. Phone Prospector div., 1978—; pres. Solar Products, Inc., Oakton, Va., 1975—; treas.-sec. Solar Film Industries, 1979—, ERG, Inc., 1980—. Mem. Newsletter Assn. Am., Apt. and Office Bldg. Assn., Fairfax County C. of C. Office: Summit Publs Inc 2936 Chain Bridge Rd Oakton VA 22124

LIGHTBODY, JAMES DAVIES, mfg. co. exec.; b. Chgo., Mar. 25, 1918; s. James Davies and Mabel (Payne) L.; B.S. in Mech. Engring. magna cum laude, Harvard U., 1940; m. Patricia Calkins, June 21, 1940; children—Thomas, Susan, John, Richard, William, Mary, George. Gen. mgr. electronic div. Clevite Corp., Cleve., 1955-60; exec. v.p., dir. McDowell-Wellman Engring. Co., Cleve., 1961-65; pres., dir. Lester Engring. Co., Cleve., 1966-69; pres., chmn., dir. Electron Inc., Cleve., 1969-75, Philway Products Co., Ashland, Ohio, 1976—. Trustee Goodrich Settlement House, Cleve., 1951-54; treas., trustee Garden Valley Neighborhood House, Cleve., 1956-62; Republican ward leader, Pepper Pike, Ohio, 1965-69; mem. welfare com. Com. Econ. Devel., 1976. Served with AUS, 1944-46. Mem. Inst. Printed Circuits, Newcomen Soc., Internat. Assn. Quality Circle, Natural History Mus. Cleve., Connemara Soc. Episcopalian. Club: Harvard (past pres.) (Cleve.). Home: 32600 Fairmount Blvd Pepper Pike OH 44124 Office: 701 Virginia Ave Ashland OH 44802

LIGHTNER, A. LEROY, JR., advt. exec.; b. Wyomissing, Pa., Apr. 26, 1921; s. Angus LeRoy and Grace Darling (Thompson) L.; A.B., Franklin and Marshall Coll., 1942; m. Betty Pauline Jenkins, July 22, 1950; children—Karen, Kevin, Laura Lightner Phillips. Prodn. supr. N.W. Ayer & Son, Inc., Phila., 1942-47, account exec., Boston, 1947-52, Phila., 1956-60, account supr., 1961-69, v.p., account supr., N.Y.C., 1970-80; nat. dir. United Meth. Ch. TV Presence and Ministry Campaign, Nashville, 1980—. Mem. Nat. Assn. Conf. Lay Leaders United Meth. Ch., 1973—; trustee Morristown Coll., 1977—; pres. alumni council Franklin and Marshall Coll., 1960-62, chmn. alumni fund, 1962-70. Mem. Geneal. Soc. Pa., New Eng. Hist. Geneal. Soc., SAR, Blue Key, Druids, Lambda Chi Alpha, Pi Gamma Mu. Methodist (lay leader Eastern Pa. Conf. 1971-74, pres. Conf. Bd. Missions and Ch. Extension, 1965-69; pres. Northeastern Jurisdiction Bd. of Laity 1979-80, lay leader No. N.J. Conf. 1976-80). Author: Jenkins-Berry Ancestry, 1970, Lightner-Thompson Genealogy, 1969. Home: 110 Surrey Hill Point Hendersonville TN 37075 Office: 810 12th Ave S Nashville TN 37203

LIGHTON, ARTHUR REID, bank design, bldg. and equipment cons.; b. Bklyn., July 6, 1918; s. Arthur McKeever and Frances Garret (Latimer) L.; student Yale U., 1938-40; m. Elizabeth Joyce Pretzfelder, May 22, 1942; children—Jeffrey Reid, Susan Brooke. Vice pres. Cunneen Co., Phila., 1950-65; asso., chief bank dept. F. D. Widersum, Architects & Engrs., Valley Stream, N.Y., 1965-75; pres. Office Reid Lighton, Inc., Port Washington, N.Y., 1975—. Served with U.S. Army, 1940-48. Mem. Can. Soc. N.Y. Episcopalian. Clubs: Can. of N.Y. (pres.), Manhasset Bay Yacht, Univ. Address: 7 Harbor View Rd Port Washington NY 11050

LIKER, JACK, ceramic co. exec.; b. N.Y.C., June 10, 1926; s. Boris and Lucy (Zerulnikova) L.; B.S. in Mech. Engring., Bridgeport U., 1958; m. Henriette Handel, Jan. 11, 1948; children—Karin, Jeffrey, Stephen. Floorman, Sloves Book Bindery, 1946-51; design engr. Burndy Corp., 1951-59; sales mgr. Molecular Dielectrics, 1959-65; sales mgr. Basic Ceramics, Hawthorne, N.J., 1965-71; v.p. sales Mykroy Ceramics, Ledgewood, N.J., 1971-72, v.p., gen. mgr., 1972-80; v.p., gen. mgr. Mykroy/Mycalex div. Spaulding Fibre Co., Clifton, N.J., 1980—; dir. Ceramic Fabricators Inc.; partner Liker Travel Agy. Cons. ceramic material dept. chem. engring. Columbia; cons. Karl Roesch Inc. Served with AUS, 1944-46. Mem. Am., Canadian, N.J. ceramic socs., Internat. Hybrid Microelectronics Soc., Soc. Aerospace Materials and Process Engrs., ASTM, Elec. Insulation Conf., Soc. Plastic Engrs. Rotarian. Patentee in field. Office: 125 Clifton Blvd Clifton NJ 07011

LILIEN, ROBERT DAVID, communications exec.; b. N.Y.C., June 25, 1926; s. Frank and Anne (Wenger) L.; A.B., Princeton U., 1949; m. Georgiana Wetherill Lewis, Feb. 19, 1955; children—Anne Cowpland, Christopher Wetherill, Robert Jarrett, Juliana Lambert. With advt. dept. Procter & Gamble Co., Cin., 1949-52; asst. advt. mgr. Whitehall Pharmacal Co. div. Am. Home Products, N.Y.C., 1952-54; asso. media dir. Bryan Houston, Inc., N.Y.C., 1955-56; with J. Walter Thompson Co., N.Y.C., 1956-76; sr. v.p. Communispond, Inc., N.Y.C., 1976—. Mem. N.Y. County Grand Jury Assn., 1965-70, bd. dirs., 1968-70. Served with USNR, 1944-45. Mem. Amagansett (N.Y.) Beach Assn. (sec. 1965—, dir. 1967-75), U.S. C. of C. (communications com. 1969-76), Princeton Alumni Assn. (trustee Princeton Tiger mag.), Newcomen Soc., Met. Squash Racquets Assn. Episcopalian. Clubs: Church, Princeton (bd. govs.) (N.Y.C.); Devon Yacht (E. Hampton, N.Y.); Charter, Nassau (Princeton). Home: 70 E 96th St New York NY 10028 Office: 485 Lexington Ave New York NY 10017

LILJEDAHL, DOUGLAS RICHARD, automotive testing co. exec.; b. St. Paul, July 23, 1938; s. Lester Lawrence and Irene (Molner) L.; student pub. schs., St. Paul; m. Sharon D. Heideman, Oct. 19, 1957; children—Lisa Gail, Douglas Richard. Lab. technician, Calif. Air Resources Bd. Lab., Los Angeles, 1963-65, Am. Motors Corp., Los Angeles, 1965-66; project engr. Automotive Research Assos., San Antonio, 1966-70; pres. Automotive Testing Labs., Inc., Aurora, Colo., 1971—, chmn. bd., 1971—. Served with USAF, 1956-60. Republican. Lutheran. Contbr. articles in field to profl. jours. Home: 2770 S Elmira St Apt 12 Denver CO 80231 Office: 19900 E Colfax Ave Aurora CO 80011

LILLER, BERNARD, internat. co. exec.; b. Milford, Del., Aug. 30, 1947; s. Francis Edward and Denise Lucienne L.; B.S., Ill. Inst. Tech., 1970; Baccalaureat, Lycee Duquesne, Paris, 1965; Swiss cert. Institut des Roches, Switzerland, 1966. Comml. attache French Consulate, Chgo., 1971-75; v.p. Izco Corp., Chgo. and Paris, 1975-77; export counselor Mavil-Serten, Paris, 1977; v.p. Pacific Project Canadian, Los Angeles, 1978, ITA Internat., Chgo., 1979—. Republican. Roman Catholic. Office: ITA Internat 70 W Hubbard St Suite 305 Chicago IL 60610

LILLEY, ALFRED, copper co. exec.; b. Belfast, No. Ireland, May 6, 1922; s. Alfred and Margaret (Rosemund) L.; came to U.S., 1957, naturalized, 1963; B. Commercial Sci., Queens U., Belfast, 1945; M.B.A., U. Utah, 1977; m. Margaret McDowell, Mar. 8, 1948. Auditor, T. Montgomery, Pub. Accountant, Belfast, 1945-47; cost accountant Sudan Rys., Atabra, Sudan, 1947-49; auditor United Africa Co., Ghana, 1949-51; sr. accountant, asst. sec. subs. cos. and joint ventures Trinidad Lease Holds Ltd. (oil), Pointe-A-Pierre, Trinidad, W. Indies, 1951-57; sr. auditor Kennecott Corp., Salt Lake City, 1957-60, mgr. systems and compliance, 1968—; comptroller, sec. Tin and Associated Minerals Ltd., Nigeria, 1960-66; sr. auditor Coopers & Lybrand, C.P.A.'s, Salt Lake City, 1967-68. C.P.A. Mem. Am. Inst. C.P.A.'s, Utah Assn. C.P.A.'s, Inst. Internal Auditors, Inst. Cost and Mgmt. Accts. (U.K.), Chartered Inst. Secs. and Adminstrs. (U.K.), Nat. Assn. Accts., EDP Auditors Assn., Data Processing Mgmt. Assn. Presbyterian. Home: 245 N Vine St Apt 902 Salt Lake City UT 84103 Office: Kennecott Corp PO Box 11299 Salt Lake Cjty UT 84147

LILLEY, THEODORE ROBERT, fin. co. exec.; b. Paterson, N.J., Jan. 11, 1923; s. Ernest R. and Antoinette E. (Hartmann) L.; B.A., N.Y. U., 1946; M.B.A., Columbia U., 1948; m. Marguerite A. Gallman, Jan. 27, 1951; children—Cheryl, Wayne, Ross. With Standard Oil Co. (N.J.), 1948-64, investment mgr., 1956-62, fin mgr., 1962-64; asst. treas. Esso Internat. Inc., 1964-69; v.p. Tchrs. Ins. and Annuity Assn. and Coll. Retirement Equities Fund, 1969-72; exec. dir. Fin. Analysts Fedn., N.Y.C., 1972-73, pres., 1972—; mem. adv. Council Fin. Acctg. Standards Bd., 1976-80. Bd. dirs. Near East Found., Ramapo Coll. N.J. (chmn.), Englewood Hosp.; bd. nat. missions United Presbyn. Ch. U.S.A. Found., 1972. Served to 1st lt. U.S. Army, 1943-46. Decorated Bronze Star, Purple Heart. Chartered fin. analyst. Mem. N.Y. Soc. Security Analysts, Inst. Chartered Fin. Analysts. Presbyterian. Club: Econ. of N.Y.

LILLEY, WILLIAM, III, communications co. exec.; b. Phila., Jan. 14, 1938; s. William and Ida Weaver (Macklin) L.; B.A. magna cum laude, U. Pa., 1959; M.A., Yale U., 1961, Ph.D., 1965; m. Eve Auchincloss, Mar. 12, 1977; children—Buchanan Morgan, Brooke

Carole, Whitman Elisa, Justin Weaver. Asst. prof. history Yale U., 1962-69; prof. govt. U. Va., 1977; co-founder, editor Nat. Jour., 1969-73; dep. asst. sec. HUD, 1973-75; dep., then dir. Council on Wage and Price Stability, 1975-77; minority staff dir. Com. on Budget, Ho. of Reps., Washington, 1977-78; v.p. govt. affairs Am. Express Co., 1978-80; v.p. CBS, Inc., Washington, 1980—. Clubs: Yale, Cosmos, Merion Cricket. Contbr. articles to profl. jours. Office: CBS Inc 1800 M St NW Suite 300 N Washington DC 20036

LILLQUIST, RICHARD ALLEN, trade assn. exec.; b. West Haven, Conn., Aug. 2, 1931; s. Arthur F. and Priscilla L.; B.A., Wesleyan U., 1954; postgrad. Columbia U., 1957; m. Pamela K. Kingan, Oct. 22, 1959; children—Erik, Christine. Spl. asst. examiner Fed. Res. Bank, N.Y.C., 1954-55; with Leahy & Co., Mgmt. Cons., N.Y.C., 1955-58; mem. staff Kraft Paper Assn., N.Y.C., 1958-66; mem. staff Aluminum Assn., N.Y.C., 1966-76, exec. sec.-treas., 1967-76; pres., chief exec. officer Flexible Packaging Assn., Cleve., 1976—. Mem. Am. Scandinavian Found., Am. Soc. Assn. Execs., Wesleyan U. Alumni Assn. Clubs: Can., Met., Bronxville Field, Cleve. Racquet. Office: 12025 Shaker Blvd Cleveland OH 44120

LILLY, JAMES ALEXANDER, constrn. co. exec.; b. Bluefield, W.Va., Sept. 1, 1918; s. Clifford Abraham and Eva Acre (Dinwiddie) L.; Engr., Bluefield Coll., 1938; B.S.M.E., Va. Poly. Inst. and State U., 1940; children—James Alexander, Pamela, Robert Clifton, Anne Martha. Field engr., gen. supt. George M. Brewster & Son Co., Bogota, N.J., 1945-49; field engr. McKenzie, Whittle Constrn. Co., Dallas, 1949-59; with Morrison-Knudsen Co., Inc., Boise, Idaho, 1959—, gen. mgr., Vietnam, 1965-68, mgr. internat. div., 1968-71, v.p. splty. div., 1971-73, exec. v.p., 1973—, dir., 1973—, exec. v.p.-domestic ops., dir., 1974—, exec. v.p.-N.Am. ops., 1976—; chmn. bd., chief exec. officer M-K Nat. Corp.; v.p., dir. Canadian Rescon Ltd., N. Western Dredging Co., Ltd., No. Constrn. Co. Ltd., High Rock Mining Co., Ltd.; v.p. Emkay Fin. Co., Inc.; dir. Internat. Engring. Co., Inc. Chpt. mem. St. Michael's Episcopal Cathedral; Served with USMCR, 1942-45. Decorated Air medal with oak leaf cluster, D.F.C. with stars; recipient Golden Beaver award, 1980. Mem. Acad. Mgmt., Alaska Pipeline Builders Assn., AAAS, ASCE, ASME, Am. Inst. Constructors, Am. Nuclear Soc., Am. Underground Space Assn., Am. Wind Energy Assn., Assn. Energy Engrs., Am. Inst. Chem. Engrs., Assn. U.S. Army, Brit. Tunnelling Soc., Internat. Tech. Inst., Nat. Acad. Scis., N.Y. Acad. Scis., IEEE, Soc. Chem. Industry, Soc. Mining Engrs. of AIME, Sunsat Energy Council, Beavers (alt. dir.), Moles (trustee, membership and awards coms.), Ground Hog Club, Nat. Audubon Soc., Nat. Trust for Historic Preservation, Nat. Geog. Soc., Nat. Hist. Soc., Met. Mus. Art, Smithsonian Assos., Nat. Wildlife Fedn., Nat. Parks and Conservation Assn., Collectors Guild, Idaho Historic Preservation Council, Internat. Game Fish Assn., Newcomen Soc. in N.Am., Internat. Platform Assn., Tau Beta Pi, Pi Tau Sigma. Clubs: Hillcrest Country, Arid, Carlton. Home: 3232 Catalina Ln Boise ID 83705 Office: One Morrison-Knudsen Plaza Boise ID 83729

LILLY, JAMES EPLING, ret. corp. fin. exec.; b. Normal, Ky., Oct. 4, 1915; s. William Webster and Hattie Glenn (Epling) L.; student Concord (W.Va.) State Coll., 1932-33, exec. program Columbia U., 1970; m. Opal Elizabeth Anderson, May 4, 1937; children—Kay Marie Lilly Cox, Franklin Brice. Adminstv. positions U.S. Forest Service, Ky., 1934-38, U.S. C.E., Ind., Ill. and Ky., 1938-43, 46-52; with Brown & Williamson Tobacco Corp., Louisville, 1952-81, successively chief auditor, budget mgr., asst. controller, 1963-67, asst. treas., 1967-69, treas., 1969-81; dir. fin. adminstrn. BATUS Inc., and predecessor corp., 1979-81; treas. Batus Inc. subs.; B&W Internat. Sales Corp., 1972-81, Brown & Williamson Industries Inc., 1980, BATUS-Wis., Inc., 1980; Gimbels-Saks Retailing Corp., 1980, Gimbel Bros., Inc., 1979-80, Saks & Co., 1979-80, Thimbles Splty. Stores, Inc., 1980, The Kohl Corp., 1979-80. Bd. dirs., past pres. Louisville Deaf Oral Sch., 1974—; trustee Louisville Deaf Oral Sch. Found., 1975—; bd. dirs., pres. Louisville-Jefferson County (Ky.) Youth Orch., 1976—; treas. City of Northfield (Ky.), 1975—; trustee United Methodist Evang. Hosp. Found., 1977—, mem. exec. and fin. coms., 1979—; trustee and mem. adminstrv. bd. Audubon Park United Meth. Ch. Served with AUS, 1943-46; ETO, PTO. Mem. Fin. Execs. Inst. (dir., past pres. Louisville chpt.), Hon. Order Ky. Cols. Methodist. Clubs: Masons, Kiwanis. Home: 6102 Stannye Dr Louisville KY 40222

LILLY, JOHN RICHARD, fin. cons.; b. St. Paul, Aug. 15, 1928; s. Richard J. and Katherine (Kaye) L.; A.B., U. Nebr., 1950; J.D., Georgetown U., 1955; m. Marcella K. Seymour, June 21, 1958; children—Marcella K., John Richard. Admitted to bar; sr. financial analyst, internat. staff Ford Motor Co., Dearborn, Mich., 1956-60; asst. to treas. overseas chem. div. W. R. Grace & Co., Boston, 1960-61, Singer Co., N.Y.C., 1961-63; exec. asst. to v.p. finance Richardson-Merrell, Inc., N.Y.C., 1964-65, treas., 1965-72; sr. v.p. finance U.S. Industries, Inc., N.Y.C., 1972-77; v.p., dir., mem. fin. and exec. coms., chief fin. officer Food Fair Inc., Phila., 1977-79; pres. J.R. Lilly Assos., Greenwich, Conn., 1979—. Served to 1st lt. AUS, 1951-53. Decorated Bronze Star. Mem. Am. Bar Assn., Fin. Council, Am. Mgmt. Assn., Delta Theta Chi, Sigma Chi. Clubs: Riverside Yacht; Treasurer's, Union League (N.Y.C.). Home: 20 Owenoke Way Riverside CT 06878 Office: Mason St Greenwich CT 06830

LIMA, PAUL EDWIN, mfg. co. exec.; b. Boston, July 17, 1945; s. Fortunato Roosevelt and Mary Louise (Machado) L.; B.S., U.S. Mil. Acad., 1967; M.A., Boston U., 1971; postgrad. U. Puget Sound, 1972-74, U.S. Army Command and Gen. Staff Coll., 1977-80; m. Maria Elena Leon, June 9, 1967; children—Paul E., Antonio M., Pedro A. With PACCAR, Inc., Bellevue, Wash., 1974—, sales adminstr. for internat. group, 1975-77, adminstrv. asst. to chmn., 1977-78, adminstrv. asst. to pres., 1978-79, spl. asst. to pres., 1979-80, dir. Latin Am. ops., 1981—; dir. Kenworth Mexicana S.A. de C.V., Kenpar S.A. de C.V. Bd. dirs. Booster Program, U. Puget Sound Sch. Law, 1977—; comdr. USAR Psychol. Ops. Co., 1977—; exec. com. Am. GI Form, State of Wash., 1977-78; dir. Hispanic Heritage program, 1977-78; bd. dirs. El Comite, 1976-77. Served with U.S. Army, 1967-72. Decorated Bronze Star with oak leaf cluster, Air medal, Meritorious Service medal with oak leaf cluster, Army Commendation medal with oak leaf cluster; recipient cert. of achievement Nat. Civil Affairs Assn., 1977. Mem. Motor Vehicle Mfrs. Assn. U.S., Soc. Internat. Devel. Republican. Roman Catholic. Home: 4606 159th Ave NE Redmond WA 98052 Office: PO Box 1518 Bellevue WA 98009

LIN, TUNG YEN, civil engr., educator; b. Foochow, China, Nov. 14, 1911; s. Ting Chang and Feng Yi (Kuo) L.; B.S. in Civil Engring., Tangshan Coll., Chiaotung U., 1931; M.S., U. Calif. at Berkeley, 1933; LL.D., Chinese U. Hongkong, 1972; m. Margaret Kao, July 20, 1941; children—Paul, Verna. Came to U.S., 1946, naturalized, 1951. Chief bridge engr., chief design engr. Chinese Govt. Rys., 1933-46; asst. and asso. prof. U. Calif., 1946-55, prof., 1955—, chmn. div. structural engring., 1960-63, dir. structural lab., 1960-63, chmn. bd. ednl. devel., 1969-70; chmn. bd. T.Y. Lin Internat., cons. structural engrs.; cons. State of Calif., U.S. Def. Dept., others. Chmn. World Conf. Prestressed Concrete, 1957, Western Conf. Prestressed Concrete Bldgs., 1960. Recipient Berkeley citation award U. Calif., 1976; Quarter Century citation NRC, 1977. Fellow ASCE (Howard medal); mem. Nat. Acad. Engring., Internat. Fedn. Prestressing (Freyssinet medal), Am. Concrete Inst. (hon.), Prestressed Concrete Inst. (medal of honor 1977), Academia Sinica. Author: Design of Prestressed Concrete Structures, 1955 (English, Spanish, Russian edits.), rev. edit., 1963; Design of Steel Structures, 1960, rev. edit. (with B. Bresler, J. Scalzi), 1968; also articles. Home: 8701 Don Carol Dr El Cerrito CA 94530

LIN, WEN-CHIAO WAYNE, mktg. exec.; b. Taiwan, Republic of China, Apr. 7, 1947; came to U.S., 1970, naturalized, 1980; s. Chuan-Hsing and Yui-Chin Lin; B.S., Nat. Tsing-Hwa U., 1969; M.S., U. Calif., Riverside, 1972; M.A., U. Calif., Berkeley, 1974; Ph.D., U. Beverly Hills, 1980; m. Mei-Huei Grace, Mar. 31, 1973; children—Emily, Gary. Research nuclear chemist Kaiser Hosp., Oakland, Calif., 1974-77; pres. ABDEC, Inc., Emeryville, Calif., 1977-80, dir., 1977—; mktg. dir. Clin. BIOResearch Corp., Emeryville; pres. EGW Internat. Corp., 1980—. Mem. Am. Soc. Clin. Chemistry. Contbr. articles to profl. jours.

LINBURN, MICHAEL RICHARD, real estate finance exec.; b. N.Y.C., Aug. 27, 1933; s. Richard Ernest and Mildred Adele (Jacobs) L.; B.S., Yale U., 1954; M.B.A., Harvard U., 1959; m. JoAnn Hopkins, Dec. 17, 1966 (div. Apr. 1976); 1 dau., Carol Evans; m. Deborah Thomas Moore, Jan. 27, 1979; 1 dau., Kimberly K. Moore. First v.p. Shearson Hammill & Co., N.Y.C., 1959-74; v.p. Oppenheimer Properties, Inc., N.Y.C., 1974-76, Whitbread-Nolan, Inc., N.Y.C., 1976-77, Pico Alexander Capital Corp., N.Y.C., 1977-78, The Balcor Co., N.Y.C., 1978—; former pres. 1125 Park Ave. Corp.; former dir. Glosser Bros., Inc. Bd. govs. Real Estate Securities and Syndication Inst. Served to 1st lt. U.S. Army, 1954-56. Licensed real estate broker, N.Y. Mem. Real Estate Bd. N.Y. Republican. Presbyterian. Clubs: Yale, Skating (N.Y.C.); Appalachian Mountain, Am. Canoe Assn. Home: 1125 Park Ave Apt 10A New York NY 10028 Office: Balcor Co 122 E 42d St 17th Floor New York NY 10168

LIND, BRUCE ELVIN, land devel. co. exec.; b. Twin Falls, Idaho, June 25, 1941; s. Wyland Herman and Helen Eileen (Bailey) L.; B.S., Utah State U., 1967, B.S. in Bus. Edn., 1968, M.S. in Mktg., 1969; m. Norma Jean Kitchen, Sept. 19, 1966; children—Billie Jean, Bonita, Ben, Katy, Tyler, Tara. Product mgr., wholesaler Boise Cascade Corp. (Idaho), 1968-70; asst. to nat. sales mgr. Trus-Joist Corp., Boise, 1970-71; founder, pres. A.M.R. Corp., Idaho Falls, Idaho, 1971—, chmn. bd., 1972—. Mem. Delta Phi Kappa. Club: Lions. Office: 2630 N Yellowstone St Idaho Falls ID 83401

LIND, CHESTER CARL, banker; b. Firesteel, S.D., Aug. 4, 1918; s. Carl L. and Dorothy (Kiehl) L.; student U. S.D., 1940, No. State Coll. Sch. Banking, U. Wis., 1951; m. Marie C. Decker, June 4, 1941; children—Karen (Mrs. Darrel Pederson), James, Stephen, John. With Dewey County Bank, Timber Lake, S.D., 1935, 1st Nat. Bank, Aberdeen, S.D., 1935-66, asst. v.p., 1947-50, v.p., 1950-54, exec. v.p., dir., 1954, pres., dir., 1954-66; exec. v.p. First Am. Nat. Bank, Duluth, Minn., 1966-68, pres., dir., 1968-75; exec. v.p. N.W. Bancorp., Mpls., 1975-79, pres., chief exec. officer, 1979-81, chmn., chief exec. officer, 1981—; tchr. bank mgmt. Minn. Sch. Banking, St. Olaf Coll.; past pres. S.D. Bankers Assn. Chmn. S.D. Indsl. Expansion Agy., 1963-64, Nat. Alliance Businessmen, Dulugh, Superior, Wis., 1970; past pres. Aberdeen C. of C.; past. v.p. bd. dirs. Upper Midwest Devel. Council. Served to maj. AUS, 1941-46. Decorated Bronze Star medal; named Outstanding Young Man, Aberdeen Jaycees, 1949, Boss of Year, 1956. Mem. Minn. Bankers Assn. (mem. council), Duluth C. of C. (past pres.). Clubs: Masons, Shriners, Elks, Mpls. Office: 1200 NW Bank Bldg Minneapolis MN 55480

LINDELL, KARL V., equipment co. exec.; b. Ashtabula, Ohio; B.S. in Mining Engring., Mich. Coll. Mines, 1928; D.Sc., (hon.), Laval U., U. Sherbrooke; D.E. (hon.), Mich. Technol. U.; m. Estelle Anita Jodouin; 3 sons, 3 daus. Immigrated to Can., 1929, naturalized, 1939. With Internat. Nickel Co. Can. Ltd., 1929-45; underground supt. Canadian Johns-Manville Ltd., Asbestos, Que., from 1945, later plant engr., mgr. Jeffrey Mine, 1950-51, then. chmn. bd.; gen. mgr. Asbestos Fibre div. Canadian Johns-Manville Ltd., 1951-71, also v.p., dir. parent Co. Johns Manville Corp.; mining cons., exec. v.p. Hazemag (Can.) Ltd., Hazemag U.S.A. Inc. Recipient Distinguished Alumnus award Mich. Tech. U. Registered profl. engr., Que. Mem. Am. Inst. Mining and Metall. Engrs., Canadian Inst. Metallurgy, Coal Mining Assn., Que. Asbestos C. of C. K.C. Club: Whitlock Golf and Country (Hudson, Que.). Home: 2699 Steeplechase Blvd Box 713 Rural Route 1 Hudson PQ J0P 1H0 Canada Office: Hazemag (Can) Ltd 98 Columbus St Pointe-Claire PQ Canada also Hazemag USA Inc Parkway West Pittsburgh PA

LINDELL, P. GRIFFITH, advt. and public relations cons.; b. Pitts., Aug. 20, 1944; s. Paul D. and Helen D. (Rizzo) L.; B.S. in Edn., Slippery Rock State Coll., 1966; M.A., Calif. State U., 1972; m. Margaret Ann Richards, Aug. 4, 1968; children—Paul Griffith, Elizabeth Ann, Richard David. Faculty, Fresno (Calif.) City Schs., 1966-74; asst. to dir./mktg. dir. Creation-Sci. Research Center, San Diego, 1974-77; co-founder Beta Book Co., San Diego, 1974-77; gen. mgr. Constrn. Div., Wolff Devel., Inc., San Diego, 1977-78; mktg./sales dir. Alban-Spear Assos., San Diego, 1978-80; advt. mgr. SPIN Physics, Inc., San Diego, 1980—; advt. and public relations cons. P. Griffith Lindell Asso., 1980—. Lic. real estate, Calif. Mem. Nat. Acad. TV Arts and Scis., San Diego Christian Businessmen's Com. (dir. 1978-80). Republican. Office: 11633 Sorrento Valley Rd San Diego CA 92121

LINDEN, MICHAEL JOHN, writer, investment advisor; b. Bristol, Eng., Oct. 17, 1946; s. John Mitchell and Kathleen (Rossiter) L.; self-educated. Editor and pub. Hard Facts, 1979—; economist, econ. philosopher, investment advisor, public speaker; also appearances on radio and TV. Mem. Newsletter Assn. Am. Buddhist. Club: Lansdowne (London). Office: PO Box 425 Jacumba CA 92034

LINDER, RODNEY, coal mining technologist, educator; b. Centralia, Ill., Dec. 22, 1941; s. Andrew B. and Mabel B. (Linder) Zack; B.S. in Mgmt., So. Ill. U., 1970; m. Marian R. Roberson, Dec. 28, 1968; children—Carla, Curtis, John. Inds. engr. Old Ben Coal Co., Benton, Ill., 1967-70; mgr. adminstrn. Coal Processing Corp., Norton, Va., 1970-71; project foreman Island Creek Coal Co., Morganfield, Ky., 1971; asst. mine mgr. Zeigler Coal Co., Johnston City, Ill., 1972; dir. coal mining Wabash Valley Coll., Mt. Carmel, Ill., 1973—; pres. fine Tech. Cons. Inc. County chmn. Young Republicans, Williamson County, 1968. Mem. Soc. Mining Engrs. of Am. Inst. Mining Engrs., Ill. Basin Manpower Council (exec. dir.). Roman Catholic. Clubs: K.C., Elks. Home: 407 Melrose St Centralia IL 62801 Office: 900 E Rexford St Centralia IL 62801

LINDLEY, DONA LOU, real estate broker; b. Shattuck, Okla., Jan. 28, 1936; d. Albert and Georgia Ima (Gillespie) Hartley; student real estate courses; m. George W. Lindley, Feb. 3, 1954; children—Wyliea Lindley Edens, George W., David L., Nancy Chloe, Dona Lisa. Owner, broker Lindley Land & Cattle Co., Ozark, Ark., 1972—; co-owner Bobby's Beauty Shop and Boutique, Ozark. Pres. Band Boosters; mem. Ozark Sch. Bd.; leader 4-H Club; active Extension Club, PTA, Girl Scouts U.S.A. designated G.R.I. (grad Realtors Inst.), C.R.S. (cert. residential specialist). Mem. Ozark C. of C. (dir. 1975-76), Nat. Fedn. Small Bus., Nat. Assn. Real Estate, Ark. Real Estate Assn., Ark. Real Estate Polit. Edn. Assn., Farm Bur., Smithsonian Assos., Bus. and Profl. Women's Club. Home: Parker Plantation Ozark AR 72949 Office: Box 531 Ozark AR 72949

LINDLEY, FRANCIS HAYNES, lawyer; b. Los Angeles, May 25, 1899; s. Walter and Florence (Haynes) L.; student Williams Coll., 1916-17; A.B., Harvard, 1922; student U. So. Calif. Law Sch., 1923-26; LL.D. (hon.), Claremont Grad. Sch.; m. Grace N. McCanne, Sept. 6, 1930; children—Francis Haynes, Walter. Admitted to Calif. bar, 1926, since practiced in Los Angeles; formerly partner Chapman, Frazer and Lindley; dep. city atty., Los Angeles, 1927-36, asst. city atty., 1936-42, 45-46. Dir. Gt. Basins Petroleum Co., 1961-63, Bolsa Corps., 1961-63, Safeco Corp., 1950-53, O.T. Johnson Corp., 1950-53, Compania Contratista de Costa Rica. Pres. Town Hall, 1952, chmn. hon. bd., 1968; mem. U.S. Regional Loyalty Bd., 1949-53; mem. Los Angeles Com. Fgn. Relations; mem. Los Angeles Bd. Water and Power Commrs., 1966-67. Pres. Haynes Found., 1937-77, chmn. bd. trustees, 1977—; bd. dirs. Christmas Seal Fund, 1950-52; former bd. dirs. Children's Bur. Los Angeles; trustee Claremont U. Center, 1954-69, hon. trustee, 1969—; trustee Whittier Coll., 1971-76; pres. Friends Claremont Colls., 1966-68; v.p., trustee Hosp. of Good Samaritan Med. Center; trustee Honnold Library Claremont Colls.; bd. dirs. Hosp. Council So. Calif., 1970-76. Mem. Am. Bar Assn. (past chmn. sect. municipal law), English Speaking Union (dir.). Republican. Clubs: California, Los Angeles Country, Men's Garden, Lincoln (Los Angeles); Harvard (So. Calif.). Home: 639 S Plymouth St Los Angeles CA 90005 Office: 530 W 6th St Los Angeles CA 90014

LINDLEY, JAMES GUNN, banker; b. Greensboro, N.C., June 13, 1931; s. Paul Cameron and Helen Marie (Gunn) L.; B.S. in Bus. Adminstrn., U. N.C., 1953; M.B.A. in Fin., N.Y. U., 1960; m. Jane Kennedy, Dec. 3, 1954; children—James Gunn, Patricia Van, Julia Anne. Sr. v.p. Mfrs. Hanover Trust Co., N.Y.C., 1953-75; pres., chief exec. officer Bankshares of N.C. and Bank of N.C., N.A., Raleigh, 1975-79, S.C. Nat. Bank, Columbia, 1979—; pres. S.C. Nat. Corp., 1979—. Served to capt. USNR, 1953-57. Office: PO Box 168 Columbia SC 29202*

LINDLEY, KEITH, oil co. exec.; b. Hutsonville, Ill., Mar. 17, 1914; s. Grover C. and Pearl (Sims) L.; B.S., U. Ill., 1937; m. Nell C. Hodgin Apr. 19, 1941; children—Robert K., Rebecca S., Sherry R. Engr., Gulf Oil Corp., Tulsa, 1937-42; dist. engr. Barnsdall Oil Co., Lake Charles, La., 1946-50; dist. prodn. mgr. Sunray DX Oil Co., Hope, Ark. and Lafayette, La., 1950-70; mgr. drilling Sun Oil Co., Lafayette, 1970—; mem. adv. com., chmn. Gulf Coast Sch. Drilling Practices U. South West La., 1963—; mem. exec. com., chmn. booth com. La. Gulf Coast Oil Exposition, 1967, mem. exec. com., co-chmn. exposition, 1968-69, mem. exec. com., chmn., 1970-71. Mem. Lafayette Humanitarian Awards Commn. Served to maj. U.S. Army, 1942-46. Recipient Good Citizenship award Sunray DX Oil Co., 1968, IADC meritorious service award, 1966; established endowment fund U. Southwestern La., 1976. Mem. Am. Petroleum Inst. (chmn. So. dist. pipe com., mem. numerous coms., Meritorious Service award 1961, citation for service award 1969), Internat. Assn. Drilling Contractors, Am. Inst. Mining Engrs., Petroleum Club Lafayette. Republican. Home: 105 Bernice St Lafayette LA 70503 Office: PO Box 3308 Lafayette LA 70502

LINDNER, CARL HENRY, II, financial holding co. exec.; b. Dayton, Ohio, Apr. 22, 1919; s. Carl Henry and Clara (Serrer) L.; m. Edith Baily, Dec. 31, 1953; children—Carl Henry, III, Stephen Craig, Keith Edward. Co-founder, United Dairy Farmers, 1940; pres., chmn. bd. Am. Fin. Corp., Cin., 1959—; pub. Cin. Enquirer; dir. Combined Communications Corp., United Brands, Fairmont Foods. Bd. advisers Bus. Adminstrn. Coll., U. Cin. Republican. Baptist. Club: Mason. Office: Am Fin Corp One E 4th St Cincinnati OH 45202*

LINDQUIST, BARBARA JEAN, trade assn. exec.; b. South Bend, Apr. 2, 1934; d. Edgar Victor and Ruth Inez (Cannon) R.; student Rockford (Ill.) public schs.; children—Loren Thomas, Kenneth Dale (dec.). Sec. to coms. Woodward Gov. Co., Rockford, Ill., 1959-61; sec., cashier, office mgr. Paul Revere Life Ins. Co., Rockford, 1963-67; exec. v.p. Ft. Collins (Colo.) Bd. Realtors, 1969-80, Denver Bd. Realtors, 1980—; lectr. secretarial seminars and exec. officer seminars. Vol. Hospice of Larimer. Recipient recognition plaque Ft. Collins Bd. Realtors. Mem. Salesmen with a Purpose Club (sec., dir.), Am. Bus. Women's Assn., Am. Soc. Assn. Execs., Nat. Assn. Realtors (gov. exec. officers seminars 1977-79, now dean, recipient recognition plaque). Republican. Presbyterian. Home: 1055 Logan St Apt 1501 Denver CO 80203 Office: 990 S Logan St Denver CO 80209

LINDSAY, DONALD PARKER, mut. savs. banker; b. Spokane, Wash., Aug. 31, 1915; s. Alexander John and Alice Maude (Kelly) L.; student U. Wash., 1934-35; m. Patricia Lally, Oct. 2, 1940; children—Karen, Bridget, Monica. Teller, Lincoln Mut. Savs. Bank, and predecessors, Spokane, 1935, appraiser, loan officer, exec. v.p., sec., 1935-50, mgr. home office, 1954-62, pres., 1962—, chief exec. officer, 1969-80, chmn. bd., 1978—; cons. AID Mission to Iran, 1964. Bd. dirs. Spokane Unltd.; mem. adv. bd. Inland Empire Goodwill Industries; mem. Spokane Arts Commn.; bus. adv. Wash. State U.; chmn. United Red Feather, 1952; trustee Spokane Mcpl. League; pres. Spokane Philharm., chmn. Champagne Charities. Served from pvt. to 1st lt., USAAF, 1942-46. Mem. Nat. Assn. Mut. Savs. Banks (dir.), Mut. Savs. Banks Assn. Wash (pres. 1979), U.S. League Savs. Assns., Nat. League Insured Savs. Assns. (gov., exec. com.), Wash. Savs. League (pres. 1961-62), Spokane Soc. Residential Appraisers (pres. 1952—), Spokane C. of C. (trustee). Clubs: Spokane, Spokane Country (past pres.), Manito Golf and Country, Empire, Univ. (past pres.). Office: W 818 Riverside Spokane WA 99201

LINDSAY, LAURENCE DUANE, foods co. exec.; b. Heber City, Utah, June 14, 1935; s. Ray and Grace Virginia (Murdock) L.; B.S., Brigham Young U., 1971; m. Shirley Ann Lee, Aug. 2, 1957; 1 son, Stanley Duane. Mem. new products devel. staff Haig Berberian Inc. div. Pet, Inc., Modesto, Calif., 1966-68, mgr. quality assurance, 1974-77, quality assurance mgr. Funsten Nut div., 1977—; supr. Wilkinson Center, Brigham Young U., Provo, Utah, 1969-71; asst. supr., food div. Salt Lake City-County Health Dept., 1971-74. Com. chmn. scout troop Boy Scouts Am. Served with anti-aircraft U.S. Army, 1954-56. Registered sanitarian. Mem. Inst. Food Technologists, Am. Soc. for Microbiology, Dried Fruit Assn. (sci. adv. bd.). Republican. Mem. Ch. of Jesus Christ of Latter-Day Saints. Home: 2517 Killarney Way Modesto CA 95355

LINDSAY, ROGER ALEXANDER, corporate exec.; b. Dundee, Scotland, Feb. 18, 1941; s. Archibald Carswell and Edith Paterson (Lindsay-Bissett) L.; Law and Econs. Queens Coll., U. St. Andrews, 1961; postgrad. Chartered Accountants Inst. (Scotland), 1964. Accountant, Sunblest Bakeries Ltd., Dundee, 1964-66; with Asso. Brit. Foods Ltd., London, Eng., 1966-71; dir. Luncheon Vouchers Ltd., London, 1969-71; sec.-treas., dir. Wittington Investments Ltd., Toronto, Ont., Can., 1971—, Wittington Properties Ltd., Wittington Devels. Ltd., Kew Securities Ltd., J.R. Booth Ltd., Wittington Leaseholds Ltd.; dir. Loblaw Cos. Ltd., Loblaws Ltd., Braemer Corp. Nat. treas. Nat. Council of Youth Fellowships (Scotland), 1964-66; treas. Scottish Youth Assembly, 1965-66; trustee, gov., sec. W.

Garfield Weston Found., 1971—, Wittington Found.; bd. dirs. United Appeal Greater Toronto, Can. 4H Council, Dr. Charles H. Best Found., Torch Ednl. Found. Fellow Brit. Inst. Mgmt. Presbyterian (elder). Home: Suite 1301 150 Heath St W Toronto ON M4V 2Y4 Canada Office: Suite 2001 22 St Clair Ave East Toronto ON M4T 2S3 Canada

LINDSAY, WILLIAM WALTER, pension and profit sharing actuary; b. Culver City Calif., Apr. 3, 1936; s. Walter J. and Elizabeth K. (Horne) L.; B.S., U. So. Calif., 1960, postgrad., 1973; m. Alice Torgerson, Apr. 20, 1969; children—William C., Robert J., Jonathan P., Elizabeth A., David W. Cons., Pension & Profit Sharing Cons. Am., Inc., Los Angeles, 1962-65; corp. analyst Conn. Gen. Life Ins. Co., Los Angeles, 1965-67; pres., chmn. bd. Lindsay & Assos. Inc., pension and profit sharing, Beverly Hills, Calif., 1967—. Bd. dirs. Russia for Christ, Inc. Served with USAF, 1961-62. Enrolled actuary U.S. Dept. Treasury. Mem. Am. Soc. Pension Actuaries, San Fernando Life Underwriters Assn. (dir.), Los Angeles Life Underwriters Assn. (Man of Year 1970), Nat. Assn. Life Underwriters, Trust Council Los Angeles, Million Dollar Round Table (life mem.), Beta Theta Pi. Republican. Presbyterian. Clubs: Jonathan, Mexican Hunting Assn. Home: 1000 Villa Grove Dr Pacific Palisades CA 90272 Office: 2029 Century Park E Los Angeles CA 90067

LINDSEY, JACK B., business exec.; b. Taft, Calif., Nov. 20, 1925; student Fresno State Coll., 1943-44; B.Applied Sci. in Elec. Engring., U. Calif., at Berkeley, 1946; M.B.A., Stanford U., 1950; m. Jean Catherine O'Brien, Jan. 24, 1948; children—Daniel Lee, David Allan. Mktg. mgr. Carnation Co., Los Angeles, 1950-59; asst. to pres. Microdot, Inc., electronics, South Pasadena, Calif., 1959-61; pres. Lindsey-Westwood Assos., mgmt. cons., Los Angeles, 1961-64; v.p. mktg. Early Calif. Foods, Inc., Los Angeles, 1964-69, pres., 1971-74; v.p. Early Calif. Industries, Inc., Los Angeles, 1964-74, dir., 1964-75; pres., pub. Clarke Pub. Co., Portland, 1969-71; pres., chief exec. officer Sun Harbor Industries, San Diego, 1974-77, Point Adams Packing Co. (Oreg.), 1974-75, Sun Harbor-Caribe, Inc., P.R., 1974-77; pres. Lindsey-Westwood Assos., mgmt. cons., 1977—; chmn. Am. Overseas Trade & Fin., Ltd., Sun Belt Energy Corp., Sun Belt Mgmt. Service, Inc., Strike Systems, Inc. Legis. sec. to gov. of Calif., 1966-67; chmn. Favorite Son Com., 1968; alt. del. Republican Nat. Conv., 1968; candidate for Congress, 1969; mem. President's Round Table; mem. bus. adv. com. to dean Sch. Bus., San Diego State U. Served to lt. (j.g.) USNR, 1943-47. San Francisco Advt. Club grantee, 1948. Mem. IEEE, Order of Golden Bear, Pres.'s Assn., San Diego C. of C. (dir.). Stanford Alumni Assn., Navy League, U.S. Naval Inst., Phi Gamma Delta. Christian Scientist. Clubs: Masons, San Diego Yacht. Home: 1594 Hacienda Dr El Cajon CA 92020

LINDSLEY, RICHARD GRAHAM, ins. co. exec.; b. Mpls., Sept. 17, 1921; s. Charles Frederick and Juanita Margaret (Miller) L.; student Occidental Coll., 1939-40; B.S., U.S. Naval Acad., 1943; postgrad. Managerial Policy Inst., U. So. Calif., 1967-68; m. Patricia Ann Winningham, June 9, 1943; children—Richard G., Michael G., Christopher B. Spl. trainee Bank of Am., Los Angeles, 1950-51; with Farmers Ins. Group, Los Angeles, 1951—, now pres., chief exec. officer; dir. Farmers New World Life Ins. Co., Ohio State Life Ins. Co. Served to lt. USN, 1943-50. Club: California. Office: 4680 Wilshire Blvd Los Angeles CA 90010

LINDSTEIN, VIGO VALDEMAR, cryptologist; b. Ljusdal, Sweden, Apr. 8, 1906; s. Axel Frans and Anna (Trygg) L.; U. Engr., Royal Tech. Coll., Stockholm, 1932; m. Maj Anna Kristina Stromgren, Sept. 26, 1937; children—Eva Marianne (Mrs. Karl-Erik Kander), Rolf Stephan, Asst. in econ. geography, Stockholm, Sweden, 1932-33; designer Hugin Cash Register, Stockholm, 1933-34; chief engr. SA Vitejust, Paris, France, 1934-35; chief engr. LM Ericsson Cash Register, Stockholm, 1935-42; works mgr. AB Cryptoteknik, Stockholm, 1942-48; prodn. mgr. AB Georg Schonander, Stockholm, 1948-52; mng. dir. AB Transvertex, Varby, Sweden, 1952-70. Mem. Swedish Tech. Assn., Am. Inst. Mgmt. Club: Par Bricole (Stockholm). Inventor field of cash registers, med. equipment, cryptology. Home: 104 Travbanevägen 60365 Norrköping Sweden

LING, SUILIN, mgmt. cons.; b. Shanghai, China, Oct. 13, 1930; s. Chunchen and Maisan (Dunn) L.; came to U.S., 1949, naturalized, 1963; B.S., U. Mich., 1952; Ph.D., 1961; m. Avril Marjorie Kathleen Button, Apr. 4, 1964; children—Christopher Charles, Charmian Avril. Mech. engr. Ebasco Services, Inc., 1953-54; with research div. Foster Wheeler Corp., 1954-64; mgmt. cons. The Emerson Cons., Inc., 1964-65; sr. economist Communications Satellite Corp., 1965-67; chief economist Northrop-Page Communication Engrs., Inc., 1967-70; founder-dir., chief economist Teleconsult, Inc., Washington, 1970—; lectr. econs. Bernard M. Baruch Sch. Bus. and Pub. Adminstrn., City Coll. N.Y. Mem. Am. Mgmt. Assn., Am. Econ. Assn., Am. Soc. M.E., Am. Acad. Polit. and Social Sci. Author: Economies of Scale in the Steam-Electric Power Generating Industry, 1964. Home: 2735 Unicorn Ln NW Washington DC 20015 Office: 2555 M St NW Washington DC 20037

LINGENFELSER, ROBERT GEORGE, hosp. ops. co. exec.; b. Savannah, Ga., Oct. 13, 1937; s. William F. and Jewel B. (Becker) L.; B.S. in Psychology, Augusta Coll., 1969; m. Rose Marie Dumas Jan. 19, 1957; children—Robert, Athena, William, Christopher, Anthony, Donna, Alicia, Billy, Alaina, Robin, Andrea. Dir. ops., asst. v.p. Charter Med. Corp., Macon, Ga., 1970-77; dir. psychiat. devel. Hosp. Corp. Am., Nashville, 1977-79; pres. Mental Health Am., Inc., Atlanta, 1979—. Sustaining mem. Republican Nat. Com. Served with USN, 1955-59. Named Family of Yr. for Augusta and 10th Dist. Ga., 1969. Mem. Fedn. Am. Hosps., Nat. Assn. Pvt. Psychiat. Hosps., Am. Coll. Hosp. Adminstrs., Nat. Assn. Mental Health Adminstrs. Roman Catholic. Club: West Paces Racquet. Home: 4960 Long Island Terr NE Atlanta GA 30342 Office: PO Box 28357 Atlanta GA 30328

LINGENFELTER, R. BRIAN, bank exec.; b. New Kensington, Pa., Aug. 29, 1944; s. Samuel Stanley and Elizabeth Avanell (Bussard) L.; B.S., Wagner Coll., 1966; M.B.A., Am. U., 1968. Asst. trust investment officer Am. Security Bank, Washington, 1969-71, trust investment officer, 1971-73, asst. v.p., 1973-80, v.p., 1980—. Mem. Washington Soc. Investment Analysts. Home: 2213 Washington Circle NW Washington DC 20037 Office: 1501 Pennsylvania Ave NW Washington DC 20013

LINK, ROBERT ALLEN, financial co. exec.; b. Detroit, July 2, 1932; s. Raymond Henry and Helen Emily (Grassley) L.; B.S., Wayne State U., 1954; J.D., U. Mich., 1957; m. Cynthia Louise Krans, June 15, 1957; children—Charles Nicholas, Frederick Allen. Admitted to Mich. bar, 1958; mem. firm Darden & Bonk, Detroit, 1958-61; pvt. practice law, Detroit, 1961-63; mem. firm Manikoff & Munde, Pontiac, Mich., 1963-64; atty. Chrysler Fin. Corp., Troy, Mich., 1964-67, sr. atty., 1967-70, corporate sec., 1970—. Mem. Am., Mich., Detroit bar assns. Home: 945 Harmon Ave Birmingham MI 48009 Office: 900 Tower Dr Troy MI 48098

LINN, EDWARD THEODORE, constrn. co. exec.; b. Peoria, Ill., Jan 14, 1933; s. Oscar and Lelia (Mellert) L.; student U. Ill., 1950-51; Northwestern U., 1953; B.S., Bradley U., 1956; m. Judith Arline Buffum, Aug. 29, 1954; children—Nancy Ann, Diana Jean, Edith Annette. Hydraulics engr. John Deere, Moline, Ill., 1956-58; pres. Linn Materials, Inc., Canton, Ill., 1958—, Canton Concrete Products, Liverpool Materials Co., Canton, 1970—, Linn Farms, Inc., Canton, 1970—, also Linn Devel. Corp. Bd. dirs. Canton Assn. Commerce and Industry, 1966-72, pres. bd., 1971. Served with USNR, 1952-54. Mem. Phi Sigma Phi. Methodist (bd. mem. 1958—). Mason (32 deg.). Club: Creve Coeur (Peoria, Ill.). Home: 150 Middle Park Dr Canton IL 61520 Office: Box 539 Canton IL 61520

LINOWITZ, SOL MYRON, lawyer; b. Trenton, N.J., Dec. 7, 1913; s. Joseph and Rose (Oglenskye) L.; A.B., Hamilton Coll., 1935, LL.D.; J.D., Cornell U., 1938; LL.D., Allegheny Coll., Babson Inst. Bus. Adminstrn., Amherst U., Colgate U., Dartmouth Coll., Ithaca Coll., U. Mich., U. Mo., Oberlin U., U. of Pacific, U. Pa., St. John Fisher Coll., St. Lawrence U., Washington U., Syracuse U., Notre Dame U., Bucknell U., Roosevelt U.; L.H.D., Am. U., Yeshiva U., Elmira Coll., Marietta Coll., Curry Coll., Jewish Theol. Sem., U. Judaism, Wooster Coll.; m. Evelyn Zimmerman, Sept. 3, 1939; children—Anne, June, Jan, Ronni. Admitted to N.Y. bar, 1938, D.C. bar, 1969; asst. gen. counsel OPA, Washington, 1942-44; partner firm Sutherland, Linowitz & Williams, 1946-58, Harris, Beach, Keating, Wilcox, Dale & Linowitz, Rochester, N.Y., 1958-66; counsel Harris Beach and Wilcox, Rochester, 1969—; sr. partner Coudert Bros. law firm, 1969—; chmn. exec. com., gen. counsel, chmn. bd. Xerox Corp., until 1966; chmn. bd., chief exec. officer Xerox Internat., 1966; dir. Pan Am. World Airways Inc.; trustee Mut. Life Ins. Co. N.Y. Ambassador to OAS, 1966-69; co-negotiator, ambassador for Panama Canal Treaty, 1977; chmn. Pres.'s Commn. on World Hunger, 1978—; spl. rep. of Pres. with rank of ambassador for Mideast negotiations, 1979—; co-chmn. organizing com. Internat. Exec. Service Corps; chmn. State Dept. Adv. Com. on Internat. Orgns., 1961-66. Vice chmn. bd. trustees John F. Kennedy Center for Performing Arts until 1970; co-chmn. Nat. Urban Coalition; trustee Hamilton Coll., Johns Hopkins U., Am. Jewish Com., Cornell U., Am. Assembly. Served to lt. USNR, 1944-46. Fellow Am. Acad. Arts and Scis.; mem. Council Fgn. Relations, Am. (pres. N.Y. State), Rochester (pres. 1952) assns. for UN, Rochester C. of C. (pres. 1958), Am., N.Y., Rochester (v.p. 1949-50) bar assns., Am. Assn. UN (dir.), Nat. Planning Assn. (trustee), Order of Coif, Phi Beta Kappa, Phi Kappa Phi. Club: Univ. Contbr. articles to profl. jours. Home: 2325 Wyoming Ave NW Washington DC 20008 Office: 1 Farragut Sq S Washington DC 20006

LINTON, ROBERT EDWARD, investment banker; b. N.Y.C., May 19, 1925; s. Adolph B. and Helen (Hirshon) Lichtenstein; grad. Phillips Exeter Acad., 1943; m. Margot R. Tishman, June 19, 1952; children—Roberta Helen, Thomas Norman, Jeffrey Robert, Elizabeth Marie. With Drexel Burnham Lambert and predecessor cos., N.Y.C., 1946—, gen. partner, 1956-72, sr. exec. v.p., 1972-77, pres., chief exec. officer, 1977—. Served to 2d lt. USAAF, 1943-45. Mem. Securities Industry Assn. (dir.), N.Y. Soc. Security Analysts. Club: Century Country. Office: 60 Broad St New York NY 10004

LIPES, HAZEL JOAN, mgmt. cons. co. exec.; b. Edmonton, Alta., Can., Dec. 3, 1938; d. Benjamin and Sally (Stein) Wainberg; B.A., Sir George Williams U., 1959; M.S.W., McGill U., 1961; diploma in community mental health consultation, Inst. Community Family Psychiatry, Jewish Gen. Hosp., Montreal, 1970-72; m. Arnold Lipes, Sept. 23, 1962; children—Leonard, Heidi, Stanley, Betsy. Psychiat. case worker, group therapist Jewish Gen. Hosp., Montreal, 1961-66; comptroller Packaging Automation Machinery Co. Ltd., Montreal, 1978-79, v.p., 1972—, also dir.; dir. Glopak Industries, Lumiray Mfg. Co., Supreme Investments, LaHada Realties; cons. and lectr. in field. Councillor, City of Cote Saint-Luc, Que., 1974-78, pro-mayor, 1976-77. Recipient Queens 25th Jubilee Commemorative medal, 1977. Mem. Que. Assn. Mental Health Cons. (v.p. 1972-76), Corp. Profl. Workers Que. Liberal. Jewish. Home: 6521 Merton Rd Montreal PQ H4V 1C4 Canada Office: 8350 Mountain Sights Ave Montreal PQ H4P 2C2 Canada

LIPMAN, IRA ACKERMAN, security service co. exec.; b. Little Rock, Nov. 15, 1940; s. Mark and Belle (Ackerman) L.; student Ohio Wesleyan U., 1958-60; LL.D., John Marshall U., 1970; m. Barbara Ellen Kelly Couch, July 5, 1970; children—Gustave K., Joshua S, M Benjamin. Salesman, exec. Mark Lipman Service Inc., Memphis, 1960-63; pres. Guardsmark, Inc., Memphis, 1963—, chief exec. officer, 1966—, chmn. bd., 1968—; mem. environ. security com. of pvt. security adv. council Law Enforcement Assistance Adminstrn., 1975-76. Met. chmn. Nat. Alliance of Businessmen, Memphis, 1970-71; bd. dirs. Memphis Jewish Community Center, 1974; bd. dirs. Nat. Council on Crime and Delinquency, 1975, mem. exec. com., 1976, chmn. fin. com., treas., 1978-79; bd. dirs. Greater Memphis Council on Crime and Delinquency, 1976-78; mem. young leadership cabinet United Jewish Appeal, 1973-78; mem. SE Regional Campaign Cabinet, 1980; mem. pres.'s council Memphis State U., 1975—; Shelby County chmn. U.S. Savs. Bonds, 1976; bd. dirs. Tenn. Ind. Colls. Fund, 1977-79, exec. com., 1978-79; trustee Memphis Acad. Arts, 1977—; mem. exec. bd. Chickasaw council Boy Scouts Am., 1978—; mem. President's Club, Christian Bros. Coll., 1979; mem. Future Memphis, 1979—, bd. dirs., 1980—; nat. trustee NCCJ, 1980—, bd. dirs. Memphis chpt., 1980—; mem. Union Am. Hebrew Congregations Task Force on Reform Jewish Outreach, 1979—; bd. dirs. Memphis-Shelby County unit Am. Cancer Soc., 1980—, Memphis Jewish Fedn., 1980—, Memphis Orchestral Soc., Inc., 1980—, Brooks Meml. Art Gallery, 1981; com. mem. Nat. Law Enforcement Explorer Conf., 1980; mem. Memphis State U. Visual Arts Council, 1980—. Entrepreneurial fellow Memphis State U., 1976. Mem. Internat. Assn. Chiefs of Police, Am. Soc. Criminology, Internat. Soc. for Criminology, Am. Soc. for Indsl. Security (cert. protection profl.). Republican. Clubs: Economic (dir. 1980—), Ridgeway Country, Racquet, Summit, Delta, Petroleum, B'nai B'rith (Memphis); International (Washington). Author: How to Protect Yourself from Crime, 1975; contbr. articles to profl. jours. Home: 4490 Park Ave Memphis TN 38117 also 58 W 58th St New York NY 10019 Office: 260 Madison Ave New York NY 10016 also 22 S 2d St Memphis TN 38103

LIPNER, ALAN J., lawyer, retail co. exec.; b. N.Y.C., Jan. 27, 1938; s. Leo H. and Ethel M. Lipner; B.S., Pa. State U., 1959; J.D., N.Y. U., 1962, LL.M., 1965; m. Nira Hozman, May 28, 1967; children—Diane, Ethel, David. Admitted to N.Y. bar, 1965, D.C. bar, 1980; tax acct. Olin Corp., N.Y.C., 1962-65; mgr. Coopers & Lybrand, N.Y.C., 1965-70; partner Touche Ross & Co., Brussels and Washington, 1970-79, v.p. F.W. Woolworth Co., N.Y.C., 1979—; asst. prof. Boston U., 1975—. C.P.A., N.Y. Mem. Tax Execs. Inst., Am. Bar Assn., Am. Inst. C.P.A.'s, Fin. Execs. Inst. Jewish. Club: B'nai B'rith. Contbr. articles to profl. jours. Office: 233 Broadway New York NY 10279

LIPNER, JONATHAN, health service co. exec.; b. Phila., Apr. 13, 1953; s. Benjamin and Ethel (Bleicher) L.; B.S., Phila. Coll. Textiles and Sci., 1976. Controller, 20th Street Med. Group, Inc., Phila., 1976-77; controller Morris Med. Lab., Inc., Phila., 1976-77, partner, 1978—; founder, pres. Home Health Services of South Phila., Inc., 1977—, also Glenwood Boarding Homes, Westmont Retirement Home, Biddle Properties; partner Merion Investments, Morrisville Garden Apts., Cresswood Apts. Active young adult pacesetters Allied Jewish Appeal. Jewish. Club: Masons. Home: Box 337 Bala Cynwyd PA 19004 Office: 1634 S 20th St Philadelphia PA 19145

LIPPE, MELVIN K(ARL), lawyer; b. Chgo., Oct. 21, 1933; s. Melvin M. and Myrtle (Karlsberg) L.; B.S., Northwestern U., 1955, J.D., 1958; grad. certificate Grad. Sch. Banking, U. Wis., 1965; certificate Sr. Bank Officers Seminar, Harvard, 1966; m. Sandra Matros; children—Suzanne, Michael S., Deanna. Admitted to Ill. bar, 1958; asso. D'Ancona, Pflaum, Wyatt & Riskind, Chgo., 1958-61; asst. to chmn. bd. Exchange Nat. Bank of Chgo., 1961-62, asst. v.p., 1962-64, v.p., 1964-66, sr. v.p., sec. to bd. dirs., 1966-69, exec. v.p., dir., 1969-74, vice-chmn. bd., 1974-76; exec. v.p., dir. Exchange Internat. Corp., 1972-74, vice chmn. bd., 1974-76; partner Antonow & Fink, Chgo., 1977—; instr. Ill. Inst. Tech., 1960-63. Bd. dirs. Young Men's Jewish Council, Chgo., 1960—, pres., 1971; bd. dirs. Jewish Community Centers Chgo., pres., 1980. Mem. Ill. N.G., 1959. C.P.A., Ill. Mem. Am., Ill., Chgo. bar assns., Am. Jewish Com., Phi Epsilon Pi, Beta Gamma Sigma. Jewish. Club: Standard (Chgo.). Editor: Northwestern U. Law Rev., 1957-58. Home: 180 E Pearson St Chicago IL 60611 Office: 111 E Wacker Dr Chicago IL 60601

LIPPE, NOEL RAYBURN, editor, pub.; b. Morganville, Kans., Nov. 16, 1936; s. Orville Rayburn and Erma Lavern (Good) L.; B.S. in Agrl. Journalism, Kans. State U., 1958; M.A. in Journalism, U. Mo., 1964; m. Betty Jane Larkin, Aug. 22, 1959; children—David, Darren. Field editor Packer Pub. Co., Kansas City, Mo., 1958-63; editor fin. publs. Mid-Am. Ins., Kansas City, asso. editor Bank News, 1964-69; pres. Halgo Pub., Kansas City, 1969-72; v.p. Fincom, Inc., Topeka, 1972-76; owner, pub. Rocky Mountain Industries Mag., 1971-74; pres., pub. Mid-Am. Commerce and Industry Mag., MACI, Inc., Topeka, 1976—. Served with AFNG, 1958. Mem. Sigma Delta Chi. Republican. Methodist. Club: Masons. Home and Office: 1824 Cheyenne St Topeka KS 66604

LIPPINCOTT, PHILIP EDWARD, paper co. exec.; b. Camden, N.J., Nov. 28, 1935; s. J. Edward and Marjorie Nix (Spooner) L.; B.A. with honors, Dartmouth, 1957; M.B.A. with distinction, Mich. State U., 1964; m. Naomi Catherine Prindle, Aug. 22, 1959; children—Grant, Kevin, Kerry. With Scott Paper Co., Phila., 1959—, staff v.p. corporate planning, 1968-71, div. v.p. consumer products marketing, 1971-72, corp. v.p. packaged products sales and marketing, 1972-75, sr. v.p., 1975-77, v.p., group exec., 1977-80, pres., 1980—, dir.; guest lectr. Columbia, U. Pa., Temple U., U. Del., Cheney State Coll. vice chmn. Solid Waste Council; mem. exec. com. Paper Distbn. Council. Chief Woodstream Nation, Y-Indian Guides, 1967-69. Trustee, Zurbrugg Meml. Hosp., 1980—. Served to capt. AUS, 1957-63. Mem. Am. Paper Inst. (dir., mem. exec. com. tissue div.), Assn. Nat. Advertisers (advt. policy com.), Kappa Kappa Kappa, Pi Sigma Epsilon, Beta Gamma Sigma. Mem. Soc. Friends. Club: Riverton Country. Home: 309 Highway Ave Riverton NJ 08077 Office: Scott Plaza I Philadelphia PA 19113

LIPS, ALLAN FRANK, steel equipment mfg. exec.; b. N.Y.C., Feb. 8, 1948; s. Albert F. and Alice (Scarani) L.; B.B.A. in Mktg., St. John's U., Jamaica, N.Y., 1969; m. Kathleen Newell, June 19, 1971; 1 son, Kevin Michael. With Cherry-Burrell Corp., 1969—, Eastern regional mgr., White Plains, N.Y., 1978—. N.Y. State Regents scholar, 1965-69. Mem. N.E. Ice Cream Assn., New Eng. Soft Drink Assn., New Eng. Milk Dealers Assn. Roman Catholic. Office: 77 Tarrytown Rd White Plains NY 10607

LIPSCOMB, LINDA ANN WAGNER (MRS. JOHN F. LIPSCOMB), info. scientist; b. Cleve., Feb. 10, 1943; d. Gordon N. and Ann Linda (Musgrave) Wagner; A.B., Marietta Coll., 1965; M.S., Case Western Res. U., 1966; m. John F. Lipscomb, Apr. 13, 1968. Information specialist TRW Systems Group, Redondo Beach, Cal., 1966-68, configuration and data mgmt. specialist, 1968-72, configuration and data mgmt. adminstr., 1972-74, project data mgr., 1974-79, project mgr. TRW Energy Systems Group, 1979—. Mem. Spl. Libraries Assn., Am. Soc. Info. Sci., Chi Omega, Pi Delta Epsilon. Home: 400 Hillcrest St El Segundo CA 90245 Office: R4/2120 One Space Park Redondo Beach CA 90278

LIPSCOMB, WILLIAM THOMAS, JR., sales exec.; b. Los Angeles, Apr. 7, 1945; s. William Thomas and Blanche Naomi (Wilson) L.; B.S., Howard U., 1967; postgrad. Temple U., 1971-73; m. Eleanore Laverne Warren, Nov. 28, 1970; stepchildren—Gale Bernadette Hopson, Sonya LaRaye Owens. Sales trainee Coated Abrasives and Related Products div. Minn. Mining & Mfg. Co., Phila., N.J., 1974, sales rep., Los Angeles, 1974, West Caldwell, N.J., 1977, account rep., West Caldwell, 1979—. Mem. ednl. task force Urban League of Bergen County, N.J., 1978—; mem. choir, chaplain Mt. Bethel Bapt. Ch., 1978-80, dir. Gospel Choir, 1978—, staff youth dept., 1978—. Served to capt., USAF, 1967-71, USAFR, 1976—. Decorated Air Force Commendation medal; recipient Outstanding Achievement Plaque, Upward Bound program Temple U., summers, 1972, 73. Mem. Am. Mgmt. Assn., Mgmt. Book Club Assos., Res. Officers Assn., Howard U. Alumni Assn., Alpha Phi Alpha. Democrat. Baptist. Clubs: 3M Sales (Outstanding Achievement Plaque 1976, 77), Order of Lamp (parliamentarian Ridgewood and Glen Rock, N.J. 1978-80). Home: 154 Laauwe Pl Wyckoff NJ 07481 Office: 15 Henderson Dr West Caldwell NJ 07006

LIPSTATE, EUGENE JACOB, petroleum geologist; b. Tyler, Tex., Dec. 6, 1927; s. Philip H. and Gertrude (Faber) L.; B.S., U. Tex., 1949; m. Jo Ann Davis, Feb. 26, 1950; children—James Mitchell, Betsy Ann. With Petroleum Service Co., San Antonio, 1949-50; Tex. dist. engr. Caran Bros. Engring. Co., San Antonio and Tyler, 1950-51; geologist Ryan Consol. Petroleum Corp., Dallas, 1951-52, Tex. dist. geologist, Abilene, 1953-54; geologist Midstates Oil Corp., San Antonio, 1955-58; Tenneco Oil Co., Houston, 1958-62; v.p. exploration Northwest Oil Co., Dallas and Lafayette La., 1962—; partner Tri-Ltd., Lafayette, 1977—; dir. Lipstate Creative Services, Inc., Lafayette, 1975-80; pres. Eugene J. Lipstate, Inc., Lafayette, 1978—. Served to lt. USAF, 1952-53. Mem. Assn. Petroleum Geologists, Lafayette Geol. Soc. (dir.), Gulf Coast Assn. Geol. Socs., U. Tex. Ex-Students Assn. Republican. Clubs: Lafayette Petroleum, Lafayette City, Lafayette Longhorn, Oakbourne Country. Home: 401 Shelly Dr Lafayette LA 70503 Office: PO Box 52421 Lafayette LA 70505

LIPSTEIN, MICHAEL, real estate and constrn. co. exec.; b. Bklyn., June 8, 1936; s. Phillip and Grace (Gleichenhaus) L.; student Boston U., 1954-55; A.A., Pratt Inst., 1957; student Bernard Baruch Grad. Sch. Bus. Adminstrn., CCNY, 1959, Practising Law Inst., 1959; m. Judith Anne Paulson, June 3, 1973; children—Keith, Evan, Hillary. Partner various real estate cos., N.Y.C., 1955-80; prin. Michael Lipstein Constrn. Co., N.Y.C., 1966—. Mem. various com. Fedn. Jewish Philanthropies and Fedn. Served with U.S. Army, 1955-56. Mem. Young Mens Real Estate Assn., Real Estate Bd. N.Y., B'nai B'rith Real Estate Assn. Home: 48 Potters Ln Kings Point NY 11024 Office: 136 E 56th St New York NY 10022

LIPTAK, EDWARD GEORGE, real estate broker; b. Passaic, N.J., Aug. 11, 1945; s. George Joseph and Blanch Margaret (Pierano) L.; B.A. magna cum laude in Psychology, U. Tampa, 1973, M.B.A., 1977; 1 dau., Cynthia M. Asst. v.p., br. mgr., tng. dir. Tourtelot, Inc., St.

Petersburg, Fla., 1977-79; pres. Sun World Assos., Inc., St. Petersburg, 1979-81; real estate cons., 1981—; instr. real estate St. Petersburg Jr. Coll. Served with CIC, U.S. Army, 1965-75; Vietnam. Mem. Nat. Assn. Realtors, Fla. Real Estate Exchangors, Real Estate Securities and Syndication Inst. Office: 6009 9th St N Saint Petersburg FL 33703

LIPTON, JOAN, advt. agency exec.; b. N.Y.C., July 12, 1930; B.A., Barnard Coll.; 1 son from previous marriage—David Dean. With Young & Rubicam Inc., N.Y.C., 1949-52, Robert W. Orr & Assos. advt., N.Y.C., 1952-57; with Benton & Bowles Inc., N.Y.C., 1957-64, asso. dir., London, 1964-68; with McCann-Erickson Advt., N.Y.C., 1968—, v.p., asso. creative dir., 1970-79, sr. v.p., 1979—. Mem. bus. council UN Decade for Women, 1977-78. Recipient Nat. Headliner award Women in Communications, 1976-77; named Woman of Yr., Am. Advt. Fedn., 1974; recipient Honors award Ohio U. Sch. Journalism, 1977. Mem. Advt. Women of N.Y. Found. (1st v.p. 1975-76, 78-79), Women in Communications (pres. N.Y. 1974-76). Office: McCann-Erickson Advt 485 Lexington Ave New York NY 10017

LIPTON, KENNETH ALBERT, auctioneer; b. San Antonio, Jan. 29, 1944; s. Meyer and Violet Lipton; A.S., Del Mar Coll., 1968; cert. Nat. Auction Inst., 1969; m. Mary Frances Foster, Aug. 10, 1968; children—Mark Allen, Lori Lynn. Material controller Hudson Engring., Houston, 1970-73; Austin sales br. mgr., A.I.M. Inc., Houston, 1973-75; auctioneer Grover Howell Co., Houston, 1975-76, L.A.W. Auctioneers, Alice, Tex., 1976—, also owner; pres. Lipton's Enterprises. Bd. dirs. Jim Wells County Fair Assn., 1980; counsellor Jim Wells County 4-H, 1980, pres., 1980-81; dr. chmn. United Way of Alice, 1979, sec., 1980, adv. council, 1980; show chmn. Mesquite Dist. Boy Scouts Am., 1979, 80; pres. St. Elizabeth's Parents Club, 1979-80. Served with U.S. Army, 1961-62. Recipient Spl. Recognition, Boy Scouts Am., 1970, 79, Cert. of Appreciation, Jim Wells County Fair Assn., 1979. Mem. Nat. Auctioneers Assn., Tex. Auctioneers Assn., Am. Entrepreneurs Assn., Alice C. of C. (dir., 1979-80). Jewish. Clubs: Jaycees (dir. Pasadena, Tex. 1970, pres. Bellaire, Tex. 1973-74, dir. Austin, Tex. 1975, Alice, Tex. 1976-77, internat. v.p. 1977-80, Key Man award Bellaire 1973, named Jaycee of Yr. Bellaire, 1973), Rotary Internat. (dir. Alice 1979—, named Outstanding Mem., Alice, 1978). Home: 1014 E 4th St Alice TX 78332 Office: 209 S Reynolds Alice TX 78332

LIPTON, WILLIAM LAWRENCE, real estate analyst and cons.; b. Jamaica, N.Y., Oct. 8, 1944; s. William Lawrence and Agnes Margaret (Ryan) Schreck; B.S. in Indsl. Arts, N.Y. U., 1968; M.B.A. in Acctg. (Saul Hertz scholar), Pace U., 1974; m. June Ann Schilowsky, Jan. 22, 1966; children—Seth Alexander, Samantha Bryl. Real estate broker, N.Y.C., 1966—; estate and property mgr. Bernard Lipton, Esq., N.Y.C., 1968-70; dir. Park Mgmt. Inc., real estate holding, N.Y.C., 1970-77; property mgr. fin. and adminstrn. Vorelco, Inc., Englewood Cliffs, N.J., 1977-78; pres. Be Our Neighbor Real Estate Ltd., N.Y.C., 1974—; chmn. Dahshur Constrn. Co., Trinidad, 1977—; sr. partner Lawrence Enterprises, real estate, N.Y.C. and Harrington, Maine, 1975—. Democrat. Jewish. Club: N.Y. U. Office: Box 134 Harrington ME 04643

LISKA, DARIN VLADIMIR, engring. exec.; b. Chotebor, Czechoslovakia, Nov. 12, 1915; s. Vladimir and Emilie (Zavorka) L.; M.Engring., U. Engring., Prague, Czechoslovakia, 1939; m. Millie Oresko, Dec. 20, 1950; 1 son, Peter. Came to U.S., 1965, naturalized, 1970. Partner constrn. co., Chotebor, 1945-49; head dept. spl. structures State Inst., Prague, 1949-64; design engr., Vienna, Austria, 1964-65, U.S., 1965-81; civil-structural cons. Recipient Czechoslovakian State award design heavy industry. Mem. Am. Concrete Inst., Prestressed Concrete Inst., Post Tensioning Inst., ASCE, Nat. Soc. Profl. Engrs. Patentee in field. Address: 14015 Briarworth Dr Houston TX 77077

LISKA, ROGER WILLIAM, educator; b. Rockford, Ill., June 19, 1943; s. William and Emily (Sandrik) L.; B.S. in Civil Engring., Mich. Tech. U., 1965; M.S. in Civil Engring., Wayne State U., 1967; m. Joyce Rotman, June 20, 1965; children—Theresa, Rebecca. Structural engr. Nat. Steel Corp., Detroit, 1965-67; plant engr. Ford Motor Co., Detroit, 1967-69; founds. engr. Chgo. Bridge & Iron Co., Oakbrook, Ill., 1969-71; asst. provost Coll. of DuPage, Glen Ellyn, Ill., 1971-73; prof. bldg. sci. Auburn (Ala.) U., 1973—; cons. structural engring and continuing edn., owner N.C. Vacation & Retirement Community, 1971—; dir. edn. nat. staff Asso. Builders and Contractors, Inc., Washington, 1980—. Danforth Community Coll. Found. fellow.; registered profl. engr., N.C., Ill., Ala. Mem. Am. Inst. Constructors, Am. Council Constrn. Edn., ASCE, Sigma Lambda Chi, Chi Epsilon.

LISKIEWICZ, ROBERT STEPHEN, mech. engr.; b. Norwich, Conn., Sept. 24, 1954; s. Robert Samuel and Lorraine Marie (Zigaro) L.; B.S. cum laude in Mech. Engring., U. Conn., 1976; M.B.A., Western New Eng. Coll., 1980; m. Pamela Jane Prior, Sept. 28, 1979. Prodn. supr. Union Carbide Corp., Hartford, Conn., 1976; project engr. Monsanto Co., Springfield, Mass., 1977-80, safety and property protection specialist, 1980—. U.S. savs. bond campaign canvasser, 1978; United Way canvasser, 1978; presenter at Showcase, Springfield Ednl. TV pledge dr., 1978-79. Mem. Western Mass. Safety Council, Am. Soc. Safety Engrs., Pi Tau Sigma, Tau Beta Pi. Club: Monsanto Social/Athletic Orgn. Home: 16 Old Mill Rd Agawam MA 01001 Office: 730 Worcester St Indian Orchard MA 01151

LISS, NORMAN RICHARD, ins. co. exec.; b. Bronx, N.Y., May 29, 1947; s. Jacob Melvin and Terry Ruth (Stoppler) L.; student Athens (Ala.) Coll., 1965-67, U. Albuquerque, 1967; m. Orlinda P. Olivas, Apr. 11, 1970; children—Maria, Jacqueline Melissa. With First Nat. Life Ins. Co., Albuquerque, 1969-70; founder, pres. Ins. Planners of N.Mex., Albuquerque, 1970—. Active Heart Fund, United Way, Arthritis Found., Boy Scouts Am. Served with USAF, 1967-69. Recipient various ins. sales awards. Mem. Assn. Life Underwriters (local sec.-treas., bd. dirs.), Million Dollar Round Table. Republican. Jewish. Home: 11433 Nassau Dr NE Albuquerque NM 87111 Office: JML Profl Bldg 3644 Thaxton SE Albuquerque NM 87108

LISS, STANLEY, life ins. underwriter; b. N.Y.C., Feb. 14, 1921; s. Max and Anne (Bleecker) L.; B.S. in Commerce, Ohio U., 1942; m. Shirley Waranch, Mar. 12, 1980; children by previous marriage—Ellen Siegel, Robert. Life ins. underwriter N.Y. Life Ins. Co., N.Y.C., 1948—; dir. Qonaar Corp., Elk Grove Village, Ill.; pres. N.Y. Life Agts. Adv. Council, 1968. Served as aviator USN, 1942-45. C.L.U. Mem. Am. Soc. C.L.U.'s (past regional v.p.), N.Y.C. Assn. C.L.U.'s (past pres.), Estate Planning Council N.Y.C. (past pres.). Republican. Club: Middle Bay Country (past pres.) (Oceanside, N.Y.). Home: 200 E 66 St New York NY 10021 Office: 90 Park Ave New York NY 10016

LISSER, MORTON SAMUEL, furniture co. exec.; b. N.Y.C., Feb. 6, 1922; s. Jacob David and Bella (Newman) L.; B.B.A., CCNY, 1942; LL.B., N.Y. U., 1957; m. Martha Schultz, Dec. 24, 1946; children—Justine, Amy. Staff, Herman J. Dobkin & Co., C.P.A.'s, N.Y.C., 1947-54; pvt. practice as C.P.A., N.Y.C., 1954-56; v.p., treas. John Stuart Inc., N.Y.C., 1956—, also dir.; asso. Columbia U. Seminar on Orgn. and Mgmt., 1975—. Chmn. bd. trustees Encampment for Citizenship, N.Y.C., 1974-77. Served with U.S. Maritime Service, 1942-46. Admitted to N.Y. State bar, 1973, C.P.A. Mem. N.Y. State Soc. C.P.A.'s, Am. Inst. C.P.A.'s. Home: 4601 Henry Hudson Pkwy New York NY 10471 Office: John Stuart Inc 979 3d Ave New York NY 10022

LISTER, HARRY JOSEPH, fin. exec.; b. Teaneck, N.J., Jan. 27, 1936; s. Harry and Arline A. (Pinera) L.; B.S., Lehigh U., 1958; C.F.P., Coll. Fin. Planning, 1979; m. Erika A.M. Englisch, Sept. 3, 1960; children—Harry Joseph, Karen, Leslie, Andrea, Michael. Officer, Calvin Bullock, Ltd. and N.Y. Venture Fund, N.Y.C., 1959-72; v.p., dir., sec. Johnston, Lemon & Co., Inc., Washington, 1972—; pres., dir. JL Fin. Services, Inc.; exec. v.p., dir., sec. WMIF Mgmt. Corp.; exec. v.p. Washington Mut. Investors Fund, Inc.; cons. The Capital Group, Inc., Los Angeles. Bd. regents Coll. Fin. Planning (Denver); bd. dirs. Central Bergen chpt. ARC, 1968-72, also mem. exec. com.; former vice chmn. Westwood (N.J.) Planning Bd.; formerly mem. Westwood Zoning Bd. Mem. Investment Co. Inst. (chmn. pension com. 1975—), Inst. Cert. Fin. Planners, Internat. Assn. Fin. Planners. Republican. Roman Catholic. Home: Citation Ct Reston VA 22091 Office: 835 Southern Bldg Washington DC 20005

LITKE, ARTHUR LUDWIG, govt. ofcl.; b. Torrington, Conn., Apr. 4, 1922; s. Gustav and Julian (Weiman) L.; B.S. in Econs., Trinity Coll., 1944; M.B.A., U. Pa., 1947; postgrad. George Washington U., Harvard U.; m. Stephanie Eleanor Lojewski, June 9, 1951; children—A. Lawrence, Suzanne Elizabeth. With GAO, Washington, 1946-64; chief accountant FPC, Washington, 1964-73; mem. Fin. Accounting Standard Bd., Stamford, Conn., 1973-78; asso. adminstr. Econ. Regulatory Adminstrn., Dept. Energy, Washington, 1978—; cons. regulatory ops. GAO, 1978—; faculty Cath. U. Am.; professorial lectr. George Washington U.; mem. faculty U. Colo. Mem. Am. Arbitration Assn., Am. Accountants Assn., Am. Inst. C.P.A.'s, Assn. Govt. Accountants (nat. pres. 1972-73), Fin. Analysts Fedn., Nat. Assn. Accountants, Nat. Economists Club, Nat. Soc. Rate of Return Analysts. Lutheran. Home: 1422 Lady Bird Dr McLean VA 22101 Office: 441 G St NW Washington DC 20548

LITMAN, RAYMOND STEPHEN, banker; b. Kingston, Pa., Nov. 2, 1936; s. Stephen Vincent and Mary Helen (Wisnewski) L.; B.S. in Commerce and Fin., Wilkes Coll., 1961; m. Ann Mae Kosik, Nov. 24, 1960; children—Raymond Stephen, A. Christine. Credit mgr. Sears Roebuck & Co., eastern div., 1961-66; banking officer Phila. Nat. Bank, 1966-69; dir. Decision Dynamics Corp., Marlton, N.J., 1969-71; asst. v.p. Bankers Trust Co., N.Y.C., 1971-75; sr. banking officer Girard Bank, Phila., 1975-77; pres. World Wide Cons. Services, Plymouth Meeting, Pa., 1977-78; asso. dir. bank card div. Am. Bankers Assn., Washington, 1978—. Mem. Citizens Adv. com. of Montgomery County (Pa.) Planning Commn., 1975—. Served with USN, 1954-57; ETO. Mem. Internat. Assn. Credit Card Investigators (pres. Del. Valley chpt. 1976-77, dir. internat. bd. 1976-77, life mem.), Nat. Police Res. Officers Assn., Montgomery County Police Chiefs Assn., Police Chiefs Assn. S.E. Pa., Am. Soc. Indsl. Security, Internat. Assn. Credit Card Investigators (exec. adv. bd. 1978—), Plymouth Meeting Hist. Soc., VFW, Frat. Order of Police. Republican. Roman Catholic. Home: 2057 Sierra Rd Plymouth Meeting PA 19462 Office: 1120 Connecticut Ave NW Washington DC 20036

LITTEN, REGINALD KEITH, soap co. exec.; b. Phillipsburg, Ohio, Mar. 11, 1929; s. Floyd Wendell and Ruth Dawn (Goodyear) L.; grad. Dayton Art Inst. Sch., 1951; m. Marlene Ann Henry, Jan. 28, 1953; 1 dau., Yolanda Dawn Ann. Staff artist Dayton (Ohio) Jour. Herald, 1949-51; civilian illustrator USAF, Dayton, 1951-52; interior designer Rike Dept. Store, Dayton, 1953-56; ast dir., creative services mgr. Hewitt Soap Co., Inc. Dayton, 1956—. Recipient award Nat. Paper Box Assn., 1969, 70, 72. Mem. Ohio Assn. for Artistic Publs. (state rep.), Dayton Soc. Painters and Sculptors (pres. 1979-80), Art Center Dayton, Cin. Art Club, Milestone Car Soc. Club: Shriners. Home: 221 Greenmount Blvd Oakwood Dayton OH 45419 Office: 333 Linden Ave Dayton OH 45403

LITTLE, DONALD BAKER, hardware co. exec.; b. Charlotte, N.C., Aug. 30, 1944; s. Farris Richard and Mabel Baker L.; B.S., Clemson U., 1967; m. Vicki Jo Molyneaux, Aug. 21, 1965; children—Shanna Joy, William Reed. Div. sales mgr. Mennen Co., Morristown, N.J., 1971-75; mktg. mgr. Scripto, Inc., Atlanta, 1975-78; gen. mgr. Bostik Consumer div. Emhart Corp., Reading, Pa., 1979—. Mem. Am. Mktg. Assn., Am. Mgmt. Assn. Home: 1793 Reading Blvd Wyomissing PA 19610 Office: 4408 Pottsville Pike Reading PA 19605

LITTLE, FREED SEBASTIAN, petroleum equipment mfg. co. exec.; b. Ft. Smith, Ark., May 4, 1926; s. Jess Edward and Floy Kimbrough (Witt) L.; B.A., U. Ark., 1950; m. Jana V. Jones, Dec. 9, 1951 (div.); 1 son, Mark McKenna. With Gilbarco Inc., Houston, 1964—, central area mgr., Chgo., 1969-73, Western regional mgr., Houston, 1974—. Patron, Houston Mus. Fine Arts. Served with USAAF, 1945-46. Mem. Am. Petroleum Inst., Petroleum Equipment Inst., Am. Mgmt. Assn., Sigma Alpha Epsilon. Presbyterian. Clubs: Houston City, Memorial Dr. Country. Home: 10121 Valley Forge Houston TX 77042 Office: 6405 Richmond Ave Suite 300 Houston TX 77057

LITTLE, GRETCHEN (DOHM), librarian; b. High Bridge, N.J., Nov. 7, 1913; d. James L. and Gretchen B. (Dohm) L.; A.B., Duke U., 1936; B.S. in L.S., Drexel Inst. Tech., 1949. Asst. librarian devel. dept. Uniroyal 1936-37; tech. librarian Mead Corp., 1937-43, Atlas Powder Co. (name changed to ICI Americas Inc.), Wilmington, Del., 1943-78; cons. for spl. libraries, 1979—. Mem. AAAS, Am. Chem. Soc., Spl. Libraries Assn. (v.p. 1953-54, pres. 1954-55, chmn. sci-tech. div., chmn. 50th anniversary conv., Hall of Fame award 1979). Address: 1600 Sunset Ln Wilmington DE 19810

LITTLE, JAMES KELLY, JR., investment exec.; b. Memphis, Feb. 23, 1925; s. James K. and Lillian R. (Fuller) L.; student Hampton Inst., 1943, Northwestern U., 1946, Roosevelt U., 1947, Ill. Inst., 1947. Founder, dir. Met. Boys Clubs Chgo., 1947-55; policeman, juvenile officer, Chgo., 1947-56; dir. pub. relations Fuller Products Co., Chgo., 1956-60; pub., editor N.Y. Courier, 1960-66; cons. in field; former mgmt. tng. instr. and unit supr. commodity operations clearing Merrill Lynch, Pierce, Fenner & Smith, Inc.; former exec. asst., confidential aide Office Equal Opportunity, HUD; now spl. cons. housing assistance, sr. citizen specialist N.Y.C. Dept. for Aging. Bd. dirs. Vocat. Guidance and Workshop Center, N.Y.C.; mem. adv. council N.Y. Urban League, Harlem Hosp. Center, 1966—. Recipient Distinguished Community Service award Alpha Kappa Alpha, Outstanding Citizen award F. & M. Schaefer Brewing Co., 1967; named hon. lt. col. aide-de-camp Ala. State Militia. Mem. Nat. Urban League Guild, N.Y. Urban League, Nat. Council Negro Women (hon.), Alpha Phi Alpha. Home: 45 W 132d St New York NY 10037 Office: 280 Broadway New York NY 10007

LITTLE, RICHARD JOSEPH, mktg. exec.; b. Balt., Dec. 13, 1945; s. Harry A. and Ruth M. (Gettier) L.; B.A., John Hopkins U., 1967; M.B.A., U. Md., 1970; m. Elizabeth Ecton, May 30, 1970; children—Sarah, Bradley. Mktg. rep. IBM, Balt., 1970-76; sales mgr. McCormick Grocery Products div., Chgo., 1976-77, sales planning mgr., Balt., 1977-78, product mgr., Flavor div., Hunt Valley, Md., 1978—, mem. corporate multiple mgmt. bd., 1979—. Served with USAR, 1968-74. Roman Catholic. Club: Balt. Country. Home: 2110 Woodfork Rd Timonium MD 21093 Office: 204 Wight Ave Hunt Valley MD 21031

LITTLE, WILLIAM D., JR., newspaper exec.; b. Ada, Okla., May 22, 1921; s. William Dee and Willie (Faust) L.; grad. McCallie Sch., Chattanooga, 1938; A.B., East Central State Coll., Ada, 1942; m. Mary Louise Osborne, Sept. 13, 1942; children—Helen Jane, Linda Brooks, William D. III. With News Pub. & Printing Co., Ada, 1942—, v.p., bus. mgr., 1947-66, pres., pub., 1966-80; dir. Home Fed. Savs. & Loan Assn., Ada, Okla. Gas & Electric Co. Mem. Gov.'s Capital Expenditures Adv. Council, 1967-68; Ark.-Verdigris Waterway Spl. Study Commn., 1970-72; pres. exec. bd. Valley View Hosp., Ada, 1963-64, trustee, 1958-78; chmn. E. Central Okla. Bldg. Authority, 1965—; mem. Okla. Econ. Adv. Council, 1963-66, Okla. State Health Planning Agy., 1968-71; v.p. Okla. Health Scis. Found., 1965-77; mem. Okla. Heritage Found., bd. dirs., exec. com., 1977—; treas. Okla. Soc. Crippled Children, 1975—; trustee, v.p. Okla. Newspaper Found., 1967—, East Central (U.) Found., Inc.; adv. bd., past pres. Salvation Army. Recipient Disting. Alumnus award East Central U., 1979. Mem. Okla. Asso. Press Mng. Editors Assn. (pres., 1958), U.S., Ada (pres. 1954), Okla. (pres. 1975) chambers commerce, East Central Coll. Alumni Assn. (pres. 1949), Scis. and Natural Resources Found. Okla. (bd. mem. Ada 1961—), Am., So. (dir. 1969-72) newspaper pubs. assns., Okla. Press Assn., Newcomen Soc. N.Am. Episcopalian. Home: South-on-Jack Fork POB 596 Ada OK 74820 Office: 116 N Broadway Ada OK 74820

LITTLEFIELD, DONALD BRUCE, r.r. exec.; b. Sturgis, Mich., Sept. 27, 1946; s. John William and Ruth J. (Moffett) L.; B.S., Mich. State U., 1968; M.A., Central Mich. U., 1976; grad. Coll. Advanced Traffic, Dearborn, Mich., 1972; m. Mary Ann Wojcik, Sept. 14, 1968; children—Jennifer Michelle, Donald Bruce. Grad. trainee Ford Parts div. Ford Motor Co., Dearborn, Mich., 1969-70, analyst, 1970-72, staff import vehicle coordinator transp., automotive assembly div., 1972-73, supr. transp. methods group, 1973-74, sr. div. auditor transp., 1974-75; mgr. phys. distbn. Bendix Corp., Southfield, Mich., 1975-77; corp. mgr. phys. distbn. and transp. Bendix Forest Products Corp., San Francisco, 1977-79, corp. dir. materiel, 1980—; sec.-treas. Amador Central R.R., 1980—. Registered practitioner ICC. Mem. Assn. ICC Practitioners, Nat. Council Phys. Distbn. Mgmt., Delta Nu Alpha. Roman Catholic. Home: 32 Regency Dr Clayton CA 94517 Office: Bendix Forest Products Corp Exec Offices 2740 Hyde St San Francisco CA 94119

LITTLEJOHN, EDWARD, diversified industry exec.; b. Sydney, Australia, Nov. 26, 1916; s. Albert and Linda (Teece) L.; student U. Sydney, 1934; B.Sc. in Econs., London Sch. Economics and Polit. Sci., 1938; A.M., Harvard U., 1941; m. Ellen Mandzik, Oct. 29, 1960; children—Christina, Christopher, Alexandra; came to U.S., 1939, naturalized, 1949. Procurement officer Australian div. Brit. Purchasing Commn., N.Y.C., 1941-42; procurement officer Commonwealth of Australia War Supplies Procurement, Washington, 1942-45; Australian vice consul, N.Y.C., 1945-48; 3d sec. Australian embassy, Washington, 1948; asso. dir. pub. relations Burroughs Corp., Detroit, 1951-55, dir. pub. relations, 1955-59; asst. mgr. pub. relations dept. Standard Oil Co. (N.J.), N.Y.C., 1959-61; mgr. pub. relations dept. Humble Oil and Refining Co., Houston, 1961-64, exec. asst. to bd. dirs., 1963-64; v.p. pub. relations Internat. Exec. Service Corps., N.Y.C., 1964-65; v.p. pub. affairs Pfizer Internat. Inc., N.Y.C., 1965-68, dir. pub. affairs Pfizer Inc., 1968-71, v.p. pub. affairs, 1971—. Mem. com. multinat. enterprises and investment U.S. council Internat. C. of C., 1978—; bd. dirs. Fund for Multinat. Mgmt. Edn., N.Y.C., 1978, Ethics and Public Policy Center, Washington; mem. public affairs research council Conf. Bd.; trustee Intercollegiate Studies Inst., Phila. Mem. NAM (internat. econ. affairs com. 1971—), Nat. Planning Assn. (trustee, exec. com. 1977—, com. on changing internat. realities 1972—), Phila. Soc. (trustee). Home: 8 Lafayette Rd W Princeton NJ 08540 Office: 235 E 42d St New York NY 10017

LITTLER, DONALD, mfg. co. exec.; b. Pao Ting Fu, China, Oct. 6, 1930; s. Harold and Nellie (Fisher) L.; came to U.S., 1948, naturalized, 1954; student Coll. of Marin, 1950-51; B.S., U. Calif. at Berkeley, 1957; postgrad. San Jose State U., 1958-60, exec. program Stanford, 1976; m. Gwen U. Davis, Aug. 13, 1955; children—Ralph, Raymond, Robert. Devel. engr. Sperry Gyroscope Co., Sunnyvale, Calif., 1957-63, R.S. Electronics, Sunnyvale, 1963; with Sylvania Electronic Systems, Mountain View, Calif., 1963—, dept. mgr., 1968—, bus. area mgr., 1977—. Bd. dirs. Casols Sch., Los Gatos, 1974—; asst. cubmaster Boy Scouts Am., San Jose, Calif., 1968-69. Served to staff sgt. AUS, 1951-54. Mem. IEEE, Assn. Old Crows, Am. Def. Preparedness Assn. Republican. Lutheran. Patentee in field. Office: PO Box 188 Mountain View CA 94042

LITTMAN, DOUGLAS ALAN, ins. agt.; b. Greenville, Ohio, May 9, 1949; s. Alan Verl and Janet E. L.; B.S. in Bus. Adminstrn., Miami U., Oxford, Ohio, 1971; m. Victoria L. Harshbarger, June 12, 1971; children—Heather N., Erica L. Partner, Littman-Thomas Agy., Greenville, 1971—. Recipient Bronze Key, Ohio State Life Ins. Co., 1973, award of excellence, Ivy trophy, Westfield, Cos., 1979. Mem. Ind. Ins. Agts. Assn. Darke County (pres. 1978-80), Ind. Ins. Agts. Assn. Ohio, Nat. Assn. Ind. Ins. Agts., Nat. Rifle Assn., Darke County Fish and Game Assn. Democrat. Mem. United Ch. of Christ. Clubs: Masons, Shriners, Kiwanis (pres. 1978-79, dir. 1973-78). Home: 102 Redwood Dr Greenville OH 45331 Office: 515 E Main St Greenville OH 45331

LITTMAN, HAROLD, printing co. exec.; b. N.Y.C., Oct. 3, 1922; s. Henry and Fanny L.; B.A., SUNY, Brookport, 1975; M.A., Montclair State Coll., 1979; m. Annette Stein, June 8, 1947; children—Joshua, Jonas, Abigail, Jeremy, Jonathan. Gen. mgr. Faultless Press, 1948-54; founder, pres. Seaward Edison Corp., N.Y.C., 1954-69; pres. Serga Corp. div. P&F Industries, L.I. City, N.Y., 1969-73, corp. v.p., dir., 1969-73; v.p. Lasky Co., Millburn, N.J., 1973—. Trustee Temple Sharfy Tefilo, East Orange, N.J. Served to 1st lt. USAAF, 1942-45. Mem. Am. Arbitration Assn., Craftmens Club, Phi Kappa Phi. Club: B'nai Brith (West Orange, N.J.). Home: 24 Clonavor Rd West Orange NJ 07052 Office: Lasky Co 67 E Willow St Millburn NJ 07041

LITTMAN, LEONARD BARRY, mfg. co. exec.; b. Newark, Dec. 27, 1942; s. Herman Max and Lydia (Bamdas) L.; A.A., Am. U., 1962; diploma Inst. Modern Procedures, Falls Church, Va., 1969; postgrad. U. Md., 1975; m. Donna Joy Cialone, Jan. 16, 1970. Sales agent United Airlines, Washington, 1962-68; salesman Morris Miller Liquors, Silver Spring, Md., 1968-69; sect. supr. Computing & Software, Seabrook, Md., 1969-73; mgr. prodn. and ops. Computer Scis.-Technicolor Assos., Seabrook, 1973-76; cons. Gen. Electric, Sunnyvale, Calif., 1976-77, math analyst computer applications, 1977; mgr. ops. systems Cubic Corp., San Diego, 1977—. Vice-pres. pastor's bd. St. Kilian's Ch., Mission Viejo, Calif., 1979—. Mem. Nat. Mgmt. Assn., Am. Mgmt. Assn. Roman Catholic. Office: 9233 Balboa Ave San Diego CA 92123

LITTNER, MARIAN LIN, accountant; b. Taiwan, Sept. 14, 1940; d. Hsui-ting and Yueh-O (Shih) Lin; came to U.S., 1969; B.A., Chung-hsing U., Taiwan, 1964; M.B.A., Ind. U., 1973. Tchr., Iou-wu Middle Sch., Taiwan, 1964-66; payroll clk. Mobil China Allied Chem.

Indsl. Ltd., Taiwan, 1966-69; jr. accountant Abbott Labs., North Chicago, Ill., 1973-74; distbn. analyst dept. 291, 1974-76; sr. accountant Square D Co., Milw., 1976—; pres. Marian Fin. Services, Milw., 1980—. Chmn., Chinese Group, Milw. Folk Fair, 1979-80. Taiwan Govt. research scholar Nat. Research Inst., Taipei, 1968. Mem. Orgn. Chinese Ams., Chinese-Am. Civic Club Milw. (treas. 1978-79, dir. 1979—). Author: You Are What You Eat, 1978. Home: 3985 W College Ave Milwaukee WI 53221

LIU, DAVID T., system engring. co. exec.; b. Shanghai, China, Apr. 1, 1930; came to U.S., 1950, naturalized, 1961; s. N.Y. and C.T. Liu; M.S. in Aeros. and Astronautics, Mass. Inst. Tech., 1961; B.S. in Aero. Engring., U. Mich., 1954; m. Agnes, May 30, 1952; children—Mark, Dwight. Mem. tech. staff Cessna Aircraft Co., Wichita, Kans., 1954-57; research staff Curtiss-Wright Corp., Caldwell, N.J., 1958-59; engring. specialist Allied Research Assos., Cambridge, Mass., 1959-61; research staff Mass. Inst. Tech., 1961-62; dynamics group head AVCO Research & Devel. Co., Wilmington, Mass., 1962-64; project head, task leader Hughes Aircraft Co., El Segundo, Calif., 1964-67; chief stability and control Hughes Tool Co., Culver City, Calif., 1967-69; program mgr. Northrop Electronics Co., Hawthorne, Calif., 1970-72; pres. Liu & Assos., tech. cons., Palos Verdes, Calif., 1968—, System Innovation & Devel. Corp., Torrance, Calif., 1972—; tchr. spl. grad. systems U. Calif., Los Angeles. Mem. Am. Helicopter Soc., AIAA, Am. Def. Preparedness Assn., Sigma Xi, Sigma Gamma Tau. Republican. Home: 28717 Cedarbluff Dr Palos Verdes CA 90274 Office: 23850 Madison St Torrance CA 90505

LIU, FRANK H. M., mfg. co. exec.; b. China, June 12, 1943; came to U.S., 1977, naturalized, 1978; s. Nan Ping and Chen Hwa (Chao) L.; B.S., Chinese Air Force Acad., 1965; M.S., No. Ill. U., 1968; m. Karen Fu Liu, Apr. 9, 1972; children—Jay, Amy, Kerry, Wade. Project mgr. Chung Shan Inst. Sci. and Tech., Taiwan, 1970-76; v.p. Victron Electronic Co., Taipei, Taiwan, 1976-77; pres. Telestar Internat. Corp., Los Angeles, 1977—. Mem. Internat. Trade Assn. South Bay, Long Beach Area C. of C., Am. Mgmt. Assn. Office: 849 Westchester Pl Los Angeles CA 90005

LIVANIS, CONSTANTINE, mgmt. cons.; b. N.Y.C., Nov. 6, 1934; s. Limberios and Elefteria (Hanos) L.; B.S., N.Y. U., 1958; m. Katherine Pattakos, Oct. 5, 1963; children—Terri, Jason. Mfg. engr. Polarad Electronics Corp., Long Island City, N.Y., 1960-61, asst. prodn. mgr., 1961-62; sr. systems and procedure analyst ITT Fed. Labs., Nutley, N.J., 1962-66; systems and procedure analyst Metal Flo Corp., Stamford, Conn., 1966; corp. supr.-systems Amerace Corp., N.Y.C., 1966-67, div. materials mgr. Swan Hose div., Bucyrus, Ohio, 1967-72, plant gen. mgr., 1972-73, corp. mgr. material resources, N.Y.C., 1974, v.p. materials and systems, elastimold div., Hackettstown, N.J., 1974-76; dir. materials Aircraft Radio and Controls div. Cessna Corp., Boonton, N.J., 1976-77; v.p. ops. F & S Central div. Buildex Corp., Bklyn., 1978-79; pres. Astrotrade Internat. Co., Closter, N.J., 1979—. Chmn. indsl. com. Bucyrus United Fund, 1973; bd. dirs. JOBS, Ohio, 1973. Served with AUS, 1958-59. Mem. Purchasing Mgmt. Assn., Soc. Mfg. Engrs., Am. Prodn. and Inventory Control Soc. Greek Orthodox. Club: Elks. Home: 52 Alpine Dr Closter NJ 07624 Office: 52 Alpine Dr Closter NJ 07624

LIVAS, BASIL LOUIS, mgmt. cons.; b. Melrose, Mass., Mar. 8, 1929; s. Frank John and Adah Catherine (Clark) L.; B.S. cum laude (NROTC scholar), Tufts U., 1951; m. Janet Adams Blood, Oct. 25, 1970; children by previous marriage—Mark Basil, Ann Elizabeth. Field sales mgr., mgr. prodn. planning and control Hitchiner Mfg. Co., Inc., 1954-58, mgr. prodn. and sales Permattach Diamond Tool div. Milford, N.H., 1958-59; mgr. mfg. services Varian Assos., Beverly, Mass., 1960-66; mgr. materials Microwave Assos., Burlington, Mass., 1966-69; owner, pres. B.L. Livas Assos., North Hampton, N.H., 1969—; dir. Info, Inc. Mem. N.H. State Occupational Info. Adv. Bd., 1972-73; mem. Internat. Exec. Service Corps; trustee Wilson Coll., Chambersburg, Pa. Served with USN, 1951-54; capt. USNR. Mem. Am. Soc. Metals, U.S. Naval Inst., Tau Beta Pi. Office: 32 Hobbs Rd North Hampton NH 03862

LIVINGSTON, DAVID ROBERT, leasing co. exec.; b. St. Johns, Mich., Sept. 14, 1943; s. Eugene Alden and Doris (Payne) L.; B.S., Mich. State U., 1966, M.B.A., 1967; m. Sheryl Lynn Romence, June 10, 1967; children—Kristin, Tadd. Mem. mktg. staff IBM Co., Detroit, 1967-72, mgr. edn., Chgo., 1972-73; mktg. rep. Itel Co., Detroit, 1973-75, dist. mgr., 1975-77, v.p. San Francisco, 1977-78; owner, pres. Starwood Corp., Birmingham, Mich., 1979—, also chmn. bd. Mem. Computer Dealers Assn. Republican. Presbyterian. Address: 1527 N Glengarry Rd Birmingham MI 48010

LIVINGSTON, LEE FRANKLIN, real estate and recreation cons. co. exec.; b. Boston, Feb. 20, 1942; s. William and Frances (Turner) L.; student Sch. Visual Arts, 1959-62, Georgetown U., 1964; m. Elaine Wiesenfeld, June 9, 1968; children—Eli, Jed. With pub. relations and promotion dept. Cowles Communications Co., N.Y.C., 1961-62, Newsweek, N.Y.C., 1965-70; exec. mng. dir. Carolier Lanes, North Brunswick, N.J., 1970—, dir., 1971-79; exec. mng. dir. Anasarca Corp., North Brunswick, 1971—; pres. Imperial Consultants, Inc., North Brunswick; dir. Aramis Constrn. Co.; cons. on charitable rund raising to various tournaments, 1971—. Active charities for autistic children. Served with C.E., U.S. Army, 1962-64. Mem. N.J. Soc. for Retarded Citizens, Mu Sigma. Democrat. Club: Glenwood Country. Home: 12 Derby Ln RD 4 North Brunswick NJ 08902 Office: Imperial Cons Ins care Carolier Lanes US Hwy 1 North Brunswick NJ 08902

LIVINGSTON, PATRICIA ANN (PAT MURPHY), mfg. co. exec.; b. Manila, July 30, 1934; d. Marion Michelin and Phoebe (Nelson) Karolchuck; B.A., Reed Coll., 1955; m. Johnston R. Livingston, Sept. 4, 1965; adopted children—Henry, Ann, Jane, David. With George Washington U. Office Human Resources Research, 1955-58; asst. sec.-treas. Bus. Equipment Mfg. Assn., N.Y.C., 1958-60; fin. writer N.Y. Post, 1961-62, Chgo. Daily News, 1962-66; fin. columnist Dallas Morning News, 1966-71, also syndicated by Newsday, 1968-69; v.p. fin. Enmark Corp., Denver, 1971—; also dir. Trustee Colo. Womens Coll.; bd. dirs. U. Denver Theatre Assn. Episcopalian. Club: Denver. Home: 869 Vine St Denver CO 80206 Office: 5070 Oakland St Denver CO 80239

LIVINGSTON, RICHARD FRANKLIN, banker; b. Daytona Beach, Fla., 1919. Chmn., chief exec. officer Sun Banks of Fla., Inc.; dir. Sun First Nat. Bank of Orlando, Sun Bank/Southwest. Office: Sun Banks of Fla Inc Sun First Nat Bank Bldg Orlando FL 32802*

LIVINGSTONE, JAMES GEORGE, petroleum co. exec.; b. Toronto, Ont., Can., June 8, 1920; s. George C. and Marione Lenore L.; B.A.Sc. in Chem. Engring., U. Toronto. Joined Imperial Oil Ltd., 1942, asst. gen. mgr. mfg. dept., 1957-63, coordinator bus. devel., 1965-67, gen. mgr. mfg., 1967-69, v.p., dir., 1969-76, v.p., dir., 1976-79, pres., dir., 1979—, on loan to Standard Oil Co. (N.J.), 1963-64. Mem. Assn. Profl. Engrs., Am. Petroleum Inst., Can. Inst. Mining and Metallurgy. Office: 111 Saint Clair Ave W Toronto ON M5W 1K3 Canada

LLEWELLYN, PHILIP MICHAEL, constrn. co. exec.; b. Danville, Ill., Sept. 28, 1947; s. James Burr and Hilda Mae (Livengood) L.; B.A., Kalamazoo Coll., 1969; M.A., Western Mich. U., 1971, postgrad., 1972; m. Theresa Ann Bergstrom, June 28, 1969; children—James Hugo, Audrey Ann. Teaching asst. Western Mich. U., Kalamazoo, 1970-71; pres. Llewellyn Lumber Co., Danville, Ill., 1972-73; constrn. mgr. Kalamazoo div. Edward Rose and Sons, 1973—. Republican. Home: 11036 Hawthorne Dr Galesburg MI 49053 Office: 6100 Newport Rd Kalamazoo MI 49081

LLEWELLYN, ROBERT JOSEPH, traffic signal equipment mfg. co. exec.; b. Houston, Sept. 9, 1926; s. Raymond Henry and Mary Ellen (Arns) L.; E.E., U. Houston, 1955; m. Bertha Mae Llewellyn, Nov. 28, 1946; 1 dau., Kay Lynn. With Houston Light & Power Co., 1946-52; with elec. div. City of Houston, 1952-63, asst. city electrician, 1960-63; exec. dir. Internat. Mcpl. Signal Assn., Houston, 1963-68; regional mgr. Econolite, Los Angeles, Fort Worth, Tex., 1968-75, pres., owner Traffic Signal Equipment, Inc., Fort Worth, 1975—; exec. dir. Internat. Mcpl. Signal Assn., 1979—. Served with U.S. Army, 1944-46. Mem. Inst. Transp. Engrs. Roman Catholic. Club: K.C. Office: 3121 Forest Ave Fort Worth TX 76112

LLOYD, CHARLES PASHLEY, indsl. co. ofcl.; b. Camden, N.J., Oct. 8, 1939; s. Charles Pashley and Esther Victoria (Wright) L.; student Greenville Coll., 1959-60; m. Nancy Louise Elling, July 14, 1961; children—Cynthia Louise, Marcella Dianne, Nancy Lynn. Sheet metal helper Metal Assemblies Co., Camden, 1958-59; press operator, sheet metal mechanic and inspector G.R. Garvey and Sons, Hammonton, N.J., 1960-64; with frame div. Budd Co., Phila., 1964-65, successively assembly inspector, receiving inspector, press inspector, layout inspector, statis. quality control analyst, quality control supr., asst. gen. supr. customer liaison, stamping div., Phila., 1965—. Lt., then capt. Berlin Fire Co. No. 1, 1966-69; active N.J. Exempt Firemen's Assn., 1969. Mem. Am. Soc. Quality Control (arrangements chmn. annual symposium Phila. Sect. 1972-74). Republican. Baptist. Home: 245 Parsons Dr Avon Lake OH 44012 Office: Ford Motor Co 650 Miller Rd Avon Lake OH 44012

LLOYD, DONNA MAE, banker; b. Barron, Wis., May 11, 1932; d. Herman and Sigrid (Solie) Lemler; student U. Minn., 1951, also banking courses; m. Charles F. Lloyd, Oct. 8, 1955; 1 son, Steven Jeffrey (dec.). With Erickson's Store, Barron, 1951-54; with 1st Nat. Bank of Barron, 1953—, auditor, 1979—, asst. v.p., 1977—; local sec. Nat. Mut. Benefit Ins. Co., Madison, Wis., 1955-80. Treas., Barron County Heart Fund, 1965-78, co-chmn., 1978—; leader Boy Scouts Am., 1967-69; permanent chmn. reunion com. Barron High Sch. Mem. Nat. Assn. Bank Women. Democrat. Lutheran. Home: Route 2 Barron WI 54812 Office: 1st Nat Bank Barron Box 159 Barron WI 54812

LLOYD, KATE RAND, editor, writer; b. Mpls.; d. Rufus Randall and Helen (Chase) Rand; B.A. cum laude, Bryn Mawr Coll., 1945; m. John Davis Lloyd, Feb. 25, 1950; children—Kate Angeline, Ann Elizabeth, John Rand. Staff writer Vogue Mag., N.Y.C., 1945-51, feature writer, 1951-54, sr. editor, 1963-67, feature editor, 1967-74, mng. editor, 1974-77; feature editor Glamour Mag., 1954, mng. editor, 1954-63; editor in chief Working Woman Mag., N.Y.C., 1977—; adj. lectr. Columbia U. Sch. Journalism, 1975—. Mem. council Hunger Project, 1977—; bd. dirs. Planned Parenthood Fedn. Am., 1978—; mem. Nat. Commn. Working Women, 1979—; adv. bd. Nat. Black Theatre, 1980—; adv. bd. Inst. Edn. and Research on Women and Work, Cornell U., 1980—; mem. adv. bd. Nat. Women's Polit. Caucus; adv. bd. Erhard Seminars Tng. Recipient 1st prize Vogue Prix de Paris, 1945; named Woman of Achievement, YWCA, N.Y.C., 1978. Mem. Women's Forum Inc., Am. Soc. Mag. Editors, Women's Econ. Round Table, Women in Communications, Inc. Democrat. Club: Colony (N.Y.C.). Editor: Glamour Magazine Party Book, 1965; Vogue Beauty and Health Guide, 1975, 76; editorial supr. Vogue's Book on Etiquette, rev. ed., 1969; Real-Life Fashion Guide, 1976. Office: 1180 Ave of Americas New York NY 10036

LLOYD, NANNELLYN WHITESTONE, chemist; b. Johnstown, Pa., Aug. 19, 1934; d. Llewellyn Edward and Alice (Bailey) Lloyd; B.S. in Chemistry, Chestnut Hill Coll., 1956; postgrad. U. Del. With E.I. duPont de Nemours & Co., Wilmington, Del., 1956—, now patent agt. Legal Dept. Vol. staff Henry Francis duPont Winterthur Mus. Mem. Phila. Patent Law Assn., Del. Ornithol. Soc., Am. Birding Assn., Hilton Head Audubon Soc., U.S. Tennis Assn. Republican. Roman Catholic. Clubs: Del. Soc. Mayflower Descs., DuPont Country, Skating of Wilmington. Home: PO Box 3927 400 Old Kennett Rd Greenville DE 19807 Office: Legal Dept E I duPont de Nemours & Co Wilmington DE 19898

LLOYD, STANLEY ROLAND, fin. cons.; b. South Bend, Ind., Nov. 27, 1946; s. Bill and Katie L.; student pub. schs., South Bend, Ind. Employed with Seat Cover Charlie, South Bend, Ind., 1965-68, Indsl. Transmission Equipment Co., South Bend, 1968-70, Packaging Corp., South Bend, 1970-73, Marcel's Auto Upholstery, Las Vegas, 1973-76; fin. and diamond broker, 1980—; mgr. Stanley R. Lloyd Fin. Cons., 1980—. Mem. Nat. Assn. Fin. Cons., Kashbuilder Internat., Jaycees. Baptist. Club: Toastmasters. Office: 121 S Iowa St South Bend IN 46619

LLOYD, STUART RALPH, mgmt. cons. and systems analysis firm exec.; b. Trenton, N.J., Nov. 23, 1943; s. Fred and Mae M. (Abramson) L.; B.S. in Bus. Adminstrn., Am. U., 1965, postgrad. 1976-78; m. Rebecca S. Petrou, Sept. 3, 1965; children—Adam M., Jennifer R. Auditor, Def. Contract Audit Agy., Silver Spring, Md., 1965-71; controller Presearch Inc., Arlington, Va., 1971-79, treas., 1971—, also dir.; dir. Control Concepts Corp. Treas. Chaddsford Civic Assn., 1971-72. C.P.A., Md. Mem. Am. Inst. C.P.A.'s, Assn. Govt. Accts. Home: 13844 Turnmore Rd Silver Spring MD 20906 Office: 2361 S Jefferson Davis Hwy Arlington VA 22202

LLOYD, TERRY DEAN, parcel delivery co. exec.; b. Chgo., June 16, 1939; s. Sam and Weetor L.; student drafting Ill. Inst. Tech.; m. Carol K. Rogers, Dec. 27, 1964; children—Phyllis, Terrance G. With United Parcel Service, Chgo., 1966—, supr., 1968-70, mgr., 1970-73, div. mgr., 1973—; v.p. Fashionably Yours Inc., 1978—; owner, pres. Outwest Corp., clothing chain, Chgo., 1979—. Served with arty. U.S. Army, 1963-65. Democrat. Mem. Apostolic Ch. Home: 10150 S Indiana Ave Chicago IL 60628 Office: 1400 S Jefferson St Chicago IL 60628

LLOYD, WILLIAM JOSEPH, graphic design and mktg. exec.; b. South Bend, Ind., Sept. 15, 1937; s. John Henry and Georgina (Lamy) L.; B.S., Ind. U., 1961; m. Nora M. Moore, July 29, 1972; children—W. Joseph, Melissa P. With Ind. U. Press, 1962-65; art dir., designer Robert Vogele, Inc., Chgo., 1965-66; mgr. of design Container Corp. Am., Chgo., 1966-71; with Unimark Internat., Chgo., 1971-72; self-employed graphic designer, Chgo. and Denver, 1972-74; art dir. Young & Rubicam, Chgo., 1974-75; v.p., dir. design Source, Inc., Chgo., 1975-76; pres. Lloyd Design Assos., Chgo., 1976—. Bd. dirs. Youth Guidance. Served with U.S. Army, 1961-62. Mem. N.Y., Chgo. art dirs. clubs, Am. Inst. Graphic Arts, Soc. Typographic Arts, Chgo. Press Club, Chgo. Ad Club. Club: Lake Shore. Home: 260 E Chestnut St Chicago IL 60611 Office: 200 E Ontario St Chicago IL 60611

LO, ALLEN KWOK-WAH, tech. co. exec.; b. Vietnam, Sept. 2, 1937; s. Kwong Man and Po Chun (Lee) L.; Indsl. Designer, Hong Kong Tech. Coll., 1960; m. Che Amy, Jan. 18, 1964; 1 son, David. Indsl. designer NCR, Hong Kong, 1959-64; asst. mgr. 3-D Arts Indsl. Ltd., Hong Kong, 1964-67; dir. research and devel. Ashahi Ltd., Tokyo, 1967-70; vice chmn., dir. tech. Nimslo Tech., Inc., Atlanta, 1970—; dir. Nimslo Ltd., London. Dir., Chinese-Am. Inst. Atlanta, 1976-78, pres., 1977-78. Mem. Soc. Photog. Scientists and Engrs. Office: 2403/C Johnson Ferry Rd Chamblee GA 30341

LO, HANG HSIN, chemist, consumer products co. exec.; b. China, Feb. 22, 1937; came to U.S., 1961, naturalized, 1974; s. Chu Tsai Lo and Jane Chiao Wang; B.S. in Chem. Engring., Nat. Taiwan U., 1959; M.S. in Chemistry, Case Inst. Tech., 1965, Ph.D. in Phys. Chemistry (NSF fellow), 1967; m. Pallas May-Jon Sun, Sept. 9, 1967; children—Serena Charlotte, Elliot Hugo. Sr. research chemist Diamond Shamrock Corp., Painesville, Ohio, 1967-68; fellow, research asso. Mass. Inst. Tech., Cambridge, 1968-71; asst. tech. dir. McKesson Lab., Fairfield, Conn., 1971-72; group leader analytical instrument lab. Chesebrough-Pond's Inc., Trumbull, Conn., 1972-77, mgr. specifications, formula control and computer applications, 1978-80; sect. leader pharm. analysis Purdue Frederick Co., 1980—. Mem. Am. Chem. Soc., Soc. Applied Spectroscopy, AAAS, Phi Lambda Upsilon. Club: Mass. Inst. Tech. Faculty. Contbr. articles to chem. jours. Home: 20 Old Still Rd Woodbridge CT 06525 Office: Purdue Frederick Research Center Saw Mill River Rd Yonkers NY 10701

LO, STANLEY TSAI, travel co. exec.; b. Yun-Nan, China, July 11, 1944; s. Chi Ming and Eng (Chang) L.; B. Polit. Sci., Tunghai U., 1965; B.E.E., San Jose State Coll., 1971; m. Ellen Tchang, Aug. 29, 1971; children—Maximillian, Justin, Celeste. Came to U.S., 1966. Owner, Tradewinds Travel, Burlingame, Calif., 1971-73; mktg. mgr. Homeland Imports, Mountain View, 1971-73; partner East West Products, Mountain View, 1971—; chmn., pres. OC Tours Corp., Burlingame, 1977—, Four Seas Center Inc.; pres. Dyna-Trek, Inc., Burlingame, 1979—; owner, mgr. La Baie Restaurant; chmn. Four Seas Airline. Bd. dirs. Asian Study League, 1971—. Served to 2d lt. Mil. in Taiwan, 1965-66. Recipient Honor Plaque for contbns. to Asian community, City of Los Angeles, 1972. Mem. Bay Area Chinese Student Assn., Chinese Students in So. Calif., Chinese C. of C., Mountain View C. of C. Clubs: Stanford Area Chinese (Palo Alto, Calif.); Chgo. Chinese. Home: 1320 Marlborough Rd Hillsborough CA 94010 Office: Four Seas Group Tradewinds Travel 800 Airport Blvd Burlingame CA 94010

LOACH, JEAN CALANTHE, bus. cons.; b. Chgo.; d. George Winwood and Mary (Sipes) Loach; Mus.B., Mundelein Coll. Hostess Jean Loach TV Show, also women's editor WXYZ-TV, Detroit, 1950-60; pres. Jean Loach & Assos., Miami Beach, Fla., and N.Y.C., 1960-70, 72—; pres. Future Record Co., 1962—; dir. advt. and pub. relations Sheraton Park Hotel, Sheraton Carlton Hotel, Washington, 1971-72; chmn. bd. Jean Loach Assos. Corp., Washington, 1972—. Mem. adv. bd. Salvation Army, Miami, Fla., 1973; bd. dirs. Univ. Concert Series Seminars, 1970. Decorated as dame (Gt. Britain). Mem. AFTRA, ASCAP, Screen Actors Guild, Am. Fedn. Musicians, Am. Women in Radio and TV. Mem. Order Eastern Star, Daus. of Nile, Order of White Shrine. Clubs: Women's City (Detroit); Brickell Bay, Viscayans (Miami, Fla.); Curzon House (London). Composer: Paree Still Seems the Same to Me, 1958; Where There's A Will There's A Way, 1966; Lucky, Lucky Me, 1973; A Mom Like Mine, 1973. Home and Office: 555 Plaza Venetia at NE 15th St Miami FL 33132

LOBB, D. L., SR., geologist; b. Green County, Ky., Sept. 17, 1937; s. Oscar and Mary E. (Jones) L.; student Campbellsville Coll., 1958-60, U. Ky., 1962-63; B.S., Eastern Ky. U., 1970; m. Nancy Gardner, June 12, 1956; children—D. L., Charlene M. Pres., D.L. Lobb & Assos. Inc., Lexington, Ky., 1977—, U.S. Land & Energy Inc., Lexington, 1973—, Del Constrn. Co. Inc., Lexington, 1973—; v.p. Del Coal Co. Inc., Lexington, 1975—. Mem. Am. Assn. Petroleum Geologists, Ky. Profl. Engrs. and Land Surveyors, Am. Congress Surveying and Mapping. Mem. Ch. of Nazarene. Address: Box 1974 Lexington KY 40508

LOCHAK, BORIS, former engring. co. exec.; b. Russia, Oct. 6, 1901; s. Efim S. and Dora (Pesako) L.; degree in math. Sorbonne, Paris, France, 1921; civil engr. degree, Nat. Sch. Bridges and Hwys., Paris, 1924; m. Rose Perlmuter, Aug. 11, 1928; children—Paul, Dorita (dec.). Came to U.S., 1941, naturalized, 1948. Engr., Found. Co., Paris, 1926-29, chief engr., 1929-33; pvt. cons. engr., Paris, 1934-39; with Gibbs & Hill, Inc., engrs. and constructors, N.Y.C., 1942—, dir. fgn. ops., 1945-57, v.p., chief engr., 1957-61, sr. v.p., 1961-68, asst. to pres., 1968-73. Served with French Army, 1939-40. Registered profl. engr., N.Y., N.J., D.C. Fellow ASCE. Home: 52 Ave Foch Paris 16 France Office: 393 7th Ave New York City NY 10001

LOCHNER, STEPHEN CARL, public warehousing firm exec.; b. Elmhurst, Ill., Sept. 28, 1942; s. Harry W. and Dorothy Hediger L.; B.A., Yale U., 1964, M.City Planning, 1966; M.B.A., Harvard U., 1970; m. Hannah Morgan Lochner, July 30, 1966; children—Laura K., Stephen C., Katherine M., Erich W. Regional planner Spindletop Research Center, Lexington, Ky., 1967-68; v.p. Investments, Inc., South Charleston, W.Va., 1970-71; pres. STI Corp., Sandusky, Ohio, 1971—; dir. Wagner Quarries Co.; v.p., dir. Sawmill Indsl. Park, Inc.; mem. adv. bd. Sandusky Area Bank, Ohio Nat. Bank. Trustee Good Samaritan Hosp., Firelands Coll. Mem. Am. Warehouseman Assn. Republican. Episcopalian. Clubs: Rotary, Plum Brook Country (dir.). Home: 614 Chippewa Pl Huron OH 44839 Office: PO Box 2303 Sandusky OH 44870

LOCHRIDGE, JAMES FREDERICK, chem. co. exec.; b. Amarillo, Tex., Feb. 18, 1923; s. Charles F. and Lelia L.; B.S., U. Ill., 1947; m. Dorothy Harms, July 10, 1945; children—Linda, Sally. Tech. dir. internat. div. Ferro Corp., Cleve., 1950-54; tech. mgr. Ferro Enamel Mex., Mexico City, 1954-59; sales mgr. Ferro Enamel Argentina, Buenos Aires, 1959-64; mng. dir. Ferro Enamel Española, Bilbao, Spain, 1964-69, 74-75, Ferro Enamel Argentina, Buenos Aires, 1970-74; v.p. internal ops. Ferro Corp., Cleve., 1976—; dir. Ferro Can., Ferro Australia. Founder, pres. sch. bd. Am. Sch. Bilbao, 1967-69. Served with U.S. Army, 1943-45. Mem. Am. Ceramic Soc., Nat. Inst. Ceramic Engrs. Club: Chagrin Valley Country. Office: 1 Erieview Plaza Cleveland OH 44114

LOCKARD, JAMES ERNEST, stockbroker; b. Akron, Ohio, June 9, 1936; s. Myron Eugene and Clara Olive (Rusk) L.; student Ohio State U., 1954-55, Akron U., 1955-60, Kent State U., 1956-58, N.Mex. A&M U., 1956-57, Tampa Coll., 1973-76; m. Jane Ann Devereux, June 14, 1958 (dec.); children—Timothy J., Cheri L., Kristy D.; m. 2d, Darlene Jane Peeler, Jan. 1, 1979. Mfrs. rep. Ames Co., div. Miles Lab., Akron, 1959-65, Merrill Lynch Inc., Honolulu and Akron, 1965-70; asso. v.p. Dean Witter Reynolds, Inc., Tampa, Fla., 1975—. Chmn. Ohio State Camp Out Nat. Campers and Hikers Assn., 1967, conservation dir., 1964-68; precinct chmn., dist. chmn. Republican

Com. Hawaii, floor leader state conv., 1971. Served with AUS, 1955-57. Mem. Stock and Bond Club St. Petersburg, Stow Jaycees (charter), Stow Aways Campers (charter). Clubs: Masons (32 deg.), Shriners, Toastmasters (past area gov., pres.). Home: 1307 Ranchwood Dr E Dunedin FL 33528 Office: 1311 N Westshore Blvd Tampa FL 33607

LOCKE, CHARLES STANLEY, mfg. co. exec.; b. Laurel, Miss., Mar. 5, 1929; s. Richard C. and Florence (Parker) L.; B.B.A., U. Miss., 1952, M.S., 1955; m. Nora Fulkerson, Mar. 15, 1952; children—Cathy, Stanley, Lauren, Pamela. With Corvey Engring. Co., Inc., Washington, 1952, Price Waterhouse & Co., C.P.A.'s, New Orleans, 1955-58, Westvaco, Inc., 1958-64; controller A.E. Staley Mfg. Co., 1964-69; v.p. Brown Co., Pasadena, Calif., 1969-73, also dir., mem. exec. com.; sr. v.p. Allen Group Inc., Melville, N.Y., 1973-75; v.p. fin. dir. Morton-Norwich Products, Inc., Chgo., 1975-80, chmn. bd., pres., chief exec. officer, 1980—; dir. Avon Products, Inc. Served with AUS, 1952-54. Mem. Nat. Assn. Accountants, Financial Execs. Inst., Beta Alpha Psi. Methodist. Clubs: Sunset Ridge Country, Mid-Am., Tower, Met., Sky, Chgo., Econ. Office: Morton-Norwich Products Inc 110 N Wacker Dr Chicago IL 60606

LOCKE, NORMAN, personnel cons.; b. Bklyn., Mar. 30, 1929; s. Charles and Ruth L.; B.A., N.Y. U., 1962, M.A., 1967; m. Barbara Ann Marks, July 8, 1972; children—Donna, Joey, Melissa, Sean, David. Personnel cons. Dependable Personnel, N.Y.C., 1958-67; personnel cons. Kent Personnel, N.Y.C., 1967-71; pres. Norman Locke Personnel, Inc., N.Y.C., 1971—, Norman Locke Temporary Services, Inc. Served with U.S. Army, 1947-49, 50-53. Decorated Purple Heart with 2 clusters, Bronze Star for gallantry, Silver Star. Mem. Assn. Personnel Agts. N.Y. Clubs: Chappaqua Pool and Tennis, Briarcliff Racquet. Home: 19 Glen Terr Chappaqua NY Office: 11 E 44th St New York NY 10017

LOCKE, RICHARD VAN DE SANDE, investment banker; b. Flushing, N.Y., Apr. 17, 1937; s. Homer F. and Ruth E. (Rosenlund) L.; B.S., Bucknell U., 1958; m. Patricia A. Casey; children—Elizabeth Denmead, Richard van de Sande III. With Kidder, Peabody & Co., investment bankers, N.Y.C., 1958-64; gen. partner Eastman, Dillon, Union Securities & Co., Inc., N.Y.C., 1964-72; exec. v.p., dir. Blyth Eastman Dillon & Co. Inc., 1973-75; exec. v.p., dir. E.F. Hutton & Co., 1975—. Mem. New York, Am. stock exchanges; dir. Council on Mcpl. Performance; bd. dirs. Watchung Area council Boy Scouts Am. Served to 1st lt. U.S. Army, 1958-59, 61-62. Mem. N.Y.C. C. of C., Municipal Forum N.Y., Municipal Finance Officers Assn., Internat. Bridge, Turnpike and Tunnel Assn., Airport Operators Council Internat., Municipal Forum Washington, Soc. Am. Magicians, Internat. Brotherhood Magicians, Antique Automobile Club Am., Municipal Bond Club N.Y., Nat. Eagle Scout Assn., Lambda Chi Alpha, Theta Alpha Pi. Clubs: India House, The Club, City Midday (N.Y.C.). Office: One Battery Park Plaza New York NY 10004

LOCKE, THEODORE FRELINGHUYSEN, JR., univ. ofcl.; b. Trenton, Aug. 29, 1920; s. Theodore Frelinghuysen and Gertrude May (Fuller) L.; student Drexel Inst. Tech., 1938-39; B.S. in Indsl. Engring., Pa. Mil. Coll., 1942; M.B.A., Syracuse U., 1957; m. Grace White Hosler, Nov. 11, 1942; children—Theodore Frelinghuysen III, Walter Roy, Lillian Hosler. Commd. 2d lt. U.S. Army, 1942, advanced through grades to lt. col., 1966; chief program mgmt. sect. Army Mgmt. Sch., Ft. Belvoir, Va., 1961-65, asst. dir. instrn., 1963-64, dir. instrn., 1964-65; dep. comptroller 7th Army, Stuttgart, W. Ger., 1965-66; ret., 1966; sales engr. Stanley Works, New Britain, Conn., 1946-48; asst. to dean Sch. Engring., Widener Coll., Chester, Pa., 1966-71, asso. prof. mgmt., 1969-74, asst. to v.p., 1971-73, asso. dir. fiscal affairs and ops., 1973-74, asso. v.p. for fiscal affairs, 1974-78, v.p. for planning and budgeting, 1978-80, v.p. adminstrn., 1981—; instr. Creative Problem Solving Inst., SUNY, Buffalo, 1963, 64, 67, 69, 71; lectr. Am. Mgmt. Assn., 1966-67. Sec., Chester-Widener Community Commn., 1980. Decorated Army Commendation medal. Mem. Nat. Assn. Coll. and Univ. Bus. Officers, Ret. Officers Assn. Republican. Presbyterian. Co-author: Army Management, 1964. Home: 813 Ridge Ln Media PA 19063 Office: Widener U 14th St and Chestnut Chester PA 19013

LOCKETT, DONALD RAYE, broadcast engr.; b. Norfolk, Va., July 5, 1947; s. Isaac and Hettie Bess L.; B.S. in Electronics Tech., Va. State U., 1969; M.S. in TV and Radio, Syracuse U., 1973; m. Anita Ruscelia Clayton, Oct. 5, 1977. Site supr. Western Union operated switching center Def. Communications Agy. Automatic Digital Network, Hancock AFB, North Syracuse, N.Y., 1969-70; sect. chief Western Electric, Balt., 1970-73; broadcast engr. Sta. WCNY-TV-FM, Liverpool, N.Y., 1973-74; producer/dir. Sta.-WJZ-TV, Balt., 1974-75; asst. chief engr. Sta. WHUR-FM, Washington, 1975-78, chief engr., 1979—. Served with Med. Service Corp., U.S. Army, 1970-72. Mem. Soc. Broadcast Engrs., Audio Engring. Soc. Democrat. Mem. Christian Ch. (Disciples of Christ). Office: 2600 4th St NW Washington DC 20059

LOCKHART, EARL JAMES, acct.; b. Duluth, Minn., May 29, 1918; s. Earl James and Margaret Kathrine (Dodd) L.; B.B.A., U. Minn., 1947; m. Bernice Irene Hagan, Jan. 10, 1945; children—Jeanne M., Margaret A., James B., Mary P., Thomas M., John G., Caroline L. Sr. acct. Peat Marwick Mitchell & Co., Mpls., 1947-49; partner Pedrizetti, Graving, Honigman, Grover & Lockhart, C.P.A.'s, Duluth, Minn., 1949-68; partner in charge Main Hurdman & Cranstoun, Duluth, 1968—; chmn. Minn. State Bd. Accountancy. Chmn. bd. trustees St. Mary's Hosp.; dir., treas. YMCA, Benedictine Health Center; chmn. adv. bd. U. Minn., Duluth. Served with AUS, 1942-45. Mem. Nat. Assn. C.P.A. Examiners (pres.), Am. Inst. C.P.A.'s, Minn. State Soc. C.P.A.'s. Roman Catholic. Clubs: Kitchi Gammi, Northland Country, Serra. Home: 2610 E 3d St Duluth MN 55812 Office: 700 Missabe Bldg Duluth MN 55802

LOCKHART, GAYLORD LEE, banker; b. Dailey, W.Va., July 16, 1935; s. Beryl Russell and Virginia Pearle (Mundell) L.; student W.Va. U., 1956-58, Fairmont State Coll., 1959; LL.B., LaSalle U., 1976; m. Melinda Diane Gerkin, Nov. 17, 1957; children—Teresa Diane, Susan Gayle, Kelly Christine. With Household Fin. Corp., Chgo., 1958-65, dist. mgr., 1964-65; asst. v.p. Parkersburg Nat. Bank, (W.Va.), 1965-70; v.p. Bank of W.Va., Charleston, 1970-73; pres., chief exec. officer Elk Nat. Bank, Big Chimney, W.Va., 1973—. Treas. March of Dimes, 1965-70; 1st v.p. YMCA, 1969-70; asst. treas. Frank Pick Meml. Hosp., 1970-79. Served with U.S. Army, 1954-56. Named Man of Yr., Jaycees, 1969. Mem. Independent Bankers Assn., Bank Mktg. Assn., W.Va. Bankers Assn., Bank Adminstrn. Inst., W.Va. Ind. Banks Assn. (dir.), Am. Inst. Banking (pres. 1969). Republican. Presbyterian. Clubs: Lions, Elks. Home and Office: PO Box 758 Big Chimney WV 25302

LOCKWOOD, FRANK JAMES, mfg. co. exec.; b. San Bernardino, Cal., Oct. 30, 1931; s. John Ellis and Sarah Grace (Roberts) L.; student S.E. City Coll., 1955, Ill. Inst. Tech., 1963-64, Bogan Jr. Coll., 1966; m. Deborah Sue Samples, 1981; children—Fay (Mrs. Mark Huegelmann), Frank, Hedy (Mrs. Michael Machala), Jonnie, George, Katherine, Bill, Dena, Kevin, Michael, Tony Potmas. Gen. foreman Hupp Aviation, Chgo., 1951-60; dept. head UARCO, Inc., Chgo., 1960-68; pres. Xact Machine & Engring. Co., Chgo., 1968—, also chmn. bd., dir.; pres. Lockwood Engring., Inc., Ill. Nat. Corp. Cons. engr. Served with USNR, 1948-50. Named Chicago Ridge (Ill.) Father of Year, 1964. Mem. Ill. Divers Assn. (pres. 1961-62). Mason (32 deg., Shriner). Patentee in field. Home: Rural Route 1 Texico IL 62889 Office: 7011 W Archer Ave Chicago IL 60638

LOCKWOOD, KAREN KING, sales rep.; b. Indpls., Mar. 3, 1950; d. John P. and Margie W. King; B.A., U. Tex., 1972; M.A., Ind. U., 1976. Sales rep. Liberty Mut. Ins. Co., Indpls., 1976-77; sales rep. Commerce Clearinghouse, Inc., Indpls., 1977; dist. mgr. Elaine Powers Figure Salons, from 1978; now sales rep. John H. Harland Co.; guest lectr. Ind. U.-Purdue U., Indpls. Mem. Am. Mgmt. Assn., Nat. Assn. Female Execs., Network of Women in Bus., Ind. State Symphony Soc., Marion County Hist. Soc. Republican. Episcopalian. Home: 6344 Central Indianapolis IN 46220

LOCKWOOD, LEIGH WILLARD, periodical co. exec.; b. New Rochelle, N.Y., Oct. 16, 1947; s. Robert Arthur and Ellen Estelle (Willard) L.; B.A., U. Pacific, 1969; postgrad. Am. Grad. Sch. Internat. Mgmt., 1972, Stanford Exec. Program for Smaller Cos., 1979; m. Carol Ann Settle, Sept. 9, 1970; children—Erin, Lisa. Procedures analyst Doubleday & Co., N.Y.C., 1973; asst. mgr. Distribuldorá de Impresos S.A., Mexico, 1974-76; gen. mgr., 1977—. Mem. Am. Sch. Found., Mex. Served with U.S. Army, 1969-71. Decorated Joint Sèrvice Commendation medal. Office: Mariano Escobedo 218 Mexico 17 DF Mexico

LOCKWOOD, MOLLY ANN, communications co. exec.; b. London, Sept. 19, 1936; d. Warren Sewell and Ann Frances (Gleason) L.; B.S., Pa. State U., 1958. With exec. tng. program Lord & Taylor, N.Y.C., 1958-60; asso. merchandising editor House & Garden Mag., N.Y.C., 1960-65; advt. dir. Status Mag., N.Y.C., 1965-70; merchandising dir. Holiday Mag., N.Y.C., 1970; account mgr. Ladies' Home Journal Mag., N.Y.C., 1970-72; adv. dir. Girl Talk Mag., N.Y.C., 1972-74; mktg. dir./asso. pub. East/West Network Mag., N.Y.C., 1974-77; v.p., treas., chief operating officer partner Catalyst Communications, Inc., N.Y.C., 1977—; mktg. and sales dir. Museum Mag., 1979—. Mem. Advt. Women N.Y., Kappa Kappa Gamma Alumnae Assn. Home: 1133 Park Ave New York City NY 10028 Office: Catalyst Communications Inc 260 Madison Ave New York City NY 10016

LOCKYER, CHARLES WARREN, JR., comml. printing co. exec.; b. Phila., Apr. 6, 1944; s. Charles Warren and Mary Alice (Underwood) L.; B.A., Fordham U., 1966; M.A., Princeton U., 1968, Ph.D., 1971; m. Karen A. Damiani, Jan. 22, 1966; children—Charles Warren III, Larissa A., Daphne M. Vice pres. Fidelity Bank, Phila., 1970-79; v.p., chief fin. officer Pubco Corp., Glenn Dale, Md., 1980—; dir. Gulfstream Land & Devel. Corp., Plantation, Fla. Trustee Jeanes Hosp., Phila., 1973—; dir. Foulkeways at Gwynedd (Pa.), 1975-80; mem. adv. com. classics Princeton U., 1978—. Woodrow Wilson fellow, 1966. Mem. Phi Beta Kappa. Club: Princeton (N.Y.); Union League (Phila.). Office: 11200 Prospect Hill Rd Glenn Dale MD 20769

LODGE, WILLIAM DUNKIN, communications equipment mfg. co. exec.; b. Bridgeport, W.Va., July 3, 1927; s. John Dunkin and Mary Tirzah (Hayes) L.; B.S., W.Va. U., 1951; M.B.A., N.Y. U., 1965; m. Pauline Marie Haskins, Aug. 6, 1950; children—David, Linda, Thomas, Daniel. With Western Electric Co. Inc., 1954—, staff mgr., N.Y.C., 1962-68, mgr. So. Tex. area, Houston, 1968—. Chmn. Harris County Com. Employment of Handicapped; trustee United Fund; exec. com. Jr. Achievement of Southeast Tex.; mem. Miller Theatre Adv. Council. Served with USNR, 1945-46, AUS, 1951-54. Mem. Am. Mgmt. Assn., IEEE, Sigma Nu. Kiwanian. Home: 9204 Clover Valley Dallas TX 75243 Office: 1800 N Mason Rd Katy TX 77450

LOEB, JOHN LANGELOTH, JR., investment banker; b. N.Y.C., May 2, 1930; s. John Langeloth and Frances (Lehman) L.; grad. Hotchkiss Sch., 1948; A.B. cum laude, Harvard, 1952, M.B.A., 1954; children—Nicholas, Alexandra. With Loeb, Rhoades & Co., N.Y.C., 1956—, gen. partner, mem. mgmt. com., 1959-73, mng. partner, pres., 1971-73, chmn., ltd. partner, 1973—; chmn. bd. Holly Sugar Corp., Colorado Springs, Colo., 1969-71; past dir. Denver & Rio Grande Western Railroad, Metro-Goldwyn-Mayer, John Morrell & Co. Spl. adviser on environ. matters to Gov. Nelson A. Rockefeller, 1967-73; chmn. Gov. N.Y. Council Environ. Advisers, 1970-75. Trustee Montefiore Hosp. and Med. Sch., Museum City N.Y. Winston Churchill Found., Frances and John L. Loeb Found.; mem. vis. com. of bd. overseers to Grad. Sch. Bus. Adminstrn., Harvard U. Served as 1st lt. USAF, 1954-56. Clubs: Recess, City Midday, St. Nicholas Soc. (N.Y.C.); Century Country, Sleepy Hollow (Westchester, N.Y.); Brooks's, Buck's (London, Eng.); Royal Swedish Yacht (Stockholm); Lyford Cay (Nassau, Bahamas). Home: Ridgeleigh Anderson Hill Rd Purchase NY 10577 Office: care of Loeb Rhoades & Co 375 Park Ave New York NY 10022

LOEB, THOMAS FREDERICK, investment mgmt. exec.; b. Phila., July 24, 1947; s. Richard Ferdinand and Marianne (Schorr) L.; B.S. in Econs., Fairleigh Dickinson U., 1969; M.B.A. in Fin., U. Pa., 1971. Asst. mgr. investment services Blyth, Eastman Dillon Inc., N.Y.C., 1971-72; v.p., mgr. index fund group Wells Fargo Investment Advs., San Francisco, 1973—; speaker on passive investment mgmt. Fin. Analysts Fedn. Instnl. Investor mag., 1974—. Contbr. chpt. to Investment Manager's Handbook, 1979. Office: 475 Sansome St San Francisco CA 94144

LOENING, WERNER, mgmt. cons.; b. Berlin, Aug. 27, 1928; s. Alfons and Alma (Hollern) L.; came to U.S., 1955, naturalized, 1960; B.S. in Physics, Tech. U. Berlin, 1950, M.S. in Mech. Engring., 1952, M.B.A., 1952; m. Brigitte Schnase, Apr. 17, 1954; children—Peter, Cynthia. Engr., Fritz Werner A.G., Berlin, 1950-53, Vereinigte Aluminum Werke A.G., Bonn, W.Ger., 1953-55; sr. engr. Raytheon Mfg. Co., Wayland, Mass., 1955-58; dept. mgr. Perkin-Elmer Corp., Norwalk, Conn., 1958-70; v.p. automatic signal div. LFE Corp., Norwalk, 1970-73; v.p. engring. Gen. Telephone & Electronics, Stamford, Conn., 1973-76; mgmt. cons., 1976—. Registered profl. eng., Conn., Mem. ASME, Armed Forces Communications and Electronics Assn., Am. Arbitration Assn. Republican. Mem. adv. bd. Jour. Research and Devel., 1974. Home and Office: 65 Ryders Ln Wilton CT 06897

LOEPER, WILLIAM JOSEPH, accountant; b. Ashland, Pa., Mar. 19, 1935; s. Peter Frank and Ruth Evelyn Loeper; B.S., Mt. St. Mary's Coll., 1960; postgrad. U. So. Calif., 1962-63; M.B.A., Loyola U., New Orleans, 1966; m. Cappock, Sept. 10, 1960; children—Joseph M., Catherine M., Ruth A. Group treas. Union Carbide Singapore, 1972-74; div. controller Computer Sci. Corp., Tehran, Iran, 1975-77; controller, chief exec. officer JEM Mgmt. Corp., Fresno, Calif., 1977-79; dir. fin. services Garrett Freightlines, Inc., Pocatello, Idaho, 1979—. Head fin., mem. sch. bd. Singapore Am. Sch., 1972-74. Served with U.S. Army, 1953-56. Mem. Nat. Assn. Accts. (dir., v.p. fin. and adminstrn.). Republican. Roman Catholic. Club: Elks. Home: 1780 Lance Dr Pocatello ID 83201 Office: 2055 Garrett Way Pocatello ID 83201

LOEWE, LESLIE F., apparel co. exec.; b. 1922; married. Vice pres. allied ops. Angelica Corp., St. Louis, 1940-63, exec. v.p. gen. mgr. ops., 1973-76, corp. exec. v.p., corp. group officer, pres. Angelica uniform group, 1976-80, pres., chief exec. officer, 1980—. Office: 10176 Corporate Sq Dr Saint Louis MO 63132*

LOFGREEN, PAUL EUGENE, JR., med. research co. mgr.; b. Stockton, Calif., June 18, 1946; s. Paul E. and Helen W. (Fotes) L.; student U. Utah, 1965-73; A.A., Thomas Edison Coll., 1975; cert. Center for Real Estate Studies, 1976; m. Clementina Maria Accinno, Aug. 10, 1979. Asst. unit mgr. operating room, dept. surgery U. Utah, Salt Lake City, 1966-67, asst. heart-lung pump technician, 1967-69, operating room technician, 1969-70; supr. inbred rodent colony dept. pathology U. Utah, Salt Lake City, 1970-71, contract adminstr., 1971-75; ops. adminstr. Basic Research Program, Frederick (Md.) Cancer Research Center, 1975-76, sr. tech. ops. mgr. animal prodn. area, 1977—; real estate cons. Imperial Realty Co., Salt Lake City, 1976-77; fiscal mgr. Utah Native Am. Consortium, 1977. Served with USN, 1965-66. Mem. Soc. Research Adminstrs., Internat. Mgmt. Council (chmn. edn. com. 1980—), Am. Assn. Lab. Animal Sci. (parlimentarian 1978-79, co-chmn. nat. capital area br. exhibitors com. 1979, chmn. com. 1980—; editorial adv. bd. Lab Animal mag. 1979—), Assn. Gnotobiotics. Baptist.

LOFTUS, DANIEL PAUL, health adminstr.; b. Scranton, Pa., June 1, 1946; s. Joseph and Marie Theresa (Byron) L.; B.S. in Psychology, U. Scranton, 1968; M.S.W., Marywood Coll., Scranton, 1974, M.S., 1980; m. Patricia Haen, Dec. 28, 1968; children—Brian, Kevin. Caseworker, Lackawanna County Bd. Assistance, Scranton, 1970-71; caseworker, then dep. dir. base service unit Luzerne-Wyoming County Mental Health Center, Wilkes Barre, Pa., 1971-78, asso. adminstrv.-coordinator, 1978—; v.p., bd. dirs. United Neighborhood Services, 1977-80; active United Cerebral Palsy Lackawanna County; adj. instr. bus. dept. Marywood Coll., 1980—. Mgr. Little League, Dandy Lion Baseball Assn. Served with AUS, 1968-70; Vietnam. Decorated Bronze Star with 2 oak leaf clusters, Army Commendation medal with 2 oak leaf clusters. Mem. Acad. Certified Social Workers, Nat. Assn. Social Workers, Assn. M.B.A. Execs., Pa. Assn. Community Mental Health-Mental Retardation Providers, Pa. Assn. Retarded Citizens, Hosp. Fin. Mgmt. Assn., Lackawanna Mental Health Assn. (pub. affairs com.), Northeastern Pa. Soc. Crippled Children and Adults, Common Cause. Democrat. Author monograph. Office: 103 S Main St Wilkes Barre PA 18701

LOGAN, HENRY VINCENT, transp. co. exec.; b. Phila., Nov. 7, 1942; s. Edward Roger and Alberta (Gross) L.; student Drexel U., 1960-70; B.S. in Commerce, De Paul U., 1975, postgrad. Grad. Sch. Bus., 1977-78; postgrad. Grad. Sch. Bus., U. Chgo., 1976; m. Mary Genzano, Sept. 28, 1963; children—Michele Leah, Maureen Laura, Monica Lynn. Acct., Ins. Co. N.Am., 1961-62; with Trailer Train Co., Chgo., 1962—, mgr. gen. acctg., 1968-70, dir. corp. acctg. and taxes, 1970-71, controller, 1971-78, dir. fin. planning, 1978—. Mem. Nat. Assn. Accts., Fin. Execs. Inst., Assn. Am. Railroads. Home: 23 W 220 Cambridge Ct Glen Ellyn IL 60137 Office: Trailer Train Co 300 S Wacker Dr Chicago IL 60606

LOGAN, ROBERT RALPH, banker; b. Farmersville, Tex., Mar. 16, 1930; s. Newt and Louie (Roberts) L.; B.S. in Agr., N.Mex. State U., 1952; m. Shirley Reynolds, Aug. 3, 1951; children—Robert Michael, Scott Allen, Steven Wayne. Exec. trainee, salesman Gen. Mills, Inc., Oklahoma City, San Antonio, 1953-55; salesman, dist. sales mgr. CIT Corp., San Antonio, Houston, 1956-67; exec. v.p., adv. dir. Chem. Bank, Houston, 1967-70; pres., dir. Peoples Bank, Houston, 1970—; organizer, dir. Heritage Nat. Bank, Houston, 1972-75; vice chmn. bd. Allied Meml. Bank, Houston, 1979—; cons. Allied Bancshares, Inc., Houston. Served with inf. U.S. Army, 1952-54; Korea. Mem. Tex. Bankers Assn., Houston, Spring Branch Meml. (pres. 1974) chambers commerce. Republican. Mem. Ch. of Christ. Clubs: Springwoods Booster (pres. 1974), Kiwanis (Outstanding Citizens award 1974). Home: 2019 Hollow Hook Houston TX 77080 Office: 8400 Long Point Houston TX 77055

LOGELIN, EDWARD CHARLES, educator, former steel co. exec.; b. Chgo., Aug. 19, 1910; s. Edward Charles and Lena (Wilhelm) L.; student pub. schs.; L.H.D., Ill. Wesleyan U., 1955; m. Eleanor Messner, Sept 7, 1940; children—Edward Charles III, Eleanor. With U.S. Steel Corp. 1930-75, asst. dir. pub. relations, 1941-46, dir. pub. relations, 1946-54, v.p. Midwest, 1954-75; Goodyear Exec. prof. bus. adminstrn. Kent (Ohio) State U., 1975-78, interim dean Coll. Bus. Adminstrn., 1977-78. Mem. citizens' bd. U. Chgo., 1957—; mem. Hosp. Council Met. Chgo., 1957-65, Chgo. Crime Commn., 1955-78. Bd. dirs. Community Fund Chgo., 1954-60, Jr. Achievement, 1954-75, John Crerar Library, Mus. Sci. and Industry; chmn., trustee, dir. Union League Found., 1968-77, Boys' Clubs. Mem. Ill. Mfrs. Assn. (dir., treas. 1962-75), Chgo. Assn. Commerce and Industry (dir., pres. 1962-63), Assn. U.S. Army (pres. 1971-74, chmn. bd. trustees 1974-77). Presbyn. (mem. bd. nat. missions 1956-66, vice moderator Gen. Assembly 1962). Clubs: Economic (dir.), Civic Federation, Executives (chmn. Chgo. plan commn. 1965-68), Commercial, Chicago, Urban League (Chgo.). Home: 1757 S Wilson Lake Forest IL 60045

LOGES, CLAYTON NEAL, bus. exec.; b. Yakima, Wash., Mar. 21, 1946; s. Russell Wilbur and Margaret Elizabeth (Purchase) L.; B.A. in Polit. Sci., U. Puget Sound, 1968; B.A. in History, U. Wash., 1975. Dir. pub. relations Action for Wash., Seattle, 1969; mktg. rep. data processing IBM, Honolulu, 1970-71; with Wash. Mut. Savs. Bank, Seattle, 1973-77, officer, mgr. bus. devel. and implementation new services, 1975-77; film producer, mgr. Pacific NW div. Corporate Prodns., Inc., Los Angeles, an affiliate Kaye-Smith Enterprises, Seattle, 1977-78; chmn. bd., dir. Speedi-Lube, Inc., 1977—; partner First Home Consulting; lectr. Am. Inst. Banking. Mem. Seattle Municipal League. Home: 3515 46th Ave NE Seattle WA 98105 Office: Univ Village 2500 NE 49th St Seattle WA 98105

LOGIE, IAN M., elec. contractor; b. New Rochelle, N.Y., Nov. 27, 1942; s. Norman and Adelade (Moore) L.; student Fairfield U.; m. Karen Marlene Stoever, Oct. 20, 1967; Elec. apprentice New Eng. Electric Co., Bridgeport, Conn., 1965-66; apprentice Hawley Electric, Danbury, Conn., 1966-68, supt., 1968-71; v.p. Johnson Electric, Bridgeport, 1972-74, owner, pres., 1974—. Served with USMC, 1959-63. Mem. Elec. Contractors Assn., Brotherhood of Elec. Workers, Nat. Contractors Assn. Club: Masons. Contbr. articles to profl. jours. Home: 60 Palmer St Stamford CT 06907 Office: 255 Hathaway Dr Stratford CT 06497

LOGSDON, H. GLENN, engring. exec.; b. Ottawa, Ill., Sept. 28, 1929; s. Hillard T. and Marie K. (Hanson) L.; B.S., Olivet Coll., Kankakee, Ill., 1952; postgrad. U. Fla., 1955-57; m. Christine B. Carter, Aug. 6, 1950; 1 dau., Angela Marie. Mech. engr. Pullara, Bowen & Watson, Tampa, Fla., 1957-59; head mech. engring. Pullara & Watson, Tampa, 1960; v.p. Bedingfield & Assos., cons. engrs., Tampa, 1960-69; chief engr., dir. research Aeronca, Inc., environmental control group, Pineville, N.C., 1969-70, dir. engring., 1971-73, chief engr., 1973-76; v.p. engring. Metal Industries, Inc., Clearwater, Fla., 1976-79; v.p. Environ. Techs. Inc., Largo, Fla., 1979—. Served with AUS, 1952-54. Mem. ASTM (mem. tech. coms.),

Am. Soc. Heating, Refrigeration and Air Conditioning Engrs. (tech. coms.), Nat., N.C., Fla. socs. profl. engrs., Nat. Fire Prevention Assn., Air Conditioning and Refrigeration Inst., Sertoma Internat. (sec. Interbay club Tampa 1961-63, chmn. bd. 1964). Methodist. Patentee air distbn., sound control and heat recovery systems. Home: 1456 Maple Forest Dr Clearwater FL 33516 Office: POB 4490 Clearwater FL 33518

LOHMEYER, PAUL FRANCIS, importing co. exec.; b. Pitts., July 23, 1922; s. William J. and Sarah (McKeating) L.; B.A., U. Pitts., 1943; m. Martha McCullough, Jan. 21, 1944; children—Susan, James, Thomas (dec.), Barbara. Tng. officer U.S. VA, Pitts., 1946-48; asst. to dean men U. Pitts., 1948-50; asst. to pres. in charge mktg. Pitts. Brewing Co., Pitts., 1950-58; exec. v.p. Red Raven Corp., Oakmont, Pa., 1959; v.p. mktg. Carling Brewing Co., Cleve., 1959-66; dir. advt., sales promotion Am. Can Co., N.Y.C., 1966-69; dir. mktg. P. Ballantine & Sons Brewers, Newark, 1969-70; pres. All Brand Importers, Inc. div. Beverage Group, Standard Brands Inc., Roslyn Heights, N.Y., 1971—; dir. Assn. Nat. Advt., 1963-66. Trustee St. Josephs Church, Bronxville, N.Y., 1977—. Served with U.S. Army, 1943-46. Mem. Nat. Assn. Beverage Importers (dir.), U.S. Brewers Assn. Roman Catholic. Office: All Brand Importers Inc 99 Powerhouse Rd Roslyn Heights NY 11577

LOHN, KENNETH JENS, mktg. co. exec.; b. Fargo, N.D., Nov. 26, 1933; s. Jens L. and Barbara Fern (McLaughlin) L.; student U. Minn., 1951-52, N.D. State U., 1955-56; m. Betty Jo Dobbs, May 20, 1972. Pres., PWI, Inc., mgrs. computer control accessories, Winston-Salem, N.C., 1961-63; founder, owner, mgr. Ken Lohn & Assos., advt., Mpls., 1963-72; founder, chmn., pres. Ranger Aviation, Inc., agrl. helicopter spraying services, Mpls., 1967—, KaBeeLo Lodge, Ltd., resort, Ear Falls, Ont., Can., 1972—, KaBeeLo Airways, Ltd., Ear Falls, 1975—, The Wintergreen Corp., computerized mktg. co. for tourist and resort industry, Mpls., 1979—. Active Jr. Achievement. Served with U.S. Army, 1952-55; Korea. Named Salesman of Yr., Sales and Mktg. Execs. Club, 1961. Mem. VFW. Clubs: U. Minn., Elks. Author: Electronic Brains: How They Think and Remember, 1963; contbr. chpt. to Advertising by Engel. Home: 5215 Hanrehan Blvd Prior Lake MN 55372 Office: Box 145 Prior Lake MN 55372

LOHNES, JOHN E., exec. search co. exec.; b. Sycamore, Ill., Dec. 22, 1928; s. E. G. and Elizabeth M. (Jacques) L.; B.A., Yale U., 1951; M.B.A., Stanford U., 1953; m. Joan Hamilton, Sept. 30, 1950; children—John, Christopher, Elizabeth, Timothy, Mary Grace, Luke, Frances. Mgmt. trainee No. Trust Co., Chgo., 1953-55; gen. mgr. Poole Bros., Chgo., San Francisco, 1955-59; v.p. Booz, Allen & Hamilton, San Francisco, Los Angeles, 1959-68; mgmt. cons., Los Angeles, 1968-71; mng. dir. Eastern region Korn/Ferry Internat., N.Y.C., 1971—, also dir.; dir. First Women's Bank, N.Y.C., Korn/Ferry S.A., France, Korn/Ferry N.V., Belgium. Bd. dirs. Urban League, Fairfield County, Conn., 1977-79, Yale U. Alumni Fund, 1976-81. Republican. Episcopalian. Clubs: Met., Yale (N.Y.C.); Tokeneke. Home: 11 Tokeneke Trail Darien CT 06820 Office: 277 Park Ave New York NY 10017

LOHR, ROGER WAYNE, oil and gas well tool mfg. co. exec.; b. Linton, Ind., Dec. 20, 1946; s. Carl Edison and Ruby (Knowles) L.; B.S. (award), No. Ariz. U., 1975. With Reed Tool Co. (name now Reed Rock Bit Co.) 1976—, sales rep., South Tex., 1977, tech. services rep., Houston, 1977-78, dist. sales mgr., Great Bend, Kans., 1978-79, tech. services cons., Houston, 1980—. Served as sgt. USAF, 1966-70. Mem. Kans. Ind. Oil and Gas Assn., Am. Petroleum Inst., Am. Mgmt. Assn., Soc. Petroleum Engrs., No. Ariz. U. Alumni Assn. (life), U.S. Racquetball Assn., Delta Sigma Pi. Club: Exec. Racquet. Home: 9303 Hammerly Unit 903 Houston TX 77080 Office: 15702 W Hardy St Suite 220 Houston TX 77060

LOHRE, JOHN OWEN, leasing co. exec.; b. Vermillion, S.D., Apr. 21, 1932; s. George Herman and Sanna (Nelson) L.; B.S., U. S.D., 1954; M.B.A., Harvard U., 1959; m. Mary Belle Biggert, Aug. 6, 1960; children—Kathryn, Philip. With Chgo. Bridge & Iron Co., 1959-65; v.p. First Nat. Bank of Chgo., 1965-74; with First Mcpl. Leasing Corp., Englewood, Colo., 1974—, pres., 1980—. Treas., Community Renewal Soc., Chgo., 1973-74. Served to 1st lt. U.S. Army, 1955-57. Republican. Presbyterian. Clubs: Univ. (Chgo.); Harvard (N.Y.C.); Harvard Bus. Sch. of Colo. (v.p. 1979-80). Home: 4330 S Alton Way Englewood CO 80111 Office: 7840 E Berry Pl Englewood CO 80111

LOHRMAN, JOHN J., mfg. co. exec.; b. Ellsworth, Iowa, Mar. 4, 1920; s. Joseph A. and Elizabeth (Crosley) L.; B.Sc., Creighton U., Omaha, 1941; postgrad. U. Pa., 1946-47; m. Natalie M. Anderson, Aug. 26, 1978; children—James B., Kristine M., David C. Anderson, Andrea L. Anderson. Indsl. relations asst., then asst. controller Phila. Transp. Co., 1946-55; asso. McKinsey & Co., N.Y.C., 1955-57; with Russell, Burdsall & Ward, Inc., Mentor, Ohio, 1957-77, v.p. adminstrn., 1961-69, exec. v.p., 1969-73, pres., chief exec. officer, 1973-76, chmn. bd., chief exec. officer, 1976-77; chmn. bd., chief exec. officer Mangel Stores Corp., 1977, Russell, Burdsall & Ward Corp., 1977—; dir. Lake Nat. Bank, Inarco Corp. Bd. govs. Asso. Industries of Cleve., 1980—; bd. dirs. Cleve. Jr. Achievement, 1976—; trustee Hillcrest Hosp., Lake Erie Coll.; chmn. governing bd. Indsl. Fasteners Inst., 1978. Served to maj. U.S. Army, 1941-46. Recipient Creighton U. Alumni Merit award, 1980. Clubs: Westchester Country, Kirtland Country, Hillbrook, Ocean Reef, Union. Home: Cedar Rd Gates Mills OH 44040 Office: 8100 Tyler Blvd Mentor OH 44060

LOIELLO, LAWRENCE PAUL, bus. and real estate broker; b. Freeport, N.Y., Nov. 1, 1934; s. Rosario Paul and Mary Agnes (Butler) L.; B.S., Fordham U., 1956; postgrad. Ind. State U., 1957, Boston Coll., 1959, Hofstra U., 1960; M.B.A., N.Y. U., 1965; m. Joan Marie Gannon, June 23, 1956; children—Lawrence E., Diane M., Maureen A. Contract adminstr. Nat. Electronics, Inc., Boston, 1959-60; supr. client accounting Young & Rubicam, Inc., N.Y.C., 1960-66; mgr. client accounting Benton & Bowles, Inc., N.Y.C., 1966-67; asst. treas. Ogilvy & Mather, Inc., N.Y.C., 1967-71; v.p. fin. Peters, Griffin, Woodward, Inc., N.Y.C., 1971-76, sr. v.p., 1976-77, exec. v.p., 1977-80, exec. com., dir., 1972-80; bus. and real estate broker, 1980—; dir. Mini-Pak, Inc. Served to 1st lt. USAF, 1957-59. Mem. Am. Mgmt. Assn., Broadcast Credit Corp. (past pres., dir.), Sta. Reps. Assn. (chmn. fin. com. 1974-79), Broadcast Fin. Mgmt. Assn., Am. Assn. Advt. Agys. Republican. Roman Catholic. Clubs: N.Y. Athletic, Murray Hill Racquet and Tennis. Home: 13 Oxford Pl Massapequa NY 11758

LOKEY, GEORGE HARRISON, oil co. exec.; b. Amarillo, Tex., Mar. 25, 1935; s. Ted Henry and Stella Alice (Yeatts) L.; B.A. in Bus. Adminstrn., U. Okla., 1957; m. Sheri Darlynn Mims, Nov. 2, 1968; 1 son, Alexander David. With Ted Lokey Oil Co., Amarillo, 1960—, v.p., gen. mgr., 1962-63, pres., chief exec. officer, 1963—; v.p. Ted Lokey Tire Co,, Amarillo, 1963-80; dir. Tascosa Broadcasting Co., 1974-79; developer skiing and tennis real estate properties in no. N. Mex. Chmn. Amarillo Bicentennial Commn., Amarillo Bd. Conv. and Visitors Activities; pres. Amarillo Zool. Soc., Panhandle Heritage Found.; bd. dirs. Discover Tex. Assn., Tex. Tourist Council, Greater S.W. Music Festival; bd. dirs. Tex. Panhandle council Boy Scouts Am. Served as 1st lt. USMCR, 1957-60. Named Outstanding Young Texan. Garland A. Smith Assos., 1976. Mem. Nat. Oil Jobbers Council (dir., mem. exec. com.), Tex. Oil Marketers Assn. (pres. 1978-79), W. Tex. C. of C., C. of C. (dir.), Les Amis du Vin (regional dir.), Confrerie des Vignerons de Saint Vincent de Macon, Confrerie de la Chaine des Rotisseurs (Bailli de Amarillo), Sigma Alpha Epsilon. Presbyterian. Clubs: Amarillo, Amarillo Country, T Bar M Racquet, Taos Ski and Cricket, Taos Tennis Ranch, Angle Fire Country, Amarillo Am. Bus. (past pres., past gov.). Home: 2801 S Hughes St Amarillo TX 79109 Office: 314 W 8th St PO Box 2627 Amarillo TX 79105

LOLLAR, ROBERT MILLER, environ. affairs cons.; b. Lebanon, Ohio May 17, 1915; s. Harry David and Ruby (Miller) L.; Chem.E., U. Cin., 1937, M.S., 1938, Ph.D., 1940; m. Dorothy Marie Williams, Jan. 1, 1941; children—Janet Ruth (Mrs. David Schwarz), Katherine Louise (Mrs. James Punteney, Jr.). Cereal analyst Kroger Food Found., Cin., 1935-37; devel. chemist Rit Product div. Corn Products, Indpls., 1937-39, 40-41; asso. prof. U. Cin., 1941-59; tech. dir. Armour & Co., Chgo., 1959-73; pres. Lollar & Assos., environ. affairs cons., 1973—; research prof. U. Cin., 1975—. Dir. OSRD, 1942-45. Recipient Alsop award Am. Leather Chemists' Assn., 1954. Mem. Am. Leather Chemists Assn. (pres., editor-in-chief jour.), Inst. Food Technologists, also mem. Am. Chem. Soc. (nat. councillor), Am. Soc. Quality Control, Sigma Xi, Tau Beta Pi, Alpha Chi Sigma. Home and office: 5960 Donjoy Dr Cincinnati OH 45242

LOM, MAX J., travel agy. exec.; b. Prague, Mar. 29, 1920; came to U.S., 1959, naturalized, 1966; s. Maximilian and Emily (Faltus) L.; B.A., Charles U., Prague, 1945; grad. Sch. Economy, Prague, 1947; m. Gerta Lifshitz, Nov. 21, 1945; children—Helen, John, Ann. With Czechoslovak Fgn. Service, 1947-50; bus. exec., Cuba, 1952-59, Nassau, Bahamas, 1960-65; mgr. Rocky Mountain br. Trans Globe Travel Bur., Denver, 1965-75; v.p., gen. mgr. Trans Globe Tours, Inc., Denver, 1976—; dir. RSI-Reservation System Inc., Des Plaines, Ill; instr., lectr. travel courses U. Colo., 1971—, U. N.Mex., 1974—. Mem. Am. Soc. Travel Agts., Am. Mgmt. Assn., ACLU, Colo. Humane Soc. Unitarian. Contbr. articles to trade publs. Home: 1616 Fairfax St Denver CO 80220 Office: 2828 E Colfax Ave Denver CO 80220

LOMBARD, DAVID FRANKLIN, publs. cons., restaurant owner; b. Portland, Maine, July 22, 1943; s. Arthur Franklin and Louise (Perkins) L.; B.B.A., Nichols Coll., 1965; m. Susan Davidson, Sept. 13, 1969; children—Bethany Eileen, Derek Franklin. Publs. cons. T. O'Toole & Sons, South Norwalk, Conn., 1965-72; publs. cons. Josten's, Mpls., 1972—; owner Olde Grist Mill Restaurant, Kennebunkport, Maine, 1965—. Trustee Nichols Coll., Dudley, Mass. Mem. Nat. Restaurant Assn. Republican. Congregationalist. Clubs: Shriners. Home: 51 Patricia Dr Dalton MA 01226 Office: Olde Grist Mill Kennebunkport ME 04046

LOMBARD, JOHN JAMES, JR., lawyer; b. Phila., Dec. 27, 1934; s. John James and Mary R. (O'Donnell) L.; B.A. cum laude, La Salle Coll., 1956; J.D., U. Pa., 1959; m. Barbara E. Mallon, May 9, 1964; children—John James III, William M., James Garrett, Laura Keating, Barbara E. Admitted to Pa. bar, 1960; asso. firm Obermayer, Rebmann, Maxwell & Hippel, Phila., 1960-65, partner, 1966—, fin. partner, 1972—; sec., dir. Airline Hydraulics Corp., Conwell Heights, Pa., 1969—; sec. ad hoc com., security transfers, N.Y. Stock Exchange, 1970-71. Mem. Whitpain Twp. (Pa.) Planning Commn., 1972-79, chmn., 1976-79; bd. dirs. Redevel. Authority Montgomery County, Pa., 1980—; bd. dirs. pres.'s council Gwynedd-Mercy Coll., Gwynedd Valley, Pa. Served with USNG, 1959-60. Named Outstanding Young Man Am., U.S. Jaycees, 1969. Mem. Phila. Bar Assn. (chmn. probate sect. 1972), Pa. Bar Assn. (Ho. of Dels. 1979-81), Am. Bar Assn. (membership chmn. sect. for real property, probate and trust law 1978—, mem. council 1979—), Am. Bar Found. Republican. Roman Catholic. Club: Union League (Phila.). Home: 660 Belfry Dr Center Square PA 19422 Office: 14th Floor Packard Bldg Philadelphia PA 19102

LOMBARDI, FRANK JAMES, govt. health care fin. adminstr.; b. Balt., Feb. 5, 1935; s. Nicola Anthony and Elvira L.; student U. Balt., 1953-54, Johns Hopkins U., 1957-58, U. Md., 1966-67; m. Bonnie Virginia Royston, May 29, 1959; children—Gina Marie, Frank Thomas, Sheri Ann, Teri Ann. Technician, Bendix Corp., Towson Md., 1957-58, Bendix Field Engrs., Columbia, Md., 1958-62; computer specialist NASA, Goddard Space Flight Center, 1962-73; teleprocessing systems analyst, br. chief Social Security Adminstrn., HEW, Balt., 1973-79, computer systems analyst, div. chief Health Care Financing Adminstrn., Balt., 1979—. Pres., Franklin Jr. High PTA, 1973-75, Cedarmere Elemen. Sch., 1974-75. Served with U.S. Army, 1955-56. Recipient Spl. Achievement award NASA, 1970. Roman Catholic. Clubs: K.C. (grand knight 1974-75), Square Dance. Home: 28 Caraway Rd Reisterstown MD 21136 Office: 1710 Gwynn Oak Ave Room 100 Belmont Baltimore MD 21207

LOMBARDO, GAETANO, mfg. co. exec.; b. Salemi, Italy, Feb. 4, 1940; came to U.S., 1947; s. Salvatore and Anna Maria L.; Sc.B., Brown U., 1962; Ph.D., Cornell U., 1971; m. Nancy B. Emerson, Sept. 2, 1967; children—Nicholas Emerson, Maryanne Chilton. Sr. staff Arthur D. Little Inc., Cambridge, Mass., 1967-77; v.p. logistics Morton Salt Co., Chgo., 1977-78; dir. logistics and distbn. Gould Inc., Chgo., 1978—; vis. prof. ops. mgmt. Boston U., 1973. Contbr. articles to profl. jours. Home: 210 Maple Hill Rd Glencoe IL 60022 Office: Gould Center Rolling Meadows IL 60004

LONDEAU, HAROLD JOSEPH MERRILL, airline exec.; b. Renfrew, Ont., Can., June 22, 1921; s. Adnos and Ethel (Southern) L.; B.A.Sc., Toronto U., 1949; M.Sc., Coll. Aeros. Engring., 1954; B.Comm., Sir George Williams U., Montreal, 1964; m. Madeline Beaumont, Oct. 24, 1942; children—Carolyn Gae Londeau McKay, Deborah Fae Londeau Snyder, Harold James. Commd. flying officer RCAF, 1942, advanced through grades to lt. col., 1957; fighter pilot; test pilot; chief maintenance NATO 4ATAF, Ramstein, Germany, 1969-71; ret., 1971; chmn. dept. bus. adminstrn. and commerce Dawson Coll., Montreal, 1971-73; asst. v.p. maintenance and engring. Nordair Ltd., Montreal, 1973-78; v.p. maintenance and engring. Air New Eng., Inc., Hyannis, Mass., 1978—. Chartered engr., Eng.; profl. engr., Can. Asso. fellow Canadian Aero. Space Inst., Inst. Petroleum; mem. Royal Aero. Soc. Anglican. Home: 22 Westminster Rd Centerville MA 02632 Office: Barnstable Mcpl Airport Hyannis MA 02601

LONDEN, JACK WINSTON, ins. co. exec.; b. Indpls., July 27, 1929; s. Jack Williford and Irene (Long) L.; student U. Colo., 1948-53; m. Doris May Isaacson, Sept. 7, 1951; children—Jack W., Thomas A., Larry D., Ronald C. Chmn., pres. Green Shield Plan, Inc., Boulder, Colo., 1956-62; chmn., pres. Londen Ins. Group, Inc., Phoenix, 1963—; dir. City Bank of Ariz.; chmn. Lincoln Heritage Life Ins. Co.; pres., chmn. Allegheny Nat. Life Ins. Co., Accredited Trust Life Ins. Co., West States Ins. Co. Bd. dirs. Camelback Hosp. Found., Maricopa County ARC; Republican nat. committeeman for Ariz., 1980—; elder 1st Christian Ch. Clubs: Phoenix Country, Plaza. Home: 33 Biltmore Estates Phoenix AZ 85016 Office: 4808 N 22d St Phoenix AZ 85016

LONDON, JOSEPH WAYNE, oil co. exec.; b. Denver, Dec. 15, 1925; s. John Thomas and Frances Estelle (Heifner) L.; B.S. in M.E., U. Calif., Berkeley, 1946; M.B.A., U. San Francisco, 1969; m. Sylvia Mary Manbey, Feb. 24, 1946; children—Lynn London Watts, David Wayne. Mech. engr. Shell Chem. Co., Houston, 1946-54; supr. purchasing, 1961-64; buyer Shell Oil Co., San Francisco and Los Angeles, 1954-61; mgr. purchasing Shell Devel. Co., Emeryville, Calif. and Houston, 1969—. Served with USNR, 1944-45. Cert. purchasing mgr., materials mgmt. profl. Mem. Nat. Assn. Purchasing Mgrs., Internat. Materials Mgmt. Republican. Episcopalian. Office: 3333 Hwy 6 S Houston TX 77082

LONES, ELAINE AVERY, computer software exec.; b. Richfield, Utah, Nov. 18, 1940; d. Gilbert and Wanda (Washburn) Avery; B.A. in Math., San Diego State U., 1963; children—Loren, Lance. Systems analyst U. Calif., San Diego, 1964-69; owner, operator L&L Systems, computer software firm specializing in devel. of software for mortgage banking industry, San Diego, 1969—. Home: 3429 Hill St San Diego CA 92106 Office: PO Box 7513 San Diego CA 92107

LONETTO, JOSEPH PAUL, comml. credit and collection co. exec.; b. N.Y.C., Dec. 2, 1944; s. Joseph Louis and Carmela Marie (Costa) L.; student St. John's Jr. Coll., 1964, St. John's U., 1966, Grad. Sch. Bus. Adminstrn., Washington U., 1980; m. Joanne Marie Galizia, July 9, 1966; children—Joseph, Sherry, Kristine. Credit reporting supr. Retail Credit Co., N.Y.C., 1966-67; credit and collections staff HFC Corp., Astoria, N.Y., 1967-68; v.p., sr. account exec., gen. mgr. Stanley Tulchin Assos., Garden City, N.Y., 1968—; v.p. Collection Clearing Corp., Garden City, 1968—; sec., dir. Lumber and Bldg. Materials Credit Assn., Garden City, 1979—; instr. C. W. Post Coll., 1979—; notary public. Mem. Whirporwil PTA, 1974—; vice pres. Richwood civic Assn., 1977—; com. chmn. Hauppauge Cub Scouts Pack, Boy Scouts Am., 1978-79. Lic. tchr. pvt. schs., N.Y. State. Mem. N.Y. Inst. Credit (faculty; asso.), Nat. Inst. Credit (asso.). Democrat. Roman Catholic. Office: 591 Stewart Ave Garden City NY 11530

LONEY, CAROLYN PATRICIA, banker; b. N.Y.C., June 16, 1944; d. Daniel and Edna Louise (Williams) L.; B.S., Morgan (Md.) State Coll., 1969; M.B.A., Columbia U., 1971. Research worker N.Y. Senate, N.Y.C., 1967; field auditor Human Resources Adminstrn., 1966, 67; rater and coder auto policies Royal Globe Ins. Co., N.Y.C., 1962-65; br. mgr. NAACP, N.Y.C., 1965; corporate lending officer Citibank, N.A., N.Y.C., 1971-77; spl. asst. bank supervision and regulations function Fed. Res. Bank of N.Y., 1977-78; asst. v.p. Citibank, N.A., 1978—; cons. Interracial Council Bus. Opportunities; instr. cons. Nat. Puerto Rican Forum; lectr. adult bus. edn. N.Y. Community Coll. Named Outstanding Instr. of Year, Interracial Council Bus. Opportunities, 1974. Mem. Nat. Bankers Assn., Nat. Assn. Accountants, Urban Bankers Coalition, Nat. Credit and Fin. Women's Orgn., Harlem YWCA. Democrat. Home: 122 Belmont St Englewood NJ 07631

LONG, ALFRED B., former oil co. exec., cons.; b. Galveston, Tex., Aug. 4, 1909; s. Jessie A. and Ada (Beckwith) L.; student S. Park Jr. Coll., 1928-29, Lamar State Coll. Tech., 1947-56, U. Tex., 1941; m. Sylvia V. Thomas, Oct. 29, 1932; 1 dau., Kathleen Sylvia (Mrs. E.A. Pearson, II). With Sun Oil Co., Beaumont, Tex., 1931-69, driller geophys. dept., surveyor engring. dept., engr. operating dept., engr. prodn. lab., 1931-59, regional supr., 1960-69, cons., 1969—. Mem. Jefferson County Program Planning Com., 1964; mem. tech. adv. group Oil Well Drilling Inst., Lamar U., Beaumont. Mem. Soc. Petroleum Engrs., Am. Petroleum Inst., Am. Assn. Petroleum Geologists, IEEE, Houston Geol. Soc., Gulf Coast Engring. and Sci. Soc. (treas. 1962-65), U.S. Power Squadron, Soc. Wireless Pioneers. Inventor various oil well devices. Home: 8510 Calder Rd Beaumont TX 77706 Office: PO Box 7266 Beaumont TX 77706

LONG, ALVIN WILLIAM, title ins. co. exec.; b. Steubenville, Ohio, Oct. 9, 1923; s. Roger H. and Emma (Reilley) L.; J.D., John Marshall Law Sch., 1949, LL.D., 1977; M.B.A., U. Chgo., 1955; m. Ethelle Sherman, Jan. 1, 1944; children—Roger H., Sherry (Mrs. John S. McBain, Jr.). Admitted to Ill. bar, 1950; v.p. Chgo. Title & Trust Co., 1960-63, sr. v.p., 1966-69, pres., chief adminstrv. officer, 1969-71, pres., chief exec. officer, 1971-81, chmn., pres., chief exec. officer, 1981—, also dir.; sr. v.p. Chgo. Title Ins. Co., 1963-66, pres., 1967—, chmn. bd., 1981—, also dir.; dir. Lincoln Nat. Corp. Bd. dirs. Bradner Central Co., Chgo. Theol. Sem.; bd. dirs. Chgo. Central Area Com., pres., 1980—; bd. dirs. United Way of Met. Chgo., Ill. Cancer Council, Protestant Found. Greater Chgo.; trustee John Marshall Law Sch., Northwestern Meml. Hosp.; bd. dirs. Ill. Childrens Home and Aid Soc., pres. 1975-77; mem. citizens bd. and alumni council U. Chgo.; mem. bus. adv. council Chgo. Urban League. Served to 1st lt. USAAF, 1943-45. Recipient Distinguished Alumni citation John Marshall Law Sch., 1968. Mem. Am., Ill., Chgo. bar assns., Am. Land Title Assn. (pres. 1970-71), Law Club Chgo., Northwestern U. Assos., Chgo. Assn. Commerce and Industry (v.p. comml. and indsl. devel., dir. 1967—), Ill. C. of C. (dir.). Clubs: Economic, Executives, Carlton, Commercial, Chicago, Mid-Day (Chgo.); Flossmoor (Ill.) Country; Quail Ridge (Fla.) Country. Home: 1110 Lake Shore Dr Chicago IL 60611 Office: 111 W Washington St Chicago IL 60602

LONG, ANNE TENNEY (MRS. RICHARD DURBIN LONG), banker; b. N.Y.C., June 2, 1923; d. Frederick William and Rose Elizabeth Haworth Tenney; B.A., Antioch Coll., 1945; postgrad. Pace Coll., 1947; M.S., Columbia, 1955; postgrad. N.Y. U., 1957-59, Rutgers U., 1966; m. Richard Durbin Long, Nov. 1, 1943; children—Mary (Mrs. William Fitch), Richard. Staff accountant Barrow, Wade, Guthrie & Co., C.P.A.'s, N.Y.C., 1945-47; instr. Davis Bus. Coll., Toledo, 1951-53; security analyst N.J. Bank & Trust Co., Paterson, 1955-62, asst. treas., 1962-63, asst. v.p., 1963-69; asst. investment officer Bank of New York, N.Y.C., 1969-71, investment officer, 1971—, asst. v.p., 1976—; organizing dir. Intercounty Community Bank, South Plainfield, N.J., 1974-75. Thesis examiner Rutgers U. Stonier Grad. Sch. Banking, 1968-72. C.P.A., N.J. Mem. Am. Womans Soc. C.P.A.'s (past dir.), Nat. Assn. Bank Women (past dir.), Am. Inst. C.P.A.'s, N.J. Soc. C.P.A.'s, Am. Soc. Women Accountants (past pres. Toledo chpt.), N.Y. Soc. Security Analysts, Inst. Chartered Financial Analysts. Republican. Unitarian. Clubs: Ridgewood College (N.J.); Arcola Country (Paramus, N.J.); New York University. Author weekly column Women's Financial World, Passaic Herald News, 1960-70. Home: 484 Ackerman Ave Glen Rock NJ 07452 Office: 530 Fifth Ave New York City NY 10036

LONG, BARRY FREDERICK, steel co. exec.; b. London, Sept. 11, 1932; came to U.S., 1969, naturalized, 1975; s. Leslie William and Gladys Mary (Pibworth) L.; B.Sc. in Naval Architecture, Durham (Eng.) U., 1956; m. Audrey Mildred Nash, July 7, 1956; children—Timothy, Elisabeth, Helen, Philip, Janet, Susan. Shipbldg. apprentice Thompsons Shipyard, Sunderland, Eng., 1951-56; asst. planning mgr., asst. to gen. mgr. Cammell Laird & Co., Birkenhead, Eng., 1958-65; tech. mgr. Can. Vickers Co., Montreal, Que., 1965-69; supt. planning Sparrows Point (Md.) yard Bethlehem Steel Corp., 1969-74, asst. gen. mgr. shipbldg. Beaumont (Tex.) yard, 1974—. Mem. exec. com. Goals for Beaumont, 1978—; bd. dirs. Beaumont Goodwill Industries, Jr. Achievement; deacon Baptist Ch. Served with Royal Navy, 1956-58. Fellow Royal Instn. Naval Architects; mem.

Soc. Naval Architects and Marine Engrs., Gideons Internat., Tex. Assn. Bus., Beaumont C. of C., Mensa. Club: BPM (Beaumont). Home: 5845 Pinkstaff St Beaumont TX 77706 Office: Box 3031 Beaumont TX 77704

LONG, CHARLES FARRELL, ins. co. exec.; b. Charlottesville, Va., Nov. 19, 1933; s. Cicel Early and Ruth Elizabeth (Shifflett) L.; C.L.U., The Am. Coll., 1972; m. Ann Tilley, May 28, 1960; children—C. Farrell, Linda. Founder, pres. Casualty Underwriters Inc., Charlottesville, 1959-72; founder, pres. Group Underwriters Inc., Charlottesville, 1959—; trustee P.A.I. Ins. Trust. Mem. Assay Commn. of U.S., 1975. Bd. dirs. Heart Assn. Served with U.S. Navy, 1954-58. Mem. Central Va. Estate Planning Council, Am. Soc. C.L.U.'s, Central Va. C.L.U.'s Assn. (dir.), Va. Press Assn., Va. Assn. Life Underwriters, Million Dollar Round Table. Creator Queen's medal for Queen Elizabeth, 1976. Home: 1400 W Leigh Dr Charlottesville VA 22901 Office: Ivy Sq Ivy Rd Charlottesville VA 22901

LONG, HARRY (ENG ON-YUEN), chemist; b. Passaic, N.J., June 22, 1932; s. Eng Yick and Yue York (Ng) L.; B.S., N.J. Inst. Tech., 1959; m. Linda Lai-king Yu, Sept. 18, 1960; 1 son, Steven (Eng Park-ning). With Uniroyal Inc., Passaic, 1959-71, asst. devel. engr., belts and splty. products, 1959-62, devel. engr., 1962-67, sr. process engr. hose and expansion joints, 1967-71; chief devel. engr. hose products Raybestos/Manhattan Inc., Passaic, 1971-72; chief chemist Goodall Rubber Co., Trenton, N.J., 1972-76, tech. mgr., 1976—. Mem. Am. Chem. Soc., Phila. Rubber Group, ASTM, AAAS.

LONG, HENRY ARLINGTON, real estate exec.; b. Arlington, Va., May 18, 1937; s. William Armstead and Emily Pearl (Garland) L.; B.S., Va. Poly. Inst., 1959; m. Betty Mae Horner, Dec. 28, 1963; children—Andrea Denise, Elissa Michell, Elizabeth Kristen, Henry Arlington. Ind. comml. real estate sales, Va. and Washington, 1965-68; co-owner Long & Foster, Inc., Fairfax, 1979—; mng. gen. partner Manassas Forum Assos. (Va.), 1973—, Snowden Village Assos., 1972—, Eskridge Indsl. Assos., 1974—, Reston Racquet Club Assos., 1976—; dir. No. Va. Bd. Realtors, 1973, 74. Trustee, The Potomac Sch., 1979—. Served as pilot SAC, USAF, 1959-65, USAFR, 1966-70. Recipient award for Mil. Merit, Chgo. Tribune, 1959; Distinguished Service award No. Va. Bd. Realtors, 1972, 73. Mem. Nat. Assn. Realtors, Nat. Assn. Homebuilders, Realtors Nat. Mktg. Inst., Real Estate Securities and Syndication Inst., Pi Delta Epsilon. Episcopalian. Clubs: Jaycees, Kiwanis (dir. Fairfax chpt. 1970-71). Producer, dir. TV film Moulders of Men, 1960. Home: 11214 Country Pl Oakton VA 22124 Office: 4085 University Dr Fairfax VA 22030

LONG, HING WING, bus. services co. exec.; b. Canton, China, Nov. 15, 1937; s. Yee S. and Wah F. (Wong) L.; B.S., UCLA, 1967, M.S., 1968; m. Pui Ng, Jan. 2, 1959; children—Epin, Siu, Ping. Auditor, Kenneth Leventhal & Co., Los Angeles, 1968-71, tax specialist, 1971-73, tax mgr., 1973—. Mem. Calif. Taxation Com., Town Hall of Calif. C.P.A., Calif. Mem. Am. Inst. C.P.A.'s, Calif. Soc. C.P.A.'s (real estate com., savs and loan com.), Beta Alpha Psi. Home: 505 W Avenida de la Merced Montebello CA 90640

LONG, HOWARD WINFRED, food processing co. exec.; b. Piedmont, Ohio, Sept. 4, 1934; s. Robert H. and Dorothy (Surratt) L.; student public schs. Ohio County; m. Emma Gene Barker, Apr. 3, 1953; children—Lorna Gene, Howard Dennis. Founder, pres. Coronet Foods, Inc., Wheeling, W.Va., 1965—, LDL Investments, Inc., Salinas, Calif., 1976—; owner, pres. Weimer Packing Co., Wheeling, 1975—. Office: Coronet Foods 15th and McColloch Sts Wheeling WV 26003

LONG, LAWRENCE LESLIE, JR., glove mfg. co. exec.; b. Chillicothe, Mo., Jan. 4, 1931; s. Lawrence Leslie and Beatrice Marie (Anderson) L.; student public schs., Chillicothe; m. Dorothy Louise Wood, June 15, 1951; children—Deborah Lynn, Linda Lou. Glove cutter Boss Mfg. Co., 1949-50; glove cutter Lambert Mfg. Co., Chillicothe, 1950-52, 54-56, asst. plant mgr., 1956-59, plant mgr., 1959-61; co-founder, v.p., plant mgr. Midwest Glove Corp., Chillicothe, 1961-69, pres., owner, 1969—. Served with U.S. Army, 1952-53; Korea. Mem. Work Glove Mfg. Assn. (dir.). Republican. Methodist. Clubs: Rotary, Masons, Shriners. Home: 906 Summit Dr Chillicothe MO 64601 Office: 835 Industrial Rd Chillicothe MO 64601

LONG, LEE EDWARD, mfg. co. exec.; b. Belleville, Ill., Oct. 3, 1946; s. Buford Edward and Edna Anna Long; student Belleville Community Coll., 1965-67, McKendree Coll., 1967-68; B.S. in Bus. Adminstrn., So. Ill. U., 1970; children—Jacqueline Michele, Jeffrey Schuyler. Dir. tax reduction dept. R. Rowland & Co., St. Louis, 1971-73; v.p. Econ. Counselors, St. Louis, 1973-74; sales mgr. Turco Mfg. Co., DuQuoin, Ill., 1974-77; v.p. sales Cardinal Home Products, Cleve., 1977-79; v.p. mktg., sales Tarco, Inc., Chgo., 1979-80; gen. sales mgr. Club Products Co., Jacksonville, Ark., 1980—. Bd. dirs. Miss. River Festival Inc., 1970—. Served with U.S. Army, 1968. Mem. Smithsonian Assn. Republican. Club: Met. (Chgo.). Home: 153 Tree Hill Loop Eugene OR 97405 Office: 1100 Redmond Rd Jacksonville AR 72076

LONG, MARY LOUISE, govt. contracting officer; b. Macon, Ga., Aug. 25, 1922; d. Willie and Sarah (Sparks) Tyson; A.B., Morris Brown Coll., Atlanta, 1946; m. Samuel F. Long, Apr. 14, 1962. Supervisory procurement clk. Dept. Def., N.Y., 1954-62, purchasing agt. Phila. Procurement Dist., 1962-64, Army Electronic Command, Phila., 1964-66, Med. Directorate, Def. Personnel Support Center, Phila., 1966-75, contracting officer, 1975—. Mem. NAACP, YWCA, Beta Omicron, Iota Phi Lambda. Congregationalist. Home: 617 E Mount Airy Ave Philadelphia PA 19119 Office: 2800 S 20th St Philadelphia PA 19101

LONG, MATTIE LEE, telephone co. adminstr.; b. Collins, Miss., Jan. 12, 1948; d. Cleveland Cooper and Ruby Mae (Sullivan) Burnell; A.A., (Blain scholar), Delta Coll., 1967; B.B.A., Saginaw Valley State Coll., 1973; M.A. in Econs., Central Mich. U., 1979; postgrad. in econs. Wayne State U., 1980. Asst., fgn. lang. lab. Delta Coll., University Center, Mich., 1965-67; with Mich. Bell Telephone Co., Saginaw, 1967—, office staff supr., 1974-77, staff service supr., 1977—. Mem. NAACP, NAUW, Alpha Beta Kappa. Democrat. Mem. Pentecostal Ch. Editor jour. Women's Liberation, 1973. Home: 1948 Caldwell St Saginaw MI 48601 Office: 1365 Cass Ave Room 710 Detroit MI 48226

LONG, MICHAEL CLARK, grocery exec.; b. St. Louis, Feb. 5, 1947; s. Adrian Clark and Kathryn Jane (Walsh) L.; B.S. in Bus. Adminstrn., Washington U., St. Louis, 1969; M.S., 1971; m. Margaret Ann Ciarleglio, Apr. 19, 1969; 1 dau., Tricia Ann. With Schnuck Markets, 1963—, pricing coordinator, St. Louis, 1974-77, grocery mdsg. analyst, 1977—; guest lectr. Washington U. Bus. Sch., Forest Park Community Coll., Meramec Community Coll. Mo. State scholar, 1965. Mem. Am. M.B.A. Execs., Allied Food Club. Republican. Episcopalian. Home: 1514 Kraft St Saint Louis MO 63139 Office: 12921 Enterprise Way Bridgeton MO 63044

LONG, REBECCA JANE, chem. mfg. co. exec.; b. Pittsboro, Miss., May 18, 1935; d. Thomas J. and Minnie A. (Keenum) L.; B.S. in Microbiology and Chemistry, Miss. State U., 1963; M.S., Memphis State U., 1969. Staff technologist dept. chemistry, lab. surp. Bapt. Meml. Hosp., Memphis, 1962-68; teaching supr. Hamilton Meml. Hosp., Dalton, Ga., 1968-69; tech. specialist Hycel, Inc., Houston, 1969-70; dir. med. lab. technician program Dalton Jr. Coll., 1970-72; lab. examiner Center for Disease Control, Atlanta, 1972-75; tech. specialist Searle Analytic, Inc., Atlanta, 1975-76; tech. specialist E.I. duPont de Nemours & Co., Claremont, Calif., 1976-77, product release chemist, Glasgow, Del., 1977-78, southeastern region tech. rep., Doraville, Ga., 1978—; rep. Bio-Sci. Labs., Van Nuys, Calif., 1980—. Mem. Am. Soc. Med. Technologists, Am. Public Health Assn., Am. Soc. Clin. Pathology, Sigma Xi. Presbyterian. Home: 6612 Point Comfort Ln Pineville NC 28134 Address: PO Box 240315 Charlotte NC 28224

LONG, RON, mktg. exec.; b. Chgo., Mar. 26, 1937; s. Williard Hector and Gloria Patricia (Pommerville) L.; student Ind. U., 1955-56, Miliken U., 1956-58; m. Karen Keller, Dec. 20, 1978; 1 dau., Corinne; 1 child by previous marriage, Dana; 1 stepson, Tom. Regional pacemaker specialist Medtronic Sales, Inc., Mpls., 1970-75; dir. mktg. and sales Am. Tech., Inc., Northridge, Calif., 1975-78; mgr. mktg. services Pacesetter Systems, Inc., Sylmar, Calif., 1978—. Served with U.S. Army, 1960-64. Mem. Am. Assn. Med. Instrumentation, Am. Mgmt. Assn., Continuing Med. Edn. Address: 3262 Galveston St Simi CA 93063

LONGBRAKE, WILLIAM ARTHUR, govt. economist; b. Hershey, Pa., Mar. 15, 1943; s. William Van Fleet and Margaret Jane (Barr) L.; B.A., Coll. Wooster, 1965; M.A., U. Wis., 1968, M.B.A., 1969; D.B.A., U. Md., 1976; m. Martha Ann Curtis, Aug. 23, 1970; children—Derek Curtis, Mark William, David Robert. Jr. Asst. planner Northeastern Ill. Planning Commn., Chgo., 1966; instr. Coll. Bus. and Mgmt., U. Md., 1969-71, lectr., 1976, 79—; financial economist Fed. Deposit Ins. Corp., Washington, 1971-75, sr. planning specialist Office Corp. Planning, 1975-76; asso. dir. banking research div. Office Comptroller of Currency, Washington, 1976, dep. dir. econ. research and analysis div., 1976-77; spl. asst. to chmn., acting controller FDIC, Washington, 1977-78; dep. comptroller for research and economic programs Office Controller of Currency, Washington, 1978—. Small bus. cons. Mem. College Park (Md.) Citizens Adv. Com. on Code Enforcement, 1973-74, cons., 1975. Recipient Kenneth E. Trefftz prize Western Fin. Assn., 1971; cert. of recognition William A. Jump Meml. Found., 1978. Mem. Am., So. econ. assns., Am., Eastern finance assns., Fin. Mgmt. Assn. (dir. 1978-80), Coll. of Wooster Alumni Assn. (pres. Washington chpt. 1976). Presbyterian (trustee 1973-75, chmn. 1975 elder 1979—, clk. 1980). Asso. editor Financial Mgmt., 1974-78; mem. editorial adv. bd. Issues in Bank Regulation, 1977—, Jour. Econs. and Bus., 1980—. Contbr. articles to profl. jours. Home: 5901 Bryn Mawr Rd College Park MD 20740 Office: 490 L'enfant Plaza E Washington DC 20219

LONGO, JOSEPH JOHN, business exec.; b. Morristown, N.J., May 20, 1927; s. John R. and Christina (Giordano) L.; B.S. in Elec. Engring., N.J. Inst. Tech., 1951; m. Madeline Di Donna, Feb. 11, 1956; children—Joseph Michael, Maria Rose. Design engr. Bogue Electric Mfg. Co., Paterson, N.J., 1951-53; partner J.R. Longo & Sons, Morristown, N.J., 1953-59; pres. J.R. Longo & Sons, Morris Plains, N.J., 1959—; pres., chmn. bd. Longo Industries Cos., Morris Plains, 1967—; dir. Fidelity Union Trust Co. N.A., Morristown, N.J. Mem. Morris County Constrn. Bd. Appeals; pres. Fathers and Friends, Delbarton Sch., Morristown, 1978-79; mem. bus. adv. bd. Fairleigh Dickinson U., Madison, N.J. Served with U.S. Mcht. Marine, 1945-46. Registered profl. engr., N.J. Mem. IEEE, Am. Inst. Plant Engrs., Internat. Assn. Elec. Inspectors, Nat. Soc. Profl. Engrs., N.J. Soc. Profl. Engrs., Elec. Apparatus Service Assn. (internat. mgmt. com.), Morris County C. of C. (dir.), Tau Beta Pi. Clubs: Rotary, Spring Brook Country (Morristown). Office: Longo Industries Cos 1775 Route 10 Morris Plains NJ 07950

LONGTIN, RAYMOND EDDY, wholesale floor covering co. exec.; b. Montreal, Que., Can., Aug. 9, 1934; s. Donat Denis and Addy (Ethier) L.; grad. St. Viateur Coll., Montreal, 1952; postgrad. U. Montreal, 1952-53; m. Pierrette Deguire, June 23, 1956; children—Johanne, Josee, Robert. Mgr., Beneficial Fin., Edmunston, N.B., Can. and Lachine, Que., 1954-57; sec., treas. Zenith Enterprises Co. Ltd., Montreal, 1957-73; pres. Zenith Floor Covering Distbr. Ltd., Montreal, 1973—; dir. A-1 Securities Inc. Mem. St. Leonard C. of C., Que. Floor Covering Inst. (sec. 1960). Roman Catholic. Club: Ste-Dorothee Golf. Office: 6125 Metropolitan Blvd E Montreal PQ H1P 1X7 Canada

LONIE, DAVID DONALD, JR., real estate developer; b. Bay City, Mich., Nov. 16, 1924; s. David Donald and Ellen Marie (Lind) L.; B.S., U. Oreg., 1947; m. Virginia Mae Peterson, Oct. 18, 1947; children—Stephen Peter, Diane Cynthia, Thomas Edward, Nancy Madeline. Printing salesman Statesman Publishing Co., Salem, Oreg., 1947-48; asst. prodn. mgr. Joseph R. Gerber Advt., Portland, Oreg., 1948-50; editor N. Lincoln County News Guard, Lincoln City, Oreg., 1950-51; asst. advt. mgr. First Nat. Bank Oreg., Portland, 1951-53; with public relations dept. Portland Gen. Electric Co., 1953-55; sales mgr. sta. KPTV, Portland, 1955-57; owner Lonie Co., public relations, Portland, 1957-72; propr. Lonie Co., real estate devel., Honolulu, 1972—; pres. Oreg. Advt. Club, 1956. Served with USNR, 1943-46. Mem. Hawaii C. of C. (vice chmn. planning com.), Hawaii Hotel Assn., U. Oreg. Alumni Assn. (past pres.). Republican. Presbyterian. Clubs: Portland Golf, Arlington (Portland); Oahu Country, Honolulu Press, Outrigger Canoe, Plaza (Honolulu); Shriners. Home: 4999 Kahala Ave Honolulu HI 96816 Office: PO Box 124 Honolulu HI 96810

LONTZ, CLIFFORD GUY, systems analysis exec.; b. Bloomington, Ill., Mar. 19, 1921; s. E. Edgar and Minnie Pearl (Taylor) L.; m. Evelyn Doorn, Nov. 20, 1941; children—Clifford Donald, Kenneth Wayne, Janet (Mrs. Thomas Boomsma), Eva Lynn (Mrs. Darrell Prine), Edfred Dorn. Mgr. data processing Combustion Engring. Inc., N.Y.C., 1953-55; mgr. adminstrn. Continental Can Co., N.Y.C., 1955-58; regional mgr. retail automation Monroe Sweda div. Litton Industries, Niles, Ill., 1958-65; owner Illiana Bus. Systems, Lansing, Ill., 1965-67, pres. Illini Bus. Systems Inc., Lansing, 1967—. Deacon, Reformed Ch. in Am. Served with Armed Forces, 1941-42. Mem. Nat. Machine Accountants Assn., Lansing C. of C. Patentee in field. Home: 2704 Ridge Rd Lansing IL 60438 Office: PO Box 51 Lansing IL 60438

LOOG, JOHN EARLE, food co. exec.; b. Phila., Nov. 19, 1915; s. Sidney and Mary E. (Mellodew) L.; B.A., Pa. State U., 1937; postgrad. Temple Law Sch., 1937-38, Washington and Lee U., 1942, U. Pa., 1945-47; m. Patricia Ann Bock, Sept. 7, 1946; children—Cynthia, Stephanie, John, Jr. Nat. advt. mgr. RCA Victor, Cherry Hill, N.J., 1954-57, radio-TV producer, 1957-61; advt., sales promotion mgr. Proctor-Silex Corp., Phila., 1961-63; independent film producer, N.Y.C., also Hollywood, Calif., 1963-67; pres. Double Kay Products Co., St. Petersburg, Fla., 1967-76; exec. v.p., chief exec. officer Roy Clark's Dieter's Choice, Las Vegas, 1976-77, also dir.; pres. Mgmt. Assos., Los Angeles, 1977—; dir. Mellmont Foods, St. Petersburg. Radio and TV advisor to Gov. Underwood of West Va., 1960, Gov. Scranton of Pa., 1962. Served with Signal Corps, AUS, 1942-46. Mem. Alpha Tau Omega. Episcopalian. Clubs: Poor Richard (Phila.); New York Athletic (N.Y.C.); Canoe Brook Country (Summit, N.J.); Bath (Redington Beach, Fla.). Home: 247 N Kenter Ave Los Angeles CA 90049 Office: 9701 Wilshire Blvd Beverly Hills CA 90212

LOOK, KENNETH WILLIAM, pharm. co. exec.; b. Appleton, Wis., Apr. 17, 1939; s. Arthur Clarence and Lorraine Elizabeth (Radder) L.; B.S. in Pharmacy, U. Wis., 1961, M.S. in Pharmacy Adminstrn., 1968, Ph.D. in Pharmacy Adminstrn., 1974; postgrad. (Rotary Found. fellow), U. Nottingham (Eng.), 1962-63; m. Virginia Lee Bailey, Feb. 8, 1975. Retail and hosp. pharmacist, Wis. and Tex., 1963-69; teaching asst. U. Wis., Madison, 1968-69; dir. corporate marketing research G.D. Searle & Co., Skokie, Ill., 1969-79; dir. bus. research and acquisitions Searle Pharms., Skokie, 1979—. Served to capt. AUS, 1963-65. Mem. Am. Pharm. Assn., Am. Marketing Assn., Rho Chi, Kappa Psi, Sigma Phi Epsilon. Home: 638 Onwentsia Ave Highland Park IL 60035 Office: 4930 Oakton St Skokie IL 60076

LOOMIS, HOWARD KREY, banker; b. Omaha, Apr. 9, 1927; s. Arthur L. and Genevieve (Krey) L.; A.B., Cornell U., 1949, M.B.A., 1950; m. Florence Porter, Apr. 24, 1954; children—Arthur L. II, Frederick S., Howard Krey, John Porter. Mgmt. trainee Hallmark Cards, Inc., Kansas City, Mo., 1953-56; sec., controller, dir. Mine Service Co., Inc., Ft. Smith, Ark., 1956-59; controller, dir. Electra Mfg. Co., Independence, Kans., 1959-63; v.p., dir. The Peoples Bank, Pratt, Kans., 1963-65, pres., 1966—; pres., dir. Gt. Plains Leasing, Inc., Pratt, 1966-80, Central States Inc., Pratt, 1970-76, Krey Co. Ltd., Pratt, 1978—; dir. Fed. Res. Bank, Kansas City, Mo., Garland Coal & Mining Co., Ft. Smith, All Ins., Inc., Pratt, Kans. Devel. Credit Corp., Topeka, 1974—. Past pres. Pratt County United Fund; bd. dirs., past chmn. Cannonball Trail chpt. ARC; past pres. Kanza council Boy Scouts Am. Served with AUS, 1950-52. Mem. Kans. (chmn. transp. council, dir.), Pratt Area (past pres., dir.) chambers commerce, Financial Execs. Inst., Kans. Bankers Assn. (past dir.), Sigma Delta Chi, Chi Psi. Republican. Presbyterian. Elk, Rotarian. Club: Park Hills Country (past pres.). Home: 502 Welton St Pratt KS 67124 Office: The Peoples Bank 222 S Main St Pratt KS 67124

LOOMIS, PHILIP CLARK, govt. ofcl., fin. analyst; b. Plainville, Conn., Sept. 24, 1926; s. Winfield Hathaway annd Lucy (Clark) L.; B.A., Yale U., 1949; M.B.A., Wharton Sch. Fin. and Commerce, U. Pa., 1950; m. Greta Elaine Gustafson, Nov. 27, 1970; children—Philip Clark, Leslie J., Martha L. Trust investment specialist No. Trust Co., Chgo., 1950-54; investment officer Hartford Ins. Group (Conn.), 1954-61; dir. research and gen. partner Eastman Dillon Union Securities & Co., N.Y.C., 1961-66; partner-in-charge research services div. E.I. duPont de Nemours & Co., N.Y.C., 1967-70; v.p. research Dean Witter & Co., N.Y.C., 1971-72; v.p. Reynolds Securities Inc., N.Y.C., 1973-78; dir. Office Securities Markets Policy, Dept. Treasury, Washington, 1979—. Served with USN, 1944-45. Mem. N.Y. Soc. Security Analysts, Fin. Analysts Fedn. Home: 130 East End Ave New York NY 10028 Office: Suite 953 Washington Bldg 1435 G St NW Washington DC 20220

LOONEY, H. RAY, glass co. exec.; b. Caldwell, Idaho, June 6, 1935; s. Harry Francis and Margie Grace L.; A.B. in Econs., Stanford U., 1957, M.B.A., Columbia U., 1961; m. Maryanne Vandervelde, July 7, 1962; 1 son, Spencer. Div. controller Hewelett-Packard, Palo Alto, Calif., 1961-64; dir. fin. analysis, sr. dir. mktg. TWA, N.Y.C., 1964-70; v.p. Indian Head, N.Y.C., 1971-74; exec. v.p. Northwestern Glass Co., Seattle, 1975-77, pres., 1977—; dir. Lane Mt. Silica Co., Madera Glass Co. Bd. dirs. Evergreen Safety Council, Mercer Island Boys and Girls Club, 1975—. Served to 1st lt., AUS, 1957-59. Mem. Indsl. Conf. Bd. (trustee 1977-79). Clubs: Rainier, Harbor, Mercer Island Country.

LOONEY, WILTON D., automotive supplies co. exec.; b. 1919; married. With Genuine Parts Co., Atlanta, 1938—, in charge N.Y. wholesale ops., 1954-55, pres., 1955-64, pres., chief exec. officer, 1964-73, chmn. bd., chief exec. officer, 1973—, also dir. Served with U.S. Army, World War II. Office: 2999 Circle 75 Pkwy Atlanta GA 30339*

LOOSEMORE, CRAIG STEVEN, securities co. exec.; b. N.Y.C., Aug. 17, 1947; s. John R. and Lottie M. (Balon) L.; B.B.A., U. Miami, 1970; postgrad. Fla. Internat. U., 1974. Founding and gen. partner Loosemore, Loosemore & Co., off-floor traders and dealers, Miami, Fla., 1974—, Loosemore Bros., real estate investments, Miami, 1978—; chmn., treas. Arbitrage Investment Mgmt., Inc., portfolio mgrs. and mng. partner Loosemore, Loosemore & Co., Miami, 1980—. Mem. Securities Industry Assn., Antique Automobile Club Am., New Eng. MGT Register Ltd., Train Collectors Assn. Home and office: 7150 SW 5th Terr Miami FL 33144

LOOSEMORE, KEVIN MICHAEL, securities co. exec.; b. N.Y.C., May 13, 1952; s. John R. and Lottie M. (Balon) L.; B.B.A. magna cum laude, U. Miami, 1974. Founding and gen. partner Loosemore, Loosemore & Co., off-floor traders and dealers, Miami, Fla., 1974—, Loosemore Bros., real estate investments, Miami, 1978—; pres. Arbitrage Investment Mgmt., Inc., portfolio mgrs. and mgr. partner Loosemore, Loosemore & Co., Miami, 1980—. Mem. Securities Industry Assn. Home and office: 7150 SW 5th Terr Miami FL 33144

LOOSIGIAN, ALLAN MALCOLM, investment co. exec.; b. Methuen, Mass., May 12, 1938; s. Allan and Mary (Kachadorian) L.; grad. Phillips Acad., Andover, Mass., 1955; B.A. magna cum laude, Princeton U., 1959; postgrad. (Fulbright scholar) Munster U., Westphalia, W. Ger., 1959. Research analyst, account exec. Merrill Lynch, Pierce, Fenner & Smith, Inc., N.Y.C., 1961-69; founder A.M. Loosigian & Co., Stamford, Conn., 1971, pres., chief exec. officer, 1971—; lectr. fin. Fairfield U. Mem. Stamford Area Commerce and Industry Assn., Friends of Westport Library. Clubs: Princeton of N.Y.; Landmark (Stamford). Author: Interest Rate Futures - A Market Guide for Hedgers and Speculators, 1979; Foreign Exchange Futures—A Guide to International Currency Trading, 1981; also articles in profl. jours., newspapers. Home: 5 Washington Ave Westport CT 06880 Office: 5 Landmark Sq Stamford CT 06901

LOPER, JAMES LEADERS, television exec.; b. Phoenix, Sept. 4, 1931; s. John D. and Ellen (Leaders) L.; B.A., Ariz. State U., 1953; M.A., U. Denver, 1957; Ph.D., U. So. Calif., 1966; m. Mary Louise Brion, Sept. 1, 1955; children—Elizabeth Margaret, James Leaders. Asst. dir. Bur. Broadcasting Ariz. State U., 1953-59; news editor, announcer KTAR, Phoenix, 1955-56; dir. ednl. TV Calif. State U., Los Angeles, 1960-64; v.p. Community Television So. Calif. Los Angeles, 1962-63, asst. to Pres. KCET ednl. tv. sta., 1963, sec., 1965-66, v.p., gen. mgr. ednl. services, 1964-65, asst. gen. mgr., 1965-66, v.p., gen. mgr., 1966-69, exec v.p., gen. mgr., 1969-70, pres., gen. mgr., 1971-77, pres., chief exec. officer, 1977—; mem. NET Affiliates Council, 1968-70; chmn. bd. Pub. Broadcasting Service, 1969-72, Pres. Asso. Otis Art Inst., Los Angeles, 1975-77; chmn. bd. visitors Annenberg Sch. Communications, U. So. Calif., 1975—, v.p. Los Angeles Civic Light Opera Assn., 1975—, trustee Polytech. sch., Pasaena, Calif., 1976—, Sears-Roebuck Found., Chgo., 1976-79, bd. dirs. Performing Tree, Los Angeles, 1976—. Named One of Outstanding Young Men

Am., 1966; recipient Outstanding Alumni award U. So. Calif., 1975. Mem. Acad. TV Arts and Scis. (v.p. Hollywood chpt. 1975-77, nat. trustee 1974-77), Western Radio-Television Assn. (past pres.), Blue Key, Phi Sigma Kappa (past v.p.), Phi Delta Epsilon, Alpha Delta Sigma. Home: 735 Holladay Rd Pasadena CA 91106 Office: 4401 Sunset Blvd Los Angeles CA 90027

LOPERFIDO, JAMES G., mfg. co. exec.; b. Auburn, N.Y., Sept. 13, 1951; s. Patrick J. and Rose M. L.; A.A.S., Auburn Community Coll., 1972; student Cornell U., 1974, Syracuse U., 1980; m. Nancy Casamassima, Mar. 22, 1969; children—Lori Ann, James, Rose. Sales rep. Columbian Rope Co., 1970-78; pres. local Amalgamated Clothing and Textile Workers Union, Auburn, 1973-77; controller, asst. to pres. E.D. Clapp Corp., Auburn, 1978—. Bd. dirs. United Way; chmn. bd. Neighborhood Settlement House. Mem. Nat. Assn. Accts., Indsl. Relations Research Assn., Am. Inst. Corp. Controllers. Democrat. Roman Catholic. Club: Elks. Home: 15 Lafayette Pl Auburn NY 13021 Office: Quarry Rd Auburn NY 13021

LOPEZ, DAVID, lawyer; b. N.Y.C., May 9, 1942; s. Damaso and Carmen (Gonzalez) L.; A.B., Cornell U., 1963; J.D., Columbia U., 1966; m. Nancy Mary Cea, Aug. 29, 1964; children—David, Jonathan. Admitted to N.Y. State bar, 1966; asso. firm Leon, Weill & Mahoney, N.Y.C., 1966-67, Bressler & Meislen, N.Y.C., 1967-70; individual practice law, N.Y.C., 1970—; chmn. bd. Am. Temps, Inc., N.Y.C., 1979—, A.P.M.C. Assos., Inc., N.Y.C., 1979—, Selwyn Proprietary Holdings, Inc., N.Y.C., 1979—; dir. Nancy Lopez, Inc., N.Y.C. Mem. Am. Bar Assn., N.Y. State Bar Assn. Club: Atrium (N.Y.C.). Home: 111 E 85th St New York NY 10028 also Edge of Woods Rd Southampton NY 11968 Office: 115 E 57th St New York NY 10022

LOPEZ, ROBERT COY, mfg. co. exec.; b. McAllen, Tex., July 19, 1950; s. Ramon and Virginia Ellen L.; A.S. in Electronic Engring., N. Am. Tech. Inst., 1973; cert. in applied math. in electronics Nat. Radio Inst., 1975; m. Greta Gail Hanshaw Parker, June 4, 1977; stepchildren—Andrea Anderson, Mark Parker, David Parker. Asst. mgr. Head Ltd., Albuquerque, 1973; asst. plant mgr. Spectrum Sound, Albuquerque, 1974; journeyman electrician BoMur Systems Devel., Albuquerque, 1974-77; supr. repair center P.C.C. Service div. Pertec Computer Corp., Albuquerque, 1977-81; account exec. Westmark Consultants, Albuquerque, 1981—. Mem. electronics adv. bd. Albuquerque Tech. Vocat. Inst. Lic. 2d class radio telephone with radar endorsement, FCC; class 2 electrician, N.Mex. Cert. diamond counselor. Mem. Internat. Platform Assn. Club: Toastmasters. Home: Star Route Box 30 Tijeras NM 87059 Office: 5400 Phoenix NE Albuquerque NM 87110

LORD, JOHN RICHARD, elevator mfg. co. exec.; b. Buffalo, Jan. 30, 1944; s. Glenn Richard and Betty Lathbury (Pusey) L.; A.B. in Econs., Bowdoin Coll., 1966; postgrad. U. So. Calif., 1966-67; M.B.A., UCLA, 1968; m. Wendy Elizabeth Vieth, Aug. 7, 1965; children—John Richard, Kerry. Asst. mgr. market research Hewitt-Robins div. Litton Industries, 1968-69, mgr. market research Power Transmission div., Hartford, Conn., 1969-70, product mgr. Power Transmission div., Chgo., 1970-72; planner Northrop Corp., Hawthorne, Calif., 1972-73; product mgr. Prescolite div. U.S. Industries, San Leandro, Calif., 1973-75; mgr. bus. planning Power Systems div. U.T.C., Farmington, Conn., 1975-76, asst. to pres. Otis Elevator div., N.Y.C., 1976-77, v.p. planning and adminstrn. Otis Elevator div., N.Y.C. and Farmington, 1977-78, v.p. mktg. Otis Elevator div., Farmington, 1978—. Mem. Am. Mgmt. Assn., Beta Gamma Sigma. Republican. Congregationalist. Home: 361 Bushy Hill St Simsbury CT 06070 Office: Otis Elevator Div U T C One Farm Springs Farmington CT 06032

LOREN, PAMELA, internat. telecommunications co. exec.; b. Paris, Jan. 11, 1944; d. Theodore and Mattie (Ephron) Loren; B.S. in Sociology, Columbia U., 1964; M.S. in Sociology, U. Madrid, 1968, M.S. in Langs., 1970; m. Morton P. Levy, June 2, 1963; children—Cristopher Aram, Stirling Brett, Cristina Sahula. Pres., Pamela Loren, Ltd., N.Y.C., 1964-74, Loren Communications Internat., Ltd., N.Y.C., 1972-74; chmn. bd. Loren Communications Internat., Caracas, Venezuela, London, Milan, Italy and N.Y.C., 1974—; exec. v.p. Cinnamon World Trade Corp., 1974—; dir. Panda Internat. Export Corp., Durable Housing Internat., Crespi, Rosann & Ponti; speaker on interdependence of medicine and communications. Recipient Humanitarian award Community Service Soc., 1972, Burden Center for Aging, 1977, Soc. Order Helpers, 1978. Mem. Am. Arbitration Assn., Am. Mgmt. Assn., Soc. Latin-Am. Bus. Owners, N.Y. Assn. Women Bus. Owners, Women's Econ. Round Table. Club: Columbia University. Author: The Generation In-Between, 1977; Looking Ahead to Thirty-Five, 1978. Home: 1095 Park Ave New York NY 10028 Office: 235 E 57th St New York NY 10022

LORENTZSEN, NORMAN M., transp. and natural resource co. exec.; b. Horace, N.D., Nov. 29, 1916; s. Ivar A. and Antonette (Olson) L.; B.A., Concordia Coll., 1941; postgrad. Am. U., 1965, Harvard U., 1968; m. Helen O. Broten, Sept. 20, 1943; children—Thomas, Mary, Katherine. With N.P. Ry. (name now Burlington No. Inc.), 1936—, trainmaster, asst. to gen. mgr., St. Paul, 1953-54, supt. Rocky Mountain div., 1954-57, supt. Idaho div., 1957-64, gen. mgr., Seattle, 1964-67, v.p. ops., St. Paul, 1968-70, v.p. ops. parent co., 1970-71, exec. v.p. parent co., 1971-73, pres. transp. div. parent co., 1973-76, pres., 1977-80, chief exec. officer, 1978-80, chmn. bd., 1980—; dir. Burlington No. Air Freight, Inc.; dir. Burlington No. Inc., BN Transport Inc., Colo. & So. Ry. Co., Ft. Worth & Denver Ry. Co., Oreg. Electric Ry. Co., Twin City Fed. Savs. & Loan Assn.; trustee Oreg. Trunk Ry. Bd. dirs. Luth. Brotherhood, Mpls., N.W. Area Found., St. Paul Found.; bd. regents Concordia Coll., Moorhead, Minn. Served with USNR, 1941-45. Clubs: Minn., Town and Country, Pool and Yacht (St. Paul). Office: 176 E 5th St Saint Paul MN 55101

LORENZO, FRANCISCO A., airlines co. exec.; b. N.Y.C., May 19, 1940; s. Olegario and Ana (Mateos) L.; B.A., Columbia U., 1961; M.B.A., Harvard U., 1963; m. Sharon Neill Murray, Oct. 14, 1972. Financial analyst TWA, 1963-65; mgr. fin. analysis Eastern Airlines, 1965-66; founder, chmn. bd. Lorenzo, Carney & Co., fin. advisers, N.Y.C., 1966—; chmn. bd. Jet Capital Corp., fin. advisers, Houston, 1969—; pres. Tex. Internat. Airlines, Inc., Houston, from 1972, chmn., pres., chief exec. officer, 1980—. Served with AUS, 1963. Office: 8451 Lockheed St Houston TX 77061*

LORING, DAVID CHARLES, lawyer; b. Los Angeles, Mar. 29, 1942; s. Charles A. and Ruth (Jenkins) L.; B.A. in Econs., Pomona Coll., 1964; J.D., Stanford U., 1967. Admitted to Calif. bar, 1968, N.Y. bar, 1972; law clk. firm Zuckert, Scott & Rasenberger, Washington, 1970; chief justice Calif. Supreme Ct., 1970-71; atty. Office of Gen. Counsel, Gen. Motors Corp., N.Y.C., 1971-78; internat. counsel Avon Products, Inc., N.Y.C., 1978—; sr. internat. atty. Atlantic Richfield Co., Los Angeles; vis. prof. comml. law U. Costa Rica, 1967-69. Stanford U. Law Sch. grantee, 1969-70. Member Am. Bar Assn., Inter-Am. Bar Assn., N.Y.C. Bar Assn., Calif. Bar Assn. Office: ARCO Tower 515 S Flower St Los Angeles CA 90071

LORINSKY, LARRY, scrap metal co. exec.; b. New Britain, Conn., July 31, 1944; s. Jacob and Bernice Edythe (Horn) L.; B.A., U. Conn., 1966, M.A., 1968; m. Laurie Clark Griffin, June 9, 1968; children—Michael Bliss, Jennifer Bartlett, Jessica Clark. Ops. mgr., then trading mgr. Norwich Iron & Metal Co. (Conn.), 1965-75; ferrous export mgr. Comml. Metals Co., Dallas, 1975-77, br. mgr., San Francisco, 1977—, West Coast area mgr., 1980—. Mem. Nat. Inst. Scrap Iron and Steel (nat. export council), Nat. Assn. Recycling Industry, Brisbane (Calif.) C. of C. (dir. 1977-81). Democrat. Jewish. Club: Masons. Office: 555 Tunnel Ave San Francisco CA 94134

LORTON, DONALD MARTIN, appliance mfg. co. exec.; b. La Harpe, Ill., Dec. 6, 1930; s. James A. and Velma A. L.; B.S., U. Ill., 1957; M.B.A., Mich. State U., 1970; m. Lila K. Weinberg, June 10, 1956; children—Kyle, Kevin, Nancy, Jeb. With Whirpool Corp., 1957-79, dir. corp. planning, Benton Harbor, Mich., 1972-74, gen. mgr., Danville, Ky., 1974-79; pres. Jenn Air Corp., Indpls., 1979—. Chmn. bd. dirs. Ephriam McDowell Hosp., Danville, 1978-79; mem. adv. council U. Ky. Sch. Commerce, 1977-79; adv. bd. Jr. Achievement, Indpls., 1980. Served with USAF, 1951-55; Korea. Mem. Danville C. of C. (pres. elect 1979-80), Laporte Jaycees. Republican. Presbyterian. Clubs: Rotary, Masons, Shriners. Home: 520 Southampton Ct Noblesville IN 46060 Office: 3035 Shadeland Ave Indianapolis IN 46226

LOSCALZO, FRANK ROBERT, banker; b. Hartford, Conn., May 27, 1942; s. Rocco Anthony and Marie C. (Taddei) L.; B.A., Williams Coll., 1964; M.S., U. Wis., also Ph.D. in Computer Sci.; m. Carol Anne Russo, Aug. 29, 1964; children—Karen Beth, Robert Frank. Mem. tech. staff Bell Telephone Labs., Whippany, N.J., 1968-70; v.p. Citicorp, 1970—. Fellow Math. Research Center, U. Wis., 1967-68. Mem. Direct Mail/Mktg. Assn., Ops. Research Soc. Am., Inst. Mgmt. Scis. Home: 6 Twin Oaks Dr Montvale NJ 07645 Office: 399 Park Ave New York NY 10043

LOTH, CLARK BALDWIN, investment banker; b. Brockton, Mass., June 17, 1941; s. Elburt Clark and Louise Baldwin (Bailey) L.; grad. Mt. Hermon Sch., 1959; B.S. (Arthur Ashley Williams Found. grant), Tufts U., 1966; spl. courses Harvard, 1962-64; m. Susan Ashby Neer, July 22, 1972 (div. 1976). With Hooper-Holmes, Inc., Boston, 1962-66, Hayden, Stone, Inc., investment brokers, Boston, 1966-70; with W.E. Hutton & Co., (now Thomson & McKinnon Auchincloss Kohlmeyer Inc.), Boston, 1970-75, instnl. investment broker, 1974-75; with Smith, Barney & Co., Boston, 1975—; pres., treas., dir. Verifacts Corp., Boston, 1971—; dir. Devel. Mgmt. Corp., Boston, 1970-78, Brit Inc., 1974-77, Vapor-Mid/Can. Ltd., Boston, 1978—, Tregony Inns, Inc., 1978—. Adviser Mass. Jaycees Charitable Trust, 1972-75; sponsor Boston Center for Arts. Bd. dirs., chmn. fin. com. Ogunquit Music Center, 1974-75; trustee Clean Environment Found., 1970-72; bd. dirs. Vols. in Corrections, Inc., 1974—. Recipient Presdl. award of honor Boston Jr. C. of C., 1972, Outstanding Jaycee of Yr. award, 1973. Mem. Assn. Financial Planners, Boston Investment Club, Aircraft Owners and Pilots Assn., Boston Jr. C. of C. (dir. 1968-69, exec. v.p. 1970-72), Mass. Jr. C. of C. (state v.p. 1973-74, mem. exec. com. 1973-75), S.A.R. (state pres. 1974-75, chmn. bd. mgrs. 1974-75, trustee Mass. soc. 1975—), Newcomen Soc., Navy League. Republican. Episcopalian. Clubs: 76, Tennis and Racquet (both Boston). Home: One Memorial Dr Watertown MA 02172 Office: Smith Barney Harris Upham & Co One Federal St Boston MA 02110

LOTKER, JACK MYRON, food co. exec.; b. N.Y.C., Dec. 25, 1943; s. George Kenneth and Grace (Reinstein) L.; B.A. in Psychology, Queens Coll., 1965; M.B.A., L.I. U., 1973; m. Charlotte A. Weiner, Nov. 14, 1965; children—Marc Alan, Amy Beth. Mgr. compensation and benefits Bristol Myers Co., 1969-75; dir. personnel and compensation Norton Simon, Inc., 1975-78; v.p. personnel Arnold Bakers Inc. and Oroweat Foods Co., Greenwich, Conn., 1978—. Served to 1st lt. USAR, 1966-69; Vietnam. Decorated Bronze Star. Office: 10 Hamilton Ave Greenwich CT 06830

LOTMAN, HERBERT, food processing co. exec.; b. Phila., Oct. 9, 1933; s. Samuel Meyer and Gertrude L.; m. Karen Levin, Apr. 6, 1957; children—Shelly Hope, Jeffrey Mark. Pres., chmn. bd. Keystone Foods Corp., Bryn Mawr, Pa., 1951, pres., 1960, chmn. bd., dir., 1960—. Bd. dirs. Nat. Juvenile Diabetes Found. Served with U.S. Army, 1952-54. Mem. Young Pres.'s Orgn. Office: Keystone Foods Corp 931 Haverford Rd Bryn Mawr PA 19010*

LOTT, DAVID WARREN, bank exec.; b. Waycross, Ga., Sept. 10, 1951; s. Arthur Bernard and Isabel Edith (Shackford) L.; B.S. in Indsl. Mgmt., Ga. Inst. Tech., 1972; m. Deborah Ann Willis, Jan. 27, 1973; children—Andrew David, Michael Dennis. Operations trainee Trust Co. Bank, Atlanta, 1972-73; ops. mgr. Lenox Square Br. Trust Company Bank, Atlanta, 1973-76, mgr. T 24 Dept., 1976-80, asst. v.p., mgr. EFT ops., 1980—; cons. automated teller machine program for affiliated banks, 1978—. Mem. Am. Inst. Banking, Delta Sigma Pi. Roman Catholic. Office: PO Box 4418 Atlanta GA 30302

LOTTO, JACK (JESSE), publisher; b. Bklyn., Oct. 19, 1920; s. Morris and Sarah L.; student pub. schs., Bklyn.; m. Eva Lotto; children—Susan, Lori, Marla. Reporter, Kings County Chronicle, Bklyn., 1939, Civil Service Leader, N.Y.C., 1940-41; reporter Internat. News Service, N.Y.C., 1946-58, successively editor, night news editor, day news editor, columnist, 1953-58; columnist King Features Syndicate, N.Y.C., 1959-64; mng. editor PR Wire Service, N.Y.C., 1961-71; pub. Disclosure Record, Floral Park, N.Y., 1972—; chmn. Newsfeatures, Inc., N.Y.C., 1958—. Served with USN, 1943-46. Recipient numerous profl. awards. Mem. Newspaper Reporters Assn. N.Y., Silurians, Publicity Club N.Y. Home: 85-11 249th St Bellerose NY 11426 Office: Disclosure Record PO Box 639 Floral Park NY 11001

LOTZ, BENNO PAUL, corp. exec.; b. Braunschweig, Germany, May 6, 1931; came to U.S., 1976; grad. engr. Coll. Wolfenbüttel, 1956; m. Waltraud Schulz, Dec. 21, 1957; children—Benno, Andreas, Constantin. Apprentice, Volkswagen, Corp., 1952-54; mgmt. asst. Eckold, St. Andreasberg, W. Ger., 1956-60; tech. dir. Ortopedia, Kiel, W. Ger., 1961-69, mng. dir., 1970-75; bd. chmn. Orthopedic Equipment Co. Inc., Bourbon, Ind., 1975—; chmn. bd. OEC Europe, London, Eng.; pres. OEC Internat. Inc., Bourbon, Ind., 1979—. Home: 38 Fairlane Dr Warsaw IN 46580 Office: Quad/Ecker St Bourbon IN 46504

LOTZ, JOHN JACOB, bldg. contractor; b. Phila., Aug. 19, 1922; s. William F. and Amelia (Albright) L.; B.S. in Civil Engring., Lehigh U., 1947; D.H.L., Combs Coll., 1970; m. Evelyn L. Buckley, Sept. 16, 1944; children—Joan Lotz Subotnick, Mary Lotz Dare. Pres., Lotz Designers, Engrs., Constructors, Horsham, Pa. Past mem. Cheltenham Twp. Bd. Edn., Sch. Authority Abington Twp.; bd. dirs. Am. Oncologic Hosp., Fox Chase Center for Cancer Care, Spring Garden Coll.; past pres. Carptenters' Co. Phila. (Carpenters Hall). Served with Combat Engrs. U.S. Army, World War II. Benjamin Franklin fellow Royal Soc. Arts, London, 1976; named Engr. of Yr., Delaware Valley Engring. Soc., 1977. Mem. Gen. Bldg. Contractors Assn. Phila. (dir.), Montgomery County Indsl. Devel. Corp. (dir.), Soc. Am. Mil. Engrs. (dir.), Nat. Assn. Indsl. and Office Parks (past pres.), Northeast Mfrs. Assn. (past pres.), Engrs. Club Phila., ASCE, Am. Concrete Inst., Northeastern Ind. Devel. Assn., Am. Indsl. Devel. Council, Indsl. Developers Research Council, Prudential Bus. Campus Assn. (past pres.), Soc. Indsl. Realtors, Council Urban Econ. Dirs., Beta Theta Pi (past chpt. pres.). Clubs: Masons, Shriners, Kiwanis, Seaview Country, Mfrs. Country. Contbr. articles to profl. jours.; nat. lectr. on balanced econ. growth, environ. concerns and economic need, indsl. and office park devel. Home: 1846 Hemlock Circle Abington PA 19001 Office: 215 Witmer Rd Horsham PA 19044

LOUCHHEIM, FRANK PFEIFER, mgmt. cons.; b. Phila., Aug. 6, 1923; s. Stuart Fleisher and Julia Louise (Pfeifer) L L.; B.E., Yale U., 1945; m. Betty Jane Meinel, Sept. 13, 1947; children—Stuart M., John P., Anna L. West. Salesman, Motor Parts Co., 1946-56; sales mgr. Peirce Phelps, Inc., 1956-66; sales mgr., mktg. mgr. Philco Ford Corp., Phila., 1966-69; pres., chief exec. officer Liquid Dynamics Corp., 1970-74; v.p. Haldane Assos., Phila., 1974-80; pres., chief exec. officer Right Assos., Phila., 1980—. Bd. dirs. Hist. Soc. Pa., Fleisher Art Meml. Served with USNR, 1943-46. Republican. Christian Scientist. Clubs: Union League, Yale (Phila.). Home: 1333 Gravel Hill Rd Southampton PA 18966 Office: 12 S 12th St Philadelphia PA 19107

LOUCKS, RALPH BRUCE, JR., investment co. exec.; b. St. Louis, Dec. 10, 1924; s. Ralph Bruce and Dola (Blake) L.; B.A., Lake Forest Coll., 1949; postgrad. U. Chgo., 1950-52; m. Lois Holloway, June 4, 1949; children—Elizabeth, Mary Jane. Investment fund mgr. No. Trust Co., Chgo., 1950-53, Brown Bros. Harriman & Co., Chgo., 1953-55; investment counsel, chmn. Trenholm, Loucks & Grannis, Chgo., 1955—. Bd. dirs. Ill. Epilepsy League, Epilepsy Found. Served with 11th Armored Div., AUS, 1943-45. Decorated Bronze Star medal, Purple Heart. Mem. Investment Analysts Soc., Investment Counsel Assn. Am., Huguenot Soc. Ill. (pres. 1960-61), Soc. Colonial Wars. Clubs: Economic, Racquet, University (Chgo.). Office: 134 S LaSalle St Chicago IL 60603

LOUCKS, VERNON REECE, JR., hosp. supply co. exec.; b. Evanston, Ill., Oct. 24, 1934; s. Vernon Reece and Sue Pearl (Burton) L.; B.A., Yale U., 1957; M.B.A., Harvard U., 1963; m. Linda Olson, May 12, 1972; children—Charles, David, Eric, Kristi, Greg, Susan. Sr. staff cons. George Fry & Assos., Chgo., 1963-65; with Baxter Travenol Labs., Inc., Deerfield, Ill., 1966—, corp. v.p. mktg., 1971-72, pres. Baxter/Travenol div., 1972-73, corp. sr. v.p., 1973, corp. exec. v.p., 1973-76, pres., chief operating officer, 1976—, chief exec. officer, 1980—, also dir.; dir. Dun & Bradstreet Cos., Inc., Emerson Electric Co., Marshall Field & Co., Continental Ill. Corp.; mem. sr. council James S. Kemper & Co. Bd. dirs. John L. and Helen Kellogg Found., Protestant Found.; trustee Rush, Presbyn. St. Lukes Med. Center, Kemper Ednl. and Charitable Fund, Yale Corp.; chmn. suburban campaigns Met. Crusade Mercy, 1977; asso. Northwestern U. Served to 1st lt. USMC, 1957-60. Clubs: Chicago, Onwentsia, Commonwealth, Comml., Econ. (dir.), Mid-Am. (Chgo.). Office: One Baxter Pkwy Deerfield IL 60015

LOUD, DOUGLASS NELSON, fin. cons.; b. N.Y.C., Oct. 27, 1941; s. Nelson Montgomery and Kathryn Jane (Douglass) L.; A.B., Yale U., 1964; J.D., U. Calif., Berkeley, 1967; m. Anne Elizabeth Douglass, Sept. 9, 1972; children—Douglass Nelson, Elizabeth Anne. Admitted to Hawaii bar, 1968, N.Y. bar, 1976; asso. Dillingham Corp., 1967-69, Morgan Guaranty Trust Co., 1969-70; pres. Loud Venture Capital Corp., Garden City, N.Y., 1972—, Loud Cons. Corp., Garden City, 1970—, Roll & Loud, Inc., Locust Valley, 1976-79; v.p. Peter B. Roll, Inc., Locust Valley, 1976-79; dir. nat. Pallet Leasing Systems, Inc. Trustee, Fay Sch.; treas. Locust Valley Library. Mem. Am., N.Y. State, Hawaiian bar assns. Clubs: The Creek, Yale of N.Y. Home: One Great Meadow Rd Locust Valley NY 11560 Office: 600 Old Country Rd Garden City NY 11530

LOUD, RONALD CHARLES, bank exec.; b. N.Y., Aug. 1, 1942; s. Richard E. and Dorothy Mae L.; ed. Hofstra U., Am. Coll., Pa., C.W. Post Coll., SUNY; cert. Nat. Assn. Life Underwriters, 1967-70; m. Grace Bonante, May 18, 1968; children—Roni Nicole, Michael Craig Cons., Met. Life Ins. Co., Ozone Park, N.Y., 1967-69; agent, registered rep. John Hancock Life Ins. Co., Ozone Park, 1969-74; mgr. N. N.Y. Savs. Bank, White Plains, 1974-76; mgr. Roosevelt Savs. Bank, Garden City, N.Y., 1976—. Pres. Cypress Hills Vol. Ambulance Corp., Bklyn., 1973-75; founder, pres. Bklyn.-Queens Emergency Ambulance Back-up Assn., 1973-75; mem. Farmingville Fire Dept. Mem. Am. Mgmt. Assn., Nat. Assn. Life Underwriters, Savs. Bank Life Ins. of N.Y., Mgrs. Forum (exec. com.), Pulaski Assn. Police Dept. City N.Y. Clubs: Kiwanis, K.P. Office: 1122 Franklin Ave Garden City NY 11530

LOUD, STEWART NELSON, JR., mfg. co. exec.; b. Detroit, Sept. 13, 1940; s. Stewart Nelson and Martha Stevens (Woodruff) L.; B.B.A., U. Mich., 1963; m. Susan Wilson Conway, Apr. 6, 1963; children—Heather Susan, Gordon Stewart. With Piedmont Products Inc. subs. Owens-Corning Fiberglas Corp., 1963—, program dir., Toledo, 1973—. Mem. Soc. for Advancement of Materials and Process Engring., Soc. Plastics Engrs., Soc. Plastics Industry (best papers award 1979), Nat. Contract Mgmt. Assn. Republican. Methodist. Club: North Cape Yacht (La Salle, Mich.). Home: 6817 Williamsburg Dr Sylvania OH 43560 Office: Fiberglas Tower CP5 Toledo OH 43659

LOUDERBACK, PETER DARRAGH, cons.; b. N.Y.C., July 16, 1931; s. Darragh and Constance (Clemens) L.; B.A., U. Vt., 1955; m. Roberta Wildow, Jan. 7, 1978; children by previous marriage—John, Jim, Susan, Tom. With Bell Telephone of Pa., Phila., 1955-61, supr. revenue accounting, 1959-61; cons. Peat, Marwick, Mitchell & Co., Newark, 1962-71, partner, 1971-79, partner in charge comml. bank cons. practice, 1979—. Served to capt. U.S. Army, 1961. Republican. Episcopalian. Home: 518 Teal Plaza Secaucus NJ 07094 Office: 150 John F Kennedy Pkwy Short Hills NJ 07078 also 345 Park Ave New York NY 10154

LOUGEE, VIRGINIUS BRYAN, III, business exec.; b. 1926; B.S. in Indsl. Engring., N.C. State U., 1950; married. With Am. Brands Inc., N.Y.C., 1951—, pres., chief operating officer, 1981—, also dir.; pres., chief exec. officer Am. Tobacco Co., 1978—; dir. Am. Tobacco Co. of Orient. Office: American Brands Inc 245 Park Ave New York NY 10017

LOUGHRAN, JAMES MICHAEL, importing co. exec.; b. N.Y.C., Sept. 17, 1948; s. John F. and Pauline (Lesniewski) L.; B.B.A., Bernard Baruch Coll., 1971, M.B.A., 1976; m. Jacqueline Sadowski, June 11, 1972; children—James Michael, Stephanie. Traffic mgr. Rainbow Indsl. Products Co., Flushing, N.Y., 1971-73, salesman, 1973-75, sales mgr., 1975-78, v.p., 1978—. Mem. Fgn. Trade Soc. Home: 21 Hartford Ave Staten Island NY 10310 Office: Rainbow Indsl Products Co 53-23 Metropolitan Ave Flusning NY 11385

LOUGHRIGE, ALAN CRAIG, r.r. adminstr.; b. Cumberland, Md., Dec. 24, 1946; s. Rayburn Dewey and Emma Catherine (Hershberger) L.; B.S. in Engring. Mgmt., U. Mo., Rolla, 1969; M.B.A., Drury Coll., 1976; m. Patricia Eloise Gooch, June 12, 1971; 1 son, Brian Craig. Sales engr. Columbia Laundry Machinery Co., Kansas City, Mo.,

1969-70; with St. Louis-San Francisco Ry. Co., Springfield, Mo., 1970—, field engr., 1970-76, asst. engr. cost and design, 1976, gen. supr. material and stores, 1976-77, purchasing agt., 1977-81; purchasing agt. Burlington No., St. Paul, 1981—; tchr. U.S. Med. Center for Fed. Prisoners, Springfield, 1977, Drury Coll., Springfield, 1978-80. Active Boy Scouts Am.; deacon Southminster Presbyterian Ch., Springfield, 1977—, stewardship chmn., 1976, 77; sponsor Jr. Achievement. Recipient cert. of appreciation U.S. Med. Center for Fed. Prisoners, 1977; named knight St. Patrick, U. Mo., Rolla, 1969. Mem. Ry. Automotive Mgmt. Assn., Transp. Materials Mgmt. Forum, Am. Soc. Engring. Mgmt., Mensa, Tau Kappa Epsilon. Home: 2845 Icerose Ln Stillwater MN 55082 Office: 176 E 5th St Saint Paul MN 55101

LOUKS, DAVID JERROLD, corp. exec.; b. Grand Rapids, Mich., May 13, 1927; s. Harry Benjamin and Marguerite Mary (Lemon) L.; B.B.A., U. Mich., 1950; m. Ruth Mae Barthel, July 28, 1950; children—David, Janet, Daniel, Jeffrey. Internal auditor Rexall Drug Co., Los Angeles, 1953-54; mgr. Alexander Grant & Co., C.P.A.'s, Los Angeles, 1954-63; corp. controller Lear Siegler, Inc., Santa Monica, Calif., 1963—, v.p., 1971—; mem. So. Calif. adv. bd. Liberty Mut. Ins. Co. Served with USNR, 1945-46, 51-52. C.P.A., Calif. Mem. Calif. Soc. C.P.A.'s, Am. Inst. C.P.A.'s, Nat. Assn. Accts., Am. Acctg. Assn., Acctg. Council Machinery and Allied Products Inst. Republican. Home: 17011 Avenida de Santa Ynez Pacific Palisades CA 90272 Office: 3171 S Bundy Dr Santa Monica CA 90406

LOUNSBERRY, JACK WOODS, ins. exec.; b. San Diego, Mar. 2, 1928; s. Chancel Ray and Gladys Palmer L.; A.B., U. Calif., Berkeley, 1949; m. Ann Irvine, May 5, 1956; children—David W., Katherine A. With John Burnham & Co., San Diego, 1956—, v.p., 1980—. Served as aviator U.S. Navy, 1950-54; lt. comdr. Res. ret. Decorated Air medal. Mem. San Diego Ins. Agts. Assn. Republican. Presbyterian. Clubs: Lions (past pres.), Toastmasters (past pres.), Masons, Shriners. Home: 1141 Sapphire St San Diego CA 92109 Office: 1555 6th Ave San Diego CA 92101

LOVATT, ARTHUR KINGSBURY, JR., mfg. co. exec.; b. Ventura, Calif., Mar. 12, 1920; s. Arthur Kingsbury and Flora (Mercedes) L.; B.S., U. So. Calif., 1941; M.B.A., Queens U., 1943; m. Juanita Gray, Feb. 1, 1946; children—Sherry Lynn, Tim Arthur. Leaseman, Shell Oil Co., Los Angeles, 1946-51; dir. indsl. relations Willys-Overland Motors, Inc., Los Angeles, 1952-55; asst. to pres. and gen. mgr. Pastushin Aviation Corp., Los Angeles, 1955-57; pres. Lovatt Assos., Los Angeles, 1957-66; chmn. bd., pres., gen. mgr. Lovatt Tech. Corp., Santa Fe Springs, Calif., 1966—, also dir.; dir. Lovatt Industries, Inc., others. Mem. Calif. Republican State Central Com., 1964—. Served with AUS, 1943-45. Mem. Am. Legion (post comdr. 1946), AAAS, Nat. Space Inst., Am. Soc. Metals, Los Angeles C. of C., U. So. Calif. Alumni Assn. (life), Nat. Hist. Soc. (founding asso.), Internat. Oceanographic Found., Smithsonian Assos., Am. Ordnance Assn. Mason (past master; Shriner). Inventor, developer Banadizing, Timadizing and Sheradizing, Banacolor, Embadize processes. Home: 13649 E Valna Dr Whittier CA 90602 Office: 12120 Altamar Pl Santa Fe Springs CA 90670

LOVE, BENTON F., banker; b. 1924; B.B.A., U. Tex., 1947; married. Founder Gift-Wraps, Inc., 1948-62, pres. Gift-Wraps Inc. div. Gibson Greeting Card Co., 1962-65; pres. River Oaks Bank & Trust Co., Houston, 1965-67; sr. v.p. Tex. Commerce Bank Nat. Assn., 1967-68, exec. v.p., dir., 1968-69, pres., dir., 1969-72, chmn. bd., chief exec. officer, 1972-77, sr. chmn., chief exec. officer, 1977-80; pres. Tex. Commerce Bancshares, Inc., 1971-72, chmn. bd., chief exec. officer, 1972—; dir. Proler Internat. Corp., Hughes Tool Co., Cox Broadcasting Corp., A.P.S., Inc., El Paso Co., Capital Nat. Bank, Austin, Tex., Pan Am World Airways, Inc. Office: 712 Main St Houston TX 77001

LOVE, CHARLES ALLEN, med. service adminstr.; b. Gettysburg, S.D., Feb. 13, 1924; s. Allen Ambrose and Ruth Beatrice (Barham) L.; student U. Oreg., 1942, Mont. State U., 1943, Willamette U., 1946, Multnomah Coll., 1952, Internat. Accts. Soc., 1960, Portland State U., 1966, U. Pa., 1977-79; m. Lovedy Janice Wolf, Oct. 20, 1946; children—Michael Stephen, Christine Ann Love Boatright. With Oreg. Physicians' Service, Portland, 1946—, beginning as janitor and stock boy, successively claims clk., claims examiner, chief clk. claims, claims supr., chief acct., asst. treas., treas., v.p., 1946-76, sr. v.p., 1976—, treas., 1971—; coordinator Western Conf. Prepaid Med. Service Plans for Internal Ops.; treas. Health Maintenance of Oreg., Inc. Pres. Hayesville P.T.A., 1954; v.p. Salem chpt. UN Assn., 1953; area dist. commr. Mt. Hood dist. Boy Scouts Am., 1965; fin. sec. Montavilla Methodist Ch., 1969, treas. bldg. fund, 1978-80; bd. dirs. United Cerebral Palsy Assn. of N.W. Oreg., 1979, treas., 1980. Served with USAAF, 1943-46. Recipient Outstanding Achievement award Soc. Med. Care Plan Adminstrs., 1976. Mem. Fin. Execs. Inst., Indsl. Relations Research Assn., Inst. Internal Auditors (pres. Portland chpt. 1971), Inst. Acctg. and Statis. Assn. (pres. Portland chpt. 1969), Oreg. Accident and Health Claims Assn. (pres. Portland chpt. 1964). Republican. Methodist. Clubs: Barn Own Square Dance (pres. 1973), Elks. Author: Cannery Production Line for Pears, 1942; Digital Filing, 1958; Magnetic Tape Billing and Premium Collection, 1972; Front End Microfilming of Claims, 1975; Microfilming Active Files, 1969. Home: 3550 SW 23d St Gresham OR 97030 Office: 619 SW 11th St Portland OR 97205

LOVE, FRANKLIN SADLER, trade assn. exec.; b. Rock Hill, S.C., Nov. 9, 1915; s. Franklin Sadler and Edna (Hull) L.; A.B., Presbyn. Coll., Clinton, S.C., 1937; m. Jessie Huggins, Apr. 10, 1943; children—Judith Love Freeman, Beverly Love Highfill, Franklin Sadler, Glenn. Sec., Cotton Mfrs. Assn. S.C., Clinton, 1937-42, Am. Cotton Mfrs. Assn., Charlotte, N.C., 1946-49; sec.-treas. Am. Textile Mfrs. Inst., Charlotte, 1949-79, v.p., 1979-80. Formerly mem. Charlotte adv. bd. Salvation Army; formerly bd. dirs. Charlotte Council on Alcoholism. Served to capt. Ordnance Dept., AUS, 1942-46. Recipient Alumni citation for outstanding achievement Presbyn. Coll., 1955; cert. of merit Ala. Textile Mfrs. Assn., 1972. Mem. Def. Supply Assn. (pres. Carolina chpt. 1950), Am. Trade Assn. Execs., Phi Psi. Presbyn. Clubs: Rotary (pres. Charlotte 1961-62, internat. del. 1961), City, Westport Country, Cowans Ford Country, Goodfellows (Charlotte). Home: 139 Island View Ct Denver NC 28037

LOVE, HOWARD MCCLINTIC, steel co. exec.; b. Pitts., Apr. 5, 1930; s. George Hutchinson and Margaret (McClintic) L.; B.A., Colgate U., 1952; M.B.A., Harvard U., 1956; m. Jane Vaughn, June 9, 1956; children—Marion Perkins, George Hutchinson, Howard McClintic, Jane Vaughn, Victoria Elizabeth. Mgmt. trainee Gt. Lakes Steel div. Nat. Steel Corp., Ecorse, Mich., 1956-58, operating mgmt. Gt. Lakes Steel div., 1958-63, asst. gen. mgr. sales Midwest Steel div., 1963-64, Gt. Lakes Steel div., 1964-65, asst. to pres., 1965-66, pres. Midwest Steel div., 1966—, pres. Granite City (Ill.) Steel div., 1972—, corporate pres., chief operating officer, 1975—, chief exec. officer, 1980—, also dir., mem. exec. com.; chmn. bd. Nat. Pipe & Tube Co. subs. Nat. Steel Corp., 1974—; dir. Monsanto Co., St. Louis, Gould Inc., United Fin. Corp. Calif., Trans World Corp. Trustee Colgate U., Hamilton, N.Y., Children's Hosp. Pitts., Pitts. Ballet Theatre, Inc.; mem. exec. com. Allegheny Conf. Community Devel.; bd. dirs. United Way Allegheny County, Pitts. Symphony, Pitts. Regional Planning Assn.; mem. exec. bd. Allegheny Trails Area council Boy Scouts Am.; Pa. bus. rep. on adv. bd. Coalition Northeastern Govs., 1979—. Served with USAF, 1952-54. Mem. Am. Iron and Steel Inst. (exec. com.), Met. Opera Assn., Beta Theta Pi. Republican. Episcopalian. Club: Masons. Home: 1440 Bennington Ave Pittsburgh PA 15217 Office: 2800 Grant Bldg Pittsburgh PA 15219

LOVE, JOHN EDWARD, agr. and forestry equipment mfg. co. exec.; b. Vaughn, Wash., Nov. 11, 1932; s. James Edward and Stella (Batey) L.; B.A., Whitworth Coll., 1954; postgrad. Minn. Sch. Art, 1955; m. Susan Ann Oliver, Mar. 15, 1954; children—James Allen, Keith Edward, Jerry Lee, Julia Ann. Interior, exterior decorator John's, Spokane, Wash., 1953-54; with J.E. Love Co., Garfield, Wash., 1957—, sales mgr., 1957-62, gen. mgr., 1962—, pres., 1964—; pres. Nepelo Inc., Garfield, 1966; dir. Bank of Whitman, Colfax, Wash., Farm Indsl. Equipment Inst., Chgo.; mem. adv. bd. Wash. State Dept. Commerce and Econ. Devel. Active Boy Scouts Am. Bd. dirs. Sch. Dist. 302 Garfield, Wash. Internat. Trade Fair, Inland Empire Water Way, Seattle, Eastern Wash. U. Found. Served to capt. USNR, 1980—. Mem. Navy Res. Officers Assn., Garfield C. of C. Elk. Clubs: Empire, Spokane, Broken Propeller Aviation, Inland Empire World Trade (v.p.) (Spokane). Home: 1002 Spokane St Garfield WA 99130 Office: 203 California St Garfield WA 99130

LOVE, JOSEPH WILLIAM, JR., oil co. exec.; b. Tulsa, Mar. 31, 1928; s. Joseph William and Eva Elizabeth (Henderson) L.; student Okla. State U., 1945-47; B.S., U. Tulsa, 1949; postgrad. U. Houston, 1957-60. Sales rep. Tex. Gas Corp., Houston, 1956-60, credit mgr., 1960-61, mgr. credit and personnel, 1961-63; credit mgr. Union Tex. Petroleum div. Allied Chem. Corp., Houston, 1963-65, mgr. mfg. adminstrn., 1965-68, mgr. mktg. ops. analysis, 1968-73, mgr. mktg. services, 1973-77, mgr. mktg. planning and devel., 1977-80, mgr. planning and evaluation, internat. producing ops., 1980—. Served to capt., USAF, 1951-55. Decorated Air Medal. Recipient Distinguished Service certificate Adminstrv. Mgmt. Soc., 1972; licensed real estate broker, Tex. Mem. Houston Bd. Realtors, Adminstrv. Mgmt. Soc. (chpt. v.p. 1971-72), Nat. Assn. Bus. Economists, No.Am. Soc. Corp. Planning, Nat. LP Gas Assn., Gas Processors Assn., Internat. Platform Assn., Sigma Phi Epsilon. Methodist. Home: 34 Lana Ln Houston TX 77027 Office: PO Box 2120 Houston TX 77001

LOVE, ROBERT MERRILL, banker; b. Jacksonville, Ala., Aug. 8, 1929; s. Robert T. and Grace (Harris) L.; student St. Anselms Coll.; m. Dina B. Nicholas, Aug. 7, 1949; children—Linda, Donna, Laura, Robert Merrill. Br. mgr. Mchts. Acceptance Corp., Worcester, Mass., 1950-66; v.p. Claremont Savs. Bank (N.H.), 1966-70, pres., treas., 1977—; v.p. Mchts. Savs. Bank, Manchester, N.H., 1970-77; pres. New Eng. Non Profit Housing Devel. Corp. Pres., Land Use Found. N.H., 1972-74, Consumer Fin. Assn. N.H., 1954-57; treas. Am. Baptist Chs. N.H. Served with USAF, 1946-49. Democrat. Baptist. Club: Lions (pres. 1967-69). Office: 145 Broad St Claremont NH 03743

LOVE, ROBERT MITCHELL, mfg. exec.; b. Chgo., Aug. 7, 1928; s. Quill Horace and Jemma (Mitchell) L.; student Monterey Peninsula Jr. Coll., 1960-61, Inst. for Orgn. Mgmt. U. Houston, 1966, 67, Tex. Christian U. Advanced Mgmt. Studies, 1968-70; m. Shari Lee Cook, Dec. 12, 1964; children—Mark, Gregory, Wendi. Customer service agt. Am. Airlines, Memphis, 1951-55, customer service mgr., Washington, 1955-59, mgr. mil. traffic office, San Francisco, 1959-63; mgr. customer service and operations Mohawk Airlines, N.Y.C., 1963-65; mgr. conv. and visitors bur. Little Rock C. of C., 1965-67; exec. v.p., gen. mgr. Jonesboro (Ark.) C. of C., 1967-71; dir. indsl. services Knoxville (Tenn.) C. of C., 1971-72; exec. v.p. Melton Hill Regional Inds. Devel. Assn., 1972-73; exec. v.p., sec. Indsl. Devel. Bd. Scott County (Tenn.), 1974-79; pres. Cumberland Wood Products, Inc., 1976—. Served with AUS, USAF, 1946-51. Decorated Bronze Star, Purple Heart. Mem. Am. Indsl. Devel. Assn., So. Indsl. Devel. Council, East Tenn. Indsl. Council, Tenn. Indsl. Devel. Council. Methodist. Mason. Home: Ponderosa Estates Oneida TN 37841 Office: Box 496 Oneida TN 37841

LOVEJOY, LEE HAROLD, investment co. exec.; b. Aurora, Mo., July 19, 1936; s. Harold B. and Lorene E. (Spangler) L.; B.S., Drake U., 1958; m. Carol L. Nellis, Feb. 14, 1976; children by previous marriage—Steven Lee, Kristin Ann. With Paine Webber Jackson & Curtis, St. Paul, 1965-68, mgr. Twin Cities instl. dept., Mpls., 1968-72, v.p./mgr. New Eng., Boston, 1972-74, sr. v.p./mgr. nat. instl. equity dept., 1974-77; sr. v.p., dir., chief adminstrv. officer, nat. sales mgr. Paine Webber Mitchell Hutchins Inc., N.Y.C., 1977—. Mem. St. Paul Mayor's Legal and Fin. Adv. Com. Bd. dirs. Presbyn. Homes Found.; trustee Drake U. Served to capt. USAF, 1958-65. Mem. Internat. Golf Sponsors Assn., Security Industry Assn., Boston Security Traders, Boston Investment Club, Security Traders N.Y., Sigma Alpha Epsilon, Omicron Delta Kappa, Arnold Air Soc. Republican. Presbyterian. Home: 238 Oak St W Ramsey NJ 07446 Office: 140 Broadway New York NY 10005

LOVEJOY, RICHARD HERBERT, ins. exec.; b. S. Portland, Maine, Mar. 1, 1934; s. James Albert and Helen Elsie (Welch) L.; student Univ. Schs., 1957; children—Richard Herbert, Gayla M., Daryl S., Scott A., Dawn A., Serena L. Insp., New Eng. Fire Ins. Rating Assn., Portland, 1957-61; spl. agt. Maine Bonding & Casualty Co., Portland, 1961-66; ins. agt. W.C. Ladd & Sons, Inc., Rockland, Maine, 1966—, v.p., sec., Mgr. Marine & Life Dept., 1980—; registered rep. Nat. Assn. Securities Dealers. Incorporator, Penobscot Bay Med. Center, Rockland, 1980. Served with USAF, 1953-57. Recipient Dale Carnegie Sch. Highest Achievement award, 1960. Mem. Rockland C. of C., Nat. Assn. Life Underwriters. Clubs: Masons (Shriner), Elks, Rotary (pres. 1975-76), Rockland Yacht (commodore 1970-71). Home: 101 N Main St Rockland ME 04841 Office: 14 School St Rockland ME 04841

LOVELACE, JON B., JR., investment mgmt. co. exec.; b. Detroit, Feb. 6, 1927; s. Jonathan Bell and Marie (Andersen) L.; A.B. cum laude, Princeton, 1950; m. Lillian Pierson, Dec. 29, 1950; children—Carey, James, Jeffrey, Robert. Personnel asst. Pacific Finance Co., 1950-51; with Capital Research & Mgmt. Co., Los Angeles, 1951—, treas., 1955-62, v.p., 1957-62, exec. v.p., 1962-64, pres., 1964-75, chmn. bd., 1975—, also dir.; chmn. bd. Investment Co. Am.; dir. Capital Research Co., 1967—; chmn. bd. Am. Mut. Fund, Inc., 1968—; pres., dir. New Perspective Fund; mem., chief exec. officer Capital Group, Inc.; dir. Capital Group, Inc. Trustee Claremont Men's Coll., Calif. Inst. Arts, Santa Barbara Med. Found. Clinic; vice-chmn. bd. fellows Claremont Univ. Center. Mem. Sierra Club. Clubs: Princeton, Univ. (N.Y.C.); Calif. (Los Angeles). Home: 800 W 1st St Los Angeles CA 90012 also 780 El Bosque Rd Santa Barbara CA 93108 Office: 333 S Hope St Los Angeles CA 90071

LOVELL, STANLEY EDWIN, retail pharmacy chair exec.; b. Oshawa, Ont., Can., Jan. 26, 1927; s. Edwin Arthur and Ruby Louise (Felt) L.; B.A., U. Toronto, 1947; m. Wilma C. Down, Aug. 26, 1950; children—Diana, Arthur, Linda. Sec.-treas. Anglo Can. Drug Co. Ltd., Oshawa, 1950-59; pres. Lovell Drugs Ltd., Oshawa, 1962—; Lovell Holdings Lts., Oshawa, 1964—, Jury & Lovell Ltd., Oshawa, 1970—; mem. Can. adv. bd. Liberty Mut. Ins. Co. Trustee Oshawa Bd. Edn., 1962-69, chmn., 1966-69; trustee Durham Bd. Edn., 1969-72, chmn., 1969-70; bd. dirs. Oshawa Gen. Hosp., chmn., 1971-76; provincial council pres. Boy Scouts Can. 1972-74, mem. nat. fin. com., recipient Silver Wolf, 1977; bd. dirs. Ont. Hosp. Assn.; bd. govs. Durham Coll., 1968-76, chmn., 1975-76. Mem. Am. Mgmt. Assn., Met. Toronto Bd. Trade. United Ch. Clubs: Rotary, Oshawa Golf, Granite, Masons. Home: 399 Simcoe St N Oshawa ON L1G 4T7 Canada Office: 52 1/2 Simcoe St N Oshawa ON L1G 4S1 Canada

LOVETT, CRISTINE LOUISE, electronics mfg. mgr.; b. Las Animas, Colo., Aug. 8, 1951; d. Ivan Eugene and Rosalee (Pemberton) Brenton; B.S. in Journalism (Scripps-Howard scholar), U. Colo., Boulder, 1972, spl. student in engring. design and econ. evaluation, 1975; M.B.A. in Fin., U. Colo., Denver, 1980; m. Daryle A. Lovett, May 19, 1972. Documentation clk. Valleylab, Inc., Boulder, 1973-74; v.p. mktg. OWL Tech. Assos., Inc., Longmont, Colo., 1974—; polit. reporter Tri-City Jour., Broomfield, Colo., 1977-78, Lafayette (Colo.) News, 1978. Recipient public service award U.S. Navy, 1973; cert. purchasing mgr. Mem. Colo. Mining Assn., M.B.A. Assn., Am. Soc. Exec. and Profl. Women, Denver Exec. and Profl. Women's Council (founding mem.), Nat. Assn. Female Execs. (local dir.). Home: 1260 Centaur Village Ct Lafayette CO 80026 Office: 1111 Delaware Longmont CO 80501

LOVETT, MARK LAWRENCE, furniture retailer; b. Corona, Calif., Nov. 26, 1955; s. Frank Owen and Gwen L.; student public schs., San Diego. With stock and inventory control dept. Calif. Electric Works, San Diego, 1972-73; foreman heliport constrn. Mardinus Inc., Augusta, Ga., 1974-76; with inventory mgmt. control dept. ITT Cable Hydrospace Co., National City, Calif., 1977-78; owner, mgr. The Wicker Palace, Lakeside, Calif., 1978—; bus. mgmt. cons., 1978—. Mem. Gas Lamp Orgn., planners San Diego downtown redevel.

LOVETT, RALPH ELMER, JR., fin. cons.; b. Moline, Ill., Sept. 13, 1952; s. Ralph Elmer and Patricia Ann (Wilson) L.; B.A.B.A., Augustana Coll., 1973. Asst. mgr. Credit Cos. Am., Gt. Falls, Mont., 1973-75; mgr. Quint City Credit Assn., Davenport, Iowa, 1975-77; pres. Lovett & Assos.—Fin. Cons. Ltd., Rock Island, Ill., 1977—. Pres. Rock Island County (Ill.) Young Democrats, 1968-72; mem. Ill. State Young Dems. Leadership Bd.; bd. dirs. Ill. Assn. Christian Schs. Mem. Ill. Assn. C.P.A.'s, PTA (life), Ill. Notary Assn., Friends of LBJ Library. Baptist. Clubs: Elks, Moose. Office: 208 18th St Suite 200 Rock Island IL 61201

LOVIE, PETER MARSHALL, civil engr.; b. Glasgow, Scotland, Nov. 21, 1940; came to U.S., 1967; s. Peter and Elizabeth (Harrower) L.; B.Sc.C.E., U. Glasgow, 1962; M.Applied Mechanics (Fulbright grantee), U. Va., 1964; 1 son, Marshall. Engr., Cameron Iron Works, Houston, 1967-68, Offshore Co., Houston, 1969; pres. Engring. Tech. Analysts, Inc., Houston, 1970-75, Lovie & Co., Houston, 1970—. Chmn., Futures of Houston. Recipient Outstanding Steel Structure award French Soc. Steel Structures, 1979; registered profl. engr., Tex. Mem. Royal Inst. Naval Architects, Inst. Civil Engrs. (U.K.). Contbr. articles tech. jours. Patentee in field.

LOVING, GRAHAM, investment banker; b. Washington, Sept. 1, 1925; s. Graham and Helen (Briggs) L.; B.A., Georgetown U., 1944, LL.B., 1948; postgrad. Tex. U. Law Sch., 1944-45; children—Jennifer, Graham, Candace. Admitted to D.C. bar, 1948, Okla. bar, 1952; trial atty. Treasury Dept., N.Y.C., 1949-51, tax div. Dept. Justice, 1951-52; partner firm Mosteller Fellers Andrews & Loving, Oklahoma City, 1952-59; partner investment banking firm Lomasney Loving & Co., N.Y.C., 1959-61; co-founder, pres. Equity Research Assos., N.Y.C., 1962-66; founder, sr. partner Graham Loving & Co., N.Y.C., 1967-74; investment banker, Aspen, Colo., 1974—; dir. Am. Home Shield, Dublin, Calif., Am. Felt & Filter, Newburgh, N.Y. Democrat. Unitarian. Club: Columbia Country (Chevy Chase, Md.). Home: 886 Roaring Fork Rd Aspen CO 81611

LOVITZ, DAVID DANIEL, mfg. co. exec.; b. Chgo., Mar. 16, 1920; s. Benjamin and Dora (Cohen) L.; student Herzl Jr. Coll., 1936-38, Walton Sch. Commerce, 1938-40; m. Florence Lifschutz, July 19, 1943; children—Sandra Eileen, Fred Steven. Plant mgr. Nat. Press, Chgo., 1937-45; sales mgr. Harlich Mfg. Co., Chgo., 1946-48; v.p. sales BECO Mfg. Co., Chgo., 1949-59; gen. mgr. Midwest Region Hartz Mountain Products Co., Chgo., 1960-65; pres. Aquarium Supply Co. div. Sternco Industries, Inc., Harrison, N.J., 1965-73; exec. v.p., chief operating officer, dir. Hartz Mountain Corp., Harrison, 1973-79, pres., chief operating officer, dir., 1979—. Served with inf. U.S. Army, 1943-45. Decorated Purple Heart, Bronze Star. Jewish. Clubs: B'nai Brith; Shackamaxon Golf and Country (Westfield, N.J.). Home: 1 Rolling Hill Rd Short Hills NJ 07078 Office: Hartz Mountain Corp 700 S 4th St Harrison NJ 07029

LOVRIEN, PHYLLIS ANN, food co. exec.; b. Birmingham, Ala., Dec. 26, 1941; d. James Keith and Phyllis M. Lovrien; B.S., Iowa State U., 1963; postgrad. U. Wis., 1967-73; With Oscar Mayer & Co., Madison, Wis., 1963—, asst. corp. relations mgr., 1973-77, corp. v.p. consumer affairs, 1977—; dir. United Bank; prof. U. Wis. Mem. Soc. Consumer Affairs Profls. (dir.), Grocery Mfrs. Am., Am. Meat Inst. Office: PO Box 7188 Madison WI 53707

LOW, JOSEPH THOMPKINS, diversified co. exec.; b. Glen Ridge, N.J., Aug. 29, 1934; s. Joseph T. and Elizabeth (Putnam) L.; B.A., Duke U., 1956; grad. Advanced Mgmt. Program, Harvard, 1975; m. Ann Legare Padgett, Aug. 20, 1955; children—Catherine, Joseph Thompkins, Rebecca, Michael. Audit mgr. Price Waterhouse & Co., N.Y.C., 1960-71; corporate controller IC Industries, Chgo., 1971-79; chief fin. officer Am. Invsco Corp., Chgo., 1979—. Elder, First Presbyterian Ch., Wilmette, Ill.; mem. fin. com. Loyola U., Chgo. Served with USAF, 1957-60. C.P.A., N.Y. Mem. Am. Inst. C.P.A.'s, N.Y. Soc. C.P.A.'s, Am. Mgmt. Assn., Fin. Execs. Inst. Clubs: Economic, Mid-Am., Execs. (Chgo.); Wilmette Sailing. Home: 1111 Sheridan Rd Wilmette IL 60091 Office: 120 S LaSalle St Chicago IL 60603

LOWE, EDMUND W., photog. chems. mfg. co. exec.; b. Dover, Minn., July 28, 1905; s. John and Mary Alice (Chermak) L.; B.S., Hamline U., 1926; M.Sc., U. Chgo., 1929, Ph.D., 1930; m. Elsie Traynor, Nov. 17, 1932; children—Henry Allan, Veronica Mary, Virginia Ann. Instr. chemistry Hamline U., 1926-27; nat. research fellow in med. chemistry U. Chgo., 1930-34; founder, pres. Edwal Labs., Chgo., 1934-50; pres. Edwal Sci. Products Corp., Chgo., 1950—. Fellow Nat. Press Photographers Assn.; mem. Photog. Soc. Am. (asso.), Am. Chem. Soc., Soc. Profl. Scientists and Engrs., Nat. Rifle Assn. Mem. Brethren Ch. Club: Quadrangle. Author: What You Want To Know about Developers, 1939; Modern Developing Methods, 1939. Office: 12120 S Peoria St Chicago IL 60643

LOWE, GEORGE WASHINGTON, JR., transp. and traffic cons.; b. Columbia, Ky., Mar. 18, 1919; s. George Washington and Fannie Sophronia (Faulkner) L.; student Lindsey Wilson Jr. Coll., 1936-37, Draughan's, Dwyer's Consol. Bus. Colls., 1943-50, Pearson Music Sch., 1941-45; Ind. U., 1944-45, Central Beauty Coll., 1961-62, Famous Writers Sch., 1966-67. Office mgr. United Laundries and Dry Cleaners, 1943-46; asst. traffic mgr. Republic Creosoting, 1947-48; rate analyst I.R.C. & D., Carolina Motor Express, 1948-56; rate analyst United Trucking, Middlestates Motor Freight, Consol. Freightways, Inc., 1956-69; rate analyst accountant Ryder Truck Lines, Inc., 1969-76; chmn. bd., pres. Lo-Jac Traffic Service Inc., Brownsburg, Ind., 1976-80; transp. and traffic cons., 1980—; pvt. tchr. piano and organ, Brownsburg, 1972-80. Ward chmn. Republican party, Marion County, Ind., 1954-55. Mem. Am. Theater Organist Soc., Internat. Platform Assn., Mid Am. Rate Council, Ind. Theatre Organists Soc. Club: Toastmasters. Author: Octave Theory, 1972. Home and Office: 1311 NE 125 St #301 North Miami FL 33161

LOWE, MITCHELL, accountant; b. Birmingham, Ala., Apr. 24, 1923; s. Ishmeal and Edna (Creen) L.; diploma Knapp Bus. Coll., 1964; A.A., Ft. Steilacoom Community Coll., 1975; B.A., Evergreen State Coll., 1977; postgrad. Golden Gate U., 1980; m. Ruth B.V. Lowe, Feb. 22, 1946; children—Frederich H., Karl J., Mitchell E., R.K. Joined U.S. Army, 1941, advanced through grades to CWO-3, 1960; ret., 1962; thereafter engaged in real estate, taxation, acctg. and constrn.; tax adv., accountant Real Estate Exchange, 1975; tax advisor, 1975—; pres. Nest Homes Corp., 1978—. Mem. Ft. Lewis Officers Club, Omega Psi Phi. Home: 3102 N Claremont Pl Tacoma WA 98407 Office: 7012 Pacific Ave Tacoma WA 98407

LOWE, PHIL O., fabricated tubing mfg. co. exec.; b. Ft. Wayne, Ind., June 15, 1924; s. Murland V. and Naomi Lowe; B.A., Wabash Coll., 1949; m. Mary Louise Svelzer, June 12, 1948; children—Michael, John, Anita, Jim, Richard, Marty, Susan, Sharon, Thomas, Mary, Phil, Joseph. Chemist, U.S. Rubber Co., Ft. Wayne, 1949-52, Internat. Harvester Co., Ft. Wayne, 1952-55; with Whitley Products, Inc., Pierceton, Ind., 1955—, chmn. bd., 1975—. Pres., Warsaw Aviation Bd., 1976-80. Served with USAAF, 1942-45. Decorated Air medal with three oak leaf clusters. Mem. U.S. C. of C., Ind. Mfg. Assn., Warsaw C. of C. (pres. indsl. div. 1963-65). Am. Legion, VFW. Clubs: Elks, Tippecanoe Lake Country. Home: 2814 E Patterson Rd Warsaw IN 46580 Office: Whitley Products Inc Box 154 Pierceton IN 46562

LOWE, ROBERT CLINTON, steel products co. exec.; b. St. Louis, Oct. 6, 1918; s. Robert M. and Eunice (Coates) L.; B.S., U. Pitts.; m. Pauline C. Artz, Oct. 5, 1940; children—Robert Clinton, Paula Carol, Diane Louise. Asst. sec.-treas. Coates Steel Products Co., 1940-52, exec. v.p., treas., 1952-60, pres., chief exec. officer, 1960—; dir. First Nat. Bank. Chmn., Greenville Airport Authority. Mem. Soc. Mining Engrs. Am. Inst. Mining, Metall. and Petroleum Engrs., Am. Soc. Metals, Kappa Sigma. Presbyn. Clubs: Glen Echo Country, Greenbriar Country, Sunset Hills Country, Mo. Athletic (St. Louis); Lehigh Country (Allentown, Pa.); Burning Tree Country (Washington); Union (Cleve.). Home: 442 E Main St Greenville IL 62246 Office: Box 100 Greenville IL 62246

LOWE, WALTER ARCHELOUS, restaurant chain exec.; b. Canton, N.C., Mar. 6, 1928; s. Walter W. and Olivia Marie (Nicholson) L.; B.S., U. N.C., 1949, M.B.A., 1956; m. Margaret June Buckner, Sept. 2, 1950; children—James Walter, Jeffrey Paul. Acct., Gen. Motors Acceptance Corp., Asheville, N.C., 1949-52; sr. auditor Coopers & Lybrand, C.P.A.'s, Pitts., 1956-59; tax specialist Genesco Inc., Nashville, 1959-62; tax supr. Ernst & Whinney, C.P.A.'s, Nashville, 1962-69; asst. treas. Ky. Fried Chicken Corp., Louisville, 1969-73; v.p., sec. JRN Chicken Stores, Inc., Columbia, Tenn., 1973—. Served with USAF, 1952-55. C.P.A., N.C. Mem. Nat. Acctg. Assn. Baptist. Home: 305 W 6th St Columbia TN 38401 Office: 201 W 7th St Columbia TN 38401

LOWE, WILLIAM DOUGLAS, oil co. exec.; b. Glen Cove, N.Y., May 29, 1949; s. William Woodrow and Winifred Virginia (Ringeisen) L.; A.B. with honors, Georgetown U., 1971; M.B.A., Columbia, 1973; m. Brenda Janice Jorgensen, Sept. 2, 1972; 1 dau., Alexandra Noelle. Fin. analyst, treas.'s internat. div. Mobil Oil Corp., N.Y.C., 1973-74, asst. to treas., East region, 1974-75, sr. supply asso. econ. analysis unit, 1976-77, treas. Mobil Oil Japan, 1977—. Pres. Red Cross Youth, N.Y.C., 1967. Served to capt. U.S. Army. Mem. Am. Mgmt. Assn., Am. C. of C. in Japan (vice chmn. banking and fin. com.). Clubs: Princeton; Tokyo Lawn Tennis; Fgn. Corrs. Home: 1 8 10 Kamineguro King Homes Apt 502 Tokyo Japan Office: 150 E 42d St New York City NY 10017

LOWELL, EDWARD OTHMAN, mfg. co. exec.; b. Lansing, Mich., Sept. 18, 1914; s. Elbridge G. and Jessie (Lewis) L.; B.A., U. So. Calif., 1939; postgrad., 1939-41; m. Kate Eunice Winder, Nov. 26, 1934 (dec. Apr. 1974); children—Ann Lowell Leatherbury, Mark Howard; m. 2d, Marion Lucille Jernegan, Jan. 3, 1975. Salesman, Equitable Life Assurance Soc., Pasadena, Calif., 1933-35, Ducommun Metal & Supply Co., Los Angeles, 1935-36; with Angelus San. Can Machine Co., Los Angeles, 1936—, dir., 1945—, v.p., 1953-63, pres., 1963—; accountant Gaffers & Sattler, Los Angeles, 1938-40, controller, 1940-42; partner Sierra Growers, Los Angeles, 1953—, Southwest Co., 1958—; dir. Jack Loew Premium Co., N. County Truck Co. Pres., bd. dirs. Henry L. Guenther Found., 1958—; trustee Food Processors Inst., 1973—, chmn., 1976-79; asst. dist. commr. San Luis Rey dist. San Diego County council Boy Scouts Am., 1966-70. Mem. Canning Machinery and Supplies Assn. (dir. 1962-65, v.p. 1965-67, pres. 1967-69), Nat. Canners Assn. (adv. bd. 1973—), Calif. Assn. Nurserymen. Presbyterian. Home: PO Box 566 Fallbrook CA 92028 Office: 4900 Pacific Blvd Los Angeles CA 90058

LOWERY, BILL WALTER, tech. co. exec.; b. Los Angeles, Nov. 27, 1947; s. Leroy and Joyce Louella (Paulson) L.; B.S., Calif. Poly. State U., 1974; M.B.A., U. Portland (Oreg.), 1978; m. Donna Joyce Coffer, Oct. 22, 1973; 1 dau., Shannon Rene. Sci. programmer/analyst Tektronix Inc., Beaverton, Oreg., 1974-75, mgr. microprocessor support, 1975-76, mgr. microprocessor/data base applications support, 1976-79; mktg. engr. advanced microcomputer systems Intel Corp., Aloha, Oreg., 1979-80; dir. mktg. Cogitronics Corp., Portland, Oreg., 1980—; lectr. in field. Chmn. bd. dirs. Carlin Homeowners Assn., 1978-79. Served with U.S. Army, 1968-70; Vietnam. Mem. Am. Legion, IEEE Computer Soc. (vice-chmn. Portland chpt. 1980—), Phi Kappa Phi. Republican. Home: 20831 SW Zurich Ct Aloha OR 97007 Office: 5470 NW Innisbrook Place Portland OR 97229

LOWERY, EARL GENE, tax preparation co. exec.; b. Elgin, Ill., Apr. 22, 1951; s. Herbert Vernon and Delores Ruth (Raddatz) L.; student Ill. Coll., Jacksonville, 1969-71, No. Ill. U., DeKalb, 1971-72; m. Linda Sue Hoke, June 17, 1972; children—Kimberly Sue, Jennifer Ruth. With H. & R. Block Inc., Elgin, 1967—, asst. city mgr., 1971, satellite dir., 1972, dist. mgr., 1972—; tchr. income tax preparation co. schs., 1974—. Mem. fin. com. Faith United Meth. Ch., Elgin, 1969—, mem. nominations and personnel, adminstrv. bd., edn. commn., 1978—, mem. endowment fund and learning center exec. bd., 1980—. Mem. Hilltoppers Theatre Group, Icthus, Phi Alpha Lit. Soc. Home: 464 Gertrude St Elgin IL 60120 Office: 692 Villa St Elgin IL 60120

LOWERY, TERRY B., data processing co. ofcl.; b. Lafayette, La., Aug. 8, 1940; s. James H. and Ruby M. Lowery; B.A., Cameron U., 1970; M.B.A., U. Okla., 1971. Grad. asst. U. Okla.; programming supr. Halliburton Services Co., Duncan, Okla., 1974-76, ops. mgr., 1976-79, application systems supr., 1979—. Mem. Duncan C. of C., Phi Kappa Phi, Phi Mu Epsilon. Republican. Baptist. Club: Elks.

LOWERY, WILLIAM HERBERT, lawyer; b. Toledo, June 8, 1925; s. Kenneth Alden and Drusilla (Pfanner) L.; Ph.B., U. Chgo., 1947; J.D., U. Mich., 1950; m. Carolyn Dodge Broadwell, June 27, 1947; children—Kenneth Latham, Marcia Mitchell. Admitted to Pa. bar, 1950; asso. Dechert, Price & Rhoads, Phila., 1950-58, partner, 1958—, mng. partner, 1970-72; permanent mem. Jud. Conf. 3d Circuit Ct. Appeals. Counsel, S.S. Huebner Found. for Ins. Edn., 1970—. Chmn. zoning hearing bd. Tredyffrin Twp., Chester County, Pa., 1959-75. Regional chmn. Mich. Law Sch. Fund, 1966-70; bd. dirs. Paoli Meml. Hosp., 1964—, pres., 1972-75; mem. task force S.E. Pa. Regional Comprehensive Health Planning, 1968-72; mem. trustees adv. com. Hosp. Assn. Pa., 1970-76. Trustee Clin. Biochemistry and Behavioral Research Inst. Served to lt. USAAF, 1943-46. Mem. Am. (ins. law sect., vice chmn. life ins. law com.) Pa., Phila. bar assns., Am., Pa. socs. hosp. attys., Juristic Soc., Phi Gamma Delta, Phi Delta Phi. Republican. Presbyn. (elder 1968-72). Clubs: Urban (Phila.); Waynesborough Country (Paoli, Pa.). Home: 542 Tory Hill Rd Devon PA 19333 Office: 3400 Centre Sq West 1500 Market St Philadelphia PA 19102

LOWNDES, TASKER GANTT, banker; b. Cumberland, Md., Oct. 1, 1913; s. Lloyd and May (Quinn) L.; ed. Yale, 1937; m. Marjorie Trowbridge, Nov. 28, 1942 (dec.). With Lowndes Bank, Clarksburg, W.Va., 1968—, chmn. bd., 1968—; pres. T.G. Lowndes Corp., N.Y.C., 1968—. Bd. dirs. Cumberland (Md.) Fair Assn. Served to capt. USAAF, 1941-44. Clubs: Racquet and Tennis, Yale (N.Y.C.); Everglades, Bath and Tennis (Palm Beach, Fla.). Home: 25 Sutton Pl S New York NY 10022

LOWRANCE, DAVID WILLIAM, fin. exec.; b. Mooresville, N.C., Sept. 23, 1947; s. David Erwin and Alda (Barber) L.; B.S. in B.A., U. N.C., 1970; postgrad. U. Pa., 1975, U. Chgo., 1977; m. Margaret E. Bullard, Sept. 4, 1973. Sr. auditor Coopers & Lybrand, Phila., 1970-74; asst. group controller ITE Imperial Corp., Spring House, Pa., 1974-76; asst. to treas. Gould, Inc., Rolling Meadows, Ill., 1976-78; treas.-internat. Ingersoll-Rand Co., Woodcliff Lake, N.J., 1978-79, mgr. corporate fin., 1979—, mem. polit. action com., 1979—. Adv. for acctg. career Explorer Post, Rolling Meadows, 1977-78. C.P.A., Pa. Mem. Pa. Inst. C.P.A.'s, Chamber Commerce and Industry of No. N.J., Am. Inst. C.P.A.'s, Fin. Execs. Inst. Republican. Presbyterian. Club: Meadow. Office: 200 Chestnut Ridge Rd Woodcliff Lake NJ 07675

LOWRANCE, MURIEL EDWARDS, data analyst; b. Ada, Okla., Dec. 28, 1922; d. Warren and Mayme E. (Barrick) Edwards; B.S. in Edn., E. Central U., Ada, 1954; divorced; 1 dau., Kathy Lynn Lowrance Gutierrez. Elementary sch. tchr., 1968-74; acct., adminstrv. asst. to bus. mgr. E. Central U., 1950-68; asst. adminstrv. officer N.Mex. Regional Med. Program, U. N.Mex. Sch. Medicine, Albuquerque, 1972-75, grants and contracts specialist, 1968-72, data analyst dept. orthopaedics, 1975—. Bd. dirs. Amigos de las Americas, Vocat. Rehab. Center, Inc. Cert. profl. contract mgr. Mem. Am. Bus. Women's Assn. (past chpt. pres.; chpt. Woman of Year 1974), AAUW. Democrat. Methodist. Club: Pilot Internat. (pres. Albuquerque 1979-80). Home: 3028 Mackland Ave NE Albuquerque NM 87106 Office: Dept Orthopaedics Univ New Mex Sch Medicine Albuquerque NM 87131

LOWREY, JOSEPH LANEY, retail exec.; b. Many, La., Oct. 16, 1942; s. Robert Louis and Merrill Josephine (Laney) L.; B.S., La. State U., 1963; m. Mary Elkins Vernon, June 10, 1963; children—Ann, Patricia, John, Carolyn. Engaged in retail automobile bus., 1965—; pres. Lowrey Chevrolet, Inc., Many, 1969—, Lowrey Trucks, Inc., 1978—, Triad Truck Leasing, Inc., 1978—, Ark-La-Tex Ford Trucks, Inc., 1981— (all Shreveport); v.p. Nunnelee Truck Rental, Inc., Shreveport, 1980—; partner Lowrey Devel. Co., Many; dir. Sabine State Bank & Trust Co., Many. Chmn. Sabine Parish Planning Com., 1969-80. Served as officer USAR, 1963-65. Mem. Nat. Automobile Dealers Assn., Am. Truck Dealers Assn., La. Automobile Dealers Assn. (dir. 1977-79), La. Truck Dealers Assn. (chmn. 1978-79), Many C. of C., Phi Kappa Phi, Beta Gamma Sigma, Phi Gamma Delta. Democrat. Roman Catholic. Club: Lions. Home: 1085 Kenilworth Ave Many LA 71449 Office: 520 W San Antonio Ave Many LA 71449

LOWRY, DAVID DOUGLAS, computer software co. exec.; Portland, Oreg., Apr. 19, 1944; s. David B. and Mary L. Lowry; B.S.C., U. Santa Clara, 1966; M.B.A., U. Oreg., 1967; m. Mary T. Weyer, July 6, 1968. Mgmt. asso. Western Electric Co., Sunnyvale, Calif., 1968-69; cons. Mgmt. Sci. Am., Palo Alto, Calif., 1969-73; founder, pres., prin. owner Data Design Assos., Inc., Santa Clara, Calif., 1973—. Republican.

LOWRY, LEO ELMO, petroleum exec.; b. Utopia, Kans., Dec. 4, 1916; s. Nim Roderick and Marticia (Veach) L.; B.A., Okla. A. and M. Coll., 1937; m. Elizabeth Watson, Sept. 5, 1940; children—Richard Clark, John Christopher, Janet Kaye. With Creole Petroleum Corp., Caracas, Venezuela, 1937-71, exec. v.p., 1961-64, pres., 1964-71; pres. Esso Inter-Am., Inc., Coral Gables, Fla., 1971-77.

LOWY, RUDOLPH JACOB, devel. co. exec.; b. Brussels, Belgium, Apr. 30, 1948; came to U.S., 1949, naturalized, 1956; s. Marcus and Mina L.; B.S.E. cum laude, UCLA, 1969, M.B.A., 1971; m. Esther Rose Freilich, June 4, 1974; children—Elliot Bennett, Edward Nathan. With Lesny Devel. Co., Beverly Hills, Calif., 1970—, exec. v.p., 1978—; chmn. bd. Developers Ins. Co., 1979—; vice chmn. bd. Atlas Capital Corp. Mem. Bldg. Industry Assn. (pres. 1980-81), Nat. Assn. Home Builders (dir.). Jewish. Office: PO Box 5526 Beverly Hills CA 90210

LOYND, RICHARD B., corp. exec.; b. 1927; student Cornell U., 1950. With sales and engring. depts. Lincoln Electric Co., 1950-55; asst. to v.p. sales Emerson Electric Co., St. Louis, 1955-60, v.p. electronics and space div., 1960-64, pres. Emerson Builders Products div., 1964-68; v.p. ops. Gould Inc., 1969-71; exec. v.p. operations Eltra Corp., N.Y.C., 1971-73, pres., 1973—, also dir.; group v.p. Allied Chem. Corp., 1979—. Office: PO Box 10135 Morristown NJ 07960

LOZANO, IGNACIO EUGENIO, JR., newspaper publisher, former ambassador; b. San Antonio, Jan. 15, 1927; s. Ignacio Eugenio and Alicia (Elizondo) L.; B.A. in Journalism, U. Notre Dame, 1947; m. Marta Eloisa Navarro, Feb. 24, 1951; children—Leticia Eugenia, Jose Ignacio, Monica Cecilia, Francisco Antonio. Asst. pub. La Opinion, Los Angeles, 1947-53, editor, pub., 1953-76, 77—; pres. Lozano Enterprises, Inc., 1958-76; ambassador to El Salvador, 1976-77; dir. Bank of Am. NT & SA, Pacific Lighting Corp., Walt Disney Prodns. Trustee, Orthopaedic Hosp., Occidental Coll.; bd. dirs. Community TV of So. Calif., Mex.-Am. Legal Def. and Ednl. Fund, Santa Anita Found., Nat. Park Found., Youth Opportunities Found. Mem. Am. Fgn. Service Assn., Calif. Press Assn., Cath. Press Council So. Calif., Inter Am. Press Assn. (dir.), Town Hall of Calif. (dir.), Los Angeles World Affairs Council (dir.), Los Angeles Philharmonic Assn. (dir.), NCCJ (dir. So. Calif. region), Los Angeles C. of C., Sigma Delta Chi. Clubs: Press, California, Transpacific Yacht, Los Angeles Country (Los Angeles); Santa Ana Country, Newport Harbor Yacht; Balboa de Mazatlan. Address: 1436 S Main St Los Angeles CA 90015

LUBIN, ROGER, mgmt. cons.; b. Santa Monica, Calif., Aug. 4, 1938; s. James and Thelma (Brodsky) L.; B.S. with honors, L.I. U., 1960; M.B.A., Pepperdine U., 1974. Program, project analyst Dept. Fin., State of Calif., Sacramento, 1963-69; cons. Charles Wells & Assos., Berkeley, Calif., 1970-71; budget dir. Pasadena (Calif.) Sch. Dist., 1972-73; mgmt. cons. Kapner, Wolfberg & Assos., Los Angeles, 1974-75; asst. city mgr., tech. agt. City of Little Rock, 1976-77; program dir. Public Tech., Inc., Washington, 1978-79; dir. state and local govt. cons. services Hay Assos., Washington, 1980—; pres. Atlantic Heritage Corp., Gaithersburg, Md., 1979—. Pres., Sacramento Young Republicans, 1965-66. Served with U.S. Army, 1960-61. Mem. Tech. Transfer Soc., Western Govtl. Research Assn., Am. Soc. Public Adminstrn., Am. Soc. Polit. and Social Sci., Mensa. Home: 2505 Walter Reed Dr Arlington VA 22206 Office: 1100 17th St NW Washington DC 20036

LUBIN, S. JACK, purchasing adminstr.; b. Hartford, Conn., Dec. 21, 1931; s. Irving Jonathan and Nellie Helen (Rubenstein) L.; B.A. in Pub. Adminstrn., U. Fla., 1954; m. Ruth Clein, Aug. 10, 1954; children—Deborah L. Bonnardel, David Sholem, Michael Zev, Seth Daniel. Chief navigator, chief of procurement, personnel, equipment Dept. Commerce, Miami, Fla., 1959-73; buyer Fla. Power & Light, Miami, 1973-74, supr. purchasing, 1974-80; corp. dir. purchasing DWG Corp., Miami Beach, Fla., 1980—. Pres., Temple Or Olom Brotherhood, Miami, 1969, pres. Temple Or Olom, 1972, 79-81, bd. dirs., 1976—; bd. dirs. Jewish Community Centers, 1974—. Served in USAF, 1955-59, to lt. col. Res. Recipient Outstanding Achievement award U.S. Govt., 1971, Superior Performance award, 1972; Outstanding Acad. Achievement award Wall St. Jour., 1978. Mem. Nat. Assn. Purchasing Mgrs. (dir. 1976, named Mgr. of Yr., So. Fla. chpt. 1979). Home: 2151 SW 87th Ct Miami FL 33165

LUBOW, HOWARD, real estate exec.; b. Bronx, N.Y., Aug. 13, 1927; s. George J. and Annette (Rosenblatt) L.; B.S., Ohio State U., 1951; J.D., Salmon P. Chase Coll. Law, Cin., 1971; m. Henrietta R. Torf, June 15, 1952; children—Cheryl Ann, Jeffrey Samuel, Barry Louis, Judith Gail. Comml. salesman, asst. property mgr. Beerman Realty Co., Dayton, Ohio, 1951-52; comml. and residential salesman George P. Huffman, Inc., Dayton, 1952-57; salesman John L. Stotter & Herb Simon, realtors, Dayton, 1957-60; pres. Lubow Realty Co., Dayton, 1960—, lectr. Ohio State U., Sinclair Community Coll., Dayton; admitted to Ohio bar, 1971. Mem. planning, allocations and research council United Way Dayton, 1980; past bd. dirs., treas. Council Retarded Citizens Montgomery County. Served with AUS, 1945-47. Named VA Broker of Yr., Mem. Nat. Assn. Realtors (dir.), Realtors Nat. Mktg. Inst. (gov., counselor mktg. mgmt. council), Ohio Assn. Realtors (dist. v.p., trustee), Dayton Area Bd. Realtors (dir., past pres. fed. credit union; Realtor of Yr. award 1979), Omega Tau Rho. Jewish. Club: B'nai B'rith. Contbr. articles profl. jours. Home: 6257 Freeport Dr Dayton OH 45415 Office: 2128 E Whipp Rd Dayton OH 45440

LUBY, JOSEPH MATTHEW, investment banking exec.; b. Kansas City, Mo., Jan. 17, 1922; s. William Arthur and Agnes Catherine (Koehler) L.; student U. Kans., 1940-41; m. Rita Phyllis Crooks, Jan. 11, 1947; children—Barbara, Thomas, Daniel, Patrick. Partner, Barret, Fitch, North & Co., Kansas City, 1949-56; v.p. Commerce Trust Co., Kansas City, 1956-60; sr. v.p., dir. Paine, Webber, Jackson, Curtis, Inc., N.Y.C., 1960-77; exec. v.p. H.I. Hennan & Co., Inc., Ft. Lauderdale, Fla., 1977-78; sr. v.p. Shearson Hayden Stone, Inc., Ft. Lauderdale, 1978-79, M. G. Lewis & Co., Inc., investment bankers, Pompano Beach, Fla., 1980—. Mem. Summit Housing Authority, 1975-77. Served to capt. AUS, 1942-46. Mem. Municipal Bond Club N.Y. Home: 2364 NE 30th Ct Lighthouse Point FL 33064 Office: 1620 S Federal Hwy Pompano Beach FL 33062

LUCANDER, HENRY, investment banker; b. Helsinki, Finland, Dec. 21, 1940; came to U.S., 1965, naturalized, 1974; student Groneschе Handelsschule, Hamburg, W. Ger., 1961-62, Pontificia Universidade Católica, Rio de Janeiro, 1963-64; diploma Brazilian Coffee Inst., Rio de Janeiro, 1965; M.B.A., Columbia U., 1968. With Schenkers Internat. Forwarders, Inc., N.Y.C., 1965-66; coffee merchandizer Anderson Clayton & Co., Inc., N.Y.C., 1966-68; with Smith Barney & Co., Inc., N.Y.C., 1968-69, Kidder Peabody & Co., Inc., N.Y.C., 1969-70; with Lucander & Co., Inc., investment bankers, N.Y.C., 1970—, pres., 1972—. Served to lt. Finnish Army, 1960-61. Home: E Mount Airy Rd Croton-on-Hudson NY 10520 Office: Lucander & Co Inc 40 Wall St X538 New York NY 10005

LUCAS, DONALD LEO, pvt. investor; b. Upland, Calif., Mar. 18, 1930; s. Leo J. and Mary G (Schwamm) L.; B.A., Stanford U., 1951, M.B.A., 1953; m. Lygia de Soto Harrison; children—Nancy, Alexandra, Donald A. Asso. corp. finance dept. Smith, Barney & Co., 1956-59; gen. and ltd. partner Draper, Gaither & Anderson, pvt. investors, Palo Alto, Calif., 1959-66; pvt. investor in venture capital activities, Menlo Park, Calif., 1967—; dir. Data Card Corp., HBO & Co., Liconix, Microform Data Systems, Inc., Tri-Data Corp., Relational Software, Inc., Robinton Products, Inc., Tracor Inc. Bd. regents Bellarmine Coll.; bd. regents emeritus U. Santa Clara. Served to 1st lt. Med. Service Corps, U.S. Army, 1953-55. Mem. Stanford U., Stanford U. Grad. Sch. Bus. alumni assns., Zeta Psi. Clubs: Commonwealth (San Francisco); Stanford Buck; Menlo Country, Menlo Circus. Home: 224 Park Ln Atherton CA 94025 Office: 3000 Sand Hill Rd Menlo Park CA 94025

LUCAS, MURRAY CHARLES, investment co. exec.; b. Abilene, Tex., Dec. 26, 1926; s. Robert Oliver and Ruth (Earl) L.; student U. So. Calif.; m. Elsie May Davis, Jan. 1, 1967. Exec. asst. to pres. Martin Wells, Inc.. Los Angeles, 1948-52; self-employed, 1952-60; organizer, gen. sales mgr. Hallmark Industries, Inc., Dallas, 1961-64; v.p. sales, Marble Industries, Houston, 1964; organizer, v.p., gen. mgr. Century Marble, Baton Rouge, La., 1965-66; dist. mgr. Ark. and Okla., Ency. Brit., 1967-75; pres. Video Center, Inc., Houston, 1978-79; mng. dir. Investors Guarantee & Trust Co., Houston, 1979—. Served with USNR, 1944-46. Recipient various sales awards. Republican. Baptist. Office: 9898 Bissonnet St Suite 100 Houston TX 77036

LUCAS, REGINA AGNES, advt. exec.; b. Monongahela, Pa., Oct. 28, 1949; d. George Stnaley and Agnes Lillian Lucas; student U. So. Calif., 1967-68; B.A. in English, Duquesne U., 1971, M.B.A., 1976, postgrad. Grad. Sch. Liberal Studies, 1980—; m. Dennis G. McAteer, July 8, 1972. Asst. buyer Gimbels, Pitts., 1972; account exec. Spenley Newspapers, Pitts., 1972-74; account exec. Observer Pub. Co., Washington, Pa., 1974-78; advt. account exec. Pittsburgher Mag., 1978-80, Pitts. Press, 1980—; guest speaker Washington and Jefferson Coll., Women in Communications seminars and symposia. Mem. Women in Communications (v.p. chpt. 1978-79), AAUW, Motor Bd., Delta Zeta. Home: 864 E McMurray Rd Venetia PA 15367 Office: 34 Blvd of Allies Pittsburgh PA 15230

LUCE, CHARLES FRANKLIN, utilities co. exec.; b. Platteville, Wis., Aug. 29, 1917; s. James Oliver and Wilma Fisher (Grindell) L.; B.A., LL.B., U. Wis., 1941; postgrad. (Sterling fellow), Yale, 1941-42; m. Helen G. Oden, Oct. 24, 1942; children—James O., Christina

Mary, Barbara Anne, Charles Franklin. Admitted to Wis. bar, 1941, Oreg. bar, 1945, Wash. bar, 1946; law clk. Justice Hugo L. Black, U.S. Supreme Ct., 1943-44; gen. practice law, Walla Walla, Wash., 1946-61; adminstr. Bonneville Power Adminstrn., Dept. Interior, Portland, Oreg., 1961-66, under sec. interior, Washington, 1966-67; chmn. bd., chief exec. officer Consol. Edison Co. of N.Y., Inc., 1967—; dir. Met. Life Ins. Co., UAL, Inc., United Air Lines, Inc., GAB Bus. Services, Inc. Trustee Columbia U., The Conf. Bd. Mem. Am., Oreg., Wash., Wis. bar assns., Order Coif, Phi Beta Kappa. Episcopalian. Office: 4 Irving Pl New York NY 10003

LUCE, MELVIN GEOFFREY, ins. co. exec., lawyer; b. N.Y.C., Jan. 25, 1924; s. Arthur and Freda (Corey) L.; B.A., Washington Sq. Coll., 1948; M.A., N.Y. U., 1951, J.D., 1957; m. Dorothy Strasheim, Sept. 4, 1955. Admitted to N.Y. bar, 1961, U.S. Supreme Ct. bar, 1970; asst. firm T.J. Flood, N.Y.C., 1960-68; Gillies & Mahoney, N.Y.C., 1969; asst. sec. Excess & Treaty Mgmt. N.Y.C., 1970-72; v.p. claims, dir. Agency Mgrs., Inc., N.Y.C. and v.p. claims Dominion Ins. Co. Am., N.Y.C., 1972-75; v.p. claims Gerling Global Offices, Inc., 1975—; dir. Seamens & Internat. House, N.Y.C., 1976—, v.p., 1978. Served with USAF, 1943-46. Mem. Am., N.Y. State bar assns., N.Y. State Trial Lawyers Assn., N.Y. County Lawyers Assn., Internat. Assn. Ins. Counsel, Fedn. Ins. Counsel, Reins. Assn. Am., Excess and Surplus Lines Assn., Phi Delta Phi. Lutheran. Club: Drug and Chem. (N.Y.C.). Home: 170 Emerson Ave North Babylon NY 11703 Office: 717 Fifth Ave New York NY 10022

LUCHT, JOHN CHARLES, mgmt. cons., exec. recruiter; b. Reedsburg, Wis., June 1, 1933; s. Carl and Ruth L.; B.S., U. Wis., 1955, LL.B., 1960; m. Catherine Ann Seyler, Dec. 11, 1965. News dir. Sta. WISC, Madison, 1952-55; merchandising dir. Bartell Group, radio and TV stas., Milw., 1955-56; instr. legal writing U. Wis. Law Sch., Madison, 1959-60; admitted to Wis. bar, 1960, N.Y. bar, 1961; TV contracts exec., account exec. J. Walter Thompson Co., N.Y.C., 1960-64; product mgr., new products supr., dir. new products mktg. Bristol Myers Co., N.Y.C., 1964-69; dir. mktg. W.A. Sheaffer Pen Co., Ft. Madison, Iowa, 1969-70; gen. mgr. Tetley Tea div. Squibb Corp., N.Y.C., 1970-71; asso., then v.p. Heidrick & Struggles, N.Y.C., 1971-77; founder, pres. John Lucht Consultancy, Inc., N.Y.C., 1977—; lectr. on bus. mgmt. and exec. selection. Recipient Radio and TV News award H.V. Kaltenborn Found., 1954. Mem. State Bar Wis., Assn. Exec. Recruiting Cons., Phi Beta Kappa, Phi Kappa Phi, Phi Eta Sigma, Phi Delta Phi, Sigma Alpha Epsilon. Clubs: Met., Canadian (N.Y.C.). Home: 54 Riverside Dr New York NY 10024 Office: The Olympic Tower 645 Fifth Ave New York NY 10022

LUCIANO, ROBERT ANTHONY, cons. engr. in packaging machinery; b. Orange, N.J., July 15, 1934; s. Anthony A. and Rose L. (Borrelli) L.; B.S.M.E., Newark Coll. Engring., 1963, M.S., 1966; m. Lorraine C. Chennette, Nov. 27, 1955; children—Susan, Robert A., Lawrence. Design engr. Colgate Palmolive Co., Jersey City, 1960-64; project engr. Ortho Pharm. Corp., Raritan, N.J., 1964-68, mgr. packaging engring., 1964-72; pres. Robert A. Luciano Assos., Lebanon, N.J., 1972—; seminar leader, N.Y. U., 1972-78; instr. Rutgers U., New Brunswick, N.J., 1979—. Pres., Bd. of Health, Warren Twp., 1967-69, mem. planning bd., 1970—. Mem. Packaging Inst., N.J. Soc. Profl. Engrs. (lic. profl. engr.), Pi Tau Sigma. Editor, Modern Packaging, 1975-78; patentee in field; contbr. articles to profl. jours. Address: RD 2 Bissell Rd Lebanon NJ 08833

LUCIANO, SALVATORE PETER, research and devel. co. exec.; b. Boston, Jan. 26, 1930; s. Antonio and Helen Virginia (Ippolito) L.; B.S., Northeastern U., 1952; postgrad. Boston U., 1955; m. Florence Bergamasco, July 13, 1952; children—Richard Louis, Cheryl A. Auditor, Touche Ross & Co., 1954-55; supervisory auditor Dept. Def., 1955-60; controller Allied Research Assos., 1960-61; v.p. Bolt Beranek and Newman Inc., Cambridge, Mass., 1961—; dir. East Boston Savs. Bank. Served with U.S. Army, 1952-54. Registered public acct., Mass. Mem. Nat. Assn. Accts., Fin. Execs. Inst., Assn. Govt. Accts., Nat. Contract Mgmt. Assn., Cambridge C. of C. (v.p., dir. 1978—). Club: Rotary (dir.) (Cambridge). Home: 8 Rodney Rd Peabody MA 01960 Office: 50 Moulton St Cambridge MA 02138

LUCKEN, JACK AUGUSTUS, economist, educator; b. London, June 27, 1929; came to U.S., 1964, naturalized, 1971; s. Jack Augustus and Edith Florence (Burgess) L.; B.Sc. in Physics, King's Coll., U. London, 1952, M.Sc. in Applied Math., 1955; Ph.D. in Econs., Boston Coll., 1972; children—Rosalind Jane, Andrew John. Research physicist Elec. and Musical Industries, Ltd., Hayes, Eng., 1952-64; research engr. Microwave Assos., Inc., Burlington, Mass., 1964-68; asst. prof. Grad. Sch. Mgmt., Rutgers U., Newark, 1972-76, asso. prof., 1976—; cons. economist. Served with Royal Navy, 1947-49. Mem. Royal Econ. Soc. (life), Am. Econ. Assn. (life), Eastern Econ. Assn. (life), Econometric Soc., Am. Statis. Assn. Contbr. articles to various publs. Home: 244 Conway Ct South Orange NJ 07079 Office: Grad Sch Mgmt Rutgers U 92 New St Newark NJ 07102

LUCKER, GILES WESLEY, real estate broker; b. Wheeling, W.Va., Nov. 22, 1934; s. Walter B. and Maude Ann (Leyland) L.; student Wittenberg U., 1934-35; m. Mary A. Baldy, Jan. 23, 1947; 1 dau., Linda L. (Mrs. Thomas McCord Paris). Owner, mgr. Lucker Realty Co., Mpls., 1947—; pres. Fairview Realty & Investment Co., Mpls., 1955—, Trenton Properties, Mpls., 1969—, Equitable Mortgage Investment Co., Mpls., 1963—, Wesley Investment Co., 1975—, Rekcul Investment Co., 1975—. Served with C.E. AUS, 1943-46. Decorated Purple Heart. Mem. Soc. Exchange Counselors, Mpls. Bd. Realtors, Minn. Property Exchangers, Uptown Business Men's Assn., Nat. Inst. Certified Bus. Counselors. Republican. Lutheran. Clubs: Masons, Shriners, K.T. Home: 4120 Parklawn Ave Edina MN 55435 Office: 1406 W Lake St Minneapolis MN 55408

LUCKEY, GEORGE PAUL, ret. business exec.; b. Ontario, Calif., Apr. 4, 1891; s. George W.A. and Bertha (Musson) L.; A.B., U. Nebr., 1910, M.A., 1912, D.Engring. (hon.), 1952; postgrad. U. Goettingen, Germany, 1912-14; m. Olive Lehmer, July 12, 1922; children—George William, Helen L. Staff, Mt. Wilson Solar Obs., Pasadena, Calif., 1915; Charles E. Brush fellow Nela Research Lab., Cleve., 1916; physicist Westinghouse Research Lab., East Pittsburgh, Pa., 1917-1919-20; physicist, instrument and equipment sect. McCook Field, Dayton, Ohio, 1920-26, asst. chief equipment sect., 1926-27; with Hamilton Watch Co., Lancaster, Pa., 1927-54, head tachometer div., 1927-30, dir. research, asst. gen. supt., 1930-33, factory mgr., 1933-40, v.p. charge mfg., 1940-52, pres., chmn. bd. dirs., 1952-54, dir., 1947-54, ret., 1954. Mem. adv. bd. Phila. Ordnance Dist., 1950-54. Served with AC, U.S. Army, 1918. Recipient certificate of appreciation Joint Chiefs of Staff, 1951. Mem. A.A.A.S., Am. Ordnance Assn., Horological Inst. Am. (hon.), Am. Phys. Soc., Winter Park C. of C., Sigma Xi. Clubs: Orlando Country; University (Winter Park, Fla.). Patentee in field. Home: 461 Virginia Dr Winter Park FL 32789

LUCKHARDT, STUART WALTER, livestock breeder exec.; b. New Hamburg, Ont., Can., Sept. 9, 1926; s. Lorne Lincoln and Eva June (Kennel) L.; 1st class cert. Stratford (Ont.) Tchrs. Coll., 1947; m. Elfrieda Elizabeth Kuhl, July 31, 1948; children—Samuel, Peter, John, James, Valerie, Mark, Heather. Prin. rural schs., 1947-60; salesman Excelsior Life Co., Linwood, Ont., 1948-52, Cooperators Ins. Co., Breslau, Ont., 1953-61; pres. Luckholm Holsteins Ltd., Owen Sound, Ont., 1971—; dir. United Coop. of Ont.; vice chmn. Grey-Bruce Farm Labour Pool, 1979. Chmn. council Our Saviours Luth. Ch., 1974. Mem. Ont. Fedn. Agr., Ont. Plowman's Assn. (dir. 1980—). Address: Rural Route 6 Owen Sound ON N4K 5N8 Canada

LUCKING, BERNARD LOUIS, ins. co. exec.; b. St. Paul, Nov. 20, 1941; s. Bernard August and Florence Lucy (Schaffer) L.; B.S., U. Minn., 1968; m. Margaret Alice Wildman, June 30, 1980; children—Laura, Jerome, Elizabeth, James, Lynn, Erika Vanderwulp. Asst. treas. Gt. No. Ry. Clks. Credit Union, St. Paul, 1962-68; with Aetna Life & Casualty Ins. Co., various locations, 1968—, supr., Toledo, 1973-75, mgr., Toledo, 1975-78, mgr., Seattle, 1978—. Vice pres. Old Orchard PTA, 1975-76, pres., 1976-77, 77-78. Mem. Health Ins. Assn. Am. (dir. N.W. Ohio consumer and pub. relations). Home: 19615 SE 23d St Issaquah WA 98027 Office: 900 Washington Bldg Seattle WA 98101

LUCKMAN, STANLEY, poultry co. exec.; b. N.Y.C., Dec. 25, 1922; s. Morris and Anna (Brown) L.; student Kans. State U., 1940-42; B.S. in Commerce and Fin., Bucknell U., 1948; m. Rosalyn Shapiro, Aug. 20, 1949; 1 daau., Elizabeth. Dir. research and devel. Zion Kosher Provisions Co. N.Y.C., 1966-70; v.p., dir. research and devel. Empire Kosher Poultry, Inc., Mifflintown, Pa., 1970—; cons. in field. Served as lt. (j.g.) USN, 1942-46; ETO. Recipient merit award Union Carbide Corp.; Canner Packer award New Product Contest, 1977. Mem. Inst. Food Technologists, N.Y. Acad. Scis., Packaging Inst. U.S.A., Nat. Geog. Soc., Kennedy Center for Performing Arts, Audubon Soc., Met. Opera Guild, Smithsonian Inst., Sigma Alpha Mu. Jewish. Clubs: Hershey Racquet, B'nai B'rith. Home: 2853 Vista Circle Camp Hill PA 17011 Office: RD 3 PO Box 165 Mifflintown PA 17059

LUDDEN, JOHN DAVID, computer co. mktg. exec.; b. Cleve., Jan. 17, 1932; s. John C. and Georgia L. L.; B.S.B.A. summa cum laude (Simon Lazarus scholar, Gen. Elec. scholar), Ohio State U., 1954; postgrad. U. Chgo., 1974; m. Marilyn A. Schlueter, Sept. 5, 1953; children—Stephen, Robert, James, Thomas, Theresa, Suzanne. Mgr. fin. analysis new bus. devel. ops. Gen. Electric Co., Schenectady, N.Y., 1964-68, mgr. bus. analysis Info. Systems div., Phoenix, 1968-70; dir. bus. analysis N. Am. ops. Honeywell Info. Systems, Inc., Waltham, Mass., 1970-73; controller central mktg. ops., Chgo., 1973-75, controller field engring. div., Newton, Mass., 1975-78; v.p. mktg. services Prime Computer, Inc., Wellesley, Mass., 1978—. Served with U.S. Army, 1955-56. Recipient award Ohio Soc. C.P.A.'s, 1953. Mem. Nat. Commerce Honor Soc. Office: Prime Park Natick MA 01760

LÜDERS, GERD, elec. engr.; b. Thorn, Germany, Dec. 21, 1943; s. Gerhard and Anni (Albrecht) L.; Civil Elec. Engr., U. Chile, 1967; M.S., Yale U., 1971, M.Phil., 1972, Ph.D., 1973; postgrad. Boston U., 1974—; m. Carmen Fernández, Oct. 19, 1968. Analyst engr. Empresa Nacional de Electr., Santiago, Chile, 1968-70; asst. prof. U. Chile, 1970; devel. engr. Pub. Service Electric & Gas Co., Newark, 1971; devel. engr. Brown Boveri & Cie, Mannheim, W. Ger., 1972; sr. project engr. Analytic Scis. Corp., Reading, Mass., 1974-79, div. staff analyst, 1979—. IBM fellow, 1972-73. Mem. Chilean Soc. Profl. Engrs., IEEE, Power Systems Soc., Control Systems Soc. Contbr. articles to profl. jours. Home: 25 Landers Rd Reading MA 01867 Office: 6 Jacob Way Reading MA 01867

LUDLAM, JAMES EDWARD, III (TED), ins. co. exec.; b. Los Angeles, Jan. 9, 1943; s. James Edward and Jane Bremen (Hyde) L.; B.A. in Econs., Claremont Men's Coll., 1965; M.B.A., U. So. Calif., 1967; m. Patricia McVee, Apr. 12, 1969; children—James Edward IV, Erin Catherine. With Prudential Ins. Co. Am., Florham Park, N.J., 1968—, v.p. group pensions, 1979—. Democrat. Presbyterian. Home: 12 Beech Ct Chatham Township NJ 07928 Office: Prudential Ins Co Am 71 Hanover Rd Florham Park NJ 07932

LUDWIG, JAY LEWIS, fin. exec.; b. Bklyn., Dec. 17, 1941; s. Michael William and Sylvia (Lesser) L.; B.S. in Acctg., Bklyn. Coll., 1963; M.B.A., Fairleigh Dickinson U., 1966; m. Helene Milden, Mar. 3, 1963; children—Wendy Michelle, Brian Keith. With Schering-Plough Corp., Kenilworth, N.J., 1964—, treas., internat. div., 1977—; dir. fin. Essex Nippon K.K., Osaka, Japan, 1967-70; regional fin. mgr. for Far East, Essex Asia, Hong Kong, 1971-76. Office: 2000 Galloping Hill Rd Kenilworth NJ 07033

LUDWIG, MYLES ERIC, publisher; b. Bklyn., Apr. 12, 1942; s. Solomon and Muriel (Levine) L.; student U. Conn., 1961; B.A., U. N.C., Chapel Hill, 1967, M.A. in Mass Communications, 1969; m. Hendrieka Van Riper, Aug. 3, 1963 (div. 1969); 1 dau., Lindsay Anne; m. 2d, Marsha Clayton Daniel, May 15, 1970 (div. 1976). Editorial dir. Art Direction mag., N.Y.C., 1970-73; creative dir. Penthouse-Viva Internat., N.Y.C., 1973-75; cons. art dir. Larry Flynt Publs., Velvet mag.; design dir. You mag., N.Y.C., 1976-77; creative dir. Swank mag., N.Y.C., 1978—; co-pub., editorial dir. Olympic, ofcl. mag. of 13th Winter Olympics, 1980; lectr. N.Y. Inst. Advt., CCNY. Recipient Thomas Wolfe Meml. award, 1966, others. Mem. Soc. Publ. Designers (v.p.). Author: A Blaze of Passion, 1968; Golem, 1970; Creativity I, 1971; The Detectives, 1978. Address: 20 Waterside Plaza New York NY 10010

LUDWIG, ROBERT CARL, recording co. exec.; b. Savannah, Ga., Dec. 11, 1944; s. Robert Forcier and Beatrice (McClellan) L.; B.Mus., Eastman Sch. Music, Rochester, N.Y., 1966, postgrad., 1967; children—Erika Lynne, Alexandra A. Announcer, Sta. WBBF-FM, Rochester, 1966; prin. trumpet Utica (N.Y.) Symphony Orch., 1967; rec. engr. A&R Rec. Co., N.Y.C., 1968; v.p. Sterling Sound, Inc., N.Y.C., 1969; exec. v.p., chief engr. Masterdisk Corp., N.Y.C., 1976—; guest tchr. Inst. Audio Research. Receipient Grammy award, over 100 Gold and Platinum records. Mem. Audi-Engring. Soc. Home: 60 W 66th St New York NY 10023 Office: Masterdisk Corp 16 W 61st St New York NY 10023

LUEDECKE, WILLIAM HENRY, engring. co. exec.; b. Pittsburg, Tex., Apr. 5, 1918; s. Henry Herman and Lula May (Abernathy) L.; B.S., U. Tex., 1940; m. Mary Anne Copeland, June 3, 1939; children—William Henry, John Copeland. Mech. engr. Columbian Gasoline Corp., Monroe, La., 1940-41; supr. shipbldg., mech. engr. USN, Orange, Tex., 1941-42; gen. supr. factory mgrs. N. Am. Aviation Co., Dallas, 1944-46; mech. engr., charge Chrysler Airtemp. div. Chrysler Corp., Los Angeles, 1946-50; owner Luedecke Engring. Co., Austin, Tex., 1950—, also Luedecke Investment Co.; chmn. bd. dirs. Mut. Savs. Instn., Austin; dir. City Nat. Bank, Austin, 1st Tex. Fin. Corp., Dallas. Bd. dirs. Travis County Heart Fund, Austin YMCA. Named Man of Year, Tex. Barbed Wire Collectors Assn.; registered profl. engr., Tex. Mem. Am. Soc. Heating, Refrigerating and Air Conditioning Engrs. (dir., pres. Austin chpt.), Tex., Nat. socs. profl. engrs., C. of C., Econ. Devel. Council, Better Bus. Bur., Nat. Fedn. Ind. Bus. (nat. adv. council). Lutheran. Clubs: Rotary, Westwood Country (treas., dir.). Home: 3403 Foothills Pkwy Austin TX 78731 Office: 1007 W 34th St Austin TX 78705

LUERSSEN, FRANK WONSON, steel co. exec.; b. Reading, Pa., Aug. 14, 1927; s. George V. and Mary Ann (Swoyer) L.; B.S. in Physics, Pa., State U., 1950; M.S. in Metall. Engring., Lehigh U., 1951; m. Joan M. Schlosser, June 17, 1950; children—Thomas, Mary Ellen, Catherine, Susan, Ann. Metallurgist research and devel. div. Inland Steel Co., East Chicago, Ind., 1952-54, mgr. various positions, 1954-64, mgr. research, 1964-68, v.p. research, 1968-77, v.p. steel mfg., 1977-78, pres., 1978—. Trustee, Calumet Coll., Whiting, Ind., 1972—; v.p., dir. Munster (Ind.) Med. Research Found., 1972—; trustee, sec., treas. Munster Sch. Bd., 1957-66. Served with USNR, 1945-47. Fellow Am. Soc. Metals, Nat. Acad. Engring.; mem. AIME, Am. Iron and Steel Inst., Metals Soc. Gt. Britain. Author various articles on steelmaking tech. Office: Inland Steel Co 30 W Monroe St Chicago IL 60603*

LUETGER, CHARLES LINDBERGH, motor common carrier co. exec.; b. Burlington, Iowa, Oct. 29, 1927; s. Louis Edward and Flossie Ella (McDaniel) L.; B.S. in Bus. Adminstrn., Century U., Beverly Hills, Calif.; m. Katheryn Anne Kennedy, Feb. 14, 1950; children—Theresa, Steven, Timothy, Matthew. With BN Transport, Inc., Burlington, Iowa, 1946-49, Galesburg, Ill., 1949-73, v.p. mgmt. services, Denver, 1973-78, v.p. adminstrn., 1978—; exec. v.p., gen. mgr. Hart Motor Express, Inc., St. Paul, 1978—; also dir. Mem. Am. Mgmt. Assn., Assn. Computer Users, Adminstrv. Mgmt. Assn. Home: 4171 S Verbena St Denver CO 80237 Office: 6775 E Evans Ave Denver CO 80222

LUFTGLASS, MURRAY ARNOLD, mfg. co. exec.; b. Bklyn., Jan. 2, 1931; s. Harry and Pauline (Yaged) L.; B.S., Ill. Inst. Tech., 1952; M.S., U. So. Calif., 1959; M.B.A., U. Conn., 1972; m. Naomi Stessel, Sept. 14, 1952; children—Paula Jean, Bryan Keith, Robert Andrew, Richard Eric. Project leader Shell Chem. Co., Torrance, Calif., 1955-60, market devel., N.Y.C., 1960-61, lab. and tech. dir., Wallingford, Conn., 1961-64, product devel. group leader, Torrance, 1964-66, process devel. sr. engr., N.Y.C., 1966-67, mgr. thermoplastic rubber operations, 1967-69; asst. gen. mgr. Westchester Plastics div. Ametek, Inc., Mamaroneck, N.Y., 1969-75; dir. corp. devel. Ametek, Inc., N.Y.C., 1975-76, v.p., 1976—; Instr. survey modern plastics Soc. Plastics Industry, Los Angeles. Bd. dirs. Sunny Hill Children's Center. Served to lt. (j.g.) USN, 1952-55. Mem. NAM, Soc. Plastics Industry, Assn. Corp. Growth, Soc. Plastics Engrs., Tau Beta Pi, Beta Gamma Sigma, Phi Lambda Upsilon. Club: University (N.Y.C.). Contbr. articles to profl. jours., publs. Patentee in field. Home: Hickory Pass Bedford Village NY 10506 Office: 410 Park Ave New York NY 10022

LUHRS, HENRY RIC, toy mfg. co. exec.; b. Chambersburg, Pa., Mar. 22, 1931; s. Henry E. and Pearl (Beistle) L.; B.A., Gettysburg Coll., 1953; m. Grace Barnhart, June 12, 1973; children by previous marriage—Stephen Frederick, Christine Michelle, Terri Ann, Patricia Denise. With The Beistle Co., Shippensburg, Pa., 1948—, pres., 1962—, chmn., 1978—; dir. Commonwealth Nat. Bank; gemologist, 1977—; owner Luhrs Gem Testing Lab., 1977—, Luhrs Jewelry, 1976—. Pres. Shippensburg Public Library, 1964-66, 70-72, 76-78, bd. dirs., 1963—; pres. Community Chest, 1965, dir., 1963-72; pres. Shippensburg Area Devel. Corp., 1966-72; bd. dirs., trustee Carlisle (Pa.) Hosp., 1967-71, Chambersburg (Pa.) Hosp., 1969-75; mem. consumer advisor council Capital Blue Cross, 1976-78. Served to capt. USAF, 1953-59. Mem. Shippensburg Hist. Soc. (dir. 1968), Nat. Sojourners, SAR (life), C. of C. (pres. 1965, dir. 1964-65), Toy Mfrs. Assn. (dir. 1968-71), Nat. Small Businessmen's Assn., Nat. Rifle Assn. Am., Shippensburg Fish and Game Assn. (pres. 1963), Am. Legion. Lutheran. Mason (32 deg., K.T., Shriner), Elk. Clubs: Industrial Management, York of Printing House Craftsmen. Home: Box B Shippensburg PA 17257 Office: 14-18 E Orange St Shippensburg PA 17257

LUIGS, CHARLES RUSSELL, business exec.; b. Evansville, Ind., Apr. 4, 1933; s. Charles Anthony and Agnes (Russell) L.; student St. Edwards U., 1951-52; B.S. in Petroleum Engring., U. Tex., 1957; m. Mary M. McClaine, Sept. 7, 1957; children—Charles Edwin, James Russell, Carol Lynn, Susan Nadine, Michael Alan. With U.S. Industries, various locations, 1957-76, v.p., 1969, exec. v.p., 1971-74, pres., 1974-76, dir., 1971-76; pres., chief exec. officer, dir. Global Marine, Inc., 1977—. Mem. Nat. Soc. Profl. Engrs., Am. Inst. Mining Metall. and Petroleum Engrs., Internat. Assn. Drilling Contractors (dir. 1978—). Home: 31 Willowron St Houston TX 77024 Office: 811 W 7th St Los Angeles CA 90017 also 7500 San Felipe Suite 1000 Houston TX 77063

LUING, LARRY L., ednl. adminstr.; b. Rhodes, Iowa, Apr. 24, 1930; s. Donald A. and Ethel I. (Dodd) L.; B.S. with honors, U. Iowa, 1951; m. Mildred Joan Bona, Sept. 19, 1959; children—Kevin, Larry, Randy Brent, Timothy Donald, Brian Dodd. Asst. buyer Denver Dry Goods, 1953-55; mgr. collegiate bus. edn. dept. McGraw-Hill, Inc., N.Y.C., 1955-65; pres. The Berkeley Schs., Little Falls, N.J., 1965—. Mem. exec. bd. Westchester (N.Y.) Better Bus. Bur., 1969-71. Served with U.S. Army, 1951-53. Mem. N.J. Bus. Edn. Assn. (pres. 1969-70), Assn. Ind. Colls. and Schs., Nat. Bus. Edn. Assn., Eastern Bus. Edn. Assn. (pres. 1977-78, dir. 1971-73, 76—), United Bus. Schs. Assn. (Disting. Service award 1968). Republican. Office: Drawer F Little Falls NJ 07424

LUKASH, SETH MAYER, mfg. co. exec.; b. N.Y.C., Apr. 19, 1946; s. Alvin and Selina (Berlowitz) L.; B.B.A., U. Miami, 1967. With Carter, Berlin, Weil, N.Y.C., 1968-73; pres. S.M.L. Assos., N.Y.C., 1973-75; with Hi-G, Inc., Windsor Locks, Conn., 1975—, dir., 1978—, sr. vp., 1979—. Vice pres. Selina Lukash Found. Mem. Assn. Corp. Growth, Young Men's Philanthropic Soc. Clubs: Jockey, Cricket, Grove Isle, Turnberry Yacht and Racquet (Miami, Fla.); Curzon House (London). Home: 10 Ironwood Ln West Hartford CT 06117 Office: 580 Spring St Windsor Locks CT 06096

LUKE, DAVID LINCOLN, III, paper co. exec.; b. Tyrone, Pa., July 25, 1923; s. David Lincoln and Priscilla Warren(Silver) L.; B.A., Yale U., 1945; LL.D. (hon.), Juniata Coll., 1967, Lawrence U., 1976; m. Fanny R. Curtis, June 11, 1955. Mem. staff Arthur Andersen & Co., 1948-49, Am. Research & Devel. Corp., Boston, 1949-52; with Westvaco Corp., N.Y.C., 1952—, exec. v.p., 1957-62, pres., 1962-80, chief exec. officer, 1963-80, chmn. bd., chief exec. officer, 1980—, also dir.; dir. B.F. Goodrich Co., Irving Bank Corp., Irving Trust Co., Clupak Inc. Trustee, past chmn. bd. Hotchkiss Sch., Lakeville, Conn.; bd. dirs. Josiah Macy Jr. Found., N.Y.C. Served to capt. USMCR, 1942-43. Mem. Am. Paper Inst. (chmn. 1971-73, trustee 1966—, exec. com. 1969—), Inst. Paper Chemistry (chmn. 1973-75, trustee 1968—, exec. com. 1970—). Clubs: Links, Union League (N.Y.C.); Piping Rock (Locust Valley, N.Y.); Seawanhaka Corinthian Yacht (Oyster Bay, N.Y.); Megantic Fish and Game Corp (Coburn Gore, Maine). Office: 299 Park Ave New York NY 10017

LUKE, DOUGLAS SIGLER, JR., securities co. exec.; b. Middletown, N.Y., Oct. 1, 1941; s. Douglas Sigler and Joanne (Benton) L.; B.A., U. Va., 1964; M.B.A., Darden Grad. Sch., 1966; children—Haven Roosevelt, David Russell, Lindsay Hall. Partner, K.S. Sweet Assos., Columbus, Ohio and Phila., 1972-74; partner, exec. v.p. Vanderkloot, Luke & Assos., Columbus and N.Y., 1975-76; chmn., pres. Central Ohio Beverage Co., Columbus, 1976-80; v.p. New Court Securities Corp., N.Y.C., 1979—; dir. Burkhart Petroleum Corp; chmn., dir. Santa Rosa Enterprises. Bd. dirs. condrs. com. Columbus Symphony Orch., to 1973, Young Republicans Ohio, to 1975; trustee Columbus Acad., to 1979. Republican. Episcopalian.

Clubs: Brook (N.Y.C.); Rocky Fork Hunt and Country (Columbus); Seabrook Island (Charleston). Home: 1172 Park Ave New York NY 10028 Office: New Court Securities Corp 1 Rockefeller Plaza New York NY 10020

LUKE, STANLEY, diversified mfg. co. exec.; b. Butler, N.J., Dec. 16, 1913; s. George W. and Viola (Osborne) L.; A.B., Union Coll., Schenectady, 1939; postgrad. in law and mgmt. Harvard U., Ind. U., 1939-42, Cornell U., 1943; m. Ethel M. Kipp, Sept. 11, 1937; 1 dau., Linda Ann Luke Trismen. Instr. mgmt. Ohio State U., 1943-44, Notre Dame U., 1944-45; with ITT, 1945—, asst. v.p., 1952-63, v.p., 1963-67, sr. v.p., 1967-76, exec. v.p., 1976—; dir. Bell & Gossett Corp., Gen. Controls Co., Cannon Electric Co., Gilfillan Inc., Aetna Fin. Co., Jabsco Pumpi Co., Electro Physics Labs., Jaspen Blackburn Corp., Pa. Glass Sand Corp., ITT Continental Baking Co., ITT Courier Terminal Systems Inc., OM Scott & Sons Co. Republican. Mem. Reformed Ch. Office: 320 Park Ave ITT New York NY 10022

LUKE, WARREN K. K., investment co. exec.; b. Honolulu, May 22, 1944; s. Kan Jung and Beatrice (Lum) L.; B.S. in Bus. Adminstrn., Babson Inst. Bus. Adminstrn., 1966; M.B.A., Harvard U., 1970; m. Carolyn Ching, 1970; children—Kevin James, Catherine, Bryan, Joanne. Pres., dir. Indsl. Investors, Inc., Honolulu, 1970—; exec. v.p., dir. Hawaii Nat. Bank, Honolulu, 1972—; v.p., dir. Bancard Assn. Hawaii Inc., 1976—; treas., dir. Computer Systems Internat. Inc.; v.p., sec., dir. KJL, Inc., Honolulu, 1974—; v.p., treas., dir. Loyalty Devel. Co., Ltd., Honolulu, 1970—; pres., dir. Mgmt. Resources Cons., Inc., Honolulu, 1973—; dir. Loyalty Enterprises, Ltd., Honolulu, Loyalty Ins. Co., Ltd., Honolulu, Barclay Corp., Honolulu. Vice pres. Hawaii State chpt. ARC, 1972-77, pres., 1977-78, mem. Pacific div. adv. council, chmn. western field office adv. council, 1979-80; treas., exec. com. mem. Community Scholarship Program, Honolulu, 1974—; mem. Gov.'s Task Force Jobs for Vets., 1975-76; trustee Honolulu Jr. Acad., 1979—, Hawaiian Meml. Park Cemetery Assn., Honolulu, 1975; mem. deans adv. council U. Hawaii Coll. Bus. Adminstrn., 1975—. Mem. Navy League U.S. (treas. Honolulu council 1974-76, dir. 1973-76, adv. com. 1977—), Chinese C. of C. (dir. 1980—). Office: 84 N King St Honolulu HI 96817

LUKOW, NEIL BURTON, institutional food service exec.; b. Bklyn., July 5, 1933; s. Nat and Ada (Gold) L.; Asso. in Applied Scis., Paul Smiths Coll., 1953; B.S., Fla. State U., 1955; M.B.A., U. Md., 1959; m. Elaine Logvin, May 19, 1956; children—Brian, Jo-Ann and Cindi (twins). Pres., Cookies Unltd. Inc., Amityville, N.Y., 1961—; food service dir. Wantagh (N.Y.) pub. schs., 1960—; pres. Facul-Tea & Coffee Service, Inc., Amityville, 1973—; tchr. food service courses. Served with U.S. Army, 1956-58. Mem. L.I. Food Service Execs. Assn. (v.p. 1977-78, scholarship chmn. 1968-78, pres. 1979-80, Food Service Exec. of Year 1965), Sch. Lunch Dirs. Assn. (past pres.), Tau Epsilon Phi. Jewish. Clubs: Carefree Tennis, Jaguar of N. Am. Home: 1621 James St Merrick NY 11566 Office: 672 Albany Ave Amityville NY 11701

LULL, ROBERT ADELBERT, mgmt. cons.; b. North Wales, Pa., June 18, 1931; s. Richard A. and Marybelle (Brooks) L.; evening student Russell Sage Coll., Albany, N.Y., 1954-57; m. Berta T. Fett; children—Michael T., Robert G., Lynn S., Patrick P.; m. 2d, Maria Campione, Sept. 26, 1970. Chief engr. Alexander Proudfoot Co., Chgo., 1956-60; v.p. Handley-Brooks Co., Westwood, N.J., 1960-66; pres., chief exec. officer Brooks Internat. Corp., Montvale, N.J., 1966—. Served with USN, 1950-54. Mem. Inst. Dirs. (London), Assn. Productivity Specialists (chmn.), Nat. Council Profl. Service Firms (dir.), Pres.'s Assn. Home: 30 Amy Ct Woodcliff Lake NJ 07675 Office: 50 Craig Rd Montvale NJ 07645

LUM, HOMER C., JR., hotel exec.; b. DuBois, Pa., Feb. 27, 1937; s. Homer C. and Aleda Viola (Abrahamson) L.; student pub. sch., N. Tonawanda, N.Y.; grad. Lewis Hotel Sch., Washington, 1962; m. June Lynne Kearly, Aug. 14, 1965; children—Keith Homer, Troy Michael. Mgmt. cons. R.B.C., Rochester, N.Y., 1968-69; gen. mgr. Gotham Motor Inn, Syracuse, N.Y., 1969-70, Horizon Hotel, Utica, N.Y., 1970-71; food and beverage dir. Sheraton Inn Hopkins, Cleve., 1971-74; dir. food and beverage Motor Inn div. Hospitality Motor Inns, Cleve., 1974-77; dir. food and beverage ops. analyis Harpendau Hotels, Cin.; mem. adv. panel Restaurant Bus. Mag., Cleve., 1974-76. Mem. Cleve. State Adv. Com. Continuing Edn., 1971-74. Served with USMC, 1955-58. Mem. Nat. Restaurant Assn. Presbyterian. Clubs: Elks, Masons. Home: 7444 Chinook Dr West Chester OH 45069 Office: Harpenau Enterprises 8001 Reading Rd Cincinnati OH 45237

LUMADUE, DONALD DEAN, hobby and crafts exec.; b. El Reno, Okla., Sept. 30, 1938; s. Harry Basil and Muriel Ellen (Craven) L.; student U.S. Coast Guard Acad., 1956-57; m. Joyce Anne Hayes, June 28, 1958; children—Dawnia, Donald, Robert, Ronald. Lab. technician Charles Pfizer & Co., Groton, Conn., 1957-60; indsl. engr. Sonoco Products, Mystic, Conn., 1960-67; partner Joydon's, New London, Conn., 1958—, House of Leisure, New London, 1965—; Hobby Crafts, New London, 1968—; pres. NEI, Inc., New London, 1968—. Mem. New Eng. (pres. 1973-74), Am. (dir. wholesaler bd. 1974—, chmn. wholesaler nat. bd. 1976-77, 77-78), hobby industry assns., Nat. Assn. Wholesalers (trustee 1976—), Wholesalers of Hobby Industry Assn. Am. (dir.), Indsl. Mgmt. Club S.E. Conn. (pres. 1961-62, 77-78). Office: 12-18 Masonic St New London CT 06320

LUMPKIN, ROBERT PIERCE, author, educator; b. Culpeper, Va., Mar. 16, 1913; s. Robert Pierce and Inez (King) L.; B.A., U. Richmond, 1948; M.A., Harvard U., 1950, Ph.D., 1955; m. Katherine Willis Green, Apr. 4, 1947; children—Margaret Ruth Lumpkin Forrester, Robert Pierce, Willis Green, Richard King. Sr. economist Fed. Res. Bank of Richmond, 1952-60; prof., chmn. econs. dept. Va. Commonwealth U., 1961-68; cons. economist Bank of Va., 1960-68; sr. v.p. Bank of Va. Co., Richmond, 1968-78; vis. prof. econs. U. Richmond, 1978—. Mem. Gov.'s Commn. on Port Unification, 1969, Gov.'s Commn. on Port Financing, 1971. Bd. dirs., treas. Richmond Better Bus. Bur., 1974-77; chmn. Henrico (Va.) Indsl. Devel. Authority; mem. Va. Advisory Commn. Career Edn. Served with AUS, 1942-46. Mem. Va. C. of C. (chmn. edn. com.). Club: Harvard of Va. Author: (with Harold Leith) Economics USA, 1968. Investments editor: United States Banker, 1977—. Home: 8414 Yolanda Rd Richmond VA 23229

LUNDEEN, ROBERT WEST, chem. engr.; b. Astoria, Oreg., June 25, 1921; s. Arthur Robert and Margaret Florence (West) L.; B.S., Oreg. State U., 1942; student Inst. Meteorology, U. Chgo., 1942-43; m. Betty Charles Anderson, Dec. 26, 1942; children—John Walter, Peter Bruce, Nancy Patricia. Research and devel. engr. Dow Chem. Co., Pittsburg, Calif., 1946-51, process design, project supr., 1951-56, mgr. planning Western div., 1956-61, mem. staff Dow Chem. Internat., Midland, Mich., 1961-63, dir. bus. devel., 1963-66, pres. Dow Chemical Pacific, Hong Kong, 1966-78, pres. Dow Chem. Latin America, 1978, exec. vice-pres. The Dow Chem. Co., Midland, Mich., 1978—, also dir.; bd. dirs. Dowell Schlumberger, Asahi-Dow Ltd., Chemical Bank & Trust Co. of Midland. Chmn., Concord (Calif.) City Planning Commn., 1960-61. Served with USAAF, 1942-46. Decorated Bronze Star medal. Mem. Am. Inst. Chem. Engrs., Am. Chem. Soc., Soc. Chem. Industry. Republican. Clubs: Midland Country, Hong Kong Club, Royal Hong Kong Yacht. Office: 2030 Dow Center Midland MI 48640

LUNDEGARD, JOHN THOMAS, merchandising exec.; b. Mpls., June 9, 1931; s. Harold George and Gertrude (Stene) L.; B.B.A., U. Minn., 1953; P.M.D., Harvard U. Grad Sch. Bus., 1965; m. Lucy Liggett, Aug. 8, 1953; children—Lucy Ann, David Liggett. From exec. asst. to chmn. bd. Dayton Hudson Corp., Mpls., 1956-68; various positions to pres., chief exec. officer Venture Stores May Dept. Stores, St. Louis, 1968-79; chmn. bd., chief exec. officer Western Auto Supply Co., Kansas City, Mo., 1979—. Planner Stanford Sch. Bus. Served with AUS, 1953-56. Mem. Am. Mgmt. Assn. (pres.'s roundtable). Office: Western Auto Supply Co 2107 Grand Ave Kansas City MO 64108

LUNDQUIST, LOUIS M., stockbroker; b. Tulsa, Oct. 11, 1928; s. Harry M. and G. Erla (Bartlett) L.; B.A., U. Tulsa, 1950, B.S. in Bus. Adminstrn., 1951; M.B.A., Stanford U., 1956; m. Joegil Krogh, Jan. 4, 1958; children—David, Jeannie. Security analyst Pacific Northwest Co., Seattle, 1956-63, security analyst/salesman, 1963-67; with Kidder, Peabody & Co., Seattle, 1967—, stockbroker/portfolio mgr., 1967—, v.p., 1972—; dir. Skipper's, Inc., 1969—. Trustee, Bush Sch., 1974—. Served to lt. (j.g.), 1951-54. Chartered fin. analyst. Mem. Seattle Soc. Fin. Analysts (dir. 1973-78, pres. 1975-76). Republican. Clubs: Seattle Tennis, Rainier. Home: 8621 NE 6th St Bellevue WA 98004 Office: 2600 Seattle First Nat Bank Bldg Seattle WA 98154

LUNDY, LLOYD P., motel exec.; b. Vinita, Okla., Dec. 28, 1920; s. William Edward and Matilda May (Herod) L.; student pub. schs., Vinita; m. Ida M. Simms, Dec. 25, 1947; children—Connie Jean Lundy Norris, Jane Ann Lundy Matlock. Mgr. lessee Sands Best Western Motel, Salina, Kans., 1961-66; mgr. co-owner Vagabond Best Western, Hays, Kans., 1966—; gen. mgr. co-owner Continental Inn Best Western, Manhattan, Kans., 1967—; co-owner Friendship Inn Vagabond II, Salina, Best Western Jayhawk Third, Junction City, Kans., Friendship Inn Villa, Hays, Best Western LaFonda Motel, Liberal, Kans.; dir. Jayhawk Investments. Bd. dirs., past pres. Homer B. Reed Tng. and Adjustment Center, Hays. Served with USAAF, 1942-46. Mem. Kans. Lodging Assn. (dir. 1968—, pres. 1971-72, Man of Yr. 1974), Nat. Innkeeping Assn., Hays C. of C. (dir. 1968-72, 78—), Kans. Hotel/Motel Assn. (dir. 1980-81), Am. Legion (past comdr.). Methodist. Clubs: Rotary, Masons, Shriners. Home and office: 2524 Vine St Apt 2 Hays KS 67601

LUNEY, PERCY ROBERT, JR., univ. adminstr., lawyer; b. Hopkinsville, Ky., Jan. 13, 1949; s. Percy Robert and Alice Charlene (Woodson) L.; A.B., Hamilton Coll., 1970; J.D. (Thomas J. Watson fellow), Harvard U., 1974; m. Gwynn Teresa Swinson, Feb. 18, 1979; 1 dau., Jamille. Admitted to D.C. bar, 1975, Tenn. bar, 1977, U.S. Supreme Ct., 1979; asst. prof. econ. geology Cornell U. Coll. Engring., 1974-75; atty. adv. Office of Solicitor, Dept. Interior, Washington, 1975-77; spl. asst. to pres., gen. counsel and dir. Urban Affairs Inst., Fisk U., 1977-79; asso. firm Birch, Horton, Bittner and Monroe, Washington, 1979-80, of counsel, 1980—; asst. dean, asst. prof. law N.C. Central U. Sch. Law, 1980—; adj. prof. environ. law Antioch Sch. Law, Washington, 1980; participant Aspen Inst. Humanistic Studies Exec. Seminar, 1974, Texaco Faculty Forum, 1977; dir. MESBIC Internat. Project Mgmt. Corp., Inc. Mem. Tenn. Bar Assn., D.C. Bar Assn., Nashville Bar Assn., Fed. Bar Assn., Am. Bar Assn., Delta Upsilon. Congregationalist. Office: NC Central U Sch Law Durham NC 27707

LUNN, WALLACE EDWARD, JR., boiler supply co. exec.; b. Nashville, Nov. 12, 1949; s. Wallace Edward and Gladys Elizabeth (Hunter) L.; B.A. in Music, Baylor U., 1972; m. Saralu Thompson, Dec. 29, 1970; children—Leigh Marie, Wallace Edward III. Corp. sec. Boiler Supply Co., Inc., Nashville, 1971-78, pres., 1978—; pres. ComTech Inc., Nashville; partner Belle Investments, Nashville. Bd. dirs. Tenn. chpt. Cystic Fibrosis, 1976-79, v.p. Nashville br., 1976-79; v.p. Nashville Booster Club; deacon Belmont Heights Baptist Ch.; dir. Phi Mu Alpha Sinfonia, 1969-72. Mem. ASHRAE (v.p.), Nashville Area C. of C., Tenn. Bus. Men's Assn. Clubs: Nashville City (1st v.p.), Kiwanis (dir. Nashville club 1976-78). Contbg. composer Good News, 1968; co-composer Happening Now, 1970. Home: 518 Shenandoah Dr Brentwood TN 37027 Office: 490 Craighead St Nashville TN 37204

LUNTZ, HARRY ADAM, fin. exec.; b. Pitts., July 19, 1946; s. Henry Adam and Dorothy Marie (Hallstein) L.; B.B.A. cum laude, Drake Coll. of Fla., 1969; grad. Duff's Bus. Inst., 1966-67; m. Diana A. Conicella, July 19, 1969; children—Eileen Marie, Erica Ann, John Michael. Internal auditor H.K. Porter Co., Inc., Pitts., 1969; chief acct. Banks-Miller Supply Co., Huntington, W.Va., 1970-77; acctg. mgr. Tidewater Supply Co., Huntington, 1977—; mem. credit com. West vasamco Fed. Credit Union. Mem. Huntington Area Postal Customers Council, 1980-81. Mem. Am. Mgmt. Assn. Republican. Lutheran. Home: Route 2 PO Box 584 South Point OH 45680 Office: PO Box 1358 Huntington WV 25715

LUPBERGER, EDWARD WILLIAM, ins. co. exec.; b. Rolla, Mo., July 8, 1917; s. William K. and Helen P. (Mueschke) L.; B.S. in Bus. Adminstrn., U. Mo., 1942; postgrad. Wharton Sch., U. Pa., 1946-47; m. Mary Margaret Mead, Aug. 6, 1944; children—Anne, Kent, David. Acct., Lybrand Ross Bros. and Montgomery, St. Louis, 1947-50; regional bus. mgr. Kaiser Frazer, St. Louis, 1950-51; comptroller Hazelwood Engring., Kirkwood, Mo., 1951-53; adminstrv. mgr. Cambridge Corp., Denver, 1953-54; with Nat. Farmers Union Property & Casualty Co., Denver, 1954—, v.p. investments, 1967—. Served to maj. U.S. Army, 1942-46. Chartered fin. analyst. Mem. Denver Soc. Fin. Analysts, Inst. Chartered Fin. Analysts, Bus. Economists. Democrat. Presbyterian. Home: 26 S Hudson St Denver CO 80222 Office: 12025 E 45th St Denver CO 80251

LUPER, ARCHIE WILLIAM, food service adminstr.; b. Elk City, Okla., Jan. 12, 1912; s. William Andrew and Elizabeth Sarah (Sharp) L.; student pub. schs., student Montana Hotel and Restaurant Sch., Lucerne, Switzerland; m. Francile Janet Sands, Jan. 20, 1941; children—Denese Rhea, Archie William. Propr., mgr. Loop's Restaurant, Ventura, Calif., 1947—; propr., mgr. Loop's Restaurants, Cafeterias and Bakeries, So. Calif. area; propr. Motor Hotel, Calif.; chmn. bd. Luper Enterprises, Inc., Ventura, Calif.; speaker at various colls. and Bible schs. in U.S. Chmn. Ventura County Heart Assn.; Bible sch. tchr. Ch. of Christ, also missionary; bd. dirs. Freed-Hardeman Coll., Tenn., Blue Ridge Encampment, Inc., N.C., Boys Club Am., Ventura chpt. Elected to Am. Restaurant Mag. Hall of Fame, 1960; seven awards Elsters. Mem. So. Calif. Restaurant Assn. (dir.). Republican. Mem. Ch. of Christ. Contbr. articles to religious publs.; editor: Loop's Gourmet Cook Book. Home: 215 Lang St Ventura CA 93003 Office: 3159 East Main Ventura CA 93003

LUPTON, ELMER CORNELIUS, JR., packaging co. exec.; b. Balt., Aug. 8, 1945; s. Elmer Cornelius and Leoni (Potucek) L.; B.S., Mass. Inst. Tech., 1965; M.Phil., Yale U., 1967, Ph.D., 1969; m. Claire Turner Cook, June 8, 1968; 1 dau., Katherine Lent. Applications research mgr. Allied Chem. Co., Morristown, N.J., 1973-76, industry mgr. packaging, govt., 1976-79; pres. Composite Container Co., Medford, Mass., 1979—. Dist. chmn., exec. bd. Morris Sussex Area council Boy Scouts Am., 1977—, mem. nat. scout com., 1975—, Northeast Region scout com., 1975—. Served to capt. USAF, 1969-73. Mem. Packaging Inst., Am. Chem. Soc., Soc. Plastic Engrs., Sigma Xi, Phi Lambda Upsilon. Roman Catholic. Contbr. articles to profl. jours. Patentee in plastics tech. Home: 15 Cobb Rd Mountain Lakes NJ 07046 Office: 330 Middlesex Ave Medford MA 02155

LUSARDI, JOAN MARGARET, mktg. cons.; b. Rochester, N.Y., June 9, 1933; d. Alfred Louis and Leisl Marion (Spencer) L.; B.S., U. Rochester, 1968. Tchr., N.Y. and Calif., 1955-64; sales exec. Hoffman-LaRoche Co., Nutley, N.J., 1964-69; mem. tech. devel. and benefits adminstrn. staff Xerox Corp., Rochester, 1969-77, mktg. cons., 1977-79, product mktg. mgr., 1979—; pension cons., 1975—; mem. adj. faculty Rochester Inst. Tech. Vol. Rochester Area United Fund; bd. dirs., mem. exec. com. Hillside Children's Center; mem. exec. com. Genesee Valley council Girl Scouts U.S.A. Republican. Roman Catholic. Home: 46 Selborne Chase Fairport NY 14450 Office: Xerox Sq Rochester NY 14644

LUSCHER, JOHN EDMOND, furniture mktg. exec.; b. Charleston, W.Va., Nov. 8, 1942; s. Harold Theodore and Mary Kathleen (Walls) L.; B.S., W.Va. U., 1964; M.B.A., Am. Grad. Sch. Internat. Mgmt., 1972; m. Judith Ann Corsino; 1 dau., Jaclyn Conti. With Procter & Gamble, Cin., 1964-65; dir. internat. ops. Pier I Imports, London, Paris and Sydney, Australia, 1972-77; exec. v.p. Tech Furniture Mfg., Shelton, Conn., 1977-80, Children's Design Center, Saratoga Springs, N.Y., 1980—; dir. vol. worker with retarded children Sunnyside Sch., Phoenix, 1971-72; mem. Republican Nat. Com., 1979-80. Served to lt. comdr., USN, 1965-71; Vietnam. Decorated Silver Star, D.F.C. (2), Air medals (32), Purple Heart, Bronze Star; Vietnamese Air Cross of Gallantry. Mem. Am. Mgmt. Assn., So. Furniture Mfrs. Assn., Nat. Assn. Furniture Mfg., Alumni Assn. Valley Forge Mil. Acad., Alumni Assn. Am. Grad. Sch., Aircraft Owners and Pilots Assn. Home: Geyser Rd Route 4 Saratoga Springs NY 12866

LUSCINSKI, STEVEN MICHAEL, fin. investment cons.; b. Boston, Nov. 4, 1951; s. Anthony Paul and Agnes Veronica (Nawoichek) L.; B.S.C.E., Northeastern U., 1974; M.S.C.E., M.I.T., 1976; M.B.A., Cornell U., 1980. Owner, pres. co., Boston, 1971; structural engr. Stone & Webster Engring. Corp., Boston, 1972-78; guest researcher, cons. Brookhaven Nat. Lab., Upton, N.Y., 1979-80; corp. fin. and strategic planning asso. UGI Corp., Valley Forge, Pa., 1980—; cons., dir. Entek Research, N.Y., 1980—. Active Big Brother Assn., 1974—. Recipient various scholarships and awards. Registered profl. engr., R.I.; lic. real estate broker, Mass. Mem. Am. Concrete Inst., Assn. M.B.A. Execs. Club: Rotary. Home: 1665 Washington St Walpole MA 02081 Office: UGI Corp PO Box 858 Valley Forge PA 19482

LUSKIN, KEITH JOSEPH, electronics co. exec.; b. Escanaba, Mich., Oct. 10, 1936; s. August A. and Margaret E. (Nontelle) L.; A.A. in Engring. Electronics, Valparaiso (Ind.) Tech. Inst., 1961; m. Darlene D. Kravets, Sept. 3, 1960; 1 son, Kevin A. Dist. sales mgr. Amphenol-Borg Electronics Co., Denver, 1961-65; indsl. sales mgr. Chgo. Miniature Lamp Works, 1965-68; v.p. mktg. Shelly/Datatron Co., Santa Ana, Calif., 1968-71; pres. Marutaka America, Torrance, Calif., 1971-73; exec. v.p. Indsl. Electronic Engrs., Inc., Van Nuys, Calif., 1973—, also dir.; pres. DTL, Singapore; dir. Souriau, Inc. Served with USAF, 1954-58. Mem. Am. Electronics Assn., Am. Mgmt. Assn., Soc. Info. Display. Republican. Roman Catholic. Club: Aero So. Calif. Home: 4808 Highgrove Ave Torrance CA 90505 Office: 7740 Lemona Ave Van Nuys CA 91405

LUSTER, RONNIE LEE, mfr.'s rep.; b. Kingsport, Tenn., Nov. 19, 1947; s. Lee George and Hazel B. (Smith) L.; B.S., East Tenn. State U., 1973. With Young' Supply Co., Boone & Lamont, Johnson City, Tenn., 1976-77; bus. mgr., controller Lancaster Assos., Johnson City, 1977—. Served with USMCR, 1966-69. Mem. Am. Fin. Assn., Adminstrv. Mgmt. Soc., Japan Karate Orgn. Methodist. Club: Elks. Home: Fairway Apts Apt 13 Johnson City TN 37601 Office: 74 Wilson Ave Box 1100 Johnson City TN 37601

LUSTGARTEN, ELI S., securities analyst; b. Bklyn., June 10, 1945; s. Samuel and Elsie (Cohen) L.; B.S.E.E., Poly. Inst. Bklyn., 1966; M.S.E.E., U. Pa., 1968; M.B.A., Harvard U., 1972; m. Jacqueline Siegel, Apr. 12, 1970; 1 son, Ephram Lloyd. Design engr., program mgr. Raytheon Co., 1968-71; v.p. Paine Webber Mitchell, Hutchins, Chgo., 1972—. Ford Found. fellow, 1967-68. Mem. N.Y. Soc. Securities Analysts, Machinery Analyst Group N.Y., Basic Industries and Natural Resources Group Chgo. Club: Harvard, Harvard Bus. Sch. Office: Paine Webber Mitchell Hutchins 2 1st National Plaza Chicago IL 60603

LUTERMAN, GERALD, mfg. co. exec.; b. Montreal, Que., Can., Jan. 5, 1944; s. David and Rachel (Kramer) L.; came to U.S., 1967; B.Comm. with honors in Econs., McGill U., 1965; M.B.A. magna sum laude (Baker scholar, Kresge fellow), Harvard, 1969; m. Lillian Berry, June 24, 1969; children—Jennifer Anne, Jessica Danielle. Auditor, McDonald Currie, Montreal, 1965-67; asso. Booz, Allen & Hamilton, Cleve., 1969-71; v.p. finance Xomox Corp., Cin., 1971-76, v.p., gen. mgr., 1976-77, exec. v.p. fin., 1978—; dir. Norwood Express & Drayage Co. Bd. dirs. United Appeal Agy., 1974-76. Mem. Fin. Execs. Inst., Canadian Chartered Accountant Assn. Home: 5495 Firethorn Ct Cincinnati OH 45242 Office: 4444 Cooper Rd Cincinnati OH 45242

LUTES, MARYBELLE PEARSON, mfrs. rep.; b. Chgo., Apr. 12, 1921; d. Carlo Arnold and Annie Laura (Fasten) Pearson; student U. Wis., 1937; m. John R. Lutes, June 20, 1941 (dec.); children—Jacqueline Karen, John. Sec., Ind. Rating Bur., South Bend, 1949-52; legal sec. to atty., Dowagiac, Mich., 1952-64; sec.-treas. John R. Lutes Co., Niles, Mich., 1952—, sec.-treas. Mem. Election Canvas Bd., Niles, Mich., 1963-70. Republican. Home: 1205 Sassafras Ln Niles MI 49120 Office: 1400 Chicago Rd Niles MI 49120

LUTHER, JON LYLE, food service mgmt. co. exec.; b. Tonawanda, N.Y., Oct. 20, 1943; s. Lyle L. and Kathryn Marie (Peterman) L.; student Canisius Coll., 1961-63; A.A.S., Paul Smith Coll., 1967; m. Sharon L. Dickman, Nov. 26, 1966; children—Jonathan L., Tiffany L. With Service Systems Corp.; with ARA Services, Inc., now corp. v.p. mktg. bus. and industry sector, Phila.; adj. instr. Paul Smith Coll. Mem. Soc. Food Service Mgmt., Nat. Automatic Merchandising Assn. Office: Independence Sq W Philadelphia PA 19106

LUTHER, RICHARD RICE, retail food co. exec.; b. Phila., May 10, 1942; s. William A. and Mildred V. (Rice) L.; B.S. in Bus. Adminstrn., Temple U., 1967, M.B.A., 1970; m. Mary Anne Colussi, July 18, 1970; 1 dau., Kelly Anne. Pension trust mgr. Aetna Life & Casualty, Phila., 1968-70; risk and ins. specialist Upjohn Co., Kalamazoo, 1970-73; mgr. corp. ins. Crown Zellerbach, San Francisco, 1973-75; mgr. corp. ins., safety and loss control, v.p. Berda Devel. Ltd. div. T.J. Lipton, Inc., Englewood Cliffs, N.J., 1975-79; dir. pension investments and risk mgmt., pres., dir. St. Pancras Co. Ltd. div. Gt. A & P Tea Co., Montvale, N.J., 1979—; instr. Ins. Edn. Assn., 1974-75. Asst. chief Ind. Fire Co., Jenkintown, Pa., 1964-66, sec., 1965-67, trustee, 1965-70; mem. River Vale (N.J.) Vol. Fire Dept. Mem. Risk and Ins.

Mgmt. Soc., Captive Ins. Cos. Assn. (dir.), Am. Mgmt. Assn. (planning council 1980—). Roman Catholic. Home: 577 Colonial Rd River Vale NJ 07675 Office: 2 Paragon Dr Montvale NJ 07645

LUTIN, DAVID LOUIS, real estate devel. and finance cons.; b. East Hartford, Conn., Apr. 18, 1919; s. Solomon and Esther (Newman) L.; A.B., Ohio No. U., 1946; M.B.A., Syracuse U., 1949; m. Dorothy Marmor, Dec. 3, 1944; children—Gary, Marnie (Mrs. George Wittig). Housing economist and field rep. HHFA, Washington, 1950-57; dir. urban renewal City of Brookline, Mass., 1957-58; cons. on urban renewal and housing Com. for Econ. Devel., N.Y.C., 1958-59; propr. David L. Lutin Assos., real estate devel. and fin. cons., Rye, N.Y. and Scottsdale, Ariz., 1959-73, 75—; v.p. real estate and mortgages Am. Bank and Trust Co., N.Y.C., 1973-75. Research asso. Albert Farwell Bemis Found., Mass. Inst. Tech., 1951-52. Served to capt. AUS, 1942-46. Decorated Purple Heart. Mem. Am. Econ. Assn., Am. Planning Assn., Ariz. Planning Assn., Nat. Assn. Housing and Redevel. Ofcls., Urban Land Inst., Nat. Assn. Home Builders, Mortgage Bankers Assn., Am. Statis. Assn., Ariz. Assn. Housing and Redevel. Ofcls. Contbr. articles and reports on econs., housing and urban devel. to profl. jours. Home and office: 11423 Century Ln Scottsdale AZ 85254

LUTMAN, MARLENE ELIZABETH, constrn. co. exec.; b. Newark, Dec. 1, 1933; d. Abraham and Shirley (Janow) Carnow; B.S. in Commerce and Fin., Bucknell U., 1955; m. Stanley Kramer, Aug. 7, 1955 (dec. 1967); children—Deborah Frances, Elizabeth Anne; m. 2d, Martin Lutman, Aug. 27, 1969. Asst. research dir. Modern Materials Handling Co., Boston, 1955-57; econ. analyst, project adminstr. United Research Co., Cambridge, Mass., 1957-58; free lance tech. writer, econ. analyst, 1958-66; asst. mgr. survey planning and market research IBM, White Plains, N.Y., 1967-69; mgr. research services McKinsey & Co., Cleve., 1969-72; v.p., dir. Am. Custom Homes, Cleve., 1971—; dir. Liberty Builders, Inc., Cleve., 1973—; part-owner, v.p., dir. Am. Custom Builders Inc., Cape Coral, Fla., 1978—, Market St., Inc., N. Ft. Myers, Fla., 1980— sec., dir. SW Fla. Bldg. Corp., Cape Coral, 1979—. Mem. Econ. and Indsl. Devel. Task Force, City of Cape Coral, 1979. Mem. Nat. Assn. Homebuilders, Bldg. Industry Assn., Constrn. Industry Assn. Home: 1624 Palaco Grande Pkwy Cape Coral FL 33904 Office: Am Custom Builders Inc 2706 Del Prado Blvd Cape Coral FL 33904

LUTZ, FRANK ANTHONY, indsl. chems. co. exec.; b. McKees Rocks, Pa., Jan. 5, 1949; s. Anthony Dominick and Deetza (Cherpes) L.; B.S., U. Dayton, 1970. Sales rep. Calgon Corp., Pitts., 1971-72, regional hosp. sales mgr., Atlanta, 1972-74, manpower devel. and tng. mgr., St. Louis, 1974—. Mem. Nat. Soc. Sales Tng. Execs., Am. Soc. Tng. and Devel., Meeting Planners Internat. Home: 1735 Russet Valley Dr Saint Louis MO 63141 Office: Calgon Corp Box 147 St Louis MO 63166

LUTZ, KENNETH VIVIAN, constrn. equipment co. exec.; b. Anselmo, Nebr., Oct. 28, 1913; s. Wilbur Edward and Daisy Victoria (Tomlinson) L.; student U. Wash., 1943; m. Dorothy Carolyn Lewis, June 24, 1935; children—David Lee, Donald Alan. Welder various constrn. and oil field firms, 1937-39; welder Bremerton (Wash.) Navy Yard, 1939-41; sr. insp. ships constrn. Bur. Ships, Seattle, 1942-45; shop foreman Ferrcfix Welding, Seattle, 1945-47; salesman Welders Supply Co., Seattle, 1947-48; salesman, regional mgr., sales mgr., v.p. All-State Welding Alloys Co., Inc., White Plains, N.Y., 1959-69; divisional mgr., v.p. Resisto-Loy Co., Inc., Grand Rapids, Mich., 1957-70; owner, mgr., pres. Kenco Welding Supplies, Inc., Cupertino, Calif., 1958-70; owner, pres. Kenco Engring., Inc., Campbell, Calif., 1970-77, Roseville, Calif., 1977—. Served with U.S. Navy, 1933-37. Mem. Nat. Asphalt Paving Assn., Family Motor Coach Assn., Roseville C. of C. (dir.). Clubs: Masons, Shriners, Los Gatos Camel Herders; Good Sam Travel; Roseville Shrine; No. Calif. Antique Car, Vogue Country. Home: 3820 Clover Valley Rd Rocklin CA 95677 Office: 2155 PFE Rd Roseville CA 95678

LUTZ, WALTER STANLEY, JR., investment casting co. exec.; b. Phila., Oct. 13, 1940; s. Walter Stanley and Anne Frances (Wingert) L.; B.S. in Metall. Engring., Lafayette Coll., 1962; m. Sylvia Rae Kreider, Oct. 20, 1967; children—Michael G., Sherri A., Wendy L. With Stellite div. Cabot Corp., Kokomo, Ind., 1962-74, mfg. mgr., 1971-73, engring. mgr., 1973-74; with Signicast Corp., Milw., 1974—, exec. v.p., 1976-78, pres., chief operating officer, 1978—, also dir. Mem. Investment Casting Inst. (dir. 1976—, pres. 1979-81). Republican. Club: Tripoli Country. Home: 934 Hawthorne Ln Cedarburg WI 53012 Office: Signicast Corp 9000 N 55th St Milwaukee WI 53223

LYCHE, IVER, fin. exec.; b. Oslo, Norway, Oct. 17, 1923; came to U.S., 1945, naturalized, 1952; s. Einar and Helga (Aaby) L.; student U. Oslo, 1940-42; B.S. in B.A., U. Calif., Berkeley, 1948, M.B.A., 1949; m. Joan Shuman, Feb. 10, 1950; children—Helga, Karen, Sylvia, Iver. With Fiberboard Corp., San Francisco, 1950; pres., chmn. bd. Shuman, Agnew & Co., Inc., San Francisco, 1953-77; a mng. dir. Morgan Stanley & Co., Inc., San Francisco, 1977—; chmn. bd. Pacific Med. Center, San Francisco, 1978—; dir. Overseas Shipping Co., San Francisco, Ampco Foods, Inc., San Francisco; dir. N.Y. Stock Exchange, 1975-78. Bd. dirs. Family Service Agy., San Francisco, 1968-70, Edgewood Children's Home, San Francisco, 1968-71, Internat. House, U. Calif., Berkeley, 1975-77. Served with Royal Norwegian Air Force, 1942-45. Mem. Norwegian Am. C. of C. (Western div. pres. 1975—). Clubs: Burlingame Country (pres. 1978—), Pacific-Union, Bohemian, San Francisco Golf. Home: 101 New Pl Hillsborough CA 94010 Office: 650 California St San Francisco CA 94108

LYET, JEAN PAUL, mfg. co. exec.; b. Phila., May 6, 1917; s. Louis F. and Elizabeth (Fortune) L.; grad. U. Pa. Evening Sch. Accts. and Fin., 1941; m. Dorothy Lillian Storz, Sept. 29, 1945. Pub. accountant Ernst & Ernst, C.P.A.'s, Reading, Pa., 1940-43; with New Holland (Pa.) div. Sperry Corp., and predecessor, 1943-71, pres., 1969-71, asst. treas. Sperry Corp., 1955-67, exec. v.p., dir., 1970-71, pres., 1971-72, chmn. bd., chief exec. officer, 1972—; dir. Armstrong World Industries, Inc., Hershey Trust Co., Eastman Kodak Co., Continental Group, NL Industries, Inc. Mem. exec. com. Machinery and Allied Products Inst.; mem. Pres.'s Export Council, Emergency Com. for Am. Trade, Bus. Council; trustee Com. Econ. Devel., U. Pa., Lancaster Country Day Sch., Elizabethtown Coll. Mem. Am. Inst. C.P.A.'s. Episcopalian. Clubs: Lancaster Country, Hamilton (Lancaster); Elk River Yacht (Md.); Blind Brook, Links; Siwanoy; Clove Valley (N.Y.); Laurel Valley Golf (Ligonier, Pa.). Office: 1290 Ave of Americas New York NY 10019

LYETH, MUNRO L(ONGYEAR), banker; b. N.Y.C., Oct. 28, 1915; s. J.M. Richardson and Judith (Longyear) L.; A.B., Harvard, 1937, LL.B., 1940; m. Josephine Clifford Good, June 28, 1939, m. 2d, 1963 (dec. 1967); children—Munro L., Judith; m. Marian Neal Rubey, Feb. 17, 1968; stepchildren—William B. Rubey, Jr., Marian S. Mitchell, Robert N. Rubey, Christina C. Rubey. Asso. Spence, Windels, Walser, Hotchkiss & Angell, 1940-41; trust officer U.S. Nat. Bank of Denver, 1946-52; pres., dir. Cherry Creek Nat. Bank, 1952—, chmn. bd., 1961-74, hon. chmn. bd., 1974—; dir. Cyclo Mfg. Co., Longyear Realty Corp., Mountain Banks Ltd. Bd. dirs. Central City Opera House Assn., Music Assos. of Aspen. Served as comdr. USNR, 1941-46. Fellow Aspen Inst. Humanistic Studies; mem. Newcomen Soc. N.Am. Clubs: Denver, Denver Country; Garden of the Gods (Colorado Springs, Colo.). Home: 556 S Elizabeth St Denver CO 80209 Office: PO Box 1560 Aspen CO 81612

LYNCH, BETTY STEVENS, accountant, business exec.; b. Bridgeport, Conn., Jan. 9, 1935; d. Fred Isaac and Emma Marie (Andersen) Stevens; B.S. summa cum laude in Bus. Adminstrn. and Acctg., Sacred Heart U., 1975, postgrad., 1978—; m. John J. Lynch, Jr., July 11, 1953; 1 dau., Cynthia Jean. Clk., Westport (Conn.) Bank & Trust, 1953-54, Conn. Nat. Bank, Westport, 1954-58; from clk. to head teller Peoples Savs. Bank, Westport, 1958-64; broker White & White Real Estate, Westport, 1964-65; owner Betty S. Lynch Real Estate, Weston, Conn., 1965; jr. accountant Nat. CSS, Inc., Wilton, Conn., 1974-75, accountant, gen. ledger coordinator, 1975-76, sr. accountant, 1977-78, mgr. corp. cash disbursements, 1978-79, treas., dir. Employees Credit Union, 1976—; mgr. mgmt. info. systems State Nat. Bank Conn., Bridgeport, 1979—. Bd. dirs. Soc. to Advance the Retarded, 1960-63, treas., 1959; active Westport United Fund, 1962-64, Girl Scouts U.S.A., 1977; active Republican politics. Mem. Bank Adminstrn. Inst., Nat. Assn. Accountants, Nat. Assn. Bank Women, Nat. Assn. Female Execs. Congregationalist. Office: 305 Black Rock Turnpike Fairfield CT 06430

LYNCH, CHARLES ALLEN, food service co. exec.; b. Denver, Sept. 7, 1927; s. Laurence J. and Louanna (Robertson) L.; B.S., Yale U., 1950; m. Linda Bennet, June 14, 1952; children—Charles Allen, Tara O'Hara, Casey Alexander. Dir. mktg., fabrics and finishes dept. E. I. duPont de Nemours & Co., Wilmington, Del., 1950-69; v.p., group pres. mfg. SCOA Industries, Inc., Columbus, Ohio, 1969-72; exec. v.p. W.R. Grace & Co., N.Y.C., 1972-78; pres., chief exec. officer Saga Corp., Menlo Park, Calif., 1978—, also dir. Bd. dirs. Bay Area Council, 1979—; trustee Hill Sch., Pottstown, Pa., San Francisco Ballet; nat. trustee YMCA; bd. dirs. San Francisco YMCA. Served with USN, 1945. Mem. Am. Footwear Inst. (chmn. 1974-75), Calif. Roundtable. Republican. Roman Catholic. Clubs: Ponte Vedra Beach and Tennis, (Ponte Vedra Beach, Fla.); Coral Beach and Tennis (Bermuda). Office: 1 Saga Ln Menlo Park CA 94025

LYNCH, CHARLES MARTIN, petroleum co. exec.; b. Lewes, Del., Jan. 10, 1922; s. Robert Augustus and Florence Gertrude (Mitchell) L.; student U. Ga., 1941-42; m. Catherine Agnes Brawders, Nov. 4, 1943; children—Karen Ann, Charles Martin, Eileen Patricia, Joann Marie. Master ships officer Sinclair Refining Co., 1946-53, mgr. safety tng., 1953-58, mgr. ops., 1958-66, gen. mgr. marine dept., 1967-69; mgr. marine transp. Atlantic Richfield Co., Los Angeles, 1969-75, v.p. marine transp., 1975-79; pres. ARCO Marine, Inc., Los Angeles, 1980—; dir. Am. Inst. Mcht. Shipping, 1975-77. Recipient award for outstanding contbn. to marine field Am. Petroleum Inst., 1973; named Marine Man of Yr., Hague Post of Am. Legion, N.Y.C., 1979. Mem. Am. Bur. Shipping (bd. mgrs.), Oil Cos. Internat. Marine Forum-Central (mem. exec. com.), Nat. Propeller Club, Permanent Internat. Assn. Navigation Congresses, Soc. Naval Architects and Marine Engrs. Republican. Roman Catholic. Clubs: Masons; Palos Verdes Golf. Home: 30806 Marne Dr Palos Verdes Peninsula CA 90274 Office: 515 S Flower St Los Angeles CA 90071

LYNCH, DALE L., supermarket chain exec.; b. Long Beach, Calif., 1921; student Long Beach City Coll., Los Angeles State Coll. With Safeway Stores, Inc., Oakland, Calif., 1940—, v.p., mgr. Seattle retail div., 1972-75, v.p., mgr. N.W. region, 1975-76, v.p. adminstrn., 1976-77, pres., 1977—, also dir. Office: 201 Fourth St Oakland CA 94660*

LYNCH, DEBRA TAYLOR, jeweler; b. Wilmington, Del., Feb. 24, 1951; d. Harold Nathaniel and Selma Henrietta (Weidenfeld) Taylor; B.A., U. Md., 1975; m. Francis M. Lynch, Apr. 1, 1978. Retail sales staff Md. Diamond Exchange, Rockville, 1976-77; owner, operator The Gold Mine, Hyattsville, Md., 1978—, instr. gemology, 1978—. Recipient Cert. of Appreciation, St. Elizabeth's Hosp., Washington, 1974. Mem. Retail Jewelers Assn., Gemological Inst. Am., U. Md. Alumni Assn. (life), Zionist Orgn. of Am. (life). Club: Hadassah (life, recipient Public Service award 1980). Office: 3500 East-West Hwy Hyattsville MD 20782

LYNCH, FRANK WILLIAM, aerospace co. exec.; b. San Francisco, Nov. 26, 1921; s. James Garfield and Med (Kelly) L.; A.B., Stanford U., 1942, postgrad, 1946-48; m. Marilyn Leona Hopwood, June 24, 1950; children—Kathryn Leona, Molly Louise. Research engr. Boeing Airplane Co., Seattle, 1948-50; mgr. engring. dept. Northrop Corp., Hawthorne, Calif., 1950-57; div. v.p. engring. Lear-Siegler Corp., Anaheim, Calif., 1957-59; with Northrop Corp., Los Angeles, 1959—, sr. v.p., 1975—, tactical and electronic systems group exec., 1980—. Served with AC, U.S. Army, 1942-46. Mem. IEEE, AIAA, Assn. U.S. Army, Am. Def. Preparedness Assn. Club: Balboa Yacht (Newport Beach, Calif.). Office: 1800 Century Park E Los Angeles CA 90067

LYNCH, GERALD JOHN, corp. exec.; b. Detroit, Feb. 22, 1906; s. Patrick John and Julia (O'Meara) L.; A.B., Wayne U., 1929, M.A., 1935; J.D., U. Detroit, 1933; D.B.A. (hon.), U. Dayton, 1963; m. Mary Romaine Livernois, July 20, 1937; children—Terence, Rose Mary Lynch Mitchell, Laura Lee Lynch Foley, Gerald John, Julie Anne. Admitted to Mich. bar, 1933, pvt. practice, Detroit, 1933-42; dir. war contract adminstrn. dept. Fisher Body div. Gen. Motors Corp., 1942-46; with Ford Motor Co., 1946-62, successively dir. war contract adminstrn. dept., exec. asst. controller, dir. Washington office, exec. asst. to group exec. Tractor and Internat. Group, dir. Office Def. Products and Govtl. Relations, 1946-56, pres. Aeronutronic Systems, Inc. subs., 1956-59, v.p., gen. mgr. aero. div., 1959-62, group v.p. def. products, 1960-62; chmn. Menasco, Inc., Burbank, Calif., 1962—; dir., group v.p. Colt Industries Inc. dir. Lloyds Bank Calif., Los Angeles. Bd. dirs. United Way; trustee Calif. Museum Found. Clubs: Met. (Washington); Calif. (Los Angeles); Annandale Golf (Pasadena, Calif.); Century II (Fort Worth). Home: 920 Avondale Rd San Marino CA 91108 Office: 805 S San Fernando Blvd Burbank CA 91510

LYNCH, HARRY WOLFE, III, mfg. co. exec.; b. Bridgeport, Conn., Feb. 25, 1949; s. Harry Wolfe, Jr. and Mary Elizabeth (Trimble) L.; B.A., U. Va., 1971; M.B.A., Inst. pour L'Etude des Methodes de Direction de l'Enterprise, Lausanne, Switzerland, 1974; M.B.A., Harvard U., 1976; m. Dana Freeman, June 12, 1971. Research asso. Inst. pour L'Etude des Methodes de Direction de l'Enterprise, 1975; planning analyst, then sr. planning analyst Philip Morris Inc., N.Y.C., 1976-79; mgr. planning Philip Morris Internat., N.Y.C., 1979—. Trustee Stanwich Congl. Ch., Greenwich, Conn., 1980—. Served with USNR, 1971-73; Vietnam. Decorated Navy Commendation medal. Mem. Am. Mgmt. Assn. Republican. Club: Union League (N.Y.C.). Author curriculum materials. Home: 567 Stanwich Rd Greenwich CT 06830 Office: Philip Morris Internat 100 Park Ave New York NY 10017

LYNCH, JAMES CHARLES, security guard co. exec.; b. Newark, Jan. 15, 1919; s. Bernard and Bridget (Fitzsimmons) L.; B.S. in B.A., Rutgers U., 1940; cert. Indsl. Coll. of Armed Forces, 1964; m. Mary Delia Powell, June 29, 1959; 1 son, Brian Joseph; 1 stepdau., Maria Nannette. Insp. P. Ballantyne & Son, Newark, 1940-42; investigator Retail Credit Co., Newark, 1946; night mgr. Robert Richter Hotel, Miami Beach, 1946-47, night auditor, 1947-48; hotel asst. mgr. Sans Souci Hotel, Miami Beach, Fla., 1948-50; pres., chmn. bd. Asset Protection Assos., Inc., Huntsville, Ala., 1973—; chief Intelligence and Security div. Redstone (Ala.) Arsenal, 1950-60; security adv. NATO Hawk Prodn. Orgn., Paris, 1960, security program chief, until 1964; security specialist U.S. Army Missile Command, Redstone Arsenal, 1964-68; chief Security Office, U.S. Army Safeguard Systems Command, Huntsville, Ala., 1968-72; guest lectr. U. Ala., Birmingham, 1979-80, Jefferson State U., Birmingham, 1979-80. Served with U.S. Army, 1942-46; ETO. Decorated Silver Star with oak leaf cluster, Bronze Star medal with oak leaf cluster, Purple Heart. Cert. protection profl., 1978. Mem. Huntsville-Madison County C. of C. (chmn. internat. trade com. 1976-78), Am. Soc. Indsl. Security (past bd. dirs., past nat. treas.), Assn. U.S. Army, Smithsonian Assos., Am. Security Council, VFW, Am. Legion, Security and Intelligence Assn. Republican. Roman Catholic. Clubs: Huntsville Country, Burning Tree Country, Elks, K.C. Contbr. articles to profl. jours. Home: 403 Zandale Dr Huntsville AL 35801 Office: 101 Governor's Dr Suite 406 Huntsville AL 35801

LYNCH, JAMES FRANCIS, sales exec.; b. Cohoes, N.Y., May 30, 1921; s. Frederick J. and Anne (Byrnes) L.; B.S., Siena Coll., 1952; M.B.A., U. Buffalo, 1955; postgrad. N.Y. U., 1952-53, Siena Coll., 1953-54, Xavier U., 1967-68; m. Catherine E. Dolon, June 1, 1946; children—James Francis, Mary J., Edward J., Catherine A., Robert P. Chief indsl. engr. Watervliet Arsenal, 1947-52; plant mgr. Am. Locomotive Co., Schenectady, 1952-58; dist. mgr., nat. sales mgr. Ladish Co., Milw., 1958-68; plant mgr. W. J. Baker Co., Newport, Ky., 1968-77, spl. asst. to pres., 1978-81; sales staff Western Stress, Inc., Cin., 1981—; tchr. adult edn. State N.Y., 1948-52. Rector, founder Curcillo de Christianity, Cin., Louisville, Memphis, Columbus, Ohio, Kansas City, Mo., Covington, Ky. Served with U.S. Army, 1942-45; ETO. Decorated D.F.C. with one cluster, Bronze Star with two clusters, Silver Star with one cluster, Air medal with six clusters, Purple Heart (3). Mem. Am. Mktg. Assn., Am. Mgmt. Assn., Assn. Tool and Mfg. Engrs. Democrat. Roman Catholic. Clubs: Nat. Rifle Assn., Ohio Gun Collectors, Cin. Revolver, Village Indian Hill Gun. Home: 1282 Aldrich Ave Cincinnati OH 45231 Office: PO Box 31122 Cincinnati OH 45231

LYNCH, JAMES RICHARD, lawyer; b. Tampa, Fla., Oct. 2, 1925; s. Virgil A. and Flora E. (Knight) L.; B.A., Calif. State U., Sacramento, 1950; J.D., Loyola U., New Orleans, 1969; m. Mary Alice White, Apr. 25, 1946; children—Robert Bruce, Daniel Mark. Mgr. mgmt. reporting aerospace div. Boeing Co., New Orleans, 1963-69; mgr. contracts adminstrn. Ingalls Shipbuilding, Pascagoula, Miss., 1969-73; dir. adminstrn. Equitable Equipment Co., New Orleans, 1973-74; mgr. contract Dresser Industries, IVO, Alexandria, La., 1974—; teaching cons. Mather AFB, parochial schs., Sacramento. Loaned exec. United Fund of New Orleans, 1966; pres. Improved Order of Redmen, Sacramento, 1950. Served with USNR, 1942-46. Recipient Bancroft awards in contracts and obligations, 1965, 66. Mem. La. Bar Assn., Am. Bar Assn. Republican. Home: 3107 Madonna Dr Alexandria LA 71301 Office: PO Box 1430 Alexandria LA 71301

LYNCH, JOSEPH P., mgmt. cons.; b. Grand Rapids, Mich., May 27, 1919; s. Joseph Patrick and Ellen Joan (Lynch) L.; student Northwestern U., 1939-41, Harvard Grad. Sch. Bus., 1968; m. Patsy Elizabeth Ashbolt, Apr. 29, 1944; children—Joseph P. III, Michael L., David, Pamela E., Anthony J. Mdse. mgr. asst. to advt. mgr., promotion mgr. Grand Rapids Press, 1946-54; promotion mgr. Washington Post, 1954-61, classified advt. mgr., 1961-67, advt. mgr., 1967-68, v.p. advt., 1969-74; pvt. practice mgmt. cons., 1974—. Active Boy Scouts Am. Bd. dirs. Cath. Youth Orgn., Met. Boys Club. Served to 1st lt. AUS, 1941-43. Mem. Internat. Newspaper Promotion Assn. (past pres.), Am. Newspaper Pubs. Assn. (plans bd. bur. advt.), Internat. Newspaper Advt. Execs. (dir.), Advt. Council (dir.), Assn. Newspaper Classified Advt. Mgrs. (past v.p.). Clubs: University, Burning Tree, Talbot. Home: 5215 Portsmouth Rd Washington DC 20016 Office: New Scotland Farm Route 2 Box 88 Trappe MD

LYNCH, RUSSELL VINCENT, oil and gas co. exec.; b. N.Y.C., Nov. 14, 1922; s. Francis R. and Helen Adams (Barrett) Lynch; B.A., Yale U., 1947; m. Nell Orand, Oct. 4, 1958; children—C. Bruton, Peter Francis, Joseph Barrett Orand; children by previous marriage—Rose P., R. Vincent, Alexander P. Chmn., chief exec. officer Lane-Wood, Inc., Dallas, 1962-75, dir., 1975—; owner, mng. partner R.V. Lynch & Co., Dallas, 1975—; chmn. bd. Riata Oil & Gas Co., Inc., 1978—, Lynch Locke Corp., 1980—; dir. Richardson Savs. Bank. Past sr. warden St. Michael's and All Angels Ch.; past pres. Episcopal Retreat and Conf. Center, Flower Mound, Tex. Served with USNR, 1942-45. Decorated Air medal. Episcopalian. Clubs: Houston; Brook Hollow Golf, City (Dallas); Fishers Island Country (N.Y.); Ocean Reef (Miami); Chevy Chase (Washington). Home: 9436 Meadowbrook St Dallas TX 75220 Office: 912 One Main Pl Dallas TX 75250

LYND, WILLIAM, computer co. exec.; b. Boston, Nov. 24, 1942; s. Joseph Mearle and Alice (Campbell) L.; A.A., Menlo Coll., 1963; B.S. in Indsl. Mgmt., U. Calif., San Jose, 1965; B.S. in Elec. Engring., Lawrence U., 1965; M.B.A., Pacific Northwestern U., 1968; M.S., Bruckner U., 1969, Ph.D., 1969; m. Nancy Helman Herman Lynd, July 3, 1973; children—Allyn David, Barry Henry, Bradford Joseph. Project analyst U. Calif., 1962-64, salesman Control Data Corp., Palo Alto, 1964-67; regional mgr. DPF & G Co., Westwood, Calif., 1967-71; v.p. sales, founder Logicon Intercomp, Torrance, Calif., 1971-75; dir. mktg./sales MacAro div. MacDonald Douglas Co., Carson, Calif., 1975-77; founder, 1977, then exec. v.p. MRP, Inc., Santa Ana, Calif., 1977-80; pres. M-Systems, Santa Ana, 1980—, also dir.; dir. CIT, Inc., Santa Ana; lectr. U. Calif., Irvine, 1979-80, Saddleback Coll., 1977-79. Mem. Am. Prodn. and Inventory Control Soc. (cert.). Home: 11321 Cielo Pl Santa Ana CA 92705 Office: 1232 A S Village Way Santa Ana CA 92705

LYNHAM, JOHN MARMADUKE, lawyer; b. Washington, Feb. 19, 1908; s. Edgar Hardwick and Mera Elsie (Marmaduke) L.; B.S. in Govt., Am. U., 1935; J.D., George Washington U., 1931, LL.M., 1932; m. Adele Radolph Pugh, May 22, 1947; children—Adele Cameron, John Marmaduke, Mary Hardwicke, Gale Randolph. Admitted to D.C. bar, 1931; partner firm Drury, Lynham & Powell, Washington, 1939-69; v.p., trust officer Nat. Savs. & Trust Co., Washington, 1969-80, cons., 1980—; individual practice law, Washington, 1980—. Chmn. bd. dirs. Landon Sch., 1967-74. Served to comdr. USNR, 1941-45. Fellow Am. Bar Found.; mem. Am. Bar Assn., Am. Judicature Soc., Instn. Jud. Adminstrn., Bar Assn. D.C., D.C. Bar Assn., Md. Bar Assn. Episcopalian. Clubs: Chevy Chase (pres. 1955), Metropolitan (pres. 1973), Lawyers (pres. 1981) (Washington). Author: The Chevy Chase Club, A History, 1958. Home: 14 Oxford St Chevy Chase Village MD 20015 Office: 719 15th St NW Washington DC 20005

LYNN, EUGENE MATTHEW, ins. co. exec.; b. Kansas City, Mo., Nov. 6, 1918; s. Eugene M. and Marthield (Ellis) L.; John B. Stetson U., 1937-39; m. Mary E. Spoors, Mar. 12, 1947 (dec.); 1 dau., Diane E.; m. 2d, Christine E. Koppl, Jan. 19, 1980. Pilot Trans World

Airlines, 1944-47; v.p. U.S. Epperson Underwriting Co., Boca Raton, Fla., 1949-55, pres., 1955—; pres. LIG Ins. Agy., Inc., Boca Raton, 1978—; v.p. Lynn Insurance Group, Kansas City, 1949-55, pres., 1955—; v.p. Universal Underwriters Ins. Co., Kansas City, 1949-55, pres., 1955—; underwriter Universal Underwriters Lloyds, Dallas, 1948—; pres. Universal Underwriters, Inc., Kansas City, 1955—, Universal Underwriters Life Ins. Co., Kansas City, 1960—; dir. United Mo. Bank of Kansas City, N.A., Gulfstream Bank & Trust Co. N.A., Boca Raton, Fla., chmn. bd., chief exec. officer Boca Raton Community Hosp. Mem. Am. Reciprocal Ins. Assn. (pres., dir.). Clubs: Kansas City, Mission Hills Country, River (Kansas City, Mo.); Boca Raton Hotel and Club, Bankers, Royal Palm Yacht and Country, Broken Sound (Boca Raton, Fla.); Delray Beach (Fla.); Ocean Reef (Key Largo, Fla.); Jockey (Miami, Fla.). Home: 565 Alexander Palm Rd Boca Raton FL 33432 Office: 5115 Oak St Kansas City MO 64112 also 2501 N Military Trail Boca Raton FL 33431

LYNN, JOHN WARREN, mcht.; b. Bklyn., Mar. 4, 1921; s. Thomas Robert and Olga (Clemens) L.; student Syracuse U., 1939-41; m. Adele Grant, Feb. 5, 1944; children—Suzanne (Mrs. Dick Falkenbush), Dianne (Mrs. Philip Nofi), Robert, Thomas. Vice pres. Mid-Atlantic region F.W. Woolworth Co., 1965-68, Northeastern region, 1968-69, v.p. sales and advt., N.Y.C., 1969-70, v.p. merchandising, 1970-74, sr. v.p. merchandising, 1975-76, exec. v.p., 1977—, dir., 1970—, sr. exec. v.p. Woolworth Corp., 1978—, chmn. exec. com., vice chmn. bd., 1980—, pres. Woolworth-Woolco Div., 1978—; dir. F.W. Woolworth Co. Ltd. (Can.), F.W. Woolworth & Co. Ltd. (U.K.), Borden Inc., Kinney Shoe Co., Richmond Clothing Co. Served with USAAF, World War II. Decorated Purple Heart, Air medal with 8 oak leaf clusters. Mem. Newcomen Soc. Office: 233 Broadway New York NY 10279

LYNN, KARYL V., JR., mfg. co. ofcl.; b. Bklyn., Mar. 20, 1922; s. Karyl V. and Hazel M. (Wendell) L.; B.B.A. with distinction, U. Mich., 1948, M.B.A. with distinction, 1949; m. Lorraine W. Mullen, July 21, 1946; children—Kevin V., Keith J., Kathleen A. Personnel dir. Dairypak, Inc., Cleve., 1949-54; personnel mgr. Gen. Mills Corp., Mpls., 1954-56; plant mgr. Dairypak, Inc., Toledo, 1956-63, Mercury Packaging Co., Toledo, 1963-66; group dir. indsl. relations Hoover Ball Bearing Co., Ann Arbor, Mich., 1966-67, Crucible Steel Corp., Pitts., 1967-68; dir. personnel adminstrn. Colt Industries, Inc., N.Y.C., 1968—; lectr. indsl. relations John Carroll U., Cleve., 1949-54; mem. steering com. Mgmt. Compensation Services, Scottsdale, Ariz., 1975—; mem. adv. com. T.P.F.&C. Compensation Data Bank, N.Y.C., 1977—; seminar speaker. Served with USAF, 1943-46. U. Mich. Club scholar, 1947-48, 49. Mem. Northwestern Ohio Tennis Assn. (chmn. jr. devel. 1965-66), Am. Soc. Personnel Adminstrn., Am. Compensation Assn., Assn. Practical Tng. (chmn. bd. 1979—), Am. Mgmt. Assn., Beta Gamma Sigma, Phi Kappa Phi. Republican. Unitarian. Club: Kiwanis of Downtown Toledo (dir. 1963-64). Contbr. articles to profl. jours. Home: 203 Forest Dr Hillsdale NJ 07642 Office: 430 Park Ave New York NY 10022

LYNN, STEPHEN ROGER, outdoor products mfg. co. exec.; b. Pasadena, Calif., Jan. 17, 1949; s. William Thomas and Marvis Anne (Rogers) L.; B.S., Brigham Young U., 1971; M.B.A., Calif. State Coll., Dominguez Hills, 1974; m. Patricia Lubniewski, June 2, 1970; children—Jennifer Laura, Kristin Anne, Jeffrey Alan, Karen Marie, Julie Anne. With Rockwell Internat., Los Angeles, 1971-74, Wilson Sporting Goods Co., River Grove, Ill., 1974-77; dir. mfg. services Roper Outdoor Products, Bradley, Ill., 1977—. Mem. Soc. Mfg. Engrs. (sr.), Am. Mgmt. Assn. Republican. Mormon. Office: 195 E Broadway Bradley IL 60915

LYON, GEORGE POWELL, mgmt. cons.; b. Phila., Dec. 15, 1928; s. Harold Vinton and Florence (Eagin) L.; B.A., Coll. William and Mary, 1951; m. Frances Chaffee, June 11, 1955; children—Janette, Laura, Pamela. Asst. personnel mgr. Am. Meter Co., Erie, Pa., 1954-55, asst. mgr. indsl. relations, Phila., 1955-56, plant mgr., Wyalusing, Pa., 1956-57; supr. product planning Sylvania Home Electronics div. Sylvania Electric Products, Inc., Batavia, N.Y., 1957-60, mktg. adminstrn., 1960-61, v.p. mktg. services, 1961-63; v.p. E.A. Butler Assos., Inc., Phila., 1963-73, pres., dir. N.Y.C., 1973-79; prin. George P. Lyon Assos., Doylestown, Pa., 1980—; dir. White Hall Mut. Ins. Co., Doylestown. Mem. Council, Borough of Doylestown, 1977—, v.p., 1978—. Served to 1st lt. USMC, 1951-53. Mem. Am. Mktg. Assn. Republican. Presbyterian. Home: 7 Juniper Dr Doylestown PA 18901 Office: 105 N Broad St Doylestown PA 18901

LYON, JAMES BURROUGHS, lawyer; b. N.Y.C., May 11, 1930; s. Francis Murray and Edith (Strong) L.; B.A. magna cum laude, Amherst Coll., 1952; LL.B., Yale U., 1955. Admitted to Conn. bar, 1955; asso. firm Murtha, Cullina, Richter & Pinney, and predecessors, Hartford, 1956—, partner, 1961—. Mem. Amherst Alumni Assn. Conn., 1956—, sec., 1956-66; Conn. chmn. capital program Amherst Coll., 1962-65, mem. exec. com. Alumni Council, 1963-69, chmn., 1968-69, chmn. com. deferred gifts and bequests, 1977-80; bd. dirs. Kingswood-Oxford Sch., West Hartford, chmn., 1975-78, gen. chmn. capital program, 1969-72; bd. dirs. Wadsworth Atheneum, Hartford, v.p., 1972—; bd. dirs. Noah Webster Found. and Hist. Soc., Inc., West Hartford, 1965-79; bd. dirs. Conn. Bar Found., 1974—; bd. dirs. Fidelco Found., Bloomfield, Conn., 1971—; advisory com. Walks Found., Hartford, 1977—. pres. Yale Law Sch. Assn. Hartford and Eastern Conn., 1966; mem. adv. com. Inst. Fed. Taxation, N.Y. U., 1975—; councilor-at-large New Eng. Assn. Museums, 1980—; corporator Mt. Sinai Hosp., Hartford, 1972—, Hartford Hosp., 1975—, St. Francis Hosp., Hartford, 1976—, Hartford Public Library, 1979—, Hartford Art Sch., 1979—; trustee Old Sturbridge (Mass.) Village, 1974—, Ella Burr McManus Trust, Hartford, 1980—; pres. No. Conn. chpt. Nat. Football Found. and Hall of Fame, 1966-69; nat. chmn. Friends of Trinity Coll., 1977-78. Recipient Amherst Coll. eminent service medal, 1967. Mem. Am., Conn., Hartford County bar assns., Assn. Bar City N.Y., Greater Hartford C. of C. (chmn. sports and recreation com. 1978—, Newcomen Soc. N.Am., Phi Beta Kappa, Phi Delta Phi, Theta Delta Chi. Clubs: Yale (v.p. 1965), Hartford, University (pres. 1976-78), Tennis (dir. 1971-74), Twentieth Century (pres. 1980—), Hartford Golf (dir. 1972-75) (Hartford, Conn.); Yale, Union (N.Y.C.); Dauntless (Essex, Conn.); Yale Golf (New Haven); Limestone Trout (East Canaan, Conn.). Home: 25 Bishop Rd West Hartford CT 06119 Office: 101 Pearl St Hartford CT 06103

LYON, PAUL RUSHMER, fin. exec.; b. Middleburgh, N.Y., Apr. 20, 1942; s. Donald Rich and Alice Louise (Rushmer) L.; B.A., Cornell U., 1964; M.B.A., U. Laval, 1972; m. Louise Labbé; 1 dau., Natasha. Comptroller, Bank of N.S., Que. region, 1972-78; dir. adminstrv. services Fédn. des Caisses d'Etablissement du Qué., 1978—; pres. Paul R. Lyon Services, Inc., 1979—. Vice-pres. internat. Cornell U. Class of 1964, 1979—. Served with USN, 1964-70. Mem. Exptl. Aircraft Assn. (treas. 1979—), Order of Land Surveyors of Que. (dir. 1980), Union des Artistes, Société Lyrique d'Aubigny. Methodist. Home: 1049 du Seigle St-Augustin PQ G0A 3E0 Canada Office: 580 Grande Allee Est Quebec PQ G1R 4R2 Canada

LYON, RICHARD GRANT, lawyer; b. Wilmington, Del., July 13, 1946; s. Donald Wilkinson and Martha (Crane) L.; A.B., Haverford Coll., 1968; J.D., Harvard U., 1971. Admitted to N.Y. State bar, 1972; asso. firm Sullivan & Cromwell, N.Y.C., 1971—. Mem. campaign com. Haverford Coll., 1975—. Served with U.S. Army, 1972. Mem. Assn. Bar City of N.Y. (library com.), Harvard Law Sch. Alumni Assn., ACLU. Democrat. Clubs: The Recess, Metropolitan Opera. Home: 411 West End Ave New York City NY 10024 Office: 125 Broad St New York City NY 10004

LYON, ROGER ADRIAN, banker; b. Phillipsburg, N.J., June 28, 1927; s. Howard Suydam and Mildred (Derry) L.; B.A., Princeton U., 1950; M.B.A., Rutgers U., 1954, postgrad. in banking, 1957-59; m. Mary Woodford, June 17, 1950; children—Nancy Carol, Roger Adrian. With Chase Manhattan Bank, 1950-76, sr. v.p. Bank Portfolio Group, 1969-72, exec. v.p., 1972-76; pres., chief adminstrv. officer Valley Nat. Bank of Ariz., Phoenix, 1976—; instr. Stonier Grad. Sch. Banking, 1960-72; mem. adv. bd. Mountain Bell Telephone Co. Nat. bd. trustees YMCA, 1964-76; chmn. dean's adv. council Ariz. State U. Coll. Bus.; bd. dirs. Ariz. State U. Found.; b. trustees, exec. com. Heard Mus.; chmn. Western Regional Council, Am. Grad. Sch. Internat. Mgmt.; chmn. Gov.'s Fuel Conservation Com. Served with USMC, 1945-46, 51-52. Mem. Am. Bankers Assn. (treas. 1975-77), Ariz. Bankers Assn., Assn. Res. City Bankers, Pacific Basin Econ. Council, Council Fgn. Relations, Internat. Monetary Conf., Nat. Alliance Bus. (Met. Phoenix chmn. 1979). Republican. Episcopalian. Author: Commercial Bank Investment Portfolio Management, 1960. Office: 241 N Central Ave Phoenix AZ 85004

LYON, SHERMAN ORWIG, chem. co. exec.; b. Greenwich, Conn., Sept. 4, 1939; s. James R. and June K. (Orwig) L.; B.S. in Chem. Engring., Purdue U., 1961; m. Nell Collar, June 15, 1968; children—Jeffrey, Michelle. Successively process engr., process supr., prodn. supt., mktg. mgr. Monsanto Co., St. Louis, 1961-72; gen. mgr. catalyst div. Mallinckrodt, Inc., St. Louis, 1972-75, gen. mgr. indsl. chems. div., 1975-77, gen. mgr. chem. div., 1977-78, v.p. splty. chems., 1978-80; group v.p. Celanese Corp., Chatham, N.J., 1980—. Mem. Am. Inst. Chem. Engrs., Tau Beta Pi, Omicron Delta Kappa, Sigma Phi Epsilon, Iron Key. Presbyterian. Home: 5 Quaker Ridge Rd Morristown NJ 07960 Office: Celanese 26 Main St Chatham NJ 07928

LYONS, BILL, bank exec.; b. N.Y.C., June 26, 1937; s. William Patrick and Lucy Ann (Flatley) L.; B.B.A., Manhattan Coll., 1962; M.B.A., N.Y. U., 1968; m. Noreen Corkerry, June 26, 1965; children—Kerry, Luann, Nora, William, Siobhan. Gen. partner Wellington & Co., N.Y.C., 1971-78; v.p., treas. Cantor, Fitzgerald & Co., Inc., Beverly Hills, Calif., 1978-80; pres. Security Trust Co., Los Angeles, 1980—; instr. Fordham U., 1975-77. Pres., PTA, Most Beloved Sacrament Ch., Franklin Lakes, N.J., 1976. Served with USMC, 1954-57. C.P.A., Calif., N.Y. Mem. Am. Inst. C.P.A.'s, Calif. Soc. C.P.A.'s, N.Y. Soc. C.P.A.'s. Office: 1 Wilshire Blvd Los Angeles CA 90017

LYONS, DUDLEY EMERSON, food co. exec.; b. N.Y.C., Feb. 20, 1941; s. Albert McKinley and Beatrice Mary (Leek) L.; B.A., Amherst Coll., 1962; M.B.A., Harvard U., 1965; m. Volina Valentine, June 25, 1965; children—Victoria, Gregory. Product mgr. Gen. Foods Corp., White Plains, N.Y., 1965-70; bus. group mgr. Church & Dwight Co., N.Y.C., 1970-73; with Topps Chewing Gum Inc., Bklyn., 1973—, sr. v.p., 1974-76, exec. v.p., 1976—, also dir. Home: 390 Riverside Dr New York NY 10025 Office: Topps Chewing Gum Inc 254 36th St Brooklyn NY 11232

LYONS, LOUIS CLAYTON, acct.; b. Gulfport, Miss., Dec. 17, 1941; s. Louis Thaddeous and Mamie Myrtle (Read) L.; B.B.A., U. Miss., 1964; m. Karen Lynne Nevling, Nov. 29, 1980; children—Louis Clayton, Mary Beth. Sr. accountant Peat Marwick, Mitchell & Co., C.P.A.'s, Jackson, Miss., 1964-68, Ernst & Ernst, C.P.A.'s., Jackson, 1969; controller Mossy Oldsmobile Co., Houston, 1970-71; sr. accountant Andrew G. Shebay & Co., C.P.A.'s, Houston, 1972; systems analyst Marathon Mfg. Co., Houston, 1973, controller battery div., Waco, Tex., 1974-75; div. v.p. fin., controller Carey-McFall div. Marathon Mfg. Co., Montoursville, Pa., 1976; corp. controller Richmond Tank Car Co., Houston, 1977-79; pvt. practice C.P.A., Houston, 1979—. C.P.A., Miss., Tex. Mem. Am. Inst. C.P.A.'s, Miss., Tex. socs. C.P.A.'s, Nat. Assn. Accts., Beta Alpha Psi. Republican. Presbyterian. Home: 1922 B Upland Houston TX 77043 Office: 11211 Katy Freeway Houston TX 77079

LYONS, ROBERT LEROY, energy conservation co. exec.; b. Windham, Maine, Apr. 20, 1946; s. Malcolm L. and Mary L. L.; student U. Maine, 1964-67; B.S. in Mktg., N.H. Coll., 1976; m. Mary Victoria Law, Nov. 20, 1970; children—Amy Adrienne, Kate Victoria. New Eng. dist. mgr. Upson Co., Lockport, N.Y., 1970-76; dist. sales rep. New Eng. and N.Y., Thermtron Products, Inc., 1976-77; owner, operator Energy Conservation Systems, Sebago Lake, Maine, 1977—; cons.; tchr. energy conservation No. Essex Community Coll., 1978. Served with USAR, 1976. Mem. Maine Insulation Contractors Assn., Aircraft Owners and Pilots Assn. Roman Catholic. Home and Office: RFD 2 Box 52-A Sebago Lake ME 04075

LYONS, ROBERT RONDELL, fin. exec.; b. Bremerton, Wash., July 15, 1944; s. Rocky R. and Shirley E. (Poynter) L.; B.S. magna cum laude, U. Colo., 1971; M.B.A., U. Tex., 1979; m. Joan G. Curreri, Apr. 1, 1967; children—Krista D., Wendy J., Suzanne N. Mgmt. cons. Peat Marwick Mitchell & Co., Denver, 1972-73; corporate auditor Xerox Corp., Rochester, N.Y., 1973-75; v.p. adminstrn. Church's Fried Chicken Inc., San Antonio, 1975-78; treas., controller Monier Resources, Inc., San Antonio, 1979—. Served to capt. USMC, 1961-69. Decorated Purple Heart, D.F.C.; C.P.A., Colo., Tex.; cert. internal auditor. Mem. Am. Mgmt. Assn., Am. Mktg. Assn., Inst. Internal Auditors, Tex. Soc. C.P.A.'s, Assn. M.B.A. Execs., U. Colo. Alumni Assn. Club: Woodlake Country. Home: 10310 Severn St San Antonio TX 78217 Office: 11100 Osgood San Antonio TX 78233

LYONS, WILLIAM RICHARD, grocery distbn. co. exec.; b. Milford, Del., June 17, 1937; s. Vernon Lee and Helen Mae (Wiley) L.; A.A.S., So. Colo. State U., 1966; M.S. in B.A., Pacific So. U., 1977; B.A. in B.A., Chgo. State U., 1976; m. Patricia Marie Morrison, June 17, 1979; children by previous marriage—Kenneth, Ronald, Patrick. Bookkeeper, Chevron Oil Co., Pueblo, Colo., 1966-70; mgr. bulk oil plant Standard Oil Co., Pueblo, 1970-73; warehouse mgr. Asso. Grocers of Colo., Denver, 1963-76; researcher in acctg., fin. Seaford, Del., 1980—. Served with U.S. Army, 1959-63. Mem. Nat. Ministers Assn., Am. Mgmt. Assn., Phi Theta Kappa. Democrat. Mem. Assemblies of God. Office: PO Box 67 Seaford DE 19973

LYONS, WILLIAM WATSON, energy co. exec.; b. Lansing, Mich., Jan. 3, 1935; s. Edward Thomas and Martha Grace (Watson) L.; B.A. in Econs. and History, Mich. State U., 1959; m. Mary Elizabeth Long, Jan. 31, 1959; children—Lisa Ann, Laura Elizabeth, Sarah O'Neil, Bridget Riley. Dist. mgr. Oldsmobile div. Gen. Motors Corp., Portland, Great Falls, Seattle and Los Angeles, 1959-66; regional planner Appalachian Regional Commn., Washington, 1968-70; with U.S. Dept. Interior, Washington, 1966-68, asst. to sec., 1970-71, dep. asst. sec., 1971-73, dep. under sec., 1973-77; v.p. resource devel./regulatory affairs Nerco, Inc., Portland, Oreg., 1977—. Bd. dirs. Providence Med. Center, Portland, 1977—; mem. Council Oreg. Mus. Sci. and Industry, 1979—. Served with U.S. Army, 1955-57. Mem. Mining and Reclamation Council Am. (dir., exec. com., chmn. govt. affairs com.). Club: Univ. (Portland). Home: 10260 SW Daphne Pl Portland OR 97219 Office: 111 SW Columbia Suite 800 Portland OR 97201

LYSONS, HARRY PHILIP DAN, advt. agy. exec.; b. London, Jan. 12, 1940; came to U.S., 1967, naturalized, 1976. s. Henry Dan and Sylvia Francesca (Treffry) L.; ed. St. Edmunds, Canterbury, Kent, Eng. Med. lab. technologist County Hosp., Redhill, Eng., 1956-61; med. rep. Merrell-Nat. Labs., London, 1961-67, William S. Merrell Co., N.Y.C., 1967-69; account exec. William Douglas McAdams, N.Y.C., 1970-76; v.p., account supr. Kallir Philips Ross, N.Y.C., 1976—. Mem. Pharm. Advt. Council N.Y., Inst. Med. Lab. Tech. (U.K.), N.Y. Power Squadron. Home: 101 E 16th St New York NY 10003 Office: 605 3d Ave New York NY 10158

LYTLE, SUSAN LEE, lawyer, investment banker; b. Ft. Warren, Wyo., Oct. 23, 1945; d. James Rholon and Bette Jane (Carper) L.; A.B. cum laude, U. Miami, 1967, J.D. cum laude, 1970; L.L.M., Harvard U., 1971. Admitted to Fla. bar, 1970; asso. firm Greenberg, Traurig, Hoffman, Lipoff & Quentel, Miami, Fla., 1971-76; mem. firm, 1976-77; asso. mergers and acquisitions Goldman, Sachs & Co., 1977-80, v.p., 1980—; instr. law Boston U., 1970; instr. law U. Miami, 1969, mem. adj. faculty, 1974-77. Mem. Am., Fla. bar assns. Democrat. Editor-in-chief U. Miami Law Rev., 1970. Home: 215 E 68th St New York NY 10021 Office: 55 Broad St New York NY 10006

LYTLE, WILLIAM ORLAND, JR., camera co. exec.; b. Pitts., Jan. 1, 1937; s. William Orland and Mary Elizabeth (Taylor) L.; B.S., Yale U., 1958, M.I.A., 1962; postgrad. Boston U., 1978—. Personnel specialist Esso Research & Engring. Co., Linden, N.J., 1962-65; mgmt. devel. specialist Polaroid Corp., Cambridge, Mass., 1965-68, tng. mgr., camera div., 1968-71, sr. orgn. devel. cons., 1971—; instr. evenings Rutgers U., 1963, 64. Loaned exec. tng. dir. United Way Mass. Bay, 1976, 77. Served with USN, 1958-60. Mem. Internat. Assn. Applied Social Scientists (cert.), Orgn. Devel. Network. Democrat. Home: 205 Mount Auburn St Cambridge MA 02138 Office: Polaroid Corp 750 Main St Cambridge MA 02139

MAAGDENBERG, RONALD RICHARD, automated control systems corp. exec.; b. Amsterdam, Netherlands, July 23, 1931; s. Richard Willem Alexander and Wilhelmina Cornelia (Mos) M.; came to U.S., 1956, naturalized, 1973; B.S. in Marine Engring., Mcht. Marine Acad. (Netherlands), 1952; M.B.A., LaSalle U., 1966; LL.B., Pepperdine U.; m. Rosemarie Moreno Maagdenberg-Orozco, Dec. 28, 1967. Third engr. Netherlands Steamship Co., Rotterdam, 1954-56; chem. technician Hoffman La Roche Pharm. Inc., Roche Park, Nutley, N.J., 1956-62; prodn. supr. Fairchild Semicondr. Corp., Mountain View, Calif., 1962-66, sr. MOS-IC supr., 1968-70; sr. prodn. supr. semicondrs. div. ITT, West Palm Beach, Fla., 1965; sr. prodn. supr. Philco Microelectronics Corp. div. Ford Motor Co., Santa Clara, Calif., 1966-68; process engr. Solitron Devices, Inc., San Diego, 1970-72; sr. supr. Signetics Corp., Sunnyvale, Calif., 1971-73; customer service engr. Unicorp, Inc., Sunnyvale, 1973-74; cons., co-owner Automotive Service Center, Mountain View, 1971-73; pres., chief exec. officer, ACS, Inc., Sunnyvale, 1974—. Served with Spl. Forces, Netherlands Army, 1952-54. Decorated Service Cross (Korea); UN War medal; Royal Mil. Combat medal, Juliana Service medal (Netherlands). Lic. radioactive material, Dept. Pub. Health, Calif. Mem. Nat. Bus. Adminstrn. Assn., Am. Mgmt. Assn. Clubs: VFW Vets. Legion (Amsterdam); Orgn. Capts. and Officers in Royal Mcht. Marine (Hague, Netherlands); Masons. Patentee silicon nitride and silicon wafer cleaning process. Home: PO Box 61389 Sunnyvale CA 94088

MAAHS, WERNER H., foods co. exec.; b. Milw., Jan. 15, 1927; s. William H. and Marie (Mueller) M.; grad. high sch.; m. Gladys M. Anderson, June 24, 1950; children—Sandra Marie, Nancy Jean, Christine Lynn, David Werner, Judy Annette. Patrolman, White Fish Bay (Wis.) Police Dept., 1950-54; pres. Alto Shaam, Inc., Milw., 1955-59; v.p. Chicken Delight, Inc., Rock Island, Ill., 1956-64; pres. Chicken Delight of Calif., Los Angeles, 1959-64; pres., dir. Franchise Devel. Corp., Los Angeles, 1962-64; chmn. bd. Chicken Delight Eastern, Inc., Paterson, N.J., 1962-64; partner Linkletter, Maahs, Bolte & Assos., Inc., 1965—; pres. Buffalo Bill's Steak Village, Inc., 1965-70, Buffalo Bill's Wild West, Inc., Los Angeles, 1967-70, Buffalo Bill's Properties Inc., 1968-70; v.p. Fitzgerald, Maahs & Miller Assos., 1965-70; v.p. Alto Shaam Inc.; pres. M & M Enterprises, Inc.; regional dir. Chicken Delight, Inc., Los Angeles; dir., producer Adventure Prodns., Inc., 1969; sales mgr. Hanna Industries, Inc., 1970-71; gen. mgr. franchise sales TraveLodge Internat., Inc., 1971-73; v.p. Energy Savs. Appliances Corp., 1977-80, A.W. Huss Co., 1980, Alto Shaam Internat.; pres. Natural Lite Food Products Corp., 1979; dir. Computoreturn Tax Preparation Service, Captain Tim's Seafood Galley, Chicken Delight Southwestern, Inc., Dallas, Rewdco Distbg. Co. Mem. ethics com. Internat. Franchise Assn., 1959-64; del. White House Conf. on Small Bus., 1980. Mem. Nat. Assn. Food Equipment Mfrs. Lutheran (pres. council). Home: N63 W 33959 Lakeview Dr Oconomowoc WI 53066 Office: 6040 Flint Rd Milwaukee WI 53209

MAAS, NORMAN HOWARD, chem. co. exec.; b. N.Y.C., Feb. 11, 1950; s. Rudolf Martin and Elizabeth (Kohnstamm) M.; B.A., U. Pitts., 1972; M.B.A., U. Miami, 1975. Account underwriter Allstate Ins. Co., Harrison, N.Y., 1972-74; asst. to pres. H. Kohnstamm & Co., Inc., N.Y.C., 1975-80, dir. personnel, 1976-80, asst. treas., 1979-80; sales adminstr. export newsprint Central Nat. Corp., N.Y.C., 1980—. Recipient Merit award United Fund of N.Y., 1976. Mem. Am. Mgmt. Assn., Synthetic Organic Chem. Mfrs. Assn., Dry Color Mfrs. Assn. Home: 3671 Hudson Manor Terr Riverdale NY 10463 Office: 100 Park Ave New York NY 10017

MAASRY, NADEEM GEORGE, banker; b. Aley, Lebanon, Feb. 8, 1940; came to U.S., 1967; m. George Nemr and Mary (George) M.; B.A., Am. U. Beirut, 1961, M.A., 1963; B.A., M.A., Johns Hopkins U., 1969; m. Anne Marie L. Drost, Oct. 14, 1978; 1 son, George Nicholas. With First Nat. Bank of Washington, 1969-70; with Internat. Bank, Washington, 1970-77, v.p., 1975-77; v.p. Fin. Gen. Bankshares, Inc., Washington, 1978—; dir. Credit European Bank, Luxembourg, Kuwait Fin. Centre, S.A.K. Mem. Nat. Press Club. Club: City Tavern (Washington). Office: 1701 Pennsylvania Ave NW Washington DC 20006

MABIE, RUTH MARIE, realtor; b. Pueblo, Colo., Feb. 7; d. Newton Everett and Florence Ellen Allen; student San Diego State U., 1957-60, Grossmont Jr. Coll., 1970-71, U. Calif., San Diego, 1970, 72; M.B.A., La Jolla U., 1980; m. Richard O. Mabie, Nov. 29, 1947; 1 son, Ward A. Mgr., LaMont Modeling Sch., San Diego, 1962; tchr. Am. Bus. Coll., San Diego, 1964-66; free-lance modeling, 1960-72; owner, broker Ruth Mabie Realty, San Diego, 1972—; asst. v.p. Skil-Bilt, Inc., 1976—; dir. Mabie & Mintz, Inc. Bd. dirs. Multiple Sclerosis Dr., 1971—. Mem. San Diego Bd. Realtors. Republican. Office: 6280 Riverdale St San Diego CA 92121

MABIRE, KENNETH EARL, bank cons.; b. Pensacola, Fla., Jan. 8, 1946; s. Daniel Edward and Loralee (Hollingsworth) M.; B.S., U. W. Fla., 1968; M.S., Rollins Coll., 1976; m. Erica Frazier, Aug. 24, 1968. Instr. mgmt., faculty marketing Savannah (Ga.) Tech., 1970-72; claims adminstr. U.S. Fidelity & Guaranty Co., Orlando, Fla., 1972-74; asst. v.p. Flagship Banks, Inc., Orlando, Fla., 1974-77, v.p., Jacksonville, 1977-78, dir., West Orlando, Fla., 1975-77; pres. Fin. Mktg. Assos., Inc., Winter Park, Fla., 1978—; dir. Jacksonville Bus. Devel. Center, Inc.; pres., dir. Investors Life Fla. 1978—. Mem. Orlando C. of C., Jacksonville C. of C., Fla. Bankers Assn., Am. Bankers Assn., Bank Marketing Assn., Am. Soc. Personnel Adminstrn. Methodist. Club: Rotary. Home: 814 Laurel Ave Orlando FL 32403 Office: 400 N New York Ave Winter Park FL 32789

MABRY, HARRY COOPER, lawyer; b. Carlisle County, Ky., Feb. 16, 1895; s. Jesse J. and Onie (Nance) M.; grad. summa cum laude, Southwestern Coll., 1916; LL.B., Yale U., 1923, J.D., 1971; m. LaVerne Dages; children—Dorothy Mabry Chambers, Marjorie Mabry Howard, Elizabeth Mabry Rhodes. Supt., Moorewood Pub. Schs., 1913-15; admitted to Calif. bar, 1924, also U.S. Supreme Ct. bar, since practiced in Los Angeles; former spl. counsel Boulder Dam project, Boulder Dam power line, Mono Basin Water Devel.; former local counsel Mfrs. Trust Co., N.Y.C.; spl. counsel Supt. Banks of Calif.; personal counsel for heirs or claimants to estates of Lady Mendl, Don Lee, Jacob H. Wood, Lupe Velez, Jesse E. Anderson, Theodore Kosloff, William Cornell Greene, Mary Greene Wiswall, Frank Borzage, Edna Saks McKinnon, others. Regional rep. Yale Law Sch., 1928-36; bd. govs. Yale Pub. Assn., 1933-38; class reunion chmn. Yale 1938, 63, 68, 73; mem. Nat. Yale Law Sch. Grad. Bd., 1957—; Yale class sec., 1962—; mem. Yale alumni bd., 1968—. Served as 1st lt., aviator U.S. Army, World War I. Named hon. Indian chief Pacific Internat. Expn., San Diego, 1936; hon. col. staff Gov. Thomas J. Mabry of N.Mex., 1950. Mem. Am. (standing com. on resolutions over 20 yrs., chmn. 1963-64), Calif., Los Angeles County bar assns., Calif. State Bar, Am. Judicature Soc., Chancery Club Am. (pres. 1929-30), Los Angeles World Affairs Council, Am. Legion (post comdr. Los Angeles 1938-39), S.A.R. (pres. Los Angeles chpt. 1942-50), Calif. Jr. C. of C. (pres. 1929-30), ASCAP, Soc. Authors and Composers of Mexico (hon.), Phi Alpha Delta, Pi Kappa Delta, Tau Kappa Epsilon (hon.), Book and Gavel (Yale). Clubs: Yale of So. Calif. (pres. 1934-36); Los Angeles Athletic; Masons, Scottish Rite, Shriners. Author: Road to Yale; Romance and Results in the Development of Water and Power Resources of Los Angeles; Americanism and the Great American, Will Rogers; The Spirit and the Sword; Decision; Just Barely; Will Contests; Oral Agreements to Provide by Will; Impossibilities in Decedent Estate Litigation, Apparent or Real; Disputing Indisputable Presumptions, Revoking Irrevocable Trusts, Breaking Unbreakable Wills, and Enforcing Unenforceable Agreements. Lyricist-composer: Alleluia; Yosemite; Catalina Isle; Dear Old Western Home: Rainbow of Hawaii; A Smile is Worth a Million; White Christmas Snow; I Could Cry Over You; Back to Mexico, (Volver A Mexico); Calypso and Limbo, Los Angeles (City of the Angels), Catalina Isle, Yosemite, others. Address: 2226 N New Hampshire Ave Los Angeles CA 90027

MAC ALEESE, JOHN ELMER, engring. co. exec.; b. Tupper Lake, N.Y., Oct. 31, 1932; s. David Rice and Louise Harriet (Elmer) MacA.; student Clarkson Coll., 1950-53, 55-56; B.S. in Mech. Engring., Tri-State Coll., 1957; m. Mary Elizabeth Walrath, May 8, 1954; children—George, Michael, Anne Marie, Lisa, John. With Newton Falls Paper Mill, Inc. (N.Y.), 1956-76, plant engr., 1964-71, v.p. engring. and maintenance, 1971-76; v.p. engring. and constrn. Stebbins Engring & Mfg., Watertown, N.Y., 1976—. Justice of Peace, Town of Clifton, N.Y., 1958, supr., 1974-76. Bd. mgrs. Clifton-Fine Hosp., Star Lake, N.Y. Served with AUS, 1953-55. Recipient Bausch-Laumb Math. and Sci. award, 1950; Rensselaer Poly. Inst. Math. and Sci. award, 1950—. Registered profl. engr., N.Y. Mem. T.A.P.P.I., Knotty Pine Ednl. Assn. (pres. 1971—). Lion. Home: 444 Barben Ave Watertown NY 13601 Office: Stebbins Engring & Mfg Watertown NY 13601

MACALLISTER, SCOTT DOUGLAS, fin. exec.; b. Ft. Wayne, Ind., Jan. 14, 1952; s. David William and Evelyn Marie (Krueger) MacA.; B.S. cum laude in Bus. Adminstrn., Butler U., 1974; m. Angela Gayle Horsley, Sept. 16, 1978. With MacAllister Machinery Co., Inc., Indpls., 1974—, sec.-treas., 1980—, dir., 1977—. Presbyterian. Club: Rotary. Home: 44 E 52nd St Indianapolis IN 46205 Office: 7515 E 30th St Indianapolis IN 46206

MAC ALPINE, RUTH CHANDLER, mgmt. trainer; b. Plainsboro, N.J., Oct. 11, 1918; d. Clarence H. and Julia (Leavitt) Chandler; B.S., Trenton State Coll., 1939; M.A., N.Y. U., 1962; m. Donald D. MacAlpine, June 22, 1943; 1 dau., Kim Irene. Various secretarial positions, 1949-56; instr. N.Y. U., 1963-67; legal sec., 1968-69; adminstrv. asst. to v.p. Apollo Chem. Corp., Whippany, N.J., 1974; propr., dir. Summit Mgmt. Tng. Service (N.J.), 1975—; mem. faculty Morris County Coll., Dover, N.J., 1976—. Mem. Am. Soc. Tng. and Devel. Clubs: Canoe Brook Country, Forsgate Country, Skytop, Ekwanok Country, Soroptimist Internat. (1st v.p. Summit 1979-80, pres. 1980—). Address: 157 Bellevue Ave Summit NJ 07901

MACARANAS, FEDERICO MEGINO, economist; b. Manila, Sept. 26, 1947; s. Jose C. and Fanny (Megino) M.; A.B. cum laude, U. Philippines, 1967; M.A. (Fulbright-Hays grantee 1969-70), Purdue U., 1970, Ph.D., 1975. Asst., Office of Pres., Republic of Philippines, 1968-69; research asst., then instr. Krannert Grad. Sch. Indsl. Adminstrn., Purdue U., 1969-72; research tutor, instr. Center for Research and Communication, Manila, 1972-73; dir. policy coordination office Nat. Econ. and Devel. Authority of Philippines, 1973-74; asst. prof. econs. and fin. Manhattan Coll., Riverdale, N.Y., 1976—, dir. Sch. Bus. Research Inst., 1978-79, chmn. dept. econs. and fin., 1979—; adj. asst. prof. Fordham U. and Columbia U., 1979, 80; cons. Clemente Capital, Inc. Pres., Philippine Forum N.Y., 1979. Econs. project fellow U. Philippines, 1968; scholar Asia Found., 1972; grantee Asia Found.-Ford Found., 1974-75; scholar-in-residence Asian Am. Research Center, 1977-78. Mem. Assn. Asian Studies (exec. council Philippine study group), Assn. Social Econs., Nat. Assn. Asian Am. and Pacific Edn. Author research papers in field; exec. editor Ningas mag., 1968-69. Office: Econs Dept Manhattan Coll Riverdale NY 10471

MACARTHUR, DIANA TAYLOR, bus. exec.; b. Santa Fe, July 7, 1933; d. Antonio J. and Elizabeth (Steele) Taylor; student U. Geneva, 1953-54, B.A., Vassar Coll., 1955; children—Elizabeth, Alexander Tschursin; m. 2d, Donald Malcolm MacArthur, Mar. 31, 1962. Cons economist Checchi & Co., Washington, 1957-61; v.p. Thomas J. Deegan Co., dir. Washington office, 1961-62; dep. chief W. Africa, Peace Corps, 1963, regional program officer N. Africa, Near E., S. Asia, 1964, dir. div. pvt. and internat. orgns., 1965-66; coordinator Nat. Youth Conf. on Natural Beauty and Conservation, 1966-68; self-employed cons. pub. affairs to corps., assns., govt., Washington, 1968-76; pres. Consumer Dynamics, Inc., 1976—; dir. Dynamac Corp., 1978—, v.p., 1980—. Mem. citizens adv. bd. Pres.'s Council on Youth Opportunity, 1968-69. Trustee Menninger Found., Topeka; Bd. dirs. Washington Area Council Alcoholism and Drug Abuse, chmn. bd., 1974. Mem. Phi Beta Kappa. Home: 5103 Cape Cod Ct Washington DC 20016 Office: Dynamac Bldg 11140 Rockville Pike Rockville MD 20852

MAC ARTHUR, DONALD MALCOM, sci. and engring. cons. exec.; b. Detroit, Jan. 7, 1931; s. Donald John and Margaret MacAulay MacA.; B.Sc., St. Andrews U., 1954; Ph.D., U. Edinburg (Scotland), 1957; m. Diana L. Taylor, Mar. 31, 1962. Lectr., U. Conn., Storrs, 1958-59; dir. chemistry and life scis. div. Melpar, Inc., Falls Church, Va., 1959-65; dep. dir. research and engring. Dept. Def., Washington, 1966-70; pres. Enviro Control, Inc., Rockville, Md., 1970—; dir. Diversitron, Inc., 1970-73, Module Systems, Inc., Washington, 1971-73, Consumer Dynamics, Inc., Washington, 1975— Borriston Research Labs., Washington, 1976—; chmn. bd. Dynamac Corp., Inc., Washington, 1976—; cons. in field. Trustee Nat. Grad. U., 1970-72. Mem. Chem. Soc., AAAS, Nat. Assn. Life Sci. Industries (dir. 1979—). Presbyterian. Contbr. articles to profl. jours. Home: 5103 Cape Cod Ct Washington DC 20016 Office: 11140 Rockville Pike Rockville MD 20852

MAC ARTHUR, ROBERT STUART, exec. cons.; b. Lausanne, Switzerland, Mar. 16, 1925 (parents Am. citizens); came to U.S., 1933; B.S., St. Lawrence U., 1949; postgrad. Harvard Bus. Sch., 1949-50; m. June Laurenberg Hill, Apr. 6, 1969; children—Kimberly, Duncan, Keturah, Richard. With Polaroid Corp., 1950-58; pres., chmn. Stocker & Yale, 1958-65; pres. Inflated Products Co., North Adams, Mass., 1977-79, Lexington Industries, Inc., Balt., 1976—; treas. Dynatran, Lincoln, R.I., 1974-76; treas. Antilles Yachting Corp., St. Thomas, V.I., 1969—, pres., 1979—; pres. North Country Corp., Cambridge, Mass., 1979—; sr. cons. Regenesis; officer, dir. various other corps.; tchr. Boston U. Bd. dirs. Mass. North Shore chpt. ARC, 1962. Served to lt. USNR, 1943-47. Episcopalian. Club: Harvard (Boston). Home: 106 Appleton St Cambridge MA 02138 Office: Box 193 Cambridge MA 02138

MACARTHUR, WILLIAM HEYWOOD, lawyer, internat. fin. and legal cons.; b. Boston, May 7, 1941; s. Harvey H. and Jean G. (Whittier) MacA.; B.A., Yale U., 1963; LL.B., Columbia U., 1967; m. Marjorie E. Eldredge, July 29, 1967; children—Andrew C., Sarah W. Admitted to N.Y. State bar, 1967; asso. firm Patterson, Belknap & Webb, N.Y.C., 1967-69, Anderson, Mori & Rabincwitz, Tokyo, 1969-71; v.p. Am. Express Internat. Banking Corp., N.Y.C., 1972-78; pres. Transar Capital Corp., N.Y.C., 1978—; dir. Trans-Arabian Investment Bank, Bahrain; mng. dir. Trans-Arabian Devel. Co., Bahrain. Mem. N.Y. State Bar Assn. Home: 26 Barclay Rd Scarsdale NY 10583 Office: 430 Park Ave New York NY 10022

MAC AVOY, THOMAS COLEMAN, glass mfg. co. exec.; b. Jamaica, N.Y., Apr. 24, 1928; s. Joseph V. and Edna M. MacA.; B.S. in Chemistry, Queens Coll., 1950; M.S. in Chemistry, St. John's U., 1952, D.Sc. (hon.), 1973; Ph.D. in Chemistry, U. Cin., 1952; m. Margaret M. Walsh, Dec. 27, 1952; children—Moira MacAvoy Brown, Ellen, Christopher, Neil. Chemist, Charles Pfizer & Co., Bklyn., 1957-60; mgr. electronics research Corning Glass Works (N.Y.), 1960-64, dir. phys. research, 1964-66, v.p. electronic products div., 1966-69, v.p. tech. products div., 1969-71, pres., 1971—, also chief exec. officer, dir.; dir. Quaker Oats Co. Trustee Corning Community Coll., Corning Found., Corning Mus. Glass; pres. N.E. region Boy Scouts Am. Served with USN, 1946; with USAF, 1952-53. Recipient Silver Antelope award Boy Scouts Am., 1976, Silver Beaver award, 1975. Mem. Am. Mgmt. Assn., Elec. Mfrs. Club, Greater Corning Area C. of C. Roman Catholic. Club: Univ. (N.Y.C.). Patentee in field; contbr. articles to tech. jours. Office: Corning Glass Works Corning NY 14830*

MACCHI, EUGENE EDWARD, package co. exec.; b. Kearney, N.J., July 20, 1926; s. Louis Robert and Teresa D. (Maher) M.; student Army spl. tng. program, Carnegie Inst. Tech., 1943-44; student Swarthmore Coll., 1945-47; B.A., Kalamazoo Coll., 1948; m. Josephine M. Towle, May 5, 1951; children—Eugene E., Michael S., Mary Jo, Karen M., Robert C., Thomas J., Charles J. Sales supr., Wyandotte Chems. Corp. (Mich.), 1948-54; mgr. Eastern div., Hankins Container div. Flintkote Co., Union, N.J., 1954-62; pres., chmn. bd. Continental Packaging Corp., Kenilworth, N.J., New Castle, Pa., 1962-75, also dir. Cons. Domestic Policy Analysis Staff Dept. Commerce, 1974-75; pres., chmn. bd. Ind. Corrugated Container Corp. Am., Paterson, N.J., 1975—. Founder, chmn. Ho-Ho-Kus Citizens Com., 1961-63; commr. N.W. Bergen County Sewer Authority, 1966—, chmn., 1967—. Mem. exec. com. Ho-Ho-Kus Democratic Club, 1964—. Served with USAAF, World War II. Mem. Eastern Corrugated Box Mfrs. (pres. 1973-76), C. of C., Nat. Honor Soc., Young Presidents Orgn., Assn. Ind. Corrugated Converters (pres., dir. 1975—), Met. Pres.'s Orgn., Phi Sigma Kappa. Contbr. articles to trade mags. Home: 63 Arbor Dr Ho-Ho-Kus NJ 07423 Office: 55 Jersey St Paterson NJ 07501

MACCHIA, VINCENT MICHAEL, lawyer; b. Bklyn., Dec. 30, 1933; s. Vincent and Lina Rose (Celli) M.; B.S., Fordham U., 1955, LL.B., 1958; LL.M., N.Y. U., 1967; m. Irene Janet Audino, Feb. 27, 1965; children—Lauren, Michele, Michael. Admitted to N.Y. bar, 1958; asso. firm Bernard Remsen Millham & Bowdish, N.Y.C., 1959-60; atty. Equity Corp., N.Y.C., 1961-63, Pfizer, Inc., N.Y.C., 1964, Trans World Airlines, Inc., N.Y.C., 1964-66; mem. firm Gifford, Woody, Palmer & Serles, N.Y.C., 1966—. Served with U.S. Army, 1958-59. Mem. Am., N.Y. State bar assns. Republican. Roman Catholic. Club: St. Andrew's Golf. Mem. editorial staff Fordham Law Rev., 1956-58. Home: 4 Greentree Dr Scarsdale NY 10583 Office: 14 Wall St New York NY 10005

MACCIO, KATHLEEN ANNE, analytical chemist; b. Yonkers, N.Y., Apr. 9, 1948; d. P. Carmine Joseph and Annette Ann (Darmiento) M.; B.S., Coll. Mt. St. Vincent, 1970. Sr. analytical chemist Vick Research and Devel., Mt. Vernon, N.Y., 1970—. Mem. Am. Chem. Soc., New Rochelle Bus. and Profl. Women's Club. Roman Catholic. Office: 1 Bradford Rd Mount Vernon NY 10553

MACCORKLE, GLENN ANDREW, fin. exec.; b. Phila., July 12, 1938; s. Orrin Clyde and Marjorie Lillian (Frey) MacC.; B.S. in B.A., U. R.I., 1960; M.B.A., Seattle U., 1972; m. Nancy Lee Manowski, June 20, 1964; children—Staci Kathleen, Sean Christopher, Molli Elizabeth. Field rep. Aetna Casualty & Surety, Seattle, 1960-65; mgr. spl. accounts Johnson & Higgins, Seattle, 1965-70; ins. mgr. Kaiser Cement & Gypsum Corp., Oakland, Calif., 1972-76; risk mgr. planning and adminstrn. United Technologies Corp., Hartford, Conn., 1976—; lectr. in field. Cantor/lector, St. Mary's Ch., Simsbury, Conn., 1977—. Served with U.S. Army, 1961-63. C.P.C.U.; asso. in risk mgmt. Mem. Soc. C.P.C.U.'s (chpt. dir. 1978—), Risk and Ins. Mgmt. Assn. (v.p. 1980), Am. Risk and Ins. Assn., Res. Officers Assn., Sigma Pi. Republican. Roman Catholic. Club: Bohemian of San Francisco. Home: 61 Winterset Ln Simsbury CT 06070 Office: 1 Financial Plaza Hartford CT 06101

MAC DONALD, DONALD JOSEPH, lab. exec.; b. New Glasgow, N.S., Can., May 3, 1943; s. Ronald Joseph and Mary Jessie (MacMillan) MacD.; B.S., St. Francis Xavier U., 1965; postgrad. McGill U., 1965; m. Danielle, Dec. 2, 1967; children—Cindy, Jason. Chemist, Canadian Arsenals Ltd., Ville Le Gardeur, Que., 196—, chief chemist, 1977-78, supr. labs., 1978—. Mem. Can. Inst. Chemistry, Assn. Chem. Profession Ont., Order Chemists Que., ASTM. Home: 7 Calcourt Ville Le Gardeur PQ J5Z 2T8 Canada Office: 5 Mtee des Arsenaux Ville Le Gardeur PQ J5Z 2P4 Canada

MACDONALD, JAN PENDEXTER, II, investment banker; b. Chgo., Oct. 19, 1942; s. Jack and Anna Jeanne (Pendexter) M.; A.B., Harvard, 1967. Analyst, John Hancock Ins. Co., 1967-69; portfolio mgr. Strand & Co., 1969-70; mgr. multi-industry group Salomon Bros., N.Y.C., 1970-71, 72-79, v.p., 1977-79; analyst Dean Witter & Co., San Francisco, 1971-72; 1st v.p. Blyth Eastman Dillon, 1979-80; prin. GB Mgmt., Gold Bar, Wash., 1980—. Served with U.S. Army, 1961-64. Mem. Assn. Computing Machinery, Fin. Analysts Fedn. (mem. program com.), N.Y. Soc. Securities Analysts, Diversified Cos. Analysts Group (co-founder). Episcopalian. Clubs: D.U. (Cambridge, Mass.); Tennis and Racquet (Boston); University (N.Y.C.). Home and Office: PO Box 666 Gold Bar WA 98251

MACDONALD, JOYCE CAROLYN, electronics industry exec.; b. Seattle, Dec. 27, 1931; d. John McKee and Francis Faye (Howe) Rathbun; student U. Oreg., 1949-51; m. Robert Anderson, Feb. 16, 1952; children—Brad, Wendy, Curtis, Laurie; m. 2d, Thomas C. Macdonald, Sept. 20, 1972. With Tektronix Co., Beaverton, Oreg., 1962—, group mgr. integrated circuits packaging, 1973-75, personnel adminstr. human resources div., 1975-79; mgr. Tek Circles, Mfg. Engring., 1979—; adv. com. Sch. Dist. 48, 1968-70; bd. dirs. Flexible Ways to Work, 1978—; condr. workshops. Mem. Washington County Pub. Affairs Forum, 1977-78. Republican. Club: Multnomah Athletic (Portland, Oreg.). Home: 18355 SW Division St Aloha OR 97005 Office: Tektronix PO Box 500 Beaverton OR 97005

MAC DONALD, KIRKPATRICK, investment banker; b. San Francisco, Oct. 21, 1940; s. Graeme Kirkpatrick and Phyllis Welch (Heinle) M.; B.Sc., Yale, 1962; M.A., Oxford (Eng.) U., 1964; postgrad. U. Geneva, 1964-67; m. Beatrice Clément, July 4, 1964; children—Cybille Alicia, Bryce Eduard Alan, Alexis Alexandra. Asso., Lehman Bros., N.Y.C., 1969-71, Blyth & Co., Inc., N.Y.C., 1971; treas.-sec. Conpar Inc. (affiliate Loeb Rhoades & Co.), N.Y.C., 1971-73; asst. vp. Morgan Guaranty Internat. Fin. Corp., N.Y.C., 1974-76; mng. partner MacDonald & Cie., N.Y.C., 1976—, MacDonald & Partners, N.Y.C., Park City Investment Co., Park Sta. Assos., W. 71st St. Assos.; dir. Glengarry Land Corp., N.Y.C. Bd. dirs. N.Y.C. Citizens Com., W. Side C. of C., Confrerie des Chevaliers du Tastevin, Commanderie de Bordeaux, Leonardo Acad. Arts and Sci. (sec.-treas.). Clubs: Bohemian (San Francisco); Univ., Down Town, Paris-Am. (N.Y.C.). Home: 114 W 78th St New York City NY 10024

MACDONALD, ROBERT WILLIAM, ins. co. exec.; b. Rochester, N.Y., Feb. 11, 1944; s. Robert Ruben and Rosemary (McPhee) MacD.; ed. Loyola U., Los Angeles, 1961-65, Western State Coll Law, Fullerton, Calif., 1970-74, Am. Coll., 1975-76; m. Patricia K. Crean, Feb. 17, 1968; children—Ryan, Brandy, Piper, Colin, Braden, Robert. Field underwriter New Eng. Life Ins. Co., Los Angeles, 1965-70; regional agy. mgr. Jefferson Standard Life Ins. Co., Los Angeles, 1970-75; v.p. mktg. devel. State Mut. Life Ins. Co., Worcester, Mass., 1975-77; sr. v.p., dir. mktg. ITT Life Ins. Corp., Mpls., 1977-79, exec. v.p., 1979-80, pres., chief exec. officer, 1980—. Mem. Nat. Assn. Life Underwriters, Am. Soc. C.L.U., Gen. Agts. and Mgrs. Assn., Young Presidents Assn., Mpls. C. of C. Republican. Roman Catholic. Club: Rotary. Office: 600 S County Rd Suite 18 Minneapolis MN 55426

MAC DONALD, RONALD BARBERIE, furniture mfg. exec.; b. Campbellton, N.B., Can., May 1, 1945; s. Ronald Wyers and Agnes Audrey (Barberie) MacD.; engring. diploma St. Francis Xavier U., 1968; B.S., St. Mary's U., 1969, B.Commerce, 1971; m. Margret Marie Pauline Cavanagh, May 11, 1968; children—Shawn Andrew, Kevin Ronald. Comptroller, Thruway Moter Inns Ltd., Campbellton, 1972-73; br. mgr. Central & Eastern Trust Co., Campbellton, 1973-76; comptroller N.E. Pine Products Ltd., Campbellton, 1976-77, gen. mgr., 1977-80, exec. v.p., 1980—; prof. Gaspe (Que., Ont.) Community Coll., 1969-70. Bd. dirs. Campbellton Nursing Home, 1972—, v.p., 1976-77; pres. Restigouche Credit Granters Assn., 1974-75. Named Mgr. of Yr., St. Francis Xavier U., 1968. Mem. Campbellton C. of C. (dir. 1973-76, pres. 1974-75). Club: Campbellton Rotary (treas. 1973-74). Home: 11 Dufferin St Campbellton NB E3N 2N3 Canada Office: PO Box 940 Campbellton NB E3N 3H3 Canada

MAC DONALD, SCOTT DOUGLAS, urban devel. cons.; b. Berwyn, Ill., June 4, 1947; s. Walter Bingham and Bernice (Corson) MacD.; A.B., Ind. U., 1970; M.Regional Planning, U. N.C., 1972; m. Jill Weitzen. Sr. asso. Gladstone Assos., Washington, 1972-75; mgr. market research and product devel. W.R. Grace Properties, Phila., 1975-76; project dir. Zuchelli-Hunter, Annapolis, Md., 1976-78; mgr. econs. div. Barton-Aschman Assos., Evanston, Ill., 1978—; mem. adj. faculty George Washington U., 1972-78; speaker on urban issues. Served with USMC, 1968-69. Mem. Urban Land Inst., Am. Soc. Planning Ofcls., Internat. Council Shopping Centers, Blue Key, Pi Kappa Alpha. Presbyterian. Home: 1624 Ashland Ave Evanston IL 60201

MAC DONALD, WILLIAM ESTES, telephone co. exec.; b. Columbus, Ohio, Oct. 14, 1918; s. William and Caroline (Mueller) MacD.; B.S.B.A., Ohio State U., 1940; m. Ruth Foster, June 28, 1941; children—William E., John A. With comml. dept. Ohio Bell Telephone Co., Cleve., 1941-51; engr. AT&T, N.Y.C., 1953; gen. comml. supr. Ohio Bell Telephone Co., Columbus, 1955-59, traffic supr., 1959-60, comml. mgr., 1960-63, v.p., gen. mgr., Cleve., 1963-64, v.p.-ops., 1964-78, pres., 1978—, also dir.; dir. BancOhio Corp., Lamson & Sessions Co., Brush Wellman, Inc., Gray Drug Stores, Inc. Pres., chief exec. officer United Way Cleve., 1979—; trustee Musical Arts Assn. Cleve., Cleve. Clinic, 1979—, Lutheran Med. Center; bd. dirs. Greater Cleve. Growth Assn.; vice chmn. bd. trustees Ohio State U. Devel. Fund. Served to lt. USN, 1942-45. Clubs: Clevelander, Country, Fifty, Pepper Pike, Union (Cleve.); Columbus (Ohio); Rolling Rock (Ligonier, Pa.); Castalia Trout (Ohio). Office: 100 Erieview Plaza Cleveland OH 44114

MACDOUGAL, GARY EDWARD, indsl. products mfg. co. exec.; b. Chgo., July 3, 1936; s. Thomas William and Lorna Lee (McDougall) MacD.; B.S. in Engring., U. Calif. at Los Angeles, 1958; M.B.A. with distinction, Harvard, 1963; m. Julianne Laurel Maxwell, June 13, 1958; children—Gary Edward, Michael Scott. Cons., McKinsey & Co., N.Y.C., also Los Angeles, 1963-68, partner, 1968-69; chmn. bd., chief exec. officer Mark Controls Corp. (formerly Clayton Mark & Co.), Evanston, Ill., 1969—, also pres., 1971-75; dir. United Parcel Service Am., Inc., N.Y.C., Union Camp Corp., Wayne, N.J., Maremont Corp., Chgo.; dir., mem. exec. com. Sargent Welch Sci. Co., Skokie, Ill. Instr. U. Calif. at Los Angeles, 1969. Asso., Northwestern U., Evanston. Trustee U. Calif. at Los Angeles Found., 1973-79. Served to lt. USNR, 1958-61. Mem. Kappa Sigma. Episcopalian. Clubs: Harvard of N.Y.; Economic of Chicago, Harvard Business School (Chgo.). Contbr. articles to profl. jours., chpts. to books. Home: 591 Plum Tree Rd Barrington Hills IL 60010 Office: 1900 Dempster St Evanston IL 60204

MAC DOWELL, WILLIAM DUNLAP, seed mfg. co. exec.; b. Bronxville, N.Y., Dec. 2, 1931; s. John Watson and Ruth Weld (Dunlap) MacD.; B.A., Oberlin Coll., 1953; M.B.A., Harvard U., 1955; m. Jane Kemmerer, July 3, 1954; children—Anne, W. Douglas, Edward W. Sates mgmt. Procter & Gamble Distbg., Boston, 1955-57, N.Y.C., 1957-59, Cin., 1960, Balt., 1960-62; mktg. mgr. J.H. Filbert Inc., Balt., 1963; mktg. and venture mgr. Gen. Foods Corp., White Plains, N.Y., 1963-70; pres., chief exec. officer W. Atlee Burpee Co., Warminster, Pa., 1970—, also dir.; dir. Luther Burbank Seed Co., James Vick's Inc., Fertl Inc. Mem. Am. Seed Trade Assn. (dir.), Pa. Hort. Soc. (dir.), Nat. Jr. Hort Assn. (dir.), Nat. Assn. Conservation Dists. Office: W Atlee Burpee Co 300 Park Ave Warminster PA 18974*

MACEDON, GEORGE G., mfg. co. exec.; b. Tucson, Ariz., July 31, 1940; s. George G. and Victoria G. (Zuccala) M.; B.S., Ariz. State U., 1966, M.S.W., 1968. Owner restaurants, Phoenix, El Paso, 1968-73; mfr.'s rep., 1972-75; sales mgr. Western states Broadmoor Industries, 1975-77; nat. sales mgr. Sampo Corp. of Am., Elk Grove Village, Ill., 1977-80; v.p. sales and mktg. Bohsei USA, Chatsworth, Calif., 1981—. Republican. Roman Catholic. Home: 2335 W Nopal Ave Mesa AZ 85202 Office: Bohsei USA 20501 Plummer St Chatsworth CA 91311

MACFARLANE, A. IAIN R., advt. agt. exec.; b. Sydney, Australia, Mar. 7, 1940; came to U.S., 1978; s. Alexander Dunlop and Margaret Elizabeth (Swan) M.; B.Econs. with honors, U. Sydney, 1961; A.A.S.A., Australian Soc. Accts., 1962; M.B.A., U. Hawaii, 1964; postgrad., Columbia U., 1963-64; A.M.P., Harvard U., 1977; m. Madge McCleary, Sept. 24, 1966; children—Douglas, Dennis, Robert, Jeffrey. Comml. cadet B.H.P. Ltd., Australia, 1958-62; product mgr. H.J. Heinz Co., Pitts., 1965-66; gen. mgr. new products div., Melbourne, Australia, 1967-72; partner, dir., gen. mgr. Singleton, Palmer & Strauss McAllan Pty. Ltd., Sydney, 1972-73; dir., gen. mgr. Doyle Dane Bernbach Internat., Sydney, 1973-77, group sr. v.p., N.Y.C., 1978—; lectr. Monash U., Melbourne, 1970-71; chmn., dir. St. Peters Sporting Goods Pty. Ltd., Australia, 1977—; mgmt. cons., 1970-72. Vice pres. Waverley Dist. Cricket Club, 1975-77. Australian Commonwealth scholar, 1958-61; Australian Steel Industry scholar, 1958-61; U.S. Fed. East-West Center fellow, 1962-64. Asso. fellow Australian Inst. Mgmt.; mem. Australian Soc. Accts. Club: Whippoorwill Country. Contbr. articles to profl. jours. Home: 2 Whippoorwill Rd Chappaqua NY 10514 Office: 437 Madison Ave New York NY 10022

MACFERRAN, WILLIAM SEWALL, banker; b. Topeka, Kans., Aug. 25, 1924; s. William and Helen Roland (Estey) Macferran; B.S. in Bus., U. Kans., 1948; grad. Sch. of Banking, Madison, Wis., 1960; m. Doris Jean Macferran, Oct. 3, 1969; 1 son, William Francis. Salesman, Nat. Cash Register Co., 1948; with First State Bank & Trust Co., Topeka, Kans., 1949—, pres., trust officer, 1973—. Served to 2d lt. USAAF, 1943-45. Republican. Presbyterian. Club: Topeka Country. Home: 1610 Plass Ave Topeka KS 66604 Office: PO Box 2429 Topeka KS 66601

MACFIE, RONALD ALASTAIR BUTE, service co. exec.; b. Cheltenham, Eng., Oct. 13, 1926; came to U.S., 1966; s. Ronald Bute and Monica Enid (Taylor) M.; B.Sc., Imperial Coll. Sci. and Tech., London, 1953; m. Jean Mary Weller, June 26, 1954; children—Helen Lindsay, Elizabeth Jane. Flight test engr. Weybridge div. Brit. Aircraft Corp., 1953-65, dep. flight test mgr., 1965-66; flight test team leader Lockheed Ga. Co. and Lookheed Calif. Co., 1966-73; pres. Furmanite, Inc., Virginia Beach, Va., 1973—. Bd. dirs. Jr. Achievement Tidewater. Served with RAF, 1943-47. Mem. Internat. Dist. Heating Assn., U.S. C. of C., Brit.-Am. C. of C., Virginia Beach C. of C., Norfolk C. of C. Episcopalian. Club: Norfolk Yacht & Country. Home: 1527 Bolling Ave Norfolk VA 23508 Office: Furmanite Inc 525 Viking Dr Virginia Beach VA 23452

MAC GUFFIE, JOHN VROOMAN, data processing co. exec.; b. Phila., Aug. 28, 1934; s. Charles Irving and Dorothy (Turnbull) MacG.; B.M.E., Cornell U., 1957; m. Carolyn Stoup, Dec. 22, 1962; children—Scott, Stephen. Asst. buyer IBM, Endicott, N.Y., 1957-58, indsl. engr., 1959-60, sr. account rep., Bridgeport, Conn., 1960-65; dir. corp. systems InSci Inc., Montvale, N.J., 1965-71; founder, pres. Program Products Inc., Montvale, 1971-76, now dir.; pres. InSci Internat., Montvale, 1976-80; pres., chief exec. officer Sales Productivity Systems, Inc., 1980—. Mem. exec. com. Saw Mill Valley Civic Assn.; pres. bd. dirs. Castlerock Village. Served with U.S. Army, 1959-60. Mem. Assn. Data Porcessing Services Orgns. Republican. Congregationalist. Contbr. articles to profl. jours. Home: 75 Worthington Rd White Plains NY 10607 Office: 2121 Saw Mill River Rd White Plains NY 10607

MACHLE, JERRY PHILIP, electronics co. exec.; b. Dayton, Ohio, Mar. 2, 1937; s. Edward Philip and Carol Irene (Heald) M.; B.S. in Bus. cum laude, Miami U., Oxford, Ohio, 1958; M.B.A., Harvard, 1964; m. M. Sue Schneider, Aug. 31, 1963; children—Paul Edward, Jeffrey Philip. Accountant, mem. audit staff Touche Ross & Co., Dayton, 1958-62; mem. controllers dept. FMC Corp., San Jose, Calif., 1964-66; founder Develco, Inc., Sunnyvale, Calif., 1966, v.p., treas., sec., 1966-75; group controller med. group Varian Assos., Palo Alto, Calif., 1975—; dir. Environment Monitoring Systems, Inc., Time & Frequency Tech., Inc., Develco, Inc. C.P.A., Calif., Ohio. Mem. Am. Inst. C.P.A.'s, Calif. Soc. C.P.A.'s, Phi Beta Kappa. Clubs: Woodland Vista Swim and Racquet (dir.); Harvard Bus. Sch. of No. Calif. Home: 2295 Mimosa Ct Los Altos CA 94022 Office: 611 Hansen Way Palo Alto CA 94304

MACIOCE, THOMAS MATTHEW, lawyer, merchandising exec.; b. N.Y.C., Jan. 2, 1919; s. Anthony and Angelina (Vodola) M.; B.A., Columbia U., 1939. LL.B., 1942; m. Francesca Paula Spinelli, June 25, 1944; 1 dau., Francesca Lee. Admitted to N.Y. bar, 1946, U.S. Supreme Ct. bar, 1966; asst. sec. Flintkote Mines, Ltd., 1948; v.p., dir. Bloomsburg Mills, Inc., 1952-56; pres., dir. L. F. Dommerich & Co., 1956-60; corp. v.p. Allied Stores Corp., N.Y.C., 1960-69, sr. v.p., 1969-70, pres., 1970, pres., chief exec. officer, 1972—, also dir.; dir. Hercules Inc., Mfrs. Hanover Trust Corp., Am. Broadcasting Cos. Inc., Penn Central Corp. Bd. dirs., chmn. Tax Found.; trustee Columbia U. Served to lt. comdr. USNR, World War II. Recipient Theodore Roosevelt Assn. Meml. award; Brainard Meml. prize, 1939; Brotherhood award NCCJ; Israeli Prime Minister's medal; Order of Merit (Italy). Mem. Young Pres.'s Orgn., Acad. Polit. Sci. (dir., treas.). Home: Quaker Ridge Dr Brookville NY 11545 Office: 1114 Ave of Americas New York NY 10036

MAC IVER, DONALD STUART, chem. co. exec.; b. Cambridge, Mass., Oct. 3, 1927; s. Charles P. and Elizabeth P. (Adams) MacI.; B.S. summa cum laude, Boston U., 1952; Ph.D., U. Pitts., 1957; m. Eleanor Smith, May 8, 1947; children—Nancy MacIver Ivanov, Bruce. Dir., Western Research Center, Richmond, Calif., 1967-74; mgr. St. Gabriel Caustic Chlorine Complex, St. Gabriel, La., 1971-73; v.p., gen. mgr. Stauffer Chem. Co. Wyo., San Francisco, 1974-78; v.p., asst. gen. mgr. Agrl. Chem. div. Stauffer Chem. Co., Westport, Conn., 1978—. Served with USMC and USNR, 1945-47. Mem. Am. Chem. Soc., Phi Beta Kappa, Sigma Psi, Phi Lambda Upsilon. Club: Family (San Francisco). Contbr. articles to tech. jours. Office: Stauffer Chemical Co Westport CT 06880

MACK, DEAN THOMAS, electronics co. exec.; b. Milw., Apr. 9, 1934; s. E. Edward and Marion N. (Spitzer) M.; B.S. in Engring., U. Calif. at Los Angeles, 1956; m. Faith Peoples, Nov. 11, 1961; children—Stephen, Gregory, Hope. Indsl. engring. mgr. Semicondr. div. Fairchild Camera & Instrument, San Rafael, Calif., 1960-63, mgr. systems group Instrumentation div., Sunnyvale, Calif., 1963-68; v.p. ops. Microform Data Systems, Mountain View, Calif., 1969-70, pres., 1970-78, also dir.; pres., dir. Equatorial Communications Co., Sunnyvale, 1978—; dir. Sci. Micro Systems Inc., Mountain View, Boles & Co., Menlo Park, Calif. Served to lt. (j.g.) USNR, 1957-60. Home: 2740 Wemberly Dr Belmont CA 94002 Office: 1294 Lawrence Station Rd Sunnyvale CA 94086

MACK, EDWARD GIBSON, business exec.; b. Toronto, Ont., Can., Dec. 4, 1917; s. Edward Gibson and Marion Margaret (Ward) M.; grad. Pickering Coll., 1938; student Syracuse U., 1938-40, U. Pa., 1945-46; m. Ruth Harriett Davies, Aug. 3, 1940 (dec. 1978); children—Edward D., Carol H. (Mrs. Donald Shaw), Susan D. (Mrs. Philip Vassel); m. 2d, Isolde Maderson, Sept. 30, 1978. Investment analyst trust dept. Syracuse Trust Co., 1939-43; accountant Hurdman & Cranstoun, Syracuse, 1943-44; asst. cashier Bank of Am., Los Angeles, 1946-48; dist. sales mgr. to dir. mktg. and prodn. research Easy Washing Machine Corp., Los Angeles and Syracuse, N.Y., 1948-55; dir. research Avco Corp., Connersville, Ind., 1955-58; exec. sec. planning and policy bd. Aeronca Mfg. Corp., Middletown, Ohio, 1958-60; pres., dir. E.D.I., State College, Pa., 1960-62, Sherman Indsl. Electronics Inc.; exec. Richards Musical Instruments, Inc., Elkhart, Ind., 1962-65; mgr. supply and distbn. plastic products Union Carbide Ltd., Lindsay, Ont., 1965-68; corporate sec. Dominion Dairies Ltd., Toronto, 1968-73, v.p., sec., 1973—; dir. Sealtest (Can.) Ltd. Mem. rep. council Pickering Coll. Served with AUS, World War II. Mem. Am. Legion, Inst. Chartered Secs. and Adminstrs. (affiliate), Am. Mktg. Assn., Sigma Chi. Republican. Clubs: Elks, Toastmasters. Home: 1862 Bathurst St Penthouse 3 Toronto ON M5P 3K8 Canada Office: 235 Walmer Rd Toronto ON M5R 2Y1 Canada

MACK, JAY ORD, JR., metallurgist; b. Wilkinsburg, Pa., May 2, 1922; s. Jay Ord and June (Shupe) M.; B.S. in Metall. Engring., Carnegie Inst. Tech., 1942, M.S. in Metall. Engring., 1950; postgrad. Pa. State U., 1945-47, U. Pitts., 1950-51; m. Nyla McCrory, May 22, 1943; children—Nyla Jane, Debra Lee. Metall. Laborer, observer Edgar Thomson works U.S. Steel Corp., Braddock, Pa., 1941-42, supervising technologist applied research labs., Monroeville, Pa., 1947-51, chief control and devel. metallurgist Fairless works, Fairless Hills, Pa., 1951-59, chief steel prodn. metallurgist, 1959-64, asst. chief metallurgist, 1964-70, chief metallurgist, 1970-77; mgr. process metallurgy U.S. Steel Corp., Pitts., 1977-80, mgr. tech. services, Baytown, Tex., 1980—; welding engr. Naval Research Lab., Washington, 1943-45; research asst. Pa. State U., 1945-47. Registered profl. engr., Pa. Mem. Am. Soc. Metals (John A. Roebling award 1976), Am. Inst. Metall. Engrs., Assn. Iron and Steel Engrs. Contbr. articles to profl. jours. Office: US Steel Corp Box 29 Baytown TX 77520

MACK, JOSEPH, II, automotive, agrl. and indsl. product components co. exec.; b. Detroit, Jan. 15, 1921; s. Thomas Henry and Maude (Packer) M.; student Ford Apprentice Sch., 1939-41, Lawrence Inst. Tech., U. Detroit, evenings, 1939-46; m. Marilyn Rae Law, Feb. 2, 1962; children—Catherine Packer, Joseph III, Michael, Patricia Ann. Apprentice tool maker Ford Motor Co., 1939-41; tool, spl. machine designer Allen Engring. Co., Detroit, 1941-42; project engr. product engring. dept. Detroit Transmission Div., Gen. Motors Corp., 1943-46; sales engr. Timken Roller Bearing Co., 1946-62; truck sales mgr. auto div. Kelsey-Hayes Co., Romulus, Mich., 1962-63, asst. gen. sales mgr., 1963, gen. sales mgr., 1963-64, v.p. sales, 1964-69; v.p. automotive operations Lear Siegler, Inc., Detroit, 1969-73; pres., chief exec. officer NEAPCO, Inc., Pottstown, Pa., 1973-78; v.p. mktg. Fruehauf Corp., Detroit, 1978—; dir. Perfect Equipment Co., Murfeesboro, Tenn. Served with USAAF, 1942-43. Mem. Soc. Automotive Engrs., Engring. Soc. Detroit, Automotive Oldtimers, Am. Ordnance Assn., Am. Mgmt. Assn. Clubs: Detroit Athletic, Recess (Detroit); Oakland Hills Country; Bloomfield Hills Country; Phila. Country (Gladwyne, Pa.). Home: 328 Barden Rd Bloomfield Hills MI 48013 Office: Freuhauf Corp Detroit MI

MACK, WALTER MERRIMAN, automobile co. owner; b. Chgo., July 22, 1925; s. Walter Adams and Viola Antionette (Merriman) M.; B.A., U. Chgo., 1948; m. Suzanne Charbonneau, Nov. 20, 1948; children—Elaine, Linda, Stephen. Owner, Mack Cadillac Corp., Chgo., 1946-64, Mt. Prospect, Ill., 1964—; owner Mack Leasing Co., Chgo., 1956-64, Mt. Prospect, Ill., 1964—; owner M & M Enterprises, Inc., Mt. Prospect, Ill., 1971—. Dir. C.L.C. Corp. Owner, WEXI-FM, Arlington Heights, Ill., 1967-72. Served with AUS, 1943-46. Mem. Chgo. Auto Trade Assn. (dir. 1965-69), Delta Kappa Epsilon. Roman Catholic. Clubs: Glen View (Ill.), Shoreacres, Chicago, Metropolitan; Lyford Cay (Bahamas). Office: 333 W Rand Rd Mount Prospect IL 60056

MACKASEY, BRUCE STUART, Can. govt. ofcl.; b. Quebec City, Que., Can., Aug. 25, 1921; s. Frank S. and Ann (Glover) M.; student McGill U., Sir George Williams U.; m. Margaret Cecilia O'Malley, Feb. 13, 1942; children—Brenda, Bryan, Michael, Susan. Former alderman City of Verdun, also chmn. Verdun Sports Commn.; mem. Can. Ho. of Commons, 1962-76, 80—; parliamentary sec. to minister nat. health and welfare, 1965; apptd. parliamentary sec. to minister labor, 1966; mem. Privy Council, 1968; minister labor, 1968-72; minister manpower and immigration, 1972; apptd. postmaster gen., 1974, minister consumer and corp. affairs, 1976; mem. Que. Nat. Assembly, 1976-78; chmn. Air Can., 1979. Mem. Liberal Party. Roman Catholic. Office: House of Commons Room 733-CB Ottawa ON K1A 0A6 Canada

MACKELPRANG, ALONZO JULIUS, educator; b. Kanab, Utah, Feb. 28, 1941; s. Willard and Maurine (Brinkerhoff) M.; A.S., So. Utah State Coll., 1964; B.S., Utah State U., 1965; M.A., U. Iowa, 1967, Ph.D., 1972; m. Sandra Marie Griffiths, July 30, 1965; children—Darren, Darla, Alan. Research asso. U. Iowa, 1967-70; asst. prof. pub. adminstrn. Am. U., 1970-72; asst. prof. U. Del., 1972-74; mgmt. analyst Office of Mgmt. and Budget, Exec. Office of Pres., Washington, 1974-75; asso. prof. mgmt. and pub. adminstrn. U. Denver, 1975—; coordinator Pub. Adminstrn. Field Service Program for Energy-Impacted Communities; cons. in field. NSF grantee, 1973-74, Del. Humanities Forum, 1974; recipient U.S. Civil Service Commn. Merit citation, 1972. Mem. Am. Soc. Pub. Adminstrn., Denver C. of C. (taxation com. 1976-77), Phi Alpha Theta, Pi Alpha Alpha, Phi Kappa Phi. Mormon. Home: 4740 S Lipan St Englewood CO 80110

MACKENTHUN, ERIC CHARLES, bus. exec.; b. Paris, Sept. 7, 1940; s. Marcel Henri and Marie Alice (Barthe) M.; Ingenieur Civil du Genie Maritime, Ecole Nationale Superieure du Genie Maritime, Paris, 1965; M.S. in Mgmt., Stanford U., 1977; m. Anne-Marie Palu, June 27, 1964; children—Marianne, Olivier. Field engr., then project engr. Sofresid, Paris, 1965-67; head marine br. Flopetrol, Paris, 1967-70; sr. engr. SEAL, London, 1970-71; br. head, U.S. coordinator, San Francisco, 1972-73, br. head ops., Houston, 1973, gen. services mgr., London, 1974-75; chmn. bd., chief exec. officer Technique 2000, Paris, 1978—, Societe Anonyme de Furnitures d'Entreprises (S.A.F.E.), Paris, 1980—. Mem. Soc. Petroleum Engrs., ASME (French tech. liaison petroleum div.), Association Francaise des Techniciens du Petrole, Association Technique Maritime et Aeronautique. Club: Stade Francais (Paris). Home: 20 blvd Suchet Paris France 75016 Office: 6 Ave Charles de Gaulle Le Chesnay France 78150

MACKENZIE, IAN RODERICK, fin. co. exec.; b. N.Y.C., May 27, 1940; s. Walter P. and Dolina C. (Williamson) M.; B.S., Washington and Lee U., 1963; m. Eugenie Tsvietkova, June 17, 1972; 1 dau., Alexandra. Arbitrage analyst Bache & Co., N.Y.C., 1964-67; arbitrageur Goldman Sachs & Co., N.Y.C., 1967-69; mng. dir. Am. & Overseas Asset Services Corp., N.Y.C., 1969—; gen. partner Pinecliff Assos., N.Y.C., 1972—; dir. Intermarket Fund I, S.A., Luxembourg. Clubs: Brook, Regency Whist (N.Y.C.); Tuxedo (Tuxedo Park, N.Y.). Home: 7 Gracie Sq New York NY 10028 also West Lake Rd Tuxedo Park NY 10987 Office: 345 Park Ave New York NY 10022

MACKENZIE, ROBERT PECK, investment co. exec.; b. Boston, May 9, 1945; s. Donald Hershey and Hope Martha (Peck) M.; student Bentley Coll., 1962-63; Am. Inst. Banking, 1968-71; m. Veronica Margaret Allan, Dec. 22, 1964; children—Andrew Donald, Sandra Hope. Investment officer govt. bond dept. Shawmut Bank, Boston, 1968-74; investment officer govt. bond dept. Hartford Nat. Bank, 1974-75; institutional salesman Blyth, Eastman, Dillon Capital Mkts Co., Hartford, 1975-79; instnl. rep. Merrill Lynch, Pierce, Fenner & Smith, N.Y.C., 1979—. Served with USAF, 1963-67. Mem. Conn. Investment Bankers Assn., Investment Soc. Northeastern N.Y., Appalachian Trail Conf., New Eng. Govt. Bond Club, Hartford Stockbrokers Club, Sierra Club. Clubs: We Few, Rand Class, Masons. Home: 30 Ralph Rd Manchester CT 06040 Office: 799 Main St Hartford CT 06103

MACKEY, JAMES WESTON, exec. search cons.; b. New Albayn, Ind., Dec. 15, 1933; s. Hugh Weston and Kathleen (Snyder) M.; B.S. in Indsl. Edn. and Mgmt., Purdue U., 1956; m. Mary Janet Kirkhoff, Aug. 6, 1955; children—James V., Helena M., Valene, Jeffery. Engring. adminstr. Electromotive div. Gen. Motors Corp., LaGrange, Ill., 1956-67; corp. personnel mgr. Barnes & Reinecke, Chgo., 1967-69; exec. search cons. Fry Cons.'s, Chgo., 1969-71; v.p. Eastman & Beaudine, Inc., Chgo., 1971—; dir. IILC. Republican. Roman Catholic. Clubs: Union League (Chgo.); Elks. Office: 111 W Monroe St Suite 2150 Chicago IL 60603

MACKEY, JOHN JANVRIN, investment broker; b. Rochester, N.Y., June 3, 1930; s. Stuart Jones and Margaret Marion (Browne) M.; B.A., Wesleyan U., Conn., 1952; M.P.A., Syracuse U., 1953; m. Marie Louise Langbein, June 25, 1955; children—Louise Janvrin, Elizabeth Timm, John Stuart. Budget examiner N.Y. State Exec. Div. Budget, Albany, 1953-56; pres. Langbein Giftwares, Bklyn., 1956-70; investment advisor, broker Dean Witter Reynolds, Inc., N.Y.C., 1970—; adj. prof. fin. Adelphi U., 1973—; mgr. fin. St. Andrews Soc. N.Y., Am. Scottish Found., 1974—, Clan Mackay Assn. N.Am., 1981—. Fund solicitor Wesleyan Alumni Fund, 1955—; pres. United Way Larchmont-Westchester, 1973-75, treas., 1975—. Mem. Internat. Soc. Registered Reps., Nat. Gift and Art Assn. (dir. 1968-70), Nat. Assn. Security Dealers, Phi Beta Kappa, Beta Theta Pi. Republican. Presbyn. (deacon 1967-70, trustee investment 1977—, elder 1981—). Home: 61 Echo Ln Larchmont NY 10538 Office: 40 W 57 St New York NY 10019

MACKEY, LEONARD B., lawyer, multinat. corp. exec.; b. Washington, Aug. 31, 1925; s. Stuart and Margaret (Browne) M.; B.E.E., Rensselaer Poly. Inst., 1945; J.D., George Washington U., 1950; m. Britta Beckhaus, Mar. 2, 1974; children—Leonard B., Cathleen C., Wendy F. Admitted to D.C. bar; patent examiner U.S. Patent Office, Washington, 1947-50; electronics engr. USN Bur. Ships, Washington, 1950-51; atty. Gen. Electric Co., Schenectady and N.Y.C., 1953-60; dir. licensing, asst. sec. IT&T, N.Y.C., 1960-73, v.p., gen. patent counsel, dir. licensing, 1973—. Mem. Rye (N.Y.) City Council, 1970-71, Recreation Commn., 1966-67, Planning Commn., 1967-70, 72-75. Served with USN, 1943-45, to lt., 1951-53. Mem. Am. Patent Law Assn. (2d v.p. 1980, bd. mgrs. 1968-70), Licensing Execs. Soc. (pres. 1978), Am. Bar Assn., Eta Kappa Nu. Republican. Presbyterian. Clubs: Am. Yacht (sec. 1968-70), Masons. Home: 19 Turner Dr Greenwich CT 06830 Office: 320 Park Ave New York NY 10022

MACKEY, THOMAS STEPHEN, metals, minerals cons. engring. exec.; b. Weehawken, N.J., July 14, 1930; s. Thomas Patrick and Delia (Dunlea) M.; B.S., Manhattan Coll., 1952; M.S., Columbia U., 1956; Ph.D., Rice U., 1972; J.D., S. Tex. U., 1976; m. Catherine A. Fagan, Apr. 23, 1955; children—Thomas, Karen, Doris, Susan, Kathleen, Michael, Ellen. With Key Metals & Minerals Engring. Corp., Texas City, Tex., 1970—, pres., 1974—; admitted to Tex. bar, 1977; partner firm Shirley, Shirley & Mackey, 1977—. Named Outstanding Sr. Citizen, Texas City/La Marque C. of C., 1967, Silver Beaver award, St. George medal Boy Scouts Am., 1967, adm. Tex. Navy. Fellow Instn. Mining and Metallurgy (Eng.), Am. Inst. Chemists; mem. Am. Inst. Profl. Geologists, AIME (chmn. com. on lead-zinc-tin 1967-74), Nat. Soc. Profl. Engrs., Tex. Soc. Profl. Engrs., Am. Iron and Steel Inst., AAAS, Am. Math. Soc., ASTM, Am. Soc. Metals, Geochem. Soc. Am., Australasian Inst. Mining and Metallurgy, Metall. Soc. Home: 1210 Sunset Ln Texas City TX 77590 Office: Key Metals & Minerals Engring Corp 710 5th Ave N Texas City TX 77590

MACKEY, WILLARD CLYDE, JR., advt. exec.; b. Rockford, Ill., Oct. 18, 1922; s. Willard Clyde and Anna B. (Bertog) M.; B.A., Beloit (Wis.) Coll., 1947; m. Lois Eileen Wilson, Sept. 8, 1945; children—Barbara Mackey Seagle, William C., David. Copywriter, Howard H. Monk, Rockford, 1947-50; product advt. mgr. Swift & Co., Chgo., 1950-53; product mgr. Gen. Foods Corp., White Plains, N.Y., 1953-56; v.p., account supr. Sullivan, Stauffer, Colwell & Bayles, N.Y.C., 1956-63; sr. mgmt. officer McCann-Erickson, Inc., Atlanta, 1964-66; exec. v.p., dir. Marschalk Co., Inc., Atlanta, 1967; sr. v.p. Inter-pub. Group Cos., Inc., Atlanta, 1968; v.p., internat. dir. mktg. Coca-Cola Co., Atlanta, 1969-70; chmn. bd., chief exec. officer Marschalk Co., Inc., N.Y.C., 1970-75; pres. McCann-Erickson Worldwide, N.Y.C., 1975-79; pres., chief exec. officer McCann-Erickson Internat., N.Y.C., 1979—. Trustee, Episcopal Radio/TV Found. Served to 1st lt. USMCR, 1943-46. Decorated Silver Star, Purple Heart. Mem. Phi Kappa Psi. Clubs: Woodway Country (Darien, Conn.); Piedmont Driving, Peachtree Golf (Atlanta); New Canaan (Conn.) Country. Home: 1211 Smith Ridge Rd New Canaan CT 06840 Office: 485 Lexington Ave New York NY 10017

MACKIE, PETER FEARING, bank exec.; b. Englewood, N.J., May 19, 1941; s. John Milton and Ruth Anewalt (Gomery) M.; B.A., Trinity Coll., 1964; m. Sara Ann Ewart, June 27, 1964; children—Stewart Andrews, Thomas Ives, Elisabeth Turlay. With Bankers Trust Co., N.Y.C., 1964—, asst. v.p., 1972-79, v.p., 1979—. Sr. warden Christ the Redeemer Episcopal Ch., Pelham Manor, N.Y., 1980—, jr. warden, 1977-80; bd. dirs. Pelham Day Care Center, 1976—, pres., 1978—; bd. dirs. United Way of Pelham, 1977—, residential chmn., 1978; coach Pelham Youth Soccer League, 1978—.

Served with U.S. Army, 1967. Republican. Clubs: Men's (dir. 1975-78, pres. 1977-78), N.Y. Athletic; Lake Paupac (Greentown, Pa.). Home: 514 Pelham Manor Rd Pelham Manor NY 10803 Office: 280 Park Ave New York NY 10017

MACKINNON, MALCOLM CHARLES, paint co. exec.; b. Washington, Aug. 10, 1934; s. Malcolm C. and Elizabeth (McGerr) MacK; B.C.E., Cornell U., 1957; postgrad. Harvard, 1973; m. Barbara Payne, Apr. 25, 1959; children—Karen, Douglas. Sales engr. Ingersoll-Rand, N.Y.C., 1957-59; salesman United Gilsonite Labs., Conn., 1960-63, sales mgr., Scranton, Pa., 1963-70, exec. v.p., 1970-77, pres., 1978—; dir. Third Nat. Bank, Scranton, 1976—. Bd. dirs. Jr. Achievement, Inc., N.Y.C., 1971-78; pres., dir. Jr. Achievement NE Pa., Scranton, 1969—; bd. dirs. Jr. Achievement Found., N.Y.C., 1980—. Served with U.S. Army, 1958. Clubs: Scranton (dir. 1980—); Waverly (Pa.) Country (dir. 1971—). Home: 115 Old Orchard Rd Clarks Summit PA 18411 Office: Box 70 Scranton PA 18501

MACKINTOSH, ELWIN LEE, med. group adminstr.; b. Tacoma Park, Md., Jan. 22, 1937; s. James Thomas and Evelyn (Collins) M.; B.S., High Point Coll., 1960; M.A., Appalachian State U., 1980; m. Elizabeth Jane Greene, Apr. 13, 1968; children—Kristin Nicole, Todd Fortescue, Bonnie Blythe. Supr. mfg. dept. R.J. Reynolds Tobacco Co., Winston-Salem, N.C., 1961-70; registered rep., mgr. local office, partner Planned Securities Inc., High Point and Winston-Salem, 1970-72; asst. cashier, br. mgr. First Citizens Bank & Trust Co., Winston-Salem, 1972-74; loan officer, mbr. mgr. Bank of N.C., Winston Salem, 1974-79; adminstr. Family Dental Care Assos., Inc., Lorain, Ohio, 1981—. Dist. chmn., mem. exec. com. Old Hickory Council Boy Scouts Am.; chmn. finance child center Centenary Meth. Ch. Served with N.C. Nat. Guard, 1960-68. Recipient Alumni of Year award High Point Coll., 19—. Mem. Winston Salem Jr. C. of C. (state dir., spark plug award, speak up award), Am. Inst. Banking, Med. Group Mgmt. Assn. Republican. Clubs: Toastmaster, Forsyth. Home: 4691 Forestmanor Dr Winston Salem NC 27103 Office: 1300 Cooper Foster Park Rd Lorain OH 44053

MACLAREN, DAVID SARGEANT, pollution control equipment co. exec.; b. Cleve., Jan. 4, 1931; s. Albert Sargeant and Theadora Beidler (Potter) MacL.; A.B., Miami U., Oxford, Ohio, 1955; children—Alison, Carolyn, Catherine. Mgr. Jet Aeration Co., Cleve., 1958-60, chmn. bd., pres., 1961—; founder, chmn. bd., pres. Air Injector Corp., Cleve., 1958-78; founder, pres. Fluid Equipment, Inc., Cleve., 1962-72, chmn. bd., 1962-72; founder, pres. T&M Co., Cleve., 1963-71, chmn. bd., 1964-71; founder, pres. Alison Realty Co., Cleve., 1965—, chmn. bd., 1967—; founder, pres. Mold Leasing, Inc., Cleve., 1968-71; founder, chmn. bd., pres. Sargeant Realty, Inc., 1979—; dir. MWL Systems. Mem. tech. com. Nat. Sanitation Found., Ann Arbor, Mich., 1967—. Mem. Republican State Central Com., 1968-72, Cuyahoga County Republican Central Com., 1968-72; registered legislative agt. 110th Ohio Gen. Assembly, 1973-74. Served with arty. AUS, 1955-58. Fellow Royal Soc. Health (London, Eng.); mem. Nat., Ohio environ. health assns., Nat. Precast Concrete Assn., Am., Ohio pub. health assns., Nat. and Ohio water pollution control fedns., Am. Mgmt. Assn., Mercedes Benz Club N.Am. (pres. 1968), U.S. Martial Arts Assn. (black belt, instr.), Jiu-Jitsu/Karati Black Belt Fedn., Scottish Tartans Soc., Clan MacLaren Soc., Vintage Sports Car Club, Nat. Audubon Soc., Ferrari Club Am., Cleve. Animal Protective League, Highland Heights Citizens League, S.A.R., Fraternal Order Police, H.B. Leadership Soc. (headmaster 1976-78, devel. com.), Delta Kappa Epsilon (nat. dir. 1974—; dir. chpt. assn. 1969—). Clubs: Mentor Harbor Yachting; Cleve. Skating; Union League, Yale, Deke (N.Y.C.). Patentee in field. Home: West Hill Dr Gates Mills OH 44040 Office: 750 Alpha Dr Cleveland OH 44143

MACLAUCHLAN, DONALD JOHN, JR., real estate co. exec.; b. S.I., N.Y., Mar. 2, 1935; s. Donald John and Alice Lucy (Macklin) MacL.; B.A. magna cum laude, Harvard U., 1957; m. Mary Eleanor Manor, Oct. 14, 1967; children—Douglas Laird, Phyllis Ann, Donald John III. Mortgage analyst Conn. Gen. Life Ins. Co., Hartford, 1957-60; mortgage broker James W. Rouse & Co., Balt., 1960-62; devel. mgr. Devel. & Constrn. Co., Inc., Balt., 1962-66; v.p. Nat. Homes Corp., Lafayette, Ind., 1966-75; pres., dir. The Criterion Group, Lafayette, 1975—. Elder, Central Presbyn. Ch., Lafayette, 1971—; mem. gen. council Presbytery of Wabash Valley, 1976-78. Mem. Lafayette Bd. Realtors, Greater Lafayette C. of C., Ind. Apt. Assn. (dir. 1980—), Tippecanoe County Apt. Assn. (dir. 1977—, pres. 1980). Republican. Clubs: Lafayette Country, Romwell Foxhounds (joint master). Office: PO Box 275 Lafayette IN 47905

MACLAUGHLIN, CHARLES ANDREWS, indsl. machinery co. exec.; b. Fort Lewis, Wash., June 5, 1931; s. John Andrews and Ruth Charshee (Hill) MacL.; grad. Balt. Poly. Inst., 1949; student Johns Hopkins U., 1949-51; B.S. in Civil Engring. (Dresser scholar 1955), Tri-State U., 1956; postgrad. Harvard U., 1981; m. Myrle Stewart Gorgas, July 12, 1958; children—Susan Andrews, Anne Stewart, Elizabeth Hill. Civil engr. Howard, Needles, Tammen & Bergendoff, 1956-59; Eastern sales mgr., advt. mgr. Hilti, Inc., 1960-66; v.p. James A. Ford Advt., Stamford, Conn., 1966-67; mktg. services mgr. Ramset div. Olin Corp., New Haven, 1967-72; Eastern regional mgr. Sweco, Inc., subs. Emerson Electric, Florence, Ky., 1972-75, nat. sales mgr., 1975-76, div. mgr. finishing equipment div., 1976-79, v.p., gen. mgr. finishing equipment div., 1979—, also dir. Vestryman, Episcopal Ch., 1971-72; active various community drives. Served to 1st lt. U.S. Army, 1952-54. Decorated Bronze Star; recipient Distinguished Alumnus award Tri-State U., 1971, Merit award State of R.I., 1964. Mem. Soc. Mfg. Engrs., Nat. Machine Tool Builders Assn., Phi Gamma Delta. Republican. Episcopalian. Clubs: Amateur Fencers League Am., Queen City Racquet. Home: 15 Dorino Pl Wyoming OH 45215 Office: 8040 US Hwy 25 Florence KY 41042

MACLEAN, JOHN ALBERT, JR., mfg. co. exec.; b. Wilmette, Ill., Jan. 22, 1905; s. John Albert and Margaret Louise (Barry) MacL.; ed. public schs.; m. Dorothy Jean Barker, May 3, 1930; children—John Albert III (dec.), David Barker, Barry Lee. With MacLean-Fogg Co., Mundelein, Ill., 1928—, pres., 1938—, chmn. bd., 1972—. Mem. Indsl. Fasteners Inst. (chmn.), Ry. Supply Assn. (pres.), Yale Engring. Assn. Republican. Episcopalian. Clubs: Univ. Chgo. Curling, Skokie Country. Office: MacLean Fogg Co 1000 Allanson Rd Mundelein IL 60060

MACLEAY, DONALD, lawyer; b. Tacoma, Dec. 27, 1908; s. Lachlan and Mabel (Nye) M.; J.D., U. Colo., 1931; m. Elizabeth Hall Fesser, Jan. 27, 1934; children—Donald Macleay, Linda Macleay Dewell, Murdo Lachlan. Admitted to Colo., Ill., D.C. bars, 1931-33; com. prevention, punishment of crime Chgo. Assn. Commerce, 1931-32; gen. practice of law, 1933—; with Esch, Kerr, Woolley, Taylor & Shipe, and successor firm Kerr, Shipe & Macleay, also Turney, Rives & Macleay; partner, now counsel firm Macleay, Lynch, Bernhard and Gregg, and predecessors, 1946—. Served as lt. USNR, 1943-45. Mem. Am., D.C. bar assns., Am. Judicature Soc., Assn. Interstate Commerce Practitioners, Maritime Law Assn. U.S., Phi Delta Phi, Chi Psi. Episcopalian. Clubs: Univ., Propeller (Washington); Belle Haven Country. Home: 1800 Edgehill Dr Belle Haven Alexandria VA 22307 Office: 1625 K St Washington DC 20006

MAC LEOD, DONALD SHEA, lawyer; b. Buffalo, Mar. 16, 1922; s. Alexander D. and Lorraine (Shea) MacL.; A.B. magna cum laude, U. Rochester, 1942; LL.B., Harvard, 1948; m. Florence Magnuson, July 26, 1952; children—Laura, Scott. Admitted to N.Y. bar, 1949, Ill. bar, 1950, Pa. bar, 1967; atty. Richards & Coffey, Buffalo, 1949-50; asso., partner Carney, Crowell & Leibman (now Sidley & Austin), Chgo., 1950-59; v.p., sec., gen. counsel Am. Photocopy Equipment Co. (now APECO Corp.), Evanston, Ill., 1959-65; v.p., gen. counsel N. Am. Rockwell Corp. (formerly Rockwell-Standard Corp.), Pitts., 1966-67, v.p., gen. counsel comml. products group, 1967-68, v.p. adminstrn. comml. products group, 1968-69, exec. v.p. comml. products group, 1969-70, v.p., chief adminstrv. officer comml. products group, 1970-71, corp. v.p. adminstrn., 1971-73, corp. v.p. investor relations, 1973-76, v.p., asst. to chmn. bd. for public affairs, 1976-79, cons. Rockwell Internat. Corp., 1979-80; pres., chief exec. officer, dir. The Upson Co., Lockport, N.Y., 1980—; dir. APECO Corp., Evanston, Ill. Served to lt. USNR, 1942-46. C.P.A., Ill. Mem. Am., Pa., Allegheny County bar assns. Home: 231 Thorn St Sewickley PA 15143 Office: Upson Co Lockport NY 14094

MACLEOD, NORMAN ANGUS, optical co. exec.; b. Providence, Feb. 16, 1900; s. John Alexander and Sarah (MacLeod) MacL.; L.H.D. (hon.), New Eng. Coll. Optometry, 1977; m. Berthe Marie Nelson, June 4, 1927; children—Norman Angus, Wallace Nelson. Founder, McLeod Optical Co. Inc., Warwick, R.I., 1922, chmn. bd., 1977—; pres. I Gard Ltd., Warwick, 1970; pres. Am. Bd. Opticianry, 1954-56. Served with U.S. Army, 1917-19; ETO. Mem. Better Vision Inst. (pres. 1965-66), Optical Labs. Assn. (pres. 1947-49), Nat. Acad. Opticianry. Baptist. Clubs: Warwick Country, Rotary, Brit. Empire, Masons, Shriners, Jesters. Home: 220 Crestwood Rd Warwick RI 02886 Office: McLeod Optical Co Inc 100 Jefferson Park Warwick RI 02888

MAC MAHON, HAROLD BERNARD, electro-mech. device mfg. co. exec.; b. Newton, Mass., Nov. 15, 1917; s. Harold A. and Alma (McCabe) MacM.; B.S. in Edn., Boston U., 1940; m. Mary M. Savage, Jan. 1, 1942; 1 dau., Karen D. MacMahon Levisay. Plant mgr. Bassick Div. Stewart-Warner Corp., Spring Valley, Ill., controller Alemite & Instrument div., Chgo., 1966-73, asst. gen. mgr., 1973-74, gen. mgr. Hobbs div., Springfield, Ill., 1974—, v.p. corp., 1976—; dir. Springfield Marine Bank; mem. Sangamon County Pvt. Industry Council. Mem. adv. council St. John's Hosp. Served with AUS, 1943-45. Mem. Soc. Automotive Engrs., Greater Springfield C. of C. (dir.). Home: 1525 W Ash St Springfield IL 62704 also 260 E Chestnut St Chicago IL 60611 Office: Stewart Warner Corp Yale Blvd and Ash St Springfield IL 62705

MACMASTER, DOUGLAS JOSEPH, JR., pharm. co. exec.; b. Boston, Sept. 20, 1930; s. Douglas Joseph and Margaret Ann (Rankin) MacM.; B.A., St. Francis Xavier U., 1953; LL.B., Boston Coll., 1958; m. Joan Marie MacLellan, Sept. 8, 1956; children—Douglas J., Donald F., Heather A., Alexander M., Karen J. Admitted to N.Y. State bar, 1960; mem. firm Kelly, Drye, Newhall & Maginnes, N.Y.C., 1958-61; atty. Merck & Co., Inc., Rahway, N.J., 1961-65; atty. Merck Sharp & Dohme (Eng.), 1965-67, sr. atty. Merck Sharp & Dohme Internat., N.Y.C., 1967-69; counsel Merck Sharp & Dohme Research Labs., Rahway, N.J., 1969-71, exec. dir. research adminstrn. and planning, 1971-73, dir. corp. licensing, 1973-75; mng. dir. Merck Sharp and Dohme, Sydney, Australia, 1975-77, regional dir. Merck Sharp & Dohme Internat., Australia, N.Z., 1977-78, sr. v.p. Merck Sharp & Dohme, Phila., 1978—. Trustee Overlook Hosp., Summit, N.J. Served with U.S. Army, 1953-55. Mem. Am. Bar Assn., N.Y. State Bar Assn. Roman Catholic. Clubs: Phila. Cricket, Beacon Hill. Office: Merck Sharp & Dohme Div of Merck & Co Inc West Point PA 19486

MACNAB, ROBERT EDWARD, elec. contracting co. exec.; b. Cleve., June 5, 1918; s. Edward J. and Thelma A. (Shoos) MacN.; student Wittenberg U., 1938-39; m. Dorothy Ismond, Dec. 9, 1944. With Hatfield Electric Co., Cleve., 1945—, vice-chmn., chief exec. officer, 1974—; pres. Midwest Property Investors Inc., Cleve., 1976—, Phoenix Homes Inc., Cleve., 1977—, Hatfield Investment Corp., Cleve., 1974—, P.S. Ops. Inc., Cleve., 1976—. Bd. dirs., v.p. Boys Clubs Cleve. Served with AC, U.S. Army, 1941-45. Clubs: Chagrin Valley Country, Cleve. Athletic, Hillbrook. Home: 121 Pheasant Ln Chagrin Falls OH 44022 Office: 2149 Fairhill Rd Cleveland OH 44106

MAC NAUGHTON, ANGUS ATHOLE, mfg. co. exec.; b. Montreal, Que., Can., July 15, 1931; s. Athole Austin and Emily Kidder (MacLean) MacN.; student Lower Can. Coll., 1947-48, McGill U., 1949-54; m. Penelope Bower Lewis, Mar. 2, 1957; children—Gillian Heather, Angus Andrew. Auditor, Cooper & Lybrand, Montreal, 1949-55; with Genstar Ltd., various locations, 1955—, pres., 1973-76, vice chmn., chief exec. officer, 1976—; dir. Sun Life Assurance Can., Can. Pacific Enterprises Ltd., Dart Containerline Inc., Can. Comml. Corp., Royal Trustco Ltd. Bd. govs. Lakefield Coll. Sch. Clubs: Mount Royal, St. James's, Montreal Badminton and Squash; Pacific Union, World Trade (San Francisco). Office: 3 Embarcadero Center San Francisco CA 94111

MAC NAUGHTON, D. ROGER, data communications and computer cons.; b. Grosse Pointe, Mich., Aug. 26, 1923; s. William James and Ann Louise (Kahn) MacN.; B.B.A., U. Mich., 1948; m. Madalyn T. Born, Sept. 16, 1944; children—George M., W. James, Ann L., Katherine L. Sales rep. IBM Corp., Detroit, 1948-58; mktg. mgr. GTE Sylvania Co., Boston, 1959-64; corp. staff, program mgr. Xerox Corp., Rochester, N.Y., 1964-68; v.p. Magnavox Co., N.Y.C., 1969-73; pres. Bus. Devel. Internat., Franklin Lakes, N.J., 1973—. Served to lt. (j.g.) USNR, 1942-46. Democrat. Presbyterian. Author: Facsimile Communications in the U.S., 1977; Maintenance of Computers and Data Communications, 1980; Electronic Mail and Message Systems, 1981. Home: 380 Atwood Place Wyckoff NJ 07481 Office: 808 High Mountain Rd Franklin Lakes NJ 07417

MACNAUGHTON, MALCOLM, bus. exec.; b. Portland, Oreg., Mar 9, 1910; s. Ernest Boyd and Gertrude Hoyt (Hutchinson) MacN.; B.S., Stanford U., 1931, postgrad. Grad. Sch. Bus., 1933; LL.D. (hon.), Pepperdine U., 1974; m. 2d, Winifred Sperry Rathstatter, Apr. 11, 1952; children—Alice, Kathleen, Daniel; adopted children—Joseph, Sperry; m. 3d, Sarah E. Brophy, Jan. 1963. Salesman, Norris, Beggs & Simpson, real estate, San Francisco, 1933-34; statistician N. Am. Investment Co., 1934-36; salesman, then asst. mgr. E. F. Hutton & Co., San Francisco, 1930-40; salesman Kaiser & Co., San Francisco, 1940-42; with Castle & Cooke, Ltd., San Francisco and Honolulu, 1942—, exec. v.p., 1957-59, pres., 1959-73, chmn. bd., chief exec. officer, 1973-75, chmn. bd., 1975—; pres. Waialua Agrl. Co., Ltd., Hawaii, 1959—, also dir.; with Kohala Sugar Corp., Hawaii, 1946—, v.p., 1957-59, pres., 1959—, also dir.; pres., dir. Hawaiian Tuna Packers, Honolulu, 1951-56; pres., dir. Hawaiian Equipment Co., Ltd., Honolulu, 1946-55, chmn. bd., dir., 1955—; dir. Dole Co., Hawaiian Airlines, Bank of Hawaii, Wells Fargo Bank, Wells Fargo Realty Advisors, Bumble Bee Seafoods, Hawaiian Trust Co., Ltd. Bd. dirs. Nat. Health and Welfare Retirement Assn., Queen's Med. Center, Honolulu, Aloha United Fund; chmn. bd. govs. Iolani Sch.; trustee Hawaii Pacific Coll. Recipient Merit medal Pres. Philippines, 1980. Mem. Bus. Council, NAM (dir.). Episcopalian. Clubs: Pacific, Waialae Golf (Honolulu); Bohemian, Pacific-Union (San Francisco). Office: Castle & Cooke Inc PO Box 2990 Honolulu HI 96802

MACNULTY, JAY FALLON, mktg. exec.; b. Troy, N.Y., Dec. 2, 1936; s. John Fallon and Loretta Ann (Shea) MacN.; B.S.S., Georgetown U., 1958; postgrad. Albany Law Sch., 1959-60; m. Patricia Rohn, June 11, 1960; 1 son, Rohn. Sec.-treas. J.F. MacNulty, Inc., Albany, N.Y., 1960-68; mktg. services mgr. Matthew Bender Co., Inc., 1969-75, sales adminstrn. mgr., N.Y.C., 1975—. Capt., United Way, New Canaan, Conn., 1978; active Republican Party campaigns in Rensselaer County, N.Y., Town of New Canaan; bd. dirs. New Canaan Day Care Center. Served with U.S. Army, 1961-62. Clubs: Sales Exec., Woodway Country, Exchange. Home: 14 Kelley Green New Canaan CT 06840 Office: 235 E 45th St New York NY 10017

MACOMBER, JOHN D., chem. co. exec.; b. Rochester, N.Y., Jan. 13, 1928; s. William Butts and Elizabeth Currie (Ranlet) M.; B.A., Yale U., 1950; M.B.A., Harvard U., 1952; m. Caroline Morgan, Oct. 21, 1955; children—Janet Morgan, Elizabeth Currie, William Butts II. Dir., mem. mng. com. McKinsey & Co., N.Y.C., 1954-73; pres., dir. Celanese Corp., N.Y.C., 1973—, chief exec. officer, 1977—, chmn. bd., 1980—; dir. Chase Manhattan Bank, R.J. Reynolds Industries, Inc., Bristol-Myers Co. Vice chmn. N.Y. Philharm. Orch.; bd. dirs. Lincoln Center for Performing Arts, Center for Inter-Am. Relations; trustee Joint Council on Econ. Edn., Com. for Econ. Devel., New York Zool. Soc. Served to 1st lt. USAF, 1952-54. Mem. Conf. Bd., Internat. C. of C. (dir.), Council on Fgn. Relations, Bus. Roundtable (taxation task force), Bus. Com. for Arts, Pilgrims of U.S. Club: Econ. (trustee). Office: Celanese Corp 1211 Ave of Americas New York NY 10036

MACON, DAL RANDALL, health care products co. exec.; b. Cottle County, Tex., Mar. 17, 1926; s. Claude Princeton and Bertie Beatrice (Powell) M.; B.S. in Bus. Adminstrn., Northwestern U., 1946; M.B.A., U. Wis., Milw., 1977; m. Doris M. Wenger, May 31, 1947; children—Dal Randall, John S., Paul M. Office mgr. Goodyear Tire & Rubber Co., Des Moines, 1946-48; salesman Younker Bros., Inc., Des Moines, 1948-54; div. mgr. Shampaine Industries, St. Louis, 1954-61; gen. mdse. mgr. Sherwood Med. Industries, St. Louis, 1961-69; v.p., gen. mgr. Kansas City White Good Mfg. Co. (Mo.), 1969-72; pres. Tek Products, Inc., Racine, Wis., 1972-73, Macon & Co., Milw., 1973—; exec. v.p. Will Ross, Inc., Milw., 1973-77; lectr. Grad. Sch., U. Wis., Milw. Bd. dirs. N.W. Gen. Hosp.; mem. Milw. Republican Com. Served with USN, 1944-46, 50-52. Mem. Weber Exec. Alumni Assn. (U. Wis.-Milw.) (dir.). Presbyterian. Home: 4647 N Ardmore Ave Milwaukee WI 53211 Office: 4385 N Greenbay Milwaukee WI 53209

MACPHERSON, CULLEN H(EASLET), mfg. co. exec.; b. San Mateo, Calif., Dec. 6, 1927; s. (John) Hugh and Margaret Ann (Barnes) M.; A.A., Menlo Coll., 1944; A.B., Stanford U., 1948, M.A., 1951; A.B., San Jose State Coll., 1949; m. Elaine M. Hallberg, Sept. 12, 1951; children—Elizabeth E., Louise A., Cullen J.G. Instr. U. Kans. Med. Sch., Lawrence, 1951-52; research asso. biophysics U. Minn., Mpls., 1952-53; mgr. reproducing components div. Electro Voice, Inc., Buchanan, Mich., 1953-55; biophysicist Tektronix, Inc., Beaverton, Oreg., 1955-75; pres. Argonaut Assos., Inc., Beaverton, 1960—; cons. biophysicist Oreg. Regional Primate Center, Beaverton, 1964—; chief research engr. Temperature Controls div. Eaton Corp., Beaverton, 1975—; dir. Western Geophys. Instrument & Exploration Co., Portland, Interface Assos., Inc., Portland, San Francisco. Mem. Audio Engrs. Soc., AAAS, Acoustical Soc. Am., IEEE (biomed. engring. group; chmn. 1964-65, 70-71, legis. adv. com. 1979—), Am. Assn. Physics Tchrs., Am. Inst. Physics, Sigma Xi, Phi Sigma. Home: 2677 NW Westover Rd Portland OR 97210 Office: Box K Beaverton OR 97005

MACPHERSON, DONALD REID, sales and mktg. exec.; b. Peterborough, Ont., Can., Oct. 13, 1932; s. James Franklyn and Amelia (Reid) MacP.; student U. Syracuse, 1964, Stanford U., 1970; m. Theresa Harriet McFee, June 25, 1955; children—Donna Amelia, Heather Jane. Vice pres., gen. mgr. Lufkin Rule Co. of Can., Ltd., 1964-68; v.p., gen. mgr. Lufkin div. Cooper Group, Raleigh, N.C., 1968-70, v.p., gen. mgr. internat. ops., 1970-78, sr. v.p. sales and mktg., 1978—; chmn. bd. Cooper Tool Group (U.K.); pres. Cooper Tool Group Can. Mem. Am. Hardware Mfrs. Assn. Presbyterian. Clubs: North Ridge Country, Capital City (Raleigh). Home: 8704 Stage Ford Rd Raleigh NC 27614 Office: 3535 Glenwood Ave Raleigh NC 27622

MACRAE, JOHN, III, editor, publisher; b. N.Y.C., Nov. 21, 1931; s. John, Jr. and Anne (Hinton) M.; A.B., Harvard U., 1954; m. Frances Arthur Cummins, May 18, 1957 (div. 1976); children—John Yancey, Elizabeth Hinton, Phebe Barber, Annabel Cummins. Engaged in sales and mktg. Owens-Corning Fiberglas Corp., 1957-60; with Harper & Row, 1960-67, exec. editor, dep. dir. trade complex, 1965-67; editor-in-chief, v.p., mng. dir. E.P. Dutton Co., 1968-69, pres., editor, 1969—; dir. Childcraft Corp. Mem. com. reading Am. Book Pubs. Council, 1968-69; mem. Van Wyck Brooks Lit. Award Com. Del. White House Conf. Natural Beauty, 1965; co-dir. Hudson River Valley Conservation Commn. Trustee Palisades (N.Y.) Free Library, 1966-70, pres., 1967-68; bd. dirs. Soc. Family of Man; trustee, bd. dirs. Roger Klein Award, Editorial 1969—. Served with U.S. Army, 1954-56. Mem. P.E.N. (treas. 1973—, dir. translation com.), Mid-Atlantic Conservation Council, Am. Mus. Natural History (vice chmn. pub. 1973—). Democrat. Clubs: Porcellian (Harvard); Century Assn. Office: EP Dutton 2 Park Ave New York NY 10016*

MACRI, GREGORY J(OSEPH), JR., chem. and chem. equipment co. exec.; b. Brockton, Mass., June 2, 1928; s. Gregorio Joseph and Adelaide (Tyler) M.; student public Schs., Weymouth, Mass.; m. Betty-Ann Corrigan, July 23, 1950; children—Lynn-Diana, Cheryl-Ann, Gregory Joseph III, Glen, Garrison. Truck driver Boston Sand and Gravel Co., 1948-52; salesman Magnus Chem. Co., Garwood, N.J., 1952-66; founder, pres. Keene Products Co. (became div. Consol. Foods Corp. 1970), Keene, N.H., 1966—; Bd. dirs. Fall Mountain YMCA, Bellows Falls, Vt., 1976-80; pres. Dollars for Scholars, Walpole, N.H., 1977, chmn. bd. dirs., 1978; incorporator Cheshire Hosp., Keene, 1976-80; mem. governing bd., chmn. audit and fin. com. Citizens' Scholarship Found. Am.; mem. Walpole (N.H.) Bicentennial Fund Raising Com., 1976. Mem. TAPPI, Paper Indsl. Mgmt. Assn., Antique Automobile Club Am. Republican. Clubs: Lions (pres. club 1964) (Walpole); Elks, Masons, Shriners (co-and asso. gen. chmn. Maple Sugar Bowl Game 1973-80). Office: 47 Victoria St Keene NH 03431

MACTAVISH, ROY DREXEL, mgmt. specialist; s. Roy L. and Velma G. MacT.; A.B., Juniata Coll., 1936; A.M., U. Pitts., 1938; Ph.D., Cornell U., 1953. Exec. asst. to dir. disaster relief ARC, Washington, 1936-38, asst. nat. dir. personnel, 1940-43; asst. prof. Ohio U., Athens and vis. prof. Kent (Ohio) State U., 1938-40; adminstr. UN Orgn., U.S. Zone Germany, 1945-51; exec. devel. coordinator Cornell U., Ithaca, N.Y., 1951-53; ednl. project dir., mgmt. programmer Am. Mgmt. Assn., Inc., N.Y.C., 1953-56; corporate mgr. tng. and personnel devel. Am. Radiator & Standard San. Corp., N.Y.C., 1956-58; pvt. practice ednl. and mgmt. cons.,

1967—; prof. bus. adminstrn. specializing in mgmt. Monmouth Coll., W. Long Branch, N.J.; adj. faculty Inter-Agency Inst. Fed. Hosp. Adminstrs., Dept. Def. armed forces and civilian mgmt. programs, Fort Monmouth (N.J.) Officer's Mgmt. Sch. Served with inf. U.S. Army, 1943-45. Certified social worker, N.Y. Mem. Internat., Am. mgmt. assns. Democrat. Baptist. Club: Masons. Home: RFD 2 Box 205 Englishtown NJ 07726 Office: Office Bus Adminstrn Dept Monmouth Coll West Long Branch NJ 07764

MACUMBER, JOHN PAUL, ins. co. exec.; b. Macon, Mo., Jan. 21, 1940; s. Rolland Deardorf and Althea Villa (Cason) M.; B.A., Central Meth. Coll., Fayette, Mo., 1962; Asso. in Risk Mgmt., Ins. Inst. Am., 1978; m. Marilyn Sue Ashe, Nov. 10, 1962; children—Leanne, Cheryl. Casualty underwriter U.S. Fidelity & Guaranty Co., St. Louis, 1962-66; automobile underwriter Am. Indemnity Co., Galveston, Tex., 1966-69; auto casualty underwriter St. Paul Cos., New Orleans, 1969-73; sr. comml. casualty underwriter Chubb/Pacific Indemnity, Portland, Oreg., 1973-75; casualty underwriter Interstate Nat. Corp., Los Angeles, 1975-76, underwriting supr., 1976-78, v.p., br. mgr., Mpls., 1978—, also v.p. subs. Chgo. Ins. Co. Served with USAF, 1962-68. Nat. Methodist scholar, 1958. Mem. Minn. Assn. Spl. Risk Underwriters. Republican. Mem. Unity Ch. (sec. bd. dirs. 1979). Clubs: Optimists (charter pres. 1968) (Friendswood, Tex.); Kiwanis (charter pres. 1979), Ins., Blue Goose (Mpls.). Home: 3716 Canterbury Dr Bloomington MN 55431 Office: 5001 W 80th St Minneapolis MN 55437

MACWILLIAMS, JOHN J., ins. co. exec.; b. Syracuse, N.Y., Apr. 30, 1929; s. John J. and Marion (Klock) MacW.; grad. Phillips Acad., 1947; B.A. in English, Hobart Coll., 1951; m. Lee Elliott, May 16, 1953; children—John J. III, William Brewster, Peter Huntington, Cameron Lee. With Aetna Life & Casualty Co., 1954-68, dir. internat. dept., 1966-68; pres. Colonial Penn Life Ins. Co., 1968-72, chmn. bd., 1968—; pres. Colonial Penn Ins. Co., 1969-72, chmn. bd., 1969—; chmn. bd. Colonial Penn Ins. Co., 1971—; chmn. bd., chief exec. officer Colonial Penn Group, Inc., 1969—; dir. Provident Nat. Bank, Provident Nat. Corp., Old Phila. Corp. Mem. Mus. Assos. and assos.' com. Phila. Mus. Art; mem. Phila. Orch. Assn.; bd. dirs. World Affairs Council; trustee Drexel U. Served to capt. U.S. Army, 1951-53. Mem. Ins. Fedn. of Pa. (dir.), Greater Phila. C. of C. (dir.). Clubs: Nat. Golf Links, Pine Valley Golf, Univ. of N.Y.; Phila., Merion Racquet Cricket, Phila. Racquet (Phila.); Gulph Mills Golf; Quogue (L.I.) Field, Quogue Beach, The Courts, Mill Reef. Home: 1234 Country Club Rd Gladwyne PA 19035 Office: 5 Penn Center Plaza 30th Floor Philadelphia PA 19103

MADDALENA, SAMUEL ANTHONY, communications co. exec.; b. Sicily, Italy, May 11, 1923; s. Alfonse and Rosaria (Termini) M.; B.S., Fordham U., 1952; M.B.A., N.Y. U., 1955; D.P.S., Pace U., 1979; m. Louise Lucy Laneri, Apr. 2, 1944; children—Rosemary, Michael. With Western Electric Co., 1941-62, dept. chief-personnel, 1961-62; costs engr. overseas AT&T long lines, N.Y.C., 1962-75; mgr. Transoceanic Cable Ship Co., 1975—; instr. Stevens Inst. Tech., Hoboken, N.J., 1954-63; adj. prof. mgmt. Montclair (N.J.) State Coll., 1978-79. Pres. St. Thomas Acquinas Baseball League, Bklyn., 1962-63; chmn. St. Thomas Acquinas Home-Sch. Assn., 1973. Served with USAAF, 1942-46. Republican. Roman Catholic. Home: 46 Lake Shore Dr Montville NJ 07045 Office: 201 Littleton Rd Morris Plains NJ 07950

MADDEN, EDWARD B., mobile home mfg. co. exec. Pres., chief exec. officer Guerdon Industries, Inc., Louisville. Office: PO Box 35290 Louisville KY 40232*

MADDEN, JOHN FRANCIS, pub. accountant, editor, pub.; b. Evansville, Ind., Apr. 22, 1902; s. William Martin and Veronica (Keller) M.; student parochial and pub. schs., Indpls.; m. Geneva Louise Stalcup, July 24, 1924; children—John William, Charles Edward, Francis Joseph. Asso. W.M. Madden & Co., C.P.A.'s, Indpls., 1921—, sole owner, 1954—; publisher Ind. Cath. and Record, 1933-56; editor, pub. Marion County Mail; pres. Shield Press, Inc., Mail Printing & Pub. Corp. C.P.A., Ind. Mem. Newcomen Soc. N.Am., Ind., Marion County hist. socs., Indpls. Art Assn. Republican. Roman Catholic. Home: 10770 Crooked Stick Ln Carmel IN 46032 also 1545 Moonridge Rd Tucson AZ 85718

MADDEN, JOHN WILLIAM, JR., silver mfg. co. exec.; b. Cambridge, Mass., Oct. 19, 1941; s. John William and Doris G. (Fraser) M.; B.B.A., U. Mass., 1963; postgrad. exec. mgmt. program U. Kans., 1976; m. Patricia A. Cummins, June 23, 1964; children—Colleen, Laura, John W. III. With Hallmark Cards Inc., Kansas City, Mo., 1967-78, creative mktg. mgr., 1972-73, dir. new product devel., 1974-75, product mgr., 1975-76, group product mgr., 1976-78; dir. mktg. Gorham-Textron Co., Providence, R.I., 1978—. Served with USMC, 1963-66. Mem. Sterling Silversmith's Guild (steering com.), Tau Kappa Epsilon. Roman Catholic. Office: 333 Adelaide Ave Providence RI 02907

MADDEN, RICHARD BLAINE, forest products co. exec.; b. Short Hills, N.J., Apr. 27, 1929; s. James L. and Irma (Twining) M.; B.S., Princeton, 1951; J.D., U. Mich., 1956; M.B.A., N.Y. U., 1959; m. Joan Fairbairn, May 24, 1958; children—John Richard, Lynn Marie, Kathryn Ann, Andrew Twining. Admitted to Mich. bar, 1956, N.Y. bar, 1957; gen. asst., treas.'s dept. Socony Mobil Oil Corp., N.Y.C., 1956-57, spl. asst., 1958-59, fin. rep., 1960; asst. to pres. Mobil Chem. Co., also dir. Mobil Chems. Ltd. of Eng., 1960-63; exec. v.p., gen. mgr. Kordite Corp., also v.p. Mobil Plastics, 1963-66, v.p. Mobil Chem. Co., N.Y.C., 1966-68, group v.p., 1968-70, asst. treas. Mobil Oil Corp., 1970-71; chmn. Mobil Estates Ltd., 1970-71; chmn., chief exec. officer Potlatch Corp., San Francisco, 1971—; dir. Pacific Gas Electric Co., Del Monte Corp., AMFAC Inc.; from lectr. to adj. asso. prof. fin. N.Y. U., 1960-63. Bd. dirs. Am. Paper Inst.; chmn. Am. Enterprise Inst.; bd. govs. San Francisco Symphony Assn.; bd. dirs. San Francisco Opera; vice chmn. Bay Area Council; mem. distbn. com. San Francisco Found. Served to lt. (j.g.) USNR, 1951-54. Mem. N.Y., Mich. bars. Roman Catholic. Clubs: Univ. (N.Y.C.); Lagunitas Country, Pacific Union (San Francisco). Office: PO Box 3591 San Francisco CA 94119

MADDEN, RUSSELL CADWALADER, acct.; b. North Wales, Pa., Mar. 4, 1923; s. John and Mary Wilson (Cadwalader) M.; Asso. Sci., Peirce Coll., 1950; student Ursinus Coll., 1966-69; m. Julia Dowiak, June 15, 1946; children—Nancy Susan Madden Craig, John Keith. Acct., Colver & Co., Pottstown, Pa., 1948-50; mgr. Philco-Ford, Lansdale, Pa., 1950-70; controller Granite Knitting Mills Inc., Souderton, Pa., 1970-75, T.M. Landis, Inc., 1975—. Bd. dirs. Elm Terr. Gardens, 1980; treas. N.Penn Vis. Nurse Assn., 1980; mem. Lansdale Borough Council, 1966-78, pres., 1966-68; v.p. Montgomery County Borough Assn., 1974-76. Served with U.S. Army, 1941-44. Decorated Combat Inf. Badge; recipient PhilcoFord Community Service award, 1967, Ford Citizen of Yr. award, 1969, Disting. Service award Pa. C. of C., 1978, citation Pa. Ho. of Reps., 1976. Mem. Am. Inst. Corp. Controllers. Republican. Baptist. Clubs: Shriners, Masons, Lehigh Consistory. Home: 701 Delaware Ave Lansdale PA 19446 Office: 47 Main Mainland PA 19451

MADDEN, WILLIAM LEWIS, textile machinery sales exec.; b. Laurens, S.C., Oct. 22, 1933; s. John Walter and Emma Nelle Madden; B.S. in Textile Mfg., Clemson (S.C.) U., 1956; m. Sara Elledge, July 3, 1954; 1 son, John Lewis. Prodn. supr. Monsanto Textiles Co., Greenwood, S.C., 1961-63; sales mgr. Fayco Machinery Co., Gastonia, N.C., 1965-69; pres. Madden-Carman, Inc., textile machinery sales, Greenville, S.C., 1969—. Served to capt. U.S. Army, 1956-58. Mem. Greenville C. of C. Baptist. Club: Elks. Address: 8 Coventry Rd Greenville SC 29615

MADDOCKS, DOUGLAS WILLIAM, banker; b. Cumberland, Md., Dec. 1, 1938; s. Robert William and Elizabeth (Babst) M.; A.A., Glendale Coll., 1973; B.S., Calif. State U., 1977, M.B.A., 1980; m. Marylee Woodard, Oct. 17, 1964; children—Deborah Sue, Patricia Lynn. Mgmt. asso. J.C. Penney Co., San Diego, Calif., 1960-62; loan rep. Household Fin. Corp., West Covina, Calif., 1962-63; br. ops. supr. Security Pacific Nat. Bank, Los Angeles, 1963-64, protection specialist, 1965-73, investment ops. mgr., 1973-80, v.p., div. mgr., 1980—. Served with U.S. Navy, 1956-59. Mem. Securities Industry Mgmt. Assn. So. Calif., Dealer Bank Assn., Beta Gamma Sigma. Republican. Baptist. Office: 333 S Hope St Los Angeles CA 90071

MADDOX, JACK DOUGLAS, utility mgr.; b. Poplar Bluff, Mo., July 17, 1945; s. Deloy Floyd and Dena Lucille (Sparkman) M.; A.S., Coll. Sch. Ozarks, Point Lookout, Mo., 1965; B.S.Ch.E., Washington U., St. Louis, 1968; M.S.N.E., U. N.Mex., Albuquerque, 1969; m. Peggy L. Clifford, July 3, 1965. Research engr., Monsanto Co., St. Louis, 1965-68, Babcock & Wilcox, Lynchburg, Va., 1973-74; chemonuclear cons. engr. Babcock & Wilcox, 1974; engr. nuclear systems Pub. Service Co. N.Mex., Albuquerque, 1974-76, supr. resource analysis, 1976-78, project mgr. Baca geothermal demonstration power plant, 1978—. Exec. com. Inst. adv. bd. N.Mex. Energy Inst., 1976—; pres. Forest Park (N.Mex.) Coop. Assn., 1977-78. Served to 1st lt. USAF, 1970-73; Vietnam. Decorated Commendation medal; NSF fellow, 1968-69; registered profl. engr., N.Mex. Mem. Nat. Soc. Profl. Engrs., Am. Nuclear Soc., Am. Inst. Chem. Engrs., Electric Power Research Inst., Porsche Club Am. Research solar repowering of fossil plants, geothermal energy, chem. processes nuclear and non-nuclear applications. Office: PO Box 2267 Albuquerque NM 87103

MADERA, VICTOR MIGUEL, elec. co. exec.; b. San Juan, P.R., Dec. 4, 1929; s. Bautista Madera and Deadina Bauza; B.E.E., U. P.R., 1951; m. Ruth Ortiz; children—Victor, Jose, Juan, Adlin. Pres., gen. mgr. Schlumberger div. Weston P.R., Inc., 1953-71; v.p., plant mgr. Westinghouse Controls, Inc., 1972-74; pres., gen. mgr. Westinghouse Toa Baja Complex, P.R., 1974-76; mfg. planning dir. Westinghouse Elec. Corp. for P.R. ops., San Juan, 1976—. Served with Signal Corps, AUS, 1951-53. Mem. Am. Soc. Personnel Adminstrs., Am. Soc. Quality Control (pres., chief proctor quality control engr. exams.), Am. Prodn. and Inventory Control Soc. (v.p. P.R. chpt.), P.R. Mfg. Assn., P.R. Electronic Industries Assn. Club: Rotary Internat. Office: Westinghouse Electric Corp Suite 200 1590 Ponce de Leon Ave Rio Piedras Juan PR 00926

MADIGAN, FRANCIS WALTER, JR., contractor; b. Worcester, Mass., Sept. 5, 1930; s. Francis Walter and Mildred Lucile (LeMoyne) M.; B.S., Worcester Poly. Inst., 1953, postgrad., 1956-57; postgrad. Clark U., 1956-57; m. Mary Jane Baggan, June 18, 1955; children—Kathleen, Francis III, Mary Frances, Margaret, James, Ellen. Treas., F.W. Madigan Co., Inc., Worcester, 1962—, chief exec. officer, 1970—. Bd. mgrs. YMCA Worcester, 1969-75; gifts adv. Bishops Fund Worcester, 1975-80; chmn. corp. fund Assumption Coll. Tomorrow, 1980—. Served with U.S. Army, 1954-56. Mem. Worcester Tech. Alumni Assn. (pres. 1970), Assn. Gen. Contractors Mass. (dir. 1964—, pres. 1972-73), Worcester Gen. Bldg. Contractors Assn. (pres. 1970—), Assn. Gen. Contractors Am. (dir. 1970— trustee Edn. and Research Found.), ASCE, Constrn. Specification Inst., Am. Inst. Constructors (dir.), Cons. Constructors Council Am., Roman Catholic. Clubs: Rotary, Worcester. Home: 15 Mary Jane Circle Worcester MA 01609 Office: PO Box 586 Worcester MA 01613

MADIGAN, JOSEPH EDWARD, food co. exec.; b. Bklyn., June 26, 1932; s. James Peter and Mildred (Goldman) M.; B.B.A. cum laude, Baruch Coll., 1958; M.B.A., N.Y. U., 1963; m. Catherine Cashman, July 26, 1980; children—Kerri Ann, Kimberly Ann, Jeffrey Charles, Elizabeth Ann. Adminstrv. asst. Asso. Metals & Minerals Corp., N.Y.C., 1961-63; fin. analyst fgn. exchange trader, copr. portfolio, also trader Amax, Inc., N.Y.C., 1963-65; mgr. corp. portfolio, dir. cash mgmt., asst. treas. Trans World Airlines, Inc., N.Y.C., 1965-68; treas. Borden, Inc., N.Y.C., 1968-80, v.p., 1976-80; exec. v.p., chief fin. officer Wendy's Internat., Inc., Dublin, Ohio, 1980—. Served with USNR, 1951-55. Mem. Fin. Execs. Inst., Investor Relations Assn., Nat. Investor Relations Inst., Assn. Corp. Growth, Am. Mgmt. Assn., N.Y. U. Fin. Club, City U. N.Y. Alumni Assn., N.Y. U. Alumni Assn., Treas.'s Club, Beta Gamma Sigma. Republican. Roman Catholic. Clubs: N.Y. U., Manhattan (N.Y.C.).

MADOLE, DONALD WILSON, lawyer; b. Elkhart, Kans., July 14, 1932; student Kans. State Tchrs. Coll., 1950-52; B.S., U. Denver, 1959, J.D., 1959; m. Juanita M. Weisbach, July 12, 1975. Vice pres. Mountain Aviation Corp., Denver, 1958-59; admitted to Colo. bar, 1960, D.C. bar, 1971; trial atty. FAA, Washington, 1960-62; sr. warranty adminstr. Am. Airlines, Tulsa, 1962-63; chief hearing and reports div., atty. adviser CAB, Washington, 1963-66; partner firm Speiser, Krause & Madole, N.Y.C. and Washington, 1966—. Pres., Aerial Application Corp., Burlingame, Calif., 1968-69; v.p. Environmental Power Ltd., Pitts., 1972—; dir. Phazar Inc., San Francisco, 1969-73, Mills Estate Realty, San Francisco, 1958-72, Unitrade Ltd., Washington, Bus. Ins. Mgmt. Inc., Bethesda, Md., Environmental Power Ltd., Pitts., Pa. Pocahontas Coal Co., Pitts., 1972-76. Entertainment Capitol Corp., N.Y.C.; gen. counsel Nat. Aviation Club, 1978—, Internat. Soc. Air Safety Investigators, 1977; mem. blue ribbon panel on airworthiness Nat. Acad. Sci., 1979. Adviser, U.S. Govt. delegation Internat. Civil Aviation Orgn., 1965; U.S. Govt. rep. Aircraft Inquiry, Montreal, Que., Can., 1964. Mem. alumni com. U. Denver, 1973—. Served to comdr. USNR, 1953-57. Recipient Outstanding Performance award FAA, 1961; Meritorious Achievement award Am. Airlines, 1962; Outstanding Performance awards CAB, 1963-65; Fed. Govt. Outstanding Pub. Service award, Jump-Meml. Found., 1966. Mem. D.C., Fed., Am., Colo. bar assns., Am. Trial Lawyers Assn., Lawyer-Pilots Assn., Nat. Aviation Club, Nat. Press Club, Phi Delta Phi, Phi Mu Alpha. Club: Congressional Country. Author: Textbook of Aviation Statues and Regulations, 1963; International Aspects of Aircraft Accidents, 1963; CAB, Aircraft Accident Investigation, 1964. Home: 2800 Jenifer St NW Washington DC 20015 Office: 1216 16th St NW Washington DC 20036

MADRIGAL, ROBERTO, oil co. exec.; b. Medellin, Colombia, Feb. 8, 1946; s. Alfonso and Judith (Quevedo) M.; came to U.S., 1976; B. Indsl. Engring., Jesuit U., Caracas, Venezuela, 1971; postgrad U. Paris., 1971-73; m. Patricia Lynn Pinedo, Dec. 20, 1970; children—Ivan Esteban, Cristina Elena. Ops. mgr. Hideca, Caracas, 1974, oil trading mgr., 1974-77; pres. Hideca Petroleum Corp., Houston, 1977-79; dir. internat. products transp. and supply Langham Petroleum Corp., Houston, 1979-80; pres. Crystal Energy Corp. of Tex., 1980—; prof. world energy econs. Central U. Venezuela; U.S. corr. Semana Venezuelian polit. weekly mag. Mem. Am. Mgmt. Assn. Research in olygopolistic structure in oil bus. and its effect on energy supply and distbn. Home: 1201 Krist St Houston TX 77055 Office: Three Riverway Suite 1380 Houston TX 77056

MADSEN, BERNHARDT, packaging co. exec.; b. Colonia, N.J., Mar. 25, 1932; s. Axel E. and Elizabeth (Kasper) M.; B.S., Rutgers U., 1963; m. Marianne Woelfel, Feb. 15, 1958; children—Diane, Bernhardt. Laborer, Celotex Corp., Metuchen, N.J., 1949; lab. technician Merck & Co., Rahway, N.J., 1951-55; merchandiser Storecast Co., Jersey City, 1955-56, asst. div. mgr., 1956-58; salesman Crompton, Knowles & Readington, Westfield, N.J., 1962-64; field sales mgr. Abbott Macht div. DCA Corp., Scranton, Pa., 1964-65, gen. mgr., 1965-72, v.p. U.S. packaging, 1972-73; gen. mgr. Control Print div. Dennison Mfg. Co., Fairfield, N.J., 1973-75; pres., chief exec. officer Robert Bosch Packaging Corp., Piscataway, N.J., 1975—, also dir.; pres., chief exec. officer, dir. Robert Bosch Tech. Products Corp., Piscataway, 1980—. Served with Signal Corps, U.S. Army, 1952-54. Recipient key for extra-curricular activities Rutgers U., 1963. Mem. Packaging Inst., Am. Mktg. Assn., Kappa Upsilon. Republican. Episcopalian. Joint holder machine patent. Home: 46 Village Way Somerville NJ 08876 Office: 15 Seeley Ave Piscataway NJ 08854

MADSEN, RAYMOND WOODROW, mgmt. analyst; b. Hampton, Nebr., Jan. 12, 1919; s. Hans Marius and Lydia Belinda (Henriksen) M.; B.S., Tex. Christian U., 1959; M.B.A., U. Calif. at Long Beach, 1971; m. Georgialee Stephens, July 3, 1941; children—Linda Gail, Don Ray, Karl Stephen, Sylvia Louise. Milling machine operator Convair div. Gen. Dynamics Corp., Fort Wort, 1942-44, 46-48, machine shop foreman, 1949-61; machine shop supt. Lear-Siegler Corp., El Segundo, Calif., 1962; mfg. and statis. analyst Space div. Rockwell Internat., Downey, Calif., 1963-64, supr. program adminstrn., 1965-70, budgets and forecasts advisor, 1970—. Pres., 1st Luth. Ch., Torrance, Calif., 1972-76; mem. long-range planning commn. Am. Luth. Ch., 1974—; bd. dirs., chmn. Southland Luth. Home Geriatric Center, 1978—. Served with U.S. Army, 1944-46. Republican. Home: 14603 Wadkins Ave Gardena CA 90249 Office: 12218 Lakewood St Downey CA 90241

MADUZIA, EDWARD F., mfg. co. exec.; b. Chgo., May 15, 1940; s. Robert Thomas and Meridal Lois (Schmidt) M.; B.A., Northwestern U., 1962; M.B.A., U. Chgo., 1963; m. Catherine Anna Tolan, June 7, 1962; children—Kimberly, Jennifer, Robert, Kenneth. Mgmt. trainee Covell Mfg. Co., Chgo., 1963-64, account exec., 1964-66; account exec. Kagle Mfg. Co., Chgo., 1966-70, dir. sales, 1970-74, v.p. sales, 1974—. Active Boy Scouts Am.; mem. Lombard (Ill.) Library Redevel. Council, 1974—, chmn. bus. com., 1977—; mem. Lombard Vol. Fire Dept., 1974—. Mem. NAM. Democrat. Methodist. Club: Butterfield Country (Oak Brook, Ill.). Address: 4505 N Manor Chicago IL 60625

MAESTRE, JOSE MARIA, marketing, ednl. and mgmt. cons.; b. Allentown, Pa., Nov. 1, 1929; s. Jose Maria and Anna Ingeborg (Linde) M.; B.A. in English cum laude, Rutgers U., 1960; postgrad. Temple U., 1962-65; postgrad. in marketing and finance U. Calif. at Berkeley Extension, 1968, in marketing U. Golden Gate, San Francisco, 1968-71; M.A. in Bilingual Vocat. Edn., U. San Francisco, 1979, postgrad. in multicultural vocat. edn., 1979—; m. Theodora Joan Racin, Sept. 11, 1962; children—Lauren Margaret, Rebekka, Gwynnd Delaen. Accounting clk. Johns Manville Products Corp., Manville, N.J., 1947-56; supr. publs. Electro-Mech. Research, Princeton, N.J., 1957-65; product mgr., advt. mgr. Warner-Lambert Pharm. Co., Richmond, Calif., 1965-67; asst. to v.p. mktg. Pacific Press & Shear Corp., Oakland, Calif., 1968; mgr. mktg. services Lex Computer Systems, Palo Alto, Calif., 1969-71; nat. marketing mgr. Concord Communications Systems, Farmingdale, N.Y., 1972-73; pres. Learning Tools, Inc., Oakland, Calif., 1971-79; owner P.M. Prodns., Oakland, 1971—; instr. mktg. for small bus. Downtown Community Coll., San Francisco, 1980—; instr. Mission Community Coll., San Francisco, U. San Francisco, 1978-79; pres. Learning Tools, 1971-78, ednl. cons. minority bus. edn. projects, 1975-77; cons. migrant edn. Calif. Office Edn., 1976-77. Mem. adv. bd. Oakland Bi-Lingual Edn. Project, 1971-72. Served with AUS, 1951-53. Recipient Advt. award Reinhold Pub. Co., 1966. Mem. Internat. Tape Assn. (mem. adv. bd. 1972), Internat. Inst. Gen. Semantics, Rutgers Alumni Assn., Designed (with wife) proprietary math manipulatives; created 5 x 13 wall mural art deco motif commissioned by Shoong Found. and installed Paramount Theatre Arts; developer, condr. proprietary program Presentation Techniques for Minorities in Job Acquisition and Career Devel., 1980; contbr. articles on marketing to tech. jours. Home: 6986 Park Blvd Oakland CA 94611

MAEWEATHER, KAREN SUE, telephone co. exec.; b. Indpls., Oct. 19, 1949; d. James W. and Katie L. (Segraves) Tanner; B.S. in Mktg., Calif. State U., Los Angeles, 1975; M.B.A., Pepperdine U., 1978; m. Thomas R. Maeweather, Apr. 30, 1977. With Gen. Telephone of Calif., Santa Monica, 1969—, mgmt. devel., 1973-74, personnel research mgr., 1974-77, bus. strategies mgr., 1977—, also product mgr. residential services and direct sales. Mem. Am. Mktg. Assn., Personnel Women of Los Angeles, Internat. Assn. Personnel Women) bd. dirs. Los Angeles chpt.), Personnel and Indsl. Relations Assn. (bd. dirs.). Democrat. Baptist. Condr. research project on Flextime, 1976. Home: 2032 Brentwood Dr West Covina CA 91792 Office: 100 Wilshire Blvd Santa Monica CA 90401

MAFFEI, NATALE SERIO, savs. and loan assn. exec.; b. Lucca, Italy, Oct. 14, 1921; s. Michele and Maria (Dal Porto) M.; grad. Stockton Coll. Commerce, 1941; student La. State U., 1943, U. So. Calif. Sch. Bus., 1965; m. LaVerne Virginia Simi, Jan. 13, 1946; children—Natale Serio, Dennis A., Bruce A., Jon A. Asst. cashier Bank of Am., Stockton, Calif., 1946-49; mgr. Gen. Finance Co., also v.p., dir. San Joaquin Investment Co., San Joaquin Real Estate Co., Stein Real Estate Co., Stockton, Calif., 1949-60; sr. v.p., sec. San Joaquin First Fed. Savs. & Loan Assn., also v.p., dir. First Plaza Corp., Stockton, 1960—. Real estate broker, pub. accountant, 1954—. Served with AUS, 1943-46. Mem. Soc. Savs. and Loan Controllers, Am. Savs. and Loan Inst., Comml. Exchange Club. Democrat. Roman Catholic. Elk. Office: PO Box 191 Stockton CA 95202

MAFFEO, THOMAS EDWIN, container co. exec.; b. New Haven, Sept. 4, 1931; s. Thomas Benjamine and Loretta Veronica (Ferguson) M.; B.S. in Indsl. Engring., U. Conn., 1954; M.S. in Indsl. Engring., Clarkson Coll. Tech., 1961; m. Marvis June Meador, Apr. 7, 1956; children—Kathleen, Michelle, Caroline. Indsl. engr., prodn. supr. Aluminum Co. Am., Massena, N.Y., 1957-62; indsl. engr., corporate staff Dart Industries, Los Angeles, 1962-64; asst. controller, dir. engring., materials mgr., gen. mgr. mfg., gen. mgr. mfg./distbn. services, v.p. distbn. Rexall Drug div., 1964-72, v.p. mfg. and distbn. Vanda Beauty Counselor div., 1972-74; exec. v.p., gen. mgr. Heil Process Equipment Co. div., 1974-79, pres., 1975-77, v.p. ops. Fiberglass Equipment div., 1978-79; div. mgr. Sewell Plastics Inc. div. Dorsey Corp., Havre De Grace, Md., 1979—. Served to 1st lt. S.C. AUS, 1954-56. Mem. Am. Inst. Indsl. Engrs., Metal Finishers Soc. Am., Soc. Plastics Industry, Cleve. Engring. Soc. Republican. Roman Catholic. Home: 112 Duncannon Rd Bel Air MD 21014 Office: 350 Old Bay Ln Havre De Grace MD 21078

MAFFEO, VINCENT ANTHONY, lawyer, telecommunications exec.; b. Bayonne, N.J., Jan. 22, 1951; s. Michael Anthony and Marie M.; B.A. summa cum laude, Bklyn. Coll., 1971; J.D., Harvard U., 1974; m. Debra Manzella, Dec. 16, 1972. Admitted to N.Y. State bar, 1975; asso. firm Simpson Thacher & Bartlett, N.Y.C., 1974-77; legal counsel Communications Systems div. ITT, Hartford, Conn., 1977-79, v.p., gen. counsel Bus. Communications div., Des Plaines, Ill., 1979—. Served to lt. Judge Adv. Gen. Corps, USNR, 1975. Mem. Am. Bar Assn., N.Y. State Bar Assn., Phi Beta Kappa. Office: 2000 S Wolf Rd Des Plaines IL 60018

MAG, ARTHUR, lawyer; b. New Britain, Conn., Oct. 11, 1896; s. Nathan Elihu and Rebecca (Goldberg) M.; A.B., Yale U., 1918, J.D., 1920; LL.D., U. Mo. at Kansas City, 1974; m. Selma Rothenberg, Nov. 7, 1925 (dec. Oct. 6, 1930); children—Josephine Selma, Helen Louise; m. 2d, Charline Weil, Nov. 24, 1932. Admitted to Conn. and Mo. bars, 1920, since practiced in Kansas City, Mo.; partner Stinson, Mag & Fizzell, 1924—; chmn. exec. com. Host Internat., Inc., Los Angeles; chmn. bd. Schutte Lumber Co.; dir. Marley Co., First Nat. Bank Kansas City, Standard Milling Co., Gold, Inc., Denver, Rival Mfg. Co., Helzberg Diamond Shops, Inc., L. B. Price Merc. Co., Hereford Redevel. Corp., 1st Nat. Charter Corp., Rothschild & Sons, Inc., Price Candy Co., Z Bar Cattle Co. Mem. Nat. Adv. Council Mental Health, 1955-59, Gov.'s Citizens Com. on Crime and Delinquency, 1966-68, Met. Coordinating Com. Regional Med. Program, 1952-56, Mo. Com. White House Conf. Aging; co-chmn. Gov.'s Task Force on Role Pvt. Higher Edn. in Mo., 1970; mem. Mayor's Commn. on Civil Disorder in Kansas City, 1968; mem. adv. bd. Kansas City Area council Boy Scouts Am; trustee, v.p. Mo. Bar Found., Sadie Danciger Trust, U. Mo.-Kansas City, Carrie J. Loose Fund, Harry Wilson Loose Trust, Frederic Ervine McIlvain Trust, Edward F. Swinney Trust, Kansas City Assn. Trusts and Founds., Carl W. Allendoerfer Meml. Library, Menorah Found. for Med. Research; hon. chmn. bd. Menorah Med. Center; hon. trustee Menninger Found., Topeka; pres. Greater Kansas City Mental Health Found., 1952-55; bd. curators Stephens Coll., 1967-72; mem. exec. com. Midwest Research Inst. Served in U.S. Navy, 1918. Recipient Pro Meritis award Rockhurst Coll., 1960; Law Day award U. Mo., 1966, Chancellor's medallion, 1966; named Mr. Kansas City, 1964; recipient Brotherhood award NCCJ, 1965; Civic Service award Hebrew Acad. Greater Kansas City, 1975; Hall of Fame award Jr. Achievement, 1980; award Greater Kansas City Mental Health Found. Fellow Am. Bar Found., Order of Coif, Am. Coll. Hosp. Adminstrs. (hon.); mem. Am., Mo., Kansas City bar assns., Lawyers Assn. Kansas City, Assn. Bar City of N.Y., Yale Law Sch. Assn. (exec. com.), Mo. Acad. Squires. Republican. Clubs: Standard (Chgo.); Yale, Lawyers (N.Y.C.); Kansas City, Oakwood Country (Kansas City); Reform (London); Grad. (New Haven). Author: Trusteeship, 1948; mem. bd. Yale Law Jour., 1919-20. Home: 5049 Wornall Rd Kansas City MO 64112 Office: Ten Main Center PO Box 19251 Kansas City MO 64141

MAGDELAIN, BERNARD LOUIS, banker; b. Bryn Mawr, Pa., Sept. 21, 1944; s. Philippe M. and Elisabeth W. (Woodward) M.; B.S., Lehigh U., 1966; M.B.A., N.Y. U., 1970; m. Dec. 28, 1967; children—Christopher, Jennifer. With Morgan Guaranty Trust Co., 1967—, now v.p. div. internat. banking; mem. faculty Manhattanville Coll. Treas., European Republican Com., 1976. Served with USN, 1963-65. Club: Apawamis Golf. Office: 23 Wall St New York NY 10015

MAGEE, JAMES HENLY, bus. developer; b. Bethesda, Md., Mar. 15, 1948; s. Thomas George and Jane R. (Frier) M.; B.S., U. Md., 1971; m. Barbara J. Jernigan, Feb. 14, 1976. With Airborne Freight Corp., Alexandria, Va., 1971-75; dist. mgr. Associated Air Freight, Atlanta, 1975-76; owner, pres. Atlanta Auto Classics, Inc., 1976-80, Rolling Stock Investment Co., Inc., Atlanta, 1979—, Opportunity Plus, 1980—; appraiser collector cars Lloyds of London. Mem. Classic Car Club Am. Clubs: Toastmasters (pres. Pershing Point chpt. 1980), Jaguar, Shelby, Mercedes, Mustang. Author: Collector Cars of the Seventies, 1981; columnist, Car Collector mag. Home: 3891 Wieuca Rd NE Atlanta GA 30342 Office: 2881 Buford Hwy Atlanta GA 30329

MAGEE, JOHN, investment counsellor; b. Malden, Mass., Nov. 24, 1901; s. John and Louise (Church) M.; grad. Pomfret Sch., 1920; student Mass. Inst. Tech., 1920-23; m. Alice Eleanor Alderson, Oct. 20, 1928 (div. Dec. 1933); 1 son, Alderson; m. 2d, Elinor Averre Trafford, July 2, 1936; children—John IV, Louise Cynthia, Abigail Anne. Asst. to sales mgr. vacuum cleaner dept. B. F. Sturtevant Co., Hyde Park, Mass., 1924-25; cost estimating, spl. prodn. dept. Stanley Works, New Britain, Conn., 1925-27; advt. mgr. Maxim Silencer Co., Hartford, Conn., 1927-28; account exec. William B. Remington Advt. Agy., Springfield, Mass., J.D. Bates advt. agy., Springfield, 1928-30; pres. Lewis & Magee, Inc., Springfield, 1930-35; owner Trafford Co., Springfield, 1935-42; investment counsellor, market research, Springfield, 1942—; sr. technician Stock Trend Service, Springfield, 1953-56; pres., treas. John Magee, Inc., 1960—. Mdse. design cons. Brooks Bank Note Co., Springfield; editor-in-chief Our Home Town; dir. radio program The Voice of Springfield; staff mem., tech. adviser Future Springfield, Inc. Mem. Republican City Com., 1944-48; pub. relations com. Springfield, 1944-45. Bd. dirs. East Forest Park Civic Assn., 1942-49. Author: (also illustrator) The General Semantics of Wall Street, 1958; (with Robert D. Edwards) Technical Analysis of Stock Trends, 1948; Wall Street—Main Street—And You, 1972. Home: 96 Maplewood Terr Springfield MA 01108

MAGEL, GERALD ALLEN, paper mcht.; b. St. Paul, Nov. 25, 1942; s. Ben and Ann M.; A.A., Los Angeles City Coll., 1970; B.A., Calif. State U., 1973, M.A., 1975; m. Susan Yellin, Sept. 1, 1968; children—Stephanie Ann, Sandra Joyce. Prodn. planner Continental Airlines, Los Angeles, 1965-68; asst. gen. mgr. Smith Pacific Bookbinders, Los Angeles, 1969-70; promotion mgr. La Salle Paper Co., Vernon, Calif., 1970—; lectr. U. So. Calif., UCLA. Mem. Los Angeles Jr. C. of C., Am. Mktg. Assn., Art Dirs. Club Los Angeles, Prodn. Mgrs. Club Los Angeles. Jewish. Club: B'nai B'rith (pres.) (Woodland Hills). Home: 6749 N Corie Ln West Hills CA 91307 Office: 4170 Bandini Ave Vernon CA 90023

MAGGARD, WOODROW WILSON, JR., mgmt. cons.; b. Quincy, Ill., Feb. 5, 1947; s. Woodrow Wilson and Claire Lorene (Lyons) M.; B.A., Brigham Young U., 1971; M.P.A., Consortium of Calif. State U., 1978; m. Linda Margaret Davis, Dec. 30, 1967; children—Jared Isaac, Erin Leigh-Taylor, Solveig Kirsten, Christian Heinrich, Anica May. Div. mgr. Sears, Roebuck & Co., Provo, Utah and Ventura, Calif., 1967-74; adminstrv. officer County of Ventura (Calif.), 1974-78; founding partner Maggard, Maughan, Gress and Assos., Ventura, 1976—; v.p. econ./bus. devel. Dineh Coops., Inc., Chinle, Navaho Nation, Ariz., 1978-80; dir. econ. devel. City of Scottsdale (Ariz.), 1980—. Active Boy Scouts Am.; youth dir. Ch. of Latter-Day Saints, 1976—. Mem. Am. Soc. Pub. Adminstrn., Nat. Assn. Indsl. and Office Parks, Nat. Assn. Rev. Appraisers, Nat. Council on Urban Devel. Democrat. Home: 8549 E Mitchell Dr Scottsdale AZ 85251 Office: City of Scottsdale Scottsdale AZ 85251

MAGLIANA, JOHN ANTHONY, computer systems co. exec.; b. Rome, Italy, July 2, 1935; s. Michael Frederick and Anna Maria (DiCresce) M.; B.S.E.E., St. Louis U., 1956; M.S., U. Calif., Los Angeles, 1967. Asst. to pres. indsl. products div. ITT, Los Angeles, 1960-62; dep. project mgr. Intelstat III, TRW Systems, Redondo Beach, Calif., 1966-68, dir. European activities, 1968-71; v.p. internat. Trivex, Orange County, Calif., 1971-74; pres., chief exec. officer Datasaab Systems, Inc., N.Y.C., 1974—, also dir.; dir. Saab-Totem, Seattle; cons. Concord Electronics, 1974-75, Muzak, 1974—. Mem. Swedish Am. C. of C. (dir.), Pres. Assn., Chevalier de Tastevan. Roman Catholic. Office: Datasaab Systems Inc 21 E 63d St New York NY 10021

MAGNE, LOUIS EDOUARD, petroleum service co. exec.; b. St. Pierre de Frugie, France, Dec. 8, 1912; s. Jean M. and Marie J. (Brunet) M.; grad. engring. Arts and Metiers Coll., Angers, France, 1933; m. Angela B. Ambard, July 8, 1939; 1 son, Lawrence E. Came to U.S., 1945, naturalized, 1951. Engr. Schlumberger, Venezuela and Trinidad, 1935-44, dist. mgr., 1945-47, div. mgr., San Antonio, 1947-56, region mgr., Houston, 1956-59, v.p. operations, exec. v.p. Eastern hemisphere, Paris, 1959-65, worldwide coordinator, Houston, 1965-66, pres. C. and S.Am. subs., Caracas, Venezuela, 1967-71, corporate v.p., Houston, 1971, pres. Schlumberger Well Services (N.Am.), Houston, 1972-78; pres. Lemco, Inc., Houston, 1978—; dir. Vector Cable Co., Surenco, Caracas; ret., 1978. Bd. dirs. Jr. Achievement, Tex. Research League. Served to lt. French Air Force, 1934-35. Mem. Alliance Francaise de Houston (pres. 1974—), Am. Inst. Mech. Engrs., Am. Assn. Petroleum Geologists, Am. Petroleum Inst., Petroleum Equipment Suppliers Assn., Tex. Ind. Producers Orgn., Ind. Producers Assn., Pi Mu Omega. Clubs: Petroleum, Univ., Houston Racquet, River Oaks Country. Home: 5555 Del Monte #1806 Houston TX 77056

MAGNELL, STEFFEN INGVAR, machinery mfg. co. exec.; b. Stockholm, Sweden, June 8, 1945; s. Otto Percy and Anne Johanna (Nilsson) M.; came to U.S., 1950, naturalized, 1957; B.A., U. Minn., 1968; M.B.A., St. Thomas Coll., 1977; m. Patricia Anne Drew, Dec. 28, 1968; children—Christian, Marget. Auditor, Sears Roebuck & Co., Mpls., 1961-68; with legal and tax dept. Northrup King & Co., Mpls., 1969; mgmt. position Conn. Gen., Inc., Edina, Minn., 1970-72; partner S M I Co., St. Louis Park, Minn., 1972-75; v.p. Continental Machines, Inc., Savage, Minn., 1975-79, sr. v.p., 1979—; dir. Greenlee Diamond Tool Co. Mem. St. Thomas M.B.A. Alumni Assn. Republican. Lutheran. Clubs: U. Minn. Alumni, Interlachen Country, Decathlon. Home: 15700 Dawn Dr Minnetonka MN 55343 Office: Continental Machines Inc Savage MN 55378

MAGNER, RACHEL HARRIS, banker; b. Lamar, S.C., Aug. 5, 1951; d. Garner Greer and Catherine Alice (Cloaninger) Harris; B.S. in Fin., U. S.C., 1972; postgrad. U. Calif., Los Angeles, 1974, Calif. State U., 1975; m. Fredric Michael Magner, May 14, 1972. Mgmt. trainee Union Bank, Los Angeles, 1972-75, comml. loan officer, 1975-77; asst. v.p. comml. fin. Crocker Bank, Los Angeles, 1978, factoring account exec. subs. Crocker Comml. Services, Inc., 1978—. Mem. Los Angeles Bank Creditmen's Assn., NOW, Wilshire Women's Bus. and Profl. Assn., Los Angeles Women's Profl. Bank Assn. Home: 2200 Pine Ave Manhattan Beach CA 90266 Office: 742 S Hill St Los Angeles CA 90015

MAGNIER, PHILIPPE JEAN MARIE, oil co. exec.; b. Paris, Apr. 19, 1930; came to U.S., 1975; s. Pierre and Gabriella (Naeder) M.; B.S., U. Paris, 1953, M.S., 1956; degree in chemistry Paris Sch. Chemistry, 1953; degree in geology geophysics, French Petroleum Inst., 1955; m. Genevieve Noel, Apr. 24, 1956; children—Elizabeth, Ann, Benoit, Caroline, Sophie, Maïween. Geologist, Compagnie Française des Petroles, Spain, Libya, 1957-63, chief geologist, Australia, 1963-67, regional geologist and exploration adv., Paris, 1967-71, exploration mgr., Indonesia, 1971-75; v.p. exploration prodn. Total Petroleum Co., Inc., Houston, 1975—. Served with French Army, 1953-54. Mem. Am. Assn. Petroleum Geologists. Roman Catholic. Club: Petroleum. Home: 818 Piney Point Houston TX 77024 Office: 2950 1 Allen Center Houston TX 77002

MAGOWAN, PETER ALDEN, retail exec.; b. N.Y.C., Apr. 5, 1942; s. Robert and Doris (Merrill) M.; B.A., Stanford U., 1964; M.A., Oxford (Eng.) U., 1966; postgrad. Johns Hopkins Sch. Advanced Internat. Studies, 1966-68; m. Jill Tarlau, June 25, 1965; children—Kimberley, Margot, Hilary. Dist. mgr. Safeway Stores, Inc., Houston, 1970-71, retail ops. mgr., Phoenix, 1971-73, div. mgr., Tulsa, 1973-76, intl. div., Toronto, Ont., Can., 1976-78, Western regional mgr., San Francisco, 1978-80, chmn. bd., chief exec. officer, 1980—. Mem. adv. council Johns Hopkins Sch. Advanced Internat. Studies. Mem. Hudson Inst. (dir.), Council Fgn. Relations, Bus. Roundtable, U.S. C. of C. (dir.). Office: Safeway Stores 4th and Jackson Sts Oakland CA 94660

MAGUIRE, THOMAS HARLAN, JR., data communications co. exec.; b. Portland, Oreg., Feb. 26, 1924; s. Thomas Harlan and Ruth Rae (Riley) M.; B.S. in Mech. Engring., U. Wash., Seattle, 1948; m. Margaret Lamping, June 20, 1947; children—Maureen, Monica; m. 2d, Joan Barber, July 4, 1973; children—Drake, Steven, Jessica, Carolyn. With Gen. Electric Co., 1948-67, office mgr., Madison, Wis., 1960-66, regional computer specialist, N.Y.C., 1966-67; v.p. mktg. Communitype Corp., N.Y.C., 1967-69; chmn. bd., pres. T.H. Maguire & Assos., Inc., Westport, Conn., 1969—; pres., treas., dir. Nat. Teleprocessing Products, Inc., Westport, 1977—; leader data communications seminars, 1972—. Pres. Skyline Drive Community Assn., 1962-66; bd. mgrs. Brooklawn Park Assn., 1973; mem. Fairfield (Conn.) Republican Town Com., 1980. Served with AUS, 1942-45. Mem. ASME, IEEE, Data Processing Mgmt. Assn., Nat. Soc. Profl. Engrs., Delta Kappa Epsilon. Republican. Christian Scientist. Clubs: Black Rock Yacht, Shorewood Hills Country, Engrs. (N.Y.C.), Conn. Rep. Keyman.

MAHAFFY, REID ALEXANDER, mfg. co. exec.; b. Argyle, N.Y., Aug. 30, 1914; s. David Alexander and Susan Ester (Williams) M.; B.S., Northeastern U., 1938; postgrad. Bklyn. Poly. Inst., 1946-47; m. Margaret E. Fardelmann, Dec. 30, 1944 (div.); children—Evann Sue, Anne, Margaret, Reid Alexander, Susan; m. 2d, Josephine B. Ives, Oct. 16, 1971. Asst. mgr. packaging machinery dept. Union Camp, N.Y.C., 1946-49; dir. engring. Standard Packaging Corp., N.Y.C., 1949-56; pres. Mahaffy & Harder Engring. Co., Totowa, N.J., 1956-75, chmn. bd., 1975—; tech. guest speaker Am. Mgmt. Assn., 1971. Served to lt. (j.g.) USNR, 1943-46. Mem. ASME. Clubs: Montclair (N.J.) Golf; Orient (N.Y.) Yacht. Patentee in field. Home: 52 Warren Pl Montclair NJ 07042 Office: Furler St Totowa NJ 07512

MAHAN, JACK LEE, JR., bus. exec., behavioral scientist; b. Springfield, Mo., Oct. 2, 1941; s. Jack L. and Verna Jane (Wright) M.; A.A. in Psychology, Palomar Coll., 1961; B.A. in Exptl. Psychology, San Diego State U., 1964, M.A. in Exptl. Psychology, 1966; postgrad. in Sociology, Internat. Grad. Sch. U. Stockholm, 1966-67; Ph.D. in Human Behavior (Dr. Edwin T. Olson scholar), U.S. Internat U., 1970; M.B.A., Nat. U., 1978, M.B.A. in Real Estate Mgmt., 1979; m. Ronna Clair Ward, June 27, 1964. Psychology aid sect. tuna behavior U.S. Bur. Comml. Fisheries, La Jolla, Calif., 1962-63, psychologist, 1963-64; teaching asst. in psychology San Diego State U., 1964; research psychologist Naval Med. Neuropsychiat. Research Unit, San Diego, 1965-66, 67-69, research psychology personnel tng. research lab., 1969; research psychologist U. Stockholm, 1966-67; interdisciplinary programs officer Salk Inst., La Jolla, 1969-70; trainee devel. officer Peace Corps, Hawaii, 1971; exec. v.p., sec. bd. dirs. JAMACO Community Developers, Inc., Escondido, Calif., 1971-73; prin. Mahan & Assos., Archtl. Research and Behavioral Planning, Escondido, 1974—; v.p. Mahan Custom Homes, Inc., Escondido, 1978—, Jack L. Mahan, Jr. Co., real estate devel., 1977—, Milestones Awards Co., 1979—; instr. Palomar Coll., 1974—; mem. faculty Calif. Sch. Profl. Psychology, 1976—. Mem. Escondido Planning Commn., 1975-77; mem. San Diego Mayor's Task Force on Urban Design, 1975—; bd. dirs., pres. Escondido Regional Arts Council. Recipient letter of commendation UN FAO Hdqrs., Rome, 1964. Mem. Am. Psychol. Assn., AIA (Spl. award Urban Design 1976), UN Assn. U.S., San Diego Zool. Soc., Environ. Design Research Assn., Assn. Study Man-Environment Relations, Calif. Assn. Realtors, World Future Soc. (pres. 1970-71). Contbr. articles to profl. publs. Home: 1982 Craigmore Ave Escondido CA 92027 Office: PO Box 27218 Escondido CA 92027

MAHAR, ROBERT LEO, lawyer; b. Bklyn., Feb. 27, 1934; s. William Joseph and Marie C. (Byrne) M.; B.B.A., Manhattan Coll., 1956; LL.B., N.Y. U., 1959, LL.M., 1968; m. Mary Sharon Leahy, Apr. 25, 1970; children—Megan, Katherine, Christopher. Admitted to N.Y. bar, 1960, U.S. Supreme Ct. bar, 1964; asso. firm Kirlin Campbell & Keating, N.Y.C., 1960-62, Dow & Stonebridge, N.Y.C., 1962-65; partner firm Freehill, Hogan & Mahar, N.Y.C., 1966—. Mem. Assn. Bar City N.Y., Am., N.Y. State bar assns., Assn. Average Adjusters U.S., Maritime Law Assn., English Speaking Union. Clubs: Downtown Athletic, Westhampton Country. Office: 21 West St New York City NY 10006

MAHER, CLEM L., acctg. firm exec.; b. O'Fallon, Mo., July 2, 1920; s. Edgar A. and Katherine M. (Tochtrop) M.; B.S. in Commerce and Fin., St. Louis U., 1949; J.D., Washington U., St. Louis, 1952; m. Patricia J. Sweeney, Dec. 28, 1946; children—Kathleen, Sharon, Jacqueline, Peggy. Cost acct., asst. mgr. retail feed store Ralston Purina Co., Columbia, S.C., 1940-42; sr. acct. Cornell & Co., C.P.A.'s, 1945-49; lectr. tax and acctg. courses Washington U., 1949-58; admitted to Mo. bar, 1952; asst. controller, atty. Wohl Shoe Co., St. Louis, 1952-53; with Price Waterhouse & Co., St. Louis, 1954—, partner in charge tax practice, 1962—. Served as pilot USAAF, 1942-45; ETO. Decorated Air medal with six oak leaf clusters. Recipient Acctg. award St. Louis U., 1972, Alumni Merit award, 1975; C.P.A., Mo. Mem. Am. Inst. C.P.A.'s (council 1971-72, 76-79), Mo. Soc. C.P.A.'s (pres. 1972-73), Mo. Bar Assn., Order of Coif. Clubs: Old Warson Country, Noonday (treas. 1975-76), St. Louis. Contbr. articles to profl. jours. Home: 9826 Waterbury Dr Saint Louis MO 63124 Office: 1 Memorial Dr Saint Louis MO 63102

MAHER, JOHN FRANCIS, investment banker; b. Berkeley, Calif., April 25, 1943; s. Edward J. and Emilia (Radovan) M.; B.S., Menlo Coll., 1965; M.B.A. (Joseph Wharton fellow), U. Pa., 1967; m. Helen Stillman, March 20, 1976; children by previous marriage—E. John, Elizabeth Ann. First v.p. Blyth Eastman Dillon, Inc. and gen. partner Eastman Dillon Union Securities Co., N.Y.C., 1967-73; exec. v.p. fin. adminstrn. Great Western Fin. Corp., Beverly Hills, Calif., 1973-76, now dir.; exec. v.p. Blyth Eastman Dillon, Los Angeles, 1976-79, also dir., mem. exec. com.; mng. dir. Lehman Bros. Kuhn Loeb Inc., Los Angeles, 1979—. Bd. dirs. ARC, Big Bros. of Greater Los Angeles, YMCA Met. Los Angeles; trustee St. John's Hosp. and Health Center Found. Clubs: Bel Air Bay, Calif., Los Angeles Country. Office: 445 S Figueroa St Suite 2900 Los Angeles CA 90071

MAHER, LAVERNE JOSEPH, newspaper pub.; b. Plankinton, S.D., May 9, 1918; s. William L. and Catherine (Theis) M.; B.S., S.D. State U., 1942; m. Doris Grace Keefe, Nov. 5, 1949; children—Brian, Patricia, Thomas, Kevin, Sean. Advt. salesman Daily Plainsman, Huron, S.D., 1946-50; advt. mgr. Huron (S.D.) Pub. Co., 1950-52, v.p., 1952—, asst. pub., 1952-68, asso. pub., 1968-80, pub., 1980—; dir. Farmers & Mchts. Bank, Huron, 1975—. Bd. dirs. Miss. Valley Assn., 1958-62; pres. S.D. Reclamation Assos., 1965-66, Greater Huron Devel. Corp., 1965-66; chmn. United Fund, Huron, 1969. Served to maj. U.S. Army, 1942-46; PTO. Recipient Outstanding Journalist award, Sigma Delta Chi, 1942. Mem. Huron C. of C. (dir. 1951-62, pres. 1963), Inland Daily Press Assn., S.D. Press Assn. (dir. 1975-77, pres. 1978-79). Republican. Roman Catholic. Clubs: Huron Country, Elks, Am. Legion. Editorial writer Daily Plainsman, 1963—. Home: 432 18 St SW Huron SD 57350 Office: 49 3rd St SE Huron SD 57350

MAHER, WILLIAM JAMES, entertainment industry exec.; b. Chgo., Feb. 23, 1937; s. Alexander E. and Merle G. (Ammann) M.; B.B.A., Marquette U., 1961. Merchandising exec. Montgomery Ward & Co., Inc., Chgo., 1962-68; mgmt. cons. Cresap, McCormack & Paget, N.Y.C., 1968-69; v.p., treas. Solar Prodns., Inc., Hollywood, Calif., 1969; v.p., sec., treas. Creative Mgmt. Assos., Los Angeles, 1972-74; v.p. Marvin Josephson Assos., Inc., Los Angeles, 1974—, also dir. Home: 1930 N Beverly Dr Beverly Hills CA 90210 Office: International Creative Management 8899 Beverly Blvd Los Angeles CA 90048

MAHL, MARSHALL, mgmt. cons.; b. N.Y.C., Dec. 5, 1944; s. Harry and Florence (Chasnov) M.; A.B., Bklyn. Coll., 1966; m. Anne Lois Herrick, Dec. 19, 1965; children—Robert, Lisa, Dana. With Itel Corp., L.I., N.Y., 1969-76, mktg. mgr., 1970-71, br. mgr., 1971-73, dist. mgr. for N.Y. and N.J., 1974-75, Western regional mgr., Los Angeles, 1975, v.p. mktg. Western region, 1975-76; v.p. Sorkin & Mahl, Santa Monica, Calif., 1976—. Home: 4661 Blackfriar Rd Woodland Hills CA 91364 Office: Sorkin & Mahl 606 Wilshire Blvd Santa Monica CA 90401

MAHLER, DAVID, chem. co. exec.; b. San Francisco; s. John and Jennie (Morgan) M.; Ph.C., U. So. Calif., 1932; children—Darrell, Glenn. Pres., United Drug Co., Glendale, Calif., 1934-37, Blue Cross Labs., Inc., North Hollywood, Calif., 1937—. Active Fund for Animals, Friends of Animals, Com. for Humane Legislations; patron Huntington Hartford Theatre, Hollywood, Calif. Mem. Packaging and Research Devel. Inst. (hon.), Anti-Defamation League, Skull and Daggar, Rho Pi Phi. Office: 7376 Greenbush Ave North Hollywood CA 91605

MAHON, LAWRENCE JOSEPH, fuels co. exec.; b. South Bend, Ind., June 23, 1948; s. Joseph Thomas and Patricia Jean (Kintz) M.; B.A., U. Notre Dame, 1970; J.D., Ind. U., 1975; m. Patricia Susan Brown, May 22, 1976. Legis. asst. Ind. Ho. of Reps., 1973-74; admitted to Ind. bar, 1975; atty. Gen. Motors Corp., Detroit, 1975-76; gen. counsel, dir. govt. relations Campbell-Ewald Co., Detroit, 1976-79; v.p., asst. sec., counsel Indsl. Fuels Corp., Troy, Mich., 1979-80; sr. counsel coal div. Peter Kiewit Sons Inc., 1980—. Deacon Grosse Pointe Meml. Ch., 1977-80. Mem. Am. Bar Assn., Am. Soc. Corp. Secs., Ind. Bar Assn. Republican. Clubs: Grosse Pointe Yacht, Hillcrest Country. Home: 9925 Harney Pkwy S Omaha NE 68114

MAHONEY, CORNELIUS MICHAEL, ins. co. exec.; b. Bronx, N.Y., Sept. 29, 1937; s. Cornelius Michael and Mary Veronica (Neenan) M.; B.S. in Acctg., Fordham Sch. Bus., 1961; student Bernard Baruch Grad. Sch. Bus., 1961-64; m. Ellenjane Theresa Ryan, June 4, 1960; children—Joan Ann, Neil Gerard, Kevin, Brian, Ryan. Various underwriting adminstrv. positions Great Am. Ins. Co., N.Y.C., East Orange, N.J., Silver Spring, Md., 1955-73; asst. regional mgr. San Francisco Great Am. Ins. Co., 1973-75; gen. mgr. Orange (Calif.) Met. Property and Liability Ins. Co., 1975-76; asst. v.p. adminstrv. services Met. Property and Liability Ins. Co., Warwick, R.I., 1976—. Pres., Saints John and Paul Home Sch. Assn., 1977-79, Parish Council, 1980—, Prout Parents Council, 1979-80. Mem. Chartered Property and Casualty Underwriters, Adminstrv. Mgmt. Soc. Home: 132 Wood Cove Dr Coventry RI 02816 Office: Met Property and Liability Ins Co 700 Quaker Ln Warwick RI 02887

MAHONEY, DAVID, corp. exec.; b. N.Y.C., May 17, 1923; s. David J. and Laurette (Cahill) M.; grad. LaSalle Mil. Acad., 1941; B.S., U. Pa., 1945; student Columbia, 1946-47; LL.D., Manhattan Coll.; m. Barbara A. Moore, May 12, 1951 (dec.); children—David Joseph III, Barbara; m. 2d, Hildegarde Ercklentz Merrill, June 24, 1978. Advt. v.p. Ruthrauff & Ryan, Inc., N.Y.C., 1949-51; founder, pres. David J. Mahoney, Inc., N.Y.C., 1951-56, also dir.; pres., dir. Good Humor Corp., 1956-61; exec. v.p., dir. Colgate Palmolive Co., 1961-66; pres., chief exec. officer Canada Dry Corp., 1966-68; pres. Norton Simon, Inc., 1968-77, pres., dir., chief exec. officer, 1969—, chmn. bd., 1970—; dir. N.Y. Telephone Co.; mem. adv. bd. Continental Airlines. Chmn. Am. Revolution Bicentennial Commn., 1970. Chmn. bd. trustees Am. Health Found.; chmn. bd. dirs. Phoenix House, Charles A. Dana Found.; bd. dirs. Nat. Urban League; trustee Tuskegee Inst., U. Pa. Served in U.S. Army, World War II. Recipient Torch of Liberty award Anti-Defamation League, 1970. Patriot's award Congl. Medal of Honor Soc., 1972, Applause award Sales Exec. Club, 1973, U.S. Marines Leatherneck award, 1975, Corporate Leadership award Girl Scouts, 1976, Horatio Alger award, 1977, Nat. Brotherhood award NCCJ, 1979, Flame of Truth award Fund for Higher Edn., Man of Achievement award Anti-Defamation League; named Man of Year Advt. Age, 1972, Man of Year Wharton Sch. Bus., 1972, Hon. mem. Boys Club N.Y. Alumni Assn., 1978. Mem. Young Pres.'s Orgn. Office: Norton Simon Inc 277 Park Ave New York NY 10017

MAHONEY, JOHN AIDAN, engr.; b. Montreal, Que., Can., Aug. 31, 1935; s. Hugh R. and Patricia (Kenehan) M.; B.S. cum laude, Loyola Coll., 1956; B.E.E., McGill U., 1958; m. Karin E. Ohlson, June 6, 1959; 1 dau., Sharon E. With No. Telecom Ltd. (formerly No. Electric Co., Ltd.), 1958—, switching systems standards engr., instr. systems engring. tng. center, dept. chief electronic switching programme engr., 1958-64, dept. chief software engring. and processing dept., 1965-66, mgr. electronic switching software, 1966-67, mgr. computer application engring., 1967-69, mgr. long range planning, 1969-70, mgr. product planning, 1970-71, mgr. installation engring., 1971, mgr. electronic switching engring., 1971-72, mgr. mktg., 1972-74, dir. mktg., 1974-75, product line mgr., 1975-76, div. gen. mgr., 1975-77, div. gen. mgr. Digital Switching div., 1977-78, asst. v.p. switching mktg., 1978-79, v.p. and gen. mgr. DMS 10 div., 1979—; v.p. and gen. mgr. AT&T Switching div., 1979. Mem. Corp. Engrs. Que., Assn. Profl. Engrs., Ont., IEEE (sr.), Raleigh (N.C.) C. of C. Home: 7400 Grist Mill Rd Raleigh NC 27609 Office: 1000 Wade Ave Raleigh NC 27605

MAHONEY, JOHN JOSEPH, bus. exec., educator; b. Chattanooga, Nov. 9, 1921; s. John J. and Helen M. (Armstron) M.; B.S. in Bus. Adminstrn., The Citadel, 1946; M.S. in Indsl. Mgmt., Ga. Inst. Tech., 1967; m. Elizabeth Dubose Porcher, June 25, 1949. Instr. dept. bus. adminstrn. The Citadel, Charleston, S.C., 1947-50, asst. prof., 1967—; founder, pres. Carolina Vending, Inc., 1947-67, Shamrock System, Inc., 1960-67; pres., gen. mgr. Carolina Vending, Inc., Charleston, 1947-67; dir. Charles F. Cates & Sons, Inc. Pickle Co., Faison, N.C., 1970—. Pres. Catholic Charities, 1958—; bd. dirs. Charleston Devel. Bd., 1957-60, United Fund, Charleston, 1955-56, Family Agy. Charleston, 1956-60. Served to lt. inf., AUS, 1943-46. Recipient Disting. Service award Charleston Jaycees, 1956. Mem. So. Mgmt. Assn., Fellowship Cath. Scholars, Charleston C. of C. (dir. 1957-59), Hibernian Soc., Soc. Francaise. Republican. Roman Catholic. Club: Carolina Yacht. Office: The Citadel Charleston SC 29409 also 276 East Bay Ct Charleston SC 29401

MAHONEY, MICHAEL JOHN, ins. co. exec.; b. Bklyn., Sept. 29, 1934; s. John Edward and Catherine (Cummingham) M.; B.S. in Math., 1956; m. Patricia McLaughlin, Aug. 6, 1960; children—Eileen, Catherine, Nancy. Vice pres. group pensions Met. Life, N.Y.C., 1958-76; sr. v.p. Woodward, Ryan, Sharp & Davis, N.Y.C., 1976—; cons. actuary Milliman and Robertson, 1978—, prin., 1980—. Served with USMC, 1956-58. Fellow Soc. Actuaries (exam. vice chmn. 1972-73, chmn. 1974, cons. employee retirement plans 1977, pensions com. 1976—, vice chmn. 1977, chmn. 1978—); mem. Am. Acad. Actuaries, Internat. Assn. Cons. Actuaries, Internat. Actuarial Assn., Actuaries Club of N.Y.C. (continuing edn. com.), Am. Pension Conf., Roman Catholic. Home: 6 Coventry Circle Princeton NJ 08540 Office: 355 Lexington Ave New York NY 10017

MAHONY, JAMES PATRICK, money mgr.; b. Kew Gardens, N.Y., Mar. 4, 1938; s. James P. and Agnes C. M.; B.B.A., St. Bonaventure U., 1963. Trader, B.J. Conlon & Co., N.Y.C., 1960-70; trader, mgr. trading dept. Edwards & Hanly, N.Y.C., 1970-76; pvt. investor, mgr. family assets, 1976-79; salesman, trader, money mgr. Laidlaw, Adams & Peck, N.Y.C., 1979-80, Bruns, Nordeman & Rea, 1980—. Served with USMC, 1957-59. Mem. Security Traders Assn. N.Y. Republican. Roman Catholic. Clubs: N.Y. Athletic, Kiwanis. Home: 48 Sherwood Ln East Hampton NY 11937 Office: 115 Broadway New York NY 10006 also PO Box 360 Montauk Hwy Water Mill NY 11976

MAHRT, CLIFFORD EUGENE, ins. exec.; b. Colome, S.D., Aug. 12, 1923; s. William George and Genevieve Viola (Soper) M.; journalism student Morningside Coll., Sioux City, Iowa, 1941-46; C.L.U., Am. Coll. Life Underwriters, 1961; m. Shirley Jean Hebbe, June 16, 1944; children—Larry J., Barbara J., Michelle M. Sports writer Sioux City Jour., 1941-43; agt. N.Y. Life Ins. Co., Sioux City, 1945-49, gen. mgr., Ft. Dodge, Iowa, Waterloo, Iowa and Kansas City, Mo., 1949-64, gen. mgr., Madison, Wis., 1964—. Served with USAAF, 1943-45. Decorated D.F.C., Air medal with 2 oak leaf clusters. Mem. Sales Execs. Eastern Iowa (charter), Sales Execs. Kansas City, Sales Execs. Madison. Republican. Lutheran. Clubs: Nakoma Golf, Pen and Mike. Home: 9 S Rock Rd Madison WI 53705 Office: 4646 Frey St Madison WI 53705

MAI, WALTER ALLEN, oil field service co. exec.; b. Great Bend, Kans., Sept. 11, 1943; s. Walter A. and Florence O. (Nuss) M.; B.S. in Fin., Fort Hays (Kans.) U., 1966; B.B.A., U. Houston, 1974, M.B.A., 1976; m. Nancey Ann Tyndall, June 5, 1966; children—Darren, Melissa, Chad. Cost analyst, controller Rockwell Internat., Tulsa, Okla., 1966-71; corporate finance mgr. Anderson Clayton, Houston, 1971-75; dir. fin., planning Reed Tool Co., Houston, 1976-79; v.p. fin. and adminstrn. Baker Well Service, Dallas, 1978-80; v.p. mktg. Baker Prodn. Services, 1980—. Bd. dirs. YMCA, 1972; youth dir. Little League, 1972-75. Served with U.S. Army, 1961-62. Recipient Rockwell Outstanding Employee award, 1969, award Soc. Petroleum Engrs., 1979. C.P.A., Tex. Mem. Soc. Petroleum Engrs. Republican. Lutheran. Club: Raveaeaux Country (Houston). Home: 16103 Maplehurst St Spring TX 77373 Office: 350 Northbelt Houston TX 77060

MAIBACH, BENJAMIN CARL, JR., constrn. co. exec., clergyman; b. Bay City, Mich., May 24, 1920; s. Benjamin Carl and Lucile (Harbourne) M.; student U. Detroit, U. Mich., 1938-44; m. Lorene Mae Belsley, June 25, 1944; children—Kathleen Ann, Benjamin Carl III, Alan A., Connie Lucile, Beverly J., Cynthia M., Sheryl B., Douglas L. Ordained to ministry, Apostolic Christian Ch. Am., 1949, ordained bishop, 1969, dir., Ill., 1949—; vice chmn. Apostolic Christian Ch. Am.; sec.-treas. Apostolic Christian Mission Fund; with Barton-Malow Co., Detroit, 1938—, v.p. and dir. field ops., 1949-53, exec. v.p., 1953-60, pres., 1960-76, chmn. bd., 1976—; pres. Cloverdale Equipment Co., Oak Park, Mich., 1963-78, chmn. bd., 1978—; pres., dir. Sarasota Chrysler-Plymouth, Inc., Fla., 1976—, S-C-P Leasing Corp., Fla., 1977—; dir., mem. exec. com. Mich. Mutual Liability Co.; dir. Asso. Gen. Life Ins. Co., Associated Gen. Ins. Co., Seven-Seven Corp., Fla. Chmn. bldg. com., dir., mem. exec. com. ARC, SE Mich. chpt., 1978—; bd. dirs. United Fund 1967—; trustee Greater Detroit Safety Council, 1970—, New Detroit, 1975—. Recipient Mich. Minuteman award Associated Gen. Contractors, 1967. Mem. Engring. Soc. Detroit, Am. Arbitration Assn. (arbitrator), Econ. Club, Newcomen Soc. N.Am., Mich. Assn. Osteopathic Physicians and Surgeons (hon. lay mem.). Clubs: Renaissance, Recess. Home: 14726 Fox St Redford MI 48239 Office: 13155 Cloverdale Oak Park MI 48237

MAIDIQUE, MODESTO (MITCH) ALEX, educator; b. Havana, Cuba, Mar. 20, 1940; s. Modesto and Hilda (Rodriguez) M.; came to U.S., 1958; B.S. in Elec. Engring., Mass. Inst. Tech., 1962, M.S. in Elec. Engring., 1964, Ph.D. in Solid State Physics, 1969; grad. Program Mgmt. Devel., Harvard Bus. Sch., 1975; m. Eulalia Avellanet, Nov. 29, 1964 (div. Dec. 1980); children—Ana Teresa, Mark Alex. Staff mem. Lab. Insulation Research, Mass. Inst. Tech., Cambridge, 1962-66; design cons. pvt. corps., 1967-69; mgr. integrated circuit design Transitron, Inc., Wakefield, Mass., 1966-67; v.p.-engring., dir. Nova Devices, Inc., Wilmington, Mass., 1969-72; v.p. ops. Nova div. Analog Devices Co., Wilmington, 1972-74, v.p./gen. mgr. semiconductor div., Wilmington, 1974-76, dir. corp. component bus. sector, 1976; dir. V.A. Metal Products of Fla., 1973—; asst. prof. Harvard Bus. Sch., 1976-81; asso. prof. Stanford U., 1981—; exec. v.p. Collaborative Research, Inc., Waltham, Mass., 1981—. Mem. Mass. Task Force for Econ. Devel., 1976—; v.p. Cuban Cultural Soc., 1975-76, pres., 1977-78; pres. Internat. Com. Cuban Intellectuals, 1980-81. Ford Found. fellow, 1967-69; Grass Instrument Co. fellow, 1964. Mem. IEEE, Am. Mgmt. Assn. Contbg. author: Designing with Linear Integrated Circuits, 1969, Integrated Circuit Operational Amplifiers, 1979, others; co-author: Energy Future, 1978; also articles. Patentee in field. Home: 10 Minola Rd Lexington MA 02173 Office: Morgan 239 Harvard Bus Sch Soldiers Field Rd Boston MA

MAIDMAN, RICHARD HARVEY MORTIMER, lawyer; b. N.Y.C., Nov. 17, 1933; s. William and Ada (Seegle) M.; grad. Hebron (Maine) Acad., 1951; B.A., Williams Coll., 1955; J.D., Yale U., 1959; postgrad. N.Y. U., 1960, grad. sch. law, 1977; m. Lynne Rochelle Lateiner, Apr. 3, 1960; children—Patrick Seth, Mitchel Aron, Dagny Carol. Dir., The Central Foundry Co., mem. N.Y. Stock Exchange, Holt, Ala., 1963-71; dir. Microbiol. Scis., Inc., mem. Boston Stock Exchange, Providence, R.I., 1971—, sec., 1971—; pres. MBS Equities, Inc., N.Y.C., 1975—; gen. partner Barcelona Hotel Ltd., Miami Beach, Fla., 1975—; asso. firm Saxe, Bacon & O'Shea, N.Y.C., 1962-64; partner Weiner, Maidman & Goldman, N.Y.C., 1964-67; pvt. practice law, N.Y.C., Fla., 1968—; of counsel Shwal, Thompson & Bloch, N.Y.C. and Geneva, Switzerland, 1976—; gen. counsel N.Y. Young Republican Club, 1969. Mem. Am. Bar Assn., N.Y. Bar Assn., Fla. Bar Assn., Assn. Bar City of N.Y., Bankruptcy Lawyers Assn. of N.Y.C. Contbr. articles to profl. jours. Home: Steamboat Landing Sands Point NY 11050 Office: 485 Madison Ave New York NY 10022

MAIER, BRUCE RICHARD, mfg. exec.; b. St. Louis, June 14, 1943; s. Arthur Russell and Mary Virginia Maier; B.S., Central Meth. Coll., 1965; M.S., U. Ark., 1968; Ph.D., U. Mo. Med. Sch., 1971; Asst. prof. U. Mo. Med. Sch., 1970-74; pres. Discwasher, Inc., Columbia, Mo., 1971—, also chmn. bd.; mktg. cons.; cons. maj. rec. cos. Active, Mo. Planned Parenthood Assn.; bd. dirs. Central Meth. Coll. Recipient Nat. Med. Sci. Student Research award, 1970; NIH Research fellow, 1972; NCI Research fellow. Mem. Columbia C. of C., Audio Engring. Soc., Am. Soc. Microbiologists, AAAS, Electronics Industries Assn., Inst. High Fidelity, Phi Beta Kappa, Sigma Xi. Patentee comml. hi-fi accessories. Office: 1407 N Providence Rd Columbia MO 65201

MAIER, CORNELL C., aluminum and chem. co. exec.; b. 1925; B.S., U. Calif. at Berkeley, 1949. With Kaiser Aluminum & Chem. Corp., Oakland, Calif., 1949—, v.p., mgr. European region Kaiser Aluminum Internat., 1963-68, v.p., gen. mgr. Mill Products div. parent co., 1969, v.p., gen. mgr. N.Am. aluminum ops., 1969-70, exec. v.p., 1970-72, gen. mgr. in charge day-to-day ops., 1971-72, pres., chief exec. officer, 1972—, chmn. bd., 1978—, also dir.; dir. Comalco Industries Pty. Ltd., Melbourne, Australia; chmn. bd. Fed. Res. Bank San Francisco, 1980—. Mem. Calif. C. of C. (bd. dirs.), Nat. Urban League (trustee), Bus. Roundtable. Office: Kaiser Aluminum & Chemical Corp Kaiser Center 300 Lakeside Dr Oakland CA 94643

MAIER, SHELDON MERRILL, fin. co. exec.; b. Miles City, Mont., Feb. 17, 1951; s. Gottlieb John and Helen Rose M.; B.S. summa cum laude, Jamestown Coll., 1972; postgrad. Tulane U., 1972-73; m. Kathryn Ann Roy, Nov. 22, 1975. Auditor/accountant Schauer, Fuchs & Bartholomay, C.P.A.'s, Jamestown, N.D., 1974-75; dir. internal audit Gate City Savs. & Loan Assn., Fargo, N.D., 1975-77, corp. controller, 1978—. Mem. Fin. Mgrs. Soc. for Savs. Instns., Am. Mgmt. Assn., Inst. Internal Auditors, Alpha Chi, Gamma Sigma. Club: Southgate Racquet. Home: 1353 4th St North Fargo ND 58102 Office: 500 2nd Ave North Fargo ND 58102

MAIERHOFER, RONALD PAUL, profl. soccer club exec.; b. Buffalo, Aug. 28, 1935; s. Edward and Bertha (Koepp) M.; B.S., Cornell U., 1960; postgrad. Xavier U., 1962, Wharton Sch., U. Pa., 1977; grad. Advanced Exec. Mktg. Program, Harvard U., 1978; m. Barbara Ruth Louis, Jan. 21, 1961; children—Scott, Jeff, Tim, Craig. With Exxon Co., 1960; salesman Carborundum Co., 1961-63; nat. sales mgr. Roper Industries, Dayton, Ohio, 1963-68; pres. Kitty Hawk Assos., Dayton, 1968-71; v.p. sales Info. Handling Services/Indianhead Co., Englewood, Colo., 1971-77, v.p. mktg., 1978—, v.p. ops., 1979—; pres., mng. gen. partner Denver Profl. Indoor Soccer Club. Officer various soccer assns., Dayton, Denver, Los Angeles, Dallas; state soccer coach, Tex., 1976, Colo., 1977; mem. U.S.A. Olympic Soccer Team, 1960, U.S.A. Pan Am. Soccer Team, 1959. Served with U.S. Army, 1955-57. Mem. Nat. Account Mgrs. Assn., Nat. Micrographics Assn., Am. Mgmt. Assn., Sales Mktg. Exec. Assn. Republican. Roman Catholic. Home: 6364 E Dorado Circle Englewood CO 80111 Office: Box 1154 Englewood CO 80110

MAILLOUX, MAURICE VICTOR, foundry exec.; b. Ste. Paul, Alta, Can., Sept. 21, 1916; s. Edmond Joseph and Martha Payette) M.; student St. Johns Coll., Edmonton, 1930-36; m. May 4, 1946; children—Fernande, Marcel, Victor, Marc, Yolande, Louis, Denis. Pres., mgr. Ste. Paul Foundry Ltd. (Alta.), 1950—; pres. Elk Point Gas Co., 1978—. Dist. coordinator War Supplies Agy., 1955-75. Served to lt. Can. Army, 1942-46, with Can. Militia, 1946-52. Mem. St. Paul C. of C. (exec. 1946—, past pres., sec.), Can. Legion. Roman Catholic. Club: K.C. Office: PO Box 8 Ste Paul AB T0A 2A0 Canada

MAIMAN, GEORGE, accountant, fin. cons.; b. Hungary, Aug. 30, 1939; s. Al and Anna (Stern) M.; B.A., Concordia U., 1965, Bernard Baruch Coll., City U. N.Y., 1975; m. Edith Schwartz, Nov. 13, 1966; children—Ronald E., Andrew D. Controller, Unimet Corp., N.Y.C., 1973-75, Pickwick Internat. Inc., Woodbury, N.Y., 1975-77; prin. Maiman & Co., C.P.A.'s, N.Y.C., 1977—; cons. C.P.A., N.Y. State. Mem. Am. Inst. C.P.A.'s. Office: Maiman & Co 250 W 57th St New York NY 10019

MAINES, CLIFFORD BRUCE, ins. co. exec.; b. Tacoma, Aug. 14, 1926; s. Clifford McLean and Ida Vera (Wardall) M.; student Central Coll., Fayette, Mo., 1944-45, U. Mich., 1945-46; B.S. in Law, U. Wash., 1948, J.D., 1949; m. Mary Jean Marshall, Sept. 4, 1948; children—Molly, Janet Lynn. Admitted to Wash. bar, 1950; with SAFECO Ins. Co., Seattle, 1950—, v.p., gen. counsel, 1968-74, exec. v.p., 1974-77, pres., 1977—, chief exec. officer, 1977—; sr. v.p. SAFECO Corp.; pres., chief exec. officer Gen. Ins., First Nat. Ins., SAFECO Nat., also dir. Served with USN, 1944-46. Mem. Seattle-King County Bar Assn., Wash. State Bar, Am. Bar Assn., Property/Casualty Ins. Council, Pacific Ins. and Surety Conf. (exec. com.), Seattle C. of C. Methodist. Club: Lions. Contbr. articles to profl. jours. Home: Seattle WA 98115 Office: SAFECO Plaza Seattle WA 98185

MAIORISI, CATHERINE THERESA, data processing cons. co. exec.; b. Hackensack, N.J., Mar. 23, 1938; d. George and Helen (Spagnuolo) M.; B.A. in Econs., Douglass Coll., 1960; M.A. in Econs. magna cum laude, Fairleigh Dickenson U., 1966. Project leader Colgate-Palmolive, N.Y.C., 1966-70; asst. v.p. Group Health, Inc., N.Y.C., 1970-76; mng. cons. Data Architects Inc., Waltham, Mass., 1976-79; pres. Computer Concepts, Inc., N.Y.C., 1979—. Mem. Soc. for Mgmt. Info. Systems, Assn. for Systems Mgmt. Office: 924 Broadway New York NY 10010

MAISEL, MELVIN LEO, employee benefit and ins. cons.; b. Bklyn., May 15, 1924; s. Abraham and Ida (Ravitch) M.; B.S. in Bus. Mgmt., N.Y. U., 1947; m. Selma Abramsky, June 8, 1946; children—Marc, David, Naomi Maisel Duker. Vice pres. Fiberoid Doll Products Corp., N.Y.C., 1947-58; agent New England Mut. Life Ins. Co., 1959-68; pres. Stabilization Plans for Bus., Inc., White Plains, N.Y., 1964—; v.p. Nat. Pension Service, Inc., White Plains, 1969—; co-chmn. adv. com. Iona Coll. Tax Inst.; guest lectr. in field at univs., industry and trade meetings. Served with U.S. Army, 1943. Named Rookie of Yr., New Eng. Life Ins. Co., 1960, Nat. Leading Agt., Guardian Life Ins. Co., 1970, 71, 74, 75, 76, 77, 78. Mem. Assn. Advanced Life Underwriting, Nat. Assn. Life Underwriters (charter and qualifying mem. of Five Million Dollar Forum and Top of the Table Million Dollar Round Table, life and qualifying mem. of Million Dollar Round Table; Nat. Quality award, 1961—, Nat. Sales Achievement awards 1966—), Nat. Assn. Health Underwriters (registered), Life Underwriters City N.Y., Life Underwriters Assn. Westchester (County), Profl. Planners Forum Ltd. (charter), Estate Planning Council West Chester (charter) (pres. 1969), Pension and Profit Sharing Inst. (charter). Contbg. author: How to Save Taxes and Increase Your Wealth with a Professional Corporation, How to Use Tax Shelters Today; contbr. articles to profl. publs. Home: 36 Birchwood Dr Greenwich CT 06830 Office: 1 N Broadway White Plains NY 10601

MAISEL, MICHAEL, shoe designer and mfr.; b. Newark, Oct. 19, 1947; s. Irving and Betty Elizabeth (Markin) M.; B.S. in Mktg., B.A. in Gen. Bus. Adminstrn., Ariz. State U., 1969; m. Marilyn Betty Schier, July 1, 1972 (div. 1978); children—Ian Albert, Alicia Beth; m. 2d, Anette Maisel, 1980. Asst. sales mgr. Mid-Atlantic Shoe Co. div. Beck Industries, N.Y.C., 1969-71; dir. imports Felsway Corp., Totowa, N.J., 1972-73; exec. v.p. Carber Enterprises, N.Y.C., 1973-80, pres., 1980—; pres. S.R.O. div. Canessa, N.Y.C., 1980—; cons. in field. Mem. 210 Shoe Industry (life), Nat. Shoe Retailers Assn. (dir.), Nat. Shoe Mfrs. Assn. Republican. Jewish. Designer Calber's shoe, displayed in Met. Mus. Art; nominated for Coty design award, 1974, 78. Home: 696 Westover Rd Stamford CT 06902 Office: 4 W 58th St New York NY

MAISONROUGE, JACQUES G., business machines co. exec.; b. 1924; ed. Ecole Centrale (France); married. With IBM, 1948—, asst. gen. mgr. IBM Europe, 1959-62, pres., 1964-67, 74—; pres. IBM World Trade Corp., N.Y.C., 1967-73, chief exec. officer, 1973—, chmn. bd., 1976—; sr. v.p. IBM Corp., 1972—; chmn. bd., chief exec. officer IBM World Trade Europe/Middle East/Africa Corp., 1974—; dir. Air Liquid Corp. Office: 360 Hamilton Ave White Plains NY 10601

MAIZE, JAMES HINDMAN, III, copper mining co. exec.; b. San Diego, Feb. 3, 1923; s. James Hindman, Jr. and Clara (Stone) M.; m. Janet E. Wharton, Nov. 7, 1947; children—Cheryl L., James C. Radio and TV newsman, announcer, Santa Fe, 1947-52, Tucson, 1952-60; with Ray Mines div. Kennecott Copper Corp., Hayden, Ariz., 1960—, dir. pub. relations, 1961—. Chmn. Pinal County Devel. Bd., 1963, 71, 77; sec. Pinal/Gila County Air Pollution Hearing Bd., 1968—; chmn. Pinal County Fair Commn., 1964-73; chmn. bd. dirs. Ariz. Automobile Assn., 1977-78, 78-79. Served with USMCR, 1940-47. Pub. affairs fellow Brookings Instn., 1967. Mem. Pub. Relations Soc. Am. (past pres. So. Ariz. chpt.). Republican. Clubs: Tucson Press; Phoenix Press. Clubs: Rotary (dist. gov. 1980-81), Elks (Kearny). Home: 315 Bristol Rd PO Box 15 Kearny AZ 85237 Office: PO Box 8 Hayden AZ 85235

MAJEWSKI, ALEXANDER FRANCIS, lawyer; b. Bridgeport, Conn., Aug. 27, 1943; s. Alexander Francis and Florence Marian (Plonski) M.; B.S., U. Bridgeport, 1965, M.B.A., 1969; J.D., Ill. Inst. Tech.-Kent Coll. Law, 1972; LL.M. in Taxation, John Marshall Law Sch., 1980. Admitted to Ill. bar, 1974; sr. tax cons. Wolf & Co., Chgo., 1970-71; sr. tax analyst Gould Inc., Rolling Meadows, Ill., 1972-73; treas. Mail Tax Corp., Chgo., 1973-74; of counsel firm Kantor & Mattenson Ltd., Chgo., 1974—; corporate tax and ins. dir. Quasar Electronics Corp., Franklin Park, Ill., 1974—. Vice pres., dir. Quasar Credit Union, 1975—. Mem. Am., Ill., Chgo. bar assns., Risk and Ins. Mgmt. Soc. Home: 1524 Forest Ave River Forest IL 60305 Office: 9401 W Grand Ave Franklin Park IL 60131

MAJOR, BERRY FRANKLIN, JR., co. exec.; b. Sebree, Ky., Dec. 12, 1938; s. Berry F. and Dorothy May (Corumn) M.; B.S., Ky. Wesleyan U., 1960; M.B.A., U. Wis., Whitewater, 1977; m. Linda C. Beyke, Nov. 20, 1970; children—Robert Charles, Mitchell Corumn, Sarah Jane. Instr., Hopkins County Bd. Edn., Madisonville, Ky., 1960-61; supr. aerial chem. spray crew Stull Bros., Inc., Sebree, Ky., 1961; ind. sch. supplies vendor, 1961; quality control engr. tube products dept. Gen. Electric Co., Owensboro, Ky., 1968-69, mfg. systems engr., 1969-70, components engr., 1970-71, supr. purchased material quality control, 1971-72, mgr. heavy machining home laundry products dept., 1972, mgr. machining and die cast Gen. Electric Appliance Park, Louisville, 1973-75, mgr. image tube prototype lab., med. systems bus. div., radiology systems programs dept., Milw., 1975-76, mgr. image intensifier tube operation, radiology systems engring. dept., 1976-77, mgr. x-ray components mfg., med. systems, mfg. dept. 1977-80; mgr. Ky. plant IMO Pump div. Transam. Delaval, Inc., Columbia, 1980—, dir. ops. U.S. Controls Corp. Bd. chmn. Summitt Heights United Methodist Ch., 1974-75, dist. lay leader, 1974-75. Served with USAF, 1961-68. Mem. Am. Soc. Quality Control (past chpt. chmn.), Air. N.G. Assn., Sigma Phi Epsilon, Keys. Democrat. Clubs: Masons, Civitan. Home: 605 Crestview Loop Columbia KY 42728 Office: 7 Frontage Rd Columbia KY 42728

MAKADOK, STANLEY, mgmt. cons.; b. N.Y.C., Mar. 30, 1941; s. Jack and Pauline (Speciner) M.; B.M.E., Coll. City N.Y., 1962; M.S. in Mgmt. Sci., Rutgers U., 1964; m. Lorraine Edith Dubin, Aug. 24, 1963; 1 son, Richard. Bus. systems analyst Westinghouse Electric Corp., Balt., 1964-65; project engr., corporate cons. Am. Cyanamid Corp., Pearl River, N.Y., Wayne, N.J., 1965-68; v.p., bus. devel. and planning Pepsico Inc. and affiliates, Purchase, N.Y., Miami, Fla., 1968-75; mgr. fin. and planning cons. Coopers & Lybrand, N.Y.C., 1975-77; pres. Century Mgmt. Cons., Inc., N.Y.C., 1977—. Contbr. articles to profl. jours. Home: 37 Grandview Ave Glen Rock NJ 07452

MAKHANI, MADAN PAL SINGH, foundry exec.; b. Amritsar, India, Oct. 23, 1937; s. Gulzar Singh and Mohinder (Kaur) M.; A.T.S. (Ednl. scholar), Machine Tool Prototype Factory, Bombay, 1957; A.M.I.B.F., City and Guilds London Inst., 1958; m. Betty Jean Lowder, June 10, 1972; children—Madana Marie, Indera, Jogi Patrick. In charge pattern shop and quality control New Haven Foundry (Mich.), 1964; gen. mgr. Old South Forge, Inc., Waycross, Ga., 1965-66; pres. Am. Casting Co., Inc., Tulsa, 1966—, also Am. Investment Casting Co. Inc., Am. Alloy Casting Co. Inc., Am. Foundry Group Inc. Prof. Artisan Tng. Sch., India, 1957. Mem. Am. (dir. Tri-state 1973-75, vice chmn. Tri-state 1976-77, chmn. Tri-state 1977-78), Brit. foundryman socs., Patternmakers League N.Am. (treas. 1968-72), Soc. Mfg. Engrs., Tulsa Mfrs. Club (dir. 1980-81), Purchasing Mgmt. Tulsa. Elk. Home: 7212 E 64th Pl Tulsa OK 74133 Office: 10041 E 52d St Tulsa OK 74133

MALACARNE, GUIDO, business exec.; b. 1924; B.S., Clarion State Coll., 1949; M.M., U. Pitts., 1951; married. Tchr., guidance counselor, football coach Reynoldsville Area Schs., 1951-58; with Penn Traffic Co., 1958—, corp. v.p., pres. Riverside div., 1976-78, pres., 1978—, chief operating officer, 1978-79, chief exec. officer, 1979—, also dir. Served with USN, 1942-46. Office: 319 Washington St Johnstown PA 15907*

MALATESTA, JOHN THOMAS AQUINAS, II, exec. recruiting exec.; b. Los Angeles; s. John B. and Mildred F. (DeFina) M.; B.S., U. Santa Clara, 1966; m. Beverly Ann Hermann, June 18, 1977; 1 son, John Thomas III. With Procter & Gamble, Inc., Los Angeles, 1965-68; advt. sales mgmt. staff Time, Inc., Los Angeles and N.Y.C., 1968-70; partner Malatesta Assos., Inc., Los Angeles, 1970—; partner, sr. asso. Korn/Ferry, 1972-74; pres. Malatesta Assos., Inc., Washington, 1974-78; v.p., mng. partner Boyden Assos., Washington, 1978—. Candidate for U.S. Senate from Calif., 1974; exec. com. Republican Central Com. Los Angeles County, 1968-74; dir. Holy Family Adoption Service, 1970-74. Mem. Assn. Exec. Recruiting Cons., Greater Washington Bd. Trade, Am. Soc. Assn. Execs., Fed. City Council. Roman Catholic. Office: 815 Connecticut Ave NW Suite 810 Washington DC 20006

MALCOLM, GERALD LINDBURG, elec. co. exec.; b. Genola, Utah, Dec. 18, 1927; s. John Leo and Rhoda (Steele) M.; student U. Utah, Salt Lake City, 1957-59; m. Edith Jackson, Oct. 4, 1952; children—Guy David, Roger Allan, JoAnn, Tracy Dale, Gerald Leo, Edith Christine. Electrician, Excel Neon Sign Co., Salt Lake City, 1946-48; owner, operator Malcolm Electric Co., Santaquin, Utah, 1948-52; journeyman electrician Dept. Army, Dugway Proving Grounds, Utah, 1952-60; sr. constrn. foreman A, Thiokol Chem. Corp., Tremonton, Utah, 1960-62; electrician leader VA Med. Center, Salt Lake City, 1962-73, constrn. mgr., 1973—; owner, operator Malcolm Electric Co., Salt Lake City, 1965—; instr. Utah Tech. Coll., Salt Lake City, 1974-76; lectr. in field. Active Soil Conservation, Utah County, U.S. Dept. Agr., 1950-51. Master electrician, Utah, also elec. contractor license. Mem. Ch. Jesus Christ Latter-Day Saints. Home: 1549 S 1300 W Salt Lake City UT 84104 Office: 500 Foothill Dr Salt Lake City UT 84113

MALIN, PAUL SAMUEL, tire and rubber co. exec.; b. N.Y.C., Oct. 29, 1943; s. Henry and Ruth (Pheffer) M.; B.S. in Biology, Pa. State U., 1965; postgrad. Baruch Sch. Bus., Coll. City N.Y., 1965-66; m. Gayle Ruth Scheinbach, Oct. 1, 1967 (div. 1976); children—Scott Hunter, Tobi Beth. With Broadway Tire & Rubber Co., Inc., River Edge, N.J., 1966—, v.p., 1973-78, pres., 1978—. Jewish. Home: 151 Prospect Ave Apt 4B Hackensack NJ 07601 Office: 555 Hackensack Ave River Edge NJ 07661

MALIN, THOMAS ROBINSON, III, banking systems co. mgr.; b. Dallas, July 20, 1942; s. Thomas Robinson and Elizabeth Hill M.; student E. Tex. State U., 1960-64, So. Meth. U., 1965; m. Lois Ann Brockles, Feb. 14, 1976; children—Thomas Edwin, Stephen Christopher, Angela Renee. Ins. salesman Prudential Life Ins. Co. Am., 1963, 65; with Clarke Checks, Mesquite, Tex., 1965-80, area sales mgr. N. Tex.-La.-Ark.-Dallas div., 1974-80; mktg. mgr. Electronic Banking Systems Corp., Richardson, Tex., 1980—; cons. to banks. Mem. Bank Mktg. Assn. (1st v.p. N. Tex. chpt. 1979-80, pres. chpt. 1980-81), Corvette Club Tex. (past pres.). Methodist. Club: Masons. Home: 605 Trailwood Ct Garland TX 75043 Office: 1200 Executive Dr E Suite 130 Richardson TX 75081

MALINSKI, ARTHUR MICHAEL, lawyer, data processing co. exec.; b. Pearl River, N.Y., June 3, 1938; s. Joseph and Marjorie Orette (Westover) M.; student Northeastern U., 1956-59, Fairleigh Dickinson U., 1961-67; B.A., Shaw U., 1974; J.D., Western State U., 1979; m. Phyllis Ablondi, Apr. 30, 1960; children—Mark Randall. Programmer, St. Regis Paper Co., Nyack, N.Y., 1965; cons. Computing Tech., Inc., Boston, 1965-68; project mgr. Digital Equipment Corp., Maynard, Mass., 1968; cons. Arthur D. Little, Inc., Cambridge, Mass., 1968-73; v.p., mgr. Western Bancorp Data Processing Co., Los Angeles, 1976—. Served with U.S. Army, 1961-64. Mem. Data Processing Mgmt. Assn., Computer Law Assn., Aircraft Owners and Pilots Assn. Republican. Home: 18601 Avolinda Dr Yorba Linda CA 92686 Office: Union Tower Suite 700 21515 Hawthorne Blvd Torrance CA 90503

MALITZ, ISAAC, computer software co. exec.; b. Cleve., Dec. 1, 1947; s. Myron D. and Ileen (Jacobson) M.; B.A., Oberlin Coll., 1970; Ph.D. in Math. Logic, U. Calif., Los Angeles, 1976. Instr. philosophy U. Calif., Los Angeles, 1976; v.p. research and devel. Soft-Pack Inc., North Hollywood, Calif., 1976-77, pres., 1977—. Home: 2301 Roscomare St Bel Air CA 90024 Office: 4605 Lankershim St Suite 350 North Hollywood CA 91602

MALIZIA, DONALD JOHN, indsl. hose distbg. co. exec., lawyer; b. Chester, Pa., Sept. 23, 1946; s. Dominic Francis and Josephine (Skubasheski) M.; B.A. in Acctg., Pa. Mil. Coll., 1968; J.D., Villanova U., 1979. Founder, owner Flotran, Chester, until 1976; ops. mgr. Bevco Industries, Inc., Aston, Pa., 1976-78, gen. mgr., 1978—, v.p., 1980—; tax and bus. cons., 1970—; instr. grad. bus. law Villanova, 1978—; admitted to Pa. bar, 1979. Served with USN, 1969-71. Recipient award Rotary Internat., 1964. Mem. Aston Twp. Businessmen's Assn. Home: 1522 Woodland Rd West Chester PA 19380 Office: Bevco Industries Inc Box 2209 Aston PA 19014

MALLEK, JAMES RUDOLPH, counsellor; b. Neenha, Wis., Apr. 3, 1926; s. Rudolph and Ann M.; B.A., San Diego State U., 1959; M.A., UCLA, 1966, M.S.W., 1969; J.D., Western State U., 1976; 1 son, James Randolph. Enlisted U.S. Army, 1943, intelligence agt., Washington, 1949, Los Angeles, 1956, Berlin, 1961; ret., 1964; supr. dep. probation officer Los Angeles County Probation Dept., 1965—; lectr. criminal justice Cerritos Coll., 1972—. Mem. Calif. Probation, Parole and Correctional Assn. (vice-chairperson Los Angeles chpt.), Nat. Assn. Social Workers, Nat. Alliance Family Life, Am. Assn. Marriage, Family and Child Therapy, Am. Correctional Assn., Nat. Council Crime and Delinquency, Am. Soc. Polit. Sci. Clubs: Masons, Shriners. Home: PO Box 2142 Downey CA 90242 Office: 9150 E Imperial Hwy Downey CA 90242

MALLEY, JOSEPH ANTHONY, mgmt. cons.; b. Boston, Oct. 27, 1935; s. Joseph Anthony and Agnes Elizabeth (Guerin) M.; B.A., Dartmouth Coll., 1957; m. Dorothy Ann Nickerson, Sept. 25, 1957; children—Kevin, Karen, Keith. Systems analyst, ops. officer 1st New Haven Nat. Bank, 1960-63, ops. analyst, ops. mgr. Nat. Shawmut Bank, Boston, 1964-66; mgmt. cons. Peat Marwick Mitchell & Co., Boston, 1967-73; prin., mgmt. advisory services Laventhol & Horwath, Phila., 1974-78; mgr. internat. mgmt. cons. services Burns Internat. Security Services, Inc., Briarcliff Manor, N.Y., 1979—; mem. acctg. adv. com. for controller City of Phila., 1974-77. Mem. advisory bd. trustees Eastern State Sch. and Hosp., Trevos, Pa., 1975. Served with USMC, 1957-59. Cert. mgmt. cons., mgmt. acct. Mem. Am. Inst. Indsl. Engrs. (sr.), Inst. Mgmt. Cons., Inst. Mgmt. Accts. Democrat. Catholic. Clubs: Dartmouth (N.Y.C.), Tuck. Contbr. articles to profl. jours. Home: 2660 Broadview Yorktown NY 10598 Office: 320 Old Briarcliff Rd Briarcliff Manor NY 10510

MALLINGER, MICHAEL JOSEPH, semicondrs. mfg. co. exec.; b. Ft. Dodge, Iowa, Nov. 14, 1940; s. Thomas Michael and Eloise Catherine (Benoit) M.; B.S.E.E., Iowa State U., 1966; m. Jenik Esrailian, Feb. 10, 1973; children—Michelle, Gregory. Product engr. Fairchild Semicondr. Co., Mountain View, Calif., 1966-67, mktg. mgr., 1967-69; dir. mktg. and sales Communications Transistor Co., San Carlos, Calif., 1969-78; v.p., founder Acrian Inc., Cupertino, Calif., 1978—. Served with Air N.G., 1959-66. Mem. Am. Mgmt. Assn. Home: 13039 Ten Oak Way Saratoga CA 95070 Office: Acrian Inc 10131 Bubb Rd Cupertino CA 95014

MALLON, JOHN LAWRENCE, II, railroad exec.; b. Seattle, Jan. 25, 1946; s. John Thomas and Alice (Archibald) M.; B.A. in Econs., Seattle U., 1971; A.A. in Real Estate, Shoreline Community Coll., 1977; M.B.A. candidate U. Puget Sound, 1979—. Various positions Bank Calif., Seattle, 1966-67; auditor Best Western Motel, Seattle, 1969-73; acct. Burlington No. R.R., Seattle, 1973-74, supr. acctg., 1974, mgr. acctg., 1975, dir. adminstrn. natural resources, 1976—; cons. taxes. Served with USMC, 1967-69. Mem. Am. Mgmt. Assn., Internat. Platform Assn., Am. Forestry Assn. Republican. Roman Catholic. Club: Bellevue Golf. Home: 2665 168th Ave SE Bellevue WA 98008 Office: Burlington No RR 650 Central Bldg Seattle WA 98104

MALLON, THOMAS FRANCIS, JR., fgn. exchange broker; b. N.Y.C., Jan. 2, 1944; s. Thomas Francis and Rose Marie (McDonnell) M.; B.B.A., Manhattan Coll., 1966; postgrad. Hofstra U., 1966-71; m. Elizabeth Ann Kiely, June 4, 1966; children—Eileen Elizabeth, Erin Cristin. Accounting clk. Exxon, N.Y.C., 1965-66; fgn. exchange clk., dealer Brown Bros., Harriman & Co., N.Y.C., 1966-69; chief fgn. exchange dealer Banca Nazionale del Lavoro, N.Y.C., 1969-70; asst. cashier, fgn. exchange dealer Security Pacific Internat. Bank, 1970-71; owner, pres. Thomas F. Mallon Assos., N.Y.C., 1971-72; pres., dir. Kirkland Whittaker & Mallon, 1972-75; sec.-treas., dir. Mallon & Dorney Co., Ltd., 1975—, Mallon & Dorney Co. (Can.) Ltd., 1978-79; lectr. fgn. exchange Am. Inst. Banking, N.Y.C., 1970-72; guest speaker U. S.C., 1979. Mem. Fgn. Exchange Brokers Assn. N.Y.C. (past sec.). Roman Catholic. Club: Downtown Athletic. Home: 22 Bagatelle Rd Dix Hills NY 11746 Office: 11 Broadway New York NY 10004

MALLORY, GEORGE BARRON, lawyer, corp. exec.; b. Port Chester, N.Y., Apr. 25, 1919; s. Philip Rogers Mallory and Dorothea (Barron) Lillie; grad. magna cum laude Kent Sch., 1937; B.A. with high honors, Yale, 1941, LL.B., 1947; m. Eleanor Moore Davis, July 12, 1941 (div. Feb. 1970); children—Peter D., George Barron, Mary R., Elizabeth P.; m. Margaret Pierson Leary, Feb. 22, 1972. Admitted to Conn. bar, 1947, N.Y. bar, 1948, Ind. bar, 1959; asso. firm Brown, Wood, Fuller, Caldwell & Ivey, N.Y.C., 1947-54, partner, 1954-58; adminstrv. v.p. P.R. Mallory & Co. Inc., Indpls., 1958-60, pres., 1960-68, chmn. bd., 1968-71, also dir., mem. audit com., until 1979; counsel Jacobs Persinger & Parker, N.Y.C., 1972—; dir. Am. Fletcher Corp., Indpls. Trustee Com. for Econ. Devel., also mem. research and policy com. Served to lt. comdr. USNR, 1941-45; Res. ret. Mem. Ind., Conn. bar assns., Assn. Bar City N.Y., Electronics Industries Assn. (life), Trust for Historic Preservation, IEEE, Mystic Seaport Mus. (trustee, mem. membership and edn. coms.), Zeta Psi, Phi Delta Phi. Clubs: Downtown Assn., Union, Yale (N.Y.C.); Apawamis (Rye, N.Y.); Mill Reef (Antigua, W.I.). Home: 1 Sutton Pl S New York NY 10022 Office: 70 Pine St New York NY 10005

MALLORY, TROY L., accountant; b. Sesser, Ill., July 30, 1923; s. Theodore E. and Alice (Mitchell) M.; student So. Ill. U., 1941-43, Washington and Jefferson Coll., 1943-44; B.S., U. Ill., 1947, M.S., 1948; m. Magdalene Richter, Jan. 26, 1963. Staff sr., supr. Scovell, Wellington & Co., C.P.A.'s, Chgo., 1948-58; mgr. Gray, Hunter, Stenn & Co., C.P.A.'s, Quincy, 1959-62, partner, 1962—. Mem. finance com. United Fund, Adams County, 1961-64; bd. dirs. Woodland Home for Orphans and Friendless, 1970—, v.p., 1978—. Served with 84th Inf. Div. AUS, 1942-45. Decorated Purple Heart, Bronze Star. Mem. Am. Inst. C.P.A.'s, Ill. Soc. C.P.A.'s, Quincy C. of C. (dir. 1970-76). Club: Rotary (dir. Quincy 1967-70, pres. 1978-79). Home: 51 Wilmar Dr Quincy IL 62301 Office: 200 Quincy Peoples Bldg Quincy IL 62301

MALM, EARLE ANDREW, II, telephone systems services co. exec.; b. Cleve., July 6, 1949; s. Earle Andrew and Marie (Kutina) M.; B.S., Bowling Green State U., 1971; m. Evelyn Ann Malm, July 24, 1971; children—Earle Andrew III, Marly Jayne. Mgmt. trainee Stouffer Frozen Foods Co., Cleve., 1971-72; br. sales mgr. RCA Service Co., Warrensville Heights, Ohio, 1972-73, regional sales mgr., Cleve., 1973-75, field sales mgr., Cherry Hill, N.J., 1975-76, nat. sales mgr., 1976-77, dir. consumer products mktg., 1977-80, v.p. div. telephone systems and comml. products, 1980—. Home: 112 Headwater Dr RD 5 Medford NJ 08055 Office: Bldg 203-3 Route 38 Cherry Hill NJ 08358

MALM, RITA PELLEGRINI, personnel service exec.; b. May 8, 1932; d. George Peter and Helen Marie (Woodward) Pellegrini; student Packard Jr. Coll., 1950-52, N.Y. Inst. Fin., 1954, Wagner Coll., 1955; m. Robert J. Malm, Apr. 19, 1969. Sales asst. Dean Witter & Co., N.Y.C., 1959-63, asst. v.p., compliance dir., 1969-74; v.p., dir. Securities Ind. Assos., N.Y.C., 1969-72; resident br. mgr. Kelly Services, Inc., N.Y.C., 1974-78; br. mgr. Manpower Inc., N.Y.C., 1978—; art mktg. cons. Mem. Women's Bond Club N.Y. (dir., pres., program chmn.), Am. Cancer Soc. Home: 1172 Park Ave New York NY 10028 Office: 100 E 42d St New York NY 10017

MALONE, EDWARD H., elec. mfg. co. exec.; b. Forest Hills, N.Y., Nov. 11, 1924; s. Edward H. and Gertrude (Gibson) M.; B.S., Columbia, 1949; M.B.A., N.Y.U., 1950; m. Margaret A. Rakers, Sept. 8, 1951; children—Mary M. Tilney, Edward P., Patricia J., Jo-Ann. Bank examiner Fed. Res. Bank N.Y., N.Y.C., 1949-52; trust officer Lincoln Rochester Trust Co., 1952-55; with Gen. Electric Co., N.Y.C., 1955—, mgr. co. trust portfolios, 1961-67, mgr. trust investment operations, 1967-70, v.p., 1970—; dir. Gen. Electric Credit Corp.; trustee Prudential Savs. Bank, 1966-78. Mem. Presdl. Commn. on Fin. Structure and Regulation, 1970-71; chmn. N.Y. State Comptroller's Investment Adv. Com.; adj. trustee, mem. investment com. Rensselaer Poly. Inst. Served with USAAF, 1943-45. Clubs: Woodway Country (Darien, Conn.); Landmark (Stamford, Conn.). Home: 9 Old Parish Rd Darien CT 06820 Office: 112 Prospect St Stamford CT 06904

MALONE, JEAN ARDELL, retail store exec.; b. Wisconsin Dells, Wis., Mar. 13, 1930; d. Hans Arnold and Isla Marie (Stafford) Kneubuhler; B.S., U. Wis.-Madison, 1964; m. Francis William Malone, June 10, 1971; 1 dau., Tara. Tchr. home econs. West Bend (Wis.) Sch. Dist., 1964-65; owner, pres. Elsie's Inc., Burlington, Wis., 1965—; dir. Bank of Burlington. Bd. dirs. United Fund; bd. dirs. Human Resource Center, chmn., 1978-79. Mem. Burlington C. of C. (pres. 1973), Nat. Retail Mchts. Assn., Wis. Mchts. Fedn. Congregationalist. Office: Burlington WI

MALONE, JOHN F., mgmt. cons.; b. Huntington, N.Y., Nov. 16, 1947; s. Harold F. and Marie L. (Rutledge) M.; B.S. in Mktg., U. Dayton, 1969; M.B.A., 1972; m. Kathleen A. Purcell, Feb. 14, 1970; children—Jeffrey, Megan. Cons., Ohio Bell Telephone Co., Dayton and Toledo, 1969-72, sales mgr., 1972-76; market strategist AT&T, N.Y.C., 1976-77, market mgr., 1977-78; pres. Eastern Mgmt. Group, Morris Plains, N.J., 1978—. Mem. Inst. Mgmt. Cons. Author: Catching the Right Economic Signals—An Analysis of Market Downturns on the Communications Industry, 1980. Office: 520 Speedwell Ave Morris Plains NJ 07950

MALONE, MICHAEL GREGORY, human services corp. exec.; b. Evansville, Ind., Oct. 27, 1942; s. Eugene, Jr. and Norma Louise M.; B.S. in Polit. Sci., U. Evansville, 1974; 1 son, Malik; m. Nanette Marie, July 19, 1980; 1 dau., Stephanie Nicole. Quality control technician Ingleheart Ops., Evansville, 1966-68; dir. Unity House, then dir. Community Services Community Action Program, Evansville, 1968-72, exec. dir. program, 1972—; bd. dirs. Gov. Ind. Council on Aging, Gov. Ind. Council on Addictions; mem. Mayor Evansville Council Community Devel.; mem. exec. bd. Buffalo Trace council Boy Scouts Am., 1976—. Served with U.S. Army, 1964-66. Recipient Gov. Ind. Community Service award, 1976; Outstanding Black Men's Community Affairs award Evansville Black Expo, 1978. Mem. Nat. Council Transp. Disadvantaged (charter), Am. Mgmt. Assn., Nat. Assn. Social Workers, So. Ind. Soccer Ofcls. Assn., Southwestern Ind. Civil Liberties Union (pres. 1975-76). Lutheran. Clubs: Masons, Downtown Civitans. Home: 764 S Kentucky Ave Evansville IN 47714 Office: 906 Main St Evansville IN 47708

MALONE, RODNEY PHIL, economist, educator; b. Albertville, Ala., Feb. 28, 1946; s. Monice Raymond and Irene Susan (Jones) M.; B.S., Berry Coll., 1968; Ph.D., U. Fla., 1974; m. Charlotte Kathleen Lee, June 11, 1971. Asst. prof. fin. U. Miss., 1973-79, asso. prof., 1979—; cons. in field. Served with U.S. Army 1968-70. Dana scholar, 1965-68; NDEA Title IV fellow, 1970-73. Mem. Fin. Mgmt. Assn., Am. Fin. Assn., Eastern Fin. Assn., So. Fin. Assn., Southwestern Fin. Assn., Beta Gamma Sigma. Methodist. Contbr. articles to profl. jours. Home: PO Box 113 University MS 38677 Office: Conner Hall U Miss University MS 38677

MALONE, THOMAS K., JR., banker. Chmn., First Va. Bank, Falls Church. Office: 1 First Va Plaza 6400 Arlington Blvd Falls Church VA 22046*

MALONE, WALLACE DAVIS, JR., bank holding co. exec.; b. Dothan, Ala., Aug. 3, 1936; B.S., U. Ala., 1957; M.B.A., U. Pa.; m. Ocllo S. Malone; 3 children. Pres., dir. So. Bancorp. of Ala., Birmingham, 1972—, chmn., 1980—. Baptist. Office: PO Box 2554 Birmingham AL 55223*

MALONE, WILLIAM ROBERT, communications co. exec.; b. Terre Haute, Ind., Apr. 15, 1936; s. Leander Alonsonand Dorothy Alice (Reveal) M.; A.B., Harvard U., 1958, J.D., 1962; m. Jane H. Foulkes, June 25, 1959; children—Elizabeth, David, Christina. Admitted to Ind. bar, 1962, D.C. bar, 1963; law clk. to judge U.S. Ct. Appeals for D.C., 1962-63; asso. firm Covington & Burling, Washington, 1963-70; resident atty. Gen. Telephone & Electronics Corp., Washington, 1970-72, v.p., 1972—. Served with Signal Corps, U.S. Army, 1959. Mem. Am. Bar Assn., Fed. Bar Assn., Fed. Communications Bar Assn., Computer Law Assn. (dir.). Republican. Presbyterian. Clubs: Internat., Harvard (chmn. schs. and scholarships com.) (Washington). Author: Broadcast Regulation in Canada, 1962. Home: 7205 Masters Dr Rockville MD 20854 Office: 1120 Connecticut Ave Suite 900 Washington DC 20036

MALONEY, CLEMENT GARLAND, internat. marketing and financial cons.; b. Hot Springs, Ark., July 4, 1917; s. James C. and Dorothy (Clement) M.; student Northwestern U., 1937-40; 1 son, Thomas C. Dep. dir. Chgo. unit War Assets Adminstrn., 1946-48; chief major procurement USAF, Washington, 1948-51; chief aircraft div. office Asst. Sec. Def., Washington, 1951-53, program adminstr., Paris, 1953-55; spl. asst. for financial control air force resources to asst. sec. Air Force, 1955-58; spl. asst. to pres. Hoffman Electronics, Los Angeles, 1958-60; spl. asst. to pres. for govt. ops. Gen. Dynamics-Electronics div. Gen. Dynamics Corp., N.Y., 1960-61; v.p. charge govt. mktg. Kollsman Instrument Corp., Elmhurst, N.Y., 1961-64; cons. to U.S. sec. def., 1964-66, 67-69; internat. mktg. cons. Philco Corp. div. Ford Motor Co., 1966-67; internat. mktg. cons. to sec. Def., 1967-69; spl. asst. to pres. Control Data Corp., 1969-72; internat. mktg. and fin. cons., 1972—. Served to col. USAAF, World War II. Recipient Exceptional Civilian Service award USAF. Mem. Air Force Assn., Nat. Security Indsl. Assn., Am. Def. Preparedness Assn., Am. Mgmt. Assn., Res. Officers Assn. (pres. chpt. 12 Long Beach), Mil. Order of Carabao. Clubs: Capitol Hill (Washington), Elks. Home: 2999 E Ocean Blvd Apt 2040 Long Beach CA 90803

MALONEY, JOHN PHILIP, banker; b. San Antonio, 1918; grad. Millsaps Coll., 1940; edn. U. Miss., 1946. Pres., Deposit Guaranty Corp.; chmn., chief exec. officer Deposit Guaranty Nat. Bank, Jackson, Miss.; dir. Jackson Packing Co., Miss. Power & Light Co., Mississippi Valley Title Ins. Co. Office: Deposit Guaranty Corp 210 E Capitol St Jackson MS 39205*

MALONEY, LEONARD JOHN, ins. co. exec.; b. Phila., June 24, 1941; s. John J. and Anne (Hettel) M.; B.A., Xavier U., 1963; m. Frances H. Suder, Oct. 26, 1963; children—Matthew, Tracey Ann. Claim supr. Employers Ins. of Wausau, Phila. and Pitts., 1965-71; div. claims mgr. Argonaut Ins. Co., Phila., 1971-78; sr. v.p. claims Vaughan Ins. Group, Phila., 1978-80; ins. cons., Broomall, Pa., 1980—. Pres., Babe Ruth Baseball, 1979-81; commr. Hilltop Baseball, 1977-78; active Boy Scouts Am., 1975-76; pres. Hilltop Civic Assn., 1975, Bryn Mawr Hills Civic Assn., 1980; bd. dirs. Vassar Assn.; asst. ward leader Havertown (Pa.), 1977-78. Served with USMCR, 1962-68. Recipient various awards. Mem. Del-Chester Claim Assn., Lower Bucks Claim Assn., Pa. Def. Inst., Phila. Claim Mgrs. Council. Home: 604 Heather Ln Bryn Mawr PA 19010

MALOTT, R.H., mfg. co. exec.; b. Boston, Oct. 6, 1926; s. Deane W. and Eleanor (Thrum) M.; A.B., Kans. U., 1948; M.B.A., Harvard U., 1950; student N.Y. U. Law Sch., evenings 1953-55; m. Elizabeth Harwood Hubert, June 4, 1960; children—Elizabeth Hubert, Barbara Holden, Robert Deane. Asst. to dean Harvard Grad. Sch. Bus. Adminstrn., 1950-52; asst. to exec. v.p. Chems. div. FMC Corp., 1952-55, controller Niagara Chem. div., Middleport, N.Y., 1955-59, controller Organic Chems. div., N.Y.C., 1959-62, asst. div. mgr., 1962-63, div. mgr., 1963-65, v.p., mgr. film ops. div. Am. Viscose div., 1966-67, exec. v.p., mem. pres.'s office, 1967-70, mgr. machinery divs., 1970-72, pres., 1972-77, chief exec. officer corp., 1972—, chmn. bd., 1973—, also dir.; dir. Continental Ill. Bank, Chgo., Continental Ill. Corp., Standard Oil Ind., Bell & Howell, United Techs. Corp. Trustee Kans. Endowment Assn., U. Kans., Orchestral Assn., Chgo. Served with USNR, 1944-46. Mem. Machinery and Allied Products Inst. (exec. com.), Chem. Mfrs. Assn., Bus. Council, Bus. Roundtable, Phi Beta Kappa, Beta Theta Pi, Alpha Chi Sigma. Clubs: Indian Hill (Kenilworth, Ill.); Links, Explorers (N.Y.C.); Bohemian (San Francisco); Econ., Mid-Am. (Chgo.). Office: FMC Corp 200 E Randolph Dr Chicago IL 60601*

MALOY, STEPHEN FRANCIS, diagnostic equip. co. exec.; b. Cambridge, Mass., Dec. 1, 1947; s. Charles Augustin and Anne Marie (Sullivan) M.; student Northeastern U., 1965-67, 73-75, Lowell Tech. Inst., 1968; 1 dau., Daphne Lea. Pres., S.F. Maloy Co., Inc., Woburn, Mass., 1970-79, dir., 1970—; chief exec. officer Mariner Enterprises, Inc., Woburn, 1976—, chmn. bd., 1977—; exec. v.p. Diagnostic Equipment Service Corp., Woburn, 1979—, also dir. Served with USAFR, 1967-73, with USCG Aux., 1976—. Recipient Membership Tng. award, USCG Aux., 1977, Flotilla Achievement award, 1978. Republican. Mem. Niscience Ch. Author: Tax Advantages for Everyone, 1978. Office: 260 New Boston Park Woburn MA 01801

MALOZEMOFF, PLATO, mining exec.; b. Russia, 1909; student U. Calif., 1931, Mont. Sch. Mines, 1932. Chmn., chief exec. officer Newmont Mining Corp., N.Y.C.; pres., dir. Resurrection Mining Co., Newmont Exploration Ltd., Carlin Gold Mining Co.; chmn. Newmont Proprietary Ltd.; chmn., dir. Newmont Mines Ltd., Idarado Mining Co.; v.p., dir. Newmont Exploration Can., Ltd.; vice chmn., dir. Magma Copper Co.; dir. Bethlehem Copper Corp., Browning-Ferris Industries, Inc., Peabody Coal Co., Peabody Holding Co., Highveld Steel & Vanadium Corp. Ltd., O'Okiep Copper Co., Cassiar Asbestos Corp., Ltd., So. Peru Copper Corp., Sherritt Gordon Mines, Ltd., Atlantic Cement Co. Inc., Bankers Trust Co., Palabora Mining Co., Ltd., Tsumeb Corp., Ltd., Foote Mineral Co. Office: 300 Park Ave New York NY 10022

MALPAS, ROBERT, chem. process technology research co. exec.; b. Birkenhead, Eng., Aug. 9, 1927; came to U.S., 1978; s. Cheshyre and Louise M. M.; B.Sc. in M.E. with honors, Durham (Eng.) U., 1948; m. Effie Josephine Dickenson, June 30, 1956. With ICI, Ltd., Millbank, London, 1948-78, also dir.; pres. Halcon Internat., Inc., N.Y.C., 1978—. Decorated comdr. Order Brit. Empire; recipient Order of Civil Merit, Spain, 1967. Fellow Council Engring., Instn. Chem Engrs., Inst. Mech. Engrs.; mem. Inst. Dirs. Clubs: River (N.Y.C.); Royal Automobile de Espanan Golf (Madrid). Home: 870 UN Plaza New York NY 10017 Office: 2 Park Ave New York NY 10016

MANAHAN, MICHAEL LARRY, community relations mgr., land devel. exec.; b. Los Angeles, Nov. 6, 1923; s. John Robert and Gertrude Jane (Nelson) M.; student Calif. State U., Los Angeles, 1942-43; profl. designation in public relations UCLA, 1980; m. Ruth Virginia Crosby, May 15, 1949; children—Mark Steven, Stacy Anne. Sales supr. Farmers Ins. Group, Ind., Wis. and Mich., 1949-56, dist. agy. owner, Los Angeles, 1957-64; pres. Manahan & Eggers, Inc., Corona del Mar, Calif., 1965-69; mgr. community relations The Irvine Co., Newport Beach, Calif., 1969—. Pres. Orange County Industry/Edn. Council, 1976; chmn. U. Calif. (Irvine) Pub. Relations Council, 1976; bd. Coastline Regional Occupation Program, 1973-76; bd. dirs. Irvine Master Chorale, 1976, Salvation Army Orange County, 1972-76, Orange County United Way, 1976; pres. Boys Club Harbor Area, 1971; mem. adv. bd. council econ. edn. Calif. State U., Long Beach. Recipient Spirit award Irvine Women's Club, 1972, civic leadership award Salvation Army, 1976, Silver Anchor award Newport Harbor C. of C., 1976; Community Leadership award Girl Scouts U.S.A., 1977; Chancellor's citation for merit; U. Calif. at Irvine, 1978. Mem. Pub. Relations Soc. Am. (accredited; pres. chpt. 1980), U. Calif. Interfaith Found. Republican. Presbyterian (elder). Clubs: Corona del Mar Kiwanis (pres. 1972), Masons (master 1965), Shriners, Orange County Press, Merced Toastmasters (pres. 1953). Office: 550 Newport Center Dr Newport Beach CA 92663

MANCHER, RHODA, govt. ofcl.; b. N.Y.C., Sept. 28, 1935; d. Joseph and Hannah (Karpf) Ross; student Wellesley Coll., 1953-55; B.S., Columbia U., 1959; M.S. in Ops. Research, George Washington U., 1978; m. Melvin Mancher, May 27, 1962; children—Amy Meg, James Marc. Head biol. data processing system Nat. Cancer Inst., NIH, Bethesda, Md., 1966-74, asst. br. chief program analysis br., 1971-73; chief fuels br. div. systems design and programming Fed. Energy Adminstrn., Washington, 1974-75, dep. dir. for programming support, 1975-77; spl. asst. Office Spl. Asst. to Pres. for Mgmt. Info., The White House, Washington, 1977-79; dir. info. systems devel. div. Office Adminstrn., Exec. Office Pres., Washington, 1979; dir. Office Systems Devel., Social Security Adminstrn., Balt. 1979-80; dep. asst. atty. gen. for adminstrn. Office Litigation and Mgmt. Systems, Dept. Justice, 1980—; chmn. Interagy. Info. Exchange. Contbr. articles to profl. publs. Home: 7602 Granada Dr Bethesda MD 20034 Office: 425 I St NW Room 4100-CAB Washington DC 20530

MANCINELLI, JACOB EMIL, corp. exec.; b. Smock, Pa., Oct. 1, 1919; s. Joseph and Claudia (Di Russo) M.; B.A., Harvard U., 1948; children—Teresa Ann, Kathryn Jean, Robin. With fin. dept. Gen. Electric Co. and G.E. C.C., Louisville, 1948-62; sr. v.p. U.S. Leasing Corp., San Francisco, 1962-69; sec., dir. Silver State Leasing Corp.; v.p., dir. Air Lease Corp., Barrel Leasing Corp., Cargo Vans Ltd., Comml. Pacific Corp., Fleet Leasing Corp., San Francisco, 1962-69; pres., dir. Compass Fin. Corp. (formerly Whittaker Leasing Corp.), Burlingame, Calif., 1969-73; pres., dir. TRE Fin. Corp., San Mateo, Calif., 1973-74; chmn. bd., pres. Dome Fin. Corp., Burlingame, 1974—; chmn. bd. Highridge, Inc., Redwood City, Calif., 1974—; owner The Dome Co., Burlingame, 1980—; instr. U. Calif. Extension. Pres., Foster City (Calif.) Home Improvement Assn., 1964-66; mem. Foster City Park and Recreation Commn., 1968—; chmn. Foster City Com. for Better Govt., 1973—; exec. bd. San Mateo council Boy Scouts Am.; bd. dirs. Foster City Community Assn., 1972—, pres., 1973—. Served as officer USAF, 1939-54. Decorated Air medal with 4 clusters, Presdl. citation. Mem. Nat. Comml. Fin. Conf. (dir. 1967—), Greater San Francisco (municipal legis. com. 1967-69), Foster City (dir. 1972) chambers commerce. Roman Catholic (council 1972—). Clubs: Commonwealth of Calif., Marina Point Tennis (pres.). Author: Love Thoughts and Other Things, 1980. Home: 1111 Compass Ln Foster City CA 94404 Office: PO Box 4294 Burlingame CA 94010

MANCUSO, JAMES VINCENT, automobile dealer; b. Batavia, N.Y., June 18, 1916; s. Benjamin J. and Laura (LaRussa) M.; student Gen. Motors Inst., Flint, Mich., 1949; m. Clarissa R. Pope, Sept. 8, 1945; children—Richard J., Robert P., Linda M., Laura Lee. Auto salesman C. Mancuso & Son, Inc., 1934-39, gen. mgr., 1939-42; gen. mgr. Batavia Motors (N.Y.), 1945-49; sales rep. Cadillac Motor Car div. Gen. Motors Corp., 1950-53; pres., gen. mgr. Mancuso Chevrolet, Inc., Skokie, Ill., 1953-74, chmn. bd., 1974—; pres. Mancuso Cadillac/Honda, Inc., Barrington, Ill., 1974-76, chmn. bd., 1976—; pres. Genesee Corp.; adv. council Consol. Am. Life Ins. Co.; dir. Lake States Life Ins. Co.; mem. faculty Chevrolet Acad., Wayne State U., 1964; dir. Auto Industries Hwy. Safety Com. Chmn. Niles Twp. Jud. Reform Com.; gen. mgr. Niles Twp. Community Fund, 1955; trustee Skokie Valley Community Hosp.; chmn. Skokie's All Am. City Com., 1961. Served from pvt. to maj. USAAF, 1942-46. Mem. Am. Legion, Nat. Auto Dealers Assn. (dir. 1963—, chmn. pub. relations com.), Chgo. Better Bus. Bur. (dir.), Asso. Employers Ill. (dir.), Skokie C. of C. (pres. 1956), Chgo. Auto Dealers Assn. (dir. 1959—), Chgo. Auto Trade Assn. (v.p. 1959-60), Chgo. Met. Chevrolet Dealers Assn. (pres. 1957-59), Chgo. Chevrolet Dealers Advt. Assn. (pres. 1969-70). Roman Catholic. Clubs: Rotary (pres. 1960-61), Evanston Golf (pres. 1969-70). Home: 17 Longmeadow Rd Winnetka IL 60093 Office: 4700 Golf Rd Skokie IL 60076

MANCUSO, ROBERT POPE, automobile dealership exec.; b. Chgo., Feb. 2, 1951; s. James Vincent and Clarissa Rosary (Pope) M.; A.B. in Psychology, Princeton U., 1973. Spl. asst. to pres. Mancuso Chevrolet, Inc., Skokie, Ill., 1969-73; pres. Mancuso Cadillac, Inc., Barrington, Ill., 1974—; pres. Consumer Concepts, Ltd., 1980—, RPM Systems, Inc., 1980—; chmn. advt. com. Chicagoland Cadillac Dealers. Career advisor Barrington Bd. Edn. Recipient Nat. Auto Dealers Edn. award, 1977. Mem. Nat., Barrington (past pres.) auto dealers assns., Cadillac Dealers Assn. (exec. com. 1979—), Honda Dealers Assn. (pres. 1980—), Barrington C. of C. (treas. 1976-77, pres. 1979—), Chgo. Auto Trade Assn. Roman Catholic. Club: Rotary (pres. 1981—). Office: 1445 S Barrington Rd Barrington IL 60010

MANDELL, STEPHEN ELLIOT, computer co. exec.; b. Bklyn., Apr. 28, 1944; s. Herman and Estelle (Minchenberg) M.; B.S. in Mech. Engring., N.Y. U., 1965, M.B.A., 1978, Ph.D./ABD, 1978; M.S. in Mgmt. Sci., Stevens Inst. Tech., 1971; m. Barbara Cooper, Dec. 31, 1971; children—David Herman, Iris Morrisa. Engr. in tng. Combustion Engring. Inc., Windsor, Conn., 1965-66; project engt. Bendix Corp., Teterboro, N.J., 1966-67; successively project engr., mgmt. cons., chief mgmt. scientist U.S. Army Material Command, Dover, N.J., 1967-76; mgr. ops. Operating Group Citibank, N.A., N.Y.C., 1976-77, mgr. fin. ops. Investment Mgmt. Group, 1977-78; dir. NE Health Survival, Inc., Maplewood, N.J., 1977—, Health & Survival Inc., Modesto, Calif., 1980—; founder, pres. Medicom, Inc., 1979—; cons. in field. U.S. Army fellow, 1971-73. Mem. Inst. Mgmt. Scis., Assn. Computing Machinery, Omega Rho (nat. sec.), Beta Gamma Sigma (past pres.). Clubs: Game Point Racquet, Scuba. Home: Box 6097 Modesto CA 95355 Office: 1700 McHenry Village Way Suite 10 Modesto CA 95350

MANDL, ALEXANDER JOHANN, mfg. co. exec.; b. Vienna, Austria, Dec. 14, 1943; s. Otto William and Charlotte J. (Peshek) M.; came to U.S., 1958, naturalized, 1968; B.A., Willamette U., 1967; M.B.A., U. Calif. at Berkeley, 1969; m. Nancy J. Scott, June 10, 1967; 1 dau., Melanie. Fin. analyst Boise Cascade Corp. (Idaho), 1969, asst. mgr. internat. 1970, dir. internat. fin., 1971, asst. treas., 1973-76, fin. chmn., 1976-80; sr. v.p.-fin. Seaboard Coast Line Industries, Inc., Jacksonville, Fla., 1980—; lectr. in field. Mem. Bogus Basin Assn., Am. Mgmt. Assn., Fin. Execs. Inst., Treas.'s Club San Francisco, Soc. Internat. Treas.'s. Clubs: Hillcrest Country, Arid (Boise). Office: Seaboard Coast Line Industries 500 Water St Jacksonville FL 32202

MANFRED, ROGER LEE, hotel exec.; b. Goulburn, New South Wales, Australia, May 9, 1930; s. Lee Cooper and Maisie Manfred; came to U.S., 1969; m. Joy Wicks, Sept. 27, 1953 (div. July 1970); 1 dau., Nicole Leone. Partner pub. accounting firm Manfred & McCallum, Coulburn, 1953-60; group gen. mgr. TraveLodge Australia Ltd., 1960-68; mng. dir., chief exec. officer TraveLodge Internat., Inc., San Diego, 1969—, now also pres., dir.; dir. TraveLodge Fiji Ltd., TraveLodge N.Z. Ltd. Fellow Australian Soc. Accountants, Australian Inst. Mgmt., Inst. Dirs. Eng.; mem. Am. Mgmt. Assn. Office: 250 S Cuyamaca Box 308 El Cajon CA 92022*

MANFRO, PATRICK JAMES, broadcaster; b. Kingston, N.Y., Dec. 30, 1947; s. Charles Vincent and Anna Agnes (Albany) M.; A.A.S. in Accounting, Ulster County Community Coll., 1968; diploma Radio Electronics Inst., 1969; A.A. in Computer Sci., St. Clair Coll., 1978; postgrad. in fin. N.Y. State U., 1977—; m. Janice Lynn Truscott, July 5, 1975; 1 son, Wesley Patrick. Program dir., radio artist Sta. WKNY, Kingston, 1966-70; radio artist Sta. WPTR, Albany, N.Y., 1970, Sta. WPOP, Hartford, Conn., 1970, Sta. WOR-FM, N.Y.C., 1971-72; radio artist Sta. CKLW, Detroit, 1970-71, radio announcer, 1972-79, asst. program dir., 1978-79, program dir., 1980—; pres. Holiday Prodns., Windsor, Ont., Can.; pres., chief exec. officer Internat. Data Corp., Wilmington, Del.; adviser New Sch. Contemporary Radio, Albany. Judge Miss Mich. Universe Pageant, 1971. Served with U.S. N.G., 1968-74. Runner up Billbd. mag Air Personality Awards, 1971; radio, telephone lic., FCC. Mem. AFTRA, Screen Actors Guild, Broadcast Music Inst., Songwriter's Guild, Assos. Smithsonian Inst. Republican. Roman Catholic. Clubs: Dominion Golf, Country, Windsor Press. Home: 1637 Goyeau St Windsor ON N8X 1L1 Canada Office: 26400 Lahser Rd Southfield MI 48076

MANGELS, JOHN DONALD, banker; b. Victoria, B.C., Can., Apr. 14, 1926; (parents Am. citizens); s. August H. and Marguerite E. (McRae) M.; B.A., U. Wash., 1950; m. Mary Ann Hahn, Nov. 25, 1954; children—Susan, Meg., John. With Rainier Nat. Bank and affiliates, Seattle, 1950—, vice-chmn. Rainier Bancorp., 1975—, pres. Bank, 1976—; dir. PEFCO. Active United Way, Downtown Seattle Devel. Assn., Corp. Council for Arts. Served in USAAF, 1944-46. Mem. Robert Morris Assos. (nat. officer), Assn. Res. City Bankers, Am. Bankers Assn., Am. Inst. C.P.A.'s. Presbyterian. Clubs: Rotary; Rainier; Broadmoor Golf and Country, Bellevue (Wash.) Athletic. Office: 1301 Fifth Ave Seattle WA 98124

MANGES, JAMES H., investment banker; b. N.Y.C., Oct. 8, 1927; s. Horace S. and Natalie (Bloch) M.; B.A., Yale U., 1950; M.B.A., Harvard U., 1953; m. Joan Brownell, Oct. 1969 (div.); m. 2d, Mary Seymour, Mar. 28, 1974; children—Alison, James H. With Kuhn, Loeb & Co., N.Y.C., 1954-77, partner, 1967-77, mng. dir. Kuhn Loeb Inc., 1977; mng. dir. Lehman Brothers Kuhn Loeb Inc., 1978—; dir. Metromedia, Inc. Served with CIC, AUS, 1946-48. Clubs: Bond, Yale (N.Y.C.); City Midday, Century Country (Purchase, N.Y.). Home: 875 Park Ave New City NY 10021 Office: 55 Water St New York NY 10041

MANGIERI, ROBERT PAUL, ins. cons.; b. N.Y.C., May 20, 1941; s. Frank and Gussie (D'Martini) M.; B.A., CCNY, 1965; certificate York Coll., 1974, Pohs Inst., 1972. Spl. cons. youth affairs Office of Mayor of N.Y., 1969; legis. asst. N.Y. City Council, 1971-73; ins. cons. Marsh & McLennan, N.Y.C., 1973-76, ind., 1976—. Exec. sec., chmn. transp. Community Planning Bd. 9, 1975—; past pres. Queensboro Young Republicans Assn.; mem. Bicentennial Adv. Com., 1975-76; chmn. public relations Marine Corps Scholarship Found.; chmn. civic and polit. com., past mem. parish council Roman Catholic Ch. Served with USMCR, 1965-69. Named Hon. Fire Chief, N.Y. State Fire Fighters Assn., 1975. Mem. Native New Yorker's Hist. Assn. (v.p.), Alumni Assn. City Coll. Club: Moose. Home: 82-60 116th St Kew Gardens NY 11418 Office: 201 E 50th St New York NY 10022

MANGIERO, GEORGE ANTHONY, educator, elec. engr.; b. Staten Island, N.Y., Apr. 23, 1947; s. Anthony J. and Joan Mangiero; B.E.E. (Regents scholar), Manhattan Coll., 1969; M.E. (Univ. fellow), Rensselaer Poly. Inst., 1970; M.B.A. in Fin., St. John's U., Jamaica, N.Y., 1977; postgrad. N.Y. U., 1980—; m. Judith Arlene Holmes, Feb. 15, 1972. With Am. Electric Power Service Corp., 1970-80, group leader supervisory control and data acquisition group, 1975-78, head system measurements sect., N.Y.C., 1978-80; asst. prof. fin. and bus. econs. Iona Coll., 1980—. Mem. IEEE, Edison Electric Inst., Nat. Assn. Bus. Economists, Mensa, Eta Kappa Nu (founder, 1st pres. indsl. chpt. 1974), Omicron Delta Epsilon, Beta Gamma Sigma. Clubs: Staten Island Athletic; Downtown Athletic (N.Y.C.). Home: 36 Piedmont Ave Staten Island NY 10305 Office: 2 Broadway New York City NY 10004

MANGO, RALPH PHILLIP, fin. co. exec.; b. East Orange, N.J., Dec. 29, 1946; s. Vincent A. and Marie F. Mango; B.S. in Accounting, Rutgers U., 1974; m. Mary Elizabeth Finucane, May 27, 1967; children—Kristin Elizabeth, Nicole Marie, Allyson Marie. Analytical reporter Dun & Bradstreet, Freehold, N.J., 1968-71; dist. credit mgr. Goodyear Tire & Rubber Co., North Brunswick, N.J., 1972-74; credit mgr. plastic machinery, pulp machinery and environ. divs. Ingersoll-Rand Co., Nashua, N.H., 1974-76; Atlantic region mgr. Ingersoll-Rand Fin. Corp., King of Prussia, Pa., 1976-80, Western region mgr., San Leandro, Calif., 1979-80; asst. v.p. Citicorp Indsl. Credit Inc., San Francisco, 1980—. Mem. Nat. Assn. Credit Mgmt., Am. Mgmt. Assn., Nashua C. of C. (pres. council 1975-76). Delta Upsilon. Office: 44 Montgomery St Suite 3785 San Francisco CA 94104

MANGRAVITE, FRANCIS JOSEPH, JR., splty. chems. mfg. co. exec.; b. N.Y.C., Nov. 7, 1945; s. Francis Joseph and Olga M. (Duray) M.; B.S. in Chemistry, Clarkson Coll. Tech., 1967, M.S. in Chemistry (fellow), 1971, Ph.D. in Phys. Chemistry (fellow), 1972; m. Arlene R. Bartlett, July 4, 1969; 1 dau., Lara Michelle. Research asso. Calgon Corp., Pitts., 1972-74; research scientist, sr. research scientist, group leader polymer applications group Betz Labs., Trevose, Pa., 1974-79; product mgr. liquid/solids separations ARCO Performance Chems. Co., Phila., 1979—. Served with U.S. Army, 1970. Mem. Am. Chem. Soc. (div. colloid and surface chemistry), Am. Water Works Assn. (adv. com. on coagulation), Water Pollution Control Assn. Presbyterian. Contbr. articles to profl. jours.; patentee in field. Office: 1500 Market St Philadelphia PA 19101

MANILLA, JOHN ALLAN, office furniture co. exec., elevator co. exec.; b. Sharon, Pa., July 17, 1941; s. Vito John and Helen Elizabeth (Papai) M.; B.S., Youngstown State U., 1966; postgrad. Duquesne U., 1967-68, Aquinas Coll., 1979—; m. Paula Gale Jurko, Nov. 26, 1960; children—Jacqueline Lee, John Paul, Paul Allan, Bradley James. Sr. staff asst. Elevator Co., Westinghouse Electric Corp., Pitts., 1966-68, salesman I, 1968-70, salesman II, Union, N.J., 1971, Miami, Fla., 1971-72, dist. mgr., Indpls., 1973-77, regional mgr. archtl. systems div., Grand Rapids, Mich., 1977-79, splty. sales mgr., 1979—; v.p. Yankee Lake Amusement Co., Yankee Lake Village, Ohio, 1961-66, 70-71; elevator cons. architects, engrs., bldg. mgr., contractors. Chief, YMCA Indian Guides, Allison Park, Pa., 1970; asst. scoutmaster Boy Scouts Am., Dania, Fla., 1971-72; asst. to Boys Scouts Am., Ind. Sch. for Blind, Indpls., 1973; jr. high sch. prin., instr. Christian Doctrine, St. Ursula Ch., Allison Park, 1968-70, St. Sabastion Ch., Masury, Ohio, 1970-71; pres. bd. edn. Our Lady of Mt. Carmel Sch., Carmel, Ind., 1973-76; mem. Carmel Dad's Club, 1973-74. Recipient First in Performance award Westinghouse Electric Corp., 1972, 120 Club Honor Roll, 1968, 69, 70, 71, 72. Mem. Bldg. Owners and Mgrs. Assn., Constrn. Specification Inst., Assn. Gen. Contractors Ind., Am. Water Ski Assn., West Mich. Water Ski Assn. Clubs: Rotary, Indpls. Athletic; Yankee Lake (Ohio) Water Ski (pres.); Renaissance (Detroit). Home: 1924 Lockmere SE Kentwood MI 49508 Office: 4300 36th St SE PO Box 8367 Grand Rapids MI 49508

MANKES, ROBERT OWEN, water treatment co. exec.; b. Bklyn., July 12, 1942; s. Edward John and Ann (Dunford) M.; B.A., Ricker Coll., 1965; M.S., Incarnate Word Coll., 1967; m. A. Louise Nilsen, July 11, 1970; children—Kari, Kyle. Tchr. high sch. biology and physics, San Antonio, 1967-69; v.p. mktg. Delta Sci. Corp., 1969-76; pres. Internat. Mktg. Co., 1977-78; v.p. mktg. Pure Cycle Corp., Boulder, Colo., 1978—. Served with USAF, 1965-67. Mem. Am. Water Works Assn., Water Pollution Control Fedn., Nat. Environ. Health Assn. Contbg. author to Manual of Practice for Water Pollution Control, 1976. Home: 17 3000 Broadway Boulder CO 80302 Office: 1668 Valtec Ln Boulder CO 80302

MANLEY, ALBERT EARL, utility ofcl.; b. Riga, N.Y., Sept. 7, 1932; s. Gilbert Earl and Ruby Pearl (Smith) M.; A.A.S., SUNY, Alfred, 1952; B.S. in Accounting, U. Rochester, 1966; m. Joyce Ann Wyand, July 10, 1954; children—Joan Marie, Mark Alan. Mgr. printing, microfilm and records mgmt. Rochester Gas & Electric Co. (N.Y.), 1956—. Treas., Lutheran Ch. of the Good Shepherd, 1966—. Served with USAF, 1952-56. Certified data processor Data Processing Mgmt. Assn. Mem. Assn. Systems Mgmt. (past pres. Rochester chpt., chmn. Div. III council Upper N.Y. State, merit award for service 1973, Achievement award 1980), Assn. Records Mgrs. and Adminstrs. (pres. Rochester chpt. 1980—), Improvement Inst. (founding mem.). Club: Irondequoit Squares (past pres.). Home: 294 Brett Rd Rochester NY 14609 Office: 89 East Ave Rochester NY 14649

MANLEY, MARSHALL, lawyer, title co. exec.; b. Newark, May 3, 1940; s. Nathan and Faye (Rosen) M.; student Bklyn. Coll., 1962; J.D. cum laude, N.Y. U., 1965; m. Tonya Lee Nordyke, Dec. 12, 1975; 1

child, Chase. Admitted to Calif. bar, 1966, D.C. bar, 1972; asso. firm McKenna & Fitting, Los Angeles, 1965-70, partner, 1970-73; partner firm Manatt, Phelps, Rothenberg, Manley & Tunney, Los Angeles, 1973-78; partner firm Finley, Kumble, Wagner, Heine, Underberg & Manley, N.Y.C., Miami and Los Angeles, Washington, 1978—; chmn. bd. So. Pacific Title Co., Santa Ana, Calif., 1978—; dir. Minoco Group of Cos., Los Angeles, First Profl. Realty Co., Beverly Hills, Calif. Mem. Calif. Motion Picture Devel. Council, 1977—, Commn. of Californians, 1978—. Mem. Am., D.C., Calif., Los Angeles County bar assns. Office: Suite 2600 2029 Century Park E Los Angeles CA

MANN, ALAN EDWARD, steel fabricating co. exec.; b. Phoenix, Aug. 14, 1950; s. Edward O'Brien and Elaine (Petersen) M.; student U. N.D., 1966-68; B.S. in Acctg. (scholar), Brigham Young U., 1973; m. Lorinda Lee Becker, Dec. 1, 1972; children—Catrina Louise, Heather Noel, Sarah Nicole, Christina May. Controller, Fin. Data Systems, Inc., Denver, 1974; mem. tax staff Ernst & Ernst, Denver, 1974, Arthur Young & Co., Denver, 1975; mem. staff Rocky Mountain Acctg. Co., Denver, 1976; controller Wisdom Mfg., Inc., Merino, Colo., 1976—, also dir.; dir. Midway Leasing, Inc., Signwise, Inc., Wisdom Internat., Inc.; instr. genealogy Northeastern Jr. Coll., 1980—. Republican. Mormon. Home: 1525 Westview Dr Sterling CO 80751 Office: 3758 County Rd 23 7 Merino CO 80741

MANN, GORDON LEE, JR., ins. exec.; b. Taylor, Tex., May 5, 1921; s. Gordon L. and Ruth (Kirkpatrick) M.; student U. Calif. at Los Angeles, 1939, Sch. Law, Loyola U., Los Angeles, 1961. Claims mgr. Traders and Gen. Ins. Co., Los Angeles, 1948-52, Fireman's Fund Am. Ins. Cos., 1952-70; account exec., claims cons. Behrendt-Levy Ins. Agy., 1970-72; asst. div. mgr. Argonaut Ins. Co. Los Angeles, 1972-79; v.p. Frank B. Hall & Co., Los Angeles, 1979—. Served to lt. USNR, 1946. Recipient Meritorious Pub. Service citation Dept. Navy, 1965; Nat. Scroll of Honor, Navy League, 1968. C.P.C.U. Mem. Am. Soc. C.P.C.U.'s (pres. Los Angeles chpt. 1972, gen. chmn. nat. conv. 1970), Navy League U.S. (nat. dir. 1963-75, v.p. for adminstrn. 11th region 1974-75. pres. Los Angeles council 1962, state pres. 1965), Am. Legion (past comdr.), Nat. Soc. Colonial Wars (gov. Cal. soc. 1967, nat. dep. gov. gen. 1969), Children Am. Revolution (past nat. com. chmn.), S.R. (treas. Calif. soc.), Mil. Order World Wars, Naval Order, Men of All Saints Soc. (pres.). Republican. Episcopalian (past vestryman). Mason. Club: Los Angeles. Speaker and writer on ins. and patriotic subjects. Home: 435 S Curson Ave Los Angeles CA 90036 Office: 3200 Wilshire Blvd Los Angeles CA 90010

MANN, JOHN C., lawyer; b. Latham, Ill., Oct. 12, 1898; s. Frank and Josephine (Canary) M.; student James Millikin U., 1917-19; J.D., U. Ill., 1922; m. Irene Watkins, Mar. 26, 1927; 1 dau., Linda. Admitted to Ill. bar, 1922; practiced law in Decatur, Ill., 1923-34; law dept. Chgo. Title & Trust Co., Chgo., 1934-63, asso. gen. counsel, 1960-63. Served as pvt. U.S. Army, World War I. Mem. Ill., Chgo. bar assns., Chgo. Law Inst., Order of Coif, Sigma Alpha Epsilon, Phi Delta Phi. Club: Glen Oak Country. Author: Title Examinations Involving Chancery Proceedings, 1948; Illinois Chancery Procedure and Forms, 1960; Escrows: Their Use and Value, 1975; Joint Tenancies Today, 1956; Is Joint Tenancy the Answer, 1953; Joint Tenancies in Estate Planning, 1975. Editor: (with John Norton Pomeroy, Jr.) Pomeroy's Specific Performance of Contracts, 3d edit., 1926. Contbr. various articles to legal publs. Home: 515 N Main St Unit 3-C-S Glen Ellyn IL 60137 Office: 111 W Washington St Chicago IL 60602

MANN, LOWELL KIMSEY, mfg. exec.; b. LaGrange, Ga., June 28, 1917; s. Otis A. and Georgia B. (Mundy) M.; grad. Advanced Mgmt. Program, Harvard U., 1962; m. Helen Margaret Dukes, Feb. 11, 1944; 1 dau., Margaret Ellen. Formen, Callaway Mills, LaGrange, 1935-39, indsl. engr., 1939-42; div. engr. Blue Bell, Inc., Greenboro, N.C., 1946-52, chief indsl. engr., 1952-61, v.p. engring., 1961-62, v.p. mfg., 1962-68, dir., 1963—, exec. v.p., 1968-73, exec. com., 1968—, pres., 1973—, chief exec. officer, 1974—; dir. Shadowline Inc., Morganton, N.C., Wachovia Bank & Trust Co., Greensboro; mem. So. adv. bd. Arkwright-Boston Ins. Co., 1975—. Bd. dirs. Learning Inst. N.C., 1967-76, treas. bd., 1969-76; mem. presdl. bd. advisers Campbell Coll., 1968-72; bd. dirs. United Community Service, Greensboro, 1974; trustee N.C. Council Econ. Edn., 1975—, Southeastern Legal Found., Inc., 1977—; adv. bd. trustees Guilford Coll., 1964-71; bd. dirs. United Fund of Greensboro, 1964-67. Served to capt. AUS, 1942-46. Mem. Piedmont Asso. Industries (dir. 1962-70, pres. 1966-68), Am. Apparel Mfrs. Assn. (dir. 1972-78, exec. com. 1976-78), Soc. Advancement Mgmt. (adv. council 1971), NAM (dir. 1977—), Nat. Alliance Bus. Men (adv. bd. 1971), Greensboro C. of C. (dir. 1969—), Nat. MS Soc., Civitan Internat. Democrat. Baptist. Club: Sedgefield Country (dir. 1973-76). Office: 335 Church Ct Greensboro NC 27401

MANN, MAURICE, banker; b. Peabody, Mass., Feb. 22, 1929; s. Abram S. and Jennie (Goldberg) M.; B.A., Northeastern U., 1951, LL.D. (hon.), 1977; M.A., Boston U., 1952; Ph.D., Syracuse U., 1955; m. Betty M. Melnick, Sept. 6, 1953; children—Deborah Ellen, Pamela Sue. Asst. prof. econs. Ohio Wesleyan U., 1955-58; financial economist Bur. Old Age and Survivors Ins., Balt., 1958-60; sr. economist Fed. Res. Bank Cleve., 1960-62, sr. monetary economist, 1962-63, v.p., gen. economist, 1963-69; asst. dir. Office Mgmt. and Budget, Washington, 1969-70; exec. v.p. Equibank (formerly Western Pa. Nat. Bank), Pitts., 1970-73; pres. Fed. Home Loan Bank San Francisco, 1973-78; vice chmn., dir. Becker Warburg Paribas, Inc., 1978—, A.G. Becker Inc., 1978—. Mem. nat. alumni council Northeastern U., Boston, 1969—; bd. advisors Applied Fin. Econs. Center, Claremont Men's Coll.; mem. policy advisory bd. Joint Center for Urban Studies Mass. Inst. Tech. and Harvard. Ford Found. fellow, summer 1956. Recipient Alumni citation Northeastern U., 1973, Chancellor's Medal for distinguished achievement in banking Syracuse U., 1977; Distinguished lectr. Claremont Men's Coll., 1978. Mem. Am. Econ. Assn., Am. Finance Assn., Nat. Assn. Bus. Economists, Nat. Economists' Club. Clubs: Commonwealth, Bankers of San Francisco, Concordia-Argonaut. Contbr. articles to profl. jours. Home: 3255 Jackson St San Francisco CA 94118 Office: 555 California St San Francisco CA 94104

MANN, WESLEY PARKER, JR., hobby co. exec.; b. Arlington, Mass., Apr. 23, 1935; s. Wesley Parker and Beatrice Irene (Young) M.; A.B., Northeastern U., 1958; m. Adina Richards, Sept. 14, 1958; children—David Parker, Rhonda Lee. Researcher, Stop & Shop, Inc., Boston, 1958-60; dir. research Elm Farm Foods, Boston, 1960-62; product mgr. Rust Craft Greeting Cards, Dedham, Mass., 1962-66; mgr. H.E. Harris & Co., Inc., 1966-73, pres., 1973—. Bd. dirs. Northeastern U., Adelphi U., Boston council Boy Scouts Am.; trustee C.S.P. Mus. Served with S.C. AUS, 1958. Mem. Am. Stamp Dealers Assn. (past dir.), Am. Acad. Philately, (dir.), Soc. Philatelic Ams., Am. Philatelic Soc., Philatelic Press Club. Home: Curtis Rd Boxford MA 01921 Office: 645 Summer St Boston MA 02210

MANNING, FARLEY, pub. relations counsel; b. Shelburne Falls, Mass., Oct. 30, 1909; s. John Farley and Bessie (Learmont) M.; student Northeastern U., 1927-29, Boston U., 1929-31; m. Ruth Fulton Koegel, Jan. 23, 1932; 1 dau., Toni Ruth. With various New Eng. papers, 1932-43; with Dudley-Anderson-Yutzy, 1946-54; pres. Farley Manning Assos., N.Y.C., 1954-72; pres. Manning, Selvage & Lee, 1972-73, chmn. bd., 1973—; bd. chmn. G & M Creative Services, Inc. 1958—; dir. Bankers Fed. Savs. & Loan Assn. Served to maj. USAAF, 1943-46. Mem. Pub. Relations Soc. Am. Clubs: N.Y. Yacht, Sleepy Hollow Country, Overseas Press. Contbr. articles on dog care and tng. to nat. mags.

MANNING, KENNETH MATELAND, transp. economist; b. Washington, Dec. 2, 1942; s. Everett Mateland and Vera (James) M.; B.B.A., George Washington U., 1964, M.B.A., 1970; m. Geraldine Ann Bell, June 1, 1968; children—Gina Mary, Lisa Margaret. Heavy truck mktg. analyst Ford Motor Co., Washington, 1964-70; chief fin. data analysis Am. Trucking Assn., Washington, 1970-72; dir. econ. research and cost analysis Middle Atlantic Conf., Riverdale, Md., 1972-75; pres. Kenneth M. Manning & Assos., Washington, 1975—, Z-M Corp., Bethesda, Md., 1979—; dir. Diplomat Nat. Bank, Washington, 1978-79, chmn. audit com., 1978-79. Sec., Transp. Research Forum, Washington, 1977-78. Mem. Md. Acctg. and Fin. Council (pres. 1978-80), Nat. Assn. Bus. Economists, Transp. Research Forum, Nat. Acctg. and Fin Council (Assos. prize for best paper 1978), George Washington U. Alumni Assn., Am. Orchid Soc., Phi Eta Sigma, Sigma Chi, Alpha Sigma Epsilon. Clubs: Potomac Tennis, Alfa-Romeo Owners. Contbr. articles to profl. jours. Office: 703 World Center Bldg 918 16 St NW Washington DC 20006

MANNING, KENNETH PAUL, corporate exec.; b. N.Y.C., Jan. 18, 1942; s. John Joseph and Edith Helen (Hoffmann) M.; B.M.E., Rensselaer Polytechnic Inst., 1963; M.B.A., Am. U., 1968; m. Maureen Lambert, Sept. 12, 1964; children—Kenneth J., John J., Elise A., Paul, Carolyn, Jacqueline. Salesman, IBM, 1967-69; prin. CMP Cons., 1969-73; with W.R. Grace & Co., N.Y.C., 1973—, pres. Ednl. products div., 1976-79, pres. real estate div., 1979—. Served to lt. with USNR, 1963-67. Mem. U.S. Naval Inst. Clubs: Union League (N.Y.C.); East India (London). Office: WR Grace Co 1114 Ave Americas New York NY 10036

MANNING, MICHAEL RICHARD, physicist; b. Philadelphia, Mar. 7, 1941; s. Valentine R., Jr. and Frances Bertha (Blanch) M.; B.A. in Physics, Temple U., 1963; Ph.D., U. Pa., 1967. Transmitter engr. CBS, 1960-67; sr. scientist Exide Corp., Yardley, Pa., 1967—; v.p. B.C.A.C. Inc., 1979—. Registered profl. engr., Pa. Mem. Electrochem. Soc., Soc. Automotive Engrs., Eastern Electric Vehicle Assn., Vincent Owners Club, Sigma Pi Sigma. Republican. Roman Catholic. Contbr. articles to profl. jours. Home: 10875 Crestmont Ave Philadelphia PA 19154 Office: 19 W College Ave Yardley PA 19067

MANNING, WILLIAM MARTIN, mfg. co. exec.; b. Yoakum, Tex., Nov. 24, 1922; s. Luey Raymond and Annie Celina (Samora) M.; student Cost Acctg., Baldwin Bus. Coll., Yoakum, 1947-50; m. Aileen Marie Weigelt, Nov. 4, 1942; children—Ralph W., Carolyn Elaine Manning Petru. Shipping clk. Tex. Tan Western Leather Co., Yoakum, 1941-43, mgr. dept. customer service, 1946-63, prodn. mgr., 1963-75, pres., 1975—; dir. Tandy Brands, Inc., Ft. Worth. Served with U.S. Army, 1943-46. Decorated Bronze Star. Mem. Western and English Mfrs. Assn. (dir. 1979-80), Yoakum C. of C. (dir. 1961). Democrat. Roman Catholic. Clubs: Rotary, K. C. Home: 813 Nelson St Yoakum TX 77995 Office: 100 Hickey St Yoakum TX 77995

MANOOGIAN, RICHARD ALEXANDER, mfg. co. exec.; b. Long Branch, N.J., July 30, 1936; s. Alex and Marie (Tatian) M.; B.A. in Econs., Yale U., 1958. Pres. Masco Corp., Taylor, Mich., 1968—, also dir. Clubs: Grosse Pointe Yacht, Grosse Pointe Hunt; Country of Detroit, Detroit Athletic. Home: 204 Provencal Rd Grosse Pointe Farms MI 48236 Office: 21001 Van Born Rd Taylor MI 48180

MANOS, JOHN GEORGE, banker, mayor; b. Paterson, N.J., Oct. 13, 1927; s. George and Katherine (Andrews) M.; student U. Mich., 1947-50, Stonier Grad. Sch. Banking, Rutgers U., 1961-63; m. Anna Konnon, June 6, 1954; children—George, Maria. With Atlantic Bank N.Y., N.Y.C., 1951-69, v.p., 1967-69, sec., 1965-69; v.p. Israel Discount Bank, N.Y.C., 1970-73, sr. v.p., 1973—. Lectr. N.Y. State Banking Dept. Mem. City Council Tenafly (N.J.), 1973-75, mayor, 1976-79. Served with AUS, 1945-47. Recipient Abraham Lincoln Brotherhood award JFK Library for Minorities, 1974, Presidents award St. John the Theologian Greek Orthodox Ch., 1975. Mem. Hellenic Am. C. of C. (dir.), N.Y. Creditmens Assn., Am. Hellenic Ednl. Progressive Assn. (past pres.). Republican. Greek Orthodox. Home: 74 Stonehurst Dr Tenafly NJ 07670 Office: 511 Fifth Ave New York NY 10017

MANSFIELD, RICHARD BLANTON, constrn. co. exec.; b. Greenwood, Miss., Feb. 10, 1938; s. Howard Blanton and Dora Elizabeth Mansfield; B.S. in Accounting, La. State U., 1962; m. Marolyn Sue Orsborn, Feb. 15, 1959; children—Stacey Elizabeth, Richard Blanton. Auditor, Allison Kolb, C.P.A., Baton Rouge, 1962-64; accountant Owen Corning Fiberglas Co., Kansas City, Kans., 1964-65; controller Ted Wilkerson Constrn. Co., Kansas City, Kans., 1965-68, Redman Industries, Kansas City, Kans., 1968-69, Alodex Corp., Memphis, 1969-72, Daniel Internat. Co., San Juan, P.R., 1972-74; owner Osborn-Mansfield Constrn. Co., Memphis, 1974-75; controller H.H. Hall Constrn. Co., East St. Louis, Ill., 1975-78; v.p. fin. Frederick Quinn Group of Constrn. Cos., Arlington Heights, Ill., 1978-79; corp. sec., controller Moritz Corp., Effingham, Ill., 1979—. Served with USMCR, 1957-59. Mem. Nat. Assn. Accountants, Belleville C. of C. Republican. Methodist. Home: 1000 Holly Dr Effingham IL 62401 Office: S 4th Street Rd Effingham IL 62401

MANTELL, KEITH CHARLES, chem. co. exec.; b. N.Y.C., May 3, 1939; s. Charles Letnam and Adelaide Marie Mantell; B.Chem.Engring., Poly. Inst. Bklyn., 1965; m. Leticia M. Carriedo, June 20, 1970; children—Kevin Phillip, Charles Edward. Chem. engr. Air Reduction Co., Middlesex, N.J., 1965-67, Refined Products Co., Lyndhurst, N.J., 1967-68, Clorox Corp., Jersey City, 1968-70; cons. chem. engr., 1970—; pres., dir. Isogenics, Inc., Westwood, N.J., 1973—. Registered profl. engr., N.J., Pa. Mem. AAAS. Republican. Congregationalist. Address: 451 Ridgewood Rd Westwood NJ 07675

MANUEL, BERNARD MARC, electronics mfg. co. exec.; b. Paris, June 9, 1947; s. Andre Alexis and Jeanine (Steel) M.; came to U.S., 1971; M.S. cum laude in Mathematics, U. Paris, 1968, cum laude in Econs., 1970; M.B.A. with high distinction (Baker scholar), Harvard U., 1973; m. Valerie Braunschweig, July 6, 1974; children—Gregory, Vladimir. Lectr. econs. U. Paris, 1968-70; investment analyst Louis-Dreyfus S.A., Paris, 1970-71, asst. to pres. Louis-Dreyfus Corp., N.Y.C., 1973-77; pres. Portescap U.S. Inc., N.Y.C., 1977—. French Govt. scholar, 1971-73, Loeb Rhodes fin. fellow, 1971-72; Melvin T. Copeland awardee, 1971-72. Club: Meadow Brook. Home: 1025 Fifth Ave New York NY 10028 Office: Portescap US Inc 730 Fifth Ave New York NY 10019

MANZI, ALBERT PETER, elec. corp. exec.; b. Lawrence, Mass., Aug. 11, 1917; s. Michael and Angela (Grillo) M.; student Franklin Tech. Inst., 1938, Lowell Tech. Inst., 1941; D.C.S. (hon.), Merrimack Coll., 1962; m. Anna L. Mikolajczyk, Oct. 6, 1951; children—Albert, Annmarie, David, Paul, Lisa. With engring. dept. Pacific Mills, 1935-41, U.S. Naval Shipyard, Pearl Harbor, Hawaii, 1941, planning and engring., Boston, 1941-45; pres., gen. mgr. Manzi Elec. Corp., Lawrence, 1945—; dir. Arlington Trust Co. Lawrence; past incorporator Lawrence Savs. Bank. Pres., Greater Lawrence Bus. Devel. Corp., 1959-66; past mem. adv. bd. Merrimack Coll.; past pres. Lawrence Boys' Club. Decorated Knight of Malta, Knight of Holy Sepulchre (Roman Cath.). Mem. Lawrence C. of C. (dir.), IEEE (sr. mem.), Soc. Am. Mil. Engrs., Nat. Soc. Profl. Engrs., Bon Secours Hosp. Guild. Lion. Home: 440 Great Pond Rd North Andover MA 01845 Office: 217-221 Elm St Lawrence MA 01841

MANZI, LOUIS JOSEPH, found. exec.; b. Riverside, N.J., Nov. 20, 1950; s. William and Frances Angelina (Rizzo) M.; B.A., St. Mary's Sem. Coll., 1972; m. Patricia A. Albano, Nov. 5, 1977. Clk., Public Service Gas & Electric Co., Burlington, N.J., 1972-74; field rep., exec. dir. Am. Cancer Soc., Union, N.J., 1974-78; exec. v.p. Arthritis Found., Phila., 1978—; fund raising cons. Arthritis Found. Reinboth scholar, 1979. Mem. Nat. Soc. Fund Raising Execs., Nat. Pilots Assn. Home: 35 Wellington Pl Burlington NJ 08016 Office: 311 S Juniper St Philadelphia PA 19107

MANZO, SALVATORE EDWARD, univ. adminstr.; b. Bklyn., Oct. 23, 1917; s. Salvatore and Mary (Sireci) M.; B.S., U.S. Mil. Acad., 1939; m. Flournoy Davis, Mar. 11, 1960; children—Janeen, John, Joanne, Molly. Commd. 2d lt. USAF, 1939, advanced through grades to col., 1944, ret., 1962; v.p. C.H. Leavell & Co., El Paso, 1962-65; exec. dir. Met. Airlines Com., N.Y.C., 1965-67; dir. aviation City of Houston, 1967-69; pres. Trans-East Air Inc., Bangor, Maine, 1969-70; aviation mgmt. cons., Bangor, 1970-72, Sao Paulo, Brazil, 1972-74; exec. asst. to pres. Hidroservice, Sao Paulo, 1974-77; asso. Charter Fin. Group, Inc., Houston, 1977-79; dir. exec. devel. Jesse H. Jones Grad. Sch. Adminstrn., Rice U., Houston, 1979—; dir. Ad-Vantage Pub. Co., Houston. Pres., El Paso Indsl. Devel. Corp., 1965; vestryman Christ Ch. Cathedral, Houston, 1979-81. Decorated Silver Star, Legion of Merit, D.F.C. (2), Soldier's medal, Air medal (5), Commendation medal (2); Croix de Guerre with palm (France). Mem. ASCE, Am. Assn. Airport Execs., El Paso C. of C. (pres.). Republican. Episcopalian. Home: 1005 Barkdull St Houston TX 77006 Office: Rice U PO Box 1892 Houston TX 77001

MAR, STEVE, banker; b. Seattle, Nov. 30, 1948; s. Albert K. and Pamalai (Tze) M.; B.A. in Bus., U. Wash., 1971; M.B.A. in Fin., Seattle U., 1977; m. Betty S. Lam, June 12, 1950; 1 son, Andrew M. With First Nat. Bank of Oreg., Portland, 1971-74; EDP auditor Seattle-First, 1974-75, sr. EDP auditor, 1975-78, asst. v.p., 1978-80, v.p., mgr. tech. audit services dept., 1980—. Minority affairs cons. Bellevue (Wash.) Sch. Dist., 1977, chmn. affirmative action advt. com., 1978-79; mem. Citizen Transit Adv. Com. Met. Seattle. Cert. data processing auditor, EDP Auditors Assn. Mem. Alpha Sigma Mu. Office: PO Box 1810 Seattle WA 98111

MARA, WILLIAM FRANCIS, accountant; b. N.Y.C., Sept. 2, 1927; s. John J. and Margaret (Coyne) M.; student Cathedral Coll. of Immaculate Conception, Bklyn, 1945-47; B.B.A., St. John's U., 1954. Clk. accounting dept. Desks, Inc., N.Y.C., 1947-50, 52-54; staff accountant, sr. tax accountant Harris, Kerr, Forster & Co., N.Y.C., 1954-66, supr., 1966, 73-75; tax mgr. Patterson, Teele & Dennis, N.Y.C., 1967-69; tax supr. Alexander Grant & Co., N.Y.C., 1969-72, Hurdman and Cranstoun, N.Y.C., 1972-73; tax mgr. Sperduto, Priskie, Spector & Vanacore, N.Y.C., 1975-77; tax supr. Oppenheim, Appel, Dixon & Co., N.Y.C., 1977-80, Mann, Brown & Baumann, P.C., N.Y.C., 1980—. Served with AUS, 1950-52. Mem. Am. Inst. C.P.A.'s, N.Y. State Soc. C.P.A.'s (pres. Richmond County chpt.), Am. Accounting Assn., Cath. Accountants Guild (pres.), Soc. for Advancement Mgmt., Internat. Platform Assn. Democrat. Home: 1 Lincoln Plaza 20 W 64th St New York NY 10023 Office: Mann Brown & Baumann PC 630 Fifth Ave New York NY 10011

MARANDA, GERALD OMER, banker; b. New London, Conn., Aug. 2, 1936; s. Joseph Marcel and Yvonne Alice (Blain) M.; A.S., Mitchell Coll., 1971; B.A., Conn. Coll., 1975; student Am. Inst. Banking, 1976; m. Janice Ruth Gregory, May 21, 1966; 1 son, Todd Philip. Police officer City of New London (Conn.), 1962-68; asst. treas. Conn. Bank & Trust Co., Hartford, 1968-79; asst. v.p. Peoples Bank, Providence, 1979-80, v.p., regional mgr., 1980—. City councilor, Groton, Conn., 1977—; vice chmn. adv. bd. Salvation Army, 1976—; v.p. Groton Bank Hist. Assn., 1975—; deacon First Ch. of Christ Congl., 1979—; chmn. bd. dirs. Am. Heart Assn., 1973; mem. Groton Rep. Town Com., 1975-77. Served with USN, 1956-60. Mem. R.I. C. of C., Am. Inst. Banking (pres. 1972-74). Republican. Congregationalist. Clubs: Rotary, Lions (pres. 1971-74), Masons, Elks. Home: 97 Church St East Greenwich RI 04818 Office: 145 Westminster St Providence RI

MARASCO, LOUIS JOSEPH, Realtor; b. Jersey City, July 24, 1946; s. Joseph and Maria Josephine (Parisi) M.; B.A., U. Pitts., 1968; postgrad. Hofstra U., 1973; m. Rosemary Lee D'Acunto, July 31, 1971; children—Michelle Marie, Louis Joseph. Personnel adminstr. 1st Nat. City Bank, N.Y.C., 1968-70; adminstr. real estate investment trust Chase Manhattan Bank, N.Y.C., 1970-72; pres. Ramlaw Bldg. Corp., Island Park, N.Y., 1972—; v.p. Walmer Realty, Island Park, 1976—. Licensed real estate broker, N.Y. Mem. Nat. Assn. Real Estate Brokers, L.I. Bd. Realtors, L.I. Builders Assn., N.Y. Realtors Assn., Internat. Platform Assn. Club: Masons. Home: 225 Merrifield Ave Oceanside NY 11572 Office: 4043 Long Beach Rd Island Park NY 11558

MARASH, STANLEY ALBERT, mgmt. cons., corp. exec.; b. Bklyn., Dec. 18, 1938; s. Albert and Esther (Cunio) M.; B.B.A., Coll. City N.Y., 1961; M.B.A., Bernard M. Baruch Coll., 1970; m. Muriel Sylvia Sutchin, June 24, 1961; children—Judith Ilene, Alan Scott. Statistician, Gen. Dynamics/Electric Boat, Groton, Conn., 1961-62, Idaho Nuclear Energy Lab., Idaho Falls, 1962-63; statistician Memory Systems Operation, RCA, Needham, Mass., 1963-64, mgr. quality assurance, Needham, 1964-65; cons. engr. Astro Electronics Div. RCA, Princeton, N.J., 1965-66; corp. mgr. quality assurance, Ideal Corp., Bklyn., 1966-68; mgr. quality assurance, Gen. Instrument, Signalite, Neptune, N.J., 1968; pres. STAT-A-MATRIX, Inc., Edison, N.J., 1968—; pres. STAT-A-MATRIX-INTERNAT., Inc., Edison, 1975—, trustee, mng. dir. STAT-A-MATRIX-INST., 1975—, indsl. tech. and quality tech. adv. coms.; adj. prof. Middlesex County Coll., 1971—; chmn. indsl. adv. com. for statistics dept., Rutgers U., 1977-78; vis. prof. Madrid Poly. U., 1975, Inst. Atomic Energy, U. Sao Paulo, 1974, 75, 77; instr. courses U.S., Am. Mgmt. Assn., 1972—; FDA expert; IAEA; mem. exec. standards council Am. Nat. Standards Inst.; tchr. courses on basic food and drug law FDA; cons. Fellow Am. Soc. Quality Control (chmn. met. sect. 1970-72, founder, edn. chmn. nuclear div., lead speaker biomed. div., mem. examining com., advisor met. sect.); mem. IEEE (sr., condr. courses U.S.), Am. Statis. Assn., ASME, Am. Nuclear Soc., ASTM. Author textbooks: Quality Assurance for the Nuclear Power Industry, 1972, Statistical Quality Control, 1972. Industrial Quality Programs, 1976, Managing Quality Costs, 1975, Nuclear Quality Assurance, 1975, Auditing Nuclear Quality Assurance, 1975, (with Louis I. Korn) Reliability in Nuclear Power Generating Stations, 1974; contbr. articles to profl. jours., presentations to profl. confs. Office: PO Box 2152 Menlo Park Station Edison NJ 08817

MARASHLIAN, RICHARD, real estate cons., appraiser; b. Newark, Jan. 6, 1930; s. Abkar Soukias and Mary (Baghsarian) M.; B.A., Rutgers U., 1951, M.B.A., 1957; m. Nevart Chorbajian, June 29, 1958; children—Richard, Edward, Paul. Sales rep. J.I. Kislak, Inc., 1955-57; real estate sales rep. Parmies-Morristown, 1957-58; pres. R. Marashlian & Co., Verona, N.J., 1958—; adj. prof. real estate Rutgers U., Upsala Coll. Mem. Am. Inst. Real Estate Appraisers, Soc. Real Estate Appraisers, Nat. Assn. Review Appraisers, AAUP, Nat. Assn. Realtors, N.J. Assn. Realtors. Club: Rotary. Home: 32 Brookdale Ave Verona NJ 07044

MARBLE, JAMES WARREN, dairy co. exec.; b. Spencerport, N.Y., Nov. 20, 1912; s. George Butler and Frances Julia (Slayton) M.; student public schs., Syracuse, N.Y.; m. Barbara Lois Faulder, Apr. 9, 1938; 1 dau., Barbara Marble Tagg. Retail milk bus., Syracuse, 1932-40; pres. Marble Farms Dairy, Inc., Syracuse, 1950—; dir. adv. bd. Skaneateles Savs. Bank, 1972-74; dir. Eastern adv. bd. Lumbermen's Mut. Casualty Co., 1970—; dir., sec. Dairy, Food and Nutrition Council, 1973-75; dir., v.p. Dairy Council Central N.Y., 1968-73; pres. Syracuse Milk Distbrs. Bargaining Agy., 1951-57. Mem. Onondaga Indsl. Devel. Corp., 1963—, Metrol. Devel. Assn., 1965-75; trustee Rescue Mission, 1952—, Oakwood Cemetery, 1975—; v.p., trustee N.Y. Council Chs., 1972-80; dir. Americanization League, 1952-75, ARC, 1974-80; pres. bd. trustees 1st Presbyn. Ch., 1975-77, ruling elder, 1971-77; bd. dirs. Meals on Wheels, Syracuse, 1958-78, Community Found., 1976-78; bd. govs. Citizens Found., 1979-80; pres. bd. trustees Big Moose Chapel, 1969-70; pres., chmn. bd. dirs. Urban League, 1962-64; pres. Midtown Hosp., 1957-62, Parents Orgn., Syracuse U., 1968-69; gen. campaign chmn. United Fund, 1967; hon. vice chmn. Onondaga County Republican com., 1964-68; Gov. Averill Harriman appointee to N.Y. State Com. on Refugee Resettlement, 1956; chmn. Syracuse Area Refugee Resettlement Com., 1954-56; bd. govs. Citizens Found., 1950-52; mem. Mayor's Commn. on Crime Study and Law Enforcement, 1965-66; v.p. Syracuse Area Council Chs., 1956-58; chmn. bldg. and expansion fund campaign First Presbyn. Ch., 1954-56, deacon, 1938-42; mem. Inter-Ch. Center Devel. Com., 1966-67. Recipient Outstanding Service award C. of C., 1965; Outstanding Man of Yr. award Syracuse Herald Jour., 1965, Syracuse C. of C., 1965; Syracuse Rotary Club award for community service, 1965; Layman of Yr. award West Genesee Meth. Ch., 1956; Silver Cow award Dairy Industry, 1977, others. Mem. N.Y. Milk Distbrs. (pres., dir. 1978-80), Mfrs. Assn. Syracuse, N.Y. Milk Sanitarians, Syracuse C. of C., Hotel-Motel Assn., N.Y. State Dairy Foods (pres. 1976-80), SAR. Clubs: Kiwanis, Men's, Masons, Syra-Can. Fish and Game (Que.). Home: 107 Windcrest Dr Camillus NY 13031 Office: 1122 Grand Ave PO Box 952 Syracuse NY 13201

MARC-ANTHONY, JAMES FRANCIS, banker; b. Bklyn., Dec. 30, 1937; s. Benjamin and Frances (Boyce) M.; certificate bus. banking Am. Inst. Banking, 1963; B.B.A. in Fin., Pace U., 1969; m. Phyllis Fuoco, May 23, 1964; children—Phyllis, Michael, Patrick, Roseann. Jr. clk. to ofcl. asst. Citicorp, N.Y.C., 1955-69; asst. mgr. Chase Manhattan Bank, N.Y.C., 1969-72, asst. treas., 1972-75, 2d v.p., 1975—. Founder, 1st pres. Chambers-Canal Civic Assn. Inc., N.Y.C., 1974-75, now hon. dir.; pres. O'Brien Assn. Bay Ridge Inc., Bklyn., pres., 1976—. Served with USAR, 1960-65. Republican. Roman Catholic. Home: 1474 76th St Brooklyn NY 11228 Office: Chase Manhattan Bank 1441 Broadway New York City NY 10018

MARCELLE, ALFONSO JAMES, steel co. exec.; b. South Bethlehem, N.Y., 1926; ed. Sienna Coll., 1945, U. Buffalo, 1948. Pres., Callanan Rd. Improvement Co. Inc., 1950-71; pres., chief exec. officer Callanan Industries Inc., 1971—; chmn. bd. Penn-Dixie Industries, Inc., 1977—; chmn. Penn-Dixie Steel Corp. Office: Penn-Dixie Steel Corp 111 S Main St Kokomo IN 46901*

MARCH, NICO D., investment co. exec.; b. Locarno, Switzerland, Sept. 24, 1924; s. Pietro and Julia Marcionni; student U. Zurich, 1944-48; came to U.S., 1948, naturalized, 1950; m. Marion Dispeker, Sept. 1, 1948; children—Michele Dia, Nico Frank. With Merrill Lynch, Pierce, Fenner & Smith, Hollywood, Calif., 1950—, mgr., 1969-70, v.p., 1970—. Office: 450 N Roxbury Dr Beverly Hills CA 90210

MARCHI, JON, investment brokerage exec.; b. Ann Arbor, Mich., Aug. 6, 1946; s. John Robert and Joan Trimble (Toole) M.; student Claremont Men's Coll., 1964-65; B.S., U. Mont., 1968, M.S., 1972; m. Mary Stewart Sale, Aug. 12, 1972; 1 dau., Aphia Jessica. Sec., treas. Marchi Marchi & Marchi, Inc., Morris, Ill., 1968-69; account exec. D. A. Davidson & Co., Billings, Mont., 1972-75, asst. v.p., office mgr., 1976-77, v.p. mktg. and adminstrn., Great Falls, Mont., 1977—; sec., dir. D. A. Davidson Realty Corp., Great Falls, 1978—; dir. Taurus Oil Corp., Denver, Big Sky Airlines, Billings. Served with U.S. Army, 1969-71. Mem. Securities Industry Inst. Episcopalian. Clubs: Glacier Racquet, Ski, Mont., Rotary, Helena Wilderness Riders. Home: 1926 Cherry Dr Great Falls MT 59404 Office: D A Davidson & Co 16 3d St N Great Falls MT 59401

MARCHMAN, RAY ELLIS, JR., banker; b. Miami, Fla., Oct. 19, 1933; s. Ray Ellis and Mabel (Parr) M.; B.A., Emory U., 1955; J.D., U. Miami, 1961. Admitted to Fla. bar, 1961; legal asst. Gov. Fla., Tallahassee, 1961; practiced in Miami, 1961-62; asst. sec. trust dept. No. Trust Co., Chgo., 1962—, 2d v.p., 1965-68, v.p. charge personal fin. planning div., 1968-77; exec. v.p., head trust dept. 1st Nat. Bank Atlanta, 1977—. Mem. faculty Nat. Trust Sch., Evanston, Ill. Treas., Chgo. Easter Seal Soc., 1964, pres., 1973-77, now dir.; mem. adv. bd. Morehouse Coll.; trustee U. Miami (Fla.); vice chmn. Atlanta Ballet. Served to 1st lt. USAF, 1955-57. Mem. Am. Judicature Soc., Ill., Chgo. bar assns., Am. Bankers Assn. (mgmt. com.), Bank Mktg. Assn., Trust Council (chmn.), Atlanta Estate Planning Council (dir.), Omicron Delta Kappa, Alpha Tau Omega, Pi Sigma Alpha, Wig and Robe, Delta Theta Phi. Clubs: Chgo. Athletic Assn.; Capital City (Atlanta). Home: 4269 Sentinel Post Rd NW Atlanta GA 30327 Office: 2 Peachtree St Atlanta GA 30303

MARCRUM, JAMES ALEX, chem. co. exec.; b. Evansville, Ind., Dec. 20, 1944; s. Mearyon Leonard and Julia Ann (Johnson) M.; student Gen. Motors Inst., 1963-64; A.B., Ind. U., 1968; m. Jane Alice Chaffin, Feb. 12, 1977; children—Monica Lyn, J. Alex. With Reilly Tar & Chem. Co., Indpls., 1966-67; service technician Betz Labs., Kokomo, Ind., 1967-68, dist. engr., area salesmgr., Louisville, 1968-73, dist. mgr., Pitts., 1973-75; sales mgr. Betz Entec, Houston, 1975-77; exec. v.p. Thermionics, Inc., Doylestown, Pa.; cons. to water treatment service cos. Recipient award Ind. Soc. Profl. Engrs. Mem. AIME, Iron and Steel Soc., Nat. Assn. Plant Engrs., Eastern States Blast Furnace and Coke Oven Assn. Club: Champions Golf (Houston). Home: PO Box 1039 Flemington NJ 08822 Office: Thermionics Inc 100 Doyle St Doylestown PA 18901

MARCUM, JOSEPH LARUE, ins. co. exec.; b. Hamilton, Ohio, July 2, 1923; s. Glen F. and Helen A. (Stout) M.; B.A., Antioch Coll., 1947; M.B.A. in Fin., Miami U., Oxford, Ohio, 1965; m. Sarah Jane Sloneker, Mar. 7, 1944; children—Catharine Ann, Joseph Timothy, Mary Christina, Sarah Jennifer, Stephen Sloneker. With Ohio Casualty Ins. Co. and affiliated cos., Hamilton, 1947—, pres., dir. all cos. Mem. library bd.; mem. Human Relations Bd. Butler County. Served to capt., inf. U.S. Army, 1943-46. C.P.C.U. Mem. Soc. C.P.C.U. (past nat. dir.), Am. Inst. Property and Liability Underwriters (trustee), Ohio C. of C. (v.p.). Presbyterian. Clubs: Queen City, Bankers (Cin.); Canadian, Met. (N.Y.C.); El Dorado Country (Indian Wells, Calif.); Little Harbor, Walloon Lake Country. Home: 475 Oakwood Dr Hamilton OH 45013 Office: Ohio Casualty Ins Co 136 N 3d St Hamilton OH 45025

MARCUS, ALAN C., public relations cons.; b. N.Y.C., Feb. 26, 1947; s. Percy and Rose (Fox) M.; student Hun Sch., Princeton, 1966; m. Judith Lamel, June 21, 1979. Dir. pub. relations Bergen County Republican Com., Hackensack, N.J., 1968; clk. N.J. Gen. Assembly, Trenton, 1969, sec. to majority party of assembly, 1970; pres. Alan C. Marcus Assos., Newark, 1971—, The Marcus Group, Inc., Newark, 1976—. Trustee Nat. Leukemia Assn., 1976—, Hun Sch. of Princeton, 1977—, Passaic River Coalition, 1980—, Garden State Ballet Found. Recipient Youth Enterprise award Jim Walter Corp., 1972. Mem. Pub. Relations Soc. Am. (N.J. chpt. pres.'s award 1975, past pres. and dir. N.J. chpt. 1976-77), N.J., Greater Newark chambers commerce, N.J. Broadcasters Assn., N.J. Press Assn. Clubs: Capitol Hill (Washington); Essex; Apple Ridge Country. Office: 60 Park Pl Newark NJ 07102

MARCUS, BRUCE WILLIAM, fin. cons. co. exec., author; b. N.Y.C., July 18, 1925; s. Louis David and Pauline (Lewis) M.; B.A. in Philosophy and Econs., New Sch. Social Research, 1951; m. Mana Balter, Nov. 27, 1962; children—David, Michael, Jonathan, Joseph, Lucy. Sr. asso. Ruder & Finn, Inc., N.Y.C., 1958-65, Mobil Corp., N.Y.C., 1965-67; pres. Bruce W. Marcus Co., N.Y.C., 1967-72, Campbell-Marcus, Inc., N.Y.C., 1968-71; sr. v.p. Fin. Relations Bd., Inc., N.Y.C., 1972-77; pres. QOT Corp., N.Y.C., 1973-77; v.p., dir. 333 West End Ave. Corp. dir. ESP, Inc. Mem. mayor's adv. com. emergency housing, N.Y.C., 1972. Served with USAAF, 1941-46. Recipient Silver Anvil award Pub. Relations Soc. Am., 1957, Lucy Stoner award, 1959. Mem. New Sch. Social Research Alumni Assn. (dir.). Author: Competing for Capital, 1976, rev., 1980; Living With Pension Funds, 1981; Business Today, 1981; The Prudent Man, 1978; The Capital Markets, 1981; The President's Task Force Report on Women Business Owners, 1978; Marketing for Professional Services in Real Estate, 1981. contbr. articles to mags. Home: 333 West End Ave New York NY 10023

MARCUS, TERRY LEE, concrete mfg. co. exec.; b. Charles Town, W.Va., Dec. 9, 1946; s. Charles Calvin and Vivian Wenonah (McKee) M.; B.S. in Bus. Adminstrn. and Accounting, W.Va. U., 1970; m. Glenda Felyce Behar, Sept. 5, 1971 (dec. 1975); 1 son, Heath Lance; m. 2d, Judy Ann Walker, Dec. 17, 1978. Staff accountant Dan Harmon & Assos., Martinsburg, W.Va., 1970-71; pres. Turf Enterprises, Inc., Charles Town, 1971—; sec., dir. So. Courts, Inc., 1970—, Panhandle Devel. Corp., 1973—; sec., dir. Sales Devel. Corp., 1974—; pres., dir. Fox Glen Utilities, Inc., 1976—; partner Panhandle Investment Assos., 1973—. Mem. Jefferson County Economic Devel. Corp., 1977—. Mem. Charles Town Jaycees (treas., dir. 1971-73), Nat. Ready-Mix Concrete Assn., Nat. Home Builders Assn., Builders Supply Assn. W.Va., Jefferson County C. of C. Democrat. Episcopalian. Home: 813 Belvedere Dr Charles Town WV 25414 Office: 608 E Washington St Charles Town WV 25414

MARDER, WILLIAM ZEV, mech. engr., engring. co. exec.; b. Phila., Nov. 4, 1947; s. Isadore Myron and Nancy Annette (Segall) M.; B.S. in Mech. Engring., U. Pa., 1970, B.A., 1970; m. Mona Marlene Kaufman, June 28, 1970. Div. mgr. Kulicke and Soffa Industries, Horsham, Pa., 1972-74; pres. Zevco Enterprises, Inc., Penllyn, Pa., 1974—; sr. devel. engr. Air Shields, Inc., Hatboro, Pa., 1977-78; mem. tech. staff RCA, Princeton, N.J., 1978—. Patentee self-priming centrifugal pump, knife sharpener. Home and office: 147 S Main St Pennington NJ 08534

MARDIAN, SAMUEL, JR., constrn. exec., city ofcl.; b. Pasadena, Calif., June 24, 1919; s. Samuel Z. and Akabe (Lekerian) M.; A.A., Pasadena Jr. Coll., 1941; B.C.S., Southwestern U., 1941; m. Lucy Keshian, Dec. 1, 1942; children—Samuel, James Kenneth, Carol Ann, Douglas David, Steven Kermit. Auditor, Haskins & Sells, C.P.A.'s. 1947; exec. v.p. Mardian Constrn. Co., pres., 1978-79, chmn., chief exec. officer, 1979—; sec.-treas. Glen-Mar Door Mfg. Co., 1947-72, pres., 1972-79, chmn. bd., 1979—; dir. 1st Nat. Bank Ariz. Campaign mgr. Gov. Pyle, Republican party, 1954; mayor City of Phoenix, 1960-64; chmn. campaign com. U.S. Senator Paul Fannin, 1964, 70; chmn. Ariz. Com. for Re-election Pres., 1972; bd. dirs., mem. exec. com. YMCA of Phoenix and Valley of the Sun, 1951-71, pres., 1965-67, mem. Pacific S.W. area bd., 1957-66, pres. Pacific S.W. area council, 1962-63, mem. nat. council, 1962-66; mem. internat. com. of U.S. and Can., 1954-59; chmn. research com. Ariz. Acad. Pub. Affairs, 1968-72, mem. exec. com., 1968-75; treas. Citizens Assn. Ariz. Cts., 1968—; trustee Madison sch. dist., 1957-59; bd. dirs. Phoenix Symphony Assn., 1959-71, v.p., 1962-64; exec. bd. Roosevelt council Boy Scouts Am.; trustee Phoenix Fine Arts Assn., 1965-76, treas., 1968, v.p., 1970-76; pres. Valley Beautiful Citizens Council, 1967-69; v.p. Valley Forward Assn., 1969-75, pres., 1975-77, chmn. bd., 1977-79; trustee Haigazian Coll., Beirut, 1964—; bd. dirs. Ariz. Kidney Found., 1964-67, State Compensation Fund Ariz., 1969-71, Hosp. Devel. Assn. Maricopa County, 1964-65; bd. dirs. Combined Phoenix Met. Arts, 1966-76, chmn. gifts com., 1970-72, pres., 1972-74; chmn. Maricopa County Citizens Action Com., 1971-73, Ariz. State Salary Commn., 1980—; mem. dean's adv. council Coll. Bus. Adminstrn., Ariz. State U., 1968-71; mem. Ariz.-Mex. Commn., 1972—, Phoenix Salary Commn., 1979—. Served from pvt. to capt. Signal Corps, USAAF, 1941-46. Mem. Phoenix Met. C. of C. (dir. 1970—, v.p. 1971-72, pres. 1973-74), Am. Municipal Assn. (exec. com. 1962-63, chmn. personnel com. 1962-63), Newcomen Soc. N. Am., Ariz. Acad., Beta Gamma Sigma (hon.). Club: Valley of the Sun Kiwanis (dir. 1959). Methodist (exec. com., chmn. fin. commn.; pres. bd. trustees 1960-62, chmn. ofcl. bd.). Home: 7310 N 4th Dr Phoenix AZ 85021 Office: 3815 N Black Canyon Hwy Phoenix AZ 85015

MARGOLIS, DAVID ISRAEL, corporate exec.; b. N.Y.C., Jan. 24, 1930; s. Benjamin and Celia (Kosofsky) M.; B.A., Coll. City N.Y., 1950, M.B.A., 1952; postgrad. N.Y. U., 1952-55; m. Barbara Schneider, Sept. 7, 1958; children—Brian A., Robert M., Peter I., Nancy P. Security analyst Josephthal Co., 1952-56; asst. treas. Raytheon Co., 1956-59; treas. ITT, N.Y.C., 1959-62; now pres., dir. Colt Industries, Inc. Mem. N.Y. State Emergency Fin. Control Bd., N.Y.C., 1975-77. Bd. dirs. Istel Fund, Inc. Mem. Fin. Execs. Inst. Office: 430 Park Ave New York NY 10022

MARIC, MILE MIKE, elec. engr.; b. Becanj, Yugoslavia, Oct. 21, 1943; s. Momir and Rada (Glisic) M.; B.A.S., Pacific Western U., 1980; postgrad. Windsor U., 1980-81; m. Danica Stankovic, Aug. 16, 1964; children—Sanja, Don, Susan. Plant maintenance supt. Kelsey-Hayes, Windsor, Ont., Can., 1969-79; pres., dir. Miles Electric Co., Windsor, 1973-77; sr. elec. engr. GM Can., Windsor, 1979—. Cert. engring. technologist and technician. Mem. Soc. Mfg. Engrs., IEEE, Profl. Engrs. Can., Engring. Soc. Detroit, Robotic Internat. (Soc. Mfg. Engrs.), Pacific Western U. Alumni Assn., Can. Royal Legion. Orthodox. Office: GM Canda 1487 Walker Rd Windsor ON N8W 2N8 Canada

MARIK, J. EUGENE, ins. broker; b. E. Bernard, Tex., July 15, 1928; s. John I. and Josephine (Spacek) M.; B.S. in Commerce, St. Edwards U., 1950; m., May 29, 1952; children—Melinda, John Patrick, Celeste, Marshall. Owner Marik Ins. Agy., East Bernard, Tex., 1950—. Lic. real estate broker, life ins. broker. Mem. Ind. Ins. Agts. Assn., East Bernard Chamber of Commerce and Agriculture (pres. 1968-70). Democrat. Roman Catholic. Clubs: East Bernard Recreation, K.C. Office: Marik Insurance Agency 707 S Main St East Bernard TX 77435

MARIN, GEORGE EDWARD, computer systems engr.; b. Phila., Aug. 29, 1950; s. George Anthony and Evelyn Lorraine (Harbert) M.; A.A.S., Montgomery County Coll., 1971; B.S. cum laude, Point Park Coll., Pitts., 1973; postgrad. Lehigh U., Bethlehem, Pa., Villanova (Pa.) U.; m. Susan Clare Nolan, June 27, 1970; children—Steven William, Michael Frederick. Dir. Rotelle Mgmt., Inc., Spring House, Pa., 1973—, mgr. info. systems, 1977—. Mem. Eastern Montgomery County Area Vocat. Tech. Sch. Data Processing Craft Com., 1974—. Mem. Data Processing Mgmt. Assn. (past chpt. sec.). Designer computer systems. Home: 1332 Highland Ave Fort Washington PA 19034 Office: Rotelle Mgmt Inc Bethlehem Pike Spring House PA 19477

MARINO, FRANK JOSEPH, sales and mktg. exec.; b. N.Y.C., May 7, 1937; s. Joseph and Gemma (D'Onofrio) M.; student L.I. U., 1955-57, Pratt Inst., 1958, Windward Community Coll., 1975-76; m. Irene Cheselka, Sept. 9, 1967; 1 dau., Catherine. Adminstrv. asst. Internat. Minerals & Metal Corp., N.Y.C., 1958-66; v.p. Princess Prestiege Corp., Lynbrooke, N.Y., 1966-72; pres. Maci Home Products Co., Ridgewood, N.Y., 1972-74; v.p. Habilitat Sales & Mktg., Kaneohe, Hawaii, 1974—. Chmn., Aikahi Park Fee Assn., 1979—. Served with U.S. Army, 1954-55. Mem. Advt. Splty. Inst., Splty. Advt. Assn. Internat., Sales and Mktg. Inst., Kaneohe Bus. Group, C. of C., Better Bus. Bur. Roman Catholic. Author: Success in Sales, 1975; also composer songs. Home: 223 Aiokoa St Kailua HI 96734

MARION, ELLIOT, mag. publishing exec.; b. Bklyn., Mar. 27, 1925; s. Benjamin and Fay (Dunaier) M.; student N.Y. U., 1946-48; B.A., Queens Coll., 1962; m. Barbara Shapiro, Oct. 30, 1955; children—Scott Fredric, David Laurence, Amy Beth. Sales rep. Jr. League Mag., N.Y.C., 1952-55, Seventeen Mag., N.Y.C., 1955-60; retail sales mgr. Glamour Mag., N.Y.C., 1960-72; pub. New Ingenue Mag., N.Y.C., 1973-75; adv. dir. Brides's Mag., N.Y.C., 1975-77; Mademoiselle Mag., N.Y.C., 1977—. Active Cub Scouts Am., Jericho, N.Y., 1963-65; v.p., mgr. Jericho Little League, 1965-69; v.p. Temple Or'Elohim, 1968-73. Served with USN, 1943-46. Home: 21 Montgomery Pl Jericho NY 11753 Office: 350 Madison Ave New York NY 10017

MARION, RICHARD ARTHUR, corp. fin. exec.; b. Cornwall, Ont., Can., Sept. 28, 1944; s. Emile Ludger and Blanche Albina (Brunet) M.; R.I.A., C.P.M. in Indsl. Acctg., McMaster U., Hamilton, Ont., 1973; m. Denise Lavictoire, Oct. 28, 1967; children—Daniel, Dominique. Chief acct. Woodland div. Domtar, Ltd., Cornwall, Ont., 1965-69, div. acct. Trucking div., Montreal, Que., 1970; office supr. USS Cons. of Can. div. U.S. Steel, Montreal, 1971; property investment acct. Standard Life Assurance Co., Montreal, 1972-75; dir. fin. Trans-Que. Realties, Inc. and Affiliates, Montreal, 1976—; officer, dir. 14 cos.; instr. acctg. Registered indsl. acct.; cert. property mgr. Mem. Soc. Indsl. Accts. (past dir. Montreal chpt.), Inst. Real Estate Mgmt. (past v.p.), Montreal Real Estate Bd., Can. Inst. Real Estate Mgmt., Assn. des administrateurs immobiliers du Quebec. Home: 85 Elgin Crescent Villa 559 Beaconsfield PQ H9W 2B3 Canada Office: 505 Sherbrooke St E Montreal PQ H2L 1K2 Canada

MARK, RICHARD CLINTON (DICK), realty exec., home builder developer, farmer; b. Cedar Falls, Iowa, July 21, 1940; s. Wayne Clinton and Dorothy Alice (Durham) M.; A.B. in Psychology, Westmar Coll., 1962; M.Div., Garrett-Evang. Theol. Sem., 1972; postgrad. Sch. Bus., U. No. Iowa; m. Peggy Marie Irving, June 8, 1966; children—Andrew, Jonathan, Christopher. With Mark Realty, Inc., Cedar Falls, 1962—, owner, pres., 1976—; owner, pres. Castle Corp., Cedar Falls, 1977—; pres. Woodland Homes Ltd., Cedar Falls, 1978—; v.p., partner Tree Farm, 1978—; owner, operator Mark Farms, 1976—; bus. cons. Inst. Cultural Affairs, Chgo. Pres. Hansen Sch. PTA, Cedar Falls, 1977-78; pres. Cedar Falls PTA Council; state dir., program coordinator Town Meeting, Iowa Program; mem. Black Hawk Assn. for Retarded Citizens. Grad. Realtor Inst. Iowa; cert. residential specialist, real estate brokerage mgr.; recipient leadership award Nat. PTA, Iowa's Outstanding PTA Unit, 1978. Mem. Nat., Iowa assns. Realtors, Waterloo-Cedar Falls Bd. Realtors, Iowa Farm and Land Inst., Realtors Nat. Mktg. Inst., Profl. Farms Am., Cedar Falls C. of C., Nature Conservancy, Soil Conservationists Am., Profl. Builders, Cedar Falls Hist. Soc. Mem. Christian Ch. (Disciples of Christ). Clubs: Cedar Falls Rotary, Beaver Hills Country, Order Eastern Star, Masons, Shriners, K.T. Home: 5829 N Union Rd Cedar Falls IA 50613 Office: 419 Washington St Cedar Falls IA 50613

MARK, SIDNEY CARL, broadcasting exec.; b. N.Y., Feb. 27, 1914; S. Henry and Sarah (Berkowitz) M.; B.A., Coll. City N.Y., 1934; M.A. in English, U. Tulsa, 1974; m. Patricia Greenfield, Jan. 18, 1946; children—Priscilla, Jonathan Greenfield, Mary Alice, Sarah Edna, Henry Greenfield. Announcer, producer radio sta. WHN, N.Y., 1935; spl. events prodn. mgr., radio sta. WHK-WCLE, Cleve., 1937-43; radio-TV dir. Al Paul Lefton Co., 1943-48; pres., gen. mgr., radio sta. WTTM, Trenton, N.J., 1948-53; pres. Swern & Co. (Lit Brothers), Trenton, 1954-62; chmn., pres. Mark/way, Inc. (Radio Stas. KAKC-AM and KBEZ-FM in Tulsa, 1962-80, KFUN-AM, KLVF-FM in Las Vegas, N.Mex.); dir. Bankers Bond & Mortgage Co. Am.; dir. Broad St. Nat. Bank, Trenton, 1957-63, Bonwit Teller Co., Phila., 1957-62; instr. radio-TV announcing and prodn. Western Res. U., also City Coll. N.Y., 1937-53. Chmn., Trenton Planning Bd., 1955-59; v.p. Trenton Philharm. Soc., 1953-63, Del. Valley United Fund, 1954-56; bd. dirs. Greater Phila.-S. Jersey Council, 1949-53; trustee Greater Trenton Council, 1956-62; bd. dirs. Tulsa chpt. ARC, Tulsa Recreation Center for Physically Ltd., Tulsa Philharmonic Soc., Inc., Downtown Tulsa Unlimited, Arts and Humanities Council Tulsa; trustee Tulsa Performing Arts Center Trust; bd. dirs., v.p. Jr. Achievement Tulsa, Tulsa Better Bus. Bur.; pres. Concertime Tulsa; chmn. Tulsa Met. YMCA; pres. Tulsa Ballet Theater, Inc.; finance chmn. Boy Scouts; mem. adv. council Salvation Army, Tulsa; mem. Jewish Community Council; trustee Fenster Gallery Jewish Art. Pres. N.J. Broadcasters Assn., 1951-52. Mem. Mensa. Clubs: Tulsa, Tulsa Petroleum, Tulsa Tennis, Tulsa Rotary. Home: 6766 S Columbia Ave Tulsa OK 74136

MARK, STEPHEN, street light brackets mfg. co. exec.; b. Evanston, Ill., July 1, 1920; s. Clayton and Gladys Agnes (Stevens) M.; student U. Va., 1938-40; M.E., Ill. Inst. Tech., 1942; m. Ann Sternberg, Nov. 11, 1944; children—Stephen, Clayton Louis. Asst. engr. Clayton Mark & Co., well supplies, 1942-45; civil engr. Sternberg Dredging Co., 1945-48; civil engr. Inland Steel Co., Indiana Harbor, Ind., 1948-58; civil engr. expressway bridges, dredging City of Chgo., 1958-63; v.p., sec. Kram Metal Products Co., Glenview, Ill., 1963-66, pres., treas., 1966—. Mem. Chgo., Glenview chambers of commerce, Field Mus. Natural History, Sigma Alpha Epsilon. Republican.

Methodist. Clubs: Masons, Mid America, Valley Lo. Home: 327C Greenleaf Ave Wilmette IL 60091 Office: PO Box 10 3148-C W Lake St Glenview IL 60025

MARKARIAN, NOUBAR, textile co. exec.; b. Larnaca, Cyprus, Dec. 15, 1922; s. Paul and Gulenia (Torikian) M.; came to U.S., 1938; student Coll. S. Murat, Sevres, France, 1935-38; B.S., Sch. Engring., Columbia, 1944; m. Judith Armistead Isley, Feb. 23, 1946; children—Judy, Beverly, Linda, Nancy, Amy, Richard. Partner, v.p. Mark Knitting Mills, Bergenfield, N.J., 1945—; v.p. Valette Undergarments, Inc., Fajardo, P.R., 1958-61; sec.-treas. Johnson Corp., Bergenfield, N.J., 1961—. Vice chmn. bd. dirs., No. Valley chpt. A.R.C.; v.p. bd. trustees Dwight Sch., Englewood, N.J. Mem. Internat. House Assn. Episcopalian. Clubs: Bay Head (N.J.) Yacht; Englewood (N.J.) Field; Rotary (pres. Bergenfield 1962-63), Columbia Alumni of Bergen County (pres. 1957-58); Columbia of N.Y.; Mantoloking (N.J.) Yacht. Home: 71 Franklin St Englewood NJ 07631 Office: 26 Palisade Ave Bergenfield NJ 07621

MARKEN, CLINTON CRAY, mfrs. sales rep.; b. Hampton, Iowa, Aug. 2, 1945; s. Gideon A. and Cleone M.; student Area 10 Community Coll., 1967-69; B.S., Iowa State U., 1971; m. Diane C. Marken; children—Melanie Anne, Brandi Christen. Seedman, Com. Agrl. Devel., Iowa State U., Ames, 1971-72; field man Arco Chem. Co., Grafton and Rockwell, Iowa, 1972-73, plant mgr., 1973; sales rep. FMC Corp., Hampton, Iowa, 1973—. Served with USAF, 1963-67. Mem. Iowa Cattle Assn., Am. Quarter Horse Assn., Iowa State U. Alumni Assn. Home: Rural Route 2 Box 50 Hampton IA 50441

MARKHAM, CHARLES ROLLA, convenience stores exec., frozen pizza mfg. co. exec.; b. East St. Louis, Ill., Nov. 28, 1935; s. L.D. and Eleanor Louise (Collins) M.; student John Carroll U., 1955-59; grad. in mgmt. Ga. State U., 1967-72; m. Claire E. Cochran, June 29, 1957; children—Michelle, Leslie, Larry, Michael, Sharon. Tng. mgr. Munford Inc., Atlanta, 1967-68, dist. mgr., 1968-69, adminstrv. dir., 1970-74; ops. mgr. Unico Majik Markets Inc., State College, Pa., 1975-77, v.p., 1977-79; exec. v.p. ops. Unico Corp., State Coll., 1980—, also dir.; dir. Economy Wholesale, Altoona, Pa. Pres., State College PTA, 1979-80. Mem. Nat. Assn. Convenience Stores, Frozen Food Mfg. Inst., S.C. Area Booster Club, Toastmasters Internat. (past pres.). Republican. Roman Catholic. Home: 1743 Circleville Rd State College PA 16801 Office: Unico Corp 477 E Beaver St State College PA 16801

MARKHAM, PHILIP NATHAN, chem. co. exec.; b. Corning, Kans., Mar. 11, 1930; s. Robert Smith and Ethel Mabel (Miles) M.; children—Robert Smith II, Scott Dean. Public acct. Carl L. Kopp & Co., Cleve., 1952-59; office mgr. Universal Paint & Varnish, Inc., Bedford, Ohio, 1959-63; div. controller Am. Petrochem. Corp., Wooster, Ohio, 1964-69; group staff asst. coating and chems. group Whittaker Corp., Mpls., 1969-75, div. gen. mgr. Colton Coatings and Chem. div. (Calif.), 1975—. Mem. City Council, Zoning Commn., Betterment Fedn., Macedonia, Ohio, 1961-63. Served with USCG, 1950-53. Office: Colton Coatings and Chem div Whittaker Corp PO Box 825 1231 S Lincoln Colton CA 92324

MARKHAM, STEPHEN CHARLES, fin. co. exec.; b. Derby, Conn., May 29, 1927; s. Stephen David and Pauline Mary (Rumble) M.; B.Ed., U. Miami, 1952; grad. Exec. Program, Grad. Sch. Mgmt., UCLA, 1976; m. Mary Ellen Donovan, Jan. 27, 1962; children—Colleen, Mary Kate, Megan. Regional mgr. Electro Technology, N.Y.C., 1966-70; asso. pub. Wire & Wire Products, N.Y.C., 1970-71; exec. v.p., dir. Job Market Publs., Inc., N.Y.C. and Phila., 1971-73; pres. Sports Digest, Inc., Greenwich, Conn., 1973-74; v.p. indsl. and community relations Litton Data Systems, Inc., Van Nuys, Calif., 1974-80; v.p. planning and devel. Pension Home Loan Corp., Torrance, Calif., 1980—, also dir.; guest lectr. UCLA, 1977—, pres. bd. dirs. Exec. Program Assos., 1979-80. Community bd. dirs. Northridge (Calif.) Hosp. Served with USN, 1945-46. Mem. Am. Mktg. Assn., U. Miami Alumni Assn., Friendly Sons St. Patrick of Los Angeles, UCLA Alumni Assn. Republican. Roman Catholic. Clubs: Westlake Yacht; Crockford's Empress (London); So. Calif. Yachting Assn. Home: 32136 Beachfront Ln Westlake Village CA 91361 Office: 21535 Hawthorne Blvd Suite 300 Torrance CA 90503

MARKIDES, GEORGE MICHAEL, hotel exec.; b. Nicosia, Cyprus, Feb. 3, 1924; s. Michael S. and Helen (Charalambous) M.; diploma Samuel's Practical Comml. Sch., Nicosia, 1942, R.R.C. Inst. Hotel Mgmt., London, Eng., 1947; diploma with profl. tng. Ecole Hoteliere de la S.S.H., Lausanne, Switzerland, 1951; m. Martha (Minouche) J.B. Caviezel, Jan. 12, 1952; children—Helena, Michael. Gen. mgr., organizer Govt. Hotels, Island of Rhodes, Greece, 1952; gen. mgr. Hotel Le Capitole, also project mgr. Hotel Beirut, Commodore, Beirut, Lebanon, 1955-57; mgmt. indoctrination Hilton Hotels Internat., N.Y.C., Houston, Hartford, Conn., 1957-58; with Inter-Continental Hotels Corp., 1958-73, mgr. Hotel Jaragua Inter-Continental, Dominican Republic, 1958-59, gen. mgr. Hotel Curacao Inter-Continental, Willemstad, Curacao, 1959-67; mng. dir. Inter-Continental Hotels (Netherlands Antilles) N.V., 1966-67; gen. mgr. Hotel Inter-Continental Quito (Ecuador), 1967-68, Hotel Inter-Continental Manila (Philippines), 1968-70, Hotel Inter-Continental Paris (France), 1970-72, Portman Inter-Continental, London, Eng., 1972-73; v.p. Canadian Pacific Hotels Ltd., 1973-76, sr. v.p., 1976-79; pres., chief exec. Amber Internat. Hotels, 1979-80; hotel cons., 1980—. Bd. govs. Chamber of Tourism, Philippines, 1969-70. Decorated comdr. Sovereign Greek Order St. Dennis of Zante; knight Greek Orthodox Order Holy Sepulchre; Medaille d' Honneur (Argent) de la Société d'Encouragement au Progrès, Paris, 1972; chevalier de l'Ordre des Coteaux de Champagne; recipient Gold medal Société de l'Excellence Européenne. Mem. Caribbean Hotel Council (pres. 1961-62), Caribbean (hon. mem., v.p. 1962-67), Curacao (founder pres. 1967), Inter-Am., Internat. hotel assns., Caribbean Travel Assn. (hon. mem., dir. exec. com. 1964-67), Hotel Assn. Philippines (v.p. 1969-70), Brit. Hotel and Restaurant Assn., Confrérie des Chevaliers du Tastevin, Confrérie de la Chaine des Rotisseurs, Hotel Sales Mgmt. Assn., Comite de Patronage de l'Ecole Hotelière de Lausanne, l'Association des Anciens Elèves de L'Ecole Hotelière de la S.S.H. (Lausanne), Lausanne Hotel Mgmt. Sch. Assn. U.S.A.; allied mem. Am. Soc. Travel Agts. Club: Rotary. Address: Avenue Juste Olivier 23 CH-1006 Lausanne Switzerland

MARKLEY, HERBERT EMERSON, bearing co. exec.; b. Elmore, Ohio, Oct. 5, 1914; s. Henry J. and Amelia (Wilde) M.; B.S. in Bus. Adminstrn., Miami U. Oxford, Ohio, 1938; LL.B., William McKinley Sch. Law, Canton, Ohio, 1943; m. Nancy Mulligan. June 22, 1946; children—Sheila, Herbert James, Maura, Noreen. Admitted to Ohio bar, 1943; with Timken Co., Canton, 1938—, exec. v.p., 1959-68, pres., 1968-79, chmn. exec. com., 1979—; dir. Firestone Tire & Rubber Co., Am. Electric Power Co. Trustee, Case Western Res. U. Served with AUS, 1943-46. Mem. NAM (dir. 1967—, chmn.), Conf. Bd. (sr.) Republican. Methodist. Clubs: International (Washington); Congress Lake (Hartville, Ohio); Union (Cleve.); Downtown Athletic (N.Y.C.); Canton Brookside Country (Canton); Ocean Reef (Fla.). Office: Timken Co 1835 Dueber Ave SW Canton OH 44706*

MARKOWITZ, GAIL EUNICE, advt. and sales exec.; b. N.Y.C., July 20, 1937; d. Morris and Barbara (Schwartz) Schechter; B.A., Queens Coll., 1959; children—Matt, Jami. Vice-pres. sales Fla. Atlantic Devel. Corp., Forest Hills, N.Y., 1973-75; v.p. Fla. Atlantic Advt., Inc., Forest Hills, 1973-75, Webb Realty, Inc., Forest Hills, 1973-75; pres. advt. firm, Jericho, N.Y., 1975; v.p. Minieri Communities, Inc., Met-Com Mktg., Inc., Hicksville, N.Y., 1975—; cons. advt., sales promotion, Jamaica Estates, N.Y., 1959—; v.p. Fla. Atlantic Devel. Corp., 1973-75, Minieri Communities Corp., 1975-78; speaker, cons. on Fla. Housing for Minieri; pres., owner, broker operator GJM Realty, Inc., Flushing, N.Y., 1978—, GM Mktg., Inc., Flushing, 1978—; sales dir. N.Y. model home program Gen. Devel. Corp., N.Y.C., 1980—. Pres., PTA, 1967-69; v.p. Orgn. for Retarded Children, 1965-73; chmn. Israel Bonds, 1969. Mem. Advt. Women N.Y., Com. 100, Nat. Home Builders Assn., Nat. Bd. Realtors, N.Y. Bd. Realtors, L.I. Bd. Realtors. Republican. Jewish. Contbr. articles to profl. publs. Home: 184-50 Hovenden Rd Jamaica Estates NY 11432 Office: 190-19 Union Turnpike Flushing NY 11366

MARKS, ALBERT AUBREY, JR., broker; b. Phila., Dec. 19, 1912; s. Albert A. and Edythe (Lilian) M.; grad. Harrisburg (Pa.) Acad., 1928; student Williams Coll., 1928-30; B.S., U. Pa., 1932; m. Elizabeth Merriel Cramer, Jan. 20, 1939; children—Albert Aubrey III, Christina M., Robert B.; m. 2d, Mary Kay Marks. Gen. partner Newburger & Co. (now Newburger div. Advest Co.), Phila., 1934-42, Atlantic City, 1946—; dir. Guarantee Bank & Trust Co., Atlantic City, Anchor Savs. & Loan Assn. Allied mem. Am., N.Y., Phila., Balt. stock exchanges. Vice pres. N.J. Mid-Atlantic Farm Show, 1952-54; dir. Atlantic City Conv. Bur., 1951-54, treas., 1962—; chmn. Atlantic County Improvement Authority, 1975—; pres. Miss Am. Pageant, 1962-64, chmn. bd., 1966—; chmn. Boardwalk Adv. Commn., mem. Bd. Edn., Margate, N.J.; vice chmn. Com. Adult Edn. So. N.J.; pres. Atlantic County Community Chest and Welfare Council, 1953; gen. campaign chmn. Community Chest, 1956; former pres. 4-Club Council; mem. exec. council Boy Scouts Am., Atlantic County; trustee So. N.J. Devel. Council, 1951-54; mem. N.J. Legislative Study Commn., Securities Adv. Com. N.J. State, Conflict Interest Com.; chmn. Com. of Fifty, 1970-74. Bd. govs. Betty Bacharach Rehab. Center. Served from 2d lt. to lt. col. USAAF, 1942-46. Named Citizen of Year, Atlantic City, 1967. Mem. Investment Bankers Assn., Security Traders Assn., Nat. Assn. Security Dealers, Assn. Stock Exchange Firms, Atlantic City (pres. 1952-53, So. N.J. (chmn. devel. council 1951-54) chambers commerce, Atlantic City Centennial Assn. (v.p. 1953-54), Mil. Order World Wars (companion), Res. officers Assn., Air Force Assn., Newcomen Soc., Pa. Soc. Episcopalian. Mason. Clubs: Kiwanis (pres. 1954), Press. Haddon Hall Racquet, Osborne Beach; Williams, Marco Polo (N.Y.C.). Home: 1 N Osborne Ave Margate NJ 08402 Office: 20 S Tennessee Ave Atlantic City NJ 08401

MARKS, EDWIN S., securities dealer; b. N.Y.C., June 3, 1926; s. Carl and Edith R. (Smith) M.; student Princeton U., 1944-45; B.S., U.S. Mil. Acad., 1949; m. Nancy Lucille Abeles, June 21, 1949; children—Carolyn Gail, Linda Beth, Constance Ann. Commd. 2d lt. U.S. Army, 1949, 1st lt., 1951, ret., 1953; v.p. Carl Marks & Co., N.Y.C., 1958-61, pres., 1961—, also dir.; exec. v.p., dir. CMNY Capital Co., Inc., 1962—. Mem. fin. com. Lincoln Center, 1978-79; trustee Hofstra U., 1974-79, Sarah Lawrence Coll.; asso. trustee North Shore Univ. Hosp., Manhasset, N.Y. Mem. Nat. Assn. Securities Dealers (mem. fgn. com.), West Point Soc., N.Y. Bd. Trade, Mexican, Philippine-Am. chambers commerce. Club: Harmonie (N.Y.C.). Author: What I Know About Foreign Securities, 1958. Home: 15 Eagle Point Dr Kings Point NY 11024 Office: 77 Water St New York NY 10005

MARKS, HOWARD LEE, advt. exec.; b. Cleve., Feb. 7, 1929; s. Archie M. and Belle (Parets) M.; student Ohio State U., 1946-48, Western Res. U., 1948-50; children—Melissa R., Andrew D. Pres. Howard Marks Advt., Inc., Cleve., 1956-64; pres. Howard Marks Advt., Norman Craig & Kummel, Inc., N.Y.C., 1964-68; v.p. Norman, Craig & Kummel, Inc., N.Y.C., 1964-68; pres. Howard Marks Advt., Inc., N.Y.C., 1968—; chmn. Marks/Aucoin Prodns., Inc., N.Y.C., 1972—; pres. Hicks Marks Advt., Inc., London, Eng., 1971—; pres. Silver Mint Inc.; pres. Glickman/Marks Mgmt. Corp., N.Y.C., 1976—. Chmn., United Appeal, Cleve., 1963, Cleve. Jewish Welfare Fund Campaign, 1962-64. Trustee Cleve. Jewish Community Fedn.; bd. dirs. Cleve. Jewish Community Center, Cleve. Jewish Vocational Service, Cleve. Community Fund, United Appeal. Served with AUS, 1951-53. Mem. Zeta Beta Tau, Am. Jewish Com. Mem. B'nai B'rith. Home: 254 E 68th St New York NY 10021 Office: 655 Madison Ave New York NY 10021

MARKS, JAMES JOHN, restaurateur, developer; b. Chgo., Aug. 23, 1911; s. Nicholas John and Stella (Koufogiani) M.; B.S., U. Mich., 1936; m. Christine Constance Tampary, Nov. 11, 1939; children—Lianna Sandra, James John. Forestry technician U.S. Forestry Service, Ava, Mo., 1934; forest supr. Mich. Conservation Dept., Lansing, 1934-35; cons. forester, Ann Arbor, Mich., 1936-37; owner Martine's Restaurant, Pensacola, Fla., 1942—, Martine's Ice Cream Co., Pensacola, 1942—; pres. Esquire House, Warrington, Fla., 1934—, Martine's, Pensacola, 1947—, Marwood Motors, Pensacola, 1955—, Ky. Fried Chicken, Biloxi and Gulfport, Miss., 1964—, Ky. Fried Chicken, Mobile, Ala., 1964—, New Orleans, 1967—, Col. Sanders Ky. Fried Chicken Corp., 1970—; sec.-treas. Circle Sanitation, Pensacola, 1959—. Mem. adv. bd. Fla. Hotel and Restaurant Commn., 1961-62; mem. bd. Fla. Hospitality Edn. Program, 1962-63; chmn., pres. Fla. Tourism Council, 1962-63; mem. Fla. Council of 100, 1963—, mem. exec. com.; mem. council advisors U. W.Fla., 1975—; advisor to council advisors Univ. System Fla.; mem. Baptist Hosp. Health Care Found., 1975—, vice chmn. exec. com., 1976—. Served to comdr. USNR, 1937-45. Named Outstanding Fla. Restaurateur, 1964. Mem. Am. Restaurants Hall of Fame, 1961. Mem. Nat., Fla. (pres. 1961-62) restaurant assns., Sales Execs. Club. Mem. Hellenic Christian Orthodox Ch. (v.p. parish council 1976). Rotarian (past local pres., Paul Harris fellow). Clubs: Toastmasters; Mobile Country; Pensacola Country. Home: 4002 Marlane Dr Pensacola FL 32506 Office: 4101 Mobile Hwy Pensacola FL 32506

MARKS, RICHARD HAROLD, banker; b. N.Y., May 16, 1945; s. Leonard Kenneth and Hermina M.; B.S., Cornell U., 1967, M.B.A., 1968; m. Carol Anne Cummings, Sept. 26, 1970; children—Lenore Anne, Rose Arnold. Fin. analyst Ford Motor Co., 1968-70, mktg. coordinator, 1970-72; various positions Citibank N.A., N.Y.C., 1973-76; v.p., fin. controller Citibank AG, Frankfurt, W. Ger., 1977—. Office: Grosse Gallusstrasse 16 6000 Frankfurt am Main 1 Federal Republic Germany*

MARKS, SOHIER DAVID, bullion mcht.; b. Boston, Mar. 3, 1931; s. Abe and Ida (Davidson) M.; B.S., Tufts U., 1952; postgrad. Grad. Sch. Design, Harvard, 1953; M.B.A., Northeastern U., Boston, 1963; m. Elaine Brody, June 30, 1957; children—Rebekah, Erik. Div. mgr. Texas Instruments, Inc., Attleboro, Mass., 1965-72; pres. Pramecta Corp., Walpole, Mass., 1972-74; v.p. Mocatta Metals Corp., N.Y.C., 1974—. Chmn. parents council U. Rochester (N.Y.), 1980—; conservation commr., Westwood, Mass., 1967-73. Served with AUS, 1954-56. Registered profl. engr., Mass. Mem. Silver Inst. (dir.), Gold Inst. (dir.). Clubs: Williams, Sheldrake Yacht. Office: 4 World Trade Center New York NY 10048

MARKSON, EDWARD ELDAR, computer co. exec.; b. Boston, Apr. 14, 1933; s. Robert T. and Marion (Rosenfeld) M.; B.S.A.E., Rensselaer Poly. Inst., 1955; M.S.A.E., So. Meth. U., 1961; children—Edward E., Charles B. Engr., Convair, Ft. Worth, 1957-61; sr. engring. specialist Martin Co., Balt., 1961-65; sr. mem. tech. staff System Scis. Corp., Falls Church, Va., 1965-66; tech. dir. Geonautics, Inc., Washington, 1966-69; center dir. Computer Scis. Corp., Jacksonville, Fla., 1969-79; pres. Computerias, Ltd., 1979—; vis. lectr. George Washington U.; mem. adj. faculty U. North Fla. Contbr. articles to tech. jours. Home: 4208 San Servera Dr S Jacksonville FL 32217

MARKWORT, LOTHAR, rehab. center exec.; b. Auerbach, Germany, Dec. 19, 1927; came to Can., 1952, naturalized, 1957; s. Gerhard Max and Elisabeth (Wolfrum) M.; student Nat. Inst. on Mental Retardation; m. Ingeborg Schebitz, Feb. 3, 1954; 1 dau., Patricia. Psychiatric nurse Alta. Hosp., Edmonton, 1952-61, psychiat. social worker, 1961-70; dir. Sheltered Workshop, Mental Health Services, Edmonton, 1970—; German-Can. radio program dir. CHFA, Edmonton, 1955-62. Served with German Army, 1944-45. Mem. Provincial Council Psychiat. Nurses Assn. Alta. (registrar 1972—), Alta. Assn. Rehab. Centres (treas./chmn. edn. com.). Lutheran. Clubs: Schlaraffia Internat., Friends of Berlin, Masons (32 deg.). Home: 26 Andrew Crescent Saint Albert AB T8N 2V3 Canada Office: 7305 99th St Edmonton AB T6E 3R7 Canada

MARLAS, JAMES CONSTANTINE, mfg. co. exec.; b. Chgo., Aug. 22, 1937; s. Constantine J. and Helen (Cotsirilos) M.; A.B. cum laude, Harvard, 1959; M.A. Jurisprudence, Oxford U., 1961; J.D., U. Chgo., 1963; m. Kendra S. Graham, Aug. 24, 1968 (div. 1971). Admitted to Ill. bar, 1963, N.Y. bar, 1966; asso. firm Baker & McKenzie, N.Y.C. and London, Eng., 1963-66; exec. v.p. S.E. Commodity Corp., N.Y.C., 1967-68; chmn. Union Capital Corp., N.Y.C., 1968—; vice chmn. Mickelberry Corp., N.Y.C., 1970-71, dir., pres., chief exec. officer, 1972—; chmn., chief exec. officer Newcourt Industries, Inc., 1976—; chmn. bd. Bowmar Instrument Corp. Bd. dirs. N.Y.C. Opera, AMIC-Manhattan Sch., Blue Cross Blue Shield Greater N.Y. Mem. Am. Fgn. Law Assn., Young Pres.'s Orgn., UN Assn. U.S.A. Clubs: Execs. (Chgo.); American, Boodle's (London); Racquet and Tennis (N.Y.C.). Editor: Univ. Chgo. Law Rev., 1962-63. Office: 405 Park Ave New York NY 10022

MARLER, JOHN ROBERT, fin. co. exec.; b. Amarillo, Tex., Nov. 18, 1944; s. John Roscoe and Betty Ione (Ames) M.; B.S. in Criminology, W.Tex. State U., 1966, M.B.A., 1969; m. Sally Ann Tubman, May 1, 1971; children—John Lee, James Gary, Joshua Robert. Regional mgr. Apache Airlines, Las Vegas, Nev., 1971-73, Litton Industries Premiercol div., 1973-76; pres. chmn. bd. Credicom Corp., Campbell, Calif., 1976—; chmn. bd. Marcomp, Inc., 1977—, Micromark, Inc., 1979—. Bd. dirs. BFAE Internat. Served to capt. U.S. Army, 1969-71. Mem. Comml. Law League Am. Republican. Mem. Christian Ch. Asso. editor Kilobaud mag., 1978. Home: 6351 Almaden Rd San Jose CA 95120 Office: 100 W Rincon Ave Campbell CA 95008

MARLETT, DE OTIS LORING, real estate exec.; b. Indpls., Apr. 19, 1911; s. Peter Loring and Edna Grace (Lombard) M.; B.A., M.A., U. Wis., 1934; postgrad. Northwestern U., part time 1934-39; postgrad. Harvard U. (Littauer fellow in econs. and govt.), 1946-47; m. Ruth Irene Pillar, Apr. 10, 1932 (dec. Feb. 1969); children—De Otis Neal, Marilynn Ruth; m. 2d, Marie Manning Ostrander, May 1, 1970. Staff mem. Ill. Commerce Commn., 1934-39; lectr. in econs. and pub. utilities Northwestern U., part time 1936-39; staff mem. Bonneville Power Adminstrn., U.S. Dept. Interior, 1939-45, asst. adminstr., 1945-52; acting adminstr. Def. Electric Power Adminstrn., 1950-51; asst. to v.p., also gen. mgr. Dicalite and Perlite divs. Gt. Lakes Carbon Corp., 1952-53, v.p., also gen. mgr. Mining and Mineral Products div., 1953-62, v.p. Property Investment dept., 1962—; pres., dir. Del. Amo Properties Co.; dir., pres. Great Lakes Properties, Inc.; dir., v.p. Rancho Palos Verdes Corp., G.L.C. Bldg. Corp.; v.p. Gt. Lakes Carbon Internat. Ltd.; gen. mgr. Palos Verdes Properties; dir. Immobiliaria Nazarena, S.L. Past mem. Calif. State Mining Bd.; mem. Western Govs. Mining Adv. Council; bd. govs. western div. Am. Mining Congress, chmn. div., 1962-63. Past bd. dirs. United Cerebral Palsy Assn. Los Angeles County; nat. trustee, bd. dirs., past co-chmn. So. Calif. region NCCJ; past bd. dirs. So. Calif. Choral Music Assn.; trustee City of Hope; dir., past pres. Los Angeles area council, past vice chmn. regional com. Region XII, past chmn. Western region relationships com. Boy Scouts Am., now pres. Western region, also mem. nat. exec. com.; bd. dirs. United Way. Recipient Distinguished Service medal U.S. Dept. Interior, 1952; named knight Order of Crown (Belgium); commd. Ky. Col. Mem. Fin. Execs. Inst., Los Angeles World Affairs Council, Wis. Alumni Assn., Perlite Inst. (past pres., dir.), Am. Inst. Mining and Metall. Engineers, Los Angeles C. of C. (past dir., chmn. mining com.), Mining Assn. So. Calif. (past pres., dir.), Calif. Mine Operators Assn. (dir.), Bldg. Industry Assn., UN Assn. U.S.A., Town Hall, Phi Kappa Phi, Beta Gamma Sigma, Phi Beta Kappa, Beta Alpha Psi. Democrat. Clubs: Rotary, Calif., Portuguese Bend (pres.), Cave des Roys, Internat., Rolling Hills Country. Contbr. articles and reports on public utility regulation, operation and management, 1935-39. Home: 3200 W LaRotonda Dr #318 Rancho Palos Verdes CA 90274 Office: 3838 Carson St Suite 220 Torrance CA 90503

MARLOW, BRUCE ABBEY, communications co. exec.; b. Hartford, Conn., Dec. 1, 1946; s. George Henry and Wilma Ruth (Dubin) M.; grad. Loomis Sch., 1965; A.B. cum laude, Tufts U., 1969; M.B.A., Columbia, 1971. Dir. merchandising and product mgmt. RCA Records, N.Y.C., 1971-73; dir. mktg. Novo Corp., N.Y.C., 1973-74; exec. v.p., chief ops. officer Novo Communications, Inc., N.Y.C., 1974-76, pres., chief exec. officer, 1976-79; chmn., chief exec. officer Starcom, Inc., N.Y.C., 1979—. Mem. Am. Mgmt. Assn., Am. Mktg. Assn., Columbia U. Club. Home: 319 E 85th St New York NY 10028 Office: Starcom Inc 45 Sutton Pl S Suite 10 New York NY 10022

MARLOW, HAROLD JAMES, contract archtl. bldg. material co. exec.; b. Redfield, S.D., July 11, 1934; s. Harold LeRoy and Gladys Irene (Larson) M.; B.S., S.D. Sch. Mines and Tech., 1961; m. Marlys Frances Smith, Sept. 1, 1957; children—Harold James, Michael Francis, Deborah Kay. Prodn. engr. Remington Rand Univac, St. Paul, 1961-63; package engr. 3M Co., St. Paul, 1963; contract hardware mgr. Midwest Builders Supply Co., Rapid City, S.D., 1963-65; div. mgr. archtl. products div. R & S Lumber Co., Rapid City, 1965-67; pres., gen. mgr. Engring. Specialities, Inc., Rapid City, 1967—, also dir.; partner R & E Enterprises, Rapid City, 1975—. Served with USAF, 1952-56. Mem. Nat. Assn. Wholesalers, Asso. Gen. Contractors Assn., Rapid City C. of C. Republican. Presbyterian. Club: Arrowhead Country, Optimist. Home: Suburban Route Box 174 Rapid City SD 57701 Office: Box 538 Industrial Blvd Rapid City SD 57709

MARMALUK, JOSEPH, business exec.; b. Jermyn, Pa., Sept. 28, 1929; s. Efrem and Mary (Wartonick) M.; B.S., U. Scranton, 1955; m. Delores L. Wilcha, Sept. 5, 1953; children—Gregory J., Daria A. Sr. mgr. Price Waterhouse & Co., Pitts., 1955-67; dir. financial controls Crucible Steel Co., Pitts., 1967-69; sr. v.p., dir. Korman Corp., Jenkintown, Pa., 1969-74; pres. Shelter Mgmt. Inc., 1974-78; mng. partner Investors Group Ltd., Phila., 1974-78; pres., chief exec. officer Life Care Soc. of Am., Inc., 1978—. Served with U.S. Army, 1951-53. C.P.A., Pa. Mem. Am. Inst. C.P.A.'s, Pa. Inst. C.P.A.'s. Home: 3922 Bradford Rd Huntingdon Valley PA 19006 Office: 115 E State St Doylestown PA 18901

MAROPIS, NICHOLAS, metal fabricating co. exec.; b. Slovan, Pa., May 14, 1923; s. Speros N. and Argero (Skinakis) M.; A.B. in Physics and Math., Washington and Jefferson Coll., 1949; postgrad. U. Md., 1950-51, U. Del., 1956-57; M.S. in Engring., Pa. State U., 1967; children—Samuel, Colin, Janice, Michelle. Physicist Naval Ordinance Lab., White Oak, Md., 1950-53; physicist, project engr. R.M.Parsons Co., Ft. Dietrich, Md., 1953-55; project engr., v.p., Aeroprojects, Inc., West Chester, Pa., 1955-72; v.p. engring. Uniform Tubes, Inc., Collegeville, Pa., 1972-76; v.p. UTI Inc., 1976—; instr. physics Am. U., 1952; cons. AEC, NASA, 1967-70. Active Methodist Ch., PTA, 1960-65. Served with USAF, 1943-45. Recipient commendations moon program NASA, 1966, Ultrasonic Engrs. Soc., 1971. Mem. Acoustical Soc. Am., Franklin Inst., Am. Phys. Soc. Democrat. Condr. research high powered ultrasonic energy; patentee fields of ultrasonic equipment and electronic circuitry. Home: 715 W Phillip Dr Phoenixville PA 19460 Office: 200 W 7th Ave Collegeville PA 19426

MAROUS, JOHN CHARLES, JR., elec. mfg. co. exec.; b. Pitts., June 9, 1925; s. John Charles and Mary Ellen (Ley) M.; B.S. in Elec. Engring., U. Pitts., 1949, M.S., 1953; m. Lucine O'Brien, May 25, 1957; children—Julia, John, Leslie. With Westinghouse Elec. Corp., 1949—, gen. mgr. 5 divs., 1970-72, exec. v.p. constrn. group, 1973-79, pres. Westinghouse Elec. Corp. Internat. Co., Pitts., 1979—. Bd. dirs. Allegheny County chpt. ARC. Served with AUS, 1943-46. Mem. Bus. Council Internat. Understanding (vice chmn., dir.), Council Fgn. Relations (dir.), Nat. Fgn. Trade Council (dir.), Internat. C. of C. (trustee U.S. council), Fgn. Policy Assn. (asso.), World Affairs Council Pitts., Conf. Board (internat. council), U. Pitts. Engring. Alumni Assn. (pres.). Republican. Roman Catholic. Clubs: Allegheny, Duquesne, Pitts. Field, Congressional Country, Laurel Valley Golf. Author papers in field. Office: Westinghouse Elec Corp Westinghouse Bldg Pittsburgh PA 15222

MARQUARD, WILLIAM ALBERT, diversified mfg. co. exec.; b. Pitts., Mar. 6, 1920; s. William Albert and Anne (Wild) M.; B.S., U. Pa., 1940; m. Margaret Thoben, Aug. 13, 1942; children—Pamela, Suzanne, Stephen. With Westinghouse Electric Corp., Pitts. and Mexico City, 1940-52; with Mosler Safe Co., Hamilton, Ohio, 1952-67, sr. v.p., 1961-67, pres., 1967-70; with Am. Standard Inc., N.Y.C., 1967—, sr. exec. v.p., 1970, pres., chief exec. officer, 1971—, chmn. bd., 1979—; dir. Chem. N.Y. Corp., Chem. Bank; Shell Oil Co., NL Industries Inc., N.Y. Life Ins. Co. Trustee, Citizens Budget Commn., N.Y.C., Com. Econ. Devel., U. Pa., N.Y. Infirmary-Beckman Downtown Hosp.; bd overseers Wharton Sch.; mem. Bus. Com. for the Arts; bd. dirs. Nat. Minority Purchasing Council; mem. Corp. for Support Pvt. Univs. Mem. Conf. Bd. (sr.), Brit.-N-Am. Com. Home: Gen Delivery Quoque NY 11959 Office: 40 W 40th St New York NY 10018

MARQUIS, DONALD KENNETH, mfg. co. exec.; b. Toronto, Ont., Can., Jan. 13, 1926; s. Donald MacLachlan and Dorothy Emily (Vaughan) M.; chartered acct., 1949; children by previous marriage—Donald Blake, Grant Lawrence. Mgr., Touche Ross Co., 1949-55; v.p. fin. Carling O'Keefe Ltd., Toronto, 1955-70; v.p. adminstrn. Guaranty Trust Co., Toronto, 1970-73; v.p. fin. Dominion Bridge Ltd., Montreal, Que., Can., 1974-76; owner, pres. Burrowes Mfg. Ltd., Toronto, 1977—. Pres., Red Cross Toronto, 1968, Goodwill Soc., 1966; trustee O'Keefe Centre, 1968-74, Scarboro Centenary Hosp., 1962—. Fellow Inst. Chartered Accts. Conservative. Anglican. Clubs: Rosedale Golf, Scarboro Golf and Country. Home: 241 Cassandra Blvd Don Mills ON M3C 1V3 Canada Office: 65 Bellwoods Ave Toronto ON M6J 287 Canada

MARRA, JAMES EDWARD, fin. economist; b. Albany, N.Y., Oct. 21, 1948; s. Harry W. L. and Sara Edna (Rothermel) M.; B.A., Johns Hopkins U., 1970; M.B.A., Am. U., 1973; cert. Inst. in Arts Adminstrn., Harvard U., 1973. Asst. to chmn. bd. Sun Life Ins. Co. Am., Balt., 1970-71; dir. pub. affairs Mktg. Policy Inst., Washington, 1974-75; dir. Internat. Econs. and Fin. Inst., Washington, 1976-79; dir. The Potomac Found., Inc., McLean, Va., 1980—. Founder, chmn. Music Forum, internat. music ednl. orgn., Washington, 1977—.

MARRAZZO, JOSEPH GENNARO, life ins. agy. exec.; b. Steelton, Pa., Oct. 15, 1935; s. Giuseppe and Angelina (Librandi) M.; student Harrisburg (Pa.) Area Community Coll., 1975, 76; C.L.U., 1977; m. Nancy J. Wheaton, Jan. 29, 1955; children—Joanne M., Joseph Gennaro, Michael J., David W., Stephen A., Paul R. Salesman, Electrolux Sales Corp., 1956-60; debit agt., then ins. cons. salesman Met. Life Ins. Co., 1960-73; pres. Profl. Adv. Corp., Harrisburg, 1973—. Fin. chmn. St. Catherine Athletic Assn., Harrisburg, 1968-72, pres., 1973, wrestling commr., 1974—, pres. Legion of Mary, 1966-72; pres. Bishop McDevitt High Sch. Athletic Assn., 1980-81. Mem. Gen. Agts. and Mgrs. Conf. (pres. 1981-82), Harrisburg Assn. Life Underwriters, Harrisburg Assn. C.L.U.'s, Estate Planning Council Harrisburg, Harrisburg Area C. of C. Democrat. Roman Catholic. Author articles. Office: 4905 Derry St Harrisburg PA 17111

MARRIE, THOMAS PHILLIP, banker; b. N.Y.C., Feb. 13, 1938; s. Thomas Philip and Mary Astrid M.; B.E.E., Manhattan Coll., 1960; M. Engring., Yale U., 1962; M.S. in Indsl. Mgmt., M.I.T., 1964; m. Elizabeth Scheeman, June 11, 1971. Asst. to pres. W.R. Grace Co., 1964-67; econ. adv. Rockwell Internat., 1967-69; dir. fin. analysis Fireman's Fund Ins. subs. Am. Express Co., 1969; dir. fin. analysis Am. Express Co., N.Y.C., 1970-71, v.p. planning, 1972-76; with Am. Express Internat. Banking Corp., N.Y.C., 1977—, sr. v.p., chief fin. officer, 1979—. Office: Am Express Internat Banking Corp American Express Plaza 125 Broad St New York NY 10004

MARRINGA, JAKOB-JACQUES LOUIS, mfg. co. exec.; b. Rotterdam, Netherlands, Aug. 8, 1928; came to U.S., 1965; s. Jakob and Christine Antoinette (Van Der Valk) M.; Degree in Econs., Erasmus U., Rotterdam, 1949, Degree in Bus. Adminstrn. 1954; m. Joan Kathryn Potter, Oct. 23, 1965; children—Jakob W., Robert H., Kathryn J. Asst. regional dir. N.V. Philips, 1956-61; product line mgr. ITT, Brussels, N.Y.C., 1961-70; v.p., dir. internat. ops. Elco Corp., Willow Grove, Pa., 1970-72, Crouse Hinds Co., Syracuse, N.Y., 1972-77; v.p. Water Treatment and Internat. divs. Sta-Rite Industries, Inc., Milw., 1977—; pres. Sta-Rite Overseas Corp., Delavan, Wis., 1977—. Served with Royal Dutch Army, 1949-51. Clubs: Milw. Country; White Lake Yacht. Home: 2520 W Dean Rd River Hills WI 53217 Office: Sta-Rite Industries Inc 777 E Wisconsin Ave Milwaukee WI 53202

MARRIOTT, JOHN WILLARD, restaurant and motel exec.; b. Marriott, Utah, Sept. 17, 1900; s. Hyrum Willard and Ellen (Morris) M.; grad. Weber Coll., Ogden, Utah, 1922; A.B., U. Utah, 1926; LL.D. (hon.), Brigham Young U., 1958; m. Alice Sheets, June 9, 1927; children—John Willard, Richard Edwin. Franchise holder A. & W. Root Beer Co., Washington, 1926-28; pres. Marriott Corp. (formerly Hot Shoppes, Inc.), 1928-64, now chmn., dir.; dir. Am. Motors Corp., Detroit, Riggs Nat. Bank, Chesapeak & Potomac Telephone Co. Mem. commrs. adv. planning bd. Fed. City Council. Bd. govs. United Service Orgns. Recipient Hall of Fame award Am. Restaurant Mag., 1954; Achievement award Advt. Club, 1957; award Am. Mktg. Assn., 1959; U. Utah, 1959; Chain Store Age award, 1961; Businessman of Yr. award Religious Heritage Am., 1971; Capt. of Achievement award Am. Acad. Achievement, 1971; Mem. NAM (dir.), Com. for Econ. Devel. (trustee), Washington Bd. Trade (dir.), Nat. (pres. 1948), Washington (pres. 1939, 43) restaurant assns. Mem. Ch. of Jesus Christ of Latter-Day Saints (pres. Washington stake 1948-57). Clubs: Burning Tree (Bethesda, Md.); Indian Creek Country (Miami Beach, Fla.); Bald Peak Colony (Melvin Village, N.H.); Columbia Country (Chevy Chase, Md.); Paradise Valley Country (Ariz); Washington Admirals, Capitol Hill (Washington). Home: 4500 Garfield St NW Washington DC 20007 Office: care of Marriott Corp 5161 River Rd Bethesda MD

MARRON, DONALD BAIRD, investment banker; b. Goshen, N.Y., July 21, 1934; s. Edward Joseph and Ethel (Baird) M.; student Baruch Sch. Bus., 1949-51, 55-57; m. Gloria Swope, June 19, 1961; children—Jennifer Ann, Donald Baird. Investment analyst N.Y. Trust Co., N.Y.C., 1951-56, Lionel D. Edie Co., N.Y.C., 1956-58; mgr. research dept. George O'Neill & Co., 1958-59; pres. D.B. Marron & Co., Inc., N.Y.C., 1959-65; co. combined with Mitchell, Hutchins & Co., Inc., 1965, pres., former chief exec. officer; chmn. bd. Data Resources, Inc., Lexington, Mass.; now pres., chief exec. officer Paine Webber Inc., N.Y.C. Bd. dirs. N.Y. Stock Exchange; trustee, chmn. exec. com. Mus. Modern Art; trustee Calif. Inst. Arts, Valencia, Dana Found., Trust for Cultural Resources of N.Y.C. Mem. Council Fgn. Relations, Securities Industry Assn. (former dir.), Young Presidents Orgn. Clubs: Economic Down Town Assn., Recess, Bond, Regency Whist, Maidstone, (East Hampton, N.Y.); River (N.Y.C.). Home: 791 Park Ave New York NY 10021 Office: 140 Broadway New York NY 10005

MARROW, HARVEY LEWIS, equipment co. exec.; b. Le Fore, Okla., Sept. 17, 1934; s. John L. and Cleo (Anderson) M.; student schs., Panama, Okla.; m. Darlene Eather, 1955; children—Kathlene, Deborah. Office supplies salesman, Reno, Nev., 1955-57; constrn. worker, San Francisco, 1957-73; mgr. Equipment Sales & Rental, Sacramento, 1973-80; pres. Bay-Cal Equipment, Livermore, Calif., 1980—. Served with USAF, 1951-55. Clubs: Rotary, Elks. Home: 2580 Pendleton Dr El Dorado Hills CA 95630 Office: 5328 Naylor St Livermore CA 94550

MARRUS, STEPHANIE KRISTINA, mgmt. cons.; b. N.Y.C., Apr. 25, 1947; d. Rick and Elsie M.; A.B., Cornell U., 1968; M.A., Columbia U., 1969. Market research analyst Gen. Foods Co., White Plains, N.Y., 1969-70; project supr. Haug Assos., Los Angeles, 1970-72; dir. mktg. and sales support, sr. mktg. analyst Dart Industries, Los Angeles, 1972-74; mgr. product planning and devel. TRW Info. Services, Long Beach, 1974-76, mgr. nat. accounts, profit center mgr., 1975-76; mgmt. cons. Arthur D. Little Co., Cambridge, Mass., 1976-78; dir. market planning Ogden Food Service Corp., Boston, 1978-80; mgr. market devel. Atex, Inc., Bedford, Mass., 1980—. Home: 9 Warren St Winchester MA 01890 Office: 15 Wiggins Ave Bedford MA

MARSH, DON E., supermarket exec.; b. Muncie, Ind., Feb. 2, 1938; s. Ermal W. and Garnet (Gibson) M.; B.A., Mich. State U., 1961; m. Marilyn Faust, Mar. 28, 1959; children—Don Ermal, Arthur Andrew, David Alan, Anne Elizabeth, Alexander Elliott. With Marsh Supermarkets, Inc., Yorktown, Ind., 1961—, pres., 1966—, also dir.; officer, dir. Nationwide Land, Inc., Am. Guaranty, Inc., Universal Tank & Iron Works, Inc., Circle Valley Farms, Marsh Drugs, Inc., Mundy Realty, Kokomo Land, Inc., Mchts. Nat. Bank Muncie, Village Pantry, Inc.; officer Kokomo Land, Inc. Bd. dirs. Ball State U. Found.; officer, bd. dirs. Central Ind. Retail Council, Food Industry Good Govt. Mem. Ind. C. of C. (dir.), Delaware County C. of C., Newcomen Soc. N.Am., Internat. Assn. Food Chains, Ind. Retail Grocers Assn., Nat. Assn. Convenience Stores, Am. Mgmt. Assn. (gen. mgmt. council), Young Pres.'s Orgn., Food Merchandisers Edn. Council, Food Mktg. Inst., Ind. Soc. Chgo., Am. Bus. Club, Phi Sigma Epsilon, Lambda Chi Alpha. Presbyterian. Clubs: Columbia (Indpls.); Delaware Country (Muncie); Rotary, Masons, Elks. Home: 1250 Warwick Rd Muncie IN 47304 Office: Marsh Supermarkets Inc POB 155 Yorktown IN 47396

MARSH, FRANK, state treas. Nebr.; b. Norfolk, Nebr., Apr. 27, 1924; s. Frank and Delia (Andrews) M.; grad. CD Coll., Nat. Parole Inst.; B.S., U. Nebr., 1950, hon. degree in Commerce, 1974; m. Shirley Mac McVicker, Mar. 5, 1943; children—Sherry Anne Marsh Tupper, Stephen Alan, Dory Michael, Corwin Frank, Mitchell Edward, Melissa Lou Marsh Fisher. Sec. of state Neb., 1953-71, lt. gov., 1971-75, treas., 1975—. Bd. dirs. Nebraskaland Found.; v.p. Lincoln Chamber Orch.; pres. Am. Youth Hostels Inc.; mem. Niehardt Found., Mayor's Com. Internat. Friendship. Served with AUS, 1943-46; ETO. Recipient Service award Am. Youth Hostels Council, 1977, Alumni Achievement award U. Nebr., Good Govt. award Jaycees. Mem. Am. Legion, VFW, DAV, Nebr. Beef Promotion Found., Central States Corrections Assn., Combined Orgn. Police Services, Nat. Assn. Unclaimed Property, Nat. Assn. State Treasurers (past pres.), Capitol City Footprinters, U. Nebr. Alumni Assn. (life), Alpha Phi Omega. Republican. Methodist. Clubs: Polemic, Lincoln Stamp, Lincoln Gem and Mineral. Office: Capitol Bldg Lincoln NE 68509

MARSH, KENNETH STANLEY, shoe mfg. co. exec.; b. St. Albans, Eng., May 17, 1925; s. Cecil Stanley and Lucy (Tucker) M.; came to U.S., 1964, naturalized, 1973; ed. Kings Coll. Cambridge U., 1943-44, Royal Air Force Coll., Cranwell, Eng., 1944, Street (Eng.) Tech. Inst., 1953-54; m. Jeanne Carol Fink, Oct. 24, 1962; 1 son, Andrew Kenneth Laidlaw. Sr. indsl. engr. C & J Clark Ltd., Street, Eng., 1949-51, asst. prodn. mgr., 1951-53, chief tng. officer, 1953-64; chief engr. Hanover Shoe Inc. (Pa.), 1964—; mem. nat. council Brit. Boot and Shoe Instn., 1961-64; mem. edn. adv. com. Shoe and Allied Trades Research Assn., 1960-64; mem. edn. adv. com. Shoe and Allied Trades Research Assn., 1960-64; mem. edn. com. Brit. Footwear Mfrs. Assn., 1963-64; examiner City and Guilds of London, 1961-64. Bd. govs. Street Tech. Inst., 1957-64; Strode Tech. Coll., 1962-64; v.p. York-Adams council Boy Scouts Am., 1973-81. Served with RAF, 1944-49, 51. Registered profl. engr., Pa., W.Va. Fellow Brit. Boot and Shoe Instn., Brit. Inst. Mgmt.; mem. Constrn. Specifications Inst., ASHRAE, Assn. Energy Engrs., Guild of Cordwainers, Am. Def. Preparedness Assn., Am. Inst. Indsl. Engrs. (sr.), Nat. Soc. Profl. Engrs., Am. Mgmt. Assn., Internat. Platform Assn. Episcopalian. Clubs: Royal Nat. Rose Soc., Am. Rose Soc., Internat. Wine Food Soc., Rotary, Hanover Country. Contbr. articles to profl. jours: author/editor tng. manuals for shoemakers, indsl. engrs., prodn. controllers, craft apprentices, pattern and last makers, other. Home: 990 McCosh St Hanover PA 17331

MARSH, LARRY G., mfg. co. exec.; b. Johnstown, Pa., Sept. 2, 1945; s. Donald Bruce and Linda Lee (Sopranzi) M.; B.S. in Psychology, U. Pitts., 1972; postgrad. in psychology Indiana U. Pa., 1973-74; m. Betty J. Kocher, Nov. 29, 1969; 1 dau., Heather Dawn. Account exec. Moore Bus. Forms, Inc., Johnstown, 1967-70; account exec. Coleman Co., Inc., Somerset, Pa., 1970-71, mgr. order processing, 1971-73, regional sales mgr., 1973-80, dir. mktg. and nat. accounts, 1980—. Mem. Am. Mgmt. Assn. Republican. Lutheran. Office: PO Box 111 Somerset PA 15501

MARSH, QUINTON NEELY, banker; b. Omaha, July 1, 1915; s. Arthur J. and Rose L. (Baysel) M.; B.C.S., Benjamin Franklin U., Washington, 1949, M.C.S., 1950; student Am. Inst. Banking, 1945-46, Am. U., 1950-51; diploma Sch. for Bank Adminstrn., U. Wis., 1959; m. Thelma May Beck, Nov. 24, 1944. With Western Electric Co., Omaha, 1935-37, Lamson Bros. & Co., Omaha, 1937-39, C.A. Swanson & Sons, Omaha, 1939-42; with Am. Security & Trust Co., Washington, 1946-77, asst. auditor, 1956, auditor, 1958, security officer, after 1968, gen. auditor, after 1969, v.p., gen. auditor, 1972, then sr. officer in charge auditing and security; sr. v.p., cashier Bank of Columbia N.A., Washington, 1977-79; sr. v.p. United Nat. Bank of Washington, 1979-80; ind. cons., 1980—; lectr. banking schs., profl. convs., seminars, law enforcement groups. Served with USNR, 1942-45. Chartered bank auditor, 1968; cert. internal auditor, 1973; cert. protection profl., 1977. Mem. Bank Adminstrn. Inst. (pres. D.C. 1966-67, auditing commn. 1968-70), Inst. Internal Auditors (pres. Washington 1962-63), Am. Soc. Indsl. Security, Am. Legion, Am. Def. Preparedness Assn., U.S. Naval Inst., Internat. Assn. Chiefs Police. Mason (Shriner). Contbr. articles to profl. jours. Home and Office: 4801 Connecticut Ave NW Apt 312 Washington DC 20008

MARSH, ROBERT EDWARD, animal and pet food co. exec.; b. Wilmington, Del., Mar. 21, 1940; s. Albert Rice and Josephine (Viands) M.; B.A. in History, Duke U., 1962; postgrad. Jefferson Med. Coll., Phila., 1962-63, Acad. Advanced Traffic, Phila., 1965-66; m. Marie Ann Kelly, Sept. 26, 1964; children—Robert Edward, Matthew Emmett, Amy Elizabeth, Katherine Marie. With Pa. R.R., 1964-71, regional mgr. trailer-on-flatcar sales, Chgo., 1970-71; pres. AllWays Service, Chgo., 1971-72; traffic mgr., then distbn. mgr. Allied Mills, Inc., Chgo., 1973-78, material control mgr., Everson, Pa., 1978—; sec.-treas. Marsh Enterprises, Inc. Pres., LaGrange Park Little League, 1975. Served with USAF, 1963. Mem. Assn. ICC Practitioners, Nat. Council Phys. Distbn. Mgmt., Traffic Club Chgo. Office: Allied Mills Inc Old Route 119 Everson PA 15631

MARSH, ROBERT HARRY, mfg. co. exec.; b. Camden, N.J., Sept. 6, 1946; s. Harry Louis and Margaret Charlotte (Starke) M.; B.A., B.S. in Mech. Engring., Rutgers U., 1969; M.B.A. in Mgmt. and Fin., Temple U., 1980; m. Margaret Sammartino, Mar. 20, 1970. From mech. engr. to mech. specialist and project engr. Rohm & Haas Engring., Bristol, Pa., 1969-76; from staff engr. to sr. engring. specialist Hercules, Inc., Wilmington, Del., 1976-80, sr. fin. analyst for corp. strategic planning, 1980—; in corp. planning and fin. analysis, Haddonfield, N.J., 1977—. Active Haddonfield civic affairs. Mem. ASME (nat. power com. 1977—, vice chmn. awards com. 1980), Nat. Soc. Profl. Engrs., Beta Gamma Sigma, Engrs. Club Phila. Club: Hercules Country. Contbr. articles to profl. jours. Home: 433 Maple Ave Haddonfield NJ 08033 Office: 910 Market St Wilmington DE 19899

MARSHALL, ALVIN FREDERICK, food distbn. co. exec.; b. Waterbury, Conn., Mar. 26, 1926; s. Isadore Joseph and Gertrude M.; B.S., Boston U., 1948; postgrad. Northeastern U., 1974-78; m. Florence Sonia Cushing, Nov. 5, 1950; children—Steven P., David M., Janet L. Asst. to pres. Baron-Peters Co., Inc., Boston, 1948-53; controller Musler-Liebeskind, Waterbury, 1953-59; controller, v.p. Consol. Foods, Inc., Nashua, N.H., 1959-65, v.p., 1966-76, pres., 1976—. Mem. adv. bd. St. Joseph Hosp., 1976—; bd. dirs. Salvation Army, 1977—; dist. committeeman Explorer div. Boy Scouts Am., 1972—. Served with USN, 1944-46. Mem. New Eng. Wholesale Food Distbrs. Assn. Jewish. Clubs: Rotary, Masons. Home: 54 Wood St Nashua NH 03060

MARSHALL, CHARLES RICHARD, railroad equipment exec.; b. Elizabeth, N.J., Aug. 19, 1929; s. Charles A. and Jean (Gormley) M.; A.B., U. Notre Dame, 1951; M.B.A., U. Pa., 1953; m. Angela Casey, Feb. 7, 1959; 1 dau., Susan. Adminstrv. asst. Marshall Ry. Equipment, Inc., N.Y.C., 1953-54, asst. to pres., 1954-60, located Scranton, Pa., 1957—, pres., dir., 1962—; partner John H. Neafie Co., N.Y.C., 1955—; pres., dir. Marshall Air Brake Co., Scranton, 1957—; dir. Metz Hat Corp., N.Y.C., Midwest Corp., Scranton, Eureka Security Printing Co., Scranton, Wyoming Sand & Gravel Co., Tunkhannock, Pa. Trustee U. Scranton; mem. Pa. Republican State Com. Republican. Roman Catholic. Clubs: Country of Scranton, Scranton (pres., dir.); Waverly Country; N.Y. Athletic. Author: Economics of Freight Car Construction Industry, 1953. Home: RD 3 Dalton PA 18414 Office: Connell Bldg Scranton PA 18503

MARSHALL, CLYDE THOMAS, mgmt. cons.; b. Winthrop, Iowa, Feb. 20, 1908; s. Arthur T. and Leta Marshall; student Cornell Coll., Iowa, 1926-28, Northwestern U., 1930-31; m. Beth Cole, Mar. 26, 1932; 1 son, John Cole. Div. v.p. Gen. Electric Co., Providence, 1928-50; gen. mgr. Agr. Chem. div. Comml. Solvents Corp., N.Y.C., 1951-59; exec. v.p. Balt. Bus. Forms, Inc., 1960-61; chmn. Coffay, Marshall Assos., Inc., Balt., 1962—. Mem. Md. Republican Central Com., 1970—; vice chmn. Balt. City Com., 1978—; del. Rep. Conv., 1976. Served with USNR, 1942-45. Mem. Assn. Mgmt. Cons. (past pres.), Exec. Assn. Balt. (past pres.), Inst. Mgmt. Cons. Elder, Presbyterian Ch. Clubs: Mchts., Hillendale Country. Home: 5313 St Albans Way Baltimore MD 21212

MARSHALL, DUANE LEROY, real estate escrow and closing service exec.; b. Sioux City, Iowa, Dec. 7, 1938; s. Vern E. and Juanetta E. (Denham) M.; B.S. in Accounting, U. Colo., 1969; m. Patricia Ann Short, Sept. 1, 1957; children—Lori Lee, Lynn Patricia, Kelly Ann, Jeffery Duane. Gen. and cost accountant FTS Corp., Denver, 1960-63; fin. dir. Adco Improvement Assn., Brighton, Colo., 1963-68; fin. and budget dir. Adams County Govt., Brighton, 1968-71; controller and v.p. fin. Nationwide Trucking Co., Brighton, 1971-77; controller and office mgr. Brooks Scanlon Inc., Denver, 1977-78; controller, fin. exec. Escrow Services, Inc., Denver, 1979—. Served with USN, 1956-59. Mem. Nat. Assn. Accountants, Nat. Assn. Credit Mgrs., Am. Inst. C.P.A.'s, Rocky Mountain Credit Assn., Colo. Horsemans Assn. Democrat. Lutheran.

MARSHALL, E. PIERCE, oil co. exec.; b. San Francisco, Jan. 12, 1939; s. J. Howard, II and Eleanor M. (Pierce) M.; B.A., Pomona Coll., 1961; m. Elaine Tettemer, July 24, 1965; children—Pierce, Preston L. Engring. trainee Gen. Motors Corp., Warren, Mich., 1962; securities analyst Loeb, Rhoades & Co., N.Y.C., 1965-66; adminstrv. asst. J. H. Marshall, II, Houston, 1967-70; sec.-treas., chief operational officer Marlor Enterprises, Inc., Houston, 1971-75; mgr. purchasing Koch Industries, Inc., Wichita, Kans., 1976-79; asst. to pres., treas. Internat. Oil & Gas Corp., Dallas, 1979, v.p. fin., 1979—;

dir. Electron Corp., Littleton, Colo. Served with USNR, 1962-64. Office: 3303 Lee Pkwy Suite 406 Dallas TX 75219

MARSHALL, HENRY CARPENTER, JR., investment banker; b. N.Y.C., Oct. 26, 1942; s. Henry Carpenter and Margaret Virginia (Sommer) M.; A.B., Dartmouth Coll., 1964; M.B.A., N.Y. U., 1970; m. Jean Smith, Oct. 2, 1970; children—Whitner H., Allison P. Regional salesman Procter & Gamble Distbg. Co., 1964-66; asst. cashier Citicorp, 1966-70; v.p., dir. Merrill Lynch Leasing, Inc., 1975-78; v.p., mng. dir. Merrill Lynch White Weld Capital Markets Group, 1970-78; mng. dir. Hunter Keith Marshall & Eaton, Inc., N.Y.C., 1978—; dir. Waterways Transp., Inc. Republican. Episcopalian. Club: N.Y. Athletic. Home: 214 Lawrence Hill Rd Cold Spring Harbor NY 11724 Office: 1 Penn Plaza Suite 2430 New York NY 10001

MARSHALL, IRL HOUSTON, JR., service co. exec.; b. Evanston, Ill., Feb. 28, 1929; s. Irl H. and Marjorie (Greenleaf) M.; A.B., Dartmouth, 1949; M.B.A., U. Chgo., 1968; m. Barbara Favill, Nov. 5, 1949; children—Alice Louise Vogler, Irl Houston III, Barbara Carol, Susan Jean. Gen. mgr. Duraclean Internat., Deerfield, Ill., 1949-61, pres. and gen. mgr., 1977—; pres. Houston Advt. Agency, Skokie, Ill., 1959-61; mgmt. Montgomery Ward, Chgo., 1961-77. Trustee, bd. dirs. Highland Park (Ill.) Hosp., 1971-80, treas., 1977-80; bd. dirs. Chgo. Suburban Chamber Music Soc., 1972—. Clubs: Exmoor, Exec., Univ., Cliff Dwellers (dir. 1976-78, treas. 1976, pres. 1977). Home: 1248 Ridgewood Dr Northbrook IL 60062 Office: 2151 Waukegan Rd Deerfield IL 60015

MARSHALL, MARION HOWARD, household products mfg. co. exec.; b. Lima, Ohio, Oct. 17, 1937; s. Harry Lee and Melba Hale (Hardin) M.; B.Ch.E., Ohio State U., 1960; student U. Cin., 1964-69; m. Lynne Louise Feigh, Dec. 23, 1960; children—Judith Louise, Melba Anne, Joseph Lee, Jeffrey Lisle. Mech. planning mgr. Procter & Gamble Co., Cin., 1964-65, prodn. planning mgr., 1965-66, dentifrice mfg. mgr., 1966-67, warehouse and shipping distbn. mgr., 1967-68, pkg. soap and detergent mfg. brand mgr., 1968-70, personnel devel. mgr., Jackson, Tenn., 1970—; instr. Jackson State Community Coll., 1972—. Vol. club leader Young Life of West Tenn., 1971—; pres. bd. dirs. Jackson Mental Health Center; trustee Western Mental Health Inst.; chmn. indsl. program adv. com. Jackson State Community Coll. Served with U.S. Army, 1960-64. Mem. Jackson Area C. of C., Internat. Transactional Analysis Assn. Presbyterian. Club: 4-H (adult advisor, leader). Home: 333 Law Rd Jackson TN 38301 Office: 1306 Hwy 70 Bypass Jackson TN 38301

MARSHALL, RAY, educator, former sec. of labor; b. Oak Grove, La., Aug. 22, 1928; s. Thomas J. and Virginia (Foster) M.; B.A., Millsaps Coll., 1949; M.A., La. State U., 1950; Ph.D., U. Calif., Berkeley, 1954; m. Patricia Williams, Nov. 27, 1946; children—Jill, Susan, John, Sarah. Asst. prof. econs. U. Miss., 1953-57; asso. prof. econs. La. State U., 1957-62; prof. econs. U. Tex., 1962-67; prof. econs., dept. chmn. U. Ky., 1967-69; prof. econs., dir. Center Study of Human Resources, U. Tex., 1969-77, 81—, chmn. dept., 1970-72; sec. of labor, Washington, 1977-81; chmn. Fed. Commn. on Apprenticeship, 1974-76; pres. Nat. Rural Center; dir. Task Force So. Rural Devel.; mem. Nat. Manpower Policy Task Force, 1969-76. Served with USNR, 1943-46. Fulbright research scholar, 1955-56; Ford Found. faculty fellow, 1954-55; Wertheim fellow in indsl. relations, 1960. Mem. Indsl. Relations Research Assn. (pres.), Am., So. (pres. 1973-74) econ. assns., Am. Arbitration Assn., AAUP, Beta Gamma Sigma, Omicron Delta Kappa, Phi Kappa Phi. Presbyterian. Author: The Negro and Organized Labor, 1965; The Negro Worker, 1967; (with Vernon Briggs) The Negro in Apprenticeship, 1967; Labor in the South, 1967; (with Lamond Godwin) Cooperatives and Rural Poverty in the South, 1971; Rural Workers in Rural Labor Markets, 1974; (with Allan Cartter) Labor Economy: Wages, Employment and Trade Unions, 1976; (with Brian Rougeling) The Role of Unions in the American Economy, 1976. Office: Lyndon B Johnson Sch Public Affairs U Texas Austin TX

MARSHALL, ROBERT DUANE, computer services specialist; b. Amsterdam, N.Y., Sept. 9, 1940; s. Kenneth and Lois Elizabeth (Shelmandine) M.; student Utica Coll., 1961; m. Janice M. Chinoweth, Dec. 6, 1968; children—James, William, Ross, Dean. Programmer, analyst Spl. Metals Corp., Utica, N.Y., 1961-68; dir. central services Oneida County (N.Y.), 1968; mgr. mfg. systems Mohaw Data Scis., Herkimer, N.Y., 1968-70; mgr. computer services O'Brien & Gere, Engrs., Inc., Syracuse, N.Y., 1970-79; dir. computer services Edwards & Kelcey, Inc., Livingston, N.J., 1979—; cons. to various civil engring. firms. Mem. Soc. Computers in Engring. Planning and Arch. (dir.), Data Processing Mgrs. Assn., Assn. Systems Mgrs. Republican. Roman Catholic. Home: 15 Bedminster Rd Randolph NJ 07869 Office: 70 S Orange Ave Livingston NJ 07039

MARSTON, ALFRED J., economist; b. Silesia, Poland, July 22, 1924; s. Aloysius and Martha (Von Stackberg) M.; Ph.D., Universite De Paris, 1950; postgrad. Ecole Des Sci. Politiques, 1945-47; m. Vilma Mercaldi, Nov. 30, 1956. Analyst, Internat. Pub. Opinion Research, N.Y.C., supr. European research operation, 1951-52; analyst, research supr. UNGRAN, N.Y.C., 1953-55; econ. analyst terminals Port of N.Y. Authority, 1956-60, asst. transp. economist, 1961-62, economist, 1962-79; v.p. Inversion, Inc., N.Y.C., 1980—; dir. Chatham Towers Inc. Vice pres. Downtown Manhattan Community Council, N.Y.C. Chmn. bd., mem. community adv. bd. Beekman Downtown Hosp., N.Y.C., also trustee; mem. Community Planning Bd. Manhattan, N.Y.C., also chmn. transp. com.; vice-chmn. Manhattan Area Health System Agy. Served with French Army, 1943-45. Mem. Am. Econ. Assn., Am. Statis. Assn., AAAS (com. mem.), Am. Acad. Scis. (transp. research bd.), Internat. Platform Assn., Urban and Regional Info. System Assn. (chmn. internat. group). Author: The French Legion in Haiti, 1952. Research and articles in field. Home: Indian Neck Peconic NY 11958 Office: 170 Park Row New York NY 10038

MARTIN, ARTHUR VICTOR, mech. contracting co. exec.; b. Fall River, Mass., May 19, 1948; s. Arthur and Evelyn (Santos) M.; student New Eng. Inst. Tech., 1973, Northeastern U., 1977; m. Marjorie Anne Bucher, Nov. 10, 1973; children—David Christopher, Kevin Michael. Serviceman to pres. ABCO Engring., Pawtucket, R.I., 1973-74; service/installation man A&M Engring. Co., Fall River, 1974-75; systems service and installation technician Lutz Engring. Inc., Providence, 1976; pres. All-Temp Mech., Inc., Plainville, Mass., 1977—; cons. town housing authority. Mem. Plainville Indsl. Devel. Commn. Mem. New Eng. Solar Energy Assn., Refrigeration Service Engrs. Soc., Refrigerating Engr. and Technicians Assn., Assn. Energy Engrs., ASHRAE, N. Attleboro Jaycees (dir.). Home and Office: 9 Cooney Ave Plainville MA 02762

MARTIN, CHARLES E., fin. exec.; b. Chgo., Aug. 5, 1920; s. Charles E. and Dorothy (Libman) M.; A.B., Cornell U., 1942; M.B.A., Harvard U., 1949; m. Valerie Buchsbaum, Apr. 26, 1949; children—Victoria, Virginia, Catherine; m. 2d, Norine Marsh, Oct. 31, 1969. Vice pres., dir. mktg. Ill. Meat Co., Chgo., 1946-58; pres. Calif. Frozen Juice Co., Beverly Hills, Calif., 1953-62; fin. v.p. TF, Inc., Beverly Hills, 1953-67; pres. 9944 Bldg. Co., Beverly Hills, 1959-61; chmn. exec. com., dir. Cosmopolitan Life Ins. Co., Beverly Hills, 1960-63, Working Capital, Inc., 1962—; pres Ft. Knox Co., Los Angeles, 1963-67; pres., dir. Hermitage Fin. Group, 1968-71, H.C.C. Acceptance Corp., 1968-71, Hermitage Capital Corp., 1968-71, Career Tng. Fund, Inc.; chmn. bd., pres. Financial Facilities, Inc., 1971—; pres., dir. Check Recovery Corp., 1972-78, Check-A-Check, Inc., 1974-78; chmn. bd. E-R-G Capital Corp. and E-R-G Mgmt. Corp., 1978—; mng. dir. Econometric Research Group; dir. Portuguese Am. Corp., Mortgage Guarantee Corp., Western Daily Asset Fund, Inc.; gen. partner Fresno Investors, Ltd., Hillcrest 79, Ltd., Tempe Vista I, II and III, also 6 other Vista ltd. partnerships. Served from pvt. to maj. USAF, World War II. Mem. Nat. Yacht Racing Union, Air Force Assn. Clubs: Saddle and Sirloin, Chgo. Yacht, Cornell (Chgo.); Cornell (N.Y.); Sand and Sea (Santa Monica, Calif.); Beverly Hills. Office: Financial Facilities Inc PO Box 2136 Santa Monica CA 90406

MARTIN, CLARENCE WILLIAM, cattle feed yard exec.; b. Elk City, Okla., Jan. 31, 1930; s. Calvin William and Lela Blanche (Baxter) M.; student public schs., Friona, Tex.; m. Martha Wynona Carter, June 22, 1947; children—Martha Ann, Larry, Mike, Greg, Keith, Kathy. Rancher, Colo., S.D., N.M., Tex., various dates; with Farwell Feed Lot (Tex.), 1958-63; with Hi Plains Feed Yard, Inc., Friona, Tex., 1967-81, pres., gen. mgr., 1963-81; v.p. W. Friona Grain, Dnc., 1969-81, Tri-County Elevator Co., Inc., 1980—. Mem. Friona C. of C. (dir. 1968-70, 78—), West Tex. C. of C. (dir. 1972-81, chmn. agr. and ranching com. 1978-81), Tex. Cattle Feeders Assn., Tex. Southwestern Cattle Raisers, Nat. Cattleman's Assn. Address: Rural Route 2 Friona TX 79035

MARTIN, DENNIS RAY, mfr. control systems; b. Saginaw, Mich., Mar. 10, 1949; s. Glenn Ray and Alice Rosealla (Spencer) M.; B.S., U. Mich., 1972; grad. Mich. Police Acad., 1976; m. Jacquelyn Ann Terlewski, Mar. 9, 1968; children—Denise Raygina, Jennifer Marie. Dep. sheriff Saginaw County, Micy., 1975—; pres., owner Denmar Engring. and Control Systems Inc., Saginaw, 1977—; dir. Community Emergency Patrol Systems Inc., 1975—; legis. agt. State of Mich., 1972-79; mem. Police Community Relations Commn., 1976—; mem. United Community Action Com. Prevention Crime, 1975—. Mem. parent council adv. bd. Saginaw Public Schs., 1977-79. Recipient Luther Christman award Nat. Male Nurse Assn., 1976; Health and Services award Mich. State U., 1976; Officer of Year award Exchange Club Saginaw, 1977; Liberty Bell award Saginaw County Bar Assn., 1979. Mem. Am. Assn. Correctional Facility Officers (pres. 1977), Dep. Sheriff Assn. (pres. 1977), Nat. Male Nurse Assn. (pres. 1971-79), Am. Assn. Trauma Specialists (dir.), Mich. Health Council (dir.), Saginaw C. of C. Republican. Baptist. Clubs: Tri-City Ski, Bridgeport Country, Saginaw Health. Author articles in field. Home: 6562 E Curtis Rd Bridgeport MI 48772 Office: 2309 State St North Office Saginaw MI 48602

MARTIN, DONALD JAMES, broadcasting co. exec.; b. Brantford, Ont., Can., May 2, 1928; came to U.S., 1960, naturalized, 1965; s. Norman Wilfred and Leeta Maude (Woodley) M.; Ph.B., Northwestern U., 1954; postgrad. in bus. adminstrn. U. Chgo., 1965-66; m. Annette Roselyn Mills, Aug. 25, 1952; children—Paul Stuart, Cheryl Anne. Account rep. J. Walter Thompson Co., Toronto, Ont., 1951-56, mgmt. supr., São Paulo, Brazil, 1956-60, v.p., Chgo., 1960-66; dir. corp. relations Kraft, Inc., N.Y.C., 1966-71, Chgo., 1971-73; v.p. Scott Paper Co., Phila., 1973-76, Conrail Co., Phila., 1976-78; pres. Martin Broadcasting, Inc., Vineland, N.J., 1978—; instr. internat. mktg. Northwestern U., 1963-67, U. Wis., 1964, Mich. State U., 1965, U. Ill., 1965, Ind. U., 1966; asst. prof. communications Mercer (N.J.) Coll., 1980—. Mem. N.J. Broadcasters Assn. (dir.), Broadcast Pioneers (dir.), Public Relations Soc. Am., Vineland C. of C., Northwestern U. Alumni Assn. (pres. N.Y.C., 1968-69, dir. 1969-74). Clubs: Waynesborough Country (Paoli, Pa.); Union League (N.Y.C.); Rotary. Office: Box 810 Vineland NJ 08360

MARTIN, E. THOMAS, advt. co. exec.; b. Long Beach, Calif., May 11, 1943; s. Edward Thomas and Florence Judith (MacFarlane) M.; B.S. in Chemistry (scholar), Gonzaga U., 1965; M.B.A., U. So. Calif., 1971; m. Patricia Ann Wyatt, Sept. 5, 1964; children—Laura Lee, Julia Marie. With Mattel Inc., Hawthorne, Calif., 1966-73, chemist, toy designer, dir. research and devel., 1973-76; dir. domestic corp. mktg. Mattel Inc., Hawthorne, 1976—; pres. Martin Outdoor Advt. Co., Lancaster, Calif. Treas., mem. exec. com. Sou South Bay Children's Health Center, 1975-80; chmn. II Ann, Tracy Austin Pro-Celebrity Benefit, 1979, III, 1980; coach, commr. Am. Youth Soccer Orgn., 1973-80. Mem. Traffic Audit Bur., Calif. Assn. Outdoor Advertisers, Am. Mgmt. Assn., Am. Advt. Fedn., Toy Mfrs. Am., So. Calif. Assn. Food Chemists (pres. 1970), Mattel Mgmt. Assn. (pres. 1974). Republican. Roman Catholic. Patentee novel materials in toy industry. Home: PO Box 2597 Paso Robles CA 93446 Office: PO Box 829 Lancaster CA 93534

MARTIN, FRANK LEONARD, mfg. co. exec.; b. Scunthorpe, Eng., Jan. 2, 1927; came to Can., 1957, naturalized, 1962; s. Leonard and Florence Martin; b. Metallurgy, Sheffield (Eng.) U., 1952; m. Florence Mary Swallow, Mar. 17, 1951; children—Lynne, Andrew David, Nadine Dawn. Research metallurgist Appleby-Frodingham Steel Co., Eng., 1952-57; various mgmt. positions Dosco, steel co., Can., 1957-67; works mgr. Pilkington Bros. Can. Ltd., Toronto, Ont., 1968-73; mfg. mgr. Dominion Chain, Stratford, Ont., 1973-74, v.p., gen. mgr., 1974—, also dir. Served with Royal Air Force, 1949-52. Mem. Canadian Standards Assn. Home: 98 Parklane Dr Stratford ON N5A 5B9 Canada Office: PO Box 578 617 Douro St Stratford ON N5A 6V5 Canada

MARTIN, FRANK WARREN, constrn. co. exec.; b. Charlottesville, Va., June 9, 1925; s. William Herbert and Rose Lillian (Roberts) M.; student U. Va., 1946; m. Charlotte Anne Kennedy, June 21, 1947; children—W. Gregory, Gayle M. Longley, F. Michael, Susan A. Wood, Sherry L. Hughes, William Scott. With Conquest, Dunn & Potter, Charlottesville, 1946-47; with Edward van Laer, Inc., Charlottesville, 1947-79, pres., 1971-79; pres. Martin/Horn, Inc., Charlottesville, 1979—. Mem. Charlottesville Planning Commn., 1976—, vice chmn., 1979, mem. bd. archtl. rev., 1978—; mem. Historic Landmarks Commn., 1977—; mem., chmn. Bldg. Code Bd. Appeals, Charlottesville, 1970—. Served with USMC, 1943-46, 50-51. Decorated Air medal. Mem. Asso. Gen. Contractors Am., Asso. Gen Contractors Va. (pres. 1979), Am. Legion (dep. vice comdr. 1963). Lutheran. Office: PO Box 590 Charlottesville VA 22902

MARTIN, HULBERT, investment brokerage co. exec.; b. Chg o., Aug. 31, 1939; s. Charles Francis and Elizabeth (Wyant) M.; B.A., Swarthmore Coll., 1961; M.A., U. Pa., 1962; credential U. Calif., Berkeley, 1970; m. Amalia Kaye Contino, Aug. 17, 1974; children—Jennifer, Naomi, Amalia. Instr., Ind. U., Bloomington and Oakland (Calif.) Public Schs., 1962-73; fin. tchr. Econ. Survival Resources, Mill Valley, Calif., 1973-75; account exec. Reynolds Securities Co., Oakland, Calif., 1975-78, Blyth, Eastman, Dillon Co., San Francisco, 1978-79; pres. Hugh Martin & Co., San Francisco, 1979—; lectr. fin. planning to corps. and community colls., 1976—. Registered securities prin., fin. and ops. prin., investment adv.; cert. fin. planner; lic. in real estate, commodities, ins.; teaching credentials, Calif. Mem. Nat. Assn. Securities Dealers, Internat. Assn. Fin. Planners, Mensa. Club: Commonwealth. Home: 203 Princess Ln Mill Valley CA 94941 Offfice: 1140 Taylor St San Francisco CA 94108

MARTIN, JAMES ERNEST, mag. publishing co. exec.; b. Raleigh, N.C., Jan. 15, 1950; s. Charles Edmund and Mildred (Gurley) M.; B.A., Pa. State U., 1971; m. Raymonde Veronique Morgan, Mar. 28, 1980. Regional media planner Asch Advt., N.Y.C., 1972; asso. media dir. Cunningham & Walsh Advt. Agy., N.Y.C., 1973-75; v.p. sales Combined Communications Corp., Los Angeles, Detroit, 1975-77; Detroit advt. mgr. Golf Digest/Tennis mag. div. N.Y. Times Co., 1977-78; N.Y. advt. mgr. Tennis mag. div. N.Y. Times Co., N.Y.C., 1978-80, asso. advt. mgr., 1980—. Mem. Am. Mgmt. Assn. Episcopalian. Club: Vertical (N.Y.C.). Office: 488 Madison Ave New York NY 10022

MARTIN, JAMES ROBERT, sign co. exec.; b. Indpls., Mar. 31, 1943; s. Walter and Helen (Snider) M.; M.B.A., Ind. U., 1965; m. Judith Gardiner, Jan. 24, 1970; children—Julia A., Justin James. Various staff positions with TRW Systems Group, Redondo Beach, Calif., 1967-70; fin. analyst Internat. Industries, Beverly Hills, Calif., 1970; v.p. fin., treas. A & E Plastik Pak Co., Inc., Los Angeles, 1970-74, now mem. exec. com.; exec. v.p. A & E Plasti-Line, Knoxville, Tenn., 1975-76, pres., 1976—; dir. 1st Tenn. Bank, Knoxville. Bd. dirs. Signage Research Inst., Knoxville Symphony Soc., pres., 1978—; bd. dirs. United Way, Jr. Achievement, Arts Council of Knoxville; trustee Knoxville Coll. Mem. Fin. Execs. Inst., Knoxville C. of C. (dir.), Delta Tau Delta. Clubs: Cherokee Country; Jonathan (Los Angeles); Knoxville Rotary. Home: 1029 Scenic Dr Knoxville TN 37919 Office: A & E Plasti-Line PO Box 5066 Knoxville TN 37918

MARTIN, JAMES RUSSELL, life ins. co. exec.; b. Peoria, Ill., Dec. 3, 1918; s. Ray and Gertrude Irene (Tilley) M.; B.S. in Bus. Adminstrn., U. Ill., 1940; m. Minnie Woodward Faucett, Mar. 6, 1942; children—Sally Lee, James Phillip. With Home Life Ins. Co. N.Y., 1940-41, 46-51, mgr., Rochester, N.Y., 1950-51; with Mass. Mut. Life Ins. Co., Springfield, 1951—, 2d, v.p., 1958-62, v.p. agy. sales, 1962-67, sr. v.p., 1967-68, pres., chief exec., 1968-74, chmn. bd., 1974—, chief exec. officer, 1974-80; dir. Mo. Pacific Corp., Stanley Home Products, Textron, Inc. Corporator, Springfield Coll., Child Guidance Springfield; trustee YMCA Retirement Fund, Springfield United Fund; bd. dirs. Bus. Fund for Arts; chmn. bd. regents Mass. Public Higher Edn. Served to lt. col. USAAF, 1941-46. Mem. Nat. Assn. Life Underwriters, Am. Mgmt. Assn. (dir.), Health Ins. Assn. Am. (dir.), Kappa Sigma. Republican. Office: 1295 State St Springfield MA 01111

MARTIN, JOSEPH JOHN BAXTER, govt. telecommunications ofcl.; b. Rochester, N.Y., Aug. 19, 1943; s. Joseph J. and Merrylin Louise (Baxter) M.; B.A., DePauw U., 1965; M.A. (scholar 1970-71), Monterey Inst. Fgn./Internat. Studies, 1971; M.B.A. in Internat. Bus., Golden Gate U., 1980, M.B.A. in Telecommunications Mgmt., 1980; m. Giselle Paris, Dec. 23, 1977. Tchr., Clay County Bd. Edn., Fla., 1967-69; ins. mgr./broker Home Life of N.Y., Jefferson Standard Life, Allstate Ins. Co., Planned Estates Assos., San Francisco, 1972-76; telecommunications sales/mktg. exec. ITT, San Francisco, 1977-78; with GSA, 1978—, telecommunications mgr., San Francisco; lectr. Golden Gate U., San Francisco, 1980—. Mem. Valley Christian Center, Dublin, Calif., 1978—, Nat. Tax Limitation Com., 1979—; sec. Nat. Alumni Bd., Monterey Inst. Fgn./Internat. Studies, 1979—. Mem. Tele-Communications Assn., Trans-World Radio, World Affairs Council. Republican. Methodist. Home: 182 Caldecott Ln Oakland CA 94618 Office: USG/GSA/ADTS 525 Market St San Francisco CA 94105

MARTIN, JOSEPH PATRICK, JR., constrn. materials co. exec.; b. Elizabeth, N.J., Jan. 24, 1943; s. Joseph Patrick and Helen Elizabeth M.; B.S. in Elec. Engring., N.Y. U., 1965, M.S., 1966. Engr. on tech. staff TRW Systems Inc., 1966-76; pres., chmn. bd. G.S.I. Ltd./Dale Andrews Assos. Inc., Denver, 1976—. Gen. Motors scholar, 1963-66; fellow Hebrew Inst. Tech., 1965-66; grantee NSF, 1963-65. Mem. Tau Beta Pi, Eta Kappa Nu. Republican. Roman Catholic. Office: PO Box 8688 1337 18th St Denver CO 80201

MARTIN, KATHERINE A., county ofcl.; b. Jamaica, N.Y., June 9, 1947; d. James Thomas Martin and Kathleen (Howson) M.; B.A., SUNY, New Paltz, 1970; M.S., U. Utah, 1976; children—Dove Francoise Gordon, Sky Martin-Green. Organizer, Ulster County Community Action, Inc., Highland, N.Y., 1971-72; dir. Ulster County Friends of Farm Workers, Kerhonkson, N.Y., 1972-73; youth counselor, then program coordinator Dutchess County Neighborhood Youth Corps, Poughkeepsie, N.Y., 1973-74; manpower services specialist Rensselaer/Columbia Bd. Coop. Ednl. Services, Castleton, N.Y., 1974-75; project dir. Program Funding, Inc., Rochester, N.Y., 1975-77; grants adminstr. County of Ulster, Kingston, N.Y., 1978—; cons. Chmn. bd. dir. Wawarsing Econ. Opportunity Center, 1971-75; mem. Gov.'s Adv. Bd. on Migrant Workers and Rural Poor, 1976-78; sec. bd. dirs. Ulster County Community Action Com., 1973-76. Mem. Am. Mgmt. Assn., Am. Soc. Public Adminstrn., Nat. Assn. Counties, N.Y. State Assn. Counties, LWV, Assn. Native Americans. Mem. Liberal Party. Home: 60 Old Ford Rd New Paltz NY 12561 Office: Office of Grants Adminstrn County Office Bldg 244 Fair St Kingston NY 12401

MARTIN, NELSON JOHN, JR., med. instrument co. exec.; b. Dayton, Ohio, Apr. 21, 1941; s. Nelson J. and Helen (Rusche) M.; B.A., U. Dayton, 1963, M.B.A., 1968; postgrad. Law Sch. U. Cin., 1964; exec. program Amos Tuck Sch. Bus. Adminstrn., Dartmouth Coll., 1978; m. Joanne Gibbons; children—Bradley N., Louis S. Mgmt. trainee E.F. MacDonald Co., Dayton, 1964-65; mgr. new product mktg. devel. St. Regis Paper Co., Troy, Ohio, 1965-66; mgr. mktg. services Cyprus Indsl. Minerals Co., Trenton, 1968-71; dir. new bus. devel. Narco Sci. Industries, Fort Washington, Pa., 1971-75; v.p. mktg., div. officer Air Shields Inc. div. Narco Sci., Hatboro, Pa., 1975-79, v.p., gen. mgr. Narco Diagnostics, 1979—. Chmn., Twp. Spl. Com.; mem. Twp. Adv. Com. on Planning. Mem. Health Industry Mfrs. Assn., Alumni Assn. U. Dayton, Am. Mgmt. Assn., Am. Mktg. Assn. Home: 1505 N Fiedler Rd Ambler PA 19002 Office: 330 Jacksonville Rd Hatboro PA 19040

MARTIN, REX, sales and distbn. co. exec.; b. Elkhart, Ind., Oct. 4, 1951; s. Lee and Geraldine Faith Martin; student Albion Coll., 1970-72; B.A. in English, Ind. U., 1974. Field salesman NIBCO S.W., Houston, 1975-76; prodn. supr. NIBCO, La Junta, Colo., 1977, sales mgr. plumbing products, Elkhart, 1978; now dir.; pres. PVF Mktg., Inc., Columbus, Ohio, 1979—, chmn. bd., 1978—. Mem. Ind. U. Alumni Assn., Wellhouse Soc., Culver Legion. Club: Elks. Home: 1000 Urlin Ave Apt 2018 Columbus OH 43212 Office: PO Box 28227 Columbus OH 43228

MARTIN, ROBERT CHARLES, pub. co. exec.; b. Stockton, Calif., Sept. 8, 1937; s. William Charles and Emily Pearle (Biehl) M.; B.A., Stanford U., 1959; m. Luisa Lee Kramer, June 22, 1963; children—Christopher, Alyssa. Ops. mgr. Emporium, San Francisco, 1961-64; editor bus., fin. and math. Prentice-Hall, Englewood Cliffs, N.J., 1964-70; gen. mgr. edn. products div. Phillip Morris-Milprint, 1970-71; pres. N.Y. Inst. Fin., N.Y.C., 1972-76, chmn., 1976—; pres.

Inst. Bus. Planning, Englewood Cliffs, 1977—. Bd. dirs. Glen Rock/Ridgewood council Boy Scouts Am. Mem. Bay Area Shippers (dir. 1962-64), Wall St. Tng. Dirs. (dir.). Club: Brookside Racquet. Home: 389 Beechwood Rd Ridgewood NJ 07450 Office: IBP Plaza Englewood Cliffs NJ 07632

MARTIN, ROBERT WESLEY, mfg. co. exec.; b. Los Angeles, Dec. 11, 1932; s. David Laurie and Dorothy Adele (Kitts) M.; student Valley Coll., 1950-52; M.S.E., U. Calif., 1955; B.S., U. So. Calif., 1967, M.B.A., 1969; m. Barbara L. Torres, June 7, 1952; children—Cynthia Ann, Mark Aaron, Traci Michelle. Engr. mgmt., subsidiary pres. Tech. Instrument Corp., Acton, Mass., 1955-59; product line mgr., mgr. planning ITT, Los Angeles, 1959-62; dir. corp. planning Tamar Electronics, Anaheim, Calif., 1962-64; program dir. Whittaker Corp., Los Angeles, 1964-66; dir. corp. planning, div. gen. mgr. Actron Industries, Monrovia, Calif., 1966-72; fin. and gen. mgmt. cons., Los Angeles, 1972-74; dir. corp. planning TRW, Inc., Cleve., 1974-80; dir. corp. devel. Data Gen. Corp., Westboro, Mass., 1980—; dir. Sports Inc.; instr. fin. and mgmt. Calif. State U. Mem. IEEE, Beta Gamma Sigma. Patentee in field. Contbr. articles to profl. jours. Office: Data General Corp Rte 9 Westboro MA 01581

MARTIN, ROBLEE BOETTCHER, cement mfg. co. exec.; b. St. Louis, Apr. 21, 1922; s. Henry W. and Esther K. (Boettcher) M.; B.S. in Chem. Engring., Columbia U., 1943, M.S. in Chem. Engring., 1947; D.Sc. in Bus. Adminstrn. (hon.), Cleary Coll., 1962; m. Lillian Seegraves, July 15, 1940; children—Mary Katherine, Bruce Daniel, Amy Lee. Prodn. supt. Monsanto Chem. Co., St. Louis, 1946-49; dir. research and devel. Miss. Lime Co., Ste. Genevieve, Mo., 1949-59; pres. Dundee Cement Co. (Mich.), 1959-69; v.p. corp., gen. mgr. bldgs. div. Fruehauf Corp., Detroit, 1969-72; pres. Pres.'s Assn. div. Am. Mgmt. Assn., N.Y.C., 1972-74; pres. insulation div. Keene Corp., Princeton, N.J., 1974-76; pres., chief exec. officer Keystone Portland Cement Co., Allentown, Pa., 1976—, also dir.; dir. Miller Industries, Inc., Miami, Fla.; chmn. Mich. Indsl. Devel. Commn., 1961-64, Mich. World Trade Adv. Council, 1964-66. Chmn. Mich. Indsl. Ambassadors, 1960-64; trustee Alma Coll., 1962-68. Served to lt. (j.g.) USNR, 1944-46. Named Wolverine Frontiersman, Indsl. Devel. Commn. Mich. Mem. Am. Inst. Chem. Engrs., Sigma Xi, Tau Beta Pi, Phi Lambda Upsilon. Baptist. Home: 1214 Knossos Dr Apt 3 Whitehall PA 18052 Office: 2200 Hamilton St PO Box 1785 Allentown PA 18105

MARTIN, RONALD JOSEPH, bank exec.; b. Green Bay, Wis., Mar. 14, 1949; s. Joseph E. and Virginia L. (Schuh) M.; B.B.A. in Acctg., U. Wis., Whitewater, 1971, M.B.A. in Fin., Oshkosh, 1978; m. Susan M. Vandenack, Jan. 2, 1971; children—Dean R., Nichole M. Mem. acctg. and audit staff Citizens Bancorp., Sheboygan, Wis., 1971-73, gen. acctg. supr., 1974-75, fin. control mgr., 1976-77, controller, 1977-79; controller Ill. Nat. Bank, Springfield, Ill., 1979—. Mem. Am. Inst. C.P.A.'s, Ill. Soc. C.P.A.'s. Home: 2304 Bates Ave Springfield IL 62704 Office: 1 Old Capitol Plaza N Springfield IL 62701

MARTIN, STANLEY ALLAN, r.r. exec.; b. Secor, Ill., July 31, 1937; s. Harold R. and Laura L. (Yergler) M.; B.S., U. Ill., 1968; M.A., U. Iowa, 1969; m. Karen Sue Siebenthal, Mar. 31, 1963; children—Steven Allen, Kathleen Sue, Kelly Suzanne. Sr. accountant Filbey, Summers, Abolt, Good & Kiddoo, Champaign, Ill., 1966-71; div. controller Wesley-Jessen, Inc., Chgo., 1971-73; with Union Pacific R.R., Omaha, 1973—, mgr. fin. services, 1975-76, mgr. customer acctg. research, 1976-78, dir. revenue acctg., 1978—. Served with U.S. Army, 1961-64. C.P.A., Ill. Mem. Am. Inst. C.P.A.s, Ill. Soc. C.P.A.s (adminstrv. officer Eastern Ill. chpt. 1971-72), Nat. Accounting Assn. Methodist. Clubs: Union Pacific R.R. Jr. Oldtimers, West Omaha Soccer (pres. 1976), Omaha Westside Swim (dir., membership chmn.). Home: 2115 S 130th St Omaha NE 68144 Office: 1416 Dodge St Omaha NE 68179

MARTIN, THOMAS BROOKS, corp. communications cons.; b. Butler, Pa., Nov. 24, 1920; s. James Campbell and Pauline (Brooks) M.; student Millersville State Tchrs. Coll., 1940-41, Carnegie Inst. Tech., 1941-42; B.S. in Commerce, Grove City Coll., 1947; m. Helen B. Spicer, May 31, 1947; 1 son, Thomas Brooks. Indsl. engr. Armco Steel Co., Butler, Pa., 1941-44; household products salesman S.C. Johnson & Son, Inc., Phila., 1947-50, service products supr., 1950-53, service products dist. mgr., 1953-55, sales tng. dir., 1955-58, advt. and merchandising dir., 1958-63, pub. relations dir., 1963-64, v.p. pub. and personnel relations, officer, 1967-70, v.p. pub. affairs, 1970-78; pres., gen. mgr. Johnson Waxway Centers, Inc., Racine, Wis., 1965-67; pres. Century Corp., Racine, Johnson Real Estate Corp.; dir. Meadow Lake Realty Co., Inc., Heritage Bank, Racine. Mem. task force Nat. Urban Coalition; bd. dirs. Pub. Affairs Council, Racine Environment Com., Racine Environment Com. Non-Profit Housing Corp.; trustee Prairie Sch., Johnson Wax Fund. Republican. Presbyn. Clubs: Racine Country, Somerset. Home: 26 Twilight Dr Granby CT 06035

MARTIN, VERNON ANTHONY, realtor; b. Worcester, Mass., June 12, 1928; s. Lewis Orin and Anna (Sorel) M.; student Boston U., 1948-52; m. Yolanda Elso, Dec. 16, 1949; children—David, Karen, Cynthia, Michele. Pres., Vernon A. Martin, Inc., Lynn, Mass., 1952—; dir. Mass. Realtors Nat. Inst.; tchr., lectr., cons. real estate. Bd. dirs. Jr. Achievement Eastern Mass., 1966-70, chmn. Greater Lynn, 1966; state dir. Am. Cancer Soc., 1966-69; mem. exec. bd. North area div. United Community Services, 1966-68. Mem. Mayor's Adv. Com., 1968-69. Bd. dirs. Greater Lynn chpt. ARC, Union Hosp. Served with AUS, 1946-48. Named Realtor of Year Greater Lynn Bd. Realtors, 1969. Mem. Greater Lynn C. of C. (pres. 1969), Greater Lynn Bd. Realtors (pres., dir. 1970), Internat. Real Estate Fedn., Mass. Assn. Real Estate Bds. (dir.), Greater Boston, Greater Salem (dir. 1977-78). Republican. Office: New England Office Parks 239 Newburyport Turnpike Topsfield MA 01983

MARTIN, WAYNE MALLOTT, lawyer, real estate co. exec.; b. Chgo., Jan. 9, 1950; B.A., Drake U., 1972; J.D., De Paul U., 1977; m. JoAnn Giordano, Mar. 1978. Admitted to Ill. bar, 1978; sales dir., atty., financing Inland Real Estate Corp., Chgo., then Oak Brook, Ill., 1977—; loan officer Clyde Savs. & Loan Assn., Chgo., 1972-75, Am. Nat. Bank, Chgo., 1976-77. Mem. Am., Ill., Chgo. bar assns. Home: 219 Golfview Terr Palatine IL 60067 Office: Inland Real Estate Corp 1919 Midwest Rd Oak Brook IL 60521

MARTIN, WILFRED SAMUEL, mgmt. cons.; b. Adamsville, Pa., June 11, 1910; s. Albert W. and Elizabeth (Porter) M.; B.S., Ia. State U., 1930; M.S., U. Cin., 1938; m. Elizabeth Myers, July 9, 1938; children—Peter W., Judith A. (Mrs. Peter Kleinman), Nancy E. (Mrs. Richard Foss), Paula J. Chem. engr. process devel. dept. Procter & Gamble Co., Cin., 1930-50, mgr. drug products mfg. 1950-51, asso. dir. chem. div., 1952-53, dir. product devel., soap products div., 1953-63, mgr. mfg. and product devel., food products div., 1963-71, sr. dir. research and devel., 1971-75; mgmt. cons., 1975—. Mem. Wyoming (Ohio) Bd. Edn., 1961-69, pres., 1965-68. Bd. dirs., pres. Indsl. Research Inst., 1970-71: trustee, v.p. Ohio Presbyn. Homes, 1965-69, 73-79, chmn. bd., 1976-78; chmn. bd. Pikeville Coll., 1977-79; trustee Pikeville (Ky.) Coll. 73—; mem. arts and scis. adv. com. Clarkson Coll., Potsdam, N.Y., 1975—. Mem. Am. Chem. Soc. Am. Inst. Chem. Engrs., A.A.A.S., Am. Mgmt. Assn. (research adv. council 1973—), Soc. Chem. Industry, Am. Oil Chemists Soc., Engring. Soc. Cin. (dir.), N.Y. Acad. Sci. Club: Wyoming Golf (Cin.). Home: 504 Hickory Hill Ln Cincinnati OH 45215

MARTIN, WILLIAM FREDERICK, oil co. exec.; b. Blackwell, Okla., Mar. 31, 1917; s. Fred and Emma (Buchholz) M.; B.S., U. Okla., 1938; m. Betty Jean Randall, Mar. 24, 1941; children—Sharol Ann, William Scott. With Phillips Petroleum Co., Bartlesville, Okla., 1939—, gen. clk. treasury dept., 1939-50, asst. sec., asst. treas., 1950-59, sec., asst. treas., 1959-60, treas., 1960-62, sec.-treas., 1962-65, sr. v.p., 1965-68, exec. v.p., 1968-71, pres., 1971-74, chief exec. officer, 1973-80, chmn. bd., 1974—, also dir.; dir. 1st Nat. Bank, Bartlesville, Bank of Okla., Tulsa. Served to 1st lt. USAAF, 1942-44. Named to Okla. U. Alumni Hall Fame, Helms Basketball Hall Fame, Okla. Hall of Fame. Mem. Bartlesville C. of C. (dir.), Am. Legion, Am. Petroleum Inst. (dir., mem. exec. com.), Nat. Petroleum Council, Phi Delta Theta, Beta Gamma Sigma. Clubs: Masons, Shriners, Jesters. Office: Phillips Bldg Bartlesville OK 74004

MARTIN, WILLIAM WOODROW, tractor co. exec.; b. Ottawa, Kans., June 19, 1924; s. Charles Henry and Mary Elizabeth (Koontz) M.; B.S. in Indsl. Mgmt., U. Kans., 1949; m. Betty Louise Chubb, Dec. 20, 1947; children—Gregory Jennings, Janet Louise, Judith Ellen. Propr., W.W. Martin Constrn. Co., Fort Scott, Kans., 1946-49; pres. Martin Tractor Co., Inc., Topeka, 1957—; chmn. bd. Martin Co. Inc., Topeka, 1967—; dir. First Nat. Bank Topeka, Southwestern Bell Telephone Co., St. Louis, Gas Service Co. Inc., Kansas City, Mo. Vice chmn. Topeka Urban Renewal Agy., 1960-64; mem. State of Kans. Pooled Money Investment Bd.; chmn. Gov.'s Task Force on Effective Mgmt. Precinct committeeman Republican Party, Topeka; mem. exec. com. Kans. Rep. Com.; chmn. 2d Congressional Dist. Republican. Exec. bd. Kans. U. Sch. Bus.; alumni bd. Kans. U.; exec. com. Kans. U. Endowment Assn.; bd. dirs. Nat. Media Inst., Bipartisan Indsl. Polit. Action Com. Served with Q.C., AUS, 1943-46; PTO. Mem. Kans. Assn. Commerce and Industry (past chmn. bd., pres., dir.), N.A.M. (dir.), Greater Topeka C. of C. (past pres.), Asso. Industries Kans. (pres. 1968-70), Kans. U. Alumni Assn. (pres.), Phi Delta Theta. Methodist (trustee 1971-76). Mason (32 degree, Shrine, Jester), Rotarian (past pres. Topeka). Home: 3162 Shadow Ln Topeka KS 66604 Office: 1737 SW 42d St Box 1698 Topeka KS 66601

MARTINEAU, FRANCIS EDWARD, editor and pub., assn. exec.; b. Attleboro, Mass., Jan. 15, 1921; s. Edward Francis and Yvonne Marie (Langlois) M.; student Attleboro pub. schs.; m. Dorothy May Clanfield, May 26, 1945; children—Jane E., Jill F., Gail K., Paul F. Reporter, Attleboro Sun, Pawtucket (R.I.) Times, Woonsocket (R.I.) Call, 1938-46; pres. Frank Martineau Inc., Providence and Woonsocket, 1946-66; exec. dir. Aircraft Owners and Pilots Assn. Air Safety Found., 1967-69; dir. pub. relations Air Line Pilots Assn., 1969-71; gen. mgr. Nat. Assn. Counties, 1972; cons. to assn. mgmt., Washington, 1973—; editor, pub. Assn. Trends, 1973—; pres. Martineau Corp., Washington, 1973—. Pres. Woonsocket Citizens League; v.p. Woonsocket City Council; Republican candidate for Congress, 1958; gov.'s aide, state chief safety edn., 1959-60; active Boy Scouts Am., recipient Silver Beaver award. Served as pilot RCAF, 1941-44; with USAAF, 1944-46; col. Res. ret. Mem. Am. Soc. Assn. Execs. (certified), Pub. Relations Soc. Am. (accredited), Aviation/Space Writers Assn., Air Force Assn., Res. Officers Assn., Ret. Officers Assn., N.G. Assn., Aircraft Owners and Pilots Assn., World Future Soc., Nat. Assn. Execs. Club of Washington. Roman Catholic. Clubs: Kiwanis (past local pres., past lt. govt. internat.), Elks. Home: Bethesda MD Office: 7204 Clarendon Rd Washington DC 20014

MARTINEK, FRANK JOSEPH, chem. co. exec.; b. Cleve., Apr. 10, 1921; s. Michael Joseph and Sophie Anna (Fortuna) M.; B.S. in Chemistry, Ohio State U., 1950; m. Julianne Christine Radics, Oct. 9, 1954; children—Frank Joseph, Janet Arlene. Chemist, Diamond Alkali Co., Painesville, Ohio, 1950, Sherwin Williams Co., Cleve., 1950-52; group supr. Sherwin Williams, Cleve., 1953-63, tech. mgr., 1964-72; pres. Mar-Bal, Inc., Cleve., 1972-78; pres. Mid-Am. Chem. Corp., Cleve., 1978—. Served with AUS, 1942-45. Decorated Bronze Star (2). Mem. Am. Chem. Soc., Soc. Plastics Industries. Roman Catholic. Home: 7419 Stonybrook Dr Middleburg Heights OH 44130 Office: 12500 Elmwood Ave Cleveland OH 44111

MARTINEK, OTTO CHARLES, savs. and loan exec.; b. Chgo., Jan. 14, 1922; s. Vincent and Anna (Vachuda) M.; student Ind. U., 1943, Northwestern U., 1949; m. Grace Jane Andreasen, Jan. 26, 1952; 1 son, Robert Charles. With Olympic Savs. & Loan Assn., Berwyn, Ill., 1946-72, exec. v.p., 1965-72; pres., chief exec. officer, dir. Republic Savs. & Loan Assn., Chgo., 1972-75; sr. v.p. 1st Fed. Savs. and Loan Assn., Chgo., 1975—, pres. Republic Fed. div., 1975—. Bd. dirs. Boys Clubs of Cicero (Ill.), 1960-73. Served to sgt. Signal Corps, USAAF, 1942-46. Mem. Savs. Inst. Marketing Soc. of Am., Savs. Assn. Council (founder, pres. 1970-72), Soc. Savs. and Loans Controllers, Insured Savs. Assns. (pres. Chgo. area council 1977-78), Pub. Relations Soc. Am. (pres. 1965-66), Chgo. C. of C. (v.p. 1972-73), Amvets, Am. Legion. Methodist (trustee 1952-55). Mason (Shriner), Elk. Home: 4125 Howard St Western Springs IL 60558 Office: 1 S Dearborn St Chicago IL 60603

MARTINELLI, ALFRED WALTER, petroleum co. exec.; b. Hackensack, N.J., Feb. 19, 1928; s. John and Marie (Grasso) M.; B.S. in Accounting and Fin. magna cum laude, Seton Hall U., 1951; postgrad. N.Y. U.; m. Aline Sgueglia, Sept. 27, 1953; children—Susan Mary, Deborah Jane, David John. Staff asst. controller Standard Brands, N.Y.C., 1951-59; asst. controller to v.p. fin. Buckeye Pipe Line Co., Macungie, Pa., 1959-69, exec. v.p., Radnor, Pa., 1974-76, pres., 1976—; asst. v.p. finance Penn Central Transp. Co., Phila., 1969-71; sr. v.p. adminstrn. Pennco, Co., N.Y.C., 1971-74; pres., chief exec. officer The Penn Central Energy Group, Inc. (includes Buckeye Pipe Line Co., Buckeye Gas Products Co., Edgington Oil Co., Buckeye Petrofuels Co.), Radnor, Pa., 1979—; dir. Everglades Pipe Line Co., Indsl. Valley Bank and Trust Co. Served with U.S. Army, 1946-47. Mem. Am. Petroleum Inst., Assn. Oil Pipelines, Fin. Execs. Inst. Roman Catholic. Clubs: Overbrook Golf; Phila. Country, Union League (Phila.). Home: 7 Harvey Ln Newtown Square PA 19073 Office: Suite 400 201 King of Prussia Rd Radnor PA 19087

MARTINELLI, JACK JEROME, telephone installation co. exec.; b. Jamaica, N.Y., Jan. 7, 1951; s. Jack Joseph and Jean Dorothy (Zoldak) M.; grad. high sch. Installer, N.Y. Telephone Co., N.Y.C., 1970-72, ComTech Telephone Contractors, N.Y.C., 1972-75; owner Martinelli Telephone Co., West New York, N.J., 1976—. Served with M.C., U.S. Army, 1969. Roman Catholic. Home and Office: 7002 Blvd E Suite 38G Guttenberg NJ 07093

MARTINEN, JOHN A., travel exec.; b. Sault Ste. Marie, Mich., June 26, 1938; s. John Albert and Ina H. (Jarvi) M.; B.A., Mich. State U., 1960; LL.B., N.Y. U., 1963. With Grace Line, N.Y.C., 1963-69; cons. Empresa Turistica Internat., Quito, Ecuador, 1969-70; regional mgr. Globus-Gateway Tours, Group Voyagers, Inc., Forest Hills, N.Y., 1971-73, v.p., 1974-76, exec. v.p., 1977-78, pres., 1979—. Mem. Am. Soc. Travel Agents. Democrat. Home: 366 Broadway New York NY 10013 Office: 105-14 Gerard Pl Forest Hills NY 11375

MARTINEZ, ALFRED EDWARD, soft drink co. exec.; b. Sacramento, Nov. 28, 1949; s. Felix and Elvera M.; B.S. in Applied Behavioral Sci., U. Calif., Davis, 1972; M.B.A., George Washington U., Washington, 1977. With corp. employees relations mgmt. program Gen. Elec. Co., N.Y.C., 1972-74; personnel adminstr. U.S. Nuclear Regulatory Commn., Washington, 1974-77; mgr. manpower planning and devel. Gould, Inc., Phila., 1977-80; corp. dir. recruiting and placement PepsiCo Inc., Purchase, N.Y., 1980—; nat. adv. com. Dept. Transp., Urban Mass Transit Authority, Washington, 1979. Mem. San Jose (Calif.) Human Relations Commn., 1972; chmn. Davis Affirmative Action Com., 1972; mem. Yolo County Housing Adv. Com., Woodland, Calif., 1972. Recipient Outstanding Instr. award Gen. Elec. Co., Schenectady, N.Y., 1974. Mem. Personnel Mgmt. Assn. Aztlan (nat. dir.), Am. Soc. Personnel Adminstrn., Mfg. Assn. Del. Valley. Home: 511 E 86th St New York NY 10028 Office: PepsiCo Inc Purchase NY

MARTINEZ, BETTY ELNORA, chem. co. exec.; b. Oklahoma City, Jan. 7, 1937; d. Jim and Jewell Frances Smith; B.S., Oklahoma City U., 1974, M.B.A., 1975; m. June 29, 1956 (div. July 1968). Pvt. booking agt. and bus. mgr., rock and roll bands, Okla., Colo., 1960-67; with Kerr McGee Corp., Oklahoma City, 1965—, accountant, 1974-76, solvent sales rep., from 1975, now asso. sales rep. Del. Okla. Democratic Conv., 1972. Mem. M.B.A. Club Oklahoma City U. (pres. 1975), ACLU. Home: 4033 33d St NW Oklahoma City OK 73112 Office: Kerr McGee Center Oklahoma City OK 73125

MARTINEZ, HERMINIA S., banker; b. Havana, Cuba; d. Carlos Manuel and Amelia (Santana) Martinez; student Salem Coll., 1961-62; B.A. in Econs. with honors, Am. U., 1965; M.S. in Fgn. Service (Univ. fellow), Georgetown U., 1967; student Nat. U. Mexico, summers 1963, 64. Came to U.S., 1960, naturalized, 1972. Prof. Spanish, George Mason Coll. U. Va., Fairfax, 1967-68; researcher internat. trade div. and indsl. econ. div. IBRD (World Bank), Washington, 1967-69, indsl. economist, indsl. div., 1969-71, loan officer Central Am. and Caribbean dept., 1971-73, loan officer Latin Am. and Caribbean regional office, Mexico, 1973-74, Venezuela and Ecuador, 1974-76, economist, sr. loan officer Panama, Dominican Republic, 1976-80, sr. loan officer Latin Am. Regional Office, 1980—. Mem. Am. Econ. Assn., Soc. for Internat. Devel., Brookings Instn. Latin Am. Discussion Group. Contbg. author: Economic Growth of Colombia Problems and Prospects. Home: Apt 712 2801 New Mexico Ave NW Washington DC 20007 Office: 1818 H St Washington DC 20433

MARTINEZ, JOSEPH ANTHONY, plastics co. exec.; b. Havana, Cuba, May 2, 1944; s. Tiburcio and Francisca Maria M.; came to U.S., 1961, naturalized, 1971; B.S. in Econs., Fairleigh Dickinson U., 1968; m. Helen Bender, June 19, 1965; children—Jennifer Lynn, Suzanne Beth. Sales mgr. Snark Products, Inc., North Bergen, N.J., 1968-69, v.p. mfg., 1969-72, sr. v.p., bus. devel., 1972-74; exec. v.p., chief operating officer, dir. Dynaric Inc., Englewood Cliffs, N.J., 1974-78, pres., dir., 1978—; dir. Dainippon Ink & Chem. Co. Mem. Soc. Plastic Engrs., Packaging Inst., Am. Inst. Profl. Indsl. Engrs. Home: 10 Garber Hill Rd Blauvelt NY 10913 Office: 560 Sylvan Ave Englewood Cliffs NJ 07632

MARTINEZ, LOUIS, electronic engr.; b. Detroit, Mar. 9, 1931; s. Leo and Guadalupe (Romero) M.; student U. Mich., 1952-53; B.S. in Physics, Wayne State U., 1954; m. Betsy Maruko Hayashida, June 24, 1952; children—Susan, Steven, Donna, Karen. With research insts. U. Mich. and Wayne State U., 1953-54; research engr. Bendix Corp., 1955-56; asso. mgr. radar dept. Motorola Research Lab., 1956-60; pres. Pantronic, Inc., 1960-64; mem. tech. staff Aerospace Corp., 1965-68, 73-75; pres. Karlton Instruments, Inc., 1968-72; v.p. Alarm Device Mfg. Co., Ademco, 1976-77; pres. Altran Electronics affiliate Research-Cottrell, Hahbor City, Calif., 1977—; cons. USAF, 1967-68, USN, 1971-72, Justice Dept., 1974-75; adv. FCC, 1980. Served to 1st lt. USAF, 1948-52; Korea. Democrat. Inventor, patentee communications and electronics. Home: 18939 Milmore Ave Carson CA 90746 Office: Altran Electronics Inc 1400 W 240th St Harbor City CA 90710

MARTINEZ, ROMAN, IV, fin. exec.; b. Santiago, Cuba, Dec. 29, 1947; came to U.S., 1960, naturalized, 1971; s. Roman and Virginia G. (Gomez) M.; B.S., Boston Coll., 1969; M.B.A., U. Pa., 1971; m. Helena Hackley, Dec. 20, 1974; 1 son, Roman. Asso., Kuhn Loeb & Co., N.Y.C., 1971-73, v.p., 1974-77; corp. v.p. Lehman Bros. Kuhn Loeb Inc., N.Y.C., 1977, mng. dir., 1978—. Republican. Roman Catholic. Clubs: Racquet and Tennis, Links, River, Piping Rock. Home: 1172 Park Ave New York NY 10028 Office: 55 Water St New York NY 10041

MARTINEZ, WILFRED JULIAN, pharm. co. exec.; b. Bern, Switzerland, Jan. 7, 1939; s. W.A. and J.M. (Gurruchaga-Duprez) M.; came to U.S., 1960, naturalized, 1964; B.A. in Bus. Sci., Havana (Cuba) U., 1958; M.S. in Social and Polit. Sci., Sorbonne, 1959; m. Evelyn M. Pedrosa-Ugalde, May 24, 1963; children—Wilfred, Woltan, Barbara. Acctg. systems analyst Prudential Ins. Co., N.Y.C., 1964-69; sr. internal auditor Schering Corp., Bloomfield, N.J., 1969-71; from asst. to v.p. fin. and treas. to asst. corp. controller Schering-Plough Corp., Kenilworth, N.J., 1972-78; group controller G.D. Searle & Co., Skokie, Ill., 1979, v.p. bus. planning and control, 1979—. Served with USAR, 1961-64. Mem. Am. Mgmt. Assn., Inst. Internal Auditors, Inst. Fin. Execs. Republican. Roman Catholic. Club: K.C. Office: 4930 Oakton St Skokie IL 60077

MARTINO, FRANK NILSON, apparel co. exec.; b. Dallas, Mar. 29, 1929; s. James Frank and Edla Dorothea (Nilson) M.; B.B.A., U. Tex., 1949; m. Betty Jean Newman, July 23, 1949; children—James B., David C., Frank Nilson, Richard D. Trainee, Clark Mfg. Co., Meridian, Miss., 1949, salesman, 1949, office mgr., 1950-53, prodn. mgr., 1953-60; v.p. mfg. Russell-Newman Mfg. Co., Inc., Denton, Tex., 1960-70, pres., 1970—; v.p. Robison Realty Co.; dir. Martino Realty Co., 5M & R Ranch, Golden Triangle Indsl. Park; mem. adv. bd. KAAM-KAFM Radio. Chmn. Denton County Program Bldg. Com.; chmn. pres.'s council Tex. Women's U.; past. pres. Denton County United Fund; past chmn. Denton County Republican Party; past dhmn. Adv. Com. for Occupational and Tech. Edn., Denton Pub. Schs.; chmn. Denton 80's Directions and Decisions Com. Recipient Disting. Service award Order of Golden Hart, 1971. Mem. Denton C. of C. (pres. 1978), Sigma Phi Epsilon (past nat. dir., treas., trustee Found.). Republican. Mormon (bishop). Club: Kiwanis (past pres.) (Denton). Home: 1222 Emerson St Denton TX 76201 Office: 2306 Denton TX 76201

MARTINSON, ROBERT DELMAR, distbn. co. exec.; b. McKenna, Wash., Oct. 8, 1923; s. Wilhelm and Lena (Sholseth) M.; student Knapp Bus. Sch., Tacoma, 1946; m. Ruth Marie Brackman, Sept. 22, 1946; children—Steven Delmar, Kenneth Neil. With Queen City Grocery, Puyallup, Wash., 1934-55; produce man Safeway Stores, Inc., Tacoma, 1953-54; produce man Carrs' Food Center, Anchorage, 1955, gen. mgr., 1955-65; pres. Alaska Party Sales, Inc. (Tupperware for Alaska), Anchorage, 1965—. Served with U.S. Army, 1943-45. Decorated Purple Heart. Republican. Lutheran. Home: 2815 E Tudor Anchorage AK 99507 Office: Alaska Party Sales Inc 2801-2815 E Tudor Anchorage AK 99507

MARTNER, HILDEGARDE MARIE SEIBT, fin. exec.; b. Dresden, Germany; d. Hermann and Marie (Froeberg) Seibt; naturalized U.S. citizen, 1943; m. John G. Martner, May 1, 1948. With Eastman Kodak Co., 1943-76; sr. partner Martner Co., St. Charles, Ill., 1970—. Mem. Am. Mgmt. Assn., Tri-County Apt. Assn. Office: PO Box 292 Brookfield CT 06804

MARTUCCI, GLORIA MARTHA, educator; b. Bronx, N.Y., Dec. 19, 1934; d. Thomas Angelo and Martha Marie (De Marco) M.; B.A., Fla. State U., 1960; M.S., State U. N.Y. at New Paltz, 1973; cert. of mgmt. Mercy Coll., Yorktown Heights, N.Y. Tchr. French and history, Bunnell, Fla., 1960-62, Dept. of Army, Okinawa, 1962-63, U.S. Air Force, Itazuke, Japan, 1963-64; tchr. langs. Yorktown Jr. High Sch., Yorktown Heights, N.Y., 1965; tchr. French and bus. Mahopac (N.Y.) Sr. High Sch., 1966-78, Mahopac Jr. High Sch., 1979—. Pinellas County (Fla.) teaching scholar, 1958-60. Mem. Am. Assn. Tchrs. French, N.Y. State Assn. Fgn. Lang. Tchrs., Nat. Bus. Edn. Assn., Bus. Tchrs. Assn. N.Y., Order Sons of Italy. Republican. Roman Catholic. Club: Single Profls. Westchester (2d v.p. 1978-79). Home: 45 Belvedere Rd Beacon NY 12508 Office: Mahopac Jr High Sch Baldwin Place Rd Mahopac NY 10541

MARTYN, J(AMES) MICHAEL, mfg. co. exec.; b. Oshkosh, Wis., Aug. 11, 1938; s. James McDowell and Blanche Lillian (Tyriver) M.; B.S., U. Wis., 1964, B.B.A., 1964; M.B.A., Wayne State U., 1969; m. Gayle Ann Briggs, Aug. 26, 1967; children—Lynn Michelle, Matthew James. Programmer, analyst Oscar Mayer Co., Madison, Wis., 1964; mgmt. systems analyst Burroughs Corp., Plymouth, Mich., 1964-69, mgr. market mgmt. systems, Detroit, 1969-71, mgr. econ. and product planning systems, 1971-72, group mgr. mgmt. systems, Rochester, N.Y., 1972-78, dir. mgmt. systems, 1979—. Served with AUS, 1961-62. Mem. Soc. Mgmt. Info. Systems, Assn. Computing Machinery, Data Processing Mgmt. Assn. (chpt. sec., v.p., pres.), Eta Kappa Nu, Sigma Phi Epsilon. Lutheran. Home: 38 Rosewood Dr Pittsford NY 14534 Office: 1150 University Ave Rochester NY 14607

MARUCCI, MATHEW MICHAEL, mktg. co. exec.; b. Orange, N.J., Sept. 19, 1946; s. Mathew Michael and Madge G. (Haney) M.; B.S., Campbell Coll., 1969; M.A., Fairleigh Dickinson U., 1976; m. Annette Stanislao, Dec. 9, 1973; 1 son, Brandon Mathew. Pharm. scientist, Ciba-Geigy, Summit, N.J., 1973-74, coordinator regulatory compliance, 1974-76, mgr. regulatory compliance, 1976-79, product mgr. mktg. devel. products mgmt., 1979-80, product dir. mktg. devel. products mgmt., 1980—. Mem. Regulatory Affairs Profl. Soc. Address: 15 Woodbine Rd Florham Park NJ 07932

MARUMOTO, WILLIAM HIDEO, mgmt. cons.; b. Los Angeles, Dec. 16, 1934; s. Harry Yuichiro and Mary Midori (Koyama) M.; B.A., Whittier Coll., 1957; postgad. U. Oreg., 1957-58; m. Jean Masako Morishige, June 14, 1959; children—Wendy Hideko, Todd Masao, Lani Misako, Jenni Tomiko. Dir. alumni relations Whittier Coll., Calif., 1958-65; asso. dir. devel. and alumni U. Calif. Los Angeles, 1965-68; v.p. planning and devel. Calif. Inst. Arts, Los Angeles, 1968-69; sr. cons. Peat, Marwick, Mitchell & Co., Los Angeles, 1969; asst. to sec. HEW, Washington, 1969-70; spl. asst. to pres. U.S. White House, Washington, 1970-73; pres. The Interface Group, Ltd., Washington, 1973—. Mem. nat. speakers bur. Boy Scouts Am.; trustee Japan Am. Soc. Washington, 1979—, Whittier Coll., 1979—, Council for Advancement and Support of Edn., 1980—. Recipient 20 nat. awards Am. Alumni Council and Am. Coll. Pub. Relations Assn.; named Nisei Man of Yr., The Rafu Shimpo, 1970; Distinguished Pub. Service citations Japanese Am. Citizens League, Nat. Chinese Welfare Council; Alumni Service award Whittier Coll. Alumni Assn., 1978. Club: Regency Racquet. Home: 8808 Brook Rd McLean VA 22102 Office: 1212 Potomac St NW Washington DC 20007

MARUSI, AUGUSTINE RAYMOND, former food processing exec.; b. N.Y.C., Nov. 30, 1913; s. Dante R. and Victoria (Sacchi) M.; B.S. in Chem. Engring., Rensselaer Poly. Inst., 1936; m. Ruth Sinclair Travis, Aug. 31, 1940; children—Frederic, Raymond, Margo. Chemist, Catalin Corp. of Am., N.Y.C., 1938-39; sales engr. Chem. div. Borden Co., N.Y.C., 1939-42, So. regional mgr., 1945-47, dir., gen. mgr. Alba S.A., Sao Paulo, Brazil, 1947-52, v.p. Chem. div., 1952-54, pres., 1954-59; pres. Borden Chem. Co. div. Borden Co., 1960-67, v.p. Borden Co., 1956-67, pres., 1967-73, chmn. bd., chief exec. officer, 1968-79, also dir. Borden, Inc. Served lt. USN, 1942-45. Mem. Am. Inst. Chemists, Soc. Plastics Industry, Phi Epsilon Phi. Club: Union League (N.Y.C.). Office: 277 Park Ave York NY 10017*

MARVIN, EARL, lawyer; b. N.Y.C., Mar. 17, 1918; s. Benjamin and Rose Lillian (Salmow) M.; B.A., Harvard U., 1938, LL.B., 1941, J.D., 1969; m. Eleanor Dreyfus Heymsfeld, June 14, 1964; children—Peter, Benjamin, Elizabeth. Admitted to Mass. bar, 1941, N.Y. bar, 1942; asso. firm Goldwater & Flynn, N.Y.C., 1946-48; asso. firm William Weisman, N.Y.C., 1948-53; individual practice law, 1954-67; of counsel Goldstein, Schrank, Segelstein & Shays, N.Y.C., 1967—; dir. Superior Surg. Mfg. Co. Inc., Bleyer Industries Inc., Royce Hosiery Mills Inc. Served with USNR, 1944-46. Mem. N.Y. County Lawyers Assn. Democrat. Jewish. Club: Harvard (N.Y.C.); Inwood Country, Countryside County. Home: 185 Alden Rd Woodmere NY 11598 Office: Goldstein Schrank Segelstein & Shays 99 Park Ave New York NY 10016

MARVIN, WILBUR, real estate co. exec.; b. Jamaica, N.Y., Apr. 8, 1921; s. Benjamin and Rose L. (Salmow) M.; B.A., Harvard, 1941; postgrad. U.S. Naval Acad., 1941; m. Livia M. Seijo, 1980; children—Michael F., Ann E., Richard A. Pres., chief exec. officer Comml. Properties Devel. Corp., Baton Rouge, 1951—; lectr. Tulane U.; past state dir., trustee Internat. Council Shopping Centers. Served to lt. comdr. USNR, 1941-45. Decorated Purple Heart. Mem. Comml. Property Owners and Developers of La., Miss., Ala., Fla., Tenn., N.Y., P.R., Navy League. Mason. Clubs: Bocage Tennis, City of Baton Rouge, Camelot (Baton Rouge); Racquet (San Juan, P.R.); Rock Tennis. Contbr. articles to trade jours. Ho-e: 1127 Longwood Dr Baton Rouge LA 70806 Office: 1762 Dallas Dr Baton Rouge LA 70806 also 1606 Ponce de Leors Santurce PR 00910

MARX, WILLIAM THOMAS, mfg. co. exec.; b. N.Y.C.; s. William and Anna (Lahr) M.; student CCNY, 1932-34, Pace Coll., 1935-37, Columbia U., 1938-41; m. Anna C. Costello, July 4, 1942. Dir. employee relations and orgn. Raytheon Mfg. Co., Waltham, Mass., 1957-59; sr. v.p. ITT, N.Y.C., 1959-63; exec. v.p. Gt. Lakes Carbon Corp., N.Y.C., 1963-66; exec. v.p., dir. Celanese Corp., N.Y.C., 1966-72; U.S. rep. Imetal, Paris, 1972—; cons. to diversified businesses, N.Y.C., 1972—; dir. Prentice-Hall, Copperweld Corp., Coleman Co., New Court Partners, Fairchild Industries. Served to 1st lt. USAAF, 1942-45. Clubs: Winged Foot Golf (N.Y.C.); Turf and Field. Office: 450 Park Ave 25th Floor New York NY 10022

MARZOCCO, LEONARD JOSEPH, real estate exec.; b. Bklyn., Dec. 17, 1942; s. Joseph and Rose (Parisi) M.; B.S., Poly. Inst. N.Y., 1964; m. Shelby Lynn Moore, 1972; children—Joseph, Leonard Joseph. Bldg. automation engr. Johnson Controls Co., Long Island City, N.Y., 1966-70; real estate broker Breslin Realty, East Meadow, N.Y., 1971-75; dir. real estate and devel. Stackler & Frank, Hicksville, N.Y., 1975—, Mid Island Fashion Plaza, 1975—; partner Indsl. Park Shopping Center, Flushing, N.Y. Served to 1st lt. C.E., AUS, 1964-66. Mem. Internat. Council of Shopping Centers, L.I. Assn. Commerce and Industry, L.I. Bd. Realtors. Home: 913 Park Ave Huntington NY 11743 Office: 358B Mid Island Plaza Hicksville NY 11802

MARZULLO, FRANK N., physician; b. N.Y.C., Jan. 11, 1916; s. Nunzio and Margaret M.; B.S., CCNY, 1936; M.D., U. Rome, 1943; m. Evelyn Selnick, June 21, 1947; children—Michelle Jamie Marzullo Kirzner, Neil. Intern, Israel Zion Hosp., Bklyn., 1945-46; resident Caledonian Hosp., Bklyn., 1947; practice medicine, specializing in family practice, N.Y.C., 1947-72; asso. attending physician Caledonian Hosp.; asso. med. dir. N.Y. Stock Exchange, N.Y.C., 1974—; med. dir. Bank of N.Y. Clinic, N.Y.C., 1974—. Fellow Am. Acad. Family Practice; mem. N.Y. State, Kings County med. socs., Am. Occupational Med. Assn., Phi Lambda Kappa. Clubs: Masons, Physicians Square. Home: 1207 Ditmas Ave Brooklyn NY 11218 Office: Executive Health Examiners 777 3d Ave New York NY 10017

MAS, JEAN-BERNARD, banker; b. Constantine, Algeria, Nov. 18, 1938; came to U.S., 1978; s. Georges and Fridah (Cozette) M.; degree in engring. Ecole Polytechnique, Paris, 1957; m. Sylvie Guillaume, July 7, 1967; children—Stephanie, Capucine, Ludovic. Civil servant Institut National de la Statistique et des Etudes Economiques, seconded to Ministere de la Cooperation, Paris, 1963-67; prof. econometrics U. de Dakar, Senegal, 1964-65; mgr. Bureau de Developpement Industriel, Abidjan, Ivory Coast, 1967-69; adv. econ. and indsl. research dept. Societe Generale, Paris, 1970-72, account mgr., 1973-74, area mgr. internat. dept. N. Am. and Gt. Britain, 1975-78, dep. gen. mgr., exec. v.p., N.Y.C., 1978—. Mem. French-Am. C. of C. in U.S. (councillor). Roman Catholic. Office: 50 Rockefeller Plaza New York NY 10020

MASCERA, LAWRENCE, JR., drug mfg. co. exec.; b. Glen Ridge, N.J., Feb. 3, 1942; s. Lawrence and Antoinette M.; B.S. in Chem. Engring. (N.J. State scholar), Newark Coll. Engring., 1964, M.S. in Mgmt., 1971; m. Ruth Ann Shea, Oct. 13, 1968; children—Michael, Matthew, Lawrence. Devel. engr. Am. Cyanamid, Pearl River, N.Y., 1964-67, fermentation production engr., 1967-71; vitamin C production supr. Hoffman-LaRoche, Inc., Belvidere, N.J., 1972-75, fermentation sr. production supr., 1975-78, fermentation products production mgr., 1978-80, mgr. chem. prodn., 1980—. Mem. Hope Twp. Planning Bd. Mem. Am. Inst. Chem. Engrs., Am. Chem. Soc. (microbial & biochem. tech. div.). Clubs: Slate Belt Shooting Assn., Roche Trap, White Game. Office: PO Box 238 Belvidere NJ 07823

MASCI, RONALD DOMINICK, securities exec.; b. Englewood, N.J., Dec. 21, 1938; s. Nicholas and Caroline L. (Petrillo) M.; B.S., Coll. William and Mary, 1960; m. Patricia Ann Piper, Nov. 20, 1960; children—Robin Cara, Cara Kristin. Credit reporter Dun & Bradstreet, Miami, Fla., 1960-61; account exec., resident mgr. Reynolds Securities, Arlington, Va., 1965-78; v.p., resident mgr. Dean Witter Reynolds, Washington, 1978—; tchr. Wharton Sch. Advanced Studies of Securities Industry Inst. Bd. dirs., chmn. activities Arlington (Va.) C. of C., 1974-78. Served to lt. (j.g.), USCG, 1961-65. Mem. Bond Club Washington. Club: Westwood Country (dir.). Author manuals. Home: 2057 Kedge Dr Vienna VA 22180 Office: Dean Witter Reynolds 1850 K St NW Washington DC 20006

MASDEO, SUZANNE PAULINE LETTIS, med. instrumentation co. exec.; b. Watsonville, Calif., Nov. 7, 1951; d. Lloyd Anthony and Myrtle Effie Lettis; B.A., U. Calif., Berkeley, 1972, M.B.A., 1981; m. Dan Lester Masdeo, Feb. 22, 1975 (dec. Dec. 1980). Sales mgr. Macy's, San Francisco, 1972-73, asst. buyer Macy's Calif. Stores, 1973, mgr. selling services, 1974; real estate salesperson Better Homes Realty, Hayward, Calif., 1975; product mgr. Berkeley Bio Engring., San Leandro, Calif., 1975-79, Cooper Med. Devices, San Leandro, 1979—. Mem. Am. Mktg. Assn., Bay Area Med. Mktg. Assn., Alameda County Assn. Realtors, Phi Beta Kappa. Democrat. Home: 544 Alcalde Way Fremont CA 94538 Office: 600 McCormick St San Leandro CA 94577

MASKA, EDWIN CHESTER, railroad exec.; b. Pittsfield, Mass., Nov. 5, 1929; s. Frank and Anna Maska; B.S. in Econs., Wharton Sch., U. Pa., 1953; LL.B., George Washington U., 1960; m. Geneil Clay, July 30, 1955. Accounting trainee Gen. Electric Co., Pittsfield, 1947-49; investigator subcom. welfare and pension funds U.S. Senate Com. Labor, 1955-56; spl. rep. Presdl. Commn. Govt. Security, 1956-57; dir. tax rev. So. Ry. Co., Washington, 1957—; dir. State Univ. R.R. Co.; admitted to D.C. bar, 1961. Treas. Citizens for Better Govt., Fairfax County, Va., 1967-68. Served to capt. USMC, 1953-55. Mem. Tax Execs. Inst., Am. Bar Assn. Presbyterian. Club: Belle Haven Country. Home: 8419 Doyle Dr Alexandria VA 22308 Office: 920 15th St NW Washington DC 20013

MASKET, EDWARD SEYMOUR, TV exec.; b. N.Y.C., Mar. 3, 1923; s. Isadore and Jennie (Bernstein) M.; B.S., CCNY, 1942; LL.B., J.D., Harvard U., 1949; m. Frances Ellen Rees, June 11, 1958; children—Joel Daniel, Johanna Rees, Kate Isobel. Admitted to N.Y. State bar, 1949; atty., dir. bus. affairs, v.p. bus. affairs ABC, N.Y.C., 1951-68; v.p., sr. v.p., exec. v.p. Columbia Pictures TV, Burbank, Calif., 1968—, exec. v.p. adminstrn., 1978—; mem. adminstrv. com. Burbank Studios. Served as 2d lt. AUS, 1942-46. Mem. Assn. Motion Picture and TV Producers (bd. dirs., chmn. exec. com.), Acad. TV Arts and Scis., Hollywood Radio and TV Soc., Phi Beta Kappa. Office: Colgems Sq Burbank CA 91505

MASLAND, BRUCE WALTON, gas and electric co. exec.; b. Amsterdam, N.Y., Feb. 18, 1931; s. Floyd Aldrichand Charlotte Mary (Buff) M.; B.E.E., Rensselaer Poly. Inst., 1956; postgrad. Johns Hopkins U., 1957—; m. Dorothy P. Tompkins, Dec. 20, 1952; 1 son, Kevin Tompkins. Jr. engr. Balt. Gas & Electric Co., 1956-63, meter engr., 1963-65, sr. engr., 1965-67, supr. meter engring., 1967-68, prin. engr., 1968-77, corp. planning analyst, 1977-79, gen. supr. planning and budgets, 1979—. Active Balt. City Sch. and Community Resource Program, 1974-77; mem. Speakers Bur., United Way, 1977-79; precinct capt. and exec. Balt. Republican Com.; pres. Balt. Community Assn. Served with U.S. Army, 1948-52; Korea. Named Community Man of Yr., Riderwood Hills, 1966; registered profl. engr., Md. Mem. Nat. Soc. Profl. Engrs. (Meritorious Service to Engring. award 1979), Md. Soc. Profl. Engrs. (edn. com.), IEEE, Power Engring. Soc. (chpt. chmn., sect. chmn., 1st chmn. public affairs dept., adminstrv. com.), Engring. Soc. Balt., Am. Mgmt. Assn., Corp. Speakers Bur. Episcopalian. Club: Toastmasters (Outstanding Toastmaster of Yr. 1977). Home: 1024 Donnington Circle Baltimore MD 21204 Office: Balt Gas & Electric Co PO Box 1475 Baltimore MD 21203

MASLAND, FRANK ELMER, III, carpet mfg. co. exec.; b. Carlisle, Pa., Aug. 23, 1921; s. Frank Elmer and Mary Virginia (Sharp) M.; A.B., Princeton U., 1944; M.B.A., Harvard U., 1948; LL.D. (hon.), Grove City Coll., 1971; m. Marie Perry, May 22, 1943; children—Ellen C. Masland Anderson, Frank E. IV, Jonathan L. Vice pres., gen. mgr. C.H. Masland & Sons, Carlisle, 1956-61, pres., gen. mgr., 1961-71, pres., chmn. bd., 1971—; dir. Dauphin Deposit Bank, Harsco Corp., Orianna Devel. Corp. Bd. dirs. YMCA, Carlisle Hosp.; pres. bd. trustees Pennsylvanians for Effective Govt.; trustee Grove City Coll. Served with U.S. Army, 1943-46. Decorated Bronze Star. Mem. Carpet and Rug Inst. (dir.), Nat. Assn. Mfrs. Republican. Methodist. Clubs: Princeton (N.Y.C.); Tavern (Chgo.); Racquet (Phila.). Home: RD 6 Box 147 Carlisle PA 17013 Office: PO Box 40 Carlisle PA 17013

MASLIN, CHARLES WALTER, business exec.; b. Port Chester, N.Y., July 31, 1930; s. Walter Adrian and Dorothy Alice (Hepworth) M.; A.B. in Econs., Brown U., 1952; m. Joann Foster, Aug. 22, 1953; children—Edward, Richard, James, John, Elizabeth. With Gen. Electric Co., 1956-65, Singer Co., 1965-74; dir. materials mgmt. Henkel Inc., Teaneck, N.J., 1974-78; dir. purchasing Diamond Internat. Corp., N.Y.C., 1978—. Active Boy Scouts Am. Served with USN, 1952-55. Mem. Purchasing Mgmt. Assn. N.Y. (dir. 1974—), Traffic Club N.Y., Am. Prodn. and Inventory Control Soc., Nat. Council Phys. Distbn. Mgmt., Am. Mgmt. Assn., Nat. Eagle Scout Assn., Beta Theta Pi. Republican. Episcopalian. Clubs: Masons, Shriners. Asso. editor: Purchasing Handbook, 3d edit. Mem. publ. bd. Met. Purchaser. Home: 535 Tremont Ave Westfield NJ 07090 Office: 377 Third Ave New York NY 10017

MASLIN, HARVEY LAWRENCE, temporary help service co. exec.; b. Chgo., Oct. 22, 1939; s. Jack and Shirley M.; B.S. in Pub. Adminstrn., U. Ariz., 1961, J.D., 1964; m. Marcia Silberman, Aug. 21, 1960; children—Elaine, Shelley, Bonnie. Admitted to Ariz. bar, 1964, Calif. bar, 1966; jr. partner firm Maslin, Rotundo & Maslin, Sherman Oaks, Calif., 1966-67; gen. counsel, asst. sec. Western Temporary Services, Inc., San Francisco, 1967-71, v.p., mgr. internat. dept., 1972-78, sr. v.p., sec., 1979—; dir. Western Staff Services (U.K.) Ltd., London, Western Staff Services Pty. Ltd., Sydney, Western Staff Services (N.Z.) Ltd., Aukland; v.p., sec. Western Videotape Prodns., Inc., San Francisco, 1977—. Mem. Am., Calif., Ariz. bar assns., Zeta Beta Tau, Phi Alpha Delta. Republican. Clubs: Commonwealth, Calif., British Am. Author publs. in field. Home: 611 Creekmore Ct Walnut Creek CA 94598 Office: Western Temporary Services World Hdqrs Bldg 101 Howard St San Francisco CA 94105

MASLIN, ROBERT SEYMOUR, III, banker; b. Balt., Mar. 7, 1944; s. Robert Seymour and Ann May (Hodges) M.; B.S. in Bus. Mgmt., U. Balt., 1972; m. Jan Clay Davis, Dec. 31, 1966; children—Lisa Ann and Laura Ashley (twins). Portfolio mgr. trust dept. Union Trust Co. Md., Balt., 1965-73; portfolio mgr. trust dept. Md. Nat. Bank, Balt., 1973-79, sr. investment officer, 1979—. Mem. Balt. Security Analysts Soc., Balt. Econ. Soc. Club: Paint and Powder (2d v.p., gov.). Office: Md Nat Bank 10 Light St Baltimore MD 21203

MASON, CHARLES CULBERSON, JR., petroleum co. exec.; b. Quiriquire, Venezuela, Feb. 25, 1936; s. Charles Culberson and Marjorie (O'Bannon) M. (parents Am. citizens); B.A., U. Tex., 1958, J.D., 1960; postgrad. Grad. Sch. Bus. Adminstrn., Tulane U., 1970; m. Joyce Baldridge, Apr. 17, 1976; children—Stephen, Catherine. Admitted to Tex. bar, 1960; atty., land dept. Exxon Corp., New Orleans, 1963-74; atty., land mgr. Goodhope Refineries, Houston, 1974-75; mgr. of land Amax Petroleum Corp., Houston, 1975-77; exec. Kilroy Co., Houston, 1977-80; pvt. practice law, 1980—. Served to capt. JAGC, U.S. Army, 1961-63. Mem. Am., Tex., Houston bar assns., Am. Assn. Petroleum Landmen, Mid-Continent Oil and Gas Assn., Internat. Platform Assn. Baptist. Home: 12003 Sugar Springs Dr Houston TX 77077 Office: 1200 Commerce Bldg Houston TX 77002

MASON, E. GILBERT, housing-devel. co. exec.; b. Vernon, Tex., Jan. 8, 1909; s. William Edward and Verna Cecil (Birch) M.; student Columbia U., 1927-28, Grand Central Art Sch., summer 1928, Beaux Arts Inst. Design, 1929-30; m. Maria Cellia Perez, Jan. 17, 1960; 1 dau., Leslie Ellen. Owner, E. Gilbert Mason & Assos., design engrs., N.Y.C., 1932-35; set designer M.G.M. Motion Pictures, Los Angeles, 1935-36; owner E. Gilbert Mason & Assos., design engrs. and housing developers, Los Angeles, Ft. Worth and Houston, 1936-42, 48-54; chief interiors design engr. Douglas Aircraft Co., Santa Monica, Calif., 1942-45, cons., 1945-48; dir. design Am. Airlines, N.Y.C., 1954-60; pres. Teco Inc., Burbank, Calif., 1960-64; cons. design and sales promotion Douglas Aircraft Co., Long Beach, Calif., 1964-68; pres. Masonbilt Homes, Inc., Fillmore and Paso Robles, Calif., 1969—; cons. in field; dir. Masonbilt Homes, Inc., Teco, Inc. Recipient 25 Year Service award Soc. Automotive Engrs., 1969; 25 Year Contbn. award Advancement of Arts, Scis. and Tech. of Aeros. and Astronautics, 1970; registered profl. engr., Calif. Mem. Soc. Automotive Engrs., AIAA, Indsl. Designers Soc. Am., Nat. Aero. Assn. Clubs: Caballeros de los Robles, El Ranchito Polo. Contbr. articles to profl. jours. Home: PO Box 1436 Rio Robles Rancho Paso Robles CA 93446 Office: 603 12th St Town and Country Center Paso Robles CA 93446

MASON, ELVIS LEONARD, bank holding co. exec.; b. Vivian, La., Oct. 4, 1933; s. Alvin J. and Ellie (Stanfield) M.; B.B.A., Lamar U., 1959; grad. Stonier Grad. Sch. Banking; m. Joan Baker; children—Ross R., Gregory E., Jo Ellen. Asst. to pres., exec. v.p., pres., chmn. bd. First Security Nat. Bank, Beaumont, Tex., 1963-73; chmn. bd., chief exec. officer First Security Nat. Corp., Beaumont, 1972-73, pres., chief exec. officer, 1976-78; chmn. bd., chief exec. officer First Internat. Bancshares, Inc., Dallas, 1978—. Served to 1st lt. U.S. Army. Office: 1201 Elm St Dallas TX 75270*

MASON, EMORY EUGENE, lawyer, business exec.; b. Ashville, N.C., Dec. 5, 1930; s. Ralph Hedges and Olga (Shaw) M.; B.B.A., So. Methodist U., 1952, LL.B., 1956, postgrad., 1958-59; m. Ann M. Sharpe, June 16, 1956; children—Caroline, Elizabeth. Admitted to Tex. bar, 1956, D.C. bar, 1959, Pa. bar, 1961; asso. lawyer Smith, Bickley & Pope, Abilene, Tex., 1956-58, Sutherland, Asbill & Brennan, Washington, 1958-60; partner firm Stradley, Ronon, Stevens & Young, Phila., 1960-67, Ringe, Peet & Mason, Phila., 1967-69, Mason & Ringe, Phila., 1970-72, Stassen, Kostos & Mason, Phila., 1972—; chmn., pres. Energy Sources, Inc., 1973—. Chmn. fin. com., trustee Randolph-Macon Woman's Coll. Served to 1st lt. USAF, 1952-54. Mem. Am. Bar Assn., Kappa Sigma, Phi Alpha Delta. Republican. Episcopalian. Clubs: Congressional Country (Washington); Union League, Merion Cricket (Phila.); Seaview Country (Absecon, N.J.); Metropolitan (N.Y.C.). Home: 260 Chamounix Rd Saint Davids PA 19087 Office: 2300 Two Girard Plaza Philadelphia PA 19102

MASON, FRANKLIN ROGERS, fin. exec.; b. Washington, June 16, 1936; s. Franklin Allison and Jeannette Morgan (Rogers) M.; B.S. in Engring., Princeton U., 1958; M.B.A., Northwestern U., 1959; m. Aileen Joan Larson, July 29, 1961; children—William Rogers, Elisa Ellen. With Ford Motor Co., 1960-75, finance mgr., Portugal, 1969-72; fin. analysis mgr. Ford subs. Richier S.A., France, 1972-75; sr. group v.p. finance Raymond Internat. Inc., Houston, 1975-78, sr. v.p.-fin., 1978—; dir. First City Nat. Bank-Westheimer, Houston; bd. dirs. Minority Enterprise Small Bus. Investment Corp., Houston, 1976-79. Served with arty. U.S. Army, 1960. Mem. Fin. Execs. Inst., Assn. Corp. Growth, Am. Mgmt. Assn., Princeton U. Alumni Assn., Alliance Francaise, Houston-Nice Sister City Assn. Republican. Episcopalian. Clubs: University, Racquet (Houston); Princeton (N.Y.C.). Home: 420 Chapelwood Ct Houston TX 77024 Office: 5065 Westheimer Suite 1225 Houston TX 77056

MASON, JOSEPH D., architect, real estate developer; b. N.Y.C., Nov. 11, 1939; s. Joseph and Rose Maisano; B.S., CCNY, 1961, B.Arch., 1967; m. Arlene J. Goldberg, Mar. 5, 1962; children—Pamela, Samantha. Staff architect Rutgers State U., New Brunswick, N.J., 1967-70; chief architect N.J. Housing Fin. Agy., Trenton, 1970-73; v.p. Concept Bldg. Industries, Inc., Keyport, N.J., 1973; pres. Joseph D. Mason, Architect, Freehold, N.J., 1973—, Mason Devel. Group Inc., Freehold, 1975-79, Mason Plowfield Devel. Co., Inc., Phila., 1980—. Served with AUS, 1961. Mem. AIA, N.J. Soc. Architects, Nat. Assn. Home Builders, N.J. Builders Assn. Republican. Home: 62 Townsend Dr Freehold NJ 07728 Office: 1303 Memorial Dr Asbury Park NJ 07712

MASON, LEON VERNE, fin. planner; b. Lawrence, Kans., Jan. 13, 1933; s. Thomas Samuel and Mabel Edith (Hyre) M.; B.S. in Engring. with honors, U. Kans., 1955; M.S. in Mgmt. with honors, U. Colo., 1970; m. Martha Harryann Sippel, Aug. 26, 1955; children—Mark Verne, Kirk Matthew, Erik Andrew. Engr., Pittsburg Des Moines Steel Co., 1955-56; with IBM Corp., 1958—, sr. engr., San Jose, Calif., 1975-77, Boulder, Colo., 1977—; sr. engr. on loan, dir. capital campaign Vols. of Am., 1980—. Pres., Boulder Interfaith Housing; dir. Golden West Manor, 1978-80; dir. Retire Sr. Vol. Program, 1979-80; chmn. elders 1st Christian Ch., Boulder, 1977-79. Served with USAF, 1955-57; col. Res. Cert. fin. planner; registered profl. engr. Mem. Internat. Assn. Fin. Planners, Am. Soc. Quality Control, Soc. Mfg. Engrs. Club: Kiwanis. Home: 660 S 42d Boulder CO 80303

MASON, PETER LEONARD, real estate broker; b. Toronto, Ont., Can., July 4, 1944; s. W. Leonard and Ida Margaret (Moir) M.; degree York U., 1971; m. Dorothy Joan Jarvis, July 1, 1966; children—Sandra, Andrea, Joanna, Lesley. Accountant, Royal Bank Can., Toronto, 1963-65; appraisal and sales staff Webb & Mason, Ltd., Toronto, 1965-67; founder, pres. Peter L. Mason Ltd., Don Mills, Ont., 1967—; mem. Ont. Comml. Registration Appeal Tribunal, 1980-81. pres. Toronto Real Estate Bd., 1977, chmn. fin. com., 1976. Fellow Real Estate Inst. Can.; mem. Ont. Real Estate Assn. (chmn. polit. affairs com. 1980-81, 1st v.p. 1981), Can. Real Estate Assn. (chmn. legis. com., dir. 1981), Met. Toronto Bd. Trade, Assn. Ont. Land Economists. Clubs: Osler Bluff Ski, Markham Rotary; York Downs Golf and Country (Unionville, Ont.). Home: Rural Route 2 Gormley ON Canada Office: 1 Valleybrook Dr Suite 401 Don Mills ON M3B 2S7 Canada

MASON, RAYMOND K., diversified co. exec.; b. Jacksonville, Fla., 1927; grad. U. N.C., 1949. Chmn., pres. Charter Co., Jacksonville, Fla.; chmn. Charter Mortgage Co., Beach Fed. Savs. & Loan Assn.; dir. Fla. First Nat. Bank of Jacksonville. Office: Jacksonville Nat Bank Bldg Jacksonville FL 32202*

MASON, RICHARD GORDON, lawn and garden tool mfg. co. exec.; b. Woonsocket, R.I., Dec. 5, 1930; s. Stephenson and Marion Irons (Cook) M.; B.S., Yale U., 1952; M.B.A., Harvard U., 1957; m. Joan Elizabeth Morrison, June 28, 1957; children—Lydia Gordon, Jonathan Whitcomb, James Stephenson. With Stanley Works, New Britain, Conn., 1957-62, 65-75, v.p. mfg., 1970-75; prodn. supt. Thomas Smith Co., Worcester, Mass., 1962-65; exec. asst. to pres. Ames, a McDonough Co., Parkersburg, w.Va., 1975, v.p., 1975-78, pres., 1978—; dir. McDonough Co. Bd. dirs. Parkersburg Community Found. Served with USN, 1952-55. Mem. Hand Tools Inst. (dir.), Am. Hardware Mfrs. Assn. (dir.), Parkersburg C. of C. (dir.). Republican. Episcopalian. Club: Parkersburg Rotary. Home: 43 Lake Dr Parkersburg WV 26101 Office: Box 1774 Parkersburg WV 26101

MASSANISO, PETER ANTHONY, investment counselor; b. Phila., Aug. 18, 1936; s. Frank Paul and Emily Elena (Finocchiaro) M.; A.B., Williams Coll., 1958; M.B.A. in Finance, Wharton Sch. of U. Pa., 1961. Sr. investment analyst, comml. and indsl. loan dept. Prudential Life Ins. Co., 1961-65; v.p. securities Ind. Life and Accident Ins. Co., Jacksonville, Fla., 1965-69; pres. Bus. and Fin. Mgmt., Inc., Jacksonville, 1969-71; v.p. corporate planning, dir. Fisco, Inc., ins., Phila., 1971-74; pres. Profl. Capital Mgmt., Inc., Jacksonville, 1974—; dir., mem. exec. com. Hickory Furniture Co. (N.C.), Presco Holding Corp., Chgo. Mem. adv. bd. and trust fund com. North Fla. council Boy Scouts Am.; bd. dirs., chmn. investment com. Jacksonville Mus. Arts and Scis. Served with Pa. N.G., 1958-61. Mem. Phila., Jacksonville fin. analysts socs., Nat. Assn. Securities Dealers, Delta Kappa Epsilon. Clubs: Tournament Players; Ponte Vedra, River, Sawgrass (Jacksonville); Palm Bay (Miami, Fla.); LeClub (N.Y.C.). Contbr. articles to profl. jours. Home: 17 Lake Julia Dr Ponte Vedra Beach FL 32082 Office: 3303 Independent Sq Jacksonville FL 32202

MASSENGILL, WILLIAM WAYNE, mfg. co. exec.; b. Brownsville, Tenn., Sept. 10, 1933; s. L. C. and E. Lucille (Boggs) M.; B.S. in Chem. Engring., Auburn U., 1954; M.B.A., Harvard U., 1962; m. Nancy Hilker, Dec. 27, 1964; children—Dana Elizabeth, Julie Suzanne, David Christopher. Tech. sales and service rep. Dupont Co., Wilmington, Del., 1954-60; bus. analyst Geigy Chems. A.G., Basel, Switzerland, summer 1961; with Kaiser Aluminum & Chem. Corp., Oakland, Calif., 1962—, mgr. planning and control, chem. and spl. metals group, 1969-70, mgr. corp. diversification planning, 1971-76, dir. corp. devel., 1976—. Active youth activities. YMCA, Oakland. Served as pilot, capt. USAF, 1955-57. Mem. Assn. Corp. Growth, Corp. Planners Assn., N.Am. Soc. Corp. Planning, Planning Execs. Inst., Harvard Bus. Sch. Alumni Assn. Republican. Clubs: Commonwealth of Calif., Harvard (San Francisco). Office: 2083 Kaiser Center 300 Lakeside Dr Oakland CA 94643

MASSEY, JACK C., hosp. co. exec.; b. Sandersville, Ga., 1904; grad. U. Fla., 1925. Chmn. exec. com., dir. Hosp. Corp. Am., Nashville; chmn. Vol. Capital Corp.; dir. Thomas Nelson Publishers, Nashville City Bank & Trust Co., Cummings Inc., Enterprise Fabricators, Inc. Trustee Montgomery Bell Acad. Office: PO Box 550 Nashville TN 37203*

MASSEY, JAMES EDWARD, elec. contracting co. exec.; b. Olney, Ill., Sept. 23, 1923; s. William Iraand Jean S. (Higgins) M.; B.S., U. Detroit, 1950; m. Patricia A. Curry, Jan. 28, 1950; children—James P., Thomas M., Daniel B., Mary Beth, Maureen Ann. Vice pres. mktg. and sales Pulte-Strang Inc., Ft. Myers, Fla. and Detroit, 1960-63; pres. Cullen-Massey Inc., Detroit, 1963-76, Hall Engring. Co., Detroit, 1976—. Chmn. U. Detroit Alumni Fund, 1960-61. Served with U.S. Army, 1943-45. Mem. Nat. Assn. Elec. Contractors (Southeastern chpt.), Iron and Steel Assn., Plant Engring. Soc. Detroit. Republican. Roman Catholic. Clubs: Detroit Athletic, Western Golf and Country, Errol Estates Country. Office: 12644 Marion Detroit MI 48239

MASSEY, JAY RICHARDSON, fin. exec.; b. Phila., Dec. 30, 1938; s. Jay Richardson and Marian Virginia (Boles) M.; A.B. with honors, Coll. of Holy Cross, 1960; M.A., Bryn Mawr Coll., 1962. Stockbroker, Reynolds & Co., Phila., 1962-65; market analyst Smith Kline Overseas Corp., Phila., 1965-68; 1st v.p. Drexel Burnham Lambert, Phila., 1968—. Chmn., Friends Phila. Mus. Art, 1977—, trustee ex-officio; pres. Fabric Workshop, 1976—. Served to ensign USN, 1960-61. Rotary Traveling fellow, Chile, 1968; chartered fin. analyst. Mem. Fin. Analysts Fedn. Roman Catholic. Clubs: Phila., Racquet, Print (v.p. 1971-78) (Phila.). Home: 2017 Waverly St Philadelphia PA 19146 Office: 1500 Walnut St Philadelphia PA 19102

MASSEY, RICHARD WESLEY, mech. engr.; b. Ballston Spa, N.Y., Jan. 18, 1930; s. Wesley Fulton and Margaret Jeannette (Levey) M.; B.M.E., Purdue U., 1953; student U. Calif. at Los Angeles, 1960, Rensselaer Poly. Inst., 1962-64; m. Suzanne LeBourveau, July 7, 1956 (div. Mar. 1979); children—Deborah Anne, Bruce Richard, Scott Howard; m. 2d, Jungmi Massey, Dec. 22, 1979. Supervising test devel. engr. Gen. Electric Co., Schenectady, N.Y., Burlington, Vt., Pittsfield, Mass., 1953-57, 61-65; supervising test devel. engr. Hughes Aircraft Co., El Segundo, Calif., Newport Beach, Calif., Fullerton, Calif., 1957-61, 65-67; cons. engr., project dir., mfg. engr. TRW Systems, Inc., Redondo Beach, Calif., 1967-71; arty. weapons engr. Joint U.S. Mil. Assistance Group, Seoul, Korea, 1976-78; value analysis engr. Watervliet (N.Y.) Arsenal, 1971-76, 78-79; task mgr. high energy laser program Pacific Missile Test Center, Port Mugu, Calif., 1979—. Transp. coordinator Sam Sung Orphanage, Seoul, 1976-78. Mem. Am. Def. Preparedness Assn., Am. Security Council (nat. adv. bd.), U.S. Embassy Assn., Am. Mgmt. Assn., Soc. Am. Mil. Engrs. Club: Masons. Home: 1821 Evangeline Pl Oxnard CA 93030 Office: Pacific Missile Test Center Port Mugu CA 93042

MASSEY, SHELBY D., processed food and cotton merchandising co. exec.; b. Mt. Hope, Ala., 1933; grad. Athens Coll., 1961. With Red Hat Poultry Co., to 1970; corp. v.p., mgr. foods div., corp. sr. v.p. Valmac Industries Inc., 1970-75, exec. v.p., 1975-76, pres., 1976-80, chief exec. officer, 1979—, chmn., 1980—, also dir.; dir. Conwood Corp. Office: 2 S Front St Memphis TN 38103*

MASSICK, JAMES WILLIAM, heavy equipment mfg. co. exec.; b. Seattle, Jan. 19, 1932; s. Peter James and Annetta Jean (Dormier) M.; B.S., U. Wash., 1954; M.B.A., U. Calif. at Los Angeles, 1966; m. Joyce Allair Puckey, Apr. 7, 1973; children—Scott, Christopher, Kit, Timothy, Nina, Sally, John, Jill. Constrn. engr. Kaiser Engrs., Oakland, Calif., 1957-60; project mgr. Ralph M. Parsons Co., Los Angeles, 1960-65; engring. mgr. Weyerhauser Co., Tacoma, 1965-68; operations mgr. Western Gear Corp., Everett, Wash., 1968-70; pres. Truckweld Corp., Truckweld Equipment Co., Truckweld Utilities, Inc.; dir. Truckweld Corp., Puget Sound Lease Co., Pacific N.W. Utility & Supply Co., Big Bud Tractors Inc. Served to capt. USNR, 1950, 54-57. Decorated Navy Cross, Silver Star, Legion of Merit, Purple Heart. Mem. Am. Soc. C.E., Soc. Am. Mil. Engrs., Seattle C. of C., Seattle Municipal League, Theta Delta Chi. Episcopalian. Clubs: Overlake Golf and Country, Harbor. Patentee in field. Home: 11451 SE 326th Pl Auburn WA 98002 Office: 8639 S 190th St Kent WA 98031

MASSMAN, JOHN THOMAS, constrn. co. exec.; b. Kansas City, Mo., Aug. 26, 1935; s. Henry Joseph and Cecelia Mary (Nangle) M.; student Rockhurst Coll., 1951-52; B.S. in C.E., U. Notre Dame, 1956; m. Carolyn Sue Pfeifer, Oct. 18, 1958; children—Carol, Karen, John Thomas, James, Joseph, Kay, Kim. With Massman Constrn. Co., Kansas City, Mo., 1956—, v.p., 1960-70, sr. v.p., 1970-80; pres. John Massman Contracting Co., Kansas City, 1980—; dir. Continental TV Inc. Mem. engring. adv. council U. Notre Dame, 1974—; bd. govs. Am. Royal Assn., 1958-78; bd. dirs. Starlight Theatre Assn., 1965—; pres. AGC Flood Control Br., Memphis, 1969, Mo. AGC, 1975; v.p. Rockhurst Hon. Dirs., 1980—; pres. alumni bd. Rockhurst High Sch., 1977—. Served with U.S. Army, 1958. Recipient Cert. of Honor, Rockhurst Coll., 1978; named Man of Yr., Notre Dame U., 1974. Fellow ASCE; mem. Heavy Contrn. Assn. (pres. 1965-66), Am. Soc. Mil. Engrs., Am. Public Works Assn., Mo.-Ark. Flood Control Assn., Nat. Waterways Conf. (dir. 1973-79), Truman Library Inst. Roman Catholic. Clubs: Kansas City, Mission Hills Country, K.C. (3 deg.). Office: 521 E 63d St Kansas City MO 64110

MASSRY, MORRIS, real estate co. exec.; b. Bklyn., Apr. 22, 1929; s. Isaac and Jane (Zalta) M.; student pub. schs., Niagara Falls, N.Y.; m. Esther Franco, Jan. 16, 1949; children—Jane, Marilyn, Linda, Norman, Sheila, Lisa. Pres., Massry Realty Corp., Albany, 1958—, Tri-City Rentals, Albany, 1966—. Pres., Daus. of Sarah Nursing Home, 1976-78, Troy Jewish Community Center, 1974-76; chmn. Doane Stuart Sch., 1978; gen. chmn. Salvation Army Bd., United Way Campaign, 1978-79; pres. Troy Jewish Community Council; bd. dirs. St. Mary Hosp., Jr. Achievement Capitol Dist., Mohawk Hudson Community Found.; v.p. Mohawk Hudson United Way; bd. dirs., chmn. 1979 fund raising Boy Scouts Am., bd. dirs. Gov. Clinton council. Republican. Jewish. Clubs: Colonie Country, Univ., Masons, K.P. (past chancellor). Office: 41 State St Suite 608 Albany NY 12207

MASSUNG, RONALD RAYMOND, retail exec.; b. McKeesport, Pa., Sept. 8, 1947; s. Raymond F. and Dorothy M.; student Pa. State U., 1969-74; 1 son by previous marriage—Ronnie A. Apprentice cabinetmaker Decor Cabinet Co., McKeesport, 1966-69; cabinetmaker foreman Murry Kitchen Center, Murrysville, Pa., 1970-71; owner, cabinetmaker Massung Cabinet Co., White Oak, Pa., 1971—. Served with AUS, 1967. Mem. Am. Inst. Kitchen Dealers, Pitts. C. of C., Jaycees. Roman Catholic. Office: 3026 Stewartsville Rd White Oak PA 15131

MAST, FREDERICK WILLIAM, constrn. co. exec.; b. Quincy, Ill., Jan. 3, 1910; s. Christian Charles and Jessie Minnie (Pape) M.; B.S., U. Ill., 1933; m. Kathryn Mary Boekenhoff, Sept. 15, 1932 (dec. Jan. 17, 1975); children—Robert Frederick, Janet (Mrs. James Austin Jones), Susan (Mrs. Edward Hoskins Wilson), Linda (Mrs. William Frederick Bohlen), Teresa Ann (Mrs. Charles Edward Connell); m. 2d, Elaine Ellen Thies Driver, Feb. 14, 1976. Hwy. engr. Adams County (Ill.) Hwy. Dept., Quincy, 1929-33; jr. engr. Ill. Div. Hwys. Rd. Office, Springfield, 1933-35, asst. hwys. architect, 1935-39; estimator Jens Olesen & Sons Constrn. Co., Waterloo, Iowa, 1939-41, v.p., 1941-54, exec. v.p., 1954-65, pres., 1965-76, chmn. bd., 1970-80; owner Frederick W. Mast & Assos., Waterloo, 1946-60; pres. Broadway Bldg. Co., 1951—, Kimball Shopping Center, Inc., 1964-78. Mem. Council Constrn. Employers, Washington, 1968-72, chmn., 1969; ofcl. U.S. del. to Soviet Union under U.S./USSR Exchanges Agreement, 1968-69; del. 8th and 9th sessions bldg., civil engring. and pub. works com. ILO, Geneva, 1971, 77; sr. builder specialist Tech. for the Am. Home Exhibit USIA, USSR, 1975. Mem. Iowa Bldg. Code Council, Des Moines, 1947-50; mem. Bd. Zoning Adjustment, Waterloo, 1947-59; mem. City Plan and Zoning Commn., Waterloo, 1955-78; chmn. Community Devel. Bd., City of Waterloo, 1959-70. Finance chmn. Black Hawk County Republican Central Com., 1958-60; chmn. Waterloo-Cedar Falls Symphony Orch. endowment fund dr., 1977-79, St. Francis Health Care Found., 1980—; chmn. bd. dirs. St. Francis Hosp., 1976-78; chmn. contractors adv. com. Iowa Coll. Found., 1972-73. Served to col., C.E., AUS, 1941-46. Decorated Legion of Merit; recipient Distinguished Service award Waterloo C. of C., 1962; Ky. Col. Registered architect, Ill., Iowa. Mem. Assn. Gen. Contractors Am. (dir. 1956—, mem. exec. com. 1959-62, 66-72, nat. pres. 1968, SIR award Nev. chpt. 1970), Am. Inst. Constructors, Contractors Mut. Assn. Washington (dir. 1971—, chmn. exec. com. 1971-73), Iowa Engring. Soc., Nat. Soc. Profl. Engrs., Soc. Am. Mil. Engrs., Waterloo Tech. Soc., Amvets, Am. Legion, Phi Eta Sigma, Sigma Phi Epsilon, Tau Beta Pi, Tau Nu Tau, Theta Tau. Roman Catholic. Elk, Kiwanian. Club: Sunnyside Country. Home: 3309 F Inverness Rd Waterloo IA 50701 Office: PO Box 575 Waterloo IA 50704 also 321 W 18th St Waterloo IA 50702

MASTERS, PHILIP JEROME, vending machine mfg. co. exec.; b. Des Moines, Apr. 8, 1950; degree in Bus., Am. Inst. Bus., 1970. Nat. sales dir. Fed. Machine Corp., Des Moines, 1970—. Office: 100 104 SW 4th St Des Moines IA 50309

MASTERSON, ADRIENNE CRAFTON, real estate exec.; b. Providence, Mar. 6, 1926; d. John Harold and Adrienne (Fitzgerald) Crafton; student No. Va. Community Coll., 1971-74; m. Francis T. Masterson, May 31, 1947 (div. Jan. 1977); children—Mary Victoria Masterson Powers, Kathleen Joan, John Andrew, Barbara Lynn. Mem. staff Senator T.F. Green of R.I., Washington, 1944-47, 54-60; mem. staff U.S. Senate Com. on Campaign Expenditures, 1944-45; clk. Ho. Govt. Ops. Com., 1948-49, Ho. Campaign Expenditures Com., 1950; asst. appointment sec. Office of Pres., 1951-53; with Hubbard Realty, Alexandria, Va., 1962-67; owner, mgr. Adrienne Investment Real Estate, Alexandria, 1968—. Exec. sec., legis. chmn. Richmond Diocesan Council Cath. Women. Mem. No. Va. Bd. Realtors, Va., Nat. assns. Realtors, Am. Soc. Profl. and Exec. Women, Nat. Assn. Female Execs., Mcht. Broker Exchange (London), Alexandria C. of C., Friends of Kennedy Center (founding), Nat. Hist. Soc., Nat. Trust Historic Preservation. Democrat. Home: 8200 Rolling Rd Springfield VA 22153 Office: PO Box 1271 421 King St Suite 218 Alexandria VA 22313

MASTIN, FREDERICK AUGUSTINE, JR., bus. exec.; b. Mineola, L.I., N.Y., Mar. 28, 1939; s. Frederick A. and Ann (McMahon) M.; B.S. in Fin., Siena Coll., 1961; m. Donna M. Markum, Nov. 25, 1966; children—Meredith, Whitney. Asst. product mgr. Vick Chem. Co. div. Richardson-Merrell Inc., N.Y.C., 1967-69; product mgr., div. sales mgr. Avon Products, Inc., N.Y.C., 1969-74; nat. sales mgr. Bell & Howell, Chgo., 1974-75; pres. Sales Consultants Fairfield, Inc., Southport, Conn., 1976—. Served to maj., USMCR, 1962-67. Mem. Southport C. of C. (dir. 1977—), Fairfield Univ. President's Circle. Republican. Roman Catholic. Home: 761 Round Hill Rd Fairfield CT 06430 Office: 3695 Post Rd Southport CT 06490

MASTRAN, JOHN LEO, orgn. and mgmt. counsel; b. Peekskill, N.Y., Mar. 29, 1920; s. John and Mary (Costella) M.; B.S. in Commerce, U. Va., 1942; Indsl. Adminstrn. degree, Harvard Grad. Sch. Bus. Adminstrn, 1943; m. Carol Ann Righter, Oct. 7, 1950; children—Mary Isabel Mastran Paterson, Elizabeth Righter Mastran Small. Orgn. planning adviser RCA, Camden, N.J., 1943-49, asst. to v.p. and to gen. plant mgr. RCA Electron Tube div., Harrison, N.J., 1949-53, mgr. orgn. planning and mgmt. devel., Camden, 1953-67, dir. orgn. planning and mgmt. devel., 1967-71, dir. orgn. planning, 1971-80, staff v.p. orgn. planning, 1980—; orgn. planning adviser 3d Internat. Conf. Mfrs., NAM, 1956; chmn. adv. council on orgn. planning Nat. Indsl. Conf. Bd.; mgmt. course guest speaker Am. Mgmt. Assn. Mem. Orgn. Devel. Council (chmn., pres.), Harvard Bus. Sch. Assn., Beta Gamma Sigma, Alpha Kappa Psi. Clubs: Moorestown Field (pres.); Harvard, Netherland (N.Y.C.). Home: 508 Stanwick Rd Moorestown NJ 08057 Office: RCA Bldg 30 Rockefeller Plaza New York NY 10020

MASUCCI, CARMINE, engring. exec.; b. Bklyn., Jan. 29, 1923; s. Anthony and Luigia (Capozzi) M.; B.E.E., Coll. City N.Y., 1944; postgrad. Poly. Inst. Bklyn., 1948-55; m. Carmela Marie Greco, July 14, 1951; children—Marylou, Melinda. Asso. gen. mgr. intelligence system dept. CBS Labs., Stamford, Conn., 1960-69, v.p. tech. ops. sequential info. systems, Elmsford, N.Y., 1969-70; mgr. advance electro optical systems Astro Electronics div. RCA, Hightstown, N.J., 1970-72; gen. mgr. govt. and indsl. ops. CBS Labs., Stamford, 1973-75; v.p., gen. mgr. Epsco Labs., Wilton, Conn., 1975-76; v.p. engring. Izon Corp., Stamford, 1976-79, New Brunswick Sci. Co., Inc., Edison, N.J., 1979—; cons. CM Engring. Inc., MRD, Inc., DeBera Elec., Inc. Pres. parents council Manhattanville Coll.; asso. dir. Poly. Inst. N.Y. Alumni Assn. Served with USNR, 1944-46. Mem. IEEE, Soc. Photog. Instrumentation Engrs., Soc. Photog. Scientists and Engrs., Air Force Assn. Roman Catholic. Contbr. articles profl. jours. Home: 64 Hickory Hill Rd Eastchester NY 10709 Office: 44 Talmadge Rd Edison NJ 08817

MASVIDAL, RAUL PABLO, banker; b. Havana, Cuba, Nov. 14, 1941; s. Raul Armando and Maria (Jury) M.; A.B., U. Miami, 1965; M.I.M., Am. Grad. Sch. Internat. Mgmt., 1966; children—Raul Pablo, Pablo Alberto. With Citibank, N.A., 1966-74, resident v.p., P.R., 1967-74, Madrid, Spain, 1974; pres. Royal Trust Bank, Miami, Fla., 1974-77; pres., chmn. bd. Biscayne Bank, Miami, 1977—. Mem. citizens bd. U. Miami; bd. patrons Greater Miami Opera; bd. dirs. Lowe Art Mus.; bd. dirs., v.p. Fla. Philharmon.; mem. Hispanic Council Fgn. Affairs; bd. dirs. City of Miami Com. on Ecology and Beautification Bd. Served with U.S. Army, 1972-73. Mem. Am. Mgmt. Assn., Dade County Bankers Assn., Fla. Bankers Assn. Roman Catholic. Clubs: Surf, Palm Bay, Grove Isle, Bankers, American. Office: 350 Biscayne Blvd Miami FL 33132

MATAYA, ROBERT JOHN, mfg. co. exec.; b. Chgo., Aug. 21, 1942; s. Joseph Vincent and Stephanie Helen Mataya; B.S. in Bus. Adminstrn., Loyola U., Chgo., 1964; M.B.A., Northwestern U., 1968; m. Patricia Steiner, Apr. 23, 1967; 1 dau., Allison. Sales analyst Internat. Harvester Co., Chgo., 1964-66; salesman Glidden Co., Chgo., 1966-68, Celanese Co., Chgo., 1968-70; dir. mktg. C.G. Conn Ltd., Oak Brook, Ill., 1971—. Served with USAR, 1966. Home: 1130 Chillem St Batavia IL 60510

MATEJIC, DENISE MARIA, family fin. mgmt. cons.; b. Vienna, Austria, Mar. 9, 1935; d. Otmar and Alice (Ulbrich) Buttoraz; came to U.S., 1962; student City of London Coll., 1954-55, U. Vienna Sch. Law, 1955-56; M.B.A., Sch. Commerce and Bus. Adminstrn. Vienna, 1960; postgrad. N.Y. Inst. Fin., 1968-70; m. Milorad B. Matejic, Apr. 7, 1960; 1 dau., Sandra D. Adminstrv. asst. Bauvag A.G., 1961-62; partner Trendicator Assos., investment cons., Elizabeth, N.J., 1970-71; agt. Sentry Ins. Co., Morristown, N.J., 1971; pvt. practice teaching, lecturing personal, family fin. mgmt., Morris Plains, N.J., 1970-71; specialist family resource mgmt., prof. Coop. Extension Service, Cook Coll., Rutgers U., New Brunswick, N.J., 1971—; curriculum cons.; mem. Nat. Extension Adv. com. Am. Council Life Ins., Washington, N.J. Ford Consumer Appeals Bd., N.J. Bell Consumer Adv. Com.; mem. ad hoc adv. com. AT&T; v.p. Consumers League N.J., 1978-79, bd. dirs., 1978-80. Recipient Merit award Rutgers U., 1977; citation Library of Congress, ERIC System, others. Mem. Am. Council Consumer Interests, AAUP, N.Y. Regional Council for Industry-Edn. Cooperation and Specialists Assn.-Rutgers U. (sec. 1978-80); asso. mem. Am., N.J. home econs. assns. Roman Catholic. Author: Your Money Matters; Personal and Family Finances; Planning and Managing Community Programs. Home: 1 Greenwood Rd Morris Plains NJ 07950 Office: Coop Extension Service Cook Coll Rutgers U PO Box 231 New Brunswick NJ 08903

MATERS, HANS WILLEM S., packaging co. exec.; b. Groningen, Netherlands, Feb. 15, 1940; s. Jan Cornelis and Hendrike Catherina (Deuling) M.; came to U.S., 1964, naturalized, 1970; HBS-A, Zeist Netherlands, 1960; student Amsterdam U., 1962-63; postgrad. N.Y. U., 1966-69; S.M.P., Harvard U., 1979; m. Karen Carver Skawden,

Dec. 30, 1967; children—Susan Caroline, John Carver. Comml. asst. Allied Products div. Philips Lamp Co., Netherlands, 1963-64; with Westvaco Corp., N.Y.C., 1965-74, sales and service supr. container board div., 1970-74; export mktg. sales mgr. pulp and paper div. CFI, N.Y.C., 1974-77; mktg. and sales mgr. internat. forest products ops. Europe, Owens-Ill. Internat., Geneva, 1977-79, gen. mgr. internat. forest products ops. Europe, 1979, v.p. and gen. mgr. Owens-Ill. Internat. S.A., Geneva, 1979—. Served with Netherlands Army, 1960-62. Mem. Am. Mgmt. Assn., Newcomen Soc. N.Am., European Fedn. Corrugated Box Mfrs. Club: Am. Internat. (Geneva). Home: 15 Chemin des Buclines 1224 Chene Bougeries Geneva Switzerland Office: 48 Route des Acacias 1227 Carouge Geneva Switzerland

MATESA, LAWRENCE GEORGE, mergers and acquisitions co. exec.; b. Dearborn, Mich., Feb. 26, 1931; s. George G. and Caroline (Krusac) M.; student Henry Ford Community Coll., 1950-54, Wayne State U. and Wayne State Law Sch., 1956; m. Lois Watkins Gregor, Nov. 17, 1978; children—Kelly, Michelle. Vice pres. F. J. Winckler Co., Detroit, 1956-64; salesman Manley Bennett McDonald, N.Y. Stock Exchange, Detroit, 1964-66; v.p. First Detroit Securities Corp., stock brokers and underwriters, Detroit, 1966-74; pres. Mich. Eagle Corp., Detroit, 1974—; dir. Ind. Liberty Life Ins. Co., Grand Rapids, Mich., 1963—, mem. audit com., 1979—; guest speaker Focus Radio Show, WJR, Detroit, 1966-71. Republican. Clubs: Detroit Yacht; Great Oaks Country (Rochester, Mich.); University (Flint, Mich.). Home: 447 Antoinette St Rochester MI 48063 Office: 933 Penobscot Bldg Detroit MI 48226

MATHE, JOHN L., acct.; b. Highland Park, Ill., Aug. 29, 1943; s. Harold O. and Vivian R. (Shelk) M.; B.S. in B.A., Elmhurst Coll., 1975. Acct., Jewel Food Stores, Melrose Park, Ill., 1969-74; fin. analyst Baxter Labs., Deerfield, Ill., 1974-78; controller Internat. Cargo Containers, Inc., Chgo., 1978—. Served to 1st lt., Ordnance Corps, U.S. Army, 1966-69. Mem. Nat. Assn. Accts. Unitarian. Home: 1270 St Johns Ave Highland Park IL 60035

MATHENY, TOM HARRELL, lawyer; b. Houston; s. Whitman and Lorene (Harrell) M.; B.A., Southeastern La. U., 1954; J.D., Tulane U., 1957; LL.D., Centenary Coll., 1979, DePauw U., 1979. Admitted to La. bar, 1957; partner firm Pittman & Matheny, Hammond, La., 1957—; v.p. Edwards & Assos., So. Brick Supply, Inc.; trust counsel 1st Guaranty Bank; former mem. faculty Southeastern La. U., Holy Cross Coll. of New Orleans. Pres. jud. council United Methodist Ch., 1976-80; pres. Nat. Assn. of Conf. Lay Leaders, 2 yrs.; conf. lay leader La. ann. conf. United Meth. Ch., 1966—, trustee La. ann. conf.; del. World Meth. Conf., London, 1966, Denver, 1971, Dublin, 1976; del. Gen. Conf. United Meth. Ch., 1968, 70, 72; trustee Scarritt Coll., Centenary Coll.; hon. trustee John F. Kennedy Coll.; chmn. bd. Wesley Found.; hon. sec. U.S. com. Audenshaw Found.; chmn. advancement com. Hammond council Boy Scouts Am., 1960-64, mem. dist. council, 1957-66, exec. bd. Istrouma Area council, 1966—; campaign mgr. Democratic candidate for gov. La., 1959-60, 63-64; bd. dirs. Tangipahoa Parish chpt. ARC, 1957-67, Hammond United Givers Fund, 1957-68, La. Council Chs., La. Interch. Conf. Recipient Man of Year award, Hammond, 1961, 64, also La. State Jaycees, 1964. Mem. Am. (probate com.), La. (chmn. com. legal aid, com. prison reform), 21st Jud. Dist. (past sec.-treas.; v.p. 1967-68, 71—) bar assns., Comml. Law League Am. (past mem. com. ethics), La. Alumni Council (pres. 1963-65), Acad. Religion and Mental Health, Internat. Platform Assn., La. Assn. Claimants' Compensation Attys., Southeastern La. Coll. Alumni Assn. (dir., pres. 1961-62, bd. spl. fund 1959-62, dir. Tangipahoa chpt.), Tulane Alumni Assn., UN Assn., Am. Trial Lawyers Assn., Am. Judicature Soc., Law-Sci. Inst., World Peace Through Law Acad. (conciliation com.), Am. Acad. Polit. and Social Sci., Am. Acad. Law and Sci., Hammond Assn. Commerce (dir. 1960-65), Phi Delta Phi, Phi Delta, Phi Alpha Delta. Democrat. Clubs: Masons, Shriners, DeMolay (dist. dep. to Supreme Council 1964—; Legion of Honor), Kiwanis (v.p., dir.). Home: PO Box 221 Hammond LA 70404 Office: 401 E Thomas St Hammond LA 70401

MATHEOS, HARRY, archtl. engr.; b. Kandila, Greece, Feb. 11, 1942; s. Peter George and Dina N. (Valkanou) M.; came to U.S., 1951, naturalized, 1960; B.Arch., U. Ill., 1968; m. Maria Scouloudi, Jan. 26, 1970; children—Peter Alexander, Stella Louisa. Project engr. Litton Devel. Corp., Athens, Greece, 1968-69; project architect McGaughy, Marshall & McMillan, Norfolk, Va. and Athens, 1969-74; chief architect PAE Internat., Los Angeles, 1974-76; project mgr. USDA-SEA, Peoria, Ill., 1977-78, head engring. design and constrn. fed. research N.E. region, Beltsville, Md., 1978—. Mem. Constrn. Specifications Inst., Am. Soc. Agrl. Engrs., Assn. Energy Engrs., Energy Conservation Cons. Council, Plant and Bldg. Energy Conservation Council, Solar Engring. Council, Wind Power Engring. Council, Engring. and Constrn. Council, Energy Engrs. in Govt. Council, New Energy Resource Devel. Council, Energy Mgmt. Council, Transp. Systems Energy Conservation Council, Energy Edn. Council, Computer Programs for Energy Analysis Council. Democrat. Greek Orthodox. Home: 14142 Castle Blvd Silver Spring MD 20904 Office: Nat Agrl Library Bldg Beltsville MD 20705

MATHER, ALBERT GRAY, JR., printing co. exec.; b. Denver, Dec. 12, 1934; s. Albert Gray and Esther (MacIver) M.; B.S.E., Princeton U., 1956; M.B.A., Harvard U., 1960; m. Nancy Spiers, Jan. 28, 1962; children—Laura Elizabeth, Jennifer Leslie, Robert Gray. Salesman, Procter & Gamble Co., Chgo., 1956-57; mktg. exec. Gen. Foods Corp., White Plains, N.Y., 1961-70; v.p. Bowne & Co., N.Y.C., 1970—. Served with AUS, 1957. Republican. Presbyterian. Club: Wilton (Conn.) Riding. Home: 40 Branch Brook Rd Wilton CT 06897 Office: 345 Hudson St New York NY 10014

MATHER, HAL FREDERICK, engring. cons.; b. London, Oct. 2, 1935; came to U.S., 1966, naturalized, 1978; s. Stanley Arthur and Elizabeth (Gibson) M.; grad. Southall Tech. Coll., 1956; m. Jean Richardson, Oct. 6, 1956; 1 dau., Carol Ann. Project engr. Nat. Research Corp., 1966, quality control mgr., 1967, prodn., inventory control mgr., 1967-69, adminstr. mfg. systems Gilbarco Inc., Greensboro, N.C., 1969-73; pres. Hal Mather Inc., Atlanta, 1973—. Mem. Am. Prodn. and Inventory Control Soc., Soc. Mech. Engrs., Nat. Speakers Assn., Inst. Mech. Engrs. Author: (with George Plossl) Master Production Scheduling Book, 1975. Home: 5428 Fieldgreen Dr Stone Mountain GA 30088 Office: Hal Mather Inc PO Box 20161 Atlanta GA 30325

MATHERNE, ALBERT RAY, accountant; b. Paulina, La., Sept. 21, 1943; s. Curtis J. and Lena M. (DeBate) M.; B.S. in Accounting, San Diego State U., 1973; M.B.A., Pepperdine U., 1977; m. Marilyn Kent Meek, Sept. 15, 1967; children—Marisa, Michael. Controller, San Diego Padres Baseball Club, 1968-73, Solitron Devices, Inc., San Deigo, 1973—; instr. accounting Nat. U., San Diego. Served with USN, 1962-65. Mem. Nat. Assn. Accountants (dir.), Planning Execs. Inst. Home: 9935 Bourbon Ct San Diego CA 92131 Office: 8808 Balboa Ave San Diego CA 92123

MATHESON, WALLACE ALEXANDER, publishing co. exec.; b. Montreal, Que., Can. July 29, 1931; s. Alexander George and Grace Deflandres (Wallace) M.; B.A., Acadia U., 1953; m. Martha Ann Driscoll, May 25, 1957; children—Heather Ann, Alexander James, Martha Jean. Can. field rep. Prentice-Hall Inc., Montreal, 1953-58, Can. dist. mgr., Eastern Can., 1958-61; v.p. Prentice-Hall of Can. Ltd., Scarborough, Ont., 1961-65, pres., 1965—; dir. Prentice-Hall Inc., 1976—; bd. dirs. Can. Book Design Com., 1975-76, chmn., 1973-74; bd. dirs. Montreal Internat. Book Fair, 1974-75; gov. Can. Copyright Inst., 1973-74. Mem. Assn. for Export Can. Books (dir. 1973), Can. Book Pubs. Council (pres. 1972-73). Office: 1870 Birchmount Rd Scarborough ON M1P 2J7 Canada

MATHESON, WILLIAM ANGUS, JR., farm machinery mfg. co. exec.; b. Oregon City, Oreg., Dec. 6, 1919; s. William Angus and Maude (Moore) M.; B.S. in Bus. Adminstrn., Lehigh U., 1941; m. Jeanne Elyse Manley, Feb. 14, 1942; children—Jeanne Sandra, Susan Manley, Bonnie Ann. Procurement engr. Office of Chief of Ordnance, 1942-43; mgr. contract sales Eureka-Williams Corp., Bloomington, Ill., 1946-49; dist. sales mgr. Perfex Corp., Milw., 1949-51; v.p. sales Internat. Heater Co., Utica, N.Y., 1951-53; sales mgr. heating div. Heil Co., Milw., 1953-55; v.p. sales, dir. Portable Elevator Mfg. Co. div. Dynamics Corp. Am., Bloomington, Ill., 1955-70, exec. v.p., dir., 1971-75, pres., dir., 1975—. Bd. dirs. Jr. Achievement Central Ill., 1959-71, pres. Bloomington dist., 1964—. Served to lt. U.S. Army, 1943-46. Mem. Farm Equipment Mfrs. Assn. (dir. 1961-80, pres. 1969, treas. 1970-80), McLean County Assn. Commerce and Industry (pres. 1974), Truck Equipment and Body Distbrs. Assn. (co-founder 1963), Ill. State C. of C. (dir. 1978—), Chi Phi. Republican. Presbyterian. Clubs; Rotary (pres. 1963), Bloomington Country, Flying Farmers, Masons, Shriners. Home: 1404 E Washington St Bloomington IL 61701 Office: PO Box 2847 Bloomington IL 61701

MATHEW, THOMAS PARAYANTHARA, service co. exec.; b. Kerala, South India, May 19, 1945; emigrated to Can., 1968, naturalized, 1974; s. Varughese Thomas and Kunjamma P. Thomas; B.A. in Econs., Kerala U., 1967; postgrad. St. Thomas Coll., Kerala, 1971; m. Rachel K. Mathew, Apr. 3, 1971; children—Manoj T., Manjula Sara. Mgr., Sun Taxi Ltd., Fort McMurray, Alta., 1975-76; mgr., pres. Forum Express, Fort McMurray, Alta., 1976—. Pres. Alta. Malayalee Assn., 1974. Mem. Am. Mgmt. Assn., Canadian Can. Overseas Fund for Edn. and Rehab. Pentecostal. Author: Martin Luther King Jr., 1972. Home and Office: PO Box 5024 Fort McMurray AB T9H 3G2 Canada

MATHEWS, LAWRENCE TALBERT, airline co. exec.; b. Michigan City, Ind., Oct. 12, 1947; s. Samuel and Cassie Mae (Thomas) Hairston; A.A., Flint Jr. Coll., 1967; B.A., U. Mich., Flint, 1969; M.B.A., U. Detroit, 1975; m. Beverly Ann Hoze, May 31, 1975. Audit sr. Arthur Young & Co., Detroit, 1972-75; controller, treas. Comml. Credit/McCullagh Leasing Co., Roseville, Mich., 1975-78; v.p. fin. Mich. Peninsula Airways, Ltd., Miami, Fla., 1978—; exec. v.p. Mich. Peninsula Airways, Inc., Miami, 1980—, also dir.; vice chmn. bd. dirs. Tri-Graphic Recovery Systems, Detroit, 1975—. Served to 1st lt. U.S. Army, 1969-72. Named Outstanding Alumnus, U. Mich., Flint, 1980; C.P.A., Mich. Mem. Nat. Assn. Black Accts. (treas. Detroit chpt. 1975-77, 1st v.p. 1977-79, pres. 1979—, nat. treas. 1977-79), Am. Inst. C.P.A.'s. Baptist. Home: 24680 Thorndyke Southfield MI 48034 Office: PO Box 523228 Miami FL 33152

MATHEWS, VICTOR WILLIAM, JR., mfg. co. exec.; b. Oakland, Calif., May 16, 1952; s. Victor William and Elizabeth Jane (Foley) M.; A.A., Ohlone Jr. Coll., 1972; B.S. in Mktg., Calif. State U., Hayward, 1975; m. Juanita Patricia Hernandez, Apr. 6, 1974. Asst. buyer H.C. Capwell Co., Oakland, 1975; buyer Peterbilt Motors Co., Newark, Calif., 1976-77; sr. buyer Stanford Linear Accelerator Center (Calif.), 1977-79; purchasing mgr. Branson Internat. Plasma Corp., Hayward, Calif., 1979—. Mem. Nat. Assn. Purchasing Mgrs. Democrat. Roman Catholic. Home: 6252 Madelaine Dr Newark CA 94560

MATHIASON, TAUNCE H., banker; b. Aberdeen, S.D., July 27, 1940; s. Milton and Avis M.; B.S., U. S.D., 1963, M.S., Northern State Coll., 1969; m. Mary M. Gutz, Dec. 22, 1963; children—Patrece, Kari. Tchr., Parker (S.D.) Public Schs., 1963-66; tchr. Miller (S.D.) Public Schs., 1966-69; with First Nat. Bank of Miller (S.D.), 1969-74; with Ainsworth State Bank (Iowa), 1974-76; pres. The National Bank of Washington (Iowa), 1976—, also dir. Mem. Iowa Bankers Assn., Washington C. of C. (dir., pres.), Am. Bankers Assn., Am. Mgmt. Assn. Republican. Methodist. Clubs: Masons, Kiwanis, Lions. Office: 300 S Iowa St Washington IA 52363

MATHIESON, PETER MATHIAS, oil co. exec.; b. Vancouver, B.C., Can., May 2, 1931; s. Olav and Margery Agnes (Cowper) M.; m. Dorothy Broadfoot, May 26, 1956; children—David, Heather, Paul, Donald. Partner, Beaton, Mathieson & Co., C.A.'s., Calgary, Alta., 1956-65, McDonald, Currie & Co., C.A.'s, Calgary, 1965-69; pres. Norse Explorations Ltd., Calgary, 1969-80; pres. Trojan Petroleum, 1980; dir. Tricentrol Corp. Group. Mem. B.C., Alta. insts. chartered accountants, Petroleum Club. Anglican. Club: Canadian. Home: 2932 Park Ln Calgary AB T2S 2L7 Canada Office: 1070 Elveden House Calgary AB T2P 0Z3 Canada

MATHIESON, ROBERT FRANCIS, demand analyst; b. N.Y.C., Aug. 11, 1932; s. Oliver and Loretta (Coleman) M.; B.A., Hunter Coll., 1960; M.A., N.Y. U., 1962; m. Mary J. McCaffery, Sept. 6, 1952; children—Christine, Michael, Kevin. Div. chief Fed. Res. Bank of N.Y., 1964-66; mgr. corp. planning Gen. Electric Co., N.Y.C., 1966-68; sr. v.p. Scudder Stevens & Clark, N.Y.C., 1968-73; v.p. econs. Merrill Lynch, N.Y.C., 1973-76; mgr. demand analysis AT&T, N.Y.C., 1976—; adj. prof. internat. mgmt. Pace U.; mem. econ. adv. com. U.S. Dept. Commerce. Named to Hunter Coll. Hall of Fame, 1974. Mem. U.S. C. of C. (Can.-U.S. relations com.), Soc. Applied Econs., N. Am. Soc. Corp. Planning. Club: Union League (N.Y.C.). Office: 195 Broadway New York NY 10007

MATHIEUX, OLIVIER CHARLES, optical products distbn. exec.; b. Lyon, France, July 4, 1942; came to U.S., 1965, naturalized, 1969; s. Pierre P. and Anne (Blehaut) M.; M.Communications Scis., Inst. des Relations Publiques, Paris, 1965; M.B.A., Northwestern U., 1969; m. Lucia M. Warslewski, Aug. 20, 1966; children—Geoffroy, Douglas. Account exec. Compton Advt., Chgo., 1965-68; with A.T. Kearney, mgmt. cons., Chgo. and Paris, 1969-72; mktg. dir. Feudor, Lyon, 1972-76; mktg. and sales dir. Am. continent Essilor Internat., Paris, 1977-79; pres. subs. Multi Optics Corp., Foster City, Calif., 1979—; dir. Amsa Co., Mexico City. Served with French Army, 1963-64. Mem. French Am. C. of C., Am. Mgmt. Assn. Club: Chantilly (France) Golf. Office: 1153D Triton Dr Foster City CA 94404

MATHIS, FRANK, assn. exec.; b. Fort Valley, Ga., Aug. 4, 1937; s. Otis and Laura (Lockhart) M.; student Fort Valley State Coll., 1955-59, Nat. Tng. Sch. for Profl. Scouters. Dist. exec. Boy Scouts Am., Macon, Ga., 1959-63, Savannah, Ga., 1963-71, Greensboro, N.C., 1971-72; exec. dir. Savannah Area Minority Contractors Assn., Inc., 1972—. Recipient Citizenship award Ga. Beautification Assn., 1974, Benedictine medal of excellence Benedictine Mil. High Sch., 1971, St. George award Diocese of Savannah, 1971. Mem. Nat. Assn. Minority Contractors, Alpha Phi Omega. Club: Sertoma. Home: 911 W 37th St Savannah GA 31401 Office: 630 E Henry St Savannah GA 31401 also 1803 Gloucester St Brunswick GA 31520

MATHIS, JACK DAVID, advt. exec.; b. La Porte, Ind. Nov. 27, 1931; s. George Anthony and Bernice (Bennethum) M.; student U. Mo., 1950-52; B.S., Fla. State U., 1955; m. Phyllis Dene Hoffman, Dec. 24, 1971; children—Kane Cameron, Jana Dene. With Benton & Bowles, Inc., 1955-56; owner Jack Mathis Advt., 1956—; creative cons. film That's Action!, 1977. Mem. U.S. Olympic Basketball Com. Recipient citation Marketing Research Council N.Y. Mem. Alpha Delta Sigma. Author: Valley of the Cliffhangers. Home: Libertyville IL 60048 Office: Box 714 3501 Woodhead Dr Northbrook IL 60062

MATHIS, JAMES FORREST, petroleum co. exec.; b. Dallas, Sept. 28, 1925; s. Forrest and Martha (Godbold) M.; B.S. in Chem. Engring., Tex. A&M U., 1946; M.S., U. Wis., 1951, Ph.D., 1953; m. Frances Ellisor, Sept. 4, 1948; children—Alan Forrest, Lisa Lynn. Research engr. Humble Oil & Refining Co., Baytown, Tex., 1946-49, 53-61, mgr. research and devel., 1961-63, mgr. Splty. products planning, 1963-65; v.p. Exxon Research & Engring. Co., Linden, N.J., 1966-68; sr. v.p., dir. Imperial Oil Ltd., Toronto, Ont., Can., 1968-71; v.p. technology Exxon Chem. Co., Florham Park, N.J., 1971-80; v.p. sci. and tech. Exxon Corp., N.Y.C., 1980—. Bd. dirs. Chem. Industry Inst. Toxicology, 1975—, treas., 1977-80, chmn., 1980—. Served with AC, USNR, 1944-45. Fellow Am. Inst. Chem. Engrs. (chmn. mgmt. div.); mem. Am. Chem. Soc., AAAS, Sigma Xi, Phi Lambda Upsilon, Tau Beta Pi. Presbyterian. Home: 96 Colt Rd Summit NJ 07901 Office: 1251 Ave of Americas New York NY 10020

MATHIS, VIOLETTE ELEANOR, sauna and hydrotherapy mfg. exec.; b. Kouts, Ind., Feb. 14, 1933; d. Benjamin John and Elnora (Egli) Kaufmann; student Kellberg Inst. Phys. Therapy, 1952-53, No. Bapt. Sem., 1954-55, U. Calif., 1955-57; m. Cleo Donald Mathis, Nov. 5, 1961. Youth dir. 1st Bapt. Ch., Garden Grove, Calif., 1955-57; pvt. practice phys. therapy, Long Beach Calif., 1957-59; owner Rita LeRoy franchise, Long Beach, 1959-60; partner Otto C. Klaye Real Estate Investments, Encino, Calif., 1960-61; co-founder, exec. v.p. Vico Products Mfg. Co. Inc., South El Monte, Calif., 1961—; v.p., mng. officer Ultra Sauna No. Calif., 1973—; partner Ultra Jet Co., 1974—; cons. sauna and hydrotherapy to archtl. and mech. engring. firms. Mem. Bldg. Industry Assn. Republican. Composer designer tech. manuals in field. Home: 609 Howard St Montebello CA 90054 Office: 1808 Potrero St South Elmonte CA 91733

MATLINS, STUART M., mgmt. cons.; b. N.Y.C., July 25, 1940; s. Louis Karl and Lillian (Keit) M.; student London Sch. Econs., 1958-59; B.S., U. Wis., 1960; A.M., Princeton U., 1962, postgrad., 1962-63; m. Andrea Cines, June 20, 1960 (div.); children—Seth, Andrew; m. 2d, Antoinette Leonard, Oct. 9, 1977. Internat. economist Bur. Internat. Commerce, U.S. Dept. Commerce, Washington, 1963-66; cons. Booz Allen & Hamilton, Inc., N.Y.C., 1966-67, asst. to pres./adminstrv. dir., 1967-70, v.p. internat. ops., 1970-71, v.p./mng. officer, instl. and pub. mgmt. div., 1971-74; pres. Stuart Matlins Assos., Inc., mgmt. cons., N.Y.C., 1974—; chmn. bd., dir. Risk Insights, Inc.; dir. Health Insts., Inc. Bd. dirs. Princeton Grad. Alumni Assn. Woodrow Wilson fellow, 1960-61; Herbert O. Peet fellow, 1961-62; Phillip A. Rollins fellow, 1962-63. Mem. Am. Econ. Assn. Club: Princeton (N.Y.C.). Office: 115 E 64th St New York NY 10021

MATSCHULLAT, WAYNE EMIL, retail exec.; b. Page, Nebr., Jan. 18, 1917; s. Otto F. and Elizabeth M.; B.S., U. Nebr., 1940, J.D., 1942; m. Harriet J. Bowman, Apr. 1942; children—Dale, Robert, Bettiann (Mrs. Patrick Cassidy), Kay. Mgmt. trainee to met. mgr. Los Angeles retail stores Sears Roebuck & Co., 1947-68; v.p. North Central states Montgomery Ward & Co., Chgo., 1968-72, also dir.; pres., chief exec. officer dir. Gamble-Skogmo, Inc., Mpls., 1972—; instr. marketing Drury Coll. Active Jr. Achievement, Boy Scouts Am., various fund drives. Served with AUS, 1942-46. Rotarian (v.p.). Office: 5100 Gamble Dr Minneapolis MN 55481*

MATSON, WAYNE ROBERT, assn. exec.; b. Duluth, Minn., Aug. 21, 1941; s. Charles Axel and Vera Ann (Herrick) M.; B.S. (CAP flight/coll. scholar 1961), U. Minn., 1963; M.A., No. Ariz. U., Flagstaff, 1966; Ed.D., NASA grantee 1971-73), Okla. State U., 1973; m. Merridee Lynn Berg, Aug. 27, 1966; children—Ann Marie, Matthew Charles. Asst. prof. aerospace studies Central Wash. U., Ellensburg, 1969-71; asso. dir. public affairs Aerospace Industries Assn., Washington, 1973-79; founder, exec. dir. Am. Soc. Aerospace Edn., Washington, 1976—, Nat. Council Aerospace Edn.; mem. nat. adv. com. aviation exploring Boy Scouts Am., 1975—; nat. adv. com. aerospace edn. Nat. 4-H Program, 1978—; pres. FAI Internat. Council Aerospace Edn., 1976—; del. nat. and internat. confs., speaker in field. Class rep. Class 1963, U. Minn., Duluth, 1973—; mem. CAP, 1955—. Recipient Aviation Edn. award Aviation Distbs. and Mfrs. Assn., 1975. Mem. Fedn. Aeronautique Internat. (pres. internat. council aerospace edn. 1976—; Niles Gold medal 1975), Nat. Aero. Assn. (exec. com. 1976—; Frank G. Brewer trophy 1975), Nat. Edn. Educators Press Assn., Phi Delta Kappa. Author: An Introduction to Aerospace Education, 1977; editor: The Book of Aerospace Education, 1977, Aerospace Education at the Elementary Level, 1977; tech. adv.: Air Transport, 1975, founder, editor-in-chief: Directory of Aerospace Education, 1975, Jour. Aerospace Edn., 1974—; asso. editor Aerospace Mag.; founder, editor-in-chief Aviation/Space Mag.; contbr. articles to profl. publs.

MATTA, JOSEPH FRANCIS, mfg. co. exec.; b. Lansford, Pa., Apr. 7, 1934; s. Joseph Francis and Mary Catherine (Knies) M.; B.S., Balt. Coll., 1969; m. Catherine Jane Haughton, Jan. 15, 1954; children—Joseph Francis, Gary. Treas. Dover Downs Racing (Del.), 1975-77; controller Jackson Rope div. Dyneer Co., Reading, Pa., 1973-77; chief fin. officer Sensor Tech. Inc., Chatsworth, Calif., 1977—. Pres., Brookside (Del.) Activities Council, 1969-70; asst. scout master local Boy Scouts Am., 1971-74. Served with AUS, 1951-54. Mem. Nat. Assn. Accts. Republican. Mem. Assembly of God Ch. Address: 21012 Lassen St Chatsworth CA 91371

MATTER, DANIEL RICHARD, fast food co. exec.; b. Harrisburg, Pa.; s. Gordon Richard M.; B.S. in Bus. Adminstrn., Calif. State U., Northridge, 1963; m. Madora Garrett; children—Daniel, Deanna, Tamara, Debora. Mem. staff Arthur Andersen & Co., C.P.A.'s, Los Angeles, 1963-64; acct. Lockheed Aircraft Co., Burbank, Calif., 1964-68; partner Alexander Grant & Co., C.P.A.'s, Van Nuys, Calif., 1968-79; pres. D & M Foods, Inc., Woodland Hills, Calif., 1979—; cons. Bd. dirs. Mid Valley YMCA, 1975—. C.P.A., Calif. Mem. Am. Inst. C.P.A.'s, Calif. Soc. C.P.A.'s. Club: Rotary (pres. 1976-77) (Van Nuys). Office: 23123 Ventura Blvd Woodlands Hills CA 91364

MATTERN, ROBIN DONALD, fin. mgr.; b. San Francisco, Apr. 16, 1950; s. John Donald and Jean Adrienne (Page) M.; student Boston U., 1968-70, U. Calif. Coll. Environ. Design, 1970-72; m. Cecelia Lee Musulin, Oct. 11, 1980. Office asst. U.S. Senator Gaylord Nelson, Washington, 1972; asst. to pres. Mattern Constrn., San Francisco, 1972-73; archtl. design asst. John Carl Warnecke & Assos., Washington, 1973-74; mktg. rep. STSC, Inc., N.Y.C., 1974-76, sr. fin. modeling cons., White Plains, N.Y., 1976-79, product mgr., Bethesda, Md., 1979—. Recipient Pres.'s award STSC, Inc., 1978. Episcopalian. Author articles; developer fin. reporting system. Home: 7806 Briardale Terr Rockville MD 20855 Office: 7316 Wisconsin Ave Bethesda MD 20014

MATTESON, BARBARA ANN, nun; b. Everett, Wash., July 31, 1939; d. Clair Anthony and Geraldine Ann (Donovan) M.; M.A., Seattle U., 1969; M.B.A., U. Wash., 1976. Elementary sch. tchr. Seattle Cath. Schs., 1962-69, elementary sch. adminstr., 1969-70; elementary sch. prin. Oakland Cath. Schs., San Leandro, Calif., 1970-73; joined Dominican Sisters Congregation Holy Cross, 1957, corporate treas., Edmonds, Wash., 1977—, treas. Health Services Consortium, 1980—, chmn. sisters salary and ministry com., intercommunity com. on retirement needs; mem. archdiocesan budget and funding com. Treas., bd. dirs. Health Services Consortium; bd. dirs. Ch. Council Greater Seattle. Mem. Conf. Religious Treas. (chmn. region XV), Hosp. Fin. Mgmt. Assn. Home: 1515 N 150th St Seattle WA 98133 Office: PO Box 280 Edmonds WA 98020

MATTESON, LEWIS WHITFORD, JR., business exec.; b. Houston, Nov. 24, 1924; s. Lewis Whitford and Lillian (Hall) M.; B.S. in Elec. Engring., Rice U., 1949; m. Betty Irene Dykes, Dec. 16, 1954; children—Sherry Adelman, Whit, Debbie Wood, Ricky. Partner, Matteson Southwest Co., Houston, 1950-62, v.p., 1962-67; chmn. bd., 1967-71; founder, owner, chmn. bd., pres. Matteson Transformers Inc., Houston, 1957-72; v.p., sec.-treas., dir. Plaza Lincoln-Mercury, Inc., Houston, 1971-79, pres., chmn. bd., 1979—; owner Matteson Devel. Co., Houston, 1970—; owner, pres. Matteson's Motorcycles, Inc., Kerrville, Tex., 1973-77. Served with Signal Corps, AUS, 1943-46. Mem. Am. Theater Organ Soc., Houston Area Theatre Organ Soc. (dir., v.p., treas.), AGO, Phi Theta Kappa. Episcopalian. Club: Racquet (Houston). Home: 211 Paul Revere Dr Houston TX 77024 also Casa del Rio Hunt TX 78024 Office: 2955 Kirby Dr Houston TX 77098

MATTEUCCI, DOMINICK VINCENT, real estate developer; b. Trenton, N.J., Oct. 19, 1924; s. Vincent Joseph and Anna Marie (Zoda) M.; B.S., Coll. William and Mary, 1948; B.S., M.I.T., 1950; m. Emma Irene DeGuia, Mar. 2, 1968; children—Felisa Anna, Vincent Eriberto. Owner, Matteucci Devel. Co.; pres. Nat. Investment Brokerage, Newport Beach, Calif. Lic. gen. bldg. contractor, real estate broker, Calif.; registered profl. engr., Calif. Home: 2104 Felipe Newport Beach CA 92660 Office: PO Box 8328 Newport Beach CA 92660

MATTHEW, DAVID CHARLES CAMERON, assn. exec.; b. Kans. City, Mo., Nov. 21, 1944; s. David Charles Cameron and Jewell (Cameron) M.; B.A. (Nat. Merit scholar), Columbia U., 1966, M.A., 1967, Ph.D., 1974; m. Marie Louise Nickerson, July 26, 1968; children—Elizabeth Constance Adams, Sayre Cameron Adams. Adminstrv. asst. Morningside Heights, Inc., N.Y.C., 1965-69; lectr. Bronx (N.Y.) Community Coll., 1968-70; instr. N.Y. Inst. Tech., 1970-71, City Coll. N.Y., 1971-74; editor Sagarin Press, N.Y.C., 1975; devel., mktg. cons. Model Decisions Corp., Breton Assos., Corporate Reporting Services, Rainhill Group Inc., N.Y.C., 1975—; program dir. Penton Pub. Co., N.Y.C., 1976-79; mgr. technol. product devel. Am. Mgmt. Assns., N.Y.C., 1979—; v.p., dir. Internat. Tech. and Comml. Services, Inc., 1978—; editor Squash News, 1978—; lectr. Volunteer promotional work state, local, fed. election campaigns, State of N.Y., 1966-68. Recipient Outstanding Sci. Student award A.T. & T.; writing award Nat. Inst. Arts and Humanities; Bausch & Lomb Sci. medal. Mem. IEEE, Assn. Computing Machinery, Am. Soc. Testing and Devel., Nat. Trust Hist. Preservation. Democrat. Club: Manhattan. Author numerous mag. and newspaper articles, manuals, brochures. Home: 425 Riverside Dr New York NY 10025 Office: 135 W 50 St New York NY 10020

MATTHEWS, A. BRUCE, corporate exec.; b. Clarksburg, W.Va., Dec. 11, 1923; s. Ezra Wilson and Hilma (Nelson) M.; B.S., Ohio U., 1945; m. Marjorie Phillips, 1944 (div. 1962); children—Bruce, Thomas, Jennifer, David, Michelle, Bradford, Christopher; m. 2d, Marjorie Nelson, Dec. 31, 1963. Partner, Arthur Andersen & Co., Detroit, 1945-65, gen. partner, 1956, mng. partner, Denver, 1956-65; v.p. fin. and adminstrn. Communications Satellite Corp., Washington, 1965-70; pres., dir. Bliss & Laughlin Industries, Inc., Oak Brook, Ill., 1970-71; sr. v.p. CNA Fin. Corp., Chgo., 1972-75; chmn. bd., pres. Larwin Group, Inc., Beverly Hills, Calif., 1974-75; chmn. bd., dir. Healthco, Inc., 1972-75, First Healthcare Corp., 1972-75, CNA Mgmt. Corp., 1973-75, Coaxial Communications, Inc., 1973-75; pres. The Matthews Group, Washington, Cairo, Egypt and London, Eng., 1975—; chmn. bd. Washington Communication Group, 1977—, Coaxial Communications, 1979—; dir. Gen. Fin. Corp., Employee Benefit Consultants, CNA Investors Group Ltd., 1972-75. Pres., Jr. Achievement Met. Denver, 1960-62, chmn. bd., 1962-64, chmn. bd. Western region, 1964-66, nat. exec. com., 1962—; pres. bd. trustees Graland Country Day Sch., Denver, 1960-61, trustee, 1959-65; treas. Denver Symphony Soc., 1964-65, trustee, 1958-65; chmn. Red Rocks Music Festival, 1960-61; trustee Nat. Symphony Orch., Washington, 1966-70; trustee Avery Coonley Sch., 1971-74, pres., 1973-74; bd. govs. Chgo. Symphony Orchestral Assn., 1972-75; treas., dir. Chgo. Crime Commn., 1970-72; bd. dirs. Health Edn. Inst., 1973-75. Served with AUS, 1942-43. Mem. Fin. Execs. Inst., Am. Inst. C.P.A.'s, Am. Inst. Aeros. and Astronautics, Am. Mgmt. Assn. (Pres.'s Assn.), Nat. Assn. Bus. Economists, Newcomen Soc., Econ. Club Chgo. Clubs: Chicago, Mid-Am., Union League (Chgo.); Hinsdale Golf; Metropolitan, Congl., Internat. (Washington); Sky (N.Y.C.). Home: 4970 Rockwood Pkwy NW Washington DC 20016

MATTHEWS, ALLYN SAMUEL, computer mfg. co. ofcl.; b. Balt., Nov. 1, 1947; s. George Albert and Helen (Johnson) M.; A.A., Community Coll. Balt., 1972; B.S., Morgan State Coll., 1974; postgrad. (gen. scholar) U. Pa., 1974-75; m. Peggy Annette Anderson, May 20, 1972; 1 dau., Alyssa Helen. Mgmt. intern Procter & Gamble Co., Cin., 1973; mktg. rep. IBM, Milw., 1974-77, Rockford, Ill., 1977-80, adv. instr., Los Angeles, 1980—; counselor, cons. SBA, 1977—. Founder, adminstr. IBM tutorial program North Division High Sch., Milw., 1974-77; account exec. United Way, Rockford, 1979; instr. Project Bus., 1980. Senatorial scholar, 1972-74; Consortium fellow, 1974-75. Mem. Data Processing Mgmt. Assn., Assn. Systems Mgrs., Alpha Kappa Mu. Home: 23113 Pamplico Dr Valencia CA 91355 Office: IBM-DPD HQ System Sci Inst 3d Floor 3550 Wilshire Blvd Los Angeles CA 90010

MATTHEWS, CORNELIA WILLIAMS, business exec.; b. Norene, Tenn., Nov. 16, 1920; d. Horace Vale and Willette (Thompson) Williams; student pub. schs., Watertown, Tenn.; m. William Hayes Matthews, Dec. 13, 1946; 1 son, William Hayes, Jr. With First Am. Nat. Bank, Nashville, 1942-63; mgr. customer service div. Nat. Cash Register Co., Nashville, 1965-71; asst. v.p., tng. coordinator Third Nat. Bank, Nashville, 1971-75; adminstrv. officer, asst. mgr. main office div. First Am. Nat. Bank, 1975-78; v.p., mgr. Bank Systems div. Bus. Machines, Inc., Nashville, 1978—; instr. Am. Inst. Banking, Nashville State Tech. Inst. Past pres. Nashville Mental Health Assn.; bd. dirs. Jr. Achievement Nashville, 1977—; mem. adv. bd. Bus. and Indsl. Inst., Vol. State Community Coll. Recipient Service award Tenn. Bankers Assn., 1976; Disting. Sales award Sales and Mktg. Assn. Nashville, 1979. Mem. Nat. Assn. Bank Women, Am. Inst. Banking, Am. Bus. Women's Assn. (past pres. Tannansie chpt.), Internat. Platform Assn. Republican. Methodist. Club: Capitol (Nashville). Author tng. manuals. Home: 616 Skyview Dr Nashville TN 37206 Office: Bus Machines Inc 304 Space Park S PO Box 110376 Nashville TN 37211

MATTHEWS, DOROTHEA ELIZABETH, lawyer; b. Englewood, N.J., June 12, 1947; d. John Clark and Dorothea (Kidd) Matthews; A.B. cum laude, Smith Coll., 1969; J.D., Fordham U., 1974. Admitted to N.Y. bar, 1975, U.S. Ct. Appeals, 1975, U.S. Dist. Ct., 1975; asso. firm Reid & Priest, N.Y.C., 1974—. Mem. exec. com. Met. Republican Club; committeewoman New York County Rep. Com. Mem. Bar of the State of N.Y., Am. Bar Assn., Smith Coll. Alumnae Assn., English-Speaking Union. Presbyterian. Office: 40 Wall St New York NY 10005

MATTHEWS, EDWARD JOSEPH, JR., food co. exec.; b. N.Y.C., Oct. 20, 1935; s. Edward Joseph and Regina Theresa (Taylor) M.; B.A. in Econs., Dartmouth Coll., 1957; M.B.A. in Fin. and Acctg., Amos Tuck Sch., 1959; m. Michelle McQueeny; children—Edward Joseph, IV, Peter M., Paul T., Margot Lynn. Sr. accountant Haskins & Sells, C.P.A.'s, N.Y.C., 1959-64; v.p. fin. Strawberry Hill Press Inc., N.Y.C., and Asheville, N.C., 1964-69; asst. controller Inmont Corp., N.Y.C., 1969-70, v.p., gen. mgr. Inmont Confections Co., N.Y.C., 1970-71; asst. treas., Inmont Corp., N.Y.C., 1971-73; asst. treas. Nabisco, Inc., N.Y.C., 1973-75, treas., 1975-78, v.p. corp. devel., 1978—; dir. Morris County Savs. Bank. Served with USMCR, 1959-60. C.P.A. Mem. Am. Inst. C.P.A.'s, N.Y. State Soc. C.P.A.'s, Fin. Execs. Inst., Morris County C. of C. (chmn.), Beta Theta Pi. Republican. Clubs: Roxiticus Golf, Mantoloking Yacht; Yale (N.Y.C.). Address: Nabisco Inc East Hanover NY 07936

MATTHEWS, JOHN L., mfg. co. exec.; b. Atkins, Ark., 1914; s. John Jefferson and Naomi L. (Gipson) M.; B.S. in Banking and Fin., U. Ark., 1932; m. Mary Beth Higby, June 13, 1939; children—John Lannes, Nancy D., Jill K. Mgr., S. H. Kress Co., Oklahoma City, 1932-34; nat. sales mgr. Sears Roebuck, Chgo., 1937-40; owner Matthews Constrn. Co., Kansas City, Mo., 1945-49; pres. Van Brunt Machinery, Kansas City, 1946-49; pres. Airosol Co., Inc., Neodesha, Kans., 1949—; dir. Merc. Bank and Trust, Kansas City-St. Louis, Racon Co., Wichita, Kans. Served with U.S. Army, 1941-45; ETO. Decorated Legion of Merit, Bronze Star; Croix de Guerre with gold star. Mem. Nat. Aerosol Packers Assn. (pres. 1976-80), Chem. Spltys. Mfg. Assn. Republican. Methodist. Clubs: Kansas City, Independence, Kansas Country, Elks, Masons, Shriners. Home: 1100 N 5th St Neodesha KS 66757 Office: 525 N 11th St Neodesha KS 66757

MATTHEWS, KENNETH C. cons.; b. Cin., Aug. 18, 1924; s. William Earle and Mosella (Cragg) M.; B.S. in Chem. Engring., 1945; m. Sandra Virda Marcum, Dec. 24, 1970; children—Bruce, Mark, Scott, Eric, Britt. Former chmn. bd. Henry P. Thompson Co., Cin.; pres. Rep-Aid Corp.; dir. E & I Corp., Katadyn USA, Unifilt, Tay River Petroleum, EPI Corp. Served with U.S. Navy, 1942-45. Home: 5616 Bayberry Dr Cincinnati OH 45242 Office: PO Box 42272 Cincinnati OH 45242

MATTHEWS, LEO LEWIS, constrn. equipment co. exec.; b. Cleve., Aug. 4, 1939; s. Leo Edward and Mildred Ann (Lewis) M.; B.A., Ohio Wesleyan U., 1961; m. Charlotte Sweeder, Sept. 29, 1962; children—Mark, Elizabeth. Staff acct. Arthur Andersen & Co., Cleve., 1961-67, audit mgr., 1967-69; controller Allied Steel & Tractor Products, Inc. (subs. Chgo. Pneumatic Tool, 1973), Cleve., 1969-72, asst. gen. mgr., 1972-76, v.p., gen. mgr., 1976-78, pres., 1978—. Served with U.S. Army, 1962. C.P.A., Ohio. Mem. Am. Inst. C.P.A.'s, Nat. Assn. Accts., Constrn. Industry Mfrs., Asso. Equipment Distbrs., Nat. C. of C., Ohio Wesleyan Assos. Home: 34630 Sherbrook Park Dr Solon OH 44139 Office: 5800 Harper Rd Solon OH 44139

MATTHEWS, LUTHER WHITE, III, r.r. exec.; b. Ashland, Ky., Oct. 5, 1945; s. Luther White, Jr., and Virginia Carolyn (Chandler) M.; B.S., Hampden-Sydney (Va.) Coll., 1967; M.B.A. in Fin. and Gen. Mgmt., U. Va., Charlottesville, 1970; m. Mary Jane Hanser, Dec. 30, 1972; children—Courtney Chandler, Brian Whittlesey. Fin. cons. Chem. Bank, N.Y.C., 1970072, asst. sec., 1972-74, asst. v.p., 1974-75, v.p., 1975-77; treas. Mo. Pacific Corp., St. Louis, 1977—, also v.p. fin. lMo. Pacific R.R. Co., St. Louis, 1979—; dir. Trailer Train Co. Trustee, Hampden-Sydney Coll., 1978—; treas. Samuel Cupples House Found., St. Louis, 1977—. Served with USCGR, 1967-73. Clubs: St. Louis Country; Union League (N.Y.C.); Chicago.

MATTHEWS, M. D., gas co. exec.; b. Mt. Vernon, Ark., 1924; B.A., U. Ark., 1948. Asst. controller Tex. Gas Transmission Corp., 1948-56; v.p., sec., treas. Fish Service Corp., 1956-58; with Internat. Pipeline Constrn. S.A., Panama, 1958-62; pres. Fish Internat. of Argentina, 1962-63; v.p. Valley Gas Prodn. Inc., 1963-64; asst. to pres. Houston Natural Gas Corp., 1964-65, v.p., asst. treas., 1965-67, v.p., treas., 1967-69, sr. v.p., treas., 1969-73, vice chmn. bd. fin. and adminstrn., 1973-74, chmn. exec. com., vice chmn. bd., 1974—, also dir.; vice chmn., dir. various subsidiaries; vice chmn., dir. Liquid Carbonic Corp., Pott Industries, Inc., Valley Piple Lines, Inc., Intratex Gas Co. Served with U.S. Army, World War II. Office: PO Box 1188 Houston TX 77001*

MATTHEWS, MILTON THOMAS, JR., foods co. exec.; b. Lakewood, N.J., Mar. 1, 1946; s. Milton Thomas and Doris May M.; B.S. in Mktg. (Albert Alvino award), U. Md., 1967; B.S., Long Beach State U., 1973; postgrad. Pa. State U., 1975; m. Rebecca Mary Beck, Mar. 2, 1973; children—Michael Milton, Stephen Thomas. With Hershey Foods Corp. (Pa.), 1972—, field sales rep., Los Angeles, 1972-74, sales coordinator, Hershey, 1974-76, mgr. sales planning, 1976-79, mgr. sales devel., 1979—. Served to capt. USMC, 1968-72; Vietnam. Decorated 52 air medals; named M Club Man of Yr., 1968. Mem. Nat. Assn. Tobacco Distbrs. (dir./treas. young execs. div.; Y.E.D. Achievement award 1980), Nat. Candy Wholesalers Assn. (dir. young exec. div.). Republican. Presbyterian. Clubs: Derry Township Rep., Kiwanis, Md. Terrapin. Contbr. articles to profl. jours. Home: 921 Greenlea Rd Hershey PA 17033 Office: Hershey Foods 19 Chocolate Ave Hershey PA 17033

MATTHEWS, ROY MELVIN, utility co. exec.; b. Fredonia, Kans., May 18, 1921; s. Roy M. and Georgia A. (Randel) M.; B.S., U. Kans., 1946; m. Sheila Stryker, Mar. 8, 1947; children—Randall, Shelia, Milburn. C.P.A., Arthur Andersen & Co., Kans. City, Mo., 1948-51; v.p. Collins Radio Co., Dallas, 1951-74; sr. v.p., Ark. La. Gas Co., Shreveport, La., 1974—; dir. Protection Mut. Ins. Co., Park Ridge, Ill., Sigmaform Corp., Santa Clara, Calif. Served with U.S. Army, 1943-45. Decorated Flying Cross, Air medal. Mem. Fin. Execs. Inst., Am. Inst. C.P.A.'s.

MATTHEWS, STUART, aircraft mfg. co. exec.; b. London, May 5, 1936; came to U.S., 1974; s. Bernard De Lides and Daisy Vera (Woodcock) M.; chartered engr., Hatfield Coll. Advanced Tech., 1958; m. Kathleen Hilary Adams, Jan. 12, 1974; children—Anthony, Caroline, Joanna. Apprentice, de Havilland Aircraft Ltd., Hatfield, 1952-53; aircraft project design engr. Hawker Siddeley Aviation Ltd., Hatfield, 1953-64; with mktg. dept. Brit. Aircraft Co., Bristol, 1964-67; gen. mgr. planning Brit. Caledonian Airways, London, 1967-74; v.p. N.Am. div. Fokker-VFW Internat., Washington, 1974-80; pres. Fokker Aircraft USA, Arlington, Va., 1980—; chmn. asso. mem. group Commuter Airlines Assn. Am., 1979-80. Fellow Royal Aero. Soc.; mem. Inst. Transp., AIAA. Clubs: Aero, Nat. Aviation (Washington); Wings (N.Y.C.); Lions (pres. Engleside, Va. 1977-78). Home: 9218 Volunteer Dr Alexandria VA 22309 Office: 2361 Jefferson Davis Hwy Arlington VA 22202

MATTHEWS, WILLIAM MCGILL, V, dept. store exec.; b. Gastonia, N.C., July 17, 1940; s. Henry Belk and Evelyn (McArver) M.; B.S., Presbyn. Coll., 1962; m. Frances Augusta Flournoy, Sept. 10, 1966; children—William McGill, Evelyn Flournoy, Carson Henry Belk. With Belk Matthews Co., dept. stores, Macon, Ga., 1964—, sec.-treas., 1966—, v.p., 1972—, also dir.; v.p., sec.-treas., dir. stores in Warner Robins, Milledgeville, Dublin, Cordele and Vidalia, Ga.; dir. First Bank & Trust Co., Macon. Chmn., Macon Downtown Council, 1971; bd. visitors Presbyn. Coll., chmn., 1978—; bd. dirs. Mus. Arts and Scis., Macon Goodwill Industries, Bibb County unit Am. Cancer Soc. Served with AUS, 1962-64. Mem. Macon C. of C. (dir. 1972—, treas. 1979), Presbyn. Coll. Nat. Alumni Assn. (pres. 1974), Kappa Alpha. Presbyn. (deacon 1971-79, trustee day sch.). Clubs: Rotary, Idle Hour Country (Macon). Home: 3185 Vista Circle Macon GA 31204 Office: Macon Mall 3661 Eisenhower Pkwy Macon GA 31205

MATTHIAS, RUSSELL HOWARD, lawyer, corp. exec.; b. MilW., Aug. 7, 1906; s. Charles G. and Lena (Martin) M.; A.B., Northwestern U., 1930, J.D., 1932; m. Helene Seibold, Dec. 28, 1932; children—Russell Howard, William Warrens, Robert Charles. Admitted to Ill. bar, 1933, Okla. bar, 1941, D.C. bar, 1949, Fla. bar, 1979; spl. asst. to atty. gen. U.S., R.R. Retirement Act, 1934-35; sec. Ill. Fraternal Congress, 1935-40, 45-60; partner firm Meyers and Matthias, Chgo., 1951-78, pres., treas., dir., sole shareholder, 1978-80; partner firm Matthias & Matthias, 1980—; dir. Kemper Total Return Fund, Inc., Kemper Summit Fund, Inc., Kemper Growth Fund, Inc., Kemper Income and Capital Preservation Fund, Inc., Kemper Money Market Fund, Inc., Kemper High Yield Fund, Inc.; v.p., gen. counsel, dir. Bankers Mut. Life Ins. Co.; gen. counsel, dir. United Founders Life Ins. Co. Ill., United Founders Life Ins. Co. Okla., Wesco, Inc.; chmn bd., dir. Old Orchard Bank & Trust Co.; dir. Republic Nat. Life Ins. Co., Dallas. Mem. drafting com. Ill. Ins. Code, 1938, annotating com., 1940; mem. La. Ins. Code Drafting Com., 1948. Mem., v.p., dir., gen. counsel Lutheran Brotherhood; trustee Luth. Gen. Hosp., Valparaiso U. Law Sch., Deaconess Hosp. Served to lt. col. AUS, 1942-46. Recipient Alumni award Northwestern U., 1973. Mem. Internat. Assn. Life Ins. Counsel, Phi Delta Theta. Republican. Lutheran. Clubs: Indian Hill Country; Univ., Mid-Day (Chgo.), Kenilworth (Ill.); Army and Navy (Washington); Mpls.; Country of Orlando, Citrus (Orlando, Fla.). Home: 1500 Sheridan Rd Wilmette IL 60091 Office: 230 W Monroe St Suite 2200 Chicago IL 60606 also 501 N Magnolia Ave Suite A Orlando FL 32802

MATTINGLY, JAMES WILLIAM, JR., apparel mfg. co. exec.; b. Lexington, Ky., Nov. 9, 1920; s. James William and Geneva (White) M.; A.B., U. Ky., 1949; m. Kitty Richardson, Oct. 6, 1950; children—John Basil, Laura Lee, Todd Davenport. With Cowden Mfg. Co., Lexington, 1951—, salesman, 1954-61, account exec., 1961-67, v.p. merchandising, 1968—, also dir. Served with USMCR, 1942-45. Episcopalian (vestryman). Clubs: Lafayette, Lexington Country, Lansdowne (Lexington). Home: Route 5 Hill Gate Evans Mill Rd Lexington KY 40511 Office: 300 New Circle Rd NW POB 12500 Lexington KY 40501

MATTIS, DAVID STANLEY, JR., machine tool mfg. co. exec.; b. Phila., Sept. 22, 1944; s. David Stanley and Helen LeVisa (Cline) M.; B.S. in Bus. Adminstrn., St. Joseph's Coll., Phila., 1967; m. Paula Karen Johnson, Aug. 20, 1966; children—Kimberly, William, Kelly. Mgmt. trainee Americold Compressor div. White Consol. Industries, Inc., Cullman, Ala., 1971-72, plant controller Franklin Laundry div., Jefferson, Iowa, 1972-73, v.p. fin. King Press div., Joplin, Mo., 1973-74, staff controller Corp. Offices, Cleve., 1974-75, v.p. fin. Blaw-Knox Constrn. div., Mattoon, Ill., 1975-77, White-Sundstrand Machine Tool Co. div., Belvidere, Ill., 1977-80, pres. Fayscott div., Dexter, Maine, 1980—. Served to capt. USAF, 1967-71. Recipient award for excellence in bus. adminstrn. Middle Atlantic Fin. Instn., 1967. Mem. Fin. Execs. Inst. Republican. Roman Catholic. Home: 26 High St Dexter ME 04930 Office: 225 Spring St Dexter ME 04930

MATTISON, PATRICK BARTON, newspaper exec.; b. Rockford, Ill., Sept. 13, 1933; s. Philip Lawrence and Jean (Patrick) M.; student Northwestern U., 1951, 53, Western Ill. Coll., 1952; B.A. in Econs., Beloit Coll., 1958; B.A. in Fgn. Trade, Am. Inst. Fgn. Trade; m. Nancy Shappert, Aug. 12, 1961; children—Katherine, Jody, Steven, John. Sales engr. Mattison Machine Works, Rockford, 1951-62; pres., asso. pub. Belvidere Daily Republican (Ill.), 1962—; v.p., dir. Shappert Engring. Co. Bd. dirs. United Givers of Boone County, 1969-70; pres. YMCA of Belvidere, 1970-71; bd. dirs. Central region YMCA; mem. bd. counselors Rockford Coll.; mem. Heritage Days Com., Boone County; chmn. Boone County (Ill.) Health Steering Com.; mem. Ill. Children's Home and Aid Bd.; mem. Belvidere State St. Action Com.; mem. Republican Precinct Com., Winnebago County, 1962-63. Served with U.S. Army, 1954-56. Named Jaycee Boss of Yr., Belvidere Jaycees, 1967. Mem. Inland Daily Press Assn. (Disting. Service award 1977), Am. Newspaper Classified Advt. Mgrs. Assn., No. Ill. Newspaper Assn. Republican. Episcopalian. Clubs: Rotary; Delavan Lake Yacht; Inland Lake Yacht Assn; Univ. Office: 401 Whitney Blvd Belvidere IL 61008

MATTOX, DONALD OTIS, drug co. exec.; b. Welborn, Kans., Jan. 9, 1933; s. Alva Otis and Mary Pearl (Everett) M.; ed. public schs.; m. Beverly Jean Siebert, July 24, 1964 (div. 1978) children—William Edward, Julie Ann, Jennifer Lee; m. 2d, Rebecca Fasha Kingery, Sept. 9, 1978. Dept. mgr. Katz Drug Co., Kansas City, Kans., 1950-57; asst. mgr. Bruce Smith Drugs, Prairie Village, Kans., 1957-63; store mgr. Parkview Drugs, Overland Park, Kans., 1963-65; dist. mgr. Jack Eckerd Drug Co., Deerfield Beach, Fla., 1965—. Mem. South Dade C. of C., Hollywood C. of C., Greater Miami C. of C. (trustee), West Palm Beach C. of C. Republican. Baptist. Clubs: Boca Del Mar, Lago Mar, Jacaranda, Center Court. Home: 15311 Kingfielo Dr Houston TX 77084 Office: 10790 Bellaire Blvd Houston TX 77072

MATTSON, GEORGE, farmer; b. Chester, Mont., Sept. 6, 1918; s. Andrew Albert and Minnie E. (Johnson) M.; student public schs., Chester; m. Mary E. Plank, Sept. 24, 1949; children—Carl R., Jodi C. With Walden Bros. Hardware Store, Chester, 1935-38, Keith Service Sta., Chester, 1939-40; farm laborer Math Thiltges Farm, Chester, 1941, Father's Farm, Chester, 1941-42; pres., gen. mgr. George Mattson Farms, Inc., Chester, 1973—. Clk., Sch. Dist. 6, Chester, 1949-62; precinct committeeman Democratic Party, 1950-52; mem. Liberty County TV Dist., 1955-58; chmn. Cemetery Bd., 1959-62. Served with U.S. Army, 1942-45. Mem. Smithsonian Soc., Farmers Union, Dist. 4 Human Resource Council, others. Democrat. Lutheran. Clubs: Elks, VFW (nat. council of adminstrn. 1966-67, 68-69).

MATTSON, WALTER EDWARD, communications co. exec.; b. Erie, Pa., June 6, 1932; s. Walter Edward and Florence Evelyn (Anderson) M.; B.S., U. Maine, 1955; A.S., Northeastern U., 1959, D.C.S., 1980; postgrad. Harvard U. Advanced Mgmt. Program, 1973; m. Geraldine Anne Horsman, Oct. 10, 1953; children—Stephen, William, Carol. Printer various cos., 1948-53; advt. mgr. Anderson Newspapers Co., Oakmont, Pa., 1954; asst. prodn. mgr. Boston Heral

Traveler, 1955-58; cons. Chas. T. Main Co., Boston, 1959; with N.Y. Times Co., N.Y.C., 1960—, sr. v.p., 1972-74, exec. v.p., 1974-79, pres., chief operating officer, 1979—. Bd. dirs. nat. council Northeastern U. Served with USMCR, 1951-52. Named Distinguished Alumni Northeastern U., 1974. Mem. ANPA (vice chmn. prodn. mgmt. com.). Office: NY Times Co 229 W 43d St New York NY 10036

MATTSSON-BOZE, DANIEL WINSTON, ins. exec., importing co. exec.; b. Chgo., Apr. 8, 1943; s. Joseph Daniel and Daga A. M.-B.; B.A., U. Ill., 1965; M.S. in Edn., No. Ill. U., 1968; m. Ingrid O. Brink, Apr. 26, 1969; children—Peder, Karl, Katrina. Sch. tchr., Chgo., 1966-72, Stockholm, 1974-75; pastor Christian Center Ch., Paris, Ill., 1972-74; tchr., S. Tex., 1975-76; field underwriter N.Y. Life Ins. Co., Mission, Tex., 1976—; sec.-treas., dir. Scandinavian Trade Inc., Houston, 1978—; dir. Scandinavian Design Inc. Bd. dirs. Herald of Faith World Missions, 1978—. Recipient Maverick Achievement award, 1978, Nat. Quality award, 1978-79, Nat. Sales Achievement award, 1977-80. Mem. Nat. Assn. Life Underwriters, Tex. Leader Round Table. Home: Route 4 Box 196X Mission TX 78572 Office: NY Life Ins Co 600 Bldg Corpus Christi TX 78403

MATUSZAK, STEPHEN ANTHONY, banker; b. Erie, Pa., Jan. 18, 1931; s. Stephen J. and Elizabeth K. M.; B.S., U.S. Mil. Acad., 1955; M.B.A., N.Y. U., 1963; m. Violet Marques, June 11, 1955; children—Nanciann, Stephen, Donna Marie, David. With Value Line Investment Survey, N.Y.C., 1959-62; with Nat. Bank Westchester (now div. Lincoln First Bank), White Plains, N.Y., 1962—, pres., chief exec. officer; dir. PM Life Ins. Co., Armonk, N.Y. Chmn., Westchester chpt. ARC, 1975; campaign chmn. United Way of Westchester, 1979-80. Served with U.S. Army, 1950-51, 55-59. Mem. Fin. Execs. Inst., Fin. Analysts Fedn. Clubs: Westchester Country, Landmark. Author: Modern Investment Guide, 1959. Office: 31 Mamaroneck Ave White Plains NY 10601

MATZ, H. RADWAY, II, printing co. exec.; b. Chgo., Oct. 13, 1907; s. H. Radway and Amelia G. (Thronsen) M.; student L.L. Cook Engring. Inst., 1924-26; children—H. Radway, III, Helene Ramelia. Pub., Midweek News, Chgo., 1932-34; founder, pres. Matz Corp., Chgo., 1931-47; owner, operator H.R. Matz-Printer, Oakland, Calif., 1958-69, Dunsmuir, Calif., 1969—; owner, operator H.R. Matz Motors, Matz Firearms, Matz Rental Properties, Matz Bargain Center, Matz Movie Entertainment Service, Dunsmuir, 1973—; lectr., researcher in health. Served with F.A., U.S. Army, 1928-30. Mem. Nat. Health Fedn. (life mem.), Baron Soc. Internat., U.S. Tennis Assn., Home: 1001 Crag View Dr Dunsmuir CA 96025

MATZ, JOHN EDWIN, life ins. co. exec.; b. Hamburg, Pa., Sept. 2, 1916; s. Harry L. and Florence (Smith) M.; M.A., Pa. State U., 1939; m. Phoebe Land, July 4, 1941; children—Susan Eugenia, John Edwin. With John Hancock Mut. Life Ins. Co., Boston, 1949—, v.p., 1961-65, sr. v.p., 1965-67, exec. v.p., 1967-72, sr. exec. v.p., 1972-73, pres., chief ops. officer, 1974-78, chmn., chief exec. officer, 1979—, also dir.; dir. Shawmut Bank Boston N.A., Shawmut Corp. Trustee Tax Found., Inc., Am. Coll. Life Underwriters; mem. corp., trustee Northeastern U.; trustee New Eng. Colls. Fund; mem. vis. com. Harvard U. Grad. Sch. Bus. Adminstrn. Fellow Soc. Acutaries; mem. Am. Council Life Ins. (dir.), Sr. Actuaries Club, Phi Beta Kappa. Clubs: Commercial (Boston), St. Botolph, Algonquin, University, Weston Golf; Bald Peak Colony (N.H.). Office: John Hancock Pl Box 111 Boston MA 02117

MATZEN, ROBERT THOMAS, ins. co. exec.; b. Grand Island, Nebr., May 30, 1924; s. Thomas Adolph and Lois Miriam (Eddy) M.; student U. Nebr., 1942-43; B.A. in Econs., Duke U., 1947; m. Frances Evelyn Udeen, Mar. 1, 1950; children—Mark, Todd, Jan, Jena. Dist. mgr. Western U.S., Hiram G. Gardner, Inc., 1947-50, dist. mgr. Tex., 1951-53, dist. mgr. Oreg., Wash., 1953-54, asst. v.p., Denver, 1954-63, v.p., 1963-72, pres., 1972-73, v.p., 1974; pres. Ins. Protectors, Inc., Denver, 1975—; dir. Heritage Fund, Denver, 1972-73. Mem. Am. Reciprocal Ins. Assn. (dir. 1973-74), Colo. Assn. Fire and Casualty Ins. Cos. (pres. 1973-75), Ind. Ins. Agts. Am., Ind. Insurors Colo. Served with USN, 1943-46. Republican. Club: Athletic (Denver). Home: 3801 S Quebec St Denver CO 80237 Office: 900 E Louisiana St Suite 110 Denver CO 80210

MAU, WILLIAM KOON HEE, financier, developer; b. Honolulu, Apr. 25, 1913; s. Wah Hop and Ho Yau (Mau) M.; student pub. schs.; LL.D. (hon.), Pacific U., 1969; m. Jean Rachel Lau, Oct. 17, 1936; children—Milton, Cynthia, Lynette, Leighton, Letitia. Owner, pres. Waikiki Bus. Plaza, Inc., Top Of Waikiki revolving restaurant, Ambassador Hotel Waikiki; pres. Waikiki Shopping Plaza Inc., Aloha Motors Properties, Aloha Motors, Inc., Tropical Enterprises, Ltd., Far East Tropical Land Investment, Ltd. (Hong Kong); Dir. Am. Security Bank, Honolulu, 1956-69, chmn., chief exec. officer, 1962-67, chmn. bd., 1967-69; mem. exec. com. Coca-Cola Bottling Co. Honolulu, Inc., 1963-68, First Hawaiian Title, Inc. Vice chmn. State Hawaii Bd. Land and Nat. Resources, 1959-63; past mem. Hawaii Gov.'s Com. Low Cost Housing, Hawaii Gov.'s Trans-Shipment Center Hawaii; v.p., bd. dirs. Downtown Improvement Assn., 1962-64; mem. exec. bd. Aloha council Boy Scouts Am., 1962-64; bd. dirs., life mem. Chinese Cultural Found. Hawaii; bd. dirs. Waikiki Improvement Assn., chmn. redevel. and urban renewal task force; bd. dirs. Aloha United Fund, 1966-69, 74, United Chinese Soc.; trustee Kauikeolani Children's Hosp., 1959-61. Recipient Wisdom Award Honor Wisdom Hall of Fame, 1969; named Business Man of Yr. Hawaii Bus. and Industry Mag., 1966. Mem. Internat. Platform Assn., UN Assn. Am., Newcomen Soc. N.Am., Honolulu (ann. progress award 1966), Chinese (past dir., past auditor) chambers commerce, Am. Acad. Achievement (gov., mem. exec. com.), Tsung Tsin Assn. (dir.), Hawaii Hotel Assn. Club: Mau of Hawaii (past pres.). Home: 3938 Monterey Pl Honolulu HI 96816 Office: 2270 Kalakaua Ave Honolulu HI 96815

MAUCK, EARL GRIGSBY, former drug co. exec.; b. Princeton, Ind., Nov. 5, 1918; s. Earle L. and Isabelle (Grigsby) M.; B.S. in Bus. Adminstrn., Ind. U., 1940; student Northwestern U. Inst. for Mgmt., 1952; m. Betty Jane Spilman, Mar. 8, 1941; children—Cynthia A., Thomas C. Accountant Eli Lilly and Co., Indpls., 1940-42; asst. mgr. cost dept., 1946-48, mgr. budget dept., 1948-52, asst. treas., 1952-57, asst. to exec. v.p., 1957-59, dir. personnel planning, 1959-64, corp. dir. purchasing, 1964-78, ret., 1978. Mem. allocations com. United Fund, 1953-61, admissions com., 1961-67. Bd. dirs., pres. Christamore Settlement House, 1956-64; bd. dirs. Home Care Agy.; bd. govs. Orchard Country Day Sch. Served from ensign to lt. USNR, 1942-46; PTO. Mem. Planning Execs. Inst. (past nat. pres.), Ind. U. Sch. Bus. Alumni Assn. (exec. council, pres. 1963-64) Indpls. C. of C., Delta Tau Delta. Republican. Methodist. Clubs: Univ., Meridian Hills Country (dir.). Home: 5272 N Meridian St Indianapolis IN 46208 Office: Eli Lilly and Co Indianapolis IN 46206 Died June 30, 1979.

MAULDEN, JERRY L., power and light co. exec.; b. North Little Rock, Ark., 1936; B.S. in Acctg., U. Ark., Little Rock, Ark., 1936; B.S. in Acctg., U. Ark., Little Rock, 1963; married. Acct., Dyke & Assos. Inc., 1959-61; sr. auditor James Madigan & Co., C.P.A.'s, 1961-62; asst. controller Dillard Dept. Stores Inc., 1962-65; with Ark. Power & Light Co., Little Rock, 1965—, sec., treas., 1973-75, v.p. fin. services, sec., treas., 1975-79, pres., chief exec. officer, 1979—; pres. Middle South Services Inc.; v.p., treas., asst. sec., dir. Middle South Utilities Inc.; treas., asst. sec. Middle South Energy Inc., System Fuels, Inc. Office: PO Box 551 Little Rock AR 72203*

MAULTSBY, GUS L., co. exec.; b. Maxton, N.C., Apr. 11, 1939; s. W. A. and Pearl Maultsby; B.A., A. and T. State U., Greensboro, N.C., 1962; m. Regenia Bass, Nov. 29, 1969; 1 son, Randy Scott. Personnel supr. Warnaco, Inc., Bridgeport, Conn., 1967-70; div. mgr. Greater Waterbury (Conn.) C. of C., 1970-72; pres. Exec. Shopps, Ltd., Stamford, Conn., 1972-74; gen. mgr. Sports Internat. Promotions, N.Y.C., 1974-76; exec. dir. Westchester/Opportunities Industrialization, Port Chester, N.Y., 1976—. Bd. dirs. Port Chester YMCA; steward St. Frances A.M.E. Zion Ch., Port Chester. Served with U.S. Army, 1962-64. Recipient Key to City, Greensboro, N.C., 1960; named Man of Yr., Bridgeport Jaycees, 1970. Mem. Am. Mgmt. Assn., Exec. Dirs. Assn. Opportunities Industrialization Center Am. (v.p. region II), Nat. Alliance Businessmen (loan exec.). Club: Rotary (Port Chester). Home: 45 Stafford Rd Stamford CT 06902 Office: 72 Westchester Ave Port Chester NY 10573

MAUNSBACH, KAY BENEDICTA, ins. co. exec.; b. N.Y.C., Apr. 25, 1933; d. Eric and Katherine M.; B.A. magna cum laude, Hunter Coll., 1961. Jr. security analyst Vilas & Hickey, N.Y.C., 1960-62; v.p. investment services Loeb, Rhoades & Co., N.Y.C., 1962-73; with Manhattan Life Ins. Co., N.Y.C., 1974—, v.p., dir. corp. communications, 1978—. Fellow Fin. Analysts Fedn.; mem. N.Y. Soc. Security Analysts, Life Advertisers Assn., Life Ins. Council N.Y., Public Relations Soc. Am., Nat. Assn. Bus. Economists, Nat. Investor Relations Inst., Life Underwriters Assn. N.Y., Internat. Assn. Bus. Communicators, N.Y. Bus. Communicators, Fin. Communications Soc., Ins. Women of N.Y., Women's Econ. Roundtable. Office: 111 W 57th St New York NY 10019

MAUPIN, KENNETH EUGENE, bank exec.; b. Arrowsmith, Ill., Apr. 10, 1944; s. Ola Otis and Effie Caldona (Roy) M.; student Ill. State U., 1962-66; m. Marjorie Jane Ringo, June 19, 1966; children—Jeffery Lynn, Rebecca Jane. Teller, Nat. Bank Bloomington (Ill.), 1967-70, head teller, 1970-72, mgr. data processing, 1972-73, dir. data processing, 1973-78; asst. cashier, fin. systems rep. City Nat. Bank of Kankakee (Ill.), 1978—; instr. data processing Am. Inst. Banking, 1975. Mem. Central Ill. Fin. Computer Uses Group, N.Am. Fin. Uses Group. Home: Rural Route 2 Box 219624 Kankakee IL 60901 Office: City Nat Bank Kankakee IL 60901

MAURER, CHARLES FREDERICK WILLIAM, 3D, food brokerage co. exec.; b. Jersey City, July 12, 1939; s. William and Daisy L. (Knight) M.; B.A., Va. Mil. Inst., 1961; m. Shon Hooker, June 6, 1964; children—Melissa, Adam. With Marshall Research Found., 1961-62; adminstrv. sec. Morse, Maurer & Kopple, Englewood Cliffs, N.J., 1965-72; v.p. instl. sales HMM&K, Englewood Cliffs, 1972-78; v.p. Maurer & Kopple, Englewood Cliffs, 1978—; v.p. Instn. and Indsl. div. M&H Co., White Plains, N.Y., 1978—. Pres., Park Ridge (N.J.) Bd. Health, 1980-81; v.p. Park Ridge Sr. Citizen Adv. Council. Served to maj., inf., U.S. Army, 1962-64. Mem. Nat. Food Brokers, N.Y. Inst. Food Technologists, Co. Mil. Historians, Pascack Hist. Soc. (pres. 1978-80), N.Y. Knights of Grip. Methodist. Club: Masons. Author: Third Continental Dragoons Diary, 1776-1784, 1979. Home: 3 Tulip Ct Park Ridge NJ 07656

MAURER, MARK KENNEDY, city ofcl.; b. New Brunswick, N.J., Dec. 27, 1949; s. Mark Kennedy and Jane (Curry) M.; B.S. in Community Devel., Pa. State U., 1973; children—Kelly Marie, Jessica Victoria. Fin. advisor New Brunswick (N.J.) Housing Authority, 1973-76; adminstrv. analyst, 1976-78; interim bus. adminstr. City of New Brunswick, 1978-79; dir. planning and devel. Housing Urban Devel., New Brunswick, N.J., 1979—; lectr. to various groups including LWV, HUD, Newark Office on Fiscal and Housing Policy. lMem. Stone Street Block Assn. Mem. Pa. State Alumni Assn., Nat. Assn. Housing and Redevel. Ofcls. Democrat. Roman Catholic. Club: K.C. Home: 19 Stone St New Brunswick NJ 08901 Office: 303 George St Room 308 New Brunswick NJ 08901

MAURIELLO, JOSEPH, accountant; b. Bklyn., Sept. 25, 1944; s. Salvatore and Rose (Tegone) M.; B.B.A., St. John's U., N.Y.C., 1966, M.B.A., 1972; m. Mary DiPrima, July 31, 1966; children—Claudine, Eric. With Peat, Marwick, Mitchell & Co., N.Y.C., 1966—, audit partner Bank dept., N.Y.C., 1974—. Lic. acct., N.Y., La., N.C. Mem. Am. Inst. C.P.A.'s, N.Y. State Soc. C.P.A.'s. Club: City Midday (N.Y.C.). Home: 52 Thornley Dr Chatham NJ 07928 Office: 345 Park Ave New York NY 10022

MAURIN, JAMES EDWARD, real estate devel. exec.; b. Baton Rouge, Jan. 23, 1948; s. Robert Anthony and Lillian (Abels) M.; M.B.A., Tulane U., 1972; B.M.E., La. State U., 1971; m. Lillian Crosby, June 6, 1970; children—Carla Elizabeth, Caroline Crosby, Margaret Lillian. Student engr. Boeing Co., New Orleans, 1969; research and devel. Atlantic Richfield Refining Co., Dallas, 1970; grad. research asst., instr. mgmt. sci. and fin. Tulane Grad. Sch. Bus., New Orleans, 1971-72, mem. fin. faculty, instr. managerial fin., 1973; sr. acct. Ernst & Ernst, C.P.A.'s, New Orleans, 1973-75; v.p., treas., dir. Maurin-Ogden, Real Estate Devel., Inc., New Orleans, Hammond, 1975—; dir. So. States Mgmt. Corp. Bd. dirs. Reynolds Inst. Registered profl. engr., La.; C.P.A. Mem. Omicron Delta Kappa, Phi Eta Sigma, Tau Beta Pi, Beta Gamma Sigma, Phi Kappa Phi, Kappa Sigma. Democrat. Roman Catholic. Clubs: Boston (New Orleans); Oak Knoll Country (Hammond); Essex, Exchange. Home: 45 Oak Ridge Estates Hammond LA 70401 Office: Maurin Ogden Inc 904 W Coleman Ave Hammond LA 70401

MAURO, GEORGE THEODORE, mgmt. cons.; b. N.Y.C., Mar. 7, 1938; s. Peter Terzo and Bella (Cohn) M.; B.A., U. N.H., 1959; M.B.A., Wharton Sch., U. Pa., 1972; m. Mary Ann Stoehr, Feb. 15, 1964; children—Mary Patricia, Christine T. Sr. cons. Booz, Allen & Hamilton, Phila., 1972-75, v.p., 1975-77; dir. asset value analysis U.S. Ry. Assn., Washington, 1977-79; sr. asso. Temple, Barker & Sloane, Boston, 1979—. Served with USAF, 1960-70. Decorated Meritorious Service medal Dept. Def., 1970; USAF Commendation medal; recipient Wellman trophy U. N.H. Mem. Inst. Mgmt. Consultants, Inst. Transp. Engrs., Transp. Research Forum, Beta Gamma Sigma, Tau Kappa Alpha, Psi Chi, Pi Kappa Alpha. Home: 112 Bertwell Rd Lexington MA 02173 Office: 33 Hayden Ave Lexington MA 02173

MAVRIS, NICHOLAS BENNIE, pipe line co. exec.; b. Oklahoma City, Nov. 23, 1923; s. George and Ada Virginia (Diles) M.; B.S. in Mech. Engring., Okla. State U., 1948, M.S., 1949; m. Elizabeth Ann Shaver, July 3, 1943; children—Virginia Ann Mavris Humes, George Samuel, Kathryne Ann Mavris Newton, Nicola Ann. Instr., Okla. State U., 1948-49; engr. Interstate Oil Pipeline Co., 1949-51; asst. regional mgr. Rocky Mountain region Continental Oil Co., 1963-67, mgr. transp., 1967-68; with Continental Pipe Line Co., 1951-63, 68—, pres., chief exec. officer, Houston, 1969—, also dir.; v.p., dir. Seaway, Inc.; chmn. bd., dir. Seadock, Inc., 1972—; dir., pres. Yellowstone Pipe Line Co., 1969-76; dir. Platte Pipe Line Co., West Shore Pipe Line Co.; chmn. bd. Explorer Pipeline Co., 1979—, also dir. Bd. dirs. Okla. State U. Devel. Found., 1976-77, trustee, 1975-78. Served with AUS, 1943-46. Named to Engring. Hall of Fame, Okla. State U., 1979; Disting. Service award Okla. State U., 1980. Mem. Rocky Mountain Oil and Gas Assn. (dir.), Am. Petroleum Inst. (div. transp. central com. 1968—), Assn. Oil Pipe Lines (exec. com.), Okla. State U. Alumni Assn. (dir. Houston br. 1973-77). Clubs: Sugar Creek Country, Houston Petroleum. Home: 703 Montclair Blvd Sugarland TX 77478 Office: PO Box 2197 Houston TX 77001

MAVROS, DIMITRI GEORGE, economist; b. Athens, Greece, 1943; s. George D. and Nikoleta C. (Pantelaiou) M.; student Athens Coll., 1952-62; B.A., Brandeis U., 1965; M.B.A., Coll. City New York, 1967, postgrad., 1967-71; m. Ariadni Kalpini, July 31, 1969. Dir. statis. publs. Am. Paper Inst., N.Y.C., 1967; researcher Nat. Bur. Econ. Research, N.Y.C., 1968-69; dir. research Spot & Assos., Athens, 1969-70; lectr. econs. City U. N.Y., Baruch Coll., 1970-71; exec. dir. Planning & Research Cons. Ltd., Athens, 1971—; sr. v.p., dir. research Spot Advt. Ltd., 1971-75; mng. dir. PRC/EMRB European Market Research Bur. Ltd., 1975—; partner, adminstr., dir. mktg. Spot-Thompson Advt. Ltd., 1975—; partner, dir. Movielab Ltd., 1975—; mng. dir. Technol. Systems Co.; dir. Applied Biochem. Scis. Co. Fulbright scholar, 1962-65. Mem. Am. Econ. Assn., Internat. Soc. for Devel., Greek Mgmt. Assn., Greek Mktg. Assn. (gen. sec. 1977-78, vice chmn. 1978—), Market Research Soc. U.K., European Soc. Market Research, Greek Am. C. of C. Club: Propeler. Home: 52 Theologou Athens 624 Greece Office: 17 Valaoritou and Amerikis Athens 134 Greece

MAWICKE, ALBERT THOMAS, business exec.; b. Chgo., July 16, 1921; s. Henry J. and Margaret (Mann) M.; student Northwestern U., 1943, U. Chgo., 1956; m. Dorothy Harris, Oct. 16, 1943 (dec.); children—Jeffrey J., Paul D., Ann M.; m. 2d, Grayce Bostic Cahoon, May 15, 1977; stepchildren—Kathryn Cahoon, Susan Schmitz. With Pontiac Graphics Corp., Chgo., 1946-50, salesman, 1950-52, sales mgr., v.p., 1952-59, sales mgr., v.p., div. mgr., 1959-63; with World Book-Childcraft Internat., 1963-68, regional mgr., 1966-68, asst. sales mgr., 1968-69, sales mgr. zone 5, 1969-70, sales mgr. zone 1, 1970-73, zone 6, 1974-75, br. mgr., 1975-79; v.p. Graphic Mgmt. Services, Elmhurst, Ill., 1979—; lectr., cons. Printing Industry Ill., Northwestern U., Craftsmen Clubs, various printers, mfrs., art groups. Served from pvt. to capt. AUS, 1942-46; ETO. Decorated Bronze Star. Mem. Phi Kappa Sigma. Home: 526 Grimes Ave Naperville IL 60565 Office: 102 Haven Elmhurst IL 60126

MAX-NEEF, NORBERT, bank and bus. exec.; b. Valparaiso, Chile, Mar. 18, 1927; s. Hermann and Magdalene (Neef Rave) Max Coers; came to U.S., 1962; B.A., U. Chile, 1945; diploma in money and banking Inst. High Banking Studies, Santiago, Chile, 1955; cert. in mgmt. scis. Montgomery Coll., 1975; cert. in devel. fin. Am. U., 1976; m. Maria Angela Ojeda Vargas, Apr. 5, 1954; children—Alejandro, Maria Angelica. Sect. chief Central Bank of Chile, Santiago, 1950-55; sec. gen., asst. to pres. Panam. Bank, Santiago, 1955-59; gen. mgr. Panam. Steel Corp., Santiago, 1959-62; with Interam. Devel. Bank, Washington, 1963—, sr. ops. officer, 1977—; chmn. Essex Motor Corp., 1980; del. Panam. Conf. for Sci. Orgn.. 1956-57. UN grantee, 1955. Mem. Am. Mgmt. Assn., Nat. Hist. Soc. Roman Catholic. Club: Bretton Woods Internat. Contbr. articles in field to profl. jours. Office: 808 17th St NW Washington DC 20577

MAXON, DON CARLTON, constrn. co. exec., mining co. exec.; b. Downers Grove, Ill., Dec. 23, 1914; s. Norman T. and Agnes M. (Matteson) M.; student public schs., Barrington, Ill.; m. Mary T. Quirk, June 14, 1941; children—Maureen, Don, Paul, Anne, Lee; m. 2d, Ella Luanne Roy, Dec. 10, 1971. Founder, pres. Maxon Constrn. Co., Tucson, 1936—, Gen. Mining & Devel. Co., Tucson, 1967—. Served with Seabees, USN, 1942-45. Recipient awards for designing family communities Parents' mag., 1953, 59, 60. Mem. Nat. Assn. Home Builders (Nat. Homes Pres.'s Land Planning award 1954). Democrat. Roman Catholic. Research on methods for testing and extracting gold from complex ores. Home: 6211 N Campbell Ave Tucson AZ 85718 Office: 2030 E Speedway Suite 105 Tucson AZ 85719

MAXSON, ALBERT LEROY, airline exec.; b. Erie, Pa., Dec. 27, 1935; s. Walter LeRoy and Emily (Sabol) M.; B.S., Pa. State U., 1957; M.B.A., Ga. State U., 1973; postgrad. Advanced Mgmt. Program, Harvard U., 1976; m. Linda Kay Kiger, Apr. 18, 1964; children—Barbara, Janet, Patricia. With Price Waterhouse & Co., Pitts., 1957-66; v.p. fin., treas., dir. So. Airways, Inc., Atlanta, 1966-79; v.p., treas. Republic Airlines, Inc., Mpls., 1979-80, sr. v.p. fin., 1980—. C.P.A., W.Va., Pa. Mem. Fin. Execs. Inst., Am. Inst. C.P.A.'s. Office: 7500 Airline Dr Minneapolis MN 55450

MAXSON, GARY ELDON, real estate exec.; b. Covina, Calif., Aug. 1, 1940; s. Willis Sheldon and Marion Elizabeth (Shuck) M.; A.B., U. So. Calif., 1964; m. Sharron Lynne Noble, Apr. 10, 1965 (div.); children—Melinda Lynne, Mark Noble. Asst. dir. alumni affairs U. So. Calif., Los Angeles, 1965-67, mem. bd. women's athletics; stockbroker F.I. duPont, Los Angeles, 1967-68; instl. stockbroker John Nuveen & Co., Los Angeles, 1968-69; instl. stockbroker Paine Webber, Los Angeles, 1969-77, v.p., mgr. inst. dept., 1977—; pres., chief exec. officer Carriage Real Estate Group, Inc. Mem. Los Angeles Bond Club, Town Hall, Commerce Assos., U. So. Calif. Assos., World Affairs Council. Republican. Presbyterian. Club: Jonathan. Home: 12 Dapplegray Ln Rolling Hills Estates CA 90274

MAXWELL, DONALD STANLEY, publishing co. exec.; b. Los Angeles, May 30, 1930; s. Harold Stanley and Margaret (Trenam) M.; student Long Beach City Coll., 1948-50; B.B.A., Woodbury Coll., 1956; m. Martha Helen Winn, Dec. 5, 1952; children—Sylvia Louise, Cynthia Lynn, Bruce Stanley, Bradley Erl, Walter James, Wesley Richard, Amy Bernice. Partner, Robert McDavid & Co., C.P.A.'s, Los Angeles, 1955-61; controller Petersen Pub. Co., Los Angeles, 1961-68, v.p. finance, 1969; controller Los Angeles Times, 1969-79, v.p., 1977-79, v.p. fin., 1979—; asst. treas. Times Mirror Co., 1971—. Adv. bd. Woodbury U., 1978—. Served with AUS, 1950-52. C.P.A., Calif. Mem. Fin. Execs. Inst. (dir. 1979—; dir. Los Angeles chpt. 1968-76, chpt. pres. 1973-74), Am. Inst. C.P.A.'s, Calif. Soc. C.P.A.'s, Inst. Newspaper Controllers and Fin. Officers (dir. 1978—, v.p. 1979—), Am. Horse Council. Republican. Baptist. Club: Friendly Hills Country (Whittier, Calif.). Home: 2160 Le Flore Dr La Habra Heights CA 90631 Office: Times Mirror Sq Los Angeles CA 90028

MAXWELL, EUGENE OLIVER, mfg. co. exec.; b. Ft. Worth, Apr. 22, 1941; s. Eugene Oliver and Nellie (Lockette) M.; M.E.T., U. Tex., Arlington, 1962; m. Terry Dawn Mayfield, June 12, 1972; children—Janna Lynn, Zxane Ian, Karen Jeanette. With Precision Mfg. Co., Ft. Worth, 1959-63, Gen. Dynamics, Ft. Worth, 1963-70; owner Comml. Wood Products, Ft. Worth, 1970-76; sales mgr. Ft. Worth S & S Distbn. Co., 1976-78; dir. mfg. Am. Optic Lite Corp., Ft. Worth, 1979-81; mgmt. info. mgr. Pengo Industries, Cleburne, Tex., 1981—; chmn. bd. Zane Corp., Ft. Worth, 1976-79. Mem. Utilities Commn., City of Briar Oaks, 1980. Mem. Illuminating Engring. Soc. N. Am., Tex. Assn. Bus., Nat. Fire Protection Assn., Nat. Hot Rod Assn. Patentee in field. Home: 116 S Briar Oaks Rd Burleson TX 76028 Office: 423 Vaughn Rd W Cleburne TX 76031

MAXWELL, JACK ERWIN, automobile co. exec.; b. Cleve., July 17, 1926; s. Fred A. and Gertrude F. (Haug) M.; B.S. in Mech. Engring., Case Inst. Tech., 1949; M.B.A., Harvard, 1952; children by previous marriage—Laura Jane, Fredric, Elizabeth Grant, Carla Moore, Linda

Hanson; m. 2d, Martha Jane Miller, Dec. 28, 1966. Indsl. engr. Lincoln Electric Co., Cleve., 1952-53; mgr. purchase analysis Ford Motor Co., Dearborn, Mich., 1953-57; v.p. Booz, Allen & Hamilton, Inc., Detroit, 1957-69; v.p. corp. devel. Am. Motors Corp., Detroit, 1969-71, v.p. adminstrn., 1971-76, v.p. non-automotive subsidiaries, 1976-79, v.p. diversified ops., 1979—. Served with USNR, 1944-46. Mem. Harvard Bus. Sch., Case Inst. Tech. alumni assns., Blue Key, Tau Beta Pi, Theta Tau. Presbyn. Clubs: Harvard Business School, Detroit Economic, Detroit Athletic, Detroit Yacht. Home: 3541 Bradway Blvd Birmingham MI 48010 Office: 27777 Franklin Rd Southfield MI 48034

MAXWELL, RICHARD ANTHONY, retail exec.; b. N.Y.C., Apr. 1, 1933; s. Arthur William and Mary Ellen (Winestock) M.; student N.Y. U., 1957-58, Acad. Advanced Traffic, 1959; m. Jacqueline Ann Creamer, Oct. 27, 1962. Import ops. mgr. Asso. Merchandising Corp., N.Y.C., 1950-52, 56-65; divisional v.p. Asso. Dry Goods Corp., N.Y.C., 1965—, sr. v.p. mktg., 1980—. Served with USAF, 1952-56. Recipient Silver medal for contbns. to trade expansion Republic of China, 1980. Mem. Am. Importers Assn. (pres., dir.), Shippers Conf. Greater N.Y. (past pres., dir.), Nat. Com. Internat. Trade Documentation (past vice chmn. gen. bus. com.), Transp. Assn. Am., Italy-Am. C. of C. (sec., dir.). Home: 47 Hardenburgh Ave Demarest NJ 07627 Office: 417 Fifth Ave New York NY 10016

MAY, ALBERT EDWARD, trade assn. exec.; b. Washington, Mar. 4, 1927; s. Albert and Margaret (Jahn) M.; A.B., Georgetown U., 1950, J.D., 1955; m. Helen Marie O'Neill, Apr. 19, 1958; children—Albert Edward, Helen O'Neill, Carolyn Carlson, Alexander Jahn. Admitted to D.C. bar, 1955; asso. firm MacLeay, Lynch and MacDonald, Washington, 1955-59; asst. exec. dir. Com. of Am. S.S. Lines, 1959-68; v.p., counsel Am. Inst. Mcht. Shipping, 1969-77; exec. v.p. gen. counsel Council of Am.-Flag Ship Operators, Washington, 1977—. Served to lt. USCG, 1950-52. Mem. Nat. Bar Assn., D.C. Bar Assn., Maritime Law Assn., Maritime Advminstrv. Bar Assn., Nat. Def. Transp. Assn., Propeller Club U.S., Am. Oceanic Orgn. (v.p.), Transp. Assn. Am. (dir.). Roman Catholic. Clubs: Univ. (Washington); Columbia Country (Chevy Chase, Md.); Sherwood Forest (Annapolis, Md.). Home: 7213 Bybrook Ln Chevy Chase MD 20015 Office: Council Am-Flag Ship Operators 1625 K St NW Suite 1200 Washington DC 20006

MAY, DONALD STEWART, investor; b. Bklyn., Oct. 27, 1926; s. Adam and Mabel (Stewart) M.; B.M.E., SUNY, 1949; m. Barbara A. Weber, Aug. 19, 1956; children—Scott W., Duncan W., Kevin R., Maryellen A. Cadet USAAC, 1944; midshipman U.S. Navy, 1946, advanced through grades to lt. comdr., ret., 1970; dir. plant ops. devel. ServiceMaster Industries, Inc., Downers Grove, Ill., 1970-76; v.p. facilities engring., Am. Mgmt. Services div. Am. Hosp. Supply Corp., Denver, 1976-79. Mem. U.S. Naval Inst., Am. Soc. Hosp. Engring., Ret. Officers Assn. Home: 8471 S Grizzly Way Evergreen CO 80439

MAY, FRANK BRENDAN, JR., lawyer; b. Bronx, N.Y., Oct. 17, 1945; s. Frank Brendan and Margaret M.; B.A. in Econs., N.Y. U., 1973, postgrad., 1973-75; J.D., John Marshall Law Sch., Chgo., 1978; m. Mary Frances Fitzsimmons, June 19, 1976. Admitted to Ill. bar, U.S. Circuit Ct. Appeals bar, U.S. Dist. Ct. bar; legal document clk. IBM Corp., White Plains, N.Y., 1972-73, firm Kane, Dalsimer, Kane Sullivan & Kurucz, 1973-74; ter. sales mgr. Baxter Labs., Deerfield, Ill., 1973-75; legal intern State's Atty.'s Office, Chgo., 1977-78, Wheaton, Ill., 1977-78; sr. asso. firm Lillig, Kemp, & Thorsness, Ltd., Oak Brook, Ill., 1978-81; asso. gen. counsel Coldwell Banker, Oak Brook, 1981—. Served with USAF, 1963-67. David Davis Meml. scholar, 1969-71. Mem. Am. Bar Assn., DuPage County Bar Assn., Am. Trial Lawyers Assn., Ill. Trial Lawyers Assn., Phi Alpha Delta, Phi Gamma Delta. Composer: Five Will Get You Ten, 1967. Office: 1225 W 22d St Oak Brook IL 60521

MAY, JAMES CARY, tractor co. exec., mgmt. accountant; b. Washington, May 26, 1946; s. Cary Lynwood May and Mary Stuart (Quaintance) May Bain; student Bradley U., 1964-65; B.S., Am. U., 1968; m. Karen Field Robinson, Sept. 2, 1967; children—Pamela Jane, Tiffany Lynn. With Caterpillar Tractor Co., 1968—, cost accounting supr. spl. corporate planning project, tech. facilities, Mossville, Ill., 1974-76, pre-production cost supr. Davenport plant (Iowa), 1976—. Treas. Central Ill. chpt. Cystic Fibrosis Found., 1973-74, dir., 1974-76, chmn. by laws com., 1975-76; co-chmn. Heart of Ill. Jaycee Operation Threshold, 1976. Recipient Ann. Scholarship award Washington chpt. Nat. Assn. Govt. Accts., 1968; named Outstanding 1st Yr. Jaycee, Peoria (Ill.) Jaycees, 1975, Outstanding Bd. Mem. of Yr., 1976. Mem. Nat. Assn. Accountants (asso. dir. profl. devel. Peoria chpt. 1973, asso. dir. communications Peoria chpt. 1975), Davenport Jaycees (pres. 1978-79, chmn. bd. 1979-80, Project Chmn. of Yr. 1977, Bd. Mem. of Yr. 1978), Iowa Jaycees (Outstanding State Dir. award 1978, regional sec.-treas. 1979-80, dist. dir. 1980, adminstrv. dir. 1980-81), Jr. Chamber Internat. (senator), Davenport C. of C. (nat. legis. com. 1977—). Republican. Baptist. Home: 2615 E 29th Ct Davenport IA 52803 Office: PO Box 2790 Davenport IA 52809

MAY, JOHN WILLIAM, motel and restaurant exec.; b. Middletown, Ohio, June 6, 1935; s. Leonard Lee and Zella Grace (Sorrell) M.; student Sinclair Coll., 1953-54, U. Dayton, 1954-55; m. Sarah Louise Allen, Nov. 6, 1954 (div.); children—Joseph Allen, Michael Lee. Model maker Nat. Cash Register Co., Dayton, Ohio, 1953-68; sales engr. J.R. Kuntz Co., Dayton, 1968-77; v.p., chief ops. officer Heritage Inns, Inc., Lebanon, Ohio, 1977—, chmn. bd., 1977—; pres., chief ops. officer Apollo Restaurants, Inc., Q-Jays, Inc., Orlando, Fla., 1978—, chmn. bd., 1978—. Pres., Springboro Alumni Assn., 1957, Lebanon Parents Recreation Assn., 1962-63, Lebanon PTA, 1963; committeeman Lebanon Democratic Precinct Com., 1963-66. Served with USAF, 1954. Named Ky. col., 1979. Mem. Soc. Mfg. Engrs., Lebanon C. of C. (dir. 1978-80), Orlando C. of C. Methodist. Club: Elks. Home: 901 Clover Ave Lebanon OH 45036 Office: 20 N Broadway Lebanon OH 45036 also 3125 W Colonial Dr Orlando FL 32808

MAY, PETER WILLIAM, mfg. co. exec.; b. N.Y.C., Dec. 11, 1942; s. Samuel D. and Isabel M. M.; A.B., U. Chgo., 1964, M.B.A., 1965; m. Leni Finkelstein, Aug. 16, 1964; children—Jonathan, Leslie. With Peat, Marwick, Mitchell & Co., N.Y.C., 1965-72, mgr. audit dept., 1972; v.p. fin. Flagstaff Corp. (now Trafalgar Industries, Inc.), N.Y.C., 1972-74, exec. v.p., treas., 1974—, also dir.; exec. v.p., sec. Coffee-Mat Corp., N.Y.C., 1975—, also chmn.; dir. Ethical-Fieldston Fund, N.Y.C. Active Little League, Cub Scouts Am. C.P.A., N.Y. Mem. Am. Inst. C.P.A.'s, N.Y. Soc. C.P.A.'s, Fin. Execs. Inst., U. Chgo. Alumni Assn. N.Y. Clubs: City Athletic, New Milford (Conn.) Racquet. Office: 600 Madison Ave New York NY 10022

MAY, SHIRLEY S., health assn. exec.; b. Plainfield, N.J., May 17, 1922; d. Morris and Anna (Barishaw) Steinberg; B.S. in Edn., Jersey City State Coll., 1942; postgrad. N.Y. U.; m. Robert C. May, May 8, 1943 (dec.); children—Michael L., Carol S. Exec. dir. N.W. N.J. Am. Heart Assn., 1974—. Pres. bd. dirs., exec. cons. Masterwork Mus and Art Found., 1974—; mem. Morris County adv. council Regional Health Planning Council. Mem. N.J. Pub. Health Assn., Morris County Council Social Welfare Agys., Soc. Heart Assn. Profl. Staff. Home: 23 Pleasant Valley Rd Whippany NJ 07981 Office: 669 Littleton Rd Parsippany NJ 07054

MAY, TEDDY RONALD, designer and contractor; b. Las Vegas, June 25, 1938; s. Ted and Louise (Matter) M.; student Los Angeles Trade Tech, 1959, Compton City Coll., 1960, San Bernardino Valley Coll., 1961; m. Nancy Ann Hinman, May 6, 1955; children—Teddy Michael, Toni Marie, Tracy Michelle, Philip Allen, Timothy Mark, Alvin Daryl. Archtl. draftsman Shubin & Tolstoy, Los Angeles, 1960-61, Hunsaker, Covina, Calif., 1961-64; archtl. designer Teddy May & Assos., West Covina, Calif., 1964-69, Collins Bros., Las Vegas, 1969-73; archtl. designer and contractor Teddy May & Assos., Las Vegas, 1973—. Democrat. Home: 1096 Tan O'Shanter East Las Vegas NV 89109 Office: 1515 E Tropicana Ave #690 Las Vegas NV 89109

MAY, WILLIAM FREDERIC, univ. dean; b. Chgo., Oct. 25, 1915; s. Arthur W. and Florence (Hartwick) M.; B.S., U. Rochester, 1937; grad. Advanced Mgmt. Program, Harvard U., 1950; m. Kathleen Thompson, June 14, 1947; children—Katherine Hartwick May Bickford, Elizabeth Shaw May Jessen. Research worker E.I. Du Pont de Nemours Co., 1937-38; with Am. Can Co., 1940—, mgr., Chgo., 1957-58, exec. v.p., 1964-65, vice chmn. bd., 1965, chmn., chief exec. officer, 1965-80, also pres., dir., mem. exec. com.; dean Grad. Sch. Bus. Adminstrn., N.Y. U., 1980—; dir. N.Y. Times Co., Johns Manville Co., N.Y., Envases, Columbtangs, Colombia, Engelhard Mineral & Chem. Co., Bankers Trust Co., Bus. Internat. Trustee U. Rochester, Poly. Inst. N.Y.; bd. dirs. Lincoln Center, Columbia-Presbyn. Hosp., Am. Mus. Natural History; bd. overseers Dartmouth Coll. Mem. NAM (dir.), Phi Beta Kappa. Clubs: Union League, River, Econ., Links (N.Y.C.); Blind Brook; Round Hill; Coral Beach; Nat. Golf Links Am. Office: American Ln Greenwich CT 06830

MAYALL, ROBERT LYON, cons. internat. trade and fin.; b. Southamton, N.Y., Nov. 23, 1936; s. Herschel James and Caroline Cox (Lyon) M.; student Harvard U., 1955; B.A., Johns Hopkins U., 1958; certificate U. Hong Kong, 1962, N.Y. Inst. Fin., 1968; M.A., Columbia U. East Asian Inst., 1966. Mgr. corp. fin. Liggett Group Inc., N.Y.C., 1970-73; v.p., fin. group mgr. Bell & Stanton, Inc., N.Y.C., 1974-76; sr. v.p., internat. group mgr. Manning, Selvage & Lee, Inc. (merged with Bell & Stanton, Inc.), N.Y.C., 1976-79; pres. The Gray Cons. Group, Inc., also mng. dir. R.L. Mayall Capital, Ltd., N.Y.C., London, 1979—; cons. in field. Dir. Asian Info. Service, Ltd., Hong Kong. Served to maj. U.S. Army. Mem. Fgn. Policy Assn., Japan Soc., China Inst., Asia Soc., Assn. for Asian Studies. Republican. Episcopalian. Author: New Fires from Old Ashes; Southeast Asia Since World War II, 1964; Yaun Shi-Kai, The Chinese Republic and The International Banking Community, 1966; Japan's Trade Surplus with the U.S.; Causes and Cures, 1978. Home: The Claridge House New York NY 10028 Office: The Gray Group Inc 77 Water St New York NY 10005

MAYBORN, FRANK WILLIS, newspaper editor, publisher; b. Akron, Ohio, Dec. 7, 1903; s. Ward C. and Nellie C. (Welton) M.; B.A., U. Colo., 1926. With Dallas News, 1926, N. Tex. Traction Co., Ft. Worth, 1927-29; bus. mgr. Temple (Tex.) Telegram, Bell Pub. Co., 1929-45, editor, pres., pub., owner, 1945—; founder, 1936, operator, pres. radio sta. KTEM, Bell Broadcasting Co., Temple, 1936-70; founder, pres., 1953—, since operator, owner KCEN-TV, Temple; pres. Sherman (Tex.) Democrat, Red River Valley Pub. Co., 1945-77; owner, pres. Killeen Pub. Co., operator Killeen (Tex.) Herald, 1952—; founder, operator radio sta. WMAK, Nashville, 1947-54; pres., owner County Developers, Inc., 1967—; pres. FWM Properties, 1965-75, Community Enterprises Inc., 1959-74; dir. 1st Nat. Bank Temple. Mem. Ft. Hood Civilian Adv. Com., 1963-75, Tex. Hist. Survey Com., 1966-69, Tex. Council for Higher Edn.; bd. dirs. Temple Indsl. Found., pres., 1963; trustee Central Tex. Med. Found., 1970—; pres. Kingsolving Youth Center, 1971-72; chmn. Scott and White Adv. Bd., 1956-61; bd. dirs. Tex. Indsl. Commn.; mem. adv. council Tex. A. and M. U. Dept. Journalism, 1958-59, U. Tex. Journalism Found., 1964-66; mem. broadcast adv. council Baylor U., 1964-65; adv. bd. Scott & White Hosp., Temple, 1973; bd. dirs. Waco Symphony Assn., 1968-69, Temple Boys Choir, 1969, Tex. Hist. Found., 1967-68, Frank W. Mayborn Found., 1964—; life trustee Vanderbilt U., Nashville. Mem. Tex. Democratic Exec. Com., 1948. Served from pvt. to maj. AUS, 1942-45; ETO. Decorated Bronze Star medal; recipient Outstanding Jaycee Citizens award, Temple, 1948, Citizenship award Jr. C. of C., 1951, Tex. award for outstanding service VFW, 1955; Centex Soil Conservation Dist. award, 1959; 4-H award for outstanding service to 4-H Clubs, 1971; named Jaycee Man of Yr. award, 1971. Mem. Tex. Daily Press League (dir. Tex. Sunday comic sect.), Temple C. of C. (pres. 1939-40, dir. 1953-55, 58-60, 70—), Retail Mchts. Assn. Temple, Tex. Daily Newspaper Assn. (pres. 1941), Am. (fed. laws com.), So. (pres. 1962, chmn. 1963, past dir.) newspaper pubs. assn., Assn. U.S. Army (life mem.; certificate achievement 1969, Gen. Creighton W. Abrams award 1979), Am. Soc. Newspaper Editors, Broadcast Pioneers, Phi Kappa Psi, Sigma Delta Chi. Presbyterian (elder). Clubs: Masons, Rotary; Nat. Press (Washington); Advertising (past pres.) (Ft. Worth); Dallas Athletic, Lancers (Dallas); Temple (Tex.) Country; Headliners (Austin, Tex.). Home: Hwy 36 Temple TX 76501 Office: 10 S 3d Temple TX 76501

MAYER, HAROLD MAX, meat packing co. exec.; b. Chgo., Mar. 18, 1917; s. Oscar G. and Elsa (Stieglitz) M.; B.S., Cornell U., 1939; m. June Sirotek, Nov. 16, 1963; children—Harold F., Richard A., Robert O. With Oscar Mayer & Co., 1939—, trainee Madison (Wis.) plant, 1939-41, plant mgr., Chgo., 1953-61, v.p., 1948-66, sec., 1962—, dir., 1951—, exec. v.p., 1966—, vice chmn. bd., 1973-77, chmn. exec. com., 1977—, chmn. bd., 1980—; pres. Kartridg Pak Co., 1953-73, chmn. bd., 1973-77; past v.p., dir. Chgo. Profl. Basketball Team; past dir. Gen. Life Ins. Co., Milw., Williams Bros. Paper Box Co., St. Joseph, Mich. Mem. Chgo. Com. Alcoholism, 1957—, v.p., 1959, exec. v.p., 1960, vice chmn., 1972. Bd. dirs. Skokie Valley Community Hosp, St. Francis Hosp., Evanston, Ill., 1980—; trustee Elmhurst (Ill.) Coll., 1978—; past trustee U. Chgo. Cancer Found., Ill. Children's Home Aid Soc. Served to maj. AUS, 1942-46. Mem. Chgo. Assn. Commerce and Industry (dir.), Young Pres.'s Orgn. (past chpt. chmn.), Ill. C. of C., Chgo. Pres.'s Orgn. (pres. 1967-68), Cornell Alumni Assn., Cornell Soc. Hotelmen. Mason (Shriner). Clubs: Executives, Economic, Mid-Am., Metropolitan, Chgo., Yacht (Chgo.); Meadow (Rolling Meadows, Ill.); Imperial Golf (Naples, Fla.); North Shore Country (Glenview, Ill.). Office: 5725 E River Rd Chicago IL 60631

MAYER, WILLIAM EMILIO, investment banker; b. N.Y.C., May 7, 1940; s. Emilio and Marie M.; B.S., U. Md., 1966, M.B.A., 1967; m. Katherine M. Deichler, May 16, 1964; children—Kristen Elizabeth, William Franz. Mng. dir. The 1st Boston Corp., N.Y.C., 1967—, chief adminstrv. officer in charge adminstrv., fin. and operational activities, 1979—; dir. Modular Computer Systems, Inc. Mem. dean's adv. council, exec.-in-residence Coll. Bus., U. Md., 1975—. Served to 1st lt. USAF, 1961-65. Mem. Am. Mgmt. Assn., Securities Industry Assn., Investment Assn. N.Y., Bond Club N.Y. Clubs: Wall Street, Manhasset Bay Yacht. Home: 47 Delafield Island Rd Darien CT 06820 Office: 20 Exchange Pl New York NY 10005

MAYES, DWIGHT JAMES, housing exec.; b. Norway, S.C., Nov. 23, 1951; s. Charles Herman and Ellen Arilen (Bell) M.; B.A., Am. U., 1976. With Nat. Corp. Housing Partnerships, Washington, 1975-77, project developer, 1977-79, sr. project developer, 1979—; multifamily housing cons. City New Orleans and D.C. Youth coordinator city council campaign, Washington, 1978; bd. dirs. Coop. Housing Services Info. Project, Met. Washington Planning and Housing Assn., 1978-79. Mem. Met. Washington Contractors Assn. (asso.). Democrat. Roman Catholic. Office: 1133 15th St NW Nat Corp Housing Partnerships Washington DC 20005

MAYO, GERALD EDGAR, ins. co. exec.; b. Boston, Aug. 12, 1932; B.A., Boston U., 1953; children—Sharon E., Gerald E. With New Eng. Mut. Life Ins., Boston, 1956-68, 2d v.p., to 1968; with Midland Mut. Life Ins., Columbus, Ohio, 1968—, exec. v.p., 1974-76, exec. v.p. mktg., 1976-80, pres., 1980—, also dir. Trustee Riverside Meth. Hosp., 1972—, vice chmn., 1979; trustee Central Ohio Transit Authority, 1973—, v.p., 1975-76, pres., 1976-77; treas. Columbus Acad., 1978-79. Served with U.S. Army, 1954-56. Mem. Life Office Mgmt. Assn., Life Ins. Mktg. and Research Assn., Nat. Assn. Life Underwriters. Clubs: Columbus Country, Athletic. Office: 250 E Broad St Columbus OH 43215

MAYO, RALPH ELLIOTT, chemist; b. Greenville, N.C., May 9, 1940; s. William Louis and Mattie Lenora (Harris) M.; student East Carolina U., 1958-61; B.S., Emory U., 1963, Ph.D., 1966; m. Tommie Nelda Humphries, Dec. 21, 1964; children—Jonathan, Jane-Margaret. Sr. research chemist Perkin Elmer Corp., Norwalk, Conn., 1966-68; supr. method devel. lab. Air Products and Chems., Inc., Linwood, Pa., 1968-78, mgr. analytical services, 1978—. Mem. Am. Chem. Soc., AAAS, Soc. Applied Spectroscopy, Catalyst Soc. Contbr. articles tech. jours. Home: 1231 Hawthorn Ln West Chester PA 19380 Office: PO Box 427 Marcus Hook PA 19061

MAYO, ROBERT PORTER, banker; b. Seattle, Mar. 15, 1916; s. Carl Asa and Edna Alberta (Nelson) M.; A.B. magna cum laude, U. Wash., 1937, M.B.A., 1938; m. Marian Aldridge Nicholson, Aug. 28, 1942; children—Margaret Alice, Richard Carl, Carolyn Ruth (Mrs. Gregory Brown), Robert Nelson. Research asst., auditor Wash. State Tax Commn., 1938-41; economist U.S. Treasury, 1941-47, asst. dir.; office of tech. staff, 1948-53, chief debt div. analysis staff, 1953-59; asst. to sec. Treasury Dept., 1959-60; v.p. Continental Ill. Nat. Bank & Trust Co. of Chgo., 1960-69; chmn. Boye Needle Co., 1963-67; staff dir. Pres. Commn. on Budget Concepts, 1967; dir. U.S. Bur. of Budget, 1969-70; counsellor to Pres. U.S., 1970; pres. Fed. Res. Bank of Chgo., 1970—. Chmn. mng. bd. YMCA, Chgo.; mem. bus. advisory council Grad. Sch. Bus. U. Wis. Mem. Chartered Financial Analysts, Chgo. Assn. Commerce and Industry (sr. council), Am. Econ. Assn., Am. Fin. Assn., Phi Beta Kappa. Presbyterian. Clubs: Cosmos (Washington); Bankers, Comml. Execs., Econ. (Chgo.); Galena (Ill.) Ter. Office: 230 S LaSalle St Chicago IL 60604

MAYOZ, RAFAEL, elec. mfg. co. exec.; b. Barcelona, Spain, July 6, 1938; s. Rafael and Wenceslada (Valencia) M.; came to U.S., 1957, naturalized, 1966; B. Indsl. Engring., U. Fla., 1962; M.E., U. South Fla., 1967; m. Gloria Alonso, Nov. 21, 1958; children—Rudy, Gloria. Methods and practices engr. Gen. Telephone of Fla., Tampa, Fla., 1962-65, sr. plant extension engr., 1965-67; systems analyst Westinghouse Electric Corp., Tampa, 1967-69, sr. systems analyst, 1969-74, supr. computer ops., 1974, mgr. mgmt. systems, 1974—; instr. engring. U. South Fla., Tampa, 1968-71. Mem. bd. dirs. Centro Asturiano Hosp. Registered profl. engr., Fla. Roman Catholic. Home: 5021 Homer Ave Tampa FL 33609 Office: 6001 S Westshore Blvd Tampa FL 33616

MAYS, WILLIAM CLARKE STEVENS, JR., mfg. co. exec.; b. Providence, Apr. 9, 1917; s. William Clarke and Alice Agnes (Hill) M.; student Bryant Coll., 1936-37, U.S. Maritime Sch., 1944; m. Ruth L. Prendergast, Feb. 15, 1941 (div. June 1961); m. 2d, Eugenia Louise Pesuit, June 30, 1965; children—William Clarke Stevens III, James H., Robinson D., Curtis, Eugenia Louise. Asst. marine supt. Wilmore Steamship Co., Boston, 1944-45; asst. marine supt. U.S. Lines Co., N.Y.C., 1945-46; sec. Writing Instrument Mfrs. Assn., Washington, 1946-58; pres. Mays Assos., Inc., Providence, 1946-48; pres. Marshall & Meier Co., Inc., N.Y.C. and Providence, 1956—, Mays Mfg. Co., Inc., Warwick, R.I., 1960—; treas. Hopkins Hollow Cemetery Corp., Greene, R.I., 1970—; pres. Mays Internat., Inc., 1975—; dir. Amica Mut. Ins. Co., Amica Pension Fund, Amica Life Ins. Co., Amica Credit Co., Providence. Mem. U.S. Dept. Commerce Nat. Export Expansion Council, 1969-72. Mem. planning bd., Warwick, 1945-50. Mem. Seamen's Ch. Inst. N.Y.C., Internat. Center New Eng., Jr. Achievement R.I.; trustee Naval War Coll. Found.; trustee Kent County Meml. Hosp., Warwick. Served with USCG, 1941-43. Recipient Presdl. citation Dept. Commerce, 1967, E Star award, 1976. Mem. Collier County Conservancy (trustee 1971), U.S. Naval Inst., Greater Providence C. of C., Steamship Hist. Soc. Am., Marine Hist. Assn., Western Coventry Hist. Soc., Navy League (dir. 1970), Naval Civilian Council (mem. exec. com. 1966-78), Mfg. Jewelers and Silversmiths Am., Inc., Am. Assn. Indsl. Mgmt., Assn. Naval Aviation, Tailhook Assn. Republican. Episcopalian. Clubs: Hope, Squantum Assn., Turks Head (Providence); N.Y. Yacht (N.Y.C.); Newport Reading Room, Newport Clambake, Quindecim Soc. (Newport); Masons, Shriners. Home: Hidden Hollow Farm Greene RI 02827 Office: Mays Mfg Co PO Box 328 Warwick RI 02887

MAZUREK, KEITH PETER, automotive exec.; b. Brantford, Ont., Can., Apr. 26, 1924; came to U.S., 1949, naturalized, 1979; s. Peter and Alice M.; B.M.E., McGill U., 1949; M. Automotive Engring., Chrysler Inst., 1951; m. Betty C. Smith, Jan. 6, 1945; children—Jane, Jill, Judy. With Chrysler Corp., Can. and U.S. 1949-69, gen. mgr. Export/Import div., 1960-67, exec. v.p. Chrysler Can., 1967-69; pres. truck div., pres. components group Internat. Harvester, 1969-79; pres. White Motor Corp., Farmington Hills, Mich., 1980—. Served with RCAF, 1942-45. Mem. Soc. Automotive Engrs., Profl. Engrs. Ont. Office: 34500 Grand River Ave Farmington Hills MI 48024

MC ADAMS, HERBERT HALL, II, banker; b. Jonesboro, Ark., June 6, 1915; s. Herbert Hall and Stella (Patrick) McA.; B.S., Northwestern U., 1937; postgrad. Harvard, 1937-38, Loyola U., Chgo., 1938-39; J.D. with honors, U. Ark., 1940; m. 2d, Shelia Wallace, Nov. 27, 1970; 1 dau., Nicole Patrick Mc Adams; children by previous marriage—Judith (Mrs. Walter A. DeRoeck), Sandra (Mrs. Robert C. Connor), Hall, Penny (Mrs. Tim Hodges). Admitted to Ark. bar, 1940; chmn. bd., chief exec. officer Citizens Bank, Jonesboro, 1959—, Citizens Bancshares Corp., 1980—, Union of Ark. Corp., 1980—, Union Nat. Bank, Little Rock, 1970—; dir. Fed. Res. Bank, Little Rock, 1974-77, Ark. La. Gas Co., Shreveport, La., 1964-74, 76—. Mem. Ark. Indsl. Devel. Commn., 1964-73, chmn., 1967-72. Bd. dirs. Ark. Arts Center, 1968-74, Ark. Baptist Found., 1975-77; bd. visitors U. Ark., Little Rock, 1978—; chmn. bd. govs. Ark. State U. Found., 1977; mem. nat. citizens adv. com. Assn. Am. Med. Colls., 1980; bd. govs., chmn. exec. com. Ark. State Fair and Livestock Show Assn., 1976—; trustee Ark.-Baptist Med. Center System, 1975-78, Ark. Bapt. Med. Center System Real Estate Corp., 1977—. Served to lt. (j.g.) USNR, World War II. Decorated Purple Heart; recipient Top Mgmt. award, 1972—. Mem. Am., Ark. bar assns., Am., Ark. bankers assns., Met. C. of C., Sigma Nu. Clubs:

Country of Little Rock, Little Rock, Capital, Pleasant Valley, Rotary (Little Rock). Home: 47 Edgehill Rd Little Rock AR 72207 Office: 1 Union Nat Plaza Little Rock AR 72201 also Citizens Bank Bldg Jonesboro AR 72401

MCAFEE, HORACE J., lawyer; b. Heflin, La., July 17, 1905; s. J.U. and Annie (Reeves) McA.; A.B., So. Methodist U., 1926; J.D., Columbia, 1931; m. Kathryn Gage, July 6, 1931 (dec. Nov. 1972); children—Mary Ann (Mrs. James N. Baxter), William Gage, Stuart Reeves; m. Jane Harrison Shaffer, Aug. 17, 1974. Admitted to N.Y. bar, 1932; with Simpson Thacher & Bartlett, N.Y.C., 1931-75, partner, 1944-54, sr. partner, 1954-75; hon. dir. Sybron Corp. Mem. Irvington (N.Y.) Zoning Bd. of Appeals, 1951—, chmn., 1955—; sec. Irvington Pub. Library, 1948-61, pres., 1961-62. Mem. Assn. Bar City N.Y., Am., N.Y. State bar assns., New York County Lawyers Soc., Am. Judicature Soc. Episcopalian. Clubs: Ardsley Country, Ardsley Curling; Church, Camp Fire of America (N.Y.C.). Home: Stoneleigh Matthiessen Park Irvington-on-Hudson NY 10533 Office: 1 Battery Park Plaza New York NY 10004 also 350 Park Ave New York NY 10022

MC AFEE, JERRY, petroleum co. exec.; b. Port Arthur, Tex., Nov. 3, 1916; s. Almer McDuffie and Marguerite (Calfee) McA.; B.S. in Chem Engring., U. Tex., 1937; Sc.D. in Chem. Engring., Mass. Inst. Tech., 1940; m. Geraldine Smith, June 21, 1940; children—Joe R., William M., Loretta M., Thomas R. Research chem. engr. Universal Oil Products Co., Chgo., 1940-45; tech. specialist Gulf Oil Corp., Port Arthur, Tex., 1945-49, v.p. engring., Pitts., 1955-60, v.p., exec. tech. adviser, 1960-64, dir. planning and econs., 1962-64, chmn. bd., chief exec. officer, 1976—, also dir.; dir. Chemistry div. Gulf Research & Devel Co., Harmarville, Pa., 1950-51, asst. dir. research, 1951-53, v.p., asso. dir. research, 1954-55; sr. v.p. Gulf Oil Corp., 1964-67, coordinator Gulf Eastern Co., London, 1964-67; exec. v.p. Brit. Am. Oil Co., Ltd., Toronto, Ont., 1967-69; pres., chief exec. officer, dir. Gulf Oil Can. Ltd., Toronto, 1969-76; dir. Mellon Bank. Active Regional Indsl. Devel. Corp. of Southwestern Pa.; pres. Allegheny Conf. Community Devel.; bd. dirs. Aspen Inst. Humanistic Studies, Pitts. Symphony. Mem. Am. Inst. Chem. Engrs. (v.p. 1959, pres. 1960), Nat. Petroleum Council, Am. Petroleum Inst. (dir.), Am. Chem. Soc., Nat. Acad. Engring., Greater Pitts. C. of C. Clubs: Duquesne (Pitts); Toronto, York (Toronto); Laurel Valley Golf; Fox Chapel Golf; Rolling Rock; Links (N.Y.C.). Office: PO Box 1166 Pittsburgh PA 15230

MC AFEE, RALPH LAVERNE, lawyer; b. Barry, Tex., Oct. 20, 1914; s. Jesse Urban and Annie (Reeves) McA.; student Southwestern U., 1931-33; B.S., Columbia, 1936, J.D., 1939; m. Carolyn Jane McDonell, June 25, 1946; children—Carolyn Jane, Horace Michael, Marc Charles. Admitted to N.Y. bar, 1940, since practiced in N.Y.C.; law asst. N.Y. County Dist. Attys. Office, 1939-40; asso. firm Cravath, Swaine & Moore and predecessor, N.Y.C., 1940-52, mem. firm, partner, 1952—. Served to maj. AUS, 1940-45; CBI. Fellow Am. Coll. Trial Lawyers, Am. Bar Found., N.Y. Bar Found.; mem. Am., N.Y. State, N.Y.C. bar assns., Fed. Bar Council, Am. Judicature Soc., N.Y. Law Inst., N.Y. County Lawyers Assn., Phi Delta Phi. Clubs: Wall Street (N.Y.C.); Sleepy Hollow Country (Scarborough, N.Y.); Shinnecock Hills Golf (Southampton, N.Y.); Metropolitan, Nat. Lawyers (Washington). Home: 22 Lakeview Ave North Tarrytown NY 10591 Office: 1 Chase Manhattan Plaza New York City NY 10005

MC ALLISTER, CYRUS RAY, JR., cons.; b. Portland, Oreg., Apr. 22, 1922; s. Cyrus Ray and Edna Marion (Parks) McA.; B.A. magna cum laude, U. Minn., 1948; M.A., U. Oreg., 1951; m. Mary Ruth Carter, Sept. 28, 1953; children—Sharon Louise, Cyrus Ray III, Mark Ross. Teaching asst. U. Minn., 1948; Instr. U. Ida., 1948-50; teaching fellow, grad. asst. U. Oreg., 1950-52; analyst Dept. Def., Washington, 1952; staff mem., mathematician Sandia Corp., Albuquerque, 1952-57, cons., 1957; sr. research scientist Nuclear div. Kaman Aircraft Corp., Albuquerque, 1957-59, cons., Colorado Springs, Colo., 1959-60; cons. Hamilton Watch Co., Lancaster, Pa., 1960; pres. tech. dir. McAllister & Assos., Inc., Albuquerque, 1960-63; research dir. Booz, Allen Applied Research, Inc., Los Angeles, 1963-68, Aerospace Corp., 1968-72; consultant, 1966—. Cons. mem. Joint Am. Soc. Quality Control—I.E.E.E. Task Force on Systems Reliability, 1961. Served with USAAF, 1940-45; ETO. Mem. Am. Meteorol. Soc., Am. Math. Soc., Soc. Indsl. and Applied Math., Math. Assn. Am., A.A.A.S., Am. Statis. Assn., Soc. Engring. Sci., A.I.M., N.Y. Acad. Scis., Phi Beta Kappa, Sigma Xi, Pi Mu Epsilon. Contbr. articles to profl. jours. Home: 4729 Libbit Ave Encino CA 91316

MCALLISTER, HARRY HALLECK, ins. co. exec.; b. Mt. Union, Iowa, Apr. 28, 1919; s. Harry H. and Hazel E. (Kester) McA.; B.S.C., State U. Iowa, 1940; m. Edwina M. Gause, June 28, 1975; children by previous marriage—Susan, James; stepchildren—John, Debbie, Chris. With Central Life Assurance Co., Des Moines, 1940—, v.p. product devel., 1979—. Served with USN, 1942-46. Mem. Am. Soc. C.L.U.'s, Nat. Assn. Life Underwriters, Nat. Assn. Securities Dealers, Des Moines C. of C. Republican. Methodist. Contbr. articles to profl. jours. Home: 6816 Northwest Dr Des Moines IA 50322 Office: 611 5th Ave Des Moines IA 50306

MC ALLISTER, JAMES HERSCHEL, savs. and loan exec.; b. Rochelle, Ga., Jan. 21, 1918; s. John Martin Colombus and Birdie Alma (Mason) McA.; student Middle Ga. Coll., 1936-39, U. Ga., 1940-41; m. Frances Dea Landram, July 26, 1947; children—James Martin, Christopher Jon. Tchr. pub. schs., Abbeville, Ga., 1939-40; bookkeeper Trust Co. Ga., Atlanta, 1940-41; teller Bank Am., Merced, Calif., 1946-48; bus. mgr. Gilbert & Siebel, Merced, 1948-52; mgr. Penn Mut. Ins. Co., Merced-Bakersfield, Calif., 1952-58; div. mgr. Prudential Ins. Co., Bakersfield-Oxnard, 1958-69; v.p. Guardian Savs. & Loan Assn., Oxnard, 1969-75, Mercury Savs. and Loan Assn., Huntington Beach, Calif., 1975-77; real estate devel. mgr. Finance America, Panorama City, Calif., 1977-78; v.p. Citizens Savs. & Loan Assn., San Francisco, 1978—. Instr., Life Underwriters Tng. Council, Bakersfield Coll., 1955-57. Pres., Oxnard Conv. and Visitors Bur., 1972-75; adviser Oxnard Broadbill Tournament, 1974-77. Bd. dirs. Oxnard Ambassadors, pres., 1977—; bd. dirs. Oxnard Boys Club. Served with USAAF, 1941-45. Decorated Bronze Star with oak leaf clusters; named Ambassador of Year, Oxnard, 1980. Mem. Oxnard C. of C. (dir.), Ventura County Life Underwriters Assn., Calif. Savs. and Loan League (chmn. mktg. com. 1972-74), Savs. Instns. Mktg. Soc. Am., Ventura County Advt. Club (charter pres. 1974—), Orange County Advt. Fedn., Calif. Trade Clubs Assn. (Trader of Year 1980; vice-chmn. 1981), Orange County C. of C. Kiwanian (charter pres. 1971). Clubs: Oxnard Trade (charter pres. 1969, pres. 1977— dir.), Oxnard Optimist Morning (pres. 1963). Home: 3020 Peninsula Rd 645 Oxnard CA 93030 Office: 345 Esplanade Dr Oxnard CA 93030

MCALLISTER, RICHARD LOUIS, environ. service co. exec.; b. Indpls., Feb. 27, 1931; s. Robert William and Lillian G. (Askine) McA.; B.A. in Chemistry, Ind. U., 1953; m. Margaret A. Kos, July 26, 1952; children—Debra, Michael, Richard. Salesman, product mgr., internat. sales mgr. Spencer Chem. Co., 1954-63; regional mgr. Borg-Warner Chems., 1963-69, gen. sales mgr., 1969-70, gen. mktg. mgr., 1970-71, gen. mgr. splty. chems., 1972-73, v.p. chems., 1974-77, pres. Kemron div., Marietta, Ohio, 1977—. Corp. mem. Marietta Meml. Hosp. Recipient award of merit Am. Soc. Electroplated Plastics, 1977. Mem. Air Pollution Control Assn., Marietta C. of C. Republican. Roman Catholic. Clubs: Parkersburg (W.Va.) Country, Rotary. Office: 235 2d St Marietta OH 45750

MCALPIN, CLAY C., retail exec.; b. Elk City, Okla., July 7, 1933; s. Lawrence Edward and May Marie (Woods) McA.; student U. So. Calif., 1973; m. Betty Ann DeLilo, Mar. 14, 1956; children—Cathie Ann, Claydean Tehresa, Clarinda Patricia. Mgr., C.R. Anthony Co., dept. store, Stanton, Calif., 1956-61, Stevens Dept. Store, Stanton, 1961-62; with Tanne Apparel div. Lucky Stores, 1962—, ops. mgr., 1967-79, v.p., dir. ops., Pico Riveria, Calif., 1979—. Planning commr. City of Stanton, 1962-64, Served with USNR, 1952-56. Mem. U. So. Calif. Alumni Assn. Republican. Presbyterian. Home: 6082 Ronald Circle Cypress CA 90630 Office: 4901 Gregg Rd Rico Riveria CA 90660

MC ALPINE, GORDON ALEXANDER, computer design engr., co. exec.; b. Highland Park, Mich., Nov. 6, 1921; s. Alexander and Anna (Heelke) McA.; B.S.M.E., Lawrence Inst. Tech., Southfield, Mich., 1949; m. Ethel M. Hilborn, Dec. 25, 1943; children—Susan, David, Steven, Nancy. Asst. to v.p. Ex-Cell-O Corp., Detroit, 1940-60; sales mgr. indsl. div. RCA, Plymouth, Mich., 1960-71; dir. mktg. indsl. and automation systems ITT Corp., Plymouth, 1971-76; v.p. indsl. div. Pioneer Engring. & Mfg. Co., Warren, Mich., 1977-79; dir. Computer Graphics Time Engring. div. Gros-Ite Industries, Troy, Mich., 1979—; cons. in field. Pres. Franklin (Mich.) Community Assn., 1961. Registered profl. engr., Calif. Sr. mem. Soc. Am. Value Engrs., Soc. Mfg. Engrs. (cert.). Author papers, articles in field. Home: 32750 Romsey St Franklin MI 48025 Office: 1522 E Big Beaver St Troy MI 48084

MCANDREWS, JAMES PATRICK, lawyer; b. Carbondale, Pa., May 11, 1929; s. James Patrick and Mary Agnes (Walsh) McA.; B.S. in Acctg., U. Scranton, 1949; LL.B., Fordham U., 1952; cert. in real estate, N.Y. U., 1972; m. Mona Marie Steinke, Sept. 4, 1954; children—James P., George A., Catherine M., Joseph M., Michael P., Anne Marie, Edward R., Daniel P. Admitted to N.Y. bar, 1953, Ohio bar, 1974; asso. firm James F. McManus, Levittown, N.Y., 1955; atty. Emigrant Savs. Bank, N.Y.C., 1955-68; counsel Tchrs. Ins. and Annuity Assn., N.Y.C., 1968-73; asso. firm Thompson, Hine & Flory, Cleve., 1973-74, partner, 1974—; mem. law faculty Am. Inst. Banking, 1968-69. Served as officer USAF, 1952-54. Fellow Am. Bar Found. Mem. Am. Coll. Real Estate Lawyers, Am. Bar Assn., Am. Land Title Assn., Mortgage Bankers Assn., Urban Land Inst., Internat. Council Shopping Centers, Nat. Assn. Corp. Real Estate Execs., Am. Judicature Soc., Nat. Trust Historic Preservation, Ohio Bar Assn., Bar Assn. Greater Cleve. (chmn. real estate law sect. 1980-81), Am. Legion, Delta Theta Phi. Roman Catholic. Clubs: Rotary, K.C. Contbr. articles to profl. pubs. Home: 2971 Litchfield Rd Shaker Heights OH 44120 Office: 1100 National City Bank Bldg Cleveland OH 44114

MCANDREWS, JOHN PATRICK, sporting goods and ammunition co. exec.; b. Owensboro, Ky., June 12, 1925; s. Patrick William and Ruth Louise (Pelligrin) McA.; B.S., U. Notre Dame, 1944, M.S., 1947; m. Margaret Ellen Stier, Aug. 23, 1952; children—Mary Ellen, Lawrence John, Kevin Francis, Brian Patrick, Christopher Lee. Chem. engr. E.I. duPont de Nemours & Co., 1947-57, mgr. Marshall Research Lab., 1957-60, mgr. sales devel. Lab., Flint, Mich., 1960-62, gen. sales mgr. consumer product div., 1964-66; with Remington Arms Co., Bridgeport, Conn., 1966—, asst. gen. mgr., from 1974, dir., 1976—, pres., 1978—; dir. Conn. Nat. Bank, Bridgeport. Dir., United Way Eastern Fairfield County; trustee Fairfield U.; mem. adv. council Coll. Sci. U. Notre Dame; dir. St. Joseph's Manor. Served to lt. USNR. Mem. Sporting Arms and Ammunition Mfrs. Inst. (exec. com.), Wildlife Mgmt. Inst., Nat. Security Indsl. Assn. (dir.). Club: Brooklawn Country (Fairfield, Conn.). Office: Remington Arms Co 939 Barnum Ave Bridgeport CT 06602

MCARTHUR, JOHN HECTOR, univ. dean; b. Vancouver, B.C., Can., Mar. 31, 1934; came to U.S., 1957; s. Hector and Elizabeth Lee (Whyte) McA.; B.Comm., U. B.C., 1957; M.B.A., Harvard U., 1959, D.B.A., 1962; m. Netilia Ewasiak, Sept. 15, 1956; children—Jocelyn Natasha, Susan Patricia. Prof. bus. adminstrn. Harvard U., 1963—, dean Bus. Sch., 1980—; dir. Rohm & Haas Co., Chase Manhattan Corp. Office: Harvard Business School Boston MA 02163

MCATEER, OWEN JOSEPH, reliability physics engr.; b. Frostburg, Md., Mar. 28, 1935; s. Owen C. and Margaret A. (Greene) McA.; B.S.E.E., Johns Hopkins U., 1965, M.S.E.E., 1969; m. Carole Ann Single, Feb. 11, 1960; foster children—John Joseph Corrigan, Eugene Francis Corrigan (dec.), Mary Ellen Dewitt. With Westinghouse Elec. Corp., Balt., 1959—, design engr., 1962-64, asso. design engr., 1964-66, engr. radar troubleshooting team, 1966-67, sr. reliability engr., 1967-73, supervisory engr. microanalysis lab., 1973-74, mgr. reliability physics, 1974-76, adv. engr., 1976—. Served with AUS, 1955-58; Korea. Recipient Johns Hopkins award Westinghouse Elec. Corp., 1959, Outstanding Presentation award EOS/ESD Symposium, 1979. Mem. IEEE (sr.), Am. Legion. Democrat. Film producer: Static Havoc, 1979; contbr. articles to tech. jours. Office: PO Box 647 MS 454 Baltimore MD 21203

MC AULIFF, DAN, elec. mfg. co. exec.; b. Dallas, Dec. 19, 1926; s. Cornelius Francis and Margery Hazel (Sparks) McA.; B.S., So. Meth. U., 1948; m. Lorraine Maxine Schmitz, June 15, 1948; children—Susan Marjorie, Donald William, Leslie Ann. Project design engr. Sangamo Electric Co., Springfield, Ill., 1948-59, various positions engring. mgmt., 1959-68, dir. engring. Power Equipment div., 1968-73, dir. engring. and quality assurance Oconee plant, West Union, S.C., 1973-76; v.p. and gen. mgr. Oconee plant, Sangamo Weston Inc. subs. Schlumberger Ltd., West Union, 1976-80; v.p. ops. devel. Sangamo Weston, West Union, 1980—; chief U.S. del. Com. SC-13A Internat. Electrotech. Commn., Toronto, Ont., Can., 1972, Warsaw, Poland, 1976; lectr. instruments and controls electric utility in energy crisis. Trustee 1st Congl. Ch., Springfield, 1970-73. Served with Signal Corps, U.S. Army, 1945-47. Mem. IEEE (sr.), Nat. Elec. Mfrs. Assn. (chmn. watt-hour meter tech. com. 1968-69, 76-77, dir. power equipment div. 1980). Republican. Presbyterian. Patentee in field. Home: 512 Hillandale Rd Seneca SC 29678 Office: Sangamo Weston Inc PO Box 75 West Union SC 29696

MCAULIFFE, JAMES MICHAEL, garden products exec.; b. Multnomah, Oreg., Oct. 24, 1936; s. James Patrick and Helen Marie McA.; student pub. and pvt. schs., Seattle; married; children—James, Micheal, John, Anthony, Daniel, Elizabeth. Constrn. worker, Alaska, 1957-59; with East Side Disposal, Bellevue, Wash., 1960-64; owner, pres. Topsoils, Inc., Bothell, Wash., 1967—; pres. Plant Soil Products, Inc., Bothell, 1976—, Ecolo Recycle, Inc., Bothell, 1974-77; owner, pres. Jim McAuliffe Landscaping; owner Penny Creek Nursery. Mrm. Bothell Park Bd., 1972-80; mem. Shoreline Hearing Bd., Bothell; active local and state polit. campaigns; bd. dirs. Bothell YMCA. Served to sgt. U.S. Army, 1961-62. Mem. Seattle Escoffier Soc., Seattle Master Builders, U.S. Jaycees, Ecol. Soc. Pacific N.W., Sons Italy Wine Festival, Am. Legion. Clubs: Mill Creek Country, Elks. Home: 17617 88th St NE Bothell WA 98011 Office: 14002 35th Ave SE Bothell WA 98011

MC BEE, FRANK WILKINS, JR., electronic mfg. co. exec.; b. Ridley Park, Pa., Jan. 22, 1920; s. Frank Wilkins and Ruth (Moulton) McB.; B.S.M.E., U. Tex., Austin, 1947, M.S.M.E., 1950; m. Sue Brandt, Apr. 10, 1943; children—Marilyn, Robert Frank. Instr. in mech. engring. U. Tex., Austin, 1946-50, asst. prof. mech. engring., 1950-53, supr. mech. dept. Def. Research Lab., 1950-59; with Tracor, Inc., Austin, 1955—, exec. v.p., 1967-70, pres., chief exec. officer, 1970—, chmn. bd., 1972—; dir. Merc. Tex. Corp. Sr. mem. U. Tex. Engring. Found. Adv. Council; mem. U. Tex. Marine Sci. Inst. Adv. Council; trustee Center Internat. Bus., Dallas, S.W. Tex. Public Broadcasting Council; bd. dirs. Tex. Ind. Coll. Fund, Dallas, Paramount Theatre Performing Arts, Austin. Served with USAAF, 1943-46. Named Disting. Grad., Coll. Engring. U. Tex., Austin, 1978. Mem. Nat. Soc. Profl. Engrs., Tex. Soc. Profl. Engrs., U. Tex. Ex-Students Assn. (life), Austin Heritage Soc. (life), Nat. Trust Hist. Preservation, Sigma Xi, Tau Beta Pi, Pi Tau Sigma. Clubs: Headliners, Austin Yacht (former commodore). Office: 6500 Tracor Ln Austin TX 78721

MC BRIDE, FRANK VINCENT, mech. contracting co. exec.; b. Paterson, N.J., Apr. 5, 1906; s. Frank A. and Alice (Nevin) M.; A.B., Holy Cross Coll., 1925; m. Margaret Mary Sweeney, Apr. 23, 1935; children—Frank Vincent, Daniel J., Mary Virginia, Timothy B. With Frank A. McBride Co., mech. contracting, 1925—, now chmn. bd., chief exec. officer; dir. 1st Nat. Bank of N.J., Paterson; past chmn. bd. N.J. Mfrs. Ins. Co., Trenton. Decorated Knight of St. Gregory (Pope Pius XII). Mem. Mech. Contractors Assn., Am. (nat. pres. 1961-62, trustee), N.J. (past chmn. bd.) mfrs. assns. Home: 335 Algonquin Rd Franklin Lakes NJ 07417 Office: 233 Central Ave Hawthorne NJ 07506

MC BRIDE, H. COLIN, lawyer; b. Edmont, Alta., Can., May 21, 1945; came to U.S., 1946, naturalized, 1968; s. Harry T. and Veronica Louise (Cole) McB.; A.B., Bates Coll., 1967; J.D., Boston U., 1974; m. Mary Jo LaRochelle, Jan. 25, 1969; children—Cami Kristen, Terrence Cole. Admitted to N.Y. State bar, 1975; asso. firm Fine, Tofel & Saxl, N.Y.C., 1974-77; employee benefits counsel Emhart Corp., Farmington, Conn., 1977-79; asst. counsel R.J. Reynolds Industries, Inc., Winston-Salem, N.C., 1979—. Served to lt. USN, 1968-71. Republican. Roman Catholic. Home: 4101 Allistair Rd Winston-Salem NC 27104 Office: R J Reynolds Industries Inc Reynolds Blvd Winston-Salem NC 27102

MC BRIDE, JAMES JOSEPH, fin. exec.; B.S.C.E., M.B.A.; married; 4 children. Engr., supr. in constrn., 1934-42; engaged in constrn., also ind. oil operator, Houston, 1947—; now chief exec. officer Fresno Industries Corp., holding co. with subs. in energy, devel., fin., constrn. and lubrication, Houston; chmn. bd. devel. co., dredging co. Served with C.E., U.S. Army, 1943-46; CBI. Lic. pilot. Mem. aviation orgns. Republican.

MC BRIDE, LLOYD MERRILL, lawyer; b. Corydon, Iowa, July 20, 1908; s. Ernest Eugene and Jeannie (Randolph) McB.; A.B. cum laude, Carleton Coll., 1930, LL.D. (hon.), 1979; postgrad. Harvard U., 1931-32; J.D., Northwestern U., 1934; m. Alice Rowland, June 8, 1935; children—Patricia Ann, Barbara Jean. Admitted to Ill. bar, 1934, since practiced in Chgo.; with firm Stearns & Jones, 1934-41; partner Stearns & McBride, 1941-43, McBride & Baker, 1943-58, McBride, Baker, Wienke & Schlosser, 1958—; sec., dir. Vermillion Corp., SMI Investments Co., FRC Investments Co., Ryder Types, Inc., Bayou Corp.; dir., chmn. exec. com. Wallace Bus. Forms, Inc.; mem. exec. com. Morton-Norwich Products, Inc.; sec. NOR-AM Agrl. Products Inc.; pres., dir. 1550 State Pkwy. Condominium Assn.; dir. Stenning Industries, Inc. Trustee, sec. Morton Arboretum, Lisle, Ill.; trustee Carleton Coll., Northfield, Minn., 1970-79, trustee emeritus, 1979—, chmn. capital campaign, 1976-78; trustee Chgo. Latin Sch., 1951-59. Mem. Am. Bar Assn., Ill. Bar Assn., Chgo. Bar Assn., Phi Beta Kappa, Delta Sigma Rho. Republican. Clubs: Mid-Am., Tower, Racquet (Chgo.). Home: 1550 N State Pkwy Chicago IL 60610 Office: 110 N Wacker Dr Chicago IL 60606

MC BRIDE, LOUIS MARCELL, banker; b. Haywood County, Tenn., Oct. 21, 1924; s. Louis K. and Floy Ann (Springer) McB.; ed. West Tenn. Bus. Coll., U. Wis. Grad. Sch. Banking; m. Albertine Booth, Feb. 2, 1947; children—Brenda, Gary. Vice pres. Browder Milling Co., Inc., Fulton, Ky., 1946-62; pres. City Nat. Bank, Fulton, 1962—. Mem. Fulton C. of C. (pres., Citizen of Yr. award 1971). Democrat. Baptist. Clubs: Rotary (pres.), Fulton Country. Office: 308 Lake St Fulton KY 42041

MC BURNEY, GEORGE WILLIAM, lawyer; b. Ames, Iowa, Feb. 17, 1926; s. James William and Elfie Hazel (Jones) McB.; B.A., State U. Iowa, 1950, J.D., 1953; m. Georgianna Edwards, Aug. 28, 1949; children—Hollis Lynn, Jana Lee, John Edwards. Admitted to Iowa bar, 1953, Ill. bar, 1954; practiced in Chgo., 1953—; with firm Sidley & Austin, and predecessor, 1953—, partner, 1964—. Mem. Chgo. Crime Commn., 1966—. Trustee, pres. Old Peoples Home City Chgo.; trustee, v.p., counsel The Georgian, Evanston, Ill. Served with inf. AUS, 1944-46. Fellow Am. Coll. Trial Lawyers; mem. Am., Ill., Chgo. bar assns., Am. Judicature Soc., Law Club Chgo., Legal Club Chgo., Bar Assn. 7th Fed. Circuit, Am. Arbitration Assn. (panel), Nat. Coll. Edn. (bd. assos.), Phi Kappa Psi, Omicron Delta Kappa, Delta Sigma Rho, Phi Delta Phi. Republican. Presbyn. Clubs: Union League, Mid-Day (Chgo.); Westmoreland Country (Wilmette, Ill.). Editor: Iowa Law Rev., 1952-53. Home: 1110 13th St Wilmette IL 60091 Office: One First National Plaza Chicago IL 60603

MCCABE, LYNN AMSDEN, food mfg. ofcl.; b. Morristown, N.J., Nov. 13, 1922; s. Ray Link and Mary Amsden (Densmore) McC.; B.S. with highest honors, Yale U., 1943; M.B.A. with distinction, U. Pa., 1952; m. Sue Dale, Aug. 24, 1952; children—Elizabeth Ann, Lynn Amsden. Engr., Gen. Elec. Co., Schenectady, N.Y., 1943-44; prodn. engr. Tenn. Eastman, Oak Ridge, 1944-45; mgmt. cons. George S. Armstrong, N.Y.C., 1945-47; methods analyst Deering Milliken, N.Y.C., 1947-49; systems analyst Great Lakes Carbon, N.Y.C., 1949-50; methods analyst DuPont, Wilmington, Del., 1952-54; mgr. mgmt. info. systems Campbell Soup Co., Camden, N.J., 1954—; adj. prof. Camden County Coll., Burlington County Coll.; mem. Camden County Data Processing Adv. Bd. Cert. data processor. Mem. Soc. Mgmt. Info. Systems, Assn. Computing Machinery, Phi Beta Kappa, Sigma Xi, Tau Beta Pi, Beta Alpha Psi. Presbyterian. Home: 45 Oak Ridge Dr Haddonfield NJ 08033 Office: Campbell Pl Camden NJ 08101

MCCAFFREY, FRANK JOSEPH, electronic mfg. co. exec.; b. N.Y.C., Feb. 18, 1923; s. Patrick J. and Catherine (Kavanagh) McC.; B.S. in Bus. Adminstrn., Hofstra U., 1958; M.B.A., San Jose State U., 1974; m. Ann M. Owens, Sept. 10, 1949; children—Ann Marie, Kathleen, Patricia Josephine, Joan Frances, Robin Elizabeth, Jill Diane. Systems Sales rep. McBee Co., N.Y.C., 1945-47, zone sales mgr., 1947-49, area sales mgr., 1950-55; dir. sales promotion and sales tng. Royal McBee Corp., N.Y.C., 1955-61; dist. sales mgr. computer services Litton Automated Bus. Services, San Francisco, 1961-65, regional mgr., 1966-67, nat. accounts mgr., 1967-69; founder, v.p. mktg. Novar Corp. div. Gen. Tel. & Elec., Mountain View, Calif., 1969, v.p. mktg. 1970-73; v.p. mktg. Trendata Corp., 1973-74; founder, v.p. mktg. AzurData Inc., 1974-78; pres., founder Winners

Group, Inc., 1978—, also dir. Served with USNR, 1943-45. Mem. Sales Honor Club, 1947-67; recipient top sales dist. award Litton Automated Bus. Systems, 1966. Mem. Nat. Assn. Accountants, San Francisco C. of C., Hosp. Fin. Mgmt. Assn. Am. Mgmt. Assn. Roman Catholic. K.C. Home and office: 19796 Oakhaven Dr Saratoga CA 95070

MC CAFFREY, JAMES DAVID, physician; b. Pawtucket, R.I., May 16, 1920; s. James P. and Louise E. (Cassidy) McC.; student Brown U., 1950; M.D., Washington U., St. Louis, 1952; m. Shirley A. Dulong, Feb. 15, 1952; children—James David, Roger, Elizabeth. Intern, Miami Valley Hosp., Dayton, Ohio, 1952-53; practice medicine, Dayton, 1953-59; partner Johnston Gendel Med. Clinic, occupational med. services, Anaheim, Calif., 1959-78; cons. practice medicine specializing in occupational medicine, Fullerton, Calif., 1978—; mem. staff Anaheim Meml. Hosp., Martin Luther Hosp.; hosp. adminstr. Canyon Gen. Hosp., 1979—, also chmn. bd. dirs.; pres. Canyon Gen. Hosp., Inc.; med. dir., cons. various coms. Served with Med. Adminstrv. Corps, U.S. Army, 1941-46. Lic. physician, Calif., Ohio, Mo. Diplomate Am. Bd. Preventive Medicine. Fellow Am. Occupational Med. Assn., Am. Coll. Preventive Medicine; mem. AMA, Calif., Orange County med. assns., Am., Western (past chmn.) occupational health confs., Western Occupational Med. Assn. (past chmn.), Am. Acad. Occupational Medicine. Roman Catholic. Home: 1525 Camino Loma Fullerton CA 92633

MC CAFFREY, JOSEPH EDWIN, paper co. exec.; b. Savannah, Ga., Feb. 27, 1930; s. Joseph Edwin and Ruby Elizabeth (Johnston) McC.; A.A. in Sci., Belmont Abbey Coll., Belmont, N.C., 1951; B.S. in Chemistry, Marquette U., 1953; B.S. in Pulp and Paper Tech., N.C. State U., 1955; postgrad. Ouachita U., 1968-72; M.S. in Counseling Psychology, Henderson State U., 1976, postgrad., 1976—; m. Betty Kimler, Apr. 25, 1953; children—Joseph, Patrick, Michael, Timothy, Shaun, Colleen. With Internat. Paper Co., 1955—, asst. tech. supt., Camden, Ark., 1965-69, supt. quality control, 1969-73, supt. tech. services, 1973-78, mgr. tech. and environ. services, 1978—. Asst. dist. commr. Des DeSota Area council Boy Scouts Am., ElDorado, Ark., 1969-70. Mem. Am. Personnel and Guidance Assn., TAPPI, Pulp and Paper Found., Phi Theta Kappa, Xi Sigma Pi. Republican. Roman Catholic. Clubs: K.C., Kiwanis. Home: 1112 Westwood Rd Camden AR 71701 Office: PO Box 2045 Cullendale Station Camden AR 71701

MC CAFFREY, NEIL, pub. co. exec.; b. Rye, N.Y., Aug. 29, 1925; s. Cornelius T. and Anastasia Frances (Waterman) M.; B.A., Fordham U., 1950; m. Joan Melervey, Apr. 10, 1950; children—Maureen, Neil, Eugene V., Roger A., Eileen, Susan. Editor, copywriter Doubleday Pub. Co., N.Y.C., 1955-61; mgr. mail order Macmillan Publ. Co., NYC, 1961-64, dir. advt., 1963-64; pres. Arlington House Publs., New Rochelle, N.Y., 1964-78, Conservative Book Club, 1964-78, Nostalgia Book Club, 1968-78, Arlray Advt., 1972-78; pres. Movie/Entertainment Book Club, Harrison, N.Y., 1978—, Harrison Assos., advt. agy., 1979—; dir. Nat. Review, 1968-71; cons. on direct mail Republican Congl. Com., 1963-71; dir. Am. Conservative Union, 1970-72. Served with USCG, 1943-46. Republican. Roman Catholic. Club: N.Y. Athletic. Office: 15 Oakland Ave Harrison NY 10528

MC CAIN, WARREN EARL, supermarket bus. exec.; b. 1925; A.A., Ore. State U., 1948; Supr. sales Mountain States Wholesale Co., 1951-59; with Albertson's Inc., owner, operator supermarkets, 1959—, became mgr. non-foods, 1959, mgr. store, 1962, supr. merchandise, 1965, dir. intermountain region, 1967, v.p. operations, 1968, exec. v.p., 1972, now pres., chmn. bd., chief exec. officer, also dir. Office: 250 Parkcenter Blvd Boise ID 83726

MCCALEB, JOHN HENRY, real estate broker; b. Saline County, Ark., Feb. 17, 1934; s. William Harvey and Laura Mildred (McCright) McC.; B.S., U. Ark., 1956; m. Annette Woodard Watts, Oct. 23, 1962; children—Jonathan J., Suzanna E., Sarah L. Engr. U.S. Army C.E., Little Rock, 1958-65; owner John H. McCaleb Constrn. Inc., Little Rock, 1965—. Dir. Quadrangle Enterprises, Inc., Little Rock, 1971-80, Minerva Enterprises, Inc., Little Rock, 1971-80. Webelos scout leader, 1974-75. Mem. Pulaski County Democratic Com., 1978; pres. Pulaski County Property Owners Assn. Served with USNR, 1956-58. Registered profl. engr. Ark. Mem. ASME. Home and Office: 4600 Annette Ln Little Rock AR 72206

MCCALLISTER, RICHARD ANTHONY, bus. cons. co. exec.; b. Newark, Ohio, Apr. 10, 1937; s. Ward C. and LeDema McC.; B.S., Ill. State U., 1960; postgrad. U. So. Calif., 1960-62; m. Trina D. Gordon, Sept. 1, 1979; children—Todd, Mark. Indsl. cons. Sci. Research Assos., 1964-66; v.p. Mgmt. Psychologists, Inc., Chgo., 1966-68; dir. Price Waterhouse & Co., Chgo., 1968-75; pres. William H. Clark Assos., Inc., Chgo., 1975—; dir. House of Vision. Pres. Dist. 113 Bd. Edn., Deerfield, Ill.; bd. dirs. Grant Hosp., Chgo. Republican. Clubs: Glen View; Chgo., Racquet (Chgo.). Office: 200 E Randolph Dr Suite 7912 Chicago IL 60601

MC CANDLESS, JACK EWING, rubber co. exec.; b. Mangum, Okla., Mar. 1, 1921; s. Cecil R. and Leah Marjorie (Yeager) McC.; B.S., Northwestern U., 1944; m. Catherine J. Christian, June 16, 1943; children—Steven Rob, Kris. Merchandising specialist, hardware sales Gates Rubber Co., Denver, 1948, indsl. sales, 1950-55, bus. research staff, 1955-59, v.p., gen. mgr. Nat. Products div., 1959-70, dir. corp. relations, 1970, v.p. corp. pub. relations, 1971—, dir. credit union. Treas., Gates Found.; mem. community vol. awards com. Mayor's Commn. on Community Relations; mem. adv. panel Denver Research Inst.; bd. dirs. Jr. Achievement Met. Denver, Denver Conv. and Visitors Bur., Colo. Council Econ. Edn.; trustee Loretto Heights Coll., Denver; pres. Student Leadership Inst., Boulder, Colo. Served with USAAF, 1943-45. Mem. Denver C. of C., Greater South Denver C. of C., Colo. Assn. Commerce and Industry (chmn. pub. relations com. Project Confidence), NAM, U.S. Ski Assn., Rubber Mfrs. Assn. Am. Clubs: Country of Colo., Rotary, Athletic. Home: 171 S Jasmine St Denver CO 80224 Office: Gates Rubber Co 999 S Broadway Denver CO 80217

MC CANN, DANIEL, banker; b. Worcester, Mass., Nov. 16, 1936; s. James Cole and Katherine (Connolly) McC.; B.S. in Econs., Holy Cross Coll., 1960; M.B.A., Babson Inst., 1962; m. Judith Hunter, Nov. 3, 1962; children—Judith, Hunter, Hilary, Caleb. Asst. to v.p. Western Hemisphere, Am. Export Isbrandtsen Lines, 1966-68; mgr. mktg. planning and research Millers Falls subs. Ingersol Rand, Greenfield, Mass., 1968-70; mgmt. cons. Rath & Strong, Lexington, Mass., 1970-71; sr. v.p. strategic planning, mktg. and adminstrn. Worcester Bancorp, 1971—; resource person Young Pres.'s Orgn., 1980. Treas., bd. dirs. Worcester County Music Assn., 1974—, Worcester County Mechanics Assn., 1971—, Worcester Taxpayers Assn., 1974—; founder, bd. lt. USNR, 1963-65. Mem. Planning Execs. Inst., Am. Mktg. Assn., Bank Mktg. Assn., Bank Adminstrn. Inst., Am. Bankers Assn., Mass. Bankers Assn., Worcester Econ. Club. Clubs: Bohemian of Worcester, Holy Cross Coll. Varsity. Home: 34 Monadnock Rd Worcester MA 01609 Office: 446 Main St Worcester MA 01608

MC CANN, JOHN JOSEPH, lawyer; b. N.Y.C., Feb. 4, 1937; s. John and Katherine (McKeon) McC.; A.B., Fordham U., 1958; LL.B., Columbia U., 1961; m. June M. Evangelist, Oct. 16, 1965; children—Catherine Anne, John Bernard, Robert Joseph, James Patrick. Admitted to N.Y. State bar, 1962, U.S. Supreme Ct. bar, 1966, N.J. bar, 1975; asso. firm Donovan Leisure Newton & Irvine, N.Y.C., 1962-71, mem. firm, 1971—. Served with U.S. Army, 1961. Mem. Internat., Am., N.J., N.Y. State bar assns., Am. Law Inst., Assn. Bar City N.Y. Clubs: Univ., Hemisphere, Canoe Brook, Beacon Hill. Office: 30 Rockefeller Plaza New York NY 10020

MC CARDELL, ARCHIE RICHARD, machinery mfg. co. exec.; b. Hazel Park, Mich., Aug. 29, 1926; s. Archie and Josephine (Gauthier) McC.; B.B.A., U. Mich., 1948. M.B.A., 1949. With Ford Motor Co., 1949-60, finance exec., Dearborn, Mich., 1960; sec.-treas. Ford of Australia, 1960-63; dir. finance Ford of Germany, 1963-66; group v.p. for corporate service Xerox Corp., Rochester, N.Y., 1966-68, exec. v.p., 1968-71, pres., 1971-77, chief operating officer, 1977-78, also dir.; pres., chief operating officer Internat. Harvester Co., 1977—, chief exec. officer, 1978—, chmn. bd., 1979—, also dir.; dir. Am. Express Co., Am. Express Internat. Banking Corp., Harris Trust & Savs. Bank, Harris Bankcorp, Inc., Honeywell, Inc., Gen. Foods Corp.; Mem. adv. council Stanford U. Grad. Sch. Bus.; trustee U. Chgo., Orchestral Assn., Bus. Council, Conf. Bd., Bus. Roundtable, Nat. Council for U.S.-China Trade. Served with USAAF, 1943-45. Mem. Motor Vehicle Mfrs. Assn. (trustee), Chgo. Council on Fgn. Relations (Chgo. com.). Office: 401 N Michigan Ave Chicago IL 60611

MCCARROLL, EARL LUCAS, banker; b. Holly Springs, Miss., May 2, 1915; s. John Ramsey and Marie Hill (McKie) McC.; student Rutgers U. Grad. Sch. Banking, 1947-49; m. Helen Shannon, Oct. 15, 1938; children—Earl Lucas, Eileen McCarroll McDonald, Michael Shannon. Asst. v.p. Union Planters Nat. Bank, Memphis, 1933-52; pres. 1st Nat. Bank of Little Rock, 1952-59, Union Nat. Bank, Little Rock, 1959-68, Farmers Bank & Trust Co., Blytheville, Ark., 1968—; dir. Memphis br. Fed. Res. Bank of St. Louis; instr., pres. Memphis chpt. Am. Inst. Banking; mem. adv. com. to comptroller of currency. Treas. Little Rock Sch. Dist., 1956-64; trustee U. Ark., Little Rock, 1961-68, Little Rock Fifty for the Future, 1963-68; pres. Blytheville United Way, 1971-72, Blytheville Unltd., 1977. Mem. Am. Inst. Banking, Am. Bankers Assn., Ark. Bankers Assn. (exec. council), Assn. Res. City Bankers, Little Rock C. of C. (pres. 1961). Episcopalian. Clubs: Blytheville Rotary, Blytheville Country. Office: 400 W Main St Blytheville AR 72315

MC CARRON, THOMAS EDWARD, investment banker; b. Chgo., Nov. 5, 1939; s. Walter Edward and Bernice Marie (Rohm) Mc.; student Marquette U., 1957-59; B.B.A., Loyola U., 1961; m. Julia Anne Bailey, July 9, 1972; 1 dau., Elizabeth Ann. Mgr., Lincoln Finance Co., Chgo., 1961-64; sr. v.p. Shearson Loeb Rhoades, Inc., Chgo., 1964—. Vice chmn. Ill. Securities Adv. Commn.; trustee Catholic Charities, Chgo. Mem. Chgo. Assn. Stockbrokers. Republican. Roman Catholic. Clubs: Chgo. Athletic Assn., Mid-Day, North Shore Country. Home: 2665 Cherry Ln Northbrook IL 60062 Office: 72 W Adams Chicago IL 60603

MC CARTER, DENNIS PAUL, mgmt. cons.; b. Chgo., May 31, 1944; s. Richard and Shirley McC.; B.A. in English, U. Oreg., 1965; M.B.A., U. Wash., 1968; postgrad. in fin., Northwestern U., 1968. Mgr. mgmt. services Arthur Young & Co., Los Angeles, 1968-73; exec. v.p. McSweeney & Assos., Newport Beach, Calif., 1973-76; pres. The Newport Group, Irvine, Calif., 1976—; dir. Equity Mktg. Systems. Mem. Nat. League Savs. and Loans, Savs. Inst. Mktg. Soc. Club: Balboa Bay. Contbr. articles to trade jours. Office: 18009 L Sky Park Circle Irvine CA 92714

MC CARTER, JAMES THOMAS, engring. co. exec.; b. Greenville, S.C., Sept. 24, 1932; s. Thomas Avery and Emily (Street) McC.; B.M.E., Clemson U., 1954; m. Patricia Marie Hood, Feb. 14, 1959; children—Steven Thomas, Bruce Hood, David Christopher. Engr., Western Electric Co., Burlington, N.C., 1954-55, J.E. Sirrine Co., Engrs., Greenville, 1957-58; resident engr. U.S. Army, Charlotte, N.C., 1958-59; project engr. Davis Mech. Contractors, Greenville, 1959-64; v.p. Piedmont Engrs., Architects and Planners, Greenville, 1964-73, exec. v.p., 1973-77, also dir.; exec. v.p. Universal Services of S.C. Inc., Greenville, 1977—; mem. regional pub. adv. panel archtl. and engring. services GSA. Served to 1st lt. AUS, 1955-57. Registered profl. engr., S.C., N.C., Ga., Ala., Tenn., N.J., Maine, Fla., N.Y., Ill., Pa., Va. Mem. ASME (vice-chmn. chpt. 1962-63, chmn. 1963-64), ASHRAE (chpt. treas. 1964-65, 2d v.p. 1965-66, 1st v.p. 1966-67, pres. 1967-68), Nat. Soc. Profl. Engrs. (chpt. treas. 1965-66, sec. 1966-67, v.p. 1967-68, pres. 1968-69, state treas. 1969-70, sec. 1970-71, 2d v.p. 1971-72, 1st v.p. 1972-73, pres. 1973-74, nat. dir. 1976—), S.C. Council Engring. Socs. (del. 1971-74, pres. 1972-73), Phi Kappa Phi, Tau Beta Pi. Baptist (deacon 1965—). Patentee in field. Home: 228 McSwain Dr Greenville SC 29615 Office: PO Box 6997 Greenville SC 29606

MC CARTER, THOMAS N., III, investment counseling co. exec.; b. N.Y.C., Dec. 16, 1929; s. Thomas N., Jr. and Suzanne M. (Pierson) McC.; student Princeton, 1948-51; m. Nancy Kohler Alker, Sept. 23, 1955 (div.); 1 dau., Nancy A.; m. 2d, Renate Bohne von Boyens, June 22, 1976. Sales exec. Mack Trucks, Inc., N.Y.C., 1952-59; partner Kelly, McCarter, D'Arcy Investment Counsel, N.Y.C., 1959-62; v.p., sec., dir. D'Arcy, McCarter & Chew, N.Y.C., 1962-66; v.p., dir. Trainer, Wortham & Co., Inc., N.Y.C., 1967-71, exec. v.p., 1971-75; chmn. bd., dir. Island Security Bank Ltd., 1976-78; pres. Knottingham Ltd., N.Y.C., 1976—; gen. partner W.P. Miles Timber Properties, New Orleans; cons. Laidlaw Adams & Peck Inc., N.Y.C., 1976—; dir. Sepradyne Corp., Haber Inc.; mem. I.R.E.X. Nat. Bus. Council. Chmn. bd. trustees Christodora Found., Inc., N.Y., N.Y.C.; charter trustee Dalton Sch., N.Y.C., 1968-76, v.p., 1972-76; v.p., trustee Am. Soc. Prevention Cruelty to Animals; pres. Loyal Legion Found., N.Y.C.; trustee, chmn. investment com. Children's Aid Soc. N.Y.C., Joffrey Ballet, Found. for Am. Dance, 1973-77; pres.'s council Mus. City N.Y. Chartered investment counselor. Mem. Loyal Legion U.S. (comdr. N.Y. State 1964-66, nat. comdr. in chief 1977-80). Clubs: Racquet and Tennis, Brook, Links, River (treas., gov.), St. Nicholas Soc., Pilgrims of U.S. (N.Y.C.); Coral Beach (Bermuda); Ivy (Princeton, N.J.). Home: 823 Park Ave New York NY 10021 Office: Knottingham Ltd care Laidlaw Adams and Peck 20 Broad St New York NY 10005

MC CARTHA, WALTER HAYNE, civil engr.; b. Batesburg, S.C., May 13, 1908; s. Walter Jacob and Henryetta (Towill) McC.; B.S. in Civil Engring., The Citadel, 1930, C.E., 1936; postgrad. in econs. George Washington U., 1930-31, in architecture, 34-35; postgrad. U. Mo. at Rolla, 1963, 64, 68, U. Md., 1962, CSC, 1966, USPHS, 1969; m. Virginia Jean Ritchhart, June 3, 1957. Valuation engr. aide ICC Washington, 1930-31; archtl. engr. Pub. Bldgs. Service, Washington, 1931-40; engr., chief materials engring. group, 1950-57; chief specifications engr. for constrn. VA, Richmond, Va., 1946-49; archtl. gen. engr. charge specification standards for constrn. Directorate of Civil Engring., Hdqrs. U.S. Air Force, Washington, 1957-74, ret., 1974. Dir. Joint Bd. on Sci. Edn., Washington, 1955-64, 72—, chmn., 1958-59; mem. tri-services com. for constrn. research Nat. Bur. Standards, 1971-74, chmn., 1973-74, mem. utilization program Materials Resource Council, Washington, 1975-76; mem. Bldg. Research Adv. Bd. for Tech. Assessment. Served to col. USAAF, 1940-46. Recipient Civil Engring. Meritorious Achievement award USAF, 1962. Registered profl. engr., D.C. Mem. Nat., D.C. (pres. 1954-55, dir. 1963-66) socs. profl. engrs., Soc. Am. Mil. Engrs., Washington Soc. Engrs. (dir. 1969-70, 74-75, 1st v.p. 1972, pres. 1973), D.C. Council Engring. and Archtl. Socs. (chmn. 1956-57), ASTM. Baptist. Mason (32 deg., Shriner). Club: Bolling AFB Officers (Washington). Contbr. constrn. chpts. Air Force Manuals, 1960, 61, 64-74. Home: 3804 14th St N Arlington VA 22201

MCCARTHY, EARL JAMES, mining co. exec.; b. Butte, Mont., May 25, 1938; s. Earl J. and Ann A. (Lubick); B.S. in Metall. Engring., Mont. Sch. Mines, 1963; M.S. in Engring. Adminstrn., U. Utah, 1966; Mineral Processing Engr. honoris causa, Mont. Coll. Mineral Sci. and Tech., 1977; m. Vivian McCarthy, Feb. 17, 1960; children—Teresa Lynne, Michael J. Mill supt. Pima Mining Co., Tucson, 1968-70; metall. supt., project engr. Hecla Mining Co., Casa Grande, Ariz., 1971; mgr. metallurgy Marcopper Mining Corp., Sta. Cruz, Marinduque, Philippines, 1971-75; pres. Earl J. McCarthy & Assos., metall. and instrumentation engrs., Makati, Manila, Philippines, 1975-79; sr. v.p., gen. mgr. North Davao Mining Co., Makati, 1979—; dir. Itogon-Suyoc Mines, Tuscany Condominium Corp., Samar Mining Corp., Asian Internat. Automotive, Inc. Served with USN, 1957-59. Mem. AIME (dir. Philippines). Roman Catholic. Clubs: Canlubang Golf; Alabang Golf and Country, Army-Navy (Manila); Elks (Butte). Home: 6751 Ayala Ave Makati Metropolitan Manila Philippines 3117 Office: 104 Gamboa St Makati Metropolitan Manila Philippines 3117

MCCARTHY, FREDERICK WILLIAM, investment banker; b. Boston, Nov. 25, 1941; s. Frederick William and Josephine Leona (Pannier) McC.; B.A. magna cum laude, Harvard U., 1963, M.B.A. with high distinction, 1967; m. Jeanette B. Champion, Sept. 2, 1967; children—Daniel Arthur, Frederick William III, Kathryn Elizabeth. Mgmt. cons. Booz Allen & Hamilton Inc., Chgo., 1967-70; 1st v.p. investment banking Shearson, Hammill & Co. Inc., N.Y.C., 1970-72, Chgo., 1972-74; mng. dir. Drexel, Burnham, Lambert Inc., Boston, 1974—. Served to 1st lt. U.S. Army, 1963-65. Home: 80 Whitelawn Ave Milton MA 02186 Office: Drexel Burnham Lambert Inc 1 Federal St Boston MA 02110

MC CARTHY, GERALD PATRICK, state ofcl. Va.; b. N.Y.C., Mar. 23, 1943; s. Patrick J. and Marie F. (Fitzgerald) McC.; B.Engring. in Elec. Engring., Manhattan Coll., 1965; M.S.Engring. in Nuclear Engring., U. Wash., 1967. Program mgr. physics br. USAF Weapons Lab., Albuquerque, 1966-70; exec. dir. Va. Gov.'s Council on Environment, Richmond, 1970-74, chmn., adminstr. Council on Environment Commonwealth of Va., 1974-77; exec. dir. Va. Environ. Endowment, Inc., 1977—; adj. prof. urban studies Va. Commonwealth U. Bd. dirs., treas., v.p. Richmond-First Club, 1979-81; bd. dirs. Church Hill Assn., 1980-81. Served to capt. USAF, 1966-70. Mem. AAAS. Roman Catholic. Club: Twenty-Three Hundred (Richmond). Home: 2616 E Grace St Richmond VA 23223 Office: 700 E Main St Box 790 Richmond VA 23206

MCCARTHY, HAROLD CHARLES, ins. co. exec.; b. Madelia, Minn., Dec. 5, 1926; s. Charles and Merle (Humphry) McC.; B.A., Carleton Coll., Northfield, Minn., 1950; postgrad. Butler U., Indpls., 1969-70; m. Barbara Kaercher, June 24, 1949; children—David, Susan. With Federated Mut. Ins. Co., Owatonna, Minn., 1950-67; with Meridian Ins. Co., Indpls., 1967—, v.p. ops., 1971-72, exec. v.p., 1972-75, gen. mgr., 1974-75, pres., 1975—; also dir., dir. subs.; dir. Conf. Casualty Ins. Cos. Served with USNR, 1944-46. Recipient Boy Scouts Am. Vet. award. Mem. Ins. Inst. Ind. (dir., exec. com., chmn.), Nat. Assn. Ind. Insurers (bd. govs.), Pres.'s Assn., Met. Devel. Commn., Newcomen Soc., Am. Mgmt. Assn., Indpls. C. of C., Ind. C. of C., U.S. C. of C. Republican. Presbyterian. Clubs: Kiwanis, Columbia, Hillcrest Country. Office: 2955 N Meridian St Indianapolis IN 46207

MC CARTHY, JOHN MICHAEL, investment co. exec.; b. Bklyn., Apr. 9, 1927; s. Michael Francis and Catherine (McCarthy) McC.; B.A., St. Francis Coll., 1951; M.B.A., N.Y. U., 1953; m. Mary Agnes Hickey, Sept. 8, 1951; children—Stephen J., Neil M., Tara Anne, Laurette E. Sr. research officer trust dept. Citibank, N.Y.C., 1951-59; sr. research analyst, then dir. research Lord Abbett & Co., N.Y.C., 1960-72, partner, 1972—; v.p., portfolio mgr., then exec. v.p. Affiliated Fund Inc., N.Y.C., 1972-77, pres., dir., 1977—; dir. Lord Abbett Bond Debenture Fund, Lord Abbett Developing Growth Fund, Lord Abbett Income Fund. Served with USAAF, 1945-47. Recipient Paper award Investment Bankers Assn., 1962, 63. Mem. N.Y. Soc. Security Analysts, Elec. and Electronic Analysts Group N.Y.C. (past pres.), Hist. Soc. Garden City. Republican. Roman Catholic. Clubs: Recess (N.Y.C.); Cherry Valley (Garden City). Office: Affiliated Fund Inc 63 Wall St New York NY 10005*

MCCARTHY, JOSEPH JAMES, trade co. exec.; b. N.Y.C., Oct. 29, 1923; s. James and Anna (O'Brien) McC.; B.S., Fordham U., 1947. Traffic mgr. Cardinal Export Corp., N.Y.C., 1947-48; dept. mgr. Muller & Phipps (Asia) Ltd., Manila, 1948-49; sales mgr. Far East, Rourke Export Co., Hong Kong, 1949-50; propr. Automotive Supply Co., N.Y.C., 1950—, N.Y.C. Export Internat. Co., 1959—, Export Internat. Komak Corp., N.Y.C., 1972—. Served with U.S. Army, 1943-46. Decorated Purple Heart. Roman Catholic. Home: 204 8th Ave New York NY 10011 Office: 1133 Broadway New York NY 10010

MC CARTHY, WALTER JOHN, JR., utility exec.; b. N.Y.C., Apr. 20, 1925; s. Walter J. and Irene (Trumbland) McC.; B.M.E., Cornell U., 1949; student Oak Ridge Sch. Reactor Tech., 1951-52; m. Alice Anna Ross, Sept. 3, 1947; children—Walter, David, Sharon, James, William. Engr., Public Service Elec. & Gas Co., Newark, 1949-56; sect. head Atomic Power Devel. Assos., Detroit, 1956-61; gen. mgr. Power Reactor Devel. Co., Detroit, 1961-68; project mgr. Detroit Edison Co., 1968-71, mgr. engring., 1971-73, mgr. operations, 1973-74, v.p. operations, 1974-75, exec. v.p. operations, 1975-77, exec. v.p. divs., 1977-79, pres., chief operating officer, dir., 1979—; dir. Detroitbank Corp., Wolverine Aluminum Corp., Edison Elec. Inst., Elec. Vehicle Council. First v.p. Detroit area council Boy Scouts Am. bd. dirs. Boys Clubs Detroit, Cranbrook Inst. Sci., Detroit Symphony Orch.; trustee New Detroit; pres., bd. dirs. Police Athletic League; bd. visitors Sch. Econs. and Mgmt. of Oakland U.; adv. bd. United Found. Named one of 5 outstanding young men in Mich., 1958. Fellow Am. Nuclear Soc., Engring. Soc. Detroit; mem. ASME, Am. Nuclear Energy Council (dir.). Methodist. Clubs: Detroit Athletic, Detroit, Renaissance. Contbr. articles on nuclear engring. to profl. jours. Office: 2000 Second Ave Detroit MI 48226

MC CARTHY, WILLIAM JOHN, mfg. co. exec.; b. Ashtabula, Ohio, July 23, 1938; s. William Joseph and Winifred (Miller) McC.; A.B., U. Notre Dame, 1960; M.B.A. with honors, George Washington U., 1966; student Northwestern Trust Sch., 1966, Rutgers Stonier Grad. Sch., 1974; m. Mary Evelyn Latchaw, June 15, 1963; children—Anne, Molly, Julie. With trust dept. Am. Security & Trust Co., Washington, 1960-66; v.p. Farmers Nat. Bank, Ashtabula,

1966-75, pres., dir., 1975-77; pres., chief exec. officers ABS Industries, Ashtabula, 1977—; dir. Univ. Services Inst. of Cleve., Farmers Nat. Bank & Trust Co. Campaign chmn. Civic Devel. Corp., 1975, Fine Arts Center, 1974, United Way Campaign, 1972; bd. dirs. YMCA, 1979-80. Mem. Cycle Parts and Accessories Assn. (pres. 1980). Republican. Roman Catholic. Clubs: Ashtabula Country (pres. 1976), Ashtabula Rotary (pres. 1972-73). Home: 4453 Shore Dr Ashtabula OH 44004 Office: 1635 E 6th St Ashtabula OH 44004

MC CARTY, EMIL STEDMAN, mgmt. cons.; b. Sikes, La., July 24, 1921; s. John Elias and Jessie Beatrice (Montgomery) McC.; B.S., La. State U., Baton Rouge, 1948, M.S., 1952, Ph.D., 1957; m. June Catherine Gorton, Oct. 1975; children—Pamela B., Katherine M., Gerald E. Tchr., Bienville (La.) Parish Schs., 1947-66; engring. and mgmt. postions with Sperry-Rand Co., 1946-70, Humana, Inc., 1972-77; prin. E.S. McCarty and Assos., Inc., mgmt. spealists, Midlothian, Va., 1977—. Served with AUS, 1942-46. Mem. Am. Mgmt. Assn. Baptist. Address: 13214 Court Ridge Ct Midlothian VA 23113

MCCAUSLAND, THOMAS JAMES, JR., investment banker; b. Cleve., Nov. 27, 1934; s. Thomas James and Jean Anna (Hanna) McC.; B.A. in Econs., Beloit (Wis.) Coll., 1956; m. Kathryn Margaret Schacht, Feb. 9, 1957; children—Thomas James, III, Andrew John, Theodore Scott. With A.G. Becker & Co., Inc., 1959-74, v.p. instl. dept., 1959-74; v.p. instl. and block depts. Chicago Corp., Chgo., 1974-78, sr. v.p., dir., mem. exec. com., mgr. asset mgmt. div., 1975—; partner Kathom Interests. Bd. dirs. McCormick Theol. Sem., Chgo., 1971-79, Presbyn. Home, Evanston, Ill., 1970-76; trustee United Presbyn. Found. Served to lt. USNR, 1956-60. Mem. Securities Industry Assn., Bond Club Chgo. (dir.). Republican. Presbyterian. Clubs: Union League (Chgo.); Skokie Country. Office: 208 S LaSalle St Chicago IL 60604

MCCLEARY, PAUL FREDERICK, relief agy. exec.; b. Bradley, Ill., May 2, 1930; s. Hal C. and Pearl (Aeicher) McC.; A.B., Olivet Nazarene Coll., Kankakee, Ill., 1952; M.Div., Garrett-Evang. Sem., Evanston, Ill., 1956; M.A., Northwestern U., 1972; D.D., MacMurray Coll., Jacksonville, Ill., 1970; m. Rachel Timm, Jan. 26, 1951; children—Leslie Ann, Rachel Mary, John Wesley, Timothy Paul. Ordained to ministry United Methodist Ch., 1956; missionary in Bolivia, 1957-68; exec. sec. structure study commn. United Meth. Ch., 1969-72, asst. gen. sec. to Latin Am., 1972-75; exec. dir. Ch. World Service, N.Y.C., 1975—; bd. dirs. Coordination in Devel., Internat. Vol. Service, Meals for Millions Found., Techno-Serv.; vice moderator comm. interch. aid World Council Chs.; pres. Am. Council Vol. Agys. in Fgn. Assistance; pres. bd. Interfaith Hunger Appeal. Mem. Am. Soc. Missiology, Hastings Center, AAAS, Acad. Polit. Sci., N.Y. Acad. Scis., Latin Am. Studies Assn., Alpha Kappa Lambda. Democrat. Club: Masons. Author: Global Justice and World Hunger, 1978; co-author: Quality of Life in a Global Society, 1978; contbr. articles to mags. Home: 19 Fairmount Ave Montclair NJ 07043 Office: 475 Riverside Dr New York NY 10027

MC CLELLAN, JACK LOVE, petroleum geologist; b. Lubbock, Tex., June 15, 1927; s. Dewey Johnstone and Anne Bertha (Howell) McC.; B.S., Tex. Tech. U., 1950, postgrad., 1950-52; m. Barbara Ann Walden, Apr. 3, 1953; children—Suzanne, Mark, Lisa. Petroleum geologist Gulf Oil Corp., Midland, Tex., 1952-54, Hobbs, N.Mex., 1955-56, Roswell, N.Mex., 1956-57, Franklin, Aston & Fair Co., Roswell, 1957-58; cons. geologist, Roswell, 1958-70; petroleum geologist McClellan Oil Corp., Roswell, 1972-76, pres., 1972—; pres. Cortez Drilling Corp., Roswell, 1966—. Mem. adv. bd. Oil Field Tng. Center, Eastern N.Mex. U. Served with USNR, 1945-46. Mem. Am. Assn. Petroleum Geologists (cert. petroleum geologist), Ind. Petroleum Assn. Am. Inst. Profl. Geologists (nat. bd. dirs. 1974-75, public lands com. 1975—), Tex. Tech. U. Alumni Assn. (trustee, dir. 1967-70), Roswell Geol. Soc., Ind. Petroleum Assn. N.Mex. (dir.), Gideons, Phi Delta Theta. Republican. Methodist (ofcl. bd. 1977-80). Clubs: Rotary, Masons, Shriners. Home: 3106 N Montana Roswell NM 88201 Office: 1000 Security Bank Bldg PO Drawer 730 Roswell NM 88201

MC CLELLAN, VAL J, bus. cons. co. exec., educator, author; b. Butte, Mont., Feb. 24, 1924; s. Oscar Alma and Nora (Riggs) McC.; B.S., U. Calif., 1956; M.A. (fellow), U. N.H., 1963; m. Lois Maxene Smith, Mar. 17, 1978; children—Robert Ensign, Valarie Jean, Brad D., Gary Lyn, Jeffrey Scot, Clark Alma. Office mgr. U.S. Employment Service, Roosevelt, Utah, 1945-47; served with USAF, 1947-65; dir. Greene County (Ohio) Econ. Opportunity Com., Xenia, 1966, exec. dir. Lorain County (Ohio) Econ. Opportunity Com., 1966-67; procurement cons. Research Assos. Ohio State U., Columbus, 1967-75; mgr. Val-Mac Assos., Jamestown, Ohio, 1975—; pub. Western Pubs., Jamestown, Ohio, 1978—; instr. U. Dayton (Ohio), 1964-65, U. Philippines, Clark AFB, 1960-63. Served with USAAF, 1943-45. Decorated Air medal with four oak leaf clusters; recipient Service plaque Lorain County Economic Opportunity Com. Author: This Is Our Land, 2 vols., 1977; author or co-author texts and case studies govt. procurement and contracting. Home: 4 S Maple St Jamestown OH 45335

MC CLENDON, CHARLES ALFRED, aircraft mfg. co. exec.; b. Warren, Ark., Aug. 11, 1938; s. Alfred Thornton and Harriett (Hankins) McC.; student Ark. Coll., 1957-59; B.S. Bus. Adminstrn., U. Ark., 1962, M.B.A., 1963; m. Marion Hackney Phillips, Mar. 1, 1963; children—Lesley Suzanne, Charles Bradley. Supervisory auditor GAO, St. Louis, 1964-71; sr. accountant Rhea and Ivy, C.P.A.'s, Memphis, 1971-72; mgr. audits and taxes Ingalls Shipbldg. div. Litton Industries, Pascagoula, Miss., 1972-74; corp. mgr. internal audit Royal Crown Cola Co., Atlanta, 1974-77; corporate audit staff Mobil Oil Corp., Dallas, 1977-78; controller Rollins, Inc., Atlanta, 1978-79; supr. fin. acctg. Lockheed-Ga. Co., Marietta, 1979—. Served with U.S. Army, 1963-64; capt. Res. C.P.A., Ill.; certified internal auditor. Mem. Inst. Internal Auditors, Am. Inst. C.P.A.'s, Nat. Assn. Accountants, Mensa. Club: Toastmasters Internat. Home: 11280 Cranwood Cove Roswell GA 30075 Office: 86 S Cobb Dr Marietta GA 30063

MC CLESTER, JOHN RICHARD, fin. co. exec.; b. Butler, Pa., Oct. 16, 1923; s. Robert Howard and Verna (Shull) McC.; B.A., Washington and Jefferson Coll., 1944; m. Jean Donaldson, Nov. 29, 1946; children—John Richard, Martha L. McClester Sandberg. Mem. treasury dept. Westinghouse Elec. Corp., Pitts., 1953-64; v.p. Westinghouse Credit Corp., Pitts., 1965-70, pres., dir., 1970—; dir. Westinghouse Leasing Corp. Trustee Mt. Lebanon United Presbyterian Ch., Washington and Jefferson Coll., 1979—. Served with AUS, 1944-46. Republican. Clubs: Allegheny, Duquesne, Sewickley Heights Golf (dir.). Office: Three Gateway Center Pittsburgh PA 15222

MCCLINTIC, JANICE LEE, acct.; b. Pawtucket, R.I., Dec. 10, 1949; d. George F. and Jeannette A. (Doyon) Day; A.A., R.I. Jr. Coll., 1970; B.S., Bryant Coll., 1981. Bus. mgr. trainee Mass. Mutual Life Ins. Co., Providence, R.I., 1970-73; jr. acct. Bankcard Assn. R.I., Providence, 1973-74, acctg. supr., 1974-76, mgr. corp. acctg., 1976-79, asst. treas., 1979-80; controller Eastern region Eastern div. Tymshare Transaction Services, Inc., 1980—. Mem. Nat. Assn. Accts. (dir. communications Providence chpt.). Home: 38 Florence St North Providence RI 02904 Office: 15 Westminster St Providence RI 02903

MCCLINTOCK, DENNIS ALLEN, public relations exec.; b. Kankakee, Ill., Nov. 30, 1950; s. Fred Leroy and Edwina Mable (Goll) McC.; student Northwestern La. State U., Natchitoches, 1968-70, U. Md. Extension, W. Ger., 1972, La. State U., Baton Rouge, 1974; m. Mary Douglas, June 1972; 1 son, David Allen. With Sta. KALB Radio-TV, Alexandria, La., 1973-75; retail clothes mgr. Gus Kaplan, Alexandria, 1974-75; gen. mgr. Brazos Mall, Lake Jackson, Tex., 1975-78; dir. public relations Intermedies Inc., Freeport, Tex., 1978—. Bd. dirs. United Way Brazoria County, div. chmn., 1978-79; bd. dirs. Jr. Achievement Brazoria County, past treas., exec. bd.; exec. com. Brazoria County Fat Stock Rodeo and Fair Assn.; gen. chmn. Brazosport area Muscular Dystrophy Assn., 1976—; bd. dirs. Freeport League, Brazosport Art Center Planetarium. Recipient Service awards Muscular Dystrophy Assn., United Way. Mem. Brazosport C. of C. (hon. life, dir.). Clubs: Riverside Country (entertainment com.), Rotary. Roman Catholic. Served with U.S. Army, 1970-73. Home: 52 Plantation Ct Lake Jackon TX 77566 Office: 240 Tarpon Inn Village Freeport TX 77541

MC CLINTOCK, ROBERT SMITH, business exec.; b. Memphis, Dec. 16, 1924; s. Robert Smith and Mary Frances (Mixon) McC.; B.S., M.I.T., 1948; postgrad. N.Y. U., 1968—; m. Sarah Louise Mohr, 1948 (div. 1974); children—Margaret Wood and Mary Louise (twins), Sarah Lee; m. 2d, Riva Blanche Sztejnberg, 1976. Asst. plant mgr. Union Carbide Corp., Singapore, Sao Paulo, Brazil, 1948-54; indsl. project mgr. W.R. Grace & Co., N.Y.C., 1954-59; asst. to pres. in charge mfg. Nat. Can. Corp., Chgo., 1959-61; mng. dir. Corning Glass Corp., Sao Paulo, 1961-63; pres. R.S. McClintock Co., Summit, N.J., 1963-65; area mgr. Latin Am. Hooker Chem. Corp., Stamford, Conn., 1965-73; v.p. Carrier Internat. Corp., Syracuse, N.Y., 1973-77, also dir.; pres. McClintock Corp., Miami, Fla., 1977—. Chmn., Lay Com. on Edn., Summit, 1959; deacon Presbyterian ch., 1964-67; mem. Municipal Facilities Com., Summit, 1964-65. Served with C.E., AUS, 1944-46. Mem. ASHRAE, Phi Eta Sigma, Phi Delta Theta. Republican. Jewish. Club: Rotary. Office: 7000 SW 62d Ave Suite 410 Box 430980 Miami FL 33143

MCCLOSKEY, JON JUSTIN, state govt. ofcl.; b. Johnson City, N.Y., Aug. 21, 1946; s. John and Inez Justine (Chamberlin) McC.; A.A.S., SUNY, Cobleskill, 1966; B.S. in Public Acctg., SUNY, Albany, 1969, M.A. in Econs., 1972. Auditor, N.Y. State Dept. Audit and Control, Albany, 1969-72; budget examiner N.Y. State Div. of Budget, Albany, 1972-75; asso. fiscal economist N.Y. State Assembly Ways and Means Com., Albany, 1975-78; exec. dir. Joint Legis. Task Force to Study and Evaluate Pari-Mutuel Racing and Breeding Industry in N.Y. State, Albany, 1978—; adj. instr. govtl. acctg. Hudson Valley Community Coll. (Troy, N.Y.). Served with AUS, 1969-70. Mem. Am. Econ. Assn., Am. Mgmt. Assn., Am. Statis. Assn. Democrat. Club: Univ. (Albany). Home: 101 Ten Eyck Pl Apt 2 Guilderland NY 12084 Office: 1 Columbia Pl Albany NY 12207

MC CLOUD, JO ETTA YANKEY, banker; b. Boyle County, Ky., Jan. 13, 1942; d. James Debo and Lora Mae (Gibson) Yankey; grad. Schs. of Banking, La. State U., 1975, U. Ky., 1971; m. Robert Webster McCloud, Sept. 26, 1959; 1 son. Robert Gregory. With State Bank & Trust Co., Harrodsburg, Ky., 1963—, cashier, 1970-75, exec. v.p., 1975—, also dir.; mem. adv. bd. dirs. Lexington Data Center affiliate Citizens Fidelity Bank & Trust Co., 1974—; dir., treas. Farmers Tobacco Warehouse Co., Inc. Bd. dirs. Fort Harrod Drama Prodns., 1973—, finance chmn., 1973—; bd. dirs., treas. Cancer Soc., 1970—; treas. Arthritis Found., 1970, chmn., 1972-73; treas. Mercer County PTA, 1974-76, Mercer County Democrats, 1980—, Cystic Fibrosis Soc., 1970—; mem. adv. bd. Ky. Ednl. TV; mem. spl. adv. com. Haggin Meml. Hosp.; bd. dirs. Pioneer Opportunity Workshop, Inc. Named Woman of Year, Ky. Fedn. Bus. and Profl. Women's Clubs, 1978; Ky. col. Mem. Nat. Assn. Bank Women, Ky. Fedn. Bus. and Profl. Women's Clubs (pres.), Am. Inst. Banking, Mercer County C. of C. Beptist. Home: 228 N East St Harrodsburg KY 40330 Office: 211 S Main St PO Box 128 Harrodsburg KY 40330

MCCLUNG, LUTHER THERMAN, oil operator, rancher; b. Kerens, Tex., Oct. 30, 1909; s. Luther T. and Carrie J. (Miller) McC.; student pub. schs., Dallas; m. Evelyn Louise Loe, Aug. 6, 1927; children—Lucian Louise (Mrs. Murl R. Richardson), Barbara Ann (Mrs. John Loveless). Circulation mgr. Courier-Times, Tyler, Tex. and Ft. Worth Press, 1927-40; asst. bus. mgr. Longview (Tex.) News-Jour., 1927-40; gen. contractor Luther T. McClung and McClung Constrn. Co., 1940-48; pres. McClung Oil Corp., 1958—; pres. Western States Equipment Co., Midland, Tex.; owner, operator Luther T. McClung 4M Ranch, Kiowa, Okla. and Comanche County, Tex., 1948—. Mem. Am. (dir. 1950-56), Tex. (pres. 1950, dir. 1948-52) Angus assns. Home: Route 2 Box 99X Comanche TX 76442 Office: Executive Plaza Bldg Fort Worth TX 76102

MC CLURE, CHARLES FRANKLIN, JR., data processing exec.; b. Pelzer, S.C., Sept. 26, 1947; s. Charles Franklin and Frances (Saylors) McC.; B.A., U. S.C., 1970, M.A., 1973; M.B.A., Ga. State U., 1978. Asst. store mgr. K-Mart Corp., Atlanta, 1973-74, Greenville, S.C., 1974-77; customer service rep. Nat. Data Corp., Atlanta, 1978-79; with policy mgmt. systems div. Seibels, Bruce and Co., Columbia, S.C., 1979—. Active Cyclorama Restoration, Inc., Atlanta, 1975—. Mem. Assn. M.B.A. Execs., Am. Mgmt. Assn., Univ. S.C. Alumni Assn., Jaycees. Republican. Presbyterian. Home: 1520 Senate St Apt 19C Columbia SC 29201 Office: 1321 Lady St Columbia SC 29201

MC CLURE, HAROLD A., ops. cons.; b. Syracuse, N.Y., Mar. 14, 1949; s. Zell Murray and Carol Ann (Clemens) McC.; A.S. in Oceanography, San Diego Mesa Coll., 1973; m. Janice Ann Kujawa; 1 son, Zebediah. Asso. pub. Ridgewood (N.Y.) Times, 1969-71; chemist Kelco Corp., San Diego, 1972-74; quality control mgr. Kimberly-Clarke Corp., Elizabeth, N.J., 1974-76; project mgr. Syn-Cronamics, Inc., Englewood Cliffs, N.J., 1976—; ops. cons. Westinghouse Electric Corp., Johnson & Johnson, Allied Mills, Inc., others. Sr. adv. Jr. Achievement of Elizabeth, N.J., 1975-76. Served with USN, 1967-69. Mem. Internat. Oceanographic Found., Nat. Space Inst., L-5 Soc. Home: 2213 Pennview Ln Schaumburg IL 60194

MCCLURE, WILLIAM EARL, investment advisor; b. Tuscaloosa, Ala., Mar. 26, 1946; s. James William and Julie Savannah McC.; student U. Ala., 1964-66; B.A. cum laude, Harvard Coll., 1970, M.B.A., 1976; m. Alison Todd, Apr. 17, 1971; children—Guerin James, Summer Scripps, Elizabeth Hope. Lending officer Inter-Am. Devel. Bank, Washington, 1971-74; sr. v.p. Royal Trust Bank, Miami, 1976-77; pres. Macdavin Internat., Miami, 1977-78; pres. Synervest Corp., Monticello, Ill., 1978-80; v.p. Roe, Martin & Neiman, Atlanta, 1980—. Served with USAR, 1970-76. Mem. Real Estate Securities and Syndication Inst., Airplane Owners and Pilots Assn. Clubs: World Trade, Atlanta City (Atlanta). Home: 193 Laurel Forest Circle NE Atlanta GA 30342 Office: Suite 1700 Cain Tower Peachtree Center 229 Peachtree St Atlanta GA 30303

MC CLUSKY, MILDRED B., die casting co. cons.; b. Solvay, N.Y., Sept. 22, 1922; d. Ben and Anna (Rychter) Kazel; ed. public schs.; m. Benny McClusky, May 2, 1942 (dec. Nov. 1963); 1 son, Adam. Insp., Frazier & Jones, Solvay, 1940-42; head insp. Easy Washer, Syracuse, N.Y., 1942-45; office mgr., bookkeeper Syracuse Die Casting & Mfg. Co., Inc., 1950-62, pres., chief exec. officer, 1963-77, cons., 1977—. Mem. Soc. Die Casting Engrs., Syracuse C. of C. Roman Catholic. Home: 50 Hardwick Dr Syracuse NY 13209 Office: 2101 Teall Ave Syracuse NY 13206

MC COLL, HUGH LEON, JR., banker; b. Bennettsville, S.C., June 18, 1935; s. Hugh Leon and Frances Pratt (Carroll) McC.; B.S.B.A., U. N.C., Chapel Hill, 1957; m. Jane Spratt, Oct. 3, 1959; children—Hugh Leon, John Spratt, Jane Bratton. With N.C. Nat. Bank, Charlotte, 1959—, v.p., 1965-68, sr. v.p. and nat. div. exec., 1968-70, exec. v.p. in charge internat., nat. and corr. banking, 1970-73, vice-chmn., 1973-74, pres., 1974—, dir., 1973—; dir. Korf Industries, Inc., Sonoco Products Co., Ruddick Corp., Dickerson, Inc., Bank of Ft. Mill (S.C.). Chmn. bd. Charlotte Latin Sch., 1978; bd. mgrs. Charlotte Meml. Hosp., 1973; bd. dirs. Heineman Med. Research Center, 1973, U. S.C. Sch. Bus., 1980. Served with USMC, 1957-59. Mem. Assn. Res. City Bankers, Am. Bankers Assn., N.C. Bankers Assn. Democrat. Clubs: Charlotte Country, Charlotte City, Charlotte Athletic; Quail Hollow Country; Augusta Nat. Golf. Office: NC Nat Bank One NCNB Plaza Charlotte NC 28255

MC COLLISTER, STEPHEN ALLAN, mfg. co. exec.; b. Wilmington, Del., Sept. 14, 1952; s. Oden Clay and Anna Mae McC.; B.A., U. Del., 1974; m. Adonica F. Lambert. With EEOC project Del. Dept. Labor, 1974-76; pres. S.A. McCollister & Assos., Inc., personnel and mgmt. cons., Wilmington, 1975—; personnel mgr. Nat. Liberty Corp., Valley Forge, Pa., 1976; affirmative action cons. Met. Property and Liberty Co., R.I. and N.Y., 1976-78; br. ops. supr. Avon Products, U.S.A., Newark, Del., 1979; dir. Del. Affirmative Action, 1979—; tchr., cons. in field. Del. Summer fellow, 1973. Mem. Am. Mgmt. Assn., Internat. Personnel Mgmt. Assn., Del. Affirmative Action Assn., Phi Sigma Alpha. Author papers, reports in field. Office: 820 N French St 11th Floor Wilmington DE 19801

MC COLLOUGH, HELEN LOUISE, marine retail co. exec.; b. Sour Lake, Tex., Mar. 9, 1929; d. Emory Bland and Cora Lee (Frederick) Smith; B.A., Southwestern Bus. Coll., 1952; m. Apr. 30, 1967; children—Harold Wayne Stockdale, Charlotte Elizabeth Stockdale, Thomas Waters; m. Jack D. Noell, Jan. 1981. Clk.-steno Humble Oil Refinery, Tomball, Tex., 1956-58; prodn. clk. Superior Oil Co., Conroe, Tex., 1958-63; bus driver Conroe Ind. Sch. Dist., 1967—; owner Conroe Marine Inc., 1967—, owner, pres., 1977—; agt. Tex. Parks and Wildlife, 1974—. Mem. Tex. Tchrs. Assn., Conroe Tchrs. Assn., Bus. and Profl. Club, Marine Retailers Assn. Am., Am. Soc. Profl. and Exec. Women, Boating Trades Assn. Tex., Boating Trades Assn. Met. Houston, Nat. Fedn. Ind. Bus., Am. Soc. Notaries, Internat. CB Radio Operators Assn. Baptist. Home: 413 Oak Hill Dr Conroe TX 77304 Office: Conroe Marine Inc 1100 Wilson Rd Conroe TX 77301

MC COLLOUGH, WILLIAM HUGH, petroleum co. exec.; b. Pryor, Okla., May 28, 1930; s. William Hugh and Eva P. (James) McC.; B.S., U. Okla., 1949, LL.B., 1951; m. Mary Lou Midkiff, May 31, 1950; children—William R., Martha, Katherine. Admitted Counsel, Gt. Lakes Pipe Line Co., Kansas City, 1951-59; gen. mgr. products pipe line div. Tex. Eastern Corp., 1959-68, v.p., N. Am. div., 1968-75, v.p., group exec. petroleum group, London, 1978—. Mem. Am. Petroleum Inst., Assn. Oil Pipelines, Natural Gas Processors Assn., Republican. Unitarian.

MC COLLUM, HUGH EVAN, chem. co. exec.; b. Deadwood, S.D., Dec. 2, 1942; s. Eldon Lundy and Mary D. McC.; B.S. in Chem. Engring., Mass. Inst. Tech., 1965, M.S., 1966; m. Carol Sherman Abbott, June 17, 1978. Devel. engr. Amicon Corp., Lexington, Mass., 1966-68; mgr. chem. products Kollmorgen Corp., Glen Cove, N.Y., 1968-74; product mgr. Oxy Metal Industries Corp., Nutley, N.J., 1974-77; mgr. bus. devel. Union Carbide Corp., N.Y.C., 1977-78; mgr. new venture devel. Akzona, Inc., Asheville, N.C., 1978—. Mem. Am. Chem. Soc., Sigma Xi. Republican. Episcopalian. Clubs: Asheville Racquet, Asheville City. Home: 16 Deva Glen Rd Asheville NC 28804 Office: Akzona Inc Asheville NC 28802

MC COLLUM, OTIS ROBERTS, banker; b. Reidsville, N.C., Oct. 8, 1930; s. Henry Edgar and Hattie Jane (Roberts) McC.; B.S., U. N.C., 1952; M.B.A., N.Y. U., 1962; grad. Stonier Sch. Banking, Rutgers U., 1966; m. Hilda Hutchins, June 18, 1960; children—Courtney Roberts, Bradley Curtis. Asst. to mgr. Mitchell Hutchins & Co., N.Y.C., 1955-56; with Mfrs. Hanover Trust Co., N.Y.C., 1956-62; v.p. and trust officer The Nat. Bank of Washington, 1963—; dir. Beitzell & Co., Inc. Bd. dirs. St. Patrick's Episcopal Day Sch., Washington; pres. Spring Valley Wesley Heights Citizens Assn., Washington, 1975-77. Served with U.S. Army, 1952-54. Mem. D.C. Bankers Assn., D.C. Estate Planning Council, Met. Washington Bd. Trade. Republican. Presbyterian. Clubs: Univ., Columbia Country, Capitol Hill. Home: 6200 Brookside Dr Chevy Chase MD 20015 Office: 4340 Connecticut Ave NW Washington DC 20008

MC COLOUGH, CHARLES PETER, bus. equipment exec.; b. Halifax, N.S., Can., Aug. 1, 1922; s. Reginald Walker and Barbara Teresa (Martin) McC.; LL.B., Dalhousie U., Halifax, 1947; M.B.A., Harvard, 1949; m. Mary Virginia White, Apr. 25, 1953. Came to U.S., 1951, naturalized, 1956. Sales mgr. Lehigh Nav. Coal Co., Phila., 1951-54; gen. mgr. Xerox Processing labs. Haloid Co., Chgo., 1954-56, asst. to v.p. sales Haloid Co., Rochester, N.Y., 1956-58, mktg. mgr., 1958-60, gen. sales mgr. Haloid Xerox, also v.p. sales Xerox Corp., Rochester, 1960-63, exec. v.p., 1963, pres., 1966, chief exec. officer, 1968—, chmn. exec. com., 1971—, chmn. bd., 1971—, also dir.; dir. Citibank, N.A., Citicorp, Union Carbide Corp.; joint pres. bd. dirs. Rank Xerox Ltd., London, Eng.; dir. Fuji-Xerox Co. Ltd., Tokyo, Japan; bd. dirs. N.Y. Stock Exchange. Chmn. exec. com. Internat. Exec. Service Corps; chmn. President's Commn. on Pension Policy; trustee Com. for Econ. Devel., U. Rochester, U.S. council Internat. C. of C.; bd. dirs. USSR Trade and Econ. Council; mem. advisory bd. Sch. Orgn. and Mgmt. Yale. Served as naval airman Fleet Air Arm, Royal Navy, World War II. Mem. Bus. Council, Bus. Round Table, Council Fgn. Relations (dir.), C. of C. of U.S. (dir.). Clubs: Rochester Country, Genesee Valley (Rochester); Econ. (dir.), Harvard (N.Y.C.); Stanwich, Greenwich Country, Belle Haven (Greenwich, Conn.). Office: Xerox Corp Stamford CT 06904

MC COMACK, WILLIAM CLARENCE, uranium, coal and oil co. exec.; b. Eunice, N.Mex., Aug. 18, 1939; s. Herman Bertis and Mildred Era McC.; B.B.A., Hardin Simmons U., 1961; m. Jo Verl Everett, June 1, 1960; children—Micki Elayne, Mindi Evonne. Sr. petroleum accountant Amerada Petroleum Co., 1965-68; adminstrv. asst. Sunset Internat. Petroleum Co., Midland, Tex., 1968-69; exec. v.p., dir. McComack Drilling, Inc., Salt Lake City, 1969-72; treas. Nuclear Dynamics, Inc., Phoenix, 1972-80, v.p. adminstrn., 1980—. Republican. Baptist. Home: 1128 W Northview Phoenix AZ 85021 Office: 2871 Sky Harbor Blvd Phoenix AZ 85034

MC COMBS, DONALD DWAIN, real estate securities exec.; b. Eureka, Mont., Jan. 26, 1922; s. William Elmer and Olive (Schroth) McC.; student U. Calif., Berkeley, 1941-42; children—William Henry, David Christopher. Pres., McCombs Securities Co. Inc., Santa Ana, Calif., 1960—; chmn. bd. D & R Properties Inc., Santa Ana, 1970—; chmn. bd. McCombs Corp. Trustee, pres. bd. Pomona (Calif.) Unified Schs., 1966-71. Served to lt. USAF, 1942-45. Home: 30462 Paseo del Valle Laguna Niguel CA 92677 Office: 2392 E Morse Ave Irvine CA 91714

MC COMIC, R. BARRY, real estate developer; B.S., Union U.; LL.B., Tulane U.; postgrad. in law (Friedrich Ebert Found. scholar), U. Freiburg, Germany, Hague Internat. Acad. Law. Admitted to N.Y. State bar, Calif. bar, Tenn. bar; asso. firm Donovan, Leisure, Newton & Irvine, N.Y.C.; acquisitions counsel Avco Corp., 1970-73; successively exec. v.p., pres., chief exec. officer, dir. Avco Community Developers, Inc., San Diego, Calif., 1973—. Regional chmn. United Negro Coll. Fund; mem. bd. devel. Children's Hosp.; bd. dirs. San Diego Symphony Orch. Assn., La Jolla Mus. Contemporary Art. Mem. San Diego Bldg. Contractors Assn. (past treas. dir.), Chancellor's Assn. of U. Calif. at San Diego, Order of Coif. Address: 16770 W Bernardo Dr PO Box 28199 San Diego CA 92127

MC COMMAS, ALEX MONROE, business exec.; b. Bynum, Tex., Nov. 26, 1918; m. Alexander Monroe and Lettie R. (Robbins) McC.; student petroleum engring. Kilgore Coll., 1936-37, Texas A. and M. U., 1938-39; m. Nancy S. Steger, May 25, 1941; children—Alexander, Barbara McCommas Smith, Ray Douglass, Donald. With Farm and Ranch Pub. Co., Dallas, 1938-49; Southwestern mgr. Holland's Mag., Dallas, 1938-49; pub. Farmer-Stockman Mag. Dallas, 1949-78; pres. All Span Steel Bldgs. of Tex., Inc., 1978—. Served with C.E., AUS, 1942-46. Mem. Dallas Ad League, Agrl. Pubs. Assn. (dir. 1974—), Nat. Agri-Mktg. Assn. Clubs: Dallas Agrl. (pres. 1961), Tex. Antique Region Auto (pres. 1964). Home: 6519 Linden Lane Dallas TX 75230 Office: 6350 LBJ Freeway Dallas TX 75240

MC CONKY, WALTER BRADLEY, banker; b. Phila., Mar. 19, 1937; s. Kenneth W. and Helen T. (Bradley) McC.; B.A., Bowdoin Coll., 1959; postgrad. Pace Coll., 1962, N.Y. U. Grad. Sch. Bus. Adminstrn., 1963; m. Nancy Bowser, Sept. 30, 1967; children—Elizabeth Patterson, David Bradley. With Bankers Trust Co., N.Y.C., 1962-71, asst. mgr., 1966-67, asst. treas., 1967-71; account officer 1st Nat. City Bank, N.Y.C., 1972-73, Citicorp Factors Inc., N.Y.C., 1973; asst. v.p. Citytrust, Bridgeport, 1973, v.p., mgr. real estate lending dept., 1974-76, dept. head, v.p. real estate lending dept., 1976-80; v.p., sr. loan officer Dartmouth Savs. Bank, Bridgeport, 1981—; lectr. Urban Reinvestment Task Force, 1978—. Bd. dirs. George Jr. Republic, N.Y.C., 1968-71, asst. treas., 1968-71; bd. dirs. Bridgeport Neighbor Housing Services, 1975-77, treas., 1975-76. Served as 1st lt. Intelligence Corps, U.S. Army, 1960-62, to capt. Res., 1962-66. Mem. Conn. Bankers Assn. (mortgage com. 1973-80, ad hoc com. on clear lang. 1978—, chmn. 1979-80, mem. joint banking com. on alt. mortgage 1978), Mortgage Bankers Assn. (urban investment com.), Nat. Assn. Review Appraisers (sr. mem.), Soc. Real Estate Appraisers (asso.), New Eng. Land Title Assn., Internat. Orgn. Real Estate Cons. (sr. mem.), Am. Coll. Real Estate Cons. (sr. mem.), Theta Delta Chi. Republican. Congregationalist. Home: The Meeting House Redding CT 06875 Office: 981 Main St Bridgeport CT 06602

MC CONNAUGHEY, GEORGE CARLTON, JR., lawyer; b. Hillsboro, Ohio, Aug. 9, 1925; s. George Carlton and Nelle (Morse) McC.; B.A., Denison U., 1949; J.D., Ohio State U., 1951; m. Carolyn Schlieper, June 16, 1951; children—Elizabeth, Susan, Nancy. Admitted to Ohio bar, 1951, since practiced in Columbus; partner firm George, Greek, King, McMahon & McConnaughey, 1967-79, McConnaughey, Stradley, Mone & Moul, 1979—; gen. counsel, sec., dir. Mid-Continent Telephone Corp., Hudson, Ohio, North Am. Broadcasting Co. (WMNI Radio), Columbus; dir. Newark Telephone Co. (Ohio). Asst. atty. gen. Ohio, 1951-54. Pres., Upper Arlington Bd. Edn., 1967-69, Columbus Town Meeting Assn., 1974-76. Chmn. Ohio Young Republicans, 1956; U.S. presdl. elector, 1956. Trustee Buckeye Boys Ranch, Ohio Council Econ. Edn. Served with AUS, 1943-45; ETO. Mem. Am., Ohio, Columbus bar assns., Sigma Chi, Phi Delta Phi. Presbyn. (elder). Mason. Clubs: Columbus, Scioto Country, Columbus Athletic (Columbus). Home: 1969 Andover Rd Upper Arlington OH 43212 Office: 100 E Broad St Columbus OH 43215

MCCONNAUGHY, JOHN E., JR., energy and environ. control exec.; b. Pitts., May 9, 1929; s. John E. and Laura (Remly) McC.; A.B., Denison U., 1950; M.B.A., Harvard U., 1952; m. Carolyn Saxton, Oct. 10, 1977; children by previous marriage—John E. III, James R., Lynne Ann. Asst. mgr. fin. planning Elec. Appliance div. Westinghouse Elec. Corp., Mansfield, Ohio, 1956-58, mgr. adminstrv. services Portable Appliance div., 1958-62, dir. mgmt. services, Pitts., 1962-63; controller Consumer Products div. The Singer Co., N.Y.C., 1963-66, Eastern regional dir., 1966; pres. Singer Co. of Can., Ltd., Montreal, 1967; v.p. European ops. Singer Sewing Machine Co., London, 1968-69; chmn. bd., chief exec. officer Peabody Internat. Corp., Stamford, Conn., 1969—; dir. Mgmt. Assistance, Inc. (N.Y.C.), lst Bank of New Haven, Gram Industries, Inc. (West Haven, Conn.). Served to lt. (j.g.), USNR, 1953-56. Recipient chief exec. awards for environ. industry Fin. World Mag., annually, 1975-79. Mem. NAM, Am. Mgmt. Assn., Conf. Bd., Nat. Coal Assn. Clubs: Queens (London); Harvard, N.Y. Athletic (N.Y.C.); Woodway Country (Darien, Conn.). Office: 4 Landmark Sq Stamford CT 06901

MC CONNELL, JOHN EDWARD, power systems engring. exec.; b. Minot, N.D., July 28, 1931; s. Lloyd Waldorf and Sarah Gladys (Mathis) McC.; B.S. in Mech. Engring., U. Pitts., 1952; M.S., Drexel Inst. Tech., 1958; m. Carol Claire Myers, July 4, 1952; children—Kathleen Anne, James Mathis, Amy Lynn. With mktg. and design depts. Westinghouse Electric Corp., Lester, Pa., 1954-60, 63-67, Pitts., 1960-63; mgr. power generation product activities in U.S. and regional mgr. power products activities Middle Atlantic, Southeastern U.S. regions ASEA Inc., White Plains, N.Y., 1967-79, mgr. turbine generator dept., 1979—; speaker, writer on energy and electric power topics; adviser on energy matters to U.S. congressman 1968-74. Served to 1st lt. C.E., U.S. Army, 1952-54. Registered profl. engr., Pa. Mem. IEEE (sr.; energy com., chmn. subcom. cogeneration), Power Engring. Soc. (sr.; govtl. activities com., chmn. subcom. chpts. public affairs), ASME, TAPPI (energy mgmt. com., steam and power com.). Republican. Home: 173 Remington Rd Ridgefield CT 06877 Office: 4 New King St White Plains NY 10604

MC CONNELL, RAYMOND THOMAS, investment co. exec.; b. N.Y.C., Apr. 3, 1949; s. Thomas and Ruby McC.; B.B.A., Pace U., 1977. With E.F. Hutton & Co., Inc., N.Y.C., 1968—, v.p. commodity accounting and ops., dir., treas. Hutton Commodity Internat., Ltd., 1978—. Mem. Nat. Assn. Black Accts., Futures Industry Assn. (treas. ops. div.), One Hundred Blackmen. Home: 30 Lincoln Plaza New York NY 10023

MC CORMACK, BURKE PATRICK, bank exec.; b. Jersye City, Jan. 2, 1949; s. Hubert Joseph and Mary (Burke) McC.; B.S., Cornell U., 1971; M.B.A., Columbia U., 1976. Asst. v.p., account officer Mfrs. Hanover Trust, N.Y.C., 1976—; lectr. Internat. Study and Research Inst. Served to lt. USNR, 1971-74. Mem. Irish Am. Cultural Inst., Am. Turkish Soc. (dir., v.p.). Home: 111 E 85 St New York NY 10028 Office: 350 Park Ave New York NY 10028

MC CORMACK, CAROL HARTFORD, mgmt. cons., business exec.; b. Redfield, S.D., Jan. 15, 1920; s. Elliott Hartford and Inger Dorthea (Stapp) M.; B.S., Drake U., 1953; certificate Sch. of Banking, La. State U., 1957; m. Virginia Dare Rothgeb, June 12, 1946; 1 dau., Patricia Ann. Dist. mgr. Universal CIT Credit Corp., Des Moines, 1946-50; v.p., comptroller La. Nat. Bank, Baton Rouge, 1953-56; mgr. Ernst & Ernst, St. Louis, 1956-59; exec. v.p., dir. Am. Nat. Bank, Portsmouth, Va., 1959-60; gen. treas. Merc. Mortgage Co., St. Louis, 1960-62; sr. industry analyst IBM, N.Y.C, 1962-67; fin. v.p. Waddell & Reed, Inc., Kansas City, Mo., 1967-68; individual practice as cons. C.H. McCormack & Assos., Inc., Houston, 1968—; lectr. in field. Served to capt. U.S. Army, 1942-46. Certified mgmt. cons. Author: Bank Investment Portfolio, 1964; Bond Trade Analysis, 1964; Optimum Bond Bidding, 1966; Accounting for Debt Securities, 1972; Managing and Trading Debt Securities, 1972; Portfolio Mgmt. and Control System, 1975; contbr. articles to profl. jours. Home: 811 Patchester Houston TX 77079 Office: Suite 130 800 W Belt S Houston TX 77042

MCCORMACK, HAROLD DENNIS, textile supply co. exec.; b. Clarksburg, W.Va., Aug. 20, 1942; s. Paul Donald and Lorena Mae (Thompson) McC.; B.S., U.S. Mil. Acad.; m. Margaret E. Gussman, Feb. 20, 1965; children—Paul T., Michael L. Sales mgr. Stein Hall & Co., 1969-71; group account mgr. Celanese Corp., 1971-76; salesmgr. Cone Mills Corp., 1976-79; pres. Transfertex Am., Ltd., N.Y.C., 1979—. Bd. dirs. Am. Printed Fabrics Council, Internat. Transfer Print Inst. Served in U.S. Army, 1964-69; Vietnam. Decorated Bronze Star (2). Mem. Textile Distbrs. Assn., West Point Soc. N.Y. Republican. Office: 1071 Ave of Americas New York NY 10018

MCCORMACK, JOHN HENRY, JR., banker; b. Pensacola, Fla., Oct. 25, 1926; s. John Henry and Lillian (Toner) McC.; B.S. in Commerce, Washington and Lee U., 1950; grad. Banking Sch. of South, La. State U., 1961; m. Julia Ellen Armstrong, June 27, 1953; children—John H., Paula, Julia, Margaret, Vincent. Sales rep., ty. mgr. Armstrong Cork Co., Atlanta and Jacksonville, Fla., 1950-57; 1st v.p., Atlantic Nat. Bank, Jacksonville, 1969-73, exec. v.p., 1973-74, chmn. bd., 1974—; v.p., regional adminstr. NE Region, Atlantic Bancorp., 1978. Chmn. Lay adv. bd. St. Vincent's Med. Center, 1979; Served with USN, 1944-64. Recipient Top Mgmt. award Sales and Mktg. Execs. of Jacksonville, 1974, Silver Medallion Brotherhood award NCCJ, 1974. Mem. Fla. Bankers Assn., Assn. Res. City Bankers, Am. Bankers Assn., Jacksonville C. of C. (pres. 1976). Democrat. Roman Catholic. Office: Atlantic Nat Bank Jacksonville 200 W Forsyth St Jacksonville FL 32203

MC CORMICK, BROOKS, ret. mfg. exec.; b. Chgo., Feb. 23, 1917; s. Chauncey and Marion (Deering) McC.; B.A., Yale U., 1940; m. Hope Baldwin, 1940. With Internat. Harvester Co., 1940—, mfg., sales positions various locations U.S. and Gt. Britain, 1940-54, dir. mfg., 1954-57, exec. v.p., 1957-68, pres., 1968-71, pres., chief exec. officer, 1971-77, chmn. bd., 1977-79, chmn. exec. com., 1979-80, ret., 1980, also dir.; dir. 1st Nat. Bank Chgo., Commonwealth Edison Co., Chgo. Bd. dirs. Nat. Safety Council, 1964-67; trustee Art Inst. Chgo., Ill. Inst. Tech., 1962-75; trustee Rush-Presbyn.-St. Luke's Hosp., 1956-75, life trustee, 1975—; chmn. bus. adv. council Chgo. Urban League, 1967-76; chmn. Crusade of Mercy, 1961; pres. United Way Met. Chgo., 1976-77. Mem. Motor Vehicle Mfrs. Assn. (dir., chmn. 1973-74, 79-80). Clubs: Chgo., Comml. (pres. 1976-77) (Chgo.). Office: 410 N Michigan Ave Chicago IL 60611

MC CORMICK, PETER HERDIC, food service co. exec.; b. Williamsport, Pa., Apr. 9, 1930; s. William Carl and Dorothy (Rentz) McC.; B.A., Lafayette Coll., Easton, Pa., 1952; postgrad. Columbia U.; m. Joan O. White, June 17, 1965; children—Pamela, Peter Herdic, Deborah. Gen. mgr. dairy div. Sealtest Foods Co., Phila., 1954-65; v.p., gen. mgr. Hawthorn Mellody Inc., Chgo., 1965-70; with ARA Food Services Co., 1970—, regional v.p. Western area, Fairbanks, Alaska, 1974-76, pres. Western area, Los Angeles, 1976—. Served to 1st lt. AUS, 1952-54; Korea. Decorated Bronze Star. Mem. Calif. Automatic Vendors Council. Office: 1 Continental Plaza Suite 490 El Segundo CA 90245

MC CORMICK, RALPH EUGENE, stationery engraving co. exec.; b. Nashville, May 11, 1948; s. Mildred Marie (Wells) McC.; A.S., King's Coll., 1972, acctg. cert., 1971; m. Eugenia Keitt, Aug. 24, 1974; 1 dau., Darby Eugenia. Acct., Mercy Hosp., Charlotte, N.C., 1972-73; acct. W. A. Buening & Co., Inc., Charlotte, 1973-75, controller, 1975-77, treas., from 1977, now v.p. fin. and adminstrn., also dir. Served with U.S. Army, 1966-69. Mem. Nat. Assn. Accts., Am. Mgmt. Assn., Am. Soc. Personnel Adminstrn. Home: 1430 Biltmore Dr Charlotte NC 28207 Office: 2518 Dunavant St Charlotte NC 28203

MC CORMICK, SANFORD ELLIOTT, oil and gas co. exec.; b. N.Y.C., July 18, 1931; s. Robert Elliott and Helen (Roberts) McC.; B.A. in History, Yale U., 1953; Certificat d'Etudes Politique, Ecole des Politiques, Paris, 1955; m. Balene Cross, Dec. 31, 1956; children—Peter E., Carolyn I. Landman oil and gas cos., Tex., 1956-65; ind. oil and gas operator, 1965-69; founder, chmn. bd., pres. McCormick Oil & Gas Corp., privately held stock co., ind. drilling and producing, Houston, 1969-79, became public and changed name to McCormick Oil & Gas Co., 1980, chmn. bd., pres., dir., 1980—; dir. Fannin Bancshares, Inc., Houston; speaker at various energy and fin. investment seminars, 1968—. Bd. visitors, bd. govs. St. John's Coll., Santa Fe; trustee Houston Ballet Found.; bd. dirs. Inst. Ophthalmology, Tex. Med. Center, St. Joseph's Hosp., Houston, Houston Mus. Fine Arts. Served with USAF, 1954-56. Mem. Mid-Continent Oil and Gas Assn., Tex. Producers Assn., Phi Beta Kappa. Republican. Contbr. articles to various industry publs. Office: Two Allen Center Suite 3600 Houston TX 77002

MC CORMICK, WILLIAM M., fin. exec.; b. Hartford, Conn., Aug. 21, 1940; s. Ernest W. and Esther R. (Mallory) McC.; B.S., Yale U., 1962; M.S., George Washington U., 1967; m. Jennifer M. Landale, Oct. 31, 1970; children—James William Landale and Skye Margaret (twins). Nuclear engr. on staff of Adm. Rickover, AEC, 1962-67; mgmt. cons. McKinsey & Co., N.Y.C., 1967-72; investment banker Donaldson, Lufkin & Jenrette, 1972-74; sr. v.p. fin. Am. Express Internat. Banking Corp., N.Y.C., 1974-78, sr. v.p. Am. Express Card Div., 1978-79, pres. Travel Div., 1979-80, pres. Card Div. and sr. v.p. Am. Express Co., 1980—. Bd. dirs. VITA, Washington, 1972, Manhattan Theater Club, 1980; bd. overseers N.Y. U. Bus. Sch. Served to lt. USN, 1962-67. Clubs: Yale, Links (N.Y.C.). Home: 122 E 82d St New York NY 10028 Office: AMEX Plaza New York NY 10004

MC CORQUINDALE, DEREK HARRY, trade assn. exec.; b. Bukinghamshire, Eng., June 1, 1933; s. Harry and Beryle (Renyolds) McC.; diploma in Bus. Mgmt., LaSalle Ext. U., 1968; m. Mar. 25, 1954; children—John, Paul, Alexander. Police officer London Met. Police, 1952-59; police officer, Calgary, Alta., Can., 1959-66; fin. reporter, salesman Dun & Bradstreet of Can. Ltd., 1966-70; exec. dir. Mech. Contractors Assn. Alta., Calgary, 1970—. Mem. Inst. Assn. Execs. (nat. dir., 2d v.p. Can.), Am. Soc. Assn. Execs. Anglican. Clubs: Toastmasters Internat., Kiwanis. Office: 608 25th St NW Calgary AB T2N 2S8 Canada

MC COURT, JAMES EDWARD, fin. co. exec.; b. Kansas City, Mo., Apr. 2, 1944; s. Charles Michael and Edna Cecil (Wright) McC.; B.S. in Bus. Adminstrn., B.S. in Phys. Scis. and Statistics, Kans. State U., 1966; M.B.A., UCLA, 1967, Ph.D. in Fin. and Econs., 1969. Research asso. Midwest Research Inst., 1962; dean's asst. Kans. State U., 1965; economist Hughes Aircraft Corp., 1968; staff cons. Coldwell Banker & Co., 1970; v.p. PFO Capital Corp., 1971; dean Sch. Bus., U. West Angeles, 1977; sr. v.p., dir. Am. Interfin. Corp., Marina Del Rey, Calif., 1973—; mng. editor Middle East Econ. Rev. Active local Boy Scouts Am.; humane officer State of Calif. Served with USAF, 1963-64; col. CAF. NDEA fellow, 1967; Regents fellow, 1969; fellow Kansas City Assn. Trusts and Founds., 1962; Byron R. Lewis fellow, 1965—. Mem. Middle East Econ. Assn., Nat. Rifle Assn., U.S. Seaplane Pilots Assn., Delta Mu Delta, Alpha Kappa Psi, Beta Gamma Sigma, Sigma Iota Epsilon, Phi Chi Theta, Alpha Phi Omega. Club: Westwind Yacht. Editor: Middle East Oil: Economic and Political Reality, 1979. Nat. rifle champion, 1961; mem. Nat. Civilian High Power Rifle Team, 1962. Address: 13900 Marquesas Way Suite 500 Marina del Rey CA 90291

MC COWN, GEORGE EDWIN, forest products co. exec.; b. Portland, Oreg., July 1, 1935; s. Floyd C. and Ada E. (Stephens) McC.; B.M.E., Stanford, 1957; M.B.A., Harvard, 1962; m. Jean Ray McKaig, Nov. 16, 1956; children—Taryn, Daniel, David. With Boise Cascade Corp. (Idaho), 1963—, gen. mgr. Housing Group, Boise, 1970-71, v.p. and gen. mgr. Boise Cascade Realty Group, Palo Alto, Calif., 1971-74, sr. v.p. Boise Cascade Realty Group, pres. Boise Cascade Home & Land Corp., Palo Alto, 1974-79, sr. v.p. Bldg. Material Group, Boise, 1976—; chmn. The Villa, Inc., The Palomar Group; partner Univ. Mgmt. Assos.; vice chmn. policy adv. bd. Harvard-Mass. Inst. Tech. Joint Center Urban Studies; dir. Center for Real Estate and Urban Econs.; dir. Impell Corp., Woodmark Corp.; mem. fed. legis. com. Nat. Council of Housing Industry. Trustee, N.W. Outward Bound Sch., also v.p. for Idaho; trustee Stanford U.; chmn. crusade for Ada County, Am. Cancer Soc., 1980. Mem. Urban Land Inst., Bay Area (Calif.) Council (dir.), Young Presidents Orgn., Greater Boise C. of C. (dir., chmn. aviation com., mem. select com. on regional carrying capacity), Stanford Alumni Assn. (past pres.). Office: Boise Cascade Co 1 Jefferson Sq Boise ID 83728

MCCOY, CHARLES WALLACE, banker; b. Marietta, Ohio, Feb. 5, 1920; s. John H. and Florence (Buchanan) Mc.C.; B.A., Marietta Coll., 1942; M.B.A., Stanford U., 1944; postgrad. Rutgers U., 1947; m. Ruth Zimmerman, July 20, 1946; children—Melissa, Charles Brent, Shelley. Trainee, Utica Savs. Bank (Ohio), 1939-41; with City Nat. Bank, Columbus, Ohio, 1944-59, also dir.; sr. v.p. La. Nat. Bank, Baton Rouge, 1959-61, pres., 1961-79, chmn., chief exec. officer, 1979—, also dir.; dir. Jefferson Standard Life Ins. Co., Greensboro, N.C., Jefferson Pilot Corp., Greensboro. Bd. dirs. Council for Better La.; mem. La. Exposition Bd. World's Fair for New Orleans; trustee Marietta (Ohio) Coll., 1981—. Mem. Am. Bankers Assn. (chmn. bank regulatory task force com. 1979—), La. Bankers Assn. (pres. elect 1980—), Res. City Bankers Assn., Conf. Bd. (voting and sr. mem.). Episcopalian. Clubs: Baton Rouge, County, City of Baton Rouge, Camelot, Rotary, Mason, Shriner. Office: 451 Florida St Baton Rouge LA 70801

MCCOY, GARDNER, heavy engring. co. exec.; b. Middletown, Ohio, Mar. 2, 1915; s. James W. and Florence (Peterson) McC.; student U. Cin., 1933-38; m. Muriel Marshall, Sept. 25, 1940; children—Kristin, Melissa. With Armco Steel Corp., Middletown, 1933-38, Australia, 1938-56; with firm Gardner L. McCoy and Assos., Australia, 1956-62; mng. dir. McCoy Internat., Sydney, New South Wales, Australia, 1962—, Bliss Welded Products, Sydney, Australia, 1966—; dir. Indsl. Ops. Pty. Ltd. Bd. dirs. YMCA, Wollongong. Fellow Inst. Dirs. Australia; asso. mem. Mech. Engrs. Australia; mem. Iron and Steel Engrs. U.S.A. (life), Am. C. of C., Australian Inst. Mgmt., Co. Dirs. Assn. Australia, Metal Trades Industry Assn. Australia. Republican. Home: Highland Park Mount Pleasant Balgownie New South Wales Australia Office: 333 Old South Head Rd Watsons Bay Sydney Australia

MC COY, GENE GUY, advt. exec.; b. Oskaloosa, Iowa, May 11, 1926; s. Guy Gene and Edith (Seaman) McC.; B.B.A., U. Wis., 1951; M.A. in Mktg., State U. Iowa, 1952; m. Idella Marie Brown, Aug. 8, 1947; children—Gene Guy, Vicki V., Randi R., S. Sherman. Advt. mgr. W.M. McAllister Co., Sycamore, Ill., 1952-53; account exec. Gerald T. LeFever & Assos., Little Rock, 1953-55, partner, 1956-57; pres. Ad Craft of Ark., Inc., Little Rock, 1958-78, chmn. bd., 1978—; asst. prof. advt. and pub. relations, chmn. dept. advt. U. Ark. at Little Rock, 1962—. Mem. Ark. Atty. Gen.'s Study Com. for Consumer Protection Legis.; cons. Model Cities Program; lobbyist Ark. Gen. Assembly. Chmn. bd. dirs. Better Bus. Bur. Ark., 1974. Served with AUS, 1944-47. Recipient Outstanding Service award Ark. Dept. Edn., 1965, 67, 68, 69; Ark. Traveller award, 1969; Outstanding Advt. Educator G.D. Crain Found., 1972; certificate of Merit, State of Ark., 1974. Mem. Public Relations Soc. Am. (accredited, del. nat. assembly 1980— counselor; v.p. Ark. chpt. 1974, pres. 1975, nat. edn. com. 1975-77, nat. liaison officer to Am. Acad. Collegiate Schs. Bus. 1975-77; recipient Ark. Aluminum award 1981), Am. Advt. Fedn. (dir. 10th dist. 1958-67, 1st lt. gov. 1968-69, gov. 1969-70, nat. dir. 1969-70, Silver medal 1966, Advt. Educator of Year 1972, Sterling service award 1974), Little Rock Advt. Club (pres. 1958-60), AIM (pres.'s council), Am. Mktg. Assn., Southwestern Assn. Advt. Agys., Ams. Working for Advt. Knowledge and Edn. (chmn.), Am. Acad. Advt., Found. Pub. Relations Research and Edn., Internat. Pub. Relations Assn., Nat. Fedn. Ind. Bus., Direct Mail Mktg. Assn., East African Wildlife Soc., Alpha Delta Sigma (regional v.p. 1969-70, Aid to Advt. Edn. award 1969, nat. v.p. 1971-72), Alpha Kappa Psi, Sigma Alpha Epsilon. Episcopalian. Home: 12000 Rivercrest Dr Little Rock AR 72207 Office: 1122 W 3d St Little Rock AR 72203

MC COY, JOHN DAVID, fin. co. exec.; b. Bainbridge, Ohio, Dec. 1, 1935; s. Frank Branson and Louise (Campbell) McC.; student Ohio U., 1953-55, U. Dayton, 1956; m. Mary Ann Sharp, Oct. 20, 1956; children—Christine, Lori, Susan, John David. Prodn. control specialist Wood Shovel & Tool, Piqua, Ohio, 1956; sales mgr. U.S. Credit Corp., Ohio, 1956; collection mgr., mgr. adminstrn. Hobart Corp., Troy, Ohio, 1970-76, mgr., br./agency accounts, customer fin., 1976-79, gen. credit mgr., 1979—. Served with USAF, 1961-62. Mem. Nat. Assn. Credit Mgmt., Am. Mgmt. Assn., Dayton Assn. Credit Mgmt. Republican. Roman Catholic. Clubs: K.C., Esquire. Home: 1106 Scudder St Piqua OH 45356 Office: Hobart Corp Grant St S Troy OH 45373

MCCOY, JOHN LUMAN, fin. exec.; b. Mpls., Dec. 17, 1939; s. John L. and Margaret L. (Clark) McC.; B.S., Regis Coll., 1961; postgrad. U. Minn., 1969; m. Charlene McDonald, Sept. 3, 1960; children—Deborah, Patty, John. With Bendix, Milw., 1961, Ford Motor Co., Mpls., 1962-69; with Kidder, Peabody & Co., Mpls., 1969—, v.p., 1978—. Roman Catholic. Club: Mpls. Athletic. Home: 5525 Hillside Circle Edina MN 55435 Office: 1650 IDS Center Minneapolis MN 55402

MC COY, LEE BERARD, paint co. exec.; b. Ipswich, Mass., July 27, 1925; d. Damase Joseph and Robena Myrtle (Bruce) B.; student U. Ala., Mobile, 1958-60; m. Walter Vincent de Paul McCoy, Sept. 27, 1943; children—Bernadette, Raymond, Joan, Richard. Owner, Lee's Letter Shop, Hicksville, L.I., N.Y., 1950-56; mgr. sales adminstrn. Basila Mfg. Co., Mobile, Ala., 1957-61; promotion mgr., buyer Mobile Paint Co., Inc., Theodore, Ala., 1961—. Curator, Shepard Meml. Library, 1972—; bd. dirs. Monterey Tour House, Mobile, 1972-78, Old Dolphin Way Assn., 1977-79, Friends of Mus., Mobile, 1978-81, Miss Wheelchair Ala., 1980—; del. Civic Roundtable, 1977-78, 1st v.p., 1980-81; pres. Gov.'s Com. Employment of Handicapped, 1981; active Mobile Area Retarded Citizens, Am. Heart Assn. Recipient Honor award Civic Roundtable, 1979, 80; Service award Women's Com. of Spain Rehab. Center, State of Ala., 1980. Mem. Spectromatic Assos., Nat. Paint Distbrs., Hist. Preservation Soc., English Speaking Union. Republican. Methodist. Clubs: Quota (charter mem. Mobile chpt., dir. 1977-81, pres. 1978-80), chmn. numerous coms., recipient Service award Dist. 8, 1979, Internat. award for serving club objectives, 1980, editor Care-Gram, Weekly newsletter for nursing homes 1980—). Home: 1553 Monterey Pl Mobile AL 36604 Office: 4775 Hamilton Blvd Theodore AL 36582

MCCOY, MILLINGTON FLENTGE, exec. search cons.; b. Cape Girardeau, Mo.; d. Milling Howard Hanscom and Mary Helen (Kinder) Flentge; B.A. with distinction, U. Mo., 1962; certificate in bus. adminstrn., Harvard U.-Radcliffe Coll., 1963; m. W. David McCoy, Dec. 23, 1966; 1 son, Daniel Phipps. Field research analyst Procter & Gamble Co., 1962-63; market research analyst Gardner Advt. Agy., 1964-65; research asso. Handy Assos., N.Y.C., 1965-70, asst. v.p., 1970-73, v.p., 1974-77; partner Gould & McCoy, N.Y.C., 1977—. Bd. mgrs. N.Y. Jr. League, 1971-73. Mem. Mortar Bd., Phi Beta Kappa. Club: Harvard Bus. Sch. Greater N.Y. (dir. 1974-77, 81-84). Office: 375 Park Ave New York NY 10152

MC COY, ROBERT BAKER, publisher; b. Arrowsmith, Ill., Mar. 26, 1916; s. Robert Benton and Charlotte (Miller) McC.; B.S., Northwestern U., 1950, M.S., 1951; postgrad. U. Ill. extension. Various positions with branches U.S. Govt., 1939-51; mng. editor book dept. Popular Mechanics Mag. Co., Chgo., 1951-60; mng. editor high sch. textbook div. J.B. Lippincott Co., Chgo., 1960-62; owner, pres., chmn. bd. Rio Grande Press, Inc., pubs. non-fiction Western Americana books, Chgo., 1962—. Lectr. on Western history. Served with AUS, 1941-45. Mem. N.Mex., Ariz., Calif., Tex. hist. socs., Santa Fe Westerners, Westerners Internat. Baptist. Contbr. articles on Am. Indian, ornithology, travel. Office: La Casa Escuela Glorieta NM 87535

MC CRACKEN, HAROLD MACKENZIE, former mfr.; b. Farmington, Mich., Feb. 3, 1904; s. Harry Norton and Isabella Florence (MacKenzie) McC.; A.B., Albion Coll., 1926; student U. Mich. extension courses; m. Helene Charlotte Sooy, June 10, 1933. Teller, Nat. Bank Commerce 1926-28; tax clk. Oakland County Mich., 1928-29; treas. Gray Marine Motor Co., 1930-47; co-founder, past sec. MP Pumps, Inc., Detroit, 1942-69, dir., 1942-75; co-founder, past chmn. bd. dirs. Am. Community Mut. Ins. Co., 1938—, now dir.; partner McBee Investors, 1944-76. Past mem. citizens adv. com. sch. needs in Detroit; past mem. nat. council Camp Fire Girls, Inc. Mem. bd., past pres. Am. Lung Assn. Southeastern Mich. Mem. Nat. Assn. Accountants, U.S. Power Squadron, Internat. Platform Assn., S.A.R., Tau Kappa Epsilon. Presbyterian. Clubs: Detroit Yacht, Rotary (Detroit), Masons, K.T. Home: 295 Stephens Rd Grosse Pointe Farms MI 48236

MC CRENSKY, JONATHAN ALLEN, advt. agy. exec.; b. Providence, Apr. 23, 1939; s. Leo and Dora (Fishman) McC.; B.S., Boston U., 1961; m. Patricia Mende; children—Paige Sue, Toby Lea, Glen Mende, Debra Ann, Robert P., Scott. Retail exec. Gimbels-Macy's-Bamberger for Hartz Mountain Corp., N.Y.C.; account exec. Bo Bernstein Advt., Providence; account exec. Bloom Advt., Dallas; dir. advt. sales promotion, marketing Edward Trauner, Inc., Zodiac, Clebar & Vacheron Constantine watch cos.; v.p. marketing Edward G. Coyne, Inc., N.Y.C.; accounts supr. Rabin Advt., Valley Stream, N.Y.; pres. Jonathan Allen Advt., Upper Brookville, N.Y., Mall Traffic Inc., Upper Brookville, Symbol Am. Corp.; sales rep. for The Ams., Symbol internat. mag. adj. prof. Suffolk Community Coll. Served to capt. USAFR. Home and office: Lawn Ln Upper Brookville NY 11771

MCCRINK, DONALD GERARD, fin. exec.; b. Bklyn., Jan. 28, 1946; s. James and Clarice (Reilly) McC.; A.A., Adelphi U., 1979; m. Bridget McGuane, July 13, 1968; children—Michelle, Kathleen, Erin. Credit analyst Meinhard Comml. Corp., N.Y.C., 1965-72; retail credit mgr. Bankers Trust Co., Los Angeles, 1979—. Past pres., Factors Retail Credit Group. Mem. Textile Profl. Orgn. Clubs: Progressive Credit (founder, pres. 1972-74), Future Credit. Home: 629 Camaritas Dr Diamond Bar CA 91765 Office: 110 E 9th St Los Angeles CA 90079

MC CUE, FRANK WILLIAM, orgn. exec.; b. London, Aug. 29, 1935; s. Francis William and Doris Edith McC.; came to U.S., 1960, naturalized, 1970; B.S., Columbia U., 1968; m. Nora R. O'Malley, June 12, 1961; children—David, John, Deirdre. Auditor, audit mgr. Knox, Cropper & Co., London, 1953-60; audit sr. Peat, Marwick, Mitchell & Co., London, 1960; budget mgr., acctg. mgr. Ford Found., N.Y.C., 1960-76; treas. AFS Internat./Intercultural Programs, Inc., N.Y.C., 1976—. Home: 7110 Eighth Ave New York NY 11228 Office: 313 E 43d St New York NY 10017

MCCULLOCH, WILLIAM ALEXANDER, III, exec. search co. exec.; b. West Point, N.Y., Oct. 24, 1926; s. William Alexander, II and Florence Alexander (Sumner) McC.; B.S. in Indsl. Engring., Lehigh U., Bethlehem, Pa., 1951; m. Helen Adele Kraus, June 25, 1952; children—Judith, Andrew, Scott, Mark. Nat. placement mgr. Coopers & Lybrand, C.P.A.'s, N.Y.C., 1960-67; mgr. recruiting Singer Co., N.Y.C., 1967-68; mgr. manpower planning/mgmt. devel. Amax, Inc., N.Y.C., 1968-70; pres. William McCulloch Assos., Inc., exec. search, N.Y.C., 1970—. Served to 2d lt. C.E., AUS, 1946-48. Republican. Mem. United Ch. Christ. Home: 91 Hillside Ave Chatham NJ 07928 Office: 20 E 46th St New York NY 10017

MC CULLOUGH, DONALD FREDERICK, textile co. exec.; b. Montclair, N.J., May 6, 1925; s. Willis Gerald and Viola (Mock) McC.; B.S. in Indsl. Adminstrn. and Engring., Yale U., 1945; Hon. Dr. Textile, Phila. Coll. Textiles and Sci., 1969; m. Mary Jane Whipple, Dec. 1951 (Dec. 1962); children—Gregory, Nina, Tracey, Sally; m. 2d, Louise C. Voorhees, July 23, 1963. Exec. apprentice Collins & Aikman Corp., N.Y.C., 1946-50, automotive-fabric sales rep., 1950-53, dir., 1950—, asst. to v.p. sales, 1953-55, exec. v.p. sales, 1955-61, pres., chief exec. officer, 1961—, chmn. bd., 1970—; dir. Bankers Trust Co., Bankers Trust N.Y. Corp., Mass. Mut. Life Ins. Co., Melville Corp., Chesebrough-Ponds, Inc. Served to lt. USNR, 1944-46, 51-53. Recipient Ann. Textile award N.Y. Bd. Trade; Brotherhood award NCCJ. Mem. Am. Textile Mfrs. Inst. (dir., past pres.). Clubs: N.Y. Yacht, Riverside Yacht, Storm Trysail, Lyford Cay (Nassau, Bahamas), Round Hill, Union League. Office: 210 Madison Ave New York NY 10016

MCCULLOUGH, FREDA JANE, brokerage co. exec.; b. Bklyn., Sept. 12, 1946; d. Sam and Blanche Lillian (Porter) Ginsberg; student C.W. Post Coll., 1964-66. Trader, Phillips Appel & Walden, N.Y.C., 1972-76; v.p. Fairfield Group Inc., N.Y.C., 1976-78; trader A.G. Becker Co., N.Y.C., 1978-79; pres. Boston Securities Assos., Inc., N.Y.C., 1979—. Home: 33 Gold St New York NY 10038 Office: 115 Broadway Suite 1108 New York NY 10006

MC CULLOUGH, JOHN PHILLIP, mgmt. cons., educator; b. Lincoln, Ill., Feb. 2, 1945; s. Phillip and Lucile Ethel (Ornellas) McC.; B.S., Ill. State U., 1967, M.S., 1968; Ph.D., U. N.D., 1971; m. Barbara Elaine Carley, Nov. 29, 1968; 1 dau., Carley Jo. Adminstrv. mgr. McCullough Ins. Agy., Atlanta, Ill., 1963-68; ops. supr. Stetson China Co., Lincoln, 1967; asst. mgr. Brandtville Service, Inc., Bloomington, Ill., 1968; instr. in bus. Ill. Central Coll., 1968-69; research asst. U. N.D., Grand Forks, 1969-71; asso. prof. mgmt. West Liberty State Coll., 1971-74, prof., 1974—, chmn. dept. mgmt., 1974—, dir. Small Bus. Inst., 1978—; mgmt. cons., Triadelphia, W.Va., 1971—; instr. Am. Inst. Banking, 1971—; lectr. W.Va. U., 1971—; adj. prof. Wheeling Coll., 1972—; profl. asso. Inst. Mgmt. and Human Behavior, 1975—; v.p. West Liberty State Coll. Fed. Credit Union, 1976—; rep. W.Va. Bd. Regents Adv. Council of Faculty. Team leader Wheeling div. Am. Cancer Soc.; coordinator Upper Ohio Valley United Fund, 1972-74; instr. AFL-CIO Community Services Program, Wheeling. Recipient Service award Bank Adminstrn. Inst., 1974, United Fund, 1973; Acad. Achievement award Harris-Casals Found., 1971. Mem. Soc. Humanistic Mgmt. (nat. chmn.), Orgn. Planning Mgmt. Assn. (exec. com.), Spl. Interest Group for Cert. Bus. Educators (nat. dir.), Soc. Advancement Mgmt. (chpt. adv.), Acad. Mgmt., Adminstrv. Mgmt. Soc. (cert.), Am. Soc. Personnel Adminstrn. (cert.), Nat. Bus. Honor Soc. (Excellence in Teaching award 1976, dir. 1974—), Alpha Kappa Psi (Dist. Service award 1973, Civic award 1977, chpt. adv. 1971—), Delta Mu Delta, Delta Pi Epsilon, Delta Tau Kappa, Phi Gamma Nu, Phi Theta Pi, Pi Gamma Mu, Pi Omega Pi, Omicron Delta Epsilon. Author: (with Howard Fryette) Primer in Supervisory Management, 1973; contbr. articles to profl. jours. Home: 68 Elm Dr Triadelphia WV 26059

MC CULLOUGH, JOSEPH LEE, indsl. psychologist; b. Bryn Mawr, Pa., Oct. 3, 1945; s. Leo Francis and Margaret Mary (Hart) McC.; A.B., Villanova U., 1967; M.A., Ohio State U., 1968, Ph.D., 1971; m. Bonnie R. Goldberg, Jan. 14, 1979. Teaching asst. Ohio State U., 1967-68, research asso., 1968-69; asso. O.P.S. Assos., Columbus, 1970-71; asso., sr. asso. prin. Hay Assos., N.Y.C., 1971-78, sr. prin., 1980—. Served with AUS, 1972. NSF fellow, 1969; NDEA Title IV fellow, 1970; Univ. Dissertation Year fellow, 1971. Mem. Am., Eastern, Pa., Met. psychol. assns. Author: (with others) The Acquisition of Information Across Cultures: Persuasive Role Play Counter Argument and Attitude Change, 1970; The Use of a Measure of Net Counterargumentation in Predicting the Influence of Mass Communications, 1970; (with others) Repetition of Highly Similar Messages and Attitude Change, 1974. Home: 16 Merion Pl Lawrenceville NJ 08648 Office: One Dag Hammarskjold Plaza New York NY 10017

MC CULLOUGH, SAMUEL ALEXANDER, banker; b. Pitts., Nov. 10, 1938; s. Alexander and Mary Ruth (Brady) McC.; B.B.A., U. Pitts., 1960; m. Katharine Graham, Sept. 23, 1967; children—Bonnie S., Elizabeth C., Rebecca D., Anne D., Mary D. With Mellon Bank, N.A., Pitts., 1956-75, asst. cashier, 1964-68, asst. v.p. nat. dept., 1968-71, v.p., 1971-75; sr. v.p. corporate banking group Am. Bank & Trust Co. of Pa., Reading, 1975-77, exec. v.p. corporate banking group, 1977-78, pres., chief exec. officer, 1978—; dir. Am. Bus. Credit Corp. and subs. Am. Venture Capital Corp., Berks Title Ins. Co. Bd. dirs. Easter Seal Soc. Berks County, Wyomissing Property Corp., United Way of Berks County, Public Sch. Employees Retirement System; trustee St. Joseph Hosp., Albright Coll. Mem. Am., Pa. bankers assns., Am. Inst. Banking, Berks County C. of C. (chmn. bd.). Republican. Presbyterian. Clubs: Allegheny Country (Sewickley, Pa.); Berkshire Country (Reading); Moselem Springs (Fleetwood, Pa.). Office: 35 N 6th St Reading PA 19601

MC CUNE, WILLIAM JAMES, JR., mfg. co. exec.; b. Glens Falls, N.Y., June 2, 1915; s. William James and Brunnhilde (Decker) McC.; S.B., M.I.T., 1937; m. Janet Waters, Apr. 19, 1940; 1 dau., Constance (Mrs. Leslie Sheppard); m. 2d, Elisabeth Johnson, Aug. 8, 1946; children—William Joseph, Heather H.D. With Polaroid Corp., Cambridge, Mass., 1939—, v.p. engring., 1954-63, v.p., asst. gen. mgr., 1963-69, exec. v.p. after 1969, now pres., chief exec. officer, dir.; dir. Haemonetics Corp.; trustee Mitre Corp. Mem. corp. Boston Mus. Sci.; mem. corp. devel. com. M.I.T.; trustee Mass. Gen. Hosp. Fellow Am. Acad. Arts and Scis.; mem. Nat. Acad. Engring. Office: Polaroid Corp 549 Technology Sq Cambridge MA 02139

MC CURDY, JOHN GRIBBEL, JR., communications co. exec.; b. San Francisco, July 6, 1949; s. John G. and Anne S. (Costello) McC.; B.S. in Communications, Ithaca (N.Y.) Coll., 1971. Asst. chief engr. Sta. WAXC, Rochester, N.Y., 1972-73; mem. engring. staff CBS Radio, 1973; newsman Westinghouse Broadcasting Co., Phila., 1973-80; mgr. network electronic journalism NBC-TV, N.Y.C., 1980—; pres. McCurdy Assos., Phila., 1973—. Recipient award for heroism Miami Legion of Honor, 1977. Mem. AFTRA. Clubs: Phila. Cricket, Pen & Pencil. Office: 30 Rockefeller Plaza New York NY 10020

MCCURDY, LARRY WAYNE, mfg. co. exec.; b. Commerce, Tex., July 1, 1935; s. Weldon Lee and Eula Bell (Quinn) McC.; B.B.A., Tex. A&M U., 1957; m. Anna Jean Ogle, June 2, 1956; children—Michael, Kimberly, Laurie. Jr. acct. Tenneco Inc., Houston, 1957-60; sr. acct. Tenneco Oil Co., Houston, 1960-64; acctg. supr. Tenneco Chems. Co., Houston, 1964-69, div. controller, Saddle Brook, N.J., 1970-72, corp. controller, 1972-74, v.p. fin., from 1974; sr. v.p. Tenneco Automotive Co., from 1978; now pres. Walker Mfg. Co. div. Tenneco Inc., Racine, Wis. Served to capt., Air Def., U.S. Army Res., 1958-66. Office: Walker Mfg Co 1201 Michigan Blvd Racine WI 53402*

MC CURE, JOANNE, mgmt. cons.; b. Joliet, Ill., July 8, 1936; d. James Joseph and Johanna Rose (Kubin) McC.; B.S., Coll. St. Francis, Joliet, 1976; cert. dental asst., Am. Dental Assts. Assn., 1967. Dentist's asst. and office mgr., Joliet, 1956; cons. Profl. Budget Plan, Madison, Wis., 1959-62; propr. Joanne McCure Assos., mgmt. cons. to physicians and dentists, N.Y.C., 1963—; pres. Conf. Dynamics, Inc., 1980, 265 Owners Corp. Coop., 1980; guest lectr. N.Y. U., Columbia U., Yeshiva U., others. Mem. Soc. Profl. Bus. Cons., Met. Research Inst., Am. Dental Assts. Assn., N.Y. Dental Mgmt. Soc. (hon.). Roman Catholic. Author articles in field. Address 265 W 93d St New York NY 10025

MCCUSKER, JOHN, automotive co. exec.; b. Bklyn., May 28, 1939; s. John Michael and Helen Frances (Sweeney) McC.; B.B.A., St. John's U., 1961; m. Brenda Ann Caprio, June 27, 1964; children—John Christian, Joseph Andrew, David Douglas. Sr. acct. Haskins & Sells, N.Y.C., 1961-67; asst. dir. fin. planning Colt Industries, Inc., N.Y.C., 1967-69; dir. fin. planning Shearson Hammill & Co., N.Y.C., 1969-70; dir. fin. analysis The Allen Group, Inc., Melville, N.Y., 1971-73; asst. corporate controller, 1973-76, v.p., controller, 1976—. Bd. dirs., Huntington (N.Y.) Hosp., Family Service League Suffolk County, Huntington, N.Y. Served with U.S. Army, 1963. C.P.A., N.Y. Mem. Am. Inst. C.P.A.'s, N.Y. State Soc. C.P.A.'s. Republican. Roman Catholic. Home: 4 Harborview Dr Huntington Bay NY 11743 Office: 534 Broad Hollow Rd Melville NY 11747

MC CUTCHEON, LUTHER NEWTON, II, banker; b. Richwood, W.Va., Nov. 25, 1931; s. Bernard Newton and Nola Susan (Dotson) McC.; B.S. in Bus. Mgmt., W.Va. Inst. Tech., 1957; postgrad. W.Va. Sch. Banking, 1966, Southwestern Grad. Sch. Banking, So. Meth. U., 1969; m. Linda Davis, Aug. 3, 1978; children—James Michael, Rebecca Susan, Margaret Ann. Salesman, Burroughs Corp., Charleston, W.Va., 1957-60; v.p. Dodson McCutcheon Office Equipment, Morgantown, W.Va., 1960-64; asst. v.p. Nicholas County Bank, Summersville, W.Va., 1964-69, v.p., 1969-72, pres., chmn. bd., 1972—; bd. dirs., adv. bd. SBA; instr. Am. Inst. Banking. Bd. dirs. Summersville Meml. Hosp.; mem. Summersville Community Council, also mayor. Served with AUS, 1951-54. Mem. Am. (dir.), Summersville (pres.) chambers commerce, Am., W.Va. bankers assns., Ind. Bankers Am., Ind. Bankers W.Va. (Banker of Yr. 1972), VFW, Am. Legion. Republican. Presbyterian. Home: Groves Rd Canvas WV 26651 Office: Box 400 Summersville WV 26651

MCDANIEL, JAMES DAVID, bus. exec.; b. Ardmore, Okla., July 20, 1935; s. Hervey Alison and Rose Armenta (Jenkins) McD.; B.S., Central State U., Edmond, Okla., 1957; M.S., Oreg. State U., 1963; postgrad., U. Oreg., 1970-76; m. Mercedes F. Altizer, Aug. 8, 1975; children—James D., Arthur Dean Matin, Bruce, Adell, Russell, Elden. With Lebanon (Oreg.) Public Schs., 1957—, dir. community services, 1964—; with Bar J M Ranches and Farms, Lebanon, 1964—; pres. H.U.I., Inc., Lebanon, 1970—; owner Sta. KFIR, Sweet Home, Oreg., 1979—; dir. S.U., Inc. Chmn., Park Com., Elks Scholarship Com., 1960—; chmn. Library Com., 1962-70, Planning Commn., 1968-80, Strawberrians, 1967; mem. Mayor's Safety Com., 1968-74; bd. dirs. Lebanon Boys and Girls Club, Linn County chpt. ARC, R.S.V.P. Rotary fellow, 1968. Mem. C. of C. (dir.). Republican. Mem. Unity Ch. Clubs: Optimists, Elks, Moose. Home: 32849 Berlin Rd Lebanon OR 97355 Office: PO Box 602 Lebanon OR 97355

MCDANIEL, JOHN LESTER, aircraft corp. exec.; b. Guin, Ala., Sept. 13, 1918; s. Lumon Monto and Clemmie (Burleson) McD.; B.S., Berry Coll., 1939; M.S., U. Ala., 1972; D.Sc., Auburn U., 1972; LL.D., Athens State U., 1975; m. Helen Blankenship, July 16, 1949; children—John Lester, Mark, Nancy, Bonnie, Willy. Tech. dir. Army Ballistics Missile Agy., U.S. Army Redstone Arsenal, Huntsville, Ala., 1960-62, tech. dir. Army Missile Command, 1962-76, dep. comdr., tech. dir. U.S. Army Research and Devel. Command, 1976-77; sr. cons. to pres. Hughes Aircraft Co., Culver City, Calif., 1977—; adj. prof. U. Ala., 1971—, Auburn U., 1972—. Chmn., Manpower Area Planning Council, Huntsville, Ala., 1968-74. Served with USNR, 1944-46. Recipient Dept. Def. Disting. Civilian Service award, 1966. Mem. Assn. U.S. Army (chmn. Tennessee Valley chpt. 1971-72), Am. Def. Preparedness Assn. Contbr. numerous articles to profl. jours. Patentee in field guidance and control. Home: Apt 1146 4335 Marina City Dr Marina del Rey CA 90291 Office: Hughes Aircraft Co Mail Sta A126 Bldg 1 Culver City CA 90230

MCDANIEL, PRESTON WOODS, fin. planner; b. Fortuna, Mo., Aug. 31, 1916; s. Jesse Preston and Lora Woods (Atkeson) McD.; B.S., U. Mo., 1939; C.L.U., 1956; m. Gloria Ouida Dubus, Dec. 27, 1944; children—Preston Woods, Elizabeth Gayle. Farm mgr., Fortuna, 1939-41; mgr. suplus property disposition Fed. Land Bank St. Louis, 1945-46; instr., asst. to dean agr. U. Mo., 1946-47; editor Polled Hereford World, 1947-49; field rep. U.S. C. of C., 1949-50; life ins. agt., 1950-58; ind. broker-cons., life ins. agt. and fin. planner, Memphis, 1958-71; pres., owner P.W. McDaniel Co., Memphis, 1971—; lectr., condr. seminars in field. Trustee, Collins Chapel Hosp., Memphis, 1974; Republican precincy chmn., 1974-75; supt. ch. sch. Mullins United Methodist Ch., Memphis, 1978-79. Served to lt. comdr. USNR, 1941-45. Decorated D.F.C., Air medal. Mem. Internat. Assn. Fin. Planners, Inst. Cert. Fin. Planners, Am. Soc. Pension Actuaries, Am. Soc. C.L.U.'s, Photog. Soc. Am., Nat. Assn. Life Underwriters, Ret. Officers Assn., U. Mo. Alumni Assn. Clubs: Memphis Agrl., Summit, Memphis Runners and Track. Home: 5449 Normandy Ave Memphis TN 38119 Office: 5050 Poplar St Memphis TN 38157

MC DERMID, RALPH MANEWAL, lawyer; b. Chgo., Feb. 7, 1909; s. Ralph and Lillian (Manewal) McD.; Ph.B., U. Chgo., 1935; LL.B., Harvard, 1938; m. Alice Connell, Nov. 28, 1931; children—Ralph Manewal, Jr., Jane (Mrs. Anders Wiberg), Michael Metcalf, John Fairbanks. Admitted to Ill. bar, 1938, N.Y. bar, 1938, then practiced in N.Y.C.; sr. and mng. partner firm Reid & Priest, N.Y.C., 1942-73; now engaged in practice of law Fed. Cts. Central Fla. Mem. project advisory bd. Jr. League Winter Park-Orlando; bd. dirs. Morse Gallery of Art Assos. Mem. Am. Arbitration Soc. (Life Time award), Assn. Bar City N.Y., County N.Y. Bar Assn. Episcopalian. Clubs: Scarsdale Golf, Fox Meadow Tennis (Scarsdale); Harvard (N.Y.C.); Capitol Hill (Washington); Racquet, Stag, University (fin. com.) (Winter Park, Fla.). Home: 1445 Granville Dr Winter Park FL 32789 Office: 210 Park Ave N Winter Park FL 32789

MC DERMOND, JOSEPH WILLIAM, JR., indsl. traffic adminstr.; b. Carlisle, Pa., Oct. 3, 1948; s. Joseph William and Bertha Florence (Barrick) M.; A.A., Goldey Beacom Coll., 1977; m. Connie Louise Vaughn, Jan. 27, 1968; children—Joseph W. (dec.), Ami Nicole. Traffic clk. C.H. Masland & Sons, Carlisle, 1968, 69-71; traffic clk. Hercules Inc., Wilmington, Del., 1971-73, sr. rate specialist, 1973-74, asst. rate analyst, 1974-75, mgr. rate div., 1975-79, mgr. rates, 1979, mgr. traffic services, 1979—; cons. in field. Served with U.S. Army, 1968-69. Decorated Bronze Star. Mem. Traffic Club Wilmington, Shippers Nat. Freight Claim Council, Fertilizer Inst. (transp. com.), Pulp Chem. Assn. (transp. com.), 101st Airborne Div. Assn. Republican. Lutheran. Club: Captain's Cove Golf and Yacht. Home: 18 Lochcarron Dr Newark DE 19711 Office: 910 Market St Wilmington DE 19899

MC DERMOTT, IDARUTH MITCHELL (MRS. EDWARD BRIAN MCDERMOTT), business exec.; b. Hingham, Mass., Oct. 9, 1921; d. Henry Forrester and Rebecca (Gerrold) Mitchell; B.A., Radcliffe Coll., 1938; postgrad. N.Y. Inst. Fin., 1940, Am. Inst. Banking, 1942; m. Edward Brian McDermott, Feb. 11, 1939; children—Brian Emerson, Bruce Burnham, Diane Lee. Acting head investment dept., adminstrv. asst. to the trust officer Comml. Nat. Bank & Trust Co., N.Y.C., 1939-49; adminstrv. asst. to the dir. sales promotion 1966-70, adminstrv. asst. to pres., 1970-74, corporate sec.-treas. Specialized Components, Inc.; owner McDermott's Surgi-Clip, Inc. Mem. N.Y. Soc. Security Analysts, Nat. Soc. DAR. Address: 23 Flower Ln Manhasset NY 11030

MC DERMOTT, ROBERT HOGAN, ins. co. exec.; b. Mpls., May 22, 1931; s. James Francis and Corrine Marie (Hogan) McD.; B.A., U. Minn., 1953; postgrad. Georgetown U., 1953-57; m. Caroline I. Hewson; children—Timothy Forbes, Martha Levering. Pres., chief exec. officer McDermott Ins., Inc., Washington, 1959—; mem. Lloyd's of London. Mem. central com. D.C. Republican Com., 1975-77, chmn. fin. com., 1976-77; alt. del. Rep. Nat. Conv., 1976.

Served with USNR, 1955-57. Mem. Met. Washington Assn. Ins. Agts., Sigma Alpha Epsilon. Roman Catholic. Clubs: Met., Congressional Country. Home: 1601 28th St NW Washington DC 20007 Office: McDermott Ins Inc 888 17th St NW Washington DC 20008

MC DEVITT, DANIEL BERNARD, fin. exec.; b. Pocatello, Idaho, Apr. 14, 1927; s. Bernard Aloysius and Margaret Helen (Gallagher) McD.; student Idaho State U., 1944, 46-47; B.S., U. Idaho, 1950; Sc.D. (hon.), U. Karachi, 1966, Riyadh U., 1977; m. Mary Ann Bohrer, June 14, 1952. Engr., Gen. Electric Co., Erie, Pa., 1950-54, systems sales engr., Cleve., 1954-56, central region mgr. power and control systems, Cleve. and Chgo., 1956-59; mgr. mktg. Nelson Electric, Tulsa, 1959-62; partner Dan B. McDevitt & Assos., Tulsa, 1962—; pres. I-C Computer Corp., N.Y.C., 1967-69; exec. partner Manhattan-McDevitt Progress Engring. & Wallace Ltd., Tulsa, 1975—; pres. Research & Devel. Inst. U.S., Tulsa, 1965—; chmn., pres. ICM Computer Corp., Tulsa, 1970—; chmn., chief exec. officer Ethanol Mktg. & Refining Ltd., Tulsa, 1979—; pres. Progress Engring. & Cons. Enterprises, Tulsa, 1965—; treas. Ace-Hi Equipment, Tulsa and Oklahoma City, 1978—; partner Saudi-Am. Metal Fabricating Co., Al-Jubail, Saudi Arabia, 1978—; chmn. King Khalid City Devel. Co., Ar-Riyadh, Saudi Arabia, 1976—; dir. Saudi-Am. Constrn. Co., Saudi-Am. Woodworking Co., Saudi-Am. Transp. Co., Saudi-Am. Equipment Co.; cons. Econ. Devel. Adminstrn., 1966-67, State Dept., 1962-66, AID, Pakistan, 1963-64. Chmn., First Select Acad., Govt. and Bus. Regional Conf., 1966-67, U.S. Council on Environ., 1970—, Coalition for Clean Air, 1970—; mem. bd. Okla. Commn. on Re-Orgn. State Exec., 1971-74; mem. evaluation council Commn. on Re-orgn. Okla. Computers and Communications, 1972-74. Served with USMCR, 1944-46, 50-51. Recipient spl. commendation King Feisal Air Acad., 1975; registered profl. engr., Ark., Okla., Tex. Mem. IEEE, Nat. Soc. Profl. Engrs., AAAS. Democrat. Roman Catholic. Clubs: Petroleum, Elks, K.C. Contbr. articles to profl. jours. Office: PO Drawer 7220 Tulsa OK 74105

MC DONALD, ALONZO LOWRY, bus. exec.; b. Atlanta, Aug. 5, 1928; s. Alonzo Lowry and Lois (Burrell) McD.; A.B., Emory U., 1948; M.B.A., Harvard, 1956; m. Suzanne Moffitt, May 9, 1959; children—Kenneth Alexander, Denise Carrie, Jennifer Wynn, Hans Peter Lowry. Asst. to sales mgr. air conditioning div. Westinghouse Electric Corp., Staunton, Va., 1956-57, Western zone mgr., St. Louis, 1957-60; asso. N.Y. Office, McKinsey & Co., Inc., 1960-64, prin. London Office, 1964-66, mng. prin. Zurich Office, 1966-68, mng. dir. Paris Office, 1968-73, mng. dir. firm, N.Y.C., 1973-76, dir. N.Y. office, 1976-77; dep. spl. trade rep., also ambassador in charge U.S. del. Tokyo round of Multilateral Trade Negotiations in Geneva, 1977-79, acting spl. trade rep., 1979; asst. to pres. U.S., White House staff dir., 1979-81; sr. lectr. Grad. Sch. Bus. Adminstrn., Harvard U., 1981—. Vis. com. on adminstrn. Harvard U. Served with USMCR, 1950-52. Mem. Council on Fgn. Relations, Com. for Econ. Devel. (trustee), U.S. Council of Internat. C. of C. (exec. com.), Adv. Council on U.S.-Japan Econ. Relations. Home: 3228 Woodley Rd NW Washington DC 20008 Office: Morgan 204 Harvard Bus Sch Soldiers Field Boston MA 02163

MC DONALD, AUBREY BARTON (MRS. JONAS BARENHOLTZ), jewelry co. exec.; b. LayFayette, Tenn., Aug. 7, 1911; d. William Dobson and Dona May (Miller) Barton; student Murfreesboro State U., 1933-34, Watkins Bus. Coll., Nashville, 1937-38, Vanderbilt Extension Sch., 1939-40; m. Paul Roy McDonald, Dec. 23, 1933 (div. Apr. 1955); 1 dau., Judy (Mrs. Duane Barnes); m. 2d, Jonas Barenholtz, Oct. 7, 1969. Co-founder Fashion Two Twenty, Inc., cosmetics firm, Aurora, Ohio, 1962, exec. v.p., 1962-76; chmn. bd. Paradise Jewelry, Inc., 1977—. Club: Akron Woman's. Home: 80 N Portage Path Akron OH 44303 Office: 565 Wolf Ledges Pkwy Akron OH 44311

MC DONALD, CLARENCE JACKSON, lawyer, mfg. co. exec.; b. Junction, Tex., Dec. 12, 1926; s. Clarence Grenville and Minnie Ila (Dunning) McD.; B.S., Trinity U. at San Antonio, 1950; J.D., So. Meth. U., 1966; m. Barbara June Kennon, May 9, 1950; children—Zane J., Laurie Jill. Electronics engr. San Antonio Air Material Command, 1950-54; chief engr. Mathes Co., Marble Falls, Tex., 1954-62; exec. v.p. Folsom Co., Dallas, 1962-66; admitted to Tex. bar, 1966, since practiced privately in Dallas; pres., co-founder Electric Products Mfg. Corp., Mesquite, Tex., 1968-74; gen. mgr. Sundial plant Square D Co., 1974-78; chmn. bd. Planned Energy Systems, Inc., Mesquite, 1979—. Served with USNR, 1942-44; PTO. Mem. IEEE. Methodist. Clubs: Masons, Shriners, Kiwanis. Patentee in field. Home: 1100 Lakeshore Dr Mesquite TX 75149 Office: 2211 Gross Rd Mesquite TX 75150

MC DONALD, DAVID THOMAS, found. exec.; b. Teaneck, N.J., May 23, 1933; s. John Francis and Mary Agnes (Flannigan) McD.; B.S. in Mktg., St. Peter's Coll., Jersey City, 1955; postgrad. Pace Coll., Seton U. Grad. Sch. Bus.; m. Janice Faye McFarland, May 14, 1977; children—David Francis, Damian Wylie. Public mcpl. auditor Conroy Smith & Co., C.P.A.'s, N.Y.C., 1957-60; from mgmt. trainee to agt. Allstate Ins. Co., Murray Hill, N.J., 1960-66; with Ford Found., 1966—, dir. taxes and ins., risk mgr., N.Y.C., 1973—. Served to 1st lt. AUS, 1955-57. Mem. Risk and Ins. Mgmt. Soc.; asso. Ins. Inst. Am. Republican. Episcopalian. Home: Lexington House Fort Hill Village Scarsdale NY 10583 Office: 320 E 43d St New York NY 10017

MC DONALD, FRANCIS JAMES, automobile co. exec.; b. Saginaw, Mich., Aug. 3, 1922; s. Francis J. and Mary C. (Fordney) McD.; grad. Gen. Motors Inst., 1944; student Yale U.; m. Betty Ann Dettenthaler, Dec. 27, 1944; children—Timothy Joseph, John Thomas, Marybeth McDonald Pallas. With Saginaw Malleable Iron Plant (Mich.); works mgr. Pontiac Motor div. Gen. Motors, Pontiac, Mich., 1965, dir. mfg. ops. Chevrolet Motor div., gen. mgr. Pontiac Motor div., v.p., 1969, mem. adminstrn. com., 1969, gen. mgr. Chevrolet Motor div., 1972, exec. v.p., dir., 1974, mem. exec. com., with power products group, 1978—, mem. fin. com., 1979, pres., chief operating officer, Detroit, 1981—; bd. dirs., mem. exec. compensation and audit coms. H. J. Heinz Co. Chmn., Research Inst., William Beaumont Hosp., Royal Oak, Mich.; exec. v.p. bd. trustees hosp., Troy, Mich.; v.p. Boys' Clubs; bd. dirs. Up with People; chmn. bd. visitors Sch. Econs. and Mgmt., Oakland U., Rochester, Mich. Served to lt. (j.g.) U.S. Navy, 1944-46. Mem. Soc. Automotive Engrs., Engring. Soc. Detroit, Detroit Athletic Club, Tau Beta Pi. Office: 3044 W Grand Blvd Detroit MI 48202

MC DONALD, HUGH RODERICK, lawyer; b. Brookville, Ont., Can., Mar. 31, 1929; s. Alexander Joseph and Margaret Isobel (McHenry) McD.; B.Comm., U. Ottawa, 1954; Barrister-at-law, Osgoode Hall, 1960; m. Joan Dorothy Gourley, Oct. 6, 1962; 1 son, Patrick Joseph. Called to bar, 1960; asso. firm Low, Honeywell, Murchison, Burns, 1960-70; individual practice law, Nepean, Ont., 1970-78; partner firm McDonald & Landry, Nepean, 1978—. Mem. Nepean Twp. Hydro Commn., 1968-76, chmn., 1971; alderman City of Nepean, 1978—; sec. Ottawa-Centre Liberal Assn., 1962-79. Served to Lt. Royal Can. Navy, 1946-51, 54-56. Mem. Can. Bar Assn., Law Soc. Upper Can., Carleton County Law Assn., Nepean C. of C., Delta Chi. Liberal Party. Roman Catholic. Clubs: Kiwanis, Can. Home: 5 Tower Rd Nepean ON K2G 1E2 Canada Office: 1511 Merivale Rd Nepean ON K2G 3J3 Canada

MC DONALD, JACK HENRY, fin. cons.; b. Pratt, Kans., July 16, 1910; s. John Dennis and Florence (Krieger) McD.; A.B., Kans. U., 1933; m. Loraine Cameron; children—Sara, Sally, William D., Sandra. Partner, Fink Abstract & Title Co., Fredonia, Kans., 1933-36; sec. Home Bldg. & Loan Assn., Fredonia, 1936-42; sec. Investors Savs. & Loan Assn., 1946-49, pres., 1950-61, chmn., 1961-72; pres. Imperial Corp. of Am., 1966-72, chmn. bd., dir., 1972-73; pres. Jack H. McDonald Co., La Jolla, Calif.; partner Chamorro Gardens, Guam; dir. Investors Mortgage Ins. Co., Boston, Burnham Am. Fund San Diego, Center City Corp., San Diego; chmn. bd. Western Security Fin. Inc., Irvine, Calif. Bd. dirs. Tournament of Roses. Served as lt. comdr. USNR, 8th Fleet, N. African-Mediterranean waters, 1942-45. Mem. Los Angeles County Group Savs. and Loan Execs. (past pres.), Nat. Savs. and Loan League (past dir.), Calif. Savs. and Loan League (past dir.), Kappa Sigma. Clubs: Univ., Annandale Golf (Pasadena); Shady Oaks Country (Ft. Worth); Calif. (Los Angeles); La Jolla Country. Home: 1001 Genter La Jolla CA 92037 Office: 8552 MacArthur Blvd Suite 300 Irvine CA 92715

MC DONALD, JOHN JOSEPH MACALLISTER, process control co. exec.; b. Chgo., Sept. 1, 1922; s. John Joseph MacAllister and Mary Inez (O'Brien) McD.; B.S., U. Chgo., 1939; B.S. in Elec. Engring., Ill. Inst. Tech., 1940; spl. courses bus. adminstrn. Harvard, 1950-52; m. Marie Elenore Vorder, Sept 7, 1942. Regional mgr. Consol. Electrodynamics Corp., Pasadena, Cal., 1950-52, dir. systems div., 1952-54; v.p., asst. gen. mgr. Consol. Systems Corp., Monrovia, Calif., 1954-61; v.p., gen. mgr. computer div. Packard Bell Electronics, Los Angeles, 1961-66; pres. Canterbury, Inc., Alhambra, Cal., 1966-68; gen. mgr. aircraft instrument div. Bissett-Berman Corp., Santa Monica, Calif., 1968—; v.p., gen. mgr. United Process Control Systems, Santa Fe Springs, Calif., 1970—; v.p. Cavitron Corp., 1970-76; pres. Britt Corp., 1976—; cons. Borg-Warner Computer Control Corp. Fellow Instrument Soc. Am. (sect. pres. 1962-63, dist. v.p. 1964-65, nat. v.p. sci. and industries 1966-67). Contbr. articles to profl. jours. Home: 610 Canterbury Rd San Marino CA 91108 Office: 9419 Ann St Santa Fe Springs CA 90670

MCDONALD, MALCOLM WALKER, bus. exec.; b. Dedham, Mass., Aug. 4, 1920; s. James Francis and Maria Genevieve (McLane) McD.; student pub. schs.; m. Mary P. Lally, June 28, 1947; children—John Patrick, Peter Jude, Mary Louise, Sara Ann, Paula. With the Boston (Mass.) Naval Base, 1939-48; salesman Nat. Telephone Directory Corp. (formerly Von Hoffmann Corp.), Boston, 1948, sales mgr., 1948-53, gen. sales mgr. N.J., 1953-58, v.p., 1958-63, exec. v.p., 1963-66, pres., 1966—, also dir.; pres., dir. Victory Broadcasting Corp., N.J., 1968-78. Served from pvt. to capt., AUS, 1942-46, ETO. Clubs: Seaview Country (Absecon, N.J.), Oyster Harbors (Osterville, Mass.); Tavistock Country (Haddonfield, N.J.). Home: 340 Knoll Top Ln Haddonfield NJ 08033 Office: 1050 Galloping Hill Rd Union NJ 07083

MC DONALD, MARSHALL, utility exec.; b. Memphis, Mar. 30, 1918; s. Marshall and Nadine (Hardin) McD.; B.S. in Bus. Adminstrn., U. Fla., 1939, LL.B., 1941; M.B.A., Wharton Grad. Sch. U. Pa., 1947; m. Florence Harris, Jan. 10, 1952 (dec. Nov. 1963); m. 2d, Lucille Smoak Collins, May 7, 1965 (dec. Sept. 1980); children—Mary Linda (Mrs. Donald Caton), Charles M. Collins, Cynthia (Mrs. H.T. Langston, Jr.), Marshall III, Roger Collins, Davis James D. Admitted to Fla. bar, 1941; Tex. bar, 1949; accountant, Houston, 1947-49; atty., Houston, 1950-52; treas. Gulf Canal Lines, 1953-54; pres. Investment Co. Houston, 1955-58; v.p., Sinclair Oil & Gas Co., Tulsa, 1959-61; v.p., gen. mgr. Oil Recovery Corp., Tulsa, 1962-63; asst. to pres. Pure Oil Co., Palatine, Ill., 1964-65; dir. affiliated cos. Union Oil Co., Los Angeles, 1966-68; pres. Sully-Miller Contracting Co., Los Angeles, 1968-71; pres., chief exec. officer Fla. Power & Light Co., Miami, 1971-79, chmn. bd., chief exec. officer, 1979—. C.P.A., Tex. Served with AUS, 1941-46. Mem. Am. Bar Assn., Am. Inst. C.P.A.'s, Alpha Tau Omega. Republican. Presbyn. Mason. Office: 9250 W Flagler St Miami FL 33174 also PO Box 529100 Miami FL 33152

MCDONALD, PEYTON DEAN, stockbroker; b. Kansas City, Kans., Feb. 6, 1936; s. Charles H. and Myra (Miller) McD.; student Bucknell U., 1954-58, Inst. Fin., 1967-68; m. Frances B. Beighley, June 14, 1958; children—Peyton D., Todd B. Sales rep. Sprout Waldron & Co., Inc., Muncy, Pa., 1958-67; office mgr. Blair & Co., Inc., Williamsport, Pa., 1967-69; v.p., mgr., dir., analyst Hugh Johnson & Co., Inc., Williamsport, 1969-78; v.p. and mgr. E.F. Hutton & Co., 1978—. Campaign chmn. Lycoming United Way, 1975, pres., 1979, 80; pres. Vis. Nurses Assn., Soc. for Mentally Retarded, Sch. of Hope; trustee Covenant Central Presbyn. Ch., also sec., pres. session. Served to 1st lt., inf., AUS, 1958-59. Republican. Clubs: Williamsport, Ross. Home: 1545 Grampian Blvd Williamsport PA 17701 Office: 213 W 4th St Williamsport PA 17701

MC DONALD, WARREN J., health care exec.; b. St. Louis, Jan. 11, 1951; s. John Hall and Mary Louise (Acree) McD.; B.A. in Psychology, U. Ark., 1974, M.B.A. in Fin., 1978. Juvenile probation officer Washington County (Ark.), 1972-73; paramedic Washington Regional Med. Center, Fayatteville, Ark., 1973-78, dir. emergency med. services, 1978-79; dir. Central Emergency Med. Service, Fayetteville Ark., 1980—; bd. dirs. Mid-Am. State Rural Emergency Med. Services Council; dir. N.W. Ark. Resource Coordination Center; chmn. adv. bd. Washington County Emergency Service; adv. bd. Home Health Services Ark.; bd. dirs. Vis. Nurses Assn. Ark.; mem. bd. control N.W. Ark. Spl. Olympics. Mem. Nat. Registry Emergency Med. Technicians, Sigma Iota Epsilon, N.W. Ark. Ducks Unlimited. Clubs: Washington County Razorback, U. Ark. Alumni, Lambda Chi Alpha Alumni. Home: 1419 N Leverett St Fayetteville AR 72701 Office: 614 N College Ave Fayetteville AR 72701

MC DONELL, HORACE GEORGE, JR., electronics co. exec.; b. N.Y.C., Sept. 23, 1928; s. Horace Gustave and Anabel (Armstrong) McD.; A.B., Adelphi Coll., 1952; postgrad. Harvard, 1962; m. Eileen Romar, Sept. 6, 1952; children—Victoria, Diane, Horace. Engr., Sperry Gyroscope Co., N.Y.C., 1952; with Perkin-Elmer Corp., Norwalk, Conn., 1963—, mgr. instrument group, 1967-77, v.p., 1966-69, sr. v.p., 1969-77, exec. v.p., 1977-80, pres., chief operating officer, 1980—, also dir.; dir. Hitachi-Perkin Elmer, Ltd. (Japan), Perkin-Elmer Ltd. (U.K.), Perkin Elmer Internat., Inc. Mem. adv. task force on export controls U.S. Def. Sci. Bd., 1975—, chmn. instrumentation subcom., 1975—. Mem. Bd. Edn., Ridgefield, Conn., 1969. Bd. dirs. Conn. Sci. Fair. Trustee, bd. dirs. Danbury (Conn.) Hosp. Served with AUS, 1946-48. Mem. Sci. Apparatus Makers Assn. (dir., chmn. analytical instrument sect.), Am. Inst. Physics, AAAS, Instrument Soc. Am. Home: Powder Horn Dr Ridgefield CT 06877 Office: Perkin-Elmer Corp Main Ave Norwalk CT

MC DONELL, WILLIAM FRANCIS, mfg. co. exec.; b. Los Angeles, June 10, 1950; s. Myron Alexander and Beatrice Lucille (Klatt) McD.; A.A. in Electronics, Rio Hondo Coll., 1971; B.S. in Indsl. Tech., Calif. State U., Long Beach, 1973, cert. in facilities ops., 1980; postgrad. U. So. Calif., 1975. Grad. mfg. rotation program Hughes Aircraft Co., El Segundo, Calif., 1973-74, mfg. engr., 1974-77, facilities planning engr., Fullerton, Calif., 1977-79; facilities mgr. Printronix, Inc., Irvine, Calif., 1979—. Republican. Roman Catholic. Club: Columbian (past pres., v.p. 1973-75). Home: 104 Orchard St Irvine CA 92714 Office: PO Box 19559 Irvine CA 92713

MCDONNELL, JAMES JOSEPH, design and constrn. co. exec.; b. Erie, Pa., Oct. 30, 1952; s. Thomas Joseph and Violet Mary (Roncevic) McD.; student Villa Maria Coll., 1980. Salesman, W.T. Grant Co., Erie, 1970-71, dept. mgr., 1971-73, mgr. trainee, 1973-74, sect. mgr., 1974, asst. store mgr., 1975-76; v.p., treas. Swim Town, Inc., Erie, 1978—. Recipient Cert. of Achievement, W.T. Grant Co., 1973, 75, Nat. Jaycees, 1979. Mem. Nat. Fedn. Ind. Bus., Nat. Swimming Pool Inst. Republican. Roman Catholic. Home: 2916 Berkley Ave Erie PA 16506 Office: 1028 W 22d St Erie PA 16502

MCDONNELL, SANFORD NOYES, aircraft co. exec.; b. Little Rock, Oct. 12, 1922; s. William Archie and Carolyn (Cherry) McD.; B.A. in Econs., Princeton, 1945; B.S. in Mech. Engring., U. Colo., 1948; M.S. in Applied Mechanics, Washington U., St. Louis, 1954; m. Priscilla Robb, Sept. 3, 1946; children—Robbin (Mrs. Hallock), William Randall. With McDonnell Douglas Corp., St. Louis, 1948—, v.p., 1959-66, pres. McDonnell Aircraft Co. div., 1966-71, exec. v.p. parent co., 1971, pres. parent co., 1971—, chief exec. officer, 1972—, also dir.; dir. 1st Union, Inc. Mem. nat. exec. bd. Boy Scouts Am.; active United Fund. Fellow AIAA; mem. Aerospace Industries Assn. (gov.), Tau Beta Pi. Presbyterian (elder). Office: McDonnell Douglas Corp PO Box 516 Saint Louis MO 63166

MC DONOUGH, HENRY CARROLL, fin. mgmt. cons.; b. Balt., Mar. 24, 1948; s. John Martin and Norton (Carroll) McD.; B.A., Princeton U., 1970; M.B.A., U. Va., 1978. Registered rep. C.T. Williams & Co., Balt., 1971-73; instl. securities analyst Alex, Brown & Sons, Balt., 1973-75; pres. McDonough & Co., Inc., Balt., 1978—. Club: Cap and Gown. Home: 14936 Carroll Rd Sparks MD 21152 Office: #3000 2322 N Charles St Baltimore MD 21218

MC DONOUGH, JAMES EDWIN, internat. sales and mktg. exec.; b. Bremerton, Wash., Dec. 5, 1922; s. James E. and Delia Augusta (Ewing) McD.; student U. Wash., 1941-43; student U. Mich., 1943-44; m. Sara Barringer Andrews, Aug. 15, 1944; children—James Edwin, William A., Barri B., Robert M. Gen. mgr. Barclay & Co., Japan, 1948-56; Far East rep. Seagram Overseas Sales Co., Hong Kong, 1956-63, dir. export, Montreal, 1963-65, v.p., N.Y.C., 1965-68, pres., N.Y.C., 1968—; former pres., dir. Far East-Am. Council Commerce and Industry; dir. numerous Seagram affiliated cos.; mem. com. comml. policy N.Y. Regional Export Expansion; mem. council U.S. Dept. Commerce. Served to lt., M.I., AUS, 1942-48; PTO. Mem. Internat. C. of C. (U.S. council), Distilled Spirits Inst. Republican. Episcopalian. Clubs: Tokyo Am., Hong Kong Golf, Sheko o Golf and Country. Office: 375 Park Ave New York NY 10152

MC DONOUGH, ROBERT EMMETT, JR., health services co. exec.; b. Washington, July 6, 1950; s. Robert Emmett and Elsa May (Carlson) McD.; B.A., Occidental Coll., Los Angeles, 1973; J.D.L. (Univ. fellow, Nat. Lawyers Guild grantee, Editorial scholar, U. San Diego, 1976; m. Jadwiga Praksa, Sept. 19, 1971; 1 son, David John. Admitted to Calif. bar, 1976; asst. counsel Nat. Treasury Employees Union, San Francisco, 1976-77; counsel Tempo Temp. Services, San Juan Capistrano, Calif., 1977-79; counsel, corp. adminstr., dir. Remedy Temp. Services, also Remedy Home and Health Care, San Juan Capistrano, 1979—; v.p. Remedy Health Services, 1980—. Mem. Am. Bar Assn., Calif. Bar Assn. Roman Catholic. Office: 32122 Camino Capistrano San Juan Capistrano CA 92675

MC DOUGALL, GEORGE DOUGLAS, cons.; b. Indpls., July 20, 1930; s. Shirley Alton and Deborah Cleveland (Hall) McD.; student Asbury Coll., 1949-51, Mt. San Antonio Coll., 1960-61, Milw. Sch. Engring., 1977, Calif. State Poly. U., 1978; m. Maria Celia Velasquez, Aug. 4, 1956. Surveyor, Tidelands Exploration Co., Houston, 1954; with Vard, Inc., Pasadena, Calif., 1954-60, Gen. Dynamics, Pomona, Calif., 1960-62; researcher Aerojet Gen. Corp., Azusa, Calif., 1962-68; engr. Davidson Optonics, West Covina, Calif., 1968-69; mfg. mgr. Angeles Metal Systems, Los Angeles, 1969-79; cons. Fremont Gen. Corp., Los Angeles, 1979—; mem. automation research project Inst. Indsl. Relations, U. So. Calif., 1966-68. Adv. bd. Automobile Club So. Calif., 1966-71; bd. dirs. St. Martha's Episcopal Sch., West Covina, 1978-79; lic. lay reader Episcopal Diocese of Los Angeles; vestryman St. Martha's Episc. Ch., West Covina, 1969-70, 77-79, 81—; gen. conv. del. Episc. Diocese of Los Angeles, 1970-78; instnl. rep. Boy Scouts Am., 1978-79, coordinator San Gabriel Valley council, 1978-79. Served with JAGC, AUS, 1951-53; Korea. Cert. in mfg. engring., Canadian Council Profl. Cert., 1977; lic. profl. engr., Calif. Mem. Soc. Mfg. Engrs. (cert.), Nat. Soc. Profl. Engrs., Calif. Soc. Profl. Engrs., Computer and Automated Systems Assn. (charter), St. Andrews Soc. Los Angeles, Town Hall Calif., S.A.R. Republican. Clubs: Masons, Shriners. Home: PO Box 848 Azusa CA 91702 Office: 1709 W 8th St Los Angeles CA 90017

MCDOWELL, ANGUS, cons.; b. Redhill, Eng., Mar. 28, 1946; came to U.S., 1974; s. Horace John and Una (Ferguson) McD.; A.C.A., Inst. Chartered Accts. in Eng. and Wales, 1969; M.S. in Bus. Policy, Columbia U., 1978. From articled clk. to sr. acct. Ernst & Whinney, London, 1964-70; mgmt. acct. P&O Steam Navigation, London, 1971; chief acct. travel and transp. div. Grindlays Internat. Banking Group, London, 1972-74; treas., gen. mgr., dir. M&J Comml., Inc., N.Y.C., 1974-79; partner AECC (Am. European Cons. Co.), N.Y.C., 1980—. Fellow Inst. Chartered Accts. Eng. and Wales; mem. N.Y. Assn. Chartered Accts. (co-founder; chmn. 1980—), Am. Mgmt. Assn. C.P.A., N.Y. Office: AECC 300 E 40 St New York NY 10016

MCELRATH, LENZA, constrn. co. exec.; b. Cleve., Dec. 23, 1930; s. Roy and Anna Bell (Cunningham) McE.; student Fenn Coll., 1957-59, Case Western Res. U., 1970; m. Lula Embry, Dec. 5, 1957; children—Grace, Jeannette, Belinda, Lenza, Kenneth, Ronald, Gloria, Lenee, Lawerence, Lambert. With H.K. Ferguson, Cleve., 1956, Austin Co., Cleve., 1958, Turner Constrn. Co., Cleve., 1963-70; founder, owner, pres. Mac's Constrn. Co., Cleve., 1970—; chmn. bd. L-Mac Enterprises, Inc. Leader, Democratic Ward Com., 1965-69; supt. Sunday Sch., 1960-72. Served with AUS, 1950-56. Mem. Cleve. constrn. Assn. (past dir.), Cleve. Minority Contractors (past dir.), Cleve. Bldg. Trade Employers Assn., Cleve. Bus. League. Clubs: Masons, Old Angle Athletic (chmn. bd.), 21st Congl. Dist. Caucus, Inc. Home: 1737 Cumberland Rd Cleveland Heights OH 44118 Office: 1115 E 114th St Cleveland OH 44108

MC ELVAIN, DAVID PLOWMAN, capital goods corp. exec.; b. Chgo., Oct. 16, 1937; s. Carl R. and Ruth P. (Plowman) McE.; B.B.A., U. Ariz., 1961, M.B.A., 1962; m. Mary Rosalind Hysong, Dec. 20, 1961; children—Jana, Jodi. Consolidation accountant, exec. div. Dresser Industries, Inc., Dallas, 1962-67, corporate fin. controller, 1973-76, dir. fin. services, 1976-78, staff v.p. fin. service and risk mgmt., 1978—, controller crane, hoist & tower div., Muskegon, Mich., 1967-73. Mem. Nat. Assn. Accountants (pres. Dallas chpt.), Inst. Mgmt. Acctg. (regent), Beta Gamma Sigma, Phi Delta Theta. Episcopalian. Home: 3806 Beverly Dallas TX 75205 Office: PO Box 718 Dallas TX 75201

MCELWAIN, JOHN ALLEN, printing co. exec.; b. Chgo., July 7, 1901; s. Frank and Bertha (Thompson) McE.; student Dartmouth Coll., 1920-22, Northwestern U., 1923; m. Jane Catherine McKenna, Apr. 3, 1926; children—Edward Frank, Phyllis Jane (Mrs. Richard Forward), John Allen IV. Tool draftsman Miehle Printing Press Corp., Chgo., 1923-24; rodman Chgo. North Shore & Milw. R.R., Chgo., 1924; circulation mgr. Toys and Novelties, Am. Artisan, Chgo., N.Y.C., 1925-27; sales engr. U.S. Gypsum Co., Chgo., 1927-33; owner John A. McElwain & Co., Chgo., 1933—. Trustee Hinsdale (Ill.) San. Dist., 1949—, pres., 1957—, Regional Water Reclamation Facility named in honor, 1978; chmn. DuPage County Drainage Com., 1955-56; precinct committeeman DuPage County Republican Com., 1940-60. Mem. Ill. Assn. San. Dist. Trustees (pres. 1960-61, 79-80, recipient Ill. award 1979), Chgo. Tennis Assn. (dir. 1942-52, pres. 1949), Kappa Sigma. Club: Hinsdale (Ill.) Golf Home: 714 S Washington St Hinsdale IL 60521 Office: 231 S Green St Chicago IL 60607

MCELWEE, JOHN GERARD, life ins. co. exec.; b. Port Bannatyne, Scotland, Dec. 19, 1921; s. James and Margaret (Fitzgerald) McE.; came to U.S., 1925, naturalized, 1935; student Boston Coll., 1939-42, LL.B., 1950; grad. advanced mgmt. program Harvard U. Sch. Bus., 1960; m. Barbara Sullivan, Mar. 31, 1951; children—Neal, Janet, Sheila, Brian. With John Hancock Mut. Life Ins. Co., Boston, 1945—, asst. sec., 1957-61, 2d v.p., 1961-65, v.p., 1965-71, sr. v.p., sec., 1972-74, exec. v.p., sec., 1974-79, pres., 1979—, dir., 1976—; dir. New Eng. Merchants Nat. Bank Boston, New Eng. Merchants Co., Cooper Industries, Inc.; dir., past chmn. Ins. Inst., Northeastern U. Trustee Univ. Hosp., Citizenship Tng. Group, Inc., Boston Coll., Radcliffe Coll.; mem. trustee council Boston U. Med. Center; past dir., past pres. Big Brother Assn. Boston. Served with USN, 1941-45. Roman Catholic. Clubs: Algonquin, Winchester Country; Univ., Comml. (Boston). Office: John Hancock Pl PO Box 111 Boston MA 02117

MC ENROE, PATRICIA SOLON, land mgmt. investor; b. Algona, Iowa, Nov. 19, 1922; d. John Edward and Kathryn Leone (Solon) McE.; student Briar Cliff Coll., 1942-44; B.M.E., Northwestern U., 1948. With Iowa Sch. for Braille and Sight Saving, Vinton, 1948-51, Chgo. Day Sch., 1951-52, Chgo. Bd. Edn., 1952-54; tchr. music and sci. Dover (Minn.) Consol. Schs., 1954-55; music supr. Fountain (Colo.) Pub. Schs.; rep. Chgo. Archdiocese, Chgo. Pub. Schs., 1965-70; investor land in Iowa, Ariz., Calif. and Fla., also investor oil explorations. Recreational dir., Evanston, Ill., 1948, Algona, 1951; founder Kossuth County Democratic Women's Club, 1962; participant Iowa Women's Polit. Caucus. Mem. AAUW, Kossuth County Hist. Soc., Themis Soc., Delphian Soc., NOW, Dorian Soc., Rochester Civic Music Guild. Roman Catholic. Clubs: Ill. Cath. for Women, Sheil. Composer: Rhapsody Ragtime Blues, 1973. Home: 408 N Thorington St Algona IA 50511

MC EVERS, ROBERT DARWIN, banker; b. Washington, May 18, 1930; s. John Henry and Beatrice (Holton) McE.; B.S. with distinction, U.S. Naval Acad., 1952; M.B.A. with distinction, Harvard, 1958; m. Joan Manning, Mar. 29, 1954; children—Robert Darwin, Allison Holton. With First Nat. Bank of Chgo., 1958-61; spl. asst., exec. offices Trans Union Corp. (formerly Union Tank Car Co.), Chgo., 1961-64, gen. mgr. Canadian subs., Toronto, Ont., 1964, asst. to pres., Chgo., 1964-65, v.p., gen. mgr. Tank Car div., 1965-70, pres., 1970-73; v.p. Trans Union Corp., 1965-73, dir., 1966-73; sr. v.p. First Nat. Bank Chgo., 1973-75, head trust dept., 1974-77, exec. v.p., 1975—, head exec. dept., 1977-81, head bldg./security dept., 1981—; pres. Fort Dearborn Income Securities, Inc., 1973-77; dir. Marquette Co., Cooper Industries, Inc., Reading Industries, AMFUND. Bd. dirs. YMCA Community Coll. Served to 1st lt. USAF, 1952-56. Mem. Am. Mgmt. Assn., Chgo. Council Fgn. Relations, Newcomen Soc. N.Am., Beta Theta Pi. Clubs: Economic, Mid-Am., University (Chgo.); Army-Navy Country (Arlington, Va.); Kenilworth (Ill.); Indian Hill (Winnetka, Ill.). Home: 48 Kenilworth Ave Kenilworth IL 60043 Office: 1 First National Plaza Chicago IL 60670

MC EVOY, CHARLES LUCIEN, printing co. exec.; b. Bradford, Pa., Sept. 2, 1917; s. L. Carle and Mary Ellen (McMahon) McE.; A.B., Xavier U., 1938; postgrad. Georgetown U., 1938-41; J.D., Chgo. Kent Coll. Law, 1950; m. Rosemary C. Rocca, Sept. 2, 1947. With Neo Gravure Co. Chgo., 1947-54, gen. mgr., 1952-54; v.p. sales Cuneo Press, Inc., Chgo., 1954-67, exec. v.p., 1967-73, pres., 1973—, also dir. Served with AUS, 1942-46; PTO. Clubs: Chgo. Athletic Assn., Chgo. Golf; N.Y. Athletic. Home: 3000 N Sheridan Dr Chicago IL 60657 Office: Two N Riverside Plaza Suite 1160 Chicago IL 60606

MC EVOY, RICHARD FRANKLIN, forest products co. exec.; b. Litchfield, Ill., Dec. 27, 1946; s. John William and Genevieve-Ann (McCarthy) McE.; B.A., Lehigh U., 1968; A.P., Sloan Sch. Mgmt., 1970; m. Margaret Ruth Drummond, Dec. 27, 1977. Retail rep. Shell Oil Co., Scarsdale, N.Y., 1968-72; mktg. mgr. Sunset Life Ins. Co., Olympia, Wash., 1972-73; quality audit supr. Weyerhaeuser Co., Springfield, Oreg., 1974-77; asst. gen. mgr. Miller Redwood Co., Crescent City, Calif., 1978-80; asst. pres. Stimson Lumber Co., Portland, Oreg., 1980—; forest industry cons., govtl. affairs and product efficiency; mem. Oreg. and Calif. forest products industry govtl. affairs groups. Bd. dirs. Oreg. Evergreen, N.Y. Urban Coalition. Mem. Western Wood Products Assn., Am. Plywood Assn., Associated Oreg. Industries, Oreg. Forest Industries Council, Oreg. Bus. Planning Council, Calif. Protective Assn., Calif Redwood Assn., Pacific Legal Found. Republican. Presbyterian. Home: PO Box 192 Forest Grove OR 97116 Office: 315 Pacific Bldg Portland OR 97204

MC EWAN, DONALD R(OBERT), aerospace exec.; b. College Point, N.Y., Nov. 13, 1932; s. Alexander and Ernestine M. (Lotz) Mc E.; B.S.E.E., Worcester Poly. Inst., 1954; m. Lorraine Drennan, June 12, 1954; children—Pamela, Jeffrey, Donald R. With ITT Avionics Div., Nutley, N.J., 1956—, dir. program mgmt., 1973-74, v.p., 1974-76, dir. ops., 1976-77, pres., gen. mgr., 1977—. Served with USMC, 1954-56. Mem. Navy League U.S., Armed Forces Communications and Electronics Assn., Assn. U.S. Army, Am. Def. Preparedness Assn., Aerospace Industries Assn., Nat. Security Indsl. Assn., Assn. Old Crows, Soc. Logistics Engrs. Office: 390 Washington Ave Nutley NJ 07110

MC EWEN, JOSEPH, distbg. co. exec.; b. Rahway, N.J., June 20, 1921; s. Joseph ahd Thora (Thompson) McE.; student Newark Coll. Engring., Temple U.; children—Joseph, Jacquelyne, Anne, Susan. Test engr. Wright Aero. Co., 1941, Lawrence Engring. Co., 1941-43; sales engr. Rapistan of Pa., 1946-55; with Modern Handling Equipment Co., Bristol, Pa., 1955—, pres., 1960—, chmn. bd., 1978—. Served to 2d lt. U.S. Army, 1943-45. Mem. Internat. Material Handling Soc., Nat. Assn. Wholesalers and Distbrs. (pres. 1976), Pa. C. of C. (dir.), Material Handling Distbrs. Assn. (pres. 1966). Club: Mfrs. Golf and Country. Home: 2230 Huntingdon Rd Huntingdon Valley PA 19006 Office: 2501 Durham Rd Bristol PA 19007

MC FADDEN, THOMAS J(OSEPH), lawyer; b. S.I., N.Y., May 1, 1900; s. Frank J. and Annie G. (McMenamin) McF.; A.B., Cornell U., 1922, J.D., 1925; postgrad. Yale Law Sch., 1927-28. Admitted to N.Y. bar, 1928, D.C. bar, 1934; spl. asst. to atty. gen. Dept. Justice, 1928-29; counsel, mgr. Nat. Paint, Varnish and Lacquer Assn., Washington, 1929-33; partner firm Donovan, Leisure, Newton & Irvine, N.Y.C., 1934—; lectr. Practising Law Inst. Served with U.S. Army, 1918; lt. comdr., naval air liaison officer, Sicily Invasion with 45th Inf. Div., USNR 1942-45; chief Pacific Far East Morale Ops., OSS, Washington, 1943-44. Mem. Soc. Internat. Law, Am., Fed., N.Y. State bar assns., N.Y. Cath. Lawyers Guild, English Speaking Union, Nat. Lawyers Club. Clubs: Cornell, Yale (N.Y.C.). Home: 183d St and Pinehurst Ave Apt J33 New York NY 10033 Office: 30 Rockefeller Plaza New York NY 10020

MC FARLAND, EMERSON LEE, nuclear engr.; b. Beech Grove, Ind., Apr. 19, 1946; s. Paul Emerson and Laura Belle (McClain) McF.; B.S.M.E., Purdue U., 1968; M.S. in Nuclear Engring., Mass. Inst. Tech., 1970; m. Cynthia Jude Rose, July 30, 1972; children—Jennifer Lee, Melissa Ann, Andrew Weston. With Commonwealth Edison Co., Chgo., 1971-73; sr. nuclear engr. Bechtel Power Corp., San Francisco, 1973—, also chmn. chugging subcom. Mark II Owners Group, spl. asst. to project engr. Mem. Am. Nuclear Soc., Mensa, Tau Beta Pi, Pi Tau Sigma. Home: 4 Ketelsen Dr Moraga CA 94556 Office: 50 Beale St San Francisco CA 94119

MC FARLAND, H(AROLD) RICHARD, food co. exec.; b. Hoopeston, Ill., Aug. 19, 1930; s. Arthur Bryan and Jennie (Wilkey) McF.; B.S.A., U. Ill., 1952; m. Sarah Forney, Dec. 30, 1967. Asst. purchasing agt. Campbell Soup Co., Camden, N.J., 1957-60, mgr. purchasing, 1960-67; dir. procurement Keebler Co., Elmhurst, Ill., 1967-69; v.p. purchasing and distbn. Ky. Fried Chicken Corp. div. Heublein, Inc., Louisville, 1969-74; v.p. food services, sales and distbn., 1974-75; pres., dir. Mid-Continent Carton Co., Louisville, 1974-75, KFC Mfg. Co., Nashville, 1974-75, McFarland Foods Corp., Indpls., 1975—; dir. Fountain Trust Bank, Covington, Ind., Covington Services Corp.; pres., dir. Central Ind. Ky. Fried Chicken Advt. Coop., 1976—; pres. Gt. Lakes Ky. Fried Chicken Franchise Assn., 1979-80. Served to 1st lt. USAF, 1952-54; Korea. Named hon. chief police Louisville, 1970; recipient Pres.'s award Ky. Fried Chicken, 1970. Mem. Ind. Restaurant Assn., Nat. Broiler Council (dir. 1972-75), Am. Shorthorn Cattle Assn., Delta Upsilon. Presbyterian. Club: Wildwood Country. Home: 6361 Avalon Ln E Indianapolis IN 46220 Office: 6314 N Rucker St Suite A Indianapolis IN 46220

MC FARLAND, MILTON CLAY, marine electronics engring. co. exec.; b. North Powder, Oreg., Feb. 11, 1924; s. Ira Jay and Alice Leona (Pennington) McF.; student U. Wash., 1941-44; B.E.E., U.S. Naval Acad., 1948; M.S. in Fin. Mgmt., U.S. Naval Postgrad. Sch., 1966; postgrad. Mass. Inst. Tech., 1974; m. Wanda Geraldine Goodhart, Nov. 12, 1949; children—Robert Bruce, Laurie Elizabeth, Alan Scott, Jocelyn Kirstie, William Gregg, Sally Jeanne. Enlisted U.S. Navy, 1943, advanced through grades to capt., 1969; submarine officer, 1950-75; ret., 1975; v.p. and tech. dir. Analysis & Technology, Inc., North Stonington, Conn., 1976; asst. mgr. New Eng. ops. Marine Systems div. Rockwell Internat. Corp., Groton, Conn., 1977-78, mgr. New Eng. ops. Autonetics Marine Systems div. Electronic Systems group, 1978—; vice chmn. sec. Navy's Undersea Warfare Council, 1974; mem. Navy Research Advisory Com., 1972-75. Chmn. mil. affairs com. S.E. Conn. C. of C., 1978—; mem. exec. bd. Indian Trails council Boy Scouts Am., 1975—, U.S.S. Massachusetts Meml. Com., 1975—. Mem. Am. Def. Preparedness Assn., Nat. Security Indsl. Assn., Navy League U.S. (bd. dirs. E. Conn. council). Republican. Anglican. Club: Rotary. Contbr. articles to profl. jours. Home: 52 Pearl St Mystic CT 06355 Office: 1028 Poquonnock Rd Groton CT 06340

MCFARLAND, RICHARD M., exec. recruiting cons.; b. Portland, Maine, Sept. 10, 1923; s. George Fiske and Phillys C. (Macomber) McF.; B.Chem. Engring., Rensselaer Poly. Inst., 1944; postgrad. U. Mich., 1946-47; m. Virginia Fitz-Randolph Ripley, Dec. 7, 1947; children—Richard Macomber, Kirk, Jane. Mgr. agrl. chem. market research Brea Chem. (Calif.) subsidiary Union Oil Co., 1953-55; product mgr. chem. div. FMC Corp., N.Y.C., 1955-59; mgr. mktg. devel. Tex. Butadiene & Chem., N.Y.C., 1959-60; pres. Cumberland Chem. Corp., N.Y.C., 1960-67; gen. mgr. inorganic div. Wyandotte Chem. Co. (Mich.), 1967-69; with Heidrick & Struggles, Inc., N.Y.C., 1969—, v.p., 1972—. Served as ensign USNR, 1943-45, lt. comdr., 1951-53. Mem. Comml. Devel. Assn., Am. Chem. Soc., Soc. Plastic Engrs., Lambda Chi Alpha. Clubs: Federal, Cornell (N.Y.C.). Patentee in field. Home: 16 Clover Ln Westport CT 06880 Office: 245 Park Ave New York NY 10017

MC FARLAND, TERRY LYNN, constrn. co. exec.; b. Knoxville, Tenn., July 8, 1947; s. Jacob E. and Virginia Kay (Allen) McF.; student Ind. U., 1969-70; m. Hazel C. Davis, Nov. 1, 1975; 1 dau. by previous marriage, Laurie Lynn. Prodn. control staff R.R. Donnelley & Sons, Warsaw, Ind., 1965-68; insp. Bendix Corp., South Bend, Ind., 1968-69; mgr. Wickes Bldgs. div. Wickes Corp., Argos, Ind., 1970-71, Crawfordsville, Ind., 1971-73, Macon, Ga., 1973-76, dist. mgr. Ill., Ind., Mich., Wis., 1976-79, mgr. Wickes bdgs. ops. in S.C., 1979-80; v.p., gen. mgr. Douglass Bldg. Service, Inc., Columbia, S.C., 1980—. Served with U.S. Army, 1966-68; Korea. Mem. Am. Legion, Nat. Geog. Soc. Democrat. Clubs: Moose, Masons, Shriners. Home: 2012 Laurie Circle Florence SC 29501 Office: 1831 Airport Rd PO Box 837 Cayce SC 29033

MC FARLANE, SAMUEL, mfg. exec.; b. Lonaconing, Md., May 21, 1916; s. Samuel Barber and Elizabeth (Stevenson) McF.; B.S., U. Md., 1939; postgrad. Poly. Inst. N.Y., 1948-50; m. Alice Louise Beck, Oct. 7, 1944; children—Carolyn, Elizabeth Jane, Barbara Ann. Research chemist Celanese Corp. Am., Cumberland, Md., 1939-47, sect. head research, Summit, N.J., 1947-52, asst. mgr. Summit Research Lab., 1952-55, lab. mgr., 1955-57, mgr. fiber research, 1957-58; v.p., tech. dir. Onyx Oil & Chem. Co., Jersey City, 1958-60; corp. v.p. research and devel. Sun Chem. Corp. N.Y.C., 1960-68; founder, pres. ElectroPrint, Inc., Palo Alto, Calif., 1969-76; asso. mgr. U.S. ERDA, San Francisco, 1976-77; mgr. Denver office U.S. Dept. Energy, 1977-79; pres. Internat. Brands, Inc., Los Gatos, Calif., 1979—. Fellow Am. Inst. Chemists; mem. Soc. Chem. Industry, Soc. Photog. Scientists and Engrs., Chemists Club, A.I.M., AAAS, Sci. Research Soc. Am., N.Y. Acad. Scis., Tech. Assn. Graphic Arts, Am. Chem. Soc., Sigma Xi, Alpha Chi Sigma, Alpha Rho. Presbyn. Editor: Technology of Synthetic Fibers, 1953. Contbr. articles to profl. publs. Home: 13631 Verde Vista Ct Saratoga CA 95070 Office: 100 Albright Way Los Gatos CA 95030

MC FARLIN, HARRY HUGG, ins. broker, savs. and loan exec.; b. Phila., Oct. 5, 1911; s. Harry H. and Edith (McMillan) McF.; student Drexel Inst. Tech., 1936-37; m. Mary Louise Crocker, Nov. 5, 1966. Owner, McFarlin Ins. Agy., 1939—; pres. John Hanson Savs. and Loan Assn., Riverdale, Forestville, Laurel and Oxon Hill, Md., 1968—. Pres. Young Men's Democratic Club, Riverdale, 1966-68; commr. Town of Henlopen Acres, Del., 1972-76, 78-80. Served with USAAF, 1943-46. Mem. Md. Ins. Agts. Assn. (pres. 1956-57), Montgomery-Prince Georges Ins. Agts. (charter pres.). Methodist. Lion (pres. 1957-58), Tall Cedars, Elk. Clubs: Columbia Country (Washington); Henlopen Acres (Del.) Country; Rehoboth Beach (Del.) Country; John's Island (Vero Beach, Fla.). Home: 3310 Shirley Ln Chevy Chase MD 20015 also Island House John's Island Vero Beach FL Office: 7610 Pennsylvania Ave Forestville MD 20028

MCGANNON, DONALD HENRY, broadcasting exec.; b. N.Y.C., Sept. 9, 1920; s. Robert E. and Margaret (Schmidt) McG.; B.A., Fordham U., 1940, LL.B., 1947, L.H.D., 1964; L.H.D., U. Scranton, 1963, Creighton U., 1965, Emerson Coll., 1966, Fordham U., 1964, Fairfield U., 1967, Temple U., 1971, Georgetown U., 1980, St. John's U., 1980; D.Sc. (hon.), St. Bonaventure U., 1965; m. Patricia H. Burke, Aug. 22, 1942. Admitted N.Y., Conn. bars, 1947; practiced in N.Y.C., 1947-50, Norwalk, Conn., 1947-51; asst. to dir. broadcasting DuMont TV Network, 1951-52, gen. mgr., asst. dir. broadcasting, 1952-55; pres. chmn. bd. Westinghouse Broadcasting Co., Inc. Ind., Md., Del., 1955; chmn. bd. TV Advt. Reps., Inc., Radio Advt. Reps., Inc., WBC Prodns., Inc., Broadcast Rating Council, Inc. Adviser to Pontifical Commn. for Communications Media; chmn. Conn. Commn. for Higher Edn.; mem. broadcasting adv. council Emerson Coll.; chmn. advt. council Coll. Liberal Arts U. Notre Dame, Coll. Arts and Scis. Georgetown U.; mem. communications com. N.Y. Urban Coalition. Trustee, pres. Nat. Urban League; trustee Ithaca Coll., N.Y. Law, Sch., N.Y. U.; hon. Fordham U.; founder, dir. trustee Sacred Heart U.; bd. dirs. Georgetown U., Acad. TV Arts and Scis. Found., Radio Advt. Bur.; chmn. Advt. Council, Inc. Served as maj. CAC, AUS, 1941-46. Recipient Distinguished Service award Nat. Assn. Broadcasters, 1964; Spl. Emmy award, 1968; Trustees award Nat. Acad. TV Arts and Scis., 1967-68. Clubs: Duquesne (Pitts.); Union League (N.Y.C.). Office: 90 Park Ave New York NY 10016

MC GARY, CARLTON DOW, bank exec.; b. Farmington, Maine, Mar. 15, 1927; s. George Boardman and Freda Louise (Dow) McG.; B.A., U. Maine, 1950; m. Beverly Babb Green, Aug. 29, 1948; children—Deborah Lee, Alan David, Carlton Scott. Mgmt. trainee First Nat. Bank Farmington, 1950, asst. cashier, 1951-60, cashier, 1960-65; v.p. First Nat. Bank & Trust Co., Ithaca, N.Y., 1966-67; v.p. Depositors Trust Co., Augusta, Maine, 1968-74, pres., 1974—, also dir.; dir. Depositors Corp. Served with USN, 1945-46. Mem. Maine Bankers Assn., Am. Bankers Assn., Robert Morris Assos. Republican. Methodist. Club: Masons. Office: 286 Water St Augusta ME 04330

MC GAVNEY, PHILIP JOHN, shipping repair co. exec.; b. Dunfermline, Scotland, Sept. 7, 1941; s. F. Philip and Jean McG.; came to Can., 1967; student Rosyth Dockyard Coll., Scotland, 1957-62; m. Catherine Sproul; children—Kenneth, Elaine, Ian Bruce. Tech. officer Dept. Nat. Def. U.K., Rosyth, 1957-67; supr. new constrn. Marystown (Nfld.) Shipyard, 1967-69; project mgr. oil rig constrn. Halifax (N.S.) Shipyards, 1969-76; asst. gen. mgr. Halifax Industries Ltd., Dartmouth, 1978-80, gen. mgr., 1980—. Commr., Halifax Dartmouth Port, 1980—. Mem. Dartmouth C. of C. (chmn. port and transp. 1980, chmn. offshore oil and gas 1980-81), Soc. Naval Architects and Marine Engrs., Can. Inst. Marine Engrs. Club: Dartmouth Yacht. Home: 95 Collins Grove Dartmouth NS B2W 4G3 Canada Office: PO Box 1477 Halifax NS B3K 5H7 Canada

MC GAVOCK, POLLY P(OLLITT), realtor; b. Walton, Ky., Feb. 7, 1904; d. Flor S. and Shirlie (Tucker) Pollitt; student Marshall Coll., 1921-22; A.B., Randolph-Macon Women's Coll., 1925; m. John Fulton McGavock, June 9, 1925 (div.); 1 dau., Shirley McGavock McConnell. Asso. H.T. Van Nostrand & Co., 1948; realtor, 1948—. Mem. exec. bd. Charlottesville ARC, 1943-46, chmn., 1947-48; co-chmn. Community Chest Campaign, 1955; mem. bd. Charlottesville div. Am. Cancer Soc.; asso. U. Va. Library. Head ARC Motor Corps, World War II. Named Most Ethical Realtor Va., 1973. Mem. Charlottesville, Albermarle County (pres.) real estate bds., Va. Real Estate Assn. (dir.; v.p. 1961, state chmn. standard forms com. 1964), Nat. Assn. Real Estate Bds., Nat. Assn. Real Estate Appraisers (mem. women's council), Nat. Inst. Real Estate Brokers, Nat. Inst. Farm and Land Brokers, Va. Assn. Realtors, Internat. Real Estate Fedn., Kappa Delta. Episcopalian. Clubs: Boar's Head Sports, Farmington Country (Charlottesville). Home: 314 Kent Rd Charlottesville VA 22903 Office: 3 Boar's Head Ln Charlottesville VA 22901

MC GEE, DEAN A., petroleum exec., geologist, engr.; b. Humbolt, Kans., Mar. 20, 1904; s. George Gentry and Gertrude Hattie (Sayre) McG.; B.S., Kans. U., 1926; LL.D. (hon.), Oklahoma City U., 1957; D.Sc. (hon.), Bethany Nazarene Coll., 1967; D.Eng. (hon.), Colo. Sch. Mines, 1968; D.H.L. (hon.), Okla. Christian Coll., 1975; m. Dorothea Antionette Swain, June 28, 1938; children—Marcia Ann, Patricia Dean. Instr. engring. geology U. Kans., 1926-27; petroleum geologist Phillips Petroleum Co., Bartlesville, Okla., 1927-37; chief geologist, 1935-37; v.p. charge prodn. and exploration Kerlyn Oil Co. (now Kerr-McGee Corp.), Oklahoma City, 1937-42, exec. v.p., 1942-54, pres., 1954-67, chmn. bd., chief exec., 1963—; pres., dir. Kerr-McGee Bldg. Corp.; v.p. Downtown Airpark, Inc.; dir. Sunningdale Oils Ltd., Kerr-McGee Oil (U.K.) Ltd., Kerr-McGee Iranian Oil Co., Mine Contractors, Inc., Kerr-McGee Chem. Corp., Kerr-McGee Australia, Ltd., Kerr-McGee Tunisia Ltd., Kerr-McGee Coal Corp., Kerr-McGee Nuclear Corp., Southwestern Oil & Refining Co., Southwestern Refining Co., Inc., Transworld Drilling Co., Transworld North Sea Drilling Services Ltd., Internat. Creosoting & Constrn. Co., Triangle Refineries, Inc., Fidelity Bank; dir. emeritus Gen. Electric Co.; owner McGee-Keesee Ranch. Chmn. Gulf Dist. com. for selection Rhodes Scholarships, 1968-74; mem. Okla. Ambassadors Corps, 1965. Chmn. exec. com. Okla. Health Scis. Found.; trustee Okla. Industries Authority; bd. dirs. Ark. Basin Devel. Assn., Oklahoma City chpt. NCCJ; trustee Kans. U. Endowment Assn., Midwest Research Inst., Kansas City, Mo.; bd. dirs. Okla. Med. Research Found., Okla. Safety Council, Oklahoma City U. Found., Inc.; trustee Calif. Inst. Tech.; pres. bd. dirs. Kerr-McGee Found., Inc.; trustee S.W. Research Inst., Sci. and Natural Resources Found. Okla., Presbyn. Hosp., Inc., Oklahoma City Indsl. and Cultural Facilities Trust; bd. dirs. Okla.-Ark. Presbyn. Found., Inc.; mem. adv. bd. Coll. Bus. U. Okla., Okla. Med. Scis. Hall Fame, Okla. Hall Fame; trustee, mem. exec. com., also hon. life mem. Nat. Cowboy Hall of Fame and Western Heritage Center; mem. Okla. City Arts Council, Okla. Hist. Soc.; pres., dir. McGee Found. Inc.; trustee Okla. Eye Found.; mem. Okla.'s Future, Inc.; dir. Com. of 100; trustee, vice chmn. exec. com., bd. trustees Oklahoma City U.; trustee emeritus Am. Assn. Petroleum Geologists Found.; mem. governing bd. Okla. Center Scis. and Arts; mem. Rockefeller U. Council. Recipient Erasmus Haworth Distinguished Alumni award in geology, Distinguished Alumni citation U. Kans., 1951; Outstanding Okla. Oil Man award Okla. Petroleum Council, 1970; Nat. Brotherhood citation NCCJ, 1961; Outstanding Civilian Service award Dept. Army, 1965; Okla. U. Distinguished Service citation, 1966; Industrialist of Year award Headliner award Oklahoma City Press Club, 1968; Golden Plate award Am. Acad. Achievement, 1969; 17th Ann. citation Midwest Research Inst., 1973; Oklahoma City Beautiful award, 1973; Bennett Disting. Service award Okla. State U., 1974; Disting. Service award Oklahoma City Advt. Club, 1976, U. Tulsa Coll. Engring. and Phys. Scis. Hall of Fame award, 1976; Nat. Petroleum Hall of Fame Disting. Service award, 1977; John Rogers award Southwestern Legal Found., U. Tex., Dallas, 1980; Disting. Service award Oklahoma City U., 1980; Okla. Disting. Salesman award, 1980, others; named World's Most Outstanding Chief Exec. Officer in Coal and Uranium Industry, Fin. World, 1980. Fellow AAAS, U. Okla. Acad. Fellows, Okla. Acad. Scis., Am. Inst. Mining Metall. and Petroleum Engrs. (hon. mem.), Am. Assn. Petroleum Geologists (Pub. Service award 1974, Sidney Powers award 1975, hon. life mem.); mem. Am. Petroleum Inst. (dir.), Am. Inst. Profl.

Geologists, Ind. Petroleum Assn. Am. (dir.), Nat., Okla. socs. profl. engrs., Atomic Indsl. Forum, Am. Mining Congress, AIA (hon. life Okla. chpt.), Oklahoma Zool. Soc. (trustee), Tex. Mid-Continent Oil and Gas Assn. (dir., Distinguished Service award 1975), Mid-Continent Oil and Gas Assn., Nat. Petroleum Council, Oklahoma City Geol. Soc. (hon. life), Soc. Econ. Paleontologists and Mineralogists, Okla. Heritage Assn., All Am. Wildcatters, Colo. Sch. Mines Alumni Assn. (hon.), Oklahoma City C. of C. (dir.), Oklahoma County Hist. Soc., Oklahoma City Symphony Soc. (life), Newcomen Soc. N.Am., Sachem, Sigma Xi, Delta Sigma Pi (hon.), Tau Beta Pi, Theta Tau, Pi Epsilon Tau (hon), Beta Gamma Sigma (Hon.). Democrat. Presbyterian. Mason (Shriner), Acacia. Clubs: Touchdown, Petroleum, Men's Dinner, Sirloin, Whitehall, Beacon, Oklahoma City Golf and Country; Twenty-five Year Club of Petroleum Industry; Oklahoma City Press. Contbr. articles to profl. jours. Office: Kerr-McGee Center POB 25861 Oklahoma City OK 73125

MCGEE, GEORGE WILLIAM, farmer; b. Logan County, Ill., Apr. 12, 1921; s. William Roy and Maurine Ellen (Lucas) McG.; student Bradley Poly. Inst., 1939-40; m. Gloria Faye Lewis, Sept. 7, 1947; children—Mark William, Sara Faye. Farmer, Mt. Pulaski, Ill., 1940—; part-owner, operator cash grain farm, Mt. Pulaski, 1953—; dir. 1st Nat. Bank of Mt. Pulaski. Mem. Mt. Pulaski Sch. Bd., 1958-67, pres., 1965-66; mem. Logan County Extension Council, 1978-80. Mem. Logan County Farm Bur. (dir. 1969-78), Land of Lincoln Soybean Assn., Ill. Corn Growers Assn. Republican. Clubs: Masons, Shriners. Home and office: Route 2 Mount Pulaski IL 62548

MC GEE, JOHN W., sales rep.; b. Cherokee, Okla., July 24, 1939; s. John Dale and Minnie Matilda (Shellhammer) McG.; B.S., Kans. State U., 1962; m. Mary Lynn Lewis, Feb. 10, 1968; children—John Gregory, Christopher Jay. Mktg. trainee Burroughs Corp., Hutchinson, Kans., 1973, mktg. rep., group 1 operating mgr., 1974, ter. mgr., 1974-77; sales rep. Berry Material Handling, Inc., 1977—. Asst. cubmaster Kanza council Boy Scouts Am. Served with USMC, 1962-73; capt. Kans. Army N.G. Mem. Hutchinson C. of C., Kans. State U. Alumni Assn. Methodist. Home: 2312 N Jackson St Hutchinson KS 67501 Office: 500 W 20th St Suite 100 Hutchinson KS 67501

MC GIBBON, EDMUND LEAVENWORTH, lawyer; b. Grand Rapids, Mich., May 27, 1908; s. William and Franc (Leavenworth) McG.; A.B., Dartmouth, 1929; J.D., Northwestern U., 1933; m. Catherine Jean Klink, Aug. 29, 1941; children—William A., Catherine Jean, Bonnie Laurie. Admitted to Ill. bar, 1934, since practiced in Chgo.; asso. Robertson, Crowe & Spence, 1934-38; partner Robertson & McGibbon, 1947-53, Williston, McGibbon, Stastny & Borman, 1953-62, Williston, Mc Gibbon & Stastny, 1962-66, Williston & McGibbon, 1966-70, Williston, McGibbon & Kuehn, 1970—. Chmn. bd. Santa Rita Ranch, Inc., Green Valley, Ariz. Bd. govs. Scottish Old Peoples Home. Served from lt. to comdr. USN, 1940-45, comdg. officer destroyer escort; capt. USNR (ret.). Mem. Am., Ill., Chgo. bar assns., Nat. Rifle Assn. (life), Am. Nat. Cattlemen's Assn., Ariz. Cattle Growers Assn., Aircraft Owners and Pilots Assn., Ill. St. Andrew Soc. (past pres.), Phi Kappa Psi, Phi Alpha Delta. Republican. Episcopalian. Clubs: University, Chicago (Chgo.); Barrington Hills (Ill.) Country; Tucson (Ariz.) Country, Old Pueblo; Guadalajara (Mexico) Country. Home: Ridge Rd Barrington IL 60010 also Santa Rita Ranch Box 647 Green Valley AZ 85614 Office: 102 N Cook St Barrington IL 60010

MC GILL, CHARLES HARRY, III, mgmt. cons.; b. Bridgeport, Conn., Jan. 2, 1942; s. Charles Harry, Jr., and Shirley Elizabeth (Haynes) McG.; B.A., Trinity Coll., Hartford, Conn., 1963; M.B.A., Dartmouth Coll., 1969; m. Patricia Crean, July 24, 1971; children—Amy Crean, Charles Carlin Haynes. Sr. asso. Cresap, McCormick & Paget, N.Y.C., 1969-72; v.p. W.R. Grace & Co., N.Y.C., 1972-77; v.p. Ogden Food Service Corp., Boston, 1977-80; dir. Mgmt. Cons. Services Group, Coopers & Lybrand, Boston, 1980—. Served to lt. USNR, 1964-67. Recipient Freedom Found. award, 1968. Office: 100 Federal St Boston MA 02110

MCGILL, ROBERT ERNEST, III, chem. and materials mfg. co. exec.; b. San Francisco, Apr. 30, 1931; s. Robert Ernest and Madeleine Melanie (Ignance) McG.; B.A., Williams Coll., 1954; M.B.A., Harvard U., 1956; m. Daphne Urquhart Driver, Apr. 26, 1958; children—Robert Ernest, Meredith Louise, Christina Elizabeth, James Alexander. With Morgan Stanley & Co., investment bankers, N.Y.C., 1956-63; mem. fin. staff, then dir. corp. planning and devel. Air Products & Chems., Inc., Allentown, Pa., 1963-68; v.p., then exec. v.p. Gen. Interiors Corp., N.Y.C., 1968-73; v.p. fin. Ethan Allen, Inc., Danbury, Conn., 1973-75; v.p. fin., sec. Dexter Corp., Windsor Locks, Conn., 1975—; dir. Pratt-Read Corp., Travelers Equities Fund, Inc.; bd. mgrs. Travelers Funds Variable Annuities; trustee Hartford Easter Seal Rehab. Center. Mem. N.Y. Soc. Security Analysts. Clubs: Williams (gov. 1960-76), Harvard Bus. Sch. (N.Y.C.). Office: 1 Elm St Windsor Locks CT 06096

MC GILLICUDDY, JOHN FRANCIS, banker; b. Harrison, N.Y., Dec. 30, 1930; s. Michael J. and Anna (Munro) McG.; A.B., Princeton, 1952; LL.B., Harvard, 1955; m. Constance Burtis, Sept. 9, 1954; children—Michael Sean, Faith Burtis, Constance Erin, Brian Munro, John Walsh. With Mfrs. Hanover Trust Co. subsidiary Mfrs. Hanover Corp., N.Y.C., 1958—, v.p., 1962-66, sr. v.p., 1966-69, exec. v.p., asst. to chmn., 1969-70, vice chmn., dir., 1970, pres., 1971—, chmn., pres., chief exec. officer, 1979—; dir. Cities Service Co., Dart & Kraft Inc., Sperry & Hutchinson Co., Westinghouse Electric Co., Continental Corp., AMF. Bd. dirs. Nat. Multiple Sclerosis Soc., 1969—, treas., 1969-77, pres., 1977—, chmn., 1979; bd. dirs. St. Lukes-Roosevelt Hosp., 1973, N.Y. Public Library, 1979—, Mus. Natural History, 1978—. Served to lt. (j.g.) USNR, 1955-58. Mem. Assn. Res. City Bankers. Roman Catholic. Clubs: Westchester County (Rye, N.Y.); Pine Valley, Augusta Nat.; Blind Brook (Port Chester, N.Y.); Princeton (N.Y.C.). Office: 350 Park Ave New York NY 10022

MCGINITY, RICHARD CHARLES, mgmt. cons.; b. Pratt, Kans., Jan. 29, 1944; s. Frank Joseph and Catherine Marie (Wheelihan) McG.; A.B., Princeton U., 1966; M.B.A., Harvard U., 1973, D.B.A., 1980; m. Mary Dianne Phelps, Apr. 13, 1973. With McKinsey & Co., Inc., Dar-es-Salaam, Tanzania, 1972; research asso. Harvard U. Bus. Sch., 1974-77; asso. Agribus. Assos., Wellesley, Mass., 1976-77; agribus. projects mgr. Parsons Brinckerhoff Quade & Douglas, Inc., N.Y.C., 1978-79; dir. corp. devel. Parsons Brinckerhoff, Inc., N.Y.C., 1979—. Served as aviator USN, 1966-71; Korea, Vietnam. Decorated Air medal (2). Mem. Am. Soc. Agrl. Cons. Clubs: Princeton (N.Y.C.); Univ. Cottage (Princeton). Author: Agribusiness Management for Developing Countries: Southeast Asia, 1979; editorial bd. Agribus. Worldwide mag. Office: Parsons Brinckerhoff Inc One Penn Plaza 250 W 34th St New York NY 10119

MC GINN, WILLIAM DONALD, ins. exec.; b. Milford, Mass., Feb. 17, 1934; s. Charles T. and Eunice R. (Granger) McG.; B.A., Trinity Coll., Hartford, Conn., 1957; m. Nancy Ann Fuller, Dec. 2, 1961; children—Maureen, Melanie, William, Scott. Asst. v.p. Northwestern Nat. Ins. Co., Milw., 1969-72, v.p., 1972-74, pres., dir., 1977—; pres. Universal Reins. Corp., 1974-77, now dir. Bd. dirs. Wis. Soc. Prevention Blindness. Served with AUS, 1957-59. Roman Catholic. Clubs: Milw. Athletic, Westmoor Country. Office: 731 N Jackson St Milwaukee WI 53201

MCGINNIS, BERNARD WILLIAM, mfg. co. exec.; b. Honesdale, Pa., Mar. 18, 1924; s. Frank Lawrence and Florence (Miller) McG.; B.S. magna cum laude, Marist Coll., Poughkeepsie, N.Y., 1974, M.B.A., 1977; divorced; children—Terrence J., Valerie. With Bendix Corp., Sidney, N.Y., 1952-56; with IBM Corp., 1956—, sr. asso. engr., Poughkeepsie, 1974—, mfg. engr., East Fishkill, N.Y., 1980—. Served with USNR, 1943-45. Mem. Soc. Mfg. Engrs., VFW (dep. insp. N.Y. State 1954-55). Democrat. Roman Catholic. Author, patentee in field. Home: 10 Wendover Dr Poughkeepsie NY 12601 Office: Dept 08E IBM Corp East Fishkill NY 12533

MC GINNIS, THOMAS PETER, real estate and ins. agt. broker; b. Honesdale, Pa., June 29, 1933; s. Charles Peter and Verlo Ruth (Getz) McG.; B.S., Pa. State U., 1955: m. Patricia Marie Schmidt, Oct. 17, 1959; children—Peter Thomas, Craig Charles, Kevin Paul, Kimberly Marie, Jill Ann. Vice pres., dir. Sandy Shore Co., Inc., Lake Wallenpaupack, Pa., 1957—; owner, mgr. Thomas P. McGinnis Ins. and Real Estate Co., Honesdale, 1967—; pres., treas. Khee Land, Inc., Honesdale, 1969—, Seven Mountains, Inc., Honesdale, 1972—; pres. Beach Glen, Inc., Honesdale, 1972—; dir. Citizens Savs. Assn. Scranton (Pa.). Vol., Protection Engine Co. No. 3, Honesdale; former team mgr. Honesdale Little Baseball Assn., now treas. Served with U.S. Army, 1955-57. Licensed real estate broker, N.Y., Pa., ins. agt., Pa., casualty and fire ins. broker, Pa., N.Y. Mem. Pa. State U. Alumni Assn., Phi Sigma Kappa. Roman Catholic. Clubs: Eagles, Lions, Honesdale, Golf, Honesdale Booster. Home: PO Box 167 RD 3 Honesdale PA 18431 Office: 809 Main St Honesdale PA 18431

MC GINNIS, WILLIAM JOHN PATRICK, JR., mgmt. cons. co. exec.; b. Beach Haven, N.J., Jan. 11, 1946; s. William John Patrick and Katherine Gertrude (Ginnelly) McG.; B.S. in Bus. Adminstrn., LaSalle Coll., 1967; M.A. in Labor Relations, Rutgers U., 1980; m. Jeanette M. Pugliese, June 14, 1969; children—William John Patrick III, Colleen, Erin. Pres., McGinnis Assos., mgmt. consultants, Brant Beach, 1965—, Olde Brigade Mfg. Co., Phila., 1971—; vis. lectr. Appalachian State U., 1978. Pres., Long Beach Island Regular Republican Orgn. Club, 1978—; corr. sec. Ocean County Regular Rep. Council, 1979—; mem. mil. staff gov. State of Ky., 1977—; mem. bd. commrs. Twp. of Long Beach, 1980—. Mem. Inst. Mgmt. Cons., Soc. Profl. Mgmt. Consultants (v.p., publs. chmn., editor all publs. 1979—), Indsl. Relations Research Assn., Internat. Public Personnel Mgmt. Assn., So. N.J. Public Employer Negotiators Assn. (Profl. Cons. award 1960), Am. Soc. Notary Public, World Wild Geese Assn., Ancient Order Hibernians (div. 100). Roman Catholic. Clubs: Beach Haven Exchange (publicity chmn.), Long Beach Island Kiwanis (citizenship chmn.), Long Beach Island Men's Garden. Author: Labor Relations Guidelines for Public Sector Management, 1980; editor: Negotiators Bull. Newsletter, 1975-80; Mgmt. Guidelines, 1976-80; Sales Management Handbook, 1980. Home and office: 27 W 45th St Brant Beach NJ 08008

MC GLASSON, CHRISTINE LOUISE, mktg. exec., mgmt. cons.; b. Glendale, Calif., Nov. 13, 1944; d. Howard Allen and Christine (Fee) McGlasson; B.A. in Radio and TV, Fla. State U., 1966; M.A. in Communications, Calif. State U., 1980, student Am. Acad. of Dramatic Arts, 1964. Asst. dir. of news program Sta. WFSU-TV, Fla. State U., Tallahassee, 1965-66, radio announcer Sta. WFSU-FM, 1964-66; copywriter and programming asst. Sta. WSB-AM-FM, Atlanta, Ga., 1966; continuity dir., announcer and promotion dir. Sta. KCTC, Sacramento, Calif., 1968-76; copy supr. and account exec. Brown, Clark & Elkus Co., Sacramento, 1972-73; writer and comml. producer for Sta. KCRA-TV, Sacramento, 1974-75; propr., creative dir. Sound Thinking Communications Consultants, Sacramento, 1973—; mktg. dir. Rancho Murieta Properties, Inc., near Sacramento, 1976—, also gen. mgr. Rancho Murieta Country Club, 1977-78; pres. Chris McGlasson & Assos., 1980—; guest lectr. on communications and broadcasting to local secondary schs. and jr. colls., 1972—; mgmt. cons. to various clubs and tng. seminars in Calif., 1977—; dir. Sacramento Better Bus. Bur., 1975-76. Broadcast chmn. Sacramento Red Cross, 1970-73; publicity chmn. Soc. for the Prevention of Cruelty to Animals, 1976-77; music festival chmn. Sacramento Symphony Assn., 1977—; mem. publicity com. Sacramento Opera Guild, 1977—. Served to capt. USAF, 1966-70; maj. with Calif. State Info. Office Air NG, 1972—. Recipient Sacramento C. of C. award, 1970; Nat. Retail Advt. award, 1972; Am. Radio/TV Commls. awards (Clios), 1972-73; Am. Advt. Fedn. award, 1973; Calif. Assn. Realtors award (3), 1978; Superior Calif. Builders Assn. awards (3), 1978, named Mktg. Dir. of Yr., 1979; Appreciation awards for pub. service by various community and civic orgns., 1973-77; named Sacramento Advt. Person of Yr., 1974. Mem. Am. Acad. of Advt., Sacramento Advt. Club (past pres.; 40 awards 1971, 72, 73, 74, 75, 77), Sacramento Women in Media, Sacramento Women in Advt., Women in Communications, Internat. Communications Assn., Sacramento Press Club, Internat. Brotherhood of Elec. Workers, Nat. Guard Assn., Sell Overseas Am. Episcopalian. Contbr. feature articles to local publs. Home: 2805 Adirondack Way Sacramento CA 95827 Office: 818 19th St Sacramento CA 95814

MC GLASSON, MOREY CLAYWELL, sales tng. material co. exec.; b. Plainview, Tex., May 8, 1925; s. Morey Claywell and Irene (Lamb) McG.; B.B.A. in Econs., Baylor U., 1950; M.S. in Fin., La. State U., 1971; m. Janette Bell, Mar. 18, 1948; 1 son, Russ Davis. Tchr., adminstr. Odessa (Tex.) Public Schs., 1950-54; life ins. agt., mgr. Am. Gen. Life Ins. Co., Waco, Tex., 1954-60, Security Life of Denver, 1960-68; dir. Inst. Ins. Mktg. La. State U., Baton Rouge, 1968-76; v.p. mktg. Acacia Mut. Life Ins. Co. and Acacia Fin. Co., Washington, 1976-79; pres. Rusty McGlasson & Co., Richardson, Tex., 1979—, People in Pursuit Of., Inc., Richardson, 1978—; mem. Washington Bd. Trade, 1976—. Bd. dirs. Goodwill Industries, Waco, Tex. Served with USAF, 1943-45. Mem. Am. Soc. C.L.U.'s, Beta Gamma Sigma. Author monthly column in Life Ins. Selling mag. Home: 16340 Lauder Ln Dallas TX 75248 Office: PO Box 5240 Richardson TX 75080

MC GLINSKY, ROBERT GENE, environ. cons. co. exec.; b. Dayton, Ohio, Dec. 10, 1938; s. Alfred Michael and Margaret Ann (Craport) McG.; B.S. in Indsl. Engring., U. Dayton, 1965; m. Rose Ann Knoebel, June 6, 1964; children—Darin Robert, Mark Andrew, Michael Alfred, Cindy Marie, Amy Renee, Lea Diane. Regional sales engr. Am. Air Filter Co., Louisville, 1965-69, mgr. indsl. sales, Mpls., 1969-77; v.p. Contamination Control Corp., Chaska, Minn., 1977-78, pres., chmn. bd., Maple Plain, Minn., 1978—. Mem. Soc. Indsl. Engrs. (pres. 1964-65), Nat. Soc. Profl. Engrs. (pres. 1964-65), Joint Council Engrs. (chmn. 1963-65), Am. Indsl. Hygiene Assn., Exptl. Aircraft Assn., Minn. Pollution Control Assn. (charter). Democrat. Roman Catholic. Researcher, inventor, developer waste control, air pollution control equipment; hazardous waste control. Home: 1951 Lakeside Ln Mound MN 55364 Office: 5469 US Hwy 12 Maple Plain MN 55359

MCGLOHON, LOONIS, broadcasting co. exec.; b. Ayden, N.C., Sept. 29, 1921; s. Max Cromwell and Bertha (Andrews) McG.; B.S., East Carolina U., 1942; m. Nan Lovelace, June 19, 1943; children—Reeves, Fan, Laurie. With Jefferson Pilot Broadcasting Co., Charlotte, N.C., 1949—, music dir., 1954—, dir. community relations, 1972—; dir. spl. projects WBTV; freelance producer, 1950—; composer numerous compositions and works, including many recorded jazz and popular pieces; various commns. for religious works; film scores; new mus. version of Land of Oz, 1970-73; syndicated TV feature mus. scores, including Come Blow Your Horn, 1966, others; score for symphonic drama The Hornets Nest, 1965; guest performer N.C. Symphony. Organizer N.C. agy. Big Bros. Am., 1972, v.p., 1972-73; producer, chmn. March of Dimes Telerama, 1972. Bd. dirs. Cultural Arts Com. of Charlotte, NCCJ, Easter Seal Soc., Big Bros. Served with USAAF, 1942-45. Recipient Peabody award, 1977. Mem. ASCAP, Broadcast Music Inc., Pub. Relations Soc. Am. Club: Charlotte Athletic. Home: 222 Wonderwood Dr Charlotte NC 28211 Office: 1 Julian Price Pl Charlotte NC 28208

MC GLYNN, JOHN FRANCIS, x-ray co. exec.; b. Binghamton, N.Y., July 28, 1930; s. Charles James and Helen L. (O'Brien) McG.; B.S., Syracuse U., 1952; m. Marilyn O'Connell, Sept. 8, 1956; 1 dau., Clare. Fin. trainee, advt. and sales promotion mgr., mktg. mgr. med. x-ray products GAF Corp., 1955-70; mgr. mktg. services Photo Repro. div., mktg. mgr. micrographic products and audiovisual products IPCO Hosp. Supply Corp., 1970-77; pres. Low X-Ray div., pres. Agfa-Gevaert Rex, Inc., White Plains, N.Y., 1978—; chmn. bd. XRC, Inc., Hialeah, Fla., 1976-77, Coronary Care Systems, Inc., 1979—; dir. Air Express Internat., Stamford, Conn. Served with Army Security Agy., 1952-55. Mem. Sigma Chi. Republican. Roman Catholic. Club: Camp Fire of Am. Author: Teaching Techniques for X-Ray Technology, 1964. Inventor disposable tape cord thermometer. Home: 333 Jay St Katonah NY 10536 Office: 925 Westchester Ave White Plains NY 10604

MCGOLDRICK, DAVID THOMAS, luggage corp. exec.; b. Sherman, Conn., Oct. 8, 1932; s. William Francis and Margaret Ellen (Lillis) McG.; B.S., Coll. of Holly Cross, 1954; M.S., Niagara U., 1955; m. Nancy Pearl Couch, June 23, 1956; children—Anne, Kathleen, Colleen, David, Teresa, Michael, Irene. Sales rep. Berlin & Jones Envelope Mfrs., N.Y.C., 1955-57; salesman, sales mgr. Gen. Electric Co., Bridgeport, Conn., 1957-64, sales planning, merchandising, 1964-65, bus. planning, 1965-67, product, mktg. mgmt., Syracuse, N.Y., 1967-72; v.p. mktg. toy div. Samsonite Corp., 1972-73, dir. mktg. new bus. ventures, luggage div., 1973, v.p. mktg., furniture div., 1973-76, pres., gen. mgr. furniture div., 1976-80, pres., gen. mgr. luggage div., 1980—; pres. luggage and personal accessories group Beatrice Foods, Denver, 1980—; Treas., Homeowners Assn., 1975-76; pres. parish council Ch. of Risen Christ, Denver, 1977-78, chmn. long-range planning com., 1978-80, spl. minister, 1979-80. Mem. Colo. Diversified Industries (dir. 1979—). Office: Samsonite Luggage Corp 11200 E 45th Ave Denver CO 80239

MC GOVERN, KEVIN MICHAEL, lawyer, corporate exec.; b. N.Y.C., July 16, 1948; s. Thomas E. and Margaret E. (Smith) McG.; student U. London, 1968; B.A., Cornell U., 1970; J.D., St. John's U., 1975; m. Lisa Camerota, Nov. 21, 1979. Sales coordinator Plastics div. ICI Am., Stamford, Conn., 1971-72; law clk. REA Express, N.Y.C., 1972-75; admitted to Conn. bar, 1975; asso. firm Ivey Barnum & O'Mara, Greenwich, Conn., 1975-77; asst. gen. counsel Clabir Corp., Greenwich, 1977, asso. gen. counsel, head inside counsel, 1977-79; partner firm Duel & Holland, Greenwich, 1979—. Profl. chmn. Greenwich United Way, 1976-77, chmn. spl. gifts, 1977—; co-chmn. Stamford (Conn.) Tng. Career Council, 1977—. Mem. Am., Conn., Greenwich bar assns., Am. Judicature Soc. (dir. 1974-75), Stamford Jaycees. Alpha Tau Omega. Home: 58 Janice Rd Stamford CT 06905

MC GOWAN, ALAN HUGH, sci. info. exec.; b. N.Y.C., Sept. 27, 1935; s. Frank Hugh and Evelyn (Hunt) McG.; B.Engring., Yale U., 1957; m. Rochelle Schiff, Apr. 10, 1960; children—David Michael, Nina Rachel. Engr., Am. Electric Power Co., N.Y.C., 1957-59; tchr. pub. high schs., N.Y.C., 1960-69; sci. adminstr. Washington U. Center for Biology Natural Systems, St. Louis, 1969-74; pres. Scientists' Inst. for Pub. Info., N.Y.C., 1973—; trustee, v.p. Inst. Environ. Edn., Cleve., 1971—; chmn. subcom. on alt. energy sources N.Y. State Gov.'s Task Force on Energy Problems, 1975-76. Mem. N.Y.C. Mayor's Energy Policy Adv. Group, 1978—, N.Y. State Energy Research and Devel. Authority, 1979—; mem. exec. bd. Yale Sci. and Engring. Assn., 1977—. Mem. AAAS, Sigma Xi. Home: 66 W 94th St New York NY 10025 Office: 355 Lexington Ave New York NY 10017

MC GOWAN, E(DGAR) L(EON), state ofcl.; b. Conway, S.C., June 1, 1920; s. Edgar L. and Francis (Mishoe) McG.; student U. Ala., 1938-41; B.S., U. S.C., 1947, M.S., 1950, LL.B., 1957, J.D., 1965; m. Mildred Parris, Apr. 3, 1941; 1 son, E. Linden. Instr. U. S.C., 1946-50, asst. prof., 1950-57, asso. prof., 1957-71; pvt. accounting practice, Columbia, S.C., 1947-57; atty. at law, 1957-71; v.p., dir. Investment Life & Trust Co., Mullins, S.C.; commr. labor State of S.C., 1971—. Recorder City of Forest Acres (S.C.), 1963-64, councilman, 1965-71; sec.-treas. S.C. Democratic Com., 1966-72. Mem. Internat. Assn. Govt. Labor Ofcls. (pres. 1976-77), Am., S.C., Richland County bar assns. Methodist. Mason (Shriner). Clubs: Lions, Palmetto. Home: PO Box 11517 5067 Hillside Rd Columbia SC 29206 Office: 3600 Forest Dr Columbia SC 29206

MC GOWN, RICHARD ALBERT, oil co. exec.; b. Jefferson County, Tex., Nov. 16, 1949; s. Richard Albert and Una Ellen (White) McG.; B.S., Sam Houston State U., 1973. Owner, operator McGown Oil Co. (name now McGown Petroleum Inc.), Huntsville, Tex., 1974—. March of Dimes scholar, 1967-68. Mem. So. Gulf Oil Distbrs. Assn., Tex. Oil Marketers Assn., Delta Tau Delta. Methodist. Republican. Club: Rotary. Home: 1523 22d St Huntsville TX 77340 Office: McGown Petroleum Inc FM 3411 PO Box 928 Huntsville TX 77340

MC GRATH, EDWARD PATRICK, mining co. exec.; b. N.Y.C., Dec. 8, 1929; s. Edward Patrick and Elizabeth (Breen) McG.; B.S. in Journalism, N.Y. U., 1958; M.A. in English, Bklyn. Coll., 1960; m. Phyllis Ruth Scher, May 28, 1967; children by previous marriage—Cynthia Elizabeth, Deborah Wayland. Editorial asst. N.Y. Herald Tribune, 1948-50; editor McGraw-Hill Pub. Co., 1953-67; asst. mgr. editorial services Am. Petroleum Inst., 1961-67; dir. advt. and pub. relations Allied Maintenance Corp., 1967-69; dir. Kennecott Copper Corp., N.Y.C., 1969—. Vice chmn. Weston (Conn.) Library Bd., 1978—. Served with AUS, 1950-52; Korea; lt. col. Res., 1952-76. Recipient 1st award for series of articles Asso. Bus. Publs., 1957. Mem. Nat. Environ. Devel. Assn. (exec. com., dir. 1978—), Co. of Mil. Historians. Republican. Presbyterian. Home: 12 Godfrey Rd W Weston CT 06883 Office: 161 E 42d St New York NY 10017

MCGRATH, THOMAS EDWARD, discount mortgage purchasing co. exec.; b. Jersey City, May 30, 1948; s. Thomas Joseph and Helen Cecilia (Ruane) McG.; B.S. in Econs., Rutgers U., 1972; m. Pamela Ann, Aug. 5, 1978. Sec., Hollivet Corp., Secaucus, N.J., 1974-79, pres., 1979—; pres. McGrath & McGrath Bus. Service Inc., 1976—. Served with USMC, 1968-70. Mem. Rutgers Alumni Assn., VFW (Kearny, N.J.). Home: 348 Maple St Murray Hill NJ 07974 Office: 232 Belleville Pike Kearny NJ 07032

MCGRATTY, CHRISTOPHER F., real estate financier; b. Bklyn.; Jan. 14, 1943; s. Frank Lee and Virginia Marie (Ward) McG.; B.S. in Economics, Coll. of the Holy Cross, 1964; grad. in law trusts and taxation Am. Coll. Life Underwriters, 1965; grad. courses I, II, VI, Am. Inst. Real Estate Appraisers, 1975; m. Caren McCammon. 1 son, Christopher Stewart. Agt., Penn Mut. Life Ins. Co., N.Y.C., 1962-67; gen. sales mgr., asst. to pres. The Carey Cos., N.Y.C., 1967-68; pres. Environ. Leisure, Inc., N.Y.C., 1968-70; v.p., div. officer Eastdil Realty, Inc., N.Y.C., 1970-78; v.p., dir. Merrill Lynch Hubbard, Inc., N.Y.C., 1978—; guest lectr. various profl. orgns. Election capt. John V. Lindsay mayoral campaign, 1965, assembly dist. coordinator, 1969; co-coordinator Borough of Manhattan, Nelson A. Rockefeller gubernatorial campaign, 1969. Served with USMC, 1964. Mem. Real Estate Bd. N.Y. Republican. Roman Catholic. Home: Route 3 Box 276 Pound Ridge NY 10576 Office: One Liberty Plaza 19th Floor New York NY 10080

MC GRAW, HAROLD WHITTLESEY, JR., publisher; b. Bklyn., Jan. 10, 1918; s. Harold Whittlesey and Louis (Higgins) McG.; grad. Lawrenceville (N.J.) Sch., 1936; A.B., Princeton, 1940; m. Anne PerLee, Nov. 30, 1940; children—Suzanne, Harold Whittlesey III, Thomas Per Lee, Robert Pearse. With G. M. Basford, advt. agy., N.Y.C., 1940-41, Brentano's Bookstores, Inc., 1946; with McGraw-Hill Book Co., Inc., N.Y.C., 1947—, successively promotion mgr., dir. co. advt. and trade sales, 1947-55, dir. c.p. charge trade book, indsl. and bus. book depts., co. advt., 1955-61, sr. v.p., 1961-68, pres., 1968-74; chmn., pres., chief exec. officer McGraw Hill, Inc., 1974—. Pres. Princeton U. Press. Served as capt. USAAF, 1941-45. Club: University (N.Y.C); Blind Brook (Purchase, N.Y.); Wee Burn (Darien, Conn.). Office: 1221 Ave of Americas New York NY 10020

MC GRAW, JOHN LAURENCE, retail exec.; b. Chgo., Aug. 11, 1954; s. Donald Frederick and Barbara Lee (Bedsworth) McG.; B.S., Olivet Nazarene Coll., 1976; m. Rhonda Lynn White, June 25, 1977; 1 son, Jesse Laurence. Sales rep. Aetna Life & Casualty Co., Dayton, Ohio, 1976; mgr. trainee Jaccard's Jewelers, Springfield, Ohio, 1976-77; with Warehouse Paint Center, Kettering, Ohio, 1977-79, asst. mgr., 1978-79, mgr., 1979; asst. buyer Payless Cashways Inc., Kansas City, Mo., 1979—. Named Ky. Col. Mem. Jason Coward Chastain Hist. Soc. Mem. Ch. of Nazarene. Home: 1017 S 57th St Kansas City KS 66106 Office: 3100 Broadway Suite 1000 Penntower Bldg Kansas City MO 64111

MC GREEVY, MARTIN KENNETH, ins. co. underwriting exec.; b. Central Falls, R.I., Jan. 17, 1931; s. John Martin and Elizabeth Mary (Coderre) IfcG.; A.B., Providence Coll., 1952; A.M., Boston U., 1953; m. Amy Whitfield Jones, Feb. 19, 1955; children—Brian Kenneth, Marion Elizabeth. Ins. agt., Atlanta, 1956-60; with Am. Mut. Fire Ins. Co., Charleston, S.C., 1960-78, v.p., 1967-73, sr. v.p., 1973-78; dir. comml. lines underwriting Prudential Property & Casualty Ins. Co., Holmdel, N.J., 1978—; lectr. at industry seminars, meetings. Served to 1st lt. U.S. Army, 1953-55. Recipient S.C. Windstorm Underwriting Assn. award, 1978. Holy Trinity Ch. award, 1978. Mem. Soc. C.P.C.U.'s (chpt. pres. 1970-72, chmn. nat. research activities com. 1975, chpt. award 1972), Nat. Hist. Soc., Monmouth County Hist. Soc. Episcopalian. Clubs: Channel (Monmouth Beach, N.J.). Contbr. articles to ins. pubs. Home: 24 Borden Pl Little Silver NJ 07739 Office: 23 Main St PO Box 419 Holmdel NJ 07733

MC GREGOR, DONALD SCOTT, mortgage banker; b. St. George, Utah, Feb. 25, 1944; s. Alpine Watson and Berneice (Holt) McG.; student Dixie Coll., 1962-63; B.S., Brigham Young U., 1970; postgrad. U. Utah, 1970-71, N.Y. U., 1971-72, LaSalle U., 1972-73; m. Diane Mehew Melchin, June 1, 1967; children—Gregory, Carolyn Travis, Christopher, Sally, Timothy. Partner, Doolin Constrn. Co., Las Vegas, Nev., 1971; pres. McGregor Devel. Corp., St. George and Salt Lake City, 1972-75, Land Tech. Inc., St. George and Salt Lake City, 1972-76, First Am. Morgage Corp., mortgage bankers, Salt Lake City and Vancouver, B.C., Can., 1973-77, First Am. Growth Resources, Inc., investment bankers, Salt Lake City and Vancouver, B.C., 1974-77, Vista Ambassador, Salt Lake City, 1975—; income property loan officer Western Mortgage Loan Corp., Salt Lake City, 1978—; chmn. bd. Guaranty Mortgage Corp. Am., 1978—, Fed. Fin. Corp., Salt Lake City, 1979—; dir. Motion Pictures Internat., Salt Lake City, Curtis Co., Salt Lake City. Mem. Washington County (Utah) Planning Commn., 1973-74; elder Ch. of Jesus Christ of Latter-day Saints, Salt Lake City. Recipient service award Boy Scouts Am., 1974. Republican. Editor, writer Econ. Forecast, 1973-74. Home: 1141 E Oakridge Ln Bountiful UT 84010

MC GREGOR, FRANK BOBBITT, lawyer; b. Houston, Nov. 22, 1922; s. Joel Ira and Martha Louise (Bobbitt) McG.; B.A., Baylor U., 1947, M.A., 1950, LL.B., 1948; m. Doris Mason, June 30, 1942; children—Dusty, Martha, Bobbitt. Admitted to Tex. bar, 1948; partner firm McGregor & McGregor, Waco, Tex., 1949-57; sr. partner firm McGregor, Sessions, Cowden & Wallace, Waco, 1957-62; individual practice law, Waco, 1962-64, Hillsboro, Tex., 1964-68, 70-72, 76-79; dist. atty. Hill County, Hillsboro, 1968-70, 72-76; sr. partner firm McGregor & McGregor, Hillsboro, 1980—; gen. counsel Bock Constrn. Co., Dallas, 1964—; instr. polit. sci. Baylor U., 1949-61, McLennan Community Coll., 1966-67. Mem. Tex. Ho. of Reps., 1950-62; drive chmn. Hill County chpt. Am. Cancer Soc., 1967-68. Served to lt. col. USAF, World War II. Named Outstanding Rural Legislator, Tex. Vocat. Agr. Tchrs. Assn., 1959. Mem. Tex. Bar Assn., Hill County Bar Assn. (v.p. 1971), VFW, Am. Legion. Democrat. Baptist. Club: Shriners. Author: McGregor Act, public works and liens legislation. Office: South Side Sq PO Box 366 Hillsboro TX 76645

MCGREGOR, JACK E., energy investment exec.; b. Kittanning, Pa., Sept. 22, 1934; s. Russell A. and Leah H. McG.; B.S., Yale U., 1956; LL.B., U. Pitts., 1962; m. Carol Dargerfield, Nov. 23, 1955; children—Nancy, Douglas, Elisabeth, Heather. Admitted to Pa. bar, 1963, D.C. bar, 1971; asso. firm Reed, Smith, Shaw & McClay, Pitts. and Washington, 1963-68, 70-71; asst. legal adv. State Dept., 1971; gen. counsel U.S. Pay Bd., 1971-72, v.p., Potomac Electric Power Corp., Washington, 1972-74; sr. v.p., gen. counsel Carey Energy, N.Y.C., 1974-75, exec. v.p., 1975-79; pres. Hampton-Douglas Corp., Bedford, N.Y. and N.Y.C., 1979—; pres., co-founder Pitts. Penguins Hockey Club, 1967-70. Pa. state senator, 1962-70; dir., corp. sec. Seven Springs Center, Mt. Kisco, N.Y., 1980. Served with USMC, 1956-59. Mem. Pa. Bar Assn., D.C. Bar Assn. Republican. Clubs: Bedford Golf and Tennis, Racquet and Tennis, F Street, Chevy Chase. Home: E Middle Patent Rd Bedford NY 10506 Office: Village Green Bedford NY 10506

MC GRORY, WILLIAM HENRY, bldg. contractor; b. Phila., Aug. 3, 1944; s. Henry William and Catherine Claire (Lloyd) McG.; B.S. in Accounting, St. Joseph's U., Phila., 1967, M.B.A., 1978; m. Maureen Catherine Rose, Oct. 30, 1965; children—Colleen, William Henry, Amy Lynn, Matthew. Auditor, Peat Marwick, Mitchell & Co., Phila., 1967-71; asst. treas. Irwin & Leighton Inc., King of Prussia, Pa., 1971-73, treas., 1973-79, v.p., 1980—; dir. I & L Equipment Co., Telmark Mgmt. Co. Mem. Nat. Assn. Accts., Am. Mgmt. Assn., Inst. Mgmt. Acctg., Gen. Bldg. Contractors Assn., St. Joseph's Coll. Alumni Accounting Soc. Democrat. Roman Catholic. Office: Irwin Bldg King of Prussia PA 19406

MCGUANE, HARRY HOUSE, veneer co. exec.; b. Olympia, Wash., June 18, 1918; s. Harry H. and Sue Elisabeth (Moore) McG.; B.A., U. Wash., 1940; m. Molly Mattecheck, Oct. 22, 1960; children—Maggie, Mike, Mark, Matthew. Mem. prodn. and sales staff U.S. Plywood Corp., Seattle, 1939-41; founder Constrn. Products Industries, Seattle, 1946, pres., 1946—, founding owner C.P.I. Veneers, Kirkland, Wash., 1947—, C.P.I. Boards, 1955-61. Served to lt., USNR, 1941-46. Mem. Hardwood Plywood Mfrs. Assn. (veneer com. 1968-75), Forest Product Research Soc., Am. Plywood Assn., Internat. Wood Collectors Soc., Peru Trade Council, Seattle Art Mus., Alpha Delta Sigma, Alpha Sigma Phi. Clubs: Seattle Yacht (sec. 1960), Coll. Seattle (dir. 1958-61), Central Park Tennis. Home: 13000 NE 61st Pl Kirkland WA 98033 Office: CPI Veneers 13000 NE 61st Pl Kirkland WA 98033

MC GUINNESS, ADELAIDE HELEN, sales exec.; b. Yonkers, N.Y., Mar. 19, 1932; d. James John and Adeline Isabelle (Kern) Kavanaugh; ed. Pa. State U.; div.; children—Kevin, Darcy. Sales coordinator Coppercraft Guild subs. Armor Bronze & Silver, Taunton, Mass., 1960-62; co-founder, sales mgr. Princess House, North Dighton, Mass., 1962-64, nat. v.p. sales, 1964—; former dir. G.A. Rogers Inc., North Dighton, Bay Bank United Mass. Mem. Direct Selling Assn. (women and minorities com.), Internat. Platform Assn. Home: 501 Fletcher Rd North Kingstown RI 02852 Office: 455 Somerset Ave North Dighton MA 02764

MC GUIRE, HUBERT EVERETT, constrn. and devel. co. exec.; b. Littlefield, Tex., Dec. 6, 1927; s. Albert Roger and Maude (Hutton) McG.; B.S. in Elec. Engring., Tex. Tech. U., 1952; m. Marilyn Swanson, Sept. 27, 1948; children—Thomas Michael, Dianna (Mrs. Michael Thomas Wright). Project engr. Melpar, Inc., Fairfax, Va., 1953-58; with Martin-Marietta Corp., Orlando, Fla., 1958-67, engring. mgr., 1961-66, NASA program mgr., 1966-67; v.p., gen. mgr. Ground/data Corp., Fort Lauderdale, Fla., 1967-71, pres., chief exec. officer, 1971-76, also dir.; pres., chief exec. officer, treas. Charmec Corp., Fort Lauderdale, 1976—, also dir.; dir., v.p. Airtronics Internat. Corp., Fort Lauderdale, 1966; dir. Atlantic Ventures Inc., Fort Lauderdale, 1969-71; owner McGuire Properties, Fort Lauderdale; pres., treas., dir. McGuire Devel. Corp., 1973—. Scoutmaster Cub Scouts Am., Fairfax, Va., 1958; chmn. steering com. Sky Crest Civic Assn., Orlando, 1964. Served with USNR, 1946-48. Recipient Outstanding Sci. Achievement award Martin-Marietta Corp. 1964. Patentee in field. Home: 5780 SW 4th Court Plantation FL 33314 Office: 4750 N Federal Hwy Fort Lauderdale FL 33308

MC GUIRE, JAMES SHERWOOD, computer co. exec.; b. Boston, Dec. 29, 1943; s. Edward Gerard and Shirley Ford (Chatfield) McG.; B.A. in Econs., Coll. of Holy Cross, 1965; M.B.A., U. Conn., 1976; m. Marilyn Flynn, May 23, 1970; 1 dau., Nancy. Mktg. rep. IBM, Washington, 1967-68; br. sales mgr. Computer Sciences, White Plains, N.Y., 1969-71; sales and product mktg. mgr. Nat. CSS, Norwalk, Conn., 1971-77, pres. computer div., 1977—. Mem. Hist. Dist. Commn. Westport, Conn., 1978-79. Served with USN, 1965-67. Contbr. articles to profl. publs. Home: 3 Stonybrook Rd Westport CT 06880 Office: 542 Westport Ave Norwalk CT 06851

MCGUIRE, PATRICK MICHAEL, health fitness club exec.; b. Vancouver, B.C., Can., Aug. 6, 1945; s. Robert Stokes and Joan Olive (Marynowski) McG.; student Psychiat. Nurse program Sask. (Can.) Hosp., North Battleford, 1964-66. Psychiat. student nurse Sask. Hosp., North Battleford, 1963-66; warehouseman Western Grocers, North Battleford, 1966-67; propr. M & J Appliance Repair, Red Deer, Alta., Can., 1968; appliance technician, asst. mgr. Sunbeam Appliance Co., Saskatoon, Sask., 1969-76; pres. Saskatoon Health-Fitness Studio Ltd., 1975—. Mem. Saskatoon Bd. Trade, Canadian Fedn. Ind. Bus., Sask. Retail Mchts. Assn. Mem. Ch. of God. Club: Saskatoon Writers. Home: Suite 1 701 Victoria Ave Saskatoon SK S7N 0Z3 Canada Office: 205-135 Robin Crescent Saskatoon SK Canada

MCGUIRE, RICHARD ALLEN, ins. co. exec.; b. Queens, N.Y., June 9, 1946; s. George and Marion R. McGuire; student Armed Forces Inst., 1966-68; B.S. in Engring., U. Md., 1968. Ins. agt. N.Y. Life Ins. Co., N.Y.C., 1969-72; pres., chief exec. officer Richard A. McGuire Assos., Inc., Bayshore, N.Y., 1972—; lectr. Sch. of Bus., City U. N.Y., 1978-80. Chmn., David Levy Meml. Scholarship Fund, Freeport, 1975-77. Served with USAF, 1965-69. Named Man of Yr., N.Y. Life Ins. Co., 1970, 71. Mem. Nat. Assn. Life Underwriters (nat. quality award annually 1971-79, v.p. Nassau chpt. 1974), Nat. Assn. Risk Mgmt., L.I. Gen. Agts. and Mgrs. Assn., Ind. Agts. Assn., Profl. Inst. Agts. Assn., Tax and Ins. Inst., Bayshore C. of C. (v.p. 1979-80), L.I. Assn. Advancement of Commerce and Industry, Am. Legion, VFW. Clubs: Elks, K.C. Home: 1714 August Rd N Babylon NY 11703 Office: Richard A McGuire Assos Inc 1510 Fifth Ave Bay Shore NY

MCGUIRK, WILLIAM EDWARD, JR., bank holding co. exec.; b. N.Y.C., Dec. 31, 1917; s. William Edward and Loretta Beatrice (Lanigan) McG.; B.S., U.S. Naval Acad., 1939; postgrad. Postgrad. Sch. Bus. Adminstrn., Harvard U., 1940; m. Mary Tolfree Paige, Aug. 2, 1941; children—Michael, Peter Patrick, Julia Paige, William Edward III, Mary Edey, Sheila Mary, Gerard Derek, Joseph Marion, Jonathan Douglas, Mary Terrence, Ann Mary, Mary Kate, Hugh Desmond, Mary Andrea, Ian. Syndicate mgr. Kuhn, Loeb & Co., N.Y.C., 1945-54; with AEC, 1950-52; exec. v.p. Davison Chem. Co., Balt., 1954-56, pres., 1956-65; chmn. exec. com. Merc.-Safe Deposit & Trust Co., Balt., 1965-67, vice chmn. bd., 1967-68, chmn., 1968-76, also dir.; chmn. bd. Merc. Bankshares Corp., Balt., 1970—, also dir.; dir. A.S. Abell Co., Kirk-Stieff Co., Louisville & Nashville R.R. Co., Seaboard Coast Line Industries, Inc., Seaboard Coast Line R.R. Co. Trustee Johns Hopkins Hosp., chmn., 1972-77. Served to lt. comdr. USNR, 1941-45. Decorated Silver Star. Roman Catholic. Clubs: Md., Links. Home: 2211 Pennington Rd Bel Air MD 21210 Office: PO Box 2257 Baltimore MD 21203

MC GUIRT, WAYNE ROBERT, pub. co. exec.; b. Englewood, N.J., May 19, 1943; s. Wayne Paul and Helen Elaine (Rinaldi) McG.; B.A., Fordham U., 1965; M.B.A., Columbia U., 1972; postgrad. in mktg. N.Y. U., 1975—; m. Lisa Berger, Sept. 12, 1975. Computer ops. mgr. CIT Fin. Co., N.Y.C., 1966-68; fin. leasing specialist Efficient Leasing Corp., Ft. Lee, N.J., 1968-71; comptrollers asst. Time Inc., N.Y.C., 1972-73; asso. dir. circulation fin. dept., Time Inc., N.Y.C., 1975-77, bus. mgr. U.S. edit. Time Mag., N.Y.C., 1977-78; asst. bus. mgr. Sports Illustrated, N.Y.C., 1973-75; dir. planning Dow Jones & Co., Inc., N.Y.C., 1978—. Bank of N.Y. fellow, 1971-72. Mem. Planning Execs. Inst., N.Am. Soc. Corp. Planning, Beta Gamma Sigma. Republican. Roman Catholic. Clubs: Downtown Athletic. Home: 19 Great Hill Rd Darien CT 06820 Office: 22 Cortland St New York NY 10007

MC GURGAN, MILDRED LOUISE, stockbroker; b. Campbell, Mo., Oct. 16, 1933; d. Charles Harvey and Margaret Bertha (Baker) Bryant; secretarial diploma Patricia Stevens Career Coll., 1961; B.B.A., U. Detroit, 1975; postgrad. N.Y. Inst. Finance; m. Anthony M. McGurgan (div. 1974); children—Patricia, Carolyn, Mary, Antoinette. Telephone salesperson Formost McKesson, St. Louis, 1951-61; sec. to v.p. fin. AMT Corp., Troy, Mich., 1962-69; account exec. Merrill Lynch, Pierce, Fenner & Smith, Detroit, 1969—. Active Girl Scouts U.S.A.; mem. student council for evening sch. U. Detroit, 1973-74; mem. pres.'s cabinet Recipient Dean's award, U. Detroit, 1975, Pres.'s award, 1980. Mem. U. Detroit Alumni Council (pres. evening bus. adminstrn. div. 1980), U. Detroit Alumni Assn. (dir. 1979), Phi Gamma Nu (pres. Zeta chpt. 1973, 74, 75). Roman Catholic. Clubs: U. Detroit Investment, Merrill Lynch Exec. Home: 13 Smith St Box 876 Mount Clemens MI 48043 Office: 200 Renaissance Center Suite 3100 Detroit MI 48243

MC GURK, JAMES HENRY, cons. co. exec.; b. Phila., July 24, 1936; s. James Henry and Ednah Mae (Kleinsmith) McG.; B.S., Pa. State U., 1957; postgrad. in Econs., Temple U., 1960-62; m. LaVerne M. Kraynek, 1960; children—Heather, Melanye. Cons. mfg., various states, 1968-72; ops. chief mfg. cons. Manatech Internat., Westmont, N.J., 1970-72, A.T. Oxford Inc., N.Y.C., 1972-74; mem. corporate staff mfg. cons. Aspro Inc., Westport, Conn., 1974-77; with LHM, Inc., cons., Rochester, Mich., 1977—, also dir.; exec. v.p. Morse Hemco Inc., Holland, Mich., 1978—, also dir. Served with USAF, 1957-59. Mem. Am. Mgmt. Assn. Democrat. Home: 39 Forest Hills Dr Holland MI 49423 Office: 455 Douglas Ave Holland MI 49423

MCHALE, WARREN EDWARD, fluid power co. exec.; b. Detroit, Sept. 13, 1932; s. William Lester and Elizabeth Amilia (Henneman) McH.; B.S.E.E., Lawrence Inst. Tech., 1962; postgrad. Western Mich. U., 1965-68; m. Carol Lee Pearson, Feb. 25, 1952; children—Linda, Lawrence, Bruce. Project engr. Fischer Body div. Gen. Motors Corp., 1960-62; application engr. Vickers div. Sperry Rand Corp., 1962-65; market mgr. Hydreco-Gen. Signal Corp., 1965-69; exec. v.p. Fluid Controls, Inc., Mentor, Ohio, 1969-77; pres. Meriam Instrument div. Scott & Fetzer Co., Cleve., 1977-79; gen. mgr. Manatrol div. Parker Hannifin Corp., Elyria, Ohio, 1979—. Pres. Lake County Health and Welfare Council, 1975-76; trustee Willoughby Sch. Fine Arts, 1977—, Lake County Mental Health Center, 1977—. Served with USAF, 1952-56. Mem. Instrument Soc. Am. Home: 9275 Creekwood Dr Mentor OH 44060 Office: 520 Ternes Ave Elyria OH 44035

MC HARGUE, WAYNE ORVAL, ins. agt.; b. Brazil, Ind., Feb. 17, 1937; s. Raymond D. and Cathern L. (Maxwell) McH.; student Ind. U., 1955-59; B.S. in Bus. Adminstrn., Ind. State U., 1961; m. Edwina; 1 dau., Kristi Ellen. Asst. to dean of men Ind. State U., 1960-61; mgmt. trainee Ind. Nat. Bank, Indpls., 1962-65; sales rep. Am. United Life, Indpls., 1965—; estate and fin. planner. Mem. exec. council Indpls. Mus. Art, 1971-73, spl. gifts div. chmn., 1971-72; div. chmn. United Way of Greater Indpls., Inc., 1966, pres. Loaned Exec. Club, 1967. Recipient Nat. Sales Achievement award Nat. Assn. Life Underwriters, 1970, Nat. Quality award, 1967; Health Ins. Quality award Nat. Assn. Health Underwriters, 1975; registered Nat. Assn. Health Underwriters. Mem. Estate Planning Council Indpls., Indpls., Am. socs. C.L.U.'s, C.L.U. Found., Am. United Life Presidents Club, Indpls. Assn. Life Underwriters (dir., pres.-elect 1980-81), Life Underwriter Polit. Action Council Century Club, Indpls. Jaycees (dir.; Key Man award 1967; Outstanding Service award 1962), Delta Sigma Pi Alumni Club (pres. 1961-62), Phi Kappa Psi Alumni Club (pres. 1966-67). Republican. Methodist. Club: Sertoma (pres. 1974-75, chmn. bd. 1975-76) (Indpls.). Home: 8201 Castleton Blvd Indianapolis IN 46256 Office: 6535 E 82d St Suite 106 PO Box 50189 Indianapolis IN 46250

MCHUGH, PETER BROOKS, lawyer; b. Washington, Oct. 17, 1944; s. Joseph Weir and Eleanor (Hayward) McH.; B.A., Colgate U., 1966; J.D., Albany Law Sch., 1973; postgrad. London Sch. Econs., 1966; m. Marie-Louise Daulte, Jan. 9, 1971; children—Samuel B., Emily D. Admitted to N.Y. bar, 1974; law clk. Schenectady County Ct., 1973-75; asso. firm Englert & Reilly, Schenectady, 1973-77; partner firm Englert, Reilly & McHugh, P.C., Schenectady, 1977—. Bd. dirs. Dominion House; bd. dirs., founding mem. Schenectady Local Devel. Corp., Old Songs, Inc. Served with USNR, 1967-79; Vietnam. Mem. N.Y. State, Schenectady County bar assns., Capital Dist. Trial Lawyers Assn. Democrat. Home: 135 Willow St Guilderland NY 12084 Office: 144 Barrett St Schenectady NY 12305

MC HUGH, THOMAS JOSEPH, investment co. exec.; b. N.Y.C., Sept. 5, 1931; s. Joseph and Josephine Veronica (Cantlon) McH.; B.S., St. Joseph's Coll. 1954; m. Patricia Curry Silcox, Dec. 29, 1956; children—Thomas Joseph, Mary Love, Josephine Patricia, Edmund Howard, Allegra Churchill. Investment analyst, fiduciary counsel, N.Y.C., 1954-56; investment analyst Fidelity Phila. Bank & Trust Co., 1956-59; investment mgr. Reliance Ins. Co., Phila., 1959-64; with Pitcairn Inc., Jenkintown, Pa., 1964—, v.p., 1964-66, sr. v.p., investment dir., 1967—, also dir.; dir. P.P.G. Industries, Rouse Corp., Keydata Corp., Evans Pitcairn Co. Mem. N.Y. Soc. Security Analysts, Phila. Soc. Security Analysts, Phila. Security Assn. Republican. Roman Catholic. Clubs: Duquesne, Union League (Phila.); Overbrook Country, Ironwood Country (Palm Desert, Calif.). Office: 101 Greenwood Ave Jenkintown PA 19046

MC ILHANY, STERLING FISHER, publishing co. exec.; b. San Gabriel, Calif., Apr. 12, 1930: s. William Wallace and Julia (Fisher) M.; B.F.A., U. Tex., 1953; student U. Calif. at Los Angeles, 1953-54, 55-57, Universita per Stranieri, Perugia, Italy, 1957; Rotary fellow Accademia delle Belle Arti, Rome, 1957-58. Teaching asst. art history U. Calif. at Los Angeles, 1953-54, 55-57; art supr. Kamehameha Prep. Sch., Honolulu, 1954-55; instr. Honolulu Acad. Arts 1955; asso. editor Am. Artist mag., N.Y.C., 1958-61, editor, 1969-70; condr. network series Books and the Artist, WRVR, N.Y.C., 1961-62; sr. editor Reinhold Book Corp., N.Y.C., 1962-69; pres. Art Horizons, Inc., N.Y.C., 1959—; instr. Sch. Visual Arts, N.Y.C., 1961-69. Recipient First award tour European art centers Students Internat. Travel Assn., 1952. Author: Banners and Hangings, 1966; Art as Design-Design as Art, 1970; Wood Inlay, 1972; Simbari, 1975; also articles. Address: 52 Morton St New York NY 10014

MC ILRATH, DAN M., steel co. exec.; b. Carrol County, Ind., May 18, 1928; s. L. L. and Mabel P. (Patty) McI.; B.S., Purdue U., 1952; m. Martha Agnes McCord, Dec. 27, 1948; children—Marie, David, Elinor, James, Beth, Robert, Rebecca. With Continental Steel Co. (now Penn-Dixie), Kokomo, Ind., 1952-74; resident mgr. Midstates Steel & Wire div. Keystone Consol. Industries, Inc., Greenville, Miss., 1974, mgr. ops., Greenville and Jacksonville, Fla., 1975-76, v.p. operations, Greenville, Jacksonville, Sherman, Tex. and Crawfordsville, Ind., 1976-78, dir. wire ops. Keystone Group, 1978-79, plant mgr., 1979—. Served with USN, 1946-48. Named Wireman of Yr., Wire Industry News, 1976. Mem. Wire Assn., Ind. Mfrs. Assn., Miss. Mfrs. Assn., Am. Inst. Steel Engrs., Crawfordsville C. of C. Republican. Roman Catholic. Clubs: Country, Rotary, Elks. Home: Rural Route 5 Crawfordsville IN 47933 Office: PO Box 392 Crawfordsville IN 47933

MC ILVEEN, WALTER, engr.; b. Belfast, Ireland, Aug. 12, 1927; s. Walter and Amelia (Thompson) McI.; came to U.S., 1958, naturalized, 1963; M.E., Queens U., Belfast, 1948; H.V.A.C., Borough Polytechnic, London, 1951; m. Margaret Teresa Ruane, Apr. 17, 1949; children—Walter, Adrian, Peter, Anita, Alan. Mech. engr. Davidson & Co., Belfast, 1943-48; sr. contract engr. Keith Blachman Ltd., London, 1948-58; mech. engr. Fred S. Dubin Assos., Hartford, Conn., 1959-64; chief mech. engr. Koton & Donovan, W. Haven, Conn., 1964-66; prin., engr. Walter McIlveen Assos., Avon, Conn., 1966—. Mem. IEEE, Illuminating Engring. Soc., ASME, Hartford Engring. Club, Conn. Engrs. in Pvt. Practice, ASHRAE. Mem. Ch. of

Ireland. Home: 3 Valley View Rd Weatogue CT 06089 Office: 195 W Main St Avon CT 06001

MCILWAIN, WILLIAM THOMPSON, automobile co. exec.; b. Fort Pierce, Fla., June 2, 1941; s. William Thompson and Virginia (Ware) McI.; B.B.A., U. Miami, 1965; m. Johnann F., Dec. 1, 1972. Mgr., Deloitte Haskins & Sells, C.P.A.'s, Miami, Fla., 1965-70; controller, Southeast Banking Corp., Miami, 1970-75; sr. v.p. First Bancshares of Fla., Inc., Boca Raton, Fla., 1975-77; pres. Basic Food Industries Inc., Ft. Lauderdale, Fla., 1977-79; pres. and chief exec. officer Griffith Co., Ft. Lauderdale, 1979—; dir. Beacon Leasing Co., Palm Beach, Fla., 1976—, Gulfstream Bank & Trust Co. of Ft. Lauderdale, 1976—. Treas., Connally for Pres., Broward County, 1979-80. Office: Griffith Co 3213 N Ocean Blvd Fort Lauderdale FL 33308

MC INNES, DONALD GORDON, r.r. exec.; b. Buffalo, Nov. 6, 1940; s. Milton Gordon and Blanche Mae (Clunk) McI.; B.A. in Econs., Denison U., 1963; M.S. in Transp., Northwestern U., 1965; certificate in transp. Yale, 1965; m. Betsy Campbell, Mar. 18, 1967; children—Campbell Gordon, Cody Milton. Budget mgr. operating Atchison, Topeka & Sante Fe Ry. Co., Chgo., 1969-71, asst. trainmaster, San Bernardino, Calif., 1971-73, trainmaster, Temple, Tex., 1973-76, asst. supt., Carlsbad, N.Mex., 1976-77, supt. Eastern div., Emporia, Kans., 1978-79, Los Angeles div., San Bernardino, Calif., 1979—. Chmn. indsl. div. United Way, 1978. Mem. St. Francis Episcopal Sch. Bd. Edn., Temple, 1975-76; bd. dirs. Temple United Fund, 1976; mem. long-range planning com. San Bernardino United Way, 1980; vestryman St. John's Episcopal Ch. Served to lt. USAF, 1965-67, to capt. U.S. Army, 1967-69; Vietnam. Decorated Bronze Star. Mem. Lambda Chi Alpha. Clubs: Rotary of San Bernardino; Arrowhead Country. Home: 4851 David Way San Bernardino CA 92404 Office: 1170 W 3d St San Bernardino CA 92401

MCINNIS, JAMES ABERNETHY, electronic products co. exec.; b. Washington, Aug. 4, 1932; s. William Donald and Helen Campbell (Abernethy) McI.; student Ind. Inst. Tech., 1955-59; m. Yvonne F. Goldschmidt, July 24, 1975; children—Gordon MacDonald, Deborah Irene, Jennifer Helen. With Magnavox Corp., 1959—, dir. internat. ops., Ft. Wayne, Ind., 1961-75, v.p. European ops., St. Gallen, Switzerland, 1975—. Served with USAF, 1951-55. Mem. Assn. U.S. Army, Armed Forces Communications and Electronics Assn., Aircraft Owners and Pilots Assn., Swiss-Am. C. of C. Home: Ahornstrasse 7 CH-9032 Engelburg Switzerland Office: Bogenstrasse 14 Ch-9000 Saint Gallen Switzerland

MC INTOSH, JAMES BOYD, mut. ins. co. exec.; b. Milton, Mass., Feb. 18, 1920; s. James A. and Margaret (Wilkie) McI.; B.B.A., Boston U., 1950; m. Frances Glading, Feb. 20, 1943; children—Judith McIntosh Carr, Gaye, Linda, James Boyd. With New Eng. Mut. Ins. Co., 1945-67, exec. v.p., 1964-67; pres. Midland Mut. Ins. Co., Columbus, Ohio, 1967-79, chmn. bd., 1980—, also dir.; dir. Lifetime Communities, Inc., Wenwest, Inc., Orange Co., Inc.; trustee Griffith Found. Ins. Edn., Boston U., Center Sci. and Industry, Franklin County Hist. Soc., Columbus, Children's Hosp., Columbus, Columbus Symphony, Ohio Dominican Coll. Served to capt. USAAF, World War II. Decorated Silver Star, D.F.C., Purple Heart, Air medal with 4 oak leaf clusters. Mem. Am. Council Life Ins., Assn. Ohio Life Ins. Cos. (past pres.), Life Office Mgmt. Assn. (dir., chmn.), Gen. Agts. and Mgrs. Assn., Ohio C. of C. (dir.). Republican. Episcopalian. Clubs: Columbus, Columbus Country, Columbus Athletic, University (Columbus); Dedham (Mass.) Country and Polo. Author: The Pearl of the Midwest, 1973. Office: 250 E Broad St Columbus OH 43215

MC INTURF, FAITH MARY, engring. corp. exec.; b. Grand Ridge, Ill., Aug. 22, 1917; d. Lynne E. and Margaret (Garver) McInturf; grad. high sch. With The J. E. Porter Corp., Chgo., 1963-65, v.p., 1951-65, sec., 1951-65, also dir.; v.p., sec. Potomac Engring. Corp., 1941—; sec.-treas., dir. Chgo. Harness Racing Inc., 1967-72, sec., dir., 1974-78; sec.-treas., dir. Balmoral Jockey Club, Inc., Horse Racing Promotions, Inc., 1967-72, sec., dir., 1974-78; sec.-treas., dir. Balmoral Park Trot, Inc., 1967-72. Mem. Art. Inst. Chgo. Roman Catholic. Home: 1360 Lake Shore Dr Chicago IL 60610 Office: 720 N Michigan Ave Chicago IL 60611

MC INTURF, JAMES LEE, ins. agency exec.; b. Zanesville, Ohio, July 22, 1945; s. Kenneth L. and Dorothy McI.; B.B.A., Ohio U., 1967; m. Sally A. Lee, Sept. 4, 1966; children—James, Cindy, Marianne. Ins. adjuster Travelers Ins. Co., Zanesville, 1967-71; ins. agent, v.p. Alan L. Rankin Ins., Zanesville, 1971-75; owner, mgr. James L. McInturf Ins., Zanesville, 1975—. Active Little League, 1974. Mem. Zanesville C. of C., Am., Ohio ind. ins. agts. Republican. Lutheran. Home: 5071 Cliffrock Dr Zanesville OH 43701 Office: 963 Adair Ave PO Box 2868 Zanesville OH 43701

MC INTYRE, JOHN WILLIAM, banker; b. Valdosta, Ga., Sept. 14, 1930; s. James A. and Julia (Norton) McI.; B.B.A., Emory U., 1951; Exec. Mgmt. Program, Stamford U., 1966; m. Joan Pruitt, Oct. 8, 1955; children—Anna, John William, Martha, Michael. With Citizens & So. Nat. Bank, Atlanta, 1951—, exec. v.p. trust, 1969-72, gen. v.p. trust and asset mgmt., 1972-77, gen. v.p., 1977-79, pres., dir., 1979—; dir. Larkin Coils, Inc. Bd. dirs. Atlanta Speech Sch.; adv. bd. dirs. Ga. State U.; bd. visitors Emory U.; pres., bd. dirs. Ga. Soc. Prevention of Blindness; bd. sponsors Atlanta Symphony; trustee The Lovett Sch. Served with AUS, 1952-54. Mem. Assn. Res. City Bankers, Ga. C. of C. (dir.). Baptist. Clubs: Piedmont Driving, Cherokee Town and Country, Commerce. Office: 35 Broad St NW Atlanta GA 30303

MCINTYRE, ROBERT ALLEN, JR., mfg. co. exec.; b. Gettysburg, Pa., Jan. 6, 1940; s. Robert Allen and Leona Hazel (Stoner) McI.; student U. Portland, 1962-63, U. Md., 1963-64, York Coll., 1969-71, U. Wis., 1972-74, also numerous profl. courses; m. Rosemary Holland, Mar. 25, 1967; children—Nicole, Brian. Field salesman L.E. Smith, Inc., Gettysburg, 1958-61; with Black & Decker Mfg. Co., Hampstead, Md. and Beloit, Wis., 1965-75, engring. and service mgr., Beloit, 1974-75; with Dover Corp., Rochester, N.Y. and Beecher, Ill., 1975-78, v.p. engring. Bernard div., Beecher, 1977-78; v.p., gen. mgr. Marvel Lighting div. Am. Brands, Mullins, S.C., 1978, exec. v.p., 1979, pres., 1979-80, exec. v.p. Swingline Inc. div. Long Island City, N.Y., 1980-81, pres., chief exec. officer MCM Products, Inc. div., N.Y.C., 1981—; chmn., dir. W.R. Case & Sons Cultery Co., Bradford, Pa., 1981—, Marvel Lighting Corp., Mullins, 1981—, Marson Corp., Chelsea, 1981—; pres., dir. Marson Sales, Inc., Chelsea, Mass., 1981—, Marson Corp. of P.R., 1981—; trustee C&L Realty Trust, Chelsea. Served with USAF, 1961-65; Vietnam. Mem. Marion C. of C. Office: 245 Park Ave New York NY 10167

MC INTYRE, ROBERT DUGALD, lawyer; b. Toronto, Ont., Can., Dec. 13, 1938; s. Archibald Campbell and Lucy Mood (MacLeod) McI.; B.A., U. Western Ont., 1960; LL.B., Osgoode Hall Law Sch., Toronto, 1964; LL.M., U. London, 1967; m. Louana Joy Armstrong, July 24, 1965; children—Scott Robert, Kyle Armstrong. Called to Ont. bar, 1966, queen's counsel, 1979; with firm Beatty, Bowyer Greenslade, Brampton, Ont., 1966-70; self-employed, 1971-75; partner firm McIntyre, Moon, Brampton, 1976—. Fellow Found Legal Research Can.; mem. Can. Bar Assn., Am. Bar Assn., Upper Can. Law Soc., York Law Assn., Peel Law Assn. Clubs: Brampton Rotary, Bentham, Brampton Bd. Trade. Home: Beechwood Acres 15 Cedar Dr Caledon ON L0N 1C0 Canada Office: 181 Queen St E Suite 200 Brampton ON L6W 2B3 Canada

MC IVER, ANDREW CHARLES, dental mfg. co. exec.; b. Santa Monica, Calif., Oct. 1, 1953; s. Angus Albert and Catherine (Louvain) McI.; stepson of G.O. Hartzell; B.S., U. Calif. at Berkeley, 1975; M.A. in Mgmt., U. Redlands (Calif.), 1980; student Brigham Young U., 1972. Translator, Acme Stores, Milpitas, Calif., 1970; with G. Hartzell & Son, Concord, Calif., 1970—, distbn. mgr., 1974-75, salesman, 1975-76, gen. mgr., 1977—, v.p., 1978—. Mem. Am. Mgmt. Assn., Calif. Berkeley Alumni Assn. Republican. Home: 300 Ranger Pl Danville CA 94526 Office: PO Box 5988 Concord CA 94520

MCKANE, DAVID BENNETT, personal care products co. exec.; b. Salem, Mass., July 10, 1945; s. Vernon Wilson and Barbara Inez (Bennett) McK.; B.A., Dartmouth Coll., 1967, M.B.A., 1969; m. Wilson Lineburgh, Apr. 16, 1977; stepchildren—Taylor, Lee, Paige. Product mgr. Church & Dwight Co. Inc., N.Y.C., 1969-72; v.p. NTA Inc., Nanuet, N.Y., and N.Y.C., 1972-75; v.p., exec. asst. to chmn. Schick Inc., Westport, Conn., 1975-77, sr. v.p., 1977-79, exec. v.p., chief operating officer, 1979—; treas., dir. Demline Nav. Ltd., Savannah, Ga. Mem. New Eng. Soc. in City N.Y., Mass. Soc. Mayflower Descs. Republican. Episcopalian. Clubs: Union (N.Y.C.); Fairfield County Hunt (Westport, Conn.). Home: 48 Owenoke Park Westport CT 06880 Office: Schick Inc 33 Riverside Ave Westport CT 06880

MC KASSON, ROBERT EDWARD, JR., ins. co. exec.; b. Los Angeles, Feb. 3, 1945; s. Robert E. and Verda C. (White) McK.; A.A., Fullerton Coll., 1967. Salesman various life ins. cos., 1967—; pres., chmn. bd. Ind. Bankers Ins. Services, Santa Ana, Calif., 1977—. Recipient Gold medal ins. sales awards, Bronze medal Investors Guaranty Life, 1976; others. Club: 20-30. Home: 124 31st St Newport Beach CA 92663 Office: 1833 E 17th St Santa Ana CA 92701

MC KAY, THOMAS NELSON, electronics co. exec.; b. Queens, N.Y., Oct. 26, 1927; s. Alexander Dunbar and Elise Viola (Nelson) McK.; B.A., Hofstra U., 1951; m. Eleanor Marie Diener, Sept. 10, 1950; children—Dwight D., Stuart S. Agt., Met. Life Ins. Co., 1951-54; sales engr. Exide Corp., 1954-58; subcontract buyer Grumman Aircraft Engring. Corp., 1958-69; with CCTV sales, 1969-71; subcontract adminstr. PRD Electronics div. Harris Corp., Syosset, N.Y., 1972—. Exec. v.p. Nassau County Fish and Game Assn., 1962-69; dist. scout commr. Boy Scouts Am., 1972—. Served with USN, 1946-47. Mem. Nat. Rifle Assn. (life). Presbyterian. Club: Masons. Home: 356 Piping Rock Seaford NY 11783 Office: Harris Corp PRD Electronics Div 6801 Jericho Turnpike Syosset NY 11791

MCKAY, WILLIAM IVOR, engring. co. exec.; b. Victoria, B.C., Can., May 22, 1920; s. Neil Eliott and Edith Mae (Hancock) McK.; A.B. in Physics, San Francisco State Coll., 1941; grad. degree in meteorology M.I.T., 1943; m. Marilyn Lewis, June 16, 1943; children—Patricia Ann, Kenneth Lewis, Kathleen. Sr. engr. Bechtel Corp., 1948-53; with Fluor Corp., Irvine, Calif., 1954—, now group v.p., dir.; pres. Fluor Constructors Internat., Inc. Served to capt. USAAF, 1942-46. Registered lic. mech. engr., Calif. Republican. Clubs: Eldorado Country (Palm Desert, Calif.); El Niguel Country (Laguna Niguel, Calif.). Office: 3333 Michelson Dr Irvine CA 92730

MC KEE, ALLEN PAGE, internat. fin. cons.; b. Los Angeles, July 26, 1941; s. Norman C. and Eleanor (Page) McK.; B.A. in Econs., U. Mich., 1964; M.B.A., U. Calif., Berkeley, 1971. Area relations officer of internat. div. Bank of Am., San Francisco, 1967-70; investment officer Bamerical Internat. Fin. Corp., San Francisco, 1971-73; v.p. and dir. internat. investments Union Bank, San Francisco, 1973-74; pres. Montgomery Assos., Inc., San Francisco, 1975—, dir., 1977—. Served to lt. USN, 1964-67; Vietnam. Mem. World Affairs Council No. Calif., Soc. Calif. Pioneers, Calif. Bus. Alumni Assn., Delta Kappa Epsilon. Republican. Club: Commonwealth of Calif. Home: 18 Chaucer Ct Mill Valley CA 94941 Office: 601 Montgomery St Suite 1725 San Francisco CA 94111

MC KEE, DONALD DARRELL, ret. ins. and real estate broker; b. Highland, Ill., July 20, 1932; s. Earl Michael and Leta Evelyn (Dresch) McK.; grad. high sch.; m. Emma A. Becker, Aug. 28, 1956; children—Dale Michael, Gail Ann. Sales clk. C. Kinne & Co., Highland, 1952-63; salesman Lowenstein Agy., Inc., Highland, 1963-69; owner Don Mc Kee Ins., 1970-79; owner Don McKee Realty, Highland, 1969-75; tchr. real estate So. Ill. U., Edwardsville, 1974-80, Lewis and Clark Community Coll., Godfrey, Ill., 1973-77, pres. Real Estate Inst., 1973-80; exec. officer Edwardsville-Collinsville Bd. Realtors, 1975. Mem. So. Ill. Tourism Council, 1969-78. Recipient Nat. Health Quality award, 1978. Mem. So. Ill. Ind. Ins. Agts. (pres. 1974-75), Edwardsville-Collinsville (pres. 1974), Ill. (v.p. dist. 1977) bds. realtors, Highland C. of C., Highland Hist. Soc. (dir.), Helvetia Sharpshooters Soc., St. Louis Art Mus., Mo. Bot. Gardens, Friends of Lovejoy Library, Friends of Latzer Meml. Library. Club: Highland Country. Contbr. articles to profl. jours. Home: 1403 Pine St Highland IL 62249 Office: 825 Main St Highland IL 62249

MC KEE, JAMES WILSON, JR., mfg. co. exec.; b. Pitts., Aug, 19, 1922; s. James Wilson and Mary Isabel (Welch) McK.; B.Comm., McGill U., 1942; m. Jayne Finnegan, July 27, 1947; children—Bettina, James Wilson, Sheila. C Cost acct. Italian affiliate Corn Products Co., Milan, 1947-50, fin. mgr. Brazilian affiliate, Sao Paulo, 1950-58, pres. Cuban affiliate, Havana, 1958-59, mng. dir. Brazilian affiliate, 1959-64, comptroller Corn Products Co., N.Y.C., 1964-65, v.p. fin., 1965-67, v.p. fin., personnel and adminstrn., 1967-69, pres., chief adminstrv. officer CPC Internat., Inc., Englewood Cliffs, N.J., 1969-72, pres., chief exec. officer, 1972-79, chmn. bd., chief exec. officer, 1979—; dir. Marine Midland Banks, Inc., Singer Co., Melville Corp. Served as pilot USAAC, World War II. Decorated Cruzeiro do Sul (Brazil), 1965. Mem. Internat. C. of C. (trustee U.S. council), Council of Americas (trustee), Com. Econ. Devel. (trustee), Conf. Bd. (trustee). Clubs: Univ., Econ., Sky, Treas.'s (N.Y.C.) Office: CPC Internat Inc International Plaza Englewood Cliffs NJ 07632

MC KEE, WILLIAM BLANCHARD, investment co. exec.; b. Orlando, Fla., Jan. 24, 1946; s. Seth Jefferson and Sarah Helen (Parshall) McK.; B.S., U.S. Air Force Acad., 1968; M.A., UCLA, 1970; m. Florence Pendleton Nowlin, Dec. 29, 1973; children—Sarah Elizabeth, Robert Blanchard. Comml. loan officer Ariz. Bank, Phoenix, 1974-76, asst. v.p., mgr., 1976-77, v.p., mgr. regional loan office, 1977-79; v.p., mgr. Venture Equities, Inc., Scottsdale, Ariz., 1979—; dir. Western I/O, Inc., Tele-Graphic Computer Systems, Inc.; lectr. U. Phoenix. Pres., bd. dirs. Scottsdale Girls Club, 1979-80; deacon Presbyterian Ch. Recipient appreciation plaque Scottsdale Girls Club, 1980. Mem. Nat. Assn. Small Bus. Investment Cos., Scottsdale C. of C. Clubs: Paradise Valley Country; Rotary (Scottsdale); Phoenix 100. Office: Venture Equities Inc 6900 E Camelback Rd Scottsdale AZ 85251

MC KEEHAN, LARRY OLIVER, JR., corp. exec.; b. Atlanta, Oct. 22, 1921; s. Luther O. and Pauline (Campbell) McK.; student public schs., Miami, Fla.; m. Florence L. Lumpkin, Jan. 1, 1980; children by previous marriage—Kathy, Larry; step-children—Karen, Debra, Roy. Vice pres. sales One-Der Frame Corp., Birmingham, Ala., 1948-56; dist. and regional sales mgr. Steelcraft Mfg. Co., Birmingham, 1956-68; gen. sales mgr. Steelcraft/Am.-Standard, Cin., 1968-72, v.p. sales, 1972-76, dir. mktg. bldg. spltys., group, 1976-79, v.p. bus. planning, 1976-79, v.p. sales and mktg., 1979—. Trustee, Union Twp. Homeowners Assn., 1975-78. Served with Army Transport Service, U.S. Mcht. Marine, 1942-44. Mem. Nat. Council Housing Industry (trustee 1979-82), Sales and Mktg. Execs. Internat. (dir. chpt. 1978-81, pres. chpt. 1979-80), Producers Council Ins. (nat. mktg. mgrs. coms. 1976-80). Republican. Protestant. Club: Glen Ridge Lake Inc. (dir. 1970-78, pres. 1977-78). Home: 11283 Marlette Dr Cincinnati OH 45242 Office: 9017 Blue Ash Rd Cincinnati OH 45242

MCKEEL, R. BRUCE, investment banking co. exec.; b. Oregon City, Oreg., Apr. 13, 1942; s. Ralph Orman and Gladys Anna (Palmer) McK.; B.A., U. Oreg., 1964; m. Lynn E. Mackey, Feb. 14, 1976. Investment banker Davis Skaggs & Co., San Francisco, 1968-73; v.p. HBE Leasing Corp., San Francisco, 1973-75; v.p. leverage leasing Equilease Corp. subs. Eltar Corp., San Francisco, 1975-77; pres., founder, dir. Qartel Corp., San Francisco, 1977-79; v.p. leverage leasing, spl. fin. project Prescott Ball & Turben, San Francisco, 1979—; spl. project fin. cons. to various nat. cos., 1979—. Vice chmn. spl. gifts United Crusade, 1978. Recipient cert. distinction N.Y. Inst. Fin., 1968. Mem. Western Assn. Equipment Lessors (past officer, dir.), Am. Assn. Equipment Lessors. Republican. Episcopalian. Clubs: Olympic of San Francisco, Family. Home: 560 Hayne Rd Hillsborough CA 94010 Office: One Sutter St San Francisco CA 94104

MC KEEN, GREGORY BRENT, accountant; b. Klamath Falls, Oreg., May 12, 1938; s. Charles Harold and Ida Jewel (Roote) McK.; student So. Oreg. Coll., 1965, Golden Gate Coll., 1968; m. Linda McKeen; children—Lila Jewel, Gregory Brent. Mgr., Western Union Telegraph Co., Klamath Falls, 1958-65, Lambie & Molatore, C.P.A.'s, Alturas, Calif., 1966-70; controller Radio Medford, Inc. (Oreg.), 1971; accountant Yergen & Meyer, C.P.A.'s, Medford, 1972; prin. Gregory B. McKeen, C.P.A., Medford, 1973—; pres. Learning Experiences, Unltd., Rainbow's End Prodns. and Flying M Prodns.; lectr. in field. C.P.A., Oreg., Calif. Mem. Oreg. Soc. C.P.A.'s (pres. So. Oreg. chpt. 1977), Am. Inst. C.P.A.'s, Nat. Theatre Critics Assn., Am. Film Inst., Internat. Platform Assn. Democrat. Methodist. Clubs: Elks, Lions (v.p. 1975). Home: 925 Janes Rd Medford OR 97501 Office: 4117 S Pacific Hwy Medford OR 97501

MC KEEVER, IRA EVERETT, coal co. exec.; b. Kit Carson, Colo., June 27, 1927; s. Ira Everett and Anna Jeanette (Reuter) McK.; Geol. Engring. degree, Colo. Sch. Mines, 1952; m. Linda Kay Padgett, Dec. 15, 1975; children—M. Christine, Scott I., Bonita L., Walter A. Vice-pres. sulphur ops. Tex. Gulf Sulphur Co., Houston, 1952-68; v.p. Gulf Resources & Chem. Corp., Houston, 1968-72; pres. Gulf Sulphur Corp. subs. Gulf Resources & Chem. Corp., Houston, 1968-72; pres. mining div. W.R. Grace & Co., N.Y.C., 1972-76; pres., gen. mgr. Colowyo Coal Co., Craig, Colo., 1976—. Served with USN, 1945-46. Recipient Van Diest Gold medal Colo. Sch. Mines, 1967. Mem. AIME, Am. Assn. Petroleum Geologists. Republican. Methodist. Clubs: Houston; Sky (N.Y.C.). Home: PO Box 787 Craig CO 81625 Office: 5731 State Hwy 13 Meeker CO 81641

MC KELL, ROBERT, telephone co. exec.; b. Boston, July 30, 1923; s. William Scott and Estelle (Coward) McK.; B.S. in Elec. Engring., U. Colo., 1944; m. Amy Hardcastle Story, June 9, 1945; children—Phoebe Hardcastle McKell Currier, Alice Lockwood (Mrs. Vernon J. Roden), Robin Story, William Scott. Asst. mgr. Chillicothe Telephone Co. (Ohio), 1946-50, v.p., asst. mgr., 1950-62, pres., 1962—; treas. Chief Logan Corp., Chillicothe, 1957—; pres. Chillicothe Telcom, Inc., 1964-74; dir. Huntington Bank of Chillicothe (formerly Savs. Bank Co.), 1946—, mem. exec. com., 1958—, chmn., 1958-70; pres. Bus. Telephone Systems, Inc., Chillicothe, 1971-75. Dir. communications Ross County Civil Def., 1952-55; mem. Union-Scioto Bd. Edn., Chillicothe, 1960-71, pres., 1962-63; adv. bd. Salvation Army, Chillicothe, 1948-60, chmn. 1958; mem. Ohio Ednl. TV Network Commn., 1963-71, 75—, exec. com., 1968-71, 76—, sec., 1980—; chmn. Ohio U.-Chillicothe Regional Council; mem. human resources council Carver Community Center, 1971-75. Served to 2d lt. Signal Corps AUS, 1944-46. Mem. U.S. (broad-band services com. 1964-79, dir. 1970—, chmn. expanded services planning com.), Ohio (pres. 1964-65, dir. 1962-75, exec. com. 1967-71), Ind. telephone assns., Ind. Telephone Pioneers Assn., Chillicothe-Ross C. of C. (bd. dirs. 1978—, treas. 1979—). Episcopalian. Clubs: Cavalier (pres. Chillicothe 1953), Rotary. Home: 443 Sandusky Blvd Chillicothe OH 45601 Office: PO Box 480 Chillicothe OH 45601

MC KENNA, JAMES, JR., mgmt. cons.; b. Cliffside Park, N.J., Feb. 6, 1939; s. James K. and Caroline Ellen (Petrillo) McK.; B.A. with honors in Polit. Sci. and History, St. Peter's Coll., 1960; children—Sue Ellen, Kelly Marie. Data processing rep. IBM Corp., N.Y.C., 1962-68; mktg. mgr. Compumedic Controls Corp., N.Y.C., 1968-69; br. mgr. Marshall Data Systems, N.Y.C., 1969-70; v.p. Computer Planning Corp., N.Y.C., 1970-72; program group mgr. Mgmt. Systems div. Am. Mgmt. Assn., N.Y.C., 1973-76; v.p. The Pres.'s Assn. div., 1977—; chmn. bd. Vista Warehousing, Inc., Hoboken, N.J., 1979—; dir. A.G. Ganz, Inc., Los Angeles. City councilman, Cliffside Park, N.J., 1964-66. Recipient Murray medal St. Peter's Coll., 1960; Merit award Assn. Systems Mgmt., 1975. Mem. Data Processing Mgmt. Assn. (past dir. N.Y. chpt.), Assn. Systems Mgmt. (past v.p. Met. chpt.). Contbr. articles to profl. jours. Home: 128 Central Park S New York NY 10019 Office: 135 W 50th St New York NY 10020

MCKENNA, JAMES A(LOYSIUS), JR., lawyer, broadcaster; b. Poughkeepsie, N.Y., July 1, 1918; s. James Aloysius and Eleanor Frances (Mahoney) McK.; student Manhattan Coll., 1934-35; B.S., Cath. U. Am., 1938; LL.B., Georgetown U., 1942; m. Rebekah Ann Rial, Sept. 1, 1941; children—Michelle Marie Nassif, James Aloysius, Dennis M., Matthew M., Marc W., Aileen. Admitted to D.C. bar, 1941; counsel Civil Aeros. Bd., 1941-42; asst. to gen. counsel Office Alien Property Custodian, 1942-44; individual practice law, Washington, 1946—; mem. Haley, McKenna & Wilkinson, 1948-52; partner firm McKenna, Wilkinson & Kittner, 1952—; pres., dir., radio stas. KQRS and KQRS-FM, Mpls., radio sta. WCMB and WSFM, Harrisburg, Pa., WWQM and WWQM-FM, Madison, Wis. Served as lt. (j.g.), USNR, 1944-46. Recipient medal for distinguished service Mt. St. Mary's Coll., 1966; Annual Alumni Achievement award in law/communications Cath. U. Am., 1978. Mem. IEEE, FCC Bar Assn., Georgetown U. Alumni Assn., Delta Theta Phi. Clubs: Internat., Army and Navy, Broadcasters (Washington). Home: 5219 Oakland Rd Chevy Chase MD 20015 Office: 1150 17th St NW Washington DC 20036 also Annandale Rd Emmitsburg MD 21727

MCKENNA, JOHN DENNIS, environ. testing co. exec.; b. N.Y.C., Apr. 1, 1940; s. Hubert Guy and Elizabeth Ann (Record) McK.; B.S. in Chem. Engring., Manhattan Coll., 1961; M.Chem.Engring., Newark Coll. Engring., 1968; M.B.A., Rider Coll., 1975; m. Christel

Klages, Dec. 26, 1964; children—Marc, Michelle. Tech. asst. to pres. Eldib Engring. & Research Co., Newark, 1964-67; program mgr. Princeton Chem. Research, Inc. (N.J.), 1967-68; projects dir. Cottrell Environ. Systems, Bound Brook, N.J., 1968-72; v.p., then pres. Enviro-Systems & Research, Inc., Roanoke, Va., 1973-79; pres. ETS, Inc., Roanoke, 1979—. Mem. Air Pollution Control Assn., Am. Inst. Chem. Engrs. Roman Catholic. Contbr. chpts. to books, articles to profl. jours. Home: 4118 Chaparral Dr SW Roanoke VA 24018 Office: ETS Inc Suite C-103 3140 Chaparral Dr SW Roanoke VA 24018

MCKENNA, QUENTIN CARNEGIE, tool co. exec.; b. Claremont, Calif., Sept. 2, 1926; s. George Alexander and Lillian Frances (Street) McK.; B.A. cum laude, Pomona Coll., 1948; postgrad. Stanford U. (Hewlett Packard fellow), 1948-50, U. So. Calif., 1951-53, UCLA, 1968-69; m. Barbara Louise Williamson, Sept. 12, 1948; children—Candace, Megan, Carl, Erin. Mem. tech. staff guided missile div. Hughes Aircraft Co., 1950-52; with Indsl. Electronics, 1952-55; with Hughes Aircraft Co., 1955-78, asst. group exec. missile systems group, 1977-78; pres. Kennametal, Inc., Latrobe, Pa., 1978-79, pres. chief exec. officer, 1979—. Mem. Los Angeles County Central Republican Com., 1953-58, mem. state central com., 1956-58, chmn. 46th Assembly Dist., 1956-58; bd. dirs. St. Paul's Cathedral, Los Angeles, 1975-78; bd. dirs. San Antonio Water Conservation Dist., 1974-75. Mem. Phi Beta Kappa, Sigma Xi. Episcopalian. Patentee in field. Office: 1 Lloyd Ave Latrobe PA 15650

MCKENNA, THOMAS ADAM, JR., analytical chemist; b. Natchez, Miss., Mar. 14, 1922; s. Thomas Adam and Blanche (Korndorffer) McK.; student Copiah-Lincoln Jr. Coll., 1938-39; B.S. in Chemistry, La. State U., 1944; student U. Miss., 1955, Podbielniak Inst., 1956; m. Peggy Marie McCrosky, June 2, 1949; children—Mary Lucille, Thomas Adam III, Michael Gerard, Patrick Joseph. With Motor Fuels Lab., Dept. Revenue, State La.; with Firestone Tire & Rubber Co., Orange, Tex., 1944—, shift control chemist, spl. problems chemist, lab. mgr. and chief chemist, 1956—; owner, dir. work Marian Labs., Lake Charles, La., 1955—. Lectr. gas chromatography Lamar Coll. Tech., 1963. Mem. dist. advancement com. Boy Scouts Am.; pres. St. Mary's Home and Sch. Assn., 1963-64; active Community Concert Assn. Fellow Am. Inst. Chemists; mem. Gulf Coast Spectroscopic Group (chmn.), Am. Soc. for Quality Control (sr. mem.; area dir. S. Tex. sect. 1959—), Am. Chem. Soc. (chmn. S.W. La. sect. 1954—, sec. Tex.-La.-Gulf sect. 1961-62), Am. Soc. Testing Materials (chmn. com. D-2 of sect. D), AAAS, Alpha Tau Omega. K.C. Editor: The Newsletter, 1949-54. Contbr. numerous articles to profl. jours. Home: 312 W Pine Ave Orange TX 77630 Office: PO Box 1269 Orange TX 77630

MC KENNA, WILLIAM FRANCIS, lawyer; b. Meriden, Conn., May 14, 1910; s. Francis Joseph and Alice (Downes) McK.; Ph.B., Yale, 1930, J.D., 1932; m. Catherine Agnes Donahue, June 25, 1935; children—William Francis (dec.), Daniel Joseph. Admitted to Conn. bar, 1932; with Buckley, Creedon & Danaher, Hartford, 1932-35; counsel, acting chief pub. loans sect. legal div. RFC, Washington, 1935-42; counsel Def. Supplies Corp., 1942; chief airports br. War Assets Adminstrn., 1945-47; counsel com. banking and currency U.S. Senate, 1947-57, U.S. Joint Com. Def. Prodn., 1950-51; adminstrv. asst. U.S. Senator William Benton, 1950; asso. Ford Motor Co., Washington office, 1957-58; house counsel Nat. Assn. Mut. Savs. Banks, N.Y.C., 1958-59; dir.-counsel Washington office, 1959-63; gen. counsel Nat. Savs. and Loan League, Washington, 1963-75, v.p., 1971-75, sec., 1973-75; editor mgrs. manual, author league legal bulls., 1970-75; sec. Nat. League Internat., 1974-75; asso. firm. Silver, Freedman, Housley, Taff & Goldberg, Washington, 1976—; dir. Knickerbocker Fed. Savs. and Loan Assn., N.Y.C., 1975—, chmn. exec. com., 1980—; former v.p., dir. Savs. & Loan of Sierra Leone, Ltd.; lectr. savs. and loan topics. Del. Inter-Am. Savs. and Loan Confs., Latin Am. Comdg. officer USNR Law Co. 5-11, Washington, 1956-57, 64-65. Pres. Conn. Dems. D.C., 1939-40; extraordinary minister St. Michael's Roman Catholic Ch., Silver Spring, Md.; lector, server St. Matthew's Cathedral, Washington. Served from lt. (j.g.) to lt. USNR, 1943-45; capt. Res. ret. Mem. Inter-Am., D.C., Md. bar assns., Bar Assn. D.C. (vice chmn. liaison com. Inter-Am. Bar Assn. 1978, chmn. ann. reception for Latin Am. ambassadors 1966, 78, mem. legis. com. 1978—, mem. D.C. affairs sect. 1980—), Yale Law Sch. Assn., U.S. Senate Assn. Adminstrv. Assts. and Secs., Assn. Former Senate Aides, Lambda Alpha. Democrat. Clubs: Yale (N.Y.C.); University, Exchequer (Washington); Men's (Silver Spring, Md.). Home: 8004 Park Crest Dr Silver Spring MD 20910 Office: 1800 M St NW Washington DC 20036

MC KENNEY, WALTER GIBBS, JR., lawyer, publishing co. exec.; b. Jacobsville, Md., Apr. 22, 1913; s. Walter Gibbs and Mary (Starkey) McK.; student Williamsport Dickinson Sem., 1935-37; Ph.B., Dickinson Coll., 1939; J.D., U. Va., 1942; LL.D. (hon.), Dickinson Sch. Law, 1964; m. Florence Roberta Rea, July 17, 1939. Admitted to Md. bar, 1942, since practiced in Balt.; partner firm McKenney, Thomsen & Burke; partner, gen. mgr., editor Taxes and Estates Pub. Co., Balt., 1946—; chmn. trust co. Equitable Trust Co.; dir. Lutherville Supply & Equipment Co., Equitable Trust Co., Equitable Bancorp., Alban Tractor Co. Lectr., Southwestern Grad. Sch. Banking, 1964-76. Pres., Kelso Home for Girls; pres. bd. child care Balt. Conf. Methodist Ch., 1961-64. Bd. dirs. Balt. Civic Opera Co.; 1964-68; trustee Goucher Coll., Dickinson Coll., Lycoming Coll., Wesley Theol. Sem., Franklin Sq. Hosp. Served to lt. USNR, 1942-45. Mem. Am., Md., Balt. bar assns. Republican. Methodist. Editor: Taxes and Estates, 1946—, Minimizing Taxes, 1946—, The Educator, 1965—, The Patron, 1968—. Home: 102 Estes Rd Baltimore MD 21212 Office: Munsey Bldg Baltimore MD 21202

MCKENNON, JOHN EARLE, JR., hotel exec.; b. Kansas City, Mo., Aug. 28, 1949; s. John Earle and Mary Fracise (Henney) McK.; student in bus. adminstrn. Santa Ana Coll., 1967-68; student in hotel and restaurant adminstrn. Wash. State U., 1969-70; m. Edith Paule Boucher, Aug. 28, 1970; children—Katia Ann, John Earle. Dir., Saddle Back Inns Mgmt. Co., Santa Ana, Calif., 1972-74; divisional dir. ops. Rodeway Inns, Dallas, Tex., 1974-76; mng. dir. St. Thomas Sheraton Hotel & Marina (V.I.), 1976-78; gen. mgr. Westwater Inn, Olympia, Wash., 1978-79; v.p. U.S. ops. Westwater Hotels, Inc., Olympia, 1979—; instr. in hotel and restaurant adminstrn. Orange Coast Coll., 1971-72; bd. dirs. Visitor-Conv. Bur., Dallas, 1974-76, St. Thomas, 1976-78, Olympia, 1978—. Named Hon. Citizen, Ky., 1975, Ark., 1975, Baton Rouge, 1975, Indpls., 1975, V.I., 1978; recipient Outstanding Service award U.S. Naval Base, Roosevelt Rds., P.R., 1978, United Way of Ark., 1975, Distbv. Ednl. Clubs Am., 1974. Mem. Calif., Wash., Bakersfield (pres. 1972-73), V.I. (pres.-elect 1978—) hotel assns., Am. Hotel-Motel Assn. (Calif. legis. council 1972-73), Hotel Sales Mgmt. Assn., Greeters Internat., Baniface Internat. (pres. Calif. chpt. 1971-72), Olympia C. of C. (dir.), Hotel-Motel Assn. Ark., Hotel-Motel Assn. U.S. V.I., Am. Restaurant Assn., Sigma Iota. Republican. Roman Catholic. Club: Rotary. Home: 7009 44th Ct SE Olympia WA 98503 Office: 2300 Evergreen Park Dr Olympia WA 98502

MCKENNY, JERE WESLEY, geol. engring. firm exec.; b. Okmulgee, Okla., Feb. 14, 1929; s. Jere Claus and Juanita (Hunter) McK.; B.S. in Geol. Engring., U. Okla., 1951, M.S. in Geol. Engring., 1952; m. Anne Ross Stewart, May 4, 1957; children—Jere James, Robert Stewart. With Kerr-McGee Corp., Oklahoma City, 1953—, mgr. oil and gas exploration, 1968-69, v.p. oil and gas, 1969-74, v.p. exploration, 1974-77, vice chmn. bd., 1977—. Mem. alumni adv. council Sch. Geology and Geophysics U. Okla. Served with U.S. Army, 1953-55. Mem. Am. Assn. Petroleum Geologists, Am. Petroleum Inst., Houston Geol. Soc., Oklahoma City Geol. Soc., Sigma Xi, Sigma Gamma Epsilon. Episcopalian. Clubs: Oklahoma City Golf and Country, Whitehall. Office: 123 Robert S Kerr Oklahoma City OK 73125*

MC KENZIE, HILTON EUGENE, construction co. exec.; b. Berlin, Pa., Sept. 5, 1921; s. Enoch Joeseph and Nellie Savilla (Colefleish) McK.; M.S.C.E. and M.E., M.I.T., 1941; B.S.C.E., Va. Poly. Inst., 1939; m. Dorothy Elyea, May 19, 1949; children—Carol, Deborah, Cynthia, Hilton. Sr. cons. Bank Bldg. Corp., St. Louis, 1950-72; sec.-treas. Fin. Bldg. Cons., Atlanta, 1972-75; pres., chmn. Fin. Structures Inc., Atlanta, 1975—; instr. Cornell U., Ithaca, N.Y., 1976. Served to lt. col. U.S. Army, 1940-45. Decorated Bronze Star, Purple Heart. Mem. Nat. Soc. Profl. Engrs., N.C. Soc. Engrs., Soc. Am. Mil. Engrs. Protestant. Club: Elks. Home: Route 1 Mansfield GA 30255 Office: 2310 Parklake Dr Atlanta GA 30345

MC KENZIE, JOSEPH ARTHUR, mfg. co. exec.; b. Princeton, W.Va., Dec. 27, 1934; s. Arthur Modoc and Lily Catherine (Mandeville) McK.; B.S. in Aero. Engring., Va. Poly. Inst., 1957; M.B.A., Xavier U., 1971; m. Wilma Jean Teel, June 9, 1956; children—Deborah Lynn, Jeffrey Arthur, Jennifer Jean. Project engr. United Aircraft Co., East Hartford, Conn., 1957-61; major test project engr Gen. Electric Co., Evendale, Ohio, 1961-63, advanced project engr., 1963-67, mgr. test engring., 1967-74, sr. engr., data systems program, 1974-77, sr. engr. evaluation engring. analysis, 1977-79, mgr. structures and life extension programs mktg., 1979—. Chmn. City Planning Commn.; elder Lebanon United Presbyn. Ch.; vice chmn. Greater Cin. United Appeal. Mem. Elfun Soc., AIAA. Club: Optimist. Office: k96 Cincinnati OH 45215

MCKIBBEN, KENNETH DARRELL, metal reclamation corp. exec.; b. Continental, Ohio, Dec. 24, 1935; s. Wilbert Henry and Zella Ada (Prowant) McK.; B.Indsl. Engring., Gen. Motors Inst., 1957; m. Betty Ellen Richard, June 9, 1956; children—Craig Kenneth, Scott Richard, Michael Terricks. Supt. Central Foundry div. Gen. Motors Corp., Defiance, Ohio, 1963-69, plant engr., 1969-71; pres. Dampco Inc., Defiance, 1971-72; mgr. mfg., engring. Engineered Cast Products div. Gen. Electric Co., Eria, Pa., 1972-73; v.p. mfg. Isaac Corp., Bryan, Ohio, 1973—. Mem. Am. Foundrymen's Soc., Am. Welding Soc., Gen. Motors Inst. Alumni Assn. Lutheran. Clubs: Ayersville Athletic Booster, Elks, Moose, Masons. Patentee in field. Home: 325 Shamrock Ln Defiance OH 43512

MC KINLEY, JIMMIE JOE, business exec.; b. Bertram, Tex., July 23, 1934; s. Joseph Crofford and Velma Anne (Barnett) McK.; B.J. cum laude, U. Tex., 1955; M.S., U. Ky., 1964. Asst. librarian Bethel Coll., McKenzie, Tenn., 1961-63, reference librarian, 1966-70, acting head librarian, 1970-71; owner, mgr. Longview Book Co. (Tex.), 1974—. Bd. dirs. Longview-Piney Woods chpt. ARC; trustee Bethel Coll., 1977—. Mem. A.L.A., Sigma Delta Chi. Presbyn. Home: PO Box 2106 Longview TX 75606

MC KINLEY, JOHN KEY, oil co. exec.; b. Tuscaloosa, Ala., Mar. 24, 1920; s. Virgil Parks and Mary Emma (Key) McK.; B.S. in Chem. Engring., U. Ala., 1940, M.S. in Organic Chemistry, 1941, LL.D. (hon.), 1972; grad. Advanced Mgmt. Program, Harvard, 1962; LL.D. (hon.), Troy State U., 1974; m. Helen Heare, July 19, 1946; children—John Key, Mark Charles. With Texaco Inc., 1941—, chem. engr., Port Arthur, Tex., 1941-53, asst. supr. cracking research, 1953-54, supr., 1954-57, asst. dir. research, Beacon, N.Y., 1957-59, asst. to v.p. research and tech. dept., 1959-60, mgr. comml. devel., 1960, gen. mgr. petrochem. dept., N.Y.C., 1960-67, v.p. petrochem. dept., v.p. in charge supply and distbn., 1967-71, sr. v.p. worldwide refining, petrochems., also supply and distbn., N.Y.C., 1971, pres., dir., 1971—, chief operating officer, 1980—; chmn. bd. Texaco Devel. Corp., 1971—; dir. Burlington Industries, 1977—. Served as maj. AUS, 1941-45; ETO. Decorated Bronze Star; recipient George Washington Honor medal Freedoms Found., 1972; Andrew Wellington Cordier fellow Columbia U. Registered profl. engr., Tex. Fellow Am. Inst. Chem. Engrs.; mem. Am. Petroleum Inst. (dir.), Am. Chem. Soc., Sigma Xi, Tau Beta Pi, Gamma Sigma Epsilon, Kappa Sigma. Clubs: Wee Burn Country (Darien, Conn.); N.Y. Yacht, The Brook (N.Y.C.); Blind Brook Country (Port Chester, N.Y.). Patentee in chem. and processing field. Office: 2000 Westchester Ave White Plains NY 10650

MCKINNEY, JOHN ADAMS, diversified mining, mfg. and forest products co. exec.; b. Huntsville, Tex., Nov. 9, 1923; s. Andrew Todd and Myra (Adams) McK.; B.S., U.S. Naval Acad., 1945; J.D., Georgetown U., 1951; m. Cleo Turner, Aug. 31, 1946; children—John Adams, II, Todd T. Admitted to D.C. bar, 1951, Colo. bar, 1976; patent examiner U.S. Patent Office, Washington, 1947-51; with Johns-Manville Corp., 1951—, sr. v.p. legal services, Denver, 1973-76, pres., 1976-79, chief exec. officer, 1977—, chmn. bd., 1979—, also dir.; dir. Public Service Co. Colo. Mem. bus. adv. council U. Denver Sch. Bus.; mem. council coll. resources Coll. Law, U. Denver; nat. bd. dirs. Jr. Achievement, Inc. Served to ensign USN, 1945-47. Mem. Am. Bar Assn., Am. Patent Law Assn., Bar D.C., Colo. Bar Assn., Conf. Bd. Bus. Roundtable (energy task force). Office: Ken-Caryl Ranch Denver CO 80217

MC KINNEY, JOHN BRADLEY, communications co. exec.; b. Jacksonville, Fla., May 16, 1918; s. George and Alice Catherine (Larson) McK.; student U. Tenn., 1936-39; LL.B., So. Law Sch., 1942; M.B.A., Harvard U., 1961, grad. Advanced Mgmt. Program, 1969; M.Internat. Affairs, George Washington U., 1965; m. Marsha Bond, June 14, 1946. Dep. collector IRS, 1939-42; admitted to Tenn. bar, 1942; individual practice law, Memphis, 1946-51; commd. 2d lt. U.S. Army, 1942, advanced through grades to col., 1962; ret., 1969; v.p. and dir. engring. ITT World Communications, N.Y.C., 1969-74, sr. v.p. and exec. dir. ops., 1974-77, exec. v.p. and gen. mgr., 1977-79, pres., 1980—. Pres., Tenn. Jaycees, 1948-49. Served in U.S. Army, 1942-46, 51-69. Decorated Legion of Merit with three oak leaf clusters, Bronze Star with three oak leaf clusters, Air medal, others; recipient George Washington Honor medal Freedoms Found. at Valley Forge, 1968. Mem. Harvard Bus. Sch. Assn. N.Y.C. Clubs: Masons; Shrewsbury River Yacht, Whitehall, Harbor View. Editor U.S. Army War Coll. Commentary, 1965-67; asso. editor Mil. Rev., 1965-67. Home: 119 Bamm Hollow Rd Middletown NJ 07748 Office: 67 Broad St New York NY 10004

MCKINNEY, JOSEPH FRANCIS, co. exec.; b. Phila., May 3, 1931; s. George Dennis and Helen B. McK.; B.S., St. Joseph's Coll., 1952; M.B.A., Harvard U., 1957; m. Clare Mercedes Kelley, Sept. 19, 1959; children—Mary Eileen, Maria Clare. Successively mgr. research dept. Reynolds & Co., Phila., regional mgr. corp. fin. Goodbody & Co., Dallas, pres., dir. Electro-Sci. Investors, Inc., Dallas; now pres., chmn., chief exec. officer Tyler Corp., Dallas; dir. First Nat. Bank, Dallas, Kidde, Inc., Cronus Industries, Inc. Dir., So. Meth. U. Found. for Bus. Adminstrn.; mem. Pres.' Council on Phys. Fitness and Sports; mem. exec. com. Cath. Found., Diocese of Dallas. Served with USNR, 1952-55. Mem. Young Pres.' Orgn., Alpha Sigma Nu. Republican. Office: 3100 Southland Center Dallas TX 75201

MCKINNEY, N(ORMAN) KENNETH, elec. mfg. co. exec.; b. Abington, Pa., Oct. 18, 1939; s. Norman and Sylvia Agnes (Surman) McK.; student La Salle Coll., 1961; m. Carolyn Virginia Harrar, Oct. 26, 1963; children—Sharon, Kristine, Kimberly. Production mgr. Mack Elec. Devices, Inc., Wyncote, Pa., 1960-64, v.p., gen. mgr., 1964-79, pres., 1979—; pres., dir. Reliable Instrument Co., Inc.; v.p., dir. Pentad, Inc.; partner B.H.M.T. Co.; gen. partner Eckenroth/PITS/Group. Mem. Council, Jenkintown, Pa., 1973-77, v.p., 1976, 77; bd. mgrs. YMCA, 1979-80; bd. dirs. Eckenroth Found. Served with U.S. Army, 1957-60. Recipient Pub. Service award Borough of Jenkintown, 1977. Clubs: Mfrs. Golf & Country, Rotary (Elkins Park, pres. 1973-74, Service award 1974). Home: 215 Summit Ave Jenkintown PA 19046 Office: 1 North Ave Wyncote PA 19095

MC KINNEY, ROBERT HURLEY, lawyer; b. Indpls., Nov. 7, 1925; s. E. Kirk and Irene (Hurley) McK.; B.S., U.S. Naval Acad., 1946; J.D., Ind. U., 1951; m. Arlene Frances Allsopp, Nov. 28, 1951; children—Robert, Marni, Kevin, Kent, Lisa. Admitted to Ind. bar, 1951, since practiced in Indpls.; sr. partner Bose McKinney & Evans, 1963—. Pres., chmn. bd. Jefferson Corp. and subsidiaries, Indpls., 1961-77, 79—; chmn. First Fed. Savs. & Loan Assn. Indpls., 1961-77, 79—; chmn. Fed. Home Loan Mortgage Corp., Fed. Home Loan Bank Bd., Washington, 1977-79; vice chmn., dir. Jefferson Nat. Life Ins. Co.; dir. Fed. Nat. Mortgage Assn., Washington, 1979—. Bd. dirs. Indpls. Legal Aid Soc., Children's Mus. Indpls.; bd. dirs., mem. exec. com. Brebeuf Prep. Sch., 1970—; trustee Indpls. Community Hosp.; trustee, chmn. fin. com. Marian Coll., Indpls. Del., Democratic Nat. Conv., 1968, 72, 76, 80. Served to lt. comdr. USNR, 1946-49, 51-53. Mem. Am., Ind., Indpls. bar assns., Young Presidents Orgn. (nat. chmn. for econ. edn. 1968-69, pres. Ind. chpt. 1973-74). Club: Knights of Malta. Home: 647 Somerset Dr Indianapolis IN 46260 Office: Jefferson Bldg Indianapolis IN 46204

MC KINNEY, ROBERT SALTER, chem. co. exec.; b. N.Y.C., Apr. 24, 1941; s. Elmer Ellsworth and Caroline Elizabeth (Clancy) McK.; B.S. in Mech. Engring., U.S. Mcht. Marine Acad., 1962; M.S. in Mgmt., Columbia U., 1966; postgrad. Advanced Bus. Inst., Harvard U., 1977; m. Carroll Geraldine Driscoll, Aug. 14, 1962; children—Robert S., Richard, James, Glenn. Engr., Moore-McCormack Lines, Inc., 1962-63; engr. Western Electric Co., N.Y.C., 1963-66; mktg. rep. IBM, N.Y.C., 1966-73, account mgr., 1973-76, product mgr., 1976-77; controller bus. services dept. Union Carbide Corp., N.Y.C., 1977-79, dir. mgmt. cons., 1979—. Mem. Assn. Internal Mgmt. Cons. Republican. Episcopalian. Club: Redding Country. Office: Union Carbide Corp 270 Park Ave New York NY 10017

MC KINNON, ROBERT HAROLD, ins. co. exec.; b. Holtville, Calif., Apr. 4, 1927; s. Harold Arthur and Gladys Irene (Blanchar) McK.; B.S., Armstrong Coll., 1950, M.B.A., 1952; m. Marian Lois Hayes, Dec. 18, 1948; children—Steven Robert, Laurie Ellen, David Martin. Regional sales mgr. Farmers Ins. Group, Austin, Tex., 1961-68; dir. life sales Farmers New World Life, Los Angeles, 1966-68; v.p. mktg. Warner Ins. Group, Chgo., 1968—, v.p. Underwriters Ins. Co., subs., Chgo., 1975—; mem. dairy adv. com. Canners Exchange. Served with U.S. Army, 1944-45. Mem. Soc. C.P.C.U.'s, Am. Mgmt. Assn., Internat. Ins. Seminars. Episcopalian. Club: Anvil (East Dundee, Ill.). Home: 974 Williamsburg Park Barrington IL 60010 Office: 4300 Peterson Chicago IL 60646

MCKNIGHT, JERRY JAMES, accountant, city ofcl.; b. Las Vegas, Nev., Dec. 23, 1949; s. Lawrence Wilson and Della Louise (Effinger) McK.; B.S. in Bus. Adminstrn., U. Nev., 1974; m. Susan Whitaker, Aug. 22, 1972; children—Jason Larry, Kerry Ann, Sheldon Jerry. Mgr., Caribou Four Corners, Inc., Fallon, Nev., 1970-74; accountant Kafoury, Armstrong, Turner, Inc., Fallon, 1974-77; pres. Agro-Chem Farm Supply, Inc., 1977-78; auditor, clk., treas. City of Fallon, 1979—. tax cons. C.P.A. Nev. Mem. Am. Inst. C.P.A.'s, Nev. Soc. C.P.A.'s. Republican. Mormon. Home: 3030 Soda Lake Rd Fallon NV 89406 Office: 55 W Williams St Fallon NV 89406

MC KONE, DON T., corp. exec.; b. Jackson, Mich., 1921; grad. U. Mich., 1947. Chmn. bd., chief exec. officer, dir. Libbey-Owens-Ford Co., Toledo; dir. Ohio Citizens Bancorp, Inc., Hayes-Albion Corp., Consumers Power Co., Nat. Bank Detroit. Office: Libbey-Owens-Ford Co 811 Madison Ave Toledo OH 43695

MC LANE, HELEN J., exec. search cons.; b. Indpls.; d. Alvin R. and Ethel (Ranck) McLane; B.S. with distinction, Northwestern U., 1951; M.B.A., 1965. Pub. relations writer Chgo. Assn. Commerce and Industry, 1952-53; press dir. Community Fund, Chgo., 1953-56; asso. Beveridge Orgn., Inc., Chgo., 1956-61, v.p., 1961-66; pub. relations cons. Internat. Harvester Co., Chgo., 1966-69, asst. to dir. pub. relations. 1969-70; asso. Heidrick & Struggles, Chgo., 1970-74, v.p., 1974—. Mem. Nat. Assn. Investment Clubs (dir. 1957-69, trustee 1969-72, adviser 1972—). Author: (with Patricia Hutar) The Investment Club Way to Stock Market Success, 1963; Selecting, Developing and Retaining Women Executives, 1980. Home: 124 Robsart Rd Kenilworth IL 60043 Office: 125 S Wacker Dr Chicago IL 60606

MC LANE, JAMES WOODS, investment banker; b. New Canaan, Con., Jan. 27, 1939; s. William Lawrence and Elizabeth Fish (Benjamin) McL.; B.A., Yale U., 1961; M.B.A., Harvard U., 1967; m. Fay Sargent, Apr. 27, 1963 (div. 1980); children—James W., Benjamin S. Cons., Booz, Allen & Hamilton, N.Y.C., 1967-69; exec. asst. to sec. HEW, Washington, 1969-70; staff asst. to Pres. U.S., White House, 1971-72; dep. dir. Cost of Living Council, Washington, 1972-74; v.p., head group mgmt. office for mcht. banking group Citibank N. A., N.Y.C., 1974-76, v.p. and head mergers and acquisitions and fin. adv. services, 1976-79, v.p. and head corp. fin. div., 1980—; speaker, panelist in field. Mem. alumni council St. George's Sch., 1968-70; campaign mgr. re-election Mass. Gov. Sargent, 1970; class rep. Assn. Yale Alumni, 1973-75, sec. Class of 1961, 1976—; mem. hon. degrees com. Yale U., 1973-74; bd. dirs. Yale Alumni of Greenwich, 1976—, treas., 1978-80; bd. dirs., spl. gifts chmn. Greenwich Helth Assn., 1979-80, v.p. and campaign chmn., 1980—. Served in USN, 1961-65; Vietnam. Congregationalist. Clubs: Yale of N.Y.; Rocky Point (Old Greenwich); Greenwich Skating (head hockey program 1978-80). Office: 399 Park Ave Citibank NA New York NY 10043

MCLARNAN, DONALD EDWARD, savs. and loan assn., corp. exec.; b. Nashua, Iowa, Dec. 19, 1906; s. Samuel and Grace (Prudhon) McL.; A.B., U. So. Cal., 1930; grad. Southwestern U., 1933; m. Virginia Rickard, May 5, 1939; children—Marilyn, Marcia, Roxane. Trust appraiser, property mgr. Security-First Nat. Bank, Los Angeles, 1935-54; regional dir. SBA, for So. Calif., Ariz., part of Nev., Los Angeles, 1954-61, area adminstr. for Alaska, Wash., Ore., Ida., Calif., Nev., Ariz., Hawaii, Guam, Samoa, U.S. Trust Ty., 1969-73; pres. Am. MARC, Inc., offshore oil drillers and mfr. diesel engines, 1961-63; pres. Terminal Drilling & Prodn. Co., Haney & Williams Drilling Co., Western Offshore Drilling and Exploration Co., 1961-63; v.p., dir. Edgemar Dairy, Santa Monica Dairy Co., 1954-70; founder, pres.

chmn. bd. Mission Nat. Bank, 1963-67, Coast Fed. Savs. & Loan Assn., 1954—; cons. numerous corps. Guest lectr. various univs. Chmn. fed. agys. div. Community Chest, 1956; nat. pres. Teachers Day, 1956. Bd. councillors U. So. Calif.; mem. real estate adv. bd. Los Angeles City Coll.; founder, chmn., pres. Soc. Care and Protection Injured Innocent, Recipient Los Angeles City and County Civic Leadership award, 1959. Mem. Skull and Dagger, Delta Chi. Mason (K.T., Shriner). Clubs: Los Angeles, Jonathan (Los Angeles). Author articles on mgmt., finance. Home: 135 S Norton Ave Los Angeles CA 90004 Office: 1101 S Crenshaw Blvd Suite 201 Los Angeles CA 90019

MC LAUGHLIN, ALEXANDER CHARLES JOHN, oil co. exec.; b. N.Y.C., June 3, 1925; s. Alexander and Margaret (Percival) McL.; B.S., Va. Poly. Inst., 1946; postgrad. Columbia, 1947-48; m. Joan Kosak, June 10, 1950; 1 dau., Jena Hilary. With Standard Vacuum Oil Co., N.Y.C., Shanghai, China, Manila, Saigon, Indochina, Hongkong, Yokohama, Japan, 1946-50; with Trans Arabian Pipeline Co., Turaif, Saudi Arabia, 1951; with Andean Nat. Corp., Cartagena, Colombia, 1952-54; practice civil engring., N.Y.C., 1954-55; chief project engr. mktg. Am. Oil Co., N.Y.C., chief engr. South Atlanta, sr. head engr., Chgo., 1955-64; sr. process engr. mfg. and marketing dept. Amoco Internat. Oil Co., Europe, S.A., Asia, N.Y.C., Chgo., 1963-72; mgr. distbn. Singapore Petroleum Co., 1972-73; constrn. supr. Iran Pan Am. Oil Co., 1973, onshore/offshore supr., 1974-75; sr. staff engr. Amoco Internat. Oil Co., Chgo., 1975—. Vol. fireman Long Beach Fire Dept., 1955-63; tng. officer USCG Aux., 1962; Eagle scout, scoutmaster, troop com. mem. Nassau County N.Y. council Boy Scouts Am., 1946-49. Decorated Order White Cloud. Fellow ASCE; mem. Nat. Soc. Profl. Engrs., Nat. Assn. Corrosion Engrs., Internat. Platform Assn., Omicron Delta Kappa. Republican. Club: Pathfinders (London, Eng.); Columbia Country (Shanghai); Singapore Swim, Singapore Petroleum, Singapore American; Tehran American; Moose. Home: 3106 Cedar Knolls Dr Kingwood TX 77339 Office: 2 Greenspoint Plaza PO Box 4381 16825 Northchase Dr Houston TX 77210

MCLAUGHLIN, BRIAN A., real estate devel. co. exec.; b. Lowell, Mass., July 14, 1942; s. Hubert Leo and H. Madeline McLaughlin; B.A. magna cum laude, Harvard U., 1964, M.B.A. with distinction, 1973; M.S.A., George Washington U., 1971; m. Maura Ann Martin, July 12, 1969; 1 dau., Caragh Megan. Instr., Franklin Inst., Boston, 1965-67; asst. to chmn. bd. Sea Pines Co., Hilton Head Island, S.C., 1973-74; exec. v.p. Hilton Head Plantation Co., Hilton Head Island, 1974-77; exec. v.p., chief operating officer The Hilton Head Co., Hilton Head Island, 1977-80; pres. B.A. McLaughlin Co., Hilton Head Island, 1980—; chmn. Hilton Head Bus. Diversification Com., 1977—. Mem. adv. bd. Hilton Head Inst. Arts, 1974-76; trustee Sea Pines Acad., 1977—, chmn. bd., 1979—; founder Hilton Head Island Conservatory and Center for Arts, 1979. Served with USN, 1967-71. Mem. Recreational Devel. Council, Urban Land Inst., Am. Mgmt. Assn., Hilton Head Island C. of C. (dir. 1977—). Clubs: Century; Harvard (Lowell Mass. and S.C.). Home: 18 Mallard Rd Hilton Head Island SC 29928 Office: PO Drawer 5969 Hilton Head Island SC 29928

MC LAUGHLIN, GLEN, computer co. exec.; b. Shawnee, Okla., Dec. 21, 1934; s. Champe and Mattie Bet (Jenkins) McL.; B.B.A., U. Okla., 1956; M.B.A., Harvard, 1964; m. Ellen Marr Schnake, Aug. 29, 1964; children—Helen Elizabeth, Glen Wallace. Asst. treas. Foremost-McKesson, Inc., San Francisco, 1964-69; exec. v.p., dir. MacFarlane's Candies, Oakland, Calif., 1969-70; dir. fin. and adminstrn. Memorex Corp., London, Eng., 1970-71; v.p. fin. Four-Phase Systems, Inc., Cupertino, Calif., 1971—; pres., chmn. Four-Phase Fin., Inc., Cupertino, 1977—; chmn. bd. Four-Phase Systems, Ltd., Toronto, Ont., Can., 1977, Four-Phase Systems Internat., Inc., Four-Phase Systems Ltd., Marlow, Eng., 1976—, De Anza Ins. Co. Ltd., Cayman Islands, 1979—; dir. Computer Optics, Inc., Bethel, Conn. Bd. dirs., pres. Jr. Achievement Santa Clara County; guarantor San Francisco Civic Light Opera Assn.; mem. internat. adv. council Golden Gate U.; mem. working council Santa Clara County Mfg. Group. Served to 1st lt. USAF, 1956-62. Recipient Bronze Leadership award Jr. Achievement, 1980. Mem. Nat. Assn. Accountants, Data Processing Mgrs. Assn., Fin. Execs. Inst., Planning Execs. Inst., English Speaking Union, Nat. Geneal. Soc., Beta Gamma Sigma, Sigma Alpha Epsilon. Clubs: Commonwealth, Harvard Bus. Sch. No. Calif. Home: 20264 Ljepava Dr Saratoga CA 95070 Office: 10700 N DeAnza Blvd Cupertino CA 95014

MCLAUGHLIN, JAMES CURTIS, II, investment banker; b. Mpls., Jan. 25, 1940; s. James C. and Elizabeth M. (Niemela) McL.; B.S., U. So. Calif., 1964; m. Sharon Linkletter, Feb. 14, 1967 (div.); children—Kelly Ann, Stacy Kathleen. Stock broker Schwabacher & Co., San Francisco, 1967-69, Blyth & Co., Los Angeles, 1969-71, W.E. Hutton & Co., Los Angeles, 1971-73, Loeb, Rhoades & Co., Los Angeles, 1973-76, A.G. Becker & Co., Los Angeles, 1976-77; corp. fin. exec. MacDonald, Krieger, Bowyer & Beyenka, Inc., Beverly Hills, Calif., 1977-78; co-founder, gen. partner The Resource Partners, Investment Bankers, Beverly Hills, 1978—. Served with U.S. Army, 1958-60. Mem. Inst. Energy Devel. Republican. Clubs: Ducks Unltd., Petroleum, Stock Exchange. Home: 856 Devon Ave Los Angeles CA 90024 Office: 433 N Camden Dr Suite 412 Beverly Hills CA 90210

MC LAUGHLIN, PETER JOSEPH, paper co. exec.; b. N.Y.C., July 21, 1928; s. Peter J. and Amelia (Greenochle) McL.; B.B.A., Pace Coll., 1954; J.D., Fordham U., 1960; m. Helen Anne Wollak, Jan. 20, 1951. Admitted to N.Y. bar, 1961; with Union Camp Corp. (formerly Union Bag-Camp Paper Corp.), N.Y.C., 1945—, asst. comptroller, 1962-65, comptroller, 1965-69, v.p. finance, dir., 1969-72, exec. v.p., dir., 1972-77, pres., 1977—, chief exec. officer, 1980—; dir. Mut. Benefit Life Ins. Co., First Nat. State Bank N.J. Served with AUS, 1954-56. Mem. Am. Bar Assn., Fordham U. Law Alumni Assn. (sec. Nassau-Suffolk 1964-65). Office: 1600 Valley Rd Wayne NJ 07470

MC LAUGHLIN, WILLIAM EARLE, banker; b. Oshawa, Ont., Can., Sept. 16, 1915; s. Frank and Frankie L. (Houlden) McL.; B.A., Queen's U., Kingston, Ont., 1936; m. Ethel Wattie, July 20, 1940; children—William, Mary. With Royal Bank of Can., 1936—, mgr. Montreal br., 1951-53, asst. gen. mgr., 1953-59, asst. to pres., 1959-60, gen. mgr., 1960—, pres., 1960, chmn., pres., 1962-77, chmn., chief exec. officer, 1977, chmn. bd., 1979-80; dir. chmn. bd. Sun Alliance Ins. Co.: Adela investment Co. S.A.; trustee Sun Alliance & London Ins. Group, Canadian Staff Pension Plan; dir. Ralston Purina Can., Inc., Algoma Steel Corp., Ltd., Power Corp. Can., Ltd., Standard Brands, Inc., Genstar, Ltd., Met. Life Ins. Co., Continental Reins, Shawinigan Industries, Ltd., Adela Investment Co. S.A., Canadian Pacific Ltd., Can. Pacific Enterprises Ltd., Allied Chem. (Can.) Ltd., Royal Bank of Can. Trust Corp., Ltd., Gen. Motors Corp., Trans-Can. Corp. Fund, L'Air Liquide, Textron (Can.) Ltd. Bd. govs. Royal Victoria Hosp.; trustee Queen's U. Clubs: Engrs., Royal Montreal Golf, Royal Montreal Curling, Univ., Mount Royal, Forest and Stream, St. James. Montreal; Seigniory (Montebello); Toronto, York (Toronto); Mt. Bruno Golf; Rideau (Ottawa, Can.); Canadian (N.Y.); Lyford Cay (Nassau); Mid-Ocean (Bermuda). Office: Royal Bank of Can 1 Place Ville Marie 3d Floor West Wing Montreal PQ H3C 3A9 Canada

MCLAUGHLIN, WILLIAM FOOTE, land devel. and property mgmt. cons.; b. Chgo., July 16, 1929; s. Frederic and Irene Castle (Foote) McL.; B.S. in Bus. Adminstrn., Hofstra U., 1951; M.B.A., U. Ark., 1957, Ph.D., 1962; m. Delores Feliu, July 29, 1950 (div. 1961); 1 dau., Irene Castle; m. 2d, Dorothy Begier, July 3, 1975; 1 son, David Lee. Vice pres., dir. W.F. McLaughlin Co., Chgo., 1957-68; mktg. adminstr. Mid-Western Instruments, Tulsa, 1964; economist, planning analyst Skelly Oil Co., Tulsa, 1968-72; exec. v.p., chief operating officer Main Place Corp., Tulsa, 1972-76; pres. Koppel Devel. Co., Bartlesville, Okla., 1977-78; mgr. corp. facilities and real estate Western Co. N.Am., Ft. Worth, 1979-81; dir. property mgmt. Kiawah Island Co. (S.C.), 1981—; instr. econs. and real estate U. Ark., 1957-61, Tulsa Jr. Coll., 1974-78; real estate cons., 1971—. Mem. Mayor's Community Devel. Com., Tulsa, 1972—. Mem. Bldg. Owners and Mgrs. Assn. (Man of Yr. award 1976), Nat. Assn. Corp. Real Estate Execs., Am. Planning Assn. (asso.), Nat. Assn. Bus. Economists, Am. Econs. Assn., Nat. Assn. Fin. Adminstrs., Cert. Rev. Appraisers, Inst. Real Estate Mgmt., Culver Legion, Co. Mil. Historians, Sons. of Confederates, S.A.R., Sigma Chi. Episcopalian. Home: 235 Sparrow Hawk Rd Kiawah Island SC 29412

MC LAUGHLIN, WILLIAM GAYLORD, metal products mfg. co. exec.; b. Marietta, Ohio, Sept. 28, 1936; s. William Russell and Edna Martha (Hiatt) McL.; B.S. in Mech. Engring., U. Cin., 1959; M.B.A., Ball State U., 1967; children by previous marriage-Debora, Cynthia, Leslie, Teresa, Kristin, Jennifer. Plant engr. Kroger Co., Marion, Ind., 1959-62; with Honeywell, Inc., Wabash, Ind., 1962-75, mgr. metal products ops., 1971-72, gen. mgr. ops., 1972-75; pres. MarkHon Industries Inc., Wabash, 1975—; dir. Frances Slocum Bank & Trust Co., Wabash, 1974-77. Pres. Wabash Assn. for Retarded Children, 1974-75; gen. chmn. United Fund Drive, 1971; treas. Young Republicans Wabash, 1968-70; bd. dirs. Youth Service Bur., Sr. Citizens, Jr. Achievement, Wabash County Arts Council, Wabash Valley Dance Theater; regional chmn. UN Day Activities. Named Outstanding Young Man of Year, Wabash Jr. C. of C., 1972; recipient Ind. Jefferson award for public service, 1979, Alumni award Ball State U. Coll. Bus., 1979. Mem. Young Pres.'s Orgn., Indsl. C. of C. (pres. 1973-74), Wabash Area C. of C. (pres. 1976), Cincinnatus Soc., Am. Metal Stamping Assn. (dir.). Methodist (adminstrv. bd. 1978—, pres. Methodist Men 1975-76). Clubs: Wabash Country (v.p. 1972-76), Columbia, Rotary (pres. 1970-71, dist. youth exchange officer 1974-77, dist. gov. 1979-80), Masons. Patentee design electronic relay rack cabinet. Home: 141 W Maple St Wabash IN 46992 Office: 200 Bond St Wabash IN 46992

MCLEAN, W. F., packing co. exec.; b. Toronto, Ont., Can., 1916; ed. U. Toronto, 1938. Pres., dir. Can. Packers, Ltd. (name now Can. Packers, Inc.), Toronto, to 1980, chmn. bd., chief exec. officer, 1980—; v.p., dir. Canadian Imperial Bank Commerce; dir. Canadian Gen. Electric Co. Ltd., Steel Co. Can. Ltd. Bd. govs. Ont. Research Found. Office: 95 St Clair Ave W Toronto ON M4V 1P2 Canada*

MCLEAN, WILLIAM L., III, publisher; b. Phila., Oct. 4, 1927; s. William L., Jr. and Eleanor Ray (Bushnell) McL.; B.A., Princeton U., 1949. With Evening & Sunday Bull., Phila., 1949-80, v.p., 1969-74, sr. v.p., 1974-75, editor, pub., 1975-80; pres. Independent Pubs. Inc., Bryn Mawr, Pa., 1975—, chmn. bd., 1980—. Mem. Pa. Newspapers Pubs. Assn. (chmn. finance com., pres. 1964). Episcopalian. Club: Blooming Grove (Pa.) Hunting and Fishing. Office: Independent Publs Inc 945 Haverford Rd Bryn Mawr PA 19010

MCLELLAN, HUGH HENDRY, lawyer; b. St. John, N.B., Can., May 25, 1948; s. Hendry Ogilvy and Catherine MacL.; B.A., U. N.B., 1967, LL.B., 1969; m. Judith Ruthanne Parent, July 12, 1969; children—Catherine, David, Lloyd, Thomas, Lynn. Admitted to N.B. bar, 1969, N.S. bar, 1975, Ont. bar, 1976, Nfld. bar, 1977; partner firm McLellan & McLellan, St. John, 1969-75; sr. partner firm McLellan, Allaby, Allman & Holland, St. John, 1975—. Chmn. Ch. of St. John and Stephen Home, 1972-78; pres. N.B. Assn. Non-Profit Nursing Homes, 1978-80. Served to maj. Canadian Armed Forces Communication Res., 1965—. Mem. St. John Law Soc., Barristers Soc. N.B., N.S. Barristers Soc., Law Soc. Upper Can., Law Soc. Nfld., Canadian Bar Assn., Canadian Tax Found., Def. Research Inst., Found. for Legal Research, Canadian Maritime Law Assn., Royal Canadian Military Inst., Canadian Inst. Internat. Affairs, Canadian Inst. Strategic Studies, United Services Inst. N.B., N.B. Amateur Radio Assn., Canadian Forces Communications and Electronics Assn. Conservative. Presbyterian. Clubs: Union of St. John, Riverside Country. Home: 23 Crescent Dr Saint John NB E2H 1E5 Canada Office: 107 Germain St PO Box 218 Saint John NB E2L 3Y2 Canada

MC LENDON, HENRY LEWELLYNN, real estate broker; b. Valdosta, Ga., Feb. 16, 1908; s. Henry Kirk and Lila (Sharp) McL.; student U. Miami, 1927, U. Ky., 1928-29; m. Mary Louise Plummer, May 27, 1938; children—Vicky Lu, Judy, James Clifford. Sec., treas. Zanesville Devel. Co., 1947—. Mem. Zanesville Exchange Club. Home: 804 Maple Ave Zanesville OH 43701 also 615 Rabbit Rd Sanibel Island FL 33957 Office: 330 Main St Zanesville OH 43701

MC LEOD, GEORGE CURTIS, automobile dealer; b. Elmira, N.Y., May 3, 1931; s. Robert M. and Clara Elizabeth (Curtis) Diggs; A.B., Hamilton Coll., 1954; postgrad. U. Va., 1957-58; m. Beverly Ann Kranz, Aug. 23, 1958; children—Jennifer Ann, George Curtis, Elizabeth Gordon. With Curtis Foods, Elmira, N.Y., 1958-67, gen. sales mgr., 1962-67, v.p., 1964-67; v.p. H. R. Amacher & Sons, Inc., Horseheads, N.Y., 1967-69: preas., treas. G. C. McLeod, Inc., Horseheads, 1969—; mem. Volkswagen Regional Adv. Council, 1970-71; mem. Hamilton Coll. Vocat. Adv. Plan, 1977—. Mem. vestry Grace Episcopal Ch., Elmira, N.Y., 1966-72, warden, 1973-77: bd. dirs. Elmira YMCA, 1972-79, pres., 1977, pres. bd. trustees, 1979—; mem. Town Elmira Bd. Appeals, 1975-79, chmn., 1977-79. Served with U.S. Army, 1952-55. Named Layman of Year, Elmira YMCA, 1975. Mem. Nat., N.Y. State (mem. legis. com. 1976—) auto dealers assns., Am. Imported Automobile Dealers Assn. (regional rep. 1974-75), N.Y. State Volkscar Assn., Chemung County Auto and Truck Dealers Assn. (pres. 1972, 78), C. of C. of Chemung County (dir. 1970-73, mem. legis. com., chmn. 1973-79, chmn. transp. com. 1979—). Republican. Episcopalian. Clubs: Country, City, Newtown Soc. (v.p.) (Elmira); Fur, Fin and Feather, Inc. of Chemung County; Seneca Lake Sailing Assn. (dir. 1973-79). Home: Dr C Strathmont Park Elmira NY 14905 Office: 1101 Grand Central Ave Horseheads NY 14845

MC LEOD, ROBERT BRUCE, real estate devel. co. exec.; b. Cleve., Sept. 22, 1941; s. Donald Lee and Anita Margaret (Wagner) McL.; B.S., U. Calif., Berkeley, 1965; student U. So. Calif., 1966, Alliance Francais, Paris, 1969; m. Sherri Michelle Cornell, Dec. 11, 1976; children—Alex Robert, Michelle Kathleen. Dist. mgr. Chrysler Corp., Los Angeles, 1965-69; mgr. Earle Ike Dodge, Inglewood, Calif., 1969-70; mgmt. cons. University Industries, San Diego, 1970-72: v.p. Mondex, Inc., Miami, Fla., 1972—; mgmt. cons. Vice chmn. Ormond Beach (Fla.) Cultural Council, 1979—. Mem. Nat. Assn. Home Builders, Daytona Beach Area Home Builders Assn., Community Assns. Inst., Daytona Beach Area C. of C., Ormond Beach C. of C., Daytona Beach Area Com. of 100. Republican. Presbyterian. Home: 3 Old Trail Ormond FL 32074 Office: 595 N Nova St Ormond FL 32074

MC LOUTH, CHARLES E., polymer chem. co. exec.; b. Franklinville, N.Y., Aug. 18, 1917; s. Earl A. and Georgia McL.; student Alfred U., 1935; B.S., U. Buffalo, 1938; m. Eloise Miller, July 9, 1966; children—Patricia G., Diane B. Salesman, Upjohn Co., Olean, N.Y., 1941-51, sales supr., Canton, Ohio, 1966-77, nat. sales mgr. polymer chem. div., Deer Park, Tex., 1977—. Mem. Tex. Republican Club, 1977—. Served with USNR, 1941-44. Mem. Am. Mgmt. Assn., Soc. Plastics Industries. Republican. Mem. Christian Ch. Club: Masons. Office: Upjohn Co Battleground Rd Deer Park TX 77571

MC MACKIN, BERNARD PATRICK, JR., publishing co. exec.; b. Brockway, Pa., Apr. 6, 1924; s. Bernard Patrick and Gertrude (Mullany) McM.; B.B.A., St. Bonaventure U., 1949; m. Patricia Catherine Devine, June 10, 1950; children—Bernard Patrick, Kevin A., Thomas K., Susan M., Mary C. Spl. agt. The Home Ins. Co., N.Y.C., 1949-51; asst. editor The Fire, Casualty & Surety bulls. The Nat. Underwriter Co., Cin., 1951-59, asso. editor, 1959-61, editor, 1961-69, editorial dir., 1969-72, pres., 1972—. Served with U.S. Army, 1943-45. Mem. Am. Risk and Ins. Assn. Home: 2901 Montana Ave Cincinnati OH 45211 Office: 420 E 4th St Cincinnati OH 45202

MC MAHAN, JOHN WILLIAM, real estate investment advisor; b. San Antonio, Aug. 4, 1937; s. John William and Lena Margaret (Coleman) McM.; A.B., U. So. Calif., 1959; M.B.A., Harvard U., 1961; m. Jacqueline Mary Cardozo, Sept. 22, 1973; children—Cathy, Jason by previous marriage; 1 son, Justin. Dir. feasibility studies Charles Luckman Assos., 1961-63; founder, prin. Devel. Research Assos., Los Angeles, 1963-70; v.p. real estate services Booz, Allen & Hamilton, N.Y.C., 1970-73; mem. faculty Stanford Grad. Sch. Bus., 1974—; founder, prin. John McMahan Assos. Inc., San Francisco, 1976—. Mem. Urban Land Inst., Am. Econ. Assn., Am. Inst. Planners, Lambda Alpha, Royal Town Planning Inst. U.K. Club: Jonathan. Author: Property Development: Effective Decision Making in Uncertain Times, 1976; McGraw Hill Real Estate Pocket Guide, 1979; editor: Ency. of Urban Planning, 1973. Office: 201 California St San Francisco CA 94111

MCMAHAN, JOSEPH WILLIAM, textile co. exec.; b. Greenville, S.C., Aug. 24, 1928; s. Henry G. and Annie Sara (Tate) McM.; B.S., Clemson U., 1950; m. Mildred L. Bridges, Mar. 19, 1950; children—Kendrick B., Patricia L. With Burlington Industries, Inc., 1950—, v.p. planning Burlington House Fabrics, 1971-76, v.p. ops. Burlington House Fabrics Group, N.Y.C., 1976—. Republican. Home: 10 Hereford Dr Princeton NJ 08550 Office: 1345 Ave of the Americas New York NY 10019

MCMAHON, JAMES D(ENNIS), banker; b. Anaconda, Mont., Jan. 20, 1926; s. Hugh A. and Mary Ann (Shannon) McM.; B.A. in Bus. Adminstrn., U. Mont., 1950; m. Amelia Blazina, Nov. 3, 1951; children—Mary Pat, James M., Jean M., Michael D., Daniel H. Asst. cashier Daly Bank & Trust Co., Anaconda, Mont., 1951-58; v.p., cashier First Nat. Bank, Minot, N.D., 1958-63; regional v.p. First Western Bank, Sacramento, 1963-65; pres. Santa Clarita Nat. Bank, Newhall, Calif., 1965—; dir. Fed. Res. Bank, Los Angeles, 1978—. Bd. dirs. Henry Mayo Meml. Hosp., Valencia, Calif. Served with AC, U.S. Army, 1943-46. Mem. Western Ind. Banker Assn. (dir., chmn. legis. com.), Calif. Bankers Assn. (chmn. fed. govt. relations com.), Am. Bankers Assn. (governing council), So. Calif. Ind. Bankers Assn. (pres. 1974-75). Republican. Roman Catholic. Clubs: K.C. (past grand knight); Newhall-Saugus Kiwanis (pres. 1973), Elks (Newhall). Office: 23620 Lyons Newhall CA 91320

MCMAHON, JOSEPH EINAR, retail co. exec.; b. Chgo., Aug. 26, 1940; s. Reynold Bernard and Dorothy Marie (Oftedahl) McM.; A.B. with honors, Denison U., 1962; J.D., U. Mich., 1965. Admitted to Mass. bar, 1968; asst. Atty. Gen. & Senator Edward Brooke, Boston, Washington, 1965-67; exec. asst. to Lt. Gov. Francis Sargent, Boston, 1968-69; v.p. Bedford Stuyvesant D & S Corp., Bklyn., 1969-73; dir. govt. regulations Westinghouse Electric Corp., Washington, 1974-78; v.p. corp. affairs Federated Dept. Stores, Inc., Cin., 1978—. Trustee, Denison U., 1972—; mem. emeritus com. visitors U. Mich. Law Sch., 1973—; bd. dirs. Cin. Urban League, 1979—, Center for Urban Environ. Studies, Washington, 1977— Community affairs adv. bd. Xavier U., Cin., 1979—. Mem. Am. Bar Assn., Mass. Bar Assn., Cincinnatus Assn. Republican. Lutheran. Clubs: Union Boat (Boston); Capitol Hill, (Washington), Queen City (Cin.), Cin. Office: Federated Dept Stores Inc 7 W Seventh St Cincinnati OH 45202

MC MANUS, JOHN WARREN, mfg. co. ofcl.; b. Beaumont, Tex., May 25, 1950; s. Harold James and Myrtle Marie (McDaniel) McM.; grad. U. So. La., 1974; m. Bette Jane Galik, Aug. 9, 1975. Owner Le Bonheur Supper Club, Lafayette, La., 1974-75; with Cameron Iron Works, New Iberia, La. and Houston, 1975-78; with Coflexip Services Inc., 1978—, sales standard application N. Am., Houston, 1979—. Mem. Petroleum Inst., Internat. Assn. Drilling Contractors. Democrat. Club: Masons (32 degrees). Home: 11135 Cedarhurst St Houston TX 77096 Office: 4242 Southwest Freeway Houston TX 77027

MC MICKLE, JAMES RICHARD, elec. contracting co. exec.; b. Washington, July 15, 1948; s. Eugene Henry and Lois Imagene (Southwood) McM.; grad. ABC Apprenticeship Sch., 1975; m. Deborah Ann Bausum, Sept. 19, 1970; children—Lisa Kristine, Carolyn Denise. Clk., Md. Dept. Motor Vehicles, 1966-67; credit mgr. Sherwin Williams Co., Annapolis, Md., 1967-70, br. mgr., Laurel, Md., 1970-71; field electrician Bausum & Duckett Electric Co., Inc., Edgewater, Md., 1971-75, purchasing agt., 1975-77, estimator, 1977—, project mgr., 1977—, v.p., 1977—, also dir.; dir. Planned Design Systems; tchr. ABC Apprenticeship Sch., 1975-77. Bible sch. tchr. Heritage Bapt. Ch., Annapolis, 1979-80. Lic. master electrician. Mem. Asso. Ind. Elec. Contractors Assn. (pres. Chesapeake chpt. 1979-80), Master Electricians Assn. Anne Arundel County (dir. 1979—). Republican. Home: 2714 Riva Rd Annapolis MD 21401 Office: 3481 Pike Ridge Rd Edgewater MD 21037

MCMILLAN, BENJAMIN EARL, purchasing specialist; b. Okmulgee, Okla., Apr. 29, 1936; student Okla. U., 1957-60; B.S., Central State U., 1966; M.B.A., Pepperdine U., 1973; 1 son, Michael Alan. Computer programmer FAA, Oklahoma City, 1961-66; with Gen. Dynamics, 1966—, now computer systems acquisitions specialist, St. Louis. Served with U.S. Army, 1954-57. Mem. Am. Mgmt. Assn. Office: 12101 Woodcrest Executive Dr Saint Louis MO 63141

MC MILLAN, BRUCE, chem. co. exec.; b. Phila., Dec. 30, 1950; s. David and Flora T. (Gavin) McM.; student Phila. Coll. Pharmacy and Sci., 1968-69; B.S. in Biology, Lincoln U., 1973; m. Shirley Shockley, Feb. 26, 1977. With Imperial Chem. Industries, Inc., 1973—, asst. lab. mgr. for quality control Atlas point plant, Wilmington, Del., 1973-77, tech. sales rep. for indsl. and oil field chems., Dallas, 1978—; vis. prof. various colls. and univs. Recipient cert. of appreciation Nat. Urban League, 1979. Mem. Am. Chem. Soc., Kappa Alpha Psi. Home: 904 Druid Dr Plano TX 75075 Office: Rohm & Haas Chem Industries Inc 4585 Simonton Rd Dallas TX 75234

MC MILLAN, GEORGE MICHAEL, lawyer; b. Salt Lake City, Nov. 30, 1921; s. Verl Fayette and Eudora (Watts) McM.; student U. Utah, 1939-41; LL.B., George Washington U., 1947; m. Wilma Smith, Feb. 27, 1946; children—Nancy Gayle, Courtney Michael. Admitted to D.C. bar, 1946, Utah bar, 1947, U.S. Supreme Ct., 1959; practiced in Salt Lake City; mem. firm McKay & Burton, 1947-58, McMillan, Cannon & Browning, 1958-65; partner firm McMillan & Browning, 1965-80; of counsel firm VanCott, Bagley, Cornwall & McCarthy, 1981—; gen. counsel KUTV, Inc., Salt Lake City, 1958—, asst. sec., 1970—; gen. counsel Standard Corp. (Ogden Standard Examiner), 1953—; gen. counsel, asst. sec. Kans. State Network, Inc.; gen. counsel, dir. Nat. TeleMation, Inc., Salt Lake City, Communications Investment Corp., Salt Lake City, Roosevelt Unit, Inc. Mem. Salt Lake County, Utah, Fed. bar assns. Democrat. Club: Fort Douglas. Home: 960 Shirecliff Rd Salt Lake City UT 84108 Office: 50 S Main St Suite 1600 Salt Lake City UT 84144

MC MILLAN, HUGH DIX, JR., mfrs. rep.: b. Shreveport, La., Sept. 15, 1925; s. Hugh Dix and Edna (Self) McM.; B.S., Tex. A. and M. Coll., 1947; m. Dorothy Jean Sawyer, May 10, 1952; children—Hugh Dix III, Janet Lynn. Design engr. Coastal Equipment Co., Houston, 1947-48; design and sales engr. D & S Sales, Inc., 1948-49: sales engr. J.R. Dowdell & Co., 1949-55; pres. McMillan Equipment Co., 1955—; dir. Tex. Commerce Bank, Katy. Dir. F.E. Giesecke Meml. Fund, Austin, Tex. Served with AC, AUS, 1944-45. Mem. Am. Soc. Heating, Refrigerating and Air Conditioning Engrs. (past pres. Houston chpt., past nat. dir., regional chmn., nat. treas. 1976-77, nat. v.p. 1977-78, pres.-elect 1978-79, nat. pres. 1979-80), Am. Assn. Engrng. Socs. (exec. com. 1980), Pres.'s Assn., Am. Mgmt. Assn., Mfrs. Agts. Nat. Assn., Houston Engrng. and Sci. Soc., Nat., Tex. socs. profl. engrs. Baptist. Mason (Shriner). Club: Pine Forest Country. Home: 13302 Apple Tree Houston TX 77079 Office: 16720 Park Row Houston TX 77084

MCMILLAN, LEON, investment co. exec.; b. Detroit, Mar. 28, 1937; s. Lyle and Grace I. (Gardner) McM.; B.S., Wayne State U., Detroit, 1960; M.B.A., N.Y. U., 1961; m. Phyllis A. Nevitt, July 3, 1961. Trainee, Thomson & McKinnon Co., N.Y.C., 1961-63; investment analyst Nat. Bank Detroit, 1963-65, First Mich. Corp., 1965-66, Robert W. Baird Co., Milw., 1966-67; sr. investment analyst Supervised Investors Services, Chgo., 1967-71, Lincoln Nat. Investment Mgmt. Co., Chgo., 1971—. Mem. Investment Analysis Soc. Chgo., Chgo. Sci. Analysts (past pres.), Chicagoland Old English Sheepdog Club (past pres.). Home: 480 Lee Rd Northbrook IL 60062 Office: 111 W Washington St Chicago IL 60602

MC MILLON, FLOYD ALLEN, fin. exec.; b. Poplar Bluff, Mo., Oct. 20, 1946; s. Paul J. and Thelma K. (Transue) McM.; B.A., Mid-Am. Nazarene Coll., 1975; student Washington U., 1973; postgrad. U. Pa., 1976. With Mercantile Mortgage Co. and First Nat. Bank of Clayton (Mo.), 1966-70; acct. Washington U., St. Louis, 1973; exec. v.p., founder Nat. Inst. Cert. Tax Accts., 1975—; corporate pres., chmn. bd. F.A. McMillon & Co., Olathe, Kans., 1975—; exec. dir. Taxpayer's Success Inst.; guest speaker various bus., tax, fin. seminars, schs.; cons. in field. Served with USAF, 1966. Cert. tax acct., Kans. Mem. Nat. Inst. Cert. Tax Accts., Polit. Action Group, Nat. Assn. Accts., Nat. Soc. Public Accts., Assn. Tax Cons., Olathe Area C. of C. Republican. Mem. Christian Ch. Home: 1001 S Lindenwood Olathe KS 66062 Office: 1620 E Rogers Rd Olathe KS 66061

MC MILLON, REGNAL LUTHER, ins. co. exec., pub. speaker; b. Guion, Tex., Apr. 23, 1921; s. James Luther and Tennessee Jones (Haynie) McM.; student Tarleton State Coll., 1938; m. Elsie Eugenia Roberts, Dec. 14, 1941; children—Toni Karen, Steven Grant. Internat. speaker for convs., clubs, other orgns.; with Bus. Men's Assurance Co., Abilene, Tex., 1946-71, dist. mgr., 1956-60, br. mgr., Abilene, 1961-71; gen. agt. Washington Nat. Ins. Co., Lubbock, Tex., 1971—. Dir. Nat. Gen. Agts. and Mgrs. Conf.; trustee Life Underwriters Tng. Council U.S., pres., 1965-66. Served with USAAF, 1942-46. Named Ins. Field Man of Yr. in Life Ins. in U.S., 1962; Internat. Health Ins. Man of Yr., 1965; recipient Harold R. Gordon Meml. award Internat. Assn. Health Underwriters, 1965, Distinguished Service award Vocat. Agr. Tchrs. Tex., 1965; John Newton Russell award, 1967. Mem. Nat. (pres. 1961-62), Tex. (pres. 1956-57) assns. life underwriters, Tex. Assn. Health Underwriters (pres. 1954-55), Author numerous articles on selling, human relations. Home: 7003-B Hartford St Lubbock TX 79413 Office: 2321 50th St Lubbock TX 79412

MC MULLEN, JOHN JOSEPH, naval architect, transp. cons., maritime co. exec.; b. Jersey City, May 10, 1918; s. Charles S. and Isabella V. (Oxley) McM.; B.S., U.S. Naval Acad., 1940; M.S. in Naval Constrn. and Engrng., Mass. Inst. Tech., 1945; Dr. Tech. Sci., Swiss Fed. Inst. Tech., Zurich, 1950; m. Jacqueline Joy Everhart, Dec. 10, 1955; children—Peter Stuart, Catherine Joy, John Joseph. Commd. ensign U.S. Navy, 1940, advanced through grades to comdr., 1954; ETO, NATOUSA, PTO; resigned, 1954; chief office ship constrn. and repair Maritime Adminstrn., U.S. Dept. Commerce, Washington, 1954-57; pres. John J. McMullen Assos., Inc., N.Y.C., 1957-68, chmn. bd., 1971—; pres., chief exec. officer Burmah Oil Tankers Ltd., 1975; chmn. bd., pres., chief exec. officer U.S. Lines, Inc., N.Y.C., 1968-70; gen. partner Houston Astros Baseball Club; dir. Norton, Lilly & Co., Inc., Cornell & Underhill, Inc., Hudson Engrng. Co., Perth Amboy Dry Dock Co., MPR Assos., Inc., Pacific Marine Corp. Trustee, Georgian Court Coll., Lakewood, N.J., Boston Coll., Chestnut Hill, Mass. Decorated Am., Nat. Def. service medals, Silver Life Sav. medal; recipient Akroyd Stuart award Inst. Marine Engrs., London, 1957, 59, Disting. Service medal citation Robert L. Hague Mcht. Marine Industries post Am Legion. Mem. Am. Soc. Naval Engrs., Navy League U.S., Am. Bur. Shipping (bd. mgrs.), Soc. Naval Architects and Marine Engrs. Clubs: Whitehall Lunch, India House, Madison Square Garden, World Trade Center (N.Y.C.); Pine Valley (N.J.) Golf; River Oaks (Tex.) Golf; Montclair (N.J.) Golf; Oslo (Norway) Golf; Grasshopper (Zurich, Switzerland); Swiss Acad. Ski. Contbr. numerous articles to profl. jours. Home: 53 Undercliff Rd Montclair NJ 07042 Office: John J McMullen Assos Inc 1 World Trade Center Suite 3047 New York NY 10048

MCMURREN, WILLIAM HENRY, contractor; b. Ontario, Oreg., Oct. 20, 1927; s. Serene Elbert and Louise Gertrude (Baker) McM.; B.S., Tex. A&M U., 1950; m. Carlyn D. Stenberg, Oct. 17, 1953; children—Catherine Lynn, John Henry. With Morrison-Knudsen Co., Inc., Boise, Idaho, 1955—, exec. v.p., dir., 1969-72, pres., chief exec. officer, dir., 1972—; dir. Idaho 1st Nat. Bank, Nat. Steel & Shipbuilding Co., San Diego, H. K. Ferguson Co., Cleve., Internat. Engrng. Co., Inc., San Francisco, Emkay Devel. & Realty, Newport Beach, Calif. Served to 1st lt. C. E., U.S. Army, 1945-46, 50-53. Mem. Soc. Am. Mil. Engrs. (dir.), Am. Inst. Constructors, Newcomen Soc. Clubs: Hillcrest Country (Boise); Houston; Internat., Georgetown (Washington); Moles (N.Y.C.); Beavers (Los Angeles). Office: One Morrison Knudsen Plaza Boise ID 83729

MCMURTRIE, JOHN BENNETT, banker; b. Williamsport, Pa.; s. Arthur John and Virginia Heinin (Clinger) McM.; B.S. magna cum laude, Lehigh U., 1959; m. Ronna Stitely, Sept. 26, 1959; children—Cindy, Elise, John, Bennett. Pres., Milton Machine Works, Milton, Pa., 1959-75, Milton Steel Supply, 1964-75; pres. No. Central Bank, Williamsport, 1975—, chmn. bd., 1978—. Bd. dirs. Lycoming County (Pa.) United Way, Lycoming County Housing Devel. Corp.; pres., mem. exec. bd. Susquehanna council Boy Scouts Am.; chmn. Hall of Fame com. Little League Baseball, South Williamsport; trustee Williamsport YMCA, Robert Packer Hosp., Sayre, Pa.; mem. Williamsport Mcpl. Authority; mem. Lycoming County Republican Fin. Com.; mem. Covenant Central Presbyterian Ch., Williamsport, 1975—, pres. bd. trustees, 1979-80. Registered profl. engr., Pa. Mem. Pa. Bankers Assn. (exec. com. Group IV). Clubs: Rotary, Williamsport Country (Williamsport); Turbot Hills Country. Office: 102 W 4th St Williamsport PA 17701

MC NALLY, ANDREW, III, printer, publishing co. exec.; b. Chgo., Aug. 17, 1909; s. Andrew and Eleanor (Vilas) McN.; A.B., Yale U., 1931; m. Margaret Clark MacMillin, Nov. 20, 1936; children—Betty Jane, Andrew, IV, Edward Clark. With Chgo. factory Rand McNally & Co., 1931, N.Y. sales office v.p., dir., 1933, pres., 1948-74, chmn. bd., 1974—; dir. Nat. Ry. Publ. Co., N.Y.C. Past pres. Graphic Arts Tech. Found. Served as capt., C.E., Army Map Service, 1942-45. Mem. Chgo. Hist. Soc. (trustee, past pres.). Office: PO Box 7600 Chicago IL 60680

MC NALLY, ANDREW, IV, publishing co. exec.; b. Chgo., Nov. 11, 1939; s. Andrew and Margaret C. (MacMillin) McN.; grad. Hill Sch., Pottstown, Pa., 1958; B.A., U. N.C., 1963; M.B.A., U. Chgo., 1969; m. Jeanine Sanchez, July 3, 1966; children—Andrew, Carrie, Ward. Bus. mgr. edn. div. Rand McNally & Co., Chgo., 1967-70, exec. v.p., sec., from 1970, now pres., chief exec. officer, dir.; dir. Harvey Hubbell Co. Mem. fin. com. Printing Industries Am., 1970—. Trustee Hill Sch., Chgo. Latin Sch.; mem. aux. bd. Art Inst. Chgo. Mem. Air Force N.G., 1963-69. Clubs: Chicago, Saddle and Cycle, Commonwealth (Chgo.); Glen View Golf. Home: 16 Canterbury Ct Wilmette IL 60091 Office: PO Box 7600 Chicago IL 60680

MCNALLY, JACK REGINALD MOORE, sci. instruments co. exec.; b. Luton, Bedfordshire, Eng., Dec. 15, 1916; s. Alfred and Caroline (Alexander) Hawkins; Higher Nat. certificate in electronics and mechanics, Woolwich Polytech. Inst., 1936-41; m. Lena Medcraf, Dec. 23, 1939. Apprentice, Dental Mfg. Co., Woolwich, London, 1936-38; jr. engr. Standard Telephones and Cables, Woolwich, 1938-41; electronic equipment engr. Telephone Mfg. Co., Orpington, Kent, 1941-46; works supt. Asso. Elec. Industries, Covent Garden, London, 1946-50; works mgr. Electrothermal Engrng. Ltd., Upton Park, London, South End, Essex, 1950-58, also asst. mng. dir. plastic moulding Bendix & Herbert, Rochester, Kent, South End, Essex, 1953-58; gen. mgr. Beckman Instruments Ltd., Fife, Scotland, 1958-63, mng. dir., 1963—, chmn., 1976—; chmn. Sci. Documentation Ltd., Dunfermline, Fife, Vivian Industries Ltd., Beckman Instruments (Holdings) Ltd., Beckman Riic, Beckman France, Beckman Italy, G&R Internat. Group of Cos., Triad Tech. & Indsl. Services Ltd.; mem. Glenrothes Devel. Corp. Justice of Peace Co. of Fife, Scotland; mem. Fife Region Health Bd., Fife Children's Panel; Justice of Peace. Vice-chmn. bd. dirs. Glenrothes Tech. Coll.; mem. adv. com., com. European community studies Edinburgh U. Served to lt. Home Guard, 1940-45. Decorated Order Brit. Empire; freeman City of London. Fellow Soc. Comml. Accountants, Inst. Dirs., Instn. Works Mgrs., Royal Soc. Arts; mem. Brit. Inst. Mgmt., Assn. Supervising Elec. Engrs., Scottish Indsl. Sports Assn. (v.p. 1966-72, pres. 1972—), Brit. Assn. Advancement Sci. (v.p. physics, math.), Edinburgh C. of C. (dir. 1968—), Confedn. Brit. Industries (exec. com.). Episcopalian. Mason, Rotarian (pres. 1968-69). Clubs: Glenrothes Golf (v.p. 1967—), St. Andrew's Golf, Royal Automobile, Master Worshipful Co. of Sci. Instrument Makers City of London. Co-author: Introduction to Spectroscopy, 1967. Patentee in field. Home: Roseacre Orchard Dr Glenrothes Fife Scotland Office: Queensway Glenrothes Fife Scotland

MC NALLY, TIMOTHY JAMES, equipment co. exec.; b. Pontiac, Mich., Sept. 26, 1947; s. Thomas Michael and Lucille Rose (Zarend) McN.; B.B.A., Ohio U., 1969; postgrad. Bowling Green State U., 1971; M.B.A., Xavier U., 1975. Bus. equipment specialist Bell & Howell, Inc., Toledo, 1970-71; sales and mktg. Prentice-Hall, Inc., Cin., 1971-76; asst. to v.p. mktg. Litton Unit Handling Systems div. Litton Industries, Florence, Ky., 1976-79, sales engr., 1979—. Mem. Cin. Indsl. Advertisers, Am. Mgmt. Assn., Cin. Office: One Campbell Ave Suite 96 West Haven CT 06516

MC NAMARA, FRANCIS JOSEPH, JR., lawyer; b. Boston, Nov. 30, 1927; s. Francis Joseph and Louise (English) McN.; A.B., Georgetown U., 1949, LL.B., 1951; m. Noreen E. O'Connor, June 18, 1953; children—Francis Joseph, Moira Patricia, John Allen, Kathleen Louise, Martha Jeanne, Mark Jeffrey. Admitted to Conn. bar, 1952; asso. firm Pullman, Comley, Bradley & Reeves, 1953; asst. U.S. atty. Dist. Conn., 1953-57; asso. firm Cummings & Lockwood, Stamford, Conn., 1957—, partner, 1959—. Mem. pres.'s council Fairfield (Conn.) U., 1967-69, trustee, 1968—; mem., dir., chmn. bd. Charles E. Culpeper Found.; trustee Charles E. Culpeper Trust. Served with USNR, 1946- 51-53. Fellow Am. Bar Found.; mem. Am., Fed., Conn. bar assns. (ho. of dels. and bd. govs. 1978—; chmn. fed. judiciary com. 1976—) U.S. bar assns., Phi Delta Phi, Knights of Malta, Navy League U.S. Republican. Roman Catholic. Clubs: Univ. (N.Y.C.); Midtown, Landmark (Stamford); Wee Burn Country Noroton Yacht (Darien, Conn.). Home: 16 Allwood Rd Darien CT 06820 Office: 10 Stamford Forum Stamford CT 06904 also 866 United Nations Plaza New York NY 10017

MC NAMARA, J(OHN) DONALD, lawyer, business exec.; b. Bridgeport, Conn., Feb. 28, 1924; s. John T. and Agnes (Keating) McN.; B.A., Dartmouth Coll., 1945; M.A. in Govt., Harvard U., 1947, LL.B., 1950; m. Shirley Addison Holdridge, Nov. 5, 1960. Admitted to N.Y. and Conn. bars, 1951; asso. firm Hall, Haywood, Patterson & Taylor, N.Y.C., 1951-53, 55-56; asst. U.S. atty. So. Dist. N.Y., 1953-55; asso. firm Wickes, Riddell, Bloomer, Jacobi & McGuire, N.Y.C., 1956-57; asso., then partner firm Nottingham & McEniry, and successor, N.Y.C., 1957-59; sec., gen. counsel Interpublic Group of Cos., Inc., N.Y.C., 1960-79, dir., 1965—, sr. v.p., 1966-73, exec. v.p., 1973-79, pres., 1980—, mem. exec. com., 1967—, mem. fin. com., 1980—. Chmn. U.S. Nat. Tennis Championships, 1965. Served to lt. (j.g.) USNR, 1943-46. Mem. Am. (com. fgn. and internat. bus. law 1971-80), Internat. bar assns. Clubs: River, Univ., Met. Opera (N.Y.C.); West Side Tennis (pres. 1964-66, 79-80, gov. 1962-66, 78-80); International (Washington); Ocean Reef (Key Largo, Fla.). Home: 350 E 57th St New York NY 10022 also Ethan Allen Rd Peru VT 05152 Office: 1271 Ave of Americas New York NY 10020

MCNAMARA, MICHAEL JAMES, computer services co. exec.; b. Denver, Dec. 15, 1946; s. Ralpha A. and Jacqueline R. (Bidel) McN.; student public schs., Glendale, Calif.; m. Judith Michele Polimeni, Sept. 21, 1969; children—Michael James, Melissa Michele. Dist. mgr. DATA 100, Los Angeles, 1976-77, region mgr., N.Y.C., 1978-79; region mgr. Nixdorf Computer Corp., N.Y.C., 1979—. Served with USN, 1964-70. Home: 1420 Round Hill Rd Fairfield CT 06430

MC NAMARA, MICHAEL ROBERT, accountant; b. Rockford, Ill., Oct. 5, 1948; s. Robert Timothy and Donna May (Sarver) McN.; A.A., Rock Valley Coll., 1968; B.S., No. Ill. U., 1970; m. Warrene Susan Westphal, June 21, 1969; children—Traci Sue, David Michael. With Gen. Electric Co., Schenectady, 1970-79, mgr. bus. analysis, 1979—. Mem. No. Ill. U. Alumni Assn. (life). Home: 5221 Bridle Pathway Schenectady NY 12303 Office: Bldg 2 Room 740 One River Rd Schenectady NY 12345

MC NAMARA, ROBERT STRANGE, ofcl. World Bank; b. San Francisco, June 9, 1916; s. Robert James and Clara Neil (Strange) McN.; A.B., U. Calif., 1937, LL.D.; M.B.A., Harvard U., 1939, LL.D.; LL.D., U. Mich., Columbia, George Washington U., 1962, Princeton U., Williams Coll., N.Y. U., Notre Dame U. Ohio U., U. Aberdeen, U. Ala., Amherst Coll.; m. Margaret Craig, Aug. 13, 1940; children—Margaret Elizabeth, Kathleen, Robert Craig. Asst. prof. bus. adminstrn. Harvard U., 1940-43; with Ford Motor Co., 1946-61, asst. gen. mgr. Ford div., 1953-55, v.p., gen. mgr., 1955-57, group v.p. car divs., 1957-60, pres. co., 1960-61, co. dir., 1957-61; sec. of Def., 1961-68; pres. World Bank, Washington, 1968—; spl. cons. War Dept, 1942. Bd. dirs. Brookings Instn.; trustee Urban Inst., Rockefeller U., Calif. Inst. Tech.; former trustee Ford Found. Served as lt. col. USAAF, 1943-46; col. Res. Decorated Legion of Merit. Mem. Phi Beta Kappa. Author: The Essence of Security, 1968; One Hundred Countries, Two Billion People, 1973.

MC NAUGHT, STEPHEN ROBERT, ins. co. exec.; b. Boston, May 29, 1947; s. John Joseph and Beatrice Cecelia (Maloney) McN.; B.S.B.A., Boston Coll., 1970; M.B.A., Suffolk U., 1978; m. Beverly Frances DeCoste, Aug. 1, 1970; children—Jeannine Renee, Jerelyn Michelle, Suzanne Denise. Underwriter, Employers Comml. Union Ins. Co., Boston, 1971-72; mgr. O'Donoghue Ins. Agy., Arlington, Mass., 1972-74; asst. dir. actuarial dept. Comml. Union Ins. Co., Boston, 1974-79, dir. mktg. personal lines, 1979—; condr. corp. seminars, telephone mktg. cons. Coach Melrose (Mass.) Youth Hockey; active Amateur Hockey Assn. Mem. Assn. M.B.A. Execs., Am. Mgmt. Assn., Am. Heart Assn., Boston Coll. Alumni Assn., U.S. Golf Assn., Suffolk U. Alumni Assn. Clubs: Hon. Order Blue Goose, Elks. Home: 8 Philips Rd Stoneham MA 02180 Office: 1 Beacon St Boston MA 02108

MC NAY, JOSEPH CLAUDIUS, investment co. exec.; b. Butler, Mo., Jan. 15, 1934; s. John Leeper and Ruby Ann (McCall) McN.; B.A., Yale U., 1956; M.B.A., U. Pa., 1959; m. Beth Pheiffer, Dec. 28, 1978; children—Joanna, Colin, Alice, Kate. Investment officer Old Colony Trust Co., Boston, 1961-66; v.p. Mass. Co., Boston, 1966-67; exec. v.p., dir. endowment Mgmt. and Research Corp., Boston, 1967-76; pres., chmn. bd., dir. Essex Investment Mgmt. Co., Boston, 1976—; dir. Child World, Inc., Cullinane Corp. Trustee, Diocesan Investment Trust Boston, 1965—, Boston U. Med. Center, 1967—, Children's Hosp. Med. Center, 1967—. Served with USAF, 1959-60. Mem. N.Y. Soc. Security Analysts, Boston Soc. Security Analysts. Episcopalian. Clubs: Brookline Country, Union Boat, Longwood Cricket. Office: Essex Investment Mgmt Co 10 Post Office Sq Boston MA 02109

MC NEAL, BERNARD GREGORY, mfg. co. exec.; b. Portsmouth, Va., June 24, 1949; s. Jesse Lawrence and Edna (Harmon) McN.; B.S. in Acctg. magna cum laude, Morgan State U., 1975; M.S.M., Purdue U., 1977; m. Nov. 11, 1978. In-charge auditor Ernst & Whinney, Balt., 1977-79; asst. tax mgr. McCormick & Co., Hunt Valley, Md., 1979—; instr. acctg. Morgan State U., Balt., 1978; mem. Md. State Bd. Accountancy. Bd. dirs. Martin Luther King Parent and Child Care Center, Balt., 1979-80. Served with USAF, 1968-72. Decorated Air Force Commendation medal; C.P.A. Mem. Inst. Mgmt. Accts., Nat. Assn. Accts., Am. Inst. C.P.A.'s, Nat. Assn. Black Accts., Assn. M.B.A. Execs. Democrat. Baptist. Address: 11350 McCormick Rd Hunt Valley MD 21031

MCNEAL, JAMES HECTOR, JR., mfg. co. exec.; b. Dover, Del., Nov. 22, 1927; s. James Hector and Elizabeth Vickers (Hodgson) McN.; B.S., U. Del., 1951; m. Lucy Cooper Finn, June 16, 1951; children—James Hector, Edwin Howell, Sarah Elizabeth. With Budd Co., 1951—, v.p. mfg. services, Troy, Mich., 1972-73, group v.p. automotive products, 1973-74, pres., chief exec. officer, 1974—, also dir.; dir. Automotive Co. of Can. Ltd. Bd. dirs. Detroit Area council Boy Scouts Am. Served with USNR, 1945-46. Mem. Econ. Club Detroit. Clubs: Bloomfield Hills Country; Oakland Hills Country; Detroit Athletic. Office: 3155 W Big Beaver Rd Troy MI 48084

MC NEAL, R(ALPH) RICHARD, ins. cons.; b. Oakville, Iowa, Aug. 19, 1925; s. Ralph Vincent and Zella Barr (Wright) McN.; student U. Minn., 1943, Coll. St. Thomas, 1943-44; B.C.S., Drake U., 1948; m. Ruth Lucille Morgan, Aug. 31, 1947; children—Michael, Deborah (Mrs. Richard D. Wood), Nancy (Mrs. Jack Burtch). Mktg. rep. Aetna Life & Casualty Co., St. Louis, 1948-54; operator Kennesaw Land & Ins. Co., Atlanta, 1954-59; operator W. Lyman Case & Co., Columbus, Ohio, 1959-64; pres. R. Richard McNeal Assos., Co., Columbus, 1964—. Speaker to various mgmt. groups. Served with USNR, 1943-45. Recipient Young Man of Yr. award, Jr. C. of C., Cobb County, Ohio, 1958; Salesman of Yr. award Upper Arlington Civic Assn., 1972. Mem. Soc. of Ins. Research, Am. Assn. Risk Analysts (trustee 1969-74), Am. Mgmt. Assn. Lion. Clubs: Athletic (Columbus); Arlington (Upper Arlington, Ohio); Optimist (Atlanta). Contbr. articles to profl. jours. Home: 2171 Pinebrook Pd Columbus OH 43220 Office: 1880 Mackenzie Dr Columbus OH 43220

MC NEAL, RALPH LEROY, financial exec.; b. London, Ohio, Sept. 8, 1935; s. Walter McKinley and Mary Marie Brown; B.S., Central State U., Wilberforce, Ohio, 1957; postgrad. Seton Hall U., South Orange, N.J., 1965-66, Rutgers U., 1967-68; m. Shirley Jane Lowery, Nov. 15, 1957: children—Ralph LeRoy, Scott Damon, Erika Marie. Field agt. IRS, Cleve., 1957-58; accountant, hearing examiner N.J. Pub. Utilities Commn., Newark, 1961-62; budget examiner City of Newark, 1962-65; budget coordinator, ops. analyst Schering-Plough Internat., Bloomfield, N.J., 1965-67; corp. budget mgr. Wakefern Food Corp., Elizabeth, N.J., 1967-69; dir. fin. City of Englewood, N.J., 1969-71; prin. mgmt. analyst Offtrack Betting Corp., N.Y.C., 1971-72; pres. Coalition Venture Group, N.Y.C., 1972-76, Ralph L. McNeal & Co., mgmt. cons., 1976-78, North St. Capital Corp., White Plains, N.Y., 1978—; v.p., dir. Crayton Co. Inc., Cleve., 1978—; dir. REM Transport Co. Inc., Tulsa, Uniworld Group, Inc., N.Y.C. Bd. chmn. South Ward Little League, Newark, 1969-75. Served with U.S. Army, 1958-60. Mem. Planning Execs. Inst., Am. Assn. Minority Enterprise Small Bus. Investment Cos. (dir., Washington 1974, 79), Nat. Assn. Small Bus. Investment Cos., Omega Psi Phi. Home: 42 Weequahic Ave Newark NJ 07112 Office: 250 North St White Plains NY 10625

MC NEEL, SYNOTT LANCE, ins. co. exec.; b. Galveston, Tex., June 5, 1923; s. John Marshall and Ann Mae (Fox) McN.; B.B.A., Baylor U., 1944; m. Evelyn Marie Schoenberg, Aug. 18, 1943; children—Linea, Peggy, Synott Lance, Kathleen. Sr. v.p., treas., dir. Am. Indemnity Co., 1970—, Am. Fire and Indemnity Co., 1970—, Tex. Gen. Indemnity Co., 1970—, Am. Indemnity Fin. Corp., Galveston, 1973—, Am. Computing Co., Galveston, 1971—. Mem. O'Connell Sch. Bd., 1974—; bd. dirs. Water Dist. 4, 1973—, Tex. Auto Ins. Plan. Served with Signal Corps, U.S. Army, 1943-45; PTO. Mem. Galveston C. of C., Ins. Accounting and Statis. Assn. (internat.

pres. 1971-72), Nat. Office Mgmt. Assn. (pres. Galveston chpt. 1958), Assn. Fire and Casualty Cos. Tex. Roman Catholic. Clubs: Galveston Arty., Galveston Racquet, Galveston Yacht, Galveston Country; Headliners Austin. Home: 2513 Gerol Dr Galveston TX 77551 Office: One American Indemnity Plaza Galveston TX 77553

MC NEELY, E.L., mcht.; b. Pattonburg, Mo., Oct. 5, 1918; s. Ralph H. and Viola (Vogel) McN.; student U. Mo., 1936-37; B.A., N.E. Mo. State Coll., 1940; student Bus. Coll. Kansas City, 1935-36; postgrad. Rockhurst U., 1942, Northwestern U., 1943; m. Alice Hall, Sept. 18, 1948; children—Sandra (Mrs. Ronald Gessl), Gregory, Mark, Kevin. With Montgomery Ward and Co., 1940-64, West Coast mdse. mgr., 1959-61, nat. deptl. mdse. mgr., 1961-64; dir. marketing Wickes Corp., Saginaw, Mich., 1964-65, sr. v.p. all retailing and bldg. activities, 1965-69, dir., 1965—, pres., chief exec. officer, 1969-75, chmn. bd., chief exec. officer, 1975—; dir. Fed. Mogul Corp., Dayco Corp., Pacific Tel. & Tel., Trans Am. Corp., San Diego Econ. Devel. Corp., San Diego. Mem. Com. for Econ. Devel. Bd. dirs. YMCA, 1969—, Scripps Inst., City of Hope; trustee Boys Clubs Am. Served to lt. (j.g.) USNR, 1942-46. Service scholar in journalism, 1938-40. Mem. Newcomen Soc., Alpha Phi Omega. Republican. Presbyn. Clubs: Saginaw; La Jolla Country; Cuyamaca (San Diego); Metropolitan, Union League (Chgo.). Office: Wickes Cos Inc 1010 2d Ave San Diego CA 92101

MC NEIL, HENRY SLACK, pharm. exec.; b. Phila., Apr. 22, 1917; s. Robert Lincoln and Grace F. (Slack) McN.; B.S., Yale, 1939; LL.D., Phila. Coll. Pharmacy and Sci.; m. Lois A. Fernley, Oct. 4, 1941; children—Henry Slack, Barbara Joan McNeil Jordan, Marjorie Fernley McNeil Findlay, Robert Douglas. With McNeil Labs., Phila., 1940-79, pres., 1955-60; v.p., dir. Johnson & Johnson, 1959-77; chmn. bd. Claneil Enterprises Inc.; dir. Bluebell Assos., Remington Rand Corp., South Eleuthera Properties, Ltd., Penguin Industries, Inc. Mem. adv. bd. Valley Forge council Boy Scouts Am., mem. Nat. council; mem. fine arts com., chmn. fin. com. diplomatic reception rooms U.S. Dept. State; pres. Pa. Acad. Fine Arts; mem. nat. adv. council Multiple Sclerosis Soc.; mem. devel. bd. Yale; trustee Henry Francis duPont Winterthur Mus.; mem. council Am. Mus. in Britain. Recipient gold medal Pa. Acad. Fine Arts. Mem. Hist. Soc. Pa., Pa. Council on Arts, Clan Macneil Assn. Am., Newcomen Soc., Confrerie des Chevaliers du Tastevin, Nat. Trust Historic Preservation (dir.), Omicron Delta Kappa (hon.). Clubs: St. Elmo (New Haven); Yale, Racquet, Phila. Cricket, Union League, St. Andrew's Soc., Sunnybrook, Corinthian Yacht, Phila. Aviation Country; (Phila.); Metropolitan (N.Y.C.); Metropolitan, Capitol Hill (Washington); Wilmington (Del.); Royal Danish Yacht (Copenhagen). Home: Plymouth Meeting PA 19462 Office: 1 Plymouth Meeting Plymouth Meeting PA 19462

MC NEIL, M. KATHERINE, women's apparel co. exec.; b. Oakland, Calif., Oct. 4, 1952; d. Wilfred James and Patricia R. (McGlinchy) McN.; B.F.A. in Apparel Design with honors (Design award high fashion men's wear 1976), R.I. Sch. Design, 1976. Pres., designer Nonchalance Ltd., Newport, R.I., 1976-78, San Francisco, 1978—; Norwegian purchasing agt./exporter men's and women's apparel, 1980—. Mem. San Francisco Museum Soc., Fashion Group (San Francisco chpt.). Address: 2645 Franklin St San Francisco CA 94123

MC NEIL, WALTER HARVE, sales rep.; b. Harlan, Ky., Apr. 21, 1920; s. John Charles and Marie E. (McBrayer) McN.; grad. Pikeville Coll. Acad., 1937, Air Command and Staff Coll., Gunter AFB, Ala.; student Pikeville Coll., 1956-58; m. Nellie Dean, June 1, 1946; children—Kay Francis McNeil Runyon, Paula Jean McNeil Branham. With Sycamore Coal Corp., Patterson, Va., 1937-42; enlisted U.S. Army, 1942, commd. 2d lt., 1943, advanced through grades to capt., 1946; staff communication officer Hdqrs. ETO; transferred to USAF Res., 1946, advanced through grades to lt. col., 1967; liaison officer Air Force Acad. coordinator W.Va., Ky., So. Ohio, 1961-70; ret., 1970; with Foster Thornburg Hardware Corp., Huntington, W.Va., 1946-61; sales rep. Tidewater Supply Co., 1961—; owner Ky. Screen Service. Pres., Pikeville Rotary Club, 1960-61. Named Outstanding Acad. Coordinator for South, Air Force Acad., 1965. Mem. Armed Forces Communications and Electronics Assn. (charter life), Air Force Assn., U.S. Capitol Hist. Soc., U.S. Air Force Hist. Found. (life), Assn. U.S. Army, Res. Officers Assn., Ret. Officers Assn. (life), Met. Opera Guild, Inc. Democrat. Baptist (deacon, lay leader). Clubs: Masons; Lafayette (Lexington, Ky.). Weekly columnist Pike County News, 1976—; contbr. articles to religious pubs. Home: 508 5th St Pikeville KY 41501 Office: PO Box 2097 Pikeville KY 41501

MC NEILL, CARMEN MARY, bus. broker; b. Charles City, Iowa, July 16; d. Benjamin T. and Mary (Orvis) McN.; M.B.A., U. Chgo., 1957. Sec.-treas., Old Rep. Life Ins. Co., 1943-62; cons., officer life cos., 1962-70; broker-finder, owner Am. Cons.'s, Chgo., 1970—; dir. Tower Life and Accident Ins. Co., 1980—. Methodist. Home: 918 Argyle Ave Flossmoor IL 60422 Office: Suite 1314 30 N Michigan Ave Chicago IL 60602

MC NEILL, WILLIAM PAUL, city ofcl.; b. Brighton, Mass., Oct. 6, 1929; s. James E. and Mona M. (McLaughlin) McN.; A.A., Boston Coll., 1950; B.A., Suffolk U., 1954, postgrad. 1955-57; m. Helen C. Burns, June 18, 1955; children—Brian W., James E., William J., Gary B. Adminstrv. asst. to mayor's office City of Boston, 1957-60, sr. budget analyst, adminstrv. services, 1960-72, dir. budgets, 1973—; with state treas.'s office Commonwealth of Mass., 1972-73; dir. pres. City of Boston Credit Union, 1960-61. Democratic state del. and ward chmn., 1954—; pres. Brighton Central Little League, 1962. Served with U.S. Army, 1950-52. Recipient Brighton-Allston Outstanding Citizen award, 1964; Man of Yr. award Exchange Club Boston, 1979. Mem. Am. Mgmt. Assn., Mcpl. Fin. Officers Assn., Mass. Assn. Auditors and Accts., Mass. Mcpl. Assn. Democrat. Roman Catholic. Clubs: K.C. (grand knight 1960-61), Needham Golf, Boston Harbor Tennis, VFW (comdr. 1962-63), Elks, Goodwill of Brighton (pres. 1960-64). Home: 54 Deerfield Rd Needham MA 02192 Office: Rm 703 City Hall Budget Dept City of Boston MA 02201

MCNERNEY, WALTER JAMES, assn. exec.; b. New Haven, June 8, 1925; s. Robert Frances and Anna (Shanley) McN.; B.S., Yale U., 1947; M.H.A., U. Minn., 1950; m. Shirley Hamilton, June 26, 1948; children—Walter James, Peter Hamilton, Jennifer Allison, Daniel Martin, Richard Hamilton. Research asst. Labor-Mgmt. Center, Yale U., 1947-48; adminstrv. resident R.I. Hosp., Providence, 1949-50; asst. to coordinator hosp. and clinics Med. Center, U. Pitts., 1950-53, instr., asst. prof. hosp. adminstrn., asst. prof. hosp., med. adminstrn., 1953-55; asso. prof., dir. program hosp. adminstrn. Sch. Bus. Adminstrn., U. Mich., 1955-58, prof., dir. Bur. Hosp. Adminstrn., 1958-61; pres. Blue Cross Assn., Chgo., 1961-78, Blue Cross and Blue Shield Assns., 1978—; dir., mem. exec. com. Nat. Health Council, 1963—, pres., 1972-73; mem. governing council Inst. Medicine, Nat. Acad. Sci.; mem. Nat. Council on Health Planning and Resources Devel., HEW; mem. nat. health policy study group Nat. Chamber Found.; dir. Internat. Execs. Service Corps; pres. Health Services Found., 1963—, bd. govs. Health Service, Inc., Chgo.; chmn. task force on medicaid and related programs HEW, 1969-70. Mem. adv. council on inst. health econs. U. Pa.; adv. council Grad. Sch. Mgmt., Northwestern U.; mem. undergrad admissions com., chmn. maj., spl. gifts com. Yale U.; bd. visitors U. Pitts. Grad. Sch. Public Health; bd. govs. VA Scholars Program. Served to lt. (j.g.) USNR, 1943-46. Named 1 of 100 Most Important Young Men and Women in U.S., Life mag., 1962; Nuffield Provincial Hosps. Trust-King's Fund fellow, Eng., 1970; recipient Sec.'s Unit citation Dept. HEW, 1970, Yale medal for Outstanding Service to Univ. Fellow Am. Hosp. Assn. (Justin Ford Kimball award 1967); mem. Royal Soc. Health, Assn. U. Programs in Hosp. Adminstrn., Assn. Tchrs. Preventive Medicine, Internat. Hosp. Fedn., Am. Mgmt. Assn. (trustee), Assn. Yale Alumni Mgmt. Execs. Soc., Am. Coll. Hosp. Adminstrs., Sigma Xi, Delta Sigma Pi. Clubs: Mid-Am., Chicago, Whitehall (Chgo.); Yale (N.Y.C.); Cosmos (Washington). Author: (with others) Hospital and Medical Economics, 1962, (with Donald C. Riedel) Regionalization and Rural Care, 1962. Office: Blue Cross-Blue Shield Assns 676 St Clair St Chicago IL 60611

MCOUAT, WALLACE GRAHAM, fin. cons.; b. Indpls., Mar. 14, 1947; s. Robert Graham and Mary (Brittain) McO.; A.B. in Math., Ind. U., 1969, M.B.A., 1971; m. Valerie Martha Lee, Mar. 29, 1969; 1 son, Travis. Mgr., Price Waterhouse & Co., Atlanta, 1971-75, N.Y.C., 1975-76, San Francisco, 1976-77; project leader Anistics div. Alexander & Alexander, Palo Alto, Calif., 1977-78; v.p. Risk Scis. Group, Inc., San Francisco, 1978—; cons. Marin Solar Village Corp., 1979—; mem. adj. faculty U. San Francisco, 1977-78; speaker, panels, coordinator numerous profl. confs., 1976—. Mem. Marin County Energy Adv. Com., 1979—; co-founder, treas. Solar Central, 1979—; treas. Yes on B Com., a solar energy adv. com., 1979. C.P.A., Ind., Ga., Calif. Mem. Am. Inst. C.P.A.'s (author, editor several courses), Calif. Soc. C.P.A.'s, Am. Assn. Accts., Phi Beta Kappa, Pi Mu Epsilon. Contbr. articles to profl. jours. Home: 516 Whitewood St San Rafael CA 94903 Office: 45 Camino Alto Suite 202 Mill Valley CA 94941

MC PARTLAND, MATTHEW F., banker; b. N.Y.C., Nov. 12, 1932; s. John Francis and Theresa (Flynn) McP.; B.B.A., CCNY, 1964; J.D., Bklyn. Law Sch., 1968; m. Marguerite Cummings; children—Maureen, Matthew, Michael, Claire. Admitted to N.Y. bar; v.p. ops. personnel Chem. Bank, N.Y.C., 1975-77, v.p. affirmative action, 1977-79, v.p. met. bank staff adminstrn., 1979—. Dep. commr. Police Dept. N.Y.C., 1978-79; dir. Criminal Justice Agy., N.Y.C., 1979—. Mem. Am. Bar Assn., N.Y. State Bar Assn. Office: 140 Broadway New York NY 10005

MC PHEE, ALEXANDER HECTOR, cons. engr.; b. Bklyn., Nov. 26, 1911; s. Alexander Hendry and Charlotte Elizabeth (Kraus) McP.; student Pratt Inst., 1928-34, Bklyn. Poly. Inst., 1935-41; m. Cynthia Rose Agar, July 26, 1947; 1 son, Alexander Hector. Asst. chief engr. Peter Clark Inc., 1934-37; engr. U.S.S. Yorktown & Enterprises Airplane Elevators, 1930-37; partner Howard V. Harding & Co., 1937-38; asst. chief engr. Lukenweld div. Lukens Steel Co., 1938-44; partner McPhee & Johnston, 1945-48; pres. Macton Machinery Co., 1947-48; cons. engr., 1948—; v.p. Hepworth Machine Co., Inc., Port Washington, N.Y., 1953-57, pres., 1957-80, chmn. bd., 1962-80, also dir.; engring. cons. mfr. movable auditorium ceiling Juilliard Sch. Music, 1967-69; mech. stage equipment John F. Kennedy Center for Performing Arts, 1968-71; v.p. Olaf Soot Assos., N.Y.C., 1979—; approved welding inspection agy. N.Y.C. Dept. Bldgs. Troop com. mem. Boy Scouts Am. Registered profl. engr., N.Y. N.J., Pa., Conn., D.C., P.R., W.Va. Mem. ASME (life), ASTM, Am. Def. Preparedness Assn., Nat. Soc. Profl. Engrs., Nassau County Grand Jurors Assn., Pi Tau Sigma (hon.). Designer 90 foot turntable for Aircraft Nuclear Propulsion Project, Idaho Falls, Idaho, 1953, 76 foot turntable Jones Beach Marine Amphitheatre; cyclotron doors Brookhaven Nat. Lab. Patentee flashwelding machine control, vertical conveyor, centrifugal machines, alert hangar door, others. Home and Office: 89 The Waterway Plandome Heights NY 11030

MCPHERSON, FRANK ALFRED, natural resources exec.; b. Stilwell, Okla., Apr. 29, 1933; s. Younce B. and Maurine Francis McP.; B.S. in Mech. Engring. and Petroleum Engring., Okla. State U., 1957; m. Nadine Wall, Sept. 10, 1955; children—David, Craig, Mark, Rebecca. Successively prodn. and drilling engr., prodn. supt., drilling supt., mgr. Gulf Coast oil and gas ops. Kerr-McGee Corp., Morgan City, La., 1960-73, pres. Kerr-McGee Coal, 1973-76, pres. Kerr-McGee Nuclear, 1976-77, vice chmn. Kerr-McGee Corp., 1977-80, pres., Oklahoma City, 1980—. Mem. adv. bd. Salvation Army; bd. dirs. YMCA. Served to capt., USAF. Mem. AIME, Soc. Mining Engrs., Atomic Indsl. Forum (dir.), Am. Mining Congress (dir.), Oklahoma City C. of C. Democrat. Baptist. Patentee in field. Office: PO Box 25861 Oklahoma City OK 73125

MCPHERSON, JOHN DALLAS, investment co. exec.; b. Inglewood, Calif., Sept. 18, 1922; s. John and Hazel (Mitchell) McP.; B.S., U. Calif., Berkeley, 1941; m. Ann Autrey, Feb. 7, 1970; children—Dallas B., John Gordon, Jacqueline Dee. Exec. trainee Gen. Electric Co., Schenectady, 1941-42; founder, pres. Airborne Freight Corp., San Francisco, 1946-69, now dir.; founder, pres., dir. Ralston Investment Corp., Burlingame, Calif., 1969—; pres. Am. Orien Travel Corp., Personal Security Life Ins. Co.; chmn. bd. Star Airline Catering, Inc., Portal Albertsen Travel Service, Inc., Dipaco, Inc., S&S Ice Vending Machine Co., Inc.; mem. adv. bd. Bay View Fed. Savs. Bd. dirs. Med. Problem Welfare Assn., Inc., U. Calif. Internat. House, Meals for Millions Found.; pres. Medic Alert Found. Internat., 1975-79. Served to lt. comdr. USNR, 1942-46. Mem. World Bus. Council (pres. 1974-75, dir. 1975—), Air Force Assn., Bay Area Peace Officers Assn., Sonoma County Trail Blazers. Presbyterian. Clubs: Commonwealth, Newcomen Soc., Masons. Office: 1275 California Dr Burlingame CA 94010

MCPHERSON, RENE C., mfg. co. exec.; b. Akron, Ohio, 1924; grad. Case Inst. Tech., 1950, Harvard Grad. Sch. Bus., 1952; married. With Dana Corp., Toledo, 1952—, chmn. bd., pres. subs. Hayes Steel Products, 1963-65, corp. v.p., 1965-66, exec. v.p., 1966-68, pres., chief operating officer, 1968-73, chmn. bd., 1973—, also dir.; dir. Brown Bros. Corp. Ltd., Gulf United Corp., Mfrs. Hanover Corp., Standard Oil Co Ohio. Office: 4500 Door St Box 1000 Toledo OH 43697*

MC PHIE, WINSTON MAXIM, govt. ofcl.; b. Trinidad, W. Indies, Aug. 23, 1943; s. Sydney C. and Rosarita C. McPhie; B.A., Howard U., 1969; M.B.A., Boston U., 1971; m. Rosella Lorena Marshall, July 9, 1979; 1 dau. by previous marriage, Anika Ayo. Budget analyst Boston U., 1969-71; mgmt. cons. Bus. Devel. Service, Trinidad, 1971-72; asst. gen. mgr. mktg. Central Mktg. Agy., Trinidad, 1972-74; sr. research asso. Match Instn., Washington, 1974-77; budget analyst UMW Trust Funds, Washington, 1976; fiscal planner Inst. Services to Edn., Washington, 1976-78; capital projects devel. officer AID, Washington, 1978-79; capital projects devel. officer, Egypt, 1979—; lectr. organizational theory and behavior. Scheft fellow, 1969-71. Mem. Am. Mgmt. Assn., Nat. Bankers Assn., Assn. M.B.A. Execs., Black M.B.A. Assn. Episcopalian. Address: US AID care US Embassy Box 10 FPO New York NY 09527/0001

MC PIKE, MARTIN JOHN, JR., steel co. exec.; b. Bklyn., June 25, 1946; s. Martin John and Neddy B. (Locco) McP.; B.S. in Mktg. and Econs., Fairfield U., 1969; M.A. in Corp. and Polit. Communications, 1974. Asst. editor R.L. White Co., Inc., Louisville, 1971-72; mortgage officer Conn. Savs. Bank, New Haven, 1972-75; mktg. analyst Internat. Vitamin Co., Union, N.J., 1975-78; dir. mktg. Superior Steel Products, Inc., Cheshire, Conn., 1979—. Mem. Am. Mktg. Assn., Fairfield U. Alumni Assn., Phi Kappa Theta.

MCQUADE, D. KEVIN, bank exec.; b. N.Y.C., Nov. 7, 1947; s. Donald P. and Mary C. McQ.; B.A., St. Francis Coll., 1969; M.B.A., St. John's U., 1973; postgrad. Amos Tuck Sch. Bus., Dartmouth Coll., 1980; m. Kathleen Maguire, Nov. 24, 1973. Loan officer nat. div. Franklin Nat. Bank, N.Y.C., 1969-74; with Mfrs. Hanover Trust Co., Bklyn., 1974—, v.p., regional loan officer, 1980—. Active fund raising ARC, 1978—, Boy Scouts Am., 1979—. Mem. St. Francis Coll. Alumni Assn. (dir. 1980—), Omicron Delta Epsilon. Roman Catholic. Office: Mfrs Hanover Trust Co 177 Montague St Brooklyn NY 11201

MCQUADE, LAWRENCE CARROLL, corp. exec.; b. Yonkers, N.Y., Aug. 12, 1927; s. Edward A. and Thelma (Keefe) McQ.; B.A., Yale U., 1950; B.A., Oxford (Eng.) U., 1952, M.A., 1956; LL.B., Harvard U., 1954; m. Margaret Osmer, Mar. 15, 1980; 1 son by previous marriage, Andrew Parker. Admitted to N.Y. bar, 1955, D.C. bar, 1968; asso. firm Sullivan & Cromwell, N.Y.C., 1954-60; asst. to asst. Sec. Def. for Internat. Security Affairs, Dept. Def., Washington, 1961-63; dep. asst. sec. Dept. Commerce, Washington, 1963-64, asst. to sec. Commerce, 1965-67, asst. sec. Commerce, 1967-69; pres. Procon, Inc, Des Plaines, Ill., 1969-75; chief exec. officer, 1971-75; v.p. Universal Oil Products Co., 1972-75; v.p. W.R. Grace & Co., N.Y.C., 1975-78, sr. v.p., 1978—; dir. Chemed Corp., W.R. Grace & Co. Trustee, Internat. House, 1976—; mem. adv. bd. Georgetown U. Law Center, 1968—; mem. adv. bd. Yale Concilium on Internat. and Area Studies, 1979—; bd. dirs. Overseas Devel. Council, 1974—, Atlantic Council of U.S., 1969—, Internat. Mgmt. and Devel. Inst., Nat. Fgn. Trade Council, 1979—. Served with AUS, 1946-47. Mem. Assn. Am. Rhodes Scholars. Clubs: Harvard, Century; (N.Y.C.); Metropolitan (Washington). Home: 125 E 72d St New York NY 10021 Office: 1114 Ave of the Americas New York NY 10036

MC QUEEN, MARVIN DUNCAN, advt. agy. exec.; b. Superior, Wis., Apr. 19, 1914; s. Angus and Mary Louise (Reineccius) McQ.; student Superior State Tchrs. Coll., 1931; B. Journalism, U. Mo., 1936; m. Maria Luisa Ordonez, July 26, 1941; children—Angus Loren, Melissa. Advt. solicitor Superior Eve. Telegram, 1929-30; advt. mgr., reporter Canby (Minn.) Press, 1931; with D'Arcy Advt. Co., St. Louis, 1936—, v.p., 1951—, dir., 1957—, chmn. adminstrv. com., asst. to pres., 1964-68, adminstrv. v.p., N.Y.C., 1968-70, exec. v.p., 1970-71; pres. Ackerman & McQueen, Inc., Tulsa, 1971—. Chmn. Freedom of Information Conf., Columbia, Mo., 1966. Bd. dirs. Ednl. Found., U. Wis.-Superior, 1960—, U. Mo. Devel. Fund, 1976—; U.S. dist. rep. Burns Fedn., Kilmarnock, Scotland, 1970—; mem. exec. com. Tulsa Philharmonic Soc., 1977—; mem. exec. com. Indian Nation council Boy Scouts Am., 1975—. Recipient Distinguished Service in Journalism medal U. Mo., 1967. Mem. U. Mo. (pres. 1965-67), U. Mo. Sch. Journalism (pres. 1965) alumni assns., Burns Soc. N.Y., St. Andrews Soc. N.Y. Republican. Lutheran. Clubs: University (Mexico City); Burns, Racquet (St. Louis); University (N.Y.C.); Tulsa. Home: 246 Center Plaza Tulsa OK 74119 Office: 123 E 5th St Tulsa OK 74103

MCQUEEN, ROBERT CHARLES, ins. co. exec.; b. Sentiago, Chile, Jan. 23, 1921 (parents Am. citizens), s. Charles Alfred and Grace Juanita (Abrecht) McQ.; B.A., Dartmouth Coll., 1943; m. Donna Marie Ikeler, Oct. 6, 1945; children—Scott, Jerry, Monte, Donald. Mathematician, Equitable Life Assurance Soc., N.Y.C., 1945-49; group actuary Union Central Life Ins. Co., Cin., 1949-57; sr. exec. v.p., chief adminstrv. officer, dir. Mut. Benefit Life Ins. Co., Newark, 1957—; chmn. bd. Mut. Benefit Fin. Service Co. Bd. dirs. Better Bus. Bur. Met. N.Y., 1974—; bd. overseers Found. N.J. Inst. Tech., 1978—; bd. trustees St. Barnabas Hosp., Livingston, N.J., 1980—. Served with OSS, AUS, 1943-45. Fellow Soc. Actuaries; mem. Am. Acad. Actuaries, Internat. Actuarial Assn., Am. Soc. C.L.U.'s. Republican. Episcopalian. Clubs: Essex, Canoe Brook Country, Quechee Lakes, East Lake Woodlands. Home: 24 Tennyson Dr Short Hills NJ 07078 Office: 520 Broad St Newark NJ 07101

MC QUILLAN, MARCY, pottery co. exec.; b. Elgin, Ill., July 12, 1919; d. Edmund Henry and Vera (Mills) Haeger; B.A., Beloit Coll., 1942; m. John McQuillan, Jr., Apr. 16, 1949 (dec. July 1976); children—John III, David, Phillip. Sec., Haeger Potteries, Inc., Dundee, Ill., 1943-50, editor of house organ, 1947-49; sec. Ruckels Potteries, Inc., White Hall, Ill., 1951—; cons., 1973—. Mem. P.E.O. (chpt. pres. 1965-67), Pi Beta Phi. Home: PO Box 744 Jacksonville IL 62651 Office: White Hall IL 62092

MC QUILLAN, WILLIAM LEO, banking exec.; b. Grand Island, Nebr., Sept. 11, 1948; s. James Michael and Mary Catherine (Clinch) McQ.; B.S. in Bus. Adminstrn., Creighton U., 1973; m. Patricia Ann Caffrey, July 12, 1975; children—William Patrick, Brian Joseph. With Omaha Nat. Bank, 1970-76, dept. head, 1974-76; officer ops. and loans Nebr. State Bank and Trust, Broken Bow, 1976-78; sr. v.p. Palisades Nat. Bank, Palisade, Colo., 1978—, also dir.; dir. City Nat. Bank, Greeley, Nebr. Served with USAR, 1970-76. Mem. Am. Inst. Banking, Bankers Adminstrv. Inst., Palisade C. of C. (pres. 1980-81), Jaycees (bd. 1977-78). Republican. Roman Catholic. Clubs: Optimists Internat. (v.p. 1977-78), K.C., Elks, Country Club (mem. com.), Lions. Home: PO Box 746 Palisade CO 81526 Office: PO Box 10 Palisade CO 81526

MCREE, KEN MARION, rubber co. exec.; b. Byers, Colo., June 14, 1932; s. Homer Herchel and Hazel Louise (McRee) McR.; B.S. in Mktg., U. Ark., 1955; m. Vyvian Cabell, Nov. 7, 1974; children—Jeff, Jill, Cathy, Jim. Owner, mgr. So. Wholesale Co., Fayetteville, Ark., 1956-64; pres. Kenco Sales Co., Rogers, Ark., 1964-68; pres. Ken McRee & Assos., Fayetteville, 1968-74; pres. GM-Tucker Duck and Rubber Co., Ft. Smith, Ark., 1974—; mgmt. cons. to various firms, 1965-74. Served with U.S. Army, 1950-53. Mem. U.S. C. of C., Am. Mgmt. Assn., Nat. Sporting Goods Assn., Furniture Mfrs. Assn. Am., Casual Furniture Assn., Fort Smith Jr. C. of C. (pres. 1958, 60, 62), Fort Smith C. of C. (mem. bd. 1964-67). Democrat. Episcopalian. Home: 5002 E Valley Rd Fort Smith AR 72901 Office: PO Box 4167 2701 Kelly Hwy Fort Smith AR 72914

MC REYNOLDS, NEIL LAWRENCE, pub. relations exec.; b. Seattle, July 27, 1934; s. Dorr Ellis and Margaret (Gillies) McR.; B.A. in Journalism with honors, U. Wash., 1956, certificate in bus. mgmt. Grad. Sch. Bus. Adminstrn., 1975; postgrad. Wharton Sch. Bus., U. Pa., 1974; m. Nancy Joyce Drew, June 21, 1957; children—Christopher D., Bonnie J. Asso. editor Bellevue (Wash.) Am., 1956-60, editor, 1960-67; press sec. Office of Gov., State of Wash., 1967-73; NW regional mgr., pub. relations/civic affairs ITT Corp., Seattle, 1973-79; v.p. communications Puget Sound Power & Light Co., Bellevue, Wash., 1980—; guest lectr. journalism and pub. relations, univs. and industry. Trustee Bellevue Community Coll., 1973-78, also former chmn. bd.; pres. bd. trustees Seattle Center Found., 1979-80; vice-chmn. Wash. Council Internat. Trade, 1979-80; v.p. Wash. Internat. Trade Fair, 1978—; mem. vis. com. U. Wash. Sch. Internat. Studies, 1974—; bd. dirs. Overlake Meml. Hosp., Seattle, 1979—; lic. lay reader Emmanuel Episcopal Ch., Mercer Island, Wash., 1975—. Named Citizen of Year City of Bellevue, 1963;

Outstanding Young Man State of Wash., 1965. Mem. Pub. Relations Soc. Am. (accredited), Seattle C. of C. (v.p. govtl. affairs 1979—), Sigma Delta Chi. Republican. Episcopalian. Clubs: Overlake Golf and Country, Rainier, Wash. Athletic, Downtown Seattle Rotary (dir. 1978—). Office: 3328 Rainier Bank Tower Seattle WA 98101

MC RICKARD, EDMUND JOSEPH, real estate co. exec.; b. N.Y.C., July 17, 1914; s. Samuel Edmund and Mary L. (Hunt) McR.; B.S., Fordham U., 1937; m. Katharine Louise Lundberg, Feb. 8, 1939; 1 dau., Wendy Ann. Asst. v.p. Ely Cruikshank & Co., N.Y.C., 1939-55; with Brooks, Harvey & Co. Inc., 1955—, dir., 1969—, chmn. exec. com., 1972-77, pres., 1976-79; trustee Emigrant Savs. Bank, Brooks Harvey Realty Investors. Mem. bus. devel. com. Village of Briarcliff Manor, N.Y., also mem. zoning bd. appeals; former mem. N.Y.C. Mayor's Realty Adv. Com.; bd. dirs. Ave. of Americas Assn. Named Realtor of Year, 1967. Mem. Am. Soc. Real Estate Counsellors (dir. 1971-77), Am. Inst. Real Estate Appraisers (dir. 1969-71, pres. N.Y. chpt. 1961), Urban Land Inst., Soc. Indsl. Realtors (dir. 1964-68), Real Estate Bd. N.Y. (pres. 1966-68). Republican. Roman Catholic. Clubs: Sleepy Hollow Country, Univ., Sky, Hemisphere (dir.), Mpls. Home: 34 Birch Rd Briarcliff Manor NY 10501 Office: 1251 Ave of Americas New York NY 10020

MCSPADDEN, PETER FORD, advt. exec.; b. Montclair, N.J., Oct. 2, 1930; s. Chester F. and Janet (Chase) McS.; A.B., Dartmouth Coll., 1952; m. Barbara Dodds, June 30, 1956; children—Douglas, Dodds, David Ford, Peter Chase. Account exec. McCann-Erickson, Inc., N.Y.C., 1956-60; with Dancer-Fitzgerald-Sample, Inc., N.Y.C., 1960—, v.p., account supr., 1965-68, sr. v.p., mgmt. supr., 1968-72, exec. v.p., 1972-74, pres., chief operating officer, 1974—, also dir.; dir. Broadstreet Communications, Inc. Pres. Greenwich (Conn.) Young Republican Club, 1966-67; campaign mgr. Congressman Lowell P. Weicker, 1968, Senator Weicker, 1970; mem. Rep. Town Com., Greenwich, 1965-68. Served to lt. (j.g.) USNR, 1952-55. Mem. Am. Assn. Advt. Agys. (gov.). Clubs: Riverside (Conn.) Yacht; Greenwich (Conn.) Country; Office: 405 Lexington Ave New York NY 10017

MC SPADEN, FRANK JAMES, tax exec.; b. Hampton, Iowa, May 8, 1932; s. James M. and Velma A. (Reed) McS.; A.B., Am. Inst. Bus., 1957; B.A., Park Coll., Kansas City, Mo., 1973; m. Beth L. Terrel, May 11, 1952; children—Cheri, Charles, Jeff. County assessor County of Delaware (Iowa), Manchester, 1967-70; chief appraiser State of Kans., Topeka, 1970-72; property tax rep. Wickes Corp., Wheeling, Ill., 1973-75; property tax staff dir. McDonald's Corp., Oak Brook, Ill., 1975—; cons., Assessor's Office Kansas City (Kans.), 1972-73; expert witness Kans. Bd. Tax Appeals, Kans. Dist. Ct. Served with USN, 1951-55. Mem. Nat. Assn. Property Tax Reps. (cert.; founder, past pres.), Am. Soc. Appraisers (cert; sr.), Internat. Assn. Assessing Officers, Iowa Govt. Appraisers Assn., Kans. Govt. appraisers Assn., Mensa, Delta Tau Kappa. Contbr. articles to profl. jours. Office: McDonalds Corp Tax Dept #3 McDonalds Plaza Oak Brook IL 60521

MC SWEEN, JAMES ANGUS, indsl. distbn. corp. exec.; b. Newton, Ala., Sept. 17, 1940; s. Jackson D. and Edna E. (Benton) McS.; B.S., Troy State U., 1966; M.B.A., Auburn U., 1969; m. Mary Ellen Bruner, Mar. 10, 1966; children—Amelia A., Steve A. Fin. analyst West Point Pepperell, Inc. (Ga.), 1966-73; ops. mgr., controller Redman Industries, Inc., Meridian, Miss., 1973-74; v.p. fin., corporate sec. Indsl. Distbrs. Am., Inc., Atlanta, 1974-79; pres. The McLeod Cos., Inc., Greenville, S.C., 1980—, Indsl. Distbrs. Am., Inc., 1980—. Served with USNR, 1958-62. Home: 10 Stone Hedge Dr Greenville SC 29615 Office: Cowgaree Rd Greenville SC 29606

MC SWEENEY, MICHAEL TERRENCE, direct mktg. execs.; b. Rockford, Ill., Jan. 28, 1937; s. John Carpenter and Julia Elizabeth (McCann) McS.; student U. Md., 1956-57; B.S.E., No. Ill. U., 1961, postgrad., 1961; m. Louise Antoinette Walters Aug. 20, 1960; children—David, Mark. Indsl. engr. Micro Switch div. Honeywell, Freeport, Ill., 1961-64; plant mgr. Metromail div. Metromedia, Inc., Mt. Pleasant, Iowa, 1964-69, v.p. ops., Westbury, N.Y., 1969-78, sr. v.p., Lombard, Ill., 1978-80; v.p. Harlequin Books, gen. mgr. Harlequin Reader Service, Don Mills, Ont., Can., 1980—; industry chmn. mailers tech. adv. com. to postmaster gen., 1977—; lectr. in field. County campaign chmn. U.S. Congress and U.S. Senate candidates; bd. dirs. St. Elizabeth's Hosp., Lincoln, Nebr., 1974-75; mem. Regional Airport Adv. Com., 1976-78; mem. Iowa Regional Transp. Adv. Com., 1977-78. Served with USAF, 1954-58. Mem. C. of C., Mfrs. Assn. (chmn. 1970-71), Direct Mail Mktg. Assn., Mail Advt. Service Assn. (dir. Chgo. chpt. 1979-80), Order of Artus, Phi Kappa Theta (nat. trustee), Am. Legion. Republican. Roman Catholic. Clubs: Kiwanis, K.C. Contbr. articles to profl. jours. Home: 7030 Webster St Downers Grove IL 60515 Office: 225 Duncan Mill Rd Don Mills ON M3B 3K9 Canada

MC SWEENY, WILLIAM FRANCIS, petroleum co. exec.; b. Haverhill, Mass., Mar. 31, 1929; s. William Francis and Mary Florence (Doyle) McS.; student Boston U., 1950; m. Dorothy Pierce, Jan. 20, 1969; children—William Francis III, Cathy Ann, Ethan Madden Maverick, Terrell Pierce. Reporter, columnist, fgn. corr. Hearst Newspapers, 1943-67; dep. chmn., dir. pub. affairs Democratic Nat. Com., Washington, 1967-68; spl. asst. to postmaster gen. U.S., Washington, 1968-69; pres. Occidental Internat. Corp., Washington, 1969—; dir. Fin. Gen. Bankshares, Inc., The Steadman Fund. Bd. dirs. Arena Stage, Meridian House Internat.; trustee Friendship Force, Capital Children's Mus.; bd. visitors Fletcher Sch. Law and Diplomacy, Tufts U.; bd. advisors Karl F. Landegger program internat. bus. diplomacy Sch. Fgn. Service, Georgetown U.; mem. nat. com. Arts for Handicapped; mem. Corp. Theatre Fund, Washington Mayor's Task Force for Internat. Affairs, Pres.'s Commn. on Exec. Exchange. Served to maj., inf., AUS, 1950-53. Decorated Combat Infantryman's badge; named Boston's Outstanding Young Man, Jr. C. of C., 1961; recipient numerous nat. 1st prizes for writings from Vietnam, Korea, Middle East. Episcopalian. Clubs: Nat. Press, Cosmos, Internat. (Washington); Lotos (N.Y.C.). Author: Go Up For Glory, 1965; Violence Every Sunday, 1966; The Impossible Dream, 1967. Writings and personal papers established Mugar Library, Boston U., 1966. Home: 5021 Millwood Ln NW Washington DC 20016 Office: 1747 Pennsylvania Ave NW Washington DC 20006

MC SWINEY, JAMES WILMER, pulp and paper mfg. exec.; b. McEwen, Tenn., Nov. 13, 1915; s. James S. and Delia (Conroy) McS.; grad. Advanced Mgmt. Program, Harvard, 1954; m. Jewel Bellar, 1940; children—Charles Ronald, Margaret Ann. Lab technician, shipping clk. Nashville div. The Mead Corp., 1934-39, asst. office mgr. Harriman div., 1939, plant mgr., Rockport, Ind., 1940, asst. office mgr. Kingsport div., 1941-44, exec. asst. to pres., Dayton, Ohio, 1954-57, v.p. devel., 1957-59, adminstrv. v.p., 1959, group v.p., gen. mgr. Mead Bd. div., 1961-64, exec. v.p., 1964-68, pres., 1968, chief exec. officer, chmn. exec. com., 1968-78, chmn. bd., 1971—, chief exec. officer, 1980—, also dir.; accountant, office mgr., asst. sec. and treas., pres. Brunswick Pulp & Paper Co. (Ga.), 1944-54, now v.p.; sr. v.p., dir. Northwood Pulp Ltd.; chmn., dir. Ga. Kraft Co.; dir. B.C. Forest Products Ltd., Dayton, Gem Savs. Assn., Dayton, Philips Industries Inc., Vulcan Materials Co., Dayton Power & Light Co., Sea Island Co., Wire Rope Industries Ltd. Chmn. United Way, Sinclair Community Coll. Served as aviation cadet USAAF, 1942-44. Mem. Am. Paper Inst. (dir., exec. com.), Inst. Paper Chemistry (chmn.). Office: Mead Corp Courthouse Plaza NE Dayton OH 45463

MCVADON, MILNER WAYNE, banker; b. Baton Rouge, Oct. 8, 1938; s. Eric A. and Nita (Gautreaux) McV.; B.A., Tulane U., 1960; grad. Sch. Banking of South, La. State U., 1971, Grad. Inst. Bank Mktg. U. So. Calif., 1978; m. Allison Claire Cook, June 3, 1960; children—Charlotte Marie, Allison Wynne, Susan Claire. Mktg. rep. IBM Data Processing Div., Baton Rouge, La., 1963-67; v.p., dir. mktg. Baton Rouge Bank & Trust Co., 1967-78; v.p., dir. mktg. Am. Bank and Trust Co., Baton Rouge, 1978—. Bd. advisors Grad. Inst. Bank Mktg.; instr. La. Banking Sch. for Supervisory Tng., U. Southwestern La.; cons. TV prodn. of fin. advtg. Finance chmn., bd. dirs. Audubon council Girl Scouts U.S., 1969-71; pres., bd. dirs. Jr. Achievement Inc. of Baton Rouge, 1971-74; mem. Greater Baton Rouge Port Commn., 1971-77, sec., 1972-73, treas., 1973-74, pres., 1974-76. Served with USN, 1960-63. Mem. Bank Mktg. Assn., La. Bankers Assn. (mem. public relations com.), Baton Rouge C. of C. United Methodist. Clubs: Baton Rouge Country, City. Home: 3080 Saratoga Dr Baton Rouge LA 70808 Office: One American Pl Baton Rouge LA 70825

MC VEY, THOMAS BERNARD, lawyer; b. N.Y.C., July 28, 1954; s. Thomas Joseph and Rita Elizabeth McV.; B.A., Columbia U., 1976; J.D., Georgetown U., 1979. Asso. firm Beinhauer, Rouhana & Pike, N.Y.C., 1979-80, Bracewell & Patterson, Washington, 1980—. Polit. campaign cons. Mem. Am. Bar Assn., N.Y. State Bar Assn., N.Y. County Lawyers Assn. Clubs: Internat. (Washington); Princeton (N.Y.C.). Author: Homo Hominus Lupus (Man is a Wolf): A Study of War Crimes in Indochina, 1975. Home: 2801 N Somerset St Arlington VA 22213 Office: 1850 K St NW Suite 400 Washington DC 20006

MCVICKERS, JACK CLELLAN, elec. co. exec.; b. Chgo., Nov. 7, 1932; s. Odis Clellan and Johanna Catherine (Decker) McV.; B.S.M.E., Ill. Inst. Tech., 1958; M.S.M.E. (fellow), U. Pitts., 1959; m. Virginia Ann O'Brien, June 11, 1955; children—Linda, Denise, Mary, Pamela. Mgr. mech. research and devel. div., dir. prodn. tech. Westinghouse Elec. Corp., Pitts., 1958-77; v.p. mfg. and engring. McGraw-Edison Co., Elgin, Ill., 1977-79; v.p., gen. mgr. distbn. apparatus div. Gould-Brown Boveri, Rolling Meadow, Ill., 1979—; tchr. Johns Hopkins U., U. Pitts., Carnegie-Mellon U. Pres. community assns., 1962-63, 70, 71, 76-77. Served with USN, 1951-54. Mem. Tau Beta Pi. Patentee in field. Home: 711 Oxbow Ln Barrington IL 60010 Office: 60 Gould Center Rolling Meadows IL 60008

MCWETHY, JOHN BERTRAND, JR., retail co. exec.; b. Sutton, N.D., Nov. 5, 1917; s. John Bertrand and Blanche Amanda (Hoff) McW.; student public schs., Carrington, N.D.; m. Christine Edith Blaber, Feb. 22, 1945; children—John Patrick, Susan Jane. Teller, Foster County State Bank, Carrington, 1935-41, asst. cashier, 1946; from asst. credit mgr. to chmn. bd. Dakota Tractor & Equipment Co., Fargo, N.D., 1946-75; v.p. Dakota Sales Agy., Inc., Fargo, 1961-74, pres., 1974-75; sec. Surplus Center, Inc., Grand Forks, N.D., 1964-75; pres., treas. Dakota Surplus, Inc., Fargo, 1975—. Mem., chmn. Fargo CSC, 1960-70; vice chmn. Minn-Kota chpt. ARC, 1970. Served with cavalry U.S. Army, 1941-45; ETO. Decorated Bronze Star medal. Mem. North Central Assn. Credit Mgmt. (pres. 1957), Fargo-Moorhead Assn. Credit Mgmt. (pres. 1956), Fargo C. of C. (dir. 1950, chmn. wholesale com. 1968), Am. Legion, VFW. Republican. Episcopalian. Clubs: Fargo Cosmopolitan (pres. 1958), Elks. Home: 2486 W Country Club Dr Fargo ND 58103 Office: 325 S 7th St Fargo ND 58103

MCWHIRTER, BARRY EVANS, real estate co. exec.; b. Montgomery, Ala., June 30, 1949; s. Thomas Fredrick and Margaret (McGinn) McW.; B.S., Ga. State U., 1972; m. Daphne Day, Aug. 21, 1971; children—Peyton, Greer, Matthew. Leasing agt. Cushman & Wakefield, Atlanta, 1971-73; v.p. office devel. Cousins Properties Inc., Atlanta, 1973-77; pres. Ackerman & Co., Atlanta, 1977—, Ackerman/Adair Brokerage Co., Atlanta, 1980—. Bd. dirs. Park Central Communities; mem. adv. bd. Scottish Hosp. Served with U.S. Army, 1969-70. Mem. Internat. Council Shopping Centers, Nat. Assn. Office and Indsl. Parks, Central Atlanta Progress. Presbyterian. Home: 5090 Hampton Farms Dr Marietta GA 30067 Office: 100 Peachtree St NW Atlanta GA 30303

MC WHITE, BENSON CARWILE, textile co. exec.; b. Abbeville, S.C., June 2, 1924; s. John Reed and Mary Harley (Carwile) McW.; B.E.E., Clemson U., 1947; m. Martha Ashley, Dec. 19, 1971; children—Mary Carla McWhite Carter, John Evans, Thomas Benson, William Loftis, Nancy Lu, John Lewis, Robert Neil, Nancy Lynn. Mgmt. trainee Abbeville Mills, Deering Milliken Corp., 1947-49, indsl. engr., 1949, cost accountant, McCormick, S.C., 1950, group adminstrn. mgr., Johnston, S.C., 1950-52, group planning mgr., Pendleton, S.C., 1953-55, supt. Excelsior finishing plant, Pendleton, 1955; group planning mgr. Amerotron Corp., Clarksville, Va., 1956-57, Raeford, N.C., 1958; div. planning mgr. Pacific Mills div. Burlington Industries, Halifax, Va., 1959, mgr. Raeford worsted plant, 1960, v.p./group mgr. Raeford Worsted div., 1960-65, v.p./dir. planning Burlington Worsted div., 1965-70, dir. planning Gayley & Lord div., Gastonia, N.C., 1970-71; planning systems dir. Deering Milliken Corp., Spartanburg, S.C., 1971-73, product planning mgr., 1973-76, market research analyst, 1977—. Served with Signal Corps, U.S. Army, 1943-46. Mem. IEEE, Am. Mgmt. Assn., Am. Prodn. and Inventory Control Soc., Nat. Assn. Cost Accountants, Advanced Computer Planning Systems Group, So. Woolen and Worsted Mfrs. Assn. (past pres.). Methodist. Clubs: Keowee Key, Foxcroft Assn., Lions. Home: 30 Queen Ann Rd Greenville SC 29615 Office: PO Box 1926 Spartanburg SC 29304

MC WILLIAMS, DAROL EUGENE, food co. exec.; b. Bellingham, Wash., Dec. 29, 1940; s. Eugene Landrum and Ardis Maxine (Bravard) McW.; B.B.A. (Standard Oil scholar, Sears Roebuck Found. scholar), Wash. State U., 1963; m. Bonnie Lee Birch, Aug. 18, 1963 (div. 1976); children—Shannon Lee, Todd Ross, Jennifer Rae; m. 2d, Carol Glumac, Mar. 4, 1978. With Green Giant Co., 1963-77, regional sales mgr., San Francisco, 1966-67, nat. sales mgr., food service dept., Mpls., 1967-71, dir. sales, food service div., Mpls., 1971-77; dir. food service div. Henri's Food Products Co. Inc., Milw., 1977—; guest speaker, food service industry problems. Office: Henri's Food Products Co Inc 2730 W Silver Spring Dr Milwaukee WI 53209

MCZIER, ARTHUR, mgmt. cons.; b. Atlanta, May 4, 1935; s. Nolan and Mamie (Gardner) McZ.; B. Sci. and Commerce, Loyola U., Chgo., 1959, postgrad., 1960-61; m. Ruby Burrows, Aug. 8, 1971; children—Sandra, Jennifer Rose. With Seeburg Corp., Chgo., 1962-66, Ford Motor Co., 1966-67; with office of fgn. investments Dept. Commerce, Washington, 1968; asst. adminstr. SBA, Washington, 1969-73; pres., chmn. bd. Gen. Bahamian Cos., Nassau, 1973-74; pres. Nat. Bus. Services Enterprises, Inc., Washington, 1975—. Mem. adv. bd. Inst. of Minority Bus. Edn., Howard U., Washington; commr. U.S. Nat. Commn. for UNESCO, 1980—. Recipient spl. achievement award SBA, 1970; City of Miami (Fla.) Econ. Devel. Center award, 1972; Public Service award Houston Citizens C. of C., 1973. Mem. Nat. Assn. Black Mfrs. (dir. 1979-80), D.C. C. of C. Home: 503 G St SW Washington DC 20024 Office: Nat Bus Services Enterprises Inc 910 16th St NW Washington DC 20006

MEACE, JEFFREY GREGORY, petrochem. co. ofcl.; b. Burnley, Eng., Nov. 25, 1941; came to Can., 1965, naturalized, 1978; s. Harry and Bertha (Hartley) M.; B.Sc. in Chem. Engring., U. Leeds, Eng., 1965; m. Joyce Gwendolyn Stone, Jan. 29, 1966; children—Cathryn Jane, Donald Alexander, Allan Gregory. Asst. supt. refining Falconbridge, Dominican Rep., 1971-74; dept. head crude and aromatics Petrosar, Sarnia, Ont., Can., 1974-78, group mgr. supply and distbn., 1978-80, group mgr. planning, 1980—. Vice pres. Sarnia Track and Field, 1979—. Progressive Conservative. Roman Catholic. Home: 603 Stafford Pl Sarnia ON N7S 3Z1 Canada Office: 785 Hill St Corunna ON N0N 1G0 Canada

MEAD, BILL O., business exec.; b. 1919; married. Pres., Mead's Fine Bread Inc., 1941-59; with Campbell Taggart Inc., Dallas, 1959—, chmn. bd., 1970—, also dir. Office: 6211 Lemmon Ave Dallas TX 75222*

MEADERS, J. BAILEY, JR., promotion exec.; b. Shreveport, La., Oct. 6, 1940; s. Jeff B. and Ada M. (Henderson) M.; B.A., Fla. State U., 1963. Promotion and publicity dir. Pab, Ltd., N.Y.C., 1965-70; convs. and meetings mgr. Schmid Labs., Little Falls, N.J., 1970-74; Eastern regional promotion mgr. Rums of P.R., N.Y.C., 1974-76; mktg. dir. Pernod div. Julius Wile Sons & Co., N.Y.C., 1976-79, nat. promotion dir., 1979—, mktg. mgr., 1981—; promotional cons. Served with AUS, 1963-65. Mem. Mktg. Communications Execs. Internat. Office: One Hollow Ln Lake Success NY 11042

MEADOR, DONALD JASON, mfg. co. exec.; b. Atlanta, May 12, 1937; s. James W. and Christine B. (Brown) M.; B.S.M.E., Clemson U., 1959; m. Nancy Vivian Dunstan, June 3, 1955; children—Christine, Diane, Mark, Carol, Lynda. Engr., Reynolds Metals Co., Richmond, Va., 1959-60, sales engr., 1960-62; salesman Tex. Instruments, Louisville and Cleve., 1962-65, sales mgr., 1965-69; v.p. sales Ind. Gen., Valparaiso, 1969-71; regional gen. mgr. ITT Grinnell, Providence, 1971-74, pres. Peninsular Supply Co., Ft. Lauderdale, Fla., 1974-77; exec. v.p. Indsl. Distbrs. Am., Atlanta, 1977-79; pres. Titeflex Corp., Springfield, Mass., 1979—. Bd. dirs. Springfield Devel. Corp., Springfield Pvt. Industry Council. Mem. Am Mgmt. Assn., Springfield C. of C. (dir.). Methodist. Office: PO Box 54 Springfield MA 01109

MEADOR, JAMES DOUGLAS, viticulturist; b. Tacoma, Wash., Sept. 15, 1940; s. Warden Russell and Ruth Ellen (Wagner) Artley; B.A. in Econs., U. Wash., Seattle, 1965; m. Shirley Bowerman, Oct. 30, 1970; children—Darren Joseph Jagla, Roni Kay Jagla. Commd. ensign, A.C., U.S. Navy, 1965, advanced through grades to lt., 1971; service in Vietnam; ret., 1972; owner Ventana Vineyards and Winery, Soledad, Calif., 1972—. Decorated Air medal with 27 oak leaf clusters, Navy Commendation medal with 7 combat Vs, Navy Achievement medal with 3 combat Vs; recipient various awards for wines. Mem. Wine Inst., Monterey County Grapegrowers Assn. (pres. 1975), Monterey Winegrowers Council (v.p. 1980). Address: Box G Soledad CA 93960

MEADORS, WILLIAM PORTER, automobile dealer; b. Clovis, N.Mex., May 1, 1946; s. Max Irby and Edelweiss (Corbin) M.; B.S. in Fin., Okla. State U., 1969; postgrad. Chevrolet Sch. Merchandising and Mgmt., 1975; m. Toni Kirkley, Apr. 1, 1967; children—Laura Michelle, Kimberley Noelle; m. 2d, Cynthia Hoopes, Jan. 17, 1981. Vice pres. Max Meadors Co., Clovis, 1966-69; pres. Bilmer Nan Corp., Clovis, 1970; chief pilot, salesman Galles Chevrolet Co., Albuquerque, 1974-75, asst. new car mgr., 1974-75, new car mgr., 1975-81; gen. mgr. Bobby Unser Chevrolet, Avondale, Ariz., 1981—. Troop leader Boy Scouts Am., Mt. Holly, N.J., 1970-72; youth dir. First Christian Ch., Albuquerque, 1975-76, bd. dirs. deacons, 1975-81; youth dir. Ch. at Litchfield Park (Ariz.). Served to capt., USAF, 1969-74. Mem. Soc. Sales Execs., Beta Theta Pi. Democrat. Home: 4680 N 105th Ave Phoenix AZ 85039 Office: 507 E Van Buren Avondale AZ 85323

MEADOWS, KIM STAN, banker; b. Des Moines, Iowa, Jan. 20, 1949; s. Roy William and Janyce Kay (Beachamp) M.; B.S., Drake U., 1971, M.B.A., 1976: 1 dau., Lee Meredith. With Iowa-Des Moines Nat. Bank, Des Moines, 1971-79, 2d v.p., 1978-79; mng. v.p. Nat. Accounts div. Central Nat. Bank, Des Moines, 1979—; instr. econ. Des Moines Area Community Coll., 1975—. Arbitrator, Better Bus. Bur., 1977—; treas. Iowa-Des Moines Polit. Action Com., 1978; treas. Meadows for State Senate, 1978; treas. Iowa chpt. Muscular Dystrophy Assn., 1973—. Mem. Robert Morris Assos. (sec.), Am. Bankers Assn., Am. Inst. Banking, Grimes Jaycees, Pi Kappa Phi, Alpha Kappa Psi, Gamma Gamma. Republican. Presbyterian. Club: Optimist of Des Moines (pres. 1976-77). Home: RFD 2 Grimes IA 50111 Office: 7th and Walnut Sts Des Moines IA 50309

MEADOWS, LAURA LOU, lawyer; b. Cin., May 10, 1932; d. Alvin Louis and Laura Marie (Fox) Muckerheide; B.A., Miami U., Oxford, Ohio, 1952; J.D., Harvard U., 1960. Tax atty. firm Choate, Hall & Steward, Boston, 1960-66, Lord, Day & Lord, N.Y.C., 1966-68, Shearman & Sterling, N.Y.C., 1969; tax counsel Mobil Oil Corp., N.Y.C., 1970-74; asst. tax dir., sr. tax counsel Merck & Co., Inc., Rahway, N.J., 1974-78; spl. counsel Cadwalader, Wickersham & Taft, N.Y.C., 1978-80; corp. dir. taxation Armco Inc., Middletown, Ohio, 1980—. Served to 1st lt. USAF, 1954-57. Mem. Am. Bar Assn. (tax sect. 1960—), N.Y. State Bar Assn. (tax sect.), Internat. Bar Assn., Assn. Bar N.Y.C. (tax com. 1971-74, 80—), Tax Execs. Inst. Methodist. Club: Harvard (N.Y.C.). Home: 351 E 84th St New York NY 10028 also 103 Bavarian Dr Apt K Middletown OH 45042 Office: 703 Curtis St Middletown OH 45043

MEADS, DONALD EDWARD, fin. and mfg. exec.; b. Salem, Mass., Sept. 23, 1920; s. Laurence Granville and Gertrude Francis (Hay) M.; A.B., Dartmouth, 1942; M.B.A., Harvard, 1947; m. Jane Lightner, June 15, 1943; children—Edward G., Robert C., Laurence G., Judith C., Suzanne M., Clifford L., Nancy E. With N.Y. Life Ins. Co., 1947-61, v.p., 1960-61, vice chmn. investment com., 1960-61; v.p. finance, chmn. investment com. Investors Diversified Services, Inc., 1961-65; dir. Investors Syndicate Life Co., 1961-65; officer, dir. Investors Syndicate Am., 1961-65; chmn. bd. Internat. Basic Economy Corp., N.Y.C., 1965-71, also chief exec. officer; exec. v.p., chief financial officer, dir. INA Corp., Phila., 1971-74, also dir. subsidiaries; chmn. bd., chief exec. officer Certainteed Products Corp., 1974-78, also chmn. exec. com.; chmn. Carver Assos., 1978—; dir. Western Savs. Fund Soc., Kaneb Services Inc., Chgo.-Milw. Corp., Purdue Farms, Inc., Singer Co., Quaker Oats Co., INA Corp. Served to capt., pilot USMCR, 1942-45. Decorated D.F.C., Air medal with 5 oak leaf clusters. Clubs: Harvard, Economic, Links, Rockefeller Center (N.Y.C.); Union League, Peale (Phila.). Home: Box 336 Uwchland PA 19480 Office: One Plymouth Meeting Plymouth Meeting PA 19462

MEADS, VINCENT JEROME, JR., businessman; b. Portsmouth, Va., Feb. 5, 1931; s. Vincent Jerome and Ruth (Sherman) M.; B.S., U. Richmond, 1953; m. Margaret Virginia Dick, Sept. 3, 1955; children—Margaret, Sandra, Vincent. Acctg. supr. Gen. Electric U.S.A., N.Y.C., 1956-60; treas. Gen. Electric Colombia, Bogota, 1960-66; gen. mgr. switch gear div. Gen. Electric Brazil, Rio de Janeiro, 1966-75; v.p. Europe and Africa div. Cutler Hammer Inc.,

Bedford Beds, Eng., 1976—; instr. Gen. Electric Fin. Tng. Program, 1968-71. Chmn. bd. Am. Sch. Rio de Janeiro, 1970. Served with U.S. Army, 1951-53. Decorated Bronze Star. Mem. Inst. Dirs., Am. C. of C. Clubs: Gavea Country (Rio de Janeiro); So. Pines Country (N.C.); Elks. Office: Elstow Rd Bedford MK42 9LH England

MEAGHER, MARK JOSEPH, communications co. exec.; b. Balt., July 9, 1932; s. Harry R. and Maria M.; B.S., U. Md., 1954; m. Patricia Essex, Aug. 8, 1951; children—Mark, Terance, Timothy, Kathleen, Robert, Christopher, Bridget, Colleen. With Price Waterhouse & Co., 1954-57, IBM Corp., 1957-58, McKinsey & Co., Inc., 1958-61; exec. v.p. McGraw-Hill Book Co., 1961-70; pres., chief operating officer The Washington Post Co., 1970—; dir. Maple Press Co., Bowater Mersey Paper Co., Ltd., subs. Washington Post Co. Trustee Federal City Council, Georgetown Prep. Sch., U. Md. Found., Washington Hosp. Center. Eisenhower fellow, 1980. Mem. Am. Inst. C.P.A.'s, Am. Newspaper Pubs. Assn., Fgn. Policy Assn. (dir.), Greater Washington Bd. Trade (dir.). Office: 1150 15th St NW Washington DC 20071

MEAGHER, ROBERT JOSEPH, tax cons.; b. New Brunswick, N.J., Feb. 21, 1932; s. Edward A. and Helen (Morris) M.; grad. St. Peter's Coll., 1958; m. Marilyn Hayden, Oct. 17, 1953 (dec. Sept. 1978); children—Karen Helene, Sherrie Ann; m. 2d, Mary Alice Lowe, July 12, 1980. Acct., Celanese Corp., Summit, N.J., 1955; sec.-treas., dir. Inmar Assos., Inc.; pres. Scientific, Inc. (formerly Scientific Chem. Treatment Co., Inc.), 1965-79, dir., 1965—; pres., dir. Kin Buc, Inc., Edison, N.J., 1966—, Mac San. Landfill Inc., Deptford, N.J., 1968—, Eastern Indsl. Corp., Phila., 1967—, Arrow Realty, Inc., Revere, Pa., 1969—; pres. Kasmar, Inc., Stroudsburg, Pa., 1980—; dir. Nann Agy., Inc., Metuchen, N.J. Served with USNR, 1951-55. Mem. Nat. Assn. Accountants, AIM. Office: RD 7 Box 7326A Stroudsburg PA 18360

MEARNS, WILLIAM MURRAY, controller; b. Westerly, R.I., Feb. 22, 1929; s. Robert and Beatrice Anne (Murray) M.; B.S. cum laude, Bryant Coll., 1951; postgrad. West Coast U., 1978-79; m. Janet F. Shortman, Sept. 12, 1959; children—W. Murray, Bonnie Jeanne, Craig Robert. Chief auditor Marine group, Gen. Dynamics Corp., 1953-67, fin. analyst corp. hdqrs., 1967-69, mgr. fin. planning, 1969-73, asst. controller Pomona div. (Calif.), 1973—. Served with U.S. Army, 1951-53. Mem. Nat. Assn. Accts., Nat. Mgmt. Assn. Presbyterian. Club: Masons. Home: 1868 N 1st Ave Upland CA 91786 Office: PO Box 2507 Pomona CA 91766

MEARS, CHARLES MARTIN, retail chain exec.; b. Niles, Ohio, Apr. 20, 1931; s. James Leo and Rose Mary (Marti) M.; B.S. in Journalism, Ohio State U., 1953; m. Debelou Issac, June 25, 1955; children—Teresa, Karen, Mary, Julie, Nancy, James. Public relations asst. E.F. MacDonald Co., Dayton, Ohio, 1955-56; asst. to advt. and sales promotion mgr. Philip Carey Mfg. Co., Cin., 1956-58; advt. and sales promotion mgr. Henlein Bros. Co., Cin., 1958-60; area advt. mgr. Inst. for Essential Housing, Princeton, N.J., 1961-62; advt. planner Western Auto Co., Kansas City, Mo., 1963—; pres. Deedco, Inc., Midvesto, Inc., Intraco, Inc. Served with U.S. Army, 1953-55. Roman Catholic. Home: 3807 E 107th St Kansas City MO 64137 Office: 2107 Grand St Kansas City MO 64108

MEATES, SUSAN CLAIRE, computer mfg. co. exec.; b. Bronx, N.Y., Apr. 10, 1950; d. Richard Fredrick and Vera Elois (Schumacher) Meates; A.B.T., U. Toledo, 1970; B.B.A. cum laude, U. Toledo, 1971; postgrad bus. Ohio State U., 1974—. With Compu-Serv Network, Inc., Columbus, Ohio, 1971-76, nat. accounts service rep., 1974-75, mgr. corp. systems services, 1975-76; systems project leader Borden Inc., Columbus, 1976-77, mgr. quality assurance chem. div., 1977-78; mgr. corporate info. systems Compu Serve, Inc., Columbus, 1978-80; exec. v.p. Diacon Systems Corp., Columbus, 1980—; mem. faculty Coll. Adminstrv. Sci. Ohio State U., 1977—; dir. Ohio Skateboard Products Inc., Software Results Corp. Mem. Assn. M.B.A. Execs., Am. Bus. Womens Assn., M.B.A. Assn., Data Processing Mgmt. Assn., Phi Alpha Kappa, Beta Gamma Sigma. Home: 3649 Kilkenny Dr Columbus OH 43220 Office: 2862 E Main St Columbus OH 43209

MEATHE, PHILIP JAMES, architect; b. Grosse Pointe, Mich., Jan. 26, 1926; s. William J. and Mary (Spears) M.; B.Arch., U. Mich., 1948; m. Jeanne Marie Munger, Oct. 14, 1950; children—Mary C., Lawrence P., James B., Carol A. Prin., Meathe, Kessler & Assos., Inc., Grosse Pointe, 1955-69; exec. v.p. Smith, Hinchman & Grylls Assos., Inc., Detroit, 1969-71, pres., 1971—; dir. 1st Fed. Savs. and Loan Assn. Bd. dirs. Harper/Grace Hosp.; chmn. Detroit Urban League, 1978-79, Pvt. Industry Council Com., 1979-80. Recipient 24 archtl. awards, including: Gold medal award Detroit chpt. AIA, 1967, Gold medal award Mich. Soc. Architects, 1969, Edward C. Kemper award, 1969; Heart of Gold award, 1980. Mem. Mich. Soc. Architects, AIA (pres. Detroit chpt. 1961-62, nat. dir. 1965-68, sec. coll. fellows 1973, chancellor coll. fellows 1976-77), Central Bus. Dist. Assn. (chmn. 1978-79), Greater Detroit C. of C. (chmn. 1979-80). Home: 329 Grosse Pointe Blvd Grosse Pointe Farms MI 48236 Office: 455 W Fort St Detroit MI 48226

MECCA, MAURO LOUIS, telecommunications exec.; b. Passaic, N.J., Oct. 29, 1935; s. Mauro and Rafaella Mecca; B.S. in Engring., B.A., Rutgers U., 1958; M.B.A., N.Y. U., 1963; m. Deanna Levonne Fisher, Oct. 11, 1959; children—Maryanne, John, Lynne. Project mgr., fin. and adminstrn. RCA Corp., Princeton, N.J., 1963-65, mfg. mgr., 1965-69, mgr. bus. control, Marlboro, Mass., 1970-72; dir. corp. devel. Gen. Telephone and Electronics Corp., Stamford, Conn., 1972-74; mktg. mgr. AT&T, Morristown, N.J., 1974-76; v.p. northeast region No. Telecom, Inc., Bloomfield, N.J., 1977-80; v.p. Gen. Dynamics Communications Co., Pine Brook, N.J., 1980—. Served to capt. USAF, 1959-62. Mem. Rutgers Alumni Assn. (mem. exec. com. 1975—), Delta Upsilon (trustee 1964-68, Alumnus of Year 1968). Roman Catholic. Club: Lake Valhalla (dir. 1976-80). Home: Fox Rd Lake Valhalla Montville NJ 07045 Office: PO Box 710 Pine Brook NJ 07058

MECHAM, LEONIDAS RALPH, mining co. exec.; b. Murray, Utah, Apr. 23, 1928; s. Leonidas DeVon and Minnie Isabella (Frame) M.; B.S., U. Utah, 1951, grad. cert. in public adminstrn., 1952; J.D., George Washington U., 1957; M.P.A. (Congressional Staff fellow), Harvard U., 1964; m. Barbara Folsom, Aug. 10, 1950; children—Mark L., Meredith, Richard O., Stephen F., Alison. Teaching and research asst. U. Utah, 1950-52; legis. asst. to U.S. Senator Wallace F. Bennett, Washington, 1952-57, adminstrv. asst., 1958-65; v.p. U. Utah, 1965-69; spl. asst. for regional econ. coordination to sec. of commerce, 1969; fed. co-chmn. Four Corners Regional Devel. Commn., 1969-70; v.p. Anaconda Co., Washington, 1970—; chmn. industry-wide Washington task force Am. Mining Congress. Vice chmn. nat. adv. council U. Utah; mem. nat. adv. council Brigham Young U. Coll. of Mgmt.; pres. Washington stake Ch. of Jesus Christ of Latter-day Saints; bd. dirs. Pro-Utah; active Boy Scouts Am.; state campaign chmn. Utah Heart Assn., 1968; bd. dirs., mem. exec. com. Intermountain Regional Med. Program, 1966-68. Recipient Abraham O. Smoot Public Service award Brigham Young U., 1976; Harvard U. fellow, 1965-66. Mem. Bus.-Govt. Relations Council, Aluminum Assn., Am. Bar Assn., Fed. Bar Assn., Utah Bar Assn., Salt Lake County Bar Assn., D.C. Bar Assn., NAM, Am. Soc. for Public Adminstrn. (dir. 1966-69, pres. Utah chpt. 1968), Phi Kappa Phi, Phi Eta Sigma. Republican. Office: Anaconda Co 1333 New Hampshire Ave NW Suite 1000 Washington DC 20036

MECKE, THEODORE HART, JR., co. dir.; b. Phila., Mar. 6, 1923; s. Theodore Hart and Genevieve (Loughney) M.; student La Salle Coll., Phila., 1941; m. Mary E. Flaherty, July 14, 1956; children—William, Theodore Hart III, John, Stephen. Mng. editor Germantown Courier, 1942-43, 46-49; with Ford Motor Co., 1949-80, v.p. pub. relations, 1963-69, v.p. pub. affairs, 1969-80; dir. Ex Cell-O Corp., Troy, Mich., Detroit Legal News Co., Detroitbank Corp., Detroit Bank & Trust Co. Bd. dirs. United Found. of Detroit. Served with AUS, 1943-45; ETO. Mem. Pub. Relations Soc. Am., Greater Detroit C. of C. Roman Catholic. Clubs: Economic (pres. 1980—), Detroit Athletic, Detroit, Country Detroit, Witenagemote, Yondotega (Detroit). Home: 296 Cloverly Rd Grosse Pointe Farms MI 48236 Office: 920 Free Press Bldg 321 W Lafayette St Detroit MI 48226

MEDBERRY, CHAUNCEY JOSEPH, III, banker; b. Los Angeles, Oct. 9, 1917; s. Chauncey Joseph, Jr. and Geneva (Raymond) M.; B.A., U. Calif. at Los Angeles, 1938; postgrad. U. Munich (Germany), 1939; m. Thirza Cole Young, Mar. 14, 1958; children—Julie Ann Young Medberry Pendergast, Ralph D. Young III, Deborah D. Young, Chauncey Joseph Medberry IV. With Bank of Am., Los Angeles, 1939—, sr. v.p., 1965-68, exec. v.p., San Francisco, 1968—, chmn. gen. fin. com., 1969—, chmn. bd., 1971—; chmn. bd. Bank Am. Corp.; dir. Getty Oil Co. Trustee Com. for Econ. Devel.; bd. overseers Huntington Library; former chmn. bd. visitors Grad. Sch. Mgmt., U. Calif. at Los Angeles. Mem. Assn. Res. City Bankers (dir.), Los Angeles Clearing House Assn. (past pres.), Am. Bankers Assn. Clubs: Bohemian, Bankers (San Francisco); Los Angeles Country (Los Angeles); Sky, Links (N.Y.). Office: Bank of America 555 S Flower St Los Angeles CA 90071

MEDINA, MANUEL DE LA CARIDAD, investment counselor; b. Matanzas, Cuba, Sept. 23, 1952; came to U.S., 1965, naturalized, 1973; s. Manuel F. and Onelia M. (Tapanes) M.; A.A., Miami-Dade Jr. Coll., 1972; B.S., Fla. Atlantic U., 1974; m. Lisette Alvarez, Apr. 24, 1976; children—Manuel D., Melissa. Mem. audit staff Price Waterhouse & Co., Miami, Fla., 1974-76; cons. investments, fins., Miami, 1976-78; pres., partner Fidelity Internat., Inc., Coral Gables, Fla., 1978—; cons. Internat. Center, Inc. Campaign exec. United Way of Dade County, 1975; cons. Youth Co-op., Inc., Miami, 1976-79; sec., vice treas. Little Havana Activities Center, Inc., Miami, 1977—. Recipient Outstanding Acad. Achievement award Miami-Dade Jr. Coll., 1972, Fla. Atlantic U., 1974; Appreciation award United Way, 1975, Little Havana Activities Center, 1979; Courtesy award City of Miami Beach, 1977; Eternal Friendship award Dominican Republic, 1978. C.P.A., Fla. Mem. Fla. C. of C., Greater Miami C. of C., Coral Gables C. of C. Republican. Roman Catholic. Pub. brochure: Greater Miami As An Investment Opportunity, 1979. Home: 220 W Rivo Alto Dr Miami Beach FL 33139 Office: 255 Alhambra Circle #100 Coral Gables FL 33134

MEDLAND, CHARLES EDWARD, investment dealer; b. Toronto, Ont., Can., July 6, 1928; s. Robert Charles and Elizabeth Winifred (Parker) M.; student St. Andrew's Coll.; B.A., U. Toronto, 1950; m. Julie Winsor Eby, Feb. 1, 1973; 1 dau., Virginia; step-children—Brian, Stephen. With Wood Gundy Ltd., Toronto, 1950—, dir., 1966—, v.p., 1968-72, pres., 1972—, chmn., chief exec. officer, 1978—; dir., chmn. Clover Meadow Creamery Ltd.; dir. Abitibi-Price, Inc., Internat. Thomson Orgn. Ltd., Interprovincial Pipe Line Ltd., Irwin Toy Ltd., Seagram Co. Ltd. Bd. dirs. Donwood Inst., Wellesley Hosp. Mem. Investment Dealers Assn. Can. (chmn. 1979-80, dir.), Jr. Investment Dealers Assn. Anglican. Clubs: Toronto, York, Toronto Golf, Rosedale Golf, Badminton and Racquet, Mount Royal, Craigleigh Ski. Office: Wood Gundy Ltd Royal Trust Tower PO Box 274 Toronto Dominion Centre Toronto ON M5K 1M7 Canada

MEDLIN, JOHN GRIMES, JR., banker; b. Benson, N.C., Nov. 23, 1933; s. John Grimes and Mabel (Stephenson) M.; B.S., U.N.C., Chapel Hill, 1956. With Wachovia Bank and Trust Co. N.A., Winston Salem, 1959—, pres., chief operating officer, 1974-77, pres., chief exec. officer, 1977—; pres., chief exec. officer, dir. Wachovia Corp.; dir. Summit Communications, Inc. Mem. N.C. Gov.'s Council Mgmt. and Devel.; trustee Research Triangle Found., Davidson Coll., Salem Acad. and Coll.; pres. bd. visitors U. N.C., Chapel Hill; bd. visitors Bowman Gray Sch./Bapt. Hosp. Med. Center. Served with USN, 1956-59. Named Most Outstanding Chief Exec. Officer State and Nat. Banks U.S., Fin. World Mag., 1978. Mem. Assn. Res. City Bankers (dir.). Club: Old Town. Office: PO Box 3099 Winston Salem NC 27102

MEDLIN, THOMAS EASTWOOD, printing co. exec.; b. Smithfield, N.C., Oct. 19, 1931; s. Ira Wade and Love (Eastwood) M.; B.S. in Bus. Adminstrn., U. N.C., 1954; B.S. in Printing Mgmt., Carnegie Inst. Tech., 1958; m. Lu Long Ogburn, Sept. 18, 1954; children—Jennifer Gail, Allison Long, Thomas Eastwood, Victor Wade. Partner, Medlin Printing Co., Smithfield, 1958-62, pres., 1962—; pres. First Fed. Savs. & Loan Assn. Smithfield, 1967—. Mem. Smithfield Town Bd. Commrs., 1970—. Served with USN, 1954-56. Democrat. Methodist. Club: Masons. Home: 826 S 2d St Smithfield NC 27577 Office: 932 Selma Rd Smithfield NC 27577

MEDNIS, JURIS M., banker; b. Riga, Latvia, Nov. 13, 1937; s. Arvids R. and Velta Mednis; A.B., Columbia Coll., 1960; m. Gita Dzelzgalvis, June 6, 1970. With Bank of N.Y., N.Y.C., 1962-75, v.p., 1971-75; pres., chief exec. officer Shore Nat. Bank, Bricktown, N.J., 1975-77; pres., chief exec. officer Howell State Bank (N.J.), 1977—. Office: Route 9 at Salem Hill Rd Howell NJ 07731

MEDSKER, STANLEY RICHARD, petroleum mktg. co. exec.; b. Dodge City, Kans., June 2, 1931; s. Hollis L. and Dorothy K. (Miller) M.; student U. Denver, 1949-52, U. Tulsa, 1957-58; B.A., U. Colo., 1956, LL.B., 1959; m. Aldah Marie Butler, Nov. 29, 1957; children—Kathleen Lynn, Michael Scott, Kimberly Michele, Cynthia Leigh. Admitted to Colo. bar, 1959, Okla. bar, 1959; v.p., sec., gen. counsel Frontier Refining Co., Denver, 1959-66; pres. Toot-n-Moo Properties, Inc., Denver, Kansas City, Mo., 1966-69; exec. v.p. Autotronic Systems, Inc., Denver and Houston, 1969-73; pres. S-M Petroleum Properties, Inc., Vail, Colo., 1976—; dir. Autotronic Systems, Inc., 1969-78, Evergreen Oil Co., 1974—. Served with U.S. Army, 1953-54. Mem. Am., Colo., Okla. bar assns., Colo. Petroleum Council, Phi Alpha Delta. Lutheran. Clubs: Denver Athletic, Denver Oilman's. Home and office: PO Box 2327 3035 Booth Falls Rd Vail CO 81657

MEDVED, JOSEPH BRUNO, indsl. hygienist, environ. engr.; b. Milw., Nov. 11, 1945; s. Frank Frank and Evelyn Frances (Poplawski) M.; B.S. in Mech. Engring., Gen. Motors Inst., 1969; M.S. in Occupational and Environ. Health and Indsl. Hygiene, Wayne State U., 1976; m. Georgeann Marie Wade, June 4, 1966. Jr. engr., foreman, mech. engr., ventilation engr., environ. engr. Buick Motor div. Gen. Motors Corp., Flint, Mich., 1964-76, divisional environ. coordinator Central Foundry div., Saginaw, Mich., 1976—. Team capt. Saginaw United Way Campaign, 1979-80. Officer res. unit Flint Police Dept., 1967-72. Registered profl. engr., Mich.; diplomate Am. Acad. Indsl. Hygiene. Mem. Am. Indsl. Hygiene Assn. (chmn. air pollution com.), Mich. Assn. Environ. Profls. (charter), Mich. Soc. Profl. Engrs. (Young Engr. of Yr. award Flint chpt. 1976), Nat. Soc. Profl. Engrs., Mich. Indsl. Hygiene Soc., Am. Foundryman's Soc. (health com.), Motor Vehicle Mfrs. Assn. (cupola safety com.). Roman Catholic. Club: K.C. Office: Central Foundry Div Gen Motors Corp Divisional Office Box 1629 77 W Center St Saginaw MI 48605

MEECE, RICHARD CHARLES, sales exec.; b. Chgo., Sept. 13, 1940; s. Brown Louis and Jessie (Harden) M.; B.B.A., U. Notre Dame, 1962. Sr. mcpl. examiner Auditor of State of Ohio, Columbus, 1970-71; adminstrv. officer Ohio River Basin Commn., Cin., 1971-73; dep. fin. dir. City of Columbus, 1973-75; health care mktg. rep. Bus. Telephone Systems, Inc., Columbus, 1975-80; sales exec. Communications, Inc., Grand Rapids, Mich., 1981—. Mem. labor relations com. Ohio Mun. League, 1974-75; exec. com. Columbus Zool. Assn., 1975; exec. com. Frankling County (Ohio) Rep. Party, 1978-79; fin. chmn. Young Rep. Nat. Fedn., 1975-76. Served with U.S. Army to capt., 1963-69. Decorated Bronze Star medal with oak leaf cluster, Army Commendation medal with 2 oak leaf clusters, Air medal; recipient awards Freedoms Found., 1965, 67, James A. Rhodes award, Ohio League of Young Reps., 1977; winner, Young Rep. Nat. Fedn. nat. speech contest, 1975; nat. sales contest winner No. Telecom, Inc., 1977. Mem. Am. Hosp. Assn., Am. Mgmt. Assn., Nat. Speakers Assn., U. Notre Dame Alumni Assn. Roman Catholic. Clubs: Toastmasters Internat.; No. Telecom Pres.'s. Office: Communications Inc 4180 44th St SE Grand Rapids MI 49508

MEEGAN, KEITH FRANCIS, transp. co. exec.; b. Buffalo, June 25, 1940; s. John J. and Cecelia (Huebbers) M.; B.S., Canisius Coll., 1962; M.B.A., U. Buffalo, 1972; m. Mary Ann Eleanor Mackay, Sept. 10, 1966; children—Sean Patrick, Ryan Michael. Controller, HRB Devel. Corp., West Senaca, N.Y., 1970-72; mgr. Fed. Express Corp., Syracuse, 1973-75; sales rep. Emery Air Freight Corp., Buffalo, 1975-77, sr. sales rep., 1977-78, sales supr., 1978—, mgr., Elmira, N.Y., 1978—; mem. faculty D'Youville Coll., 1970-72; dir. Chemung Traffic Co., 1978—. Served with USAF, 1961-65. Recipient Mktg. award Research Inst. Am., 1979. Mem. Elmira-Corning Traffic Club (sec. 1980-81), Buffalo Air Cargo Assn., Southtowns Motor Club, Delta Nu Alpha. Republican. Roman Catholic. Clubs: K.C., Moose. Patentee electronic presence sensing device. Home: 1008 Hoffman St Elmira NY 14905 Office: 1100 Sullivan St Elmira NY 14901

MEEHAN, ARTHUR HENRY, JR., banker; b. N.Y.C., Sept. 23, 1935; s. Arthur Henry and Marie (Pechin) M.; B.A. in Econs., St. Vincent Coll., 1957; postgrad. Rutgers U., 1957-58, Bernard Baruch Coll., 1962-70; m. Jeanne Marie Gibbons, Oct. 17, 1970; children—Jennifer Marie, Daniel Francis. Asst. treas. Bank of Am. Internat., N.Y.C., 1962-63, 64-67; asst. to pres. World Banking Corp., Nassau, Bahamas, 1964; asst. v.p. J. Henry Schroder Banking Corp., N.Y.C., 1967-70; successively asst. v.p., v.p., sr. v.p. New Eng. Mchts. Nat. Bank, Boston, 1970—, also dir.; pres., dir. New Eng. Mchts. Bank Internat.; mem. fgn. exchange adv. com. Fed. Res. Bank N.Y. Bd. dirs. Internat. Center New Eng., Melrose YMCA; trustee Melrose Public Library; mem. adv. com. New Eng. Fgn. Credit Ins. Assn. Served to lt. USNR, 1958-68. Mem. Dist. Export Council of Boston (chmn.), Am. Mgmt. Assn., Bankers Assn. Fgn. Trade, Forex Club. Republican. Roman Catholic. Club: Bellevue Golf. Home: 97 Ardsmoor Rd Melrose MA 02176 Office: 28 State St Boston MA 02190

MEEHLEIS, GEORGE ALLYN, data systems mfg. co. exec.; b. Los Angeles, Apr. 1, 1933; s. George W. and Pearl (Kelsey) M.; B.S., Calif. State U., Los Angeles, 1964; m. Phyllis J. Priester, Dec. 20, 1951; children—Rick W., Guy A., Dan A., Troy J. Indsl. engr. Hughes Aircraft Co., El Segundo, Calif., 1955-63; mgr. budgets and cost control guidance and control systems Litton Industries, Woodland Hills, Calif., 1963-68, mgr. production control Duluth Avionics div. (Minn.), 1968-70, dir. mfg. services Litton Ship Systems, Pascagoula, Miss., 1971-72, dir. ops. control Amecom div., College Park, Md., 1972-73, dir. mfg. Hewitt Robins, Columbia, S.C., 1973-75, dir. mfg., Data Systems div., Van Nuys, Calif., 1975-76; gen. mgr. mfg. Colo. div. Litton Data Systems, Colorado Springs, 1976—; mgr. ops. control Teledyne Casting Co., Pomona, Calif., 1970-71. Bd. dirs. Jr. Achievement, Colorado Springs; bd. dirs. U. Colo. Served as staff sgt. USAF, 1951-55; Korea. Mem. Am. Inst. Indsl. Engrs., Duluth C. of C., Nat. Assn. Accountants. Mem. Ch. Jesus Christ Latter-day Saints. Developer Automated Production Control System, Hughes Aircraft, 1960. Home: 7120 Wildridge Rd Colorado Springs CO 80908 Office: 425 E Fillmore Colorado Springs CO 80933

MEEK, JOHN LEONARD, corp. mktg. exec.; b. Kansas City, Mo., July 15, 1946; s. Jack Junior and Nadine (Monchil) M.; B.A. (scholar), Emporia State U., 1969, postgrad. Colo. State U., 1972-74, U. Colo., 1974-76; m. Mary Ellen McDorman, Oct. 22, 1978; 1 son, Andrew Jonathan. Microbiologist, Center Disease Control, Ft. Collins, Colo., 1972-74; microbiologist, lab. supr. dept. molecular, cellular and developmental biology U. Colo., Boulder, 1974-76; tissue culture specialist sci. products div. Corning Glass Works, Fairfax, Va., 1976-78, sales rep., 1978-80, cell biology product mgr. Med. and Sci. div., 1980—; cons., lectr. in field. Served with AUS, 1969-71. Recipient President's Circle award Corning Glass Works, 1978. Mem. Am. Soc. Microbiology (Mfrs. Rep. award Washington br. 1978), Tissue Culture Assn., Sports Car Club Am. (solo events driving champion 1973, 75), Porsche Club Am., Sigma Xi, Alpha Kappa Lambda. Lutheran. Contbr. articles to profl. jours. Home: 12 Knollbrook E Painted Post NY 14870 Office: MP 21-5 Corning Glass Works Corning NY 14830

MEEK, PAUL DERALD, oil and chem. co. exec.; b. McAllen, Tex., Aug. 15, 1930; s. William Van and Martha Mary (Sharp) M.; B.S. in Chem. Engring., U. Tex., Austin, 1953; m. Betty Catherine Robertson, Apr. 18, 1954; children—Paula Marie, Kathy Diane, Carol Ann, Linda Ray. Mem. tech. dept. Humble Oil & Refining Co., Baytown, Tex., 1953-55; with Cosden Oil & Chem. Co., 1955—, pres., 1968—; v.p. parent co., dir. Am. Petrofina, Inc., Dallas, 1968-76, pres., chief operating officer, 1976—. Chmn. chem. engring. vis. com. U. Tex., 1975-76; chmn. adv. council Coll. Engring. Found., U. Tex., Austin, 1979—. Named Disting. Engring. Grad., U. Tex., Austin, 1969. Mem. Am. Petroleum Inst., Am. Inst. Chem. Engrs., Mfg. Chemists Assn., Tex. Chem. Council (chmn. 1976). Contbg. author: Advances in Petroleum Chemistry and Refining, 1957. Office: Box 2159 Fina Plaza Dallas TX 75221*

MEEKER, ARLENE DOROTHY HALLIN (MRS. WILLIAM MAURICE MEEKER), mfg. co. exec.; b. Glendale, Calif., June 13, 1935; d. Haddon Eric and Martha (Randow) Hallin; grad. John Muir Jr. Coll., 1953; student Los Angeles Valley Coll., 1956-58, B.A., Whittier Coll., 1973, M.B.A., 1980; m. William Maurice Meeker, Aug. 19, 66; 1 son, William Michael. Statewide sec. pub. relations United Republicans Calif., Los Angeles, 1964; personnel specialist Sanford Mgmt. Services, Inc., Los Angeles, 1964-66; v.p. personnel Grover Mfg. Corp., Montebello, Calif., 1966-75, pres., 1975—, dir., 1969—; dir. Brit. Marine Industries, Montebello, 1969—, Grover Internat., 1969—. Mem. City of Whittier Transp. and Parking

Commn., 1976—, chmn. commn., 1977-79; council mem. Los Angeles County Art Mus., 1969-80; chmn. fine arts bd. Hillcrest Congregational Ch., mem. Ch. council, 1977—; patron KCET Ednl. TV, Action for Children's TV, Whittier Guild, Children's Hosp.; press chmn. Whittier Republican Women Federated, 1977-78, 1st v.p., 1981—; Rep. precinct capt., 1964. Mem. Docian Soc. (pub. relations chmn. 1967-68), Los Angeles World Affairs Council, AAUW. Conglist. Clubs: Newport Harbor Yacht (Newport Beach, Calif.); Friendly Hills Country (Whittier, Calif.). Home: 9710 Portada Dr Whittier CA 90603 Office: 620 S Vail St Montebello CA 90640

MEEKER, MILTON SHY, heavy duty truck mfg. co. exec.; b. Knob Noster, Mo., Nov. 9, 1933; s. David and Helen Elizabeth (Kendrick) M.; B.A., U. Calif. at Berkeley, 1955, B.S., 1959; M.B.A., U. Mich., 1963; m. Nancy Orbison, Nov. 27, 1976; 1 son, Sherwin Kendrick. With Ford Motor Co., 1959-68; dir. purchasing, mktg., research mgr. Paccar, Inc., Seattle, also Newark, Calif., 1968-71; commr. fed. supply service, commr. automated data and telecommunications, asso. dep. adminstr. GSA, Washington, 1972-75; dir. purchasing chem. group FMC Corp., Phila., 1975-77, dir. purchasing planning and adminstrn., Chgo., 1977-79; gen. sales mgr. Peterbilt Motors Co. div. Paccar, Newark, Calif., 1979-80, mktg. mgr., 1980—. Chmn., Pres.'s Com. for Purchase of Products from Blind, 1973-74; bd. dirs. Nat. Industries for the Blind. Served with U.S. Army, 1957-58. Mem. Nat. Assn. Purchasing Mgmt. Republican. Home: 254 Almeria Ave Fremont CA 94538 Office: 38801 Cherry St Newark CA 94560

MEEKIN, PETER THOMAS, data processing cons. firm exec.; b. Troy, N.Y., July 26, 1949; s. Chester C. and Madeline (Boyle) M.; B.S. cum laude, SUNY, New Paltz, 1971; m. Susan D. Halpern, May 26, 1974; 1 dau., Sarah Caitlin. Vice pres. systems Shared Ednl. Computer System, Inc., Poughkeepsie, N.Y., 1972-76; pres. COMPRO Assos., New Paltz, N.Y., 1976—. Mem. Assn. Computing Machinery. (editor jour. APL Quote Quad 1979—). Office: 7 Innis Ave New Paltz NY 12561

MEESE, FRED LEROY, ins. co. exec.; b. Pocatello, Idaho, July 20, 1949; s. Frederick Leroy and Barbara (Bitter) M.; B.S., U. Utah, 1974; m. Mary Ann Schleckman, Aug. 14, 1974; children—Nathan, Jodi, John, Becky, Matthew. Agt., ITT Life Ins. Co., Salt Lake City, 1974-76; sec.-treas. Gem State Mut. Life Ins. Co., Pocatello, 1976—; dir. Gem. State Mut. of Utah. Coach Gate City Soccer League; mem. Pocatello central council PTA. Republican. Mormon. Office: PO Box 1787 Pocatello ID 83201

MEESE, WILLIAM GILES, utilities exec.; b. Rugby, N.D., Aug. 27, 1916; s. William Gottlieb and Emma (LaPierre) M.; B.S. in Elec. Engring., Purdue U., 1941, D.Eng. (hon.), 1972; m. Mary Edith Monk, Apr. 4, 1942; children—Elizabeth Ann, Stephen William, Richard Edward. Various positions in engring. depts. Detroit Edison Co., 1941-67, v.p., 1967-69, exec. v.p. prodn., 1969-70, pres., 1970-71, pres., chief exec. officer, 1971-75, chmn. bd., chief exec. officer, 1975—, also dir.; dir. Eaton Corp., Ex-Cell-O Corp., Mfrs. Nat. Bank Detroit, Mfrs. Nat. Corp. Bd. dirs. United Found.; trustee Detroit Renaissance, Rackham Engring. Found. Served to maj. AUS, 1941-45. Decorated Bronze Star medal; recipient Distinguished Alumnus award Purdue U., 1969, Internat. B'nai B'rith Humanitarian award, 1977. Registered profl. engr., Mich. Fellow Engring. Soc. Detroit, IEEE; mem. Newcomen Soc. N.Am., Econ. Club Detroit (dir.), Conf. Internat. des Grands Reseaux Electriques, Tau Beta Pi, Eta Kappa Nu. Clubs: Detroit Athletic, Detroit. Office: 2000 2d Ave Detroit MI 48226

MEGARGEL, ROY CURTIS, tire co. exec.; b. N.Y.C., Sept. 5, 1930; s. Ralph Garfield and Nancy Elizabeth (Larlee) M.; A.B., Dartmouth Coll., 1952; LL.B., Harvard U., 1957; m. Diane Daniels, Aug. 16, 1979; children by previous marriage—Kate Julia Gray, Ralph Curtis. Admitted to N.Y. State bar, 1958; asso. firm Kirlin, Campbell & Keating, N.Y.C., 1957-62, N.J. Zinc Co. N.Y., 1962-64, Hewitt-Robins, Inc., Conn., 1964-66; v.p., gen. counsel Hewitt-Robins, Inc. div. Litton Industries, 1966-68, v.p., gen. mgr. Robins Engrs. and Constructors div. Hewitt-Robins, 1968-70; v.p., gen. counsel GTE Internat, N.Y.C., 1970-72; sr. v.p. telecommunications, 1972-77; pres. Gen. Tire Internat. Co., Akron, Ohio, 1977—, also dir.; dir. fgn. affiliates. Served with USMC, 1952-54. Republican. Clubs: N.Y. Yacht, Mentor Harbor Yacht. Office: 1 General St Akron OH 44329

MEGARRY, A. ROY, publisher; b. Belfast, No. Ireland, Feb. 10, 1937; s. Andrew Blain and Barbara (Bennett) M.; ed. U. Western Ont. (Can.); grad. mgmt. devel. course Princeton U.; m. Barbara Todd Bird Bennett, May 31, 1959; children—Andrew, Kevin, Lianne. Controller, Honeywell Ltd., Toronto, Ont., 1957-64; v.p. Daystrom (Heathkit) Ltd., Toronto, 1964-66; sr. cons. Urwick, Currie, Coopers & Lybrand Ltd., Toronto, 1966-69; v.p. fin. Internat. Syscoms Ltd., Toronto, 1969-71; v.p., gen. mgr. Blackwoods Beverages Ltd., Winnipeg, Man., Can., 1971-73; v.p. Charterways Co. Ltd., 1974; v.p. Torstar Corp., Toronto, 1974-78; pub., chief exec. officer Globe and Mail, daily newspaper, Toronto, 1978—; dir. F.P. Publs. (Eastern) Ltd.; mem. edn. bd. Cost and Mgmt. mag.; mem. planning com. TV Ont. Mem. Soc. Indsl. Accts. Can. (past dir.), Soc. Indsl. Accts. Ont. Roman Catholic. Clubs: Donalda, Nat. Office: Toronto Globe & Mail 444 Front St W Toronto ON M5V 2S6 Canada*

MEGEE, WILLIAM VIRDEN, passenger ground transp. exec.; b. Rehoboth Beach, Del., Apr. 20, 1928; s. Ernest Edward and Ressie Isabelle (Scarborough) M.; B.S.B.A., U. Del., 1950; m. Mary Adelaide Patrician, Aug. 19, 1954; children—William Virden, Linda Ann, Melissa Patrician, Andrew Patrick. Dir. procurement Rollins Leasing Corp., Wilmington, Del., 1953-68; pres. Airport Shuttle Service, Inc., Wilmington, Diamond Cab Del. Inc., and Yellow Cab...Del. Inc., Wilmington, 1968—; prin. stockholder, pres. Airport Shuttle-Cin., Inc. Mem. Mayor's Econ. Adv. Com. Served with U.S. Army, 1951-53. Mem. Airport Ground Transp. Assn. (chmn.), Internat. Taxicab Assn., Transp. Research Bd., Ground Transp. Cert. Carriers Assn. (chmn.). Republican. Home: 1219 Lakewood Dr Carrcroft Wilmington DE 19803 Office: 1227 E 15th St Wilmington DE 19802

MEGGINSON, ROBERT MITFORD, mortgage banker; b. Jackson, Miss., Aug. 2, 1932; s. Oscar Gray and Gladys (Lindsey) M.; student Millsaps Coll., 1965-66; B.S., Miss. State U., 1958; grad. Northwestern U. Mortgage Banking Sch., 1965-67; m. Joanne Jenkins, Jan. 8, 1953; children—Laurie Anne, Robert Kyle. Mem. acctg. dept. First Nat. Bank, Jackson, Miss., 1951-53; bookkeeper Ross & Hurst, C.P.A.'s, Jackson, Miss., 1958-59; mem. loan servicing, processing and acctg. dept. Reid-McGee & Co., Jackson, Miss., 1959-61; v.p. loan origination Wortman & Mann, Inc., Jackson, Miss., 1961-69; exec. v.p. Milton & Megginson Mortgage Co., Inc., Jackson, Miss., 1969—; pres. Milton, Megginson & Spencer, Inc., Jackson, Miss., 1970—; exec. v.p., dir. First Am. Savs. & Loan Assn., Clinton, Miss., 1972—; owner, pres. R.M. Megginson, Realtor-Appraiser-Builder, Jackson. Mem. adv. bd. dirs., bd. dirs. Youth for Christ, Jackson, Miss.; bd. dirs. Southwest YMCA, Forest Hill Youth Club. Served with AUS, 1953-55. Licensed Real Estate Broker, Miss. Mem. Soc. Real Estate Appraisers (chpt. v.p. 1968-69), Jackson Bd. Realtors. Nat. Assn. Real Estate Bds., Miss. Assn. Realtor Bds. Inc., Nat., Miss. assns. home bldrs., Jackson Jr. C. of C. (past v.p.; recipient Spark Plug award, Speak Up award, Spoke award), Gideons Internat. Baptist. Club: Jackson Civitan. Home: Route 9 Box 109-A Jackson MS 39212 Office: PO Box 6985 Jackson MS 39212

MEHALCHIN, JOHN JOSEPH, fin. co. exec.; b. Hazleton, Pa., Aug. 8, 1937; s. Charles and Susan M.; B.S. with honors, Temple U., 1964; M.B.A., U. Calif., Berkeley, 1965; m. Mechtild Cremer, Feb. 8, 1964; 1 son, Martin. Supr. costs Winchester-Western, New Haven, 1965-67; mgmt. cons. Booz-Allen & Hamilton, N.Y.C., 1967-68; mgr. planning TWA, N.Y.C., 1968-70; 2d v.p. Smith, Barney, N.Y.C. and Paris, 1970-74; chief fin. officer, pres. leasing co. Storage Tech. Corp., Louisville, Colo., 1974-79; sr. v.p. Heizer Corp., 1979; pres., founder Highline Fin. Services, Boulder, Colo., 1979—. Served with AUS, 1958-61. Mem. Fin. Execs. Inst., Beta Gamma Sigma, Omicron Delta Epsilon. Office: 1911 11th St Suite 205 Boulder CO 80302

MEHLENBACHER, DOHN HARLOW, phys. plant exec.; b. Huntington Park, Calif., Nov. 18, 1931; s. Virgil Claude and Helga (Sigfridson) M.; B.S. in Civil Engring., U. Ill., 1953; M.S. in City and Regional Planning Ill. Inst. Tech., 1961; M.B.A., U. Chgo., 1972; m. Barbara Ruth Stinson, Dec. 30, 1953; children—Dohn Scott, Kimberly Ruth, Mark James, Matthew Lincoln. Structural engr., draftsman Swift & Co., Chgo., 1953-54, 56-57, DeLeuw-Cather Co., Chgo., 1957-59; project engr. Quaker Oats Co., Chgo., 1959-61, mgr. constrn., 1964-70, mgr. real property, 1970-71, mgr. engring. and maintenance, Los Angeles, 1961-64; chief facilities engr. Bell & Howell Co., Chgo., 1972-73; v.p. design Globe Engring. Co., Chgo., 1973-76; project mgr. I.C. Harbour Constrn. Co., Oak Brook, Ill., 1976-78; dir. estimating George A. Fuller Co., Chgo., 1978; pres. Food-Tech Co., Willowbrook, Ill., 1979-80; dir. phys. resources Ill. Inst. Tech., Chgo., 1980—. Served with USAF, 1954-56. Registered profl. engr., Ill., N.Y., Calif. Mem. Nat. Soc. Profl. Engrs., Am. Mgmt. Assn., ASCE, Constrn. Specifications Inst., Am. Arbitration Assn. Home: 2662 Sheridan Rd Highland Park IL 60035 Office: IIT Center Chicago IL 60616

MEHLUM, JOHAN ARNT, banker; b. Trondheim, Norway, Nov. 11, 1928; s. Hans Aage and Olga (Nygaard) M.; diploma Norwegian Bus. Coll., 1946, Grad. Sch. Banking, Rutgers U., 1971; m. Ladona Marie Christensen, May 30, 1951; children—Ann Marie, Katherine, Susan Jane, Rolf Erik. Came to U.S., 1950, naturalized, 1955. Clk., Forretningsbanken, Trondheim, 1946-50, First Nat. Bank Oreg., Astoria and Corvallis, 1952-57; cashier, mgr. Bank of Shedd, Brownsville, Oreg., 1958-63; pres. Siuslaw Valley Bank, Forence, Oreg., 1963—; chmn. bd. Community Bank Creswell (Oreg.), 1970-79; dir. Siuslaw Valley Plaza, Inc., 1966—. Mayor, Dunes City, Oreg., 1973-75. Trustee Lane Community Coll. Found., 1971-78; chmn. bd. dirs. NW Intermediate Banking Sch., Lewis and Clark Coll., Portland, Oreg., 1975-77; trustee, past chmn. Western Lane County Found., 1976—. Served with Royal Norwegian Army, 1948-49. Named Jr. First Citizen, Astoria, 1955, First Citizen, Brownsville, 1962; recipient internat. relations award U.S. Jr. C. of C., 1960. Mem. Western Ind. Bankers (mem. exec. council 1970-74), Am. Bankers Assn. (mem. exec. com. community bankers div. 1976-78), Oreg. Bankers Assn. (pres.-elect 1980-81), Florence Area C. of C. (pres. 1970), Banking Profession Polit. Action Com. (state chmn. 1973-76), Sons of Norway. Elk, Rotarian (pres. 1967-68). Club: Norsemen's League (pres. 1954). Home: PO Box 131 Florence OR 97439 Office: PO Box 280 Florence OR 97439

MEHN, W. HARRISON, surgeon, utilities exec.; b. Monroe, Wis., Nov. 25, 1918; s. William Herman and Hedwig Gertrude (Butenhoff) M.; B.A., North Central Coll., Naperville, Ill., 1940; M.D., Northwestern U., 1944, M.S. in Pathology, 1944; m. Jean Belle Dorr, Sept. 23, 1945; children—Mary Ann, Judith Susan. Intern, Passavant Meml. Hosp., Chgo., 1944, resident in surgery, 1947-50, resident in pathology Children's Meml. Hosp., Chgo., 1945; Alexian Bros. Hosp., Chgo., 1946-47; resident in surgery Cook County Hosp., Chgo., 1949, asso. attending surgeon, 1949-53; clin. asst. dept. surgery Northwestern U., 1948-52, instr. surgery, 1952-53, asso. surgery, 1953-58, asst. prof. surgery, 1958-73, asso. prof., 1973-74, prof. clin. surgery, 1974—; practice medicine specializing in surgery, Chgo., 1950—; mem. staff Northwestern Meml. Hosps., VA Lakeside Hosp.; med. dir. Commonwealth Edison Co., Chgo., 1955—; mem. accident prevention com. Edison Electric Inst., N.Y.C., 1960—; participant profl. research task forces Electric Power Research Inst., Palo Alto, Calif., 1973—; mem. U.S.-USSR Coop. Agreement on UHV, 1977—, U.S.-USSR Coop. Agreement on Biologic Effects Electric Fields, 1977—. Bd. dirs. NCCJ, 1968—; mem. bd. ruling elders Northminster Presbyn. Ch., Evanston, Ill., 1971—; bd. dirs. Presbyn. Home, Evanston, 1977—. Served to lt. USN, 1945-46, to lt. comdr., 1953-55. Diplomate Am. Bd. Surgery. Mem. A.C.S. (mem. Chgo. com. on trauma, 1970—), Ill. Surg. Soc., Chgo. Heart Assn., Ill., Chgo., Western surg. socs., Soc. Surgery Alimentary Tract, Collegium Internationale Chirurgiae Digestivae, Inst. Medicine, Ill. State, Chgo. med. socs., AMA, Indsl. Med. Assn., Am. Trauma Soc., Sigma Xi, Pi Kappa Epsilon, Phi Beta Pi. Clubs: Westmoreland Country (pres.), Waupaca Country, Internationale, Anglers, Camp Fire, McGraw Wildlife Fedn. Contbr. articles to med. and sci. jours. Home: 3033 Normandy Pl Evanston IL 60201 Office: 707 N Fairbanks Ct Chicago IL 60611

MEHRA, RAVINDER, trading co. exec.; b. Lahore, India, Aug. 4, 1941; immigrated to Can., 1968, naturalized, 1976; s. Amar Nath and Shakuntala (Dhawan) M.; B.A. with honors, St. Stephen's Coll., New Delhi, 1963; m. Binny Gill, Sept. 15, 1968; children—Arjun, Arun, Deepak. With Universal Paper, Montreal, Que., Can., 1971—, pres., 1978—. Home: 10 Thompson Point Beaconsfield PQ H9W 5Y8 Canada Office: 1198 Mountain St Montreal PQ H3G 1Z1 Canada

MEHREN, LAWRENCE LINDSAY, investment co. exec.; b. Phoenix, May 26, 1944; s. Lawrence and Mary Teresa (Stelzer) M.; B.A., U. Ariz., 1966; M.A., U. Ariz., 1968; m. Lynn Athon McEvers, June 5, 1965; children—Lawrence Lindsay, John Eskridge. Bus. mgr. Rancho Santa Maria, Peoria, Ariz., 1968-69; traffic mgr. Glen-Mar Mfg. Co., Phoenix, 1969-70; account exec. Merrill Lynch, Pierce, Fenner and Smith, Inc., Phoenix, 1970-77, sr. account exec., 1977-78, asst. v.p., 1978-80, v.p., 1980—. Mem. Maricopa County Citizens Action Com.; chmn. Madison Citizens Adv. Com., 1973-74. Recipient award Ariz. Hist. Found., 1968. Mem. Nat. Securities Traders Assn., Ariz. Securities Assn., Phoenix Stock and Bond Club (dir. 1979—), Ariz. Acad. Public Affairs, Phi Alpha Theta, Beta Theta Pi. Republican. Roman Catholic. Clubs: Phoenix Country, Dons. Home: 7215 N Central Ave Phoenix AZ 85020 Office: 40 N 1st Ave Phoenix AZ 85003

MEIER, OTTO, JR., educator; b. N.Y.C., Feb. 5, 1931; s. Otto and Anna Marie (Marks) M.; B.S. in Engring. for Indsl. Mgmt., Fairleigh Dickinson U., 1960. Project coordinator Rep. Aviation Corp., Farmingdale, N.Y., 1953-57; engring. designer M. Rosenblatt & Son, N.Y.C., 1957-58; supr. product engring. services Mergenthaler Linotype Co., Plainview, N.Y., 1960-65; instr. Manhattan Tech. Inst., N.Y.C., 1965-67; lectr. tech. SUNY, Bklyn., 1967—. Bd. trustees Liederkranz Found., 1975-78, pres. Younger Mems. Group, 1980—. Recipient cert. of excellence in teaching Charvoz-Carsen Corp., 1978. Mem. N.Y. State Assn. Jr. Colls., Soc. Naval Architects and Marine Engrs., Am. Inst. Design and Drafting, Am. Vocat. Assn., U.S. Naval Inst., Am.-Scandinavian Found., N.Y. State Occupational Edn. Assn., Bklyn. Power Squadron. Mem. German Reformed Ch. Clubs: Anchor and Saber of N.Y. (dir. 1975-77, pres. 1978-79), Sport Rites. Home: 61 15 43d Ave Woodside NY 11377 Office: 470 Vanderbilt Ave Brooklyn NY 11238

MEIERS, HAROLD NORMAN, ins. agt.; b. Appleton, Wis., Apr. 18, 1943; s. Harold Paul and Lucille (Beschta) M.; B.S., U. Wis., Madison, 1967; m. Karen A. Thomson, June 27, 1980. With Union Mutual Ins. Co., Madison, Wis., 1967—, v.p. James F. McMichael & Assos., 1980—. Merit badge counselor Boy Scouts Am. Recipient Man of Yr. award Union Mut. Life Ins. Co., 1968, Disting. Sales award, 1969, 80; Nat. Quality award Nat. Assn. Life Underwriters, 1975-80, Nat. Sales Achievement award, 1975, 79; C.L.U. Mem. Nat. Assn. Life Underwriters, Madison Assn. Life Underwriters. Lutheran. Office: Union Mutual Ins Co 6314 Odana Rd Suite 12 Madison WI 53719

MEIKLE, FREDERICK CLINTON, JR., ferrous castings mfg. co. exec.; b. Santa Monica, Calif., Oct. 19, 1931; s. Frederick Clinton and Catherine Leonie (Ahonen) M.; B.S. with honors, Yale U., 1953; postgrad. Oreg. State U., 1957-60; m. Claudia Debord, Oct. 27, 1973; children—Frederick Clinton, Susan. Mng. asso. Arthur Young & Co., Los Angeles, Portland, Oreg., 1960-65; v.p. ops. and fin. Moore-Oreg., Portland, 1965-71; pres. Bancorp Leasing, Portland, 1971-74; pres. Blackwell N. Am., Beaverton, Oreg., 1974-77; pres. Van Rich Casting Corp., Portland, 1977—. Dir., mem. exec. com. Found. for Oreg. Research and Edn., 1973—; bd. dirs. Portland Opera Assn., 1973-79. Served with U.S. Army, 1954-56. Mem. Am. Inst. Indsl. Engrs., Nat. Assn. Accts., Assn. Systems Mgmt. Club: Columbia-Edgewater Country. Office: PO Box 17216 Portland OR 97217

MEINERS, GARY ALLYN, machinery dealer; b. Caledonia, Minn., Apr. 2, 1953; s. Glenn Herman and Gladys Mavis M.; student public schs., Caledonia; m. Anna Maire Hammell, Nov. 30, 1975; 1 son, Nicholaus. Mechanic, Hector Constrn. Co., Caledonia, Minn., 1971-74; mgr. Lager Farms, Caledonia, 1974-78; mgr., pres. Klinski Implement Co., Caledonia, 1978—; mem. Houston County (Minn.) Farm Bur. Mem. Retail Farm Equipment Assn. Minn. and S.D., Nat. Fedn. Ind. Bus., Caledonia C. of C. Republican. Lutheran. Clubs: Red Baron Flying, Ma-Cal-Grove Country. Home: 124 N McPhail Caledonia MN 55921 Office: PO Box 148 Hwy 44 and 76th St Caledonia MN 55921

MEINIG, PETER CARL, mfg. co. exec.; b. West Reading, Pa., July 15, 1939; s. Carl Henry and Mary Catherine (DeLong) M.; B.M.E., Cornell U., 1962; M.B.A., Harvard U., 1964; m. Nancy Elaine Schlegel, Sept. 1, 1962; children—Anne, Katheryn, Sarah. Asst. to v.p. Allegheny Ludlum Steel Corp., Pitts., 1964-66; gen. mgr. Kennamex S.A., Mexico City, 1966-70; mng. dir. Rassini Rheem S.A., Mexico City, 1970-79; pres. Indsl. Fabricating Co., Tulsa, 1979—, Gen. Screw Products Co., Houston, 1979—; dir. Rassini Rheem, Mexico City, 1979—. Pres. sch. bd. Am. Sch. Mex., 1975-80; pres. ch. council Christ Episcopal Ch., 1976-78. Mem. Automotive Industry C. of C. Mex. (dir. 1975-79), Am. C. of C. in Mex. (dir. 1978-80), Indsl. Fasteners Inst. (governing bd. 1975-80), Young Pres.'s Orgn. Home: 2010 E 46 St Tulsa OK 74105 Office: 10055 E 56 St N Tulsa OK 74145

MEINKEN, KENNETH CHARLES, JR., electronics mfg. co. exec.; b. Phila., July 15, 1921; s. Kenneth Charles and Emily Krauss (Dietz) M.; B.S. in Econs., U. Pa. Wharton Sch., 1943; m. Nancy Ramsdell, Mar. 20, 1945; children—Sayre, Kenneth Charles III. Exec. v.p. Gen. Atronics Corp., Phila., 1957-61; v.p. Gen. Instrument Corp., Newark, 1961-66; pres. Advance Transformer Co., Chgo., 1966-78; pres. Magnavox Consumer Electronics Co., Ft. Wayne, Ind., 1978—; dir. Stange Co., Chgo. Served to lt. j.g. USNR, 1943-45. Episcopalian. Clubs: Seaview Country (Absecon, N.J.); Turtle Creek (Tequesta, Fla.); Cherokee Country (Knoxville); Huntingdon Valley Country (Phila.); Bald Peak Colony (Melvin Village, N.H.). Office: Magnavox Consumer Electronics Co I-40 and Straw Plains Pike Knoxville TN 46804

MEINTZER, BENJAMIN TOWNSEND, oil co. exec.; b. Easton, Md., July 20, 1929; s. John Ells and Lillian E. (Townsend) M.; grad. high sch.; m. Mary Ellen West, June 1, 1963 (dec. 1980); children—Susan West, Benjamin Townsend. With Oxford Boatyard Co. (Md.), 1948; photographer FBI, Washington, 1948-51; v.p., co-owner J.E. Meintzer Sons, Easton, 1958—. Served with U.S. Army, 1951-53; Korea. Mem. Delmarva Oil Heat Assn., Am. Legion. Democrat. Episcopalian. Office: 400 S Aurora St Easton MD 21601

MEISEL, MARTIN HUGH, mgmt. cons. co. exec.; b. Bklyn., Jan. 31, 1933; s. Clarence A. and Seraphine S. (Sanft) M.; B.A., N.Y. U., 1954, M.P.A., 1958; postgrad. Syracuse U., 1954; m. Lola M. Preiss, June 12, 1960. Asst. salary adminstr. B. Altman & Co., N.Y.C., 1956-60; asst. dir. personnel Bache & Co., N.Y.C., 1960-62; pres. Exec. Talent Inc., N.Y.C., 1962-68, Martin H. Meisel Assn., Inc., N.Y.C., 1968—, Faith Prodns., Inc., 1977—; alt. del. N.Y. Jud. Conv., 1978—. Fund raising cons. Democratic presdl. candidates, 1968, 72, 76; mem. New York County Dem. Com., 1977—; mem. adv. bd. Am. Security Council, 1975—. Served with AUS, 1954-56. Mem. Ams. for Dem. Action (dir. 1973-78), Am. Soc. Pub. Adminstrn., ACLU, Am. Friends Service Com., Phi Beta Kappa (dir. N.Y. alumni 1980—), Pi Sigma Alpha. Club: Town. Author: Televisomania Fantasy 2050, 1950. Office: 55 E 87th St New York NY 10028

MEISELES, MURRAY JACOB, transp. co. exec.; b. Bklyn., Oct. 15, 1930; s. Arthur and Rose (Steinman) M.; B.A., Bklyn. Coll., 1952; postgrad. Coll. City N.Y., 1953; m. Ruth Peggy Appel, Sept. 2, 1951; children—Howard, Paul, Eliot. Vice pres. finance Stoll Packing Corp., N.Y.C., 1952-64; asst. to pres. W.M. Tyman & Co., N.Y.C., 1964-65; practice accounting, Rockaway, N.J., 1965-66; div. controller Farmbest, Inc. div. Farmland Industries, Denison, Iowa, 1966-67; controller Midwest Emery Freight System, Inc., Chgo., 1966-71, treas., 1971-76; treas. Rentar Industries, Inc.; dir. Little Audreys Transp. Co., Inc., Fremont, Nebr., Trans-Cold Express, Inc., Dallas, Belford Trucking Co., Inc., Miami, Fla., Ar Glen Corp., South Kearny, N.J., Couzens Warehouse & Distbrs., Inc., Chgo.; sec.-treas. Ind. Refrigerator Lines, Muncie, 1976—. Sec. Sheepshead Bay Community Council, Bklyn., 1956-60; treas. Brigham Park Fed. Credit Union, Bklyn., 1964-66. Mem. Nat. Accounting and Finance Council, Am. Trucking Assn., Nat. Assn. Accountants for Coops., Bklyn. Coll. Alumni Assn. Jewish (dir. congregation). Home: 3005 Riverside St Muncie IN 47305 Office: PO Box 552 Riggin Rd Muncie IN 47305

MEISNER, EDWARD CHARLES, mfg. exec.; b. Dayton, Ohio, Mar. 12, 1913; s. Charles Philip and Louisa (Schoettinger) M.; student Ohio State U., 1931-32; B.S. in Mech. Engring., U. Dayton, 1936; m. Martha Eileen Cull, June 13, 1945; children—Michael E., Patricia A., Geoffrey C. Head phys. testing lab., asst. metallurgist, head tool planning and processing Nat. Cash Register Co., 1936-46; chief indsl. engr., plant mgr., gen. mgr. Plant 7, Crosley div. Avco Mfg. Corp., 1946-55; gen. mgr. insulation div. Philip Carey Mfg. Co., 1955-59, div. v.p., 1959-63, co. v.p., 1963-68; mgr. mfg. engring. Nat. Cash Register Co., Cambridge, Ohio, 1968-71, mfg. devel. engr., Dayton, 1971-77;

ret., 1977. Registered profl. engr., Ohio. Mason (Shriner). Home: 10088 Tanager Ln Cincinnati OH 45215

MEISTER, GREGORY JAMES, steel co. exec.; b. Seattle, Jan. 23, 1953; s. William R. and Sharon L. (Boike) M.; B.A. in Bus. Adminstrn., U. Wash., 1975; m. Cheryl L. Gorham, Apr. 18, 1975. Staff acct. Moss Adams & Co., C.P.A.'s, Seattle, 1974-77; fin. adv. M. A. Wyman Lumber Co., Seattle, 1977—; v.p. fin., asst. sec., dir. Pacific Steel Co., Inc., Seattle, 1977-80; v.p. fin., asst. sec., dir. Stack Steel & Supply Co., Seattle, 1977—. C.P.A., Wash. Mem. Am. Inst. C.P.A.'s, Wash. Soc. C.P.A.'s. Clubs: Rainier, Wash. Athletic (Seattle); Bellevue (Wash.) Athletic. Office: 3330 Rainier Bank Tower Seattle WA 98101

MEISTER, JOHN DAVID, diversified mfg. co. exec.; b. Miami, Fla., Apr. 16, 1939; s. Clarence Raymond and Rose E. (Dasch) M.; B.S. in Elec. Engring., U. N.Mex., 1962; m. Martha Elizabeth Terwilliger, June 30, 1962; children—John David, James Christopher. Exploration geophysicist Humble Oil Co., Houston, 1962; mgr. systems engring. TRW, Inc., San Bernardino, Calif., 1965-68; program dir. Tracor, Inc., Austin, Tex., 1968—. Active U. Tex. Internat. Student Host Family Program, 1969—; adult vol. Capitol Area council Boy Scouts Am., 1972—, recipient Wood Badge; Tex. instr. Nat. Hunter Safety Program. Served to 1st lt. USAF, 1962-65. Registered profl. engr., registered public surveyor, Tex. Mem. Armed Forces Communication Electronics Assn. (founding pres. Austin-Bergstrom chpt.), Kappa Alpha. Republican. Presbyn. (deacon 1971-73). Research, publs. in systems engring. field. Home: 6815 Willamette Austin TX 78723 Office: 6500 Tracor Lane Austin TX 78721

MEITZ, A. A., mgmt. cons.; b. Fraser, Mich., July 15, 1937; s. Alfred W. and Edna (Dryer) M.; B.S.E.E., Valparaiso U., 1958; M.B.A. with honors, Stanford U., 1965; m. Karen S. Prescott, Aug. 23, 1958; children—Kori, Tani. Grad. engr. tng. program, missile div. Chrysler Corp., Warren, Mich., 1958; instrumentation engr. Martin-Marietta Co., Denver, 1959-61; field engr. Denver Research Inst., 1961-63; with Booz, Allen & Hamilton, Chgo. and Dallas, 1965—, now sr. v.p., also dir., 1979—. Trustee, Dallas Alliance for Minority Enterprise, 1972-77; mem. nat. alumni assn. bd. trustees Stanford Grad. Sch. Bus., 1973-76, pres., 1971-72. Mem. N. Am. Soc. Corp. Planning (pres. Dallas chpt. 1978-80), Republican. Lutheran. Clubs: Bent Tree Country, T Bar M Racquet. Office: 1700 1 Dallas Centre Dallas TX 75201

MELANCON, MICHAEL RAY, bus. machines co. exec.; b. Beaumont, Tex., May 29, 1950; s. Joseph Whitney and Hester Dave M.; B.B.A., Lamar U., 1972; postgrad. bus. adminstrn. Tex. So. U., 1977—; m. Gradie B. Hopper, Aug. 12, 1972; children—Leah Michelle, Ray Michael. Counselor, High Sch. Equivalency Program, Beaumont, 1971-72; acct. Ernst & Ernst, Detroit, 1972-75; account rep. IBM, Houston, from 1975, now account mgr. Adviser, Jr. Achievement, 1973-75. Mem. Nat. Assn. Accts., Nat. Assn. Black Accts., Delta Sigma Pi. Roman Catholic. Club: Toastmasters Internat. Home: 15830 Valverde Dr Houston TX 77083

MELCHER, LEROY, JR., foods co. exec.; b. Brenham, Tex., Nov. 8, 1938; s. LeRoy and Lucile (Birmingham) M.; student U. Tex., 1956-58, U. Houston, 1958-59; children—Frank Dodd, LeRoy III, Pierre Schlumberger, Marc Carroll. With UtoteM Co., Houston, 1957—, store mgr., 1959-67, v.p. Fairmont Foods Co. (merged with UtoteM Co. 1967), 1975-76, sr. v.p., 1976—, pres. UtoteM div., 1976-79; pres. Ranger Markets div. Ranger Energy Co., Inc., Houston, 1979—; partner Helicopters Unltd. Home: 9250 Sandringham Dr Houston TX 77024

MELCONIAN, JERRY OHANES, aerospace co. exec.; b. Cairo, Jan. 22, 1934; s. Melik and Zarouca (Papazian) M.; came to U.S., 1967, naturalized, 1973; B.Sc., U. London, 1957; m. Kathleen Fay DiRe, May 8, 1976; 1 son, Terran Kirk. Sect. leader Rolls Royce Engines, Derby, Eng., 1961-66; program coordinator Avco Lycoming, Stratford, Conn., 1967-74; program mgr. Gen. Electric Co., Lynn, Mass., 1974-77; dir. bus. devel. No. Research & Engring. Corp., Woburn, Mass., 1980—, gen. mgr. subs., Promec, Inc., 1978—; pres. SOL-3, Resources Inc., Wenham, Mass., 1976—. Patentee in field. Home: 76 Beaver Rd Reading MA 01867 Office: 39 Olympia Ave Woburn MA 01801

MELICAN, JOSEPH MICHAEL, JR., law firm adminstr.; b. Boston, Feb. 3, 1941; s. Joseph Michael and Margaret Mary (Tully) M.; B.S. in Bus. Adminstrn., Northeastern U., 1964, M.B.A., 1966; m. Paula J. Wilfert, July 9, 1966; children—Amy, Peter. Teaching fellow Northeastern U., Boston, 1964-66; sr. analyst public acctg. Arthur Andersen & Co., Boston, 1966-70; v.p., treas. Breck McNeish, Nagle DeLorey Inc., Boston, 1970-74; v.p., sec. Boston Stock Exchange Clearing Corp., 1974-78; v.p. New Eng. Securities Depository Trust Co., Boston, 1976-78; pres., treas., dir. Boseco Inc., Boston, 1976-78; adminstr. firm Hutchins & Wheeler, Boston, 1978—. Mem. Assn. Legal Adminstrs. (dir., treas., v.p.). Home: 98 Main St Dover MA 02030 Office: One Boston Pl Boston MA 02108

MELICHAR, ERNEST ALOIS, newspaper pub.; b. Hamilton, Ont., Can., May 24, 1936; s. Alois and Blanche Kristina (Sustek) M.; came to U.S., 1946, naturalized, 1955; A.A., Morton Jr. Coll., 1955; B.S., Northwestern U., 1957, M.S., 1958; m. Phyllis A. Dorociak, June 6, 1964; children—Joseph E., Frances Mary, Ann Louise. Co-pub., Ind. Newspapers, Wheeling, Ill., 1959-63; asst. editor Skyscraper Mgmt. Mag., Chgo., 1963-65; editor Chicagoland's Real Estate Advt., Chgo., 1965-68, pub., editor, 1968-70, pub., 1971—; dir. Clyde Fed. Savs. & Loan Assn., Nat. Baking Co., Chgo., N.W. Investment Co., Northbrook, Ill. Pres., Riverside Twp. Gold and Blue Com., 1977—; v.p. Riverside Twp. Regular Republican Orgn., 1977—, Riverside Community Fund, 1968-69. Mem. Chgo. Press Club, N.G. Assn. Ill., Moravian Cultural Soc. (founding pres. 1965-66), Chgo. Real Estate Bd., Lambda Alpha. Clubs: Rotary, Monroe. Home: 235 Maplewood Rd Riverside IL 60546 Office: 415 N State St Chicago IL 60611

MELINE, EDWARD STEVEN, mktg. and sales exec.; b. Malden, Mass., July 27, 1939; s. Samuel and Perle (Groman) M.; A.B. in Phys. Scis., Harvard U., 1961; M.B.A. in Fin., Columbia U., 1964; m. Eileen H. Hanley, Dec. 26, 1977; children—Michael, Matthew. Mgr. price analysis Philco-Ford Corp., Phila., 1969-70, nat. sales planning mgr., 1970-71, nat. mktg. mgr., 1971-75; v.p. mktg. and sales K-TRON Corp., Glassboro, NJ, 1975-78; dir. mktg. Transport Internat. Pool, Inc., Bala Cynwyd, Pa., 1978—. Home: 7 W Elm St Wenonah NJ 08090 Office: 2 Bala Cynwyd Plaza Bala Cynwyd PA 19004

MELINE, KONNIE LEE, real estate broker; b. Denver, May 13, 1947; d. Hersell Plant and LaVonne E. (Schulze) Linton; student Colo. State U., 1964-66, 68-69; m. Carl W. Meline, Apr. 16, 1966; children—Melinda Sue, Marc Tucker, Michael Scott. Real estate salesman SMR Real Estate W., Inc., Ft. Collins, Colo., 1975-76, real estate broker, 1976-79; v.p., broker asso. The Meline Co., Ft. Collins, 1979-80; broker/mgr. Rocky Mountain Realtors Gallery of Homes, Rifle, Colo., 1980—; owner Interiors by Konnie, Ft. Collins, 1979—. Grad. Realtors Inst., 1976. Mem. Ft. Collins Bd. Realtors (pres. 1980), Colo. Assn. Realtors, Multiple Listing Service (chmn. 1981), Alpha Chi Omega. Republican. Lutheran. Office: 125 W 4th St Suite 208 Rifle CO 81650

MELLAM, LEO LESLIE, leasing co. exec.; b. Comstock, Nebr., July 1, 1906; s. Charles and Jennie Myrtle (Reynolds) M.; grad. high sch.; m. Laural Darlene Carey, May 1, 1926; children—Marilyn Darlene (Mrs. Douglas Alan Rogers). Chmn. bd., chief exec. officer, dir. Flexi-Van Corp., N.Y.C., 1971—. Founder, Leo L. and Laural D. Mellam Found. Clubs: Westchester Country; New York Traffic, New York Athletic. Home: 425 E 58th St New York NY 10022 Office: 330 Madison Ave New York NY 10017

MELLEBY, ROY ALBERT, JR., mfg. co. ofcl.; b. S.I., N.Y., Jan. 22, 1946; s. Roy Albert and Gertrude Melleby; student Cath. U. Am., 1964-66; B.A. in Sociology, St. Peters Coll., 1968; M.B.A. in Mktg. and Stats., U. Oreg., 1977; m. Debra Jean Bechtold, Dec. 20, 1979. Sales rep. Procter & Gamble Co., Portland, Oreg., 1977-78, Tacoma, 1978-80, 3M Co., Seattle, 1980—. Active Jr. Achievement. Served with USN, 1968-71. Mem. MENSA. Home: Route 2 Box 509-G Tacoma WA 98424 Office: 100 Andover Park W PO Box C-34350 Seattle WA 98124

MELLISH, EUGENE DAVID, constrn. co. exec.; b. Bradys Bend, Pa., Sept. 11, 1923; s. Ludwig William and Lula Virginia (Boltz) M.; B.S. in Civil Engring., U. Conn., 1947; m. Nancy Florence Dole, June 10, 1946; children—Virginia, Sarah Alvord, Eugene David. Designer, Jackson & Moreland Engrs., Boston, 1947-50; chief engr. Fabricated Steel Products Co., Wollaston, Mass., 1950-63, Haynes, Lieneck & Smith, Fitchburg, Mass., 1963-64; v.p., chief engr. The MacMillin Co. Inc., Keene, N.H., 1964—; structural design cons., 1950—. Mem. Lincoln (Mass.) Sch. Bldg. Com., 1958; chmn. bd. trustees Unitarian-Universalist Ch., Keene, 1967, mem. investment com., 1973—; commr., chmn. Keene Housing Authority, 1969-74; mem. investment com. Vis. Nurse Assn., Keene, 1973—. Served with C.E., U.S. Army, 1943-46; PTO. Registered profl. engr., Maine, N.H., Mass.; registered fall-out shelter analyst. Mem. Asso. Builders and Contractors (apprentice com. 1972—), Asso. Gen. Contractors., Nat. Assn. Investment Clubs. Home: Gunn Rd RD 2 Box 387I Keene NH 03431 Office: 17 Elm St Keene NH 03431

MELLO, JUDY HENDRON, banker; b. Okla., July 14, 1943; d. Ed V. and Dorothy M. (Schoggen) Hendren; B.A., Muskingum Coll., 1965; postgrad. Johns Hopkins U., 1969; m. Marcus V. Ce Albuquerque e Mello, June 23, 1973. Planning officer Latin Am., 1st Nat. City Bank, 1969-72; v.p., sr. rep. Marine Midland Bank, Brazil, 1973-79, v.p. internat. treasury mgmt., 1980; pres. The First Women's Bank, N.Y.C., 1980—. Bd. dirs. Brazilian Cultural Found., Am. C. of C., Rio de Janeiro. Office: 111 E 57th St New York NY 10022

MELLOR, JAMES ROBB, electronics co. exec.; b. Detroit, May 3, 1930; s. Clifford and Gladys (Robb) M.; B.S. in Elec. Engring. and Math., U. Mich., 1952, M.S., 1953; m. Suzanne Stykos, June 8, 1953; children—James Robb, Diane Elyse, Deborah Lynn. Mem. tech. staff Hughes Aircraft Co., Fullerton, Calif., 1955-58; pres. Data Systems div. Litton Industries, Van Nuys, Calif., after 1958; sr. v.p. Litton Industries, Inc., Beverly Hills, Calif.; now pres., chief operating officer AM Internat., Inc., Los Angeles; dir. Bergen Brunswig Corp., Kerr Glass Mfg. Corp. Bd. councilors Sch. Bus. and Grad. Sch. Bus. Adminstrn., U. So. Calif.; bd. dirs. Hollywood Presbyn. Med. Center Found. Served to 1st lt., Signal Corps, U.S. Army, 1953-55. Mem. IEEE, Am. Mgmt. Assn., Computer and Bus. Equipment Mfrs. Assn. (chmn. bd. dirs.), Armed Forces Communication and Electronics Assn. (dir.), Sigma Xi, Tau Beta Pi, Eta Kappa Nu, Phi Kappa Phi. Club: Los Angeles Country. Contbr. articles to profl. publs. Patentee fields of storage tubes and display systems. Office: AM Internat Inc 1900 Ave of Stars Los Angeles CA 90067

MELNICK, MARTIN, bus. machines mfg. co. ofcl.; b. Pitts., July 16, 1949; s. Henry and Mollie M.; B.A., Pa. State U., 1970. Sales mgr. Hoover Co., Pitts., 1970-75, Royal Typewriter Co., 1975-78; product mgr. Royal Bus. Machines Co., Hartford, Conn., 1978-79, internat. product mgr., 1979—. Nat. account fund raiser Conn. Public TV, 1979. Recipient Service award Conn. Public TV, 1979. Mem. Am. Mgmt. Assn. Democrat. Pioneer in color coded keytops to electronic calculator industry. Home: 164 Whitney St Hartford CT 06105 Office: 150 New Park Ave Hartford CT 06106

MELNITCHENKO, EUGENE, investment co. exec.; b. Ukraine, Mar. 8, 1937; s. B.A., City U. N.Y., 1966; M.A., N.Y. U., 1973, M.B.A., 1973; m. Valentina, Jan. 22, 1961; children—Dereck, Mark. With U.S. Trust Co. N.Y., N.Y.C., 1961-73, 74-79, v.p., 1975-79; v.p. Eberstadt Asset Mgmt., N.Y.C., 1980—; asst. to pres. ICN Pharms., Irvine, N.Y.C., 1973-74. Served with USMC, 1955-58. Certified fin. analyst. Mem. Security Analysts, Inst. Chartered Fin. Analysts, Am. Chem Soc., Med. Group N.Y., Chem. Analysts N.Y. Home: 143 Kilburn Rd Garden City NY 11530 Office: 61 Broadway New York NY 10006

MELONAS, PETER CONSTANTINE, communications co., exec.; b. Chgo., Apr. 12 1941; s. Gust Peter and Marie (Athens) M.; B.A., DePaul U., 1964. Personnel asst. corporate coll. relations Sinclair Oil Co. (merger Atlantic Richfield Co. 1968), 1968, personnel asst., 1968-69, personnel coordinator recruitment, tng. minority affairs internat. div., 1969-72; mgr. personnel Interpublic Group Cos. Inc., N.Y.C., 1972-75, dir. mktg. recruitment, 1975-78; v.p., dir. personnel Kenyon & Eckhardt, N.Y.C., 1978-79; v.p., dir. recruitment worldwide KM&G (Ketchum, MacLeod & Grove) Internat. Inc., Chgo., 1979—. Served with Peace Corps, 1964-66. Eastern Orthodox. Club: Masons. Contbr. articles to Esquire mag. Home: 1560 N Sandburg Terr Chicago IL 60610 Office: KM&G Internat Inc 233 N Michigan Ave Chicago IL 60601

MELTON, ANDREW J., JR., investment banker; b. Bay Shore, N.Y., Mar. 4, 1920; s. Andrew J. and Alice (Lonergan) M.; B.S., Villanova U., 1942; m. Mary Ann Shanks, Sept. 18, 1943; children—Diana, Andrew, Robert, Karen, Marjorie, Michaelle, Edward. With Smith, Barney & Co. Inc., N.Y.C., 1946-72, partner, 1958-72, dir., 1974-72, sr. v.p., 1965-67, exec. v.p., 1967-72, chmn. exec. com., 1968-72; exec. v.p. Dean Witter Reynolds Inc., N.Y.C., 1972-77, vice chmn. bd., 1977, chmn. bd., chief exec. officer, 1977—, chmn. exec. com., 1977-79; mem. adv. bd. Bankers Trust Co.; mem. nominating com. Am. Stock Exchange; mem. Pacific Coast Stock Exchange, Chgo. Bd. Trade. Served with USMCR 1942-46, 51-53; maj. Res (ret.). Mem. Investment Bankers Assn. Am. (pres. 1970), Securities Industry Assn. (governing council, dir., exec. com.). Clubs: Bond, Board Room, Knickerbocker, Links, Madison Square Garden, Pilgrims, Recess (N.Y.C.); Beach, Jupiter Hills, Old Port Cove Yacht, West Palm Beach Fishing (Fla.); Dorset Field, Ekwanok Country (Vt.). Office: Dean Witter Reynolds Inc 130 Liberty St New York NY 10006

MELTON, CLAUDIS EDWARD, aerospace engr.; b. Kemp, Tex., Feb. 26, 1937; s. Robert Edward and Mary Inez (Bowers) M.; B.S., E. Tex. State U., 1960, M.S., 1964; cert. ednl. achievement in real estate U. Colo., 1974; m. Janie Glenn, June 29, 1956; 1 dau., Terri Lynn. Research scientist Douglas Aircraft, missiles and space div., Santa Monica, Calif., 1960-67; staff engr. Martin Marietta Corp., aerospace div., Denver, 1967-73; owner Sears Roebuck & Co. Catalog Store, Brush, Colo., 1974-78; owner, broker Melton Realty, Brush, Colo., 1976-78; aerospace engr. Martin Marietta Aerospace, 1980—. Campaign com. chmn. United Way, Brush dist., 1975; com. chmn. Summer Parks Program, Brush Centennial-Bicentennial, 1976. Recipient Grad. Teaching asst. award E. Tex. State U., 1960, Outstanding Profl. Achievement awards Douglas Aircraft, 1962-64. Democrat. Presbyterian. Home: 6428 S Harlan Way Littleton CO 80123

MELTON, H. BURT, banker; b. Henrietta, N.C., Apr. 9, 1942; s. Horace M. and Edna E. (James) M.; B.A., Wake Forest U., 1964; postgrad. advanced mgmt. program Harvard U., 1979; m. Phyllis Davidson, Sept. 9, 1962; children—Brooks, Patrick, Craig. Trainee, 1st Union Nat. Bank, 1966, br. mgr., Charlotte, N.C., 1966-67, comml. loan officer, 1968, head Charlotte brs., 1969, city exec., Kannapolis, N.C., 1970, Fayetteville, N.C., 1971-73, area exec., 1974-75, regional exec. v.p., 1975—. Bd. dirs. Fayetteville Planning Commn., 1973-74; v.p. United Way, Fayetteville, 1974; pres.-elect. Fayetteville Mus. Art, 1980; chmn. diaconite Highland Presbyn. Ch. Mem. Am. Bankers Assn., N.C. Bankers Assn., Fayetteville C. of C. (pres. 1975). Club: Highland Country. Office: 200 Green St Fayetteville NC 28302

MELTON, RUSSELL DEAN, mfg. co. exec.; b. Lumberton, N.C., June 3, 1945; s. Everett Dean and Edna Marian Melton; student U. Minn., 1969-72, B.A., 1977; postgrad. William Mitchell Coll. of Law, 1978—. Sr. electronics technician Control Data Corp., Mpls., 1972-78; corp. personnel dir./mgr. Camera div., Photo Control Corp., Mpls., 1978-80; safety dir./loss/control Pako Corp., Mpls., 1980—; pres. Dwarf Engring. & Mfg.; cons. in field. Served with USN, 1963-69. Mem. Am. Soc. Personnel Adminstrn., Am. Soc. Quality Control, Am. Prodn. and Inventory Control Soc., Am. Mgmt. Assn., Soc. Mfg. Engrs., Am. Soc. Safety Engrs., Am. Bar Assn., U.S. Submarine Vets. WW II, U.S. Submarine Vets. Inc. Office: 6300 Olson Memorial Hwy Minneapolis MN 55440

MELUCCI, RICHARD ALLEN, printing co. exec.; b. Detroit, Nov. 23, 1949; s. Evo Joseph and Doreen Hilda (Woodcock) M.; student Macomb County Community Coll., 1977; m. Roberta Eve Bevan, May 6, 1972; children—Scott Allen, Amy Lynn, Wendy Michelle. With Atom Print Shop Inc., Warren, Mich., 1968—, supt., 1972-73, v.p., 1973—. Mem. Tri County Printers Council (founder), Detroit Sportsmens Congress, S.E. Mich. Amateur Radio Assn., Amateur Radio Relay League. Lutheran. Office: 23045 Ryan St Warren MI 48091

MELVILLE, DONALD ROBERT, indsl. products mfg. co. exec.; b. Manchester, Eng., Nov. 18, 1926; came to U.S., 1956, naturalized, 1966; s. Robert and Minnie (Veitch) M.; B.A., Queen's Coll., Cambridge (Eng.) U., 1950, M.A., 1951; M.B.A., Harvard U., 1956; m. Mary H. Sutton, June 16, 1955; children—Wendy F., Jennifer K. Salesman, Dunlop Rubber Co., London, 1951-54; asst. to v.p. Continental Can Co., N.Y.C., 1956-60, sales mgr., 1962-67; market analysis mgr. Scott Paper Co., Phila., 1960-62; with Norton Co., Worcester, Mass., 1967—, exec. v.p., 1971-78, pres., 1979—, chief operating officer, 1979-80, chief exec. officer, 1980—, also dir.; dir. New Eng. Life Mut. Funds, Chemplast, Inc., Wayne, N.J. Chmn., Worcester City Mgr.'s Adv. Com. on Arts, 1971-77; mem. Mass. Council on Arts and Humanities, 1977—; trustee Radcliffe Coll. Served with RAF, 1945-48. Mem. Am. Mktg. Assn., Am. Mgmt. Assn., Am. Antiquarian Soc., Bus. Roundtable, Mass. Bur. Roundtable (dir.), Machinery and Allied Products Inst. (exec. com.). Office: 1 New Bond St Worcester MA 01606

MELVIN, ARTHUR FRANK, mgmt. cons.; b. Marion, Ill., Dec. 21, 1948; s. Arthur Frank and Virginia (Bracy) M.; B.S. in Econs., Purdue U., 1970; M.B.A., So. Meth. U., 1971; m. Doretha Eileen Ort, Oct. 23, 1975. Vice pres. Griffin Mgmt. Services, Inc., Tulsa, 1972-74; asst. dir. for adminstrv. computer services So. Meth. U., Dallas, 1974-79; exec. v.p. Software & Communication Concepts, Inc., Houston, 1979-80, now dir.; prin. Arthur F. Melvin Consulting, Houston, 1980—; dir. Surger Bay, Inc., Heber Springs, Ark. Mem. Data Processing Mgmt. Assn., Ind. Computer Consultants Am. Club: Nottingham Country Civic (v.p.). Office: 4801 Woodway Suite 300E Houston TX 77079

MELVIN, RICHARD HUGH, retail trade exec.; b. Pontiac, Mich., Mar. 8, 1924; s. Charles Lester and Florence Hazel (Lynch) M.; B.B.A., Gen. Motors Inst., 1952; m. Virginia Jo Gean, Feb. 26, 1949; children—Daryl Lynn, Melissa Sue, Leslie Gail. Vice-pres. Sahlin Engring. Co., Birmingham, Mich., 1954-60; divisional plant mgr. Kux Machine div. Wickes Corp., Chgo., 1960-65; pres. Melvin Corp., Bay City, Mich., 1965-70; exec. v.p., dir. Benjamin Mill & Lumber Co., Rose City, Mich., 1970-71; v.p., operating officer, dir. Melvin-Fitzgerald Homecenter, Inc., Walled Lake, Mich., 1972—, Melvin-Fitzgerald Huron Valley Hardware Inc., Melvin-Fitzgerald Supply Co. Councilman, Wolverine Lake Village, 1958-59; distributive edn. adv. com. Oakland County Schs., Pontiac, Mich., 1974; mem. Walled Lake Planning Commn., 1973-74, Walled Lake Econ. Devel. Corp., 1979-80; bd. dirs., exec. v.p. Town and Country Land Devel. Corp., Rose City, Mich., 1970-71. Served with USMC, World War II. Mem. Soc. Die Cast Engrs., Am. Mgmt. Assn., Soc. Automotive Engrs. Lutheran (pres., bldg. chmn. 1959). Patentee in field. Home: 4487 Driftwood Milford MI 48042 Office: 970 W Maple St Walled Lake MI 48088

MEMHARD, RICHARD CLOW, investment banker; b. N.Y.C., Jan. 21, 1930; s. Allen Raymond and Judith (Atwater) M.; B.A., Yale U., 1951; M.B.A., Golden Gate Coll., 1957; m. Polly Ann Hunter, Apr. 5, 1952; children—Raymond Scott, Laura, Jennifer. Asst. treas. Chem. Bank N.Y., N.Y.C., 1957-59; gen. partner Hornblower & Weeks-Hemphill, Noyes, N.Y.C., 1959-68; pres. Shelter Resources Corp., N.Y.C., 1968-71; sr. v.p. corp. fin. G.H. Walker & Co. Inc., N.Y.C., 1971-73, also dir.; founder, chmn., pres. R.C. Memhard & Co., Inc., Stamford, Conn., 1973—; dir., mem. exec. com., audit com. Mich. Gen. Corp.; dir. MKT Corp. Served with USNR, 1951-54. Mem. Conn. Venture Group. Republican. Episcopalian. Club: Riverside Yacht. Office: 22 5th St Stamford CT 06905

MEMMER, FREDERICK PHILLIP, savs. and loan exec.; b. St. Paul, June 15, 1907; s. Phillip Louis and Lillian (Hoffmann) M.; B.A., U. Minn., 1929, J.D., 1931: m. Ellen S. Dube, May 31, 1934; children—Fred J., Mary (Mrs. Marvin Stoll), Louise (Mrs. D. Sabby), Karol (Mrs. R. Manfredini), Peter. Admitted to Minn. bar, 1931, since practiced in St. Paul, sr. partner firm Memmer, Caswell, Parks and Beck; organizer Lincoln Fed. Savs. & Loan Assn., 1951, pres., 1951-76, also dir.; emeritus dir. Home Savs. Mpls. Mem. Ramsey County Welfare Bd., 1952-55. Mem. Minn. Ho. of Reps., 1939-51, chmn. judiciary com., 1943-51. Pres. Riverview Meml. Hosp., 1950-52; bd. dirs. St. Croix Rev. of Religion and Soc., Stillwater, Minn. Mem. League Minn. Savs. and Loan Assns. (pres. 1973). K.C. Home: 666 Labore Rd Saint Paul MN 55117 Office: 1590 White Bear Ave Saint Paul MN 55106

MENCHER, ALEXANDER, lawyer; b. Bklyn., Sept. 30, 1902; s. Max and Anna (Weisman) M.; A.B., Columbia, 1923, A.M., 1924; J.D., N.Y.U., 1927; m. Mildred Heidt, Sept. 7, 1934; children—Howard, Bonnie. Admitted to N.Y. bar, 1928; mem. firm Merin & Mencher, N.Y.C., 1929-32, Juhass & Mencher, 1932-34; pvt. practice, N.Y.C., 1934—; v.p., gen. counsel Internat. Patent Exchange, Ltd.; patent and engring. counsel Modern Adhesives & Electronics, Inc. Mem. N.Y., Queens County bar assns., N.Y. Patent Law Assn., Columbia Engring. Sch. Alumni. Author articles in field. Home: 69-42 Ingram St Forest Hills NY 11375 Office: 150 Broadway New York NY 10038

MENDELBAUM, GERALD BRUCE, systems analyst; b. Pitts. Feb. 23, 1953; s. Morris and Louise (Levy) M.; B.S., Carnegie-Mellon U., 1975; M.B.A., U. Pitts., 1976; m. Lynn Pamela Hochhauser, Aug. 21, 1977. Systems analyst Burroughs Corp., Piscataway, N.J., 1976-79, sr. systems analyst Peripheral Products Group Staff, Detroit, 1979—. Mem. Zeta Beta Tau. Home: 26803 Berg Rd Apt 115 Southfield MI 48034 Office: 1 Burroughs Pl Room 4F27 Detroit MI 48232

MENDELSOHN, MAX LEWIS, pharm. co. exec.; b. Balt., May 16, 1933; s. Israel Mordeci and Rose (Silverman) M.; B.S., U. Md., 1955; m. Barbara Becker, Aug. 1, 1955; children—David Alan, Jeffrey Eric, Cheryl Lynn, Melissa Beth. Pres. Barre-Nat. Inc., Balt., 1970—, also pres. subsidiaries Nat. Pharm. Mfg. Co., Barre Drug Co., 1970—. Instl. rep. Balt. council Boy Scouts Am., 1970—; mem. Young Men's Leadership Council Asso. Jewish Charities; bd. dirs. Jewish Nat. Fund, 1980—. Served with AUS, 1955-57. Named Employer of Year Asso. Jewish Charities, 1968; recipient Merit awards Assn. Jewish Charities, 1969—; Boy Power-Man Power medal Boy Scouts Am., 1970, certificate of appreciation for outstanding service, 1970. Mem. Nat. Pharm. Alliance (pres. 1973-74), Am., Md. pharm. assns. Jewish (trustee congregation, v.p. Men's Club 1973-76, pres. club 1976-78; recipient Brotherhood award 1972). Home: 2313 Sugarcone Rd Baltimore MD 21209 Office: 7205 Windsor Blvd Baltimore MD 21207

MENDELSON, LAURANS A., real estate investor, developer, C.P.A.; b. N.Y.C., July 7, 1938; s. Samuel and Blanche (Lederer) M.; A.B., Columbia Coll., 1960; M.B.A., Columbia U., 1961; m. Arlene Lobel, Sept. 18, 1962; children—Eric Arthur, Victor Howard. C.P.A., Arthur Andersen & Co., N.Y.C., 1961-66, David Berdon, N.Y.C., 1966-67, Brimberg & Co., N.Y.C., 1968; real estate investor, developer, C.P.A., Miami, Fla., 1969—; dir. Internat. Bank of Miami, N.A. Patron, Greater Miami Opera Assn. Served with U.S. Army, 1962. C.P.A., N.Y., Fla. Mem. Am. Inst. C.P.A.'s, Fla. Inst. C.P.A.'s, N.Y. Soc. C.P.A.'s. Office: 9300 S Dadeland Blvd Miami FL 33156

MENDELSON, LEWIS AARON, appliance sales exec.; b. Pitts., Apr. 11, 1935; s. Mendel B. and Florence (Goldfarb) M.; B.B.A., U. Pitts., 1956; m. Catherine Anderson, Nov. 4, 1965; children—Matthew Dana, Grant Oliver, Andrew Shephard. Partner, DeMarcellus, Knowlten & Asso., West Palm Beach, Fla., 1958-59; v.p. Pressure Pak, Inc., West Palm Beach, 1960-65; sales mgr. Jet Air Products, Dallas, 1965; v.p. sales and mktg. Dazey Products Co., Kansas City, Mo., 1966—, also dir. Served with U.S. Army, 1956. Republican. Home: 9830 Briar Dr Overland Park KS 66207 Office: 1 Dazey Circle Industrial Airport KS 66031

MENDELSON, PHYLLIS CARMEL, editor; b. Cin., Dec. 27, 1929; d. A. Gerson and Cyrilla E. (Wallace) Carmel; B.A., Wellesley Coll., 1951; student Ohio State U., 1952-53, Wayne State U., 1970-72, Oakland U., Rochester, Mich., 1971, Tex. A&M U., 1978—; children—Michael, Joan, Susan. Tchr., Oakland County (Mich.) Schs., 1968-72; editorial asst. Gale Research Co., Detroit, 1972-73, asst. editor, 1973-74, asso. editor, 1974-75, editor, 1975—; editor GEO NEWS, Coll. Geoscis., Tex. A&M U., College Station, 1977—. Founding mem., chmn. Berkley (Mich.) Youth Assistance Com., 1964-68; mem. Oakland County (Mich.) Youth Adv. Council, 1964-70; mem. Oakland County Juvenile Ct. Legis. Adv. Com., 1966-70; mem. textbook rev. com. State of Tex.; bd. dirs. local LWV, 1962-68, 77—; trustee Brazos Valley Community Action Agy., 1979—; bd. dirs. Congregation Beth Shalom, 1979—. Mem. Internat. Assn. Bus. Communicators, Adult Edn. Assn. U.S.A., Am. Personnel and Guidance Assn., AAUW, NOW, Common Cause, Womens Polit. Caucus, Council Jewish Women, Alpha Kappa Delta, Phi Delta Gamma (sec. 1980—). Club: Altrusa (pres. 1980—). Editor: (with others) Contemporary Literary Criticism, Vols. 5-8, 1975-78, 20th Century Literary Criticism, Vol. 1, 1978; mng. editor Children's Lit. Rev., Vols. 1, 2, 1975-76. Home: 3902 E 29th St D3 Bryan TX 77801

MENDELSON, RALPH RICHARD, water heater mfg. co. exec.; b. Cleve., July 11, 1917; s. Louis Ralph and Ruth Margaret (Cohen) M.; B.S. in Mech. Engring., U. Mich., 1939; m. Mary Adelaide Jones, Feb. 22, 1941; children—Walton, Philip. With The Hotstream Heater Co., Cleve., 1941-61, v.p., 1948-59, pres., 1959-61; pres. Glass-Lined Water Heater Co., Lakewood, Ohio, 1961—. Mem. vis. com. humanities and arts Case Western Res. U., 1972-80; trustee Cleve. Urban League, 1957-61, Greater Cleve. Neighborhood Centers Assn., 1976-78; bd. dirs. Merrick House; del. Ohio White House Conf. on Library and Info. Services, 1978. Served to lt. USAAF, 1942-46. Mem. Oil Heat Inst. No. Ohio (dir. 1966-73), Heights C. of C. (dir. 1953-59), Assn. Energy Engrs. (charter). Club: Play House (Cleve.). Author: Solar Energy, 1978; patentee in field. Home: 3137 Fairmount Blvd Cleveland Heights OH 44118 Office: 13000 Athens Av Lakewood OH 44107

MENDENHALL, JOHN RYAN, lawyer, accountant; b. Des Moines, Jan. 17, 1928; s. Merritt Blake and Elizabeth (Ryan) M.; B.Sc., U. Notre Dame, 1950; J.D., Harvard, 1953; m. Joan Lois Schaefer, June 20, 1953; children—Thomas, James, Jane, Julie, Robert, Jennifer. With tax dept. Arthur Andersen & Co., C.P.A.'s, Cleve., 1953-66, partner, 1963-74, dir. taxes, Chgo., 1966-70, Washington, 1970-74; partner law firm Williams, Connolly & Califano, Washington, 1975-76; v.p. taxes, gen. tax counsel Union Pacific Corp., 1976—; professorial lectr. in law George Washington U.; mem. adv. bd. Bur. Nat. Affairs; chmn. Center for Policy Research. Mem. governing com. Cook County Hosp., 1968-71; trustee Convent of Sacred Heart, Greenwich, Conn.; bd. dirs. Am. Council on Capital Formation, 1972—, Center for Continuing Edn., 1975—; mem. exec. com. Com. for Effective Capital Recovery; mem. tax adv. group Tax Found. Mem. Am. (vice-chmn. spl. com. taxation and price indexing), D.C. bar assns., Am. Petroleum Inst. (gen. com. taxation), C. of C. U.S. (taxation com. 1977—), Am. Law Inst. (tax adv. group), Assn. Am. Railroads (tax policy com.), Western Oil and Gas Assn., Nat. Tax Assn. (fed. tax com., dir.). Roman Catholic. Clubs: Harvard (N.Y.C.); Belle Haven (Greenwich, Conn.); Met. (Washington). Co-author: Reforming the Federal Tax Structure, 1973; contbr. articles to tech. tax jours. Home: 144 North St Greenwich CT 06830 Office: 345 Park Ave New York NY 10022

MENDEZ, MANNY, banker; b. Havana, Cuba, Sept. 15, 1952; came to U.S., 1956, naturalized, 1964; s. Manuel V. and Esther B. (Fernandez) M.; A.A. in Bus. and Fin., San Antonio State U., 1972; A.A. in Computer Programming, Los Angeles Valley Coll., 1975; m. Christine A. Berg, Feb. 24, 1980. Dist. fin. mgr. CITI Bank Corp., Los Angeles, 1974—, employee tng. mgr., 1974—. Served to 1st lt. U.S. Army, 1972-74; Vietnam. Decorated Congl. Medal of Honor, Purple Heart. Mem. Nat. Pilots Assn., U.S. Sky Diving Assn. Roman Catholic. Home: 6004 Cahuenga Blvd North Hollywood CA 91606 Office: CIT Financial Services 12116 Sylvan St North Hollywood CA 91606

MENENDEZ, CARLOS, banker; b. Cuba, Apr. 16, 1938; came to U.S., 1960, naturalized, 1968; s. Ramon and Rita (Leon) M.; law degree Nat. U. Cuba, 1960; B.B.A., N.Y. U., 1971; m. Teresa Moran, Oct. 28, 1960; 1 dau., Maria Teresa. With Irving Trust Co., N.Y.C., 1963—, v.p. internat. group, Latin Am. div., 1971—. Mem. N.Y. U. Alumni Assn. Roman Catholic. Home: 40 The Hemlocks Roslyn Estates NY 11576 Office: 1 Wall St New York NY 10015

MENGEL, PHILIP RICHARD, investment banker; b. Memphis, Oct. 30, 1944; s. John Philip and Marjorie Ann Mengel; A.B., Princeton U., 1968, undergrad cert. Woodrow Wilson Sch. Public and Internat. Affairs, 1968; m. Jayne E. Frutig, Dec. 20, 1980. With Fiduciary Trust Co. N.Y., N.Y.C., 1968-77, v.p., 1971-77, mem. exec. com., 1974-77; pres. Fiduciary Investment Corp., N.Y.C., 1973-77; founder, pres. Mengel, McCabe & Co., Inc., N.Y.C., 1978—. Trustee, St. Stephen's Sch., Rome, 1976—, chmn. bd. trustees, 1978—. Episcopalian. Clubs: Racquet and Tennis, Down Town Assn., Princeton (N.Y.C.). Home: 300 Central Park W New York NY 10024 Office: One Rockefeller Plaza New York NY 10020

MENGER, RICHARD ALLEN, banker; b. Victoria, Tex., Apr. 15, 1942; s. James Joffre and Lucille (Livingston) Colglazier; B.A., U. Tex., Austin, 1964; M.B.A., U. Tex., San Antonio, 1975; sr. bank officers seminar Grad. Sch. Bus., Harvard U., others; m. Mary Deborah Bass, June 3, 1966; children—Catherine B., Lucy M. With Frost Nat. Bank, San Antonio, 1968-75, v.p., mgr. mktg. research and planning, 1974-75; sr. v.p., mgr. corporate planning and devel., exec. com. Bexar County Nat. Bank, San Antonio, 1975—; instr. Coll. Bus., San Antonio Coll., 1975—, Am. Inst. Banking, 1971—. Trustee, treas. exec. com. S.W. Tex. Public Broadcasting Council, 1976-80; trustee Tex. Opera Theater; mem. San Antonio Zool. Soc., San Antonio Symphony Soc., San Antonio Art League, San Antonio Mus. Assn., Arts Council San Antonio, Tex. Arts Alliance; bd. dirs. Bexar County chpt. ARC, 1978-79. Served with USAF, 1960-62. Mem. Bank Mktg. Assn. (dir. Gulf coast chpt.), Houston Advt. Club, Republic Tex. Mktg. Council, Tex. Bankers Assn. (mktg. com.), U. Tex. Ex-students Assn., Harvard Coop. Soc. Republican. Episcopalian. Clubs: St. Anthony, San Antonio German, Christmas Cotillion, Conopus, Univ. Home: 233 Alta San Antonio TX 78209 Office: PO Box 300 San Antonio TX 78241

MENGERS, PAUL EUGENE, electronics mfg. co. exec.; b. Kenmare, N.D., May 25, 1927; s. Ethan T.C. and Catherine Emily (Jensen) M.; B.A., Dana Coll., 1950; postgrad. U. Wash., 1952-55, 56-57; m. Ardis Anine Gramps, Dec. 11, 1949; children—Pamela Anine, Kathryn Ann, Candace Louise. Research engr. Boeing Airplane Co., Seattle, 1955-58, Gen. Electric Co., Ithaca, N.Y., 1958-60; group leader Armour Research Found., Chgo., 1960-61; engring. mgr. Optics Tech., Inc., Belmont, Calif., 1961-63, Dalmo Victor, Belmont, 1963-67, Sylvania Electro-Optics Orgn., Mountain View, Calif., 1967-70; dir. product research Comml. Electronics, Inc., Mountain View, 1970-73; pres. Quantex Corp., Sunnyvale, Calif., 1973—; tech. cons., 1973—. Served with USN, 1945-46. Mem. IEEE, Soc. Photo-Optical Instrumentation Engrs. Contbr. articles in field of electro-optics to profl. jours. and trade mags.; patentee in field of electro-optics. Home: 1712 William Henry Ct Los Altos CA 94022 Office: 252 N Wolfe Rd Sunnyvale CA 94086

MENK, LOUIS WILSON, r.r. exec.; b. Englewood, Colo., Apr. 8, 1918; s. Louis A. and Daisy Deane (Frantz) M.; student U. Denver, 1937-39, Harvard, 1953, Northwestern U., 1959; LL.D., Drury Coll., 1965, Denver U., 1966, Monmouth Coll., 1967; m. Martha Jane Swan, May 30, 1942; children—David Louis, Barbara Ann. Telegraph messenger U.P. R.R., Denver, 1937-39, telegrapher, 1939-40; various positions from telegrapher to v.p., gen. mgr., Springfield, Mo., 1940-60, v.p. operations, dir. St. L.-S.F. Ry., St. Louis, 1960-62, pres., dir., 1962-65, pres., chmn., 1965; pres., chmn. exec. com. Chgo., Burlington & Quincy R.R., Colo. & So. Ry., Ft. Worth & Denver Ry., 1965-66; pres., dir. No. Pacific Ry., St. Paul, 1966-70; pres., dir. Burlington No. Inc., St. Paul, 1970-71, chmn., chief exec. officer, 1971-78, chmn., 1978-80, also dir.; dir. 1st Nat. Bank of Chgo., Gen. Mills, Inc., Mpls., Internat. Harvestor, ASARCO, Minn. Mut. Life Ins. Co., St. Paul. Trustee, U. Denver, Conf. Bd. Presbyterian. Clubs: Masons; Desert Forest (Ariz.); Chgo., Petroleum, Yellowstone Country (Billings, Mont.). Home: 2751 Gregory Dr S Billings MT 59102 Office: 1st Northwestern Bank Center Suite 600 Billings MT 59101

MENKE, JOHN D., fin. cons.; b. Amarillo, Tex., June 14, 1942; s. John D. and Mary M.; B.A., U. Tex., 1964; LL.B., Yale U., 1967; m. Nancy Gilbert, Mar. 20, 1978; children—Eric, Lara. Admitted to Calif. bar, 1968; pres. Menke & Assos., Inc., San Francisco; gen. partner silver mining partnerships. Author book; also articles. Home: 129 Calvert Ct Piedmont CA 94611 Office: 235 Montgomery St San Francisco CA 94104

MENNELLA, VINCENT ALFRED, automotive and airplane co. exec.; b. Teaneck, N.J., Oct. 7, 1922; s. Francis Anthony and Henrietta Vernard (Dickson) M.; B.A. in Acctg., U. Wash., 1948; m. Madeleine Olson, Aug. 18, 1945; children—Bruce, Cynthia, Mark, Scott, Chris. Sales and bus. mgmt. positions Ford div. Ford Motor Co., 1949-55; founder, pres. Southgate Ford, Seattle, 1955—, also exec. v.p. Flightcraft, Inc., Seattle, 1973—; pres. Stanley Garage Door Co. Former chmn. March of Dimes. Served to capt. USN, 1942-45. Republican. Roman Catholic. Clubs: Rainier Golf, Seattle Tennis, Wash. Athletic, Rotary (past pres.). Home: 1400 SW 171st Pl Seattle WA 98166 Office: 14500 1st Ave S Seattle WA 98168

MENNELLA-ZARRA, JO-ANN VICTORIA, ins. agt. and broker; b. Bklyn., Nov. 2, 1948; s. Augustine A. and Josephine (Alonge) M.; student Hofstra U., 1971-72; m. Anthony C. Zarra, Nov. 25, 1978. Sec., Continental Can Co., N.Y.C., 1968-73; textile converter Garrison Industries, N.Y.C., 1973-74, Tandem Textiles, N.Y.C., 1974-76; owner, agt.-broker Mennella Ins. Service, Middle Village, N.Y.C., 1976—. Mem. Ins. Women's Assn. Queens. Office: 65-50 Metropolitan Ave Middle Village NY 11379

MENSCHER, BARNET GARY, steel co. exec.; b. Laurelton, N.Y., Sept. 5, 1940; s. Samuel and Louise (Zaimont) M.; student Centenary Coll., 1958-59; B.B.A., U. Tex., 1963; m. Diane Elaine Gachman, June 12, 1966; children—Melissa Denise, Corey Lane, Scott Jay. Vice pres. mktg. Ella Gant Mfg., Shreveport, La., 1964-66; warehouse mgr., dir. material control Gachman Steel Co., Fort Worth, 1966-68, gen. mgr., Houston, 1968-70, v.p., sales mgr. Gulf Coast, 1971-76; pres. Menko Steel Service, Inc., Houston, 1979—; v.p., treas. Gachman Metal Co.; investment cons. D & L Enterprises, 1966—. Mem. solicitation com. United Fund, 1969-76; mem. Nat. Alliance of Businessmen Jobs Program, 1969—. Served with AUS, 1963-65. Mem. Tex. Assn. Steel Importers, Purchasing Agts. Assn. Houston, Credit Assn. Houston, Am. Mgmt. Assn., Assn. Steel Distbrs., Phi Sigma Delta, Alpha Phi Omega. Home: 314 Tealwood Dr Houston TX 77024 Office: PO Box 40296 Houston TX 77040

MENSINGER, ROBERT MICHAEL, lumber co. exec.; b. Modesto, Calif., Aug. 5, 1932; s. William Robert and Jane Marshall (Nichol) M.; student Stanford U., 1951-52; B.A., Coll. of Pacific, 1959; m. Dawn Elaine Schmid, Sept. 1, 1953; children—Stephanie Ann, Marilyn Elaine, Stephen Marshall. Pres., Valley Insulation Co., Stockton, Calif., 1956-72; sec., div. mgr. Schmid Devel., Inc., Irvine, Calif., 1972-75; treas., dir. Am. Lumber Co., Modesto, Calif., 1975—; dir., sec. Boreal Ridge Corp., Truckee, Calif., 1965-79. Pres., United Way, Modesto, 1981; mem. state aid rev. com. Modesto Unified Sch. Dist., 1979; dist. treas., council dir. Boy Scouts Am., 1978-80. Served with USAF, 1952-56. Mem. Sales and Mktg. Execs., Modesto C. of C., Stockton C. of C., Lumber Mchts. Assn. No. Calif., Builders Exchange of Stockton (past dir.). Republican. Episcopalian. Clubs: Rotary (dir. 1980—), Trade (dir. 1976—), Stockton Engrs. (pres. 1971), Masons. Home: 7018 N Parkridge Ct Modesto CA 95355 Office: 9th and M Sts Modesto CA 95354

MENTEN, THOMAS HENRY, bus. exec.; b. Chgo., Feb. 6, 1926; s. Thomas Henry and Gladys Elizabeth (Keller) M.; student Holy Cross Coll., 1943-44; B.S. in Bus. Adminstrn., Boston Coll., 1948; postgrad. Mich. State U.; m. Greer Melling, June 9, 1976; children—Thomas Grant, Lawrence Edwin, Paul Christopher, Elizabeth Holly, Eric Keller, Eugenie Grace, Nils Christian. With Swift and Co., Somerville, Mass., Omaha, N.Y.C., 1948-60, Hunt Foods and Industries, Elizabeth, N.J., 1960-61; with Dunham and Smith Agencies, Inc., Greenwich, Conn., 1961-76, product sales mgr., 1978—; with MilBrands, Stamford, N.Y., 1976-78. Served with USN, 1943-46. Recipient Founders award Swift and Co., 1955. Mem. Def. Supply Assn., Sales Execs. Club N.Y. Clubs: Rotary (chmn. program com. Greenwich 1979, dir. 1980-81). Office: Dunham and Smith Agencies Inc 39 Lewis St Greenwich CT 06830

MENTKOWSKI, LAWRENCE JOHN, mfg. co. exec.; b. Buffalo, Mar. 21, 1953; s. Leo John and Alice Stephanie (Wisniewski) M.; B.S. in Mgmt., State U. N.Y., 1975, M.B.A., 1977; m. Elizabeth Jean Gow, May 5, 1979; children—Aaron David, Brooke Elizabeth. Market research analyst Plastics div. Carborundum Co., Niagara Falls, N.Y., 1976, supr. document control Bonded Abrasives div., 1977, prodn. control mgr., 1978-79, mfg. systems and finished goods inventory mgr. Bonded Abrasives div., 1979—. Mem. Assn. M.B.A. Execs., Am. Prodn. and Inventory Control Soc., AAU, Carborundum Mgmt. Club (chpt. pres.). Home: 733 Wurlitzer Dr North Tonawanda NY 14120 Office: Carborundum Co Bldg 30H-2 Buffalo Ave Niagara Falls NY 14302

MENZ, WILLIAM WOLFGANG, research co. exec.; b. Zweibruecken, Germany, Mar., 1917; came to U.S., 1939, naturalized, 1944; s. Michael Rudolf and Rosel (Butzel) M.; B.S., U. Munich, 1937, M.S., 1939; postgrad. Ohio State U., 1949-50; m. Gertrude Weissman, May 17, 1941; children—Roberta Menz Suhrbier, Paul Fred. Br. chief intelligence dept. USAAF, Dayton, Ohio, 1946-50; editor USPHS, Cin., 1950-51; tech. info. analyst Gen. Aniline & Film Corp., Easton, Pa., 1951-52, Ethyl Corp., Detroit, 1952-57; sect. chief R.J. Reynolds Industries, Winston-Salem, N.C., 1957-70; v.p. research, exec. sec. Dairy Research Inc., Rosemont, Ill., 1970—. Served with USAAF, 1941-45. Mem. Am. Chem. Soc. (sect. chmn. 1962), Soc. Tech. Writers and Editors (pres. 1960), Am. Dairy Sci. Assn., AIAA, Sigma Xi. Home: 111 S Baybrook Dr Apt 603 Palatine IL 60067 Office: Dairy Research Inc 6300 N River Rd Rosemont IL 60018

MERAR, ERWIN JEROME, distbg. co. exec.; b. Green Bay, Wis., Jan. 19. 1924; s. Marcus C and Sadye (Rosenberg) M.; student St. Norberts Coll., 1942-43, Bard Coll., 1943-44, U. Wis., 1945-47; m. Emma Lee Stern, Jan. 5, 1952; children—David L., Robert M. Advt. mgr. Humphrey Chevrolet Co., Milw., 1947-49; dir. advt. Samson Appliance Stores, 1949-54; v.p. Standard Electric Supply Co., Milw., 1954-70; pres. Mid-Am. Acceptance Corp., 1960-70, now dir.; pres. Ader Corp., 1962—, Summit Tower Corp., 1958—, Merco Corp., 1970—, CC Refractories, 1980—. Served with AUS, 1942-45. Mem. Am. Legion, Zeta Beta Tau Alumni Club. Mason (32 deg.), Shriner. Club: Wisconsin. Home: 825 Autumn Path Ln Bayside WI 53217 Office: Merco Corp PO Box 12145 4080 N Port Washington Rd Milwaukee WI 53212

MERCER, GEORGE RILEY, JR., bus. exec., investor; b. Richmond, Va., Aug. 22, 1946; s. George Riley and Mary Rutherfoord (Rose) M.; student U. N.C., Chapel Hill, 1965-67; B.S., U. Ga., Athens, 1968, postgrad., 1968-69; m. Marsha Dale Tatum, Apr. 29, 1972; children—Tinsley Randolph, Dabney Winston. Vice pres., dir. Mercer Rug and Carpet Co. Inc., Richmond, 1969—, George-Marshall Real Estate Investment Corp., Richmond, 1970—, Victory Rug and Carpet Co. Inc., Richmond, 1970—; pres., trustee, dir. Airport Properties Co., Richmond, 1974—. Bd. dirs. Va. League Planned Parenthood, 1973—, Richmond br. English Speaking Union, 1975—, Jamestowne Soc., Richmond, 1975—, Friends of Elk Hill Boys Farm, Goochland, Va., 1977—; historian Clan Rose Soc., 1974—. Recipient Disting. Service award Va. League Planned Parenthood, 1974. Mem. West Richmond Businessmen's Assn. (dir.), Va. Hist. Soc., Assn. Preservation Va. Antiquities, Order First Families Va. 1607-1624, Descs. Most Noble Order Knights of Garter, Baronial Order Magna Charta, Ams. Royal Descent, Va. Mus., Valentine Mus., Zeta Psi. Episcopalian. Clubs: Country of Va., Commonwealth, Deep Run Hunt (Richmond); Farmington Country (Charlottesville, Va.); Rotary. Home: 4811 Cary St Rd Richmond VA 23226 Office: 3116-20 W Moore St Richmond VA 23230

MERCER, ROBERT E., tire co. exec.; b. Elizabeth, N.J., 1924; grad. Yale U., 1946; married. With Goodyear Tire & Rubber Co., 1947—, asst. to pres., 1973-74, pres. Kelly-Springfield Tire Co. subs., 1974-76, corp. exec. v.p., pres. tire div., 1976-78, corp. pres., 1978—, chief operating officer, 1980—, also dir. Served with U.S. Navy, World War II. Office: 1144 E Market St Akron OH 44316

MERCHANT, MYLON EUGENE, engr., physicist; b. Springfield, Mass., May 6, 1913; s. Mylon Dickinson and Rebecca Chase (Currier) M.; B.S. magna cum laude, U. Vt., 1936, D.Sc. honoris causa, 1973; fellow U. Cin., 1936-40, D.Sc., 1941; D.Sc. honoris causa, U. Salford (Eng.), 1980; m. Helen S. Bennett, Aug. 4, 1937; children—Mylon David, Leslie Ann, Frances Sue. Research physicist Cin. Milacron, Inc., 1940-51, asst. dir. research, 1951-57, dir. phys. research, 1957-63, dir. sci. research, 1963-69, dir. research planning, 1969—; vis. prof. mech. engring. U. Salford (Eng.), 1973—. Active Boy Scouts Am. Recipient Nat. award Am. Soc. Lubrication Engrs., 1959; Richards Meml. award ASME, 1959; Research Medal award Soc. Mfg. Engrs., 1968; Distinguished Alumnus award U. Cin., 1969; Polish Inst. Metal Cutting medal, 1971; Disting. Contbns. award San Fernando Valley Engrs. Council, 1975; George Schlesinger prize City of Berlin, 1980; AM award Am. Machinist mag., 1980; named Cin. Engr. of Year, 1955; registered profl. engr., Ohio, Calif.; certified mfg. engr. Fellow Instn. Prodn. Engrs. (U.K.) (hon.; Tribology medal 1980), Am. Soc. Metals, Ohio Acad. Scis., Inst. Advancement of Engring.; mem. ASME (hon. mem.; v.p. 1973-75), Nat. Acad. Engring., Engring. Soc. Cin. (pres. 1961-62), Internat. Inst. Prodn.

Engring. Research (pres. 1968-69), Am. Soc. Lubrication Engrs. (nat. pres. 1952-53), Soc. Mfg. Engrs. (pres. 1976-77), Belgian Soc. Mech. Engrs. (hon.), Fedn. Materials Socs. (pres. 1974), Phi Beta Kappa, Sigma Xi, Tau Beta Pi. Contbr. articles on basic and applied research on machining, friction, lubrication and wear, mfg. systems to tech. jours., sci. socs. Home: 3709 Center Ave Cincinnati OH 45227 Office: 4701 Marburg Ave Cincinnati OH 45209

MERCULIEFF, LARRY PAUL, investment exec.; b. St. Paul Island, Alaska, Nov. 3, 1949; s. John Paul and Stefanida M.; B.A., U. Wash., 1972; m. Phyllis Ann Hajny, Sept. 12, 1970; children—Leatha Nicole, Marissa Genelle. Dir., Am. Indian Edn. Program, U. Wash., 1968-71; dir. land dept. The Aleut Corp., Anchorage, 1973-75; bus. mgr. Tanadqusix Corp., St. Paul Island, 1975-79, pres., 1979—; chmn. bd. Aleut Corp. and 3 subsidiaries. Mem. Nat. Indian Edn. Adv. Bd., 1968-70, Rural Affairs Commn., 1970-74, St. Paul City Council, 1977-79, St. Paul Community Council, 1977-79; bd. trustees Alaska Native Found., 1969—. Recipient Cert. of Commn., State of Alaska Rural Affairs, 1972; cert. Aleut History and Culture Expert. Mem. Am. Mgmt. Assn. Editor: Aleut Resources Manual, 1974; (with others) Pribilof Island Tour Guide Book, 1978, Aleut History Book: Slaves of the Harvest, 1977. Home and Office: Saint Paul Island AK 99660

MEREDITH, DAVID ROBERT, personnel corp. exec.; b. Cleve., Apr. 9, 1940; s. Wilbur R. and Lillian B. M.; A.B., Colgate U., 1962; Ph.D. (Ford Found. grantee), M.I.T., 1966; student Universidad de Cuyo, 1961, Universidad de Tucuman, 1960; m. Sheila Kay Provost, Dec. 21, 1963; children—Karen, Adam, Alison. Labor cons. W.R. Meredith & Co., Cleve., 1958-65; labor asst. Mountain States Employers Council, Denver, 1965-66; prin. McKinsey & Co., Inc., N.Y.C. and Cleve., 1966-75; pres. Meredith Assos., Inc., Westport, Conn., 1975-80; chmn., chief exec. Personnel Corp. Am., Westport; dir. Canberra Industries, Inc.; chmn. bd. North Wind Power Co., 1976-78; research and teaching asst. M.I.T., 1962-66. Fin. chmn. Weston Community Center, Inc., 1977; mem. Rep. Town Com., Weston, Conn., 1979—, Weston Transit Study Commn., 1976-78; deacon Norfield Ch., 1975-81, fair chmn., 1977, treas., 1981—. NDEA fellow, 1962-65; FTES scholar, 1958-62; Williams scholar, 1960-61; recipient Osborne math. prize, Colgate U., 1962. Clubs: Conn. Golf, Aspetuck Valley Country, Cherry Hills Country, Pinacle. Contbr. articles to newspapers, bus. and profl. jours. Home: 3 Heritage Ln Weston CT 06883 Office: 16 Wilton Rd Westport CT 06880

MEREDITH, FRANK D., precision automated measurement systems mfg. co. exec.; b. Pitts., Dec. 12, 1941; s. Frank C. and Anna D. (Sobek) M.; B.A., St. Vincent Coll., 1964; M.B.A., U. Pitts., 1981; m. Mary Anne Foley, Aug. 22, 1964; children—Douglas Matthew, Anne Patricia, Mary Julia. Salesman, Union Carbide Corp., Pitts., 1965-66, Hoffman LaRoche, Inc., Pitts., 1966-72; account exec. Splty. Cons.'s, Inc., Pitts., 1972-73; area mgr. Southwestern Industries, Inc., Pitts., 1973-75; br. mgr. Fed. Products Corp., Pitts., 1975-77; owner Meredith Metrology Products, Pitts., 1977-79; eastern regional mgr. automation and measurement div. Bendix Corp., Pitts., 1979—; condr. seminars, lectr. Mem. Soc. Mfg. Engrs., Am. Soc. Quality Control. Office: PO Box 4554 4480 Steubenville Pike Pittsburgh PA 15205

MERINO, ROSE RAQUEL ELLIS, physician; b. El Paso, Tex., Dec. 13, 1924; d. Frederick and Elizabeth Ellis; B.A. in Pre-medicine, Coll. Mt. St. Vincent, Riverdale, N.Y., 1945; M.D., N.Y. Med. Coll., 1949; m. Francisco Merino, Feb. 22, 1955; children—Rosa, Margaret, Frances, Frank Joseph. Intern, St. Vincent's Hosp., N.Y.C., 1949-50, resident, 1951-52, asst., 1953-55; resident Willard Parker Hosp., 1950, N.Y. Foundling Hosp., 1951; fellow Vanderbilt Clinic, 1952-53; practice medicine specializing in pediatrics and occupational medicine, N.Y.C., 1954-74; pediatrician Dept. of Health, 1955—; clin. asst. pediatrician outpatient dept. and wards Meml. Hosp., 1967-73, adj. attending, 1980—; asst. vis. pediatrician James Ewing Hosp., 1967-73; cons. clin. pediatrician 9 E. 91st St. Eye Hosp., 1965-73, N.Y.C. Bur. Child Welfare, 1960—; asst. v.p. med. dept. Equitable Life Assurance Soc., 1978—. Diplomate Am. Bd. Pediatrics, Am. Bd. Family Practice. Mem. AMA, N.Y. State Med. Soc., N.Y. County Med. Soc., N.Y. State Soc. Indsl. Medicine. Roman Catholic. Home: 444 E 57th St New York NY 10022 Office: 1285 Ave of Americas New York NY 10019

MERK, HOWARD SEXTON, truck stop exec., lawyer; b. Greenwich, Conn., Apr. 2, 1941; s. Howard Charles and Edna Loretta (Sexton) M.; B.A., The Citadel, 1963; J.D., Yale U., 1966; m. Martha Elizabeth Beard, June 14, 1963; children—Howard Charles II, Wendy E.B., Lars M.S., J.P. Dana. Admitted to Conn. bar, 1966; asso. firm Daggett, Colby & Hooker, New Haven, 1966-67; exec. v.p., dir. Mayflower Truck Sta., Milford, Conn., 1969-80; pres. Petroleum Distbrs. North Haven, Conn. Pres. Milford Hist. Soc., 1976—: v.p. bd. dirs., exec. com. Milford Hosp., 1974—; chmn. exec. com. Milford Cemetery, 1973—. Served to capt. M.I., AUS, 1967-69. Decorated Bronze Star, Air Medal, Army Commendation Medal (U.S.); Dieu Thu (Viet Nam). Mem. Am., Conn., New Haven County bar assns., Nat. Assn. Truck Stop Operators. Democrat. Unitarian. Club: Grad. (New Haven). Research on fragmentation in urban planning. Home: 299 Gulf St Milford CT 06460 Office: 11 Universal Dr North Haven CT 06473

MERL, KURT, electronics co. exec.; b. Vienna, Austria, Apr. 9, 1929; came to U.S., 1938, naturalized, 1943; s. Leon and Heny (Hermann) M.; B.E.E., CCNY, 1952; M.E.E., Columbia U., 1960; m. Ellen B. Hirsch, Aug. 26, 1952; children—Susan Lynn, Jeffrey Stuart, Gary Michael. With Electronics Research Lab., Columbia U., 1952-53; engring. dept. head Ford Instrument Co. div. Sperry Rand, 1953-60, systems engring. mgr., strategic systems Sperry Marine Systems div., 1960-68, strategic systems mgr., 1968, v.p., gen. mgr. Microwave Systems div., 1973-75, v.p., gen. mgr. Sperry Systems Mgmt., Great Neck, N.Y., 1975—. Served with USNR, 1946-52. Mem. IEEE (sr.), Am. Def. Preparedness Assn., Navy League (life), Soc. Logistics Engrs., Am. Soc. Naval Engrs. Club: Masons. Contbr. articles on digital data communications to profl. jours.; patentee in field. Home: 5 Ives Ln Plainview NY 11803 Office: Sperry Systems Management Marcus Ave Great Neck NY 11020

MERLO, ANDREW EUGENE, real estate developer; b. Jersey City, June 14, 1942; s. John and Rose Merlo; student U. Miami, 1964, N.Y. U., 1968; divorced; 1 dau., Vanessa. Project engr. Wilbur Smith and Assos., 1966-69; corp. real estate rep. Amerada Hess Corp., 1970; mem. sales staff GAC Properties, 1970-71; with U.S. Home Communities Corp., N.J., 1971; v.p. real estate Radice Realty & Constrn. Corp., Ft. Lauderdale, Fla., 1973-78; owner, real estate cons., developer A.E. Merlo Real Estate Cons., Union City, N.J., 1978-80; dir. nat. bus. devel. DiScala Assos., Norwalk, Conn., 1980—. Mem. Nat. Assn. Corp. Real Estate. Buddhist. Home: 314 19th St Union City NJ 07087 Office: 50 Washington St Norwalk CT 06854

MEROW, JOHN EDWARD, lawyer; b. Little Valley, N.Y., Dec. 20, 1929; s. Luin George and Mildred Elizabeth (Stoll) M.; student UCLA, 1947-48; B.S.E., U. Mich., 1952; J.D., Harvard U., 1958; m. Mary Alyce Smith, June 19, 1957; 1 dau., Alison Dana. Admitted to N.Y. State bar, 1958; asso. firm Sullivan & Cromwell, N.Y.C., 1958-64, partner, 1965—; dir. Kaiser Aluminum & Chem. Corp., Kaiser Aluminum & Chem. Sales, Inc., Broad Street Investing Corp., Nat. Investors Corp., Union Capital Fund, Inc., Union Cash Mgmt. Fund, Inc., Union Income Fund, Inc.; mem. adv. council Center for Study Fin. Instns., U. Pa. Law Sch. Warden, St. Thomas Ch. (Episcopal), N.Y.C., 1971-78; trustee Protestant Episocopal Soc. for Promoting Religion and Learning in State of N.Y. Served to lt. USN, 1952-55. Mem. Am. Bar Assn., N.Y. State Bar Assn., Assn. Bar City N.Y. (chmn. com. on securities regulation 1974-77), Am. Law Inst., N.Y. Law Inst., Union Internationale des Avocats, Council on Fgn. Relations. Clubs: Links, Met. Opera, Piping Rock, Down Town, Church, Chatham Beach and Tennis. Home: 350 E 69th St New York NY 10021 Office: 125 Broad St New York NY 10004

MERRIAM, GREGORY JAY, ins. co. exec.; b. Chgo., Nov. 2, 1945; s. Jack G. and Georgia C. (Grow) M.; B.S. in Bus. Mgmt., Fairleigh Dickinson U., 1968; m. Gertrude Elizabeth Guttenburger, Nov. 24, 1974; 1 dau., Karen Lynn. Loss control engr. Sentry Ins. Co., Morristown, N.J., 1970-73, loss control mgr., Cedar Knolls, N.J., 1973-77, loss control mgr., Chgo., 1977—. Scoutmaster Morris County council Boys Scouts Am., 1967-68. Served with U.S. Army, 1969-70. Cert. safety profl., cert. hazard control mgr. Mem. Am. Soc. Safety Engrs., Nat. Fire Protection Assn., Assn. Mut. Ins. Engrs., Alliance of Am. Insurers (mem. loss control com. 1977—, chmn. comml. vehicle safety com. 1980—), Fairleigh Dickinson U. Alumni Assn. Republican. Home: 348 Green Valley Dr Naperville IL 60540 Office: 10 S Riverside Plaza Chicago IL 60606

MERRIFIELD, GORDON EDWARD, advt. and mktg. exec.; b. Cleve., Feb. 14, 1942; s. Gordon P. and Margaret (Mayhew) M.; student Kent State U., 1972-73, T.A. Edison Coll., 1975-76; m. Lisa Davidson, Feb. 28, 1973; children by previous marriage—Dean Gordon, James Lawrence. Pres., Creative Merchandising Inc., Cleve., 1964-69; v.p. advt. Mr. Gasket Co. div. W.R. Grace & Co., Cleve., 1969-74, mgr. advt. and communications Automotive Group, 1977-79; pres. Mktg. Support Inc., 1979—; mktg. and sales rep. Petersen Pub. Co., Los Angeles, 1974-77; cons. in field. Served with USN, 1961. Recipient Commendation for Civilian Assistance, USN, 1971. Mem. Cleve. Advt. Club. Methodist. Clubs: Chagrin River Yacht, Shriners. Home: 37090 Lakeshore Blvd Eastlake OH 44094

MERRILL, DONALD GENE, JR., mortgage banker; b. Lebanon, Ind., Dec. 10, 1945; s. Donald Gene and Dorthy M. (Staton) M.; student Purdue U., 1964-65; B.A. in Bus. Adminstrn., Ind. U., 1968; m. Mary Ann Schuster, Dec. 11, 1970; children—Lisa Ann, Kelly M. With Merc. Mortage Co., St. Louis, 1971-79, sr. v.p., dir., 1971-79; pres., chief exec. officer Met. Mortgage Fund, Inc., Alexandria, Va., 1979—; mem. exec. council Dominion Bankshares Corp. Mem. Mortgage Bankers Assn. Am., Soc. Real Estate Appraisers. Methodist. Clubs: Country of Fairfax (Va.); Masons, Shriners. Home: 10994 High Ridge St Fairfax Station VA 22039 Office: 500 Montgomery St Alexandria VA 22305

MERRILL, MARCELLUS S., bus. exec.; b. Carroll, Nebr., Aug. 7, 1900; s. George C. and Carrie L. (Lingelbach) M.; B.S.E.E., U. Colo., 1923, postgrad., 1936-46; m. Geraldine Robinson, Feb. 19, 1930; children—Constance Louise, M. Stanley. Engring. dept. Gen. Electric Co., Schenectady, 1923-27; chmn., owner Merrill Axle-Wheel Service, Inc., Denver and Pueblo, Merrill Engring. Labs., Inc., Denver, 1928—. Mem. ASME, Soc. Automotive Engrs. Presbyn. Clubs: Denver Press, Denver Athletic, Cactus. Patentee in field. Home: 1201 Williams St Apt 10C Denver CO 80206 Office: 2390 S Tejon Englewood CO 80110

MERRILL, RICHARD GLEN, bank exec.; b. Anaheim, Calif., Feb. 23, 1931; s. Howard Glen and Ann (Clark) M.; B.S., U. Calif. at Los Angeles, 1953; m. Grace Marilyn Hansler, Aug. 29, 1959; children—Thomas Glen, Ann Adelia, Elizabeth Mary, John Richard. Group sales rep. Prudential Ins. Co. Am., Los Angeles, Seattle, San Francisco, 1956-66, dir. group sales and service, Newark, 1966-68, v.p. group ins., 1968-70, v.p. group annuity dept., 1970-72, sr. v.p. in charge, Houston, 1972-78; pres. 1st City Nat. Bank, Houston, 1978—. Exec. bd. Sam Houston council Boy Scouts Am., 1973—, v.p. finance, chmn. council campaign fund, 1974, pres. council, 1975-76; trustee United Fund Houston and Harris County, campaign chmn., 1978; mem. exec. com. Houston Symphony, 1977—, pres., 1980; chmn. campaign for excellence U. St. Thomas, 1977, bd. dirs. univ., 1977-80; mem. exec. com., bd. dirs. Rice Center for Community Design and Research; trustee Meml. Dr. Presbyterian Ch., Interferon Found.; bd. visitors M.D. Anderson Hosp. and Tumor Inst., 1977-80; adv. bd. Bus. Sch., Tex. A. and M. U., 1980—. Served to 1st lt., inf., AUS, 1954-56. Mem. Assn. Res. City Bankers, Am. Bankers Assn., Houston C. of C. (dir.-at-large 1974, dir. 1976, 77, 78, research com. 1974-75), Alpha Tau Omega. Clubs: Houston Country, Ramada, Houstonian, Houston City, Met. Racquet (Houston). Home: 605 E Friar Tuck Ln Houston TX 77024 Office: PO Box 2557 Houston TX 77001

MERRILL, ROBERT EDWARD, spl. machinery mfg. co. exec.; b. Columbus, Ohio, Oct. 21, 1933; s. Robert Ray and Myrna Ione (Rinehart) M.; student Ohio State U., 1954-56; m. Donna Rae Bernstein, Mar. 19, 1967; children—Robert Edward, Aaron Jay, Jonathan Cyrus, Raquel Naomi. Pres., PSM Corp., San Jose, Calif., 1974—. Served with AUS, 1950-51; Korea. Patentee in pneumatic applications for indsl. press machinery. Home: 858 Fieldwood Ct San Jose CA 95120 Office: Box 5156 San Jose CA 95150

MERRILL, WILLIAM GADSDEN KING, bus. cons.; b. Charleston, W.Va., June 9, 1951; s. Robert E. and Jennie H. M.; B.S. in Bus. Adminstrn., Washington and Lee U., 1973; M.B.A., Colgate U., 1976. Salesman, Gt. Am. Silver Co., Va. and Md., 1973-75; personnel policies researcher Charter Oil Co., Jacksonville, Fla., 1975; v.p. Mgmt. Leadtime, Inc., Pitts., 1976-80; cons. internat. mktg. Champion Products Inc., Rochester, N.Y., 1981—; discussion group leader Ruff Times; econs. analyst; small bus. cons. Presdl. adv. staff Philip Crane for Pres., 1979. Mem. Am. Mgmt. Assn., Beta Gamma Sigma. Episcopalian. Home and Office: PO Box 85 Greenwood VA 22943

MERRIMAN, RICHARDSON TAYLOR, banker; b. Kansas City, Mo., Jan. 3, 1949; s. James F. and E. Jean (Richardson) M.; B.A. in Econs., Rollins Coll., 1971; M.B.A. in Finance, N.Y. U., 1975; m. Pamela Beardsley, Sept. 30, 1978; 1 son, Edward Wing. With Girard Bank, Phila., 1973—, adminstrv. officer, 1974-77, investment officer, 1977-80, sr. investment officer, 1980—. Republican. Presbyterian. Club: Merion Cricket (Haverford, Pa.). Home: 270 Rosedale Ave Strafford PA 19087 Office: Girard Bank 3 Girard Plaza Philadelphia PA 19101

MERRISS, PHILIP RAMSAY, JR., corporate banker; b. N.Y.C., June 7, 1948; s. Philip Ramsay and Elisabeth (Paine) M.; A.B. in Econs. magna cum laude, Lafayette Coll., 1970, M.B.A. (Tuck scholar, Gulf Oil fellow), Dartmouth Coll., 1972; m. Janet Henry Hylan, Oct. 27, 1973. Asso. corporate fin. dept. A.G. Becker and Co. Inc., N.Y.C., 1972-73; fin. analyst corporate banking dept. Chase Manhattan Bank, 1973, asst. treas. N.Y.C. dist., 1974-75, 2d v.p. mining and metals div., 1976-78, 2d v.p. petroleum div., 1978-79, v.p. petroleum div., 1979—. Served to capt. U.S. Army, 1978. Mem. Am. Econ. Assn., Aircraft Owners and Pilots Assn., N.Y. Road Runners Club, Phi Beta Kappa. Republican. Episcopalian. Clubs: Yale (N.Y.), Westport Athletic, Weston Gun (Conn.). Home: 100 Hills Point Rd Westport CT 06880 Office: Chase Manhattan Bank One Chase Manhattan Plaza New York NY 10081

MERRITT, EVERETT CHARLES, II, personnel exec.; b. Geneva, N.Y., Nov. 10, 1935; s. Everett Charles and Marion (Wright) M.; B.A. in Psychology, Syracuse U., 1957; M. Indsl. and Labor Relations, Cornell U., 1959; children—Douglas Everett, David Christopher. Personnel asst. Chas. Pfizer & Co., Inc., N.Y.C., 1962-65; dir. personnel, personnel cons. Rochester (N.Y.) Inst. Tech., 1965—, mem. adj. faculty, 1973—. Active ednl. TV fund raising, 1974-75, chmn. 1974. Served with USCG, 1959-62, comdg. officer Res., 1978—. Mem. Nat. Assn. Coll. and Univ. Bus. Officers, Coll. and Univ. Personnel Assn., Res. Officers Assn. (chpt. pres. 1980-81), Sigma Phi Epsilon, Tau Kappa Epsilon (adviser). Republican. Clubs: Masons, Racquet-Tennis of Rochester. Home: 55 Terrace Villa Circle Fairport NY 14450 Office: 1 Lomb Meml Dr Rochester NY 14623

MERRITT, LUCIAN GERALD, instrument mfg. co. exec.; b. Waco, Tex., Aug. 8, 1936; s. Lucian Henry and Hester Novel (Perdue) M.; B.B.A., Baylor U., 1958, M.S., 1960; postgrad. St. Mary's U., 1960-62; m. Tommie Pierce, Dec. 22, 1956; 1 dau., Lezli Diane. Mgr. div. purchasing, space and info. systems div. N. Am. Aviation, Inc., Downey, Calif., 1962-67; dir. material services Tracor, Inc., Austin, Tex., 1967-71, dir. mfg. ops., 1971-79, v.p. ops., 1979—; dir. Merritt, Inc. Past pres. Austin Gideon Camp; past bd. dirs. Campus Crusade for Christ. Served from 2d lt. to 1st lt. USAF, 1959-62; capt. Res. Mem. Am. Mgmt. Assn., Nat. Purchasing Mgmt. Assn., Gideons, Order of Artus, Alpha Chi. Home: 98 Wallis St Austin TX 78746 Office: 6500 Tracor Ln Austin TX 78721

MERRYFIELD, LYNNE FRANCES, health care mgmt. cons.; b. Richmond, Va., Nov. 3, 1942; d. Donald Norris and Rose Marie (Russell) Merryfield; student in mgmt. Simmons Coll., 1979. Bus. mgr. for Drs. Trujillo and O'Kieffe, Washington, 1971-79; pres. Med. Group Mgmt., Inc., Washington, 1980—; speaker, seminar leader, 1978—. Nat. Assn. Bus. and Profl. Women grantee, 1979. Mem. Am. Mgmt. Assn., Med. Group Mgmt. Assn., Internat. Assn. Fin. Planners, Am. Group Practice Assn., Nat. Assn. Women Bus. Owners (fin. officer, del. nat. conv. 1980), Nat. Fedn. Bus. and Profl. Women's Clubs. Office: 1629 K St NW Suite 520 Washington DC 20006

MERRYMAN, H(OLT) WALLACE, fin. co. exec.; b. Los Angeles, Nov. 26, 1927; s. Emmett and Annette Mary (Wallace) M.; B.S., UCLA, 1952; Advanced Mgmt. Sch., U. Hawaii, 1962; m. Fantine Elizabeth Holley, Apr. 24, 1949; children—Lloyd, Elizabeth Merryman Lorber, Craig. With Seaboard Fin. Co., Newport Beach, Calif., 1956—, (merged with Avco Delta Corp.) pres., chmn. bd., chief exec. officer Avco Fin. Services, Inc., 1975—; dir. Collins Foods Internat., Inc. Pres., Orange County council Boy Scouts Am., 1980; mem. U. Calif. at Irvine Chancellor Club, adv. bd. GSA Affiliates; trustee Calif. Coll. Medicine. Served with USNR, 1945-48. C.P.A. Republican. Methodist. Clubs: Balboa Bay, Big Canyon Country. Office: 620 Newport Center Dr Newport Beach CA 92660

MERSEL, MARJORIE KATHRYN PEDERSEN (MRS. JULES MERSEL), lawyer; b. Manila, Utah, June 17, 1923; d. Leo Henry and Kathryn Anna (Reed) Pedersen; A.B., U. Cal., 1948; LL.B., U. San Francisco, 1948; m. Jules Mersel, Apr. 12, 1950; 1 son, Jonathan. Admitted to D.C. bar, 1952, Calif. bar, 1955; Marjorie Kathryn Pedersen Mersel, atty., Beverly Hills, Calif., 1961-71; staff counsel Dept. Real Estate State of Calif., Los Angeles, 1971—. Mem. Beverly Hills Bar Assn., Trial Lawyers Assn., So. Calif. Women Lawyers Assn. (treas. 1962-63), Beverly Hills C. of C., World Affairs Council. Club: Los Angeles Athletic. Home: 13007 Hartsook St Sherman Oaks CA 91403 Office: Dept Real Estate 107 S Broadway Los Angeles CA

MERSZEI, ZOLTAN, oil co. exec.; b. Budapest, Hungary, Sept. 30, 1922; Architecture degree Fed. Poly. Inst. Zurich (Switzerland), 1944; LL.D. (hon.), Northwood Inst., 1976; Dr.Sci., Albion Coll., 1978; m. Ilona Eisele, May 22, 1946; children—Leslie G., Geoffery E., Karen G. With Dow Chem. Co. and subs's., 1949-79, v.p. Dow Chem. Internat. Ltd., 1961-65, pres. Dow Chem. Europe, 1965-75, mem. exec. com. Dow Chem. Co., Midland, Mich., 1971-79, exec. v.p., 1975-76, pres., chief exec. officer, 1976-79, chmn., 1978-79; vice-chmn. Occidental Petroleum Corp., Los Angeles, 1979—. Decorated Grand Cross of Order of Merit (Spain); comdr. Order Oranje Nassau (Netherlands). Clubs: Met.; Midland Country; Canadian (N.Y.C.). Office: Occidental Petroleum Corp 10889 Wilshire Blvd Los Angeles CA 90024*

MERTEN, ULRICH, chemist, oil co. exec.; b. Houston, Feb. 27, 1930; s. Eugen and Hedwig Martha Clara (Wolf) M.; B.S., Calif. Inst. Tech., 1951; Ph.D., Washington U., 1955; m. Katherine Williams, Nov. 7, 1953; children—Cynthia, Gail. Research chemist Gen. Electric Co., Schenectady, 1955-56; research mgr. Gen. Atomic Co., San Diego, 1956-70, v.p. research and devel., 1970-71; v.p. Gulf Research and Devel. Co., Harmarville, Pa., 1971—. Mem. editorial bd. Jour. of Membrane Sci., 1976—. Fellow AAAS; mem. Am. Chem. Soc., Am. Petroleum Inst. Contbr. articles to various publs. Home: 321 Wildberry Rd Pittsburgh PA 15238 Office: PO Drawer 2038 Pittsburgh PA 15230

MERTZ, FRANCIS JAMES, banker; b. Newark, Sept. 24, 1937; s. Frank E. and Marian (Brady) M.; B.A., St. Peters Coll., 1958; J.D., N.Y. U., 1961; m. Gail Williams, Apr. 11, 1964; children—Lynn, Christopher, Suzanne, David, Amy, Jonathan. Admitted to N.J. bar, 1964; with St. Peter's Coll., Jersey City, 1962-78, v.p. fin. and devel., 1970-72, exec. v.p., 1972-78; v.p., chief fin. officer N.Y. Med. Coll., Valhalla, 1978-79; dir. adminstrn., firm Sage Gray Todd & Sims, N.Y.C., 1979—; dir. Comml. Trust Co., Jersey City. Trustee Iona Coll., 1978—; mem. Watchung (N.J.) Bd. Edn., 1980—. Mem. N.J. Bar Assn., Assn. Legal Adminstrs. Roman Catholic. Clubs: Bergen Carteret, World Trade Center. Home: 60 Bayberry Ln Watchung NJ 07060 Office: Two World Trade Center 100th Fl New York NY 10048

MERTZ, GEORGE JOSEPH, charitable assn. exec.; b. San Diego, Nov. 30, 1928; s. Joseph Vincent and Elizabeth Rebecca (Baker) M.; B.B.A. in Accounting, Woodbury U., 1950; m. Mary Ellen Wilson, Apr. 6, 1951: children—Kathleen, David, Gary, Nancy. Accountant, Standard Oil Co., Los Angeles, 1950-52; chief accountant Shepherd Tractor & Equipment Co., Los Angeles, 1953-55; credit mgr., controller Tubesales, Inc., Los Angeles and N.J., 1956-69; exec. v.p., asst. treas., controller Nat. Industries for the Blind, Bloomfield, N.J., 1969—; treas. Royal Maid, Inc. (Miss.); instr. fin. and accounting courses for mgmt. of blind agencies. Served with AUS, 1946-47. Accredited in accounting Agencies Serving the Blind. Mem. Affiliated Leadership League, Am. Asso. Workers for the Blind. Methodist. Home: 153 Hope St Ridgewood NJ 07450 Office: 1455 Broad St Bloomfield NJ 07003

MERTZ, JOSEPH ROBERT, printing and office supply co. exec.; b. Gloucester City, N.J., June 6, 1927; s. Harry Walls and Emma (Markley) M.; student Phila. Printing Inst., 1948, Dale Carnegie Inst.,

1974-79; m. Jane A. Henderson, Oct. 23, 1948; children—Sandra A., James R., Richard H., Robert J. Compositor, Royal Typographers, Phila., 1948-50; plant mgr. Park Printing Service, Clementon, N.J., 1950-56; v.p. sales mgr. Chapel Co., Inc., Cherry Hill, N.J., 1966—; cons. to graphic art schs. and colls., Camden, Burlington, Gloucester counties, N.J., 1964—. Mem. Gloucester Twp. Bd. Edn., 1963-68, pres., 1965-68. Served with USMC, 1944-46. Mem. Printing Industries Am., Nat. Office Products Assn., Graphic Arts Assn. Delaware Valley, South Jersey C. of C., Cherry Hill C. of C. Republican. Methodist. Clubs: Moorestown Lions (dir., dep. dist. gov. 1971-72), Masons. Office: 1700 Chapel Ave Drawer A Cherry Hill NJ 08034

MERTZ, MICHAEL FREDERICK, JR., real estate, coal, oil and gas broker/appraiser; b. Weston, W.Va., May 17, 1931; s. Michael Frederick and Bridget Elizabeth (Mullady) M.; B.S., W.Va. U., 1955, postgrad., 1965; grad. U.S. Army Armor Officers Sch., 1956; postgrad. Rider Coll., 1970, U. Va., 1970; grad. Realtor Inst., Parkersburg Community Coll., 1975; m. Norma Janet Talbott, June 11, 1955; children—Michael, Frank, Gregory, Barbara, Mary Ann; m. 2d, Elizabeth Amy Pierce, Nov. 27, 1970; 1 son, Thomas. Land, coal, oil, gas, right-of-way appraiser, cons. and contract agt., 1957-68, 72—; land agt. Bitner Fuel Co., Uniontown, Pa. 1957-60; comml. farm owner-operator, Jane Lew, W.Va., 1960-68; right-of-way agt. Ford, Bacon & Davis Constrn. Corp., Monroe, La., 1968-69, 72-73, Coates Field Service, Oklahoma City, 1969-70; appraiser, salesman Joseph H. Martin Appraisal & Real Estate Co., Trenton, N.J., 1970-72; real estate broker, Weston and Bridgeport, W.Va., 1972—; pres. Mertz Land Co., Inc., Weston, 1972—, Mertz Realty, Inc., 1976—; sr. right-of-way agt. Colonial Pipeline Co., 1979; oil and gas broker Atlantic Richfield, 1980, Houston Oil & Minerals, Sterling Drilling & Prodn., 1981—; instr. Mertz Sch. Real Estate, 1974-79; writer, lectr. in field of land use and evaluation of right-of-ways, coal, oil and gas properties. Mem. Internat. Right-of-way Assn. (sr. designation), Am. Right-of-Way Assn. (sr. designation), Nat. Assn. Ind. Fee Appraisers (state pres. 1972-73; Ind. Fee Appraisers (sr. designation), Clarksburg Bd. Realtors (pres. 1976), W.Va. Assn. Realtors (dir. 1976-78), Weston Bd. Realtors (Realtor of Yr. 1977; pres. 1977-80), Realtors Nat. Mktg. Inst., Nat. Assn. Realtors, Alpha Gamma Rho. Address: 236 E First St Weston WV 26452

MESAROS, CHARLES, chem. co. exec.: b. McKeesport, Pa., July 12, 1933; s. Thomas and Helena (Vlad) M.; B.S. in Chem. Engring. (Senatorial scholar), U. Pitts., 1956; m. Elizabeth Mesaros, Aug. 18, 1958; children—James, Francis, Lisa Beth, Melinda Louise, Charles John. Foreman, U.S. Steel Corp., Dravosburg, Pa., 1956-59; asst. tech. dir. Dacar Chem. Co., Pitts., 1959-64; pres. Zenol, Inc., Pitts., 1964-70, Kol-Blox Co., Pitts., 1970—. Served to lt. USMCR, 1958. Mem. Am. Chem. Soc., Am. Inst. Chem. Engring., Am. Inst. Metall. Engring., Nat. Engrs. Club. Contbr. current interest articles to local newspapers; inventor in field. Home: 200 White Hampton Ln Canongate Apt 112 Pittsburgh PA 15236 Office: 2923 Brownsville Rd Pittsburgh PA 15227

MESHEL, LEON, accountant; b. Bklyn., Mar. 31, 1934; s. Irving and Laura (Sherriff) M.; B.B.A., City Coll. N.Y., 1955, M.B.A., 1967; m. Helenore Gloria Jacobs, Jan. 29, 1955; children—Andrew Hugh, Harvey Simon. Sr. auditor S.D. Leidesdorf & Co., N.Y.C., 1957-63; chief internal auditor Asso. Univs., Inc., Upton, L.I., N.Y., 1963-69; treas. Applied Digital Data Systems, Inc., Hauppauge, N.Y., 1969—, also dir. Served with AUS, 1955-57. C.P.A., N.Y. Mem. Am. Inst. C.P.A.'s, N.Y. State Soc. C.P.A.'s. Home: 15 Pheasant Run Kings Point NY 11024 Office: 100 Marcus Blvd Hauppauge NY 11787

MESHOWSKI, FRANK ROBERT, corp. exec.; b. Milw., Sept. 10, 1930; s. Frank L. and Constance (Mockus) M.; M.E., N.Y. State Maritime Acad., 1951; B.S. in Mech. Engring., Newark Coll. Engring., 1954; m. Olga Skirka, Jan. 26, 1952; children—David, Laurie, Elaine. Project mgr. Curtiss-Wright Co., Woodridge, N.J., 1952-59; v.p. sales Gulton Industries, Metuchen, N.J., 1959-68; group v.p. Nytronics Co., Alpha, N.J., 1968-72; v.p. mktg. Gulf & Western Industries, N.Y.C., 1972-79, pres. subs. Unicord, Inc., 1979—; dir. OPT Industries, Philippsburg, N.J., Aros, S.P.A., Italy, Aros, Sud, Italy. Mem. Am. Mgmt. Assn., Am. Mktg. Assn. Democrat. Roman Catholic. Address: 4 Brandywine Dr East Brunswick NJ 08816

MESSEMER, RICHARD CHARLES, paper distbn. co. exec.; b. N.Y.C., Apr. 15, 1950; s. Frank Edward and Evelyn (Williams) M.; A.A.S., N.Y.C. Community Coll., 1968, 72, postgrad. Baruch Coll., 1973; m. Marie Manganiello, May 21, 1972; 1 dau., Laura Jean. Sales promotion mgr. Daniel O. Reich, Inc., paper mills rep., Bklyn., 1972; sales rep. Nationwide Papers Co. div. Champion Internat. Co., Moonachie, N.J., 1977; pres. Foremost Paper Co. Inc., N.Y.C., 1977—; propr. R.M.A., small press printers cons., N.Y.C., 1978—. Vice chmn. Pilgrim Covenant Ch., Bklyn., 1980. Club: Masons (past master). Office: Foremost Paper Co 56 W 45th St New York NY 10036

MESSER, MERLE MILTON, steel co. exec.; b. Austin, Tex., May 23, 1916; s. Joy Clark and Leona Pearl (Wilson) M.; student Tex. Wesleyan U., 1934; m. Bonnie Nereje McWhorter, Mar. 31, 1940; children—Bonnie Merle (Mrs. Clifford Lee Thomson), Grace Leone (Mrs. Joseph John Holt), Jay Milton, Jerie Claire. Helper, welder Modern Supply Co., Austin, 1934-37; welder Brown & Root Constrn. Co., Austin, 1937-42; mgr. Cryer Corp., Austin, 1942-43; owner, pres. Modern Supply Co., Austin, 1942—. Mem. Tex. Mfg. Assn., C. of C. Baptist (deacon 1942—, Sunday sch. tchr. 1974-78). Home: 2608 McCallum Dr Austin TX 78703 Office: 316 N Lamar Blvd Austin TX 78703

MESSEROLL, JOHN ALBERT, JR., communications co. exec.; b. New Brunswick, N.J., June 15, 1940; s. John Albert and Josephine Messeroll; B.S., Rutgers U., 1974; children—John Albert III, James A., Merrie Frances, Jeffrey A. Supr. duplicating, office service mgr. Carter Wallace, Inc., Cranbury, N.J., 1960-69; dir. corp. services and purchasing Harper & Row Pubs., N.Y.C., 1969-78; pres. The Delta Group, Princeton, N.J., 1978—; editor, pub. Info. for Graphic Communications Mgmt., 1976—, Word Processing Mgmt., 1974—; asso. pub. Sports Bus., 1976—, Sports Media News, 1979—; acting exec. dir. Internat. Soc. Sports Sponsors, Princeton, 1979—; dir. Graphic Mgmt. Services. Cert. graphic communicator. Mem. Adminstrv. Mgmt. Assn., Purchasing Mgmt. Assn., Internat. Purchasing Mgmt. Assn. (internat. v.p. 1969-74). Home: 7 Grier Rd Somerset NJ 08873 Office: 245 Nassau St Princeton NJ 08540

MESSNER, ROBERT THOMAS, lawyer, retail trade exec.; b. McKeesport, Pa., Mar. 27, 1938; s. Thomas M. and Cecelia Mary (McElhinny) M.; A.B., Dartmouth, 1960; LL.B., U. Pa., 1963; m. Anne Margaret Lux, Dec. 3, 1966; children—Megan Anne, Michael Thomas. Admitted to Pa. bar, 1965; asso. firm Rose, Schmidt and Dixon, Pitts., 1965-68; asst. dir. employee relations G.C. Murphy Co., McKeesport, 1968-70, asst. sec., 1970-74, corp. sec., 1974-75, corp. sec. and gen. counsel, 1975—, v.p., 1976—; dir. G.C. Murphy Co. Found.; lectr. Nat. Investor and Fin. Relations Exec. Conf., 1977. Adv. bd. Pa. Human Relations Commn., 1968-69; registration chmn. Republican Com. Allegheny County, Pa., 1967; chmn. bd. dirs. McKeesport YMCA. Served with U.S. Army, 1963-65. Mem. Am., Pa., Allegheny County bar assns., Am. Soc. Corp. Secs. (pres. Pitts. regional group 1978-79, dir. nat. assn. 1980—), McKeesport C. of C. (dir. 1972-73). Clubs: University (Pitts.); Nat. Lawyers (Washington); Dartmouth of Western Pa. Home: 1061 Blackridge Rd Pittsburgh PA 15235 Office: 531 Fifth Ave McKeesport PA 15132

METCALF, DOUGLAS REED, banker; b. Salt Lake City, Apr. 26, 1949; s. Reed J. and Barbara Lynn (McIntire) M.; B.A. magna cum laude, U. Utah, 1972; M.B.A., Brigham Young U., 1974; m. Nancy Hellewell, Aug. 8, 1972; children—Mary Courtney, Wyatt Douglas. Security analyst Fireman's Fund Ins. Co., San Francisco, 1974-76; portfolio mgr. Crocker Nat. Bank, San Francisco, 1976-78; mgr. investment div. 1st Nat. Bank of Ariz., Phoenix, 1978—; faculty asso. Ariz. State U.; instr. Foothill Community Coll. Hinckley intern Utah State Democratic Com., 1972. Chartered fin. analyst. Mem. Fin. Analysts Fedn., Phoenix Soc. Fin. Analysts (dir.), Phi Beta Kappa. Mormon. Office: PO Box 20551 100 W Washington St Phoenix AZ 85036

METCALF, EDWARD LEE, edn. adviser; b. Paducah, Ky., June 13, 1941; s. Earl L. and Kathleen M.; A.A., Paducah Jr. Coll., 1961; B.S., Murray State U., 1964; M.S., St. Louis U., 1969, Ph.D., 1979; m. Eva Jean Wagner, July 30, 1966; 1 dau., Dawn Kathleen. Tchr. math. and physics St. Louis schs., 1964-66; tchr. sci. Beaumont High Sch., University City, Mo., 1966-69; instr. math., Fulbright grantee in math. Draussafaka Lisesi, Istanbul, Turkey, 1967-68; instr. physics and calculus St. Louis Rabbinical Coll., 1968-69; internat. computer edn. adviser IBM, Atlanta, 1969—; lectr. computer tech. Mem. Pi Mu Epsilon. Episcopalian. Home: 3903 Loch Highland Roswell GA 30075 Office: IBM PO Box 2150 Atlanta GA 30301

METCALFE, WILLIAM KENNEDY, engring. exec.; b. Carr, Colo., June 10, 1912; s. Thomas William and Ada (Kennedy) M.; student Geneva Coll., Beaver Falls, Pa.; B.S., U. Colo., 1936; Sc.D., Geneva Coll., 1965; m. Ruth Dresser, Aug. 21, 1937; children—Carolyn Marie (Mrs. David P. Mollenkopf), Robert W. With Great Western Sugar Co., Denver, 1929-31, Prouty Bros. Engring Co., Denver, 1931-32, U.S. Coast and Geod. Survey, Colo., 1934-35; with J.O. Ross Engring. Corp., N.Y.C., 1936-57, sec., 1948-56, v.p. sales, dir., 1956-57; sec., dir. Ross Midwest Fulton Corp., Dayton, Ohio, 1954-59; dir. Ross Engring Can. (Montreal), 1955-60; with J. O. Ross Engring. div. Midland Ross Corp., N.Y.C., 1957-61, v.p. sales, 1957-60, v.p. mktg., 1960-61; pres., dir. AER Corp., Ramsey, N.J., 1961—, chmn. bd., 1977—; pres., dir. AER Process Systems Ltd., Montreal, 1966—; chmn. bd., dir. AER Realty Co., Inc., 1967—; v.p., dir. AER Internat. Inc. Former state v.p. Gideons Internat.; bd. mgrs. Nat. Temperance Soc. and Publ. House; trustee Geneva Coll., Beaver Falls, Pa.; chmn. fin. com., bd. fgn. missions Reformed Presbyterian. Ch. N.A., treas. ch., N.Y.C.; bd. dirs. Reformation Translation Fellowship; supt. Bronxville Cemetery. Recipient George E. Norlin award U. Colo., 1980; registered profl. engr. N.Y., N.J. Mem. Am. Soc. Heating and Air Conditioning Engrs., TAPPI (recipient Engring. Div. award 1979), Am. Mgmt. Assn., Paper Industry Mgmt. Assn., Can. Pulp and Paper Assn. Clubs: Sag Harbor Yacht; Tarrytown (N.Y.) Boat; Town (New Castle, N.Y.); Sales Execs. N.Y. Contbr. to heating and ventilating sect. Text Book on Pulp and Paper Manufacture, 1955; articles for trade papers. Patentee in field, U.S., Eng., Can. Home: 27 Overlook Dr Chappaqua NY 10514 Office: 100 Hilltop Rd Ramsey NJ 07446

METRINKO, MICHELE BETTINA, lawyer; b. N.Y.C., Mar. 23, 1945; d. Michael J. and Elizabeth (Sedor) Metrinko; B.S. in Fgn. Service, Georgetown U., 1965, J.D., 1968, LL.M. in Taxation, 1970; m. John W. Rollins; children—Michele, Monique. Admitted to D.C. bar, 1969, Fed. bar, 1970, D.C. Ct. Appeals, 1971, U.C. Ct. Claims bar, 1971, U.S. Supreme Ct. bar, 1973, Pa. bar, 1977, Del. bar, 1980; mem. legis. research staff Rep. Seymour Halpern, Washington, 1964-65; law clk. firm Keatinge & Sterling, Los Angeles, summer 1967; mem. staff legal advisers' office Dept. State, Washington, 1967; staff atty. div. corp. regulation SEC, Washington, 1968-71; trial atty. tax div. Dept. Justice, Washington, 1971-72; spl. asst. to adminstr. EPA, Washington, 1972-74; asso. solicitor, div. conservation and wildlife Dept. Interior, Washington, 1974-77; corp. sec., asso. counsel Sun Co., Radnor, Pa., 1977-80; individual practice law, Greenville, Del., 1980—; dir. Phila. Indsl. Devel. Corp.; disc jockey, pub. affairs announcer radio sta. WGTB, Washington, 1961-65; moderator, appearances numerous TV spls. and programs; toured with Bob Hope U.S.O. troupe, Middle East and Mediterranean area, Christmas, 1963. Trustee Cabrini Coll., Radnor; pres.-elect Pres. Reagan's Task Force on Environment. Recipient oratory awards Cath. Youth Orgn., 1959, B'nai B'rith, 1960, Forensic League, 1961, Am. Legion, 1960, K.C., 1961; numerous beauty pageant titles including Miss U.S.A., 1963-64. Mem. Fed., Am. bar assns., Am. Soc. Internat. Law, Nat. Symphony Com., Nat. Steeplechase and Hunt Assn. Clubs: Blue Ridge Hunt (Boyce, Va.); Vicmead Hunt (Greenville, Del.); Wilmington (Del.) Country; Met. (Washington). Home: Walnut Green Owl's Nest Rd Greenville DE 19807 Office: PO Box 4131 Greenville DE 19807

METROKA, JULIUS JOHN, advt. exec.; b. N.Y.C., June 19, 1934; s. George L. and Mary (Adams) M.; B.A., W.Va. Wesleyan U., 1956; M.A., Columbia U., 1958; m. Carol Lee Worthington, Sept. 8, 1962; children—Laura, Julie, Mary. Traffic mgr. J. Walter Thompson Advt., N.Y.C., 1964-78; sr. account exec. Collier Graphics Co., N.Y.C., 1978-80; mng. dir. Winet Advt. Prodn.-Transp. Displays Inc., N.Y.C., 1978—; cons. seminars in field. Recipient award Graphic Arts Tech. Found., 1978, United Way, 1977, 78. Mem. Am. Mgmt. Assn., Advt. Prodn. Club. Republican. Mem. Carpatho-Russian Orthodox Ch. Home: 19 Country Club Dr White Plains NY 10607 Office: 275 Madison Ave New York NY 10017

METROPULOS, JOHN N., ins. exec.; b. Greece, July 30, 1920; s. Nicholas and Angeline (Kalamatas) M. (parents Am. citizens); student U. Ill., 1940-41; m. Velia A. Vietti, Apr. 11, 1942; children—Diane L., John N., Raymond J., Linda M., Timothy M., Anne E., James D. Successively ins. agt., gen. agt., pres. J.N. Metropulos & Assos., Inc., Park Ridge, Ill., 1946—; dir. All Am. Life & Casualty Corp. Bd. dirs. Boy Scouts Am.; former pres. St. John's Greek Orthodox Ch. Served to 1st lt. C.E., AUS, 1942-46; PTO. Mem. Ill. C. of C., Internat., Nat., Ill. life underwriters assns., All Am. Life and Casualty Co. Blue Blazers (past pres., life mem.). Clubs: Park Ridge Country, Masons, Lions, Elks. Home: 101 Cuttriss St Park Ridge IL 60068 Office: 600 Talcott Rd Park Ridge IL 60068

METTER, CHARLES W., holding co. exec. Pres., chief exec. officer Chgo. Milw. Corp., Chgo. Office: 666 Lake Shore Dr Chicago IL 60611*

METTLER, RUBEN FREDERICK, electronics and engring. co. exec.; b. Shafter, Calif., Feb. 23, 1924; s. Henry Frederick and Lydia Mettler; student Stanford, 1941-43; B.S. in Elec. Engring., Calif. Inst. Tech., 1944, M.S., 1947, Ph.D. in Elec. and Aero. Engring., 1949; m. Donna Jean Smith, May 1, 1955; children—Matthew Frederick, Daniel Frederick. Asso. div. dir. systems research and devel. Hughes Aircraft Co., 1949-54; spl. cons. to asst. sec. def., 1954-55; asst. gen mgr. guided missile research div. Ramo-Wooldridge Corp., 1955-58, pres., dir. Space Tech. Labs., Inc., Los Angeles, 1958-68; exec. v.p., dir. Thompson Ramo Wooldridge, Inc. (name changed to TRW Inc.), 1965-68, asst. pres., 1968-69, pres., 1969-77, chmn. bd., chief exec. officer, 1977—; dir. Bank Am. Corp., Goodyear Tire & Rubber Co., Merck & Co., Inc. Vice chmn. Def. Industry Adv. Council; nat. chmn. Nat. Alliance of Businessmen, 1978-79; mem. policy com. Bus. Round Table. Chmn. Pres.'s Task Force on Sci. Policy, 1970; mem. Blue Ribbon Def. Panel, 1969-70. Trustee Cleve. Clinic, Nat. Safety Council; trustee, mem. com. for econ. devel. Calif. Inst. Tech.; adv. bd. Case Western Res. U., Council Financial Aid to Edn. Named 1 of ten Outstanding Young Men of America, U.S. Jr. C. of C., 1955; So. Calif.'s Engr. of Yr., 1965; Distinguished Civilian Meritorious Service award Dept. Def., 1969. Served with USNR, 1943-46. Registered profl. engr., Calif. Fellow I.E.E.E., Am. Inst. Aeros. and Astronautics; Sci. Research Soc. Am., Calif. Inst. Tech. Alumni Assn. (dir.), Nat. Acad. Engring., Sigma Xi, Eta Kappa Nu (named nation's outstanding young elec. engr. 1954), Tau Beta Pi, Theta Xi. Author reports airborne electronic systems. Patentee interceptor fire control systems. Office: 23555 Euclid Ave Cleveland OH 44117*

METZ, DOUGLAS WILBER, trade assn. exec.; b. Port Huron, Mich., Feb. 8, 1934; s. Wilber Leroy and Doris Mabel (Hurni) M.; B.A., Colgate U., 1955; J.D., Wayne State U., 1957; m. M. Elinor Daschbach, Feb. 13, 1971; children—William D., Mary J., Kathryn L., Paula D., Bradley F. Admitted to Mich. bar, 1957; adminstrv. asst. Congressman Alexander Pirnie, Utica, N.Y., 1959-64; v.p. Booz-Allen & Hamilton, N.Y.C., 1964-74; dep. dir. Domestic Council Com. on Right of Privacy, White House, Washington, 1974-75; sr. staff ops. dir. Econ. Policy Bd., White House, Washington, 1975-76; asso. dir., gen. counsel Council on Internat. Econ. Policy, Exec. Office of Pres., Washington, 1976-77; exec. v.p., gen. counsel Wine and Spirits Wholesalers Am., Washington, 1977—; chmn. bd. Internat. Mgmt. Assos., Inc., Washington, 1977-78. Chmn. bd. Cathedral Latin Sch., Cleve., 1971-72; dir. Bethesda (Md.) Fire Bd., 1976-78; bd. dirs. Sky Ranch Found., 1978-79. Served to capt. USAF, 1957-59. Recipient Cert. of Achievement, Combined Fed. Campaign of Capitol Area, 1977. Mem. Am. Bar Assn., Phi Beta Kappa. Republican. Roman Catholic. Clubs: Internat., Capitol Hill (Washington). Home: 13 Orchard Way S Potomac MD 20854 Office: 2033 M St NW Suite 400 Washington DC 20036

METZ, RAYMOND EUGENE, bldg. materials co. exec.; b. Bklyn., May 13, 1939; s. Raymond Leonard and Winifred Ann (Mannion) M.; B.S. in Mech. Engring., Ohio U., 1962; M.B.A., U. Mo., 1969; m. Carole Elizabeth Mason; children—Raymond Michael, Regina Marie, Reneé Michelle. Indsl. engr. Owens-Corning Fiberglas Corp., Kansas City, Kans., 1966-70, corp. budget staff mem., Toledo, 1970-73, planning mgr., 1973-76, dir. corp. planning, 1976—. Pres. bd. visitors Ohio U. Coll. Bus. Adminstrn., 1979—. Served with USAF, 1962-65. Mem. Planning Execs. Inst. (past pres. Toledo chpt.), Ohio U. Alumni Assn. (dir.). Home: 883 Sandalwood Rd Perrysburg OH 43551 Office: Owens-Corning Fiberglas Corp 1 Levis Square Toledo OH 43659

METZGER, ALAN FAIRFIELD, mfr., elec. engr.; b. Montclair, N.J., Feb. 28, 1906; s. Elmer Eugene and Mina (Burgess) M.; B.S., Yale, 1929; m. Nathalie Elizabeth Whitten, June 15, 1935; children—Alan Whitten, Joan Elizabeth. Test course Gen. Electric Co., 1929-31, design engr., motors, 1931-36, application engr. New Eng. dist., 1936-43; asst. elec. engr. Electric Boat Co., 1943-45, chief elec. engr., 1945-51; v.p., dir. Ideal Windlass Co., 1951-55; pres., treas. Edward Parkingson Mfg. Co., 1956-76, chmn., 1977—, also dir.; pres. Hope Industries, 1957-62; Exec. budget com. United Fund. Mem. Am. Inst. E.E., Soc. Naval Architects and Marine Engrs., Am. Soc. Naval Engrs., Providence Engring. Soc., R.I. Soc. Profl. Engrs. (Engr. of Yr.), Marine Hist. Assn., Yale Engring. Assn., U.S. Power Squadron (tchr. navigation, piloting, boat handling 1940—), Am. Textile Machinery Export Assn. (dir. 1972-76), USCG Aux. (tchr. boating courses 1959—). Club: Wickford Yacht. Home: Pojac Point RFD 2 North Kingston RI 02881 Office: Edward Parkinson Mfg Co Esmond RI 02917

METZGER, CHARLES OTTMAR, plastic co. exec.; b. Nurenberg, Germany, Oct. 22, 1923; s. Paul Arthur and Charlotte Babett (Kann); came to U.S., 1938, naturalized, 1945; B.S. in Chem. Engring., CCNY, 1945; M.S. in Chem. Engring., Columbia U., 1948; m. Loretta Iris Castellino, Sept. 13, 1958; children—Laura, Janet, Paul, Stephen. Devel. engr. Rohm & Haas Co., Phila., 1948-50, group leader, 1950-58, sect. head arsenal research div., 1958-62, asst. gen. mgr. Rhee Industries div., 1962-66, prodn. mgr. Fayetteville Fibers Plant, 1966-71, mgr. mfg. fibers div., 1971-76, bus. mgr. nylon, 1976-77, bus. mgr. Carodel and Kemos, 1977—. Served with USAAF, 1945-47. Registered profl. engr., Ala., R.I., Pa. Mem. Am. Inst. Chem. Engrs., Am. Chem. Soc., Tau Beta Pi, Phi Lambda Upsilon. Home: 3 Wexford Ct Cherry Hill NJ 08003 Office: Rohm & Haas Co Ind Mall West Philadelphia PA 19105

METZGER, HENRY ANTHONY, mfg. co. exec.; b. Mansfield, Ohio, Apr. 8, 1933; s. Henry Abraham and Mary Barbara (Prion) M.; student W.Va. State Coll., 1965-66; m. Patricia R. Rosier, Jan. 20, 1960; children—Mark Hedrick, Lisa Marie, Pamela Ann. Sr. indsl. engr. Gravely Div., Clemmons, N.C., 1963-65, mgr. indsl. engring., 1965-71, dir. mfg., 1971-72, v.p. mfg., 1972—. Bd. dirs. Southwest Forsyth Little League. Moravian. Club: Clemmons Civic. Home: Box 815 Bermuda Run Advance NC 27006 Office: Gravery Ln Clemmons NC 27012

METZGER, IRWIN HERBERT, stock broker; b. Rockville Centre, Long Island, N.Y., Mar. 30, 1931; s. Jerome and Fay (Gerber) M.; student N.Y. U., 1949, N.Y. Inst. Fin., 1973. With New Eng. Rep. Food Co., 1950-59; v.p. Merrill Lynch & Co., N.Y.C., 1959, now v.p., sr. account exec.; weekly columnist Options Alert, 1977-79. Club: Merrill Lynch & Co. (chmn.). Contbr. articles to profl. jours. Office: 165 Broadway 20th Floor New York NY 10080

METZGER, JAMES BORCHARD, bank exec.; b. N.Y.C., Aug. 16, 1938; s. H.A. and Evelyn (Borchard) M.; B.A. in Econs., Cornell U., 1962; M.B.A., Columbia U., 1964. Portfolio mgr. investment dept. Chase Manhattan Bank, N.Y.C., 1964-66; v.p., treas. Overseas Ventures, Inc., N.Y.C., 1966-70; mgr. fgn. dept. Paribas Corp., N.Y.C., 1970-71, fin. cons., 1971-72; mini-instl. sales, internat. bus. devel. staff Laird, Inc., 1973; with U.S. Govt., 1973-75, asst. dir. Office Fgn. Direct Investments, Washington, overseas rep. Overseas Pvt. Investment Corp., spl. asst. to dir. Office Policy Devel., Dept. Commerce, Washington; v.p., treas. Borchard Mgmt. Corp., N.Y.C., 1975-77; money mkt. mgr. Banco de Bilbao, N.Y.C., 1977-79, v.p., dep. mgr., 1979-81, sr. v.p., gen. mgr., 1981—. Home: 50 E 78th St New York NY 10021 Office: Gen Motors Bldg Ste 603 767 5th Ave New York NY 10153

METZGER, JOHN FREDERIC, banker; b. N.Y.C., June 12, 1946; s. Walter and Gretl (Hirsch) M.; B.S., N.Y. U., 1972, postgrad. Grad. Sch. Pub. Adminstrn., 1972-74; m. Carol Margulies Metzger, Aug. 18, 1974; 1 son, James David. Mgmt. trainee Citibank, N.Y.C., 1972-73; controller No. Acceptance Corp., Balt., 1974-75; asst. v.p. card products div. Citicorp, N.Y.C., 1975-76; controller Citicorp Australia, Sydney, 1979—; v.p. Retail Credit Services Inc., New Orleans, 1979—. Served to 1st lt. U.S. Army, 1966-69. Clubs: N.Y. U.;

Australian-Am. (Sydney). Office: Retail Credit Services Inc 921 Canal St New Orleans LA 70112

METZGER, SHIRLEY JEAN, seafood processing equipment mfr.; b. Estes Park, Colo., May 20, 1938; d. Wallace N. and Ruth Hurt (Fikes) Merrick; children—Debra Ann, Katherine Lee. Founder, 1952, since pres. Sort-Rite Internat., Inc., Harlingen, Tex. Mem. Nat. Fisheries Inst. (Distinguished Mem. Capt.'s Table award), Nat. Fedn. Businesses, U.S. C. of C., La. Tex. shrimp assns., Tex. Assn. Bus. (Small Bus. Person award 1974), Valley C. of C. Methodist. Home: 2206 Treasure Hill Blvd PO Box 645 Harlingen TX 78550 Office: 825 W Jefferson St PO Box 1805 Harlingen TX 78550

METZLER, DAVID LEE, electric co. exec.; b. Youngstown, Ohio, Apr. 28, 1934; s. Carroll Eugene and Doris Jean (Evans) M.; student Hiram Coll., 1952-55; B.S. in Bus. Adminstrn., Kent State U., 1960; m. Linda J. Modrzejewski, July 19, 1975; children—Nancy Jean, Craig Allen. Audit mgr. Peat, Marwick, Mitchell & Co., Cleve., 1960-72; corporate audit dir. Emerson Electric Co., St. Louis, 1972—. Fin. adviser Solon (Ohio) Sch. Bd., 1968-71. Served with U.S. Army, 1955-57, capt. Res., 1958-68. C.P.A., Ohio. Mem. Am. Inst. C.P.A.'s, Mo. Soc. C.P.A.'s, Inst. Internal Auditors. Club: Norwood Hills Country. Home: 352 Diplomat Saint Louis MO 63017 Office: 8100 W Florissant Saint Louis MO 63136

MEYER, CARL EDWIN, JR., aviation co. exec.; b. Flushing, N.Y., Aug. 6, 1928; s. Carl Edwin and Eunice Clifton (Taylor) M.; B.A., Amherst Coll., 1950; M.B.A., N.Y. U., 1955. Mgr., Harris, Kerr, Forster & Co., N.Y.C., 1953-65; asst. treas. Eastern Air Lines, 1965-68; pres., chief exec. officer Trans World Airlines, 1968—, also dir.; trustee Empire Savs. Bank; dir. Hilton Internat., Canteen Corp., Trans World Corp. Trustee, Midwest Research Inst. Served with AUS, 1950-53. Mem. Am. Inst. C.P.A.'s, Air Transport Assn. (dir.). Clubs: Sky (N.Y.C.); North Hempstead Country (Port Washington). Office: 605 3d Ave New York NY 11016

MEYER, CARL SHEAFF, mgmt. cons.; b. Mineola, N.Y., Dec. 19, 1932; s. William Herman and Dorothy Gertrude (Anderson) M.; B.A. in Arch., U. Va., 1956. Archtl. specialist, govt. sales coordinator metals div. Olin Corp., 1958-60; sales adminstr., advt. mgr. Gen. Bronze Corp., 1960-61; product mgr. Barrett div. Allied Chem. Corp., 1961-64; cons. Barrington & Co., 1964-68; sr. cons., mng. asso., v.p. Lester B. Knight & Assos., N.Y.C., 1968-77; pres. William H. Meyer & Assos., N.Y.C., 1977—; lectr. Am. Mgmt. Assn. Chief, Plandome (N.Y.) Fire Dept., 1965-67; trustee Plandome Employees Fund, 1966-76; bd. dirs. Plandome Civic Assn., 1974-75. Served with USN, 1956-58, capt. Res., 1958-80. Certified mgmt. cons. Mem. Inst. Mgmt. Cons. (bd. dirs. 1979—), Am. Arbitration Assn., Assn. Mgmt. Cons.'s, Naval Reserve Assn., Bank Mktg. Assn., Theta Chi. Republican. Episcopalian. Clubs: N.Y. Yacht, Manhasset Bay Yacht, Royal Bermuda Yacht, Shelter Island Yacht, Masons, Shriners, Meadow Brook Hunt. Contbr. articles to profl. jours. Home: 78 Westgate Blvd Plandome NY 11030 Office: 666 Fifth Ave New York NY 10019

MEYER, CAROLYN ANNE, mfg. co. ofcl.; b. Abilene, Kans., Jan. 30, 1945; d. Bernard Francis and Mary Edith (Carroll) M.; student Marymount Coll., 1963-65; B.A., Wichita State U., 1969. Copywriter Crown Drug Co., Kansas City, Mo., 1969-71; freelance advt. Accent Sound, Mission, Kans., 1969-77; traffic supr., copywriter Ray Advt. Agy., Kansas City, Mo., 1971-74; advt. mgr. Adler's Kansas City, Mo., 1974-77; mgr. advt. and sales promotion Lily div. Owens Illinois, Toledo, 1977-79; communications mgr. The Fuller Brush Co. subs. Consol. Foods Corp., 1979—. Mem. Am. Advt. Fedn. (Merit award 5th dist. 1978), Toledo Advt. Club (Silver award 1978), Womens Advt. Club Toledo (dir.), Women in Communications, Toledo Press Club. Democrat. Roman Catholic. Home: 809 Coolidge Great Bend KS 67530 Office: PO Box 729 Westport Addition Great Bend KS 67530

MEYER, CAROLYN BURNHAM, ednl. adminstr.; b. Boston, Sept. 25, 1921; d. John Wicks and Martha Briney (Emmons) Cooke; B.A., Smith Coll., 1943; m. John Thomas Burnham (dec.); children—William H., Robert C.; m. 2d, John H. Meyer (div.). Sales mgr. South Shore Mirror, Scituate, Mass., 1976-78; counsel cons. United Investment Counsel, Boston, 1978-79; asst. dir. devel. Thayer Acad., Braintree, Mass., 1979—. Republican. Episcopalian. Clubs: Pilgrim Tennis (Kingston, Mass.); South Shore Smith. Home: 28 Trout Farm Ln Duxbury MA 02332 Office: Thayer Acad 745 Washington St Braintree MA 02184

MEYER, DAVID LAWRENCE, computer programmer/analyst; b. Stillwater, Okla., Nov. 28, 1954; s. Warren D. and Merlyn L. M.; B.S. in Computer Info. Systems, Ariz. State U., 1977. Asst. mgr. Dairy Queen Restaurant, Tempe, Ariz., 1976; cook Denny's Restaurant, Tempe, 1976-78; controller SW Restaurant Systems, Tempe, 1976-78; programmer/analyst El Paso Co. (Tex.), 1978—. Mem. Am. Mgmt. Assn. Republican.

MEYER, E(DMOND) GERALD, univ. adminstr.; b. Albuquerque, Nov. 2, 1919; s. Leopold and Beatrice M.; B.S., Carnegie Mellon U., 1940, M.S., 1942; Ph.D., U. N.Mex., 1950; m. Betty F. Knobloch, July 4, 1941; children—Lee Gordon, Terry Gene, David Gary. Head sci. dept. U. Albuquerque, 1950-52; dean Grad. Sch. and Div. Research, N.Mex. Highlands U., 1952-63; dean Coll. Arts and Scis., U. Wyo., Laramie, 1963-75, v.p. research, 1975—; on sabbatical with Diamond Shamrock Corp., 1980; dir. 1st Wyo. Bank, Laramie; chmn. bd. Western Regional Sci. Lab.; chmn. Consortium of Univs. for Research on Energy; cons. NSF, HEW, Dept. Energy, GAO, Diamond Shamrock Corp. Served with USN, 1942-44. Fulbright prof., Chile, 1959; sci. adviser Gov. Wyo., 1972—. Fellow AAAS, Am. Inst. Chemists; mem. Am. Chem. Soc. (council), Laramie C. of C. (dir.), Biophys. Soc. Republican. Club: Rotary. Author: Chemistry: A Survey of Principles, 1963; Biophysical Kenitics, 1973; Legal Rights of Chemists and Engineers, 1977. Contbr. articles to profl. jours. Home: 1058 Colina Dr Laramie WY 82070 Office: Univ Wyoming Box 3825 Laramie WY 82071

MEYER, EDWARD HENRY, advt. exec.; b. N.Y.C., Jan. 8, 1927; s. I. H. and Mildred (Driesen) m.; B.A. with honors in Econs., Cornell U., 1949; m. Sandra Raabin, Apr. 26, 1957; children—Margaret Ann, Anthony Edward. With Bloomingdale's, div. Federated Dept. Stores, 1949-51, Biow Co., advt. agy., 1951-56; with Grey Advt., Inc., N.Y.C., 1956—, exec. v.p., dir., mem. exec. com., 1963-68, pres., chief exec. officer, 1968—; dir. Merrill Lynch Spl. Value Fund, May Dept. Stores Co., Merrill Lynch Ready Assets Fund, Trans-Lux Corp. Bd. dirs. Asso. Y's of N.Y., Am. Health Found. Served with USCG, 1945-47. Clubs: Econ., Univ., Cornell, Century Country, Harmonie (N.Y.C.). Home: Rockwood Ln Greenwich CT 06830 also 580 Park Ave New York NY 10021 Office: 777 3d Ave New York NY 10017

MEYER, FRED WILLIAM, JR., corp. exec.; b. Fair Haven, Mich, Jan. 7, 1924; s. Fred W. and Glayds (Marshall) M.; A.B., Mich. State Coll., 1946; m. Jean Hope, Aug. 5, 1946; children—Frederick, Thomas, James, Nancy. Salesman, Chapel Hill Meml. Gardens, Lansing, Mich., 1946-47; mgr. Roselawn Meml. Gardens, Saginaw, Mich., 1947-49; dist. mgr. Sunset Meml. Gardens, Evansville, Ind., 1949-53; pres. Memory Gardens Mgmt. Corp., Lincoln Memory Gardens and Forest Lawn Memory Gardens, Indpls., Chapel Hill Meml. Gardens, S. Bend, Ind., Covington Meml. Gardens, Ft. Wayne, Ind., Chapel Hill Meml. Gardens, Grand Rapids, Mich., Hamilton Meml. Gardens, Chattanooga, Sherwood Meml. Gardens, Knoxville, Tenn., White Chapel Meml. Gardens, Huntington, W.Va., Floral Hills Meml. Gardens, Clarksburg, W.Va., Beverly Hills Meml. Gardens, Morgantown, W.Va., Tri-Cities Meml. Gardens, Florence, Ala., Woodlawn Meml. Gardens, Paducah, Ky., White Chapel Meml. Gardens, Springfield, Mo., Mercury Devel. Corp., Indpls., Quality Printers, Indpls., Quality Marble Imports, Indpls., Am. Bronze Craft, Inc., Judsonia, Ark. Mem. Nat. Assn. Cemeteries, Am. Cemetery Assn., Prearrangement Interment Assn. Am., C. of C., Nat. Sales Execs., Sigma Chi, Phi Kappa Delta. Lutheran. Clubs: Meridian Hills Country, Columbia, Athenaeum, Elks. Home: 110 E 111th St Indianapolis IN 46280 Office: 3733 N Meridian St Indianapolis IN 46208

MEYER, GEORGE BAKER, II, advt. agy. exec.; b. Houston, Nov. 20, 1933; s. George Baker and Loraine (Morris) M.; B.A., U. Tex., 1958; children—Chaille: Chet, Graham, Cynthia. Partner, J.R. Phillips Investment Co., Houston, 1958-61; pres. Meyer Investment Co., Houston, 1961-65: exec. v.p. Boone Advt., Inc., Houston, 1965—; dir. Meyerland Bank; dir., officer Meyerland Co. Vestryman, St. John the Divine Ch., 1964-66, St. Thomas Epis. Ch., 1974-76; bd. dirs. Cerebral Palsy Found. Mem. Bus./Profl. Advt. Assn. Republican. Clubs: Houston, Forest, Masons, Rotary. Office: 3121 Buffalo Speedway Suite 303 Houston TX 77098

MEYER, GEORGE MICHAEL, mech. engr.; b. Nuremberg, Ger., Mar. 28, 1935; came to U.S., 1973, naturalized, 1980; s. Hans and Marie Henriette (Amler) M.; B.S. in Mech. Engring., Tech. U. Munich, 1958, M.S., 1960; m. Ruth Elizabeth Menhofer, Dec. 7, 1974. Various engring. and mgmt. positions, W. Ger., 1958-68; gen. mgr. gas dept. German Babcock & Wilcox, 1968-74, rep. in U.S., 1973-74; ind. engring. cons., 1974-76; mgr. sales and process engring. J.F. Pritchard Co., Kansas City, Mo., 1976-77; mgr. engring., utility div. Research Cottrell Co., Somerville, N.J., 1977-79; pres. Engrs. and Energy Investment Cons., Inc., New Preston, Conn., 1979—; cons. utility and chem. industry. Recipient Bronze medal German Chem. Soc., 1969. Mem. Soc. Naval Architects and Marine Engrs. Patentee in field. Home: Marble Hill New Preston CT 06777 Office: PO Box 308 New Preston CT 06777

MEYER, HELEN, publisher; b. Bklyn., Dec. 4, 1907; d. Bertolen and Esther (Greenfield) Honig; student pub. schs.; m. Abraham J. Meyer, Sept. 1, 1929; children—Adele Meyer Brodkin, Robert L. With Popular Sci., McCall's mag., 1921-22; pres., dir. Dell Pub. Co., Inc., N.Y.C., 1923-57; pres., dir. Dell Distbg., Inc., from 1957, now chmn. bd.; pres. Dell Internat., Inc., Montville Warehousing Co., Inc.; 1957—; chmn. bd. Noble & Noble Pubs., Inc., Dell Pub. Co., Inc.; editorial cons. Doubleday & Co., Inc., 1978—. v.p. Dellprint, Inc., Dunellen, N.J.; pres. Dial Press. Mem. Assn. Am. Pubs. (dir.). Home: 231 Montrose Ave South Orange NJ 07079 Office: 245 Park Ave New York NY 10017

MEYER, IRWIN STEPHAN, lawyer; b. Monticello, N.Y., Nov. 14, 1941; s. Ralph and Janice (Cohen) M.; B.S., Rider Coll., 1963; J.D., Cornell U., 1966: m. Leslie Mazor, July 10, 1977; children—Kimberly B., Joshua A. Admitted to N.Y. bar, 1966; tax mgr. Lybrand, Ross Bros. & Montgomery, N.Y.C., 1967-71; tax atty. Ehrenkranz, Ehrenkranz & Schultz, N.Y.C., 1971-74; prin. Irwin S. Meyer, N.Y.C., 1974-77, Levine Honig Eisenberg & Meyer, N.Y.C., 1977-78, Eisenberg Honig & Meyer, 1978—. Served with U.S. Army Res., 1966-71. C.P.A., N.J. Mem. Am., N.Y. State bar assns., Am., N.Y. State assns. attys.-C.P.A.'s, Am. Inst. C.P.A.'s, N.J. Soc. C.P.A.'s. Home: 19 Woodhaven Dr New City NY 10956 Office: 270 Madison Ave New York NY 10016

MEYER, LASKER MARCEL, retail exec.; b. Houston, Jan. 8, 1926; s. Lasker and Lucile (Dannenbaum) M.; student Rice U., 1942-44; m. Beverly Goldberg, Sept. 17, 1949; children—Lynn, Susan. With Meyer Bros., Inc., Houston, 1946-58, Foley's, Houston, 1959-79; chmn. bd., chief exec. officer Abraham & Straus, Bklyn., 1980—. Served in USN, 1944-46. Jewish. Club: Houston Racquet. Office: Brooklyn NY 11201

MEYER, MARVIN JONAS, ins. agt.; b. N.Y.C., June 13, 1943; s. Morris and Claire (Goodman) M.; B.S., CCNY; 1 son, David. Agt., Bernard Mayer & Marvin Meyer Assos., N.Y.C., 1961-70, supr., 1971-74, asso. gen. agt., 1974-76, gen. agt., 1976—. Mem. Million Dollar Round Table (life), N.Y.C. Life Underwriters Assn., Gen. Agts. Assn. (exec. bd.), Gen. Agts. Mgrs. Assn. Clubs: Old Oaks Country, Ocean Reef. Office: Bernard Mayer and Marvin Meyer Assos 680 Fifth Ave New York NY 10019

MEYER, RENE L., resort exec.; b. St. Gallen, Switzerland, July 27, 1935; came to U.S., 1953, naturalized, 1959; s. Ludwig B. and Irma Meyer; student U. Md., 1959-60; B.S. in Bus. Adminstrn., Calif. State U., Los Angeles, 1962, postgrad., 1962-64; m. Diana D. Deming, Dec. 5, 1959; children—Kevin A. and Deirdre V. (twins), Stephanie A., Bradford A. Acct., Price Waterhouse & Co., Los Angeles, 1962-68; sr. v.p. Sun Valley Co., Inc. (Idaho), 1968-77; sec., treas. Yosemite Park & Curry Co. subs. MCA Inc., 1977-79; pres. Snowbird Corp. (Utah), 1979—. Bd. dirs., treas. Center Arts and Humanities, Yosemite Nat. Park, Sun Valley. Served with U.S. Army, 1958-60. C.P.A., Calif. Mem. Am. Inst. C.P.A.'s, Calif. Soc. C.P.A.'s. Republican. Lutheran. Clubs: Winter (pres. 1978-79), Rotary (pres. 1972-73) (Sun Valley). Home: 8724 S Kingshill Dr Salt Lake City UT 84121 Office: Snowbird Corp Snowbird UT 84070

MEYER, RICHARD EDWARD, fragrance and cosmetics mfg. co. exec.; b. Cin., May 8, 1939; s. Joseph H. and Dolores (Daley) M.; A.B., U. Mich., 1961; m. Judith A. Shoup, Sept. 1, 1973; children—Donna, Valerie. Auto staff mgr. Chgo. Tribune, 1961-63; account supr., v.p. London & Assos. Advt., Chgo., 1963-64; pres., chmn. bd. Richard E. Meyer, Inc., Chgo., 1965-77; exec. v.p., gen. mgr. Jovan Inc., Chgo., 1974-75, pres., chief operating officer, 1975—, also dir., Mem. Fragrance Found. (dir.), Cosmetics Toiletries Fragrance Assn. (dir.), Chgo. Advt. Club, Broadcast Advt. Club, Nat. Assn. Chain Drugstores, Delta Upsilon Internat. Club: U. Mich. Club of Chgo. (trustee, past dir.). Patentee various scents by Jovan. Office: 875 N Michigan Ave Chicago IL 60611

MEYER, RUSSELL WILLIAM, JR., aircraft co. exec.; b. Davenport, Ia., July 19, 1932; s. Russell William and Ellen Marie (Matthews) M.; B.A., Yale, 1954; LL.B., Harvard, 1961; m. Helen Scott Vaughn, Aug. 20, 1960; children—Russell William III, Elizabeth Ellen, Jeffrey Vaughn, Christopher Matthews, Carolyn Louise. Admitted to Ohio bar, 1961, Kans. bar, 1975; mem. firm Arter & Hadden, Cleve., 1961-66; pres., chief exec. officer Grumman Am. Aviation Corp., Cleve., 1966-74; exec. v.p. Cessna Aircraft Co., Wichita, Kans., 1974-75, chmn. bd., chief exec. officer, 1975—; dir. Fourth Nat. Bank & Trust Co., Wichita. Bd. dirs. Cleve. Yale Scholarship Com., 1962-74, United Way Wichita and Sedgwick County, 1975—; trustee Wichita State U. Endowment Assn., 1975—, Wesley Hosp. Endowment Assn., 1977—. Served with USAF, 1955-58. Mem. Am., Ohio, Cleve., Kans. bar assns., Gen. Aviation Mfrs. Assn. (chmn. bd. 1973-74), Wichita C. of C. (dir. 1975—). Clubs: Wichita, Wichita Country. Home: 600 Tara Ct Wichita KS 67206 Office: Cessna Aircraft Co Wichita KS 67201

MEYER, WILLIS G(EORGE), petroleum geologist; b. Bellwood, Nebr., Jan. 21, 1906; s. George David and Ella V. (Carrigan) M.; A.B., U. Nebr., 1930; A.M., U. Cin., 1933, Ph.D., 1941; m. June Allison, June 26, 1937; children—Nancy Rebecca, Ann Marie. Geologist Amerada Petroleum Corp., Tex. and Okla., 1934-38, DeGoyler & MacNaughton, Dallas, 1938-48; partner Meyer & Achtschin, Dallas, 1948-57; owner, mgr. Willis G. Meyer (formerly Willis G. Meyer and Assos.), also cons. in petroleum engring. and geology, 1957—. Fellow Geol. Soc. Am.; mem. Am. Assn. Petroleum Geologists (past v.p.), Am. Geophys. Union, AAAS, Am., Dallas (past pres.) geol. socs., Soc. Ind. Profl. Earth Scientists (past pres.), Explorers Club, Sigma Xi, Acacia. Clubs: Engrs., Dallas Country, Petroleum (Dallas). Author geol. papers. Home: 4950 Rheims Pl Dallas TX 75205 Office: PO Box 7660 Inwood Sta Dallas TX 75209

MEYERHOFF, ARTHUR EDWARD, advt. exec.; b. Chgo., Mar. 12, 1895; s. Emanuel and Jennie (Lewin) M.; student pub. schs., Chgo.; m. Madelaine H. Goldman, 1921; m. 2d, Elaine Clemens, Jan. 27, 1945; children—Jane, Arthur Edward, Joanne, William, Judith Lynn. With Hood Rubber Co., 1914-22; classified advt., circulation mgr. Wis. News, Milw., 1922-29; with Neisser & Meyerhoff, Chgo., advt. and merchandising, 1929-41; pres. Arthur Meyerhoff Assos., Inc. (formerly Arthur Meyerhoff & Co.), Chgo., 1941-65, chmn. bd., 1965—; pioneered comic page advt.; dir. Santa Catalina Island Co., Chgo. Nat. League Baseball Club, Inc.; developer Myzon products; Myzon, Inc. organized, 1951; organizer Gibraltar Industries, Inc., 1958; developer Pam, spray for cookware. Mem. adv. bd. Sta. KBIG-KBRT, Los Angeles. Served with AEF, World War I. Recipient 1st prize Marshall Field candid div., 6th ann., 3d internat. competition and salon, 1939; George Washington Honor medal Freedoms Found., 1967. Mem. Am. Assn. Advt. Agys., C. of C. Author: Strategy of Persuasion, 1965. Office: 410 N Michigan Ave Chicago IL 60611

MEYERS, DONALD WILLIAM, mfg. co. exec.; b. Chgo., Jan. 30, 1929; s. Robert Francis and Alberta Mae (McMahon) M.; B.Sc., Loyola U., Chgo., 1954; M.B.A., U. Chgo., 1967; m. Sandra Jean Young, May 28, 1971. Personnel asst. Allstate, Skokie, Ill., 1954-64; mgr. personnel Ohmite Mfg. Co., Skokie, Ill., 1964-68; mgr. indsl. relations Warner Electric, South Beloit, Ill., 1968-70; employee relations mgr. Clark Equipment, Buchanan, Mich., 1970-73; dir. employee relations, engine components Wallace Murray Corp., Indpls., 1973—. Mem. salary compensation com. City of Carmel, Ind., 1977-78; mem. workmans compensation com. State of Ind., 1977-79. Served with USN, 1946-48, 50-52. Mem. Am. Soc. Personnel Adminstrs., Ind. Personnel Assns., Indpls. Personnel Assn. Home: 10549 LaSalle Rd Carmel IN 46032 Office: Wallace Murray Corp 1025 Brookside Ave PO Box 80B Indianapolis IN 46206

MEYERS, FRANCIS HART, paint mfg. co. exec.; b. San Jose, Calif., Aug. 12, 1925; s. Charles Wilfert and Stella (Yoachum) M.; M.A., U. Calif., San Francisco, 1952; m. Carmel Gloria Dali, June 13, 1952; children—Kimberly Anne, Carol Lee. Regional mfg. mgr. Fuller Panama Corp., Mexico City, 1960-62; resident tech. dir. Fuller Pakistan, Lahore, 1963-64; joint mng. dir. Glidden-Salchi, s.p.a., Milan, Italy, 1965-69; tech. dir. Kwal Paints, Inc., Denver, 1972—, mem. operating com., 1979—; pres. Internat. Paint Cons., Denver, 1973—; overseas dir. Champion Paints Ltd., Lahore, Pakistan, 1973—. Served with USAAF, 1943-46; ETO. Decorated Air Medal. Mem. Rocky Mountain Soc. Coatings Tech. (pres. 1979-80). Republican. Home: 16702 E Kentucky Ave Aurora CO 80012 Office: 3900 Joliet St Denver CO 80239

MEYERS, GEORGE EDWARD, plastics co. exec.; b. N.Y.C., June 26, 1928; s. Sol and Ethel (Treppel) M.; student Sampson Coll., 1948-49, Columbia, 1949-50; m. Marianna Jacobson, June 12, 1955; children—Deborah Lynn, Joanne Alyssa. Technician Manhattan Project, 1944; mem. staff CIA, 1951; tech. rep. Mearl Corp., 1952-56; sales mgr. Rona Labs., 1956-59; v.p. Dimensional Pigments Corp., 1959-60; pres. Plastic Cons., Inc., Plainview, N.Y., 1959—, Tech. Machinery Corp., 1963-69; pres. Extrudyne, Inc., 1971-77, also dir.; dir. research and devel. Homeland Industries, Bohemia, N.Y., 1977-80; plastic and bus. mgmt. cons. Plastic Cons.'s, Inc., Dix Hills, N.Y., 1980—; tchr., staff cons. N.Y.C. Bd. Higher Edn., Bronx Community Coll., 1966-70; lectr. N.Y. U., Technion, Haifa, Israel. Served with CIC, AUS, 1946-48. Mem. Soc. Plastics Engrs. (v.p. N.Y. sect. 1967-68), Soc. Plastics Industry, Am. Ordnance Assn., Aircraft Owners and Pilots Assn. Contbr. articles to profl. jours. Home: 25 Penn Dr Dix Hills NY 11746 Office: 25 Penn Dr Dix Hills NY 11746

MEYERS, GERALD CARL, automobile co. exec.; b. Buffalo, Dec. 5, 1928; s. Meyer and Berenice (Meyers) M.; B.S., Carnegie Inst. Tech., 1950, M.S. magna cum laude, 1954; m. Barbara Jacob, Nov. 2, 1958. With Ford Motor Co., Detroit, 1950-51, Chrysler Corp., Detroit and Geneva, 1954-62; with Am. Motors Corp., Detroit, 1962—, v.p., 1967-72, group v.p. product devel., 1968-71, group v.p. product, 1972-75, pres., chief operating officer, 1977, now chmn., chief exec. officer, also dir. Trustee Carnegie-Mellon U., Citizens Research Council of Mich., 1980—, U.S. council Internat. C. of C.; bd. dirs. Detroit Renaissance, Detroit Symphony Orch., 1979—, United Found., 1980—. Served to 1st lt. USAF, 1951-53. Mem. Motor Vehicle Mfrs. Assn. (chmn. bd. dirs.), Econ. Club Detroit (dir.), Soc. Automotive Engrs., The Conf. Bd., Hwy. Users Fedn. (dir.), Traffic Safety Assn. of Detroit (trustee 1979—), Tau Beta Pi, Phi Kappa Phi, Omicron Delta Kappa. Office: 27777 Franklin Rd Southfield MI 48034

MEYERS, PETER G., engring. and mgmt. cons. co. exec., inventor; b. Bklyn., Sept. 27, 1932; s. Joseph and Lillian M.; B.S. in Mech. Engring., Pa. State U., 1953; M.S. in Mech. Engring., U. Conn., 1956, M.B.A., 1960; m. Gail Brotherton, Feb. 1, 1960; children—Erik, Meredith. Sr. engr. Pratt & Whitney Aircraft, 1953-61; pres. Meyers Systems and Tech. Inc., Manchester, Conn., 1961—, gen. mgr. Meyers ElectroCooling div., Manchester, 1961—, Systems Research div., 1968—; adj. instr. bus. adminstrn. Manchester Community Coll., 1975—; mem. transp. and utilities task forces Capitol Region Council Govts., 1971-74. Mem. ASME, Soc. Mfg. Engrs. Patentee in fields of energy conversion, mfg. processes, solid wastes handling, and hosp. service equipment. Contbr. articles to profl. jours. Office: 983 Main St Manchester CT 06040

MEYLER, WILLIAM ANTHONY, chem. co. exec.; b. Newark, Oct. 29, 1944; s. Raymond Francis and Margaret (Loveless) M.; B.S., St. Joseph's Coll., 1966; M.B.A., Fairleigh Dickinson U., 1974; m. Dana Irene Brennan, May 3, 1975. Sr. accountant Ernst & Ernst, Trenton, N.J., 1970; dir. accounting Baker Industries, Inc., Parsippany, N.J., 1971-72; mgr. corporate accounting Witco Chem. Corp., N.Y.C., 1973-75, asst. to controller, 1976-77, asst. controller worldwide ops., 1977-79, asst. controller maj. systems project, 1979—; asst. adj. instr. Rutgers U., fall 1975. C.P.A., N.J. Fellow N.J. Soc. C.P.A.'s; mem. Am. Inst. C.P.A.'s, Am. Acctg. Assn. Home: 30 Southview Terr S Middletown NJ 07748 Office: 277 Park Ave New York NY 10017

MEYN, THOMAS LEE, accountant; b. Cedar Rapids, Iowa, Oct. 11, 1941; s. Harold F. and Lucille K. M.; B.B.A., Coe Coll., Cedar Rapids, Iowa, 1968; m. Carolyn K. Smith, July 18, 1964; children—Tadd, Derek, Kristen. Joined McGladrey Hendrickson & Co., C.P.A.'s, 1968—, partner, South Bend, 1974-80, exec. partner, group adminstr. 6 offices, 1980—. Served with AUS, 1960-63. C.P.A. Mem. Am. Inst. C.P.A.'s, Ind. Soc. C.P.A.'s, Iowa Soc. C.P.A.'s. Republican. Presbyterian. Club: South Bend Rotary (treas., dir.). Office: 340 S Columbia St South Bend IN 46601

MEYO, FRANK COLUMBO, fin. exec.; b. Cleve., Oct. 12, 1933; s. George John and Edith (Wilkes) M.; student, U. Kans., 1955, U. Nebr., 1956-57; m. Shirley Beth Lowery, Nov. 27, 1955; children—Wyn C., Douglas, Cole A., John E. Artist, Advance Art Studio, Cleve., 1951; with Fullwell Motors, Cleve., 1951-52, Research Corp. Am., Lincoln, Nebr., 1956-57, Beneficial Fin. Co., Morristown, N.J., 1957-71; pres., chmn. bd. Indsl. Loan Investment Co., Omaha, 1972—. Chmn. Children and Youth adv. bd. to Douglas County Bd. Commrs., Omaha, 1978—. Served with U.S. Army, 1954-55. Mem. Nebr. Assn. Indsl. Loan and Investment Cos. (treas. exec. com. 1978—), Sons of Italy (fin. sec. 1976—), Mchts. and Brokers Exchange (London), Nebr. Indsl. Bankers, Entrepreneurs Assn. Am., Nat. Second Mortgage Assn., Pilots Assn. Roman Catholic. Club: K.C. Home: 1511 S 91st Ave Omaha NE 68124 Office: 3003 Dodge St Omaha NE 68131

MEYROWITZ, ALVIN A(BRAHAM), mgmt. exec.; b. N.Y.C., Dec. 16, 1917; s. Jacob Norman and Anne (Bader) M.; A.B., Cornell U., 1938; M.B.A, N.Y. U., 1941; postgrad. Law Sch., George Washington U., 1948-50; m. Ruth Liberman, Feb. 1, 1942; children—Linda Jean, Jack Norman. Asso. bus. research dept. U. Newark, 1937-38; market analyst Miller Franklin Co., 1938-41; chief copper br. Office Civilian Supply W.P.B., 1941-46; dir. basic materials NHA, 1946-49; asst. dir. copper div. NPA, 1949-51; v.p. H. Kramer & Co., gen. mgr. Calif. div., El Segundo, Calif., 1951-62, v.p. H. Kramer & Co., El Segundo, 1964—; pres. Metals Refining Co., Inc., Los Angeles, 1962-64; dir. Mchts. Petroleum Co., Calif. Tech. Systems, Inc., Glendale; bd. advisers Mfrs. Bank, Los Angeles. Cons. Copper Policy, Washington, 1951-61; exec. reservist Bus. and Def. Services Adminstrn., Dept. Commerce, 1956—; vice chmn. So. Calif. Nat. Def. Exec. Res. Trustee City of Hope, Duarte, Calif. Mem. Am. Mktg. Assn., Am. Statis. Assn., Am. Econ. Assn., Am. Ordnance Assn., Am. Inst. Mgmt., Air Pollution Control Assn., Los Angeles, El Segundo chambers commerce, Sigma Alpha Mu. Clubs: Rotary, Beverly Hills, Brentwood Country. Home: 10450 Wilshire Blvd Los Angeles CA 90024 Office: PO Box 7 El Segundo CA 90245

MEZEI, GABOR, mfg. and service co. exec.; b. Budapest, Hungary, May 18, 1935; s. Endre and Anna (Kemeny) M.; came to U.S., 1956, naturalized, 1962; B.A., Hunter Coll., 1961; M.B.A. (Samuel Bronfman fellow), Columbia, 1962; m. Margaret A. Moran, Oct. 17, 1964; children—Robert, Peter. Mgr. planning and finance Transport Group, Universal Oil Products Co., Des Plaines, Ill., 1967-70, dir. finance Aerospace div., Bantam, Conn., 1970-72, dir. planning Bostrom div., Milw., 1972-73; exec. asst. to pres. ITT Service Industries, Cleve., 1973-75, v.p., 1977—, dir. ops. and planning, 1977, comptroller, 1978-79, mgr. fin. controls ITT Corp. Hdqrs., N.Y.C., 1979—; v.p. adminstrn. and planning APCOA, Inc., Cleve., 1975-76. Mem. Nat. Assn. Bus. Economists, Nat. Assn. Accountants, Beta Gamma Sigma. Home: Reimer Rd Westport CT 06880 Office: 320 Park Ave New York NY 10022

MHATRE, NAGESH SHAMRAO, health care industry exec.; b. Bombay, India, July 26, 1932; s. Shamrao G. and Laxmibai S. (Save) M.; came to U.S., 1954, naturalized, 1967; B.S., Bombay U., 1954; M.S., Oreg. State U., 1956; Ph.D., Rutgers U., 1962; m. Shirlee Lee Girsh, Jan. 21, 1962; children—Neelan Raj, Ravi Brian. Research biochemist Chems. div. Miles Lab., Inc., Elkhart, Ind., 1962-65, sr. scientist, sect. head enzymology research lab. Ames Co. div., 1965-71; mng. dir., dir. Miles-Yeda Ltd., Rehovot, Israel, 1971-75; dir. sci. affairs Lab-Tek Products div. Miles Lab., Inc., Naperville, Ill., 1975-78, v.p. product planning, research and devel., 1978-79; dir. bus. planning, lab. group Becton Dickinson & Co., Paramus, N.J., 1979—; now pres. lab. products Europe, Becton Dickinson Europe, Meylan, France; adj. lectr. Ind. U., South Bend, 1967-68. Recipient Outstanding Exporter award State of Israel, 1974; Carnation Co. research fellow, 1959-61. Mem. N.Y. Acad. Scis., Am. Chem. Soc. Contbr. articles to profl. jours.; patentee in field. Home: 8 Allée de la Roseraie Meylan 38240 France Office: Becton Dickinson Mack Centre Dr Paramus NJ 07652

MICHAELS, GORDON JOSEPH, copper co. exec.; b. Williamsport, Pa., May 9, 1930; s. Scott Joseph and Gloria Jean M.; B.S. in E.E., Bucknell U., 1959; m. Cleo Arlene Lela Tietbohl, June 12, 1954; children—Cathryn, Cheryl, Carole. Tool engr. Ternstedt div. Gen. Motors, Warren, Mich., 1958-59, sr. facilities engr., 1959-65; div. mgr. rectifiers M & T Chem. div. Am. Can Co., Rahway, N.J., 1965-71; v.p. mfg. and engring. Ullrich Copper Co., Kenilworth, N.J., 1971—; pres. Golld Truck Inc. Bd. dirs. Tech. Machinery Inst., Union, N.J.; active Jr. Achievement, Elizabeth, N.J. Served with USAR, 1954-56. Mem. IEEE, Assn. Mining Engrs. Republican. Lutheran. Home: 31 Debmar Dr Red Bank NJ 07701 Office: 2 Mark Rd Kenilworth NJ 07033

MICHAELS, JOHN PATRICK, JR., investment banker, media broker; b. Orlando, Fla., May 28, 1944; s. John Patrick and Mary Elizabeth (Slemons) M.; grad. Jamaica Coll., Kingston, 1961; B.A. magna cum laude, Tulane U., 1966; M.A. in Communications (ABC fellow), U. Pa., 1968; student London Sch. Econs., U. London, 1964; m. Ingeborg D. Theimer, May 2, 1970; 1 dau., Kimberly Lynn. With Times Mirror Co., 1968-72, v.p. mktg. and devel. TM Communications Co., 1968-72; v.p. Cable Funding, N.Y.C., 1973; founder, sr. partner Communications Equity Assos., cable TV investment bankers, 1973—; co-owner, officer, dir. Sanlando Cablevision, Inc., Altamonte Springs, Fla., Gulfstream Cablevision, Inc., Dunedin, Fla., Atlantic Am. Capital Corp., Tampa, Fla. Tulane scholar, 1962-66; Tulane fellow, 1963-66. Mem. Nat. Cable TV Assn., So. Cable TV Assn., Community Antenna TV Assn., Am. Mktg. Assn., Phi Beta Kappa, Phi Eta Sigma. Clubs: Univ., Tampa Yacht. Contbr. articles to trade jours. Home: 3024 Villa Rosa Park Tampa FL 33611 Office: 851 Lincoln Center 5401 W Kennedy Blvd Tampa FL 33609

MICHALIK, EDWARD FRANCIS, constrn. co. exec.; b. Hartford, Conn., Apr. 4, 1946; s. Edward S. and Hellen A. (Sito) M.; B.B.A., Nichols Coll., Dudley, Mass., 1969; children—Marc Edward, Michael Donald. Cost engr. Wigton Abbott Corp., Plainfield, N.J., 1969-70; mgr. cost control John W. Cowper Co., Buffalo, 1970-73; fin. v.p. Titan Group Inc., Paramus, N.J., 1973-76; sec.-treas., v.p., dir. Lilley Resources Corp., Harrison Western Corp., Denver; officer Lilley Resources Ltd. (Can.). Mem. Asso. Gen. Contractors, The Beavers, Am. Mgmt. Assn. Republican. Office: Harrison Western Corp 1208 Quail St Denver CO 80215

MICHAUD, ALPHEE MARTIAL, bus. exec.; b. St. Quentin, N.B., Can., Nov. 13, 1938; s. Napoleon and Alpheda (Deschenes) M.; M.D., Laval U., 1965; postgrad. in econs. McGill U., 1973; m. Claudette Gingras, July 4, 1964; children—Harold, Isabelle. Intern, Hotel-Dieu and Hosp. St. Sacrement, Quebec City, Que., 1964-66; resident in internal medicine Hosp. St. Sacrement, Quebec City, 1966-67; gen. practice medicine, Caraquet, N.B., 1968-71; pres., owner Les Pharmacies Populaires Ltd., Caraquet, 1971—; pres. Les Entreprises Ami Ltd., Caraquet, 1972—; pres., sec. Radio-Acadie Ltd., Caraquet, 1976—; pres., owner weekly newspapers; dir. N.B. Devel. Corp., 1973—; owner Les Papeteries du Nord Est Ltée, 1978—. Bd. dirs. Tracadie Assn. Mental Disease, 1973-76, N.B. Indsl. Devel. Bd., 1976—; pres. Le Festival Acadien Caraquet, 1974-76. Mem. Can., N.B. med. assns., Assn. Med. De Langue Francaise, Caraquet Bd. Trade, Atlantic Provinces Bd. Trade (chmn.), Canadian C. of C. (dir. 1980—). Roman Catholic. Med. editor weekly newspaper Le Voilier, 1972-76. Home: PO Box 450 Caraquet NB E0B 1K0 Canada Office: Place Caraquet Caraquet NB E0B 1K0 Canada

MICHEAUX, RICHARD WALTER, cons. co. exec.; b. N.Y.C., Aug. 2, 1921; s. Ernest and Edna Evelyne M.; B.A., Agr. and Tech. Coll., 1943; m. Margaret Mary Faulks, Feb. 3, 1963; 1 son, Gregg Marcel. Transp. cons. 20th Century Fox Film Corp., 1946-57, Cinerama, Inc., 1957-58; ops. mgr. Western Union Internat., N.Y.C., 1959-63; partner, cons. Subs Golf Inc. & Trade Inc., N.Y.C., 1963-68; gen. mgr., treas. Micheaux Sales Co., N.Y.C., 1968-72, pres. Micheaux Sales Inc. (parent co.), 1973—; managerial asst. N.Y. Telephone. Vice pres. Hamilton Grange, N.Y.C., Children's Orgn. and Better Neighborhoods, N.Y.C., 1976—. Served with USAAF, 1942-46; PTO. Club: Eleanor Roosevelt Democratic. Home: 289 Convent Ave New York NY 10031 Office: 4770 White Plains Rd New York NY 10462

MICHELS, FRANK GEORGE, chem. co. exec.; b. N.Y.C., Nov. 26, 1931; s. Frank and Dorothy Anna (Rosenberger) M.; B.Chem.Engring., Poly. Inst. Bklyn., 1952; M.Chem.Engring., N.Y. U., 1959; m. Marie Louise Ullrich, Aug. 24, 1957; children—Kathleen, Susan, Stephen, Karen, Peter, Jeffrey. Operations and Maintenance engr. E. I. DuPont De Nemours & Co., Inc., Gibbstown, N.J., 1952-53, 55-56; with Stauffer Chem. Co., Dobbs Ferry, N.Y., 1956-78, chief engr., 1972-78; v.p., gen. mgr. Stauffer Chem. Co. of Wyo., San Francisco, 1978—. Active Boy Scouts Am., Little League. Served with Chem Corps, U.S. Army, 1953-55. Mem. Am. Inst. Chem. Engrs., Am. Mgmt. Assn., Glass Packaging Inst. Roman Catholic. Club: Bankers. Home: 100 Bando Ct Walnut Creek CA 94595 Office: 636 California St San Francisco CA 94108

MICHELS, THOMAS ERNEST, govt. agy. data processing ofcl.; b. Sioux City, Iowa, Mar. 27, 1935; s. Ernest Thomas and Gertrude (Finnell) M.; B.S., U.S. Naval Acad., 1958; M.A., U. S.D., 1960; Ph.D., Iowa State U., 1972; m. Mary-Ann Ferlauto, Aug. 29, 1964; children—David Thomas, Melinda Ann. Aerospace scientist NASA Goddard Space Flight Center, Greenbelt, Md., 1960-68; systems analyst Gen. Electric, Washington, 1968-70; asst. dir. computer network U. Nebr., Lincoln, 1972-74; chief data automation Def. Communications Agy., Washington, 1974—; adj. prof. computer sci. Georgetown U., U. Nebr. Served with USN, 1954-58. Ednl. research fellow, 1969-72. Mem. Assn. for Computing Machinery, Armed Forces Communications and Electronics Assn., IEEE, Phi Kappa Phi. Club: Toastmasters Am. Contbr. articles in field to profl. publs. Home: 705 Skyline Ct Vienna VA 22180 Office: Defense Communications Agency Washington DC 20305

MICHELSEN, JOHN ERNEST, software services co. exec.; b. New Brunswick, N.J., May 11, 1946; s. Ernest Arnold and Ursula (Hunter) M.; B.S., Northwestern U., 1969; M.S., Stevens Inst. Tech., 1972; M.B.A. with honors, U. Chgo., 1978; m. Ruth Ann Flanders, June 15, 1969; children—Nancy Ellen, Rebecca Ruthann. Real-time programmer Lockheed Electronics Co., Plainfield, N.J., 1969-72; control system designer Fermi Nat. Accelerator Lab., Batavia, Ill., 1972-75; chief system designer Distributed Info. Systems Corp., Chgo., 1975-78, v.p., 1978-79; mgr. M.I.S. adminstrn. FMC Corp., Chgo., 1979—; cons. Princeton U. Tokamak Fusion Test Reactor project, 1976. Mem. Assn. Computing Machinery, Phi Eta Sigma, Tau Beta Pi, Beta Gamma Sigma. Office: 200 E Randolph Dr Chicago IL 60601

MICHELSON, LOUIS, elec. products co. exec., physicist; b. Lynn, Mass., Mar. 24, 1919; s. Charles and Minnie (Winer) M.; B.S., M.I.T., 1940; postgrad. U. Md., 1950-51; m. Florence M. Eisenberg, Nov. 9, 1941; 1 dau., Barbara Karen. With melting dept. Corning Glass Works (N.Y.), 1940-41; elec. engr. Sanborn Instrument Co., Cambridge, Mass., 1945-46; chief engr., gen. mgr. Allied Cement and Chem. Co., Lynn, 1946-47; tech. dir. Army Ordnance Submarine Mine Lab., Naval Ordnance Lab., White Oak, Md., 1947-50, chief of mine div., 1950-51; tech. dir. Naval Underwater Ordnance Sta., Newport, R.I., 1951-55; mgr. rocket engines Flight Propulsion Lab., Gen. Electric Co., Evendale, O., 1955-60; mgr. space environment simulation facilities Missile and Space div., Phila., 1960-61, mgr. NASA programs, 1964-65, mgr. advanced requirements, 1965—; pres. Spacerays, Inc., Burlington, Mass., 1966-67; pres. Lion Precision Corp., elec. products, Newton, Mass., 1967—. Served to maj. AUS, 1941-45. Mem. Am. Rocket Soc. (pres. So. Ohio sect. 1953-54), Army Ordnance Assn., Am. Mgmt. Assn., Inst. Aeronautical Scis., I.E.E.E., Engring. Soc. R.I., AIAA (mem. spacecraft com. 1963-65), Scabbard and Blade. Patentee in field. Home: 25 Beechcroft Rd Newton MA 02158 Office: Lion Precision Corp 60 Bridge St Newton MA 02185

MICHLIN, NORMAN, chem. corp. exec.; b. Tyrone, Pa., June 22, 1922; s. John and Zelda (Solomon) M.; B.S., Rose Poly. Inst., 1943; m. Bernice Goldberg, Mar. 9, 1946; children—Robert, Jeffrey, Margie Ann. Founder, co-owner Michlin Surplus Co., Detroit, 1946—; founder, sec., treas. Mich. Indsl. Finishes, Detroit, 1948—; pres. Michlin Chem. Corp., Detroit, 1954—; founder, pres. Dannz Land Co., Detroit, 1957—; founder, pres. Universal Devel. Corp., Detroit, 1970—. Pres. Twickingham Civic Assn., 1969, Vandenberg PTA, 1962; vice chmn. Mich. Regional Adv. Bd., 1975-80. Served with Signal Corps, U.S. Army, 1943-46. Jewish. Club: B'nai B'rith. Home: 28200 Bell Rd Southfield MI 48034 Office: Michlin Chem Corp 9045 Vincent St Detroit MI 48211

MICKEL, BUCK, constrn. co. exec.; b. Elberton, Ga., Dec. 17, 1925; s. James Clark and Reba (Vaughn) M.; B.S., Ga. Inst. Tech., 1947; m. Minor Herndon, May 2, 1946; children—Minor Herndon, Buck Alston, Charles Clark. With Daniel Constrn. Co., Greenville, S.C. 1947—, exec. v.p. 1960-65, pres., 1965-74, chmn., from 1974; chmn., pres. Daniel Internat. Corp.; dir. Citizens & So. Nat. Bank S.C., Graniteville Co., Seaboard Coast Line R.R. Co., Richmond, Va., Liberty Life Ins. Co., Assos. Investments Inc., South Bend, Liberty Corp., Wachovia Realty Corp., Monsanto Corp., Fluor Corp. Past pres. Greenville YMCA; past dir. United Fund; vice chmn. bd. trustees Converse Coll., Spartanburg, S.C.; life trustee Clemson U.; trustee S.C. Found. Ind. Colls., Inc.; adv. trustee Wofford Coll., Presbyn. Coll., Clinton, S.C., Furman U.; mem. Gov.'s Commn. on Higher Edn. for Jr. Colls.; bd. dirs. S.C. Ednl. TV. Served to 1st lt. C.E., AUS, World War II. Mem. S.C. (dir.), U.S. chambers commerce, Ga. Tech. Alumni Assn. (adv. bd.), NAM (dir.), Newcomen, Soc., Sigma Alpha Epsilon. Clubs: Masons, Green Valley Country (past dir.), Greenville Country, Poinsett (past dir.), Cotillion, City (Greenville); Piedmont (Spartanburg); Commerce, Capital City (Atlanta); City (Charlotte); Weavers, Links (N.Y.C.); Augusta (Ga.) Nat. Golf. Office: Daniel Bldg Greenville SC 29602

MICKENS, EDWARD FREDERICK, traffic exec.; b. Garfield, N.J., Sept. 11, 1924; grad. Acad. Advance Traffic, 1948; B.S., Rutgers U., 1955; m. Olive T. Kowalski, Sept. 29, 1946; children—Patricia, Edward, Robert, Janet, Michael. Night supr. L.I. Transp. Co., Carlton Hill, N.J., 1945; rate specialist Chevrolet-Bloomfield div. Gen. Motors Corp., Bloomfield, N.J., 1946-51; traffic mgr. Coates Bd. & Carton Co., Inc., Garfield, N.J., also Stroudsburg, Pa., 1951-64, sales service mgr., 1960-64, gen. traffic mgr., 1964; gen. traffic mgr. Becton, Dickinson & Co., 1965-68, mgr. distbn. and gen. traffic, 1968—; substitute tchr. traffic mgmt. Fairleigh Dickinson U., Teaneck, N.J., 1959—; traffic cons., 1949—. Served with USNR, 1943-46. Mem. Nat. Indsl. Traffic League, ICC Practitioners Assn., Delta Nu Alpha (pres. Newark 1967). Club: Traffic of North Jersey (pres. Paterson 1962). Research on ICC, pub. relations in trucking industry. Home: 264 Chittendon Rd Clifton NJ 07013 Office: Rutherford NJ 07070

MIDDENDORF, ROBERT WILLIS, cosmetic co. exec.; b. Akron, Ohio, Sept. 24, 1914; s. John Wienhold and Eva Belle (Foltz) M.; student pub. schs.; m. Olga Krist, Apr. 16, 1938; children—John Karl, Kathi (Mrs. Gerald Folden), Johanna (Mrs. Joseph Ogrin), Eric, Heidi. With Bonne Bell, Inc., Cleve., 1940—, salesman, 1940-50, sales mgr., 1950-60, v.p. sales, 1960-66, v.p. sales and mktg., 1966-70, sr. v.p., 1970-75, exec. v.p., 1975—, also dir. and chmn. exec. com. Vice chmn. Cleve. Better Bus. Bur., 1971—. Trustee, Grad. Sch. Sales Mgmt. and Mktg., Syracuse U., 1968-76, chmn., 1975-76. Mem. Cleve. Sales and Mktg. Execs. Club (pres. 1967-68), Sales and Mktg. Execs. Internat. (regional v.p. 1971, 72, 73, sr. v.p. 1976-77). Republican. Mem. United Ch. of Christ (deacon, trustee). Mason (32 deg.). Club: Fairlawn Country (Akron). Home: 200 Schocalog Rd Akron OH 44313 Office: Bonne Bell Inc 18519 Detroit Ave Lakewood OH 44107

MIDDLEKAUFF, JAMES HOLAN, chem. co. exec.; b. Cleve., July 16, 1938; s. Roger David and Ella Marie (Holan) M.; B.S., Mass. Inst. Tech., 1960; M.B.A., Boston U., 1964; m. Eveline Schmidt Bowers, Aug. 26, 1979; children by previous marriage—Scott H., Lee M. Sales engr. Trane Co., Boston, 1960-64; rep. comml. devel. Am. Cyanamid Co., Wakefield, Mass., 1964-67, mgr. comml. devel., bldg. products div., 1967-68; asst. to v.p. Watts Regulator Co., Lawrence, Mass., 1968-70; mgmt. analyst comml. devel. div. Am. Cyanamid Co., Wayne, N.J., 1970-72, project coordinator internat. div., 1972-74, mgr. comml. planning med. products, 1974-75, mgr. pharm. div., 1975-76, mgr. strategic planning internat. div. 1976-80, dir. materials mgmt. and planning Cyanamid Quimica do Brasil Ltda., Rio de Janeiro, 1980—; instr. Merrimac Coll., Mass., 1968-70. Mem. Town of Lynnfield (Mass) Charter Commn., 1968-70. Served with AUS, 1961. Clubs: Road Runners of N.J., Mass. Inst. Tech. of N.J. (v.p.), Wyckoff Jr. C. of C. (v.p.), Toastmasters of Clifton (N.J.). Home: Ave Delfim Moreira 830/101 Leblon Rio de Janeiro Brazil Office: Ave Rio Branco 311 #7 Rio de Janeiro Brazil

MIDDLETON, CAROLE FOSTER, ins. broker; b. Weymouth, Mass., Dec. 24, 1946; d. David Warren and Hazel Margaret (MacRae) Foster; B.A., Coll. St. Catherine, 1968; B.S., Rutgers U., 1974; m. Finley N. Middleton, II, Mar. 23, 1974. Claims supr. Allstate Ins. Co., 1969-74; asst. account exec. Johnson & Higgins, Brazil, 1974-76; new bus. prodn. mgr. Edward Lumley & Sons, South Africa, 1976-77; asst. v.p. Johnson & Higgins, N.Y.C., 1977-81; asst. v.p. Alexander & Alexander, N.Y.C., 1981—; speaker on sales techniques and women in ins. Bd. dirs. Bklyn. YWCA, also mem. fin. com.; active Bklyn. Women's Network. Mem. Nat. Assn. Ins. Women, Adminstrv. Mgmt. Assn., Nat. Fedn. Bus. and Profl. Women, Assn. Profl. Ins. Women, Women's Econ. Round Table. Presbyterian. Club: Wall St. Bus. and Profl. Women's (pres.). Columnist Wall St. Woman, 1979-80. Home: 91 Columbia Heights Brooklyn NY 11201 Office: 1185 Ave of Americas New York NY 10036

MIDDLETON, CHARLES FRANCIS, JR., engring. co. exec.; b. Winchester, Mass., Sept. 2, 1933; s. Charles Francis and Alberta Ameilia (Schmitt) M.; m. Shirley Marie Glynn, May 3, 1959; children—Wayne Charles, Craig Charles, Jane Alison. Designer, Raytheon Co., Waltham, Mass., 1951-52, engr., Wayland and Sudbury, Mass., 1956-64; engring. mgr. ITT, Raleigh, N.C., 1964-65, Raytheon Co., Sudbury and Norwood, Mass., 1965-69; pres. Concept Formulation & Mgmt. Inc., Wayland, 1969—. Mem. com. Boy Scouts Am., Sudbury, 1975-78. Served with USAF, 1952-56. Patentee in field. Home: 18 Ames Rd Sudbury MA 01776 Office: PO Box 24 187 E Commonwealth Rd Wayland MA 01778

MIDDLETON, DERALD LLOYD, mfg. co. exec.; b. Guthrie Center, Iowa, Aug. 24, 1930; s. Harold and Myrtle Violet (Moore) M.; student public schs., Guthrie Center; m. Juanita Grace Evans, Mar. 23, 1951; children—Rick, Rita, Roger, Rhonda, Ryan. Pres., gen. mgr. Guthrie Ready Mix Co., Inc., Guthrie Center, 1959-70; pres. Circle M Enterprises, Guthrie Center, 1973-75, Interstate Tiedown Systems, Inc., Des Moines, 1977-80. Mem. Guthrie Center City Council, 1965-68; formerly active Boy Scouts Am. Mem. Guthrie Center C. of C. (pres. 1966), Full Gospel Businessmen's Fellowship Internat. Republican. Methodist. Home: 607 Brown St Guthrie Center IA 50115

MIDDLETON, FREDERICK ALEXANDER, JR., mfg. co. exec.; b. Morristown, N.J., June 27, 1949; s. Frederick A. and Carolene B.; B.S. in Chemistry, M.I.T., 1967-70, postgrad. Sloan Sch. Mgmt., 1970-71; M.B.A., Harvard U., 1973; m. Carole J. Might, 1978; children—Alexander, Jennifer. Cons., McKinsey & Co., San Francisco, 1973-75; asst. to chmn. and chief exec. officer Studebaker-Worthington, N.Y.C., 1975-77; v.p. corp. planning and devel. Chase Manhattan Bank, N.Y.C., 1977-78; v.p. fin. and adminstrn. Genentech, Inc., South San Francisco, Calif., 1978—. Recipient Alpha Chi Sigma Achievement award, 1971; Alpha Theta scholarship trophy, 1971. Mem. Am. Chem. Soc., Phi Lambda Upsilon, Sigma Chi. Clubs: Harvard, M.I.T. Contbr. articles to Sloan Mgmt. Rev., Jour. Phys. Chemistry. Office: Genentech 460 Point San Bruno Blvd South San Francisco CA 94080

MIDIRI, PHILIP DOMINICK, record co. exec.; b. Queens, N.Y., Oct. 7, 1950; s. Stephen and Mary Jane (Failla) M.; B.B.A., CCNY, 1972. Sr. auditor consumer goods and services div. Arthur Andersen & Co., N.Y.C., 1972-76; corp. audit mgr. CBS Records Internat., N.Y.C., 1976-77, dir. acctg., 1977-78, dir. mktg. adminstrn., 1978-80, dir. adminstrn. CBS Records Australia Ltd., North Sydney, 1980—. C.P.A., N.Y. Mem. Am. Inst. C.P.A.s. Home: 9/82 Raelan St Mosman 2088 NSW Australia Office: care CBS Records Australia Ltd 15 Blue St North Sydney 2060 New South Wales Australia

MIELE, ARTHUR ROBERT, metals co. exec.; b. N.Y.C., June 4, 1941; s. Albert Frederick and Marie Jean (Timpone) M.; B.A., St. John's U., 1963; M.B.A., George Washington U., 1967; m. Susan Jean Ripley, Oct. 18, 1969; children—Arthur Robert, Heather Kristen. Planning mgr. Phelps Dodge Internat. Corp., N.Y.C., 1967-72, v.p. mktg. Phelps Dodge P.R. Corp. and Phelps Dodge Steel Co., Carolina, P.R., 1972-74, pres. Phelps Dodge P.R. Corp., 1974-78, also dir.; pres. Alambres y Cables Venezolanos S.A., 1978—; v.p. S.Am. ops. Phelps

Dodge internat., Coral Gables, Fla., 1976—; dir. Alcan de Venezuela, Camara Nacional Empresas de Telecommunicaciones, Cables Electrics os Ecuatorianos C.A., Vencobre S. A., Redivenca S. A. Active Jr. Achievement. Served with U.S. Army, 1964. Recipient Alumni Achievement award George Washington U., 1978; George B. Munroe award Phelps Dodge Corp., 1980. Mem. Young Pres.'s Orgn., P.R. C. of C., Am. Mfrs. Assn., Am. Mgmt. Assn., Sales and Mktg. Execs. Assn., Phi Kappa Theta. Clubs: Toastmasters, Racquet. Home: care Alcave Apartado 62/07 Caracas Venezuela

MIELKE, FREDERICK WILLIAM, JR., utility co. exec.; b. N.Y.C., Mar. 19, 1921; s. Frederick William and Cressida (Flynn) M.; A.B., U. Calif., 1943; J.D., Stanford U., 1949; m. Lorraine Roberts, 1947; children—Bruce Frederick, Neal Russell. Admitted to Calif. bar, 1950; law clk. to Asso. Justice John W. Shenk, Calif. Supreme Ct., 1949-51; with Pacific Gas and Electric Co., San Francisco, 1951—, exec. v.p., 1976-79, chmn. bd., chief exec. officer, 1979—, also dir.; dir. Pacific Gas Transmission Co., Alta. and So. Gas Co., Eureka Energy Co., Natural Gas Corp. Calif., Edison Electric Inst. Trustee, Stanford U., 1977—, Golden Gate U., 1977-79; bd. dirs. Calif. C. of C., 1979—, San Francisco C. of C., 1977-79, Ind. Colls. No. Calif., 1969-79. Served with USN, 1943-46. Mem. Am. Bar Assn., Calif. Bar Assn., Pacific Coast Elec. Assn., Pacific Coast Gas Assn. Club: Electric of San Francisco. Office: 77 Beale St San Francisco CA 94106

MIHALAS, NICHOLAS MICHAEL, watch and clock co. exec.; b. Norfolk, Va., June 23, 1937; s. Michael and Vivian (Pitsikoulis) M.; B.Sc., Va. Poly. Inst., 1959; M.B.A., Pepperdine U., 1975; m. Elaine Zelinsky, July 2, 1966; children—Michael Joseph, Christina. Engring. mgr. Gen. Electric Co., Phila., 1960-69; cons. Aerospace Corp., Los Angeles, 1970; pres. Timex Corp., Waterbury, Conn., 1971—, dir.; dir. TMX Ltd., Conn. Econ. Devel. Corp. Trustee St. Margaret's Sch. Served with USAF, 1959. Mem. Am. Mgmt. Assn., Conf. Bd., Western Conn. Indsl. Council, Waterbury C. of C. (dir.). Republican. Waterbury Country, Copper Valley. Office: Timex Corp Waterbury CT 06720*

MIHALICK, STEPHEN CHARLES, indsl. engr.; b. Youngstown, Ohio, Aug. 7, 1954; s. Edward Emil and Elizabeth (Kohl) M.; B.S. in Edn.-Indsl. Arts, Ohio U., 1976; postgrad. in indsl. tech. Western Ill. U., 1977-79. With paint dept. Youngstown Steel Door, 1973-74; lab. asst. indsl. tech. dept. Ohio U., Athens, 1974-76; tchr. Youngstown public schs., 1976-77; grad. asst. indsl. edn. and tech. dept. Western Ill. U., Macomb, 1977-78; indsl. engr. Bailey Control Co., Wickliffe, Ohio, 1978-79; mfg. engr. instruments div. Gould Inc., Cleve., 1979—. Mem. Nat. Assn. Watch and Clock Collectors. Home: 15616 Maplewood Ave Maple Heights OH 44137

MIHALIK, FRANK MELVYN, mktg. co. exec.; b. Aliquippa, Pa., Feb. 20, 1927; s. Michael K. and Mary (Kozak) M.; student U. Wis., 1945-46; B.A., Duquesne U., 1949; m. Mona Jo Haney, Aug. 25, 1962; children—Jeffrey Mark, Marisa Ann. Sports editor Beaver Valley Times, Aliquippa, 1944-45; feature writer Pitts. Post-Gazette, 1949; publicity dir. Contest Bd., Am. Automobile Assn., Washington, 1949-51; screen writer MGM, Hollywood, Calif., 1951-52; publicity dir. Switch & Signal div. Westinghouse Air Brake Co., Pitts., 1952-53; pub. relations dir. Instrument Soc. Am., Pitts., 1953-54; sales promotion mgr. Catranel Constrn. Co., Pitts., 1954-59; v.p. real estate devel. Penn-Internat., Inc., Pitts., 1959-70; pres. Comml. Realty Mktg., Inc., Monroeville, Pa., 1970—; pres. Shortway Freeway Land Corp. Mem. Am. Mgmt. Assn., Internat. Platform Assn., Nat. Assn. Corp. Real Estate Execs. (nat. chmn. chpt. edn.), Nat. Assn. Rev. Appraisers (cert.), Urban Land Inst., Internat. Council Shopping Centers, U.S. Olympic Soc., Smithsonian Inst., Nat. Students Assn. (Pa. State chmn. 1947-48). Roman Catholic. Office: Monroe Complex Bldg 1 2510 Mosside Blvd Monroeville PA 15146

MIHELICH, DONALD LOUIS, engring. co. exec.; b. Lake Linden, Mich., Mar. 26, 1926; s. Lodi Mathew and Evelyn Ann (Thouin) M.; B.Indsl. Engring., Gen. Motors Inst., 1950; M.Indsl. Engring., Okla. State U., 1971; m. Wilma Tuma, Dec. 20, 1947; children—Michael, Kenneth, Thomas, Anne Marie. Foreman, Chevrolet div. Gen. Motors Corp., St. Louis, 1951-53; sr. mfg. engr. N. Am. Aviation Co., Los Angeles, 1953-57; prodn. mgr. Bobrick Mfg. Co., Los Angeles, 1957-59; v.p. prodn. Barber Webb Inc., Los Angeles, 1959-65; indsl. engring. specialist N.Am. Rockwell Corp., 1965-68, mgr. indsl. and facilities engring., Tulsa, 1968-71; mgr. Urban Ore div. Williams Bros. Engring. Co., Tulsa, 1971—. Bd. dirs. Neighbor for Neighbor. Served with USAAF, 1944-46. Decorated Air medal. Registered profl. engr., Okla., Calif. Mem. Am. Inst. Indsl. Engrs. (v.p. Los Angeles 1956, dir. 1956-59, treas. Tulsa 1974-76), ASTM (chmn. com. resource recovery 1978), Engrs. Soc. Tulsa, Am. Pub. Works Assn., Okla. Soc. Profl. Engrs. Patentee plastic cell liners. Home: 4344 E 72d St Tulsa OK 74136 Office: 6600 S Yale Ave Tulsa OK 74177

MIHELICH, JOHN LOUIS, metall. engr.; b. Cleve., Oct. 10, 1937; s. Joseph F. and Helen (Laurich) M.; B.S., Case Western Res. U., 1959, M.S., 1961, Ph.D., 1964; m. Donna L. Robison, Dec. 29, 1962; children—Mary L., John L. III, Michael D., Joseph R., Peggy E. With Jones & Laughlin Steel Corp., Pitts., 1964-70; with Climax Molybdenum Co., Ann Arbor, Mich., 1970—, v.p. research, Pitts., 1979—. Mem. ASTM, Am. Soc. Metals, AIME, Sigma Xi. Roman Catholic. Patentee in field; contbr. articles to profl. jours. Office: PO Box 1568 Ann Arbor MI 48106

MIHLIK, JOSEF JOHN, real estate exec.; b. Woodstock, Ont., Can., Mar. 30, 1942; s. Josef and Mary (Brinsko) M.; B.A., U. Western Ont., 1968; postgrad. Ariz. State U., evenings 1968; m. Judith Sheila Nutt, June 29, 1963; children—James John, Josef James. Came to U.S., 1966, naturalized, 1971. Staff accountant Clarkson, Gordon & Co., London, Ont., 1965, 66; sr. accountant Arthur Young & Co., Phoenix, 1966-68; controller Verco Mfg., Phoenix, 1968-69, Queen Creek Land & Cattle Corp., Phoenix, 1969-70; controller Sunshine Land & Cattle Corp., Phoenix, 1970-71, pres., 1971—; sec.-treas. Western Nat. Land Corp., Phoenix, 1971-74, pres., 1974—; pres. Republic Nat. Mortgage Corp., 1971-74, West Phoenix Properties, Inc. (formerly Litchfield Land Corp.), 1972—, Western Nat. Mortgage Corp., 1973— (all Phoenix). C.P.A., Ariz. Mem. Am. Inst. C.P.A.'s, Ariz. Soc. C.P.A.'s, Exec. Internat. Club, Platform Profls. Clubs: Valley of Sun Weimaraner (pres. 1972-73) Arizona (Phoenix). Home: 12202 N 60th Pl Scottsdale AZ 85254 Office: PO Box 4008 Scottsdale AZ

MIJARES, HUMBERTO LUIS, steel co. exec.; b. Matamoros, Mex., Jan. 11, 1926; came to U.S., 1955, naturalized, 1962; s. Antonio Mijares and Luz M. Ayala; C.E., U. Nuevo Leon, 1950; m. Hilda Martinez Gonzalez, Oct. 2, 1950; children—Humberto Luis, Hilda Marie, Carlos, Alexandra, Sandra. With Alamo Iron Works, San Antonio, 1955-59, Tex. Hwy. Dept., San Antonio, 1959-62, Hi-way Signs, Inc., Norman, Okla., 1962-66; rebar detailer Border Steel Mills Inc., El Paso, Tex., 1966-68, chief engring., 1968-75, mgr. fabrication, 1975-77, v.p. Fabricating div., 1977—. Mem. Nat. Concrete Reinforced Steel Inst., Assn. Reinforced Bar Producers. Republican. Roman Catholic. Home: 5713 Oak Cliff El Paso TX 79912 Office: PO Box 12843 El Paso TX 79912

MIKELSON, DAVID LEE, electronics mfg. co. exec.; b. South Bend, Ind., Aug. 16, 1938; s. Kermit L. and Helen (Hinkson) M.; student U. Cin., 1956-61, Miami U., Oxford, Ohio, 1962-63; B.S. in Bus., Ind. U., 1966; postgrad. Syracuse U., 1966-67; m. Patricia MacDade, Apr. 23, 1976; children—John, Dan, Sandy Mikelson, James, Tari. With McDade Blackhawk Electro-Components Inc., Bettendorf, Iowa, 1963-66; foreman RCA, Bloomington, Ind., 1966-67; mfg. engr. Gen. Electric, Syracuse, N.Y., 1967-69; mgr. engring. Philco-Ford, Phila., 1969-75; dir. ops. ITT, Brussels, Belgium, 1975-76; pres. Pleasant Valley Industries, Bettendorf, 1975-76; div. mgr. Graftek div. Exxon Enterprises, South Plainfield, N.J. and Raleigh, N.C., 1977-78; pres. Blackhawn Computers, Bettendorf, 1979—, Wire-Tech., Bettendorf, 1979—; dir. D & M Constrn., Ltd.; broker Iowa Real Estate Services, Bettendorf. Major Civil Air Patrol, 1956—. Served with USAF, 1961-62; ETO. Registered profl. engr., Calif., Can. Mem. Am. Inst. Indsl. Engrs., Soc. Mfg. Engrs. Clubs: Optimists, Moose. Home: 4480 N Newport Ct Bettendorf IA 52722 Office: 2705 E Kimberly Rd Bettendorf IA 52722

MIKESELL, SHARELL LEE, mfg. co. exec.; b. Coshocton, Ohio, Nov. 24, 1943; s. Forrest and Wilma Madeline (Axline) M.; B.A., Olivet Nazarene Coll., 1965; M.S., Ohio State U., 1968; Ph.D. (NDEA fellow), U. Akron, 1971. Chemist, Edmont-Wilson Co., Coshocton, 1965; polymer chemist Gen. Electric Co., Coshocton, 1971-72, project mgr., 1972-74, mgr. market devel. and indsl. products, 1974-75, mgr. indsl. product devel., 1975-76; mgr. textile systems lab. Owens-Corning Fiberglas Corp., Granville, Ohio, 1976-78, research dir. textile operating div. and fabric structures, 1978—. Mem. Am. Assn. Textile Chemists and Colorists, Am. Chem. Soc. Patentee in field. Office: Owens-Corning Fiberglas Corp Tech Center Box 415 Granville OH 43023

MIKULKA, BOHUSLAV EDUARD, wood products co. exec.; b. Velka Bystrice, Czechoslovakia, Apr. 7, 1925; s. Bohuslav and Anna (Langer) M.; B.S., U. Tharandt, Eberswalde, Germany, 1942-44; postgrad. U. Brno, Czechoslovakia, 1945-48; M. Forest Engring., Hochschule fur Bodenkultur, Vienna, Austria, 1951; D.Tech. Sci., Swiss Fed. Inst. Tech., Zurich, 1955; Ph.D., Inst. Wood Tech., Munich and Braunschweig, Germany, 1955; m. Maja Doris Eimer, July 25, 1956; 1 dau., Ann Elizabeth. Came to U.S., 1955, naturalized, 1961. Research asso. Swiss Fed. Inst. Tech., 1951-55; with Temple Industries, Inc., Diboll, Tex., 1956-65; with Evans Products Co., 1965—, dir. research and devel., mgr., Doswell, Va., 1969-71, mgr. tech. and engring. center, Corvallis, Oreg., 1971-77, dir. tech., 1977-79, v.p. research and devel. and environ., 1979—. Mem. tech. com. Insulation Bd. Inst., 1959-60; pres. Student Assn. Brno, 1947-49, Czechoslovakia Student Assn., Zurich, 1951-55, U. Free Europe, Strasbourg, France, 1953-55. Mem. Forest Products Research Soc., Nat. Particleboard Assn. (tech. com. 1964-65), Am. Hardboard Assn. (tech. com. 1971—). Home: 2917 NW Angelica Corvallis OR 97330

MILAVSKY, HAROLD PHILLIP, real estate devel. and constrn. mfg. co. exec.; b. Limerick, Sask., Can., Jan. 25, 1931; s. Jack and Clara (Levitsky) M.; B.Comm., U. Sask., 1953; m. Miriam R. Shugarman, Sept. 5, 1954; children—Gregory, Charlene, Roxanne, Abbie, Carrie. Chief acct. to treas. and controller Loram Internat. Ltd. (Mannix Co. Ltd.), Calgary, Alta., Can., 1956-64; v.p. and chief fin. officer Power Corp. Devels., N. Am. Recreation Ltd., 1965-69; dir., exec. v.p. Great West Internat. Equities, Ltd., 1969—; pres., chief exec. officer Trizec Corp., Ltd., Calgary, 1976—; dir. N. Can. Oils Ltd., Carena-Bancorp, Inc., Foodex, Inc., Brascan Ltd., Central Park Lodges of Can., Hatleigh Corp., Trizec Western Inc. Fellow Chartered Inst. Secs.; mem. Inst. Chartered Accts. (dir.), Calgary C. of C. Clubs: Calgary Petroleum, U. Calgary; Glenmore Racquet; Chancellor's (Sask. and Alta.). Office: 700 2d St SW Suite 3000 Calgary AB T2P 2W2 Canada

MILES, LARRY DEWAYNE, fin. broker; b. Evansville, Ind., Dec. 12, 1947; s. O. Ray and Bonnie Mae Miles; student U. Evansville, 1965-66, Ind. U., 1967-69, Ball State U., Muncie, Ind., 1969-71; m. Barbara Ann Baumeister, June 26, 1976; children—Ryan Michael, Meredith Ann. Ins. agt., 1972-75; v.p. Am. Mkgt. Assos., Indpls., 1975-78; pres., chmn. bd. Fin. Brokers Exchange, Inc., Indpls., 1978—; pres. FBE Fin. Corp., Indpls., 1980—. Mem. Internat. Assn. Fin. Planners, Internat. Entrepreneurs Assn., Nat. Assn. Fin. Cons., Nat. Alliance Bus. Brokers. Republican. Home: 495 Coventry Way Noblesville IN 46060 Office: 1111 E 54th St Indianapolis IN 46220

MILES, MARY JO LATSCH (MRS. RICHARD S. MILES), investments exec., civic worker; b. Lincoln, Nebr., May 22, 1922; d. Robert Don and Hattie (Ogden) Latsch; student Vassar Coll., 1940-41; A.B., U. Nebr., 1944; m. Richard Samuel Miles, Nov. 16, 1951 (dec.); children—Linda, Steven. Signal Corps insp. Western Electric Co., Lincoln, 1944-45; advt. mgr. Latsch Bros., Inc., Lincoln, 1945-51, sec., 1947-63; v.p. Triangle Hardware Co., Santa Barbara, Calif., 1958-61; pres. Miles Enterprises, Latsch Realty Corp., 1966-73. Gen. women's div. Lincoln Community Chest, 1951; pres. Women's Inter-Club Council, 1952-53, Lincoln Camp Fire Council, 1954; pres. Santa Barbara Summer Theatre; bd. mem. women's bd. Community Arts Music Assn., 1962-70; pres. Santa Barbara County unit Am. Cancer Soc., 1972-74; mem. bd. Cottage Hosp. Aux., 1966-67; mem. Mayor's Adv. Com. on Arts, 1966-67; mem. bd. Inter-Agy. Council on Smoking and Health, 1967-72; mem. Calif. Democratic Central Com., 1968-72; pres. Dem. Women Santa Barbara County, 1970-72. Pres. Lobero Found., 1972-75, Nat. Charity League, 1969-71, Channel City Women's Forum, Regional Med. Program, 1968-72; dir. 19th Dist. Agrl. Assn.; pres. Santa Barbara Arts Council, 1976; mem. adv. bd. Rec. for Blind, 1974-76; mem. adv. council continuing edn. Santa Barbara City Coll.; trustee Santa Barbara Art Inst., 1972-75; pres., bd. dirs. 19th Agrl. Dist., 1978—. Recipient Charles Garvin award improvement stationery industry, 1947; Brand Name Found. award, 1949; named Santa Barbara's Woman of Yr., 1975. Mem. Jr. League (bd. dirs. Santa Barbara (1958-60, 70-71), Santa Barbara Council Women's Clubs, League Women Voters, C. of C. (pres. women's div. 1950), Internat. Platform Assn., Magna Charta Dames, Descs. Noble Order of Garter, Coral Casino, Alexander House (bd. 1960-61), Sovereign Colonial Soc. Ams. Royal Descent, Kappa Alpha Theta (pres. Santa Barbara alumnae 1957-59). Club: Vassar (Santa Barbara). Home: Montecito Shores Santa Barbara CA 93108

MILES, OSCAR LANDON, III, engring. and constrn. co. exec.; b. Monroe, La., Apr. 5, 1920; s. Oscar Landon and Gladys (Skinner) M.; B.S., La. Tech. U., 1940; m. Virginia Anita Vaughan, Dec. 9, 1944; children—Margaret Ann Miles Barnes, Michael Landon. Mgr. payrolls U.S. Constrn. Q.M., Alexandria, La., 1940; chief project acct. Ford, Bacon & Davis, Monroe, 1941-61, mgr. sealants dept., 1962-67, v.p. bus. devel., 1968-77, v.p. corp. mktg. (worldwide), 1978-80, v.p. sealants dept., 1980—; v.p., dir. M & S Advt. Agy., 1978—; pres. dir. Sealants Internat., Inc., West Chester, Pa., 1965—; dir. F.B. & D., Engenharia E Construcoes Ltda., Sao Paulo, Brazil. Exec. adviser Jr. Achievement, Monroe, 1970-71; pres. Little League Baseball, Joliet, Ill., 1960; mem. exec. council Boy Scouts Am., 1975-78. Served with USNR, 1942-46; lt. comdr. Res. (ret.). Mem. TAPPI, Soc. Gas Operators, Am. Gas Assn., La. Engring. Soc., Alpha Phi Omega. Episcopalian. Clubs: Masons (32 deg.), Shriners, K.T.; N.Y. Athletic (N.Y.C.); Lotus (pres. 1969-70), Bayou De Siard Country (Monroe). Home: 4405 Belle Terre Monroe LA 71201 Office: 3901 Jackson St Monroe LA 71201

MILES, SOLOMON THOMAS, fin. planner, mortgage cons.; b. Cerro Gordo, N.C., June 12, 1934; s. Colon Ceasar and Gladys Miles; student George Washington U., 1960-61; m. Marion Pratt, Nov. 28, 1959; children—Thomasine M., Solomon Thomas. Life ins. agt., staff mgr. N.C. Mut. Life Ins. Co., 1957-69; dist. mgr. Franklin Life Ins. Co., 1969-76; area gen. agt. So. Life, 1975—; pres., chief exec. officer Solomon T. Miles & Assos., Inc., Washington, 1977—; v.p., dir. Ga. Ave. Devel. Corp. Pres. Rabaut Jr. High Sch. Home and Sch. Assn.; bd. dirs. D.C. Shaw Area Bus. Guild, 1976—. Recipient various service awards. Mem. D.C. C. of C., Nat. Assn. Fin. Consultants, Am. Entrepreneurs Assn., Soc. for Govt. Economists, Soc. Internat. Devel., Nat. Economists Club, Washington Council Lawyers, Washington Urban League, Urban Bus. Edn. Assn. Democrat. Roman Catholic. Clubs: K.C. Home and Office: 6426 W 6th St NW Washington DC 20012

MILKO, EDWARD MICHAEL, accountant; b. Rahway, N.J., July 8, 1939; s. Michael, Jr., and Veronica (Sosinski) M.; B.S., Seton Hall U., 1961; M.B.A., N.Y. U., 1964; cert. data processing Rutgers U., 1972; m. Cecilia A. Krupinskas, Dec. 3, 1966; children—Michael, John. Sr. accountant Arthur Young & Co., Newark, 1961-66; chief accountant Hoechst-Uhde Corp., Somerville, N.J., 1966-69; corp. chief accountant Am. Hoechst Corp., Somerville, 1969-73; asst. div. controller Ga. Pacific Corp., Stamford, Conn., 1973-78, controller printing papers and splty. products, 1978-79, asst. to controller, 1979-80; corp. controller William E. Wright Co., West Warren, Mass., 1980—. Served to staff sgt. F.A., AUS, 1962-68. C.P.A., N.J. Mem. Am. Inst. C.P.A.'s, N.J. Soc. C.P.A.'s, Nat. Assn. Accountants (membership dir. 1967-68, sec. 1971-72, treas. 1972-73, communication dir. 1973-74, v.p. 1974-77, pres. 1977-78, cert. of recognition 1970), Inst. Mgmt. Accounting, Data Processing Mgmt. Assn., Alpha Kappa Psi. Home: 11 Happy Hill Rd Stamford CT 06903 Office: South St West Warren MA 01092

MILLARD, FRANK WHITTEMORE, wholesale distbn. co. exec.; b. Jersey City, July 31, 1931; s. Austin Jayne and Juliette (Suter) M.; A.B. in Econs., Lafayette Coll., 1953; postgrad. N.Y. U. Sch. Bus., 1959-61; m. Suzanne Nesbitt Turtle, Oct. 1, 1960; children—John Berry, Jayne Nesbitt. Merchandising exec. Young & Rubicam Inc., N.Y.C., 1955-57; product mgr. Sterling Drug Inc., N.Y.C., 1957-65; product mgr. Lever Bros., N.Y.C., 1965-68; pres. Turtle & Hughes Inc., Linden, N.J., 1968—, also dir.; dir. Elec. Leasing Inc., Tech. Products Internat. Bd. govs. N.Y. Young Republican Club, 1959-61; justice of peace City of Norwalk (Conn.), 1966-68; rep. Greenwich (Conn.) Town Meeting, 1972-76; mem. nat. council Lafayette Coll., 1978-80. Served to lt. (j.g.) USNR, 1953-55. Mem. Nat. Assn. Wholesalers, Essex Elec. League. Republican. Episcopalian. Banjo soloist Diamonds in the Rough Band, Conn. Home: 13 Quinatard Ave Old Greenwich CT 06870 Office: 1900 Lower Rd Linden NJ 07036

MILLARD, LAVERGNE HARRIET, free-lance artist; b. Chgo., July 8, 1925; d. Lewis and Julia (Smolk) Bassmire; student Chgo. Art Inst., 1937-39; m. Bailey Millard, Mar. 9, 1958 (div.); children—Bryan Lewis Costales, Julianne Juanita Crump, Candace Lynn Millard. Cocktail waitress Verdis, Grant Street, Concord, Calif., 1955-61; mgr. used book shop Joyce Book Shop, Concord, 1964-79; now free-lance artist. Recipient ribbons local fairs, art shows. Republican. Copyright holder for pastel art work. Home and Office: 1500 Ellis St Apt 39 Concord CA 94520

MILLARD, STEPHENS FILLMORE, forest products co. exec.; b. Balt., Dec. 5, 1932; s. Lyman Clifford and Frances Louise (Stephens) M.; B.S. in Econs., U. Pa., 1955; M.B.A., Northwestern U., 1962; m. Suzanne Taylor, Nov. 2, 1957; children—Anne, Stephens, William. Dist. sales mgr. Olin Mathieson Chem. Corp., Chgo., 1958-63; Western sales mgr. Champion Papers Inc., San Francisco, 1963-70; U.S. sales mgr. MacMillan Bloedel, Ltd., Vancouver, B.C., Can., 1970-72; dir. new product devel. Crown Zellerbach Corp., San Francisco, 1972-75; Midwestern sales mgr. paper group Internat. Paper Co., Chgo., 1975-79; dir. mktg. Mead Corp., Dayton, Ohio, 1979—; founder, dir. CableData, Inc., Equatorial Communications, Telebit Inc., Packet Cable, Inc.; asso. prof. mgmt. Golden Gate U., 1970-75; vis. lectr. Simon Frazier U., 1973. Dir. alumni ann. giving Northwestern U., 1966—; trustee Severn Prep. Sch., Severna Park, Md. Served to 1st lt. U.S. Army, 1955-57. Mem. Northwestern U. Grad. Bus. Sch. Alumni Assn. (nat. pres. 1967-68), Wharton Sch. Alumni Assn. (v.p. 1975), Active Core of Execs. Republican. Episcopalian. Clubs: Dayton Racquet; Peninsula Golf (San Mateo, Calif.). Home: 745 Oakwood Ave Dayton OH 45419 Office: Mead Corp World Hdqrs Dayton OH 45463

MILLER, ALAN JAY, investment co. exec.; b. Bklyn., July 11, 1936; s. Louis and Claire (Maltz) M.; B.A., Cornell U., 1957; m. Susan Ruth Morris, Oct 29, 1961; children—Laurie Ann, Adam Louis. Pres., Analysis-in-Depth Inc., N.Y.C., 1965-67; mng. editor Value Line Investment Survey, N.Y.C., 1967-68; research dir. Emanuel Deetjen & Co., N.Y.C., 1968-69; exec. v.p., dir. Intersci. Capital Mgmt. Corp., N.Y.C., 1969-71; pres., dir. ICM Equity Fund Inc., ICM Fin. Fund, Inc., N.Y.C., 1970-71; v.p., asso. research dir. Bache & Co., Inc., N.Y.C., 1972; v.p., asso. research dir. G.H. Walker & Co., Inc., N.Y.C., 1972-73; 1st v.p., asso. research dir. Blyth Eastman Dillon & Co., Inc., N.Y.C., 1974-76; sr. v.p., research dir. E.F. Hutton & Co. Inc., N.Y.C., 1976—, dir., 1979—; adj. asso. prof. Columbia Grad. Sch. Bus., 1978—; mem. faculty N.Y. Inst. Finance, 1977—. Chartered fin. analyst. Mem. N.Y. Soc. Security Analysts, Fin. Analysts Fedn., Am. Statis. Assn., Nat., N.Y. assns. bus. economists. Office: 1 State St Plaza New York NY 10004

MILLER, ALAN MANNING, lawyer; b. N.Y.C., July 24, 1934; s. Philip and Sylvia (Lubash) M.; A.B., Syracuse U., 1955, LL.B., 1958, J.D., 1968; children—Neil, Peter, Stephanie, Douglas; m. Ferne Mayer Steckler, Jan. 13, 1978; stepchildren—Todd, Troy, Tamara, Tiffany. Admitted to N.Y. bar, 1958, U.S. Supreme Ct. bar, 1964, Mass. bar, 1970; individual practice law; adj. faculty N.Y. State Inst. Tech., Westbury, 1974-75, Nassau Community Coll., 1978—, Hofstra U. Law Sch., 1979—; mem. N.E. regional faculty Nat. Inst. Trial Advocacy. Mem. N.Y. State Democratic Com., assembly dist. leader 11th Assembly Dist., 1965-76. Mem. Am., Mass., N.Y. State, Nassau County, Criminal Courts bar assns., Nat. Assn. Criminal Def. Lawyers, Am. Arbitration Assn. Jewish. Home: 35 Wood Ln S Woodsburgh NY 11598 Office: 1 Old Country Rd Carle Place NY 11514

MILLER, ANSELM DENNIS, corp. exec.; b. Barnesville, Ohio, May 21, 1901; s. John Nicholas and Jane (Clabby) M.; Ph.B. in Commerce magna cum laude, U. Notre Dame, 1925; m. Edna Catherine Quinn, Sept. 5, 1925; children—Anselm Dennis, John Marshall, Marshall Quinn, Ann Livingston. Successively office mgr., v.p., pres. Va. Metal Mfg. Co., Inc., Roanoke, 1955-71, chmn. bd., chief exec. officer, 1972—; pres., dir. S.W. Va. Savs. & Loan Assn., 1936-63, chmn. bd., 1963—. Vice chmn. Community Fund campaign; chmn. ARC drive; co-founder NCCJ of Roanoke. Clubs: Shenandoah, Roanoke Rotary (pres., hon. mem.). Office: Virginia Metal Mfg Co Inc Box 12342 Roanoke VA 24040

MILLER, BRUCE GORTY, investment banker; b. N.Y.C., Dec. 12, 1941; s. Helmuth and Beatrice (McGorty) M.; A.B., Johns Hopkins, 1963; M.B.A., U. Chgo., 1965. Mem. corp. planning staff Inmont Corp., N.Y.C., 1965-69; v.p. corp. fin. Reynolds Securities Inc., 1969-78, Dean Witter Reynolds Inc., 1978-80, Moseley, Hallgarten, Estabrook & Weeden, Inc., N.Y.C., 1980—. Home: 1200 Fifth Ave New York NY 10029 Office: One New York Plaza New York NY 10004

MILLER, CHARLES, investment mgmt. co. exec.; b. Galveston, Tex., Feb. 13, 1934; s. Samuel and Rose M.; B.A. in Math., U. Tex., 1959; m. Beth Birdwell. Investment officer Tchr. Retirement System, Austin, Tex., 1961-66; v.p., portfolio mgr. Funds, Inc., Houston, 1966-71; pres., chief exec. officer Funds Adv. Co., Houston, 1971—; pres., chief exec. officer Criterion Mgmt. Co., Houston, 1976—; bd. dirs. State Pension Review Bd. of Tex., 1979—. Served with USN, 1957-58. Mem. Fin. Analysts Fedn., Am. Statis. Assn., Nat. Assn. Bus. Economists. Episcopalian. Clubs: Petroleum (Houston); Headliners (Austin); Ponte Vedra (Jacksonville, Fla.). Office: 333 Clay St Houston TX 77002

MILLER, CHARLES LEROY, automobile agy. exec.; b. Coffeyville, Kans., June 8, 1935; s. Charles Leo and Della (Griffith) M.; m. Sondra Carol Miller, July 15, 1955; children—Randall Sherman, Cheryl Lynn. Dealer, chief exec. officer Paul's Ford Sales, Inc., Kansas City, Mo., 1964-69; dir. retail fin. B.J. McCombs Enterprises, San Antonio, 1970-72; fin. and ins. mgr. Charlie Thomas Ford, Houston, 1972-73; pres., chief exec. officer Fin. First Group Inc., Houston, 1973-78; gen. mgr. San Pedro Chrysler-Plymouth, San Antonio, 1978—. Exec. dir. Hickman Mills Scholarship Found., 1967-68; exec. dir. Richards Giebaner Air Force Base Community Relations Council, 1968-70. Mem. South Kansas City C. of C. (pres. 1968-69). Republican. Episcopalian. Office: 5810 San Pedro San Antonio TX 78212

MILLER, DALE, housing planner, designer, developer; b. Cashmere, Wash., May 20, 1941; s. Glen W. and Vivian B. (Barden) M.; B.A. in Polit. Sci. and History, U. Puget Sound, 1964; postgrad. in Lit., Universite de Grenoble, 1964-65; M.Arch., U. Wash., 1970; m. Leslee A. Batchelder, Dec. 31, 1967; children—Damon Jove, Cameron Todd. Fin. mgr. Miller Bldg. Enterprises, Tacoma, Wash., 1962-64; archtl. designer Roland Terry & Assos., Seattle, 1968-69; coordinator The Environ. Works, Seattle, 1970-73; dir. office of housing policy City of Seattle, 1973-75; dir. Mt. Baker Housing Rehab. Program, Seattle, 1975-78; project mgr. housing and neighborhood planning and devel., corp. dir. The Phoenix Group, Inc., Seattle, 1978—; instr. housing and devel. Seattle U., 1978-79; instr. bus. law and fin. Petersons Sch. of Bus., 1967-68; prof. lit. Ecole de Gardinere, 1965-66. Pres. Madrona Neighborhood Devel. Assns., 1978—; dir. Univ. Dist. Devel. Assn., 1970-71; chmn. dist. exec. com. Group Health Coop., 1973-75. Served with USAR, 1959-60. Recipient award of excellence, Seattle King County Bd. Realtors, 1969. Mem. Am. Planning Assn., Nat. Assn. Housing and Redevel. Ofcls., AIA (asso.). Designer MITU Townhouses, 1969; author Home/Repair and Remodeling pamphlet series, 1976, Housing Rehab Operation Workbook for Public Programs, 1976. Home: 1537 38th Ave Seattle WA 98122 Office: 1139 34th Ave Seattle WA 98122

MILLER, DANIEL C(OURTNEY), lawyer; b. N.Y.C., July 8, 1915; s. Daniel Fry and Ruth (Chambers) M.; LL.B., San Francisco Law Sch., 1946; m. Shirley Whipple Froats, Jan. 3, 1977; children by previous marriage—Daniel Courtney, Adelen Ruth, Barbara Beth; 1 stepdau., Suzanne Gail Courtney Miller. Admitted to Calif. bar, 1946; chief legal dept. Gen. Am./Safeco Ins. Cos., San Francisco, 1946-53, individual practice, San Francisco, 1953—. Mem. Am. Bar Assn., Assn. Def. Counsel, Surety Claims Assn., Calif., San Francisco bar assns. Democrat. Episcopalian. Clubs: Golden Gate Yacht, Opera Guild. Author pamphlet: An Introduction to Contract Bond Claims, 1961; Mechanical and Engineering Reconstruction of Evidence in Products and Casualty Cases, 1970; Consumer's Guide to Insurance. Patentee jack for raising motor vehicle, jack and guide for loading trailers, also portable bidet. Home: Bethel Island CA Office: PO Box 7616 San Francisco CA 94104

MILLER, DEANE GUYNES, beauty salon exec.; b. El Paso, Tex., Jan. 12, 1927; d. James Tillman and Margaret (Brady) Guynes; student U. Tex., El Paso, 1944-47; m. Richard George Miller, Apr. 12, 1947; children—J. Michael, Marcia Deane. Owner three Merle Norman Cosmetic Studios, El Paso, 1967—, The Velvet Door, Inc., El Paso, 1967—; dir. Mountain Bell Telephone Co. Pres. bd. dirs. YWCA, 1967; v.p. Sun Carnival Assn., 1970; bd. dirs. El Paso Symphony Assn., El Paso Mus. Art, El Paso Internat. Airport. Named Outstanding Woman field of civic endeavor, El Paso Herald Post. Mem. Women's C. of C. (pres. 1969, now dir.), Pan Am. Round Table (dir.). Home: 1 Silent Crest St El Paso TX 79902 Office: 122 Thunderbird St El Paso TX 79912

MILLER, DEREK ELLIS, fin. exec.; b. Mt. Vernon, N.Y., Sept. 4, 1942; s. Glen Barkalow and Ann J. M.; B.A., U. Miami, 1965; postgrad. Am. U. Grad. Sch. Internat. Mgmt., 1966; postgrad. in accounting N.Y. U., 1966-69; m. Marjorie Roeser Myles, Nov. 17, 1967; children—Kimberly Ann, Alison Katherine. Mem. staff exec. program First Nat. City Bank-Citibank, N.Y.C., 1966-68; asst. v.p. corp. fin. Jesup & Lamont, N.Y.C., 1968-70; pres. Beacon Resources Corp., N.Y.C., 1972—; dir. Goddard Industries Inc., Petrol Industries Inc., Advanced Materials Systems; chmn. Universal Sporting Mdse., Inc., Railroad Systems Corp., Felton Brush, Inc. Served with U.S. N.G., 1965-70. Clubs: Am. Yacht, Fox Meadow Tennis. Home: 31 Barry Rd Scarsdale NY 10583 Office: 230 Park Ave New York NY 10017

MILLER, DOLORES JOAN JENKINS, printing co. exec.; b. Scranton, Pa., Aug. 29, 1940; d. Lemuel Bromley and Matilda Margaret (Buchanan) Jenkins; m. William F. Miller, Jr., Sept. 13, 1958. Asst. mgr. data processing dept. Clinton Milk Co., Newark, N.J., 1962-66; asst. mgr. demurrage dept. Airco, Union, N.J., 1967-69; office mgr. Pa. Life Ins. Co., Scranton, 1970-71; mgr. budget and layaway dept. Oppenheim's, Scranton, Pa., 1971-72; office mgr., exec. prodn. coordinator, traffic mgr. Scranton Lithographing Co., 1972-80; partner, v.p. Falcon Printing Co., Inc., Scranton; partner B & J Enterprises. Mem. Am. Bus. Women's Assn. (pres. Scranton chpt. 1977-79, named Scranton Businesswoman of Yr. 1979), Scott Twp. Fire Dept. Women's Aux. (pres. 1980). Democrat. Home: Route 1 Box 539 Olyphant PA 18447 Office: 262 Main St Archbald PA 18403

MILLER, DONALD BRITTON, mgmt. cons.; b. Rochester, N.Y., Apr. 10, 1923; s. Alvin Austin and Avis (Britton) M.; B.S. in Mech. Engring., U. Rochester, 1944; M.B.A., Columbia U., 1948; m. Alice Ruth Mellgard, Aug. 26, 1950; children—Christopher Donald, James Austin. Telephone design engr. Stromberg Carlson Co., Rochester, 1943-45; asst. to dean Columbia U. Sch. Engring., N.Y.C., 1947-52; lab. ops. mgr., dir. personnel, program mgr. human resources IBM, N.Y.C., Poughkeepsie and Harrison, N.Y., San Jose, Calif., 1952-78; mgmt. cons., Santa Clara, Calif., 1978—; vis. prof. mgmt. John F. Kennedy U., 1978—. Fellow Soc. Advancement Mgmt. (internat. pres. 1965-66); mem. Am. Soc. Engring. Edn. (Disting. Service award 1978), ASME, IEEE, Orgn. Devel. Network, Acad. Mgmt., Am. Soc. Tng. and Devel. Club: Saratoga Rotary. Author: Personal Vitality and Personal Vitality Workbook, 1977; Careers, 1980-81; Working With People, 1979. Home: 14600 Wild Oak Way Saratoga CA 95070 Office: Suite 185 3600 Pruneridge Ave Santa Clara CA 95051

MILLER, DONALD BURNELL, JR., utility co. exec.; b. Hanover, Pa., Jan. 1, 1942; s. Donald Burnell and Genevieve Elizabeth (Heng) M.; B.S. in M.E., Pa. State U., 1969; m. Irene Busch, June 25, 1966; children—Candace Anne, Donald Burnell III. Project engr. Boat div. Gen. Dynamics Co., Groton, Conn., 1969-70, shift test supr., 1970-73; asst. startup supr. Millstone II, Northeast Nuclear Energy Co., Waterford, Conn., 1973-76, startup supr. Millstone III, 1976-78; mgr. Midland nuclear site Consumers Power Co., Jackson, Mich., 1978—. Served with USAF, 1962-66. Home: 5605 Drake St Midland MI 48640 Office: PO Box 1963 Midland MI 48640

MILLER, DONALD CALVIN, banker; b. Geneseo, Ill. Mar. 31, 1920; s. Otto H. and Mary (Erdman) M.; A.B., U. Ill., 1942, A.M., 1943, Ph.D., 1948; m. Marjorie Grace Morgan, Dec. 18, 1943; children—Barbara Grace, Donald Calvin, Douglas Morgan. Asst. prof. econs. U. Calif. at Los Angeles, 1949-51; economist. chief govt. fin. sect. Bd. Govs. Fed. Res. System, 1951-58; 2d v.p. Continental Ill. Nat. Bank & Trust Co., Chgo., 1958-59, v.p., 1959-68, sr. v.p., 1968-72, exec. v.p., from 1972, now vice chmn. bd., treas.; dir. A.E. Staley Mfg. Co., Decatur, Ill., Royal Group Inc., Chgo.; public gov. Chgo. Merc. Exchange. Mem. faculty adminstrv. com., asso. dir. Grad. Sch. Banking, U. Wis., Madison. Bd. dirs. U. Ill. Found. Served with U.S. Army, 1943-46. Mem. Am. Bankers Assn. (govt. borrowing com.), Assn. Res. City Bankers, Nat. Tax Assn. (treas. 1961—), C. of C. U.S. (dir.). Author: Taxes, The Public Debt and Transfers of Income, 1950. Office: 231 S LaSalle St Chicago IL 60693

MILLER, DONALD HERBERT, JR., business exec.; b. N.Y.C., Apr. 7, 1914; s. Donald and Blanche (Gray) M.; A.B., Dartmouth Coll., 1937; m. Constance Hoague, June 21, 1939; children—Linda, Geoffrey; m. 2d, Claire Strauss, Feb. 25, 1949; children—Meredith, Donald III, Bruce, Sheila. Asst. circulation mgr. Honolulu Star-Bull., 1937-40, Honolulu Advertiser, 1940-41; exec. asst. to dir.-gen. Canadian Dept. Munitions and Supply, Washington, 1941-45; asso. Handy Assos., Inc., mgmt. cons., N.Y.C., 1945-46; organizer (with Gerard Piel and Dennis Flanagan), v.p., sec.-treas., dir. Sci. Am., Inc., 1947—, dir., gen. mgr., pub. mag. Sci. Am., 1946-79, now dir.; dir. AEL Industries, Inc., Phila., Ednl. Found. for Nuclear Sci., Inc., pub. Bull. Atomic Scientists, Chgo. Clubs: Mt. Kisco (N.Y.) Country; Univ. (N.Y.C.). Home: 31 Seneca Dr Chappaqua NY 10514

MILLER, DONALD KAY, life ins. co. exec.; b. Jacksonville, Fla., Dec. 7, 1935; s. James Robert and Laurel (Armstrong) M.; B.Mus., Baylor U., Waco, Tex., 1957; B.B.A., U. Ga., 1959; m. Peggy Ann Eaton, June 14, 1959; children—Donna Kay, Dee Ann, James E. With Cherokee Nat. Life Ins. Co., Macon, Ga., 1959—, exec. v.p., 1967-69, pres., 1969—; pres., dir. CNC Fin. Corp., 1972—; dir. Ga. Bancshares Co. Treas., bd. dirs. Goodwill Industries Middle Ga. C.L.U. Fellow Life Mgmt. Inst.; mem. Consumer Credit Ins. Assn. (dir.), Ga. Assn. Life Ins. Cos. (past pres.), Sigma Alpha Epsilon. Methodist. Clubs: Idle Hour Country, Elks. Office: 1122 Gray Hwy Macon GA 31213

MILLER, DONALD LEE, investigative engring. co. exec.; b. Battle Creek, Mich., June 23, 1932; s. Hollis Laverne and Signe Susanna (Peterson) M.; B.S. in Elec. Engring., Calif. Poly. U., 1959; postgrad. Long Beach State Coll., 1963-64; m. Doris A Benedict, Feb. 11, 1951 (dec.); children—Denise, Diane, Duane; m. 2d, Jacqueline A. Blake, Apr. 23, 1978. Sr. project engr. N. American, Anaheim, Calif., 1959-63; pres. Intercontinental Research Corp., Beverly Hills, Calif., 1964-65; test supr. United Aircraft, Farmington, Conn., 1966-67; dir. engring. Docutel Corp., Dallas, 1968-70; sr. consulting engr. Gen. Adjustment Bur., Chgo., 1971-75; pres., sr. investigative engr., dir. Effective Engring., Inc., Palatine, Ill., 1976—; pres., sr. engr., dir. Efficiency Systems, Inc., Kalamazoo, 1976—, Research, Devel. & Mktg., Palatine, 1977—. Served with USAF, 1951-55. Mem. IEEE. Methodist. Home: 357 Windsor Ln Barrington IL 60010 Office: 261 Woodwork Ln Palatine IL 60067

MILLER, EDGAR MARDEN, ins. co. exec.; b. Abilene, Tex., May 28, 1925; s. Acker C. and Persilla Margaret (Goodnight) M.; B.A. in Math., So. Meth. U., 1949; m. Sue Goswell, July, 1980; children by previous marriage—Dan, Mark. Employed in life ins. field, 1947—; exec. v.p. USLIFE Corp., N.Y.C., 1968-71, pres., 1971-74; pres. Gt. Nat. Life Ins. Co., Dallas, 1970-71, U.S. Life Ins. Co., N.Y.C., 1972-74; pres. Republic Nat. Life Ins. Co., Dallas, 1974-77; sr. v.p. Am. Gen. Ins. Co., Houston, 1977-79; pres., chief exec. officer Variable Annuity Life Ins. Co., Houston, 1979—. Served to ensign USN, 1943-46. C.L.U. Fellow Life Mgmt. Inst.; mem. Am. Coll. Life Underwriters, Am. Acad. Actuaries. Office: Variable Annuity Life Ins Co 2727 Allen Pkwy Houston TX 77019

MILLER, EDWARD KIRKBRIDE, investment banker; b. Balt., July 27, 1917; s. E. Kirkbride and Elizabeth (Turner) M.; B.S., Mass. Inst. Tech., 1941; M.B.A., Harvard U., 1950; m. Ann R. Hoffman, Apr. 3, 1948; children—Daniel K., Pamela Miller Gisriel. Spl. rep. N.C. Shipbldg. Co., Wilmington, 1941-42; treas. Moldcraft, Inc., Balt., 1946-50; spl. rep. Western Md. Ry., Balt., 1950-52; with T. Rowe Price Assos., Balt., 1952—, vice chmn. bd., 1972-76, chmn. bd., 1976—; chmn. bd. T. Rowe Price Growth Stock Fund, 1976—. Bd. dirs. Balt. Council Internat. Visitors, Balt. Symphony; trustee Balt. Mus. Art. Served to lt. USNR, 1942-46. Republican. Episcopalian (vestryman). Clubs: Merchants, Center. Home: 307 Overhill Rd Baltimore MD 21210 Office: T Rowe Price Assos 100 E Pratt St Baltimore MD 21202

MILLER, ELIZABETH GARR, constrn. corp. exec.; b. Indpls., Mar. 2, 1948; d. J. Irwin and Xenia S. Miller; B.A., Goucher Coll., 1970; M.A., Courtauld Inst., U. London, 1972; M.B.A., Columbia U., 1976; m. R. Alan Melting, May 3, 1980. Program dir. Archtl. League N.Y., N.Y.C., 1973-74; bus. mgr. Fawcett Books Group, CBS, Inc., N.Y.C., 1976-78; bus. mgr. Mus. Contemporary Art, Chgo., 1979; project mgr. Tishman Realty & Constrn. Co., Inc., N.Y.C., 1979—. Bd. dirs. Archtl. History Found., N.Y.C., 1977—, Irwin-Sweeney-Miller Found. (Ind.), 1978—. Chester Dale fellow Met. Mus. Art, 1972-73. Mem. Soc. Archtl. Historians. Club: Muskoka Lakes Golf and Country (Port Carling, Ont., Can.). Contbr. articles to profl. jours. Home: 565 W End Ave New York NY 10024 Office: Tishman Realty & Constrn Co Inc 666 Fifth Ave New York NY 10019

MILLER, ELIZABETH LOUISE, hypnotism inst. dir.; b. Chattanooga, Tenn., May 12, 1930; d. Cecil Carter and Carolyn Windom (Mayton) Noecker; student Mich. State Coll., 1948, Williams Inst. Hypnological Research, 1969; m. Robert A. Miller (div.); 1 dau., Pamela Kay Miller Boswinkel. Theatre exhibitor, Okla., Wis., 1949-52, Mondovl, Wis., 1952-69; womans editor, Eau Claire, Wis., 1964-65, La Crosse, Wis., 1965-69; antique dealer, Durand, Wis., 1964-66; exec. editor Skyway News, Mpls., 1969-70; promotional mgr. Barbario Corp., Mpls., 1971; pres. Hypnotism Inst. Inc., La Crosse, 1973—; asso. bus. cons. Culler & Assos.; sales dir. Ruby Cup Internat.; lectr. hypnotism. Republican. Methodist. Author: Just People of the Friendly Valley, 1965; I Am the Mississippi, 1975; author articles in field. Home: 9101 Cedar Ave S Bloomington MN 55420

MILLER, EMERSON WALDO, accountant; b. Green Island, Jamaica, W.I., Jan. 27, 1920; s. Adolphus Eustace and Catherine Sarah (Dixon) M.; student U. Toronto (Ont., Can.), 1938-41, U. Calif. at Berkeley, 1950-61; m. Olive Claire Ford, Apr. 10, 1945; children—Cheryll, Hellena, Emerson, Oliver, Donald, Selwyn. Came to U.S., 1950, naturalized, 1957. Cost accountant Poierier & McLane Corp., N.Y.C., 1941-42; prin. Emerson Miller & Co., Kingston, Jamaica, 1942-49; lectr. accounting and bus. law Jamaica Sch. Commerce, Kingston, 1945-48; tax examiner, conferee IRS, San Francisco, 1963-64; chief financial and accounting aspects transp. and communications services programs Gen. Services Adminstrn., San Francisco, 1965-70, chief maj. segment financial mgmt. activities, 1970—, instr. govt. accounting, 1966-67. Chmn. credit com. VA Regional Office Fed. Credit Union, San Francisco, 1969—. Mem. mgmt. improvement com. Fed. Exec. Bd., San Francisco, 1973-74. Recipient Commendable Service award Gen. Services Adminstrn., 1968, Spl. Achievement award, 1969. Mem. Am. Accounting Assn., Nat. Assn. Accountants, Fed. Govt. Accountants Assn. (chpt. pres. 1973-74), Am., Financial mgmt. assns., Brit. Inst. Mgmt., Am. Judicature Soc., Royal Econ. Soc. (Cambridge), U. Calif. Alumni Assn., Internat. Platform Assn., Acad. Polit. and Social Sci. Clubs: Toastmasters (Disting. Service award 1968, ednl. v.p. 1966-68) (San Francisco); No. Calif. Cricket (San Anselmo); Brit. Social and Athletic (Los Angeles). Home: PO Box 471 Berkeley CA 94701 Office: 525 Market St San Francisco CA 94105

MILLER, ERIC RUDOLPH, retail cons.; b. Columbus, Ohio, Sept. 8, 1949; s. Milburn E. and Georgia E. (Wylie) M.; B.S., Ohio U., 1968-72; m. Sharon Lynn Edison, Aug. 4, 1974; children—Kyle Christopher, Kevin Edison. With C & O R.R., Columbus, Ohio, 1968-71; mgr. Susie's Casual's, Columbus, 1972-75; mgr. Madison's Inc. of Columbus, 1975-80; retail cons., 1980—. Mem. promotion com. Eastland Mall, Columbus, 1974-75; bd. dirs. Northland Mall, 1977-78. Mem. Gahanna Jr. C. of C. (pres. 1978-79), Ohio U. Alumni Assn. Republican. Evangelical Ch. Home and Office: 644 Moss Oak Ave Columbus OH 43219

MILLER, EUGENE, financial co. exec.; b. Chgo., Oct. 6, 1925; s. Harry and Fannie (Prosterman) M.; B.S., Ga. Inst. Tech., 1945; A.B. magna cum laude, Bethany Coll., 1947, LL.D., 1969; diploma Oxford (Eng.) U., 1947; M.S. in Journalism, Columbia U., 1948; M.B.A., N.Y. U., 1959; m. Edith Sutker, Sept. 23, 1951 (div. Sept. 1965); children—Ross, Scott, June; m. 2d, Thelma Gottlieb, Dec. 22, 1965; stepchildren—Paul Gottlieb, Alan Gottlieb. Reporter, then city editor Greensboro (N.C.) Daily News, 1948-52; S.W. bur. chief Bus. Week mag., Houston, 1952-54, asso. mng. editor, N.Y.C., 1954-60; dir. pub. affairs and communications McGraw-Hill, Inc., 1960-63, v.p., 1963-68; v.p. pub. relations and investor relations, exec. com. N.Y. Stock Exchange, N.Y.C., 1968-70, sr. v.p., 1970-73; sr. v.p. CNA Financial Corp., 1973-76; v.p. U.S. Gypsum Co., 1977—; adj. prof. mgmt. Grad. Sch. Bus. Adminstrn., N.Y. U., 1963-75; prof. bus. adminstrn. Fordham U. Grad. Sch. Bus. Adminstrn., 1969-75; chmn. bus. and mgmt. dept. Northeastern Ill. U., Chgo., 1975-77; lectr. econs. pub. relations to bus. and sch. groups; author syndicated bus. column, 1964—; dir. Tech. Advisors, Inc., Ann Arbor, Mich.; cons. sec. commerce, 1961—. Alumni dir., trustee Bethany Coll.; mem. alumni bd. Columbia Sch. Journalism; pres. The U.S. Found., Inc., 1979—. Served to ensign USNR, World War II; comdr. Res. Mem. Am. Econs. Assn., Am. Finance Assn., Nat. Assn. Bus. Economists, Nat. Investor Relations Inst., Soc. Am. Bus. Writers, Pub. Relations Soc. Am., Newcomen Soc., Sigma Delta Chi, Alpha Sigma Phi. Clubs: N.Y. U. (N.Y.C.); Mid-Am. (Chgo.); Green Acres Country (Northbrook, Ill.). Author: Your Future in Securities, 1974. Contbg. editor: Public Relations Handbook, 1971; Barron's Guide to Grad. Bus. Schs., 1978, 2d edit., 1980. Home: 376 Sunrise Circle Glencoe IL 60022 Office: 101 S Wacker Dr Chicago IL 60606

MILLER, EUGENE LESLIE, internat. mfg. co. exec.; b. Tulsa, Apr. 23, 1919; s. Joseph G. and Flora (Shorten) M.; B.S. in Engring., Okla. State U., 1942; D.S. (hon.), Grove City Coll., 1969; LL.D. (hon.), Kenyon Coll., 1977; m. Doris L. Cooley, May 6, 1942; children—Melinda Miller Powell, Matthew Stillwell, Melissa Miller Rush. With Cooper Industries, 1946—, pres., 1957-67, chief exec. officer, 1959-75, chmn. bd.,1967—; dir. Varo, Inc. Bd. dirs. Houston chpt. ARC, 1971-77, Jr. Achievement S.E. Tex., 1971-75, Houston C. of C., 1975-76. Served with U.S. Army, 1942-46; ETO. Decorated Bronze Star (U.S.); Croix de Guerre (France); named to Engring. Hall of Fame, Okla. State U., 1967. Mem. Machinery and Allied Products Inst. (dir., mem. exec. com. 1966-76). Presbyterian. Office: Cooper Industries Inc Two Houston Center Houston TX 77002

MILLER, FORREST MALCOLM, bank exec.; b. Newport, Wash., June 3, 1943; s. Forrest Duane and Lois Elaine (Ownbey) M.; student U. Wash., 1961, 65-66, Withworth Coll., 1967-69; grad. Def. Lang. Inst., 1963; A.A. in Bus., Columbia Basin Coll., 1971; m. Cheryl Lynn Schellhorn, Apr. 6, 1963; children—Ryan, Heather, Kyle. Trainee, Seattle Trust and Savs., 1966; trainee Old Nat. Bank of Wash., Sunnyside, 1966, loan officer, Spokane, 1968, agr. and comml. loan officer, Pasco, 1969, mgr., Granger, 1971; loan officer Comml. Bank, Salem, Oreg., 1974, asst. v.p., 1974, v.p., mgr. Silverton (Oreg.) br., 1976-78, v.p. mortgage div., Salem, 1978—. Bd. dirs. Cascade Area council Boy Scouts Am., 1974-80, scoutmaster, 1972; bd. dirs. Twilight Courts Retirement Home, 1978; bd. dirs. United Way, 1976, 71-73, chmn., 1975, 72-73; Rep. precinct chmn., 1973; adv. bd. Columbia Basin Coll., 1970; active Bicentennial Commn., 1975-76. Served with U.S. Army, 1962-64; capt. Oreg. Air N.G. Recipient Good Citizen award, 1972, Citizenship award United Way, 1975, Bicentennial Commn. certificate of Appreciation, 1976. Mem. Am. Inst. Banking (pres. Columbia Basin chpt. 1970), Bank Adminstrn. Inst. (founder, dir. Columbia Region 1970-74; Salem real estate research com.), Oreg. Bankers Assn., Nat. Honor Soc., N.G. Assn., Oreg. N.G. Assn., Pilots Internat. Lutheran. Clubs: Elks, Rotary (treas. 1978). Contbr. tech. articles and fiction short stories to publs. Home: 4805 Woodland Dr Silverton OR 97381 Office: Commercial Bank 325 Cottage NE Salem OR 97301

MILLER, FRANCIS ROY, mfg. co. exec.; b. Elko, Minn., Nov. 6, 1926; s. Robert F. and Astrid M. (German) M.; B.A., St. Olaf Coll., 1950; m. JoAnn E. Foss, Aug. 12, 1950; children—Nancy Jo, Douglas Lee, David John. Asst. mgr. Credit Bur. of Rice County, Faribault, Minn., 1950-54; rep. State Farm Ins., Faribault, 1954-56; chief acct. Northwestern Nat. Life, Mpls., 1956-62; treas., controller Faribault Woolen Mill Co., 1962—. Mem. Faribault Area Sch. Bd., 1966-78, chmn., 1975-78; treas. United Way, 1964-69. Served with U.S. Army, 1945-46. Cert. adminstrv. mgr. Mem. Adminstrv. Mgmt. Soc., Data Processing Mgmt. Assn. Republican. Lutheran. Clubs: Faribault Country, Exchange (pres. 1980—). Home: 713 6th Ave SW Faribault MN 55021 Office: 1500 NW 2d Ave Faribault MN 55021

MILLER, FRANCIS WILLIAM, assn. exec.; b. Ringsted, Iowa, Apr. 15, 1923; s. Frank H. and Edna L. (Kummet) M.; B.A. in Econs., St. John's U., 1948; M.A. in Econs., U. Minn., 1952; m. Laila L. Held, Jan. 3, 1952; children—Tom, Susan, Kathryn, Patti. Personnel mgr. Pillsbury Inc., Hamilton, Ohio, 1952-56; dir. compensation

Honeywell Corp., Waltham, Mass., 1956-76; exec. dir. Am. Compensation Assn., Scottsdale, Ariz., 1976—; tchr. in field. Served with C.E., U.S. Army, 1942-46. Mem. Am. Soc. Personnel Adminstrn, Am. Legion. Contbr. articles to profl. jours. Office: PO Box 1176 Scottsdale AZ 85252

MILLER, G. WILLARD, JR., stock broker; b. Sacramento, Nov. 3, 1919; s. G. Willard and Ednah Miller (Simmons) M.; student Dartmouth Coll., 1936-40. Vice pres., br. mgr. Dean Witter & Co., investment brokers, San Francisco, 1946-58, gen. partner, 1958—, mgr. San Francisco office, 1961-64, asst. mgr. No. div., 1964-67, mgr. No. div., 1967-72, pres., 1972-80, vice chmn., 1980—. Active, United Bay Area Crusade; asso. mem. for fund-raising St. Francis Meml. Hosp. Served with USAAF, 1942-45. Decorated D.F.C. with three clusters, Air medal with six clusters. Mem. Nat. Assn. Securities Dealers (dist. chmn. 1967, gov. 1971-74). Clubs: San Francisco Bond, Mchts. Exchange (pres. 1974), Street Club of San Francisco (founding mem.), Bohemian, Pacific-Union, Four Leaf Clover, Claremont Country. Office: 45 Montgomery St San Francisco CA 94106

MILLER, G(EORGE) WILLIAM, sec. Treasury; b. Sapulpa, Okla., Mar. 9, 1925; s. James Dick and Hazle Deane (Orrick) M.; B.S., U.S. Coast Guard Acad., 1945; J.D., U. Calif., 1952; m. Ariadna Rogojarsky, Dec. 22, 1946. Admitted to Calif. bar, 1952, N.Y. bar, 1953; practiced law with Cravath, Swaine & Moore, N.Y.C., 1952-56; with Textron Inc., Providence, 1956-78, v.p., 1957-60, treas., 1958-59, pres., 1960-74, dir., 1960-78, chief exec. officer, 1968-78, chmn. bd., 1974-78; chmn. Fed. Res. Bd., 1978-79; sec. Dept. Treasury, Washington, 1979—. Chmn. adv. council Pres.'s Com. on Equal Employment Opportunity, 1963-65; mem. council Nat. Found. on Humanities, 1966-67; bd. dirs. Coast Guard Acad. Found., 1969-78, pres., 1973-77, chmn., 1977-78. Mem. State Bar Calif., Nat. Alliance Businessmen (dir.), Nat. Urban League (trustee 1966-69), UN Assn. U.S. (dir. 1970-74), Conf. Bd. (chmn.), Order of Coif, Phi Delta Phi. Clubs: Lyford Cay (Nassau, Bahamas); Acoaxet (Westport, Mass.); Squantum Assn., Hope, Turks Head, Univ., Agawam Hunt (Providence); Brook (N.Y.). Office: Dept Treasury Washington DC 20220

MILLER, GEORGE CRAWFORD, printing co. exec.; b. Washington, May 15, 1946; s. Louis Reed and Emilie Morrison (Crawford) M.; B.S., U. Tenn., 1968; M.B.A., Loyola Coll., 1979; m. Dianna Ruth Roach, Dec. 18, 1965; children—Matthew, Mark. With IBM Office Products, Washington, 1968-70; mktg. rep. Wallace Bus. Forms, Inc., Chattanooga, 1970-71, asst. dist. mgr., Richmond, Va., 1972; dist. mgr. Houston, 1972-73, Washington/Balt., 1973-75; mktg. mgr. Am. Standard Inc., Graphic Arts Group, Hunt Valley, Md., 1975—. Mem. Data Processing Mgrs. Assn., Am. Nat. Standards Inst. (standards com., 1977—), Bus. Forms Mgmt Assn., Direct Mail Mktg. Club Washington. Office: 11350 McCormick Rd Hunt Valley MD 21031

MILLER, GEORGE FRANCIS, ins., fin. corp. exec.; b. N.Y.C., Apr. 14, 1945; s. George F. and Mary Miller; B.B.A., CCNY, 1967; M.B.A., Pace U., 1973; m. Joan C. Mara, Oct. 29, 1977. Asst. sec. C.I.T. Fin. Corp., N.Y.C., 1968-73; sr. v.p. Mfrs. Hanover Leasing Corp., N.Y.C., 1973-80; pres., chief exec. officer John Hancock Fin. Services, Inc., Boston, 1980—. Mem. Little Neck Civic Assn., 1978-80. Served with AC, USNR, 1966-72. Mem. Am. Mgmt. Assn., Am. Assn. Equipment Lessors. Club: Douglaston.

MILLER, GEORGE WARREN, real estate exec.; b. Evanston, Ill., Mar. 7, 1924; s. Wallace L. and Georgie K. Miller; A.B., Dartmouth Coll., 1947; postgrad. Stonier Grad. Sch. Banking, 1954, Walton Sch. Commerce, 1952; m. Elizabeth Ann Wallace, May 1, 1946; children—Bruce W., Melinda M. Remley, David B., Mark W. Vice pres. First Nat. Bank of Chgo., 1947-64; pres. Bank of the Commonwealth, Detroit, 1964-69; chmn. bd. C.P. Industries, Inkster, Mich., 1971-72; pres. Nationwide Real Estate Investors, Columbus, Ohio, 1973—; v.p., gen. mgr. Nationwide Devel. Co., Columbus, 1980—; dir. Miller & Co., Chgo. Served with USN, 1943-46; PTO. Home: 2635 Clairmont Ct Columbus OH 43220 Office: Nationwide Real Estate Investors One Nationwide Plaza Columbus OH 43216

MILLER, HAROLD T., publishing co. exec.; b. New Paltz, N.Y., Jan. 5, 1923; s. Harold F. and Grace (Taylor) M.; B.S., Franklin and Marshall Coll., 1947; M.Ed., Columbia U., 1948; m. Marcheta Novak, 1947; 1 son, Harold F. Tchr., 1948-50; with Houghton Mifflin Co., 1950—, textbook salesman, 1950-57, editor in chief test dept., 1957-62, asst. mgr. edn. Midwestern office, 1962-65, mgr., 1965-71, v.p. ednl. div., 1971-73, pres., chief exec. officer, 1973—, chmn. bd., 1979—, also dir.; dir. SCA Services, New Eng. Mchts. Nat. Bank. Trustee, Babson Coll. Corp., Franklin and Marshall Coll. Mem. Assn. Am. Pubs. (dir., chmn. bd. 1977-78), Kappa Sigma. Clubs: Union, Algonquin, St. Botolph, Commercial (Boston). Office: One Beacon St Boston MA 02107

MILLER, HARRY KERN, chem. co. exec.; b. Norristown, Pa. Aug. 13, 1928; s. Harry L. and Elizabeth J. (Kern) M.; student Adm. Farragut Acad., 1941-46, U. Scranton, 1946-48; children—Michael, Steven, Brian. With Harry Miller Corp., Phila., 1953—, chemist, 1958-63, salesman, 1963-80, exec. v.p., sec.-treas., 1980—. Served with U.S. Army, 1950-53. Mem. Assn. Iron and Steel Engrs. Home: 700 Wyndale Rd Jenkintown PA 19046 Office: 4th & Bristol Sts Philadelphia PA 19140

MILLER, HARVEY, financial exec.; b. N.Y.C., Jan. 26, 1942; s. Murry and Minnie (Lieb) M.; B.S., Fordham U., 1969, M.B.A., 1973; m. Elizabeth Eleanor Murphy, Jan. 7, 1967; children—Erin Elizabeth, Alyson Dawn, Rachel Maria. Chief accountant Random House, Inc., N.Y.C., 1967-68; sr. accountant Price Waterhouse & Co., N.Y.C., 1968-72; chief fin. officer Parade Publs., Inc., N.Y.C., 1972-75; asst. corp. controller Warnaco, Inc., Bridgeport, Conn., 1975-76; corp. controller Warnaco, Inc., Bridgeport, Conn., 1977-78; corp. controller Salant Corp., N.Y.C., 1978-80; v.p. fin. and adminstrn. Murjani Internat., N.Y.C., 1980—. Served with AUS, 1964-66. C.P.A., N.Y. Mem. Am. Inst. C.P.A.'s, N.Y. State Soc. C.P.A.'s, Nat. Assn. Accountants, Fin. Execs. Inst., Am. Mgmt. Assn. Office: 925 Paterson Plank Rd Secaucus NJ 07094

MILLER, J. CARTER, SR., mfg. co. exec.; b. Goshen, Ind., Mar. 20, 1920; s. Noble H. and Letta F. (Carter) M.; B.S., Ind. State U., 1940; M.S. in M.E., Purdue U. and Ill. Inst. Tech., 1942; Ph.D., Rochford U. (Eng.); 1 son, J. Carter. With Carter Controls, Inc., 1952—, chmn. bd., pres., 1970—; chmn. bd. Carter Controls Internat., Palm Beach, Fla., 1970—. Served to col. USAAF. Mem. ASME. Patentee in field. Office: Carter Controls Inc Box 961 Palm Beach FL 33480

MILLER, J. RICHARD, factoring co. exec.; b. Kansas City, Mo., July 18, 1931; s. Sanderson Staley and Bertha Amelia (Hoeger) M.; B.S. in Econs., U. Pa., 1952; 1 dau., Jill Elizabeth. Co-founder, pres. Miller Martin & Co., Dallas, 1960—; dir. Realex Corp., Kansas City, 1st Nat. Bank of Euless (Tex.). Bd. dirs., mem. exec. bd. Circle Ten council Boy Scouts Am. Served as officer Transp. Corps, U.S. Army, 1952-55. Mem. Nat. Comml. Fin. Conf. (dir.), Sigma Chi. Clubs: City (Dallas); Rivercrest Country (Ft. Worth); Steeplechase; Phoenix (Dallas). Home: 6306 Diamond Head Circle Dallas TX 75225 Office: Suite 2677 1st Internat Bldg 1201 Elm St Dallas TX 75270

MILLER, JAMES LLOYD, paper and wood products co. exec.; b. Ga., Nov. 21, 1929; s. Roy and Rosalie M.; B.B.A., U. Ga., 1950. Cost acctg. mgr. Ampex Corp., Opelika, Ala., 1958-60; corp. acctg. mgr. Celanese Corp., N.Y.C., 1961-65; v.p. fin. and adminstrn. MacMillian Bloedel Inc., Pine Hill, Ala., 1967—. Served to lt. USNR, 1951-55. Mem. Nat. Assn. Accts. Home: Apt C-3 Thomasville AL 36784 Office: MacMillan Bloedel Inc Pine Hill AL 36769

MILLER, JAMES THOMAS, III, mgmt. cons.; b. Greenville, S.C., July 11, 1933; s. James Thomas, Jr. and Clara Louise Miller; A.B. in Sociology, Wofford Coll., Spartanburg, S.C., 1956; postgrad. Duke U. Div. Sch., 1968-70, Lutheran So. Theol. Sem., 1970-71; m. Brenda Jean Earl, Mar. 4, 1979; children—Michael David, Jeffrey Thomas, Stephen Eugene, Elisabeth Ann. Ordained to ministry United Methodist Ch., 1963; pastor chs. in S.C., 1963—; dean mgmt. sci. div. Greenville (S.C.) Tech. Coll., 1973-78; pres. Leadership Seminars Assns., Duncan, S.C., 1978—; lectr. safety mgmt. U. So. Calif., 1978—. Served with USAF, 1956-63. Mem. Am. Soc. Tng. and Devel., Am. Mgmt. Assn. Republican. Club: Masons. Author: Every Supervisor a Winner, 1979; Effective Motivation Techniques, 1980. Address: PO Drawer 536 Duncan SC 29334

MILLER, JEROME HARRY, constrn. co. and real estate investment co. exec.; b. N.Y.C., Mar. 6, 1913; s. Andrew N. and Rose (Stone) M.; LL.B., St. John's U., Bklyn., 1935; m. Katherine Pearlman, Jan. 23, 1945; 1 dau., Nancy Ellen. Pres., Miller Homes, L.I., 1936—, Iris Constrn. Co., 1953—; partner JIHL Assos., 1953—, Miller Assos., 1953—; dir. bldg. corps.; lectr. on land C.W. Post Coll., L.I. Home Builders Inst. Sch. for Builders; cons. Consol. Mut. Ins. Co., Bklyn. Co-chmn. United Jewish Appeal Builders Drive, L.I.; bd. dirs. Chronic Disease Hosp., Bklyn., Hillcrest Community Center, Boys Town of Israel, Pride of Judea, L.I. Council on Econ. Edn., C.W. Post Coll.; mem. State of Israel Prime Minister's Club; pres. Andrew N. and Rose Miller Found., Levittown, N.Y.; hon. mem. Glen Cove Police Force. Served with U.S. Army, 1942-45. Mem. Nat. Assn. Builders (dir. 10 years; Task Force Ins. award 1963), L.I. (pres., chmn. bd.) home builders assns., Spike Club (life), Alpha Phi Pi (chancellor; Gold and Silver awards). Home: 50 Merrivale Rd Great Neck NY 11021 Office: 3707 Hempstead Turnpike Levittown NY 11756

MILLER, JOHN, women's retail apparel chain exec.; b. Ralphton, Pa., July 4, 1909; s. Michael and Catherine M.; student in bus. and acctg., Columbia U., 1941-43, in real estate N.Y. U., 1937-40; m. June 27, 1932; children—Mary Esther, Joan Margaret. Store mgr. S.H. Kress & Co., N.Y.C., 1935-60, v.p., 1950-60; pres., owner Nettie Lee Shop Inc., Bristol, Tenn., 1960—, J. Miller Fashions, Wallaces. Bd. dirs. United Fund of John City, Tenn., 1965-70, C. of C. of Bristol, 1973-76. Republican. Roman Catholic. Clubs: Kiwanis (dir. club 1974-77), Bristol Country, Elks. Home: 57 Country Club Estates Bristol TN 37620 Office: 634 State St Bristol TN 37620

MILLER, JOHN ADALBERT, life ins. co. exec.; b. Wilkes-Barre, Pa., June 14, 1927; s. Joseph and Marie M. (Arenova) M.; A.B., Columbia U., 1948; postgrad. Cornell U.; m. Margaret Marie Hausler, Aug. 14, 1945; children—Cynthia Joan, Jeffrey Charles, John Joseph, Kristen Marie. Asst. adminstrv. personnel mgr. Willys-Overland Motors Co., 1948-49; with Aetna Life & Casualty Co., 1948-58, acting gen. agt., Seattle, 1957-58; with Life Ins. Agy. Mgmt. Assn., Hartford, Conn., 1958-72, v.p. co. relations, 1968-72; with Provident Mut. Life Ins. Co., Phila., 1972—, sr. v.p. agencies, 1975-76, pres., 1976-78, pres., chief exec. officer, 1978—; dir. Phila. Nat. Bank/Phila. Nat. Corp.; vice-chmn. Ins. Fedn. Pa. Chmn. bd. dirs. YMCA Phila. and Vicinity, 1978; bd. dirs. Food Distbn. Center, Phila. Drama Guild, Greater Phila. Partnership, Universal City Sci. Center; vice-chmn. Phila. Conv./Visitors Bur.; bd. mgrs. Children's Hosp., Phila. Served with USMCR, 1945-46. C.L.U. Mem. Am. Coll. Life Underwriters, Phila. C. of C. (dir.). Republican. Presbyterian. Club: Overbrook Golf. Author: What You Should Know About Permanent Life Insurance, 1962; Getting More Out of Life, 1968; others. Home: 1946 Montgomery Ave Villanova PA 19085 Office: 4601 Market St Philadelphia PA 19101

MILLER, JOHN BURKE, hardware and bldg. specialties distbg. co. exec.; b. Kansas City, Mo., Oct. 14, 1934; s. Samuel Burke and Mary Lucy M.; student U. Colo., 1955; B.A., Grinnell Coll., 1956; postgrad. U. Mo., Kansas City, 1957; m. Mary Ann Holthues, June 30, 1956; children—Tom, Ann, Kathy. With Broadway Supply Co., Kansas City, Mo., 1959—, v.p., 1964-70, pres., 1970—; dir. United Mo. Bank South, Kansas City, 1973—. Mgr., Johnson County (Mo.) 3 & 2 Baseball Team, 1970-72, Johnson County YMCA Basketball League, 1972-73; session mem. 2d United Presbyterian Ch., 1975-77; pres. Church Corp., Kansas City, Mo., 1977; host 1976 Nat. Republican Conv.; adv. trustee Research Med. Center, Kansas City, 1977—. Served with Ordnance Corps., U.S. Army, 1957-59. Mem. Door and Hardware Inst., Kansas City C. of C. Presbyterian. Club: Rotary. Office: 601 W 103d St Kansas City MO 64114

MILLER, JOHN CHARLES, corp. exec.; b. Wilkes-Barre, Pa., Jan. 20, 1940; s. John C. and Delia F. (Hardy) M.; A.B., U. Pa., 1964; m. Linda C. Williams, Apr. 22, 1967; children—Susan, Elizabeth Ann. Finance mgr. Philco-Ford, Phila., 1961-69; div. controller Hitchiner Mfg. Co., Milford, N.H., 1969-70; corporate controller Kleer-Vu Industries, Inc., N.Y.C., 1970-74; v.p., treas. Fed. Express Corp., Memphis, 1974-80, sr. v.p. fin. and adminstrn., 1980—. Bd. govs. U. Pa., 1964. Mem. Nat. Accounting Assn. (sec. 1974), Memphis Area U. Pa. Alumni Assn. (pres. 1976), Financial Execs. Inst. Office: 2837 Sprankle Ave Memphis TN 38130

MILLER, JOHN EVAN, oilfield equipment mfg. co. exec.; b. San Antonio, Tex., Aug. 24, 1944; s. Omer Allen and Grace Elizabeth M.; B.A., Mich. State U., 1966; M.B.A., U. Tex., 1974; postgrad. UCLA, 1976-77. Supr. W. Tex. fabrication center Nat. Supply Co. div. Armco, Inc., Big Spring, 1975-76, purchasing agt., Torrance, Calif., 1976-77, supr. prodn. scheduling, 1977-78, spl. assignment to nat. prodn. equipment and distbn., Houston, 1978—. Served as officer USAF, 1968-74. Mem. Nat. Purchasing Mgrs. Assn. (certified), Am. Prodn. and Inventory Control Soc. (certified), Assn. M.B.A. Execs., Soc. Mfg. Engrs., Porsche Club Am. Clubs: Univ., Officers. Home: Rt 1 Box 292 Big Spring TX 79720 Office: 604 N Owens Big Spring TX 79720

MILLER, JOHN NELSON, banker; b. Youngstown, Ohio, Sept. 15, 1948; s. W. Frederic and Julia Elizabeth (Lohman) M.; Mus. B. in Cello, Westminster Coll., 1970; M.B.A. in Finance, Wharton Sch. Finance, U. Pa., 1974; m. Lynnette McDonald, May 31, 1974. Asst. br. mgr. Mahoning Nat. Bank, Youngstown, 1970-72; asst. dir. fin. services dept. Mellon Bank N.Am., Pitts., 1974-76; a v.p., head cash mgmt. div. Md. Nat. Bank, Balt., 1976-78; v.p., mgr. corp. cash mgmt. div. N.Y. Bank of Am., N.Y.C., 1978-80; dir. cash mgmt., strategic planning, product mgmt. and tng. Bank of Am. S.F., 1980—; lectr. Wharton Grad. Sch., Am. Mgmt. Assn. cash mgmt. seminars; speaker Payment Systems Inc., Corporate EFT Seminar, Atlanta, Bank Adminstrn. Inst. Corporate Payment Conf., N.Y.C., numerous others. Chmn. ann. giving program Wharton Grad. Sch., 1977-79. Mem. Wharton Grad. Alumni Assn. (pres., local club, rep., nat. dir., mem. exec. com.), Bank Adminstrn. Inst. (mem. subcom. interindustry commn.), Am. Nat. Standards Inst., Cash Mgmt. Inst. (dir.), Omicron Delta Kappa. Clubs: Mchts., Univ. of Pitts., Rotary N.Y. Office: Bank America 299 Park Ave New York NY 10017

MILLER, JOHN RAYMOND, bakery exec.; b. St. Joseph, Mo., Jan. 2, 1939; s. Raymond Clarence and Annona Ruth (Scott) M.; B.S., N.W. Mo. State U., 1964; m. Marian Roberta Thomas, Dec. 3, 1960; children—Sean Patrick, Shannon Thomas, Stacy Lynn. Sales mgr. ITT Continental Bakery, Dallas, 1964-69; dist. sales mgr. Pepperidge Farm, Inc., 1969-76, territorial sales mgr., 1975-76, Eastern Biscuit Div. sales mgr., Norwalk, Conn., 1977—. Mem. Grocery Mfrs. Rep. Assn., Mass. Food Assn., N.Y. Food Mchts. Assn., Am. Mus. Natural History, Nat. Audubon Soc. Democrat. Baptist. Home: 51 Merwin Brook Rd Brookfield Center CT 06805 Office: Norwalk CT 06856

MILLER, JON HAMILTON, forest products co. exec.; b. Des Moines, Jan. 22, 1938; s. Victor George and Virginia Adelaine (Hamilton) M.; A.B. in Econs., Stanford U., 1959, M.B.A. in Mktg. and Fin., 1961; m. Sydney Gail Fernald, June 4, 1966; children—Emily, Sara. With Boise Cascade Corp. (Idaho), 1961—, sr. v.p. bus. products and services, packaging, Portland, Oreg., 1971-74, exec. v.p. paper and paper products, Boise, 1974-76, exec. v.p. timber/wood products/bldg. materials, 1976-78, pres., chief operating officer, dir., 1978—; dir. 1st Security Corp. Bd. dirs. St. Luke's Hosp., Boise State U. Bronco Athletic Assn. Served with U.S. Army, 1959-60. Mem. Greater Boise C. of C. (pres. 1977). Methodist. Clubs: Arid (Boise); Multnomah Athletic (Portland). Office: 1 Jefferson Sq Boise ID 83728

MILLER, JOSEPH IRWIN, mfg. co. exec.; b. Columbus, Ind., May 26, 1909; s. Hugh Thomas and Nettie Irwin (Sweeney) M.; grad. Taft Sch., Watertown, Conn., 1927; A.B., Yale U., 1931, M.A. (hon.), 1959, L.H.D., 1979; M.A., Oxford U., 1933; LL.D., Bethany Coll., 1956, Ind. U., 1958, Tex. Christian U., 1957, Oberlin Coll., 1962, Princeton, 1962, Hamilton Coll., 1964, Columbia, 1968, Mich. State U., 1968, Dartmouth, 1971, U. Notre Dame, 1972; L.H.D., Case Inst. Tech., 1966, Manchester Coll., 1973, Moravian Coll., 1976, U. Dubuque, 1977; m. Xenia Ruth Simons, Feb. 5, 1943; children—Margaret Irwin, Catherine Gibbs, Elizabeth Ann Garr, Hugh Thomas Miller II, William Irwin Miller. Vice pres., gen. mgr. Cummins Engine Co., Inc., Columbus, Ind., 1934-42, exec. v.p., 1944-47, pres., 1947-51, chmn. bd., 1951-77, chmn. exec. and fin. com., 1977—; pres. Irwin Union Bank & Trust Co., 1947-54, chmn. bd., 1954-76, dir., 1937—; chmn. exec. com. Irwin Union Corp., 1976—. Pres., Nat. Council Chs., 1960-63; mem. Commn. on Money and Credit; chmn. Pres.'s Spl. East-West Trade Commn., 1965; mem. Pres.'s Commn. on Postal Reorgn., 1967, Commn. on Urban Housing, 1967; chmn. Nat. Adv. Commn. on Health Manpower, 1966-67; vice chmn. UN Com. on Mutlinat. Corps., 1973-74; mem. study com. on U.S. policy toward So. Africa, Ford Found., 1961-79; hon. trustee Mus. Modern Art; hon. rector Dubuque U., 1967-77. Fellow Branford Coll.; hon. fellow Balliol Coll., Oxford. Served as lt. USNR aboard U.S.S. Langley, 1942-44. Recipient Rosenberger medal U. Chgo., 1977. Mem. World Council Chs. (exec. com. 1961-68), The Bus. Council, Conf. Bd., Phi Beta Kappa, Beta Gamma Sigma. Mem. Christian Ch. (Disciples of Christ). Clubs: Yale, Links, Century (N.Y.C.); Chicago (Chgo.); Indianapolis Athletic, Columbia (Indpls.). Home: 2760 Highland Way Columbus IN 47201 Office: 301 Washington St Columbus IN 47201

MILLER, KARL A, mgmt. counselor; b. Reading, Pa., Feb. 27, 1931; s. Harvey and Kathleen S. M.; B.S. Indsl. Engring, Pa. State U., 1953; M.S. Indsl. Mgmt., Mass. Inst. Tech., 1963; m. Carol Joann Mickle, July 28, 1956; children—Dawn Alison, Kevin Bryan. Bus. mgr. Gen. Electric Co., Evendale, Ohio, 1953-55, Lynn, Mass., 1956-63; asst. to pres. Burn & Roe, N.Y.C., 1964-65; cons. George Armstrong Co., N.Y.C., 1966-68; sr. cons. H.B. Maynard Co., N.Y.C., 1968-70; mng. partner Kamid Assos., Yonkers, N.Y., 1971—; lectr. fin. Bucknell U., Pa., Mercy Coll., N.Y.; speaker in field. Pres. men's brotherhood Collegiate Ch. of N.Y.C., 1970-72; pres. Westchestertowne Houses Condominium, Yonkers, 1971-76, Council of Condominiums of N.Y. State, 1972—; mem. commn. of deeds City of Yonkers, 1976, chmn. citizens' budget adv. com., 1975-76. Recipient Speak Up award Peabody (Mass.) Jr. C. of C., 1960, Minuteman citation, 1960. Mem. Yonkers C. of C. (pres's. club 1975-78), Mass. Inst. Tech. Alumni Center N.Y.C. (gov. 1970-81), Triangle Frat., Sigma Tau. Republican. Mem. Dutch Reformed Ch. Author: The Farm Machinery Market Through 1980, 1973; also articles. Editor: Jet Engine Newsletter, 1955-56. Home: 412-21 N Broadway Yonkers NY 10701 also 546 S Richards St Bedford PA 15522 Office: PO Box 63 Yonkers NY 10703

MILLER, KENNETH MICHAEL, electronics co. exec.; b. Chgo., Nov. 20, 1921; s. Matthew and Tillie (Otto) M.; student Ill. Inst. Tech., 1940-41, U. Calif. at Los Angeles, 1961; m. Dolores June Miller, Jan. 16, 1943 (dec. Dec. 1968); children—Barbara Anne Woodcock, Nancy Jeanne Hathaway, Kenneth Michael, Roger Allan; m. 2d, Sally J. Ballingham, June 20, 1970. Electronics engr. Rauland Corp., Chgo., 1941-48; gen. mgr. Lear, Inc., Santa Monica, Calif., 1948-59; v.p., gen. mgr. Motorola Aviation Electronics, Inc., Culver City, Calif., 1959-60; v.p., gen. mgr. Instrument div. Daystrom, Inc., Los Angeles, 1961; gen. mgr. Metrics div. Singer Co., Bridgeport, Conn. and Los Angeles, 1962-65; v.p., gen. mgr. Lear Jet Corp., 1965-66; pres., dir. Infonics Inc., 1967-68; v.p., gen. mgr. Computer Industries, Inc., 1968-69; dir. ops., tech. products group Am. Standard Corp., McLean, Va., also v.p., gen. mgr. Wilcox Electric div., Kansas City, Mo., 1969-71; pres., gen. mgr. Wilcox Electric, Inc. subs. Northrop Corp., Kansas City, 1971-72, v.p., dir. World Wide Wilcox, Inc. subs., McLean, Va., 1971-72; pres., chief exec. officer, dir. Penril Corp., Rockville, Md., 1973—. Mem. regional planning council Community Mental Health Services, Bridgeport, 1964; mem. Bridgeport Capital Fund Com.; trustee Park City Hosp.; bd. dirs. U. Bridgeport. Recipient Job Makers award Mfrs. Assn. Bridgeport, 1963. Fellow Radio Club Am.; mem. Aircraft Owners and Pilots Assn., Am. Inst. Aeros. and Astronautics, Am. Mgmt. Assn., Armed Forces Communications and Electronics Assn., Electronic Industries Assn., IEEE, Instrument Soc. Am., Nat. Aero. Assn., Soc. Non-Destructive Testing, Soc. Automotive Engrs., Air Force Assn., Am. Radio Relay League (life), Mfrs. Assn. Bridgeport (dir.), Bridgeport Engring. Inst., C. of C. (pres, 1964), Quarter Century Wireless Assn. (life), Soc. Wireless Pioneers. Clubs: Rolling Hills Country (Wichita); Algonquin (Bridgeport). Contbr. articles to profl. jours. Home: 16904 George Washington Dr Rockville MD 20853 Office: 5520 Randolph Rd Rockville MD 20852

MILLER, LEE, chem. co. exec.; b. Rock Island, Ill., May 5, 1931; s. Leslie H. and Emma Miller; B.A., Augustana Coll., 1952; Ph.D., U. Ill., 1955; m. Lois Magnuson, June 20, 1953; children—Randall L., Blair A., Cynthia A. With Monsanto Co., 1955—, gen. mgr. nutrition chems. and devel. div., St. Louis, 1980—. Mem. Comml. Devel. Assn., Inst. Food Tech., Am. Chem. Soc. Presbyterian. Office: 800 N Lindbergh Blvd Saint Louis MO 63166

MILLER, MARY JEANNETTE, office engr.; b. Washington, Sept. 24, 1912; d. John William and David Evengeline (Hill) Sims; student Howard U., 1929-30, U. Ill., 1940-42, Dept. Agr. Grad. Sch., 1957-59,

U. Md., 1975; m. Cecil Miller, June 17, 1934 (dec.); children—Sylvenia Delores Doby, Ferdi A., Cecil Jr. Chief mail processing unit Bur. Reclamation, Washington, 1940-57; records supr. AID, Manila, Korea, Mali, Guyana, Dominican Republic, Indonesia, Laos, 1957-71; office engr. Bechtel Assos., Washington, 1976-79; records mgmt. cons. AID, Washington, 1979—; tchr. English as 2d lang. Ministry of Edn., Seoul, Korea, 1960-61, Ministry of Fin., Laos, 1968-70. Mem. Soc. Am. Archivists, Montgomery County Bd. Realtors, Am. Fgn. Service Assn., Nat. Trust Hist. Preservation, Zeta Phi Beta. Roman Catholic. Home: 700 7th St SW Apt 802 Washington DC 20024 Office: AID Dept State Washington DC 20523

MILLER, MARY SNYDER, investment banker; b. Boston, Oct. 11, 1943; d. Wade R. and Janet (Mincher) S.; B.A., Allegheny Coll., 1965; M.P.A., SUNY, Albany, 1966; m. Leonard G. Miller, Aug. 8, 1968 (div.). Mcpl. bond analyst Am. Re-Ins. Co., N.Y.C., 1970-71; instl. salesperson McDonald & Co., Cleve., 1971-73; mcpl. bond analyst Dillon Read & Co., N.Y.C., 1973-78, asso. dept. public fin., 1978—. Aide to dir. Meadville (Pa.) Urban Renewal Agy., 1965. Mem. Soc. Archtl. Historians. Democrat. Home: 382 Central Park W New York NY 10025 Office: 46 William St New York NY 10005

MILLER, MELISSA, telecommunications cons.; b. Ill., Oct. 6, 1908; d. James Nelson and Alberta (Shepherd) Tupper; B.Sc., Wayne State U., Detroit, 1961; M.A. in L.S., U. Mich., 1965; m. Howard H. Miller, Apr. 22, 1935; children—John H., James T. Library coordinator E. Windsor (Ont., Can.) pub. schs., 1929-35; instructional materials system coordinator Warren (Mich.) consol. schs., 1961-70; mem. faculty Wayne State U., part-time 1966—; telecommunications cons., 1972—; pres. E. Windsor Edn. Assn., 1930-35; bd. dirs. Romeo (Mich.) Pub. Library, 1975—; cons. librarian First Ch. of God, Romeo. Chmn. Citizens for Regional Sewers, McComb County, 1972—; McComb County del. Mich. White House Conf. on Libraries; bd. dirs. Bruce Twp. Econ. Devel. Corp. Mem. Mich. Library Assn., U. Mich. Alumni, U. Mich. L.S. Alumni Assn., Nat., Mich. edn. assns., Mich. Assn. Study of Adolescents (charter), Internat. Platform Assn., Internat. Soc. Edn. Tech., Nat. Farm and Garden Assn., Women of World. Republican. Congregationalist. Clubs: Women's City, Boat (Detroit); Altrusa. Home: Norfolk Farm 73140 Van Dyke Rd Romeo MI 48065 Office: 67200 Van Dyke Rd Romeo MI 48065

MILLER, MELVIN NORMAN, med. instrumentation co. exec., engr.; b. N.Y.C., Nov. 9, 1936; s. Abraham and Elsie (Greenberg) M.; B.M.E., Cornell U., 1959; M.S., U. Pa., 1963, Ph.D., 1967; m. Eunice Eisenberg, May 12, 1963; children—Emily, Rachel, Deborah. Engr., Philco Corp., Blue Bell, Pa., 1959-61; pres. Melvin N. Miller Assos., Chalfont, Pa., 1967-70; founder, pres. Geometric Data Corp., Wayne, Pa., 1970—; research asso. U. Pa., Phila., 1963-67; mem. med. staff Wilmington Med. Center, 1974—. Mem. Am. Soc. Clin. Pathology, Pattern Recognition Soc., Soc. Automated Cytology. Patentee in field; contbr. articles to profl. jours. Co-developer first comml. automated white blood cell differential system. Office: 999 W Valley Rd Wayne PA 19087

MILLER, NED ARNOLD, ins. agt., employee benefit cons.; b. Mt. Vernon, N.Y., Sept. 25, 1931; B.S. in Fin., Bucknell U., 1953; postgrad. Am. Coll. Life Underwriters; m. Anita Podell, Dec. 25, 1960; children—Jonathan, Alison. Agt., Conn. Mut. Life Ins. Co., N.Y.C., 1955-76, Albuquerque, 1976—, cons. employee benefits, 1968—; nat. lectr. in field; adj. prof. ins. Pace U., 1967-75; tchr. masters' grad. course in advanced estate planning Am. Coll. Life Underwriters. Organizer, first co-chmn. Bus. Trade Fair, Albuquerque, 1977; chmn. Small Bus. Council, Albuquerque, 1977-78; co-chmn. Ambassadors, Albuquerque; bd. dirs. Albuquerque Balloon Fiesta Council, 1977-78. Served with U.S. Army, 1953-55. Named Life and Qualifying Mem., Million Dollar Round Table. Mem. Assn. Advanced Life Underwriters (chmn. 1977 N.Mex. state sales meeting), N.Y.C. Assn. Life Underwriters (v.p., bd. dirs. 1973-76), C.L.U.'s Assn. N.Mex. (bd. dirs. 1978), Estate Planning Council. Democrat. Jewish. Author: Complete Guide to Employee Benefits, 1976; author booklet: Compensating Executives, 1978; film author and subject: Executive Compensation Ideas (Best In Its Class award Ann. Ins. Advt. Conv., Montreal, 1974); author film: Employee Benefits, 1977; contbg. editor Bus. Ins., 1968-75. Home: 223 Spring Creek Ln NE Albuquerque NM 87122 Office: 4004 Carlisle Blvd NE Albuquerque NM 87107

MILLER, PATRICIA MARIA, real estate broker; b. Detroit, Feb. 10, 1933; d. John and Fannie (Pulkanin) Carberry; student U. Akron, 1968-70; m. William Farquar Miller, Sept. 8, 1950; children—William S., Lisa B., Robert J. Interviewer, Nat. Opinion Research Center, U. Chgo., 1965-66; mgr. classified advt. Falls News, Cuyahoga Falls, Ohio, 1966-67; sales asso. Frank Krause Realty, Akron, Ohio, 1967-74; sales mgr. Trail Realty, Cuyahoga Falls, 1974-75; broker, owner Century 21, PMA Realty, Inc., Cuyahoga Falls, 1975—. Sec., League Women Voters Cuyahoga Falls, 1961-63, pres., 1963-65; mem. Cuyahoga Falls Charter Rev. Commn., 1965; mem. Mayor's Adv. Commn. on Urban Renewal, 1966-67; precinct committeewoman, also sec. Cuyahoga Falls Republican Central Com., 1967-68; mem. Cuyahoga Falls Planning Commn., 1966-71; mem. Summit County Planning Commn., 1976-79, Akron Regional Devel. Bd., 1979—. Mem. Akron Area Bd. Realtors, Realtors Nat. Mktg. Inst., Cuyahoga Falls C. of C. (1st v.p.). Methodist. Home: 345 Marian Lake Blvd Cuyahoga Falls OH 44223 Office: 2427 State Rd Cuyahoga Falls OH 44223

MILLER, PAUL GEORGE, finance and ins. co. exec.; b. Louisville, Dec. 13, 1922; s. George Moore and Pauline Louise (Koob) M.; B.M.E., Purdue U., 1948; B.S., U.S. Naval Acad., 1946; B.S. in Electronics Engring., Mass. Inst. Tech., 1949, postgrad. in Nuclear Sci., 1949; m. Doris Kahl Ingram, Feb. 17, 1979; children—George, James, Randolph. Gen. mgr. control systems div. Daystrom (later acquired by Control Data Corp.), La Jolla, Calif., 1957-65; v.p., gen. mgr. communications and spl. systems group Control Data Corp., Mpls., 1965-67, v.p., group gen. mgr. computer systems and devel., 1967-69, sr. v.p., mktg. group exec., 1970-72, sr. v.p., 1973—, pres. Control Data Mktg. Co.; chmn. bd., pres., dir. Comml. Credit Co., Balt., 1975—; dir. Control Data Corp., Fed. Res. Bank, Richmond, Va. Served to lt. USN, 1946-57. Recipient Distinguished Alumnus award Purdue U., 1968. Mem. IEEE (sr.), Sigma Xi, Tau Beta Pi, Eta Kappa Nu, Delta Tau Delta. Home: Cedar Lane Farm Rd Annapolis MD 21401 Office: 300 Saint Paul Pl Baltimore MD 21202 also PO Box 9763 Annapolis MD 21012

MILLER, PAUL LUKENS, investment banker; b. Phila., Dec. 6, 1919; s. Henry C. L. and Elsie (Groff) M.: student William Penn Charter Sch., Phila., 1937; A.B., Princeton U., 1941; m. Adele Olyphant, Nov. 4, 1950; children—Paul L., Hilary, Beverly, Leslie. With First Boston Corp., N.Y.C., 1946—, v.p., 1955-64, dir., 1959—, pres., 1964-78, sr. adviser, 1978—; trustee Seamen's Bank for Savs.; dir. Cummins Engine Co., Aluminum Co. Am., Celanese Corp., Ogilvy & Mather Internat. Inc., Congoleum Corp. Served from 2d lt. to maj. F.A., AUS, 1941-46. Clubs: Ivy (Princeton); Links, Union, Recess (N.Y.C.); Duquesne (Pitts.). Home: Young's Rd New Vernon NJ 07976 Office: 20 Exchange Pl New York NY 10005

MILLER, PAUL SANFORD, investment firm exec.; b. Schenectady, Aug. 27, 1930; s. Harry and Ida G. (Goldsmith) M.; A.B., U. Rochester, 1952; M.B.A., Harvard U., 1954; m. Marilyn S. Adler, June 7, 1953; children—Deborah, Joel, Barry. Buyer, Gimbels Corp., 1956-63; mng. dir. S. Klein Dept. Stores, 1963-66; mgr. Bache Halsey Stuart Shields, Washington, 1972-79, v.p., mgr. spl.and internat. accounts, N.Y.C., 1979—. Pres., Har Shalom Congregation, Potomac, Md., 1973. Clubs: Nat. Economics, Harvard Bus. Sch. Home: 235 Spring Ridge Dr Berkeley Heights NJ 07922 Office: Bache Halsey Stuart Shields 100 Gold St New York NY 10028

MILLER, PAUL STEWART, automobile dealership exec.; b. Bridgeport, Conn., Aug. 19, 1944; s. Theodore and Evelyn M.; m. Kathleen Healey, Aug. 20, 1966; children—Gregg, Michelle, Kyle. Auto salesman Miller & Pinto, Inc., Bridgeport, 1962-64; v.p., gen. mgr. Ted Miller, Inc., Bridgeport, 1964-65; owner, mgr. Ted Miller Buick, Inc., Bridgeport, 1965—. Served with U.S. Army, 1962-63. Mem. Conn. Buick Dealers Assn. (dir.), Greater Bridgeport New Car Dealers Assn. (dir., v.p.). Jewish. Clubs: Easton Racquet (dir., treas.), Lions Club of Easton, Jewish Community Center. Home: 75 Asmara Way Easton CT 06425 Office: 930 Kings Hwy Fairfield CT 06430

MILLER, RICHARD ALLEN, chem. co. exec.; b. Rockville Centre, N.Y., May 29, 1947; s. Jacob and Nina Jean (Konchanin) M.; B.A., Colgate U., 1969; m. Olga Shkutzko, June 8, 1969; children—Alison Jane, Richard Allen. Buyer trainee J.C. Penney Co., N.Y.C., 1969, asst. buyer, 1970-74, asso. buyer, 1974-75; with Prentiss Drug & Chem. Co., N.Y.C., 1975—, v.p., 1976-80, exec. v.p., 1980—, also dir. Served with U.S. Army, 1969-70. Mem. United Pesticide Formulators and Distbrs. Assn. (dir. 1979-80), Chem. Specialties Mfrs. Assn. (dir. insecticide div. exec. bd. 1980-83). Office: 363 7th Ave New York NY 10001

MILLER, RICHARD G., JR., indsl. mfg., engring. and constrn. co. exec.; b. Chgo., 1918; grad. Marshall U., 1942. Pres., Roberts & Schaefer Co., 1963—; v.p. Elgin Nat. Industries, Inc., Chgo., 1968-72, pres., chief exec. officer, 1977—, also dir. Office: 120 S Riverside Plaza Chicago IL 60606

MILLER, RICHARD KENDALL, cons. engr., author; b. Muncie, Ind., Oct. 16, 1946; s. Robert Kendall and Ruth Mary (Beinke) M.; B.S.M.E., Purdue U., 1970, postgrad.; m. Marcia Lee Drummond, May 20, 1979. Engr., Electro-Voice, Inc., Buchanan, Mich., 1965-69; cons. L.S. Goodfriend & Assos., Cons. Engrs. in Acoustics, Cedar Knolls, N.J., 1970-72; pres. Richard K. Miller & Assos., Inc., Acoustical Cons., Atlanta, 1972—. Mem. Morgan County Cultural Center, 1978—, Madison Hist. Soc., 1978—. Mem. Acoustical Soc. Am., Archtl. Acoustics Soc. (adminstr.), Assn. Energy Engrs. (dir.), Phi Kappa Sigma (Outstanding Mem. 1969). Methodist. Author: (with A. Thumann) Secrets of Noise Control, 1974; Handbook of Industrial Noise Mangement, 1976; Industrial Noise Control, 1978; Coping with The Barking Dog Noise Problem, 1978; (with Mark D. Oviatt) City Noise Index, 1978; Noise Control Solutions for the Chemical and Petroleum Industries, 1979; Special Solutions for Punch Press Noise Control, 1979; Noise Control Solutions for Power Plants, 1979; Noise Control Solutions for the Rubber and Plastic Industry, 1979; Noise Control Solutions for the Wire Industry, 1979; Noise Control in Buffing and Polishing, 1979; Construction Noise Control, 1979; (with Wayne V. Montone) Handbook of Acoustical Enclosures and Barriers, 1978; (with David F. Barr) Basic Industrial Hearing Conservation, 1979; also numerous articles.

MILLER, RICHARD MORGAN, corp. exec.; b. Nashville, Apr. 12, 1931; s. Marvin LeRoy and Lucile Stephenson (Morgan) M.; B.A., Vanderbilt U., 1953; m. Betty Ruth Randolph, June 16, 1953; children—Richard Morgan, Ellen Randolph, Claire Elizabeth. Salesman, Dominion Ins. Agy., Nashville, 1955-58; founder, pres. Richard M. Miller & Co., Nashville, 1958-70, merged with Synercon Corp., Nashville, founding pres., chief exec. officer, 1970-76; exec. v.p., chief operating officer Corroon & Black Corp., N.Y.C., 1976-78, pres., chief operating officer, 1978—, also dir.; dir. Sports Industries Am., Nashville. Active Nashville YMCA. Served as 1st lt. USMC, 1953-55, to capt. USMCR, 1955-61. Life. asso. Owen Grad. Sch. Mgmt., Vanderbilt U. Mem. Nat. Assn. Casualty & Surety Agts., Nat. Assn. Ins. Brokers, Nat. Assn. Surety Bond Producers, Nashville Area C. of C. Republican. Methodist. Clubs: Belle Meade Country, Nashville City, Cumberland (Nashville); City Midday, N.Y. Athletic (N.Y.C.); Ponte Vedra, Sawgrass (Ponte Vedra Beach, Fla.); John's Island (Fla.). Home: 25 Sutton Pl S New York NY 10022 also 4400 Chickering Ln Nashville TN 37215 Office: Wall St Plaza New York NY 10005 also 301 Plus Park Blvd Nashville TN 37217

MILLER, RICHARD WESLEY, multi-industry fin. exec.; b. Buffalo, Nov. 22, 1940; s. John Irwin and Rose Mary (Mirco) M.; B.B.A., Case Western Res. U., 1967; M.B.A., Harvard, 1970; m. Sharon Ann Betzler, Jan. 28, 1967; children—Barbara Ann, Thomas Andrew. Various mgmt. and lending positions Nat. City Bank of Cleve., 1961-68; v.p. investments Pa. Co., N.Y.C., 1970-72; exec. v.p. Arvida Corp., Boca Raton, Fla., 1972-79, sr. v.p. fin., chief fin. officer Penn Central Corp., N.Y.C., 1979—; dir. Sav-A-Stop, Inc., 1975-80. Mem. adv. council Fla. Atlantic U., dir., 1975-79; mem. Gov.'s Commn. on Energy, 1976; mem. City of Boca Raton Housing Adv. Bd.; chmn. Econ. Council Palm Beach County (Fla.), 1978—. Mem. Harvard Bus. Sch. Assn. (dir. S. Fla., internat. pres. 1980), Urban Land Inst., Recreation Devel. Council (chmn. 1979). Clubs: Club at Citicorp Center (N.Y.C.); Club at Boca Raton Hotel. Home: 27 Normandy Ln Riverside CT 06878 Office: Penn Central Corp 245 Park Ave New York NY 10167

MILLER, RICHARDS THORN, naval architect, engr.; b. Jenkintown, Pa., Jan. 31, 1918; s. Herman Geistweit and Helen Buckman (Thorn) M.; B.S. in Naval Architecture and Marine Engring., Webb Inst. Naval Architecture, 1940; Naval Engr., Mass. Inst. Tech., 1951; m. Jean Corbat Spear, Sept. 13, 1941; children—Patricia (Mrs. Charles G. Fishburn), Linda (Mrs. John X. Carrier). Commd. ensign U.S. Navy, 1940, advanced through grades to capt., 1960; specialized work design oceanographic research ships, mine sweepers, torpedo boats, destroyers; ret., 1968; mgr. ocean engring. Oceanic div. Westinghouse Electric Corp., 1969-75, adv. engr., 1975-79; cons. naval architect and engr., 1968—; mem. com. naval architecture Am. Bur. Shipping, 1960-63, mem. tech. com., 1978—, mem. ship structure com., 1966-68. Decorated Navy Legion of Merit. Fellow Soc. Naval Architects and Marine Engrs. (chmn. S.E. sect. 1965-66, chmn. marine systems com. 1970-77, chmn. tech. and research steering com. 1977-78, v.p. tech. and research 1979—, mem. council 1976—, mem. exec. com. 1977—; Capt. Joseph H. Linnard prize 1964); mem. Am. Soc. Naval Engrs. (mem. council 1976-78), U.S. Naval Inst., Sigma Xi. Clubs: N.Y. Yacht (N.Y.C.); Sailing of the Chesapeake. Author: (with R.G. Henry) Sailing Yacht Design, 1963; also sects. in books, articles. Home: 957 Melvin Rd Annapolis MD 21403 Office: 957 Melvin Rd Annapolis MD 21403

MILLER, ROBERT, investment banker; b. Los Angeles, Mar. 26, 1947; s. Robert Martin and Marion Elizabeth (Mills) M.; m. Amparo Jaramillo Cortez. Pvt. investor, Beverly Hills, Calif., 1968-73; chmn., chief exec. officer Century City Securities Corp., Los Angeles, 1974-75, Calif. Securities Corp., Beverly Hills, 1976—; chmn. bd. Calif. Group. Chmn. bd. govs. Calif. Found. Republican. Club: Beverly Hills. Office: 9701 Wilshire Blvd Beverly Hills CA 90212

MILLER, ROBERT ERIC, engring., constrn. co. exec.; b. Jacksonville, Fla., May 4, 1919; s. Robert E. and Uldene (Sheppard) M.; student U. Ga., 1936-39; m. Lilyan James Privett, Jan. 29, 1978; children—Marsha Helen Miller Yawn, Robert Eric, Deborah Paull, Andrew Hines. Mgr. personnel and labor relations H.K. Ferguson Co., Cleve., 1941-56; v.p. Bechtel Corp., San Francisco, 1956-80; pres., dir. Pacific Internat. Computing Corp., 1973-75; pres., dir. Fluor Constructors, Inc., Irvine, Calif., 1980—. Bd. dirs. Industry Edn. Council Calif., 1974-75; trustee Golden Gate U., San Francisco, 1974-75, San Francisco Met. YMCA, 1969-71, Am. Sch. in London, 1965-67; bd. dirs., treas. The Washington Ballet, 1978-80. Mem. Asso. Gen. Contractors Am. (past v.p. Cleve.), Nat. Constructors Assn. (pres. Washington 1972). Episcopalian. Clubs: Meadow (Fairfax, Calif.); Olympic (San Francisco); 1925 F St., Univ. (Washington) Columbia Country (Chevy Chase, Md.); Georgetown (Washington). Contbr. articles to profl. jours. Home: 6 Rue Deauville Newport Beach CA 92660 Office: 3333 Michelson Dr Irvine CA 92715

MILLER, ROBERT RICHEY CONKLIN, transp. co. exec.; b. Lincoln, Nebr., Apr. 1, 1925; s. Dwight R.C. and Cora E. (Conklin) M.; B.S. in Bus. Adminstrn., U. Nebr., 1943; M.B.A. with high distinction, Harvard U., 1948; m. Kappy S. Kellogg, Jan. 16, 1944; children—David K., Robert L. Adminstrv. asst. to dean Harvard U. Bus. Sch., Boston, 1948-49; exec. trainee Crossett Co. (Ark.), 1949-52; v.p. Ashley Drew & No. Ry. Co., Crossett, 1952-54, pres., gen. mgr., dir., 1954-59; v.p. planning and devel. Consol. Freightways, Inc., Menlo Park, Calif. and Portland, Oreg., 1959-61, v.p. spl. transp., 1961-63; pres., dir. Greyhound Van Lines, Inc. and subs., Chgo., 1963-70; cons. transp., 1970-71; exec. v.p. Atlas Van Lines, Inc., Evansville, Ind., 1971-74, pres., dir. chief operating officer, 1974-80, vice-chmn., 1980—; dir. Union Fed. Savs. and Loan, Evansville. Conf. v.p. Am. Trucking Assn., 1977-79. Vice pres., bd. dirs. Buffalo Trace Council Boy Scouts Am., 1973-78; mem. Mayor's Spl. Commn. on Energy, Evansville, 1977. Served to capt. U.S. Army, 1943-46; PTO. Recipient Distinguished Service award U.S. Jr. C. of C., 1952; Silver Beaver award Boy Scouts Am., 1976. Mem. Am. Movers Conf. (treas. 1964-68, dir., exec. com. 1973—, vice chmn. 1978—), Harvard U. Bus. Sch. Club (pres. Oreg. chpt. 1962-63, Chgo. chpt. 1967-68), Ind. Soc. Chgo., Evansville C. of C. (dir., v.p. 1974-79), Alpha Kappa Psi, Phi Gamma Delta. Republican. Methodist. Clubs: Union League (Chgo.); Evansville Country, Petroleum (Evansville). Office: 1212 Saint George Rd Evansville IN 47711*

MILLER, ROBERT THOMAS, paint co. exec.; b. McMinnville, Oreg., July 1, 1940; s. Ronald V. and Marjorie E. (Jones) M.; B.S., Linfield Coll., 1962; m. Sandra L. Ballard, Nov. 11, 1961; children—Brian Lee, Lori Marie. Vice-pres., Norris Paint and Varnish Co., Salem, Oreg., 1962-71; v.p. mfg. Kelly-Moore Paint Co., San Carlos, Calif., 1971-76; gen. mgr. Imperial Paint Co., Portland, Oreg., 1976—. Mem. Com. for Citizen Involvement, City of West Linn, Oreg. Mem. Soc. Paint Tech. (sec. Pacific N.W. sect.), Nat. Paint and Coatings Assn. Democrat. Club: Elks. Home: 19481 Wilderness Dr West Linn OR 97068

MILLER, ROBERT WALTER, accountant; b. Binghamton, N.Y., Aug. 27, 1944; s. Walter L. and Hilda A. M.; B.S., SUNY, Binghamton, 1977; m. Oct 21, 1972; m. Colleen; children—Kathleen, Jody, Brian. Cost acctg. mgr. Emkay Candle Co., Syracuse, N.Y., 1976-77; sr. cost acct. Automation Services, Binghamton, 1979-80; sr. acct. Yellow Transp. Services, Binghamton, 1980—. Served with U.S. Army, 1963-69. Mem. Nat. Assn. Accts., Inst. Mgmt. Acctg. Club: Elks. Home: 29 Patch Rd RD 3 Box 209A Binghamton NY 13901 Office: 385 State St Binghamton NY 13902

MILLER, ROBERT WILSON, chem. engr.; b. Erie, Pa., July 13, 1934; s. Wilson Finley and Jane Louise (Keene) M.; B.Chem.Engring., Yale U., 1956; M.Chem. Engring. (Grad. fellow), U. Del., 1958; m. Janet Joris Brandon, June 23, 1956; children—Barbara Jane, Diane Grace, Robert Brandon, Susan Emily, Mark David. Engr. plastics div. Monsanto Co., Springfield, Mass., 1958-64; from engr. to group leader Diamond Shamrock Corp., Painesville, Ohio, 1964-77; group leader Arco polymers div. Atlantic Richfield Corp., Monaca, Pa., 1977-80, Newton Square, Pa., 1980—. Mem. Hampden Symphony Orch., Springfield, 1961-64, Beaver County Symphonic Wind Ensemble, Beaver, Pa., 1977-80; mem. Suburban Symphony Orch., Cleve., 1964-77, mem. exec. bd., 1966-77. Sr. mem. Soc. Plastics Engrs.; mem. Am. Inst. Chem. Engrs., TAPPI. Republican. Presbyterian. Patentee in field. Home: 290 Musket Ln Wayne PA 19087 Office: 3801 West Chester Pike Newton Square PA 19073

MILLER, RONALD LEE, diversified co. exec.; b. Columbus, Ohio, Aug. 17, 1940; s. Bruce Eugene and Opal Maxine (Boss) M.; B.S. in Mech. Engring., Ohio State U., 1966; M.B.A., U. Beverly Hills, 1977, Ph.D., 1979; children—Kellie Ann, Christina Lynn, Erin Nichole. Corp. engr. chems. civ. U.S. Steel Corp., Circleville, Ohio, Pitts., 1970-72; owner Quality Mold, Grand Rapids, Mich., 1972-73; v.p. Nika Plastics, Grand Rapids, 1973-75; pres. Internat. Prototypes, Grand Rapids, 1975-79; pres. Hilco Plastics, Grand Rapids, 1977—; pres., founder RLM Prodns., Hollywood, Calif., 1980—; cons. product devel. Mem. ednl. adv. com. Grand Rapids Area Colls.; mem. U.S. Senatorial Adv. Com. Served with USMCR, 1957-58. Mem. Soc. Plastics Engrs., N.Y. Acad. Scis. Republican. Roman Catholic. Author texts in field. Home: 2520-2 Fox Run Rd Wyoming MI 49509 also 4498 Woodman Ave Hollywood CA 91423 Office: 6505 S Division Grand Rapids MI 49508 also 6331 Hollywood Blvd Suite 903 Hollywood CA 90028

MILLER, RONALD LEE, fin. broker, cons.; b. Dover, Ohio, May 3, 1942; s. Richard George and Constance Arlene M.; B.S., Ohio State U., 1972; M.B.A., U. Dayton, 1975; m. Juliette Nell Gerlach, June 9, 1968; children—Jeffrey Daniel, Kristen Melissa. Mgr. material planning Hobart Corp., Troy, Ohio, 1972-76; mgr. inventory and procurement Bellows Internat., Akron, Ohio, 1976-78; mgmt. cons. R.L. Wallace, Inc., Akron, 1978-80; pres. R.L. Miller Diversified Fin. and Consulting, Akron, 1980—. Served with USN, 1962-70; Vietnam. Mem. Am. Prodn. and Inventory Control Soc., Nat. Assn. Fin. Cons., Internat. Assn. Bus. and Fin. Cons. Republican. Lutheran. Home and Office: 47 Castle Blvd Akron OH 44313

MILLER, ROSWELL CARNEGIE, bus. systems co. adminstr.; b. Berkeley, Calif., Jan. 20, 1947; s. Roswell and Anne (Brinton) M.; B.A. in Computers and Info. Sci., Colgate U., 1968; m. Wendy Hillas, July 6, 1968; children—Roswell, Jason, Wendy, Tracy. With IBM, Poughkeepsie, N.Y., 1968-79, Satellite Bus. Systems, Stamford, Conn., 1979—. Budget officer Town of Poughkeepsie, 1976, dep. supr., 1977-78; bd. dirs. Dutchess County Arts Council, 1978-79. Home: 10 Country Club Rd Darien CT 06820

MILLER, RUSSELL ROWLAND, ins. cons.; b. San Francisco, May 12, 1937; s. Joseph Hennessy and Irene (Barrett) M.; B.S. in English, U. San Francisco, 1960; M.B.A. in Fin., Columbia U., 1962; m. Ellen Kamarck, Dec. 14, 1979; children—Owen, Adrian. Underwriter, Aetna Life & Casualty Co., 1962, Crum & Forster Ins. Cos., 1963-64; agt. and broker Miller & Ames Ins. Brokers, 1964-66; asst. to

Congressman J. V. Tunney, 1966-68; dean Stuart Hall Sch., 1968-70; instr. Lone Mountain Coll., 1970; chmn., pres. Russell Miller, Inc., San Francisco, 1971—; chmn. exec. com., dir. ISU Cos., Inc., 1979—. Candidate for U.S. Congress, 1970; mem. Calif. Democratic Central Com.; mem. San Francisco County Dem. Central Com.; founder San Francisco Counselor Hosts, 1961. Served with inf. U.S. Army, 1962. Recipient various ins. awards. Mem. Am. Assn. Ins. Mgmt. Cons's., Western Assn. Ins. Brokers, Ins. Forum San Francisco, Am. Soc. Appraisers, League to Save Lake Tahoe, San Francisco Symphony Assn., San Francisco Opera Assn., San Francisco Performing Arts Center. Roman Catholic. Author: A Merger and Acquisitions Guide for Agents and Brokers, 1980; contbr. articles to profl. jours. Office: 300 Montgomery St San Francisco CA 94104

MILLER, RUSSELL TUTTLE, Realtor; b. Spokane, Dec. 10, 1922; s. Russell Tuttle and Claudia (Lewis) M.; B.S., M.I.T., 1948; postgrad. Colo. Sch. Mines, 1950; m. Georgette Thioliere, Apr. 17, 1948. Pres., New World Exploration Corp., Los Angeles, 1948-56; cons. mineral engring., Los Angeles, 1956-58; pres. Tech. Mktg. Assos., Los Angeles, 1959-73; pres. Titan Realty Corp., Los Angeles, 1959—, Worldwide Properties, Ltd., Newport Beach, Calif., 1976—, Sepol, Ltd., Irvine, Calif., 1976—. Served in U.S. Army, 1942-45. Decorated Purple Heart. Mem. AIME, Am. Inst. Chem. Engrs., Soc. Exploration Geophysicists. Episcopalian. Clubs: Calif. Yacht, Riviera Country, Marina City, Balboa Bay. Home and Office: 2 Mandarin Irvine CA 92714

MILLER, SAMUEL LEE, JR., corp. exec.; b. Maywood, Ill., Apr. 22, 1912; s. Samuel Lee and Clarissa (Buck) M.; Ph.B., U. Chgo., 1935; m. Sally Ann Walton, June 24, 1939 (dec.); 1 dau., Sally Ann (Mrs. David Roth); m. 2d, Irene A. Reed, Oct. 12, 1973. Foreman mfg. Am. Can Co., Maywood, Ill., 1933-42; adminstrv. mgr. George S. May Co., San Francisco, 1942-47; gen. sales mgr. Hunt Foods and Industries, Fullerton, Calif., 1947-58; with H.M. Parker and Son, wholesale automobile parts co., 1958-68, v.p., gen. mgr., dir., North Hollywood, Calif., 1962-68; pres. Am. Parts Systems, Inc., North Hollywood, 1968-71, regional market devel. mgr., 1971-72, gen. mgr. APS-Fairfield Distbn. Center No. Calif., 1972-76; pres. Roth & Miller Realty, Inc., 1977—. Mem. Theta Delta Chi. Republican. Methodist. Mason. Home: 248 Cheyenne Dr Vacaville CA 95688

MILLER, SHERMAN G., communications co. exec.; b. Boston, Oct. 20, 1933; s. Benjamin and Leah (Bornstein) M.; B.S. in Bus. Adminstrn. (Univ. scholar), Boston U., 1955; m. Thelma S. Shefner, June 26, 1955; children—Jordan S., Barry L., Faith J. Fin. and mfg. exec. Gen. Electric Co., Lynn and Pittsfield, Mass., 1959-63; gen. mgmt. exec. GTE Sylvania, Needham, Mass., 1963-78; v.p., chief operating officer RF Systems Inc., St. Cloud, Fla., 1978-80; founder, pres. UNICOM, mgmt., tech. and mktg. cons., 1980—; guest lectr. INTELSAT symposium on satellite communication, Munich, 1976, Athens, 1977. Mem. steering com. Sch. Mgmt., Boston U. Served to capt. USAF, 1955-58. Mem. Boston U. Alumni Assn. Contbr. articles on communications to trade jours. Office: 2483 Castlewood Rd Maitland FL 32751

MILLER, SIDNEY AARON, ins. co. exec.; b. N.Y.C., June 18, 1934; s. Leon Richard and Ann (Taxier) M.; B.A., Hunter Coll., 1957; m. Rona Lifshey, Feb. 12, 1961; children—Hugh Ian, Marc Evan, Lee Lawrence. Underwriter N.Y. Life Ins. Co., N.Y.C., 1960-78; pres. Miller Planning Corp., N.Y.C., 1972—, Great Neck Funding Corp., N.Y.C., 1975—; partner Liberty Tower of Oklahoma City, 1961—; pres. Allied Capital Corp., Stamford, Conn., 1978—; dir. Remco Internat. Corp. Mem. Nat. Assn. Life Underwriters, Am. Coll. Life Underwriters, Estate Planning Council of N.Y.C. Club: Stepping Stone Sailing. Home: 85 Station Rd Great Neck NY 11023 Office: 70 Middle Neck Rd Great Neck NY 11021

MILLER, TED ROBERT, mgmt. cons.; b. Perth Amboy, N.J., Sept. 17, 1947; s. Marvin Lester and Carolyn Ruth (Guttman) M.; B.S. in Engring., Case Western Res. U., 1968; M.S. in Operations Research, M.City Planning, U. Pa., 1970, Ph.D. in Regional Sci., 1975. Ops. research analyst U.S. Dept. Commerce, Nat. Bur. Standards and HEW, Washington, 1971-75; staff dir. task force on Nat. Blood Data Center and com. for commonality in blood banking automation Am. Blood Commn., Rosslyn, Va., 1975-77; asst. dir. urban and econ. devel. Nat. Inst. Advanced Studies, Washington, 1977-78; v.p. Granville Corp., Washington, 1978—. Mem. Bd. Proprs. Eastern N.J., 1974—; pres. Adelphi Ter. Condominium Assn., 1979—. Mem. Am. Inst. Planners, Nat. Assn. Housing and Redevel. Ofcls., Am. Public Health Assn., Ops. Research Soc. Am., Regional Sci. Assn., AAAS, World Future Soc., Pi Delta Epsilon. Democrat. Contbr. articles to profl. jours. Office: 1133 15th St NW Suite 1100 Washington DC 20005

MILLER, THOMAS JAMES, coal co. exec.; b. Johnstown, Pa., Mar. 4, 1949; s. Jay Jacob and Mary Elizabeth (Finnegan) M.; student U. Pitts., 1967-69, Indiana (Pa.) U., 1977-78; m. Anne N. Davis, Aug. 2, 1969; children—Thomas James, Randy Lee, Dennis Andrew. With W.L. Fedorko Engrs., Portage, Pa., 1969; cost accountant Pa. Electric Co., Johnstown, 1969-76; project accountant Zapata Fuels, Inc., Houston, 1976-77; controller, treas. Mears Coal Co. subs. Zapata Fuels, Inc., Dixonville, Pa., 1977-79; mgr. acctg. and adminstrn. Northwestern Resources Co., Huntsville, Tex., 1979—. Auditor fund drives ARC and Community Chest, Johnstown, Pa., 1974-76; fin. dir. Conemaugh Ch. of Brethren Bldg. Com., 1973-77. Lic. real estate, Pa. Republican. Club: Elks. Home: 226 Oaklawn Huntsville TX 77340 Office: 1300 11 St Suite 300 Huntsville TX 77340

MILLER, THOMAS LLOYD, galvanizing co. exec.; b. Wilmington, Del., June 30, 1915; s. Thomas W. and Katharine Marie (Tallman) M.; B.S., U.S. Naval Acad., 1937; m. Madeleine Bridgeford Russel, Oct. 7, 1939 (dec. Jan. 1975); children—Russel T., Lloyd, Lindsay, Bruce W.; m. 2d, Elizabeth Cooper Joy, July 18, 1975. Commd. ensign USN, 1937, advanced through grades to comdr., 1947; with submarine forces Atlantic and Pacific, 1940-47; ret., 1947; pres. Miller Ford Co., Inc., Stonington, Conn., 1950-62; pvt. investor, 1962-70; v.p., sec. U.S. Mfg. & Galvanizing Corp., Miami, 1970—. Founder, pres. Pine Point Sch., Stonington, Conn., 1948-52. Justice of the Peace, Stonington, Conn., 1950-63. Trustee Marine Hist. Assn., Mystic Seaport, Conn., 1948-78. Mem. Am. Legion, V.F.W., U.S. Naval Acad. Alumni Assn. (trustee 1950-52). Clubs: New York Yacht; Storm Trysail (Larchmont, N.Y.); Ocean Reef (Key Largo, Fla.); Biscayne Bay Yacht, Coral Reef Yacht (Miami); Ocean Racing Am. (founder). Home: 3570 Matheson Ave Coconut Grove FL 33133 Office: US Mfg & Galvanizing 7320 NW 43d St Miami FL 33166

MILLER, TIMOTHY JOSEPH, oilfield sales, mng., mktg. exec.; b. El Dorado, Kans., 1940; s. Cyril W. and Francis C. (Muth) M.; grad. pub. schs. Great Bend, Kans.; children—Sean Kelly, Kim Lynn. Owner, operator Oil Field Mfg. Warehouse, Great Bend, 1958—, chmn. bd., pres., sec.-treas. Asst. dir. Barton County CD, 1968-78. Served with USNR. Mem. Kans. Ind. Oil and Gas Assn., Am. Petroleum Inst., VFW. Republican. Roman Catholic. Clubs: Great Bend Petroleum, Elks. Home: Rural Route 2 Great Bend KS 67530 Office: 115 Patton Rd Great Bend KS 67530

MILLER, VICTOR FRANCIS, mortgage co. exec.; b. Irvington, N.J., May 11, 1920; s. Stanley Anthony and Mary Gertrude (Maier) M.; student Rutgers Coll., nights 1939; m. Barbara Ann Zwick, June 7, 1947; children—Gail Marie, John Stanley. With Underwood Mortgage Co., Irvington, 1938-47, 67-70, v.p., 1967-70; dept. head U.S. Mortgage & Guaranty Co., Newark, 1948-50; from dept. head to v.p. Bankers Mortgage Co., Clifton, N.J., 1950-66; project mgr. bldg. div. Rellim Corp., Flanders, N.J., 1966-67; with Margaretten & Co. Inc., Perth Amboy, N.J., 1971—, sr. v.p., 1975—, sec., 1975—. Served with AUS, 1941-46. Decorated Purple Heart. Mem. Mortgage Bankers Assn. Am., Mortgage Bankers Assn. N.J. (chmn. VA coms. 1972), N.J. Home Builders Assn., Middlesex Bd. Realtors, VFW. Republican. Roman Catholic. Club: K.C. Home: 8 Rehoboth Rd Flanders NJ 07836 Office: 280 Maple St Perth Amboy NJ 08861

MILLER, W(ALTER) GORDON, water conditioning co. exec.; b. Havre, Mont., July 6, 1932; s. Walter Wesley and Vivian (Vagg) M.; B.A. in Psychology, Carleton Coll., 1954; M.S. in TV, Syracuse U., 1955; m. Gayle Highberg, Dec. 29, 1954; children—Peggy, Debby, David. Pres., Culligan Water Conditioning Co., Marlette, Mich., 1958—, Swim Pool Center, Marlette, 1967—, Clean Water Corp., LaCrosse, Wis., 1974—; dir. Wolverine State Bank, Sandusky, Mich., U.S. Water Corp. of Mpls.; trustee Water Quality Assn. Nat. Ins. Trust; adv. bd. Safe Drinking Water Act, Mich. Dept. Pub. Health, 1977. Chmn., Sanilac County (Mich.) Mental Health Bd., 1971—; bd. dirs. Marlette Community Hosp., 1971—; sec. Sanilac County Bldg. Authority, 1972—. Mem. Mich. (founder, pres.), Internat. (pres.) water conditioning assns., Water Quality Assn. (internat. key award for outstanding service 1977, chmn. plumbing certification com. 1977-78, chmn. awards com. 1977-78). Republican. Presbyterian. Home: 6623 Cooper Rd Marlette MI 48453 Office: 3099 Main St Marlette MI 48453

MILLER, WALTER RICHARD, JR., banker; b. N.Y.C., Nov. 20, 1934; s. Walter Richard and Anne M. (Phelan) M.; A.B., Dartmouth, 1956; M.B.A., Columbia, 1957; Ph.D., N.Y. U., 1965; m. Joan M. Groark, June 29, 1963; children—Kathryn Anne, Margaret Elizabeth, Jennifer Marie, Walter R. III. Account exec. McCann-Erickson, Inc., N.Y.C., 1957-60; instr. mktg. N.Y. U., 1961-65, adminstr. day master's program, 1963-65, asst. to dean Grad. Sch. Bus., 1963-65; mgr. mktg. research, area devel. Mellon Nat. Bank and Trust Co. (now Mellon Nat. Corp.), Pitts., 1965-66, v.p., dir. mktg., 1966-78; also dir. mktg. Mellon Bank N.A.; sr. v.p., dir. mktg. and planning 1st Nat. Bank Atlanta, 1978—; mem. faculty Stonier Grad. Sch. Bus.; chmn. internat. com., chmn. mktg. com. Interbank, Inc.; cons. savs. banks, mktg. cons. Trustee, mem. exec. com. Cheshire (Conn.) Acad.; chmn. bd. regents Bank Marketing Sch. U. Colo. Served with USAFR, 1958. Ford Found. fellow, 1963; recipient Wall St. Jour. award. Mem. Am. Bankers Assn. (mem. savs. com. exec. com. banking div.), Am. Mgmt. Assn., Pa. Bankers Assn. (chmn. mktg. and edn. com.), Bank Mktg. Assn. (dir.), Delta Kappa Epsilon, Alpha Kappa Psi. Republican. Clubs: Capital City, Bridgehampton, Schinnecock Hills Golf, Rolling Rock. Home: 65 W Wesley Rd NW Atlanta GA 30305 Office: 2 Peachtree St Atlanta GA 30302

MILLER, WILLIAM CHARLES, lawyer; b. Jacksonville, Fla., Aug. 6, 1937; s. Charles and Mary Elizabeth (Kiger) M.; B.A., Washington and Lee U., 1958, LL.B., 1961; LL.M., N.Y. U., 1963; grad. Advanced Mgmt. Program, Harvard U., 1978; m. Hadmut Gisela Larsen, June 10, 1961; children— Monica Lee, Charles Andreas. Admitted to Fla. bar, 1961, U.S. Supreme Ct. bar, 1968; counsel to electrochem., elastomers and internat. depts. E.I. du Pont de Nemours and Co., Wilmington, Del., 1963-66; counsel S. Am. ops. Bristol-Myers Co., N.Y.C., 1967-69; internat. counsel Xerox Corp., Stamford, Conn., 1969-78, asso. gen. counsel, 1979—; prof. internat. law U. Md., Munich, Germany, 1962. Bd. dirs. Southwestern Legal Found., 1975—. Fulbright scholar, 1959-60, Ford Found. fellow, 1961-62, German Govt. grantee, 1962-63, Hague Acad. fellowship, 1963, Kappa Sigma scholar, 1959. Mem. Egypt/U.S. Bus. Council (chmn. export promotion com.), Nat. Council China/U.S. Trade (exec. dir. legal com.), Westchester Fairfield County Corp. Counsel Assn. (chmn. internat. com.; sec. and dir. 1979), Internat., Am. (chmn. joint venture subcom. of China com.), Fla., Supreme Ct. U.S. bar assns. Clubs: Mason, Elks. Home: 130 Cheese Spring Rd Wilton CT 06897 Office: Long Ridge Rd Stamford CT

MILLER, WILLIAM DAWES, metals co. exec.; b. Buffalo, Feb. 14, 1919; s. William S. and Hazel (Sands) M.; B.S. in Mech. Engring., Carnegie Inst. Tech., 1942; m. Celeste M. Fain, Nov. 20, 1943 (dec. 1970); 1 dau., Elizabeth F.; m. 2d, Anne J. Johnson, Dec. 20, 1972. Prodn. engr. Wright Aero. Corp., Cin., 1942-44; with AEC, 1944-53, dep. chief Oak Ridge Prodn. div., 1944-49, chief ops. div. Paducah Area, 1949-51, dep. mgr. Paducah Area, 1951-53; v.p., chief engr. Continental Copper & Steel Industries, Inc., N.Y.C., 1953-60; v.p. Consol. Aluminum Corp., Jackson, Tenn., 1960, exec. v.p., 1960-61, pres., chief exec. officer, dir., 1961-69; chmn. bd. AIAG Metals, Inc., Jackson, 1961-69; pres., chief exec. officer, dir. Gulf Coast Aluminum Corp., 1967-69, Independence Energy Co., Inc., 1979—; dir. mfg. planning and devel. Anaconda Co., N.Y.C., 1969-71, v.p., 1971-79; pres., dir. Anaconda Jamaica, 1971-73; v.p., dir. Anaconda Aluminum Co., 1969-73; dir. Anaconda Wire & Cable Co., 1969-73, Anaconda Am. Brass Co., 1969-73, Gen. Astrometals Corp., 1969-73, Internat. Smelting & Refining, 1969-73, Greene Cananea Copper Co., 1969-73; v.p., dir. Mitsui-Anaconda Corp., 1973-78; dir. Oak-Mitsui, Inc., 1975-78, Habanero Corp., 1976-79. Clubs: Shinnecock Hills (N.Y.) Golf; Met. (gov.), Athletic (N.Y.C.); Meadow Tennis (Southampton). Home: 35 E 75th St New York NY 10021 Office: 660 Madison Ave Fifth Floor New York NY 10021

MILLER, WILLIAM EARL, uniform rental and sales co. exec.; b. Cin., Jan. 17, 1942; s. Earl Ben and Hazel Ann (Johnson) M.; B.B.A., U. Cin., 1965; m. Joyce Elaine Clopten, June 19, 1962; children—Pamela, Gary, Penny, Patricia. Systems mgr. Southwestern Pub. Co., Cin., 1965-69; asst. gen. myr. Cintas Uniform Rental, Cin., 1969; gen. mgr. Cintas Rental Operations, Dayton and Columbus, Ohio, 1970; dist. mgr. Cintas, Cleve., 1971-78, v.p. Great Lakes region, Strongsville, Ohio, 1978—; v.p. Greater Cin. Data Processing Corp., 1967—. Com. chmn. Boy Scouts Am., 1979. Mem. Inst. Indsl. Honors Assn., Am. Mgmt. Soc. Club: Masons. Home: 9817 Hazlewood St Strongsville OH 44136 Office: 12133 Alameda Dr Strongsville OH 44136

MILLER, WILLIS LEE, rancher; b. Akron, Ohio, Feb. 3, 1921; s. William Lee and Nina Mae (Bell) M.; student U. Calif., Davis; m. Dorothy Rhea Murdy, June 22, 1945; children—William Lee, Norma Jeanne, Walter James, Dorothy Willene, Marilyn Louise, Katherine Anne, Wesley Stephen. Engaged in farming and ranching, Westminster, Calif., 1946—; owner, pres. Willis L. Miller Ranch Co., 1967—, Los Alisos Ranch Co., 1967—, Springdale Equipment Co., 1960—; dir. Riverside Asso. Fed. Land Bank, County Nat. Bank. Deacon, elder Presbyn. Ch., 1948—. Served as pilot USAAF, World War II; ETO. Decorated D.F.C. with oak leaf clusters, Air medal with 5 oak leaf clusters. Mem. Farm Bur. Republican. Address: 13070 Old Bolsa Rd Westminster CA 92683

MILLHISER, ROSS R., tobacco products co. exec.; b. Richmond, Va., 1920; B.A., Yale U, 1941; married. With Philip Morris Inc., N.Y.C., 1941—, exec. v.p., 1965-66, pres. Philip Morris U.S.A., 1966-73, pres., dir. Philip Morris Inc., 1973—, vice chmn., dir., 1978—; dir. First & Mchts. Corp., Best Products Co., Seven-Up Co., Mission Viejo Co., Philip Morris Indsl. Co.; Trustee Ind. Coll. Funds Am., Va. Found. Ind. Colls.; mem. exec. com. Tobacco Inst., Washington; chmn. Va. Found. Ind. Colls. Served as maj. U.S. Army, 1942-45. Office: Philip Morris Inc 100 Park Ave New York NY 10017*

MILLIGAN, JAMES DWIGHT, foods co. exec.; b. Harrisburg, Ill., May 28, 1940; s. Harvey Loren and Emma Jane (Stilley) M.; B.S., So. Ill. U., 1962; m. Sue B. Yost, Dec. 2, 1979; children—Michael Dana, Stephen Dwight. Account mgr. Price Waterhouse & Co., St. Louis, 1962-71; asst. gen. controller Borden, Inc., Columbus, Ohio, 1971-72, controller, foods div., 1973, v.p. ops., foods div., 1974, sr. v.p., foods div., 1975, pres. foods div., 1975—, corp. exec. v.p., 1980—. Mem. adv. bd. Capital U.; trustee Columbus Coll. Arts Design. C.P.A. Mem. Nat. Food Processors Assn. (dir.), Ohio C. of C. (dir.). Office: Borden Inc 180 E Broad St Columbus OH 43215

MILLIGAN, ROBERT LEE, JR., computer co. exec.; b. Evanston, Ill., Apr. 4, 1934; s. Robert L. and Alice (Connell) M.; B.S., Northwestern U., 1958; m. Susan A. Woodrow, Mar. 23, 1957; children—William, Bonnie, Thomas, Robert III. Account rep. IBM, Chgo., 1957-66; sr. cons. L.B. Knight & Assos., Chgo., 1966-68; v.p. mktg. Trans Union Systems Corp., Chgo., 1968-73; v.p. sales Systems Mgmt. Inc., Des Plaines, Ill., 1973—, dir., 1980—; dir. Nanofast, Inc., Chgo. Div. mgr. N. Suburban YMCA Bldg., 1967. AeraaahmArea chmn. Northfield Twp. Republican Party, 1965-71. Bd. dirs. United Fund, Glenview, Ill., 1967-69, Robert R. McCormick Chgo. Boys Club, 1974—; pres. bd. mgrs. Glenview Amateur Hockey Assn., 1974-79, gen. mgr. Glenbrook South High Sch. Hockey Club, 1973-78; bd. dirs. Chgo. Boys Clubs, 1974—. Served with AUS, 1953-55. Mem. Data Processing Mgmt. Assn., Consumer Credit Assn. (dir., sec. 1969-70), Phi Kappa Psi. Presbyn. Clubs: Northwestern (dir. 1973-75) (Chgo.); Glen View (Ill.). Home: 702 Glendale Dr Glenview IL 60025 Office: 10400 W Higgins Rd Des Plaines IL 60018

MILLIKEN, BRUCE CARROLL, mfg. co. exec.; b. Bath, Maine, Dec. 23, 1941; s. Ralph George and Effie Marie Milliken; B.A., Moncton (N.B., Can.) U., 1962; m. Michelle Marie Cazalet, May 14, 1977. Quality control engr. Haveg Industries, Winooski, Vt., 1961-65; quality control mgr. Harbour Industries, Shelburne, Vt., 1965-71, v.p. engring., 1971-76; owner, pres. MiliBride, Inc., Williston, Vt., 1976—. Mem. Nat. Electronics Mfrs. Assn., Am. Soc. for Quality Control, Williston C. of C. Roman Catholic. Club: Ethan Allen. Home: Hillspoint Rd Charlotte VT 05459 Office: MiliBride Inc Industrial Ave Williston VT 05495

MILLIKEN, FRANK ROSCOE, mining engr.; b. Malden, Mass., Jan. 25, 1914; s. Frank R. and Alice (Gould) M.; B.S. in Mining Engring., Mass. Inst. Tech., 1934; m. Barbara Kingsbury, Sept. 14, 1935; children—Frank R., David C. Chief metallurgist Gen. Engring. Co., Salt Lake City, 1936-41; asst. mgr. Titanium div. Nat. Lead Co., 1941-52; v.p. charge mining operations Kennecott Copper Corp., N.Y.C., 1952—, exec. v.p., 1958-61, dir., 1958—, pres., 1961-78, chmn., 1978-79, chief exec. officer, 1961-79; dir. Procter & Gamble. Life mem. corp. M.I.T. Recipient Robert H. Richards award Minerals Beneficiation div. AIME, 1951. Mem. Am. Mining Congress, Mining and Metall. Soc. Am., AIME, Bus. Council. Clubs: River (N.Y.C.); Wee Burn Country (Darien, Conn.); Blind Brook (Purchase, N.Y.).

MILLIKEN, ROGER, textile co. exec.; b. N.Y.C., Oct. 24, 1915; s. Gerrish and Agnes (Gayley) M.; student Groton Sch., 1929-33; A.B., Yale U., 1937; LL.D. (hon.) Wofford Coll., 1967, Rose Hulman Inst. Tech., 1978; D. Textile Industry (hon.), Clemson U. m. Justine V. R. Hooper, June 5, 1948; children—Justine V.R. Milliken Russell, Nancy, Roger, David, Weston. Pres., Milliken & Co., N.Y.C., 1947—; dir. Westinghouse Electric Corp., Citicorp, N.A., Merc. Stores Co., W. R. Grace & Co. Chmn. bd. Inst. Textile Tech., 1948—. Chmn. Greenville-Spartanburg Airport Commn. Trustee, Spartanburg Day Sch., Wofford Coll., S.C. Found: Ind. Coll.; S.C. del. Republican Nat. Conv., 1956-76. Mem. Bus. Council, Bus. Roundtable (policy com.), Textile Inst. (companion) (Eng.), Am. Textile Mfrs. Inst. (dir.), S.C. Textile Mfrs. Assn. (dir.). Episcopalian. Clubs: University, Union League, Links, Augusta Nat. Golf. Home: 627 Otis Blvd Spartanburg SC 29302 Office: 234 S Fairview Ave Spartanburg SC 29302

MILLS, EDWARD WARREN, lawyer, precision bearings and machine parts mfg. co. exec.; b. N.Y.C., Apr. 7, 1941; s. Foy Fitzhugh and Isabelle Marie (Vega) M.; B.S. in Commerce, Washington and Lee U., 1962; M.B.A., Hofstra U., 1974, J.D., N.Y. Law Sch., 1977; m. Maria Parascandolo, Sept. 19, 1971. Accountant, Wasserman & Taten, N.Y.C., 1962-69; exec. v.p. L.H. Keller Co., Inc., N.Y.C., 1969-73, Hugo P. Keller, Inc., 1969-73; pres. Gen. Ruby & Sapphire Corp., N.Y.C., 1973—, Qualistar Corp., N.Y.C., 1973—; admitted to N.Y. State bar, 1978. C.P.A., N.Y. Mem. Am., N.Y. State bar assns., N.Y. County Lawyers Assn., Am. Inst. C.P.A.'s, N.Y. State Soc. C.P.A.'s, Sigma Phi Epsilon, Phi Delta Phi. Clubs: Hofstra U., 60 East, Downtown Athletic (N.Y.C.). Contbr. to Suburban Econ. Network, 1977. Home: 271 Cold Spring Rd Syosset NY 11791 Office: 60 E 42d St New York NY 10017

MILLS, GEORGE MARSHALL, state ofcl., ins. exec.; b. Newton, N.J., May 20, 1923; s. J. Marshall and Emma (Scott) M.; B.A., Rutgers U., 1943; M.A., Columbia, 1951, Profl. Certificate, 1952; m. Dorothy Lovilla Allen, Apr. 21, 1945; children—Dianne (Mrs. Thomas McKay III), Dorothy L.A. (Mrs. Edward Sphatt). Pres. George M. Mills Inc., North Brunswick, N.J., 1946—; pres. CORECO, Inc., Newark, 1960—; risk mgr. N.J. Hwy. Authority. Bd. dirs. Alpha Chi Rho Ednl. Found.; dir. workshop March of Dimes; pres. Nat. Interfrat. Conf. Served with USNR, 1943-46. C.L.U., C.P.C.U. Mem. Am. Coll. Life Underwriters, Am. Coll. Property Liability Underwriters, Internat. Bridge Tunnel and Turnpike Assn. (chmn. risk mgmt. com.), New Brunswick Hist. Soc., English Speaking Union, Alpha Chi Rho (nat. councillor 1964-70, nat. pres. 1970-73, nat. treas. 1975—), Kappa Kappa Psi, Tau Kappa Alpha, Phi Delta Phi. Mem. Reformed Ch. Am. Club: Rutgers Alumni-Faculty (New Brunswick, N.J.). Home: 1054 Hoover Dr North Brunswick NJ 08902 Office: US Route 9 Woodbridge NJ

MILLS, JAMES THOBURN, bus. exec.; b. Balt., Nov. 30, 1923; s. Victor Garfield and Beatrice (Moore) M.; B.A., Princeton U., 1945; LL.B., Yale U., 1950; m. Frances Clagett Keller, June 16, 1951; children—Elizabeth R., Hilary F., Frances T., Margaret K. Admitted to N.Y. State bar, 1951; asso. firm Burke & Burke, N.Y.C., 1950-51, firm Mudge, Stern, Baldwin & Todd, N.Y.C., 1951-56; with Sperry & Hutchinson Co., N.Y.C., 1956-80, pres., 1978-80, chmn. bd., chief exec. officer, 1980-81, also dir., cons., 1981—; dir. Union Camp Corp. Served as 1st lt. AUS, 1943-46. Decorated Bronze Star medal, Purple Heart. Mem. Am. Bar Assn., N.Y. State Bar Assn., Assn. Bar City N.Y. Clubs: Union League, Mcpl. Golf. Office: 330 Madison Ave New York NY 10017

MILLS, JOSHUA REDMOND, importing co. exec.; b. Lynn, Mass., Aug. 30, 1936; s. Joshua and Adelaide (Redmond) M.; A.B., Harvard U., 1957; postgrad. N.Y. U. Grad. Sch. Bus. Adminstrn., 1960-65; m. Annette Aliferis Perillo, May 29, 1965; children—Carlotta, Anastasia. With Chase Manhattan Bank, N.Y.C., 1960-63, Continental Bank Internat., N.Y.C., 1963-66; v.p. Amerconsult Corp., Colombia, Peru, N.Y.C., 1966-74; pres. Joshua Mills & Co., N.Y.C., 1974—. Chmn. strategy com., mem. gen. council Presbytery of N.Y.C. Republican. Clubs: Harvard, Union League (N.Y.C.). Home: Greenwich CT Office: 415 Lexington Ave New York NY 10017

MILLS, LAWRENCE, lawyer, trucking co. exec.; b. Salt Lake City, Aug. 15, 1932; s. Samuel L. and Beth (Neilson) M.; B.S., U. Utah, 1955, J.D., 1956. With W.S. Hatch Co. Inc., Woods Cross, Utah, 1947—, v.p., treas., gen. mgr., 1963—, also dir.; admitted to Utah bar, 1956, U.S. Supreme Ct. bar, 1963; mem. motor carrier adv. com. Utah Dept. Transp., 1979. Mem. Nat. Petroleum Council, 1974-75; v.p. Utah Safety Council, 1979. Mem. Nat. Tank Truck Carriers (pres. 1974-75, chmn. bd. 1975-76, Safety Dir. award 1967), Utah Motor Transport Assn. (pres. 1974-76), Indsl. Relations Council Utah (dir. 1974—), Am. Trucking Assn. (exec. com. 1974-76), U.S., Salt Lake City chambers commerce, Salt Lake City Jaycees (life internat. senator 1969—, ambassador for life 1977, pres. state senate 1979-80), Asso. Gen. Contractors. Clubs: Silver Tank; Ambassador Athletic (Salt Lake City). Home: 77 Edgecombe Dr Salt Lake City UT 84103 Office: 643 S 800 W Woods Cross UT 84087

MILLS, REBECCA ANN, advt. exec.; b. Storm Lake, Iowa, May 11, 1950; d. Omer H. and Awanda Lucille (Mathison) Roth; student Northwestern U., summers, 1968, 70; B.S. in Journalism with honors, Drake U., 1972; m. Timothy Lemar Mills, Dec. 22, 1973; 1 dau., Sarah Rebecca. Editor house organ Des Moines Register and Tribune, 1972-73; coordinator mktg. services corp. Iowa Credit Union League, Des Moines, 1973-74; account exec. Prescott Co., Denver, 1974-75; pres. Mills Agy., Storm Lake, Iowa, 1975—; lectr. Iowa Bank Mktg. Conf., 1979, Internat. Telephone Credit Union Assn., Dallas, 1978; authored ad series for Des Moines Register (award Am. Advt. Fedn.), 1972. Winner numerous advt. awards. Mem. C. of C., Am. Soc. Exec. and Profl. Women, Women in Communication, Nat. Fedn. Ind. Bus. Republican. Presbyterian. Clubs: Order Eastern Star, D.A.R. (treas. and state page 1979-81, regent 1980-81), Keystone Reading, Des Moines Ad, Denver Ad, Sioux City Ad. Home: 131 N Emerald St Storm Lake IA 50588 Office: 612 Seneca St Storm Lake IA 50588

MILLS, ROYCE JOHNSON, automotive co. exec.; b. Rush City, Minn., Dec. 18, 1925; s. Roy J. and Myrtle B. (Johnson) M.; ed. pub. sch. Cresco, Iowa, 1937-39, Harmony, Minn., 1939-43; m. Erlene K. Strauser, Dec. 6, 1950; children—Deborah, Pamela, Tina. With Goodyear Tire & Rubber Co., 1950-70, dist. mgr., Peoria, Ill., 1966-68, Indpls., 1968-70; exec. v.p. Ameron Automotive Centers, St. Louis, 1970-75, pres., 1975-78; pres. Triangle Bandag Tire Co., Inc., Cedar Rapids, Iowa, 1978—. Served with USMC, 1945-46, 50-51. Republican. Clubs: Masons (32 deg.), Shriners. Home: 2021 Sandalwood Dr NE Cedar Rapids IA 52402

MILLS, RUDULPH, JR., ins. agy. exec.; b. Folkston, Ga., Feb. 19, 1930; s. Rudulph and Mary Ivella (Kight) M.; B.B.A., Emory U., 1952; m. Diane Dunaway, June 20, 1959; children—Lisa, Leslie, James, Michael. With Ins. Co. N.Am., 1954-58; with Mills Co., Dallas, 1958—, chmn. bd., 1978—. Served with USAF, 1950-51. Republican. Episcopalian. Clubs: Dallas Country, City. Home: 4219 Arcady St Dallas TX 75205 Office: Mills Co 800 One Main Pl Dallas TX 75250

MILLS, WILLIAM ANDREW, pub. accountant; b. Washington County, Ga., Apr. 7, 1910; s. Oscar L. and Willie Mae (Griffin) M.; B.S. in Commerce, U. Ga., 1934; m. Ruth H. Waters, Aug. 31, 1940 (dec. Jan. 1974). Staff accountant M. H. Barnes and Co., C.P.A.'s, Savannah, Ga., 1934-43, 46-47; partner Barnes, Askew, Mills and Co., C.P.A's, Savannah, 1947-61; partner Haskins & Sells, C.P.A.'s, Savannah, Ga., 1961-73; ret., 1973. Served to capt. AUS, 1943-46. Mem. Ga. Soc. C.P.A.'s, Am. Inst. Accountants, Beta Gamma Sigma, Phi Kappa Phi, Beta Alpha Psi. Kiwanian. Home: 802 E 41st St Savannah GA 31401 Office: Suite 618 CTS Bank Bldg Savannah GA 31402

MILLS, WILLIAM GARY, chem. distribution exec.; b. Wilkes-Barre, Pa., June 26, 1938; s. Lloyd Christian and Mary Virginia (Sterling) M.; A.Engring., Wyomissing Poly. Inst., 1959; m. Sandra E. Mearig, May 14, 1960; children—Susan D., Lisa A. With Textile Machine Works, Reading, Pa., 1959-63; with R.W. Eaken, Inc., Leesport, Pa., 1963—, v.p., 1967—. Chmn. bd. dirs. Goodwill Industries of Greater Berks County, 1980—. Served with U.S. Army, 1961. Mem. Berks County Mfrs. Assn. (pres. accident, safety and health group 1978—), Am. Soc. Lubricating Engrs., Pa. Environ. Council. Democrat. Lutheran. Home: RD 2186 Fleetwood PA 19522 Office: PO Box 171 Leesport PA 19533

MILLS, WILLIAM HAROLD, gen. contractor; b. Birmingham, Ala., Feb. 19, 1911; s. Charles W. and Mary (Parker) M.; student Woodberry Forest Sch. (Va.), 1928-29, U. Fla., 1929-30; B.S. in Civil Engring., Mass. Inst. Tech., 1934; m. Helen D. Cooper, Nov. 16, 1963; children—William Harold, Susan Ann, Caroline Bridget, Mary Danforth. Partner, Clarson & Mills, St. Petersburg, Fla., 1935-46; pres., chief exec. officer Mills & Jones Constrn. Co., 1946—; dir. Fla. Fed. Savs. and Loan Assn., St. Petersburg, Gen. Telephone Co. Fla., Founders Life Assurance Co. Mem. corp. Mass. Inst. Tech.; bd. dirs. St. Petersburg Episcopal Community, Inc. Mem. Fla. Council 100, St. Petersburg Com. 100, Tampa Horse Show Assn., Greater St. Petersburg C. of C. (past pres.), Suncoasters, Newcomen Soc., Delta Tau Delta. Episcopalian. Clubs: Mass. Inst. Tech. of Central Fla., Feather Sound Country, St. Petersburg Yacht, Dragon, Pasadena Golf. Home: One Beach Dr Apt 1404 St Petersburg FL 33703 Office: PO Box 1257 St Petersburg FL 33731

MILLS, WILLIAM HAROLD, JR., bldg. exec.; b. St. Petersburg, Fla., July 24, 1939; s. William Harold and Caroline (Bonfoey) M.; B.C.E., U. Fla., 1961; children—William Harold, Robert Michael, Leslie Anne. Vice pres. bus. devel. Mills & Jones Constrn. Co., St. Petersburg, 1964-68, exec. v.p., 1971—; pres. Fed. Constrn. Co., 1979—; v.p. Wellington Corp., Atlanta, 1968-71; dir. Century First Nat. Bank, St. Petersburg. Chmn. blue ribbon zoning com., City St. Petersburg, 1965-68; mem. Tampa Bay Aviation Adv. Com., 1967-68. Bd. dirs. United Fund, Pinellas County, 1966-68; chmn. bd. dirs. Pinellas Marine Inst. Served to lt. (j.g.) USPHS, 1962-64. Mem. St. Petersburg C. of C., Am. Soc. C.E., Am. Inst. Constructors, Mensa, Sigma Alpha Epsilon. Democrat. Episcopalian. Clubs: Suncoasters, St. Petersburg Yacht, Dragon (St. Petersburg); Jockey (Miami, Fla.). Home: One Beach Dr Apt 1705 Saint Petersburg FL 33701 Office: 400 23d St S Saint Petersburg FL 33731

MILLSPAUGH, MARTIN LAURENCE, JR., urban redevel. exec.; b. Columbus, Ohio, Dec. 16, 1925; s. Martin Laurence and Elizabeth (Park) M.; A.B. summa cum laude, Princeton U., 1949, cert. Woodrow Wilson Sch. Public and Internat. Affairs, 1949; m. Viola Meredith Plant, May 10, 1952; children—Elisabeth Graeme, Meredith Plant, Martin Laurence III, Thomas E.D. Reporter, news editor Richmond (Va.) News Leader, 1949-53; urban affairs writer Balt. Evening Sun, 1953-57; asst. commr. U.S. Urban Renewal Adminstrn., Washington, 1957-60; dep. gen. mgr. Charles Center Project, Balt., 1960-65; gen. mgr. Inner Harbor Renewal Program, Balt., 1965—; pres., dir. Charles-Center-Inner Harbor Mgmt., Inc., 1965—, chief exec. officer, 1975—; dir. Savs. Bank of Balt., Blue Cross of Md., Inc.; exec. group urban devel/mixed use council Urban Land Inst., 1978—; lectr. Nat. Council Urban Econ. Devel., 1980. Bd. trustees Enoch Pratt Free Library, 1966—, Gilman Sch., 1967-76, Bryn Mawr Sch., 1969-77; bd. dirs. YMCA Greater Balt. Area, 1970-72, Balt. Symphony Orch. Assn., 1965-66, Planned Parenthood Assn. Md., 1962-65; bd. dirs., former sec.-treas. Roland Park Civic League. Served with USAAF, 1944-46. Recipient Disting. Service award U.S. HHFA, 1960. Mem. Nat. Council Urban Econ. Devel., Nat. Assn. Housing and Redevel. Ofcls., Internat. Downtown Execs. Assn., Phi Beta Kappa. Democrat. Episcopalian. Clubs: Center, 14 W.Hamilton St. (Balt.); Ivy (Princeton). Author: (with Gurney Breckenfeld) The Human Side of Urban Renewal, 1958; Charles Center: A Case Study in Downtown Renewal, 1964; contbr. articles to profl. jours. Office: 1444 World Trade Center Baltimore MD 21202

MILNE, GEORGE HECTOR FANJOY, business exec.; b. New Glasgow, N.S., Can., Nov. 23, 1926; s. James Andrew and Mary Evelyn (Fanjoy) M.; B.Commerce, McGill U., 1948, B. Engring., 1953; m. Carolyn Boyd Wiseheart, Mar. 18, 1968; children—Mary Milne Pillsbury, James, Catherine, Malcolm, Christopher, Elizabeth. Came to U.S., 1961. Successively plant mgr., sec.-treas., dir. Horton Steel Works, Ltd., Ft. Erie, Ont., Can., 1953-61; controller Duriron Co., 1961-64; mgr. corp. accounting, then mgr. corp. systems and data processing Xerox Corp., 1964-69; exec. v.p., treas., dir., mem. exec. com. Scholastic mags., 1969-75; corp. v.p., treas., dir. fin. and adminstrn. IPCO Corp., 1975-80; in pvt. bus., Englewood, N.J., 1980—; dir. H.M. Boyd Co., Cheyenne, Wyo., Transnat. World Trade Corp., asso. dir. Peoples Trust Co., Hackensack, N.J. Chartered accountant, Que., Ont.; C.P.A., Ohio; registered profl. engr., Que., Ont. Mem. Nat. Assn. Accountants, Fin. Execs. Inst., Engring. Inst. Canada, ASME. Clubs: N.Y. Yacht (N.Y.C.); Palisades Yacht (Englewood, N.J.), Masons. Home and Office: 110 Summit St Englewood NJ 07631

MILNER, CHARLES FREMONT, JR., mfr.; b. Durham, N.C., July 21, 1942; s. Charles Fremont and Eloyse (Sargent) M.; B.A., Guilford Coll., 1963; M.B.A., Harvard, 1965; m. Molly Franc Wakefield, Aug. 28, 1965; children—Bernadette Ann, Eloyse Lee. Asst. to comptroller Harvard, 1965-66; instr. Northeastern U., Boston, 1965-66; with Burlington Hosiery Co. div. Burlington Industries (N.C.), 1966-71, asst. v.p., 1970-71; exec. v.p. Parklane Hosiery Co., Inc., New Hyde Park, N.Y., 1971-74, also dir.; pres. Rudin & Roth, Inc. div. NCC Industries, N.Y.C., 1974-75, also dir.; v.p. apparel group M. Lowenstein and Sons, N.Y.C., 1975-76; pres., chief exec. officer BBC Inc. and Camp Industry divs. Genesco Inc., 1976-80, gen. mgr. Johnston and Murphy Shoe Co. div., 1979—, gen. mgr. footwear mktg. and mfg. Genesco Inc., 1980—. Trustee, Friends Acad., Locust Valley, N.Y., 1974-79. Mem. Nat. Assn. Hosiery Mfrs. (dir. 1978—). Home: 612 Belle Meade Blvd Nashville TN 37205 Office: Genesco Park Nashville TN 37202

MILNER, HAROLD WILLIAM, real estate trust and hotel exec.; b. Salt Lake City, Nov. 11, 1934; s. Kenneth W. and Oliver (Schoettlin) M.; B.S., U. Utah, 1960; M.B.A., Harvard, 1962; m. Susan Emmett, June 19, 1959 (div. 1976); children—John Kenneth, Mary Sue; m. 2d, Lois Friemuth, Aug. 14, 1977; 1 dau., Jennifer Rebecca. Instr. Brigham Young U., Provo, Utah, 1962-64; v.p. Gen. Paper Corp., Mpls., 1964-65; dir. finance Amalgamated Sugar Co., Ogden, Utah, 1965-67; corp. treas. Marriott Corp., Washington, 1967-70; pres., chief exec. officer, trustee Hotel Investors, Kensington, Md., 1970-75; pres., chief exec. officer Pick Am. Hotels Corp., Chgo., 1975—; trustee Propert Capital Trust. Served as lt. AUS, 1960. Mem. Greater Chgo. Hotel Assn. (dir. 1977—), Young Pres.'s Orgn., Am. Hotel and Motel Assn. (industry adv. council). Mem. Ch. Jesus Christ Latter-day Saints. Author: A Special Report on Contract Maintenance, 1963. Home: 474 Butler Dr Lake Forest IL 60045 Office: 532 S Michigan Ave Chicago IL 60605

MILO, FRANK ANTHONY, indsl., engineered adhesives co. exec.; b. Bristol, Conn., Aug. 19, 1946; s. Frank Raymond and Helen Ellen M.; B.S. in Indsl. Engring., Gen. Motors Inst., 1970. Abrasives supr. New Departure-Hyatt Bearings div. Gen. Motors Corp., Bristol, Conn., 1964-72; sales engr. air tools Ingersoll Rand Co., Liberty Corners, N.J., 1972-74; process engr. Electric Boat div. Gen. Dynamics, Groton, Conn., 1974-75; regional sales mgr. Unbrako Chem. Products div. SPS Tech., 1975-78; nat. sales mgr. Permabond Internat., Englewood, N.J., 1978-80; v.p. sales-indsl., internat. Pacer Tech. & Resources, Campbell, Calif., 1980—. Mem. Soc. Mfg. Engrs. Democrat. Roman Catholic. Office: Pacer Tech & Resources 1600 Dell Ave Campbell CA 95008

MILOCK, SUSAN LORIMER, interior designer; b. Dayton, Ohio, July 15, 1939; d. Alexander Hoyt and Mary Katherine (Klopf) Lorimer; student U. Mich., 1957-59; B.F.A. in Design, Sch. of Art Inst. Chgo., 1962. Asst. gallery dir. Richard Feigen Galleries, Chgo., 1959-63, chief contract designer Hudson's Contract Div., Detroit, 1963-67; contract designer Silver's, Inc., Detroit, 1967-68; pres. Designs for Bus., Detroit, 1968—; exec. v.p. Wunderlich Assos., Detroit, 1974—; lectr. in field. Mem. AIA, Engring. Soc. Detroit, Carpenter Contractors Assn. Club: Woman's City. Contbr. articles to profl. jours. Home: 799 Notre Dame Grosse Pointe MI 48230 Office: 16800 Strong Dr Taylor MI 48180

MILSTEAD, WILLIAM CLYDE, bldg. material co. exec.; b. San Antonio, Apr. 30, 1926; s. Earl L. and Mattie Lee (Brown) M.; B.S., Rice Inst., 1946; m. Jacqueline Wheeler, July 16, 1955; children—William Mark, Matthew Earl. With Milstead Co. (merged into Tex. Austin Industries, Inc.), Austin, also Temple and Waco, Tex., 1946-75, v.p. sales, 1953-56, v.p., gen. mgr., 1956-64, pres., treas., 1964-75; chmn. bd. Tex. Austin Industries, Inc., 1975—; dir. Am. Nat. Bank Austin, First Fed. Savs. & Loan Assn., Austin. Mem. planning commn. City Austin, 1968-74, chmn., 1972-74; vice commodore Austin Aqua Festival, 1968-69; trustee St. David's Community Hosp.; founding trustee Austin Community Found., 1976-77, treas.; v.p. manpower Capitol Area council Boy Scouts Am., 1977, pres., 1978. Served as ensign USNR, 1943-46, lt. (j.g.), 1952. Mem. Am. Inst. Supply Assn. (past dir.), S.W. Air Conditioning and Refrigeration Wholesalers Assn. (past chmn.), Am. Soc. Heating, Air Conditioning and Refrigeration Engrs. (pres. Austin 1966), Wholesale Distbrs. Assn. Tex. (pres. 1955-56), Austin C. of C. (pres. 1971), Young Men's Bus. League (pres. 1957), Tex. Assn. Bus. (dir., vice chmn. Central Tex. chpt., chmn. 1979). Episcopalian (vestryman 1959-61). Mason (32 deg., Shriner), Rotarian (pres. Austin 1971). Home: 2516 Tanglewood Trail Austin TX 78703 Office: 701 W 5th St Austin TX 78701 also PO Box 1827 Austin TX 78767

MILSTEIN, PAUL, diversified food co. exec. Vice chmn., pres., chief operating officer United Brands Co., N.Y.C., also dir.; chmn. Starrett Housing Corp. Office: 30 Rockefeller Plaza New York NY 10020*

MILSTEIN, SEYMOUR, food co. exec.; b. N.Y.C., July 21, 1920; s. Morris and Rose (Gordon) M.; B.S., N.Y. U., 1941; m. Vivian Leiner, June 3, 1945; children—Constance Jane, Philip Lloyd. Sec.-treas. Mastic Tile Corp. Am., N.Y.C., 1945-55, dir., 1945-60, pres., 1955-60: v.p., dir., exec. com. Ruberoid Co. 1960-62, sr. v.p., 1962-67; partner One Lincoln Assos., 196C—; mem. adv. bd. Chase Manhattan Bank, 1964—; now chmn. bd., chmn. exec. com., chief exec. officer United Brands Co., N.Y.C. Clubs: Metropolis Country (White Plains, N.Y.); Harmonie (N.Y.C.). Home: 35 Ogden Rd Scarsdale NY 10583 Office: 1271 Ave of the Americas New York NY 10020

MILTON, LEONARD, electronics mfg. co. exec.; b. N.Y.C., July 26, 1917; s. Israel M. and Sadie (Kranes) M.; E.E., Pratt Inst., 1939, D.Sc., 1965; m. Hilda Lozner, Dec. 29, 1946; children—Donn, Ilo, Cindy, Rand. Chief engr. Solar Mfg. Corp., Bayonne, N.J., 1940-46; v.p., chief engr. Filtron Co., Inc., Flushing, N.Y., 1946-56, pres., 1956-70, chmn. bd., 1970—, pres., chmn. bd., Bethpage, N.Y., 1977—; chmn. bd. APC Inc., Bethpage, 1975—; dir. Starrett Housing Corp., N.Y.C., 1967—. Pres. People to People Sports Com., 1966—; pres. I. Milton Found., 1950—; bd. govs. St. Huberts Soc.; trustee Pratt Inst. Mem. N.Y. Acad. Scis., IEEE, Tau Beta Pi. Clubs: Shikar Safari, N.Y. African Safari; Glen Head Country (L.I.); Explorers, Adventurers (N.Y.C.). Author: Radio Interference in Aircraft Systems; Radio Interference in Aircraft Electrical and Electronic Systems; Electromagnetic Analysis of the Arctic; Interference Reduction Guide for Design Engineers. Patentee in field. Home: Windsor Gate Great Neck NY 11020 Office: 98 Cuttermill Rd Great Neck NY 11021

MIMNA, CURTIS JOHN, fin. exec.; b. Colorado Springs, Colo., Dec. 7, 1943; s. Curtis T. and Margaret Ann (Witchey) M.; B.S. in Econs., Va. Poly. Inst. and State U., 1965; postgrad. George Washington U., 1969-70. Urban land planner Fairfax County Planning Office, 1966-67; mktg. dir. Fairfax County Indsl. Authority, 1968-70; asst. to Fairfax County exec.; dir. market research Shaw Real Estate, Alexandria, Va., 1970-72; v.p. land devel. financing DRG Fin. Corp., Washington, 1972—. Mem. Washington Bd. Realtors, Nat. Assn. Realtors, So. Indsl. Devel. Council. Democrat. Roman Catholic. Clubs: Polo, Army-Navy Country. Home: 1819 Dalmation Dr McLean VA 22101 Office: 1909 K St NW Suite 200 Washington DC 20006

MIMS, THOMAS J., ins. co. exec.; b. Sumter, S.C., Dec. 12, 1899; s. Lazarus and Sarah Rebecca (White) M.; A.B., Furman U., 1921; m. Valma Gillespie, Dec. 14, 1926; children—Thomas J., George Franklin. With Rec. and Statis. Corp. of N.Y., 1921-29, asst. mgr., Phila., 1922-25, mgr., Indpls., 1925-27, Boston, 1927-29; salesman Burroughs Adding Machine Co., Detroit, Boston, 1929-31; ins. spl. agt. State of N.J., 1931-32; mgr. William R. Timmons Agy., Greenville, S.C., 1933—, v.p., sec., dir. Canal Ins. Co., 1942-48, pres., treas., dir., from 1948, now pres., dir.; pres., dir. Canal Indemnity Co. Bus. mgr. Greenville Little Theatre, 1951-53, 64-66, mem. council, 1951—, v.p., 1956-57, 72-73, pres., 1957-58, 73-75; pres. Greenville Found., 1973; adv. council Furman U.; mem. legis. com. to study automobile liability policies; adv. bd. S.C. Safety Council, pres., 1970-75; past bd. dirs. Met. Arts Council; bd. dirs. United Way Greenville, 1973-79, chmn. campaign, 1976, v.p., 1977, pres., 1978, chmn. bd., 1979; bd. dirs., mem. bd. mgmt. Internat. Ins. Seminars. Named Ky. col.; named Boss of Year, Greenville Jr. C. of C., 1964, Greenville Assn. Ins. Women, 1966; named Vol. of Yr., S.C. affiliate United Way, 1978; Ins. Co. Rep. of Year, Assn. Ind. Ins. Agts. S.C., 1980. Mem. AIM (fellow pres.'s council, Marquis award), Am. Mgmt. Assn. (mem. pres.' assn.), Greenville (pres. 1951-52, chmn. exec. com. 1952-53), S.C., Nat. assns. ins. agts., S.C. Motor Transp. Assn. (chmn. ins. com. 1951-63, dir. 1975), U.S. (ins. com. 1959-61, 64-70), S.C., Greenville (chmn. community relations com. 1964-69, dir. 1969-71, exec. com. 1972, pres. 1973) chambers commerce, S.C. Assn. Property and Casualty Ins. Cos. (pres. 1962-63, 72-73, exec. com. 1963—), Truck and Heavy Equipment Claims Council (charter), Internat. Platform Assn., M.B.L.S. (adv.). Baptist. Elk, Rotarian (dir. Greenville 1957-58, pres. 1963-64, pres. Rotary Charities 1964-65). Clubs: Greenville City (pres. 1965-66, chmn. bd. 1966-67), Poinsett; Greenville Touchdown (pres. 1963-64, charter); V.I.P. (charter); Palmetto, Summit, (Columbia, S.C.). Home: R-6 Knollwood Dr Greenville SC 29607 Office: 417 E North St Greenville SC 29601

MINAMI, ISAMU, farmer; b. Guadalupe, Calif., July 21, 1922; s. Henry Yaemon and Kuni (Yamasaki) M.; student Santa Maria (Calif.) Jr. Coll., 1942; m. Grace Misao Yamamoto, May 6, 1950; children—Sammy Yahe, Susan Kuniye. Engaged in vegetable farming, Guadalupe, 1944—; owner Security Farms, 1944—; pres., bd. dirs. Santa Barbara County Fair Bd. Bd. dirs. Santa Maria Assn. Retarded, Boys Club Santa Maria Valley; bd. dirs. bldg. fund Sis Sisters Hosp., Santa Maria; mem. civilian adv. bd. Vandenberg AFB; mem. spl. adv. com. Senator S.I. Hayakawa of Calif. Mem. Nisei Farmers League, United Fresh Fruit Assn., Iceberg Lettuce Research Assn. (dir.), Grower-Shippers Assn. (past pres.), Western Growers Assn. (dir.), Calif.-Ariz. Growers Assn. (dir.), Calif. Farm Bur. Assn., Calif. C. of C., Santa Barbara County Taxpayers Assn., Santa Maria Valley C. of C. (dir.; Citizen of Year award 1980), Santa Maria Valley Developers (dir.). Republican. Buddhist. Clubs: Guadalupe Rotary, 36th Congl., Republican Century, Santa Maria Elks. Office: PO Box 818 Guadalupe CA 93434

MINARD, THOMAS MICHAEL, r.r. products co. exec.; b. St. Charles, Ill., Dec. 31, 1944; s. Clarence Scott and Ruth L. (Larson) M.; grad. Coll. Advanced Traffic, 1964. Gen. mgr. Iowa Terminal R.R. Co., Mason City, 1968-70; mgr. quality control C.&N.W. Ry. Co., Chgo., 1970-73; pres., gen. mgr. Great Plains Ry. Co., Seward, Nebr., 1973-76; rail product mgr. L.B. Foster Co., Des Plaines, Ill., 1976-80, mgr. r.r. sales and procurement, 1980—. Mem. Nat. Ry. Hist. Soc., Elec. Railroaders Assn., Coll. Advanced Traffic Alumni Assn., Delta Nu Alpha. Home: 1211 N LaSalle Dr Chicago IL 60610 Office: L B Foster Co 1111 E Touhy Ave Des Plaines IL 60018

MINCHEFF, EDISON ELAINE, constrn. co. exec.; b. Winnett, Mont., July 20, 1920; s. Peter and Lota (Hooker) M.; B.S. in Mech. Engring., U. Kans., 1949; m. Evelyn Lee Moore, Nov. 4, 1943; children—Sharon Lee, Claudia Anne, Christine Marie, Marc Edison. Engr., Bendix Aviation Co., Kansas City, Mo., 1949-51; asst. chief engr. Great Lakes Pipeline Co., Kansas City, 1951-57; engr., v.p. Williams Bros. Co., Tulsa, 1957-75; v.p. Williams Internat. Group, Inc., Tulsa, 1976—; dir. Williams (Overseas) Ltd., 1967-75. Served with USNR, 1942-45. Registered profl. engr., Ill., Fla., Mo., Okla. Mem. ASME, Am. Petroleum Inst., Internat. Pipeline Assn., Pipeline Industries Guild (Eng.), Soc. Am. Mil. Engrs. Club: Masons. Contbr. articles to tech. jours. Home: 3244 S Evanston St Tulsa OK 74105 Office: 2530 E 71st St Tulsa OK 74136

MINDALA, JAMES JOHN, furniture and med. devices mfg. co. exec.; b. Cleve., Nov. 8, 1944; s. John and Ola Mindala; B.S. in Bus. Adminstrn., Bowling Green State U., 1967; m. Joanne Newton, May 22, 1976; children—Michelle Marie, Kelly Lynn, Halle Macrae. Accountant, Ernst & Ernst, Cleve., 1967-69; asst. controller Weatherhead, Inc., Cleve., 1970-73; partner Salupo & Assos., C.P.A.'s, Cleve., 1973-75; chief exec. officer Nutro Co., Inc., Cleve.,

1975-78; pres. Leisure Tan Internat., Inc., Cleve., 1979—; pres. W.T., Inc., Cleve., 1978—; instr. Lake Erie Coll., 1973-76. C.P.A., Ohio. Mem. Am. Inst. C.P.A.'s, Ohio Soc. C.P.A.'s. Republican. Home: 7614 Kinsman Rd Novelty OH 44072 Office: 9085 Freeway Dr Macedonia OH 44056

MINDELL, MARK GREGORY, mfg. co. exec.; b. Moline, Ill., Nov. 21, 1951; s. Stan Harold and Dale S. (Badner) M.; B.A., No. Ill. U., 1973; M.A., Central Mich. U., 1974; Ph.D., Kent State U., 1977; m. Lynette Sue Mindell, June 29, 1973. Sr. orgn. devel. cons. B.F. Goodrich, Akron, Ohio, 1976-79, mgr. corp. orgn. research and devel., 1979-80; mgr. mgmt. devel. Stouffer's Corp., Solon, Ohio, 1980; exec. cons. Abbott Labs., North Chicago, Ill., 1980—. Mem. Am. Psychol. Assn., Internat. Communication Assn., Acad. Mgmt., Speech Communication Assn., Nat. Orgn. Devel. Network, Internat. Communication Auditor. Author: Employee Values in a Changing Society. Contbr. articles to profl. jours. Home: 323 Thornwood S Lindenhurst IL 60046 Office: Abbott Park D-583 North Chicago IL 60064

MINDELL, MARVIN IRA, engring. co. exec.; b. Bklyn., Dec. 14, 1932; s. Joseph B. and Harriet (Covell) M.; B.E.E., Poly. Inst. Bklyn., 1954; postgrad. Columbia U., 1955-56; m. Phyllis Gross, Dec. 25, 1958; children—Joseph Andrew, David Avram. Project engr., aerial photographer Fairchild Camera & Instrument Co., L.I. City, 1954-59; project engr. aerial stabilized mounts Aeroflex Corp., Plainview, N.Y., 1959-60; chief engr., dir. Viewlex, Inc., Planetariums Unltd., Holbrook, N.Y., 1960-70, also dir.; v.p. engring.-audio visual mfg. Edn. Systems, Singer Co., Rochester, N.Y., 1970—. Mem. Nat. Audiovisual Assn. (cert. appreciation 1979), IEEE (service citation 1968, spl. service award 1969), Soc. Motion Picture and TV Engrs. (regional mgr. 1973-74), ASME, Am. Mgmt. Assn., Soc. Advanced Learning Tech., Am. Nat. Standards Inst., Soc. Photog. Scientists and Engrs., Audio Engring. Soc., Rochester C. of C. Club: Stepping Stone Sailing (pres. 1968-70) (L.I. Sound). Patentee audiovisual equipment, office copy machines, electronic circuitry. Office: 3750 Monroe Ave Rochester NY 14603

MINER, CHARLES BRADLEY, sprinkler mfg. co. exec.; b. Buffalo, Feb. 15, 1942; s. Amos Bradley and Marcella (Judson) M.; B.S. in Chem. Engring., U. Rochester, 1964; m. Margaret Louise Holbrook, June 19, 1965; children—Curtis B., Jason D. Sales engr. Trane Co., Rochester, N.Y., 1964-67, mktg. engr., LaCrosse, Wis., 1967-74; pres. Limbach Systems Co. div. Limbach Co., Pitts., 1974-77; v.p., gen. mgr. Limbach Co., Detroit, 1977-78; pres. Automatic Sprinkler Corp. Am. div. ATO, Inc., Cleve., 1979—. Registered profl. engr., Pa. Office: PO Box 180 Cleveland OH 44147

MINES, HERBERT THOMAS, exec. recruiting firm exec.; b. Fall River, Mass., Jan. 30, 1929; s. Abraham and Fanny (Lepes) M.; B.S. in Econs., Babson Inst., 1949; M.S. in Indsl. and Labor Relations, Cornell U., 1954; m. Barbara Goldberg, Oct. 23, 1960; 1 dau., Susan. Supr., asst. buyer, employment supr. G. Fox & Co., Hartford, Conn., 1949-52; adminstr. div. tng.-exec. devel. and orgn. planning R.H. Macy & Co., N.Y.C., 1954-66; v.p. personnel Neiman Marcus Co., Dallas, 1966-68, sr. v.p. personnel, 1968-70; v.p. personnel Revlon, Inc., N.Y.C., 1970-73; pres. Bus. Careers, Inc., 1973-78, chmn., 1978—; pres. Exec. Search and Cons. Div., Wells Mgmt. Corp., 1978—. Bd. dirs. Fashion Inst. Tech., Lab. Inst. Merchandising, Am. Jewish Com. Mem. Am. Mgmt. Assn. Contbr. articles to trade publs. Home: 724 Seney Ave Mamaroneck NY 10543 Office: 400 Park Ave New York NY 10022

MINIUTTI, JOHN ROBERTS, mfg. co. exec.; b. Monterey Park, Calif., Feb. 21, 1937; s. Leslie Ezio and Elizabeth May (Roberts) M.; B.S.M.E., Cornell U., 1959; M.B.A., N.Y. U., 1965; m. Ann Mather Byrne, June 15, 1959; children—Michele Roberts, John Frederick. Sales engr. Worthington Corp., East Orange, N.J., 1962-65; systems engr. IBM Corp., Savannah, Ga., 1965-68; salesman IBM Data Processing Div., Savannah, 1968-71, Chgo., 1971-76; mgr. market devel. Fiat-Allis, Deerfield, Ill., 1976-77, mgr. strategy devel., 1977-78, dir. market planning, 1978-79, mgr. sales planning., 1979-80, dir. sales adminstrn. and bus. planning, 1980—, dir., ops. mgr., 1979—. Served with USAF, 1959-62. Club: Lions (dir. 1971). Office: 106 Wilmot Rd Box F Deerfield IL 60015

MINKO, PHILIP PETER, food co. exec.; b. Troy, N.Y., Dec. 27, 1929; s. Panko J. and Catherine C. (Symbolie) M.; B.S. magna cum laude, St. Michael's Coll., 1952; M.B.A., U. Detroit, 1954; m. Dolores I. Metcalfe, Oct. 22, 1955; children—Philip Peter, David James. With Ford Motor Co., 1954-57, Chrysler Corp., 1957-61; plant controller Am. Standard Co., Detroit, 1961-63; group controller Glidden Co., Cleve., 1963-67; v.p., controller Glidden-Durkee div. SCM Corp., Cleve., 1968-76, v.p., asst. to pres. Durkee Foods div., 1976—. Mem. adv. council dept. acctg. Kent State U., 1968—; mem. bus. adv. com. John Carroll U., 1978—; dir. Jr. Achievement of Greater Cleve., 1975—, treas., 1978-80, v.p. fin., 1980—, Bronze Leadership award, 1980. Served with USN, 1948-49. Mem. Fin. Execs. Inst. (past dir., pres. N.E. Ohio chpt. nat. dir. N. Central area 1980—), Am. Mgmt. Assn., Nat. Assn. Accts., Greater Cleve. Growth Assn., Conf. Bd. Roman Catholic. Clubs: Cleve. Athletic, Westwood Country. Home: 20729 Morewood Pkwy Rocky River OH 44116 Office: 900 Union Commerce Bldg Cleveland OH 44115

MINNER, ROBERT SCHERMERHORN, advt. agy. exec.; b. Chgo., Oct. 29, 1927; s. Charles Fred and Isabel (Schermerhorn) M.; B.S. in Bus. Adminstrn., Northwestern U., 1949; m. Arleen Ruth Johnson, Feb. 3, 1951; children—Barbara Ann, Thomas Oliran. Asst. mgr. data processing Pure Oil Co., 1957-63; asst. to adminstrv. v.p., 1963-64, asst. sec.-treas., 1965; asst. sec. Union Oil Co. Calif., 1966; asst. treas. Needham, Harper & Steers, Inc., Chgo., 1967, v.p., treas., 1967-72; v.p., treas. Lien Chem. Co., 1972-74; asst. treas. Leo Burnett Co., Chgo., 1974, v.p., treas., 1975—. Home: 306 MacArthur Dr Mt Prospect IL 60056 Office: Prudential Plaza Chicago IL 60601

MINNEY, ORVAL HENSON, engring. and venture cons.; b. Duquesne, Pa., Oct. 24, 1925; s. Denon and Rosa Ada (Price) M.; student Adrian Coll., 1950-52, U. Pitts., 1956-58, Calif. Inst. Tech., 1958, Claremont Coll., 1960-61; B.S., U. Toledo, 1953; m. Jean Muriel Collins, Oct. 14, 1947; children—Martin Orval, Denon Collins (dec.), David Lee (dec.), Judith Ann, Deena Lyn; m. 2d, Alice Hansen, Dec. 24, 1970. Gen. mgr. Denon Minney Co., Pitts., 1953-57; dir. radiation safety Calif. Inst. Tech., 1958; research engr. N. Am. Aviation, Downey, Calif., 1959-61; mgr. systems safety engring. Hughes Aircraft Co., Fullerton, Calif., 1961-63; pres., dir. Bionomics Corp., Cheyenne, Wyo., 1963-65, chmn. bd. dirs., 1965—; mgr. systems effectiveness mktg. office Brown Engring. Co., Huntsville, Ala., 1965-66; asst. to v.p. and gen. mgr. research br. Varo, Inc., Garland, Tex., 1966-68; mgr. manned systems market devel. Space Tech. Center, Gen. Electric Co., Valley Forge, Pa., 1968-71; dir. planning and research Pa. Dept. Environ. Resources, 1972-75; bldgs. mgmt. engr. U.S. Postal Service, 1980—; engring. and venture cons., 1958—. Served with USNR, 1943-47. Mem. Baha'i Faith. Contbr. 21 articles to profl. jours. Home and office: 2008 Mulberry St Harrisburg PA 17104

MINNICH, SHERRY GORDON, bank exec.; b. London, Eng., Jan. 4, 1945; came to U.S., naturalized, 1948; d. George Arthur and Pamela (Bartlett) G.; student U. N.C., 1962-64, La. State U., 1978—, Am. Inst. Banking, 1969—; m. William R. Minnich, Jr., May 27, 1972. With 1st Nat. Bank of Atlanta, 1969—, Southeastern sales rep. employee benefits div., 1979—. Sec. consumer adv. council Peachtree-Parkwood Mental Health Hosp.; capt. United Negro Coll. Fund Drive, 1979. Mem. Ga. Bankers Assn., Nat. Assn. Bank Women, Am. Inst. Banking. Democrat. Episcopalian. Club: Piedmont Driving. Contbr. articles on banking to profl., popular mags. Office: 2 Peachtree St Atlanta GA 30303

MINOT, GEORGE MARSHALL, info. processing co. exec.; b. Galveston, Tex., Aug. 11, 1933; s. George Patrick and Julia May (McCollum) Prendergast; student U. Tex., 1951-56; m. Betty Jane Kraft, Nov. 4, 1961; children—Christine Anne, Steven Marshall. Sr. mktg. rep. Service Bur. Corp., St. Louis, 1960-69; v.p. mktg. Computercraft, Inc., St. Louis, 1969-70, pres., 1970-74; v.p. nat. accounts Compu-Serv, Inc., Columbus, Ohio, 1974-78; sr. v.p. Compuserve Inc., Columbus, 1978—. Presbyterian. Office: 5000 Arlington Centre Blvd Columbus OH 43220

MINSKER, ROBERT STANLEY, cons., former glass co. exec.; b. Pitts. Jan. 1, 1911; s. Theodore Koene and Isabella Lavinia (Trumbor) M.; B.S., U. Ill., 1934; postgrad. Pa. State U., 1938-39; m. Marion Elizabeth Warner, May 29, 1937; children—Norma (Mrs. Leo Jerome Brown II), Robert S., James. D. With Owens-Ill., Inc., Alton, Ill., 1934-76, personnel dir. Clarion (Pa.) plant, 1936-40, personnel dir. Columbus (Ohio) plant, 1940-44, mgr. indsl. relations Alton, 1945-72, adminstr. workmen's compensation, safety and health Ill. plants and pub. affairs, 1972-76; dir. Germania Financial Corp., 1953—, Germania Fed. Savs. & Loan Assn., 1953-81; asso. faculty So. Ill. U., 1959-64. Lectr., cons. Chmn. Madison County Savs. Bond Campaign, 1959-61; active Boy Scouts Am.; pres. Piasa Bird Council, 1949-51, mem. exec. bd., 1945—; mem. grievance com. panel State of Ill. Dept. Personnel, 1967—; vice chmn. Higher Edn. Coordinating Council Met. St. Louis, 1966-70; founder Board Pride, Inc., 1966—. Mem. Bd. Edn., 1957-70, pres. 1961-70. Bd. dirs., treas., sec., exec. com. Alton Meml. Hosp., 1969—, Jr. Achievement, United Fund.; bd. dirs. Community Chest, v.p., 1949-54, 61-66, gen. chmn., 1949-50; trustee Alton Found., sec., 1955—; trustee Lewis and Clark Community Coll., sec. bd., 1970-77. Recipient Silver Beaver award Boy Scouts of Am., 1951; recipient Achievement award U.S. Treasury Dept., 1951; Hall of Fame award Piasa Bird Council, 1969; named to Lewis and Clark Hall of Fame, 1977. Mem. Alton C. of C. (chmn. pub. relations 1951-54), Nature Conservation Assn. (a founder), Acacia, Alpha Phi Omega. Meth. Mason (32 deg.), K.T., Shriner). Home: 2018 Chapin Pl Alton IL 62002

MINTZ, GARY, health care exec.; b. Baranownch, Poland, Oct. 25, 1933; s. Harold and Ruth (Berger) M.; student acctg. and bus. mgmt. U. Calif., Berkeley, 1958; m. Celine; children—Ronald, Mark, Russell, Dana. With West Bend Aluminum, San Francisco, 1958-64; v.p. Interstate Dept. Stores, Los Angeles, 1964-74; partner Sam Nassie Co., Los Angeles, 1974-77; chief exec. officer, chmn. bd. Nu-Med Systems, Inc., Van Nuys, Calif., 1977—. Served with U.S. Army, 1953-55. Republican. Office: 6850 Van Nuys Blvd Van Nuys CA 91405

MINTZ, ROBERT BEIER, consumer package goods co. exec.; b. Phila., June 17, 1952; s. Richard A. and Marjorie I. (Thompson) M.; B.A., Ohio State U., 1974, M.A., 1976. Resident counselor Ohio Wesleyan U., 1975-76; asst. dean students Rider Coll., Lawrenceville, N.J., 1976-77; mgmt. cons. Staub, Warmbold & Assos., N.Y.C., 1977-80; corp. mgr. tng. and devel. Revlon, Inc., N.Y.C., 1980—. Mem. Am. Soc. Tng. and Devel., Am. Psychol. Assn., Am. Soc. Personnel Adminstrs., Omicron Delta Kappa, Phi Kappa Tau. Home: 346 E 87th St New York NY 10028 Office: Revlon Inc 767 Fifth Ave New York NY 10022

MINUTILLI, JOSEPH D., bus. credit and ins. co. exec.; b. Columbus, Ohio, 1928; ed. Ohio Wesleyan U., Northeastern U. With Comml. Credit Co., Balt., 1951—, sr. v.p., 1973-75, exec. v.p., 1975-79, pres., chief operating officer, 1979—, also dir. Served with U.S. Navy, 1946-48. Office: 300 St Paul Pl Baltimore MD 21202*

MIRABITO, ROBERT STEPHEN, ins. co. exec.; b. Boston, Aug. 17, 1939; s. Frank Dominic and Josephine Janet (Zanco) M.; B.A., Boston U., 1958; M.A., Harvard U., 1959; postgrad. Mass. Inst. Tech., 1959-60; m. Carol A. Iula, Oct. 29, 1962; children—Frank, Camille, Laura. Pres., W.H. Brewster Co., Boston, 1962-66; founder Mirabito Ins., Inc., Boston, 1966—, pres., chmn. bd., 1967—; dir. Minot Corp. Bank, Boston, Economy Fin. Co., Boston, 1964-70. City councillor City of Boston, 1966-68, commr., 1968-72; mem. sch. com., Reyer, Mass.; mem. Pres.'s Adv. Com. Fgn. Affairs, 1962-63. Served with USAF to lt. col., 1960-62. Decorated Purple Heart, Silver Cross, Bronze Star. Mem. Profl. Ins. Agts. Assn., Boston Bd. Underwriters, D.A.V., V.F.W., Ind. Ins. Agts. of Am. Club: Boston Yacht. Home: 169 Whittier Rd Milton MA 02186 Office: 141 Milk St Boston MA 02109

MIRANDA, JAMES MELVAN, supermarket and gen. mdse. corp. exec.; b. Nuttalsburg, W. Va., Dec. 3, 1931; s. Russell William Miranda and Fornia (Honaker) Miranda Ellman (stepson Jerry E. Ellman); B.A., Morris Harvey Coll., 1953; M.B.A., U. N.Fla., 1980; 1 dau., Sharon Gail. Corporate tng. dir., personnel mgr. Rich's Dept. Store, Atlanta, 1964-70; ops. mgr. Richway Discount, Atlanta, 1970; dir. store ops. Red Food, Chattanooga, 1971; v.p. ops. Value-Mart, Hattiesburg, Miss., 1972-75; dir. corporate projects Chatham Supermarkets, Detroit, 1976—; dir. ops. Jax Liquors, Jacksonville, Fla., 1977—. Recipient Nat. Superior Govs. award Am. Bus. Clubs, 1970, Nat. First Place For Project's award, 1970. Mem. Food Industry Council, Detroit C. of C. 1976-77. Clubs: Am. Bus. (dist. gov. Ga. 1970). Presbyterian. Home: 12943 Bearpaw Pl Jacksonville FL 32211 Office: PO Box 8743 Jacksonville FL 32211

MIRANDA, JOSEPH CHARLES, lawyer, mfg. co. exec.; b. Bklyn., Mar. 4, 1930; s. Frank M. and Josephine (Puleo) M.; A.B., Fordham U., 1951, J.D., 1957; m. Joan F. Viggiani, Aug. 7, 1954; children—Neal Joseph, Gail Mary. Admitted to N.Y. bar, 1958; asso. Kissam & Halpin, N.Y.C., 1958-62; corp. atty. Foremost-McKesson, Inc., N.Y.C., 1962-70; corp. atty., asst. sec. N.Am. Philips Corp., N.Y.C., 1970—. Served from ensign to lt. USNR, 1951-54. Mem. Am., N.Y. State bar assns., Assn. Bar City N.Y., Practising Law Inst., Fordham Law Rev. Assn., Fordham U. Alumni Fedn. (gov. 1978—), Fordham Coll. Alumni Assn. (dir. 1977—), Regis Alumni Assn. Roman Catholic (pres. Holy Name Soc. 1972-73). Clubs: West Side Tennis Forest Hills, N.Y.); Plandome (N.Y.) Country. Home: 1270 Plandome Rd Plandome Manor NY 11030 Office: 100 E 42d St New York NY 10017

MIRANDO, LOUIS PATRICK, cons., investment co. exec.; b. Buffalo, June 27, 1927; s. Pietro and Lucia (Carbone) M.; student Niagara Coll., 1948-52; m. Ada Francescutti, Jan. 15, 1949; children—Martha Louise, Louis Patrick, Victor Joseph, John Anthony, Marianne. Traffic mgr. Detroit Steel Products Co., 1948-50; mgr. Schrieber Trucking Co., Buffalo, 1950-53; sales mgr. Shirks Motor Express Corp., Lancaster, Pa., 1953-55; gen. mgr., mng. dir. Fess Transport Ltd. and Harrison Motorways Ltd., Welland, Ont., Can., 1955-63; pres. Uscan Transport, Ltd. R.R. #1, Chippawa, Ont., 1963-65; pres., chmn. bd. dirs. Internat. Scanning Devices, Inc., Fort Erie, Ont., Can., 1965—, also dir.; pres. Columbia Security & Transfer; sr. partner Columbia Bus. Cons., Inc., 1978—; dir. Intermountain Chem. Corp., Buck Printing Co., Ford Films Ltd., Electroluminesence, Inc., Columbia Security & Transfer Inc., Internat. Chem. & Devel. Inc., Columbia Autocar, Inc., Lad Electro Systems Ltd., Fess Transport Ltd., Uscan Transport Ltd., Mirland Developments Ltd., Holdings Ltd. Served with USNR, 1944-46. Mem. Canadian Pilots Assn., First Fin. Credit Assn., Nat. Geog. Soc., Delta Nu Alpha. Progressive Conservative. Roman Catholic. Clubs: Buffalo Athletic, Welland, St. Catharine's Flying. Patentee flat TV, also plastic el light sheet. Home: Rural Route 2 Stevensville ON L05 1SO Canada also 26 Virginia Pl Buffalo NY 14202 Office: 16 Dufferin St Fort Erie ON Canada

MIRCHANDANI, TIRTH MULCHAND, mech. engr.; b. Hyderabad, W. Pakistan, May 29, 1939; s. Mulchand Khanchand and Radha Mulchand M.; came to U.S., 1968, naturalized, 1973; B.E., Faculty of Tech. and Engring., Baroda, India, 1961; M.E., Stevens Inst. Tech., 1971; m. Veena Bakshi, Nov. 27, 1975; children—Sarika, Kaajal. Mech. engr. various firms, India, 1961-67; sr. mech. engr. Ebasco Services, N.Y.C., 1968-71; mech. group supr. Bechtel Power Corp., San Francisco, 1971-78; prin. engr. Kaiser Engrs. Inc., Oakland, Calif., 1978-79; mech. group supr. Bechtel Power Corp., San Francisco, 1979—. Office: 50 Beale St San Francisco CA 94119

MIRTICH, ROBERT MICHAEL, fin. exec.; b. Bklyn., Sept. 27, 1943; s. Emil A. and Rose T. (McQueeney) M.; B.B.A., Coll. Ins., 1971; M.B.A., L.I. U., 1975; m. Marie L. Demarco, June 26, 1967. Underwriter, Sun Ins. Office Ltd., N.Y.C., 1960-63; examiner N.Y. Compensation Rating Bd., N.Y.C., 1963-67; underwriter Comml. Union, N.Y.C., 1967-69, Kemper Ins., N.Y.C., 1969-71, Am. Reins. Co., N.Y.C., 1971-74; v.p. Munich Am. Reins. Co., N.Y.C., 1974—. Recipient Nat. Assn. Mut. Ins. Cos. merit award, 1976. Mem. Coll. Ins. Alumni Assn. (dir. 1977-78), Casualty and Surety Club N.Y., Soc. C.P.C.U.'s. Republican. Roman Catholic. Clubs: Haworth Country, Haworth, N.J. Office: 560 Lexington Ave New York NY 10022

MISAMORE, BRUCE KELVERN, oil co. exec.; b. Findlay, Ohio, June 20, 1950; s. Von Dale and Helen JoAnn (Ritchey) M.; B.B.A., Bowling Green State U., 1972, M.B.A., 1973; m. Janet Louise Farison, Sept. 5, 1970; children—Brian Elliott, Catherine Elizabeth. Instr. fin. Bowling Green State U., 1973-74; investments officer The Toledo Trust Co. (Ohio), 1974-76; fin. analyst Marathon Oil Co., Findlay, 1976-77, advanced fin. analyst, 1977-78, credit analysis mgr., 1978, supr. internat. banking, 1978-79, internat. fin. rep., London, Eng., 1979—. Div. chmn. United Way of Hancock County (Ohio), 1979; corp. chmn. Findlay Civic Music Assn., 1979; bd. dirs. Hancock County Regional Planning Commn., 1977-79. Kiwanian. Office: 174 Marylebone Rd London NW1 5AT England

MISAWA, MITSURU, bank exec.; b. Naganoken, Japan, Sept. 18, 1936; s. Fukuji and Kaneyo (Haba) M.; LL.B., Tokyo U., 1960; LL.M., Harvard U., 1964; M.B.A., U. Hawaii, 1965; Ph.D., U. Mich., 1967; m. Kuniko Ishii, Mar. 6, 1965; children—Anne Megumi, Marie Lei. Mgr., Indsl. Bank of Japan, Tokyo, 1960-74; exec. v.p. Indsl. Bank of Japan Trust Co., N.Y.C., 1974—. East West Center grantee, 1962-65; Fulbright grantee, 1965; Internat. Bus. fellow U. Mich., 1965-67; recipient Japan Scholarship Soc. award, 1960. Mem. Phi Kappa Phi, Pi Sigma Epsilon. Club: Harvard. Translator Bank Lending Policies (Douglas A. Hayes), 1973; contbr. articles in field to profl. jours. Home: 6 Byron Ct Westfield NJ 07090 Office: Indsl Bank Japan Trust Co 1 Wall St New York NY 10005

MISCHLER, HARLAND LOUIS, food machinery mfr.; b. Troy, Ohio, Feb. 21, 1932, s. James Jolly and Margaret (Fladd M.; B.S.c., Ohio State U., 1954; M.B.A., 1957; m. Jean Marie O'Connor, June 20, 1959; children—Marilyn West, Thomas O'Connor. Prin. Haskins & Sells, Cin., 1958-66; with Hobart Corp., Troy, 1966—, controller, 1968-75, v.p., 1975—, treas., 1977—; dir. Hobart Mfg. Co. Ltd. (Toronto); controller, dir. Hobart Export Co., Troy, Hobart Sales & Service (P.R.). Bd. dirs. Diagnostic Clinic for Mentally Retarded Children, Cin., 1966; chmn. bd. dirs. Stouder Meml. Hosp.; bd. dirs. Troy Nursing Assn., 1971, Camp Fire Girls, 1973-77; v.p., bd. dirs. Troy Improvement Council; mem. sch. com. for local joint vocat. sch. Served to capt. USAF, 1955-57. Mem. Am. Inst. C.P.A.'s, Ohio Soc. C.P.A.'s, Financial Execs. Inst. (v.p., dir.), Troy C. of C. (dir., pres.), Miami County Hosp. Assn. (pres.), Ohio State U. Alumni Assn. (pres. 1977-78), Alpha Kappa Psi, Sigma Alpha Epsilon. Episcopalian. Clubs: Troy Rotary, Troy Country. Home: 2192 Merrimont Dr Troy OH 45373 Office: World Headquarters Ave Troy OH 45374

MISHLER, DENNIS HAROLD, retail store exec.; b. South Bend, Ind., June 1, 1944; s. Harold Mervin and Rose (Hornyak) M.; B.S. in Aero. Engring., Purdue U., 1967; m. Barbara Anne Martin, Feb. 10, 1968; children—Brian, Scott. Project engr. Cornell Aero. Lab. (Calspan Inc.), Buffalo, 1967-70; sr. product engr. Carborundum Co., Niagara Falls, N.Y., 1970-72; franchise owner, pres. World Bazaar Balt., Inc., 1972—. Mem. Balt. Astron. Soc., Balt. Zool. Soc., Md. Apple Corps, Md. Racquetball Assn. (dir.). Republican. Presbyterian. Home: 1032 Lakemont Rd Baltimore MD 21228 Office: World Bazaar Security Square Mall Baltimore MD 21207

MISHOE, KENNETH LEROY, III, med. communications corp. exec.; b. Conway, S.C., Apr. 14, 1948; s. Kenneth L. and Mers W. (Bass) M.; B.S. in Econs., U. SW La., 1971; M.B.A., U. West Fla., 1972, M.A. in Psychology, 1973; m. Norma Zeiger, Dec. 22, 1968; children—Kenneth LeRoy IV, Joshua Z. Cons. personnel U.S. Navy, Pensacola, Fla., 1972, Monsanto Chem. Co., Pensacola, 1973; dir. edn. and devel. Day Cos., Atlanta, 1973-74; corporate mgr. inst. for personnel devel. B.F. Goodrich Co., Akron, Ohio, 1974—; corporate dir. organizational devel. Meredith Corp., Des Moines, 1976—; cons. S.L.S. Mental Health Center, Broadlawns Hosp. Certified jr. coll. instr., Fla. Republican. Baptist. Author: Client Behavior Analysis, 1976. Home: Rt 1 Van Meter IA 50261 Office: Meredith Corp Locust at 17th St Des Moines IA 50336

MISHRA, RAJNI RAMAN, engr.; b. Gosain Gaon, India; s. Asharfi and Bedwati M.; came to U.S., 1970, naturalized, 1978; B.Tech. with honors in Civil Engring., India Inst. Tech., 1962; M.C.E., U. Conn., 1975; m. Pratibha Jha, June 2, 1963; children—Vibha, Prakash, Vikas. Asst. engr. Hevy Engring. Corp., Ranchi, India, 1962-70; structural drafting Shepard Steel Co., Hartford, Conn., 1970-73; asso. engr. N.E. Utilities Service Co., Berlin, Conn., 1973—. Registered profl. engr., Conn.; chartered engr., India. Mem. Nat., Conn. socs. profl. engrs., Instn. Engrs. (India), IEEE. Democrat. Hindu. Home: 227 Church St Newington CT 06111

MISKOVSKY, GEORGE, SR., lawyer; b. Oklahoma City, Feb. 13, 1910; s. Frank and Mary (Bourek) M.; LL.B., J.D., U. Okla., 1936; m. Nelly Oleta Donahue, Dec. 30, 1932; children—George, Gary, Grover, Gail Marie. Admitted to Okla. bar, 1936, since practiced in Oklahoma City; sr. partner firm Miskovsky, Sullivan & Miskovsky, Oklahoma City; pub. defender Oklahoma City, 1936; county atty.

Oklahoma County, 1943-44; mem. Okla. Ho. of Reps., 1939-42; mem. Okla. Senate, 1950-60; pres., dir. Economy Sq. Inc., Penn 74 Mall Inc. Mem. Am., Okla., Oklahoma County bar assns., Am. Judicature Soc., Oklahoma City C. of C., Order of Coif, Pi Kappa Alpha, Phi Alpha Delta. Democrat. Episcopalian. Mason (Shriner). Clubs: Lions, Oklahoma City Golf and Country, Sooner Dinner, Bailli de Okla., Confrerie de la Chaine de Rotisseurs. Home: 1511 Drury Ln Oklahoma City OK 73116 Office: Hightower Bldg Oklahoma City OK 73102

MISRA, NITYANANDA, mfg. co. exec.; b. Cuttack, India, Aug. 4, 1944; s. Bhabagrahi and Saraswati (Dash) M.; B.S., U. Utkal, 1966; M.S., U. Vt., 1972; M.B.A., Clark U., 1978; m. June 8, 1969; 1 child. Asst. mech. engr. Govt. of Orissa, Bhnbeneswar, India, 1966-70; tech. support engr. Abcor Inc., Wilmington, Mass., 1972-74; plant engr. Dennison Mfg. Co., Framingham, Mass., 1974-78, corp. energy mgr., 1978—; faculty Worcester State Coll., part-time 1978—, Northeastern U., Boston, part-time 1978—. Mem. Am. Inst. Plant Engrs., Assn. Energy Engrs., Internat. Dist. Heating Assn., Milford Friends of Library. Contbr. articles to profl. jours. Address: 300 Howard St Framingham MA 01701

MITCHELHILL, JAMES MOFFAT, sugar co. exec.; b. St. Joseph, Mo., Aug. 11, 1912; s. William and Jeannette (Ambrose) M.; B.S. in Engring., Northwestern U., 1934, C.E., 1935; m. Maurine Hutchason, Jan. 9, 1937 (div. 1962); children—Janis Maurine Mitchelhill Johnson, Jeri Ann Mitchelhill Riney. With engring. dept. Chgo., Milw., St. Paul & Pacific R.R. Co., 1935-45; asst. mgr. Ponce & Guayama R.R., Aguirre, P.R., 1945-51, v.p., gen. mgr., 1969-70; mgr. Central Cortada, Santa Isabel, P.R., 1951-54; R.R. Supt. Braden Copper Co., Rancagua, Chile, 1954-63; staff engr. Coverdale & Colpitts, N.Y.C., 1963-64; asst. to exec. v.p., Central Aguirre Sugar Co. (P.R.), 1964-67; v.p., gen. mgr. Coddea Inc., Manzanillo, Dominican Republic, 1967-68; asst. to gen. mgr. Centrals Aguirre, Mercedita, and Lafayette, P.R., 1970-75, asst. to adminstr. Corporación Azucarera de P.R., Aguirre, 1976-77, asst. to exec. dir., 1977-79, asst. exec. dir. environment, 1979—. Mem. Aguirre (P.R.) Sch. Bd., 1965-77. Recipient Aguirre Sch. System Recognition award, 1976; registered profl. engr., Mont.; licensed civil engr., P.R. Fellow ASCE, Am. Geog. Soc., mem. Am. Ry. Engring. Assn., Colegio de Ingenieros y Agrimemsores de P.R., Asociacion Tecnicos Azucareros de P.R., World Expeditionary Assn. Presbyterian. Clubs: Aguirre Recreation Assn.; Explorers (N.Y.C.); Travellers Century. Home: House 106 Aguirre PR 00608 Office: PO Box 137 Aguirre PR 00608

MITCHELL, BERT NORMAN, accountant; b. Jamaica, B.W.I., Apr. 12, 1938; s. Joseph Benjamin and Edith Maud M.; B.B.A., Coll. City N.Y., 1963, M.B.A., 1968; m. Carole Harleston, Aug. 19, 1961; children—Tracey, Robbin, Ronald. Sr. accountant J.K. Lasser & Co., N.Y.C., 1963-66; comptroller Interam. Ins. Co., N.Y.C., 1966-67; asst. comptroller Ford Found., N.Y.C., 1967-69: partner Lucas, Tucker & Co., N.Y.C., 1969-73; mng. partner Mitchell, Titus & Co., N.Y.C., 1973—. Commr.'s adv. group IRS; mem. bd. edn. Roosevelt Sch. Dist. Nassau County (N.Y.), 1967; assembly dist. leader Democratic Party 12th Assembly Dist., State of N.Y., 1971-72; bd. dirs. St. Augustine's Coll., 1969-73, Nassau Community Coll., 1970-73, 100 Black Men, 1976—, Dance Theatre Harlem, 1976—; trustee Baruch Coll. Fund. Recipient Achievement award Nat. Assn. Black Accountants, 1977. C.P.A. Mem. Am. Inst. C.P.A.'s (dir. 1977—), N.Y. State Soc. C.P.A.'s (dir. 1977—), Nat. Assn. Minority C.P.A. Firms (dir. 1971—), N.Y. State Bd. Pub. Accountancy. Contbg. editor Black Enterprise, 1974—. Contbr. articles to profl. publs. Office: Mitchell Titus & Co 2 Park Ave New York NY 10016

MITCHELL, CHARLIE HOWARD, JR., cons. engr.; b. Pittsylvania County, Va., July 10, 1930; s. Charlie Howard and Nannie Mae (Waller) M.; B.S., Va. Poly. Inst., 1952; m. Malinda Beryl Branscome, June 15, 1963; children—Laura Carol, Karen Eileen, Sarah Kate. Test engr. Wright Aero. Div., Woodridge, N.J., 1952-53; design engr. Wiley & Wilson, Engrs.-Architects-Planners, Lynchburg, Va., 1955—, asst. head mech. dept., 1967-71, head mech. dept., 1971-73, project mgr., 1973—: owner lumber mill, 1978—. Co-founder Central Va. Diabetes Assn., Inc., 1972, pres., 1972-73, bd. dirs., 1974—. Served with C.E., U.S. Army, 1952-55. Registered profl. engr. Mem. Nat., Va. (past bd. dirs.) socs. profl. engrs. Baptist. Address: 3414 Plymouth Pl Lynchburg VA 24503

MITCHELL, DANIEL WERTZ, banker; b. Phoenix, Jan. 23, 1928; s. Larry Roy and Audrey Iris (Wertz) M.; B.S., Ind. U., 1950; m. Nancy E. Byrd, Feb. 12, 1950; children—Daniel L., Douglas R., Karen. With Old Nat. Bank of Evansville (Ind.), 1950—, pres., 1973-80, chmn., chief exec. officer, 1980—; dir. Warrick Nat. Bank, Boonville, Ind., 1970—, Hurst Mfg. Corp., Princeton, Ind., 1968—. Served with AUS, 1946-47. Mem. Robert Morris Assos. (nat. pres. 1976-77). Republican. Lutheran. Home: 515 Audubon Dr Evansville IN 47715 Office: 420 Main St Evansville IN 47701

MITCHELL, DAVID DEAN, accountant; b. Terre Haute, Ind., Mar. 1, 1950; s. Robert Dean and Norma Katheryn (Patton) M.; A.A., Fresno (Calif.) City Coll., 1970; B.S. in Gen. Mgmt., Purdue U., 1977; m. Marjorie Viola Weiler, July 27, 1974. Accountant, Consumers Power Co., Jackson, Mich., 1977—. Served with USN, 1972-75, Res., 1975-77. Mem. Alpha Gamma Sigma, Sigma Nu. Republican. Roman Catholic. Home: 10619 Hewitt Rd Brooklyn MI 49230 Office: Consumers Power Co 212 W Michigan Ave Jackson MI 49201

MITCHELL, DAVID NASH, bus. exec.; b. Milw., May 5, 1939; s. Ronald Nash and Dortha Madeline (Conrad) M.; B.B.A., U. Denver, 1975, M.B.A., 1977; children—David N., Kurt Conrad. Prodn. mgr. Autrey Bros. Inc., Denver, 1970-72; v.p., gen. mgr. Studio Three, Inc., Aspen, Colo., 1972-74; v.p., gen. mgr. Colo. Log Homes, Denver, 1978—; pres. Denver Bus. Cons., Ltd., 1974—; guest speaker Arapahoe Community Coll., Littleton, Colo., 1975. Contbr. award Small Bus. Inst., 1977. Mem. Nat. Assn. Bus. Economicsts. Home: 3140 S Williams St Englewood CO 80110

MITCHELL, DAVID W., bus. exec.; b. 1928. With Avon Products, Inc., N.Y.C., 1947—, v.p.-sales promotion, 1964-65, group v.p., 1965-67, sr. group v.p., 1967-68, exec. v.p., 1968-72, pres., 1972-77, chmn. bd., chief exec. officer, 1977—, also dir. Office: Avon Products Inc 9 W 57 St New York NY 10019*

MITCHELL, EDGAR LAROY, JR., energy co. mgr.; b. Claremore, Okla., Oct. 8, 1943; s. Edgar LaRoy and Margaret Evelyn (Parris) M.; B.B.A., U. Okla., 1972; m. Dorothy Sue Christenson, July 5, 1963; children—Troy Lynn, Gregory Kent. Auditor, Arthur Young & Co., Tulsa, 1972-74; asst. controller LaBardge Electronics, Tulsa, 1974-76; mgr. treasury dept. Reading & Bates Corp., Tulsa, 1976—. Mem. budget com. Tulsa Area United Way, 1977, mem. loaned exec. program, 1978. Served with AUS, 1966-68; Vietnam. Republican. Methodist. Clubs: Indian Springs Country (Broken Arrow, Okla.); Elks (Tulsa). Home: 1013 S Aspen Ct Broken Arrow OK 74012 Office: 3800 1st National Tower Tulsa OK 74103

MITCHELL, GARY RONALD, drug store exec.; b. Winnipeg, Man., Can., Sept. 19, 1940; s. David and Tobie (Silverman) M.; grad. Nutana Collegiate, Saskatoon, Sask., Can., 1958; m. Sharon Greff, Aug. 20, 1965; children—Eric Todd, Corey Blain. Owner, partner Bi-Rite Drugs Ltd., Regina, Sask., 1964—. Served with RCAF, 1962-63. Jewish. Club: B'nai B'rith. Home: 246 Plainsview Dr Regina SK S4S 6N1 Canada Office: 1308 Ottawa St Regina SK S4R 1P4 Canada

MITCHELL, GERALD BENSON, vehicular parts supply exec.; b. Goderich, Ont., Can., Aug. 29, 1927; s. Reginald and Mary Elizabeth (Sanders) M.; student U. Western Ont.; m. Stephanie Bennett Wood, Oct. 1, 1970; children—Fraser, Jamie, Briar, Michael, Melissa. Machine operator Hayes Dana Co., Toledo, 1944-63, pres., 1963-67; exec. v.p. Dana Corp., Toledo, 1967-72, pres., 1972-80, chmn. bd., chief exec. officer, 1980—; dir. Anchor Hocking Corp., Mich. Nat. Bank, Mich. Nat. Corp. Pres. bd. trustees Med. Coll. Ohio at Toledo Found.; trustee Toledo Symphony Orch., Toledo Mus. Art; mem. Toledo Labor-Mgmt.-Citizens Com. Mem. Western Hwy. Inst., Heavy Duty Truck Mfrs. Assn. Clubs: Inverness, Renaissance, Anglers, Toledo, Ocean Reef. Contbg. author: Chief Executive's Handbook, 1974. Office: PO Box 1000 Toledo OH 43697

MITCHELL, GUY PATRICK, mfg. co. exec.; b. Jonesboro, Ark., Mar. 15, 1937; s. Joseph Francis and Artie (Cook) M.; student LaSalle U., 1961; m. Patricia Ann Thurber, July 13, 1964; children—Jennifer and Juliana (twins), Richard Dale, Larry Guy, Elizabeth Ann, Alan Dane. Engring. technician Phillips Petroleum Co., Bartlesville, Okla., 1956-69; sales engr. Ameron Inc., Houston, 1969-70; gen. sales mgr. Porter Paint Co., Louisville, 1970-78; v.p. Sigma Coatings, Inc. subs. Am. Petrofina, New Orleans, 1978—; pres., dir. Vista Inc., New Orleans; dir. Sigma Internat. Marine, Protective Coatings Internat. of Amsterdam. Mem. Am. Mgmt. Assn., Nat. Assn. Corrosion Engrs., Soc. Naval Architects and Marine Engrs., Harvey (La.) Canal Indsl. Assn. Republican. Mem. Ch. of Christ. Home: 171 Wiegand Dr Westwego LA 70094 Office: 3300 River Rd Harvey LA 70058

MITCHELL, HERBERT EUGENE, mktg. cons.; b. Elkhart. Ind., July 25, 1929; s. Charles N. and Beulah (McDonald) M.; B.S., Iowa State U., 1949; postgrad. Sinclair Coll., 1954-56; m. Roberta Marie Blesie, Oct. 22, 1949; children—Robert Kent, Debra Mitchell Maul, Kimbra Mitchell Anderson, Candi Mitchell Mann, Melissa Marie. Owner, pres. J.W. Rodgers Co., Dayton, 1960-65; dir. mktg. John Henry Co., Lansing, Mich., 1965-67; dir. wholesale mktg. Jackson & Perkins/Harry & David, Medford, Oreg., 1967-69; v.p. Mktg. Telefora, Inc., Redondo Beach, Calif., 1969-75; owner, pres. Herb Mitchell Assos. mktg. and mgmt. planning floriculture industry, Costa Mesa, Calif., 1975—. Float judge Tournament of Roses Parade, 1978. Mem. Am. Acad. Florists, Am. Inst. Floral Designers (pres.), Soc. Am. Florists, Nat. Color Mktg. Group, Color Assn. of U.S. Republican. Presbyterian. (elder). Club: Toastmasters. Publisher, Floriculture Directions, 1975—; mng. editor Design for Profit, 1969-76; contbr. articles to profl. jours. Home: 1308 Mariners Dr Newport Beach CA 92660 Office: Suite 206 Pacific Plaza 234 E 17 St Costa Mesa CA 92627

MITCHELL, HERBERT LECKIE, mil. electronic co. exec.; b. Manhattan, Kans., Mar. 5, 1932; s. Walter Rankin and Nelle (Holt) M.; B.S., Kans. State U., 1954; M.S., U. Tex., 1956; Ph.D., Okla. State U., 1972; m. Patricia Jane Lacy, Sept. 7, 1963; children—James L., Amy M. Vice pres. Nat. Geophys. Co., Dallas, 1956-69; v.p., gen. mgr. Hydroscience Inc., Dallas, 1972-76; dir. electronic prodn. and devel. Valmont Industries, Valley, Nebr., 1976-78; v.p., gen. mgr. Piqua (Ohio) Engring., 1978. Registered profl. engr., Tex. Mem. Am. Inst. Indsl. Engrs., IEEE, Eta Kappa Nu, Sigma Tau, Alpha Pi Mu. Methodist. Patentee in field. Office: 234 1st St Piqua OH 45356

MITCHELL, JOHN FRANCIS, electronics co. exec.; b. Chgo., Jan. 1, 1928; s. William and Bridie (Keane) M.; B.S. in Elec. Engring., Ill. Inst. Tech., 1950; m. Margaret J. Gillis, Aug. 26, 1950; children—Catherine (Mrs. Edward Welsh III), John, Kevin. Exec. v.p., asst. chief operating officer Motorola Inc., Schaumburg, Ill., 1953-80, pres., 1980—. Served to lt. (j.g.) USNR, 1950-53. Mem. I.E.E.E. (sr.). Club: Inverness (Ill.) Country. Patentee in field. Office: 1303 E Algonquin Rd Schaumburg IL 60196*

MITCHELL, JOHN T., III, fin. exec.; b. Dayton, Ohio, Sept. 6, 1945; s. John T. Jr. and Betty Lou (Fike) M.; B.S., Fairleigh Dickinson U., 1968; M.S., Fairleigh Dickinson U., 1974; m. Pamela Carr, July 9, 1977; children—Stephen, John, David. Project engr. Austenal div. Howmet Corp., Dover, N.J., 1968-70; sr. indsl. engr. Singer Co., Elizabeth, N.J., 1970-74; corporate indsl. engr. Abex Research Center, Mahwah, N.J., 1974-78; mgr. planning and budget R.R. Products Group, Abex Corp., Mahwah, N.J., 1978—. Scouting coordinator Boy Scouts Am., Maplewood, N.J., 1979—. Served with U.S. Army, 1968-70. Mem. Am. Inst. Indsl. Engrs. Home: 682 Prospect St Maplewood NJ 07430 Office: PO Box 400 Suffern NY 10901

MITCHELL, JOHN THOMAS, JR., food co. exec.; b. Bklyn., July 14, 1929; s. John Thomas and Ella Bernadette (Neylon) M.; A.B. in History, Niagara U., 1951; postgrad. Harvard U., 1953-54; m. Marilyn Elizabeth Merolla, May 25, 1963; children—Denise Elaine, Douglas John. Salesman, Fed. Paperboard Co., N.J., 1955-58; account exec. Benton & Bowles Advt., N.Y.C., 1958-62; sales mgr. Franklin Sugar Co., Phila., 1962-66; mktg. mgr. Standard Packaging Corp., N.Y.C., 1966-69; v.p. mktg. Nabisco, Inc., East Hanover, N.Y., 1969—. Pres., Independence Day Assn., 1970-71, Village Players Community Theater, 1971-75; bd. dirs. Morris-Sussex council Boy Scouts Am., 1979—. Served with U.S. Army, 1951-53; Korea. Decorated Bronze Star. Mem. Internat. Foodservice Mfrs. Assn., Nat. Automatic Merchandisers Assn., Am. Legion. Roman Catholic. Clubs: Mountain Lakes, K.C. Home: 34 Arden Rd Mountain Lakes NJ 07046 Office: 100 DeForest Ave East Hanover NJ 07936

MITCHELL, JOSEPH NATHAN, ins. co. exec.; b. Winnipeg, Man., Can., Oct. 10, 1922; s. Edward David and Anna (Copp) M.; student UCLA, 1940-42; m. Beverly Edna Henigson, Oct. 27, 1946; children—Jonathan Edward, Jan Ellen, Karin Helene. With Beneficial Standard Life Ins. Co., Los Angeles, 1946—, exec. v.p., 1957-59, pres., 1959—, also dir.; chmn. bd., dir. Fielity Interstate Life Ins. Co., Los Angeles, 1969—; pres. Beneficial Standard Corp., Los Angeles, 1967—; mem. internat. bd. Ampal-Am. Israel Corp., N.Y.C., 1979—; dir. Pacific Lighting Corp., Los Angeles, Calif. Fed. Savs. & Loan Assn., Los Angeles, Glacier Nat. Life Ins. Co., Vancouver, B.C., Can.; chmn. exec. com. Transit Casualty Co., St. Louis; chmn. bd. Beneficial Standard Life Ins. Co., Los Angeles. Chmn., State of Israel Bonds Appeal, Los Angeles, 1967; mem. Dist. Atty.'s Adv. Council; mem. Am. com. Weizmann Inst. Sci.; co-chmn. NCCJ, 1976; bd. dirs., vice chmn. bd., mem. exec. com., chmn. audit com. Cedars-Sinai Med. Center; bd. dirs., mem. exec. com. Am. Jewish Joint Distbn. Com.; mem. Greater Los Angeles Urban Coalition; trustee, v.p. Jewish Community Found.; bd. dirs., v.p., mem. exec. com. United Way and United Crusade, gen. chmn. Los Angeles Area, 1972; bd. dirs. Los Angeles Safety Council. Served with AUS, 1942-46; ETO. Mem. Am. Technion Soc. (nat. v.p., gov.), Los Angeles Area C. of C. (dir., pres. 1979, chmn. bd. 1980), Invest-in-Am. (exec. com.), World Bus. Council. Clubs: Hillcrest Country (dir.); Los Angeles; Tamarisk Country; Tennis (Palm Springs, Calif.), 100, Lincoln. Office: Beneficial Standard Life Ins Co 3700 Wilshire Blvd Los Angeles CA 90010

MITCHELL, KEVIN ROBERT, leasing and fin. services co. exec.; b. Quincy, Mass., Oct. 23, 1948; s. Peter James and Gertrude E. (Robertson) M.; B.S. in Bus. Adminstrn., Suffolk U., 1970; M.B.A., U. Detroit, 1975; postgrad. U. Minn., 1979-80; m. Elizabeth O'Keefe, Nov. 15, 1969; children—Jennifer, Renee, Joshua, Faith. Audit rev. specialist Herbert F. French & Co. C.P.A.'s, Boston, 1968-70; mgr. planning and mgmt. reporting Ford Motor Credit, Detroit, 1970-74; asst. v.p., mgr. mktg. services FBS Fin., Mpls., 1974-75; v.p., controller Gelcofleet & Mgmt. Services Co., Eden Prairie, Minn., 1975-80; v.p. sales fin. div. Citicorp Consumer Services Group, St. Louis, 1980-81; v.p. adminstrn. Gelco Corp., Eden Prairie, Minn., 1981—. Bd. elders Jesus is Lord Fellowship, Rosemount, Minn. Mem. Nat. Assn. Accts., Am. Mgmt. Assn., Beta Gamma Sigma. Home: 1277 Dunberry Ln Eagan MN 55123 Office: 1 Gelco Dr Eden Prairie MN 55123

MITCHELL, LEE HARTLEY, investment co. exec.; b. Chgo., Dec. 10, 1941; s. Bernard A. and Marjorie E. (Iglow) M.; B.S. with honors, U. Calif., Berkeley, 1963; M.B.A., Harvard U., 1966. Partner, Hatikvah Co., Jerusalem, Israel, 1973-77; dir. mktg. research Jovan, Inc., Chgo., 1977-80; pres. Lee Mitchell & Co., Inc., Chgo., 1980—. Mem. Am. Mktg. Assn., Midwest Planning Assn., Soc. Cosmetic Chemists. Clubs: Internat. 700, Harvard U. Bus. Sch. (Chgo.). Home: 100 E Walton St Chicago IL 60611 Office: 875 N Michigan Ave Chicago IL 60611

MITCHELL, LESTER EDWARD, JR., ins. co. exec.; b. Morristown, N.J., Aug. 21, 1943; s. Lester Edward and Carrie (Ragland) M.; B.A., L.I. U., 1968, M.B.A., 1972. Account exec. CBS, N.Y.C., 1972-74; identification rep. Celanese Fibers Mktg. Co., N.Y.C., 1969-70; exec. trainee Chem. Bank. N.Y.C., 1968-69; field underwriter N.Y. Ins. Co., Jamaica, N.Y., 1975—; lectr. in field. Served with U.S. Navy, 1961-64. Mem. Nat. Assn. Life Underwriters, Council Concerned Black Execs., Black M.B.A. Assn., Million Dollar Roundtable. Home: 57 Shepard Ave Teaneck NJ 09666 Office: NY Life 97-77 Queens Blvd Rego Park NY 11374

MITCHELL, MARVIN GEORGE, steel constrn. co. exec.; b. Waycross, Ga., Dec. 24, 1916; s. Marvin G. and Minnie (Holland) M.; B.S.C.E. cum laude, Ga. Inst. Tech.; m. Margaret V. Lovelady, Sept. 24, 1942; children—Marvin George III, Margaret Nelle. With CBI Industries, Inc., Oak Brook, Ill., 1939—, beginning as jr. engr., successively field engr., contracting engr., dist. sales mgr., Atlanta, asst. gen. sales mgr., Chgo., v.p. sales, dir., sr. v.p. comml., exec. v.p., 1939-69, pres., 1969—, chmn. bd., 1973—; dir. Continental Ill. Nat. Bank, McGraw-Edison Co., R.R. Donnelley & Sons Co., Bliss & Laughlin Industries, Mitchell-Stewart Hardware Co. Nat. adv. bd. Ga. Inst. Tech., Atomic Indsl. Forum; mem. citizens bd. U. Chgo., Goodwill Industries, Beavers, Chgo. Heart Assn., Prot. Found., NAM. Mem. Steel Plate Fabricators Assn. (past pres.), Am. Iron and Steel Inst., Am. Gas Assn., Am. Petroleum Inst., Am. Water Works Assn., Am. Mgmt. Assn. Clubs: Chgo., Mid-Am., Econ., Comml., Butler Nat., Hinsdale (Ill.) Golf. Office: 800 Jorie Blvd Oak Brook IL 60521

MITCHELL, MARY LOU, dept. store exec.; b. Cherry Ridge, La., July 25, 1934; d. W.C. and Ora Mae (Henderson) Webb; student St. Louis Bus. Coll., 1961; m. Bill H. Mitchell, May 15, 1966. Women's dir., hostess Noon Show, Sta. KTHV-TV, Little Rock, 1964-73; v.p. account service Holland & Assos., advt. agy., Little Rock, 1973-76; dir. corp. broadcast advt. Dillard Dept. Stores, Inc., Little Rock, 1973—. Active United Fund, Ark. Heart Assn.; bd. dirs. Better Bus. Bur. Ark. Mem. Nat. Sales and Mktg. Execs. Assn., Little Rock Sales and Mktg. Execs. Assn., Ark. Advt. Assn. Office: Dillard Dept Stores Inc 900 W Capitol St Room 214 Little Rock AR 72203

MITCHELL, MICHAEL JOSEPH, JR., business exec.; b. Washington, May 24, 1939; s. Michael J. and Ruth (Alexander) M.; student Everett Jr. Coll., 1960-62. Electronic tech. Boeing Co., Seattle, 1959-62, engring. aide, 1962-64; owner-pres. The Mitchell Co. (U.S.) Ltd., Seattle, 1964—; partner-v.p. Northwest Avionics Co., Renton, Wash., 1964-66; pres. M.J. Mitchell & Assos., Seattle, 1972—, The Mitchell Co. (Internat.) Ltd., 1973—, Bus. & Fin. Mgmt., Inc., 1977—. Served with USNR, 1957-59. Mem. Internat. Assn. Fin. Planners, Inst. Certified Bus. Counselors, Seattle Fire Buffs Soc., Am. Mgmt. Assn. Democrat. Elk. Home: 2803 8th Ave West Seattle WA 98119 Office: 231 Summit Ave East Seattle WA 98102

MITCHELL, PAUL FREDERICK, mfg. co. exec.; b. Masontown, Pa., Feb. 12, 1919; s. Michael Paul and Ann Margaret (Fredericks) M.; B.S. in Bus. Adminstrn., W.Va. U., 1938; postgrad. Western Res. U., 1947-53; m. Marcia Feulner, Jan. 6, 1947 (dec.); children—Wayne, Douglas, Paulette, Mary. Dir. purchasing Trabon Engring. Co., Cleve., 1948-51; dir. purchasing, v.p. operations Diamond Products Co., Cleve., 1951-53, v.p. purchasing, asst. to pres., v.p. mfg., 1954-61, 65-70; cons. mfg., prodn. control Elwell Parker Electric, 1962-65, dir. mfg., 1976-77, v.p. mfg., 1977—; pres. Upson-Walton Co., Cleve., 1970-72; group v.p. crane accessories group Anvil Industries, Inc., 1973-75; bus. cons., 1975-76, 80—. Chmn. Heart Fund, 1966. Served to lt. comdr. USNR, 1941-46. Mem. Am. Mgmt. Assn. Republican. Presbyn. Clubs: Cleveland Athletic; Orchard Hills Country (Chesterland, Ohio), Canterbury Golf. Author: Scientific Aspects of Purchasing, 1963. Home: 941 E 216th St Euclid OH 44119

MITCHELL, PHILIP JAMES, banker; b. Manchester, Eng., May 23, 1930; s. David Ernest and Marie (Dilbeck) M.; came to U.S., 1954, naturalized, 1965; grad. in controllership Sch. for Bank Adminstrn. U. Wis., 1973; m. Charlotte Studer, Aug. 10, 1957 (dec. Jan. 1979); 1 son, Mark Philip. Theatre mgr. J. Arthur Rank Orgn., London, 1952-54; chief accountant Whitehall Labs., Inc., Elkhart, Ind., 1955-66; asst. controller/cashier St. Joseph Valley Bank subs. SJV Corp., Elkhart, 1966—, asst. treas. parent corp., 1976—. Bd. dirs., Elkhart County Mental Health Assn., 1967—, pres., 1973-75; bd. dirs. Mental Health Assn. Ind., 1975-77; treas. Elkhart Concert Club, Inc., 1973—. Served to sgt. Royal Corps Signals Brit. Army, 1948-52. Recipient awards for Service Elkhart County Mental Health Assn., 1975. Mem. Nat. Assn. Accountants, Bank Adminstrn. Inst. Episcopalian. Club: Lions (treas. local club 1970-76, charter Treas's. award 1970). Home: 2601 E Jackson Blvd Elkhart IN 46516 Office: 121 W Franklin St Elkhart IN 46516

MITCHELL, ROBERT GREENE, clothing co. exec.; b. Abington, Pa., July 20, 1925; s. James Henry and Nellie Edna (Greene) M.; B.S., Drexel U., 1948; m. Alma Maerker Honsberger, Mar. 6, 1948; children—Scott Craig, Donna Lynn, Sandra Lee. Dept. mgr. Internat. Playtex, Dover, Del., 1949-52, quality control mgr., 1952-59, mfg. mgr., Indsl. div., 1959-60; v.p. operations The Wool "O" Co., Phila., 1960-65; mfg. mgr. Plymouth Rubber, Canton, Mass., 1965-68; chief indsl. engr., spl. projects, Vanity Fair Mills, Monroeville, Ala., 1968-75; v.p. materials mgmt. The H.W. Gossard Co., Chgo., 1975-76, v.p. adminstrn., 1977; v.p. adminstrn., mem. exec. com. Knickerbocker Toy Co., Middlesex, N.J., 1977-79; pres. H&R Block, Prince Frederick, Md., 1979—; dir. The Wool "O" Co., 1963-65. Advanced gifts chmn., United Fund, Dover, Del., 1958-60; bd. dirs. YMCA, Dover, 1960. Served with USAF, 1943-46. Certified quality engr. Mem. Am. Soc. Quality Control (chmn. Del. sect. 1955-56, gen.

chmn. Middle Atlantic conf. 1959, chmn. textile div. 1959-60), Am. Inst. Indsl. Engrs., Am. Assn. Textile Colorists and Chemists, Am. Apparel Mfrs. Assn., Am. Prodn. and Inventory Control Soc. Clubs: Lions (dir. 1954-56, pres. 1955-56). Patentee in field. Home: 13 Laurelwood Dr Colts Neck NJ 07722 Office: 207 Pond Ave Middlesex NJ 08846

MITCHELL, ROBERT JAMES, petroleum co. exec.; b. Montour Falls, N.Y., Mar. 16, 1925; s. Robert Bowlby and Helen (Bates) M.; student Ga. Inst. Tech., 1944, U. Richmond, 1945, Sampson Coll., 1947-48; student Valparaiso U., 1948, J.D., 1953; m. Pearl Kohnken, Aug. 30, 1947; children—Susan E., LuAnne, Robert James II. Adjuster, State Farm Mut. Auto Ins., Valparaiso, 1953-54; dist. rep. life ins. Aid Assn. for Lutherans, Hoffman, Ill., 1954-57; with dept. of devel. Valparaiso (Ind.) U., 1957-58; oil producer, Hoffman, 1958-64; founder Ego Oil Co., Inc., 1964, pres., 1964—, also dir. Bd. dirs. Law Sch. Alumni Bd., 1970-73. Served with USNR, 1941-46, 50-52. Mem. Ind. Petroleum Assn. Am. (dir. 1976—), Delta Theta Phi. Rotarian. Home: PO Box 87 Hoffman IL 62250 Office: 407 First Nat Bank Bldg Centralia IL 62801

MITCHELL, ROBERT LYNNE, chem. co. exec.; b. Floresville, Tex., Oct. 25, 1923; s. Lynn Harvey and Elsa (Eschenburg) M.; B.S., Tex. A. and I. Coll., 1943; M.S., Mass. Inst. Tech., 1947; m. Alicia Jane Gross, Apr. 26, 1952; children—Mark Robert, Scot Richard, Alicia Lyn. With Celanese Chem. Co., 1947—, v.p. planning, N.Y.C., 1957-61; v.p. Celanese Internat. Corp., N.Y.C., 1961-63, Celanese Che. Co., N.Y.C., 1963-66; v.p. tech. and mfg. Celanese Chem. Co., 1966-68; v.p., gen. mgr. operations, 1968-69, exec. v.p., 1969-71, pres., 1971-73, group v.p. Celanese Corp., 1973, exec. v.p., now vice chmn., dir.; dir. Celanese Can. Inc. Served to lt. (j.g.) USNR, 1944-46. Fellow Am. Inst. Chemists, Am. Inst. Chem. Engrs.; mem. Am. Chem. Soc., Soc. Chem. Industry. Conglist. Clubs: Weston Gun, Winged Foot Golf. Research in field. Office: Celanese Corp 1211 Ave of Americas New York NY 10036

MITCHELL, ROY SHAW, lawyer; b. Sherwood, N.Y., Jan. 16, 1934; s. Malcolm D. and Ruth L. (Holland) M.; B.S., Cornell U., 1957; J.D. with honors, George Washington U., 1959; m. Nancy E. Bishop, Aug. 27, 1955; children—Mark, Jeffrey, Jennifer. Admitted to D.C. bar, 1959, Ohio bar, 1960, Va. bar, 1967, U.S. Supreme Ct. bar, 1965; asso. firm Squire Sanders & Dempsey, Cleve., 1959-61; partner Hudson & Creyke, Washington, 1961-67, Lewis, Mitchell & Moore, Washington, 1967—; sec. Transit Products, Inc., 1975—; chmn. bd., chief exec. officer Newgate Savs. & Loan, Centreville, Va., 1979-80; vice chmn. 1st Am. Savs. & Loan, Woodbridge, Va., 1980—. Mem. Am. Bar Assn. (nat. chmn. public contract law sect. 1976-77). Democrat. Presbyterian. Contbr. articles to profl. jours. Home: 8444 Sparger St McLean VA 22102 Office: 600 New Hampshire Ave NW Washington DC 20037

MITCHELL, RYAN DUNNEHOO, JR., constrn. co. exec.; b. Belton, S.C., Aug. 1, 1935; s. Ryan Dunnehoo and Laura Haynie (Boyce) M.; B.S., Clemson U., 1958; postgrad. Ga. State U., 1965, Manhattan Coll., 1966, U. Okla., 1966; m. Barbara Jean Zimmer, Sept. 16, 1954; children—Elizabeth, Pamela, Ryan. Engr., Robert M. Angas Assos., Jacksonville, Fla., 1958-63; mgr. engring. Davco Mfg. Co., Thomasville, Ga., 1963-66; dir. Rhodes Corp., Oklahoma City, 1966-69; pres. Mitchell Engring., Inc., Georgetown, Guyana, South Am., 1969-71; v.p. Lang Engring., Cora Gables, Fla., 1971-72; dir. mktg. Daniel Internat. Corp., Greenville, S.C., 1972—. Registered profl. engr., Tex., S.C., Okla., Ark. Mem. ASCE, ASME, Nat. Soc. Profl. Engrs., Am. Chem. Soc., Soc. Ind. Devel. Council, U.S. C. of C. (subcom. on internat. econ. devel.), Am. Inst. Plant Engrs., Southeastern Community Devel. Assn. Episcopalian. Clubs: Greenville Country, Pebble Creek Country. Contbr. articles to profl. publs. Patentee in field. Home: 307 Sassafras Dr Taylors SC 29687 Office: Main St Greenville SC 29601

MITCHELL, SHIRLEY WATKINS MONTGOMERY, banker; b. New Castle, Pa., June 6, 1930; d. Roy Eugene and Sally Katherine (Holland) Watkins; student New Castle Bus. Coll., 1963-64, Cleve. State U., 1972; m. Charles Mitchell, Nov. 17, 1973; children by previous marriage—Robert C. Montgomery, Marvin E. Montgomery. With New Castle News, 1964-69, Cleve. Plain Dealer, 1969-72; asso. dir. communications div. United Way Services, Cleve., 1972-79; installment loan acctg. supr. Union Commerce Bank, Cleve., 1979-80, affirmative action officer, 1980—. Mem. community-univ. relations com. Cleve. State U., 1975-78; trustee SW Gen. Hosp., 1978—; trustee People's Community Ch., 1977—, now chmn. bd. trustees; pres. North Berea (Ohio) Action Group; chmn. affirmative action adv. com. YWCA. Recipient Distinguished Service award Goodwill Industries, 1971, Cuyahoga Assn. for Retarded Citizens, 1970. Mem. Internat. Assn. Bus. Communicators (job placement dir. 1978-79), Citizens League Cleve., Cleve Employers Equal Opportunity Assn. Clubs: City (Cleve.); Zonta (pres. Berea, Ohio 1977-79). Editor N. Berea News and Views Newsletter, 1978—. Home: 687 Shakespeare Dr Berea OH 44017 Office: 917 Euclid Ave Cleveland OH 44115

MITCHELL, STEPHEN DENNIS, ednl. publisher; b. Denver, Jan. 29, 1941; s. Johnson and Louise (Bailey) M.; B.S., Pa. State U., 1964; m. Karen B. DeBoer, Jan. 16, 1965; children—Scott, Shannon. Computer sci. editor Sci. Research Assos. of IBM, Palo Alto, Calif., 1970-73, dir. mktg., 1973-77, sr. computer sci. editor, 1978; pres. Mitchell Pub., Inc., Scotts Valley, Calif., 1978—; part-time instr. computer sci. Foothill Coll., Los Altos Hills, Calif. Served with U.S. Army, 1966. Mem. Assn. Computing Machinery. Methodist. Editor: Computers and Society, 1976. Contbr. to Malice in Blunderland, 1973. Home and office: 116 Royal Oak Ct Scotts Valley CA 95066

MITTEL, JOHN J., economist, business exec., cons.; b. L.I., N.Y.; s. John and Mary (Leidolf) M.; B.B.A., U. City N.Y. Researcher econs. dept. McGraw Hill & Co., N.Y.C.; mgr., asst. to pres. Indsl. Commodity Corp., J. Carvel Lange Inc. and J. Carvel Lange Internat., Inc., 1956—, corporate sec., 1958—, v.p., 1964—; pres. I.C. Investors Corp., 1972—, I.C. Pension Adv., Inc., 1977—. Trustee, Combined Indsl. Commodity Corp. and J. Carvel Lange Inc. Pension Plan, 1962—, J. Carvel Lange Internat. Inc. Profit Sharing Trust, 1969—, Combined Indsl. Commodity Corp. and J. Carvel Lange Inc. Employees Profit Sharing Plan, 1977—. Mem. grad. adv. bd. Bernard M. Baruch Coll., City U. N.Y., 1971—. Mem. Conf. Bd., Am. Statis. Assn., Newcomen Soc. N.Am. Club: Union League (N.Y.C.). Co-author: How Good A Sales Profit Are You, 1961; The Role of the Economic Consulting Firm; also numerous market surveys. Office: Room 1206 122 E 42d St New York NY 10168

MITTELSTAEDT, ARTHUR HOWARD, JR., edn. and recreation cons.; b. N.Y.C., Sept. 25, 1936; B.S., Syracuse (N.Y.) U., 1958; M.P.A. (Hegeman scholar 1959-61), N.Y. U., 1963, Ed.D., 1977; m. Sue Carol Olsen, 1962; children—Kurt Arthur, Karen Ma 8; asst. landscape architect N.Y.C. Housing Authority, 1959; landscape architect Nassau County Dept. Public Works, 1959-62, Office Joseph Gangemi, N.Y.C., part-time 1959; landscape architect, planning cons. Urban Planning Assos., Port Washington, N.Y., part-time, 1960—, Planning Assos., Mineola, N.Y., 1961-66; chmn. bd. P.A. Edn. and Recreations Cons., Inc., leisure systems planner, West Hempstead and Bohemia, N.Y., 1966—; adj. asst. prof. N.Y. U., 1965-70, Hunter Coll., 1971, So. Conn. State Coll., 1975-77; prof. Merrimack Valley Community Coll., 1973; asso. prof. C.W. Post Center, L.I. U.; participant confs. in field. Exec. bd. Nassau County council Boy Scouts Am., 1978-80; usher, vestryman St. Stephen's Episcopal Ch., Port Washington, 1975; corp. bd. dirs. Nassau-Suffolk YMCA, 1975-78; trustee Dikaia Found., 1977-80. Served as officer USAR, 1958-59. Disting. fellow N.Y. State Recreation and Park Soc. (chmn. licensing com. 1973-76); mem. Am. Soc. Landscape Architects, Am. Inst. Planners, Council Park and Recreation Cons., Internat. City Mgmt. Assn. (asso.), Council Ednl. Facility Planners, Soc. reatio Assn. (vice chmn. council recreation and park cons. 1973), AAHPER (trustee nat. found. 1974-76), Am. Forestry Assn., Am. Camping Assn., Conservation Edn. Assn., Am. Soc. Planning Ofcls., World Future Soc., Am. Gerontol. Soc., New Eng. Gerontol. Assn., L.I. Planners, N.H. Recreation and Park Soc., N.Y. State Outdoor Edn. Assn., Md. Park and Recreation Soc., System Safety Soc., Am. Community and Sch. Safety Assn., N.Y. Soc. Health, Phys. Edn. and Recreation (pres. leisure and recreation edn. council), Pa. Park and Recreation Soc., Nassau Recreation, Park and Conservation Soc. (chmn. civic affairs com. 1970-80; profl., presdl. and hon. mention awards 1963-78). Contbr. numerous articles, reports to profl. publs. Address: 39 Shadyside Ave Port Washington NY 11050

MITTENDORF, THEODOR HENRY, paper mfg. cons.; b. Clay Center, Kans., Jan. 14, 1895; s. Theodor Henry and Antonie (Carls) M.; B.S., Okla. State University, 1917; m. Dorothy E. Solger, May 18, 1919; 1 dau., Laone M. (Mrs. D. R. Hoerl). Lectr. extension div. Okla. State U., 1917; lectr., free lance writer, 1919-20; dept. supt. Armour & Co., Chgo., 1920-22; sec., dir. sales and advt. Mid-States Gummed Paper Co., Chgo., 1922-38; v.p. charge sales Industrial Training Inst., 1938-39, v.p., gen. mgr. The Gummed Products Co., Troy, Ohio, 1940-48; v.p. charge sales Hudson Pulp and Paper Corp., N.Y.C., 1948-56, exec. v.p., 1956-58, cons., 1958—; pres. Mitt Industries, Inc., Mount Dora, Fla., 1972—; dir. 5 East 71st St. Corp. Dir. Muscular Dystrophy Assn. Served from 2d lt. F.A. to 1st lt. AS, U.S. Army, World War I, AEF. Named to Okla. State U. Alumni Hall of Fame, 1961. Mem. Kraft Paper Assn. (dir., mem. exec. com. 1951-58), Gummed Industries Assn. (pres. 1955-56). Paper Bag Inst. (pres. 1955-56), Paper Club N.Y., Am. Legion, Symposiarchs, Kappa Sigma, Alpha Zeta, Pi Kappa Delta. Republican. Methodist. Mason; mem. Order Eastern Star. Clubs: Mount Dora (Fla.) Golf, Mount Dora Yacht; Ponte Vedra (Fla.); African Safari of Fla. Home: Box 1138 Mount Dora FL 32757 Office: PO Box 1138 Mount Dora FL 32757

MITTMAN, BEN DANIEL, health care exec.; b. Newton, Kans., July 28, 1940; s. Paul Herman and Leonore Arlene (Gardner) M.; R.N., Los Angeles County Sch. Nursing, 1965; B.A., San Francisco State Coll., 1968; M.P.H., U. Calif., Berkeley, 1970; exec. mgmt. program Yale U., 1979. Asst. to adminstr. Herrick Meml. Hosp., Berkeley, 1969-70; profl. hosp. planner Arthur D. Little, Internat., Terra Linda, Calif., 1970; adminstrv. asst. Mercy Hosps. of Sacramento, 1970-71; asst. adminstr. French Hosp., San Francisco, 1971-75; adminstr., asst. dir. mgmt. services div. Nat. Med. Enterprises, Inc., Los Angeles, 1975-77; asso. adminstr. Garfield Med. Center, Monterey Park, Calif., 1977-78, adminstr., 1978-80; v.p. mktg. Nat. Med. Health Care Services, Los Angeles, 1980—. Served in maj. USAF Res. Fellow Am. Coll. Hosp. Adminstrs. Democrat. Contbr. articles to profl. jours. Home: 3868 Berry Ct Studio City CA 91604 Office: 11620 Wilshire Blvd Los Angeles CA 90025

MIYAKE, SHIGEMITSU, banker; b. Osaka, Japan, Feb. 27, 1911; s. Shigetaka and Fumi (Ito) M.; LL.B., Tokyo Imperial U., 1933; m. Hina Inoue, May 24, 1935; children—Hiroko (Mrs. Taro Kimura), Atsuko (Mrs. Tohru Nagano), Yasuo. With Bank of Japan, 1933-67, br. mgr. Okayama, 1949-51, Kyoto, 1954-56, Nagoya, 1961-63, Osaka, 1963-66, dir., 1962-67; dep. pres. Tokai Bank Ltd., Nagoya, 1967-68, pres., 1968-69, chmn. bd., pres., 1969-75, chmn., 1975—. Recipient Blue Ribbon medal, 1974. Mem. Japan (dep. pres.), Nagoya (pres.) chambers commerce and industry, Japan Mgmt. Orgns. (exec. dir.) Fedn. Japan Econ. Orgns. (exec. dir.). Home: Tsukimigaoka Mansion C-7 2-5 Ho-o-cho Chikusa-Ku Nagoya Japan Office: Tokai Bank Ltd 21-24 Nishiki 3-chome Naka-ku Nagoya Japan

MIZEL, GERALD M., loan co. exec.; b. Mitchell, S.D., Nov. 18, 1933; s. Philip and Esther (Martinsky) M.; B.B.A., U. Miami, 1957; postgrad. Law Sch., DePaul U.; m. Liora Katzengold, Nov. 1, 1966; children—Michelle, Elliana. With Midland Fin. Co., Chgo., 1957—, now exec. v.p., sec., treas., dir.; exec. v.p., sec.-treas., dir. U.S. Auto Sales Inc., Chgo. Participant, 3d Econ. Conf., Jerusalem, 1973. Office: Midland Finance Co 7541 N Western Ave Chicago IL 60645

MIZELL, ANDREW HOOPER, III, concrete co. exec.; b. Franklin, Tenn., Sept. 26, 1926; s. Andrew Hooper, Jr. and Jennie McEwen (Fleming) M.; B.A., Venderbilt U., 1950; m. Julia Yolanda Mattei, Dec. 20, 1947; children—Andrew Hooper, Julia Felming. Supt., Wescon Constrn. Co., Nashville, 1950-52; accountant McIntyre & Asso., Nashville, 1952-55; credit mgr. Ingran Oil Co., Nashville, 1955-56, v.p. and dir., 1956-60; v.p., dir. Comml. Sign & Advt. Co., Nashville, 1957-59; v.p. and dir. Gen. Properties Co., New Orleans, 1957-62; v.p. and dir. Minn. Barge & Terminal Co., St. Paul, 1957-62; mgr. real estate and devel. Murphy Corp., El Dorado, Ark., 1962-63, mgr. retail sales, 1962-63; pres. and chmn. bd. Transit Ready Mix, Inc., Nashville, 1963—. Active United Givers Fund, 1965-66; chmn. Concrete div. Office Emergency Planning, 1965—; mem. Nat. UN Day Com., 1978. Served with USNR, 1944-46. Named Ark. Traveler, 1966, Ky. Col., 1969. Mem. Nat. Ready Mix Concrete Assn. (chmn. membership com. Tenn. sect. 1971—, chmn. marketing com. Tenn. chpt. 1973—), Assn. Gen. Contractors, Tenn. Bldg. Material Assn., Nat. Fedn. Ind. Businessmen, Portland Cement Assn., Nat. Area Bus. and Edn. Radio, Assn. Builders and Contractors, Spl. Indsl. Radio Service Industry, Tenn. Road Builders, Boat Owners Assn. U.S., Nashville C. of C., U.S. C. of C., Am. Concrete Inst. Clubs: Nashville Yacht, Nashville City, Belle Meade Country, Commodore Yacht (past commodore). Home: 4340 Beekman Dr Nashville TN 37215 Office: 2319 Crestmoor Rd Nashville TN 37215

MOAK, ROGER MARTIN, lawyer; b. Bklyn., Mar. 22, 1947; s. Lester and Phoebe (Elkins) M.; B.S., Cornell U., 1969; J.D., Georgetown U., 1972; postgrad. N.Y. U., 1972-73. Research asst. extension and pub. service div. Sch. Indsl. and Labor Relations, Cornell U., Ithaca, N.Y., 1967; staff asst. labor com. Transp. Assn. Am., Washington, 1968; research analyst, indsl. relations dept. Am. Trucking Assns., Inc., Washington, 1969; law clk. firm Speiser Shumate Geoghan Krause Rheingold & Madole, Washington, 1970-72; admitted to N.Y. bar, 1974, D.C. bar, 1975, U.S. Supreme Ct. bar, 1977; asso. firm Speiser & Krause, P.C., N.Y.C., 1972-77, mem. firm, treas. corp., 1977-80; asst. gen. counsel Ins. Services Office, N.Y.C., 1980—. Mem. Assn. Bar City N.Y. (com. ins. law), N.Y. County Lawyers Assn., Am., N.Y. State bar assns., D.C. Bar, Cornell Alumni Assn. (gov. N.Y.C.). Republican. Home: 330 E 46th St New York NY 10017 Office: Legal Dept Ins Services Office 160 Water St New York NY 10038

MOBLEY, NATHAN, JR., communications corp. exec.; b. Great Neck, N.Y., Sept. 11, 1934; s. Nathan and Eleanor (Smith) M.; B.A., Yale U., 1957; M.A., Columbia U., 1966, Ph.D., 1971; m. Melinda Menzies, Dec. 29, 1970; children—Sara Anne, Rob, Mark, Jennifer, Michael. Ins. broker Marsh & McLennan, 1957-62; stock broker Eastman Dillon, N.Y.C., 1962-64; tchr. Greenwich (Conn.) Country Day Sch., 1964-70; pres. Mobley & Bingham, Inc., San Francisco, 1970—. Served with AUS, 1957-66. Address: 50 Parker Ave San Francisco CA 94118

MOCCIA, ALFRED J., equipment mfg. co. exec.; b. Wilmington, Del., 1917; grad. U. Pa., 1941; LL.B., Temple U., 1949; married. Admitted to bar; with firm Drinker, Biddle & Reath, 1935-50; tax atty. E.I. duPont de Nemours & Co., 1950-52; asst. to exec. v.p., tax mgr. Gen. Aniline & Film Corp., 1952-59; v.p., treas. Am. Airlines Inc., 1959-67; v.p. Sperry Corp., 1967-74, treas., 1967-72, chief fin. officer, 1972—, sr. v.p., 1974-79, vice chmn. bd., 1979—, also dir.; dir. European-Am. Bank Corp., European-Am. Bank & Trust Co., Franklin Savs. Bank, Western Ins. Co., Bekaert Steel Wire Corp., Asso. Dry Goods Corp. Served with USAF, World War II. Office: Sperry Corp 1290 Ave of Americas New York NY 10019

MOCERINO, VINCENT JOSEPH, mktg. exec.; b. N.Y.C., Jan. 11, 1938; s. Vincent John and Julia (Castaldo) M.; student City U. N.Y., 1957-59; B.S., Phoenix U., 1960; postgrad. N.Y. U., 1965, Cornell U., 1970; m. Theresa Dellecave, July 1, 1962; children—Susan, Vincent. Sr. financial analyst Revlon, Inc., 1963-66; with The Nestle Co., Inc., White Plains, N.Y., 1966—, marketing controller, 1967-71, asst. to gen. sales mgr., 1971-72, asst. gen. mgr., 1972-74, product mgr., 1974—, asst. treas. Wine group, nat. sales mgr. chocolate div., 1977-79; asso. partner, nat. mktg./sales mgr. J.M. Blumon Import Co., Inc., wine import firm, San Francisco, 1979-80; nat. ops. mgr. Nestle Co., Inc., White Plains, N.Y., 1980—. Served with U.S. Army, 1956. Mem. Nat. Assn. Accountants. Club: Lions. Home: 269 London Rd Yorktown Heights NY 10598 Office: 369 Pine St San Francisco CA 94104

MOCIUK, YAR WASYL, corp. exec.; b. Mylowannia, Ukraine, Jan. 26, 1927; s. Mykola and Ewdochia (Hawrysh) M.; came to U.S., 1950, naturalized, 1956; B.A., N.Y.C. U., 1957; m. Psychology' Jackson (Miss.) State U., 1968; Ph.D., World U., Tucson. 1972; L.H.D., People U., 1973; m. Irene Groch, Apr. 12, 1959; children—Daria N., Natalie M. Plant mgr. Comprehensive Service Corp., N.Y.C., 1955-65; pres. C & M Film Service Corp., 1965-73; pres. Filmtreat Internat. Corp., N.Y.C., 1973—, also chmn. bd.; asst. dean communications Peoples U. of Americas, N.Y.C. Sec. St. Michaels PTA, Yonkers, N.Y.; treas. Ukrainian Free U. Found., Inc. Mem. Soc. Motion Picture TV Engrs., Ukranian Cinema Assn. Am. (pres.), Univ. Film Assn., Ukranian Inst. Am., Greek Catholic. Patentee method and apparatus for treating film. Home: 2 Essex Pl Bronxville NY 10708

MOCK, ALBERT KARL, JR., machine mfg. co. exec., architect; b. Abingdon, Va., Sept. 1, 1928; s. Albert K. and Annette (Barker) M.; B.S. in Architecture, U. Va., 1953; student Va. Poly. Inst., 1946-48; postgrad. Va. Highlands Community Coll., 1974; m. Margaret Turner, Mar. 6, 1964 (div. 1975); children—Karl Turner, Robert Stockton. Partner Pacific House Ltd., Tokyo, 1955-57; partner and co-founder Charles E. Smith Assos., Boston, 1957-58; co-founder, pres. Internat. Marine Ltd., Yokohama, Japan, 1958-61; co-founder Iron Mountain Stoneware, Inc., Laurel Bloomery, Tenn., 1961, dir., 1961—; co-founder Enterprise Devel., Inc., Oak Knoll, Damascus, Va., 1967, pres., 1967—; co-founder Mock-Wright, Inc., Damascus, Va., 1971, pres., 1971—; co-founder Montgomery Mining Mach. Mfg. Co., Ltd., Damascus, 1977, partner, 1977—. Mem. Damascus Town Council, 1964-68; dir., chmn. fin. com. Council of So. Mountains, Berea, Ky., 1965-69. Served to 1st lt. U.S. Army, 1953-55; Korea. Eagle Scout. Mem. U.S.-China Econ. Council. Home: Oak Knoll Damascus VA 24236 Office: Montgomery Mining Co Damascus Indsl Park PO Box 700 Damascus VA 24236

MOCKLER, COLMAN MICHAEL, JR., mfg. co. exec.; b. St. Louis, Dec. 29, 1929; s. Colman Michael and Veronica (McKenna) M.; A.B., Harvard, 1952, M.B.A., 1954; m. Joanna Lois Sperry, Dec. 28, 1957; children—Colman Michael III, Joanna Lois, Emily McKenna, Andrew Sperry. With Gen. Electric Co., 1954-55; mem. faculty Harvard Grad. Sch. Bus., 1955-57; with Gillette Co., Boston, 1957—, treas., 1965-68, v.p., 1967-68, sr. v.p., 1968-70, exec. v.p., 1970-71, vice chmn. bd., 1971-74, pres., chief operating officer, 1974-76, chief exec. officer, 1975—, chmn. bd., 1976—, dir., 1971—; dir. First Nat. Boston Corp., First Nat. Bank Boston, Fabreeka Products Co., John Hancock Mutual Life Ins. Co., Raytheon Co. Bd. dirs. Greater Boston YMCA, Boston Municipal Research Bur. Boston; chmn. corp. Simmons Coll.; pres. bd. overseers Harvard Coll.; mem. corp. Mus. Sci., Mass. Gen. Hosp. Served with AUS, 1948-49. Club: Harvard (N.Y.C.). Home: 37 Draper Rd Wayland MA 01778 Office: Gillette Co Prudential Tower Bldg Boston MA 02199

MODICA, ALFRED JOSEPH, mktg. communications mgmt. co. exec.; b. Riverdale, N.Y., Jan. 22, 1925; s. Vincent J. and Agatha S. (Nicosia) M.; certificate Morton Schs. Real Estate, N.Y.C., 1963; certificate Henry George Sch. Social Sci., N.Y.C., 1966; LL.B., Blackstone Sch. Law, Chgo., 1965, J.D., 1968; B.S. in Bus. Adminstrn., Empire State Coll. State U. N.Y., 1976; M.B.A. with distinction, Long Island U., 1979; m. Teresa D. O'Donnell, Sept. 7, 1947; children—Christopher, Stephen, Eugene. Sales mgr. Electrolux Corp., N.Y.C., 1946-49; free-lance mktg. dir., 1949-54; pres., dir. Meadowstone, Inc., N.Y.C., 1954-62; marketing communications cons. on franchise programming, 1962-66; exec. v.p. Seltz Franchising Devel., Inc., N.Y.C., 1967-69; pres., dir. OFI Corp., Maspeth, N.Y., 1969—, Lee Myles Assos. Corp., Maspeth, 1970—; exec. v.p., dir. Lee Myles Corp., Maspeth, 1970—, Alfred J. Modica Assos., 1974—; prof., area dir. mgmt. Mercy Coll., 1974—, also ednl. workshop sessions for minority groups, workshop sessions and seminars for fed. and state govts., bus., 1970—; instr., seminar leader mgmt., div. bus. and mgmt. N.Y. U. Sch. Continuing Edn. Served with USMCR, 1943-46. Mem. Inst. for Applied Communications (dir.), Am. Acad. Consultants, Mid-Hudson Inst., Nat. Small Bus. Assn., C. of C. U.S., Internat. Platform Assn., Alpha Psi Omega, Kappa Delta Pi. Asso. editor Franchising Around the World mag., 1970—. Contbr. articles to profl. publs. Office: 700 Scarsdale Ave Scarsdale NY 10583

MOECKER, MICHAEL EUGENE, assn. exec.; b. Albany, N.Y., Dec. 6, 1943; s. Herman Eugene and Mildred (Busch) M.; B.S. in Advt., Syracuse U., 1965; m. Christine Kathleen Pledger, Oct. 11, 1969; children—Michael, Graham, Kelly. Mktg. rep. Lehigh Portland Co., Orlando, Fla., 1970-72, regional credit mgr., Miami, Fla., 1972-76; exec. v.p. Nat. Assn. Credit Mgmt. of So. Fla., Miami, 1976—; also editor, pub. monthly newsletter; guest lectr. U. Miami, also internat. seminars and various assn. ednl. seminars. Mem. Internat. adv. bd. U. Miami. Served to lt. USNR, 1965-69. Recipient awards U.S. Navy. Mem. Broward County C. of C. (commerce and industry task force), Phi Delta Theta. Republican. Mem. Dutch Reformed Ch. Home: 1101 NW 94th Ave Plantation FL 33322 Office: PO Box 380728 Miami FL 33138

MOEHLMAN, ROBERT STEVENS, oil and gas cons.; b. Rochester, N.Y., Feb. 23, 1910; s. Conrad Henry and Bertha (Young) M.; B.A., U. Rochester, 1931; M.A., Harvard, 1932, Ph.D. in Geology, 1935; m. Lillian Johnson, Sept. 17, 1934; children—Karen, Linda Gail. Exploration geologist for mining cos. in Can., Mex., Colo., summers 1929-35; mine geologist Anaconda Copper Mining Co.,

1936-38, at Butte, Mont., exploration geologist, Inspiration, Ariz., 1938-40, Reno, 1941-44; chief geologist S. Am. Mines Co., N.Y.C., 1945-50; exec. v.p., dir. Austral Oil Co., Inc., Houston, 1951-62; pres., dir. Newmont Oil Co., 1962-77, vice chmn. bd., 1978-79; pres., dir. Newmont Oil Co. Internat., 1962-77, vice chmn. bd., 1978-79; chmn. bd., dir. Yucca Water Co., 1962-79; chmn. bd. Can. Export Gas & Oil, 1974-76; oil and gas cons., Houston, 1979—; mem. Nat. Petroleum Council, 1973-79. Fellow Geol. Soc. Am.; mem. Ind. Petroleum Assn. Am. (v.p. 1966-68), AIME, Am. Assn. Petroleum Geologists, Houston Geol. Soc. Clubs: Houston, Petroleum (Houston); Harvard, Canadian, Mining (N.Y.C.). Home: 242 Maple Valley Rd Houston TX 77056 Office: Suite 917 600 Jefferson St Houston TX 77002

MOELLER, WARREN ELBERT, educator; b. Frederick, Okla., Oct. 12, 1926; s. Walter Edward and Rebecca (Anderson) M.; B.S. in Bus., U. Okla., 1949, M.B.A., 1950; postgrad. U. Nebr. Instr., Cumberland Coll., Williamsburg, Ky., 1950-51; asst. prof. Ga. Inst. Tech., 1950-58; research asso. Bur. Bus. Research, U. Okla., 1958-63; asso. prof bus. Midwestern State U., Wichita Falls, Tex., 1963—, chmn. dept., 1964-79; investment cons. Served with AUS, 1945-47. Mem. Fin. Mgmt. Assn., Beta Gamma Sigma, Phi Chi Theta, Sigma Nu. Republican. Presbyterian. Club: Elks. Home: 3008 Barrywood Dr Wichita Falls TX 76309 Office: Midwestern State University Wichita Falls TX 76308

MOELLERING, MELVYN WILLIAM, ret. banker; b. Florissant, Mo., Dec. 28, 1912; s. Joseph C. and Gertrude C. (Gettemeier) M.; grad. high sch.; m. Loretta E. Meyer, May 10, 1938; children—Jeanne Moellering Carney, Suzanne Moellering Sheehan, Mary R. Moellering Preuss, John J., James M. Asst. cashier Florissant Bank, 1935-40, v.p., 1948-56, pres., chmn. bd., 1956-79. Treas., Florissant Library Bd., 1942-58, Florissant Centennial Corp., 1958; chmn. Zoning and Planning Commn., City of Florissant, 1952-54, Park Bd., 1958-63. Trustee, Christian Hosp. N.W., 1963, chmn. bd., 1973-76; bd. mgrs. No. County YMCA. Named Bus. Man of Year, Jaycees of Florissant, 1961, Man of Year, Florissant Profl. Womens Club, 1971, St. Louis County Businessperson of Year Florissant C. of C., 1975. Mem. Assn. Bankers of St. Louis and St. Louis County (exec. com.). Rotarian. Club: Norwood Hills Country. Home: 2 Valley Dr Florissant MO 63031

MOFFATT, LESLIE MACK, aluminum co. exec.; b. New Orleans, Sept. 6, 1928; s. Frank Leslie and Vesta Jane (Sanders) M.; B.A., Southeastern La. U., 1949; m. Carolyn Joyce Guess, Sept. 6, 1952; children—Leslie S., Vance P., Neil S. With Gen. Electric Co., Decatur, Ill., 1950-64, mgr. bus. analysis and planning, 1960-64; exec. v.p., dir. fin. Croft Metals Co., McComb, Miss., 1964-72; pres. Better-Bilt Aluminum Co., Smyrna, Tenn., 1972—. Served with Fin. Corps, U.S. Army, 1952-54. Recipient Disting. Citizenship award Rutherford Courier, 1979. Home: 4080 Port Cleburne Ct Hermitage TN 37076 Office: Better-Bilt Aluminum Co 12th and G St Smyrna TN 37167

MOFFET, DONALD PRATT, computer co. exec.; b. St. Paul, Jan. 30, 1932; s. William Theodore and Dorothy (Pratt) M.; student Wesleyan U., 1949-50; B.B.A., U. Minn., 1953, M.B.A., 1954; m. Sally E. Hullsiek, June 1, 1955; children—Kerry, Kenneth, Mark. With Honeywell, Inc., 1957-72, mgr. bus. devel., Mpls., 1968-70, dir. computer services, 1970-72; v.p. mktg. AM Internat., Chgo., 1972-77; exec. v.p., chief operating officer Sycor, Inc., Ann Arbor, Mich., 1977-78, pres., 1978-79; corp. v.p., gen. mgr. computer systems div. Perkin-Elmer Corp., Oceanport, N.J., 1980—; dir. Wells Electronics Corp., South Bend, Ind. Served with USAF, 1955-57. Presbyterian. Club: Navesink Country. Home: 4 Broadmoor Dr Rumson NJ 07760 Office: 106 Apple St Tinton Falls NJ 07724

MOFFITT, DAVID ANDREW, oil co. exec.; b. Washburn, Wis., Jan. 10, 1927; s. Robert Hugh and Goldie Alma (Steele) M.; A.A., Duluth Jr. Coll., 1948; B.A., U. Minn., 1950; M.B.A., Pace U., 1977; m. Phyllis June Frisk, June 24, 1950; children—Robert Hugh, Patricia Lynn, Douglas David. Promotion mgr. Winona (Minn.) Daily News and radio affiliate KWNO, 1950-53: mgr. pub. relations North Central Airlines, Mpls., 1953-57; asst. to v.p. pub. relations Air Transport Assn. Am., Washington, 1957-63; dir. editorial services TWA, N.Y.C., 1963-69, dir. press relations, 1969-73; dir. corporate information and news services Conoco Inc. (formerly Continental Oil Co.), Stamford, Conn., 1973—. Served with USAAF, 1945-46. Mem. Pub. Relations Soc. Am., Aviation/Space Writers Assn., Assn. Petroleum Writers, Aircraft Owners and Pilots Assn., Kappa Tau Alpha, Sigma Delta Chi. Club: National Press (Washington). Home: Deer Hill Ln Briarcliff Manor NY 10510 Office: High Ridge Park Stamford CT 06904

MOFFITT, PETER MIDDLETON, financial cons.; b. New Haven, Apr. 16, 1926; s. John Adams and Virginia Marriott (Hellen) M.; B.A., Yale U., 1948: m. Florence F. Beach, June 24, 1962; children—Margaret, Anne, Johanna. Staff, Hanover Bank, N.Y.C., 1948-55; mgr. mktg. Conn. Hard Rubber Co., New Haven, 1955-58: exec. v.p. Conn. Devel. Credit Corp., Meriden, 1958-60; asso. Harriman Ripley & Co., Inc., N.Y.C., 1960-63; ind. cons., 1963-73: pres. Moffitt and Co. Inc., Southport, Conn., 1973—; dir. Narda Microwave Corp., Hussey Mfg. Co. Inc., E.A. Sween Co. Trustee Green Farms Acad., 1968-73, Pomfret Sch., 1978—; warden St. Timothy's Episcopal Ch., Fairfield, Conn., 1973-76. Mem. Am. Mgmt. Assn. Clubs: Yale (N.Y.C.); Pequot Yacht, Fairfield County Hunt. Home: 3632 Congress St Fairfield CT 06430 Office: PO Box 532 Southport CT 06490

MOGDIS, FRANZ JOSEPH, bus. mgmt. cons.; b. Hastings, Mich., Jan. 12, 1941; s. Joseph and Frances Lucille (Maurer) M.; student Northwestern U., 1959-61, U. Md., 1961-64; B.A., U. Mich., 1968; m. Diane L.; children—Kim, Mellissa. Dir. Bendix Applied Sci. and Tech. Div., Ann Arbor, Mich., 1970-74, gen. mgr. Bendix Energy, Environment and Tech. Office, Ann Arbor, 1974-76; pres. Chase-Mogdis, Inc., Ann Arbor, 1976—, T-Drill, Inc., Ann Arbor, 1978—; lectr. to maj. univs., U.S. Fgn. Service Inst. Pres. Urban Adv. Group, 1971-75, Ann Arbor Tomorrow, 1974-77; mem. Ann Arbor Planning Commn., 1971-75. Served with U.S. Army, 1960-63. Mem. Am. Soc. Planning Ofcls., Am. Mgmt. Assn., AAAS. Contbr. articles to profl. jours. Home: 1220 Ferdon St Ann Arbor MI 48103 Office: 204 E Washington St Ann Arbor MI 48104

MOGEL, RONALD DAVID, new products planning co. exec.; b. Washington, June 2, 1936; s. Simon Leon and Betty Harriet (Katz) M.; B.A., Duke U., 1958; m. Christie Alexander Reed, Nov. 12, 1976; children—Rondi Susan, Kristi Anne. Advt. copywriter Ayer ABH, Chgo., 1959-61; advt. copywriter Leo Burnett Co., Chgo., 1961-63; creative supr. Batten, Barton, Durstine & Osborn, N.Y.C., 1963-65, v.p., creative dir., 1965-67, chmn. new products com., 1965-67, sr. v.p., creative dir., Los Angeles, 1972-74; sr. v.p., creative dir. Rockwell & Assos., N.Y.C., 1967-69; pres. Gull Lake Conf., Inc., Mpls., 1969-72; pres. Wayne Jervis, Jr., and Assos., Los Angeles, 1974-76; pres. New Products Network, Los Angeles, 1976—. Served with USMC, 1958-59. Recipient more than 100 awards for advt. excellence, 6 nat. awards for mktg. excellence. Mem. Am. Mktg. Assn., Am. Mgmt. Assn. Home: 14020 Old Harbor Ln Marina del Rey CA 90291 Office: 2049 Century Park E Los Angeles CA 90067

MOGELEVER, BERNARD, public relations exec.; b. Newark, Oct. 15, 1940; s. Louis J. and Kate (Rosenblatt) M.; B.A., Rutgers U., 1962; m. Diane Hinkley, Feb. 19, 1966; children—Elisa, Jonathan G. News and feature writer S.I. Advance, 1965-66; public relations and advt. writer The Nat. Found., N.Y.C., 1966-68; exec. A.A. Schechter Assos., Inc., N.Y.C., 1968-73; v.p. Harshe-Rotman & Druck, Inc., N.Y.C., 1973—. Served to 1st lt. USAF, 1962-65. Office: 300 E 44th St New York NY 10017

MOGENSEN, CHARLES RAY, JR., food service adminstr.; b. Elizabeth, N.J., May 7, 1946; s. Charles Ray and Helen O. (Holland) M.; student in food service supervision Middlesex County Vocat. Coll., 1972; m. Linda Diane, Apr. 25, 1970; children—Charles Ray, Jason Christopher, Eric Stephen. Chef, St. Elizabeth Hosp., Elizabeth, N.J., 1969; food service dir. Cornell Hall Conv. Center, Union, N.J., 1970—; pvt. practice catering, 1970—. Mem. Republican Nat. Com. Served with USMC, 1964-68; Vietnam. Recipient 3d prize Food Mgmt. Mag. Recipe Contest, 1977; cert. merit Nat. Escargot Recipe Contest, 1979; dist. winner desserts Gen. Foods Recipe Contest, 1980. Mem. Internat. Food Service Execs. Assn. (cert.; pres. N.J. br. 1977-78, dir. br. 1974-77; spl. service citation 1977), VFW. Episcopalian. Clubs: Elks, Masons. Home: 33 Park Dr Kenilworth NJ 07033 Office: 234 Chestnut St Union NJ 07083

MOHLMAN, PAUL HEINZE, oil co. exec.; b. Chgo., June 5, 1949; s. John William and Myrtle (Heinze) M.; B.S. in Mech. Engring., Calif. State U., San Luis Obispo, 1972; m. Gail Ann Wells, Nov. 23, 1977. Oil well treater Getty Oil Co., 1968; asst. engr. Standard Oil Co. Calif., 1969; treater's asst. Halliburton Services Co., 1970; engr.'s asst. Rockwell Internat. Co., 1971; project engring. mgr. Mobil Oil Corp., Torrance, Calif., 1972-80; corp. process planning exec., shale, coal and synfuel planning Getty Oil Corp., Los Angeles, 1980—. Mem. ASME, Soc. Automotive Engrs., Calif. State U. Alumni Assn. (v.p. 1979). Republican. Baptist. Patentee heat exchanger. Home: 904 24th St Hermosa Beach CA 90254 Office: Getty Oil Corp 3810 Wilshire Blvd Los Angeles CA

MOHLMAN, ROBERT HENRY, container mfg. co. exec.; b. New Haven, May 29, 1918; s. Floyd William and Mary Franklin (Savage) M.; A.B., U. Chgo., 1939, J.D., 1941; M.B.A., Harvard U., 1943; m. Ina Maria Meyer, Aug. 23, 1941; children—Robert Peter, David John. Admitted to Ill. bar, 1941; mgmt. trainee Inland Steel Corp., 1941-42; with Inland Container Corp., Indpls., 1946-66; with Ball Corp., Muncie, Ind., 1966—, v.p. fin. and adminstrn., 1968-78; sr. v.p., chief fin. officer, 1978—, also dir.; dir. Merchants Nat. Bank, Muncie. Served to 1st lt. U.S. Army, 1943-46. Mem. Ind. Mfg. Assn. (dir.), Phi Delta Theta, Phi Delta Phi. Democrat. Unitarian. Home: 3405 N Vienna Woods Dr Muncie IN 47304 Office: 345 S High St Muncie IN 47302

MOHR, BOUDEWIJN, banking exec.; b. Hilversum, Holland, Sept. 4, 1940; came to U.S., 1972; s. Bernard and Helena Josephina (Heybroek) M.; LL.M., U. Leiden (Holland), 1965; M.B.A., Insead, Fontainebleau, France, 1969; m. Annette H. Schoonbeek, Feb. 19, 1966; children—Vanessa Victoria, Nadim Bernard. Asst. cashier Bank Am., Amsterdam, Holland, 1967-68; personal asst. to pres. Damco Shipping, Rotterdam, Holland, 1969-71; trainee Chase Manhattan Bank, London, 1971-72; 2d v.p., French corp. desk div. fgn. direct investment Chase N.Y., N.Y.C., 1973-78; v.p. Societe Generale for French, European, and Canadian Investments in U.S., N.Y.C., 1979—. Bd. dirs. All Children's Theatre N.Y., N.Y.C. Mem. Netherland Club N.Y., Dutch Fin. Club. Author: The Language of International Trade, 1977. Home: 111 E 80th St New York NY 10021 also Briar Creek Rd RD 1 Box 279 Otego NY 13825 Office: 50 Rockefeller Plaza New York NY 10020

MOHR, JON ERNST, mfg. co. exec.; b. Danville, Ill., Oct. 26, 1943; s. Ernst August and Eugenia Ester (Jordan) M.; B.S. in Accountancy, U. Ill., 1966, M. Com., 1973; m. Susan E. Bengry; children—Laura, Todd, Robert, Douglas. Auditor, Deere & Co., Moline, Ill., 1966-70; dir. univ. budget systems U. Ill., 1970-75; v.p., comptroller Allerton Implement Co., Sidell, Ill., 1975-79, pres., 1980—; farm mgr. JDSM Farms. Life mem. Am. Conservative Union. Cert. in food service sanitation, Ill. Mem. U.S. C. of C., Ill. Retail Farm Equipment Assn., Assn. M.B.A. Execs., Vermillon County (Ill.) Farm Bur. Clubs: Danville (Ill.) Country, Elks, Sidell Aqua 20 (dir.).

MOHR, LIONEL CHARLES, mgmt. cons.; b. N.Y., Dec. 18, 1927; s. Lionel C. and Emma Ann (Stohldrier) M.; went to Can., naturalized, 1967; A.B., Wesleyan U., 1950; M.B.A., Harvard U., 1959; m. Patricia Margaret Sinclair, Aug. 24, 1968; children—Lionel Thomas, Deborah Susan, Sharon Patricia, Deborah Anne, Douglas Tredwell, John David Edward. Retail salesman Scott Paper Co., N.Y.C., after 1950, then retail dist. sales mgr., Binghamton, N.Y., advt. staff asst., Phila., 1959-60, asst. merchandising mgr., Phila., 1960-61; mgr. consumer products div. E.B. Eddy Co., Ottawa, Ont., Can., 1961-62; product mgr. Gen. Foods, Ltd., Toronto, Ont., 1962, sales promotion mgr., 1963-64, product planning mgr., 1964, sr. product mgr., 1965; cons. Stevenson & Kellogg Co., Toronto, 1966, prin., 1967, then prin. in-charge of mktg.; dir. mktg. Toronto Star Ltd., 1971, v.p. marketing, 1974-77, dir., 1975-78; v.p., dir. Torstar Corp., 1977-79; pres. L. Mohr & Assos., Toronto, 1979—; operating bd. dirs. Canadian Opera Co., 1976—, bd. govs., 1977—, pres., 1978-79; chmn., dir. Comac Communications Ltd., 1974-79; dir. Metromarket Newspapers Ltd., 1974-78. Founding dir. Peel Family Services, 1970, dir., 1973-75, treas., 1974-75, mem. exec. com., 1974-77; mem. public info. com. Canadian Diabetic Assn., 1979—; chmn. bd. of stewards Christ Ch. United Clarkson, 1963, elder, 1964-79; nat. chmn. dept. planning assistance United Ch. of Can., 1971-72. Served to sgt., Transp. Corps, U.S. Army, 1950-52. Mem. Am. Mktg. Assn. (dir. Toronto chpt. 1965-69), Internat. Newspaper Advt. Execs. (chmn. mktg. mgmt. com. 1971-79), Canadian Daily Newspaper Pubs. Assn. (dir. 1975-79). Presbyterian. Clubs: Rotary; Niagara Falls (N.Y.) Country; Nat., Empire, Canadian, Mississauga Golf and Country. Home: 460 Mountain View Dr Lewiston NY 14092 Office: 105 Davenport Rd Toronto ON M5R 1H6 Canada

MOHR, ROBERT WOOD, toiletries co. exec.; b. Glen Gardner, N.J., Jan. 30, 1943; s. Jack Hankins and Elizabeth (Wood) M.; B.A., Bloomfield Coll., 1966; postgrad. Fairleigh Dickinson U. Sch. Bus., 1967-68. Asst. to dean students Bloomfield (N.J.) Coll., 1967-68; v.p. fin. Products of Excellence, Ltd., N.Y.C., 1968-71: pres., owner Mohr Asso. Industries, Montclair, N.J., 1971—, also divs. Perfumes of Hawaii Ltd. and SPA Bath Products, Ltd.; mktg. cons. Aide de Camp, Ltd.; dir. House of Excellence. Soccer coach Drew U., Madison, N.J., 1972—; mem. Football Found. and Hall of Fame. Served with N.J. N.G., 1966-74. Recipient Outstanding Airman award, 1969. Mem. Advt. Club, Sales Mgrs. Assn., Bloomfield Coll. Alumni Assn. (pres. 1968). Republican. Presbyterian. Club: Touchdown (N.Y.C.). Home: 483 Park St Upper Montclair NJ 07043 Office: PO Box AD Montclair NJ 07042

MOHS, BRUCE BALDWIN, mfg. co. exec.; b. Madison, Wis., Oct. 29, 1932; s. Carl Elijah and Doris (Baldwin) M.; B.B.A., So. Methodist U., 1955; m. Jeannette Marjory Hight, June 22, 1963; children—Julia Grace, Bruce Eric, Kathryn Mae. Owner-mgr., Ivy Inn Motor Hotel, Madison, 1957-79, part owner, 1979—; pres. Mohs Seaplane Corp., operators aircraft and mfrs. motor vehicles, Verone, Wis., 1970—; owner Der Deutsche Raum, restaurant, Verone, 1970—, Mohs Auto Museum, Verone, 1970—; treas. Mohs Realty Corp., 1957—; pres. Bicentennial Manned Flight-1983 Ltd., 1976—. Served as officer USAF, 1956-57. Rotary Internat. Exchange fellow, 1968. Mem. Am. Hotel and Motel Assn. Republican. Presbyterian. Clubs: Madison Rotary West, Madison Slide and Camera (pres. 1980), Shriners (past pres. Madison). Author articles on antique automobiles. Home: 5226 Hedden Circle Middleton WI 53562 Office: 2355 University Ave Madison WI 53705 also Mohs Seaplane Corp Route 9 Verone WI 53593

MOIR, DOUGLAS A., Indsl. engr.; b. Newark, Oct. 2, 1938; s. Archibald and Christina (Jeffrey) M.; B.S., Rutgers U., 1969; m. Elizabeth Ann Rice, Sept. 20, 1958; children—Margaret Jean, Sharon Marie. Computer operator Bendix Corp., Teterboro, N.J., 1964-66; jr. indsl. engr. Tung-Sol Corp., Livingston, N.J., 1966-69; indsl. engr., prodn. supr. Sandoz Pharm., East Hanover, N.J., 1969-74: sr. indsl. engr. Hoffmann-LaRoche, Inc., Nutley, N.J., 1974—. Served to aerographer's mate 1st class U.S. Navy, 1957-64. Registered profl. engr., Calif. Mem. Am. Inst. Indsl. Engrs. Democrat. Presbyterian. Clubs: Pioneer Social and Athletic (Hasbrouck Heights, N.J.), Masons. Home: 21 Fordham Rd Clifton NJ 07013 Office: 340 Kingsland St Nutley NJ 07110

MOISA, JULIO ERNESTO, export co. exec.; b. El Salvador, Dec. 30, 1949; came to U.S., 1978; s. Carlos Calileo and Concepcion (Parada) M.; Indsl. Engr. degree, Universidad Nacional de el Salvador, 1977; m. M. Riad, June 21, 1969; 1 dau., Claudia Eugenia. Gen. mgr. Corporacion Tecnica Alfa y Beta S.A., San Salvador, El Salvador, 1975-77, dir., 1977-78; under dir., head research dept. Camara Salvadorena de la Industria de la construcion, San Salvador, 1977; regional mgr. for C. Am., Semsco Internat., San Salvador, 1977-78, gen. mgr., Tampa, Fla., 1978-80; pres. Export Mgmt. Internat., Inc., Tampa, 1980—; dir. Secomsa de C.V. El Salvador. Mem. Am. Water Works Assn., ASTM, Asociacion Interamericana de Ingenieros Sanitarios. Roman Catholic. Office: PO Box AP-16000 Tampa FL 33617

MOISE, FRANCIS DAVIS, brokerage co. exec.; b. Sumter, S.C., Dec. 31, 1935; d. Francis Marion and Ella Pauline (Blanding) M.; B.S., U. S.C., 1958; postgrad. Wharton Inst. Fin., 1972-74; m. Roland Tucker Nettles; children—Helen Penina, Francis Davis, Robert Mason, Margaret Linn, John Stone. Registered rep. Bache & Co., Inc., Charlotte, N.C., 1959-70, resident mgr., Fort Worth, 1970-76, Columbia, S.C., 1976-77; v.p. instl. sales Bache Halsey Stuart Inc., 1977—; mng. partner Moise & Haritt, Sumter, S.C., 1978—; pres. The Moise Co., Sumter, 1978—, Eastside, Inc., Sumter, 1978—; advisor in field, 1978—. Solicitor United Fund, 1968-72; sect. chmn. United Way, 1973, div. dir., 1977; deacon Presbyn. Ch., 1970-76; bd. dirs. Boystown, Charlotte, 1968—, founder, 1968. Mem. Leadership Ft. Worth, 1972. Served with inf. U.S. Army, 1958. Mem. Nat. Assn. Securities Dealers, Greater Columbia C. of C. (chmn. transp. com., dir. 1977-79), Sigma Nu. Clubs: Palmetto (Columbia, S.C.); Rotary; Petroleum Ft. Worth, Charlotte Athletic. Home: 123 Reynolds Rd Sumter SC 29150 Office: Executive Bldg 410 W Liberty St Suite 200 Sumter SC 29150

MOLAN, RICHARD EDWARD, lawyer, union exec.; b. Manchester, N.H., Nov. 30, 1947; s. Edward P. and Victoria J. (Pecor) M.; B.A., U. N.H., 1969; J.D., Franklin Pierce Law Center, Concord, N.H., 1979; m. Patricia L. Quinn, Aug. 30, 1969; children—Shauna Elizabeth, Maura Ann. Asst. mgr. Brighams Inc., Arlington, Mass., 1970; field rep. State Employees Assn. N.H., Concord, 1970-73, asst. exec. dir., 1972—, chief negotiator, 1979—; admitted to N.H. bar, 1979; partner firm Cahill, Murtha & Molan, Concord, 1979—; mem. nat. collective bargaining com. Assembly Govtl. Employees; lectr. U. N.H., Plymouth State Coll., Franklin Pierce Law Center. Bd. dirs., exec. com. N.H. Council World Affairs, 1975—; pres. Acacia Frat. Bldg. Corp., 1972-76. Recipient Paul A. Gilman Alumni award U. N.H., 1971. Mem. Am. Arbitration Assn., Am. Bar Assn., N.H. Bar Assn. Democrat. Roman Catholic. Author: Simulex, 1968. Home: 90 Linda Ln Manchester NH 03104 Office: 163 Manchester St Concord NH 03301

MOLES, STEPHEN DAVID, JR., mgmt. cons.; b. Gary, Ind., Apr. 14, 1949; s. Stephen David and Rose Rita (Pustzay) M.; B.S., U. Wis., 1971; postgrad. Marquette U., Milw.; m. Linda Lee LeRoy, June 25, 1979; children—Lisa Jean, Steven Michael. Asst. to v.p., sales mgr. Amity Leather Products Corp., West Bend, Wis., 1972-74; asst. gen. mgr., recruiting mgr. Purcell Systems, Inc., Milw., 1974-76; sr. mktg. cons. C.I.M.I. Co., Milw., 1976-77; pres. Corp. Resources, Inc., exec. recruiting and gen. cons. firm, Milw., 1977-79; pres. S. David Moles Assos., mgmt. cons., Houston, 1979—; v.p., bus. devel. mgr. K.J.M. Enterprises, Inc., Houston, 1979—. Mem. Delta Upsilon (co-founder, past pres. alumni corp.). Republican. Roman Catholic. Author studies, reports in field. Home: 16630 La Avenida Dr Houston TX 77062

MOLESKI, ANTHONY GERARD, mail order co. exec., mfg. exec.; b. Feasterville, Pa., Apr. 4, 1957; s. Anthony Joseph and Claire Marie (Schoppy) M.; B.S. in Econs., Wharton Sch., U. Pa., 1979, B.A. in Public Policy, 1979. Adminstrv. aide purchasing dept. U. Pa., 1975-78; adminstrv. aide Naval Air Devel. Center, Warminster, Pa., 1978-79; internal auditor Gen. Electric Co. Space Div., 1979—; owner, pres. Gen. Merchandising Corp., 1976—. Mem. Phila. 27th Ward Republican Exec. Com., 1978—. Recipient Cert. of Achievement, Gen. Electric Co., 1980. Mem. Internat. Entrepreneurs' Assn. Republican. Roman Catholic. Home: 11 N Westview Feasterville PA 19047

MOLESSA, EUGENE JOHN, petroleum products co. exec.; b. Binghamton, N.Y., Mar. 20, 1938; s. Demetrius and Anna M.; B.A., St. Bernard's Coll., 1959, postgrad., 1963-66; postgrad. Syracuse U., 1967-68; m. Patricia M. Boyle, Feb. 27, 1970; children—Thomas, Karen. High sch. tchr., Syracuse, N.Y., 1960-61, 66-69; adminstrv. mgr. H. J. Heinz Co., Pitts., 1969-72; adminstr. Calgon Corp., Pitts., 1972-76; gen. mgr. John T. Howe, Inc., Lake Ariel, Pa., 1976—. Served with U.S. Army, 1961-63. Mem. Hawley-Lake Wallenpaupack C. of C. (pres. 1980). Roman Catholic. Office: PO Box 125 Lake Ariel PA 18436

MOLITOR, GRAHAM THOMAS TATE, lawyer, bus. exec.; b. Seattle, Apr. 6, 1934; s. Robert Franklin and Louise Margaret (Graham) M.; B.S., U. Washington, 1955; LL.B., Am. U., 1963; m. Carlotta Jean Crate, July 30, 1960; children—Graham Thomas Tate, Jr., Anne Therese, Christopher Robert. Research asst. U. Wash., Seattle, 1957; bailiff U.S. Criminal Ct. for D.C., 1958-59; admitted to D.C. bar, 1963, legis. counsel U.S. Ho. of Reps., Washington, 1961-63; dir. candidate research Rockefeller for Pres. com., 1963-64, 68; D.C. counsel, asst. dir. govt. relations Nabisco, Inc., Washington, 1964-70; dir. govt. relations Gen. Mills, Inc., Washington, 1970-77; pres., chmn. bd., chief operating officer Pub. Policy Forecasting, Inc., Potomac, Md., 1977—; adj. prof. Grad. Sch. Bus. Am. U., Washington, 1969-75; dir. research White House Conf. on Indsl. World Ahead, 1971-72; mem. White House Adv. Com. on Social Indicators, 1975-76; guest. lectr. numerous univs. Del. White Confs. on Food, Nutrition and Health, 1969-71, White House Conf. on

Youth, 1970. Served to 1st lt. U.S. Army, 1958-61. Recipient Distinguished Service award Grocery Mfrs. Am., 1974-73, Nat. Consumer Info. Center, 1974, Am. Mgmt. Assn., 1973. Mem. Washington Bus.-Govt. Relations Council, Washington Indsl. Rountable, E.D. Export Council, World Future Soc. (gen. chmn. 2d Gen. Assembly 1975, Distinguished Service award 1975), Phi Kappa Sigma, Phi Alpha Delta. Republican. Presbyterian. Club: University. Contbg. editor Food Tomorrow Newsletter, 1976-77; contbr. articles to profl. jours.; bd. editors World Food Prospects and Agricultural Production, 1977; editorial bd. Bus. Tomorrow Newsletter. Home and Office: 9208 Wooden Bridge Rd Potomac MD 20854

MOLITOR, HAROLD O., ins. exec.; b. Francesville, Ind., June 18, 1914; s. John Frank and Ferne V. (Parker) M.; student Depauw U., Greencastle, Ind., 1932; m. Mary Ann Krise, July 2, 1938; children—Harold O. II, Shirley Ann. Field rep. charge Northeastern Ind., Simmons Hardware Co., 1937-40; with Continental Casualty Co., 1940-56, spl. agt. burglary dept., 1941-46, prodn. mgr., dishonesty ins. div., 1947-53, asst. v.p., sales mgr. accident and health dept., 1953-56; mgr. inland marine dept. Transp. Ins. Co., 1941-53, prodn. and underwriting mgr., 1941-56; now co-chmn. bd., cons. Continental Agy. Co.; dir. Diversified Investment Co. Recipient U. Utah Hon. Alumnus award, 1970. Mem. Phi Delta Kappa. Roman Catholic. Clubs: Salt Lake Country, Alta, Ambassador, Rotary, Serra (past pres.). Home: 1832 Princeton Ave Salt Lake City UT 84108 Office: 320 E 4th St Salt Lake City UT 84111

MOLL, KENDALL DEAN, educator, cons.; b. Oakdale, Calif., Apr. 30, 1927; s. Leo Raymond and Erna Augusta (Schattenburg) M.; B.S., U.S. Naval Acad., 1950; M.S., Stanford U., 1952, Ph.D., 1967; m. Barbara Lucille Delphey, Sept. 2, 1951; children—Stanton, Howard, Martin. Electronic engr. U.S. Air Force, McClellan AFB, Calif., 1950-51; electronic engr. Beckman Instruments Inc., Richmond, Calif., 1952-53; sr. ops. analyst Stanford Research Inst., Menlo Park, Calif., 1953-76; dir. environ. standards Castle & Cooke Inc., San Francisco, 1976-80; econ. devel. cons. Am. Mgmt. Assn., Anchorage, 1980-81; asso. prof. Bus. Sch., San Francisco State U., 1981—; adj. prof. Bus. Schs., San Jose State U., Santa Clara U., U. Alaska, 1972-81; mem. Nat. Def. Exec. Res., 1966—. Chmn. Calif. Gov.'s Econ. Stabilization Planning Com., 1967; mem. San Mateo County (Calif.) Republican Central Com., 1978—, dist. chmn., 1979. Served with USN, 1945-50. Home: 80 Bear Gulch Dr Portola Valley CA 94025 Office: 1600 Holloway Ave San Francisco CA 94122

MOLLAN, PETER DENNIS, accountant; b. Bellingham, Wash., Feb. 12, 1932; s. Melvin Phillip and Vera Marie (Ginnett) M.; student St. Joseph Coll., 1948-50, U. San Francisco, 1950-52. Warehouseman, Denco Sales Co., Oakland, Calif., Salt Lake City, 1961-63; warehouse, order desk clerk Globe Auto Glass Co., San Leandro, San Diego, 1963-64, office mgr., sales mgr., 1964-71; office, sales mgr. Pegboard Systems, San Diego, 1972-73; tax preparer, adminstrv. asst., city mgr., dist. mgr. H & R Block, Inc., San Diego, National City, Calif., 1973-78; adminstr. H & R Block Income Tax Schs. Treas. regional assembly drug and alcohol rehab. programs, San Diego and Imperial counties, 1975-78, chmn. steering com. region 2 assembly, 1976. Served with USAF, 1952-61. Democrat. Roman Catholic. Home: 1830 E 12th St National City CA 92050 Office: 927 Highland Ave National City CA 92050

MOLLICA, THOMAS JOE, JR., sales exec.; b. Akron, Ohio, Aug. 8, 1944; s. Thomas Joe and Billie Marie M.; student Kent State U., 1962, Akron U., 1964-65; m. Martine C. Shacklett, Apr. 4, 1965; children—Thomas Joe III, Timothy William, Tamara Lynn. With United Parcel Service, 1964-67; asst. dist. sales mgr. Ric-Wil, Inc., 1967-69; v.p. R.J. Ruschell Co., Annapolis, Md., 1970-79; pres. Piping & Corrosion Spltys., Pasadena, Md., 1979—; v.p. 505 Mgmt. Co., Inc. Bd. dirs. Southgate Community Assn., 1972. Mem. ASHRAE, Nat. Assn. Corrosion Engrs. (past chmn. Balt.-Washington chpt.). Clubs: Bay Hills Golf, Annapolis Racquet. Home: 7956 Queensroad Glen Burnie MD 21061 Office: PO Box 206 Pasadena MD 21061

MOLLISON, RICHARD DEVOL, mining co. exec.; b. Faribault, Minn., June 7, 1916; s. Allan Edwin and Edna (Devol) M.; B. Mining Engring., U. Minn., 1941; m. Elizabeth Ellen Cobb, June 7, 1941; children—Steven Cobb, Ann Elizabeth, Mark Richard. Mining engr. various locations, 1941-47; with Texasgulf Inc., 1947—, v.p., mgr. exploration, 1962-64, v.p. metals div., 1964-72, sr. v.p., 1972-73, pres. and dir., 1973-79, vice chmn. and dir., 1979—; chmn. and dir. Texasgulf Can. Ltd. Mem. AIME, Lead and Zinc Inst., Silver Inst., Mining and Metall. Soc. Am., Canadian Inst. Mining and Metall. Engrs., Mining Club N.Y.C., Tau Beta Pi, Theta Xi. Republican. Clubs: Landmark, Riverside Yacht, Royal Canadian Yacht, Navy League of U.S. (dir.). Home: 13 Hendrie Dr Old Greenwich CT 06870 Office: High Ridge Park Stamford CT 06904

MOLONY, MICHAEL JANSSENS, JR., lawyer; b. New Orleans, Sept. 2, 1922; s. Michael Janssens and Marie (Perret) M.; J.D., Tulane U., 1950; m. Jane Leslie Waguespack, Oct. 21, 1951; children—Jane Leslie, Michael Janssens, Megan Elizabeth, Kevin, Sara, Brian, Ian Peter, Duncan Christopher. Admitted to La. bar, 1950; partner firm Molony & Baldwin, 1950; asso. partner firm Jones, Flanders, Waechter & Walker, 1951-56; partner firm Jones, Walker, Waechter, Poitevent, Carrere & Denegre, New Orleans, 1956-75, Milling, Benson, Woodward, Hillyer, Pierson & Miller, 1975—; instr., lectr. Tulane U. Med. Sch. and Univ. Coll., 1953-59. Asst. sec.-treas., ex-officio mem. council La. Law Inst., 1958-70; mem. Mayor's Adv. Com. on City Charter; vice chmn. Port of New Orleans Operation La. Impact Com., 1969-70; mem. Met. Area Com., New Orleans, 1970—; ex-officio mem., mem. council Goals Found., Met. New Orleans Goals Program, vice chmn. ad hoc planning com. Goals for Met. New Orleans, 1969-72; chmn. La. Gov.'s Task Force on Space Industry, 1971-73, Gov.'s Adv. Com. Met. Transp. Planning Program, 1971-77; mem. Gov.'s Task Force on Natural Gas Requirements, 1971-72; trustee Pub. Affairs Research Council La., 1970-73; mem. corporate bd. Boys' Clubs Greater New Orleans, 1969-74; bd. dirs., mem. exec. com. New Orleans Tourist and Conv. Com., 1973-75, chmn. family attractions com., 1973-75; mem. Eisenhower Legal Com., 1952; trustee Acad. of Sacred Heart, 1975-77, Gulf South Research Inst., 1980—; mem. Port of New Orleans Bd. Commrs., 1976—, pres., 1978—; mem. Met. Council for Continuing Higher Edn., 1980—. Served from aviation cadet to staff sgt., AUS, USAAF, 1942-46, PTO; capt. USAF ret. Mem. Fed., Am. (antitrust law com. 1968, mgmt. co-chmn. com. on devel. of law on union adminstrn. and procedures 1969, mem. com. on equal employment opportunity practice and procedure), La. (sec.-treas. 1957-59, gov. 1957-60, editor jour. 1957-59), New Orleans (dir. legal aid bur. 1954, chmn. standing com. on legislation 1968, vice chmn. standing com. on pub. relations 1970-71) bar assns., Am. Judicature Soc., AIM, Internat. House (dir. 1978), So. Inst. Mgmt. (a founder), U.S. (labor relations com. 1965, blue ribbon com. of lawyers for labor law reform, urban and regional affairs com. 1970-73), La. (dir. 1963-66), New Orleans Area (v.p. bus. climate div. 1966-69, dir. 1963, v.p. met. devel. and urban affairs 1969, pres.-elect 1970, pres. 1971, dir. 1963-78, exec. com. 1972) chambers commerce, Sigma Chi (pres. New Orleans alumni chpt. 1956). Roman Catholic. Clubs: Pickwick, So. Yacht, Serra, Plimsoll, Lakewood Country, Bienville (New Orleans). Home: 3039 Hudson Pl New Orleans LA 70114 Office: 1100 Whitney Bldg New Orleans LA 70130

MOLTENI, GEORGE JAMES, JR., tool mfg. co. exec.; b. Paterson, N.J., Jan. 29, 1943; s. Marco George and Emma (LaNeve) M.; B.S., Fairleigh Dickinson U., 1964; LL.B., Blackstone Law Sch., 1967, J.D., 1969; Ph.D., Calgary Coll., 1974; M.Sc.D., U. Metaphysics, 1980; m. Apr. 26, 1964 (div. Oct. 1973); children—Mark Louis, Scott Richard. Ops. coordinator, contracts dept. Kearfott div. Singer Corp., West Paterson, N.J., 1967-68; ops. and mdse. mgr. Medi Mart Drugs, Stop & Shop Corp., Wyckoff, N.J., 1968-71; Gt. Eastern Drugs, Daylin Corp., Union, N.J., 1971-72; area office mgr. Safeguard Bus. Systems, Inc., East Orange, N.J., 1972-73; with Aloris Tool Co. Inc., Clifton, N.J., 1973—, also comptroller, sec. Author: Without End...or Beginning, 1980. Office: Aloris Tool Co Inc 407 Getty Ave PO Box 1529 Clifton NJ 07015

MOLZ, PHILIP JACK, fin. exec.; b. N.Y.C., Jan. 28, 1929; s. Philip and Maria H. (Geist) M. B.S. cum laude in Math., CCNY, 1953; m. Margaret Jane Ralph; 1 dau., Philene Mae. With Gen. Electric Co., U.S., 1953-66, traveling auditor, 1958-62, treas., Brazil, 1962-66, v.p. fin. KUBA Imperial Co. subs., Wolfenbuettel, W.Ger., 1966-68; dir. fin. controls ITT, N.Y.C., 1969-70; controller and treas. Xerox Corp., Latin Am. group, 1970-74; v.p. fin. adminstrn. internat. div. Abbott Labs., N. Chicago, Ill., 1974-79; sr. v.p., chief fin. officer Macmillan Inc., N.Y.C., 1980—; pres. PMP Internat. Group, mgmt. cons. Served with CIC, U.S. Army, 1951-53. Mem. Fin. Execs. Inst., Nat. Assn. Accountants, Pharm. Mfrs. Assn. Republican. Roman Catholic. Clubs: Stamford (Conn.) Yacht, Stamford Racquet. Home: Bend of River Ln Stamford CT 06902 Office: Macmillan Inc 866 3d Ave New York NY 10022

MOMMSEN, JACK TERMAN, minerals market cons.; b. Chgo., Mar. 13, 1927; s. Terman Jens and Julianne (Schilthelm) M.; B.S., U. Ariz., 1954, M.S., 1955, Hon. Met. Engr., 1967; M.B.A., U. Santa Clara, 1965, Ph.D., 1977; m. Beverly M. Platt, July 4, 1948; children—Robert W., Jack Terman, Julianne Ida. Metallurgist, U.S. Bur. Mines, Tucson, 1954-55; engr. Gen. Electric Co., San Jose, Calif., 1955-69; v.p. Nuclear Exchange Corp., Menlo Park, Calif., 1970-75; pres. J.T. Mommsen Co., Campbell, Calif., 1975—. Served with U.S. Army, 1945-48, 50-52. Decorated D.F.C. Mem. AIME, Am. Nuclear Soc., Atomic Indsl. Forum. Home: 18641 Harleigh Dr Saratoga CA 95070 Office: 595 Millich Dr Campbell CA 95008

MONAHAN, ANGELA MARIE, real estate co. exec.; b. Battle Creek, Mich., Apr. 11, 1952; d. Robert Gordon and Martha Elizabeth (Fell) Pender; student Cambridge (Mass.) Jr. Coll., 1970-71, Bridgewater (Mass.) State Coll., 1975. Realtor, Southbrook Real Estate of Hanover, Inc. (Mass.), 1972-76, pres., prin., 1976—. Mem. Nat. Assn. Realtors, Mass. Assn. Realtors, Plymouth County Bd. Realtors (dir. 1979-80, sec.-treas. 1981), South Shore/Quincy Bd. Realtors, South Shore C. of C., Realtors Nat. Mktg. Inst. Home: 243 Winter St Norwell MA 02061 Office: 899 Washington St Hanover MA 02339

MONAHON, PHILIP CHRISTOPHER, constrn. corp. exec., cons.; b. Newton, Mass., June 4, 1929; s. Arthur Thomas and Ruth (Tulis) M.; B.S., Mass. Maritime Acad., 1952; m. Joan Skillin Mills, July 18, 1953; children—P. Christopher, Gregory, Hilary, Catherine, Laura. Pres. Monahon Corp., Watertown, Mass., 1955—; pres. Nat. Home Inspection Service New Eng., Inc., 1969—; constrn. cons. Served as lt. USNR, 1953-55; Korea, Vietnam. Recipient United Fund awards, 1965, 66; Mem. of Year award Mass. Maritime Acad. Alumni Assn., 1962. Mem. Asso. Gen. Contractors Mass. (past pres. and dir., award 1965), Asso. Gen. Contractors Am. (dir.), Am. Inst. Constructors, Am. Arbitration Assn. (arbitrator), Am. Soc. Home Insps. (nat. dir., pres. New Eng. chpt. 1977-78, exec. dir.), Ancient and Honorable Arty. Co. of Mass. Republican. Club: Lakewood Tennis (Newton). Contbr. articles and book revs. to Constructor mag. Home: Five Chester St Newton Highlands MA 02161 Office: 2 Calvin Rd Watertown MA 02172

MONBERG, JAY PETER, mfg. co. exec.; b. N.Y.C., Aug. 19, 1935; s. Carl-Johannes and Maria Anna Sophie (Haugwitz-Reventlow) Hammerich-Monberg; B.B.A., Northwestern U., 1962, M.B.A., 1968. Corp. controller Furnas Elec. Co., Batavia, Ill., 1966-67; sr. v.p., dir. Logan Mfg. Co., Chgo., 1967-72; exec. v.p. Moser Industries, Inc., Naperville, Ill., after 1972; now pres., chief exec. officer, dir. Wickman Machine Tools Inc., Elk Grove Village, Ill. Mem. dean's council Grad. Sch. Mgmt., Northwestern U., 1973—. Mem. Nat. Assn. Accountants, Financial Mgmt. Assn., Am. Accounting Assn., Am. Mgmt. Assn. Scandinavian-Am. Found., Rebild Nat. Park Soc. (v.p.), Dania Soc., Danish Nat. Com. (trustee), Sheffield Hist. Soc., Danish Am. Lang. Found. (pres.), Danish-Am. C. of C. (v.p., dir.), Chgo. Council on Fgn. Relations, Internat. Trade Club of Chgo. Clubs: Execs., Mid-Am., Internat., 100 Club of Cook County, Union League (Chgo.); Cress Creek Country (Naperville). Home: 612 Mulford St Evanston IL 60202 Office: 950 Morse Ave Elk Grove Village IL 60007

MONCARZ, ELISA SHAFRAN, accountant; b. Havana, Cuba, Oct. 10, 1947; came to U.S., 1960, naturalized, 1966; d. Benjamin and Felicia (Steinberg) Shafran; B.B.A., City U. N.Y., 1966; m. Raul Moncarz, May 31, 1973; children—Felippe Henley, Roger Jonathan. Supervising sr. acct. S.D. Leidesdorf & Co. (merged into Ernst & Ernst 1978), N.Y.C., 1966-72; audit rev. mgr. Spear, Sheldon & Safer, C.P.A.'s, Miami, Fla., 1972-74; asst. prof. acctg. Fla. Internat. U., Miami, 1974-79, asso. prof., 1979—; cons. banks, hospitality firms and others; mem. nat. steering com. 2nd Nat. Symposium on Hispanic Bus. and Economy, 1979. Bd. dirs. Community Tax Aid, Inc., N.Y.C., 1969-72. C.P.A., Fla., N.Y. Mem. Am. Inst. C.P.A.'s, N.Y. State Soc. C.P.A.'s, Fla. Inst. C.P.A.'s, Council Hotel, Restaurant and Instl. Edn., Am. Acctg. Assn., Southwestern Fin. Assn., Ernst & Ernst Alumni, Beta Alpha Psi. Contbr. articles on banking and hospitality acctg. to jours. Research on hospitality acctg. and tourism. Office: Florida International University Tamiami Trail Miami FL 33199

MONCHIN, ROBERT STANLEY, mktg. cons.; b. Kingston, N.Y., Oct. 31, 1923; s. Abraham H. and Gertrude (Gerlin) M.; B.A., N.Y. U., 1948; m. Marylin Barsky, Dec. 26, 1949; children—Jonathan, Scott. Account exec. DKG, 1949-51; dir. spl. projects Am. Visuals Corp., 1952-59; dir. advt. and public relations Arthur Wiesenberger & Co., N.Y.C., 1959-65; pres. Robert S. Menchin & Co., N.Y.C., 1966-67; pres. Wall St. Marketing and Commerce Co., N.Y.C., 1967-71; exec. v.p. Roberts; Menchin & Myers, Inc., N.Y.C., 1971; dir. mktg. So. Star Inc., Miami, Fla., 1972-77; mktg. adviser Chgo. Bd. Trade, 1977—. Served with U.S. Army, 1942-45. Mem. Public Relations Soc. Am., Fin. Planners Assn. Author: The Last Caprice, 1964; Where There's A Will, 1977; editor: Interest Rate Futures Newsletter, 1977-80. Home: 1313 Ritchie Ct Chicago IL 60610 Office: Chicago Bd Trade LaSalle at Jackson Sts Chicago IL 60604

MONFREDINI, JAMES JOSEPH, food distbn. export co. exec.; b. San Francisco, Jan. 28, 1947; s. Emil James and Eleanor Nancy Monfredini; student St. Mary's Coll. Calif., 1965-67; B.S., U. San Francisco, 1969; postgrad. Golden Gate U. Law Sch., 1969-70; m. Lee Ann Duca, June 22, 1968; children—Joshua Emil, Alexis Catherine. Exec. v.p. B.J. Holmes Sales Co., Inc., San Francisco, 1971-74; pres., chmn. bd. Pacific Agri-Products, Inc., South San Francisco, Calif., 1974—. Mem. Nat. Ind. Poultry and Food Distbrs. Assn., Southeastern Poultry and Egg Assn., Pacific Egg and Poultry Assn. Republican. Roman Catholic. Club: Guardsmen. Home: 50 San Leandro Way San Francisco CA 94127 Office: 551 Eccles Ave South San Francisco CA 94080

MONIZ, ALBERT PAUL, bus transp. co. exec.; b. Honolulu, Jan. 8, 1918; s. Joseph J. and Sophie (Rodrigues) M.; student pub. schs., Honolulu; m. Ritsuko Nakagawa, June 15, 1946; children—Albert Paul, Barbara Jean Moniz Tomita, Ann Naomi Moniz Suen, Linda Joyce Moniz Petersen. Vice pres., treas., dir. Honolulu Rapid Transit Co., Ltd., 1960-71; sec., treas., dir. Honolulu Ltd., 1960-71, Honolulu Scenic Tours, Inc., 1960-71; v.p., treas., dir. Wahiawa Transport System Inc., Honolulu, 1962-71, Fed. Enterprises Ltd., Honolulu, 1962-71; pres., gen. mgr., dir. MTL, Inc., Honolulu, 1971—. Civil service commr., Honolulu, 1955-61; bd. mgrs. Army & Navy YMCA, Honolulu, 1957-60, Central br. YMCA, Honolulu, 1978—; bd. dirs. Hawaii Med. Service Assn., Honolulu, 1979—. Mem. C. of C. of Hawaii, Portuguese C. of C. of Hawaii. Episcopalian. Club: Elks. Home: 415 Hind Dr Honolulu HI 96821 Office: 1133 Alapai St Honolulu HI 96813

MONK, ROBERT ALLEN, fabricating co. exec.; b. McKeesport, Pa., Apr. 15, 1935; s. George Allen and Helen Louise (Mushrush) M.; B.S.M.E., Purdue U., 1958; M.S. in Engring. Mgmt., Drexel U., 1968; m. Ethel Mae Windeknecht, June 4, 1956; children—Carrie Sue, Gary Allen, Peggy Lynn. Mfg. trainee Westinghouse Electric, Pitts., 1957-59; indsl. engr. Crucible Steel Co., Midland, Pa., 1959-62; with Personal Products Co., Milltown, N.J., 1962-74, prodn. supt., 1972-74; plant mgr. Ellisco, Inc., Phila., 1974-77; v.p. mfg. K.W. Muth Co., Sheboygan, Wis., 1977—; mem. faculty Rider Coll., Trenton, N.J., 1969-71. Bd. dirs. Center for Bus. and Econs., Lakeland Coll., Sheboygan. Recipient Achievement award as pres. Raritan Valley chpt. Soc. Advt. Mgmt., 1979. Mem. Soc. Advancement Mgmt. (internat. bd. rep. 1970-73, pres. Raritan Valley chpt. 1969, Achievement award 1969). Republican. Presbyterian. Home: 628 School St Kohler WI 53044 Office: 2021 North Ave Sheboygan WI 53081

MONROE, EDWIN PAUL, resort services exec.; b. Galion, Ohio, Apr. 5, 1915; s. Edwin P. and Georgia (Pavey) M.; student Ohio Wesleyan U., 1933-34; B.A., Rollins Coll., 1937; m. Virginia Lorene Hocker, Oct. 12, 1940; children—Edwin Paul III, Frederic Alan. Sales promotion mgr. Hercules Steel Products Co., Galion, 1938-42; pres., dir. Monroe Standard, Inc., Galion, 1946-65; v.p. Monroe Enterprises, Inc., Clearwater, Fla., 1968—; pres. Sea Chest Resort Properties, Treasure Island, Fla., 1949—. Vice mayor, commr. City of Treasure Island, 1951-54, chmn. planning and zoning bd., 1955-61. Served with USAAF, 1942-46. Mem. Sigma Alpha Epsilon, Pi Gamma Mu. Republican. Clubs: Rotary; St. Petersburg Yacht. Home: 8350 40th Ave N St Petersburg FL 33709 Office: 11780 Gulf Blvd Treasure Island FL 33706

MONROE, JOHN CLAYTON, JR., architect; b. Kansas City, Mo., Jan. 19, 1923; s. John Clayton and Virginia (McPherson) M.; B.S. in Architecture, U. Kan., 1949; m. Leona Wallenmeyer, Apr. 5, 1952; children—John Clayton III, Laurie K. Project architect Neville, Sharp and Simon, architects, Kansas City, Mo., 1949-53; architect, owner John C. Monroe, architect, 1953-55; pres. Monroe-Lefebvre-Ritchie Architects, Inc., Kansas City, Ten Seventeen Penn Co., Inc., 1966-72, Monroe & LeFebvre Architects, Inc., 1972—. Mem. Clay County Bd. Parks and Recreation, 1965—, chmn., 1971—; mem. Kansas City Art Commn., 1959-63; chmn. Citizens Assn., 1959; mem. Kansas City Bd. Park Commrs., 1955-56, exec. com. Starlight Theatre, 1955-56, Mayor's Recreational Adv. Commn., 1955-58, Kansas City Jud. Commn., 1966. Bd. dirs. YMCA, 1959-64. Served with USMCR, 1943-45, 50-51. Fellow AIA (chpt. pres. 1975), Mo. Arts Council; mem. Mo. Assn. Registered Architects (pres. 1959), Constrn. Specification Inst. (pres. 1963-64), Am. Legion (life), 40 and 8, Marine Corps League, Globe and Anchor Soc. Democrat. Methodist (mem. bd.). Mason (Shriner). Clubs: Univ. (pres. 1965), Vanguard (pres. 1967), Mission Hills Country. Home: 123 Greentree Lane Kansas City MO 64116 Office: 1021 Pennsylvania Kansas City MO 64105

MONROE, JOHN WILLIAM, electronics mfg. co. exec.; b. Utica, N.Y., Nov. 5, 1945; s. Charles Helfert and Florence Alice (Murray) M.; B.S. in Elec. Engring., Cornell U., 1966, M.S., 1968, Ph.D., 1970; m. Margaret Edith Warne, June 8, 1968; children—John Warne, Charles William. Sr. engr. Monsanto Co., St. Louis, 1970, Watkins-Johnson Co., Palo Alto, Calif., 1971-73; prodn. mgr. Hewlett-Packard Co., Palo Alto, 1973—; v.p. engring., treas., dir. William E. Warne Assos. Inc., Sacramento, 1975-79; v.p. Warne Walnut Wrandro, 1979—. Chmn. Palo Alto phone fundraising orgn. Cornell Fund, 1976-79, No. Calif. Cornell Fund, 1980—. Served to capt., M.I., U.S. Army, 1970. Nat. Merit scholar, 1962-66, Cornell Nat. scholar, 1962-66, Gen. Electric fellow, 1970. Mem. IEEE, AAAS, Am. Mgmt. Assn., Stanford U., Savoyards, Stanford Symphony. Contbr. articles to profl. publs. Home: 1570 Madrono St Palo Alto CA 94306 Office: 974 E Arques Ave Sunnyvale CA 94086

MONROE, MORGAN DEAN, banking exec.; b. Fremont, County, Iowa, Mar. 12, 1928; s. Reuben Jasper and Lucy Catherine (Kite) M., stepmother Lucien Marie (Doty) M.; student Grad. Sch. Banking, U. Wis., 1966, U. Chgo., 1969, Okla. U., 1974; m. Ruth Marie Biggins, June 21, 1947; children—Morgan Dean, Angela Marie Monroe Strait. With Fremont County Savs. Bank, Sidney, Iowa, 1946-54, 57-75, v.p., 1961-75, also dir.; with Security 1st Nat. Bank Los Angeles, San Fernando, Calif., 1954-56; teller Colorado Springs Nat. Bank, 1956; owner, mgr. Morgan D. Monroe Assos., Sidney, taxes, ins., realty, 1975-77; v.p., cashier, dir. Farmers Nat. Bank, Pilger, Nebr., 1977-78; pres., dir. Maxwell (Iowa) State Bank, 1978—. Mem. advt. com. Sidney Rodeo; sec.-treas. Sidney Area Devel. Corp.; chmn. bd. Meth. Ch., 1959; pres. PTA, 1960; bd. dirs. Grape Community Hosp. Served with USMC, 1945-46. Mem. Iowa Fedn. County Bankers (v.p. 1974), Am. Legion (comdr. 1961), VFW. Republican. Clubs: Masons, Lions, Toastmasters, 40 and 8, K.P. Home: Box 314 Maxwell IA 50161 Office: Maxwell State Bank Maxwell IA 50161

MONSEES, RICHARD HENRY, health care exec.; b. Sedalia, Mo., Oct. 11, 1942; s. Dietrich G. and RubyLou (Bremer) M.; B.S., U. Mo., 1964; cert. Stanford U. Grad. Sch. Bus., 1979; m. Janet Louise Hartin, Apr. 11, 1963; children—Richard Henry, Scott D., Robert M. Operator farm nr. Sedalia, 1964-69; exec. dir. Pettis County United Fund, Sedalia, 1964-65; pres. Monsees Realty Co., Sedalia, 1964—, Maplewood Service Co., pub. utility, Sedalia, 1974—, Brooking Park Geriatrics, Inc., Sedalia, 1974—, Geriatrics Mgmt., Inc., 1980—, Brooking Park Home Health Agy., Inc., 1980—; v.p., sec. A and R Industries, Ind., Sedalia, 1978—; sec., treas. Monsees Devel. Corp., Sedalia, 1975—. Mem. curriculum com. Smith-Cotton High Sch., Sedalia, 1972. Founder, pres. Pettis County Rep. Club, Sedalia, 1970; regional coordinator 4th Congl. Dist. Bond-for-Auditor Com., 1970, 4th Congl. Dist. Bond-for-Gov. com., 1972; mem. Pettis County Rep. Com., Sedalia, 1966—, chmn., 1974—; mem. Nat. Reagan Selection Com., 1979; mem. adv. bd. Exec. Program for Smaller Cos., Stanford U., 1979—. Mem. Mo. Health Care Assn. (chmn. skilled nursing facility conf. 1980—), Nat. (rural devel. com. 1974—, mem. Washington task force 1979), Mo. (chmn. rural devel. com. 1975) assns. home builders, Sedalia Bd. Realtors (pres. 1973), Nat. Inst. Real Estate Brokers, U. Mo. Alumni Assn., Sedalia C. of C. (dir. 1973-74), Mo. (community devel. chmn. 1966-67), Sedalia (dir. 1964-68) jr. chambers commerce, Alpha Kappa Psi. Methodist (bd. mem. 1965-68). Club: Walnut Hills Country (dir. 1969-73) (Sedalia, Mo.). Home: Hermosa Lake Route 2 Sedalia MO 65301 Office: Brooking Park Village Route 6 PO Box 1567 Sedalia MO 65301

MONSERRAT, ALFREDO, mfg. co. exec.; b. Gibara, Oriente, Cuba, Oct. 25, 1936; came to U.S., 1961, naturalized, 1967; s. Florencio and Maria (Ramos) M.; B.A., Purdue U., 1967; M.B.A., Loyola U., Chgo., 1973; m. Janet Ruth Hjerpe, Jan. 28, 1967; children—Andre Mark, Vanessa Lynn. Security officer Cuban Nat. Police, 1959-61; with Sherwin-Williams Co., 1968-79, mgr. systems and adminstrn., Mexico City, 1977-79; bus. systems mgr. Norton Co., Akron, Ohio, 1979-80; computer systems mgr. Stock Equipment Co., Chagrin Falls, Ohio. Republican. Quaker. Home: 395 Starrline Dr Tallmadge OH 44278 Office: PO Box 350 Akron OH 44309

MONSON, CRAIG ARTHUR, ins. co. exec.; b. Chgo., Apr. 20, 1931; s. Arthur and Gertrude (Durst) M.; student chem. engring. North Central Coll., Naperville, Ill., 1950-51; B.S. in Journalism, U. Ill., 1954; m. Nancy Norpell, Sept. 6, 1958; children—Cathleen, Michael, Sandra, Diane, Steven. Data processing sales rep. IBM, Peoria, Ill., 1954-59; asst. to pres. Indsl. Casualty Ins. Co., Bloomington, Ill., 1959-62; with Combined Ins. Co. Am., various locations, 1962—, asst. v.p. sales adminstrn. Little Giant Life, Chgo., 1971-74, v.p., chief operating officer, Hearstone div., Boston, 1974—; dir., mem. exec. com. Harbor Bank, Boston, 1976—; dir. Patriot Bank Corp. Trustee, mem. fin. com. Waltham Hosp., 1979—. Office: 111 Washington St Brookline MA 02146

MONTAG, PAUL MICHAEL, electronic co. exec.; b. Freehold, N.J., Mar. 27, 1945; s. Michael and Mary M.; B.S.E.E., B.A., Rutgers U., 1968; M.B.A., U. Santa Clara, 1972; m. Sandra McCobin, Sept. 7, 1968; 1 dau., Pamela. Project engr. Raytheon Corp., Sudbury, Mass., 1968-70; product mktg. mgr. Hewlett-Packard Co., Palo Alto, Calif., 1970-73; sr. sales engr. Tex. Instruments, Los Angeles, 1973-76; western regional sales mgr. Control Logic, Inc., Santa Ana, Calif., 1976-78; pres., chief operating officer Micro-Specialists, Inc., Hollywood, Calif., 1978—; dir. Melvic Enterprises Inc. Mem. IEEE, Am. Mgmt. Assn. (pres.'s council), Assn. M.B.A. Execs. Club: Masons. Office: 535 E Main St Tustin CA 92680

MONTE, SALVATORE JOSEPH, polymer chem. mfg. co. exec.; b. Bklyn., Sept. 18, 1939; s. Michael Salvatore and Antoinette A. (Gentile) M.; B.C.E., Manhattan Coll., 1961; M.S. in Polymeric Materials, Poly. Inst. N.Y., 1969; m. Erika Gertraud Spiegelhalder, Oct. 14, 1961; children—Michelle Marie, Deborah Frances, Denise Christine, Eric Michael. Asst. supt. Turner Constrn. Co., N.Y.C., Phila., 1961-64; project mgr. Blaize Constrn. Co., Eastchester, N.Y., 1964-66; v.p. Kenrich Petrochems., Inc., Bayonne, N.J., 1966-69, exec. v.p., 1969-79, pres., 1980—, trustee pension fund, 1976—; mgmt. trustee Oil, Chem. and Atomic Workers Local 8-406 Welfare Fund. Bd. dirs. United Fund, 1970, Jobs of Bayonne, 1980; v.p., sec. South Ganon-Forest Hills Homeowners Assn., 1971-74. Registered profl. engr., N.Y. State, N.J. Mem. Soc. Plastics Engrs. (div. dir. 1980), Soc. Plastics Industries, Am. Chem. Soc. (rubber div.), N.Y. Federated Soc. Coatings Tech., N.Y. (chmn. bd. 1976), Phila., Boston, Blue Ridge, S.E. Ohio rubber groups, Bayonne C. of C., Phi Kappa Theta, Chi Epsilon. Republican. Roman Catholic. Clubs: Richmond County Country; Bayonne Rotary (dir. 1974-77 1st v.p. 1980). Contbr. numerous articles to profl. publs. and mags., chpts. to books on interfacial tech. Patentee in U.S. and 22 fgn. countries on monoalkoxy, chelated and coordinated titanate coupling agts., cumyl phenol derivatives. Office: Foot of E 22d St Bayonne NJ 07002

MONTEMURRO, FRANK MICHAEL, mktg. exec.; b. N.Y.C., Oct. 13, 1947; s. Arthur Francis and Antoinette (Mangiapane) M.; B.A., Fordham U., 1969; M.B.A., Columbia U., 1972; m. Patricia Heidel, May 14, 1977. Campaign mgr. Senator Joseph Pisani, New Rochelle, N.Y., 1972-73; advance man Mike Roth Campaign Com., White Plains, N.Y., 1973; cons. Ted Angelus Assos., N.Y.C., 1973-76; product mgr. Miles Labs., Elkhart, Ind., 1976-78; sr. product mgr. Pharmacraft, Rochester, N.Y., 1978—. Pres., New Rochelle Young Republicans, 1973-74. Served with U.S. Army, 1970. Mem. Am. Marketing Assn. Republican. Roman Catholic. Home: 21 S Cross Trail Fairport NY 14450 Office: PO Box 1212 Rochester NY 14603

MONTEVERDE, JAMES WESLEY, ins. co. exec.; b. Pitts., Jan. 14, 1948; s. John Paul and Mary Elizabeth (Donahue) M.; B.S. in Bus. Adminstrn., U. Dayton, 1970; C.L.U., Am. Coll., 1977; m. Kathi Morter, Nov. 21, 1970; children—Brooke M., Jay, Darcy. Sales rep. Lincoln Nat. Life, Pitts., 1970-75; ins. broker, cons. James W. Monteverde C.L.U. & Assos., Pitts. (merged with Coordinated Fin. Services 1978), 1975-78, sr. partner Coordinated Fin. Services, Pitts., 1978—. Recipient Man of Yr. award Lincoln Nat. Life, 1971, 72, 73, 77. Mem. Pitts. Estate Planning Council, Pitts. Life Underwriters Assn. (v.p.), Pa. Assn. Life Underwriters (dir.), Pa. Life Underwriters Assn. (chmn. public edn. 1979-80), Allegheny Profl. Group (pres.), Pitts. C. of C., Nat. Assn. Life Underwriters. Roman Catholic. Clubs: Pitts. Athletic, Longue Vue Country. Contbr. articles to profl. jours.; lectr. Home: 218 E Waldheim Rd Fox Chapel PA 15215 Office: Mellon Bank Bldg Suite 3434 Pittsburgh PA 15219

MONTGOMERY, DONALD WEST, ins. co. exec.; b. Celina, Ohio, Aug. 14, 1925; s. C.M. and Mabel (Baxter) M.; B.A., DePauw U., Greencastle, Ind., 1947; J.D., Columbia U., 1950; children—William W., Elizabeth Montgomery McConnell, Thomas, Nancy. Admitted to Ohio bar, 1950; asst. atty. gen. State of Ohio, 1951-52; pros. asst. Mercer County (Ohio), 1953-56; with Celina Ins. Group (Ohio), 1954—, pres., chmn. bd. Celina Fin. and Ins. Group, 1969—; underwriting mem. Lloyds of London; chmn. Ill. Ins. Exchange; chmn., dir. Heartland Group, Inc.; dir. Gen. Telephone Co. Ohio. Served to lt. (j.g.) USNR, 1943-46. Mem. Am. Bar Assn., Am. Judicature Soc., Ohio Bar Assn., Allen County Bar Assn., Mercer County Bar Assn., Ohio C. of C. (pres., dir. 1973-75, chmn. bd. 1975-77, life dir. 1977—), Exec. Order Ohio Commodores. Republican. Methodist. Clubs: Shawnee Country, Metropolitan, Union League, Shriners. Address: 2775 Fort Amanda Rd Lima OH 45805

MONTGOMERY, E. WYNELL, mfg. co. exec.; b. Plainview, Tex., July 19, 1939; d. Hubert O. and Mary Ethel (McElroy) Lee; B.B.A., E. Tex. State U., 1979; divorced; children—Leanne, Curtis. Various secretarial and bookkeeping positions, 1957-68; bookkeeper Maytex Mfg. Co., Terrell, Tex., 1968-73, comptroller, 1973—; dir. Rockwall Steel Co. (Tex.), 1973-75. Mem. Tex. Assn. Bus., Beta Gamma Sigma. Home: Route 4 Box 17B Grand Saline TX 75140 Office: 1210 Airport Rd Terrell TX 75160

MONTGOMERY, HENRY DUBOSE, JR., fin. exec.; b. Hartsville, S.C., Mar. 16, 1949; s. Henry DuBose and Mary Eudora (Wells) M.; B.S. in E.E., M.I.T., 1971, B.S. in Mgmt. Sci., 1971, M.S. in E.E., 1972, M.B.A. with distinction, Harvard U., 1974; m. Nancy Kay Timmerman, Aug. 25, 1973. Researcher, Bell Telephone Labs., Inc., Murray Hill, N.J., 1969-71; asst. to pres. Computer Signal Processors, Inc., Burlington, Mass., 1972-73; mktg. cons. Wang Labs., Inc., Tewkesbury, Mass., 1974; mng. dir. Menlo Fin. Corp., Menlo Park, Calif., 1974—; dir. Waugh Controls Corp., Chatsworth, Calif., Data Electronics, Inc., San Diego, Nat. Micronetics, Inc., San Diego, The Monadnock Co., Los Angeles. Fundraiser, Children's Health Council, Palo Alto, Calif., 1978-79; mem. alumni activities bd. M.I.T., 1979—, chmn., 1980—, mem. M.I.T. nat. selection com., 1980—. NSF fellow, 1971-72; Scott Paper Found. Leadership award, 1970. Mem. Western Assn. Venture Capitalists, Nat. Assn. Small Bus. Investment Cos., Nat. Venture Capital Assn., Am. Electronics Assn. Republican. Presbyn. Clubs: M.I.T. of No. Calif. (pres. 1977-79, dir. 1977—), Peninsula Golf and Country, Harvard Bus. Sch. of No. Calif. Home: 40 Tulip Ct Hillsborough CA 94010 Office: 3000 Sand Hill Rd Menlo Park CA 94025

MONTGOMERY, JAMES FISCHER, savs. and loan assn. exec.; b. Topeka, Nov. 30, 1934; s. James Maurice and Frieda Ellen (Fischer) M.; B.S. in Accounting, U. Calif., Los Angeles, 1957; m. Linda Jane Hicks, Aug. 25, 1956; children—Michael James, Jeffrey Allen, Andrew Steven, John Gregory. Accountant, Price Waterhouse & Co., C.P.A.'s, Los Angeles, 1957-60; controller Conejo Valley Devel. Co., Thousand Oaks, Calif., 1960: asst. to pres. Gt. Western Fin. Corp., Beverly Hills, Calif., 1960-64; fin. v.p., treas. United Fin. Corp., Los Angeles, 1964-69, exec. v.p., 1969-74, pres., 1975; pres. Citizens Savs. and Loan Assn., Los Angeles, 1970-75; pres., chief operating officer, dir. Gt. Western Savs. and Loan Assn., also Gt. Western Fin. Corp., Beverly Hills, 1975—: dir. Inner City Housing Corp., Savs. Assn. Mortgage Co., Inc., Asso. Bldg. Industry, Calif. Taxpayers Assn., Savs. Assn. Central Corp. Trustee, mem. chancellor's assos., chmn. investment com. UCLA Found., Los Angeles. Served with AUS, 1958-60. Mem. Calif. Savs. and Loan League (past dir., past chmn. coms.), Young Pres. Orgn. Office: 8484 Wilshire Blvd Beverly Hills CA 90211*

MONTGOMERY, JEFF, lawyer, exploration co. exec.; b. Winfield, Tex., Jan. 11, 1920; s. Jefferson Franklin and Bertha (Hofman) M.; B.S. in Petroleum Engring., Tex. A&M Coll., 1941; postgrad. Harvard Sch. Bus. Adminstrn., 1941-42; J.D., George Washington U., 1948; m. Leonora Ryan, July 1, 1944; children—Franklin Jefferson, Bethany Rebecca, Catherine Melinda, John Noland Ryan. Admitted to Tex. bar, 1948; partner firm Klapproth, Hamilton & Montgomery, Midland, Tex., 1948-50; mgr. Tex. Crude Oil Co., Fort Worth, 1950-53; cons. petroleum engring., Fort Worth, 1953-54; v.p., dir. Murmanill Corp., Dallas, 1954-56; pres. Kirby Industries, Inc., Houston, 1956-73, chmn. bd., 1973-76; chmn. bd. Kirby Exploration Co., 1976—, Caribbean Fin. Co., 1976—; dir. Cullen Center Bank & Trust Co., Houston, 1969—. Chmn. welfare com. Salvation Army Adv. Bd., Houston, 1965-69; bd. dirs. United Fund, Houston, 1971-73, Alley Theatre, Houston, 1973-76; trustee U. St. Thomas, 1972-78, Meadville Theol. Sch., 1978—. Mem. AIME, Am. Assn. Petroleum Geologists (asso.), Tex. Mid-Continent Oil and Gas Assn. (dir., exec. com.), Natural Gas Supply Assn. (chmn.), Ind. Petroleum Assn. Am. (exec. com. 1973-75), Am. Petroleum Inst., Am. Inst. Mgmt., Am. Bar Assn., State Bar Tex., Nat. Petroleum Council, Order of Coif, Tau Beta Pi, Phi Delta Phi. Home: 2212 Del Monte Dr Houston TX 77019 Office: PO Box 1745 Houston TX 77001

MONTGOMERY, JOHN OSBORN, corp. exec.; b. Detroit, Mar. 21, 1921; s. Henry Arthur and Bessie Ellen (Henderson) M.; B.S. in Agr., Mich. State U., 1950; m. Joy Evelyn Dunlop, Mar. 2, 1946 (dec.); children—John Henry Earl, James Lawrence, Jeffrey Michael; m. 2d, Kathryn M. Vogel, Mar. 12, 1978. Mem. editorial staff Detroit Times, 1937-40, columnist state capitol bur., 1946-49; owner, operator dairy farm, Howell, Mich., 1949-52; mem. pub. relations staff Chrysler Corp., Detroit, 1952-55, dir. pub. relations Chrysler div., 1955-60, corp. mgr. news relations, 1960-74, mgr. indsl. pub. relations, 1974-79; sr. v.p. P/R Assos., Inc., 1980—. Chmn. pub. relations com., bd. dirs. ARC, Detroit, 1971—; bd. dirs., chmn. pub. relations com. Wayne County unit Am. Cancer Soc., 1974-79; chmn. pub. relations com. Boy Scouts Am., 1970-79. Trustee Greater Detroit Council on Alcoholism, 1970-74. Served with AUS, 1940-46, PTO. Mem. Pub. Relations Soc. Am. (chpt. dir. 1962-64, pres. 1970, dir. 1971, Silver Anvil award, 1957). Mich. Press. Assn., Detroit Press Club (dir. 1978—), Detroit Bd. Commerce, Detroit Hist. Soc., Founders Soc., Detroit Inst. Arts, Soc. Mayflower Desc., St. Andrews Soc. Clubs: Detroit Boat, Players, Crisis (Detroit). Home: 745 University Place Grosse Pointe MI 48230 Office: 1600 City National Bank Bldg Detroit MI 48226

MONTNEY, ROBERT PAUL, mfg. co. mgr.; b. Elktom, Mich., Feb. 28, 1939; s. Peter Byron and Ila Jenne (Yeager) M.; student Gen. Motor Inst., 1965-68; A.A.S., Flint Jr. Coll., 1969; B.S., Central Mich. U., 1970, M.A., 1971; m. Mary Francis Bielski, May 7, 1966; children—Patrick, Roberta, William. System analysis Huron Tool & Mfg. Co., Lexington, Mich., 1972-73, mgr. data processing, 1973-74; mgr. data processing Taylor Bldg Products, Detroit, 1974-80; mgr. data processing Ft. Worth Pipe & Supply div. Whittaker Corp., 1980—. Served with U.S. Navy, 1959-63. Mem. Am. Mgmt. Assn., Assn. Computing Machinery, Internat. Platform Assn., Data Processing Mgmt. Assn. Home: 3812 River Pass Dr # 108 Fort Worth TX 76109 Office: PO Box 2108 Fort Worth TX 76101

MONTZ, GEORGE ARNOLD, wholesale food service co. exec.; b. Louisville, Sept. 26, 1922; s. George Getig and Mildred (Arnold) M.; student U. Tex., Austin, 1940, U. Mo., 1966; m. Edna Francis Campbell, Dec. 17, 1943; children—George Arnold, Cynthia Lynn Montz Russ. Br. mgr. Lone Star Co., Tex., 1948-53; v.p. Nelson Davis & Son Inc., Austin, 1953-67; pres. Instnl. Sales Inc., Kansas City, Kans., 1967-73, Fleming Food Service Inc., Austin, 1973—; treas. Summerwood II, Inc., Austin, 1977—. Elder, 1st Presbyn. Ch., Austin. Served to capt. USAAF, 1940-45. Decorated Air medal. Mem. Nat. Instnl. Food Distbrs. Assn. (sec.), Tex. Wholesale Grocers Assn. (dir.), Instnl. Food Distbrs. Assn., Food Service Orgn. Distbrs., Nat. Am. Wholesale Grocers Assn., Austin C. of C. Clubs: Masons, Shriners. Office: 220 E St Elmo Rd Austin TX 78745

MOODY, ARTHUR MONROE, III, air transp. co. exec.; b. N.Y.C., Jan. 5, 1937; s. Arthur Monroe and Alice Elizabeth (Williams) M.; A.B., Kenyon Coll., 1960; m. Constance J. Renaud, May 1, 1971; children—Elizabeth Jane, Marc Renaud. Systems engr. IBM, Bridgeport, Conn., 1964-68; systems and procedures analyst Emery Air Freight, Wilton, Conn., 1968-69, regional service mgr., Wakefield, Mass., 1969-72, domestic service mgr., Wilton, 1972-75, mgr. air transp., 1975-78, dir. ops. devel., 1979—. Treas., St. Peter's Episcopal Ch., Monroe, Conn., 1975-77; alt. mem. Woodbury (Conn.) Zoning Commn., 1980—; active vol. leader Boy Scouts Am., 1965—. Served with USAF, 1960-64. Recipient Silver Beaver award Boy Scouts Am., 1977. Republican. Home: 42 Applegate Ln Woodbury CT 06798 Office: Emery Air Freight Old Danbury Rd Wilton CT 06897

MOODY, GEORGE FRANKLIN, banker; b. Riverside, Calif., July 28, 1930; s. William Clifford and Mildred E. (Scott) M.; student Riverside City Coll., 1948-50; grad. with honors Pacific Coast Banking Sch., 1963; m. Mary Jane Plank, Jan. 19, 1950; children—Jeffrey George, Jane Ellen Moody Fowler, John Franklin, Joseph William. Bus. officer U. Calif., Riverside, 1950-52; with Security Pacific Nat. Bank, 1953—, v.p., personnel dir., Los Angeles, 1970-71, sr. v.p. inland div. adminstrn., 1971-73, exec. v.p., 1973—, vice chmn., 1978—. Bd. dirs. Los Angeles YMCA, NCCJ, Hollywood Presbyterian Med. Center; chmn. Los Angeles chpt. ARC. Mem. Los Angeles C. of C. (pres., dir.), Mchts. and Mfrs. Assn. (vice chmn. bd. dirs.), Colorado River Assn. (pres.). Republican. Presbyterian. Club: Hacienda Heights Golf. Address: 333 S Hope St Los Angeles CA 90071

MOODY, J. ROGER, communication systems co. exec.; b. N.Y.C., June 23, 1932; s. Albert and Kathleen May (Cook) M.; student (Coll. scholar), Williams Coll., 1950-53; B.S.E.E. (Univ. scholar 1955-58, U.S. Rubber scholar of Yr. 1957-58), Columbia U., 1958; M.B.A. (Univ. scholar), U. Mich., 1959; m. Kathleen McEvoy, Aug. 17, 1960; children—Karen L., J. Roger, Kristina L. With IBM, 1959-72, systems mgr. consumer transaction systems, Raleigh, N.C., 1969-71, dir. multi processing systems, 1971-72; v.p., gen. mgr. Nuclear Data Co., Palatine, Ill., 1972-73; v.p., gen. mgr. U.S. and Can., Sweda Internat., Orange, N.J., 1973-74; mktg. dir. AT&T, Morristown, N.J., 1974-77; exec. v.p., dir. Teletype Corp., Skokie, Ill., 1977-79; asst. v.p. AT&T, Basking Ridge, N.J., 1979—; chmn. bd. Kay Lee Enterprises, Inc., Comdr. Bd. Advt. Co.; speaker in field. Served with U.S. Army, 1953-55. Mem. IEEE. Clubs: Roxiticus Golf (Mendham, N.J.); Whipperwill Golf (Armonk, N.Y.); Sands Point (N.Y.) Golf. Home: 60 Crest Dr Bernardsville NJ 07924 Office: 295 N Maple Ave Basking Ridge NJ 07920

MOODY, KENNETH ARTHUR, bus. cons.; b. Bklyn., Aug. 22, 1913; s. Alfred Clark and Lavinia P. Moody; B.Sc. in Edn., Bucknell U., 1936; postgrad. Nat. Tng. Lab., 1948, exec. program Pa. State U., 1968; m. Barbara Clarkson, Sept. 12, 1942 (dec.); children—Robert, Deborah. With U.S. Steel Corp., 1937-78, mgr. edn., tgn. and coll relations for raw materials, internat. and other divs., Pitts., 1964-72, mgr. gen. mgmt. devel., 1972-78; pres. Performance Improvement Assos., Inc., Santa Cruz, Calif., 1978—. Chmn. Gateway-to-Careers Project, Pitts., 1965-70. Served to lt. j.g. USN, 1943-46. Mem. Am. Soc. Tng. and Devel. (Man of Yr. award 1976, Outstanding Contbns. to Profession award 1978), Republican. Clubs: Lakeview Country, Santa Cruz Yacht. Contbr. articles to Adult Edn., Clevelander, Tng. and Devel. Jour. Home and Office: 107 Hammond Ave Santa Cruz CA 95062

MOODY, LAMON LAMAR, JR., cons. engr.; b. Bogalusa, La., Nov. 8, 1924; s. Lamar Lamon and Vida (Seal) M.; B.S. in Civil Engring., U. Southwestern La., 1951; m. Eve Thibodeaux, Sept. 22, 1954; children—Lamon Lamar III, Jennifer Eve, Jeffrey Matthew. Engr., Tex. Co., N.Y.C., 1951-52; project engr. African Petroleum Terminals, West Africa, 1952-56; chief engr. Kaiser Aluminum & Chem. Corp., Baton Rouge, 1956-63; pres., owner Dyer & Moody, Inc., Cons. Engrs., Baker, La., 1963—, also chmn. bd., dir. Chmn., Baker Planning Commn., 1961-63. Served with USMCR, 1943-46. Decorated Purple Heart. Registered profl. engr., La., Ark., Miss., Tex. Fellow Am. Soc. C.E.; mem. La. Engring. Soc. (dir., v.p. 1980-81, Charles M. Kerr award for pub. relations 1971), Profl. Engrs. in Pvt. Practice (state chmn. 1969-70), Am. Congress Surveying and Mapping (award for excellency 1972), La. Land Surveyors Assn. (pres. 1968-69 Land Surveyor of Yr. award 1975), Cons. Engrs. Council, Engrs. Joint Council, Research Council of La. (exec. com., trustee public affairs), Baker C. of C. (pres. 1977, Bus. Leader of Yr. award 1975), Nat. Soc. Profl. Engrs., Blue Key. Democrat. Baptist. Mason (32 deg.), Kiwanian (dir. 1964-65). Home: 3811 Charry Dr Baker LA 70714 Office: 2845 Ray Weiland Dr Baker LA 70714

MOODY, PAUL LAWRENCE, chemist; b. Cambridge, Mass., Oct. 24, 1924; s. Oliver Wendell and Grace Mae (West) M.; B.S., Northeastern U., 1942; M.A., M.I.T., 1954; m. Jean Chandler, Jan. 1, 1970; children—Sheryle Diane, Roland Paul. Phys. metallurgist M.I.T.-Lincoln Lab., 1955-61; mech. engr. Dept. Interior, Gloucester, Mass., 1961-65; owner Property Renewal, Inc., Boston, 1965-72; pres. Omega Systems, Inc., Dedham, Mass., 1972—. Served with U.S. Army, 1943-45. Mem. Cambridge Black Cultural Soc., Omega Psi Phi. Democrat. Episcopalian. Office: 123 East St Dedham MA 02026

MOON, M. MUNIR, corp. planning cons.; b. Karachi, Pakistan, Apr. 11, 1952; came to U.S., 1971; s. Abaumer and Khadija M.; B.S.C.E., UCLA, 1975, M.B.A. in Fin. and Mktg., 1977, M.S. in Bus. Econs., 1979; m. Samina Moon, May 27, 1980. Fin. cons., pvt. practice UCLA, 1976-77; partner Erdelyi, Moon, Mezey & Assos., Los Angeles, 1977-79; corp. planning cons. IDC-Chase Econometrics, Los Angeles, 1979—. Mem. UCLA Alumni Adv. Bd., 1976-77, UCLA Alumni Scholarship Adv. Bd., 1979-80; chmn. corp. planning conf. UCLA, 1977; mem. Program Task Force Bd., 1975-76. Registered investment advisor SEC. Mem. Nat. Assn. Bus. Economists, Am. Mgmt. Assn., Assn. M.B.A. Execs., Western Econ. Assn. Author: Financial Simulation Model for Banks, 1979. Research on diversification by mktg. new product or acquisitions. Home: 15061 D Sherman Way Van Nuys CA 91405 Office: One Wilshire Bldg Suite 1715 Los Angeles CA 90017

MOONEY, JOHN ALLEN, bus. exec.; b. Amery, Wis., May 17, 1918; s. Harry Edmon and Maybelle (Johnson) M.; student U. Wis., River Falls; m. Nettie O. Hayes, Aug. 29, 1940; children—John Allen, Suzanne, Jean, Nancy. Salesman, Reid Murdock & Co., Chgo., 1940-45, Consol. Foods Corp., Chgo., 1945-69; nat. sales mgr., v.p. M & R Sales Corp., Oak Park, Ill., 1969-78, pres., chief exec. officer, dir., 1978—; nat. sales mgr., v.p. Western Dressing, Inc., Oak Park, 1970-78, pres., chief exec. officer, dir., 1978—; dir. 1st Nat. Bank of LaGrange (Ill.), Waunakee Alloy Casting Corp. Bd. govs. Shrine Hosp. for Crippled Children, Chgo., Mpls., St. Paul; asso. bd. govs. LaGrange Meml. Hosp. Club: Masons (hon. past potentate Medinah Shrine Temple Chgo.); past potentate Zor Temple, Madison, Wis.). Home: 75 S 6th Ave La Grange IL 60525 Office: 1515 N Harlem Ave Oak Park IL 60302

MOORE, ARTHUR HOLROYD, mfg. co. exec.; b. Bridgeport, Conn., June 8, 1913; s. Arthur Hill and Ethel (Holroyd) M.; student Yale U., 1934, Syracuse U., 1933; B.S., U. Conn., 1935; m. Margaret Hawley, Apr. 3, 1937; children—Cynthia, Betsy, Sally, Curtis, Penny. With Bridgeport Metal Goods Mfg. Co. (Conn.), 1935—, pres., 1973—, also dir.; pres. Moore Products, Fairfield, Conn. Mem. Cosmetic Toiletries and Fragrance Assn. Republican. Episcopalian. Clubs: Brook Lawn Country, Fairfield Beach. Patentee in field. Office: 365 Cherry St Bridgeport CT 06605

MOORE, BENNETT FRANKLIN, electronics co. exec.; b. Cin., May 15, 1951; s. Bruce William and Bertha Jane M.; B. Gen. Studies cum laude, Ohio U., 1972; m. Betty Aileen Hanson, Apr. 3, 1976; 1 son, Jason. Staff acct. Price Waterhouse & Co., Cin., 1973-75; controller comml. devel. div. McGraw-Edison Co., Manchester, N.H. 1975-80; v.p., treas. Armtec Industries, Inc., Manchester, 1980—. Mem. audit advt. com. United Way of Greater Manchester. Mem. Am. Inst. C.P.A.'s, Ohio Soc. C.P.A.'s. Office: Armtec Industries Inc Manchester Municipal Airport Manchester NH 03103

MOORE, EARLE KENNEDY, lawyer; b. Buffalo, Dec. 8, 1921; s. Frank Charles and Velma (Kennedy) M.; A.B., Harvard, 1943, LL.B., 1948; m. Sarah Clarissa Burt, Feb. 15, 1947 (div. Nov. 1964); children—Arthur B., Frank C., Rebecca T., Elizabeth K.; m. 2d,

Katherine Fusako Muto, Feb. 3, 1968. Admitted to N.Y. bar, 1948, U.S. Supreme Ct. bar, 1954; atty. firm Goldstein, Judd & Gurfein, N.Y.C., 1948-60, partner, 1960-68; partner firm Moore, Berson & Lifflander, N.Y.C., 1968—. Dir. P & F Ind, Inc., Great Neck, N.Y. Chmn., Town and Village Com. Against Discrimination, N.Y.C., 1952; mem. Great Neck Com. on Human Rights, 1960-63, Nassau County Ethics Commn., 1963; cons. N.Y. State Temporary Commn. on Estates, 1967-68; vice chmn. Citizens Union, N.Y.C., 1967-72; chmn. Civil Service Reform Assn., N.Y.C., 1967-72; chmn. Com. Housing and Urban Devel., Community Service Soc., N.Y.C., 1975—; bd. dirs. Nat. Citizens Com. Broadcasting, 1969-77, Action for Children's TV, 1974—, Tri-State Media Ministry, 1976—, Media Access Project, 1977—; mem. media com. ACLU, N.Y.C., 1972-77. Mem. Am. Bar Assn., Fed. Communications Bar Assn., Assn. Bar City N.Y., N.Y. Law Inst. Mem. United Ch. of Christ (Churchmanship award 1969). Bd. dirs. Am. Jour. Econs. and Sociology, 1975—. Home: 185 E 85th St New York NY 10028 Office: 555 Madison Ave New York NY 10022

MOORE, EDWARD FREDERICK, investor; b. Detroit, Feb. 1, 1900; s. George Frederick and Walfrid Louisa (Brudin) M.; B.S. in Mech. Engring., U. Mich., 1922, B.A. with distinction, 1923, M.S. in Mech. Engring., 1923; postgrad. Columbia U., 1935-37, Union Theol. Sem., 1936-37. Mech. engr. Gen. Motors Corp., Detroit, 1923-26; fin. engr. natural gas pipeline financing P.W. Chapman & Co., N.Y.C., 1926-28; fin. engr. natural gas pipeline financing, W.Va., Ohio, Ky., Tex., 1928-33; asso. Dr. Alexis Carrel, 1937-41; founder, pres. Found. for Future of Man, Inc., N.Y.C., 1972—. Mem. ASME, Phi Beta Kappa, Sigma Xi, Tau Beta Pi. Republican. Congregationalist. Club: University (N.Y.C.) Author, designer Deep Water Salvage, 1923; Encyclopedia of Unknown, 1973, 77; Charting the Future, 1978. Home: 341 Mountain Rd Englewood NJ 07631 Office: 39 Broadway New York NY 10006

MOORE, GEORGE, equipment co. exec.; b. Plattsburgh, N.Y., Apr. 7, 1927; s. Carl W. and Marion E. (Bunnell) M.; student public schs., Keeseville, N.Y.; m. Shirley M. Chauvin, Feb. 7, 1946; children—Russell, Ellen, George, Roger, Carolyn, Cynthia, Donald, Philip. Constrn. steel worker, 1947-51; owner, operator George Moore Truck Equipment Co., Keeseville, 1951—; real estate investor, commodity market trader. Bd. dirs. Clinton County Area Devel. Corp. Served with U.S. Army, 1945-47. Home and Office: 32 N Sable St Keeseville NY 12944

MOORE, GEORGE ANDREW, JR., steel co. exec.; b. Easton, Pa., May 24, 1927; s. George Andrew and Alice Josephine (Speer) M.; A.B. magna cum laude, Lafayette Coll., 1950; J.D. cum laude, U. Pa., 1953; grad. Advanced Mgmt. Program, Harvard U., 1973; m. Virginia Lambert, Nov. 29, 1958; children—Jeffrey J., Valerie A. Admitted to Pa. bar, 1954, Fed. Dist. Ct. bar, 1958, U.S. Supreme Ct. bar, 1975; asso. firm Fackenthal, Teel & Dancer, Easton, Pa., 1953-56; solicitor Pa. R.R., 1956-58; with Bethlehem Steel Co., 1958—, mgr. indsl. relations, 1965-69, mgr. labor relations, 1970-73, asst. to v.p. indsl. relations, 1973-74, asst. v.p. indsl. relations, 1974-78, v.p. indsl. relations, 1978—. Chmn. bd. trustees East Stroudsburg State Coll.; mem. nat. council Lafayette Coll.; mem. ch. council St. John's Luth. Ch. Served with U.S. Navy, 1945-46. Mem. NAM, Am. Arbitration Assn. (bd. dirs.), Am. Bar Assn., Pa. Bar Assn., Northampton County Bar Assn., Am. Iron and Steel Inst., Internat. Iron and Steel Inst., Bethlehem C. of C., Order of the Coif, Phi Beta Kappa. Clubs: Saucon Valley Country, Duquesne (Pitts.); Masons. Office: Bethlehem Steel Corp Bethlehem PA 18016

MOORE, GERALD THOMAS, bldg. materials co. exec.; b. East Boston, Mass., Sept. 20, 1932; s. Henry A. and Ellen M. M.; B.S. cum laude, Boston Coll., 1960; m. June G. Stott, Apr. 23, 1955; children—Michael, Kathleen, Brian, Colleen. Nat. sales mgr., constrn. products div. Am. Cyanamid Co., Woburn, Mass., 1964-68; br. mgr., constrn. products div. W.R. Grace & Co., Chgo., 1968-73; div. mktg. mgr. Malta div. Philips Industries, Inc. (Ohio), 1973-76, v.p. sales, 1977—. Served with U.S. Army, 1953-55. Recipient Pres.'s award Constrn. Specifications Inst., 1967. Mem. Nat. Sash and Door Jobbers Assn., Nat. Assn. Home Builders, Nat. Wood Working Mfrs. Assn., Nat. Bldg. Materials Distbrs. Assn. Address: Box 397 Malta OH 43758

MOORE, GIBBS BERRY, coal mining exec.; b. Fairmont, W.Va., Mar. 13, 1928; s. James Basil and Beatrice Evangeline (Berry) M.; student Fairmont (W.Va.) State Coll., 1956-57, W.Va. U. Sch. Mines, 1960-65; m. Josephine Marianna, Torch, Mar. 28, 1953; children—David Gibbs, Susan Jo Moore Wamsley. Operator mining machine, sect. foreman Consol. Coal Co., Monongah, W.Va., 1957-70; foreman, gen. belt maintenance Florence Mining Co., Seward, Pa., 1970-73; mine supt. Ranger Fuel Co., Beckley, W.Va., 1973-74; mine supt., dist. supt. Island Creek Coal Co., Craigsville, W.Va., 1974-79; v.p. Keystone div. Eastern Associated Coal Corp., Beckley, W.Va., 1979—; mine ops. cons. Midwestern Mining Firm; mem. Coal Age Advisory Panel. Bd. dirs. Family Planning Bd., Indiana, Pa., 1971-72, Nicholas County Emergency Ambulance Authority; craft com. Nicholas County Vocat. Tech. Center. Served with arty. U.S. Army, 1950-52; Korea. Mem. Mid-State Coal Mining Inst. (v.p. 1977-79), Am. Inst. Mining, Metall. and Petroleum Engrs. Presbyterian. Club: Masons. Home: Grandview Rd Route 9 Box 300 Beaver WV 25813 Office: PO Box 70 Beckley WV 25801

MOORE, HERBERT MOFFETT, lumber co. exec.; ed. Clemson Coll., U. S.C.; m. Eleanor V. Sullivan. Founder Herbert M. Moore Hardwood Lumber, Morganton, N.C., 1933—. Served with USNR, World War II. Home: 101 Woodbine Terr Morganton NC 28655 also 2575 Peachtree Rd NW Atlanta GA 30305 also (summer) Blowing Rock NC 28605

MOORE, HOWARD DENIS, editor, publisher; b. St. Louis, July 22, 1939; s. Howard Stanley and Dorothy Ola (Woltjen) M.; student U. Mo., 1957-60, Nikon Sch. Photography, 1971, 73; m. Mary Jean Brauch, June 1, 1963; children—Michael Anthony, Mark Denis. Newsboy, St. Louis Globe Democrat, 1948-52; with St. Clair Chronicle, 1953-57, pres., editor, publisher, 1979—; advt. editor Tri County News, Sullivan, Mo., 1960-63, editor, 1963—, publisher, 1970—. Vice pres., sec., chief operating officer Moore Enterprises, Inc., Sullivan, Mo., 1966-79; also dir. vice pres. Sullivan Community Betterment, 1963-72, pres., 1972—; chmn. Sullivan Planning and Zoning Commn., 1968—; founding pres. Sullivan Indsl. Devel. Corp., 1973-74; chmn. Sullivan Police Commn., 1974-76; pres. Sullivan United Republican Club, 1972-73. Recipient Leadership award Mo. Gov., 1972. Mem. Nat. Newspaper Assn., Mo. Press. Assn., C. of C. (pres. 1973), Sigma Tau Gamma. Republican. Roman Catholic. Rotarian (pres. 1972-73). Home: 650 Crestview Dr Sullivan MO 63080 Office: 226 W Main St Sullivan MO 63080

MOORE, HUDSON, JR., realtor; b. Atlanta, May 10, 1906; s. Hudson and Tochie (Davis) M.; B.S. in Elec. Engring., U. Colo., 1927; Rhodes scholar, Oxford (Eng.) U., 1927-28; m. Alice Evans, Dec. 30, 1930 (dec. May 5, 1979); children—Hudson III, Barbara Moore Rumsey, Walter Scott Cheesman. Engr., Pub. Service Co. of Colo., 1929-34; pres. Walter S. Cheesman Realty Co., Denver, 1934-76, vice chmn. bd., 1976-78, chmn. bd., 1978—; pres. Republic Bldg. Corp., 1936-76, chmn. bd., 1976—; dir. Evans Investment Co., First Nat. Bank, Denver; dir., mem. exec. com. Mountain States Tel & Tel. Co. Mem. exec. council Denver Area council Boy Scouts Am.; former pres. Downtown Denver Improvement Assn., vice chmn. Downtown Denver Master Plan Com; former chmn. Denver Planning Bd.; former pres. Denver Bd. Water Commrs.; trustee Boettcher Found; trustee, past pres. Denver Mus. Natural History; life trustee Denver Botanic Gardens Found. Served to comdr. USNR, ret. Mem. Am. Soc. Real Estate Counselors. Clubs: Denver Country, Denver Athletic, University, Hiwan Golf, Mile High. Home: 2201 E Alameda Ave Denver CO 80209 Office: 3355 Amoco Bldg 1670 Broadway Denver CO 80202

MOORE, JAMES CLAYTON, III, retail mgr.; b. Washington, Apr. 5, 1949; s. James Clayton and Charlotte Elizabeth (Hopkins) M.; student Emory U., 1967-69; B.A., U. S.C., 1971. With Jim Moore Cadillac-Oldsmobile, Inc., Columbia, S.C., 1969—, bus. mgr., 1975-76, gen. mgr., 1976—. Bd. dirs. Boys' Clubs Greater Columbia. Mem. Columbia Auto Dealers Assn. (past v.p., pres., treas. 1979—), Central S.C. Alumni Assn. (past pres., v.p.), Sales Mktg. Execs. Internat. Clubs: Kiwanis, WildeWood, Columbia Sailing. Home: 220 Raintree Dr Irmo SC 29063 Office: 2222 Main St Columbia SC 29201

MOORE, JOHN LOVELL, JR., govt. ofcl.; b. West Palm Beach, Fla., Aug. 24, 1929; s. John Lovell and Birdie (Welker) M.; A.B. magna cum laude (E.E. Coolidge scholar), Harvard U., 1951, LL.B. magna cum laude, 1956; B.Litt. (Rhodes scholar), Oxford (Eng.) U., 1953. Asso. firm Alston, Miller & Gaines, Atlanta, 1956-61, partner, 1961-77; pres., chmn. Export-Import Bank of U.S., Washington, 1977—; past dir. Vintage Enterprises Inc., Charter Med. Corp.; past lectr. law and medicine Emory U. Sch. Law. Chmn. Ga. Task Force on Mental Health, 1971; spl. counsel on ethics and conflicts of interest Carter-Mondale Transition Group, 1976-77. Mem. Am., Atlanta bar assns., Fla., Ga. bars, Am. Law Inst., Phi Beta Kappa. Democrat. Episcopalian. Office: 811 Vermont Ave NW Washington DC 20571

MOORE, KENNETH LAWRENCE, petroleum mktg. exec.; b. Washington, Feb. 6, 1932; s. William Robert and Ruth Marion (Byron) M.; B.S.E. in Chem. Engring., B.S.E. in Metall. Engring., U. Mich., 1954; M.B.A., U. Del., 1970; m. Sally Ann Hawken, July 24, 1954; children—Christopher Byron, Bradley Hawken, Philip Brooke. Devel. engr. Atlantic Refining Co., Phila., 1954-57; corrosion engr. Tidewater Oil Co., Delaware City, Del., 1957-60, tech. group leader, 1961-65; project mgr., Sun Oil Co., Phila., 1966-67, mgr. new product planning, 1968-69, mgr. petrochems. devel., 1970-71, mgr. mktg. planning and econs., 1972-73, mgr. midwestern mktg. region, 1974-75, v.p., western mktg. area, 1975-79, v.p. sales, 1979—. Election dist. chmn. Republican Party, 1963-72. Mem. Am. Inst. Chem. Engrs., Am. Petroleum Inst., Tau Beta Pi. Presbyterian. Clubs: Union League of Phila., Wilmington Country. Home: 6 Wellington Rd Wilmington DE 19803 Office: 1845 Walnut St Philadelphia PA 19103

MOORE, RANDOLPH GRAVES, real estate exec.; b. Honolulu, Feb. 12, 1939; s. Howard Hoffman and Mary May (Philips) M.; B.A., Swarthmore Coll., 1961; M.B.A., Stanford U., 1963; m. Lynne Johnson, Nov. 8, 1979. Fin. analyst Castle & Cooke, Inc., Honolulu, 1966-68, asst. to treas., 1968-70, treas., 1970-74, group controller, 1974-77, sr. v.p. Oceanic Properties, Inc. subs. Castle & Cooke, Inc., Honolulu, 1977-78, exec. v.p., 1978—. Vol., Aloha United Way, 1966—, chmn. budget and allocations com., 1979—. Home: 59-161 Ke Nui Rd Haleiwa HI 96712 Office: 130 Merchant St Honolulu HI 96813

MOORE, RAYMOND WESLEY, acct., film co. exec.; b. Torrance, Calif., Dec. 31, 1937; s. Walter B. and Mary M.M.; B.A., Calif. Poly. U., 1964; postgrad. U. So. Calif., 1968-70; m. Sandra Benningfield, June 27, 1959; children—Susan, Catherine. Pub. acctg., 1964-65; cost acctg., 1965; with FMC, 1966; budget coordinator Pasadena div. Famous Jet Propulsion Labs., 1967-68; fin. planner marine systems div. Honeywell Co., West Covina, Calif., 1969-70; mgr. corp. acctg. Walt Disney Prodns., Burbank, Calif., 1970—; prin. R.W. Bookkeeping, Claremont, Calif., 1964—. Presbyterian.

MOORE, REID FRANCIS, JR., lawyer; b. Chattanooga, Sept. 27, 1934; s. Reid Francis and Corinne (Milton) M.; B.A., Yale, 1956; LL.B., U. Va., 1959; m. Janice Griffin, July 20, 1963; children—Allyson, Ramsey, Carter. Admitted to Fla. bar, 1959; practiced in Palm Beach, 1959-64, 69—, West Palm Beach, 1965-68; mayor West Palm Beach, 1967-68; mem. Fla. State Legislature, 1976-78. Commr., West Palm Beach, 1965-69; bd. dirs. United Fund Palm Beach County, 1966-68, YMCA, 1967-69, A.R.C., 1972—. Recipient Distinguished Service award West Palm Beach Jr. C. of C., 1965, Good Govt. award 1967; Distinguished Service award Baylor Sch. Alumni Assn., 1969. Mem. Am., Fla., Palm Beach County bar assns., C. of C. (dir. 1965-69), West Palm Beach Jaycees (pres. 1963-64), S.A.R. (chpt. pres. 1970), Phi Alpha Delta. Episcopalian. Republican. Clubs: Masons, Shriners, Yale of The Palm Beaches (pres. 1976-78). Home: 343 Seabreeze Ave Palm Beach FL 33480 Office: 350 Royal Palm Way Palm Beach FL 33480

MOORE, RICHARD ALAN, mfg. co. exec.; b. Lebanon, Ind., Oct. 24, 1949; s. Max and Dorothy Jean Moore; B.S., Ind. U., 1977; diploma horology Bowmen Tech. Sch., 1970; postgrad. Butler U.; m. Mary B. Skroch, June 14, 1980. Retail cons. Wolfe's, Terre Haute, Ind., 1972-73; retail salesman F.R. Lazarus, Indpls., 1973, 74-75, L.S. Ayres, Indpls., 1976-77; mktg. research analyst Hyster Co., Danville, Ill., 1977-79; mktg. specialist Stewart-Warner Co., Indpls., 1979—. Mem. Am. Mgmt. Assn., Ind. Watchmakers Assn., Ind. U. Alumni Assn., Sigma Pi Alpha. Republican. Home: 9507 San Miguel Dr Indianapolis IN 46250 Office: Stewart-Warner Co 1514 Drover St Indianapolis IN 46221

MOORE, RICHARD GEORGE, educator; b. Canandaigua, N.Y., June 20, 1945; s. George Clinton and Julia Elizabeth (Abraham) M.; B.E.E., Cornell U., Ithaca, N.Y., 1967, M.E.E., 1968, M.B.A., 1970; m. Kay Charlene Hansen, Apr. 1, 1967; children—Michelle, Gretchen, Jason. Electronics engr. GTE-Sylvania, Seneca Falls, N.Y., 1966-69; asst. prof. hotel adminstrn. Cornell U., 1970-76, sr. research asso., 1976—; cons. IBM, NCR, MICOR, Digital Equipment Corp., Sweda. Mem. Am. Hotel and Motel Assn., Assn. Ednl. Data Processors, Soc. Certified Data Processors. Republican. Methodist. Home: Box 575 Auburn Rd Groton NY 13073 Office: 533 Statler Hall Ithaca NY 14853

MOORE, RICHARD LEE, fin. services corp. exec.; b. Richmond, Ind., Sept. 29, 1942; s. Joseph Donald and Betty Marie (Moody) M.; B.S., Ind. U., 1964; children—Christopher Shane, Carey Justin, Sabrina Angeline. Nat. comml. mgr. Borg-Warner Acceptance Corp., Chgo., 1967-70; regional mgr. InLeasing subs. Indsl. Nat. Bank, Chgo., 1971-72; v.p. Colonial Bank & Trust Co., Chgo., 1973-76; chmn. bd. First Ill. Fin. Co., Inc., Palatine, Ill., 1976-79; pres. Fin. Industries of Ga., Inc., Atlanta, 1979—. Active boys' basketball, 1974-80. Mem. Am. Assn. Equipment Lessors. Club: Rotary. Home: 140 Marsh Glen Point Atlanta GA 30328 Office: Fin Industries of Ga Inc 15 Dunwoody Pl Atlanta GA 30328

MOORE, ROBERT BRUCE, govt. ofcl.; b. Los Angeles, June 27, 1934; s. Glenn W. and Mary E. (Sharp) M.; B.A., Rutgers U., 1959; M.S., George Washington U., 1972; m. Nancy Phyllis Hood, June 30, 1956; 1 son, Robert Hood. Asst. buyer Bamberger's, Newark, 1959-65; budget analyst Bur. Data Processing, Social Security Adminstrn., Balt., 1966-72, long range planning analyst, 1972-74, supervisory budget analyst, 1974-78, budget officer, 1978-79, budget analyst Office Mgmt., Budget and Personnel, 1979—. Served with U.S. Army, 1956-58. Recipient Social Security Adminstrn. Commrs. citation, 1975; Intergovtl. Affairs fellow, 1976. Home: 216 Longwood Rd Baltimore MD 21210 Office: 245 Altmeyer Bldg 6401 Security Blvd Baltimore MD 21235

MOORE, ROBERT LEROY, mfg. co. exec.; b. Oxford, Miss., Mar. 8, 1936; s. Robert Lawrence and Susie (Wilson) M.; B.S., Memphis State U., 1957; postgrad. U. Calif., Los Angeles, 1967-68, Inst. Mgmt. Northwestern U., 1977; m. Elizabeth Ann Tuggle, June 12, 1954; 1 son, Robert Russell. Adminstrv. asst. City of Los Angeles, 1957-58; with Lockheed Co., Burbank, Calif., 1959—, dir. govt. product support supply div., 1976-80. Fin. mgr., treas. St. Jude's Episcopal Ch., Burbank, Calif., 1969-70. Mem. Nat. Mgmt. Assn. Club: Burbank Men's Golf. Home: 1123 Vista Ridge Burbank CA 91504 Office: PO Box 551 Burbank CA 91520

MOORE, ROBERT WILLIAM, assn. exec.; b. Claysburg, Pa., June 4, 1924; s. Frank B. and Sarah A. (Edelbute) M.; B.A., Pa. State U., 1948; m. Helen Lingenfelter, July 17, 1948; children—Thomas R., Priscilla Jane. With Price Waterhouse & Co., Pitts., 1948-62, mgr., 1955-62; asst. controller Con-Gas Service Corp., Pitts., 1962-65; asst. controller Consol. Natural Gas Service Co., Inc., Pitts., 1966-72, controller, 1972-78; asst. controller Consol. Natural Gas Co., Pitts., 1968-72, controller, 1972-78; pres. Fin. Execs. Inst., N.Y.C., 1978—. Bd. dirs. Central Blood Bank, Pitts., 1960-78, treas. corp., 1962-68, chmn. fin. com. 1962-68, chmn. bd., 1969-72. Served with AUS, 1943-45. Mem. Am., Pa. insts. C.P.A.'s, Nat. Assn. Accountants, Fin. Execs. Inst., Fin. Acctg. Standards Adv. Council, Pa. State Alumni Assn. (exec. bd. Council), Pa. Soc., Delta Tau Delta. Episcopalian. Mason (32 deg.). Clubs: Pitts.; Univ. (dir. 1970—, pres. 1975-76), Union League, Bd. Rm. (N.Y.C.); Valley Brook Country (dir. 1968-70, v.p. bd. 1970). Home: 928 Bridgewater Dr Pittsburgh PA 15216 also 160 E 38th St New York NY 10017 Office: Financial Execs Inst 633 3d Ave New York NY 10017

MOORE, ROGER ALLAN, lawyer; b. Framingham, Mass., Aug. 8, 1931; s. Ralph Chester and Mabelle (Taft) M.; A.B. cum laude, Harvard, 1953, LL.B., 1956; m. Barbara Lee Wildman, July 4, 1955; children—Marshall Christian, Elizabeth Lee, Taft Hayden Davis, Allan Baron. Admitted to Mass. bar, 1956, since practiced in Boston; asso. firm Ropes & Gray, 1956-66, partner, 1967—. Chmn. bd. Nat. Rev., Inc.; clk. L.S. Starrett Co., Wrentham Steel Products Co. Former chmn. bd. dirs. Beacon Hill Civic Assn.; former mem. Bd. Fgn. Scholarships, U.S. Dept. State; bd. dirs. Historic Boston; clk. Bostonian Soc. Recipient Endicott Peabody Saltonstall prize Harvard, 1953, Boylston prize, 1952. Mem. Am., Mass., Boston bar assns., Old South Assn. Boston (dir.). Episcopalian (mem. corp., warden). Home: 26 W Cedar St Boston MA 02108 Office: 225 Franklin St Boston MA 02110

MOORE, ROGER MCEWEN, Realtor, real estate developer; b. Knoxville, Tenn., Jan. 15, 1938; s. Claude B. and Sue (Jordan) M.; B.S., U. Tenn., 1960; m. Jane Ann, Mar. 17, 1979; children—Roger, Charles Gregory, Michael David. Chmn., pres. R.M. Moore & Assos., Inc., Knoxville, 1980—; chmn. R.M. Mktg. Assos., Inc., 1980—; chmn. R.M. Moore & Assos., Inc., Knoxville, 1980—; pres. Moore Realty Investment, Inc., Knoxville, 1980—; dir. City & County Bank of Anderson County, 1979-80. Bd dirs. Jr. Achievement, Knoxville, 1978-80. Mem. Knoxville Bd. Realtors (dir., muliple-listing chmn.), Tenn. Assn. Realtors, Nat. Assn. Realtors, Nat. Life Underwriters. Episcopalian. Club: Fox Den Country.

MOORE, SHIRLEY THROCKMORTON (MRS. ELMER LEE MOORE), accountant; b. Des Moines, July 3, 1918; d. John Carder and Jessie (Wright) Throckmorton; student Iowa State Tchrs. Coll., summers 1937-38, Madison Coll., 1939-41; M.C.S., Benjamin Franklin U., 1944; m. Elmer Lee Moore, Dec. 19, 1946; children—Fay, Lynn Dallas. Asst. bookkeeper Sibley Hosp., Washington, 1941-42, Alvord & Alvord, 1942-46, bookkeeper, 1946-49, chief accountant, 1950-64, financial adviser to sr. partner, 1957-64; dir. Allen Oil Co., 1958-74; pvt. practice in accounting, 1964—. Mem. sch. bd. Takoma Acad., Takoma Park, Md., 1970—; bd. dirs. Washington Adventist Hosp., 1971—, finance chmn., 1974-76; bd. dirs. Blue Ridge Youth Camp. Recipient Disting. Grad. award Benjamin Franklin U., 1961. C.P.A., Md. Mem. Am., D.C. (pub. relations com. 1976—) insts. C.P.A.'s, Am. Women's Soc. C.P.A.'s, Am. Soc. Women Accountants (legislation chmn. 1960-62, nat. dir. 1952-53, nat. treas. 1953-54), Bus. and Profl. Women's Club (treas. D.C. 1967-68), Benjamin Franklin U. Alumni Assn. (Distinguished Alumni award 1964, charter, past dir.), D.A.R., Md. Assn. C.P.A.'s (charter chmn. membership com. Montgomery Prince George County 1963-64, chmn. student relations com. 1964-67, pres. 1968-69, mem. fed. tax com. 1971-73). Mem. Seventh Day Adventist Ch. Contbr. articles to profl. jours. Home and office: 1007 Elm Ave Takoma Park MD 20012

MOORE, SIDNEY CHESTERFIELD, fin. planning co. exec.; b. Dallas, Jan. 19, 1931; s. Henry and Hazel (Johnston) M.; B.S. in Scis., U. Tex., El Paso, 1964; m. Helen Frank Price, Dec. 12, 1950; children—Sidney Chesterfield, Frank Henry, Randal David. Chemist, Texas City Chem. Co., 1952-54; project mgr. Price McNemar Constrn. Co., 1954-62; owner, mgr. Moore Constrn. Co., El Paso, Tex., 1962-64; territorial mgr. Sterling Drug Corp., Ventura, Calif., 1964-80; mktg. mgr. Envirotron Engring. Corp., 1975-77; pres. Moore Fin. Planners, Ventura, 1978—. Pres., Ventura County Young Republicans, 1969. Mem. Internat. Assn. Fin. Planners, Inst. Cert. Fin. Planners. Mem. Ch. of Christ. Clubs: Ventura Elks, Sunrise Optimist (lt. gov. 1975-77, Disting. Lt. Gov.'s citation 1976, 77, Outstanding Lt. Gov. award 1977) (Ventura). Home: 1699 Swift Ave Ventura CA 93003 Office: 3585 Maple St Ventura CA 93003

MOORE, TERRY LOCKLIN, III, civil engr.; b. Decatur, Ala., Oct. 16, 1945; s. Terry Locklin Jr. and Harriet Irwin M.; B.S.C.E., Va. Mil. Inst.; M.S.A., George Washington U., 1975; m. Vera Elizabeth Caldwell, June 29, 1968; children—Terry Locklin IV, Serena E., Frances I. Sr. project engr. Internat. Paper Co., Mobile, Ala., 1974-76, design engr., sr. design engr., Gardiner, Oreg., 1976-80, mgr. entry level programs, N.Y.C., 1980—. Bd. dirs. S.W. Ala., Am. Lung Assn., 1976; deacon Government St. Presbyn. Ch., Mobile, Ala., 1976; elder United Presbyn. Ch., Reedsport, Oreg., 1979-80, 1st Presbyn. Ch., Stamford, Conn., 1981—. Served to capt. USAF, 1967-74. Decorated USAF Commendation medal with oak leaf cluster, USAF Meritorious Service medal. Registered profl. engr., La. Mem. ASCE, Am. Mgmt. Assn. Office: 77 W 45th St New York NY 10017

MOORE, THOMAS HUGH, trade assn. exec.; b. Morrilton, Ark., Jan. 13, 1929; s. James Thomas and Annie Nellie (Van Marion) M.; student Hendrix Coll., 1947-48; B.A. in Journalism, U. Central Ark., 1951; m. Clara Jean Jackson, Nov. 18, 1950; children—Melanie

Anne, Stephanie Suzanne, James Van. Journalist, Log Cabin Democrat, Conway, Ark., 1947-51; dir. public relations Ark. Electric Cooperatives, Inc., Little Rock, 1957-61; gen. mgr., exec. v.p. Assn. Ill. Electric Coops., Springfield, 1961—. Trustee Am. Inst. Cooperation. Served to lt. USNR, 1951-57. Mem. Ill. Farm Electrification Council (dir., past pres.), Ill. Soc. Assn. Execs. (pres. 1969), Rural Electric Statewide Mgrs. Assn. (pres. 1969), Consumer Fedn. Ill. (pres. 1968-70). Methodist. Clubs: Sangamo, Shriners. Home: 2117 Kenwood Dr Springfield IL 62704 Office: 6460 S 6th Frontage Rd Springfield IL 62708

MOORE, THOMAS JUSTIN, JR., electric co. exec.; b. Richmond, Va., Apr. 15, 1925; s. Thomas Justin and Carrie (Willingham) M.; A.B., Princeton U., 1947; LL.B., U. Va., 1950; m. Mary Elizabeth Pearson, Oct. 22, 1954; children—Mary Elizabeth, Thomas Justin. Admitted to Va. bar, 1949; asso. firm Hunton, Williams, Gay, Powell & Gibson, Richmond, 1950-54, mem. firm., 1955-67; asso. gen. counsel Va. Electric and Power Co., Richmond, 1960-67, sr. v.p., 1967-69, exec. v.p., 1969-70. pres., 1970-77, vice chmn., 1978-79, chmn., 1979—, also dir.; dir. Fidelity Banks, Inc., Philip Morris Inc.; former dir. Richmond Corp.; bd. dirs. Southeastern Elec. Exchange, Edison Electric Inst. Former campaign chmn. Richmond United Givers Fund; trustee Colonial Williamsburg Found.; bd. assos. U. Richmond; former chmn. Va. Found for Ind. Colls.; former bd. dirs. Atomic Indsl. Forum. Served to lt. (j.g.) USNR, 1943-46; PTO. Mem. Am. (mem. council pub. utility law sect. 1968-74), Va. (chmn. exec. com. 1967), Richmond (pres. 1966) bar assns., Assn. Bar City N.Y., Phi Alpha Delta, Omicron Delta Kappa. Episcopalian. Clubs: Princeton, Brook (N.Y.C.); Met. (Washington); Country Club of Va., Commonwealth, Downtown (Richmond). Home: 9 Maxwell Rd Richmond VA 23226 Office: One James River Plaza Richmond VA 23261

MOORE, WILLIAM ARTHUR, accountant; b. Roseville, Calif., Dec. 17, 1934; s. Millard P. and Mary June (Wilder) M.; B.A., Fresno State Coll., 1956; m. Dorothy Lee Reece, June 11, 1955; children—Thomas Philip, Robert Kirk, Mari Anne, Lori Anne. Acct., Muncy McPherson & Co., C.P.A.'s, San Francisco and Redding, Calif., 1957-65; pres. Moore Evanhoe Accts., Redding, 1965—. Mem. Calif. Soc. C.P.A.'s (pres. Sacramento chpt. 1979-80), Redding C. of C. (pres. 1979-80), Am. Inst. C.P.A.'s. Republican. Clubs: Elks, Masons. Home: 3500 Scenic Dr Redding CA 96001 Office: 1330 West St Redding CA 96001

MOORE, WILLIAM ESTILL, JR., land mgmt. and financial exec.; b. Bowling Green, Ky., Dec. 19, 1920; s. William E. and Carolyn (Elkin) M.; B.A., Stanford, 1947; m. Margaret Jackson Shanks, Mar. 12, 1952; children—Carrol Meteer, William Estill III, Marilyn Taylor, Thomas Edwin III, James Rogers. Asst. to pres. Tejon Ranch Co., 1947-48; v.p., 1948-59, exec. v.p., 1959, pres., 1959-70, exec. cons., 1970-73; chmn. bd. Heritage Savs. and Loan Assn., 1973—; v.p. Chandler-Sherman Corp., 1949-56, pres., dir., 1956-70; exec. cons., dir. Kings County Devel. Co., 1970—; dir., audit com., investment com. Ticor and Title Ins. & Trust Co., 1956—; dir. Rowland Land Co., Heritage Savs. & Loan Co., Pioneer Nat. Title Co. Bd. dirs. Arvin-Edison Water Dist. Kern County, 1952-71, W.R.M. Water Storage Dist., United Way Bakersfield; bd. dirs., exec. com. So. Calif. Water Conf.; bd. dirs., exec. com., policy com. Irrigation Dists. Assn. Calif.; bd. dirs. North Kern Water Dist., 1972—; bd. dirs. adviser, sec.-treas. Calif. Feather River Project Assn., League Women Voters; commr. Kern County Water Commn., 1952—, pres., 1966-76; dir., exec. com., sec.-treas. Calif. Water Resources Assn., 1962-74, pres., 1974-78, chmn. bd. dirs., 1978—; mem. Calif. Republican Central Com., 1958-59. Served from pfc. to lt. col., USMC, 1940-59. Decorated Navy Cross, Silver Star, Purple Heart. Mem. Sci. and Industry Mus., Philharmonic Assn. Los Angeles, Kern County Water Assn. (dir. 1955—, pres. 1971-74), San Joaquin Valley Oil Producers Assn. (dir.), Calif. Farm Bur., Assn. Calif. Water Dists. (dir.), Calif. Cattlemen's Assn., Greater Bakersfield (dir.), Los Angeles chambers commerce, Kern County Farm Bur., (dir.), Young Pres.'s Orgn., Inc., Navy League, U.S. (exec. com., dir., v.p. Bakersfield council). Presbyn. Clubs: Commonwealth (Calif.); Food and Wine Soc. London; Town Hall (Los Angeles); Annandale Golf (Pasadena, Calif.); San Gabriel Country; Bakersfield Country, Petroleum (Bakersfield). Home: 2930 22d St Bakersfield CA 93301 Office: 3120 18th St Bakersfield CA 93301

MOORE, WILLIAM GARRISON, communications and electronics co. exec.; b. Madison, Wis., Sept. 2, 1921; s. Sylvester and Anna Mills (Garrison) M.; A.B., Wabash (Ind.) Coll., 1942; LL.B., U. Wis., 1950; m. Marjorie Winski, Feb. 2, 1947; children—Jennifer Mills, Emily Norris, William Garrison. Admitted to D.C. bar, N.Y. bar, Conn. bar; asso. firm Covington & Burling, Washington, 1950-56; sr. counsel Reynolds Metals Co., Richmond, Va., 1956-62; partner firm Reavis & McGrath, N.Y.C., 1962-64; gen. counsel Latin Am., then asst. dir. bus. devel. Internat. Tel. & Tel. Co., N.Y.C., 1964-73; dir. bus. devel. United Technologies Co., Hartford, Conn., 1973-75; v.p. mergers and acquisitions Citibank, N.A., N.Y.C., 1975-78; v.p. bus. devel. Gen. Tel. & Electronics Corp., Stamford, Conn., 1978—. Served to lt. (j.g.) USNR, 1942-46. Episcopalian. Editor-in-chief Wis. Law Rev., 1949-50. Office: 1 Stamford Forum Stamford CT 06904

MOORE, WILLIAM GEORGE, JR., mktg. exec.; b. San Francisco, Feb. 22, 1916; s. William George and Helen Crawford (Martin) M.; B.A., Stanford, 1938; div.; children—William George III, William Walter, Elizabeth Terry. Supr., Coopers Lybrand, San Francisco, 1937-43; comptroller C.C. Bechtel McCone, S.A., Dhahran, Saudi Arabia, 1944-47; sec., comptroller Cathedral Films, Burbank, Calif., 1959-62; exec. v.p., dir. mktg. NUCO Industries, Inc., Monrovia, Calif., 1963—; pres. Holiday, Inc., Monrovia, 1972—. Producer radio and TV programs for Tex. Democratic candidates. C.P.A., Calif., Tex. Clubs: Whitehall (Chgo.); Los Angeles Turf. Home: 245 W Colorado Blvd Arcadia CA 91006 also Buzzard's Roost Ranch Buzzard's Roost Rd Round Mountain CA 96084 Office: 135 E Railroad Ave Monrovia CA 91016

MOORE, WILLIAM MERRETTE, JR., bus. cons.; b. Goldsboro, N.C., Sept. 17, 1939; s. William Merrette and Margaret Lee (Mumford) M.; B.S., U.S Naval Acad., 1961; M.B.A., U. N.C., 1967; m. Sandra Janet Phillips, July 9, 1966; children—Merrette, Hayden. Vice pres. investment banking Legg Mason Wood Walker, Washington, 1967-74; independent investor, operator various businesses, 1974-76; pres. Trident Fin. Corp., New Bern, N.C., 1976—: cons. in field. Served to lt. USN, 1961-65. Sr. mem. Am. Soc. Appraisers. Clubs: New Bern Golf and Country, Harbour Town Racquet (founder), Coral Bay (Atlantic Beach), Capital City (Raleigh, N.C.). Address: 4604 W Fairway Dr New Bern NC 28560

MOORED, KEITH W., banker; b. Burnips, Mich., May 28, 1922; s. Francis W. and Orah (Miller) M.; student Grand Rapids Jr. Coll., 1942, Baldwin-Wallace Coll., 1943, Augustana Coll., 1943; m. Joyce C. Cook, June 9, 1949; children—Jane, Keith W., Susan, Ann, David, Cindy. Sales, Avco Corp., New Idea Farm Equipment Div., Jackson, Mich., 1950-53; pres. Moored Constrn. Co., Grandville, Mich., 1954-65; pres. Grand Valley Nat. Bank, Grandville, Mich., 1964—, also dir., chmn. bd.; dir. NBD Portage Bank; dir., mem. exec. com. Words of Hope, Inc. Radio. City councilman, City of Grandville, 1964-65; mem. Kent County Pension Bd., 1976—; pres. Grandville Econ. Devel. Com. Served with USAAF, 1943-46. Mem. Grandville C. of C. (pres. 1968, 80-81), Am. Bankers Assn., Mich. Bankers Assn. Republican. Office: 3115 Wilson Ave Grandville MI 49418

MOORHEAD, THOMAS BURCH, lawyer, bus. exec.; b. Evanston, Ill., May 3, 1934; s. John William and Jane (Hendrich) M.; B.A., Yale, 1956; J.D., U. Pa., 1959; LL.M., N.Y. U., 1964; m. Christie Barnard, Dec. 31, 1966; children—Merrell Hendrich, Hannah Christie, Rachel McGill. Admitted to N.Y. bar, 1960, Conn. bar, 1971; asso. Milbank, Tweed, Hadley & McCloy, N.Y.C., 1959-63; asso. counsel, asst. sec. Hooker Chem. Corp., N.Y.C., 1963-68, dir. indsl. relations, 1968-69, v.p. indsl. relations, 1969-72; v.p. employee relations Champion Internat. Corp., N.Y.C., 1972-74; v.p. adminstrn. Beker Industries Corp., Greenwich, Conn., 1974-76; v.p. corp. affairs Esteé Lauder, Inc., N.Y.C., 1976—. Mem. New Canaan (Conn.) Republican Town Com., 1980—. Mem. Assn. Bar N.Y.C., Am. Bar Assn., Am. Soc. Internat. Law. Clubs: Met., Yale (N.Y.C.); Woodway Country (Darien, Conn.); Winter (New Canaan, Conn.). Home: 148 Ramhorne Rd New Canaan CT 06840 Office: 767 Fifth Ave New York NY 10022

MOQUIN, JOSEPH CHARLES, engring. co. exec.; b. Middleboro, Mass., July 7, 1924; s. Joseph Alfred and Sarah (Bump) M.; student Miss. State Coll., 1943-44; B.S., Washington U., 1949, postgrad., 1949, 51; m. Anita Johnson, Jan. 2, 1979; children—Michael James, Stephen Charles, Claiborne Lee, Margaret Mary, Sarah Jo, William Alfred, Paul Benedict, Thomas Joseph. Indsl. engr. Beltex Corp., St. Louis, 1949-50, Rice-Stix Co., St. Louis, 1950-52; with Rock Island (Ill.) Arsenal, 1952-56; chief mgmt. services Army Ballistic Missile Agy., Redstone Arsenal, Ala., 1956-58; chief mgmt. engring. Army Ordnance Missile Command, 1958-59; exec. v.p. Brown Engring. Co., Inc., Huntsville, Ala., 1959-66; pres. Teledyne Brown Engring., Huntsville, Ala., 1966—; dir. 1st Ala. Bank, Huntsville, 1973—; pres. Research Park Adv. Bd., 1976. Mem. Tenn. Valley Council Boy Scouts Am., 1970-72; mem. Huntsville Indsl. Expansion Com., 1965-70; mem. Mayor of Huntsville Advt. Com., 1971. Served to 1st lt. C.E., AUS, 1943-46. Mem. Am. Inst. Indsl. Engrs., Am. Def. Preparedness Assn., Assn. U.S. Army, AIAA, Ala. Soc. Profl. Engrs., Huntsville C. of C. Roman Catholic. Clubs: Huntsville Country, Turtle Point Yacht and Country, Kiwanis. Home: 122 Scenic Dr Madison AL 35758 Office: Teledyne Brown Engring Cummings Research Park Huntsville AL 35807

MORALES, WILLIE, bank exec.; b. Santurce, P.R., Jan. 16, 1946; s. Natividad and Gloria (González) M.; B.B.A. in Accounting, U. P.R., 1968; m. Ivette Martinez, Nov. 6, 1971; children—Daniel Guillermo, David Guillermo. Staff accountant Peat, Marwick, Mitchell & Co., San Juan, P.R., 1967-69, sr. accountant, 1969-71; v.p., spl. asst. to pres. Caribbean Fin. Co., Rio Piedras, P.R., 1971-75; mgr. Citibank, N.A., San Juan, 1975-76, resident v.p., 1976-78, v.p., 1978—. Mem. Nat. Assn. Accountants, Hosp. Fin. Mgmt. Assn., Sigma Delta (past treas.). Home: Flor de Lis 6 Santa Maria Rio Piedras PR 00927 Office: GPO Box 4106 San Juan PR 00936

MORALES-CORREA, JOSÉ RAFAEL, computer co. exec.; b. San Juan, P.R., Sept. 17, 1940; s. Clemente and Eulalia (Correa-Perez) Morales-Rodriguez; B.S., U. P.R., 1962; M.S., U. So. Calif., 1971; m. Clare A. Elliott, Dec. 23, 1967; 1 dau., Lea Catalina Morales-Elliott. Project mgr. EDP, Fireman's Fund Ins. Co., San Francisco, 1969-73; corporate tech. mgr. EDP Foremost-McKesson, Inc., San Francisco, 1973-77; v.p. tech. services ADP, Security Pacific Bank, Los Angeles, 1977-79; v.p. Info-Mgmt. Div., Tymshare Corp., San Francisco, 1979—; cons., lectr. in field. Served to capt. USAF, 1963-69. Mem. IEEE, Computer Soc., Telecommunications Assn. Roman Catholic. Home: PO Box 2723 San Francisco CA 94126 Office: 900 Front St San Francisco CA 94126

MORAN, ALFRED JAY, JR., business exec.; b. Washington, Aug. 1, 1943; s. Alfred Jay and Marjorie Leverich M.; B.A., U. N.C., 1967; M.B.A., Harvard U., 1969; m. Lansing Simonds, Nov. 1, 1969. Vice pres. Coenen & Co., N.Y.C., 1970-75; pres. QSR Adv. Corp., N.Y.C., 1975-78; pres. TJM Corp., New Orleans, 1978—. Clubs: Racquet and Tennis, Brook (N.Y.C.); Spouting Rock Beach Assn. (Newport, R.I.); New Orleans Country. Home: 1022 Dumaine St New Orleans LA 70116 Office: 1001 Howard Ave 35th Floor New Orleans LA 70113

MORAN, CHARLES A., investment mgmt. co. exec.; b. Chgo., Feb. 7, 1943; s. Charles W. and Rose B. (Sutcher) M.; A.B., Princeton U., 1964; J.D., U. Mich., 1967; m. Donna L. Orbach, Sept. 2, 1967; children—Scott Alan, Erin Elizabeth. Pension trust officer, adminstrv. officer, officer in charge new bus. devel., pension div. Chase Manhattan Bank, N.Y.C., 1967-70; sr. v.p., sr. adminstrv., fin. officer trust div. bank coms. Manufacturers Hanover Trust Co., N.Y.C., 1971-79, officer-in-charge employee benefit trust div., 1979-80; chmn. bd., pres. Lionel D. Edie & Co., Inc., N.Y.C., 1980—; lectr. bus., econs. Bloomfield Coll.; formerly lectr. sociology, fin. employee benefits C.W. Post Coll., L.I. U., Am. Inst. Banking; adv. council U.S. Dept. Labor; adv. bd. BNA Pension Reporter; cons. Urban Vol. Cons. Group, Inc.; mem. Employees Retirement Income Security Act of 1974 Roundtable, chmn., 1974-79. Mem. Am. Pension Conf. (treas. 1976-79), N.Y. State Bankers Assn. (employees trusts com.), Am. Bankers Assn. (chmn. employees trust com.), Internat. Found. Pension and Welfare Plans, Assn. Pvt. Pension and Welfare Plans (dir.), AAUP, N.Y. C. of C. (task force on pub. pensions). Contbr. articles to profl. jours. Office: 530 Fifth Ave New York NY 10036

MORAN, HAROLD JOSEPH, lawyer; b. N.Y.C., Feb. 21, 1907; s. Thomas J. and Leonore M.F. (Geoghegan) M.; A.B. cum laude, Holy Cross Coll., 1928; LL.B., Fordham U., 1932; J.D., 1968; m. Geraldine D. Starkey, July 12, 1956. Admitted to N.Y. bar, 1934; practiced in N.Y.C., 1934-42, Bklyn., 1949-57, Malverne, N.Y., 1977—; law dept. Title Guarantee & Trust Co., Bklyn., 1945-48; sr. atty. real property bur. N.Y. State Law Dept., Albany, 1957-63, N.Y.C., 1963-77, ret., 1977; spl. dep. atty. gen. election frauds, 1973. Title closer City Title Co., Bklyn., 1949-52; U.S., P.R. mortgage loan examiner Cadwalader, Wickersham & Taft, N.Y.C., 1952-56, 63—, 9th Fed. Savs. & Loan Assn., N.Y.C., 1971—; instr. law St. John's U. Sch. Commerce, Jamaica, N.Y., 1956-57. Served with AUS, 1942-45. Knight Holy Sepulchre. Mem. Am. Bar Assn., Bar Assn. Nassau County, Am. Judicature Soc., N.Y. County Lawyers Assn., Catholic Lawyers Guild. Democrat. Roman Catholic. Clubs: Hempstead Golf and Country, Southward Ho Country. Home: 1509 Alfred Dr Boynton Beach FL 33435 Office: 277 Hempstead Ave Malverne NY 11565

MORAN, JOHN PAUL, ins. agt.; b. Davenport, Iowa, Feb. 8, 1917; s. James Aloysius and Mary Ann (Ryan) M.; student St. Ambrose Coll., 1935-37, Cath. U., 1937-38; m. Betty L. McGonigle, Oct. 19, 1940; children—Jon Stephen, Janice Sue, Thomas James, James Michael, Mary Martha. Ins. agt. James A. Moran Agy., Rock Island, Ill., 1937-38, owner, 1938-80, partner, 1977—; pres. Ill. Casualty Co., 1949-54; coordinator Office Price Adminstrn., 1942-45; adviser, supr. Ill. Housing Authority, 1949-51. Mem. Ind. Ins. Agts. Ill. (past pres.), Rock Island Bd. Realtors (past pres.), Rock Island C. of C. Roman Catholic. Clubs: Moose, Elks, K.C. Home: 1408 21st Ave Rock Island IL 61201 Office: James A Moran Agy 1705 2d Ave Rock Island IL 61201

MORAN, JULIETTE M., chem. co. exec.; b. N.Y.C., June 12, 1917; d. James Joseph and Louise M.; B.S., Columbia U., 1939; M.S., N.Y. U., 1948. Research asst. Columbia U., 1941; jr. engr. Signal Corps Lab., AUS, 1942-43; with GAF Corp. (formerly Gen. Aniline & Film Corp.), N.Y.C., 1943—, successively jr. chemist process devel. dept., tech. asst. to N.Y. process devel. dept., tech. asst. to dir. Central Research Lab., tech. asst. to dir. comml. devel., 1953-55, supr. tech. service, comml. devel. dept., 1955-59, sr. devel. specialist, 1959-60, mgr. planning, 1961, asst. to pres., 1962-67, v.p., 1967-71, sr. v.p., 1971-74, exec. v.p., 1974-80, vice-chmn., 1980—, also dir.; dir. GAF Corp. and various subs.'s; trustee Empire Savs. Bank. Fellow A.A.A.S., Am. Inst. Chemists; mem. Am. Chem. Soc., Comml. Devel. Assn. Clubs: Econ. of N.Y., Hemisphere. Office: GAF Corp 140 W 51st St New York NY 10020

MORAN, MARGUERITE KATHERINE, chem. co. exec.; b. Pringle, Pa.; d. John V. and Anna (Brennan) M.; B.S. in Chemistry cum laude, Coll. Misericordia, 1943; M.S., Columbia U.; M.L.S., Rutgers U., 1960. Organic research chemist Reichold Chems., Inc., Elizabeth, N.J., 1943-49; tech. information supr. M&T Chems., Inc., Rahway, N.J., 1949-71, mgr. tech. information, 1971-77, dir. bus. and tech. info., 1977—. Cons. med. library Elizabeth Gen. Hosp. 1957-64. Mem. Am. Chem. Soc. (advt. mgr. chem. lit., 1962-77), Soc. Plastics Engrs. (com. guide to lit. polyvinyl chloride, 1962—), Spl. Libraries Assn. (various coms., past pres. N.J. chpt., chmn. metals-materials div.), AAUW, ASTM, Am. Soc. Info. Scientists. Co-author: Industrial Chemicals, 1975; contbr. articles in field to profl. jours. Home: 13 Longfellow Dr Colonia NJ 07067 Office: Box 1104 Rahway NJ 07065

MORAN, THOMAS HARRY, univ. adminstr.; b. Milw., Oct. 21, 1937; s. Harry Edward and Edna Agnes Moran; B.S., U. Wis., 1964, M.A., 1972, Ph.D., 1974; m. Barbara Ellen Saklad, June 10, 1969; children—David Thomas, Karen Ellen. Dir. capital budgeting Wis. Dept. Adminstrn., 1962-64; exec. dir. Wis. Higher Ednl. Aids Bd., 1964-69; spl. cons. tax policy Wis. Dept. Revenue, 1973-74; dep. dir. Wis. Manpower Council, Office of Gov., 1974-76; v.p. bus. and fin., treas. U. Detroit, 1976-78; asso. v.p. health affairs U. So. Calif., Los Angeles, 1979—. USN fellow, 1957-59; U.S. Office Edn. research fellow, 1973. Mem. Am. Mgmt. Assn., Am. Assn. Higher Edn., Phi Kappa Phi. Home: 3245 Sawtooth Ct West Lake Village CA 93631 Office: U So Calif 349 Adminstrn Bldg University Park Los Angeles CA 90007

MORAVY, GERALD JAY, transp. services co. exec.; b. Mt. Pleasant, Mich., Aug. 15, 1937; s. Herbert Lee and Ida Blanche (Ankrom) M.; student pub. schs., Mt. Pleasant; m. Evelyn Joyce Tyler, May 8, 1964; children—Steven James, Michael Wayne, Sherry Lynn, Kimberly Yvonne (dec.), Jeremy Jay. Truck driver Gordon Drilling Co., Mt. Pleasant, 1954-59; driller McClure Drilling Corp., Mt. Pleasant, 1959-61; toolpusher N.Am. Drilling Co., Mt. Pleasant, 1961-64, Moco Drilling Co., Mt. Pleasant, 1964-67) pres. Moravy Trucking Co., Mt. Pleasant, 1967—, pres. Midwest Pollution Control, Inc., 1980—. Mem. Mich. Oil and Gas Assn., Mich. Trucking Assn., Mich. Ltd. Carriers Assn. (dir. 1979-80), Independent Petroleum Assn., Liquid Indsl. Control Assn. (dir. 1979-80), Oilfield Haulers Assn., Nat. Fedn. Ind. Bus., U.S. C. of C., Mt. Pleasant Area C. of C. Baptist. Clubs: Saginaw Valley Oilmen's, Moose, Elks. Home: 2051 S Lincoln Rd Mt Pleasant MI 48858 Office: 1934 Commercial Dr Mt Pleasant MI 48858

MORE, GARY CHARLES HOWARD, tool mfg. co. ofcl.; b. Saratoga Springs, N.Y., Feb. 26, 1949; s. Charles Lewis and Ada (Benoit) M.; A.A.S., SUNY, Farmingdale, 1971; B.A. in Polit. Sci., C.W. Post Coll., L.I. U., 1973; B.B.A. in Fin., U. Ga., 1979; m. Donna Beth Howard, Jan. 10, 1979. Supr. shipping and receiving Snap-on Tools, Albany, N.Y., 1973-77, warehouse mgr., Miami Lakes, Fla., 1980—; unit coordinator trainee Armour Food Co., Atlanta, 1979-80, warehouse supr., 1979. First aid vol. ARC, Schenectady, 1976; vol. Herman Talmadge to U.S. Senate campaign, Atlanta, 1980. Republican. Roman Catholic. Office: 6051 NW 153d St Miami Lakes FL 33014

MORE, RONALD, appraisal co. exec.; b. London, July 8, 1943; came to U.S., 1961, naturalized, 1966; s. Robert Peter and Thelma Rose M.; B.A., U. Bridgeport, 1966; M.B.A. in Fin., Boston Coll., 1972; m. Eileen Marie Farrell, Sept. 17, 1966; children—Robert Joseph, Donna Marie. Dist. sales mgr. Schick Safety Razor Co., Boston, 1971-72; asst. to exec. v.p. Medallic Art Co., Danbury, Conn., 1972-76; dist. mgr. Am. Appraisal Co., Stamford, Conn., 1976—. Served as capt. USAF, 1966-71. Mem. Nat. Assn. Accts. (pres. Bridgeport chpt.), Assn. Corp. Growth, Am. Mgmt. Assn. Home: Rocky Ridge Rd Easton CT 06468 Office: Am Appraisal Co 1200 Bedford St Stamford CT 06905

MOREL, LEON, JR., foundry exec.; b. Seattle, Mar. 29, 1922; s. Leon and Rose (Knox) M.; student Cast Metals Inst., 1965, 70; m. Lena R. Merlino, June 14, 1947; children—Paul, Eugene, Stephen, Mark. Pattern maker Morel Foundry, Seattle, 1940-43, 46-48, foundry supt., 1948-81, pres., 1981—. Served with USNR, 1943-46; PTO. Mem. Wash. Gray Iron Founders (past pres.), Wash. Non-Ferrous Founders Soc. (past pres., nat. dir.), Am. Foundrymen's Soc. (nat. dir., past pres. Wash. chpt.). Club: Wash. Athletic. Home: 7705 45th St SW Seattle WA 98136 Office: 3400 26th Ave SW Seattle WA 98106

MORELAND, WILLIAM JOHN, real estate broker; b. Chgo., Feb. 21, 1916; s. James C. and Izora M. (McCabe) M.; A.B., U. Ill., 1938; student Northwestern U., 1937. With James C. Moreland & Son, Inc., real estate and home building, Chgo., 1938—, pres. 1952—; pres. Moreland Realty, Inc., Chgo., 1952-72. Builder, operator Howard Johnson Motor Lodge, Chgo., 1960-72. Helped develop model housing community, El Salvador, Central Am., 1960's. Presidential appointment to commerce com. for Alliance for Progress, 1962-64. Served to lt. USNR, 1941-46. Mem. Home Bldrs. Assn. Chicagoland (pres. 1961-62), Chgo. Assn. Commerce and Industry, Chgo., N.W. real estate bds., N.W. Bldrs. Assn., Nat. Assn. Home Bldrs. (hon. life dir. 1972—), Chi Psi. Republican. Roman Catholic. Office: 5717 Milwaukee Ave Chicago IL 60646

MORENO, FERDINAND ALBERT, engring. mgr.; b. Colorado Springs, Colo., Nov. 22, 1923; s. Hermenigildo Antonio and Ina (Fisher) M.; student La Sierre Coll., 1946, Walla Walla Coll., 1949-52; B.A., U. Wash., 1954; m. Ruby J. Jutzy, July 23, 1969; 1 son, Tony. Asst. supr. Workers Compensation Bd., Salem, Oreg., 1955-67; pub. relations rep. Mut. of Omaha Ins. Co., 1967-69; engr. Argonaut Ins. Co., Portland, Oreg., 1970-74, engring. mgr., 1974—; pres., owner F & M Industries of Beaverton (Oreg.); instr. ins. Mt. Hood Community Coll. Mayor, Aumsville, Oreg., 1966-67; mem. Marion County advisory Planning Bd., 1966; mem. Washington County Traffic Safety Commn., 1976—, chmn., 1978. Served with U.S. Army, 1943-46. Decorated Bronze Star; recipient Citizen's award Washington County Traffic Safety Commn., 1977. Mem. Am. Soc. Safety Engrs. (treas. Portland chpt., recipient pub. service awards 1975, 76), Internat. Loss Control Assn. (pres. 1977, 78), Vets. of Safety. Republican. Club: Toastmaster. Office: Argonaut Ins Co 1700 SW 4th St Portland OR 07201

MORETON, FREDERICK ALBERT, ins. co. exec.; b. Salt Lake City, Mar. 6, 1896; s. John B. and Elizabeth (Cooper) M.; student U. Utah, 1916-17; grad. Mil. Aero., Mass. Inst. Tech., 1918; m. Sarah Burton, June 8, 1920; children—Isabel (Mrs. Wally Coats), Mary (Mrs. Dale Barton), Sharee (Mrs. Paul T. Kunz), Edward B., Frederick Albert. Chmn. bd., dir. Fred A. Moreton & Co., Salt Lake City, 1924—; dir., mem. exec. com., hon. chmn. Utah Power & Light Co., Salt Lake City; adv. dir. Walker Bank & Trust Co. Served as lt. U.S. Army, 1918-19. Mem. Nat. Assn. Ins. Agts. (pres. 1943-44), C. of C. Clubs: Alta, Kiwanis. Home: 1428 Circle Way Salt Lake City UT 84103 Office: 645 E South Temple Salt Lake City UT 84102

MORETSKY, LEWIS ROBERT, telecommunications cons. co. exec.; b. Bklyn., Aug. 25, 1940; s. Samuel and Shirley (Wexelbaum) M.; B.S. in Public Acctg., N.Y. U., 1963; M.A. in Bus. with honors, Central Mo. State U., 1971; m. Rhoda L. Weisler; children—Susan Faye, David Michael. Treas. United System Supply, Inc., Westwood, Kans., North Electric Co., Lenexa, Kans.; mgr. sales Original Equipment Mfg., 1971-73, eastern regional mktg. mgr., 1973-75, nat. accounts sales rep., 1975-77; mgr. consumer products North Supply Co., Lenexa, 1977-79; chief operating officer, treas. Suma Corp., Leawood, Kans., 1979—. Served to capt. USAF, 1963-68. Home: 9015 High Dr Leawood KS 66206

MORGAN, A. HENRY, mfg. co. exec.; b. N.Y.C., Mar. 30, 1926; B.E.E., N.Y. U., 1946; postgrad. Harvard Bus. Sch., 1979. Founder, T-Bar Inc., Wilton, Conn., 1959, chmn. bd., chief exec. officer, 1959—; dir. Firing Circuits Inc., Norwalk, Conn. Mem. Norwalk Mayor's Com. for Overall Econ. Devel. Mem. Nat. Assn. Relay Mfrs. (pres. 1980—, chmn. com. edn. 1978-79), IEEE (sr.), Newcomen Soc. N.Am., Ops. Research Soc. Am., Greater Norwalk C. of C. (v.p. econ. devel., dir.), Audubon Soc., Sierra Club, Photog. Soc. Am., Mt. Kenya Safari Club. Office: T-Bar Inc 141 Danbury Rd Wilton CT 06897

MORGAN, ARTHUR CREAT, corp. exec., artist, indsl. designer; b. Cumberland, Md., Aug. 14, 1917; s. Walter C. and Leota (McFarland) M.; student pub. schs.; m. Alma J. Parker, June 9, 1938. Machine operator, research trainee Celanese Corp., Cumberland, Md., 1935-43; pres. Artmor Plastics Corp., Cumberland, 1946—. Designer-creator displays, lighting and housing for various internat. trade fairs; engring. and design cons. to textile and other industries. Mem. U.S. Dept. Commerce trade missions to 40 countries, apptd. by Md. Gov. Harry Hughes to represent State of Md. at 1st White House Conf. on Small Bus., 1980. Bd. dirs. Operation Gateway. Served with USAAF, 1943-46. Sr. mem. Soc. Plastics Engrs. (dir. chpt.). Home: Huckleberry Hill LaVale MD 21502 Office: PO Box 3187 LaVale Br Cumberland MD 21502

MORGAN, ARTHUR EDWARD, transp./control products mfg. co. exec.; b. Milw., July 3, 1929; s. Burchell Edward and Irene C. (Schneiberg) M.; B.B.A., U. Wis., 1951, M.B.A., 1960; m. Jean Ellen Nagler, Jan. 28, 1951; children—Sandra Jean Morgan Harter, Nancy Lee Morgan Lococo. With Eaton Corp., Cleve., 1951—, div. gen. mgr., 1970-78, corp. v.p., 1978, group v.p., 1978-79, pres. Instruments and Diversified Products Group, 1979—; dir. Condura de CU, SA, Nova Assos., Optimetrix, Inc. Served to lt. comdr. USNR, 1952-55. Mem. Naval Inst., Am. Electronics Assn., Semicondr. Equipment Mfrs. Inst., Aerospace Industries Assn. Office: 100 Erieview Plaza Cleveland OH 44114

MORGAN, ARTHUR THOMAS, steel co. exec.; b. Rochester, N.Y., Mar. 13, 1928; s. Joseph and Elizabeth (Perrone) Mitrano; B.S., Purdue U., 1951; M.B.A., U. Chgo., 1960; m. Heidi E. Kopper, July 23, 1960; 1 dau., Audrey Christina. Trainee, Inland Steel Co., East Chicago, Ind., 1951, tech. service metallurgist, 1952-55, research metallurgist, 1956-60, supervising research metallurgist, 1961-63, sr. research metallurgist, 1964; chief metallurgist Calumet Steel div. Borg-Warner Corp., Chicago Heights, Ill., 1964-72, works mgr., 1973-75; v.p., works mgr., dir. Calumet Steel Co. subs. BW Steel, Inc., Chicago Heights, 1975—. Mem. Am. Inst. Mining and Metall. Engrs. (chmn. Chgo. sect.), Steel Bar Mills Assn. (chmn.), Am. Soc. Metals, Assn. Iron and Steel Engrs., ASTM. Republican. Patentee in field of metall. engring. Home: 16038 S Minerva Ave South Holland IL 60473 Office: 317 E 11th St Chicago Heights IL 60411

MORGAN, BARBARA ANN, real estate broker; b. Owen County, Ky., Dec. 27, 1937; d. Lester James and Gladys Marie M.; student U. Ky., 1955-57; m. William R. Jones, Feb. 25, 1967 (div. Feb. 1971); m. 2d, John H. Gilliam, May 19, 1973 (div. Aug. 1977); 1 son, John H. II. Real estate salesman Dan Long Real Estate, Lexington, Ky., 1960-65; real estate broker Bill Jones Real Estate, Lexington, 1965-71; owner, mgr. Morgan Real Estate Co., 1971-78; partner, owner Century 21 Morgan-Gilliam Realtors, Lexington, 1978-80; owner Century 21 Barbara Morgan Real Estate, Inc., 1980—; tchr. comml. investment Lexington Tech. Inst. Cert. residential broker. Mem. Lexington Bd. Realtors (dir.), Nat. Assn. Realtors, Ky. Assn. Realtors, Women's Council (past pres.). Baptist. Home: 703 Bullock Pl Lexington KY 40508 Office: 139 Walton Ave Lexington KY 40508

MORGAN, BRUCE IAN, corp. planning co. exec.; b. Montreal, Que., Can., Feb. 10, 1931; came to U.S., 1962; s. Harry Llewellyn and Edna Rosa (Giancarlo) M.; B.A., McGill U., 1952, M.B.A., 1954; Ph.D. in Econs. and Monetary Policy, U. Edinburgh (Scotland), 1956; m. Helen Mary Lyons, Sept. 21, 1960; children—Charles J., Linda W., Helena L. Exec. v.p. Westland Equities Ltd., Oklahoma City, 1963-71; pres. Southland Investment Corp., Miami, Fla., 1971-76; dir. mergers and acquisitions One, Inc., St. Petersburg, Fla., 1977—; cons. on mktg., fin., merger and acquisitions, 1970—. Author over 300 articles and studies for pvt. corps. Home: 1021 29th St N Saint Petersburg FL 33713

MORGAN, CLAROLD FORREST, sugar refining co. exec.; b. McPherson, Kan., Dec. 31, 1936; s. Clarold Forrest and Albina Blanche (Dolecek) M.; student U. Colo., 1954-55, J.D., 1968; B.S. in Bus. Adminstrn. cum laude U. Denver, 1958; m. Sherrill Novotny, Apr. 6, 1958; children—Sherrill Lynn, Clarold Forrest III, Marcia Ann. Admitted to Colo. bar, 1968; asso. counsel Holly Sugar Corp., Colorado Springs, Colo., 1968-71, sec., corporate counsel, 1972-74, sec., gen. counsel, 1975-77, v.p., sec., gen. counsel, 1977—. Served to capt. U.S. Army, 1958-63. Mem. Am. Bar Assn. (sects. anti-trust law, corp., banking and bus. law), Colo. Bar Assn. Colo. Assn. Corporate Counsel, Colo. Trial Lawyers Assn., Am. Soc. Corporate Secs., Order of Coif, Beta Gamma Sigma, Sigma Alpha Epsilon. Republican. Presbyterian. Club: Rotary (dir. Colorado Springs 1974-81). Bd. editors U. Colo. Law Rev., 1967-68. Office: PO Box 1052 Colorado Springs CO 80901

MORGAN, CYRIL FREDERICK, bus. exec.; b. St. John's, Nfld., Can. Nfld., Can., Aug. 2, 1932; s. Samuel Frederick and Victoria Mabel (Anthony) M.; m. Patricia Kemp; 5 children. Pres., Nuport Constrn. Ltd., residential constrn., rentals, land devel., gen. constrn., St. John's, 1967—, Omega Investments Ltd., property mgmt. co., St. John's, 1979—; sec. Sealand Helicopters Ltd., St. John's. Mem. com. to revise zoning by-laws St. John's Mcpl. Council, 1977-79; pres. St. John's Table Tennis Assn., 1950-55, Nfld. Table Tennis Assn., 1967. Cert. gen. acct. Mem. St. John's Home Builders Assn. (pres. 1969, 70, 75), Housing and Urban Devel. Assn. Can. (nat. dir. 1975—, nat. sec. 1976, 77, 80, 1st v.p. 1981), Cert. Gen. Accts. Assn. Nfld. Anglican. Clubs: Rotary (St. John's N.W.); Riverdale Tennis (pres. 1966), Greenbelt Tennis (pres. 1980). Home: Box 221 Rural Route #1 Portugal Cove NF A0A 3K0 Canada Office: 120 Torbay Rd Saint John's NF A1A 2H4 Canada

MORGAN, EDWARD AIKEN, JR., naval officer; b. Hanna, Wyo., Aug. 6, 1940; s. Edward Aiken and Emma (Walker) M.; B.S., U. Wyo., 1964; M.B.A., So. Ill. U., Edwardsville, 1976; 1 adopted son, Steven Edward. Commd. ensign U.S. Navy, 1964, advanced through grades to lt. comdr., 1973; asst. supply officer U.S.S. Duluth (LPD-6), 1965-67; supply officer U.S.S. Hopewell (DD681), 1967-68; finance and accounting officer Def. Contract Services Region, Phila., 1968-70; comptroller UN Command, Korea, 1970-71; supply officer U.S.S. Mt. Vernon (LBO-39), 1971-73; budget officer Comdr. Naval Air Force, U.S. Pacific Fleet, 1973-77; comptroller Naval Air Sta., Brunswick, Maine, 1977-80; acctg. officer, comdr. Naval Air Force, U.S. Atlantic Fleet, 1980—. Decorated Joint Service Commendation medal with oak leaf cluster, Navy Commendation medal. Mem. Supply Corps Assn., Pi Kappa Delta, Delta Sigma Rho, Alpha Kappa Psi. Episcopalian. Home: 1224 Cherry Blossom Ct Virginia Beach VA 23464 Office: CNAL Code 0032 Norfolk VA 23511

MORGAN, FINIS, textile co. exec.; b. Vinemont, Ala., June 6, 1922; s. Jerry M. and Nolie (Vawter) M.; B.S. in Accounting and Econs., U. Ala., 1949; m. Marjorie Nan Johnston, June 4, 1946; children—M. Nan, J. Scott. Spl. agt. IRS, Ala. and Fla., 1949-52; partner F.C. Holle, C.P.A., Decatur, Ala., 1953-54; gen. accountant Monsanto Corp. (formerly Chemstrand), Pensacola, Fla., 1954-59, plant accountant, 1959-61, asst. controller, N.Y.C., 1961-63, mgr. mfg., Pensacola, 1963, dir. nylon mfg., 1964-67, v.p. fin., St. Louis, 1967-70; exec. v.p. fin. and adminstrn., dir. Russell Corp., Alexander City, Ala., 1971—; dir. FNB of Alexander City, Russell Lands Co. Charter mem. U. West Fla. Found., 1965—; pres. Northwest Fla. Safety Council, 1964-66, Jr. Achievement of Pensacola, 1966-67; mem. Fla. Council of 100; active Greater Pensacola United Fund, Boy Scouts Am. Bd. dirs. Asso. Industries Fla.; adv. bd. Bapt. Hosp. Served with AUS, 1942-45. Decorated Silver Star, Bronze Star, Purple Heart; C.P.A., Ala. Mem. Fin. Execs. Inst., Nat. Assn. Accts. (pres. Pensacola-Mobile chpt. 1958-59), Alexander City C. of C. (v.p. 1977—). Club: Willow Point Golf and Country (Alexander City). Home: 210 Ridgeway Dr Alexander City AL 35010 Office: Russell Corp Alexander City AL 35010

MORGAN, GRAHAM JAMES, mfg. exec.; b. Aurora, Ill., Sept. 19, 1917; s. Caradoc James and Nina Hermana (Herbrandson) M.; B.A., Carleton Coll., 1938; m. Nancy Loraine Meeker, June 15, 1940 (dec. Oct. 1948); 1 dau., Heather Lynn; m. 2d, Vernile Ann Murrin, 1952. With U.S. Gypsum Co., 1939—, successively in sales, dist. mgr., Omaha, div. mgr. Western div., Midwest div., mdse. mgr. insulation products, gen. mdse. mgr., v.p. merchandising, 1945-54, v.p., asst. to chmn. bd., 1954-59, exec. v.p., 1959-60, pres., 1960-65, pres., chief exec. officer, 1965-71, chmn., chief exec. officer, 19/1—, dir., 1958—; dir. BRB Industries, Ltd., London, Am. Hosp. Supply Co., Evanston, Ill., IC Industries, Ill. Central Gulf R.R., Ill. Bell Telephone Co., Internat. Harvester Co., Trans Union Corp.; mem. adv. bd. Kemper Ins. Co. Past mem. nat. adv. com. Housing Center; past vice chmn. Pres.'s Com. on Urban Housing. Bd. dirs. Northwestern Meml. Hosp., Chgo. Boys Clubs, Chgo. Central Area Com.; trustee Northwestern U., Mus. Sci. and Industry, Orchestral Assn.; mem. Council on Med. and Biol. Research of U. Chgo. Recipient Housing and Urban Devel. Pioneer medal U.S. Dept. Health, Edn. and welfare; (past v.p., dir.), Hardboard Assn. (past dir.), Bldg. Research Inst. (dir.). Home: 1500 North Lake Shore Dr Chicago IL 60610 Office: 101 S Wacker Dr Chicago IL 60606

MORGAN, HARRY ELBURN, diversified mfg. corp. exec.; b. Pittsfield, Mass., Aug. 2, 1918; s. William E. and Mamie (Hickingbotham) M.; B.S. in Mech. Engring., U. Calif., Berkeley, 1947; m. Elizabeth L. Davis, May 5, 1956; children—Heather A., Jane L., Susam M. Pres., Insul-8 Corp. subs. Rucker Co., San Carlo, Calif., 1968-72, 75-79; cons. C. Delachaux Corp., Gennevilliers, France, 1972-74, pres. Indsl. Electric Reels subs., Omaha, 1974-78; dir. Insul-8 U.S., 1975—, Insul-8 Can., 1975—, Insul-8 Australia, 1975—, Insul-8 Gt. Britain, 1975—. Served with USAAF, 1943-45, C.E., U.S. Army, 1950-52. Mem. Tau Beta Pi, Lambda Chi Alpha. Republican. Club: Castlewood Country. Home: 15 Golf Rd Pleasanton CA 94566 Office: Delachaux Corp 867 American St San Carlos CA 94070

MORGAN, JOHN DAVID, exec. search cons.; b. Bremen, Ga., Feb. 21, 1947; s. J.B. and Virginia Elizabeth (Baker) M.; B.S. in Indsl. Mgmt. with high honors, Ga. Inst. Tech., 1970; student West Ga. Coll., 1965-67; m. Susan Teresa Bell, July 19, 1968; children—Katherine Lea, Shani Lauren, Virginia Suzanne. Application engr. measurement and control div. Rockwell Mfg. Co., Statesboro, Ga., 1969-71; product mgr. Brooks Instrment Instrument div. Emerson Elec. Co., Hatfield, Pa., 1971-72; asst. dir. devel. Ga. Inst. Tech., Atlanta, 1972-73, dir. devel., 1973-79; exec. search cons. Billington Fox & Ellis, Atlanta, 1979—. Bd. dirs. Northside Meth. Kindergarten, 1978—, chmn., 1979—; bd. dirs. Atlanta Zool. Soc., 1981—. Mem. Assn. Exec. Recruiting Cons., Nat. Soc. Fund Raising Execs. (chpt. sec.). Methodist. Clubs: Ponte Vedra Golf and Country (Jacksonville, Fla.); Cross Creek Golf and Country (Atlanta). Contbr. articles to profl. jours. Home: 1403 Moores Mill Rd NW Atlanta GA 30327 Office: Suite 1420 Atlanta Center 250 Piedmont Ave Atlanta GA 30308

MORGAN, JOHN ROBERT, chem. co. exec.; b. Louisville, Apr. 21, 1928; s. Robert Alexander and Edna Olive (Waddell) M.; M.B.A., Pepperdine U., 1973; m. Dolores Joan Steinbrenner, Feb. 26, 1949; children—Colleen Judith, Timothy John, Daniel Robert. With Hooker Electrochem. Co., Niagara Falls, N.Y., 1947-57; with Union Carbide Corp., various locations, 1957—, supt. liquid oxygen plant, Wilmington, Calif., 1967-73, asst. to mgr. energy utilization, Tustin, Calif., 1973-74, energy consultant, Union, N.J., 1974-80, ops. mgr. Union Carbide France, Creil, 1980—. Served with USCG, 1945-46. Registered profl. engr., Calif. Mem. Instrument Soc. Am. (sr.). Roman Catholic. Home: 11 ave de Breteuil 75007 Paris France Office: Union Carbide France 4 Place des Etats Unis Silic 214 94518 Rungis Cedex France also Usine de Gaz Industriels Quai d'Aval 60100 Creil France

MORGAN, LEE LAVERNE, tractor co. exec.; b. Aledo, Ill., Jan. 4, 1920; s. L. Laverne and Gladys (Hamilton) M.; B.S., U. Ill., 1941. With Caterpillar Tractor Co., Peoria, Ill., 1946—, mgr. sales devel., 1954-61, v.p. charge engine div., 1961-65, exec. v.p., 1965-72, pres., 1972-77, chmn. bd., chief exec. officer, 1977—, also dir.; dir. 3M Co., Boeing Co., Comml. Nat. Bank, Mobile Corp. Vice chmn. European Community-U.S. Businessmen's Council; vice chmn. Adv. Council Japan-U.S. Econ. Relations; trustee conf. bd. Com. for Econ. Devel. Bd. dirs. Monmouth Coll., Proctor Community Hosp. Served to maj. AUS, 1941-46. Mem. Soc. Automotive Engrs., Bus. Council, Bus. Roundtable. Presbyterian. Clubs: Masons, Peoria Country, Creve Coeur; Chicago, Union League (Chgo.); Tucson Nat. Golf; Augusta Nat. Office: Caterpillar Tractor Corp 100 NE Adams St Peoria IL 61629

MORGAN, LEE MOREY, printing and distbg. co. exec.; b. Xenia, Ohio, Apr. 8, 1943; s. Ernest and Elizabeth (Morey) M.; B.A., Antioch Coll., 1969; m. Victoria A. Neff, Mar. 27, 1968; children—Asha, Matthew. Treas., exec. v.p. Antioch Bookplate Co., Yellow Springs, Ohio, 1968-71, pres., chief exec. officer, 1971—, also dir. Vol., Unitarian Universalist Service Com., South India, 1965-67; v.p., bd. dirs. Friends Health Care Assn.; mem. adv. com. on ednl. info. centers Ohio Bd. Regents, 1979—. Quaker. Office: 888 Dayton St Yellow Springs OH 45387

MORGAN, MARIANNE, bus. exec.: b. Muncie, Ind., Oct. 13, 1940; d. Clarence Wilson and Mary Estle (Shafer) M.; student Ball State U., 1958-61; B.A., Calif. State U., 1963; M.S., U. So. Calif., 1968; postgrad. U. Calif. at Irvine, 1970-74, So. Fla. U., 1974-75, N.Y. Inst. Photography, 1980—. Library asst. Anaheim (Calif.) Pub. Library, 1963-65, sr. library asst., 1965-68; librarian Orange Coast Coll., Costa Mesa, Calif., 1968-74, exec. v.p., partner Pine Meadow Ranch, Inverness, Fla.; dir. F.E. Brady Products, Inc., CleArwater, Fla., Brady Air Controls, Inc., Muncie. Alice M. Kitselman scholar, 1958. Mem. Faculty Assn. Calif. Community Colls., Wilderness Soc., ACLU, Sierra Club, Common Cause, Gamma Theta Upsilon, Beta Phi Mu. Republican. Home: Rt 4 1331 Appaloosa Rd Tarpon Springs FL 33589 Office: PO Box 5304 2151 Logan St Clearwater FL 33515

MORGAN, ROBERT ARTHUR, mktg. exec.; b. Toledo, May 5, 1922; s. Arthur James and Bernice Marie (Farmer) M.; B.S. cum laude in Bus. Adminstrn., Bowling Green (Ohio) State U., 1943; certificate Carnegie Mellon U., 1951; m. Betty Helen Byers, June 19, 1954; children—Todd Byers, Barbara Lee. With Westinghouse Electric Corp., 1947—, mgr. sales devel. indsl. systems div., Buffalo, 1964-66, mktg. mgr. indsl. systems div., 1967-73, mgr. mktg. services indsl. equipment div., 1973-79, mgr. bus. devel. power electronics and drive systems div., 1979—. Mem. Wilkinsburg (Pa.) City Council, 1961-65, v.p., 1964-65; co-pres. Maple Elem. Sch. PTA, 1966-67; chmn. Citizens Adv. Bd., Williamsville Central Sch. Dist., 1974-77; vestryman Calvary Episcopal Ch., 1979—. Named Man of Year, Wilkinsburg, 1965; cert. bus. communicator. Mem. Bus./Profl. Advt. Assn. (nat. v.p. 1967-69), Am. Mktg. Assn., Greater Buffalo C. of C. Clubs: Red Carpet, Am. Legion, Masons, Shriners. Contbr. articles on indsl. mktg. to profl. jours. and handbook; editor tng. manuals. Home: 80 Chaumont Dr Williamsville NY w14221

MORGAN, W. EUGENE, banker; b. Monterey, Tenn., Sept. 8, 1919; s. Walter B. and Juanita (Bugg) M.; student Tenn. Technol. U., 1940-41; m. Nelda Duer, Aug. 24, 1948; children—Nelda Gene, William Brettley. Pres., dir. Bank of Monterey, 1951-61; chmn. bd., chief exec. officer First Ala. Bank of Huntsville, 1970—; vice chmn. First Ala. Bancshares, Inc., 1970—; dir. Birmingham br. Fed. Res. Bank Atlanta. Regional chmn. U.S. Savs. Bond Program; bd. dirs., past pres. Huntsville Madison County Indsl. Devel. Assn.; chmn., pres. Huntsville-Madison County Marina and Port Authority; mem. pres.'s cabinet U. Ala., Huntsville; mem. Huntsville Army Adv. Com.; past treas. Huntsville-Madison County United Way; bd. dirs. Huntsville Better Bus. Bur., Huntsville Boys' Club; trustee Huntsville Arts Council; past mayor of Monterey, 1945-47; chmn. Monterey Planning Commn., 1950-56; mem. Cookville (Tenn.) Housing Authority, 1950-56. Mem. Am. Bankers Assn. (govt. relations council), Ala. Bankers Assn. (coms.), Ala. C. of C. (dir.), Huntsville-Madison County C. of C., Army Ordnance Assn., Tenn. Bankers Assn. (exec. council). Methodist. Clubs: Huntsville Rotary (past pres.), Masons, Shriners, Whitesburg Boat and Yacht, Valley Hill Country. Office: PO Box 680 Huntsville AL 35804

MORGAN, WILLIAM J., acctg. co. exec.; b. Bklyn., Jan. 12, 1947; s. William J. and Emma T. (Kraft) M.; B.S., St. John's U., 1968; m. Patricia A. Maltz, Mar. 23, 1968; children—Michele, Jennifer. Acctg., auditor Peat, Marwick, Mitchell & Co., N.Y.C., 1968-72, audit supr., 1972-74, audit mgr., 1974-77, adv. com., 1977-79, partner, 1977—, partner-in-charge recruiting, 1979—; mem. acctg. adv. bd. Grad. Sch. Bus., Fordham U., 1979—; mem. standardization com. Nat. Retail Mchts. Assn., 1979; mem. public meetings com. N.Y. Credit and Fin. Mgmt. Assn., 1977-79. Co-chmn. N.Y. chpt. small bus. fund drive ARC, 1978. C.P.A., N.Y. State; lic. acct., N.Y. State, La. Mem. Am. Inst. C.P.A.'s (small bus. devel. com. 1979—), N.Y. State Soc. C.P.A.'s (retail acctg. com. 1975-78, com. on edn. in colls. and univs. 1978—), Nat. Assn. Accts. (dir. manuscripts 1975-77, v.p. N.Y. chpt. 1977—, Disting. Service award 1975), Accts. Club Am. Roman Catholic. Home: 19 Westminster Rd Chatham NJ 07928 Office: Peat Marwick Mitchell & Co 345 Park Ave New York NY 10022

MORGISON, F. EDWARD, investment broker, govt. ofcl.; b. Clay Center, Kans., Oct. 4, 1940; s. Fred and Lena Edna (Chaput) M.; B.A. in Math., Emporia State U., 1963; M.S. in Bus. Adminstrn., U. Mo., Columbia, 1964; M.S. in Acctg. candidate U. Mo., Kansas City, 1981—; m. Karen Lorene Herdman, Nov. 21, 1964; 1 dau., Diana Michelle. Computer programmer U. Mo. Med. Center, Columbia, 1964-65; adminstrv. and budget analyst Urban Renewal Project, Independence, Mo., 1965-66; account exec., bank broker Stifel Nicolaus & Co., Kansas City, Mo., 1966-73; pres., chief exec. officer Will-Mor Investment Systems, Kansas City, Mo., 1973-75; br. mgr. Edward Jones & Co., 1975; editorial and exec. asst. to Morgan Maxfield, candidate for U.S. Congress, Kansas City, 1976; sr. account exec., merger and acquisitions specialist R. Rowland & Co., Kansas City, Mo., 1976-77; chmn. bd., pres., chief exec. officer Mo. Securities Inc., Kansas City, 1977-78; v.p., regional mgr. Charles Schwab & Co., Kansas City, 1978-79; v.p. Profl. Assistance, 1979-81; registered agt. Offerman & Co., Kansas City, 1979-81; chief exec. officer Morgison & Assos., Kansas City, 1979-81; fiscal dir. Housing Authority of Kansas City, 1981—; diamond counselor Internat. Diamond Corp., Kansas City, 1980—; sec., treas., dir. several Kansas City corps. Recipient Bausch and Lomb Sci. award, 1959; Sci. award Lambda Delta Lambda, 1962; registered account exec. N.Y. Stock Exchange, Am. Exchange, registered securities agt., Mo., Kans., Ill. Mem. U. Mo. (life), Emporia State U. (life) alumni assns., Nat. Rifle Assn. (life), U.S. Chess Fedn. (life), Mensa (life). Home: 1000 NE 96th Terr Kansas City MO 64155 Office: 1016 Locust St Kansas City MO 64106

MORI, FUMIKO, trade council exec.; b. Omura, City, Japan, Jan. 11, 1944; came to U.S., 1967; d. Masuo and Hisako (Yoshitake) M.; B.A., Kyoto U., 1966; M.I.A., Sch. Internat. Affairs, Columbia U., 1970; m. Richard C. Halloran, Nov. 11, 1978. Bibliographer, Japan Documentation Center, Columbia U., N.Y.C., 1970-73; program officer Japan Center for Internat. Exchange, Tokyo, 1973-76; research dir. Washington Internat. Communications, 1976-77; dir. econo-polit. research U.S.-Japan Trade Council, Washington, 1978—. Mem. Japan Commerce Assn., Arms Control Assn. Washington. Roman Catholic. Author: From the City of Washington, 1979 recipient 11th Oya Soichi Best Non-Fiction award Bungei Shunju, Tokyo, 1979); U.S.-Japan Economic Relations Year Book, 1978. Home: 2939 Van Ness St NW Washington DC 20008 Office: 1000 Connecticut Ave NW Washington DC 20036

MORIARTY, DONALD WILLIAM, JR., banker; b. Amarillo, Tex., Sept. 15, 1939; s. Donald William and Lorraine Julia (Walck) M.; student St. Benedict's Coll., Atchison, Kans., 1957-59, 60-61; B.Sc., Washington U., 1962; M.Sc., St. Louis U., 1965, Ph.D., 1970; m. Rita

Ann Giller, Nov. 28, 1964; children—Mary Kathleen, Jennifer Ann, Anne Marie, Kerry Lee, Erin Teresa. Cost acct. Emerson Electric, St. Louis, 1959-63; grad. fellow in econs. St. Louis U., 1963-65, instr., 1965-68; asst. prof. U. Mo.-St. Louis, 1968-70; with Fed. Res. Bank St. Louis, 1968—, v.p., 1971-73, sr. v.p., controller, 1974-77, 1st v.p., chief operating officer, 1977—; vis. instr. Webster Coll., 1975—; bd. dirs. Mid-Am. Payments Exchange, 1975-77; adviser City of Des Peres (Mo.). Chmn., Personnel Commn. Des Peres, 1978—, chmn. mgmt. com., 1978—. Recipient Alumi Merit award St. Louis U., 1979. Mem. Am. Econ. Assn., Am. Mgmt. Assn., Beta Gamma Sigma, Alpha Kappa Psi. Office: 411 Locust St Saint Louis MO 63102

MORIARTY, FREDERIC BARSTOW, banker; b. Butte, Mont., Aug. 7, 1940; s. Frederic Barstow and Elizabeth (Carman) M.; A.B., Harvard U., 1962; LL.B., N.Y. U., 1967; m. Suzanne Bridge, Dec. 30, 1966; children—Douglass, Elizabeth, Frederic Barstow III. With trust dept. U.S. Trust Co., N.Y.C., 1962—, sr. v.p., 1976—, head estate and trust dept., 1976—; dir. U.S. Trust London, Ltd.; admitted to N.Y. State bar, 1968. Mem. Am., N.Y. State bar assns., Estate Planning Council N.Y.C. (pres. 1977-78), N.Y. State Bankers Assn. (chmn. trust mktg. com. 1975-77). Club: Rockaway Hunting. Home: 243 White Oak Shade Rd New Canaan CT 06840 Office: 45 Wall St New York City NY 10005

MORICE, WILLIAM DANIEL, transp. mgmt. cons.; b. Washington, May 6, 1946; s. John Lowry and Evelyn Mae (Brown) M.; B.S. in Elec. Engring., U. Md., 1973; M.B.A., Emory U., 1976; m. Kay Iris Mason, June 14, 1975. Tech. rep. Xerox Corp., Washington, 1965-66, So. Ry., Atlanta, 1973; cons. Mantech of N.J., Washington, 1975; cons. aerospace, def. Peat Marwick Mitchell & Co., Newport, R.I., 1976-78, practice coordinator bus. logistics, Washington, 1978—. Asst. precinct chmn., 1971, chmn., 1980; election judge, 1972. Served with U.S. Army, 1966-69. C.P.A., Md. Mem. Nat. Indsl. Traffic League (fin. and auditing com.), Nat. Council Phys. Distbn. Mgmt. (v.p. Balt.-Washington Roundtable), Am. Inst. C.P.A.'s, Delta Nu Alpha, Beta Gamma Sigma. Republican. Episcopalian. Clubs: Terrapin, Friends of Kennedy Center (founding mem.), Tau Kappa Epsilon. Author: Motor Carriers: An Industry Profile, 1979. Office: Peat Marwick Mitchell 1990 K St Washington DC 20006

MORIN, HAROLD MYRON, printing co. exec.; b. Worcester, Mass., Mar. 11, 1927; s. Jacob and Gertrude (Greenberg) M.; A.B. in Human Relations, U. Miami, 1950; m. Shirley Cinthia Jacobson, Dec. 19, 1953; children—Carol Ann Morin Moss, Susan Jean, Daniel Robert. Mem. exec. staff Boy Scouts Am., N.Y.C., Worcester and Montclair and Alpine, N.J., 1950-69; real estate salesman, property appraiser Gustav A. Hoffmann Agy., Closter, N.J., also Hal Morin Real Estate, Closter, 1969-72; pres., treas. The Morin Press, Inc., Worcester, 1972-76; gen. mgr. I.B.A. Print Shop, Millbury, Mass., 1976—; mng. editor Dairy World Mag., 1976—; bus. mgr. Design Graphics, South Grafton, Mass., 1980—. Served with USNR, 1944-46. Mem. Printing and Pub. Council New Eng. Jewish. Clubs: Worcester Craftsmans (pres., chmn. bd. govs.), Auburn Lions (outstanding Lion dist. 33A 1974-75, Ralph Waterhouse award 1975). Home: 6 Simonds St Auburn MA 01501 Office: IBA Print Shop 19 River St Millbury MA 01527

MORISON, DAVID WILLIAM, fin. cons.; b. Otterville, Ont., Can., Nov. 29, 1915; s. David Howard and Gertrude Isabel (Holmes) M.; B.Com., U. Toronto, 1939; m. Elizabeth Enid Angus, Dec. 15, 1945; children—David Angus, Susan Elizabeth. With Royal Bank of Can., 1939-76, mgr. Toronto main br., 1962-64, asst. gen. mgr., 1964, dist. gen. mgr., Winnipeg, 1967-70, dist. gen. mgr., Toronto, 1970-72, v.p. Ont., 1972-76; chmn. Roymark Fin. Services, Ltd., Toronto, 1976—, Reed Paper Ltd., 1979—, Mack Can., Inc., Dominion Dairies Ltd., Yonge-Bloor Devel. Corp. Ltd., Columbian Chems. Can. Ltd., E.P.G. Energy Products Group Ltd., Electrohome Ltd., Headway Corp. Ltd. Served to lt. RCAF, 1941-45. Decorated D.F.C. Presbyterian. Clubs: Toronto Golf, Granite, National, Masons (32 deg.). Office: 11 King St W Toronto ON M5H 1A3 Canada

MORISON, JOHN HOPKINS, casting mfg. co. exec.; b. Milw., June 29, 1913; s. George Abbot and Amelia (Elmore) M.; A.B., Harvard, 1935; LL.D., New Eng. Coll., 1973; m. Olga de Souza Dantas, July 29, 1944; children—Maria de Souza Dantas, John Hopkins III. Various positions Bucyrus-Erie Co., South Milwaukee, Wis., U.S. and Latin Am., 1935-49; pres., dir. Hitchiner Mfg. Co., Inc., Milford, N.H., 1949—, chmn. bd., 1973—; treas. Upland Farm Inc., Peterborough, N.H.; dir. Morris Bean & Co., Pneumo Precision Inc., Markem Corp., Souhegan Nat. Bank, Cargocaire, Inc. Commr., N.H. Commn. on Arts, 1967-77; mem. regional exec. com. Boy Scouts Am., Framingham, Mass., 1970-76; mem. regional adv. com. Merrimack Valley br. U. N.H.; mem. exec. com., past pres. N.H. Council on World Affairs. Trustee Land Use Found. N.H., 1970-75, World Peace Found., Currier Gallery Art; pres. bd. dirs. Matthew Thornton Health Plan; bd. dirs. Forum on N.H.'s Future; pres., distbg. dir. N.H. Charitable Fund., 1968-79; mem. corp. MacDowell Colony; bd. govs. N.H. Pub. Broadcasting Council. Served to lt. (j.g.) USNR, 1943-46. Unitarian. Clubs: Harvard (N.Y.C.); Somerset (Boston). Home: Lyndeboro Route 2 Wilton NH 03086 Office: Elm St Milford NH 03055

MORITA, HIROSHI, internat. trading co. exec.; b. Toyama, Japan, Jan. 3, 1933; came to U.S., 1979; s. Ryoji and Kimiko Morita; B.Jurisprudence, Tokyo U., 1957; m. Shizuko Gokyu, Apr. 27, 1960; 1 dau., Keiko. With C. Itch & Co., Ltd., Tokyo, 1957—, asst. mgr. overseas affiliate dept., 1979-81, v.p. in charge subs. ops. C. Itch & Co. (Ams.), Inc., N.Y.C., 1979—; mgmt. and internat. investment cons., 1970—. Authorized mgmt. cons., Japan. Co-author: Management of the Japanese Corporations, 1979. Home: 516 5th St Mamaroneck NY 10543 Office: 270 Park Ave New York N)Y 10017

MORITZ, KENNETH CAREY, electronic co. exec.; b. Joplin, Mo., Nov. 23, 1917; s. Melvin M. and Lilly V. (Flusser) M.; A.B., N.Y. U., 1938, postgrad., 1939; postgrad. George Washington U., 1940; m. Margot Heuer, July 11, 1952. European mgr. Philco Corp., London, 1946-52, nat. sales mgr., Phila., 1952-58; mktg. mgrg. Semicondr. div. Raytheon Corp., Boston, 1958-60; v.p. Internat. div. Gen. Instrument Corp., N.Y.C., 1960-64; v.p., dir. Milo Corp., N.Y.C., 1964-66; v.p., dir. C. Tennant Corp. div. Cargill Corp., Mpls., 1966—; mem. U.S. Trade Mission to Brazil, 1967. Bd. dirs., v.p. Lakepoint Assn., Mpls. Served as officer Signal Corps, U.S. Army, 1944-46. Mem. IEEE (sr.). Clubs: Minikahda (Mpls.); Metropolitan (N.Y.C.). Home: 2950 Dean Pkwy Minneapolis MN 55416 Office: PO Box 9300 Minneapolis MN 55440

MORITZ, MILTON EDWARD, telephone co. exec.; b. Reading, Pa., Sept. 5, 1931; s. Edward Raymond and Anna May M.; student U. Md., 1950-51, Fla. State U., 1959-60; m. Elizabeth Ann Walls, June 6, 1952; children—Betsy Ann Moritz Koppenhaver, Stephen Edward, Sandra E. Moritz Ryan. Enlisted in U.S. Army, 1963, served as spl. agt. M.I.; ret., 1970; safety and security dir. Harrisburg (Pa.) Hosp., 1970-72; audit and security mgr. United Telephone Systems, Carlisle, Pa., 1972—; lectr., instr. Harrisburg Area Community Coll. Pres., Greater Harrisburg Crime Clinic, 1974. Decorated Bronze Star with oak leaf cluster. Mem. Am. Soc. Indsl. Security, Assn. Former Intelligence Officers, Inst. Internal Auditors, Internat. Narcotic Enforcement Officers Assn. Republican. Baptist. Home: 7723 Avondale Terr Harrisburg PA 17112 Office: 1170 Harrisburg Pike Carlisle PA 17013

MORITZ, WALLACE ALBERT, Realtor; b. Milw., Apr. 21, 1913; s. Leopold and Theresa (Bauer) M.; student Marquette U., 1931; m. Ruth Kalle, Jan. 2, 1945; children—Judith Moritz Phillips, Diana Moritz Hill, Arthur Lee. Founder Wallace Labs. Inc., San Angelo, Tex., 1940, now pres.; pres. W. Tex. Bus. Music Co., San Angelo, 1953; owner Wallace A. Moritz and Assos., Realtors San Angelo, 1960—. Chmn., Nat. Wool Pageant, 1958-59; pres. Crippled Children's Center, San Angelo, 1958, United Fund, San Angelo, 1963, Lighthouse, San Angelo, 1965. Pres., Tex.-Okla. Kiwanis Found., 1973-74, now trustee; bd. dirs. Scottish Rite Found. Tex. Named San Angelo Citizen of Year, 1958. Mem. Tex. Assn. Realtors (dir., pres. 1978, Realtor of Yr. 1980), San Angelo Bd. Realtors (pres. 1967). Presbyn. Mason, Kiwanian. Club: San Angelo Country. Home: 166 Moritz Circle San Angelo TX 76901 Office: 1900 Sherwood Way San Angelo TX 76901

MORK, EDWARD S., foods co. exec.; b. Bergen, Norway, Apr. 3, 1944; s. Edward and Signe (Stabel) M.; came to U.S., 1973; B. Commerce Birmingham (Eng.) U., 1967; M.B.A., European Inst. Bus. Adminstrn., Fontainebleau, France, 1968; m. Chantal Slabbaert, Dec. 17, 1970; 1 son, Patrick Robert. Corp. staff asst. CPC-Europe, Brussels, 1968-70, group product mgr., CPC-Netherlands, 1970-73; mgr. new product devel. Best Foods div. CPC-Internat. Inc., Englewood Cliffs, N.J., 1973-75, sr. product mgr., 1975-77; mgr. new business projects CPC/Europe, Brussels, 1977—. Mem. Norwegian Sivilokonom Assn., Am. Mgmt. Assn., U.S.-European Inst. Bus. Adminstrn. Alumni Assn. Home: 1 rue du Moulin 1310 La Hulpe Belgium Office: CPC/Europe 149 Ave Louise Brussels Belgium

MORLEY, HENRY BARCLAY, chem. co. exec.; b. Sydney, N.S., Can., Apr. 25, 1929; s. Clarence Gregory and Jessie Bolby (Armstrong) M.; came to U.S., 1953, naturalized, 1962; B.Sc., St. Francis Xavier U., 1948; Ph.D., U. Toronto, 1953; m. Annette Hauck, Dec. 16, 1972; children by previous marriage—Edward Bruce, Christopher Engen, Gary Stuart. Dir. Eastern Research Center, Stauffer Chem. Co., Dobbs Ferry, N.Y., 1962-67, asst. to pres., N.Y.C., 1967-68, v.p. tech., 1968-70, exec. v.p., 1970-72, pres., 1972-74, pres., chief exec. officer, Westport, Conn., 1974—, chmn. bd., 1977—; dir. Bank of N.Y., Conn. Nat. Bank, Champion Internat., Schering-Plough. Mem. Fairfield County council Boy Scouts Am.; trustee Greens Farms Acad., Nutrition Found., Inc., U. Bridgeport, Nat. Action Council for Minorities in Engring., Inc. Mem. Soc. Chem. Industry, Chem. Mfrs. Assn. Clubs: Pequot Yacht, Board Room, Blind Brook, Fairfield Country, Nutmeg Curling, Country of Darien, Algonquin, Econ. (N.Y.C.). Office: Stauffer Chem Co Westport CT 06880

MORLEY, JOSEPH FRANCIS, trade assn. exec.; b. Westerley, R.I., Aug. 11, 1931; s. Patrick Joseph and Ellen (McNicholas) M.; student Pace Coll., 1954-56; m. Roberta Ann Schilling, Feb. 27, 1954; children—Robert J., J. Scott, Curt G., Peter G. Adminstrv. asst. to v.p. corp. trust dept. Lincoln-Rochester Trust Co. (N.Y.), 1964-66; dir. gen. services Dempsey-Tegeler & Co., Inc., N.Y.C., 1966-68; v.p. ops. and state legis. Securities Industry Assn., N.Y.C., 1978—; mem. faculty N.Y. Inst. Fin., 1963—. Trustee, chmn. parents div. coll. fund Marist Coll., Poughkeepsie, N.Y.; mem. Com. Corr. Ind. Higher Edn. in N.Y. State. Served with AUS, 1952-54; Korea. Decorated Combat Inf. badge; recipient various certs. appreciation. Mem. Stock Transfer Assn., Am. Legion. Roman Catholic. Author papers in field. Office: 20 Broad St New York NY 10005

MORNEAU, GUILDO JOSEPH, ins. co. exec.; b. Estcourt, Que., May 11, 1933; m. Huguette Lavoie, Dec. 22, 1968; children—Josee, Andre. Pres., Les Agences Morneauet Assos., Inc., Montreal, Que., 1971—. C.L.U.; chartered ins. broker. Mem. Provincial Life Assn., Que. Broker Assn. Roman Catholic. Club: Epic. Office: 5925 De Jumonville Montreal PQ H1M 1R2 Canada

MORNEAULT, A. JOEL, bus. exec.; b. St. Agatha, Maine, Aug. 15, 1936; s. Leo and Catherine (Plourde) M.; B.S. in Engring., UCLA, 1967; m. Sally Street, July 29, 1961; children—Monique, A. Joel. Process engr. TFI, Los Angeles, 1967-69; devel. engr. RCA, Indpls., 1969-71; sr. tech. service rep. ICI Am., Wilmington, Del., 1971-73; dir. engring. Wabash Tape Corp., Huntley, Ill., 1973-75; founder, pres. TRI, Cary, Ill., 1975—; tech. cons. Kuwaiti Co., Kuwait. Served with USAF, 1956-60. Mem. IEEE, Dundee Bus. and Profl. Assn. (membership chmn. 1978-79). Republican. Roman Catholic. Office: 150 Chicago St Cary IL 60013

MORONE, JOHN HENRY JOSEPH, pharmacist, developer; b. Albany, N.Y., Feb. 7, 1941; s. Henry Joseph and Phyllis (Graziano) M.; B.S., Albany Coll. Pharmacy, 1963. Pharmacist, Carls Drug Co., Oneida, N.Y., 1964-65, Gem Drug Co., Syracuse, N.Y., 1966-67; part-owner Canastota Corner Drug Co. (N.Y.), 1967-72: owner, operator, dir. Morone's Colonial Pharmacy Inc., Canastota, 1972—, Morone's Colonial Shopping Center, Canastota, 1977—; dir. M.C.P. Profit Plan Trust. Served with Tank Corps, U.S. Army, 1963. Mem. Nat. Assn. Retail Druggists, Am., N.Y. State, Mohawk pharm. assns., Nat. Fedn. Better Bus., Nat. Geog. Soc. Roman Catholic. Clubs: President's of Albany Coll. Pharmacy, Canastota Civic (v.p. 1978), Canastota Devel. (v.p. 1972). Home: Route 5 Canastota NY 13032 Office: Morone's Colonial Shopping Center Routes 5 and 13 Canastota NY 13032

MOROSANI, GEORGE WARRINGTON, warehousing co. exec.; b. Cin., July 20, 1941; s. Remy Edmond and Virginia Caroline (Warrington) M.; B.A., Rollins Coll., 1964, M.B.A., 1965; m. Judith Clontz; children—Katherine Carmichael, Elizabeth Warrington. Fin. mgr. Lunar Orbitor and Minuteman Programs, Boeing Co., Cape Canaveral, Fla., 1965-68; controller Equitable Leasing Co., Asheville, N.C., 1968-69; founder, pres., treas. Western Carolina Warehousing Co., Asheville, 1969—, A Mini Storage Co., Fletcher, N.C., 1976—; gen. partner Pine Needle Apts., Arden, N.C., 1978—, Pine Ridge Apts., Skyland, N.C., 1980—; owner George W. Morosani Indsl. Realtor, Fletcher, 1981—. Bd. dirs. Jr. Achievement Greater Asheville Area, 1977—. Mem. Sales and Mktg. Execs. Asheville (dir. 1974-76, chmn. membership com. 1976-77), Western N.C. Traffic Club (dir. 1973-74, sec.-treas. 1974-76, pres. 1976-77, dir. 1977-79), Asheville Bd. Realtors, Am. Warehousemen Assn., Southeastern Warehousemen's and Movers Assn. (dir. 1977-79), N.C. Merchandise Warehousemen's Assn., Nat. Council Distbn. Mgmt., Affiliated Warehouse Cos., Asheville Area C. of C. (chmn. indsl. relations 1978-79), Western Carolina Horse Show Assn. (co-chmn. 1969-70, treas. 1968-71, 73-75). Episcopalian. Clubs: Biltmore Forest Country, Asheville Downtown City, Asheville Racquet, Civitan (dir. 1975-77). Home and office: PO Box 858 Fletcher NC 28732

MORRELL, GENE PAUL, pipeline co. exec.; b. Ardmore, Okla., Oct. 4, 1932; s. Paul T. and Etta L. (Weaver) M.; B.S. in Geology, U. Okla., 1954, LL.B., 1962; m. Jan A. Foster, Aug. 20, 1954; children—Jeffrey T., Kelly Ann, Rob Redman. Geologist, Gilmer Oil Co., Ardmore, Okla., 1957-59, atty.-geologist, 1962-63; admitted to Okla. bar, 1962, D.C. bar, 1973; practiced law, Ardmore, 1963-69; ofcl. Dept. Interior, Washington, 1969-72; v.p. Lone Star Gas Co., Washington, 1972-76; sr. v.p. United Gas Pipeline Co., Houston, 1976—; adv. dir. Lincoln Bank & Trust Co., Ardmore. City commr. Ardmore, 1967-69, vice-mayor, 1968; mem. alumni adv. bd. U. Okla. Sch. Geology. Mem. Am., Okla., D.C., Fed. Power bar assns., Am. Assn. Petroleum Geologists, Phi Alpha Delta, Sigma Alpha Epsilon. Episcopalian. Club: City Tavern (Washington). Contbr. articles to profl. jours. Office: Pennzoil Pl POB 1478 Houston TX

MORRILL, LEON LESLIE, JR., investment adv., archeologist; b. Lynn, Mass., Nov. 11, 1926; s. Leon L. and Edna (Willey) M.; B.A., New Eng. Coll., 1950; m. Marilyn J. Craig, July 16, 1949; children—Craig D., Deborah, Jeffrey C. Various positions, 1950-55; dir. tng. Automobile Legal Assn., 1955-67; v.p. sales, dir. Keystone Am. Automobile Assn., Phila., 1967-70, sales mgr. Chgo. Motor Club, 1970-76; investment adviser Fin. Alternatives, Inc., 1976—; dir. WorldWide Travel, Phila. Insurers. Bd. dirs. Heart Fund, Cub Scouts. Served with USNR, 1944-46. Mem. New Eng. Antiquity Research Assn. (dir. 1968—, research dir. 1969—, v.p. 1969—), Soc. for Early Archaeology. Republican. Christian Scientist. Club: Masons. Home: 99 Ferry Rd Newburyport MA 01950 Office: Fin Alternatives Inc 240 Commercial St Boston MA 02109

MORRIS, CALVIN MILYARD, ins. co. exec.; b. Salida, Colo., Oct. 21, 1934; s. Charles Lee and Margaret Naomi (Milyard) M.; B.A., Beloit Coll., 1953-57; M.Ed., U. Va., 1969, E.Ed., 1974; student Naval Intelligence Sch., 1960-61, Command, Staff Coll., 1968-69; m. Karen Lynn Hansen, Sept. 8, 1956; children—Diana, Calvin, Scott, James. Commd. 2d lt. U.S. Marine Corps, 1957, advanced through grades to lt. col., 1974; head academics Marine Corps Officer Candidate Sch., 1966-68; chief analyst N. Vietnam, China desk U.S. Mil. Asst. Command, Vietnam, 1969-70; asso. prof. naval sci. dept. U. Va., 1970-74; dir. Instructional Mgmt. Sch. Marine Corps Edn. Center, Quantico, 1974-77; ret., 1977; head human resources devel. div. Met. Property and Liability Ins. Co., Warwick, R.I., 1977—; dir. Met. Risk and Mgmt. Inst., Inc.; instr. grad. sch. Bryant Coll., Smithfield, R.I. Mem. Kingston (R.I.) Bd. Wardens. Decorated Bronze Star, Purple Heart. Mem. Nat. Profl. Edn. Soc., Am. Personnel and Guidance Assn., Am. Soc. Tng. and Devel., Phi Delta Kappa, Kappa Delta Pi. Home: 9 Conant Ln Kingston RI 02881 Office: 700 Quaker Ln PO Box 370 Warwick RI 02881

MORRIS, CHARLES EMMET, banker; b. Chgo., Sept. 28, 1935; s. Hugh G. and Ann M. (Connolly) M.; student Sch. of Banking, U. Va., 1968, Stonier Grad. Sch. Banking, Rutgers U., Am. Inst. Banking, 1964; m. Micki Bruno, May 5, 1962; children—Charles E., Nancy C., Jon C. With Mercantile Nat. Bank of Chgo., 1960-74, sr. v.p. comml. lending, 1968-74; sr. v.p. lending Oak Brook Bank (Ill.), 1974-76, pres., 1976—; formerly instr. Am. Inst. Banking. Mem. Bd. Edn., Dist. 44, Lombard, Ill., 1970-75, pres., 1974-75. Mem. Robert Morris Assos. Clubs: Bankers; Exec. (Chgo.); Glen Oak Country. Office: Oak Brook Bank 2021 Spring Rd Oak Brook IL 60521

MORRIS, DAVID MARTIN, relocation cons., real estate broker; b. Bklyn., Sept. 17, 1939; s. Perry and Evelyn (Charleston) M.; student The Citadel. Media dir. Bursten Phillips Co., Advt., N.Y.C., 1968-69; sr. cons. Met. Relocation Assos., N.Y.C., 1970-71; v.p. Nat. Home Settlers, Inc., N.Y.C., 1972-73; v.p. Executrans, Inc., Greenwich, Conn., 1974-76; pres. Domicile, Inc., Relocation Cons., Office Bldg. Mgmt., Westport, Conn., 1977—; dir. Universal Utilities, Inc., Great Neck, N.Y. Dir. new blood donor recruiting Westport-Weston chpt. ARC, 1980—. Served with U.S. Army, 1965-68; Vietnam. Decorated Combat Inf. Badge, Army Commendation medal with oak leaf cluster. Home: 17 Drumlin Rd Westport CT 06880 Office: 16 Taylor Pl Westport CT 06880

MORRIS, EDWIN ALEXANDER, bus. exec.; b. Concord, N.C., Aug. 13, 1903; s. William Lee and Martha Margaret (Ervin) M.; B.S. in Commerce, Washington and Lee U., 1926, LL.D. (hon.), 1980; m. Mary Ella Cannon, Nov. 1, 1933; children—Joseph E., Mary Lou. Joined Blue Bell, Inc., Greensboro, N.C., 1937, pres., chief exec. officer, 1948-66, dir., 1940—, chmn. bd., chief exec. officer, 1966—; former mem. gen. bd. Wachovia Bank & Trust Co. N.A. Winston-Salem, N.C.; former dir. Wachovia Bank & Trust Co., Greensboro. Trustee Wesley Long Hosp. Presbyterian. Club: Greensboro Country. Office: PO Box 21488 Greensboro NC 27420

MORRIS, EUGENE I., ins. exec., mus. dir.; b. Newark, Feb. 27, 1923; s. Albert James and Ida (Kalb) M.; student Christ Coll., Oxford U., 1944; B.A. in Ins., Rutgers U., 1947; m. Jocelyn Seidler, Sept. 18, 1949; children—Alison Diane, Richard Evan. With Joseph A. Morris & Co., 1946-54; with The Morris Agy., Inc., South Orange, N.J., 1954-79 (merged with O'Gorman & Young, Inc., Chatham, N.J., 1979), v.p., 1979—; pres. Survey and Analysis Corp., 1972—; founder, dir. New Eng. Fire and Hist. Mus., Brewster, Mass., 1972—; instr. ins., div. secondary sch. adminstrn. Rutgers U., 1950-51. N.J. dist. commr. Boy Scouts Am., 1966-67; co-founder Maplewood jr. football program; coach South Orange Little League; mem. Chatham Hist. Soc., 1978; mem. Chatham (Mass.) Conservation Soc., Unitarian Layman's League; pres. Fire Mark Circle of Ams., 1976-78. Served with USAAF, 1941-46; liaison staff Air Force Acad., 1965-70. Decorated Croix de Lorraine, Air medal with 2 clusters; recipient nat. quality award 10 years, State Leaders' Club N.J. Life Underwriters Assn., award Ins. Advt. Council, 1965; Freedoms Found. certification award to Fire and Hist. Mus., 1969. Mem. Nat. Assn. Ind. Ins. Agts., N.J. Assn. Ins. Agts. (v.p., 1961), Morris County Ins. Agts. Assn., Essex County Agts. Assn. (pres. 1961), Profl. Ins. Agts. Assn., New Eng. Assn. of Museums, Am. Assn. Museums, Bay State Hist. League, South Orange C. of C. (pres.). Republican. Contbr. articles to publs. Office: 159 Main St Chatham NJ 07928

MORRIS, FRANK EUGENE, banker; b. Detroit, Dec. 30, 1923; s. Frank and Beatrice (Perkins) M.; B.A., Wayne U., 1948; M.A., U. Mich., 1949, Ph.D. in Econs., 1955; m. Geraldine Elizabeth Coltharp, Dec. 22, 1944; children—Susan, Lisa, Betsy. Research dir. Investment Bankers Assn., Washington, 1955-61; asst. to sec. debt mgmt. Treasury Dept., 1961-63; v.p. Loomis Sayles and Co., Boston, 1963-68; pres. Fed. Res. Bank Boston, 1968—; teaching fellow U. Mich., 1949-51. Served to 1st lt. USAAF, 1943-45. Mem. Am. Econ. Assn. Home: Walpole St Dover MA 02030 Office: 600 Atlantic Ave Boston MA 02106

MORRIS, GEORGE (RED) ARTHUR, real estate exec., publisher, govt. ofcl.; b. Jamaica, N.Y., Apr. 6, 1939; s. George Arthur and Cathine Rita (Hefferen) M.; A., Dean Jr. Coll., Franklin, Mass., 1959; B.B.A., U. Hawaii, 1963; m. Gail Ann Bilecki, June 19, 1965; children—Traci "Lekina", Malia, Nani. Mgr. legis. dept. C. of C. Hawaii, 1963-68; exec. v.p. Honolulu Bd. Realtors and Hawaii Assn. Realtors, 1968-75; pres. G.A. Morris, Inc., Honolulu, 1975—; pub. Hawaii Tax Map Key Service, 1975—; chmn. Hawaii Real Estate Commn., 1979—. Served with USCG, 1956. Mem. Japanese C. of C., C. of C. Hawaii, Hawaii Assn. Realtors, Nat. Assn. Real Estate Lic. Law Ofcls. Roman Catholic. Club: Plaza of Honolulu. Home: 45-302 Puuloko Pl Kaneohe HI 96744 Office: 841 Bishop St Suite 2005 Honolulu HI 76813

MORRIS, GEORGE MICHAEL, retail exec.; b. Seattle, Jan. 11, 1942; s. Benjamin Martin and Irene Bernice Morris; student U. Wash., Seattle, 1963; m. Rosali K. Nelsson, June 19, 1965; children—Michael Taylor, James Martin. Supr., Bostonian Shoes, Seattle, 1968-73; v.p. mktg. Childs Corp., Pitts., 1973-79; pres. Pix Am. Corp., Miami, Fla., 1979-81, also dir.; pres., chief exec. officer Bari of Fla., Inc., 1981—; past bd. dirs. retail div. Pitts. C. of C. Mem. Volume Footwear Retailers Assn. Republican. Episcopalian. Club: Am. Yacht Racing Union. Home: 7801 SW 171st St Miami FL 33157

MORRIS, J. ROY, mfg. co. exec.; b. N.Y.C., Jan. 29, 1938; s. Lee E. and Wanda Morris; B.A., Adelphi U., 1967; m. W. Maureen Carney, Oct. 15, 1960; children—Roy, Suzanne, Wendy, Kevin, Kimberly, Tara, Ginger. Pres., chmn. bd. Cybermatics Inc., Englewood, N.J., 1968—; chmn. bd. Scanforms, Inc.

MORRIS, JOHN OSGOOD, mgmt. cons.; b. N.Y.C., 1918; s. Ray and Katharine (Grinnell) M.; B.A., Yale U., 1941; J.D., U. Va., 1948; m. Bernardine Day, 1947; children—Robert S., Bernardine S., Katharine C.; m. 2d, Mary Newton, 1978. Asso., Kirlin, Campbell & Keating, N.Y.C., 1948-51; various positions Aetna Life Ins. Co., Hartford, Conn., 1951-58, asst. counsel, 1958-65; pres. John O. Morris Assos., plain lang. cons., West Hartford, Conn., 1965—; dir. Stratton Corp., Stratton Mt., Vt. Served with USN, 1941-46. Mem. Am. Soc. Tng. and Devel., Am. Bar Assn. Clubs: Hartford Golf, Stratton Mt. Country. Author: Make Yourself Clear!, 1972, 2d edit., 1980. Home and Office: 40 Wood Pond Rd West Hartford CT 06107

MORRIS, JOSEPH PAUL, JR., sales cons.; b. Phila., Dec. 27, 1922; s. Joseph Paul and Emma (Montgomery) M.; student Haverford Coll., 1941-42, 46, 49; m. Rebecca Polk Darnall, Apr. 16, 1955; children—Sarah Polk Wistar, Martha Elizabeth. Clk., Morris, Wheeler & Co., Inc., Phila., 1947-48; sect. mgr. Strawbridge & Clothier, Phila., 1949-50; pvt. studies, writing in fgn. affairs, 1951—; clk., sales copy Lannett Co., Inc., Phila., 1955-56; clk., reporting Alan Wood Steel Co., Conshohocken, 1956-57; free-lance agt. for fgn. and domestic industry, 1958—. Mem. Morris Family Publs. Com.; mem. 1st troop Phila. City Cavalry, 1948-50; active Heart Fund drives, Haverford, Pa., 1954-59, Am. Fund for Westminster Abbey, Phila., 1954; treas. Episcopal Co-operating Com. Bd. dirs. Chinese Christian Ch. and Center, 1967-72; guarantor Bach Choir, Bethlehem, 1957; judge of elections, 1980—. Volunteer ambulance driver with Brit. Army, Am. Field Service, Middle East and Italy, 1943-45. Decorated Africa Star, Italy Star, Victory medal (Eng.). Mem. Hist. Soc. Pa., Welcome Soc. Pa., Colonial Soc. Pa., Athenaeum of Phila., Pa. Soc. N.Y., S.R., Zool. Soc. Phila., Mil. Order Fgn. Wars, Friends Independence Nat. Hist. Park, Friends of Wyck, Morris Cricket Library Assn. Episcopalian. Office: Broad Axe Box 218 Ambler PA 19002

MORRIS, LEWIS S., garment mfg. co. exec.; b. Salisbury, N.C., 1915; A.B., U. N.C., 1936; B.S., N.C. State Coll., 1937; married. With Cone Mills Corp., 1946—, asst. sec., 1952-56, sec., asst. treas., 1956-58, v.p. Revolution div., 1958-59, v.p., 1959-63, sr. v.p. mfg., 1963-65, pres., chief exec. officer, mem. exec. com., 1965-72, chmn. bd., chief exec. officer, 1972—, also dir. Served with U.S. Navy, 1941-46. Office: 120 Maple St Greensboro NC 27405*

MORRIS, MARJORIE HALE, retail exec.; b. Chattanooga, Aug. 4, 1940; d. Laurie Everett and Marjorie (Hunt) Hale; student El Camino Jr. Coll., 1958-60; 2 sons. Stewardess, Am. Airlines, 1960-62, mem. staff nat. advt. and publicity, 1961-62; mgr. Viking Ski Shop, Pacific Palisades, Calif., 1963-64; promotional adviser East Sierra Land Devel. Co., 1963-66; Pepsi Cola Corp. rep. to Republican Nat. Conv., 1964; co-owner, mgr. Ready Room Restaurant, Los Angeles, 1967; architects adviser, restaurant devel. and design, Honolulu, Dallas, Atlanta, Los Angeles, 1967-73; mgr., buyer Great Things, Honolulu, 1972-74; mgr. Braille Inst. Thrift Shop, Los Angeles, 1975-78, dir., 1978—, also adminstr. devel. office; freelance photographer, 1974—; designer floats Pacific Palisades Parade, 1965, TransPac Race Com., Honolulu, 1972. Team mother Pacific Palisades Little League, 1974-76. Mem. Am. Soc. Appraisers, Am. Soc. Profl. and Exec. Women, Internat. Platform Assn., Beverly Hills C. of C. (Outstanding Service to Community awards 1976, 77). Originator, dir. Christmas Tree Project, Beverly Hills; cover editor Calif. Yacht Club Mag., 1976. Home: PO Box 71 Pacific Palisades CA 90272 Office: 125 N Western Ave Los Angeles CA 90004

MORRIS, MICHAEL BORIS, oil co. exec.; b. Manning, Tex., Sept. 5, 1920; s. James Richard and Anna Elizabeth (Burnett) M.; B.S. in Geology, U. Tex., 1947; student Advanced Mgmt. Program, Harvard U., 1965; m. Louise Murphee, Aug. 18, 1951; children—James, Richard. Various geol. positions Conoco, Inc., 1948-57, mgr. internat. exploration, 1964-67, v.p. internat. exploration, 1967-74; asst. mgr., mgr., then v.p. Hudson Bay Oil & Gas, Calgary, Alta., Can., 1957-64; exec. v.p. Eastern Hemisphere Petroleum, 1974-75, exec. v.p. exploration, 1975-78, pres. petroleum ops., 1978—; dir. Conoco Inc., Hudson Bay Oil & Gas Co., Calgary. Bd. dirs. Tex. Research League, Houston Symphony; mem. energy com., mem. com. for arts Houston C. of C. Served with USN, 1941-45. Mem. Am. Assn. Petroleum Geologists, Am. Petroleum Inst. (dir.), Houston Geol. Soc. Clubs: Petroleum of Houston, Ramada. Office: PO Box 2197 Houston TX 77001

MORRIS, PAUL ROBERT, mfg. co. exec.; b. Sykesville, Pa., June 30, 1924; s. John J. and Mary (Skovran) M.; student Ohio State U., 1943-44; B.S.I.E., Pa. State U., 1950; postgrad. Syracuse U., 1964-65, Cornell U., 1965-67; m. Alberta N. Stinson, June 30, 1951; children—Paul Kyler, Barry, Philip Grant. Indsl. engr. Sylvania Electron Tube div. Sylvania Corp., Emporium, Pa., Reynoldsville, Pa., Huntington, W.Va., Burlington, Iowa, 1950-53, mfg. dept. mgr. Electronic Tube div., Burlington, 1953-58, indsl. relations supr., Burlington and Seneca Falls, N.Y., 1958-69; mgr. personnel and mfg. services W.M. Chace Co., Detroit, 1969-70; v.p., gen. mgr. Chace Internat. Corp., San Juan, P.R., 1970-75; v.p. new bus. and new facilities devel. GTE Sylvania, Reidsville, N.C., 1975—; dir. Chace Internat. Corp., Chace Precision Materials Corp. Mem. Selective Service Bd., 1962, 63; bd. dirs. Girl Scouts U.S.A., 1950-62; chmn. Boy Scouts Am., 1967-69; bd. dirs. Salvation Army, 1958-64. Served with U.S. Army, 1943-46; ETO. Recipient Selective Service System award, 1963. Mem. Nat. Foreman's Assn. (pres. 1953), Pa. State U. Alumni Assn., Triangle. Republican. Lutheran. Clubs: Rotary, Masons. Home: 1601 Country Club Rd Reidsville NC 27320 Office: 1704 Barnes St Reidsville NC 27320

MORRIS, RALPH FREDERICK CHARLES, bus. machine sales and service co. exec.; b. Toronto, Ont., Can., Mar. 31, 1924; s. George F. and Gladys G. (Tice) M.; student Upper Can. Coll., 1939-42, U. Western Ont., 1970-71; m. Gwendolyn J. Shore, Sept. 4, 1954; children—Brian G., Sandra. Sales rep. Justowriter Corp., Buffalo, Comml. Controls Corp., Toronto, Gray Mfg. Co., Hartford, Conn.; sales mgr. No. Electric Co. Ltd., Belleville, Seely Systems Ltd., Toronto; pres. Glomor Services Ltd., Toronto, 1957-64; dist. mgr. IBM Can. Ltd., Toronto, 1964-74; pres. Dictaphone Can. Ltd., Islington, Ont., 1974—. Served with Royal Can. Navy Vol. Res., 1942-45. Mem. Internat. Word Processing Assn., Can. Bus. Equipment Mfrs. Assn., Naval Officers Assn. Club: Blvd. Home: 980 Springhill Dr Mississauga ON L5H 1M9 Canada Office: 630 The East Mall Islington ON M9B 4B2 Canada

MORRIS, ROBERT LOUIS, food processing co. exec.; b. Phila., Aug. 24, 1932; s. Joseph Aloysius and Philomena Mary Ellen (Clauser) M.; B.S., Drexel U., 1955; M.S., U. Pa., 1957; postgrad. U. Cin., 1965-66, U. Chgo., 1969-71; m. Elizabeth Marie Smyth, Sept. 10, 1955; children—Robert L., Thomas J., Lawrence F., Elizabeth M., Mary Ellen, Richard B. Group leader Procter & Gamble Co., Miami Valley Labs., 1958-68; dir. computing services research and devel. div. Kraft, Inc., Glenview, Ill., 1968-71; dir. research and process devel. ITT Continental Baking Co., Rye, N.Y., 1971-77, v.p. tech. affairs, 1978—. tech. dir. food and chem. products ITT Inc., N.Y.C., 1977-78. Bd. dirs. Fundacion Chile, Santiago, 1978—; mem. Greenwich Rep. Town Meeting, 1977. Served with AUS, 1957. NSF fellow, 1955-56; Wilson S. Yerger fellow, 1956-57. Mem. Am. Inst. Chem. Engrs., Inst. Food Technologists, Am. Mgmt. Assn., Assn. Research Dirs., Indsl. Research Inst. Roman Catholic. Clubs: Innis Arden Golf, Stamford Racquetball. Patentee in field. Office: PO Box 731 Rye NY 10580

MORRIS, WILLIAM ALLEN, real estate exec.; b. Coral Gables, Fla., Apr. 11, 1952; s. Lonnie Allen and Ida (Akers) M.; B.S., Ga. Inst. Tech., 1975; m. Diane Yohe. Pres., chief exec. officer Allen Morris Co., Miami, Fla., 1980—; dir., mem. exec. and loan coms. Northside Bank, Miami, 1974-78; v.p., dir. Allen Morris Co. Ga., 1978—, Allen Morris Mgmt. Co., 1980—, Allen Morris Devel. Co., 1980—, Brokers Title Co., 1978—, Right Investment Corp., 1978—, Realty Leasing Corp. Ga., 1978—, Center Constrn. Co., 1978—, 1000 Brickell, Inc., 1978—, Brickell Plaza, Inc., 1978—; mng. partner Morris Investments, 1980—, KAI Properties, 1976—; v.p. and/or dir. other related cos. Vice pres., bd. dirs. Allen Morris Found.; bd. dirs. Boys Clubs Am., Campus Crusade for Christ, Miami, Dade County Citizens Safety Council, Orange Bowl Com.; bd. mgrs. Southwest YMCA, Miami, 1978—, chmn. fin. com., 1979; deacon Granada Presbyn. Ch., Coral Gables. Mem. Nat. Assn. Realtors, Fla. Assn. Realtors (dir.), Inst. Real Estate Mgmt. (cert.), Realtors Nat. Mktg. Inst. (dir.), Miami Bd. Realtors, S.A.R., Com. 100 Miami Beach. Democrat. Clubs: Miami Rotary, Riviera Country, Miami, Two Hundred Greater Miami, Bankers, Bath. Home: 1470 Mercado St Coral Gables FL 33146 Office: 2 S Biscayne Blvd 1 Biscayne Tower Suite 2600 Miami FL 33131

MORRISON, BRUCE PANNETT, banker; b. Bklyn., Sept. 13, 1942; s. William Pannett and Myra (Putney) M.; B.A. in Chemistry, Wesleyan U., Middletown, Conn., 1965; m. Dale Garrett Andrews, Nov. 24, 1973; 1 dau., Tait Whitney. Successively loan officer Eastern div., group head metals and mining, v.p. and group head, loan workout div. Bankers Trust Co., N.Y.C., 1965-66, 69—; dir. Hamilton Mortgage Corp., Atlanta, 1978-79. Served to lt. (j.g.) USNR, 1966-69. Republican. Episcopalian. Clubs: Madison (Conn.) Beach; N.Y.C. Doubles. Home: 14 Pierce Rd Riverside CT 06878 Office: 280 Park Ave New York NY 10017

MORRISON, HOWARD IRWIN, computer co. exec.; b. Bklyn., Aug. 16, 1929; s. Philip O. and Anne (Eisler) M.; B.A., George Washington U., 1951; m. Barbara May Kraut, Dec. 5, 1959 (dec. Feb. 1967); children—Peter Keith, Scott David; m. 2d, April Keil, Dec. 8, 1968 (div. Nov. 1976); 1 dau., Dina Helen; m. 3d, Joyce Simone, June 18, 1977. Research asst. Harvard Research Found., Washington, 1951; statistician U.S. Govt., Washington, 1951-52; buyer Lansburgh's Dept. Store, Washington, 1954-56; economist, adminstr. CEIR, Inc., Washington, 1956-61; pres. Computer Concepts, Inc., Washington, 1961-66; v.p. Computer Applications, Inc., N.Y.C., 1964-68, pres. Info. Scis. div., 1968-70, also dir.; pres., chmn. bd. Policy Mgmt. Systems, Inc., 1970-71; chmn. bd. Dewey, Irwin & Co., Inc., N.Y.C., 1970-71; exec. v.p., gen. mgr. Auerbach Pubs., Inc., Phila., 1971-76; pres. ADL Systems Inc., Burlington, Mass., 1976-79, Morrison Assos., Sudbury, Mass., 1979—. Served with USNR, 1952-53. Mem. Assn. Computing Machinery, Colonials, Am. Newcomen Soc., Phi Epsilon Pi, George Washington U. Alumni Assn. Office: 227 Mossman Rd Sudbury MA 01776

MORRISON, JAMES LEWIS, educator, cons.; b. London, Ont., Can., July 21, 1941; s. Gerald L. and Mary Lou (Mackie) M.; B.A., Queen's U., 1972; M.Ed., U. Ottawa, 1976; divorced; children—Michelle, Scott. Owner, pub. The No. Light News, Fraserdale, Ont., 1965-66; pres. Facilitators, Brockville, Ont., 1978-80, The Choosers' Group, Brockville, 1978-80; prin. N. Edwardsburg Public Sch., Spencerville, Ont.; instr. St. Lawrence Community Coll., Brockville, 1975—; health cons. Bd. dirs. Brock Cottage, 1977-79; chmn. Internat. Conf. on Addictions, Eastern Ont. and No. N.Y., 1978; presenter Ont. Public Health Assn., 1979; chmn. com. on addictions Tri-County Dist. Health Council, Smith Falls, Ont., 1979—; conf. leader Ont. Assn. Curriculum Devel., 1980. Mem. Can. Guidance and Counselling Assn., Ont. Public Sch. Men Tchrs. Fedn. (com. chmn.), Ont. Prins. Assn. Mem. United Ch. of Can. Home: Box 70 Brockville ON K6V 5V1 Canada Office: N Edwardsburg Public Sch Spencerville ON K0E 1X0 Canada

MORRISON, JOHN DOANE, lawyer, r.r. exec.; b. Albany, N.Y., Mar. 26, 1927; s. J. Cayce and Grace D.; student Swarthmore Coll., 1943-45; A.B., U. Pa., 1946; LL.B., Harvard, 1951; m. Barbara Lewis, June 27, 1953; children—Jeffrey Lewis, Christopher Doane. Admitted to N.Y. bar, 1952, Mich. bar, 1962, Ill. bar, 1967; atty., commerce counsel, asst. to v.p.-law N.Y. Central R.R., 1951-62; mem. firm Badgley, Domke, Morrison, McVicker & Marcoux, Jackson, Mich., 1962-67; gen. atty., gen. solicitor Ill. Central R.R., 1967-72; dir., gen. counsel Bessemer & Lake Erie R.R., 1972—, sec., 1973—; dir., gen. counsel, sec. Carbon County Ry., Duluth, Missabe and Iron Range Ry., Elgin, Joliet and Eastern Ry., Johnstown and Stony Creek R.R., Lake Terminal R.R., McKeesport Connecting R.R., Newburgh and S. Shore Ry., Northampton and Bath R.R., Union R.R., Youngstown and Northern R.R., Pittsburgh and Conneaut Dock Co., Birmingham So. R.R. Served to lt. (j.g.) USNR, 1944-47. Mem. Am. Bar Assn., ICC Practitioners Assn., Pi Gamma Mu, Phi Delta Theta. Clubs: Duquesne, Allegheny Country. Home: RD 4 Blackburn Rd Sewickely PA 15143 Office: PO Box 536 Pittsburgh PA 15230

MORRISON, JOHN JOSEPH, pharm. co. exec.; b. Richmond County, N.Y., Sept. 30, 1932; s. James Joseph and Grace Katherine (McCarthy) M.; B.S., St. Peters Coll., 1954; postgrad. Pace Coll., 1959-61; M.B.A., Wagner Coll., 1968; m. Mary Irene Graham, Jan. 28, 1967; children—Katherine, Thomas, James. Accountant, Gen. Motors Co., Bloomfield, N.J., 1956-57; credit reporter Dun & Bradstreet, N.Y.C., 1957-59; credit mgr. Gulf Oil Co., N.Y.C., 1959-64; mgmt. cons. Alexander Proudfoot, Boston, 1964; div. credit mgr. Pfizer, Inc., N.Y.C., 1964-68, asst. gen. credit mgr., 1968-72, mgr. receivables ops., 1972-76, dir. credit and receivables, 1976-79, asst. treas., 1979—; instr. Katherine Gibbs Sch., N.Y.C.; mem. credit research com. Credit Research Found., Lake Success, N.Y. Vice chmn. Summit (N.J.) Safety Council, 1974-76; with wife conducts human growth devel. program, pub. schs., Summit. Served with U.S. Army, 1954-56. Mem. Nat. Assn. Credit Mgmt., Credit Research Found., Am. Mgmt. Assn., Nat. Chem. Credit Assn. Club: St. Peters Coll. of S.I. Home: 228 Blackburn Rd Summit NJ 07901 Office: 235 E 42d St New York NY 10017

MORRISON, JOHN WILLIAM, fin. exec.; b. Hamilton, Ohio, Aug. 23, 1932; s. Michael M. and Alice L. (Board) M.; student Miami U. Oxford, 1951-52; grad. Ohio Sch. Banking, 1961; grad. Sch. Banking U. Wis., 1965; m. Antoinette Massarelli, Oct. 17, 1953; children—John J., Ann M. Comml. loan officer Second Nat. Bank, Hamilton, Ohio, asst. v.p., 1954-77; treas., fin. advisor, partner Hamilton Merchandising Co., 1955—. Past treas. Butler County March of Dimes; past trustee Greater Cinn. March of Dimes; past treas. Arthritis Found.; fin. com. St. Peter in Chains Ch., Hamilton. Served with U.S. Army, 1952-54. Mem. Ohio (trustee 1966-68), Butler County bankers assns. Republican. Roman Catholic. Clubs: New London Hills, Moose, Elks. Home: 1308 Cleveland Ave Hamilton OH 45013 Office: 844 East Ave Hamilton OH 45011

MORRISON, PETER GIFFORD, fin. cons.; b. Washington, Iowa, Sept. 2, 1948; s. G. Gifford and Sara Lu M.; student Robert Morris Coll., 1967-69; A.B., U. Iowa, 1972, postgrad., 1972. Tax cons. Morrison, Morrison & Morrison, 1966-78; fin. and investment cons. N.W. Bank & Trust Co., Davenport, Iowa, 1974-79; trust officer and affiliate mgr. Iowa-Des Moines Nat. Bank, 1979; specialist in probate and taxation Morrison Law Office, Washington, Iowa, 1980—; lectr. estate and fin. planning. Mem. Kappa Sigma. Republican. Presbyterian. Home: 215 1/2 S Iowa Ave Washington IA 52353 Office: 213 S Marion Washington IA 52353

MORRISON, RAYMOND HEWES, sch. supply co. exec.; b. Bangor, Maine, Oct. 13, 1905; s. Lewis J. and Edith Emma (Sweet) M.; B.S., U. Maine, 1928, M.S., 1932; m. Eva M. Griffin, Oct. 2, 1934; children—Hugh A., Bruce A., Elizabeth Ann, David G., Nancy, Roberta. Sales engr. Gen. Electric Co., Schenectady, N.Y., 1924-31, T.R. Savage Co., Bangor, 1932-51; sales mgr. Cascade Paper Co., North Adams, Mass., 1951-61; founder No. Supply Co. Bangor, 1961, pres., treas., 1978—; founder The Learnin' Tree, ednl. retail store, 1978, pres., treas., 1978—. Mem. Nat. Sch. Supply and Equipment Assn. Republican. Club: Masons. Home: 39 Plaisted St Bangor ME 04401 Office: 739 Odlin Rd Bangor ME 04401

MORRISON, ROBERT HUGH, financial co. exec.; b. Calif., Jan. 28, 1938; s. Charles Hugh and Sarah Inez (Morrison-Rutledge) M.: A.A., Pasadena City Coll., 1958; m. Patricia L. Seefried, Apr. 2, 1980; children—Robert Hugh, Jeri L., Donna D., Debra M., James C., Shawn C. Various engring. and accounting positions, 1957-61: pres. Fin. Mgmt. Assos., Inc., Phoenix, 1961-78, Owtward Bound, Ltd., Phoenix, 1978—. Mem. Nat. Assn. Accredited Tax Accountants. Republican. Club: Elks. Author books including: My Hobby As A Business, 1973; The Fraud Report, 1975: Why S.O.B.'s Succeed and Nice Guys Fail in Small Businesses, 1976; Contracting Out, The Pawns, The Moneylenders, The Rulemakers, Stalemate, How to Steal a Job, various others, 1977-78; How to Survive and Prosper in the Next American Depression, War or Revolution, 1979; Divorce Dirty Tricks, 1979. Home: 3933 E Rancho Dr Paradise Valley AZ 85253

MORRISON, WALTON S., lawyer; b. Big Spring, Tex., June 16, 1907; s. M. H. and Ethel (Jackson) M.; student Texas A. and M. Coll., 1926-28; J.D., Tex. U., 1932; m. Mary Bell, Dec. 19, 1932. Admitted to Tex. bar, 1932; asso. Morrison & Morrison, Big Spring, 1932-37; county atty. Howard County, Tex., 1937-39, county judge, 1941-42, 47-48; pvt. practice, 1946-47; partner Morrison and Morrison, 1949-53; pvt. practice, 1953—; city atty. Big Spring, 1949-58. Served with USAAF, 1942-46. Mem. Am. Bar Assn., State Bar Tex. Club: Rotary. Home: 1501 E 11th Pl Big Spring TX 79720 Office: 113 E 2d St Big Spring TX 79720

MORRISSEY, JAMES JOSEPH, JR., computer co. exec.; b. Phila., July 15, 1938; s. James Joseph and Adelaide E. (Emig) M.; B.S. in Elec. Engring., Drexel U., 1961; m. E. Gail Brooke, Sept. 17, 1960; children—Mark, Craig. Engr., Honeywell Co., St. Petersburg, Fla., 1961-66, mem. mktg. staff, 1966-68, sales mgr., 1968-72; regional mgr. Data Gen. Corp., Westboro, Mass., 1972-77, dir. corp. accounts, 1977-80; dir. modulation products Codex Corp., Mansfield, Mass., 1980—. Home: 24 Grove St Wayland MA 01778

MORRISSEY, MADELEINE MARIA, perfume co. exec.; b. N.Y.C., Jan. 8; d. Joseph Lawrence and Madeleine Catherine (Curran) M.; B.A. in Sociology, Notre Dame Coll., N.Y.; postgrad. N.Y. U.; m. Francis Klabouch; 1 dau., Meryn. Vice pres. Grant Advt., N.Y.C., 1960-65; copy chief consumer div. Hazard Advt., N.Y.C., 1965-69; copy supr. Ketchum, MacLeod & Grove Advt., N.Y.C., 1969-71; pres. Capricorn Communications, N.Y.C., 1971-73; dir. advt. and pub. relations Dana Perfumes Corp., N.Y.C., 1973—. Mem. parish council St. Thomas More Ch., N.Y.C., 1973—, also founder, editor-in-chief More ch. newspaper; chmn. Yorkville Cath.-Jewish Council, 1976-80; bd. dirs. Yorkville Outreach; mem. Yorkville Area Cath. Council, 1977—. Home: 60 East End Ave New York NY 10028 Office: 609 Fifth Ave New York NY 10017

MORRISSEY, THOMAS JEROME, investment banker; b. Racine, Wis.; s. Patrick William and Lillian (Mitchell) M.; Ph.B., U. Wis., 1940; postgrad. U. Ill., 1942, U.S. Naval Acad., 1942; m. Clovene Marie Nogel, Feb. 21, 1957. Merchandising trainee Vick Chem. div. Richardson-Merrill, Inc., N.Y.C., 1940-41, sales promotion asst., 1941-42, mgr. mil. sales, 1942; pvt. practice as marketing, financial cons., N.Y.C., 1952-54; dir. marketing research Pharmacraft Labs. div. Seagrams Distillers, Inc., N.Y.C., 1946-48, mgr. sales promotion, 1948-49, gen. sales mgr., 1949-52; asst. to pres. Turner-Smith Drug Co., N.Y.C., 1954-55, sales mgr., Smithtown, L.I., N.Y., 1955-57; mgr. advt. and sales Denver Chem. Mfg. Co., Stamford, Conn., 1957-58, N.Y.C., 1958-59; v.p., dir. marketing, account exec. Ralph Allum Advt. Agy., N.Y.C., 1959-67; v.p. Community Sci., Inc., 1959-67; account exec. Walston & Co., Inc., N.Y.C., 1967-74, Harris, Upham & Co., Inc., 1974-76; sr. account exec. Smith Barney Harris Upham & Co., 1976—. Served to lt. USNR, 1942-46. Decorated Silver Star medal. Mem. The Marketeers (pres. 1963-67), Astoria Park Tennis Assn. (pres. 1967-70), Eastern Lawn Tennis Assn. (del. 1967-69), Met. Badminton Assn. (del. 1968—), Sigma Chi. Clubs: Dutch Treat (chmn. 1960-61), Army and Navy (gov.), Central Badminton (pres. 1971—), West Side Tennis (Forest Hills). Research in field. Home: 865 UN Plaza New York NY 10017 Office: 120 Broadway 23d Floor New York NY 10005

MORROW, BRUCE W., data processing cons.; b. Rochester, Minn., May 20, 1946; s. J. Robert and Frances P. Morrow; B.A., U. Notre Dame, 1968, M.B.A. with honors in Mgmt., 1974, M.A. in Comparative Lit., 1975; grad. U.S. Army Command and Gen. Staff Coll., 1979. Co-mgr., Wendy's Old Fashioned Hamburgers, South Bend, Ind., 1976-77; adminstrn. mgr. Eastern States Devel. Corp., Richmond, Va., 1977; v.p. JDB Assos., Inc., Alexandria, Va., 1977-78; owner Aardvark Prodns., Alexandria, 1978-80, Servital Foods, Alexandria, Va., 1980—; sr. cons. Data Base Mgmt., Inc., Springfield, Va., 1979—; systems analyst/individual tng. officer Office of Chief Army Res., Dept. Army, Washington, 1980-81; cons. advt. writer The Miracle of Birth, Arlington, Va., 1979. Active Boy Scouts Am., 1960-69; chmn. elem. German sect. U. Notre Dame, 1973-75. Served to capt. U.S. Army, 1969-72. Decorated Bronze Star, Army Commendation medal, Parachutist's badge. Mem. Nat. Eagle Scout Assn., Internat. Entrepreneurs Assn., Va. State Sheriffs Assn., VFW (life), Am. Legion, Beta Gamma Sigma, Delta Phi Alpha. Clubs:

Friends Internat. (Am. v.p. 1969-71) (Boeblingen, Germany); Order of DeMolay. Contbg. columnist Notre Dame Mag., 1974—; composer songs. Home: 708A W Glebe Rd Alexandria VA 22305 Office: Data Base Mgmt Inc 6501 Loisdale Ct Springfield VA 22150

MORROW, DAVID WARREN, retail exec.; b. Hood River, Oreg., Aug. 11, 1931; s. Claude W. and Etta Elfreda (Brown) M.; student Coll. Idaho, 1949, exec. program Stanford U., summer 1968; m. Patricia Ann Ballard, Apr. 16, 1949; children—Kelly, Kristi, Jody. With Albertsons, Inc., Boise, Idaho, from 1949, exec. v.p., 1975-76, pres., chief operating officer, 1976-77, vice chmn., 1977; pres., chief operating officer Great Atlantic & Pacific Tea Co., Inc., Montvale, N.J., 1977—, also dir. Bd. dirs. Food Mktg. Inst. Office: Great Atlantic & Pacific Tea Co Inc 2 Paragon Dr Montvale NJ 07645*

MORROW, RICHARD MARTIN, oil co. exec.; b. Wheeling, W.Va., 1926; B.M.E., Ohio State U., 1948; married. With Standard Oil Co. (Ind.), 1948—, exec. v.p. Amoco Internat. Oil Co., 1966-70, exec. v.p. Amoco Chem. Corp., 1970-74, pres., 1974-78, pres. Standard Oil Co. (Ind.), 1978—; dir. First Chgo. Corp., First Nat. Bank Chgo. Trustee U. Chgo., Rush-Presbyn.-St. Luke's Med. Center. Mem. Am. Petroleum Inst. (dir.). Office: 200 E Randolph Dr Chicago IL 60601

MORROW, ROBERT MILES, food co. exec.; b. Bklyn., Oct. 27, 1937; s. Abraham and Mina (Kay) M.; B.Sc., Ohio State U., 1959; M.B.A., L.I.U. 1961; m. Ina Gurin, Dec. 25, 1954; children—Christopher, Rebecca. Asst. mgr. mktg. research Oxford Paper Co., N.Y.C., 1960-63; dir. mktg. Almay Cosmetics, N.Y.C., 1963-69, Revlon, Inc., N.Y.C., 1969-74; corp. v.p., dir. mktg. and new bus. devel. ITT Continental Baking Co., Rye, N.Y., 1974—; dir. Gualtney, Inc., Smithfield, Va., C&C Cola, Elmwood Park, N.J.; adj. prof. mktg. U. Conn. Grad. Sch., 1979—. Served with USAF, 1960. Recipient Achievement Award Sales and Mktg. Mgmt. mag., 1977; Merit award Art Dirs., 1978. Mem. U.S. C. of C., Grocery Mfrs. Assn., Am. Mktg. Assn., Am. Mgmt. Assn. Clubs: Twin Lakes, Landmark (Stamford, Conn.). Office: ITT Continental Baking Co Halstead Ave Rye NY 10580

MORSE, ANDREW LOUIS, finance inst. exec.; b. Northfield, Vt., Dec. 23, 1942; s. Louis Lincoln and Alice (McNamara) M.; B.B.A., Norwich U., 1965; m. Barbara Jean O'Grady, July 24, 1965; children—Megan Jean, Katherine Suzanne. Broker, br. mgr. Mut. Fund Brokers, Inc., Tucson, 1967-71; mktg. rep., regional mgr. N.Y. Inst. Fin., N.Y.C. and Chgo., 1971-75, v.p., gen. mgr., N.Y.C., 1976-77, pres., 1977—. Chmn., N.J. Norwich Devel. Campaign; bd. fellows Norwich U., 1979—. Served with AUS, 1965-67. Mem. Wall St. Tng. Dirs. (chmn. 1977-79), Internat. Assn. Fin. Planners. Republican. Office: 70 Pine St New York NY 10005

MORSE, DANIEL DUNN, fin. cons.; b. N.Y.C., Jan. 8, 1947; s. Jonathan Dean and Elaine (Dunn) M.; ed. spl. courses Am. U., Practising Law Inst., N.Y. U. Account exec. Pension and Investment Assn. of Am., Montclair, N.J., 1967-71; project devel. officer Greater Grand Rapids (Mich.) Housing Corp., 1971; dir. housing devel. services Nat. Urban League Devel. Found., Washington, 1972-73; prin. Danmor Enterprises, Silver Spring, Md., 1973—, also Danmor Fin. Mgmt. Services, Inc. chmn. Greater Washington Local Devel. Co., Inc.; founder 1st Montgomery Bank and Trust Co., Montgomery County, Md.; advisory council SBA; housing devel. specialist; del. White House Conf. on Small Bus., 1980 lectr. in field. Mem. Met. Washington Bd. Trade, Montgomery County C. of C. (dir.), Arlington C. of C. Baptist. Contbg. editor: Housing in the 70's, 1973. Home: Three Pines Farm Morse Family Estate Route 1 S South Hill VA Office: 8715 1st Ave Silver Spring MD 20910

MORSE, DONALD LAVERNE, elec. contractor; b. Freeport, Ill., July 9, 1941; s. Donald L. and Joyce E. (Woods) M.; m. Jane L. Crippen, Apr. 27, 1973; children—Lori, Kristin, Donald LaVerne, III. With Morse Electric, Inc., Freeport, Ill., 1960—, pres., 1973—. Mem. Nat. Elec. Contractors Assn. Home: 1745 W Stephenson St Freeport IL 61032 Office: 711 S Chippewa Ave Freeport IL 61032

MORSE, ELEANOR REESE (MRS. A. REYNOLDS MORSE), plastic accessory co. exec.; b. Cleve.; d. George William and Elsie Frances (Douds) Reese; Mus.B., Rollins Coll., 1935, D.F.A. (hon.), 1977; M.A. in French, Case Western Res. U., 1970; m. A. Reynolds Morse, Mar. 21, 1942; 1 son, Bradish. Bookkeeper, sec. Injection Molders Supply Co. (named changed to IMS Co. 1969), Cleve., 1949-60, sec.-treas., 1960-65, Beachwood, Ohio, 1965—. Vice pres. Salvador Dali Found.; treas. Salvador Dali Mus., St. Petersburg, Fla.; v.p. Mid-Central states Fedn. French Alliances in U.S., 1974-76. Decorated chevalier Ordre des Palmes Academiques, chevalier Nat. Order of Merit (France); recipient certificate of recognition Mayor of Cleve., 1978; Aim award, 1978. Mem. Le Cercle des Conferences Francaises (pres. 1965-67), Fedn. French Alliances (nat. council 1979—), Maison Francaise de Cleve. (pres. 1969—). Office: 24050 Commerce Park Rd Beachwood OH 44122

MORSE, JOAN BEREND, fund raiser; b. N.Y.C., Dec. 28, 1924; d. Frank H. and Anne (Bramson) Berend; student Sweet Briar Coll., 1946; m. Donald E. Gordon, Sept. 9, 1979; children by previous marriage—Ann B. and Jonathan Morse. Researcher, Frank H. Berend & Assos., Inc., N.Y.C., 1972-73, account exec., 1973-76, pres., 1976—. Mem. Nat. Soc. Fund Raising Execs. (dir. N.Y. chpt.). Democrat. Contbr. children's stories to McCall's and Children's Digest, 1950-53; sculptor, works exhibited Silvermine, Conn., 1959, White Plains, N.Y., 1966-68, Bologna, Italy, 1970. Office: 312 E 51st St New York NY 10022

MORSE, LEON WILLIAM, distbn. mgmt. exec.; b. N.Y.C., Nov. 13, 1912; s. Benjamin and Leah (Shapiro) M.; B.S., N.Y. U., 1935; grad. Acad. Advanced Traffic, 1937, 1954; D.B.A., Columbia Pacific U., 1979; m. Goldie Kohn, Mar. 30, 1941; children—Jeffrey W., Saul J. Individual bus., traffic mgmt. cons., Phila., 1950-58; gen. traffic mgr. W.H. Rorer, Inc., Ft. Washington, Pa., 1958-77; adj. prof. econs. of transp., logistics Pa. State U., Ogontz campus, 1963—; sr. partner Morse, Stoner, Travis & Assos. Served to capt. Transp. Corps, AUS, World War II. Recipient Del. Valley Traffic Mgr. of Year award, 1963; registered ICC, Fed. Maritime Commn. Mem. Traffic and Transp. Club of Phila., Traffic Club Phila., Traffic Club Norristown (Pa.), Am. Soc. Internat. Execs. (pres.), Canadian Assn. Phys. Distbn. Mgmt., Assn. ICC Practitioners, Am. Soc. Traffic and Transp. (emeritus), Nat. Council Phys. Distbn., Del Valley Drug Traffic Assos. (chmn.), Drug and Toilet Preparations Traffic Conf. (ret. chmn. bd.). Mason (Shriner). Author: Practical Handbook of Industrial Traffic Management, 1980. Home: 14086 Kelvin Ave Philadelphia PA 19116

MORSE, RICHARD DURLAND, coll. fin. adminstr.; b. Boston, Oct. 11, 1927; s. George Dresser and Ruth (Durland) M.; student Champlain Coll., 1947-49; B. Mgmt. Engring., Rensselaer Poly. Inst., 1951; postgrad. Indsl. Coll. Armed Forces Extension, 1964-65; m. Shirley Mae Baker, May 29, 1954; children—Martha, Stephenie. Trainee, Remington Rand Corp., Washington, 1953-54; sr. indsl. engr. Reynolds Metals Co., Phoenix, 1954-56, sr. staff asst., central systems dept., Richmond, Va., 1956-59; mgr. mgmt. info. systems div. RCA Global Communications, Inc., N.Y.C., 1967-68; adminstr. data systems projects RCA Electronic Components and Devices, Harrison, N.J., 1965-67; adminstr. mgmt. systems, corporate staff mgmt. engr. RCA, Camden, N.J., 1959-65; dir. adminstr. info. services div. Rutgers U., 1969-72, dir. univ. mgmt. evaluation and services, 1972-75, dir. univ. mgmt. audit, 1975-79, asst. treas., 1979—; bd. dirs. Ednl. Computing Center, Inc., New Brunswick, 1970-72. Served with AUS, 1946-47, USAF, 1951-53. Mem. Am. Inst. Indsl. Engrs. (sr.), Am. Soc. Public Adminstm., Nat. Audubon Soc. Episcopalian (vestryman). Club: 7th Regt. Rifle (life). Home: 32 Bullion Rd Basking Ridge NJ 07920 Office: Rutgers State U NJ Adminstrv Services Bldg Busch Campus New Brunswick NJ 08903

MORSE, RICHARD JAY, transp. and bldg. services co. exec.; b. Detroit, Aug. 2, 1933; s. Maurice and Belle Roslyn (Jacobson) M.; B.A. in Psychology, U. Va., 1955; teaching credential U. Calif. at Los Angeles, 1957; M.A. in Psychology, Calif. State U. at Los Angeles, 1964. With Gen. Telephone Co. of Calif., Santa Monica, 1957-68; dir. tng. and devel. Bekins Co., Los Angeles, 1968-69, dir. personnel, 1969-70, dir. personnel and organizational devel., 1970-72, v.p.-personnel, 1972-74, v.p.-adminstrn., 1974-80, v.p. human resources, 1980—; cons. organizational devel. Active City of Hope, Am. Cancer Soc. Mem. Los Angeles C. of C., Nat. Soc. Performance and Instrn. (charter), Personnel and Indsl. Relations Assn. Los Angeles, Nat. Panel Arbitrators, Am. Soc. Tng. Devel. Republican. Jewish religion. Clubs: Univ. (Los Angeles); Verdugo (Glendale, Calif.). Contbr. articles to profl. jours, chpts to books. Home: 60 Glenflow Ct Glendale CA 91206 Office: 777 Flower St Glendale CA 91201

MORSE, SCOTT QUADE, automotive exec.; b. Toledo, Jan. 4, 1931; s. William Errol and Helen Augusta (Roe) M.; student U. Albuquerque, 1952-54; B.B.A., U. Toledo, 1957; m. Mary M. Mayhall, Dec. 8, 1950; children—Susan C., Sharon K., Mary E. With Ford Motor Co., 1957-74, area indsl. relations rep. parts div., 1974; v.p. indsl. relations Volvo of Am. Corp., Rockleigh, N.J., 1974—. Served with USAF, 1951-55. Address: Volvo of America Corp Rockleigh Industrial Park Rockleigh NJ 07647

MORSE, TED ALLAN, computer and electronics co. exec.; b. Toledo, June 7, 1947; s. Leroy Eugene and Bessie Marie (Jacobs) M.; student Elmhurst Coll., 1966-67; B.B.A., U. Toledo, 1970; student exec. mgmt. seminars Harvard U., 1977-78; m. Lorraine K. Moore, 1966; children—Julie, Jenny, Ted Allan. Corp systems analyst Owens Corning Fiberglas Co., 1968-69; asst. to v.p. mktg. Am. Warming and Ventilating Co., Toledo, 1970-72; sr. sales rep. Olivetti Co., Toledo, 1970-72; corp. sales mgr. Toledo Metal Fabricators Co., 1972-74; dist. sales mgr. Docutel Corp., Toledo, 1974-76; S.E. regional sales mgr. TRW, Inc., Longwood, Fla., 1976-79; nat. sales mgr. Mosler Safe Co., Hamilton, Ohio, 1976-78; chmn. bd., prin. stockholder N.Am. Fin. Services, Inc.; partner, exec. v.p. Fla. Mgmt. Adv., Inc.; tchr., cons. in electronic funds transfer. Republican. Baptist. Clubs: Tennis, Ski, Investment. Research in future direction of electronic funds transfer and fin. consumer attitudes. Office: 1177 Louisiana Ave Suite 202 Winter Park FL 32789

MORSE, WILLIAM ALLEN, real estate developer, lawyer; b. Miami, Fla., June 15, 1927; s. Austin Raymond and Marguerite Phyllis (Lloyd) M.; J.D., U. Miami (Fla.), 1955; m. Marie Catherine Rudisill, Apr. 6, 1955; children—William Blair, Brian Raymond. Admitted to Fla. bar, 1955; partner firm Coleman Leonard Morse & Morrison, Ft. Lauderdale, Fla., 1955-68, firm Morse Beyer Moriner & Traver, Ft. Lauderdale, 1968-72; municipal judge City of Oakland Park (Fla.), 1964-66; mayor City of Tamarac (Fla.), 1964-70; chmn. bd. Blackhawk Corp., Danville, Calif., 1972—; chmn. bd., pres. Kenbill Investment Co., Tamarac, 1975—; pres. Sonoma Internat., San Francisco, 1978—; dir. Burnup & Sims, Inc., Plantation, Fla., 1977—; individual practice law, San Francisco, 1976—. Served in USCG, 1945-46, U.S. Army Res., 1948-56. Mem. Am., Fla., Calif. bar assns., Phi Delta Phi, Pi Kappa Alpha. Democrat. Home: 19 Escanyo South San Francisco CA 94080 Office: 625 Market St Suite 308 San Francisco CA 94105

MORTARA, MICHAEL PAUL, investment banking exec.; b. Torrington, Conn., Aug. 17, 1949; s. Natalino Paul and Florence Lee Mortara; B.S. in Fgn. Service, Georgetown U., 1971; M.B.A., U. Chgo., 1974; m. Virginia Lee Kolius, July 8, 1972. Mgr. Yankee bond trading Salomon Bros. Internat. Ltd., N.Y.C., 1973-75, dir. Eurobond trading, v.p., 1975-80, v.p., mgr. Ginnie Mae trading, 1980—. Bd. govs. Georgetown U. Mem. Assn. Internat. Bond Dealers, Corp. Bond Traders Club, Govt. Nat. Mortgage Assn., Securities Dealers Assn. Democrat. Home: North St Litchfield CT 06759 Office: One New York Plaza New York NY 10002

MORTEN, JAMES ERIC, printing co. exec.; b. Toronto, Ont., Can., Aug. 12, 1931; s. Charles Eric and Marjorie Isabel (Thomas) M.; came to U.S., 1965; student in graphics Western Tech. Sch., 1945-47, Ryerson Inst. Tech., 1947-49; m. Marion Lorraine Bond, Aug. 18, 1951; children—Grant, Scott, Kirk, James. Reprodn. dept. mgr. Imperial Oil Ltd., Toronto; mgr. W. Toronto Printing, 1959-65; pres., chief exec. officer, gen. mgr. Interprint Inc., Clearwater, Fla., 1965—; mem. printing adv. bd. Dixie Hollins High Sch., St. Petersburg, 1976-80. Mem. Printing Industries Fla. (dir.). Clubs: Optomist (v.p. 1965-70), Masons. Home: 6349 29th Ave N Saint Petersburg FL 33710 Office: 12350 US Hwy 19 S Clearwater FL 33516

MORTENSEN, ARVID LEGRANDE, bus. services co. mktg. exec.; b. Bremerton, Wash., July 11, 1941; s. George Andrew and Mary Louise (Myers) M.; B.S. in English and Psychology, Brigham Young U., 1965, M.B.A. in Mktg. and Fin., 1967; diploma in life ins. mktg. Life Underwriters Tng. Council, 1974; J.D. cum laude, Ind. U., 1980; m. Elaine Marie Mains, Aug. 2, 1968; 1 dau., Marie Louise. Agt., Connecticut Mut. Life Ins. Co., Salt Lake City, 1967-68, agt. and br. mgr., Idaho Falls, Idaho, 1968-74; with Research and Rev. Service Am., Inc./Newkirk Assos., Inc., Indpls., 1974—, sr. editor, 1975-79, mgr. advanced products and seminars, 1979-80, dir. mktg., 1980—; also tchr., lectr.; admitted to Ind. bar, 1980. Missionary, Ch. of Jesus Christ of Latter-day Saints, 1960-62, bishop, 11th ward, Idaho Falls, Idaho, 1969-74, mem. High Council, Indpls. North Stake, 1975—. Recipient award for outstanding legal scholarship in ins. law Am. United Life, 1980, award for service to Ind. Law Rev., Am. Fletcher Nat. Bank, 1978, award for demonstrated legal excellence Lawyers Coop., 1978, 80; C.L.U. Mem. Assn. Advanced Life Underwriting, Estate Planning Council Indpls., Am. Bar Assn. Ind. Bar Assn., Indpls. Bar Assn., Am. Soc. C.L.U.'s, Nat. Assn. Life Underwriters, Ind. Assn. Life Underwriters, Indpls. Assn. Life Underwriters. Author: Employee Stock Ownership Plans, 1975; Fundamentals of Corporate Qualified Retirement Plans, 1975, 78, 80; (with Norman H. Tarver) The IRA Manual, 1975, 76, 78, 79, 80 edits.; (with Norman H. Tarver) The Keogh Manual, 1975, 77, 78, 80 edits.; (with Norman H. Tarver) The Section 403 (b) Manual, 1975, 77, 78, 80 edits.; (with Leo C. Hodges) The Life Insurance Trust Handbook, 1980; contbr. articles to profl. jours., mags.; editor-in-chief Business Insurance Course, 1974-80, The Estate Protection Course, 1974-80, The Pensions and Profit-Sharing Course, 1974-80; bd. editors Ind. Law Rev., 1977-78. Home: 715 Sugarbush Dr Zionsville IN 46077 Office: 6213 LaPas Trail PO Box 1727 Indianapolis IN 46206

MORTENSEN, RALPH, publisher; b. Mankato, Minn., Jan. 29, 1894; s. Jacob and Christine (Strand) M.; B.A., Augsburg Coll., 1913; student Augsburg Sem., 1913-16, Oslo U, 1916-17; M.S.T., Hartford Sem., 1918, Ph.D., 1927; m. Petra Helland, June 3, 1918 (Dec. Nov. 1942); children—Ralph Helland (dec.), Agnes Carolyn (Mrs Donald Paul Mosling), Margaret Christine Anne (Mrs George Boine Anderson); m. 2d, Esther Elizabeth Tappert, Jan. 19, 1946. Tchr., Luth. Boys' Sch., Kweiteh, Honan, China, 1919-21; pub. Luth. Bd. Publ. Hankow, China, 1930-42; China rep. Am. Bible Soc., Chungking, 1944-45, Shanghai, 1945-53; pastor Bethel Luth. Ch., LaCrosse, Wis., 1921-25; asso. pastor Emanuel Luth. Ch., Manchester, Conn., 1925-27, Battle Lake Parish, Minn., 1927-30; acting pastor Community Ch., Shanghai, China, 1946, 51; rep. Am., Brit., Scottish Bible socs. as traveling sec. East Asia, 1954-58; field sec. Am. Bible Soc., N.Y.C., 1958-65, spl. sec., 1966-67, spl. rep., lectr., 1968—; v.p. Research Center for Religion and Human Rights in Closed Socs., 1976—. Mgr. Lord's Day Alliance U.S., 1959-71; lectr. Gen. sec. Internat. Red Cross for Central China, Hankow, China, 1939-41; chmn. coordinating com. Fgn. Refugees, Shanghai, China, 1948-52; chaplain, commr. SE dist. Long Rivers council Boy Scouts Am., 1976-77, Silver Beaver award, 1977. Recipient Distinguished Alumnus citation Augsburg Coll., 1964, Bronze medal Centennial Celebration, 1969; meritorious Service award to cause of free China, Inst. Chinese Culture, 1972; spl. cravat Order Brilliant Star (Republic of China), 1978; Service Above Self award Rotary Club N.Y., 1979. Fellow Hymn Soc. Am. (treas. 1967-76, Emily Swan Perkins award 1980), Royal Asiatic Soc.; mem. Am. Oriental Soc., Asia Soc., Conn. Bible Soc. (dir., mem. finance com. 1972—), Fellowship Former Overseas Rotarians (treas., sec. 1962-77, chmn. 1977-80, sec. 1980—), Nat. Audubon Soc. (dir. Quinnipiac chpt. 1978—), Tibet Soc. Republican. Rotarian. Clubs: Shanghai Tiffin (sec. 1980—), Rotary. Translator, editor: (with Stephen Pan and T.H. Tsuan) Inside Mao Tse-tung Thought by Yeh Ching (Jen Tso-hsuan), 1975. Home: Riverbound Farm on Quinnipiac 1881 Cheshire St RFD 1 Southington CT 06489 Office: 475 Riverside Dr Suite 448 New York NY 10027

MORTENSON, MARK DWIGHT, wholesale bldg. materials co. exec.; b. Seattle, Oct. 16, 1950; s. Harold Adolf and Marjorie Eileen (Honrud) M.; B A., Seattle U., 1972; m. Maria De Deus Alves, Dec. 20, 1975; children—Matthew, Michael. With Georgia Pacific, Billings, Mont., 1972-75, Oakland, Calif., 1975-76, br. mgr., Eugene, Oreg., 1976—. Republican. Home: 1020 Elm St Junction City OR 97401 Office: Georgia Pacific 3445 W 1st St Eugene OR 97401

MORTON, EDWARD JAMES, ins. co. exec.; b. Fort Wayne, Ind., Nov. 8, 1926; s. Clifford Leroy and Clara Marie (Merklein) M.; B.A., Yale U., 1949; m. Jean Ann McLernon, Apr. 30, 1949; children—Marcia Lynn, Anne. With John Hancock Mut. Life Ins. Co., Boston, 1949—, exec. v.p., 1974—. Bd. dirs. Childrens Hosp. Med. Center, Boston, Center for Blood Research. Served with USAAF, 1945. Fellow Soc. Actuaries. Office: John Hancock Pl PO Box 111 Boston MA 02117

MORTON, HUGHES GREGORY, real estate devel. exec.; b. St. Joseph, Mo., Aug. 11, 1923; s. William Marmaduke and Jeanette (Hughes) M.; B.S., Wharton Sch. U. Pa., 1947; postgrad. UCLA, 1949-50; children—William Marmaduke II, Hughes Gregory, Mary Gladys. Divisional personnel dir. Carnation Co., Los Angeles, 1950-52; contractors rep. Calif. Portland Cement Co., Los Angeles, 1959-64; v.p. Western Fed. Savs. & Loan Assn., Los Angeles, 1964-70; owner Morton and Assos., Beverly Hills, Calif., 1970—; chmn. United Housing Group, Inc., Beverly Hills, 1970—. Served as lt. (j.g.) USNR, 1941-46. Mem. Calif. Assn. Realtors. Home: 217 S Barrington Ave Los Angeles CA 90049 Office: 433 N Camden Dr Suite 400 Beverly Hills CA 90210

MORTON, JAY ROBERT, energy equipment mfg. co. exec.; b. Tarrytown, N.Y., July 24, 1914; s. Jay Daniel and Sara (Skerritt) M.; A.B., Syracuse U., 1936, M.S., 1937; advanced mgmt. course Am. Mgmt. Assn., 1967; m. Barbara Louise Tyler, Feb. 8, 1941; children—Jay Robert II, Wellington Charles, Linda Joy. With Vega Industries, Inc. (formerly San-Equip, Inc.), 1937-60, traffic mgr., 1937-46, gen. traffic mgr., 1946-58, asst. to pres., 1958-60; gen. traffic mgr. Combustion Engring., Inc., Windsor, Conn., 1960-66, dir. corporate transp. and distbn., 1966-70, v.p. corporate transp. and distbn., 1970—; dir., past exec. com. Nat. Commn. Internat. Trade Documentation. Mem. Atlantic States Shippers Adv. Bd.; pres. Myasthenia Gravis Found. Recipient Harry E. Salzberg Meml. medallion and lecture Syracuse U., 1980; John T. McCullough award Distbn. mag., 1980. Mem. Nat. Def. Transp. Assn. (regional v.p.), Traffic Club N.Y., Am. Soc. Traffic and Transp. (past regional v.p.; Joseph C. Schleen award 1980), Charter Oaks Shippers Assn., Am. Boiler Assn. (past chmn. traffic com.), Am. Mgmt. Assn., Syracuse, Hartford, N.Y. traffic clubs, Conn. Quarter Century Traffic Club, Newcomen Soc. N.Am., Stamford Area Commerce and Industry Assn. (street and hwy. policy com.), Transp. Council Asso. Industries N.Y. State, Nat. Indsl. Traffic League (past pres.), Nat. Freight Traffic Assn. (v.p.), Delta Nu Alpha (past regional v.p.), Sigma Phi Epsilon (dir.). Episcopalian (vestryman). Clubs: Masons, City (Hartford); Wampanoag Country. Home: 108 Gray Farms Rd Stamford CT 06905 Office: 900 Long Ridge Rd Stamford CT 06902

MORTON, WILKS CURTIS, wholesale auto parts co. exec.; b. Napier, Tenn., May 1, 1921; s. William Clarence and Pollie Louise (Phillips) M.; B.Mus., Stetson U., 1940; m. Claritas Morton; children—Edward E. (dec.), Cynthia E. Morton Galbraith. Salesman, Patten Sales Co., Miami, 1945-47; minister music edn. Miami Shores Baptist Ch., 1947-55; minister edn. First Bapt. Ch., Ft. Lauderdale, Fla., 1956-63; dir. advt. and sales adminstrn. Seaboard Photo Service, Ft. Lauderdale, 1963-65; exec. v.p., gen. mgr. Tom Wood Equipment Co., Miami, 1966; sales mgr. Alter Sales Co., Miami, 1966-69; gen. mgr., pres. A C Suhren Corp., Orlando, Fla., 1969-71; pres., gen. mgr. Morton Motor & Machine Inc., Melbourne, Fla., 1972—; pres., gen. mgr. Morton Sales Co. Melbourne, 1972—. Served with USAF, 1941-45. Decorated Purple Heart. Mem. Fla. Bapt. Religious Edn. Assn. Republican. Baptist. Clubs: Kiwanis, Mason. Home: 1521 Riverside Dr W Melbourne FL 32935 Office: 1395 Cypress Ave Melbourne FL 32935

MOSCATI, LEONARD FRANK, investment banker; b. N.Y.C., Apr. 2, 1949; s. Pat Vincent and Catherine (Marchese) M.; B.S. (dean's honor list) in Bus. Adminstrn., Manhattan Coll., 1970; M.B.A. in Finance, Pace U., 1973. Mgmt. auditor U.S. Gen. Accounting office, N.Y.C., 1970-71, supervisory auditor, 1971-73; fin. analyst N.Y. Stock Exchange, N.Y.C., 1973-75; v.p., mcpl. bond trader L.F. Rothschild & Co., N.Y.C., 1975—. Mem. Delta Mu Delta. Roman Catholic. Clubs: Nassau Country, N.Y. Athletic. Home: 310 E 71st St New York NY 10021

MOSCATO, NICHOLAS, JR., bank exec.; b. Bklyn., Sept. 1, 1942; s. Nicholas and Albina (Donato) M.; diploma Am. Inst. of Banking, 1966; m. Patricia G. Lipski, Apr. 25, 1965; 1 son, Matthew. Clk. internat. div. Chem. Bank, N.Y.C., 1960-65; money mgmt. officer fgn. exchange Marine Midland Bank, N.Y.C., 1965-72; pres. Lasser Bros. Internat., N.Y.C., 1973-75; exec. v.p. Lasser Bros., Inc., N.Y.C., 1972-76; v.p. Berliner Handles und Frankfurter Bank, N.Y.C.,

1976-77; sr. v.p. fgn. exchange Garvin GuyButler, N.Y.C., 1977—. Served to 1st lt., USAR. Mem. Fgn. Exchange Assn. North Am., Fgn. Exchange Brokers Assn., Republican. Roman Catholic. Home: 71 Strathmore Lane Rockville Centre NY 11570 Office: 120 Broadway New York NY 10005

MOSELEY, EMORY FRANKS, agrl. equipment sales co. exec.; b. Ebony, Va., Dec. 20, 1928; s. James Branford and Fannie H. (Reid) M.; grad. Indsl. Tng. Inst., 1948; m. Virginia Sunday, Jan. 27, 1950; children—Gary Wayne, Donna Lea, Terri Lynn. Refrigeration engr. Jones, Tompkins & Wright Co., Boydton, Va., 1948-49; with sales and service dept. Gen. Mills, Inc., Richmond, Va., 1950-53; treas. Superior Equipment & Supply Co. Inc., Richmond, Va., 1953—; pres. Dairymen's Supply Co., Inc., Richmond, 1957—, Superior Equipment & Supply Co. Inc., 1979—, Garber & Moseley Inc., 1979—; v.p. Garber & Moseley, Inc., Richmond, 1964—. Served with USN, 1946-47. Baptist. Club: Varina Charles City Sportsman and Ducks Unltd. Home: Route 5 Box 287 A Richmond VA 23231 Office: 13 N 24th St Richmond VA 23223

MOSELEY, FREDERICK STRONG, III, investment banker; b. N.Y.C., May 4, 1928; s. Frederick Strong and Jane H. (Brady) M.; B.A., Harvard U., 1951; m. Elizabeth H. Perkins, June 12, 1952; children—Frederick Strong, Elizabeth H., Cassandra H. Gen. partner F. S. Moseley & Co., Boston, 1959-70, mng. partner, 1970-73; pres. chief exec. officer, dir., F. S. Moseley, Estabrook, Inc., Boston, 1973-75; chmn., chief exec. officer Moseley, Hallgarten & Estabrook, Inc., Boston, 1976-79, Moseley, Hallgarten, Estabrook & Weeden Holding Corp., Boston, 1979—; trustee Provident Inst. for Savings. Corporator Trustees of Reservations, 1979-82, Boston Mus. of Sci., 1980—; trustee Que. Labrador Mission Found. Served to 1st lt. U.S. Army, 1953-55. Mem. Mass. Soc. for Promoting Agr. (trustee, treas. 1965), Associated Harvard Alumni (dir. 1977—), Mass. Audubon Soc. (dir. 1977—), Humane Soc. of Commonwealth of Mass. (trustee 1980—). Episcopalian. Clubs: Myopia Hunt; Links (N.Y.C.); Pine Valley (N.J.) Golf; Somerset (Boston). Home: 38 Gardner St Hamilton MA 01936 Office: 60 State St Boston MA 02109

MOSELEY, JACK, ins. co. exec.; b. Birmingham, Ala., June 21, 1931; s. Rennie J. and Clariece Ruth (Spinks) M.; B.S., Auburn (Ala.) U., 1953; m. Patsy Blake, June 21, 1953; children—Jack, Glenn E., Edward B. With U.S. Fidelity & Guaranty Co., 1953—, v.p., sr. actuary, then exec. v.p., Balt., 1969-78, pres., chief adminstrv. officer, 1978-80, chmn. bd., pres., chief exec. officer, 1980—, also dir. affiliated cos.; dir. Union Trust Co., Balt.; chmn. AIA. Trustee, Md. Inst. Coll. Arts, Balt. Symphony; bd. dirs. Greater Balt. Com. Fellow Casualty Acturaial Soc.; mem. Internat. Congress Actuaries, Am. Acad. Actuaries. Republican. Methodist. Clubs: Center, Mchts. (Balt.). Office 100 Light St Baltimore MD 21202

MOSES, HORACE CHESTER, III, pharm. co. exec.; b. Montclair, N.J., Jan. 16, 1934; s. Horace Chester, Jr. and Geraldine Louise (Stebbins) M.; B.A., Amherst Coll., 1955; m. Lela Mildred Graham, Aug. 8, 1972; children—Mary B., George S., Louise B. Various mktg. positions The Kendall Co., Chgo. and Boston, 1955-59, asst. to pres., 1959-63; mng. dir. Hoyt Labs. div. Colgate-Palmolive Co., Needham Heights, Mass., 1963—. Mem. Am. Mktg. Assn. Republican. Clubs: Needham Pool and Racquet, Sportsmen's (Needham, Mass.); Slope 'n' Shore (New London, N.H.). Home: 51 Windsor Rd Needham MA 02192 Office: 633 Highland Ave Needham Heights MA 02194

MOSES, IRVING BYRON, architect; b. Chgo., Aug. 5, 1925; s. Morris Lester and Dorothy (Berns) M.; B.S., U. Ill., 1950; m. Toby Kornfeld, June 29, 1947; children—Barbara Susan, Jack Robert, Carol Lynn. Time, motion and material study Small Homes Council Ill., Urbana, 1947; design draftsman Holsman, Holsman Klekamp & Taylor & Mies Van Der Rohe, Chgo., 1950-51; partner firm Comm & Moses, Chgo., 1951-62; prin., mgr. I. Moses & Assos., A.I.A., Chgo. and Highland Park, Ill., 1962-81, 77—; cons. architect Globe Engring. Co., Chgo., 1975-77; adj. prof. architecture Central YMCA Community Coll., 1970-78, William Rainey Harper Coll.; appearance rev. commr. City of Highland Park, 1976—; academic, curriculum advisor YMCA Community Coll. Served with USNR, 1943-46. Mem. AIA, Ill. Soc. Architects, Am. Registered Architects, Constrn. Specification Inst., Art Inst. Chgo., Nat. Council Registration Bds. Jewish. Home: 145 Blackhawk Rd Highland Park IL 60035 Office: 53 W Jackson Blvd Chicago IL 60604

MOSHER, GILES EDMOND, banker; b. Boston, Jan. 1, 1933; s. Giles Edmond and Mary A. (Downs) M.; B.S. in Bus. Adminstrn., Boston Coll., 1955; postgrad. Northwestern U. Sch. Fin. Pub. Relations, 1963; Stonier Grad. Sch. Banking, Rutgers U., 1965; m. Thelma A. Doyle, Sept. 1956; children—Mary Beth, Susan M., Michelle, Giles E., III, Alison, Caitlyn. With Bay Bank Newton (formerly Newton-Waltham Bank and Trust Co.), Waltham, Mass., 1955-79, mgr. credit dept., 1959-60, asst. treas., 1960-62, asst. v.p., 1962-64, v.p., 1964-65, sr. v.p., 1965-68, exec. v.p., 1968-70, pres., 1970-79, chmn., 1971-79; pres., chief exec. officer Bay Bank Middlesex, Burlington, Mass., 1979—; dir. Mass. Bus. Devel. Corp. Mem. fin. and adminstrn. advisory council Archdiocese of Boston; past pres. Newton (Mass.) Boys Club; adv. bd. Emmanuel Coll.; mem. pres.'s advisory council Bentley Coll.; past trustee Catholic Charitable Bur., Fessenden Sch., Newton-Wellesley Hosp.; past trustee, mem. endowment investment com. Boston Coll.; trustee, chmn. adminstrn. and finance com. St. Elizabeth's Hosp. Recipient Bronze medallion Boys Clubs of Am., 1964; Distinguished Community award Brandeis U., 1975; named Young Man of Year, City of Newton, 1960; one of Ten Outstanding Young Men of Greater Boston, 1964; one of Four Outstanding Young Men of Mass., 1965; one of Five Outstanding Young Men New Eng., 1966. Mem. Newton Bankers Assn. (past pres.), Newton Taxpayers Assn. (dir.), Boston Coll. Alumni Assn. (past pres.), Newton C. of C. (past pres.), Alpha Gamma Sigma (hon.). Clubs: Brae Burn Country (bd. dirs., chmn. fin. com.) (West Newton, Mass.). Home: 227 Windsor Rd Waban MA 02168 Office: 7 New England Executive Park Burlington MA 01803

MOSHOFSKY, WILLIAM JAMES, forest products co. exec.; b. Beaverton, Oreg., Mar. 30, 1923; s. Edward George and Sophia (Lehman) M.; B.S., U. Oreg., 1942, J.D., 1948; m. Margaret Jean Utz, Aug. 3, 1957; children—Mary Newman, Brett, Sally, Michael. Admitted to Oreg. bar, 1948; asso. firm Farrens & Maxwell, Klamath Falls, Oreg., 1948-51, Koerner, Young & Dezendorf, Portland, Oreg., 1952-59; atty. Georgia-Pacific Corp., Portland, 1959-62, asst. to pres., 1963-70, asst. to chmn., 1970-72, v.p. govt. affairs, 1972—. Chmn., Oreg. Council on Crime and Delinquency, 1961-68; pres. Inst. Public Affairs Research, Inc., 1974—. Served with U.S. Army, 1943-46, 51-52. Mem. U.S. C. of C. (dir. 1974-80). Republican. Protestant. Clubs: Arlington, City, Multnomah Athletic. Office: 900 SW Fifth Ave Portland OR 97204

MOSIER, JOHN ADELBERT, plastics co. exec.; b. East Cleveland, Ohio, May 20, 1938; s. Clifford Charles and Virginia Mae (Belville) M.; student Ohio State U., 1957-60, Cleve. State U., 1960-66, Western Res. U., 1966; m. Margaret Sabol, Nov. 12, 1960; children—Tammy, Gretchen, Wendy, John Adelbert. Field sales engr. Glastic Corp., Cleve., 1961-66, asst. sales mgr., advt. mgr., 1968-70; field sales engr. Ward Leonard, Mt. Vernon, N.Y., 1966-67, Taylor Corp., Valley Forge, Pa., 1967-68; account mgr. Rockwell Internat., Detroit, 1970-76; sales and mktg. mgr. Zehrco Plastics, Inc., Ashtabula, Ohio, 1976-79; v.p. sales and mktg. Leigh Industries, Inc., Ashtabula, 1979—. Mem. Soc. Plastics Inc., U.S. C. of C., Ducks Unltd. Contbr. articles to profl. jours. Home: 2158 W Lake Rd Conneaut OH 44030 Office: 3013 W 38 St Ashtabula OH 44004

MOSKOWITZ, ARNOLD X., economist, educator; b. N.Y.C., Jan. 27, 1944; s. Morris and Millie (Kozichovsky) M.; B.S. in Elec. Engring., CCNY, 1966; M.S. in Indsl. Mgmt., Poly. Inst. N.Y., 1970; M.Phil. in Econs. and Fin., N.Y. U., 1979; m. Marilyn Betty Goldstein, Nov. 24, 1968; children—Dara, Alex. Economist, Grumman Corp., N.Y.C., 1968-70; asso. economist Dean Witter Reynolds Inc., N.Y.C., 1970-74, 1st v.p., economist, 1974—; lectr. New Sch. for Social Research, 1978—; adj. asso. prof. fin. Pace U., 1980—; cons. to World Bank, UN, U.S. Congress, 1976—. Mem. Am. Econ. Assn., Money Marketeers, Nat. Economist Club, Nat. Assn. Bus. Economists, Atlantic Soc. Contbr. articles to profl. jours., chpts. to books including Security Selection and Active Portfolio Management; contbr. to Ency. Econs.; often quoted in Bus. Week, Wall St. Jour., others. Office: 5 World Trade Center New York NY 10048

MOSKOWITZ, MICHAEL WAYNE, computer equipment distbn. co. exec.; b. Newark, June 5, 1955; s. Victor and Charlotte (Bregman) M.; B.S., Tufts U., 1977; m. Beth Glanz, Dec. 23, 1978. Sales dept. Gamatron Corp., Framingham, Mass., 1978, pres., 1978-79; pres. Datatrend, Inc., Saugus, Mass., 1979—. Mem. Computer Dealers Assn., Nat. Fire Protection Assn. Office: 465 Essex St Saugus MA 01906

MOSLEY, LYNN H., multi-bank holding co. exec. Pres., First Ala. Bankshare, Inc., Montgomery. Office: PO Box 1448 Montgomery AL 36102*

MOSMILLER, JOSEPH WILLIAM, savs. and loan assn. exec.; b. Balt., Nov. 30, 1935; s. Charles August and Mary Margaret (Flahaven) M.; B.S., Mt. St. Mary's Coll., Emmitsburg, Md., 1958; J.D. magna cum laude, U. Md.; m. Clare Marie Synan, Aug. 10, 1957; children—Sheila, Susan John, Mark. Admitted to Md. bar; with Loyola Fed. Savs. and Loan Assn., Balt., pres., chief adminstrv. officer, 1974-77, chmn. bd., chief exec. officer, 1977—; chmn. bd. Loyola Fin. and Devel. Corp., Bay State Appraisal Corp., Del. Mortgage Service Co.; dir. United Guaranty Corp., Security Title Guaranty Corp., Hutzler Bros. Dept. Store, Fed. Home Loan Bank Atlanta. Bd. dirs. Good Samaritan Hosp. Endowment Fund, Balt., Lyric Found., Balt., Lyric Theatre Co., Balt., Md. region NCCJ. Mem. U.S. League Savs. Assn. (dir.), Md. Bar Assn. Democrat. Roman Catholic. Office: 1300 N Charles St Baltimore MD 21201

MOSS, ARTHUR HENSHEY, lawyer; b. Reading, Pa., July 26, 1930; s. John Arthur and Christine Bracken (Henshey) M.; A.B., Williams Coll., 1952; LL.B., U. Pa., 1955: 1 son, John Arthur. Admitted to Pa. bar, 1955; asso. firm Montgomery, McCracken, Walker & Rhoads, Phila., 1960-69, partner, 1969—. Chmn., Radnor-Haverford-Marple Sewer Authority, 1968—; pres. Wayne Civic Assn., 1964-65; steward, deacon Wayne Presbyn. Ch., 1963-66, ruling elder, 1966-72, 79—, clk. of session, 1971, 78—. Served to lt. USN, 1955-60. Mem. Am., Fed., Pa., Phila. bar assns. Republican. Clubs: Rittenhouse, Broadacres Trouting Assn. Editor: U. Pa. Law Rev., 1954-55. Contbr. articles to profl. jours. Office: Three Parkway Philadelphia PA 19102

MOSS, CRUSE WATSON, automobile co. exec.; b. Kent, Ohio, Apr. 7, 1926; s. Cruse Watson and Lucille M. (Shafer) M.; B.S. in Indsl. Engring., Ohio U., Athens, 1948; m. Virginia Ann Patton, Dec. 22, 1949; children—Stephen, Carol Susan, Michael. Pres., Kaiser Jeep Automotive div., also exec. v.p. Kaiser Jeep Corp., 1960-70; group v.p. Am. Motors Corp., 1970; pres., dir. AM Gen. Corp., Detroit, 1970-79; chmn. bd., chief exec. officer, dir. White Motor Corp., Farmington Hills, Mich., 1979—; dir. First Nat. Bank, Toledo. Adv. council Internat. Eye Found.; mem. founders soc. Detroit Inst. Arts. Served with USNR, 1944-46. Mem. Assn. U.S. Army (past chmn. council trustees), Am. Def. Preparedness Assn., Def. Orientation Conf. Assn., Bus. Roundtable, Motor Vehicle Mfrs. Assn. (dir., vice-chmn.), Hwy. Users Fedn., Soc. Automotive Engrs., Confrerie des Chevaliers du Tastevin, Chief Execs. Forum, Beta Theta Pi. Presbyterian. Clubs: Circumnavigators, Detroit Athletic. Home: 2205 Melrose St Ann Arbor MI 48104 Office: 34500 Grand River Ave Farmington Hills MI 48024

MOSS, EDWARD, textile co. exec.; b. N.Y.C., May 11, 1949; s. Charles and Etta (Glater) Moskowitz; A.A., Coll. Orlando, 1969, B.S., L.I. U., 1971; student Ohio State U., 1969-70; m. Mindy Moss. Advt. copywriter J.B. Ivey, Orlando, Fla., 1971-72; sales exec. Wamsutta Fabrics, N.Y.C., 1972-73, Wambel Fabrics, N.Y.C., 1973-74, Wamsutta Mills div. M. Lowenstein and Sons, Los Angeles, 1974—. Mem. St. Louis Mus. Contemporary Art Club. Democrat. Jewish. Home: 7222 Cirrus Way Canoga Park CA 91307

MOSS, JAMES BURKE, ins. co. exec.; b. Clarksburg, W.Va., Apr. 29, 1933; s. Hayward B. and Edith E. (Reeder) M.; student Defience Coll., 1951-52, Ohio State U., 1953; m. Carol M. Kuck, July 26, 1952; children—Robert, Steven, Rebecca, Kathy, Donald, Mark. Agt., Nat. Life and Accident Ins. Co., Lima, Ohio, 1953-54, staff mgr., Springfield, Ohio, 1954-57; prin. James B. Moss Ins. Agy., Lima, Springfield, Ohio, South Bend, Ind., Huntington, Ind., 1957-76; v.p. mortgage banking/savs. and loan bus. Am. Bankers Life Assurance Co., Miami, Fla., 1976-78, v.p. fin. manpower devel., 1978-80; v.p. mktg. Med. Life Ins. Co., Cleve., 1980—. Dist. chmn., bd. dirs. council Anthony Wayne Area council Boy Scouts Am., 1973-74, dist. fin. chmn. South Fla. council, 1976, dist. chmn., 1978, council tng. dir., exec. bd., 1979, chmn. membership Greater Cleve. council. Recipient numerous sales awards. Home: 5937 Ogilby Dr Hudson OH 44236 Office: Med Life Ins Co 2060 E 9th St Cleveland OH 44115

MOSS, MIKE, ins. co. exec.; b. N.Y.C., Feb. 6, 1943; s. Edward and Rose (Goldstein) M.; student Miami Dade Coll., 1961-62, U. Miami, 1963-64; m. Laurie Judd, May 4, 1969. Div. mgr. NCR, Miami, Fla., 1964-69; asst. gen. agt. Mass. Mut., Miami, 1969-74; mgr. Home Life Ins. Co. of N.Y., Coral Gables, Fla., 1974—. Active Young Pres.'s Club of Mt. Sinai Hosp., Miami Beach, Fla., 1977—. Recipient Fla. State RAM award, Fla. Gen. Agts. and Mgrs. Assn., 1979; Nat. Mgmt. award, 1976, 77, 78; C.L.U. Mem. Greater Miami Estate Planning Council, Gen. Agts. and Mgrs. Assn. (pres. 1978-79), Young Pres.'s Orgn., Miami Assn. Life Underwriters, Estate Planning Council. Clubs: Standard of Greater Miami, Jockey, Masons. Home: 212 W DiLodo Dr Miami Beach FL 33139 Office: 2600 Douglas Rd Coral Gables FL 33134

MOSS, PAUL, acctg. and data processing exec.; b. Scranton, Pa., Apr. 12, 1943; s. Elmer Paul and June Rose (Carris) M.; B.S. in Computer Sci., U. Scranton, 1980: diploma Chgo. Acctg. Sch.; Cert. Hartford (Conn.) Grad. Center; m. Annmarie Lillian Mack, Apr. 27, 1963; children—Christine, Paul Jarrod. Computer operator Intext Corp., Scranton, 1961-66; programmer analyst Asso. Transport, Inc., Scranton, 1970-73; mgr. acctg. services Consol. Molded div. Rep. Corp., Scranton, 1973—. Served with USN, 1966-70. Methodist. Home: 1131 Cedar Ave Scranton PA 18505 Office: Consolidated Molded Products Warner and Greenwood Sts Scranton PA 18505

MOSS, WALTER SCOTT, JR., banker; b. Horse Cave, Ky., Feb. 21, 1922; s. Walter Scott and Janie Pearl (Steen) M.; B.S., Ind. U., 1943; m. Nelle Corinne Bernard, Sept. 9, 1943; children—Linda Ann, Jean Carol. Exec. v.p., dir. Moss Tobacco Co., Horse Cave, 1948-68, Gen. Tobacco Co., Horse Cave, 1948-68; v.p., dir. Carrollton Redrying Co. (Ky.), 1954-68; pres. Horse Cave State Bank, 1969, chmn. bd., 1970—, also dir.; dir. Carroll Storage Co. Bd. regents Western Ky. U., 1971-75. Served with USAF, 1942-45. Mem. Burley Leaf Tobacco Dealers Assn. (pres. 1959, dir. 1958-65), Ky. Bankers Assn. (dir.) Methodist. Home: 309 Maple St Horse Cave KY 42749 Office: Horse Cave State Bank Main St Horse Cave KY 42749

MOSSING, JEROME DOUGLAS, ins. co. exec.; b. Los Angeles, Aug. 10, 1946; s. Norraine Sylvester and Marvel Mae (Smith) M.; BA., Ohio State U., 1968; postgrad. bus. U. Dayton; m. Margie Lee Siddel, June 18, 1972. Multiple lines claims rep. Nationwide Ins. Co., Columbus, Ohio, 1970-72; spl. agt. Harleysville Ins. Cos., Columbus, 1972-77; state agt. Am. Indemnity Group, Reynoldsburg, Ohio, 1977-80, br. mgr., 1980—. Served to 1st lt. FA, AUS, 1968-70; capt. Res. Decorated Bronze Star with oak leaf cluster; cert. ins. counselor. Mem. Profl. Ins. Agts. Ohio (recipient Mr. Mut. Fieldperson of Ohio award 1976), Ohio 1752 Club (pre. 1975), Ohio State U. Alumni Assn., Res. Officers Assn. Republican. Lutheran. Home: 366 Brandy Hill Ave Pickerington OH 43147 Office: 2020 Brice Rd Suite 242 Reynoldsburg OH 43068

MOTLEY, B. GERALD, comml. printing co. exec.; b. Albertville, Ala., Feb. 13, 1946; s. Medwin D. and Audrey (Baswell) Beale; student U. Houston, 1964-69; m. Robin Lyons, Mar. 11, 1972. Sales coordinator Wetmore & Co., Houston, 1965-66, asst. plant mgr., 1966-67, estimator, 1967-69, chief estimator, 1969-73, dir. planning, v.p., 1973-75, v.p. mfg., 1975-80, v.p., gen. mgr., 1980—. Co-chmn. Houston mayoral campaign, 1973; del. Tex. Republican Conv., 1976, 80; bd. dirs. Houston Livestock Show Rodeo, 1972-73; pres. Republican Men's Club West Harris County, 1976—; capt. Harris County Constable Res. Recipient award of excellence U.S. Jr. C. of C., 1972, 73, Award of Achievement, 1972, 73. Mem. Printing Industries-Gulf Coast (dir. 1980), Tex. Jaycees (nat. dir. 1973-74, adminstrv. nat. dir. 1974-75, George O. Wilson award, most outstanding local pres. award 1973), Houston Jaycees (pres. 1972-73), Houston C. of C. (dir. 1972-73). Methodist. Home: 12418 Wedgehill St Houston TX 77077 Office: 1015 S Shepherd St Houston TX 77019

MOTT, CHARLES HARVEY, financial exec.; b. Norwich, Conn., Nov. 29, 1930; s. Charles Harvey and Mabel Ellen (Lambert) M.; B.S. magna cum laude, U. Conn., 1956; M.B.A., U. Hartford, 1966; Ph.D., Am. U., 1979; m. Madeline Margaret Leary, Feb. 16, 1952; 1 dau., Karen Elizabeth. Cost accountant Pratt & Whitney Aircraft div. United Aircraft Corp. (now United Technologies Inc.), East Hartford, Conn., 1956-57, asst. chief cost accountant, Middletown, Conn., 1957-58, chief cost accountant, asst. to supr. accounting, 1958-63, budget and cost controller current engines, East Hartford, 1963-67, spl. assignment Div. Controllers Office, 1967-68; research and devel. controller Black & Decker Mfg. Co., Towson, Md., 1969-70, fin. planning and analysis mgr., profl. products, 1970-71; div. controller L. Greif & Bros. div. Genesco Inc., Balt., 1971-73, v.p. fin., 1973-75; facility controller Curtis Bay Facility, Davison Chem. Co. div. W. R. Grace & Co., Curtis Bay, Balt., 1975-76; controller, chief accounting officer Contee Resources Inc., Laurel, Md., 1976-77, treas. Contee Sand Gravel Inc., 1977—; partner firm Jeffers & Mott, C.P.A.'s, Pasadena, Md., 1975—; instr. accounting U. Balt., 1974-75, asst. prof. accounting, 1975—; instr. accounting M.B.A. program Am. U., 1978—. Bus. vol. United Fund Central Md., 1971. Served with U.S. Army, 1950-52. Recipient certificate of Merit, Nat. Assn. Accountants, 1973, Best Article in 1973 award Balt. chpt.; Conn. chpt. C.P.A. Assn. grantee, 1955; C.P.A., Md. Mem. Nat. Assn. Accountants, Planning Execs. Inst. (1st v.p. 1974), Am. Accounting Assn., Am. Inst. C.P.A.'s, Md. Soc. C.P.A.'s, Am. Inst. Corporate Controllers, Phi Kappa Phi. Democrat. Roman Catholic. Club: Randall Ridge Swimming. Contbr. articles in field to profl. jours. Home: 3904 Rayton Rd Randallstown MD 21133 Office: PO Box 1000 Laurel MD 20810

MOTT, GEORGE FOX, mgmt., internat. affairs cons.; b. Riverside, Calif.; s. George Fox and Alice (Way) M.; A.B., A.M., Stanford U.; Ph.D., U. Minn., 1938; m. Dorothy Hale Williams, Feb. 12, 1944; children—David Edward Way, Jonathan Loren Gould. Dean, prof. English and polit. sci. liberal arts colls. in San Diego and Chgo., 1933-35; asst. to pres. Hancher Orgn., Chgo., 1935-36; asst. prin., critic instr. Univ. High Sch., Coll. Edn., U. Minn., 1936-38; dean students, publicity dir. N.Mex. State U., 1938-39; cons., asst. dir. Kansas City Sch. Survey, 1939; cons. Mayors Survey Coms., St. Louis, Houston, 1939-40; chief analyst, adv. council War Assets Adminstrn., 1946-48; mng. partner, sr. cons. Mott of Washington & Assos., 1948—; chmn. Mott Research Group, 1952—; pres., chief exec. Wold Air Brush Mfg. Co., Chgo., 1977—; cons. Bilger Monorail Internat. Inc., 1975—; vis. prof. U. Md., 1949, Fla. State U., 1950; adj. prof. Am. Univ., 1964-70; internat. lectr. in field. Alt. mem. adv. council to Com. on Fund Raising within Fed. Services, 1959-66; counsellor, chmn. Greater Washington council United Bd. for Christian Higher Edn. in Asia. Bd. dirs., founding mem. Am.-Korean Found., 1952-62, spl. cons., 1962-67; hon. mem. Noyes Sch. Rhythm Found.; mem. Am. Symphony Orch. League. Mem. arty. U.S. Army, Res., 1928-63; served as col. AUS, 1940-46, with Insp. Gen.'s Office, 1941-45, insp. gen. Am. Forces-in-Korea, 1945-46. Decorated Bronze Star with cluster, Commendation Ribbon; Distinguished Service citation, Republic of Korea, 1962. Mem. A.I.M. (pres.'s council), Am. Acad. Polit. and Social Sci., Nat. Assn. Corp. Dirs., Nat. Def. Transp. Assn., Res. Officers Assn. (past dept. pres., past nat. chmn. army affairs com., nat. resolutions com.; past nat. and dept. officer, minuteman), Nat. Rifle Assn. (trustee Pinwheel Jr. Rifle Club), Mil. Order World Wars (past comdr. D.C. chpt., mem. nat. gen. staff), Sino-Am. Soc. (dir. 1966), Am. Legion (past post comdr., chmn. dept. resolutions com.), Chgo. Trade and Commerce (dir. 1976), Ill. Mfrs. Assn., Nat. Art Materials Trade Assn., Phi Delta Kappa (life). Clubs: Elks, Army and Navy. Author: San Diego Politically Speaking, 1932; History of the Middle Ages, 1933, rev., 1950; Survey of Journalism, 1937; Housing of College Students in the U.S., 1938; New Survey of Journalism, 1950, rev., 1965; U.S. Government Jobs, 1950; Survey of U.S. Ports, 1951; mil. engring. series, 1952-54; Miami's Marine Destiny, 1955. Editor: Transportation Renaissance, 1963; Transportation Century, 1967; Urban Change and the Planning Syndrome, 1973; Wold Airbrush Artist series, 1975; sr. author, editor: The Panama Canal: Today's Decision-Tomorrow's Security, A Case History From 1903 to 1977, 1977. Home: 3220 Rittenhouse St NW Washington DC 20015 Office: Dupont Circle Bldg Washington DC 20036

MOULIGNÉ, PATRICK ALAIN, reinforced plastics products distbn. co. exec.; b. Paris, Dec. 14, 1945; came to U.S., 1969, naturalized, 1976; s. Jean Marc and Yvette Marie (Briand) M.; M.Math. and Physics, Grenoble U., 1967; m. Christine M. Martin, Feb. 11, 1978; children—Tristan, Cheyenne. Tech. dir. Sugarloaf Mountain Corp., Kingfield, Maine, 1970-76; v.p. No. Reinforcements

Inc., South Hampton, N.H., 1977—; cons. in field. Served as officer French Air Force, 1965-67. Mem. Soc. Plastics Industries. Home: 97 Bayside Ave Portsmouth RI 02871 Office: Route 150 South Hampton NH 03842

MOULTON, DONNA NASH, draftswoman; b. Troy, N.Y., Jan. 15, 1946; d. Donald Elwin and Jeanne Phillis (England) Nash; m. James Moulton, III, July 4, 1973. With Gen. Electric Co., 1968-76, drafter support ops., Nuskayuna, N.Y., 1973-76; drafter research and devel. Nat. Catheter Co., Argyle, N.Y., 1976—; owner Grassroots Studio. Mem. Lower Adirondack Regional Arts Council; mem. Cossayuna (N.Y.) Vol. Fire Dept. Ladies Aux., Cossayuna Lake Improvement Assn., Council Reprographic Execs., Engring. Reprographics Soc., Am. Inst. Design and Drafting (nat. student com.). Republican. Presbyterian. Illustrator tech. books. Home: PO Box 124 Cossayuna NY 12823 Office: Nat Catheter Co Hook Rd Argyle NY 12809

MOULTON, ELLIOTT JAN, communications cons.; b. Grand Haven, Mich., Nov. 5, 1936; s. Elliott Glen and Gladys Fern (Seiler) M.; B.E.E., Clarkson Coll. Tech., 1958; M.B.A., Harvard, 1965. Mgmt. trainee ITT, Havana, Cuba, Santiago, Chile, Buenos Aires, Argentina, Rio de Janeiro, Brazil, 1958-60; audio visual engr. CBS, N.Y.C., 1960; tech. staff Thompson Ramo Wooldridge Corp., Redondo Beach, Calif., 1960-61; asst. sta. mgr. Hughes Aircraft Corp., Culver City, Calif., Lagos, Nigeria, Johannesburg, S. Africa, 1962-63; mgr. for African and Near East devel. Communications Satellite Corp., Washington, 1965-69; dir., treas., founder Teleconsult, Inc., Washington, 1970-78; pres. Elliott, Jay & Assos., Inc., Washington, 1979—; dir. Adams Travel, Inc., Washington. Mem. exec. com. Republican Party, Washington, 1967-70. Served to 1st lt. U.S. Army, 1959-66. Mem. Founders and Patriots of Am., SAR, Nat. Huguenot Soc., Tau Beta Pi, Eta Kappa Nu, Delta Upsilon. Presbyterian. Club: Harvard (N.Y.C.). Home: 1061 Thomas Jefferson St NW Washington DC 20007 Office: 2555 M St NW Washington DC 20007

MOUNTAIN, MICHAEL LINDLEY, automotive mfg. co. exec.; b. Bronx, Dec. 5, 1941; s. Harold and Antonina Giaconda (Frascona) M.; student public schs., Detroit; m. Mary Ann Vera Bommarito, Dec. 1, 1962; children—Michelle, Michael, Mary; guardian of Jeffrey M. Henning. Technician, Royal TV Co., Albuquerque, 1963-64; sr. technician Claus TV Co., Redford, Mich., 1965-71; sr. tester Hydramatic div. Gen. Motors Co., Ypsilanti, Mich., 1964-78, supr. instrumentation, photographic lab. exptl. engring., 1978—; founder, owner, operator Electronics by M. L. Mountain, 1964—; instr. electronics Detroit House Correction, Rets Electronic Sch., Detroit, 1980—. Trustee Biltmore-Meadowview Civic Assn., Livonia, Mich., 1972, v.p., 1973; extraordinary minister Our Lady of Good Counsel Ch., Plymouth, Mich. Served with USAF, 1960-64. Mem. Law Enforcement and Indsl. Security Assn. of Washtenaw County. Club: Our Lady of Good Counsel Ushers (sec. 1979—). Office: Hydramatic Exptl Engring Willow Run MI 48197

MOUNTCASTLE, KENNETH FRANKLIN, JR., stock broker; b. Winston-Salem, N.C., Oct. 8, 1928; s. Kenneth Franklin and May M.; B.S. in Commerce, U. N.C., Chapel Hill, 1950; m. Mary Katharine Babcock, Sept. 1, 1951; children—Mary Babcock, Laura Lewis, Kenneth Franklin, Katharine Reynolds. With Mountcastle Knitting Co., Lexington, N.C., 1952-55, Reynolds & Co., N.Y.C., 1955-71; with Reynolds Securities Inc. (co. name changed to Dean Witter Reynolds 1978), N.Y.C., 1971—, sr. v.p., 1974—. Trustee, New Canaan (Conn.) Country Sch., 1962-68, Ethel Walker Sch., Simsbury, Conn., 1973—, Coro Found., 1980—; pres. Mary Reynolds Babcock Found., Winston-Salem, N.C.; bd. visitors U. N.C., Chapel Hill. Served with U.S. Army, 1950-52. Republican. Presbyterian. Clubs: Country of New Canaan; Wee Burn Country (Darien, Conn.); Old Town (Winston-Salem, N.C.); Racquet and Tennis, City Midday, Bond, Stock Exchange Luncheon, Madison Sq. Garden (N.Y.C.). Home: 37 Oenoke Ln New Canaan CT 06840 Office: Dean Witter Reynolds 5 World Trade Center New York NY 10048

MOURNING, STEVEN LEWIS, hosp. found. exec.; b. Little Rock, June 2, 1947; s. Burl A. and Sybil M. (Bush) M.; B.S., U. Ark., 1969, B.A., 1970; m. Cathy Louise Plating, June 19, 1970; children—Alicia Lyn, Lauri Ann. Life ins. salesman, 1970-72; field rep. Nat. Found.-March of Dimes, Little Rock, 1972-73, exec. dir. Memphis chpt., 1974-76; dir. Methodist Hosp. Found., Memphis, 1976-78; exec. v.p. St. Joseph Hosp. Found., Denver, 1978—; fund devel. cons. SLM Cons., Inc., 1976—. Mem. Nat. Soc. Fund Raising Execs., Nat. Assn. for Hosp. Devel., Nat. Assn. Health and Welfare Ministries, Nat. Council on Philanthropy, Am. Hosp. Assn., Denver C. of C. Democrat. Methodist. Home: 4417 S Eagle Circle Aurora CO 80015 Office: 1835 Franklin St Denver CO 80218

MOURSUND, ALBERT WADEL, III, lawyer; b. Johnson City, Tex., May 23, 1919; s. Albert W. and Mary Frances (Stribling) M.; LL.B., U. Tex., 1941; m. Mary Allen Moore, May 8, 1941; children—Will S., Mary M. Admitted to Tex. bar, 1941; practice in Johnson City, 1946—; mem. firm Moursund & Sanders, 1963—; county judge Blanco County, 1953-59. Pres., dir. Moore State Bank, Llano, Tex., 1963—, also dir.; pres. Arrowhead Co., Lakeland Investment Corp., Ranchlander Corp.; pres., dir. Tex. Am. Moursund Corp., Southwest Moursund Corp.; dir. Scott Corp., Scott Plaza, Inc., Las Vegas. Mem. Tex. Parks and Wildlife Commn., 1963-67. Mem. Tex., Ho. of Reps. 1948-52. Served with USAAF, 1942-46. Mem. Am., Tex., Hill County (past pres.), bar assns., Blanco County Hist. Soc. (charter), Sons of Hermann. Democrat. Clubs: Masons, Woodman of World. Home: Johnson City TX 78636

MOUSOURAKIS, IOANNIS NIKOLAOS, fin. co. exec.; b. Canea-Crete, Greece, Aug. 5, 1944; s. Lambros and Erasmia (Lambrinakis) M.; came to U.S., 1962, naturalized, 1974; B.A., West Liberty State Coll., 1968; M.A., Vanderbilt U., 1970; J.D., Woodrow Wilson Sch. Law, 1980; m. Donna Rose, Aug. 15, 1969; children—John Steven, Mary Ann, Erasmia Elena. Officer, mgr. internat. banking dept. Commerce Union Bank, Nashville, 1969-74; v.p., mgr. internat. banking dept. Hamilton Nat. Bank, Chattanooga, 1974; internat. treas. Tuftco Corp., Chattanooga, 1975—, internat. v.p., 1978—; cons., dir. several comml. or pvt. banking cos. Served with M.C., USNR, 1963-69. Vanderbilt U. grantee, 1968-70. Mem. Internat. Law Assn., Am. Soc. Internat. Law, Middle East Inst., U.S.-Arab, U.S. Brazilian/French chambers commerce, UN Assn., Pan Am. Assn., others. Greek Orthodox. Home: Somerset Estates 9307 Wyndover St Ooltewah TN 37363 Office: 2318 Holtzclaw Ave Chattanooga TN 37404

MOYE, CHARLES MICKLE, banker; b. Cuthberg, Ga., June 5, 1936; s. Andrew Jackson and Doris Dean (Groover) M.; B.S.I.M., Ga. Inst. Tech., 1959; grad. cert. Am. Inst. Banking, 1966; grad. mgmt. devel. program Harvard U., 1968; m. Lana Ball, Nov. 24, 1962; children—Jeffrey Mickle, Charles David, Ruffin Ball. With Whitley Constrn. Co., Decatur, Ga., 1956-59, Hardware Muts. Casualty Co., Atlanta, 1959-63, Citizens & So. Nat. Bank, Atlanta, 1963-77, Southeastern Foam Products, Conyers, Ga., 1977-78; pres. Cobb Bank & Trust Co., Smyrna, Ga., 1978—. Bd. dirs. Cobb County (Ga.) C. of C., 1980-81, Salvation Army, Marietta and Cobb County; deacon Second Ponce de Leon Baptist Ch., Atlanta. Mem. Ga. Bankers Assn., Ind. Bankers Assn., Am. Bankers. Assn. Republican. Clubs: Cherokee Town and Country, Terminus Internat. Tennis (Atlanta). Office: 3030 Windy Hill Rd Marietta GA 30367

MOYER, CARLTON DREW, credit co. exec.; b. Norristown, Pa., Dec. 6, 1948; s. Carlton and Jean F. (Huber) M.; B.A. in Econs., Grove City Coll., 1970; m. Elizabeth A. Wenderoth, Jan. 31, 1975; 1 dau., Jennifer E. Asst. bank examiner Comptroller of Currency, U.S. Treasury Dept., Washington, 1970-73; various comml. lending positions Commonwealth Nat. Bank, Harrisburg, Pa., 1973-78; exec. v.p., chief exec. officer Pa. Devel. Credit Corp., Harrisburg, 1978—. Mem. Nat. Assn. Bus. Devel. Corps. (dir.), Am. Mgmt. Assn., Northeastern Indsl. Developers Assn., Pa. C. of C., Harrisburg C. of C. Republican. Lutheran. Club: The Tuesday (Harrisburg). Office: 212 Locust St Harrisburg PA 17101

MOYER, F. STANTON, banker; b. Phila., June 7, 1929; s. Edward T. and Beatrice (Stanton) M.; B.S. in Econs., U. Pa., 1951; m. Ann P. Stovell, May 16, 1953; children—Edward E., Alice E. Registered rep. Smith, Barney & Co., Phila., 1951-54; registered rep. Kidder, Peabody & Co., Phila., 1954-60, mgr. corp. dept. Blyth Eastman Dillon & Co., Inc. (formerly Eastman Dillon, Union Securities & Co.), Phila., 1960-65, instnl. sales mgr., 1965-67, gen. partner, 1967—, 1st v.p., 1971-74, sr. v.p., 1974-80, v.p., resident officer Kidder, Peabody & Co., Inc., 1980—. Trustee U. Pa., 1978—, Hosp. of U. Pa., 1978—. Mem. Bond Club Phila., Fin. Analysts Phila., Phila. Securities Assn., Delta Psi. Republican. Episcopalian. Clubs: Phila., Racquet (Phila.); Merion Cricket (Haverford, Pa.); St. Anthony (Phila.); Gulph Mills Golf (King of Prussia, Pa.). Home: Evans Ln Haverford PA 19041 Office: Fidelity Mutual Life Bldg 3 Girard Plaza Philadelphia PA 19102

MOYER, HOWARD ROY, petroleum research and devel. exec.; b. Parker, Pa., Nov. 9, 1930; s. Howard Vincent and Oma Rhoda (Kilgore) M.; B.S., Grove City (Pa.) Coll., 1952; m. Frances A. Friedberger, Apr. 18, 1953; children—Howard, Frances, Patricia, David, Joseph, Andrew, Mary. Research engr. research and devel. Sun Oil Co., Marcus Hook, Pa., 1952-61, sect. chief process devel., 1961-65, 67-73, sect. chief basic research, 1965-67, mgr. process devel., 1973-77, mgr. process devel. applied research and devel. Suntech, Inc. div. Sun Oil Co., Marcus Hook, 1977—. Mem. Am. Petroleum Inst., Am. Inst. Chem. Engrs., Am. Chem. Soc. Presbyterian. Office: Suntech Inc Box 1135 Marcus Hook PA 19061

MOYER, PAUL KENNETH, ins. co. exec.; b. Hamburg, Pa., May 29, 1936; s. Paul Frederick and Verna Marie (Miller) M.; B.B.A., Tex. Luth. Coll., 1962; postgrad. U. Houston, 1966; M.B.A., So. Meth. U., 1971; m. Betty Louise Scheffer, Aug. 25, 1962; children—Mark Kevin, Kayla Marie, Michael Christian. Auditor, Ernst & Ernst C.P.A.'s, Houston, 1962-65; asst. to asst. treas. Gulf & Western Industries, Inc., N.Y.C., 1965-68; asst. treas., 1968-69; v.p., controller UCC Fin. Corp., Dallas, 1969-73; v.p. investment services Gulf Ins. Co., Dallas, 1973-79; sr. v.p., treas. Capitol Life Ins. Co., Denver, 1979—. Mem. devel. bd. Tex. Luth. Coll., Seguin, 1972-78; referee U.S. Soccer Fedn., 1978—; mem. Nat. Intercollegiate Soccer Ofcls. Assn., 1978—; bd. dirs. Clifton (Tex.) Luth. Sunset Home, 1978-79. Served with USAF, 1954-58. C.P.A., Tex., Colo. Mem. Fin. Execs. Inst., Am. Inst. C.P.A.'s, Nat. Assn. Accountants, Colo. Soc. C.P.A.'s. Lutheran. Home: 7127 S Magnolia Circle Englewood CO 80112 Office: 1600 Sherman St Denver CO 80203

MOYER, RALPH WELLER, sch. bus. adminstr.; b. New Hanover, Pa., Feb. 22, 1926; s. Warren E. and Katie (Weller) M.; B.A., Pa. State U., 1951; postgrad Pa. State U., U. Pa.; m. Lora Lynn Riley, Sept. 15, 1951; children—Jack W., Deborah H. Mem. sales mgmt. staff Prudential Life Ins., 1953-59; with Northwestern Mut. Life Ins. Co., 1959-60, Hartford Life Ins. Co., 1960-61; bus. adminstr. pub. schs., Phoenixville Area, 1961-66, State College, Pa., 1966—. Sec., State College Area Sch. Bd., 1966—. Served with USAAF, 1944-46, USAF, 1951-53; PTO. Mem. Pa. Assn. Sch. Bus. Ofcls. (pres. 1970-71), Assn. Sch. Bus. Ofcls. U.S. and Can. (chmn. risk mgmt. com. 1975-77), Phi Delta Kappa. Republican. Presbyterian. Club: Masons. Home: 1299 Penfield Rd State College PA 16801 Office: 131 W Nittany Ave State College PA 16801

MOYER, ROBERT BRADLEY, chem. engr.; b. Berkeley, Calif., Sept. 13, 1943; s. Horace B. and Martha C. (Smith) M.; B.S. in Chem. Engring., Tri-State Coll., 1965; m. Doris L. Froman, May 15, 1965; children—Sandra Kay, Bradley Scott. Project engr. Austenal Microcast, LaPorte, Ind., 1965-67; sr. application engr. Wheelabrator-Frye, Inc., Pitts., 1967-76; mgr. fabric filter engring. Research-Cottrell, Inc., Somerville, N.J., 1976—. Mem. Inst. Certified Engrs., Indsl. Gas Cleaning Inst., Alpha Sigma Phi. Home: RD 1 PO Box 160C Asbury NJ 08802 Office: PO Box 1500 Somerville NJ 08876

MOYLE, JOHN CURTIS, metal co. exec.; b. Lock Haven, Pa., May 24, 1916; s. Walter C. and Marguerite I. (Brown) M.; student Carnegie Inst. Tech., 1935-40; m. Margaret E. Bond, Sept. 29, 1936 (dec.); children—David, Curtis; m. 2d, Jean M. Newlin, Feb. 22, 1975. Apprentice, armature winder U.S. Steel, Duquesne, Pa., 1936-41; electrician Navy Yard, Washington, 1941-42; electrician Firth Sterling Steel, McKeesport, Pa., 1942-45, maintenance foreman, 1945-52; plant mgr. Carbidie, Inc., Latrobe, Pa., 1952-60, McKeesport, 1960-69; chmn. bd., pres. Vista Metals, Buena Vista, Pa., 1969—. Mem. Carbide Engrs., Soc. Mfg. Engrs., Cemented Carbide Producers Assn., C. of C., Pitts. Zool. Soc. Lutheran (lay reader 1960—). Mason (Shriner). Clubs: Youghiogheny (McKeesport); Lakeview Country (Morgantown, W.Va.). Home: 2125 Neal Dr McKeesport PA 15135 Office: 1024 E Smithfield St McKeesport PA 15135

MOYLES, WILLIAM PHILIP, oil co. exec.; b. N.Y.C., June 1, 1930; s. William Philip and Margaret Elizabeth (Keenan) M.; A.B., Georgetown U., 1952; LL.B., Harvard U., 1957; m. Virginia Dillon Curry, Apr. 4, 1959; children—Virginia Curry, Margaret Mary, Frances Carroll. Admitted to N.Y. bar, 1958; pvt. practice law, N.Y.C., 1957-67; asso. Mendes & Mount, N.Y.C., 1957-61; counsel Prudential Lines, Inc., N.Y.C., 1961-62; asso. firm Reavis & McGrath, N.Y.C., 1962-64, Donovan Leisure Newton & Irvine, N.Y.C., 1964-67; with Control Data Corp., Mpls., 1967-73, counsel, 1967-68, v.p. corp. growth, 1969-73; with Gulf Oil Corp., Pitts., 1973—, v.p. corp. devel., 1973-76, v.p. adminstrn. and devel., 1979—; pres. Gulf Oil Real Estate Devel. Co., 1976-79. Bd. dirs. Western Pa. Sch. for Blind Children, 1979—, Pitts.-Allegheny County chpt. ARC, 1980—. Served with USAF, 1952-54. Mem. Am. Bar Assn., Assn. Bar City N.Y., Georgetown Alumni Assn. (bd. govs. 1963-66), Nat. Assn. Corp. Real Estate Execs. Republican. Roman Catholic. Clubs: Union League (N.Y.C.); Bathing Corp. (Southampton, N.Y.); Duquesne, Harvard-Yale-Princeton (Pitts.); Allegheny Country, Edgeworth (Sewickley, Pa.). Home: 335 Woodland Rd Sewickley PA 15143 Office: 439 7th Ave Pittsburgh PA 15219

MOYNAHAN, JOHN DANIEL, JR., ins. co. exec.; b. Chgo., Dec. 10, 1935; s. John D. and Helen (Hurley) M.; B.A. cum laude, U. Notre Dame, 1957; m. Virginia Thomas, Oct. 10, 1959; children—Laura, Mark, Tricia, Kate. With Met. Life Ins. Co., N.Y.C., 1957—, regional v.p. group ins., 1971-79, v.p., nat. div. group nat. accounts, 1979-80, sr. v.p. group life and health ops., 1980—. Office: One Madison Ave New York NY 10010

MOZINSKI, RICHARD THEODORE, sugar co. exec.; b. Minto, N.D., May 3, 1918; s. Lawrence Valentine and Wanda Anna (Glaner) M.; student U. N.D., 1939-41; m. Virginia May Wangsness, May 27, 1949; children—Candy Mozinski Brachle, Theresa, Richard S. Transp. specialist GAO, 1945-47; cryptoanalyst Armed Forces Security Agy., 1947-50; co-owner Lake Calhoun Drive-In Restaurant, Mpls., 1950-52; transp. specialist Great Western Sugar Co., Denver, 1952-71; ops. dispatch mgr. spl. commodities Ringsby Truck Line, Denver, 1971-73; traffic mgr. Am. Crystal Sugar Co., Moorhead, Minn., 1973—. Dist. capt. Republican party, Westminster, Colo. Served with USNR, 1941-45. Mem. Nat. Indsl. Traffic League, NW Shippers Advisory Bd., Moorhead C. of C. Roman Catholic. Home: 1208 23d Ave S Moorhead MN 56560 Office: 101 N 3d St Moorhead MN 56560

MOZIS, BYRON GEORGE, mktg. exec.; b. Mpls., Sept. 19, 1946; s. George and Grace Wilda (Dorson) M.; A.A., U. Minn., 1971, B.A., 1973, C.J.S., 1973; teaching and counseling cert. Sch. Applied Aerospace Studies, 1975; grad. Dale Carnegie, 1979. Owner, Mozis & Papouchis & Co., St. Paul, 1973-75; gen. mgr. York Steak House, Inc., Maplewood, St. Paul, 1975-76; sales rep. PCA Internat., Portland, Oreg., 1976-77; lease cons. Truck div. Nat. Car Rental, Portland, 1977-78; safety officer, mktg. mgr. Knez Bldg. Materials, Tigard, Oreg., 1978—; dir. Hobbs & Hopkins Ltd., Portland, 1979—. Vol.-counselor Tualatin Valley Mental Health Center, Portland, 1977-78; vol. inspection/safety of race cars Portland Internat. Raceway, 1979—. Served with USAF, 1966-70. Recipient Outstanding Class Mem. award, Dale Carnegie Leadership Sch. Course, 1979, Human Relations award, 1979. Mem. Am. Bowling Congress. Methodist. Clubs: Hist. Car of Oreg., Sports Car of Am., Fraternal of Rosicrucians. Home: 6323 SE Jordan Portland OR 97222 Office: 8185 SW Hunziker St Tigard OR 97223

MROZINSKI, PHILLIP DAVID, mktg. and mgmt. cons.; b. Milw., Nov. 28. 1941; s. Edmund and Mary Mrozinski; A.A., Milw. Area Tech. Coll., 1971; B.A. cum laude, U. Wis., 1973; m. Nancy Barbara Skubal, Nov. 28, 1964. Sales rep. Wis. Nat. Life Ins. Co., Oshkosh, 1964-67; office supr. Time Ins. Co., Milw., 1967; dir. pub. relations Am. Cancer Soc., Milw., 1967-69; sales rep., publicist Patrick Cudahy (Wis.), 1969-71; tchr. Milw. Area Tech. Coll., 1973-75; with Walt Peabody Advt. Service, Inc., Fort Lauderdale, Fla., top sales rep., 1974, v.p. sales and mktg., asst. to pres., 1975-77; dir. bus. devel. and ins. sales Nat. Liberty Mktg., Inc., Valley Forge, Pa., 1977—; pres. Transam. Bus. Cons., Inc., Tustin, Calif., 1978—; dir. Eastern sales mgmt. Transtate Recovery Bur., Kamper-Gide, Inc. Congressional candidate 4th Wis. Dist., 1970, 72. Served with U.S. Navy, 1959-62. Recipient Speak-Up award Milw. Jaycees, 1968; Outstanding Service award Milw. Assn. Retarded Children, 1970; lic. in securities, ins., real estate; cert. tchr., Calif. Mem. Mortgage Bankers Assn., Soc. Profl. Journalists, Businessmen's Assn., Sigma Delta Chi (pres. 1973, Golden Mike award 1966). Address: 15731 Pasadena Ave Tustin CA 92680

MRUK, EDWIN STANLEY, mgmt. cons. co. exec.; b. Coventry, R.I., Nov. 29, 1932; s. Joseph F. and Bertha M. (Stefanik) M.; B.A., Johns Hopkins, 1954; m. Cecilia Levesque, May 2, 1959; children—Gregory E., Andrew C. Vice-pres. Jerome Barnum Assos., N.Y.C., 1955-60; partner Arthur Young & Co., N.Y.C., 1960—; mng. dir. Arthur Young Exec. Resource Cons., 1979—. Bd. dirs. Jr. Achievement N.Y. Mem. Am. Soc. Personnel Adminstrn. Clubs: Marco Polo, Larchmont Yacht. Author books, contbr. articles on exec. compensation, selection, mgmt. devel. to publs. Home: 7 South Dr Larchmont NY 10538 Office: Arthur Young & Co 277 Park Ave New York City NY 10017

MSCICHOWSKI, LOIS I., ins. agent and exec.; b. Omaha, Nov. 24, 1935; d. Edward J. and Evelyn B. (Davidson) Morrison; m. Peter A. Mscichowski, Aug. 16, 1952; 1 son, Peter Edward. Ins. clk. Gross-Wilson Ins. Agy., 1955-57; ins. sec., bookkeeper Reed-Paulsen Ins. Agy., 1957-58; office mgr., asst. sec., agent Don Biggs & Assos., Vancouver, Wash., 1958—. Mem. Citizens Com. Task Force, City of Vancouver, 1976, Block Grant Rev. Task Force, 1978—; chmn. adv. com. Clark Community Coll. Mem. Ins. Women of SW Wash. (pres.), Nat. Assn. Ins. Women. Roman Catholic. Club: Soroptimist (pres. elect Vancouver). Home: Office: 835 Broadway PO Box 189 Vancouver WA 98666

MUCCHETTI, DOMENIC ANTHONY, pub. co. exec.; b. Phila., July 12, 1933; s. Albert Joseph and Sarah Marguerite (Falasca) M.; B.S., Villanova U., 1955; m. Anna G. Ciampitti, Nov. 12, 1955; children—Donna Marie, Albert Joseph. Auditor, U.S. Army Audit Agy., Phila., 1955; accountant Gulistan Carpet Co., Milltown, N.J., 1958-65; accounting mgr. McGraw Hill, Hightstown, N.J., 1965-67, budget dir., N.Y.C., 1967-69; pres. Morgan-Grampian Inc., N.Y.C., 1978—, also dir.; sec., dir. David McKay Co., Benwill Pub. Co., Boston. Served with AUS, 1956-58. Office: 2 Park Ave 4th Floor New York NY 10016

MUCEUS, JOHN ARTHUR, bishop; b. Millford, Utah, Apr. 3, 1931; s. John O. and E. Grace (Lane) M.; B.A. in Pub. Edn., Fresno (Calif.) State Coll., 1955; m. Marjorie Helen Hintz, June 14, 1953; children—Joy Lorraine, Peter John, Jeffrey Mark. Engaged in ins. bus., 1955-59; ordained to ministry Reorganized Ch. of Jesus Christ of Latter Day Saints, 1960; pastor in Calif. and Eng., 1960-69; bishop of Tex., Okla. and N.Mex., 1970-76, Orange-San Gabriel (Calif.) Stake, 1977—; dir. Buckhorn Camp; corp. treas., dir. Camp Sionito Campground Inc., 1970-76; past treas., dir. Zionic Devel. Fund Inc., W. Tex. and N.Mex. Campground Inc.; pres., chmn. bd. Casa Real Convalescent Center Inc., Casa Real Retirement Center Inc., 1980. Served with AUS, 1953-55. Mem. W. Tex./N. Mex. Camping Assn. Inc. (dir., corp. treas. 1972-76). Republican. Contbr. articles to jours. Home: 2806 Molly St Riverside CA 92506 Office: 393 S Tustin Rd Orange CA 92666

MUDD, JOHN PHILIP, real estate exec.; b. Washington, Aug. 22, 1932; s. Thomas Paul and Frances Mary (Finotti) M.; B.S.S., Georgetown U., 1954, J.D., 1956; m. Barbara Eve Sweeney, Aug. 10, 1957; children—Laura, Ellen, Philip, Clare, David. Admitted to Md. bar, 1956, D.C. bar, 1963, Fla. bar, 1964, Calif. bar, 1973; individual practice law, Upper Marlboro, Md., 1956-66; v.p., sec., corp. atty. Deltona Corp., Miami, Fla., 1966-72; sec. Nat. Community Builders, San Diego, 1972-73; gen. counsel, adviser Continental Mortgage Investors, Coral Gables, Fla., 1973-76, v.p., gen. counsel, 1976-80; v.p. Am. Hosp. Mgmt. Corp., Miami, 1980—; pres., dir. Tropic Devel. Corp., Coral Gables, 1974—; sec., dir. Nationwide Bldg. & Devel., Coral Springs, Fla., Commonwealth Continental Corp., St. Petersburg, Ocean Springs Devel. Corp., Seattle, Birchwood Farms Devel. Corp., Harbor Springs, Mich., H.M.F. Corp., Honolulu; mem. land devel. adv. com. State of N.Y., 1971-75. Mem. alumni interview com. Georgetown U. Mem. Am., Fla. (exec. com., corp. counsel com.), D.C. bar assns., State Bar Calif. Democrat. Roman Catholic. Home: 1211 Hardee Rd Coral Gables FL 33146 Office: 5915 Ponce de Leon Blvd Coral Gables FL 33146

MUDD, SIDNEY PETER, beverage co. exec.; b. St. Louis, Jan. 21, 1917; s. Urban Sidney and Hallie Newell (Perry) M.; A.B. magna cum laude, St. Louis U., 1938; L.H.D., Coll. of New Rochelle, N.Y., 1974; m. Ada Marie Herbermann, Oct. 22, 1942; children—Sidney Peter, Ada Marie, Peter, Michael, Mary, Elizabeth, Catherine. Distbr., Joyce Seven-Up Co., Chgo., 1938, sales mgr., 1939, coordinator N.Y. ops., New Rochelle, 1941, v.p. ops., 1949-51; exec. v.p. N.Y. Seven-Up Bottling Co., Inc., New Rochelle, 1951-63, pres., 1963-73, dir., 1952—, chmn. bd., 1973—; pres. Joyce Beverages, Inc., also Joyce Advt., 1973—; chmn. bd. Joyce Beverages/N.Y., N.J., Conn., Ill., Wis.; dir. Joyce Beverages/N.Y., N.J., Conn., Chgo., Washington, Wis., Ill., Joyce Assos., Westchester Fed. Savs. & Loan Assn. Past pres., trustee St. Joseph's Hosp., N.Y.C., St. Francis Hosp., N.Y.C.; past bd. lay advisers St. Agnes Hosp., White Plains; past chmn. bd. trustees Coll. New Rochelle; past bd. dirs. U.S. Cath. Hist. Soc.; former trustee St. Louis U.; pres., New Rochelle Devel. Council; chmn. Westchester County Assn.; bd. dirs. Keep Am. Beautiful, Inc.; bd. dirs., v.p. John M. and Mary A. Joyce Found. Served with USNR, 1942-46. Recipient St. Louis U. Alumni Merit award, 1967; Dr. Martin Luther King, Jr. award New Rochell Community Action Agy., 1978; New Rochelle K.C. Civic award, 1978; New Rochelle YMCA Outstanding Citizen award, 1979, numerous others; named to St. Louis U. Sports Hall of Fame, 1976. Mem. Nat. (pres. 1974-76), N.Y. State (trustee) soft drink assns., Am. Alliance Resource Recovery Interests (dir.), Theta Kappa Phi, Crown and Anchor Soc. Clubs: Sales Execs. (founder, past v.p., dir.) (Westchester); Winged Foot Golf (New Rochelle). Home: 274 Broadview Ave New Rochelle NY 10804 Office: Joyce Rd New Rochelle NY 10802

MUDGETT, DONALD FOREST, mfg. co. exec.; b. Lynn, Mass., Oct. 19, 1932; s. Carl Forest and Jennie Christine (Swanson) M.; S.B., Mass. Inst. Tech., 1959; m. Marla R., Nov. 19, 1977; children by previous marriage—Steven Forest, Roger Fowler, Charles Frederick, Troy Alan, Todd Aaron; stepchildren—Lydia Ruthann Payne, Dara Christine Payne, Theodore Robert Payne. Asst. to gen. mgr. Ingersoll-Rand Co., Phillipsburg, N.J., 1959-64; sr. cons. L.B. Knight & Assos., Chgo., 1964-68; staff cons. W. King & Assos., Chgo., 1968-70; works mgr. Cooper Bessemer, Mt. Vernon, Ohio, 1970-71; prodn. control mgr. Marion Power Shovel Co. (Ohio), 1971-72; v.p. engring. U.S. Fiber Corp., Delphos, Ohio, 1972-79, also dir.; pres., dir. Centec Fiber, Inc., Denison, Tex., 1979-81, CFI Industries, Inc., Denison, 1981—. Served to 1st lt. AUS, 1955-57. Mem. Am. Prodn. and Inventory Control Soc. (chmn. nat. membership communications 1965-66). Home: 5 Woodlake Rd Sherman TX 75090 Office: 700 W Coffin St Denison TX 75020

MUEHL, ERIC JOHN, wholesale foods co. exec.; b. Waukesha, Wis., May 6, 1945; s. Robert John and Kathryn Gertrude (Volland) M.; B.S. in Chem. Engring., U. Wis., 1968; M.B.A. (N.W. Ayer fellow), Wharton Sch., U. Pa., 1972; m. Patricia Ann Hackbarth, Dec. 7, 1968 (div. 1976); 1 son, Jeffrey Robert. Research engr. Atlantic Richfield Co., Anaheim, Calif., 1968-69, process engr., Dallas, 1969-71, corporate planning analyst, Los Angeles, 1973-74; v.p., asst. comptroller, sec. asset liability com. Union Bank, Los Angeles, 1974-77; v.p.-fin. and adminstrn. Waukesha Wholesale Foods, Inc., 1977—, also dir. Mem. Planning Execs. Inst. (v.p. programs, treas. Los Angeles chpt.), Beta Gamma Sigma. Methodist. Home: 633 Crescent Ct Wauwatosa WI 53213 Office: 900 Gale St Waukesha WI 53186

MUELLER, CARL MUTH, banker; b. Erie, Pa., June 7, 1920; s. Herman Gundert and Edna Anna (Muth) M.; B.S., Mass. Inst. Tech., 1941; postgrad. N.Y. U., 1946-48; m. Suzanne Morrison Carreau, May 22, 1948; children—Anne M. Mueller Redman, Frederick C., Elizabeth M. Mueller Wales, Charles M., Henry G. With Bankers Trust Co., N.Y.C., 1946-60, asst. v.p., 1951, v.p., 1952-60; partner Loeb, Rhoades & Co., N.Y.C., 1960-72, mng. partner, 1973-76, pres., 1977—; vice chmn., dir. Bankers Trust Co., Bankers Trust N.Y. Corp., 1977—; dir. Cabot Corp., MacMillan, Inc. Mem. corp. Mass. Inst. Tech.; trustee John Simon Guggenheim Meml. Found., Carnegie Corp. N.Y. Served from lt. to maj. USAAF, 1941-45. Mem. Sigma Xi, Tau Beta Pi. Clubs: Links, River (N.Y.C.); Nantucket (Mass.) Yacht; Larchmont (N.Y.) Yacht. Home: 435 E 52d St New York NY 10022 Office: 42 Wall St New York NY 10005

MUELLER, DONALD ROBERT, advt. co. exec.; b. Detroit, Aug. 27, 1946; s. Douglas Harold and Shirley Anne (Davies) M.; B.A., Albion Coll., 1968; M.B.A., Mich. State U., 1972; m. Nancy Chatterton, Aug. 2, 1969; 1 son, Jonathan. Copywriter, J.L Hudson, Detroit, 1968-69; media buyer Fawcett McDermott Cavanagh, Honolulu, 1972-73; v.p. Peck Sims Mueller, Honolulu, 1973—; lectr. Chaminade Coll., 1975-77. Served with U.S. Army, 1969-70. Mem. Am. Mktg. Assn. Clubs: Mid-Pacific Road Runners, Honolulu. Home: 44-023A Aina Moi Kaneohe HI 96744 Office: 1170 Waimanu Honolulu HI 96814

MUELLER, FOORMAN LLOYD, lawyer; b. Chgo., Aug. 5, 1904; s. George Edgar and Bessie Dorothy (Foorman) M.; A.B., U. Mich., 1927; J.D., Kent Coll. Law, Chgo., 1932; m. Isabel McFarland, Oct. 25, 1930; children—Georgeana (Mrs. Thomas J. McColloch), Foorman Lloyd. Admitted to Ill. bar, 1932, D.C. bar; law clk. George E. Mueller, Chgo., 1929-32, mem. firm, 1932-35; practiced in Chgo., specializing in patents and trademarks, 1935-75, Phoenix, 1975—; patent counsel Motorola, Schaumberg, Ill., 1935—. Chmn. Hinsdale (Ill.) Community Caucus, 1948, 49, Hinsdale Planning Commn., 1949-57. Mem. Am., Ill., Chgo. bar assns., Chgo. (pres. 1967), Am. (pres. 1953-54) patent law assns., Phi Gamma Delta, Phi Delta Phi. Presbyterian. Clubs: Union League (Chgo.); Hinsdale Golf; Paradise Valley Country (Scottsdale, Ariz.). Home: 6721 E Cheney Rd Paradise Valley AZ 85253 Office: 4350 E Camelback Rd Suite 250F Phoenix AZ 85018

MUELLER, JOHNNIE DEWAYNE, bank exec.; b. Burton, Tex., Nov. 21, 1933; s. John Adolph, and Ida Hedwig (Stebner) M.; grad. Blinn Coll.; grad. Southwestern Grad. Sch. Banking, 1970; m. July 19, 1958; children—Renee Ann, Jill Rachelle. With Brenham Nat. Bank (Tex.), 1958—, investment officer, to 1972, pres., 1972—, also dir. Pres., Wahington County (Tex.) Fair Assn., also chmn. exec. com.; treas. various civic orgns.; mem. ch. council Martin Luther Lutheran Ch., Carmine, Tex., pres. Brotherhood; treas. Brenham Conf. Brotherhood, So. dist. Am. Luth. Ch. Brotherhood. Served in U.S. Army, 1956-58; Germany; in U.S. N.G. Mem. Brazos Valley Bankers Assn. (dir.), Washington County C. of C. (dir. 1972-74). Office: PO Box 583 Brenham TX 77833

MUELLER, ROY CLEMENT, graphic arts co. exec.; b. Weehawken, N.J., Aug. 15, 1930; s. Adam and Bertha M.; student Rochester Inst. Tech., 1976; m. Patricia Robinson, Sept. 3, 1970; children—Eric, Janet, Debra, Gregory. Mgr. estimating/billing dept., Editors Press, Hyattsville, Md., 1962-66; v.p., gen. mgr. Peninsula Press div. A.S. Abell Corp., Salisbury, Md., 1968-70; owner, mgr. Crown Decal & Display, Co., Bristol, Tenn., 1972—; pres. Bristol Screen Inc. (Va.), 1977—. Recipient Ad award Tri City Advt. Fedn., 1975, internat. exhbn. award Screen Printing Assn., 1977. Mem. Screen Printing Assn. Internat., Am. Philatelic Soc. Republican. Lutheran. Home: 202 Forest Dr Bristol TN 37620 Office: 1608 Edgemont Ave Bristol TN 37620

MULARZ, STANLEY LEON, credit info. services exec.; b. Chgo., Apr. 11, 1923; s. Stanley A. and Frances (Baycar) M.; A.B., St. Louis U., 1944; M.A., De Paul U., 1956; M.B.A., U. Chgo., 1960; Ph.D. Loyola U., Chgo., 1971; m. Lillian M. Kammerer, Apr. 10, 1948; children—James P., Thomas E., Geraldine E., Joanne F., John F., Paul S., Donna M. Tchr., Benedictine Jr. Coll., Savannah, Ga., 1945-46, Grant Community High Sch., Fox Lake, Ill., 1946-47; fgn. corr. Continental Ill. Nat. Bank, 1947-48; tchr., adminstr. Morgan Park Mil. Acad. and Jr. Coll., 1948-51; mgr. Spiegel, Inc., 1951-52; regional credit mgr. Aldens, Inc., Chgo., 1952-54, ops. mgr., 1954-67, mgr. indsl. relations, 1967-68, credit div. group mgr., 1968-69; pres. Credit Info. Services Corp., 1969-78; v.p. Trans Union Systems Corp., Chgo., 1972—; pres. Trans Union Credit Info. Co., 1979—; lectr., adviser on consumer edn. Mem. Gov.'s Commn. Schs./Bus. Mgmt. Task Force; chmn. State Info. Systems com., 1974-76. Mem. Internat. Consumer Credit Assn. (pres. Dist. V 1975-76), Mchts. Research Council (dir., treas. 1975—), Soc. Certified Consumer Credit Execs. (dir., v.p. 1978—), Am. Statis Assn., U. Chgo. Exec. Program Club, Phi Delta Kappa (pres. chpt. 1970-71). Club: Executives. Office: 111 W Jackson Blvd Chicago IL 60604

MULBERGER, ROBERT DIVEN, JR., franchise co. exec.; b. Phila., Aug. 5, 1944; s. Robert Diven and Doris Elaine (Matthews) M.; B.A., Pa. State U., 1966; M.B.A., Drexel U., 1975; m. Ruth Ann Doane, May 15, 1976. Sales rep. Campbell Soup Co., Camden, N.J., 1966-68; v.p. franchise ops. Schneider Hill & Spangler, Inc., Phila., 1968-74; v.p. ops. Snelling & Snelling, Inc., Sarasota, Fla., 1974-78; corp. v.p., pres. Employment Service Group, Snelling & Snelling, Inc., Sarasota, 1978—. Mem. Amateur Trapshooting Assn. Home: 5545 Shadow Lawn Dr Sarasota FL 33581 Office: Snelling Plaza 4000 S Tamiami Trail Sarasota FL 33581

MULEIN, JAY H., ins. sales exec.: b. W. Palm Beach, Fla., Nov. 27, 1944; s. Warren and Jean (Wallens) M.: B.A., U. So. Calif., Los Angeles, 1968; m. Merry Carp, July 29, 1973: 1 son, Michael David. Ins. agt., 1971—; dir. corps. Served with U.S. Army. Mem. Million Dollar Round Table, Nat. Assn. Life Underwriters (Century Club mem. polit. action com.). Jewish. Club: Century. Home: 4566 Winnetka Ave Woodland Hills CA 91364 Office: 625 S Kingsley Dr Los Angeles CA 90005

MULERT, HOWARD MAX, ins. broker; b. Pitts., Feb. 19, 1929; s. Carl J. and Thelma M. (Salkeld) M.; student U. Nev., 1947-49; m. Jeanne P. Vaux, June 20, 1950; children—Sandra J., Jeffrey S. Trainee The London Assurance, N.Y.C., 1949-50; with Blahnik & Mulert, Inc. (formerly Justus Mulert Co.), Pitts., 1950-64, v.p., dir., 1955-64, pres., 1970-79, chmn., 1979—; v.p. Edwards, George & Co., Ebbert, Grant & Kakel, Pitts., 1964-66; v.p., dir. Strothman & Mock, Inc., Pitts., 1966-70; v.p. 900 Washington, Inc. Bd. dirs. Golden Triangle YMCA, 1962—, chmn. bd., 1968-70; chmn. bd. Mt. Lebanon (Pa.) Community Center, 1968-69; bd. dirs. Greater Pitts. Bus. Devel. Corp., 1977—. Past bd. dirs., v.p. adminstrn. Civic Light Opera Assn. Greater Pitts.; bd. dirs. Greater Pitts. Bus. Devel. Corp., 1977. Mem. Nat. Assn. Life Underwriters, Nat. Assn. Ins. Agents, Greater Pitts. Assn. Ind. Ins. Agents and Brokers (past v.p.), Mass Mktg. Ins. Inst. (charter; dir., past v.p.), Nat. Assn. Ins. Brokers, Pitts. Alumni Assn., Pa. Soc., Internat. Platform Assn., Sigma Alpha Epsilon (past pres.). Republican. Episcopalian. Mason (32 deg., Shriner, Jester). Clubs: Allegheny, Duquesne, St. Clair Country, Rotary, Allegheny (dir. 1971—). Home: 137 Mayfair Dr Pittsburgh PA 15228 Office: Union Bank Bldg Pittsburgh PA 15222

MULFORD, DONALD LEWIS, publisher; b. Montclair, N.J., Apr. 22, 1918; s. Vincent S. and Madeleine (Day) M.; A.B., Princeton, 1940; m. Frances Root, Aug. 9, 1940 (div. Apr. 1954); children—Marcia M., Sally E., Sandra D. (dec.); m. 2d, Josephine M. Abbott Davisson, Apr. 23, 1954 (dec. Mar. 1956); stepchildren—Lee, Joanne, Sue; m. 3d, Emily L. Enbysk, Dec. 29, 1958. With Montclair Times Co., 1940—, exec. v.p., 1950—, asso. pub., 1956-71, pres., co-pub., 1971-79, pres., pub., 1979—; pres., pub. Verona-Cedar Grove Times, 1979—. Mem. N.J. Press Assn. (pres. 1980—), Phi Beta Kappa. Rotarian. Clubs: Princeton, Overseas Press, Montclair Golf; Nat. Press (Washington); Nassau (Princeton, N.J.). Home: 260 Highland Ave Upper Montclair NJ 07043 Office: 114 Valley Rd Montclair NJ 07042

MULHALL, RONALD TIMOTHY, lawyer; b. N.Y.C., Apr. 8, 1946; s. Andrew Richard and Virginia Lee (Alley) M.; B.A., U. Tex., Austin, 1968; J.D. (scholar), Loyola U., 1972; m. Janet Rae Kastler, July 28, 1976; children—Kimberley M., Kelly L., Matthew T. Admitted to Calif. bar, 1972; individual practice law, Manhattan Beach, Calif., 1976—; sec., chief exec. officer S.M.T. Transp., Inc. Served with USAF, 1968-69. Sharon Cahn Meml. scholar, 1964-65. Mem. Am. Bar Assn., Calif. Bar Assn., South Bay Bar, Manhattan Beach C. of C. (legis. com.), St. Thomas More Honor. Soc.

MULHOLLAND, WILLIAM DAVID, JR., corp. exec.; b. Albany, N.Y., June 16, 1926; s. William David and Helen E. (Flack) M.; A.B. cum laude, Harvard, 1950, M.B.A., 1952; LL.D., Meml. U., 1972; m. Nancy Louise Booth, June 22, 1957; children—William David III, Charles Douglass, James Andrew, John Alexander, Elizabeth Helen, Madeline Louise, Sarah Alexandra, Caroline Marie, Bruce Henry. Mem. staff Morgan Stanley & Co., N.Y.C., 1952-61, gen. partner, 1962-69; pres., chief exec. officer Brinco Ltd., Montreal, Que., Can., 1970-74; pres., chmn., chief exec. officer Churchill Falls (Labrador) Corp. Ltd. 1970-74; pres. Bank of Montreal, 1975—, chief exec. officer, 1979—; vice-chmn. Altgemeins Deutsche Credit Anstalt (Frankfurt); dir. Kimberly-Clark Corp, UpJohn Co., Standard Life Assurance Co. (Edinburgh). Mem. Canadian Com., Pacific Basin Econ. Council, mem. Canadian Econ. Policy Com. Bd. dirs. Montreal Symphony. Served as officer, inf., AUS, 1944-46; PTO. Mem. Sierra Club. Roman Catholic. Clubs: Met. (N.Y.C.); Mount Royal, St. Denis, Canadian, Forest and Stream, Lake of Two Mountains Hunt, Knowlton Golf (Montreal, Que.). Home: 1296 Redpath Crescent Montreal PQ H3G 2K1 Canada Office: 129 St James St Montreal PQ Canada

MULKERN, LOUIS JOSEPH, banker; b. Cambridge, Mass., Oct. 25, 1919; s. Louis William and Josephine (Halloran) M.; B.A., Dartmouth Coll., 1949; m. Dorothy McLaughlin, June 25, 1949; children—Elizabeth, Sarah. Exec. v.p. Bank of Am., San Francisco, 1949-78; vice chmn. bd. dirs. Am. Security Bank, Washington, 1979—. Instr., Pacific Rim program U. Calif. Served with USAAF, 1941-45. Decorated Air medal with oak leaf cluster. Mem. Asia Soc., Japan Soc., World Affairs Council, Washington Inst. Fgn. Affairs. Clubs: Univ. Columbia (Chevy Chase, Md.). Office: 1501 Pennsylvania Ave NW Washington DC 20013

MULLALLY, PIERCE HARRY, steel co. exec.; b. Cleve., Oct. 6, 1918; s. Pierce Harry and Laura (Lynch) M.; student U. Western Ont., 1935; B.S., John Carroll U., 1939; M.D., St. Louis U., 1943; m. Mary Eileen Murphy, Feb. 22, 1943; children—Mary Kathleen, Pierce Harry. Intern, St. Vincent Charity Hosp., Cleve., 1943, resident surgery, 1944, 47-50, staff surgeon, 1951-62, head peripheral vascular surgery, 1963-76, dir. med. edn., 1967-73, dir. dept. surgery, 1968-75; plant physician Republic Steel Corp., Cleve., 1952-68, med. dir., 1968-76, corp. dir. occupational medicine, 1976—. Vice-chmn. Cleve. Clinic-Charity Hosp. Com. Surg. Residency Tng., 1970-78; health com. Bituminous Coal Operators Assn. Served to capt. U.S. Army, 1944-46; PTO. Diplomate Am. Bd. Surgery. Fellow A.C.S., Am. Coll. Angiology; mem. Am. Iron and Steel Inst. (chmn. health com. 1977—), Am., Ohio occupational med. assns., Cleve. Acad. Medicine, Cleve. Surg. Soc., Western Res. Med. Dirs., Soc. Clin. Vascular Surgery. Roman Catholic. Clubs: Cleve. Skating, Cleve. Playhouse, Serra. Home: 2285 Harcourt Dr Cleveland Heights OH 44106 Office: Republic Steel Corp PO Box 6778 Cleveland OH 44101

MULLAN, JACK W., real estate developer; b. Ft. Dodge, Iowa, Sept. 17, 1924; s. Paul B. and Florence (Zeller) M.; B.S., U. So. Calif., 1950; postgrad. U. J.W. Goethe, Frankfurt, Germany, 1953-54; Ph.D., San Gabriel U., 1970; m. Beverly Fortner, Feb. 8, 1951; children—Lori Lee, Jill Ann. Co-Pilot, United Airlines, 1951-53; mgr. Aero Exploration, Frankfurt, Germany, 1954-55; pres. Mullan Real Estate, and other real estate devel. cos., 1955—. Founding chmn. Orange County Econ. and Indsl. Conf., 1959, chmn., 1960; co-chmn. Orange County Econ. Devel. Conf., 1963; bd. dirs. Orange Coast Assn., Porject "21"; mem. Orange County Met. Area Com., 1963; chmn. City Newport Beach (Calif.) Air Traffic Adv. Com., 1967-68; financial steering com. Orange County Boy Scouts Am., 1959. Trustee So. Calif. Aviation Council, pres., 1979—. Served to capt. USAAF, 1942-46; PTO. Mem. Calif. Real Estate Assn. (dir. 1957-65, state chmn. indsl. and comml. div. 1961, regional v.p. 1962), Newport Harbor Bd. Realtors (pres. 1960), Aircraft Owners and Pilots Assn., So. Calif. Aviation Council (chmn. air mus. com. 1974-75), Delta Tau Delta. Co-developer 1st horizontal condominium devel. in Calif. Home: 2031 Mesa Dr Santa Ana Heights CA 92707 Office: 3400 Irvine Newport Beach CA 92660

MULLANE, DENIS FRANCIS, life ins. co. exec.; b. Astoria, N.Y., Aug. 28, 1930; s. Patrick F. and Margaret M. (O'Neil) M.; B.S., U.S. Mil. Acad., 1952; m. Kathryn M. Mullman, June 28, 1952; children—Gerard, Kevin, Denise. With Conn. Mut. Life Ins. Co., 1956—, sr. v.p., then exec. v.p., Hartford, 1972-76; pres., 1976—, also dir.; dir. Conn. Natural Gas Co.; past chmn., bd. dirs. Life Underwriters Tng. Council; mem. bus. and econ. adv. bd. Conn. Bank & Trust Co., Hartford. Bd. dirs. St. Francis Hosp., Greater Hartford Arts Council; past pres. Jr. Achievement N. Central Conn. Served to 1st lt. C.E., U.S. Army, 1948-56. C.L.U. Mem. Nat. Assn. Life Underwriters, C.L.U. Assn., U.S. Mil. Acad. Assn. Grads. (bd. dirs.). Home: 82 Stoner Dr West Hartford CT 06107 Office: 140 Garden St Hartford CT 06115

MULLE, HENRY GORDON, fin. and econ. cons. co. exec.: b. Camden, N.J., Mar. 21, 1935; s. Henry Livingston and Margaret Caroline (Gross) M.; B.S. in Econs., Franklin and Marshall Coll., 1957; M.B.A., Drexel U., 1963; m. Katherine Elizabeth Leckey, Feb. 1, 1958; children—Karen Leslie, Karl Henry, Linda Cheryl, Mark Thomas, Amy Eileen. Systems and fin. analyst Phila. Electric Co., 1957-68; treasury asst., regional treas. Am. Water Works Co., Richmond, Ind., 1968-71; sr. rate economist, asst. treas., dir. rates Gen. Waterworks Co., Phila., 1971-76; founder H.G. Mulle & Assos. (Inc. 1977), Haddonfield, N.J., 1976, pres., chief exec. officer, 1977—. Served with USAF, 1958-60. Mem. Nat. Soc. Rate of Return Analysts, Nat. Assn. Water Cos. (asso.), Am. Mgmt. Assn. Republican. Methodist. Club: Lions (Haddonfield). Home: 49 West End Ave Haddonfield NJ 08033 Office: 336 Haddon Ave Haddon Township NJ 08108

MULLEN, DAVID BERNARD, gen. constrn. co. exec., investment banker; b. Milw., Oct. 20, 1928; s. Simon Steven and Mary Josephine (McCollow) M.; A.B., Marquette U., 1951; J.D. in Internat. Law and Diplomacy, Georgetown U., 1953; degree in fin. U. Pa., 1964; m. Bernice Johnson, Apr. 16, 1955; children—Craig A., John P., Suzanne M. Mem. staff Chief Naval Ops., Washington, 1951-53; with life ins. co., Milw., 1953-61, dist. agt., 1957-61; gen. agt. Boston area life ins. co., Cin., 1961-66; organizer, pres., chmn. bd. 1st Pension Planning Corp. Am., Milw., 1966—; reorganizer R.C. Borchert Engring. & Supply, Inc., Milw., 1975, v.p., 1976-78, pres., 1978—, chmn. bd., 1979—, also dir. Mem. Milw. Fire and Police Commn., 1970-72; bd. dirs. St. Mary's Hosp., Milw., 1956-59. Recipient letter of commendation Pres. of U.S., 1953. Mem. Nat. Assn. Security Dealers (registered), Allied Gen. Contractors, Milw. Met. Assn. Commerce, Sigma Delta Pi. Republican. Roman Catholic. Club: K.C. (founder, past grand knight local council) (Milw.). Office: 606 W Wisconsin Ave Milwaukee WI 53203

MULLEN, RICHARD ALLEN, mfg. co. exec.; b. Dayton, Ohio, Feb. 13, 1942; s. Howard Allen and Mary Jane (Ellis) M.; B.B.A., U. Cin., 1965; m. Donna May Allread, June 19, 1965; children—Christine Lee, Scott Allen, Elizabeth Ann. With Mobil Oil, Milw., Detroit, 1965-68; mgr. budgets and financial analysis Philips Industries, Dayton, Ohio, 1968-70, asst. treas., 1970-72, controller mfg. housing and recreation vehicle div., 1972-73, div. v.p. fin., 1973-74, corp. v.p. fin., treas., 1974-78, pres. Lau Industries Div., 1978—. Mem. Sigma Phi Epsilon. Methodist. Club: AMBUCS. Home: 1976 Spring Tree Ct Dayton OH 45459 Office: 2027 Home Ave Dayton OH 45407

MULLEN, THOMAS MICHAEL, financial exec.; b. St. Paul, Nov. 19, 1925; s. George Aloysius and Zita Cecilia (McCallow) M.; student Wharton Sch., U. Pa., 1943-44, Harvard Bus. Sch., 1944-45; B.B.A., U. Minn., 1947, M.B.A., 1950; m. Betty Lucille Osborn, Sept. 6, 1948; children—John, Susan Mullen Rogers, Claudia Mullen Mills, Gregory, Mary Jill Mullen Boyd, Paul. Instr., U. Minn., 1948-51; cost accounting supr. Studebaker Corp., South Bend, Ind., 1951-53; asst. dir. accounting research Monsanto Chem. Co., St. Louis, 1953-57; sr. cons. A.T. Kearney & Co., Chgo., 1957-64; with Dart Industries, Inc., Los Angeles, 1964—, treas., 1970-72, v.p., treas., 1972-80, v.p. fin., 1980—. Served with USNR, 1943-46. Mem. Fin. Execs. Inst., Beta Alpha Psi, Sigma Alpha Epsilon. Republican. Roman Catholic. Home: 12 Ponderosa Ln Rolling Hills Estates CA 90274 Office: 8480 Beverly Blvd Los Angeles CA 90048

MULLENEX, SHIRLEY LEE, mobile home mfg. co. exec.; b. Dyess, Ark., Sept. 11, 1938; d. William Robert and Lillie Lee (Stringer) Metcalf; B.S., Ark. State Coll., 1961; m. George Edward Mullenex, Dec. 19, 1964. Tchr. Cash Schs., Ark., 1958-59, Jonesboro, 1959-60, Las Vegas, Nev., 1960-64; with Lakewood Industries, Inc., Gardena, Calif., 1965—, pres., 1970—. Bd. govs. T.C.A., 1974—; vice chmn. Mfg. Housing Inst.; chmn. Mobile Home Consumers Affair Council. Office: 18026 S Broadway St Gardena CA 90247

MULLENIX, GEORGE CURTIS, engring. exec.; b. Kansas City, Kans., June 2, 1939; s. George Malcolm and V. Loretta (Morris) M.; B.S. in Engring. Tech., Riverside U., 1961; M.B.A., Coll. of Notre Dame, 1976; grad. U.S. Army Command and Gen. Staff Coll., 1979; student U.S. Army War Coll. Designer, Bourns, Inc., Trimpot div., Riverside, Calif., 1961-63; chief engr. Pico Cryogenic Products, Inc., LaHabra, Calif., 1963-65; sr. engr. Lockheed Propulson Co., Redlands, Calif., 1965-72; dir. engring. Quantic Industries, Inc., San Carlos, Calif., 1972—. Served to lt. col. Calif. N.G., 1957—. Decorated Meritorious Service medal; recipient ARCOM medal, 1976, 77. Mem. AIAA, Am. Def. Preparedness Assn., Assn. Old Crows, U.S. Armor Assn. Contbr. articles to tech. jours. Home: 426

Cuesta Dr Los Altos CA 94022 Office: 990 Commercial St San Carlos CA 94070

MULLENS, JOHN DEWEY, paper and wood products mfr.; b. Aspermont, Tex., Aug. 18, 1921; s. John Mark and Frances (Ellison) M.; B.B.A., So. Meth. U., 1948; m. Marjorie Render, Apr. 18, 1946; children—Lawrence, Michael, Marjorie Elizabeth. Various mgmt. positions Olinkraft, Inc., West Monroe, La., v.p. fin., treas., dir., 1966-77, pres., chief exec. officer, 1977—; sr. v.p., dir. Johns Manville, also pres., chief exec. officer Manville Forest Products Corp., West Monroe, La.; dir. Ouachita Nat. Bank. Bd. dirs. La. State U. Found., Public Affairs Research Council. Served with USAAF, 1941-45. Decorated Air Medal, Purple Heart. Mem. Monroe C. of C. (dir.), La. Assn. Bus. and Industry (dir.), U.S. C. of C. (mem. natural resources com.), La. Forestry Assn., Pres.'s Assn. Baptist. Clubs: Bayou DeSiard Country, Lotus. Office: PO Box 488 West Monroe LA 71291

MULLER, GARY WILLIAM, ins. co. exec.; b. Queens, N.Y., Jan. 13, 1941; s. Howard Peter and Helen Rose (Tubbiola) M.; B.B.A., Fairfield U., 1962; M.B.A. (grad. asst.), St. John's U., 1964; postgrad. N.Y. U., 1965—; m. Noreen Mullen, June 6, 1964; children—Anne Marie, Nancy Elizabeth, Barbara Jeanne. Grad. asst., chmn. mgmt. dept. St. John's U. Grad. Sch. Bus. Adminstrn., Jamaica, N.Y., 1962-64; mgmt. trainee Asso. Hosp. Service of N.Y., N.Y.C., 1964-65, exec. asso. to v.p., 1965-72, asst. to exec. v.p., 1972, asst. to pres., 1972-74; asst. v.p. Subscriber Service, Blue Cross & Blue Shield of Greater N.Y., N.Y.C., 1974-77, asst. v.p. profl. benefits, 1977-78, v.p. exec. services, 1978—; adj. asst. prof. Pace U. Grad. Sch. Bus. Adminstrn., N.Y.C., 1976-77. Recipient Mgmt. award Bus. Adminstrn. Soc., 1964. Mem. Adminstrv. Mgmt. Soc. N.Y. (dir. 1975—, merit mgmt. award 1977, Man of Year 1978), Acad. Mgmt., Beta Gamma Sigma, Omicron Delta Epsilon. Roman Catholic. Contbr. articles to profl. jours. Home: 1362 E 28th St Brooklyn NY 11210 Office: 622 3d Ave New York NY 10017

MULLER, RICHARD JOHNSON, automotive corp. exec.; b. Westfield, N.J., Nov. 28, 1928; s. Julius Frederick and Ethel Mae (Johnson) M.; student Kenyon Coll., 1947-49; A.B., Bard Coll., 1951; m. Barbara Alice Reading, Oct. 11, 1952; children—Melissa Ann, Richard Johnson, David Webster. Intelligence officer CIA, 1951-54; asst. news editor Sta. WICH, Norwich, Conn., 1954-57; news dir. Sta. WHCT-TV, Hartford, Conn., 1958, Sta. WNBC-TV, West Hartford, Conn., 1959, Sta. KDKA-TV, Pitts., 1960-61; mgr. radio-TV, Chrysler Corp., Detroit, 1961-65, mgr. field pub. relations, 1965-67, dir. div. and field pub. relations, 1967-68, dir. pub. relations services, 1968-75, dir. nat. and internat. media relations, 1975, dir. pub. relations, Washington, 1976-80, dir. Washington office, 1980—; chmn. pub. relations com. Motor Vehicles Mfrs. Assn., 1974-75. Vestryman Episcopal Ch., 1972-74, lay reader, 1969-75; mem. transition team Office of Pres.-Elect, 1980. Mem. Nat. Press Club, Radio-TV News Dirs. Assn., Pub. Relations Soc. Am., Bus.-Govt. Relations Council, Aircraft Owners and Pilots Assn. Clubs: Capitol Hill, George Town (Washington); Belle Haven Country (Alexandria, Va.). Lic. pvt. pilot. Office: 1100 Connecticut Ave NW Washington DC 20036

MULLESTEIN, WILLIAM ERNEST, former steel co. exec.; b. St. Gallen, Switzerland, Aug. 22, 1911; s. Christoph and Hulda Hitz (Lehmann) M.; C.E., Cornell U., 1932; student N.Y. U. Law Sch., 1933-35; m. Louise Pforzheimer, Jan. 25, 1941; children—Mary, Linda. Constrn. engr., supt. Austin Co., N.Y.C., 1939; sec. bldg. code commn. Am. Iron and Steel Inst., N.Y.C., 1939-42; dir. constrn. div. WPB, Washington, 1942-43; asst. supt. Dewey & Almy Chem. Co., Cambridge, Mass., 1943-44; with Lukens Steel Co., 1944—, v.p. adminstrn., 1957-61, v.p., gen. mgr., 1961-69, pres., 1969-76, chief operating officer, 1969-73, chief exec. officer, 1973-78, chmn., 1974-78; dir. Ogden Corp. N.Y., Provident Nat. Bank, Phila., Carpenter Tech. Corp., Provident Nat. Corp. Mem. U.S. Strategic Bombing Survey, ETO, 1945. Mem. Brandywine Valley Assn., Cornell U. Council, Friends Hosp., Phila.; chmn. Chester County Manpower Adv. Council; mem. County Bus. and Industry Council; trustee Carpenter Found. Mem. Am. Iron and Steel Inst. (dir.), Steel Plate Fabricators Assn., Soc. Cornell Engrs., Am. Mgmt. Assn., Phila. Com. Fgn. Relations. Clubs: Tower, Statler (Cornell U.); Cornell (N.Y.C. and Phila.); Racquet, Sunday Breakfast (Phila.); Mohawk (Schenectady); Rolling Rock (Ligonier, Pa.). Home: Valley Creek Farm RD 1 West Chester PA 19380

MULLETT, JOHN MCLAUGHLIN, tobacco co. exec.; b. Pitts., Feb. 21, 1950; s. John Selwyn and Betty June (Nelson) M.; B.A. in Psychology, W.Va. Wesleyan Coll., 1972. Sales rep. Philip Morris, USA, 1973-75, mil. mgr., 1975-76, asst. div. mgr., 1976-78, div. mgr., Fargo, N.D., 1978-80, area mgr., 1980—. Sponsor, Nat. Republican Congressional Com.; mem. Rep. Nat. Com., Walker Art Center, Fargo-Moorhead Community Theater; sponsor Fargo-Moorhead Symphony. Mem. Am. Mgmt. Assn., Sales and Mktg. Execs. Assn., W.Va. Wesleyan Coll. Alumni Assn. Methodist. Clubs: Fargo Country, Southgate Racquet. Home: 237 12 1/2 Ave E West Fargo ND 58078 Office: 7901 Xerxes Ave Minneapolis MN 55431

MULLIGAN, JAMES ANTHONY, computer service co. exec.; b. Bayonne, N.J., Jan. 21, 1950; s. James Joseph and Dorothy May (Winton) M.; B.S., St. Peter's Coll., 1972; m. Joan Patricia Lillis, July 22, 1972; children—Deirdre Anne, Karen Marie, James William. Operator, programmer Kraft Corrugated Containers, 1970-72; programmer Global Terminal and Container Services, 1972-76; project leader ODS Systems, Inc., N.Y.C., 1976-78; dir. tech. support, 1978-79, v.p., 1979—. Mem. Am. Mgmt. Assn. Clubs: Jaycees (past sec.). Home: 346 Wood Ridge Ave Wood Ridge NJ 07075 Office: Wall Street Plaza New York NY 10005

MULLIGAN, RAYMOND JOSEPH, tobacco co. exec.; b. Munhall, Pa., Jan. 22, 1922; s. James Russell and Sophio (Dymsia) M.; student Duquesne U., Pitts., 1949; postgrad. U. Pitts.; m. Mary Margaret Welsh, Aug. 1947; children—David, Robert, Timothy, Terry. Salesman, Snow Crop div. Minute Maid Corp., 1948, dist. sales mgr., 1949-55; dist. sales mgr. Burry Biscuits Co., 1955-61; dir. sales and mktg. Allen Products Co., Inc., 1961-64, v.p. sales and mktg., 1964-69, pres., 1969-73; dir. Liggett Group Inc., Durham, N.C., 1970, pres., chief operating officer, 1973, pres., chief exec. officer, 1973—; dir. Wachovia Corp., Winston-Salem, N.C., Huyck Corp., Wake Forest, N.C., Allegheny Ludlum Industries, Inc., Pitts., Dynalectron Corp., McLean, Va., Amstar Corp.; mem. exec. com. Stagville Corp., Durham. Bd. dirs., mem. exec. com. N.C. Citizens Assn.; bd. dirs. Duquesne U., N.C. Engring. Found., N.C. State U., Raleigh. Served with mil., 1941-45. Mem. World Wildlife Soc. (charter), Greater Durham C. of C. (dir., mem. exec. com., past pres.), Grocery Mfrs. Am. (dir.). Clubs: Hope Valley Country, Croasdaile Country, Rotary (hon.) (Durham); New York Athletic; Saucon Valley Country (Allentown, Pa.). Office: 100 Paragon Dr Montvale NJ 07645*

MULLIKIN, HARRY LAVERNE, hotel mgmt. exec.; b. Hot Springs, Ark., Apr. 27, 1927; s. William E., Jr. and LaVerne Mahone (Harper) M.; student Wash. State U., 1947, U. Wash., 1949; m. Judith Ann Thomas, July 25, 1970; children—Michael, Patricia, Scott, Kelly. Resident mgr. Davenport Hotel, Spokane, Wash., 1953-57; gen. mgr. The Olympic, Seattle, 1957-61; asst. v.p., dir. food and beverage Western Internat. Hotels, 1961-63, v.p., also v.p., mng. dir. Century Plaza, Los Angeles, 1963-70, sr. v.p., 1970-71, exec. v.p., 1971-73, pres., chief exec. officer, dir., 1977—; dir. UAL, Inc., United Airlines, Sea-First Corp., Seattle-1st Nat. Bank. Bd. dirs. Virginia Mason Hosp.; mem. travel and tourism council Senate Com. Commerce, Sci. and Transp. Recipient Golden Plate award Internat. Foodservice Mfrs. Assn., 1972, Father Coogan Labor-Mgmt. award for outstanding contbrn. to indsl. peace and social justice, 1966, Alumni achievement award Wash. State U., 1976; named to Hall of Fame, Hospitality Mag., 1967, Penn State Man of Year, 1975. Mem. Am. Hotel and Motel Assn. (past pres.), Nat. Inst. Foodservice Industry (trustee), Seattle C. of C. (trustee). Republican. Roman Catholic. Clubs: Seattle Rotary, Seattle Golf, Rainier, Corinthian Yacht. Office: The Olympic Seattle WA 98111

MULLIN, TERRY, lumber co. exec.; b. Burbank, Calif., Aug. 25, 1921; s. Russell Bishop and Merced (Terry) M.; B.A., Stanford, 1943; m. Mary Diane King, Feb. 23, 1952; children—Mary Reilley, Thomas Kalmus, Russell Bishop II. Pres., Burbank Lumber Co., 1954—, Tarzana Lumber Co. (Calif.), 1951—, Precision Milling Co., Burbank, 1956—, Terry Bldg. Centers, Hollywood, Tarzana, Northridge, Chatsworth, and North Hollywood, Calif., 1972—, Glendale, Calif., 1979—, Flagstaff Lumber Co. (Ariz.), Verde Valley Lumber Co. (Ariz.), Blanchard Co., 1976—, Tarzana Lumber & Garden, 1976—, Terry Lumber Co., 1980—, Inland Timber Co., 1981—, Terry Investment Co., 1981—; v.p. Kingman Lumber Co. (Ariz.). Mem. Lumber Assn. So. Calif. (dir. 1963, past pres.), Nat. Lumber and Bldg. Material Dealers Assn. (pres. 1973). Club: Los Angeles Tennis (pres. 1969-70). Office: 18551 Oxnard St Tarzana CA 91356

MULLINEAUX, JOHN ALYMER, JR., mfg. co. exec.; b. Upper Darby, Pa., Feb. 2, 1950; s. John Alymer and Rita Marie (Downey) M.; B.S. in Acctg., Ithaca Coll., 1971; m. Paulette Staub, May 20, 1972; children—James P., Kimberly A. Jr. acct. Delliote Haskins & Sells, Rochester, N.Y., 1971-73, sr. acct., 1973-76; asst. treas. Arbee Corp., Manheim, Pa., 1976-78, sec.-treas., 1978—; dir. Lancaster Threaded Products Inc., IMI of Phila. Inc., TranTorque Corp. Treas. Lancaster-Lebanon council Boy Scouts Am.; treas., deacon St. Paul United Ch. of Christ. C.P.A., N.Y. State, Pa. Mem. Am. Inst. C.P.A.'s, Fin. Execs. Inst., Pa. Inst. C.P.A.'s, N.Y. State Sec. C.P.A.'s. Home: RD 1 Box 706 Manheim PA 17545 Office: Arbee Corp 311 W Stiegel St Manheim PA 17545

MULLINS, JAMES BOLL, ins. co. exec.; b. Dallas, June 19, 1934; s. Frank Morris and Alice Ophelia (Holland) M.; student Howard Payne Coll., 1952-53, Kilgore Jr. Coll., 1953-54; B.A., N. Tex. State U., 1956; postgrad. So. Methodist U. Law Sch., 1959-60; m. Joann Barnett, Aug. 6, 1954; children—Kiann, Kala-Joy. Adjuster, Allstate Ins. Co., Dallas, 1956-58, supr., 1958-60, dist. claim mgr., 1961-67, div. claim mgr., Dallas, 1967-68, St. Petersburg, Fla., 1968-69, regional claim mgr., Jackson, Miss., 1969-70, Valley Forge, Pa., 1970-76, zone claim mgr., East Zone, N.J., 1976-77; vice-pres. claims CNA Ins., Chgo., 1977—. Campaign coordinator United Fund Dallas, 1956-57; mem. Republican Nat. Com., 1979-80. Mem. Claim Mgmt. Council Tex., Fla., Field Mus. Natural History. Presbyterian. Author: Management Digest Series, 1971-80. Office: CNA Plaza Chicago IL 60685

MULLINS, WILLIAM FRANKLIN, assn. exec.; b. Ohio, Jan. 2, 1934; s. Harry Bernard and Edna Gladys (Shanks) M.; B.S., George Washington U., 1970, M.B.A., 1973; m. Mary Anna Blazina, June 27, 1958; children—Terry Ann, Courtney Ann. Enlisted in U.S. Navy, 1952, advanced through grades to lt. comdr., Med. Service Corps, 1973; service in Japan; ret., 1975; adminstr. Facey Med. Group, Inc., Granada Hills, Calif., 1975-78; dir. mgmt. services Los Angeles County Med. Assn., 1978—. Mem. Am. Assn. Med. Soc. Execs., Am. Soc. of Assn. Execs., Med. Group Mgmt. Assn., Profl. Conv. Mgmt. Assn. Roman Catholic. Home: 2277 E Calle Riscoso Thousand Oaks CA 91362 Office: 1925 Wilshire Blvd Los Angeles CA 90057

MUMA, RICHARD ALLEN, fin. exec.; b. Warren, Mich., Dec. 29, 1940; s. Forest Amber and Elizabeth Maude (Troyer) M.; B.S. in Edn., No. Mich. U., 1972; m. Dagmar Ann Brock, June 12, 1965; children—Jeffrey Michael, Cheryl Lynn, David Richard. Dir. phys. edn. Pinconning (Mich.) Area Schs., 1972-73; with Schater Chevrolet, Pinconning, Mich., 1974-76; agt. Prudential Ins. Co., Grand Rapids, Mich., 1976—, new manpower devel. mgr., 1977—. Served with USN, 1959-67. Recipient No. Star award, Prudential Ins. Co. Am., 1978, 79. Mem. Nat. Assn. Life Underwriters (life underwriters polit. action com.). Reformed Ch. of Am. Clubs: Ch. Golf League. Home: 7788 Emberly St Jenison MI 49428 Office: 161 Ottawa NW 4115 Waters Bldg Grand Rapids MI 49503

MUMBY, WILLIAM, JR., coll. ofcl.; b. Bklyn., Dec. 13, 1926; s. William and Anna Rosina (Paige) M.; B.S., Morgan State Coll., 1952, postgrad., 1975-76; postgrad. Harvard U., 1974; m. Mattie Lawson, Sept. 11, 1955; children—Wayne William, Geralyn Rosina, Kim Evette. Dir. admissions Bowie (Md.) State Coll., 1967-69, asst. to pres., 1969-73, v.p. planning and devel., 1977—; v.p. instl. planning and devel. Coppin State Coll., Balt., 1973-75; asst. to pres. Charles Center-Inner Harbor Mgmt., Inc., Balt., 1975-80. Participant Voluntary Council of Balt., 1973-78; past treas. Hilton Elementary Sch.; past v.p. Lemmel Jr. High Sch. PTA; pres. Forest Park Little League, 1965-67; bd. dirs., mem. exec. search com., chmn. agency services com. Family and Childrens Soc. Balt., 1976—; bd. dirs. Met. Bus. Resource Center, 1977-78; bd. dirs., treas. NW Health Services, 1977—; bd. dirs. Nat. Aquarium, Inc., 1977—, YMCA Greater Balt., 1979—. Served with USN, 1943-46. Mem. Soc. for U. Planning, Md. Classified Employees Assn., Afro-Am. Music Opportunities Assn., Omega Psi Phi, Theta Psi Chi. Mem. United Ch. of Christ. Home: 3610 Durley Ln Baltimore MD 21207 Office: Bowie State College Bowie MD 20715

MUMOVIC, ALEKSANDAR MLADEN, trading corp. exec.; b. Melenci, Yugoslavia, Sept. 19, 1933; came to U.S., 1974; s. Mladen and Kornelija (Krompic) M.; grad. Faculty of Law, Belgrade U., Yugoslavia, 1956. Salesman, Omnicommerce and Jugoelektro, Beograd, Yugoslavia, 1956-59; chief of export dept. Invest-Import, Beograd, 1960-64, head rep. Teheran, Iran, 1964-71, exec. dir. for coordination fgn. offices, 1971-74; pres., sr. adv. IPT Co., N.Y.C., 1975—. Mem. Assn. Yugoslav Businessmen in U.S.A. (pres. 1975-76), Assn. Yugoslaventreprises (pres. 1973-74). Socialist. Club: 60 East (N.Y.C.). Home: 245 E 40th St New York NY 10016 Office: 60 E 42d St New York NY 10017

MUMPHREY, ANTHONY JOSEPH, JR., city ofcl., educator; b. New Orleans, May 15, 1942; s. Anthony Joseph and Josephine (Trumbaturi) M.; B.S. in Civil Engring., Tulane U., 1963, M.S. (Ideal Cement fellow), 1964; M.A., U. Pa., 1971, Ph.D. (NSF research fellow), 1973; m. Kathleen McCahill, Jan. 6, 1968; children—Kathleen A., Anthony Joseph III, Benjamin L., Christina M. Civil engr. Waldemar S. Nelson & Co., Inc., New Orleans, 1963, Boh Bros. Constrn. Co., Inc., New Orleans, 1968-69; instr., research coordinator div. bus. and econ. research La. State U., New Orleans, 1969-70, faculty urban and regional planning U. New Orleans, 1973—, prof., 1978—; mayor's exec. asst. for planning and devel. City of New Orleans, 1978—; cons. energy, transp. planning Tex. So. U., 1973-78. Dir. transition for mayor-elect E.N. Morial, City of New Orleans, 1978. Served with USNR, 1964-67. Registered profl. engr., land surveyor, La. Mem. Am. Inst. Cert. Planners, Am. Planning Assn., Regional Sci. Assn., Am. Public Works Assn. Democrat. Roman Catholic. Author monographs, articles in profl. jours. Home: 7165 Crowder Blvd New Orleans LA 70127 Office: Mayor's Office City Hall New Orleans LA 70112

MUNDT, RAY BENJAMIN, indsl. conglomerate exec.; b. Appleton, Wis., Aug. 10, 1928; s. Benjamin J. and Jessie (Toft) M.; postgrad. Syracuse U., Advanced Mgmt. Program, Harvard U., 1957; m. Ruth C. Stanchik, June 15, 1953; children—R. Scott, William, Robert, Mary Mundt Klumpp. Vice pres., gen. mgr. sales Kimberly Clark Corp., Neenah, Wis., 1953-70; pres. Unisource Corp., Phila., 1970-73; exec. v.p. Alco Standard Corp., Valley Forge, Pa., 1973-75, pres., chief operating officer, 1975-80, pres., chief exec. officer, 1980—, dir., 1975—; dir. Phila. Savings Fund Soc., 1979—, Penjerdel Corp., 1976—; adv. bd. Liberty Mut. Ins., 1975—. Served with USN, 1945-49. Clubs: Univ. (Chgo.); Seaview Country, Phila. Country, Chub Cay, Masons. Home: 300 Thornbrook Ave Rosemont PA 19010 Office: PO Box 834 Valley Forge PA 19482

MUNDY, JEFFREY GORDON, real estate devel. corp. exec.; b. Princeton, Ind., Mar. 4, 1944; s. Gene Gordon and Helen Elizabeth (Frese) M.; B.A. in Econs., U. Tex., Austin, 1966, Ph.D. in Fin., 1971; M.B.A. in Fin., Harvard U., 1968; m. Deborah Schumacher; 1 son, Gregory G. Mgr., Houston regional real estate investment office Prudential Life Ins. Co. of Am., Houston, 1971-72; v.p. PIC Realty Corp. subs. Prudential Life Ins. of Am., Newark, 1972-78, v.p. Houston office, 1978-79; sr. v.p. Century Devel. Corp., Houston, 1979—; asst. prof. fin. U. Tex., Austin, 1968-71, lectr., 1980—; lectr. U. Houston, 1980—, U. Tex., Austin, 1980—; dir. Base Fin. Realty & Devel., Houston, 1979-80. Mem. tech. adv. bd. Rice Center, Houston, 1979-80; coach YMCA Youth Football, 1980. Recipient outstanding ex-student award for real estate profession U. Tex., 1980. Mem. Houston Zool. Soc., Urban Land Inst. (asso.). Presbyterian. Home: 5009 Yoakum Houston TX 77006 Office: Five Greenway Plaza Suite 1700 Houston TX 77046

MUNERA, GERARD EMMANUEL, aluminum co. exec.; b. Algiers, Algeria, Dec. 2, 1935; came to U.S., 1976; s. Gabriel E. and Laure A. (Labrousse) M.; Math. and Physics degrees Lycee Bugeaud, Algiers, 1956; M. Math., M. Physics, M. Chemistry, Ecole Polytechnique, Paris, 1956; C.E., Ecole Des Ponts Et Chaussees, Paris, 1959; m. Paule A. Ramos, July 28, 1959; children—Catherine, Phlippe, Emmanuelle, Jean-Marie. Chief county engr. Dept. Rds. and Bridges, South Algiers, 1959-62; cons. economy, long-term planning French Ministry Fgn. Affairs, Argentina, 1962-66; sr. v.p. fin. Camea group Pechiney Ugine Kuhlmann, Buenos Aires, Argentina, 1966-70, chmn., chief exec. officer, 1976-77, exec. v.p. Howmet Aluminum group, Greenwich, Conn., 1976-77, pres., chief operating officer, 1977-79, pres., chief exec. officer, 1980—; dir. Pechiney Ugine Khulmann Corp. (U.S.), Cegedur (France). Served with French Air Force, 1956-57. Decorated Commemorative medal (Algeria). Mem. French Am. C. of C. (sec.-gen.), Aluminum Assn. (exec. com., chmn. membership com.), Internat. Primary Aluminum Inst. Roman Catholic. Club: Stanwich (Greenwich). Developer, patentee low income housing system for developing countries. Office: 475 Steamboat Rd Greenwich CT 06830

MUNGER, DEXTER GAYLORD, profl. services co. exec.; b. Los Angeles, June 12, 1933; s. Stephen Ingham and Corinne (Kelly) M.; B.S., Georgetown U., 1956; m. Sandra Claire Jaeger, Apr. 26, 1956; children—Blair G., Brooks T., Lance D., Lindsey H., Meredith L. Salesman, product mgr. Rowan Industries, Red Bank, N.J., 1960-64; v.p. sales Parker Instrument Co., Stamford, Conn., 1964-67; dir. corp. fin. dept. A.L. Stamm & Co., N.Y.C., 1967-68; pres. Munger Baker & Currie, N.Y.C., 1968-70; chmn. bd., pres. John D. Kettelle Corp., Arlington, Va., 1970-74; chmn. bd. Kappa Systems Inc., Arlington, 1974—, Resource Mgmt. Corp., Arlington, 1975—, Automated Processes, Inc., Huntington, N.Y., 1976—; cons. in field; dir. Resource Mgmt., Automation Processes, Eastern Telephone Co. Bd. dirs. Danbury Health Plan, 1979—. Served to capt., USMC, 1956-60. Republican. Roman Catholic. Club: Redding Country (dir. 1977—). Office: 1501 Wilson Blvd Arlington VA 22209

MUNRO, J. RICHARD, pub. co. exec.; b. 1931; B.A., Colgate U., 1957; postgrad. Columbia U., N.Y. U.; married. With Time Inc., N.Y.C., 1957—, pub. Sports Illustrated, 1969-71, v.p. Time Inc., 1971—, dep. to group v.p., 1972-74, v.p. video ops., 1974-75, group v.p. video ops., 1975-79, exec. v.p., 1979-80, pres., chief exec. officer, 1980—, also dir.; dir. IBM Corp. Served with USMC. Office: Time and Life Bldg New York NY 10020*

MUNROE, GEORGE BARBER, business exec.; b. Joliet, Ill., Jan. 5, 1922; s. George Muller and Ruth (Barber) M.; A.B., Dartmouth, 1943; LL.B., Harvard, 1949; B.A. (Rhodes scholar), Christ Church. Oxford (Eng.) U., 1951, M.A., 1956; m. Helen Taylor, June 22, 1945 (div. 1964); children—George Taylor, Ralph W. Taylor; m. 2d, Elinor Bunin, May 30, 1968. Admitted to N.Y. bar, 1949; asso. firm Cravath, Swaine & Moore, N.Y.C., 1949; atty. Office Gen. Counsel, U.S. High Commn. Germany, Frankfort and Bonn, 1951-53; justice U.S. Ct. Restitution Appeals, Allied High Commn. Germany, Nuremberg, 1953-54; asso. firm Debevoise, Plimpton & McLean, N.Y.C., 1954-58; with Phelps Dodge Corp., 1958—, v.p., 1962-66, pres., 1966-75, chief exec. officer, 1969—, chmn. bd., 1975—, also dir.; dir. Mfrs. Hanover Corp., Mfrs. Hanover Trust Co., N.Y. Life Ins. Co., Johns-Manville Corp., So. Pacific Co., So. Peru Copper Corp. Trustee Dartmouth Coll., Met. Mus. Art, YMCA of Greater N.Y. Served to lt. (j.g.) USNR, 1943-46. Mem. Council on Fgn. Relations, Am. Bar Assn., Am. Inst. Mining, Metall, and Petroleum Engrs. (asso.), Acad. Polit. Sci. (dir.), Mining and Metall. Soc. Am., Am. Mining Congress (dir.), Phi Beta Kappa. Clubs: Brook, Mining, River, Sky, Univ. (N.Y.C.). Home: 870 United Nations Plaza New York City NY 10017 Office: 300 Park Ave New York City NY 10022

MUNSON, ALEXANDER LEE, forest products co. exec.; b. Hempstead, N.Y., Aug. 22, 1931; s. Alexander Lawrence and Bertha Louise (Geer) M.; B.A., Amherst Coll., 1953; M.B.A., with distinction, Harvard U., 1960; m. Betty Sue Shideler, Dec. 14, 1957 (div. June 1978); children—Eric Lawrence, Genevieve Sue, Anna Lee. Vice pres., treas. Crown Zellerbach Corp., San Francisco, 1972—. Served with USCGR, 1954-58. Republican. Presbyterian. Club: University. Home: 3369 Jackson St San Francisco CA 94118 Office: Crown Zellerbach Corp 1 Bush St San Francisco CA 94104

MUNSON, FLOYD EDWARD, automotive parts mfg. co. exec.; b. Lafayette, Ind., May 28, 1935; s. Floyd Irvin and Dorothea Mary (Scheumann) M.; B.M.E., Purdue U., 1957, M.S. in Indsl. Mgmt., 1958. Controller, gas turbine and elevator divs. Westinghouse Electric Corp., Phila., Millburn, N.J., 1958-69; v.p. ops. Walworth Co., Phila., 1969-71; mgmt. cons. Munson Assos., Bryn Mawr, Pa., 1971-72; dir. ops. analysis and planning, automotive products group IT&T, N.Y.C., 1972-76, pres. automotive distbrs. div., 1977-80; pres., chief exec. LeRoy Machine Co. (N.Y.), 1980—. Mem. Tau Beta Pi. Republican. Lutheran. Home: 300 E 40th St New York City NY 10016 Office: 7921 E Main Rd LeRoy NY 14482

MUNSON, FRANK WILLIAM, ins. co. exec.; b. Rockville Centre, N.Y., Jan. 18, 1928; s. Bernard and Julia (Brennan) M.; A.B., Dartmouth Coll., 1949; m. Barbara Wright, Sept. 23, 1950; children—Richard, Susan, Elizabeth, Barbara Jane, JoAnne. With Liberty Mut. Ins. Co., 1949-50; underwriter Md. Casualty Co., 1950-52; with Gen. Re-ins. Corp., Greenwich, Conn., 1954—, sr. v.p. adminstrv. services, 1968-70, exec. v.p., dir., 1970-73, pres., dir., chief operating officer, 1973—. Served with USCG, 1952-54. Mem. Underwriters Golf Assn., Sigma Chi. Clubs: Dartmouth (N.Y.C.), Univ., Winged Foot Golf, Woodway Country. Office: 600 Steamboat Rd Greenwich CT 06830

MUNSON, JOHN HENRY GLASS, investment counselor; b. Honolulu, Nov. 13, 1940; s. Henry Glass and Anna-Marie (Amundsen-Olsen) M.; student U.S. Naval Acad., 1958-61; B.S., Columbia U., 1963, postgrad., 1963-64; m. Ruth Field Blake, May 24, 1969; 1 dau., Marrianne C.A. Instl. researcher and sales W.E. Hutton & Co., N.Y.C., 1965-70, Paine-Webber Jackson & Curtis, N.Y.C., 1970-72; asst. to chmn. Baird Patrick & Co., N.Y.C., 1972-75; investment counselor A.R. Schmeidler & Co., N.Y.C., 1975—; fin. cons. Episcopal Diocese of N.Y.; mgr. bldg. fund Cathedral St. John the Divine. Sustaining mem. Republican Nat. Com., 1976—. Mem. Nat. Assn. Securities Dealers, Soc. Colonial Wars. Episcopalian. Clubs: Met. Opera, Downtown Assn., St. Anthony. Home: 1000 Park Ave New York NY 10028 Office: 555 Fifth Ave New York NY 10017

MUNSON, LEON J., portfolio mgr.; b. McGill, Nev., Dec. 14, 1939; s. Edward Ivin and Ella Jean (Jenne) M.; B.S., U. Nev., 1963; m. Carolyn Ann Donahoe, Feb. 19, 1965 (dec. Sept. 1968). Teller, First Nat. Bank Nev., Reno, 1963, mgmt. trainee, 1963-65, trust investment officer, 1965-71, head trust investments, 1971-74, asst. v.p., 1973-74; investment officer Bishop Trust Co. Ltd., Honolulu, 2d v.p., 1976-78; asst. v.p. 1st Hawaiian Bank, Honolulu, 1978-79, v.p., head trust investments, 1979—. Mem. Nat. Assn. Security Dealers (regional arbitrator 1980), Honolulu Investment Soc. (dir. 1979—), Financial Analysts Fedn., Am. Inst. Banking, Security Analysts of San Francisco, Defenders of Wildlife, Animal Protection Inst., Common Cause. Home: PO Box 3314 Honolulu HI 96801 Office: PO Box 3200 Honolulu HI 96847

MUNSON, LUCILLE MARGUERITE (MRS. ARTHUR E. MUNSON), real estate broker; b. Norwood, Ohio, Mar. 26, 1914; d. Frank and Fairy (Wicks) Wirick; R.N., Lafayette (Ind.) Home Hosp., 1937; A.B., San Diego State U., 1963; student Purdue U., Kans. Wesleyan U.; m. Arthur E. Munson, Dec. 24, 1937; children—Barbara (Mrs. Charles Papke), Judith Munson Andrews, Edmund Arthur. Staff and pvt. nurse Lafayette Home Hosp., 1937-41; indsl. nurse Lakey Foundry & Machine Co., Muskegon, Mich., 1950-51, Continental Motors Corp., Muskegon, 1951-52; nurse Girl Scout Camp, Grand Haven, Mich., 1948-49; owner Munson Realty, San Diego, 1964—. Mem. San Diego County Grand Jury, 1975-76, 80-81. Mem. San Diego Bd. Realtors. Presbyterian. Home: 3538 Esterlina Dr Fallbrook CA 92028 Office: 2999 Mission Blvd San Diego CA 92109

MUNSON, MARIE CHRISTEAN BENNETT, employment agy. exec.; b. Claremore, Okla., Apr. 1; d. Fred R. and Myrtle (Rutherford) Christean; student So. Meth. U., 1943; m. William Franklin Bennett, Jr. (dec. Apr. 1962); children—William Franklin, Mark Allen, Robert Christean; m. 2d, Hal R. Colter, Feb. 10, 1966 (div. Oct. 17, 1970); m. 3d, Craig D. Munson, Jr., July 1, 1973. Owner, mgr. Bennett Assos., Odessa, Tex., 1949-54; owner Bennett Personnel Cons., Odessa and Midland, Tex., 1954—; pres. Bennett Munson, Inc., Lubbock, Tex., 1965—; br. mgr. Kelly Services, Inc., Detroit, 1958—; registered rep. Waddell & Reed, Kansas City, Mo., 1962-69, Kelly & Morey, Inc., Denver, 1969-71, Am. Growth, 1971-80; pres. Nat. Tng. & Testing, Inc., Odessa and Midland, 1964-69. Bd. dirs. Better Bus. Bur., Salvation Army. Recipient awards including Gold Citizen of Year award Nat. Conf. Kelly Service, Inc., 1962, 63, Outstanding Performance award, 1978. Mem. Permian Basin Petroleum Pioneers (charter), St. John's Episcopal Bus. Women, Nat. Employment Assn., Nat. Assn. Women Bus. Owners, Cert. Personnel Cons.'s Soc., Presdl. Room Mus., Odessa, Midland chambers commerce, Altrusa Internat. Office: Nat Bank of Odessa Suite 111 Odessa TX 79760 also Suite 3B 3211 W Wadley Midland TX 79703

MUNTNER, MICHAEL, computer co. exec.; b. Bklyn., Nov. 11, 1940; s. Irving and Josephine (Birnbaum) M.; B.S., Poly. Inst. Bklyn., 1962, Ph.D., 1967; M.S., U. Pa., 1963; m. Judith A. Feldman, Aug. 24, 1963; children—Amy, Joshua, Paul. Mem. tech. staff Bell Telephone Labs., Holmdel, N.J., 1962-67; mem. staff Inst. for Def. Analyses, Arlington, Va., 1967-70; chief systems engring. div. Def. Communications Agy., Reston, Va., 1970-72; asst. commr. Automated Data & Telecommunications Service, Gen. Services Adminstrn., Washington, 1972-77; v.p. Internat. Computing Co., Bethesda, Md., 1977—; lectr. in field. Poly. Inst. Bklyn. sr. fellow, 1967; recipient Meritorious Service award Def. Communications Agy., 1972; Outstanding Service award Gen. Services Adminstrn., 1976. Mem. IEEE, Eta Kappa Nu, Tau Beta Pi, Sigma Xi. Contbg. Author: Computer Communications Networks, 1972; contbr. articles to profl. jours. Office: 4330 East-West Hwy Bethesda MD 20014

MUNYON, WILLIAM HARRY, JR., archtl. co. exec.; b. Panama City, Panama, Feb. 20, 1945 (parents Am. citizens); s. William Harry and Ruth (Hyde) M.; B.A., Tulane U., 1967; postgrad. U. Hawaii, 1972-73; B.Arch. with high distinction, U. Ariz., 1978; m. Nancy Jean Rearick, July 17, 1976. Elec. designer Ohlsen-Mitchell, Inc., New Orleans, 1966-67; research cons. hist. preservation U. Ariz., Tucson, 1974-75; cons. hist. preservation State of Ariz., Phoenix, 1974-75; mktg. dir., programmer, designer Architecture One, Ltd., Tucson, 1975-78; mng. prin. Artistic License II, graphics and design, 1975—; dir. mktg. Hansen Lind Meyer, P.C., Iowa City and Chgo., 1978-79; v.p. John F. Steffen Assos., Inc., subs. Turner Constrn., St. Louis, 1979-80; asso., dir. corp. devel. Rees Assos., Inc., Oklahoma City, 1980—; mktg. cons., 1979—; mem. adv. bd. Interior Design mag., 1978-79; mem. Bldg. Energy Performance Standards Adv. Panel, 1979—. Active U. Ariz. Fund for Athletic Devel., 1977—. Served with USN, 1967-73; lt. comdr. Res. Mem. AIA (asso., architecture for justice com. 1978—), Nat. Trust Hist. Preservation, Naval Res. Officers Assn., Soc. Archtl. Historians, Am. Correctional Assn., Naval Inst., Soc. Mktg. Profl. Services, Res. Officers Assn. U.S., Mensa, Lionel Collectors Club Am., Brit. Model Soldier Soc., Tulane U. Alumni Assn., Phi Kappa Phi (life), Sigma Chi (life). Roman Catholic. Founder ann. archtl. history prize U. Ariz., 1979. Home: 3305 Eton Ave Oklahoma City OK 73122 Office: 722 N Broadway Suite 500 Oklahoma City OK 73102

MURANIA, JOSEPH CHARLES, discount chain exec.; b. N.Y.C., Apr. 27, 1931; s. Charles and Jennie Murania; B.B.A., St. Johns U., 1956; M.B.A., N.Y. U., 1960; m. Joan Getko, June 20, 1959; children—Jane, Charles. Asst. controller Halle Bros. Co., Cleve., 1960-63; v.p., controller Lit Bros. Dept. Store, Phila., 1963-65; v.p. control and adminstrn. The Sperry & Hutchinson Co., N.Y.C., 1965-76; sr. v.p. store ops. Zayre Corp., Framingham, Mass., 1976—. Served with Signal Corps, U.S. Army, 1952-54; Korea. Mem. Nat. Retail Mchts. Assn., Nat. Mass Retail Inst. Home: 47 Chanticleer Rd Sudbury MA 01776 Office: Zayre Corp Framingham MA 01701

MURAWSKI, PHILLIP EDMUND, mfg. co. exec.; b. Chgo., Mar. 16, 1948; s. Edmund Anthony and Virginia Mary M.; B.A., U. Ill., 1970; m. Elaine A. Kowalczyk, June 19, 1971; 1 son, David Phillip. Structural designer Creative Displays, 1970-72; with Alkco Mfg. Co., Franklin Park, Ill., 1972—, advt. mgr., project estimator mgr., indsl. graphic designer, 1972—. Charter mem. Greenpeace Found., 1978—. Mem. Illuminating Engring. Soc. (dir. Chgo. sect.), Nat. Wildlife Fedn. Roman Catholic. Office: 11500 Melrose Ave Franklin Park IL 60131

MURCHISON, DAVID CLAUDIUS, lawyer; b. N.Y.C., Aug. 19, 1923; s. Claudius Temple and Constance (Waterman) M.; student U. N.C., 1942-43; A.A., George Washington U., 1947, J.D. with honors, 1949; m. June Margaret Guilfoyle, Dec. 19, 1946; children—David Roderick, Brian Cameron, Courtney Virginia, Bradley Duncan, Stacy Constance. Admitted to D.C. bar, 1949; with firm Dorr, Hand & Dawson, N.Y.C., 1949-50, Howrey, Simon, Baker & Murchison, Washington, 1956—; legal asst. under sec. of army, 1949-51; counsel motor vehicle, railroad equipment, textile, aircraft and ordnance and shipbldg. divs. NPA, 1951-52; asso. gen. counsel Small Def. Plants Adminstrn., 1952-53; legal adviser, asst. to chmn. FTC, 1953-55. Served with AUS, 1943-45. Mem. Am. (chmn. com. internat. restrictive bus. practices, sect. antitrust law 1954-55, sect. adminstrv. law, sect. litigation), Fed., D.C., N.Y. bar assns., Phi Delta Phi, Order of Coif. Republican. Clubs: Metropolitan, Chevy Chase. Home: 5417 Blackistone Rd Westmoreland Hills MD 20016 Office: 1730 Pennsylvania Ave Washington DC 20006

MURCHISON, JOHN PRESCOTT, JR., mortgage banker; b. Atlanta, July 5, 1926; s. John Prescott and Gertrude Ware (Burch) M.; student U. Wis., 1943-48; B.S. in Bus. Adminstrn., Am. U., 1955; m. Betty M. Bates, Aug. 14, 1948; children—Christy (Mrs. Leonardo Aden), Brett, Sheila, Betty, Venice, John III. With Murchison Bros., real estate, Washington, 1950-56, Murchison Realty Co., Washington, 1956-63; with Murchison Realty Co., Inc., Washington, 1963—, pres., 1968—; pres. Inter-City Mortgage Corp., Washington, 1968—; brs. advisory bd. Riggs Nat. Bank; chmn. Municipal Title & Escrow Co., Inc.; commr. Neighborhood Reinvestment Commn. Lectr. mortgage banking, real estate financing and licensing; ins. broker, real estate cons. and appraiser. Mem. Washington Mayor's Ad Hoc Com. Landlord Tenant Relations, City Council Adv. Panel Usury Ceilings. Served with Armed Forces, 1945-46. Mem. Nat. Assn. Real Estate Brokers, Washington Real Estate Brokers Assn. (dir., past v.p.), Nat., Washington (dir., past mem. mortgage and finance com.) bds. realtors, United, Washington mortgage bankers assns. (gov.), Mortgage Bankers Assn. Am., Fed. Nat. Mortgage Assn. (loan corr.), Govt. Nat. Mortgage Assn. (loan corr.), D.C. C. of C. (past treas.). Home: 1433 Primrose Rd NW Washington DC 20012 Office: 3007 Georgia Ave NW Washington DC 20001

MURDOCH, KEITH RUPERT, publisher; b. Melbourne, Australia, Mar. 11, 1931; s. Keith and Elisabeth Joy (Greene) M.; came to U.S., 1974; M.A., Worcester Coll., Oxford, Eng., 1953. Chmn., City Post Pub. Corp., pub. New York Post, New York mag., New West mag. and Village Voice, 1977—; chmn. News Am. Pub., Inc., pub. The Star, San Antonio Express and News, News Internat., Ltd. Group, London, Eng.; chief exec., mng. dir. News, Ltd. Group & Asso. Cos., Australia. Office: 210 South St New York NY 10002*

MURDOCH, WILLIAM FRANCIS, JR., real estate investment exec.; b. Pitts., Jan. 22, 1931; s. William Francis and Adeline Henrietta (Hrubecky) M.; B.A., Princeton U., 1952; M.B.A., Harvard U., 1956, m. Mary Robinson Cullens, Jan. 25, 1958: children—Mary Rodman, Elizabeth Patterson, Timothy Robinson, Kate Cullens. Real estate developer, Pitts., 1956-62: mgmt. cons. Booz Allen & Hamilton, N.Y.C., 1962-65; mgr. comml. devel. Columbia, The Rouse Co., Balt., 1965-68; v.p. Equity Investments, Eastdil Realty, Inc., N.Y.C., 1968-70; pres. Schroder Real Estate Corp., N.Y.C., 1970-74: pres. Hubbard Real Estate Investments, N.Y.C., 1974—. Trustee Princeton Day Sch., 1972—. Served to lt. arty. U.S. Army, 1952-54. Mem. Urban Land Inst., Nat. Assn. Real Estate Investment Trusts (gov.). Republican. Presbyterian. Home: 33 Cleveland Ln Princeton NJ 08540 Office: Hubbard Real Estate Investments 165 Broadway New York NY 10080

MURGAS, WILLIAM JOSEPH, mfg. co. exec.; b. Plainfield, N.J., Mar. 12, 1931; s. William Joseph and Caroline Josephine M.; B.S.M.E., Lafayette Coll., 1953; M.S.M.E., U. Wis., 1961. Sr. engr. steam turbine dept. Allis-Chalmers, 1953-63; with Velvac, Inc., New Berlin, Wis., 1963—, pres., 1965—. Bd. dirs. ARC; dist. vice chmn Waukesha County council Boy Scouts Am., active nat. Boy Scouts Am. Served with U.S. Army, 1954-56. Mem. ASME, Council Ind. Mgrs. (dir.), Engrs. Soc. Milw., Am. Mgmt. Assn., Ind. Bus. Assn. Wis., Nat. Assn. Emergency Med. Technicians, Wis. Emergency Med. Technicians Assn., Phi Beta Kappa, Tau Beta Pi. Club: Masons. Patentee in field. Home: 180 Stockton Ct Brookfield WI 53005 Office: 2900 S 160th St New Berlin WI 53151

MUROGA, KO, electronics corp. exec.; b. Nishinomiya, Hyogo-ken, Japan, July 20, 1928; came to U.S., 1978; s. Kunitake and Kimiko (Okumura) M.; B.E., Kyoto (Japan) U., 1952, D.Engring., 1962; M.S., M.I.T., 1954; m. Yasuko Narutomi, Jan. 3, 1956; children—Toru, Ikuko. With Nippon Electric Co. Ltd., 1954—, mgr. software devel. dept., Tokyo, 1969-75, gen. mgr. switching systems div., 1975-78, exec. v.p. NEC Am., Inc., Melville, N.Y., 1978-80, pres., 1980—. Recipient Kajii Spl. award, 1976. Mem. Inst. Electronics and Communications Engrs. of Japan, Eta Kappa Nu. Home: 1 Warton Pl Garden City NY 11530 Office: NEC America Inc 532 Broad Hollow Rd Melville NY 11747

MURPHREE, WILLIAM ROY, ins. cons.; b. Mobile, Ala., Dec. 27, 1947; s. William Henry and Grace (Moore) M.; B.S., Auburn U., 1970; A.A., Marion Mil. Inst., 1967; m. Susan Lynn Hill, Aug. 10, 1974; 1 dau., Alma Michelle. Pres., Smith-Murphree, Inc., Auburn, Ala., 1975—. Adminstrv. bd. First United Meth. Ch., Opelika, Ala., 1978—. Served as pilot U.S. Army, 1970-73. C.L.U.; registered profl. disability and health ins. underwriter. Mem. Nat. Assn. Life Underwriters (recipient 6 Nat. Quality awards, 6 Sales Achievement awards), Nat. Assn. Health Underwriters, Nat. Assn. Estate Planning Councils, Lee County Estate Planning Council (pres. 1980), Am. Soc. C.L.U.'s, Montgomery chpt. C.L.U.'s, Million Dollar Roundtable (life mem.). Republican. Methodist. Clubs: Kiwanis, Elks, Meth. Men's (v.p. 1977-79). Home: 1104 Willow Run Dr Opelika AL 36801 Office: PO Box 910 112 S Ross St Auburn AL 36830

MURPHREE, WILLIAM THOMAS, mgmt. cons. co. exec.; b. Milliken, Colo., Apr. 7, 1928; s. Edward A. and Sarah E. (Jackson) M.; A.A., San Antonio Coll., 1951; B.S. in Elec. Engring., B.S. in Bus., U. Colo., 1954; postgrad. U. Wis., 1959; m. Sherri R. Swan, June 17, 1965; children—Vana L., Duke, Carrie, Patrick, Joel. Design and devel. engr. Cutler-Hammer Co., Milw., 1954-59; prodn. mgr. Tex. Instruments Co., Dallas, 1959-61; planning engr. Martin-Marietta Co., Denver, 1962; plant mgr. Hewlett-Packard Co., 1962-64; budget dir. NASA, 1965; prin. M.P. & Assos., Omaha, 1965-80; pres. Colonna of Colo. Co., Denver, 1977—; mgmt. cons. Murphree-Palmer Advt. Group, Ltd., 1977—; instr. math. U. Wis., 1958-59, instr. profl. mgmt. devel., 1967—. Served with U.S. Army, 1946-49. Registered profl. engr., Mo., Colo. Mem. IEEE, Am. Inst. Indsl. Engrs., Am. Hosp. Assn., Hosp. Mgmt. Systems Soc., Kansas City C. of C. Clubs: Toastmasters, Elks, President's. Home: PO Box 428 Center City CO 80427 Office: 811 Lincoln St Denver CO 80203

MURPHY, ALAN CHARLES, accountant; b. Frederic, Wis., July 20, 1937; s. Edward Lester and Irene Margaret (Rogers) M.; B.B.A., U. Wis., Madison, 1959. With Stokely Van Camp, Inc., Milltown, Wis., 1955-59; partner Touche Ross & Co., Mpls./St. Paul, 1960-74; partner, dir. audit opns. Touche Ross & Co., Dayton, Ohio, 1974—. Served to capt. U.S. Army, 1959-60. C.P.A., Wis., Minn., Ohio. Recipient Citizenship award Am. Legion, 1955. Mem. Ohio Soc. C.P.A.'s, Am. Inst. C.P.A.'s, Inst. Internal Auditors, Nat. Soc. Accountants for Coops., Beta Alpha Psi. Clubs: Dayton Racquet, Sycamore Creek Country, Trailsend. Home: 4719 Wilmington Pike Kettering OH 45440 Office: 1700 Courthouse Plaza NE Dayton OH 45402

MURPHY, AUSTIN DE LA SALLE, banker, educator, economist; b. N.Y.C., Nov. 20, 1917; s. Daniel Joseph and Marie Cornelia (Austin) M.; A.B., St. Francis Coll., Bklyn., 1938; A.M., Fordham U., 1940, Ph.D., 1949; m. Mary Patricia Halpin, June 12, 1948 (dec. May 1974); children—Austin de la Salle, Owen Gerard; m. 2d, Lee Chilton Romero, Dec. 14, 1974; stepchildren—Thomas, Robert. Instr. econs. Fordham U., 1938-41, Georgetown U., 1941-42; asst. statistician, statis, controls Bd. Econ. Warfare, 1942; sr. econs. research editor N.Y. State Dept. Labor, 1947-50; lectr. econs. Fordham U. Sch. Edn., 1946-55; instr. N.Y. U. Sch. Commerce, 1950-51; dean sch. bus. adminstrn. Seton Hall U., South Orange, N.J., 1950-55; Albert T.O. Neill prof. of Am. enterprise, dean sch. bus. adminstrn. Canisius Coll., Buffalo, 1955-62; dir. edn. dept. NAM, 1962-63; exec. v.p. Savs. Banks Assn. N.Y. State, 1963-70; chmn., pres. East River Savs. Bank; trustee Erie County Savs. Bank, 1958-63; charter trustee Savs. Bank Rockland County, 1965-70; dir. MSB Fund, Inc., Drayton Ins. Co., Tiger Investors Mortgage Ins. Co., Ban-Ser Ins. Mem. Livingston (N.J.) Charter Commn., 1954-55; mem. capital expenditures com. City of Buffalo, 1957-63; bd. dirs., v.p. N.Y. council Boy Scouts Am.; vice chmn. Invest-in-America; trustee Fordham U., 1972-79; mem. adv. council Seton Hall U., Pace U. Served 1st lt. Q.M. Corps, AUS, 1942-46. Mem. NAM (chmn. ednl. aids com. 1958-63), Am. Inst. Banking (adv. council), Am. Fin. Assn., Nat. Def. Transp. Assn. (life mem.), Nat. Assn. Mut. Savs. Banks (treas., dir.), Alpha Kappa Psi, Pi Gamma Mu. K.C. Author: Social Studies Review Book (with Fleming Frasca, and Mannion), 1946; Leading Problems of New Jersey Manufacturing Industries (with Bullock and Doerflinger), 1953; Reasons for Relocation, 1955; Forecast of Industrial Expansion in Buffalo and the Niagara Frontier, 1956; Metropolitan Buffalo Perspectives, 1958. Editor: Handbook of New York Labor Statistics, 1950. Home: 1060 Bay Head Dr Mamaroneck NY 10543 Office: 26 Cortlandt St New York NY 10007

MURPHY, BRIAN THOMAS GERALD, fin. exec.; b. Toronto, Ont., Can., Sept. 29, 1940; s. Thomas R. and Alice E. (Scarlett) M.; student Inst. Chartered Accts., 1961-67; m. Carol Anne Sharland, Aug. 20, 1971; children—Marley Anne, Kerrie Elizabeth, Thomas Brent. Supr. corp. acctg. Internat. Harvester Co. Ltd., Hamilton, Ont., 1967-73; office mgr., chief acct. F.W. Fearman Co. Ltd., Burlington, Ont., 1973-74; plant controller Gen. Bakeries Ltd., Hamilton, 1974-76, asst. to corp. controller, Toronto, 1976-80; controller Dun & Bradstreet Can., Toronto, 1980—. Mem. Ont. Amputee Sports Assn. (v.p. 1977-78). Home: 250 Rambler Ct Oakville ON L6H 3A6 Canada Office: 365 Bloor St E Toronto ON M4W 3L4 Canada

MURPHY, CHARLES HAYWOOD, petroleum co. exec.; b. El Dorado, Ark., Mar. 6, 1920; s. Charles Haywood and Bertie (Wilson) M.; ed. pub. schs., Ark., pvt. tutors; LL.D., U. Ark., 1966; m. Johnie Walker, Oct. 14, 1939; children—Michael Walker, Martha, Charles Haywood, III, Robert Madison. Ind. oil producer, 1939-50; pres. Murphy Oil Corp., 1950-72, chmn., dir., 1972—, also chief exec. officer; dir. 1st Tenn. Nat. Corp., 1st Nat. Bank, El Dorado. Mem. Ark. Bd. Higher Edn., 17 yrs.; bd. govs. Oschner Med. Found.; trustee Hendrix Coll.; bd. adminstrs. Tulane U. Served as infantryman World War II. Recipient citation for outstanding individual service in natural resource mgmt. Nat. Wildlife Fedn. Mem. Am. Petroleum Inst. (exec. com.), Nat. Petroleum Council (chmn.), 25 Yr. Club Petroleum Industry (past pres.). Office: Murphy Bldg El Dorado AR 71730*

MURPHY, CHARLES W., fin. planner; b. Richmond, Va., June 22, 1944; s. Francis Patrick and Regina Mary (Morgan) M.; B.S. magna cum laude, Va. Commonwealth U., 1973; M.B.A., U. S.C., 1977; m. Judith J. Jensen, Apr. 6, 1974. Asst. dir. U. S.C. Fin. Center, 1974; account exec. Merrill Lynch, 1974-75; account exec. Bache Halsey Stuart, Columbia, S.C., 1975-77; account exec. E.F. Hutton, Columbia, S.C., 1977—, asso. mgr., 1979—; lectr. fin. planning and pension funds Va. Commonwealth U., U. S.C., Erskine Coll. Served with U.S. Army, 1967. Mem. Inst. Cert. Fin. Planners, Internat. Assn. Fin. Planners, Omicron Delta Epsilon. Republican. Methodist. Clubs: Palmetto, Bull and Bear. Home: 107 Boulters Lock Rd Irmo SC 29063 Office: 2700 Middleburg Dr Suite 200 Columbia SC 29204

MURPHY, CHRISTOPHER JOSEPH, III, banker; b. Washington, Apr. 24, 1946; s. Christopher Joseph and Jean Olive (Connelly) M.; B.A. in Govt. and Internat. Relations, U. Notre Dame, 1968; J.D., U. Va., 1971; M.B.A. with distinction in Mgmt. and Fin., Harvard U., 1973; m. Carmen Morris Carmichael, Feb. 1, 1969; children—Christopher, Sean, Kelly, Kevin, Conor, Dillon. Admitted to Va. bar, 1971, U.S. Dist. Ct. bar for D.C., 1971; area dir. Nationwide Fin. Services, St. Louis, 1974-75; v.p. Citicorp. Mgmt. Services and Nationwide Fin. Services, St. Louis, 1975-76; sr. v.p. First Bank & Trust Co., South Bend, Ind., 1976-77, pres., chief exec. officer, 1977—; pres. FBT Bancorp, Inc., South Bend, 1979—, dir., 1972—. Bd. dirs. South Bend Symphony, 1977, Midwest Pops Orch., 1977, No. Ind. Med. Edn. Found., 1978; pres. Michiana Econ. Devel. Found., 1980; mem. exec. com., mem. bd. dirs. United Way St. Joseph County, 1980, gen. chmn. campaign, 1980; mem. adv. com. John F. Kennedy Center for Performing Arts, Washington. Nat. Endowment for Arts grantee, 1968. Mem. Am. Bar Assn., Ind. Bar Assn., Robert Morris Assos. Roman Catholic. Home: 1237 E Jefferson Blvd South Bend IN 46617 Office: PO Box 1602 133 S Main St South Bend IN 46634

MURPHY, FRANKLIN DAVID, physician, publisher, educator; b. Kansas City, Mo., Jan. 29, 1916; s. Franklin E. and Cordelia (Brown) M.; A.B., U. Kan., 1936; M.D., U. Pa., 1941, D.Sc., 1957; LL.D., Park Coll., 1955, Temple U., 1956, Bucknell U., 1962, Occidental Coll., 1962, U. So. Calif., U. Notre Dame, 1967, Loyola U., 1968; L.H.D., Kans. Wesleyan U., 1953, U. Judaism, 1961, Hebrew Union Coll., 1966, Hope Coll., 1968; D.Sc., U. Nebr., 1959; m. Judith Joyce Harris, Dec. 28, 1940; children—Judith (Mrs. Walter Dickey), Martha (Mrs. Craig Crockwell), Carolyn (Mrs. Reese Milner II), Franklin. Intern, Hosp. of U. of Pa., 1941-42, instr., 1942-44; instr. in medicine U. Kans., 1946-48, became dean Sch. Medicine and asso. prof. medicine, 1948-51, chancellor, 1951-60; chancellor U. Calif. at Los Angeles, 1960-68; chmn. bd., chief exec. officer Times-Mirror Co., Los Angeles, 1968—; dir. Ford Motor Co., Hallmark Cards, Inc., Bank of Am. Pres. Samuel Kress Found. Bd. dirs. Nat. Gallery Art, Los Angeles County Mus. Art. Served to capt. AUS, 1944-46. Named One of 10 outstanding young men in U.S., U.S. Jr. C. of C., 1949. Diplomate Am. Bd. Internal Medicine. Fellow A.C.P.; mem. Phi Beta Kappa, Sigma Xi, Alpha Omega Alpha, Beta Theta Pi, Nu Sigma Nu. Episcopalian. Home: 419 Robert Ln Beverly Hills CA 90210 Office: Times Mirror Co Times Mirror Sq Los Angeles CA 90053

MURPHY, GORDON NEIL, banker; b. Spokane, Apr. 12, 1929; s. Robert Clarence and Edna Ella (Beal) M.; student Modesto (Calif.) Jr. Coll., 1947-48; m. Alice Marie Rhodes, Sept. 6, 1948; children—Christine (Mrs. Jeffrey Landes), Michael J., Deborah A. (Mrs. Nicolas Herman), Terry A. With J.M. Wade Fruit Co., Wenatchee, Wash., 1948-51, Electric Smith, Inc., Spokane, 1951-53, Seattle 1st Nat. Bank, Spokane, 1953-56, Internat. Harvester Co., Ephrata, Wash., 1956-60; with Wash. Trust Bank, 1960—, asst. v.p., br. mgr. Spokane, 1967—. Past pres. Spokane County unit Am. Cancer Soc., Spokane chpt. Amateur Athletic Union; trustee Spokane Valley Gen. Hosp. Named Boss of Year, Spokane Valley Jr. C. of C., 1969. Mem. Am. Inst. Banking (past pres. Spokane), Spokane Valley C. of C. Club: Rotary (pres. Spokane Valley 1974-75, Sunrise 1979-80). Home: 11209 E 25th St Spokane WA 99206 Office: N 100 Pines Rd Spokane WA 99206

MURPHY, JOHN JOSEPH, JR., steel service center exec.; b. Syracuse, N.Y., July 21, 1920; s. John Joseph and Mary (Ryan) M.; student Powelson Bus. Inst., 1938, Cornell Coll., Mt. Vernon, Iowa, 1945, U. Ga., 1946; m. Eileen Hennessy, Aug. 24, 1946; children—Maureen, John Joseph III, Mary Sheila, William. With Peter A. Frasec & Co. Inc., N.Y.C., 1939-53, central N.Y. sales mgr., to 1953; founder, pres. Murphy & Nolan, Inc., Syracuse, 1953—. Served with USCG, 1942-44, USN, 1944-46. Mem. Steel Service Center Inst. (govtl. affairs com.). Home: 2 Wynnridge Rd Syracuse NY 13066 Office: 340 Peat St Syracuse NY 13201

MURPHY, LYNNE ANN, commodities broker; b. N.Y.C., Oct. 22, 1947; d. Stewart Francis and Mary M.; student Katharine Gibbs, N.Y.C., 1965-66, Seattle U., 1966-68. Commodity asst. Kipnis Commodities, Santa Barbara, Calif., 1970-71; pub. relations asst. Coca Cola Bottling Co. of N.Y., 1971-73; with Shearson Hayden Stone, N.Y.C., 1973-80, asst. v.p. commodities, 1977-78, v.p., 1979-80; v.p. commodities Paine Webber, N.Y.C., 1980—. Vol. Urban Minority Coalition, Harvard Bus. Sch., 1972-73. Mem. Futures Industry Assn. (sec. tng. dirs. div. 1979). Democrat. Club: Downtown Athletic (publicity com., athletic com.). Home: 348 E 78th St New York NY 10021 Office: 120 Broadway New York NY 10004

MURPHY, MATTHEW EDWARD, ins. co. exec.; b. S.I., Oct. 1, 1944; s. John David and Mary Louise (McKeever) M.; B.S., St. John's U., Jamaica, N.Y., 1976; grad. spl. intensive course in Chinese, Yale U., 1965; m. Beverly Marie Auriemma, Feb. 4, 1978; 1 son, Matthew McKeever. Programming systems rep. IBM, N.Y.C., 1969-75; mgr. systems programming team Atlantic Co., Roanoke, Va., 1975-80; ops. support mgr. Info. Services Group, div. Mars, Inc., 1980—. Served with USAF, 1964-68, USNR, 1973-75, USAR Spl. Forces, 1976-79. USMCR, 1979—. N.Y. State Regents scholar, 1962. Mem. Data Processing Mgmt. Assn., Am. Mgmt. Assn., Am. Radio Relay League, VFW, 82d Airborne Div. Assn., Sigma Rho. Roman Catholic. Club: K.C. Home: 9 Elm Ct Long Valley NJ 07853 Office: 2 Emery Ave Randolph NJ 07869

MURPHY, MICHAEL GORDON, banker; b. Dallas, Jan. 26, 1939; s. Elbert Gordon and Mary Emma (Ford) M.; B.B.A. in Fin., So. Meth. U., 1960; J.D., U. Tex., Austin, 1963; m. Charlotte Head, July 4, 1965; children—Shannon, Marshall. Mem. trust dept. Moody Nat. Bank, Galveston, Tex., 1963-64; admitted to Tex. bar, 1963; lawyer SEC matters Tenneco, Inc., 1964-67, Tex. Eastern Transmission, 1967-70; individual practice law, 1970-73; exec. v.p. Chem. Bank, Houston, 1973-78, pres., chief exec. officer, dir., 1978—. Mem. Ind. Bankers Assn. Tex. (dir.), Am. Mgmt. Assn. (pres.'s assn.). Methodist. Office: PO Box 66549 3201 Kirby Dr Houston TX 77006

MURPHY, MORGAN G., banker; b. Arlington, Ga., July 18, 1929; s. Paul F. and Mildred (Morgan) M.; student Brevard Coll., 1947-49; grad. La. State U. Grad. Sch. Banking; m. Jacolyn Holland, Mar. 2; children—Morgan S., Cherie Lynn, Mark R., David K. Pres., First State Bank & Trust Co., Albany, Ga.; past mem. faculty Ga. Banking Sch., U. Ga., Athens. Vice chmn. Dougherty County Bd. Edn. Served with USAF. Named 1st Albany Young Man of Year. Mem. Ga. Bankers Assn. (dir.), U.S. C. of C., Small Bus. Council, Albany C. of C. (past pres.). Methodist. Clubs: Albany Rotary (past pres.); Doublegate Country. Office: PO Box 8 Albany GA 31703

MURPHY, RANDALL KENT, cons. co. exec.; b. Laramie, Wyo., Nov. 8, 1943; s. Robert Joseph and Sally (McConnell) M.; student U. Wyo., 1961-65; postgrad. So. Meth. U., 1974; m. Cynthia Laura Hillhouse, Dec. 29, 1978; children—Caroline, Scott. Dir. mktg. Wycoa, Inc., Denver, 1967-70; dir. Communications Resource Inst., Dallas, 1971-72; account exec. Xerox Learning Systems, Dallas, 1973-74; regional mgr. Systema Corp., Dallas, 1975-76; pres. Performance Assos., also pres., dir. Acclivus Corp., Dallas, 1976—. Mem. Dallas Mus. Fine Arts. Served with AUS, 1966. Mem. Am. Soc. Tng. and Devel., Sales and Mktg. Execs. Internat., U. Wyo. Alumni Assn. Roman Catholic. Author: Performance Management of the Selling Process, 1979. Co-inventor The Randy-Band, multi-purpose apparel accessory, 1968. Home: 15702 Nedra Way Dallas TX 75248 Office: 13601 Preston Rd Dallas TX 75240

MURPHY, ROBERT BLAIR, mgmt. cons. co. exec.; b. Phila., Jan. 19, 1931; s. William Beverly and Helen Marie (Brennan) M.; B.S., Yale, 1953; m. Mary Emily Eckart, June 24, 1953; children—Stephen, Emily, Julia, David, Catherine. Indsl. engr. Dupont Corp., Aiken, S.C., 1953-55; mgr. sales can div. Reynolds Metals Co., Richmond, Va., 1955-69; gen. mgr. corrugated div. Continental Can Co., N.Y.C., 1969-73; v.p. and gen. mgr. beverage div. Am. Can Co., Greenwich, Conn., 1973-75; asso. Heidrick & Struggles, Inc., N.Y.C., 1976-78, v.p., 1978; v.p., mng. dir. Stamford office Spencer Stuart & Assos., 1978—. Clubs: Round Hill, Riverside Yacht (Greenwich), Yale (N.Y.C.). Home: 11 Tomahawk Ln Greenwich CT 06830 Office: 3 Landmark Sq Stamford CT 06901

MURPHY, ROBERT FRANCIS, finance co. exec.; b. N.Y.C., Dec. 30, 1921; s. Frank J. and Mary (Neely) M.; B.S., Columbia U., 1949, Grad. Sch. Bus., 1949-50; m. Madeline L. Fleming, June 16, 1951; children—Marilyn, R. Morgan, Philip M. With Gen. Motors Acceptance Corp., 1949, treas., 1960-67, v.p. charge staff adminstrn., 1967-70, v.p. overseas ops., 1970-74, v.p. charge devel. staff, 1975-77, exec. v.p. ops., U.S., Can., overseas, 1978-80, pres., 1980—, also mem. exec. com.; chmn. bd. Motors Ins. Corp., 1980—, also dir., mem. exec. com. Office: 767 Fifth Ave New York NY 10153

MURPHY, THOMAS AQUINAS, ret. automobile co. exec.: b. Hornell, N.Y., Dec. 10, 1915; s. John Joseph and Alma (O'Grady) M.; B.S., U. Ill., 1938; m. Catherine Rita Maquire, June 7, 1941; children—Catherine Murphy Rowan, Maureen Murphy Fay, Thomas Aquinas. With Gen. Motors Corp., 1938—, asst. treas., N.Y.C., 1959-67, comptroller, Detroit, 1967-68, treas., 1968-70; v.p. in charge car and truck group, 1970-72, vice chmn., 1972-74, chmn., chief exec. officer, 1974-80, ret., 1980. Served with USNR, 1943-46. Mem. Motor Vehicle Mfrs. Assn., Fin. Execs. Inst., Nat. Assn. Accountants, Greater Detroit Bd. Commerce. Clubs: Recess (Detroit); Bloomfield Hills (Mich.) Country: Huron River Hunting and Fishing (Farmington). Office: 3044 W Grand Blvd Detroit MI 48202

MURPHY, THOMAS JOHN, metal furniture mfg. co. exec.; b. St. Paul, Dec. 9, 1937; s. Edward Charles and Appolonia Lee (Weihs) M.; B.A. in Bus. Adminstrn., Coll. St. Thomas, 1968; m. Shirley M. Dziuk, June 15, 1978. Prodn. supr. Univac div. Sperry Rand Co., 1960-72; ops. mgr. Datacraft Barbados Ltd. (W.I.), 1972-73; plant mgr. Litton Microwave Cooking Products div. Litton Co., 1973-78; v.p. mfg. Homecrest Industries Inc. div. Sperry and Hutchinson Co., Wadena, Minn., 1978—; instr. fin. Am. Mgmt. Associates. Mem. Minn. Democratic Central Com., 1968-70; chmn. Minn. Dist. 48B Dem. Com., 1968-70; alt. del. Dem. Nat. Conv., 1968. Served with U.S. Army, 1957-59; Korea. Clubs: Rotary, Elks. Home: Stocking Lake Rural Route 4 Box 175 Menahga MN 56464 Office: PO Box 350 Wadena MN 56482

MURPHY, THOMAS VINCENT, mgmt. cons.; b. Phila., Oct. 12, 1928; s. James Frances and Mary Magdeline (McLaughlin) M.; bus. certificate Columbia Bus. Coll., 1948; student Temple U., 1948-49, 49-50, Alexander Hamilton Bus. Mgmt., 1954-59; m. Patricia Ann Martin, Apr. 26, 1952; children—Thomas Vincent, John M., Richard G., David G. With Nat. Cash Register Co., Phila., 1949-50, Stewart Equipment Co., Phila., 1950-60; with Bell Equipment Corp., leasing engineered equipment to petroleum industry, Los Angeles, 1960-78, exec. v.p., 1968-78, dir., 1972-78; pres. Bell Worldwide, Inc. (now Tiger Equipment & Services Ltd.), Chgo., 1973-78; individual practice as mgmt. cons., 1978—; dir. Bell Worldwide Ltd., Bell Caribbean N.V., Soon Douglas (Pte.) Ltd. Singapore, Cons. Quebec Iron & Titanium, Tin and Asso. Minerals, Royal Dutch Shell, Colvac Internat., Pacific Tin. Alyeska Pipeline Service Co., others. Bd. dirs. United Fund, Allentown, Pa., 1950-51. Judge of elections State of Pa., Springfield, 1953-54. Served with AUS, 1944-46. Decorated Purple Heart. Mem. Am. Mgmt. Assn., Am. Material Handling So. Inc., Franklin Inst. Mech. Arts, Smithsonian Instn., Mid-Am.-Arab C. of C. Clubs: Sleepy Hollow Country (Scarsborough, N.Y.); 21 Club Soc. (London, Eng.); Vesper (Phila.); World Trade Center, N.Y. Athletic (N.Y.C.). Contbr. to profl. pubs. Patentee in field. Home: O Hara Bldg 9501 Devon Rosemont IL 60018

MURPHY, WILLIAM GEORGE, III, accountant, financial cons.; b. Greenville, S.C., Aug. 18, 1942; s. William George and Ruth Sylvia (Vath) M.; B.S., Miss. State U., 1964; m. Patricia Michele Rotolo, Aug. 24, 1968; children—William George, Ray Joseph, Sean Michael. Tax staff Arthur Andersen & Co., New Orleans, 1967-71; controller Southdown Sugars, Inc., New Orleans, 1971-72, asst. to exec. v.p., 1972-73, v.p. fin., sec.-treas., 1973-77; cons., 1977—. Served with Signal Corps, U.S. Army, 1965-67. C.P.A., Miss., La. Mem. Am. Inst. C.P.A.'s, La. Soc. C.P.A.'s, Fin. Execs. Inst. Roman Catholic. Home: 4309 N Turnbull Dr Metairie LA 70002 Office: 2900 Kingman St Suite E Metairie LA 70002

MURPHY, WILLIAM PIERCE, data processing fin. exec.; b. Boston, June 6, 1937; s. Frank J. and Catherine A. M.; B.Sc. in Acctg., Babson Coll., 1962; M.B.A. in Fin., Boston Coll., 1968; m. Sheila Lane, Nov. 4, 1964; children—William Pierce, Kimberly L., Kristin L. Fin. mgr. Raytheon Corp., Lexington, Mass., 1962-64; controller Dynatech Corp., Cambridge, Mass., 1964-67; asst. to v.p. W.R. Grace, Cambridge, 1966-67; controller Ventron Corp., Beverly, Mass., 1967-69; v.p. fin. Internat. Data Group, Inc., Newton, Mass., 1969—; dir. Knowledge Sci. Industry, Inc. (White Plains, N.Y.), Internat. Data Group Inc., Advanced Tech. Publs., Inc. Mem. Soc. Advancement Mgmt., Am. Bus. Press. Office: 60 Austin St Newton MA 01810

MURRAY, ALICE PEARL, data processing co. exec.; b. Clearfield, Pa., Aug. 4, 1932; d. James Clifford and Leah Mae (Williams) M.; B.S., Pa. State U., 1954. With IBM, 1954—, systems service rep., Pitts., 1954-56, computer test center rep., Endicott, N.Y., 1956-58, edn. devel. coordinator, Endicott, 1958-59, adv. instr., Los Angeles, 1959-63, staff instr., Los Angeles, 1963-68, exec. edn. coordinator, 1968-74, sr. instr. Systems Sci. Inst., Los Angeles, 1974—; coordinator exhibit Calif. State Mus. Sci. and Industry; guest speaker before civic and profl. groups; guest instr. various univs. and colls.; profl. lectr. Recipient Distinguished Educator award IBM, 1974, also Outstanding Professionalism award, 1975; hon. citizen Tex., Alaska. Mem. Los Angeles County Art Mus., Pa. State Alumni Assn., Opera Assos., Hancock Park Hist. Soc., Delta Delta Delta. Republican. Clubs: Wilshire Country, Order Eastern Star, 100, Banning Soc. Home: 514 S Gramercy Pl Los Angeles CA 90020 Office: 3550 Wilshire Blvd Los Angeles CA 90010

MURRAY, GILMAN YOST, engring.-constrn. co. exec.; b. Springfield, Mass., Dec. 26, 1923; s. Arthur F. and Barbara (Gilman) M.; student Lehigh U., 1941-43; B.S. in Chem. Engring., Mass. Inst. Tech., 1944, M.S. in Metallury, 1948; postgrad. Cornell U., Ithaca, N.Y., 1945, N.C. State Coll., 1945; m. Winifred Jean Tipping, June 15, 1947; children—Scott Tipping, Craig Arthur, Victoria Anne. Research engr. Allis-Chalmers Co., Milw., 1948-50, Los Angeles, 1950-52, San Francisco, 1952-54; mgr. bus. devel. Western-Knapp Engring. Co., San Francisco, 1954-61; v.p. Bradberry Assos., 1961-67, merged with Bendix Corp., 1967, v.p., 1967-68; v.p. Hallanger & Assos. subs. Zapata Orgn., San Francisco, 1968-71; v.p., gen. mgr. Fluor Utah, Inc., San Mateo, 1971-74, sr. v.p., 1974-78; sr. v.p., div. mgr., dir. Ralph M. Parsons Co., Pasadena, Calif., 1978-79; pres., dir. Lurgi Corp., Belmont, Calif., 1979—. Served to lt. (j.g.), USNR, 1943-46. Recipient award merit Colo. Mining Assn., 1959. Registered profl. engr., Calif. Mem. Am. Inst. Mining Engrs., Am. Mining Congress, Mining and Metall. Soc. Am., Mass. Inst. Tech. Club No. Calif., Sigma Xi, Alpha Chi Sigma, Delta Sigma Phi. Elk. Clubs: Monterey Peninsula Country Club (Pebble Beach, Calif.); Bankers, Commonwealth of San Francisco. Home: 12355 Stonebrook St Los Altos Hills CA 94022 Office: One Davis Dr Belmont CA 94002

MURRAY, HUGH HARGRAVE, ins. exec.; b. Wilson, N.C., Oct. 30, 1908; s. Hugh Hargrave and Kate Whitfield (Connor) M.; B.S. in Aero. Engring., N.C. State Coll., 1932; postgrad. bus. mgmt. U. N.C., 1960; m. Martha Ruth Kendall, Dec. 15, 1934 (dec. Mar. 1959); children—Hugh Hargrave III, Picket Kendall (Mrs. Robert Lillard Guthrie), Thomas Connor; m. 2d, Lillian Ellison Allen, Nov. 24, 1960. Founder, pres., chmn. Asso. Insurers, Inc., Raleigh, N.C., 1933—; elector Internat. Ins. Hall of Fame, 1965, 80. Pres. exec. program U. N.C.; mem. adv. com. Fed. Flood Adminstrn., 1956; U.S. del. Inter-Am. Council Commerce and Prodn., 1950, 53. Served with USAAF, 1932, to lt. USNR, 1942-46. Mem. Ins. Inst. Am. (life gov.), Am. Inst. Property and Liability Underwriters (life trustee, pres. 1956-58, mem. exec. com., exam. bd.), U.S. C. of C. (ins. com. 1956-60), Nat. Assn. Ins. Brokers (dir.), Nat. (pres. 1948), Carolinas (past pres.) assns. mut. ins. agts., Nat. Assn. Casualty and Surety Agts., NAM, Ins. Soc. N.Y. Republican. Episcopalian. Kiwanian. Clubs: Army Navy (Washington), Carolina Country, Hound Ears, MacGregor Downs Country, Ponte Vedra. Home: 1809 Chester Rd Raleigh NC 27608 Office: 1033 Wade Ave PO Box 25968 Raleigh NC 27611

MURRAY, JAMES ALAN, econ./fin. cons.; b. Evansville, Ind., Oct. 2, 1942; s. William Dewey and Dorothy Marie (Gleason) M.; B.S., U. N.Mex., 1964; M.B.A., Harvard U., 1969; M.A. (NDEA fellow), U. Oreg., 1971, Ph.D., 1972; children—Heidi Lynn, Paul Alan, Kendra Leigh. Dir. fin. City of Boulder (Colo.), 1972-73, dir. adminstrv. services, 1973-74; v.p. Briscoe, Maphis, Murray & Lamont, Inc., Boulder, 1974-78, pres., 1978—, also dir.; adj. asso. prof. Grad. Sch. Public Affairs, U. Colo., Boulder, 1976—; dir. Briscoe-Maphis, Inc. Mem. open space adv. com. City of Boulder, 1972-74. Mem. Am. Econ. Assn., Western Econ. Assn., Am. Soc. Pub. Adminstrn., Water Pollution Control Fedn., Kappa Mu Epsilon, Pi Alpha Alpha. Home: 722 11th St Boulder CO 80302 Office: Briscoe Maphis Murray & Lamont Inc 2855 Valmont Rd Boulder CO 80302

MURRAY, JEROME WAYNE, mgmt. cons.; b. Dallas, Dec. 10, 1940; s. Cambridge Franklyn and Lois Eleven (Patton) M.; B.S. in Psychology, U. Santa Clara (Calif.), 1971, M.A. in Counseling Psychology summa cum laude, 1973; Ph.D. in Clin. Psychology, Heed U., Fla., 1977; m. Jayne Ann Basch, Mar. 19, 1977; children by previous marriage—Craig Franklyn, Jeffrey Byron, Christine Lodell. Founder, 1967, since exec. dir. Guidance Assos., mental health clinic, San Jose, Calif.; pres. Jerome Murray Cons. Resource, mgmt. cons., Saratoga, Calif., 1977—; mgmt. cons. Hewlett Packard Corp., 1977—, U. So. Calif., 1980—; chmn. legal affairs and research com. Nat. Alliance Family Life, 1977-80; chmn. profl. adv. bd. Parents without Partners, 1968—; bd. dirs. Contact Crisis Intervention Agy., 1969—. Served with USN, 1958-61. Mem. Am. Soc. Tng. and Devel., Am. Mgmt. Assn., Am. Assn. Marriage and Family Therapists, Am. Assn. Sex Educators, Counselors and Therapists, Am. Guild Tutors, Nat. Speakers Assn., Calif. Psychol. Assn., Calif. Assn. Marriage and Family Therapists. Republican. Author books, articles and tapes. Office: 960 Saratoga Ave Suite 214 San Hose CA 95129

MURRAY, LAWRENCE, mgmt. cons.; b. N.Y.C., May 10, 1939; s. Gilbert and Edna (Blatt) M.; B.A., Cornell U., 1961; M.B.A., U. Okla., 1966; children—Robert, Stacy, David, Daniel. Account exec. Merrill Lynch, Paramus, N.J., 1965-69; chmn., pres. Murray, Lind & Co., Inc., Jersey City, 1969-72; dir. investor relations IU Internat. Corp., Phila., 1972-73, dir. spl. projects, 1974-75; dir. fin. communications ARA Services, Inc., Phila., 1975-78; chmn., chief exec. officer Century Mgmt. Corp., West Chester, Pa., 1976—; lectr. bus. orgn. and mgmt. Bergen Community Coll., 1971-72. Pres., Congregation Beth Israel, Media, Pa., 1977-78. Served to lt. arty. U.S. Army, 1963-64. Mem. Nat. Investor Relations Inst. (pres. Phila. chpt. 1976-78), Internat. Council Shopping Centers. Author: The Organized Stockbroker, 1970; contbr. articles to profl. jours. Office: 720 N Five Points Rd Westchester PA 19380

MURRAY, MICHAEL RUSSELL, bank adminstr.; b. New Castle, Ind., Oct. 20, 1953; s. Merrill Russell and EvaJean (Yergin) M.; B.S. in Bus. Adminstrn., Central Mich. U., 1975; M.B.A., Ball State U., 1976; m. Debra Ann Brinkman, Jan. 24, 1981. Grad. asst. Ball State U., Muncie, Ind., 1975-76; personnel officer Central Mich. Bank & Trust, Big Rapids, Mich., 1976-78, asst. v.p., 1978-79; personnel officer Mfrs. Nat. Bank Detroit, 1979—; mem. faculty dept. mgmt. Ferris State Coll., Big Rapids, 1977-79. Mem. Am. Mgmt. Assn., Mich. Bankers Assn. (personnel com. 1977-80). Democrat. Clubs: Order of DeMolay, Rotary. Home: 24727 Verdant Sq Farmington Hills MI 48018 Office: 411 W Lafayette St Detroit MI 48226

MURRAY, PHILIP CHASE, retail mcht.; b. Nantucket, Mass., Aug. 16, 1921; s. Philip and Alice Burdette (Chase) M.; B.A., Oberlin Coll., 1943; m. Elizabeth Rodenhizer Cumby, July 15, 1945; children—Patricia, Diana, John. Rehab. rep. Am. Legion, Richmond, Va., 1947-51; pres. Murray's Toggery Shop Inc., Nantucket, Mass., 1951—, Murray's of the Vineyard, Vineyard Haven, Mass., 1976—; dir. Pacific Nat. Bank; trustee Nantucket Savs. Bank, 1973-76. Pres. Nantucket Cottage Hosp., 1976-79, trustee, 1961—. Served to capt. U.S. Army, 1943-46. Mem. Menswear Retailers Am. Republican. Episcopalian. Clubs: Nantucket Yacht, Pacific, Miacomet Golf, Masons, Rotary Club of Nantucket (pres., 1960-61). Home: Monomoy Rd Nantucket MA 02554 Office: 62 Main St Nantucket MA 02554

MURRAY, RALPH DAY, outdoor power equipment mfg. co. adminstr.; b. Boston, Dec. 27, 1944; s. John Joseph and Alberta (Sullivan) M.; B.S. in Mktg. and Advt., Northeastern U., 1967; M.B.A., Midwestern U., 1971; m. Ingrid E. Munnick, June 29, 1968; children—Sonjia Tara, Erik Day. Sales tng. rep. Caterpillar Co., Mentor, Ohio, 1972-73, field sales rep., 1973; dist. field mgr. The Toro Co., Boston, 1973-74, nat. accounta mgr., 1974-76, dir. sales consumer products, 1976-78, dir. mktg. and sales Internat. div., 1978-79, div. v.p. mktg., 1979—. Served with USAF, 1967-71. Mem. Minn. Zool. Soc., Minn. Orithologist Union. Democrat. Roman Catholic. Home: 1736 Walnut Ln Eagan MN 55122

MURRAY, ROBERT EVANS, cons. firm exec.; b. Lansdowne, Pa., Dec. 21, 1939; s. Jess E. and Mary E. (Esham) M.; B.S., U. Pa., 1961; M.B.A., Widener U., 1971; m. Kathleen M. Mitman, Nov. 27, 1965; children—Robert Evans, J. Bradley Scott. Indsl. engr. Nat. Gypsum Corp., Lansdale, Pa., 1961-67; mgr. distbn. planning Scott Paper Co., Phila., 1967-72; cons. A.T. Kearney Inc., N.Y.C., 1972-77; dir. logistics planning Standard Brands Inc., N.Y.C., 1977-79; prin. Booz Allen & Hamilton Inc., N.Y.C., 1979—; cons., lectr. in field. Mem. West Windsor (N.J.) Planning Bd., 1977—; mem. sewer adv. bd. City of West Windsor, 1977—; chmn. West Windsor Juvenile Conf. Com., 1974—; treas. Princeton Fraternal Service Assn., 1976—. Served with M.I., U.S. Army, 1961. Mem. Nat. Council Phys. Distbn. Mgmt., Am. Inst. Indsl. Engrs., Am. Mgmt. Assn., Nat. Materials Mgmt. Soc. Clubs: Masons, Shriners. Home: 20 Lorrie Ln Box 365 Princeton Junction NJ 08550 Office: Booz Allen and Hamilton 245 Park Ave New York NY 10167

MURRAY, THOMAS JAMES, fin. planner; b. Jamestown, R.I., Mar. 26, 1924; s. Daniel P. and Margaret A. (McPartland) M.; grad. Brown U., 1946; A.B., George Washington U., 1964; m. Betty Jean Shaw, July 2, 1948; children—Thomas James, Elizabeth Jean, Margaret Carolyn, John Michael, Peter Lawrence. Commd. ensign U.S. Navy, 1944, advanced through grades to lt. comdr., 1956; service in PTO, Korea; ret., 1964; asso., v.p. Marsh Mead Hill & Assos., fin. planners, Washington, 1964-78; propr. Thomas Murray Assos., fin. and assets planning, Kensington, Md., 1978—. C.L.U. Mem. Internat. Assn. Fin. Planners, Nat. Assn. Life Underwriters, Am. Soc. C.L.U.'s, Am. Legion, Ret. Officers Assn., St. Andrews Soc. Roman Catholic. Club: Rotary. Address: 9620 E Bexhill Dr Kensington MD 20795

MURRAY, VINCENT THOMAS, business exec.; b. N.Y.C., July 22, 1923; s. Thomas William and Gwin (LeMassena) M.; B.S. in Biology, Rutgers U., 1944; postgrad. Columbia U.; m. Septima Porcher, Oct. 14, 1950; children—Allison, Vincent Thomas, Jack. Salesman, Sayford Corp., N.Y.C., 1946-49, regional sales mgr., Atlanta, 1949-62; owner Murray Sales, Inc., paper and plastic products, Atlanta, 1963—; pres. Buccaneer Brokerage, Inc., Atlanta, 1967—. Lay reader, vestryman All Saints Episcopal Ch., Atlanta; 1st pres. Big Bros. Atlanta, 1960, nat. bd. dirs., 1963-66. Served with USMCR, 1942-45; PTO. Recipient award NCCJ, 1967, Spl. Father of Year award, 1977. Mem. Mfrs. Reps. Am. (dir.), Fulton County Grand

Jurors Assn. Republican. Clubs: Cherokee Town and Country, Optimists (life; past pres. N. Fulton chpt.). Home: 2874 Alpine Rd NE Atlanta GA 30305 Office: 2143 Plasters Bridge Rd NE Atlanta GA 30324

MURRIN, THOMAS JOSEPH, elec. mfg. co. exec.; b. N.Y.C., Apr. 30, 1929; s. Thomas and Jane (Dow) M.; B.S. in Physics, Fordham U., 1951; postgrad. U. Pitts., 1952-58, U. Ga., 1958-60; m. Marie Coyne, June 9, 1951; children—Kathleen Ann, Jeanne Marie, Mary Ruth, Cecilia Joan, Theresa Louise Murrin Robbins, M. Heidi, Thomas J.C., Claire Marie. With Westinghouse Electric Corp., 1951—, mfg. engr. Sharon Transformer div., 1952-57, supt. factory planning, Athens, Ga., 1957-59, European rep., 1959-61, mgr. mfg. planning, engring. mgr. Buffalo Motor & Gearing div., 1961-63, gen. mgr., 1963-65, v.p. mfg., Pitts., 1965-67, group v.p. aerospace, def. and marine, 1967-69, exec. v.p. def., 1969-71, exec. v.p. def. and public systems, 1971-74, sr. exec. v.p. pub. systems, 1974, pres. pub. systems co., 1975—. Past mem. U.S. del. NATO Indsl. Adv. Group; mem. Fordham council; bd. dirs. Duquesne U.; bd. dirs., exec. com. Regional Indsl. Devel. Corp. S.W. Pa.; mem. bd. exec. advisors Sch. Bus. Adminstrn., U. Miami; trustee Mercy Hosp. Recipient Encaenia award Fordham U., 1956, Achievement award in bus. Fordham U., 1976. Mem. Aerospace Industries Assn. (exec. com., bd. govs.), Machinery and Allied Products Inst., Beta Gamma Sigma. Contbr. articles to profl. publs. Patentee in field. Home: 8077 Dormar Ct Pittsburgh PA 15237 Office: Westinghouse Bldg Gateway Center Pittsburgh PA 15222

MURTAGH, JAMES P., lawyer; b. N.Y.C., Feb. 26, 1911; s. Thomas and Mary (Mee) M.; A.B., CCNY, 1931; J.D., Harvard U., 1934; m. Roberta Virginia Flaherty, Aug. 30, 1947; children—Melinda, James, Robert, Hilary, Richard, Kenneth. Admitted to N.Y. bar, 1935; asst. U.S. atty. So. Dist. N.Y., 1934-36; asso., then partner Simpson Thacher & Bartlett, 1936—. Mem. N.Y.C. Bd. Higher Edn., 1948-52. Served from 2d lt. to lt. col. AUS, 1942-45. Mem. Am. Bar Assn., Bar Assn. City N.Y., N.Y. County Lawyers Assn., Delta Sigma Phi, Phi Beta Kappa. Club: Larchmont Shore. Home: 9 Huguenot Dr Larchmont NY 10538 Office: 350 Park Ave New York NY 10022

MURTAGH, THOMAS JOHN, investment banker; b. San Francisco, July 25, 1930; s. James Joseph and Teresa (Murphy) M.; B.S., U.S. Naval Acad., 1953; postgrad. bus. adminstrn. N.Y. U., 1960-62; m. Maurine M. Mills, Feb. 3, 1973; children—Sean Travis, Hugh Keenan. Vice-pres., dir. Smith Barney & Co., N.Y.C., 1959-72; mng. dir. Western Am. Bank, London, 1973-74; sr. v.p., dir. Dean Witter Reynolds Inc., N.Y.C., 1975—; dir. Puritan Bennet Corp. Served with USN, 1953-58. Clubs: Brook, Knickerbocker, Maidstone. Home: 200 E 66th St New York NY 10021 Office: Dean Witter Reynolds 130 Liberty St New York NY 10006

MUSE, EDWARD T., mfg. co. exec.; b. Ft. Worth, Sept. 24, 1942; s. Ewell H. and Mary T. Muse, Jr.; student U. Tex., 1961-64, St. Edward's U., 1964-65; student in mktg. U. Ams., 1966; m. Marie Rilling, June 30, 1957; children—Michelle, Maddox, Hunter. Account exec. Shearson Hammill Co., San Antonio, 1968-70; pres. Smoker Products, Inc., Mabank, Tex., 1970—. Served with USMCR, 1962-67. Mem. Nat. Sporting Goods Assn., Nat. Housewares Mfg. Assn., Nat. Premium Sales Execs. Assn., Barbecue Industry Assn. Republican. Methodist. Club: Cedar Creek Country. Patentee electric meat smoker, multi smoker. Home: Route 5 Box 19 Kemp TX 75143 Office: PO Drawer S Mabank TX 75147

MUSE, SCOTT THOMAS, JR., real estate investment co. exec.; b. Oklahoma City, Sept. 6, 1930; s. Scott T. and Cathren (Lowry) M.; student Southwestern Coll. at Oklahoma City, 1950; m. Lesta Lou Little, Aug. 7, 1950; children—Dan T., Pamela S., Matthew S., Mark J. Mgr., Agrl. Stablzn. and Conservation Office, U.S. Agr. Dept., Morton County, Elkhart, Kans., 1956-65; farmer, land devel., Morton County, 1954-70; v.p. Cavalier Constrn. Co., Oklahoma City, 1969—; pres. Fireside Properties, Phoenix, 1969—; pres., owner Muse Investment Co., Oklahoma City, 1968—; pres. Whale Systems, Oklahoma City, 1971—; pres. Oklahoma City Southwestern Coll., 1976-80. Pres. Sch. Bd., Rolla, Kans., 1962-70, mem. City Council, Rolla, 1963-64, mayor, 1965-66. Mem. Western Bd. Edn. Oklahoma City Southwestern Coll., 1967-72. Named Outstanding Alumnus, Oklahoma City Southwestern Coll., 1966. Home: 6201 Commodore Ln Oklahoma City OK 73132 Office: 535 N Ann Arbor St Oklahoma City OK 73127

MUSGRAVE, CLARENCE REESE, publishing co. exec.; b. Toledo, July 25, 1930; s. Clarence Shaeffer and Virginia Gay (Hamer) M.; B.A., U. Rochester, 1955; m. Sandra Elaine Saunders, Sept. 6, 1969; children—Diana Gay, William Reese, Scott David, Melissa Margaret. Mgr. zone sales Procter & Gamble Co., Balt., 1955-61; area sales mgr. Edward Dalton div. Mead Johnson Co., Balt., 1961-62; various sales mgmt. positions Lebhar-Friedman Inc., N.Y.C., 1962-71, v.p. sales, 1971—. Served with USMCR, 1950-51. Mem. Sigma Chi. Episcopalian. Clubs: Sales Execs. N.Y., Univ. N.Y., Advt. N.Y., Masons, Chgo. Press. Home: 7 Lake Rd Upper Saddle River NJ 07458 Office: Lebhar-Friedman Inc 425 Park Ave New York NY 10022

MUSHMAN, WILLIAM C., mfg. co. exec.; b. Chgo., Nov. 26, 1915; s. John William and Ella (McNellis) M.; B.S. in Mech. Engring., Purdue U., 1938; postgrad. Harvard Sch. Bus. Adminstrn., 1938-39; M.B.A., U. Chgo., 1949; m. Mary A. Swope, Dec. 22, 1945 (dec. Nov. 1975); children—William C., Catherine, Mary Ellen; m. 2d, Bettye Martin, Aug. 4, 1979; 1 stepdau., Claudia Koeze. With Imperial Brass, Chgo., 1939-41; asst. to exec. v.p. Imperial Eastman, Chgo., 1946-50, exec. v.p., 1950-58, pres., chief exec. officer, 1958-68; pres. chief exec. officer I-T-E Imperial Corp., Phila., 1968-76, also dir.; vice chmn., dir. Gould Inc., 1976—; dir. Arvin Industries, INA Investment Securities, Phila. Nat. Bank, Walgreen's, Rome Cable, Gear Inc., Wallace Bus. Forms, Carson Pirie Scott & Co.; instr. exec. program U. Chgo., 1966, guest lectr. quar., 1966-68; guest lectr. Dartmouth, 1977; Am. Mgmt. Assn. Seminars. Mem. Council, Grad. Sch. Bus., U. Chgo., pres. council Purdue U.; trustee Am. U., Fenwick High Sch., Rosary Coll., Rider Coll.; bd. dirs. Inst. Achievement Human Potential, Phila. Served with AUS, World War II. Mem. Am. Mgmt. Assn., ASME, Instrument Soc. Am., Soc. Automotive Engrs., Sigma Xi, Tau Beta Pi, Pi Tau Sigma. Clubs: Union League (Phila.); Met. (N.Y.C.); Chgo., Union League, Econ. (Chgo.); Westmoreland (Ill.) Country. Home: Northern Cross Farm Erwinna PA 18920 Office: Gould Inc Rolling Meadows IL 60008

MUSIC, JOHN FARRIS, mgmt. cons. co. exec.; b. Childress, Tex., Oct. 5, 1921; s. Rondo William and Madeline Callie (Hanson) M.; B.A. in Chemistry with honors, U. Tex., 1946, Ph.D. in Phys. Chemistry with honors, 1951; m. Barbara Ellen Isett, Sept. 20, 1942; children—Barbara Helen, Elizabeth Ann. With Gen. Electric Co., Richland, Wash., 1951-60, internal cons.-research and devel. mgmt., Schenectady, 1960-62, strategic planning for def. and space groups, King of Prussia, Pa., 1962-71; pres. Strategic Mgmt., Inc., Paoli, Pa., 1971—. Mem. Am. Chem. Soc., Am. Phys. Soc., Inst. Mgmt. Scis., Sigma Xi, Phi Beta Kappa, Phi Lambda Upsilon. Author: the Logic of Business Success...And How to Apply It, 1978. Home: 590 Bair Rd Berwyn PA 19312

MUSOLINO, JOSEPH RICHARD, banker; b. Quincy, Ill., Mar. 19, 1937; s. John and Harriett (Vanden Boon) M.; B.S. in Aero. Engring., Okla. U., 1959, M.B.S. in Bus., 1964; m. Sue Skaggs Fowler, Sept. 9, 1978; children—Camille, John Mark, Katherine Fowler. With Republic Nat. Bank of Dallas, 1964—, v.p., 1968-72, sr. v.p., 1972-74, exec. v.p., 1974-79, vice-chmn. bd., 1979-80, pres., 1980—. Bd. dirs. Baylor U. Med. Center Found., United Way Met. Dallas, N. Tex. Commn.; trustee Children's Med. Center, Dallas Garden Center, Tex. Bur. Econ. Understanding, Nat. Jewish Hosp. and Research Center, Baylor Coll. Sch. Dentistry, Nat. Asthma Center; mem. Dallas Assembly; pres. Dallas Clearing House Assn.; asso. bd. So. Meth. U. Sch. Bus.; adv. bd. Jr. League Dallas; deacon Highland Park Presbyn. Ch. Served with USN, 1960-63. Mem. Am. Bankers Assn. (nat. AIB com.), Tex. Bankers Assn., Young Pres.'s Orgn., U.S. C. of C. (banking, monetary and fiscal affairs com.). Club: Dallas Country. Office: Republic Nat Bank Pacific Ervay and Bryan Sts Dallas TX 75201

MUSSER, ROBERT DANIEL, JR., resort hotel operator; b. Circleville, Ohio, Apr. 29, 1932; s. Robert Daniel and Elizabeth (Woodfill) M.; B.A., Dartmouth Coll., 1955; m. Amelia Maverick Epler, Nov. 30, 1957; children—Robin Epler, Margaret Stewart, Robert Daniel. With Grand Hotel Co. subs. Musser-Mackinac Holding Co., Inc., Mackinac Island, Mich., 1957—, pres., chief exec. officer, gen. mgr., 1962—, pres., owner holding co., 1979—. Chmn. Mich. Tourist Commn. Served with AUS, 1955-57. Mem. Mich., Am. hotel and motel assns., Hotel Sales Mgmt. Assn., Mackinac Island C. of C. Episcopalian. Clubs: Mid-Am. (Chgo.); Mackinac Island Yacht. Home: 13855 Peacock Rd Laingsburg MI 48848 Office: Grand Hotel Mackinac Island MI 49757 also Grand Hotel Co 3401 E Saginaw St Lansing MI 48912

MUSSER, WARREN VANDYKE, diversified co. exec.; b. Harrisburg, Pa., Dec. 15, 1926; B.S. in Indsl. Engring., Lehigh U., 1949; m. Betty K. Umstad; children—Craig V., Joan V., Peter U. Salesman, Hornblower & Weeks-Hemphill Noyes, Phila., 1950-53; founder, pres. Musser and Co., Inc., Phila., 1953-65; founder, chmn., pres. Lancaster Corp., Phila., 1953-68; chmn., chief exec. officer Safeguard Industries, Inc., King of Prussia, Pa., 1968—; vice chmn., chmn. exec. com. dir. Safeguard Bus. Systems, Inc.; dir. Gino's Inc., UGI Corp. Mem. World Bus. Council, Automotive Pres.'s Council. Club: Aronimink Golf (Newton Square, Pa.). Office: 630 Park Ave King of Prussia PA 19406

MUTH, ARNOLD EDWARD, gas utility co. exec.; b. Eveleth, Minn., Sept. 13, 1919; s. Arnold John and Anna Dorothy (Langhorst) M.; student Northeastern U., 1937-39, 45, Harvard U., 1939-40, M.I.T., 1940-41, Boston Tech. Inst., 1942-43, Farnsworth Inst., 1944, Tufts U., 1948, U. Cin., 1962, Rutgers U., 1971-72; m. A. Corinne Boyd, Sept. 27, 1941 (dec.); children—Brenton A., Jeffrey B., Garry A. Engr., Holtzer-Cabot Electric, Boston, 1941-45; mgr. market devel. CHARG-A-PLATE div. Farrington Mfg. Co., Boston, 1945-47; dealer supr. Utilities Distbrs. Inc., Portland, Maine, 1947-54; with Suburban Propane Gas Corp., Whippany, N.J., 1955—, dist. sales mgr., 1955-56, regional sales mgr., 1956-59, regional mgr., 1959-65, mktg. coordinator, 1966-72, asst. dir. mktg., 1972-78, sr. research analyst, 1978—; instr. Southeastern Mass. U., 1951-53; chmn. bd. dirs. Associated Lawyers Service Inc., 1974-78; dir. Harding Assos. Inc., 1975-78. Orgn. dir. Norumbega council Boy Scouts Am., 1950-52; program chmn. N.J. Energy Council, 1978. Mem. Nat. LP Gas Assn., Ohio LP Gas Assn., Am. Mktg. Assn., Solar Energy Industry Assn. Methodist. Clubs: Merlands Country, Greenhills (Ohio) Country, Eagles, Co-author Ohio State regulations of LP gas industry, 1964, State and Nat. LP Gas Assns. affiliation agreement, 1961; adv. to media, industry, govtl. and pvt. research projects. Home: 5 Ellsworth Ave Morristown NJ 07960 Office: PO Box 206 Whippany NJ 07981

MUTH, RAYMOND ALBERT, ins. agt.; b. Newark, N.Y., May 19, 1912; s. Walter R. and Mary (Gleason) M.; student Wharton Sch., U. Pa., 1931-34; m. Ellen Van Duser, June 27, 1940; children—Walter Norris, Marilyn Louise. With George W. Muth & Son Agy., Newark, N.Y., 1935—, now pres. Past chmn. Wayne County Civil Service Commn.; chmn. major gifts div., 50 million dollar fund Geneva Presbytery, U.P. Ch., now mem. theol. edn. com. Past bd. Visitors Newark State Sch. Served with USNR, 1943-46. Named Man of Year, Newark Courier Gazette, 1965. Mem. Nat. (dir.), N.Y. State (past pres.) assns. ins. agts., Eastern Agts. Conf. (pres. 1968), Newark C. of C. (past pres.), N.Y. State Synod Council U.P. Men (past pres.). Mason, Elk, Rotarian (past pres.). Home: 109 Prospect St Newark NY 14513 Office: 105 E Miller St Newark NY 14513

MUTH, VICTOR OLIVER, engring. exec.; b. Milw., Nov. 11, 1930; s. Victor Ernst and Irene (Kurriger) M.; B.S.E.E., U. Wis., 1953, M.S.E.E., 1963; A.M.P., Harvard U., 1976; m. Ann Louise Melcher, June 20, 1953. Engr., Hamilton Standard div. UAC, Windsor Locks, Conn., 1953-56; engring. dir. Delco Electronics div. Gen. Motors Corp., Milw., 1956-71; with Xerox Corp., 1971—, v.p. engring and v.p. mfg. office products div., Dallas, 1973-76, pres. Diablo Systems, Hayward, Calif., 1976-79, v.p. Reprographic Tech. Group, Rochester, N.Y., 1979—; dir. Diablo Systems. Club: Rochester Yacht. Patentee automobile crash sensor, typewriter printing element. Home: 2 Wood Hill Rd Pittsford NY 14534 Office: 800 Phillips Rd W-105 Webster NY 14580

MUZIC, MARILYN ANN, accountant; b. New Orleans, Nov. 14, 1945; d. Roy and Sylvia Marie (Vlachovsky) Jones; B.B.A. magna cum laude, Cleve. State U., 1975, M.B.A., 1977; m. John Michael Muzic, June 27, 1964; children—John Michael, Kimberly Ann, Christine Marie. Staff acct. Cook United, Inc., Cleve., 1976-79, sr. acct., 1977-78, acctg. supr., 1978-79; acctg. mgr. Bobbie Brooks, Inc., Cleve., 1979—. Cons., Jr. Achievement, 1980—. C.P.A., Ohio. Mem. Pentelicus, Cleve. State Alumni Assn., Beta Gamma Sigma. Home: 36 Oviatt Dr Northfield Center OH 44067 Office: 3830 Kelley Ave Cleveland OH 44114

MYERHOLTZ, EARL FREDERICK, metals co. exec.; b. Oak Harbor, Ohio, Oct. 12, 1923; s. Ernest Henry and Viola Louise (Foreman) M.; B.S., Va. Poly. Inst., 1948; m. Betsy Jane Draper, June 20, 1946; children—Suzanne (Mrs. David Cameron), Pamela Jean (Mrs. Norman Brose). With Gen. Electric Co., 1948-64, mgmt. trainee, Lynn, Mass., 1948-51, mfg. mgmt., Evendale, Ohio, 1951-61, mgr. mfg. engring., 1961-64; with TRW, 1964—, dir. mfg. engring., v.p., gen. mgr., mech. products div., Cleve., 1966-71, v.p., gen. mgr. Marlin Rockwell div., Jamestown, N.Y., 1971-79, v.p., gen. mgr. Indsl. Products group, Cleve., 1979—; dir. 1st Nat. Bank Jamestown. Bd. dirs. YMCA, Jamestown, 1973—, WCA Hosp., 1976—. Served as sgt. AUS, 1942-46. Decorated Bronze Star. Mem. Anti-Friction Bearing Mfrs. Assn. (dir. 1971—, pres. 1976-78), Jamestown Mfg. Assn. (dir. 1972-74, pres. 1976-78), Am. Inst. Indsl. Engrs., Soc. Automotive Engrs. Club: Moon Brook Country (Jamestown). Home: 7540 Twin Lakes Trail Chagrin Falls OH 44022 Office: 20600 Chagrin Blvd Cleveland OH 44122

MYERS, AL, realtor, property mgmt. co. exec., mayor; b. Oakland, Calif., Aug. 6, 1922; s. Alvi A. and Emma (Thoren) M.; student Oreg. Inst. Tech., 1940-41; m. Viola Doreen Wennermark, Sept. 11, 1954; children—Susan Faye, Pamela Ann, Jason Allen. Supt.'s asst. Aluminum Co. Am., Troutdale, Oreg., 1942-44; asst. mgr. Western Auto Supply Co., Portland, 1944-46; owner, operator Al Myers Auto & Electric, Gresham, 1946-53; realtor, broker Al Myers Property Mgmt., 1954—; v.p., sec. The Oreg. Country, Inc. Ednl. rep. Oreg. Real Estate Dept. and U. Oreg.; mem. Indsl. Devel. Com. Multnomah County, Power and Econ. Devel. Commn., for Multnomah County; instr. Mt. Hood Community Coll. Mem. East Multnomah County Democratic Forum, 1955—, mem. exec. com., 1958—, now pres. Mayor, Gresham, Oreg., 1972—. Served with AUS, 1943. Mem. Portland Realty Bd., Nat. Assn. Real Estate Bds., Internat. Platform Assn., Christian Bus. Men's Com. Internat., Rho Epsilon Kappa (pres.). Mem-Evangelical Ch. (treas.). Home: 935 NW Norman Ave Gresham OR 97030 Office: 995 NE Cleveland Ave Gresham OR 97030

MYERS, CHARLES LLEWELLYN, apparel co. exec.; b. Williamstown, Pa., Nov. 27, 1928; s. Charles W. and Myrtle Irene M.; student Pa. State U.; m. Lucille Carolyn Myers, Aug. 11, 1949; children—Charles L., Lee Miles, Linda Ann Myers Eisenhower. With Ebinger Iron Works, Schuylkill Haven, Pa., 1948-51; with Van Huesen Co., 1948—, regional mgr., Brinkley, Ark., 1973-74, asst. v.p. mfg., gen. prodn. mgr., Pottsville, Pa., from 1973, v.p. mfg., to 1979, sr. v.p. mfg., Ozark, Ala., 1979—. Bd. dirs. Ozark YMCA. Mem. Am. Apparel Mfrs. Assn. Methodist. Club: Rotary. Office: 501 Roy Parker Rd Ozark AL 36360

MYERS, HAL L., export-import co. exec.; b. Holton, Ind., Feb. 28, 1925; s. Hallie L. and Beryl (Custer) M.; student Purdue U., 1942; B.A. in Internat. Relations, U. Wis., 1948; M.A. in Orgnl. Behavior (Solalinde scholar Wis.) Newport U., 1947; m. Eunice Jean Stoltenberg, June 28, 1955 (dec.); children—Mark Gregory, Stephanie Jean. Documents clk. E.C. Atkins & Co., Indpls., 1948-50; fgn. sales mgr. Shirley Corp., Indpls., 1950-52; regional sales mgr. Butler Pan Am. Corp., Kansas City, Mo., 1952-55; European sales mgr. Borg-Warner Internat. Corp., Chgo., 1955-56; mktg. mgr. Automercado, C.A., Caracas, Venezuela, 1957-59; dir. fgn. sales Thomas Industries Inc., Louisville, 1959-66; v.p. sales Mattel Pan Am. Corp., Hawthorne, Calif., 1966-71; pres. Myers Enterprises Inc., Long Beach, Calif., 1971-79; dir. product sales J.D. Marshall Internat. Inc., Skokie, Ill., 1979—. Served with combat inf. U.S. Army, 1943-45; ETO. Decorated Bronze Star, Purple Heart; recipient Exporters Presdl. E award U.S. Dept. Commerce, 1965. Republican. Presbyterian. Club: Masons (Indpls.). Office: 666 E Ocean Blvd Suite 500 Long Beach CA 90802

MYERS, JOHN DELBERT, mfg. co. exec.; b. South Bend, Ind., Aug. 21, 1933; s. Delbert Roy and Dorise (Haimbaugh) M.; student Ind. U., 1951-53; B.S. in Physics, Purdue U., 1959; postgrad. Pa. State U., 1960-61, Cornell U., 1961-62; m. Marcia Ellen Pfeifer, Dec. 28, 1978; children—Michael, David, Jeffrey, Daniel, Gregory. Research scientist Martin Marietta Corp., 1959-61, Cornell Aero. Lab., 1961-63; head research and devel. Lear Siegler Laser Systems Center, 1963-67; product mgr. lasers Owens-Ill. Co., Toledo, 1967-73; pres., chmn. bd. Kigre, Inc., Toledo, 1973—. Served with U.S. Army, 1954-56. Mem. IEEE, Sci. Research Soc. Am. Patentee optical radar, hybrid laser structure, phosphate laser glass; designer, developer 1st plane position indicating laser radar system, 1st dual-frequency laser ceilometer system, 1st gigawatt laser oscillator-amplifier system. Home: 900 Sandalwood E Perrysburg OH 43551 Office: 5333 Secor Rd Toledo OH 43623

MYERS, JOHN EDWARD, communications ofcl.; b. Taneytown, Md., May 9, 1931; s. James Casper and Maude Elizabeth (Walters) M.; student U. Md., 1949-51; m. Mildred I. Fleming, Sept. 28, 1957; children—John E. (dec.), Daniel T., Carol A. With U.S. Army Communication Command, Ft. Detrick, Frederick, Md., 1954—, chief signal div., 1962-63, communications mgr., 1961-62, foreman telephone central office, 1960-71, telephone mechanic foreman, 1971—. Neighborhood commr. Boy Scouts Am.; past capt. Taneytown Fire Police; dep. sheriff Carroll County, Md. Past pres. central Md. sec., past pres. St. Joseph's parish Holy Name Soc. Served with Signal Corps, U.S. Army, 1951-54. Mem. Am. Legion (past comdr. post 120 Md.), Pa. Fire Police Assn., Carroll County Fire Police Assn. (past pres.), Taneytown Jaycees (charter). Roman Catholic. Clubs: Taneytown Rod and Gun, K.C. Home: 49 York St Taneytown MD 21787 Office: US Army Communication Command Fort Detrick Frederick MD 21701

MYERS, LARRY VICTOR, banker; b. Nanty-Glo, Pa., June 5, 1934; s. Lawrence Victor and Marion Lamby (Caldwell) M.; student Pa. State U., 1957-58, Bank Adminstrn. Inst., U. Wis., 1965-67, U. Md., 1968-72; cert. in banking Northwestern U., 1964; m. Nancy Carole Riggs, Mar. 17, 1962. Acct., Am. Security Bank, Washington, 1959-65, asst. auditor, 1965-69, auditor, 1969-75, v.p., dep. comptroller, 1975—; lectr. Am. Inst. Banking, FBI Nat. Acad., U.S. marshalls, 1970—. Served with USMC, 1954-57. Cert. internal auditor. Mem. Bank Adminstrn. Inst. (pres. 1971-72), D.C. Bankers Assn. (chmn. audit, control and ops. 1971-72, audit com., audit com. for student loans), D.C. Bd. Trade (protective com.), Inst. Internal Auditors, Am. Soc. for Indsl. Security. Home: 10404 Kardwright Ct Gaithersburg MD 20760 Office: 1501 Pennsylvania Ave NW Washington DC 20013

MYERS, LOUIS S., diversified equipment co. exec.; b. N.Y.C., 1913. Chmn. chief exec. officer Myers Industries, Inc., Akron, Ohio; dir. Wright Tool & Forge Co. Office: 1293 S Main St Akron OH 44301

MYERS, MARSHALL NEIL, C.P.A. co. tax partner; b. Kansas City, Mo., Aug. 19, 1938; s. William and Edith Gertrude (Weiner) M.; B.S.B.A., Washington U., 1960, M.S. in Accounting, 1962; m. Sara Raskas, Sept. 3, 1961; children—Edward, Stephanie, Anne. Staff accountant William Pesmen & Co., C.P.A.'s, Kansas City, Mo., 1960-63; controller Jay Zee Inc., St. Louis, 1963-64; staff mem., partner Alexander Grant & Co., St. Louis, 1964—; lectr. taxation Washington U., 1964-76. Mem. Jewish Fedn. Leadership Devel. Council, 1973-75, mem. budget com., 1974-75, bd. dirs., 1979-81; pres. St. Louis Hillel Found., 1979-81; treas. B'nai B'rith Covenant House II, 1977-79; v.p. Congregation Shaare Zedek, 1979-81; mem. St. Louis Assn. for Retarded Children, St. Louis Kidney Found.; bd. dirs. Central Agy. for Jewish Edn., 1981—. Recipient Charles J. Stevenson Creative Writing award, U. Mo.-Kansas City, 1957. Mem. St. Louis Estate Planning Council, Am. Inst. C.P.A.'s, Mo. Soc. C.P.A.'s, Internat. Tax Inst. Clubs: Clayton, Stadium, Washington Univ. Faculty, B'nai B'rith. Editorial adv. bd. Internat. Tax Jour. Home: 12232 Kingshill Dr Saint Louis MO 63105 Office: 222 S Central Avenue Suite 300 Saint Louis MO 63105

MYERS, MICHAEL JOE, lawyer, venture capital co. exec.; b. Sterling, Ill., Aug. 8, 1940; s. Cloyd C. and Marjorie Alice (Young) M.; B.S. in Elec. Engring., U. Ill., 1962; J.D., George Washington U., 1966; M.B.A., Harvard U., 1969; m. Nancy Jeanne Tipton, Oct. 1, 1966; children—Gregory, Jennifer. Admitted to D.C. bar, 1966; asso. J.H. Whitney & Co., N.Y.C., 1969-72; v.p. Smith Barney, Harris Upham & Co., N.Y.C., 1972-76; pres. Smith Barney Venture Corp., N.Y.C., 1976—, also dir.; dir. Floating Point Systems, Inc., L. Perrigo Co., Mobex Corp., Internat. Dynetics Corp., Classics Ltd. Inc. Mem.

Nat. Venture Capital Assn., Sigma Nu. Clubs: Harvard (N.Y.C.); Springdale Golf. Home: 113 Herrontown Ln Princeton NJ 08540 Office: 1345 Ave of the Americas New York NY 10019

MYERS, MILLER FRANKLIN, mfg. co. exec.; b. Aberdeen, S.D., Sept. 26, 1939; s. Burton F. and Virginia (Miller) M.; B.S., U. Minn., 1951, LL.B., 1953; m. Janet Rylander, June 16, 1951; children—Leslie, Burton F., Claudia, Georgianna. Admitted to Minn. bar, 1953; pres. Internat. Dairy Queen, Mpls., 1965-70, chmn. bd., 1970-73; pres. Econo-Therm Energy Systems Corp., Mpls., 1974-78, chmn. bd., 1978—; dir. Redfield Cos., Variant, Inc. Delegate Republican State Conv., 1970; bd. dirs. Planned Parenthood of Minn., 1975-76; mem. adv. council U. Minn. Inst. Tech., Keller Grad. Sch. Mgmt., Chgo. Mem. U. Minn. Law Alumni Assn., Minn. Bar Assn., Minn. Execs. Assn., Am. Mgmt. Assn., World Bus. Council. Clubs: Wayzata (Minn.) Country; Hamilton (Ont., Can.) Golf & Country. Office: 11535 K-Tel Dr Minnetonka MN 55343

MYERS, ROLLAND GRAHAM, fin. exec.; b. St. Louis, Aug. 30, 1945; s. Rolland Everett and Lurilien (Graham) M.; A.B. cum laude in History and Lit. (hon. freshman scholar), Harvard U., 1966; postgrad. Faculty of Social Scis. and Law, U. Edinburgh, Scotland, 1966-67, Fondation Nationale des Sciences Politiques and Faculte de Lettres et des Sciences Humaines, U. Paris, 1967-68. Mem. 32nd spl. devel. program Chase Manhattan Bank, N.Y.C., 1968-69, comml. banker internat. dept., 1969-70, investment banker fiduciary investment dept., 1970; account exec. N.Y. sales dept. Smith Barney & Co., Inc., N.Y.C., 1971-72, account exec. internat. sales dept., 1972-74, 2nd v.p., 1975-76; v.p. Smith Barney Harris Upham & Co., Inc., N.Y.C., 1976-78; ltd. partner Croke Patterson Campbell Ltd., Denver, 1975—; pvt. investment portfolio mgr., 1978—; gen. partner Mansion Disbursements, Denver, 1979—; pres., dir. Fifty-Five Residents Corp., N.Y.C., 1980—. Vice pres., vestryman Episcopal Chaplaincy at Harvard and Radcliffe, Cambridge, 1965-66; trustee, mem. corp. Bishop Rhinelander Found., Cambridge, 1973-75; v.p., treas., dir. The Whitehill Graham Found., St. Louis, 1976—. Episcopalian. Clubs: Harvard, Hasty Pudding-Inst. of 1770. Address: 55 E End Ave New York NY 10028

MYERS, STEPHEN E., diversified equipment co. exec. Pres., Myers Industries Inc., Akron, Ohio. Office: 1293 S Main St Akron OH 44301*

MYERS, THOMAS ALDEN, diversified co. exec.; b. Akron, Ohio, Dec. 1, 1945; s. Minor and Ruth (Libby) M.; B.S. in Bus. Adminstrn., Ohio State U., 1968; M.B.A., U. Cin., 1970; postgrad. U. Akron, 1974, 75; m. Lynn Dee Ann Locke, Aug. 24, 1969; children—Emily Michelle, Timothy Alden. Fin. analyst Mid-Continent Telephone Corp., Hudson, Ohio, 1973-77, supr. fin. results, 1977-78; public relations account exec. Edward Howard & Co., Cleve., 1978-79; mgr. investor relations TRW Inc., Cleve., 1979—. Co. photographer Ohio Ballet, Akron, 1976—, trustee, 1979—. Served with U.S. Army, 1970-73. Mem. Ohio State U. Alumni Assn. Club: Ohio State U. Marching Band Alumni. Home: 156 N Highland Ave Akron OH 44303 Office: TRW Inc 23555 Euclid Ave Cleveland OH 44117

MYHRE, KJELL EINRIDE, instrumentation co. exec.; b. Addis Ababa, Ethiopia, Mar. 9, 1930; s. Peder Margido and Mathea (Ellevseth) M.; A.A. in Engring., Pasadena City Coll., 1959; m. Kay Louise Fasnacht, Sept. 29, 1973. Engring. specialist Electro-Optical Systems, Pasadena, Calif., 1963-67; engring. specialist Whittaker Corp., Pasadena, 1968-69; v.p. Micron Instruments, Inc., Los Angeles, 1969-74; pres. Century Technology Co., Inglewood, Calif., 1974—; designer implantable pressure transducer (IR 100 award Indsl. Research Mag. 1966). Mem. Am. Soc. Metals, Instrument Soc. Am., Am. Welding Soc. Patentee in field. Office: 1524 Centinela Ave Inglewood CA 90302

MYLOD, ROBERT JOSEPH, mortgage banker; b. Bklyn., Nov. 21, 1939; s. Charles Joseph and Katherine (Normile) M.; B.A. in English, St. John's U., Jamaica, N.Y., 1961; m. Monica Manieri, July 11, 1964; children—Rosemary, Robert, Kevin, Paul, Monica, Megan. Vice pres. Citibank, N.A., N.Y.C., 1965-70, Citcorp, N.Y.C., 1970-73; exec. v.p. residential loan div. Advance Mortgage Corp., Detroit, 1973-75, pres., 1975—. Bd. trustees, legis. com. Mich. Heart Assn.; trustee Detroit Symphony Orch., W. Bloomfield Center of Henry Ford Hosp. Served to lt. USN, 1961-65. Mem. Mortgage Bankers Assn. (gov.). Office: 23077 Greenfield St Southfield MI 48075

MYRICK, MARION LINDLE, banker; b. Searcy, Ark., Oct. 5, 1933; s. Eugene Wesley and Lovie Mae (Reaves) M.; ed. Am. Inst. Banking, 1976, Harvard, 1976; m. Nelda Mae Smith, Dec. 3, 1953; children—Marion Keith, Kent Aaron, Brenda Lynne. Addressograph operator Worthen Bank & Trust Co., Little Rock, 1951-55, bookkeeper, 1955-57, teller, 1957-64, br. mgr., 1964-65, purchasing agt., 1965-66, asst. cashier, dir. purchasing, 1966-69. Asst. v.p., 1969-75, v.p. adminstrv. services, 1975—; lectr. in field. Treas. Little Rock Jaycee Little League, 1957-61; active United Way, Boy Scouts Am. Cert. purchasing mgr. Mem. Nat. Assn. Purchasing Mgmt. (v.p. 1980-81), Purchasing Mgmt. Assn. Ark. (grantee 1976). Mem. Ch. of Christ. Clubs: Optimist, Little Rock Chamber Diamond (life). Home: 715 Coulter Rd North Little Rock AR 72116 Office: 200 W Capitol St Little Rock AR 72201

NABOURS, ROBERT EUGENE, cons. engring. co. exec.; b. Tucson, Nov. 27, 1934; s. James Oliphant and Dorothy Madelle (Brown) N.; B.S. in Elec. Engring., U. Ariz., 1957, Ph.D., 1965; M.S., Stanford U., 1959; m. Jane Brock Burnett, Feb. 27, 1954; children—Kathleen, Bradley, Gregory. Draftsman, A.E. Magee Cons. Engr., 1954-57; engr. Lenkurt Electric Co., 1957-58; instr. U. Ariz., 1959-63; project engr. Bell Aerosystems Co., 1963-65; chief engr., mgr. engring. Burr-Brown Research Co., 1965-68; owner, mgr. Robert E. Nabours, cons. engr., Tucson, 1968-78; sr. v.p., mgr. So. Ariz. div. Johannessen & Girand, Tucson, 1978-80, also dir.; head elec. engring. Finical & Dombrowski, Tucson, 1980—; lectr. Coll. Architecture, U. Ariz., 1973-76. Registered profl. engr., Ariz. Mem. Nat. Soc. Profl. Engrs., Illuminating Engrs. Soc., Instrument Soc. Am., IEEE, Tau Beta Pi, Sigma Pi Sigma. Republican. Anglican Catholic. Clubs: V.I.P. Breakfast, Elks. Research on solid state devices, adaptive communications. Home: 5201 Salida Del Sol Tucson AZ 85718 Office: 731 N Stone Ave Tucson AZ 85705

NACE, JOHN ALFRED, mfg. co. exec.; b. London, Ont., Can., Jan. 23, 1928; s. George Washington Fay and Dorothy Daisy (Price) N.; grad. Sir Adam Beck Collegiate Inst., London, Ont., 1947; m. Dorothea Kathleen Titus, Sept. 12, 1953; children—Janice, John, Dale, William, Marc. With Somerville Belkin Industries Ltd., 1947—, purchasing mgr., Montreal, 1961-68, quality control mgr., 1968-74, purchasing and material handling mgr., 1974-75, prodn. control mgr., 1975-77, ops. mgr., 1977-80, gen. mgr., 1980—. Mem. Can. Paper Box Mfrs. Assn. Anglican. Home: 33 Huron Rd Dollard des Ormeaux PQ H9G 2C2 Canada Office: 865 Hodge St Saint Laurent PQ H4N 2B2 Canada

NACHMAN, RICHARD JOSEPH, mgmt. cons.; b. Washington, Sept. 18, 1944; s. Joseph F. and Rosemary A. (Anderson) N.; B.A., U. Colo., 1968; m. Nancy Ruth Hodgson, Feb. 4, 1966; children—Russell James, Kirk Leslie; m. 2nd. Maria Christina Hoff, Jan. 2, 1979; 1 stepson, William Christopher. Program dir./acad. appointment Bur. Indsl. Relations, Grad. Sch. Bus., U. Mich., Ann Arbor, 1968-70; dir. Center Mgmt. and Tech. Programs, Grad. Sch. Bus., U. Colo., Boulder, 1970-74; pres. Mgmt. Research Corp., Boulder; lectr., cons. in field. Mem. Am. Soc. Tng. and Devel., Direct Mail Mktg. Assn., Am. Mgmt. Assn., C. of C. Republican. Contbr. articles to profl. jours. Home: 4814 W Moorhead Circle Boulder CO 80303 Office: 1200 Pearl St Boulder CO 80302

NADEEM, RAPHAEL GEORGE, dept. store exec.; b. Pawtucket, R.I., May 5, 1926; s. George Raphael and Adel (Samra) N.; student pub. schs., Pawtucket. Asst. display mgr. Strawbridge & Clothiers, Ardmore, Pa., 1950-55; dir. display Snellenburghs, Phila., 1955-61; dir. visual presentation Litt Bros., Phila., 1961-67; dir. display Lansburgh's Washington, 1969-73; corporate v.p. dir. visual presentation The Hecht Co., Washington. Served with USN, 1944-46; PTO. Recipient award Nat. Assn. Display Industries, 1976. Mem. Nat. Retail Mchts. Assn. (dir.). Home: 512 S Pitts St Alexandria VA 22314 Office: F St at 7th NW Washington DC 20004

NAGAMURA, TOSHIO, banker; b. Fujinomiya, Japan, Mar. 26, 1926; came to U.S., 1978; s. Masao and Chiseko N.; B.A., Tokyo U., 1947; m. Sachiyo Takamatsu, Apr. 14, 1958; children—Makiko, Massaki. Pres., chief exec. officer Calif. 1st Bank, 1978—. Mem. Japanese C. of C. of San Francisco (pres.). Office: 350 California St San Francisco CA 94104

NAGEL, MABEL HUDSPETH, property devel. exec.; b. Berryville, Ark., July 7, 1903; d. Joseph D. and Minerva (Robinson) Hudspeth; student N.Mex. State Coll., 1929-31; m. George Henry Nagel, May 26, 1931 (dec. May 1968); children—Georgia Mae (Mrs. R.T. Jenkins), James Henry. Co-owner, operator Nagel Lumber & Timber Co., Winslow, Ariz., 1950-79; pres. Nagel Lumber Co., Inc., 1951-65, Acme Lumber Co., Inc., 1966—, Nagel Devel. Corp., 1970—, also Rincon Cattle Corp.; sec. Four Corners Devel. Corp., 1966-70. Mem. Winslow City Council, 1950-54; mem. Sitgreaves Nat. Rest Adv. Com., 1952-62; police commr. Winslow, 1953-54; sec. Winslow Planning and Zoning Commn., 1954-56; pres. Winslow Youth Council, 1955-57, Winslow Bicentennial Commn., 1975-77, Winslow Enrichment Commn., 1977-78, Winslow Arts Assn., 1977-79; vice chmn. Winslow Devel. Commn., 1958-64; mem. lumber div. Ariz. Water Resources Div., 1958-71; mem. Ariz. indsl. adv. com. rural housing FHA, 1971-74; pres. Winslow Bicentennial Commn., 1975-76, Winslow Enrichment Commn., 1977-78; mem. Ariz. Forest Industry Com., 1962-68; chmn. Navajo County March of Dimes women's div., 1958-59; rep. corr. Fgn. Soroptimist Sister Club, Antwerp, Belgium, 1962-65, mem. fgn. exchange student com., 1961-64; chmn. water devel. com. Navajo County Devel. Council, 1963-65, bd. dirs., 1963-71; mem. Gov.'s Adv. Council Navajo County Welfare, 1964-66, Apache-Navajo County chmn. Statewide Art Mus. League, 1962-65, adv. bd. (charter; rec. Meml. Hosp., 1957-66; bd. dirs. Bapt. Children's Home, 1959-60, Ariz. Arts Humanities Commn.; bd. dirs. Ariz. Acad., 1964-68, sec., mem. exec. com., 1965-67; sec. bd. dirs. Indsl. Devel. Endeavor Assn., 1964-66, bd. dirs., 1974—; pres. Winslow Sr. Council, 1971-74; mem. adv. commn. Navajo County Planning and Zoning, 1973-74. Named Woman of Yr., Bus. and Profl. Women's Club, 1954-55, C. of C., 1976, Winslow Woman of Yr., 1975; recipient RSVP award No. Ariz. Council Govts., 1976. Mem. S.W. Pine Assn. (dir. 1963-64), Nat., Ariz. (rep. Navajo County) reclamation assns., Ariz. Press Women (v.p. 1967-68), Navajo County Hist. Soc. (charter; rec. sec. 1972-75, v.p. 1971-72, pres. 1973-74), Am. Assn. Ret. Persons (pres. Winslow chpt. 1972-74), C. of C. (dir. 1965, 60, 62), Ariz. Cattle Growers Assn. Clubs: Writers (sec.-treas. 1960-64), Soroptimist (pres. 1961-62). Feature writer, photographer and news corr. Home: 708 W Maple St Winslow AZ 86047 Office: Box 550 Winslow AZ 86047

NAGI, TERRY ALLEN, trade assn. exec.; b. Milw., May 24, 1939; s. Herbert B. and Emma (Eggart) N.; B.B.A. in Mktg., U. Wis., 1960, M.B.A. in Mktg., 1967; m. Barbara A. Morgan, May 18, 1979; 1 dau., Lisa Lynne. Sales adminstr. Alcoa, Pitts., 1960-61; communications cons. Wis. Telephone Co., Milw., 1961-63; Sales mgr. O. L. Schilffarth & Co., Milw., 1963-67; dir. mktg. Western Pub. Co., Racine, Wis., 1967-73; exec. dir. Printing Industries of Am., Inc., Washington, 1973-79, exec. v.p., 1980—, dir. mgmt. services, 1978-80. Served with U.S. Army, 1976-80. Mem. Am. Soc. Assn. Execs., Washington Soc. Assn. Execs., Am. Mgmt. Assn., Am. Mktg. Assn. Republican. Lutheran. Contbr. articles to profl. jours. Office: 1730 N Lynn St Arlington VA 22209

NAGIN, STEPHEN E., lawyer; b. Phila., Nov. 7, 1946; s. Harry S. and Dorothy R. (Pearlman) N.; B.B.A., U. Miami, 1969, J.D., 1974. Admitted to Fla. bar, 1974, D.C. bar, 1976, Supreme Ct. U.S., 1978; asst. atty. gen. State of Fla., Miami, 1974-75; staff atty. Atlanta regional office FTC, 1975-76, atty. advisor regional operations Office of Dir., Bur. Competition, Washington, 1976-78, trial atty. Bur. Competition, Washington, 1978-80; spl. asst. U.S. atty. D.C., 1980—. Mem. Am., Fed., Fla., D.C. bar assns., Assn. Trial Lawyers Am. Democrat. Guest editor Fla. Bar Jour., 1976, 80, 81, mem. editorial bd., 1975—, vice-chmn. editorial bd., 1979. Home: 1280 21st St NW Washington DC 20036 Office: Washington DC

NAGLE, REID, banker, economist; b. Boston, May 26, 1952; s. James Francis and Henrietta (Reid) N.; A.B., Georgetown U., 1974; M.A., Johns Hopkins U., 1978, Ph.D., 1979; m. Colleen Crahan, Dec. 8, 1979. Cons., Nat. Savs. and Loan League, Washington, 1974-75; economist U.S. Senate Budget Com., 1975-77; economist Md. Dept. Econs. and Community Devel., Annapolis, 1977-78; v.p., economist City Fed. Savs. and Loan, Somerville, N.J., 1978—. Mem. Am. Econs. Assn., Nat. Tax Assn., Nat. Savs. and Loan League. Home: 250 Hawthorne Ave Princeton NJ 08540 Office: City Fed Savs 776 Eve's Dr Somerville NJ 08876

NAGLER, LEON GREGORY, mgmt. cons.; b. Buenos Aires, Argentina, Jan. 29, 1932 (parents Am. citizens); s. Morris and Jennie (Golden) N.; B.S., Boston U., 1953, M.B.A., 1954; J.D., Cleve.-Marshall Coll. Law, 1961; m. F. Elise Charness, Dec. 20, 1953; children—Jeri Lynn, Sandra Michelle. Tchr. psychology Cameron State Agrl. Jr. Coll., Lawton, Okla., 1956-57; supr. employment and tng. Jones & Laughlin Steel Corp., Cleve., 1957-65; exec. dir. indsl. relations Charles Corp., Cleve., 1965-67; dir. personnel ITT Service Industries Corp., Cleve., 1967-72; v.p. personnel Builder Services Corp., Clearwater, Fla., 1972-73; v.p. adminstrn. Damon Corp., Needham Heights, Mass., 1973-77; pres. Nagler & Co., Wellesley Hills, Mass., 1977—. Sec. Mayfield Heights (Ohio) Zoning Bd. Appeals, 1963-65; chmn. Combined Health Fund, Mayfield Heights, 1963; pres. N.E. Ohio region, mem. nat. gov. council Am. Jewish Congress, 1972-73; bd. dirs. New Eng. region Anti-Defamation League, 1977—, Jewish Vocat. Service, Boston, 1977-78; trustee Temple Beth Avodah, Newton, 1978—, v.p., 1979. Served with AUS, 1955-57. Admitted to Ohio bar, 1961. Mem. Ohio, Cleve. bar assns., Am. Soc. Tng. and Devel., Am. Soc. Personnel Adminstrn., Boston U. Alumni Assn. (pres. N.E. Ohio 1969-73, nat. alumni council 1973—). Democrat. Club: Masons. Address: 60 William St Wellesley Hills MA 02181

NAGY, LOU, broker, investment banker; b. Warfield, Ky., Oct. 27, 1922; s. Louis and Fannie (Vizy) N.; student U. Chgo., 1941-42; B.S.E.E., U. Toledo, 1949; m. Dorothy Ellen Fallowes, June 23, 1943; children—Joel Gordon, Lora Lynn, Russell Eric. Communications engr.-mktg. Motorola Communications and Electronics, Inc., Toledo, also Ft. Lee, N.J., 1949-59; broker J.N. Russell, Cleve., 1959-65; partner Ball, Burge & Kraus/Prescott, Ball & Turbin, Stockbroker, Cleve., 1965-73; v.p. Fulton, Reid & Staples, Cleve., 1973-76; sr. v.p. Dean Witter Reynolds, Cleve., 1976-78; sr. v.p., partner Fulton, Reid & Staples investment div. William C. Roney, Cleve., 1978—, now partner parent co.; chmn. bd. Unitec Corp., Cleve.; dir. TSI, Inc., Phila. Bd. dirs. Kiwanis Found., Cleve., 1974—; trustee Ohio Synod, Luth. Ch. Am., 1973-74, Luth. Home for Aged, Westlake, Ohio, 1974—, Luther House, 1974—; chmn. bd. Tetelestai, Inc., 1978—. Served with USAF, 1942-46. Republican. Lutheran. Clubs: Cleve. Athletic, Clevelander, Kiwanis (lt. gov. 1976) (Cleve.); Lutheran Businessmen's, Torch; Westwood Country. Home: 22475 Spencer Ln Fairview Park OH 44126 Office: Bond Court Bldg 1300 E 9th St Cleveland OH 44114

NAIL, CHARLES EDWIN, JR., ins. co. exec.; b. Mansfield, Ohio, Sept. 17, 1931; s. Charles Edwin and Margaret Barry (MacLean) N.; B.A. in Polit. Sci., Amherst Coll., 1954; children—Edwin, Chip, Jack, Laetitia. With Lumbermens Mut. Ins. Co., 1954—, dir., 1963—, pres., chief exec. officer, 1972—, mem. exec. com.; pres., chief exec. officer, exec. com., dir. Ohio Hardward Mut. Ins. Co., Lumbermens Fin. Corp., Inc.; chmn. bd., chief exec. officer, exec. com. Interstate Bus. Services, Inc.; chmn. bd. Lumbermens Mut. Ins. Agy. Inc. (Ohio), Lumbermens Agy., Inc., Lumbermens Mut. Ins. Agy., Inc. (W.Va.), pres., dir. Lumbermens Mut. Agy., Inc. (all Mansfield); pres., dir. Zachary-Randolph, Inc., Greenville, S.C.; governing com. Improved Risk Muts., White Plains, N.Y.; dir. Bank One of Mansfield; bd. govs., dir. Internat. Ins. Seminars. Chmn. bd. trustees, past pres. Griffith Found. for Ins. Edn., Ohio State U., Columbus; mem. Mansfield City Charter Commn. Mem. Ohio Ins. Inst. (trustee), Ins. Fedn. Ohio (exec. com., past pres.), Ins. Hall of Fame (convocation chmn. 1972-74). Club: Rotary. Office: Lumbermens Mutual Ins Co 900 Springmill Mansfield OH 44901

NAIL, JOHN BIRNEY, JR., steel co. exec.; b. Wheeling, W.Va., Dec. 14, 1934; s. John Birney and Maude (Lynch) N.; Metall. Engr., U. Cin., 1957; m. Patricia Moser, Aug. 6, 1955; children—John James, Kenneth Edward, Cheryl Ann. Metall. trainee U.S. Steel, Homestead Works, 1957-59, metall. technologist, Chgo., 1959-60; metal. supr., Dayton, 1960-61, Malleable Research and Devel. Found.; with Wheeling Steel Corp., Yorkville, Ohio, 1962—, supr. metallurgy, 1967-75, supt. metallurgy and quality control, 1975-78; supr. process control, tin mill Weirton (W.Va.) Steel div. Nat. Steel Corp., 1978—. Mem. Am. Electroplaters Soc. (sec. Pitts.), Am. Iron and Steel Inst., ASTM, Am. Soc. Metals. Home: 3014 Denwood Dr Moundsville WV 26041 Office: Weirton Tin Mill Weirton Steel Div Weirton WV 26062

NAIL, WILLIAM ALDEN, pub. relations exec.; b. Crawford, Tex., Apr. 26, 1926; s. Benjamin Miles and Avie Maria (Harrison) N.; student Baylor U., 1943-45; B.A., U. Tex., 1946, M.A., 1948; m. Betty Young, Feb. 20, 1952; children—John Joseph, James Douglas. Instr. broadcasting Oreg. State U., Corvallis, 1948-49; program dir., broadcasting service U. Ala., University, 1949-51; program devel. officer USIA, Voice of Am., N.Y.C., 1951-53; asst. prof. English, McNeese State Coll., Lake Charles, La., 1953-54; asst. to dir. pub. relations Zenith Radio Corp., Chgo., 1954-64, asst. dir., 1964-65, dir. pub. relations, 1965—. Mem. pub. relations adv. group Council of Better Bus. Burs., 1971-79; mem. devel. council Williams Coll., 1978; charter mem. Parents Council, Williams Coll., 1975-78; vice chmn. pub. relations Chgo. Met. Crusade of Mercy, 1978, chmn., 1979; bd. dirs. Frank Lloyd Wright Home and Studio Found. Mem. Internat. Pub. Relations Assn., Pub. Relations Soc. Am. (accredited), Chgo. Pub. Relations Clinic (v.p. 1979—), Electronic Industries Assn. (pub. relations chmn. 1974-75). Democrat. Episcopalian. Clubs: Chgo. Press; Nat. Press (Washington). Home: 605 N Grove Ave Oak Park IL 60302 Office: 1000 Milwaukee Ave Glenview IL 60025

NAIMARK, GEORGE MODELL, advt. agy. and pub. exec.; b. N.Y.C., Feb. 5, 1925; s. Myron S. and Mary (Modell) N.; B.S., Bucknell U., 1947, M.S., 1948; Ph.D., U. Del., 1951; m. Helen Anne Wythes, June 24, 1946; children—Ann, Richard, Jane. Research biochemist Brush Devel. Co., Cleve., 1951; dir. quality control Strong, Cobb & Co., Inc., Cleve., 1951-54; dir. sci. services White Labs., Inc., Kenilworth, N.J., 1954-60; v.p. Burdick Assos., Inc., N.Y.C., 1960-66; pres. Rajah Press, Summit, N.J., 1963—; pres. Naimark & Barba, Inc., N.Y.C., 1966—. Served with USNR, 1944-46. Fellow AAAS, Am. Inst. Chemists; mem. Am. Chem. Soc., N.Y. Acad. Scis., Edinburgh (Scotland) Bibliog. Soc., Am. Mktg. Assn., Pharm. Advt. Council. Author: A Patent Manual for Scientists and Engineers, 1961; Communications on Communication, 1971, 2d edit., 1978. Contbr. articles in profl. jours. Home: 87 Canoe Brook Pkwy Summit NJ 07901 Office: 130 E 40th St New York NY 10016

NAJJAR, ROBERT PAUL, univ. ofcl.; b. Boston, Sept. 8, 1938; s. George John and Mabel Marion (Shaheen) N.; B.S., Northeastern U., 1961, M.B.A., 1963; m. Joyce Lucille Samia, June 23, 1963; children—Julie Anne, Gregory. Auditor, Ernst & Ernst, Boston, 1964-65; partner Roma Foods, Methuen, Mass., 1965-66; asst. dir. fin. aid office Northeastern U., 1966-69, bursar, fin. office, 1969—, sr. lectr. Univ. Coll., 1965-78; owner Robert P. Najjar Assos., bus. and mgmt. cons.; v.p. Power & Indsl. Trading Products, Inc. Mem. Nat. Assn. Coll. and Univ. Bus. Officers, Coll. and Univ. Machine Records Council. Club: Masons. Home: 8 Regis Rd Andover MA 01810 Office: 360 Huntington Ave Boston MA 02115

NAKAMURA, DENNIS MASAAKI, financial and bus. cons.; b. Berkeley, Calif., Nov. 2, 1953; s. Akira and Rurie N.; B.S. in Acctg. and Finance, U. Calif., Berkeley, 1975. Supr., D/A Assos., Orinda, Calif., 1975—; pres. Exec. Fin. Services, Inc., San Francisco, 1979—. C.L.U. Mem. Provident Mut. Leaders Assn., Million Dollar Round Table, Nat. Assn. Life Underwriters, Leading Life Producers No. Calif., Nat. Assn. C.L.U.'s, Berkeley Jaycees (pres. 1980), Estate Planning Council Diablo Valley. Republican. Club: Quail Ct. Athletic. Home: 3598 Walnut St Lafayette CA 94549 Office: Exec Financial Services Inc 44 Montgomery St 5th Floor San Francisco CA 94104

NAPIER, JAMES VOSS, telephone co. exec.; b. Ellsworth, Kans., Feb. 2, 1937; s. Nial Voss and Leonilla (Seus) N.; B.S., St. Benedict's Coll., 1959; postgrad. U. Kans., 1959; m. Mary Louise Holke, July 18, 1959; children—Laura Ann, Lisa, Miriam, Suzanne, Cynthia, Amy. Sr. acct. Western Utility Corp., San Francisco, 1959-63, asst. sec., treas., 1963-64; pres., comptroller San Joaquin Telephone Co., Manteca, Calif., 1965; dir. finance Western div., v.p., treas. Continental Telephone Co. Calif., Bakersfield, 1966-68, asst. to pres. fin., St. Louis, 1968-69, asst. v.p. fin., 1969-70, v.p. fin., 1970, v.p. fin. and adminstrn., Bakersfield, 1972-73, exec. v.p., 1974-76, pres., 1976—, also dir.; dir. Nat. Bank Ga. Mem. AIM, U.S. Ind. Telephone Assn. (dir.), Young Presidents Orgn., Sci. Atlanta (dir.). Office: Continental Telephone Corp 56 Perimeter Center E Atlanta GA 30346

NAPIER, STANLEY, JR., chemist; b. Hindman, Ky., June 18, 1948; s. Stanley and Greta (Smith) N.; A.A. with honors (Scholar), Alice Lloyd Jr. Coll., 1968; exchange student Harvard U., 1969; B.A., U. Ky., 1970; M.S., Ohio U., 1974; m. Cynthia D. Steele, June 11, 1976. Chemist, Merrell-Nat. Labs., Cin., 1970-72; chemist DuBois Chems. Research Labs., DuBois Chem. Co., Cin., 1974-75, sr. chemist, 1975-78, research asso., 1978—. Edn. Protection Def. Act fellow, 1972-74. Mem. Am. Soc. Lubrication Engrs., Soc. Mfg. Engrs. Democrat. Methodist. Home: 3787 Fox Run Dr Cincinnati OH 45236 Office: 3630 E Kemper Rd Cincinnati OH 45241

NAPLES, RONALD JAMES, mfg. co. exec.; b. Passaic, N.J., Sept. 10, 1945; s. James V. and Lee A. N.; B.S., U.S. Mil. Acad., 1967; M.A., Fletcher Sch. Law and Diplomacy, 1972; M.B.A. with distinction (Walter Heller fellow), Harvard U., 1974; m. Suzanne Lorraine Shoudy, June 17, 1967; 1 son, Regen Jeffrey. Asso. in corp. fin. Loeb Rhoades Co., 1974; White House fellow, asst. to counselor to Pres., 1974-75; exec. dir. Presdl. Task Force on Energy, Washington, 1975-76; v.p. internat. Hunt Mfg. Co., Phila., 1976, exec. v.p., 1980—, pres. Hunt Internat. Co., 1977—. Mem. regional commn. Pres.'s Com. on White House Fellows, 1977; bd. dirs. Phila. Coll. Performing Arts, Internat. Bus. Forum, Phila. Served with U.S. Army, 1967-71. Decorated Bronze Star with oak leaf cluster, Army Commendation medal with oak leaf cluster, Air medal (U.S.); Cross of Gallantry (Vietnam); recipient Mil. Order World Wars award U.S. Mil. Acad., 1967; named Outstanding Young Man Am., U.S. Jaycees, 1977. Mem. World Affairs Council, White House Fellows Assn., Assn. Grad. U.S. Mil. Acad., Harvard Bus. Sch. Alumni Assn. Club: Racquet (Phila.). Office: 1405 Locust St Philadelphia PA 19102

NARCIANDI, FERNANDO M., bar, dairy products and soft-service equipment co. exec.; b. Havana, Cuba, May 30, 1947; came to U.S., 1961, naturalized, 1969; s. Mateo and Leonor Narciandi, A.A., Spokane Jr. Coll., 1966; B.S., Woodbury U., 1971; m. Consuelo Herrera, Oct. 25, 1969; 1 son, Eric. Sect. supr. Prudential Ins. Co., Los Angeles, 1969-73; audit mgr. Signal Ins. Co., Los Angeles, 1973-75, Penn Fin. Corp., Santa Monica, Calif., 1974-75; gen. mgr., controller for employee benefits cons Penn Fin. Co., 1975-76, credit and collection mgr., 1976-77; pres., dir. Yogurt Mktg. Corp. and Glacier Products of So. Calif., Garden Grove, Calif., 1977-80; pres., owner Fiesta Enterprises Inc., Miami, 1980—; cons. in field. Served with USMC, 1966-69. Decorated Purple Heart. Mem. Inst. Internal Auditors, Am. Mgmt. Assn., Soc. Advancement Mgmt., Credit Mgrs. Assn., DAV. Republican. Roman Catholic. Club: Kings Racket and Health. Office: 4030 NW 29th St Miami FL 33142

NARDONE, DON D., fin. co. exec.; b. N.Y.C., Feb. 10, 1924; s. Sebastian and Mary (Genero) N.; B.S. in Econs. and Fin., CCNY, 1948; m. Maryalice Clark, Feb. 5, 1955; children—Karin, Michael, Nora. Account exec. Charles Plohn & Co., N.Y.C., 1962-70; v.p. Thomson McKinnon Securities, Inc., N.Y.C., 1970—; lectr. on fin. products, 1963—. Served to 1st lt. inf. U.S. Army, 1943-46. Club: Shelter Rock Tennis (Manhasset, N.Y.). Contbr. articles to profl. jours. Home: 34 Shrub Hollow Rd Roslyn NY 11576 Office: One New York Plaza New York NY 10004

NARESKI, WILLIAM JOHN, diversified mfg. and holding co. exec.; b. Hartford, Conn., Sept. 25, 1948; s. William John and Stella Marie (Pawellac) N.; B.S. in Elec. Engring., Rensselaer Poly. Inst., 1970, M.E. in Elec. Engring. (scholar), 1971; M.B.A., Harvard U., 1973; m. Nancy M. Trombini, Sept. 2, 1972; children—Nicolas, Ursula. Engr., Raytheon Inc., Bedford, Mass., 1968-71; venture analyst G.T.E. New Ventures, Stamford, Conn., 1973-74; pres. Ashley Moorehouse, Inc., Stamford, 1974-76; v.p. corp. devel. Clabir Corp., Greenwich, Conn., 1976—. Mem. N.Am. Soc. Corp. Planning, Planning Execs. Inst., Conn. Venture Capital Group, Soc. Corp. Growth, Tau Beta Pi, Eta Kappa Nu. Republican. Roman Catholic. Club: Roton Point Yacht. Home: Charcoal Rd Norwalk CT 06854 Office: Clabir Corp 1455 E Putnam Ave Old Greenwich CT 06870

NARINS, CHARLES SEYMOUR, lawyer, instrument co. exec., hosp. ofcl.; b. Bklyn., Mar. 12, 1909; s. Joshua and Sarah E. (Levy) N.; LL.B., Yale, 1932; B.S., N.Y. U., 1929; m. Frances D. Kross; children—Lyn Ross, Joyce Hedda. Admitted to N.Y. bar, 1933, Mass. bar, 1955; atty. Curtis & Glynn, N.Y.C., 1932-34, Glynn, Smith & Narins, 1934-37, Probst & Probst, 1937-47; pres., dir., counsel C. L. Berger & Sons, Inc., 1947-68; div. chmn. Berger Instruments div. High Voltage Engring. Corp., Boston, 1968-74; dir., chmn. med. planning New Eng. Sinai Hosp., Stoughton, Mass., 1974—. Trustee Boston Ballet Co., Boston Opera; bd. dirs. Boston Civic Symphony, 1975-76; bd. dirs., 1st v.p. Greater Palm Beach Symphony. Mem. corp. Norfolk House, Boston. Mem. Am., N.Y., Mass., Boston bar assns., Assn. Bar City N.Y., N.Y. County Lawyers Assn., Am. Congress Surveying and Mapping, Am. Judicature Soc., Boston C. of C., Assn. Yale Alumni (law sch. rep.), Internat. Cultural Soc., Pi Lambda Phi. Clubs: Univ., Yale (Boston); Yale, Poinciana (Palm Beach); Yale, N.Y. U. (N.Y.C.); Kernwood Country (Salem, Mass.); Palm Beach (Fla.) Country (bd. govs., sec.). Home: 150 Bradley Pl Palm Beach FL 33480 also 2 Brackett Pl Marblehead MA 01945

NAROD, ARNOLD S., fin. planner; b. Phila., Dec. 11, 1946; s. Manuel and Betty Narod; B.A., Temple U., Phila., 1968; C.L.U., 1977; diploma Coll. Fin. Planning, 1977; m. Bonnie Orlove, June 30, 1968; children—Jennifer Rose, Scott Farrell. Social worker Crime Prevention Assn. Phila., 1968-72; ins. agt., King of Prussia, Pa., 1972—; pres. Pa. Pension Cons., Inc., Haverford, Pa., 1977—, South Jersey Pension Cons., Atlantic City, 1977—; founder, 1977, since fin. planner Investment Search, Inc. Mem. Am. Soc. C.L.U.'s, Soc. Cert. Fin. Planners, Nat. Assn. Fin. Cons., Ind. Ins. Agts. Assn., Pa. Ins. Assn., Phila. Assn. Life Underwriters, Phila. Estate Planning Council, Montgomery County Estate Planning Council. Home: 726 School Line Dr King of Prussia PA 19406 Office: 1275 Drummer Ln Suite 200 Wayne PA 19087

NASH, ALAN EDWARD, communications and mktg. exec.; b. N.Y.C., May 24, 1950; s. Sol M. and Edna (Gordon) N.; B.S. in Bus. Adminstrn., Northeastern U., 1973; M.B.A., Boston U., 1979; postgrad. Rochester Inst. Tech. Accounting asst. Fairfield-Noble, Inc., Farmingdale, N.Y., 1968-69; graphic arts rep. Star Printing Co., Boston, 1970-72; adminstrv. asst. Block Engring., Inc., Cambridge, Mass., 1970-71; sales coordinator Creative Studies, Inc., Boston, 1971-72; mktg. dir. Imports Internat., Woburn, Mass., 1972—; pres., chmn. bd. Q Mktg. Ltd., Inc., Needham, Mass., 1970—, also account exec. sales Winthrop Printing, Boston, 1972-73; pres., chmn. bd. Positive Co., 1976—; dir. Datachart Computer Graphics Group; mem. Advt. Speakers Bur., 1975—. Cons. to minorities Small Bus. Resource Center, 1973—; active Boston council Boy Scouts Am., fin. chmn., 1979; chmn. Community Fund drive, 1977—. Recipient awards in advt. Mem. Advt. Club Greater Boston (certified), Am. Mktg. Assn., Art Dirs. Club Greater Boston (officer), Internat. Assn. Bus. Communicators, Boston Jaycees, Nat. Assn. Printers and Lithographers, Printing Industries New Eng., Alpha Epsilon Pi. Jewish. Clubs: Masons, Shriners. Editor, pub.: Better Living mag., 1977—. Office: 1480 Great Plain Ave Needham MA 02192

NASH, E(MANUEL) WILLIAM, JR., ins. co. exec.; b. Mansfield, Ohio, Sept. 30, 1925; s. Emanuel William and Myrtle N.; student Wheaton Coll., 1947-48; B.B.A., Emory U., 1951; exec. program bus. adminstrn., Columbia U., 1974; businessman-in-residence, Guilford Coll., 1976; m. Frances Johnston, Dec. 20, 1949; children—Emanuel William III, Katherine. With Prudential Ins. Co. Am., 1951—, pres. charge Southwestern ops., Houston, 1978—. Bd. dirs. YMCA, Univ. Cancer Found., Better Bus. Bur., Rice Center, St. Joseph Hosp. Found., Houston Symphony Soc., Houston Ballet Found., Sam Houston council Boy Scouts Am.; bd. visitors Guilford Coll.; adv. bd. trustees United Way of Houston and Harris County; founding bd. dirs. Forum Club of Houston. Served with USNR, 1943-46. C.L.U. Mem. Am. Coll. Life Underwriters, Life Ins. Mktg. and Research Assn., Houston C. of C. Methodist. Clubs: Ramada, Houstonian (Houston). Office: PO Box 2075 Houston TX 77001

NASH, ELIZABETH IVES, securities co. exec.; b. W. Chazy, N.Y., Aug. 5, 1909; d. Alfred Peabody and Eleanor Collista (Stoughton) Ives; student bus. colls.; m. Maynard Nash, Dec. 7, 1929; 1 son, Paul Ives. Sec., treas., dir. Maynard Nash, Inc., contractor, Stamford, Conn., 1950-68; stock broker, asst. v.p. Hardy, Hardy & Assos. Inc. (merged with Raymond, James & Assos. 1976) Sarasota, Fla., 1961-76, stock broker, fin. planning exec., 1976—. Mem. N.Y., Phila., Balt., Washington stock exchanges. Bd. assos. First Step, Inc., Sarasota. Mem. Mut. Fund Council, Internat. Assn. Fin. Planners. Club: Field (Sarasota). Home: 3936 Shell Rd Sarasota FL 33581 Office: 1718 Main St Sarasota FL 33577

NASH, ROBERT J., banker; b. Binghamton, N.Y., Sept. 13, 1916; s. Benjamin J. and Florence G. (Terry) N.; student Am. Inst. Banking, Dartmouth Coll.; M.S. in Banking, Rutgers U., postgrad.; m. Harriette Weir, May 17, 1942; children—Lonson W., Warren J., Vincent M. With Binghamton (N.Y.) Savs. Bank, 1934—, pres., chief exec. officer, 1971—. Bd. dirs. Valley Devel. Found., Binghamton, Conrad and Virginia Klee Found., Inc., Binghamton, New Industries for Broome; mem. N.Y. Bus. Devel. Corp.; bd. dirs. B.C. Pops. Served with U.S. Army, 1942-45. Mem. Savs. Banks Assn. N.Y. (chmn. 1979-80), Nat. Assn. Mut. Savs. Banks (dir.), Instl. Securities Corp. (dir.). Presbyterian. Home: 518 Lowell Dr Endwell NY 13760 Office: 58 68 Exchange St Binghamton NY 13902

NASHEM, LELAND O., life ins., recruiting exec.; b. Seattle; s. Oscar and Myrtle A. (Spriggs) N.; ed. U. Wash.; children—Bettie Lee, Jack Lee. Pres., Nashem Furniture Co., Inc.; sales mgr. Kaufmann Leonard Co., furniture chain stores, 1930-33; with Met. Life Ins. Co., successively agt., asst. mgr., personal asst. mgr.; with Acacia Mut. Life Ins. Co., mgr. Seattle br., asst. field v.p. home office, Washington, mgr. Chgo. br.; pres. Lee Nashem Agy. Ltd.; gen. agt. Mut. Benefit Life Ins. Co. of Newark, N.Y.C.; gen. agt., sec. U.S. gen. agts. and mgrs. council Can. Life Assurance Co., Toronto, Ont.; dir., chmn. exec. com. Life Ins. Securities Corp.; pres., chief exec. Exec. Recruiting Agy., affiliate Lee Nashem Cos.; dir. Major Pools Equipment Corp., 1st Maine Corp., Maine Indemnity Corp., Madison Finance Corp., Roger Williams Ins. Co. Mem. Nat. Assn. Life Underwriters, Life Mgrs. Assn. N.Y., Midtown Mgrs. N.Y., Nat. Sales Execs. Club. Mason (K.T., Shriner), Rotarian. Clubs: Westchester Country (Rye, N.Y.); Boulder Brook (Scarsdale, N.Y.); New York Athletic, Sales Executives (N.Y.C.); Hunt, Oak Brook Polo (Hinsdale, Ill.); Century City (Calif.). Home: 2222 Ave of Stars Los Angeles CA 90067 Office: 1901 Ave of Stars Los Angeles CA 90067

NASON, GEORGE MALCOLM, computer systems and services co. exec.; b. Spokane, Wash., Feb. 17, 1933; s. George Malcolm and Ella (Buist) N.; B.S., Calif. State Coll. at Long Beach, 1958; m. Dolores Irene Lockinger, Oct. 7, 1951; children—George Malcolm III, Scott, Lance, Natalie. Data processor, project mgr. Gen. Motors Corp., Los Angeles, 1956-65; systems mgr. dairy div. Arden Mayfair, 1965-68; dir. systems Gallo Winery, Los Angeles, Modesto, Calif., 1968-73; dir. systems and data processing Familian Corp., 1973-74; v.p. Coldwell Banker & Co., Los Angeles, 1974-78; pres. Nason & Assos., Inc., Long Beach, Calif., 1978—. Bd. dirs. Confrat. of Christian Doctrine High Sch., Long Beach, 1969-70. Served with USMCR, 1951-54. Mem. Data Processing Mgmt. Assn. Republican. Roman Catholic. Home: 4503 Pepperwood Ave Long Beach CA 90808

NASON, HOWARD KING, research exec.; b. Kansas City, Mo., July 12, 1913; s. Eber James and Florence (King) N.; student Kansas City Jr. Coll., 1929-32; A.B., U. Kans., 1934; postgrad. Washington U., 1937, Harvard Grad. Sch. Bus. Adminstrn., 1950. Chief chemist Anderson-Stolz Corp., Kansas City, 1935-36; with Monsanto Co., St. Louis, 1936-60, successively research chemist, asst. dir. research plastics div., asso. dir., dir. central research dept., asst. to v.p., research dir. organic chems. div., 1936-56, gen. mgr. research and engring. div., v.p., 1956-60; pres. Monsanto Research Corp., 1960-76; pres. Indsl. Research Inst. Research Corp., 1976-80, also cons.; mem. adv. com. isotopes and radiation devel. AEC, 1964-68; mem. Atomic Energy Labor-Mgmt. Adv. Com., 1965—; mem. President's Commn. on Patent System, 1965-68; v.p., exec. com. Atomic Indsl. Forum, 1971-73; mem. Planetarium Commn., St. Louis, 1966—; mem. patent adv. com. U.S. Patent Office, 1968-70; chmn. Aerospace Safety Adv. Panel, 1972-79; mem. ad hoc com. sci. application and coordination Nat. Materials Adv. Bd., 1972-74; mem. nat. materials adv. bd. Nat. Acad. Engring., 1973-76; mem. task force on demonstration plants ERDA, 1975-77; mem. industry task force NSF, 1976; chmn. bd. St. Louis Research Council, 1971-73; mem. investment adv. com. St. Louis County Fund, 1976—. Bd. dirs., exec. com. St. Louis Regional Commerce and Growth Assn., 1971-74; trustee-at-large Univs. Research Assn., 1973-79; trustee Charles F. Kettering Research Found., 1973—. Exec. fellow Rensselaer Poly. Inst., 1977—. Mem. U.S. C. of C. (com. on sci. and tech. 1968-71), Soc. Chem. Industry, Am. Chem. Soc., Am. Inst. Chem. Engrs., AAAS, Nat. Rifle Assn., ASTM (dir.), Am. Inst. Chemists, Mfg. Chemists Assn. (nuclear com.), Sci. Research Soc. Am. Clubs: St. Louis, Quiet Birdmen (St. Louis); Cosmos (D.C.); Washington U. Faculty Conf. Center; Commanderie de Bordeaux (maitre), Confrerie des Chevaliers du Tastevin (officier commandeur). Contbr. articles to profl. jours. Patentee in field. Office: 7800 Bonhomme Ave Clayton MO 63105

NASON, ROBERT EARL, acctg. firm exec.; b. Sioux Falls, S.D., July 29, 1936; s. Earl V. and Eileen P. Nason; B.S., U. S.D., 1958; m. Carol Ann Horton, Oct. 6, 1962; children—Steven R., Jill Renee. With Alexander Grant & Co., 1958—, mng. partner, Cleve., 1971-76, Chgo., 1976-80, nat. mng. partner, 1980—, mem. exec. com., 1978—. Active United Way Met. Chgo., 1976—. Mem. Am. Inst. C.P.A.'s, Ill. Soc. C.P.A.'s, Chgo. Assn. Commerce and Industry. Presbyterian. Clubs: Exmoor Country, Mid Am., Plaza, Econ. of Chgo., Exec. of Chgo. Office: 39th Floor Prudential Plaza Chicago IL 60601

NATHAN, EDWARD ANTON, automobile mfg. co. ofcl.; b. Trenton, N.J., July 13, 1952; s. Albert Lee and Norma Elsie N.; A.A., Northwood Inst., 1974; B.A., Fordham U., 1977, M.B.A., 1979; m. Theresa Ann Stengele, Dec. 23, 1975. Mktg. rep. Oldsmobile div. Gen. Motors Corp., N.Y.C., 1974-77; field coordinator Nat. Automobile Dealers Assn., McLean, Va., 1977-78; asst. v.p. Term Industries, N.Y.C., 1978-79; mgmt. trainee Citibank N.A., N.Y.C., 1979-80; computer sales analyst, N.Y.C. rep. Oakleaf & Assos., N.Y.C., 1980-81; mgr. data processing adminstrn. World-Wide Volkswagen Corp., Orangeburg, N.Y., 1981—. Mem. Assn. M.B.A. Execs., Nat. Assn. Underwater Instrs., Chi Alpha Mu. Republican. Jewish. Clubs: Fordham-Cornell; Bay City Hunting and Fishing Lodge (Roscomon, Mich.). Home: 80 Central Park W New York NY 10023 Office: Volkswagen Greenbush Rd Orangeburg NY 10962

NATION, OSLIN, air conditioning equipment mfg. co. exec.; b. Erie, Kans., Apr. 11, 1914; s. Howard Seth and Dorothy (Oslin) N.; B.S. in Elec. Engring., So. Meth. U.; m. Merle Nation, June 4, 1939; children—James H., Patricia R., Linda. Pres., Oslin Nation Co., Dallas, 1959—; exec. v.p. First Co., 1966—; dir. Forestwood Nat. Bank. Mem. ASHRAE, Tex. Soc. Profl. Engrs. Baptist. Clubs: Engrs., Dallas Athletic, Masons, Shriners. Office: Oslin Nation Co 2532 Irving Blvd Dallas TX 75207

NATIONS, HOWARD LYNN, lawyer; b. Dalton, Ga., Jan. 9, 1938; s. Howard L. and Eva Earline (Armstrong) N.; B.A., Fla. State U., 1963; LL.B., Vanderbilt, 1966; 1 dau., Cynthia Lynn. Admitted to Tex. bar, 1966, U.S. Supreme Ct. bar, 1969; asso. firm Butler, Binion, Rice, Cook & Knapp, Houston, 1966-71; pres. Nations & Cross, Inc., Houston, 1968—; v.p., gen. counsel Ins. Corp. of Am., Houston, 1973—; pres. NCM Trade Corp., Houston, 1974—; Delher Am., Inc., 1975—; adj. prof. law S. Tex. Coll. Law, 1968—; dir. Ins. Corp. Am. Served with U.S. Army, 1957-60. Mem. State Bar Tex., Harris County, Am. bar assns., Harris County, Tex. trial lawyers assns., Assn. Trial Lawyers Am., Harris County, Tex. Criminal lawyers assns. Presbyterian. Contbr. articles to profl. jours. Home: 122 Sugarberry Circle Houston TX 77024 Office: 3000 Post Oak Rd Suite 1500 Houston TX 77056

NATT, ROBERT LESTER, cruise co. exec.; b. Newark, May 28, 1948; s. Walter J. and Relly Seeman; B.A., Queens Coll., 1969; M.B.A., Columbia U., 1971; m. Helen Marie Mc Kerlie, May 23, 1971; children—Beth, Thomas. Prin., Arthur Andersen & Co., C.P.A., N.Y.C., 1971-76, Hurdman & Cranstoun, C.P.A., N.Y.C., 1976-78; dir. budgets Holland Am. Cruises, N.Y.C., 1975—, exec. asst. to pres., 1979-80. C.P.A., N.Y. Mem. Am. Inst. C.P.A.'s, N.Y. State Soc. C.P.A.'s, Nat. Accountants Assn. Home: 15 Pawnee Rd East Brunswick NJ 08816 Office: 2 Penn Plaza New York NY 10001

NAUERT, ROBERT W., ins. exec.; b. Boscobel, Wis., Sept. 15, 1901; s. Joseph and Matilda (Dilger) N.; student high sch.; specialized ins. training courses; m. Irene H. Huepenbecker, Sept. 5, 1923; children—Robert, Mary A., Peter W. Owner and operator gen. ins. agency, Wis., 1921-32; then with Ill. ins. cos.; chmn., chief exec. officer Pioneer Life Ins. Co. Ill., Rockford. Mem. lay bd. St. Anthony Hosp.; bd. dirs. Delavan Lake Improvement Assn. K.C. (4 deg.), Elk. Republican. Roman Catholic. Club: Forest Hills Country. Home: 1020 N 2d St Rockford IL 61107 Office: Delavan Lake WI 53115

NAUGHTON, PAUL FRANCIS, utility exec.; b. Port Monmouth, N.J., Sept. 1, 1942; s. John Paul and Gertrude (Sheehan) N.; B.S., LaSalle Coll., 1964; M.B.A., St. John's U., 1969; m. Jean Connell, Sept. 18, 1965; children—Thomas, Brian, Jacqueline Ann. Sr. analyst Dean Witter & Co., N.Y.C., 1968-70; partner, sr. analyst F.S. Smithers & Co., N.Y.C., 1970-72; v.p. 1st Boston Corp., N.Y.C., 1972-75; treas. Am. Natural Service Co., Detroit, 1975-79; v.p. Dean Witter Reynolds Inc., 1979-81; v.p. fin. Mich. Consol. Gas Co., Detroit, 1981—. Mem. N.Y. Soc. Security Analysts, Delta Sigma Pi. Clubs: Econ. (Detroit); Top of the World (N.Y.C.). Home: 4215 N Willoway Estates Ct Bloomfield Hills MI 48013 Office: One Woodward Ave Detroit MI 48226

NAUGLE, THOMAS EARL, well servicing equipment mfg. co. exec.; b. Garber, Okla., Feb. 12, 1939; s. Earl H. and Amber (Dunlavy) N.; B.S., Okla. State U., 1961; M.B.A., Harvard, 1967; m. Barbara Naugle; children—Kimberly, Rodney Bo. Prodn. engr. Union Carbide Co., Texas City, Tex., 1961-62; process econs. engr. Skelly Oil Co., Tulsa, 1963-65; planning analyst Cooper Industries, Inc., Houston, 1967-68, pres. Pa. Pump & Compressor div., 1969-72, pres. CB/So. div., 1968-69, corporate v.p. planning, 1972-74; pres. Cooper Energy Services Group, Mt. Vernon, Ohio, 1974-79; corp. sr. v.p. Cooper Industries, 1979-80; pres., chief exec. officer Cooper Mfg. Corp., Tulsa, 1980—. Home: 6699 Timberlane Rd Tulsa OK 74136 Office: Cooper Mfg Corp PO Box 3108 Tulsa OK 74101

NAUMAN, EDWARD FRANKLIN, electronics mfg. co. exec.; b. Kansas City, Mo., May 1, 1915; s. Edward Augustus and Lida (Stevens) N.; B.Sc. in Chem. Engring., Kansas City Jr. Coll., 1935; postgrad. in chemistry U. Kansas City, 1939-40; m. Elizabeth Wiles, Feb. 6, 1943 (dec. 1962); m. 2d, Jeanne Gardner, Nov. 1963 (div. 1970); children—Edward Bruce, Kent Jerome, Mark Robert; m. 3d, Eleanor Conley, Jan. 18, 1973. Chem. engr., explosives research Remington Arms Co., Independence, Mo., 1941-45; tech. dir. J.A. Folger & Co., Kansas City, Mo., 1945-54; gen. mgr. Thiokol Chem. Corp., Marshall, Tex., 1954-60, Brigham City, Utah, 1960-65, v.p., 1963-65; sr. exec. research and devel., v.p., dir. U.S. Plywood-Champion Papers, Inc., Chgo. 1965-71; pres. Disposal Systems, Inc., 1971-73; pres. Nauman Electronics Co., 1975—; chmn. bd. Disposal Tech., Inc. Chmn., Airport Adv. Bd. Harrison County (Tex.), 1958-60; active United Fund, 1951—. Mem. Am. Inst. Chem. Engrs. (v.p. E. Tex. chpt. 1959-60), C. of C. (dir. 1958-60), Am. Ordnance Assn. (v.p. Shreveport post 1959-60), Am. Rocket Soc., Am. Chem. Soc., AAAS, Assn. U.S. Army, N.Y. Acad. Scis. Clubs: Rotary, Marshall Country, Chemists of N.Y.; Union League (Chgo.). Inventions in field of extraction, heat transfer, materials handling, pigments and organic chems., electronic devices. Home: 508 Highland Blvd Brigham City UT 84302

NAUMANN, WILLIAM LOUIS, mfg. co. exec.; b. Desloge, Mo., Nov. 20, 1911; s. Jules L. and Barbara (Eichenlaub) N.; ed. pub. schs., Ill.; m. Emma H. Bottin, June 1, 1934; children—William C., Virginia L. With Caterpillar Tractor Co., Peoria, Ill., 1929—, mgr. Joliet plant, 1952-56, mgr. Peoria plant, 1956-60, v.p. charge direction domestic plants, 1960-63, v.p. charge mfg., purchasing quality control and traffic, 1963-66, exec. v.p., 1966-72, vice chmn. bd., 1972-75, chmn. bd., 1975-77, chief exec. officer, 1975—, also dir.; dir. Pekin Nat. Bank (Ill.), Jefferson Trust & Savs. Bank of Peoria, Abex Corp., IC Industries, Inc., IC Products Co., Helmerich & Payne, Inc., Hussman Refrigerator Co., No. Telecom Ltd., Verson Allsteel Press Co. Mem. adv. bd. St. Francis Hosp., Peoria; trustee Ill. Wesleyan U., Bradley U.; bd. govs. Purdue Found. Home: 3619 Sandia Dr Peoria IL 61604 Office: Caterpillar Tractor Co 100 NE Adams St Peoria IL 61629

NAUSS, JOHN FREDERICK, ins. agy. exec.; b. Glencoe, Ill., June 5, 1929; s. Louis H. and Ursula M. (Ehrlichmann) N.; grad. Concordia Tchrs. Coll., River Forest, Ill., 1951; m. Jeanette L. Schlemeyer, Sept. 8, 1950; children—Philip R., Barbara B. Tchr. elem. sch., 1951-54; ins. salesman, 1954-56; instr. life ins. tng. United of Omaha, 1956-57; div. mgr. Mut. of Omaha, Indpls., 1957-60; pres. John F. Nauss & Assos., Inc., Eau Claire, Wis., 1960—; dir. Wising Inc., Broadway Investments. Mem. Eau Claire Aviation Com., 1961-63; chmn. deferred gifts Luther Hosp. Devel. Council, 1975—. C.L.U. Mem. Gen. Agts. and Mgrs. Assn., Chippewa Valley Life Underwriters, C.L.U. Assn. Republican. Lutheran. Club: Eau Claire Golf and

Country. Home: Route 6 Box 177 Eau Claire WI 54701 Office: 1612 S Hastings Way Eau Claire WI 54701

NAVARRO, CARLOS FRANCISCO, social program adminstr.; b. El Salvador, Dec. 3, 1934; came to U.S., 1956, naturalized, 1979; s. Jose Maria and Carmen (Coto) N.; student U. El Salvador, 1954-55; B.S. in Bus. Adminstrn., U. San Francisco, 1978, M. Public Adminstrn., 1980; m. Elba Moczo, Dec. 13, 1958; children—Francisco, Rosalba, Carlos, Elvira. Clk. recorder mgr. Assessor's Office, San Salvador, El Salvador, 1951-55; various positions, Calif., 1956-59; machine operator Nachman Corp., San Francisco, 1960-67; owner, chief instr. Navarro's Kenpo Karate Studio, San Francisco, 1968-78; exec. dir. Mission Neighborhood Phys. Devel., Inc., San Francisco, 1972—. Treas., Christian Family Movement, 1964-65; chmn. Mission Coalition Orgn. Recreation Com., 1971-72; pres. Amigos of Nicaragua, 1972-74; chmn. Mission Planning Council Recreation Task Force, 1973; sec. bd. dirs. El Salvador Soccer Club, 1976; pres. Pro-Retarded Children of San Miguel, 1976-77. Recipient outstanding performance cert. in community affairs City of San Francisco, 1974; plaque of recognition San Francisco Strikers, soccer, 1978; award of Merit, Honduras Soccer Club, San Francisco, 1979; holder 5th degree black belt in Kenpo karate, oriental weapons, juijitsu, Chinese boxing and Kung-fu. Mem. Latin Am. Fedn. Karate, No. Calif. Karate Referees Assn. (dir.). Office: Mission Neighborhood Phys Devel Inc 1292 Potrero Ave San Francisco CA 94110

NAVARRO, RICARDO ANTONIO, fin. cons., structural engr.; b. Phila., Aug. 8, 1950; s. Saturnino G. and Juanita (Taylor) N.; student Northrop Inst. Tech., Calif., 1968-70; B.Structural Engring., U. Calif., Los Angeles, 1972; M.B.A., Stanford, 1975. Mem. tech. staff Rockwell Internat., Inc., Downey, Calif., 1972-73; instr. math. U. Calif., Los Angeles, 1972-73; asst. v.p. corporate fin. dept. Citibank, N.A., N.Y.C., 1975—; fin. cons. Stanford Research Inst., summer 1974. Mem. Am. Inst. Aeros. and Astronautics, Am. Mgmt. Assn., Smithsonian Instn., Met. Mus. Art. Home: 500 E 77th St New York NY 10021 Office: 399 Park Ave Corporate Finance Dept Citibank N A New York NY 10043

NAVEJA, ALBERT FRANCIS, banker; b. Queens, N.Y., Nov. 10, 1941; s. Louis P. and Violet A. (Alvarez) N.; B.S. in Mgmt., St. John's U., 1969; m. Carol Anne Testa, July 18, 1965; children—Tracy Anne, Christopher Scott. Asst. sec. Mfrs.' Hanover Trust Co., N.Y.C., 1964-71; v.p., gen. mgr. Harris Bank Internat. Corp., N.Y.C., 1971-76, v.p., div. adminstr. internat. fin. services, Chgo., 1976—, dir. Harris Bank Internat. Corp. Mem. planning com. Met. Housing and Planning Council Chgo. Served with USAF, 1960-64. Mem. Bankers Assn. for Fgn. Trade (EDGE Act com.). Naperville (Ill.) Heritage Soc. Roman Catholic. Clubs: Cress Creek Country; Internat. Trade (export expansion com.) (Chgo.). Home: 749 Bauer Rd Naperville IL 60540 Office: Harris Bank 111 W Monroe St Chicago IL 60690

NAWN, JOHN FRANCIS, mfg. co. exec.; b. Boston, Feb. 28, 1930; s. Leo J. and Louise M. (Whelan) N.; B.S., Coll. Holy Cross, Worcester, Mass., 1952; M.B.A., Colo. State U., 1976; m. JoAnne Young, Aug. 7, 1954; children—Priscilla, John Francis, Christopher, Timothy, Andrew. Vice pres., sec. Leo J. Nawn, Inc., constrn., Boston, 1956-60; with Johns Manville Sales Corp., 1961-77, nat. mktg. mgr., Denver, 1972-74, v.p., mdse. mgr., 1974-77; regional mgr. Automatic Sprinkler Corp. Am., 1978; v.p. sales Can-Tex Industries div. Harsco, Mineral Wells, Tex., 1979—. Trustee, Kent-Denver Country Day Sch., 1974-76; bd. dirs. Met.-Denver Youth Hockey Program, 1974—. Served to maf. C.E., AUS, 1952-55; Korea. Mem. Am. Water Works Assn., Water Pollution Control Fedn., Nat. Elec. Mfrs. Assn., Uni-Bell Plastic Pipe Assn. (pres. 1977). Clubs: Denver Country; Colonial Country (Ft. Worth). Address: 3709 Autumn Dr Fort Worth TX

NAYLOR, GEORGE LEROY, R.R. exec.; b. Bountiful, Utah, May 11, 1915; s. Joseph Francis and Josephine Chase (Wood) N.; student U. Utah, 1934-36; student George Washington U., 1937; J.D. (Bancroft Whitney scholar), U. San Francisco, 1953; m. Maxine Elizabeth Lewis, Jan. 18, 1941; children—Georgia (Mrs. Ralph E. Price), RoseMaree (Mrs. Glenn B. Hammer), George LeRoy II. Admitted to Calif. bar, 1954, Ill. bar, 1968; v.p., sec., legis. rep. Internat. Union Mine, Mill & Smelter Workers, CIO, Dist. Union 2, Utah-Nevada, 1942-44; examiner So. Pacific Co., San Francisco, 1949-54, chief examiner, 1955, asst. mgr., 1956-61; carrier mem. Nat. R.R. Adjustment bd., Chgo., 1961-77, chmn., 1970-77; atty. Village of Fox River Valley Gardens (Ill.), 1974-77; gen. counsel Can-Veyor, Inc., Mountain View, Calif., 1959-64. Served with AUS, World War II. Mem. Am. Bar Assn. Mem. Ch. of Jesus Christ of Latter Day Saints. Author: Defending Carriers Before the NRAB and Public Law Boards, 1969; Choice Morsels in Tax and Property Law, 1966; Underground at Bingham Canyon, 1944; Nat. R.R. Adjustment Bd. Practice Manual, 1978. Home: 8417 Klondike Rd Pensacola FL 32506

NAYLOR, PLEAS COLEMAN, JR., Realtor; b. Clareville, Tex., Nov. 22, 1914; s. Pleas Coleman and Beulah (Pettus) N.; student U. Tex., 1934-36; LL.D. (hon.), U. Tex.-San Antonio, 1969; children—Ruth (Mrs. Charles Schraedley), Ellen Ferne (Mrs. Ron L. Mooney), Patty (Mrs. Don Martin), Chester Slimp III; m. 2d, Ellen Watson, Apr. 14, 1962. Office mgr. Comml. Credit Corp., San Antonio, 1936-46; pres., owner Naylor Realty, Inc., San Antonio, 1946—; faculty mem. St. Mary's U., San Antonio, 1965-69; dir. Community Title Co.; owner, developer Tri-County Indsl. and Bus. Park; pres. N.R.E., Inc., Naylor Enterprises, Inc.; mem. Tex. Real Estate Commn., 1965-69, chmn., 1968-69; rancher. Mem. San Antonio City Council, 1971-73; campaign chmn. Alamo council Camp Fire Girls, 1971, council adviser, 1971-73. Chmn. Bexar County Democratic Com. for Election Preston Smith for Gov. Tex., 1970. Trustee S.W. Research Inst., 1970—; bd. dirs. Taxpayers League Bexar County, 1962-64, Tex. Good Rds. Assn.; bd. govs. S.W. Heart and Lung Center. Served with AUS, 1943-45. Named San Antonio Realtor of Yr., 1958; Tex. Realtor of Yr., 1968. Accredited farm and land broker; certified property mgr. Mem. Nat. (dir. 1973, regional v.p. Tex. and La. 1969), Tex. (dir.; pres. 1967) assns. Realtors, San Antonio Bd. Realtors (pres. 1950; dir. 1951-66), Soc. Indsl. Realtors, Realtors Nat. Mktg. Inst., Nat. Assn. Rev. Appraisers (sr.), Am. Polled Hereford Assn., Am. Indsl. Devel. Council, Internat. Platform Assn., Internat. Oceanographic Found., Polit. Action Com. Texans, Truman Library Inst. Nat. and State Affairs, Research and Planning Council (past pres.), Tex. Research League, Urban Land Inst., San Antonio Council Presidents, San Antonio Mus. Assn., San Antonio Livestock Exposition (life), Farm and Land Inst., Nat. Inst. Real Estate Mgmt., Tex. Property Exchangors, Tex. Soc. Farm and Ranch Mgrs. and Appraisers, Internat. Real Estate Fedn., San Antonio C. of C. (dir. 1971-73). Mason (32 deg., Shriner). Home: 327 Clubhill Dr San Antonio TX 78228 Office: 7475 Callaghan Rd Suite 200 San Antonio TX 78229

NAZARETH, VASCO PHILIP, mfg. co. exec.; b. Lisbon, Portugal, Feb. 19, 1937; s. John dePaiva and Marie C. (Serra) N.; B.A., U. Louvain (Belgium), 1959, M.B.A., 1961; diploma in Internat. Law, U. Lisbon, 1960; postgrad. Washington U., St. Louis, 1961-63; m. Jeanine Y. Mousset, Feb. 26, 1962; 1 dau., Ann M. Came to U.S., 1961, naturalized, 1966. Dir. Econ. Service Angolese Govt. (W. Africa), 1959; cons. Petrofina Oil Co. (Africa), 1960; mgmt. positions in marketing, bus. planning, internat. sales various divs. Gen. Electric Co., 1963-74; v.p. internat. mktg. and sales Joy Mfg. Co., Pitts., 1974-76; pres. Joy Mfg. Sales Ltd., N.Y.C., 1974-76, group v.p. internat. group, 1976-77; group v.p. internat. group Cooper Industries/Gardner-Denver, Dallas, 1977-78, sr. v.p., 1978-79, pres. mining and constrn. group, 1979—; mem. faculty Washington U., St. Louis, 1962. Bd. dirs. Dallas Opera, Dallas Theater Center; trustee Dallas Symphony. Decorated Order Arthus; Herman Found. fellow, 1961; Gulbenkian fellow, 1962; Ky. col., 1967. Mem. Am. Mining Congress (bd. govs.), Internat. Compressed Air Assn. (exec. com.), Omicron Delta Gamma. Author: L'Angola et son Expansion Industrielle, 1961. Contbr. articles to profl. jours. Home: 5503 Bent Tree Dr Dallas TX 75248 Office: Suite 500 8585 Stemmons Freeway Dallas TX 75247

NAZAREWICZ, WALTER, chem. co. exec.; b. N.Y.C., July 18, 1927; s. Peter and Anna (Derevlany) N.; B.Ch.E., Cooper Union, N.Y.C., 1949; M.Ch.E., N.Y. U., 1952; m. Frances R. Ziejka, Apr. 19, 1953; children—Susan Frances, Scott Peter. With research and devel. Pfizer, Inc., N.Y.C., 1949-60, dir. comml. devel., 1960-66, dir. licensing, 1966-70, pres., mng. dir. Pfizer Quigley K.K., Japan, 1970-74, v.p. mktg. MPM div., 1974-79, v.p. minerals MPM div., 1980—. Served with AUS, 1945-47. Mem. Am. Chem. Soc., Ukrainian Inst. Am., Sales Execs. Club N.Y.C. Home: 106 Split Oak Dr East Norwich NY 11732 Office: 235 E 42d St New York NY 10017

NAZEM, FEREYDOUN FRED, investment co. exec.; b. Tehran, Iran, Dec. 29, 1940; s. Hassan and Afsar N.; B.Sc. in Chemistry (merit scholar), Ohio State U., 1964; M.Sc. (fellow), U. Cin., 1967; M.B.A., Columbia U., 1971; m. Susie Gharib, Jan. 20, 1973. Sr. research chemist Matheson Coleman & Bell, Norwood, Ohio, 1967-68; asst. v.p., investment analyst Irving Trust Co., N.Y.C., 1969-74; venture capital officer, v.p. Charter N.Y. Corp., N.Y.C., 1974-75; exec. v.p. fin. Tehran Cement Co., 1975-76; mng. dir. Collier Enterprises, N.Y.C., 1976—; dir. Delmed, Inc., Newton, Mass., AMDAX Corp., Bohemia, N.Y., Control Transaction Corp., Fairfield, N.J. Mem. N.Y. Soc. Security Analysts, N.Y. Venture Capital Forum. Club: Columbia Tennis. Author: The Chemical Industry and the Energy Shortage, 1973. Contbr. articles to profl. jours.; one-man photography shows, 1963, 64, 66, 67. Home: 1185 Park Ave New York NY 10028 Office: 655 Madison Ave New York NY 10021

NEAD, RICHARD GORDON, ins. agy. exec.; b. Norwood, Mass., Dec. 19, 1925; s. Carroll Plimpton and Nadine Edith (Gustavison) N.; B.A., Tufts U., 1950; m. Carolyn Ada Nickerson, June 19, 1949; children—Judith Nickerson, Amanda Crowell. With Frank A. Morrill, Inc., Norwood, 1950—, pres., 1977—; mem. governing com. Mass. Motor Vehicle Reins. Facility, 1974-78; agts. adv. council Utica Mut. Ins. Co., Travelers Ins. Co., Excelsior Ins. Co.; bd. dirs. Ins. Inst. of Northeastern U. Trustees Norwood Hosp., 1976—, now v.p.; chmn. Norwood Bd. Public Welfare, 1953-56; former pres. Norwood ARC, March of Dimes, United Fund. Served with USNR, 1943-46. Mem. Ind. Ins. Agts. Am. (past pres. Mass.), Soc. C.P.C.U.'s (past pres. Boston chpt.), Nat. Assn. Ins. Brokers (dir. 1973-75, 77-80), Profl. Ins. Agts. New Eng., Am. Mgmt. Soc. Republican. Clubs: Rotary, Kiwanis (past pres. Norwood chpt.), Masons. Home: 2 Brookfield Rd Dover MA 02030 Office: 19 Central St Norwood MA 02062

NEADEAU, LESLIE LEROY, former lumber co. exec.; b. Atlanta, Dec. 28, 1917; s. Mark M. and Edna H. (Poque) N.; student Golden Gate Jr. Coll., 1935-36, San Francisco State Tchrs. Coll., 1936-38; m. Ruth E. Krings, Jan. 28, 1945; children—Marion Diane, Leslie Leroy II, Denise D. Vice pres. Hogan & Van Gelder Lumber Co., Inc., San Francisco, 1945-48; pres. Neadeau Wholesale Lumber Co., Inc., San Francisco, 1948-50, Big Bear Lumber Co., Inc., San Francisco, 1948-50, Mill Reps. Inc., San Francisco, 1950-63; v.p. Hedlund Lumber Sales Co., Sacramento, 1963-70; pres. Am. Lumber Species, Inc., Sacramento, 1970—, Mountain Milling, Inc., Rocklin, Calif., 1973-78, div. mgr. Forest Products Mfg. Co. subs., Rocklin, 1975-77; div. mgr. nat. div. J.E. Higgins Lumber Co., Inc., Rocklin, 1975-77; pres. Pacific Laminates, Inc., Reno, 1974-76, Surinam Gold & Minerals Co., Inc., Sacramento, 1978—; v.p. T.O.N.M. Oil & Gas Exploration Corp., Albuquerque, 1979, pres., 1979—. Bd. dirs. Ducks Unltd., Sacramento. Served to capt. USAAF, 1941-45. Lutheran (elder 1950-60). Clubs: Masons, Shriners, Commonwealth. Home: 872 Laverstock Way Sacramento CA 95825 Office: 105 Scripps Dr PO Box 255648 Sacramento CA 95825

NEAFSEY, JOHN PATRICK, oil co. exec.; b. Woodside, N.Y., Aug. 4, 1939; s. James and Mary C. (Burns) N.; B.S. in Mech. Engring. (Sloan scholar), Cornell U., 1962, M.B.A. in Fin., 1963; m. Marilla Bowman, Sept. 2, 1962; children—John P., Terence E., William C. Fin. analyst Esso Research and Engring., 1963-65; planning coordinator Standard Oil of N.J., 1965-67; mgr. corporate devel. Sun Oil Co., Radnor, Pa., 1967-68, asst. dir. internat. mktg., 1968-70, spl. assignment for exec. v.p. in products mktg., 1971-72, mgr. investor relations, 1972-74, v.p. fin. services, 1975-78, v.p. fin., 1978—; sec., treas. Sun of Pa., 1974-75; dir. Suncor, Inc. Bd. dirs. Riddle Meml. Hosp., Media, Pa., also chmn. fin. com.; mem. council Cornell U., Ithaca, N.Y., also mem. adv. council Grad. Sch. Bus. and Public Adminstrn. Mem. Am. Petroleum Inst., Pi Tau Sigma. Office: 100 Matsonford Rd Radnor PA 19087

NEAL, ROBERT EUGENE, JR., fin. and legal printing exec.; b. Lebanon, Ind., Aug. 22, 1944; s. Robert Eugene and Ruth Winifred (Medsker) N.; A.B., Wabash Coll., 1966; postgrad. Butler U., 1967-68; m. Gretchen Ann Rolfe, June 21, 1975; children—Patricia Lee, Lisa Lyn, David Christopher. With R. R. Donnelley & Sons, Chgo., 1966-69, exec. salesman, 1968-69; with Arcata Corp., Menlo Park, Calif., 1970-76, mgr. corporate planning and devel., 1975-76; pres. Bowne & Co., Inc., 1976—, Bowne of San Francisco, Inc., 1979—. Mem. Am. Soc. Corporate Secs., Printing Industries No. Calif. Republican. Clubs: Kiwanis, Tennis (San Francisco); Round Hill Golf and Country (Alamo, Calif.); Commonwealth of Calif. Home: 2644 Bridle Ln Walnut Creek CA 94596 Office: 190 9th St San Francisco CA 94103

NEALE, F. BRENT, investment banker; b. N.Y.C., Aug. 28, 1919; s. G. Brent and Sophie Hill (Hamilton) N.; student N.Y. Inst. Finance, 1938-41, St. Peter's Coll., 1950, N.Y. U. Grad. Sch. Bus., 1954-58, Coll. Fin. Planning, 1978-80; m. Elizabeth M. Rowan, Apr. 25, 1953. Asst. syndicate mgr. Loeb Rhoades Co., N.Y.C., 1945-54; syndicate mgr. Parrish & Co., N.Y.C., 1954-58; salesman Lehman Bros., N.Y.C., 1958-62; sales mgr. and v.p. Blair Granbery Marache & Co., N.Y.C., 1962-64; asso. mem. N.Y. Stock Exchange, 1962-64; asst. v.p. sales E.F. Hutton Co., N.Y.C., 1965-71; salesman Riter Pyne Kendall & Hollister, Inc., N.Y.C., 1971-72; instl. sales Hayden Stone Co., N.Y.C., 1972-74; investment banking and instl. sales Hoppin Watson Inc., N.Y.C., 1974-76; salesman Smith Barney, Harris Upham & Co., Inc., Tinton Falls, N.J., 1976-79; investment adviser, fin. planner, ins. agt.; dir. Pkwy. Plastics Co., Piscataway, N.J., 1960—, Neale Assos., 1978-79; mgr. tobacco farm, 1945-54. Chmn. Monmouth (N.J.) Ocean Damage Control Bd., 1958-64; chmn. Central Rd.-Seaview Ave.-Monmouth Beach Project, 1975—; mem. planning bd. Boro of Monmouth Beach, 1976-77, 78-81, commr. revenue and fin., 1977-78, mayor, 1978—; campaign mgr. Monmouth County Republican primary candidates, 1958, 62; trustee Ch. of Precious Blood, Monmouth Beach. Served with AUS, 1941-45. Decorated Purple Heart medal, Bronze Star medal, Combat Infantryman's Badge with 7 battle stars; recipient citations Fairleigh Dickinson U., 1954, 56, Kiwanis Internat., 1950, Internat. Lions Clubs, 1951, Catholic Action medal, 1950. Mem. Md. Soc., N.Y. Soc. (pres. 1951-54, 70-74), So. Soc. (trustee 1970-74), Wall Streeters (pres. 1958-76), SAR, Order Magna Charta (baron), Order Descs. Charlemagne, Sovereign Order Temple Jerusalem (knight), Manor Lords Md., Channel Club, City Midday Club, Money Marketeers, Soc. 1st Div., Cath. War Vets. (N.J. trustee 1948-50, comdr. Hudson County 1949-50), Monmouth Beach Bus. Men's Club. Clubs: K.C., Monmouth Beach Bath and Tennis (trustee 1972-75). Home and Office: 94 Ocean Ave Monmouth Beach NJ 07750

NEAS, JOHN THEODORE, petroleum co. exec.; b. Tulsa, May 1, 1940; s. George and Lillian J. (Kasper) N.; B.S., Okla. State U., 1967, M.S., 1968; m. Sally Jane McPherson, June 10, 1966; children—Stephen, Gregory. With accounting dept. Rockwell Internat., 1965; with controller's dept. Amoco Prodn. Co., 1966-67; mem. audit and tax staff Haskins & Sells, 1968-75; pres. Nat. Petroleum Sales, Inc., Tulsa, 1975—, Port City Bulk Terminals, Inc., Tulsa, 1976—; owner John Neas Tank Lines; asst. instr. U. Tulsa, 1974. C.P.A., Okla. Mem. Nat. Assn. Accountants (v.p. membership 1976-77), Am. Inst. C.P.A.'s, Okla. Soc. C.P.A.'s, Port of Catoosa C. of C. Republican. Lutheran. Clubs: Petroleum, Oil Marketers, Transportation (Tulsa); Propeller; Oaks Country. Home: 2943 E 69 St Tulsa OK 74136 Office: 3105 E Skelly Dr Suite 509 Tulsa OK 74105

NEBERGALL, DONALD CHARLES, bank exec.; b. Davenport, Iowa, Aug. 12, 1928; s. Ellis W. and Hilda N.; B.A., Iowa State U., 1951; m. Shirley Elaine Williams, Apr. 12, 1952; children—Robert W., Nancy L. Nebergall Bosma. With Poweschick County Nat. Bank, 1958-72, sr. v.p., to 1972; pres., dir. Brenton Bank and Trust Co., Cedar Rapids, Iowa, 1972—, dir. Brenton Banks, Inc.; dir. Telephone & Data Services Inc. Vice-pres., dir. Iowa 4-H Fedn., 1972-76; div. campaign chmn. United Way; bd. dirs. ARC, Boy Scouts Am. Served with AUS, 1946-48. Mem. Cedar Rapids Greater Downtown Assn. (pres., dir.), Delta Upsilon. Republican. Methodist. Office: Brenton Bank & Trust Co 150 1st Ave NE Cedar Rapids IA 52401

NEBO, CHINEDU OSITADINMA, mining co. exec.; b. Udi, Nigeria, June 3, 1952; s. Christopher Okeke and Francisca N.; B.S., S.D. Sch. Mines and Tech., 1978, M.S., 1979; m. July 23, 1977; children—Chidinma, Chinenye. Mgr., GESCO, Lagos, Nigeria, 1973-75; research metallurgist Duval Corp., Sahuarita, Ariz., 1979—; cons. African mineral resources and devel. Founder, Internat. Action for Africa. AMAX fellow, 1978-79. Mem. AIME, Am. Soc. Metals, Tau Beta Pi, Pi Mu Epsilon. Evangelical. Editor The Revivaltime, Nigeria, 1972-74. Office: PO Box 125 Sahuarita AZ 85629

NECKES, PAUL ROBERT, mfg. co. ofcl.; b. Boston, Dec. 27, 1932; s. Irving L. and Marion (Warshaw) N.; B.S. in Bus. Adminstrn., Boston U., 1959; m. Mary Cheverie, Nov. 25, 1972. Sportswear buyer D.M. Read Co., Bridgeport, Conn., 1959-62; mdse. coordinator Oxford Industries, N.Y.C., 1962-68; dir. purchasing Coll.-Town Sportswear, Braintree, Mass., 1968-74; product mgr. Etonic, Brockton, Mass., 1974—. Served with USAF, 1951-55. Mem. Am. Prodn. and Inventory Control Soc. Clubs: Masons, Shriners. Home: 60 Herring Weir Rd Duxbury MA 02332 Office: 147 Centre St Brockton MA 02403

NEDERVELD, TERRILL LEE, corporate mktg. mgr.; b. Hudsonville, Mich., Jan. 26, 1934; s. Fred and Clara (DeGroot) N.; student Purdue U., 1952, U. Mich., 1976; m. Ruth E. Schut, June 6, 1952; children—Courtland Lee, Valerie Lynn Nederveld Heisey, Darwin Frederick. With Packaging Corp. Am., 1953—, design mgr., 1959-67, market coordinator, Lancaster, Pa., 1967-73, mgr. market coordination, Grand Rapids, Mich., 1973-74, mktg. mgr., Grand Rapids, 1974-76, corp. mktg. mgr., 1976-79, dir. corp. mktg. services, 1980—; lectr. Mich. State Sch. Packaging, East Lansing, 1977-80, mem. indsl. adv. bd. Recipient Silver award for outstanding package devel. Mem. U.S. Power Squadron, Soc. Packaging and Handling Engrs., Sales Mktg. Execs. (1st v.p., pres. 1978-79), Pi Sigma Epsilon. Presbyterian (deacon). Clubs: Nat. Campers and Hikers, Masons (Shriner, 32 deg.). Patentee in packaging field. Office: 470 Market St Grand Rapids MI

NEDOM, H. ARTHUR, petroleum co. exec.; b. Lincoln, Nebr., Aug. 19, 1925; s. Henry Arthur and Pearle Bertrick (Swan) N.; B.S., U. Tulsa, 1949, M.S., 1950; m. Patricia Margaret Rankin, July 4, 1974; children—Nicole Christine, Richard A., Robert L. Chief engr. Amerada Petroleum Corp., Tulsa, 1961-65, v.p., 1965-71; v.p., dir. Natomas Co., San Francisco, 1971-74; pres. Norwegian Oil Co., Houston, 1974-75: pres., dir. Weeks Petroleum Ltd., Westport, Conn., 1975—; chmn. exec. com. Offshore Technology Conf., 1971; dir. Engrs. Joint Council, 1978. Served with U.S. Army, 1943-45. Decorated Bronze Star; recipient citation for service Am. Petroleum Inst., 1961; Disting. Alumni award U. Tulsa, 1972. Mem. Soc. Petroleum Engrs. (pres. 1967, dir. 1965-68, Disting. lectr. 1973, Disting. Service award 1978), Am. Inst. Mining, Metall. and Petroleum Engrs. (pres. 1977, dir. 1966-69, 76-79), Am. Assn. Petroleum Geologists, Am. Petroleum Inst., Am. Assn. Engring. Socs. (chmn. 1981). Presbyterian. Home: 21 Deerwood Ln Westport CT 06880 Office: One Sylvan Rd N Westport CT 06880

NEEB, LOUIS P., restaurants and holding co. exec. Chmn., chief exec. officer Burger King Corp. Office: Burger King Corp 7360 N Kendall Dr Miami FL 33156

NEECE, TALMADGE MACON, lawyer, ins. co. exec.; b. Pleasant Garden, N.C., Mar. 23, 1924; s. Rufus Talmadge and Anna Moleta (Macon) N.; B.S., Georgetown U., 1950; LL.B., U. Conn., 1962; m. Edith Glenn Shepherd, Sept. 11, 1948; children—Laura, Robert, Alice. With Travelers Ins. Co., Hartford, Conn., 1949-80, claims dir., 1973-80; admitted to Conn. bar, 1962; legal analyst Johnson & Higgins, N.Y.C., 1980—. Served to lt. USNR, 1944-46. C.P.C.U. Mem. Society of Friends. Contbr. articles to various publs. Office: 95 Wall St New York NY 10005

NEEDHAM, MAURICE E., printed circuits mfr.; b. Chelsea, Mass., Aug. 22, 1940; s. Maurice and Mary C. (Driscoll) N.; student U. Ala., 1960-61, Northeastern U., 1963-65, spl. courses U. Conn., 1975-77; m. Marjorie Hay, Feb. 7, 1959; children—Gary, Beth, Mark. Plant mgr. Electro Circuits, Lowell, Mass., 1963-69; pres. treas. A & M Constrn., Derry, N.H., 1974-76; pres., dir. Hadco Printed Circuits, Inc., Derry, 1969—; lectr. in field. Pres. Derry Indsl. Devel. Authority, Andover Sr. Little League; bd. dirs. So. N.H. United Way. Served with U.S. Army, 1958-61. Mem. Derry C. of C. (dir.), Am. Electro-Platers Soc., Inst. Printed Circuits. Office: Route 28 Manchester Rd Derry NH 03038

NEELLY, EDWIN C., III, banker; b. Greenwood, Miss., Oct. 2, 1939; s. E.C. and Margaret C. N.; B.B.A., U. Miss., 1961; postgrad. La. State U., 1973, Harvard U., 1975; m. Claudia Johnson, July 12,

1963; children—Edwin, Claudia Perry, Tucker McGowan. Asst. mgr. Bank of Ackerman (Miss.), 1964-66; exec. v.p., mgr. Calhoun County Bank, Calhoun City, Miss., 1966-73, Bank of Louisville, 1973-74; pres. Grenada (Miss.) Banking System, 1975—. Bd. dirs. U. Miss. Alumni Bd., 1978-81. Served with USAFR, 1963-69. Mem. Grenada C. of C. (dir.), Miss. Bankers Assn., Am. Bankers Assn. Republican. Presbyterian. Club: Rotary (past pres.). Office: PO Box 947 Grenada MS 38901

NEETZEL, RAYMOND JOHN, transit corp. exec.; b. St. Paul, Apr. 2, 1937; s. John Raymond and Alyce Irene (Berge) N.; B.A., U. Wis., Green Bay, 1973; M.B.A., St. Thomas Coll., 1978, cert. Urban Transp. Planning, 1976; m. Marlene Frances Jezierski; children—John, Michael, Thomas. Owner small bus., 1955-73; planning and devel. cons., 1979—; owner custom and handcrafted wood products co., 1979—; transit analyst Met. Transit Commn., St. Paul, 1973-76, sr. transit analyst, 1976—; guest lectr. U. Aston, Birmingham, Eng., 1972-73; cons. in field. Active Boy Scouts, community orgns. Mem. Nat. Inst. Transp. Engrs. Author: Handbook on Winter Survival Techniques, 1980. Home: 2003 James Ave Saint Paul MN 55105

NEEVES, JAMES PATRICK, chem. and consumer products co. exec.; b. N.Y.C., Apr. 6, 1937; s. Archibald Augustus and Ellen Margaret (Healy) N.; B.S., Columbia U., 1960; m. Cynthia Stone, Feb. 24, 1979. With W.R. Grace & Co., N.Y.C., 1960-69, 74—, v.p. planning, devel. Leisure Performance group, 1974-75, v.p. ops. Consumer Services group, 1976—, v.p. Gen. Devel. group Office of Strategic Projects, 1978—; exec. v.p., dir. Marine Internat. Corp., N.Y.C., 1969-73. Home: 250 E 65 St New York NY 10021 Office: 1114 Ave of Americas New York NY 10036

NEFF, CHARLES YEAGER, hose mfg. exec.; b. Sharon, Pa., Dec. 13, 1913; s. Harry C. and Helen (Yeager) N.; B.S.M.E., Cornell U., 1937; m. Mary C. Martindale, Nov. 26, 1942; children—Charles Y., Tamsey D. Sales mgr. foam div. Hewitt Robins, 1937-46; pres. Neff-Perkins Co., 1946-80, Fed. Hose Mfg. Corp., Painesville, Ohio, 1963—. Republican. Presbyterian. Clubs: Country, Rolling Rock, Lyford Cay. Office: PO Box 480 Painesville OH 44077

NEFF, FRANCINE IRVING, banker, former treas. U.S.; b. Albuquerque, Dec. 6, 1925; d. Edward Hackett and Georga (Henderson) Irving; B.A. with distinction, U. N.Mex., 1948; H.H.D. (hon.), Mt. St. Mary's Coll., N.Y., 1974; LL.D. (hon.), Am. Internat. Coll., Mass., 1975, N.Mex. State U., 1976; m. Edward John Neff, June 7, 1948; children—Sindle Neff Tomforde, Edward Vann. Nat. dir. U.S. Savs. Bonds div. Dept. Treasury, also treas. U.S., Washington, 1974-77; v.p. Rio Grande Valley Bank, Albuquerque, 1977—; dir. Hershey Foods Corp. (Pa.), E-Systems, Inc., Dallas. Pres., Inez chpt. PTA, 1960-61; Republican poll worker, Albuquerque, 1966-74; mem. N.Mex. Rep. state exec. com., 1966-74, state central com., 1966-74, 77-79; chmn. Women for Nixon, N.Mex., 1968; del. Rep. Nat. Conv., 1968, 72; nat. committeewoman, Rep. Nat. Com., 1970-74, mem. exec. com., 1973-74; pres. Rep. Women's Fed. Forum, Washington, 1975; pres. Albuquerque Rep. Federated Women's Club, 1977; Heart Sunday chmn. D.C. Heart Assn., 1975; adv. bd. Lovelace Med. Center, Albuquerque, 1979—; bd. dirs. United Way Greater Albuquerque, 1977-79, campaign chmn. profl. div., 1977; nat. bd. dirs. Camp Fire Girls, Inc., 1977-78, guardian local group, 1955-62. Recipient Exceptional Service award U.S. Dept. Treasury, 1976; Horatio Alger award Am. Schs. and Colls. Assn., 1976; Outstanding Alumni award Alpha Delta Pi, 1975, Phi Theta Kappa, 1976. Mem. Am. Bankers Assn., Nat. Assn. Banking Women, Nat. Assn. Bus. and Profl. Women, Mortar Bd. Alumnae (pres. 1966-67), Aux. N.Mex. Soc. C.P.A.'s (pres. 1961-62), Albuquerque City Panhellenic Assn. (alumnae pres. 1959-60), Greater Albuquerque C. of C. (dir. 1978—), Alpha Delta Pi (alumnae pres. 1956-57), Sigma Alpha Iota, Pi Lambda Theta, Phi Theta Kappa. Club: P.E.O. (chpt. pres. 1958-59, 63-64). Episcopalian. Office: 501 Tijeras NW Albuquerque NM 87102

NEFF, HOWARD JOSEPH, SR., restaurant chain exec.; b. Sandusky, Ohio, Dec. 20, 1923; s. Charles Joseph and Emily Teresa (Buerkle) N.; student Purdue U., 1942-43, Springfield (Mass.) Coll., 1944-45; diploma in acctg. Internat. Accts. Soc., 1950; m. Roberta Mae Schmitz, May 6, 1945; children—Joan Marie Neff Zobrist, Howard J., Dennis, Mark, Timothy, Christopher. Partner, Neff & Sons, Public Accountants, Ohio, 1945-58; exec. v.p., controller Cassano's Inc., Dayton, Ohio, 1958-75, pres., 1975—; dir. Citizens Fed. Savs. & Loan Assn. Mem. food service adv. com. Montgomery County Vocat. Sch., 1974; bd. trustees St. Elizabeth Hosp. Found.; adv. bd. Inst. Community and Orgn. Devel. of Wright State U. Served with USAAF, 1943-45. Clubs Optimists, K.C. Home: 7436 Heatherwood Ct Dayton OH 45459 Office: 1700 E Stroop Rd Dayton OH 45429

NEFF, JOHN EARLE, JR., ins. co. exec.; b. Lake Charles, La., July 30, 1924; s. John Earle and Mary Edith (Bergstedt) N.; B.S., U. Tex., Austin, 1944, B.B.A., 1946, M.B.A., 1948; diploma Inst. Ins. Mktg., So. Methodist U.; m. Barbara Louise Davis (Dec. May 1974); children—Nancy Louise, Barbara Gretchen, John Earle; m. 2d, Julie Ann Simmons, Nov. 4, 1978. With Nat. Western Life Ins. Co., and predecessors, 1950-63, v.p., dir., to 1963; pres. Am. Savers Life Ins. Co., San Antonio, 1963-67 (merged with Am. Founders Life Ins. Co., Austin 1967), sr. v.p., chmn. exec. com., 1967-68, pres., 1968—; dir. Capital Nat. Bank, Austin. Bd. dirs. Austin Better Bus. Bur.; trustee S.W. Tex. Public Broadcasting Council; mem. Austin Labor Day Telethon com. Muscular Dystrophy Assn. Served with USNR, 1943-44. Mem. Nat. Assn. Life Cos. (past dir.), Tex. Legal Res. Ofcls. Assn. (past pres., dir.), Tex. Life Ins. Assn. (v.p., dir.), Austin C. of C. (past dir.), Phi Gamma Delta (past trustee). Republican. Episcopalian. Clubs: Citadel, Headliners, Tarry House, Coronet, Admirals. Office: 6937 N Interregional St PO Box 14427 Austin TX 78761

NEFF, PETER JOHN, metals co. exec.; b. New Brunswick, N.J., Oct. 31, 1938; s. Peter and Carrie (Colasurdo) N.; B.S., Rutgers U., 1969; M.B.A., Rider Coll. Grad. Sch. Bus., 1978; m. Joan R. Knapp, June 18, 1960; children—Lisa, Kristopher, Greg. Chemist, Exxon Research, Linden, N.J., 1962-68, tech. sales rep. Exxon Chem. U.S.A., N.Y.C., 1968-70; product mgr. Standard Brands Chem. Industries, Edison, N.J., 1970-73; market mgr. St. Joe Minerals Co., N.Y.C., 1973-75, asst. div. sales mgr., 1975-77, sales mgr., 1977-79, dir. planning, 1979-80, v.p. internat., 1980—. Served with USN, 1956-59. Mem. Am. Chem. Soc., Soc. Plastics Engrs. Home: 47 Dogwood Ln Skillman NJ 08558 Office: 250 Park Ave New York NY 10017

NEFF, THOMAS JOSEPH, exec. search firm exec.; b. Easton, Pa., Oct. 2, 1937; s. John Wallace and Elizabeth Ann (Dougherty) N.; B.S. in Indsl. Engring., Lafayette Coll., 1959; M.B.A., Lehigh U., 1961; m. Susan Culver Paull, Nov. 26, 1971; children—David Andrew, Mark Gregory, Scott Dougherty. Asso., McKinsey & Co., Inc., N.Y.C. and Australia, 1963-66; dir. mktg. planning TWA, N.Y.C., 1966-69; pres. Hosp. Data Scis., Inc., N.Y.C., 1969-74; prin. Booz, Allen & Hamilton, Inc., N.Y.C., 1974-76; regional partner N. Am. and Asia, dir. Spencer Stuart & Assos., N.Y.C., 1976-79, pres., mng. partner, 1979—. Served with U.S. Army, 1961-63. Mem. Assn. Exec. Recruiting Cons.'s (dir.). Republican. Roman Catholic. Clubs: Yale, Quogue Beach, Quogue Field, Stanwich. Home: 96 Round Hill Rd Greenwich CT 06830 Office: 437 Madison Ave New York NY 10022

NEGRI, BEVERLY JOAN, banker; b. Seattle, Nov. 13, 1932; d. Tyra Owen and Julia Barbara (Franz) Blackwell; student N.W. Intermediate Banking Sch., 1977, Lewis and Clark Coll., 1977; m. Donald Warren Negri, July 14, 1951; children—James, Nancy Negri Campbell, Joan Negri Barrow, Howard, Donald Owen. Messenger, proof operator Fed. Res. Bank, Seattle, 1950-52; asst. ops. supr., br. auditor Seattle 1st Nat. Bank, 1952-75; asst. cashier Community Bank Renton (Wash.), 1976, cashier, 1976-78; with Bank of Everett (Wash.), 1978-79; v.p., Cashier Sound Bank, Federal Way, Wash., 1979—; counselor bus. adminstrn. Highline Community Coll. Mem. Nat. Assn. Bank Women, Bank Adminstrn. Inst., Wash. Bankers Assn., Am. Inst. Banking, Conf. State Bank Suprs., Pacific NW Ski Assn. Democrat. Roman Catholic. Clubs: Soroptimists, Ancient Order United Workman. Home: 4228 135th Pl SE Bellevue WA 98006 Office: 32303 Pacific Hwy S Federal Way WA 98003

NEIDERT, ANDREW REINHARDT, banker; b. Akron, Ohio, June 10, 1925; s. Andrew and Lena M. (Haas) N.; B.S., Miami U., Oxford, Ohio, 1947; postgrad. Ind. U., 1957-59; m. Ruth Purdy, Apr. 3, 1948; children—Gerald Andrew, Judith Ann, Jeffrey Alan, James Arthur. Salesman, Allen & Hartzell, Inc., Wadsworth, Ohio, 1949-52; asst. v.p. Akron Savs. & Loan Co., 1952-61; exec. v.p. First Fed. Savs. & Loan, Akron, 1961-65; pres. Standard Fed. Savs. & Loan, Cin., 1965—; pres. Standard Financial, Inc., Cin., Standard Am. Mktg., Santa Monica, Calif.; mem. Fed. Savs. and Loan Adv. Council, 1974-76; mem. adv. com. Fed. Home Loan Mortgage Corp., 1973-74; instr. Am. Savs. & Loan Inst., 1960-73; trustee Savs. & Loan Found., Washington, 1969-73, 78—; mem. UN devel. com. Internat. Union Bldg. Socs. and Savs. Assns., 1971—, mem. council, 1980—; mem. bus. adv. council Miami U., 1976-80; v.p. Dan Beard council Scouts Am.; mem. Parents Council, Lincoln, Ill., 1969, 70; trustee Cin. Rehab. Fin. Corp.; bd. dirs. Neighborhood Housing, Cin. Mem. Greater Cin. C. of C. (trustee 1973-80), Soc. Real Estate Appraisers (sr. residential appraiser), Am. Savs. & Loan Inst. (chpt. pres. 1962-63), Savs. and Loan League S.W. Ohio (pres. 1971-72), Am. Soc. Fine Arts Appraisers, Soc. Rev. Appraisers (cert.), Assn. Fed. Appraisers, Nat. Savs. and Loan League (dir.), Statesman's Club Internat. (chmn., dir. 1975—), Delta Kappa Epsilon, Phi Mu Alpha. Clubs: Masons, Shriners, Queen City, Bankers, Maketewah Country (Cin.). Home: 3310 Lamarque Dr Cincinnati OH 45236 Office: 525 Vine St Cincinnati OH 45202

NEIKIRK, JOSEPH RANDOLPH, railroad exec.; b. Max Meadows, Va., May 29, 1928; s. John W. and Bridye (Armentrout) N.; A.B., U. N.C., 1950; m. Eleanor McClure, July 29, 1950; children—John McC., Jeffrey A., Robert C., Christpher Rex. With Norfolk & Western Ry. Co., 1955-70, 74—, gen. mgr., 1968-70, gen. mgr. terminals, 1974, v.p. labor relations, 1974, v.p. adminstrn., 1975—; v.p. Erie-Lackawanna Ry. Co., 1970-72, sr. v.p., 1972-74; v.p., dir. Va. Holding Corp., 1976—; dir. Lake Erie Dock Co., No. Ohio Food Terminal Inc., Dereco, Inc., N.J., Ind. & Ill. R.R. Co. Mem. adv. bd. Roanoke Valley 4-H, 1975—, Jr. Achievement, 1977—. Mem. Roanoke Valley C. of C. (bd. dirs. 1979—, v.p.). Presbyterian. Home: 5152 Falcon Ridge Rd SW Roanoke VA 24014 Office: 8 N Jefferson St Roanoke VA 24042

NEILLY, ANDREW HUTCHINSON, JR., publisher; b. Balt., 1923; U. Rochester, 1974. Coll. sales rep. John Wiley & Sons, Inc., N.Y.C., 1947-51, asst. sales mgr., 1951-57, asst. v.p. domestic sales and promotion, 1957-61, v.p. mktg. div., 1961-67, exec. v.p., chief operating officer, 1967-71, pres., chief operating officer, 1971-79, pres., chief exec. officer, 1979—, also dir. Home: 180 Goodhill Rd Weston CT 06883 Office: 605 3d Ave New York NY 10016

NEIMARK, PHILIP JOHN, editor, fin. cons.; b. Chgo., Sept. 13, 1939; s. Mortimer William and Hortense Adrienne (Peters) N.; student U. Chgo., 1956-58, Northwestern U., 1958-59; D. Bus. Mgmt. (hon.), Ricker Coll., Houlton, Maine, 1976; children—Tanya Lee, Joshua Daniel. Mem. Chgo. Mercantile Exchange, 1968-74; owner Josephson Neimark Trading Co., Chgo., 1972-73; partner Rosenthal & Co., Chgo., 1973-77; owner, prin. Philip J. Neimark Investments, Miami, Fla., 1977-79, Chgo., 1979—; editor, pub. Philip J. Neimark Viewpoint, N.Y.C., 1976—; fin. editor Money Maker mag., 1979—; mem. Internat. Monetary Market, 1971-74, N.Y. Mercantile Exchange, 1973-74, Chgo. Bd. of Options Exchange, 1973-75. Mem. Fla. Exec. Planning Assn., South Fla. Fin. Planners Assn. Author: How to Be Lucky, 1975; contbg. editor Consumers Digest mag., 1977—. Office: 5705 N Lincoln Ave Chicago IL 60659

NEIMARK, STANLEY CALVIN, accountant; b. Chgo., May 1, 1940; s. Allan and Eva N.; B.S. with distinction, Ind. U., 1961; m. Barbara Brody, June 15, 1965; children—Lisa, Brian, Jason. Staff acct. Coopers & Lybrand, 1961-65; staff sr. Goldrich Goodman Co., Chgo., 1965-67; partner Goldman & Angell, Chgo., 1967-69 (merged with Neimark Kraus & Noparstak 1969, then merged into Kupferberg Goldberg & Neimark, 1976—), mng. partner, 1976—. Served to 1st lt. U.S. Army, 1961-63. C.P.A., Ill. Mem. Am. Inst. C.P.A.'s, Ill. C.P.A.'s Soc., Chgo. Restaurant Assn. Jewish. Home: 2426 The Strand Northbrook IL 60062 Office: 111 E Wacker Dr Chicago IL 60601

NELLES, RICHARD KENNETH, mfg. co. ofcl.; b. Boston, Nov. 26, 1936; s. Philip and Betty Nelles; B.S. in Bus. Adminstrn., Northeastern U., 1960, M.B.A., 1970; m. Carole Ann Kumins, Jan. 10, 1960; children—Steven Howard, Lisa Holly, Robin Lori, Systems service rep. Honeywell Corp., 1963-65; account rep. IBM, 1965-69; applications programming mgr. Sanders Assos., 1969-70; sr. support rep. Digital Equipment Corp., Maynard, Mass., 1970-71; sr. mktg. rep. Harris Co., Boston, 1971-77; product mktg. mgr. Wang Labs., Lowell, Mass., 1977-79; dir. mktg. Computer-Link Corp., Burlington, Mass., 1979-80; v.p. mktg. CL Systems Inc., Newtonville, Mass., 1980—; lectr. in field, 1974—. Named Man of Yr., Bus. and Profl. Women's Club, 1979. Mem. Data Processing Mgmt. Assn., Optical Character Recognition Users Assn. Club: Rotary. Home: 5 Gregory Ln Wayland MA 01778 Office: CL Systems Inc 81 Norwood Ave Newtonville MA 02160

NELLI, DONALD JAMES, bus. sch. exec., acct.; b. Seneca Falls, N.Y., Feb. 19, 1917; s. Thomas and Vits N.; B.S., Syracuse U., 1948; m. Victoria Margaret Serino, Aug. 31, 1941 (dec. May 1980); children—Thomas, Diane, Joseph, John. Staff acct. Seidman & Seidman, N.Y.C., 1948-49, Stover, Butler & Murphy, Syracuse, N.Y., 1949-55; instr. Syracuse U., 1953; instr. acctg. Central City Bus. Inst., Syracuse, 1955-58, pres., 1958—, also pvt. practice acctg., Syracuse. Served with USNR, 1943-46. Mem. Am. Inst. C.P.A.'s, N.Y. State Soc. C.P.A.'s, Am. Acctg. Assn., AAUP. Roman Catholic. Clubs: Lakeshore Yacht and Country (Clay, N.Y.), Italian Am. Athletic (Syracuse). Home: 217 1/2 Dewitt St Syracuse NY 13203 Office: 953 James St Syracuse NY 13203

NELSON, ALAN ARVID, ins. co. exec.; b. Aurora, Ill., Apr. 10, 1937; s. Arvid Benjamin and Mary Elizabeth (Reiss) N.; A.B., Harvard U., 1959, M.B.A., 1962. Vice pres. Assos. Corp. of N. Am., South Bend, Ind., 1970-73; asst. v.p. Aetna Life & Casualty, Hartford, Conn., 1973-78; v.p. Colonial Penn Ins. Co., Phila., 1978—; lectr. bus. adminstrn. Northeastern U., 1964-69. Mem. Greater Hartford Council Econ. Edn., Hartford Area Bus. Economists (past pres.), Planning Execs. Inst., Alliance Française. Republican. Congregationalist. Clubs: Harvard of N.Y.C.; Harvard Bus. Sch. of No. Conn. (past pres.); Harvard Bus. Sch. of Phila. (v.p.). Home: 226 Rittenhouse Sq Philadelphia PA 19103 Office: 5 Penn Center Philadelphia PA 19103

NELSON, ALBERT LOUIS, III, fin. exec.; b. St. Louis, Apr. 29, 1938; s. Albert Louis and Mildred Mary (Bischoff) N.; B.S. in M.E., Washington U., 1960, M.B.A., 1962; LL.B., George Washington U., 1964; m. Pamela Eakins, Mar. 14, 1970; children—Holly Reid, Amy Bischoff. Exec. v.p. Equity Research Assoc., Inc., N.Y.C., 1967-69; pres. The Westwood Group, Inc., Los Angeles, 1969-73; dir. planning chem. plastics The Gen. Tire & Rubber Co., Akron, Ohio, 1973-75; sr. v.p., dir. corp. fin. dept. Prescott, Ball & Turben, Cleve., 1975—. Served with U.S. Army, 1964-66. Club: N.Y. Stock Exchange Lunch. Home: 154 Durward Rd Akron OH 44313 Office: 900 National City Bank Bldg Cleveland OH 44114

NELSON, ALLEN F., investor relations co. exec.; b. Portland, Oreg., Oct. 17, 1943; s. Roy August and Mildred Mary (Jensen) N.; B.S., U. Iowa, 1965, M.A., 1968; m. Johanna Molenaar, Dec. 8, 1973. Vice-pres. Shareholder Communications Corp., N.Y.C., 1970-72, Trafalgar Capital Corp., N.Y.C., 1973; pres. Nelson, Lasky & Co., Inc., N.Y.C., 1974-76; account exec. Corp. Communications Inc., Seattle, 1976-77; pres. Allen Nelson & Co., Inc., Seattle, 1977—; dir. Air Film Corp., Air Film Engring. Group, Mem. Fin. Analysts Fedn., Nat. Investor Relations Inst., Nat. Security Traders Assn., Practising Law Inst., Public Relations Soc. Am. Clubs: The Rainier, Washington Athletic. Home: 5702 SW Admiral Way Seattle WA 98116 Office: Allen Nelson & Co Inc PO Box 16157 Seattle WA 98116

NELSON, ARTHUR HUNT, lawyer, research exec., engr.; b. Kansas City, Mo., May 21, 1923; s. Carl Ferdinand and Hearty (Brown) N.; B.A., U. Kans., 1943; J.D., Harvard, 1949; m. Eleanor Thomas, Dec. 27, 1954; children—Carl F., Frances, Pamela. Staff radiation lab. Mass. Inst. Tech., 1943-44; sr. engr., cons. Raytheon Mfg. Co., Boston, 1948-52; admitted to Mass. bar, 1949, practiced in Boston; v.p., treas., dir. Gen. Electronic Labs., Inc., Cambridge, Mass., 1951-64, chmn. bd., 1959-63; treas., dir. Sci. Electronics, Inc., Cambridge, 1955-64; treas., dir. Assos. for Internat. Research, Inc., 1954—, pres., 1968—; treas., dir. Victor Realty Devel., Inc., 1959—, pres., 1972—; gen. partner Prospect Hill Exec. Office Park, 1977—; dir. Internat. Data Group, Inc. Pres., trustee Tech. Edn. Research Centers, Inc., 1965—; treas., trustee Winsor Sch., Boston, 1978—. Served from ensign to lt. (j.g.) USNR, 1944-46. Mem. Am., Mass., Boston bar assns., Greater Boston C. of C., Phi Beta Kappa, Sigma Xi, Beta Theta Pi. Club: Harvard (Boston). Home: 75 Robin Rd Weston MA 02193 Office: 8 Eliot St Cambridge MA 02138

NELSON, BARRY WARREN, hosp. exec.; b. Portland, Maine, Jan. 3, 1950; s. Philip Warren and Dorothy (Dunn) N.; B.A. in Psychology, U. Louisville, 1972; postgrad. Adelphi U., Garden City, N.Y., 1972-74; m. Susan Charles, Aug. 21, 1971; children—Zachary C., Taja Maren. Research asst. Raymond Kemper and Assos., Louisville, 1968-72; research/planning analyst Exec. Dept., State of Maine, 1975-77; dir. personnel and public relations Rumford (Maine) Community Hosp., 1977-78; dir. personnel mgmt. Webber Hosp. Assn., Biddeford, Maine, 1978—; guest instr. U. Maine, Augusta, 1975-76, U. N.H., 1980; bd. dirs., exec. com., chmn. personnel com. York County (Maine) Health Services. Mem. Am. Hosp. Assn., Am. Soc. Personnel Adminstrn., Maine Hosp. Assn., Maine Soc. Hosp. Personnel Adminstrn., N.Y. Acad. Scis., Pvt. Industry Council York County. Home: 456 Ferry Rd Saco ME 04072 Office: 1 Mountain Rd Biddeford ME 04005

NELSON, CATHERINE ELEANOR, auditor; b. Washington, Aug. 18, 1938; d. Willie James and Eleanor C. (Tucker) N.; student Southeastern U., Washington, 1970-73, Toledo U., 1978, Mercy Coll., 1979, Pace U., 1980. Various adminstrv. positions Potomac Electric Power Co., Washington, 1957-66; adminstrv. positions IBM Corp., Washington, 1966-73, corp. internal auditor, 1974-76, field audit mgr., 1977-79, area audit mgr., Armonk, N.Y., 1980—. Vol. worker Big Sister program, Washington, VA Hosp., Washington. Cert. data processing auditor. Mem. Nat. Assn. Female Execs., Am. Mgmt. Assn., Inst. Internal Auditors. Democrat. Baptist. Home: 21 Winding Ct Mohegan Lake NY 10547 Office: One Barker Ave Room 620 White Plains NY 10601

NELSON, CHARLES DAVID, accountant; b. Iowa, Nov. 12, 1938; s. Harold David and Dorothy Jeanne (Clark) N.; student Tarkio (Mo.) Coll., 1957, Taft (Calif.) Coll., 1958; acctg. certificate Southwestern Bus. U., Los Angeles, 1960; m. Beverly Jean Loeb, Feb. 19, 1958; children—Tamara Lynn, Gregory Charles. Acct., McClain & Co., acctg., Taft, 1958-66, Getty Oil Co., Los Angeles, 1960; controller contract div., corp. asst. sec. Pyramid Oil Co., Taft, 1966—; cons. in field; sec.-treas., dir. Malotto Co. Inc., Taft, 1978—. City treas. City of Taft, 1974-80; treas., bd. dirs. Westside Children's Camp Assn., 1969-70; treas. bd. deacons Peace Luth. Ch., Taft, 1967-72, 74, 76, pres., 1978-80; bd. dirs. Westside Oilfield chpt. ARC, 1976. Mem. Calif. Licensed Contractors Assn., Soc. Calif. Accts., Nat. Assn. Accts. Republican. Home: 108 Village Way Taft CA 93268 Office: PO Box C Taft CA 93268

NELSON, DAVID WALTER, instrumentation and computers cons.; b. Los Angeles, Apr. 28, 1934; s. Leland Paul Burns and Elma Anita (Rosenberger) N.; B.S.E.E., Oreg. State Coll. (now Univ.), 1959; m. Susan Carolynne Kerseg, Feb. 20, 1960; children—Barbara Lee, Ross Bryan. Field engr. Tektronix, Inc., Boston, 1960-62, staff engr., 1963-64, staff field engr. Tektronix Ltd., Guernsey, Tektronix AG, Switzerland, Tektronix UK Ltd., Harpenden, Herts, Eng., 1965-67, regional export mgr., Beaverton, Oreg., 1968-72, mktg. product mgr., 1972-77; mktg. mgr. Frye Electronics, Tigard, Oreg., 1977-79; pres. Norpac Instruments, Inc., 1979—; lectr. Hearing Instruments Inst. Pres., Mt. Hood Ski Patrol, 1975-77; founding dir. Portland unit Mountain Rescue, 1977. Served with USAF, 1951-55. Recipient cert. of appreciation U.S. Sec. Commerce, 1969; lic. hearing aid cons., Oreg. Mem. Internat. Assn. Study of Pain, Assn. for Advancement of Med. Instrumentation. Clubs: Am. Alpine, Wy'East Climbers, Nat. Ski Patrol. Contbr. article to profl. jour. Home: 726 NW Skyline Crest Portland OR 97229

NELSON, DONALD CLAIR, ins. co. exec.; b. Rugby, N.D., Sept. 26, 1926; s. John A. and Lucinda Elizabeth (Whitmore) N.; B.S. in Econs., U. N.D., 1949; postgrad. U. Minn., 1950-56. Mortgage loan underwriter Lutheran Brotherhood, Mpls., 1949-62, asst. v.p. dpt. securities, 1963-77, v.p. investment div., 1977—. Served with U.S. Navy, 1944-46. Mem. Mortgage Bankers Am., Fin. Analysts Fedn. Republican. Home: 5714 Hyland Courts Dr Minneapolis MN 55437 Office: 701 2d Ave S Minneapolis MN 55402

NELSON, DONNA GAYLE, aviation co. exec.; b. Paducah, Tex., June 13, 1943; d. Jack Harold and Hazel Louise Moss (Stephens) Williams; A.B., S. Plains Coll., 1963; B.B.A., U. Tex. State U., 1965, M.B.A., 1967; children—Kellye Lou, Robert Kreg, Jack Gregory.

Tchr., Hemet High Sch., Laguna Beach (Calif.) High Sch., 1965-70; instr. Riverside (Calif.) City Coll., 1971-72; ops. coordinator Evergreen Helicopters Inc., McMinnville, Oreg., 1974-77, public relations dir., 1977-80; v.p. Evergreen Air, Inc., McMinnville, 1980—; public relations dir. Evergreen Internat. Airlines Inc., McMinnville, 1977-80. Co-founder, Poyama Land Treatment Center. Mem. Am. Mgmt. Assn., Beta Sigma Phi. Republican. Baptist. Club: Soroptomist. Home: 2150 Saint Andrews Dr McMinnville OR 97128 Office: 3850 Three Mile Lane McMinnville OR 97128

NELSON, DUANE ORRIN, oil co. exec.; b. Granite Falls, Minn., Nov. 8, 1929; s. John Edward and Marguerite Mathilda (Carlson) N.; Petroleum Engr., Colo. Sch. of Mines, 1951, hon. degree, 1976; m. Dorothy Ann Roth, May 9, 1954; children—Carrie Loren, Mark Steven. Petroleum engr. Arabian Am. Oil Co., Saudi Arabia, 1951-62; staff engr. Standard Oil Co. of Calif., San Francisco, 1962-63; v.p. prodn. Chevron Oil of Colombia, 1963-65; pres. Chevron Oil Co. of Venezuela, Maracaibo, 1965-68, Chevron Overseas Petroleum Co., San Francisco, 1968—; officer, dir. numerous operating cos. Mem. Am. Inst. Mining, Metall. and Petroleum Engrs., Soc. Petroleum Engrs. Club: Stock Exchange. Office: Chevron Overseas Petroleum Co 575 Market St San Francisco CA 94105

NELSON, EARL BENJAMIN, ins. co. exec.; b. McCook, Nebr., May 17, 1941; s. Benjamin Earl and Birdella Ruby (Henderson) N.; B.A., U. Nebr., 1963, M.A., 1966, J.D., 1970; m. Diane C. Gleason, Feb. 22, 1980; children by previous marriage—Sarah Jane, Patrick James; stepchildren—Kevin Michael Cleason, Christine Marie Gleason. Admitted to Nebr. bar, 1970; instr. dept. philosophy U. Nebr., 1963-65; supr. Dept. Ins., State of Nebr., Lincoln, 1965-72, dir. ins., 1975-76; asst. gen. counsel, gen. counsel, sec., v.p. The Central Nat. Ins. Group of Omaha, 1972-75, exec. v.p., 1976-77, pres., 1978—, chief exec. officer, 1980—, also dir.; dir. The Central Nat. Life Ins. Co. of Omaha. Bd. dirs. Legal Aid Soc., Omaha, Omaha Ballet; co-chmn. Carter/Mondale re-election campaign, Nebr., 1980. Mem. Consumer Credit Ins. Assn., Nat. Assn. Ind. Insurers, Nat. Assn. Ins. Commissioners, Nebr. Bar Assn., Am. Bar Assn. Home: 9789 Frederick St Omaha NE 68134 Office: 105 S 17th St Omaha NE 68102

NELSON, EDWARD SHEFFIELD, utility co. exec.; b. Keevil, Ark., Feb. 23, 1941; s. Robert Ford and Thelma Jo (Mayberry) N.; B.S., State Coll. Ark., 1963; LL.B., Ark. Law Sch., 1966; J.D., U. Ark., 1968; m. Mary Lynn McCastlain, Oct. 12, 1961; children—Cynthia, Lynn, Laura. Mgmt. trainee Ark. La. Gas Co., Little Rock, 1963-64, sales engr., 1964-67, sales coordinator, 1967-69, gen. sales mgr., 1969-71, v.p., gen. sales mgr., 1971-73, pres., dir., 1973-79, pres., chmn. bd., chief exec. officer, 1979—. Mem. N.G., 1957-63. Bd. dirs. Better Bus. Bur. Named Ark.'s Outstanding Young Man, Ark. Jr. C. of C., 1973; One of Am.'s Ten Outstanding Young Men, U.S. Jr. C. of C., 1974. Mem. Am., Ark., Pulaski County bar assns., Little Rock (dir.), Met. (pres. 1981) chambers commerce, Central Ark. Mktg. (pres.), Sales and Marketing Execs. Assn. (past pres.), Ark. Tennis Assn. (pres. 1980). Democrat. Methodist. Home: 42 Hickory Hill Circle Little Rock AR 72207 Office: 400 E Capitol St Little Rock AR 72201

NELSON, GEORGE DALMAN, ins. agt.; b. Junction City, La., Oct. 9, 1917; s. Noah Webster and Birdie Anne (Reynolds) N.; B.S., La. State U., 1938, J.D., 1940; m. Nell Querbes, Dec. 29, 1945; children—George Dalman, Carolyn Querbes. With FBI, 1940-47; pres. Querbes & Nelson, Inc., Shreveport, La., 1947—; pres. Life Ins. Co. La.; dir. Frost-Whited Co., Inc.; v.p., dir. La. Cos. Bd. dirs. Willis-Knighton Hosp., Inc.; chmn. bd. trustees Centenary Coll. of La.; pres. Council Better La., 1969-70; v.p., dir. La. Expo, Inc.; bd. visitors Tulane U. Recipient Clyde E. Fant Meml. award for community service United Fund, 1973. Mem. Shreveport Petroleum Club, Dallas Petroleum Club. Methodist. Clubs: Shreveport, Univ., Boston (New Orleans). Home: 2770 Fairfield Ave Shreveport LA 71104 Office: 214 Milam St Shreveport LA 71161

NELSON, JOHN BRISSMAN, fin. pub. co. exec.; b. St. Paul, Feb. 28, 1937; s. John Adolph and Mildred (Brissman) N.; B.B.A., U. Minn., 1959; m. Nancy E. Edstrom, Sept. 6, 1957; children—Lory Anne, Elizabeth Kerstin, Fieldman, Ins. Co. of N. Am., Mpls., 1959-62, Indpls., 1962-64, sr. fieldman, South Bend, Ind., 1964-66; stockbroker Thomson & McKinnon, South Bend, Ind., 1966-69; v.p. Carleton Financial Computations, South Bend, Ind., 1969—. Mem. Nat. Consumer Finance Assn., Soc. Nat. Assn. Publs. Republican. Club: South Bend Country. Home: 17633 Hansom Ct South Bend IN 46635 Office: 1801 Commerce Dr South Bend IN 46624

NELSON, JOHN C., energy co. exec.; b. McKinney, Tex., June 13, 1913; B.S. in C.E., Tex. A. & M. U., 1935, M.S. in Civil Engring., 1937; m. Ann Blos; children—Marsha, John Charles, Jr. Engr., United Energy Resources, Inc., Shreveport, La., 1951-59, supr. rates and econs., 1959-64, asst. chief engr., 1964-67, asst. dir. rates and spl. studies, 1967-69, exec. v.p., 1969-76, group v.p., Houston, 1976—, now vice chmn. bd. Served to maj. U.S. Army, 1941-48. Mem. Tex. State Bd. Profl. Engrs. Tex., La. State Bd. Profl. Engrs., Am. Gas Assn., So. Gas Assn. Episcopalian. Clubs: Houston; Warwick; Coronado; Lakeside Country. Office: PO Box 1478 Houston TX 77001

NELSON, JOHN WALTER, JR., diversified co. exec.; b. N.Y.C., Sept. 29, 1923; s. John Walter and Anna Victoria (Hanson) N.; B.Ch.E., Bklyn. Poly. Inst., 1950; m. Marie J. Hornberger, Nov. 25, 1950; children—Nancy Ann, John Walter III. Mfg. engr. Nat. Starch Co., N.Y.C., 1948-54; div. engring. head Liberty Products, Farmingdale, N.Y., 1954-57; sr. product engr. Sonotone Corp., Cold Spring, N.Y., 1957-63; asst. v.p. Chemprene div. Chem. Rubber Products, Beacon, N.Y., 1963-65; dir. pub. works, Poughkeepsie, N.Y., 1965-72; dir. Richard Solomon Assos., Wappinger Falls, N.Y., 1972-79; cons. in engring. and mgmt., 1977—. Committeeman, counselor, treas., dist. commr., mem. exec. bd. Dutchess County council Boy Scouts Am., 1971—; cons. Girl Scouts Dutchess County, N.Y., 1969-71; bd. dirs. Stony Kill Found., 1980—. Served with USNR, 1942-46. Recipient Nat. Leadership award Am. City Mag., 1966. Mem. Forest Products Research Soc., Am. Pub. Works Assn. (exec. com. 1965—, dir. sch. edn. 1970—, pres. Mid Hudson br. 1972—). Lutheran (pres., founder, trustee). Clubs: Chelsea (N.Y.) Yacht (trustee); Stonycreek (N.Y.) Rod and Gun. Editor Polytechnic Reporter, Bklyn., 1941-43; edit. writer Naval Bur. Personnel Mag., 1943-48; contbr. Forest Products Research Publ., 1948-54. Contbr. articles Am. City Mag., 1965—. Home and Office: Sky Top Dr Chelsea NY 12512

NELSON, JULIUS, publisher; b. Minsk, Russia, Aug. 15, 1910; s. Abraham and Temme Dolores (Solow) N.; B.S., Indiana U. Pa., 1932; M.A., Columbia U., 1940; m. Goldie Goldstein, Aug. 1, 1942; children—Temma Nelson Rubin, Abra Nelson Goldfarb. Tchr., Windber (Pa.) High Sch., 1932-42; field tax investigator IRS, 1943-47; instr. bus. edn. N.J. State Tchrs. Coll., Paterson, 1947-49, U. Balt., 1949-52; pres., chmn. bd. Artistic Typing Hdqrs. Inc., Balt., 1972—; lectr.in field. Bd. dirs. Hebrew Sunday Schs., Windber, 1932-41; v.p. Randallstown (Md.) Synagogue Center, 1963-64, bd. dirs. synagogues, 1961—. Recipient Outstanding achievement award Md. Vocat. Assn., 1970; charter mem. Exec. and Profl. Hall of Fame; named to Windber Hall of Fame, 1980. Mem. Eastern, Nat. bus. tchrs. assns., Alpha Phi Gamma, Gamma Rho Tau, Phi Delta Kappa, Pi Omega Pi. Jewish. Mason. Author numerous books on typewriting. Home and office: 3200 Southgreen Rd Baltimore MD 21207

NELSON, KATHLEEN VEENSTRA, public relations cons.; b. Flint, Mich., Sept. 1, 1932; d. Louis Benedict and Cynthia (Aalders) Veenstra; student Wheaton (Ill.) Coll., 1950-51; student grad. seminars, N.Y. U., U. San Francisco, Salk Inst., San Jose (Calif.) State U.; m. Wallace E. Nelson, Sept. 11, 1954. Pres. Kathleen Nelson Cons., Bainbridge Island, Wash., 1978—; spl. cons. Frank Delano & Assos., Los Angeles and Seattle, 1978—; lectr. U. Wash., Seattle, 1977-78, 80, Seattle Community Coll., 1975; panelist, speaker in communications field. Mem. Mayor Seattle Waterfront Park Com., 1969-71, Mayor Seattle St. Tree Com., 1968-71; chmn. Operation Triangle Park Com., Seattle, 1964-71; mem. Downtown Seattle Devel. Com., 1965-69; trustee Northwest Outbound Sch., Portland, Oreg., 1972-79. Recipient citation Am. Horticulture Soc., 1970, Urban Design award Downtown Seattle Devel. Assn., 1958, 60, Gov. Wash. Beautification trophy, 1970, others. Mem. Public Relations Soc. Am. (accredited), Seattle C. of C., Women in Communications, Seattle Women in Advt., Women's Network, Puget Sound Devel. Officers Assn. Clubs: Wing Point Golf and Country, Meadowmeer Golf (Bainbridge Island). Author articles in field. Address: 11194 Killdeer Ln Bainbridge Island WA 98110

NELSON, KENNETH EDWIN, ins. co. exec.; b. N.Y.C., Oct. 6, 1950; s. Lorin G. and Barbara G. (Blum) N.; B.A., Oberlin Coll., 1972; M.B.A., U. Mich., 1975. Asst. scheduling mgr. Bobbie Brooks Co., Hialeah, Fla., 1972-73; asst. to field v.p. Equitable Life Ins. Co., Ann Arbor, Mich., 1975-76, advanced seminar facilitator, Stamford, Conn., 1976-77, corp. ins. mktg. specialist, N.Y.C., 1977-79, ADP employer services tng. specialist, 1979—. C.L.U. Democrat. Home: 18 Lawson Ln Ridgefield CT 06877 Office: 405 Rt 3 Clifton NJ 07015

NELSON, LENWOOD MELVIN, fin. and ins. cons.; b. Atlantic City, Nov. 22, 1948; s. Lenwood and Dorothy Nelson; B.S., Howard U., Washington, 1971; M.A., Am. U., 1974; m. Emily Gunter, May 21, 1971; children—Saliha, Kadir, Amin, Shedia. Bus. mgr. Blackstone mag., 1972; ins. agt., 1972-74: spl. agt. Bankers Life Ins. Co. Iowa, 1974-76; pres., chmn. bd. Equity Mgmt. & Planning Corp., Washington, 1976—; pres. Market Towers, Inc., Atlantic City; dir. Belspan Assos., Washington. Mem. Million Dollar Round Table, 1978. Mem. Nat., Suburban Md. assns. life underwriters, Am. Mgmt. Assn., Life Underwriters Polit. Action Com., Provinces Civic Assn. Democrat. Islamic. Office: 11300 Rockville Pike 9th Floor Rockville MD 20852

NELSON, MARION CLAVAR, advt. exec.; b. Manti, Utah, Jan. 11, 1897; s. Andrew Clarence and Amanda (Jenson) N.; student U. Utah, 1916-17; m. Edna Anderson, Aug. 25, 1919; children—Marjory (Mrs. Robert F. Rohlfing), Russell Marion, Enid N. (Mrs. Richard H. Ogaard), Robert H. Sports editor Deseret News, Salt Lake City, 1918-21; prodn. mgr. Gillham Advt. Agy., Inc., Salt Lake City, 1922-29, pres., 1930-70, chmn. bd., 1970-75; advt. cons. investments, 1975—. Mem. Salt Lake C. of C. (pres. 1938-39). Mem. Ch. of Jesus Christ of Latter-day Saints. Clubs: Salt Lake Advertising (pres. 1931-32, Printers Ink Silver award 1965), Salt Lake Rotary (pres. 1943-44), Bonneville Knife and Fork (pres. 1947-48), Salt Lake Country, Alta. Home and office: 875 Donner Way Salt Lake City UT 84108

NELSON, PAUL FREDRICK, constrn. co. exec.; b. Stanford, Conn., Nov. 10, 1940; s. C.W. and E.R. Nelson; Asso. in Applied Sci., St. Petersburg Coll., 1964; m. Helen J. Walker, Sept. 11, 1964; children—Amanda L., Michael P., Laura L., Johanna H. Supt., White Plains Ironworks, Peekskill, N.Y., 1967-70; project mgr. Mills and Jones Constrn., St. Petersburg, Fla., 1970-76; project mgr. J.A. Jones Constrn. Co., Dallas, 1976-77, constrn. mgr., 1977-78, v.p., regional mgr., 1978—; guest lectr. engring. M.I.T., 1964. Served with C.E., U.S. Army, 1958-62. Mem. Assn. Gen. Contractors (dir. Fla. West Coast chpt.). Address: 14110 Dallas Pkwy Suite 170 Dallas TX 75240

NELSON, RICHARD ALLAN, capital equipment co. exec.; b. Chgo., Aug. 12, 1943; s. Richard Frank and Mildred (Loeck) N.; B.A., Roosevelt U., 1967; M.B.A., U. Chgo., 1976; m. Ada M. Pellegrino, May 25, 1968. Supr. prodn. and inventory control Rockwell Internat., Chgo., 1970-76; staff asst. corp. materiel Bendix Corp., Southfield, Mich., 1976-78, materiel mgr., automation and measurement div., Dayton, Ohio, 1978—. Served with U.S. Army, 1967-70. Decorated Bronze Star with two oak leaf clusters, Purple Heart, Air Medal, Army Commendation Medal. Mem. Am. Prodn. and Inventory Control Soc. (cert. practitioner in inventory mgmt.). Office: 721 Springfield St Dayton OH 45401

NELSON, RICHARD STANLEY, lawyer; b. Pitts., June 22, 1931; s. Ben and Minna (Blumer) N.; B.A., U. Mich., 1953; LL.B., U. Pitts., 1956; m. Inez Joan Krouse, Oct. 17, 1954; children—David Keith, Gary Robert, Linda Sari, Wendy Barbara. Admitted to Pa. bar, 1956, Ky. bar, 1961, U.S. Supreme Ct. bar, 1971; practiced in Pitts., 1956; spl. agt. FBI, Louisville and Covington, Ky., 1959-61; practiced in Covington, 1961—; judge protem, trial commr. Kenton County Ct., 1964-69; city atty. Ft. Mitchell, 1965-80; instr. No. Ky. Coll., 1971; adj. asst. prof. law Chase Coll. Law, 1972—. Served with AUS, 1956-59. Mem. Ky. (bd. govs.), Kenton County (pres. 1972) bar assns., Am. Arbitration Assn., Soc. Am. Magicians, Soc. Former Spl. Agts. FBI, Ky. Trial Lawyers Assn. Home: 135 Thompson Ave Fort Mitchell KY 41017 Office: 11 W 6th St PO Box 1209 Covington KY 41012

NELSON, ROBERT CHARLES, trade assn. exec.; b. LaPorte, Ind., Feb. 18, 1923; s. Joseph N. and Myrtle (Johnson) N.; B.S., Ind. U., 1949; m. Geraldine C. Smith, Sept. 6, 1947; children—Richard C., David R. With Assos. Investment Co., South Bend, Ind., 1949-54; with Ind. Bankers Assn., Indpls., 1954—, exec. v.p., 1967—. Served with AUS, 1943-46. Named hon. Ky. Col., Sagamore of Wabash. Mem. Indpls. Mus. Art, 500 Festival Assos., Econ. Club Indpls., Am. Legion, Am. Soc. Assn. Execs., Ind. Soc. Assn. Execs., State Assn. Div. Am. Bankers Assn., Ind. U. Alumni Assn., Alpha Kappa Psi. Republican. Baptist. Clubs: Indpls. Athletic, Columbia Club Indpls., Indpls. Press, Capitol Hill Club of Washington, Kiwanis (treas. 1978-79). Home: 4735 Wyandott Trail Indianapolis IN 46250 Office: 929 Electric Bldg Indianapolis IN 46204

NELSON, ROBERT HENSHAW, mfg. co. exec.; b. Detroit, Jan. 16, 1934; s. Harry Monroe and Elizabeth James (Jones) N.; B.S., Mich. State U., 1957; M.S., Kans. State U., 1960; m. Catherine Casteel Saunders, Jan. 24, 1959; 1 son, Robert Henshaw. Adminstrv. asst. to pres. Shatterproof Glass Corp., Detroit, 1960-62; sr. mktg. analyst Internat. Mineral & Chem. Corp., Skokie, Ill., 1962-64; mktg. research mgr. Cryovac div. W.R. Grace, Duncan, S.C., 1964-66; pres. Estan Mfg. Co., Troy, Mich., 1966-71; pres., owner R.A. Young Ind., Inc., Fraser, Mich., 1973—, Master Industries, Sterling Heights, Mich., 1975—; tchr. bus. orgn. Furman U., 1963-64; head bus. seminar Lawrence Inst. Tech., 1968. Served in U.S. Army, 1957-59. Mem. Engring. Soc. Detroit, Birmingham Power Squadron. Republican. Clubs: Birmingham Athletic; Birmingham Village Players, Grosse Pointe Yacht. Home: 1438 Kensington Rd Bloomfield Hills MI 48013 Office: 34190 Doreka St Fraser MI 48026

NELSON, ROGER ELLIS, minerals devel. mfg. co. exec.; b. St. Cloud, Minn., Dec. 10, 1938; s. Walter O. and Alice (Bergetta) N.; B.A., U. Minn., 1960; B.Landscape Arch., U. Calif., Berkeley, 1968; m. Rosalie Jean Davis, June 25, 1960. River basin planner Bur. Land Mgmt., U.S. Dept. Interior, Denver, 1968-71, resource specialist, Washington, 1971-73; mgr. environ. quality Utah Internat., Inc., San Francisco, 1973—. Bd. dirs. Westhaven Christian Adult Retirement, Inc., 1975—; mem. adv. council to seminar on environ. arts and scis. Thorne Ecol. Inst., 1977-79; chmn. Western Dist. Bible Conf., Evang. Free Ch. Am. Served with USN, 1960-63, comdr. Res. Mem. Am. Soc. Landscape Architects, ASCE (environ. impact analysis research council). Contbr. articles to profl. jours. Home: 1939 Oakview Dr Oakland CA 94602 Office: Utah Internat 550 California St San Francisco CA 94104

NELSON, ROGER HUGH, oil and gas exploration exec., bus. cons., educator; b. Spring City, Utah, Mar. 7, 1931; s. Hugh Devere and Maudella Sarah (Larsen) N.; B.S., U. Utah, 1953, M.S., 1953; Ed.D., Columbia U., 1958; m. DeEtte Munk, Aug. 26, 1955; children—Steven R., Deanne, Mark L. Mem. faculty U. Utah Coll. Bus., 1953—, asst. dean, 1969-74, prof. mgmt., 1970—, chmn. dept., 1976—; v.p. Computer Logic Corp., 1970-73; faculty Utah Mgmt. Inst.; pres. Am. Leisure & Sports Investment Corp., 1973—, Oil Resources, Inc., 1980—, Puma Energy Corp., 1980—; fin. and mgmt. cons. Active local Am. Heart and Am. Cancer Soc. campaigns. Recipient Westinghouse Nat. Sci. award. 1949; Danforth Teaching fellow, 1957. Mem. Acad. Mgmt., Adminstrv. Mgmt. Soc., NEA, AAUP, Phi Kappa Phi, Beta Gamma Sigma, Phi Delta Kappa, Delta Phi Epsilon. Author: Personal Money Management, 1973; also articles, reports, manuals. Inventor comml. color separation camera and related dye-transfer processes. Home: 2662 Skyline Dr Salt Lake City UT 84108 Office: Grad Sch Bus U Utah Salt Lake City UT 84112 also 926 Kennecott Bldg Salt Lake City UT 84133

NELSON, ROGER KENT, acct.; b. Denver, July 16, 1947; s. Roland O. and Evelyn D. Nelson; B.S., U. Kans., 1970; m. Deborah J. Robertson, Nov. 28, 1970; 1 son, Matthew. With Ernst & Whinney, Kansas City, Mo., 1970-77, audit supr., 1974-77; controller, asst. sec. U.S. Supply Co., Kansas City, 1977—. Served with U.S. Army, 1970. Mem. Am. Inst. C.P.A.'s, Mo. Soc. C.P.A.'s, Nat. Assn. Accts., Am. Mgmt. Assn. Presbyterian. Office: 1315 W 12th St Kansas City MO 64101

NELSON, THOMAS HARRY, SR., ins. co. exec.; b. Balt., July 23, 1945; s. Edward Joseph and Bernice Cecelia (Spears) N.; student U. Va., 1965-68; m. Sandra Lorraine Briscoe, Nov. 27, 1965; children—Eric Anthony, Gwendolyn Reneé, Thomas Harry, Valerie Nicole, Kimberly Bernice. Analyzer, expediter IBM, Gaithersburg, Md., 1968-70, accounts receivable specialist, Balt., 1970-71; trainee asso. Franklin Ins. Co., Silver Spring, Md., 1971, asso., Silver Spring, Md., 1971-72, dist. mgr., 1973, dir. tng. adn supervision, 1974, agy. mgr., College Park, Md., 1975, sr. agy. mgr., 1976-77, Bladensburg, Md., 1977—. Served with USMC, 1963-68. Mem. Nat. Assn. Life Underwriters, Md. Suburban Life Underwriters Assn., Am. Biog. Inst. Research Assn. (asso.). Democrat. Mem. Christian Ch. Club: Masons. Home: 7407 Radcliffe Dr College Park MD 20740 Office: Parkway Bldg 5801 Annapolis Rd Suite 400 Bladensburg MD 20710

NELSON, WARREN BRYANT, commodity brokerage co. exec.; b. Manhattan, Kans., Sept. 29, 1922; s. Oscar William and Eda Caroline (Hokanson) N.; B.S. cum laude in Agrl. Econs., Kans. State U., 1942, postgrad., 1950; postgrad. Am. U., 1947; m. Betty Lou Wiley, Dec. 24, 1944; children—Barbara Ann, David William, Marcia Lynn, Robert Warren. Statistician agrl. div. Bur. Census, U.S. Dept. Commerce, Washington, 1945-48, Statis. Reporting Service, U.S. Dept. Agr., Topeka, 1948-50; price analyst Longstreet Abbott & Co., St. Louis, 1951-59, partner, 1959-69; sec. Clayton Brokerage Co., St. Louis, 1959-69, exec. v.p., 1969-72, pres., 1972-77, vice chmn. bd., 1977—. Served to lt. USAAF, 1942-45. Decorated D.F.C. with 2 oak leaf clusters, Air medal with 3 oak leaf clusters. Mem. Chgo. Bd. Trade, Chgo. Merc. Exchange, Internat. Monetary Market, N.Y. Cotton Exchange, Winnipeg Grain Exchange. Republican. Lutheran. Clubs: Union League (Chgo.); St. Louis. Home: 839 Elm Tree Ln Kirkwood MO 63122 Office: 7701 Forsyth Blvd Suite 300 Clayton MO 63105

NELSON, WAYNE KEITH, proprietary drugs mfg. co. exec.; b. Chgo., Nov. 12, 1938; s. Melvin Earl and Mildred L. (Pfeifer) N.; B.S., Northwestern U., 1960, M.S.J., 1961; m. Jane Van Dellen, Aug. 20, 1960; children—Wendy, Kathryn, Peter, Julie. Brand mgr. Procter & Gamble, Cin., 1961-66; group v.p. Glendinning Cos., Westport, Conn., 1967-71; dir. product mgmt. Johnson & Johnson Health Care Div., New Brunswick, N.J., 1972-75, v.p., gen. mgr. McNeil Consumer Products div., Ft. Washington, Pa., 1975-78, pres., 1978—; v.p. Johnson & Johnson Internat.; chmn. bd. Johnson & Johnson Germany, Austria and France. 1st runner-up as Corp. Mktg. Exec. of Year, 1979. Mem. Proprietary Assn. (v.p., dir.), U.S. Council Family Health (v.p.), Young Pres.'s Orgn. Presbyterian. Club: Tavern (Chgo.). Home: 2 Elm Rd Princeton NJ 08540 Office: Camp Hill Rd Fort Washington PA 19034

NELSON, WILLIAM ANDREW, farmer; b. Williams, Iowa, Jan. 1, 1914; s. William Henry and Olive Rebecca (Blair) N.; student public schs., Dodge Center, Minn.; m. Ona Ruth Kellar, Sept. 28, 1936; children—William D., Donna M., Daryl G. Route salesman Kraft Foods Co., 1936-46, br. mgr., 1946-51, product mgr., 1951-61, mktg. mgr., 1961-67, v.p. sales and ops., 1967-73; pres. Huntsinger Farms, Inc., Eau Claire, Wis., 1973—, aldo dir.; pres. Silver Spring Gardens, Eau Claire, 1974—; dir. Am. Nat. Bank. Mem. Chippewa Valley council Boy Scouts Am. Mem. Nat. Food Distbrs. Assn. (mfrs. council). Republican. Methodist. Clubs: Masons, Shriners, Elks. Office: Huntsinger Farms Inc PO Box 360 Eau Claire WI 54701

NELSON, WILLIAM BISCHOFF, educator; b. St. Louis, Apr. 14, 1940; s. Albert Louis, Jr. and Mildred Mary (Bischoff) N.; B.S., U. Ariz., 1962, M.S., 1963; m. Julie T. McDevitt, Dec. 1, 1972; children—Keli Anne, William Bischoff. Field advt. rep. Procter & Gamble Co., 1962; Ford Motor Co., mem. mktg. staff Dearborn, Mich., 1963-66; instr. mktg. U. Ariz., 1965-70; prof. mktg., dept. head Pima Community Coll., Tucson, 1970—; cons. in mktg., 1965—. Active United Way, also numerous other civic and polit. orgns. Recipient achievement award for polit. activities Ford Motor Co., 1964; cert. bus. communicator. Mem. Internat. Newspaper Advt. Execs., Point of Purchase Advt. Inst., Bus./Profl. Advt. Assn., Am. Mktg. Assn. (emeritus), Nat. Assn. Mgmt. Edn. (v.p. 1974-77), Am. Mgmt. Assn., So. Mktg. Assn., Audit Bur. of Circulation, Nat. Bus. Edn. Assn., Acad. Mktg. Sci., Southwestern Mktg. Assn., Direct Mail Mktg. Assn., Am. Acad. Advt., Am. Film Inst., Internat. Platform Assn., NEA, AAUP, Ariz. Edn. Assn., Tucson Press Club, Pima Community Coll. Edn. Assn. (bd. govs. 1972-74), Tucson Mus. Art, Ariz.-Sonora Desert Mus., Ariz. Hist. Soc., Nat. Trust Hist. Preservation, Smithsonian Assos., Am. Mus. Natural History, Nat. Archives Trust, Delta Sigma Pi, Beta Gamma Sigma, Phi Kappa Phi. Roman Catholic. Office: PO Box 41630 Tucson AZ 85717

NELSON, WILLIAM LINTON, investment mgr.; b. Phila., Jan. 20, 1900; s. William Robert and Ella Blanche (Johnson) N.; grad. U. Pa., 1926; LL.D. (hon.), Washington and Jefferson Coll., 1975; m. Grace Mehorter Solly, Feb. 8, 1934. With Fidelity-Phila. Trust Co., 1922-29; officer, dir. Investment Corp. of Phila., 1929-41; organizer Delaware Fund, 1938, dir., 1938—, pres., 1942, 46-71, chmn. bd., 1963-77; mng. partner Delaware Co., Phila.; 1946—; chmn. bd. Decatur Income Fund, 1963-77, Delta Trend Fund, 1967-77, Delchester Bond Fund, 1970-77, DMC Tax-Free Income Trust, Pa., 1976-77, Delaware Mgmt. Co., 1952-57, 63—; trustee DMC Tax-Free Income Trust, Pa., 1977—; dir. Del. Investment Advisers, Inc., 1972-76, chmn. bd., 1972-75; dir. Decatur Income Fund, Delta Trend Fund, Delchester Bond Fund, Del. Cash Res., Del. Mgmt. Co.; dir. ops. Office Fgn. Liquidation, Dept. State, 1945. Republican Candidate for controller, City Phila., 1949; trustee Valley Forge Mil. Acad. Served in USNR, World Wars I and II, advancing through grades to rear adm. Decorated Legion of Merit, Bronze Star. Mem. Investment Co. Inst., Securities Industry Assn., Naval Res. Assn., Navy League, Nat. Assn. Security Dealers, Def. Orientation Conf. Assn. Republican. Presbyterian. Clubs: Racquet, Phila. Country, Union League, Brit. Officers, Undine Barge; Analysts (N.Y.C.). Mem. U.S. Nat. Championship Sculls, 1921, doubles crew, 1924-26; winner Can. Assn. Single Rowing Championship, 1926. Home: 1124 Stony Ln Gladwyne PA 19035 Office: 7 Penn Center Plaza Philadelphia PA 19103

NEMCEK, JOHN B., JR., steel co. exec.; b. Butler, Pa., Dec. 14, 1941; s. John and Catherine (Tishey) N.; B.S. in Math., Geneva (Pa.) Coll., 1968; m. Betty Lou Leitem, Aug. 28, 1965; children—Stacey Lynn, Jeffrey John, Rachele Rene. Indsl. engr. Am. Bridge div. U.S. Steel Corp., Ambridge, Pa., 1968-69, sr. indsl. engr., 1969-70, asst. to weld engr., 1970-71, asst. weld engr., 1971-72, weld engr., 1972-74, supt.-welding, 1974-78, supt. South Shops, 1978-79, mgr. mfg. engring., 1979-80; mgr. prodn. Am. Bridge Co., South San Francisco, Calif., 1980—; adv. Westmoreland Community Coll., Airco Tech Tng. Mem. Am. Welding Soc., Am. Soc. Non-Destructive Testing. Home: 5722 Roanwood Way Concord CA 94521 Office: Am Bridge Co South San Francisco CA 94080

NEMEC, BRUCE HAWTHORNE, hosp. supply co. exec.; b. Phila., Jan. 22, 1950; s. Joseph William and Carol Louise (Hagedorn) N.; B.A., Lafayette Coll., 1971; M.B.A., U. Va., 1973; m. Dorothea Ellen Howe, June 20, 1975. Distbn. understudy Bekins Moving & Storage Co., Washington, also King of Prussis, Pa., 1973-75; mgr. pvt. fleet ops. Sci. Products div. Am. Hosp. Supply Corp., Edison, N.J., 1975-76, fin. mgr., 1976-77, regional distbn. mgr., 1977, mgr. distbn. ops., Eastern area, 1978—. Mem. Raritan Valley Traffic Council, Pvt. Carrier Conf. of N.J. Motor Truck Assn., U. Va. Alumni Assn., Zeta Psi. Lutheran. Home: 2232 Morse Ave Scotch Plains NJ 07076 Office: 100 Raritan Center Pkwy Edison NJ 08817

NEMET, THOMAS MAYOR, automobile dealer; b. Cluj, Romania, Feb. 1, 1934; s. Morris and Lillian N.; student N.Y. U.; m. June Glantz, Oct. 16, 1960; children—Kyle Ian, Todd Douglas. With Nemet Motors, Jamaica, N.Y., 1948—, now pres.; pres. Nemet Auto Internat.; dir. Dolmatch Publs., 1980—; mem. auto industry adv. group to sec. transp., 1980—, also auto industry trade adv. group, 1980—; mem. task force on small bus. and econ. stability SBA. Pres., Jamaica Center for the Performing Arts, 1978—; advisor to Queens County pres., 1976—; bd. govs. Jamaica Hosp., 1980. Named Man of Yr., Imported Car Industry, 1961; recipient Datsun Disting. Service award 1976, 77, 78, named quality dealer, 1980; recipient Time Quality Dealer award, 1980, Sports Illustrated Dealer of Distinction award, 1980. Mem. Am. Internat. Automobile Dealers Assn. (dir. 1979—, chmn. nat. membership com. 1980, award for outstanding contbn. to imported car industry 1978), Greater N.Y. Auto Dealers Assn. (dir., v.p. 1980), Datsun Nat. Dealer Council (pres. 1978), Datsun Advt. Council (chmn. 1977), Jamaica C. of C. (bd. govs. 1979), N.Y. State Automobile Dealers Assn. (legis. com. 1980—), Nat. Automobile Dealers Assn. (indsl. relations com. 1976, service award 1979) Club: Glen Head Country (bd. govs. 1978). Office: 153-12 Hillside Ave Jamaica NY 11432

NEPPL, WALTER JOSEPH, retail store exec.; b. Halbur, Iowa, June 15, 1922; s. Frank and Anna (Halbur) N.; grad. high sch., Halbur; m. Marian Maher, Oct. 15, 1945; children—Eugenie Neppl Kauffman, Marilee Neppl Csaklos, Deborah, Thomas, John, Christina, Nancy. With J.C. Penney Co., Inc., 1940—, mgr. store, Albuquerque, 1954-55, dist. mgr., Pitts. 1955-61, store coordination mgr., N.Y.C., 1961-64, asst. to dir. dist. mgmt. dept., 1964-65, gen. mdse. mgr. hard lines, 1965-67, v.p., 1967-68, gen. sales and mdse. mgr., 1968-71, dir. merchandising, 1971-72, exec. v.p., from 1972, pres., chief exec. officer, dir., 1976—; dir. Sun Co., Fidelity Union Trust Co., Fidelity Union Bancorp. Trustee, Geraldine R. Dodge Found., Inc.; mem. corp. Morristown Meml. Hosp. Served to capt. USAAF, 1943-45. Decorated D.F.C. Roman Catholic. Clubs: Morris County Golf; Sky Top. Home: 5 Scenery Hill Dr Chatham NJ 07928 Office: 1301 Ave of Americas New York NY 10019

NERGAL MAZAR, ORY, publisher, author, editor; b. Jerusalem, Jan. 21, 1932; s. Benjamin and Dina Ben Zvi (Shimshi) Mazar; Ph.D., Hebrew U. Jerusalem, 1955; m. Helen G. Zarovich, Aug. 8, 1968; children—Adoram M., Danny M., Joseph C. Vice-pres., Internat. Pub. Corp., Jerusalem and N.Y.C., 1955-62; pres. Allied Pubs., Inc., N.Y.C., 1962-68; pres., chief exec. officer Unibook, Inc., N.Y.C., 1968-76, Houston, 1978—; author: Lincoln and the Civil War, 1953; The Pharoahs of Egypt, 1954; Poems, 1955; Geography of the Holy Land, 1950; History of the Holy Land, 1951; Crete, 1953; The Hittites, 1953; The Phoenicians and Carthagenes, 1954; (with others) Jerusalem-History of the Holy City, 1960, French edit., 1961; mng. editor: The World of the Bible, 5 vols., 1961; Illustrated History of the Jews, 1962, rev. edit., 1963; The Story of Christmas, 1961; The Story of Easter, 1970; editor-in-chief: The Israel Honorarium, 5 vols., 1968; The Biographical Encyclopedia of the U.S., 5 vols., 1969; The Hebrew Heritage, 10 vols., 1970; The Encyclopedia of American Cities, 1980; Houston: City of Destiny, 1980. Office: 2323 S Voss Rd Houston TX 77057

NESBITT, JOHN ALFRED DREAN, investment banking exec.; b. Belfast, No. Ireland, May 18, 1945; s. John and Blanche Elizabeth Margaret (Drean) N.; B.A., Oxford (Eng.) U., 1967; M.B.A., U. Pa., 1969. Econ. asst. H.M. Treasury, London, 1967-68; asso. Eastman Dillon Union Securities & Co., N.Y.C., 1969, 1st v.p. Blyth Eastman Dillon & Co. Inc., 1974, sr. v.p., 1976, mng. dir. Blyth Eastman Paine Webber Inc., 1980. Clubs: Downtown Assn., Racquet and Tennis, Links, Stanwich, Royal Belfast Golf. Home: 500 E 77th St New York NY 10021 Office: Blyth Eastman Paine Webber Inc 1 1221 Ave of Americas New York NY 10020

NESBITT, LEROY EDWARD, inventor, design specialist; b. Phila., Sept. 14, 1925; s. Lonnie Reynolds and Josephine Elvira N.; student Temple U., 1965-69; m. Vivian Elizabeth Lee, June 27, 1952; 1 son, Warren Eric. Founder, pres. Incentives, Inc., Wilmington, Del., 1975—; design specialist Sperry Univac, Blue Bell, Pa. Served with U.S. Army, 1943-46. Decorated Bronze Star (4). Home and Office: 6213 Gardenia St Philadelphia PA 19144

NESSEN, WARD HENRY, typographer; b. Empire, Mich., Nov. 29, 1909; s. Henry L. and Louise (Stecher) N.; A.B., U. Mich., 1931; J.D., John Marshall Law Sch., Chgo., 1937; course in accounting Northwestern U. Grad. Sch., 1946; m. Jane Randall, Apr. 4, 1959. Admitted to Ill. bar, 1937; trust dept. No. Trust Co., Chgo., 1934-41; sales planning Am. Home Products, 1946-51; sales exec. Permacel Tape Corp., 1951-55; pres. The Highton Co., advt. typographers, Newark, 1955-75; sr. v.p. Arrow Typographers, Newark, 1975—; chmn. Coll. Communications Seminar, 1973. Mem. Civic Clubs Council Greater Newark Area, 1957-59. Served from 2d lt. to lt. col. AUS, 1941-46; ETO, assigned SOS. Decorated Bronze Star with oak leaf cluster, Army Commendation medal. Mem. Typographers Internat. Assn. (pres. 1970-71), N.J. Typographers Assn. (pres. 1957-59), Printing Industries N.J. (pres. 1967-69), Printing Industries N.Y. (bd. govs. 1967-69), Order of John Marshall (Elmer G. Voigt award 1975), Sigma Phi. Republican. Lutheran. Clubs: Type Dirs., Pharm. Advt. (N.Y.C.); Advt. N.J. (bd. govs.); Down Town (Newark). Home: 11 Euclid Ave Summit NJ 07901 Office: 2-14 Liberty St Newark NJ 07102

NESTERENKO, DIMITRI A., civil engr.; b. Kiev, Ukraine, May 23, 1909; s. Atanazy and Maria (Mikulinski) N.; came to U.S., 1948, naturalized, 1954; C.E., Tech. State U., Warsaw, Poland, 1935; m. Herta-Maria Reichardt, Oct. 22, 1939; children—Elizabeth, Alexander. Field engr. City of Sochaczew (Poland), 1935-36; city engr. City of Otwock (Poland), 1936-44; structural design specialist Stanley Consultants Inc. (formerly Stanely Engring. Co.), Muscatine, Iowa, 1948-55, prin. and chief structural engr., 1955-77, v.p., 1972—, dir. cons. staff, 1977—; instr. structural engring. topics for civil engrs., 1970-80. Mem. Nat. Soc. Profl. Engrs., Am. Concrete Inst., Iowa Engring. Soc. Republican. Greek Orthodox. Club: Muscatine Engrs. Author: Coefficients for Analysis of 2 and 3 Span Continuous Beams of Constant Moment of Inertia, 1961, Coefficients for Analysis of 4 Span. . ., 1966; contbr. numerous articles to tech. publs. Home: 206 W 4th St Muscatine IA 52761 Office: Stanley Bldg Muscatine IA 52761

NESTLER, MARK ALAN, floor covering co. exec.; b. N.Y.C., Sept. 23, 1947; s. Arthur and Ginger (Rubinstein) N.; B.B.A., Babson Coll., 1970. Regional sales mgr. Champion Carpet Mills, 1970-72; dir. operations Stephen-Leedom Carpet Co., Inc., 1972-74, v.p. sales, 1974-75; v.p. Nestler Enterprises, Inc., N.Y.C., 1975—; mem. Floor Covering Exec. Com. Active United Jewish Appeal, Bonds for Israel, Juvenile Diabetes Found. Mem. Nat. Assn. Floor Covering Distbrs. (asso.). Office: 919 3d Ave New York NY 10022

NETCHVOLODOFF, VADIME V., steel co. exec.; b. St. Petersburg, Russia, Apr. 1, 1910; s. Vadime P. and Blanche Anna (Florin) N.; M.E., Cornell U., 1932; m. Carolyn M. Perrine, Nov. 24, 1934; children—Alexander V., Catherine V. Vice-pres. Hill Equipment Engring., 1932-55; mgr. welding machinery and equipment Vickers Electric div. Sperry Rand Corp., 1955-59; cons. engr., 1960; pres., chmn. bd. Ames Corp., St. Louis, 1960-65; v.p. engring., dir. Valley Industries and Valley Steel Products Co., St. Louis, 1965—. Mem. ASTM, Am. Welding Soc., Phi Delta Sigma, Phi Kappa Tau. Republican. Episcopalian. Office: PO Box 503 Saint Louis MO 63166

NETHERWOOD, DOUGLAS BLAKESHAW, III, real estate mgmt. and fin. co. exec.; b. Washington, Nov. 22, 1944; s. Douglas Blakeshaw and Mary Anne (Carlsen) N.; B.A., U. Md., 1973; m. Norma Jean Veneskey, Sept. 13, 1969; children—Douglas Blakeshaw, Andrea Marie, Ashley Jonathan. Systems controller Planning Research Corp., McLean, Va., 1970-73; mgr. systems adminstrn. Am. Mgmt. Systems, Inc., Arlington, Va., 1973-77; data processing mgr. AZTECH Corp., Washington, 1977-79, asst. v.p., dir. data processing, 1979-80; mgr. data center Nat. Corp. for Housing Partnerships, Washington, 1980—; cons. in field. Served with USNR, 1966-68. Mem. Data Processing Mgrs. Assn., Res. Officers Assn., U. Md. Alumni Assn. (life), U.S. Tennis Assn. Roman Catholic. Clubs: U. Md. Terrapin (College Park, Md.), Loudoun Indoor Tennis (Leesburg, Va.), Forester. Home: 31 Running Brook Ln Sterling VA 22170 Office: 1133 15th St NW Washington DC 20005

NETSCHERT, BRUCE CARLTON, economic cons.; b. Newark, Jan. 6, 1920; s. William and Julia Sanborn (Routh) N.; B.A., Cornell U., 1941, Ph.D., 1949; m. Katherine Virginia Bock, June 3, 1944; children—Juliana, Bruce James. Asst. prof. U. Minn., Duluth, 1949-50; economist with U.S. Govt., including Bur. Mines, Pres.'s Materials Policy Commn., Nat. Security Resources Bd., Office Def. Moblzn. and CIA, 1951-55; sr. research asso. Resources for the Future, Inc., 1955-61; v.p. Nat. Economic Research Assos., Inc., Washington, 1961—; advisory council Elec. Power Research Inst.; tech. advisory com. conservation of energy FPC, com. biol. effects of ionizing radiation NRC-Nat. Acad. Scis. Served to 1st lt. USAAF, 1942-46. Fellow Geol. Soc. Am., Inst. Petroleum (London); mem. Am. Economics Assn., Assn. Energy Economists, Am. Inst. Mining, Metall. and Petroleum Engrs. Club: Cosmos. Author: (with others) General Geography for Colleges, 1957, Energy in the American Economy, 1850-1975, 1960, The Future Supply of the Major Metals, 1961; The Future Supply of Oil and Gas, 1958; The Mineral Foreign Trade of the United States in the Twentieth Century, 1977. Home: 1917 Marthas Rd Alexandria VA 22307 Office: 1800 M St Washington DC 20036

NETZEL, PAUL ARTHUR, youth and family service orgn. exec.; b. Tacoma, Sept. 11, 1941; s. Marden Arthur and Audrey Rose (Jones) N.; B.S. in Group Work Edn., George Williams Coll., 1963; m. Diane Viscount, Mar. 21, 1963; children—Paul M., Shari Ann. Program dir. S. Pasadena, San Marino (Calif.) YMCA, 1963-66; exec. dir. camp and youth programs Wenatchee (Wash.) YMCA, 1966-67; exec. dir. Culver-Palms Family YMCA, Culver City, Calif., 1967-73; v.p. met. fin. devel. YMCA Met. Los Angeles, 1973-78; sr. v.p. fin. devel. YMCA, Los Angeles, 1978—; pres. bd. dirs. YMCA Employees Fed. Credit Union, 1977-80; instr., cons., fund raiser. Pres. bd. Culver City Guidance Clinic, 1971-74; mem. Culver City Bd. Edn., 1975-79, pres., 1977-78; vice mayor and mem. City Council Culver City, 1980—; bd. dirs. Los Angeles Psychiat. Service; chmn. Regional Babe Ruth Baseball Tournament. Recipient Man of Year award Culver City C. of C., 1972. Roman Catholic. Club: Rotary (Los Angeles). Office: YMCA Metropolitan Los Angeles 818 W 7th St 10th Floor Los Angeles CA 90017

NEUBAUM, FRANK EDWARD, JR., constrn. equip. co. exec.; b. Harrisburg, Pa., July 7, 1944; s. Frank Edward and Anna Catherine (Horvath) N.; B.S., Edn., West Chester State Coll., 1966; m. Jacqueline Louise Liptak, July 17, 1971; children—Bethany Christine, Sarah Lindsey. Tchr.-coach Bishop McDevitt High Sch., Harrisburg, Pa., 1966-68; marketing rep. Aetna Casualty & Surety Co., Harrisburg, 1968-72; sales mgr. Highway Equipment Supply Co., Harrisburg, 1972—. Mem. East York Lions (pres.), West Shore C. of C., Pa. Aggregates Assn., Assn. Builders & Contractors, Inc. Roman Catholic. Home: 42 N Lehman York PA 17403 Office: 4500 Paxton St Harrisburg PA 17105

NEUENSCHWANDER, FREDERICK PHILIP, business exec.; b. Akron, Ohio, Mar. 19, 1924; s. Willis L. and Esther (Mayer) N.; student Franklin and Marshall Coll., 1942-43, U. Akron, 1946-49; m. Mary Jane Porter, Mar. 19, 1948; children—Carol, Frederick, Lynn, Dean, Richard. Chief insp. Retail Credit Co., Akron, 1949-55; exec. v.p. Wadsworth C. of C., 1955-62, Wooster (Ohio) C. of C., 1962-63; dep. dir. Ohio Dept. Devel., Columbus, 1963-64, dir., 1964-70; exec. v.p. James A. Rhodes & Assos., Columbus, 1970-74; pres. F.P. Neuenschwander & Assos., 1975—; sec., dir. Jackson Iron and Steel Co. Chmn., Ohio Water and Sewer Rotary Commn., Midwest Gov.'s Adv. Com., 1967; vice chmn. Ohio Water Commn., Ohio Air Pollution Control Bd.; mem. gov.'s cabinet State of Ohio; sec. Ohio Devel. Council, 1964-70, Ohio Devel. Financing Commn., 1964—; mem. Ohio Expns. Commn.; chmn. bd. govs. Ohio Hwy. Research center; mem. exec. com., nat. adv. council Small Bus. Adminstrn.; bd. dirs. Bd. World Ministries, United Ch. of Christ, League Against Child Abuse; exec. com. Central Ohio council Boy Scouts Am. Served with AUS, 1943-46. Named Outstanding Young Man of the Year, 1958; recipient awards Gov. Ohio, 1967, Nat. Soc. Indsl. Realtors, 1966, 68. Mem. C. of C. Execs. of Ohio, Gt. Lakes State Indsl. Devel. Council, Am. Indsl. Devel. Council, Am. Assn. State Planning and Devel. Dirs., Huguenot Soc. Am., Am. Legion. Mem. United Ch. of Christ. Club: Worthington Hills Country. Home: 2066 Henderson Rd Columbus OH 43220 Office: 50 W Broad St Columbus OH 43215

NEUER, PHILIP DAVID, lawyer; b. Bklyn., May 31, 1946; s. Murray and Adele (Jacobs) N.; B.B.A., Baruch Sch., CCNY, 1968; postgrad. Boston U., 1968-69; J.D., Seton Hall U., 1976; m. Rena Donna Levine, July 30, 1972; children—Jeremy Evan, Linzy Michelle, Sari Faith. Admitted to N.J. bar, 1976; municipal law clk. Town of West Orange (N.J.), 1973-76, asst. town atty., 1976-78; individual practice law, Orange, N.J., 1976-78; asso. firm Margolis, Bergstein & Schiffman, P.A., Verona, N.J., 1978-80, firm Slavitt, Slavitt, Feldman & Marshall, P.A., West Orange, 1980—; atty. West Orange Consumer Protection and Edn. Advisory Bd., 1977—. Mem. West Orange Economic Devel. Com., 1975-76. Served with USN, 1969-73. Mem. Am., N.J., Essex County bar assns., Assn. Trial Lawyers Am., Assn. Fed. Bar N.J., Sigma Alpha Rho, Alpha Epsilon Pi. Jewish. Club: Masons. Home: 1 Edgar Rd West Orange NJ 07052 Office: 80 Main St West Orange NJ 07052

NEUHARTH, ALLEN HAROLD, media exec.; b. Eureka, S.D., Mar. 22, 1924; s. Daniel J. and Christina (Neuharth) N.; B.A. cum laude, U. S.D. 1950; student Am. Press Inst., Columbia, 1956, 62, 63; m. Loretta Faye Helgeland, June 16, 1946 (div. 1972); children—Daniel J. II, Janet Ann; m. 2d, Lori Wilson, Dec. 31, 1973. Reporter, Rapid City (S.D.) Jour., 1948; sports writer Mitchell (S.D.) Daily Republic, 1949; staff writer A.P., Sioux Falls, S.D. 1950-52; editor, pub. S.D. Sports Weekly Sioux Falls, 1952-54; with Miami (Fla.) Herald, 1954-60, asst. mng. editor, 1958-60; asst. exec. editor Detroit Free Press, 1960-63; gen. mgr. Times-Union and Democrat and Chronicle, Rochester, N.Y., 1963—; exec. v.p. Gannett Co., Inc., 1967-70, pres., 1970—, chief exec., 1973—, chmn., 1979—, also dir.; dir. numerous Gannett subsidiaries, also Marine Midland Bank. Bd. dirs. Nat. Council Better Bus. Burs.; trustee Gannett Found. Served with inf. AUS, 1943-46; ETO, PTO. Decorated Bronze Star; recipient Horatio Alger award, 1977. Mem. Am. Newspaper Pubs. Assn. (dir. 1968—, chmn., pres. 1978-80), N.Y. State Pubs. Assn. (past pres.), Sigma Delta Chi (nat. regional dir.). Clubs: Genesee Valley (Rochester); Sky (N.Y.C.); Jockey (Miami); Ocean Reef (Key Largo, Fla.); Carlton (Chgo.); International (Washington). Home: 333 S Atlantic Ave Cocoa Beach FL 32931 Office: Lincoln Tower Rochester NY 14604

NEUMAIER, GERHARD JOHN, environ. cons. co. exec.; b. Covington, Ky., July 27, 1937; s. John Edward and Elli Anna (Raudies) N.; B.M.E., Gen. Motors Inst., 1960; M.A. in Biophysics, U. Buffalo, 1963; m. Ellen Elaine Klepper, Oct. 24, 1959; children—Kevin Scott, Kirsten Lynn. Research ecologist, project mgr. Cornell Aero. Lab., Buffalo, 1963-70; pres., chief exec. Ecology and Environment, Inc., Buffalo, 1970—, also chmn. bd. Mem. Am. Public Health Assn., Air Pollution Control Assn., Internat. Assn. Gt. Lakes Research, Inst. Environ. Scis., Ecol. Soc. Am., Am. Inst. Biol. Scis., Urban Land Inst., Arctic Inst. N.Am., Nat. Parks and Conservation Assn., Defenders of Wildlife, Nat. Wildlife Fedn., Wilderness Soc., Am. Hort. Soc., Smithsonian Assos., Nat. Audubon Soc. Home: 284 Mill Rd East Aurora NY 14052 Office: 195 Sugg Rd Buffalo NY 14225

NEUMAN, LEON, banker; b. St. Louis, Sept. 12, 1920; s. Jacob and Mamie (Love) N.; student St. Louis U., 1953-54, Washington U., 1951-52, Am. Inst. Banking, 1948-50; grad., Sch. Banking, U. Wis., 1955; m. Gertrude Helen Ladinsky, Mar. 19, 1944 (dec. Sept. 1978); children—Susan H. Neuman Goldstein, Priscilla A. Neuman Alper, Marcia Sheri. Nat. bank examiner, St. Louis, 1939-48; asst. v.p., auditor State Bank & Trust Co., St. Louis, 1948-51, v.p., auditor, 1951-58, exec. v.p., 1958-61; pres., dir. Landmark North County Bank & Trust Co., St. Louis, 1961—; exec. v.p., dir. Landmark Bancshares Corp., Inc., St. Louis, 1971—. Chmn. Lewis and Clark fund Raising com. Boy Scouts Am., St. Louis, 1963; active various fund drives. Mem. pacesetters bd. Mo. Bapt. Hosp., St. Louis, 1974; bd. dirs. Gradwohl Sch. Lab. Techniques, St. Louis, 1974, United Way Greater St. Louis, 1976—; bd. dirs. St. Louis Rabbinical Coll., 1981, Man of Yr., 1980; bd. dirs. Easter Mo. chpt. Arthritis Found., 1977—, pres., 1979—; mem. adv. bd. Am. Med. Center, Denver, 1967—, dinner chmn., 1977, 78. Mem. Am. Inst. Banking (dir. 1950-52), Jennings C. of C. (dir.). Jewish (dir. temple 1956—, v.p. 1970-71). Clubs: Norwood Hills Country, Meadowbrook Country, Variety (pres. 1970, named Man of Yr. 1976), Kiwanis (pres. 1970), B'nai B'rith (St. Louis). Home: 306 N Brentwood Blvd Clayton MO 63105 Office: 9269 Lewis and Clark Blvd St Louis MO 63136

NEUMANN, ROBERT WILLIAM, auditor; b. Wasco, Calif., Oct. 9, 1943; s. Willard Isaac and Vera Florence (Johnson) N.; B.S. in B.A., LaSierra Coll., 1967; m. Lyla Mae, Aug. 21, 1966; children—Ryan Isaac, Kaarsten Patrice, Blair Justice, Evan Davis. Programmer, analyst Loma Linda (Calif.) U., 1966-68; v.p. data processing United Med. Labs., Portland, Oreg., 1968-72; program mgt. Boeing Computer Services, Seattle, 1973-75; internal auditor PACCAR, Bellevue, Wash., 1976—. Dir., mem. exec. com. Michel Found.; chmn. Explorer Scouts. Mem. Aircraft Owners and Pilots Assn. Home: 13603 NE 36th Pl Bellevue WA 98005 Office: Business Center Bldg 777 106th Ave NE Bellevue WA 98004

NEUMANN, THOMAS JORDAN, gen. contracting co. exec.; b. Dawson, Ga., Mar. 17, 1932; s. Lloyd Anthony and Chloie Pauline (Jones) N.; student public schs., Dawson, Ga.; m. Janice Mildred Brose, Dec. 5, 1959; children—Roger Allan, Costa Anthony, Thomas Jordan. Pres., T. & J. Marble & Tile Co., Oklahoma City, 1960-70; exec. v.p. Am. Superior Co., Oklahoma City, 1970-74; ops. mgr. Am. Standard Co., New Brunswick, N.J., 1974-78; pres. T.J. Neumann and Assos., Inc., Oklahoma City, 1978—. Served with U.S. Army, 1949-52. Decorated Bronze Star, Silver Star. Mem. Nat. Home Builders Assn., Central Okla. Home Builders Assn. Republican. Home: 10409 Harvest Moon Ave Oklahoma City OK 73132 Office: 8011 NW 82d St Oklahoma City OK 73132

NEUNER, GEORGE WILLIAM, lawyer; b. Buffalo, Oct. 3, 1943; s. George J. and Geraldine M. (O'Connor) N.; B.S. magna cum laude, SUNY, Buffalo, 1965; S.M. (grantee Sun Oil Co. 1966), M.I.T., 1966;

J.D. with honors, George Washington U., 1975; m. Kathleen M. Stoeckl, Aug. 28, 1965; children—George William, II, Kathleen E. With Eastman Kodak Co., Rochester, N.Y., 1966-77, patent atty., 1975-77; admitted to N.Y. State bar, 1976, Mass. bar, 1978, D.C. bar, 1976, Va. bar, 1975; asso. firm Dike, Bronstein, Roberts, Cushman & Pfund, Boston, 1977-79, partner, 1980—; arbitration panelist 4th Jud. Dept. N.Y. State, 1976-77. Mem. Am. Bar Assn., Mass. Bar Assn., Boston Patent Law Assn. (chmn. chem. practice com. 1980-81), Am. Inst. Chem. Engrs. (Student of Yr. award Western N.Y. chpt. 1965), George Washington U. Law Assn., Bisonhead, Tau Beta Pi. Club: M.I.T. (dir. Rochester 1976-77). Home: 8 Ravenscroft Rd Winchester MA 01890 Office: 120 Water St Boston MA 02110

NEUSCHEL, RICHARD FREDERICK, ret. mgmt. cons.; b. Buffalo, Mar. 3, 1915; s. Percy J. and Anna (Becker) N.; student U. Colo., 1932-33; A.B., Denison U., 1936; M.B.A. cum laude, Harvard U., 1941; m. Jean Fuller, Oct. 16, 1943; children—Robin Fuller, Debra Jean. Gen. procedures dir. Sperry Gyroscope Co., 1941-45; with McKinsey & Co., Inc., N.Y.C., 1945-74, prin., 1954-59, dir., mem. exec. com., 1959-73, mng. dir. N.Y. office, 1968-74. Trustee Denison U., 1972—, vice chmn. bd. trustees, 1975—, distinguished alumni citation, 1970. Named Systems Man of Year, Internat. Systems and Procedures Assn., 1965. Mem. Am. Mgmt. Assn. (planning council; life), Sigma Alpha Epsilon, Omicron Delta Kappa, Pi Delta Epsilon. Clubs: Sky, Harvard (N.Y.C.); Nassau Country (Glen Cove, N.Y.). Author: Streamlining Business Procedures, 1950; Management by System, 1960; Management Systems for Profit and Growth, 1976; The Chief Executive's Strategic Role and Responsibilities, 1977; contbg. author: Industrial Engineering Handbook, 1956, 63; Marketing and the Computer, 1963; Toward a Unified Theory of Management, 1964; The Arts of Top Management, 1971. Home: 14 Woodacres Rd Brookville Glen Head NY 11545 Office: 245 Park Ave New York NY 10017

NEUWIRTH, PAUL DAVID, public accountant; b. N.Y.C., July 12, 1936; s. Benjamin and Anna (Kaufman) N.; B.B.A., City U. N.Y., 1957; m. Beatrice Kleinberg, Sept. 7, 1958; children—Stephen R., James G., Richard H. Staff accountant Eisner & Lubin, C.P.A.'s, N.Y.C., 1957-61, Klein, Hinds & Finke, C.P.A.'s, 1962-68, partner, 1968-69; partner Alexander Grant & Co., 1969—; nat. dir. corporate devel., 1975-76, mng. partner, Phila., 1976—; lectr. City U. N.Y., 1962-75, N.Y. U., 1969, Wharton Sch., U. Pa., 1979—. Bd. dirs. YM-YWHA, Riverdale, N.Y., 1970-78, Ednl. Alliance, N.Y.C., 1975-76, Equity Library Theatre, 1975-76, Phila. Jewish Youth Center, 1976-77, Med. Coll. Pa., 1977—. C.P.A., Pa., N.Y., La., Mich., Va., W.Va. Mem. Am. Inst. C.P.A.'s, N.Y. State Soc. C.P.A.'s, Pa. Inst. C.P.A.'s, Accountants Club Am., Beta Alpha Psi, Beta Gamma Sigma, Sigma Alpha. Contbg. author: Attorney's Handbook of Accounting, 1971; contbr. articles in field to profl. jours. Home: 286 Barwynne Ln Wynnewood PA 19151 Office: 2000 Market St Philadelphia PA 19103

NEVIN, JOHN J., tire and rubber mfg. co. exec.; b. Jersey City, Feb. 1, 1927; s. Edward Vincent and Anna (Burns) N.; B.S., U. Calif., 1950; M.B.A., Harvard, 1952; m. Anna Filice, June 16, 1951; children—Stanley James, John Joseph, Richard Charles, Paul Edward, Gerald Patrick, Mary Anne. Various positions finance, product planning and mktg. Ford Motor Co., Dearborn, Mich., 1954-71, v.p. mktg., 1969-71; pres. Zenith Radio Corp., Chgo., 1971-76, chmn., chief exec. officer, 1976-79, also dir.; pres., chief exec. officer Firestone Tire & Rubber Co., Akron, Ohio, 1979—. Gen. chmn. Detroit United Found., 1970. Served with USNR, 1945-46. Home: 80 N Portage Path Akron OH 44303 Office: 1200 Firestone Pkwy Akron OH 44317

NEVINS, BRUCE STANLEY, mktg. co. exec.; b. Amsterdam, N.Y., July 17, 1937; Strauss & Co co. exec.; b. Amsterdam, N.Y., July 17,1937; s. Marshall S. and Emily N.; B.S., U.S. Mil. Acad., 1960; M.B.A., Stanford U., 1966. Account exec. Benton & Bowles Advt., N.Y.C., 1966-68; mktg. dir. Levi Strauss & Co., 1968-69, dir. internat., gen. mgr. Asia/Pacific/Latin Am./Can., 1969-72, pres. bus. devel. and diversified products div., 1973-74; chmn. Pony Sporting Goods, N.Y.C., 1974-75; founder, pres. Perrier - Great Waters of France, Inc., Greenwich, Conn., 1976-80; chief exec. officer Premium Products Mktg. Corp., Greenwich, 1981—. Trustee, Am. Health Found., N.Y.C., 1978—; bd. dirs. Healthy America Coalition, Washington, 1978—. Served as capt. U.S. Army, 1960-64; Laos. Recipient Mag. Grand award Sales and Mktg. Mgmt. mag., 1979. Mem. Council Natural Waters (pres. 1980), Assn. Grads. U.S. Mil. Acad. Clubs: Le Club, Vertical, N.Y. Athletic. Office: 777 W Putnam Ave Greenwich CT 06830

NEVISTICH, DRAGUTIN DOUG, camera co. exec.; b. Duvno, Yugoslavia, May 24, 1938; s. Martin and Perka N.; B.S. in Engring., Mech. Engrs. Coll., 1961, M.S. in Engring., 1965; m. Tania, Apr. 15, 1968; children—Sandra, Igor. Designer, Constructor Energoinvest Co., Yugoslavia, 1957-61; instr. engring. U. Sarajevo, Yugoslavia, 1961-65; chief tech. Rude Knocar, Yugoslavia, 1967-68; asst. supr. engring. Pyro Plastic, 1968-72; mgr. mfg. engring. and dir. plastics dept. Keystone Camera Co., Clifton, N.J., 1972—. Served with Army, 1966-67. Mem. Soc. Plastic Engring. Club: Tennis of W. Orange. Designer spl. radial drill machine. Home: 6 Dana Dr Livingston NJ 07039 Office: 420 Getty Ave Clifton NJ 07015

NEWBANKS, LLOYD LEON, army officer; b. Oswego, Kans., Apr. 5, 1950; s. Lloyd Clinton and Mildred May (Walter) N.; B.S. in B.A., Kans. State Coll., 1972; M.B.A., Golden Gate U., 1975; m. Louise Darlene Peoples, Nov. 25, 1969; children—Laura Leanne, Tonya Lashelle, Tara Louise. Commd. 2d lt. U.S. Army, 1972, advanced through grades to capt., 1976; chief mil. pay Ft. Ord, Calif., 1974-75, chief pay and exam br., 1975, cash control and disbursing officer 1st Fin. Sect., 1976, staff fin. officer 19th Support Command, Taegu, Korea, 1977-79; instr. Los Angeles Community Coll., 1976-79, U. Md., Far East Div., 1977-79; asst. prof. mil. sci. Kans. State U., Manhattan, 1979—. Decorated Army Commendation medal with oak leaf cluster. Mem. Nat. Assn. Scabbard and Blades. Republican. Methodist. Home: PO Box 504 Altamont KS 67330 Office: Kans State U Manhattan KS 66506

NEWBEGIN, WADE, farm and irrigation equipment mfg. and distbn. co. exec.; b. Portland, Oreg., Oct. 3, 1907; s. Edward C. and Susan E. (Wade) N.; B.A. in Bus. Adminstrn., U. Oreg., 1929; m. Margaret Elizabeth Hall, Nov. 30, 1929; children—Wade, Edward H., Susan Newbegin Russell. Pres., R.M. Wade & Co., Beaverton, Oreg., 1929—, chmn., 1978—, pres. Tractor Sales div., 1931—; pres. Pumps West, Inc., Beaverton, 1945—, Wade Credit Corp., Beaverton, 1979—; dir. 1st Nat. Bank of Oreg., Portland Gen. Electric Co. Mem. Nat. Assn. Wholesalers (past pres.), Farm Equipment Wholesalers Assn. (past pres.), Farm and Indsl. Equipment Inst., Irrigation Assn. (Industry Achievement award 1979), Portland C. of C. (v.p. 1960-61), Phi Beta Kappa, Beta Gamma Sigma. Republican. Congregationalist. Clubs: University (past pres.), Waverley Country (past pres.), Multnomah Athletic. Home: 4101 SW Greenleaf Dr Portland OR 97221 Office: 10025 SW Allen Blvd Beaverton OR 97005

NEWBERG, THOMAS GERALD, mfg. co. exec.; b. Chgo., June 16, 1951; s. Manfred Allen and Dorthy Mary (Tiltges) N.; B.S. in Fin., U. Ill., 1973; M.B.A., Roosevelt U., 1978; m. Sally Schancer, Dec. 21, 1973. Staff accountant Am. Hosp. Supply Corp., 1973; asst. to controller A. Epstein & Co., Chgo., 1974-75; with Internat. Harvester Corp., Chgo., 1975—, cost analyst mfg. and facility planning, supr. mfg. accounting, 1978-80, sr. fin. analyst, 1980—; part-time instr. Coll. Lake County. C.P.A.; cert. mgmt. acct. Mem. Assn. M.B.A. Execs., Nat. Assn. Accountants, Am. Inst. C.P.A.'s, Ill. Soc. C.P.A.'s, Alpha Kappa Psi. Roman Catholic. Home: 101 Austin Ct Vernon Hills IL 60061 Office: 401 N Michigan Ave Chicago IL 60611

NEWBERGER, JOSEPH MICHAEL, lawyer, tanning co. exec.; b. Chgo., Nov. 7, 1936; s. Ralph and Rebecca (Schottenstein) N.; B.S.B.A., Northwestern U., 1957; J.D., U. Chgo., 1960; m. Charlotte Malkin, Nov. 4, 1962; children—Tamar, Robin. Admitted to Ill. bar, 1960; individual practice law, Chgo., 1961—; controller Newberger Bros., Inc., Chgo., 1962-66, dir., 1966—, pres., 1972—. Bd. dirs. Hebrew Theol. Coll., Skokie, Ill., St. Nicholas Theater, Chgo.; chmn. bd. Anshe Sholom Synagogue, Chgo.; mem. commn. Camp Ramah, Wis.; chmn. bd. trustees Anshe Emet Day Sch., Chgo. Mem. Am., Ill., Chgo. bar assns. Freelance comedy writer. Club: Standard. Office: Newberger Bros Inc 230 W Lake St Chicago IL 60606

NEWBERGER, SHEL, packaging exec.; b. Chgo., Nov. 30, 1925; s. Oscar and Daisy N.; B.A., U. Chgo., 1944; m. Natalie Bernard, Oct. 22, 1946; children—Steven, Richard, David, Jill. Packaging salesman Cleary Box Co., Chgo., 1946-48, Chippewa Paper Products, Chgo., 1948-63, Lanzit Corrugated Box Co., Chgo., 1950-63, Consol. Packaging Corp., Chgo., 1960-63; pres., Apollo Containers, Inc., Evanston, Ill., 1963—, prin., pres., Boyer Corp., Evanston, 1976—. Alderman, Evanston, 1967-71; officer Evanston Recreation Bd., 1971—. Served with U.S. Army, 1944-46. Mem. Chgo. Assn. Commerce and Industry, Evanston C. of C. Home: 100 Dempster St Evanston IL 60202 Office: 2902 Central St Evanston IL 60201

NEWBOLD, MARYLOU, savs. and loan exec.; b. San Diego, Dec. 30, 1942; d. James Thomas and Marjorie Louise (Chapman) Allen; grad. in bus. adminstrn. Grossmont Coll.; grad. in econs. San Diego State U.; postgrad. Sch. Savs. and Loan, Ind. U.; m. Tony Thompson Newbold, June 26, 1959 (div. July 1971); children—Tony Thompson, Deborah Denise, Timothy Thomas, Michael L. Adminstrv. asst. Palomar Mortgage Co., San Diego, 1960-64; residential real estate salesman Joplin Realty, El Cajon, Calif., 1970-72; comml. loan officer San Diego Fed. Savs. & Loan, 1972-74, asst. loan servicing mgr., 1974-75, sr. v.p., 1980—, secondary market mgr., 1975—; dir. Fin. Scene, Inc., Cal-Gen. Mortgage Service, Inc. Mem. single parent project YMCA. Mem. Assn. Profl. Mortgage Women (founding pres. San Diego chpt. 1977-78, dir. 1978-79), Nat. Forum Exec. Women (voting mem.). Republican. Home: 2484 Kenda Way Alpine CA 92001 Office: 600 B St San Diego CA 92183

NEWBY, CHARLES DAVID, auto parts co. exec.; b. Fort Worth, Tex., Dec. 15, 1953; s. Milas E. and Ruth L. (Echols) N.; B.B.A. in Mgmt., Tex. Christian U., 1976. With Greenfield Sales Co., Fort Worth, 1969—, v.p. mktg., 1974, exec. v.p., 1979—, pres. subs. Dave's Auto Parts and Tools, 1974—. Mem. Nat. Right to Work Com. Mem. Am. Mgmt. Assn., Ind. Garagemens Assn. Democrat. Mem. Ch. of Christ. Home: 1517 Byrd St Fort Worth TX 76114 Office: 509 E 3d St Fort Worth TX 76101

NEWELL, MICHAEL PERRY, audio co. exec.; b. Nashville, Dec. 5, 1955; s. Paul Haynes, Jr. and Frances Carole (Foster) N.; student in Biomed. Engring., Tex. A. and M. U., 1972-74; student Mech. Engring., N.J. Inst. Tech., 1975-76; m. Susan Jeanne Wilkins, Sept. 15, 1979. Partner, Custom Sounds, Inc., Bryan, Tex., 1976-78, exec. v.p., chmn. bd. Custom Sounds, Inc., 1978—. Mem. Soc. Audio Cons.'s, Nat. Fedn. Ind. Bus. Republican. Mem. Ch. of Christ. Home: 2210 Dewberry Ln Bryan TX 77801 Office: Custom Sounds Inc 3806-A Old College Rd Bryan TX 77801

NEWELL, RICHARD NELSON, bank exec.; b. Toledo, June 2, 1932; s. James Reed and Florence N.; B.S. in Econs., Wharton Sch. Fin. and Commerce, U. Pa., 1955; m. Judith Dewey, July 30, 1960; children—Richard Nelson, Phillip, Elizabeth. Account exec. Merrill Lynch, Pierce, Fenner & Smith, Inc., Toledo, 1958-68; investment officer First Nat. Bank of Toledo, 1968-71, v.p. trust investments, 1971-76, v.p. bank investments, 1976—; fin. trustee Med. Coll. Ohio at Toledo Found., 1973—. Treas. St. Michael's In-the-Hills Episcopal Ch., Toledo, 1977—; chmn. fin. sect. employees div. United Way, Toledo, 1978—; mem. allocations com. Community Chest of Greater Toledo. Recipient Distinguished Guest Speaker award U. Toledo Coll. Bus. Adminstrn., 1978. Mem. Econ. Club of Detroit, Fin. Analysts Soc. Toledo (pres. 1978-79). Home: 3436 Brookside Rd Toledo OH 43606 Office: PO Box 1868 Toledo OH 43603

NEWELL, WILLIAM THOMAS, bus. exec.; b. Rochester, N.Y., July 5, 1936; s. Earl Edward and Ruth Hazel (Dorsey) N.; student Rochester Inst. Tech., 1955; m. Margret Anne Laurash, July 10, 1971. Owner, operator ChemMark Chem. Co., Miami, Fla., 1965-67, Newell & Co., sales and mktg. cons. and sales agts., Atlanta, Dallas, Ft. Lauderdale, Fla., 1967—, Keynote Music Studios, Ft. Lauderdale, 1974—; pres. Sytlewood Industries, Inc., mfg. and sales of insulated bldg. panels, Gainesville, Fla., 1977-80. Served with U.S. Army, 1959-61. Democrat. Episcopalian. Home: 2500 NE 48th Ln Fort Lauderdale FL 33308 Office: 5130 N Federal Hwy Fort Lauderdale FL 33308

NEWHALL, CHARLES WATSON, III, venture capital co. exec.; b. Washington, Nov. 18, 1944; s. Charles Watson, Jr. and Gladys (Brantley) N.; B.A. with honors, U. Pa., 1967; M.B.A., Harvard U., 1971; m. Mary Washington Marr, Oct. 14, 1967; children—Charles Ashton, Adair Brantley. With T. Rowe Price Assos., Balt., 1971-77, v.p., 1974-77; v.p. Rowe Price New Horizons Fund, 1974-77; gen. partner New Enterprise Assos., Balt., 1977—; dir. Bethesda (Md.) Research Labs., Chomerics, Inc., Boston, Vectra Corp., Dayton, Ohio. Trustee, Balt. Mus. Art. Served to 1st lt. USAR, 1967-69; Vietnam. Decorated Silver Star, Bronze Star V with oak leaf cluster, Air medal, Army Commendation medal, Purple Heart, Combat Inf. badge, Parachutist badge. Mem. Soc. Cincinnati. Republican. Episcopalian. Clubs: Green Spring Valley Hunt (Balt.); Somerset (Boston). Office: 300 Cathedral Pl Suite 110 Baltimore MD 21201

NEWHARD, HARRY WALLACE, investment banker; b. St. Louis, Aug. 19, 1930; s. Chapin Slater and Anne Kennard (Wallace) N.; B.A., Brown U., 1953; m. Sept. 1960 (div.); children—Jean H., Pennock H. With Newhard, Cook & Co., Inc., St. Louis, 1956—, pres., 1971—. Served with A.C., USNR, 1953-56. Mem. Investment Bankers Assn. (chmn. Miss. Valley Group 1970, exec. com. 1971). Republican. Clubs: St. Louis Country, Noonday (St. Louis); Union (N.Y.C.). Home: 2 Pebble Creek Rd Saint Louis MO 63124 Office: 300 N Broadway Saint Louis MO 63102

NEWHOUSE, SAMUEL I., newspaper exec. Pub. Newark Star Ledger; pres. Morning Ledger Co. L.I. Daily Press, Syracuse Herald-Journal, Syracuse Post-Standard, S.I. Advance, Harrisburg Patriot-News, Portland Oregonian, Ore. Jour., Jersey Jour., St. Louis Globe-Democrat, Birmingham News, Huntsville Times, Times-Picayune, States and Item, New Orleans. Address: Star Ledger Plaza Newark NJ 07101*

NEWKIRK, JACK ANGLE, acct.; b. Hagerstown, Md., June 29, 1947; s. Donald Harry and Frances Marian (Angle) N.; B.S., U. Md., 1976; m. Nancy Jean Shrader, June 8, 1968; 1 son, Jack Angle. Bookkeeper, Bob White Buick, Washington, 1969, Miller Buick, Inc., Rockville, Md., 1972; office mgr. Christopher R. Custer, Inc., Frederick, Md., 1972-75; comptroller Middletown Ford Sales, Inc. (Md.), 1975-76; gen. mgr. Christopher R. Custer, Inc., Frederick, Md., 1976-79 corporate sec., 1977-79, also dir.; acct. R.W. Warner, Inc., Frederick, 1979—. Served with U.S. Army, 1969-72. Mem. Am. Legion, Amvets. Democrat. Lutheran. Club: Masons. Home: 7290 Beechtree Ct Middletown MD 21769 Office: 12 E 5th St Frederick MD 21701

NEWLAND, JAMES I., stockgrower; b. Belle Fourche, S.D., Feb. 12, 1911; s. Wilbur F. and Lucille C. (King) N.; m. Velma L. Bourne, Sept. 5, 1943; children—Robert J., Wilbur H. Stockgrower, Belle Fourche, S.D. and Colony, Wyo., 1920—; pres., dir. Fed. Land Bank Assn., Belle Fourche, 1970-76. Mem. Am. Scotch Highland Breeders Assn. (past pres.), Am. Nat. Cattlemen's Assn. (past dir.), S.D. Sheepgrowers Assn., S.D. Stockgrowers Assn. (past dir.), Wyo. Stockgrowers Assn., Mont. Stockgrowers Assn., Nat. Woolgrowers Assn., Wyo. Woolgrowers Assn., Mont. Woolgrowers Assn. Democrat. Methodist. Clubs: K.P., Moose. Home: Via Belle Fourche SD 57717

NEWLIN, GEORGE WILLIAM, mgmt. co. exec.; b. Covington, Ind., July 3, 1917; s. Russell Stewart and Janet (Skene) N.; B.S., Ind. U., 1940; m. Rachel Elizabeth Meharry, Apr. 27, 1941; children—Charles R., William M., Thomas S., Esther M. Newlin Haus, David B. With Control div. Cummins Engine Co., Columbus, Ind., 1940-43; with Union Starch & Refining Co., Columbus, investment div., 1946-51, sec., 1951-56, v.p. investments, 1956-57; v.p. Union Sales Corp., 1956-57; v.p. Irwin Mgmt. Co., Inc., Columbus, Ind., 1958-60, pres., 1960—; dir. Cummins Engine Co., Inc., Compagnie Internationale de Placements et de Capitalisation, Irwin Union Corp., Irwin Mgmt. Co., Inc. Bd. dirs. Irwin-Sweeney-Miller Found.; bd. dirs. Louisville Presbyn. Theol. Sem. Served with USNR, 1943-46. Republican. Presbyterian. Home: 2920 Franklin Dr Columbus IN 47201 Office: 235 Washington St PO Box 808 Columbus IN 47201

NEWMAN, BARRY I., fin. co. exec.; b. N.Y.C., Mar. 19, 1932; s. M.A. and T.C. (Weitman) N.; B.A., Alfred U., 1952; J.D., N.Y. U., 1955; m. Jean Short, Mar. 6, 1965; children—Suzanne, Cathy, David. Admitted to N.Y. State bar, 1957, Ohio bar, 1957, U.S. Supreme Ct. bar, 1967; practiced in N.Y.C., 1957; partner firm Shapiro Persky Marken & Newman, Cleve., 1957-63; asst. v.p. Meinhard & Co. (now Meinhard Comml. Corp.), N.Y.C., 1963-65; v.p. Amsterdam Overseas Corp., N.Y.C., 1966-68; pres. No. Fin. Corp., Los Angeles, 1968-72; sr. v.p. Aetna Bus. Credit, Inc., Hartford, Conn., 1972-78; exec. v.p. Security Pacific Fin. Corp., San Diego, 1978—. Vestryman, chmn. fin. com. Christ Episcopal Ch., 1975—; treas., mem. exec. com. Avon (Conn.) Republican Town Com.; mem. Avon Bd. Fin., 1977—; justice of peace, Conn., 1977—. Served with U.S. Army, 1955-57. Recipient Distinguished Service award Cleve. Jr. C. of C., 1961. Mem. Am., N.Y. State, Ohio, San Diego bar assns., Assn. Comml. Fin. Attys., Nat. Comml. Fin. Conf. (v.p., dir. exec. com.), Financemen's Club. Republican. Clubs: Cherry Valley (Garden City, N.Y.); Avon Golf, Escondido (Calif.) Country, Masons. Home: 3308 Avenida Sierra Escondido CA 92025 Office: 10103 Carroll Canyon Rd San Diego CA 92131

NEWMAN, FRANK NEIL, banker; b. Quincy, Mass., Apr. 20, 1942; s. Robert D. and Ethel N.; B.A magna cum laude, Harvard, 1963; m. Monetta B. Wronski, June 16, 1966; 1 son, Daniel. With Corp. for Econ. and Indsl. Research, Boston, 1963-66; mgr. Peat, Marwick, Livingston & Co., Boston, 1966-69; v.p. product devel. Transaction Tech. div. Citicorp, Cambridge, Mass., 1969-73; v.p., mgr. mgmt. scis. dept. Wells Fargo Bank, San Francisco, 1973-77, sr. v.p. fin. and analysis, 1977—, sr. v.p., chief fin. officer Wells Fargo & Co., 1977-80, exec. v.p., chief fin. officer, 1980—. Mem. adv. panel San Francisco Ednl. Services. Mem. Ops. Research Soc. Am. Home: San Francisco CA Office: PO Box 44000 San Francisco CA 94144

NEWMAN, FRED COLBY, ins. co. exec.; b. Pulaski, Va., Sept. 22, 1931; s. Elmer Dexter and Mary Lydia (Gross) N.; B.S. in Bus. Adminstrn., Va. Poly. Inst., 1958; cert. Vale Tech. Inst., 1959, Am. Ednl. Inst., 1971, Coll. Ins., 1978; m. Mary Lou Meade, Aug. 6, 1955; children—Michael, Matthew, Charles. Claim trainee Glens Falls Ins. Co., 1959, claim rep., supr., br. claim mgr., exec. asst., 1959-70; staff asst. Gt. Am. Ins. Cos., Cin., 1970, exec. asst., 1971-74, dir. field claims, 1974-78, asst. v.p. claims, 1978-79, v.p. claims, 1979—; v.p. Agrl. Excess & Surplus Lines Ins. Co., Agrl. Ins. Co., Am. Nat. Fire Ins. Co. Served with USAF, 1951-55. Republican. Baptist. Club: Cin. Home: 810 Kipp Dr Cincinnati OH 45230 Office: 580 Walnut St Cincinnati OH 45202

NEWMAN, JAMES GARDNER, constrn. co. exec.; b. LaGrange, Ga., Dec. 11, 1920; s. James Rufus and Flossie Agnes (Gardner) N.; student Ga. Inst. Tech., 1937-40; m. Frankie Lee Fling, June 3, 1941; children—James Ridley, Nancy Lee (Mrs. Dan Durand), Alan Gardner, Ivy Marie (Mrs. William Jones), Agnes Ruth (Mrs. Phil Perdue), Frank Seay. With Newman Constrn. Co., LaGrange, 1946—, job. supt., 1946-48, gen. supt., 1948-51, estimator, 1951-68, treas., 1946-68, pres., 1968—; dir. C & S Bank West Ga., LaGrange. Mem. LaGrange City Council, 1952-63, mayor, 1964—; mem. LaGrange Bd. Edn., 1964—; trustee LaGrange Coll. Served to lt. comdr. USNR, 1940-46. Mem. Ga. Soc. Profl. Engrs. (asso.), Nat. Soc. Profl. Engrs., Am. Inst. Constructors, Profl. Engrs. in Constrn. Presbyterian (elder 1968—). Clubs: Rotary (pres. local club 1957-58), Gridiron, Moose, Highland Country (LaGrange). Home: 1016 Country Club Rd LaGrange GA 30240 Office: 101 Whitesville St LaGrange GA 30240

NEWMAN, LARRY ARNOLD, drilling fluids co. exec.; b. Seattle, Feb. 5, 1943; s. Malcolm A. and Gerry R. N.; student U. Tex., 1961-62, Tex. A & I U., 1962-66; m. Barbara Gutekunst, June 17, 1973; children—Gail, Jennifer, Daniel, David. Drilling fluid engr. Dresser Industries, Alaska, 1966-67, Nev. and Calif., 1967-68; founder Nova Corp., Ely, Nev., 1969, pres., 1969—; dir. Needle Exploration Co. Inc. Mem. Nev. Mining Assn., Nev. Water Well Assn. Republican. Mormon. Clubs: Rotary, Elks. Office: PO Box 143 Ely NV 89301

NEWMAN, LAWRENCE WALKER, lawyer; b. Boston, July 1, 1935; s. Leon Bettoney and Hazel W. (Walker) N.; A.B., Harvard Coll., 1957, LL.B., 1960; m. Cecilia Isette Santos, Nov. 29, 1975; children—Reynaldo W., Timothy D., Virginia I.S., Isabel B., Thomas H. Admitted to D.C. bar, 1961, N.Y. State bar, 1965; atty. U.S. Dept. Justice, 1960-61; atty. spl. study of securities markets and office of spl. counsel on investment co. act matters U.S. SEC, 1961-64; asst. U.S. atty. So. Dist. N.Y., 1965-69; asso. firm Baker & McKenzie, N.Y.C., 1969-71; partner, 1971—; dir. Norse Petroleum Inc. Mem. Am. Bar Assn., Internat. Bar Assn., Fed. Bar Council, Am. Fgn. Law Assn.,

Maritime Law Assn. U.S., Bar Assn. City N.Y. Home: 1001 Park Ave New York NY 10028 Office: 375 Park Ave New York NY 10152

NEWMAN, MOGENE D., fin. exec.; b. Covin, Ala., Dec. 28, 1920; s. Earl Mercer and Lucille (Nichols) N.; B.A., Coll. of William and Mary, 1949, M.A., 1950; m. Martha Louise Bragg, June 8, 1944; children—James Bragg, Rebecca Lynn, John Rodney. Pres., dir. Princeton Mgmt. Group, Inc., Hopewell, N.J., 1976, Livestock Breeders, Internat., Inc., Hopewell, N.J., 1977; pres., dir. PMG Ranches, Inc., Tex. and Okla., 1976—; sr. bus. analyst Internat. Mgmt. Cons. firms, Hopewell, 1964—; dir. info. IEH div. Certain-Teed Products, Inc., 1960-64. Pres., Civitan Club of Richmond (Va.), 1960-61. Served to lt. comdr., USN, 1943-46. Mem. Va. C. of C. (dir. 1955-60), Smithsonian Inst., Am. Simmental Assn. Democrat. Methodist. Club: Falconhead Ranch and Country. Home: Amwell Rd RD 1 Box 43A Hopewell NJ 08525

NEWMAN, PAMELA JANE, mgmt. cons.; b. Kalamazoo, Oct. 20, 1947; d. Arnold Edward and RoseAnn (Shaffer) Schneider; B.A., U. Mich., 1968, M.A., 1970, Ph.D., 1973; m. William A. Newman, May 19, 1974; 1 dau., Romaine Shaffer. Asst. prof. bus. Eastern Mich. U., 1972-74; mgr. dir. mgmt. devel. tng. Peat, Marwick, Mitchell & Co., N.Y.C., 1974-79; v.p. Marsh & McLennan, Inc., N.Y.C., 1979—; adj. asst. prof. Pace U.; speaker in field. Participant fellow Gen. Electric Co. Bus. and Soc. Conf., 1973. Mem. Fin. Women's Assn. (sec. 1979-80), Met. Soc. Applied Psychologists. Co-author: Organizational Communication, 1975. Home: 1165 Fifth Ave New York NY 10029 Office: 1221 Ave of Americas New York NY 10020

NEWMAN, PHYLLIS RUTH, banker; b. Bklyn., Jan. 21, 1945; d. Irving Lester and Louise Lillian (Kerzner) N.; B.A., Bklyn. Coll., 1970; M.B.A., L.I. U., 1976. Programmer, Stonehenge Computer Systems, N.Y.C., 1971-76; sr. mgmt. analyst Bowery Savs. Bank, N.Y.C., 1976-79; br. automation planning project mgr. Mfrs.-Hanover Trust Co., N.Y.C., 1979—. Mem. Am. Mgmt.Assn. Home: 170 West End Ave New York NY 10023

NEWMAN, RICHARD CLARK, bldg. products co. exec.; b. Colfax, Wis., Nov. 11, 1925; s. Charles Frederick and Inga Nina (Bodin) N.; B.S. in Forestry, U. Minn., 1950; m. Mavis Ann Reep, Mar. 20, 1948; children—Paul, Lisa, Sara. Purchasing agt. Shurtleff Co., Elgin, Ill., 1950; salesman U.S. Plywood, St. Paul, 1951-60, sales mgr., 1960-64; br. mgr. Georgia-Pacific Corp., Mpls., 1964-69, regional mgr., Chgo., 1969-75, Clifton, N.J., 1976, v.p. internat. div., Portland, Oreg., 1977—; honorarium lectr. U. Minn. Forestry Sch., 1957-58, lectr. bldg. products merchandising, 1963. Precinct chmn. Republican Party, 1967-68; trustee United Methodist Ch., Barrington, Ill., 1973-75; bd. dirs., greens chmn. Biltmore Country Club, Barrington, 1974-75; also bd. dirs. various other civic orgns. Served to sgt. USAAF, 1943-46. Mem. U. Minn. Alumni Assn. (pres. Forestry Sch., 1960), NE Lumbermen's Assn., Nat. Forest Products Assn. Clubs: Wavereley Coutry (Portland); Masons, Shriners. Office: 900 SW Fifth Ave Portland OR 97204

NEWMAN, SAMUEL, banker; b. N.Y.C., Mar. 12, 1938; s. Aaron and Rachel (Hershkowitz) N.; B.B.A., Baruch Coll., 1971; m. Carolyn Gropper, Oct. 27, 1963; children—Marci Ann, Jodi Robin, Michael David. Methods analyst Bankers Trust Co., N.Y.C., 1964-67; project leader Clark O'Neil Service Corp., Fairview, N.J., 1967-68; sr. v.p. Irving Trust Co., N.Y.C., 1968—; speaker industry confs. Served with U.S. Army, 1957-60. Mem. Am. Nat. Standards Inst. (banking com., chmn. X9E bank ops. sub-com.), Am. Bankers Assn. (ops. and automation research and planning com.), Internat. Standards Orgn. (chief U.S. del. tech., sub-coms. on banking), Soc. Worldwide Interbank Fin. Telecommunication (U.S. dir., U.S. swift steering com., chmn. U.S. swift standards subcom.). Home: PO Box 2981 Huntington Station NY 11746 Office: One Wall St New York NY 10015

NEWMAN, STEPHEN BERNARD, architect, retail exec.; b. N.Y.C., Sept. 2, 1941; s. Charles and Mildred (Rosenblum) N.; B.Arch with honors, Carnegie Inst. Tech., 1964; M.B.A. with distinction, Harvard Bus. Sch., 1966; m. Judith Lynn Robinson, Aug. 2, 1964; children—Jennifer Robinson, Charles Robinson. Dir. planning Internat. Design and Devel. Corp., Boston, 1965-66; dir. planning, asst. to pres. Chord Devel. Corp., Washington, 1966-67; partner Asso. Architects and Planners, Balt., 1967; dir. tech. services Joseph Meyerhoff Co., Balt., 1967-68; v.p., dir. The Design Store Corp., Washington, 1968-71, pres., chmn. bd., 1971—. Mem. Young Pres.'s Orgn. Club: Harvard Bus. Office: 9201 Gaither Rd Gaithersburg MD 20760

NEWMAN, WILLIAM RICHARD, III, life ins. co. exec.; b. Jackson, Miss., May 10, 1939; s. William Richard and Elizebeth Eugene (Bentley) N.; B.B.A., U. Miss., 1960, M.B.A., 1961; m. Nancy Ray Mize, June 6, 1961; children—Nancy Amelia, William Richard IV. Officer, Deposit Guaranty Nat. Bank, Jackson, Miss., 1961-64; officer Standard Life Ins. Co., Jackson, 1964—, pres., chief exec. officer, 1971—; chmn. bd. Capitol Broadcasting Co., 1977—; dir. Deposit Guaranty Nat. Bank, Jackson, Deposit Guaranty Corp., Jackson, Magna Corp., Jackson, Deposit Guaranty Mortgage Co., Jackson. Bd. dirs. YMCA, Boy Scouts Am., Jr. Achievement, United Givers Fund, Central Miss. Growth Found. Mem. Nat. Assn. Life Underwriters, Life Ins. Assn. Miss., Miss. Life Underwriters Assn., Jackson C. of C. Baptist. Clubs: Young Pres. Orgn., Jackson Country. Home: 3535 Hawthorn Dr Jackson MS 39216 Office: PO Box 1729 Jackson MS 39205

NEWMYER, ARTHUR GROVER, JR., pub. relations cons.; b. New Orleans, June 16, 1915; s. Arthur Grover and Edith (Strasburger) N.; grad. Phillips Acad., Andover, 1933; B.S., Yale, 1937; m. Alice West, Sept. 18, 1940; children—Barbara West (Mrs. Mark W. Johnson), Arthur Grover III. Newspaper work in Hartford, Conn., Washington, Phila., 1937-40; asso. Arthur G. Newmyer and Assos., Washington, 1945-55; partner Newmyer Assos., 1955-58, pres. Newmyer Assos., Inc., 1959-74, chmn., 1975—. Washington co-chmn. NCCJ, 1961-66, nat. bd. govs., 1965-78, recipient Community Service award, 1972. Bd. dirs., exec. com. Met. Washington Urban Coalition, 1968-72; trustee Pub. Relations Found. for Research and Edn., 1957-60, 67-70. Served from ensign to lt. comdr. USNR, 1940-45. Mem. Pub. Relations Soc. Am. (govt. affairs com. 1959-61, 63-70, com. on standards of profl. practice 1960-62). Jewish (past trustee congregation). Clubs: Nat. Press, Yale (Washington); Yale (N.Y.C.); Federal City; Internat. (Washington). Home: 4501 Linnean Ave NW Washington DC 20008 Office: 1000 Vermont Ave NW Washington DC 20005

NEWSOM, MICKEY BRUNSON, bus. exec.; b. Columbia, Miss., July 26, 1941; s. James Hezzie and Opal Eugenia (Prescott) N.; A.A., Hartnell Coll., 1961; B.B.A., Golden Gate U., 1964, M.B.A., 1976; m. Rose Marie Christensen, May 25, 1963. Mgr., Roy's Restaurants, Salinas, Calif., 1964-67; prin. Humboldt County Schs., Redcrest, Calif., 1967-69; educator Bur. Indian Affairs, Wide Ruins, Ariz., 1969-71; owner Western Auto Store, Columbus, Miss., 1971-76, Mickey Newsom & Co., 1976—. Polit. campaign aide Maurice Dantin for U.S. Senator Com., Jackson, Miss., 1978, John Arthur Eaves for Gov. Com., 1979, Evelyn Gandy for Gov. Com., 1979; mem. Columbus Dem. Exec. Com.; bd. dirs. East Miss. Council, Lowndes County Assn. Retarded Citizens, 1979. Mem. E. Miss. Council, New Orleans Mus. Art, Am. Acad. Polit. and Social Sci., Midcontinent Oil and Gas Assn. Clubs: Commonwealth of Calif. (San Francisco); Civitan (lt. gov. Miss. N. dist. 1978-79). Lutheran. Democrat. Home: PO Box 241 Columbus MS 39701 Office: PO Box 241 Columbus MS 39701

NEWTON, DAVID IRWIN, mgmt. cons.; b. New Haven, July 14, 1949; s. Robert Floyd and Martha Miller (Silver) N.; B.A., Williams Coll., 1973; M.S., Columbia U., 1978. Asst. to dir. univ. opns. Yale U., New Haven, 1973-75; exec. dir. Energy Task Force of Am. Council on Edn., New Haven and Washington, 1975-77; v.p., prin. Energy Resources Mgmt. Co., New Haven, 1977—; mem. faculty Coll. Bus. Mgmt. Inst., U. Ky., Lexington. Alumni dir. Hopkins Grammar Sch.; alumni rep. Williams Coll. Mem. New Haven C. of C., Nat. Assn. Colls. and Univs. Clubs: New Haven Lawn; Mory's Mory's Assn. Co-author: Impact of Administration's Economic and Energy Proposals on Non Profit Institutions, 1975, Energy Conservation—Capital Investment Needs for Building Rehabilitation, 1975; Energy Alert—The Impending Gas Crises; Energy Conservation on Campus, Vol. I-Guidelines, Vol. II-Case Studies; editor: Energy Mangement in Colleges and Universities, 1977. Home: 21 Court St New Haven CT 06511 Office: 379 Temple St New Haven CT 06511

NEWTON, GEORGE ADDISON, investment banker, lawyer; b. Denver, Apr. 2, 1911; s. George Addison and Gertrude (Manderson) N.; A.B., U. Colo., 1933; LL.B., Harvard, 1936; m. Mary Virginia Powell, Sept. 18, 1937; children—George Addison, IV, Nancy Ella, Virginia Powell. Admitted to Ill. bar, 1937, Mo. bar, 1946; asso. firm Scott, MacLeish & Falk, Chgo., 1936-42; partner G.H. Walker & Co., St. Louis, 1946-62, mng. partner, 1962-72; chmn. bd. Stifel Nicolaus & Co., Inc., St. Louis, 1973—, chief exec. officer, 1974-78. Treas., Episcopal Diocese of Mo., 1958-69, also sr. warden, trustee diocesan investment trust; bd. govs. Greater St. Louis Community Chest; mem. Council on Civic Needs; bd. dirs., pres. Episcopal Home for Children, St. Luke's Hosp., Goodwill Industries; dir. devel. fund U. Colo., 1954-55, chmn., 1955; trustee Whitfield Sch.; trustee Fontbonne Coll., 1971-80, chmn., 1974-77. Served to maj. USAAF, 1942-45; trial judge adv. Western Flying Tng. Command, 1942-43; legal officer procurement div. Wright Field, 1944-45. Recipient C. Fobb award U. Colo., 1955, alumni recognition award, 1958; named to C Club Hall Fame, 1968; silver ann. All Am. award Sports Illus., 1957; Norlin award U. Colo., 1968. Mem. Investment Bankers Assn. Am. (pres. 1961), Nat. Assn. Securities Dealers (gov. 1954-56, vice chmn. 1956), Assn. Stock Exchange Firms (gov. 1969-72), Sales Execs. Assn. (dir. 1955-60), U. Colo. Alumni Assn. (dir. 1965-67), Phi Beta Kappa, Phi Gamma Delta. Clubs: Racquet, Noonday, St. Louis, Bellerive Country (St. Louis); Denver Country; Legal (Chgo.); Boulder (Colo.) Country; Links (N.Y.C.). Home: 6428 Cecil Ave Saint Louis MO 63105 Office: 500 N Broadway St Saint Louis MO 63102

NEWTON, ROBERT DEAN, fin. services corp. exec.; b. San Diego, Dec. 1, 1945; s. Alfred James and Mary Doris (Houk) N.; B.S., Portland State U., 1970; M.B.A., U. Portland, 1973; m. Janette Marie Daniels, Mar., 1979. Regional purchasing agt. U.S. Forest Service, Portland, Oreg., 1970-73; mgmt. assistance officer SBA, Seattle, 1973-74; mgr. cost analysis and control Evergreen Helicopters Co., McMinnville, Oreg., 1974-76; div. controller Barker Mfg. Co., Portland, 1976-77; regional sales mgr. N.W. Acceptance Corp., Boise, Idaho, 1977-78; asst. credit mgr. N.W. Acceptance Corp., Portland, 1978-79; Pacific NW loan rep. CIR fin. div. Ford Motor Credit Co., 1979—; bus. cons., 1970—; notary pub. State of Idaho, 1978—. Served with USMCR, 1965-67. Mem. Fin. Mgmt. Assn., Assn. M.B.A. Execs., Alpha Kappa Psi. Democrat. Home: 14345 SW Walker Rd Beaverton OR 97006

NEWTON, ROBERT PARK, JR., engring. co. exec.; b. Jackson, Ga., Oct. 25, 1913; s. Robert Park and Bessie (Powell) N.; B.S. in Chem. Engring., Ga. Inst. Tech., 1935; m. Elizabeth Edwards, Aug. 11, 1936; children—Nancy Elizabeth, Robert Park III, William Aris. Asst. chemistry instr. Ga. Inst. Tech., 1936; research chemist Swann & Co., Birmingham, Ala., 1936-39; plant design engr. Naval Stores, Valdosta, Ga., 1940; exec. v.p. Wannamaker Chem. Co., Orangeburg, S.C., 1941-45; pres., treas. Applied Engring. Co., Orangeburg, 1946-74, chmn. bd., 1974-79; chmn. bd. Dynamatics, Inc., Tampa, Fla.; dir. 1st Nat. Bank, Orangeburg. Trustee Orangeburg Regional Hosp.; exec. com. U.S. Indsl. Council; mem. nat. alumni advisory bd. Ga. Inst. Tech. Mem. Am. Chem. Soc., S.C. C. of C. (dir.), Phi Delta Theta, Tau Beta Pi, Alpha Chi Sigma. Rotarian. Clubs: Palmetto, Summit (Columbia); Orangeburg Country; Wildcat Cliffs Country (Highlands, N.C.); Green Boundary (Aiken, S.C.). Inventor engring. devices. Home: 1120 Moss Ave Orangeburg SC 29115 Office: Carolina Bldg PO Box 506 Orangeburg SC 29115

NEWTON, ROBERT PARK, III, automotive service equipment mfg. co. exec.; b. Orangeburg, S.C., Oct. 6, 1943; s. Robert Park and Elizabeth (Edwards) N.; student Clemson U., 1963-64; m. Francine Herack, Jan. 4, 1969. Asst. dir. mktg. Western Heritage U.S.A., Ocala, Fla., 1964-66, dir. mktg., 1966-68; owner retail automotive service center, Tampa, Fla., 1968—; pres., founder Autodynamics, Inc., Tampa, 1970-78; pres.-treas., chmn., founder Ride Control Systems, Inc., 1978—; founder C.U.B.S., Inc., Tampa, 1975—. Served with USAR, 1962-70. Mem. Equipment and Tool Inst., Nat. Tire Dealers and Retreaders, Motor Equipment Mfrs. Assn., Tampa C. of C. Republican. Epsicopalian. Club: Elks. Home: 4011 Priory Circle Tampa FL 33624 Office: PO Box 15276 Tampa FL 33684

NEWTON, WARREN SANFORD, JR., ins. exec.; b. San Francisco, Sept. 29, 1938; s. Warren Sanford and Ruth Evelyn (McDaniels) N.; student U. Colo., 1956-59; m. Mary Lyn Midgett, July 10, 1978; children by previous marriage—Warren Sanford III, Taeia, Bill. Agt. to gen. agt. Grand Pacific Life Ins. Co., Honolulu, 1963-68; successively 2d v.p., v.p. and agy. dir., exec. v.p. and gen. mgr. Lincoln Nat. Life of N.Y., 1968-72; with Pan-Am. Life Ins. Co., New Orleans, 1972—, beginning as 2d v.p. career agy. sales, v.p. U.S. sales, v.p. and agy. dir., 1972-75, sr. v.p. U.S. individual ops., 1979—. Bd. dirs., exec. com. Greater New Orleans Tourist and Conv. Commn. CLU. Mem. Life Ins. Mgmt. and Research Assn., Soc. C.L.U.'s, Nat. Assn. Life Underwriters, Health Assn. Am., New Orleans C. of C. Republican. Episcopalian. Home: PO Box 1028 Lacombe LA 70445 Office: Pan Am Life Center New Orleans LA 70130

NEY, EDWARD N(OONAN), advt. exec.; b. St. Paul, May 26, 1925; s. John Joseph and Marie (Noonan) N.; B.A. (Lord Jeffrey Amherst scholar 1942), Amherst Coll., 1947; m. Suzanne Hayes, Jan. 28, 1950 (div. 1974); m. 2d, Judith Lasky, May 24, 1974; children—Nicholas, Hilary, Michelle. From exec. trainee to account exec. Batten, Barton, Durstine & Osborn, N.Y.C., 1947-51; with Young & Rubicam, Inc., N.Y.C., 1951—, v.p., 1959-63, asst. to pres., 1962, sr. v.p., 1963-67, exec. v.p., 1967-68, pres. internat. div., 1968-70, chmn., chief exec. officer, 1970—. Trustee, Amherst Coll., 1979—, Nat. Urban League, 1976—, N.Y. U. Med. Center; trustee, mem. exec. com. Com. for Econ. Devel., 1974—; bd. dirs., mem. exec. com. Radio Free Europe, 1975—; bd. dirs. Internat. Exec. Service Corps, 1975—. Served to lt. (j.g.) USNR, 1943-46. Mem. Internat. C. of C. (dir. U.S. council 1974—), Fgn. Policy Assn. (gov.), Council Fgn. Relations. Office: Young & Rubicam 285 Madison Ave New York NY 10017

NEZELEK, ANNETTE EVELYN (MRS. EDWARD NEZELEK), constrn co. exec.; b. Chgo., Feb. 16, 1921; d. Frank and Susan (Linstra) Van Howe; B.A. in History magna cum laude, Hofstra U., 1952; M.A. in Am. History, State U. N.Y. at Binghamton, 1966; m. Edward L. Nezelek, Apr. 3, 1961. Editorial asst. Salute Mag., N.Y.C., 1946-48; asso. editor Med. Econs., Oradell, N.J., 1952-56; nat. mag. publicist Nat. Mental Health Assn., N.Y.C., 1956-60; exec. dir. Diabetes Assn. So. Calif., Los Angeles, 1960-61; corp. sec., v.p., editor, public relations dir. Edward L. Nezelek, Inc., Johnson City, N.Y., 1961—; substitute tchr. high schs., Binghamton, N.Y., 1961-63. Bd. dirs. Broome County Mental Health Assn., 1961-65, Fine Arts Soc., Roberson Center for Arts and Scis., 1968-70, Found. Wilson Meml. Hosp., Johnson City, 1972—, Found. State U. N.Y. at Binghamton; bd. dirs. Broome County Community Charities, 1974—, Broome County Cancer Soc., 1973-74; trustee Broome Community Coll., 1973-78. Mem. AAUW, Am. Med. Writers Assn., LWV (dir. Broome County 1969-70), Alumni Assn. State U. N.Y. at Binghamton (dir. 1970-73), Am. Acad. Polit. and Social Sci., English Speaking Union, Alpha Theta Beta, Phi Alpha Theta, Phi Gamma Mu. Club: Acacia Garden (pres.). Editor newsletter Mental Health Assn., 1965-68, newsletter Unitarian-Universalist Ch., weekly 1967-71, History of Broome County Meml. Arena, 1972. Home: 3051 NE 55 Ln Fort Lauderdale FL 33308 Office: 6061 NE 14 Ave Fort Lauderdale FL 33308

NEZTSOSIE, DICK, Indian tribe adminstr.; b. Navajo Mountain, Utah, Nov. 11, 1948; s. Richard and Clara (Greyeyes) N.; B.S. in Bus. Mgmt., Brigham Young U., 1974; m. E. Renea Little, May 27, 1971; children—Kristin Dawn, Shawn Jayson, Marcie Leigh. Asst. purchasing dir. Navajo Tribe, Window Rock, Ariz., 1974-76, purchasing dir., 1976-77, material mgmt. dir., 1977-80; pres. Utah Navajo Industries, Blanding, 1980—, also dir.; dir. Henry Hillson Co. Mem. Nat. Assn. Purchasing Mgmt., Govtl. Purchasing Assn. Inst. Mormon. Home: PO Box 844 Blanding UT 84511 Office: PO Box 1000 Blanding UT 84511

NG, PETER ZETT, banker; b. Kwangtung, China, Oct. 20, 1946; s. You Shin and Lee Shee (Lee) Ng; B.E.E., City U. N.Y., 1971; M.B.A., Wharton Sch., U. Pa., 1975; m. Judy Mong, 1979. Loss control adminstr. Aetna Life and Casualty Co., N.Y.C., 1971-73; dir., v.p. Creative Futures, Inc., N.J., 1974; asst. treas., relationship mgr. real estate finance Chase Manhattan Bank, N.Y.C., 1975-79; asst. v.p. real estate loan div. Nat. Bank N. Am., N.Y.C., 1979—; founder, chmn. Asian M.B.A. Conf., 1974-76; chmn. bd. Asian Mgmt. Bus. Assn. Internat. Inc., 1977-78. Mem. Met. Mus. Art, N.Y.C. Clubs: Princeton, U. Pa. (gov.), Wharton Bus. Sch. (v.p.). Office: 44 Wall St New York NY 10005

NIARCHOS, DEMETRIUS GIKA, engring. co. exec.; b. Constantinople, Turkey, Feb. 24, 1916; came to U.S., 1949, naturalized, 1957; s. Gika Constantine and Angeliki (Poletis) N.; B.S. in Civil Engring., Robert Coll., 1936; M.S. in Civil Engring., Columbia U., 1950; m. Sylvia Ellis, Dec. 10, 1949; children—Mary Anne, Cathy. Field engr. John Monks & Sons—Ulen & Co., Greece, 1936-37; civil engr. Water Supply Co., Athens, Greece, 1939-47; with Atkinson, Drake & Park, Athens, 1947-48, Econ. Cooperation Adminstrn., 1948-49; sr. engr. Ford, Bacon & Davis, Inc., N.Y.C., 1951-57, project engr., 1958-63, project mgr., 1964-68, resident mgr., 1968-70, v.p., 1971—. Served with Greek Army, 1937-39, 40-41, 45-47, Brit. Army, 1943-45. Registered profl. engr., N.Y. State, Queensland (Australia). Fellow ASCE, Instn. Engrs. (Australia); mem. Nat. Soc. Profl. Engrs., N.Y. State Soc. Profl. Engrs. Greek Orthodox. Club: Brisbane (Australia). Home: 870 UN Plaza New York NY 10017 Office: Ford Bacon & Davis Inc 2 Broadway New York NY 10004

NIAZI, MUZZAMIL, agrl. machinery mfg. co. exec.; b. India, Feb. 19, 1946; s. Niaz Ahmed Khan and Tyqga (Khan) N.; B.S. in Physics and Math., U. Panjab (India), 1964; B.S.M.E., Wichita State U., 1969; M.S.I.E., U. Tex., Arlington, 1972; m. Jeri J. Roberts, Sept. 2, 1978. Structures engr. Cessna Aircraft Co., Wichita, Kans., 1966-70; with Clark Equipment Co., 1970-79, plant mgr. Niles, Mich., 1975-76, N. Am. ops. mgr., Jackson, Mich., 1978-79; v.p. mfg. N. Am., Payline group Internat. Harvester Co., Schaumburg, Ill., 1979-80, v.p., gen. mgr. worldwide crawler ops. Payline group, 1980—. Moslem. Office: 600 Woodfield Dr Schaumburg IL 60196

NICANDROS, CONSTANTINE STAVROS, oil co. exec.; b. Port Said, Egypt, Aug. 2, 1933; s. Stavros Constantine and Helen (Lianakis) N.; came to U.S., 1955, naturalized, 1963; Diplome HEC Ecole des Hautes Etudes Commerciales, 1954; licencié en droit Law Sch. U. Paris, 1954, doctorate in econs., 1955; M.B.A., Harvard, 1957; m. Tassie Boozalis, May 24, 1959; children—Steve Constantine, Vicky Ellen. With planning div. Continental Oil Co., Houston, 1957-61, N.Y.C., 1961-65, land acquisition internat. exploration-prodn. dept., N.Y.C., 1964-65, mgr. planning eastern hemisphere, N.Y.C., 1966-71, gen. mgr. supply and transp., eastern hemisphere, 1971-72, v.p. supply and transp. eastern hemisphere, 1972-74, exec. v.p. eastern hemisphere refining, mktg. and supply and transp., 1974-75, exec. v.p. worldwide supply and transp., Stamford, Conn., 1975-78, group exec. v.p. petroleum products, Houston, 1978—. Trustee, mem. exec. com. Houston Ballet Found., 1980. Mem. Am. Petroleum Inst. (dir. 1980—). Greek Orthodox. Clubs: Racquet, City, Petroleum, Univ. (Houston).

NICASTRO, MAUREEN ELLEN-JOAN (MRS. FELIX A. NICASTRO), ins. agt.; b. Jamaica, N.Y., May 10, 1937; d. Harold Joseph and Hilda S. (Evans) Voetsch; ed. pub. and ins. schs.; now student Hofstra U., Hempstead, N.Y.; m. Felix Andrew Nicastro, May 14, 1955; 1 son, Stephen Christopher. Sec., Liberty Mut. Life Ins. Co., 1954-55, Harper's Bazaar, 1955, Hearst Publs., 1956-57; nursery sch. tchr. Mother Goose Sch., 1960-64; paraprofl. tchr. Meml. High Sch., Levittown, N.Y., 1974; ins. agt. Mack Brokerage, Allstate Ins. Co., Rockville Centre, N.Y., 1975—; lectr. to high sch. on ins. and driving safety; advisor Career Day. Chmn. Nassau County (N.Y.) Bd. Elections, 1961-76; asso. committeeman Republican Party; officer Boy Scouts Am., 1965-70. Recipient citation Personal Lines Ins., 1976, Bus. Lines Ins., 1977. Mem. Nat. Assn. Life Underwriters, Allstate Agts. Assn., N.C. Assn. Ins. Women. Roman Catholic. Home: 69 Grey Ln Levittown NY 11756 Office: 279 Sunrise Hwy Rockville Centre NY 11570

NICCOLI, THOMAS CARL, retail computer chain exec.; b. Gunnison, Colo., Oct. 3, 1950; s. Albert Carl and Blanche Marie (Kapusion) N.; B.S. in Physics Engring., Regis Coll., 1972; M.S. in INdsl. Engring. cum laude, Ariz. State U., 1974; m. Mary Ann Carney, July 12, 1974. Systems engr. IBM, Phoenix, 1974-77, mktg. rep., 1977-78; pres., owner Databank, Inc., Computerland of Phoenix, 1978—; dir. Miller Edn. and Communications Corp. Recipient Regional Mgrs. award IBM, 1975, Achievement Conf. award, 1976-77, Nat. Computerland Conf. award, 1980. Republican. Roman Catholic. Club: Karate. Research on selling productivity through micro computer systems in retail environ. Home: 4558 W Laurie Ln Glendale AZ 85302 Office: 3152 E Camelback Rd Phoenix AZ 85016

NICEWANGER, WILLIAM B., III, telephone systems co. exec.; b. Indpls., Aug. 29, 1941; s. William Bernard and Gladyes Kathleen (Washburn) N.; B.S.E.E., Rose Hulman Inst. Tech., 1963; M.B.A., Ind. U., 1965. Sales supr. AT&T Long Lines, Indpls., 1965-66, dist. office supr., Columbus, Ohio, 1966-67; sales mgr. Taylor'd Sound, Inc., Columbus, 1967-70, pres., 1970-74; founder, pres. Bus. Telephone Systems, Inc., Columbus, 1974—. Bd. dirs. Columbus Central YMCA, 1972—, treas., 1976—; bd. dirs. Camp Alfred Wilson, 1981. Clubs: Masons, Shriners. Home: 324 E Sycamore St Columbus OH 43206 Office: 550 W Spring St Columbus OH 43215

NICHOLAS, DARRELL HUNT, securities corp. exec.; b. St. Petersburg, Fla., Sept. 27, 1930; s. Louis and Faye Allen N.; student public schs., St. Petersburg; m. Mary Adams, May 8, 1958; children—William D., Sally Ann. Asst. mgr. Hot Shoppes, Inc., Washington, 1954-62; ins. agt. Prudential Ins., Kingston, N.Y., 1962-67, Doolittle & Co., Kingston, 1967-68; v.p. Kingston Securities Corp., 1968—. Served with USN, 1950-54. Decorated Nat. Defense medal. Mem. Nat. Soc. Registered Reps. (charter), V.F.W. Republican. Mem. Reformed Ch. Home: 15 Overlook Dr Hurley NY 12443 Office: 224 Fair St Kingston NY 12401

NICHOLAS, LAWRENCE BRUCE, import co. exec.; b. Dallas, Nov. 9, 1945; s. J. W. and Helen Elouise (Whiteacre) N.; B.B.A., So. Meth. U., 1968; m. Virginia Pearl Farmer, Aug. 5, 1967; children—Helen Brooke, John Lawrence, Alexis Bradlee. Mem. sales staff Nicholas Machinery Co., Dallas, 1963-69; sales mgr. Indsl. and Comml. Research Corp., Dallas, 1969-74; v.p. Precision Concepts Corp., Dallas, 1974-76, gen. mgr., 1976-78, pres., Addison, Tex., 1978—, dir., 1974—; pres. INCOR Inc., Addison, 1974—, dir., 1972—. Served as officer Ordnance Corps, U.S. Army, 1968, N.G., 1968-74. Mem. Woodworking Machinery Distbrs Assn. (dir.), Nat. Archtl. Woodwork Inst., Nat. Sporting Goods Assn., Nat. Assn. Diecutters and Diemakers, Nat. Assn. Furniture Mfrs., Nat. Rifle Assn., Nat. Shooting Sports Found., Safari Club Internat, Game Conservation Internat. Club: Bent Tree Country. Office: 4200 Westgrove St Addison TX 75001

NICHOLAS, LOUIS JOSEPH, ins. agy. exec.; b. Boston, Aug. 21, 1939; s. Victor and Carmella (Umbro) N.; B.S. in Bus. Adminstrn., Boston Coll., 1962; postgrad. in bus. adminstrn. U. So. Calif., 1962. Dir. sales Mass. Gen. Life Co., Boston, 1962-70; pres. Nicholas Agencies, Inc., Balt., 1968—; chmn. Group Brokerage Services of Washington, Group Brokerage Services of Ohio, Group Brokerage Services of Fla., Group Brokerage Services of New Eng.; pres. Group Brokerage Services of Denver, Group Brokerage Services of Atlanta; chmn. bd., chief exec. officer Denta-Check Corp.; corp. sec. ALO, Inc.; pres. Group Adminstrn. Services. Recipient 68 awards from various ins. cos., 1962-77. Mem. Am. Mgmt. Assn. (officer). Republican. Home: 4000 N Charles St Baltimore MD 21218 Office: 1 N Charles St Suite 2512 Baltimore MD 21201

NICHOLAS, ROBERT BATES, ins. co. exec.; b. West Sayville, N.Y., Apr. 24, 1929; s. Robert C. and Jean (Bates) N.; B.A., Denison U., 1950; M.S., Sch. Bus., Columbia U., 1954; m. Sally Anne Macomber, June 24, 1955; children—John B., Paul M., Sally Anne. With Atlantic Richfield Co., N.Y.C., 1960-71, sec., 1965-66, mgr. fin. services, 1966-68, sec., exec. com., 1966-71, mgr. corp. planning, 1968-71; v.p. corp. planning Aetna Life & Casualty Co., Hartford, Conn., 1971-75, v.p. fin. and planning, 1976—, also sec. corp. mgmt. com., mem. fin. policy com. Treas. Delaware County Vocat.-Tech. Sch. Authority, 1966-68; bd. dirs., mem. fin. com., fin. com., former pres. Hartford Dispensary; trustee, mem. audit and fin. coms. Hartford Grad. Center; trustee Simsbury United Meth. Ch.; bd. advs. for bus. environ. and policy Sch. Bus. Adminstrn., U. Conn. Served to 1st lt. AUS, 1951-53 Mem. N.Y. Treasurers Group, Life Office Mgmt. Assn. (property-liability corp. planning com.), C. of C. U.S. (council on trends and perspectives). Club: Hopmeadow Country (dir., exec. com. 1976—). Home: 6 Apple Ln Simsbury CT 06070 Office: 151 Farmington Ave Hartford CT 06156

NICHOLL, THOMAS HILL, mfg. corp. exec.; b. Anderson, Ind., Feb. 28, 1917; s. Thomas Harry and Ruth (Hill) N.; B.S. in Mech. Engring., Case Inst. ch., 1939; postgrad. U. Houston, 1941, U. Mex., 1945, U. Calif., Berkeley, 1945, Columbia U., 1947, U. Kansas City, 1958; m. Grace Williams Morrill, Dec. 26, 1949; children—Margaret, John, Carolynn, Christine, Catherine. Heat treater Hughes Tool Co., Houston, 1939-42; instr. U. Houston, 1942-44; field welding engr., dist. mgr. San Francisco area, Lincoln Electric Co., 1947-61; pres., owner Nicholl Bros., Inc., Kansas City, Mo., 1961—; dir. Fusion, Inc.; instr. U. Calif., 1951-53, U. Mo., Kansas City, 1958; del. White House Conf. on Small Bus. Served as officer USN, 1944-46. Named Small Bus. Person, Kansas City Region, 1980; recipient Sears symbol of excellence, 1977; recipient awards Kansas City Commn. on Indsl. Devel., 1979, Jackson County Commrs., 1978, resolution, Mayor of Kansas City, 1980, proclamation, Gov. of Mo., 1980; lic. profl. engr., Kans. Mem. AAAS, AIAA, Oceanic Soc., Kansas City Astron. Soc., Am. Soc. Plastic Engrs., Mid-Continent Ind. Small Bus. Assn. (dir.), Nat. Houseware Mfrs. Assn., Nat. Sporting Goods Assn., U.S. C. of C., Kansas City C. of C. Presbyterian. Clubs: Kansas City Athletic, Sertoma (dir.) (Kansas City); Woodside Racquet (Westwood, Kans.). Contbr. papers to publs.; speaker, lectr. in field; patentee. Home: 9935 High Dr Leawood KS 66206 Office: 1204 W 27th St Kansas City MO 64108

NICHOLLS, GRANT TELFER, ins. co. exec.; b. East Meadow, N.Y., Mar. 22, 1946; s. Russell E. and Marjorie G. N.; B.S. in Edn., Lebanon Valley Coll., Annville, Pa., 1969; m. Linda Eicher, Sept. 23, 1967; children—Russell E., Debora J. Agt., agy. tng. dir. Penn Mut. Life Ins. Co., Cherry Hill, N.J., 1970-72; gen. agt. Beneficial Standard Life Ins. Co., New Lisbon, N.J., 1972-74; adminstrv. asst., dir. sales Colonial Life Ins. Co. Am., East Orange, N.J., 1974-80; supt. agys. Bankers Security Life Ins. Soc., N.Y.C., 1980—. Crew chief Pennsauken (N.J.) 1st Aid Squad; exec. bd. N.J. 1st Aid Council, 1972-74, vice chmn. 22d Dist., 1973; mem. Burlington County Adv. Council Task Force on Emergency Med. Services, 1972-74; asst. chief Presdl. Lakes 1st Aid Squad, 1973; v.p. Brown Mills Emergency Squad, 1974; mem. Warren County adv. council Regional Health Planning Agy. of No. N.J., 1978—; mem. Allamuchy Twp. Planning Bd., 1979—, vice chmn., 1980; alumni ambassador Lebanon Valley Coll., 1977—; mem. Council Allamuchy Civic Orgns., Annville Cleona Jaycees, 1967-69; mem. Comprehensive Health Planning Council South N.J.; mem. Warren County (N.J.) Solid Waste Adv. Council, 1980—. Named Man of Yr., Camden Gen. Agts. and Mgrs. Conf., 1972; recipient Health Ins. Quality award, 1973, Nat. Sales Achievement award N.J. Assn. Life Underwriters, 1973, Leaders award, 1971, 72, 73, 74, Pres.'s award Beneficial Standard Life, 1973. Mem. Newark Assn. Life Underwriters, N.J. Beekeepers Assn., Lebanon Valley Coll. Alumni Assn., Nat. Assn. Life Underwriters (nat. quality award 1972, 73). Republican. Club: Fraternal Order Police (1st v.p. 1973-74). Home: Walnut Hill Farm PO Box 168 Allamuchy NJ 07820 Office: 475 Park Ave S 20th Floor New York NY 10016

NICHOLS, CHARLES WALTER, III, banker; b. N.Y.C., Aug. 25, 1937; s. Charles Walter and Marjorie (Jones) N.; B.A., U. Va., 1959; m. Anne Sharp, Aug. 8, 1959; children—Blair, Sandra, Walter, Hope. Vice pres. Citibank, N.A., N.Y.C., 1962-78, Morgan Guaranty Trust Co. N.Y., N.Y.C., 1979—. Trustee Nichols Found., Inc., 1969—, Choate Rosemary Hall, 1972-77, Greenwich House, 1972—, Caramoor, 1974-78, Westover Sch., 1978-80, Lower Hudson (N.Y.) chpt. Nature Conservancy, 1978—, John Jay Homestead, 1980—. Served to 1st lt. U.S. Army, 1960-62. Decorated Army Commendation medal. Clubs: River (N.Y.C.); Bedford (N.Y.) Golf and Tennis, Pilgrims of U.S. Office: Morgan Guaranty Trust Co NY 23 Wall St New York NY 10015

NICHOLS, GUY W., utilities exec.; b. Colchester, Vt., Oct. 27, 1925; s. Guy W. and Gladys (Tomlinson) N.; B.C.E., U. Vt., 1947; postgrad. Worcester Poly. Inst., Sch. Indsl. Mgmt., 1953-56; M.S. in Bus. Adminstrn. (Sloan fellow), Mass. Inst. Tech., 1961; m. Shirley Hibbard, June 21, 1947; children—Pamela, Gail, Sally. With New Eng. Electric System, Westborough, Mass., 1947—, exec. v.p., 1968-70, dir., 1968—, pres., 1970—, chief exec. officer, 1972—, chmn., 1978—; chmn., dir. New Eng. Power Co., New Eng. Power Service Co., New Eng. Energy, Inc., Yankee Atomic Electric Co.; dir. Mass. Electric Co., Narragansett Electric Co., First Nat. Bank of Boston, Nashua Corp., State Mut. Life Assurance Co. Am., Conn. Yankee Atomic Power Co., Vt. Yankee Nuclear Power Co., Maine Yankee Atomic Power Co., Electric Power Research Inst., Breeder Reactor Corp.; chmn. mgmt. com. New Eng. Power Pool; exec. com. N.E. Power Coordinating Council; mem. coal industry adv. bd. Internat. Energy Agy. Trustee, Thomas Alva Edison Found.; mem. exec. com., bd. dirs. Edison Electric Inst.; mem. corp. Woods Hole Oceanographic Instn.; mem. corp. devel. com., energy lab. adv. bd., corp. vis. com. dept. elec. engring. Mass. Inst. Tech. Served with AUS, 1944-46. Home: 69 Wildwood Dr Needham MA 02192 Office: 25 Research Dr Westborough MA 01581

NICHOLS, HENRY ELIOT, lawyer, savs. and loan exec.; b. N.Y.C., Jan. 3, 1924; s. William and Elizabeth (Lisse) N.; B.A., Yale, 1946; J.D., U. Va., 1948; m. Frances Griffin Morrison, Aug. 12, 1950; children—Clyde Whitney, Diane Spencer. Admitted to D.C. bar, 1950, U.S. Ct. Appeals bar, 1952, U.S. Supreme Ct. Bar, 1969; law clk. Wellman & Smyth, N.Y.C., 1949-50; asso. Frederick W. Berens, Inc., Washington, 1950-52; practiced in Washington, 1952—; real estate columnist Evening Star, Washington, 1966—; pres., gen. counsel Hamilton Fed. Savs. & Loan Assn., Washington, 1971-74; vice chmn. bd. Columbia Fed. Savs. and Loan Assn., Washington, 1974—; pres. Century Financial Corp., Washington, 1971—; dir., mem. exec. com. Columbia Real Estate Title Ins. Co., Washington, 1968-77; regional v.p. Previews, Inc., Washington, 1972-78; dir. Dist.-Realty Title Ins. Co., Met. Washington Bd. Trade, 1974—; nat. adv. bd. Harker Prep. Sch., 1975—. Del. Pres. Johnson's Conf. on Law and Poverty, 1967; vice-chmn. Mayor's Ad Hoc Com. on Housing Code Problems, 1968-71; commr. City Council Commn. Landlord-Tenant Affairs, 1970-71; vice-chmn. Washington Area Realtor's Council, 1970; dir., mem. exec. com. Downtown Progress, 1970. Bd. dirs. Washington Mental Health Assn., 1973, Washington Med. Center, 1975, Vincent T. Lombardi Cancer Research Center, 1979—. Served to capt. USAF, 1942-46. Named Realtor of Year, Washington Bd. Realtors, 1970. Mem. Am., D.C. bar assns., Am. Land Devel. Assn., Internat. Real Estate Fedn., Nat. Assn. Realtors, Nat. Assn. Real Estate Editors, Washington Bd. Realtors (pres.), Metropolitan Washington Bd. Trade, U.S. League Savs. Assn. (mem. attys. com. 1971—), Washington Savs. and Loan League (mem. attys. com. 1971—). Clubs: Yale, St. Elmo, Antique Auto, Rolls Royce; Cosmos (Washington). Contbr. articles to profl. jours. Patentee in field. Home: 1 Kittery Ct Bethesda MD 20034 Office: 1122 Connecticut Ave NW Washington DC 20036

NICHOLS, MARILYN JACKSON, fin. planner; b. New Brunswick, N.J., Mar. 29, 1938; s. Wilfrid J. and Mabel Elizabeth (Mott) Jackson; B.A., Oberlin Coll., 1959; m. David Crane Nichols, Feb. 21, 1962; 1 dau., Deborah Kay. Asst. young adult dir. YWCA, Flint, Mich., 1959-60; sr. group mgr. Gimbel's Inc., Phila., 1960-62; registered rep. All Am. Mgmt. Corp., Springfield, Ill., 1969-73; sec. IAA of Ill., Inc., Savoy, 1968—, also dir.; pres. Money Matters, Inc., Savoy, 1975—, dir., 1975—. Mem. adv. bd. Women's program Parkland Coll., 1974-75; adv. bd. Parents Without Partners, Champaign, 1976—. Recipient Top Producer award Exec. Life Ins. Co., 1977. Mem. AAUW. Unitarian. Club: Altrusa (dir. 1977-79), Author: The Woman's Guide to Financial Planning, 1978; The Teacher's Manual for Financial Planning Courses, 1979; developer seminars, fin. planning for women, also tchr. trainer. Office: 16060 Lyndhurst Dr Savoy IL 61874

NICHOLS, RICHARD, mktg. exec.; b. Miami, Fla., May 26, 1945; s. Ray F. and Elinor (Wheeler) N.; A.S. in Bus., Miami-Dade Jr. Coll., 1965; m. Nancy Nuzum, Nov. 30, 1974; 1 dau., Terri. With Boeing Aerospace Co., Cape Kennedy, Fla., 1969-72; adminstrv. asst. to Brevard County commr., Merritt Island, Fla., 1972-74; East Coast sales mgr. Hwy. Equipment & Supply, Orlando, Fla., 1974-75; regional mktg. v.p. Fla. Mktg.-Chelsea Title & Guaranty Co., Sanford, Fla., 1975—. Mem. Titusville (Fla.) Homeowners Assn., 1975—, sec., 1976-78. Served with USAF, 1966-69. Recipient Apollo Achievement award Boeing Co.; Appreciation award Seminole County Bd. Realtors, 1977. Mem. Mid-Fla. Home Builders Assn., Titusville Home Builders Assn., Seminole County Bd. Realtors, Titusville Bd. Realtors, Sanford C. of C., Titusville C. of C. Republican. Roman Catholic. Club: Kiwanis. Home: 3432 Willis Dr Titusville FL 32780 Office: 119 W 1st St Sanford FL 32771

NICHOLS, RICHARD ALLEN, cons. engr.; b. Ottawa, Ill., Oct. 25, 1939; s. Allen Andrew and Dorothy Eline (Madsen) N.; B.S. in Sci. Engring., Northwestern U., 1963, M.S. in Chem. Engring., 1964, Ph.D. in Chem. Engring., 1966; m. Alexandra Marie Gladdys, July 4, 1973; children—Katherine, Matthew, Richard. Design engr. Airesearch Corp., Los Angeles, 1965-66; design specialist Parker Hannifin Corp., Los Angeles, 1966-69, program mgr., Irvine, Calif., 1969-71, tech. program mgr., 1971-73; pres., prin. engr. R.A. Nichols Engring., Corona del Mar, Calif., 1973—. Walter P. Murphy fellow, 1961-64; Phillipps Petroleum fellow, 1965; registered profl. engr., Calif. Mem. Nat. Fire Prevention Assn., Air Pollution Control Assn., Sigma Xi, Alpha Delta Phi. Republican. Fundamentalist. Contbr. articles in field to profl. jours.; patentee. Home and Office: 519 Iris Ave Corona del Mar CA 92625

NICHOLS, WEEDEN BENJAMIN, property mgmt. exec.; b. Horseheads, N.Y., Aug. 20, 1905; s. C.C. and Minerva (Rockwell) N.; ed. Rochester (N.Y.) Athenaeum, Mechanics Inst. Mgr., Smith-Young Tower, San Antonio, 1929-39, Hoblitzelle Properties, Dallas, 1939-46, Interstate Circuit, Inc., 1939-50, v.p., gen. mgr. Republic Nat. Bank Bldg. Co., Dallas, 1950-71. Served as col., inf. AUS, 1940-47. Decorated Legion of Merit; Order Pao Ting (China). Mem. Nat. Assn. Bldg. Owners and Mgrs. (life, past v.p. Southwest), Boat Owners Assn. U.S., U.S. Power Squadron, Res. Officers Assn. U.S., Inst. Real Estate Mgmt. (past pres. chpt.), Dallas Hist. Soc. Clubs: St. Petersburg Yacht, Variety. Office: PO Box 12841 Saint Petersburg FL 33733

NICHOLS, WILLIAM WARREN, dept. store chain exec.; b. Dandridge, Tenn., Oct. 8, 1917; s. Clyde Logan and Lela Beatrice (Carpenter) N.; student U. Tenn., 1937-39. Office clk. Knox County Water Co., 1939-40; with Ira A. Watson Co., Knoxville, Tenn., 1940—, now sr. v.p., dir.; dir. Appalachian Dist. Corp. Bd. dirs. Watson Found. Served with U.S. Army, 1942-46. Decorated Bronze Star with oak leaf cluster. Mem. Am. Soc. Mil. Engrs., Am. Def. Preparedness Assn., Mil. Order of World Wars. Methodist. Home: PO Box 5044 Knoxville TN 37918 Office: 200 Hayfield Rd Knoxville TN 37922

NICHOLSON, GORDON J., acctg. firm exec.; b. Maize, Kans., Mar. 1, 1924; s. Gordon M. and Mary Agnes (McCoy) N.; B.S., U. Wichita, 1947; M.B.A., Northwestern U., 1949; J.D., DePaul U., 1953; m. Anne Truesdale, Dec. 27,1948; children—Karen Nicholson Meeker, Steven, Patricia. With Arthur Andersen & Co., 1949—, head tax dept., dir. multinat. taxes, N.Y.C., 1965-77, partner, 1960—, mng. partner tax practice, Chgo., 1977—; admitted to Ill. bar, 1953; guest lectr. Com. Sci. and Industry in Moscow, 1973. Served with USAAF, 1943-45. Mem. Am. Inst. C.P.A.'s, (exec. com. 1969-73, chmn. com. internat. taxation 1969-73), Internat. Fiscal Assn. (officer U.S. br. 1975-78), Ill. Soc. C.P.A.'s, Chgo. Bar Assn., N.Y. Soc. C.P.A.'s. Clubs: Glen View; Mid-Am. Office: 69 W Washington St Chicago IL 60602

NICHOLSON, JAMES JOHN, lawyer, food co. exec.; b. Flushing, N.Y., Aug. 19, 1926; s. James Aloysius and Ellen (Gilmore) N.; A.B., Dartmouth Coll., 1948; J.D., St. John's U., 1955; m. Margaret Louise Cullen, Oct. 13, 1956; children—John Cullen, Louise Ellen, Jeanine Rose. With U.S./New Amsterdam Casualty Cos., 1948-55; admitted to N.Y. State bar, 1955; asso. firm Suozzi & Sordi, Glen Cove, N.Y., 1955-57; with Corn Products Co. (now CPC Internat. Inc.), Englewood Cliffs, N.J., 1957—, asst. to comptroller, 1959-62, asst. sec., 1962-67, mgr. personnel, 1967-69, asst. treas., 1969-74, treas., 1974—, dir. CPC Asia and affiliates; dir. Argo State Bank. Chmn., Pelham chpt. ARC, 1967-69; trustee Coll. of New Rochelle, 1978—; bd. dirs. Graham-Windham Services to Families and Children, N.Y.C., 1968—, pres., 1970-73; committeeman Westchester County Democratic Com., 1962—; village co-chmn. United Fund, 1971; mem. Union Free Sch. Dist. 10 Bd. Edn., Greenburgh, N.Y., 1969—. Served with USN, 1944-45. Mem. Am. Bar Assn., N.Y. Bar, Am. Soc. Corp. Secs. Roman Catholic. Clubs: Union League (N.Y.C.); Stage Harbor Yacht (Chatham, Mass.). Home: 1056 Prospect Ave Pelham Manor NY 10803 Office: Internat Plaza Englewood Cliffs NJ 07632

NICHOLSON, LUTHER BEAL, fin. cons.; b. Sulphur Springs, Tex., Dec. 15, 1921; s. Stephen Edward and Elma (McCracken) N.; B.B.A., So. Meth. U., 1942, postgrad., 1946-47, Tex. U., 1947-48; diploma Southwestern Grad. Sch. Banking, 1967; m. Ruth Wimbish, May 29, 1952; children—Penelope Elizabeth, Stephen David. Controller, Varo, Inc., Garland, Tex., 1946-55, dir., 1947-72, v.p. fin., 1955-66, sr. v.p., 1966-67, exec. v.p., 1967-70, pres., 1970-71, chmn. bd., 1971-72, cons. to bd. dirs., 1972-75; gen. mgr. Challenger Lock Co., Los Angeles, 1956-58; dir. Varo Inc. Electrokinetics div., Varo Optical, Inc., Biometrics Instrument Corp., Varo Atlas GmbH, Micropac Industries, Inc., Gt. No. Corp., Garland Bank & Trust Co. Bd. dirs., exec. v.p. Harriett Stanton-Edna Murray Found. Served with AUS, 1942-46. Mem. Fin. Execs. Inst. (past pres.), Am. Inst. C.P.A.'s, AIM, Am. Mgmt. Assn., NAM. Home: 1917 Melody Ln Garland TX 75042 Office: 610 W Garland Ave Garland TX 75040

NICHOLSON, RICHARD HINCKLEY, electronics co. exec.; b. San Diego, Feb. 23, 1922; s. Samuel N. and Laura I. (Hinckley) N.; B.S., Tex. State Tech. Inst., 1971; M.S., Nat. U., 1973; m. Beatrice Burger, Apr. 3, 1948; children—Karen Lee, Julie Ann. Aircraft and engine mechanic Ryan Aero. Co., 1939-40; with Gen. Dynamics Astronautics, Convair and Electronics div., San Diego, Cape Kennedy and Vandenberg AFB Space Launch Vehicle sites, 1940—, chief reliability control, 1957-67, mgr. quality control, 1967-71, dir. div. quality assurance, 1971—. Mem. nat. panel on consumer arbitration panel Better Bus. Bur., 1973—; asst. program chmn. San Diego Biomed. Symposium, 1974. Mem. adv. bd. San Diego City Coll. Served with USAAF, 1944-46. Recipient award of merit Toastmasters Internat., 1955. Registered profl. engr., Calif. Fellow Am. Soc. Quality Control (chmn. internat. cooperation com.; mem. European Orgn. for Quality Control, Am. Def. Preparedness Assn. (chmn. product assurance tech. div.), USN Nat. Security Indsl. Assn., Aerospace Industries Assn. Army Liaison Panel. Home: 711 Albion St San Diego CA 92106 Office: PO Box 81127 San Diego CA 92138

NICKELS, CARL EDWIN, JR., mining co. exec.; b. Cleve., Jan. 22, 1931; s. Carl Edwin and Genevieve H. N.; B.S., U. Notre Dame, 1953; J.D., Cleve. Marshall Law Sch., 1958; m. Mary Ellen Keller, June 9, 1951; children—Richard C., Paul J., Carl E., Christopher, Mary L., Caroline G. Admitted to Ohio bar, 1958; staff acct. Hanna Mining Co., Cleve., 1953-55, mem. legal dept., 1955-58, staff lawyer, 1958-65, asst. sec., 1965-74, v.p., 1974-76, sr. v.p. fin. and law, 1976-79, exec. v.p., 1979—; dir. Allendale Mutual Ins. Co., Johnston, R.I., 1977—, Pitts. and Lake Erie R.R. Co., 1975—, St. John del Rey Mining Co. Ltd., Cleve., 1979—. Mem. Cleve. Bar Assn., Ohio State Bar Assn., Am. Iron Ore Assn., Fin. Exec. Inst. Roman Catholic. Clubs: Union (Cleve.), Clevelander, Westwood Country. Office: 100 Erieview Plaza Cleveland OH 44114

NICKELSON, DONALD EUGENE, broker; b. Emporia, Kans., Dec. 9, 1932; s. Harry and Mildred B. (Nicholson) N.; m. Barbara Ruth Fronterhouse, Jan. 7, 1950; children—Marta, Nancy, Donny, Dana, Harry, Margaret, Elizabeth, James, Douglas. Mgr., Bache & Co., Beverly Hills, Calif., 1956-64; partner A.G. Edwards & Sons, St. Louis, 1964-66; sr. v.p., dir. Paine Webber Jackson & Curtis, Los Angeles, 1967—; chmn. Pacific Stock Exchange; chmn. Pacific Depository Trust. Chmn. Harris County (Tex.) March of Dimes, 1968. Mem. Securities Industry Assn. Republican. Lutheran. Clubs: Jonathan, Stock Exchange, Ramada. Office: 555 S Flower St Los Angeles CA 90071*

NICKLAS, ROBERT HEARD, lawyer, fin. exec.; b. Pitts., June 14, 1925; s. Chester John and Margaret (Spires) N.; A.B., U. Pitts., 1947; LL.B., Duquesne U., 1951. Admitted to Pa. bar, 1951; atty. CIA, Washington, 1949-66; individual practice law, fin. cons. in pvt. practice, Pitts. and N.Y.C., 1966-79; v.p., legal counsel United Am. Energy, Inc., N.Y.C., 1979—. Served with USN, 1943-46. Office: 300 Madison Ave Suite 602 New York NY 10017

NICOL, ALAN MONRO, constrn. co. exec.; b. Birmingham, Eng., Mar. 5, 1929; came to U.S., 1971; s. Douglas John and Diana Chubb (Wright) N.; M.A., U. Cambridge, 1952; m. Pamela Muir Macfarlane, Sept. 5, 1959; children—James, Heather, Jane. Trainee engr. Lemon & Blizzard, Cons. Engrs., London, 1952-56; with John Laing Ltd., Contractors, London, 1956-71, contracts mgr., 1962-67, mktg. mgr., 1967-71; pres. Laing Constrn. Services Inc., Stamford, Conn., 1971—. Served with Brit. Army, 1948-49. Mem. Instn. Civil Engrs., Brit.-Am. C. of C. (v.p. 1977—). Congregationalist. Clubs: N.Y. Yacht; Country of New Canaan (Conn.); Royal Ocean Racing (London). Home: 272 West Hills Rd New Canaan CT 06840 Office: 1346 Washington Blvd Stamford CT 06902

NICOL, WILLIAM BURKE, acctg. firm exec.; b. Lakewood, Ohio, Apr. 4, 1918; s. William Buffenmeyer and Florence Irene (Burke) N.; student Georgetown U., 1937-39; m. Mary Elizabeth Hopkins, Apr.

9, 1943; children—Nancy Ann, William Burke. With Meaden & Moore, C.P.A.s, Cleve., 1941—, mng. partner, 1964—. Served with U.S. Army, 1942-45, 51-52. Mem. Am. Inst. C.P.A.s, Ohio Soc. C.P.A.s. Presbyterian. Clubs: Union, Cleveland Athletic; Lakewood Country. Home: 23416 Lake Rd Bay Village OH 44140 Office: Meaden and Moore 1010 Union Commerce Bldg Cleveland OH 44115

NICOL, WILLIAM KENNEDY, ins. co. exec.; b. Hamilton, Ont., Can., July 20, 1922; s. William Robertson and Mae Alice (Kennedy) N.; B.A., U. Toronto, 1949; m. Jessie Thompson Helms, Jan. 18, 1974; children—Frances Mae Teague, Christine P. Dunn, Catherine Meyer. Asso. actuary Equitable Life Ins. Co. Can., Waterloo, Ont., 1949-52; asso. actuary Tchrs. Ins. Assn. Am., N.Y., 1952-55; actuary, comptroller Commonwealth Life Ins. Co., Louisville, 1955-61; with Am. Nat. Ins. Co., Galveston, Tex., 1961—, v.p., actuary ins. services, 1969, exec. v.p. ins. services, 1969-74, exec. v.p. research, 1974—; dir. Trans World Life Ins. Co. N.Y., Am. Nat. Property & Casualty Co.; v.p., dir. Am. Nat. Life Ins. Co. Tex., Standard Life & Accident Ins. Co. Okla., Am. Nat. Okla. Corp. Served with RCAF, 1941-46. Enrolled actuary. Fellow Soc. Actuaries; mem. Am. Acad. Actuaries, Can. Inst. Actuaries (corr.), Actuaries Club S.W. Office: Am Nat Ins Co 1 Moody Plaza Galveston TX 77550

NICOLSON, DONALD BEYNON, fin. and constrn. exec.; b. Long Beach, Calif., Oct. 22, 1930; s. Alexander MacIntosh and Anna Beulah (Beynon) N.; B.S., U. Calif., Santa Barbara, 1957; m. Virginia Lee Hattendorf, Jan. 15, 1977; children by previous marriage—Janet Lee, Bethany Ann. Treas., dir. Paul Hardeman, Inc., Stanton, Calif., 1960-67; controller Dillingham Corp. Calif., Los Angeles, 1967-70; v.p. TGI Corp., Los Angeles, 1970-75; pres. Mead Found., also Mead Housing Inc., Los Angeles, 1976—. Republican. Presbyterian. Home: 23910 DeVille Way Malibu CA 90265 Office: 3650 S Broadway Los Angeles CA 90007

NIEBUR, STANLEY LOUIS, food co. exec.; b. Breese, Ill., Jan. 28, 1926; s. Anton B. and Florence (Beck) N.; B.S. cum laude, St. Louis U., 1949; m. Alice Markus, Nov. 28, 1946; children—Susan Niebur Collins, Elizabeth Niebur Harris, James, Lynn. With Ralston Purina Co., St. Louis, 1948—, v.p., 1970-78, dir. consumer products group, 1973—, exec. v.p., 1978—. Served with USNR, 1944-46. Roman Catholic. Club: Mo. Athletic. Home: 12832 Huntercreek Rd Saint Louis MO 63131 Office: Checkerboard Sq Saint Louis MO 63188

NIEHAUS, WILLIAM ROGER, newspaper exec.; b. Cin., June 10, 1932; s. George Anthony and Lorine Rosemary (Bennett) N.; B.S. in Physics, Xavier U., 1954; M.S. in Physics (Univ. fellow), St. Louis U., 1956; m. Marian Camille Martinson, Oct. 21, 1961; children—Theodore, David, Jennifer, Thomas, Juliet, Natalie. Engring. cons. Allstates Design & Devel. Co., Cin., 1959-61; engring. physicist Thompson-Ramo-Wooldridge Co., Cleve., 1961; head of aerothermodynamics systems analysis Aeronca Mfg. Corp., Middletown, Ohio, 1961-65; engring. cons. Belcan Corp., Montgomery, Ohio, 1965-70; research dir. E.W. Scripps Co., Cin., 1970—. Bd. dirs. Montgomery Baseball Assn., 1972—; mem. Montgomery Recreation Commn., 1978—. Served as 1st lt. ordnance U.S. Army, 1956-58. Mem. AIAA, Am. Inst. Indsl. Engrs., Internat. Newspaper Promotion Assn., Am. Newspaper Pubs. Assn., Nat. Rifle Assn. (life), Sigma Xi. Republican. Roman Catholic. Patentee. Home: 10240 Pendery Dr Cincinnati OH 45242 Office: 1100 Central Trust Tower Cincinnati OH 45202

NIELSEN, ARTHUR CHARLES, JR., mktg. research exec.; b. Chgo., Apr. 8, 1919; s. Arthur Charles and Gertrude (Smith) N.; Ph.B., U. Wis., 1941; m. Patricia McKnew, June 24, 1944; children—Arthur Charles III, John Christopher, Elizabeth Kingsbury. Chmn., chief. exec. officer A. C. Nielsen Co., Chgo.; dir. Marsh & McLennan Corp., Republic Capital Corp., Gen. Binding Corp., Motorola, Inc., Marcor Inc., Harris Trust & Savs. Bank, Walgreen Drug Co., Hercules, Inc., Internat. Execs. Service Corps. Dir. Fair Campaign Practices Com. Cons., U.S. Govt. mission to Italy, 1952, OEEC, France, 1953, Japan, 1955, Israel, 1958, India, 1960, Middle East, 1961; mem. nat. marketing adv. com. U.S. Dept. Commerce. Asso. Northwestern U., mem. bus. adv. council Grad. Sch. Bus.; mem. nat. adv. council Peace Corps; mem. Presdl. Adv. Council Minority Enterprise, Census Adv. Com. on Privacy and Confidentiality; mem. Pres.'s Com. Health Edn.; chmn. Nat. Health Council, 1975; mem. U.S. Advisory Commn. Info. Bd. dirs. Advt. Research Found., Ill. Children's Home and Aid Soc., Northwestern Meml. Hosp., Jr. Achievement, Chgo.; trustee U. Chgo., others. Served to maj. C.E., AUS, 1941-45. Mem. Mgmt. Execs. Soc. (exec. com., past pres.), Nat. Planning Council (trustee), U. Wis. Alumni Assn. (dir.), Phi Eta Sigma, Phi Kappa Phi, Beta Gamma Sigma, Sigma Phi. Clubs: Chgo., Chgo. Commonwealth, Economic, Indian Hill, Racquet, Casino, Commercial (Chgo.). Office: AC Nielsen Co Nielsen Plaza Northbrook IL 60093*

NIELSEN, CARL FREDEGOD, metal fabricating co. exec.; b. Freeport, Ohio, Nov. 6, 1918; s. Andreas Lehman and Elizabeth Marie (Ottosen) N.; student public schs., Freeport; m. LaVerne M. Jensen, Oct. 28, 1950; children—David William, Janice Elizabeth, James Carl. Export mgr. Gould Milk & Cream Co., Mpls., 1946-48; sales rep. A.H. Arnold Co., Chgo., 1948-51; sales mgr. Owatonna Creamery Supplies Co. (Minn.), 1951-55; founder, pres. Dairy Craft, Inc. (name now DCI, Inc.), St. Cloud, Minn., 1955—; dir. Western Nat. Mut. Ins. Co., Mpls. Bd. dirs. BIPAC of Minn., 1974—, chmn., 1975-76; bd. dirs. St. Cloud Opportunities, Inc., 1976—, v.p., 1978—. Served with U.S. Army, 1941-43; with USAAF, 1943-46. Mem. Dairy and Food Industry Supplies Assn. (dir. 1974-80, pres.-elect 1980—), Minn. Assn. Commerce and Industry (dir. 1974-80, chmn. 1980), St. Cloud Area C. of C. (dir. 1972-78). Republican. Methodist. Clubs: St. Cloud Country, Sertoma, Elephant. Patentee hydraulic drive system. Home: 116 Greenock Rd Saint Cloud MN 56301 Office: 600 54th Ave N Saint Cloud MN 56301

NIELSEN, KRIS RICHARD, mgmt. cons.; b. Hartford, Conn., May 14, 1945; s. Emil Harold and Susanne Ursula (Tunger) N.; B.S.E., Princeton, 1967; J.D., George Washington U., 1970; m. Mary Jane Armour, Dec. 16, 1978; children by previous marriage—Tanya Stewart, Tara Helen. Admitted to Va. bar, 1970; project cons. Wood & Tower Inc., Princeton, 1967-70, gen. counsel, 1970-73; v.p. constrn. cons. services div. McKee Berger Mansueto Inc., N.Y.C., 1973-76, also pres. subs. Omnifirm Services Inc., 1976-77; pres. Constrn. Info. Services Inc., Ringoes, N.J., 1975—, Nielsen-Wurster Group, Inc., N.Y.C., 1976—. Served with U.S.N.G., 1971-72. Mem. Am. Arbitration Assn., Am., Va. bar assns., Am. Assn. Cost Engrs., Soc. Am. Value Engrs., ICC Practitioners Assn. Republican. Presbyterian. Clubs: Nature Conservancy; Princeton of N.Y. Home: Unionville Farm PO Box 295 Ringoes NJ 08551 Office: 275 Madison Ave New York NY 10016

NIELSEN, VERNON JAMES, brokerage exec.; b. Dawson Creek, B.C., Feb. 28, 1949; s. Svend and Hilda (Johnson) N.; B.Com., U. Calgary, 1971; diploma sales and mktg. mgmt. U. B.C., 1976; m. Wilma J. Vanlersel, Nov. 16, 1971; children—Candice, Gregory, Jennifer. Sales rep. Occidental Life Ins. Co., Vancouver, B.C., 1971-72; salesman, then dist. mgr. Gen. Foods Ltd., Vancouver, 1972-76; salesman, then sales mgr. Barry Brokerage Ltd., Calgary, Alta., 1975-78, pres., 1978—; pres. Nelcor Holdings Ltd., Edmonton, Alta., 1978—. Dir., elder St. Stevens United Ch., Vancouver, 1974-75. Mem. Alta. Food Brokers Assn. (pres. 1980), Can. Food Brokers Assn. (dir.), Nat. Food Brokers Assn., Can. Frozen Food Assn. Office: 15618 116th Ave Edmonton AB Canada

NIELSON, JAMES EDWARD, oil co. exec.; b. Cardston, Alta., Can., Apr. 2, 1931; came to U.S., 1935, naturalized, 1940; s. Glenn E. and Olive (Wood) N.; B.S. in Bus. Adminstrn., U. Wyo., 1954; m. Joanne H. Henry, Apr. 7, 1962; children—James Randall, Julia Elizabeth, John William, Jeffrey Glenn, Jay Edward. Exec. v.p., dir. Husky Oil Co., 1971-73, pres., chief exec. officer, 1973-79; mng. dir. Nielson Internat., Cody, Wyo., 1979—. Served as officer USNR, 1955-58. Mem. Am. Petroleum Inst. (dir.), Wyo. Indsl. Devel. Corp., Buffalo Bill Meml. Assn., U.S. C. of C. (Joint Can.-U.S. com.), Conf. Bd. Presbyterian. Home: PO Box 2850 Cody WY 82414 Office: PO Box 380 Cody WY 82414

NIEMANN, LEWIS KEITH, lamp co. exec.; b. Alliance, Nebr., Dec. 10; s. William Grover and Vivian Zelma (Holloway) N.; grad. with honors and distinction in mktg. (Standard Oil Co. scholar), San Diego State Coll., 1956; m. Elaine Marie Achtenhagen, Dec. 23, 1951; children—Randall Scott, Debra Lee and Denise Lee (twins). Mgr. sales planning and product devel. RCA Sales Corp., 1967-70; spl. asst. to pres. Magnavox Consumer Electronics Co., 1970-73, v.p. internat. and comml. sales, 1973-74; v.p. mktg. mfg. div. Beatrice Foods Co., 1974-75; v.p. mktg. luggage div. Samsonite Corp., 1975-78; pres. Stiffel Co., Chgo., 1978—. Bd. dirs. Jr. Achievement, Denver, 1976-78. Served with USMC, 1948-52. Recipient Clio award, 1978. Republican. Episcopalian. Office: Stiffel Co 700 N Kingsbury St Chicago IL 60610*

NIEMIEC, JEROME PETER, banker; b. Chgo., July 4, 1941; s. James J. and Marie (Celenica) N.; B.S., Ill. Inst. Tech., 1969; M.B.A., U. Chgo., 1973; grad. Stonier Grad. Sch. Banking, Rutgers U., 1980; m. Janice M. Anderson, June 24, 1967; children—Jorie, Julie. With Beverly Bank, Chgo., 1964-66; v.p. Mt. Greenwood Bank, Chgo., 1966-71, pres., 1974-77; v.p. Oak Brook Bank (Ill.), 1971-74; exec. v.p. McIlroy Bank & Trust Co., Fayetteville, Ark., 1977—. Mem. N.W. Ark. Regional Planning Commn., Downtown Fayetteville Unltd.; chmn. United Fund campaign, 1980. Served with USAR, 1964. Mem. Robert Morris Assos., Am. Mgmt. Assn., Fayetteville C. of C. (dir.). Club: Rotary. Office: Box 1327 Fayetteville AR 72701

NIEMIEC, MICHAEL JOSEPH, lawyer, accountant; b. Wyandotte, Mich., Oct. 9, 1951; s. Joseph Aloysius and Alice Mary (Mazmanian) N.; B.S. magna cum laude, U. Detroit, 1972, M.B.A., 1973, J.D., 1977. Admitted to Mich. bar, 1978; controller Wyandotte (Mich.) Auto Parts, Inc., 1972—; supr. dept. tax Ernst & Ernst, Detroit, 1973; partner Crittenden & Broderick, Southfield, Mich., 1974-75; sr. partner Niemiec, Nemes & Garwood, Southfield, 1975—; pres., dir. Michael's Family Restaurants, Inc., MJN Ltd., Starboard Systems, Inc.; lectr. Madonna Coll., Livonia, Mich., Oakland Community Coll., Farmington, Mich. Mem. So. Mich. C. of C., Am. Inst. C.P.A.'s, Mich. Assn. C.P.A.'s, Am. Bar Assn., State Bar Mich. Roman Catholic. Contbr. articles in field to profl. jours. Office: 21800 W Ten Mile Rd Suite 218 Southfield MI 48075

NIGHTINGALE, WILLIAM JOSLYN, mgmt. cons. co. exec.; b. Mpls., Sept. 16, 1929; s. William Issac and Gladys (Joslyn) N.; B.A., Bowdoin Coll., 1951; M.B.A., Harvard U., 1953; m. Carla Carroll, Jan. 26, 1958; children—Paul, Sara, William Joslyn, Margaret. Mktg. mgr. Gen. Mills Inc., Mpls., 1957-66; sr. asso. Booze, Allen & Hamilton Inc., N.Y.C., 1966-68; v.p. fin. Hanes Corp., Winston-Salem, N.C., 1969; pres. Bali Co. Inc., N.Y.C., 1970-75; pres. Nightingale & Assos. Inc., New Canaan, Conn., 1975—; dir. Vt. Weatherboard Inc., Ring's End Lumber Inc. Active numerous charitable orgns.; vestryman St. Luke's Episcopal Ch., 1975-78; mem. Darien Representative Town Meeting, 1971-74. Served to lt. (j.g.) USN, 1953-57. Republican. Clubs: Harvard (N.Y.C.); Coral Beach, Small Point, Noroton Yacht. Home: 20 Harbor Rd Darien CT 06820 Office: 135 Cherry St New Canaan CT 06840

NIKITAS, NICHOLAS MARINES, motel exec.; b. Fitchburg, Mass., Feb. 26, 1950; s. Marines Nicholas and Helen (Pappazisis) N.; A.B., Dartmouth, 1972. Owner/mgr. Howard Johnson Motor Lodge, Kingston-Plymouth, Mass. and Holiday Inn, Worcester, Mass., 1972—; pres. Nikitas Family Inns; owner apt. properties, Boston and Fitchburg, Mass.; lectr. Massasoit Community Coll., Fisher Jr. Coll. Mem. Kingston Republican Town Com., 1971-76; mem. Rep. City Com. of Boston, 1977—; bd. dirs. Plymouth (Mass.) Philharmonic Orch., Plymouth County Devel. Council; co-chmn. Am. Cancer Soc. Crusade, 1978; class agt. Dartmouth Coll. Alumni Fund; mem. North End Neighborhood Task Force; mem. steering com. Worcester Conv. Bur.; v.p., dir. Central Mass. Tourist Council; mem. Italian-Am. Found.; charter mem. U.S.S. Constitution Mus. Found., Boston; admissions and enrollment interviewer Dartmouth Coll. Recipient certificate of honor Fed. Disaster Assistance Adminstrn., 1978, award for blizzard lodging and relief effort Gov. of Mass. Mem. Waterfront Neighborhood Assn. Boston, Kingston Jaycees (past v.p.), Plymouth C. of C. (mem. tourist and cultural affairs com.), Boston Jaycees, Howard Johnson Nat. Operators Council, Mass. Hotel-Motel Assn., Nat. Tour Brokers Assn., AHEPA. Republican. Greek Orthodox. Clubs: Harvard (Boston); South Shore Dartmouth; Hub Dartmouth. Address: 484 Commercial St Boston MA 02109

NILSEN, CLIFFORD T., fin. exec.; b. Jamaica, N.Y., July 19, 1932; s. Carl and Sigrid (Aanesens) N.; B.A., Hofstra U., 1956; m. Charlene Ann Renninger, Sept. 12, 1959; children—Wendy Jean, Kurt Clifford. Security analyst Reliance Investment Co., Phila., 1962-66; v.p., sr. investment officer Savs. Banks Trust Co., N.Y.C., 1966-73; pres. Chem. Fund, Inc., N.Y.C., 1973—, Surveyor Fund, Inc., N.Y.C., 1973—, F. Eberstadt & Co. and successor firm Eberstadt Asset Mgmt., N.Y.C., 1973—; bd. trustees E. N.Y. Savs. Bank; dir. N.Y. State Mcpl. Bond Bank. Served with AUS, 1952-54. Mem. N.Y. Soc. Security Analysts. Methodist. Office: 61 Broadway New York NY 10006

NILSSEN, OLE KRISTIAN, inventor; b. Skien, Norway, June 6, 1928; s. Eigil Odd and Elizabeth Redisch (Carlsen) N.; B.S.E.E., U. Wis., 1952, M.S.E.E., 1953; m. Ellen Johanne Holmberg, Mar. 1, 1952; children—Mette Elisabeth, Richard Vegem, Linda Dorthea. Electronics engr. RCA Corp., 1953-56; prin. engr. Ford Motor Co., Dearborn, Mich., 1956-67; dir. research and devel. Motorola, Inc., Chgo., 1967-72; pres. Innovention Center Inc., Algonquin, Ill., 1972—. Mem. IEEE (founder vehicular tech. group). Patentee in field. Home: Rural Route 4 Barrington IL 60010 Office: 200 N Harrison St Algonquin IL 60102

NIMER, MELVIN DEAN, mktg. cons. co. exec.; b. Walla Walla, Wash., Feb. 25, 1950; s. Melvin Arthur and Lou Jean (Park) N.; B.S. in Acctg., Brigham Young U., Provo, Utah, 1974; m. Janet Spafford, Jan. 25, 1972; children—Michael Dean, David Earl, Janelle. Accounts payable supr. K.S.L. Inc., Salt Lake City, 1974; staff acct. Husky Oil Co., Cody, Wyo., 1974-76; controller Larsen/Bateman Inc., Santa Barbara, Calif., 1976-77, Anarad, Inc., Santa Barbara, 1978; controller, gen. mgr. acctg./data processing McNally Mountain States Steel Co., Lindon, Utah, 1978-81; pres. Nimer Enterprises, Inc., internat. mktg. cons., 1972—. Mem. citizens choice com. Goleta Valley C. of C., 1976-77. Mem. Assn. Computer Users (dir.), Data Processing Mgmt. Assn., Aircraft Owners and Pilots Assn., Utah Valley Execs. Club, Nat. Pilots Assn. Republican. Mormon. Home: 1034 N 560 E Orem UT 84057 Office: PO Box 1300 Orem UT 84057

NIMMO, OTIS DALE, fire equipment co. exec.; b. Fair Grove, Mo., June 26, 1936; s. Otis Gustus and Iverene Mahala (Gallion) N.; student S.W. Mo. State Coll., 1954-55; m. Cora Lee Batson, Mar. 24, 1956; children—Steven Anthony, Michael Andrew, Deborah Ann, Mark Allen. With Otis G. Nimmo, Springfield, Mo., 1955-56, Caterpiller Tractor Co., Joliet, Ill., 1956-57; sales mgr. A & W Appliances, Springfield, 1957-58; route salesman Manor Bread, Topeka, 1958-59, Taystee Bread Co., Topeka, 1959-60; partner L.L. Letterman Meat Co., Springfield, 1960-63; mgr. Ozark Fire Extinguisher Co., Springfield, 1963-64; pres., gen. mgr. Mozark Fire Extinguisher Co., Springdale, Ark., 1964—, also dir. Profl. chmn. Fire Extinguisher Serviceman and Installer adv. bd., Ark. Gov. David Pryor, 1978. Served with Mo. N.G., 1952-56. Mem. Nat. Fire Protection Assn. Mem. Ch. of Christ. Home: Rt 2 Blue Springs Village Springdale AR 72764 Office: 705 E Robinson Ln Springdale AR 72764

NIMTZ, RICHARD LEWIS, retail exec.; b. Omaha, Dec. 6, 1940; s. Albert and Ellenora N.; B.S., Colo. U., 1963; m. Patricia A. Marshall, May 25, 1965; children—Holly L., Richard T. With J.C. Penney, Boulder, Colo., 1963-66, nat. merchandiser cosmetics/small wares, 1966-68, mgr. spl. projects, 1968-70, buyer stationery, 1970-72, buyer automotive, 1973-75, mdse. mgr. home improvement, 1976-77; v.p. mdse. and mktg. Hoffritz for Cutlery and Edwin Jay, Inc., 1977-79; dir. mktg. Berrie & Co. W., 1979—. Active Boy Scouts Am. Served in U.S. Army, 1962. Republican. Methodist. Home: 1701 Monte Carlo St Santa Rosa CA 95405

NIOCHE, JACQUES, cosmetic co. exec.; b. Paris, France, Dec. 11, 1940; came to U.S., 1969; s. Georges Emile and Nadine (Nonroy) N.; B.S., N.Y. U., 1973; m. Brigitte Haltner, Dec. 27, 1962; 1 son, Marc. Jr. chemist Max Factor, Sydney, Australia, 1960-61; chemist Schramm Lack, Farb Fabrik Offenbach-Main, W. Ger., 1962; processing mgr. Harriet Hubbar Ayer, div. Unilever N.V., Paris, 1964-66; prodn. mgr. Helene Curtis, Montreal, 1966-69; chemist Avon, N.Y.C., 1969; asst. v.p. research and devel. Elizabeth Arden div. Eli Lilly, 1969-78; asst. v.p. cosmetic ops. l'Oreal-Lancome div. Cosmair, Inc., Piscataway, N.J., 1978—. Mem. Am. Mgmt. Assn., Piscataway C. of C. (dir.). Office: 81 New England Ave Piscataway NJ 08854

NIPPER, THOMAS EDWARD, advt. products co. exec.; b. Hollis, N.Y., Oct. 4, 1938; s. Albert C. and Frances Ann (Sarnowski) N.; B.B.A., U. Okla., 1959; postgrad. Columbia, 1960, U. Calif., Los Angeles, 1963; m. Renee A. Giglio, May 7, 1966; children—Kelly Ann, Katie Theres. With Young & Rubicam, Inc., N.Y.C., San Francisco, Chgo., Los Angeles, 1960-67; exec. v.p. fin. adminstrn. Knox Reeves Adv., Inc., Mpls., 1967-73; pres. Monterey Wine Villages, Mpls., 1973-74; v.p., sec.-treas. Mithun Enterprises, Inc., Mpls., 1974-76; pres. Asco, Inc., Winona, Minn., 1976—; pres. Frontier Broadcasting, Inc., Dallas, 1975—, Sovran Assos., Inc., Dallas, 1975—. Mem. bd. dirs. Exchange of Students in Commerce and Industry (pres. Minn. chpt. 1972—). Mem. Inst. Broadcasting Fin. Mgmt. Assns., Fin. Exec. Inst., Inst. Corporate Planning Execs., Pres.'s Council of Am. Mgmt. Assn. Republican. Roman Catholic. Home: 1365 Conrad Dr Winona MN 55987 Office: 1205 E Sanborn St Winona MN 55987

NIRENBERG, KENNETH CHARLES, computer service bur. exec.; b. Boston, Oct. 4, 1946; s. Bernard Israel and Ida (Kalish) N.; B.A. in Econs., Brandeis U., 1968; m. Charlotte Castillo, Oct. 16, 1971; children—Marc Andrew, Ronald Adrian. Vol., Peace Corps, Malaysia, 1968-71; data processing mgr. Charter Info. Corp., Austin, Tex., 1972—. Cert. data processor Inst. Cert. Computer Profls. Mem. Data Processing Mgmt. Assn., Assn. for Returned Peace Corps Vols. Democrat. Home: 12812 Poquoson Dr Austin TX 78759 Office: 2421 Rutland Dr Austin TX 78758

NISBETH, G. RICHARD, banker; b. Potsdam, N.Y., Nov. 28, 1947; s. George R. and Adriana (Bettini) N.; B.S. in Fin., Fla. Atlantic U., 1970; m. Ardith Austin, July 2, 1977; 1 son, Eric. With St. Joseph Valley Bank, Elkhart, Ind., 1973—, v.p., dir. corp. planning, 1976-78, sr. v.p., 1978—. Bd. dirs. Elkhart Water Works, Elkhart Concert Club, Big Bros./Big Sisters, Elkhart. Mem. Planning Execs. Inst., Midwest Planning Assn., Nat. Assn. Accountants, Am. Mktg. Assn., Alpha Tau Omega. Episcopalian. Home: 1507 Ash Dr W Elkhart IN 46514 Office: 121 W Franklin St Elkhart IN 46514

NISENHOLTZ, FRED, computer co. exec.; b. Paterson, N.J., June 3, 1943; s. Max and Rae N.; B.S. in Elec. Engring., Rutgers U., 1964, M.B.A., 1971; m. Joan R. West, July 8, 1967; children—Brian Scott, Judi Dale. Engr., Public Service Electric & Gas, Newark, 1964-66; sales rep., systems engr. IBM Corp., Newark and N.Y.C., 1966-71; v.p. software and systems Itel Corp., N.Y.C. and San Francisco, 1972-79; v.p. Alanthus Corp., San Francisco, 1979—. Home: 68 San Pablo Ct Moraga CA 94556 Office: 1750 Montgomery St San Francisco CA 94111

NISHIUWATOKO, TETSU, engring. corp. exec.; b. Kagoshima, Japan, Sept. 20, 1941; came to U.S., 1973; s. Jikichi and Hanae (Kamino) N.; B.A., Takushoku U., 1964; postgrad. Internat. Inst. Studies and Tng., 1971-72; m. Kazuko Murata, Nov. 21, 1965; children—Tsutomu, Mitsuru. Staff internat. div. Kajima Corp., Tokyo, 1964-68, 71-73, rep. in Okinawa, 1968-71, chief rep. in N.Y., N.Y.C., 1973—; dir. Kajima Devel. Corp. Pres., PTA, Japanese Sch. N.Y., 1979-80; mem. adminstrv. com., bd. edn. Japanese Edn. Council N.Y., 1979-80. Mem. Am. Mgmt. Assn., Real Estate Bd. N.Y., U.S.-Japan Trade Council, Japanese C. of C. of N.Y., Japan Soc. Clubs: Rotary (N.Y.), Marco Polo, Nippon. Home: 3 Horizon Rd Fort Lee NJ 07024 Office: 299 Park Ave New York NY 10017

NISSEN, ARTHUR HERBERT, air conditioning co. exec.; b. Jersey City, Oct. 12, 1929; s. Charles C. and Marie G. (Scheffler) N.; student public schs.; m. Florence E. Renfroe, Nov. 3, 1951; 1 dau., Lisa K. Service mgr. Southernaire Distbg. Co., Jacksonville, Fla., 1955-62; with Cain & Bultman, Inc., 1962—, gen. service mgr. appliance and central airconditing div., 1964—; chmn. customer assurance distbrs. conf. Whirlpool Corp., 1979-80. Adv. com. Fla. Jr. Coll., Jacksonville. Served with USAF, 1950-54. Republican. Baptist. Home: 7110 St Augustine Rd Jacksonville FL 32217 Office: 2145 Dennis St Jacksonville FL 32203

NISSEN, CARL ANDREW, JR., govt. ofcl.; b. Manhattan, Kan., June 26, 1930; s. Carl Andrew and Bernice Lydia (Varney) N.; B.A., Ohio State U., 1960; postgrad., Berkeley Bapt. Div. Sch., 1960-61; student def. basic procurement mgmt. Army Logistics Mgmt. Center, Ft. Lee, Va., 1964, def. advanced procurement mgmt., 1970. Contract asst. Def. Electronics Supply Center, Dayton, Ohio, 1963-64, procurement asst., 1964-65, procurement agt., 1965-66, contract negotiator, 1966—. Served with U.S. Army, 1950-53. Recipient George Washington Honor award Freedoms Found., 1972. Mem. Am. Def. Preparedness Assn. (life), Nat. Rifle Assn. (life), Air Force Sgts. Assn. (life), Ohio Def. Corps Officers Assn., Ohio Soc. Mayflower Descs., SAR (officer Ohio soc.), Ohio State U. Alumni Assn. (life), Alpha Phi Omega. Baptist. Home: 727 W Riverview Ave Dayton OH 45406 Office: 1507 Wilmington Pike Dayton OH 45444

NITZ, TERRY EDWIN, housing mfg. co. exec.; b. St. Joseph, Mich., May 1, 1944; s. Leonard Harry and Gloria Ann (Swope) N.; B.S. in Mktg., Ferris State Coll., Big Rapids, Mich., 1980; m. Patricia Lynn Chipman, June 7, 1971; children—Justin Mathew, Kimberly Lynn. Dock ops. supr. Squire Dingee Co., Baroda, Mich., 1962—; supr. stock dept. Heathkit Co., Benton Harbor, Mich., 1964; mgr. men's suit dept. Libin's Varsity Shop, Kalamazoo, 1971-72; mgr. men's clothing and furnishings Montgomery Ward & Co., Kalamazoo, 1972-78; sales mgr. South Park Homes, Inc., Reed City, Mich., 1978-80; mgr. Doyle's Mobile Home Center, Inc., Columbus, Ohio, 1980—. Served with USAF, 1966-70. Mem. Am. Mktg. Club, Profl. Bus. Orgn. Lutheran. Clubs: Lions, Photography, USO (v.p.). Home: 493 Knob Hill W Columbus OH 43228 Office: 6200 S High St Columbus OH 43137

NIVEN, MALCOLM P., textile co. exec.; b. Dunedin, Fla., Aug. 15, 1914; s. Percy D. and Janie Elizabeth (McLean) N.; B.S. in Bus. Adminstrn., U. Fla., 1937; postgrad. Harvard. Grad. Sch. Bus., 1962; m. Nellie Felicia Booker, Dec. 7, 1941; children—Linda (Mrs. Thomas Tiller, Jr.), Sandra, Malcolm P., Jan (Mrs. Eugene Taylor). Pres., founder Carolina Mfg. Co., Greenville, S.C., 1948—; pres. R.W. Eldridge Co., Charlotte, N.C., 1964—; pres. So. Handkerchief Co., Greenville, 1968—; v.p. Fendrich Industries, Greenville, 1971—; dir., mem. exec. com. Carolina Fed. Savs. & Loan Co., Greenville, 1970—; dir. Fendrich Industries, Evansville, Ind., exec. v.p., 1976—; dir. Bankers Trust S.C. Bd. dirs. Info. Center on Alcoholism and Drugs, Greenville County, 1970—, Boys Club, 1969—, Salvation Army, 1969—, Greenville Symphony Assn., 1969—, Met. YMCA, 1977—; trustee Montreat (N.C.)-Anderson Coll., 1968—, Presbyn. Coll., Clinton, S.C., 1967—; chmn. bd. Greenville Hosp. System, 1980—. Served to lt. col. USAAF, World War II. Mem. Nat. Assn. Tobacco Distbrs., Ret. Officers Assn. Presbyterian (elder, trustee). Clubs: Green Valley Country, Greenville Country, Poinsett (treas. 1976, dir.); Charlotte City (N.C.); Rotarian. Home: 8 Meyers Dr Greenville SC 29605 Office: Box 5497 Station B Greenville SC 29606

NIX, HOWARD WEBSTER, JR., banker; b. East Point, Ga., Dec. 20, 1929; s. Howard Webster and Ruby Mae (Smith) N.; LL.B., Atlanta Law Sch., 1951, LL.M., 1952; m. Carolyn Statham, Oct. 5, 1951; children—Deborah Anne, Howard Webster. With Bank of Ga., Atlanta, 1947-52, Citizens & So. Nat. Bank, Atlanta, 1952-60; with Comml. Nat. Bank of Pensacola (Fla.), 1960-68, pres., chmn., 1960-68; pres. Jacksonville (Fla.) Nat. Bank, 1968-69; vice-pres. Bankstock Corp. Am., Jacksonville, 1969-70; pres. Landmark Union Trust Bank, St. Petersburg, Fla., 1970—; sr. v.p., dir. Landmark Banking Corp. Mem. Fla. Council of 100, Com. of 100, Am. Bankers Assn., Fla. Bankers Assn. Baptist. Clubs: St. Petersburg Yacht, Feather Sound Country, Commerce. Office: PO Box 11388 Saint Petersburg FL 33733

NIX, JOSEPH NELSON, JR., advt., pub. relations and mktg. exec.; b. Atlanta, Dec. 18, 1942; s. Joseph Nelson and Era Marguerite (Parks) N.; B.A., U. Ga., 1965, M.A., 1970; postgrad. Yuba Coll., 1968-69; m. Carole Worfolk, Oct. 5, 1974. News dir. radio stat. WJJC, Commerce, Ga., 1969-70; corporate pub. relations coordinator Citizens and So. Nat. Bank, Atlanta, 1971; dir. pub. relations Mead Packaging, Atlanta, 1972; comml. broadcast cons., Atlanta, 1973; field account exec. N.W. Ayer ABH Internat., N.Y.C., and Richmond, Va., 1973-80, regional account supr. N.W. Ayer, Inc., 1980—. Mem., co. rep. Atlanta Internat. Council, 1972, Ga. Bus. and Industry Assn., Atlanta, also Keep Am. Beautiful, Inc., N.Y.C., Nat. Center for Resource Recovery, Washington, Jr. Achievement, Atlanta, 1971-72; committeeman United Way, Atlanta, 1971. Served to capt. USAF, 1965-69. Mem. Atlanta C. of C. (mem. com. 1972), Pub. Relations Soc. Am. (Old Dominion chpt.), Atlanta Advt. Club, Atlanta Press Club, Ga. Press Assn., Air Force Assn., Ga. Assn. Newscasters, Sigma Delta Chi (Richmond chpt.), DiGamma Kappa. Baptist. Home: 1706 Chevelle Dr Richmond VA 23235 Office: 1706 Chevelle Dr Richmond VA 23235

NOBEL, JOEL J., physician, inst. adminstr.; b. Phila., Dec. 8, 1934; s. Bernard D. and Golda R. (Nobel) Judovich; A.B., Haverford Coll., 1956; M.A., U. Pa., 1958; M.D., Thomas Jefferson Med. Coll., 1963; m. Bonnie Sue Goldberg, June 19, 1960 (div.); children—Erika, Joshua. Intern, Presbyn. Hosp., Phila., 1963-64; resident Pa. Hosp., Phila., 1964-65, U. Pa. Hosp., 1965-66; practice medicine, specializing in biomed. engring. research, Phila., 1968—; dir. research Emergency Care Research Inst., Plymouth Meeting, Pa., 1968-71, dir., 1971—; pres. Plymouth Inst.; cons. in field. Bd. dirs. Consumers Union, 1976-79, 80—. Served with USN, 1966-68. Smith Kline & French fgn. fellow, 1962; HEW grantee, 1968-72; Am. Heart Assn. grantee, 1965-66. Mem. Assn. for Advancement of Med. Instrumentation, Critical Care Med. Soc., Am. Pub. Health Assn., AMA, Pa. Med. Assn., Am. Def. Preparedness Assn. Publisher Health Devices, Health Devices Alerts; contbr. articles to profl. jours. Home: 1434 Monk Rd Gladwyne PA 19035 Office: 5200 Butler Pike Plymouth Meeting PA 19462

NOBLE, JAMES KENDRICK, JR., brokerage exec.; b. N.Y.C., Oct. 6, 1928; s. James Kendrick and Orrel (Baldwin) N.; student Princeton, 1945-46; B.S., U.S. Naval Acad., 1950; M.B.A., N.Y. U., 1961, postgrad. Grad Sch. Edn., 1962-68; m. Norma Jean Rowell, June 16, 1951; children—Anne Rowell, James Kendrick, III. Asst. to pres. Noble & Noble, Pubs., subsidiary Dell Pub. Co., N.Y.C., 1957-58, editor, 1958-60, dir. spl. projects, 1960-62, v.p., 1962-65, exec. v.p., editor-in-chief, 1965-66, dir., 1957-65; v.p., dir. Translation Pub. Co., Bronxville, N.Y., 1958-65; sr. analyst instl. investment research F. Eberstadt & Co., 1966-69; sr. analyst Auerbach, Pollak & Richardson, Inc., 1969-75, v.p., 1972-75, mgr. spl. research projects, 1973-75, also dir.; v.p. research Paine, Webber, Jackson & Curtis, Inc., 1975-77, asso. dir. research, 1976-77; v.p. Mitchell Hutchins Inc., 1977-79, 1st v.p., 1979—. Mem. Bronxville Bd. Edn., 1968-74; pres., 1970-72. Leader, 21st Republican Dist., 1961-65. Bd. dirs. Curriculum Info. Center, 1972-78; trustee St. John's Hosp., 1972—. Served to lt. USN, 1950-57; capt. Res. Fellow AAAS; mem. Nat. Inst. for Social Scis., Printing and Pub. Industry Analysts Assn. (sec. 1968-69, pres. 1969-71), Am. Inst. Chartered Fin. Analysts, Am. Ednl. Research Assn., Cum Laude Soc., N.Y. Soc. Security Analysts (dir. 1975--, v.p. 1977—), Am. Mgmt. Assn., Naval Res. Assn. (v.p. N.Y. chpt. 1968-75), Kappa Delta Pi. Clubs: Wings (N.Y.C.); Siwanoy Country (Bronxville). Author: Ploob, 1949; also articles in various kinds publs. Editor, pub.: The Years Between, 1966. Home: 45 Edgewood Ln Bronxville NY 10708 Office: 140 Broadway New York NY 10005

NOBLE, MILNER, heat exchanger mfg. co. exec.; b. Richmond, Va., Sept. 27, 1900; s. Thomas Jefferson and Susan (Wright) N.; B.S. in Mech. Engring., Va. Poly. Inst., 1922; m. Margaret Stanley Elliot, Jan. 11, 1930; 1 son, Milner Elliot. Student engr. Carrier Corp., 1922; with Aerofin Corp., Lynchburg, Va., 1923—, gen. mgr., 1939-42, pres., 1942—. Mem. WPB, 1942. Registered profl. engr., Va. Mem. Am. Soc. Heating and Ventilating Engrs., Newcomen Soc. Jamestown Soc. Clubs: Syracuse (N.Y.) University, Boonsboro Country (Lynchburg, Va.); Commonwealth of Va. (Richmond). Home: 3241 Downing Dr Lynchburg VA 24503 Office: Murray Pl Lynchburg VA 24505

NOBUKI, SABURO, publisher; b. Tokyo, Japan, May 5, 1923; s. Mokusaburo and Kiyono (Akiyama) N.; B.A. in Sociology, Tokyo U., 1946; m. Tsugiko (Suwa), Oct. 7, 1955; children—Soichiro, Haruo. Editor, writer, high sch. tchr., translator, 1946-53; sales mgr. C.E. Tuttle, 1953-61; Japan rep. Feffer & Simons, 1961-62; mng. dir. Kodansha Internat., 1962—; v.p. Kodansha Internat./ U.S.A., 1966—; mng. dir. Kodansha Famous Sch.; pres. NST Internat. Co.; dir. Kodansha Culture Indsl. Co., Kodansha Sci.; lectr. U. Tokyo, 1979. Bd. dirs. News Letter, Unesco Tokyo Developing Book Center. Mem. Japanese Animal Welfare Soc., Japan Sociol. Assn., Gakushikai, P.E.N. Club, Editorogical Soc. Japan (mem. masters exec.). Club: Tokyo Ginza Rotary. Home: 3-17-14 Akatsutsumi Setagaya-ku Tokyo 156 Japan Office: 2-12-21 Otowa Bunkyo-ku Tokyo 112 Japan

NOCHISAKI, WILLIAM S., mfg. co. exec.; b. N.Y.C., Feb. 26, 1922; s. Nisabro and Anna K. (Ericson) N.; B.S.M.E., CCNY, 1943; M.S. in Indsl. Mgmt. (Sloan fellow), M.I.T., 1960; m. Esterina Rosetti, Sept. 17, 1948; children—Eric William, Karen Aede, Lynne Susan. Aeronautical draftsman, layout engr. Chance Vough Aircraft, Stratford, Conn., 1943-46; chief mfg. services Sikorsky Aircraft div. United Tech., Stratord, 1947-66; v.p. mfg. Bell Aerospace-Textron, Buffalo, 1966-70, Rohr Industries, Chula Vista, Calif., 1970-73; v.p. ops. Homelite-Textron, Charlotte, N.C., 1973—. Chmn. bd. advisors Winthrop Coll. Sch. Bus. Adminstrn., 1978—; exec. bd. Pomperaug council Boy Scouts Am., Bridgeport Conn., 1968-70, exec. bd. Charlotte Jr. Achievement, 1976—; mem. R.H. Community Ch. council, Clover, S.C., 1978—. Served with U.S. Army, 1944-46. Named Mfg. Exec. of Yr., ASME, 1972. Mem. ASME (hon.), Beta Gamma Sigma. Clubs: Rotary, River Hills Golf and Country. Home: 20 Wood Hollow Rd Clover SC 29710 Office: PO Box 7047 14401 Carowinds Blvd Charlotte NC 28217

NODAR, MANUEL VALENTINE, power tool co. exec.; b. Schenectady, June 5, 1927; s. Manuel J. and Mary Ellen (Iacovitti) N.; B.S. cum laude, Syracuse U., 1950; m. Mildred G. Rothberg, Oct. 6, 1974; children—M. David, M. Diane, Stephen G. Vice pres. advt. and public relations Black & Decker, Towson, Md., 1966-69, v.p. product planning, 1970-72, v.p. new bus. group, 1972-73; v.p. adminstrn. McColloch Corp., Los Angeles, 1973-77, v.p., gen. mgr. engine div., 1978-79, v.p. corporate devel., sec., 1979—; dir. McColloch Mite-E-Lite, Wellsville, N.Y., 1980—. Patron, Los Angeles County Mus. of Art. Served with USNR, 1945-46. Mem. Chain Saw Mfrs. Assn., Am. Mgmt. Assn. Republican. Club: Bel Air Country, Magic Castle. Contbr. articles in field to profl. jours.; author: Advertising Department Management, 1968; contbg. author: Advertising Fundamentals, 1970. Home: Office: 5400 Alla Rd Los Angeles CA 90066

NODINE, WILLIAM EDWARD, savs. and loan exec.; b. Meadville, Pa., Oct. 27, 1929; s. Frank Ernest and Mildred L. (Hazen) N.; B.A. with high honors, U. Fla., 1950, J.D. with high honors, 1951; grad. Judge Adv. Gen. Sch., U.S. Army; m. Christine Randall, May 2, 1953; children—Donald, Thad, Bruce. Admitted to Fla. bar; partner firm Richards, Nodine, Gilkey, Fite, Meyer & Thompson, P.A., Clearwater, Fla., 1951-72; pres. Clearwater Fed. Savs. and Loan Assn., 1972—; chmn. bd. Fla. Savs. & Loan Services, Inc. Elder, Peace Meml. Presbyterian Ch., 1955-80. Served to 1st lt., JAGC, U.S. Army, 1952-54. Mem. Clearwater Bar Assn. (pres.), Fla. Bar, Am. Bar Assn., Fla. Savs. and Loan League (dir.), U.S. League Savs. Assns. Democrat. Clubs: Carlouel (commodore 1978), Kiwanis (club pres. 1963). Office: PO Box 4608 Clearwater FL 33518

NOFFSINGER, DONALD ALLEN, publishing co. exec.; b. Defiance, O., Apr. 18, 1929; s. Obert M. and Mazie V. (Etter) N.; B.S. in Commerce, Internat. Coll., 1949; postgrad. U. Calif. at San Diego, 1959-61; B.S., Ball State U., 1974, M.B.A., 1980; LL.D. (hon.), Anderson Coll., 1980; m. Birdie F. George Smith, May 21, 1955; stepchildren—Gregory L., Ronald D., Randall G.; 1 son, Mark A. With dist. accounting office Burroughs Corp., Chgo., 1949-50; accounting supr. Gen. Motors Corp., Defiance, Ohio, 1950-59; in charge financial forecasting Gen. Dynamics-Astronautics, San Diego, 1959-61; pres., dir. Warner Press, Inc., Anderson, Ind., 1961—; partner Orange Blossom Gardens Devel. Co.; 1964—; dir. Laymen Life Ins. Co.; pres., dir. Comml. Service Co., Inc., Anderson, Asso. Cos., Inc. City councilman Defiance, 1958-59; redevel. commr. City of Anderson, 1968-71, pres., redevel. commn., 1970-71. Bd. dirs. Anderson Community Hosp., Ch. Extension and Home Missions Ch. of God, Wilson Boys Clubs, Inc., Jr. Achievement Madison County, YMCA, Crossroads of Am. council Boy Scouts Am., Anderson Symphony Orch., 1978—. Served with AUS, 1947-55. Mem. Nat. Assn. Accountants, Am. Accounting Assn., Indpls. Art Assn., Anderson Urban League, Pres.'s Assn., Am. Mgmt. Assn., Anderson C. of C. Mem. Ch. of God (dir., v.p. nat. bd. ch. extensions and home missions, ch. treas., trustee), Protestant Ch. Owned Pubs. Assn. (dir., pres. 1978-80), Coop. Publ. Assn. (v.p. 1980—). Mason. Clubs: Optimist (pres. 1971-72), lt. gov. Ind. chpt. 1972-73); Anderson Country. Home: 310 Ravenview Ct Anderson IN 46011 Office: PO Box 2499 Anderson IN 46011

NOGG, ROBERT STERLING, accountant, mfg. co. exec., real estate developer; b. Omaha, July 20, 1942; s. Ezra Leo and Sarah Irene (Sterling) N.; B.B.A., U. Okla., 1964; student U. Nebr., 1977, Wharton Sch. U. Pa., 1978; children—Dana, Jennifer. Staff acct. Peat, Marwick, Mitchell & Co., C.P.A.'s, 1964-65; sr. acct. Elmer Fox, Westheimer & Co., C.P.A.'s, Omaha, 1965-67; partner, co-founder Frankel Nogg & Co., Omaha, 1968—; pres. Indsl. Label Corp., Omaha, 1974-77, Bocage Real Estate Inc., 1972—; v.p. Nogg Fruit Co., 1975-77, Ski Racquet Inc., 1976-78; partner GNF Co. Real Estate, 1973-77, Pacific Properties Co., 1974-78, Firehouse Dinner Theatre, 1973-78; guest lectr. Creighton U., U. Nebr.; adv. Open Elem. Sch., 1977; counselor SBA, 1974-76. Chmn. bd. dirs. Phillip Sher Home for Aged, 1974; mem. nat. leadership cabinet UJA, 1976; treas., bd. dirs. Omaha Civic Opera, 1976-78; co-chmn. leadership cabinet Omaha Jewish Philanthropies, 1976; bd. dirs. Temple Israel, 1975-77, Jewish Fedn.; adv. Jr. Achievement; com. mem. Loveland Sch. PTA, 1977-78. Mem. Am. Inst. C.P.A.'s, Nebr. Soc. C.P.A.'s (chmn. rev. com. 1975, ethics com. 1974), Joslyn Art Soc., Nat. Assn. Ski Dealers. Clubs: Temple Mens, Highland Country, Omaha Racquet, Tennis, B'nai B'rith, Ak-Sar-Ben. Exhbn. photography Jewish Community Center, 1978. Home: 728 Sunset Trail Omaha NE 68132

NOHA, EDWARD J., ins. co. exec.; b. 1926; B.B.A., Pace Coll.; married. With Dept. Justice, 1944-52, Met. Life Ins. Co., 1952-55; exec. v.p. Allstate Ins. Co., 1955-74; chmn. bd., pres. CNA Ins.-Continental Assurance Co., Chgo.; chmn. bd. Continental Casuality Co., Nat. Fire Ins. Co. of Hartford, Inc., Transcontinental Ins. Co. Office: Continental Assurance Co CNA Plaza Chicago IL 60685*

NOLAN, AGNES FOLK, real estate co. exec., lawyer; b. N.Y.C., Aug. 6, 1931; d. William James and Agnes (Sikora) Gilligan; B.A., Trinity Coll., 1952; LL.B., Columbia U., 1955; m. Richard Nolan, Jan. 31, 1959; children—Anthony R., Christopher Whitbread, Timothy Robert, Mariana Celeste, Katherine Hope. Admitted to N.Y. bar, 1957, U.S. Supreme Ct. bar, 1965; practice with firm Cadvalader, Wickersham and Taft, N.Y.C., 1955-60; asst. gen. counsel Kaiser-Roth Corp., N.Y.C., 1960-62; pres. Whitbread Nolan Inc., N.Y.C., 1962—, Windham Properties Ltd., 1978—. Bd. dirs., v.p. Am. Friends of Westminister Cathedral. Mem. Am. Bar Assn., Real Estate Bd. N.Y. Club: Lake George. Home: 271 Central Park West New York NY 10024 Office: 600 Madison Ave New York NY 10022

NOLAN, FRANK MICHAEL, lawyer; b. Bklyn., Sept. 21, 1902; s. Michael J. and Mary A. (Nolan) N.; A.B., Columbia, 1928; LL.B., Fordham U., 1932, J.D., 1968; m. Mary E. Flanigan, Dec. 10, 1938; children—Elizabeth C. (Mrs. George B. Arnold), Barbara F. (Mrs. Richard Ruland), Peter F. Admitted to N.Y. bar, 1933; patent counsel Eli Lilly & Co., Indpls., 1940-42; sr. atty. Alien Property Custodian, U.S. Govt., 1943; atty. Fish & Neave, N.Y.C., 1943-51; patent counsel Merck & Co., Inc., 1951-58; pvt. practice law, 1958-80. Registered profl. engr., N.J. Mem. Am. Bar Assn., Am. Chem. Soc., N.Y., N.J. patent law assns., Delta Theta Phi. Roman Catholic. Club: Nat. Lawyers (Washington). Home: 269 Forest Dr S Short Hills NJ 07078

NOLAN, JOHN JOSEPH, JR., security cons.; b. Boston, July 5, 1945; s. John Joseph and Helen Marie (Spiers) N.; student public schs. Asst. security officer Planning Research Corp., Washington, 1968-70; engaged in risk and security ins. bus., 1972—; gen. mgr. risk mgmt. services div. Met. Internat. Investigative and Security Services, Inc., Arlington, Va., 1979—; lectr., vocat. counselor in fi field. Served with U.S. Army, 1970-72. Decorated Army Commendation medal. Mem. Am. Soc. Indsl. Security, Nat. Assn. Chiefs Police, Nat. Fire Protection Assn., Nat. Safety Mgmt. Assn., Am. Legion. Republican. Roman Catholic. Author tng. manuals. Home: 3026 Wisconsin Ave NW Apt C207 Washington DC 20016 Office: 1121 Arlington Blvd Jet Space Suite 57 Arlington VA 22209

NOLAN, JOSEPH THOMAS, mfg. co. exec.; b. Waterbury, Conn., Apr. 11, 1920; s. Thomas Francis and Mary Margaret (Gaffney) N.; A.B., Holy Cross Coll., Worcester, Mass., 1942; M.A. in English, Boston U., 1945; Ph.D. in Econs., N.Y.C., 1972; m. Virginia Theodate Tappin, May 6, 1943; children—Carol Nolan Rigolot, David J. Washington corr. UPI, 1943-49; writer, editor N.Y. Times, 1949-55; mgr. editorial and press services RCA, N.Y.C., 1955-62; sr. v.p. corp. communications Chase Manhattan Bank, N.Y.C., 1962-74; prof. journalism and public affairs U. S.C., 1974-76; v.p. public affairs Monsanto Co., St. Louis, 1976—. Bd. dirs. United Way Greater St. Louis. Mem. Public Relations Soc. Am., Regional Commerce and Growth Assn. St. Louis (dir.). Author numerous mag. articles. Office: 800 N Lindbergh Blvd St Louis MO 63166

NOLAN, RICHARD THOMAS, life underwriter; b. Davenport, Iowa, Mar. 8, 1954; s. John Edward and Frances (Ready) N.; B.A. cum laude in Bus. Adminstrn., Coll. of St. Thomas, 1976. Real estate sales rep. Columbia Realty Corp., Manchester, Ind., 1975-76; real estate appraiser Shenehon, Goodlund, Taylor, Fruen Inc., Mpls., 1976-77; life underwriter, registered rep. Mut. Benefit Fin. Service Co., Newark, 1977—; chmn. Life Underwriters Polit. Action Com., 1979. Bd. dirs. Mississippi Valley Youth for Christ, 1978; life mem. president's council Coll. of St. Thomas. C.L.U. Mem. Nat. Assn. Life Underwriters, Davenport Jr. C. of C. (membership chmn. 1978, dir. 1979), Alpha Kappa Psi (life), Delta Epsilon Sigma. Roman Catholic. Home: 800 Inwood Terr Cliffside Park NJ 07010 Office: 520 Broad St Newark NJ 07101

NOLDE, GEORGE V., cons. engr.; b. St. Petersburg, Russia, Feb. 28, 1900; s. Vladislav and Maria (Rashinscaja) N.; student E. Siberia Poly. Coll., 1918-23, Moscow Tech. Sch. Higher Learning, 1927-29, diploma elec. engring., 1923, Sc.D., 1929; m. Eugenia Poliakova, Oct. 15, 1936. Staff research establishments, indsl. installations, Moscow, 1923-33; cons. engr., Los Angeles, 1934-36; research asso., photometry lab. U. Calif., 1937; devel. engr. Butte Electric & Mfg. Co., San Francisco, 1937-40; research engr. Marchant Calculating Machine Co., 1940-44; cons. engr. Dalmo Victor Co., San Carlos, Calif., 1945-46; cons. engr. in charge of research Marchant Calculators Corp., Oakland, Calif., 1946-52; computing devices engring. Radio Corp. Am., Camden, N.J., Los Angeles, 1953-61, mgr. aerospace ground support systems engring., 1961-62; sr. staff engr. Aerospace Corp. El Segundo, Calif., 1963-64, cons. engr., 1965—; cons. engr. Douglas Aircraft Co., Long Beach, Calif., Electro Optical Industries Corp., Santa Barbara, Calif., 1965-66, USN Electronics Lab., San Diego, 1966—; prof. elec. engring. U. Calif. at Berkeley, 1955-57; project engr. Airborne systems, RCA, 1957—. Mem. IEEE (sr. mem.), ASME, Calif. Acad. Scis. Writer monographs info. theory, applied math., radar tech., aerospace guidance systems. Inventor improvements of regulators, calculating machines, aviation instruments and indsl. electronics apparatus; holder of U.S. and Brit. patents. Home: 537 San Vicente Blvd Santa Monica CA 90402 Office: 910 Great Western Bldg Berkeley CA 94704

NOLF, DAVID MANSTAN, fin. exec.; b. Hartford, Conn., Nov. 25, 1942; s. Richard Alvin and Erreld Irene (Manstan) N.; B.S. in Chem. Engring., Lafayette Coll., 1964; M.B.A., U. Conn., 1968; m. Linda Joan Anderson, June 20, 1964; 1 dau., Cristina Em. Prodn. engr. Am. Cyanamid, Wallingford, Conn., 1964-66; project engr./adminstr. Gen. Dynamics, Groton, Conn., 1966-71; v.p. fin. and adminstrn. Analysis & Tech., Inc., N. Stonington, Conn., 1971—; pres., dir. A & T Constrn., Inc., N. Stonington, Conn., 1973—; v.p., dir. A & T Tech. Services, Inc., N. Stonington, 1977—; chmn. bd. Analysis & Technology, Inc., 1978—. Mem. Nat. Accountants Assn., Nat. Contract Mgmt. Assn. (chpt. treas. 1977—), Fed. Govt. Accountants Assn., Tau Beta Pi, Beta Gamma Sigma. Episcopalian. Club: Lions. Home: Meadow Rd Pawcatuck CT 06379 Office: Technology Park Route 2 North Stonington CT 06359

NOLL, THOMAS FREDRICK, mfg. co. exec.; b. Ft. Wayne, Ind., June 25, 1951; s. Martin Frank and Viola Thresa (Mestemaker) N.; A.B. in Econs., Ind. U., 1973; m. Deborah Keesling. Sales rep. paper products div. Proctor & Gamble Distbg. Co., Dallas, 1973-76; account mgr. toiletries div. Johnson & Johnson Baby Products Co., Los Angeles, 1976-77, San Diego area sales mgr. disposables div., 1977-78, Los Angeles dist. mgr., 1978-80, Chgo. dist. mgr., 1980—. Mem. Common Cause, Ind. U. Alumni Assn. Democrat. Roman Catholic. Home: 234 S Scoville Ave Oak Park IL 60302 Office: 1300 W 22 St Suite 540 Oak Brook IL 60521

NOLTE, GEORGE WASHINGTON, investment co. exec.; b. nr. Woodbury, N.J., Apr. 2, 1904; s. Harry Kircher and Anna (Porch) N.; B.S., U. Pa., 1924. Accountant, Lybrand, Ross Bros. & Montgomery, Phila., 1924-32; comptroller Atwater Kent Mfg. Co., Phila., Wilmington, Del., 1932-49, v.p., dir., 1949-67, pres., 1972—; v.p. Kent Co., Wilmington, 1972—; treas., dir. Kent Elec. Mfg. Corp., 1949-71. Cons. parks, recreation com. Bd. Chosen Freeholders, Gloucester County, N.J., 1965-66. Pres., trustee Gloucester County Conservancy, Etlon Found.; comdr. USNR, 1942-46. Recipient Distinguished Service award for outstanding community service

Woodbury Jr. C. of C., 1965. C.P.A., Pa. Mem. Am. Inst. C.P.A.'s. Home: 801 Lake Shore Dr Lake Park FL 33403 Office: 3411 Silverside Rd Wilmington DE 19810

NOONAN, EDWIN JOHN, JR., export mgmt. co.; b. Alvin, Tex., Oct. 24, 1948; s. Edwin John and Florine Diane (Wright) N.; B.A. magna cum laude, Met. State Coll., 1975; M.I.M. with honors, Am. Grad. Sch. Internat. Mgmt., 1976; m. Harriet Anne Cathcart; 1 dau., Leslie Caryn. Mktg. rep. Caterpillar Tractor Co., Peoria, Ill., 1976-77; pres. Trade Specialists Internat. Ltd., Phoenix, 1977-78; pres. Keel Internat., Steamboat Village, Colo., 1978—. Pres., Polit. Research and Devel. Project, Denver, 1974-75. Served with USN, 1966-68; Vietnam. Colo. scholar economics, 1974-75. Mem. Ariz. World Trade Assn. (dir. 1978—), Nat. Assn. Underwater Instrs., Aircraft Owners and Pilots Assn., Delta Phi Epsilon (pres. chpt. 1976).

NOONAN, PATRICK FRANCIS, orgn. exec.; b. St. Petersburg, Fla., Dec. 2, 1942; s. Francis Patrick and Henrietta Mary (Donovan) N.; A.B., Gettysburg Coll., 1965; M. City and Regional Planning, Cath. U., 1966-67; M.B.A., Am. U., 1971; m. Nancy Elizabeth Peck, Aug. 15, 1964; children—Karen Elizabeth, Dawn Wiley. Planner, Md. Nat. Capitol Park and Planning Commn., Silver Spring, 1965-68; investment counselor, real estate broker, appraiser, Washington, 1967-69; dir. ops. The Nature Conservancy, Arlington, Va., 1969-73, pres., 1973—. Mem. exec. com. Natural Resources Council Am., 1973-76; trustee Cath. Youth Orgn. Washington, 1975—, Nat. Council on Philanthropy, 1977-79; mem. Appalachian Trail adv. com. U.S. Dept. Interior; bd. visitors Duke U. Sch. Forestry; trustee Gettysburg Coll. Recipient Conservation award Am. Motors Corp., 1974, Horace Marden Albright Scenic medal Am. Scenic and Historic Preservation Soc., 1974. Mem. Am. Soc. Appraisers, Am. Inst. Cert. Planners, Nature Conservancy (life). Roman Catholic. Club: Congressional. Home: 11901 Glen Mill Rd Potomac MD 20854 Office: 1800 N Kent St Arlington VA 22209

NORD, SCOTT RUSSELL, wood products co. exec.; b. Everett, Wash., June 4, 1952; s. Robert William and Bette (Baisden) N.; B.A., U. Wash., 1970-75. With E.A. Nord Co., Everett, Wash., summers, 1969-75, full time, 1975—, exec. v.p., 1977-80, pres., 1980—. Active United Good Neighbors, Everett, 1977. Mem. Everett C. of C. (dir. 1977-78). Presbyterian. Club: Cascade. Address: 3d and Norton St Everett WA 98201

NORDLUND, DONALD ELMER, mfg. exec.; b. Stromsburg, Nebr., Mar. 1, 1922; s. E.C. and Edith O. (Peterson) N.; A.B., Midland Coll., 1943; LL.B., U. Mich., 1948; m. Mary Jane Houston, June 5, 1948; children—Donald Craig, William Chalmers, Sarah, James. Admitted to Ill. bar, 1949; with Stevenson, Conaghan, Velde & Hackbert, Chgo., 1948-55; with A.E. Staley Mfg. Co., Decatur, Ill., 1956—, v.p., dir., mem. exec. com., 1958-65, pres., dir., mem. exec. com., 1965—, also chmn., 1975—; dir. Ill. Bell Telephone Co., Amsted Industries, Inc., Citizens Nat. Bank Decatur, Sentry Ins., Sunstrand Corp. Trustee Millikin U.; mem. Grad. Dirs. Council Decatur Meml. Hosp. Served to 1st lt. AUS, 1943-46, 51-52. Mem. Am., Chgo., Decatur bar assns., Decatur Assn. Commerce, Phi Alpha Delta. Club: Legal (Chgo.). Home: 260 N Oakcrest Ave Decatur IL 62522 Office: AE Staley Mfg Co Decatur IL 62525

NORDQUIST, PAUL JOHN, satellite systems bus. mgr.; b. Providence, May 4, 1933; s. Clarence E. and Mabel M. (Sandstrom) N.; B.S. in Elec. Engring., U. R.I., 1954, M.S. in Elec. Engring., 1956; m. Shirley Ann Clarke, Dec. 28, 1957; children—Betsy, Laurie, Paula, Kristen. Engr., Sylvania, Waltham, Mass., 1958-64, engring. mgr., 1964-69; engring. mgr. GTE Internat. Systems Corp., Waltham, 1969-75, bus. mgr., 1975—; extension instr. U. R.I., 1955-56. Served with Signal Corps, AUS, 1956-58. Decorated Army Commendation Medal. Mem. IEEE, Tau Beta Pi, Sigma Psi. Lutheran. Home: 32 Greenleaf Circle Framingham MA 01701 Office: 140 1st Ave Waltham MA 02154

NOREHAD, ARMAND ORIE, fin. exec.; b. Chgo., June 16, 1934; s. Onnig M. and Christine (Kashian) N.; B.S. in Econs., Purdue U., 1956; M.B.A., Northwestern U., 1957; m. Marilyn Calderini, Aug. 18, 1961; children—David Christopher, Michael Scott, Steven John. With Union Cord Products Co., Chgo., 1958-68, Paine Webber Jackson & Curtis, N.Y.C., 1968-71; with Bear Stearns & Co., Chgo., 1971—, partner, 1975—. Served with U.S. Army, 1958. Mem. Security Traders of Chgo., N.Y. Stock Exchange, Midwest Stock Exchange. Episcopalian. Clubs: Bond of Chgo.; Skokie Country; Mid Day. Office: 230 W Monroe St Chicago IL 60606

NORENE, R(AYMOND) EUGENE, JR., mfrs. rep. firm exec.; b. Chgo., Apr. 10, 1927; s. Raymond Eugene and Nadine N.; student No. Ill. State Tchrs. Coll., 1947-48, Iowa State U., 1948-49; m. Dorothy Ann Saar, Nov. 24, 1951; children—Nancy Ann, Terilee, Raymond Eugene III, Eric Peter, Dorothy Jean. Estimator, James B. Clow & Sons, 1949-51; salesman Boston Gear Co., Chgo., 1951-53, Dodge-Chgo. Co., 1953-56, Morse Chain, Chgo., 1956-57, Milw. dist. mgr., 1957-59; pres., founder R.E. Norene & Assos., Inc., Cedarburg, Wis., 1960—. Mem. Bd. of Rev., City of Cedarburg, 1979; chmn. Ozaukee County Republican Party, 1960-64. Served with U.S. Army, 1945-46. Mem. Power Transmission Rep. Assn. (charter, pres. 1975-76, chmn. bd. 1976-77), Mfrs. Agts. Nat. Assn., Wis. Assn. Mfrs. Agts., Ind. Bus. Assn. Wis., U.S. Power Squadron. Clubs: Milw. Yacht, Milw. Athletic, West Bend Country, Great Lakes Cruising, Masons, Shriners. Office: R E Norene & Assos Inc W63 N648 Washington Ave Cedarburg WI 53012

NORGREN, C. NEIL, mfg. co. exec.; b. Silt, Colo., Aug. 23, 1923; s. Carl A. and Juliet E. (Lien) N.; student U. Colo., 1941-43; m. Carolyn Sutherland, Apr. 12, 1980; children—Jeraldine L., Carol A. Norgren Wilbur, John C., David L. With C.A. Norgren Co., Littleton, Colo., 1938—, officer mgr., 1947-49, gen. mgr., 1949-53, v.p., 1953-55, exec. v.p., 1955-62, pres., 1962—, also dir.; dir. IMI Norgren Shipston Ltd., Unitog Co., United Bank Denver, Pneumatic Norgren S.A., Argentina, Tokyo Automatic Control Co., FENSA (Mex.); chmn. bd. C.W. Morris Co., Livonia, Mich., 1974—. Bd. dirs. Denver Mus. Natural History, Western Stock Show Assn., 1975—, Bus.-Industry Polit. Action Com., 1968—. Served with USAAF, 1943-46. Mem. NAM (dir.), Colo. Assn. Commerce and Industry (dir. 1966—), Inst. Dirs. (London), Beta Theta Pi. Clubs: Cherry Hills Country, Denver Athletic, Flatirons (dir. 1966—), Pinehurst Country, Garden of Gods; Les Ambassadeurs, Curzon House (London). Home: 17 Sedgwick Dr Englewood CO 80110 Office: 5400 S Delaware St Littleton CO 80120

NORMAN, DAVID ARTHUR, market research co. exec.; b. St. Paul, Nov. 15, 1935; s. Robert Albin and Nellie (Williams) N.; B.S. in Mech. Engring., U. Minn., 1963; B.S. in Indsl. Engring. (grad. study award), Stanford U., 1966; m. M. Ruth Landrum, July 19, 1959; children—David, Susan. Lead engr. liaison engring. group Lockheed Missiles and Space Co., Sunnyvale, Calif., 1963-67; project leader, Stanford (Calif.) Research Inst., 1967-69; founder, v.p., dir. Creative Strategies, Inc., Palo Alto, Calif., 1969-71; founder, pres., chief exec. officer, dir. Dataquest, Inc., subs. A.C. Nielsen Co., Cupertino, Calif., 1971—; dir. Ungermann-Bass. Served as aviator USN, 1955-60. Republican. Office: 19055 Pruneridge Cupertino CA 95014

NORMAN, JOHN WILLIAM, oil co. exec.; b. Harrisburg, Ill., Sept. 4, 1910; s. Walter Jacob and Clarissa May (Bush) N.; student pub. schs., Saline County, Ill.; m. Marcella Mary Souheaver, July 2, 1937. Dist. mgr. Martin Oil Co., 1936-54; with Am-Bulk Oil Co. (name changed to Norman Oil Co., 1960), Lisle, Ill., 1949—, pres., 1960—; dir. 1st Ogden Corp., Bank Hinsdale, Bank Lisle, Bank Lockport. Served with USNR, 1943-44. Mem. VFW, Am. Legion. Home: 4333 Main St Lisle IL 60532 Office: 1018 Ogden Ave Lisle IL 60532

NORMAN, RONALD ALLEN, mfg. co. exec.; b. Shelby, Iowa, May 30, 1935; s. Harold A. and Opal M. (Hill) N.; B.S. in Bus. Adminstrn., U. Omaha, 1959; m. Doris Jean Lindsay, Sept. 24, 1955; children—Steven, Daniel. Steel pipe, tubing product mgr. Valmont Industries, Valley, Nebr., 1959-78; pres. Giant Mfg., Inc., Council Bluffs, Iowa, 1978—, also dir. Served with U.S. Army, 1954-56. Mem. Fremont C. of C. (dir. 1973-76), Council Bluffs C. of C., Nat. Truck Equipment Assn., Midwest Employers Council. Republican. Presbyterian. Home: 11330 Camden St Omaha NE 68134 Office: 2802 Ave B Council Bluffs IA 51501

NORMAN, THOMAS EDMUND, real estate exec.; b. Charlotte, N.C., Mar. 20, 1944; s. Theron Jesse and Jane Ellen (Taylor) N.; B.B.A., Wake Forest U., 1966; M.B.A., N.Y. U., 1970; m. Kathryn Heath, July 3, 1971; children—Anna Taylor, Thomas Heath. Mgmt. trainee Chem. Bank, N.Y.C., 1969-71; project mgr. McDevitt & Street Co., Charlotte, 1971-72; pres. LAT Purser & Assos., Charlotte, 1972—. Founder, pres., chmn. bd. Charlotte Summer Pops, 1972-75; bd. dirs., treas. Open House Counseling Service, 1974-77; bd. dirs., chmn. Dept. Social Services of Mecklenburg Country, 1979—; bd. dirs., treas. Travelers Aid Soc., 1974-79. Served to 2d lt. AUS, 1965. Mem. Mortgage Bankers Assn. Am., N.C. Income Property Assn. (dir. 1978-79), Mortgage Bankers Assn. of Carolinas, Charlotte Bd. Realtors, Nat. Assn. Realtors, N.C. Assn. Realtors. Democrat. Baptist. Clubs: Charlotte City; Charlotte Country. Home: 3821 Sedgewood Circle Charlotte NC 28211 Office: PO Box 220184 Charlotte NC 28222

NORMAN, WALLACE, pipe co. exec.; b. Houlka, Miss., Feb. 5, 1926; s. Leland Fleming and Alma Lucile (Brown) N.; student East Central Jr. Coll. 1942, U. Miss., 1946, Millsaps Coll., 1946; B.S., Oklahoma City U., 1948; m. Maurene Collums, Dec. 26, 1950; children—Wallace, Karen Jean, Emily June, Lauren Beth, John Crocker. Owner, operator Wallace Norman Ins. Agy., Houston, Miss., 1949—; pres. Norman Oil Co., Houston, 1956—, Nat. Leasing Co., Houston, 1969—, U.S. Plastics, Inc., Houston, 1969—, Calhoun Nat. Co., 1974—, Norman Trucking Co., 1975—. Chmn. Running Bear dist. Boy Scouts Am., 1971-73. Served with USNR, World War II. Mem. Miss. Assn. Ins. Agts., Miss. Mfrs. Assn., Am. Waterworks Assn., DAV, VFW, Am. Legion. Methodist. Club: Exchange. Address: PO Box 208 Houston MS 38851

NORMAN, WILLIAM STANLEY, rail transp. co. exec.; b. Roper, N.C., Apr. 27, 1938; s. James Colbitt and Josephine Cleo (Woods) N.; B.S., W.Va. Wesleyan U., 1960; M.A., Am. U., 1967; postgrad. Stanford, 1976; m. Elizabeth Patricia Patterson, May 30, 1969; children—Lisa Renee, William Stanley. Math. tchr. Norfolk (Va.) Pub. Schs., 1961; commd. ensign U.S. Navy, 1962, advanced through grades to lt. comdr., 1973; resigned, 1973; exec. dir. corporate responsibility Cummins Engine Co., Columbus, Ind., 1973-76, exec. mktg. dir., 1976-77, exec. dir. distbn. and mktg., 1977-78, v.p. Eastern div., 1978-79; v.p. mktg. Nat. Railroad Passenger Corp. (AMTRAK), Washington, 1979—; dir. Chem. Investors, Inc., Indpls., 1976-79. Chmn. Columbus Human Rights Commn., 1974-78; chmn. Community Devel. Task Force Columbus, 1975-77; bd. dirs. Quinco Endowment Found., 1974-78; chmn. bd. dirs. Laws Found., 1974-78; bd. advs. African Student Aid Fund, 1978—. Served to comdr. USNR. Decorated Legion of Merit, Air medal (4), Navy Commendation medal (2). Mem. Am. Mgmt. Assn., Council on Fgn. Relations. Club: Harrison Lake Country. Home: 1308 Timberly Ln McLean VA 22102 Office: Nat RR Passenger Corp (AMTRAK) 400 N Capitol NW Washington DC 20001

NORRIS, CHARLES HEAD, JR., mfg. exec.; b. Boston, Sept. 14, 1940; s. Charles Head and Martha Marie N.; B.A., U. Pa., 1963, J.D., 1968; M.A., U. Wash., 1965; m. Diana D. Strawbridge, July 31, 1974; 1 dau., Margaret Dorrance. Admitted to Pa. bar; mem. firm Morgan, Lewis & Bockius, Phila., 1968-77; pres., chief exec. Artemis Corp., 1978-79; chmn. bd., chief exec., 1979—; chmn. exec. com., vice chmn. bd. Remington Rand Corp., 1979—; dir. Wee Donuts, Inc., Bite-Size Meals, Inc. Trustee, Margaret Dorrance Strawbridge Found.; bd. dirs. Elesabeth Ingalls Gillet Found.; mem. Pa. Commn. Crime and Delinquency. Served with USAF, until 1959. Mem. Am. Bar Assn., Pa. Bar Assn., Am. Econ. Assn. Clubs: Phila., Knickerbocker. Office: 103 College Rd E Princeton NJ 08540

NORRIS, DAVID BALLARD, mgmt. cons. co. exec.; b. Berkeley, Calif., Dec. 15, 1922; s. Homer Alvaro and Alice Elenore (Freuler) N.; student U. Calif., Berkeley, 1940-41, U. Cin., 1946-48, U. Tenn., 1952-53, U. Calif., Los Angeles, 1954-55; B.S. in Indsl. Mgmt., Calif. State Coll., 1960; m. Bonnie Sue McNatt, Nov. 27, 1970; children by previous marriage—Teresa White Norris Fahey, Anita Alice Norris Sell, Carol Estelle Norris Luellen, Steven Varo; stepchildren—Vicki Sue Diebel Sherrard, Cathi Diebel, Scott A. Wolff. Various mgmt. positions, 1947-59; with Cresap, McCormick & Paget Co., Los Angeles, 1959-64; pres. Norris & Gottfried Inc., Los Angeles, 1964-70; mgr. A.T. Kearney, Inc., Los Angeles, 1971-72; pres. Norris Cons., Inc., Calabasas, Calif., 1973—; arbitrator Am. Arbitration Assn., 1968—. Served with U.S. Army, 1943-46. Mem. Inst. Mgmt. Consultants, Assn. Mgmt. Consultants, Am. Prodn. and Inventory Control Soc. (nat. adv. planning council, editorial bd.). Republican. Home: 5900 Clear Valley Rd Hidden Hills CA 91302 Office: PO Box 16 Calabasas CA 91302

NORRIS, FRANK WILLIAM, banker; b. Milw., Sept. 19, 1920; s. Patrick John and Mary Elizabeth (McGrath) N.; B.S.B.A., Marquette U., 1943, M.A. in Econs., 1952; m. Margaret I. Beversdorf, Sept. 12, 1953; children—Patrick, Michael, Daniel, Mary. Pres., Bank of Commerce, Milw., 1943—, Capital Investments Inc., 1959—, Time Holdings Inc., 1970-78; dir. Ken Cook Co., Waukee Engring. Co., G P & F Co., Catholic Family Life Ins. Co., (all Milw.). Served with USAAF, 1943-46. Decorated Air medal. Office: Bank of Commerce PO Box 522 Milwaukee WI 53201

NORRIS, JAMES PATRICK, trade assn. exec.; b. Chgo., Feb. 4, 1939; s. William John and Nellie (Scanlon) N.; B.Ed., Chgo. State Coll., 1960; student DePaul U., 1960-63; m. Barbara Ann Schouten, Aug. 12, 1961; children—David William, Thomas James, Leah Marie. Tchr. English, Lindblom Tech. High Sch., Chgo., 1960-64, chmn. English dept., 1961-64; dictionary editor Scott Foresman & Co., Glenview, Ill., 1964-69; exec. v.p. Air Conditioning Contractors Am., Washington, 1969—. Campaign mgr. John Wright for Congress, Tyler, Tex., 1980. Mem. Am. Subcontractors Assn. (chmn. nat. adv. council), Am. Soc. Assn. Execs., Washington Soc. Assn. Execs. Office: 1228 17th St NW Washington DC 20036

NORRIS, JAMES WARREN, accountant; b. Cushing, Okla., Dec. 13, 1928; s. Marion Ware and Esther Gladys (Schneider) N.; B.A. in Bus., U. Colo., 1949; M.B.A., U. Mich., 1951; m. Joal Lamoutte Madden, Apr. 10, 1928; children—Anne Elizabeth, Susan Madden, Paul Francis, Mary Joal. With Arthur Andersen & Co., 1954—, partner, 1965—, head worldwide retail industry practice, 1967-70, mng. partner Detroit office, 1969-75, dir., 1974—, mng. dir. industry competence programs, 1975-78, dep. vice chmn. profl. edn. div., 1978-80, head worldwide wholesale industry practice, Chgo., 1980—. Mem. Mich. Econ. Expansion Council, 1973-75; bd. dirs. Econ. Club Detroit, 1973-75, United Found. Detroit, 1973-75, Hutzel Hosp., Detroit, 1971-75, The Lambs, Inc., 1977—. Served with Supply Corps, USNR, 1951-54. Recipient Gold medal in C.P.A. exam., State of Okla., 1950. Mem. Ill. Soc. C.P.A.'s, Am. Inst. C.P.A.'s, Am. Acctg. Assn. Republican. Roman Catholic. Clubs: Union League, Met. (Chgo.); Standard (Detroit). Office: 69 W Washington St Chicago IL 60602

NORRIS, JANE PARSONS, banker; b. Lewiston, Maine, July 30, 1924; d. George Francis and Luella Louise Ernestine (Small) Parsons; B.A. in Econs., Bates Coll., Lewiston, 1946; m. Leon Manfred Norris, July 22, 1947; 1 dau., Linda Ann. Successively teller, asst. treas., corporator, trustee, treas., exec. v.p. and chief exec. officer Mechanics Savs. Bank, Auburn, Maine, 1950—; instr. Am. Inst. Banking; dir. Patrons Oxford Ins. Co. Bd. trustees Central Maine Med. Center; bd. trustees, exec. com. Bates Coll.; bd. dirs. Lewiston and Auburn YWCA; bd. trustees Maine League Hist. Socs. and Museums, Inc.; treas. Androscoggin Hist. Soc.; active Maine Hist. Soc. Mem. Nat. Assn. Bank Women, Maine Assn. Savs. Bank Women, Nat. Assn. Mut. Savs. Banks, Savs. Banks Assn. Maine. Republican. Mem. United Ch. of Christ. Author: 100 Years of Growth—A History of the Mechanics Savings Bank, 1975. Home: 93 Field Ave Auburn ME 04210 Office: 100 Minot Ave Auburn ME 04210

NORRIS, JOHN STEVEN, constrn. co. exec.; b. Chgo., Apr. 25, 1943; s. Norris Dale and Olive (Grissinger) N.; B.A., U. Ariz., 1967; B.F.T., Am. Grad. Sch. Internat. Mgmt., 1968; m. Susan Jean Armstrong, May 3, 1975; children—Lindsey Jean, Whitney Ann. Inspection officer Citicorp., Brazil, Colombia, Mexico, 1968-72, asst. cashier, N.Y.C., 1972-74; pres., gen. mgr. Phoenix Athletic Club, 1974-76; bus. mgr. Phoenix Pub. Inc., 1976-77; project mgr. Environ. Constrn., Phoenix, 1977-80; pres. AGN Devel. Corp., gen. contracting and real estate devel., Phoenix, 1980—. Mem. Phi Delta Theta. Republican. Home: 726 W Maryland Ave Phoenix AZ 85013 Office: PO Box 9831 Phoenix AZ 85068

NORRIS, NORMA ALYCE, mktg. co. exec.; b. Dallas, Mar. 8, 1921; d. Carl Augustus and Nellie Blaine (Woodson) N.; student public schs., Houston; theology student. Decorator-cons. Pinellas Lumber Co., St. Petersburg, Fla., 1943-45; exec. sec. Fla. chpt. Nat. Assn. Home Builders, 1945-49; founder, pres. Norcliffe Co., mfrs. ladies belts and accessories, Houston, 1949-56, Colonel Norcliffe Corp., mfr. dress lables and name tapes, Houston, 1952-56; asst. personnel dir. Carnation Co., Houston, 1956-58; fashion coordinator, stylist Abbott Mills, also Vogue Pattern Co., 1958-63; interior designer, 1963-64; founder, pres. Anything About Art, Inc., 1964-74; dir. mktg. Monel, Inc., Houston, 1979-80; broker Tex. Real Estate, 1980—; owner Norma Norris & Assos., Stafford, Tex., 1979—; exec. analyst, 1981—. Charter judge sch. art com. Houston Livestock Show and Rodeo Assn., 1969—; past v.p. Houston Conservative Arts Assn., Clear Creek Art League.; co-founder Clear Creek Community Playhouse, 1965. Mem. Houston Fin. Council Women (charter), Houston Bd. Realtors, Am. Soc. Appraisers (asso.), Houston C. of C. (past vice chmn. Oct. arts event), Clear Creek C. of C., Mensa. Republican. Methodist. Office: 11678 Kirkwood St Suite 11 Stafford TX 77477

NORRIS, RONALD BARRY, mfg. co. exec.; b. N.Y.C., Mar. 16, 1949; s. Gerald B. and Dorothy (Rosen) N.; B.A., Haverford Coll., 1971; M.B.A. (E.O. Cocke-TWA fellow), U. Pa., 1973; m. Fredi L. Mellitz, May 28, 1972; 1 son, Alex. Sr. acct. Arthur Young & Co., N.Y.C., 1973-76; asst. mgr. fin. reporting Goldman Sachs & Co., N.Y.C., 1976-77; dir. operations Hukapoo Sportswear, Inc., N.Y.C., 1977-79; v.p. Market Exchange div. Bobbie Brooks, Inc., N.Y.C., 1979—; asst. prof. acctg. Hofstra U., 1977—. Mem. Am. Inst. C.P.A.'s, N.Y. Soc. C.P.A.'s. Home: 949 Wenwood Dr North Bellmore NY 11710 Office: 55 W 39th St New York NY 10018

NORRIS, WILLIAM C., corp. exec.; b. Inavale, Nebr., July 14, 1911; s. William H. and Mildred A. (McCall) N.; B.S., U. Nebr., 1932; m. Jane Malley, Sept. 15, 1943; children—W. Charles, George, Daniel, Brian, Constance, Roger, Mary N., David. Sales engr. Westinghouse Electric Mfg. Co., Chgo., 1935-41; v.p., gen. mgr. Engring. Research Assos., 1946-55; v.p., gen. mgr. Univac div. Sperry Rand Corp., 1955-57; pres., chief exec. officer Control Data Corp., 1957—, now also chmn. bd.; dir. N.W. Bank Corp., N.W. Growth Fund, Tronchemics, Inc.; mem. adv. com. White House Conf. on Balanced Nat. Growth and Econ. Devel., 1978—. Trustee Hill Reference Library. Served to comdr. USNR, 1941-46. Office: 8100 34th Ave S Minneapolis MN 55415*

NORTH, MICHAEL RAY, real estate broker; b. Corpus Christi, Mar. 12, 1949; s. Jack Lane and Betty Lou (Penberton) N.; student Tex. A&M U., 1967-70; m. Delilah Sue Womack, Nov. 20, 1978; children—Mitzi Jean, Eric Ryan Jones, Justin Ray. Engaged in real estate sales and land devel., 1970—; broker, mgr. Jack North & Assos., Alpine Tex., 1974—; gen. mgr. N & N Land and Cattle Co., Alpine, 1976—; mgr. Terlingua Ranch; cons., appraiser, 1976—. Trustee, Terlingua Sch. Dist. Mem. Nat. Assn. Realtors, Tex. Assn. Realtors. Home: Terlingua Route Box 221 Alpine TX 79830 Office: Terlingua Route Box 200 Alpine TX 79830

NORTH, PHIL RECORD, bus. exec.; b. Fort Worth, July 6, 1918; s. James and Lottie N.; B.A., U. Notre Dame, 1939; m. Janis Harris, July 28, 1944; children—Phillip Kevin, Kerry Lawrence, Mairin Kathleen, Deirdre Aine. With Ft. Worth Star-Telegram, 1937-62, exec. editor, 1956-62; asst. gen. mgr., 1959-62; v.p. Carter Publs., Inc., Ft. Worth, 1949-62; with Tandy Corp., Ft. Worth, 1966—, chief exec. officer, pres., 1978-80, chmn. bd., 1978—; dir. First City Nat. Bank of Ft. Worth. Mem. The Rockefeller U., Ft. Worth Stock Show and Rodeo, MacArthur Meml. Found. Served to maj. U.S. Army, 1940-46; press aide to Gen. Douglas MacArthur. Decorated Bronze Star; knight of Malta; knight comdr. with star Order of Holy Sepulchre. Roman Catholic. Clubs: Ft. Worth, River Crest, Shady Oaks, Little Bay, Live Oak. Home: 6141 Locke St Forth Worth TX 76116 Office: 1900 One Tandy Center Fort Worth TX 76102

NORTH, WILLIAM STANLEY, mfg. co. exec.; b. Chgo., May 1, 1911; s. Francis Stanley and Julia (Morgan) N.; B.M.E., Harvard, 1934, postgrad., 1935; m. Sarah Jackson, 1934; children—Sarah Randolph, Elizabeth Holmes; m. 2d, Patricia Cathcart Armstrong, Mar. 20, 1958 (dec. Nov. 1978); 1 stepson, James Cathcart Armstrong; m. 3d, Margot Reid Donald, Dec. 11, 1979; 1 stepson, Alanson Donald. With Union Spl. Corp., Chgo., 1935—, engr. and salesman, personnel dir., 1941-44, v.p., 1944-47, asst. gen. mgr., 1947-52, pres., gen. mgr., 1952-74, chmn., chief exec. officer, 1974-76, chmn., 1976—; dir. Portec Inc.; chmn. compensation com. Signode Corp. Bd. dirs. exec. fin. com., past chmn. Lawson YMCA, Chgo.; bd.

dirs., v.p., past pres. Lyric Opera Chgo.; trustee, past pres. Allendale Sch. Boys; bd. dirs., v.p., treas. Lake Forest Open Lands Assn.; governing mem. Chgo. Symphony Orch.; mem. U.S. Srs. Golf Assn. Mem. Ill. Mfg. Assn. (past pres.), Midwest Indsl. Mgmt. Assn. (past pres.). Republican. Episcopalian (past sr. Warden). Clubs: Univ., Harvard, Campfire, Casino (past gov.), Commonwealth (past pres.), comml. (Chgo.); Onwentsia (past gov.), Old Elm (past gov.), Winter (past pres.) (Lake Forest, Ill.); Tin Whistles (Pinehurst, N.C.); Pine Valley (N.J.) Golf; Gulf Stream Bath and Tennis, Gov. Gulf Stream Golf (bd. govs.), Delray Beach Yacht (Delray Beach, Fla.); Royal and Ancient Golf of St. Andrews (Fife, Scotland). Home: 1490 N Green Bay Rd Lake Forest IL 60045 also 3224 N Ocean Blvd Delray Beach FL 33444 Office: 400 N Franklin St Chicago IL 60610

NORTHROP, JOY ANNE, sch. adminstr.; b. Pikeville, Ky., May 14, 1950; d. LeRoy M. and Linda Joyce (Stepp) N.; B.S., Trenton State Coll., 1972; M.A., Montclair State Coll., 1979. Jr. acct. Silverman-Brown Assos., West End, N.J., 1972-73; dept. chmn., programmer, data processing supr., tchr. Keyport (N.J.) public schs., 1973-78; sch. bus. adminstr., sec. bd. Galloway Twp. public schs., Pomono, N.J., 1978-79; sch. bus. adminstr. Ramapo Indian Hills Regional High Sch., Franklin Lakes, N.J., 1979—; tchr. Bergen Community Coll., Paramus, N.J., 1980—. Mem. Assn. Sch. Bus. Ofcls., N.J. Assn. Sch. Bus. Ofcls., Bergen County Assn. Public Sch. Bus. Ofcls., Nat. Council Adminstrv. Women in Edn. Republican. Presbyterian. Clubs: Wing, Bonnet Sport Car. Home: 1 River Rd Apt 2-F Nutley NJ 07110 Office: George St Franklin Lakes NJ 07417

NORTHROP, STUART JOHNSTON, bicycle mfg. co. exec.; b. New Haven, Oct. 22, 1925; s. Filmer Stuart and Christine (Johnston) N.; B.A., Yale U., 1948; m. Cynthia Stafford Daniell, Feb. 23, 1946; children—Christine Daniell, Richard Rockwell Stafford. Vice-pres. mfg. Am. Meter Co., Phila., 1961-69; pres., dir. The Buffalo Meter Co., Phila., 1968-69; founder, v.p., gen. mgr. Water Resources div. Singer Co., Phila., 1969-72; pres. The Huffy Corp., Dayton, Ohio, 1972-76, chief exec. officer, 1976—, chmn. bd., 1979—; dir. Danis Industries, Winters Nat. Bank, Duriron Corp. (all Dayton). Bd. dirs. Wynnewood Civic Assn., 1971-72, Dayton Art Inst., Center City Sch., Dayton Mus. Natural History; state ambassador Gov. Scranton's campaign for Pres., 1964; co-chmn. George Bush Fin. Com., Dayton. Served with USAAF, 1944-45. Named Chief Exec. Officer of Year, Leisure Industry, Forbes mag., 1980. Mem. Delaware Valley Investors, Interlocutors, Delta Kappa Epsilon, KOA Soc., Elihu. Clubs: Moraine Country, Dayton Racquet. Home: 3732 Blossom Heath Dayton OH 45419 Office: Byers Rd Dayton OH 45401

NORTHUP, WILLIAM CARLTON, accountant; b. Columbia, Mo., Dec. 1, 1930; s. Lansford Lionel and Elsie Rebecca (Eaton) N.; B.S. in Statistics, U. Mo., 1953, M.B.A., 1974; m. Sharon Joan Carlson, June 27, 1970; children—Richard Carlton, Karen Frances. Research asso. Mo. Crippled Children's Service, Columbia, 1968-69, asst. supt. research and records, 1969-70, supt., 1970-76; broker London Commodity House, Inc., Chgo., 1976-77; chief accountant Nat. Congress PTA, Chgo., 1977-78; mgmt. analyst fin. systems for health and hosps. Cook County Governing Commn., Chgo., 1978-79; acct. V, Cook County Hosp., 1979—; controller, dir. pub. health statistics, coordinator automatic data processing, supt. ins. Mo. Crippled Children's Service; asst. prodn. mgr., chief estimator, account exec. Am. Press; spl. advisor to Gov. Mo. on printing and pub., 1965. Mem. Columbia Fin. Study Commn., 1974, steering com. Columbia Town Meeting, 1976; bd. dirs. Camp Wannanoya, 1976; mem. steering com. Teen Auto Club, 1972; vol. probation officer Boone County Juvenile Office, 1971-72. Mem. Am. Mgmt. Assn., Am. Statis. Assn., Mo. Pub. Health Assn., Assn. M.B.A. Execs., Hosp. Fin. Mgmt. Assn., Mensa, Delta Sigma Pi. Republican. Baptist. Club: Optimist. Home: 24 Williamsburg Terr Evanston IL 60203 Office: 1835 W Harrison St Chicago IL 60612

NORTON, ALAN PAUL, comml. devel. corp. exec.; b. Calgary, Alta., Can., Feb. 22, 1943; s. Chester P. and Betty (Luxford) N.; cert. in bus. adminstrn. So. Alta. Inst., Tech., 1971; m. Lynda Diane Dunbar, June 30, 1973; 1 dau., Alana Lea. Collection supr. Calgary Gen. Credit Ltd., 1964-66; area fin. mgr. Massey-Ferguson Industries Ltd., Calgary, 1966-67; retail credit analyst Gulf Oil Canada Ltd., Calgary, 1968-70; crew tng. officer Universal Ambulance Service Ltd., Calgary, 1970; fin. corr. Allis-Chalmers Credit Corp., Calgary, 1970-71; instructional adminstr. St. John Ambulance, Calgary, 1972-73; div. credit mgr. Neonex Shelter Ltd., Calgary, 1973-77; credit mgr. Westburne divs. Engring. and Plumbing Supplies Ltd., Calgary, 1978-79, Alta. Electric Supply Ltd., 1978-79; gen. mgr. The Marsh Group of Cos., Calgary, 1979—; western regional credit mgr. Gough Electric Ltd., Calgary, 1979-80, v.p. fin. Eastlake Devel. Corp. Ltd., 1980—; chmn. area adv. com. Creditel of Canada Ltd., 1978—. Decorated Order of St. John; recipient Provincial Shield, Alta. Provincial Council of St. John Ambulance, 1971, Priory Vote of Thanks of St. John Ambulance, Gov. Gen. Canada, 1974. Notary public, Calgary, 1976—. Mem. Coalition for Life, Alliance for Life, Calgary Pro-Life Assn., Right to Life. Mormon. Home: 59 Huntford Rd NE Calgary AB T2K 3Y8 Canada

NORTON, DEWEY, mfg. co. exec.; b. Jackson, Miss., May 25, 1944; s. Dewey Mark and Ruth Brame (Smith) N.; B.A., U. Pa., 1967, M.A., 1971, M.B.A., 1971; m. Diane Cook, Sept. 28, 1968; children—Weston Dewey, Drew Hopkins. Fin. analyst, product devel. group Ford Motor Co., Dearborn, Mich., 1972-75; mgr. corp. analysis Bendix Corp., Southfield, Mich., 1976-78; mgr. acctg. and fin. analysis GKN Automotive Components Inc. subs. Guest, Keen & Nettlefolds Ltd., Southfield, 1978—. Vestryman, treas. Cathedral Ch. St. Paul, 1974—; co-chmn. Can.-Am. Friendship Com., 1974-75. Nat. Merit scholar; fellow Center for Advanced Study in Behavioral Scis., Palo Alto; fellow U. Pa. Mem. Inst. Mgmt. Acctg., Nat. Assn. Accts., Newcomen Soc., Econ. Club Detroit. Clubs: Country of Detroit, U. Pa. Alumni of Mich. (treas.), Founders Soc. Home: 1461 Oxford Rd Grosse Pointe Woods MI 48236 Office: 23800 Northwestern Hwy Southfield MI 48075

NORTON, FRANK TRACY, tennis co. exec.; b. San Francisco, Jan. 20, 1936; s. Tracy Murray and Loretta Gladys (Buchel) N.; student Internat. Corr. Schs., Alexander Hamilton Inst., LaSalle Extension U., Nat. Radio Inst.; m. Loretta Yvonne Talley, June 25, 1955; children—Lynn Dora, Lori Ann, Lisa Marie. Sr. design engr., temp. design unit supr. Pacific Gas & Electric Co., San Francisco, 1954—; pres., chmn. bd. Tennis Outings Inc., San Francisco, 1976—; exec. dir. Club Tennis, 1978—; tennis pro Meadowmont Village, Arnold, Calif., 1973—, Sequoia Woods Country Club, Arnold, 1977. Bd. dirs. indsl. div. San Francisco Recreation and Park Dept., 1972-78, v.p., 1977-78. Certified Profl. Tennis Registry. Mem. Assn. Tennis Industry, Profl. Tennis Registry, Profl. Stringers Assn., U.S. Racquet Stringers Assn., U.S. Profl. Tennis Assn. Club: Bayside Racquet. Address: 126 Madrone Ave San Francisco CA 94127

NORTON, H. GAITHER, food mktg. corp. exec.; b. Bklyn., Aug. 16, 1918; s. Dwight Fanning and Jessie (Gaither) N.; student Middlebury Coll., 1936-37, N.Y. U., 1939-40, Lafayette Coll., 1938-39, Stevens Inst. Tech., 1941; A.B. in Econs. with honors, U. Calif., Los Angeles, 1952; m. Ann Lou Allen, Mar. 15, 1941; children—Priscilla Ann, Lou Elaine; m. 2d. Laura Louise Smith, July 26, 1950; children—Craig Gaither, Laura Marjorie, Scott Clark, Ellen Louise. With Continental Can Co., 1937-41, sales trainee, 1939-41; employment interviewer, Grumman Aircraft Corp., 1941-43; USMC personnel classification and rehab. interviewer, counsellor, 1943-46; F.W.Boltz Corp., Los Angeles, 1947-48, nat. sales mgr., 1948-50; asst. div. mgr. Northeast div. Welch's Grape Juice Co., N.Y.C., 1952-54; pres. H.G. Norton Co., Inc., New Milford, Conn., 1954—. Dir., first v.p. Weantinoge Heritage Land Trust, Inc., New Milford, 1966-76, hon. dir., 1976—; zoning bd. appeals, New Milford, 1970; planning commn. to set up Commn. on Aging, New Milford, 1972; sec., dir. Sunny Valley Found., 1978-79. Served with USMC, 1943-46. Mem. Nat. Assn. Specialty Food Trade (pres., 1962-63), Nat. Assn. Splty. Food and Confection Brokers (pres., 1972-74), Nat. Food Distbrs. Assn. (dir. mfrs. council), Phi Beta Kappa, Pi Gamma Mu. Republican. Home: Sprucegate Farm W Meetinghouse Rd New Milford CT 06776 Office: PO Drawer 269 New Milford CT 06776

NORTON, JOHN WILLIAM, mgmt. cons.; b. Queens County, N.Y., June 12, 1952; s. Michael Vincent and Dorothy Winifred (Ragl) N.; student Nassau Coll., 1973; B.S. in Bus. Adminstrn., Stanford U.; m. Louise Rita Elefante. Asst. mgr. sales and mktg. Sun Life Assn. Co. of Can., Phila. and Cherry Hills, N.J., 1976-77; mgr. ops. circulation dist. Phila. Inquirer, 1977-78; pres., chief exec. officer Internat. Exec. Reports, Marlton, N.J., 1978—; mgmt. Radio Shack div. Tandy Corp., 1980—; mgmt. cons. Recipient Outstanding Sales and Mktg. award Sun Life Co., 1977. Asso. mem. Smithsonian Instn.; mem. Ind. Consultants Am., Internat. Mgmt. Council, Am. Mgmt. Assn. Democrat. Roman Catholic. Clubs: Rotary, K.C. Contbr. articles to profl. jours. Inventor electric power transfer device. Home: Allison Suite 141 North Maple Ave Marlton NJ 08053

NORTON, MAHLON ROMEO, acct.; b. Newport, N.H., Nov. 10, 1942; s. Mahlon William and Bessie Albertina (Lamson) N.; student Concord Coll., Manchester, N.H., 1972-73, Federated Tax Service, Chgo., 1978; diploma N.A. Corr. Sch. of Acctg., 1980; m. Barbara Jane Hoyt, Aug. 17, 1974 (dec. Apr. 1980). Fed. income tax preparer H & R Block, Manchester, 1978—; prin. Mahlon Norton Tax and Acctg. Service, Manchester, N.H., 1976. Served with USAF, 1960. Mem. N. Am. Students Assn. Republican. Home and Office: 3202 Brown Ave Manchester NH 03103

NORTONEN, GEORGE ROBERT, mfg. co. exec.; b. Chelsea, Mass., Feb. 10, 1944; s. George A. and Beverly A. N.; A.A., Concordia Jr. Coll., Bronxville, N.Y., 1963; B.S. in Bus. Adminstrn., U. New Haven, 1972; postgrad. mgmt. devel. program The Hartford Grad. Center, 1980; m. Janet M. Douglas, June 16, 1968; 1 dau., Kateri. Sales trainee Corbin Hardware div. Emhart Industries, Berlin, Conn., 1972; sales rep., 1972-75, sales promotion mgr., 1976-77, gen. sales mgr., 1978—. Instr. Jr. Achievement, New Britian, Conn., 1977. Served with USAF, 1966-70. Mem. Door and Hardware Inst., Alpha Chi, Pi Sigma Epsilon. Republican. Methodist. Home: 268 Ridgewood Dr Rocky Hill CT 06067 Office: 225 Episcopal Rd Berlin CT 06037

NORWOOD, SAMUEL WILKINS, III, diversified co. exec.; b. Chgo., Apr. 6, 1941; s. Samuel Wilkins and Miriam Lois (Cary) N.; student Vanderbilt U., 1959-61; B.A. in History and Econs., Tulane U., 1963; M.B.A. in Fin., U. Chgo., 1965; m. Julianne Parker Jones, June 15, 1962; children—Samuel Parker, Elizabeth Cary. Supr. appropriations and spl. studies div. Allied Chem. Corp., 1965-67; mgr. fin. analysis div. I.T.T., 1967-69; successively dir. fin. planning, group controller, asst. corp. controller, dir. planning, v.p. planning, v.p. corp. devel. Fuqua Industries, Inc., Atlanta, 1969—. Mem. Planning Execs. Inst., Assn. Corp. Growth (dir. Atlanta chpt., past chpt. pres.), So. Center Internat. Studies, Atlanta Econs. Club. Home: 330 Thornwood Dr Atlanta GA 30328 Office: 2 Peachtree St Atlanta GA 30383

NOSSAN, STEVEN, advt. exec.; b. N.Y.C., Dec. 20, 1952; s. Robert J. and Mary (Martin) N.; student St. Paul's Coll., Cheltenham, Eng.; B.A., State U Coll., Potsdam, 1974. Creative dir. Solo, Inc., N.Y.C., 1976-78, fin. cons., 1978—, art dir. Kemco Advt. Co., N.Y.C., 1976-79; asso. art dir. Sassy Mag., N.Y.C., 1978-79; artist Cavalieri-Kleier-Pearlman Advt. Agy., N.Y.C., 1979; art dir. Wolf Whitehill & Thomas Advt. Co., N.Y.C., 1979—. Mem. Art Dirs Club N.Y., Objectivist Forum.

NOTHSTEIN, ERROL RAY, automobile dealer; b. Trexlertown, Pa., Sept. 30, 1941; s. Ray Wallace and Mayola Ellen (Walbert) N.; ed. bus. sch.; m. Beverly Ann Hartman, Jan. 20, 1962; children—Errol Ray, Pamela K. Used car dealer, mgr. Nothstein Bros. Inc., Trexlertown, 1959-61; v.p., gen. mgr. Nothstein Ford Inc., Kutztown, Pa., 1961-67, pres., 1967—; dir. Kutztown Nat. Bank. Mem. Nat. Automobile Dealers Assn., Pa. Auto Assn., Kutztown Fair Assn. (dir., exec. com. 1969-74). Republican. Lutheran. Clubs: Masons, Shriners, Fraternal Order Police. Home: 3018 Pennsylvania St Allentown PA 18104 Office: 531 E Main St Kutztown PA 19530

NOTOWIDIGDO, MUSINGGIH HARTOKO, mfg. co. exec.; b. Indonesia, Dec. 9, 1938; s. Moekarto and Martaniah (Brodjonegoro) N.; B.M.E., George Washington U., 1961; M.Sc., N.Y. U., 1966, postgrad., 1970; m. Sihar P. Tambunan, Oct. 1, 1966 (dec. Nov. 1976); m. 2d, Joanne S. Gutter, June 3, 1979. Cons., Dollar Blitz & Assos., Washington, 1962-64; ops. research analyst Am. Can Co., N.Y.C., 1966-69; prin. analyst Borden Inc., Columbus, Ohio, 1969-70, mgr. ops. research, 1970-71, mgr. ops. analysis and research, 1972-74, asst. gen. controller, officer, 1974-77, corp. dir. info. systems/econ. analysis, officer, 1977—; adj. lectr. Grad. Sch. Adminstrn. Capital U. Mem. Fin Execs. Inst. (chmn. profl. devel., mem. bd. Columbus), Ops. Research Soc., Inst. Mgmt. Sci., Am. Mgmt. Assn., Nat. Assn. Bus. Economists, Long Range Planning Soc., Am. Statis. Assn., Soc. Mgmt. Info. Systems. Republican. Club: Racquet. Home: 4532 Carriage Hill Ln Upper Arlington OH 43220 Office: 180 E Broad St Columbus OH 43215

NOTTBERG, HENRY, mech. engring. exec.; b. Kansas City, Mo., Nov. 14, 1914; s. Henry and Olga A. (Bockshammer) N.; A.S. in Engring., Kansas City (Mo.) Jr. Coll., 1933; B.S. in Mech. Engring., U. Kans., 1937; m. Barbara R. Bodwell, Oct. 19, 1946; children—Henry, Don R., Martha R. Engr., estimator U.S. Engring. Co., Kansas City, Mo., 1937-41, project mgr., Parsons, Kans., 1941-42, Milw., 1942-43, successively sec., v.p., pres., Kansas City, 1946-78, chmn. bd., 1979—; dir. Mercantile Bank Kansas City (Mo.). Trustee, Research Med. Center, Kansas City, Mo.; councilman City of Mission Hills (Kans.), 1963-67, mayor, 1967-69. Served with USN, 1943-46. Mem. ASME, ASHRAE, Mech. Contractors Assn. Am. (nat. pres. 1968-69). Clubs: Kansas City, Mission Hills Country, Engrs. Home: 2825 Tomahawk Circle Shawnee Mission KS 66208 Office: 3433 Roanoke Rd Kansas City MO 64111

NOVACK, EVE, advt. agy. exec.; b. Antwerp, Belgium, Apr. 21, 1939; came to U.S., 1946, naturalized, 1954; d. Frederick and Hanny (Wassermann) N.; A.A.S., Packer Coll. Inst., 1958; B.A., Hunter Coll., 1960; postgrad. U. Nev., 1963-65; M.B.A., Fairleigh Dickinson U., 1969. Registered broker-dealer, SEC, N.Y.C., 1959-62; advt. space sales rep. Vanderbilt Enterprises, Reno, 1962-65; account exec. Century Advt. Agy., 1966-67, Diener and Dorskind, 1967-71; pres. Novack Devel. Corp., account exec., exec. v.p. Manister & Assos., 1971-73; account exec., exec. v.p. Bernard Hodes Advt., 1973-76, Newmark, Posner & Mitchell, 1976-79, World Wide Advt., N.Y.C., 1979—. Recipient Llewellen Found. annual award for creativity in print advt., 1972, Fin. and Mktg. Advt. award, 1977. Mem. Fin. Communications Soc., Advt. Women N.Y., Fin. Women's Assn. N.Y., Soaring Soc. Am., Am. Glider Pilots Assn. Contbr. articles to profl. jours. Home: 300 E 74th St New York NY 10021 also 350 Kings Point Rd East Hampton NY 11937 Office: 551 Fifth Ave New York NY 10176

NOVACK, RICHARD M., constrn. co. exec.; b. Boston, July 14, 1932; s. Lawrence and Pearl (Meirick) N.; student civil engring. U. Mass.; m. Claire Rosenfeld, Oct. 30, 1955; children—Karyn Lee, Lawrence James. Supt., engr., estimator Gil Wyner Co., Inc., Malden, Mass., 1951-52, 55-56, 58; project mgr., estimator A.R.T. Constrn. Co., Newport, R.I., 1956-57; v.p., dir. Edward R. Marden Corp., Allston, Mass., 1958-70; v.p. Hannan Co., Cleve., 1970—. Served with C.E., U.S. Army, 1953-54. Home: 24775 Hilltop Dr Beachwood OH 44122 Office: 23200 Chagrin Blvd Cleveland OH 44122

NOVAK, ALBERT JOHN WITTMAYER, electronic systems and parts mfg. co. exec.; b. Grand Rapids, Mich., Mar. 30, 1921; s. Albert Joseph and B. Joan (Wittmayer) N.; A.B. magna cum laude in Physics, Harvard, 1941; postgrad. Mass. Inst. Tech., 1944, Case Inst. Tech., 1946-48; m. Patricia M. Henline, Mar. 25, 1950 (div. Oct. 22, 1980); children—Patricia Joan, Albert John Wittmayer, David Bruce, Loren Lee. Indsl. engr. RCA, Camden, N.J., 1941-42; sales mgr. Brush Instruments div. Clevite Corp., Cleve., 1946-53, gen. mgr. Tex. div., Houston, 1955-57; mgr. sales and engring. Ansonia Wire & Cable Co., Ashton, R.I., 1957-59; gen. mgr. Electronics div. Hoover Co., Balt. and Pompano Beach, Fla., 1959-65; founder, pres., chmn. bd. Novatronics Group, Inc., Novatronics, Inc., Pompano Beach, 1965—, Novatronics of Can., Ltd., Stratford, Ont., Novatronics East, Inc., Dover, N.H., Novatronics South, Inc., Delray Beach, Fla.; dir. Fla. Coast Bank of Broward County. Chmn., Broward Indsl. Bd., 1967, 75, Broward County Community Relations Commn., 1974, S.Fla. Dist. Adv. Council, SBA, 1978; pres. Fort Lauderdale Symphony Assn., 1970-72. Bd. dirs. S. Fla. Edn. Center, 1963—, pres., 1970—; bd. dirs. United Way Broward County, 1975—, v.p., 1977—; mem. Gov.'s Mgmt. Adv. Council for Health and Rehab. Services, 1977—, chmn. Dist. X Health and Rehab. Services Adv. Council, 1977; bd. dirs. Center for Pastoral Counseling and Human Devel., 1973—, pres., 1977-79. Served to lt. comdr. USNR, 1942-46. Named Industrialist of Yr. Pompano Beach, 1966-67, 75-76; recipient Outstanding Service award Nat. Elec. Mfrs. Assn., 1967. Mem. Broward Mfrs. Assn. (pres. 1966-67), Greater Ft. Lauderdale C. of C. (dir. 1973-74), Phi Beta Kappa. Club: Harvard (pres. 1976-78) (Broward County). Home: 2214 Cypress Bend Dr S Pompano Beach FL 33060 Office: 500 SW 12th Ave Pompano Beach FL 33061

NOVAK, EUGENE FRANCIS, advt. exec.; b. Johnstown, Pa., May 4, 1925; s. John F. and Amelia (Havel) N.; B.A., U. Pitts., 1948; m. Joan Tross, Apr. 12, 1947; children—Gregory, Mark. With radio sta. WKBW, Buffalo, 1950-52; mgr. continuity dept. sta. WBEN-TV, Buffalo, 1952-54; TV writer, dir. Comstock Advt., Buffalo, 1954-58; radio-TV dir. Rumrill-Hoyt, advt., N.Y.C., 1959-69, pres., creative dir., 1969—, also chief exec. officer; pres. Parker-Rumrill Internat., Inc. Dir. Fair Campaign Practices Com., Washington, Advt. Council, Nat. Advt. Rev. Bd. Served with AUS, 1943-46; ETO. Mem. Pi Delta Epsilon. Author articles. Home: 303 E 57th St New York NY 10022 Office: 635 Madison Ave New York NY 10022

NOVAK, RAYMOND F(RANCIS), ins. co. exec.; b. Alexander, N.D., Nov. 24, 1918; s. Anton J. and Agnes (Kankerlik) N.; B.S., N.D. State U., 1941; postgrad. Cornell U., 1941; m. Anne (Barefoot), Mar. 25, 1944; children—Richard, Candyce (Mrs. Robert Karulf), Barbara. State mgr. N.D. Farmers Union Ins. and gen. mgr. Farmers Union Mut. Ins. Co., Jamestown, N.D., 1949-60; gen. mgr. Nat. Farmers Union Ins. Cos., Denver, 1960-70, pres., 1970—; dir. Nat. Farmers Union Life Ins. Co., Nat. Farmers Union Standard Ins. Co., Nat. Farmers Union Property & Casualty Co., Nat. Farmers Union Service Corp., Nat. Investors Fire and Casualty Ins. Co. Served with AUS, 1943-46. Mem. V.F.W. Methodist. Mason (Shriner), Elk. Home: 3133 S Adams Way Denver CO 80210 Office: 12025 E 45th Ave PO Box 39251 Denver CO 80251

NOVELL, EARL KENYON, ins. co. exec.; b. Bridgeport, Conn., Sept. 13, 1925; s. Michael and Allegra Nancy (Kenyon) N.; student Marysville Coll., 1944-45, U. Conn., 1947-48; m. Stephanie T. Coleman, June 21, 1959; children—Michael K. and Paula W. (twins), Stephen J. Photographer, USN Underwater Sound Lab., New London, Conn., 1949-51; asst. mgr. Retail Credit Co., Boston, 1951-61; rep. Employers Ins. of Wausau, Brockton, Mass., 1961-66; dir. ins. and safety Perini Corp., Framingham, Mass., 1966-72; mng. dir. Marta Ins. Mgrs., Atlanta, 1972-77; dir. risk mgmt. Met. Atlanta Rapid Transit, 1977-78; v.p. Molton, Allen & Williams Ins. Corp., 1979—; cons. risk mgmt. to U.S. Dept. Transp., UMTA Studies; cons. constrn. rapid transit. Mem. safety adv. bd. Transit Devel. Corp., Washington, 1973—. Served with USAAF, 1943-46. Registered profl. engr.; certified hazard control mgr.). Mem. Nat. Safety Council (exec. com. transit sect. 1977—), Am. Soc. Safety Engrs., Am. Soc. Ins. Mgmt., Am. Passenger Transit Assn., Nat. Fire Protection Assn., Inst. Rapid Transit (patron safety com. 1974-76). Clubs: The Club (Birmingham); K.C. Home: 3837 River Run Trail River Run AL Office: 1200 Watts Bldg 3d Ave N PO Box 548 Birmingham AL 35201

NOVELL, JOHN KINGSLEY, trailer mfr.; b. Spokane, June 2, 1937; s. John Amleto and Christine Edith (Austin) N.; B.A. in Econs., Wash. State U., 1959, postgrad. in econs., 1960; m. Dorothy Karen Salsbery, Apr. 1, 1961; children—Susan Elizabeth, John Austin. Bus. mgr. Alloy Mfg. Co., 1960-61; bus. mgr. Alloy Trailers, Inc., Spokane, 1961-65, treas., 1965-70, sec.-treas., 1970-79, pres., 1979—, gen. mgr., dir., 1973—; dir. H.W. Metal Products, Inc., T.W. Transport, Interior Transport, Hi-way Trailer Service, Westgate Investment Co., Fleetway Leasing Co., Alloy Mfg. Co., Western Leasing Co. Bd. dirs. Goodwill Industries, 1974, O.I.C., 1979; financier Boy Scouts Am., 1979. Served with USNR, 1955-63. Mem. Idaho Motor Transport, Assn. Wash. Bus. Roman Catholic. Clubs: Manito Golf and Country, Kiwanis (lt. gov. internat. 1969). Home: E 1215 Rockwood Blvd Spokane WA 99203 Office: PO Box 19208 Spokane WA 99219

NOVIDOR, BENJAMIN, motel exec.; b. South Danby, N.Y., Aug. 17, 1917; s. Jacob and Gussie (Shub) N.; student pub. schs.; m. Beatrice L. Carpenter, Mar. 26, 1940; children—Sharyll (Mrs. Gary P. Carlson), Stanley, Owner, mgr. New Central Meat Markets, Elmira, Elmira Heights, Corning, and Ithaca, N.Y., 1940-60, Charlesmont Constrn. Co., Elmira, 1944—, Red Jacket Motel, Elmira, 1956—, Red Jacket Restaurant, 1965; supr. constrn. Floral Estates Trailer Park, Ithaca; dir. Restaurant Bus. Adv. Panel. Mem. exec. com. World Famous Restaurants Internat. Active United Jewish Appeal drive, 1944-50. Served with USAAF, 1945. Mem. N.Y. State Hotel and Motel Assn., N.Y. State Motel Assn. (dir. 1960-64), Elmira C. of C. Mem. B'nai B'rith. Home: 579 Maple Ave Elmira NY 14904 Office: PO Box 489 Elmira NY 14902

NOVINA, TRUDI (MRS. CHARLES E. COAKLEY), pub. relations exec.; b. Bklyn., Dec. 8; d. Isidor and Lilian (Greenberg) N.; B.A., Bklyn. Coll., 1950; M.B.A., Fordham U., 1981; m. Leo H. Papazian, June 24, 1956 (dec. 1964); children—Lyssa D., Gregory M.; m. 2d, Charles E. Coakley, Apr. 27, 1968. Reporter, N.Y. World Telegram & Sun, N.Y.C., 1950-54, asst. woman's editor, 1954-57, home furnishings editor, 1957-60; free-lance writer, 1960-64; account exec., dir. home fashions publicity Donald Degnan Assos., N.Y.C., 1964-69; publicity mgr. fibers & plastics co. Allied Chem. Corp., N.Y.C., 1969—. Mem. Am. Inst. Interior Designers, Nat. Home Fashions League (chpt. v.p. 1972-73), Fashion Group. Club: Overseas Press (N.Y.C.). Editor: House and Garden Decorating Book, 1965; contbr. articles to various mags. Home: 34 W 89th St New York NY 10024 Office: 1411 Broadway New York NY 10018

NOWEL, RICHARD JOHN, bank exec.; b. Hackensack, N.J., Oct. 12, 1942; s. Edward August and Emily (Rupinski) N.; B.S., Seton Hall U., 1965; M.B.A., Fairleigh Dickinson U., 1974; postgrad. N.Y. U./Pace U., 1974-75; m. Maureen S. Roach, Apr. 23, 1966; children—Stephen, Kristen, Kathleen. Asst. v.p. Garden State Nat. Bank, Hackensack, N.J., 1969-72; v.p. Heritage Bank, Morristown, N.J., 1972-75; v.p./dir. mktg. BayBank Newton-Waltham Trust Co., Waltham, Mass., 1975-76; pres., chief exec. officer Garden State Bank of Ocean County, Jackson, N.J., 1976—; asst. prof. County Coll. of Morris, 1973-75. Bd. dirs. Framingham Union Hosp., Am. Heart Assn. Greater Boston, ARC; sec.-treas., N.J. Health Care Facilities Fin. Authority; v.p. Ocean County council Boy Scouts Am. Served to 1st lt. AUS, 1966-67. Mem. Am. Mgmt. Assn., Bank Mktg. Assn., Mass. Bankers Assn., Am. Mktg. Assn., Am. Bankers Assn., West Milford Jaycees. Home: 36 Elm St Jackson NJ 08527 Office: West County Line Rd and Bennetts Mills Rd Jackson NJ 08527

NOWFEL, CAMILLE, business cons.; b. Beirut, Lebanon, June 19, 1922; came to U.S., 1951, naturalized, 1954; s. Shukri Milhem and Hneini Hanna (Madi) N.; student Am. U. Beirut and Middle East Coll., 1939-44; B.A., Columbia Union Coll., 1948; postgrad. U. Md., 1952-53; m. Dixie Joan Webb, June 13, 1948 (div.); 1 son, Ronald C. Instr., Fgn. Service Inst., Dept. State, Washington, 1951-53, interpreter div. lang. services, 1953-54, Arabic specialist, sr. diplomatic interpreter, 1956-77; scriptwriter, sr. news editor Voice of Am., USIA, 1954-56; cons. U.S. bus. firms with interests in Arab World. Recipient cert. meritorious honor award USIA, 1967; Commendable Service award Dept. State, 1958. Mem. Am. U. Beirut Alumni Assn., Columbia Union Coll. Alumni Assn., Pi Sigma Alpha. Office: 730 24th St NW Washington DC 20037

NOWICKI, NORBERT JOHN, multiemployer trust fund adminstr.; b. Hamtramck, Mich., June 23, 1935; s. Adam Lubicz and Clara Jane (Siwanowicz) N.; B.B.A.; M.P.A.; m. Sara Joseph, Nov. 1, 1958; children—Renee Jaunty, Richard Ethan. Enlisted as pvt. USMC, 1953, advanced through grades to capt., 1968; service in Israel, Vietnam, Japan, Morocco as adj. personnel officer, ret., 1973; engaged in estate planning and real estate investing, 1974-75; exec. dir. Engrs. and Gen. Contractors Assn., San Diego, 1975-77; adminstr. San Diego County Constrn. Laborers Benefit Funds, San Diego, 1977—; mem. Constrn. Industry Coordinating Council, 1975-76; instr. employee benefits and social ins. Nat. U. San Diego; cons. in field. Chmn. energy task force San Diego Overall Econ. Devel. Program, 1975-79. Decorated Bronze Star, Navy Commendation medal. Mem. Internat. Found. Employee Benefit Funds, Am. Soc. Personnel Adminstrn., Adminstrv. Mgmt. Soc., Western Pension Conf., Ret. Officers Assn. Home: 6551 Green Gables Ave San Diego CA 92119 Office: 4161 Home Ave San Diego CA 92105

NOWKA, CHERYL ANN, real estate broker; b. Hydro, Okla., Jan. 17, 1948; d. Carl Robert and Lucille Iona (Arthurs) Hamons; student Southwestern State Coll., 1966, Southwestern Union, 1973, N.Mex. U., 1977; m. Paul Terry Nowka, Apr. 28, 1973; children—Jason Paul, Kevin Logan. Mem. Tex. Cowgirls profl. basketball team, 1966; owner, operator recreation center, Weatherford, Okla., 1967-70; broker, owner, operator N.Mex. Solar Real Estate, Grants, N.Mex., 1977—. Mem. N.Mex. Realtors Assn., Nat. Realtors Assn., Grad. Realtors Inst. (cert.), Miss Okla. Sorority. Home and Office: 832 Houston Grants NM 87020

NOYCE, STEPHEN FRANK, mgmt. cons.; b. Norfolk, Nebr., Dec. 1, 1940; s. Donald Clark and Mercy Bernice (Burlingame) N.; B.A. in Tech. Journalism, Colo. State U., 1963; m. Vera Elaine Malone, June 11, 1960; children—Kevin Alexander, Justine Marie. Br. mgr. Auto Tronix Universal Corp., Denver, 1968-70; v.p. Fisher Pub. Co., Denver, 1970-71; sr. cons. Applied Mgmt. Corp., Denver, 1971-73; mgr. info. systems Idaho Transp. Dept., Boise, 1973-78; prin. S.F. Noyce & Assos., mgmt. consultants in planning, organizational devel. and info. systems, Boise, 1978-79; chief Bur. of Mgmt. Info. Systems, Idaho Dept. Health and Welfare, Boise, 1979—. Mem. Data Processing Mgmt. Assn., Assn. Systems Mgmt. Democrat. Roman Catholic. Club: Boise Wranglers. Home: 2624 N 36th St Boise ID 83703 Office: 450 W State St Boise ID

NOYES, ROBERT EDWIN, publisher, author; b. N.Y.C., June 22, 1925; s. Clarence A. and Edith (LaDomus) N.; B.S. in Chem. Engring., Northwestern U., 1945; m. Janet Brown, Mar. 24, 1952 (div. June 1963); children—Keith, Steven, Mark, Geoffrey; m. 2d, Mariel Jones, July 1964; children—Rebecca, Robert. Chem. engr. Am. Cyanamid Co., Pearl River, N.Y., 1947; sales exec. Titanium Pigment Corp., N.Y.C., 1948-55; market research mgr. U.S. Indsl. Chem. Co., N.Y.C., 1956-58; sales mgr. atomic energy Curtiss Wright Export, N.Y.C., 1958-60; pres., founder, chmn. bd. Noyes Data Corp.; pub. Noyes Press, Park Ridge, N.J., 1961—. Served to lt. (j.g.) USNR, 1945-47. Mem. Am. Chem. Soc., Am. Inst. Chem. Engrs., Chemists Club, Pi Mu Alpha. Episcopalian. Author numerous books in field of internat. finance, devel., tech. Home: 224 W Saddle River Rd Saddle River NJ 07458 Office: Noyes Bldg Park Ridge NJ 07656

NOZNESKY, HARRY JOSEPH, battery mfg. co. exec.; b. Kennett Sq., Pa., Dec. 21, 1909; s. Jacob and Anna J. (Gralitzer) N.; B.Fgn. Service, Georgetown U., 1933, LL.D., 1974; m. Serena Graul, May 5, 1932; children—Peter H., Serena V. (Mrs. John Morrissey), Philip A. Clk., Pa. Co. Banking and Trust, Phila., 1933-35; dist. sales mgr. U.S. Rubber Co., 1935-49; v.p. sales Fox Products Co., 1949-50; chmn. emeritus, dir. Gen. Battery Corp., Reading, Pa., 1950—; dir. Chit Chat Farms. Bd. dirs. Reading AA Eastern Baseball League, Li'l Phils Baseball Club, Hawk Mountain council Boy Scouts Am.; bd. govs. Georgetown U.; bd. visitors Sch. Fgn. Service; trustee Albright Coll., Reading, 1979—. Mem. Battery Council Internat. (dir., past pres.), Soc. Automotive Engrs., C. of C. Reading and Berks County (dir. 1964), Sch. Fgn. Service Georgetown U. (v.p.). Home: 1198 Reading Blvd Wyomissing PA 19610 Office: General Battery Corp Reading PA 19603

NUETZEL, JOHN ARLINGTON, JR., indsl. laser specialist; b. St. Louis, Feb. 28, 1947; s. John Arlington and Sally (Bowman) N.; student St. Louis U., 1965, DePauw U., Greencastle, Ind., 1966-67; m. Janet Ann Schwanbeck, May 4, 1968; children—Jennifer Alice, Sarah Kistner, Dorothy Nehls. Self-employed broker indsl. and aviation risk mgmt., St. Louis, 1967-71; pres. Midwestern Module, Inc., St. Louis, 1972; sec. Nuetzel Machinery Co., St. Louis, 1972-78; regional mgr.-Midwest, Coherent Laser div. Coherent, Inc., Palo Alto, Calif., 1978-79, regional mgr., automotive specialist, Mich., 1979—. Mem. Warson Woods (Mo.) City Council, 1971-75; chmn. bd. Chesterfield (Mo.) Incorp. Study Com., Inc., 1977-79; pres. River Bend Assn., Inc., Chesterfield, 1979-80. Recipient Freedom Guard award U.S. Jaycees, 1972. Mem. Mensa. Republican. Roman Catholic. Address: 11035 Indianola Ave Hamburg MI 48139

NUGENT, JOHN HILLIARD, fin. exec.; b. Paterson, N.J., Aug. 20, 1944; s. James Joseph and Jacqueline Anne (Storms) N.; B.A., Columbia U., 1970; M.S., Southeastern U., 1978; postgrad. Internat. Inst. Advanced Studies, 1979; m. Mary Elizabeth Maher, June 3, 1967; 1 dau., Jill Frances. Sr. personal trust adminstr. Chase Manhattan Bank, N.Y.C., 1970-71; analyst U.S. Dept. Army, Washington, 1971-72; sr. auditor Fin. Gen. Bankshares, Inc., Washington, 1972-73; corp. auditor Internat. Trust Co. of Liberia, Monrovia, 1973-75; asst. treas. Liberian Services, Inc., N.Y.C., 1975-79; v.p., dir. Adminstrv. Control Services, Inc., Reston, Va., 1979—; chmn. bd. Strategic Planning & Research Corp.; mem. faculty dept. acctg. No. Va. Community Coll. Served with USMC, 1962-66. Mem. Nat. Assn. Accountants, Computer Security Inst. Home: 2327 Archdale Rd Reston VA 22091 Office: 1870 Michael Faraday Dr Reston VA 22090

NUGENT, JOSEPH C., stock broker; b. N.Y.C., Sept. 25, 1903; s. Henry J. and Mary Henrietta (Clark) N.; A.B. in Econs., Columbia, 1925; L.H.D., Marymount Manhattan Coll., 1970; m. Kathleen M. Dolan, Nov. 19, 1927 (dec.); children—Barbara (Mrs. Donald P. Bovers), Constance (Mrs. James R. McQuade), Joseph C.; m. 2d, Mrs. John V. Mara, Feb. 14, 1980. With Whitney & Co., stocks and bonds, 1925-38; with Mabon & Co. (firm name changed to Mabon, Nugent & Co. 1965), N.Y.C., 1938—, partner, 1941, later sr. and mng. partner, now ltd. partner. Former mem. N.Y. State Banking Bd. Vice pres. Cardinal's Com. of Laity; former chmn. bd. trustees Marymount Manhattan Coll.; trustee Cath. Youth Orgn., N.Y.; trustee N.Y. Med. Coll., Corp. Cath. Charities. Decorated knight comdr. Order of Holy Sepulchre of Jerusalem, Knight of Malta. Mem. Friendly Sons of St. Patrick (past pres.), John Jay Assos. of Columbia. Clubs: Bond; Spring Lake Golf; Spring Lake Bath and Tennis. Home: 16 Sutton Pl New York NY 10022 Office: 115 Broadway New York NY 10006

NUNGESSER, WILLIAM AICKLEN, food co. exec.; b. New Orleans, Sept. 30, 1929; s. Harold John and Isabel (Aicklen) N.; m. Ruth Amelia Marks, May 5, 1956; children—Nancy, William, Eric, Heidi. Founder, Algiers Canning & Sales Co., New Orleans, 1954—, also pres., chmn. bd.; pres., chmn. bd. Gen. Marine Catering Co., Inc., 1971—; chmn. bd. Nunco Food Co., Inc.; chief exec. asst. to gov. La., 1980—. Pres. Adv. Com. on Fisheries; treas. Orleans Parish Republican Polit. Action Com., 1972-76; bd. dirs. Met. New Orleans Crime Commn., 1974-76, Internat. House, New Orleans; mem. La. Republican Central Com.; treas. Dave Treen for Gov. Served with USMCR, 1950-53. Mem. U.S. C. of C., New Orleans Tourist Commn., La. Shrimp Assn. (dir.) La. Restaurant Assn., New Orleans Hotel Assn. Home: 5740 Durham Dr New Orleans LA 70114 Office: 300 Homer St New Orleans LA 70114

NUNN, DONNA MAE SMULAND, small bus. devel. cons.; b. Edmonton, Alta., Can., Dec. 24, 1946; d. Henry and Elma (Lehman) Smuland; came to U.S., 1951, naturalized, 1956; B.A. in Adminstrn. and Communications, U. Washington, 1977; student Cascade Coll., 1965-67, Portland State U., 1967-70. Community organizer YMCA, Portland, Oreg., 1965-66; advt. asst. Fred Meyer's, Portland, 1966-68; phys. therapist Rehab. Inst. Oreg., Portland, 1968-71; apt. mgr. Don Philita Apts., Seattle, 1971-73; dept. head phys. therapy Moderncare Convalescent, Seattle, 1972; indsl. therapist Wash. State Dept. Labor and Industries, Buckner Center, 1972-75; clinic mgr. Columbia Clinic, Seattle, 1976-77; gen. mgr. Natural Learning Center-Dynamics of Teamwork, Seattle, 1977-79; founder, dir. Women's Bus. Exchange, Seattle, 1979—; bd. dirs. Women Plus Bus., 1979-81; corp. recruiting coordinator Women Plus Bus. Conf., 1980; rep. to White House Conf. on Small Bus., 1979. Recipient Perseverance award for devel. of public info. project Wash. State Dept. Labor and Industries, Buckner Center, 1975. Mem. Nat. Assn. Female Execs., Women's Polit. Caucus, Planetary Citizens, Seattle C. of C., Pres.'s Club. Office: 314 Lloyd Bldg 6th and Stewart Sts Seattle WA 98101

NUNN, PHILIP CLARK, III, environmentalist; b. Cin., Apr. 4, 1933; s. Philip Clark and Frances Kay (Patton) N.; student Kenyon Coll., 1951-53; B.A., Aquinas Coll., 1969; postgrad. Western Mich. U., 1970-78; m. Hildegarde Loretta Bauer, Jan. 17, 1953; children—Annette, Catherine, Margaret, Christopher. With Lear Siegler, Inc., Grand Rapids, Mich., 1957-70, devel. project coordinator, 1962-70; mgr. environ. systems devel. Nat. Sanitation Found., Ann Arbor, Mich., 1970-74; dir. urban and environ. studies inst. Grant Valley State Colls., Allendale, Mich., 1974-80; internat. coordinator research and devel. Amway Corp., Ada, Mich., 1980—; adj. prof. F. E. Seidman Grad. Coll. Bus. and Adminstrn., 1976—. Health dir. Cin. area Boy Scout Camp, 1952; regular panel mem. Soundings weekly radio program WOOD-AM and FM, Grand Rapids, 1973—; vice chmn. community health planning sect. W. Mich. Health Systems Agy., 1976—; mem. central planning com. W. Mich. Comprehensive Health Planning Unit, 1973-76; chmn. environ. simulation sect. Summer Computer Simulation Conf., 1972; bd. dirs. Kent County Conservation League, 1964-65. Served with USAF, 1953-57. Kenyon Coll. scholar, 1951. Mem. AAAS, Soc. Gen. Systems Research (chmn. orgn. and mgmt. studies 1970-74), Soc. for Computer Simulation, Alpha Delta Phi. Episcopalian. Contbr. articles in field to profl. jours. Home: 201 Netherfield St Comstock Park MI 49321 Office: Amway Corp Ada MI 49355

NUNN, RALPH LEO, appliance co. exec.; b. Cedar Rapids, Iowa, May 10, 1923; s. Earl Love and Florence Pearl (Doyle) N.; B.A., State U. Iowa, 1948; m. Marilyn M. Coleman, Feb. 1, 1946; children—James R., Nancy M., Jerald R. Asst. advt. mgr. Micro Switch Corp., Freeport, Ill., 1948; mem. advt. dept. staff The Maytag Co., Newton, Iowa, 1948-50, asst. advt. mgr., 1950-52, advt. mgr., 1952-68, asst. vice-pres. mktg., 1968-70, vice-pres. mktg., 1970—, also dir. Served with USAAF, 1943-46. Mem. Assn. Home Appliance Mfrs. (dir.), Newton C. of C. (dir.). Republican. Congregationalist. Club: Newton Country. Office: 403 W 4th St N Newton IA 50208

NUNNALLY, H. MCKEE, investment banker exec.; b. Atlanta, June 7, 1918; s. Winship and Jessie (McKee) N.; student U. Ga., 1938-40; m. Betty Yopp, Nov. 25, 1939; children—McKee, Martha Nunnally O'Callaghan. With Dean Witter Reynolds, Inc. (formerly Courts & Co.), Atlanta, 1946-69, managing partner, 1957-69, v.p., from 1973, now sr. v.p., dir., 1976—; partner Reynolds & Co., 1970-73; mem. advisory bd. Citizen & So. Nat. Bank, Atlanta. Bd. dirs., pres. Am. Cancer Soc., Atlanta; trustee U. Ga. Found., Athens, Ga., Piedmont Hosp., Atlanta. Served with USNR, 1944-46. Republican. Presbyterian. Clubs: Rotary, Piedmont Driving; Capital City, River, Cat Cay, Del Ray Beach Yacht, Key Largo Anglers. Home: 670 W Paces Ferry Rd NW Atlanta GA 30327 Office: Suite 800 100 Peachtree St Atlanta GA 30303

NUNNIKHOVEN, THOMAS SPENCE, paper co. exec.; b. Burlington, Iowa, June 19, 1947; s. Antonie Aart and Margaret Lois (Spence) N.; B.A. in Math., U. Iowa, 1968, M.S. in Statistics, 1971; M.S., Case Western Reserve U., 1973, Ph.D. in Ops. Research, 1975; m. Kathleen Mae Smalley, Dec. 28, 1974; 1 dau., Amy Kathleen. Ops. research analyst Standard Oil Co., Cleve., 1973-74; sr. ops. research analyst Hammermill Paper Co., Erie, Pa., 1975—; lectr. Behrend Coll. of Pa. State U., Erie, 1979—. Served with U.S. Army, 1969-71. Mem. Am. Statis. Assn., Inst. Mgmt. Sci. Contbr. articles in field to profl. publs. Home: 519 Margo Ct Erie PA 16505 Office: PO Box 1440 Erie PA 16505

NUPEN, HARLAN CLARENCE, shooting range operator, shooting sports supply co. exec.; b. Hudson, S.D., Oct. 30, 1936; s. Clarence Harry and Honore Hildg (Benjamson) N.; B.S., S.D. State U., 1958, M.Ed., 1980; m. Colleen Rose Brown, June 29, 1958; children—Valerie, Monae, Amber. Commd. 2d lt. USAF, 1958, advanced to grades to lt. col., 1974; ops. officer, 1968-74; squadron comdr., 1975-76, wing exec. officer, 1977-78; ret., 1978; founder, dir. Black Hills Counseling Service, Rapid City, S.D., 1977—; incorporator, sec. Rushmore Range & Supply, Inc., Rapid City, 1978—, also dir. Bd. dirs. Big Bros., Big Sisters Black Hills. Decorated D.F.C. with 1 oak leaf cluster, Air medal with 13 oak leaf clusters. Mem. Nat. Rifle Assn. (endowment mem.), Am. Numismatic Assn. (life), South African Numismatic Soc. (life), Am. Personnel and Guidance Assn., West River Personnel and Guidance Assn., Nat. Assn. Christian Marriage Counselors, S.D. Shooting Sports Assn. (life). Republican. Wesleyan. Club: Cosmopolitan. Home: 4602 Baldwin St Rapid City SD 57701 Office: 429 Kansas City St Rapid City SD 57701

NUSBAUM, MORT, investment mgr.; b. Rochester, N.Y., Aug. 10, 1914; s. Lester and Belle (Goldstein) N.; B.A., U. Rochester, 1935; m. Virginia Lee Smith, Feb. 16, 1954. Broadcaster, Rochester, 1936-42; radio dir. 20th Century Fox Films, N.Y.C., 1943-44, pub. relations, 1944; sales mgr. Sta. WQQW, Washington, 1945; broadcaster Sta. WROC-TV, Rochester, 1946-74, TV financial commentator, 1961-74; investment mgr. Mort Nusbaum Investment Mgmt., Rochester, 1961—; tchr. investments Rochester Inst. Tech. Extended Services 1961—; investment counselor, 1961—; fin. editor Sta. WNWZ-FM, 1976-77; fin. commentator Sta. WVOR, Rochester. Past pres. Jewish Home and Infirmary, Rochester. Recipient Civic medal VFW, 1941, citation Rochester Police Athletic League, 1952. Mem. Soc. Am. Bus. Writers (charter), Rochester Soc. Security Analysts, Fin. Analysts Fedn., Radio Pioneers, Genesee Conservation League. Republican. Jewish. Clubs: Circus Saints and Sinners (past pres.), Rochester Police Locust (hon.). Fin. columnist Upstate Bus. Jour., 1972—. Home: 265 Forest Hills Rd Rochester NY 14625 Office: Midtown Plaza Rochester NY 14604

NUTTALL, ARNOLD JODELL, med. services adminstr.; b. Safford, Ariz., June 14, 1943; s. Dewain Floyd and Lydia Ellen Nuttall; student U. Ariz., 1961-62, 70-71, Ariz. State U., 1962-64; m. Danna Colette Sherwood, Dec. 17, 1971; children—Rachel Sophia, Rebecca Amy, David Abraham, Jonathan Lester. Chief orderly Mesa (Ariz.) Luth. Hosp., 1963-66, Good Samaritan Hosp., Phoenix, Ariz., 1966-67, pulmonary technician, 1967-68; cardiopulmonary biochemist U. Utah Hosp., Salt Lake City, 1968-70; chief technologist cardiology U. Ariz., Tucson, 1970-71; staff research asso. II U. Calif. Med. Center, San Diego, 1971-73; chief technologist cardiology VA Hosp., La Jolla, Calif., 1973-74; mgr. dept. head Meml. Hosp. Med. Center, Long Beach, Calif., 1974-78; mgr. cardiology services Walter E. Boswell Hosp., Sun City, Ariz., 1978—. Pres., PTA, Lindberg Sch., 1980-81. Recipient Superior Performance award VA Hosp., 1974. Mem. Am. Coll. of Sports Medicine (cert. exercise specialist), Nat. Soc. of Cardiopulmonary Technologists (pres. Ariz. chpt. 1979-80, mem. internat. platform com.). Republican. Mormon. Home: 1317 Flower Mesa AZ 85204 Office: 10401 Thunderbird Blvd Sun City AZ 85372

NWUKE, EJI I., mfg. co. exec.; b. Nigeria, Apr. 5, 1950; s. Jonas E. and Roseannah N.; B.S., Metro State Coll., Denver. Accounts exec. Mersten Mfrs., Denver, 1974-77; accounts exec. Tex. Refinery Corp., Denver, 1978; now pres., owner Nwuke Enterprises, Aurora, Colo., Frankfurt, Ger., also Nigeria. Office: 707 Uvalda St Aurora CO 80011

NYKIEL, FRANK PETER, diversified co. exec.; b. Chgo., Dec. 30, 1917; s. Joseph and Ann (Jerz) N.; B.S. in Accounting, U. Ill., 1941; m. Marie Papa, Mar. 1, 1942; children—Carol Ann (Mrs. Thomas J. Barta), Frank Peter II. With Arthur Andersen & Co., C.P.A., Chgo., 1947-52, sr. accountant, 1951-52; with Consumers Co., Chgo., 1952-60, exec. v.p., 1959-60; v.p., treas. Miss. Valley Barge Line Co., St. Louis, 1960-62, exec. v.p., dir., 1962—, (merger Miss. Valley Barge Line Co. and Chromalloy Am. Corp. to Valley Line Co., 1968), v.p. marine-finance, dir. Chromalloy Am. Corp., 1968-70, vice chmn. bd. finance, dir., 1970-80, pres., chief exec. officer, 1980—; chmn. bd., chief exec. officer, dir. Water Treatment Corp., 1968-71. Served with USAAF, World War II. C.P.A. Clubs: Mo. Athletic; Sunset Country. Office: Chromalloy Am Corp 120 S Central Ave Saint Louis MO 63105*

NYLEN, DAVID WALKER, bus. educator; b. Providence, R.I., May 3, 1931; s. C. Victor and Caroline G. (Daly) N.; A.B., Duke U., 1952; M.B.A. with distinction, Harvard U., 1954; Ph.D., U. Fla., 1969; m. Carlene Powers, Mar. 3, 1956; children—Peter, Matthew, Caroline. Research asso. Harvard Bus. Sch., 1958-59; v.p., account supr. Needham, Harper & Steers, Inc., N.Y.C., 1959-65; asst. to pres. 1st Nat. Bank of St. Petersburg (Fla.), 1965-67; asst. prof. mktg. Stetson U., DeLand, Fla., 1968-72, prof. mktg., dean Sch. Bus. Adminstrn., 1979—; asso. prof. U. North Fla., Jacksonville, 1972-74; v.p. Booz, Allen & Hamilton, Inc., N.Y.C., 1975-79. Served to lt. USNR, 1954-57. Mem. Am. Mktg. Assn., Acad. Mktg. Sci., So. Bus. Adminstrn. Assn., West Volusia Com. of 100, Phi Beta Kappa. Baptist. Club: Rotary. Author works in field. Office: Sch Bus Adminstrn Stetson Univ DeLand FL 32720

OAKES, WILLIAM ELWOOD, banker; b. Wichita, Kans., Mar. 26, 1934; s. Elwood William and Rose Marie (Wolverton) O.; B.S., U. Wichita, 1955; m. Jacqueline Claire LaPorte, Apr. 8, 1955; children—Bradford W., Lesley C. Pres., chmn. bd. State Exchange Bank, Yates Center, Kans., 1958—; dir. 1st Nat. Bank of Chanute (Kans.), Home Savs. Assn., Chanute, Strawn State Bank, New Strawn, Kans.; chmn. Kans. BankPac. Trustee, Mid-Am., Inc., former pres. Served with USAF, 1955-57. Mem. Kans. Bankers Assn. Republican. Presbyterian.

OAKES, JOHN DAVID, savs. and loan assn. exec.; b. Middletown, Ind., July 29, 1941; s. John Daniel and Nell Easter (Sanders) O.; B.S., Ball State U., 1964, M.A., 1965; m. Linda S. Graybiel, Dec. 22, 1962; children—John Paul, Dawn Anne. Tchr. pub. schs., Ind., 1964-69; owner, operator Oakes Constrn. Co., Anderson, Ind., 1964-69; asst. sec. 1st Savs. & Loan Assn., Anderson, 1969-70, asst. v.p., 1970-72, v.p., 1973, sr. v.p. ops., 1974—; lectr. in field. Vice-pres. bd. dirs. Wilson Boys' Club, 1974-75. Served with USMCR, 1963-64. Mem. Anderson C. of C., Anderson Home Builders Assn., Anderson Bd. Realtors, U.S. League Savs. Assns., U.S. League Ednl. Inst., Mortgage Bankers Assn., Sigma Phi Epsilon. Republican. Clubs: Lions,

Anderson Country, Masons, Shriners. Home: 904 Northwood St Anderson IN 46015 Office: 33 W 10th St Anderson IN 46015

OAKLEY, GRAYCE A., real estate broker; b. Bellwood, Nebr., May 19, 1937; d. Everett E. and Ella A. (Hahn) Allen; B.Mus. Edn., Oberlin Conservatory of Music, 1958; postgrad. Alaska Meth. U., 1967-68; grad. Realtors Inst., 1975; m. Lawrence W. Oakley, Aug. 6, 1962; children—Raymond M., Brenda J. Tchr. pub. schs., Parma, Ohio, 1958-61, Anchorage, Alaska, 1961-63, 69-72; real estate sales asso. Totem Realty, Anchorage, 1972-73; partner Denali Realty, Anchorage, 1973—, owner, broker, 1977—. State adv. March of Dimes, 1978—; bd. dirs. Anchorage Cancer Assn., 1977—, sec., 1980; bd. dirs. Anchorage Civic Opera, 1978—, pres., 1979-81. Named Realtor of the Yr., Anchorage Bd. Realtors, 1976, Alaska Assn. Realtors, 1979; recipient Gov.'s Cert. of Appreciation for outstanding vol. service, 1978, 79. Mem. Anchorage Bd. Realtors (dir. 1976-79, pres. 1978), Alaska Assn. Realtors (dir. 1978-79, 81), Alaska Realtors Inst. (dean bd. govs. 1978-79), NEA, Nat. Assn. Realtors (dir. 1981), Anchorage C. of C. Republican. Presbyterian. Club: Soroptimist. Address: 2458 Sprucewood St Anchorage AK 99504

OAKS, ROBERT LEE, accountant; b. South Gate, Calif., May 25, 1938; s. Roger J. and Mildred L. Oaks; student public schs., Kerman, Calif.; m. Jacqueline A. DeRouchey, June 25, 1958; children—Deborah, Rodney, Russel, Ricky. Bookkeeper, Serria Meat Co., Fresno, Calif., 1959-62; office mgr. Noble Land & Cattle Co., Kerman, 1962-70; owner, mgr. Oaks Bookkeeping & Tax Service, Kerman, 1970—. Mem. Nat. Assn. Tax Cons., Nat. Notary Assn., Nat. Soc. Public Accts. Club: Lion. Office: 562 S Madera Ave Kerman CA 93630

OANCEA, ROD JOHN, corp. exec.; b. Bucharest, Romania, Nov. 15, 1937; s. John and Elena (Bratianu) O. (Am. citizen); B.S. in Elec. Engring., U. Pitts., 1961, postgrad. 1965; M.B.A., Purdue U., 1972. Designer, Houser and Carafas Engring. Co., Pitts., 1958-63; engr. Swindell Dressler, Pitts., 1963; design engr., constrn. engr., project mgr. U.S. Steel Corp., Pitts., 1964-75; cons. engr. Altos Hornos del Mediteraneo-Madrid (Spain), 1975; pres. Enterprise T. & E.S. Co., Pitts. and Chgo., 1975—. Active Chgo. Council on Fgn. Relations, Internat. Visitors Center-Chgo., Art Inst. Chgo., Nat. Soc. Hist. Preservation. Served with USAF, 1961. Mem. Nat. Soc. Profl. Engrs., Internat. Trade Club, IEEE, Iron and Steel Assn., Chgo. Hist. Soc., Am. Security Council, Am. Def. Preparedness Assn., Internat. Entrepreneurs Assn., Secretariat OAS. Republican. Clubs: Good Fellowship, Univ., Toastmasters Internat. Office: PO Box 8259 Chicago IL 60680 also PO Box 9679 Pittsburgh PA 15256

OATES, JAMES BART, fin. co. exec.; b. Brownwood, Tex., June 10, 1945; s. John Bart, Jr., and Bernadette M. (Kane) O.; B.B.A. in Acctg., So. Meth. U., 1967, M.B.A. in Acctg., 1969. Sr. acct., office mgr. Edward P. Thompson, C.P.A., Dallas, 1965-69; mgr. Alexander Grant & Co., Dallas, 1969-73; treas. Hill. Consol. Corp., Hillco Mgmt., Hill Realty, Inc. and Interiors by Jeanie, Dallas, 1973-75; v.p., treas. Pearcy-Christon, Inc., Dallas, 1975—; treas., dir. PCH Dog House, Inc.; dir. D.R. Titus, Inc.; sec., dir. Greater Garland Community Credit Union. Bd. dirs. Oak Cliff Jaycees. C.P.A.; lic. real estate broker, Tex. Mem. Am. Inst. C.P.A.'s, Tex. Soc. C.P.A.'s, Real Estate Execs. Assn., Ind. Cattlemen's Assn., Alpha Beta Psi. Home: 16810 Preston Bend Dr Dallas TX 75248 Office: 5429 LBJ Freeway Dallas TX 75240

OATMAN, JAMES MARIS, computer services co. exec.; b. Lancaster, Pa., Aug. 29, 1939; s. Ray and Rachel Elizabeth O.; A.Indsl. Engring., Pa. State U., York campus, 1960; B.S. in Math., Millersville State U., 1964; M.S. in Computer Sci., Pa. State U., 1968; m. Sally Sue Templeton, June 9, 1962; children—Michael James, Steven John. Data processing mgr. Trojan Yacht Co., Lancaster, 1968-71; sr. systems cons. Whittaker Corp., Los Angeles, 1971-72; gen. mgr. Computer Services Internat., Lancaster, 1975-78; pres. Oatman Enterprises, Lancaster, 1972—; owner Bird-in-Hand Moped Tours; pres. Oatman Computer Resources; dir. Alex Riverbank Assos.; instr. Pa. State U. Judge elections, Lancaster County, 1969-78; ofcl. world team tennis, collegiate football. Recipient awards for acad. achievement Engring. Soc. York, 1959, 60. Mem. Pa. Dutch Visitors Bur., Assn. Computing Machinery, Assn. Systems Mgmt. Republican. Clubs: Conestoga Country, Pegasus Travel, Masons, Shriners, Rotary (dir. local club 1977-78, dist. com. girls' leaders camp 1978-79) (Lancaster). Research on simulation of prodn. line with fluctuating product mix, 1968. Home: 3300 Nolt Rd Lancaster PA 17601 Office: 20 E Walnut St Lancaster PA 17604

OAXACA, FERNANDO, communications exec.; b. El Paso, Tex., Aug. 8, 1927; s. Angel and Lucinda (Nevarez) O.; B.S.E.E., U. Tex., 1950; m. Bertha Candelaria, Oct. 4, 1968. With various cos. constrn. industry, 1950-53; with Lockheed, Burbank, Calif., 1953-57, Douglas Missiles, Santa Monica, Calif., 1957-60; project dir. Aerospace Corp., El Segundo, Calif., 1960-67; program mgr. TRW Systems, Redondo Beach, Calif., 1967-69; sr. v.p. Ultrasystems, Inc., Newport Beach, Calif., 1969-75, dir., 1969—; asso. dir. Office of Mgmt. and Budget, Exec. Office of Pres., 1975-77; pres. Resource for Communications, Inc., Los Angeles, 1977-80; chmn. bd. Coronado Communications, Los Angeles, 1979—; chmn. bd. Bel Air Mgmt. & Investment Corp., 1978—. Adv. council Grad. Sch. Bus., Stanford U., 1973-76; mem. exec. com. Republican Nat. Com., 1979-81; nat. chmn. Rep. Nat. Hispanic Assembly, Washington, 1979. Served with U.S. Army, 1946-47. Recipient U.S. Office Edn. Spl. Recognition award, 1976; Nat. Congress of Hispanic Orgn. spl. ann. award, 1975. Mem. Nat. Assn. Latino Elected Ofcls. (dir. 1980—), Hispanic Council on Fgn. Affairs (nat. chmn. 1981—), Coalition of Spanish-Speaking Mental Health Orgns. (dir. 1980—). Roman Catholic. Office: 9255 Sunset Blvd 8th Floor Los Angeles CA 90069

OAXACA, VIRGINIA C., savs. and loan assn. exec.; b. El Paso, Tex., Dec. 30, 1940; d. Angel and Lucinda (Nevarez) O.; B.S. in Edn., U. Tex., 1962, M.S. in Counseling and Psychology (NDEA fellow 1969), 1969; Sloan-Merrill fellow Stanford U. Grad. Sch. Banking, 1974. Personnel mgr. Master Charge div., then asst. v.p. employee relations United Calif. Bank, Los Angeles, 1974-76; dir. personnel Rockwell Internat. Space Co., Downey, Calif., 1976-77; sr. v.p. Gibraltar Savs. & Loan Assn., Beverly Hills, Calif., 1977—. Mem. Mayor Los Angeles Bicentennial Com., 1976. Recipient Woman of Yr. award for bus. and industry Los Angeles YWCA, 1978. Mem. Women in Bus. (pres. bd. dirs. 1978), Orgn. Women Exevs., Alumni Assn. Stanford U. Grad. Sch. Bus. (dir.). Republican. Roman Catholic. Address: 305 Ardmore St Hermosa Beach CA 90254

O'BANNON, DONA CAROLE, cons. firm exec.; b. Washington, Apr. 13, 1943; d. H.A. and E. Kay (Kessel) O.; B.S. in Fgn. Service cum laude, Georgetown U., 1965. Spl. asst. to Congressman Sam Gibbons from Fla., 1963-74; partner Alcalde, Henderson, O'Bannon & Bracy, Ltd., govt. and pub. affairs cons. firm, Rosslyn, VA., 1974—. Mem. adv. council Cornell U. Grad. Sch. Bus. and Pub. Adminstrn.; pres. Nat. Found. for Women Bus. Owners. Mem. Nat. Assn. Women Bus. Owners (named Entrepreneur of Year 1977, pres., 1977-78), AAUW, Phi Beta Kappa. Club: Nat. Press. Contbr. articles to profl. mags. Home: 3409 Prospect St NW Washington DC 20007 Office: 1901 N Ft Myer Dr Suite 1204 Rosslyn VA 22209

OBER, STUART ALAN, investment cons., pub.; b. N.Y.C., Oct. 2, 1946; s. Paul and Gertrude E. (Stollerman) O.; B.A., Wesleyan U., Middletown, Conn., 1968; postgrad. U. Sorbonne, U. Paris, 1970, Baruch Coll., CUNY, 1976. Pres., editor-in-chief, chmn. bd. Beekman Pubs., Inc., N.Y.C., 1973—; investment cons., 1972—; tax shelter specialist Loeb, Rhoades & Co., 1976-77; div. dir. tax investment dept. Josephthal & Co., Inc., 1977-78; mgr. tax shelter dept. Bruns, Nordeman, Rea and Co., 1978-80; fin. cons., 1980—. Author: Everybody's Guide to Tax Shelters, 1980; also articles. Home: 38 Hicks St Brooklyn Heights NY 11201 Office: 38 Hicks St Brooklyn Heights NY 11201

OBERMAN, LAWRENCE, food co. exec.; b. Newark, Oct. 13, 1940; s. Sigmund and Miriam O.; B.S. in Elec. Engring., Fairleigh Dickinson U., 1963; children by former marriage—Randi, David, Julie. Staff Weston Inst., Newark, 1963, Exide Battery Co., West Orange, N.J., 1964; exec. v.p. Aster Nut Products Inc., Newark, 1965—; v.p. Ashton Food Machinery Co., Newark, 1965—. Office: Aster Nut Products Inc 1455 McCarter Hwy Newark NJ 07104

OBERMAN, MOISHE DAVID, mag. pub.; b. Springfield, Ill., Mar. 3, 1914; s. Harry and Ida (Guralnik) O.; student St. Louis Coll. Pharmacy, 1931-33; m. Bobbye Friedman, Oct. 8, 1939; children—Michael Alan, Martin Jay, M.H. William, Marjorie Ann. Scrap metals broker, Springfield, 1937-41; founder Scrap Age Mag., 1944, Mill Trade Jour., 1963, Waste Age Mag., 1969, Encyclopedia of Scrap Recycling, 1976; pres., editor, pub. 3 Sons Pub. Co., 1944; pres. Emde Realty Devel. Corp., Springfield, 1957-63; exec. sec. Midwest Scrap Dealers Assn., Springfield, 1941; treas. North Shore Investments, Highland Park, Ill., 1968; exec. dir. Springfield Area Devel. and Tourist Commn., 1963-68; mem. Ill. Inst. Environ. Quality Solid Waste Task Force Com., 1971. Pres. Ill. Assn. Jewish Centers, 1934-40; editor congregation publs., treas. North Suburban Synagogue Beth El. Mem. War Production Bd., 1942-44. Recipient Meritorious Service award for outstanding contbrs. iron and steel industry St. Louis Steel Assn., 1961. Mem. Nat. Solid Waste Mgmt. Assn., Am. Pub. Works Assn. (solid waste mgmt. task force), Execs. Inc. (pres. 1963-67), Am. Soc. Assn. Execs., Internat. Platform Assn., Nat. Press Club, Springfield Jr. C. of C. (pres. 1946-47), Springfield Assn. Execs., Springfield Assn. Commerce and Industry. Jewish. Club: B'nai B'rith (sec. 1935-39, pres. 1942-45). Home: 857 Stonegate Dr Highland Park IL 60035 Office: 6311 Gross Point Rd Niles IL 60648

OBERMAN, SAMUEL EUGENE, employee relations cons. co. exec.; b. Titusville, Pa., Sept. 8, 1933; s. Max Phillip and Bessie (Krause) O.; B.S., U. Pa., 1955; M.B.A., U. Mich., 1958; m. Judith P. Meshberg, Apr. 3, 1966; children—Scott Evan, Amy Lisa. Mgr. personnel relations CBS, N.Y.C., 1958-60; asst. dir. personnel N.Y. Hosp., 1960-64; dir. personnel Meth. Hosp. Bklyn., 1964-66; v.p. Don Rowe Assos., N.Y.C., 1966-69, exec. v.p., 1969-71, pres., chief exec. officer, 1971—; lectr. in field. Founder, chmn. Greater Westbury (N.Y.) Community Coalition, 1971—; pres. L.I. chpt. Am. Jewish Com., 1976-78; chmn. U. Pa. Alumni Giving L.I., 1974-76; bd. dirs. YMCA L.I., 1974-78, Greater Westbury Arts Council, 1978—; chmn. Cub Scouts Am., 1978—. Served with USN, 1955-57. Recipient Human Relations award Am. Jewish Com., 1979. Mem. L.I. Assn., AIM (pres.'s council). Clubs: Wharton of N.Y., Rotary. Home: 532 Rockland St Westbury NY 11590 Office: 155 Mineola Blvd Mineola NY 11501

OBERT, MARK JOHN, heavy duty truck mfg. co. exec.; b. Camden, N.J., Oct. 1, 1940; s. Maximilian John and Louise Elizabeth (Yost) O.; A.A., Valley Forge Jr. Coll., 1960; B.A., Mich. State U., 1963; M.B.A., U. Minn., 1966; m. Susan Jean Keller, May 26, 1973; children—Karen Elizabeth, Michael John, John Patrick, Mchelle Joan, Jennifer Susan. Zone sales mgr. Ford div. Ford Motor Co., Mpls., 1963-67; mktg. services and distbn. mgr. Marquette Corp., St. Paul, Minn., 1967-70; gen. mgr. EV power systems, new bus. div. Gould Inc., Chgo., 1973-76; dir. mktg. AM Gen. Corp., Detroit, 1976-79; v.p. truck mktg. White Motor Corp., Detroit, 1979—. Mem. Soc. Automotive Engrs., Am. Mktg. Assn., Am. Mgmt. Assn. Office: 35129 Curtis Blvd Eastlake OH 44094

OBLEY, ROSS PATTERSON, real estate exec.; b. West Newton, Pa., Dec. 22, 1928; s. Harold Jacob and Sarah Rebecca (Kelley) O.; B.S., U. Pitts., 1951; M.B.A., Am. U., 1958, postgrad., 1958-60; m. Cora Pancereve, Aug. 31, 1951; children—Ross Patterson, Janine Kelley, Curtis Jay. With Westinghouse Electric Corp. & Subs., 1951-72, dep. mgr. Oceanic Div., Annapolis, Md., 1969-71, exec. asst. corp. hdqrs., Pitts., 1971-72; pres. Urban Systems Devel. Corp., Coral Springs, Fla., 1973-78, Coral Ridge-Collier Properties, Inc., Naples, Fla., 1978—; dir. Citizens Nat. Bank, Naples, 1979—. Trustee Collier County Econ. Devel. Commn., 1978—, Collier County Conservancy, 1978—. Served to lt. (j.g.) USCGR, 1952-54. Recipient Westinghouse Order of Merit, 1979. Mem. Urban Land Inst. (dir. fed. policy council 1979-80), Am. Real Estate and Urban Econs. Assn., Pelican Bay of Naples Found. (dir., pres. 1978-80), Theta Chi. Republican. Presbyterian. Clubs: Pelican Bay (pres. 1979-80), Imperial Golf; Univ. Pitts. Golden Panthers. Home: 6554 Ridgewood Dr Naples FL 33940 Office: Coral Ridge-Collier Properties Inc 5801 Pelican Bay Blvd Naples FL 33940

O'BLOCK, ROBERT PAUL, distbg. and warehousing co. exec., mgmt. cons.; b. Pitts., Mar. 9, 1943; s. Paul Joseph and Mary Elizabeth (Galicic) O'B.; B.S.M.E., Purdue U., 1965; M.B.A. (Research fellow), Harvard, 1967. Research and teaching fellow in fin., econs. and urban mgmt., Harvard, 1967-70; asso. in real estate mgmt. and fin. McKinsey & Co., Inc., N.Y.C., 1969-78, prin., 1979—; gen. and mng. partner Freeport Center, Clearfield, Utah, 1971—; vis. lectr. urban econs. Yale Law Sch., Princton; cons. Mass., N.J. housing fin. agencies, Rockefeller Assos., HUD; chmn. mgmt. com. Snowbird Lodge (Utah), 1974—. Mem. nat. adv. bd. Snowbird Arts Inst., 1977—; mem. budget com. N.Y. Pub. Library. Roman Catholic. Clubs: River, Harvard (N.Y.C.); Devon Yacht, Maidstone (East Hampton, N.Y.); Nat. Golf Links Am. (Southampton, N.Y.); Alta (Salt Lake City); Ogden (Utah) Golf. Contbr. articles to profl. jours. Home: 415 E 52d St New York NY 10022 Office: Bldg 1A Box 1325 Clearfield UT 84016

O'BRIEN, CHARLES PATRICK, ins. co. exec.; b. Winnipeg, Man., Can., Dec. 10, 1936; s. Charles Arthur and Viola Helen (Burns) O'B.; B.Comm., Sir George William U., Montreal, 1959; m. Maryse Bernard, Sept. 9, 1961; children—Lorrinda, Geoffrey, Christopher. Agt., London Life, Can., 1961-63; program dir. Life Ins. Mktg. and Research Assn., Hartford, Conn., 1963-66; dir. agys. Sun Life of Canada, Wellesley, Mass., 1966-76; pres., chief exec. officer Reliance Standard Life Ins. Co., Phila., 1976—; pres., dir. Reliance Life Ins. Co., Phila.; dir. United Pacific Life Ins. Co., Tacoma, Wash. Philadelphia County crusade chmn. Am. Cancer Soc., 1979-81. Mem. Am. Soc. C.L.U., Am. Coll. Life Underwriters (founder Golden Key soc.). Clubs: Union League of Phila., Waynesborough Country. Office: 4 Penn Center Plaza Philadelphia PA 19103

O'BRIEN, CYRIL CORNELIUS, research co. exec.; b. Halifax, N.S., Can., Mar. 22, 1906; s. Arthur Michael and Mary Jane (Buchanan) O'B.; B.A., St. Mary's U., 1926; academic diploma Nova Scotia Normal Coll., 1929; postgrad. Halifax Conservatory Music, 1927-28; Dalhousie U., 1930-32; L.Mus., McGill U., 1931; M.A., M. Allison U., 1932; B.Pd., U. Toronto, 1934; D.Pd., U. Montreal, 1937; D.Mus., 1950; B.Mus., Laval U., 1937; Ph.D., U. Ottawa, 1944; m. Madeleine Agatha Jones, July 4, 1939, (dec. Aug. 1946); children—Maureen Louise, Terry Michael, Christopher Joseph; m. 2d, Mary Patricia Florence Davison, July 27, 1957. Came to U.S., 1947, naturalized, 1956; re-established Can. citizenship, 1972. Prin. schs. Waterville, Kings County, N.S., 1927; tchr., prin. Halifax Pub. Schs., 1927-47; head dept. psychology Maritime Acad. Music, Halifax, 1935-47; lectr. St. Mary's U., 1942-46; cons. psychologist The Allis-Chalmer Mfg. Co., Milw., 1948-63; asst. prof. Marquette U., 1947-54, asso. prof., 1954-59, prof., 1959-63; dir. research The Alcoholism Found. Alta., Edmonton, 1963-68, Alta. Div. Alcoholism, Edmonton; cons. psychologist Franciscan Sisters, N.Y., 1964-68; pres. Adan Research Co., Ltd., Edmonton, 1969—; v.p., dir. Interpersonal Communications, Inc., Chgo., 1961—; dir. Prince of Peace Research Inst., Mundare, Alta., 1980—; lectr. indsl. psychology U. Alta., 1968-77. Research cons. Alta. Alcoholism and Drug Abuse Commn., 1970-72. Served with Can. Officers Tng. Corps, 1942-46. Named Hon. Fellow dept. physics, U. Wis., 1950; named to Gallery of Living Catholic Musicians, 1948; recipient Silver Certificate award Acoustical Soc. Am., 1973; decorated knight comdr. Order St. Briget of Sweden; decorated knight, then knight comdr. Equestrian Order Holy Sepulchre Jerusalem (Vatican). Fellow Am., Mass. psychol. assns., Royal Statis. Soc., Royal Soc. Arts, AAAS, Internat. Inst. Arts and Letters (life), Internat. Acad. Forensic Psychology; mem. Wis. Acad. Scis. Arts and Letters (past v.p.), L'Accademia Tiberina (corr. academician), Assn. Littéaire et Artistique Internationale, Midwestern Psychol. Assn. (life), Internat. Philo-Byzantine Acad. and U. Valencia (hon. Venezuela), N.S. Music Tchrs. Assn. (past pres.), Royal Canadian Coll. Organists (past v.p.), Assn. Pontificial Knights (Paris). Author books and articles. Home: Clandonald AB T0B 0X0 Canada Office: PO Box 666 Edmonton AB Canada

O'BRIEN, JOHN WILLIAM, JR., securities co. exec.; b. Bronx, N.Y., Jan. 1, 1937; s. John William and Ruth Catherine (Timon) O'B.; B.S., Mass. Inst. Tech., 1958; M.S., U. Calif. at Los Angeles, 1964; m. Jane Bower Nippert, Feb. 2, 1963; children—Christine, Andrea, Michael, John William III, Kevin Robert. Sr. asso. Planning Research Corp., Los Angeles, 1962-67; dir. financial systems group Synergetic Scis., Inc., Tarzana, Calif., 1967-70; dir. analytical services div. James H. Oliphant & Co., Los Angeles, 1970-72; chmn. bd., chief exec. officer, pres. O'Brien Assos., Inc., Santa Monica, Calif., 1972-75; v.p. A.G. Becker Inc., Los Angeles, 1975—. Served to 1st lt. USAF, 1958-62. Recipient Graham and Dodd award Financial Analysts Fedn., 1970. Mem. Delta Upsilon. Home: 231 Surfview Dr Pacific Palisades CA 90272 Office: One Century Plaza Los Angeles CA 90067

O'BRIEN, JOHN WILLIAM VINCENT, mgmt. cons.; b. N.Y.C., Apr. 9, 1922; s. Patrick Joseph and Anne (Gibbons) O'B.; B.S. in Econs., Wharton Sch., U. Pa., 1948; m. Mary Anne Kelly, Nov. 19, 1955; children—Padric Kelley, Catherine Mary, Colleen Anne, John Michael. Asst. comptroller's dept. Am. Can Co., 1948-56; gen. mgr. finance div. Am. Mgmt. Assn., 1956-58; v.p. finance Hadson Pulp & Paper Corp., 1965-66, sales mgr. consumer and comml., 1958-66; sr. v.p., chief financial officer Brown Co., N.Y.C., 1966-69; chief financial officer Susquehanna Corp., Alexandria, Va., 1969-70; exec. v.p. Statler Industries Inc., Medford, Mass., 1970-73; pres. J.W.V. O'Brien Assos., Inc., Jacksonville, Fla., 1973—. Served to lt. (j.g.) USNR, 1942-46. Mem. Beta Gamma Sigma. Home: 8014 Hollyridge Rd Jacksonville FL 32216 Office: JWV O'Brien Assos Jacksonville FL 32216

O'BRIEN, RAYMOND FRANCIS, transp. and mfg. co. exec.; b. Atchison, Kans., May 31, 1922; s. James C. and Anna M. (Wagner) O'B.; B.S. in Bus. Adminstrn., U. Mo., 1948; grad. Advanced Mgmt. Program, Harvard, 1966; m. Mary Ann Baugher, Sept. 3, 1947; children—James B., William T., Kathleen A., Christopher R. Accountant-auditor Peat, Marwick, Mitchell & Co., Kansas City, Mo., 1948-52; controller-treas. Riss & Co., Kansas City, Mo., 1952-58; regional controller Consol. Freightways Corp. of Del., Indpls. and Akron, Ohio, 1958-61, dir., 1966—, pres., 1973-75, now chmn.; with Consol. Freightways, Inc., San Francisco, 1961—, controller-treas., 1962-63, v.p., treas., 1963-67, v.p. finance, 1967-69, exec. v.p., 1969-75, pres., 1975—, chief exec. officer, 1977—, chmn. bd., 1979—, also dir.; pres., dir. Freightways Terminal Co.; chmn. bd., dir. Can. Freightways Ltd., Centron Ltd., CF Air Freight, Inc., CF Data Services, Inc., Consol. Metco, Inc., Freightliner Corp., Freightliner Credit Corp., Freightliner Market Devel. Corp. Mem. bus. adv. bd. U. Calif., Berkeley, Northwestern U., Chgo.; bd. regents St. Mary's Coll. Calif., 1979. Served to 1st lt. USAAF, 1942-45. Mem. Am. Trucking Assn. (exec. com., dir.), Transp. Assn. Am. (dir.), Western Hwy. Inst. (treas.), Calif. C. of C. (dir.). Clubs: World Trade, Commonwealth (San Francisco); Palo Alto Hills Golf and Country; Congl. Country; Burning Tree. Home: 26347 Esperanza Dr Los Altos Hills CA 94022 Office: 601 California St San Francisco CA 94108

O'BRIEN, THOMAS HENRY, bank exec.; b. N.Y.C., June 19, 1944; s. Leo Francis and Alice (Beatty) O'B.; B.S., Fordham U., 1966, M.B.A., 1976; m. Carmen Gandara, Apr. 26, 1969; children—Thomas, Sean, Dennis. Acct., Shell Oil Co., N.Y.C., 1966, Price Waterhouse & Co., N.Y.C., 1967-74; v.p.-corp. acctg. and reporting Bankers Trust Co., N.Y.C., 1974-77, v.p. and controller London br., 1977-80; v.p., dep. controller BTNY Corp., 1980—. Served as 2d lt. USAF, 1966-67. C.P.A., N.Y. Mem. Am. Inst. C.P.A.'s, N.Y. Soc. C.P.A.'s. Catholic. Club: Downtown Athletic (N.Y.C.). Home: River Vale NJ Office: Bankers Trust Co 1 Bankers Trust Plaza New York NY 10015

O'BRYAN, WILLIAM HALL, ins. co. exec.; b. Tulia, Tex., June 15, 1919; s. Barnett and Goldie Sharp (Hall) O'B.; student Hills Bus. U., 1937, Tulsa Law Sch., 1939; m. Marjorie Wayland, Apr. 14, 1961; children—Richard, Clelie. With Okla. Compensation Rating Bur., 1937; v.p. Tri-State Ins. Group, 1937-62; pres. Occidental Fire and Casualty Co., Denver, 1961-73; pres., chmn. Prime Ins. Corp., Denver, 1973-74, exec. v.p., 1974-77; dep. ins. commr., State of Colo., 1974-77; pres. Mo. Profl. Liability Ins. Assn., Jefferson City, 1977—. Served to capt. AUS, 1942-46. Decorated Bronze star (3). Mem. Hosp. Ins. Forum, Nat. Assn. Mut. Ins. Cos. Republican. Episcopalian. Club: Rotary. Office: PO Box 1498 Jefferson City MO 65102

OBST, GEORGE JAY, med./dental employment and office services exec.; b. Bklyn., Mar. 21, 1939; s. Joseph Jay and Pearl Louise (Newmark) O.; B.A., Alfred U., 1960; M.S., L.I. U., 1963; m. Carol Adler, June 24, 1961; children—Amy, Pamela, Matthew. Social investigator N.Y.C. Dept. Welfare, 1960-62; asst. v.p. Chem. Bank, N.Y.C., 1962-70; v.p. ops. Heritage Dental Labs. div. Sybron Corp., Romulus, Mich., 1970-79; pres. Dental Lab. div., Codesco Inc., Phila., 1979-80, Met. Med. Placement, Mpls., 1980—. Served with U.S. Army, 1961-62. Home: 6936 Moccasin Valley Rd Edina MN 55435 Office: 7250 France Ave S Edina MN 55435

OCCHIPINTI, VINCENT MICHAEL, electronics and computer co. exec.; b. Cheyenne, Wyo., Jan. 4., 1940; s. Saverio and Lillian R. O.; student U. Calif., Berkeley, 1961-62 postgrad. in bus. adminstrn.; B.A. in Econs. with honors, Stanford U., 1963; m. Catherine Ann Crane, Sept. 3, 1960; children—Mari, Cynthia, John, Michael. With C.P.A. firms Peter G. Hart & Assos. and Charles A. Bock & Assos., Oakland, Calif., 1958-63; gen. agt. Fidelity Union Life Ins. Co., Oakland, 1963-65; product div. mgr. Levi Strauss Co., San Francisco, 1965-68; v.p. mktg. Mobility Systems, Inc., Santa Clara, Calif., 1968-74; prin. founder, pres., chief exec. officer Logisticon, Inc., Sunnyvale, Calif., 1974—. Trustee Woodside (Calif.) Village Sch., 1973-79, Woodside Village Ch., 1978-80. Mem. Am. Electronics Assn., Material Handling Inst., Electronics Assn. Calif., Stanford Alumni Assn., Mounted Patrol San Mateo County. Contbr. articles to profl. jours.

OCHILTREE, NED A., JR., metals mfg. co. exec.; b. Omaha, Dec. 23, 1919; s. Ned A. and Garnett (Briggs) O.; B.S., Purdue U., 1942; m. Isabel Hayden, Oct. 25, 1946; 1 dau., Judith Herseth. Research engr. Gen. Motors Research Labs., 1942-47; with Ceco Corp., Cicero, Ill., 1947—, exec. v.p. mfg., 1964-70, exec. v.p. sales and prodn., 1970-71, pres., 1971-76, pres., 1976-80, chief exec. officer, 1976—, chmn. bd., 1979—, also dir.; dir. Oak Park Trust & Savs. Bank (Ill.). Mem. Chgo. Crime Commn. 1966—. Presbyterian. Clubs: River Forest Tennis; Oak Park Country; Univ., Econ. (Chgo.). Home: 74 Briarwood Circle Oak Brook IL 60521 Office: 1400 Kensington Rd Oak Brook IL 60521

O'CONNELL, FRANCIS V(INCENT), mfr.; b. Norwich, Conn., July 8, 1903; s. Thomas Francis and Isabelle (Gelino) O.'C.; LL.B., Blackstone Coll. Law, 1932, J.D., 1940, LL.M., 1942; m. Marie Louise Lemoine, Nov. 7, 1940. Textile screen printer U.S. Finishing Co. Norwich, 1921-30; foreman Ahern Textile Print Co., Norwich, 1930-36; pres., owner Hand Craft Textile Print Co., Plainfield, Conn., 1936—. Roman Catholic. Home: 25 14th St Norwich CT 06360 Office: Bishop's Crossing Plainfield CT 06374

O'CONNELL, MICHAEL VINCENT, ins. co. exec.; b. Los Angeles, May 13, 1935; s. John W. and May Elizabeth (Diffley) O'C.; student U. Ariz., 1953-54, Auburn U., 1955-56; m. Patricia Jeanette Moran, Oct. 10, 1959; children—Kathleen Carol, Eileen Marie. Claims adjuster Liberty Mut. Ins. Co., Southeastern U.S., 1957-62, claims supr., Los Angeles, 1963-66; asst. claim mgr. Republic Indemnity Co., Los Angeles, 1966-67; home office claim mgr. Employers Self Ins. Service, Los Angeles, 1969; asst. claim mgr. Firemens Fund Ins., Los Angeles, 1970-76; asst. v.p., home office claims dept. Mission Ins. Co., Los Angeles, 1976-79, v.p., 1979—; claims cons. United Surg. Service City of Glendale, Calif. Licensed self ins. adminstr., Calif. Mem. Calif. Workers Compensation Inst. (claim com.), Indsl. Claims Assn. Republican. Roman Catholic. Club: K. of C. Home: 10038 Swinton Ave Sepulveda CA 91343 Office: 2601 Wilshire Blvd Los Angeles CA 90057

O'CONNELL, PHILIP R., lawyer, mfg. co. exec.; b. Woodside, N.Y., June 2, 1928; s. Michael J. and Ann C. (Blaney) O'C.; B.A., Manhattan Coll., 1949; LL.B., Columbia U., 1956; postgrad. Advanced Mgmt. Program, Harvard U., 1967; m. Joyce McCabe, July 6, 1957; children—Michael, Kathleen, Jennifer, David. Admitted to N.Y. State bar, 1956, U.S. Supreme Ct. bar, 1961; asso. firm Dewey, Ballantine, Bushby, Palmer & Wood, N.Y.C., 1956-61, 62-64; sec., gen. counsel Laurentide Fin. Corp. Calif., San Francisco, 1961-62; gen. counsel, div. mgr. Wallace-Murray Corp., N.Y.C., Indpls., Phila., 1964-70; pres. Universal Papertech Corp., Hatfield, Pa., 1970-71; v.p., sec. Champion Internat. Corp., Stamford, Conn., 1972—; trustee, Champion Internat. Found., 1979—. Served with USN, 1951-54. Mem. Am. Bar Assn. Clubs: Fairfield County Hunt, Landmark. Office: One Champion Plaza Stamford CT 06921

O'CONNOR, FRANK XAVIER, jewelry mfg. co. exec.; b. N.Y.C., Aug 15, 1925; s. Daniel J. and Lillian (Hayes) O'C.; m. Mary C. McAvinue, Mar. 1, 1968. Diamond sorter and salesman Baumgold Bros., N.Y.C., 1943-46; buyer Ollendorff Watch Co., N.Y.C., 1946-54; diamond buyer Wilkens Co., Pitts., 1954-60; ops. mgr., buyer Apco/Macy's, N.Y.C., 1960-70; div. mgr. Finlay/Gimbels, Pitts., 1970-74; v.p., chief exec. officer Busch Jewelry Co., N.Y.C., 1974-78; v.p., D.I.A. Trading Ltd., N.Y.C., 1978-79; v.p. Aurea Jewelry Creations, N.Y.C., 1979—; dir. Flavia div. of Aurea. Mem. Diamond Trade Assn. Office: 580 5th Ave New York NY 10036

O'CONNOR, JAMES ALBERT, mgmt. cons., former aerospace co. exec.; b. Brainerd, Minn., May 8, 1922; s. Francis C. and Emma B. O'Connor; B.S., Loyola Marymount U., Los Angeles, 1951; M.B.A., Calif. State U., 1975; m. Ruth Evangeline Buckley, Aug. 27, 1949; children—James F., John T., Maureen, Mary Ann. With Hughes Aircraft Co., 1951-78, head labor relations and wage adminstr. mfg. div., El Segundo, Calif., 1970-73, supt. space and communications fabrication shop Space and Communications div., 1973-78; mgmt. cons., 1979—. Chmn. Centinela Valley Com. for Employment of Handicapped, Inglewood, 1976-78; mem. Calif. Gov.'s Com. for Employment of Handicapped, 1976-78. Served with U.S. Navy, 1942-46. Mem. Soc. Mfg. Engrs. Democrat. Roman Catholic. Home: 8181 San Vincente Ave South Gate CA 90280

O'CONNOR, JAMES FRANCIS, JR., chocolate mfg. co. exec.; b. Phila., June 3, 1943; s. James Francis and Dorothy Winefred (Dietz) O'C.; student Pa. State U., 1965-67; B.S. in Acctg., LaSalle Coll., 1972; m. Rita Anne Boyle, Sept. 16, 1972; 1 son, James Francis 3d. Cost acct. ITT Nesbitt, Phila., 1967-70; acct. Certain-Teed Products, Valley Forge, Pa., 1970-74; acctg. mgr. Ward Chocolate Co., Inc., Phila., 1974-78, controller, 1978—. Served with USN, 1961-65. Mem. Nat. Assn. Accts. Office: Ward Chocolate Co Inc 4530 Tacony St Philadelphia PA 19137

O'CONNOR, JAMES JOHN, utility exec.; b. Chgo., Mar. 15, 1937; s. Fred J. and Helen E. (Reilly) O'C.; B.S. in Econs., Holy Cross Coll., 1958; M.B.A., Harvard, 1960; J.D., Georgetown U., 1963; m. Ellen Lawlor, Nov. 24, 1960; children—Fred, John, James, Helen Elizabeth. Admitted to Ill. bar, 1963; comml. mgr. Commonwealth Edison Co., Chgo., 1966, asst. v.p., 1967-70, v.p., 1970-73, exec. v.p., 1973-78, pres., 1978—, chmn. bd., 1980—; dir. Talman Fed. Savs. and Loan Assn., Chgo., Borg-Warner Corp., Esmark. Bd. dirs. Lyric Opera, Chgo. Assn. Commerce and Industry, Spl. Children's Charities, Chgo. Central Area Com., Chgo. Boys' Clubs, Chgo. Urban League, Assos. of Harvard U. Grad. Sch. Bus. Adminstrn., Reading is Fundamental, Chgo. Conv. and Tourism Bur., Arthritis Found., Cath. Charities Chgo.; bd. dirs. Chgo. unit Am. Cancer Soc., chmn., 1971-73; bd. dirs., v.p. Leadership Council Met. Open Communites; v.p. bd. advisers Mercy Hosp., Chgo.; chmn. Citizenship Council Met. Chgo.; trustee Mus. Sci. and Industry, Michael Reese Med. Center, Ill. Children's Home and Aid Soc., Adler Planetarium, Northwestern U., St. Xavier Coll. Field Mus.; exec. bd. Boy Scouts Am.; mem. citizens' bd. U. Chgo.; exec. v.p. Hundred Club of Cook County. Served with USAF, 1960-63. Mem. Am., Ill., Chgo. bar assns. Clubs: Chicago Commonwealth, Commercial, Chicago, Economic (Chgo.); Hundred of Cook County (exec. v.p.). Home: 9549 Monticello Ave Evanston IL 60203 Office: PO Box 767 Chicago IL 60690

O'CONNOR, JOHN THOMAS, mfg. co. exec.; b. Oakland, Calif., Feb. 9, 1944; s. John Charles and Mervyne (Hinske) O'C.; B.S. in Econs., U. Pa., 1966; postgrad. George Washington U., 1967-69; m. Barbara Orlando, Feb. 4, 1967; children—Thomas Stephen, Michael John, Lauren Barbara. Fed. mgmt. intern Dept. Def., Washington, 1967-68; aerospace group staff exec. Textron Inc., Washington, 1968-71; with IU Internat., Phila., 1971-80, pres., chief exec. of various subsidiaries, 1973-80; group mgr. planning and devel., indsl. electronics Gen. Electric Co., Charlottesville, Va., 1980—; instr. econs. Coll. No. Va., 1967-68; cons. in field.

O'CONNOR, LAWRENCE, fed. agy. ofcl.; b. Nome, Alaska, Apr. 13, 1948; s. John W. and Blanche Walters; student Sheldon Jackson Jr. Coll., 1968-69; m. Maggie Marie Fagerstrom, Dec. 30, 1972; children—Kimberley Alice, Dawn Marie, Floyd John. Air traffic control specialist FAA, Nome, 1970—; chmn. bd. Grand Alaska Industries, 1977—; dir. Bering Straits Native Corp., chmn. bd., 1978-79; v.p. Bering Straits Credit Union, 1979—. Coordinator Iditarod Basketball, 1975-79; pres. City League Basketball, 1976-79. Home: PO Box 1152 Nome AK 99762 Office: Fed Aviation Adminstrn Box 340 Nome AK 99762

O'CONNOR, LORETTA SINGLER, sales exec.; b. Point Pleasant, N.J., Apr. 23, 1955; d. Paul Vanston and Helen M. (Swain) Singler; B.S., Fairleigh Dickinson U., 1976; m. Lawrence V. O'Connor, III, June 12, 1976. With Sayrewood Jewelers, Brocktown, N.J., 1971-74, Littman Jewelers, Livingston, N.J., 1976-77; asst. to dir. Center for Women, Fairleigh Dickinson U., Rutherford, N.J., 1976; asso. account mgr. Burroughs Corp., Bloomfield, N.J., 1977-80, account mgr., 1980—. Recipient Profl. Achievement award Burroughs Corp., 1977, Legion of Honor, 1979, 80; Century Club award, 1977, 78. Mem. Phi Omega Eqsilon, Phi Chi Theta. Roman Catholic. Club: Spring Brook Country. Home: 53 Meadow Brook Rd Randolph NJ 07869 Office: 465 Bloomfield Ave Bloomfield NJ 07006

O'CONNOR, MATTHEW JAMES, chem. co. exec.; b. N.Y.C., July 31, 1940; s. Francis Patrick and Dorothy (Hayes) O'C.; B.S., Calif. State U., Long Beach, 1970; M.S., 1972; m. Geraldine Josephine Anello, July 1, 1967; children—Kelly, Stacy. Computer operator Vitro Labs., West Orange, N.J., 1963-64; analytical technician Shulton Inc., Clifton, N.J., 1964-65; supr. analytical and quality assurance labs. Chromizing Co., Gardena, Calif., 1965-72; mgr. analytical and quality assurance labs. Apollo Chem. Corp., Whippany, N.J., 1972-74, dir. tech. services, 1974-76, asst. v.p. Tech. Services div., 1976-79, v.p. mktg., 1979—. Served with USN, 1961-63. Mem. Am. Chem. Soc., ASTM, Air Pollution Control Assn. Patentee in field. Home: 157 Ironia Rd Mendham NJ 07945 Office: 35 Jefferson Rd Whippany NJ 07981

O'CONNOR, RICHARD DONALD, advt. co. exec.; b. Nyack, N.Y., Dec. 29, 1931; s. James Patrick and Sophie Kathryn (Hensel) O'C.; B.A., U. Mich., 1954. With Campbell-Ewald Co., Detroit, 1956—, exec. v.p., chief operating officer, 1975-76, pres., 1976-79, vice chmn., chief exec. officer, 1979—, also dir. Mem. acad. adv. council Walsh Coll., Troy, Mich., 1976-77; promotion chmn. United Found. Torch Drive, 1976; mem. adv. com. Mich. Cancer Found., 1976-77; bd. dirs. Detroit Better Bus. Bur., 1977—, Am. Assn. Advt. Agys.; trustee Northwood Inst., Detroit Country Day Sch., Bloomfield Hills Acad. Served with U.S. Army, 1954-56. Recipient Robert E. Healy award Interpub. Group Cos., 1974. Mem. Adcraft Club Detroit (past pres.), Detroit Advt. Assn. Republican. Roman Catholic. Clubs: Recess, Bloomfield Hills, Detroit Athletic, Duquesne, Hundred. Office: 30400 Van Dyke St Warren MI 48093

O'CONNOR, THOMAS WILLIAM, electronics co. exec.; b. Evanston, Ill.; s. Joseph Patrick and Florence Mary (Donohoe) O'C.; B.S. in Econs., U. Tampa; postgrad. in bus. adminstrn. George Washington U., 1972-75. Mgr. mortgage sales dept. Percy Wilson Mortgage & Fin. Corp., Chgo., 1960-65; chief exec. officer Aviation Transport Co., Kans. and Vietnam, 1966-69; command and control systems analyst Dept. Def., Washington, 1969-75; mktg. mgr. Collins Govt. Telecom Co. div. Rockwell Internat., Dallas, 1975-77, ITT Def. Space Group, Nutley, N.J., 1977-80; eastern regional mgr. Collins Avionics Group, Rockwell Internat., Arlington, Va., 1980—. Served to lt. col. U.S. Army, 1951-58. Decorated Legion of Merit, Bronze Star, D.F.C., Air medal (10). Mem. Army Aviation Assn. (life), Assn. U.S. Army, Armed Forces C-E Assn., Nat. Economists Club, Omicron Delta Epsilon. Editor tech. books on aviation, air traffic control, flight navigation and communications. Office: Rockwell-Collins 1745 Jefferson Davis Hwy Arlington VA 22202

O'CONNOR, WALTER JOSEPH, mfg. co. exec.; b. East Pittsburgh, Pa., Feb. 3, 1903; s. Walter Walker and Nora (O'Toole) O'C.; LL.D., Grove City Coll., 1959; m. Edith M. Thompson, Nov. 17, 1930. Chief engr. Homestead Ice & Brewing Co., 1930-38; plant engr. Stoner-Mudge Co., Pitts., 1938-43; prodn. mgr., v.p. Gilling Mfg. Co., 1943-46; founder-pres. Arcweld Mfg. Co., Grove City, Pa., 1946-61; pres., treas. Pinegrove Devel. Co., 1953—; with Della Robbia Prodns., Grove City, Pa., 1978—; treas. Calsicat Co., from 1958; dir. Grove City Nat. Bank; developer indsl. and comml. townsite, London, Pa. Bd. dirs. Grove City Devel. Council, Community Chest, Grove City Hosp., Grove City Library; treas. Geo. Jr. Republic. rehab. center for boys, 1970-75. Mem. Am. Ordnance Assn., Am. Vacuum Soc. Clubs: Rotary, Aero, OX5 (Pitts.); Grove City Country. Patentee in mech. and elec. field. Home and office: 412 W Washington Blvd Grove City PA 16127

O'DAY, DANIEL JAMES, petroleum equipment mfg. exec.; b. Fargo, N.D., Feb. 16, 1924; s. Leo John and Elizabeth Mary (Hopkins) O'Day; student N.D. State U., 1942; B.S. in C.E., Purdue U., 1946; m. Levon A. Merchant, Nov. 8, 1947; children—Susan, Margaret, James, Jean, Anne. Engr., United Engrs. and Constructors, Phila., 1947-48; with O'Day Equipment, Inc., Fargo, N.D., 1949—, pres., 1965—; dir. Bank N.D., Bismarck, Fargo Nat. Bank and Trust Co.; pres. Fargo Cass County Indsl. Devel. Corp., 1980. Served with USMC, 1943-45. Mem. Petroleum Equipment Inst. (pres. 1974), Steel Tank Inst. (v.p., dir. 1975), Am. Legion. Roman Catholic. Clubs: Elks; Eagles; Fargo Country; Ocean Reef. Office: 2500 Main Ave Fargo ND 58102

O'DEA, MARIE, publisher, freelance writer; b. Norfolk, Va., Nov. 12, 1900; d. Nicholas Francis and Nora (Tyers) O'Dea; student Johns Hopkins, 1919-20; A.B., George Washington U., 1923, M.S., 1923; postgrad. Columbia, 1926. Lab. asst. Dept. Agr., Washington, 1918-19; chemist Balt. Butterine Co., 1919-20, sales promotion mgr., corporate sec., 1926-34; instr. chemistry George Washington U., 1923-26; partner O'Dea Co., 1934-36; sales promotion mgr. Rennert Hotel, Balt., 1936-37; free-lance writer, 1937-41; asso. editor Herald-Argus weekly paper, Catonsville, Md., 1941-43, editor, 1943-64, asso. editor Catonsville Times & Herald-Argus, 1965-71; advt. mgr. Charles A. Skirven, Inc., realtor, Catonsville, 1967-76; pres. Caton Publs., Inc., 1977—. Mem. Md. Gov.'s Juvenile Delinquency Commn., 1940; founder, pres. Cath. Library, Balt., 1940-43; founder Catonsville Fourth July celebrations, 1947. Mem. Nat. League Am. Pen Women (pres. Balt. br. 1972-74) Catholic Golden Age, Am. Assn. Ret. Persons, Catonsville Hist. Assn., Friends Catonsville Library, George Washington U. Alumni Assn., Iota Sigma Chi, Phi Mu, Pi Delta Epsilon. Democrat. Roman Catholic. Clubs: Soroptimist (charter pres. Catonsville 1951-53, life mem.), Women's Advt. Balt. (pres. 1933-34, life mem.). Home and Office: Village Oaks Apts 801 Winters Ln Apt 440 Catonsville Baltimore MD 21228

ODER, FREDERIC CARL EMIL, space satellite co. exec.; b. Los Angeles, Oct. 23, 1919; s. Emil and Katherine Ellis (Pierce) O.; B.S. in Sci., Calif. Inst. Tech., 1940, M.S. in Meteorology, 1941; Ph.D., UCLA, 1952; postgrad. exec. program Stanford U.; m. Dorothy Gene Brumfield, July 2, 1941; children—Frederic Emil, Barbara Katherine Oder Debes, Richard William. Commd. U.S. Army Air Force, 1940, ret., 1960; asst. dir. and program mgr. for research and engring., apparatus and optical div., Eastman Kodak Co., 1960-66; v.p., gen. mgr. space systems div. Lockheed Missiles & Space Co., Sunnyvale, Calif., 1966—, corp. v.p. Lockheed Corp. Decorated Legion of Merit. Fellow AIAA; mem. Nat. Acad. Engring., Sigma Xi. Episcopalian. Club: Masons. Office: 1111 Lockheed Way Sunnyvale CA 94086

ODLE, IRA C., fire and safety equipment co. exec.; b. South Bend, Ind., Jan. 10, 1925; s. Ralph E. and James Henry (Ringstaff) O.; B.S., Butler U., 1949; m. Edith Louise Read, May 19, 1951; children—Patricia Ann, Stanley Reed. Salesman, Ind. Fire Prevention Co., Indpls., 1949; with Midwest Fire and Safety Co., Indpls., 1949-56, pres., 1953-56; pres., Safety Corp., Indpls., 1956—. Mem. exec. bd. Indpls. Safety Council, 1959-69. Trustee Ind. Soldiers and Sailors Children's Home. Served with AUS, 1943-45. Decorated Purple Heart. Mem. Safety Equipment Distbrs. Assn. (pres. 1969-71), Nat. Fire Equipment Distbrs. Assn. (pres. 1974-76), Nat. Assn. Wholesale Distbrs. (trustee 1974—), Am. Soc. Safety Engrs. (pres. Central Ind. chpt. 1972-73). Presbyn. (deacon 1963-69). Mason (Shriner), Rotarian. Club: Heather Hill's Country (Indpls). Home: 6625 E 9th St Indianapolis IN 46219 Office: 2716 E Michigan St Indianapolis IN 46201

ODOK, ADNAN M., aluminum co. exec.; b. Diyarbakir, Turkey, Apr. 21, 1925; came to U.S., 1956, naturalized, 1964; s. Cemal Ibrahim and Emine Odok; Dipl. El. Ing., Swiss Fed. Inst. Tech., 1949, Dr. sc. techn., 1955; m. Dora Magdalena Schaeppi, Aug. 29, 1950; children—Handan, Haydar, Selma, Sinan. Lectr., Swiss Fed. Inst. Tech., Zurich, 1949-50; specialist orgn. and mgmt. Sumerbank, Ankara, 1950-51; group leader Lect. machine devel. Oerlikon Engring. Co., Zurich, 1952-56; cons. engr. Louis Allis Co., Milw., 1956-57; mgr. transp. dept. physics and applied math. labs. Gen. Electric Co., Erie, Pa., 1957-61, project leader space weapons, Santa Barbara, Calif., 1961-63; prin. scientist Martin Co., Balt., 1963-64; group dir. advanced planning Aerospace Corp., El Segundo, Calif., 1964-69; v.p. research and devel. Swiss Aluminum Ltd., Zurich, 1969—; dir. Alusuisse Caster Corp.; lectr. Swiss Fed. Inst. Tech., Gannon Coll., Erie, also Behrend campus Pa. State U. Served with Turkish Navy 1951-52. Contbr. articles to profl. jours. Home: 11 Freudacherstrasse Herrliberg Switzerland 8704 Office: 16 Badische Bahnhofstrasse Neuhausen Switzerland 8212

ODOM, JOANNA BETH, accountant; b. Indpls., May 7, 1949; d. Ralph Harold and Betty Ruth (Marcum) Slaughter; B.S. in Bus., Ind. U., 1971, postgrad., 1975—; m. John Odom, Feb. 23, 1968; children—Cara, Lora. Office mgr. First Holding Corp., Indpls., 1968-74; sr. bookkeeper Firstmark Fin. Corp., Indpls., 1974-76; accountant Mallory Timers Co., Indpls., 1976—; cons. tax matters small businesses. Active ARC; coach jr. girls softball team. C.P.A., Ind. Mem. Am. Mgmt. Assn., Mensa. Home: 236 E North St Westfield IN 46074 Office: 3029 E Washington St Indianapolis IN 46206

O'DONNELL, DOUGLAS ALLEN, veterinarian; b. Richmond, Calif., May 31, 1949; s. Albert Roger and Carole Ann Leapley (Tilden) O'Donnell; B.S. Animal Biology, Wash. State U., 1971, B.S. in Vet. Sci., 1973, D.V.M., 1975; m. Candyce Star Bumstead, Feb. 4, 1968; children—Douglas Allen (Butch), Karie Ann-Marie. Veterinarian, Wheaton Way Vet. Clinic and Animal Hosp. Central Kitsap, Bremerton, Wash., 1975—, partner, 1978—; also veterinarian Belfair Animal Hosp. First v.p. North Kitsap Peewee Assn., 1978—; active Boy Scouts Am., bd. dirs. N. Kitsap Sch. Bd. Mem. Am., Wash. State, S. Puget Sound vet. med. assns., Wash. State Orthopedic Soc. Clubs: Rotary (dir. Bremerton Olympic 1977—, treas. 1980—), Bremerton Tennis and Swim, Wash. Racquetball Assn. Home: 1106 NE State Hwy 308 Poulsbo WA 98370 Office: 1220 Sheridan Rd Bremerton WA 98310

O'DONNELL, EDWARD BAXTER, JR., fgn. service officer; b. Memphis, May 19, 1946; s. Edward Baxter and Velma Ruth (Hensley) O'D.; B.A., So. Methodist U., 1968; M.A., Am. U., 1974; postgrad. econs. Heidelberg (Germany) U., 1971-72; m. Beth Nichols Beal, June 22, 1974; children—Christina, Susannah, Bradley. Internat. lending rep. Mfrs. Hanovers Trust Co., N.Y.C., 1974-75; fgn. service officer U.S. Dept. State, 1975; asst. comml. attache Am. Embassy, Bogota, Colombia, 1975-77; comml. officer, vice-consul Am. embassy, Asuncion, Paraguay, 1977-78; internat. economist Latin Am. Bur., Dept. State, Washington, 1978-79; spl. asst. to dir. policy planning staff Dept. State, Washington, 1979—. Served to capt. U.S. Army, 1968-72. Teagle Found. grantee, 1964-68. Mem. Am. Mgmt. Assn., Am. Fgn. Service Assn., Assn. Comml. Attaches in Colombia, Am. Soc. Bogota, Phi Kappa Phi, Phi Alpha Theta. Methodist. Home: 9309 Marycrest St Fairfax VA 22030 Office: US Dept State S/P Rm 7311 Washington DC 22030

O'DONNELL, EDWARD M., JR., warehouses co. exec.; b. Syracuse, N.Y., Dec. 24, 1935; s. Edward M. and Florence (Feeney) O'D.; B.A., Georgetown U., 1959; m. Catherine Phillips, Jan. 27, 1962; children—Maureen, Edward M., Patrick. Stockbroker, Foster and Adams, N.Y.C., 1960-62; pres., gen. mgr. O'Donnell Distbrs. Inc., Syracuse, 1962-69; pres. Gt. No. Warehouses, Inc., Syracuse, 1962—; pres. E. M. O'Donnell Co. Inc., Syracuse, 1962—. Mem. parents council Westhill Sch. Dist., 1977-80, pres., 1980. Served with U.S. Army, 1960. Roman Catholic. Clubs: Bellevue Country (dir. 1968-74), Thunder Bird Ski (dir. 1972-78, pres. 1975-77), Syracuse Dist. Golf Assn. (mem. scholarship com. 1972—). Home: 208 Rockwood Pl Syracuse NY 13215 Office: 301 Erie Blvd Syracuse NY 13201

O'DONNELL, JOHN WILLIAM, mfg. co. exec.; b. Hamilton, Ont., Can., Feb. 26, 1934; s. Frederick William and Jean Marie (Hossack) O'D.; B.A., U. Toronto, 1954; A.M.P., Harvard U., 1978; m. Nancy Innes, Aug. 27, 1955; children—Megan, Victoria, John, Charles, Joseph, Melissa. With Lever Bros. Ltd., Toronto, Ont., 1955-69, mktg. dir. Lever Detergents Ltd., 1969-70; pres. Monarch Fine Foods Co. Ltd., Rexdale, Ont., 1970—; dir. Riviera Foods Ltd. Mem. Grocery Products Mfrs. Assn. Canada, Met. Toronto Bd. Trade, Inst. Edible Oil Foods. Roman Catholic. Club: Mississauga Golf and Country. Home: 223 Trelawn Ave Oakville ON L6J 4R3 Canada Office: 6700 Finch Ave Rexdale ON M9W 1G9 Canada

O'DONNELL, MARTIN THOMAS, food co. exec.; b. Chgo., Feb. 20, 1937; s. Martin and Barbara (Flaherty) O'D.; B.S., Loyola U., Chgo., 1960; M.B.A., U. Chgo., 1964. Math. tchr. Chgo. pub. schs., 1961-62; bus. analyst Exxon Corp., Baton Rouge, 1964-65; staff analyst sales and fin. depts. Inland Steel Corp., Chgo., 1966-70;

diversification analyst G.D. Searle & Co., Skokie, Ill., 1970-74; corporate devel. specialist Libby, McNeill & Libby, Inc., Chgo., 1974, mgr. real estate, 1974-76, asst. to treas., 1976-78, asst. treas., 1978—. Mem. Met. Housing and Planning Council. Served to lt. U.S. Army, 1960-61. Mem. Chgo. Council Fgn. Relations, Cash Mgmt. Practitioners Assn., Assn. Corporate Growth, Midwest Planning Assn., Planning Execs. Inst., N.Am. Soc. Corporate Planning, Nat. Assn. Corporate Real Estate Execs., Indsl. Devel. Research Council. Roman Catholic. Home: 2820 W Chase St Chicago IL 60645 Office: 200 S Michigan Ave Chicago IL 60604

O'DONNELL, ROBERT JOHN, lawyer; b. Worcester, Mass., Aug. 3, 1943; s. Joseph Charles and Nellie (Baltrukaitis) O'D.; B.S. in Bus. Adminstrn., U. Calif., Berkeley, 1965; certificate of completion (fellow) Coro Found., San Francisco, 1966; J.D., Boston Coll., 1969; m. Joyce I. Samonek, May 31, 1969; children—Gary Thomas, Shaun Kenric. Admitted to Vt. bar, 1970; clk. Black & Plante, White River Junction, Vt., 1969-70, asso. firm, 1970; individual practice law, Woodstock, Vt., 1970—; pres. Unican Corp., Shrewsbury, Mass., 1974-75; justice peace, Hartland, Vt., 1979. Mem. vestry St. James Episcopal Ch., Woodstock, 1973-76; vestryman, lay reader St. Paul's Episcopal Ch., Windsor, Vt., 1978—; chmn. Woodstock chpt. ARC, 1975—, mem. New Eng. div. advisory council, 1975-78; mem. Bd. Civil Authority, Hartland, Vt., 1979, Pomfret (Vt.) Planning Commn., 1980—. Mem. Am., Vt., Windsor County bar assns., Woodstock C. of C. (dir.), Older Golder Bears, Phi Phi, Phi Kappa Sigma, Alpha Phi Omega. Republican. Clubs: Masons, Order of Eastern Star, Commonwealth, Order Golden Bear, Calif. (San Francisco). Home: Stage Rd S Pomfret VT 05067 Office: Five The Green Woodstock VT 05091

O'DONOHUE, BRIAN FRANCIS, audio products mfg. co. exec.; b. N.Y.C., Dec. 24, 1944; s. Timothy J. and Nora O'D.; B.A. (N.Y. State Regents scholar), Iona Coll., 1966; M.B.A., Boston Coll., 1968; m. Kathleen Meehan, June 10, 1967; children—Jennifer, Timothy. Fin. analyst Itek Corp., Lexington, Mass., 1968-72; controller Litho Systems div., 1972-75; controller Ventron Corp., Beverly, Mass., 1975-77; v.p. fin. ops. KLH Corp., Westwood, Mass., 1979—; notary public, Mass. Mem. Nat. Assn. Accts., Fin. Execs. Inst. Home: 29 Louise Rd Belmont MA 02178 Office: 145 University Ave Westwood MA 02090

O'DRISCOLL, JEREMIAH JOSEPH, railroad exec.; b. Galveston, Tex., Dec. 8, 1925; s. Jeremiah Joseph and Natie Alice (Jones) O'D.; student Southwestern La. U., 1943-44; B.B.A., U. Tex., 1950; m. Marie Louise McCormack, Feb. 7, 1953; children—Maureen Immaculata, Sharon Maura, Jeremiah Joseph, Maria, Paul, Kathleen, Jonathan. Explosives safety engr. U.S. Naval Ordnance Lab., White Oak, Md., 1954-56; mgr. safety and security Catalyst Research Corp., Balt., 1956-59; mgr. corp. safety and loss prevention Atlas Chem. Industries, Wilmington, Del., 1959-69; mgr. planning and safety So. Rwy. System, Atlanta, 1969-79, dir. hazardous materials and safety, 1979—; pres. Jody Inc., 1977—; lectr. in field; mem. chem. reactivity panel Com. on Hazardous Materials, Nat. Acad. Scis., 1974-76. Served to lt. USNR, 1943-46, 50-54. Certified safety profl., Ill.; registered profl. engr., Calif. Mem. Am. Soc. Safety Engrs., Hazardous Materials Adv. Council, Phi Kappa Sigma. Roman Catholic. Author: Emergency Action Plan for Accidents Involving Hazardous Materials, 1969, Transportation Emergency Action Guide for Hazardous Materials Incidents, 1977; contbg. author: Safety and Accident Prevention in Chemical Operations, 1965. Contbr. articles profl. jours. Home: 505 Valley Hall Dr Dunwoody GA 30338 Office: 185 Spring St SW Atlanta GA 30303

ODWAK, ROGER KEITH, fin. exec.; b. N.Y.C., Mar. 27, 1940; s. Clifford Ira and Julia (Jawitz) O.; B.S., N.Y. U., 1966; m. Nancy Ruth Blacher, Nov. 3, 1968. With Robinson Humphrey, Ft. Lauderdale, Fla., 1975-76, Drexel Burnham, Ft. Lauderdale, 1976-78; v.p. Oppenheimer & Co., Los Angeles, 1978—; tchr. investment courses. Served with U.S. Army, 1962-63. Home: 100 S Doheny Dr Los Angeles CA 90048 Office: 2029 Century Park E Los Angeles CA 90067

OEHLERKING, ARMOND DEAN, heavy equipment mfg. co. exec.; b. Omaha, Sept. 8, 1934; s. Albert F. and Julia A. O.; B.S. Elec. Engring., U. Nebr., 1956; M.S. in Bus. Adminstrn., No. Ill. U., 1964; m. Judith A. Lawrence, July 2, 1954 (dec. Sept. 1972); children—Cynthia, Julie, Sharon; m. 2d, Mryna J. Jung, Aug. 30, 1974. Engr., Honeywell, Mpls., 1956-60; project engr. Ideal Industries, Inc., Sycamore, Ill., 1960-67; engring. mgr. elec. products div. Joy Mfg. Co., New Philadelphia, Ohio, 1967-73; pres. Dakota Mfg. Co. Inc., Mitchell, S.D., 1973—. Regents scholar U. Nebr., 1952; registered profl engr., S.D. Patentee elef. and mech. devices. Home: 94 N Harmon Dr Mitchell SD 57301 Office: Dakota Mfg Co Inc Box 1188 Mitchell SD 57301

OEHMLER, GEORGE COURTLAND, corp. exec.; b. Pitts., May 6, 1926; s. Rudolph Christian and Virgia Sylvia (Stark) O.; B.S. in Indsl. Engring, Pa. State U., 1950; m. Martha Jane Swagler, July 3, 1954; children—Wendy Lynn, Christy Ann, Geoffrey Colin. Indsl. egnr. Allegheny Ludlum Steel Corp., Pitts., 1953-54, salesman, 1954-60, mgr. export sales, 1960-67, mgr. flat rolled products, 1967-68, asst. to chmn., 1968-73, v.p. internat., 1973-75, v.p. internat. Allegheny Ludlum Industries, Inc., Pitts., 1975—. Mem. exec. bd. Pa. State U. Alumni Council, 1976—. Served with U.S. Army, 1944-46, 51-52. Mem. Am. Iron and Steel Inst., Assn. Iron and Steel Engrs., Machinery and Allied Products Inst. (internat. ops. council), NAM, Internat. Econ. Affairs Com., World Affairs Council Pitts. (pres. 1980—, dir.), Pitts. Council for Internat. Visitors (dir. and pres. 1976-78), Greater Pitts. C. of C. Republican. Presbyterian. Clubs: Duquesne, Longue Vue, Pitts. Athletic. Home: 321 Braddsley Dr Pittsburgh PA 15235 Office: Two Oliver Plaza Pittsburgh PA 15222

OETH, PETER JOHN, mgmt. cons.; b. Chgo., Dec. 9, 1934; s. Cle Francis and Marie Cecilia (Shea) O.; B.S. (Bd. Trustees scholar), Drexel U., 1959; M.A., Temple U., 1964; m. Linda Lowell, Nov. 25, 1960; children—Lee, David, Paul. Systems engr. IBM, 1961-64; computer salesman Gen. Electric Info. Systems, 1964-67; nat. sales mgr. Gen. Electric Resource Service, 1968-69; exec. v.p. Western Data Scis., Inc., Phoenix, 1969-73, now dir.; dir. EDP cons. practice for Orange County, Arthur Young & Co., Santa Ana, Calif., 1973-75; partner McSweeney & Assos., Newport Beach, Calif., 1975—; lectr., instr. in field, 1973—. Served with U.S. Army, 1959-62. Mem. IEEE. Republican. Club: Balboa Yacht (Newport Beach). Contbr. numerous articles on productivity improvement, uses of automation in various industries to profl. publs. Office: 1550 N Bristol St Newport Beach CA 92660

O'FARRELL, JOHN FRANCIS, investment co. exec.; b. Alpena, Mich., Dec. 4, 1939; s. John A. and Helen A. (Widdis) O'F.; B.A., U. Mich., 1963; postgrad. George Washington U., 1967; m. Jeannine Joy Elowsky, Sept. 28, 1968; children—John, Carmen, Shannon, Brennan. Vice pres. Reynolds Securities, Washington, 1969-77, Dean Witter, Washington, 1978, Merrill Lynch, Washington, 1979—. Served with U.S. Navy, 1963-69. Roman Catholic. Office: Suite 200 1111 19th St NW Washington DC 20036

O'FARRELL, ROBERT LOUIS, med. exam. service exec.; b. Bay City, Mich., Feb. 28, 1937; s. Louis A. and Madeline Cecilia (Maxson) O'F.; A.A., Bay City Jr. Coll., 1958; married, Aug. 2, 1958; children—Katherine, Lisa, Rebecca, Jamie. Supr. Coca Cola Bottling Co., Bay City, 1956-59; sales rep. Cook Coffee Co., Mt. Pleasant, Mich., 1959-60, 7-Up Bottling Co., Bay City, 1960-64; agt. Allstate Ins. Co., Bay City, 1964-72; ind. ins. agt., Bay City, 1972-75; owner, mgr. Med. Exam. Service, Bay City, 1975—, also O'Farrell Enterprises. Served with USNR, 1954-58. Mem. Bay City Life Underwriters, Am. Agts. and Brokers, Mich. Life Underwriters, Bay Med. Center. Roman Catholic. Clubs: Bay Valley Raquette Ball, Sports Illustrated Ct. Home: 57 Bay Shore Dr Bay City MI 48706 Office: 405 State Park Dr Bay City MI 48706

O'FARRELL, STEPHEN THOMAS, petroleum mfg. co. exec.; b. Quebec City, Que., Can., Aug. 18, 1937; s. John Patrick and Alma (Simard) O'F.; D.Eng., St. Francis Xavier U., 1957; B.S. in Chem. Engring., McGill U., 1959, D.B.A., 1969; cert. in Mgmt., U. Western Ont., 1977; m. Julie Ann Fothergill, June 24, 1971; children—Susan, Michael. With Texaco Can. Inc., Donn Mills, Ont., 1963—, asst. div. mgr., 1969-71, dist. mgr. 1971-73, div. mgr., 1973-76, regional mgr., 1976-77, asst. gen. mgr., 1977-80, dir. computer and info. systems dept., 1980—; pres. Ind. Petroleum Co. Ltd., Montreal, 1973-76, also dir. Served with Can. Army, 1959-63. Mem. Inst. Profl. Engrs. Ont., Order Engrs. Que., Am. Inst. Chem. Engrs., Que. Petroleum Assn. (v.p. 1973-74, pres. 1975-76), Ont. Petroleum Assn. (v.p. 1976-77). Clubs: Montreal Athletic, Bloor Park, Parkview Racquet. Home: 40 Alexander St Penthouse L Toronto ON M4Y 1B5 Canada Office: 90 Wynford Dr Don Mills ON M3C 1K5 Canada

OFFENSTEIN, CLARENCE FRANK, mergers, acquisitions and real estate co. exec.; b. Wichita, Kans., Jan. 23, 1913; s. Barney Christian and Anna Marie (Pale) O.; student Wichita State U., 1929-31, U. So. Calif., 1953; student real estate law U. Kans. Extension, 1971; m. Elsie G. Gottschalk, Oct. 23, 1937; 1 dau., Sonya Sue Beardsley. Asst. treas. Santa Fe Trail Transp. Co., Wichita, 1936-37, chief clk., personnel dir., 1940-45, gen. mgr., 1955-68; asst. v.p., asst. gen. mgr. Atchison, Topeka and Santa Fe R.R., Wichita, 1945-68; pres. Affiliated Bus. Brokers, Inc., Wichita, 1969—; dir., cons. Carlson Mfg. and Hydraulics, Inc. Active Founders Club, Cerebral Palsy Research Endowment Assn. Lic. real estate broker, Kans. Mem. Wichita Ind. Bus. Assn. (dir.), Wichita State U. Alumni Assn. Republican. Clubs: Shocker, Hatch Cover. Office: 567 S Roosevelt St Wichita KS 67218

OFFUTT, GEORGE QUENTIN, wooden pallet mfg. co. exec.; b. Knox City, Tex., May 2, 1940; s. Lonnie D. and Sara L. Offutt; B.S. in Acctg., Abilene Christian U., 1961; m. Linda Nell Guinn, May 27, 1960; children—Bradley, Brian. Staff acct. Ben M. Davis and Co., 1961-66; chief fin. officer, dir. various corps. controlled by McGlothlin family, including N. Am. Petroleum Corp., E-Z Serve, Inc., Abilene, Tex., 1966-79; chief fin. officer Mulberry Lumber Co., Abilene, 1966-79, chmn. bd., 1979—, dir., 1966-79. Mem. adv. bd. Abilene Christian U.; pres. Bowie Elem. Sch. PTA, 1978-79. C.P.A., Tex. Mem. Fin. Execs. Inst., Am. Inst. C.P.A.'s, Tex. Soc. C.P.A.'s, Abilene Estate Planners, Abilene C. of C. Mem. Ch. of Christ. Clubs: Petroleum, Abilene Country, Fairway Oaks Country, Cactus Lions (treas.) (Abilene). Office: PO Box 3658 Abilene TX 79604

OGDEN, PEGGY A., personnel exec.; b. N.Y.C., Mar. 21, 1932; d. Stephen A. and Margaret (Stern) Ogden; B.A., Brown U., 1953; M.A., Trinity Coll., 1955. Asst. personnel dir. Inst. Internat. Edn., N.Y.C., 1956-59; personnel adviser Girl Scouts U.S.A., N.Y.C., 1959-61; personnel mgr. Ohrbach's Westbury (L.I., N.Y.), 1961-66, store mgr., 1966-73; dep. dir. adminstrn. and personnel dir. N.Y.C. Tech. Coll., 1974—; vis. lectr. Nassau Community Coll. Chmn., N.Y. State Adv. Bd. Distributive Edn. Mem. Am. Psychol. Assn., Internat. Assn. Personnel Women, N.Y. Personnel Mgmt. Assn. Home: 1100 Park Ave New York NY 10028 Office: 300 Jay St Brooklyn NY 11201

OGG, ROBERT DANFORTH, business exec., inventor, author; b. Gardiner, Maine, June 10, 1918; s. James and Eleanor B. (Danforth) O.; A.A., San Francisco Jr. Coll., 1941; student U. Calif. at Berkeley, 1946-47; m. Phyllis Idun Aasgaard, Nov. 23, 1946 (div. 1963); children—Richard Aasgaard, Robert Danforth, James Erling; m. 2d, Catherine O'Neill Zamore, Sept. 14, 1963; children—Christopher Hale, Daniel Benton, Ann Brooke, Thomas H.; m. 3d, Nancy Foote Bechtel, Oct. 21, 1978. Utilities engr. State of Calif., 1947-49; research engr., sales mgr. Danforth Anchors, East Boothbay, Maine and Berkeley, Calif., 1949-51, gen. mgr., Berkeley, 1951-56, pres., 1956-61, also dir.; mng. dir. Danforth div. The Eastern Co., mfrs. marine products, weather, yacht racing instruments, Portland, Maine, 1961—; dir. Brewers Boatyard, West Southport, Maine, Eastern Co., H.R. Hinckley & Co., boat builders, Manset, Maine; pres. OEG Ocean Systems. Bd. dirs. Arlington Ave. Community Center Council Kensington, 1954-57, chmn. bd., 1956-57; sr. warden St. Ann's Episcopal Ch., Windham, Maine, 1976—; mem. Internat. Oceanographic Found.; asso. Woods Hole Found. Served as lt. comdr. USNR, 1941-46. Mem. Nat. Marine Products Assn. (pres. 1961-63), Nat. Assn. Engine and Boat Mfrs., Am. Boat and Yacht Council, I.E.E.E., Am. Geophys. Union, Boating Industry Assn., N.Am. Yacht Racing Union, Soc. Naval Architects and Marine Engrs., Am. Soc. Naval Engrs., Navy League (pres. Casco Bay council), Boating Industry Assn., Portland Marine Soc., U.S. Naval Inst., Mayflower Soc., Sierra Club. Clubs: Elks; Outboard Boating (Maine); Card Ledge Yacht; St. Croix Country (dir. 1973—, v.p. 1974—), Portland Yacht, Cumberland (Portland, Maine); N.Y. Yacht. Author: Compasses and Compassing; Anchors and Anchoring. Contbr. to McGraw Hill Handbook of Ocean Engineering, Chapman's Piloting Seamanship and Small Boat Handling; also many articles in field. Inventor and patentee anchors, compasses, gas detectors, others. Home: Box 160 Kentfield CA 94914 also Estate Sprat Hall Frederiksted Saint Croix VI 00840 Office: 500 Industrial Pkwy Portland ME 04103 also Kentfield CA 94904

OGG, WILSON REID, lawyer, real estate investment cons.; b. Alhambra, Calif., Feb. 26, 1928; s. James Brooks and Mary (Wilson) O.; student Pasadena Jr. Coll., 1946; A.B., U. Calif. at Berkeley, 1949, J.D., 1952. Asso. trust dept. Wells Fargo Bank, San Francisco, 1954-55; admitted to Calif. bar; pvt. practice law, Berkeley, 1955—; real estate broker, 1974—; research atty., legal editor dept. continuing edn. bar U. Calif. Extension, 1958-63; psychology instr. 25th Sta. Hosp., Taegu, Korea, 1954; English instr. Taegu English Lang Inst., 1954. Trustee World U., 1976—, treas., 1979—. Served with AUS, 1952-54. Fellow Internat. Acad. Law and Sci., World-Wide Acad. Scholars; hon. fellow Harry S. Truman Library Inst. Nat. and Internat. Affairs; mem. State Bar Calif., San Francisco Bar Assn., Am. Arbitration Soc. (nat. panel arbitrators), AAAS, Center for Study Presidency, World Future Soc., Am. Mgmt. Assn., Am. Bar Assn., Am. Acad. Polit. and Social Sci., Am. Soc. for Psychical Research, Calif. Soc. Psychical Study (pres., chmn. bd. 1963-65), Mechanics Inst., Internat. Platform Assn., Lawyers in Mensa, Am. Mensa, Suomi Soc., Soc. for Psychical Research (London), Mensa Psychic Sci. Spl. Interest Group, Parapsychol. Assn. (asso.). Unitarian. Mason, Elk. Clubs: Faculty (U. Calif.), City Commons (Berkeley); Press (San Francisco); Commonwealth of Calif., Town Hall of Calif. Editor: Legal Aspects of Doing Business under Government Contracts and Subcontracts, 1958, Basic California Practice Handbook, 1959. Office: 8 Bret Harte Way Berkeley CA 94708

OGONOWSKI, GEORGE ROMAN, bldg. contractor; b. Mineola, N.Y., May 28, 1929; s. Kazmer and Stella (Raymond) O.; student N.Y. Elec. Sch., 1949, Pace Coll., 1951-52, Hofstra Coll., 1954; m. Shirley Jean Fisher, Aug. 23, 1969; 1 dau., Vicki. Owner, George R. Ogonowski Constrn. Co., Roman Investment Co., Tucson, 1954—; pres. Govoso Corp., Sierra Madre Devel. Co. Served with C.E., AUS, 1951-52. Mem. So. Ariz. Home Builders Assn. (dir.), Tucson C. of C. Roman Catholic. K.C., Elk. Club: Sertoma. Home: 5373 Gleneagles Dr Tucson AZ 85718 Office: 4615 N 1st Ave Tucson AZ 85704

O'GRADY, BEVERLY TROXLER, investment analyst; b. Greensboro, N.C., Nov. 26, 1941; d. Robert Andrew and Beverly Beam (Barrier) Troxler; B.A., St. Mary's Coll., Notre Dame, Ind., 1963; M.A., Columbia U., 1965; m. Robert Edward O'Grady, Aug. 6, 1966. Chmn. English dept. Cardinal Spellman High Sch., Bronx, N.Y., 1964-72; asst. v.p. Dudley & Wilkinson, Inc., N.Y.C., 1973-80, v.p., 1980—. Clubs: Women's Bond; Princeton (N.Y.C.). Office: Dudley & Wilkinson Inc 521 Fifth Ave New York NY 10017

O'GREEN, FREDERICK W., multinat. corp. exec.; b. Mason City, Iowa, Mar. 25, 1921; s. Oscar A. and Anna (Heikkinen) O'G.; student Mason City Jr. Coll., 1939-40; B.S. in Elec. Engring., Iowa State U., 1943; M.S. in Elec. Engring., U. Md., 1949; LL.D. (hon.), Pepperdine U., 1977; m. Mildred G. Ludlow, Mar. 21, 1943; children—Susan Renee, Jane Lynn O'Green Koenig, John Frederick, Eric Stephen. Project engr. Naval Ordnance Lab., White Oak, Md., 1943-55; dir. Agena D project Lockheed Aircraft Co., Sunnyvale, Calif., 1955-62; v.p. Litton Industries, Inc., Beverly Hills, Calif., 1962-66, sr. v.p., 1966-68, exec. v.p., 1968-74, pres., chief operating officer, 1974—. Area chmn. United Crusade, 1965. Served with USNR, 1945. Recipient Meritorious Civilian Service award U.S. Navy, 1954; Outstanding Achievement award Air Force Systems Command, 1964; Distinguished Achievement citation Iowa State U., 1973. Mem. AIM, Am. Inst. Aeros. and Astronautics, U.S. C. of C., Assn. U.S. Army (dir.), Phi Kappa Psi, Phi Mu Alpha. Republican. Lutheran. Office: Litton Industries Inc 360 N Crescent Dr Beverly Hills CA 90210

O'HARA, CLIFFORD BRADLEY, port authority exec.; b. Newark, Jan. 2, 1918; s. Ralph Leslie and Edna (Brangs) O'H.; B.A., Princeton, 1939; M.B.A., N.Y. U., 1956; m. Helen Elizabeth Hanford, Apr. 26, 1941; children—Hanford, Helen Elizabeth (Mrs. D.J. White), Susan Bradley, Jane Loving, Clifford Bradley. With Pa. R.R., 1939-48, spl. rep. office v.p. traffic, 1943-48; supr. traffic dept. Shell Oil Co., N.Y.C., 1948-53; chief port commerce Port of N.Y. Authority, 1953-62, dir. port commerce, 1962—. Vice chmn. N.Y. World Trade Week Com., 1963-68, chmn., 1969-73; mem. supervisory bd. Panama Canal Commn. Served to lt. (j.g.) USNR, 1944-46. Mem. N. Atlantic Ports Assn. (pres. 1961-64), Am. Assn. Port Authorities (pres. 1979—), Assn. ICC Practitioners, Nat. Freight Traffic Assn., Containerization Inst. (chmn. 1978—), Nat. Def. Transp. Assn. (v.p. N.Y. 1960-64, pres. 1964-66, nat. v.p. 1965—) Traffic Club N.Y.C., Fgn. Commerce Club N.Y.C. Episcopalian. Clubs: Riverside Yacht, Princeton (N.Y.C.). Home: 19 Indian Head Rd Riverside CT 06878 also Pocomo Nantucket MA 02554 Office: 1 World Trade Center New York City NY 10048

O'HARA, DAVID MICHAEL, lawyer; b. Springfield, Ill., Mar. 31, 1940; s. James Dennis and Angela Maud (Becker) O'H.; B.S. in Civil Engring., Bradley U., 1962; J.D., U. Calif., 1969; m. Sharon F. LePage, Feb. 19, 1977. Admitted to Calif. bar, 1970; asst. legal counsel Castle & Cooke, Inc., San Francisco, 1968-69; with firm Danaher, Fletcher & Gunn, Palo Alto, Calif., 1969-70, Quaresma, Avera, Benya, Hall & Haun, 1970—. Tchr. real estate law Ohlone Coll., Fremont, Calif., 1972—; legal council Calif. Jaycees, 1973-74. Bd. dirs. Operation Amigo, Riverside, Calif., 1973-74, Calif. Jaycee Found., 1973-74, Community Drug Council, Fremont, 1971—. Served to lt. comdr. USNR, 1962-66. Recipient Outstanding Young Men of Am. award 1972-74, Nat. Am. Legion Citizenship award, 1958. Mem. Calif., Alameda County, San Francisco, Washington Twp. bar assns., Sierra Club, Internat. Platform Assn., Mensa. Clubs: Barristers, Commonwealth, Lawyers (San Francisco); Berkeley Yacht. Author: Nuclear Biological and Chemical Warfare-Offense, 1966; Nuclear Biological and Chemical Warfare-Defense, 1967; The Incarceration and Persecution of the Atom, 1969. Contbr. articles to law jours. Home: 986 Seville Pl Fremont CA 94538 Office: Quaresma Avera Benya Hall & Haun 37323 Fremont Blvd Fremont CA 94536

O'HARA, JOHN STEPHEN, state govt. statistician; b. Emmett, Mich., Sept. 28, 1918; s. John C. and Mable Catherine (Mittig) O'H.; B.S., U. Fla., 1946; m. Ann Theresa Rhoads, Feb. 26, 1949; children—John Stephen, Janis Elaine, Victoria Louise, Deborah Ann, David Bruce, Suzanne Denise, Ellen Carol, Cathy Elizabeth, Rebecca Alayne. Statistician, Office Research and Statistics, Fla. Dept. Commerce, Tallahassee, 1946-55, asst. research and statistics dir., 1955-68, dir. research and statistics, 1968—. Cubmaster, troop com. mem. Suwamee River Area council Boy Scouts Am. Served with USN, 1942-45. Mem. VFW, Fla. Employees Assn. (dir. 1968-72), Internat. Assn. Personnel and Employment Security. Democrat. Roman Catholic. Clubs: Tallahassee Travelers Camping (pres. 1976), Tallahassee Twirlers, Square Dance, K.C. Home: 1021 Carrin Dr Tallahassee FL 32301 Office: Bur Research and Analysis Fla Dept Labor and Employment Security Tallahassee FL 32304

O'HARA, PATRICK JOHN, finance co. exec.; b. N.Y.C., June 18, 1932; s. Patrick John and Anna Theresa (Clifford) O'H.; student LaSalle U., 1958-59, N.Y. Inst. Fin., 1959-61; m. Mary E. Mortimer, Apr. 19, 1958; children—Kathleen, Maureen, Annmarie. Receive and deliver clk. Dominick & Dominick, N.Y.C., 1955-57; supr. receiving and delivery L.M. Marks & Co., N.Y.C., 1957-59; ops. cashier Faulkner, Dawkins & Sullivan, N.Y.C., 1959-66; mgr. lending and borrowing program Mabon, Nugent & Co., N.Y.C., 1966—. Served with U.S. Army, 1952-54. Decorated Combat Infantryman's badge, Bronze Star. Mem. Security Industries Assn., Assn. Stock Loan Reps. (exec.), VFW (comdr. post 1962-63), Am. Legion. Democrat. Roman Catholic. Clubs: K.C., Marine Park Gold Dunes. Office: Mabon Nugent & Co 115 Broadway New York NY 10006

O'HARE, DEAN RAYMOND, ins. co. exec.; b. Jersey City, June 21, 1942; s. Francis and Ann O'H.; B.S., N.Y. U., 1963; M.B.A., Pace Grad. Sch. Bus. Adminstrn., 1968; m. Kathleen T. Walliser, Dec. 2, 1967; children—Dean, Jason. Trainee, Chubb Corp., N.Y.C., 1963-64, tax adv., 1964-67, asst. v.p., mgr. corp. fin. devel., 1968-72, sr. v.p., mgr. corp. fin. devel. dept., 1979—; dir., vice chmn. Bellemead Devel. Corp., 1973—; chmn. Colonial Life Ins. Co. Am., 1980—, United Life & Accident Ins. Co., 1980—; dir. Touchette Corp., Fed. Bus. Products. Mem. Urban Land Inst. Clubs: India House, Hanover Square. Office: 100 William St New York NY 10038

O'HARE, EMMETT NELSON, assn. exec.; b. Pitts., July 15, 1945; s. Emmett P. and Thelma (Nelson) O'H.; student Duquesne U., 1964-66, 68; B.S. cum laude in Aviation Mgmt., Embry Riddle Aero U., 1970; M.S. in Transp. Planning and Engring., Poly. Inst. N.Y., 1977; Ph.D. in Transp. Systems, Am. Internat. U., 1981; m. Elinor Nock; 1 son, Brian James. Elec. contractor O & T Electric Co.,

Homestead, Pa., 1968-70; airport mgr. Deland (Fla.) Mcpl. Airport, 1971-74; mgr. airport requirements, eastern region Air Transport Assn., Valley Stream, N.Y., 1974-78, dep. regional dir., eastern region, 1978—; aviation cons. U.S. Dept. Transp. Study on Transp. System Safety; transp. cons. for nuclear power plant evacuation planning; mem. transp. systems safety com. Transp. Research Bd. Merit badge counsellor Boy Scouts Am.; safety officer Freeport (N.Y.) Fire Dept.; instr. radiol. monitoring Nassau County CD, 1974-80; first aid instr. ARC, 1968-75; mem. Freeport Community Devel. Com., 1979—; pres. Methodist Men's Club, 1971-72, dist. v.p., 1973-74; mem. ch. fin. com., 1971-74, 79—; mem. ch. exec. bd., 1970-74, 79—. Served with USNR, 1966-68; Vietnam; capt. Transp. Corps, USAR. Mem. Am. Assn. Airport Execs. (accredited), ASCE, Inst. Transp. Engrs., Internat. Soc. Air Safety Investigators, DAV, Alpha Phi Omega (life). Club: Elks. Home: 117 Southside Ave Freeport NY 11520 Office: Suite 601 181 S Franklin Ave Valley Stream NY 11581

OHLENDORF, HAROLD FRED, banker, farmer; b. Freeburg, Ill., Feb. 7, 1909; s. Diedrich and Annie (Schmidt) O.; A.B., Southwestern U., Memphis, 1931; LL.D. (hon.), U. Ark., 1963; m. Frances Margaret Jones, May 2, 1934; children—Sherwood, June Ohlendorf Kizer. Farmer, Mississippi County, Ark., owner Ohlendorf Farms, Osceola, Ark., 1935—; chmn. bd. dirs. First Nat. Bank, Osceola, 1946, First Nat. Bank, W. Memphis, Ark., 1954; pres., dir., Ohlendorf Investment Co., 1951—, Osceola Broadcasting Co., 1949—, Midway Farms, Inc., 1962—; sec., dir. Delta Products Co., Wilson, Ark., 1946—; dir. Farmers Gin Co., Joiner, Ark., 1968—, Southwestern Bell Telephone Co., St. Louis, 1959—, St. Louis-San Francisco Railway Co., St. Louis, 1970—; trustee Northwestern Mut. Life Ins. Co., 1969—. Trustee Ark. Coll., Batesville, 1956—, Miss. County Community Coll., Blytheville, Ark., 1975—; trustee, treas. Miss. County Library, Osceola, 1951—; dir., chmn. Ark. Good Roads/Transp. Council, Little Rock, 1976—; dir., sec. Miss. County Hosp. Systems, Blytheville and Osceola, 1952—; dir., treas. Osceola Port Commn., 1972—; dir., Ark. Community Found., Inc., Little Rock, 1976—, Ark. Free Enterprise Assn., Inc., Little Rock, 1952—, Ark. Indsl. Devel. Commn., Little Rock, 1970—, Mid-South Communities, Memphis, Tenn., 1971—, Osceola Devel. Com., 1966—, Osceola Sch. Bd., 1948—; mem. advisory group Ark. Regional Med. Planning Program, 1968—, devel. council U. Ark., Fayetteville, 1973—, U. Ark. Found., Fayetteville, 1974—, Resources Com. Southwestern U., Memphis, Tenn., 1976—. Recipient Master Farmer award, State of Ark., 1950, Outstanding Citizen award, Osceola C. of C., 1950, award Ark. Assn. for Mentally Retarded Children, 1974, Osceola and Miss. County awards for indsl. health care, ednl. devel., 1972; named Man of Yr. in Service to Agr. for Ark., Progressive Farmer, 1961. Mem. Sigma Nu, Omicron Delta Kappa. Deomcrat. Presbyterian. Clubs: Univ., Summit, Memphis County, Memphis Exec., Economic (Memphis, Tenn.), Five Lakes Outing (Hughes, Ark.), Menesha (Turrell, Ark.), Greasy Slough (Jonesboro, Ark.). Home and Office: PO Box 248 Osceola AR 72370

OHM, MERVIN ROBERT, mfg. exec.; b. Olney, Ill., Nov. 30, 1939; s. John Francis and Anna Margaret (Harper) O.; student Chosun U., Kyung Hee U.; B.S. in Bus. Adminstrn., Franklin U., 1963; postgrad. Feng Chia U. Mil. adviser to Republic of China, 1964-66; ops. engr. Am. Bridge div. U.S. Steel Co., Gary, Ind., 1966-67; sr. supr. prodn. Uniroyal, Joliet (Ill.) Army Ammunition Plant, 1967-70; co-owner Tip Top Motel, Olney, 1970-75; asst. advt. dir. Olney Daily Mail, 1975-78; contract procurement and prodn. specialist Opportunity Center, Inc., 1978-80; prodn. planning and control exec. Union Fronderburg Corp., 1980—; v.p. Oleon Coins, Inc., Joliet, 1967-70. Dist. chmn. Am. Ind. Party, 1972-76. Served with AUS, 1957-66. Mem. Am. Legion, Olney C. of C. (legis. com. 1971-76), Franklin U. Alumni Assn., Epsilon Delta Chi. Club: Eagles. Home: 1501 E York St Olney IL 62450 Office: 515 E Main St Olney IL 62450

O'KEEFE, BERNARD JOSEPH, tech. co. exec.; b. Providence, Dec. 17, 1919; s. John B. and Christina (McNee) O'K.; B.E.E., Cath. U. Am., 1941; D.Sc. (hon.), Boston Coll., 1980, Curry Coll., 1980; D. Humanities (hon.), New Eng. Sch. Law, 1980; m. Madeline M. Healey, Nov. 21, 1942; children—Geraldine, Thomas, Kathleen, Carol. With EG & G, Inc., Wellesley, Mass., 1947—, pres., chief exec. officer, 1965-78, chmn. bd., chief exec. officer, 1972—; dir. Boston Edison Co., Dennison Mfg. Co., John Hancock Life Ins. Co., LFE Corp., New Eng. Mchts. Nat. Bank. Chmn. Gov.'s Mgmt. Task Force; trustee Lahey Clinic, Mus. Sci. Served to lt. (j.g.), USNR, 1943-46. Mem. NAM (vice chmn.). Office: 45 William St Wellesley MA 02181

O'KEEFE, GERALD JAMES, plastics office accessories mfg. co. exec.; b. Springfield, Mass., Dec. 11, 1937; s. Gerald Edward and Mildred (Brown) O'Keefe; student Bridgewater State Coll., 1955-57; B.A., U. Mass., 1957-59; m. Susan M. Lyons, June 20, 1970; children—John Ryan, William Neil. Sales rep. Calif. Chem. div. Standard Oil of Calif., 1961-66, Mercedes Benz Co., 1966-70; European del. cons. Lowery Corp., Hartford, Conn., 1970-71; sales rep. Papermate div. Gillette Co., New Eng., N.Y.C., 1971-75; sales rep. Gates Paper div. SCM Corp., Marion, Ind., 1975-77; sales mgr. for East Coast, Eldon Office Products Co., Glastonbury, Conn., 1977-80; gen. mgr. Arlac Werk, Hamburg, W. Ger. and Branford, Conn., 1980—. Active Glastonbury Service Club. Mem. Nat. Office Products Assn. Home: 47 Delmar Rd Glastonbury CT 06033 Office: Route 139 McDermott Rd Branford CT 06405

O'KEEFE, WANDA LYDIA, food industry ofcl.; b. North Bergen, N.J., Aug. 8, 1926; d. David Charles and Ida Josephine (Del Nero) Viola; grad. schs. Englewood, N.J.; m. Arthur Robert O'Keefe, Sr., Nov. 6, 1948; children—Arthur Robert, Barbara Ann, Charles James. Asst. to frozen food buyer N.Y. region, Grand Union Co., Elmwood Park, N.J., 1964, sec. to merchandise mgr. N.Y. region, 1968-71, mgr. customer relations, 1971-75, mgr. customer communications, 1975—. Mem. Soc. Consumer Affairs Profls. (Nat. and N.Y. chpts.), Nat. Assn. Food Chains (steering com. consumer affairs), N.J. Food Council (consumer affairs com.), N.Y. State Food Mchts. Assn. (consumer affairs com.). Home: 209 Wilson St Saddle Brook NJ 07662 Office: Grand Union Co 100 Broadway Elmwood Park NJ 07407

O'KEEFE, WILLIAM FRANCIS, trade assn. exec.; b. Washington, Nov. 8, 1938; s. William Francis and Mildred Elizabeth (Porter) O'K.; B.S. in Bus. Adminstrn., Southeastern U., 1965; postgrad. Am. U., Catholic U., 1966-68; m. Margaret Ann Narsted, June 6, 1959; children—Shawn, Lynn, Michael, John. Head tech. documents Ops. Evaluation Group, Arlington, Va., 1956-62; successively systems analyst, asst. to pres., personnel dir., dir. adminstrn. Center for Naval Analyses, Arlington, 1962-74, also sec. bd. overseers; v.p. Am. Petroleum Inst., Washington, 1974—; cons. planning and evaluation to asst. sec. HEW. Bd. dirs. Washington Center for Learning Alternatives, Nat. Council for Career Women. Mem. Am. Econ. Assn., World Petroleum Congress (nat. com.), World Energy Conf. (nat. com.), U.S. C. of C., Inst. for Contemporary Studies. Roman Catholic. Home: 3503 Redwood Ct Fairfax VA 22030 Office: 2101 L St NW Washington DC 20037

OKEKE, KEVIN CHUKWUEMEKA EJIMOFOR, bus. analyst; b. Enugu, Nigeria, Nov. 26, 1948; s. Francis E. and Regina Okeke; ind. study univs. Nebr., Lincoln, Wis.; Regent External Degree, SUNY, Albany. Audit clk. Akintola Williams & Co., Chartered Accts., Lagos, Nigeria, 1967-70; sr. accounts clk. Internat. Inst. Tropical Agr., Ibadan, Nigeria, 1970-73, acctg. asst., 1973-80, bus. analyst, spl. projects accounts exec., N.Y.C., 1980—. Mem. Internat. Assn. Systems Mgmt., Brit. Inst. Mgmt., Cert. Internal Auditors (asso.), Smithsonian Instn. Roman Catholic. Office: care UN Plaza 809 IITA Joan Murray New York NY 10017

O'KELLEY, HAROLD E., data processing systems co. exec.; b. Jacksonville, Fla., 1925; grad. Auburn U., 1947; postgrad. U. Fla., 1952. Chmn., pres., chief exec. officer Datapoint Corp., San Antonio; chmn. Computer and Communication Industry Assn. Office: 9725 Datapoint Dr San Antonio TX 78284*

OKINAGA, SAM, savs. and loan exec.; b. Honolulu, Nov. 26, 1926; s. Sohei and Hatsu (Kakimoto) O.; B.A., U. Hawaii, 1949; postgrad. U. Ind., summers 1969-71; m. Genevieve N. Takemoto, Aug. 20, 1949; children—Garner, Mia. Asst. to pub. Rural Oahu Reporter, 1949-50; office mgr. Engring. Equipment Co., 1950-53; chmn. bd., dir. State Savs. & Loan Assn., Honolulu, 1953—; chmn. mgmt. com. Mid-Pacific TV Assos.; pres. Ten-Tel Assos., Inc., Honolulu; pres., dir. Gt. State Financial Corp., Kahili Investment Co., Inc., 1974-77. Pres. Hawaii council Camp Fire Girls, Inc., 1962, Friends of Library, 1974, Council Social Agys., 1966; treas. Friends of Sparky, 1972—; bd. dirs. Kuakini Hosp., 1966-68; trustee U. Hawaii Found., 1973-80; mem. Hawaii Bicentennial Commn., 1974-76. Named Outstanding Young Man of Year, Jaycee Chpts. in Honolulu, 1961. Mem. Savs. and Loan League of Hawaii (pres. 1973-74), Savs. and Loan Controllers (pres.), Am. Savs. and Loan Inst. (pres.), U.S. League of Savs. Assn. (dir. 1976-79), Honolulu Japanese Jr. C. of C. (pres. 1959-60). Home: 2980 Laukoa Pl Honolulu HI 96813 Office: 180 S King St Honolulu HI 96813

OKOJIE, CHRISTOPHER ISIKHUEME, mktg. cons.; b. Lagos, Nigeria, Jan. 25, 1952; came to U.S., naturalized, 1970; s. Christopher Gbelokoto and Olufunke Olayemi (Phillips) K.; B.A. in Biology, CUNY, 1974; M.B.A. in Mktg., L.I. U., 1979. Pres., Crisire Assos., Inc., Bronx, N.Y., 1975—. Mem. Assn. M.B.A. Execs. Office: Crisire Assos Inc 1718 Purdy St PO Box 488 Bronx NY 10462

OKWUMABUA, BENJAMIN NKEM, corp. exec.; b. Issele-Uku, Nigeria, June 20, 1939; s. Daniel Ikeduba and Nwaonogwu Emily O.; came to U.S., 1963, naturalized, 1978; B.S., Central State U., 1967; M.B.A., Mich. State U., 1974, M.Labor and Indsl. Relations, 1971, Ph.D. (doctoral fellow), 1974; m. Constance Lee, Mar. 16, 1968; children—Benjamin Nkem, Obiamaka Patricia, Richard Ikeduba. Prof., Saginaw Valley State Coll., Saginaw, Mich., 1971-75, dept. chmn., 1971-75; sales mgr. Oldsmobile div. Gen. Motors Corp., Buffalo, 1975-78; pres., chief exec. officer AFRO-Lecon, Inc., Jamestown, N.Y., 1978—. Mem. Acad. Mgmt., Am. Mgmt. Assn., Am. Mktg. Assn., Indsl. Relations Research Assn., Beta Gamma Sigma, Sigma Iota. Democrat. Baptist. Club: Rotary. Researcher in field. Home: 505 Chautauqua Ave Jamestown NY 14701 Office: 335 Harrison St Jamestown NY 14701

OLAFSON, HAROLD STANLEY, engring. and research exec.; b. Los Angeles, July 1, 1939; s. Stanley Theodore and Margaret (Seapy) O.; B.A. in Econs., U. Calif., Los Angeles, 1963, M.B.A. in Finance (H.J. Hagge fellow), 1965; certificate of achievement Advanced Mgmt. Program, U. N.Mex., 1977; m. Barbara Jean Hall, June 24, 1967. Financial analyst Philco-Ford Corp., Newport Beach, Calif., 1965-71, mem. corporate finance staff, financial controls and accounting office, 1971-72, financial analysis mgr., aeronutronic div., 1972-74; staff financial analyst Los Alamos Sci. Lab., 1974-75, asst. div. leader electronics div., 1975-80, asso. div. leader electronics, 1980—; small bus. cons. Served with U.S. Army, 1957-63. Mem. Nat. Contract Mgmt. Assn., Santa Fe Bd. Realtors (asso.). Club: Kiwanis. Home: Box 95 El Porvenir Route Montezuma NM 87731 Office: PO Box 1663 MS 450 Los Alamos NM 87545

OLAFSSON, THOMAS ROBERT, chem. co. exec.; b. Boston, Oct. 9, 1932; s. Hogni Peter and Katherine (Savage) O.; B.S. in Chemistry, Tufts U., 1959; M.B.A., Babson Coll., 1977; m. Barbara L. Soley, June 20, 1959; children—Thomas Robert, Michael. Tech. sales rep. Celanese Corp. Am., 1959-61; new bus. devel. specialist Carter's Ink Co., Cambridge, Mass., 1962-64; pres., founder Chromex Chem. Corp., Bklyn., 1964-72, Butler Labs., Inc., N.Y.C., 1971-72; v.p., gen. mgr. Brotherhood Corp., Washingtonville, N.Y., 1972-73; founder, pres. Environex Corp., Boston, 1973—; pres. Olafsson Assos., Inc., Boston, 1979—; founder, dir. Diversified Chem. Corp., Union, N.J., 1977; dir. Beautiline, Inc., N.Y.C. Served with Mil. Police Corps, AUS, 1953-55. Mem. Am. Chem. Soc., Am. Mgmt. Assn., Inst. Mgmt. Acctg. Club: N.Y. Athletic. Home: 180 St Paul St Brookline MA 02146 Office: 84 State St Boston MA 02109 also 329 Main Ave Stirling NJ 07980

OLANDER, FINN, paint mfr.; b. Copenhagen, July 30, 1930; came to U.S., 1970, permanent resident, 1975; s. Paul H. and Ruth A.K. (Rasmussen) O.; B.A., Niels Brock Comml. Coll., Copenhagen, 1959; grad. Program Mgmt. Devel., Harvard Bus. Sch., 1976; m. Majken Holst, Dec. 7, 1963; children—Jacob T., Nina H. With Hempel's Marine Paints Inc., 1970—, exec. v.p., N.Y.C., 1970-78, pres., chief exec. officer, 1978—; hon. consul of Denmark in Kobe, Japan, 1969-70. Chmn. paint industry div. N.Y.C. chpt. Assn. Help Retarded Children, 1980-81. Served with Danish Navy, 1955-56. Mem. Nat. Paint and Coatings Assn. (past chmn. marine coatings div. 1975-77), Soc. Naval Architects and Marine Engrs., Nat. Assn. Corrosion Engrs. Clubs: Harvard Bus. Sch., Whitehall Lunch (N.Y.C.); Doolittle (Norfolk, Conn.). Home: 9 Shady Acres Rd Darien CT 06820 Office: 65 Broadway New York NY 10006

OLAYAN, STANLEY ROY, Realtor; b. Honolulu, Aug. 25, 1947; s. Leonard and Josephine (Raquel) O.; student Honolulu Bus. Coll. Sch. Automation, 1967; grad. Realtors Inst. Hawaii, 1977; m. Florence Diane Asis, Feb. 24, 1968; children—Roxanne M., Ryan S. Sales rep., div. consumer products Theo H. Davies & Co., Honolulu, 1968-70; mfr.'s rep. Helene Curtis, Royal Supply Co., Honolulu, 1970-71; sales mgr. Yuruki Agy., Franklin Life Ins. Co., Honolulu, 1971-76; sales mgr.-projects Servco Pacific-Service Realty, Honolulu, 1976-78; Realtor-residential sales V. DeLaCruz Realty, Honolulu, 1978-79; sales mgr. Banyan Realty div. Consol. Fin. Services, Inc., Honolulu, 1979-81; Realtor, A.E. LePage (Hawaii) Realtors, Ltd., Honolulu, 1981—; partner, real estate broker Venus Realty Inc. Served with USAF, 1967. Mem. Nat. Assn. Realtors, Hawaii Assn. Realtors, Honolulu Downtown Jaycees (dir. 1977, v.p. individual devel. 1978, pres. 1980-81). Home: 1315 Arsenal Rd Honolulu HI 96819 Office: Grosvenor Center Suite 1465 733 Bishop St Honolulu HI 96813

OLDFATHER, GAIL EDWARD, cable TV co. exec.; b. Miami, Ind., Mar. 18, 1935; s. Gail Frederick and Madelyn (Turner) O.; B.S. in Merchandising and Bus. Adminstrn., Ind. State U., 1959; m. Helen Isobel Hughes, Sept. 12, 1961; children—Jennifer Sue, Jonathan Edward. With Economy Fin. Corp., Indpls., 1959-71, asst. v.p., 1963-65, v.p., 1965, head communications fin. div., 1965-71; exec. v.p., chief exec. officer Televents, Inc., Walnut Creek, Calif., 1971-72, pres., 1972—. Served with USNG, 1958, USRC, 1961-62. Mem. Nat. Cable TV Assn. (dir. 1976-80), Calif. Community TV Assn. (past pres., dir. 1972—). Republican. Methodist. Home: 721 Snowdon Ct Walnut Creek CA 94598 Office: 2855 Mitchell Dr Suite 250 Walnut Creek CA 94598

OLDHAM, DOROTHY CLOUDMAN, advt. agy. exec., editor; b. Detroit; d. Philip Horace and Mabel (Rigg) Cloudman; student Albion Coll., Mich.; B.A., U. Mich.; m. Robert Price Oldham (div. 1955); 1 dau., Carol Cloudman. Successively ad service mgr. Simons Michelson Advt. Co., Detroit; fashion editor Detroit Free Press, account exec. W. B. Doner & Co., Detroit; owner-pres. Cloudman Oldham Advt., Inc. (Mich. corp.), Cloudman Oldham Advt. and Pub. Relations, Bal Harbour, Fla., 1975—; editor Detroit & Suburban Life, 1967-72. Chmn., Fashion Careers Lectr. Series, Wayne U., 1965. Chmn., Women Out Working for Romney for Gov., 1966; pres. Republican Bus. and Profl. Women, 1966-67. Mem. Nat. Home Fashions League (v.p. jour. sales 1977-78), Women in Communications, Advt. Fedn. Greater Miami, Fashion Group Miami, South Fla. Builders' Assn., Am. Soc. Interior Designers (public relations mem.), Met. Miami Art Center. Inventor, patentee Magic-Balance Checks System. Home and office: 261 Bal Cross Dr Bal Harbour FL 33154

OLDHAM, FRANK PUGH, mfg. co. exec.; b. Lockport, N.Y., Apr. 2, 1945; s. Frank Somers and Genevieve Gertrude (Pugh) O.; B.A., Brevard Coll., 1967; M.E., Tri-State Coll., 1968. Sales mgr. Cocker Saw Co. Inc., Lockport, 1967-69, v.p. sales, 1969-71; exec. v.p. U.S. Saw Corp., Burt, N.Y., 1970—; pres. Oldham Saw Co., Inc., Burt, 1970—; dir. United Bank of N.Y., Liberty Nat. Bank-Niagara Orleans Genesee Region; officer Nat. Hardware Show Packaging Expn. Served with U.S. Army, 1963-65. Recipient Packager of Yr. award Nat. Hardware Show, 1971. Mem. Am. Hardware Mfrs. Assn. (pres. young exec. club), Nat. Hardware Retail Assn., Nat. Wholesale Hardware Assn., Nat. Hardware Mktg. Council. Presbyterian. Club: Young Execs. (officer). Office: 2084 Lockport-Olcott Rd Burt NY 14028

OLDSHUE, JAMES YOUNG, equipment co. exec.; b. Chgo., Apr. 18, 1925; s. James and Louise (Young) O.; B.S. in Chem. Engring., Ill. Inst. Tech., 1947, M.S., 1949, Ph.D., 1951; m. Betty Weirsema, June 14, 1947; children—Paul F., Richard J., Robert W. Chem. engr. Los Alamos Labs., 1945-46; devel. engr. Mixing Equipment Co., Rochester, N.Y., 1950-52, head devel. engring., 1952-54, dir. research, 1954-63, tech. dir., 1964-70, v.p. mixing tech., 1970—; instr. U. Rochester, 1954-57; lectr. Rochester Inst. Tech., 1976. Chmn. YMCA, Irondequoit, N.Y., 1960-62; bd. dirs., chmn. internat. com. Rochester YMCA, 1974—; bd. dirs. Genesee Ecumenical Ministries. Served with AUS, 1944-46. Registered profl. engr., N.Y. Fellow Am. Inst. Chem. Engrs. (pres. 1979, past dir.); mem. Am. Chem. Soc., Nat. Acad. Engring., Am. Assn. Engring. Socs. (exec. com.), Rochester Council Sci. Socs., Internat. Platform Assn., Sigma Xi, Tau Beta Pi. Contbr. articles to profl. jours. Research in field. Home: 141 Tyringham Rd Rochester NY 14617 Office: 135 Mt Read Blvd Rochester NY 14611

O'LEARY, JACK ARNOLD, electric co. exec.; b. Johnstown, Pa., Dec. 20, 1931; s. Patrick Joseph and LaVina (Betts) O'L.; student U. Pitts., 1954-57, 62-63, Pa. State U., 1974-75; m. Dorothy Gertrude Keelan, Nov. 7, 1959; children—David Brian, Leslie Ann. With Pennsylvania Electric Co., Johnstown, 1964—, dir. safety and work methods, 1978—. Instr. cardiopulmonary resuscitation; instr. multimedia first aid ARC, 1975—; del. Am. Heart Assn., 1975—; asso. advisor Penn's Woods council Boy Scouts Am., 1976—. Served with USNR, 1952-55. Mem. Am. Soc. Safety Engrs., Nat. Safety Mgmt. Soc. Democrat. Roman Catholic. Clubs: Elks, K.C. Home: 36 Reed Ct Johnstown PA 15902 Office: 1001 Broad St Johnstown PA 15907

O'LEARY, JOHN JOSEPH, accounting co. exec.; b. N.Y.C., Aug. 27, 1940; s. Daniel and Bridget (Ruane) O'L.; B.B.A., Iona Coll., 1962; m. Maureen D. McKee, Sept. 5, 1964; children—John D., Tracy A., Meredith K., Faith D., Jennifer N. Audit mgr. Arthur Andersen & Co., N.Y.C., 1962-75; audit partner Alexander Grant & Co., N.Y.C., 1975—. C.P.A., N.J., N.Y. Mem. Am. Inst. C.P.A.'s, N.J. Soc. C.P.A.'s, N.Y. State Soc. C.P.A.'s. Roman Catholic. Home: 242 Walnut St Dunellen NJ 08812 Office: Alexander Grant & Co 400 Lanidex Pl Parsippany NJ 07054

O'LEARY, THOMAS HOWARD, railroad exec.; b. N.Y.C., Mar. 19, 1934; s. Arthur J. and Eleanor (Howard) O'L.; A.B., Holy Cross Coll., 1954; postgrad. U. Pa., 1959-61; m. Barbara A. McDonough, Aug. 13, 1977; children—Mark, Timothy, Thomas, Denis, Daniel, Mary Frances. Asst. cashier First Nat. City Bank, N.Y.C., 1961-65; asst. to chmn. finance com. Mo. Pacific R.R. Co., 1966-70, v.p. finance, 1971-76, dir., 1972—, chmn. fin. com., 1976—; treas. Mo. Pacific Corp., St. Louis, 1968-71, v.p. finance, 1971-72, exec. v.p., 1972-74, dir., 1972—, pres., 1974—; chmn. bd. Mississippi River Transmission Corp., 1974—; dir. Merc. Trust Co., Merc. Bancorp., The Kroger Co., Interco Inc. Trustee St. Louis U., 1974—. Served to capt. USMC, 1954-58. Clubs: Blind Brook, Wall Street (N.Y.C.); Chgo. Office: 9900 Clayton Rd Saint Louis MO 63124

OLEKSY, DANIEL DAVID, wholesale distbg. co. exec.; b. Jackson, Mich., Oct. 2, 1949; s. Stanley Peter and Alma Jean (Pieper) O.; grad. Ranken Tech. Sch., St. Louis, 1971; m. Linda Rose Harrison, Feb. 28, 1976; 1 son, Jeffrey Michael. Warehouse mgr. Mesa N.O. Nelson Co. (Ariz.), 1974, salesman, 1974-76, purchasing agt., sec.-treas., 1976—; pres. Lakeside N.O. Nelson Co. (Ariz.), 1976-79; pres. John Fox Solar, Inc., Mesa, 1980—; comml. sales distbr. Amfac Mech. Supply, 1980—. Mem. Pacific S.W. Distbrs. Assn. (chmn. young exec. com.), Am. Supply Assn. Republican. Roman Catholic. Club: Racquet. Home: 2254 E Contessa St Mesa AZ 85203 Office: 737 W 2d Ave Mesa AZ 85202

OLENDER, TERRYS T. (MRS. EDWARD GLICK), lawyer, author; b. San Francisco; d. Julius and Mollie Olender; B.A., U. Calif. at Berkeley; postgrad. U. So. Calif. Law Sch.; m. Edward Glick, May 26, 1952. Admitted to Calif. bar, 1932, Fed. bar, 1932; practiced law in Los Angeles, 1933-41, 50—, San Francisco, 1942-49; dep. dist. atty. Los Angeles County, 1933-38; fgn. corr. Overseas News Agy., Mediterranean area, 1949-50; land subdivider, developer, 1955—; program coordinator radio and TV, producer, 1959—; film-drama editor Calif. Jewish Press; guest numerous interview and panel shows. Del., Internat. Fedn. Women Lawyers to ECOSOC, Geneva, 1962. Mem. mayor's adv. com. Juvenile Delinquency and Narcotic Coms.; President's Com. to Maintain Hotel Rent Control, San Francisco, 1948; an organizer, liaison officer No. Calif. br. Am. Christian Palestine Com., 1947-49, liaison officer, Los Angeles, 1950-59; founder, pres. Olender Found., 1966—; founder, chmn. So. Pacific region ZOA Youth Mitzvah Fund, 1968—. Bd. dirs. Los Angeles chpt. Am. Assn. UN; trustee Inst. Cancer and Blood Research. Recipient joint awards Los Angeles Bd. Suprs. and Los Angeles City Council, 1961; Western mem. adv. bd. U.S. Wheelchair Sports Fund; sponsor Calif. Wheelchair Athletic Club. Named Woman of Year, Zionist Orgn. Am., 1964; Woman of Achievement, Calif. Press Women, 1967, 1968-69, Los Angeles Press Women, 1968-69. Mem. Los Angeles Bar Assn., So. Calif. Women Lawyers, Internat. Fedn. Women Lawyers, Acad. Television Arts and Scis. (judge Emmy awards Los Angeles area 1964), Radio and TV Women So. Calif., Nat. Fedn. Press Women, Profl. Writers League, World Affairs Council,

Am. Bar Assn., Calif. State Bar, Brit. Anti-Slavery Soc., Nat. Assn. Women Lawyers. Democrat. Clubs: Greater Los Angeles Press, Hollywood (Calif.) Foreign Press. Author: For The Prosecution: Miss Deputy D.A.; Delitto Prequidizio; My Life in Crime (autobiography), 1966. Legal tech. adviser motion picture The Long Rope, 1961. Contbr. articles newspapers, mags.; feature columnist Los Angeles Daily Jour., Athens (Greece) Daily Post, Tico Times, San Jose, Costa Rica. Syndicated column, Hollywood Oddities, Legal Oddities. Office: 450 N Rossmore Ave Los Angeles CA 90004

OLENICK, THOMAS ZALMAN, holding co. exec.; b. Winnipeg, Man., Can., Nov. 7, 1921; s. Zalman and Anna (Tessler) O.; B.Sc., U. Man., 1943; B.A., U. Man., 1944; m. Mindel Rady, June 11, 1947; children—Gail Olenick Wagner, Debra Olenick Hirsch, Roberta. Pres. Garry Fin. Corp. Ltd., Winnipeg, 1950—; v.p. Summit Resources Ltd., Calgary, Alta., 1972—, Memrad Holdings Ltd., Winnipeg, 1974—; sec. treas. Project Holding Ltd., Winnipeg, 1969—. Mem. Man. Human Rights Commn., 1976—; bd. dirs. YMCA, 1976—; past pres. Robert H. Smith Home and Sch. Assn., Mem. Chem. Inst. Can., Man. Environ. Research Com. (former gov.). Progressive Conservative. Jewish. Clubs: Maple Leaf Curling, U. Man. Alumni. Home: 155 Waverley St Winnipeg MB R3M 3K3 Canada Office: 201-228 Notre Dame Ave Winnipeg MB R3B 1H7 Canada

OLIVAS, NATHAN JOSEPH, seed co. exec.; b. San Jose, Calif., Aug. 27, 1937; s. Nathan Calvin and Julia Vecinta (Lopez) O.; student Hartnell Coll., 1957; B.S., Calif. State Poly., San Luis Obispo, 1960; m. Jere Lee Steidley, Aug. 16, 1957; children—Cindy Lynn, Nathan Khristian, Nancy Elizabeth. Prodn. and research technician Pieters-Wheeler Seed Co., Gilroy, Calif., 1961-64; pres., gen. mgr. Harnish-Brinker Seed Co., Five Points, Calif., 1965-67, Quali-Sel, Inc., Salinas, Calif., 1968—. Mem. Am. Soc. Agronomy, Am. Seed Trade Assn., Calif. Seed Assn. (dir. 1972, 73, 74), Western Growers Assn., Grower-Shipper Assn. Central Calif. Republican. Roman Catholic. Developer seven varieties of lettuce, 1968-78. Office: Quali-Sel Inc 11 W Laurel Dr Suite 125 Salinas CA 93906

OLIVER, ALVIN E., trade assn. exec.; b. Sterling, Mich., Nov. 4, 1918; s. Hugh and Blanche (Knight) O.; B.S. with honors, Mich. State U., 1943, M.S., 1948; m. Jean Stanton, Aug. 6, 1943; children—Dale, Donald, Richard, James. Tchr. public schs. in Mich., 1936-39; asst. prof. Mich. State U., East Lansing, 1946-54, coordinator grain elevator tng. program; asst. v.p. Nat. Grain and Feed Assn., Washington, 1954-55, exec. mgr., 1955-56, exec. v.p., 1956—. Mem. adv. com. on wheat and feed grain U.S. Dept. Agr., 1961-63; del. Pres.'s Summit Conf. on Inflation, 1974; mem. Pres.'s Food for Peace Council, 1963; active 4-H Service Club. Served with U.S. Army, 1943-45. Decorated Bronze Star with cluster; recipient Nat. Disting. Service award Future Farmers Am., 1972, Hon. Am. Farm award, 1974. Mem. Agr. Assn. Execs. Council, Am. Assn. Assn. Execs. (chmn. food group 1960-61), Washington Trade Assn. Execs., Alpha Zeta, Kappa Delta Pi. Methodist. Club: Univ. (Washington). Home: 1700 River Farm Dr Alexandria VA 22308 Office: 725 15th St NW Washington DC 20005

OLIVER, ELIZABETH MURPHY, newspaper editor; b. Brazil, Ind., June 25, 1914; d. Jacob Berdette and Rose (Murphy) O.; A.B., Fisk U., 1935; M.Ed., Ind. State Tchrs. Coll. Tchr. public schs., Ind., Balt.; city editor Balt. Afro-Am.; librarian Afro Archives. Named Top Negro Women reporter Nat. Assn. Negro Bus. and Profl. Women; recipient 4 awards of honor NAACP; Freedom Heritage award Lillie Carroll Jackson Mus., 1979. Presbyterian. Author several books. Office: 628 N Eutaw St Baltimore MD 21201

OLIVER, JAMES JEROME, real estate co. exec.; b. Pueblo, Colo., Nov. 30, 1934; s. Glenn William and Rebekah (Deal) O.; B.S., U. Colo., 1962; m. Betty Lucille Nielsen, Apr. 26, 1959; children—James, Christine Marie. Sr. acct. Price Waterhouse & Co., Denver, 1962-66; controller Leprino Co., Denver, 1966-67; mgr. audit services Mobil Chem. Co., Richmond, Va., 1967-68, mgr. fin. analysis, 1968-69, controller agr. chem. div., 1969; controller hosiery div. J.P. Stevens & Co., Hickory, N.C., 1970-71; controller McCall Pattern div. Norton Simon, Inc., N.Y.C., 1971-74, v.p. fin., 1975, exec. v.p., 1975-77, pres. Notions div., 1977-79; v.p. devel. Merrill Lynch Realty Assos., Stamford, Conn., 1980—; prin. Nielsen Assos.; dir. Bour Internat. Leader Greenwich council Boy Scouts Am., Riverside, Conn., 1973—; gen. chmn. Riverside Park Assn., 1975-80; vestryman St. Paul's Ch., Riverside, 1980—. C.P.A., Colo. Mem. Am. Inst. C.P.A.'s, Planning Execs. Inst., Nat. Assn. Accts. Club: Innis Arden Golf. Office: One Landmark Sq Stamford CT 06901

OLIVIERI, JOSEPH J., banker; b. Chgo., Oct. 20, 1923; s. Joseph and Isola (Menconi) O.; student Chgo. Tech. Coll., 1941-43; m. Adelaide T. Leonard, Feb. 7, 1948; children—Joseph J., Linda R., Michael H., Evelyn T., Thomas J. Owner, officer Olivieri Bros. Inc., Chgo., 1947-63; pres. East Side Bank & Trust Co., Chgo., 1960—. Served with C.E., U.S. Army, 1943-46. Mem. Ill. Bankers Assn. (sr. v.p. Group 1), South Side Bankers (pres. 1978), East Side C. of C. (pres. 1976-77). Clubs: Flossmoor Country, Lions, K.C. Office: 10635 Ewing Chicago IL 60617

OLKER, NICHOLAS RAYMOND, printing co. owner; b. Chgo., May 11, 1927; s. John P. and Johanna C. (Pascaly) O.; grad. high sch.; m. Charlotte Wood, June 16, 1951; children—Stephen, Christina, Thomas, Charles. Mgr. printing dept. Conal Pharm. Co., Chgo., 1949-63; pres. Forrest Press, Inc., Barrington, Ill., 1963—. Served with Signal Corps, AUS, 1945-47. Mem. Barrington C. of C. K.C. Club: Biltmore Country. Home: 470 Brookside Rd Barrington IL 60010 Office: 1010 W Northwest Hwy Barrington IL 60010

OLLADA, FELIPE B., pub. accountant; b. Caba, P.I., Apr. 27, 1901; s. Miguel M. and Petrona (Bacudo) O.; B.B.A., U. Manila (P.I.), 1929; M.B.A., Northwestern U., Evanston, Ill., 1934; Ph.D. meritissimus, U. Santo Tomas, Manila, 1939; m. Pacita Zalasar; children—M. Teresita (Mrs. Leonard A. Ona, Jr.), M. Elisa (Mrs. Benito Lacson). Tchr. elementary schs., 1920-22; clk.-bookkeeper Manila R.R. Co., 1922-31; asst. auditor Insular Sugar Refining Corp., 1939-44; prof. accounting U. Santo Tomas, U. Manila, Areliano U., 1941-45; mem. Bd. Accountancy, 1941, chmn. bd., 1942-54; exec. chmn. Bds. Examiners, 1950-54, Manila; prof., head dept. accounting U. of East, 1955—; partner Felipe B. Ollada & Assos., Manila; owner agrl. devel., Sipocot, Camarines Sur, P.I. Chmn. profl. group Philippine Nat. Red Cross and Community Chest; exec. v.p. Good Govt. League. Named knight of St. Sylvester by Pope, 1960; recipient plaque as Outstanding Auditor, United Commentators, 1965. C.P.A. Mem. Ilocandia Profls. (pres.), Philippine Inst. C.P.A.s (dir., plaque outstanding profl. contbn. 1975, named to Accountancy Hall of Fame 1980). World Neighbors, Inc. (dir.), Am. Inst. C.P.A.'s, Am. Acad. Polit. and Social Sci., AAUP, Nat. Assn. Accountants, Inst. Internal Auditors, Internat. Soc. Tax Consultants, Australian Soc. Accountants, Philippine Columbian Assn., Philippine Affairs Assn., World Peace Congress (auditor), Philippine Constn. Assn. (gov.-auditor), Timpuyod Ti Ameanan (pres.). Author simplified accounts and tax records for various businesses, 1946—; amendments to Nat. Internal Revenue Code. Home: 1451-3 Gov Forbes Blvd Santa Cruz Manila Philippines Office: Martinez Bldg 378 Dasmarinas St Manila Philippines

OLLIS, HESTER GREY, ins. agency exec.; b. Eldorado, Okla., Mar. 19, 1914; d. Embry G. and Gladys Gertrude (Wood) West; m. Lawrence Woodbridge Ollis, Oct. 21, 1934; children—Ronald Arkwright, Hester Elizabeth Ollis Massey. Partner, sec. Ollis and Co., Springfield, Mo., 1955-60, v.p., 1960-70, pres., 1970-72, v.p., dir., 1972—. Treas. steering com. Goals for Springfield, 1972-73; membership chmn. Community Concert Assn., 1970-71; pres. St. Anne's Guild, St. John's Episcopal Ch. Mem. Springfield Assn. Ind. Ins. Agts (sec. treas). Republican. Club: Soroptimists Internat. Home: 3745 E Monroe Springfield MO 65804 Office: 2274 E Sunshine Springfield MO 65804

OLM, CARL PAUL, mfg. co. exec.; b. Cumberland, Md., May 1, 1930; s. Carl Paul and Mildred Pauline (Gurley) O.; B.S.I.E., U. Pitts., 1963; children—David, Richard, Tom, Mary E. Indsl. engr. USS Steel, Pitts., 1957-63; plant mgr. Corning Glass Works, Shawnee, Okla., 1963-70; v.p. mktg. Pitts. Corning, 1970—, dir. subs. Served with U.S. Army, 1950-57. Decorated Bronze Star, Purple Heart. Mem. Nat. Roofing Contractors Assn., Nat. Insulation Contractors Assn., Internat. Assn. Refrigeration Warehouses. Republican. Home: 401 Hunting Creek Rd Canonsburg PA 15319 Office: 800 Presque Isle Pittsburgh PA 15239

OLMSTEAD, FRANCIS HENRY, JR., glass industry exec.; b. Corning, N.Y., June 21, 1938; s. Francis Henry and Josephine (Andolino) O.; B.S., Detroit U., 1960; M.S., Purdue U., 1962; postgrad. program for mgmt. devel. Harvard, 1976; m. Mary Helen Nelson, Sept. 2, 1961; children—Kathleen, Ann, John. Foreman, Corning Glass Works, 1962, sect. foreman, 1963-64, dept. foreman, 1965-66, prodn. supt., 1967-69, plant mgr., 1970-71, mgr. mktg., 1972-73, gen. sales and mktg. mgr., 1973-75, bus. mgr. lighting products, 1976-79, bus. mgr. TV products, 1979—; instr. bus. adminstrn. Elmira Coll., 1972-73; vis. lectr. Purdue U., 1973. Mem. exec. bd. Steuben area council Boy Scouts Am., 1975—, v.p. fin., 1977-79, pres. Steuben Area council, 1979—. Served to capt. U.S. Army, 1961-62. Mem. Electronic Industries Assn. (bd. dirs. tube div.), Corning C. of C., Tau Beta Pi, Pi Tau Sigma. Republican. Roman Catholic. Club: Corning Country. Home: 121 Weston Ln Painted Post NY 14870 Office: Corning Glass Works Houghton Park Corning NY 14830

OLMSTED, JONATHAN, communications cons.; b. Boston, Aug. 27, 1942; s. James Warren and Harriet Towle (Atwood) O.; B.A. in Architecture, Stanford U., 1965; m. Janet Farrel Simpson, July 31, 1971; children—Spencer Peck, Whitney Simpson. Profl. entertainer, part-time, 1960-70; v.p. Bankers Trust Co., N.Y.C., 1965-79; prin., dir. Cameron Communications Corp., Darien, Conn., 1979—. Clubs: Racquet and Tennis (N.Y.C.); Tokeneke (Darien). Home and Office: 338 Middlesex Rd Darien CT 06820

OLMSTED, SPALDING MAXINE, real estate devel., mktg. and sales co. exec.; b. San Francisco, Aug. 17, 1946; d. Joel Burleson and Maxine (Blakemore) O.; B.S. in Home Econs. and Bus., Ariz. State U., 1968, M.S. in Family Counseling and Child Devel. Retail mgr., asst. buyer, dept. mgr. Emporium-Capwell Co., San Francisco, 1968-70; asst. to dir. housing Ariz. State U., 1970-72; advt. dir., account exec. Spring Air Mattress Co., Phoenix, 1972-73; individual real estate practice in mktg., promotion and sales, Phoenix, 1973-75; dir. mktg. and sales Fiesta Inn, Tempe, 1975-77; project mgr. indsl. real estate sales and mktg. C.W. Jackson Co., Tempe, 1977-78; dir. mktg. and sales Interwestern Mgmt. Corp., Tempe, 1978—; soloist Phoenix Dance Theater, 1976-78; owner, dir. Dancin' Machine; tchr. dance and exercise classes, 1978—; mem. advisory bd. Ariz. Women's Pages, Inc.; pres. Olmsted Assos.; speaker Women's Investment Group; chmn. bd. dirs. House Corp. of Phi Beta Phi. Mem. advt. sales and promotion com. Devereaux Ann. Charity Celebrity Tennis Tournament, Scottsdale, Ariz., 1977-78; co-chmn. Maricopa County (Ariz.) div. Am. Heart Assn., Annual Charity Golf Tournament, 1977. Mem. Tempe C. of C. (chmn. tourism com. 1976-77), Ariz. Home Econs. Assn. (chmn. subject matter sect. and dir. 1976-77), Ariz. Home Economists in Bus. (treas., membership chmn. 1973-77), Ariz. State U. Alumni Assn. (homecoming com. 1977-79). Republican. Episcopalian. Home: 3312 E Camelback St Phoenix AZ 85018 Office: 2100 S Priest Dr Tempe AZ 85282

OLOFSON, TOM WILLIAM, business exec.; b. Oak Park, Ill., Oct. 10, 1941; s. Ragnar V. and Ingrid E. O.; B.B.A., U. Pitts., 1963; m. Jeanne Hamilton, Aug. 20, 1960; children—Christopher, Scott. Various mgmt. positions Bell Telephone Co. of Pa., Pitts., 1963-67; sales mgr. Xerox Corp., Detroit, 1967-68, nat. account mgr., Rochester, N.Y., 1968, mgr. govt. planning, Rochester, 1969, mgr. Kansas City (Mo.) br., 1969-74; corp. v.p. health products group Marion Labs., Inc., Kansas City, Mo., 1974-78, sr. v.p., 1978-80; exec. v.p., dir. Electronic Realty Assn., Inc., 1980—; dir. Optico Industries, Kalo Labs., Am. Stair-Glide, Marion Health and Safety, Marion Sci., Marion Internat. Mem. Menninger Found. Mem. Omicron Delta Kappa, Sigma Chi. Republican. Presbyterian. Club: Kansas City. Home: 4808 W 87th St Prairie Village KS 66207 Office: 4900 College Blvd Overland Park KS 66207

OLSEN, FLORENCE JOHANNA, machinery mfg. and roll leaf mfg. exec.; b. Bklyn., July 3, 1924; d. Samuel Matthew and Bertha Eva (Woodruff) Olsen; B.S., N.Y. U., 1943, postgrad., 1943-45. Research asst. Outdoor Advt., Inc., N.Y.C., 1943-44; media research Batten, Barton, Durstine & Osborne, N.Y.C., 1944-48; copy research v.p. Bur. Advt., Am. Newspaper Pubs. Assn., 1948-65; sec. corp., charge advt. Kensol-Olsen Mark, Inc., Melville, N.Y., 1965—; v.p. charge advt. Whiley-Kensol, 1972—, sec. corp., charge advt. Foilmark, Inc., Melville, and R.J.O., Amesbury, Mass., 1977; pres. E.M.F., Melville, N.Y., 1978. Nurses aide, motor corps driver ARC, 1940-45; asso. Lincoln Center Performing Arts, 1965—. Mem. Met. Opera Guild, Am. Advt. Fedn. Advt. Women N.Y., N.Y. University Alumni Assn. Contbr. articles to profl. jours. Home: 896 Lincoln Ave Baldwin NY 11510 Office: 40 Melville Park Rd Melville NY 11747

OLSEN, JOHN BRIAN, banker; b. Chgo., Sept. 6, 1942; s. John Oscar and Angeline Olsen; B.A. (scholar), U. Ill., 1964; M.S. in Mgmt. (Grad. fellow), Case Western Res. U., 1973. Asst. to city admnstr. City of Fountain Valley (Calif.), 1964; asst. exec. dir. Council for Econ. Opportunities in Greater Cleve., 1965-67; sr. project mgr. Booz-Allen & Hamilton, Cleve., 1969-71; asst. dir., chief fin. and admnstrv. officer Cleve. Found., 1971-73; dir. budget and mgmt. Gov.'s Cabinet, State of Ohio 1973-75; dir. corp. planning Mellon Bank, Pitts., 1975—, v.p., 1978-79, sr. v.p., 1979—; lectr. in fin., pub. adminstrn. and urban affairs Cleve. State U., 1974, U. Md., 1968-69, Kent (Ohio) State U., 1966; lectr. corp. planning U. Mich. Grad. Sch. Bus., 1978—. Mem. vis. com. Case Western Res. U., Cleve., 1973-77. Served to capt. U.S. Army, 1967-69. Mem. Com. for Progress in Allegheny County (dir. 1976-78), N.Am. Soc. Corp. Planning (exec. com. Pitts. chpt. 1975—, pres. 1978—), Planning Execs. Inst., Am. Soc. Pub. Admnstrn., Inst. Pub. Affairs. Club: Duquesne. Home: 1411 Grandview Ave Pittsburgh PA 15211 Office: Mellon Bank Mellon Sq Pittsburgh PA 15230

OLSEN, KENNETH HARRY, mfg. co. exec.; b. Bridgeport, Conn., Feb. 20, 1926; s. Oswald and Svea (Nordling) O.; B.S. in Elec. Engring., Mass. Inst. Tech., 1950, M.S., 1952; m. Eeva-Liisa Aulikki Value, Dec. 12, 1950; children—Ava-Lisa Eleanor, Glenn Charles, James Jonathan. Elec. engr. Lincoln Lab., Mass. Inst. Tech., 1950-57; founder, 1957, since pres. Digital Equipment Corp., Maynard, Mass.; dir. Polaroid Corp., Cambridge, Mass., Shawmut Corp., Boston, Ford Motor Co., Dearborn, Mich. Former mem. computer sci. and engring. bd. Nat. Acad. Scis.; mem. Pres.'s Sci. Adv. Com., 1971-73; mem. Mass. Gov.'s Mgmt. Task Force; trustee, mem. corp. Joslin Diabetes Found.; mem. corp. Mus. Sci., Boston, Wentworth Inst., Boston; trustee Gordon Coll., Wenham, Mass.; deacon Park St. Ch., Boston. Served with USNR, 1944-46. Named Young Elec. Engr. of Year, Eta Kappa Nu, 1960, Businessman of Year, Bay State Bus. World, 1970, Exec. of Year, Boston chpt. Soc. for Advancement Mgmt., 1970; recipient Pres.'s award New Eng. chpt. Electronic Reps. Assn. Fellow IEEE, Am. Acad. Arts and Scis.; mem. Nat. Acad. Engring. Patentee magnetic devices. Home: Weston Rd Lincoln MA 01773 Office: Digital Equipment Corp 146 Main St Maynard MA 01754

OLSEN, MERVYL OLINUS, indsl. devel. exec.; b. Schaller, Iowa, May 8, 1924; s. Olinus and Margola (Kyle) O.; grad. Nat. Sch. Aeros., 1941, Tex. A. & M. U., 1974, U. Okla., 1975; m. Ruby Bruggeman, Jan. 8, 1944; children—Gary, Delores, Diane. Technician, Continental Motors Corp., Detroit, 1942-49; prin. Olsen Body Service, Cherokee, Iowa, 1952-73, Olsen Rentals, Cherokee, from 1958; now asst. dir. Indsl. Devel. div. Iowa Devel. Commn., Des Moines; pres. Cherokee Indsl. Corp., 1968-74. Mem. Cherokee Airport Commn., 1964-68; councilman, Cherokee, 1968-75. Served with USAAF, 1943-46. Mem. Iowa Profl. Developers. Republican. Presbyterian. Club: Toastmasters. Home: 6408 Crocker Des Moines IA Office: Iowa Devel Commn 250 Jewett Bldg Des Moines IA 50309

OLSEN, NORMAN OSCAR, mgmt. cons.; b. Wilmington, Del., Mar. 25, 1930; s. Oscar E. and Viola P. (Pace) O.; student public schs., Phila.; m. Dorothy Jensen, Nov. 15, 1974. Product mgr. AMP Inc., Harrisburg, Pa., 1954-64; regional mgr. Photocircuits Corp., Glen Cove, N.Y., 1965-68; acquisition cons. Winmic Jones Walker Co., N.Y.C., 1969-70; pres. The Mgmt. Meeting Co., Inc., Clearwater, Fla., 1970—. Mem. U.S. Yacht Racing Assn. Club: Clearwater Yacht (dir.). Home: 600 Ponce De Leon Blvd Clearwater FL 33516 Office: 600 Cleveland St Clearwater FL 33516

OLSEN, ROBERT ARTHUR, educator; b. Pittsfield, Mass., June 30, 1943; s. Arthur Anton and Virginia O.; B.B.A., U. Mass., 1966, M.B.A., 1967; Ph.D., U. Oreg., 1974; m. Maureen . Joan Carmell, Aug. 21, 1965. Security analyst Am. Inst. Counselors, 1967-68; research asso. Center for Capital Market Research, U. Oreg., 1972-74; asst. prof. fin. U. Mass., 1974-75; asso. prof. fin. Calif. State U., Chico, 1975—; cons. U.S. Forest Service. Stonier Banking fellow, 1971-72; Nat. Assn. Mut. Savs. Banks fellow, 1975-76. Mem. Am. Fin. Assn., Western Fin. Assn. (Trefftzs award 1974), Southwestern Fin. Assn., Fin. Mgmt. Assn., Sierra Club. Office: Calif State U Sch Bus Chico CA 95929

OLSEN, ROBERT JOHN, savs. and loan assn. exec.; b. N.Y.C., July 8, 1928; s. Christian Marinius and Agnes Geraldine (Jensen) O.; B.S., Strayer Coll., D.C., 1956; children—Duanne Mara, Bradley Stephen, Russell John. Supervisory agt. Fed. Home Loan Bank Bd., N.Y.C., 1956-65; pres., dir. Keystone Savs. & Loan Assn., Asbury Park, N.J., 1965—, also chmn.; pres. Rapid Money Service, Inc., Deal, N.J.; dir. Central Corp. of Savs. & Loans, Newark, Fed. Home Loan Bank N.Y., 1974-77. Councilman, Borough of Oceanport, N.J., 1971-73, 77—, council pres., 1979; v.p. Econ. Devel. Corp., Asbury Park, N.J., 1972—, Oceanport, N.J., 1974-77; mem. Zoning Bd. of Adjustment, Oceanport, 1969-70; mem. Citizens Adv. Council, Oceanport, 1975-76; dir. Monmouth and Ocean Devel. Council, Eatontown, N.J., 1974—; trustee Savs. and Loan Found. of Washington; chmn. N.J. Electronic Funds Transfer Com., 1971-80. Served with USMC, 1946-48, 1950-56. Mem. N.J. Savs. League (pres. chpt. 1966-67), U.S. Savs. League (vice chmn. com. on internal ops., chmn. remote service unit com.), Nat. Soc. Controllers and Fin. Officers (adv. council), Nat. Assn. Savs. and Loan Suprs., Nat. Soc. Fin. Examiners, Monmouth County, Ocean County realtors assns., C. of C. of Asbury Park, Navy League, Assn. U.S. Army. Clubs: Rotary; World Trade (N.Y.C.); Channel (Monmouth Beach, N.J.); Provost Marshals Guild (Ft. Monmouth, N.J.); Wheelmans (Asbury Park). Home: 28 Riverside Ave Red Bank NJ 07701 Office: 440 Cookman Ave Asbury Park NJ 07712

OLSEN, SAMUEL RICHARD, JR., printing co. exec.; b. Hamilton, Ohio, May 1, 1938; s. Samuel Richard and Hazel Mildred (Berg) O.; Asso. Applied Sci., Rochester Inst. Tech., 1961; children—Kristin, Erika, Samuel Richard III, Lonnie; m. 2d, Roberta Apa, June 1, 1974; 1 son, Erik. Vice-pres. mfg. Datagraphic N.Y., Inc., Rochester, N.Y., 1965-68; pres., chief exec. officer Form Service, Inc., Schiller Park, Ill., 1968—; pres., chief exec. officer Dealers Press, Inc., Schiller Park, 1973—, also dir. Served with USMC, 1960-63. Mem. Nat. Bus. Forms Assn. (certified forms cons.; dir.), Forms Mfg. Credit Interchange (chmn. 1973-74), Printing Industries Am., Nat. Assn. Printers and Lithographers. Home: 772 Halbert Ln Barrington IL 60010 Office: 9555 Ainslie St Schiller Park IL 60176

OLSEN, THEODORE ANDREW, mech. engr.; b. Rhinelander, Wis., Nov. 8, 1943; s. Andrew Edwin and Theodora Sylvia (Helgeson) O.; B.Aero. Engring., U. Minn., 1966. Engring. sci. specialist McDonnell Douglas Astronautics Corp., Huntington Beach, Calif., 1967-78; mech. engr. Dynalectron Corp., Albuquerque, 1978—. Democrat. Lutheran. Home: 5600 Gibson St SE Albuquerque NM 87108 Office: Box 18068 Air Flow Simulator Kirtland AFB Albuquerque NM 87115

OLSHEVER, HERBERT MORTON, retail furniture co. exec.; b. Bklyn., Jan. 2, 1933; s. Samuel and Rae (Solomon) O.; B.A., Bklyn. Coll., 1954; M.S., Columbia, 1959; m. Dorothy H. Jaslow, July 3, 1960; children—Steven B., Tracy E. Asst. buyer Abraham & Straus, Bklyn., 1959-60, buyer, 1960-67, div. group mgr., 1967-70, div. mdse. mgr., 1970-74; v.p., gen. mdse. mgr. William H. Block Co., Indpls., 1974-78; chmn. bd., pres. Connersville Furniture Co. Inc. (doing bus. as Guttman's) (Ind.), 1978—. Pres. Mount Sch. PTA, Stony Brook, N.Y., 1969-71. Served with USAF, 1955-57. Mem. Bklyn. Coll. Alumni Assn., Columbia U. Sch. Bus. Alumni Assn. Jewish. Clubs: Connersville Country, Connersville Kiwanis. Home: 536 Oakwood Dr Indianapolis IN 46260 Office: 815 Eastern Ave Connersville IN 47331

OLSKI, JERRY, mfg. co. exec.; b. Oswego, N.Y., Oct. 12, 1919; s. Francis Michael and Eva (Turay) O.; student Syracuse U., 1946-55, Harvard U., 1944, Stanford Exec. Inst., 1977; m. Marilyn Gayle Tetzlaff, Sept. 4, 1976; children—Susan, Anne, Joseph. Unit mgr. radio and TV div. Gen. Electric Co., Syracuse, N.Y., 1947-63; factory mgr. Litton Guidance & Control Systems, Woodland Hills, Calif., 1963-68; dir. ops. Datagraphix, San Diego, 1968-73; dir. ops. McDonnell Douglas Astronautics Co., Monrovia, Calif., 1973—. Served to lt. comdr. USN, 1940-45, ETO, 52-54, Korea. Mem. Air Force Assn., Ret. Officers Assn., Am. Electronics Assn., UN Assn. Republican. Roman Catholic. Home: 110 Oak Forest Circle Glendora CA 91740 Office: 700 Royal Oaks Dr Monrovia CA 91016

OLSON, DIANE FAYE, psychologist; b. Mpls., Jan. 11, 1946; d. Douglas Donald and Mabel Dorothy (Hagen) Christensen; B.A. magna cum laude, U. Minn., 1968, Ph.D., 1972; 1 dau., Emily S.L. Sr. clin. psychologist Hennepin County Gen. Hosp., Mpls., 1970; dir. patient hospitalization unit Abbott-Northwestern Hosp., Mpls., 1972; sr. clin. psychologist Pilot City Health Center, Mpls., 1974; exec. v.p. Dor & Assos., Inc., Mpls., 1978—; adj. asst. prof. U. Minn. Mem. allocation panel Mpls. United Way; pres., bd. dirs. Northside Settlement Services, Mpls.; mem. nat. accreditation team United Neighborhood Centers. Recipient Disting. Bd. Mem. award Northside Settlement Services, 1978. Mem. Am. Mgmt. Assn., St. Anthony's Comml. Assn. (bd. dirs.), Am. Psychol. Assn., Minn. Psychol. Assn., Assn. Labor Mgmt. Adminstrs. and Cons. Alcoholism (pres. Minn. chpt. 1980). Democrat. Lutheran. Club: Blaisdell Women's Health (chmn. bd. 1978). Home: 169 Seymour Ave SE Minneapolis MN 55414 Office: 416 H Hennepin St Suite 216 Minneapolis MN 55414

OLSON, FORREST WILLIAM, JR., accountant; b. Stillwater, Okla., Aug. 9, 1950; s. Forrest William and Shirley Ailene (Shire) O.; student Central State U., 1968-70, Okla. State U., 1971; B.B.A., Okla. U., 1972, postgrad., 1972-74; m. Pamela Jo Mathis, Dec. 18, 1971; children—Ashley Elizabeth, Forrest William III. Pres. Jones, Penn & Co., Oklahoma City, 1974-79, Forrest W. Olson, C.P.A., Inc., Oklahoma City, 1979—. C.P.A., Okla. Mem. Am. Inst. C.P.A.'s, Okla. Soc. C.P.A.'s. Republican. Baptist. Home: 10101 Midfield Cross Oklahoma City OK 73159 Office: Forrest W Olson 2200 Classen Blvd Oklahoma City OK 73106

OLSON, GEORGE CHARLES, banker; b. Boston, May 19, 1930; s. Charles Lewis and Mary Alice (Navin) O.; B.S., Boston U., 1952, M.B.A., 1956; children—George Charles, Kristin A., Jennifer J. Vice pres. State St. Bank & Trust Co., Boston, 1955-67; sr. ops. officer Western States Bankcard, San Francisco, 1967-70; sr. v.p., treas., trustee, corporator Home Savs. Bank, Boston, 1974—; treas., dir. Mass. Savs. Investment Corp., Mass. Savs. Realty Corp.; dir. Savs. Mgmt. Computer Corp. Bd. dirs. Arch Found. Served to capt. AUS, 1952-55. Mem. Security Officers Assn., Savs. Bank Officers Assn., Fin. Execs. Inst. Club: Mason. Home: 9 Temple St Boston MA 02114

OLSON, H. EVERETT, mfg. co. exec.; b. Chgo., Ill., 1906; grad. Northwestern U., 1927. With Carnation Co., 1931—, treas., 1948-54, v.p. fin., 1954-63, pres. 1963-71, chmn. exec. com., 1965-71, dir., chmn. bd., pres., chief exec. officer, from 1971, now chmn. bd., chief exec. officer. Office: Carnation Co 5045 Wilshire Blvd Los Angeles CA 90036*

OLSON, JANET LEE M., conveyor systems mfg. co. exec.; b. Chgo., Nov. 26, 1943; d. Clarence and Mary Ann (Borgia) Knicker; student DePaul U., 1961-62; m. Charles E. Olson, Mar. 3, 1963 (div. Jan. 1973); children—Charles E. Jr., Camille Marie, James Frederick. With Sears Roebuck Co., 1962, Am. Steel Foundries, 1963, Peoples Auto Parking Co., 1964; from bookkeeper to asst. controller Gen. Felt Industries, 1966-68; asst. controller in charge Standard Electronics div. Gulton Industries, Chgo., 1968-70; acting controller Chgo. Circuit Drilling, 1970-73; controller Automotion, Inc., Worth, Ill., 1973—; tax cons., 1973—. Mem. Republican Caucus. Mem. Am. Mgmt. Assn., Nat. Hist. Assn. Roman Catholic. Home: 10720 S Laramie Ave Oak Lawn IL 60453 Office: 11743 S Mayfield St Worth IL 60482

OLSON, KAREN LOUISE, life ins. agt.; b. Chgo., Jan. 5, 1944; d. Ervin Carl and Jeanette (Henss) O.; B.A., CCNY, 1969; C.L.U., 1977; 1 dau., Robin. Life ins. agt. Aetna Life & Casualty Co., 1973-76, Home Life Ins. Co., N.Y.C., 1976—; condr. seminars. Mem. Nat., N.Y. State assns. life underwriters, N.Y. Soc. Ins. Women (founder, 1st pres. 1974-76), N.Y. Assn. Women Bus. Owners (founder, pres. 1977-79). Publisher Compleat Women's Classified, 1976. Office: 770 Lexington Ave New York NY 10021

OLSON, MAYNARD WILLIAM, retail farm equipment co. exec.; b. La Crosse, Wis., Oct. 4, 1930; s. John and Lillian Mae (Kolstad) O.; student public schs.; m. Shirley Ann Scheidegger, June 7, 1951; children—Nancy, Judy, Ronald, Mary Ann, Carol, William. With Scheidegger Implement Co., Waumandee, Wis., 1949—, owner, 1976—. Instr. tractor project 4-H Club, 1965-76; sec., treas. Fire Dept., 1963-80; trustee St. Boniface Ch., 1980—; hunter safety instr.; boating safety instr. Served with N.G., 12 yrs. Mem. Wis. Power Equipment Retailers, Nat. Fedn. Ind. Bus. Club: Rod and Gun (past pres.). Address: PO Box 60 Waumandee WI 54622

OLSON, MELVIN NATHAN, agrl. microbiols. mfg. co. exec.; b. Marshfield, Wis., Apr. 10, 1932; s. Carl Frederick and Dorothy Hannah (Rowley) O.; B.A., Seattle Pacific U., 1955; M.Th., Western Evang. Sem., 1959; M.Ed., U. Portland, 1960, Ed.D., 1969; m. Mary Harder, July 26, 1969; 1 son, Michael David. Instr., Western Evang. Sem., Portland, Oreg., 1960-62; asso. prof. psychology Cascade Coll., Portland, 1962-67, pres., 1967-70; pres. Microbial Products div. Pioneer Hi-Bred Internat., Inc., Portland, 1970—. Mem. Nat. Feed Ingredients Assn., Am. Mgmt. Assn., Presidents Assn. of Am. Feed Mfrs. Assn. Republican. Baptist. Clubs: City, Multnomah Athletic (Portland). Home: 6415 SW Parkhill Way Portland OR 97201 Office: 3930 SW Macadam Ave Portland OR 97201

OLSON, O(SCAR) WILLIAM, corp. exec.; b. Oak Park, Ill., Feb. 1, 1927; s. Oscar William and Eudora (Landstrom) O.; A.B., DePauw U., 1949; J.D., John Marshall Law Sch., 1953; m. Margaret G. Olson; children—Peter W., Stephen W., Martha L. Admitted to Ill. bar, 1953; chmn. bd. Safeway Precision Products, Pompano Beach, Fla., 1968—; pres. Intercontinental Steel Corp., Chgo., 1969—; chmn. bd., pres., chief exec. officer South Suburban Safeway Lines, Inc., Harvey, Ill., 1970—; chmn. bd. Safeway Enterprises, Inc., Chgo.; pres. Dahltron Corp., Intercontinental Services, Ltd., Intercontinental Sales Ltd., Maran Mfg. Corp., Illectric Industries, Inc., Barr Industries, Inc. (all Chgo.). Served with USAAF, 1944-46; ETO. Mem. Am., Ill., Chgo. bar assns. Clubs: Union League, Chgo. Athletic Assn., Monroe, Executives, Nordic Law, Plaza (Chgo.); Edgewood Valley Country (LaGrange, Ill.). Home: 15W121 81st St Hinsdale IL 60521 Office: 111 W Washington St Chicago IL 60602

OLSON, OSCAR DONALD, investment co. exec.; b. Pueblo, Colo., Feb. 9, 1917; s. Oscar and Iva (Ackerman) O.; B.A., U. Chgo., 1941, M.B.A., 1948; m. Bonnie B. Waggoner-Breternitz, May 17, 1944; children—Pamela Lynne, Douglas Donald. With No. Trust Co., Chgo., 1941-54; asst. personnel dir., 1947-54; with Exchange Nat. Bank, Colorado Springs, Colo., 1954-72, v.p., 1959-63, sr. v.p., 1964-66, pres., 1967-72; pres., dir. Air Acad. Nat. Bank, 1966-71; pres. Warehouses, Inc., 1975-79, O.D. Olson & Assos.; chmn. bd., pres. Citizens' Nat. Bank, Colorado Springs, 1976-77. Mem. Phillips Andover Acad. Parents' Giving Com.; mem. parents com. Harvard; Ill. regional adviser Small Bus. Adminstrn. Served with USAAF, 1942-45; now maj. gen. Res. (ret.). Decorated Silver Star medal, Legion of Merit, D.F.C., Air medal; recipient Man of Year Nat. Air Force Assn. award, 1960, Alumni citation U. Chgo., 1961. Mem. Am. Bankers Assn. (past pres.), C. of C. (past pres.), Air Force Assn. (past dir.), Newcomen Soc., Order Daedalians, Urban League, Sigma Chi. Clubs: El Paso, Garden of Gods, 100 USAF Academy. Home: 2110 Hercules Dr Colorado Springs CO 80906 Office: PO Box 700 Colorado Springs CO 80901

OLSON, WALTER JUSTUS, JR., utility co. exec.; b. Paterson, N.J., July 27, 1941; s. Walter Justus and Viola P. (Trautvetter) O.; Sc.B., A.B., Brown U., 1964; M.B.A., Columbia U., 1967. Design engr. Rockwell Internat., Inc., Downey, Calif., 1964-65; fin. officer CIA, Washington, 1969-73; sr. cons. Booz, Allen & Hamilton, Inc., Washington, 1973-78; corp. planning coordinator Washington Gas Light Co., Springfield, Va., 1978—. Served to 1st lt. USAF, 1967-69. C.P.A., Md. Mem. Am. Inst. C.P.A.'s, D.C. Inst. C.P.A.'s, No. Am. Soc. Corp. Planning. Republican. Episcopalian. Home: 7348 Dartford Dr McLean VA 22102 Office: Washington Gas Light Co 6801 Industrial Rd Springfield VA 22151

OLSSON, LARS OLOF, air pollution control co. exec.; b. Orebro, Sweden, Feb. 27, 1928; s. Gustav Hugo and Edith Lovisa (Sundh) O.; came to U.S., 1973; B.Sc. in Engring., Orebro Tech. Coll., 1949; m. Marta Birgitta Andersson, Oct. 30, 1953; 1 dau., Kristina. With Flakt Group, 1950—, pres. Flakt Can. Ltd., Vancouver, B.C., 1963-65, Montreal, Que., 1965-73, pres. Flakt, Inc., Old Greenwich, Conn., 1973—, dir. Flakt Can. Ltd., Flakt, Inc. bd. dirs. Indsl. Gas Cleaning Inst., Inc. Bd. dirs. Swedish-Am. C. of C., 1977—. Registered profl. engr., Conn. Mem. Am. Inst. Mining, Metall. and Petroleum Engrs., Air Pollution Control Assn., Canadian Pulp and Paper Assn., Pul, Paper Machinery Mfrs. Assn., TAPPI. Club: Innis Arden Golf (Old Greenwich). Home: 15 Stanwich Rd Greenwich CT 06830 Office: 1500 E Putnam Ave Old Greenwich CT 06870

O'MALLEY, EDWARD JOSEPH, JR., ednl. adminstr.; b. Flushing, N.Y., Jan. 4, 1942; s. Edward Joseph and Elsie Anne (Ende) O'M.; B.S., Widener Coll., 1963; M.B.A., St. Johns U., Jamaica, N.Y., 1976; m. Iris Theresa Hill, Aug. 10, 1975; stepchildren—James, Marc. Ins. agt. Liberty Mut. Ins. Co., N.Y.C., 1966-67; supr. group home Children's Village, Bayside, N.Y., 1967-69; unit head N.Y. Narcotic Addiction Control Commn., N.Y.C., 1970-71; exec. dir., sch. dist. drug and alcohol abuse program, Howard Beach, N.Y., 1971—. Past chmn., sec. N.Y.C. Coalition Sch. Based Drug Prevention Programs; past vice chmn. Comprehensive Health Planning Agy., Queens, N.Y.; mem. Queens Community Planning Bd.; past v.p. Flushing (N.Y.) Boys Club; past chmn. bd. dirs. Regular Democratic Club, Rockaway, N.Y.; mem. N.Y. State Dem. Com.; mem. Parish Council St. Camillus Ch.; mem. Chancellor N.Y.C. Bd. Edn. Task Force on Drug Abuse; bd. dirs. Queens chpt. ARC, N.Y.C. Health Systems Agy., Rockaway Task Force on Arts, Far Rockaway chpt. NAACP; chmn. Anti-Redlining Com. of Rockaways; vice chmn. Com. for Casino Gambling in Rockaways, Surfside Housing Assn. for Tenants; mem. N.Y. State Urban Coalition Task Force Drug Abuse. Mem. Emerald Assn. L. I. Beta Gamma Sigma. Club: Rockaway Kiwanis (past pres.). Home: 107 10 Shore Front Pkwy Rockaway Park NY 11694

O'MALLEY, PATRICK ANTHONY, beverage co. exec.; b. Phila., June 22, 1942; s. Thomas F. and Helen C. (Passe) O'M.; B.S., Villanova U., 1964; LL.B., Blackstone Sch. Law, 1968, J.D., 1974; m. Lynne M. Marmaduke, Nov. 27, 1965; children—Karen Elisabeth, Patrick Thomas, Michael Christopher. Account exec. Gen. Electric Co., Dallas, 1967-70; nat. sales mgr. Bob Philips Assos., Dallas, 1970-73; regional mgr. Advance Machine Co., Overland Park, Kans. 1973-77; nat. mktg. mgr. Midland Internat. Co., Kansas City, Kans., 1977-80; gen. mgr. John P. Ward & Son, Inc., 1980—. Served to capt., parachutist, USMC, 1964-70. Decorated Purple Heart (5), Bronze Star, Air medal; Vietnamese Cross of Gallantry; 1st degree black belt Kempo Karate; nat. Ryukyu Kata champion. Mem. Nat. Speakers Assn., U.S. Yachting Assn., Boating Industry Assn. Roman Catholic. Club: K.C. (4th degree). Home: 13030 W 104th St Overland Park KS 66215

O'MALLEY, PATRICK LAWRENCE, corp. exec.; b. Boston, Jan. 2, 1911; s. Matthias and Bridget (Sweeney) O'M; student Harvard, 1930-31; hon. degrees St. Joseph Coll., Mundelein Coll., St. Procopius Coll., Bryant Coll.; m. Helen Lee, Oct. 29, 1933; 1 son, Patrick Lawrence. With Employers Liability Assurance Co., 1930, Western Electric Co., 1931; salesman Coca-Cola Bottling Co., Boston, 1932-35, mgr., 1935-42; tech. observer Coca-Cola Export Corp., 1942-45; with Coca-Cola Bottling Co., Stamford, Conn. 1946-48. Oshkosh, Wis., 1948-52, v.p., then pres. Chgo., 1952-60; v.p. nat. sales Coca Cola Co., Atlanta, 1960-62; chmn., dir., chief exec. officer Canteen Corp. (formerly Automatic Canteen Co. Am.), Chgo., 1962—; chmn., dir. Casualty Ins. Co., Michigan Ave. Nat. Bank; dir. Transworld Airlines, Stone Container Corp., Del Webb Corp. Bd. dirs. Better Bus. Bur. Chgo., Chgo. Conv. and Tourism Bur., Regional Transp. Authority; trustee Roosevelt U., Mundelein Coll., Chgo.; mem. adv. council Coll. Bus. Adminstrn. U. Notre Dame; chmn. exec. adv. bd. St. Joseph Hosp., Chgo.; pres. Chgo. Park Dist. Recipient outstanding bus. award Oshhosh Jr. C. of C., 1950; Horatio Alger award; Great Am. Award B'nai B'rith; Golden Plate award Am. Acad. Achievement, others. Mem. Nat. Inst. Food Service Industry (past pres.), Nat. Restaurant Assn. (past pres.), Ill. Coca Cola Bottlers Assn. (pres.), Chgo. Sales Marketing Execs. (pres. 1960), Quincy (Mass.) C. of C. (v.p.), Atlantic Council of U.S. (dir.). Elk, K.C. Clubs: Beverly Country (Chgo.); Oshkosh Rotary (pres. 1952). Office: Canteen Corp 1430 Merchandise Mart Chicago IL 60654*

ONAL, HASAN FEHMI, mfg. co. exec.; b. Istanbul, Turkey, Feb. 22, 1925; came to U.S., 1960, naturalized, 1970; s. Faik and Fatma (Manizade) O.; B.S. in Mil. Sci., Mil. Coll., Ankara, Turkey, 1948; M.E., Inst. Tech., Stockholm, 1955; children—Linda, John. Sr. engr., project mgr. Byron Jackson Pumps, Los Angeles, 1960-70; v.p. Hydro-Jet Corp., Oceanside, Calif., 1970-74; product mgr. Fluid Handling div. Sundstrand Corp., Denver, 1974-75; pres. Hydro-Tech Corp., Pueblo West, Colo., 1975—; cons. on centrifugal pumps to Worthington Pump Corp., Mercury Marine Co., Stewart & Stevenson Services, Inc., 1975—; tech. adv. Turkish consulate, Los Angeles, 1968-69. NSF grantee, 1974. Mem. ASME (dir. 1968-69). Republican. Muslim. Club: Elks. Contbr. articles to profl. jours.; patentee in field centrifugal pumps in U.S. and fgn. countries. Home: 4722 S Idalia St Aurora CO 80015 Office: PO Box 7331 716 Industrial Blvd Pueblo West CO 81007

ONDEK, VIOLET CECILIA HUGHES, ins. and investment co. exec.; b. Phila.; d. Lewis Rhodes and Cecilia Regina (Gerhard) Winnemore; student pub. schs., Colwyn-Darby, Pa.; m. Steve Michael Ondek, June 29, 1963; children—Joan Elaine Hughes Wolfe, George Blaine Hughes. Corr. Phila., Bull., 1949-51, Upper Darby News, 1948-51; mem. advt. dept. Gettysburg (Pa.) Times and News, 1951-53; owner, operator V.C. Hughes Co., residential constrn., Biglerville, Pa., 1953-72; co-founder, sec.-treas., dir. Corporate Investment Co., Biglerville, 1970—; sec.-treas., dir. Corporate Life Ins. Co., Corporate Land Investment Co.; sec.-treas. Doylestown (Pa.) Inn. Inc. Mem. adv. council U.S. SBA, 1976—; mem. Gov. Thornburg's Council on Small Bus.; mem. Republican Council Women. Mem. Adams County Home Builders Assn. (charter), Adams County Hist. Soc., Music Box Soc. Internat. Presbyterian. Clubs: Woman's of Colwyn, Woman's of Gettysburg. Home: Guernsey Rd Rural Delivery 2 Biglerville PA 17307

O'NEAL, ARL RANKIN, farmer services exec.; b. Miss., June 15, 1926; s. Eugene Bryon and Lissie Louvenia (Bond) O'N.; student public schs.; m. Carolyn Gracia Berry, Jan. 3, 1945; children—Barbara, Reita, Sheila, Judith, Arl Rankin. Engaged in logging bus., 1946-49; with Rouse Pontiac Co., Wiggins, Miss., 1949-58, gen. mgr., 1958; postmaster, Perkinston, Miss., 1958-73; pres., gen. mgr. Magnolia Purchasing Service, Inc., Hattiesburg, Miss., 1973—; chmn. bd. Deep South Land and Cattle Co., Inc., 1974—. Active local PTA, Boy Scouts Am. Served with AUS, 1944-46; ETO. Decorated Bronze Star (2), Purple Heart; recipient various service awards. Mem. Deep South Farm Equipment Dealers Assn., Better Bus. Bur. Hattiesburg, Miss. Forestry Assn., Miss. Peace Officers Assn., Am. Legion, VFW. Club: Kiwanis.

O'NEAL, KIRKMAN, steel co. exec.; b. Florence, Ala., June 17, 1890; s. Emmet and Elizabeth (Kirkman) O'N.; student State Tchrs. Coll., Florence, 1905-09; B.S., U.S. Naval Acad., 1909-13; m. Elizabeth Paramore, Oct. 9, 1917; children—Emmet, Elizabeth (Mrs. David H. White). Commd. ensign USN, 1913, resigned, 1913, recalled to serve as lt. (s.g.), 1917-19; prodn. engr. Chickasaw Shipbldg. Co., 1919-20, Ingalls Iron Works Co., 1920-21; founder, 1921, pres. O'Neal Steel, Inc., Birmingham, Ala., 1921—, now chmn. bd., pres. Ga., Tenn. and Miss.; chmn. bd. O'Neal Steel, Inc., Del.; dir. Indsl. Paint Co. Bd. dirs., finance com. local chpt. A.R.C.; bd. dirs. Birmingham Civic Symphony, Jr. Achievement of Am., Emmet O'Neal Library. pres., bd. dirs. Kirkman O'Neal Found. Mem. U.S., Ala., Birmingham chambers commerce, Am. Inst. Steel Constrn., Am. Warehouse Assn., S. Structural Steel Bd. of Trade, Ala. Hist. Soc., Nat. Indsl. Conf. Bd., N.A.M., Newcomen Soc. N.Am. Presbyn. Clubs: Relay House, Mountain Brook Country, Birmingham Country, Redstone, The Club. Home: 2500 Mountain Brook Pkwy Birmingham AL 35223 Office: 744 N 41st St Birmingham AL 35202

O'NEIL, C. RODERICK, ins. co. exec.; b. N.Y.C., Jan. 26, 1931; s. Charles A. and Elizabeth (Whyte) O'N.; B.A., Princeton U., 1953; M.B.A., U. Chgo., 1957; m. Nancy Galante, Nov. 25, 1950; children—Brian, Sarah, Timothy, Kevin, John, Anne. Asst. mgr dept. investment No. Trust Co., Chgo., 1953-59; v.p. H.M. Byllesby & Co., Chgo., 1959-62, A.G. Becker & Co., Chgo., 1962-64; with Mfrs. Hanover Trust, N.Y.C., 1964-77, exec. v.p., head trust div., 1970-77; chmn. fin. com. Travelers Ins. Cos., Hartford, Conn., 1977—, also dir.; mem. investment adv. bds. N.Y. State Tchrs. and N.Y. State Employees Retirement System; mem. investment policy panel Pension Benefit Guaranty Corp. Bd. dirs. St. Francis Hosp., Hartford; trustee Meml. Dr. Trust, Cambridge, Mass. Mem. Inst. Chartered Fin. Analysts, Fin. Analysts Fedn., N.Y. Soc. Security Analysts, Hartford Soc. Security Analysts, Victorian Soc. in Am. (dir.), Greater Hartford Arts Council (dir.). Office: 1 Tower Square Hartford CT 06115

O'NEIL, EUGENE JOSEPH, chem. co. exec.; b. Akron, Ohio, Dec. 8, 1909; s. William James and Catherine Elizabeth (Tobin) O'N.; B.A., U. Akron, 1936; m. Katherine Alice Bream, Sept. 18, 1937; children—Eugene Joseph, Catherine Tobin. Latex research mgr. Firestone Tire & Rubber Co., Akron, 1936-45; co-founder Tigron Latex Corp., 1945, pres., 1945—; founder, pres. Tigron Latex & Chem. Corp., Stoughton, Mass., 1950; pres., dir. O'Neil Investment Corp., Babson Park, Mass., 1957—, O'Neil Securities Corp., Babson Park, 1969—. Mem. exec. bd. parents assn. Lawrence (Mass.) Acad. Mem. Am. Chem. Soc., N.A.M. (govt. expenditure com.), Asso. Industries Mass., Boston Rubber Group, Pi Kappa Epsilon. Republican. Roman Catholic. Clubs: Algonquin of Boston, Wellesley (Mass.) Country. Home: 52 Clarke Circle Needham MA 02192 Office: PO Box 27 Babson Park MA 02157

O'NEIL, JAMES F., ret. publisher; b. Manchester, N.H., June 13, 1898; s. Joseph H. and Mary E. (Dalton) O'N.; M.A., U. N.H., 1947; LL.D., St. Anselm's Coll., 1948; m. Edythe Graf, Sept. 7, 1925; children—Kenneth G., J. Russell. City editor Union & Leader, Manchester, N.H., 1924-34; chief police Manchester, 1937-50; publisher Am. Legion Mag., N.Y.C., 1950-78, emeritus, 1978—. Dir. Civil Def., 1939-42; mem. Mcpl. Airport, Golf Course, Stadium Bd., 1928-37. Spl. asst. to Sec. Navy, 1944-46; pres. Truman's Amnesty Bd., 1946-47. Trustee MacArthur Meml. Found., Norfolk, Va., 1959—. Served with U.S. Army, 1916-17, Mexican border, A.E.F., 1917-19. Decorated French Legion Honor, Croix de Guerre with palm. Mem. Am. Legion (nat. comdr., 1947-48), Newcomen Soc. Republican. Roman Catholic. K.C. Club: Dutch Treat (N.Y.C.). Home: 10 Holder Pl Forest Hills NY 11375

O'NEIL, JOHN JAMES, rubber co. exec.; b. Akron, Ohio, June 24, 1917; s. William and Grace Agnes(Savage) O'N.; A.B., Holy Cross Coll., 1938; LL.B., Harvard U., 1941; S.T.L., Cath. U. Am., 1954; m. Helene Connellan, May 27, 1959; children—Helene, John, Ann, Jane. Fin. analyst The Gen. Tire & Rubber Co., Akron, Ohio, 1946-48, treas., 1948-50, fin. advisor, 1955-60, chmn. fin. com., 1960—, dir., 1949-50, 55—, chmn. investment bds., 1956. Served with USCG, 1942-46. Clubs: Portage Country, Burning Tree, Columbia Country, Kenwood Country, Bath, Knights of Malta, Knights of Holy Sepulchre, K.C. Office: 1 General St Akron OH 44329

O'NEIL, MICHAEL GERALD, bus. exec.; b. Akron, Ohio, Jan. 29, 1922; s. William Francis and Grace (Savage) O'N.; A.B., Coll. of Holy Cross, 1943; postgrad. Sch. Bus., Harvard, 1948; LL.D., U. Akron, 1962, Ashland, Coll., 1967; m. Juliet P. Rudolph, Jan. 7, 1950; children—Michael, Gregory, Jeffrey, Shawn, Julie, Nancy, Susan. With Gen. Tire Co., 1947—, staff inter-plant ops., Venezuela, 1947-48, dir., 1950—, exec. asst. to pres., 1951-60, pres., 1960—, chmn. bd., 1981—, mem. exec., finance coms.; dir., chmn. bd. Aerojet-Gen. Corp.; dir. 1st Nat. Bank of Akron. Served as lt. USAAF, 1944-45. Clubs: Portage Country, Akron City; Detroit Athletic, Sharon Golf. Office: One General St Akron OH 44329

O'NEIL, THOMAS FRANCIS, broadcasting and rubber co. exec.; b. Kansas City, Mo., Apr. 18, 1915; s. William and Grace Agnes (Savage) O'N.; A.B., Holy Cross Coll., 1937; m. Claire Miller McCahey, June 15, 1946; children—Shane, Eileen, Mark, Conn, Claire, Liam, Grace, Carol, Owen. With Gen. Tire & Rubber Co., Akron, Ohio, 1937-41, 46—, dir., 1948—, v.p., 1950-60, vice chmn. bd., 1960, chmn., 1961—; v.p., dir. The Yankee Network, Boston, 1948-51; pres., dir. RKO Gen., Inc., N.Y.C., 1955-66, chmn. bd., 1966—, dir., 1981—; dir. Frontier Airlines, Inc. Served to lt. USCG, World War II. Office: Gen Tire & Rubber Co One General St Akron OH 44329*

O'NEILL, DONALD EDMUND, pharm. co. exec.; b. Port Angeles, Wash., Feb. 10, 1926; s. Edward I. and Christine (Williamson) O'N.; B.S., U. Wash., 1949; m. Violet Elizabeth Oman, June 12, 1948; children—Shelley O'Neill Lane, Erin O'Neill Kennedy and Shawn (twins). Sales rep. Calif. Bay area G.D. Searle & Co., 1950-53, sales rep., Seattle, 1953-59, div. mgr., 1959-62, regional sales dir., 1962-64, dir. med. service, 1964-68, dir. mktg., 1968-71; pres. Warner/Chilcott div. Warner-Lambert Co., 1971-74, pres. Softcon products, 1973-74, pres. profl. products group, corp. v.p., 1974-76, pres. Parke, Davis & Co. div., 1976-78, exec. v.p. pharm. group Warner-Lambert Co., 1977-78, pres. health care group, 1978—, pres., exec. dir. Parke-Davis research div., 1978-79, corp. v.p., 1974—; bd. dirs. Cert. Med. Reps. Inst., Inc., 1979—. Bd. dirs. United Way Morris County, 1980—;

trustee Morris Mus. Arts and Scis. Served with USAAF, 1944-46. Mem. Pharm. Mfrs. Assn. Club: Morris County Golf (Convent Station, N.J.). Office: Warner-Lambert Co 201 Tabor Rd Morris Plains NJ 07950

O'NEILL, FRANCIS JAMES, mgmt. cons.; b. Syracuse, N.Y., May 26, 1936; s. Frank Halsey and Cecilia Marie (Gannon) O'N.; B.S., Holy Cross Coll., 1958; grad. Program for Mgmt. Devel., Harvard U., 1971; children—Lisa, Brian, Kevin. Mem. mktg. mgmt. staff Procter & Gamble Co., Cin., 1959-60; with Vick Chem. div. Richardson-Merrell Inc., Wilton, Conn., 1960-64, new products dir., 1962-64; product mktg. mgr., consumer products div. Am. Cyanamid Co., Wayne, N.J., 1964-66; asst. to pres. Vick Chem. div. Richardson-Merrell Inc., 1966-68, mng. dir. Can., 1968-70, dir. mktg. services, 1970-71; pres. Strategic Devel. Inc., Westport, Conn., 1972-77, 80-81; v.p. Eastman & Beaudine, Inc., N.Y.C., 1977-80; dir. mktg. Generix Drug Corp., Hollywood, Fla., 1981—. Served to lt. U.S. Army, 1958-59. Roman Catholic. Clubs: Met. (N.Y.C.), Harvard Bus. Sch. Home: Fairway 5A 4006 Inverrary Blvd Lauderhill FL 33319 Office: 3001 N 29th Ave Hollywood FL 33020

O'NEILL, GEORGE DORR, investment co. exec.; b. N.Y.C., Dec. 27, 1926; s. Grover and Catherine G. (Porter) O'N.; B.A., Harvard U., 1949; m. Abby R. Milton, June 22, 1949; children—George Dorr, Abby, David, Catherine, Wendy, Peter. With Harris Upham & Co., 1949-53, Chase Manhattan Bank, 1953-58, Equity Corp., 1959-63, Train Cabot & Assos., N.Y.C., 1963-76; pres. Meriwether Capital Corp., N.Y.C., 1977—; dir. Anatar Industries, Fin. Gen. Bankshares, Statesman Group Inc. Trustee Colonial Williamsburg, 1966—, Webster Coll., 1967-73, Vassar Coll., 1978—; pres., trustee Community Found. of Oyster Bay, 1966—, Youth and Family Counselling Agy., 1970—. Club: Harvard (N.Y.C.); Piping Rock. Office: 30 Rockefeller Plaza Room 4528 New York NY 10020

O'NEILL, THOMAS HOWARD, JR., oil and gas co. exec.; b. Buffalo, Aug. 14, 1941; s. Thomas Howard and Helen Jeanette (Voss) O'N.; B.S., Canisius Coll., 1963; M.S., SUNY, Buffalo, 1974. Vice pres. Venture Tech., Inc., Buffalo, 1972-75; pres. BerVent, Inc., Buffalo, 1976—, also dir.; pres. Berea Oil & Gas Corp., Buffalo, 1976—, also dir. Mem. Ohio Oil and Gas Assn., W.Va. Oil and Gas Assn., Tenn Oil and Gas Assn. Office: Berea Oil and Gas Corp 69 Delaware Ave Buffalo NY 14202

O'NEILL, TIMOTHY JAMES, office supplies and equipment exec.; b. Cadillac, Mich., Dec. 14, 1948; s. Jack Whyte and Dorothy Ann (Kroth) O'N.; A.A., Regis Coll., 1969; B.A. in Bus. Adminstrn., Aquinas Coll., 1971; m. Mary Diane Stilwell, June 27, 1970; children—Molly Ann, Brian James. With O'Neill Co., real estate holding co., Cadillac, 1976—, pres., 1977—; dir. O'Neill Ace Hardware, Inc., Cadillac; pres. O'Neill Office Centers, Inc., Cadillac. Mem. St. Ann Sch. System Bd. Edn., 1979—; bd. dirs. Cadillac Police/Fire Pension Fund, pres., 1978—. Recipient 1st award for store design Geyer's Dealer Topics mag., 1979. Mem. Cadillac Area C. of C., Cadillac Area Retailers Assn., Nat. Office Machine Dealers Assn., Nat. Office Products Assn., Mich. Retail Hardware Assn., Nat. Fedn. Ind. Bus. Republican. Roman Catholic. Clubs: Cadillac Rotary (pres. 1976-77), Moni Investment (pres. 1974-75). Home: 515 Oak St Cadillac MI 49601 Office: 116 W Harris St Cadillac MI 49601

O'NEILL, WILLIAM JAMES, leasing and transp. co. exec.; b. Cleve., Sept. 21, 1906; s. Hugh and Louise (Berchtold) O'N.; A.B. magna cum laude, U. Notre Dame, 1928; m. Dorothy Kundtz, May 28, 1932; children—William James, Dorothy (Mrs. John Donahey), Kathleen (Mrs. William France), Molly (Mrs. George Sweeney), Timothy. Operating mgr. Superior Transfer Co., 1928-30, Motor Express, Inc., 1928-30; v.p., chief operating officer over-the-road carrier subsidiaries U.S. Truck Lines, Inc. of Del., 1930-37; founder, owner, pres., chief exec. officer Niagara Motor Express, Inc., 1938-59; chmn. bd., pres., chief exec. officer Transp. Fin. Corp., 1954—; founder, chmn. bd. Lease Plan Internat. Corp., N.Y.C., 1959-61; pres., chief exec. officer Leaseway Ltd. (Can.), 1959-75; founder, pres., chief exec. officer Leaseway Transp. Corp., 1961-69, chmn. bd., chief exec. officer, 1969-75; chmn. bd., chief exec. officer Leaseway Intercontinental (LEASECO) S.A., Zug, Switzerland, 1962-72; founder 7 fin. leasing cos. in Europe, Mex. and Can.; partner N.Y. Yankees; dir. Portec, Inc. Pres., trustee O'Neill Bros. Found.; trustee Sherwick Found., W.J. and D.K. O'Neill Fund; bd. dirs. Villa Dorado Owners Assn., Dorado Beach, P.R.; 1st lay pres. Gilmour Acad., Gates Mills, Ohio; hon. trustee Robinson Sch., West Hartford, Conn.; trustee, mem. distbn. com. The Cleveland Found. Mem. Newcomen Soc. N.Am. Clubs: Metropolitan (N.Y.C.); The Country (Pepper Pike, Ohio); Chagrin Valley Hunt (Gates Mills); Union (Cleve.). Home: Clanonderry Ct Daisy Hill RD 3 33917 Hackney Rd Chagrin Falls OH 44022 Office: 3733 Park East Dr Suite 101 Cleveland OH 44122

O'NEILL, WILLIAM JAMES, JR., transp. co. exec.; b. Cleve., Aug. 28, 1933; s. William James and Dorothy (Kundtz) O'N.; B.S. cum laude, Georgetown U., 1955; J.D., Harvard, 1958; m. Deborah J. Baker, Oct. 22, 1966; children—Alec M., Sara L., Jessie A., Laura E. Admitted to Ohio bar, 1958; gen. counsel Leaseway Transp. Corp. and subsidiaries, 1961-67, East Coast group head, Phila., 1967-68; v.p. East Coast group, Phila., 1968-69, sr. v.p., Cleve., 1969-74, pres., chief operating officer, 1974—, also dir. Trustee, Dyke Coll. Corp., O'Neill Bros. Found., Gilmour Acad., Bluecoats (all Cleve.). Served to capt. USAF, 1958-61. Recipient Air Force Commendation medal with oak leaf cluster; named Man of Yr., Gilmour Acad., 1974. Mem. Am. Bar Assn., Am. Trucking Assn., Truck Renting and Leasing Assn. (pres. 1980—), Pvt. Truck Council Am. Roman Catholic. Clubs: Chagrin Valley Hunt, Country, Cleveland Polo, Park East Racquet. Home: Hunting Valley OH 44022 Office: 3700 Park East Dr Cleveland OH 44122

ONG, JOHN DOYLE, rubber products co. exec.; b. Uhrichsville, Ohio, Sept. 29, 1933; s. Louis Brosee and Mary Ellen (Liggett) O.; B.A., Ohio State U., 1954, M.A., 1954; LL.B., Harvard, 1957; m. Mary Lee Schupp, July 20, 1957; children—John Francis Harlan, Richard Penn Blackburn, Mary Katherine Caine. Admitted to Ohio bar, 1958; asst. counsel B.F. Goodrich Co., Akron, 1961-66, group v.p., 1972-73, exec. v.p., 1973-74, vice chmn., 1974-75, pres., dir., 1975-77, pres., chief operating officer, dir., 1978-79, chmn. bd., pres., chief exec. officer, 1979—; asst. to pres. Internat. B.F. Goodrich Co., Akron, 1966-69, v.p., 1969-70, pres., 1970-72; dir. Cooper Industries, The Kroger Co. Vice-pres. exploring Great Trail council Boy Scouts Am., 1974-77; v.p. Akron Community Trusts. Trustee Akron Regional Devel. Bd., Mus. Arts Assn., Cleve., Bexley Hall Sem., 1974—; trustee Hudson (Ohio) Library and Hist. Soc., pres., 1971-72; trustee Western Res. Acad., Hudson, 1975—, pres. bd. trustees, 1977—; nat. trustee Nat. Symphony Orch., 1975—; mem. bus. adv. com. Transp. Center, Northwestern U., 1975-78, Carnegie-Mellon U., 1978—; mem. adv. bd. Blossom Music Center. Served with JAGC, AUS, 1957-61. Mem. Ohio Bar Assn. (bd. govs. corp. counsel sect. 1962-74, chmn. 1970), Rubber Mfrs. Assn. (dir. 1974—), Conf. Bd., Phi Beta Kappa, Phi Alpha Theta. Episcopalian. Clubs: Portage Country, Akron City; Union (Cleve.); Links, Union League (N.Y.C.); Country of Hudson (Ohio); Georgetown (Washington); Rolling Rock (Ligonier, Pa.); Castalia Trout. Office: B F Goodrich Co 500 S Main St Akron OH 44318*

ONO, NAGAHISA, devel. co. exec.; b. Tokyo, Feb. 8, 1938; s. Takeshi and Kaoru (Kajima) O.; came to U.S., 1974; B.A., Keio U. (Japan), 1960; M.B.A., U. Pa., 1967; m. Yumiko Yano, Mar. 17, 1970; children—Takashisa, Takehiko. Field officer Kajima Co., Tokyo, 1960-63, system analyst, chief of mgmt. info. system, 1967-74; v.p. East West Devel. Co., Los Angeles, 1974—; mgr. mktg. and planning Kajima Internat., Los Angeles, 1974—. Gen. chmn. Nisei Week Japanese Festival. Mem. Am. Mgmt. Assn., Los Angeles C. of C. Buddhist. Clubs: Riviera Country (Los Angeles); Takanodai Country (Tokyo). Home: 1015 A 21st St Santa Monica CA 90403 Office: 250 E 1st St Suite 612 Los Angeles CA 90012

ONTHANK, JOHN BONTIES, candy and soft drink co. exec.; b. Greenwich, Conn., Apr. 12, 1936; s. Pierce and Nancy (Fuller) O.; B.A. in Econs., Yale, 1957; m. Judy Howse, Nov. 2, 1957; children—Robert Pierce, Christopher Howse, John Bonties. Mktg. exec. Can. Dry Corp., N.Y.C., 1960-68, Coca-Cola U.S.A., Atlanta, 1968-71, mktg. exec. Schweppes U.S.A., Stamford, Conn., 1971-75, pres., 1976—; pres. Cadbury Schweppes U.S.A. Inc., Stamford, 1976-78, also dir.; pres. Schweppes N.Am., 1977—, Rondo Beverage Corp., 1978—. Served to lt. USN, 1957-60. Mem. Am. Mgmt. Assn., Pres.'s Assn. Republican. Episcopalian. Club: Wilton Riding. Home: 18 Turner Ridge Ct Wilton CT 06897 Office: 1200 High Ridge Rd Stamford CT 06905

OPEL, JOHN ROBERTS, bus. machines co. exec.; b. Kansas City, Mo., Jan. 5. 1925; s. Norman J. and Esther (Roberts) O.; A.B., Westminster Coll., 1948; M.B.A., U. Chgo., 1949; m. Julia Carole Stout, Dec. 28, 1953; children—Robert, Nancy, Julia. Mary, John. Salesman, various mktg. posts IBM, Armonk, N.Y., 1949-66, mem. mgmt. com., 1967, v.p. corp. fin. and planning, 1968-69, sr. v.p. fin. and planning, 1969-72, group exec. data processing group, 1972-74, pres., mem. corp. office, 1974—, chief exec. officer, 1981—; dir. Pfizer, Inc., Fed. Res. Bank of N.Y. Trustee, Inst. Advanced Study, Westminster Coll.; bd. govs. United Way Am., Wilson Council. Served with AUS, 1943-45. Mem. Bus. Council, Bus. Roundtable. Office: IBM Corp Old Orchard Rd Armonk NY 10504

OPOTOWSKY, BARBARA BERGER, lawyer, non-profit corp. exec.; b. N.Y.C., Aug. 31, 1945; d. Alexander and Adele (Brooks) Berger; B.A. in Polit. Sci., U. Pa., 1967; J.D., Fordham U., 1971; m. Stuart Opotowsky, Aug. 3, 1972; 1 dau., Sasha. Admitted to N.Y. bar; asso. firm Stroock & Stroock & Lavan, N.Y.C., 1971-74; asst. commr. N.Y.C. Dept. Consumer Affairs, 1974-78; pres. Better Bus. Bur. Met. N.Y.C., 1978—. Mem. Bar Assn. City N.Y. (com. consumer affairs, com. product liability). Mem. Fordham Law Rev., 1969-71. Office: 257 Park Ave S Ave S New York NY 10010*

OPPENHEIM, E. MAGNUS, investment counsel and analyst, economist; b. Hamburg, Ger., Jan. 28, 1933; came to U.S., 1938, naturalized, 1944; s. Fred Werner and Gerda P. O.; A.B. cum laude, CUNY, 1956; M.A. in Econs. Columbia U., 1957, M.B.A. in Fin., 1959; postgrad. N.Y. U., 1960-66; m. Rachel Eldad, July 31, 1972; children—Michelle, Simeon, Jay Joshua. Sr. analyst Reynolds & Co., Oppenheimer & Co., Shearson Hammill & Co., Econometric Inst., 1959-67; asso. David J. Greene & Co., N.Y.C., 1967-69; gen. partner S.D. Cohn & Co., N.Y.C., 1969-71; partner E. Magnus Oppenheim & Co., Investment Counsel, N.Y.C., 1971-78, mng. partner, 1979—; dir. Apollo Plastic Corp., Jersey City; observer White House Conf. on Balanced Nat. Growth and Econ. Devel., 1978. Mem. N.Y.C. Port Council on Devel. and Promotion; mem. 66th Assembly Dist. Democratic County Com., N.Y. County; alt. to Jud. Dist. Conv., N.Y.C. Dem. Party; mem. exec. bd. Lexington Dem. Club, N.Y.C., 1977-81, v.p., 1979-80; chmn. fin. com. Salute to Israel Parade, N.Y.C.; mem. nat. bd. dirs. Union Orthodox Jewish Congregations Am.; mem. council Wall St. Synagogue, N.Y.C. Recipient N.Y. Found. award, 1956; Eibschultz scholar, 1956. Fellow Fin. Analysts Fedn.; mem. N.Y. Soc. Security Analysts. Contbr. articles to profl. jours. Office: 366 Madison Ave New York NY 10017

OPPENHEIM, JUSTIN SABLE, business exec.; b. N.Y.C., Aug. 17, 1923; s. Ferdinand S. and Esther D. (Hirsch) O.; B.S., N.Y.U., 1943; postgrad. Cambridge U., 1945, New Sch. for Social Research, 1963; m. Joyce Marrits, June 26, 1949; children—Janet Wexler, Judy, Jeffrey. Vice pres. Consol. Mercantile Industries, N.Y.C., 1946-52; adminstrn. and mgt. Norden div. United Aircraft Co., 1952-60; pres., gen. mgr. Potentiometer div. Litton Industries, Inc., Floral Park, N.Y., 1960-68, pres. Office Products Centers div., 1968-70, v.p., 1970—; v.p. Litton Industries Inc., 1971—, Litton Bus. Systems, Inc., Litton Bus. Equipment Ltd., Can., Standard Desk Ltd., Can.; pres., dir. Streator Industries Ltd., Can.; dir. Atal Societe Anonyme, France. Lectr. on advt. N.Y.U., Coll. City N.Y., 1954-57; mem. adv. com. N. Hempstead Housing Authority, 1956-59. Mem. Nassau County Republican Com., 1961-73. Served with AUS, 1943-45. Hon. Adm. Tex. Navy, 1969. Mem. S.A.R., Actor's Fund (life), Alpha Epsilon Pi. Jewish religion. Mason (32 deg.). Clubs: Lambs, Governors (N.Y.). Contbr. articles to profl. jours. Home: 14 Sherwood Ln Roslyn Heights NY 11577 Office: 125 Community Dr Greater Neck NY 11021

OPPENHEIM, RICHARD KENNETH, accountant; b. N.Y.C., July 17, 1942; s. Henry and Selma (Citron) O.; B.S. in Accounting, U. Pa., 1964; postgrad. in bus. adminstrn. N.Y. U., 1964-67; m. Susan Irene Peyser, Aug. 18, 1968; children—Donald Scott, Allyson Michele. Staff accountant Peat Marwick & Mitchell, N.Y.C., 1964-66, Oppenheim, Appel, Dixon, N.Y.C., 1966-68; staff accountant Mgmt. Services, N.Y.C., 1968-74, partner, 1974—; lectr. Mem. Blind-Brook Rye Union Free Sch. Dist. Bd. Edn., 1978-80; adj. prof. N.Y. U. Grad. Sch. Bus. Adminstrn. C.P.A., N.Y. Mem. Am. Inst. C.P.A.'s, N.Y. State Soc. C.P.A.'s. Office: 1 New York Plaza New York NY 10004

OPPENHEIM, ROBERT, beauty industry exec.; b. N.Y.C., May 21, 1925; s. Hyman and Hannah (Lieberman) O.; B.S. cum laude, Syracuse U., 1950; m. Ruth Weiler, Feb. 7, 1954; children—Nancy Ellen, David Paul, Howard P. Product sales specialist McKesson & Robbins, Yonkers, N.Y., 1950-55; asst. sales mgr. Clairol, Inc., N.Y.C., 1955-60; dir. marketing Haircolor div. Revlon, Inc., N.Y.C., 1960-68, dir. marketing and sales Salon div., 1968-70; exec. v.p. Milton R. Barrie Co., Inc., 1970-71; mgmt. cons., 1971-76; pub. Beauty Salon Newsletter, N.Y.C., 1971—; pres. Salon div. Clairol, Inc., N.Y.C., 1976—. Served with AUS, 1942-44; ETO. Mason. Home: 241 Sickletown Rd West Nyack NY 10994 Office: 345 Park Ave New York NY 10022

OPPENHEIMER, FRANZ MARTIN, lawyer; b. Mainz, Germany, Sept. 7, 1919; s. Arnold and Johanna (Mayer) O.; B.S., U. Chgo., 1942; student U. Grenoble (France), 1938-39; LL.B. cum laude, Yale, 1945; m. Margaret Spencer Foote, June 17, 1944; children—Martin Foote, Roxana Foote, Edward Arnold. Research asst. com. human devel. U. Chgo., 1942-43; law clk. to Judge Swan, U.S. Circuit Ct. of Appeals, N.Y., 1945-46; asso. atty. Chadbourne, Wallace, Parke & Whiteside, N.Y., 1946-47; atty. Internat. Bank for Reconstrn. and Devel., Washington, 1947-57; individual practice law, 1958; partner Leva, Hawes, Symington, Martin & Oppenheimer, 1959—. Bd. dirs. Internat. Student House; founding mem. Co. of Christian Jews; trustee Com. of 100 on the Fed. City, Chatham Hall, Inst. Empirical Econ. Research, Berlin, West Germany. Mem. Am. Psychol. Assn., Am., Fed. bar assns., Am. Soc. Internat. Law, Council Fgn. Relations. Episcopalian. Clubs: Yale (N.Y.C.); Federal City, City Tavern, Metropolitan (Washington). Note editor: Yale Law Jour., 1945. Contbr. articles to profl., other jours. Home: 3248 O St NW Washington DC 20007 Office: 815 Connecticut Ave NW Washington DC 20006

OPPENHEIMER, HENRY NATHAN, ednl. firm exec.; b. Germany, Jan. 25, 1932; s. Max and Nellie O.; came to U.S., 1937; B.E.E., Coll. City N.Y., 1954; M.S. in Elec. Engring., Columbia U., 1958; M.B.A., U. Conn., 1970; doctorate in Mgmt., Pace U., 1980; m. Kay Flacks, June 5, 1955; children—Charles, Lisa. Engr., A.B. DuMont Labs., Clifton, N.J., 1954-59; project mgr. Gen. Precision Labs., Pleasantville, N.Y., 1959-64; asso. engring. dept. mgr. CBS Labs., Stamford, Conn., 1964-69; founder, pres. MGI Mgmt. Inst. (formerly Mgmt. Games Inst.), Larchmont, N.Y., 1969—. Mem. IEEE (past chmn. met. chpt. Engring. Mgmt. Soc.), Soc. Engring. Edn., Adult Edn. Assn., Beta Gamma Sigma, Eta Kappa Nu, Tau Beta Pi. Democrat. Jewish. Author: Management Games Seminar, 1968; Management Games Seminar II, 1970; Advanced Financial Management, 1974; People Management, 1976. Home: 198 E Garden Rd Larchmont NY 10538 Office: 2 East Ave Larchmont NY 10538

OPPERMAN, DANIEL WILLIS, computer systems specialist; b. Findlay, Ohio, Dec. 19, 1943; s. Willis Henry and Anna Mary (Bartlett) O.; B.S., Bowling Green State U., 1965; m. Denise J. Nolan, Apr. 30, 1975; children—Christopher Denis, Sarah Anne, David Daniel, Rebecca Sue. Supr., programming and ops. Inmont Corp., Clifton, N.J., 1966-69, mgr. systems devel., 1969-72, gen. mgr. systems devel., 1972—. Mem. Am. Prodn. and Inventory Control Soc., Soc. Cert. Data Processors, Data Processing Mgmt. Assn. Office: 16 Hillman St Clifton NJ 07011

OPPERMAN, DWIGHT DARWIN, lawyer, publishing co. exec.; b. Perry, Iowa, June 26, 1923; s. John H. and Zoa L. (Bickal) O.; student Dakota Wesleyan U., Mitchell, S.D., 1947-48; LL.B., J.D., Drake U., 1951; m. Jeanice Wifvat, Apr. 22, 1942; children—Vance K., Fane W. Admitted to Minn. bar, 1951, U.S. Supreme Ct. bar, 1976; editor West Pub. Co., St. Paul, 1951-60, asst. editorial counsel, 1960-64, mgr. reporter and digest depts., 1964-65, v.p., 1965-68, asst. to pres., 1967-68, pres., 1968—, chief exec. officer, 1978—, also dir. Bd. dirs. Mpls. Soc. Fine Arts, 1969-74, Jerome J. Hill Reference Library, 1972-80, United Way St. Paul, 1974-79. Served with U.S. Army, 1942-45. Recipient Alumni Disting. Service award Drake U. and Nat. Alumni Assn., 1974. Mem. Am. Bar Assn., Fed. Bar Assn. (v.p. Twin City chpt. 1978-80, dir. 1977-80), Am. Judicature Soc. (exec. com., v.p. 1979-80), Supreme Ct. Hist. Soc. (founding), St. Paul C. of C. (dir. 1971-75), Nat. Assn. Businessmen (chmn. 1973-74), Drake U. Law Sch. Alumni Assn., Order of Coif. Clubs: Minnesota (pres. 1975-77, dir. 1974-80); Nat. Lawyers, Capitol Hill (Washington). Home: 3100 N Chatsworth St Saint Paul MN 55113 Office: PO Box 3526 50 W Kellogg Blvd Saint Paul MN 55165

OPPERMANN, DAVID WELLS, travel agy. exec.; b. Saginaw, Mich., Oct. 22, 1937; s. Peters and Martha (Smith) O.; B.A., Denison U., 1959; children—Jeffrey, Darby, Jennifer. TV news anchorman sta. WNEM-TV, Saginaw, Mich., 1964-66; sales rep. John Henry Co., Lansing, Mich., 1966-68; pres. Entertainment Assos., Inc., Saginaw, 1968-75, Oppermann Travel, Saginaw, 1975—; mem. faculty Central Mich. U., 1979. Vice chmn. Tri-City Joint Air Com., Saginaw, 1978—. Mem. Am. Soc. Travel Agts., Am. Pyrotechnics Assn. (exec. dir.). Congregationalist. Club: Rotary. Office: 120 N Washington St Saginaw MI 48605

O'QUINN, MILTON LAFAYETTE, bus. machines co. mgr.; b. Chgo., Apr. 19, 1944; s. John William and Cleodia L. (Dawkins) O'Q.; B.A., Houston-Tillotson Coll., 1967; postgrad. U. Chgo. Grad. Sch. Bus., 1968-71; m. Helen Inez Boatner, Dec. 25, 1965; children—Lynn, Milton Lafayette, John, Lisa. Sales rep. Lever Bros., 1967; account rep. Procter & Gamble, 1968-71; account rep. Xerox Corp., Chgo., 1971-73, systems specialist, Mpls., 1974-76, sales mgr., 1976-78, br. mgr. sales, 1978-80, regional sales ops. mgr., Des Plaines, Ill., 1980—. Br. dir. Chgo. Youth Centers, Altgeld-Roseland, 1975-77. Bd. dirs. South Shore Community Center, Chgo., Marcy-Newberry Assn.; v.p. West Side Assn. for Community Action, 1974-75; co-founder O'Quinn Royal Gladiators Drum and Bugle Corp. Mem. Bloomington C. of C., Am. Legion, Kappa Alpha Psi. Home: 2240 Hassell Rd Hoffman Estates IL 60195 Office: 3000 Desplaines Ave Desplaines IL 60018

ORAN, GARY CARL, retail exec.; b. Kearney, Nebr., July 5, 1948; s. Carl Franklin and Bernice Merideth (Grosh) O.; B.S., Kearney State Coll., 1978; m. Janet Marie Petersen, Sept. 6, 1969; 1 dau., Jenny Marie. Electronics service technician Finke TV Service, Kearney, 1964-69; appliance salesman Sears, Roebuck & Co., Kearney, 1969-70, carpet and TV salesman, 1970, div. mgr. installed home improvements, 1971, service mgr., 1971-79, service mgr., Springfield, Mo., 1980—. Scoutmaster, Boy Scouts Am., Kearney, 1971-73, dist. membership chmn., 1975-77, dist. commr., 1977-78, exec. bd., 1979; United Way rep., 1977-79. Served with Nebr. N.G., 1966—. Recipient Cert. in Distributive Edn., 1975-79. Mem. Nebr. N.G. Assn., N.G. Assn. of U.S. Club: Elks. Office: 541 E St Louis St Springfield MO 65806

ORAZIO, JOAN POLITI, fin. planning co. exec.; b. N.Y.C., Mar. 24, 1930; d. Joseph and Anna B. Politi; B.S., Mercy Coll., 1975; cert. fin. planner Coll. Fin. Planning, 1979; m. Louis D. Orazio, Aug. 24, 1952; children—Louise, Joanne, Paul, Phyllis. Vice pres. Gary Goldberg & Co., Spring Valley, N.Y., 1977—; instr. Rockland Community Coll., 1977—; workshop leader, speaker various colls. and community orgns., 1970—. Mem. Internat. Assn. Fin. Planners, Inst. Cert. Fin. Planners, Rockland County Bus. and Profl. Women. Roman Catholic. Club: Soroptimist. Home: 17 Wilder Rd Suffern NY 10901 Office: 14 E Central Ave Spring Valley NY 10977

ORDONEZ, GEORGES, cons. geologist; b. Mexico, D.F., Mexico, Mar. 20, 1907; s. Ezequiel and Margarita (Jullian) O.; E.M., Colo. Sch. Mines, 1929; m. Angelina Cortes, Dec. 1, 1938; children—Georges E., Paul A., L. Philip. Gas engr. Lago Petroleum Corp., Maracaibo, Venezuela, 1929-30; asst. field supt. Huasteca Petroleum Co., Tampico, Mexico, 1931-32; asst. field supt. Mexican Petroleum Co., 1933-35, field supt., 1936-38; geologist Cananea Cons. Copper Co., Mexico, 1939-41; pvt. practice as cons. geologist, Mexico, D.F., 1941-44; field engr. Kennecott Copper Corp., Silver City, N.M., 1944-50, asst. chief geologist, N.Y.C., 1951-52, chief geologist, 1952-54; mgr. Cia. Minera Kenmex, S.A., Mexico, D.F., 1954-61; instr. U. Mexico, Mexico, D.F., 1960-62, Guanajuato (Mexico) Sch. Mines, 1960-62; now geol. cons.; dir. Fox Mexicana, Minera Frisco, S.A. Mem. Geol. Soc. Am., Soc. Econ. Geologist, Sociedad Geologica Mexicana, Asociacion de Ingenieros de Minas, Metalurgistas, Petroleros y Geologos de Mexico. Roman Catholic. Office: Sierra Gorda 54 Mexico 10 DF Mexico

ORDOVER, BENJAMIN, advt. co. exec.; b. N.Y.C., Sept. 10, 1931; s. Joseph and Bertha (Fromberg) O.; B.S. in Bus. Adminstrn. magna cum laude, Syracuse U., 1953; m. Barbara Miriam Ordover, Aug. 31, 1958; children—Mark Bennett, Diane Susan. Pres. pub. div. FAS Internat., N.Y.C., 1961-70; v.p., account supr. Wunderman, Ricotta

& Kline, N.Y.C., 1970-72; pres. Columbia House div. CBS, Inc., N.Y.C., 1972—. Served to lt. USAF, 1953-55. Mem. Am. Mktg. Assn., Direct Mail Advt. Assn., Beta Gamma Sigma. Home: 2988 Bond Dr Merrick NY 11566 Office: 1211 6th Ave New York NY 10019

ORECHIO, FRANK ANTHONY, publisher; b. Somerville, N.J., June 12, 1917; s. Pasquale and Rose (Cocchiola) O.; certificate bus. administrn. Rutgers U., 1938; m. Edith Johnson, July 5, 1953. Self-employed accountant, Nutley, N.J., 1945-51; pres. OK Electronic Corp., Nutley, 1951-58; pub. Sunbank Newspapers, Nutley, including Nutley Sun, Belleville Times-News, Newark Record, Accent Suburbia, 1970—; pres. Orechio Broadcasting Co., 1979—, Orechio Communications Co., 1979—, Orechio Industries, Inc., 1980—. Chmn., North Jersey dist. Water Supply Commn. N.J., 1966—. Chmn., N.J. Young Republicans, 1947-49; campaign dir. U.S. Senator Clifford P. Case, 1954; del. Rep. Nat. Conv., 1972; Essex County campaign mgr. Com. Re-election Pres. Nixon. Served with AUS, 1941-43. Mem. Nutley (past pres.), Belleville (past chmn. bd.) chambers commerce. Clubs: Le Club (N.Y.C.); Le Club International. Home: 777 Bloomfield Ave Nutley NJ 07110

OREFFICE, PAUL FAUSTO, mfg. co. exec.; b. Venice, Italy, Nov. 29, 1927; s. Max and Elena (Friedenberg) O.; came to U.S., 1945, naturalized, 1951; B.S. in Chem. Engring., Purdue U., 1949, D. Engring. (hon.), 1976; m. Franca Giuseppina Ruffini, May 26, 1956; children—Laura Emma, Andrew T. With Dow Chem. Co., 1953—, fin. v.p., Midland, Mich., 1970-75; pres. Dow U.S.A., 1975-78, pres., chief exec. officer, 1978—, also dir.; dir. Dow Corning, Conn. Gen. Ins. Corp., First Midland Bank & Trust. Bd. dirs. Purdue Research Found., also found. bd. govs. nat. bd. dirs. Jr. Achievement. Served with AUS, 1951-53. Mem. Mfg. Chemists Assn. (dir.). Home: 5400 Siebert St Midland MI 48640 Office: 2030 Dow Center Midland MI 48640

O'REILLY, ANTHONY JOHN FRANCIS, food co. exec.; b. Dublin, Ireland, July 5, 1936; came to U.S., 1971; s. John Patrick and Aileen (O'Connor) O'R.; B.C.L., U. Coll. Dublin; postgrad. U. Bradford (Eng.), Wharton Bus. Sch. Overseas, 1965; LL.D. (hon.), Wheeling (W.Va.) Coll., Trinity Coll., Dublin, Rollins Coll., Fla.; D.C.L. (hon.), Ind. U., Terre Haute, 1979; Ph.D., U. Bradford, Yorkshire, Eng., 1980; m. Susan Cameron, May 5, 1962; 6 children. Indsl. cons. Weston Evans, 1958-62; personal asst. to chmn. Suttons Ltd., Cork, Ireland, 1960-62; dir. Robert McCowen & Sons, Tralee, Ireland, 1961; gen. mgr. An Bord Bainne/Irish Dairy Bd., 1962-66; dir. Agrl. Credit Corp. Ltd., 1965-66, Nitrigin Eireann Teo, 1965-66; mng. dir. Comhlucht Suicre Eireann Teo and Erin Foods, Ltd., 1966-69; joint mng. dir. Heinz-Erin Ltd., 1967-70; dir. Allied Irish Investment Bank Ltd., 1968-71; mng. dir. H. J. Heinz Co. Ltd., U.K., 1969-71; dir. Thyssen-Bornemisza Co., Rotterdam, Netherlands, 1970-71; sr. v.p. N. Am. and Pacific, H.J. Heinz Co., Pitts., 1971-72, exec. v.p., chief operating officer, Pitts., 1972-73, pres., chief operating officer, 1973-79, pres., chief exec. officer, 1979—; chmn. Fitzwilton Ltd., Ind. Newspapers Ltd., Dublin; partner Cawley Sheerin Wynne & Co. Solicitors, Dublin; dir. Mobil Oil Corp., N.Y.C., Bankers Trust Corp., N.Y.C., Ulster Bank Ltd., Belfast, No. Ireland. Bd. dirs. Nat. Assn. Deaf, Am. Irish Fedn.; trustee U. Notre Dame, Harvard U. Bus. Sch., Duquesne U., U. Pitts. Fellow British Inst. Mgmt.; mem. Inst. Dirs., Inc. Law Soc. Ireland. Clubs: St. Stephen's Green, Dublin, Kildare, University (Dublin); Reform, Annabels (London); Union League (N.Y.C.); Duquesne, Allegheny, Fox Chapel Golf, Pitts. Golf (Pitts.); Rolling Rock (Ligonier, Pa.); Lyford Cay (Bahamas). Office: PO Box 57 Pittsburgh PA 15230

O'REILLY, PHILIP F., cable TV co. exec.; b. Bklyn., Feb. 27, 1941; s. Edward F. and Theresa A. (Hoenninger) O'R.; B.S. in Bus. Adminstrn., Georgetown U., 1963; postgrad. in bus. adminstrn. Pace U., 1973-75; m. Caryl Ann Maloy, July 11, 1964; children—Philip F., Meegan E., Matthew C., Brooke A., Lindsay C. Sr. acct. Schumaker & Yates, C.P.A.'s, Washington, 1961-63; acct. Fed. Systems div. IBM, Bethesda, Md., 1963-66; mgr. Main, Hurdman & Cranstoun, N.Y.C., 1966-75; treas. Cablevision Systems Corp., Woodbury, N.Y., 1975—; instr. Pace U., 1973-76, N.Y. U. Grad. Sch. Bus., 1974-76. Adv., Jr. Achievement, N.Y.C., 1972-73; mem. exec. council family faculty fellowship St. Joseph Hill Acad., 1978—. C.P.A., N.Y., D.C. Mem. Am. Inst. C.P.A.'s, N.Y. State Soc. C.P.A.'s, Am. Acctg. Assn., Am. Mgmt. Assn. Roman Catholic. Club: Cedar Grove Beach (gov. 1972—, v.p. 1976-77, pres. 1978-79). Home: 8 Murray Pl Staten Island NY 10304 Office: 1 Media Crossways Dr Woodbury NY 11797

OREM, CHARLES ANNISTONE, ret. mil. officer, nuclear engr., marine and hydraulic products co. exec.; b. Bryn Mawr, Pa., Apr. 1, 1929; s. Howard Emery and Elizabeth Clements (Stone) O.; B.S. in Engring., U.S. Naval Acad., 1950; postgrad. George Washington U., 1968-69; M.E.E., U.S. Navy Postgrad. Sch., 1960; m. Gerry Morgan Wellborn, June 15, 1951; children—Nancy Elizabeth, Catherine Stone, Sarah Annistone. Commd. ensign U.S. Navy, 1950, advanced through grades to comdr.; commd. U.S.S. Seawolf, 1957; navigator U.S.S. Abraham Lincoln; exec. officer U.S.S. Thomas Jefferson; comdr. U.S.S. Simon Bolivar, 1965-68; submarine specialist Office of Chief of Naval Ops., 1968-70; ret., 1970; various mgmt. positions Babcock & Wilcox Co., Barberton, Ohio, 1970-77, dir. corporate planning and devel., N.Y.C., 1977-79; exec. v.p. Bird-Johnson Co., Walpole, Mass., 1979-80, pres., 1980—; lectr. mgmt. prins. Am. Mgmt. Assn. Recipient 6 Polaris Patrol award U.S. Navy, 1968; recipient Meritorious Service medal USN, 1970. Mem. IEEE, Soc. Naval Architects and Marine Engrs., Am. Soc. Naval Engrs., Am. Mgmt. Assn. (mfg. council 1974—), Am. Inst. Aeros. and Astronautics, Machinery and Allied Products Inst. (mktg. council 1979—), Navy League, Ret. Officers Assn., Sigma Xi (asso.). Republican. Clubs: Wellesley Country, Army-Navy City, Army-Navy Country. Home: 25 Saddlebrook Rd Sherborn MA 01770 Office: 110 Norfolk St Walpole MA 02081

ORENDORFF, WILLIAM RADCLIFFE, banker; b. Kirksville, Mo., Dec. 21, 1949; s. Joseph Richard and Evelyn Gertrude (Radcliffe) O.; B.S. in Bus. Adminstrn., U. Mo., Columbia, 1971; m. Judith Ann McCune, July 19, 1969; 1 son, Edward Charles. Visual mdse. mgr. Sears, Roebuck & Co., Lawton, Okla. and Columbia, Mo., 1971-73; communications cons. Gen. Telephone Co. of Midwest, Columbia, Mo., 1973-74; sales rep. Equitable Life Assurance Soc. of U.S., 1974-75; asst. trust officer First Nat. Bank, Kirksville, 1977—; mem. student loan com. Mo. Dept. Higher Edn. Bd. dirs. Spring Lake Inc., Kirksville Community Center, Kirksville Cardio-Pulmonary Resuscitation Tng. Center; chmn. Adair County Heart Assn.; capt. retail div. Adair County United Fund Campaign; bd. dirs., treas., chmn. finance com. Kirksville Family YMCA. Served with U.S. Army, 1975-77. Mem. Kirksville C. of C., Kirksville Jr. C. of C. (dir.). Methodist. Home: Spring Lake PO Box 306 Kirksville MO 63501 Office: First Nat Bank PO Box 289 Kirksville MO 63501

ORENSTEIN, FRANKLIN LEONARD, freight shipping co. exec.; b. N.Y.C., July 27, 1931; s. Max and Gussie O.; student night classes, CCNY, 1950-51; m. Harriet Kirschenbaum, Mar. 21, 1959; children—Marlene, Mitchell. Messenger, Transworld Shipping Corp., 1950-51; documentation clk. Intra Mar Shipping Corp., 1952-53; asst. traffic mgr. UN Shipping Corp., 1954-55; v.p. Franoren Shipping Corp., N.Y.C., 1956-70, pres., 1971—. Office: 140 Cedar St New York NY 10006

ORENT, GERARD MAURICE, publishing co. exec.; b. Bklyn., Jan. 28, 1931; s. Nathan and Sylvia Lenore O.; B.B.A., Hofstra U., 1954; m. Sally Elaine Cardon, Sept. 6, 1953; children—Andrew Mark, Eric Scott. Systems analyst Met. Life Ins. Co., N.Y.C., 1956-60; with McGraw Hill Book Co., N.Y.C., 1960—, dir. inventory mgmt., 1967-70, v.p. mfg. and inventory mgmt., 1970-80; v.p. resource mgmt. McGraw Hill Inc., N.Y.C., 1980—. Trustee, Babylon (N.Y.) Public Library, 1976—. Served to 1st lt. Ordnance Corps, USAR, 1954-56.

ORGERA, ADAM, retail exec.; b. N.Y.C., Dec. 18, 1920; s. Joseph and Elvira (Galassi) O.; grad. U.S. Coast Guard Acad., 1944; student seminar on acctg. Wharton Sch., U. Pa.; m. Louise Wooldridge, June 27, 1947; children—Raymond Edward, Michael Adam, Elvira Ann, Donna Marie. Trainee, Sears, Roebuck and Co., Mobile, Ala., 1946-47, div. mgr., 1947-48, floor mgr., New Orleans, 1948-50, mdse. mgr., Greenville, Miss., 1950-52, asst. mgr., Meridian, Miss., 1952-54, asst. mgr., Portsmouth, Va., 1954-60, store mgr., Meridian, 1960-62, Spartanburg, S.C., 1962-63, Greensboro, N.C., 1963-66, Virginia Beach, Va., 1966-69, group mgr., Nashville, 1969-73, regional mgr., New Orleans, 1973—; lectr. in field. Bd. dirs. Metro Area Com.; chmn. adv. bd. New Orleans Mus. Art. Served as lt. jg. USCG, 1946. Recipient award Merit, George Peabody Coll. Devel. Council, 1973, Levinson Inst., 1972. Mem. La. Assn. Bus. and Industry, Pub. Affairs Research Council La., Better Bus. Bur., Econ. Devel. Council (dir.), Greater New Orleans Tourist Commn., Met. Area Council (dir.), C. of C., La. Retailers Assn. (dir.). Episcopalian. Clubs: Internat. House, New Orleans Country, Rotary, Sandestin Country (Destin, Fla.). Office: PO Box 7790 Metairie LA 70010

ORKAND, DONALD SAUL, mgmt. cons.; b. N.Y.C., Mar. 2, 1936; s. Harold and Frances (Wolfson) O.; B.S. summa cum laude, N.Y. U., 1956, M.B.A., 1957, Ph.D., 1963; m. Lindsay Day Porter, May 8, 1971; children—Dara Sue, Katarina Day. Statistician, Western Electric Co., N.Y.C., 1956-58; group v.p. Ops. Research, Inc., Silver Spring, Md., 1960-69; pres. Ops. Research Industries, Ltd., Ottawa, Ont., Can., 1968-69; pres., chief exec. officer Orkand Corp., Silver Spring, 1970—. Served with Ordnance Corps, U.S. Army, 1958-60. Mem. Am. Econs. Assn., Am. Statis. Assn., Ops. Research Soc. Am. Contbr. articles to profl. jours. Home: 5260 Pooks Hill Rd Bethesda MD 20014 Office: 8630 Fenton St Silver Spring MD 20910

ORKIN, LOUIS H., lawyer; b. Cleve., Dec. 30, 1930; s. William H. and Dorothy K. (Kaspy) O.; J.D., Boston U., 1954; m. Charlotte Simon, July 10, 1959; children—Linda, Laura, Steven. Admitted to Ohio bar, 1954; asst. atty. gen. State of Ohio, 1957-59; individual practice law, 1959-60; asst. law dir. and pros. atty. Cleveland Heights (Ohio), 1961-64; partner firm Weiner, Orkin, Abbate & Suit, and predecessor firms, Beachwood, Ohio, 1964—; law dir., prosecutor City of Bedford (Ohio), 1964-73; pros. atty. Shaker Heights (Ohio), 1964—; law dir., prosecutor City of Beachwood, 1973—; acting judge Cleveland Heights Municipal Ct., 1969-72; prosecutor Hunting Valley (Ohio), 1977—; Village Solicitor Orange Village (Ohio), 1977—, Woodmere Village (Ohio), 1979—; Spl. Counsel to state atty gen.; asst. to pres., gen. counsel Peoples Bldg. & Loan Co.; adj. prof. mcpl. law Cleve. State Law Sch., 1974—. Mem. Am. Bar Assn., Ohio Bar Assn., Cleve. Bar Assn., Cuyahoga County Bar Assn., Nat. Assn. Mcpl. Law Officers, Ohio Assn. Attys. Gen., Am. Soc. Hosp. Attys. (charter mem.), Am. Trial Lawyers Assn., Ohio Acad. Trial Lawyers, Cuyahoga County Law Dirs. Assn., Suburban East Bar Assn. (v.p.). Home: 23400 Ranch Rd Beachwood OH 44122 Office: 24200 Chagrin Blvd Beachwood OH 44122

ORLOFF, MALCOLM KENNETH, splty. chems. mfg. co. exec.; b. Phila., Feb. 26, 1939; s. Leonard and Anne Harriet (Schlaff) O.; B.A., U. Pa., 1960, Ph.D., 1964; postgrad. (fellow) Yale U., 1964-65; m. Phoebe Zimmerman, Aug. 21, 1960; children—Amy, Lisa, David. Sr. research chemist Am. Cyanamid Co., Stamford, Conn., 1965-76, product mgr. for dyes, 1976-77, mktg. mgr. for color, textile and intermediate chems., 1977-78; v.p. research and devel. Buffalo Color Corp., West Paterson, N.J., 1978—. Fellow Am. Inst. Chemists; mem. Am. Chem. Soc., Phi Beta Kappa. Contbr. articles to sci. jours., chpt. to Modern Quantum Chemistry. Home: 333 Mt Airy Rd Basking Ridge NJ 07920 Office: One Garret Mountain Plaza West Peterson NJ 07424

ORLOFF, MONFORD ARTHUR, mfg. co. exec.; b. Omaha, Mar. 29, 1914; s. Samuel and Hannah (Masters) O.; A.B., Stanford U., 1937; LLB., Harvard U., 1940; m. Janice Diamond, Feb. 2, 1941; children—Jonathan Harris, Carole Sue, Chester Lloyd. With Evans Products Co., Portland, 1961—, pres., 1968—, chief exec. officer, chmn. bd., 1964—, also dir.; dir. Pacwest Corp., Precision Castparts. Bd. dirs. Oreg. Grad. Center, Oreg. Symphony Soc.; bd. dirs., vice chmn. Oreg. Community Found.; trustee Reed Coll., Portland Art Assn. Served with AUS, 1941-46. Mem. Phi Beta Kappa. Office: 1121 S W Salmon St PO Box 3295 Portland OR 97208

ORLOWSKI, JOHN, chem. engr.; b. Passaic, N.J., Oct. 4, 1952; s. Antoni W. and Katherin (Szponar) O.; B.S. in Chem. Engring., N.J. Inst. Tech., 1977. Asst. staff engr. marine div. Drew Chem. Corp., Boonton, N.J., 1975-77, tech. specialist water and waste div., 1977-78, sr. project engr. mfg. div., 1978—. Mem. Am. Inst. Chem. Engrs. Roman Catholic. Office: 1 Drew Chem Plaza Boonton NJ 07005

ORMSBY, ROBERT BENZEIN, JR., mfg. co. exec.; b. Winston-Salem, N.C., Aug. 13, 1924; s. Robert Benzein and Ruth Olive (Hart) O.; B.S. in Aeros., Ga. Inst. Tech., 1945; postgrad. Stanford U. Grad. Sch. Bus.; m. Margarett Williams, May 17, 1947; children—Marka Robin, Robin Patricia. Aerodynamicist, Glenn L. Martin Co., 1945-47; dep. div. head U.S. Navy, Bur. Aeros., 1947-54; with Lockheed-Ga. Co., Marietta, 1954-74, 75—, v.p. maj. engring. and ops. programs, until 1974, pres., 1975—; v.p., gen. mgr. research and devel. Lockheed Missiles & Space Co., 1974-75; sr. v.p. Lockheed Corp., 1975—; chmn. bd. LockheedGa. Internat. Services, Inc. Mem. alumni adv. bd. Sloan Sch., Stanford U.; mem. aeros. and space engring. bd. NRC. Bd. dirs. Ga. Motor Club, United Way Met. Atlanta. Recipient Silver Knight Mgmt. award, 1976; hon. dir. Ga. Engring. Found. Asso. fellow AIAA; mem. Air Force Assn., Am. Def. Preparedness Assn., Assn. U.S. Army, Nat. Assn. Remotely Piloted Vehicles, Navy League, Soc. Automotive Engrs., Soc. Logistics Engrs., Soc. Material Processing Engrs., Ga. C. of C. (dir.), Atlanta C. of C. (dir.). Club: Marietta Kiwanis.

ORNST, ARTHUR ALBERT, gen. contractor; b. Milw., Jan. 8, 1903; s. Julius and Lena O.; student, U. Wis.; m. Jan. 29, 1928; children—Robert A., Susan Ornst Young. With Theodore Stark & Co., Milw., 1928-30; with Selzer-Ornst Co., Wauwatosa, Wis., 1930—, now chmn. bd., sec.-treas. Mem. Gen. Contractors Assn. (pres.). Clubs: Wis., Kiwanis, Masons. Home: 2024 Underwood Ave Wauwatosa WI 53213 Office: 6222 W State St Wauwatosa WI 53213

ORONA, ERNEST JOSEPH, real estate and constrn. co. exec.; b. Belen, N.Mex., Oct. 5, 1942; s. Joseph B. and Melinda (Sanchez) O.; B.A. in Latin Am. Affairs and Spanish, U. N.Mex., 1968; m. Margaret M. Guinan, Aug. 22, 1964; children—Mary Melinda, Marie-Jeanne. Vol. community devel. Peace Corps, Colombia, S. Am., 1962-64; instr. Peace Corps tng. U. Mo., Kansas City, summer 1964, Baylor U., Waco, Tex., summer 1965, also U. Ariz., N.Mex. State U., Las Cruces, 1966, U. N.Mex., Albuquerque, 1966; exec. dir. Mid-Rio Grande Community Action Project, Los Lunas, N.Mex., 1965-66; community devel. cons. Center for Community Action Services, Albuquerque, 1967-68; project dir. Peace Corps Tng. Center, San Diego State U., Escondido, Calif., 1968-70; propr., developer GO Realty and Constrn. Co., Albuquerque, 1970—. Mem. Nat. Bd. Realtors, Albuquerque Bd. Realtors Albuquerque C. of C., Albuquerque Com. on Fgn. Relations. Roman Catholic. Home: 908 Sierra SE Albuquerque NM 87108 Office: 10601 Lomas NE Suite 112 Albuquerque NM 87112

ORR, DARRELL CLARK, mfg. co. fin. exec.; b. Grand Forks, N.D., Sept. 29, 1938; s. Raymond Clark and Bernice (Anderson) O.; B.S. in Indsl. Mgmt., U. N.D., 1960; M.B.A. in Fin. Mgmt., Loyola U., Chgo., 1972; m. Maureen Scully, Jan. 30, 1960; children—Julie, Suzanne, Jeffrey. Asst. plant controller Nat. Can Corp., 1963-66, plant controller, 1966-67, group controller, 1967-68, mfg. methods specialist, 1968-70, adminstrv. asst., 1970-71, asst. plant mgr., 1971-72; corp. mgr. ops. analysis ATO Inc., 1972-73, div. controller George J. Meyer div., 1973-76, v.p., controller George J. Meyer Mfg. div., 1976-77, v.p. fin. and Latin Am. ops., 1977-79, v.p. fin. and internat. ops., 1979; dir. acctg. and adminstrn. Heil Co., Milw., 1979—. Bd. dirs. Trinity Meml. Hosp. Found., Cudahy, Wis., 1975. Served to 1st lt. U.S. Army, 1960-63. Mem. Nat. Assn. Accountants, Fin. Execs. Inst. Home: 12003 W Burdick Ave West Allis WI 53227 Office: 777 E Wisconsin Ave Suite 2800 Milwaukee WI 53202

ORR, DENNIS MARK, mfg. and retail exec.; b. Winamac, Ind., Jan. 12, 1940; s. Mark Ulysses and Clara Belle (Riley) O.; A.B., Ind. U., 1962; m. Edna Ann Winckelbach, Aug. 18, 1962; 1 son, Colin Patrick. Vice-pres., Investments in Real Estate, Denver, 1968-72; sr. v.p. The Lincoln Cos., Denver, 1972-74; pres. Cotter-Orr Devel. Co., Littleton, Colo., 1974-76, Duffy Storage & Moving, Denver, 1976-78; chmn. bd., chief exec. officer Poor Richards Ltd., 1978—; dir. Interiors by Heloise. Chmn. Littleton City Planning Commn., 1975—; chmn. leadership Denver, 1975; mem. Gov.'s I-470 Ad Hoc Commn., 1975-76; Republican precinct committeeman. Served to capt. USAF, 1962-67. Named Outstanding Young Republican Male of Colo., Young Rep. League, 1971. Mem. Denver C. of C. (dir. 1975—), Am. Mgmt. Assn., S. Suburban Bd. Realtors, Am. Trucking Assn., Crane and Rigging Assn. (bd. govs. 1977), Nat. Fedn. Ind. Bus. (Colo. adv. council), Phi Sigma Kappa. Republican. Clubs: Univ., Arapahoe Men's (pres. 1968-73). Home: 1004 W Peakview Circle Littleton CO 80120 Office: 650 S Cherry St Denver CO 80222

ORR, JAY BRYANT, sch. ofcl.; b. Dallas, Oct. 11, 1945; s. Green Jackson and Geraldine (Leach) O.; B.B.A., Tex. Tech. U., 1968; M.Ed., Stephen F. Austin State U., 1980; m. Elizabeth Anne Lynch, Aug. 26, 1967; 1 dau., Heather Dalaine. Tchr., Spade (Tex.) Ind. Sch. Dist., 1968-69, Roosevelt Ind. Sch. Dist., Lubbock, Tex., 1970; tchr., coach, elementary prin. Spade Ind. Sch. Dist., 1971-75, prin. 1976; bus. mgr. Hallsville (Tex.) Ind. Sch. Dist., 1976—. Mem. Tex. Assn. Sch. Bus. Ofcls. (chpt. pres. 1977-78), Assn. Tex. Profl. Educators. Methodist. Club: Lions (pres. 1979-80). Office: PO Box 247 Hallsville TX 75650

ORRIS, GLENN WILLIAM, sales exec.; b. Manhasset, N.Y., Apr. 7, 1947; s. William Winston and Patricia Richmond (Proskauer) O.; B.A., U. Colo., 1969; Mktg. Mgmt. Certificate, Grad. Sch. Bus., Columbia U., 1976; m. Linda Gayle Alexander, Sept. 16, 1972. With Dun and Bradstreet, Inc., N.Y.C., 1969—, jr. account exec., 1969-70, account exec., 1970-71, sr. account exec., major accounts, 1971—; lectr. Grad. Sch. Bus., Fairleigh Dickinson U., Teaneck, N.J.; mem. Dun and Bradstreet Presdl. Adv. Council. Republican. Home: 14 Millbrook Ct Livingston NJ 07039 Office: 99 Church St New York NY 10007

ORT, PAUL LANNING, appraiser, cons.; b. Hackettstown, N.J., May 31, 1917; s. Charles C. and Jeanette E. (Gulick) O.; grad. Jordon Engring. Sch., Phila., 1938; D.B.A. (hon.); m. Mildred H. Vey, June 25, 1938; children—Michael P., Thomas W. With Thomas Motors, Hackettstown, N.J., 1938-40, William G. Vey & Sons, 1940-42; propr. Paul L. Ort, Hackettstown, 1945—; real estate counselor; chmn. adv. bd. Hackettstown br. Nat. Community Bank N.J. Chmn., Hackettstown Parking Authority, 1956—, Hackettstown Planning Bd., 1960-68; chmn. Juvenile Conf. Commn., Hackettstown, 1955-58; past pres. 1st Aid and Rescue Squad; past chmn. Hackettstown Zoning Bd. Adjustment, Hackettstown Planning Bd.; mem. adv. council N.W. County unit N.J. Planning Ofcls. Bd. dirs. Warren County unit Retarded Children Assn.; pres. Heath Village. Served with USCGR, World War II. Mem. Nat. Inst. Real Estate Brokers (dist. rep.), Nat. Assn. Real Estate Appraisers, Nat. Assn. Ind. Fee Appraisers, Warren County Bd. Realtors (past pres.), Nat. Assn. Review Appraisers, Nat. Assn. Real Estate Counselors, Internat. Platform Assn., N.J. Assn. Real Estate Bds. (past v.p.), V.F.W. (past comdr.). Presbyn. (elder; past dir. N.J. Presbyn. Homes). Rotarian (past pres. Hackettstown). Clubs: Warren County Country, Panther Valley Country, Vista Royale. Home and Office: 410 Moore St Hackettstown NJ 07840

ORTHWEIN, JAMES BUSCH, advt. exec.; b. St. Louis, Mar. 13, 1924; s. Percy J. and Clara H (Busch) O.; student Washington U., St. Louis; m. Katherine B. Gatch, May 9, 1945 (div. 1964); children—Katherine G., Percy J. II, James Busch; m. 2d, Romaine Milford Haven, July 10, 1964 (dec. 1975); 1 dau., Romaine Clara Busch; m. 3d, Ruth R. O'Connor, May 3, 1975; stepchildren—Robin O'Connor, Pamela O'Connor. Pres. D'Arcy-MacManus & Masius, Inc., 1970—, chmn. bd., 1976—; dir. Anheuser-Busch, Inc., Merc. Trust Co. Trustee U.S. Naval War Coll. Named So. Advt. Markets Man of Yr., 1979. Clubs: Deer Creek, Brook, Bridlespur Hunt, Spouting Rock Beach, Bogey, Clambake, Old Warson Country; Racquet (N.Y.C. and St. Louis). Home: 35 Squires Ln Huntleigh Village Saint Louis MO 63131 Office: D'Arcy-MacManus & Masius Inc 1 Memorial Dr Saint Louis MO 63102

ORTIZ-MONASTERIO, FELIPE, investment banker; b. Mexico City, Sept. 6, 1952; s. Juan M. and Carlota (Ugarte) Ortiz-Monasterio; B.A. in Econs. summa cum laude, Instituto Tecnologico Autonomo de Mex., 1975; M.B.A., Harvard Bus. Sch., 1977. Mem. exec. tng. program Multibanco Comermex S.A., Mex., 1973, economist, staff mem., 1974-75, v.p. investment banking, 1977—; dir. Adamex, S.A., Mex., 1977—, Volkswagen Leasing, SA, Mex., Internat. Harvester, Mex., 1979—, Pescatun S.A. de C.V.; prof. internat. fin. Instituto Tecnologico Autonomo de Mex., 1977-78, prof. investment banking, 1978—. Mem. Instituto Tecnologico Autonomo de Mex. Alumni Assn. Clubs: Jockey Club Mexico City; Centro Hipico Morelos (Cuernavaca). Home: Sierra Madre 415 Mexico 10 D F Mexico Office: Plaza Comermex Piso 17 Mexico 10 D F Mexico

ORTON, RUSSELL CLARK, indsl. resource devel. co. exec.; b. Boston, May 9, 1922; s. Leon Martin and Harriett Phoebe (Clark) O.; B.S. in Mech. Engring., U. N.H., 1948; M.B.A., Harvard U., 1953; m. Janet Crabbe Ballou, May 29, 1954 (dec.); children—Leslie Janet, Piper Starr, Janet Chase, Clark Edward. Engr., Allis Chalmers, Milw.,

1948-51; sales & engring. mgmt. asso. Scott Williams, Inc., Laconia, N.H., 1953-60; chief engr. Acme Staple Co., Franklin, N.H., 1960-67; dir. State Resource Clearinghouse, U. N.H., Durham, 1967-71; dir. New Eng. Indsl. Resource Devel., Inc. Durham., 1977—; lectr. U. N.H. Leader, commr. Boy Scouts Am., 1956-62; Republican city and county chmn., 1964-68; trustee Gunstock Jr. Coll., 1970, Laconia Hosp., 1970-72; chmn. adv. bd. N.H. Vocat. Coll., Laconia, 1973-74; police commr. Laconia, 1973-74; bd. dirs., mem. exec. com. Squam Lakes Sci. Center, 1978—. Served with U.S. Army, 1943-46. Decorated Silver Star, Bronze Star, others; recipient Outstanding Service award State of N.H., 1974; registered profl. engr., N.H. Mem. N.H. Bd. Profl. Engrs., Am. Soc. Metals, New Eng. Bus. & Econ. Assn., Smaller Bus. Assn. of New Eng., New Eng. Solar Energy Assn., N.H. Solar Energy Assn., U.S. Ski Assn. (dir. 1973-74). Republican. Episcopalian. Clubs: Scott Fish & Game, Masons. Contbr. articles in field to profl. jours. Home: RD 3 Old Parade Rd Laconia NH 03246 Office: Pettee Brook Offices Durham NH 03824

ORVIS, IRA DUDLEY, indsl. exec.; b. Jackson, Mich., Feb. 18, 1924; s. Howard A. and Harriet A. O.; B.S.M.E., U. Mich., 1945, M.B.A., 1948; m. Elizabeth J. Batten, May 2, 1953; 1 dau., Margaret Elizabeth. Indsl. engr. Clark Equipment Co., Jackson, 1958-51; factory mgr. Teer-Wickwire Co., Jackson, 1951-56; gen. mgr. The Dynex Co., Pewaukee, Wis., 1956-62; group v.p. Leesona Corp., Warwick, R.I., 1962-70; group pres. Dresser Industries, Inc., Houston, 1970—. Served with USNR, 1943-46. Methodist. Club: Houston. Home: 15010 Benfer Rd Houston TX 77069 Office: 601 Jefferson St Houston TX 77002

OSANN, RICHARD, printing co. exec.; b. White Plains, N.Y., July 12, 1921; s. Frederick and Ada (Reiner) O.; A.B., Princeton U., 1943; m. Priscilla Stearns, Sept. 7, 1946; children—Timothy (dec.), Kathryn, David, Sally, Richard S., Paul. Sales trainee Robert W. Kelly Pub. Corp., 1946-47; v.p. sales, dir. Lincoln Engraving & Printing Corp., 1947-59; v.p., sales mgr. Bowne & Co., Inc., N.Y.C., 1960-72; v.p., dir. Bowne of N.Y.C., Inc., 1960-72; v.p. mktg. U.S. Banknote Co., N.Y.C., 1973-74; chmn., pres. Osann/Shaw, Inc., Stamford, Conn., 1975-78; v.p., mktg. mgr. Sorg Printing Co., N.Y.C., 1978—. Vestryman, St. Pauls Episcopal Ch., Riverside, Conn., 1953-56, 73-76, clk., 1976-78. Served to lt. USNR, 1943-46. Mem. Printing Industries Am. (chmn. sales mgmt. and mktg. com. 1969-70, mem. mktg. subcom. 1979-80), Young Printing Execs. N.Y. (pres. 1962-63). Republican. Club: Princeton (N.Y.C.). Home: 66 Winthrop Dr Riverside CT 06878 Office: Sorg Printing Co 111 8th Ave New York NY 10011

OSBORN, JOHN STEPHEN, acct.; b. Searcy, Ark., Jan. 10, 1951; s. John Elmer and Geneva Maye (Harden) O.; B.S. in B.A., Henderson State U., 1978; student Harding Coll., 1969-73; m. Nancy Horner, Aug. 20, 1971; children—Stephanie Lynn, Adam Blake. Owner, H & R Block Income Tax Service, Searcy, Ark., 1973-76, Osborn Acctg. Service, Searcy, 1973-76; mgr. Texarkana Bookkeeping Service, Texarkana, Tex., 1978; pvt. practice pub. acctg., Searcy, 1978—. Sec.-treas. White County Sheriff's Patrol, 1979; lt. Searcy Police Res., 1980; deacon Cloverdale Ch. of Christ. Lic. profl. acct., Ark. Mem. Ark. Soc. C.P.A.'s, Nat. Soc. Profl. Accts. Club: Lions. Contbr. articles to profl. jours. Home: 1206 Hwy 267 S Searcy AR 72143 Office: 100 S Spring St Searcy AR 72143

OSBORN, PRIME FRANCIS, III, lawyer, r.r. ofcl.; b. Greensboro, Ala., July 31, 1915; s. Prime Francis and Anne (Fowlkes) O.; J.D., U. Ala., 1939, LL.D., 1970; m. Grace Hambrick, Aug. 30, 1939; children—Prime Francis IV, Mary Anne. Admitted to Ala. bar, 1939, Ky. bar, 1952, N.C. bar, 1959, also Fed. Cts., ICC, U.S. Supreme Ct. bar; asst. atty. gen., Ala., 1939-41; atty. G. M. & O. R.R., 1946-51, commerce atty., 1950-51; gen. solicitor L. & N. R.R., 1951-57; v.p., gen. counsel, dir. A.C.L. R.R., 1957-67, S.C. Pacific R.R. Co., Atlantic Land & Improvement Co.; v.p. law, dir. Seaboard Coast Line R.R. Co., 1967-69, pres., 1969-78, chmn. bd., chief exec. officer, 1978—; pres. SCL Industries, Inc., 1970-78, chmn., chief exec. officer, 1978—; pres., chief exec. officer Louisville & Nashville R.R. Co., 1972-78, chmn. bd., chief exec. officer, 1978—; dir. Columbia, Newberry & Laurens R.R. Co., Alico Land Devel. Co.; pres. Duval Connecting R.R.; dir. Winston-Salem Southbound Ry. Co., Winston-Salem Terminal Co., Clinchfield R.R. Co., Atlantic & East Coast Terminal Co., Richmond, Fredericksburg & Potomac R.R., S.C. Pacific Ry. Co., Savannah River Terminal Co., Augusta Union Sta. Co., 1st Ky. Nat. Corp., 1st Nat. Bank Louisville, 1st Ky. Trust Co., 1st Ky. Co., Fla. Fed. Savs. & Loan Assn., Jacksonville, Fla., Carrollton R.R., Monon Transp. Co., Barnett-Winston Investment Trust, S.C.L. R.R. Co., Central R.R. S.C., Tampa & Gulf Coast R.R. Co., Haysi R.R., Richmond-Washington Co. Exec. reservist Office Emergency Transp. Dept. Transp.; nat. council, regional exec. com., chmn. nat. exploring com., regional chmn. Boy Scouts Am., 1965-69. Bd. overseers, bd. dirs. Sweet Briar Coll., Jacksonville U., Jacksonville Episcopal High Sch., chmn. nat. adv. bd. Salvation Army; mem. ho. deps. Gen. Conv. P.E. Ch. Am., provincial chmn. Episc. Ch. Found. Served from 2d lt. to lt. col. atty., AUS, 1941-46. Decorated Bronze Star; named Man of Year, Duval County, Fla., 1962; recipient Silver Beaver, Silver Antelope, Silver Buffalo awards Boy Scouts Am. Mem. Am. Bar Assn., Bar Assn. City N.Y., S.C.V., Newcomen Soc. N. Am., Nat. Def. Transp. Assn., Episc. Men of Ky. (past pres.), Episc. Men of Ala. (past pres.), Jacksonville Area (pres. 1971—, com. of 100), Louisville Area (dir. 1972-74) chambers commerce, Sigma Alpha Epsilon, Omicron Delta Kappa, Tau Kappa Alpha, Alpha Kappa Psi (hon.). Democrat. Episcopalian (exec. counsel 4th Province, vestryman, nat. exec. council). Clubs: Rotary; Ponte Vedra (Fla.) Beach; River, Florida Yacht, Timuquana Country, Union League (N.Y.C.); Met., Army and Navy (Washington); Pendennis, Jefferson, Harmony Landing, Louisville Country (Louisville); Augusta Nat. Golf; Laurel Valley Country (Ligonier, Pa.). Home: 5005 Yacht Club Rd Jacksonville FL 32210 Office: 500 Water St Jacksonville FL 32202

OSBORN, RICHARD SCOTT, civil engr.; b. Eau Claire, Wis., Apr. 8, 1948; s. Clyde N. and Ferne E. (Clough) O.; B.S. in Civil Engring., U. Wis., Platteville, 1975. Project mgr., civil engr., surveyor McClure Engring. Assos., East Moline, Ill., 1980—. Registered profl. engr., Wis., Ill. Mem. ASCE, Am. Congress Surveying and Mapping, Nat. Soc. Profl. Engrs., Wis. Soc. Profl. Engrs. and Land Surveyors, Jaycees. Lutheran. Club: Lions. Address: 3504 70th St Apt 104 Moline IL 61265

OSBORN, TERRY WAYNE, research co. exec.; b. Roswell, N.Mex., May 17, 1943; s. Woodrow Edward and Wilma Marie (Meador) O.; A.A., Ventura Coll., 1967; B.S., U. Calif., Riverside, 1969, Ph.D. (Chancellors fellow, Deans Spl. fellow), 1975. Research scientist McGaw Labs., Irvine, Calif., 1976, research scientist, project leader, 1976, research scientist, project team leader, 1976-77, group leader, research scientist, 1978-79, group leader/sr. research scientist, 1979, clin. research mgr., 1980—; tchr. chemistry Riverside City Coll., San Bernardino Valley Coll., 1974-76. Served with 101st Airborne div. U.S. Army, 1962-65. Mem. Am. Chem. Soc., Inst. Food Technologists, Am. Oil Chemists Soc., U.S. Ski Assn., Sigma Xi, Alpha Gamma Sigma. Contbr. articles to profl. jours. Club: Tyrolean Ski. Home: 639 Rhine Ln Costa Mesa CA 92626 Office: 2525 McGaw Ave Irvine CA 92714

OSBORN, WILLIAM O., banker; b. Culver, Ind., Jan. 27, 1885; s. John and Ora Osborn; m. Minnie L. Shilling, Apr. 9, 1906; 1 dau., Frances Osborn Butler. Cashier, State Exchange Bank, Culver, 1906-51, pres., chmn. bd., 1951—; admitted to Ind. bar. Bd. dirs. DePauw U., Greencastle, Ind., Culver Mil. Acad. Recipient award Ancilla Coll., Donaldson, Ind., 1975; named Sagamore of Wabash. Mem. Am. Bar Assn., Marshall County Bar Assn. Democrat. Methodist. Office: PO Box 71 Culver IN 46511

OSBORNE, ARTHUR ELLSWORTH, JR., dept. store exec.; b. Chgo., May 21, 1920; s. Arthur Ellsworth and Esther Irene (Harrison) O.; student, Grinnell (Ia.), 1942; m. Barbara Jane Rupp, May 21, 1943; children—Arthur Ellsworth III, Richard Harrison, David Charles. Asst. to dir. personnel Marshall Field & Co., 1945-46, group mgr. fine jewelry, 1947-65, v.p. women's apparel, 1966-71, v.p., gen. mgr., after 1972, now corp. exec. v.p., dir.; dir. upper Ave. Nat. Bank, 1972—. Chmn. Chgo. crusade Am. Cancer Soc., 1975, Ill. crusade, 1978; chmn. State St. Council, 1972-73, 77-78; bd. dirs. Evanston Hosp., 1974—; trustee Chgo. Boys' Club, Chgo. Crime Commn., Chgo. Hist. Soc. Served to capt. USAAF, 1942-45. Decorated D.F.C., Purple Heart, Air medal, Presdl. Citation. Mem. Nat. Retail Merchants Assn. (exec. com. 1973). Episcopalian (vestry). Clubs: Chgo., Glen View, Carlton, Mid-Am. Home: 935 Woodland Dr Glenview IL 60025 Office: 25 E Washington Chicago IL 60690

OSBORNE, BASIL ROYSTON, garment mfg. and travel co. exec.; b. Jamaica, W.I., Sept. 22, 1938; s. Conrad Constantine and Millicent Zara (Campbell) O.; came to U.S., 1970; student Jamaica schs.; m. Lucille Joyce Ferron, July 8, 1978; children—Suzanne, Wayne; children by previous marriage, Dawn, Sheldon, Rose-Marie. Jr. clk. Bybrook Sugar Factory, Bog-Walk, Jamaica, 1957-58; asst. internal auditor Univ. Hosp. W. Indies, Mona, 1958-59; sr. accounting clk. Jamaica Cooling Store, Myers Wharf, 1959-61; accountant Leslie H. Moodie & Sons, Kingston, 1961-64; owner Timepiece Bus. Service, Kingston, 1962-68, Welcome Aboard Tours, Miami, Fla., 1970—, Kingston Harbour Luxury Services, 1975—; pres. Resort Fashions, Inc., 1977—, Travel & Resort Fashions (Ja) Ltd., 1977—. Mem. Airline Passengers Assn., Small Bus. Assn. Jamaica. Baptist. Home and Office: 4635 NW 27th Ave Miami FL 33142 Office: Shop 14 7th Ave Plaza Kingston 10 Jamaica

OSBORNE, LAWRENCE THOMAS, banker; b. Brookville, Pa., Apr. 30, 1934; s. Lawrence James and Kathryn Mary (Larsen) O.; B.A., U. Pacific, 1955, postgrad., 1955-56, 58; B.F.T., Am. Grad. Sch. Internat. Mgmt., 1959; m. Phyllis Mae Grimm, Sept. 18, 1960; children—Karen Louise, John Robert. Overseas trainee 1st Nat. City Bank, N.Y.C., 1959-61; with Bank of Monrovia (Liberia), 1961-66; asst. cashier 1st Nat. City Bank, N.Y.C., 1967, asst. mgr., Dubai, Trucial States, 1967-69, asst. mgr., mgr., Maghreb, Morocco, 1969-71; v.p., head Europe, Africa and Middle East Area, Internat. div. Crocker Nat. Bank, San Francisco, 1973-75, mgr. internat. div. personal banking, 1975-79, Corp. Western/Internat. Group, 1979—. Served with U.S. Army, 1956-58. Mem. World Affairs Council San Francisco, Stock Exchange Club. Republican. Methodist. Club: Masons. Office: 1 Montgomery St San Francisco CA 94104

OSBORNE, PHILIP DEAN, engring. co. exec.; b. Riverdale, Mich., June 20, 1920; s. Rutherford Leo and Helen Muriel (Schaeffer) O.; B.S., Fremont Coll., 1955; m. Ruth M. Hummel, Mar. 3, 1946; children—Gary, Anne Osborne Herskowitz, Devon, Thomas, John. Commd. 2d lt. USAAF, advanced through grades to col. USAF, 1966; ret., 1967; group dir. engring. services Commonwealth Engring. Services, 1967-68, 71-77; dir. procurement Cons. Services Vietnamese Govt., Saigon, 1968-71; dir. procurement service Gilbert Assos. Inc., Reading, Pa., 1977—; cons. in field. Decorated D.F.C., Air medal, Commendation medal; Distinguished Service medal (Vietnam). Mem. Nat. Assn. Purchasing Mgmt., Pub. Utility Buyers Assn., Def. Supply Agy. Republican. Home: 18 Nassau Circle Reading PA 19607 Office: Box 1498 Reading PA 19603

OSGOOD, PETER GREER, public relations agy. exec.; b. Waltham, Mass., Dec. 26, 1940; s. Ernest Hamilton and Katherine (Greer) O.; B.A., Syracuse U., 1965; m. Theodora J. Stewart, July 2, 1966; children—Greer, Blaire. With Newsome & Co., Inc., Boston, 1965—, pres., 1975—. Trustee Joslin Diabetes Found., 1979—, Newton-Wellesley Hosp., 1978—; bd. dirs. Big Bros. Assn. Boston, 1977—. Served with AUS, 1959-62. Named Outstanding Citizen, Sudbury, Mass., 1962. Mem. Nat. Investor Relations Inst. (pres. 1979-80, dir. 1977-80), Public Relations Soc. Am. Editor: Smaller Bus. Assn. New Eng., 1967-68. Home: 94 Elmwood Rd Wellesley MA 02181 Office: Newsome & Co Inc 225 Franklin St Boston MA 02110

O'SHEA, JOHN, lawyer, C.P.A.; b. N.Y.C., May 3, 1928; s. William and Margaret (Heffron) O'S.; B.S., N.Y. U., 1952; LL.M., 1966; J.D., St. John's U., 1955; m. Mary Ward, May 25, 1963. Admitted to N.Y. State bar, 1955, U.S. Supreme Ct. bar, 1964; mem. audit staff Haskins & Sells, 1955-58, Lopez, Edwards Co., 1958, S.D. Leidesdorf & Co., 1958; tax specialist J.K. Lasser & Co., 1958-65; tax. supr. Ernst & Ernst, 1965-68, Hurdman & Cranstoun, 1968-72; tax mgr. Louis Sternbach & Co., 1972-74, Sperduto, Priskie Co., 1974, George F. Sheehan & Co., 1947-77, Price, Waterhouse & Co., 1977-80, Kaufman, Nachbar & Co., 1980— (all N.Y.C.); Faculty Bank, Found. Acctg. Edn.; lectr. in field. Served with USMC, 1946-48. C.P.A., N.Y. State. Mem. New York County Lawyers Assn., Am. Inst. C.P.A.'s, N.Y. State Soc. C.P.A.'s, Am. Assn. Atty.-C.P.A.'s. Roman Catholic. Club: Strathmore-Vanderbilt Country. Contbr. articles to profl. jours. Home: 305 Mill Spring Rd Manhasset NY 11030 Office: 225 W 34th St New York NY 10022

O'SHEA, JOHN DANIEL, banker; b. Toledo, Aug. 13, 1942; d. Michael B. and Florence A. (McPartland) O'S.; B.S. in Fin., Xavier U., Cin., 1964; M.B.A. in Mgmt., Ind. U., 1966; m. Kathleen E. Lyons, Nov. 25, 1967; children—Erin Eileen, Katie Coleen, Molly McPartland, Bridget Lyons. With City Nat. Bank, Columbus, Ohio, 1966-77, comml. leading officer, 1970-77; exec. v.p. charge lending Bank One of Coshocton N.A. (Ohio), 1977—. Bd. dirs. United Way Coshocton, Echoing Hills Village, Downtown Revitalization Com. Coshocton. Recipient Wall St. Jour. award, 1964, cert. of merit SBA, 1977. Mem. Am. Inst. Banking, Ohio Bankers Assn., Coshocton C. of C. Home: 1982 Fulton St Coshocton OH 43812 Office: 120 S 4th St Coshocton OH 43812

O'SHEA, LYNNE EDEEN, capital goods co. exec.; b. Chgo., Oct. 18, 1945; d. Edward Fisk and Mildred (Lessner) O'Shea; B.J., U. Mo., 1968, B.A., 1968, M.A., 1971; Ph.D., Northwestern U., 1977; m. James David Thybony, Dec. 22, 1973. Writer, The Columbia Missourian, 1965-68; writer/editor Mo. Regional Med. Program, Columbia, 1967-68; pres. O'Shea Advt. Agy., Dallas, 1968-69; exec. asst. U.S. Hos. of Reps., Washington, 1969-70; teaching asst. U. Mo., Columbia, 1970-71; brand mgr. Procter & Gamble, Cin., 1971-73; account exec. Foote, Cone & Belding, 1973-76; account supr. The First Nat. Bank of Chgo., 1976-78; v.p. Foote, Cone & Belding, Chgo., 1978-79, Internat. Harvester, 1980—; vis. faculty Mich. State U., E. Lansing, 1978, Northwestern U., Evanston (Ill.), 1978, Wayne State U., Detroit, 1979; lectr. mktg. U. Chgo., 1980. Cons., Voluntary Action Center, United Way of Chgo., 1973-75; founder, chmn. Ill. Women's Olympic Com., 1976—; Ill. del. U.S. Olympic Com., N.Y.C., 1978—; cons. YWCA, Chgo., 1978—; advt./campaign mgr. various Rep. Congressional campaigns, 1968-72; bd. dirs. Off-the Street Club, Chgo., 1978—. Recipient numerous Eagle Fin. Advt. awards, Chgo., 1978; Am. Assn. Advt. Agencies research grantee U. Mo., 1970-71. Mem. World Future Soc., Chgo. Advt. Club, Public Relations Soc., Am. Assn. Public Opinion Research, Women's Forum, Chgo. Network. Council on Fgn. Relations. Republican. Episcopalian. Clubs: Execs., Women's Athletic, Econ. Author: A Q-Methodological Approach to the Use of Advertising in Politics, 1971; Adam's Apple: A Q-Study of the Value Congruences that are Shaping Mankind's Future, 1977. Home: 525 Hawthorne St Chicago IL 60657 Office: 401 N Michigan Ave Chicago IL 60611

O'SHEA, MARTIN LESTER, investment banker, real estate investor; b. San Francisco, Dec. 6, 1938; s. Adolph Martin and Maria Carola (Bergmann) O'S.; B.A., Stanford, 1959; postgrad. (Fulbright scholar), Oxford (Eng.) U., 1959-61; M.B.A., Harvard, 1963; m. Barbara Ann Behn, Aug. 2, 1969; children—Laura Elizabeth, Amy Susanna, Amanda Catherine. Asso., Dean Witter & Co., N.Y.C., 1963-66; v.p. First Calif. Co., Inc., San Francisco, 1966-69; pres. O'Shea & Co., Inc., San Francisco, 1970—; trustee First Eastern Realty Trust Boston, 1963-67; partner Gen. Western Co., San Francisco, 1967—. Pres., St. Francis Republican Assembly, 1972-74, 76-78, dir., 1973—; dir. San Francisco County Coordinating Rep. Assembly, 1970—; mem. San Francisco County Republican Central Com., 1972-74, 76—, chmn., 1979—; treas. Rep. County Chmn.'s Assn. Calif., 1979—; mem. Electoral Coll., 1980; bd. dirs. Cow Hollow Improvement Assn., 1975—. Mem. Phi Beta Kappa Assn. No. Calif., Delta Sigma Rho. Clubs: Harvard (N.Y.C.); Commonwealth (chmn. sect. on law enforcement 1971-75, pension fund and investment coms. 1978, bd. govs. 1975-78), Harvard (sec. 1972-74), Harvard Bus. Sch. (San Francisco). Author: Tampering with the Machinery: Roots of Economic and Political Malaise, 1980. Home: 2863 Pacific Ave San Francisco CA 94115 Office: 235 Montgomery St San Francisco CA 94104

O'SHIELDS, RICHARD LEE, natural gas co. exec.; b. Ozark, Ark., Aug. 12, 1926; s. Fay and Anna (Johnson) O'S.; B.S. in Mech. Engring., U. Okla., 1949; M.S. in Petroleum Engring., La. State U., 1951; m. Shirley Isabelle Washington, Nov. 8, 1947; children—Sharon Isabelle (Mrs. Stanley R. Boles), Carolyn Jean (Mrs. Dennis L. Turney), Richard Lee. Instr. petroleum engring. La. State U., 1949-51; prodn. engr. Pure Oil Co., 1951-53; sales engr., chief engr., v.p. Salt Water Control, Inc., Ft. Worth, 1953-59; cons. engr. Ralph H. Cummins Co., Ft. Worth, 1958-60; with Anadarko Prodn. Co. and parent co. Panhandle Eastern Pipe Line Co., 1960—, pres. Anadarko Prodn. Co., 1966-68, dir., 1966—; exec. v.p. Panhandle Eastern Pipe Line Co., 1968-70, pres., chief exec. officer, 1970-79, chmn., chief exec. officer, 1979—; pres., chief exec. officer Trunkline Gas Co., 1970—, chmn., chief exec. officer, 1979—; dir. Nat. Distillers, First City Nat. Bank Houston. Bd. dirs. Tex. Research League, Midwest Research Inst. Served with USAAF, 1945. Registered profl. engr., Kan., Tex. Mem. Am. Petroleum Inst. (dir.), Soc. Petroleum Engrs., Mid Continent Oil and Gas Assn. (dir.), Ind. Natural Gas Assn. Am. (dir.), Ind. Petroleum Assn. Am. (dir.), Tau Beta Pi. Republican. Baptist. Mason. Home: 3320 Chevy Chase Houston TX 77019 Office: PO Box 1642 Houston TX 77001

OSIAS, RICHARD ALLAN, internat. financier, investment, fin. and real estate exec., city ofcl.; b. N.Y.C., Nov. 13, 1936; s. Harry L. and Leah (Schenk) O.; student Columbia U., 1951-63; m. Alexandra Stuart Currey, Sept. 22, 1962; children—Alexandra Stuart Kimberly, Alexandra Elizabeth. Founder, Osias Orgn., Inc., N.Y.C., also Ft. Lauderdale, Fla., St. Clair, Mich., San Juan, P.R., 1953, chmn. bd., chief exec. officer, 1953—; pres., chmn. bd. Venture Capital Corp. Am. Mem. North Lauderdale (Fla.) City Council, 1967—; vice-mayor and police commr. North Lauderdale, 1967—. Active Royal Dames Nova U., Ft. Lauderdale Mus. Art, Ft. Lauderdale Symphony Soc., Tower Council of Pine Crest Prep. Sch., Ft. Lauderdale, Boys Clubs Broward County; mem. U. Miami Founders Soc. Served with USAF, 1953. Recipient Am. House award Am. Home Mag., 1962, Westinghouse award, 1968; named Builder of Year, Sunshine State Info. Bur. and Sunshine State Sr. Citizen, 1967-69. Mem. Ft. Lauderdale Better Bus. Bur., Offshore Power Boating Assn., Lauderhill (Fla.) Fraternal Order Police Assn. (pres.), Fla., Margate, Ft. Lauderdale chambers commerce. Clubs: Tower, Bankers Top of First (San Juan); Quarter Deck (Galveston, Tex.); Boca Raton (Fla.) Hotel and Country; Jockey, Le Club Internat. (Miami). Prin. works include city devel., residential and apt. units, residential housing communities, shopping centers, country clubs, golf courses, hotel chains, comprehensive housing communities. Home: Bay Colony 71 Compass Island Fort Lauderdale FL 33308 also Chateau de Vincy Gilly Switzerland Office: 1700 N Dixie Hwy West Palm Beach FL 33407

OSIPOV, GEORGE JURI, info. systems corp. exec.; b. Tagil, USSR, Apr. 12, 1937; came to U.S., 1951, naturalized, 1958; s. Grigori Constantinovich and Olga Trachaniatovskata O.; B.S. in Elec. and Electronic Engring., Ind. Inst. Tech., 1961; m. Judith Swan, Jan. 2, 1961; children—Robert Gregory, Theresa Lucille, Debra Joann. Owner, GVG Electric, New Brunswick, N.J., 1957-62; logic and circuit designer IBM, Poughkeepsie, N.Y., 1961-66; computer energy systems mgmt. Honeywell, Waltham, Mass., 1966-69; dir. mfg. and fin. systems Morgan Constrn. Co., Worcester, Mass., 1969-75; installer fin., engring. and project control systems Amtel/Litwin, Paris, 1975-77; dir. H.P. Hood Inc., Boston, 1977—; lectr. in field; hon. prof. Clark U., Worcester, 1973-75, Worcester State Coll., 1973-75. Mem. traffic and communication com. Town of Holden (Mass.), 1973-74. Mem. Assn. Systems Mgmt., Data Processing Mgmt. Assn., Soc. Adminstrv. Mgmt. Republican. Greek Orthodox. Clubs: Worcester Country, Maxines, Masons, Elks. Home: 35 Laurelwood Holden MA 01520 Office: 500 Rutherford Boston MA 02129

OSSIP, JEROME J., restaurateur; b. N.Y.C., Mar. 15, 1920; s. Harry A. and Fannie O.; B.S., U. Ill., 1940; M.B.A., N.Y. U., 1949; m. Audrey A. Herman, May 30, 1949; children—Dale Ava, Brad Henry, Michael Ian. Pres. Bards Systems, Inc., N.Y.C., 1950-73; pres. Churchills Enterprises, Inc., N.Y.C., 1953-58; Cambridge Inns, Inc., Paramus, N.J., 1960-72, Greentree Restaurants, Inc., N.Y.C., 1974—; chmn. Guardian Food Service Corp., N.Y.C., 1974—. Bd. govs. Nat. Democratic Club. Served to capt. USAF, 1943-46. Mem. N.Y., Nat. restaurant assns., N.Y. Vis. Conv. Bur., Chemists Club. Clubs: Ridgeway Country (bd. govs.). Editor: 509th Composite Group, 1946. Home: 8 Glen Dr Harrison NY 10528 Office: 630 Fifth Ave New York NY 10020

OSTEN, JAMES ARTHUR, energy economist; b. Milw., July 24, 1946; s. Harvey Arthur and Alfreda Mary (Evanson) O.; B.A., U. Wis., Milw., 1971, postgrad., 1971-73; postgrad. Boston Coll., 1978-80; m. Susan Ruth Searing, June 24, 1972; children—Elizabeth, Mary Ruth. Petroleum economist Data Resources, Inc., Lexington, Mass., 1974-75, sr. energy economist, 1975-77, dir. drilling service, 1978-79, dir. Can. energy service, 1979—; speaker confs. Energy Bur., 1978-80. Served to capt. U.S. Army, 1966-69, to capt. USNG, 1972-73. Mem. Am. Econ. Assn., Internat. Assn. Energy Economists,

Can. Econ. Assn., Internat. Assn. Drilling Contractors, U.S. Chess Fedn. (life). Contbr. articles to profl. jours. Home: 63 N Hancock St Lexington MA 02173 Office: 29 Hartwell Ave Lexington MA 02173

OSTENDORF, EDGAR LOUIS, JR., real estate co. exec.; b. Cleve., July 30, 1934; s. Edgar Louis and Mary Martha (McConnell) O.; B.S. Bus. Adminstrn., John Carroll U., 1957; m. Joan Marie Donahue, Feb. 10, 1962; 1 dau., Mary E. Salesman real estate Ostendorf-Morris Co., Cleve., 1959-68; pres. First Commerce Realty Co., Mentor, Ohio, 1968-70; owner Ostendorf Assos., Cleve., 1970—. Mem. Citizens League, 1964—, speakers com. United Appeal, 1966-70; occupational planning com. Welfare Fedn., 1965-67; v.p. council smaller enterprises Cleve. Growth Assn., 1973—. Served with AUS, 1957-59. Mem. Real Estate Securities and Syndication Inst. (pres. Ohio chpt. 1976), Nat., Ohio (trustee), Cleve. (trustee) bds. realtors, Nat. Assn. Real Estate Appraisers. Clubs: Chagrin Valley Hunt, Union. Home: 3425 Roundwood Rd Chagrin Falls OH 44022 Office: 28349 Chagrin Blvd Cleveland OH 44122

OSTER, MERRILL JAMES, publisher, farmer, author, lectr.; b. Cedar Falls, Iowa, May 30, 1940; s. Harland James and Pearl Rosetta (Smith) O.; B.S. in Agrl. Journalism (Sears and Roebuck scholar, Spokesman scholar), Iowa State U., 1961; M.S. in Agrl. Journalism, U. Wis., 1962; m. Carol Jane Dempster, June 1, 1962; children—David, Leah Jane. Grad. asst. U. Wis., 1961; asst. radio-TV farm dir. Sta. WKOW, Madison, 1961-62; asst. editor Crops and Soils mag., Madison, 1962, Ford Farming and Ford Almanac mags., 1964-67; editor Top Farmer Intelligence, Woodstock, Ill., 1967-69; pres. Communication Consultants, Cedar Falls, 1969—, Oster Farms and Pork Pro, Inc., Cedar Falls, 1971—, Hometowner, Inc., Cedar Falls, 1976—, Cedar Terrace Developers, Inc., Cedar Falls, 1977—; pres., pub. Commodities Mag., Inc., Cedar Falls, 1975—; lectr. Land and commodity futures Profl. Farmers Inst., 1973—; instr. Grad. Sch. Banking, U. Wis., 1976—. Trustee, Emmaus Bible Sch., Oak Park, Ill.; pres. bd. dirs. Christian Heritage Sch., 1977-79; chmn. bd. trustees Downing Avenue Gospel Chapel; mem. alumni achievement fund com. Iowa State U. Named Outstanding Young Alumnus, Iowa State U., 1975. Mem. Am. Assn. Agrl. Editors, Nat. Assn. Agrl. Marketers, Am. Soc. Farm Mgrs. and Rural Appraisers (instr.), Profl. Farmers Am. (founder, pres. 1973—), Cedar Falls C. of C. (dir. 1975-78), Alpha Zeta, Sigma Delta Chi. Republican. Clubs: Rotary; Sunnyside Country (Waterloo, Iowa); Beaver Hills Country (Cedar Falls). Author: Commodity Futures for Profit, 1978; Multiply Your Money Through Commodity Trading, 1979; contbr. numerous articles, bulls. and spl. reports on food, agr., commodity futures to profl. publs. Home: Rural Route 4 Cedar Falls IA 50613 Office: 219 Parkade Cedar Falls IA 50613

OSTERGARD, PAUL MICHAEL, elec. mfg. co. exec.; b. Akron, Ohio, Apr. 1, 1939; s. Paul and Jannette Beryl (Laube) O.; A.B., Western Res. U., 1961; J.D., U. Mich., 1964; M.Pub. Adminstrn., Harvard, 1969; Admitted to Ohio bar, 1964, U.S. Ct. Mil. Appeals, 1965; atty. U.S. Steel Corp., Pitts., 1967-69; gen. atty. TWA, N.Y.C., 1969-71; sec., counsel Pa. Co., N.Y.C., 1971-74; v.p., counsel Buckeye Pipe Line, N.Y.C., 1971-74; pub. affairs exec. Gen. Electric Co., Fairfield, Conn., 1974—; dir. Pullman Co., 1971-74, Penn Towers, Inc., 1971-74, Clearfield Bituminous Coal Corp., 1971-74. Served to capt. USAF, 1965-67. Decorated Bronze Star medal. Mem. Phi Beta Kappa, Omicron Delta Kappa. Clubs: Atrium, Harvard (N.Y.C.); Fort Orange (Albany). Home: 115 Roseville Rd Westport CT 06880 Office: 3135 Easton Turnpike Fairfield CT 06431

OSTERHOLT, WALTER BERNARD, ins. co. exec.; b. Fort Recovery, Ohio, Dec. 5, 1918; s. Bernard John and Johanna (Wenning) O.; m. Luella C. Hartings, Aug. 21, 1943; children—Mary Jane, Ruth Ann, Audrey Rose, Nancy Alfredia, Theresa Marie, Karen Alice, Agnes Cecilia. Appliance sales Wolf & Dessauers, 1946-53; sales staff, dir. The Place, Inc., 1953-60; agt., estate planner N.Y. Life Ins. Co., Fort Wayne, Ind., 1960—. Bd. dirs. Bishop Luers Cath. High Sch., Fort Wayne, 1971-73; bd. dirs. St. Anne Home, 1966-68; bd. dirs. Fort Wayne Home Rescue Mission; bd. dirs. St. Vincent's Children's Service of Fort Wayne, 1972-79; bd. trustees St. Hyacinth's Cath. Ch., 1950-79. Served with AUS, 1941-46; served to lt. col. U.S. Army Res. Decorated Purple Heart. Mem. Nat., Ind. (past dir.), Fort Wayne (past pres.) assn. life underwriters, Fort Wayne Estate Planning Council, Am. Soc. C.L.U.'s, V.F.W., Res. Officers Assn. (past pres. local chpt., pub. relations officer Ind.). Club: Optimist (past bd. dirs., Pres.). Home: 3025 Reed St Fort Wayne IN 46806 Office: 220 Insurance Ave Fort Wayne IN 46825

OSTERMILLER, RONALD L., accountant; b. Bayard, Nebr., Oct. 30, 1942; s. Henry K. and Mary Ostermiller; B.A. in Bus. and Acctg., Calif. State U., Fullerton, 1968; m. Donna Scalzo, July 26, 1969. Staff acct. Touche Ross & Co., Los Angeles, 1968-71; v.p. fin., controller Travel Queen Industries, 1971; owner, mgr. Ronald L. Ostermiller, C.P.A., San Clemente, Calif., 1972—; guest lectr. on income, estate taxation and planning. Served with U.S. Army, 1964-66. C.P.A., Calif. Mem. Am. Inst. C.P.A.'s, Calif. Soc. C.P.A.'s, Soc. Calif. Accts. Republican. Roman Catholic. Club: Kiwanis. Home: 25861 Paseo de Juanita San Juan Capistrano CA Office: 102 Avenida Algodon Suite 5 San Clemente CA 92672

OSTRONIC, FRANCIS JAMES, computer co. exec.; b. Omaha, Aug. 3, 1929; s. Frank J. and Helen K. O.; student Creighton U., 1947-49; B.S., U.S. Naval Acad., 1953; postgrad. Duquesne U., 1959-60; M.B.A., Am. U., 1965; m. Judith Mary Nugent, Sept. 11, 1954; children—Francis P., Thomas D., Michael J., Ellen M., Mary J., John F., Judith M. Mgr., Westinghouse Elec. Corp., Washington, 1958-64, Hoffman Elec. Corp., Washington, 1964-65; program mgr. Univac/Fed. Systems Div., Washington, 1965-68; v.p. program devel. Computer Scis. Corp., Falls Church, Va., 1968—. Served with USN, 1953-58, to capt. USNR, 1958-77. Mem. Electronic Industries Assn., Armed Forces Communications and Electronics Assn., Assn. U.S. Army. Home: 11308 Tara Rd Potomac MD 20854 Office: 6565 Arlington Blvd Falls Church VA 22046

OSTROW, JOHN BRUCE, lawyer; b. Bklyn., Oct. 19, 1944; s. Allen Abraham and May (Brown) O.; B.A., Fla. Atlantic U., 1965, M.Ed., 1966; J.D. cum laude (research asst. 1968-69), Fla. State U., 1970; m. Jane Roth, Apr. 15, 1973; children—Stephen Asher, Jason Lee. Admitted to Fla. bar, 1970; atty. Fla. Ho. Reps., 1970; law clk. to U.S. dist. judge, Miami, 1970-72; asso. firms in Ft. Lauderdale and Miami, 1972-78; individual practice, Miami, 1978—; mem. Fla. Bd. Bar Examiners. Recipient commendation Fla. Ho. Reps., 1970. Mem. Am. Bar Assn., Am. Trial Lawyers Assn., Fla. Bar Assn. Jewish. Editor Fla. State U. Law Rev., 1969-70. Address: 200 SE 1st St Miami FL 33131

OSTROW, KENNETH PAUL, computer co. exec.; b. Painesville, Ohio, Dec. 15, 1941; s. Stanley S. and Viola (Rockefellar) O.; B.M.E., Ohio State U., 1965; M.B.A., Northeastern U., 1970; m. Judith Rodgers, July 3, 1965; children—Christy, Kerry. Sales engr. Reliance Electric Co., Boston, 1965-68; mktg. mgr. Whitely Hydraulics Inc., Melrose, Mass., 1968-70; with Measurex Corp., various locations, 1970-80, v.p. field ops., Portland, Oreg., 1974-75, v.p., mgr. Pulp and Paper div., Cupertino, Calif., 1975-76, v.p. U.S. sales and service, 1976, v.p. mktg., sales and service, 1977-78, sr. v.p. sales and service for U.S., Japan, Latin and S. Am., 1978-80; pres. Impact Systems, Inc., 1980—; partner KNOW Enterprises; dir. Sturm's Meats Co. Vice pres., then pres. Oaklin Park Homeowners Assn., 1968-70. Bd. dirs. Pulp and Paper Found., N.C. State U., 1977. Mem. Paper Industry Mgmt. Assn., TAPPI, Am. Mgmt. Assn. Republican. Roman Catholic. Contbr. articles to profl. jours.

OSWALD, JAMES MARLIN, educator; b. Plainview, Tex., Aug. 17, 1935; s. James Buchanan and Eula Bea (Marlin) O.; B.S., W. Tex. State Coll., 1957, M.A., 1958; Ed.D., Stanford U., 1970; m. Dorothy Anne Veigel, Dec. 27, 1956; children—Richard, Ramona, Roberta. Tchr., supr. Salt Lake City pub. schs., 1958-66; curriculum specialist Am. Insts. Research, 1966-68; staff asso. Nat. Council Social Studies, 1968-69; asst. prof. social studies and social sci. edn. Syracuse (N.Y.) U., 1969-72; researcher-writer Am. Univs. Field Staff, 1972-75; asst. supt. instrn. East Penn Sch. Dist., Emmaus, Pa., 1975-78; field coordinator citizen edn., also dir. global edn. projects. Research for Better Schs., Phila., 1978—; instrnl. developer Community Coll. Phila.; propr. Main Line Stove and Self-Sufficiency Products, 1978—; pres. N.Y. State Council Social Studies, 1971-72. Served with AUS, 1957-58. Recipient Service to Mankind award Salt Lake City, 1966; grantee NSF, U.S. Office Edn., Inst. Internat. Studies, Henry Newell fellow, 1966-68, Fulbright-Hays SEAsia Study Program fellow, 1968. Mem. AAAS, Nat. Council Social Studies, Assn. Supervision and Curriculum Devel., Am. Assn. Sch. Adminstrs., Tex. Panhandle-Plains Hist. Soc., Utah Hist. Soc., Phi Delta Kappa. Author: The Monroe Doctrine: Does It Survive?, 1969; Research in Social Studies and Social Science Education, 1972; co-author, Earthship, 1974; Planet Earth, 1976; Our Home, the Earth, 1980. Home: 333 Bryn Mawr Ave Bala Cynwyd PA 19004 Office: 3450 11th St Philadelphia PA 19107 also 147 Montgomery Ave Bala Cynwyd PA 19004

OSWALD, WILLIAM JACK, financial investor; b. Chgo., Feb. 10, 1927; s. Jeho and Maria Jeanette (Van Calcar) O.; student Ill. Inst. Tech., 1943-44, U. Wis., 1944-45; B.S., Barry Coll., 1978; m. Delores Jean Kipple, Dec. 6, 1958; 1 son, William Randolph. Pres. Star Corps., Chgo., 1953-74, chmn. bd., 1964-74; pres. Interam. Car Rental, Inc., 1976—; chmn. bd. Capital & Devel. Control Corp., Coral Galbes, Fla., 1975—; dir. Ostar, Inc., Am. Autolet Corp. Served with USAAF, 1945-46. Certified employment cons. Am. Inst. Employment Counseling. Home: 2200 S Ocean Ln Fort Lauderdale FL 33316

OTANI, HENRY HIDEO, contracting co. exec.; b. Hilo, Hawaii, Jan. 29, 1943; s. Hideyoshi and Matsue (Okuno) O.; B.S. in Engring., U. Hawaii, 1966; m. Carole Mae Fumie Sugimoto, Apr. 4, 1964; children—Michele Leinaala Tamiko, Brandon Keoni Kiyoshi. With Fair Contracting Co. Ltd., Hilo, 1966—, dir., 1967—, v.p., mgr., 1971-77, pres., mgr., 1977— Instl. rep. Boy Scouts Am., 1965—, recipient 10 Year Vet. award, 1976; pres. Kaumana Sch. PTA, 1968-69, treas. Hawaii Dist. 1, 1971—; pilot, 2d lt. CAP and USCG Aux., 1972—; bd. dirs. Boy's Club Am., 1975—; conv. chmn., coordinator PTA, 1975; sect. rep. Mauka Kaumana Kumiai, 1975, pres 1976; Democratic precinct capt. for candidate Hawaii Ho. of Reps. campaign, 1972, com. chmn. for candidate's campaigns, 1974, 76; del. White House Conf. on Small Bus., 1980. Mem. Constrn. Industry Legis. Orgn., Hilo Contractors Assn. (sec. 1974, 2d v.p. 1977-79, pres. 1979—), Aloha Arborist Assn. (v.p. 1977), Kanoelehua Indsl. Area Assn. (v.p. 1978-79, pres. 1979-80). Buddhist. Clubs: Lions (Lion of Year award 1970, pres. Hilo 1976-77, Liontamer, dir., v.p.), Tailtwisters. Home: 1503 Kaumana Dr Hilo HI 96720 Office: 133 Makaala St Hilo HI 96720

OTHMER, DONALD FREDERICK, chem. engr., educator; b. Omaha, May 11, 1904; s. Frederick George and Fredericka Darling (Snyder) O.; student Ill. Inst., Chgo., 1921-23; B.S., U. Nebr., 1924, D.Eng. (hon.), 1962; M.S., U. Mich., 1925, Ph.D., 1927; D.Eng. (hon.), Poly. Inst. N.Y., 1977, N.J. Inst. Tech., 1978; m. Mildred Jane Topp, Nov. 18, 1950. Devel. engr. Eastman Kodak Co. and Tenn. Eastman Corp., 1927-31; instr. Poly. Inst. N.Y., 1932-33, prof., 1933—, head dept. chem. engring., 1937-61, sec. grad. faculty, 1948-58, distinguished prof., 1961—. Hon. prof. U. Conception, Chile, 1952; licensed chem. engr. in N.Y., N.J., Ohio, Pa.; dir. various engring., mfg. corps.; cons. chem. engr. and licensor of process patents, numerous cos., govtl depts., lectr. U.S., Can., Mex., Cuba, P.R., Central and S.Am., Norway, Sweden, Finland, Denmark, Germany, France, Eng., Belgium, Switzerland, Italy, Spain, South Africa, India, Burma, Yugoslavia, Korea, Japan, Taiwan, P.I., Dominica, Poland, Middle East, in fields of chem. mfg., petroleum, petro-chem. fermenting, pharms., solvents, acetic acid, acetylene, distilling, synthetic fuels, wood utilization, wallboard, pigments, salt, engring. equipment, synthetic rubber, solar energy utilization, pulping liquor recovery, plastics, synthetic fibers, sugar refining, sewage and waste treatment, extractive metallurgy, zinc, titanium, aluminum, pipe line heating, saline water conversion; cons. to UN, WHO, Office Saline Water, U.S. Dept. Interior, Chem. Corps. and Ordnance Dept., U.S. Army, Spl. Devices Div., USN, WPB, U.S. Dept. Health, Edn. and Welfare, Dept. of State, sci. adv. bd. U.S. Army Munitions Command, other depts. of U.S. govt., financial instns.; mem. nat. materials adv. bd. NRC. Bd. regents L.I. Coll. Hosp.; bd. dirs. various ednl. and philanthropic instns. Recipient Tyler award Am. Inst. Chem. Engrs., 1958; Barber-Coleman award Am. Soc. Engring. Edn., 1958; Honor Scroll award Am. Inst. Chemists, 1970; Distinguished Service award Assn. Cons. Chemists and Chem. Engrs., 1975; Golden Jubilee award Ill. Inst. Tech., 1976, Profl. Achievement award, 1978; Pioneer Chemist award Am. Inst. Chemists, 1977; E.V. Murphree Exxon award Am. Chem. Soc., 1978; Perkin medal Soc. Chem. Industry, 1978. Fellow AAAS, N.Y. Acad. Scis. (chmn. engring. sect. 1973-74, hon. life), Am. Inst. Cons. Engrs., Am. Inst. Chemists (dir. 1950), Am. Inst. Chem. Engrs. (chmn. N.Y. sect. 1944, dir. 1956-59), ASME (chmn. processes div. 1948-49), Inst. Chem. Engrs. London (hon. life), mem. Am. Chem. Soc. (council 1945-47, hon. life), Soc. Chem. Industry, Newcomen Soc., Japan Soc. Chem. Engrs., Societe de Chimie Industrielle (pres. Am. sect. 1973-74), Chemurgic Council (dir. 1963—, chmn. research com.), Engrs. Joint Council (dir. 1957-59), Am. Soc. Engring. Edn., Am. Arbitration Assn. (panel mem.), Deutsche Gesellschaft fur Chem. Appar. (hon. life), Sigma Xi, Tau Beta Pi, Phi Lambda Upsilon, Iota Alpha, Alpha Chi Sigma, Lambda Chi Alpha. Clubs: Chemists (pres. 1974-76), Norwegian, Rembrandt. Designer of plants and processes for numerous corps. U.S., fgn. countries. Holder over 125 U.S., fgn. patents; del. numerous internat. engring., sci. and petroleum congresses. Co-author: Fluidization and Fluid-Particle Systems, 1960. Contbr. numerous articles to tech. jours. Editor: Fluidization, 1956; co-editor Kirk-Othmer Ency. Chem. Tech., 17 vols., 1947-60, 2d edit., 24 vols., 1963-72, 3d edit., Vols. 1-11, 1977-80, Spanish edit., 16 vols., 1960-65; tech. editor UN Report-Desalination of Water, 1964; editorial adv. bd. 3d edit. Chem. Engr.'s Handbook. Home: 140 Columbia Heights Brooklyn NY 11201 also Coudersport PA 16915 Office: 333 Jay St Brooklyn NY 11201

OTIS, JOHN EDWARD, III, banker; b. N.J., Jan. 31, 1936; s. John Edward and Linda Helen (Walser) O.; A.B., Dartmouth Coll., 1958; M.B.A. cum laude, Fairleigh Dickinson U., 1967; m. Carol Dornemann, June 6, 1959; children—John, Greg, Sarah. Credit mgr. Nustone Products Co., Tenafly, N.J., 1958-59; pres. Otis Industries, Inc., Wayne, N.J., 1963-69; v.p. Bank of N.Y., N.Y.C., 1969—; dir. John E. Otis, Inc.; instr. Am. Inst. Banking. Served with USMC, 1959-63. Clubs: Whitehall, Morris County Country. Office: Bank of NY 48 Wall St New York NY 10005

O'TOOLE, JOHN E., advt. exec.; b. Chgo., 1929; B.S. in Journalism, Northwestern U., 1950; m. Phyllis O'Toole, 1955; children—Sally, Ellen. With Foote, Cone and Belding, 1954—, v.p., 1961-68, creative dir. Los Angeles office, 1964-67, creative dir. Chgo. office, 1967-68, sr. v.p., 1968-69, pres., 1969—, also dir.; pres. Foote, Cone & Belding Communications, Inc., 1970-80, chmn., 1981—. Trustee, Greenwich Acad., Am. Ballet Theatre. Served to capt. USMCR, 1951-56. Mem. Am. Assn. Advt. Agys. (dir.), Advt. Council (dir.). Office: 200 Park Ave New York NY 10017

O'TOOLE, PAUL THOMAS, JR., mfg. co. exec.; b. Worcester, Mass., Oct. 17, 1949; s. Paul Thomas and Irene Mary O'Toole; B.B.A. in Acctg., Coll., Dudley, Mass., 1971; M.B.A. in Fin., Anna Maria Coll., Paxton, Mass., 1977. Auditor, Goff & Cagan, C.P.A.'s, Worcester, Mass., 1971-72, George A. Smith & Co., Worcester, 1972-77; acctg. supr. Parker Mfg. Co., Worcester, 1977—; cons. in field. Mem. Delta Mu Delta. Roman Catholic. Home: 6 Bryant Ave Shrewsbury MA 01545 Office: 149 Washington St Worcester MA 01613

OTT, GILBERT RUSSELL, JR., lawyer; b. Bklyn., Apr. 15, 1943; s. Gilbert Russell and Bettina Rose (Ferrel) O.; B.A., Yale U., 1965; J.D., Columbia U., 1969, M.B.A., 1969. Admitted to N.Y. State bar, 1970; asso. firm Chadbourne, Parke, Whiteside & Wolff, N.Y.C., 1969-72, LeBoeuf, Lamb, Leiby & MacRae, N.Y.C., 1972-78; asso. gen. counsel, asst. sec. Kidder, Peabody & Co., Inc., N.Y.C., 1978—, asst. v.p., 1978-79, v.p., 1979—; v.p. Webster Cash Res. Fund, Inc., 1980—. Mem. Assn. Bar City N.Y. Clubs: Piping Rock; University (N.Y.C.). Home: 4 E 89th St New York NY 10028 Office: 10 Hanover Sq New York NY 10005

OTTAVIANO, VICTOR BENEDICT, energy cons.; b. Bklyn., May 31, 1934; s. Lawrence John and Lucia (Palmesino) O.; B.S., St. John's U., 1958; m. Ann Marie Dee, July 1, 1961; children—Deanne, Lawrence John. Sales engr. Arco Fuel Oil Corp., N.Y.C., 1959-61; v.p., sales engr. Air-Ideal, Inc., Roslyn, N.Y., 1961-72; pres. Ottaviano Tech. Services, Inc., Melville, N.Y., 1972—; mem. faculty N.Y. U., 1969-70, U. Wis., Madison, 1975—; energy memt. cons. various cos. Served with U.S. Army, 1959. Recipient Cert. of Energy Conservation, Fed. Exec. Bd., Dept. of Energy, 1979; Cert. of Appreciation, U. Wis., 1980. Mem. Assn. Energy Engrs. (chmn. 1st World Energy Congress, named Energy Engr. of Yr. 1980), ASHRAE, Air Conditioning Contractors Am. Roman Catholic. Author: National Mechanical Estimator, 1972; Energy Management Manual, 1976; (with Marvin Hubert) National Plumbing Estimator and Solar Energy Manual, 1976. Office: 150 Broad Hollow Rd Melville NY 11747

OTTE, KARL HENRY, research engr.; b. Chgo., Feb. 20, 1904; s. Paul C. and Mileta (Olbert) O.; B.S., Armour Inst. Tech., 1926, M.E., 1933; S.M., Mass. Inst. Tech., 1928; m. Maxine Muriel Roehl, June 10, 1950. Mech. engr. F. J. Littell Machine Co., 1926-27; mech. engr. on foundry devel. Hawthorne Plant, Western Electric Co., 1928-32; sr. indsl. engr., supr. devel. of improved methods E. J. Brach & Sons, 1933-41; mech. engr. on research in printing equipment R. R. Donnelley & Sons, Inc. (all Chgo.), 1942; bldg. process engr. supervising process engring. dept. Milw. Ordnance Plant of U.S. Rubber Co., 1942-43; mech. engr. supervising engring. research and devel. of equipment Purity Bakeries Service Corp., and successor co. Am. Bakeries Co., Chgo., 1943-63; asst. prof. mech. engring. U. Ill., Chgo., 1963-74. Lectr. in machine design, Lewis Inst. Bd. dirs. St. Paul's House (home for aged). Registered profl. engr., Ill. Fellow Am. Soc. M.E. (v.p.); mem. Profl. Engrs., Am. Mgmt. Assn. Clubs: University, Massachusetts Institute Technology (Chicago). Holder three British, two Canadian, two Am. patents. Home: 1005 S Knight Ave Park Ridge IL 60068

OTTEN, MICHAEL, data processing exec.; b. N.Y.C., Apr. 19, 1942; s. Louis and Marjorie O.; B.S.E., Princeton U., 1963; M.S., Columbia U., 1965; M.B.A., Harvard U., 1967; Ph.D., Am. U., 1972; m. Evelyne Bonnem, Aug. 5, 1965; children—Sylvie, Daniel, Marc. Computer research engr. NIH, Bethesda, Md., 1967-69; with IBM, various locations, 1970—, mgr. data requirements plans and controls, North Tarrytown, N.Y., 1979—. Pres. bd. trustees Green Chimneys Sch., Brewster, N.Y., 1979—. Served to lt. comdr. USPHS, 1967-69. Mem. IEEE, Assn. Computing Machinery. Clubs: Harvard Bus. Sch., Princeton Alumni of Westchester. Home: 37 Stonehouse St Scarsdale NY 10583 Office: A/FE HQ Rockwood Rd North Tarrytown NY 10591

OTTENFELD, MARSHALL, mktg. research co. exec.; b. Chgo., Jan. 15, 1937; s. Leo and Sadie (Patt) O.; B.A., U. Chgo., 1959; M.A., Roosevelt U., 1968; m. Gloria Jean Zilke, Dec. 28, 1960; children—David Joel, Jonathan Lawrence, Jennifer Lynn, Heather Anne. Study dir. Chgo. Tribune, 1962-64; project dir. Gardner Advt. Co., N.Y.C., 1964-65; research asso. Advt. Research Found., N.Y.C., 1965-66; research asso. pharm. products div. Abbott Labs., North Chicago, Ill., 1966-70; sr. v.p., dir. mktg. research D'Arcy-MacManus & Masius, Inc., Chgo., 1970—; pres. Mid-Am. Research, Chgo., 1970—; lectr. mktg. Roosevelt U. Asst. scout master Boy Scouts Am., Deerfield, Ill., 1978—. Served with AUS, 1961-62. Mem. Am. Mktg. Assn., Advt. Research Found., Research Practices Council, Qualitative Research Council, Am. Assn. Public Opinion Research, Midwest Assn. Public Opinion Research, Am. Acad. Polit. and Social Sci., Zeta Beta Tau. Jewish. Club: Internat. Home: 1050 Summit Dr Deerfield IL 60015 Office: 200 E Randolph Dr Chicago IL 60015

OTTENSTEIN, ARTHUR BENJAMIN, heavy machinery mfg. co. exec.; b. Bklyn., Apr. 8, 1935; s. Nathan and Shirley (Gilman) O.; B.B.A., Coll. City N.Y., 1957; m. Rosalie Wininger, June 9, 1956; children—Thomas, Nancy, James. Audit supr. Touche Ross & Co., N.Y.C., 1961-65; asst. comptroller Studebaker-Worthington, Inc., N.Y.C., 1965-69; v.p. Masonelilan Internat., Norwood, Mass., 1969-78, sr. v.p., 1978—; pres. Masoneilan Regulator Co., Norwood, 1972—; dir. Niigata Masoneilan Ltd. (Japan) Masoneilan (S.E.A.) Pvt. Ltd., Singapore, Masoneilan Ltd. (Eng.), Masoneilan Australia Pty. Ltd. C.P.A., N.Y., N.J. Mem. Financial Execs. Inst. (mem. accounting prins. com.). Office: 63 Nahatan St Norwood MA 02062

OTTERY, WILLIS DEE, JR., mfg. co. exec.; b. Fond du Lac, Wis., July 7, 1927; s. Willis Dee and Irene Elizabeth (Sampson) O.; B.S. in Agr., U. Wis., 1950; m. RuEllen Serina Hjella, Jan. 28, 1950; children—Faith Debra, Noel Christine, Theresa Adrienne, Willis Dee. Sales rep. Aermotor Co., Chgo., 1950-52; area sales rep. Internat. Harvester Co., Grand Island, Nebr., 1952-57, service supr., 1957-60, supr. sales promotion, Mpls., 1960-62, project supr. creative services, Chgo., 1962-64, product sales supr. hay and cotton equip., 1967-71, mgr. dealer devel., St. Louis, 1964-67, sales mgr., Harrisburg, Pa., 1971-73, mgr. market planning, Albany, N.Y., 1973-78, hay and forage market mgr., Davenport, Iowa, 1978—; advisor Milford Trade Sch. Pres., coach Plainsmen Jr. Football League, Clifton Park, N.Y., 1976-78; mem. indsl. and profl. advisory council Coll. Agrl. Engring. Pa. State U. Served with U.S. Army, 1945-46. Recipient Golden Spear award Sales Promotion Execs. Assn., 1964; Civic award for community service Internat. Harvester, 1978. Mem. Am. Mgmt. Assn., Pa. Farm Equipment Mfg. Assn. (v.p.), Am. Soc. Agrl. Engrs., Nat. Agrl. Mktg. Assn., Wis. Alumni Assn., Uncas Shenendehowa Booster Club (pres.), Alpha Gamma Rho. Republican. Episcopalian. Home: 4450 Norfolk Ct Bettendorf IA 52722

OTTESON, SCUYLER FRANKLIN, univ. dean; b. Mondovi, Wis., July 17, 1917; s. Hans and Elizabeth (Meyer) O.; Ph.B., U. Wis., 1939; M.B.A., Northwestern U., 1940; Ph.D., Ohio State U., 1948; m. Marie Lila Rothering, June 21, 1940; children—Judith Marie, Martha Jean, Karn Wilma, John Christian. Asso. dir. Sch. Bus., Ind. U., 1947-49, dir., 1954-60; editor Bus. Horizons, 1957-66, chmn. dept. mktg., 1960-65, chmn. D.B.A. program, 1965-71, dir. internat. bus. Reserach Inst., 1968-71, acting dean, 1971-72, dean, 1973—, also prof. bus. adminstrn,; pres. Center Leadership Devel., 1976—. Bd. dirs. Bloomington Boys Club, 1974—. Recipient Sagamore of the Wabash award Gov. of Ind., 1956, Leader medal Sigma Delta Chi, 1960. Mem. Am. Assembly Collegiate Schs. Bus. (pres. 1980-81), Am. Mktg. Assn. (nat. pres. 1965-66), Am. Econ. Assn., Am. Statis. Assn., Ind. Acad. Social Scis. (pres. 1967-70, sec. 1956-60), Midwest Econ. Assn., Beta Gamma Sigma (gov.). Methodist. Clubs: Indpls. Athletic, Indpls. Columbia. Author: (with William G. Panschar and James M. Petterson) Marketing: The Firm's Viewpoint, 1964; editor: Marketing, Current Problems and Theories, 1952. Office: Sch Bus Ind U Bloomington IN 47405

OTTLEY, EDWARD GRANGER, mfg. co. exec.; b. N.Y.C., March 31, 1930; s. James Henry and Margaret (Deeble) O.; A.B., Williams Coll., 1951; m. Carolyn Lissner, Aug. 6, 1953 (separated); children—Elizabeth, Henry, James. Vice pres. mktg. Polyplastex United, Inc., Union, N.J., 1953-66; pres. Aries Corp., N. Bergen, N.J., 1966—; mem. adv. bd. 1st Jersey Nat. Bank. Pres., Tenafly Community Chest, 1970-71, Dwight Englewood Sch., 1970-75; sr. warden Ch. of the Atonement, Tenafly, N.J., 1973-79; v.p. Youth Consultation Service, Newark, 1976; bd. dirs. Bergen County council Girl Scouts U.S.A., 1976—; trustee, v.p. Palisades Gen. Hosp., North Bergen, N.J., 1978—; trustee Episcopal Fund, Newark Diocese, 1979—. Served in USAF, 1951-53. Mem. Wallcovering Mfrs. Assn. Episcopalian. Clubs: Englewood Field, Bay Head Yacht. Home: 111 Meadow Ave Bayhead NJ 08742 Office: 2029 83d St North Bergen NJ 07047

OUDINE, JOHN ALBERT, editor; b. West Orange, N.J., May 15, 1916; s. John and Susan (Maunas) O.; B.A., Columbia, 1937, M.S., Sch. Journalism, 1938; m. Elaine Farrimond Weston, Jan. 29, 1948; children—John Mark, Jennifer Susan. Asst. mgr. World Letters, Inc., E. Aurora, N.Y., 1938-39; overseas reporter, photographer Keystone View Co., Meadville, Pa., 1939-40; mem. Washington editorial staff Time, Inc., 1940-42; information officer UNRRA, China, 1946-47; mng. editor Navy Dept. The Naval Reservist, Washington, 1947-51, news editor All Hands Mag., 1951, mng. editor, 1951-62, editor, 1962-76; editorial cons., 1976—. Chmn. parks and recreation North Springfield (Va.) Civic Assn., 1960-72. Served to lt. USNR, 1942-46. Mem. Columbia U. Alumni Assn. Lutheran. Editorial cons. World Book Ency., 1964—; contbg. editor Am. Gazette, 1976. Home: Lake of the Woods VA 22508

OUER, J. KATHRYN, interior designer; b. Paterson, N.J., Aug. 10, 1918; d. James and Jessie Grant-Frazer (Garside) Ratcliffe; A.Interior Design with distinction, Ind. U., 1975; m. Raymond Frederick Ouer, July 4, 1943; 1 dau., Mona Rae Ouer Sprott. Legal sec. Judge Milton Schamach, Paterson, N.J., 1937-39, 43-45; sec. Wright Aeronautical Corp., Paterson N.J. and Los Angeles, 1939-42, expediter, 1942-43; exec. sec. Golden Gate Fields, Berkeley, Calif., 1948-52; exec. sec. and design cons. Orchard Nursery & Florist, Lafayette, Calif., 1956-59; interior designer Interiors Inc., Auburn, Ind., 1976—; lectr. in field; cons. in field. Program chmn. Lafayette (Calif.) Forum, 1953-54; mem. fund raising com. DeKalb Meml. Hosp., Auburn, 1962-68; mem. Auburn Improvement Assn., 1976-78; bd. dirs. Community Center, Lafayette, 1954-58. Mem. Ft. Wayne Mus. Art, Ft. Wayne Art Inst. Presbyterian. Clubs: Auburn Garden, Ladies Literary, Ft. Wayne Women's.

OULTON, PATRICIA TOBIN, hosp. adminstr.; b. Washington, Oct. 21, 1945; d. John Henry and Frances Kathryn (Tkaczyk) Tobin; B.A., U. Chgo., 1968; postgrad U. Buffalo, 1972; M.B.A., Bernard Baruch Coll., 1976. Civil service rep. Dept. Civil Service State of N.Y., Buffalo, 1968-70; sr. personnel adminstr. W. Seneca Devel. Center, Buffalo, 1970-72; personnel officer S. Beach Psychiat. Center, S.I., N.Y., 1972-75, bus. officer, 1975-76, dep. dir. adminstrn., 1976—, acting dir., 1979—; lectr. Baruch Coll.; guest lectr. N.Y. U.; chmn. com. continuing edn. Baruch-Mt. Sinai Sch. Medicine. Mem. Am. Coll. Hosp. Adminstrs., N.Y. Assn. Mental Health Adminstrs. (dir.). Home: 19 Sherman St Brooklyn NY 11215 Office: 777 Seaview Ave Staten Island NY 10305

OUNG, KIN, shipping co. exec.; s. Tun Hla Oung and Kin Kin E.; b. Nov. 10, 1923; student Rangoon U., Burma, 1943-44; m. Patricia Thaung Sein, Mar. 4, 1976; children—Kin Oo, Tun Hla. Served to lt. (s.g.) Burma R.N.V.R. and Burma Navy, 1945-52; dir. Mackinnon MacKenzie & Co. of Burma Ltd., 1952-69; v.p. Thai Mercantile Marine Ltd., Bangkok, Thailand, 1971-79; owner's rep. Ocean Shipping and Enterprises Ltd. Group, Hong Kong, 1972—. Decorated Burma Star, War medal and Star (Gt. Britain); Liberation Star, Independence Star, Good Service medal (Burma). Mem. Australian Inst. Export, Young Men's Buddhist Assn. Club: Star of Burmah Lodge and chpt. Cyrus. Home: 6050 Blvd East Apt 18 West New York NJ 07093 Office: 17 Battery Pl New York NY 10004

OUSSANI, JAMES JOHN, stapling co. exec.; b. Bklyn., Jan. 3, 1920; s. John Thomas and Clara (Tager) O.; B.M.E., Pratt Inst., 1938-42; m. Lorraine G. Tutundgy, Apr. 25, 1954; children—James J., Gregory P., Rita C. Dir. research, mfg. Supertronic Co., N.Y.C., 1943-46; sr. partner Perl-Oussani Machine Mfg. Co., N.Y.C., 1946-49; founder The Staplex Co., Bklyn., 1949, pres., 1949—; exec. dir. Lourdes Realty Corp.; dir. Junios Corp., Gregrita Realty Corp., Republic Nat. Bank N.Y., Republic N.Y. Corp. Producer air sampling equipment for radioactive fallout AEC, 1951—. Mem. Bur. Research Air Pollution Control, Pres.'s Council on Youth Opportunity, Cardinal's Com. for Edn.; trustee Ch. of Virgin Mary; founder, dir. The Oussani Found.; mem. cardinal's com. of laity, bishop's com. of laity. Recipient Blue Ribbon Mining award, Sch. Mgmt. award, Aerospace Pride Achievement award. Mem. Adminstrv. Mgmt. Soc., Office Adminstrn. Assn., Nat. Stationery and Office Equipment Assn., Office Execs. Assn., Nat. Office Machine Mfg. Assn., Nat. Office Machine Dealers Assn., Nat. Office Products Assn., Bus. Equipment Mfrs. Assn., Our Lady Perpetual Help Holy Name Soc., Knight of Holy Sepulchre. Clubs: Knights of Malta; Rotary, Salaam (N.Y.C.); Mahopac Golf (Lake Mahopac, N.Y.). Inventor automatic electric stapling machine. Patentee in field. Office: 777 5th Ave Brooklyn NY 11232

OVERCASH, REECE A., JR., financial co. exec.; b. Charlotte, N.C., June 15, 1926; s. Reece A. and Mary Louise (Daniel) O.; B.B.A., U. N.C., Chapel Hill, 1946; m. Christa Lee Anderson; children—Susan Kay, Mary Ann, Sarah Lee, Alex. With Am. Credit Corp., Charlotte, 1952-75, pres., 1970-75; pres. Assos. Corp. N. Am., Dallas, and N.Y.C., 1975—; dir. Duke Power Co., First Nat. Bank, Dallas; chmn. exec. com. Nat. Consumer Fin. Assn., 1979—; mem. N.Tex. Commn. Mem. Dallas Citizens Council; campaign chmn. Dallas United Way, 1979. Served with inf., AUS. World War II. Named Man of Yr. in Charlotte, 1972. Mem. Dallas C. of C. (dir.). Presbyterian. Clubs: Myers Park Country, City (Charlotte); Petroleum (Dallas). Office: Associates Corp NAm 1 Gulf & Western Plaza New York NY 10023*

OVERHOLSER, J. HOMER HAROLD, financial co. exec.; b. Springfield, Ohio, June 18, 1914; s. Alden Earl and Nora Liscilla (Hartman) O.; student Wittenberg Coll., 1932-34; m. Marian Lee Whelan, Nov. 10, 1939; children—James Allan, Sharyl Ann. Design engr. Nat. Supply Co., Springfield, 1935-36; devel. engr. Chrysler Airtemp Div., Dayton, Ohio, 1936-38; project engr. Vultee Aircraft Corp., Downey, Calif., 1938-39; engring. supr. Northrop Aircraft Corp., Hawthorne, Calif., 1939-43; chief engr. Hydro-Aire, Inc., Burbank, Calif., 1943-46, exec. v.p., 1946-53; v.p., dir. Skyline Catering Corp., Santa Monica, 1952-62, Poly Industries, Inc., Pacoima, Calif., 1959-60, Buckingham Palace Corp., Los Angeles, 1961-63, Wesco Industries, Inc., Burbank, 1961-63, Precision Dipb Van Nuys, Calif., 1961-67, Nat. Post-Pak Systems, Hollywood, 1962-63, Woodlake Realty, Inc., Woodlan 1962—, Intercontinental Engring. and Mfg. Corp., Tex., 1963-64, E.M.C. Instrumentation, Inc., Van N 66, S.O.M. Corp., Woodland Hills, 1964—; asst. gen. mgr. Pacific div. Bendix Corp., N. Hollywood, 1953-58; pres., chmn. bd. Hydrodyne Corp., N. Hollywood, 1953-58, Solar Systems, Inc., N. Hollywood, 1961-62, Woodland Savs. & Loan, Woodland Hills, 1961-63, Aero Spacelines, Inc., Van Nuys, 1963-65, Aqua Systems, Inc., N. Hollywood, 1968-70, Sierra Pacific Fin. Corp., Los Angeles, 1969-70, Royal Pacific Fin. Corp., Los Angeles, 1970—, Hotel Devel. Corp., Santa Ana, 1970—, Dynamatics Corp., Burbank, 1960-61; exec. v.p., dir. U.S. Systems, Inc., Los Angeles, 1961-62; pres. Corp. Service, Inc., Beverly Hills, 1961-63, Am. Investment Co., N. Hollywood, 1962-63, Jaco Mgmt. Corp., Tarzana, 1963-69; exec v.p., dir. Am. Hydrocarbon Corp., Dallas, 1963-64, Brush-Away Corp., 1976-77; pres., dir. Basic Industries, Compton, Calif., 1963-64, Calif. Time Airlines, Burbank, 1965-66, Palm Springs Mobile Country Club, Palm Springs, 1967-70; dir. Independence Bank, Canoga Park, 1963—; chmn. bd. Clerke Technicorp., Santa Monica, Clerke Recreation Corp., Santa Monica, Sierra Western Life Ins. Co. Calif., Los Angeles, Sierra Western Life Ins. Co. Ariz., Phoenix, J.Y.S. Corp., Honolulu, Royal Catfish Industries, Inc., Twin Falls, Internat. Houseboat and Recreation, Inc., Los Angeles, Western Resources, Inc., Denver, Sierra Pacific Devel. Corp., Honolulu, Georgetown Assos., Inc., Denver, So. Calif. Hotel Corp.; chmn. bd., sec. Varadyne, Inc., Santa Monica, 1966-69; sec., dir. Interdyne, Inc., Santa Monica, 1967-70; chmn. bd., v.p. Zolomatics, Inc., Hollywood, 1967-70; sec., dir. Microwave Sensor Systems, Inc., Downey, Calif., 1968-70; chmn. bd., dir. United Optical Systems, Inc., Oxnard, Calif., 1968-70; sec., dir. chmn. fin. com. Varadyne Industries, Inc., Santa Monica, 1969—; chmn. bd., pres. Highland Assos., Inc., Alphatec Internat. Inc., 1977—, Nat. Golf Products, Inc., 1977—; chmn. bd., exec. v.p. Nat. Golf Media, Inc., 1977—, Lyricard Corp. Am., 1978—; partner O.K. Enterprises, Tarzana, 1960—, Southridge Devel. Co., Palm Springs, 1961-70, Ratran, Ltd., Encino, 1963-67, Am. Investment Co., N. Hollywood, 1962-64, H & O Co., Fullerton, 1964—, Hotel Devel. Co., Santa Ana, 1970—, sec., chmn. fin. com., dir. Varadyne Industries, Inc., 1969—; pres. Brush Away Vending Corp., 1976—. Industry chmn. Los Angeles County March of Dimes, 1954-55; mem. nat. voter adv. bd. Am. Security Council, 1970—. Recipient Freedom Season Pioneer award Woodland Hills C. of C., 1963, Million Miler award United Airlines, 1959; registered profl. engr., Calif. Mem. Inst. Aero Scis., Am. Ordnance Assn., ASME, AIM, Am. Helicopter Soc., Am. Soc. Air Affairs, Air Force Assn., Assn. U.S. Army, Soc. Automotive Engrs. (com. 1946-51), Internat. Platform Assn., North Hollywood, Los Angeles (com. 1955-56), Hollywood chambers commerce, San Fernando Wine and Food Soc. (chmn. bd. 1969-70). Republican. Mem. Ch. of God. Clubs: Masons (32 deg.), Shriners; Lakeside Golf (Toluca Lake, Calif.); Deauville Golf (Tarzana); Woodland Hills Shrine (Woodland Hills). Patentee in field. Home: 4961 Palomar Dr Tarzana CA 91356 Office: 5955 DeSoto Ave Suite 252 Woodland Hills CA 91367

OVERS, RONALD ROLAND, inventor, mfg. co. exec.; b. Buffalo, Nov. 18, 1931; s. Charles F. and Beatrice O.; student St. Bonaventure U., 1951, U. Buffalo, 1953; m. Barbara Quane, 1969; children—April, Cheryl, Randall, Lauren, Ronald Roland, Gordon, Ingrid, Audrey. Dist. sales mgr. J.C. Virden Co., Cleve., 1954-58; pres. Overs Assos. Inc., Williamsville, N.Y., 1958—; pres. Electro Marine Systems, Inc., East Amherst, N.Y., 1970—, Electro Marine Systems Internat., Inc., East Amherst, 1973—; v.p. Overs, Ltd., Toronto, Ont., Can., 1974—; pres. Emsco Electronics, Inc., Buffalo, 1973—; cons. Hoovercraft Bell Aerospace, 1976 and 1980 Olympics. Recipient President's award J.C. Virden Co., 1956, 57. Mem. IEEE, Boating Industry Assn., Internat. Yacht Racing Assn., Buffalo Zool. Soc., Fox Hunt Farms Civic Assn., Aircraft Owners and Pilots Assn., Exptl. Aircraft Assn. Clubs: Buffalo Yacht, Buffalo Canoe, Rolls Royce Owners, Smithsonian Instn. Patentee marine instruments; designer cardiac med. equipment. Home: 96 Fox Hunt Ln East Amherst NY 14051 also Pompano Beach, Fla.

OVERSTREET, JAMES WILTON, mfg. co. exec.; b. Beckville, Tex., Oct. 10, 1936; s. Roy Wilton and Lydia K. Overstreet; B.B.A., North Tex. State U., 1958; m. Bronwyn Coon, June 21, 1975. Auditor, loan officer Agts. Acceptance Corp., Dallas, 1962-66; adminstr. Collins Radio Co., Dallas, 1966-70; acctg. mgr. UTL Corp., Dallas, 1970-75; controller Optic-Electronic Corp., Dallas, 1975—; cons. on acctg. and tax matters, 1974—. Home: 2920 Shalimar Dr Plano TX 75023 Office: 11477 Pagemill Rd Dallas TX 75243

OVERSTREET, WARREN LUCK, mfg. co. exec.; b. Roanoke, Va., July 18, 1922; s. James Crowder and Emma (Patton) O.; B.S. in Elec. Engring., Va. Mil. Inst., 1947; m. Evelyn Fariss, May 23, 1943; children—James Thomas, Joyce Marie. Electrician, Jefferson Electric Co., Roanoke, 1941-42; asst. to power distbn. mgr. Appalachian Electric Power Co., Roanoke, 1942-43; test engr. Gen. Electric Co., Lynn, Mass., 1947-49, mfg. trainee, Lynn, 1949-50, machine shop foreman, 1950-52, salesman, 1950-58, product planner, Lynchburg, Va., 1958-63, product mgr., Auburn, N.Y., 1964-68, mktg. mgr. refractory metals products dept., Cleve., 1968-78, mgr. sales programs refactory metals products dept., 1978—. Served to lt. U.S. Army, 1943-47. Clubs: Masons, Shriners. Home: 7201 Taft St Mentor OH 44060 Office: 21800 Tungsten Rd Cleveland OH 44117

OVERTON, GEORGE W., lawyer; b. Hinsdale, Ill., Jan. 25, 1918; s. George Washington and Florence Mary (Darlington) O.; A.B., Harvard, 1940; J.D., U. Chgo., 1946; m. Jane Vincent Harper, Sept. 1, 1941; children—Samuel Harper, Peter Darlington, Ann Vincent. Admitted to Ill. bar, 1947; prin. Overton, Schwartz & Fritts Ltd. Chmn., Ill. Inst. Continuing Legal Edn., dir., 1979-80; bd. dirs. Chgo. Bar Found.; pres. Open Lands Project. Mem. Am., Ill., Chgo. bar assns., Assn. Bar City N.Y. Home: 5648 S Dorchester St Chicago IL 60637 Office: 30 N LaSalle St Chicago IL 60603

OVERTON, JOSEPH ALLEN, JR., mining exec.; b. Parkersburg, W.Va., Apr. 17, 1921; s. Joseph Allen and Edith (Wharton) O.; J.D., Washington and Lee U., 1946; m. Bette Crosswhite, May 15, 1943; children—Joseph Allen III, Rebecca A., Mallory E. Admitted to W.Va. bar, 1947; mem. firm Handlan, Overton & Earley, Parkersburg, 1949-54; spl. asst. to gen. counsel Dept. Commerce, 1955-56, dep. gen. counsel, 1956-59; mem. U.S. Tariff Commn., 1959-62, vice chmn., 1959-60; adminstrv. v.p. Am. Mining Congress, Washington, 1962, exec. v.p., 1963-71, pres., 1972—, pub. Mining Congress Jour., 1963—. Prin. adviser fgn. trade matters U.S. del. negotiations GATT. Mem. W.Va. Legislature, 1948-50. Served to 1st lt. USAAF, 1941-46. Mem. Am., W.Va., Fed. bar assns., Phi Kappa Psi. Episcopalian. Elk. Home: 4677 N Dittmar Rd Arlington VA 22207 Office: 1920 N St NW Washington DC 20036

OVERTON, ROSILYN GAY HOFFMAN, stockbroker, economist; b. Corsicana, Tex., July 10, 1942; d. Billy Clarence and Ima Elise (Gay) Hoffman; B.S. in Math., Wright State U., Dayton, Ohio, 1972, M.S. in Applied Econs. (fellow), 1973; postgrad. N.Y. U. Grad. Sch. Bus., 1974—; m. Aaron Lewis Overton, Jr., July 2, 1960 (div. Mar. 1975); children—Aaron Lewis III, Adam Jerome. Research analyst Nat. Security Agy., Dept. Def., 1962-67; bus. reporter Dayton Jour.-Herald, 1973-74; economist First Nat. City Bank, N.Y.C., 1974, A.T. & T. Co., 1974-75; broker Merrill Lynch, N.Y.C., 1975-80; asst. v.p. E.F. Hutton & Co., N.Y.C., 1980—; adj. faculty Marymount Manhattan Coll., 1977—. Mem. N.Y.C. Mayor's Commn. on Status of Women. Named Businesswoman of Yr., N.Y.C., 1976. Mem. Met. Econ. Assn., Nat., N.Y. assns. bus. economists, Nat. Fedn. Bus. and Profl. Women, Nat. Economists Club, Women's Econ. Roundtable, Gotham Bus. and Profl. Womens Club (pres.), Wright State U. Alumni Assn. (dir.), Mensa. Methodist. Author: (with John Treacy) Measuring Externalities of Strip Coal Mining via Property Tax Assessment, 1973; editor: Monthly Economic Letter, First Nat. City Bank, 1974; contbr. articles to profl. jours. Home: 115 E 9th St New York NY 10003 Office: 605 3d Ave New York NY 10016

OVERTON, WILLIAM WARD, JR., former banker; b. Kansas City, Kans., Apr. 30, 1897; s. William Ward and Ella Mae (Barnes) O.; student Kansas City U., Tex. U.; m. Evelyn Lucas, June 10, 1924 (dec.); children—Nancy (Mrs. Mark Lemmon), William T. (dec.), Thomas N. Dir. Tex. Bank & Trust Co. (name formerly 1st City Bank of Dallas), 1936—, chmn. bd., 1947-71, pres., 1961-65, chmn. exec. com., 1971—; past pres., exec. com. Downtown Improvement & Property Owners Assn., Inc.; dir., mem. finance com. Southland Corp., 1966-67; hon. dir. Southwestern Life Ins. Co.; dir. Dallas Tex. Corp. Past mem. adv. bd. Internat. Mgmt. Congress; nat. membership chmn. A.R.C., 1954, vice chmn. nat. fund, 1963, chmn. nat. conv., 1967, past mem. internat. com., del. conf. Internat. Socs., New Delhi, India, hon. life dir. Dallas chpt.; council mem.-at-large Boy Scouts Am.; past nat. chmn. Nat. Bible Week, Layman's Nat. Com., 1962, bd. dirs., 1964-67, mem. council, 1967; mem. finance com. Com. for Econ. Devel. 1965-66; adv. com. Bus. Execs. Research Com.; mem. nat. council Action, Inc.; founding mem. chancellor's council U. Tex., 1966-67; active YMCA, Dallas Baptist U., U. Dallas, Boys Club Dallas, Children's Med. Center, Council Social Agys. Dallas, numerous others; v.p., past dir. Greater Dallas Planning Council; chmn. regional adv. council, past trustee, past chmn. bd., life councillor Nat. Conf. Bd.; bd. dirs., treas. Dallas Theater Center; mem. bd. So. Meth. U. Bd. Devel.; bd. govs. Dallas Found.; pres., past chmn. bd. Caruth Meml. Rehab. Inst.; bd. dirs. Tex. Law Enforcement Found., 1967, Dallas Crime Commn., Citizens Traffic Commn., United Fund and Council, Met. Opera, Dallas Citizens Council, Dallas Mus. Contemporary Arts, State Fair Tex.; trustee St. Paul's Hosp., Southwestern Med. Found.; trustee, trustee of exec. com. Tex. Research Found.; bd. govs. Dallas Found. Served with USN, World War I. Recipient Distinguished Service Plaque, Dallas County chpt. A.R.C.; Kudos Coll. award, Dallas. Mem. Tex. (dir.), Dallas (trustee) hist. socs., Dallas Zool. Soc. (dir.). Home: 4830 Cedar Springs Dallas TX 75219

OVERTURF, CARROLL GARY, roller skating industry exec.; b. Lucas County, Iowa, June 7, 1935; s. Delmer V. and Mamie B. (Doll) O.; student U. Iowa, 1955; B.S. in Bus. Adminstrn., Mo. State U., 1957; postgrad. N.Y. Inst. Fin., 1962, Am. Mgmt. Assn., 1971-72, U. Ill., 1973; m. Judith Brown, Apr. 21, 1961; children—Lisa, Natalie, Todd. Stock broker Quail & Co., 1961-62; sales and office mgr. Squibb, 1962-66; personnel devel. ofcl. Ill. Power Co., Decatur, 1967-76; pres., owner Great Skate, Inc., Decatur, 1974—, Disco Skate, Inc., 1977—, Sportmaster, Inc., Decatur, 1976—; owner, operator Skelly Skate Co., Inc., 1980—. Chmn. bd. Jefferson County United Way, 1970-71; chmn. Small Bus. Council, 1979-80; mem. Decatur Planning Commn., 1980—; deacon Christian Ch. Served to 1st lt. USMC, 1969-72. Mem. Roller Skating Rink Operators Assn., Roller Skating Mfrs. Assn., Decatur C. of C. (dir.). Contbr., cons.: The Complete Book of Roller Skating, 1979; Roller Disco, 1979; contbr. articles to trade publs. Inventor Discoskate and other products in field. Home: 4035 Grace's Ln Decatur IL 62621 Office: 625 W Imboden Dr Decatur IL 62525

OVERTURF, WILLIAM HOWARD, JR., financial cons. co. exec.; b. St. Louis, July 18, 1932; s. William Howard and Ethel Bert (Hulen) O.; A.B., Washington U., St. Louis, 1953, M.B.A., 1961; m. Jeanette Marie Fahnster, Oct. 15, 1960; children—William H. III, Susan D., Christopher M. Mem. sales mgmt. staff NCR, St. Louis, 1956-60, Honeywell EDP, St. Louis, 1960-66; bus. analyst Alex Proudfoot Co., Chgo., 1966-72; pres., chief exec. officer Janbe & Assos., St. Louis, 1972—. Dist. officer St. Louis area council Boy Scouts Am., 1974—; sustaining mem. Republican Nat. Com. Served to 1st lt. U.S. Army, 1953-56. Decorated Order of Arrow, Boy Scouts Am. Fellow Am. Bus. Analysts and Consultants; mem. Am. Security Council (nat. adv. bd.), Smithsonian Assos., Nat. Assn. Life Underwriters, Mo. Assn. Life Underwriters, St. Louis Life Underwriters Assn. Office: Box 721 Fenton Plaza Fenton MO 63026

OWADES, JOSEPH LAWRENCE, chemist; b. N.Y.C., July 9, 1919; s. Samuel Abraham and Gussie (Horn) O.; B.S., CCNY, 1939; M.S., Poly. Inst. N.Y., 1944, Ph.D., 1950; m. Ruth Markowitz, Sept. 7, 1969. Chemist, Standard Brands, N.Y.C., 1948-50; chief chemist Schwarz Labs., Mt. Vernon, N.Y., 1950-59; v.p., tech. dir. Rheingold Breweries, N.Y.C., 1959-67; tech. coordinator Anheuser-Busch, St. Louis, 1968-70; v.p., tech. dir. Carling Brewing Co., Waltham, Mass., 1970-74; dir., cons. Center for Brewing Studies, Quincy, Mass., 1974—. Mem. Master Brewers Assn. Am., Am. Soc. Brewing Chemists, Inst. Food Technologists, Am. Soc. Enologists, N.Y. Acad. Sci., Inst. of Brewing (London). Contbr. numerous articles to profl. jours.; patentee in field. Home: 1575 Tremont St Boston MA 02120 Office: 5 Hayward St Quincy MA 02171

OWEN, ARCHIBALD ALEXANDER, mfg. co. exec.; b. Nashville, Oct. 4, 1932; s. Archibald Alexander and Elizabeth Fairchild (Spyker) O.; B.S., in Chem. Engring., Bucknell U., 1954; M.B.A., George Washington U., 1968; m. Glenn Allen Brown, Dec. 30, 1958; children—Archibald Alexander, Carter Brown, Henry Spyker. With Celanese Corp., 1959-71, prodn. mgr., Lanaken, Belgium, 1963-65, devel. supt., Rock Hill, S.C., 1966-71; mgr. mfg. Gen. Electric Co., Selkirk, N.Y., 1971-73, Pittsfield, Mass., 1973-74; mgr. mfg. FMC Corp., Parkersburg, W. Va., 1974-75, dir. mfg. film, Phila., 1975-78;

plant mgr. Kurz-Hastings, 1979—; instr. marine engring. U.S. Naval Acad., Annapolis, 1957-59. Served with USN, 1954-59. Mem. Am. Inst. Chem. Engring (sec. Carolinas sect. 1967-68), Toastmasters Internat. (pres. local chpt. 1969-70, regional gov., 1970-71, named Man of Year S.C., 1970), Bucknell Engring. Alumni Assn. (dir. 1971—, pres. 1977—). Republican. Presbyterian. Home: 225 Mystic Ln Media PA 19063 Office: Datton Rd Philadelphia PA 19154

OWEN, H. MARTYN, lawyer; b. Decatur, Ill., Oct. 23, 1929; s. Honore Martyn and Virginia (Hunt) O.; grad. Phillips Exeter Acad., 1947; A.B., Princeton, 1951; LL.B., Harvard, 1954; m. Candace Catlin Benjamin, June 21, 1952; children—Leslie Woodruff, Peter Hunt, Douglas Parsons. Admitted to Conn. bar, 1954; asso. with firm Shipman & Goodwin, Hartford, 1958—, partner, 1961—. Dir. Cushman Industries, Inc. Mem. Simsbury Zoning Bd. Appeals, 1961-67, Simsbury Zoning Commn., 1967-79; sec. Capitol Region Planning Agy., 1965-66; dir. Symphony Soc. Greater Hartford, 1967-73. Trustee Renbrook Sch., W. Hartford, Conn., 1963-72, treas., 1964-68, pres., 1968-72, hon. life trustee, 1972—; trustee Simsbury Free Library, Hartford Grammar Sch., Corp. Inst. Living, Hartford. Served to lt. with Supply Corps, USNR, 1954-57. Clubs: Hartford; Princeton (N.Y.C.); Ivy (Princeton, N.J.). Republican. Episcopalian. Home: 44 Pinnacle Mountain Rd Simsbury CT 06070 Office: 799 Main St Hartford CT 06103

OWEN, JOHN LAVERTY, mfg. co. exec.; b. Mayfield, Ky., July 28, 1923; s. John Clarence and Lydia (Laverty) O.; B.A. magna cum laude, Westminster (Mo.) Coll., 1944; postgrad. Purdue U., 1945; M.S. in Psychology, Pa. State U., 1951; m. Marjory Clara Wallace, June 29, 1946; children—John Wallace, David William, Jeffrey Daniel. With Hamilton Watch Co., Lancaster, Pa., 1946—, staff personnel services dir., 1963-70, corporate employee relations dir. HMW Industries, Inc., 1970-77, dir. human resources, 1977-79; v.p. human resources and public relations Hamilton Tech., Inc., 1980—. Bd. dirs. Lancaster County chpt. United Way, to 1978, Lancaster chpt. Nat. Urban League. Licensed psychologist, Pa. Mem. Am., Eastern, Pa. psychol. assns., Am. Mgmt. Assn., Am. Soc. for Personnel Adminstrn. (accredited exec.), Am. Soc. Tng. and Devel., Lancaster Assn. Commerce and Industry, Omicron Delta Kappa, Psi Chi, Phi Kappa Phi, Delta Tau Delta. Republican. Presbyn. Home: 948 Pleasure Rd Lancaster PA 17601 Office: PO Box 4787 Lancaster PA 17604

OWEN, NATHAN RICHARD, mfg. co. exec.; b. Burnt Hills, N.Y., May 3, 1919; s. George H. and Mildred T. (Sharpley) O.; B.M.E., Mass. Inst. Tech., 1941, M.S., 1942; m. Janet M. Smith, Sept. 26, 1942; children—Patricia O. Smith, David G., Lorinda L. With Chase Brass and Copper Co., 1946-47; with J. H. Whitney & Co., N.Y.C., 1947-62, partner, 1951-62; dir. Marine Midland Banks, Gen. Reins. Corp., Gt. No. Nekoosa Corp.; chmn. bd. Gen. Signal Corp., 1962—. Trustee Clarkson Coll., Technoserve, Inc. Served with USNR, 1942-46. Clubs: Bd. Room, Univ., River (N.Y.C.); Landmark, Indian Harbor Yacht, Greenwich Country. Home: 680 Steamboat Rd Greenwich CT 06830 Office: High Ridge Park Stamford CT 06904

OWEN, STEPHEN COOKE, apparel co. exec.; b. Providence, June 6, 1933; s. Stephen Cooke and Katherine Llewelyn (Jones) O.; B.A., U. N.C., 1956; m. Evelyn Diane Bates, Jan. 17, 1958; children—Evelyn, Stephen, Ted. Salesman Beacon Mfg. Co., N.Y.C., 1957-62, sales mgr., 1962-68, v.p. mktg., 1968-71; sr. corp. planning asso. Nat. Distillers, N.Y.C., 1971-72; gen. mgr. Beacon Mfg. Co. div. Nat. Distillers, 1972-74; group pres. Genesco Inc., N.Y.C., 1974-78, v.p. pub. affairs and govt. relations, 1978—; dir. Partners Oil Co., Houston, Eagle Growth Fund, N.Y.C., Sirocco Co., N.Y.C. Served with USCGR, 1956-57. Republican. Episcopalian. Club: Rockaway Hunting (Lawrence, N.Y.). Home: 19 E 72d St New York NY 10021

OWEN, THOMAS LLEWELLYN, investment exec.; b. Patchogue, N.Y., June 24, 1928; s. Griffith Robert and Jeanette Roberts (Hatfield) O.; A.B. in Econs., Coll. William and Mary, 1951; postgrad. Columbia U., 1952, N.Y. Inst. Fin., 1960-62; M.B.A., N.Y. U., 1966. Exec. trainee Shell Oil Co., N.Y.C. and Indpls., 1951-59, supr., 1958-59; petroleum and chem. investment analyst Paine, Webber, Jackson & Curtis, N.Y.C., 1959-62; sr. oil investment analyst DuPont Investment Interests, Wilmington, Del., N.Y.C., 1962-66, asst. dir. research, 1964-66; with Nat. Securities & Research Corp., N.Y.C., 1966-75, v.p., sr. investment officer, mem. policy, investment coms., 1969-75; investment exec., v.p., portfolio mgr. F. Eberstadt & Co. and Eberstadt Asset Mgmt., Inc., N.Y.C., 1975—, mem. policy com., 1979—. Mem. N.Y. Soc. Security Analysts, Oil Analysts Group N.Y., Am. Econ. Assn., Investment Assn. N.Y., Am. Petroleum Inst., Nat. Assn. Petroleum Investment Analysts, Internat. Assn. Energy Economists. Contbr. chpt. on oil and gas industries to Financial Analysts Handbook, 1975. Home: 251 E 32d St New York NY 10016 Office: Eberstadt Asset Mgmt Inc 61 Broadway New York NY 10006

OWENS, HARRY STEPHEN, financial exec.; b. Bridgeton, N.J., Jan. 10, 1949; s. Harry Lemuel and Dorothy Eleanor (Buzby) O.; B.S. in Acctg., Villanova U., 1970; m. Mary Jo Klug, Aug. 30, 1969; children—David E., Douglas E. Jr. acct. Touche Ross & Co., Phila., 1970-71, sr. acct., 1971-74; dir. fin. Thomas Jefferson U. Hosp., Phila., 1979—; condr. seminars on health care fin. C.P.A. Mem. Hosp. Fin. Mgmt. Assn., Am. Inst. C.P.A.'s, Pa. Inst. C.P.A.'s, Am. Hosp. Assn. Home: 28 Doncaster Ct Cherry Hill NJ 08003 Office: 11th and Walnut Sts Philadelphia PA 19107

OWENS, HUGH FRANKLIN, govt. ofcl.; b. Muskogee, Okla., Oct. 15, 1909; s. James Francis and Elizabeth (Turner) O.; A.B., U. Ill., 1931; LL.B., U. Okla., 1934; m. Louise Simon, Dec. 27, 1934; 1 dau., Julie. Admitted to Ill. Bar, 1934, Okla. bar, 1934, Tex. bar, 1952, also U.S. Supreme Ct. bar; asso. mem. firm Cummins, Hagenah & Flynn, Chgo., 1934-36, Rainey, Flynn, Green & Anderson, Oklahoma City, 1936-48; partner firm Hervey May & Owens, Oklahoma City, 1948-51; div. atty. Superior Oil Co., Midland, Tex., 1951-53; gen. counsel Nat. Asso. Petroleum Co., Tulsa, 1953; pvt. practice, Oklahoma City, 1953-59; adminstr. Okla. Securities Commn., 1959-64; commr. SEC, Washington, 1964-73, acting chmn., 1971; chmn. Securities Investor Protection Corp., Washington, 1973—, also dir.; mem. faculty Oklahoma City U. Law Sch., 1957-64. Bd. dirs. Salvation Army, Oklahoma City Community Fund, 1938-41. Served to lt. comdr. USNR, World War II; PTO. Mem. Okla. Bar Assn., Kans. Bar Assn. (hon.), U.S. Jr. Jaycees (v.p. 1940-41, dir.), Oklahoma City C. of C. (dir. 1938-40), Nat. Assn. R.R. and Utility Commrs. (exec. com. 1964-73), Phi Delta Phi, Sigma Chi. Democrat. Roman Catholic. Clubs: Met., Chevy Chase (Washington); Men's Dinner (Oklahoma City). Office: 900 17th St NW Washington DC 20006

OWENS, JOHN CARROLL, accountant; b. Lexington, Ky., Mar. 28, 1927; s. John Deward and Grace Louise (Creed) O.; B.S. in Commerce, U. Ky., 1950; m. Mary Roberts Crafton, Apr. 24, 1953; children—John Robert, Mary Creed, Martha Carol. Accountant, John D. Owens, Lexington, 1950-53; partner Owens & Owens, Lexington, 1953-60, Owens, Owens & Hisle, Lexington, 1960-64; mng. partner Owens, Potter & Hisle, Lexington, 1964-69; pres. Dynafacts, Inc., 1969-71; mgmt. cons., 1971-73; v.p. fin. Nat. Mines Corp., Lexington, 1973-78; partner Owens & Co., C.P.A.'s, 1978—; dir. Bank of Lexington. Bd. dirs. United Way of Bluegrass, 1975-77, U. Ky. Alumni Bd., 1974-80. Served with USAAF, 1945-46. C.P.A., Ky.; multi-engine instrument rated pilot. Mem. Ky. Soc. C.P.A.'s (past dir.), Am. Inst. C.P.A.'s, Ky. Coal Assn., So. Golf Assn. (treas. 1977—), U. Ky. Alumni Assn. (pres. 1979). Methodist. Clubs: Lexington Country, Idle Hour Country, Lafayette, Lexington Rotary (treas. 1972-75). Ky. state golf champion, 1963, 64; quarterfinalist U.S. Amateur Golf Championship, 1963, Brit. Amateur Golf Championship, 1974. Home: 116 Chinoe Rd Lexington KY 40502 Office: 101 E Vine St Suite 302 Lexington KY 40507

OWENS, JOHN FRANKLIN, health care adminstr., govt. ofcl.; b. Slatington, Pa., May 19, 1935; s. William and Goldie Irene (Zerfass) O.; student Orange County Community Coll., 1954-55; Pa. State Extension, 1964, U. Pa., 1967; grad. Middletown State Hosp. Sch. Nursing, 1957; m. Shirley Ann Spade, June 15, 1956; children—Terri Ann, Rick Todd. Nursing supr., instr. Easton (Pa.) Hosp., 1961-65, dir. in-service edn., 1963-65; dir. services Northampton County Homemaker Service, Bethlehem, Pa., 1965-67; exec. dir. Homemaker-Home Health Aide Services, Bucks County, Inc., Doylestown, Pa., 1967-72; zone mgr. So. N.J., Upjohn Healthcare Services, Inc., Kalamazoo, 1972-73, govt. adminstr. Conn., Del., Md., Mass., Maine, Mich., N.H., N.Y., Pa., R.I., Vt., Va., W.Va., N.J., and Washington, 1973-79, Fla. mgr., 1979—; cons. to various nursing homes, 1961-67; chmn. profl. advisory com. Bucks County Dept. Pub. Health, Pa., 1970-72; chmn. by-laws com. Greater Delaware Valley Regional Med. Program, 1970-72. Mgr. Little League Baseball, Doylestown, Pa., 1968-72; mem. advancement com. Lenape council Boy Scouts Am., 1969-72; bd. dirs. Central Bucks YMCA, 1969-72, pres. 1971-72. Served with U.S. Amry, 1953-54. Recipient Upjohn Spl. Schievement award, 1975. Mem. Am. Pub. Health Assn., Am., N.J. State nurses assns., Nat. Council for Homemaker-Home Health Aide Services, Doylestown Area Jaycees (pres. 1970-71, Key Man award 1969, named Outstanding Young Man 1970-71). Club: Warriors Hockey (mgr. 1974-78). Author: Pennsylvania Training Guide for Homemaker-Home Health Aides, 1972. Office: 3118 Gulf-to-Bay Blvd Suite 300 Clearwater FL

OWENS, ROBERT MASTERSON, JR., fin. co. exec., economist; b. Bklyn., Jan. 20, 1943; s. Robert M. and Marjory (Sheehan) O.; student N.Y. U., 1962-67, 69-73. Sales rep. Dow Jones News Service, N.Y.C., 1969-71; Eastern mgr. SRI Internat. Co., N.Y.C., 1971-73; dir. mktg. Chase Econometrics Assos. Inc., N.Y.C., 1973-77; dir. research mktg. Morgan Stanley & Co. Inc., N.Y.C., 1977—. Served with U.S. Army, 1967-68. Decorated Bronze Star. Democrat. Roman Catholic. Home: 103 W 69th St New York NY 10023 Office: Morgan Stanley & Co Inc 1251 Ave of Americas New York NY 10020

OWENS, WILLIAM ROBERT, mfg. co. ofcl.; b. Syracuse, N.Y., May 12, 1932; s. William James and Florence Elizabeth (Haar) O.; B.B.A., Lemoyne Coll., 1953; grad. student Syracuse U., 1957-60; m. Lois Ruth Gumprecht, Apr. 7, 1956; children—William Michael, Robert Joseph, Steven Patrick. Service technician Carrier Corp., Syracuse, 1953, Porter-Cable Power Tool Co. div. Rockwell Mfg. Co., Syracuse, 1955-61; mgr. corp. systems devel. Crouse-Hinds Co., Syracuse, 1961-80, dir. corp. mgmt. systems, 1980—; instr. Sair Aviation Flight Sch., Syracuse 1975—; instr. systems and data processing Auburn (N.Y.) Community Coll., 1967—, cons. data processing adv. com., 1969-75; guest lectr. Syracuse U. Sch. Mgmt., 1977. Served with U.S. Army, 1953-55. Recipient Merit award Assn. Systems Mgmt., 1970, Nat. Achievement award, 1971; certified flight and ground sch. instr., N.Y. Mem. Assn. Systems Mgmt. (pres. Central N.Y. chpt. 1968-69), CAP (asst. squadron comdr. 1975-76), Central N.Y. Pilots Assn. (pres. 1973-74), Syracuse Systems Execs. Assn. (co-founder 1971). Author booklet on aviation, 1978. Home: 4062 Pawnee Dr Liverpool NY 13088 Office: c/o Crouse-Hinds Co Wolf at 7th N St Syracuse NY 13201

OWINGS, MALCOLM WILLIAM, packaging co. exec.; b. Cin., Feb. 5, 1925; s. William Malcolm and Margaret (Benvie) O.; B.S. in Bus. Adminstrn., Miami U., Oxford, Ohio, 1950, LL.D., 1976; m. Margie M. Gehlker, Sept. 4, 1948; children—Lynn A., Sandra S., Wendy K., Cheryl M. With Continental Can Co., 1950—, sales rep., Milw., 1950-58, dist. sales mgr., Mpls., 1959-61, Milw., 1963-66, div. product sales mgr., Chgo., 1961-63, asst. gen. mgr. sales, Chgo., 1966-67, gen. mgr. sales, Chgo., 1967-69, gen. mgr. So. metal div., Altanta, 1969-71, v.p., gen. mgr. gen. packaging div., Chgo., 1971-73, v.p., gen. mgr. beverage div., 1973-76; v.p. pub. affairs Continental Can Co. U.S.A., 1976—; dir. Mako-Inc.; adviser to Am. del. Internat. Tin Council, 1978—. Dean's asso., exec. in residence Miami U. Sch. Bus., 1973. Village trustee Thiensville, Wis., 1956-59; mem. alumni council Miami U., 1958-65, pres.'s devel. council, 1965—; bd. dirs. Barrington Area Devel. Council, 1974—, Sales Mgmt. Execs. Grad. Sch., Am. Soc. for Environ. Edn., 1976—, Keep Am. Beautiful, 1980-81. Served with USNR, 1942-44; N. Africa, ETO. Recipient certificate of meritorious service Miami U., 1967, named Alumnus of Yr., 1970; 1st Am. recipient Order of Apteryx, Earth Awareness Found., 1971. Mem. Ill. C. of C. (dir. 1976—), Miami U. Alumni Assn. (nat. pres. 1964-65), Omicron Delta Kappa, Sigma Chi, Delta Sigma Pi. Clubs: Cherokee Town and Country (Atlanta); Barrington (Ill.) Hills Country; Pinehurst Country. Home: 115 Old Oak Dr Barrington IL 60010 Office: O'Hare Plaza Chicago IL 60631

OWOROETOP, JOSEPH DAVIES, investment co. exec.: b. Ikot-Obon, Nigeria, July 15, 1943; s. Davies and Jannie (Akpan) O.; came to U.S., 1972, naturalized, 1976; A.A., Wayne County Community Coll., 1975; B.B.A., Walsh Coll., Troy, Mich., 1977; m. Jacqueline Falconer, Dec. 20, 1975; children—Ime, Imo Jawara. Subscription sec., then hon. sec. Ikoi Club, Lagos, Nigeria, 1964-70; with Simpson-Sears Ltd., Toronto, Can., 1971-72, Chrysler Corp., Detroit, 1973-77; pres. Investment Funding Internat., Detroit, 1978—, also dir.; trader, dir. Global Enterprises Co. Ltd., Detroit, 1978—. Mem. Internat. Traders Assn., Detroit Bus. and Civic League, Cross River State in Am. Assn., Orgn. Nigerian Citizens in U.S.A. Unitarian. Address: 4635 Beaconsfield Ave Detroit MI 48224

OXFORD, RICHARD ORRVILLE, bus. exec.; b. El Paso, Nov. 19, 1937; s. Orrville O. and Elizabeth (Gladney) O.; B.S., U. So. Calif., 1959, M.B.A., 1962; m. Isabel M. Oxford, Dec. 29, 1962; children—Sidney Richard, Sandra Isabel. Exec. trainee Western Electric Co., Los Angeles, 1959-61; cons. Kintner Assos., Los Angeles, 1962-64, McKinsey & Co., Los Angeles, 1966-68; project leader Transam. Corp., 1964-66; pres. Dial Industries, Inc., Los Angeles, 1968—; v.p., dir. Dial Internat.; dir. Commerce Assos. Active YMCA, pres. Downtown Y's Men's Club, 1967. Mem. Am. Mktg. Assn., U. So. Calif. M.B.A. Assn. (pres. 1969, chmn. 1976), Beta Gamma Sigma, Phi Kappa Phi, Alpha Kappa Psi, Alpha Tau Omega. Democrat. Presbyn. Toastmaster (pres.). Club: Jonathan. Home: 2248 N New Hampshire Ave Los Angeles CA 90027 Office: 1538 Esperanza St Los Angeles CA 90023

OXNER, EDWIN STORY, semicondr. mfg. co. exec.; b. Chgo., Mar. 28, 1928; s. Edwin Kaulbach and Sarah Ellen (Story) O.; B.S. in Elec. Engring., Tri-State Coll., 1948; diploma Moody Bible Inst., 1959; m. Carol Ann Rothenberg, Jan. 14, 1950; children—Cynthia Oxner Peck, Sheila Oxner Johnston, Todd, Peter. Employee, U.S. Civil Service, 1948-52; sr. research engr. Trans-Sonics, Inc., 1952-54; sr. engr. Hughes Aircraft Co., 1954-56; mem. tech. staff Armour Research Found., 1956-59, Fairchild Semiconductor, 1963-64; engring. supr. Varian Assos., 1959-63; field engring. mgr. Melabs, Palo Alto, Calif., 1964-69; application mgr. Intradyne Systems Co., Sunnyvale, Calif., 1969-70; with Siliconix Inc., Santa Clara, Calif., 1970—, mgr. spl. projects engring., 1976—; tech. adv. Am. Radio Relay League, 1979—. Mem. IEEE (Sr.), Joint Electron Device Engring. Com. Contbr. chpts. to books, articles to electronics jours. Patentee. Home: 1337 Glen Haven Dr San Jose CA 95129

OXTOBY, ROBERT BOYNTON, lawyer; b. Huron, S.D., May 8, 1921; s. Frederic Breading and Frieda (Boynton) O.; B.A., Carleton Coll., 1943; J.D., Northwestern U., 1949; student Ill. Coll.; m. Carolyn Bartholf, Feb. 25, 1956; children—Michael, Thomas, Susan. Admitted to Ill. bar, 1949, since practiced in Springfield; partner Van Meter & Oxtoby & Funk; asst. state atty., Sangamon County, 1950-53; asst. U.S. atty., 1953-57; spl. asst., atty. gen., 1957-61, 69—; pres. Downtown Park, Inc.; dir. Ill. Nat. Ins. Co., Inland Nat. Ins. Co., Springfield, dir. N.H. Ins. Co., Manchester; dir., mem. exec. com. Ill. Nat. Bank. Mem. Ill. Capital Devel. Bd.; chmn. bd., mem. exec. com. Meml. Med Center. Served to 1st lt. USMCR, 1943-46. Mem. Am., Ill., Sangamon County bar assns. Republican. Presbyterian (trustee), Mason (Shriner). Clubs: Sangamo (pres. 1965, dir.); Illini Country. Home: 1933 Outer Park Dr Springfield IL 62704 Office: Illinois Nat Bank Center Springfield IL 62705

OZIER, CECIL RUSSELL, constrn. exec.; b. Cumberland County, Ill., July 1, 1900; s. Richard Simms and Lena Lottie (Webber) O.; student pub. schs. Cumberland County and Greenlaws Bus. Coll., Flora, Ill.; m. Gleena Morefield, Apr. 16, 1921 (died 1957); children—Darrell Simms, Mervyn Watts; m. 2d, Dorothy A. Seeber, Nov. 19, 1958. In bldg. industry, 1925—, as individual propr., 1925-47, bldg. homes in Champaign-Urbana, Ill.; pres., dir. Ozier-Weller, Inc., developers Garden Park, other sub-divs., in Ill., 1947—. Community Homes, Inc., Bel Air Builders, Inc., Danville Community Builders, Inc., 1950—; pres. Ozier Homes, Inc., Fairlawn Village, Inc.; sole owner Ozier-Weller Homes, Inc. Fl., 1950—; developer land in P.R.; chem. experimentation, mining, refining rare earths for use in def., Cin., Colorado Springs, Laramie, Wyo.; active in oil and gas prodn., Ill.; lectr. U. Ill., mortgage bankers groups, builders. Mem. Operations Trade Group, on tour Europe, 1956. Active YMCA. Methodist (ofcl. bd., past lay leader). Home: 608 W John St Champaign IL 61820 Office: 2000 N Mattis Ave PO Box 581 Champaign IL 61820

PAAL, KATHERINE BAYS, educator; b. Shreveport, La., Dec. 31, 1953; d. Robert Payne and Lilburn (Sandoz) Bays; B.A. in Econs., Roanoke Coll., 1975; M.B.A. in Mktg., Loyola Coll., Balt., 1978; m. Rutland Beard Paal, June 28, 1975; 1 son, Rutland Beard. Mgmt. trainee First Nat. Bank Md., Balt., 1975-76, sr. mktg. research analyst, 1976-78; instr. Towson State U. (Md.), 1978—; cons. in field. Mem. Am. Mktg. Assn., Am. Bus. Women's Assn., Balt. Econ. Soc. Home: 11 Huntress Ct Timonium MD 21093 Office: Towson State U Bus Adminstrn Dept Towson MD 21204

PABARCIUS, ALGIS, investment co. exec.; b. Telsiai, Lithuania, May 1, 1932; s. Vacius and Brone (Ziuryte) P.; came to U.S., 1950, naturalized, 1956; B.S., U. Ill., 1955; M.S., Ill. Inst. Tech., 1958, Ph.D., 1964; postgrad. Technische Hochschule Muenchen, Germany, 1962; m. Eleanor A. Rakovic, Aug. 18, 1956; children—Nina, Lisa, Algis. Engr., Esso Research & Engring. Co., Linden, N.J., 1955-56; instr. U. Ill., Chgo., 1956-59, asst. prof., 1959-64; partner Zubkus, Zemaitis & Assos., Architects and Engrs., Chgo., Washington, 1959-67; v.p. Garden Hotels Investment Co. and Whitecliff Corp., Lanham, Md., 1967-75; pres. Aras Investment Corp., 1975-79, Colony Funding Corp., Chevy Chase, Md., 1979—. Profl. engr. Ill., D.C.; structural engr. Ill. Danforth Found. grantee, 1960-61, NSF faculty fellow, 1961-62. Mem. ASCE, Sigma Xi, Tau Beta Pi, Sigma Tau, Chi Epsilon, Phi Kappa Phi. Home: 5909 Tudor Ln Rockville MD 20852 Office: 5550 Friendship Blvd Chevy Chase MD 20015

PACCHIANO, ANTHONY, banker; b. Naples, Italy, Sept. 6, 1946; s. Felice and Frances (D'Apice) P.; B.S. in Econs. and Fin., St. Johns U., 1969; M.B.A. in Fin., Fordham U., 1972; m. Linda Cardillo, May 8, 1976. Internal auditor Bowery Savs. Bank, N.Y.C., 1969-71; mgr. accounting fin. Am. Express Co., N.Y.C., 1971-74; mgr. fin. analysis ABC, N.Y.C., 1974-75; v.p. and controller Citibank N.Y., N.Y.C., 1975—. Mem. Am. Econ. Assn., Am. Mgmt. Assn. Home: Six Squirrel Run Morristown NJ 07960

PACCO, CHARLES BERNARD, credit union exec.; b. Corinth, N.Y., Apr. 17, 1918; s. Charles P. and Agnes M. (Cohan) P.; grad. high sch.; m. Mary Agnes Mooney, Sept. 14, 1943; children—Jeanne, Richard, Carol, Loraine, Paul. Asst. dept. supr. Internat. Paper Co., 1940-54; treas.-mgr. Hudson River Fed. Credit Union, Corinth, 1954—. Mem. Saratoga County Selective Service Bd., 1962-74; treas. Town of Corinth Indsl. Devel. Agy., 1977—. Mem. Credit Union Assn. (dir. Adirondack dist. 1957-79), N.Y. State Credit Union League (dir. 1958-79, past pres.), Empire State Credit Union Execs. Soc., Mgrs. Soc., Eastern N.Y. Golf Assn. (past pres.). Clubs: Elks, Rotary. Home: RD 1 Box 55 Corinth NY 12822 Office: 312 Palmer Ave Corinth NY 12822

PACE, CARL RICHARD, fin. co. exec.; b. N.Y.C., May 13, 1944; s. Carl C. and Margaret (Farah) P.; B.S.B.A., Bucknell U., 1966; postgrad. Fla. State U., 1967; postgrad. in bus. adminstrn. Baruch Coll., Coll. City N.Y., 1968-70; m. Mary M. Heywood, Mar. 24, 1974; children—Richard H., Gergory C. Project mgr. overseas div. Internat. Paper Co., London, 1970-71; mgr. Export Credit Corp., N.Y.C., 1971-73, asst. v.p., N.Y.C., 1973-75, v.p. London-Am. fin. group subs. Midland Bank Eng., N.Y.C., 1975—; dir. Euro Dollar Credits Corp., London. Served to 1st lt. U.S. Army, 1966-68. Mem. Am. Mgmt. Assn. (speaker), World Trade Inst. (speaker). Club: N.Y. Athletic. Contbr. articles, letters to Bus. Week, N.Y. Times and trade publs. Home: 8 Chapel Ln Riverside CT 06878

PACE, CAROLINA JOLLIFF (MRS. JOHN MCIVER PACE), book co. exec.; b. Dallas, Apr. 12, 1938; d. Lindsay Gafford and Carolina (Juden) Jolliff; student Holton-Arms Jr. Coll., 1956-57: B.A. in Comparative Lit., So. Meth. U., 1960; m. John McIver Pace, Oct. 7, 1961. Fashion cons., lectr. Nancy Taylor Sch., Dallas, 1959-61; promotional adv., dir. season ticket sales Dallas Theatre Center, 1960-61; exec. sec. Dallas Book and Author Luncheon, 1959-63; promotional and instnl. cons. Henry Regnery-Reilly & Lee Pub. Co., Chgo., 1962-65: pub. trade rep. various cos., institutional rep. Don R. Phillips Co., Southeastern area, 1965-67; Southwestern rep. Edl. Reading Service, Inc.-Troll Assos., Mahwah, N.J., 1967-72; v.p., dir. multimedia div. Melton Book Co., Dallas, 1972-79; v.p. mktg. Webster's Internat., Inc., Nashville, 1980—; mem. adv. bd. Nat. Info. Center of Spl. Edn. Materials; mem. materials rev. panel Nat. Media Center for Materials of Severely-Profoundly Handicapped, 1981. Mem. Womens Nat. Book Assn., Nat. Audio Visual Assn., Assn. Ednl. and Communications Tech., Assn. Spl. Edn. Tech. (nat. dir., v.p. publicity 1980-82), Dallas Press Club, Dallas Central Bus. Dist. Assn., Council Exceptional Children (dir. exhibitors com., chmn. publ. com. 1979 conf., conf. speaker 1981), DAR, Dallas Civic Opera Assn., ALA, Dallas Art Assn., Alpha Delta Pi. Presbyn. Home: 4524 Lorraine Ave Dallas TX 75205

PACE, STANLEY CARTER, aero. engr.; b. Waterview, Ky., Sept. 14, 1921; s. Stanley Dan and Pearl Eagle (Carter) P.; student U. Ky., 1939-40; B.S., U.S. Mil. Acad., 1943; M.S. in Aero. Engring., Calif. Inst. Tech., 1949; m. Elaine Marilyn Cutchall, Aug. 21, 1945; children—Stanley Dan, Lawrence Timothy, Richard Yost. Commd. 2d lt. USAAF, 1943, advanced through grades to col., 1953; pilot, flight leader B-24 Group, 15th Air Force, 1943-44; chief power plant br., procurement div. Hdqrs. Air Materiel Command, Wright-Patterson AFB, Ohio, 1945-48, assignments, procurement div., 1949-53, dep. chief prodn., 1952-53; resigned, 1953; with TRW, Inc., Cleve., 1954—, successively sales mgr., asst. mgr., mgr. West Coast plant, mgr. jet div. Tapco plant, Cleve., asst. mgr. Tapco group, 1954-58, v.p., gen. mgr. Tapco group, 1958-65, exec. v.p. co., 1965-77, pres., chief operating officer, 1977—, also dir.; dir. Republic Steel Corp., Lamson & Sessions Co., Nat. City Bank of Cleve. Trustee, Western Res. Hist. Soc., Musical Arts Assn., United Way Services, Leadership Cleve.; pres. Greater Cleve. council Boy Scouts Am.; active Jr. Achievement; past chmn. bd. trustees Denison U. Decorated Air medal with oak leaf clusters. Mem. AIAA, NAM (past vice-chmn., dir., exec. com.), Am. Inst. Mgmt., Nat. Aeros. Assn., Soc Automotive Engrs., Delta Tau Delta. Clubs: Union, Pepper Pike, Tavern, Country, Rolling Rock. Office: 23555 Euclid Ave Cleveland OH 44117

PACE, WILLIAM MARK, mktg. communications cons.; b. Yonkers, N.Y., Mar. 5, 1931; s. Nicholas E. and Catherine (Fagan) P.; B.A., Syracuse U., 1953; m. Lesley Bullen; children—Mark, Leslie Ann. Advt. supr. Sylvania Electric div. GTE, N.Y.C., 1956-60; sales promotion mgr. Remington Rand Office Systems, N.Y.C., 1960-63; with Time mag., N.Y.C., 1963-73, mgr. bus.-indsl. mktg., 1967-73; with sr. public relations staff United Aircraft, Hartford, Conn., 1973-75; prin. Bill Pace Assos. Inc., Chester, Conn., 1975—. Cert. bus. communicator. Mem. Bus. and Profl. Advt. Assn., Co. Mil. Historians, Co. Fifers and Drummers, Alpha Delta Sigma, Alpha Tau Omega, Alpha Phi Omega. Clubs: Grads. Yale (New Haven); Elks. Home: 68 Spring St Chester CT 06412 Office: 91 Main St Chester CT 06412

PACHETTI, RENATO MATTEO, TV co. exec.; b. Massa Carrara, Italy, Aug. 26, 1925; s. Ulderico and Angela (Ariani) P.; came to U.S., 1970; grad. in Pharm. Chemistry, U. Modena (Italy), 1950; m. Diane Finney, Dec. 29, 1965; children—Alex, Nicholas, Edward. Fgn. news editor RAI-Radio-TV Italiana, Rome, 1955-60; corr. RAI UN, N.Y.C., 1960-62; dir. radio programs RAI, Rome, 1963-69; exec. v.p. and gen. mgr. RAI Corp., N.Y.C., 1970-80, pres., 1980—. Decorated grand officer Order Merit Republic of Italy. Mem. Fgn. Press Assn. (pres. 1972-73), Internat. Council TV Arts and Scis. (chmn. bd. 1978-81), Am.-Italy Soc. (v.p. 1976-81), Gruppo Esponenti Italiani (pres. 1977-81), Italy-Am. C. of C. (v.p. 1981). Clubs: Met., Mid-Atlantic. Home: 525 Park Ave New York NY 10021 Office: 1350 Ave of Americas New York NY 10019

PACINI, LAUREN RICHARD, human resource cons. co. exec.; b. Manchester, N.H., Aug. 26, 1943; s. Richard and Elizabeth Lynn (Anderson) P.; student public schs., Cleve.; m. Martha Sue Blackledge, Mar. 26, 1966; children—Lauren Richard, Elizabeth Ann, Christopher Knox, Jeffrey Barnett. Regional mgr., internat. metals trader Century Steel Co., Inc., West Long Branch, N.J., 1970-73; account exec., dept. mgr. Sales World, Inc., Cleve., 1973-77; cons. Alexander & Sterling, Cleve., 1977-78; pres. Resource Unltd., Inc., Cleve., 1978—; human resource cons., 1973—; del. Ohio coalition Washington Presentation on Small Bus., 1980. Mem. steering com., chmn. small bus. task force plan for continuing edn. for working adults Cuyahoga Community Coll. Served with Spl. Forces, U.S. Army, 1964-70. Decorated Bronze Star, Air medal, Commendation medal; cert. employment cons. Mem. Am. Prodn. and Inventory Control Soc., Greater Cleve. Growth Assn., Council Smaller Enterprises (dir.). Home: 3566 Lytle Rd Cleveland OH 44122 Office: PO Box 22597 Cleveland OH 44122

PACK, HARRY SAMUEL, banker; b. N.Y.C., June 7, 1943; s. Eugene and Yetta (London) P.; B.S., L.I. U., 1963; LL.B., Harvard, 1966; LL.M., N.Y. U., 1967; m. Rebecca Mistriel, Sept. 18, 1971; children—Edmond E., Simon M., Avery L. Admitted to N.Y. State bar, 1966; practiced in N.Y.C., 1966-74, Watertown, N.Y., 1975—; asst. prof. bus. adminstrn. L.I. U., Bklyn., 1966-70; pres., chmn. bd. Jefferson Nat. Bank and predecessor firms, LaFargeville, 1970—. Jewish. Clubs: Black River Valley (Watertown, N.Y.). Home: 1214 Harris Dr Watertown NY 13601 Office: Outer Washington St Watertown NY 13601

PACK, HOWARD M., vice chmn. bd., chmn. exec. com. Seatrain Lines, Inc., 1951-80, chmn. bd., 1980—. Office: Seatrain Lines 1 Chase Manhattan Plaza New York NY 10005*

PACKARD, DANIEL ABBOTT, motor carrier co. exec.; b. Denver, Feb. 23, 1927; s. Daniel Abbott and Caroline Edith Packard; B.A., Jacksonville State U., 1949; m. Catherine R. Smith, July 2, 1950; 1 son, Daniel A. Asst. dir. indsl. relations Am. Trucking Assn., Washington, 1950-61; asst. v.p. ops. Norwalk Truck Lines (Ohio), 1961-63; v.p. personnel and labor relations Asso. Truck Lines, Grand Rapids, Mich., 1964-80, sr. v.p., 1980—. Vice-pres. United Way of Kent County; bd. dirs. Home Health Care Services. Served with U.S. Army, 1943-46.

PACKARD, DAVID, electronic co. exec.; b. Pueblo, Colo., Sept. 7, 1912; s. Sperry Sidney and Ella Lorna (Graber) P.; B.A., Stanford U., 1934, E.E., 1939; Sc.D., Colo. Coll., 1964; LL.D., U. Calif., Santa Cruz, 1966, Catholic U., 1970, Pepperdine U., 1972; Litt.D., So. Colo. State Coll., 1973; D.Engring., U. Notre Dame, 1974; m. Lucile Salter, Apr. 8, 1939; children—David Woodley, Nancy Ann (Mrs. Robin Burnett), Susan (Mrs. Franklin M. Orr, Jr.), Julie Elizabeth. With vacuum tube engring. dept. Gen. Electric Co., Schenectady, 1936-38; co-founder partner Hewlett-Packard Co., Palo Alto, Calif., 1939-46, pres., 1947-64, chmn. bd., chief exec. officer, 1964-68, chmn. bd., 1972—; dep. sec. Def. Dept., 1969-71; dir. Caterpillar Tractor Co., Standard Oil Co. Calif., Boeing Co. Trustee, Hoover Found., 1972—, also Am. Enterprise Inst., Inst. Ednl. Affairs; mem. Palo Alto Bd. Edn., 1947-56; mem. Univs. Research Assn., 1965-69; mem. Trilateral Commn., Wilson Council; trustee Stanford U., 1954-69, pres., 1958-60, 1st v.p., 1960-67; dir., exec. com. Stanford Research Inst., 1958-69; bd. dirs. Alliance to Save Energy, Found. for Study Presdl. Terms; dir. Nat. Merit Scholarship Corp., 1963-69; trustee Colo. Coll., 1966-69, U.S. Churchill Found., 1965-69; chmn. bd. regents Uniformed Services U. Health Scis.; bd. dirs. Atlantic Council, 1972-80; trustee Nat. Symphony Assn., 1973-80. Decorated Grand Cross Merit (Fed. Republic Germany); recipient numerous awards; named Bus. Statesman of Year Harvard U., 1973, Industrialist of Year, Calif. Mus. Sci. and Industry, 1973; also from World Trade Club San Francisco, 1976, Am. Cons. Engrs. Council, 1977, Ency. Brit., 1977, Nat. Acad. Engring., 1979. Fellow IEEE; mem. Nat. Acad. Engring., Am. Mgmt. Assn. (dir. 1956-59, Calif. v.p. at large 1959-69), Instrument Soc. (life), Calif. State C. of C. (dir.), Bus. Council (chmn. 1972-74), Bus. Roundtable, Phi Beta Kappa, Sigma Xi, Tau Beta Pi, Alpha Delta Phi. Clubs: Links (N.Y.C.); Commonwealth, Engineers, Pacific Union, World Trade Bohemian (San Francisco); Calif. (Los Angeles); Alfalfa, Capitol Hill (Washington); Executive (Chgo.). Office: 1501 Page Mill Rd Palo Alto CA 94304

PACKO, JOSEPH JOHN, industrialist; b. Toledo, Mar. 9, 1925; s. Joseph Steve and Mary (Toth) P.; student in thermodynamics engring. John Carroll U., U. N.C., 1943-44; B.S. in Physics, Math., Bus. Adminstrn., Fin., Bowling Green State U., 1948; postgrad. in nuclear chemistry Toledo U., 1950; Ph.D. in Comml. Sci., Southeastern Mass. U., 1969; m. Bette Throne, July 10, 1948; children—Jo Anne, Mark. With Packo Industries, Ft. Lauderdale, Fla., 1953—; pres. J.J. Packo Mortgage Corp., 1954-69; pres. Packo Enterprises, 1955—, S. Fla. Asphalt Co., 1956-65; pres., chmn. Am. Dynamics Internat., Inc. 1967-73, Packo Internat., 1978—. Mem. Trade Mission, West Berlin, 1965; adv. panel Dept. Army, 1974-78. Bd. dirs. Fla. chpt. Nat. Soc. Prevention Blindness, Holy Cross Hosp., Nova U. Alumnae Assn., A.R.C. Served with USNR, 1943-45. Mem. Opera Guild Ft. Lauderdale, Young Presidents Orgn. (vice-chmn., sec.-treas. Fla. chpt.), Am. Mgmt. Assn., A.A.A.S., Symphony Soc., Asphalt Inst., Nat. Bd. Realtors, Nat. Mortgage Bankers Assn., Nat. Bituminous Assn., Bowling Green U. Alumni, Southeastern Mass. U. Alumni, Navy League, Sigma Xi. Clubs: Lago Mar Country, Capitol Hill; Onion Creek Country (Austin). Patentee in field. Home: 30 Pelican Isle Fort Lauderdale FL 33301

PADNOS, SEYMOUR KANTOR, scrap iron processing and brokerage co. exec.; b. Grand Rapids, Mich., Oct. 17, 1920; s. Louis and Helen (Kantor) P.; B.A., Hope Coll., 1943; m. Esther Roth, June 20, 1948; children—Mitchell W., Shelley E., William R., Cynthia B. With Louis Padnos Iron & Metal Co., Holland, Mich., 1938—, pres., chief exec. officer, 1961—, pres., chief exec. officer affiliated firms. Founding dir. Windmill Island Mcpl. Authority. Served with USAAF, 1943-45. Mem. Inst. of Scrap Iron and Steel (dir.), Nat. Fedn. Ind. Scrap Yard Processors (pres., chmn.), Bur. International de la Recouperation (v.p.), Nat. Assn. Recycled Industries, Mick. C. of C. Club: Macatawa Bay Yacht (past commadore). Office: Louis Padnos Iron & Metal Co River Ave and Bayside Dr Holland MI 49423

PAETKAU, WALTER HENRY, community services exec.; b. Bassano, Alta., Can., May 4, 1935; s. Peter H. and Maria (Harder) P.; B.Ed., U. Alta., 1960; postgrad. Interdenominational Theol. Center, Atlanta, 1963-64; M.Div., Mennonite Bibl. Sem., Elkhart, Ind., 1966; m. Mabel E. Lauver, Dec. 27, 1960; children—Trevor, Kevin. Tchr., Edmonton, Alta., 1956-58, 60-62; nat. ch. adminstr. Mennonite Ch., Kans., 1964-65, Ind., 1965-66, B.C., Can., 1966-70; exec. dir. Matsqui-Abbotsford Community Services, Abbotsford, B.C., 1971—; seminar leader mgmt. workshops, 1972—. Vice chmn. local congregation Mennonite Ch., 1979, chmn., 1980—; chmn. Regional Adv. Council for Retarded; adv. com. Nat. Poverty Council, Mennonite Ch., 1975-79. Mem. B.C. Assn. Social Workers (pres. 1972), Social Planning and Rev. Council B.C. (pres. 1979—, exec. com. 1974-78). Author: Start Where You Are, 1965. Home: 2364 Cascade St Abbotsford BC V2T 3G3 Canada Office: 2420 Montrose St Abbotsford BC V2S 3S9 Canada

PAGAN, RAFAEL DAVID, JR., former army officer, food co. exec.; b. Ponce, P.R., Dec. 7, 1928; s. Rafael D. and Ana Maria (Ayala) P.; B.S. in Biology and Chemistry, U. P.R., 1960; B.A. in History and Econs., U. Tex., 1962; M.A. in Internat. Relations and Trade, U. Md., 1966, postgrad., 1967-71; m. Hazel Jean Burns. Commd. 2d lt. U.S. Army, 1948, advanced through grades to col., 1970; various command and staff positions U.S. Army in Asia, Latin Am., Europe, 1950-55; gen. staff officer Dept. Def., Washington, 1959-70, mem. various govt. policy coms., ret., 1970; exec. rep. in charge internat. relations Internat. Nickel Co., Inc., N.Y.C., 1970-74; v.p. govt. and industry affairs Castle & Cooke Foods Co., San Francisco, 1975-80; pres. Nestle Coordination Center for Nutrition, Inc., Washington, 1980—; cons. Latin Am. affairs Universal Oil Products Co., 1973-74, Baer Foods Co., 1973-74; adviser to P.R. Govt., 1963-68; lectr. seminars on internat. trade and relations, 1970-74. Bd. dirs. Fund for Multinat. Mgmt. Edn., Food for Millions Found., Arriba Juntos. Decorated Bronze Star, Legion of Merit. Mem. Council of the Americas, Pub. Affairs Council (internat. com.), Pan Am. Soc. (dir.), Philippine-Am. C. of C. (dir. 1975-76), World Affairs Council (adv. com.), Latin Am. Area Specialists Assn. Clubs: Univ., Nat. Press. Home: 10024 Kendale Rd Potomac MD 20854 Office: 1200 17 St NW Washington DC

PAGE, CAROL LORRAINE, export exec.: b. Denver, Nov. 28, 1942; d. John Nathan and Fay Lorraine (Thurman) Hopkins; B.A. cum laude in Chinese Lang. and Lit., U. Wash., Seattle, 1974, M.A. in Internat. Communications, 1978. Editor, Central Kitsap Reporter, Silverdale, Wash., 1965-67, Snoqualmie (Wash.) Valley Record, 1970-71; faculty U. Wash., 1974-76; owner, pres., mgr. export co. PAGECO: Progress and Growth East Co., Seattle, 1976—. Henry M. Jackson scholar, U. Wash., 1972-73, Alumnae scholar, 1972-73, Wash. Presswomen scholar, 1973-74, John Reid Meml. scholar, 1973-74. Mem. Mensa, Intertel, Theta Sigma Phi, Mortar Bd., Phi Theta Kappa, Sigma Delta Chi. Club: Seattle Folklore Soc. Address: 4902 N Phinney Ave Seattle WA 98103

PAGE, DONALD DEROSEAR, constrn. co. exec.; b. Harrisburg, Ill., Mar. 20, 1932; s. Orval Derosear and Edna Earle (Dillon) P.; student schs., Anna, Ill.; m. Betty Jean Worful, Apr. 27, 1973; 2 daus., 3 stepsons. Partner, Page's Auto Home Supply, Anna, 1953-57; estimator, office mgr. Rader Constrn. Co., Hopkinsville, Ky., 1957-61; project engr. Laurel Co., Nashville, 1961-62; engr. John Woodruff Constrn. Co., Inc., Cadiz, Ky., 1962-63; estimator Hal Perry Constrn. Co., Inc., Benton, Ky., 1963-65; v.p. J.A. Hill Constrn. Co. Inc., Benton, 1965-68; project mgr. Charles E. Story Constrn. Co., Inc., Wickliffe, Ky., 1968-77; pres., owner Donald D. Page & Assos., Inc., Wickliffe, 1977—. Served with U.S. Army, 1951-53. Mem. Associated Gen. Contractors Western Ky., Builders Orgn. Labor Together (mgmt. rep.). Democrat. Home: Route 10 Box 321 Paducah KY 42001 Office: PO Box 606 Wickliffe KY 40287

PAGE, GARY WAYNE, banker; b. Wilmington, N.C., Feb. 2, 1944; s. Daniel and Edith Graham (Williams) P.; B.S., U. Tenn., 1966; student Asheville Biltmore Coll., 1962-64; m. Cynthia Caroline Cash, Jan. 13, 1979; children—Karen, David. Asst. cashier Valley Fidelity Bank & Trust Co., Knoxville, Tenn., 1964-67; sr. v.p. compliance control div. Bankers Trust S.C., Columbia, 1967—; mem. faculty Midlands Tech. Coll., evenings, 1976-80. Treas., Carolinians for Godd Govt. Fund, 1977—; coach Minor League Baseball. Mem. Nat. Assn. Bus. Polit. Action Coms., Bank Fin. Mgmt. Forum (chmn.), Bank Adminstrn. Inst. (past pres. S.C. chpt.), N.Am. Soc. Corp. Planners, Planning Execs. Inst., Am. Inst. Banking. Home: 2050 Waterworks Pl Columbia SC 29210 Office: PO Box 448 Columbia SC 29202

PAGE, ROBERT WESLEY, constrn. co. exec.; b. Dallas, Jan. 22, 1927; s. Arow Cleo and Zelma Maggie Page; B.S., Tex. A. and M. U., 1950; m. Sept. 21, 1952; children—Wes, David, Mark, Meg. Project mgr. Aramco, 1953-55; mgr. Internat. Bechtel, 1957-65; asst. prof. U. Beirut, 1955-57; v.p. Rockfeller Bros., N.Y.C., 1965-72; pres. George A. Fuller, N.Y.C., 1972-76, Rust Engring., Birmingham, Ala., 1976—; dir. Metro Bank. Active Birmingham Boy Scouts Am.; mem. nat. Girl Scouts U.S.A. Served with USNR, 1944-46. Mem. ASCE, Am. Soc. Mil. Engrs. Clubs: Rotary, Apsusmis Country, Vestonia Country, Relay, Met. Office: PO Box 101 Birmingham AL 35201

PAGE, WALTER HINES, former banker; b. Huntington, L.I., N.Y., July 7, 1915; s. Arthur W. and Mollie H. (Hall) P.; grad. Milton (Mass.) Acad., 1933; A.B., Harvard, 1937; m. Jane N. Nichols, Jan. 24, 1942; children—Jane N., Walter Hines, Mark N. With J. P. Morgan & Co., Inc., N.Y.C., 1937-59; bank merged with Guaranty Trust Co., 1959; v.p. Morgan Guaranty Trust Co., N.Y.C., 1959-64, sr. v.p., 1964-65, exec. v.p., 1965-68, vice chmn. bd., 1968-71, pres., 1971-77, chmn., chief exec. officer Morgan Guaranty Trust Co. and J.P. Morgan & Co., 1978-79; pres., dir. J.P. Morgan & Co., Inc., 1971-77, chmn. bd., 1978-79; dir. Morgan Guaranty Trust Co., J.P. Morgan & Co., Inc., U.S. Steel Corp., Royal Group, Inc., Saudi Internat. Bank. Chmn., Cold Spring Harbor Lab. Office: 23 Wall St New York NY 10015

PAGEL, GARY CHARLES, chem. co. exec.; b. Fond du Lac, Wis., June 18, 1943; s. Charles Gary and Violet (Baker) P.; B.S. in Chemistry, Case Inst. Tech., 1965; M.S. in Bus. Adminstrn., Purdue U., 1966; children—Christopher G., Nathaniel S. Nat. mktg. mgr. Hooker Chem. Corp., Houston, 1973-75, mgr. planning, 1976, dir. devel., 1977-79, mem. mgmt. com., 1977—, dir. bus. devel. Occidental Geothermal div., 1980—. Mem. Comml. Devel. Assn., Am. Chem. Soc. Roman Catholic. Clubs: River Oaks Country, K.C. Home: 727 Bunker Hill Rd Houston TX 77024 Office: PO Box 4289 Houston TX 77024

PAGET, ALLEN MAXWELL, investment co. exec.; b. Karuizawa, Japan, Sept. 12, 1919 (parents Am. citizens); s. Allen Maxwell and Mary (Baum) P.; B.S. in Bus. Adminstrn., Lehigh U., 1941; m. Dorothy A. Lord, Dec. 22, 1941. With C. L. Emmert & Co., 1955-58; with Waddell & Reed, Inc., 1958-68, investment mgr., distbr. united group of mutual funds, 1958-68, regional mgr., resident v.p., Harrisburg, Pa., 1961-68; v.p. Mark Securities, Inc., Harrisburg, Pa., 1968—; pres., treas., dir. Penn-Ben, Inc., 1969—, also chmn. bd.; chmn., bd., pres., treas., dir. Paget-San Enterprises, Inc. (Benihana of Tokyo), 1973—; v.p. Gamma Lambda Corp., 1973-78. Served to comdr. Supply Corps, USN, 1941-55; capt. Res. (ret. 1972). Mem. Am. Philatelic Soc., Navy League U.S., Res. Officers Assn. (pres. Central Pa. chpt. 1972-73), Mil. Order World Wars (comdr. Central Pa. chpt. 1979—), Internat. Assn. Financial Counselors (charter), Navy Supply Corps Sch. Alumni Assn. (founding mem.), Mid Atlantic Shrine Clowns Assn., Internat. Shrine Clown Assn., Harrisburg, West Shore Area chambers commerce, Nat. Sojourners, Heros of '76, Brown Key Soc., Lambda Mu Sigma (founder), Pi Kappa Alpha (treas.), Alpha Phi Omega, Pi Delta Epsilon. Presbyn. (trustee). Clubs: Rotary (dir.), Mason (Master 1968, K.T., Shriner, pres. Pa. Shrine Assn. 1978-79, Potentate, Zembo Temple 1978, Tall Cedars of Lebanon, Ancient Accepted Scottish Rite, Legion of Honor, antique and classic car unit Zembo Clowns), Mid-Atlantic Shrine Assn. (v.p. 1980—); Central Pa. Lehigh (pres. 1966); Zembo Luncheon; Shrine (Adams County, Pa.); Shrine (Cumberland County, Pa.); Shrine (Hershey, Pa.); Shrine (Lancaster County, Pa.); Shrine (Lebanon County, Pa.); Shrine (Perry-Juniata County, Pa.), Shrine (Upper Dauphin County, Pa.), Shrine (Waynesboro, Pa.); Shrine (York County, Pa.). Home: 308 Lamp Post Ln Pine Brook Camp Hill PA 17011 Office: 2517 Paxton St Harrisburg PA 17111

PAGET, JOHN ARTHUR, mech. engr.; b. Ft. Frances, Ont., Can., Sept. 15, 1922; s. John and Ethel (Bishop) P.; B.Applied Sci., U. Toronto, 1946; m. Vicenta Herrera Nunez, Dec. 16, 1963; children—Cynthia Ellen, Kevin Arthur, Keith William. Chief draftsman Gutta Perch & Rubber, Ltd., Toronto, Ont., 1946-49; chief draftsman Viceroy Mfg. Co., Toronto, 1949-52; supr., design engr. C.D. Howe Co. Ltd., Montreal, Que., Can., 1952-58, sr. design engr. combustion engring., Montreal, 1958-59; sr. staff engr. Gen. Atomic Co. Inc., La Jolla, 1959—. Registered profl. engr., Calif., Ont. Mem. Am. Soc. M.E., Am. Nuclear Soc., Inst. Nuclear Engrs., Profl. Engrs. Ont., Soc. for History Tech., Inst. Mech. Engrs., Soc. Am. Mil. Engrs., Newcomen Soc., Brit. Nuclear Energy Soc. Patentee in field. Home: 3183 Magellan St San Diego CA 92154 Office: Gen Atomic Co PO Box 81608 San Diego CA 92138

PAGET, JOHN GEORGE, JR., fin. and mktg. exec.; b. Detroit, Apt. 7, 1942; s. John George and Shirley (Nicholas) P.; B.S. in Mktg., Calif. Western U., 1980, M.B.A. in Fin., 1981; m. Celia A. Iacampo, May 8, 1971; children—Cleve Geoffrey, Nicholas John, Annmarie. Mktg. rep. Univac div. Sperry Rand Corp., Cleve., 1967-70; sales mgr. Midwestern div. Ampex Computer Products Corp., 1971-72; sales mgr. Ohio area Mohawk Data Scis. Corp., 1972-74; regional sales mgr. Midwestern div. Data Transmission Corp., 1974-75; v.p., gen. mgr. Traveletter Corp., Bellevue, Wash., 1975—. Served with U.S. Army, Mem. Am. Mgmt. Assn., Wash. Council on Fgn. Trade, U.S. Parachute Assn. (cert. instr., class D license). Club: Sons of Italy (trustee) (Bellevue). Home: 4701 Somerset Pl SE Bellevue WA 98006

PAGET, SAM STUART, chem. mfg. co. exec.; b. Bridgeport, Conn., Jan. 9, 1947; s. Louis S. and Edith S. P.; B.S. in Bus. Adminstrn., Lehigh U., 1968; m. Cathy Shogan; children—Jonathan, Wendy. Auditor, Brout Isaacs & Co., C.P.A.'s, Bridgeport, Conn., 1969-71; v.p. Qonaar Corp., Elk Grove Village, Ill., 1971-79; v.p. Bell Chem. Co., Chgo., 1979-81, chief operating officer, 1981—. Served with U.S. Army. Office: 411 N Wolcott Ave Chicago IL 60622

PAHLMANN, GENE ARTHUR, ceramic engr., engring., constrn., energy conservation cons.; b. Alton, Ill., July 27, 1946; s. Herman William and Verna Naomi Pahlmann; B.S. in Ceramic Engring., U. Mo., Rolla, 1969, M.S. in Ceramic Engring., 1970; m. Pisamai Kwangkratoke, Sept. 15, 1973; children—Montana, Gene Arthur. Ceramic engr. Drakenfield div. Hercules, Inc., Washington, Pa., 1970-71; mech. and indsl. engr. Hdqrs. Armament Command, U.S. Army, Rock Island, Ill., 1974-77; chief indsl. engr. Directorate Indsl. Ops., Ft. Leonard Wood, Mo., 1977—; owner, mgr. Pahlmann Enterprises, consultants, Newburg, Mo., 1977—. Mem. solar resource adv. panel Mo. Dept. Natural Resources, 1979—. Served with Ordnance Corps, U.S. Army, 1971-74; Vietnam. Registered profl. engr., Ill., Mo. Lutheran. Home: Route 1 Box 24 Newburg MO 65550

PAIER, ADOLF ARTHUR, JR., automotive parts and bus. systems mfg. co. exec.; b. Branford, Conn., Oct. 27, 1938; s. Adolf Arthur and Margaret Mary (Almond) P.; A.A., Quinnipiac Coll., 1958; B.S. in Econs., U. Pa., 1960; m. Geraldine Shnakis, Sept. 17, 1966; children—Nathaniel Jason, Andrew Joseph, Alena Catherine. Audit mgr. Touche Ross & Co., Phila., 1960-67; sr. v.p., treas., dir. Safeguard Industries, Inc., King of Prussia, Pa., from 1967, now pres.; dir. Morlan Internat., Inc., Phila. Mem. Am., Pa. insts. C.P.A.'s, Fin. Execs. Inst., Nat. Assn. Accountants. Office: Safeguard Industries 630 Park Ave King of Prussia PA 19406

PAIGE, MIREILLE, cosmetic co. exec.; b. Montreal, Que., Can., June 11, 1936; d. Polydore Joseph and Gilberte Marie (Rose) Roy; came to U.S., 1956, naturalized, 1959; B.A., Coll. St. Nom de Jesus et Marie, Montreal, 1956; m. Edward Louis Paige, June 13, 1956; children—Edward Vincent, Curtis Andrew. Tchr., Commn. Scolaire du Que., Montreal, 1955-56; sales rep. Elizabeth Arden, N.Y.C., 1963-67; cons. Revlon Co., N.Y.C., 1967-71; nat. sales dir. Dermetics Co., Gt. Neck, N.Y., 1971-73, v.p., from 1973; founder, pres., chief exec. officer Mireille Paige Corp., 1979—. Fund raising St. Jude's Children's Hosp. Named Cosmetic Woman Achiever of Yr., 1978.

Mem. Am. Assn. Esthetics and Make-up, Fragrance Found. Assn., Cosmetic Career Women. Contbr. articles to skin care analysis jours., trade mags. Home: 15 Pound Ridge Rd Plainview NY 11803

PAIGE, RICHARD E., inventor; b. N.Y.C., Dec. 30, 1904; s. Louis and Florence (Elias) P.; student Voltaire Sch. Music, Grand Central Sch. Art; m. Evelyn Kitz, Apr. 26, 1931. Profl. musician, orchestra leader, sometimes radio sta. WHN, N.Y.C., vaudeville performer; composed and sold some of earliest theme songs and singing commls.; mem. Band of a Thousand Melodies, WJZ, N.Y.C.; salesman Reproduction Products, Bklyn., 1929-31; idea man, constrn. expert Display Finishing Co., L.I. City, N.Y., 1931; created profession of cardboard engr.; granted the only basic patents in field of paper manufacture, inventions introduced through Gen. Electric Co., Coty, Seagram, Calvert, Colgate, Gen. Foods, other nat. advts., 1931-34; entered field of folding boxes, 1934; v.p. Display Finishing Co., 1936-40; established Richard E. Paige Co., N.Y.C., 1940; guest lectr. New Sch. Social Research, Pratt Inst., Am. Mgmt. Assn., 1970; exhibit New Frontiers of Modern Design, Pratt Inst.; inventor instructional sighting device used by U.S. Army, USMC, World War II; founded Paige Tng. Aids, 1944; founded Paige Lab., 1946, The Paige Co., 1948, Paige Co. Internat.; developed can carriers Container Corp. Am. developed corrugated floor display stands; with Hallmark Cards, Inc., 1960-70; chmn. bd. Paper Products Devel. Corp., 1964—; research steel foil Bethlehem Steel Co., 1964-65; tech. cons. Procter & Gamble Co., Ivorydale Tech. Center, 1970. Recipient Bronze Plaque, Advertising Club of Greater Providence C. of C., 1956; Top Design award Design Mag.; named to Packaging Hall of Fame, 1975. Mem. Point of Purchase Advt. Inst.; Inventors Workshop Internat. (hon. mem., guest lectr.). Club: Advertising (N.Y.C.). Author: Complete Guide to Making Money with Your Ideas and Inventions. Patentee in field, U.S. and abroad. Home: 800 Fifth Ave New York NY 10022 Office: 432 Park Ave S New York NY 10016

PAILEY, WILLIAM JOHN, JR., bus. planning and services co. exec.; b. Boston, May 5, 1940; s. William John and Ruth E. Pailey; A.B., Brown U., 1962; M.B.A., Columbia U., 1964; m. Maryann Brahos, Nov. 24, 1973; 1 dau., Joann Ruth. Sr. cost analyst Bruning div. Addesssograph Co., 1964, sr. market analyst, 1965, econ. planner, 1966; cons. A.T. Kearney & Co., Chgo., 1966-70; v.p., treas. Memory Gardens Cemetery Inc., Arlington Heights, Ill., 1970—; gen. partner Pailey Computer Spltys., Arlington Heights, 1974—; pres. Automated Planning Systems Inc., Arlington Heights, 1979—. Mem. MICRU Internat. of Microdata Users Group (founding mem., dir., treas.), Nat. Assn. Cemeteries, Ill. Cemetery Assn., Met. Chgo. Cemetery Ofcls. Office: 2501 E Euclid Ave Arlington Heights IL 60004

PAINE, THOMAS HALLSTEN, goldsmith, jeweller, gemmologist; b. Everett, Wash., Jan. 30, 1947; s. Rowell Everett and Shirley Margaret (Hallsten) P.; A.A. with high honors, Everett Jr. Coll., 1967; B.S. in Chemistry magna cum laude, U. Wash., 1969; postgrad. Wash. State U., 1969-71. Owner, operator Thomas Paine, Fine Jewels of the World, Everett, 1973-79, Thomas H. Paine, cons. in gemmology, Everett, 1980—. Recipient Scholastic Award Everett, Area C. of C., 1967. Mem. Am. Chem. Soc. (certified 1970), Gemological Inst. Am. (Diamond Certificate 1975), Gemological Assn. Gt. Brit., Phi Beta Kappa, Phi Theta Kappa, Phi Lambda Upsilon. Clubs: Masons. Home: 1343 Madrona Ave Everett WA 98203 Office: 2806 Colby Ave Everett WA 98201

PAINE, THOMAS OTTEN, aerospace exec.; b. Berkeley, Calif., Nov. 9, 1921; s. George Thomas and Ada Louise (Otten) P.; A.B. in Engring., Brown U., 1942; M.S. in Phys. Metallurgy, Stanford, 1947, Ph.D., 1949; m. Barbara Helen Taunton Pearse, Oct. 1, 1946; children—Marguerite Ada, George Thomas, Judith Janet, Frank Taunton. Research asso. Stanford, 1947-49; with Gen. Electric Co., 1949-68, 70-76, GE Research Lab., Schenectady, mgr. center advanced studies, Santa Barbara, Calif., 1963-68, v.p., group exec. power generation, 1970-73, sr. v.p. tech. planning and devel., 1973-76; pres. Northrop Corp., Los Angeles, 1976—; dep. adminstr., then adminstr. NASA, 1968-70; dir. Eastern Air Lines. Trustee Occidental Coll., Brown U., Harvey Mudd Coll., Asian Inst. Tech. Served to lt. USNR, World War II. Decorated Submarine Combat insignia with stars, USN Commendation medal; grand ufficiale della Ordine al Merito (Italy); recipient Distinguished Service medal NASA, 1970, Washington award Western Soc. Engrs., 1972; John Fritz medal United Engring. Socs., 1976, Faraday medal Inst. Elec. Engrs. (London), 1976. Mem. Nat. Acad. Engring., N.Y. Acad. Scis., Am. Phys. Soc., IEEE, Inst. Strategic Studies (London), AIAA, Explorers Club, U.S. Naval Inst., Sigma Xi. Clubs: Lotos, Sky (N.Y.C.); Cosmos, Army and Navy (Washington); Calif. (Los Angeles). Contbr. articles to tech. publs. Co-inventor lodex R magnets. Home: 765 Bonhill Rd Los Angeles CA 90049 Office: 1800 Century Park E Los Angeles CA 90067

PAINTER, HOWARD ORRIN, JR., electronics co. exec.; b. Bloomfield, Conn., Apr. 22, 1936; s. Howard O. and Cecilia K. (Brady) P.; B.S.E.E., Worcester Poly. Inst., 1958; postgrad. Northeastern U., 1977, Harvard U., 1979; m. Carole A. Flynn, June 27, 1959; children—Edward M., Helen C. Applications engr., mktg. mgr., Japan mgr. Digital Equipment Corp., Maynard, Mass., Washington and Tokyo, 1962-71; v.p. advanced devel. Gen Rad, Inc., Bolton, Mass., 1971—; cons. Mktg. mgr., Zurich, Switzerland gen. mgr. service products div., Phoenix, 1980—. dir. Glamour Care, Inc. Corporator Emerson Hosp., 1979—; mem. Stow (Mass.) Fin. Com., 1978—, Stow Conservation Com., 1970-73; bd. dirs. Aquinas Assn. Worcester; active Worcester Poly. Inst. Alumni Fund. Served to capt. Signal Corps, AUS, 1958-59. Mem. IEEE, Sci. Apparatus Mfrs. Assn. (exec. com.). Home: 10 W Country Gables Dr Phoenix AZ 85023

PAINTER, JUDITH HARTRIDGE, builder, designer; b. Denver, Feb. 17, 1941; d. George Gadsden and Margaret Catharine (Todd) Hartridge; B.A., Wellesley Coll., 1962; B.Arch. with honors, U. Calif., Berkeley, 1972; postgrad. Stanford U., 1965-66, U. Calif., Davis, 1978; M.A., Mills Coll., 1973; m. James David Painter, Aug. 31, 1968. Tchr., Mayflower Sch., Nigeria, 1963-64; city planner City of Hayward (Calif.), 1968-70; archtl. draftsman William C. Glass, Hayward, 1971; property developer Painters' Properties, Hayward, 1969-74; constrn. program liaison Regional Transit, Sacramento, 1974-77; responsible mng. officer Paintridge Design and Devel., Inc., Davis, 1976—, sec.-treas., 1977—; asst. dir. U. Calif. Inst. Appropriate Tech., 1977-79. Recipient Suntherm award for design Pacific Gas and Electricity. Mem. alumnae assns. Wellesley Coll., Mills Coll., U. Calif. Berkeley Author: Sun Ridge: Passive Solar in Practice. Home: 220 Jubilee Way Rio Linda CA 95673 Office: 6432 2d St Rio Linda CA 95673

PAJAK, JOHN STEVEN, constrn. co. exec.; b. Chgo., Nov. 6, 1947; s. John and Florence (Merrick) P.; computer programmer cert. Mayfair Coll., 1971, Asso. Applied Sci., 1972; B.S., DePaul U., 1978; m. Cheryl Trelka, July 11, 1970. Customer service mgr. Transo Envelope Co., Chgo., 1965-68; asst. controller Electro Engring. Products Co., Chgo., 1968-70; controller Midwesco Inc., Niles, Ill., 1970-80, Blinderman Constrn. Co., Inc., Glenview, Ill., 1980—. C.P.A., Ill. Mem. Am. Inst. C.P.A.'s, Ill. C.P.A. Soc., Chgo. Midwest Credit Mgmt. Assn. Home: 1652 Smith Ct Streamwood IL 60103 Office: Blinderman Constrn Co Inc 1701 E Lake Ave Glenview IL 60025

PAJERSKI, BERNARD MICHAEL, cleaning co. exec.; b. Pitts., July 23, 1949; s. Michael Matthew and Nellie E. (Landowski) P.; student Community Coll. Allegheny County (Pa.), 1967-69, 71-72, U. Pitts., 1972-74; m. Sandra Jean. Mem. ground crew 3 Rivers Stadium, Pitts., 1971-76; owner, mgr. CIR Cleaning, Verona, Pa., 1974—. Active, Verona Firemen's Relief Fund. Served with U.S. Army, 1969-71. Decorated Bronze Star. Mem. C. of C., Bldg. Service Contractors Assn., VFW. Club: Kiwanis (dir.). Home: 440 Arch St Verona PA 15147 Office: 5238-5240 Verona Rd Verona PA 15147

PALAZZOLO, RUSSELL MICHAEL, electronic co. exec.; b. Geneva, N.Y., Sept. 28, 1938; s. Nicola R. and Ines (Nicocia) P.; grad. Coll. Advanced Traffic, Chgo., 1966; B.S., Mankato State U., 1976; m. Diane Elise Wheater, Dec. 4, 1964; children—Mark Andrew, Guy Andrew. With Gen. Electric Co., various locations, 1963—, mgr. transp., Portsmouth, Va., 1966-68, distbn. mgr., Charleston, S.C., 1968-72, divisional distbn. mgr., 1972—. Mem. adv. bd. So. Shippers, Atlanta, 1968—. Mem. adv. bd. San Jose City Coll. Mem. Nat. Indsl. Transp. League, Calif. Mfrs. Assn., Atomic Indsl. Forum, Delta Nu Alpha. Home: 6147 Encinal Dr San Jose CA 95119 Office: 175 Curtner Ave San Jose CA 95115

PALENCHAR, ROBERT EDWARD, diversified indsl. co. exec.; b. Detroit, Apr. 8, 1922; s. John Peter and Irene Ann (Repicky) P.; A.B., U. Notre Dame, 1942; m. Ethel Lindsey, Sept. 10, 1942; children—Patricia (Mrs. Richard K. Atchinson), James Lindsay. Vice-pres. indsl. relations automotive div. Budd Co., Detroit, 1962-66; v.p., dir. employee relations Sunbeam Corp., Chgo., 1966-69; v.p. personnel and pub. relations Esmark, Inc., Chgo., 1969-77, v.p. corp. affairs and personnel, 1977—; dir. Estech, Inc., Internat. Playtex, Inc., STP, Swift & Co., Chgo. Econ. Devel. Corp. Pres., Esmark Found.; bd. dirs. Chgo. Alliance Businessmen Manpower Services. Mem. Ill. State C. of C., Conf. Bd., Orgn. Planning Council, Indsl. Relations Assn. Chgo., Notre Dame Alumni Assn. Chgo. Assn. Commerce, Better Bus. Bur., Am. Mgmt. Assn. (Human Resource Council), Bus. Roundtable (labor mgmt. com.). Clubs: Glen Oak Country (Glen Ellyn, Ill.); Mid-Am. (Chgo.). Home: 64 Joyce Ct Glen Ellyn IL 60137 Office: 55 E Monroe St Chicago IL 60603

PALEY, WILLIAM S., corp. exec.; b. Chgo., Sept. 28, 1901; s. Samuel and Goldie (Drell) P.; grad. Western Mil. Acad., Alton, Ill., 1918; student U. Chgo., 1918-19; B.S., U. Pa., 1922, LL.D., 1967; LL.D., Adelphi U., 1957, Bates Coll., 1963, Columbia U., 1975, Brown U., 1975, Pratt Inst., 1977; m. Dorothy Hart Hearst, May 11, 1932; children—Jeffrey, Hilary; m. 2d, Barbara Cushing Mortimer, July 28, 1947; children—William Cushing, Kate Cushing. Vice pres., sec. Congress Cigar Co., Phila., 1922-28; pres. CBS, Inc., 1928-46, chmn. bd., 1946—. Mem. com. for White House Conf. on Edn., 1954-56; chmn. President's Materials Policy Commn. which produced report Resources for Freedom, 1951-52; mem. exec. com. Resources for Future, 1952-69, chmn., 1966-69, hon. dir., 1969—; chmn. N.Y.C. Task Force Urban Design, 1967; chmn. N.Y.C. Urban Design Council, 1968-71; pres., dir. William S. Paley Found., Greenpark Found. Inc.; bd. dirs. North Shore Univ. Hosp., 1949-73, co-chmn. bd. trustees, 1954-73; founding mem. Bedford-Stuyvesant D and S Corp., 1967-72; trustee Mus. Modern Art, 1937—, pres., 1968-72, chmn., 1972—; life trustee Columbia U., 1950-73, trustee emeritus, 1973—; dir. Internat. Exec. Service Corps; founder, chmn. bd. trustees Mus. Broadcasting, 1976—; life trustee Fedn. Jewish Philanthropies N.Y.; mem. Commn. on Critical Choices for Am., 1973-77, Commn. for Cultural Affairs, N.Y.C., 1975-78. Served as col. AUS, World War II, dep. chief psychol. warfare div. SHAEF, dep. chief Info. Control Div. of USGCC. Decorated Legion of Merit, Medal for Merit (U.S.); Croix de Guerre with palm, officer Legion of Honor (France); comdr. Order Merit (Italy); asso. comdr. Order St. John Jerusalem; recipient Medallion of Honor of City of N.Y., 1965; Gold Achievement medal Poor Richard Club; Keynote award Nat. Assn. Broadcasters; Spl. award Broadcast Pioneers; Concert Artist Guild award; Skowhegan Gertrude Vanderbilt Whitney award; Gold medal award Nat. Planning Assn. Mem. Council on Fgn. Relations, Econ. Club N.Y., France Am. Soc., Acad. Polit. Scis., Nat. Inst. Social Scis., Pilgrims U.S. Clubs: Economic, River (N.Y.C.); Met. (Washington); Turf and Field, Nat. Golf, Links Golf, Deepdale Golf, Meadowbrook, Century Assn.; Lyford Cay (Nassau, Bahamas); Bucks (London). Office: 51 W 52d St New York NY 10019

PALFREYMAN, RICHARD WARWICK, fin. exec.; b. Payson, Utah, Aug. 14, 1942; s. Warwick Charles and Ione (Averett) P.; B.S., U. Utah, 1966, M.B.A., 1967; m. Lindy Olson, June 9, 1966; children—Mandi, Scott, Michael, Matthew, Timothy. Fin. analyst Kaiser Aluminum & Chem., Oakland, Calif., 1967-68, mgr. lease financing, 1968-70, mgr. banking and staff services, 1971-72; treasury analyst Natomas, San Francisco, 1972-73; treas. analyst and asst. treas. 1973—; leasing officer First Security Corp., Salt Lake City, 1973. Mem. Risk and Ins. Mgmt. Soc., San Francisco Treasurers Club. Republican. Mem. Ch. of Jesus Christ of Latter Day Saints. Home: 123 Highland Ave Piedmont CA 94611 Office: 601 California St San Francisco CA 94108

PALLEIJA, PETER A., export mktg. exec.; b. Bayamo, Ote, Cuba, Mar. 26, 1934; s. Pedro A. and Elena P.; B.B.A., Havana U., 1955; postgrad. Rutgers U., 1964, Fashion Inst. Tech., 1968, Upsala Coll., 1959; m. Martha Jane Harrop, May 1, 1976; children—Pamela Ann, Melinda Ann. Internat. sales corr. Worthington Corp., 1959-62; asst. export mgr. Rutger Fabrics Corp., 1962-66; mgr. Caribbean sales J.P. Stevens & Co., N.Y.C., 1969-77; dir. textile sales Beaunit Internat., N.Y.C., 1969-77; export mgr. Blue Ridge Winkler Co., N.Y.C., 1977-79; dir. export mktg. Guilford Mills, Inc., N.Y.C., 1979—; dir. Skyline Terrace Corp., S.I.; Guilford Mills Inc. rep. to joint Dept. Commerce-Knitted Textiles Assn. econ. mission to U.K., France, W. Ger., Belgium. Served with USMC, 1955-59. Mem. N.Y.C. Ballet Soc., S.I. Arts Soc. Republican. Home: Staten Island NY 10301 Office: 180 Madison Ave New York NY 10016

PALM, EDWARD BERT, tool mfg. co. exec.; b. Cleve., Feb. 11, 1944; s. Bert and Harriett (Winburn) P.; student Ohio State U., 1962-64, Cleve. State U., 1964-66; m. Patricia Dennis, June 11, 1967; children—Merritt B., Justin D. Designer comml. kitchens Midwest Design Service, Cleve., 1964-66; sales rep. splty. chems. Diamond Alkalin Co., Cleve., 1966-67, fluid power components Alkan Products, Wayne, N.J., 1967-68; various positions, then v.p. sales Stilson div. KMS Industries, Roseville, Mich., 1968-73; pres. Detroit Tap & Tool Co., Warren, Mich., 1974—; dir. Detroit Tool Industries Corp. Mem. Soc. Mfg. Engrs., Cutting Tool Mfrs. Assn. Republican. Presbyterian. Clubs: Crescent Sail, Grosse Pointe Yacht. Home: 282 Moran Grosse Pointe Farms MI 48236 Office: 8615 E Eight Mile Rd Warren MI 48090

PALME, LENNART ALEXANDER, JR., commodity exchange exec.; b. Port Chester, N.Y., Sept. 30, 1935; s. Lennart A. and Jessica Burt (Colvin) P.; student U. Calif., Santa Barbara, 1952-53; B.A., Stanford, 1956, M.B.A., 1958; m. Virginia Ann Fisher, Dec. 23, 1977; children by previous marriage—Theodore Colvin, Pamela Esterly, Christopher Alexander. Supr. agrl. mktg. Kern County Land Co., Bakersfield, Calif., 1958-64; agrl. economist Armour & Co., Chgo., 1964-67; livestock economist Hayden Stone Co., Chgo., 1967-70; mgr. Clayton Brokerage Co., Santa Barbara, Calif., 1971-76; mgr. livestock mktg. Allied Mills, Inc., Chgo., 1976-78; mgr. agrl. research Chgo. Mercantile Exchange, 1978—; instr. Santa Barbara Coll., 1973-74. Regional v.p. Calif. Young Republicans, Bakersfield, 1964; chmn. Kern County (Calif.) Goldwater for Pres., Bakersfield, 1964; campaign mgr. Crane for Congress, Northbrook, Ill., 1969. Mem. Chgo. Agrl. Economists Club, Nat. Cattleman's Assn., Stanford Alumni Assn. Republican. Christian Scientist. Club: Oak Brook Bath and Tennis. Contbg. author The Feedlot, 1972. Home: 1008 Merry Ln Oakbrook IL 60521 Office: 444 W Jackson Blvd Chicago IL 60606

PALMER, CHARLES JOSEPH, computer services co. exec.; b. New Bedford, Mass., May 22, 1945; s. Charles Richard and Florence Rita (McDonald) P.; B.S. in Econs., Boston Coll., 1966; m. Martha L. Lanagan, Aug. 6, 1966; children—Maureen, Charles, James. With Burroughs Corp., 1967-69, Cogar Corp., 1969-70; sales mgr. Rapidata Inc., Boston, 1970-76; br. mgr. Camshare Inc., Wellesley. Mass., 1976—. Mem. Assn. Time-Sharing Users, Data Processing Mgmt. Assn., Am. Mgmt. Assn. Home: 79 Boyles St Beverly MA 01915 Office: 60 William St Wellesley MA 02181

PALMER, HARRY WARREN, digital equipment mfg. co. exec.; b. Clinton, Mass., Sept. 17, 1944; s. Harry Lewis and Maxine Elizabeth (White) P.; A.A., Mt. Wachusett Community Coll., Gardner, Mass., 1977; m. Deborah May Eden, Nov. 30, 1974; children—Aimee Beth, Jared Warren. With Digital Equipment Corp., 1969—, distbn. mgr., Westminster, Mass., 1975-77, materials service mgr., 1977—. Loaned exec. United Way of Central Mass., 1979-80. Served with U.S. Army, 1965-69; Vietnam. Mem. Greater Fitchburg (Mass.) C. of C. (dir.), Nat. Council Phys. Distbn. Mgmt., Warehouse Edn. and Research Council, Internat. Material Mgmt. Soc. Club: Masons. Home: 149C Beaman Rd Princeton MA 01541 Office: 1 Digital Dr Westminster MA 01473

PALMER, JAMES ROBERT, electronic mfg. exec.; b. Elm Creek, Nebr., Dec. 13, 1923; s. Charles Andrew and Margaret Eleanor (Mitchell) P.; B.S., Iowa State U. 1944; postgrad. U.S. Navy Officers PreRadar and Radar Schs., Bowdoin Coll., Mass. Inst. Tech.; postgrad. advanced engring. program Gen. Electric Co. 1947; m. Barbara M. Raeder, Aug. 21, 1948; children—Janet Palmer Lipcon, David, Charles. Project engr. Gen. Electric Co., Phila. 1946-51; elec. engr. United Engrs. and Constructors, Inc., 1951-53; project engr. Haller, Raymond and Brown, Inc., State College, Pa. 1953-56; pres. Centre Video and subs., State College, 1956-72, C-COR Electronics, State College, 1956—. Bd. dirs. Allegheny Ednl. Broadcast Council, 1966-74. Registered profl. engr., Pa. Mem. Nat. Cable TV Assn. (dir. 1965-68, chmn. various coms.), Pa. Community Antenna Assn. (pres. 1966-67, dir. 1960-66), IEEE (sr.), Tau Beta Pi, Eta Kappa Nu, Phi Kappa Phi. Presbyterian (elder). Patentee in field. Home: 324 Homan Ave State College PA 16801 Office: 60 Decibel Rd State College PA 16801

PALMER, JOHN ALLEN, screen and door mfg. co. exec.; b. Phila., Dec. 7, 1942; s. John Allen and Dorothy (Simpson) P.; B.S. in Mktg. and Bus. Adminstrn., Rider Coll., 1965; m. Carol Desoline Peri, Aug. 7, 1965; children—Elizabeth Allen, Melissa Ann. Salesman, U.S. Steel Corp., 1965-68, Revere Copper & Brass Co., N.Y.C., 1968-73, Consol. Aluminum Corp., St. Louis, 1973-75; v.p. Am. Screen & Door Co., Inc., Memphis, 1975-76, pres., chief exec. officer, 1976—, also dir.; Served with USAR, 1965-72. Republican. Episcopalian. Club: Germantown Kiwanis (dir. officer). Office: 490 Cumberland St Memphis TN 38112

PALMER, JOHN CANNON, comml. printing and office supplies co. exec.; b. N.Y.C., May 11, 1932; s. John Joseph and Margaret (Cannon) P.; B.A. in Philosophy and Psychology, St. John's U., N.Y.C., 1960; grad. Exec. Mgmt. Program, Pa. State U., 1974, 76; m. Sandra Schmitt, Sept. 16, 1954; children—Cynthia Anne, Lynn Anne, John Cannon, Christopher Thomas, Jennifer Hai. Asst. to traffic mgr. Asiatic Petroleum Corp., N.Y.C., 1955-60; successively sales rep., sales mgr., gen. mgr. Internat. Paper Co., N.Y.C., 1960-77; pres., prin. Am. Corrugated Containers, Cherry Hill, N.J., 1977-78; pres., chief exec. officer Edwards & Broughton Co., Raleigh, N.C., 1979—. Bd. dirs. My Friend's House, Boston, 1974-74, Family to Family, Council Bluffs, Iowa, 1975—. Served with USMC, 1950-54; Korea. Mem. Sales Execs. of Am., Graphic Arts Tech. Assn., Printing Industries of Carolinas, Power Squadron Am. Roman Catholic. Club: Raleigh Kiwanis. Home: 11621 Coachman's Way Raleigh NC 27614 Office: 1821 N Boulevard Raleigh NC 27611

PALMER, JOHN LEWIS, lawyer, plumbing mfr.; b. Milw., Nov. 22, 1921; s. John Lewis and Florence Margaret (Schneider) P.; B.A., Beloit (Wis.) Coll., 1947; J.D., U. Wis., 1949; m. Virginia Frances Smith, July 15, 1944; children—Michael John, Steven Peter. Admitted to Wis. bar, 1949; partner firm Whyte & Hirschboeck, Milw., 1949-71; exec. v.p., gen. counsel, sec., dir. Bradley Corp. and subsidiaries, Menomonee Falls, Wis., 1971-79, pres., dir., 1979-80, chmn. bd., chief exec. officer, dir., 1980—; dir. Imperial Marble Corp., Pelton Casteel, Inc., KSM Industries, Inc., Kieckhefer Assos., Inc., Eilcar Corp., Alpha Cellulose Corp. Alumni trustee Beloit Coll., 1972-75. Served to capt. USMCR, 1943-46. Mem. Am., Wis., Milw. bar assns., Order of Coif, Phi Beta Kappa. Republican. Congregationalist. Clubs: Milw. Country, Tucson Nat. Golf. Contbr. articles to profl. jours. Home: 780 E Ravine Ln Milwaukee WI 53217 also 7939 N Tuscany Dr Tucson AZ 85704 Office: PO Box 446 Menomonee Falls WI 53051

PALMER, ROBERT JOSEPH, advt. exec.; b. Queens, N.Y., July 16, 1934; s. Patrick J. and Irene M. (O'Brien) Prignano; m. Lorraine E. Wittmer, Sept. 27, 1958; children—Linda, Katherine, Lori-Anne, Barbara. Page ABC-TV, N.Y.C., 1949-52; trainee Kenyon & Eckhart Advt., N.Y.C., 1952-54; buyer media, v.p., asso. dir. media, dir. TV programming, mgr. new bus. Cunningham & Walsh Advt., N.Y.C., 1954-70; pres. Kelly Nason, Inc., N.Y.C., 1970-78, also chief exec. officer; chmn. bd. Davis Communications; pres. 42d St. TV Programming, Telecators, Inc., 1979—, Robert J. Palmer, Inc., 1979—, N.Y.C. Address: 575 Madison Ave New York NY 10022*

PALMER, ROBERT TOWNE, lawyer; b. Chgo., May 25, 1947; s. Adrian Bernhardt and Gladys (Towne) P.; B.A., Colgate U., 1969; J.D., U. Notre Dame, 1974; m. Ann Therese Darin, Nov. 9, 1974; 1 son, Justin Darin. Admitted to Ill. bar, 1974; law clk. to judge Ill. Supreme Ct., 1974-75; atty. firm McDermott, Will & Emery, Chgo., 1975—; adj. faculty Chgo.-Kent Sch. Law, 1975-77, Loyola U. Law Sch., 1976-78. Mem. Am. Bar Assn., Ill. State Bar, D.C. Bar Assn., Chgo. Bar Assn., Mensa. Episcopalian. Clubs: Chgo., University, Saddle and Cycle. Contbr. articles to legal jours. Home: 5555 N Sheridan Rd Chicago IL 60640 Office: 111 W Monroe St Chicago IL 60603

PALMER, RUSSELL E., accounting co. exec.; b. Jackson, Mich., Aug. 13, 1934; s. Russell E. and Margarite M. (Briles) P.; B.A. with honors, Mich. State U., 1956; D.C.S. (hon.), Drexel U., 1980; m. Phyllis Anne Hartung, Sept. 8, 1956; children—Bradley Carl, Stephen Russell, Russell Eugene, III, Karen Jean. With Touche Ross & Co.,

C.P.A.'s, 1956—, mgr., 1964-66, partner, 1966—, partner in charge Phila. office, 1968-72, mng. partner, chief exec. officer, N.Y.C., 1972—, also bd. dirs., exec. coms. Trustee Fin. Accounting Found., pres., 1979—; trustee Accounting Hall of Fame, Carnegie Hall Corp., Greenwich Country Day Sch., Com. Econ. Devel.; mem. Bus. Com. Arts, Joint Council Econ. Edn.; bd. dirs. UN Assn., United Fund Greater N.Y.; mem. Pres.'s Mgmt. Improvement Council, 1979-80; adv. bd. Salvation Army, N.Y. U. Grad. Sch. Bus.; adv. council Stanford U. Grad. Sch. Bus.; bd. visitors U. Conn. Sch. Bus. Adminstrn. Recipient Gavin Meml. award Beta Theta Pi, 1956. Presbyterian. Clubs: Links, Union League, Merion Cricket, Field of Greenwich, Round Hill, N.Y. Athletic. Office: 1633 Broadway New York NY 10019

PALMER, STANLEY LEMOYNE, accountant, union exec.; b. Benkelman, Nebr., Sept. 6, 1947; s. William LeMoyne and Cleo Emmareta (White) P.; B.S. in Bus. Adminstrn. and Acctg., So. Colo. State Coll., 1975; student Pikes Peak Community Coll., 1979—. Data collection technician U.S. Postal Service, Colorado Springs, Colo., 1966—; pvt. practice tax acctg., 1975—; treas. Colorado Springs Area local 247 Am. Postal Workers Union, 1978—. Served with USMC, 1970-72. Democrat. Roman Cathdlic. Home: PO Box 15444 Colorado Springs CO 80935

PALMER, TED WAYNE, mfg. co. exec.; b. Cabool, Mo., Sept. 7, 1933; s. R.W. and Rosa (Derry) P.; A.A., Boise State U., 1954; B.S. in Chem. Engring., Oreg. State U., 1957; children—Ted Wayne, Thomas W., Laura, Alison, Mary. With The Dow Chem. Co., Midland, Mich., 1957-70, bus. mgr. organic chems. until 1970; pres., chmn. bd. Kalama Chem., Inc., Seattle, 1971—. Mem. Young Pres.'s Orgn., Nat. Petroleum Refiners Assn. Republican. Episcopalian. Clubs: Rainier, Seattle Yacht, Washington Athletic. Home: 8885 Woodbank Dr Bainbridge Island WA 98110 Office: 1110 Bank of Calif Seattle WA 98164

PALMER, WHITFIELD MCRORY, JR., stone co. exec.; b. Ocala, Fla., Mar. 28, 1929; s. Whitfield McRory and Margaret (Eddins) P.; student U. Fla., 1948-51; m. Polly Martorell, July 28, 1952; children—Henry E., Margaret Palmer Smith, Whitfield McRory III, Susan Eddins, Thomas Martin. With Dixie Lime and Stone Co., Ocala, 1951-70; with Fla. Crushed Stone Co., Leesburg, 1972—, now chmn. bd.; dir. Ft. Myers So. R.R. Co., Sun Bank of Ocala, Sikes Corp., Jacksonville br. Atlanta Fed. Res. Bank Bd. Past mem. Fla. Jr. Coll. Bd.; past pres. U. Fla. Found.; past campaign chmn. United Way of Ocala; past chmn. City of Ocala Planning Bd. Recipient Disting. Alumnus award and Pres.'s medallion U. Fla., 1975. Mem. Nat. Lime Assn., Fla. Lime Rock Inst., Fla. Aggregates Assn., Nat. Limestone Inst., NAM, Fla. C. of C., Young Pres.'s Orgn., Nat. Crushed Stone Assn., U. Fla. Alumni Assn. (past pres.), Ocala-Marion County C. of C. (past mem. exec. com.). Episcopalian. Clubs: Elks (Ocala); Golden Hills Golf and Turf. Home: 5910 SW 27th Ave PO Box 367 Ocala FL 32671 Office: 1616 S 14th St PO Box 317 Leesburg FL 32748

PALMER, WILLIAM K., III, investment banker; b. Oak Park, Ill., Oct. 16, 1926; s. William K. and Sonja (Johnson) P.; student Mich. State U., 1944-45, U. Ill., 1946-47; m. Nancy Helen Thomsen, Mar. 19, 1947; children—Linda J. (Mrs. Morton), Thomas W., Sally L., William R. Sec.-treas., William Palmer, Inc., Oak Park, 1947-55; registered rep. Paine, Webber Jackson & Curtis, Chgo., 1955-64, gen. partner, 1965—, now v.p. Served with USAAF, 1945. Mem. Newcomen Soc., Securities Industry Assn. Republican. Presbyn. Mason, Rotarian. Club: Sedona Racquet. Home: Drawer 4040 West Sedona AZ 86340 Office: Vista del Norte Bldg Rural Route 2 Sedona AZ 86336

PALOMBO, MICHAEL ANTHONY, ins. exec.; b. Pitts., Mar. 31, 1947; s. Domenico and Sophia Catherine (Belotti) P.; Asso. Sci., Allegheny Community Coll., 1971; B.S., Pa. State U., 1973; m. Bernadette Marie Jones, June 4, 1971; 1 son, Domenic Michael. With The Bakery, Inc. (formerly Dolly Donuts), Rancho Cucamonga, Calif., 1973-80, owner, 1974-80; salesman Prudential Ins. Co., 1980—; small bus. cons. Mem. Rancho Cucamonga City Council, 1977—, city finance dir., 1977-78; mem. CETA Regional Council, West Valley Transp. Com., Public Safety Commn. of League of Calif. Cities. Mem. Nat. Fedn. Ind. Bus., U.S. C. of C. Democrat. Roman Catholic. Clubs: Kiwanis (dir. 1976-77, sec.-treas. 1979-80), Elks. Home: 7501 Cerrito Rojo Rancho Cucamonga CA 91730 Office: 675 W Foothill Blvd Suite 201 Claremont CA 91711

PALUMBO, JOHN SAMUEL, fiber and fabric mfg. co. exec.; b. Tampa, Fla., Dec. 18, 1951; s. Norman A. and Caterina P.; student U. So. Miss., 1969-70; B.A., U. South Fla., 1973. Acct., Price, Waterhouse & Co., C.P.A.'s Atlanta, 1973-76; controller Snapfinger Sportswear Co., Atlanta. 1976-79; controller Gen. Fibers & Fabrics, Inc., LaGrange, Ga., 1979—. C.P.A. Club: Kiwanis. Office: 709 Lee St LaGrange GA 30240

PAMPLIN, ROBERT BOISSEAU, JR., agrl. co. exec.; b. Augusta, Ga., Sept. 3, 1941; s. Robert Boisseau and Mary Katherine (Reese) P.; student in bus. adminstrn. Va. Poly. Inst., 1960-62; B.S. in Bus. Adminstrn., Lewis and Clark Coll., 1964, B.S. in Acctg., 1965, B.S. in Econs., 1966; M.B.A., U. Portland, 1968, M.Ed., 1975, LL.D. (hon.), 1972; M.C.L., Western Conservation Bapt. Sem., 1978; cert. in wholesale mgmt., Ohio State U., 1970; cert. in labor mgmt. U. Portland, 1972; certificate in advanced mgmt., U. Hawaii, 1975; m. Marilyn Joan Hooper; children—Amy Louise, Anne Boisseau. Pres. R. B. Pamplin Corp., Portland, Oreg., 1964—; chmn. bd., pres. Columbia Empire Farms, Inc., Lake Oswego, Oreg., 1976—; pres. Twelve Oaks Farms, Inc., Lake Oswego, 1977—; lectr. bus. adminstr. Lewis and Clark Coll., 1968-69; adj. asst. prof. bus. adminstrn., U. Portland, 1973-76; lectr. in bus. adminstrn. and econs. U. Costa Rica, 1968. Mem. Nat. Adv. Council on Vocat. Edn., 1975—; mem. Oreg. State Scholarship Commn., 1974—, chmn., 1976-78; mem. Portland dist. adv. council SBA, 1973-77; mem. Rewards Review Com., City Portland, 1973-78, chmn., 1973-78; bd. regents U. Portland, 1971-79, chmn. bd., 1975-79, regent emeritus, 1979—; trustee Lewis and Clark Coll., 1980—, Oreg. Episcopal Schs., 1979—. Named distinguished alumni, Lewis and Clark Coll., 1974; recipient Air Force ROTC Distinguished Service award, U.S.A.F., 1974. Mem. Acad. Mgmt., Delta Epsilon Sigma. Republican. Episcopalian. Clubs: Waverley Country, Arlington, Multnomah Athletic, Rotary. Editor Oreg. Mus. Sci. and Industry Press, 1973, trustee, 1971, 74—; editor Portrait of Oregon, 1973; co-author: A Portrait of Colorado, 1976; author (with others) Three in One, 1974, The Storybook Primer on Managing, 1974; editor (with others) Oregon Underfoot, 1975. Address: 3131 W View Ct Lake Oswego OR 97034

PAN, BINGHAM YING KUEI, chem. engr.; b. Hunan, China, Feb. 11, 1925; s. Tsai-How and Chow (Shih) P.; B.S., Ordnance Engring. Coll., Chungking, China, 1947; M.S., Va. Poly. Inst., 1956, Ph.D., 1959; m. Terry Ti-wei Liu, Nov. 12, 1949; children—Kim K.T., Karl K.Y., Shirley L. Came to U.S., 1955. Engr. 23d Arsenal, Szechwan, China, 1947-49; instr. chem. engring. Ordnance Sch. & Hwalien (Taiwan) Engring. Inst., 1949-52, group leader design and research The Ordnance Service, Taipei, Taiwan, 1952-55; teaching asst., fellow Va. Poly Inst., 1955-59; with Monsanto Co., Texas City, Tex., 1959-74, research engr., 1959-60, sr. research engr., 1961-65, sr. process engr., 1965-66, process specialist, 1966-74; group leader Occidental Research Corp., Irvine, Calif., 1974—. Mem. Am. Chem. Soc., Am. Inst. Chem. Engrs., N.Y. Acad. Scis., Phi Lambda Phi, Phi Kappa Phi. Toastmaster. Contbr. articles to profl. jours. Patentee in field. Home: 2442 N San Fernando Ct Claremont CA 91711 Office: Occidental Research Corp 2100 Main St Irvine CA 92714

PAN, PETER NAW YANK, mfg. co. exec.; b. N.Y.C., Feb. 1, 1942; s. Wen Yuan and Julia W.T. Pan; B.E.E., Rensselaer Poly. Inst., 1963, M.E.E., 1965; Ph.D. in Physics, Tex. Christian U., 1970; postgrad. Harvard U. Bus. Sch., 1975; m. Carolyn L. Benjamin, July 23, 1963; children—Victoria, Michael, William. Sr. research scientist Continental Group Inc., Chgo., 1970-72, mgr. research and devel., 1972-77; v.p. Paxall Inc., Chgo., 1977—; exec. v.p., gen. mgr. Thiele Engring. Co., Mpls., 1979—; dir. PHP Inc., Mpls. Bd. dirs. Country Club Hills (Ill.) Library Bd., 1970-72; mem., pres. Sch. Dist. 160 Bd., 1971-77. Recipient Humanitarian of Yr. award Jaycees, 1970. Mem. IEEE, Tex. Acad. Sci., Soc. Mfg. Engrs., Am. Inst. Physics, Sigma Xi. Contbr. articles to profl. jours.; patentee in field. Home: 18408 Timber Ridge Dr Minnetonka MN 55343 Office: 7225 Bush Lake Rd Minneapolis MN 55435

PANAGAKO, JOHN PETER, real estate devel. co. exec.; b. Hartford, Conn., Mar. 23, 1944; s. Peter John and Bessie (Paganakis) P.; B.S. in Bus. Adminstrn., U. R.I., 1966; m. Janice Kapos, June 7, 1970; children—Peter John, Michael John. With Medi Mart div. Stop & Shop, 1968-69; controller community mgmt. div. Devel. Corp. Am., 1969-70; dir. property mgmt. Tern Mgmt. div. Pastan Constrn., Winthrop, Mass., 1973-76; dir. devel. Kelly & Picerne, Inc., Cranston, R.I., 1979-80; pres. Consol. Devel., Bristol, R.I., 1980—. Bd. dirs. Bristol Highlands Improvement Assn. Served with USAF, 1966-68. Mem. Inst. Real Estate Mgmt., Nat. Assn. Homebuilders, Real Estate Securities and Syndication Inst., R.I. Realtors. Office: 44 Gibson Rd Bristol RI 02809

PANCERO, JACK BLOCHER, restaurant exec.; b. Cin., Dec. 27, 1923; s. Howard and Hazel Mae (Blocher) P.; student Ohio State U., 1941-44; m. Loraine Fielman, Aug. 4, 1944; children—Gregg Edward, Vicki Lee. Partner, Howard Pancero & Co., Cin., 1948-66; stockbroker Gradison & Co., Cin., 1966-70; real estate asso. Parchman & Oyler, Cin., 1970-72; v.p. Gregg Pancero, Inc., Kings Mills, Ohio, 1972—. Methodist. Clubs: Western Hills Country, Cin., Engrs. Table, Masons, Shrine; Wilderness Country (Naples, Fla.). Home: 5730 Pinehill Ln Cincinnati OH 45238 Office: Kings Island Columbia Rd Kings Mills OH 45034

PANCOE, WALTER, fin. exec.; b. Chgo., Oct. 18, 1923; s. Morris A. and Florence (Lidsker) P.; B.S. in Mech. Engring., U. Wis., 1947; m. Carolyn S. Imig, Dec. 21, 1975; children—Patricia G., Peggy C. Pancoe Rosoff, Polly A.; stepchildren—Cheri L. Brasser, Richard C. Brasser. Pres., dir. Standard Stationery Supply Co. (named changed to 1020 Corp. 1972), Chgo., 1947—, Imperial Fastener Co., Chgo., 1952-72, 1616 Bldg. Corp., 1965-72, Walart Mgmt. Co., Chgo., 1965—; gen. partner Northcrest Assos., 1976—, Mountain View Futures Fund, 1976—; developer Sand Caper, Sun Caper, Caper Beach Club, Boardwalk Caper condominiums, Ft. Myers Beach, Fla.; pres. Caper Beach Corp.; mem. faculty, trustee Fox Valley Coll. Trustee U. Wis. Student Union, 1967—. Served to ensign USNR, World War II; PTO. Mem. Alpha Delta Sigma, Pi Lambda Phi. Clubs: Zorine's (Chgo.), Cape Fear Country (Wilmington, N.C.). Author: (with Mitchell S. Rieger) Word Trap, 1955. Office: 1020 S Wabash Ave Chicago IL 60605

PANDYA, NAVINCHANDRA N., cons. civil engr.; b. Mangrol, India, Jan. 30, 1928; came to U.S., 1957, naturalized, 1967; s. B. and Rambhaben N. (Joshi) P.; B.E.Civil, Gujarat U., 1954; M.S. in Civil Engring., Watne State U., Detroit, 1959; postgrad. U. Mich., 1959-63; m. Snehlata P. Joshi, Apr. 29, 1954; children—Sonal, Pranav, Prashant. Chief civil engr. Atul Products Co., Bulsar, India, 1954-57; instr. Wayne State U., 1959-62; with Giffels Assos., Inc., Southfield, Mich., 1962—, dir. computer applications, 1973-78, dir. advanced tech., 1978—; partner Real Investment Co., Universal Investment Co., CPPZ Co.; part-time vis. and teaching prof. Wayne State U., U. Detroit, Lawrence Inst. Tech. Vice pres. Baratiya Temple, Detroit. Mem. ASCE (br. pres. 1975), Am. Concrete Inst., Cultural Soc. India (pres. 1975). Club: Toastmasters (pres. Detroit 1979). Author papers in field. Home: 27460 Everett St Southfield MI 48076 Office: 25200 Telegraph Rd Southfield MI 48076

PANFELD, ARTHUR JAY, acct.; b. Bklyn., Mar. 15, 1927; s. Peter M. and Rose (Goodrich) P.; B.B.A. cum laude St. Mary's U., San Antonio, 1950; m. Shirley L. Schwartz, Oct. 27, 1957; children—Kenneth, Michael, Jeanie. Asst. mgr. Ernst & Ernst, San Antonio, 1950-62; asst. controller Acme Brick Co., Ft. Worth, 1962-64; partner Karpel, Panfeld & Edelman, C.P.A.'s, San Antonio, 1964-78; partner Panfeld, Edelman & Stein, C.P.A.'s San Antonio, 1979—. Bd. dirs. Temple Beth-El, San Antonio, 1973—, treas., 1974-76, 3d v.p., 1980-81. Recipient Outstanding Service award San Antonio chpt. Tex. Soc. C.P.A.'s, 1978-79; C.P.A., Tex. Mem. Tex. Soc. C.P.A.'s (dir. San Antonio chpt. 1977-79), Am. Inst. C.P.A.'s. Jewish. Home: 3615 Rockview San Antonio TX 78230 Office: 1800 NE Loop 410 Plaza W Suite 300 San Antonio TX 78217

PANG, JOSHUA KEUN-UK, trade co. exec.; b. Chinnampo, Korea, Sept. 17, 1924; s. Ne-Too and Soon-Hei (Kim) P.; came to U.S., 1951, naturalized, 1968; B.S., Roosevelt U., 1959; m. He-Young Yoon, May 30, 1963; children—Ruth, Pauline, Grace. Chemist, Realemon Co. Am., Chgo., 1957-61; chief-chemist chem. div. Bell & Gossett Co., Chgo., 1961-63, Fatty Acid Inc., div. Ziegler Chem. & Mineral Corp., Chgo., 1963-64; sr. chemist-supr. Gen. Mills Chems. Inc., Kankakee, Ill., 1964-70; pres., owner UJU Industries Inc., Broadview, Ill., 1971—, also dir. Bd. dirs. Dist. 92, Lindop Sch., Broadview, 1976—; chmn. Proviso Area Sch. Bd. Assn., Proviso Twp., Cook County, Ill., 1976-77; bd. dirs. Korean Am. Community Services, Chgo., 1979. Mem. Am. Chem. Soc., Am. Inst. Parliamentarians (regional treas. 1979—), Internat. Platform Assn., Nat. Speakers Assn., Ill. Sch. Bd. Assn., Chgo. Area Parliamentarians. Toastmaster (dist. gov. 1970). Home: 2532 S 9th Ave Broadview IL 60153 Office: PO Box 351 Broadview IL 60153

PANKEY, EDGAR EDWARD, rancher, developer; b. Irvine, Calif., May 22, 1916; s. John Henry and Emma Jane (Bercaw) P.; B.A., Pomona Coll., 1938; m. Elizabeth Libby Searles, Feb. 4, 1939; children—Victor Searles, James Henry, Roberta Lynn Pankey Jones, Peter Searles. Owner, operator Pankey Ranches Inc., So. Calif. and Ariz., 1945-78; owner, dir. Tustin East Corp., 1967-78, Pankey Blower Investment Corp., Riverside, Calif., 1963-76; v.p. Maricopa Mining Co., 1977—; owner, operator Pankey Plaza, Thoner-Pankey; co-owner Pankey Kern County, Challenge Grove Pty. Ltd., South Australia; partner Calif. Best Hydrofarms; chmn. bd. Bank of Irvine; dir. Pyrotonics, Inc., Orange County Dist. Exchange. Pres. Orange County Sch. Bds. Assn., 1958-59; mem. study mission to European Common Market, 1963; pres. trustees Tustin Presbyterian Ch., 1955-58; fin. chmn. Children's Hosp. Orange County; asso. dir. Santa Ana-Tustin Community Hosp.; mem. pres.'s council Chapman Coll. Served to capt USAAF, World War II. Mem. World Affairs Council Orange County (pres. 1976-78, chmn. bd. 1978-80), Irvine Valencia Growers (v.p. 1970—), Yuma Mesa Fruit Growers, Orange County C. of C., Baja Bush Pilots, U.S. Scuba Divers, Aircraft Owners and Pilots Assns., Orange County Farm Bur. Republican. Club: Elks. Home: 320 W Main St Tustin CA 92680

PANKRATZ, JOHN ROBERT, tree farmer, lumber and flooring distbr.; b. Seattle, Sept. 6, 1935; s. John Simpson and Josephine Lurinthia (Gilmore) P.; B.S., Stanford, 1958; m. Noriene Louise Wagner, May 11, 1974; children by previous marriage—Jeff, John, Jay, Joanie. Test engr. Boeing Co., Seattle, 1958-60; mng. partner Pankratz Lumber Co., Seattle, 1960—; pres., chief exec. officer Pankratz Forest Industries, 1960—, Kelly-Goodwin Hardwood Co., 1969—, Greater Seattle Floors, 1980—; mem. Master Resources Council Internat. Fin. chmn. Lakeside Sch., Seattle, 1965-70, also trustee; fin. chmn. Seattle-Stanford U., 1968—; fin. chmn. Univ. Congl. Ch., 1970-73, also trustee; Stanford pres. rep. Seattle Pacific Coll. Investiture, 1968. Named Outstanding Grad., Lakeside Sch., 1953. Mem. ASME, U.S. Power Squadron, Nat. Assn. Wholesale Distbrs., Nat. Soc. Profl. Engrs., Maple Flooring Mfrs. Assn., World Trade Club, Stanford Assos., Seattle C. of C. Clubs: Masons, Seattle Rotary, Edmonds Yacht, Seattle Golf, Seattle Yacht, Rainier. Home: 155 N 145th St Seattle WA 98133 Office: 320 Terry Ave N Seattle WA 98109

PANNABECKER, ROBERT TSCHANTZ, utility ofcl.; b. Puyang, Honan, China, Oct. 9, 1925; s. Samuel Floyd and Sylvia Lydia (Tschantz) P.; B.S. in Bus. Adminstrn., Bluffton (Ohio) Coll., 1949; m. Deborah Bishop, May 19, 1951; children—Leslie, David. Sales rep. N.W. Airlines, Inc., 1949-54; Far Eastern sales mgr. Wyeth Internat., Ltd. subs. Am. Home Products Corp., 1954-61; various ins. positions, Honolulu, 1961-67; dir. ins. and claims Hawaiian Elec. Co., Inc., Honolulu, 1967—. C.P.C.U.; asso. in risk mgmt. Mem. Soc. C.P.C.U.'s, Risk and Ins. Mgmt. Soc. (past pres. Hawaii chpt., legis. rep.), Edison Elec. Inst. Republican. Episcopalian. Office: PO Box 2750 Honolulu HI 96840

PANNY, WILLIAM PAUL, corp. exec.; b. N.Y.C., Apr. 18, 1928; s. Frank and Rose (Petz) P.; B.M.E., Pratt Inst., 1951; M.Automotive Engring., Chrysler Inst. Engring., 1953; m. Lillian Dragosits, Aug. 4, 1951; children—Gail Susan, Lynn Diane, Karen Michele, William Robert. Jr. engr. Fairchild Guided Missiles div. Fairchild Engine & Airplane Co., 1951; with Chrysler Corp., 1951-60, asst. chief engr. trucks; with Pioneer Engring. & Mfg. Co., Warren, Mich., 1960-66, exec. v.p., 1962-66; v.p., gen. mgr., dir. Paramount Engring. Co., Madison Heights, Mich., 1966-68; v.p. engring. automotive ops. Rockwell Internat. Corp., 1968-70, v.p., gen. plants mgr., 1970-71, pres. Rockwell-Standard div., 1971-74, exec. v.p. automotive ops., 1974, pres., 1975-76, exec. v.p. parent co., 1976-77; chief operating officer Bendix Corp., Southfield, Mich., 1977—, vice chmn., 1977-79, pres., chief operating officer, 1979—; instr. mech. engring. Lawrence Inst. Tech., 1953-55. Mem. adv. bd. United Found.; trustee Rackham Engring. Found., Marygrove Coll., Citizens Research Council Mich. Served with USMC, World War II. Named Outstanding Young Engr. of Yr., Engring. Soc. Detroit, 1958. Registered profl. engr., Mich. Mem. Soc. Automotive Engrs. (mem. fin. com.), Nat. Security Indsl. Assn., Engring. Soc. Detroit (mem. bd., past pres.), Am. Soc. Body Engrs., Am Def. Preparedness Assn., Automotive Orgn. Team, Soc. Mfg. Engrs., Am. Mgmt. Assn., Hwy. Users Fedn. (dir.), Soc. Plastic Industries, Nat. Rifleman Assn., Assn. U.S. Army, Western Hwy. Inst. (dir.), Am. Trucking Assn., Tau Beta Pi. Clubs: Detroit Athletic, Renaissance (Detroit); Hunters Creek (Metamora, Mich.); Bloomfield Hills Country; Ducks Unltd.; Turtle Lake (Hillman, Mich.). Office: Bendix Corp Bendix Center Southfield MI 48037*

PANOFF, CHARLES E., wholesale hosp. supply co. exec.; b. Bklyn., Dec. 27, 1942; s. Irving E. and Madeline R. Panoff; student Syracuse U., 1962: 1 dau., Jamison Elizabeth. Transp. cons. Star Maintenance Co., N.Y.C., 1968; lighting cons. Luxor Lighting Co., N.Y.C., 1965-66; career counselor Careers Unltd. Inc., N.Y.C., 1967-68: dir. mktg. Nuclear Research Assos., Gt. Neck, N.Y., 1968-69; pres. Stanley Hosp. Supply Corp., Elmsford, N.Y., 1969—; tchr., lectr. Am. Mgmt. Research Assos., 1971. Served with USAF, 1967-68. Mem. Nat. Assn. Wholesaler-Distbrs. (trustee), Am. Surg. Trade Assn., U.S. Power Squadron, U.S. Coast Guard Aux. (vice comdr. flotilla 63), Tau Epsilon Phi. Clubs: Rotary (Elmsford); Huguenot Yacht (New Rochelle, N.Y.); Orienta Beach Yacht, Sheldrake Yacht (Mamaroneck, N.Y.) Office: 13 Havens St Elmsford NY 10523

PANZENHAGEN, BERNARD HARRY, supermarket chain exec.; b. N.Y.C., Oct. 7, 1935; s. Herbert Ludwig and Marie (Albohn) P.; student Fairleigh Dickinson U.; m. Ann Claire Hennessy, Sept. 26, 1956; children—Jean Marie, Robert Bernard. Gen. mgr. Super Excelsor Food Mart Inc., 1958-66, pres., Paramus, N.J., 1966—; founder, pres. Panbro Excelsior Companies Inc., Paramus, 1968—; pres. Super Excelsior Trucking Co., 1971-74; dir. Twin County Grocers Inc., Foodtown Stores Inc.; sec. Foodtown Stores Inc. Mem. Supermarket Inst., N.J. Food Counsel, Supermarket Inst. (operating exec. com.). Home: 575 Ramapo Valley Rd Oakland NJ 07438 Office: 54 Rt 17 Paramus NJ 07652

PAOLINO, RICHARD FRANCIS, precision automated measurement systems mfg. co. exec.; b. Fall River, Mass., Feb. 16, 1945; s. Emelio and Sylvia (Fasciani) P.; A.B. in Engring. Sci., Dartmouth Coll., 1967; M.B.A. in Mktg. and Fin., U. Chgo., 1973; m. Elizabeth Jane Maloney, Sept. 9, 1973; children—Christopher Matthew, Kathryn Elizabeth. Plant engr. Polaroid Corp., Cambridge, Mass., 1967; from salesman to asst. br. mgr., Chgo., Fed. Products Corp., 1967-74; area mgr., nat. accounts mgr., Chgo. and Toronto, Can., Husky Injection Molding Systems, 1974-76; v.p. mktg. Quality Measurement Systems Inc., Penfield, N.Y., 1976-78; dir. mktg. domestic ops. Automation and Measurement div. Bendix Corp., Dayton, Ohio, 1978—; condr. seminars, lectr. in field. Served to 1st lt. USMCR, 1967-69. Mem. Soc. Mfg. Engrs. (chmn. quality assurance tech. council), Soc. Quality Control. Home: 321 Shafor Blvd Oakwood OH 45419 Office: PO Box 1127 721 Springfield St Dayton OH 45401

PAONESSA, PHILIP JOSEPH, state ofcl., accountant; b. Peeksill, N.Y., May 25, 1917; s. Joseph and Maria (DeSantis) P.; B.B.A. cum laude, Niagara U., 1951; diploma bus. adminstrn. Bryant and Stratton Bus. Coll., 1937; m. Florence Presti, Sept. 3, 1945; children—Maria Ann, Joseph P., Philip John. Office mgr. Diffine's Quality Dairy, Inc., Niagara Falls, N.Y., 1939-41; pvt. practice acctg., Niagara Falls, 1940—; asst. to purchasing agt. Vanadium Corp., Niagara Falls, 1941-44; acct. D.F. Cubello, C.P.A., Niagara Falls, part time 1944-51; milk accounts examiner Niagara Frontier Milk Mktg. Area, Buffalo, 1944-58, sr. milk accounts examiner, 1958-71, asso. acct., 1971-75, adminstr. mktg. area, 1975—; sec., dir. Cataract Furniture Inc.; acct., comptroller Alonge's Floor Covering; instr. acctg. Niagara County Community Coll., evenings 1964-66. Mem. Democratic City Com., 1958—; mem. Niagara County Dem. Exec. Com., 1964-65; mem. parish council Our Lady of Mt. Carmel Catholic Ch., 1974-75. Mem. Niagara U. Alumni Assn. (dir. 1966-67), Empire State Assn. Pub. Accts., N.Y. State Soc. Ind. Accts., Nat. Soc. Pub. Accts., Assn. Enrolled Agts. Club: K.C. Home: 524 30th St Niagara Falls NY 14301 Office: 125 Main St Buffalo NY 14203

PAPA, ALFRED VINCENT, JR., strategic planning, mktg. cons.; b. New Castle, Pa., July 5, 1946; s. Alfred Vincent and Susan Patricia (Cook) P.; B.A., Geneva Coll., 1969; M.Ed., Slippery Rock State Coll., 1971; M.A., U. Akron, 1973; D.B.A., Pacific Western U., 1980; m. Marilyn Joan Armstrong, Mar. 1, 1975; 1 son, Vincent James. Research asst. Slippery Rock State Coll., 1970-72; research asso. Center for Urban Studies, U. Akron, 1972-73; mgr. spl. mktg. projects Pa. Dept. Agr., 1973-75; spl. asst. for econ. devel. Pa. Dept. Commerce, 1975-78; sr. cons., project mgr. Day and Zimmermann, Inc., Phila., 1978—; condr. mgmt. tng. seminars for small businesses; named to Community Leadership Tng. Programs, Wharton Sch., U. Pa., 1980. Del. UN World Food Conf., Rome, 1974; co-leader Internat. Mktg. Tour of Sweden and Netherlands, 1975. Mem. Am. Mgmt. Assn. Democrat. Roman Catholic. Clubs: Glenhardie Country, Peale. Author: Cost-Benefit Analysis of Public Institutions, 1973; Steel and the Economy, 1978. Office: Day and Zimmermann Inc 1818 Market St Philadelphia PA 19103

PAPADIMITRIOU, DIMITRI BASIL, economist, coll. adminstr.; b. Salonica, Greece, June 9, 1946; s. Basil John and Ellen (Tacas) P.; came to U.S., 1965, naturalized, 1974; B.A., Columbia U., 1970; M.A., New Sch. Social Research, 1974, postgrad., 1974—, now Ph.D. candidate; m. Vasiliki Fokas, Aug. 26, 1967; children—Jennifer E., Elizabeth R. Vice pres., asst. sec. ITT Life Ins. Co. N.Y., N.Y.C., 1970-73; sr. v.p., sec., treas. William Penn Life Ins. Co. N.Y., N.Y.C., after 1973, also dir.; now exec. v.p., chief operating and fin. officer Bard Coll., Simon's Rock Early Coll.; adj. lectr. econs. New Sch. Social Research, 1975-76, Bard Coll., 1978—, Simon's Rock Early Coll., 1980—; dir. Bankers & Shippers Ins. Co. N.Y., Wm. Penn Life Ins. Co. N.Y. Vice pres. Hellenic Soc. of Columbia, 1966-67, treas., bd. dirs. Catskill Ballet Theatre. Mem. Am. Econ. Assn., Royal Econ. Soc., Am. Fin. Assn., Atlantic Econ. Soc. Club: Hellenic Univ. Home: PO Box 40 Annandale-on-Hudson NY 12504 Office: Bard Coll Annandale-on-Hudson NY 12504

PAPADOPOULOS, GEORGE, automotive products and services co. exec.; b. Polikastron, Greece, May 8, 1949; came to U.S., 1967, naturalized, 1970; s. Ioannis and Irini (Moyratidis) P.; student De Vry Inst., 1971-73; m. Shirley A. Coakley, July 24, 1969; children—Tina-Marie, Raina E. Owner, operator Central Shell Service, Milford, Mass., 1970-77, Midtown Motor Works, 1977—, Franklin Shell, 1977—, Medway Shell (Mass.), 1977—, Marlboro Shell (Mass.), 1977—; pres., chief exec. officer G.P. Enterprises, Inc., Medway, 1979—. Mem. Medway Bus. Council. Served with U.S. Army, 1969-71. Recipient various service and sales awards. Mem. Nat. Inst. Service Excellence, Am. Legion, VFW, Smithsonian Assos., Am. Mgmt. Assn., Internat. Entrepreneurs Assn. Home and Office: 5 Mann St Medway MA 02093

PAPAJOHN, JOHN, bus. services co. exec.; b. Amsterdam, N.Y., Mar. 15, 1927; s. George Christopher and Foto (Mayakis) P.; student Syracuse (N.Y.) U., 1948-50, 52-53; M.S., U. Calif. at Los Angeles, 1965; m. Margaret Priscilla Mattson, Feb. 27, 1954; children—George Alexander, Christopher Gus. Pres., gen. mgr. Haltom Mfg. Co., Dallas, 1967; dir. mktg. Volt Tech. Corp., El Segundo, Calif., 1968-69; pres. Datatemp Corp., Los Angeles, 1969-70; mgr. contract adminstrn. Xerox Corp., El Segundo, 1972—; asso. mgmt. cons. Traversi & Assos., San Diego, 1966—; dir. Consol. Data Industries. Active youth athletics. Served with U.S. Navy, 1944-47, 50-52; ETO. Mem. Nat. Contract Mgmt. Assn., Nat. Mgmt. Assn. Republican. Greek Orthodox. Clubs: Xerox Mgmt., Xerox Duplicate Bridge, Masons. Home: 4013 Merrill St Torrance CA 90503 Office: 701 S Aviation Blvd El Segundo CA 90245

PAPITTO, RALPH RAYMOND, mfg. co. exec.; b. Providence, Nov. 1, 1926; s. Joseph and Maria (David) P.; B.S. in Fin., Bryant Coll., 1946; children—Andrea J Papitto Crump, Aurelia J., David John. With Arthur Andersen & Co., 1948-51; v.p. fin. Ritz Products, Inc., 1951-55; founder, pres. GTI Corp., 1956-66; chmn. bd. Hi-G, Inc., 1965-66; chmn. bd. Nortek, Inc., Cranston, R.I. Bd. dirs. Providence Indsl. Devel. Corp.; trustee Roger Williams Coll. Clubs: Jockey, Surf, Rolling Hills (Fla.); Alpine Country, Turks Head. Office: 815 Reservoir Ave Canston RI 02910

PAPONE, ALDO, bus. exec.; b. Genoa, Italy, Aug. 16, 1932; came to U.S., 1956, naturalized, 1956; s. Alexander and Ines (Mantegazza) P.; B.B.A., U. Genoa, 1955; m. Sandra Cataleta, July 2, 1955; 1 dau., Renata. With R.H. Macy Co., N.Y.C., 1956-74, v.p., asst. gen. mdse. mgr., 1971, sr. v.p. 1972, dir. exec. com., chmn. mdse com., 1972-74, sr. v.p., gen. mgr. travel div., 1974; dir., sr. v.p. Am. Express Internat., Inc., N.Y.C., 1974-80, pres., 1975, sr. v.p., 1974-80, pres. card div., 1979-80; dir., pres. Am. Express Co. of Egypt Ltd. and Spain, 1974-80; dir., chmn. Am. Express Co. of Greece, 1974-80; pres. Am. Express SAI, Italy, 1974-80; exec. v.p. Dayton Hudson Corp., Mpls., 1980—; dir. Club Med, Inc., N.Y.C., 1976-80, Warner Amex Cable Communications Corp., 1979-80. Mem. United Cerebral Palsy Assn. campaign com., 1976-79; vice chmn. travel and tourism industry adv. council Commerce Com., U.S. Senate, 1979—; chmn. adv. bd. Congl. Travel and Tourism Caucus, 1980—; trustee Minn. Opera, 1980—; bd. dirs. St. Paul Chamber Orch., 1980—. Roman Catholic. Contbr. articles to profl. jours. Home: 2950 Dean Pkwy Minneapolis MN 55416 Office: 777 Nicollet Mall Minneapolis MN 55402

PAPP, LASZLO GEORGE, architect; b. Debrecen, Hungary, Apr. 28, 1929; s. Joseph and Gizela (Szoboszlai) P.; Archtl. Engr., Poly. U. Budapest, 1955; M.Arch., Pratt Inst., 1960; m. Judith Liptak, Apr. 12, 1952; children—Andrea, Laszlo-Mark (dec.). Came to U.S., 1956, naturalized, 1963. Architect-designer Inst. for Residential Devel., Budapest, Hungary, 1951-56; designer Harrison & Abramovitz, Architects, N.Y.C., 1958-63; partner Whiteside & Papp, Architects, White Plains, N.Y., 1963-67; prin. Papp Assos., Architects, White Plains, 1968—; pres. L.P. Design, Inc., White Plains. Vice chmn. New Canaan (Conn.) Planning and Zoning Commn., 1971—. Mem. AIA (chpt. dir. 1967-69, treas. 1971-73, pres. 1975-76), N.Y. State Assn. Architects (v.p. 1978-80, pres. 1980-81), Energy Resources Devel. Inst. (dir. 1979—), Hungarian U. Assn. (pres. 1958-60), Am.-Hungarian Engrs. Soc. (dir. 1978—), White Plains C. of C. (dir. 1968-71). Home: 1197 Valley Rd New Canaan CT 06840 Office: 222 Mamaroneck Ave White Plains NY 10605

PAPPAJOHN, JOHN GEORGE, investment banker; b. St. Luke's, Greece, July 31, 1928 (parents Am. citizens); s. George and Maria (Zanios) P.; student N.Iowa Community Coll., 1946-48; B.C.S., U. Iowa, 1952; m. Mary Limberis, Sept. 10, 1961; 1 dau., Ann Mary. Partner, Pappajohn Ins. Agy., Mason City, Iowa, 1953-58; gen. agt. Occidental Life Ins. Co., Mason City, 1958-62; pres. Guardsman Ins. Investors, Inc., Des Moines, 1962-69, also exec. v.p. Guardsman Life Ins. Co.; pres. Equity Dynamics, Inc., Des Moines, 1969—, founder-chmn., 1969—; v.p. Jotelso, Inc., Mason City 1967—; pres. Evia, Ltd., Des Moines, 1966—, Equimatics, Inc., Des Moines, 1969—, State St. Investments Corp., Mason City; pres. Fedinco, Inc., Des Moines; gen. partner Growth Equities Ltd., Des Moines, 1971—, John Pappajohn & Assos.; pres., partner Ashworth Plaza Ltd.; mng. partner Hickman Village Ltd., Des Moines; dir. Tech-S, Detroit, Key Labs. and Thermal Energy Storage, Inc., both San Diego, Home Health Care of Am., Irvine, Calif., Am. Trencher, Inc., Delhi, Iowa, Shirlamar, Inc., Des Moines, Curries Mfg. Co., Mason City, Data Law, Denver, Bion Corp., Denver, Computer Applications, Ames, Iowa. Bd. dirs. Big Bros. Am., Des Moines; treas., trustee Des Moines Art Center, Consultants Com. of 100. Mem. Iowa Investment Bankers, Soc. Fin. Analysts, Nat. Assn. Life Underwriters, Internat., Nat. assns. merger and acquistion consultants, Nat. Assn. Life Cos., Soc. Advancement Mgmt., Assn. for Corp. Growth, Inst. Bus. Appraisers, Internat. Soc. Fin. Planners, C. of C., U. Iowa Alumni Assn., Order of Ahepa, Phi Gamma Delta. Republican. Greek Orthodox. Mason (Shriner). Clubs: Des Moines (trustee), Embassy, Golf and Country (Des Moines); University (Iowa City). Home: 7301 Benton Dr Des Moines IA 50322 Office: 2116 Financial Center Des Moines IA 50309

PAPPAS, MIKE J., candy co. exec., mayor; b. Canea, Crete, Greece, July 5, 1934; s. James M. and Katherine (Tornazakis) P.; B.S., B.A., U. Denver, 1956; m. Joy Ann Walker, Aug. 27, 1962; 1 dau., Anne Marie. Jr. accountant Arthur Young and Co., 1956-57; city clk. City of Raton (N.Mex.), 1957-58; pres. Sweet Shop, Inc., Raton, 1958—; pres. Joy's, Inc.; city commr. City of Raton, 1977—, mayor, 1978—. Mem. Raton C. of C., Beta Alpha Pi, Sigma Chi. Mason (Shriner). Elk. Patentee. Home: 304 S 6th St Raton NM 87740 Office: 1201 S 2d Raton NM 87740

PAPPAS, PETER DINO, restauranteur, real estate developer; b. Norwich, Conn., Jan. 1, 1949; s. Dino Peter and Helen Peter (Sellas) P.; B.S. in Indsl. Engring., Lowell Tech. Inst., 1970; M.B.A., Northeastern U., 1971. Corp. troubleshooter VLN Corp., 1971-73; mgr. indsl. engring. Leece-Neville, Brownsville, Tex., 1973-75; v.p., co-owner Dino Pappas, Inc., Norwich, 1975—; real estate developer; dir. New Eng. Retail ICP Cream and Sandwich Shop Operators Assn. Asst. chief Groton Long Point Vol. Fire Co. Named Employer of Yr., Conn. Govs.'s Com. on Employment of Handicapped, 1975. Mem. Associated Restaurants of Conn. Republican. Club: Mystic Marlin and Tuna. Home: 33 Island Circle S Groton Long Point CT 06340 Office: 47 Town St Norwich CT 06360

PAPPONE, FRANK NICHOLAS, purchasing exec.; b. N.Y.C., Nov. 14, 1923; s. Frank and Angela (Orlando) P.; student public schs.; m. Florence Musso, Sept. 6, 1948. Mgr. Rayco Auto Stores, 1961-73; v.p. Biddle Co., N.Y.C., 1973—. Served with USAAF, 1942-45. Decorated D.F.C., D.S.C., Air medal with 3 oak leaf clusters, presdl. citation with oak leaf cluster. Address: Biddle Co 225 Broadway New York NY 10007

PAQUETTE, DONALD ANTHONY, mfg. co. exec.; b. Attleboro, Mass., July 27, 1945; s. Arthur A. and Louise V. (Bourbeau) P.; B.S. in Bus. Adminstrn., Bryant Coll., 1967; m. Sanda M. Stemmler, May 24, 1969 (div. Dec. 1979); children—Robin Marie, David Arthur. Staff acct. Price Waterhouse & Co., Hartford, Conn., 1967-70, sr. acct., 1970-72; asst. mgr. corp. acctg. Loctite Corp., Newington, Conn., 1972-75, mgr. corp. acctg., 1975-77, asst. corp. controller, 1977—. Treas., Marlborough Vol. Fire Dept., 1976-79. C.P.A., Conn. Mem. Am. Inst. C.P.A.'s, Conn. Soc. C.P.A.'s, Nat. Assn. Accts. Republican. Roman Catholic. Home: 163 C-4 Cynthia Ln Middletown CT 06457 Office: 705 N Mountain Rd Newington CT 06111

PARACHA, SAIFULLAH ABDULLAH, internat. trading and fin. co. exec.; b. Sargodha, Pakistan, Aug. 17, 1947; s. Hafiz M. and Khadija A. (Paracha) Abdullah; came to U.S., 1971, naturalized, 1974; B.S., N.Y. Inst. Tech., 1972. Pres., Zissa Internat. Inc., N.Y.C., 1974—. Muslim. Home: 83-09 Midland Pkwy Jamaica Estates NY 11432

PARADIS, ROGER, communications co. exec.; b. Quincy, Mass., Dec. 12, 1944; s. Lionel De L'Etoile and Florence (Carr) P.; B.S., U.S. Naval Acad., 1967; M.S., U.S. Naval Nuclear Power Sch., 1968; M.B.A., Harvard, 1974; m. Maureen O'Connor, July 2, 1967; children—Melissa, Suzanne. Cons., Resource Planning Assn., Cambridge, Mass., 1971-74; area mgr. Raychem Corp., Menlo Park, Calif., 1974, Hingham, Mass., 1975; planning mgr. AT&T, Basking Ridge, N.J., 1975—; dir. Cambridge Bus. Research. Served with USN, 1967-71. Mem. Am. Mgmt. Assn., Harvard, U.S. Naval Acad. alumni assns., Sigma Xi. Republican. Roman Catholic. Author: The Language of Business, 1973, 75. Home: 3 Rolling Hill Dr Morristown NJ 07960 Office: AT&T 295 N Maple Ave Basking Ridge NJ 07960

PARADIS, THOMAS LEE, pub. co. exec.; b. Rochester, N.H., June 9, 1947; s. Lionel DeLetoile and Florence (Carr) P.; B.B.A., U. Mass., 1969; J.D., U. Denver, 1975; m. E. Paulette, Aug. 9, 1980; children—Marc DeLetoile, Jeffrey, Terry. Asst. dir. continuing legal edn. U. Denver, 1973-75; cons., rep., cons. fin. planning, Service Bur. Co., Phila., 1976-77; pres. U/Stat Inc., gen. partner U/Stat Ltd., Denver, 1977—. Served to capt. USAF, 1969-73; Vietnam. Republican. Roman Catholic. Office: 2300 Walnut St Suite 431 Philadelphia PA 19103

PARADISE, ROBERT CAMPBELL, banker; b. N.Y.C., July 28, 1928; s. Robert Campbell and Elizabeth Janeway (Scudder) P.; B.A., Yale U., 1951; postgrad. N.Y. U., 1953-58; m. Mary Louise Meenan, Mar. 7, 1975; children—Robert C., James F., Elizabeth J. With Citibank N.A., N.Y.C., 1952—, v.p., 1966—, v.p. chems. dept. N. Am. banking group, 1977—. Served with U.S. Army, 1951-52. Club: Riverside (Conn.) Yacht. Home: 3 Game Cock Rd Greenwich CT 06830 Office: 399 Park Ave New York NY 10022

PARADISE, STEVEN SANDER, ins. agy. exec.; b. Bronx, N.Y., Mar. 19, 1944; s. Lionel P. and Jean S. (Sander) P.; B.S. cum laude in Commerce and Fin., Wilkes Coll., 1965; m. Jane Klein, June 12, 1966; children—Gregg, Jeffrey. With J.B. Paradise & Co., Inc., Valley Stream, N.Y., 1965—, now v.p. C.P.C.U. Mem. Ind. Ins. Agts. Am., Ind. Ins. Agts. N.Y., Ind. Ins. Agts. Nassau County (pres.), Profl. Ins. Agts. Am., Profl. Ins. Agts. N.Y., Downstate Ins. Agts. Council (sec.), Wilkes Coll. Alumni Assn. (treas. 1976—). Club: Masons. Home: 128 Lincoln Blvd Merrick NY 11566 Office: JB Paradise & Co Inc 108 S Franklin Ave Valley Stream NY 11582

PARASCOS, EDWARD THEMISTOCLES, utilities exec.; b. N.Y.C., Oct. 20, 1931; s. Christos and Nina (Demitrovich) P.; B.S. in Mech. Engring., Coll. City N.Y., 1956, M.S., 1958; postgrad. ops. research N.Y. U., 1964—; m. Jenny Morris, July 14, 1978; 1 dau., Jennifer Melissa. Design engr. Ford Instrument, 1957-61; reliability engring. supr. Kearfott div. Gen. Precision Inc., 1961-63; staff cons. Am. Power Jet, 1963-64; reliability mgr. Perkin Elmer Corp., 1964-66; dir. system effectiveness CBS Labs., Stamford, Conn., 1966-72; pres. Dipar Cons. Services Ltd., East Elmhurst, N.Y., Lapa Trading Corp.; quality assurance and reliability cons. Consol. Edison Co., N.Y.C., 1972—; pres., chmn. bd. RAM Power Engring. Consultants Ltd.; instr. human factors in engring. CBS Labs., 1968-70; chmn. 1st Reliability Engring. Conf. Electric Power Industry, 1974, also 4th conf.; lectr. in field. Registered profl. engr., Calif. Mem. Am. Soc. Quality Control (vice chmn. 1968-70, sr. mem.), Am. Mgmt. Assn., ASME, Am. Statis. Assn., Inst. Environ. Scis. Home: 34-47 88th St Jackson Heights NY 11372 Office: 30-02 83d St East Elmhurst NY 11370 also 4 Irving Pl New York NY 10003

PARBURY, C(HARLES) ALAN, mgmt. cons. firm exec.; b. Palo Alto, Calif., Aug. 13, 1947; s. Charles B. and Ethel N. Parbury; B.S.C., U. Santa Clara, 1970; postgrad. Coll. San Mateo, 1972-73; m. Sandra Wanderer, June 1978; children—Cynthia J., Holly R. Sales and ops. mgr. Grantree Corp., San Francisco, 1970-74; mgmt. cons. G.S. May, Internat., Park Ridge, Ill. and BWA, Ltd., San Francisco, 1974-78; corp. pres. Alameda Joe's Inc., Alameda, Calif., 1978—. Mem. Am. Bus. Assn., Internat. Platform Assn., Assn. Mgmt. Consultants, Bay Area Restaurant Assn., Alameda C. of C. Republican. Roman Catholic. Clubs: Kiwanis, Elks. Office: Alameda Joe's Inc 300 Park St Alameda CA 94501

PARENTEAU, JEROME FRANCIS, paint and coatings mfg. co. exec.; b. Rochester, N.Y., Feb. 8, 1924; s. Charles Anthony and Elvera (Born) P.; student U. Mich., 1941-42, U. Minn., 1943; A.B., Syracuse U., 1948; m. Lois Scott, Nov. 29, 1946; children—Richard, Ellen. Account rep. William H. Reed, Niagara Falls, N.Y., 1948-49; mgr. advt. and communications Varcum Chem. Corp., Niagara Falls, N.Y., 1949-51; div. advt. mgr. Nat. Gypsum Co., Buffalo, 1951-54; mgr. advt. and pub. relations Seidlitz Paint & Varnish Co., Kansas City, Mo., 1954-62; v.p. advt. and pub. relations Conchemco, Inc., Kansas City, Mo., 1962-69, Seidlitz Paints Div., 1962-69, Nashua Homes Div., 1965-69, exec. v.p. Colony Paints Div., 1969-73; mgr. finance and adminstrn. coatings group Conchemco Inc. (now Valspar Corp.), Lenexa, Kans., 1973-75, v.p. finance and adminstrn. coatings group, 1975-77, v.p., gen. mgr. coatings eastern div., 1977-79, plant mgr., 1979—. Mem. pub. relations council Mid-Continent council Girl Scouts U.S.A., 1968-70. Served with USAAF, 1943-46. Mem. Nat. Paint, Varnish and Lacquer Assn., Pub. Relations Soc. Am. (chpt. dir. 1968-69), Am. Marketing Assn. (chpt. dir. 1966-70, chpt. v.p. 1969-70), Am. Mgmt. Assn., Mensa, Alpha Delta Sigma, Theta Beta Phi, Kappa Sigma. Republican. Presbyn. Mason. Contbr. articles to profl. jours. Home: 2 Clubview Ln Sunnybrook Phoenix MD 21131 Office: 1401 Severn St Baltimore MD 21230

PARFET, RAY T., JR., pharm. co. exec. Bd. dirs. Upjohn Co., 1958—, v.p., 1958-59, exec. v.p. charge research, legal, financial and personnel activities, 1960-62, pres., gen. mgr., 1962-69, chmn. bd., chief exec. officer, 1969—; dir. 1st Nat. Bank & Trust Co. Mich., Kalamazoo, Gilmore Bros. Dept. Store, Kalamazoo, Union Pump Co., Battle Creek, Mich. Bell, Detroit, Aro Corp., Bryan, Ohio, 1st Am. Bank Corp., Kalamazoo. Trustee, Bronson Meth. Hosp., Kalamazoo. Mem. Pharm. Mfrs. Assn. (past dir., past chmn.), Internat. Fedn. Pharm. Mfrs. Assns. (past dir.). Office: 7000 Portage Rd Kalamazoo MI 49001

PARGAS, NATALIE JEAN, pub. exec.; b. Palmerton, Pa., Mar. 7, 1943; d. John Murray and Natalie (Brown) Murray; student Am. U., 1960-67; m. Rafael Pargas, Mar. 28, 1964; children—Jonathan Rafael, David Lee, Jennifer Michelle. With Food Chem. News, Washington, 1964—, asst. to editor, 1970—, bus. mgr., 1975—, editor Food Chem. News Guide, 1974—. Home: 11500 Hearthstone Ct Reston VA 22091 Office: 777 14th St NW Rm 400 Washington DC 20005

PARIKHAL, JOHN REZA, media cons.; b. Guildford, Eng., Feb. 13, 1947; naturalized Canadian citizen, 1957; s. Reza and Betty (Dell) P.; B.A. with honors, U. Western Ont., 1969; M.A., U. Toronto, 1972, A.B.D., 1977. Sociocultural analyst specializing in econs. Canadian Govt., 1971-75; free-lance media cons., Toronto, Ont., Can., 1975-77; creative dir. I.W.C. Communications, Toronto, 1977; partner, sr. media cons. Joint Communications Corp., media cons., lifestyle research, predictions on future of media and culture, Toronto, 1977—, also dir.; cons. NBC, N.Y.C. Ont. grad. fellow, 1972-73; Can. Council doctoral fellow, 1973-75. Editor: Folio, 1969; research on impact of electronic media on Islamic countries and emerging cultures, 1979. Office: 191 John St Toronto ON M5T 1X3 Canada

PARISH, H(AYWARD) CARROLL, educator, bus. exec.; b. Pasadena, Calif., Feb. 13, 1920; s. Hayward Carroll and Gertrude I. (Riggs) P.; A.B., UCLA, 1943, M.A., 1950, Ph.D., 1958. Los Angeles County Youth commr., 1938-42, pres. commn., 1938; asst. prof. naval sci. U. Calif., 1946-47, 52-53, asso. prof. 1954, asst. dean, 1957-62, asso. dean, 1962-76, dean, 1966-71; provost, trustee Miller Community Coll., 1971—; adj. prof. polit. sci. U. La Verne, 1976—; v.p. Environ. Design Assos., 1966—; pres. Kapa Co., 1969—; attache Calif. State legislature, 1947; Fulbright research fellow Waseda U. Tokyo, 1958-59; engaged in property mgmt.; lectr. Asiatic Studies, U. So. Calif., 1961; collaborator Inst. Internat. Relations, Aoyama Gakuin U., Tokyo, 1960—. Mem. scholarship adv. com. Calif. State Scholarship and Loan Commn., 1964-71; cons. U.S. Office Edn., 1969-71; cons. Time-Life Books Inc. Sec. citizens ind. vice investigating com. which initiated successful recall against corrupt Los Angeles adminstrn., 1938; mem. exec. com. Los Angeles Co. Coordinating Councils, 1939-41; 1st v.p. Japanese Am. Cultural Center. Served USNR, World War II Korea; capt., 1964; comdg. officer Naval Res. Officers Sch., 1965-68. Twice decorated for combat service Pacific area; for valor at Okinawa when ship was hit by Kamikaze plane; for meritorious service as flag-sec. to comdr. assault transport div. Decorated Order Golden Merit, Japanese Red Cross; knight grand officer Order St. John The Bapt. Am.; knight comdr. Hospitaller Order St. John of Jerusalem; knight comdr. Mil. and Hospitaller Order St. Lazarus of Jerusalem; comdr. Order of Merit; chancellor Grand Priory of Am.; Knight of honor Venerable Order of Rose of Lippe. Fellow Institut International des Arts et des Lettres (life), AAAS, Augustan Soc.; mem. Am. Legion (mem. Nat. Security Commn. 1950-53), Am. Polit. Sci. Assn., Founders and Patriots Am. (gov. gen.), Soc. Colonial Wars, S.R., Internat. Polit. Sci. Assn., Assn. Asian Studies (chmn. Pacific Coast regional conf. 1967), Am. Coll. Personnel Assn. (chmn. commn.), Assn. Ind. Colls. and Schs. (com. chmn.), Coll. Scholarship Service, Com. on Fgn. Students, Navy League (life), Asia Soc., Am. Siam Soc. (pres.), Siam Soc. (life), Nat. (pres. 1971, distinguished service award 1971), Western (pres. 1970, distinguished achievement award 1971) assns. student financial aid adminstrs., Associated Japan Am. Socs. U.S. (vice-chmn.), Japan Am. Soc. So. Calif. (council chmn.), Phi Eta Sigma, Alpha Mu Gamma, Pi Sigma Alpha, Pi Gamma Mu (chancellor Western region, nat. honor Key 1973). Episcopalian. Clubs: Jonathan (Los Angeles); Internat. House of Japan (Tokyo). Author: Canada and the United Nations, 1950. Co-author: Thailand Bibliography, 1958. Contbr. articles on internat., Far East, S. E. Asian Affairs to profl. jours. Home: 633 24th St Santa Monica CA 90402

PARISH, PRESTON SEITER, pharm. co. exec.; b. Chgo., Nov. 10, 1919; s. Preston and Louise (Vesley) P.; A.B., Williams Coll., 1941; m. Suzanne U. DeLano, Apr. 17, 1948; children—Barbara Parish Gibbs, Katharine Parish Miller, P. William, Preston L., David. Salesman, Am. Flange and Mfg. Co., N.Y., Chgo., Los Angeles, 1946-47, resident mgr. Can. subs., 1947-49; prodn. engr. Upjohn Co., Kalamazoo, Mich., 1949-55, dir., 1955-58, v.p., dir., 1958-60, exec. v.p., dir., 1960-69, vice chmn. bd., chmn. exec. com., 1969—; dir. Am. Nat. Bank and Trust Co., Kalamazoo, Am. Nat. Holding Co., Kalamazoo; chmn. Kal-Aero, Inc., Kalamazoo; trustee W.E. Upjohn Unemployment Trustee Corp., Kalamazoo, 1963—, chmn., 1976—. Trustee Bronson Methodist Hosp., 1959—, Williams Coll., Williamstown, Mass., 1965—, Holderness Sch., Plymouth, N.H., 1968-76; chmn. Kalamazoo Aviation History Mus., 1978—; mem. nat. bd. Jr. Achievement, 1979—; adv. bd. Found. Student

Communication, Inc., Princeton, N.J., 1973—. Served to maj. USMC, 1941-46, col. Res. ret. Decorated Bronze Star. Mem. Nat. Alliance of Businessmen (past chmn.), Food and Drug Law Inst. (dir., chmn.), Conf. Bd. Office: 7000 Portage Rd Kalamazoo MI 49001

PARISI, MICHAEL SALVATORE, electronics co. exec.; b. Providence, Aug. 31, 1930; s. Michael Salvatore and Anna (Ragno) P.; A.S. in Elec. Engring., Worcester Jr. Coll., 1959; m. Elizabeth Joan Lombardi, Jan. 1, 1953; children—Michael, Ronald, Debra, Jacquelyn, Thomas. Cook, various restaurants, Providence, 1948-51; assembly worker Draper Corp., Hopedale, Mass., 1955-56; with Fenwal Electronics Co., Framingham, Mass., 1956—, sr. design engr., 1967-68, group leader design engring., 1968-75, chief engr., 1975-76, v.p. engring., 1976—. Mem. Bellingham (Mass.) Zoning Bd. Appeals, 1963-68, chmn., 1964-68; chmn. Bellingham Planning Bd., 1968-71, chmn., 1970-71; mem. Bellingham Bd. Selectmen, 1971-73, chmn., 1972-73; mem. Bellingham Fin. Com., 1973-74; mgr. Little League, 1961-67. Served with USAF, 1951-55. Mem. ASTM, Am. Ceramic Soc., Electronic Industries Assn. Democrat. Roman Catholic. Club: Kiwanis (charter pres., lt. gov. div. 9, dir.). Home: 25 Shadowbrook Ln Apt 5A Milford MA 01757 Office: Fenwal Electronics Co 63 Fountain St Framingham MA 07701

PARK, GEORGE COOLIDGE, engring. cons.; b. Concord, Mass., Mar. 30, 1917; s. George Coolidge and Harriet Maybel (Hawkes) P.; A.B., Middlebury Coll., 1939; m. Nancy Stalker, Jan. 11, 1941; children—George Coolidge, Suzanne, Kathleen, Bradford S., Alexander H., William H.; m. 2d, Barbara J. Weir, Oct. 2, 1971. Pres., Hersey Paper Co., Melrose, Mass., 1949-63, Barrier Coatings Inc., Lawrence, Mass., 1963-73; engring. cons. Bolton-Emerson, Inc., Lawrence, 1973—. Served to lt. col. U.S. Army, 1940-45. Decorated Silver Star, Bronze Star; Order of Alexander Nevsky (USSR); recipient plaque for contbn. to coating industry TAPPI, 1980. Mem. TAPPI. Republican. Contr. numerous articles to trade mags.; patentee coating methods and apparatus, U.S. and fgn. countries; developer method and machinery for applying thermoplastics, aqueous and other liquids to moving webs. Home: Star Route Bristol NH 03222 Office: 9 Osgood St Lawrence MA 01842

PARK, ROY HAMPTON, communications exec.; b. Dobson, N.C., Sept. 15, 1910; s. I. A. and Laura Frances (Stone) P.; B.S. in Bus. Adminstrn., N.C. State U. at Raleigh, 1931; L.H.D., Keuka Coll., 1967; H.H.D. (hon.), N.C. State U., 1978; m. Dorothy Goodwin Dent, Oct. 3, 1936; children—Roy Hampton, Adelaide Hinton (Mrs. Charles August Gomer III). Dir. pub. relations N.C. Cotton Growers Coop. Assn., Farmers Coop. Exchange, Raleigh, 1931-42; sr. editor Rural Electricification Adminstrn., 1936-37; founder, editor, pub. Farm Power, also Coop. Digest, Raleigh, 1939-42, Ithaca, N.Y., 1942-66; pres. Hines-Park Foods, Inc., Ithaca, 1949-50, v.p., dir., 1956-63; pres. Hines-Park Foods (Can.) Ltd., 1949-56, v.p., dir., 1956-63; pres. Duncan Hines Inst., Inc., 1949-56, dir., 1956-63; pres., dir. Park Broadcasting Inc., Ithaca, 1962—, Roy H. Park Broadcasting, Inc., Greenville, N.C., WNCT-TV-AM-FM, 1962—, Roy H. Park Broadcasting Tenn., Inc., WDEF-TV-AM-FM, Chattanooga, 1963—, Roy H. Park Broadcasting Tri-Cities, Inc., WJHL-TV, Johnson City, Tenn., 1964—, Roy H. Park Broadcasting Va., Inc., WTVR-TV-AM-FM, Richmond, 1965—, Roy H. Park Broadcasting Birmingham, Inc., WBMG-TV, 1973—, Roy H. Park Broadcasting Midwest, Inc., WNAX-AM, Yankton, S.D., 1968—, Roy H. Park Broadcasting Utica-Rome, Inc., WUTR-TV, 1969—, Roy H. Park Broadcasting Roanoke, Inc., WSLS-TV, 1969—, KWJJ Radio, Contemporary FM, Inc., KJIB-FM (both Portland, Oreg.), 1973—, Roy H. Park Broadcasting of Minn., Inc., KRSI-AM, Roy H. Park Broadcasting Lake Country, Inc., KFMX-FM (both St. Louis Park, Minn.), 1974—, Roy H. Park Broadcasting Syracuse, Inc., WHEN-AM, 1976, Roy H. Park Broadcasting Finger Lakes, Inc., WONO-FM, Syracuse, N.Y., 1977, Roy H. Park Broadcasting Wash., Inc., KEZX-FM, Seattle, 1975, RHP Inc., Ithaca, 1945—, Park Outdoor Advt. and Park Displays, Ithaca, 1964—, Park Newspapers, Inc., Ithaca, 1972—, Park Newspapers Ga., Inc., 1972—, Warner Robins (Ga.) Sun Inc., 1972—, Park Newspapers Va., Inc., 1972—, Prince William Pub. Co., Manassas, Va., 1973—, RHP Newspapers, Ithaca, 1973—, Lockport Publs. Inc. (N.Y.), 1973—, Park Newspapers Nebr., Inc., 1975—, Park Newspapers Fla., Inc., 1975—, Park Newspapers St. Lawrence, N.Y., Inc., 1975—, Park Newspapers Ind., Inc., 1977, Park Newspapers Norwich, Inc., 1977, Avalon Citrus Assn., Inc., Orlando, Fla., 1962—, Cobb House of Rock Hill, Inc. (S.C.), 1967—, Windup, Inc., Ithaca, 1970—, Park Newspapers of Okla., Inc., News-Capital & Democrat, McAlester, 1978; vice chmn. Kannapolis Pub. Co. (N.C.), 1977, Park Newspapers of Ill., Inc., 1979, State and Aurora, Inc., Broken Arrow, Okla., 1979, Southside Publs., Inc., 1979, WNC, Inc., Sapulpa, Okla., 1979, Park Newspapers of Newton, Inc., 1979, Park Newspapers of Morganton, Inc., 1979, Park Newspapers of Statesville, Inc., 1979, Park Newspapers of Concord, Inc., 1980, Park Newspapers of Perry, Ga., Inc., 1980; dir., mem. exec. com., chmn. audit com. Raymond Corp., Greene, N.Y.; dir., chmn. exec. com. ConAgra, Inc., Omaha; dir., mem. exec. com. Security N.Y. Corp., Rochester; dir. Molinos de P.R., Santurce, 1957, First Nat. Bank & Trust Co., Ithaca, Wachovia Bank & Trust Co., Raleigh. Dir. Tompkins County Area Devel. Corp., Ithaca, First Research Devel. Corp., Ithaca; pres., dir. Upstate Small Bus. Investment Co., Ithaca, 1960-66; trustee N.C. State U., 1977; asso. chmn. laymen's nat. Bible com. Nat. Bible Week, 1972; chmn. pub. relations N.C. State U. Devel. Council, 1963-72, vice-chmn. devel. com., 1964-72, chmn., 1972-78, bd. dirs. Found., 1962-66; trustee Ithaca Coll., 1973—, Endowment Funds N.C. State U.; chmn. bd. trustees N.Y. State Newspapers Found., Syracuse, 1978. Recipient spl. citation for distinguished service to agr. Am. Inst. Coop., 1947, Distinguished Service award Tompkins County United Fund, 1961, Meritorious Service award N.C. State U. Alumni Assn., 1970, Abe Lincoln award So. Bapt. Radio-TV Commn., 1971; named Country Squire Gov. N.C., 1953, hon. citizen New Orleans, 1958, hon. citizen Tenn., 1961, Ky. col., 1963, adm. Gt. Navy Nebr., 1961, Soc. Prodigal Son. Mem. N.Y. State Publishers Assn. (dir. Syracuse, pres. 1980—), Pub. Relations Soc. Am., Am. Agrl. Editors' Assn., N.C. State U. Alumni Assn. (dir., chmn. spl. gifts div. 1957-62, pres. 1960-61, chmn. gen. fund 1962), Agrl. Relations Council, Friends Ithaca Coll., Lucullus Circle, Les Amis D'Escoffier Soc., Confrerie de la Chaines des Rotissuers, Va., N.C., Nat. assns. broadcasters, Am., So. newspaper pubs. assns., Ga. Press Assn., Phi Kappa Phi, Phi Sigma Epsilon, Alpha Phi Gamma, Pi Phi Pi. bd. 1961-62, gen. fund chmn. 1962, meritorious service award 1970), Tompkins County C. of C. (v.p. 1962-63, pres. 1963-64), Am. Hotel Assn. (allied membership div. adv. com.), Clubs: Nat. Press, Capitol (Washington); N.Y. Athletic, Cornell, Marco Polo, Union League, Sales Execs. (dir. 1980—) (N.Y.C.); City, Sphinx (Raleigh); Ithaca Country; Statler (Cornell U.); Commonwealth (Richmond); Shenandoah (Roanoke). Presbyn. (ruling elder 1969—). Home: 205 Devon Rd Ithaca NY 14850 Office: Terrace Hill Ithaca NY 14850

PARKE, ROBERT LEON, cartage co. exec.; b. Jersey City, Aug. 28, 1940; s. Edwin Gager and Alice Elizabeth (Servis) P.; student pub. schs., Jersey City; m. Geraldine R. Pavlick, Sept. 2, 1967; children—Cheryl Lynn, Tracy Ann, David Scott. Asst. bookkeeper Snow-Kist Frozen Foods Co., Jersey City, 1964-67; supr. accounts receivable Swift Line Transfer Co. Inc., North Bergen, N.J., 1967-69; controller Imperial Cartage Co., Inc., Jersey City, 1969—; corp. sec. Imperial Warehouse Co. Inc., Jersey City, 1968—; v.p. Cole Foods Inc., Jersey City, 1974—; corp. sec. Arbe Transfer Co. Inc., Jersey City. 1968—. Mem. Pemberton Twp. Zoning Bd., 1977-79; trustee, dir. Browns Mills Improvement Assn., 1974—; trustee Rebecca Wolf Meml. Fund, 1976—, Pemberton Community Library Assos., 1978-79. Mem. Am. Mgmt. Assn. Home: PO Box 1878 Kissimmee FL 32741 Office: PO Box 352 Jersey City NJ 07303 also Walt Disney World PO Box 40 Lake Buena Vista FL 32830

PARKER, ABNER, mgmt. cons.; b. Russia, July 25, 1902; s. Morris and Miriam (Mushkin) P.; came to U.S., 1906, naturalized, 1913; B.Comml.Sci., N.Y. U., 1923; m. Frances Ness, July 23, 1926; children—Nessa (Mrs. Loewenthal), Michael. Gen. mgr. Milgrims, Inc., Chgo., 1924-29; exec. v.p., gen. mgr. Sally Chain Stores, Inc. (merged into Spiegels), Chgo., 1929-46; pres. Los Angeles Warehouse Co., 1946-47; mgmt. cons. specializing in reorgn. troubled cos., Los Angeles, 1946—; chmn. bd., chief exec. officer, cons., dir. Pacific Coast Properties, Santa Monica (now subs. Cenvill Communities, Fla.), 1974-77; dir., cons., mem. audit com. Terminal Data Corp., Woodland Hills, Calif.; cons. United Convalescent Hosps. (merged into Hillhaven, Inc.), Tacoma, Wash.; cons. on devel. Lakewood (Calif.) Shopping Center. Chmn. juvenile com. Los Angeles County Grand Jury, 1963; mem. planning com., bd. mem. research bur. Jewish Welfare Fedn.; former v.p. and mem. bd. Jewish Big Bros. Assn.; chmn. emeritus Camp Max Straus (for boys); pres. Camp Max Straus Found.; mem. Calif. Atty. Gen.'s Adv. Council, Dist. Atty.'s Adv. Council; trustee emeritus Am. Contract Bridge League Charity Found. Jewish. Mem. Phi Sigma Delta (now Zeta Beta Tau), Delta Mu Delta. Author: Problems of the Modern Specialty Shop, 1928. Home and Office: 1121 Somera Rd Los Angeles CA 90024

PARKER, CHARLES WALTER, JR., equipment co. exec.; b. nr. Ahoskie, N.C., Nov. 22, 1922; s. Charles Walter and Minnie Louise (Williamson) P.; B.S. in Elec. Engring., Va. Mil. Inst., 1947; m. Sophie Nash Riddick, Nov. 26, 1949; children—Mary Parker Hutto, Caroline Davis, Charles Walter III, Thomas Williamson. With Allis-Chalmers Corp., 1947—, dist. mgr., Richmond, Va., 1955-57, Phila., 1957-58, dir. sales promotion industries group, Milw., 1958-61, gen. mktg. mgr. new products, 1961-62, mgr. mktg. services, 1962-66, v.p. mktg. services and pub. relations, 1966-70, v.p., dep. group. exec., 1970-72, staff group exec., 1972—; dir. Heritage Wis. Corp., Internat. Gen. Ins. Corp. Mem. Greater Milw. Com.; gen. chmn. United Fund Greater Milw. Area, 1975; mem. exec. bd. Boy Scouts Am., Milw., Jr. Achievement Milw. Bd. dirs. Better Bus. Bur., 1976; trustee Univ. Sch. Milw., Carroll Coll.; bd. regents Milw. Sch. Engring. Served to capt. AUS, 1943-46; ETO. Decorated Bronze Star. Mem. Am. Mktg. Assn. (dir. 1976-78), Wis. C. of C. (pres. 1975), IEEE (asso.), Sales and Mktg. Execs. Internat. (pres., chief exec. officer 1974-75), Pi Sigma Epsilon, Kappa Alpha. Home: 2907 E Linnwood Ave Milwaukee WI 53211 Office: PO Box 512 Milwaukee WI 53201

PARKER, EDWARD ARTHUR, chem. co. exec.; b. Hebron, Ill., Nov. 3, 1908; s. George Arthur and Carrie Johanna (Stratton) P.; B.S., U. Ill., 1930, M.S., 1932, Ph.D., 1937; m. Ruth Engler Graver, Aug. 9, 1941; 1 son, George Arthur. Chemist, Am. Comml. Alcohol Co., Pekin, Ill., 1930-31, L.I. Biol. Lab., Cold Spring Harbor, N.Y., 1937-39, A. Kenneth Graham Assos., Phila., 1941-42, Alrose Chem. Co., Providence, 1942-44; tech. dir. Technic, Inc., Providence, 1945-50, sec., 1945—, v.p., 1962-64, exec. v.p., 1964—; sec., dir. Technic Precious Metals (Can.), Ltd., Toronto, Ont., 1968—; v.p. Barberry Corp., Providence, 1979—. Textile Found. fellow, 1934-37; Atlas Powder fellow, 1939-41. Fellow Inst. Chemists; mem. Am. Chem. Soc., Electrochem. Soc., Inst. Metal Finishing (London), ASTM, Am. Electroplaters Soc. (Heussner Gold medal 1952, editorial bd. 1948-52, del. 1948-72, chmn. research bd. 1970, bd. mgrs. New Eng. council 1952-66, 75— sec.-treas. New Eng. council, 1970—, named Nat. Hon. Mem. 1969), Sigma Xi. Contbg. author: Gold in Modern Electroplating, 1963. Contbr. articles to profl. jours. Patentee in Field. Home: 172 Belvedere Dr Cranston RI 02920 Office: Technic Inc 88 Spectacle St Cranston RI 02910

PARKER, FRANCIS TROOST, III, moulding co. exec.; b. Charlottesville, Va., Oct. 9, 1937; s. Francis Troost and Marion McElroy (Pendleton) P.; B.A., Williams Coll., 1960; M.B.A., U. Va., 1962; m. Tove Erichsen Nordness, June 16, 1962; children—Karin Nordness, Elizabeth McElroy. Adminstrv. asst. to dean Darden Sch., U. Va., Charlottesville, 1964-65; systems engr., data processing mktg. rep. IBM, Richmond, Va., 1965-71; co-founder, v.p. and sec.-treas. Ivy Industries, Inc., Charlottesville, 1971—, also dir.; dir. Fidelity Am. Bank, Charlottesville, Bellemead Devel. Corp., Tomoka Peat & Rock Co. Trustee, mem. exec. com. Va. Mus. Fine Arts, 1976—. Served with Fin. Corps, U.S. Army, 1962-64. Mem. U. Va. Darden Sch. Alumni (treas., dir.). Episcopalian. Clubs: Farmington Country (dir. 1979—), Boar's Head Sports; Rotary (Charlottesville). Home: 701 Flordon Dr Charlottesville VA 22901 Office: PO Box 7747 Charlottesville VA 22906

PARKER, FRANK PARISH, JR., shopping center developer; b. Harrisburg, Ill., Nov. 29, 1928; s. Frank Parish and Helen (Robb) P.; student Wentworth Mil. Acad., 1947, Murray State Coll., 1948; m. Mary Ann Murphy, Feb. 6, 1954; children—Frank Parish II, Charles P., Mary Helen, Colleen. Pres., Parker Shopping Plaza, Harrisburg, 1968—; dir. Harrisburg Nat. Bank, First Trust Assn. Served with USMCR, 1950. Mason (32 deg., Shriner), Kiwanian. Home: 101 S Webster St Harrisburg IL 62946 Office: PO Box P Route 45 S Harrisburg IL 62946

PARKER, HARRY LYNN, textile co. exec.; b. Knoxville, Tenn., Oct. 30, 1930; s. Harry Lynn and Evelyn (Irwin) P.; B.S., Clemson Coll., 1953; m. Sandra Ellen Speare, Sept. 15, 1961; children—Andrew Lynn, David Harry, Gordon Speare. Textile dyestuff sales rep. Blackman-Uhler Co., Spartanburg, S.C., 1953-67; founder, chief exec. officer, pres., dir. Palmetto Knitting, Inc., Spartanburg, 1967—. Mem. Spartanburg Mental Health Bd., 1966-69; bd. dirs. Spartanburg Jr. Achievement, 1974-78, Spartanburg YMCA, 1979—; coach YMCA Boys Basketball; mem. Republican Steering Com.; elder 1st Presbyterian Ch. Served to 1st lt. Signal Corps, U.S. Army, 1953-55. Home: 106 Juniper Ct Spartanburg SC 29302 Office: PO Box 5771 Spartanburg SC 29304

PARKER, J(ACK) ROYAL, engring. exec.; b. N.Y.C., Apr. 25, 1919; s. Harry and Clara (Saxe) P.; student Bklyn. Poly. Inst., 1943; D.Sc., Pacific Internat. U., 1956; m. Selma Blossom, Dec. 8, 1946; children—Leslie Janet, Andrew Charles. Instr., Indsl. Tng. Inst., 1938-39; engr. Brewster Aero Corp., 1939-40; pres. Am. Drafting Co., 1940; design engr. U.S. Navy Dept., 1941-44, also supervising instr. N.Y. Drafting Inst., 1941-43; cons. Todd Shipyards Corp., 1947-54; tech. adviser to pres. Rollins Coll., 1949-50; v.p. Wattpar Corp., 1947-54; pres. Parco Co. of Can., Ltd., 1951-55; partner, dir., chief project mgr. Parco Co., N.Y.C., 1947—; pres. Parco Chem. Services, Inc., 1965—, Guyana Oil Refining Co., Brit. Guiana, 1966-67; pres., dir. Parco Internat., 1965-70, Peruviana Del Sur, S.A., 1965-68; pres. Royalpar Industries, Inc., also chmn. bd., 1971-75; former pres., sec.-treas., dir. Vernitron Corp.; former v.p., dir. Amsterdam Fund, European Securities Publ., Inc., Internat. Capital Devel. Ltd., Nassau, B. W. I.; v.p., a founder Refinadora Costarricense de Petroles, S.A. (partnership with Allied Chem. Corp.), San Jose, Costa Rica, 1963—; dir. Career-Mgmt. World-Wide Personnel Consultants, Inc. Cons. to pres. Republic of Costa Rica, 1964-65; cons. Malta Indsl. Devel. Study Co., Ltd., 1965-67, mgmt. cons. Stone & Webster Engring. Corp., 1967-75; gen. mgr. Kellex Power Services, Pullman Kellogg Co., 1975-77; pres. J. Royal Parker Assos., Inc., 1977—; pres., dir. Delaware Valley Fgn. Trade Zone, Inc., 1978-80. Mem. drafting commn. N.Y.C. Bd. Edn.; trustee Coll. Advanced Sci., Canaan, N.H., 1958-60. Fellow A.A.A.S.; mem. Inst. Engring. Designers (London), Am. Petroleum Inst., Am. Ordnance Assn., Soc. Am. Mil. Engrs., Am. Inst. Chem. Engrs., Am. Inst. Design and Drafting, Marine Technol. Soc. Mason, Knights of Malta. Clubs: Marco Polo (N.Y.C.); Royal Automobile (London). Author: Gasoline Systems, 1945. Contbr. articles tech. jours. Patentee in field; inventor Lazy Golfer. Home: 106 The Mews Haddonfield NJ 08033 Office: 900 Haddon Ave Collingswood NJ 08108

PARKER, JACK STEELE, corp. exec.; b. Palo Alto, Calif., July 6, 1918; s. William L. and Mary I. (Steele) P.; student Menlo Jr. Coll., 1935-37, B.S., Leland Stanford Jr. U., 1939; LL.D., Clark U.; D.B.A., S.E. Mass. Inst. Tech.; m. Elaine Simons, 1946; 1 dau., Kaaren Lee. Mech. engr. Western Pipe & Steel Co. Calif., San Francisco, 1939-40; marine surveyor Am. Bur. Shipping, Seattle, 1940-42; asst. gen. supt. Todd Shipyards, Inc., Houston, 1942-44, gen. supt. outfitting, San Pedro, Calif., 1944-46; asst. chief engr. Am. Potash & Chem. Co., Irona, Calif., 1946-50; asst. mgr. design and constrn. Gen. Electric Co., Richland, Wash., 1950-52, ops. mgr. aircraft nuclear propulsion project, Cin., 1952-53; gen. mgr. small aircraft engine dept., Lynn, Mass., 1953-54, gen. mgr. aircraft gas turbine div., Cin., 1955-57; v.p. Gen. Electric Co., 1956-68, v.p. relations services, exec. office, 1957-61; v.p., group exec. aerospace and def. group, 1961-68, exec. v.p., 1968, vice chmn. bd., exec. officer, 1968-80; dir. Continental Group, TRW Inc., So. Pacific Co., J.G. Boswell Co., Utah Internat., Pan American World Airways. Trustee, St. Louis U., 1967-69, Am. Enterprise Inst., Rensselaer Poly. Inst., Grand Central Art Galleries (pres. 1972—), Conf. Bd. (chmn. 1972-74); bd. overseers Hoover Instn., chmn., 1973-76; chmn. Wildlife Mgmt. Inst., 1979—; mem. adv. council Stanford Grad. Sch. Bus. Asso. fellow Royal Aero. Soc.; fellow Am. Inst. Aeros. and Astronautics (sr.), Inst. Jud. Adminstrn., ASME; mem. NAM (dir. 1958-62), Nat. Acad. Engring., Aerospace Industries Assn. (chmn. bd. govs. 1966), Nat. Security Industry Assn. (trustee), Soc. Automotive Engrs., Air Force Assn., Newcomen Soc., Conquistadores Del Cielo. Clubs: Augusta Nat. Golf; Burning Tree, (Washington); Commonwealth, Queen City, Comml. (Cin.); Econ., Univ., Links, Sky (N.Y.C.); Question, Blind Brook, Desert Forest Golf, Camp Fire Am., Round Hill, Clove Valley Rod and Gun, Boone and Crockett, Bohemian (San Francisco). Home: Round Hill Club Rd Greenwich CT 06830 Office: 3135 Easton Turnpike Fairfield CT 06431

PARKER, JAMES JOHN, elec. engr.; b. Oak Park, Ill., June 16, 1947; s. John J. and Marjorie (Grohmann) P.; B.S. in E.E., Marquette U., 1971; B.S. in B.A., Elmhurst Coll., 1980; m. Mary P. Nash, Oct. 21, 1972; children—Elizabeth Ann, John James. Student engr. Motorola Consumer Products, Franklin Park, Ill., 1968-70, engring. asso., 1972-74; co-op engr. Warwick Electronics, Niles, Ill., 1971-72; engr. Quasar Electronics, Inc., Franklin Park, 1974-76; sr. project engr. Motorola Data Products, Carol Stream, Ill., 1976-79; sr. project engr. Zenith Radio Co., 1979—; faculty Wright Jr. Coll., Chgo., part-time 1975—. Advisor, Jr. Achievement, Chgo., 1972-75. Mem. Elmhurst Jr. C. of C. Editorial adv. bd. Electronic Products Mag., 1976-77. Home: 421 Berkeley Ave Elmhurst IL 60126 Office: 1000 Milwaukee Ave Glenview IL 60025

PARKER, JAMES MITCHELL, mktg. co. exec.; b. Chgo., Sept. 3, 1931; s. Robert Barnett and Bonnie (Mitchell) Chidester; student Wilson Jr. coll., 1949-51; B.S., U. Ill., 1955; M.B.A., U. Chgo., 1969; 1 dau., Ginger. Asso. producer Lee Parker Prodns., Chgo., 1955-59; sales exec. Borg-Warner Corp., Chgo., 1959-65; account supr. Perrin & Assos., Chgo., 1966-69; pres. Parkton Corp., Ellsworth, Kans., 1969-72; v.p. Dynamark Corp., Chgo., 1972-77; pres. United Mktg. Corp., Chgo., 1977—. Served to lt. U.S. Army, 1951-53. Mem. Exec. Club, Exec. Program Club. Clubs: Chgo. Athletic; Flossmoor Country. Patentee improved lawn mower. Home: 1117 Leavitt Ave Flossmoor IL 60422 Office: 35 E Wacker Dr Chicago IL 60601

PARKER, JOHN HAMILTON, microbiologist; b. Bath, N.Y., Oct. 7, 1939; s. Leland Charles and Laura Virginia (Hamilton) P.; A.B. in Gen. Sci., U. Rochester, 1961, Ph.D. in Radiation Biology, 1968; postgrad. Albany Med. Coll., 1962-64; m. Marcia Ellen Witters, June 30, 1962; children—Lisa, Lindsay, David. Nat. Cancer Inst. postdoctoral fellow Johns Hopkins U. Sch. Medicine, Balt., 1967-69; asst. prof. SUNY, Buffalo, 1969-72; research microbiologist Miles Labs., Inc., Elkhart, Ind., 1972-77, sr. research scientist, 1977-78; asst. dean Coll. Sci., Nat. Tech. Inst. for Deaf, Rochester (N.Y.) Inst. Tech., 1978-80; sr. project microbiologist Merck, Sharp and Dohme div. Merck Inc., West Point, Pa., 1980—; instr. Notre Dame (Ind.) U., 1975-77. NSF grantee, 1970-72. Mem. AAAS, Am. Soc. Microbiology, Soc. Indsl. Microbiology, Genetics Soc. Am., Am. Assn. Univ. Adminstrs., N.Y. Acad. Scis., Sigma Xi. Mennonite. Contbr. articles to profl. jours., chpts. to books. Home: 885 Weikel Rd Lansdale PA 19446 Office: Biol Products Tech Service Merck Sharp and Dohme West Point PA 19486

PARKER, JOHN MALCOLM, utility co. exec.: b. Halifax, N.S., Can., June 13, 1920; s. Charles Fisher and Mabel (Hennigar) P.; came to U.S., 1936, naturalized, 1942; m. Irene Wilson Davis, Oct. 11, 1942; 1 dau., Bette Elane (Mrs. William E. Sewell). Accounting clk. Standard Oil Co. N.J., Charlotte, N.C., 1941; accounting supr. Duke Power Co., Charlotte, 1941-42; office mgr. So. Bell Tel. & Tel. Co., Charlotte, 1946-50, Atlanta, 1950-60, gen. internal auditor, 1960-68; gen. internal auditor South Central Bell Telephone Co., Birmingham, Ala., 1968—. Chmn. Empty Stocking Fund, Atlanta, 1952-54; bd. mgrs. Birmingham YMCA. Served with AUS, 1942-46. Certified internal auditor. Mem. Nat. Assn. Accountants (pres. chpt. 1972-73, dir.), Am. Mgmt. Assn., Inst. Internal Auditors (pres. chpt. 1978-79, dist. v.p. so. region 1975—), Internat. Platform Assn. Republican. Presbyn. (commr. gen. assembly Presbyn. Ch. of U.S. 1968, 76). Home: 3520 Belle Meade Ln Birmingham AL 35223 Office: 600 N 19th St Birmingham AL 35201

PARKER, JOHN RICHARD, mfg. co. exec.; b. Three Rivers, Mich., Sept. 9, 1917; s. Guy E. and Esther (Fulcher) P.; B.S.M.E., U. Mich., 1939; m. Roberta Irene Chissus, Nov. 2, 1940; children—Robert A., Joan E., Ann B., Richard G. With A. O. Smith Corp., Milw., 1939—, beginning as detail draftsman, successively exec. engr. aircraft landing gears, chief product engr. auto div., dir. sales and engring. auto div., v.p. automotive and r.r. products, group v.p. contract products, 1939-75, pres., dir., 1975—, also dir. subs.'s; dir. Briggs & Stratton Corp., Koehring Co., Marine Corp., Marine Nat. Exchange Bank. Trustees, Citizens Govt. Research Bur., Milw. Boys' Club; adv. council U. Wis.-Milw. Sch. Bus. Adminstrn.; mem. Greater Milw. Com.; bd. dirs. Luth. Hosp., Metro Milw. Assn. Commerce, United Way Greater Milw. Mem. Soc. Automotive Engrs., Machinery and Allied Products Inst. (exec. com.), Wis. Soc. Profl. Engrs. Clubs: Chenequa Country, Milw. Athletic, Milw. Yacht, Univ., Rotary. Office: 3533 N 27th St Milwaukee WI 53216

PARKER, JOSEPHUS DERWARD, corp. exec.; b. Elm City, N.C., Nov. 16, 1906; s. Josephus and Elizabeth (Edwards) P.; A.B., U. of South, 1928; postgrad. Tulane U., 1928-29, U. N.C., 1929-30, Wake Forest Med. Coll., 1930-31; m. Mary Wright, Jan. 15, 1934 (dec. Dec. 1937); children—Mary Wright (Mrs. Mallory A. Pittman, Jr.), Josephus Derward; m. 2d, Helen Hodges Hackney, Jan. 24, 1940; children—Thomas Hackney, Alton Person, Derward Hodges, Sarah Helen Parker Smith. Founder, chmn. bd. J.D. Parker & Sons, Inc., Elm City, 1955—, Parker Tree Farms, Inc., 1956—; founder, pres. Invader, Inc., 1961-63; pres. dir. Brady Lumber Co., Inc., 1957-62; v.p., dir. Atlantic Limestone, Inc., Elm City, 1970—; owner, operator Parker Airport, Eagle Springs, N.C., 1940-62. Served to capt. USAAF, 1944-47. Episcopalian, Moose, Lion. Club: Wilson (N.C.) Country. Address: PO Box 905 Elm City NC 27822

PARKER, LARRY, accountant; b. Paris, Sept. 3, 1928; s. Lawton S. and Beatrice (Snow) P. (parents Am. citizens); came to U.S., 1940; B.S., Northwestern U., 1951: M.B.A., City U. N.Y., 1970; m. Yukie M. Momose, Nov. 5, 1961; children—Yuka-Marie, David Aki. Asst. controller Iwai, Inc., N.Y.C., 1965-68; sr. auditor Eisner & Lubin, N.Y.C., 1968-73: controller Miller & Fink Corp., Darien, Conn., 1973-77; acting treas. Miller & Fink Corp., 1977-78; sec.-treas. Patient Care Publs., Inc., Darien, 1978—, dir. Patient Care Internat., Inc. (Del.), dir. Mark Powley Assos. (New Canaan, Conn.), Publs. Prodn. Service, Inc. (Darien). Treas., Citizens for Informed Choices on Marijuana, 1979—; bd. dirs. Career Life Council, Inc., Darien. Served with C.I.C. U.S. Army, 1951-53. Mem. Am. Inst. C.P.A.'s, N.Y. State Soc. C.P.A.'s, Nat. Assn. Accountants, Sigma Nu. Office: Patient Care Publications Inc 16 Thorndal Circle Darien CT 06820

PARKER, LEE MERKEL, ins. co. exec.; b. Birmingham, Ala., Mar. 14, 1939; s. Delmer Frederick and Lois Izetta (Merkel) P.; B.S., U. Oreg., 1960, M.S., 1962; M.A., Harvard U., 1965; m. Dorothy Joan Montgomery, June 12, 1961; children—Susan Dorothy, Bethany Lee, Camber Cathleen, Lee Montgomery. Account exec. Dean Witter & Co., Reno, 1965-70; v.p., research dir. Resource Mgmt Cons., Portland, Oreg., 1970-71; v.p. investments Willamette Mgmt. Assos., Portland, 1971-72; mng. editor N.W. Investment Review, Portland, 1971-72; dir. corp. services TransPacific Fin. Corp., Portland, 1972-74; v.p. corp. affairs First Farwest Corp., Portland, 1974-78; v.p. investor relations Am. Family Corp., Columbus, Ga., 1978—. Bd. dirs. Irvington Community Assn., 1976-78; mem. bd. edn. Madeleine Parish, 1975-77. Recipient Merit award Fin. World Annual Report, 1977, 78, 79, 80. Mem. Nat. Investor Relations Inst. (dir. 1979—, founder, pres. Pacific N.W. chpt. 1977), Internat. Assn. Bus. Communicators. Republican. Episcopalian. Club: Columbus Country. Home: 2929 Fleetwood Dr Columbus GA 31906 Office: 1932 Wynnton Rd Columbus GA 31906

PARKER, MARILYN MORRIS, entertainment cons. co. exec.; b. St. Louis, Jan. 2, 1935; d. Walter Louis and Viola (Morris) Priebe; tchrs. certificate Kroeger Sch. Music, 1951; B.B.A., Washington U., St. Louis, 1954, M.B.A., 1955; m. H. Virgil Parker, Mar. 11, 1971. With IBM Corp., various locations, 1957-77, mgr. aids, Los Angeles, 1971-75, mgr. performance evaluation, San Jose, 1976-77; v.p. Cherokee Creek Enterprises, Los Angeles and San Jose, 1973—. Co founder, pres. Am. Indian Scholarship Fund, 1971-76, regional dir. No. Calif., 1977; mem. Santa Clara County Alcoholism Adv. Bd.; bd. dirs. TRY Found., Los Angeles. Mem. Am. Harp Soc., Washington U. Alumni Council, Bus. and Profl. Women's Club, Am. Indian Edn. Assn. Lutheran. Office: 5600 Cottle Rd San Jose CA 95193

PARKER, NORMAN FRANCIS, electronics co. exec.; b. Fremont, Nebr., May 14, 1923; s. Frank Huddleston and Rose Johanna (Launer) P.; student W.Va. U., 1943-44; B.S. in Elec. Engring. (George Westinghouse scholar), Carnegie-Mellon U., 1947, M.S. in Elec. Engring., 1947, D.Sc. in Engring. (Buhl fellow), 1948; m. Carol Hope Watt, June 12, 1949; children—Leslie Ann, Kerry Irene, Sandra Jean, Noel Louise. Engr., Westinghouse Electric Corp., East Pittsburgh, Pa., summer 1941, Bloomfield, N.J., summer 1942, U. Calif. Radiation Lab., Oak Ridge, 1944-45; with Autonetics div. N.Am. Aviation, Inc., Anaheim, Calif., 1948-67, asst. chief engr., 1956-59, v.p., gen. mgr. Data Systems div., 1959-62, exec. v.p., 1962-66, pres. autonetics div., 1966-67, v.p., N.Am. Aviation, Inc., 1966-67; exec. v.p., dir. Bendix Corp., 1967-68; pres., dir. Varian Assos., 1968—, chief exec. officer, 1972—; dir. System Devel. Corp. Life trustee Carnegie-Mellon U., mem. bus. adv. com. Grad. Sch. Indsl. Adminstrn. Served with AUS, 1943-46. Fellow IEEE, AIAA; mem. Nat. Acad. Engring., Sigma Xi, Tau Beta Pi, Eta Kappa Nu, Phi Kappa Phi, Pi Mu Epsilon. Patentee curve follower and gyroscopes. Office: 611 Hansen Way Palo Alto CA 94303

PARKER, PATRICK S., bus. exec.; b. Cleve., 1929; A.B., Williams Coll.; M.B.A., Harvard; married. With Parker-Hannifin Corp. and predecessor, Cleve., mgr. Fittings div., 1957-63, mgr. Aerospace Products div., 1963-65, v.p., 1967-69, pres., dir., 1969—, chief exec. officer, 1971—, chmn. bd., 1977—; dir. Soc. Nat. Bank, Cleve., Acme-Cleve. Corp., Reliance Electric Co., Sherwin Williams Co. Trustee, Salvation Army, Coll. of Wooster, Woodruff Hosp., Kolff Found. Served with USNR, 1954-57. Office: 17325 Euclid Ave Cleveland OH 44112*

PARKER, ROBERT AMOS, ins. agt.; b. Bragg City, Mo., June 3, 1935; s. Ira Clofic and Lizzie Bell (Holmes) P.; B.S., Ark. State U., 1958; M.P.H., U. N.C., 1962; m. Mon; 1 dau., Natasha. Adminstrv. asst. dist. 4, Mo. Div. Health, Poplar Bluff, 1958-61; asst. health officer East Orange (N.J.) Health Dept., 1962-66; asst. regional dir. regional office VII, Office Comprehensive Health Planning, HEW, Kansas City, Mo., 1966-69; vis. faculty dept. health care adminstrn. Washington U., St. Louis, 1969-74; exec. dir. Alliance for Regional Community Health, Inc., St. Louis, 1969-76; v.p. fin. mgmt. concepts Gerald Siegel & Assos., St. Louis, 1976-81; gen. agt. Continental Assurance Co., St. Louis, 1981—. Bd. dirs. Family Planning Council, 1977-79, mem. exec. com., 1978-79. Served to 2d lt. U.S. Army, 1958-60, capt. Res., 1966-69. Mem. Am. Public Health Assn., Nat. Assn. Life Underwriters, Mo. Public Health Assn., Am. Comprehensive Health Planning Assn., St. Louis Soc. Assn. Execs. Home: 1971 Beacon Grove Saint Louis MO 63141 Office: 1971 Beacon Grove Saint Louis MO 63141

PARKER, ROLLAND S., cons. psychologist; b. N.Y.C., Dec. 31, 1928; s. Irving and Stella (Sandau) P.; A.B., N.Y. U., 1948, Ph.D., 1959. Cons. psychologist, N.Y.C., 1959—; v.p. Exec. Research Internat., N.Y.C., 1971-72; asso. cons. Dunlap & Assocs., N.Y.C., 1967-70; dir. Center for Emotional Common Sense, N.Y.C., 1971—; instr. N.Y. U., 1978—, Marymount Manhattan Coll., 1978; pres. Exec. Effectiveness, Inc., 1980—. Served to maj. with USAR, 1948-67. Diplomate Am. Bd. Profl. Psychology; licensed psychologist, N.Y., N.J.; recipient Founders' Day award N.Y. U.; Holocaust Meml. award, N.Y. Soc. Clin. Psychologists, 1974. Fellow Soc. Personality Assessment; mem. AAAS, Am., N.Y. State psychol. assns., Am. Group Psychotherapy Assn., N.Y. Soc. Clin. Psychologists, N.Y. Acad. Sci. Author, editor 5 books; contbr. numerous research papers in field to profl. jours., chpts. to books.

PARKER, STANTON HOWARD, univ. bus. ofcl.; b. Nevada, Iowa, May 30, 1933; s. Adolphus Howard and Alice Bernice (Carlson) P.; B.A., Loma Linda (Calif.) U., 1955; postgrad. UCLA, 1963-65; m. Dolly Louise Gregory, Feb. 5, 1953; children—Linda Louise, Sandra Mae, Shirley Ann, Lori Kay. Mgr., Preferred Ins. Agy., Riverside, Calif., 1952-56; mgr. Western br. Gen. Conf. Seventh-day Adventist Ins. Service, Riverside, 1956-75; dir. risk mgmt. Loma Linda U., 1975—; speaker in field. Sec., La Sierra Community Services Dist., Riverside, 1954-56. William Randolph Hearst scholar, 1947; chartered property casualty underwriter. Mem. Am. Soc. Hosp. Risk Mgmt. (dir. 1979-81), Am. Risk and Ins. Assn., Univ. Risk and Ins. Mgmt. Assn. (dir. 1981—), Risk and Ins. Mgmt. Soc. (past pres. Los Angeles Chpt.), Calif. Soc. Hosp. Risk Mgmt. (pres. 1981). Republican. Home: 34979 Holly St Yucaipa CA 92399 Office: Loma Linda U University Arts Suite 103 Loma Linda CA 92350

PARKER, TERRY HOWARD, architect; b. Bklyn., Jan. 13, 1941; s. Jack and Sylvia (Alexander) P.; B.Arch., Rensselaer Poly. Inst., 1964; m. Frida Gerry Feldman, Jan. 26, 1969 (div. Sept. 1979); children—Michael Andrew, Matthew David. Chief designer Frederick N. Fischer, Linden, N.J., 1964-65; designer Pomerance & Breines, N.Y.C., 1965-67; project architect Gruzen & Partners, N.Y.C., 1967-69, Quinlivan, Pierik & Krause, Syracuse, N.Y., 1969; prin. Terry H. Parker, Architect, Montclair, N.J., 1969—. Registered architect, N.Y., N.J., Pa.; registered profl. planner, N.J. Mem. N.J. Soc. Architects, AIA, Bldg. Ofcls. and Code Adminstrs. Internat., N.J. Solar Energy Assn. (sec.). Home: 110 High St Montclair NJ 07042 Office: 17 Academy St Newark NJ 07102

PARKER, W. GARY, banker; b. Hattiesburg, Miss., June 26, 1944; s. Charles P. and Nell M. P.; B.S. in Bus. Adminstrn., U. Ariz., 1966; postgrad. Armstrong Coll., 1975; M.B.A. in Banking, Golden Gate U., 1978; m. Judith K. Merkle, Dec. 6, 1973; stepchildren—James, John. Area mgr. Reading Dynamics, 1966-70; sales mgr. Burroughs Corp., Oakland, Calif., 1970-74; with Bank of Am., Corp. Electronic Banking, Chgo., 1974—, sales mgr., 1980. Mem. exec. bd. Boy Scouts Am., 1978; bd. dirs. Anchorage Handicapped Workshop; fund raiser United Way; vol. worker Home for Handicapped Children. Mem. Bank Mktg. Assn., Jaycees, C. of C. Republican. Club: Toastmasters.

PARKER, WHILDEN SESSIONS, lawyer; b. Baton Rouge, La., Jan. 27, 1936; s. Fred C. and Laverne S. Parker; B.S., La. State U., 1960; J.D., George Washington U., 1970; m. Diane E. Vance, Aug. 3, 1963; children—Pamela, Elaine, Vance. Admitted to Va. bar, 1970, D.C. bar, 1971, Fla. bar, 1979; law clk. U.S. Ct. Claims, Washington, 1970-71; asso. law firm Sellers, Conner & Cuneo and Pettit & Martin, Washington, 1971-75; adminstrv. judge Armed Services Bd. Contract Appeals, Alexandria, Va., 1975-76; v.p., counsel Pratt & Whitney Aircraft Group, Govt. Products div. United Technologies Corp., West Palm Beach, Fla., 1976—. Served with USMC, 1960-70. Decorated Air medal. Mem. Am. Bar Assn., Va. State Bar, D.C. Bar, Fla. Bar. Republican. Office: PO Box 2691 West Palm Beach FL 33402

PARKER, WILLIAM ANDERSON, JR., investment co. exec.; b. Atlanta, Aug. 10, 1927; s. William A. and Emmy Johnson (Nixon) P.; B.S., Emory U., 1950; LL.B., Atlanta Law Sch., 1952; m. Nancy Jean Fraser, May 9, 1952; children—William Anderson, Isobel Fraser, Richard Carlyle. Dir. Genuine Parts Co., Atlanta, 1969—; v.p. Beck & Gregg Industries, Atlanta, 1957-63, pres., 1963-77; chmn. bd. Cherokee Investment Co., Atlanta, 1977—; dir. So. Co., Ga. Power Co., 1st Union Real Estate Investments, Life Ins. Co. Ga. Bd. dirs. Atlanta YMCA, 1967-77, trustee, 1978—; trustee Emory U., A.G. Rhodes Home, John B. Campbell Found., Luther C. Fischer Found., L.H. Beck Found., Westminster Schs. (chmn. bd.), Atlanta Med. Center. Served with USNR, 1945-46. Mem. Nat. (exec. com.), So. (exec. com.) wholesale hardware assns., Chi Phi. Baptist. Clubs: Rotary (Atlanta), Capital City, Piedmont Driving. Home: 1880 Garraux Rd Atlanta GA 30327 Office: Cherokee Investment Co 1380 W Paces Ferry Rd Suite 260 Atlanta GA 30327

PARKER, WILLIAM EDWARD, electronic co. exec.; b. New Haven, June 18, 1924; s. Charles I. and Florence Anna (Ohr) P.; B.S. in Chemistry, Brown U., 1950; Ph.D. in Phys. Chemistry, U. Kans., 1956; m. E. Constance Nash, Sept. 6, 1947; children—William Edward II, Robert N., Nancy J. Vice pres. tech. Airco Electronics, Niagara Falls, N.Y., 1959-77; pres. PFC Components, Great Neck, N.Y., 1977-79; exec. v.p., chief operating officer Statek Corp., Orange, Calif., 1979—; gen. chmn. Electronic Component Conf., 1975. Served with AUS, World War II. Mem. IEEE, Am. Electronics Assn., Internat. Soc. Hybrid Mfrs. Contbr. articles to sci. jours. Office: 512 N Main St Orange CA 92668

PARKER, WILLIAM JAMIESON, constrn. co. exec.; b. Guelph, Ont., Can., Aug. 14, 1929; s. William and Ruth Mary (Jamieson) P.; diploma Guelph Coll. and Vocat. Inst., 1949; grad. Ryerson Poly. Inst., Guelph, 1951; m. Catharine Joan Steinmann, Sept. 22, 1956; children—Elizabeth Jane, William Richard. Estimator, William Parker Constrn. Ltd., Guelph, 1951-63, sec., treas., mgr., 1963-69, pres., owner, 1969—; pres. Wilpak Constrn. Industries Ltd., Guelph. Bd. govs. St. John's Sch., Elora, Ont., 1972-80, vice chmn., 1976-78, chmn., 1978-80; mem. adv. bd. Conestoga Coll., 1976-80. Mem. Canadian Constrn. Assn., Ont. Gen. Contractors Assn., Grand Valley Constrn. Assn., Constrn. Specifications Can., Inst. Profl. Designs, London, Engrs. Club Toronto. Anglican. Clubs: Rotary (pres. 1975-76), Guelph Country, Masons. Home: 23 Woodlawn Rd E Guelph ON N1H 7G6 Canada Office: 70 Preston St PO Box 607 Guelph ON N1H 6L3 Canada

PARKER, WILLIAM THOMAS, advt. exec.; b. Wilson, N.C., July 7, 1943; B.A., Shaw U., 1965; postgrad. Rochester Inst. Tech., 1975-76; m. Dolores Parker. Asst. to dep. dir. Presidential Inaugural Com., Washington, 1964-65; asst. to operations mgr. Union Carbide Corp., 1965-67; with consumer markets div. Eastman Kodak Co., Rochester, N.Y., 1967-78, sales promotion exec., 1978-80; mktg. mgr. E. & J. Gallo Winery, Modesto, Calif., 1978—; pres. The Mktg. Forum, Inc., advt. agy., Atlanta, 1980—; dir. Eltrex Industries, Inc. Vice pres. Rochester Urban League, Inc., 1976-78; pres. Contact of Rochester, Inc., 1970-71. Mem. Nat. Assn. Market Developers. Democrat. Home: 3440 Somerset Trail Atlanta GA 30331 Office: 230 Peachtree St Suite 500 Atlanta GA 30343

PARKINSON, HOWARD EVANS, retail exec., financial cons.; b. Logan, Utah, Nov. 3, 1936; s. Howard Maughan and Valeria Arlene (Evans) P.; B.S., Brigham Young U., 1961; M.B.A., U. Utah, 1963; m. Lucy Kay Bowen, Sept. 21, 1960; children—Blake, Gregory, Dwight, Lisa, David, Rebecca. Mgmt. intern AEC, Richland, Wash., 1963-65; v.p. Belstar, Inc., Rexburg, Idaho, 1965-71, dir., 1966-76, pres., 1971-76; v.p., dir. Grand Targhee Resort, Inc., Rexburg, 1967-69; v.p., dir. Fargo-Wilson-Wells Co., Pocatello, Idaho, 1974-76; equity qualified agt. Equitable Life Assurance So. U.S., Idaho Falls, Idaho, 1977-79, mem. nat. council sales group, 1978; dist. mgr. Mass. Mut. Ins., Idaho Falls, 1980—; fin. cons. small bus. Bd. dirs. Little League Baseball, 1974-75; coach Little League Basketball, 1975-76; high councilman Rexburg Stake, Ch. of Jesus Christ of Latter-day Saints, 1976-77, bishop, 1981—. Mem. Million Dollar Roundtable. Republican. Club: Toastmasters (past pres.). Home: 264 S 2d W Rexburg ID 83440 Office: 1650 S Woodruff Idaho Falls ID 83401

PARKINSON, JAMES THOMAS, III, investment cons.; b. Richmond, Va., July 10, 1940; s. James Thomas and Elizabeth (Hopkins) P.; B.A., U. Va., 1962; M.B.A., U. Pa., 1964; m. Molly O. Owens, June 16, 1962; children—James Thomas, Glenn Walser. Trainee, Chem. Bank, N.Y.C., 1964-66; asso., corporate fin. dept. Blyth & Co., Inc., N.Y.C., 1968-69; v.p., corporate fin. dept. Clark Dodge & Co., Inc., N.Y.C., 1969-74; pvt. practice investment mgmt., N.Y.C., 1974—; dir. Thetford Corp., Ann Arbor, Mich., 1170 Fifth Ave. Corp., N.Y.C.; trustee Empire Savs. Bank, N.Y.C.; bd. mgrs. Am. Bible Soc., N.Y.C.; instr. corporate fin. Ind. U., 1966-68. Sr. warden Ch. of Holy Trinity, N.Y.C., 1978-79. Served with AUS, 1966-68. Republican. Episcopalian. Clubs: Univ., Church (N.Y.C.); Va. Country (Richmond). Office: 22 E 67th St New York NY 10021

PARKINSON, THOMAS IGNATIUS, JR., lawyer; b. N.Y.C., Jan. 27, 1914; s. Thomas I. and Georgia (Weed) P.; A.B., Harvard, 1934; LL.B., U. Pa., 1937; m. Geralda E. Moore, Sept. 23, 1937; children—Thomas Ignatius III, Geoffrey Moore, Cynthia Moore. Admitted to N.Y. bar, 1938, since practiced in N.Y.C.; asso. Milbank, Tweed, Hope & Hadley, 1937-47, partner, 1947-56; pres. Mar Ltd., 1951—, Breecom Corp., 1972—; dir., exec. com. Pine St. Fund, Inc., N.Y.C. Trustee State Communities Aid Assn., 1949—; dir. Fgn. Policy Assn., 1949-53; bd. dirs., exec. com. Milbank Meml. Fund. Mem. Am. Bar Assn., Assn. Bar City N.Y., Pilgrims U.S.A., Brit. War Relief Soc. (officer), Met. Unit Found., Phi Beta Kappa. Clubs: Down Town Assn., Knickerbocker, Union, Piping Rock. Home: 215 Lakeview Ave Brightwaters NY 11718 Office: 75 E 55 St New York NY 10022

PARKISON, ED HOYT, research engr.; b. Ventura, Calif., Feb. 10, 1932; s. Hoyt S. and Hila (Clifford) P.; B.S. in Mech. Engring., U. Wyo., 1953; J.D., U. Md., 1962; m. Shirley Regina Dixon, Dec. 4, 1954; children—Mark Hoyt, Regina Ann, David Clifford. Test engr. Koppers Co., Balt., 1955-57, sr. test engr., 1957-59, supr. sound control lab., 1959-61; sr. engr. Martin Marietta Corp., Balt. Div., 1961-64, mgr. support ops. RIAS Div., 1964-74, mgr. engring. Martin Marietta Labs., 1974-77, prin. engr., 1977—. Treas., Catonsville PTA, 1964-66, 72-74, v.p., 1966-67; treas. Hillcrest PTA, 1967-70, pres., 1970-71; treas. Pub. Edn. Nominating Com. Balt. County, 1973—. Served with AUS, 1953-55. Recipient Martin Marietta Exceptional Achievement prize, 1974. Mem. ASME (dir. 1965-67, treas. 1969-70, sec. 1970-71, vice chmn. 1971-72, chmn. 1972—), Acoustical Soc. Am., Inst. Noise Control Engrs. (noise control com.), Aluminum Assn. (chmn. 1975-77), Md. Acad. Sci. (sci council), Md., Catonsville hist. socs., Kappa Sigma. Mem. Ch. of Jesus Christ of Latter-day Saints. Editor: Colonial History of Catonsville; developed isotope ratio mass spectrometer for extra-terrestrial life detection, 1966; developed upper atmospheric gun launched probe for project HARP, 1967; developed noise suppression systems for U.S. Army, 1973-74; invented, developed mineral benefication process, 1972-74. Home: 1211 Brandford Rd Baltimore MD 21228 Office: 1450 S Rolling Rd Baltimore MD 21227

PARKS, JAMES NICHOLAS, rec. co. exec.; b. Manchester, N.H., Oct. 31, 1924; s. Nicholas D. and Angela (Boritsos) Psarakis; student Columbia U., 1948, 49; Asso. Bus. Sci., N.H. Coll. Accounting and Commerce, 1952; m. Georgette Poirier Psarakis. Song plugger Lewis Music Pub. Co., N.Y.C., 1947-49; gen. mgr. Marvel Records, 1949-50; freelance producer London Records, 1950-53; Am. rep. W & G Record Processing Co. Pty. Ltd. Australia, 1953-58, v.p. Am. operations, 1958-61, exec. v.p. Am. ops., 1961-68, dir. W & G Group; control dir. Internat. Jaspar Music Group Ltd., 1967; state indsl. agt. at large Office of Indsl. Devel., 1967-68; supr. fgn. trade and comml. devel. resources and econ. devel., 1968—; dir. Taylor Industries Ltd., Toronto, Ont., Can.; personnel mgr. The Brandywine Singers and Mar-Vels, 1964—, The Seekers, 1965-68, Danny Gravas, Bambi Lynn, 1967-75, Marc Denny, 1968—; writer column Record Round Up, N.H. Sunday News, 1955-73. Served with USNR, 1945-46. Mem. Internat. Record Mfrs. Assn. (sec. 1958), Am. Hellenic Ednl. Progressive Assn., A.F.M. (hon. life), N.H. Indsl. Agents Assn., Northeast Indsl. Devel. Assn., Profl. Musicians Union Australia (hon. life), League of Greek Orthodox Stewards. Mem. Greek Orthodox Ch. (dir.). Clubs: NOA, Lions. Home: 188 Highland St Manchester NH 03104 Office: 852 Elm St Manchester NH 03101

PARKS, LLOYD LEE, oil co. exec.; b. Kiefer, Okla., Dec. 9, 1929; s. Homer H. and Avis Pearl (Motes) P.; student Okla. State U., 1948-50, Tulsa U., 1951; A.M.P., Harvard Bus. Sch., 1965; m. Mary Ellen Scott, Aug. 20, 1948; children—Connie, Karyn, Becky. Accountant, Deep Rock Oil Co., Tulsa, 1951-54; sec., treas. Blackwell Oil & Gas Co., Tulsa, 1954-62; v.p. finance Amax Petroleum Corp., Houston, 1962-68, pres., 1969—, v.p. Amax Inc., Houston, 1975—; dir. Adobe Oil Co., Midland, Tex. Bd. dirs. Town & Country Bank, Houston. Served with U.S. Army, 1946-48. Republican. Clubs: Cherry Hills Country (Denver), Lakeside Country (Houston), Houston. Home: 11321 Greenvale Houston TX 77024 Office: 1300 West Belt PO Box 42806 Houston TX 77042

PARKS, THOMAS AQUINAS, corp. exec.; b. Cleve., Nov. 4, 1929; s. Jonathan B. and Marian Mae (Campbell) P.; B.A., State U. Iowa, 1954; postgrad. U. Ill., 1965; m. Judith Fausch, Dec. 31, 1973; children by previous marriage—David Jonathan, Sandra Anne. Dept. head internat. sales div. Collins Radio Co., Cedar Rapids, Iowa, 1954-58; asst. export sales mgr. Amana Refrigeration, Inc. (Iowa), 1958-62; export sales mgr. Cedar Rapids Engring. Co., 1962-64, gen. sales mgr., 1964-65, v.p. sales, dir., 1966-68, pres., treas., 1968—; pres., treas. parent co. Kwik-Way Industries, 1969—; chmn. bd. Line-O-Tronics, Inc., Rock Island, Ill., 1973—, Kwik-Way Mfg. of Can., Toronto, 1980—; pres. Kwik-Way Mfg. Co., Marion, Iowa, 1976—, Danvir Cons., Inc., Chgo., 1978—; dir. A/L Sports, Inc., Niles, Ill., 1979—. Fgn. affairs speaker Speakers Bur., Cedar Rapids C. of C., 1958—, chmn. Fgn. Trade Bur., 1956-62; bd. dirs. Hawkeye Area council Boy Scouts Am., Cedar Rapids Childrens Home, Cedar Rapids Symphony Assn.; trustee Coe Coll., 1977—. Served with USAF, 1951-53. Mem. Cedar Rapids C. of C. (dir.). Republican. Club: Cedar Rapids Country. Home: Timberlake Estates Swisher IA 52338 Office: 701 American Bldg Cedar Rapids IA 52406

PARMAN, FRITZ QUINN, JR., retail tire co. exec.; b. Corbin, Ky., Dec. 22, 1942; s. Fritzie Quinn and Dorothy (Williams) P.; student U. Fla.; m. Patricia Sue Paul, Mar. 6, 1968; children—Fritz Quinn III, Cynthia Dorlyn, Robert Edward, Jessica Sue. Pres., Big Chief's Tire Co., Inc., Jacksonville, Fla. Mem. Jacksonville Tire Dealers Assn., Jacksonville Area C. of C. Episcopalian. Home: 9330 Parman Rd Jacksonville FL 32222 Office: Big Chief's Tire Co Inc 5444 Normandy Blvd Jacksonville FL 32205

PARNELL, CHARLES ALVIN, mfg. co. ofcl.; b. Eastport, Maine, Aug. 9, 1948; s. Anthony J. and Elinore (Cheverie) Parrinello; A.A.S. in Data Processing, Monroe Community Coll., 1969; m. Diane M. Kocan, July 21, 1972. Programmer, Security Trust Co., Rochester, N.Y., 1969-72; programmer Pennwalt Corp., Rochester, 1972-73, sr. programmer, 1973-76, programming mgr., 1976—; pres. C&M Assos., Rochester, 1973—; v.p. Tee Pee Foto's, Rochester, 1978—. Mem. Assn. for Systems Mgmt., Computer Systems Assn. Home: 266 Miramar Rd Rochester NY 14624 Office: Pennwalt Corp 755 Jefferson Rd Rochester NY 14623

PARO, TOM EDWARD, broadcasting co. exec.; b. Belleville, Ill., July 7, 1923; s. Edward Westermann and Alice Jane (Price) P.; B.J., U. Mo., 1948; m. Aileen Nance, Oct. 1, 1955: children—Jeffrey, Daniel, Kathleen. With MBS, 1948-54; with sales dept. NBC, 1955-59; dir. sales WRC-TV, Washington, 1960-62, sta. mgr., 1962-65, gen. mgr., 1969-78; sta. mgr. WNBC-TV, 1966-69; v.p. Nat. Broadcasting Co., 1969-77; pres. Maximum Service Telecasters, Inc., 1978—; adv. bd. Riggs Nat. Bank. Bd. dirs. Meridian House, Boy Scouts Am. Served to lt., AUS, 1943-46; ETO; to capt., 1951-53. Kiwanian. Clubs: International; Burning Tree; Congressional Country; National Broadcasters (dir.). Home: 5913 Searl Terr Washington DC 20016 Office: 1735 DeSales St NW Washington DC 20036

PARR, OWEN ANTHONY, leasing co. exec.; b. Havana, Cuba, Sept. 5, 1932; came to U.S., 1959, naturalized, 1967; s. Owen Gordon and Otilia Clara (Ramos) P.; LL.D., U. Havana, 1954; m. Agneta K. Klint, Dec. 14, 1963; children—Nancy, Vivian, Anthony, Michael. Atty., Havana, Cuba, 1954-59; dist. mgr. Avis RAC, N.Y.C. and San Juan, P.R., 1960-68; mgr. VW Interamericana, San Juan, 1968-70, v.p. leasing Caribbean, 1970-76; group v.p. internat. automotive group Pepsico Leasing Corp., San Juan and Mexico City, 1976-78; v.p. internat. leasing div. Gelco Corp., Mpls., 1978-79; cons., 1979—; exec. v.p. Hansord Leasing Inc., Mpls., also dir. Mem. Am. Automotive Leasing Assn., Car and Truck Rental and Leasing Assn. Republican. Roman Catholic. Club: Wayzata Country. Home: 1190 Heritage Ln Wayzata MN 55391 Office: 5353 Wayzata Blvd Minneapolis MN 55416

PARRIOTT, JAMES DEFORIS, JR., oil co. exec.; b. Moundsville, W. Va., Aug. 21, 1923; s. James D. and Bessie (Sadler) P.; student Ohio Wesleyan U., 1941-43; LL.B., U. Colo., 1949; m. Marynette Sonneland, Aug. 3, 1946; children—James Deforis III, Sara. Admitted to Colo. bar, 1949; practice in Denver, 1949-53; asst. city atty., Denver, 1950-51; asst. atty. gen., Colo., 1952-53; chief counsel Bur. Land Mgmt., Dept. Interior, 1953, asso. solicitor lands and minerals, 1954-56; atty. Ohio Oil Co., Washington, 1956-60, Findlay, O., 1960-62; mgr. employee relations Marathon Oil Co., 1962-69, dir. pub. affairs, 1969-74, dir. pub. and govt. affairs, 1974—. Council pres. Boy Scouts Am. Served as pilot, 2d lt., USAAF, 1943-46. Mem. Am., Fed. bar assns., Phi Alpha Delta, Phi Gamma Delta. Republican. Clubs: University (Washington); Findlay Country. Home: 1932 Queenswood Dr Findlay OH 45840 Office: Marathon Oil Co 539 S Main St Findlay OH 45840

PARRISH, ARTHUR, economist; b. Bklyn., Nov. 23, 1946; s. Joseph Thomas and Marion Diane Parrish; B.A. summa cum laude in Econs., L.I. U., 1971; M.A. in Econs., Bklyn. Coll., CUNY, 1975; m. Anne De Biase, June 27, 1970. Asst. supr. Ins. Services Office, N.Y.C., 1968-72; sr. econ. cost analyst Consol. Edison, N.Y.C., 1972-73; commodity research analyst Louis Dreyfus Corp., Stamford, Conn., 1973-79; sr. grains and oilseed analyst Bache & Co., N.Y.C., 1979-80; sr. grains analyst E.F. Hutton & Co., N.Y.C., 1980—. Served with USN, 1967-68. Mem. Am. Econ. Assn., Futures Industry Assn., Am. Statis. Assn., Am. Mus. Natural History. Roman Catholic. Home: 58 Greenway Circle Ryetown NY 10573 Office: One Battery Park Plaza New York NY 10004

PARRISH, CHRIS GLENN, bus. services co. exec.; b. Laurel, Miss., Sept. 9, 1931; d. Ivie and Katie (Coley) Glenn; m. Oct. 19, 1969 (div.); children—Billy, Cheryl, Joan, Leslie. Mgr. House of Cachet, Laurel, Miss., 1973-74, Waldorff's, Biloxi, Miss., 1974-75, Lerner Shops, Gulfport, Miss., 1974-78, Meridian, Miss., 1978-79, Jackson, Miss., 1979-81, Gautier, Miss., 1981—; mem. staff gov. Miss., 1968-72; tchr. bridge classes. Mem. Gulfport C. of C., Downtown Mchts. Assn. Methodist. Clubs: Bath and Racket, Am. Contract Bridge, Garden (pres. 1964-65). Home: Beach Front Dr Ocean Springs MS 39564 Office: 2800 US Hwy 90 Singing River Mall Gautier MS 39553

PARRISH, EDWARD, lawyer; b. Adel, Ga., Nov. 21, 1911; s. C. E. and Nona (Rountree) P.; grad. Young Harris (Ga.) Coll., 1930; m. Jeannette Crane. Admitted to Ga. bar, 1931, since practiced in Adel; county atty. Cook County, Ga., 1938-42; city atty. city of Adel, 1940-42, 46—, also city atty. Sparks, Ga.; solicitor-gen. Alapaha Jud. Circuit, 1949-73; dir. Cook-Berrien Service Corp., Cook County Fed. Savs. and Loan Assn. of Adel, Guaranty Fed. Savs. and Loan Assn. of Adel. Served with AUS, 1942-45. Mem. Am. Legion, V.F.W., Woodmen of World. Club: Adel Lions. Home: 201 E 8th St Adel GA 31620 Office: Del-Cook Bldg Adel GA 31620

PARRISH, JAMES DUDLEY, JR., steel co. mktg. exec.; b. Port Arthur, Tex., Sept. 9, 1931; s. James Dudley and Addie Pearl (Wigley) P.; B.B.A., U. Houston, 1954; m. Dorothy Collins, Sept. 9, 1952; children—Mark Kent, David Kevin. Spl. agt. Office of Naval Intelligence, Oklahoma City, 1956-61; account exec. Merrill Lynch, Pierce, Fenner & Smith, Inc., 1961-69; regional rep. Wellington Mgmt. Co., Houston, 1969-72; mktg. mgr. T.B.I. Steel, Paducah, Ky., 1975—. Pres. Parents Assn. Transylvania U., 1975-77. Served to capt. AUS, 1954-56. Recipient Century III Honorary, Transylvania U., 1976. Mem. Steel Service Center Inst., Am. Inst. Econ. Research, SAR, SCV, Sons Republic of Tex., St. George's Soc., Order of Lafayette. Republican. Baptist. Clubs: Elkins Lake Country, Old Capitol (Houston); Masons, Shriners, Rotary. Home: 265 Alben Barkley Dr Paducah KY 42001 Office: 2425 S 4th St Paducah KY 42001

PARRISH, LOWE LOWE, III, pharm. co. exec.; b. Spartanburg, S.C., Feb. 25, 1947; s. Lowe Lowe and Nelle Irene (Elmore) P.; B.S., Augusta Coll., 1969; postgrad. (NSF scholar) Med. Coll. Ga., 1969-70; Pharmacy Degree, U. Ga., 1972, M.B.A., 1973; postgrad. Ga. State U., 1972-73, Old Dominion U., 1973-74. Mgr. pharm. mfg., registered pharmacist Grady Meml. Hosp., Atlanta, 1972-73; pharm. rep. Eli Lilly Co., Indpls., 1973-75; eastern regional sales mgr. R.P. Scherer Corp., Detroit, 1975-76; dir. mktg. and spl. projects Paco Packaging, Pennsauken, N.J., 1976-77; nat. sales mgr. Kolar Labs., Chgo., 1977-78; dir. sales and mktg. Paco Labs., Lakewood, N.J., 1978—; exec. v.p. Realaw Assos., Inc., 1980—. Served with USAR, 1969-75. Mem. Drug, Chem. and Allied Trades, Sales Assn. of Chem. Industry, Cosmetic, Toiletries and Fragrance Assn., Pharm. Mfrs. Assn., Am. Pharm. Assn., Soc. Cosmetic Chemists. Republican. Methodist. Clubs: Society Hill, Woodlake Country. Home: PO Box 413 Haddonfield NJ 08033 Office: 1200 Paco Way Lakewood NJ 08701

PARRISH, NORMAN CHARLES, mech. engr.; b. Los Angeles, Feb. 28, 1912; s. George C. and Estella (Lay) P.; B.S. in Mech. Engring., U. So. Calif., 1942, M.S., 1965; m. Margaret Pierce Smith, Dec. 31, 1944 (div. Nov. 1969); 1 dau., Margaret Candace; m. 2d, Dorothy Dalley Caswell, Jan. 16, 1971. Research engr. Lockheed Aircraft Co., Burbank, Calif., 1938-42; project engr. Gilfillan Bros., Los Angeles, 1942-43; engring. adv. to pres. Saval Co., Vernon, Calif., 1944-45; cons. indsl. field engr. So. Calif. Edison Co., 1946-53; research engr. Northrop Aircraft Co., 1950-55, Lockheed Missiles & Space Corp., Sunnyvale, Calif., 1957-62; mem. tech. staff Hughes Aerospace Co., El Segundo, Calif., 1962-70; on leave to U. Calif., Berkeley, 1966-70, chief engr. environ. physiology White Mountain research and NASA project, U. Calif., Berkeley, 1966-72; staff scientist Lawrence Berkeley Labs., 1976-81; tech. cons. Dept. Energy, Nat. Bur. Standards, 1980—; dir. Parthay Devel., Inc., Lawndale, Calif., 1950-60, Parlin Engring. Co., Moraga, Calif., 1948-72, Echo, Ltd., Berkeley, 1970-76, Candace Corp., Los Angeles, 1958-78; cons., instr. in field. Registered profl. engr., Calif. Mem. ASME, Soc. Automotive Engrs., ASTM, AIAA, Bio-Med. Engring. Soc., Sigma Xi. Author: Micro Diaphragm Pressure Transducers, 1964; Inventors Source Book, 1977; also articles; patentee in field. Office: PO Box 158 Rheem Valley CA 94570

PARROTT, TIMOTHY JOHN, aircraft distbg. co. exec.; b. Monterrey, Calif., July 1, 1947; s. William G. and Mary (Pitney) P., Jr.; student U. Colo., 1965-66; m. Jennifer Lee Jensen, Apr. 1, 1977; children—Troy, Carrie, Amy. Dist. mgr. Horizon Property Corp., Ft. Worth, 1970, gen. mgr., 1971; sales mgr. Western Airmotive Co., Oakland, Calif., 1972-74, v.p. mktg., 1975-78, exec. v.p., 1978-80, pres., 1980—. Served to chief warrant officer U.S. Army, 1967-69; Vietnam. Decorated Air medal with oak leaf cluster, Vietnamese Cross of Gallantry. Mem. Nat. Bus. Aircraft Assn. Roman Catholic. Club: Burlingame Country. Office: Oakland Airport PO Box 2445 Oakland CA 94614

PARSONS, ALLAN FOWLER, mfrs. rep.; b. Hartford, July 5, 1916; s. Robert Smith and Alice Gertrude (Southwick) P.; B.A., Colgate U., 1938; m. Sally Skinner Newbold, Jan. 2, 1943; children—Elizabeth, Bruce, Craig, Alice, Keith. Sales engr. IBM, New Eng., 1938-41; sales clk. Marsh & McLennan, Inc., San Francisco, 1946-48; adminstrv. asst. to treas. FMC Corp., San Jose, Calif., 1948-50; pres. Robert S. Parsons & Son, Inc., West Hartford, 1950—. Served to lt. (s.g.) USNR, 1941-46. Mem. Conn. Soc. Genealogists, SAR (life), Delta Kappa Epsilon. Republican. Baptist. Club: Masons. Address: 102 Walden St West Hartford CT 06107

PARSONS, JAMES FREDERICK, mfg. co. exec.; b. N.Y.C., Feb. 8, 1920; s. James Franklin and Anne Marie (McGill) P.; M.E., Stevens Inst. Tech., 1942; m. Adrienne M. Morris, Dec. 16, 1944; children—Edwina Mary, Meredith Ann, Adrienne Mary. Gen. sales mgr. Econ. Machinery Co., Worcester, Mass., 1952-62; v.p. mktg. George J. Meyer Mfg. Co., Milw., 1962-68; pres. SS Systems div. ATO, Inc., Milw., 1968-75; v.p., gen. mgr. Simplicity Engring. Co., Durand, Mich., 1975-80; group v.p. Gen. Steel Industries, Inc., St. Louis, 1980—; cons. ATO, Inc., 1976. Counselor, Jr. Achievement, 1969-70; chmn. fin. lay com. Milw. Roman Catholic Archdiocese, 1970-71. Served with USN, 1942-45; PTO. Registered profl. engr., Mass. Mem. Packaging Inst., TAPPI, Am. Foundrymen's Assn., Conveyor Equipment Mfrs. Assn., Inst. Scrap Iron and Steel, ASME, Master Brewers Assn. Clubs: Univ. (Milw.); Oakland Hills Country. Home: 2627 Covington Pl Birmingham MI 48010 Office: 11 S Meramec Ave Saint Louis MO 63105

PARSONS, THEODORE METCALF, stockbroker; b. New Rochelle, N.Y., Aug. 17, 1929; s. Theodore Chandler and Elizabeth Brunette (Metcalf) P.; B.S., Mass. Inst. Tech., 1952; M.B.A., Harvard, 1956; m. Betty Jean Bryant, July 24, 1954; children—Theodore C., Susan B. Limited partner, Oscar E. Dooley & Co., Miami, Fla., 1960-63; asst. v.p. Kidder Peabody & Co., N.Y.C., 1963-67; v.p. E.F. Hutton Co., N.Y.C., 1967-71; asst. to chief fin. officer GAC Corp., Miami, 1971-72; account exec. Merrill Lynch, Miami, 1973—. Served to 1st lt. USAF, 1952-54. Republican. Episcopalian. Clubs: Colo. Mountain, Biscayne Bay Yacht, Riviera Country, Miami, Univ. Home: 900 Hardee Rd Coral Gables FL 33146 Office: One Biscayne Tower Miami FL 33131

PARTNOY, RONALD ALLEN, firearms co. exec.; b. Norwalk, Conn., Dec. 23, 1933; s. Maurice and Ethel Marguerite (Roselle) P.; B.A., Yale, 1956; LL.B., Harvard, 1961; LL.M., Boston U., 1965; m. Diane Catherine Keenan, Sept. 18, 1965. Admitted to Mass. bar, 1962, Conn. bar, 1966; atty. Liberty Mut. Ins. Co., Boston, 1961-65; asso. counsel Remington Arms Co., Inc., Bridgeport, Conn., 1965-70, gen. counsel, 1970—. Served with USN, 1956-58, to capt. USNR. Mem. Sporting Arms and Ammunition Mfrs. Inst. (chmn. legis. and legal affairs com. 1971—), U.S. Navy League (pres. Bridgeport council 1975-77, state pres. 1977—), Am., Conn., Bridgeport bar assns., Westchester Fairfield Corp. Counsel Assn., Am. Judicature Soc. Clubs: Chancery; Harvard (Boston); Yale (N.Y.C.). Home: 135 Parkwood Rd Fairfield CT 06430 Office: 939 Barnum Ave Bridgeport CT 06602

PASCARELLA, PERRY JAMES, mag. editor; b. Bradford, Pa., Apr. 11, 1934; s. James and Lucille Margaret (Monti) P.; A.B., Kenyon Coll., 1956; postgrad. William and Mary Coll., 1957, George Washington U., 1958; m. Carol Ruth Taylor, May 4, 1957; children—Cynthia, Elizabeth. Credit reporter Dun & Bradstreet, Cleve., 1956, 60; asst. editor Steel mag., Cleve., 1961-63, asso. editor, 1963-67, bus. editor, 1968-69, mng. editor, 1969; mng. editor Industry Week mag., Cleve., 1970-71, exec. editor, 1971—; lectr. in field. Served to lt. comdr. USNR, 1957-60. Recipient Distinguished Service award Kenyon Coll., 1975; Carnegie scholar, 1952-56. Mem. N.E. Ohio Kenyon Alumni Assn. (trustee 1975-76), Soc. Profl. Journalists, Nat. Assn. Bus. Economists, World Future Soc., Am. Teilhard Assn. Future of Man, AAAS. Presbyn. (elder). Author: Technology-Fire in a Dark World, 1979; Humanagement in the Future Corporation, 1980; contbr. articles to profl. publs. Home: 29701 Wolf Rd Bay Village OH 44140 Office: Industry Week Mag Penton Plaza 1111 Chester Ave Cleveland OH 44114

PASCH, KENNETH WALTER, trucking co. exec.; b. Niagara Falls, N.Y., Dec. 4, 1924; s. Herbert Emil and Floradora P.; B.S. in Acctg. with distinction, U. Buffalo, 1950; m. Lois Marie Donato, June 12, 1948; children—Kathleen Pasch Phalen, Kenneth, Cynthia, Eileen Pasch Allen, Christopher, Amy, Timothy, Mary. Acct., Robert P. Schermerhorn & Co., 1951-54; lectr. U. Buffalo and Niagara U., 1955-58; pvt. practice acctg., 1956-63; controller Graphite Products div. Carborundum Co., 1964-66, Red Star Express, 1966-69; controller Motor Freight Express, York, Pa., 1969-71, treas., 1972-73, v.p. fin., 1973-74, exec. v.p., 1975-76, pres., 1977—, also dir. Chmn. transp. div. Nat. Bible Week. Served with USMC, 1943-45. Mem. Am. Inst. C.P.A.'s, N.Y. State Soc. C.P.A.'s (Acctg. medal 1950), Middle Atlantic Conf. (dir.), Eastern Central Motor Carriers Assn. (trustee), Am. Trucking Assn. (dir.), York C. of C., Beta Gamma Sigma. Republican. Roman Catholic. Home: 15 Hunting Park Ct York PA 17402 Office: Motor Freight Express Arsenal Rd and Toronita St York PA 17402

PASH, GEORGE KINNEAR, investment co. exec.; b. Whittier, Calif., Feb. 7, 1938; s. George Maxwell and Helen Francis (Kinnear) P.; B.S., UCLA, 1960, M.B.A., 1961; m. Deborah Tacy Allen, Mar. 6, 1975; children—Nanette Jeanee, George Kinnear. Investment analyst Occidental Life Ins. Co., Los Angeles, 1961-66; v.p. Putnam Mgmt. Co., Boston, 1967-70; sr. v.p. Gardner & Preston, Moss, Boston, 1970—. Served with USCGR, 1958-59. Mem. Inst. Chartered Fin. Analysts, Boston Security Analysts Soc., Inc. Home: 32 Gloucester St Boston MA 02115 Office: One Winthrop Sq Boston MA 02110

PASHLEY, RICHARD DANA, semicondr. co. exec.; b. Ft. Belvoir, Va., Sept. 15, 1947; s. Walter Alexander and Jane Louise (Kraft) P.; B.A., U. Colo., 1969; M.S., Calif. Inst. Tech., 1970, Ph.D., 1974. Circuit design engr. Intel Corp., Santa Clara, Calif., 1973-74, group project mgr., 1975-76, H-MOS program mgr., 1976-77, tech. devel. program mgr., 1977—, dept. mgr., 1978—. Served as 2d lt. USAF, 1973. Tektronix fellow, 1972-73, NSF Trainee, 1969-71. Mem. IEEE, Bohmische Physikalische Gesellschaft, Phi Beta Kappa, Sigma Xi. Contbr. papers to tech. publs. Patentee in field. Home: 784 Pear St Sunnyvale CA 94087 Office: 3065 Bowers St Santa Clara CA 95051

PASKERIAN, CHARLES KAY, JR., plastics co. exec.; b. Medford, Mass., Mar. 18, 1933; s. Charles Kay and Gertrude (Russian) P.; B.A. in Econs., Tufts U., 1954; M.B.A., Stanford, 1959; m. Susan Eileen Poland, Jan. 4, 1958; children—Michael Charles, Matthew Wayne. Salesman kordite div. Mobil Chem. Co., Los Angeles, 1959-60; dist. sales mgr., 1960-64; Western sales mgr. Webster Ind. div. Chelsea, Ind., Los Angeles, 1964-66; pres. Flexi-Pac, Inc., Santa Ana, Calif., 1966—, also dir. Pub. mem. speech pathology and audiology examining com. Calif. Bd. Med. Examiners, 1973—. Mem. bd. edn. Santa Ana Unified Sch., 1969—, pres., 1971-72. Trustee Holy Family Adoption Service, Rancho Santiago Coll. Served to capt. USAF, 1954-58. Mem. Indsl. Devel. Assn. (dir.), Soc. Plastics Engrs., Inc., Santa Ana C. of C. (dir. 1971—), Zeta Psi. Republican. Conglist. (chmn. bd. trustees). Mason. Home: Newport Beach CA 92661 Office: 2020 S Hathaway St Santa Ana CA 92706

PASKOWITZ, IRVING FRANK, banker; b. Bklyn., July 1, 1936; s. Morris and Gladys (Schneider) P.; B.S. in Accounting, Bklyn. Coll., 1958; m. Susan Linda Gerofsky, Feb. 25, 1961; children—David Scott, Richard Jay. Pvt. practice accounting, N.Y.C., 1958-63; audit mgr. Comml. Fin. Co., N.Y.C., 1963-67, loan officer, 1973-75; chief fin. officer Royal Detective Agency, N.Y.C., 1967-73; loan officer, audit mgr. Bankers Trust Co., N.Y.C., 1975-80; sr. account officer Continental Ill. Bank, Chgo., 1980—; lectr. on fraud monitoring and control; mem. faculty Nat. Comml. Fin. Conf. Tng. Sch. Football, baseball and basketball coach Marlboro (N.J.) Civic Assn.; treas. Marlboro First Aid and Rescue Squad, 1976-77. Registered emergency med. technician N.J. Dept. Health. Mem. Comml. Fin. League (treas. 1975-79), Tau Alpha Omega. Democrat. Jewish. Clubs: Pop Warner Football, K.P. Home: 1839 Cavell Ave Highland Park IL 60035 Office: Continental Ill Bank 231 S LaSalle Chicago IL

PASSAGE, RICHARD JR., exec. recruiting co. exec.; b. Calif., Oct. 9, 1942; s. Richard James and Alice Elizabeth Passage; B.A. in Bus. Adminstrn., Wash. State U., 1966; m. Geraldine M. Johnson, Aug. 2, 1964; children—Lisa, Jennifer. With Price Waterhouse & Co., Seattle, 1966-74, audit mgr., 1974-78; v.p. fin. Laser Link Corp., Seattle, 1974-77, pres., 1977-78; partner Passage & Assos., Seattle, 1978—; mem. adv. com. to bd. dirs. Steinberg Bros. Vice pres. Job Therapy, 1975—. C.P.A., Wash. State. Mem. Am. Inst. C.P.A.'s, Wash. State Soc. C.P.A.'s. Lutheran. Clubs: Rainier, Seattle Yacht. Home: 20415 12th Pl NW Seattle WA 98177 Office: 2121 4th Ave Suite 1300 Seattle WA 98121

PASSALACQUA, SALVATORE ANTHONY, mfg. co. exec.; b. Wyandotte, Mich., Apr. 26, 1949; s. Joseph and Nancy Mary (Randazzo) P.; B.B.A., Eastern Mich. U., 1971; m. Susan M. Vettraino, Oct. 26, 1973; children—Marc, Jason, Nicholas. Supr., Touche Ross, Detroit, 1971-77; controller, v.p. fin., treas., Jack Haines, Detroit, from 1977, now v.p., gen. mgr. C.P.A., Mich. Mem. Am. Inst. C.P.A.'s, Mich. Soc. C.P.A.'s, Detroit Tooling Assn. Republican. Roman Catholic. Club: Detroit Athletic. Office: 2761 Stair St Detroit MI 48209

PASSINO, JACQUE HAROLD, mfg. co. exec.; b. Toledo, Sept. 4, 1920; s. Harold Maurice and Lucille (Merickel) P.; B.S., U. Toledo, 1942, Mech. Engring., 1948; m. Florenne Henderson, Aug. 31, 1946; children—Jacque Harold, Ralph Herickel, Ann Henderson, Andrew Lee. With Willys Overland Export Corp., 1948-56, v.p. adminstrn., 1954-56; spl. vehicles activity mgr. Ford Motor Co., 1957-70; pres. Rectrans div. White Motor Co., 1971-73; account exec. C.E. Greene, Southfield, Mich., 1973-75; partner Autorep Inc., mfrs. rep., Troy, Mich., 1975-79; v.p. mktg. Irvin Industries, Madison Heights, Mich., 1979—. Served with USAAF, 1942-46. Club: Pine Lake Country (Orchard Lake, Mich.). Home: 4480 Commerce Rd Orchard Lake MI 48033 Office: 29235 Stephenson Hwy Madison Heights MI 48071

PASSOLT, JAMES CYRUS, parcel delivery co. exec.; b. Mpls., Apr. 23, 1944; s. James Clifford and Dory Elizabeth (Mashek) P.; B.B.A., Tex. Wesleyan Coll., 1969; J.D., U. S.D., 1972; m. Ronnie J. Bounds, Aug. 23, 1974; children—James Cyrus, III, Jessica Southard. Admitted to Nebr. bar, 1972; asst. to pres. Seldin Devel. & Mgmt. Co., Omaha, 1972-73; with United Parcel Service, 1973—, real estate mgr. West region, Omaha, 1976-79, Pacific region, Garden Grove, Calif., 1979—. Bd. dirs. Douglas-Sarpy Counties (Nebr.) Heart Assn., 1972-77, chmn. corp. gift drive, 1973. Mem. Am. Bar Assn., Nat. Assn. Corp. Real Estate Execs., Nebr. Bar Assn., Phi Beta Lambda (pres. 1969). Roman Catholic. Clubs: Young Republicans (pres. 1969), Shriners. Home: 25055 Costeau St Laguna Hills CA 92653 Office: 12822 Garden Grove Blvd Garden Grove CA 92643

PATE, JAMES LEONARD, economist, oil co. exec.; b. Mt. Sterling, Ill., Sept. 6, 1935; s. Virgil Leonard and Mammie Elizabeth (Taylor) P.; student U. Md., 1957-58; A.B., Monmouth Coll., 1963; M.B.A., U. Ind., 1965, Ph.D., 1968; m. Donna Charlene Pate, Oct. 23, 1955; children—David Charles, Gary Leonard, Jennifer Elizabeth. Prof. econs. Monmouth (Ill.) Coll., 1965-68; sr. economist Fed. Res. Bank Cleve., 1968-72; chief economist B.F. Goodrich Co., Akron, Ohio, 1972-74; asst. sec. Dept. Commerce, Washington, 1974-76; spl. adviser to White House, Washington, 1976; v.p., chief economist Pennzoil Co., Houston, 1976—. Fellow Royal Econ. Soc.; mem. Am. Econ. Assn., Soc. Social Polit. Scientists, Nat. Assn. Bus. Economists, Pi Gamma Mu. Republican. Contbr. articles to profl. jours. and text books. Home: 3822 Point Clear St Missouri City TX 77459

PATEL, MAHENDRAKUMAR ASHABHAI, mech. engr.; b. Dantali, India, Feb. 1, 1946; s. Ashabhai Ranchhodbhai and Funaben Ashabhai P.; came to U.S., 1970, naturalized, 1972; M.S. in Mech. Engring., Worcester Poly. Inst., 1972; m. Sarlaben, Dec. 14, 1969; children—Nishit, Viraj. Designer, E.H.L. Cons. Engr., Thornhill, Ont., 1972-73; designer Imperial Oil Co., Winnipeg, Man., 1973; sr. project engr. Tembec Inc., Temiscaming, Que., 1974—. Registered profl. engr., Ont. Mem. Can. Pulp and Paper Assn., Order Engrs. Que. Hindu. Home: 56 Thorne Ave PO Box 682 Temiscaming PQ J0Z 3R0 Canada Office: PO Box 700 Temiscaming PQ J0Z 3R0 Canada

PATIL, MILIND, mgmt. cons.; b. Bombay, India, June 8, 1948; s. Dattaram and Hirabai (Pathare) P.; came to U.S., 1969, naturalized, 1974; B.S. in Elec. Engring., Ind. Inst. Tech., 1970; M.S. in Elec. Engring., Carnegie-Mellon U., 1971; M.S. in Pub. Affairs, U. Tex., 1973. Project dir., Indian Electronics, Bombay, 1968; chief tech. exec. Air-Frame Products, Bombay, 1969-70, v.p. world mktg., 1970-73; dir. mgmt. Dept. Human Resources, Austin, Tex., 1973-76; dir. budget and planning Tex. Comptroller Office, Austin, 1976-77, asst. dir. Data Services, 1977-80; sr. v.p., cons. Patil & Covington Cons. Co., Austin, 1976—; sr. v.p. Rational Systems, Austin, 1977—; v.p. mktg. UBQ Imports, Austin, 1978—; mgr. systems and procedures Agy. Records Control, 1980—. Campaign worker in state and nat. elections, 1972, 76; mem. student govt. coms., 1975-76. L.B.J. fellow,

1971-73. Mem. IEEE, AAAS, Am. Pub. Health Assn., Am. Polit. Sci. Assn., Am. Statis. Assn. Home: PO Box 88206 Atlanta GA 30338 Office: 219 Perimeter Center Pkwy Atlanta GA 30346

PATOCKA, BARBARA ANNE, oil co. exec.; b. N.Y.C., Apr. 23, 1946; d. Joseph William and Jennie (Vokolek) P.; B.A., Coll. Mt. St. Vincent, 1968; postgrad. City U. N.Y., 1968-71, in bus. adminstrn. N.Y. U., 1974—; m. Everett B. Mattlin, Sept. 28, 1975; 1 son, Jeffrey Lee Mattlin. With Instl. Investor Systems, N.Y.C., 1971-75, mng. editor, 1973, sr. editor, 1973-75; investment adviser Mobil Oil Corp., N.Y.C., 1976-77, asst. mgr. corp. investments, 1977-78, mgr. benefit plans coordination-fin., 1978-80, asst. treas. Mobil South, 1980—; guest lectr. Columbia U. Sch. Journalism. Recipient Fin. Journalism award U. Mo., 1973. Mem. Fin. Women's Assn., Women's Econ. Roundtable. Contbr. articles to Instl. Investor Mag., Pensions Mag., Town & Country mag., London Times. Home: 65 Mayapple Rd Stamford CT 06903 Office: 150 E 42d St New York NY 10017

PATOTZKA, OWEN BERT, accountant; b. Houston, Aug. 8, 1939; s. Edward Henry and Bertha Owen (Wilson) P.; A.A., Pasadena City Coll., 1958; student Pomona Coll., 1958-59; B.S., UCLA, 1961; m. Barbara Lee Neese, Sept. 20, 1965; children—Debra Lee, Douglas Owen. Staff acct. Touche Ross & Co., Los Angeles, 1961-70, partner, 1970—. Bd. dirs. Planned Parenthood Fedn. Am. Served with U.S. Army, 1962. Mem. Calif. Soc. C.P.A.'s,(dir.), Am. Inst. C.P.A.'s, Life Ins. and Trust Council Los Angeles. Republican. Clubs: Los Angeles Tennis, Los Angeles Athletic. Office: 3700 Wilshire Blvd Suite 600 Los Angeles CA 90010

PATOUHAS, DENNIS HARRY, automobile co. exec.; b. New Rochelle, N.Y., Mar. 30, 1948; s. Harry Costas and Nancy (Blanner) P.; A.S. in Acctg., Norwalk Community Coll., 1968; B.S. in Acctg., U. Bridgeport, 1973; m. Marian E. Topping, Apr. 28, 1973; 1 son, Brian. Supr. portfolio acctg. Chestnutt Corp., Greenwich, Conn., 1968-71; fund acct. Greenwich Mgmt. Co., 1971-72; with Computer Investors Group, N.Y.C., 1972-79, controller, 1975-78, v.p. corp. devel., 1978-79; asst. to chmn. DeLorean Motor Co., N.Y.C., 1979-80, controller, 1980—. Greek Orthodox Ch. Home: 39 Nutmeg Dr Greenwich CT 06830 Office: 280 Park Ave New York NY 10017

PATRICELLI, ROBERT E., ins. exec.; b. Hartford, Conn., Dec. 8, 1939; s. Leonard J. and Lydia E. Patricelli; A.B., Wesleyan U., 1961; Fulbright scholar, U. Paris, 1961-62; LL.B. cum laude, Harvard U., 1965; m. Susan Schaffer, Sept. 6, 1961; children—Alison, Thomas. Admitted to N.Y. bar, 1965; White House fellow Dept of State, Washington, 1965-66; minority counsel U.S. Senate Subcom. on Employment Manpower and Poverty, 1966-69; dep. asst. sec. for planning and evaluation, spl. asst. to Sec. for Urban Affairs Council, HEW, Washington, 1969-70, dep. under sec. for policy coordination, 1970-71; v.p. Greater Hartford Process, Inc., and Greater Hartford Community Devel. Corp., Inc., 1971-75; adminstr. Urban Mass Transp. Adminstrn., Dept. of Transp., Washington, 1975-77; v.p. Conn. Gen. Life Ins. Co., Hartford, 1977-80, sr. v.p., 1980—; dir. Greater Hartford Ridesharing Corp., Hartford Fed. Savs. & Loan Assn. Bd. trustees Loomis Chaffee Sch. (Windsor, Conn.); corporator Hartford Hosp.; chmn. transp. subcom. Council on Human Concerns, Republican Nat. Com.; mem. Simsbury (Conn.) Rep. Town Com. Recipient Outstanding Achievement award Sec. of Transp., 1977; named Engring. News Record Constrn. Man of Yr., 1976. Mem. Greater Hartford C. of C., Phi Beta Kappa. Home: 6 Cedar Hill Rd West Simsbury CT 06092 Office: Connecticut General Life Insurance Co Hartford CT 06152

PATRICK, CHARLES EDWARD STEWART, mfg. co. exec.; b. Lancashire, Eng., June 19, 1938; came to U.S., 1975; s. William Leonard and Josephine Mary (Watkin) P.; B.A. in Natural Scis., Cambridge U., 1961, M.A., 1974; M.B.A. with distinction (fellow Sci. Research Council 1968), Wharton Sch., U. Pa., 1979; m. Gillian Anne MacDonald Smith, May 25, 1963; children—Nicholas James, Rupert Charles. Indsl. engr. ICI Fibres Ltd., 1961-68; mgmt. cons. McKinsey & Co., Inc., N.Y.C. and London, 1970-77; dir. exec. and internat. compensation Continental Group Inc., N.Y.C., 1977-78; dir. personnel adminstrn. Pepsico Internat., Purchase, N.Y., 1978—; lectr. indsl. engring. Constantine U., Middlesbrough, Eng., 1963-68. Served as 2d lt. Brit. Army, 1956-58. Mem. Brit. Grads. Assn. Club: Am. Yacht (Rye, N.Y.). Home: 97 Apawamis Ave Rye NY 10580 Office: 700 Anderson Hill Rd Purchase NY 10577

PATRICK, LORAN BLAINE, bldg. contractor; b. Arthur, Ill., Oct. 26, 1926; s. Troy Foreman and Florence May (Fulk) P.; student Bradley U., Peoria, Ill., 1944-45, U. Ill., Champaign-Urbana, 1945; m. Jeannine Marie Houser, Feb. 25, 1949; children—Connie, Kathy, Diane, Gary, David. Engaged in farming, Hammond, Ill., 1949—; self-employed bldg. cotractor, Patrick Home Bldg., Hammond, 1971—; bd. dirs. LaPlace Coop. Grain Co., 1969—, sec. 1970-80; mem. bd. Farmer Home Adminstrn., 1970-73, Multrie Soil and Water Conservation Bd., 1967-74, Piatt County Extension Service, 1967-70. Elder, Ch. of Christ, Hammond, 1966—. Served to 1st lt. C.E., AUS, 1945-48. Mem. Stephen Decatur Rose Soc. Home: RFD 1 Hammond IL 61929 Office: 1st St Hammond IL 61929

PATTEE, GORDON BURLEIGH, investment banker; b. San Francisco, Apr. 13, 1948; s. William Burleigh and Dorothy Elizabeth (Evans) P.; B.A., Stanford U., 1970; M.B.A., Harvard U., 1975; m. Dailey Jones, Dec. 1, 1972. Loan officer Bank of Calif., San Francisco, 1971-73; asso. White, Weld & Co., Inc., N.Y.C., 1974; asst. v.p. corporate finance Kuhn Loeb & Co., Inc., N.Y.C., 1975-77; asso. in corporate finance Lehman Bros., Kuhn Loeb, N.Y.C., 1977—; dir. Great Western Coca-Cola Bottling Co., Houston. Clubs: Racquet & Tennis, Piping Rock (N.Y.C.); Univ. (San Francisco); Burlingame Country (Calif.). Home: 660 Park Ave New York NY 10021 Office: 1 William St New York NY 10004

PATTERSON, CHARLES FORREST, JR., banker; b. Boston, Nov. 24, 1933; s. Charles Forrest and Martha (Orr) P.; B.S. in Commerce, Washington and Lee U., 1955; postgrad. Grad. Sch. Consumer Banking, U. Va., 1963-65, Nat. Comml. Lending Sch., U. Okla., 1979; m. Mary Louise Robinson, Apr. 19, 1958; children—Catherine, Charles Forrest III, James, Robert. With Trust Co. Bank, Atlanta, 1957—, asst. treas., 1964-65, asst. v.p., 1965-69, v.p., 1969-72, group v.p., 1972—, regional br. adminstr., 1976—. Sect. chmn. United Way, Atlanta, 1970; v.p., bd. dirs. Ga. Soc. for Prevention Blindness, 1979-80; voting mem. Nat. Soc. for Prevention Blindness, 1979; coach Murphy Candler Little League, 1976-80; bd. dirs. Atlanta Consumer Credit Counseling Service, 1971-75; trustee Grad. Sch. Consumer Banking, U. Va., 1978—. Served with Transp. Corps, U.S. Army, 1955-57. Mem. Consumer Bankers Assn. (exec. com. 1976—, pres. 1978-79), Am. Bankers Assn. (adv. bd. 1969-72), Atlanta Consumer Credit Assn. (pres. 1968-69). Presbyterian. Clubs: Cherokee Town and Country, Phoenix Soc. Mem. editorial bd. Jour. Retail Banking, 1979-80. Home: 4173 Ashwoody Trail NE Atlanta GA 30319 Office: 25 Park Pl Atlanta GA 30303

PATTERSON, DESSIE FINCH, rental co. exec.; b. Bastrop County, Tex., July 21, 1912; d. Olive N. and Rebecca M. Finch; student San Marcos State Tchrs. Coll.; m. Frank Patterson, June 27, 1936; children—Frank, Myrna Sue, Rebecca Ann, James Wayne. Sec., Asso. Mech. Contractors, Houston, 1948-49, Am. Fore Ins. Group, Houston, 1949-53; ins. agt., Houston, 1953-68; treas. Aladdin Rents, Inc., San Antonio, 1970-80. Recipient awards for ins. sales. Republican. Baptist. Home: 206 Shadywood St San Antonio TX 78216 Office: Aladdin Rents Inc 6635 San Pedro St San Antonio TX 78216

PATTERSON, HARLAN RAY, educator; b. Camden, Ohio, June 27, 1931; s. Ernest Newton and Beulah Irene (Hedrick) P.; B.S., Miami U., 1953, M.B.A., 1959; Ph.D., Mich. State U., 1963; m. Carol Lee Reighard, July 31, 1970; children—Kristan Lee, Lisa (previous marriage), Leslie, Nolan Gene. Asst. prof. fin. U. Ill. at Urbana, 1962-66; asso. prof. fin. Ohio U., Athens, 1968-77, prof. fin., 1977—; fin. cons. Research projects for Bank of Am., Morgan Guaranty Trust, Am. Investment Corp., City Pub. Service Bd. of San Antonio. Chmn. Athens adv. bd., chmn. Ohio State scholarship com. Rainbow for Girls. Served with USN, 1953-56. Stonier fellow, 1961; Found. Econ. Edn. fellow, 1965, 67, 69, 71; vis. prof., fellow Chgo. Merc. Exchange, 1971; fin. cons. Mem. Phi Beta Kappa, Beta Gamma Sigma, Phi Eta Sigma, Omicron Delta Epsilon, Pi Kappa Alpha, Alpha Kappa Psi. Republican. Mason (32 deg., Shriner). Contbr. articles to profl. and acad. jours. Home: 17 LaMar Dr Athens OH 45701

PATTERSON, JAMES DWIGHT, real estate co. exec.; b. Tulsa, Dec. 29, 1931; s. John Ashley and Anna Lois (Pearson) P.; B.A., Tulsa U., 1955; M.S., Purdue U., 1958; div.; children—Brett Ashley, Erin Wyn. Adminstr. mgmt. devel. and tng. NBC, Burbank, Calif., 1958-61; account exec. KVOO-TV, Tulsa, 1961-62; sales mgr. Continental Industries, Tulsa, 1962-65; nat. sales tng. mgr. Xerox Corp., Rochester, N.Y., 1965-69; dir. adminstrn. Midas-Internat., Chgo., 1969-70; pres. Midas-Internat., Ltd., Toronto, Ont., Can., 1970-71; v.p. mktg. and fin. Innerspace Environs., San Francisco, 1971-74, now dir.; pres. Woodfield Properties, Kentfield, Calif., 1974—, also dir. Mem. Am. Mgmt. Assn., Nat. Assn. Realtors, Calif. Assn. Realtors, Marin County Bd. Realtors, San Francisco Bd. Realtors. Home: 12 Rosebank St Kentfield CA 94904 Office: 919 Sir Francis Drake Blvd Kentfield CA 94904

PATTERSON, JAMES MARTIN, machinery mfg. co. exec.; b. Highland Park, Mich., Nov. 24, 1941; s. James R. and Margaret Louise (Drollinger) P.; B.A., Gannon Coll., 1963; m. Lynda Joanne Evans, Mar. 2, 1968; children—Melinda Louise, Evan James. Market analyst, bus. planner Gen. Elec. Co., Burlington, Vt., 1969-71; product planning engr., mgr. advance material planning and control, Erie, Pa., 1971-78; mgr. div. purchasing planning and programs Borg Warner Corp., York, Pa., 1973-76; field sales mgr. HydroTurbine div. Allis Chalmers, York, 1976—. Bd. dirs. Jaycees, 1970-71; scoutmaster Boy Scouts Am., 1968-69, committeeman, 1970-71. Served to capt. AUS, 1963-69. Decorated D.F.C. (2). Republican. Roman Catholic. Office: Box 712 York PA 17405

PATTERSON, JERRY EUGENE, editor; b. Fort Worth, May 2, 1931; s. Charles Edward and Lois (Pruitt) P.; B.A., U. Tex., 1952, M.A., 1955; postgrad. Yale, 1955-57, Columbia, 1958-60. Asst. editor Hispanic Am. Hist. Rev., 1954; manuscript div. librarian Yale U. Library, 1955-57; cataloguer Edward Eberstadt & Sons, N.Y.C., 1958-61; with Parke-Bernet Galleries, N.Y.C., 1962-68, asst. v.p., 1964-65, v.p., 1965-68; U.S. rep. Christie, Manson & Woods, London, 1968-71; sr. v.p. Sotheby Parke Bernet, 1980—; cons. Library of Congress, 1964-67. Mem. N.Y. Hist. Soc. (Pintard fellow 1967), bibliog. socs. Am., Eng., Va., Oxford, Cambridge. Republican. Episcopalian. Contbg. editor Auction Mag., 1970-72, Art News Mag., 1973-78; mng. editor Artnewsletter, 1975-78. Author: Autographs, a Collector's Guide, 1973; Collector's Guide to Relics and Memorabilia, 1974; Antiques of Sport, 1975; The City of New York, 1978; Porcelain, 1979. Contbr. articles on rare books and manuscripts to Am. and fgn. periodicals. Home: 176 E 77th St New York NY 10021

PATTERSON, JOHN H., steel co. exec.; b. Chgo., June 27, 1922; s. Howard Lorraine and Isabel Mary (Cronin) P.; B.B.A., U. Richmond, 1950; m. Sara Powers, May 27, 1967; children—John Howard (dec.), Patrick C. (dec.), Tralene L., Cheryl A., Meredith L. Gen. mgr., Reco Tanks, Inc., West Columbia, S.C., 1950-58, v.p., 1958-62; pres. Midland Steel Corp., Columbia, 1962—; mem. nat. indsl. adv. bd. Underwriters Lab., Inc. Bd. dirs. Cola ARC. Served with USNR, 1942-45. Mem. Soc. Heating, Ventilating and Refrigerating Engrs., S.C., Columbia, West Columbia-Cayce chambers commerce. Presbyterian. Clubs: Kiwanis (chmn. vocat. guidance com.), Palmetto (Columbia). Home: 14 Ludwell Rd Columbia SC 29209 Office: 1940 Shop Rd Columbia SC 29201

PATTERSON, JOSEPH CROMWELL, financial co. exec.; b. Detroit, Nov. 21, 1928; s. Walter Rodney and Mildred Lona (Cromwell) P.; student Ohio State U., 1953; B.A., Ohio Wesleyan U., 1954; m. Anne Elizabeth Ferrall, Jan. 19, 1952; children—J. Sean, Kevin B., Michael B., Mary A., Kathleen M., Julia M., Susan E., Margaret A., Patrick D., Jane M. Pres., Med. Mgmt. Inc., Dayton, Ohio, 1954-60; exec. staff Research Inst. Am., N.Y.C., 1960-62, 62-64; cons. E.F. MacDonald Co., Dayton, 6 mos.; pres. Financial Mgmt. Inst., Dayton, 1964-72, Fiscal Concepts Inc., Newport Beach, Calif., 1972—; cons. in field. Served with USAAF, 1946-49, 51-52. Mem. Am. Mgmt. Assn., Am. Soc. Mgmt. Cons.'s, Am. Profl. Practice Assn. (editor ofcl. jour. 1966-68), Internat. Assn. Financial Planners. Republican. Roman Catholic. Editorial adviser Med. Econs. mag., 1956-60.

PATTERSON, ROBERT WILLIAM, cons. engr.; b. Ravinia, Ill., Aug. 24, 1922; s. James B. and Benice A. (Cummings) P.; B.S. in Mech. Engring., Northwestern U., 1947; m. Rae F. Spahr, Sept. 24, 1955; children—Carol L., John H. With Sargent & Lundy, cons. engrs., Chgo., 1947—, partner, 1964—, dir. engring., 1973-77, sr. partner, 1977—. Served with U.S. Army, 1943-45; ETO. Decorated Purple Heart; registered profl. engr. 14 states, including Calif., Ill., Ind., and State of Israel. Mem. Am. Nuclear Soc., ASME, Atomic Indsl. Forum, Western Soc. Engrs., Chgo. Assn. Commerce and Industry (dir.). Clubs: Chgo., Union League of Chgo., Park Ridge (Ill.) Country. Contbr. articles to trade press. Office: 55 E Monroe St Chicago IL 60603

PATTERSON, S. DAVID, savs. and loan exec.; b. Trask, Mo., Dec. 23, 1931; s. Harvey Jonas and Vera Leola (McGuire) P.; B.S.B.A., S.E. Mo. U., 1958; m. Jo Evelyn Kinder, Sept. 9, 1949; children—Marc, Kelly, John. Joined Colonial Fed. Savs. & Loan Assn., Cape Girardeau, Mo., 1958, exec. v.p., 1963-71, pres., chief exec. officer, 1971—, dir., 1966—. Pres. Cape Girardeau Jaycees, 1961, Greater Cape Devel. Corp., 1980. Served with USAF, 1951-55; ETO. Mem. Mo. Savs. and Loan League (dir.), U.S. League Savs. Assns., Cape Girardeau C. of C. (dir. 1977). Republican. Roman Catholic. Club: Rotary (pres. 1974). Office: PO Box 1000 Cape Girardeau MO 63701

PATTISON, JAMES ALLEN, consumer services co. exec.; b. Saskatoon, Sask., Can., Oct. 1, 1928; s. Chandos W. and Julia Blue (Allen) P.; student U. B.C., 1947-50; m. Mary Ella Hudson, June 30, 1951; children—James Allen, Susan Mary Ann, Cynthia Lee. Owner, pres., chmn., chief exec. officer Jim Pattison Industries Ltd., Neonex Internat. Ltd., Jim Pattison Enterprises Ltd., chmn. bd., pres., dir. Crush Internat., Ltd., Toronto, Ont., Can. Mem. Young Pres.'s Orgn. Club: Terminal City (Vancouver). Office: Crush Internat Ltd 1590 O'Connor Dr Toronto ON M4B 2V4 Canada*

PATTON, DAVID A., JR., mgmt. cons.; b. Yakima, Wash., Aug. 15, 1951; s. David A. and Belen (Asumendi) P.; B.S. in Commerce, U. Va., 1973; postgrad. Va. Theol. Sem., Georgetown U. Cons., Peat, Marwick, Mitchell & Co., Washington, 1973-76, Arthur Andersen & Co., Washington, 1976; budget dir. Pres. Ford Com., Washington, 1976; mgr. Program Resources, Inc., 1977—. Adv. del. Presbyn. Nat. Gen. Assembly, 1974, candidate Va. Ho. of Dels., 1975; patron Jefferson Soc. U. Va.; treas., dir. Circle Condominiums, 1974-76; exec. bd. Arlington County Republican Com., 1976-77, also rep., 1977—; pres. Arlington Young Reps., 1976-77; bd. dirs. Companions in World Mission, 1978—; treas. No. Va. Young Reps., 1979-80; vestryman St. John's Episcopal Ch., Georgetown, 1980—. Recipient Jefferson Soc. award 1973. Mem. Data Processing Mgmt. Assn., English Speaking Union, Jefferson Soc., U. Va. Alumni Assn. (life), Mensa. Episcopalian. Contbr. articles to profl. jours. Home: 2030 N Adams St Arlington VA 22201

PATTON, FARREL LEON, mfg. co. exec.; b. San Diego, Sept. 9, 1931; s. Farrel Leon and Delphine Elizabeth (Lopez) P.; B.S. in Acctg., San Diego State U., 1964; m. Jane Lynn Casey, Feb. 19, 1951; 1 dau., Gail M. With Gen. Dynamics Corp., 1959—, successively mgr. budgets electronics div., mgr. fin. analysis shipbldg. div., controller data systems service div., mgr. logistics adminstrn. Ft. Worth Aerospace div., mgr. estimating internat. aircraft services div. Served with USAF, 1950-54. Mem. Planning Execs. Inst., Nat. Mgmt. Assn. Republican. Address: 7151 Tamarack Rd Fort Worth TX 76116

PATTON, ROBERT LAWRENCE, operations research analyst; b. Tulsa, Dec. 20, 1921; s. Harry Allen and Berintha (Mendenhall) P.; B.A., U. Tulsa, 1942, M.S., Okla. State U., 1955; postgrad. U. Chgo., Northwestern U., Boston U., U. Calif. at Los Angeles, San Jose State Coll.; m. Alva Lee Wakefield, Dec. 24, 1941; children—Lurose, Milton Lawrence, Lisa Ruth, Leelyn Zoe. Instr., U. Tulsa, 1946-48; sales and systems analyst Monroe Calculating Machine Co., 1952-55; staff mem. Mass. Inst. Tech., Lincoln Lab., 1955-57; computer systems spl. RAND Corp. and Systems Devel. Corp., Santa Monica, Calif., 1957-59; group engr. Douglas Aircraft, 1959-63; engring. specialist ITT, Western Test Range, 1963-66; sr. systems engr. RCA, White Sands missile range, 1966: cons., dir. Alva Lee Mgmt. Services, 1966—; cons. ops. research, statistics, command-control systems, computer systems. Founder Project Peace. Served with USNR, 1945-46, 50-52. Home: 431 Bishop Ave Pacific Grove CA 93950 Office: PO Box 772 Pacific Grove CA 93950

PATTON, THOMAS JAMES, pharm. co. exec.; b. Port Deposit, Md., Feb. 1, 1933; s. Gordon Sexton and Ellen Robins (Whaley) P.; B.A., Princeton U., 1955; m. Jean Douglas Welliver, May 19, 1962; children—Catherine Anne, Elizabeth Allyn. With Wyeth Labs., Phila., 1958—, now dir. med. mktg. Wyeth Internat., Ltd. Served with CIC, U.S. Army, 1955-57. Club: Radnor Hunt. Home: 330 Spring House Ln West Chester PA 19380 Office: PO Box 8616 Philadelphia PA 19101

PATZMAN, STEPHEN NARR, ins. co. exec.; b. Kansas City, Mo., Feb. 19, 1942; s. Kenneth J. and Kathryn (Narr) P.; B.A. in Math., U. Colo., Boulder, 1964; m. Kathleen G. Stephens, Dec. 30, 1965; children—Heather, Rick, Marlies. Agt., Patzman Ins. Agy., Tucson, 1966-67; sr. actuarial asst. Aetna Life and Casualty Co., Hartford, Conn., 1968-77; v.p., chief life actuary Mut. Service Life Ins. Co., St. Paul, 1977-79; v.p., actuary USAA Life Ins. Co., San Antonio, 1979—. Served to 1st lt. U.S. Army, 1964-66. Fellow Soc. Actuaries; mem. Am. Acad. Actuaries, Internat. Actuarial Assn., Actuaries' Club of S.W. Home: 10111 N Manton Ln San Antonio TX 78213 Office: USAA Bldg 9800 Fredericksburg Rd San Antonio TX 78288

PAUL, DAVID LEWIS, real estate developer; b. N.Y.C., May 1, 1939; s. Isadore and Ruth (Goldstein) P.; B.S. in Econs., U. Pa., Isadore and Ruth (Goldstein) P.; B.S. in Econs., Wharton Sch., U. Pa., 1951; M.B.A., Columbia U., 1965, J.D., 1967; Ph.D. in Planning, Harvard U., 1968; children—David J., Michael M. Developer Hawthorne Towers, Montclair, N.J., 1967, Colony House, Lakewood, N.J., 1968, Pequannock (N.J.) Shopping Plaza, 1969, Townhouse of Amherst (Mass.), 1971, Brandywine Village, Amherst, 1972, Shrewsbury Mass., 1973, Regency Hyatt House, Sarasota, Fla., 1974, Tall Oaks Village, Weymouth, Mass., 1975, Somerset Village, Ft. Lauderdale, Fla., 1977, Green Knolls, Brockton, Mass., 1977, Am. Furniture Mart, Chgo., 1979, others. Trustee, Mt. Sinai Med. Center, N.Y.C., U. City N.Y., Mt. Sinai Hosp., N.Y.C., Mt. Sinai Sch. Nursing and Neustadter Convalescent Center, N.Y.C.; bd. dirs., governing mem. Lincoln Center Repertory Theatre, N.Y.C. Clubs: Standard, Mid-Am. (Chgo.). Author: The Effect of the AFL-CIO Merger on Centralization, 1961; Progressive Architecture, 1967. Office: 666 N Lake Shore Dr Chicago IL 60611

PAUL, GABRIEL GABE, profl. baseball club exec.; b. Rochester, N.Y., Jan. 4, 1910; s. Morris and Celia (Snyder) P.; ed. pub. schs., Rochester; m. Mary Frances Copps, Apr. 17, 1939; children—Gabriel, Warren, Michael, Jennie Lou, Henry. Reporter, Rochester Democrat and Chronicle, 1926-28; publicity mgr., ticket mgr. Rochester Baseball Club, 1928-34, traveling sec., dir., 1934-36; publicity dir. Cin. Baseball Club, 1937, traveling sec., 1938-48, asst. to pres., 1948-49, v.p., 1949-60, gen. mgr., 1951-60; v.p., 1949-60; v.p., gen. mgr. Houston Baseball Club, 1960-61; gen. mgr. Cleve. Baseball Club (Cleve. Indians), 1961-63, pres., treas., 1963-72, v.p., gen. mgr., 1972-73; pres. N.Y. Yankees, 1973-77; pres., chief exec. officer Cleve. Indians, 1978—. Dir. or trustee various charitable instns. Served with inf. AUS, 1943-45. Named Major League Exec. of Yr., Sporting News, 1956, 74, Milw. chpt. Baseball Writers Assn., 1976, Sports Exec. of Yr., Gen. Sports Time, 1956, Baseball Exec. of Yr., Boston chpt. Baseball Writers Assn., 1974, 76, Maj. League Exec. of Yr., United Press, 1976; recipient J. Lewis Comiskey Meml. award Chgo. chpt. Baseball Writers Assn. Am., 1961, Judge Emil Fuchs Meml. award Boston chpt., 1967, Bill Slocum Meml. award N.Y. chpt. Baseball Writers Assn. Am., 1975, Sports Torch of Learning award, 1976. Clubs: Palma Ceia Country (Tampa); Shaker Heights (Ohio) Country, Cleve. Athletic; Skyline Country (Tucson, Ariz.). Home: 5700 Mariner Dr Tampa FL 33609 also 2112 Acacia Park Dr Lyndhurst OH 44114 Office: Cleveland Indians Cleveland Stadium Cleveland OH 44114

PAUL, HERBERT MORTON, lawyer, accountant; b. N.Y.C., July 17, 1931; s. Julius and Gussie Paul; B.B.A., Baruch Coll., 1952; J.D., Harvard, 1955; M.B.A., N.Y.U., 1956, LL.M., 1960; children—Leslie Beth, Andrea Lynn. Partner, N.Y. dir. tax services, N.Y., asso. nat. dir. tax services, exec. nat. service dir.-CSO, Touche, Ross & Co., N.Y.C., 1957—; prof. N.Y. U.; mem. adv. bd. Bur. Nat. Affairs-Tax Mgmt.; chmn. adv. com. N.Y. Inst. on Taxation; adv. com. Internat. Inst. Tax, mem. bus. planning com. trusts and estates Rockefeller U. Trustee Asso. Y's N.Y.; co-chmn. accountants div., adminstrv. com. Fedn. Philanthropies; adv. bd. Fin. and Estate Planning Reporter, Profl. Practice Mgmt. Mag.; adv. panel Tax Shelter Insider's Publ. Served with AUS, 1954-56. Mem. N.Y. State Soc. C.P.A.'s (chmn. com. fed. taxation, chmn. gen. tax com., com. relations IRS, chmn.

furtherance com.), Am. Inst. C.P.A.'s (taxation div.), N.Y.U. Tax Study Group, N.Y. U. Tax Soc. (v.p., chmn. com. tax shelters), Nat. Assn. Accountants, Empire State C. of C. (tax com.), Am. Bar Assn., N.Y. County Lawyers Assn., Pension Club, Estate Planning Council N.Y. (dir.), Alumni Assn. Grad. Sch. Bus. N.Y. U. (v.p., treas.). Clubs: Accountants of Am., Wall Street, City Athletic. Author: Ordinary and Necessary Expenses. Contbr. articles to profl. jours., books. Contbg. editor Federal Income Taxation of Banks; adv. tax editor The Practical Accountant. Home: 775 Oakleigh Rd North Woodmere NY 11581 Office: 1633 Broadway New York NY 10019

PAUL, HERMAN LOUIS, JR., valve mfg. co. exec.; b. N.Y.C., Dec. 30, 1912; s. Herman Louis and Louise Emilie (Markert) P.; student Duke, 1931-32, Lehigh U., 1932-33; m. Janath Powers; children—Robert E., Charles Thomas, Herman Louis III. Power plant engr. Paul's Machine Shop, N.Y.C., 1935-43; pres., chief engr. Paul's Machine Shop, N.Y.C., 1943-48; v.p., chief engr. Paul Valve Corp., East Orange, N.J., 1948-54; pres., chief engr. P-K Industries, Inc., North Arlington, N.J., 1954-59; v.p., dir. research Gen. Kinetics, Englewood, N.J., 1959-62; engring. cons., N.Y.C., 1962-65; v.p., dir. Hudromatics, Inc., Bloomfield, N.J., 1965-67; with P.J. Hydraulics, Inc., Myerstown, Pa., 1967—, pres., chief engr., 1968-80, dir. and stockholder, 1980—; cons. to Metal Industries Devel. Center, Taiwan, 1979; engring. cons. valves and complimentary equipment, 1980—. Vice chmn. Nat. UN Day Com., 1977, 78, 79. Mem. ASME, Instrument Soc. Am., Am. Soc. Naval Engrs., Internat. Platform Assn., Nat. Contract Mgmt. Assn. Club: Heidelberg Country (Bernville, Pa.), Quentin (Pa.) Riding. Patentee in field. Home: 370 Dogwood Ln RD 5 Lebanon PA 17042

PAUL, JEFFREY WILLIAM, apparel co. exec.; b. Los Angeles, Sept. 11, 1946; s. Jerome Otto and Doris Sidney (Jacobson) P.; B.S. in Bus. Adminstrn., U. Calif., Berkeley, 1968; M.S. in Fin., UCLA, 1970; m. Nancy J. Sockett, Oct. 14, 1979. Mgmt. trainee Security Pacific Nat. Bank, Los Angeles, 1968-69; fin. analyst Citibank N.A., N.Y.C., 1970-71; asst. treas. Cyprus Mines Corp., Los Angeles, 1971-79, mgr. planning and project evaluations, 1979-80; dir. fin. The Olga Co., Van Nuys, Calif., 1980—. Served with U.S. Army, 1971. Mem. Risk and Ins. Mgmt. Soc., Cash Mgmt. Club So. Calif., UCLA Sch. Mgmt. Alumni Assn., Calif. Alumni Assn. Republican. Jewish. Clubs: Town Hall (Los Angeles); Hillcrest Country. Home: 3701 Longview Valley Rd Sherman Oaks CA 91423 Office: The Olga Co 7900 Haskell Ave Van Nuys CA 91409

PAUL, PHILIP FRANKLIN, JR., mgmt. cons.; b. Chgo., Feb. 1, 1941; s. Philip Franklin and Dorothy (Hite) P.; B.S. in Indsl. Mgmt., U. So. Calif., 1963; grad. exec. program, Dartmouth Coll., 1976; m. Anne Catherine Rush, June 12, 1960; children—James Franklin, Philip Franklin III, Patricia Joy. Pres., Communications Equipment Co., Beverly Hills, Calif., 1960-63; supr. communications engring. Autonetics div. N.Am. Rockwell, 1963-66; mgr. field mktg. Honeywell Info. Systems, 1966-70, dir. product and strategic planning, 1970-74, dir. systems mgmt. and engring., 1974-78; mgmt. cons. to electronics industry, Sudbury, Mass., 1979—; mem. faculty Northeastern U., Poly. Inst. N.Y. Sr. mem. IEEE (past chmn. communications group). Author: Management Systems for Planning, 1975. Office: 29 Juniper Rd Sudbury MA 01776

PAUL, RICHARD L., banker; b. Frankfort, Ind., Sept. 16, 1932; B.A., Earlham Coll., 1954; student Stonier Grad. Sch. Banking, Rutgers U., 1969; m. Evelyn K. Kellum; children—Teresa Elizabeth, Mary Katherine. Vice-pres. met. dept. Am. Fletcher Nat. Bank, Indpls., 1956-70; v.p., head banking div. Winters Nat. Bank, Dayton, 1970-73; sr. v.p. Louisville Trust Bank, 1973-74, exec. v.p. 1974-76, pres., 1976—; pres. United Ky. Bank, 1980—, exec. v.p. parent co. United Ky. Inc. Pres., Old Ky. Home council Boy Scouts Am., 1979—; sec. Ky. Council on Econ. Edn., 1977—. Bd. dirs. Louisville YMCA, Methodist Evang. Hosp., Louisville. Served with AUS, 1954-56. Club: Hunting Creek Country. Office: PO Box 34000 Louisville KY 40233

PAUL, ROBERT, 'awyer; b. N.Y.C., Nov. 22, 1931; s. Gregory and Sonia (Rijock) P.; B.A., N.Y. U., 1953; J.D., Columbia, 1958; m. Christa Molz, Apr. 6, 1975; 1 dau., Gina. Admitted to Fla. bar, 1958, N.Y. bar, 1959; partner Paul Landy Beiley & Harper, Miami, 1964—, Morrison, Paul & Bailey, N.Y.C., 1970—; counsel Republic Nat. Bank Miami, 1967—. Bd. dirs., past pres. Fla. Philharm., Inc., 1978—; pres. citizens bd. U. Miami, 1977—, also trustee. Mem. Am., N.Y., Fla., Inter-Am. bar assns. Home: 700 Alhambra Circle Coral Gables FL 33134 Office: 200 SE 1st St Miami FL 33131

PAUL, ROBERT ARTHUR, steel co. exec.; b. N.Y.C., Oct. 28, 1937; s. Isadore and Ruth (Goldstein) P.; A.B. with honors, Cornell U., Ithaca N.Y., 1959; J.D., Harvard, 1962, M.B.A. with distinction, 1964; m. Donna Rae Berkman, July 29, 1962; children—Laurence Edward, Stephen Eric, Karen Rachel. With Ampco-Pitts. Corp. (formerly Screw and Bolt Corp. of Am.), 1964—, v.p., 1969-73, exec. v.p., 1973-79, pres., chief operating officer, 1979—, also dir.; v.p., dir. Steel Trading Corp., Dover Securities, Inc.; v.p., asst. treas., dir. Parkersburg Steel Corp.; v.p., asst. sec., asst. treas., dir. Louis Berkman Co., Follansbee Steel Corp., Louis Berkman Realty Co.; gen. partner Romar Trading Co.; dir. 1st Nat. Bank of Washington (Pa.), First Fin. Group, Inc.; instr. Carnegie Mellon U. Sch. Indsl. Adminstrn., 1966-69. Trustee, H.L. Louis Berkman Found., Montefiore Hosp., Pitts.; trustee, v.p. YM-YWHA; trustee, vice chmn. Vocat. Rehab. Center Allegheny County; trustee, treas. Ampco-Pitts. Found. Mem. Am., Mass. bar assns., Soc. Security Analysts. Republican. Jewish. Clubs: Concordia, Pitts. Athletic, Harvard-Yale-Princeton (Pitts.); Westmoreland Country (Export, Pa.); Harvard (Boston and N.Y.C.). Home: 1236 Squirrel Hill Ave Pittsburgh PA 15217 Office: 700 Porter Bldg Pittsburgh PA 15219

PAUL, ROLAND ARTHUR, lawyer; b. Memphis, Jan. 19, 1937; s. Roland and Hattye (Mincer) P.; B.A. summa cum laude, Yale U., 1958; LL.B. magna cum laude, Harvard U., 1961; m. Barbara Schlesinger, June 10, 1962; children—Deborah Lynn, Arthur Eliot. Admitted to N.Y. bar, 1961, Mich. bar; law clk. to Hon. Sterry R. Waterman, U.S. Ct. Appeals, 1961-62; fgn. affairs officer, spl. asst. to gen. counsel Dept. Def., 1962-64; asso. firm Cravath Swaine & Moore, N.Y.C., 1964-69; counsel U.S. Senate Fgn. Relations Subcom. on Security Commitments, 1969-71; asso. firm Simpson Thacher & Bartlett, N.Y.C., 1971-73; v.p., gen. counsel Howmet Turbine Components Corp., Greenwich, Conn., 1976—; dir. New Eng. Aircraft Products Co., Microfusion, S.A. Mem. Council Fgn. Relations, Am. Bar Assn., Mich. State Bar Assn. Democrat. Jewish. Author: American Military Commitments Abroad, 1973. Home: 8 Ellery Ln Westport CT 06880 Office: 475 Steamboat Rd Greenwich CT 06830

PAUL, SOMIR K., mech. engr., business exec.; b. Nov. 14, 1951; B.S. with distinction (Merit scholar), U. Delhi (India), 1973; M.S.M.E., Pa. State U., 1979; M.B.A., Sam Houston State U., 1980. Indsl. trainee Indian Airlines, India, 1972; from mgmt. trainee to sr. devel. engr. Shriram Refrigeration Industries/Westinghouse Electric Co., India, 1973-78; staff cons. Braintrust Inc., Houston, 1980—. Mem. ASME, Indian Instn. Indsl. Engrs., Machine Tool Tech. Group (India).

PAULSEN, BERNIECE MARIE, data processing co. exec.; b. Wallace, Idaho, June 5, 1940; d. Arthur Thomas and Edith Goldie (Bryan) Morgan; A.E. in Elec. Engring. Tech., Oreg. Inst. Tech., 1972, A.E. in Electro-Mech. Engring. Tech., 1972, B.T. in Computer Systems Engring. Tech., 1973; m. Charles LeRoy Paulsen, Sr., Mar. 2, 1958; children—Charles, Keith, Corinne. Programmer, analyst Computer Service of Klamath Falls, Oreg., 1973-77; programmer, analyst Klamath County, Oreg., 1977, sr. programmer, analyst, 1977-78, systems program mgr., 1978-79, dir. data processing, 1979—. Mem. Am. Bus. Women's Assn. (hospitality chmn. 1979-80, scholarship com. 1980, treas. 1980), Data Processing Mgmt. Assn., NCR Users' Group, Alpha-Micro Users' Group. Democrat. Lutheran. Club: Quota. Home: 2527 Link St Klamath Falls OR 97601 Office: Court House Klamath Falls OR 97601

PAULSEN, CAMILLE ANTHONY, mgmt. cons.; b. Marshfield, Wis., July 8, 1946; d. Douglas Howard and Marie Elizabeth (Helish) Anthony; B.S., U. Wis., Madison, 1968; m. Norman Paulsen, Jr., Feb. 9, 1980. Asst. to pres. Emporium Dept. Store, Madison, Wis., 1967-68; asst. personnel mgr. Frito-Lay, Inc., Madison, 1968-69; White House liaison Nat. Liaison of Businessmen, Washington, 1969-70; coordinator to Wis. Atty. Gen., Madison, 1970-75; pres. Consumer Concepts, Milw., 1975—; bd. dirs. H.C. Prange's. Bd. dirs., past pres. Wis. Consumers League. Mem. Am. Council on Consumer Interests, Conf. Consumer Orgns., Nat. Consumers League, NOW, Am. Home Econs. Assn., Internat. Assn. Bus. Communicators, Met. Milw. Assn. Commerce (dir.), Nat. Soc. Consumer Affairs Profls. in Bus. (dir.), Milw. Better Bus. Bur. (dir.). Republican. Contbr. articles to mags. Office: 733 N Van Buren St Milwaukee WI 53202

PAULSEN, JOSEPH CHARLES V., publishers' rep.; b. N.Y.C., Nov. 30, 1925; s. Frank J. and Mary (Weaffer) P.; student Birmingham So. Coll., 1943-44, St. John's U., 1945-48, City Coll. N.Y., 1949; m. Ann D. Moore, Sept. 17, 1949; children—Brad, Joann, Nancy, Amy. Researcher, Hearst Advt. Service, 1949; advt. salesman N.Y. Jour.-Am., 1949-51; account exec. Robert Bories Co., 1951-52; v.p. Austin LeStrange Co., N.Y.C., 1952-57; Eastern mgr. Oklahoma Pub. Co., N.Y.C., 1957-65, advt. dir., Oklahoma City, 1965-67; pres. J. Paulsen, Inc., N.Y.C., 1967—; cons. to mag. pubs.; guest speaker Nat. Assn. Radio-TV Farm Dirs.; dir. Agr. Public Reports. Active Hartsdale Republican Club; v.p. Hartsdale Civic Assn.; v.p., past chmn. Community Chest. Mem. Mensa, Farm Publ. Men. N.Y. (past pres.), Agrl. Pubs. Assn. (past dir.), State Farm Paper Bur. (dir.), Nat. Agrl. Mktg. Assn. (v.p. SW). Roman Catholic. Clubs: Orient Yacht (vice commodore), K.C. Contbr. articles to mags. Home: 23 Woodland Pl Chappaqua NY 10514 Office: 420 Lexington Ave New York City NY 10017

PAULSON, C(ARL) ROBERT, mktg. and creative services cons., film/TV writer-dir.; b. Brockton, Mass., Mar. 11, 1923; s. Bror Ragnar and Astrid Viola (Anderson) P.; A.B., Dartmouth Coll., 1948; M.S. in Elec. Engring., Thayer Sch. Engring., Hanover, N.H., 1949; mgmt. studies U. Calif. at Berkeley, 1959; m. Marjorie Nocross, Sept. 9, 1945; children—Alan B., Kirk R., Nancy C., Carla T. Asst. dir. Fred Waring's Pennsylvanians, 1950-52; dist./sales/mktg./div. mgr. Ampex Corp. Audio Video Products, Redwood City, Calif., 1952-63: nat. sales mgr. Precision Instrument Co., Palo Alto, Calif., 1963-66; mktg. mgr., systems devel. div. EG&G Inc., Bedford, Mass., 1966-71; v.p. mktg. TV Microtime, Inc., Bloomfield, Conn., 1971-74; mng. partner AVP Communication, Westborough, Mass., 1974—; instr. Menlo Coll. (Calif.) Sch. Bus. Adminstrn., 1963-64; cons. to TV equipment mfrs.; lectr. and seminar leader; film/TV writer-dir. Active local theatre and ch. Served as 1st lt. Signal Corps, U.S. Army, 1942-46. Mem. IEEE, Soc. Motion Picture and TV Engrs. (video disk study group chmn.), Audio Engring. Soc., Soc. Broadcast Engrs. (certified), Internat. TV Assn., Info. Film Producers Assn., Am. Soc. for Tng. and Devel., Armed Forces Communications and Electronics Assn. Republican. Congregationalist. Author: ENG/EFP/Electronics Post-Production Handbook, 1976, 80; articles to profl. jours. Home: 15 Kay St Westborough MA 01581 Office: PO Box 454 Westborough MA 01581

PAULSON, RICHARD, mgmt. cons.; b. Erie, Pa., Feb. 10, 1920; s. Oscar and Martha Paulson; 1 dau. by previous marriage, Kathy Ann. Field test engr. Convair-Astronautics, 1953-63; sr. cons. Bruce Payne Assos., 1963-65; self-employed mgmt. cons., 1965-72; founder, pres. O.N. Eno Co., mgmt. cons., Fresno, Calif., 1972—. Served with USAAF, 1943-45. Author, pub.: The ABC's of Time Study. Contbr. articles on mgmt. to bus. jours.; also composer, songwriter, inventor and designer of toys. Office: PO Box 11032 Fresno CA 93771

PAULUS, JOHN DOUGLAS, pub. relations and advt. exec.; b. Canton, Ohio, July 6, 1917; s. James and Helen (Pateas) P.; B.A., U. Pitts., 1936; postgrad. Georgetown U., Washington; m. Mildred Hankey, Dec. 4, 1937. Sports editor Washington Post, 1936-40; editorial exec., Pitts. Press, 1940-45; promotion dir., asso. pub. Bklyn. Eagle, 1945-47; sr. account exec., Ketchum Inc., 1947-51; dir.-pub. relations and advt. Jones & Laughlin Steel Corp., Pitts., 1951-57; dir. pub. relations Firestone Tire & Rubber Co., 1957-58; pres. Hankey, Paulus & Co., pub. relations, fund raising, advt.; lectr. editing, pub. relations, U. Pitts., 1945-53; v.p. pub. relations Allegheny Ludlum Steel Corp., 1958-70; v.p. pub. relations and pub. affairs Allegheny Ludlam Industries, Inc., 1971—. Book editor Am. Metal Market, daily newspaper, 1960-70, Mid-Continent Feature Syndicate, 1953—. Cons., Task Force on Water Resources and Power, 2d Hoover Commn., 1953-55. Trustee Mercy Hosp., Pitts., Duquesne U., Pitts., Pitts. Ballet Theater, ARC, Pitts. Council Internat. Visitors, Point Park Coll., Pitts., Seton Hall Coll., Greensburg, Pa. Recipient Putman medal for advt., 1954, Golden Quill, 1962. Mem. Internat. Iron and Steel Inst. (com. on pub. affairs and pub. relations 1968—, chmn. com. 1971—), Am. Iron and Steel Inst. (sr. v.p. 1970-71), Sigma Delta Chi, Omicron Delta Kappa. Episcopalian. Clubs: Duquesne, University, Press. Author: Pittsburgh in Music, 1949; Our Dollar in Danger, 1961; For Whom the (Steel) Bell Tolls, 1962; Rome Wasn't Bilked in a Day, 1963; House Organs—Sour Notes and Lullabies, 1966; Carrying Kumquats to Khartoum, 1972; The Curious Case of the Busted Back, 1973; Toward Economic Chaos-Via Majority Vote, 1973; Of Sheiks and Shahs and Commissars, 1974; Whither Trade Unionism in Industrial Democracies?, 1977; The Me Generation and the Winds of Change, 1978; Prospects and Promises—the Decades of the 80's, 1979; Will the Real Ayatollah Please Stand Up, 1980. Home: 826 N Meadowcroft Ave Pittsburgh PA 15216 Office: 2 Oliver Plaza Pittsburgh PA 15222

PAULUS, PETER VIRGIL, chemist; b. Newark, Feb. 14, 1914; s. James and Helen (Pateas) P.; student Carnegie Inst. Tech., 1931-33; A.B., Ohio State U., 1937; M.A., U. Cin., 1939, Ph.D., 1941; m. Sara Josephine Thompson, Mar. 13, 1943; 1 dau., Marsha Lynn. Research chemist Mine Safety Appliances Co., Pitts., 1941-46; pres., gen. mgr. Paulus, Inc., Connellsville, Pa., 1946-53; with The Standard Products Co., Port Clinton, Ohio, 1953—, tech. dir., 1953-55, chief engr., 1955-60, factory mgr., 1960-66, asst. gen. mgr., 1966-68, corporate dir. research and devel., 1968-72, v.p. product devel., Dearborn, Mich., 1972—. Bd. dirs. Boy Scouts Am. Candidate for U.S. Congress, 1958; mem. Ottawa County, Dem. Central Com. Mem. bd. advisers Bowling Green State U., 1967. Mem. Nat. Forensic League, Sigma Xi, Phi Lambda Upsilon. Clubs: Kiwanis (pres.), Order of Ahepa (supreme pres. 1979-80). Research and devel. in elastomers, plastics, adhesives, flocking, automotive body sealing and plastic decorative trim, pollution saving devices. Home: 1511 Riverwood Ln Coral Springs FL 33065 Office: Standard Products Co 2401 S Gulley Rd Dearborn MI 48124

PAVIA, CHARLES NICHOLAS, art and graphic supplies co. exec.: b. Bklyn., Apr. 16, 1946; s. Vito Angelo and Frances Jean (Abruzzo) P.; B.S. in Mktg. (Mktg. Student of Year), Calif. State Poly. U., 1967: M.B.A., U. So. Calif., 1968. Market planning analyst Chartpak Co., Santa Ana, Calif. and Leeds, Mass., 1968-71, product mgr., Leeds, 1972-73, dir. planning, 1973-75; mktg. mgr. Pickett Industries, Irvine, Calif., 1975-78; dir. planning and devel. Chartpak Pickett, Irvine, 1978-79, v.p. planning and devel., 1980—; cons. mktg. Porter & Goodman Design Assos., 1968-69. Served with USN, 1969-71. Mem. Assn. Corp. Growth, U. So. Calif. M.B.A. Alumni Assn., Beta Gamma Sigma. Republican. Roman Catholic. Home: 6466 Horse Shoe Ln Yorba Linda CA 92686 Office: 19700 Fairchild Suite 230 Irvine CA 92715

PAVLIDES, CONSTANTINE CHRIS, internat. banker; b. Athens, Greece, Dec. 5, 1946; came to U.S., 1969, naturalized, 1975; s. George and Catherine (Kafejoglou) P.; Mech. Engring. A.D., Poly. U., Athens, 1969; B.A. in Econs., Pa. State U., 1973; M.B.A. in Fin. summa cum laude, U. City N.Y., 1975; postgrad. in fin. N.Y. U.; m. Charlotte Lydia Nagy, June 29, 1975; 1 dau., Elizabeth Juliann. Overseas investment analyst Ford Motor Co., Dearborn, Mich., 1974-75; asst. treas. Am. Express Internat. Banking Corp., N.Y.C., 1975-80; 2d v.p. World Trade Banking Group, Chase Manhattan Bank, N.Y.C., 1980—; dir. Investment Mgmt. Internat. Co., Hellenic Engrs. & Architects Ltd. Recipient Highest Achievement award U. City N.Y., 1975. Mem. Am. Econ. Assn., Am. Mgmt. Assn., Am. Inst. Banking (advanced cert. 1976), Assn. M.B.A. Execs., Scotch Plains Sportsmen's Assn., Beta Gamma Sigma. Greek Orthodox. Club: Scotch Plains (N.J.) Country. Home: 506 Westfield Rd Scotch Plains NJ 07076 Office: 1 World Trade Center 78th Floor New York NY 10048

PAWE, JOEL JOHN, real estate investment co. exec.; b. Brussels, Belgium, Apr. 17, 1942; came to U.S., 1956, naturalized, 1963; s. Joseph and Sonia (De Bain) P.; B.A., Hunter Coll., 1965; cert. N.Y. Inst. Fin., 1966; m. Yuta Zednicek, Sept. 14, 1968. With Julien J. Studley Inc., N.Y.C., 1966-67; v.p. E.R. Frank Internat., Inc., Paris, 1967-74; pres. Internat. Property Ops. Ltd., N.Y.C., 1975—; cons. real estate investment field. Republican. Club: Am. (Paris). Author: World Wide Study of Commercial Space (booklet), 1969. Office: 3 W 57th St New York NY 10019

PAWEK, HUGO JOHN, forester, lumber co. exec.; b. Wilmot, S.D., July 17, 1907; s. William Henry and Caroline (Stearns) P.; B.S. in Forestry, U. Minn., 1930; m. Helen Keever, Sept. 1, 1932; children—David E., Alicia M. (Mrs. Graham E. Norwood). Field asst. forest entomology and forestry S.E. Forest Expt. Sta., U.S. Dept. Agr., Asheville, N.C., 1930-31; field and research asst. forestry dept. Duke, Durham, N.C., 1931-33; project supt., state insp., state dir., staff asst. Civilian Conservation Corps program, N.C., 1933-42; adminstrv. asst. Aircraft Warning System, Ala., 1942-43; timber mgmt. asst., asst. forest supr. U.S. Forest Service, Ga., Ala., 1946-54; forester Bonnie Doone Plantation, Ritter, S.C., 1954-57, Williams Furniture Corp., Ritter, 1957-60; v.p., forester Mower Lumber Co., Durbin, W.Va., 1960-74, pres., forester, 1974—, also dir.; forestry cons. S.C. Forest Mgmt. Service. Served with C.E., AUS, 1943-45; CBI. Mem. Soc. Am. Foresters. Home: Box 84 Durbin WV 26264 Office: Mower Lumber Co Durbin WV 26264

PAWELEC, WILLIAM JOHN, electronics co. exec.; b. Hammond, Ind., Feb. 15, 1917; s. John and Julia (Durnas) P.; B.S. in Accounting, Ind. U., 1939; m. Alice E. Brown, May 30, 1941 (dec. Dec. 1970); children—William John, Betty Jane Pawelec Conover; m. 2d, June A. Shepard, Nov. 27, 1976 (div. June 1980). Statistician, Ind. State Bd. Accounts, 1939-41; with RCA, 1941—, mgr. accounting and budgets internat. div., 1957-61, controller internat. div., 1961-68, corporate mgr. internat. finance operations and controls, 1968-75, mgr. corp. accounting, 1975-77, dir. internat. accounting, 1977—; controller RCA Internat., Ltd., Electron Ins. Co., 1977, RCA Credit Corp., 1979. Active, Westfield United Fund, 1967—. Mem. Nat. Assn. Accountants (past nat. v.p.), Watchung Power Squadron, N.J. State C. of C., Commerce and Industry Assn. N.Y., Stuart Cameron McLeod Soc., Ind. U. Alumni Assn. (pres. N.J. chpt.), Beta Gamma Sigma, Sigma Epsilon Theta. Club: Echo Lake Country. Home: 86 New England Ave Summit NJ 07901 Office: RCA Corp 30 Rockefeller Plaza New York NY 10020

PAWLIK, JOHN MICHAEL, II, investment banker; b. Buffalo, Dec. 6, 1954; s. John Joseph and Marie Rita (Luthi) P.; B.S., SUNY, Buffalo, 1975; M.B.A., U. Pa., 1979; J.D., Buffalo Law Sch., 1980. Investigative asso. N.Y. State Commn. on Jud. Conduct, Buffalo, Albany, N.Y.C., 1976-77; research fellow Higher Edn. Fin. Research Inst., U. Pa., Phila., 1979-80; admitted to Pa. bar, 1980; asso. John Nuveen & Co., Inc., Chgo., 1980—; adj. asst. prof. Glassboro (N.J.) State Coll., 1978-79; lectr. Medaille Coll., 1976-77. Mem. Mayor's Adv. Bd. of Buffalo Environ. Mgmt. Commn., 1975; mem. govt. structures task force Greater Buffalo Devel. Found., 1976-77. Mem. Wharton Grad. Alumni Assn., Beta Gamma Sigma, Omicron Delta Epsilon. Republican. Roman Catholic. Club: Wharton (Phila.). Opinion editor Wharton Jour., 1979-80. Office: 209 S LaSalle St Chicago IL 60604

PAXSON, JAMES MALONE, livestock feed mfg. co. exec.; b. St. Louis, May 14, 1912; s. Alfred Pryor and Elsa (Malone) P.; student U. Nebr., 1931-33; LL.B., George Washington U., 1967, LL.D., 1975. Admitted to Nebr. bar, 1967; asst. city atty., Omaha, 1947-53; with Standard Chem. Mfg. Co., Omaha, 1953—, v.p., 1955-60, pres., chief exec. officer, 1960—. Mem. nat. adv. council Salvation Army, 1980—; bd. dirs. Nebr. Meth. Hosp., 1974—, pres., 1977-78; bd. dirs. Omaha Home for Boys, pres., 1975; chmn. adv. com. Booth Hosp., 1970-80; fin. chmn. Nebr. Republican Party, 1977-78. Mem. Nebr. Bar Assn. Presbyterian. Clubs: Omaha, Plaza, Masons (33d degree), Shriners. Home: 3722 Pacific St Omaha NE 68105 Office: 701 S 42d St Omaha NE 68105

PAYNE, ARTHUR JAMES, mfg. co. exec.; b. Chgo., Aug. 9, 1931; s. Arthur Lawrence and Virginia Laura (Baum) P.; B.S. in Bus. Adminstrn., U. Ill., 1957; m. Kay Ellen Reinert, Aug. 13, 1955; children—James Arthur, Pamela Maureen, Victoria Kay, Robert Clifford. With Am. Can Co., 1957-69, corp. mgr. exempt employment, 1968-69; with ITT Corp., 1969-74, group v.p., dir. personnel, St. Louis, 1971-74; dir. exec. placement and mgmt. devel. Gen. Instrument Corp., Clifton, N.J., 1974-77; dir. manpower planning and devel. Parker Hennifin Corp., Cleve., 1978—. Chmn. Outstanding Citizen award program U.S. Jaycees, 1958-61. Served with USNR, 1950-54; Korea. Mem. Am. Soc. Tng. and Devel., Employment Mgrs. Assn., Coll. Placement Council, Nat. Assn. Corp. Profl. Recruiters. Club: Tanglewood Country. Office: 17325 Euclid Ave Cleveland OH 44112

PAYNE, DENNIS KEITH, mfrs. rep., cons. mgmt.; b. Seattle, July 13, 1944; s. James Keith and Callie Jean (Mount) P.; B.A., U. Wash., 1966; m. Leslie Joan Crawley, Dec. 11, 1971; children—Megan April, David Keith, Stefanie Joan. Editor/ copywriter Boeing Co., Seattle, 1966-67; various managerial positions The Denver, dept. store, 1967-69; gen. mgr. Tot Lines Inc., Kirkland, Wash., 1969-74; mfr.'s rep., Seattle, 1974—; mgmt. cons. mktg. apparel industry. Served with U.S. Army, 1965-66. Mem. Pacific NW Apparel Assn. Republican. Episcopalian. Clubs: Wash. Athletic, Bellevue Athletic. Office: Suite 3323 2601 Elliott Ave Seattle WA 98121

PAYNE, JAMES ELMER, mgmt. cons.; b. Des Moines, Mar. 14, 1942; s. James Herndon and Ann Elizabeth (Barker) P.; student Grinnell Coll., 1960-62, Iowa State U., 1962-63; B.A. in Econs., Golden Gate U., 1968; M.B.A. in Managerial Econs., U. Calif. at Berkeley, 1970; m. Donna Jean Edwards, July 12, 1966; children—Jason Kirby, Amber Elizabeth. With Northwestern Bell Telephone Co., Des Moines, 1964, Bechtel Corp., San Francisco, 1967-68, Pacific Telephone Co., San Francisco, 1968; asso. Arthur D. Little, San Francisco, 1969—; mng. partner Payne-Maxie Consultants, Berkeley, Calif., 1969—; instr. Golden Gate Coll., 1969. Bd. dirs. San Francisco Local Devel. Corp., 1971-73, Paltenghi Youth Center, 1972-75; mem. adv. bd. Calif. Office Small Bus. Devel., 1977-79; mem. adv. com. Emergency Sch. Assistance Act, Berkeley Unified Sch. Dist., 1978-79. Served with USNR, 1964-67. Journey for Perspectives world study tour fellow, 1969. Mem. Nat. Assn. Minority Cons. and Urbanologists (dir. 1972-75). Home: 20 Alta Rd Berkeley CA 94708 Office: 1510 E Walnut St Berkeley CA 94708

PAYNE, JAMES LEROY, fin. exec.; b. Carthage, Mo., Oct. 8, 1936; s. Leonard Wilson and Faye Emma (Brooks) P.; B.S., U. Mo., 1958; m. Virginia Marlene Cowan, Aug. 11, 1957; children—Robert James, Catherine Marlene. Tab supr. Southwestern Bell Telephone Co., St. Louis, 1959-60; sr. accountant Peat, Marwick Mitchell & Co., Kansas City, Mo., 1960-63; v.p. fin. Kansas City (Mo.) Star Co., 1963—. Served with arty. AUS, 1958-59. C.P.A.; certified data processor. Mem. Nat. Assn. Accountants (asso. dir. Kansas City chpt. 1965-66, 69-70), Inst. Newspaper Controllers and Fin. Officers, Beta Gamma Sigma. Republican. Baptist. Home: 13400 E 53d St Kansas City MO 64133 Office: 1729 Grand Ave Kansas City MO 64108

PAYNE, ROSLYN BRAEMAN, real estate exec.; b. Kansas City, Mo., Apr. 1946; d. Aaron and Sophie (Pincus) Braeman; B.B.A., U. Mich., 1968; M.B.A. (Mortar Bd. fellow 1968-69, Edith Stedman fellow 1969, 70), Harvard U., 1970; m. Lisle W. Payne, Dec. 27, 1973; 1 son, Matthew Lisle. Trainee, First Nat. Bank of Chgo., 1968, Coopers & Lybrand, N.Y.C., 1969; with Eastdil Realty Inc., N.Y.C. and San Francisco, 1970—, v.p., 1971—; v.p. Eastdil Equities Inc., N.Y.C., 1972; dir. 1st Am. Title Guaranty Co., Oakland, Calif. Mem. Women's Forum West, Bay Area Mortgage Assn. (v.p. programs). Clubs: Commonwealth; Harvard Bus. Sch.; Harvard (San Francisco and N.Y.C.); Peninsula Golf and Tennis, Menlo Circus. Home: 3616 Jackson St San Francisco CA 94118 Office: Eastdil Realty Inc 555 California St San Francisco CA 94104

PAYNE, WILLIAM NORMAN, petroleum refining and chem. mfg. exec.; b. Vicksburg, Miss., Dec. 15, 1942; s. Robert Emmitt and Edith Zoe (McDaniel) P.; B.S., Miss. State U., 1966; m. Jane Elizabeth Beeland, Sept. 4, 1965; children—William Brian, David Norman. Cost accountant Garan, Inc., garment mfrs., Starkville, Miss., 1966-67; plant accountant Gen. Foods Corp., Jacksonville, Fla., 1967-68; chief accountant Amax Chem. Co., Vicksburg, 1969-71; cost accounting mgr. Kershaw Mfg. Co., heavy equipment, Montgomery, Ala., 1971-73; controller Vicksburg Chem. Co., 1973-75, sec.-treas., 1975-78; controller and officer Vicksburg Refining, Inc., 1978—. Mem. ofcl. bd. Crawford St. United Methodist Ch., Vicksburg, 1975. Mem. Inst. Internal Auditors, Nat. Assn. Accountants (chpt. dir.), Miss. State U. Alumni Assn. (dir.). Address: 104 Montaign Dr Vicksburg MS 39180

PAYNE, WILLIAM TAYLOR, JR., word processing-tech. publs. cons.; b. Bradshaw, W.Va., Mar. 15, 1930; s. William Taylor and Clara Mae (Horn) P.; student various USAF tech. courses, 1948, 49, 51, 52, Keio U., 1949, Sch. Electronics, Balt., 1953, Comml. Radio Inst., Balt., 1954-55; m. Joan M. Reinhardt, Mar. 11, 1954; children—Susan C., William Taylor III, Karen L. Publs. engr. Westinghouse Electric Corp., Balt., 1953-56, Collins Radio Co., Cedar Rapids, Iowa, 1956-58; supr. tech. publs. Gen. Dynamics Corp., Rochester, N.Y., 1958-60; supr. engring. writing Curtiss Wright Corp., East Patterson, N.J., 1960-61; mgr. tech. publs. ACF Industries, Riverdale, Md., 1961-65; services mgr. tech. publs. Bechtel Power Corp., Gaithersburg, Md., 1965-77. Served with USAF, 1947-52; Japan. Mem. Internat. Word Processing Assn., Research Inst. Am., Internat. Assn. Tech. Communication for Co. Communicators, Nat. Assn. Govt. Communicators, Soc. Tech. Communication. Contbr. articles to profl. jours. Home: 8312 Cathedral Ave New Carrollton MD 20784

PAYTON, JAMES YELVERTON, computer co. exec.; b. Los Angeles, Feb. 7, 1930; s. Louis E. and Frances A. (Dunn) P.; B.S. in Engring., UCLA, 1956, M.S., 1962; m. Annabelle Burnett, Apr. 12, 1953; children—Karen, David. Mem. tech. staff Hughes Aircraft Co., Los Angeles, 1956-57; design engr. Nat. Cash Register Co., Hawthorne, Calif., 1957-58; dept. mgr. Litton Industries, Woodland Hills, Calif., 1958-65; v.p. Xerox Data Systems, 1965-71; exec. v.p. Century Data Systems, Anaheim, Calif., 1972-75, pres., 1979—; sr. v.p. Calif. Computer Products, 1972-79. Served with USAF, 1951-55. Mem. Am. Mgmt. Assn., Sigma Pi. Contbr. articles in field to profl. jours.; patentee in field. Home: 1819 Via Coches Palos Verdes Estate CA 90274

PAYTON, ROBERT LEE, builder, developer; b. Bolivar, Mo., Nov. 15, 1919; s. Colen Bert and Elsie Nora (Neuhart) P.; student Ventura (Calif.) Coll., 1939-41, U. Mont., Missoula, 1943; m. Paulina Myrl Samples, June 6, 1954; 1 son, Robert Lee. With U.S. Civil Service, Naples, Italy, 1946-47; gen. bldg. contractor, 1949—; propr. Paytons Research and Devel. Co., Ventura, 1977—; inventor constrn. concept, energy concept, novelty ideas. Served with USAAF, 1942-46. Mem. Ventura County Contractors Assn. (dir. 1960-62). Democrat. Mem. Foursquare Gospel Ch. Address: 3700 Dean Dr Apt 3202 Ventura CA 93003

PEABODY-BROWN, CHARLES DAN, bookseller; b. Mahopac, N.Y., Nov. 1, 1947; s. George Dan and Jane Marie (Melgaard) Peabody-B.; m. Maria Estela Villalva Hernandez, Dec. 13, 1975; 1 son, Luis Alberto. With Bear, Stearns & Co., N.Y.C., 1967-68; propr. Aspen Bookshop, 1963—. Bd. dirs. Lorien Found., Aspen, Colo., 1970—. Mem. Am. Booksellers Assn. Clubs: Aspen, Sons of Fedaykia (Aspen); 519 (Boulder, Colo.); Dull Men's (San Francisco). Home: Box 11075 Aspen CO 81611 Office: 205 S Mill St Aspen CO 81611

PEACE, JOHN H., advt. exec.; b. N.Y.C., Nov. 20, 1922; s. Thomas G. and Ella (Curry) P.; m. Agnes Cross, Mar. 7, 1942; children—Kathleen, Ellen, John, Mary, James, William. With William Esty Co., Inc., N.Y.C., 1941—, successively v.p., media dir., account exec., 1st v.p., 1941-58, chmn. operating com., 1958-60, pres., 1960-67, chmn. bd., 1967-74, chmn. exec. com., 1974—. Clubs: Siwanoy, Bronxville (N.Y.); Spring Lake (N.J.) Golf and Country; Sky (N.Y.C.); Turf and Field. Office: William Esty Co 100 E 42d St New York NY 10017*

PEACOCK, D. GRANT, fin. cons., lawyer; b. Pitts., Feb. 8, 1938; s. Dundas and Agnes (Ritchie) P.: B.A., Ohio Wesleyan U., 1959; J.D., Dickinson Sch. Law, 1966; m. Nancy Bair, Oct. 7, 1967; children—Bradley, Douglas, Craig. Audit staff Price Waterhouse & Co., Pitts., 1959-62; tax mgr. Lybrand, Ross Bros. & Montgomery, Pitts., 1962-69; admitted to Pa. bar, 1969; tax mgr. Arthur Andersen & Co., Pitts., 1969-71; v.p., mgr. corp. fin. dept. Moore, Leonard & Lynch, Investment Bankers, Pitts., 1971-74; chmn. Grant Peacock & Co., Inc., Pitts., 1974—. Bd. dirs. Pitts Symphony Orch., 1975—, Allegheny Gen. Hosp., 1975—. Mem. Am. Inst. C.P.A.'s, Pa. Inst. C.P.A.'s, Am., Pa. bar assns. Presbyterian. Clubs: Duquesne, Fox Chapel Golf. Office: 1460 US Steel Bldg Pittsburgh PA 15219

PEAHUFF, JIMMY WILLIAM, mfg. co. exec.; b. Greenville County, S.C., Oct. 31, 1934; s. Daniel William and Lucille (Sanders) P.; A.S. in Bus. Mgmt., LaSalle Extension U., 1974; student N.C. State U., 1965, Cleve. State Coll., 1968-70; m. Betty Center, July 8, 1955. Lab. supr. So. Bleachery, Taylors, S.C., 1961-65; quality control mgr. Rockwood Hosiery Mills, (Tenn.), 1965-68; process control mgr. Cleveland Woolens (Tenn.), 1968-71; supr. quality engring. M. Lowenstein Corp., Lyman, S.C., 1978—. Served with U.S. Army, 1956. Registered profl. engr., S.C.; cert. mfg. engr. Mem. Am. Soc. Quality Control. Baptist. Club: Sertoma. Home: 107 Lakeland Dr Greer SC 29651 Office: M Lowenstein Corp Lyman SC 29365

PEAKE, ROBERT WESTLAKE, communications co. exec.; b. Cardiff, Wales, Apr. 12, 1927; s. George Frederick and Mary Eileen (Cavill) P.; student Cardiff Wireless Coll., 1946-47, U. B.C. (Can.), 1972-75; married. Radio officer Marconi Internat. Marine, 1946-53; sound equipment engr. Rediffusion Ltd., Wales, 1953-57; chief engr. Tru-Vu TV Ltd., Vancouver, B.C., 1957-62; chief engr. Vancouver Cablevision, 1971-75; v.p. engring. Premier Cablevision, Vancouver, 1973-75, gen. mgr., 1974-77; v.p. ops. Premier Communications, Vancouver, 1977—; dir. Victoria Cablevision Ltd., Oakville Cablevision Ltd., Albion Cablevision, Wirevisions Ltd., Marlin Communal Antennas Ltd., Radiant Cable TV, Camas, Wash., Northwest Entertainment Industries, Portland, Premier Communication Network Inc., San Francisco, others; cons. in field. Served with Royal Signals, 1945-46. Recipient Cert. Achievement Ameco Inc., 1965. Mem. Nat. Assn. Ednl. Broadcasters, Vancouver Bd. Trade, Western Soc. Cable TV Engrs., Soc. Motion Picture and TV Engrs. Clubs: Univ. (Vancouver); Point Grey Golf and Country, Canadian Power Squadrons, Vancouver Flying, Masons. Office: 200-1090 W Georgia St Vancouver BC V6E 3Z7 Canada

PEARCE, J(OHN) JAMES, JR., research co. exec.; b. Cin., Apr. 4, 1943; s. John James and Louise Martha (Weinberg) P.; B.S.E., Princeton U., 1965; M.B.A., Harvard U., 1967; m. Carol Quisno, Aug. 13, 1966; children—Melissa, Sarah. Technician, Procter & Gamble, 1963-65; product mgmt. intern Dow Chem. Co., 1965; dir. automated systems Hill Top Labs., 1967-68, v.p., gen mgr., 1969-70; v.p. Am. Biomed. Corp. of Ohio, Inc., 1970-74, v.p. clin. labs., 1975-78; v.p., treas. Hill Top Research, Inc., Cin., 1978-79, pres., 1979—. Class agt. Princeton U., 1965-70, chmn. N. Tex. Ann. Giving, 1977-78; chmn. transp. study group Social Planning Council, Greater Cin. Community Chest; alumni trustee Woodward High Sch., 1970-75; deacon Knox Presbyterian Ch., 1972-74, head usher, 1973-74; chmn. Sycamore Sch. Bd. Tax Levy, 1980. Mem. Queen City Anglers Guild. Club: Princeton of S.W. Ohio (dir. 1968-72). Home: 8140 Millview St Cincinnati OH 45242 Office: PO Box 42501 Cincinnati OH 45242

PEARCE, MICHAEL BARRY, financier; b. Rawlins, Wyo., Jan. 31, 1947; s. R. Warren and M. Elaine (Kienath) P.; B.S., Calif. State U., 1973; M.B.A., Rutgers U., 1979; m. Susan Stabbert, Oct. 18, 1969; children—Corrin, Allison. Mgr. ops. control and analysis Singer Co., 1972-76; v.p., bus. mgr. Citibank, N.Y.C., 1976-79; v.p. corp. banking Rainier Bank, Seattle, 1979-81; pres. Bell Fin. Corp., Kirkland, Wash., 1981—. Republican. Home: 4029 169th SE Bellevue WA 98008 Office: 552 S Lake View Dr Kirkland WA

PEARCE, PHYLLIS LOIS YOCUM, archtl. firm exec.; b. East Chicago, Ind., June 18, 1938; d. Elmer A. and Ledora (McSwain) Yocum; grad. cum laude, Hammond (Ind.) Bus. Coll., 1957; student spl. courses Ind. U., U. Wis.; m. Alton Pearce, Jr., Aug. 4, 1957; children—Dawn Alane, Alton III. Adminstrv. asst. to exec. dir. Purdue-Calumet Devel. Found., East Chicago, 1957-66; office mgr. Wendell Campbell Assos., Inc., Chgo., 1966-71, Campbell & Macsai Architects, Inc., Chgo., 1971-75; asst. to pres., chief profl. mgr. Wendell Campbell Assos., Inc., 1975—; mktg. and sales cons.; pub. relations cons. Life mem. NAACP, sec. Gary br., 1977-78, 81-82, sec. Ind. Conf. Branches labor and industry com., 1977-78, mem. Conf. Black Politics, 1978. Recipient Meritorious Service citation and plaque NAACP, 1977, 78; Progressive Literary and Art Club scholar. Mem. Nat. Assn. Exec. Secs., Am. Mgmt. Assn., Profl. Services Mgmt. Assn., Coalition of Black Feminists. Baptist. Clubs: Ida M. Walker Household of Ruth, Odd Fellows. Organist, pianist. Home: 688 Cass Ct Gary IN 46403 Office: 180 N Michigan Ave Chicago IL 60601

PEARL, JOHN JOEL, consumer products co. exec.; b. Orange, N.J., July 28, 1936; s. Jacob and Bertha Mary (Slaseman) P.; B.S., Fairleigh Dickinson U., 1961; M.B.A., Seton Hall U., 1965, postgrad. Law Sch., 1965-67; m. Sheila Slade, May 25, 1962; children—Jamie, Jill. With Pepsico, 1967—, dir. personnel Frito-Lay, Inc., Dallas, 1971-74, dir. employee relations Pepsi-Cola Co., Purchase, N.Y., 1974-75, v.p. personnel Pepsi-Cola Co. and Pepsi-Cola Bottling Group, Purchase, 1975—; cons., lectr. personnel labor relations. Served with U.S. Army, 1955-57. Mem. Am. Arbitration Assn., Am. Mgmt. Assn., Phi Alpha Delta. Club: Rolling Hills Country. Office: Pepsi Cola Co Anderson Hill Rd Purchase NY 10577

PEARLMAN, ELLIOT STUART, steel container co. exec.; b. Chgo., Mar. 31, 1941; s. Philip Allen and Sally (Liebowitz) P.; B.S. in Chem. Engring., U. Mich., 1962; M.B.A., DePaul U., 1966; children—Jennifer, David. Treas., Acme Barrel Co., Chgo., 1962—; pres. Acme Steel Container Inc., Chgo., 1979—. Vice pres. Better Boys Found., Chgo., 1971. Mem. Nat. Barrel and Drum Assn. (v.p. and fin. chmn. 1972). Home: 1958 N Mohawk St Chicago IL 60614 Office: 2300 W 13 St Chicago IL 60608

PEARSON, ANDRALL EDWIN, beverage mfr.; b. Chgo., June 3, 1925; s. Andrall E. and Dorothy M. (MacDonald) P.; B.S., U. So. Calif., 1944; M.B.A., Harvard, 1947; m. Joanne Pope, Mar. 2, 1951; 1 dau., Jill Lee. Marketing mgr. Standard Brands, Inc., N.Y.C., 1948-53; asso. to prin. McKinsey & Co., Inc., N.Y.C., 1953-70, dir., 1965-70; exec. v.p. Pepsico, Inc., Purchase, N.Y., 1970-71, pres., 1971—, also dir.; dir., mem. exec. com. TWA, TWC. Trustee, Wesleyan U., 1977-79. Served as lt. (j.g.), USNR, 1943-46. Mem. Ref. Ch. of Bronxville (elder). Clubs: Harvard Bus. Sch. of N.Y. (dir.), Bronxville Field, Blind Brook, River (N.Y.C.). Contbr. articles to profl. jours., chpt. to handbook. Office: Pepsico Inc Purchase NY 10577

PEARSON, CARL ALFRED, JR., ins. co. exec.; b. Brockton, Mass., Apr. 6, 1925; s. Carl Alfred and Ellen E. (Mara) P.; B.S. in Bus. Adminstrn., Carthage Coll., 1964; m. Doris E. Lundin, June 21, 1946; children—Bruce, Donald, Timothy. Served to 1st class petty officer U.S. Navy, 1942-45; enlisted as sgt. U.S. Army, 1947, advanced through grades to maj., 1964; ret., 1966; field engr. Travelers Ins. Co., New Orleans, 1966-68, asst. mgr. San Francisco office, 1968-69, asst. supt. home office, Hartford, Conn., 1969-71, asst. dir. engring. div., 1971—, seminar dir. for customers, 1971—. Mem. Am. Soc. Tng. and Devel. Republican. Lutheran. Clubs: Masons (C.Z.); Elks (Hartford). Home: 59 Pine Glen Rd Simsbury CT 06070 Office: 1 Tower Sq Hartford CT 06115

PEARSON, DONALD WILLIAM, telephone co. exec.; b. Rochester, N.Y., Mar. 1, 1924; s. Frank William and Marian Ann (Luckman) P.; B.S. in Bus. Adminstrn., U. Rochester, 1951; m. Edna David, Feb. 1, 1947; children—Donna Pearson Werner, Michael, Mark, Steven. With Rochester Telephone Corp. (N.Y.), 1953—, dept. head computer ops., 1965-67, controller, 1967-70, v.p. adminstrn., 1970-75, v.p. fin., treas., sec., 1975—; dir. Central Trust Co. Mem. exec. bd. Otetiana council Boy Scouts Am.; past bd. dirs. Assn. for Blind of Rochester and Monroe County, N.Y.; mem. Com. to Re-evaluate County Govt., 1969-72. Served with USMC, 1942-46. Decorated Purple Heart. Mem. U.S. Ind. Telephone Assn. (investor relations com.), Nat. Assn. Accountants (past dir.), Fin. Execs. Inst., Rochester Soc. Security Analysts, Am. Soc. Corporate Secs., Better Bus. Bur. Rochester and Monroe County (dir., past chmn. bd. dirs.), Rochester C. of C. Republican. Lutheran. Clubs: City Midday (N.Y.C.). Home: 94 Sunset Trail W Fairport NY 14450 Office: 100 Midtown Plaza Rochester NY 14646

PEARSON, GEORGE BERNARD, business exec.; b. Mercedes, Tex., Feb. 19, 1938; s. Bernard and Agatha (Peterson) P.; B.A., U. Tex., 1959, M.B.A., 1961; m. Margaret Jean Royall, May 1, 1965. Statistician, Bur. Bus. Research, U. Tex., Austin, 1959-60; sales engr. IBM Corp., Endicott, N.Y., also Dallas, 1959; lead engr. Ling-Temco-Vought, Inc., Dallas, 1961-65, engring. specialist, 1965-67; mgr. finance Pan Am. World Airways, Inc., N.Y.C., 1967-69, mgr. operations research and system planning, 1969-72, dir. system planning, 1972, dir. operating plans and system devel., 1972-74, dir. planning systems and adminstrn., 1974-75; v.p. planning and research Beneficial Mgmt. Corp., 1975—, mem. mgmt. com., 1977—. Mem. U. Tex. Alumni Assn. Lutheran. Contbr. articles to profl. jours. Home: 100 Carriage House Rd Bernardsville NJ 07924 Office: 200 South St Morristown NJ 07960

PEARSON, GERALD LEON, meat processor; b. Mpls., June 24, 1925; s. Perry and Lillian (Peterson) P.; student Mpls. public schs.; m. Beverly Mary Schultz, Nov. 10, 1946; children—Steven, Perry, Liecia. Treas., sales mgr. Trimont Packing Co., 1946-52; treas., sales mgr. Spencer Packing Co. (Iowa), 1952-53, v.p., sales mgr., 1953-68; pres. Spencer Foods, 1968—; dir. Spencer Nat. Bank. Served with USNR, 1943-46. Mem. Nat. Meat Assn. (dir. 1966-80), Nat. Hide Assn. (dir.). Congregationalist. Office: Box 1228 Spencer IA 51301

PEARSON, GLEN MARTIN, engring. co. exec.; b. Eston, Sask., Can., Feb. 15, 1933; s. Arthur G. and Emelia (Duckert) P.; B.S.M.E., U. Sask., 1955; cert. in adminstrn. U. Regina, 1977. Design engr. J. Klassen Consulting, Ottawa, Ont., 1955-56; asso. engr. Douglas Michalenko & Dupuis, Saskatoon, Sask., 1956-62; prin. Douglas, Pearson, Daniels-Fossey, Saskatoon, 1962-72; pres., gen. mgr. Saskmont Engring., Regina, Sask., 1972—. Mem. Assn. Consulting Engrs. Can. (treas. 1979-80, pres. elect 1980—), Assn. Profl. Engrs. Sask. (councillor 1971-73), Sask. C. of C. (dir. 1975-76), Engring. Inst. Can., Can. Soc. Mech. Engrs., ASHRAE. Clubs: Assiniboia, Regina Flying (past dir.), Wascana Golf. Office: 500-2400 College Ave Regina SK S4P 2C2 Canada

PEARSON, NATHAN WILLIAMS, fin. cons.; b. N.Y.C., Nov. 26, 1911; s. James A. and Elizabeth (Williams) P.; A.B., Dartmouth Coll., 1932; M.B.A., Harvard U., 1934; LL.D. (hon.), Thiel Coll., Greenville, Pa., 1972; m. Kathleen McMurtry, Apr. 9, 1947; children—James S. (dec.), Nathan Williams. With U.S. Steel Corp., 1939-42; mgr. research Matson Navigation Co., 1946-47; controller Carborundum Co., 1947-48; v.p. T. Mellon and Sons, Pitts., 1948-70; fin. exec. Paul Mellon Family interests, 1948—; dir. Aluminum Co. Am., Gulf Oil Corp., Mellon Nat. Corp., Mellon Bank N.A., Pitts., Hanna Mining Co., Koppers Co., Inc., Fed. St. Fund, Inc., Ampex Corp. Bd. dirs. Met. Ednl. Sta. WQED-TV, Pitts. Theol. Sem. Served to comdr. USNR, 1942-46. Republican. Presbyterian. Clubs: Laurel Valley Golf; Rolling Rock (Ligonier, Pa.); Duquesne, Allegheny Country (Pitts.); Racquet and Tennis (N.Y.C.); Edgeworth, Harvard-Yale-Princeton. Home: 10 Woodland Rd Sewickley PA 15143 Office: PO Box 1138 Pittsburgh PA 15230

PEARSON, NELS KENNETH, mfg. exec.; b. Algonquin, Ill., May 2, 1918; s. Nels Pehr and Anna (Fyre) P.; student pub. schs.; m. Louise Mary Houston Lenox, June 28, 1941; children—Lorine Marie, Karla Jean. Assembler, Oak Mfg. Co., Crystal Lake, Ill., 1936-38, machine operator, assembly line foreman, 1938-43, apprentice tool and die maker, 1946-50; co-founder, pres. Wauconda Tool & Engring. Co., Inc., Algonquin, Ill., 1950—; co-founder, treas. Kenmode Tool & Engring. Co., Inc., Algonquin, 1960-72; co-owner Martinetti's Restaurant, Crystal Lake, v.p., 1975-78. Mem. McHenry County Edn. and Tng. Com., 1961—, treas., 1961—. Served with AUS, 1943-46. Mem. Am. Soc. Tool and Mfg. Engrs., Ind. Order Vikings. Moose. Clubs: Antique Auto, Classic Car, Veteren Motor Car, Horseless Carriage. Home: 125 Dole Ave Crystal Lake IL 60014 Office: Huntley Rd Algonquin IL 60102

PEARSON, NORMAN, cons. co. exec., planner; b. Stanley, Eng., Oct. 24, 1928; came to Can., 1954, citizen, 1962; s. Joseph and Mary (Pearson) P.; B.A. with honors in Town and Country Planning, U. Durham (Eng.), 1951; M.B.A., Pacific Western U., 1980; Ph.D. in Land Economy, Internat. Inst. Advanced Studies, 1979; m. Gerda Maria Josefine Riedl, July 25, 1972. Cons., Stanley Urban Dist. Council, 1946-47; planning asst. Accrington Town Plan and Bedford County Planning Survey, U. Durham Planning Team, 1947-49; planning asst. to Allen and Mattocks, cons. planners and landscape designers, Newcastle upon Tyne, Eng., 1949-51; adminstrv. asst. Scottish div. Nat. Coal Bd., 1951-52; planning asst. London County (Eng.) Council, 1953-54; planner Central Mortgage and Housing Corp., Ottawa, Ont., Can., 1954-55; planning analyst City of Toronto Planning Bd., 1955-56; dir. planning Hamilton (Ont.) Wentworth Planning Area Bd., 1956-59; dir. planning Burlington (Ont.) and Suburban Area Planning Bd., 1959-61, commr. planning, 1961-62; planning cons., London, Ont., 1962—; pres. Tanfield Enterprises Ltd., London, Ont., 1976—; life mem. U.S. Com. for Monetary Research and Edn., 1976—; spl. lectr. in planning McMaster U., Hamilton, 1956-64, Waterloo (Ont.) Lutheran U., 1960-63; asst. prof. geography and planning U. Waterloo, 1963-67; asso. prof. geography U. Guelph (Ont.) and chmn./dir. Centre for Resources Devel., 1967-72; prof. polit. sci. U. Western Ont., London, 1972-77; mem. social scis., econs. and legal aspects com. Research Adv. Bd., Internat. Joint Commn., 1972-76; cons. City of Waterloo, 1973-76, Province Ont., 1969-70; adv. Georgian Bay Regional Devel. Council, 1968-72; real estate appraiser Province Ont., 1976—; Can. v.p. Gt. Lakes Tomorrow,

1976-77; mem. Communities and Large-Scale Devel. Council, Urban Land Inst. U.S., 1979—. Pres., Unitarian Ch. Hamilton, 1960-61. Served with RAF, 1951-53. Fellow Royal Town Planning Inst. (Bronze medal award 1957), Royal Econ. Soc. (life), Am. Geog. Soc. (life), Atlantic Econ. Assn. (life); mem. Internat. Soc. City and Regional Planners, Am. Inst. Planners, Can. Inst. Planners, Can. Polit. Sci. Assn., Am. Inst. Cert. Planners. Clubs: Masons, Empire, Ont., Univ. (London, Ont.). Author: (with others) An Inventory of Joint Programmes and Agreements Affecting Canada's Renewable Resources, 1964; editor and co-author: Regional and Resource Planning in Canada, 1963, rev. edit., 1970; editor: (with others) The Pollution Reader, 1968; contbr. numerous articles on town planning to profl. jours., chpts. to books; editorial bd. Jour. Gt. lakes Research, 1973-79; editor Ont. Land Economist, 1978-81. Home: 223 Commissioners Rd E London ON N6C 2S9 Canada Office: PO Box 5362 Sta A London ON N6A 4L6 Canada

PECAUT, ROBERT EUGENE, banker; b. Sioux City, Iowa, June 16, 1932; s. John Harold and Ethel Lillian (Horne) P.; B.A., Morningside Coll., 1958; LL.B., U. S.D., 1960; m. Janice Claire Metcalf Spencer, Feb. 24, 1956; children—Gregory Spencer, Mark Allen. Admitted to Iowa bar, 1960, S.D. bar, 1960, Fed. bar, 1960; trust officer First Nat. Bank, Sioux City, 1960-63, v.p., sr. trust officer, 1963-70; v.p., sr. trust officer Northeast Bank & Trust Co., Bangor, Maine, 1970-73; sr. v.p. Harvard Trust Co., 1973-77: v.p. Hempstead Bank, 1977-80, sr. v.p., 1980—; v.p. Northeast Bankshare Assn., Lewiston, Me., 1970-73; trust officer Peninsula Nat. Bank, 1980—; mem. N.Y. State Bank Trust Edn. Com., L.I. Tax Com.; former dir. Harbeck Footwear, Grants Dairy Co., Rathbun Co., Rathbun Realty Co., Rathbun Lumber Co. Guest lectr. U. S.D. Law Sch., 1965-67. Chmn., Speakers Bur., Sioux City, 1964-65; mem. adv. bd. St. Joseph Hosp., 1968-70; mem. Bangor Dist. Nurses Adv. Bd.; chmn. finance com. Bangor Half-Way House; treas., mem. investment com. Community Girl Scouts; scoutmaster Boy Scouts Am. Mem. investment adv. com., City of Bangor, 1970-73. Former mem. bd. dirs. Harriett Ballou New Hope Center, Siouxland Assn. for Retarded Children, Sioux City Council Chs.; past pres. Siouxland Estate Planning Council; mem. deferred giving com. United Way. Served with USAF, Intelligence Service, 1952-56. Mem. Am. (probate, pension and profit sharing com.), Iowa bar assns., Am. Bankers Assn. (mem. community banks com., chmn. subcom. on community banks), Sudbury Pub. Health Nursing Assn. (past dir.), Mass. Bankers Assn. (chmn. edn. com.), Sudbury Minute Militia (capt.), State Bar S.D., Tax and Estate Planning Council of L.I., Suffolk County Estate Planning Council, C. of C., Jr. C. of C. (dir.), Pi Kappa Delta (past pres.), Delta Theta Phi. Republican. Lutheran (past trustee). Mason. Club: Exchange. Home: 8 Tower Pl Smithtown NY Office: 1035 Stewart Ave Garden City NY

PECHERSKY, MARTIN JAY, research labs. exec.; b. Pitts., July 29, 1943; s. Louis and Mildred (Kaplan) P.; B.S.M.E., Pa. State U., 1965; M.S.M.E., Carnegie Mellon U., 1969, Ph.D., 1971; m. Carole Frank, Jan. 5, 1970; children—Julie, Kara, Dana. Asso. engr. Bettis Atomic Power Lab., W. Mifflin, Pa., 1966-69; sr. engr. Westinghouse advanced reactors div., Waltz Mill, Pa., 1972-74, sr. engr. research and devel. labs., 1974—. Registered profl. engr., Pa. Mem. Am. Phys. Soc., Sigma Xi. Democrat. Jewish. Contbr. research publs. in field. Home: 109 Drake Dr Monroeville PA 15146 Office: 1310 Beulah Rd Pittsburgh PA 15235

PECK, CLAIR LEVERETT, JR., constrn. co. exec.; b. Los Angeles, Nov. 18, 1920; s. Clair Leverett and Viola (Curtis) P.; B.S.C.E. cum laude, Stanford, 1942; m. Linda H. Haggin, Jan. 2, 1974; children—Nancy Peck Birdwell, Suzanne Peck Worthington, Clair Leverett. Owner, chmn. bd. C.L. Peck, Contractor and Real Estate Developer, Los Angeles, 1945—; dir. Fed. Res. Bank San Francisco, Farmers Ins. Group, Investment Co. Am., AMCAP Fund, Inc., J.G. Boswell Co., Northrop Corp., 1966-76, Technicolor Corp., 1967-76, DiGiorgio Corp.; constrn. cons. to various firms. Chmn. bd. YMCA Met. Los Angeles; past bd. dirs. So. Calif. Visitors Council, Los Angeles Visitors Bur.; bd. dirs. Doheny Eye Found.; vice-chmn. Ear Research Inst.; bd. med. counselors U. So. Calif.; trustee Mead Housing Trust, Harvey Mudd Coll., House Ear Inst., Huntington Library, Brentwood Sch.; chmn. Santa Anita Found. Served to lt. USNR, 1941-45. Mem. ASCE, Associated Gen. Contractors. Clubs: California, Chaparral, Bohemian, Los Angeles Country, Eldorado Country, Calif. (Los Angeles). Home: 710 N Alta Dr Beverly Hills CA 90210 Office: 3303 Wilshire Blvd Los Angeles CA 90010

PECK, JOSEPH RICHARD, constrn. co. exec.; b. Lexington, Ky., Oct. 1, 1947; s. Bob K. and Joy (Freeman) P.; B.A., U. Ky., 1969; m. Susan Pelton, May 18, 1968; children—Mercedes Kirsten, Robert Richard. Product mgr. Sight & Sound Internat., Milw., 1971-72; dir. mktg. Hal Leonard Publ. Corp., Milw., after 1972, then dir. product devel.; now gen. mgr. Sturgeon Constrn., Pompano Beach, Fla., Quadrangle Racquetball Complex, Coral Springs, Fla. Baptist. Contbr. articles to profl. jours. Office: 8408 NW 35th St Coral Springs FL 33065

PECK, ROLAND BRYAN, designing co. and profl. agy. exec.; b. Valparaiso, Nebr., Aug. 28, 1932; s. Roland Bryan and Christine Louise (Wilcox) P.; B.S.M.E., Ariz. State U., 1958; m. Mary Ellen Mansfield Sharpe, Aug. 25, 1956; children—Jeffrey Bryan, Stephanie Mansfield, Justin Mason. Supt. maintenance and engring. Midland Ross Corp., Phoenix, 1960-65, chief engr. indsl. castings div., Chgo., 1965-70; engring. cons. Lester B. Knight & Assos., Inc., Chgo., 1970-71, sr. v.p. Keller & Gannon subs., San Francisco, 1971-78, v.p. Lester B. Knight Internat., Chgo., 1971-78; v.p., dir. engring. Ace Designing Co., San Francisco, 1978—, pres., dir. Geneva Profl. Agy., San Francisco, 1978—; dir. Downes Assos., Washington. Mem. vestry St Paul's Episcopal Ch., San Rafael, Calif., 1973-75, 77-81. Served with USMA, 1954-56. Registered profl. engr., Calif. Mem. West Point Assn. Grads. and Former Cadets (life), Am. Inst. Mining and Metall. Engrs., AIA (asso.). Republican. Research and patentee in field. Home: 95 Wimbledon Way San Rafael CA 94901 Office: 580 Market St San Francisco CA 94104

PECKRON, HAROLD STEPHEN, lawyer; b. St. Louis, Apr. 5, 1946; s. Charles James and Amelia Rose (Riska) P.; B.S. in Bus. Adminstrn., Marquette U., 1970; M.B.A., Loyola U., Chgo., 1972; J.D. with honors, Drake U., 1976; LL.M., Georgetown U., 1979; m. Koudelka, Aug. 6, 1966. Admitted to Iowa bar, 1976, Hawaii bar, 1980; tax research intern Office Atty. Gen., Iowa Dept. Revenue, Des Moines, 1974-76; tax cons. Ernst & Whinney, Chgo., 1976; tax atty. Office Chief Counsel-Treasury Tax Ct. Litigation Div., Washington, 1977-78; atty.-adv. U.S. Tax Ct., Washington, 1978-80; tax atty. Case, Kay & Lynch, Honolulu, 1980—; tax cons., 1977—; dir. grad. acctg. and taxation program Southeastern U., Washington, 1977—; adj. prof. law Cath. U. Columbus Sch. Law, 1979—, U. Hawaii, 1980—. Bd. dirs., legal counsel Atlantic Found., Washington, 1978-79, Hawaii Performing Arts Co., 1981; active United Way, Honolulu, 1980; mem. staff Arts Council Hawaii. Mem. Am. Bar Assn., Hawaii Bar Assn., Iowa Bar Assn., Fed. Bar Assn. (tax editor Jour. Washington chpt. 1977-80, sec. Hawaii chpt. 1981—), Honolulu C. of C. (tax com., energy com.), Phi Alpha Delta. Club: Lawyers (Fed. Bar). Author: Law Office Management, 1977, Business Government Relations and Corporate Public Affairs, 1979, Accounting and Tax Aspects of Corporate Acquisitions, 1980; asso. tax editor Tax Lawyer, 1979-80; contbr. Federal Tax Deductions, 1980; columnist Hawaii Real Estate Investor; contbr. articles to profl. jours. Home: 225 Queen St Honolulu HI 96813 Office: 1100 1st Hawaiian Bank Bldg PO Box 494 Honolulu HI 96809

PECOR, RAYMOND CHARLES, JR., ferry boat service exec.; b. Burlington, Vt., May 18, 1939; s. Raymond C. and Lorraine T. (Tupper) P.; student Nichols Coll. Bus. Adminstrn., 1959, U. Vt., 1961; m. Jean Gianarelli, Sept. 15, 1962; children—Stacey, Raymond Charles III. Pres., Ray's Mobile Homes, Inc., Burlington, Vt., 1961—, Ray's Devel., Inc., Burlington, 1962—, Ray's Motor Sales, Inc., Burlington, 1947—; pres. Ray's Mobile Homes, Ltd., St. John's, N.B., Can., 1971-76, Can. Mobile Home Bus., St. Johns, 1971—, Lake Champlain Transp. Co., Burlington, 1976—; dir. McAuliffe, Inc., Mchts. Bank, Burlington. Bd. dirs., pres. Greater Burlington Indsl. Corp., 1975—; bd. dirs. YMCA, United Way; trustee Vt. State Colls. Mem. Greater Vt. Assn., New Eng. Mobile Home Assn. (dir.), U. Vt. Alumni Assn. (dir. 1969—), Young Pres.'s Orgn. Methodist. Clubs: Ethan Allen, Burlington Country (Burlington). Home: Pine Haven Shore Shelburne VT 05482 Office: King St Dock Burlington VT 05401

PECUKONIS, ALFRED BERNARD, computer programmer; b. Pringle, Pa., Dec. 16, 1937; s. Alfred Bernard and Mary Ann (Chisko) P.; B.S., Elizabethtown (Pa.) Coll., 1976; m. Barbara Watkins, Jan. 30, 1959; children—Diane, Laurie. EAM supr. Bethlehem Steel Co. (Pa.), 1960-66; asst. ops. mgr. Aries Corp., Fairfield, N.J., 1966-68; data processing cons. Sperry Univac, Ind., Ill. and Pa., 1968-76; computer specialist U.S. Navy, Mechanicsburg, Pa., 1976—; pres. PMF Software Assos. Inc., 1980—; dir. Gallion Data Systems, Inc. Treas. Community Action Party, Lindenhurst, Ill., 1972. Served with USAF, 1956-59. Mem. Assn. Computer Users. Roman Catholic. Club: K.C. (4 deg.). Office: 6427 Carlisle Pl Mechanicsburg PA 17055

PEDERSON, BURTON CARL, accountant, bus. exec.; b. Virginia, Minn., Jan. 22, 1947; s. Carl Olaf and Elsie Sylvia P.; B.S. in Accounting, No. Ariz. U., 1974; postgrad. Grad. Sch. Bus. Adminstrn., U. So. Calif., 1975. Internal and electronic data processing auditor Northrop Corp., Los Angeles; v.p. adminstrn. and fin. Road & Show Publs., Inc., Hollywood, Calif., also dir. Served with USMC, 1966-70. Decorated Air medal with 3 oak leaf clusters. Mem. Electronic Data Processing Auditors Assn. Home: 320 S Ardmore Apt 321 Los Angeles CA 90020 Office: 4307 1/2 Melbourne Los Angeles CA 90027

PEDRICK, THEODORE KENNETH, caterer; b. Somers Point, N.J., Dec. 6, 1946; s. Frederick Maximillion and Thelma Evelyn (Crismond) P.; student Coll. of Emporia, 1965-66, U. Md., 1967-69, 76-77; A.A.S., No. Va. Community Coll., 1975; m. Marjorie Dianne Day, June 24, 1978; children—Kenneth Douglas, Kimberly Dawn; stepchildren—Charles W., Jennifer L. and Emily Jane Mathis. Asst. mgr. Gino's, Inc., No. Va., 1970-72, Arby's Roast Beef, College Park, Md., 1972-73; mgr. Fatted Calf Restaurant, Washington, 1973-74; owner Pedrick's Gen. Store, South Dennis, N.J., 1972—; co-founder, pres., chmn. bd. T & M Gourmet Caterers, Inc., 1979—. Served with USAF, 1966-70; Vietnam. Mem. Internat. Food Service Exec. Assn. (treas. Washington chpt.), Prince George's County C. of C. (econ. devel. com.). Home: 8511 Schultz Rd Clinton MD 20735 Office: PO Box 458 Clinton MD 20735

PEEBLER, CHARLES DAVID, JR., advt. exec.; b. Waterloo, June 8, 1934; s. Charles David and Marry E. (Barnett) P.; student Drake U., 1954-56; m. Susie Jacobs, June 5, 1958 (div. 1977); children—David Jacobs, Mark Walter; m. Tonita Worley, Nov. 12, 1979. Asst. to exec. v.p. J.L. Brandeis & Sons, Omaha, 1956-58; with Bozell & Jacobs, Inc., 1958—, v.p., mem. plans. bd. 1960-65, pres. mid-continent operations, Omaha, 1965-67, pres., chief exec. officer, 1967—, also chmn. bd.; dir. Storer Broadcast System, United Nat. Bank. Mem. Covered Wagon council Boy Scouts Am., 1962—; asso. chmn. Coll. Worlds Series, 1966; co-chmn. primary gifts div. Creighton U. New Goals Program, 1963; chmn. Omaha area Drake U. Bldg. Fund drive, 1960, 72. Bd. dirs. United Community Services Omaha, 1963—, drive chmn. 1966-67; bd. dirs. United Funds and Councils of Am., 1967, chmn. pub relations adv. com., mem. exec. com., 1968; bd. dirs. Omaha Jr. Achievement, 1964—, treas., mem. exec. com., 1965-66, pres., 1972-74; bd. dirs. Omaha chpt. Nat. Conf. Christians and Jews, 1962-65, chmn. ann. dinner, 1963; trustee Creighton-Omaha Regional Health Care Corp., 1972-73; pres. trustees Brownell-Talbot Sch., bd. govs. United Way, 1980—. Mem. Young Pres.'s Orgn. (internat. dir.), Omaha Advt. Club (dir. 1964—), Omaha C. of C. (chmn. edn. com. 1962-64, dir. 1965—), Omaha Indsl. Mgmt. Club (adv. bd. mgmt. 1960-62), Omaha Sales and Marketing Execs. (dir. 1962), Ad Sell League Omaha (pres. 1972, chmn. exec. bd.), Nebr. Wildlife Fedn. (pres.). Clubs: Marco Polo (N.Y.C.); Bermuda Dunes Country (Palm Springs, Calif.); Omaha Press, Omaha Plaza, Highland Country (Omaha). Home: 12 E 76th St New York NY 10021 Office: Bozell & Jacobs One Dag Hammarskjold Plaza New York NY 10017

PEEKEMA, GEORGE THOMAS, steel fabrication co. exec.; b. San Francisco, June 19, 1928; s. George Thomas and Carolyn Louise (Mayer) P.; B.S. in Civil Engring., U. Calif., Berkeley, 1951; M.B.A., Columbia U., 1956; m. Joanne Beckett, Sept. 15, 1956. Engr., Crown Zellerbach Corp., 1956-63, St. Regis Paper Co., 1963-67, Ga. Pacific Corp., 1967-78; pres. Stevens Equipment Co., Salem, Oreg., 1978—; owner, operator ranches and tree farms. Served to 1st lt. C.E., U.S. Army, 1951-53. Registered profl. engr., Calif., Wash., La. Republican. Home: 7519 NE 69th St Vancouver WA 98662 Office: PO Box 12006 Salem OR 97309

PEI, T'ING CHUNG, city planner, real estate developer, b. Princeton, N.J., Nov. 10, 1944; s. Ieoh Ming and Eileen (Loo) P.; A.B., Harvard U., 1965: M.City Planning, Mass. Inst. Tech., 1967; m. Marianne Margaret Magocsi, Mar. 6, 1976; 1 son, Stephen Shih-Feng; 1 dau. by previous marriage, Alyssa Shih-Ying. Various positions with govt. N.Y.C., 1967-71; dir. civic devel. div. N.Y. State Urban Devel. Corp., N.Y.C., 1971-74; v.p., corp. sec. Sefrius Corp., N.Y.C., 1974—. Mem. Manhattan Community Planning Bd. #8, 1970; mem. community adv. com. 59th St. Area Task Force, Manhattan, 1976—; v.p., dir. Miami (Fla.) World Trade Center, Inc., 1977—; pres. Ivy Network, Inc., New Haven, 1965-66; bd. dirs. Harvard Radio Broadcasting Co, Inc., 1964-65; guest lectr. Columbia U., Yale U., Cornell U., U. Calif. at Berkeley, Harvard Bus. Sch., Pratt Inst.; panelist numerous confs.: cons. HEW, 1969, Regional Plan Assn., 1971-72, Société d'Etudes Financières et de Réalisations Immobilières, Paris, 1974. Mem. Am. Inst. Cert. Planners, Am. Planning Assn., Urban Land Inst., Regional Plan Assn., Archtl. League N.Y., Citizens Housing and Planning Council. Democrat. Clubs: Harvard of Boston; Hasty Pudding. Co-author: Project Metran, 1966. Home: 325 E 57 St New York NY 10022 Office: 600 Madison Ave New York NY 10022

PEIRCE, FREDERICK GRADAN, food distbn. co. exec.; b. Hinsdale, Ill., Aug. 17, 1955; s. Sumner Lloyd and Margot Smith (Hillberg) P.; student Berklee Coll. Music, 1973, U. Pa., 1974-76; m. Debra Lynn Dietrich, Aug. 21, 1976. With Selas Corp. Am., Dresher, Pa., 1973-74; with Rohelle, Inc., Spring House, Pa., 1974—, dir. personnel, 1978—, also dir. Mem. North Penn Indsl. Relations Assn. Republican. Office: PO Box 273 Bethlehem Pike Spring House PA 19477

PEIRCE, THOMAS SEELEY BRICE, constrn. exec.; b. Toledo, Ohio, Nov. 29, 1939; s. Richard Howell and Elizabeth (Seeley) P.; B.A., DePauw U., 1961; m. Deborah DeSilva, July 20, 1968; children—Michael, David, Paige, Lara, Patricia; stepchildren—Christopher, Carin. Purchasing agt. Peirce Constrn. Co., Toledo, 1961; v.p. Bellevue Trucking Corp., Holland, Ohio, 1962-63; pres., 1964-67; v.p., equipment mgr. Peirce Constrn. Co., Holland, 1968-73, dir., 1969—, v.p. sales, 1974—. Mem. adv. bd. Sch. Constrn. Tech., Bowling Green State U., 1979—; trustee Ohio Operating Engrs. Health and Welfare Plan, 1971—; bd. dirs. Ohio chpt. Nat. Found. Ileitis and Colitis, 1972-76, Am. Council Econ. Devel., 1979—. Mem. Ohio Contractors Assn. (chmn. Toledo chpt. 1974, labor exec. bd. 1971-76, chmn. heavy hwy. sect. 1975, chmn. 1976, bd. dirs. 1976-79), U.S. Indsl. Council (dir. 1975—). Episcopalian. Home: 6528 Abbey Run Sylvania OH 43560 Office: 1049 S McCord Rd Holland OH 43528

PEIZER, MAURICE SAMUEL, med. advt. cons.; b. Hartford, Conn., Aug. 21, 1912; s. David I. and Mary (Pomerantz) P.: B.A., U. Pa., 1933; postgrad. in Journalism, Columbia U., 1945, 49, 50; m. Marjorie Knowlton, Aug. 25, 1951; children—Miriam Frances, Jessica Cathleen (dec.). Asst. to acting chief POW dept. U.S. Office of Censorship, N.Y.C., 1943-45: med. advt. writer Paul Klemtner & Co., Inc., Newark and N.Y.C., 1946-52, asst. copy chief, 1952-53, tech. dir. of copy, 1953-57, tech. dir., 1957-58, copy chief, 1958-62; sr. writer, pharm. copy chief, Hutchins Advt. Co., Rochester (N.Y.), 1962-67; group copy supr. William Douglas McAdams Inc., N.Y.C., 1967-78, assa. creative dir./copy, 1978-79, copy dir., 1979-80; now med. advt. cons. Pres. Nutley (N.J.) Little Theatre, 1957-59; co-founder Penfield (N.Y.) Players, pres., 1967; mem. publicity com. Nutley (N.J.) Citizens for Kennedy, 1960; mem. ofcl. bd. Methodist Ch., Penfield, N.Y., 1963-67; chmn. missions com. Community Ch., Cedar Grove, N.J., 1969-71, long-range planning com., 1972-74. Fellow Am. Med. Writers Assn. (pres. Met. N.Y. chpt. 1975-76, dir. 1973-80, exec. com. 1977-80, dir. dept. membership affairs 1977-80; award 1978); mem. Pharm. Advt. Council of N.Y., AAAS, N.Y. Acad. Scis. Cons. editor AMWA Chpt. Exchange, 1977-79. Home: 135 Sunrise Terr Cedar Grove NJ 07009

PEKAREK, ROBERT CHARLES, indsl. psychologist; b. Cleve., Sept. 9, 1938; s. Thomas and Johanna (Miller) P.; B.S., Purdue U., 1963, M.S., 1967, Ph.D., 1969; m. Mary Ann Hulburt, Nov. 29, 1969; children—Kristina Lynn, Brian Thomas, Robert Christopher. Asst. Purdue U., 1965-67; pvt. practice marriage and family counseling, 1969-73; dir. student activities and orgns. Fla. State U., Tallahassee, 1967-69; Fla. dir. White House Confs. on Children and Youth, Tallahassee, 1969-71, follow-up dir., Washington, 1971-73; indsl. psychologist Medina & Thompson, Inc., Chgo., 1973-78; pres. Indsl. Psychology, Ltd., Chgo., 1978—; dir. N. Am. Biols., Inc. Served with USAF, 1963-65. Mem. Am. Psychol. Assn., Alpha Tau Omega, Phi Delta Kappa, Kappa Delta Pi. Author: Florida's Children and Youth, 1970, A Year Later, 1971. Home: 1220 Wild Rose Ln Lake Forest IL 60045 Office: 444 N Michigan Ave Penthouse Level Chicago IL 60611

PELANDINI, THOMAS FRANCIS, bank exec.; b. Vallejo, Calif, Jan. 6, 1938; s. Francis Lee and Betty (Tucker) P.; B.A., U. Wash., 1961; m. Sandra Lee Holmes, Sept. 17, 1961; children—Jennifer Lynn, Beth Ann. Div. dir. public relations Pepsi-Cola Co., N.Y.C., Chgo., 1966-68; account supr. Patton Agy., Phoenix, 1968-70; v.p. Hill & Knowlton, Los Angeles, 1970-72; dir. communications Avco Corp., Greenwich, Conn., 1972-75; v.p. public affairs Crocker Nat. Bank, San Francisco, 1975—. Bd. dirs. San Francisco Forward, 1979—, No. Calif. chpt. Cystic Fibrosis Found., 1980—. Served with USAF, 1962-66. Mem. Public Relations Soc. Am. Clubs: Bankers (San Francisco); Diablo Country. Office: One Montgomery St San Francisco CA 94105

PELIO, WILLIAM LAWRENCE, accountant; b. Garfield, N.J., Feb. 26, 1912; s. Lawrence and Julia (Shirak) P.; B.C.S., N.Y. U., 1934; m. Joan Ann Holdnik, Nov. 11, 1950; 1 son, Earl William. Partner, Pelio & Pelio, C.P.A.'s, 1936—; city comptroller City of Garfield, 1943-73; twp. auditor, Saddle Brook, N.J., 1954-66, Lyndhurst, N.J., 1970-80; borough auditor, Wollington, N.J., 1954-61; sch. auditor Garfield Bd. Edn., 1954-79. Chmn., Garfield YMCA, 1964-65; mem. Garfield Golden Jubilee, 1967, Garfield Youth Com.; commr. Garfield Housing Authority, 1953-75; pres. Garfield Babe Ruth League, 1974—. Bd. dirs. Garfield Boys Club. C.P.A., N.Y., N.J. Mem. Internat. Platform Assn., Finance Officers Assn. N.J., U.S. Capitol Hist. Soc., N.J., N.Y. socs. C.P.A.'s. Home: 460 Massey Ct Wyckoff NJ 07481 Office: 114 Palisade Ave Garfield NJ 07026

PELL, ANTHONY DOUGLAS, fin. mgmt. co. exec.; b. Washington, July 2, 1938; s. Robert Thompson and Thecla Caroline (Barker) P.; A.B., Princeton, 1960; J.D. with honors, George Washington U., 1966; m. Katharine Murphey, Sept. 27, 1962; children—Theodore, Katharine. Admitted to N.Y. bar, 1966, Washington bar, 1966; atty., firm Coudert Bros., N.Y.C., 1966-68, firm Cadwalader, Wickersham & Taft, N.Y.C., 1968-72; v.p. The Boston Co., 1972-75, sr. v.p. fin. strategies, 1975—; exec. v.p., treas., dir. Pell, Rudman & Co.; pres., dir. Union Wharf Securities; exec. v.p., dir. CFI, Inc.; dir. Fin. Strategies, Inc., Boston. Mem. Weston (Mass.) Planning Bd., 1976—, chmn., 1980, bd. dirs. Fort Ticonderoga Mus. Served to lt. USN, 1960-64. Episcopalian. Clubs: Ausable (N.Y.C.); Country Club (Boston). Home: 2 Willow Rd Weston MA 02193 Office: 108 Union Wharf Boston MA 02109

PELLETIER, JOSEPH ANTHONY, energy co. exec.; b. Chgo., Dec. 18, 1922; s. Joseph A. and Margaret A. (Liston) P.; student St. Ambrose Coll.; B.S.M.E., Iowa State U., 1949; m. Martha I. vonSchrader, May 26, 1944; children—Joseph, Norman, Monica, Martha, Karen. With No. Ind. Public Service Co., Hammond, 1949-72, v.p. engring., constrn. and research, 1972; exec. v.p. Gasco, Inc. subs. Pacific Resources, Inc., Honolulu, 1972-78, pres., 1978—; v.p. Pacific Resources, Inc., Honolulu, 1973-74, sr. v.p., 1974, exec. v.p., 1974-79, pres., chief operating officer, 1979—. Bd. dirs. Jr. Achievement Hawaii, 1973—, ARC, 1980-81; bd. dirs., mem. exec. com. Hawaii Employers Council, 1974—; mem. Hawaii Dist. Export Council, 1977—; trustee Hawaii Army Mus. Soc., 1977—; chmn. energy recovery com. Hawaii Energy Conservation Council, 1978—; mem. exec. com., council commr. Aloha council Boy Scouts Am. Served to 1st lt., inf., U.S. Army, 1943-46, ETO, Korea. Recipient Silver Beaver award Boy Scouts Am.; registered profl. engr., Hawaii, Ind. Mem. Am. Gas Assn., Am. Nuclear Soc., ASME, Assn. U.S. Army, IEEE, Navy League U.S., Oahu Devel. Conf., Pacific Coast Gas Assn. Roman Catholic. Clubs: Oahu Country, Outrigger Canoe, Pacific, Plaza, Rotary (Honolulu). Office: PO Box 3379 Honolulu HI 96842

PELLING, LLOYD LAWRENCE, constrn. co. exec.; b. Chgo., Nov. 3, 1924; s. Lloyd Lawrence and Ruth Teresa (Johnson) P.; B.S., Northwestern U., 1948, M.B.A., 1949; m. Jillian Linnea Breding, June 17, 1950; children—Jill, Victoria, Karen. Asst. to exec. v.p. Container

Corp. Am., Chgo, 1949-53; with L.L. Pelling Co., Inc., Iowa City, 1953—, pres., 1963—; pres., L.L. Pelling Equipment Leasing Corp., 1964—; v.p., dir. Cedar Rapids Asphalt & Paving Co. (Iowa). Bd. dirs. Cedar Rapids-Iowa City area council Girl Scouts U.S. Served with C.E., AUS, 1943-46. Mem. Asphalt Paving Assn. Iowa (dir. 1965-71, pres. 1970), Tau Beta Pi, Beta Gamma Sigma, Alpha Delta Phi. Presbyn. Elk, Rotarian. Club: University Athletic (Iowa City). Home: 2617 Bluffwood Ln Iowa City IA 52240 Office: 2401 Scott Blvd Iowa City IA 52240

PELOQUIN, PAUL EDWARD, personal products mfg. co. exec.; b. Manchester, N.H., Jan. 29, 1945; s. Isidore Edward and Emillienne Josephine (Brisbois) P.; B.S., U. N.H., 1967; m. Lorette R. Duford, Jan. 28, 1967; children—Sara, Matthew. Various systems and programming positions Johnson and Johnson, New Brunswick, N.J., 1967-80; dir. mgmt. info. services Becton Dickinson Consumer Products, Rochelle Park, N.J., 1980—. Cert. data processor. Home: 33 Kory Dr Kendall Park NJ 08824 Office: 365 Passaic St Rochelle Park NJ 07662

PELTIER, PAUL J., mfg. co. exec.; b. St. Louis, Mar. 9, 1919; s. Paul Joseph and Emma (Smith) P.; B.S. in Metall. Engring., Rensselaer Poly. Inst., 1940; grad. Command and Staff Sch., Montgomery, Ala., 1954; M.B.A., George Washington U., 1963; grad. Indsl. Coll. Armed Forces, 1963; m. Edna Lorna Syska, Jan. 3, 1948; children—Peter J., Michael R., Susan M. Metallurgist, Youngstown S & T (Ohio), 1940-41; served with U.S. Air Force, 1941-46, commd. 2d lt., 1951, advanced through grades to col., 1957; air staff officer Pentagon, 1963-66; ret., 1966; pres. Permag Northeast, Waltham, Mass., 1967-77, chmn. parent co. Hicksville, N.Y., 1977—, also treas.; mng. partner Phylss Realty Co., Mchy Co. Decorated Air Force Commendation medal with oak leaf cluster. Home: 2341 Gulf Shore Blvd Naples FL 33940

PELTZ, NELSON, diversified co. exec.; b. N.Y.C., June 24, 1942; s. Maurice Herbert and Claire (Wechsler) P.; student Wharton Sch. Fin., U. Pa., 1960-62; children by previous marriage—Andrew, Brooke. Pres., chief exec. officer APS Food Systems, Inc., N.Y.C., 1970-72, Flagstaff Corp., N.Y.C., 1972-78, Coffee-Mat Corp., Kenilworth, N.J., 1975-76 (merged with Flagstaff Corp. 1976); now pres., chmn. bd., chief exec. officer Trafalgar Industries, N.Y.C.; gen. partner Brook Fund. Trustee, U.S. Olympic Ski Team, 1975—. Mem. Young Pres.'s Orgn. Clubs: Madison Sq. Garden, Old Oaks Country, City Athletic. Office: 600 Madison Ave New York NY 10022

PELTZER, DOUGLAS LEA, semicondr. device mfg. co. exec.; b. Clinton, Ia., July 2, 1938; s. Albert and Mary Ardelle (Messer) P.; B.A., Knox Coll., 1960; M.S., N.M. State U., 1964; m. Nancy Jane Strickler, Dec. 22, 1959; children—Katharine, Eric, Kimberly. Research engr. Gen. Electric Co., Advanced Computer Lab., Sunnyvale, Calif., 1964-67; large scale integrated circuit engr. Fairchild Camera & Instrument, Research & Devel. Lab., Palo Alto, Calif., 1967-70, supervisory engr. bipolar memory devel., Mountain View, Calif., 1970-73, process engring. mgr., bipolar memories div., 1973—, tech. dir., 1977—. NSF fellow, 1962-63; recipient Sherman Fairchild award for tech. excellence, 1980. Mem. AAAS, Sigma Pi Sigma. Inventor in field; patentee in field. Home: 10358 Bonny Dr Cupertino CA 95014 Office: 464 Ellis St Mountain View CA 94040

PENDER, JOHN HURST, ins. co. exec.; b. Washington, May 25, 1930; s. Paul Soloman and Augusta Caroline (Hurst) P.; B.S. in Commerce, St. Louis U., 1952; m. Virginia Mary Woodward, May 11, 1963 (div. 1973); 1 son, David. Investment analyst St. Louis Union Trust Co., 1952-55; portfolio mgr. Am. Asso. Ins. Co., St. Louis, 1955-56; v.p. Baker, Fentress & Co., Chgo., 1956-69; asst. to pres. Union Pacific Corp., N.Y.C., 1969-71; v.p. investments Reliance Ins. Co., Phila., 1971-74; pvt. cons., Phila., 1974-76; sr. v.p. fin. Aid Assn. for Lutherans, Appleton, Wis., 1976—. Trustee Carthage Coll., Kenosha, Wis.; bd. dirs. Appleton Meml. Hosp., 1978—, Fox Cities Arts Alliance; dir. Appleton Devel. Council, 1978—, pres., 1980—. Fellow Fin. Analysts Fedn.; mem. Fox Cities C. of C. (dir.). Lutheran. Clubs: Union League (N.Y.C.); Univ. (Chgo.). Home: 1213 Woodland Ct Appleton WI 54911 Office: 4321 N Ballard Rd Appleton WI 54919

PENDER, MICHAEL ROGER, county ofcl.; b. Bklyn., Feb. 18, 1926; s. Horace G. and Lilian Frances (Higgins) P.; A.B., Dartmouth, M.S. in Civil Engring., 1950; m. Francina Joan Krosschell, June 4, 1949; children—Michael Roger, William J., Robin Jane, Richard A., John A. Project engr. Madigan-Hyland, Inc., N.Y.C., 1950-60; dep. exec. v.p., dir. state exhibits N.Y. World's Fair, N.Y.C., 1960-65; commn. pub. works, Hempstead, N.Y., 1966-74, commn. Gen. Services, 1974-77; commr. pub. works Nassau County, N.Y., 1978—; sec. Hempstead Local Indsl. Devel. Corp., 1967—; treas. Hempstead Indsl. Devel. Agy., 1973—, Nassau County Local Devel. Corp., 1978—; mem. Nassau-Suffolk Bi-County Planning Bd. Served with U.S. Army, 1945-46. Registered profl. engr., N.Y., N.H.; named one of 10 top publ. works ofcls. in U.S., 1973, Met. Civil Engr. of Yr., 1979, N.Y. State Engr. Mgr. of Yr., 1979; recipient Distinguished Service award Town of Hempstead Local Devel. Corp., 1974. Fellow ASCE, Inst. Transp. Engrs.; mem. N.Y. State Assn. Traffic Safety Bds. (past pres.), N.Y. State Assn. County Hwy. Supts., N.Y. State Soc. Profl. Engrs. (pres.), Am. Public Works Assn. (dir.), Am. Water Works Assn., Nat. Assn. County Engrs., N.Y. State Assn. Indsl. Devel. Agys., Inst. Municipal Engrs. (past pres.). Republican. Episcopalian. Clubs: Mineola-Garden City Rotary, Dartmouth Alumni Assn. of L.I., Univ. of L.I. Contbr. articles to profl. jours. Home: 148 Poplar St Garden City NY 11530 Office: 1 West St Mineola NY 11501

PENDER, POLLARD EUGENE, retail exec.; b. Montgomery, La., Feb. 5, 1931; s. Ralph Louis and Ann Marie (Carter) P.; student Northwestern State Coll., Natchitoches, La., 1948-50, Centenary Coll., Shreveport, La., 1950-52; m. Vera Lynelle George, May 4, 1950; children—Jeffrey Scott, Gary Warren. Accountant, Pak-a-Sak Service Stores, Inc., Shreveport, 1950-52, sec.-treas., dir., 1952-71; div. controller Southland Corp., Shreveport, 1971-72, asst. corp. controller, Dallas, 1972, corp. controller, 1973-80, v.p., controller, 1981—; pres. Penro Mobile Homes, Inc.; sec.-treas., dir. Highland Furniture Center, Inc.; dir. United Mercantile Bank; sec.-treas., dir. So. Research Co., Inc. Bd. dirs. Shreveport Mental Health Center, 1964, Shreveport Better Bus. Bur., 1971. Recipient Amelia Earhart Aviation award Zonta Club, 1971; C.P.A., La., Tex. Mem. Soc. C.P.A.'s, Am. Inst. C.P.A.'s, Fin. Execs. Inst. Democrat. Episcopalian. Club: Masons. Home: 7215 Lavendale Circle Dallas TX 75230 Office: 2828 N Haskell St Dallas TX 75204

PENDERGAST, HOWARD EDWARD, indsl. mfg. co. exec.; b. Norwood, Mass., July 23, 1925; s. Raymond Gerard and Marion Josephine (Ortla) P.; B.S. in Chem. Engring., M.I.T., 1950; m. Patricia Shaw, Aug. 26, 1951; children—Margaret S., Mark D., Michael E. Gen. mgr. The Rex Corp., Acton, Mass., 1950-61; v.p. Compo Chem. Co., Waltham, Mass., 1961-64; group v.p. Borden Chem. div. Borden Inc., Columbus, Ohio, 1964-79; v.p. Am. Biltrite Inc., Cambridge, Mass., 1979—; pres. Boston Met. Airport Inc., 1970—. Served with USAAF, 1943-46. Decorated D.F.C., Air medal with four oak leaf clusters. Home: PO Box 525 Waquoit MA 02536 Office: 575 Technology Sq Cambridge MA 02139

PENDERGRAST, ROBIN FRAZIER, public relations co. exec.; b. Oak Park, Ill., June 3, 1945; s. Delbert and Patricia (Frazier) P.; B.A., Bradley U., 1967; M.S., Northwestern U., 1969; numerous continuing edn. courses. With Sta. WMBD-TV-AM, Peoria, Ill., 1965-67; press relations officer Keystone Steel & Wire Co., 1967-68; writer public relations dept. R.J. Reynolds Tobacco Co., Winston-Salem, N.C., 1969-70; v.p. Edelman, Inc., Chgo., 1970-73; account supr. Zylke & Affiliates, Glenview, Ill., 1973-76; exec. v.p. Dienhart Steen Pendergrast, Chgo., 1976—; speaker on public relations, 1974—; free-lance photographer, 1972—. Paramedic, fireman City of Winnetka (Ill.), 1973—, City of Northfield (Ill.), 1978—. Recipient life-saving commendation Village of Northfield, 1979. Mem. Public Relations Soc. Am., Ill. Fireman's Assn. Episcopalian. Contbr. numerous articles on public relations and paramedic/fire dept. fields to profl. publs. Home: 1726 Mount Pleasant St Northfield IL 60093 Office: One E Superior St Chicago IL 60611

PENDSE, KISHOR BALWANT, mfg. co. exec.; b. Poona, India, Nov. 28, 1954; s. Balwant S. and Nirmala B. (Dixit) P.; came to U.S., 1977; B.Tech., Indian Inst. Tech., 1976; M.S. in Indsl. Adminstrn., Carnegie Mellon U., 1979. Engr., Mukand Iron & Steel Works, Bombay, India, 1973; adminstrv. asst. Jaya Jeewan Sdn. Bhd., Kuala Lumpur, Malaysia, 1975; prodn. planning engr. Pressure Cookers & Appliances, Bombay, 1976-77; mktg. analyst KSM div. Omark Industries, Moorestown, N.J., 1978; mfg. analyst J.H. Williams div. TRW Inc., Buffalo, 1979—. Advisor, Jr. Achievement of Western N.Y., 1979—. Recipient Cert. of Recognition, Jr. Achievement. Mem. Nat. Assn. Accts., Assn. M.B.A. Execs. Republican. Hindu. Home: PO Box 22 Hiler Branch Buffalo NY 14223 Office: 400 Vulcan St Buffalo NY 14207

PENICK, EDWARD MOORE, bank exec.; b. Little Rock, Jan. 2, 1922; s. James H. and Mary (Worthen) P.; B.S. in Bus. Adminstrn., U. Ark., 1947, LL.B., 1949; postgrad. Stonier Grad. Sch. Banking Rutgers U., 1954-56, Sch. of Fin. Public Relations, Northwestern U., 1954-56; m. Evelyn; children—Edward M., George, Charles, Lydia. With Worthen Bank & Trust Co., N.A., Little Rock, 1948—, pres., 1961-74, chief exec. officer, 1966-81, chmn., 1974—; pres. First Ark. Bankstock Corp., Little Rock, 1968—, chief exec. officer, chmn., 1974—. Bd. dirs. Central Ark. Radiation Therapy Inst., Inc., 1970-71, Ark. Orch. Soc., 1972-73, Ark. State C. of C., 1972-73, 50 for the Future, 1975-76, Indsl. Devel. Co. of Little Rock, 1975-76; bd. visitors U. Ark., Little Rock, 1975-76; chmn. Metro Centre Mall Improvement Dist. Commn., 1975-76; trustee Trinity Cathedral Parrish. Served with USAF, 1941-45. Decorated D.F.C., Air medal with 3 oak leaf clusters. Mem. Ark. Bankers Assn. (pres. 1967-68), Bank Public Relations & Mktg. Assn. (pres. 1967-68), Assn. Res. City Bankers, Am. Bankers Assn., Assn. Bank Holding Cos.

PENNA, GILBERTO AFFONSO, publishing co. exec.; b. Minas Gerais, Brazil, Dec. 29, 1916; s. Affonso, Jr. and Marieta (Pinto) P.; LL.B., U. Brazil, 1938; m. Wanda Batista, Jan. 26, 1946; children—Maria Beatriz, Gilberto Affonso, Antonio Augusto, Ana Maria. Practiced law, Rio de Janeiro, 1938-43; dir. Radiocomunicacoes-Aerovias Brazil, Rio de Janeiro, 1943-45; consultor Tecnico de Radio-Linha Aerea Transcontinental Brasileira, 1945-47; dir. Responsavel-Revista Antenna, 1941—; founder, dir. Responsavel-Revista Electronica Popular, 1956—; sr. mng. dir. Antenna Edicões Técnicas Ltda., 1956—. Vice pres. Conselho Fed. de Telecomunicacoes, 1961. Pres. Associacao Brasileira de Telecomunicacoes, 1953-54. Recipient Golden Plate award Escola Comunicações Exército, 1976, Ministério das Comunicações, 1980. Mem. Soc. for Tech. Communication (sr.), Liga de Amadores Brasileiros de Radio Emissao Labre (life), Associacao de Radioamadores de Petropolis (benemerit), Group Priano de CW (medal of merit), Associacao Brasileira de Normas Tecnicas, Associacao Brasileira de Imprensa, Ordem dos Advogados do Brasil. Clubs: Ubatuba Iate, Xadrez de Araruama. Author, editor: ABC do Radio, 1948; Curso Pratico de Televisao, 1953; O Transistor E Assim, 1968; Guia Pratico do Reparador de TV, 1955; Artigos Técnicos de Eletrônica, 1979; numerous others. Office: 143 Ave Mal Floriano Rio de Janeiro RJ 20080 Brazil

PENNELL, CARROLL EDWARD, II, bank exec.; b. Brunswick, Maine, Aug. 12, 1934; s. Andrew Simpson and Alice Maria (Coffin) P.; A.B., Bowdoin Coll., 1956; M.B.A., N.Y. U., 1973; m. Nancy Wheelan Sutliff, Sept. 3, 1966; children—Andrew Sutliff, Samuel Stuart. Project supr. Cole, Layer-Trumble Co., Dayton, Ohio, 1959-63; adminstrv. asst. Investors Central Mgmt. Corp., N.Y.C., 1963-64; chief real estate appraiser Empire Savs. Bank, N.Y.C., 1964-73; real estate officer New England Merchants Nat. Bank, Boston, 1973-79; chief appraiser comml. real estate, partner C.W. Whittier and Bro., Boston, 1979—; instr. Univ. Coll. Northeastern U., Boston; dir. Unit-Nat. Assos.; cons. in field. Served with U.S. Army, 1957-58. Mem. Columbia Soc. Real Estate Appraisers, Beta Theta Pi. Republican. Congregationalist. Clubs: St. Bartholomew's Community; Sons of Am. Revolution, Bowdoin (Boston); Royal Ascot Soc. Home: 12 Cottonwood Rd Wellesley MA 02181 Office: 1 Federal St Boston MA 02110

PENNELLA, FRANCIS JOHN, banker; b. Port Chester, N.Y., Oct. 6, 1943; s. Francis R. and Florence C. (Covino) P.; B.S., Ithaca Coll., 1968; M.B.A., Fordham U., 1972; m. Barbara Jacoby, Nov. 6, 1971. Mgmt. trainee Marine Midland Bank, N.Y.C., 1968-70, research and devel. officer, 1970-71, asst. v.p., 1971-74, v.p., 1974-78, v.p. and dir. human resources Eastern region, 1978-80, adminstrv. v.p., 1980—. Bd. dirs. Archeus Found., N.Y.C.; v.p., treas. Iconn Erie Found. Mem. N.Y. State Bankers Assn. (com. on personnel policies), N.Y. Personnel Mgrs. Assn. Clubs: Whippoorwill, City Midday. Home: 54 Tamarack Rd Port Chester NY 10573 Office: Marine Midland Bank 140 Broadway New York NY 10015

PENNELLA, WILLIAM ANDREW, marine transp. and terminal co. exec.; b. Newark, Mar. 30, 1945; s. William Rocco and Marie Theresa (Rastelli) P.; B.A. in Psychology, Rutgers U., 1968; m. Joan Bukovez, June 1, 1968; children—William, Jennifer, James. Mgr. salary adminstrn. Sea-Land Service, Inc., Elizabeth, N.J., 1968-71; personnel dir. Global Terminal & Container Services, Inc., Jersey City, 1971-73, dir. adminstrv. services, 1973-77, v.p. corporate services, 1977—. Bd. trustees Christ Hosp., 1979—, Nat. Alliance of Bus., 1975-80, Jersey City Mayor's Adv. Com., 1978-79. Served with USAR, 1968-74. Recipient Meritorious award Nat. Alliance of Bus., 1977; Disting. Service to Bus. and Edn. award Jersey City State Coll., 1979. Mem. Am. Mgmt. Assn., Conf. Bd., Am. Soc. Indsl. Security, Hudson County C. of C. (trustee). Club: Masons. Home: 5 Meadowbrook Ln Freehold NJ 07728 Office: PO Box 273 Jersey City NJ 07303

PENNER, ELMER JOHN, aircraft and missile mfg. co. exec.; b. Wolf Point, Mont., Aug. 10, 1923; s. Peter Edward and Eva (Vogt) P.; B.T., Tex. State Tech. Inst., 1971; M.B.A., Nat. U., San Diego, 1975; m. Louise H. Nickel, May 3, 1946; children—Carolyn, Ronald, Steven, Susan. With Convair div. Gen. Dynamics, San Diego, 1942—, mgr. prodn. engring. 1975—. Served with USAAF, 1943-46; PTO. Registered profl. engr., Calif. Mem. Nat. Mgmt. Assn. Republican. Home: 5674 Raymar Ave San Diego CA 92120 Office: 3302 Pacific Hwy San Diego CA 92138

PENNEY, CHARLES RAND, lawyer, civic worker; b. Buffalo, July 26, 1923; s. Charles Patterson and Gretchen (Rand) P.; B.A., Yale, 1945; LL.B., U. Va., 1951; J.D., U. Va., 1970. Admitted to Md. bar, 1952, N.Y. bar, 1958; U.S. Supreme Ct. bar, 1958; law sec. to U.S. Dist. Judge W.C. Coleman, Balt., 1951-52; dir. devel. office Children's Hosp., Buffalo, 1952-54; sales mgr. Amherst Mfg. Corp., Williamsville, N.Y., 1954-56, also Delevan Electronics Corp., E. Aurora, N.Y.; mem. firm Penney & Penney, Buffalo, 1958-61; individual practice, Niagra County, N.Y., 1961—. Hon. bd. mgrs., mem. art com. Meml. Art Gallery, U. Rochester (N.Y.); mem. Niagara Council Arts. Served to 2d lt. U.S. Army, 1943-46. Life mem. Albright-Knox Art Gallery, Buffalo, Patteran Artists (hon.), Niagara County Hist. Soc., Buffalo Museum Sci., Buffalo and Erie County Hist. Soc.; mem. Niagara County Bar Assn., Assn. Am. Artists, Historic Lockport (life), Nat. Trust Historic Preservation, Gallery Assn. N.Y., Kenan Center, Archives of Am. Art, Historic Lewiston, Victorian Soc. Am., Asso. Art Museums Western N.Y., Buffalo Soc. Artists (hon. trustee), Met. Mus. Art N.Y., Mus. Modern Art N.Y., Smithsonian Instn., Old Fort Niagara Assn. (life), Niagra Falls Area C. of C., Calif. Palace of Legion of Honor, Asian Art Mus. San Francisco), Cobblestone Soc., Internat. Mus. Photography, Rochester (N.Y.) Hist. Soc., Chautauqua (N.Y.) Art Assn., Nat. Archives of U.S., Mark Twain Soc. (hon.), Asia Soc., Japan Soc., Pierpont Morgan Library, Am. Mus. Natural History, Cooper-Hewitt Mus., Columbus (Ohio) Mus. Art, Community Music Sch., Mus. Am. Folk Art, Solomon R. Guggenheim Mus., M.H. DeYoung Meml. Mus., Chi Psi, Phi Alpha Delta. Presbyterian (deacon). Clubs: Zwicker Aquatic (Lockport); Niagara County Antiques (hon. life); Automobile; Intrepids; U. Iowa President's Club. Editorial bd. Art Gallery Mag. Address: 343 Bewley Bldg Lockport NY 14094

PENNINGTON, BRUCE CARTER, mgmt. communications cons.; b. Kansas City, Mo., Oct. 22, 1932; s. Dwight Hillis and Esther Helena (Carter) P.; B.A., Kenyon Coll., 1953; postgrad. U. So. Calif., 1957; m. Gloria Anne Artinian, July 1, 1960; children—Bruce Carter, Juliet Jean, Adam Dwight. Feature writer, book reviewer Kansas City Star, 1947-62; brakeman Santa Fe R.R., 1952; TV story editor Universal Studios and Four-Star Studios, Los Angeles, 1956-59; writer Time Mag., Beverly Hills, Calif., 1959; feature writer CBS-TV Network, Los Angeles, 1960-63; free-lance writer, producer, Los Angeles, 1963-65; dir. new TV programs Benton & Bowles, Los Angeles, 1964-65; dir. TV program devel. Grey Advt., N.Y.C., 1966-67; dir. TV spls. BBDO, N.Y.C., 1967-68; producer Sesame Street, 1969; TV program mgr. Needham, Harper & Steers, N.Y.C., 1969-70; communications cons., TV producer NAM, Washington, 1971-73; communications cons. career edn. Office of Edn., HEW, Washington, 1973-74; communications cons., dir. mgmt. communications Am. Can Co., Greenwich, Conn., 1974-76; founder, v.p., mng. dir. corp. communications div. Young & Rubicam, Inc., 1976-77; v.p., partner Chester Burger & Co., N.Y.C., 1978—. Officer, Hastings-on-Hudson Vol. Fire Dept. Served with U.S. Army, 1953-55. Recipient award U.S. Indsl. Film Festival, 1977, award Freedoms Found., 1954; fellow Cambridge Inst. Applied Research, 1975. Mem. Public Relations Soc. Am., Mensa, Beta Theta Pi. Episcopalian. Home: 41 S Driveway Hastings-on-Hudson NY 10706 Office: 275 Madison Ave New York NY 10016

PENNINGTON, MALCOLM WHITTIER, mgmt. cons.; b. Cleve., Mar. 12, 1930; s. Gordon Riddle and Ruth Whittier (Duffie) P.; B.A., Cornell U., 1952; M.B.A., Columbia U., 1961; m. Jean Anne Zimmer, Oct. 10, 1964; 1 dau., Deborah Dukes. Systems analyst IBM Corp., 1957-59; asso. Joel Dean Assos., 1961-62; v.p. Bus. Internat. Corp., 1962-65; v.p. Golightly & Co. Internat., Inc., N.Y.C., 1965-70; pres. Mktg. and Planning Group, Inc., N.Y.C., 1971—; dir. Kikkoman Foods, Inc., Walworth, Wis. Pres., dir. Jose Limon Dance Co., N.Y.C., 1979—. Served to maj. USAF, 1952-57. Mem. Soc. Applied Econs. (pres. 1980), N.Am. Soc. Corp. Planning (v.p. 1981—). Club: Union League. Editor Planning Rev., 1973—. Address: 160 W 77th St New York NY 10024

PENNINGTON, TERRY LEE, cons., lectr.; b. Sioux City, Iowa, Aug. 5, 1939; s. Lee Earl and Florence M. (Orr) P.; student Portland State Coll., 1957-58, 62-64, U. Minn. Extension Div., 1958-62; m. Karyn Ann Boom, Aug. 12, 1960; children—Julie Ann, Terry Lee, Edward Lee. Exec. mgmt. trainee, supr. San Francisco Fed. Res. Bank, Portland (Oreg.) br., 1963-64; sr. fin. clk. Steelcase of Oreg. Inc., Portland, 1964-65; fin./adminstrv. mgr. McCann-Erickson, Inc., Portland, 1966-68, Los Angeles, 1969-71; treas. Chiat/Day, Inc., Los Angeles, 1972-73; v.p. Mealer & Emerson, Inc., Whittier, Calif., 1973-75; pres. Terry L. Pennington & Co., Inc., Fullerton, Calif., 1975-80; mktg. and communications cons., 1980—; lectr. on mktg. communications Calif. State U., Fullerton. Alt. del. Calif. Republican Central Com., 1976-78. Served with USN, 1958-62. Mem. Western States Advt. Agy. Assn. (pres. 1977-79, chmn. bd. 1979-80, organizer Inst. at Calif. State U. extension div., Fullerton 1978; recipient various service awards); founder, organizer, treas. Western States Advt. Agency Assn. Fed. Credit Union 1973-74, also recipient various service awards), Adminstrv. Soc. (dir. Los Angeles chpt. 1974-75). Home: 1201 W Northwood Ave Brea CA 92621 Office: PO Box 1237 Brea CA 92621

PENNOCK, DONALD WILLIAM, engr.; b. Ludlow, Ky., Aug. 8, 1915; s. Donald and Melvin (Evans) P.; B.S. in M.E., U. Ky., 1940, M.E., 1948; m. Vivian C. Kern, Aug. 11, 1951; 1 son, Douglas. Stationary engring., constrn. and maintenance Schenley Corp., 1935-39; mech. equipment design engr. mech. lab. U. of Ky., 1939; exptl. test engr. Wright Aero. Corp., Paterson, N.J., 1940, 1941, investigative and adv. engr. to personnel div., 1941-43; indsl. engr. Eastern Aircraft, div. Gen. Motors, Linden, N.J., 1943-45; factory engr. Carrier Corp., Syracuse, N.Y., 1945-58, sr. facilities engr., 1958-60, corporate material handling engr., 1960-63, mgr. facilities engring. dept., 1963-66, mgr. archtl. engring., 1966-68, mgr. facilities engring. dept., 1966-78. Staff, Indsl. Mgmt. Center, 1962, midwest work course U. Kan., 1959-67. Mem. munitions bd. SHIAC, 1950-52. Elected to Exec. and Profl. Hall of Fame, 1966. Registered profl. engr., Ky., N.J., D.C. Mem. Soc. Advancement Mgmt. (life mem., nat. v.p. material handling div. 1953-54), Am. Soc. M.E., Am. Material Handling Soc. (dir. 1950-57, chmn. bd., pres. 1950-52), Am. Soc. Mil. Engrs., Nat. Soc. Profl. Engrs., Am. Mgmt. Assn. (men. packaging council 1950-55, life mem. planning council), Nat. Material Handling Conf. (exec. com. 1951), Tau Beta Pi. Protestant. Mng. editor Materials Handling Engring. (mag. sect.), 1949-50; mem. editorial adv. bd. Modern Materials Handling (mag.), 1949-52. Contbr. articles to tech. jours. Contbg., cons. editor: Materials Handling Handbook, 1958. Home: 24 Pebble Hill Rd Dewitt NY 13214

PENROSE, GILBERT QUAY, financial planning co. exec.; b. Robinson, Pa., Sept. 8, 1938; s. Albert Snyder and Olive Jeanette (Boring) P.; B.S. in Chem. Engring., Pa. State U., 1960; m. Anna Mae Riffle, Aug. 22, 1959; children—Kim Denise, Kevin Lee, Kara Lynn. Registered rep. Investors Diversified Services, 1969-70, div. mgr., Huntington, W.Va., 1972-73, Miami, 1973-76; regional mgr. S. Fla., Westamerica Fin. Corp., Miami Lakes, 1976—; pres. Gilbert Penrose & Assos., Inc., Certified Fin. Planners, Miami, 1976—, South Pitts. Mgmt. Co., So. Fla. Mgmt. Co., Inc.; pres., chmn. bd. Three K Investments, Inc., B.P.R., Inc., Five Star Concepts, Inc., Columbus Mgmt. Co. Inc., Pitts. Mgmt. Co. Inc., Penrose Internat., Inc.; chmn.

bd. Exec. Investments & Ins. Group, Inc. Bd. dirs. Miami Lakes Civic Assn., 1975-76. Certified fin. planner; registered investment adviser SEC. Mem. Internat. Assn. Fin. Planners, Assn. Certified Fin. Planners. Home: 17531 SW 68th Ct Fort Lauderdale FL 33331 Office: Suite 510 1840 W 49th St Hialeah FL 33012

PEPE, JOHN MICHAEL, mfg. co. exec.; b. N.Y.C., June 17, 1939; s. Michael P. and Lillian M. (Martini) P.; B.B.A., St. John's U., 1960; M.B.A., Am. Internat. Coll., 1979; m. Patricia DeMaio, Apr. 28, 1962; children—John (dec.), Elizabeth, Lorraine, Christopher. Auditor, Arthur Andersen & Co., N.Y.C., 1960-64, Hartford, Conn., 1964-67; asst. controller Am. Bosch div. Ambac Industries, Springfield, Mass., 1967-70; controller Diesel & Fluid Power Group, Ambac SpA, Castenedolo, Italy, 1970-76; controller Schrader Bellows Automation Products Group, Scovill Inc., Akron, Ohio, 1976—. Mem. Am. Inst. Corp. Controllers. Home: 91 Mayfield Ave Akron OH 44313 Office: 200 W Exchange St Akron OH 44309

PEPER, CHRISTIAN B(AIRD), lawyer; b. St. Louis, Dec. 5, 1910; s. Clarence F. and Christine (Baird) P.; A.B., Harvard, 1932; LL.B., Washington U., 1935; LL.M. (Sterling fellow), Yale, 1937; m. Ethel C. Kingsland, June 5, 1935; children—Catherine K., Anne C., Christian B. Admitted to Mo. bar, 1934, since practiced in St. Louis; partner Peper, Martin, Jensen, Maichel & Hetlage; lectr. various subjects Wash. U. Law Sch., 1943-61; partner A.G. Edwards & Sons, 1945-67; chmn. St. Louis Steel Casting Inc., Hydraulic Press Brick Co. vis. com. Harvard Divinity Sch., 1964-70; trustee St. Louis Art Mus. Mem. Am., Mo., St. Louis bar assns., Order of Coif, Phi Delta Phi. Roman Catholic. Clubs: Noonday, University, Harvard (St. Louis); East India (London). Contbr. articles to law jours. Home: 1454 Mason Rd St Louis MO 63141 Office: 720 Olive St St Louis MO 63101

PEPITONE, JOSEPH PHILIP, beverage co. exec.; b. Bklyn., Oct. 22, 1944; s. Philip Anthony and Santina Teresa (LoGelfo) P.; student Fullerton Jr. Coll., 1965-66, Nassau Community Coll., 1966-67; B.B.A., Hofstra U., 1969; m. Ellen Shaw, July 31, 1969; children—Jason Scott, Morgan Lance. Budget coordinator/asst. account exec. Ogilvy & Mather Advt., Inc., N.Y.C., 1970-71; account exec. Schweppes U.S.A. Ltd., Ogilvy & Mather Advt., Inc., N.Y.C., 1971-72; pres. Beverage King, Inc., beverage-convenience store franchise chain, Ft. Lauderdale, Fla., 1972—; pres. World of Beverages Inc., Ft. Lauderdale, 1978—, Subway Systems of Oakland Park Inc. (Fla.), 1979—; v.p. Diversified Beverages Inc., Ft. Lauderdale, 1977—, Equipment Solution Group Inc., Ft. Lauderdale, 1979—; cons. in field. Voting mem. Boca Raton (Fla.) Acad., 1976—. Mem. Nat. Hist. Soc., Nat. Geog. Soc., Sigma Alpha Mu. Club: Boca Del Mar Golf and Country. Contbr. articles to profl. jours. Home: 22247 Alyssum Way Boca Raton FL 33432 Office: 1545 E Commercial Blvd Fort Lauderdale FL 33334

PEPONIS, JAMES ARTHUR, telephone co. exec.; b. Chgo., Sept. 28, 1934; s. Arthur H. and Ethel A. (Karambis) P.; B.S., Northwestern U., 1956, M.B.A., 1979; m. Catherine Coulolias, Aug. 22, 1959; children—Nancy Ellen, Arthur James. With Linde div. Union Carbide Corp., Chgo., 1956-59, Plaza Cleaners & Dyers, Inc., Chgo., 1959-62; div. mgr. Ill. Bell Telephone Co., Chgo., 1962—, mktg. dir., 1978—. Dist. chmn., exec. bd. Chgo. council Boy Scouts Am., 1965-68; mem. archdiocesan council Greek Orthodox Archdiocese of N. and S.Am., 1977—; mem. exec. com. United Hellenic Am. Congress, 1979—; gen. chmn. Greek Heritage Week, 1980; bd. dirs. Wilmette Baseball Assn., 1980. Served with inf., U.S. Army, 1958-59, to lt. USNG, 1958-66. Recipient Erickson trophy Army N.G. Bur. of U.S., 1961, award of Merit, Boy Scouts Am., 1968. Mem. Western Soc. Engrs., Am. Mktg. Assn. Greek Orthodox. Club: Masons. Home: 723 Sheridan Rd Wilmette IL 60091 Office: HQ9A 225 W Randolph St Chicago IL 60606

PEPPER, DONALD GENE, banker; b. Cambridge, Ohio, Mar. 27, 1931; s. Cecil Calvert and Clara Hazel (Pryor) P.; B.A. in Social Scis., Ohio State U., 1956; postgrad. U. Mich., 1957, Xavier U., 1958; m. Joan Irwin Busby, June 10, 1952; children—Andrea Jane, Dawn Elnora. With Park Nat. Bank, Newark, Ohio, 1949-51, Huntington Nat. Bank, Columbus, Ohio, 1954-56; with Fifth Third Bank, Cin., 1957—, sr. v.p. adminstrn., treas., 1968—; instr. Am. Inst. Banking. Served with Fin. Corps, U.S. Army, 1951-54. Mem. Am. Soc. for Indsl. Security, Bank Adminstrn. Inst., Am. Inst. Banking, Fin. Execs. Inst., Delta Sigma Pi (hon.). Club: Bankers (Cin.). Office: Fifth Third Bank 38 Fountain Square Plaza Cincinnati OH 45202

PEPPLER, ALICE STOLPER, publishing co. exec.; b. Saginaw, Mich., Mar. 14, 1934; d. Lothar E. and Hulda M. (Koenig) Stolper; B.S., Concordia Tchrs. Coll., River Forest, Ill., 1956; postgrad. U. Ill., 1966-67; children—Jeanne, Jon, Jan. Elementary sch. tchr., librarian, music dir. Bethany Lutheran Sch., Chgo., 1956-63; editor lang. arts materials Scott, Foresman & Co., Chgo., 1963-71; sr. editor lang. arts materials Lyons & Carnahan, Chgo., 1972-74; mktg. mgr. lang. arts, fgn. langs. and social studies Rand McNally & Co., Chgo., 1974-77, also ednl. cons. coordinator; mktg. mgr. lang. arts Scott, Foresman & Co., Chgo., 1977—; piano tchr., 1956-63; condr. workshops, 1970—. Organist, music dir. First Luth. Ch. of the Trinity, 1967-76; organist, choir dir. Mt. Olive Luth. Ch., Chgo., 1976—. Mem. Internat. Reading Assn., Nat. Council Tchrs. English, Nat., Luth. edn. assns., Author: Bible Children I Know, 1971; God's Love for Everyone, 1971; Why Jesus Came, 1972; Divorced and Christian, 1974; Single Again—This Time With Children, 1981; also articles, poems, monograph; editor Luth. Edn. Assn. Yearbook, 1972-74. Home: 5851 W Henderson St Chicago IL 60634 Office: 1900 E Lake Ave Glenview IL 60025

PERANSKI, ROBERT ZIGMUNT, ins. exec.; b. San Diego, Nov. 20, 1935; s. Zigmunt T. and Velma N. (Patterson) P.; A.B., San Diego City Coll., 1959; m. Virginia A. Bianchi, Dec. 1, 1955; children—Lawrence R., Stephen M., Richard A. With Hartford Life Ins. Co., Boston and San Francisco, 1961-67; dir. mktg. adminstrn. New Eng. Life, Boston, 1967-76; asst. v.p. Life Ins. Co. of Va., Richmond, 1976-79; v.p. 1st Farwest Life Ins. Co., Farwest Am. Assurance Co., Portland, Oreg., 1979—. Served with USAF, 1954-57. Recipient Heritage award United Way of Mass. Bay, 1975. Mem. Portland (Oreg.) Assn. Life Underwriters, Nat. Assn. Life Underwriters. Republican. Roman Catholic. Clubs: Kiwanis, Rock Creek Country. Home: 15520 SW Bristol Ave Beaverton OR 97007 Office: 400 SW 6th Ave Portland OR 97208

PERCHICK, L. STEPHAN, wig importing co. exec.; b. Phila., Aug. 21, 1941; s. George and Sylvia (Cohen) P.; Asso. Sci., Temple U., 1961, B.S., 1964, M.B.A., 1967; m. Rochelle Toll, June 26, 1965; children—Tracey, Gregg. Nat. sales mgr. N. Wagman & Co., Phila., 1966-71; pres. L. Stephen Perchick Sales Agy. Inc., Phila., 1971-80; territorial rep. Wild Oats Jeans Co., Phila., from 1977; distbr. Revlon Gen. Wig Co., Phila., from 1976; East Coast, So. territorial rep. Fashion Leader Products, 1978; East Coast rep. André Douglas Line, 1979; chmn. Amekor Industries, Conshohocken, Pa., 1980—. Dir. elections dist. 4, City of Phila.; adv. Greater Phila. Korean Assn., 1979-80. Served with U.S. Army, 1966. Mem. Am. Mktg. Assn., Am. Wig Assn. (Man of Yr. award 1979), Internat. Entrepreneurs Assn., Phila. Jaycees. Contbr. articles to Phila. Inquirer, Phila. Bull., Daily News. Office: 3 Union Hill Rd West Conshohocken PA 19428

PERCHICK, MITCHELL, dental lab. exec.; b. Bklyn., Apr. 25, 1947; s. Hyman and Blanche (Lotus) P.; A.A.S., N.Y. Community Coll. Applied Arts and Scis., 1966; m. Paula Joan Zeppenick, Mar. 28, 1970; 1 dau., Heather Lynn. Technician, Tri-Tech Dental Lab., Bklyn., 1966-70; gold technician Charles Blechner Dental Lab., N.Y.C., 1970-72; ceramic gold technician Magna Dental Lab., N.Y.C., 1972-75; owner, v.p. Progressive Dental Labs., Inc., N.Y.C., 1975—. Mem. N.Y. Dental Lab. Assn. (cert. dental technician), Nat. Assn. Dental Labs., N.Y. Guild Dental Craftsmen. Office: Progressive Dental Labs 57 W 57th St New York NY 10019

PEREDA, EUGENE FALERO, antenna co. exec.; b. Juncos, P.R., Dec. 25, 1909; s. Clemente Pereda Santisteban and Juana Falero Robles; B.S. in Math., George Peabody Coll., 1937; B.S. in Elec. Engring., U. Tenn., 1951; postgrad. Drexel U., 1956-57, Syracuse U., 1955-56, U. N.Mex., 1959-66; m. Clementina Santisteban, Apr. 24, 1950; 1 dau., Maria. Engr., Submarine Base, Kittery, Mass., 1951-52; radar engr. Gen. Electric Co., Syracuse, 1952-54, Rome Air Devel. Center (N.Y.), 1954-56; engr. Martin Co., Balt., 1957-58; asst. prof. elec. engring. U. S.W. La., 1958-59; scientist, Kirtland AFB, Albuquerque, 1959-66; engr. Bell Aerosystems, Ft. Huachuca, Ariz., 1966-67; missile engr. U.S. Naval Weapons Center, Seal Beach, Calif., 1967-72; ret., 1972, pres., owner, operator Sky-Slot Antenna Design Co., Albuquerque, 1972—; cons. in field. Served with USNR, 1942-46. DuPont scholar, 1932-33. Mem. IEEE, AIAA, Nat. Soc. Profl. Engrs., Am. Assn. Med. Instrumentation, AAUP. Democrat. Patentee; inventor liquid air engine. and Office: 11621 Hughes Ave NE Albuquerque NM 87112

PEREIRA, RONALD MANUEL, petroleum co. exec.; b. Sandusky, Ohio, Sept. 20, 1938; s. Antonio and Helen (Miller) P.; B.A., Cornell U., 1960; M.B.A., Columbia U., 1965; B.S. in Acctg., U. Miami (Fla.), 1976; m. Carolyn Kenney, Mar. 28, 1962; children—Charles Manuel, William Wyatt. Corporate internal auditor The Singer Co., N.Y.C., 1965, cost acctg. supr., Power Tool Div., Pickens, S.C., 1966; fin. analyst Esso InterAm., Coral Gables, Fla., 1967-69; fin. mgr. Esso Paraguay, Asuncion, 1970-72; sr. acct. Esso Caribbean, Coral Gables, 1973-76; ops. acct., 1977—. Active Coconut Grove Civic Club, Miami, 1972-79. Served with USN, 1960-63; to lt. comdr. USNR, 1977-79. Recipient Danforth Found. award, 1956; Delta Upsilon Leadership award, 1960; Navy ROTC scholar, 1956-60; C.P.A., Fla. Mem. Coconut Grove C. of C., Nat. Assn. Accts., Fla. Soc. C.P.A.'s, Am. Inst. C.P.A.'s, Naval Reserve Assn., Fla. Hort. Soc., Rare Fruit and Vegetable Council Broward County, Delta Upsilon. Republican. Episcopalian. Clubs: Rare Fruit Council, Internat. Fairchild Tropical Garden; Miami Men's Garden. Home: 111 Prospect Dr Coral Gables FL 33133 Office: 396 Alhambra Circle Coral Gables FL 33134

PERELLE, IRA B., psychologist; b. Mt. Vernon, N.Y., Sept. 16, 1925; s. Joseph Yale and Lillian (Schaffer) P.; student U. Tex.; postgrad. RCA Inst., 1951; B.S., M.S., Ph.D., Fordham U.; m. Mar. 17, 1946 (div. 1956); children—Ronnie Jean, Robert Jeffrey. Prodn. mgr. Arden Jewelry Case Co., 1946-49; became chief engr. Westlab Electronic Engrs., 1949; partner Westlab, 1954; pres. Westlab, Inc., 1955-64, chmn. bd., 1956; dir. Teleponce Inc., Ponce, P.R.; exec. dir. Atlantic Research Inst.; pres. Westchester Research and Devel. Labs.; exec. dir. Interlink, Ltd.; dir. Mid-Hudson Inst., 1975—; cons. ednl. tech. Fordham U., Bayamon (P.R.) Central U., World U.; research cons. Bd. Coop. Ednl. Services, Westchester County, N.Y., Mt. Vernon Public Schs., Readers Digest; mem. faculty Mercy Coll., Dobbs Ferry, N.Y., N.Y. U., L.I. U., SUNY, Purchase; former mem. faculty Fordham U. Mem. N.Y. State Edn. Com. Assn. Mem. staff Civil Def., 1954-72. Served as radio instr. USAAF, 1943-46. Mem. I.E.E.E., N.Y. Zool. Soc., Audio Engring. Soc., Acoustical Soc. Am., Am. Inst. Physics, Am. Psychol. Assn., Am. Ednl. Research Assn., Assn. Ednl. Communication and Tech., Am. Genetic Assn., Animal Behavior Soc., N.Y. Acad. Sci., Kappa Delta Pi, Psi Chi, Delta Mu Delta. Author: A Practical Guide to Educational Media for the Classroom Tchrs., 1974. Contbr. articles to profl. jours. Home: 1234 Midland Ave Bronxville NY 10708 Office: Mid-Hudson Inst 555 Broadway Dobbs Ferry NY

PERELMAN, LEON JOSEPH, paper mfg. co. exec.; b. Phila., Aug. 28, 1911; s. Morris and Jennie (Davis) P.; B.A., La Salle Coll., 1933; postgrad. Law Sch. U. Pa., 1933-35; L.H.D., Dropsie U., 1976; m. Beverly Waxman, Jan. 27, 1945 (div. Apr. 1960); children—Cynthia, David. Partner Am. Paper Products Co., Phila., 1935-42, 45—; pres. Am. Paper Products Inc., Phila., 1968—; pres. Am. Cone & Tube Co. Inc., Phila., 1953—; v.p. Esslinger Inc., Phila., 1961-64, United Ammunition Container, Inc., Phila.; vice chmn. bd. Belmont Industries, Phila.; pres. Dropsie U., 1976-77. Fin. chmn. Valley Forge council Boy Scouts Am., 1969; founder, dir. Perelman Antique Toy Museum, Phila. Bd. dirs. Akiba Hebrew Acad., United Hias Service; trustee, pres. West Park Hosp., Phila. Served to 1st lt. USAAF, 1942-45. Recipient citation Jewish Theol. Sem., 1965; Beth Jacob award, 1966; Soc. Fellows award, 1969. Mem. Am. Ordnance Assn., Franklin Inst., Am. Assn. Museums, Nat. Trust Historic Preservations. Jewish religion. Clubs: Masons, Shriners, Union League (Phila.). Home: 339 Winding Way Merion PA 19066 Office: 2113-41 E Rush St Philadelphia PA 19134

PERERA, PHILLIPS, investment banker; b. Boston, Sept. 26, 1933; s. Guido Rinaldo and Faith (Phillips) P.; A.B., Harvard, 1955; diplôme in Indsl. Mgmt., Centred' Etudes Industrielles, 1961; m. Frederica Plimpton Drinkwater, Dec. 22, 1962; children—Phillips, Frederica Sophia, Christopher Davis, Alexander Lorenzo. Trainee Morgan et Cie., Paris, Am. Export Lines, N.Y.C., First Nat. Bank of Boston, 1958-63; indsl. economist Arthur D. Little Inc., Cambridge, Mass., 1963-68; dir. authorizations and acting dep. dir. ops. Office of Fgn. Dir. Investment, Dept. Commerce, Washington, 1968-69; pres. Internat. Liquidities Inc., fin. cons., Washington, 1971-72; v.p. corporate devel. Am. Express Co., N.Y.C., 1972-74; sr. v.p., dir. Donaldson, Lufkin, Jenrette and Co., N.Y.C., 1975; pres. Phillips Perera & Co., Inc., pvt. investment bankers, N.Y.C., 1976—; former dir. Am. Express Investment Mgmt. Co., 1972-74; dir. Club Med. Inc., 1972-74; spl. cons. UN, 1967-68, AID, 1969; cons. Orgn. Am. States on Devel. Fin., 1976. Served to capt. USAF, 1956-58. Clubs: Knickerbocker (N.Y.C.); Met. (Washington); Somerset (Boston). Contbr. articles to profl. jours.; author: Development Finance-Institutions, Problems and Prospects, 1968. Home: 150 Sarles St Mount Kisco NY 10549 Office: Suite 270 200 Park Ave New York NY 10017

PEREYO, MIGUEL ANGEL, mech. engr.; b. Humacao, P.R., Nov. 23, 1941; s. Jose F. Pereyo and Luz Pereyo Torrellas; B.S. in Mech. Engring., U. P.R., 1963; M.B.A., Catholic U. P.R., 1974; m. Ivonne Negron, Apr. 8, 1967; children—Ivonne Elizabeth, Miguel Jose, Roberto Jose. Field service engr. Babcock & Wilcox Co., N.Y.C., 1965-67; plant supt. Fibras Ceramicas, Inc., Ponce, P.R., 1967-69; pres., treas. Fibras Ceramicas, Inc./Productos De Caolin, Ponce, 1969-77, dir., 1969—; mgr. ceramic fibers Babcock & Wilcox Co., Augusta, Ga., 1977—. Bd. dirs. Dr. Pila Health Hosp., Ponce, 1975-77. Served with AUS, 1963-65. Mem. ASME, Thermal Insulation Mfrs. Assn. Roman Catholic. Clubs: West Lake Country (Augusta); Ponce Yacht. Address: 4 Fox Creek Dr North Augusta SC 29841

PEREZ, JOSE ANTONIO, savs. and loan exec.; b. Rio Piedras, P.R., Nov. 23, 1942; s. Jose Antonio and Nemy (Torres) Perez-Fiz; B.B.A., U. P.R., 1964; m. Margarita Jimenez de Perez, Sept. 4, 1965; children—Jose Antonio, Tomas E., Maria Margarita, Isabel M. Loan officer United Fed. Savs. & Loan Assn., San Juan, P.R., 1964-74, v.p., 1971-74; pres., dir. Pan Am. Fed. Savs. & Loan Assn., Rio Piedras, P.R., 1974—. Served with Nat. Guard P.R., 1963-64. Mem. P.R. Loan Officers Assn. (dir. 1972-76), P.R. Savs. and Loan League (dir., treas. 1976-77, mem. com. on Fed. Home Loan Bank system 1977, pres. 1978-80). Clubs: Rotary, Caparra Country. Home: 1-5 Alhambra and Madrid Sts Guaynabo PR 00657 Office: PO Box 29067 65th Infantry Sta Rio Piedras PR 00929

PEREZ, PAUL ESTEBAN, computer co. exec.; b. Havana, Cuba, Dec. 26, 1943; came to U.S., 1945, naturalized, 1947; s. Pablo and Isela (Fraga) P.; B.S. in E.E., U. Fla., 1965; M.S. in E.E., Drexel Inst. Tech., 1968; m. Linda Jean Stout, Dec. 3, 1980; children—Cheryl, Stephen. Design engr. RCA, Moorestown, N.J., 1965, United Aircraft, Southampton, Pa., 1966-68; systems engr. Radiation Inc., Melbourne, Fla., 1968-69; systems engr. NCR, Dayton, Ohio, 1969-74; with Rockwell Internat., Anaheim, Calif., 1974-75; v.p. mktg. and sales Internat. Teleprocessing, Inc., Santa Clara, Calif., 1975-76; pres. West Coast Computer Exchange, Sunnyvale, Calif., 1976—. Mem. IEEE. Roman Catholic. Office: 248 Sobrante Way Sunnyvale CA 94086

PEREZ-VILLAMIL, JOSE RAMON, econ. cons.; b. San Juan, P.R., May 29, 1945; s. Marcelino M. and Carmen M. (Rodriguez) Perez-V.; B.B.A., U. P.R., 1966; Ph.D. in Econs., U. Mich., 1973; m. Lourdes Riera, Dec. 26, 1966; children—Marimar, Jose R. Research asst. FDIC, Washington, 1967; instr. econs. Cath. U. P.R., Bayamon, 1968; supr. Bus. Census of P.R., San Juan, 1968; instr. econs. Inter-Am. U., Hato Rey, P.R., 1970-72; econ. cons. P.R. Planning Bd., 1973-74, Pub. Service Commn. of P.R., San Juan, 1974—; asst. prof. econs. U. P.R., 1977, chmn. econs. dept., 1978; dir. Jocama Investment Corp. Trustee, St. John's Sch., San Juan, 1976—; mem. fin. adv. com. Colegio San Ignacio, San Juan, 1976—; mem. Ateneo Puertorriqueno, 1974-76; vol. traffic policeman, 1974. Mem. Am. Econ. Assn., Population Assn. Am., AAAS, Am. Acad. Polit. and Social Sci., Nu Sigma Beta. Office: Calle Riera 528 Santurce San Juan PR 00909

PERFALL, ARTHUR GEORGE, banker, communicator, journalist; b. Jamaica, N.Y., Apr. 26, 1927; s. Arthur Anthony and Helen E. (Guldhardt) P.; B.A., Hofstra U., 1951; children—Alison Ellen, Arthur Clayton, Faye Francesca. Reporter, L.I. (N.Y.) Daily Press, 1948-50; asst. city editor Nassau Daily Rev. Star, Rockville Centre, N.Y., 1950-51; organizer, staff writer Seafarers Internat. Union AFL, N.Y.C., 1951-54; with Newsday, Inc., Garden City, N.Y., 1954-72, fgn. corr., feature editor, picture editor, mng. editor; sr. v.p. Franklin Nat. Bank, N.Y.C., 1972-74; sr. v.p. European-Am. Bank & Trust Co., 1974-77; dir. public affairs N.Y. State Met. Transp. Authority, 1978—; adj. lectr. journalism C.W. Post Coll., L.I. U., 1962-64; chmn. L.I. region Nat. Alliance Businessmen. Bd. dirs. Day Care Council Nassau County, Nassau County Manpower Council. Served with USNR, 1944-46. Recipient numerous awards including Pulitzer Prize for community service, 1970. Mem. Acad. Polit. Sci., Am. Acad. Social Polit. Scis., Bank Marketing Assn., Am. Marketing Assn., Pub. Relations Soc. Am., Nat. Headliners Club, Sigma Delta Chi. Clubs: Overseas Press; University, Deadline (N.Y.C.); Indian Hills Country. Contbr. to various mags. Home: 1 Haig Dr Dix Hills NY 11746 Office: 1700 Broadway New York City NY 10019

PERIS, JEFFREY SCOTT, pharm. products co. exec.; b. Pitts., Apr. 13, 1946; s. Bernard and Sylvia Ruth (Scott) P.; B.S., U. Pitts., 1966, M.Sc., 1967, Sc.D., 1969; M.B.A., Rutgers U., 1975; m. Eleanor Sue Levinson, June 25, 1967; children—Marshal David, Jonathan Stuart, Rachel Ellen. Statis. cons. Hays Army Ammunition Plant div. Levinson Steel Co., Pitts., 1966-70; lectr. biostatistics U. Pitts., 1969-70; epidemiological biostatistician dept. clin. epidemiology Upjohn Co., Kalamazoo, 1970-72; sr. biometrician, clin. biostatistics and research data systems-med. affairs internat. Merck Sharp & Dohme Research Labs., Merck & Co., Rahway, N.J., 1972-73, mgr. clin. biostatistics, 1973-75, asso. dir. clin. bio statistics and research data systems, 1975-76, dir. mktg. research internat., 1976-79, mktg. planner Merck Sharp & Dohme Ltd., Hoddesdon, Herts, Eng., 1978, exec. dir. mktg., vaccines, internat., Rahway, N.J., 1979, exec. dir. mktg., vaccines and antibiotics, 1979-80, exec. dir. mktg. intelligence internat., 1980—; dir. Levinson Steel Co., Pitts. Bd. dirs. Community Concert Series, 1970-72; active PTA, Scotch Plains, N.J., 1972—. Senatorial scholar, 1963-66; NIH fellow, 1966-70. Mem. Am. Statis. Assn., Am. Public Health Assn., Internat. Pharm. Mktg. Research Group, Am. Pharm. Assn., Am. Soc. Clin Pharmacology and Therapeutics, Biometric Soc. Contbr. articles to profl. jours. Home: 12 Heritage Ln Scotch Plains NJ 07076

PERKES, DANIEL, news agency exec.; b. Bklyn., Feb. 17, 1931; s. A. and Edith Perkes; student Amarillo, Tex., Jr. Coll., 1952-54; B.A. in Journalism, Tex. Tech. U., 1957; m. Norma Jean O'Mary, Dec. 6, 1952; children—Kimberly, Daniel. Newsman, Morning Avalanche, Lubbock, Tex., 1954-57; with AP, 1957—, newsman, Lincoln, Nebr., 1957, statehouse reporter, Des Moines, 1958-62, corr., Pierre, S.D., 1962-64, bur. chief, Oklahoma City, 1964-67, chief of bur. Iowa-Nebr., 1967-69, gen. editor AP Newsfeatures, N.Y.C., 1967-79, asst. gen. mgr. AP, in charge of Newsfeatures and Wide World Photos, 1979—. Served with USAF, 1950-54. Mem. Am. Assn. Sunday and Feature Editors, Sigma Delta Chi. Clubs: N.Y. Athletic, Masons. Author: Eyewitness to Disaster, 1976; project dir. various AP books including: AP Sports Almanac, Century of Sports, Century of Champions, AP news annuals, 1969-77, Footprints On The Moon. Home: 21 Lawrence Pl Pelham Manor NY 10803 Office: 50 Rockefeller Plaza New York NY 10020

PERKIN, MARTIN JACK, real estate investment trust co. exec.; b. Phila., Dec. 9, 1939; s. Louis and Rose (Shapiro) P.; B.S., Pa. State U., 1961; postgrad. Temple U. Law Sch., 1962; m. Barbara S. Melnick, June 24, 1962; children—Beth, Jody, Wendy. 1st v.p. N. Am. Mortgage Investors, N.Y.C., 1971-79; pres. Bayswater Realty & Investment Trust, N.Y.C., 1979—; dir. Peterson-Craig Psychol. Clinic; lectr. U. Pa., Yale U., Columbia U. Sch. Law, also public-pvt. seminars, 1972—. Founder Bay County Children's Fund. Office: 25 Broadway New York NY 10004

PERKINS, CURTIS GRAHAM, ins. and surety exec.; b. Danville, Va., May 25, 1942; s. Walter Graham and Edith (Rutledge) P.; B.S. in Math., Va. Poly. Inst., 1965; m. Francis Myrtle Crowder, Mar. 8, 1971; children—Charles Graham, Elizabeth. Bus. lines account rep. Liberty Mut. Ins. Co., Roanoke, Va., 1966-68; pres., dir. Perkins and Assos., Inc., Bethesda, Md., 1969-79, chmn. bd., 1979—; pres., dir. Investment Consultants, Inc., Bethesda, 1971-76, Atlantic Mining Co. of W.Va., Inc., Beckley, 1974-77; v.p., treas., dir. Eastern Contracting Co., Inc., Lexington, Ky., 1974-78; pres., treas., dir. Eastern Indemnity Co. of Md., Bethesda; pres., dir. EHC Assos., Inc., Las Vegas, Nev.; v.p., dir. AFP & Co., Inc., Vienna, Va.; corp. dir. Design Bus. Interiors, Inc., Roanoke, Columbia (Md.) Distbrs., Inc., A & G Ins. Services, Inc., Bethesda, Homeowner Warranty Corp., Washington, Omega Enterprises, Inc., Arlington, Va., Eastern Contracting Co., Inc., Lexington, Investment Consultants, Inc.,

Bethesda. Chmn. Camp Echo Lake, Balt., 1977; mem. steering com. Holton-Arms Sch., Bethesda, 1980. Mem. Montgomery-Prince George's Ind. Agts. Assn., Md. Ind. Agts. Assn., Nat. Assn. Ind. Agts., Md. Surety Assn., D.C. Homebuilders Assn., No. Va. Builders Assn., Heavy Constrn. Contractors Assn. Clubs: Watergate, Gaslight, Robert F. Kennedy Stadium, Polo, Bethesda Kiwanis (pres. 1972-76). Contbr. articles to trade jours. and mags. Office: 4340 East West Highway Bethesda MD 20014

PERKINS, DONALD SHELDON, diversified retailing co. exec.; b. St. Louis, Mar. 22, 1927; s. Arthur and Edna Ann (Meinert) P.; B.A., Yale, 1949; M.B.A., Harvard, 1951; m. Phyllis Elizabeth Babb, June 9, 1951; children—Elizabeth Perkins Hill, Jervis, Susan Perkins Getzendanner. With Jewel Cos., Inc., 1953—, v.p., gen. mgr. routes dept., 1961-63, dir., 1962—, exec. v.p. 1963-65, pres., 1965-70, chmn., 1970—, chmn. exec. com., 1980—; dir. Inland Steel Co., Cummins Engine Co., Corning Glass Works, Aurrera, S.A. (Mexico City), G.D. Searle & Co., Freeport Minerals Co., AT&T, Time, Inc.; internat. council Morgan Guaranty Trust Co. Trustee Ford Found.; bd. dirs. Harvard Bus. Sch. Assos., LaSalle St. Fund; trustee Brookings Inst., Ford Found., Northwestern U.; chmn. United Way/Crusade of Mercy, Chgo. Mem. Bus. Council. Clubs: Chicago, Economic, Commonwealth, Commercial (Chgo.); University (N.Y.C.); Glen View (Golf, Ill.); Old Elm (Sheridan, Ill.). Office: Jewel Cos Inc One First Nat Plaza Chicago IL 60603

PERKINS, GEORGE FREDERICK, JR., internat. publishing co. exec.; b. N.Y.C., Apr. 12, 1936; s. George Frederick and Lucia King (Fly) P.; B.A., Princeton U., 1958; M.A., Columbia U., 1967, grad. internat. exec. mgmt. program Grad. Sch. Bus., 1980; m. Alice Bernstein Cannon, Oct. 28, 1972; 1 dau., Rebecca. Sales rep. Ginn & Co., 1961-65, internat. sales mgr., 1966-67; program mgr. RTAC/AID, Buenos Aires, 1967-70; mng. dir. McGraw-Hill do Brasil São Paulo, 1970-74; pub. ESL/EFL programs McGraw-Hill Internat. Book Co., N.Y.C., 1974, v.p. Ibero-Am. Group, 1974—; dir. Libros McGraw-Hill de Mex., McGraw-Hill Latinoamericana, McGraw-Hill de España, McGraw-Hill do Brasil, EPASA/Guatemala, McGraw-Hill de Portugal. Served with USMC, 1960-61. Mem. Assn. Am. Pubs. Congregationalist. Clubs: Princeton (N.Y.C.); County Tennis (Westchester, N.Y.). Home: 19 Gorham Rd Scarsdale NY 10583 Office: 1221 Ave of Americas New York NY 10020

PERKINS, GEORGE WILLIAM, II, financial services co. exec.; b. Salem, Mass., Sept. 10, 1926; s. George William and Daisy Almira (Chase) P.; student Northeastern U., 1944-49; B.Sc., Curry Coll., 1952; postgrad. Boston U., 1964; certified fin. planner Coll. Fin. Planning, Denver, 1974; m. Mildred Boyle, Oct. 6, 1951; children—George William, Clifton Alfred Dow, Mark Paige. Commn. accountant John Hancock Ins. Co., Boston, 1946-47, agt., supr., sr. agt., 1962; gen. agt. Union Mut. Ins. Co., Andover, Mass., 1963; brokerage supr. Hartford Life Ins. Co., 1964-65; New Eng. mgr., life dept. Nat. Life Ins. Co.-Can., 1968-69; br. mgr. Equity Funding Corp., Boston, 1970-71; regional mgr. equity sales United Life & Accident Ins. Co., Burlington, Mass., 1972, nat. dir. equity sales and tng., 1973; regional v.p. Western Res. Life Assurance Co. of Ohio, 1974-75; pres., chmn. bd. Fin. Mktg. Systems, Inc., Nashua, N.H. 1976—; New Eng. div. mgr. Calif. Pacific Corp., 1977-79; dir. Sonolite Corp., Fin. Cons. Mgmt. Corp., 1979—; registered prin. Fin. Cons., Inc.; former prof. bus. adminstrn. and fin. Curry Coll.; cons., advisor small bus.; lectr. in field. Chmn., Ins. Com. Town of Lynnfield (Mass.), 1970—; trustee Curry Coll., 1963—. Served with USNR, World War II; PTO. Recipient prodn. awards Hartford Life Ins. Co., 1964, Nat. Life Ins. Co. of Can., 1968; Nat. Sales Achievement award Nat. Assn. Life Underwriters, 1969. Mem. Internat. Assn. Fin. Planners (founding pres. No. Mass. chpt.), Inst. Cert. Fin. Planners, Merrimack Valley Life Underwriters (v.p., dir.), Nashua (N.H.) Life Underwriters Assn., Boston Life Underwriters Assn., Advt. Club Greater Boston, New Eng. Businessmen's Assn. Clubs: Masons; Rotary (past charter pres.) (Chelmsford, Mass.). Contbr. articles to profl. jours. Designer largest portable cinemascope motion picture screen. Home: 278 Lowell St Lynnfield MA 01940 Office: Gatepoint II 157 Main Dunstable Rd Nashua NH 03060

PERKINS, JAMES SECOR, indsl. engr., prodn. mgmt. cons.; b. Oak Park, Ill., Mar. 16, 1911; s. Augustus Thompson and Emily Charlotte (Secor) P.; student engring. Cornell U., 1930-31; B.S. in Bus. Adminstrn., Northwestern U., 1939; m. Helen Dorchak, May 29, 1958; children—Diane Lea Kulik, Sandra Lea Merin. Indsl. engr. Bauer & Black Co., Chgo., 1934-35; cons. in plant layout Berger div. of Republic Steel Corp., Canton, Ohio, 1936; cons. cost accountant Barco Mfg. Co., Chgo., 1936; cons. indsl. engring. Belmont Radio Corp., Chgo., 1936; indsl. engr. Western Electric Co., Chgo., 1936-46; chief indsl. engr. Ball Bros. Co., Muncie, Ind., 1946-48; plant supt. Courier-Citizen Co., Chgo., 1948-52; v.p. mfg. Wallace Bus. Forms Corp., Chgo., 1952-60; gen. mgr. Rec. & Statis. Corp., Danville, Ill., 1960-63; dir. prodn. mgmt. Printing Industries Am., Inc., Arlington, Va., 1963-71; pres. mgmt. cons. Perkins Assos., Bethesda, Md., 1971-77, Savannah, Ga., 1977—: instr. prodn. mgmt. Northwestern U., Evanston, 1941; instr. indsl. engring. night sch. Ill. Inst. Tech., Chgo., 1941-46. Recipient Excellence in Indsl. Engring. Chgo. Coll. Indsl. Engring., 1946. Mem. ASME, Am. Inst. Indsl. Engrs. (Graphic Arts award 1980), Soc. Advancement Mgmt. (Gilbreth Gold medal award 1945), Graphic Arts Assn. Execs., Sigma Ch. Clubs: Marshwood/Landings Golf and Country (Savannah); Cornell (dir. 1964-65). Author: The Original Films of Frank B. Gilbreth, 1969 (film); contbr. numerous articles on mgmt. to printing trade mags. Address: 3 Middleton Rd The Landings on Skidaway Island Savannah GA 31411

PERKINS, JOHN HAROLD, banker; b. Chgo., Aug. 28, 1921; s. Harold Reed and Roschen (Baker) P.; B.S., Northwestern U., 1943; m. Len Welborn, June 24, 1944; children—John Harold, Robert G., Reed F. With Continental Ill. Nat. Bank & Trust Co., Chgo., 1946—, asst. cashier, 1949-52, 2d v.p., 1952-56, v.p., 1956-65, sr. v.p. adminstrv. services, 1965-66, exec. v.p., dir., 1968-71, vice chmn., 1971-73, pres., 1973—; instr. fin. dept. Northwestern U., 1950-54; dir. Continental Bank Internat., Continental Internat. Finance Corp., Pillsbury Co., Pvt. Export Funding Corp.; trustee Underwriters Labs., Inc.; pub. adviser, gov. Midwest Stock Exchange. Trustee Northwestern U., Episcopalian Diocesan Found. Chgo., Chgo. Symphony Orch., Michael Reese Hosp. and Med. Center, Com. for Econ. Devel.; chmn. Chgo. Econ. Devel. Com.; chmn. adv. council, also chmn. devel. Fin. and Investment Council, Ill. Dept. Commerce and Community Affairs. Served with USNR, 1943-46. Mem. Econ. Club, Am. Bankers Assn. (dir., govt. relations council, pres.), Assn. Res. City Bankers (govt. relations com.), U.S. C. of C. (fin. com.), Phi Beta Kappa, Delta Tau Delta. Clubs: Univ., La Salle St., Chgo., Comml., Carlton, Bond, Bankers, Met. (Chgo.); Met. (Washington); Wall St. (N.Y.C.): Indian Hill (Winnetka); Old Elm (Ft. Sheridan); John Evans of Northwestern Univ. (pres.). Office: 231 S LaSalle St Chicago IL 60693

PERKINS, RICHARD BURLE, real estate broker; b. Rockville, Ind., July 1, 1923; s. Walter Mac and Olevia Maude (Vinson) P.; student Ball State U., 1941-42, Oberlin Coll., 1944-45, U. Mich., 1946; B.A., DePauw U., 1947; m. Mariam Catherine Jamail, Aug. 1, 1959; children—Richard Burle II, Mele Angelique. Territory mgr. P & G Edible Oils, Tex., La., Okla., 1947-53; dist. mgr. Southwest U.S. DCA Food Industries, spl. flours, mixes and machinery, Houston, Tex., 1953-62; pres. Gold Seal Donuts, Houston, 1962-63; div. mgr. Nat. Oats Co., Houston, 1963-68; mgr. apt. mng. systems Office Services, Inc., Houston, 1970—: owner Dick Perkins Co., realtor, Houston, 1970—; registered securities rep. Waddel & Reed, Houston, 1970-71; gen. mgr. Seven-Up Bottling Corp., Houston, 1969. Chmn. orgn. and extension com. Sunset dist. Boy Scouts Am., 1970: com. chmn. Cub Scout Pack 855, 1968—; coach, sponsor Spring Branch Little League Baseball, 1967—. Served with USMC, 1942-46. Mem. Pi Sigma Alpha. Club: Meml. Plaza Civic (pres. 1968) (Houston). Home: 6503 Rippling Hollow Spring TX 77379 Office: 5211-YFM 1960 West Houston TX 77069 also 13027 Champions Dr Suite C Houston TX 77069

PERKINS, TERRY RICHARD, ins. co. exec.; b. Salt Lake City, Feb. 20, 1947; s. Dean Alvin and Colleen (Wallace) P.; B.A. magna cum laude, U. So. Calif., 1969, J.D. with honors, Gould Sch. Law, 1972; m. Laurie Jean Garner, Nov. 27, 1976. Spl. liaison Los Angeles City Adminstrv. Office and City Atty., 1971; cons. fin. planning services Pacific Mut. Life Co., Newport Beach, Calif., 1972-76, sr. cons., 1976—, dir., 1979—. Bd. dirs. panel, speaker Hoag Meml. Hosp. Support Group, Newport Beach. Mem. Nat. C.L.U.'s Orange County (Calif.) C.L.U.'s, Newport Beach Estate Planning Council (pres.), Orange County Estate Planning Council, Phi Beta Kappa. Republican. Office: 700 Newport Center Dr Newport Beach CA 92660

PERKINS, THOMAS JAMES, venture capital investor; b. Oak Park, Ill., Jan. 7, 1932; s. Harry H. and Elizabeth (Henseler) P.; B.S.E.E., M.I.T., 1953; M.B.A., Harvard U., 1957; m. Gerd Thune-Ellefsen, Dec. 9, 1961; children—Tor, Elizabeth. Gen. mgr. Computer div. Hewlett-Packard Co., 1965-70, dir. corp. devel., 1970-72; gen. partner Kleiner & Perkins, 1972-80, Kleiner Perkins Caufield & Byers, 1978-80, Kleiner Perkins Caufield & Byers II, San Francisco, 1980—; chmn. bd. Tandem Computers, 1975—, Genentech, 1976—; dir. Spectra Physics. Bd. dirs. San Francisco Ballet. Mem. Nat. Venture Capital Assn. (pres.), Western Venture Capital Assn. (pres. 1974-75). Clubs: N.Y. Yacht, St. Francis Yacht. Early innovator field of laser tech. Office: 2 Embarcadero Center 2900 San Francisco CA 94111

PERKOWSKI, JOSEPH CHARLES, environ. scientist; b. N.Y.C., Dec. 23, 1949; s. Alexander Peter and Isabel Monica (Mankauskas) P.; B.S. in Elec. Engring. with highest honors, Manhattan Coll. Sch. Engring., 1971; Ph.D. with highest honors in Environ. Systems Mgmt., M.I.T., 1977. Mem. research staff Study of Man's Impact on the Climate, M.I.T., Cambridge, summer 1971; summer intern Council on Environ. Quality, Exec. Office of Pres., Washington, 1972; coordinator of staff study on prediction of potential marine pollutants Ocean Affairs Bd., Nat. Acad. Scis., Washington, summer, 1973; summer research intern Brookhaven Nat. Lab., ERDA, 1975; mem. faculty environ. mgmt. seminar Centre d'Etudes Industrielles, Geneva, 1975; cons. water resource data analysis in arid environments Devel. Analysis Assos., Inc., Cambridge, 1976; staff cons. M.I.T. Workshop on Alternative Energy Strategies, 1975-77; environ. mgmt. cons. to sr. adviser to pres. for environ. and social affairs Petro-Can., Calgary, Alta., 1976-77, sr. research officer environ. and social affairs dept., 1977-79; v.p. engring. Oxford Devel. Group Ltd., Edmonton, Alta., 1979—. Mem. Am. Nuclear Soc., IEEE, ASCE, Sigma Xi, Tau Beta Pi (pres. N.Y. chpt. 1970-71), Epsilon Sigma Pi, Chi Epsilon, Eta Kappa Nu. Republican. Roman Catholic. Contbr. articles on environ. sci. and tech. to profl. jours. Home: RD 3 Evergreen Ln Box 84 Port Jervis NY 12771 Office: care Oxford Devel Ltd 2300 Royal Trust Tower Edmonton AB T5J 3A4 Canada

PERLBERG, WILLIAM, chem. co. exec.; b. N.Y.C., July 30, 1933; s. Samuel and Pearl (Pulver) P.; B.S. in Chemistry, Coll. City N.Y., 1954, M.B.A., 1963; m. Muriel Rhoda Spiegel, Nov. 21, 1954; children—Mark Craig, Elyssa Laine. Research chemist Colgate Palmolive Co., Jersey City, 1956-50; mgr. product devel. Airkem, Inc., 1960-64; asst. dir. research Revlon Inc., 1964-68; v.p. research and devel. control Airwick Industries, Inc., Carlstadt, N.J., 1968-73, also dir.; corporate v.p., Hartz Mountain Corp., 1973—; lectr. consumer product tech., disinfectant tech., govt. regulation of consumer products. Served with AUS, 1954-56. Mem. Am. Pub. Health Assn., Air Pollution Control Assn., Am. Chem. Soc., Cosmetic Chemists, Royal Soc. Health. Patentee in fields of chemistry and engring. Office: 700 S 4th St Harrison NJ 07481

PERLMAN, LAWRENCE, lawyer, bus. exec.; b. St. Paul, Apr. 8, 1938; s. Irving and Ruth (Mirsky) P.; B.A., Carleton Coll., 1960; J.D., Harvard U., 1963; m. Medora Scoll, June 18, 1961; children—David, Sara. Admitted to Minn. bar, 1963; law clk., fed. judge, 1963-64; asso. partner, firm Fredrikson, Byron, Colborn, Bisbee Hansen & Perlman, and predecessor firms, Mpls., 1964-75; v.p., sec., gen. counsel Medtronic Inc., Mpls., 1975, exec. v.p., 1975-78; sr. partner firm Oppenheimer, Wolff, Foster, Shepard and Donnelly, Mpls., St. Paul, and Brussels, Belgium, 1978-80; v.p., gen. counsel, sec. Control Data Corp., 1980—; adj. prof. law U. Minn., 1974-76, 79—; lectr. Minn. Continuing Legal Edn. Chmn., Minn. Fgn. Policy Assn., 1972; mem. Mpls. Bd. Estimate and Taxation, 1973-75; chmn. Mpls. Municipal Fin. Commn., 1978-79; bd. dirs. Walker Art Center, 1975—, Hennepin Center for Arts, 1977—, Mpls. Urban League, 1972-74, Hennepin County chpt. ARC, 1976-79. Mem. Am., Minn. (vice chmn. banking, corp. and bus. law sect.), recipient Outstanding Author award, 1975), Hennepin County bar assns., Health Industries Mfrs. Assn. (past dir.), Am. Judicature Soc., Am. Law Inst., Phi Beta Kappa. Club: Minneapolis. Home: 2366 W Lake of Isles Pkwy Minneapolis MN 55405 Office: Control Data Corp Box O Minneapolis MN 55440

PERLSTEIN, HARRIS, bus. exec.; b. N.Y.C., N.Y., Aug. 18, 1892; s. Abram and Betsy (Cohen) P.; B.S., in Chem. Engring., Armour Inst. Tech., Chgo., 1914; LL.D., Ill. Inst. Tech., 1965; m. Anne Agazim, Mar. 11, 1929 (dec. Sept. 1956); children—Betsy Ann Perlstein Cowan, Lawrence A.; m. 2d, Florence L. Weiss, Oct. 23, 1960 (dec. Sept. 1973). Chemist, engr., 1914-18; partner Singer Perlstein Co., cons. engrs., Chgo., 1918-24; treas., dir. Premier Malt Products Co., Peoria, Ill., 1924-27, pres. 1927-32, co. merged with Pabst Brewing Co., 1932, pres., dir. Pabst Brewing Co. Chgo., 1932-54, chmn., pres., dir., 1954-56, chmn., dir., 1956-72, chmn. exec. com., dir., 1972-79, chmn. emeritus, 1979—. Mem. adv. hosp. council Ill. Dept. Pub. Health, 1961-71. Bd. dirs. Ill. Mfrs. Assn., 1945-55, 58-59; hon. chmn., life trustee, past chmn. bd. Ill. Inst. Tech.; pres., bd. dirs. Peristein Found.; past pres., dir. Jewish Fedn. Met. Chgo.; mem. Ill. Bd. Pub. Welfare Commrs., 1949-53. Mem. Am. Chem. Soc., Pi Delta Epsilon. Mason (Shriner). Clubs: Lake Shore Country, Northmoor Country, Standard (Chgo.); Chemist (N.Y.C.). Home: 1440 N Lake Shore Dr Chicago IL 60610 Office: 1 E Wacker Dr Chicago IL 60601

PERREAULT, NORMAND, service co. exec.; b. Montreal, Que., Can., Sept. 26, 1945; s. Lionel and Madeleine (Faucher) P.; student Saint Denis Coll., Montreal, 1962-64, U. Montreal, 1964-66; m. Judith Cruchet, Oct. 7, 1972; 1 son, Eric. Founder, owner, pres. Transpobec Enr, Saint Bruno, Que., 1972—; adviser Diamond Ltd., Belair Ins. Ltd. Pres. Cugnet Homeowners Assn., St. Bruno; dir. Ile Aux Bois Blanc Recreational Corp., Repentigny, Que. Served with Royal Can. Navy, 1961-64. Mem. Diamond Assn. Liberal. Roman Catholic. Clubs: Sani-Sport, Club De Petancles de St Bruno. Office: 1915 Cugnet St Suite 1001 Sainte Bruno PQ J3V 5H7 Canada

PERRELLA, ANTHONY JOSEPH, telecommunication mfg. co. exec.; b. Boulder, Colo., Sept. 16, 1942; s. Anthony Vincent and Mary Dommica (Forte) P.; B.S., U. Wyo., 1964, postgrad., 1965; postgrad. U. Calif., San Diego, 1966-67, U. Calif., Irvine, 1968-70. Flight engr. U.S. Naval Tng. Devices Center, San Diego, 1965-67; with Rockwell Internat. Corp., Newport Beach, Calif., 1967-78, group head, 1970-74, engring. mgr., 1974-78; systems engr. mgr. ARGO Systems, Sunnyvale, Calif., 1978, program mgr., 1978—; v.p. research and devel. Things Unlimited Inc. Laramie, Wyo., 1965-72, pres., 1972-75. Mem. Am. Mgmt. Assn., IEEE, AAAS, Tau Kappa Epsilon. Republican. Roman Catholic. Contbr. articles in field. Office: 884 Hermosa Ct Sunnyvale CA 94086

PERRETTE, JEAN RENE, banker; b. Dinan, France, May 24, 1931; s. Rene Jean and Marie Cecile (Ollivier) P.; came to U.S., 1961; HEC Bus. Sch. Paris, 1953; LL.D., U. Paris, 1955; D. Econs., 1959; m. Virginia Moore Schott, Sept. 8, 1962; children—Virginie-Alvine, Clarisse, Jean-Briac, Julien-Yannick. Asst. to gen. mgmt. Worms CMC, Paris, 1959-61, U.S. rep. N.Y.C., 1961-65; U.S. rep. Banque Worms, N.Y.C., 1965—; pres. Permal Internat. Inc., U.S. reps. Messrs. Worms & Cie., Paris, other European cos., N.Y.C., 1965—; dir. several cos.; cons. French pub. group, 1967-71. Served with French Navy, 1956-59. Mem. HEC Bus. Sch. U.S. Alumni Assn. (pres. 1975-76), French C. of C. in U.S. (exec. com. 1975—). Club: Union (N.Y.C.). Home: 14 E 90th St New York NY 10028 Office: 919 Third Ave New York NY 10022

PERRI, PASQUALE JOSEPH, JR., hosp. fin. adminstr.; b. Westerly, R.I., July 7, 1939; s. Pasquale Joseph and Emily Theresa (Sposato) P.; B.S. in Bus. Adminstrn., U. R.I., 1962; m. Louann C. Cluny, Oct. 29, 1976; children—Michael, Karen, Gayle, Mark. Cost/budget analyst Electric Boat div. Gen. Dynamics Corp., 1962-67; silver controller Yardney Electric Corp., Pawcatuck, Conn., 1967-71; accountant Westerly (R.I.) Hosp., 1971-75, controller, 1975-77, dir. fiscal affairs, 1977—; trustee Haricomp. Mem. Am. Hosp. Assn., Hosp. Fin. Mgmt. Assn., Nat. Assn. Accts., Am. Mgmt. Assn. Home: 4 Hardwood Ln Westerly RI 02891 Office: Westerly Hosp Wells St Westerly RI 02891

PERRIN, ANDREW E., plastic molding co. exec.; b. Maplewood, Mo., Mar. 23, 1918; s. Peter Joseph and Emma (Ettling) P.; m. Beatrice Meta Riemann, May 23, 1942. Pres., Compression Molding Co., 1947-50; v.p. Koch Mfg. Co., Jackson, Mo., 1950-55; v.p. Lenco, Inc., Jackson, 1955-77, pres., 1977—; dir. Jackson Exchange Bank & Trust Co. Chmn. Jackson Library Bd., 1959-71. Mem. Soc. Plastic Engrs. Republican. Roman Catholic. Clubs: Kimbleland Country, K.C. Home: 1647 Cherokee St Jackson MO 63755 Office: 319 W Main St Jackson MO 63755

PERRIN, MARJORIE EVELYN, Realtor; b. Atlantic, Iowa, May 3, 1924; d. Wolmer and Helen Ruth (Gardner) Jensen; student pub. schs., Iowa; grad. Realtor Inst., 1975; m. Donald J. Crane, Dec. 1942 (dec. May 1966); children—Kenneth O., Gary D., Peggy Crane Rosener, Judith Crane Heitink; m. 2d, Charles D. Perrin, Nov. 3, 1969. Nurses' aide Atlantic Hosp., 1942-53; clk. Ted's Pen and Party Shop, Omaha, 1956-58; broker Crane Realty, Council Bluffs, Iowa, 1962-63; agt. Woodmen Accident & Life Ins. Co., Lincoln, Nebr., 1962-70; broker, owner Perrin Real Estate, Atlantic, 1970—. Mem. Life Underwriters Assn., Nat., Iowa, Atlantic real estate assns., Realtors Nat. Mktg. Inst., Bus. and Profl. Women. Lutheran. Club: Soroptimist (treas., dir. 1972—). Home: 1403 Olive St Atlantic IA 50022

PERRINE, BEAHL THEODORE, lawyer; b. Monticello, Iowa, July 4, 1902; s. John H. and Minnie (Ryan) P.; student U. Mich., 1922-27, J.D., 1927; m. Irene L. Hall, Oct. 27, 1934. Admitted to Iowa bar, 1927, since practiced in Cedar Rapids; former mem. firm Simmons, Perrine, Albright, & Ellwood, from 1943; asst. atty. Linn County, 1942-44; former chmn. bd., dir. Iowa Mfg. Co.; sec., dir. Amana Refrigeration, Inc.; regional War Bond dir. Treasury Dept., World War II. Bd. dirs. Mercy Hosp., Mercy Hosp. Found.; bd. dirs., chmn. Hall Found., Inc.; trustee Cedar Rapids YMCA, Herbert Hoover Presdl. Library Assn. Inc. Mem. Am., Iowa, Linn County (pres. 1936) bar assns., Am. Judicature Soc., Cedar Rapids C. of C., Alpha Kappa Lambda, Delta Theta Phi. Clubs: Pickwick, Elks, Cedar Rapids Country. Home: 2222 First Ave NE Cedar Rapids IA 52402 Office: 1200 Merchants National Bank Bldg Cedar Rapids IA 52401

PERRY, ALAN STODDARD, mgmt. cons.; b. Malden, Mass., Mar. 27, 1923; s. Howard Stoddard and Lois Gertrude (Maraspin) P.; student N.Y. U., 1949-50, Art Students League, 1953-54, Silvermine Guild, 1961-62; B.A., Bowdoin Coll., 1943; M.B.A., Harvard U., 1948; m. Nancy Blood, Sept. 14, 1946; children—Lizabeth, Christine, Michele. Account exec. Doherty Clifford, Steers & Shenfield, N.Y.C., 1948-50, Dancer-Fitzgerald-Sample, N.Y.C., 1950-54; account exec., account supr. Young & Rubicam, N.Y.C., 1954-60; v.p. account supr. Batten, Barton, Durstine & Osborn, N.Y.C., 1960-64; v.p., account group supr. Cunningham & Walsh, N.Y.C., 1964-68; v.p., mktg. dir. Inst. Outdoor Advt., N.Y.C., 1968-79; v.p., partner Devine, Baldwin & Peters, N.Y.C., 1979—. Dist. leader Republican Party, New Canaan, Conn., 1960-65; mem. Republican Town Com., 1961-68. Served to lt. (j.g.) U.S. Navy, 1943-46. Republican. Congregationalist. Clubs: Bowdoin, Harvard (N.Y.C.); Harvard (Fairfield County); Country Club of Darien (Conn.). Home: 9 Whiffletree Lane New Canaan CT 06840 Office: 250 Park Ave New York NY 10177

PERRY, CHARLES E., bus. exec.; b. Holden, W.Va., July 25, 1937; s. Lester and Ethel (White) P.; B.A. with honors, B.S. (Distinguished Service grad.), M.A., L.H.D., Bowling Green State U.; postgrad. U. Mich.; LL.D., Bethune-Cookman Coll.; m. Betty Laird, Sept. 17, 1960; children—Thomas Edward, Lynnette Eleanor. Tchr. English and history East Detroit pub. schs.; admissions counselor Bowling Green State U., 1959-61, dir. admissions, 1961-64, dir. devel., 1964-67, asst. to pres., 1965-67; spl. asst. to gov. Fla. for edn., 1967-68; vice chancellor Fla. U. System, 1968-69; pres. Fla. Internat. U., 1969-75; pres., pub. Family Weekly mag., 1976; pres. Golden Bear, Inc., 1977—, Golforce, Inc.; partner Jack Nicklaus & Assos.; chmn. bd. dirs. Golden Bear Communications; chmn., chief exec. CEPCO; dir. Am. Bankers Life Assurance Co., Jack Nicklaus Eyeware, Inc., B.C. Devel. Corp., Orange Bowl. Past exec. dir. Fla. Commn. Quality Edn.; past chmn. Gov. Fla. Edn. Adv. Council; past dir. So. Regional Edn. Bd.; past chmn. Council Fla. Jr. Coll. Affairs; past chmn. Fla. Edn. Council, Fla. del. Edn. Commn. States; past mem. Select Council Post High Sch. Edn.; past chmn. com. on internat. programs Am. Assn. State Colls. and Univs.; past mem. Nat. Com. Utilization Ednl. TV, Southeastern Ednl. Lab. Council, Commn. Latin Am. Affairs, Miami Commn. Fgn. Relations, Dade Marine Inst., UN U. U.S.A., UN World Edn. Commn., U.S. commn. UNESCO; past mem. exec. com. Fla. Am. Revolution Bicentennial Commn., James E. Scott Community Assn. Past trustee Cultural Alliance Greater Miami, United Way Dade County, Council Internat. Visitors, Fla. Council 100, Internat. Center, Miami, Fla. Hist. Soc., Community

TV Found. S. Fla., Third Century U.S.A., Mus. Sci. and Space Transit Planetarium; past mem. planning adv. bd. Capital Improvement Commn. Met. Dade County. Named Outstanding Young Man of Bowling Green, 1966; One of 10 Outstanding Young Men of Am., U.S. Jr. C. of C., 1971, Outstanding Young Man of Achievement, 1965; recipient Silver Anvil award Pub. Relations Soc. Am., 1964; Spl. Appreciation award for outstanding contbns. to Fla., 1968; Certificate of Merit award Edinboro State Coll., 1972; Diamond Jubilee Celebration award City of Miami, 1971; 1st Ann. Service award N.O.W.; Man of Year award Phi Delta Kappa, 1972; Community Service award Christian Migrant Assn., 1973; Medal of Honor, Acción Pro Darien Soc., Colombia, 1973; Distinguished Service award Marshall U. Alumni Assn., 1973; Distinguished Alumnus award Bowling Green State U., 1975. Mem. Am. Assn. Higher Edn., Internat. Assn. U. Pres.'s, Young Pres.'s Orgn., So. Assn. Colls. and Schs., Fla. C. of C., Pi Sigma Alpha, Alpha Kappa Delta, Phi Delta Kappa. Address: Golden Bear Inc 1208 US Hwy #1 North Palm Beach FL 33408

PERRY, DAVID, lawyer, ins. co. exec.; b. Phila., Nov. 13, 1940; s. Harry J. and Alice M. (Heller) P.; B.A. in English Lit., Carleton Coll., 1962; LL.B., U. Pa., 1965, M.A. in Econs., 1972, Ph.D. in Econs., 1974; m. Sherryl Frances Rosenbaum, June 24, 1962. Law clk. firm Freedman, Borowsky and Lorry, Phila., 1964-65; admitted to Pa. bar, 1965; atty. HUD, Phila., 1965-67; practice law, Phila., 1967-72; sr. fin. and planning analyst INA Corp., Phila., 1972-74; exec. asst. to pres. Certain-teed Products Corp., Valley Forge, Pa., 1974; dir. capital budgeting INA Corp., Phila., 1974-75, asst. treas., 1975—, v.p., 1979-80, pres. Phila. Investment Corp. subs. INA Corp., 1980—. Brookings Instn. research fellow, 1968-69. Mem. Phila. Bar Assn., Am. Econ. Assn. Home: 431 Boxwood Rd Rosemont PA 19010 Office: INA Corp 1600 Arch St Philadelphia PA 19101

PERRY, DENZEL LAFAYETTE, feed mill and bulk plant exec.; b. Great Falls, Mont., June 3, 1936; s. Clarenc H. and Theresa A. (Anderson) P.; B.S. in Engring., Mont. State U., 1958; M.B.A., Tex. Christian U., 1971; m. Donna G. Curtis, Dec. 28, 1958; children—Clayton Loren, Michelle Renne, Curtis Dean. Rancher, Choteau County, Mont., 1961-66; program controller missile programs Boeing Co., 1966-77, also internat. ops. mgr. and analyst, new bus. mgr., analyst, Seattle; owner, mgr. Perry's Outfit, Kent, Wash., Western States Industries, Inc., Choteau, Mont., 1977—. Served with ordnance, AUS, 1959-61. Home and Office: Box 1206 Choteau MT 59422

PERRY, EDWARD THOMAS, constrn. and bldg. materials cons.; b. Attleboro, Mass., June 7, 1898; s. Charles Henry and Elizabeth (Murray) P.; student Brown U., 1923-26; m. Lisabella Clare, Apr. 7, 1921. Adminstrv. v.p., dir. New Haven Trap Rock Co. (Conn.), 1951—; dir. Dunning Sand and Stone Co., Wauregan, Conn., Foxon Concrete Co., New Haven, M.F. Roach Co., North Eastham, Mass. Served with U.S. Army, World War I. Mem. Nat. Hwy. Research Bd., Washington, R.I. Road Builders Assn. (past sec., hon. dir.), R.I. Hwy. Assn., Nat. Asphalt Pavement Assn. (hon. mem.; bd. govs., chmn. awards com.), Conn. Bituminous Concrete Assn. (past pres., hon. mem.), Conn. Crushed Stone Assn. (past pres.). Clubs: Quinnipiack, New Haven Country (New Haven); N.Y. Yacht; Wannamoisett Country (East Providence, R.I.), Triton (Que., Can.). Home: 3205 Diamond Hill Rd Cumberland RI 02864 Office: 1199 Whitney Ave Hamden CT 06514

PERRY, JAMES EDWARD JOSEPH, fin. cons.; b. Cambridge, Mass., Dec. 11, 1944; s. Joseph Jesse and Mary Catherine (Corcoran) P.; B.S., Boston Coll., 1966; M.B.A., Babson Inst., 1968; Ph.D., U. Okla., 1976; m. Thelma Bridgett Long, May 5, 1979; children—Christopher James, Amy Michelle, Jennifer Lynn. Fin. analyst, Gen. Electric Co., 1966-68; acct. Bruno & Drankwater, C.P.A.'s, Arlington, Mass., 1968-72; asst. dean, asst. prof. fin. Oklahoma City U., 1971-77; vis. asst. prof. acctg. and fin. U. Hawaii, 1976; dean Sch. Bus. Central State U., Edmond, Okla., 1977—; fin. cons., Edmond, 1977—. Mem. Oklahoma City C. of C., Edmond C. of C., Soc. Advancement Mgmt., Econ. Club Okla., Nat. Assn. Accts., Southwestern Fin. Assn., Southwestern Fedn. Adminstrv. Disciplines. Democrat. Roman Catholic. Contbr. articles to profl. jours. Office: 100 N University Ave Edmond OK 73034

PERRY, JAMES EUGENE, data processing co. exec.; b. Decorah, Iowa, May 16, 1949; s. Eugene Albert and Mary (Limkeman) P.; B.S., Bethany Nazarene Coll., 1973; M.B.A., Phillips U., 1980; m. Carol F. Dittmeyer, Aug. 21, 1970; children—Christina Janette, Julie Dawn, April Janee. Computer programmer, acct. Atwood Warehousing Corp., Enid, Okla., 1976-77; acct. Carey's Acctg. and Tax Service, Oelwein, Iowa, 1977; controller Atwood Distributing, Enid, 1977-79; systems analysis Enid Data Systems, 1979—. Served with USAF, 1971-73. Republican. Clubs: Ambucs, Kiwanis. Home: Route 3 Box 446 Enid OK 73701 Office: 1st National Bank Bldg Enid OK 73701

PERRY, JAMES MEREDITH, mfg. co. exec.; b. Sparta, Wis., Sept. 3, 1944; s. James Russell and Dorothy (Jayne) P.; B.S. in Bus. Adminstrn., U. Del., 1973; m. Vicki Sue Larkin, Aug. 1, 1970; children—Barbara Lynn, Melinda Sue. With Johnson & Johnson, 1973—, mgr. orthopedics, 1976-79, mgr. personnel quality of work life program, New Brunswick, N.J., 1979—. Served to capt. USAR, 1966-70; Vietnam. Decorated Army Commendation medal, Purple Heart, Bronze Star. Mem. Am. Mgmt. Assn., Monroe Twp. Jaycees. Address: Johnson & Johnson 501 George St New Brunswick NJ 08903

PERRY, JESSE LAURENCE, JR., investment mgr., financier; b. Nashville, Oct. 15, 1919; s. Jesse Laurence and Mamie Lucretia (White) P.; B.A. magna cum laude, Vanderbilt U., 1941; M.B.A., Harvard, 1943; postgrad. edn. retarded children George Peabody Coll., summer 1953; m. Susan Taylor White, Nov. 5, 1949 (dec. Mar. 1972); children—Robert Laurence, Judith Foulds; m. 2d, Sarah Kinkead Stockell, Apr. 6, 1974. Treas., J.L. Perry Co., Nashville, 1947-48, v.p., 1949-54, pres., 1954-73, also dir.; pres., chmn. bd. Perry Enterprises, Nashville, 1973—; chmn. bd. 1st So. Savs. & Loan Inc., 1973—; pres. PortersField, Inc., Nashville, 1971—. Pres., Police Assistance League, 1973-74; mem. Tenn. Dept. Agr. Pest Control Licensing Bd., 1971-74; a.d.c. gov.'s staff, 1962-74; 1st v.p. Tenn. Assn. for Retarded Children, 1954-62; mem. Tenn. Mental Retardation Adv. Council, 1966-72; bd. advisers Salvation Army, 1958-72; founder, sec. Tenn. Bot. Garden and Fine Arts Center, 1958—; hon. col., staff Gov. Tenn., 1962-74. Chmn., 5th dist. Republican. Exec. Com., 1950-54; vice chmn. Tenn. Rep. State Exec. Com., 1956-70; Middle Tenn. campaign mgr., 1956, 60, 66; state mgr. Pub. Service Com. Campaign, 1964; mem. spl. com. on urban devel. Rep. Nat. Exec. Com., 1962; del. Rep. Nat. Exec. Com., 1960, vice chmn. Tenn. delegation, 1960, alternate del., 1968; dist. mem. Rep. State Exec. Com., 1954-75; state chmn. Rep. Capitol Club, 1971-73; Tenn. Rep. party state committeeman, 1956-74. Bd. govs. U. So., Sewanee Acad., 1968-74. Served to capt. AUS, 1943-46. Decorated knight hospitaller Order St. John of Jerusalem, chevalier Ordo Constantini Magni. Mem. Episcopal Churchmen Tenn. (v.p. 1956), Am. Ch. Union (v.p. 1958), S.A.R. (chpt. pres. 1977—), Nat. Young Pres.'s Orgn., U.S. C. of C., Nat. Office Mgmt. Assn. (pres. Nashville chpt. 1958-59), Am. Legion, Nat. Assn. Wholesalers, English Speaking Union, Westerners Internat. (sheriff Nashville chpt.), Magna Charta Barons, Phi Beta Kappa, Omicron Delta Gamma, Pi Kappa Alpha. Elk. Clubs: Nashville Exchange; Nashville Sewanee, Harvard, Nashville City, Cumberland (Nashville); Capitol Hill (Washington); Lakeview Country (Marshall, Tex.). Home: Rokeby 3901 Harding Rd Nashville TN 37205 Office: 16th Floor 1st Am Center Nashville TN 37238

PERRY, LEE ROWAN, lawyer; b. Chgo., Sept. 23, 1933; s. Watson Bishop and Helen (Rowan) P.; B.A., U. Ariz., 1955, LL.B., 1961; m. Barbara Ashcraft Mitchell, July 2, 1955; children—Christopher, Constance, Geoffrey. Admitted to Ariz. bar, 1961; clk. Udall & Udall, Tucson, 1960-61; practiced in Phoenix, 1961—; mem. firm Cunningham, Carson, Messinger, 1961-62, Carson, Messinger, Elliott, Laughlin & Ragan, 1962—. Mem. law rev. staff U. Ariz., 1959-61. Mem. Bd. Edn. Paradise Valley Elementary and High Sch. Dists., Phoenix, 1964-68, pres., 1968; bd. dirs. Florence Crittenton Services Ariz., 1967-72, treas., 1969, pres., 1970-72; bd. dirs. Family Service Assn. Ariz., 1975-76, Florence Crittenton div. Child Welfare League Am., 1976—, Vol. Bur. Maricopa County, 1977—, Am. Cancer Soc., 1978-80; pres., bd. dirs. Child Abuse Center, 1978-80; mem. nominating com. Cactus-Pine council Girl Scouts Am., 1978. Served to 1st lt. USAF, 1955-58. Mem. State Bar Ariz. (gen. conv. chmn. 1972), Am., Maricopa County bar assns., U. Ariz. Alumni (pres. Phoenix chpt. 1969-70), Phi Delta Phi, Phi Delta Theta (pres. 1954). Republican. Episcopalian (warden 1969-70). Clubs: Rotary (pres. 1975-76), Ariz., Plaza. Home: 10838 N 38th Pl Phoenix AZ 85028 Office: PO Box 33907 Phoenix AZ 85067

PERRY, MERVYN FRANCIS, investment co. exec.; b. Brockton, Mass., Feb. 20, 1923; s. Mervyn E. and Marie A. (Therrien) P.; A.B., Boston U., 1950, J.D., 1951; children—Cynthia, Richard, Susan, Janet. Mgr., Conn. Gen. Life Ins. Co., Cleve., 1954-62; v.p., dir., founder Mass. Gen. Life Ins. Co., Boston, 1962-65; pres., dir. Mass. Co. Distbrs., Inc., Boston, 1965-69; pres., chief exec. officer, dir. Mass. Co., Boston, 1969-77, also pres., chief exec. officer Mass. Fund; pres., chief exec. officer, chmn. bd. Independence Fund, Freedom Fund, MassCo Investment Mgmt. Corp., Boston, 1969-77, Mass. Fund for Income, 1973-77, Ready Reserves Trust, 1975-77; pres., chief exec. officer, chmn. bd. Fiduciary Investment Co., Boston, 1975-77; chmn. bd., chief exec. officer Investment Mgmt. Assos., Englewood, Colo., 1978—. Served with USNR, 1942-45, USAAF, 1946-68. C.L.U., Colo. Mem. Coll. Life Underwriters, Internat. Assn. Fin. Planners, Boston U. Alumni Assn. (Collegium of Disting. Alumni). Episcopalian. Clubs: Aspen (Colo.), Pinehurst Country (Denver), Union (Boston), University (Boston). Home: 4725 W Quincy Ave 1108 Denver CO 80236 Office: Investment Mgmt Assos Inc 7409 S Alton Ct Englewood CO 80112

PERRY, ROBERT PRESLEY, JR., soft drink co. exec.; b. Chattanooga, Feb. 20, 1928; s. Robert P. and Ida Alafair (Morrow) P.; B.S., U. Tenn., 1963; m. Charlotte Ann Coffelt, July 15, 1950; children—Elizabeth, Galyn. Asst. controller soil pipe div. Combustion Engring. Co., Chattanooga, 1960-63; controller Chattanooga Coca-Cola Bottling Co., 1963-65; adminstrv. asst. to pres. Crawford Johnson & Co., Inc., Birmingham, Ala., 1965-71; v.p. fin., treas. Coca-Cola Bottling Co. United, Inc., Birmingham, 1971—. Served with USAF, 1951-55. C.P.A., Tenn. Mem. Tenn. Ala. socs. C.P.A.'s, Am. Inst. C.P.A.'s. Mem. Ch. of Nazarene. Clubs: Downtown (Birmingham), The Club, Riverchase Country. Home: 865 Cable Dr Birmingham AL 35226 Office: 4600 E Lake Blvd Birmingham AL 35217 also PO Box 2006 Birmingham AL 35201

PERRY, RUSSELL H., ins. exec.; b. Cornell, Ill., Nov. 8, 1908; s. Walter O. and Mabel (Hilton) P.; student N.Y.U., 1937; J.D. cum laude, Bklyn. Law Sch., 1940; m. Phoebe Sherwood, June 2, 1956. Clk., Chgo. Fire and Marine Ins. Co., 1925-32; underwriter Republic Ins. Co., N.Y.C., 1934-38, charge eastern dept. underwriting, 1939-42, asst. to v.p., 1942-43, spl. agt. for L.I. and Westchester, 1943-44, mgr. eastern dept., 1945-47, resident sec., 1947-49, v.p., 1949-59, exec. v.p., 1959-61, pres., 1961-72, chmn. bd., chief exec. officer, 1972—, also dir.; chmn. bd., dir. Republic Financial Services, Inc., 1961—, Republic Ins. Co.; dir., mem. exec. com. Allied Finance Co.; trustee Murray Mortgage Investors, Dallas; dir. Union Bank & Trust Co., Bonanza Internat., Met. Savs. & Loan Assn., Taca, Inc., Dallas, Ins. Info. Inst., N.Y.; bd. govs. Internat. Ins. Seminars. Bd. dirs., mem. exec. com. Dallas Citizens Council; mem. exec. adv. council Coll. Bus. Adminstrn., N. Tex. State U.; bd. dirs. Tex. Research League, KERA-TV, Dallas, Am. Cancer Soc., Better Bus. Bur. Met. Dallas, Greater Dallas Planning Council, Nat. Center Public Interest; chmn. Dallas div. Salvation Army; pres. Tex. Bur. Econ. Understanding; chmn. bd. trustees, mem. exec. com. Dallas Community Chest Trust Fund; mem. devel. bd. Dallas Bapt. Coll.; bd. dirs. Tex. Good Rds. Assn., Big Bros./Big Sisters Am., Citizen' Choice, Washington; pres. Trinity Improvement Assn.; trustee Center Internat. Bus.; chmn. exec. com. Dallas Postal Customers Council; chmn. Gt. Plains Legal Found., Tex. Right to Work Com.; mem. adv. council Airline Passengers Assn.; dir. Tex. Soc. Prevention Blindness. Recipient G. Mabry Seay award Dallas Assn. Ins. Agts., 1970; Headliner of Year award Press Club Dallas, 1975; Distinguished Salesman of Dallas award Sales and Mktg. Execs. Dallas, 1977; orchid for uncommon support free enterprise Students in Free Enterprise, So. Meth. U., 1977; Person of Vision award Tex. Soc. Prevention Blindness, 1977; Linz award, 1978; Torch of Liberty award, 1979; named Boss of Year, Ins. Women of Dallas, 1976. Mem. Philonomic Soc., Am. Bar Assn., N.Y. Bar Assn., Dallas Bar (trustee), State Bar Tex., Tex. Ins. Adv. Assn. (exec. com.), La. Ins. Adv. Assn. (exec. com.), Am. Ins. Assn. (dir.), Assn. Fire and Casualty Ins. Cos. Tex. (exec. com.), Dallas (dir.), East Tex. (dir.), Tex. (dir.), N.Y., U.S. (dir., mem. pub. affairs com.) chambers commerce, Nat. Assn. Casualty and Surety Execs. (pres.), Tex. Catastrophe Property Ins. Assn. (alt. dir.), Tex. Property and Casualty Ins. Guaranty Assn. (chmn.), Navy League U.S. (adv. dir. Dallas chpt.), Newcomen Soc. N.Am. Tex. Assn. Taxpayers (dir.), Dallas Council on World Affairs (dir., chmn. bd., mem. exec. com.), Dallas Postal Customers Council (chmn. exec. com.), Delta Theta Phi. Rotarian. Clubs: N.Y. University, Insurance (past pres., dir.), Petroleum, Lancers, Knife and Fork (dir., exec. com.), Country (Dallas); Austin (Tex.). Home: 2817 Park Bridge Ct Dallas TX 75219 Office: 2727 Turtle Creek Blvd Dallas TX 75219

PERRY, STEPHEN CLAYTON, petroleum co. exec., former mayor; b. Atlanta, Feb. 9, 1942; s. Clayton Henry and Elizabeth Hill (Staples) P.; B. Indsl. Engring. (Ethyl Corp. scholar), Ga. Inst. Tech., 1964; M.B.A. (Pillsbury fellow), Harvard, 1968; m. Bonnie Janet Bentley, Nov. 27, 1965; 1 dau., Beverly Elizabeth. Indsl. engr. Union Carbide Corp., Columbia, Tenn., 1964; systems analyst, metals and controls div. Tex. Instruments, Attleboro, Mass., 1967; with Exxon Corp., 1968—, ops. mgr. ACS group Reliance Electric Co., affiliate Exxon Corp., Branchburg, N.J., 1980—. Mem. Berkeley Heights Twp. (N.J.) Com; 1977-79, dep. mayor, police commr., 1978, mayor, 1979. Served to capt., inf., AUS, 1964-66. Republican. Presbyterian. Home: 88 Valley Rd Berkeley Heights NJ 07922 Office: 59 Chubb Way Branchburg NJ

PERRY, THOMAS MANLEY, apparel retail exec.; b. Yankton, S.D., Mar. 22, 1942; s. Donald Edward and Elinor Celestine (Slowey) P.; B.A. in Bus. Adminstrn., B.S. in Psychology, Coll. of St. Thomas, St. Paul, 1964; postgrad. U. Minn., 1964-65; m. Barbara Annabelle Heisler, Feb. 1, 1969; children—Megan Colleen, Michael Langan. Asst. to pres. Dayton's Dept. Stores, Mpls., 1964-68; asst. to v.p. research and planning Donaldson's Dept. Stores, Mpls., 1968, buyer sportswear, 1969-71; v.p., gen. merchandise mgr. Braun's Fashions, Inc., Mpls., 1971-74; chmn. bd., pres. Perry Enterprises, Inc., Denver, 1975—; dir. S.D.S. Fashions Inc., Denver. Active, Denver Center Theatre Co., Denver Symphony Assn., Denver Art Mus. Mem. Alliance for Contemporary Art, Am. Adventurers Assn., Rocky Mountain Big Horn Soc., Sierra Club, Nat. Rifle Assn., Alpha Kappa Psi. Republican. Roman Catholic. Club: Watkins (Colo.) Gun. Home: 1293 S Williams St Denver CO 80210 Office: 701 W Hampden Ave Englewood CO 80110

PERRYMAN, BRUCE CLARK, savs. and loan assn. exec.; b. Laramie, Wyo., Jan. 28, 1939; s. Homer F. and Phyllis Coltharp (White) P.; student Colo. State U., 1957-58; fgn. lang. diploma Syracuse U., 1959; B.A., U. Wyo., 1965, B.A.in Bus. Edn., 1965, M.S. in Bus. Edn. (Wyo. State Tchrs. scholar), 1966, postgrad., 1970-71; m. Sharon Lynn Lungren, June 28, 1958; children—Kimberly Jo, Bruce Homer. Grad. research and teaching asst. U. Wyo.,1965-66; research info. specialist Wyo. State Dept. Edn., Cheyenne, 1966-67, dir. research coordinating unit, 1968-69, state dir. vocat. edn., 1969-71; asst. prof. bus./mktg. Adams State Coll., 1967-68; pres., exec. dir. Mountain Plains Edn., Inc., Glasgow, Mont., 1971-77; field underwriter N.Y. Life Ins. Co., Worland, Wyo., 1977-79; v.p., mgr. United Savs. & Loan Assn., Worland, 1979—; cons. career edn. Alt. del. Wyo. Republican Conv., 1980; mem. Worland Bd. Public Utilities; Soc.; pres. Zion Lutheran Ch. Consistory, Worland; mem. Worland Recreation Bd. Worland Sch. Bd., 1981. Served with USAF, 1958-62; ETO. U. Wyo. football scholar, 1957; Nat. Inst. Edn. grantee, 1971-76. Mem. U.S. League Savs. Assn., Nat. Assn. Life Underwriters, Nat. Assn. Home Builders, Am. Mgmt. Assn., NEA (life), U. Wyo. Alumni Assn. (life), Am. Vocat. Assn., Am. Vocat. Edn. Research Assn., Am. Assn. Sch. Adminstrs., Am. Assn. Community and Jr. Colls., Farm Bur. Fedn., Phi Delta Kappa. Clubs: Rotary (club dir.), Elks, Masons. Contbr. articles to profl. publs. Home: 404 S 18th St Worland WY 82401 Office: United Savs & Loan Assn 15th and Big Horn Worland WY 82401

PERSKY, JOSEPH H., lawyer, fin. co. exec.; b. Cleve., Dec. 7, 1914; s. Abraham E. and Sylvia (Meisel) P.; A.B. magna cum laude, Case-Western Res. U., 1936, LL.B., 1938; m. Roselyn Diamondstone, Sept. 8, 1940. Admitted to Ohio bar, 1938; mng. asso. firm Persky, Marken, Konigsberg and Shapiro Co., Cleve., 1938—; pres. A.J. Armstrong Co., Inc. of Ohio, Cleve., 1960—; v.p., sec., dir. Magnetics Internat., Inc.; sec., dir. Horizons Research, Inc.; sec., dir. Clark Consol. Industries, Inc., Kidron Body Co. Pres., Cleve. Coll. Jewish Studies, Fairmount Temple; trustee Jewish Community Fedn. Served to lt. USCGR, 1942-45. Mem. Am. Bar Assn., Ohio State Bar Assn., Bar Assn. Greater Cleve., Order of Coif, Phi Beta Kappa. Republican. Jewish. Clubs: Beechmont Country, Commerce, Masons. Office: 900 One Public Sq Cleveland OH 44113

PERSONEUS, ARLINGTON M., chem. and plastics co. exec.; b. Grand Gorge, N.Y., Oct. 2, 1926; s. Lester and Hattie (Barringer) P.; B.C.E., Union Coll., Schnectady, 1949; m. Jacqueline J. Post, Nov. 26, 1949; children—Linda J., Mark A., Kim E., Neal B. Field salesman U.S. Gypsum Co., Chgo., 1949-54, dist. mgr., 1954-61, div. mgr., 1961-64, mktg. services mgr., 1965-66; nat. sales mgr. Gen. Tire & Rubber Co., Akron, Ohio, 1966-70, dir. mktg. services, 1970-71, v.p., chem. plastics div., 1971—; pres. GTR Wallcovering Co. Served with USNR, 1944-45. Mem. Wallcovering Mfrs. Assn. (v.p., dir.), Chem. Fabrics Film Assn. Republican. Home: 22 Linda Dr Allendale NJ 07401

PERSONS, (AGNES) MADELYN MORONEY, sales exec., educator, author; b. St. Paul; d. Patrick M. and Katherine (Cunningham) Moroney; student Coll. St. Catherine, St. Paul; B.A., U. Minn.; postgrad. Columbia U., UCLA; M.S., U. So. Calif., 1949; m. Ralph C. Persons, Feb. 11, 1933 (div.). Music and drama editor Minn. Daily, 1925-26; contbr. interviews and spl. stories Mpls. Tribune, St. Paul Pioneer-Press, 1925-26, N.Y. World, 1926-28; advt. mgr. Phillips-Hambaugh Realty & Constrn. Corp., Los Angeles, 1929-30; sales promotion Barker Bros., Inc., Los Angeles, 1930-31; editor The Firing Line, Richfield Oil Corp., Pacific Coast advt. dept. and asst. editor The Richfield Salesman, 1932-34; partner in charge advt. and sales promotion nationally, 1934-44; sole owner The Persons Co. (nat. pub. relations), Los Angeles, 1945—; treas. Bellemont Industries, Inc., Bellemont, Ariz.; part-time instr. Los Angeles Pub. Sch. System, 1944—; investor securities, real estate. Dir. in charge publicity Calif. Arthritis Found., 1962; active Nat. Council on Alcoholism, Pres.'s Council on Phys. Fitness: dir. charge publicity So. Calif. Republican Women, 1940-44, Los Feliz Rep. Women, 1954-58; legis. chmn. Loma-Portal Rep. Women Federated, 1976-77, 78-79. Recipient Lulu award Los Angeles Advt. Women in publicity, 1947, in pub. relations, 1950. Mem. Los Angeles C. of C. (dir. charge publicity, 1944-52), Theta Sigma Phi (chmn. publicity; mem. Fashionations com., 1956, editor, advt. mgr. Fashionations 1958). Roman Catholic. Home: 3205 Whittier St San Diego CA 92106 Office: PO Box 81052 San Diego CA 92138

PERTSCHUK, MICHAEL, chmn. FTC; b. London, Jan. 12, 1933; s. David and Sarah (Baumander) P. (parents Am. citizens); B.A., Yale U., 1954, LL.D., J.D., 1959; m. Carleen Joyce Dooley, Sept. 1954 (div. Dec. 1976); children—Mark, Amy; m. 2d, Anna Phillips Sofaer, Apr. 1977. Asst. in instruction Yale U. Law Sch., 1957; admitted to Oreg. bar, 1959; law clk. to U.S. Dist. Ct. Judge Gus O. Solomon, Portland, Oreg., 1959-60; asso. firm Hart, Rockwood, Davies, Biggs & Strayer, Portland, 1960-62; legis. asst. to Senator Maurine B. Neuberger of Oreg., 1962-64; trade relation counsel Senate Commerce Com., Washington, 1964-68, chief counsel, staff dir., 1968-77; chmn. FTC, Washington, 1977—; professorial lectr. Am. U.; adj. prof. Georgetown U. Sch. Law; lectr. pub. law seminars Brookings Instn.; pub. mem. Nat. Interagy. Council Smoking and Health, 1973-76; commr. Nat. Commn. Product Safety, 1967-70; mem. council Adminstrv. Conf. U.S.; mem. Nat. Commn. for Rev. of Antitrust Laws and Procedures. Mem. Nat. Acad. Pub. Adminstrn. Served with AUS, 1954-56. Office: FTC Pennsylvania Ave at 6th St NW Washington DC 20580*

PERUGINI, THOMAS FRANCIS, fin. exec.; b. Phila., July 14, 1934; s. Rocco Ralph and Lydia (Julian) P.; B.S. cum laude, LaSalle Coll., 1960; postgrad. Temple U., 1961-62; m. Bernice Theresa Kelly, Sept. 10, 1960; children—Lisa Kathleen, Thomas Francis II, Patrick James, Michael R. Vice pres., comptroller Lamp div. ITT, Lynn, Mass., 1968-71, mgr. fin. controls, N.Y.C., 1971-72, v.p., dir. fin. ITT Grinnell Corp., Providence, 1976—; v.p. CitiBank N.A., N.Y.C., 1972-76. Mem. Fin. Execs. Inst. Republican. Roman Catholic. Clubs: R.I. Country, K.C. Office: 260 W Exchange St Providence RI 02903

PERULLO, LOUIS CHRISTOPHER, JR., retail splty. chain exec.; b. Boston, July 23, 1939; s. Louis Christopher and Ferma Florence (Fiore) P.; B.A., Dartmouth Coll., 1960; m. Karen Telesco, May 7, 1976; 1 dau., Laura. Asst. media buyer Grey Advt., N.Y.C., 1960-63; media dir. Chirurg & Cairns, Boston, 1962-64; account supr. Arnold & Co., Boston, 1964-66; dir. advt. Thom McAn Shoe Co., Worcester,

Mass., 1966-74; v.p. advt., display and constrn. Kay Jewelers, Alexandria, Va., 1974—; performing mem. Potomac River Jazz Club. Served with U.S. Army, 1960-62. Recipient cert. of appreciation USMC-Toys for Tots, 1970, 73, cert. of merit for lyric composition Am. Song Festival, 1976; named Outstanding Driver, Md. Internat. Raceway, 1976. Mem. Nashville Song Writers Assn., Art Dirs. Club Washington, Nat. Hot Rod Assn., Am. Fedn. Musicians. Roman Catholic. Club: Italian Am. Citizens (life). Poem Bix Beiderbecke included in Best Loved Contemporary Poems, 1979. Home: 707 S Lee St Alexandria VA 22314 Office: 320 King St Alexandria VA 22314

PETCHENIK, EDWARD F., chem. co. ofcl.; b. St. Louis, Sept. 9, 1933; s. Roger Owens and Johanna Alice (St. Denis) P.; B.A., Dartmouth Coll., 1956; M.S. in Mktg., Columbia U., 1958; m. Susan Roth, Nov. 3, 1960; children—Alice, Susan, Martin. Mfr.'s rep. Smith Clothing Co., N.Y.C., 1960-64; with Acme Chem. Co., 1964—, asst. v.p., 1968-70, v.p., 1970-76, pres., 1976—, chmn. bd., 1978—, also dir. Served with AUS, 1958-60. Mem. Am. Chem. Soc., Assn. U.S. Army. Address: 335 Lincolnwood Rd Highland Park IL 60035

PETER, PHILLIPS SMITH, elec. product co. exec.; b. Washington, Jan. 24, 1932; s. Edward Compston and Anita Phillips (Smith) P.; B.A., U. Va., 1954, J.D., 1959; m. Jania Jayne Hutchins, Apr, 8, 1961; children—Phillips Smith Peter Jr., Jania Jayne Hutchins. Admitted to Calif. bar, 1959; asso. mem. firm McCutchen, Doyle, Brown, Enerson, San Francisco, 1959-63; with Gen. Electric Co. and subsidiaries, various locations, 1963—, v.p. corp. bus. devel., 1973-76, v.p., Washington, 1976—. Mem. leadership com. United Fund, Darien, Conn., 1974—, finance com. Republican Town Com., Darien, 1974—. Served with Transp. Corps, U.S. Army, 1954-56. Mem. Calif. Bar. Assn., Elfun Soc., Order Coif, Omicron Delta Kappa. Episcopalian. Clubs: Wee Burn (Darien); Eastern Yacht (Marblehead, Mass.); Farmington Country (Charlottesville, Va.); Ponte Vedra (Fla.); Lago Mar (Fort Lauderdale, Fla.); Racquet (Miami Beach, Fla.); Landmark (Stamford, Conn.); Congressional Country (Potomac, Md.); Georgetown, F Street (Washington); Coral Beach and Tennis (Bermuda). Mem. edit. bd. Va. Law Rev., 1957-59. Home: 10805 Tara Rd Potomac MD 20854 Office: 777 14th St NW Washington DC 20005

PETERHANS, LOUIS RAYMOND, JR., aluminum products mfg. co. exec.; b. Evanston, Ill., Oct. 14, 1949; s. Louis R. and Rosemary (Rudersdorf) P.; B.A., St. Thomas Coll., 1971; M.B.A., Loyola U., Chgo., 1972; m. Mary Carol Toebber, June 1, 1974; 1 dau., Megan Lynn. Fin. planning mgr. Nichols-Homeshield, Aurora, Ill., 1977—; instr. quantitative methods St. Thomas Coll., St. Paul, 1969-71. Vice-pres., bd. dirs. Holy Cross Parish Credit Union, 1979, chmn. bd., 1980. Served with USAF, 1973-77. Mem. Assn. of M.B.A. Execs., Batavia Jaycees (treas.). Home: 214 N Lincoln St Batavia IL 60510 Office: 1470 Farnsworth Ave Aurora IL 60507

PETERS, ALEC, mktg. and mfg. co. exec.; b. Queens, N.Y., Sept. 28, 1934; s. George and Sophie (John) P.; B.S. in Chemistry, Adelphi U., 1958; m. Martha Kyriakos, Oct. 7, 1957; children—Alec, Nicholas. Dist. mgr. Equitable Life Ins. Co., N.Y.C., 1960-65; pres., dir. Omnicard Systems Inc., N.Y.C., 1965-70, Transam. Color Labs Ltd., N.Y.C., 1972-76; v.p., dir. Gen. Film Devel. Corp., Southport, Conn., 1970-72; v.p., dir. Omni Industries Corp., Maspeth, N.Y., 1968—; cons. mktg. dir. Colvac Internat. Corp., N.Y.C., 1976—; fin. and mktg. cons. Electro-Photo Systems Inc., Anaheim, Calif., 1970—. Served with U.S. Army, 1954-56. Patentee 1st photo identification card compatable for computer input. Home: 250 Garth Rd Scarsdale NY 10583

PETERS, JOSEPH HARLAN, savs. and loan exec.; b. Coffeyville, Kans., Feb. 21, 1920; s. Phillip John and Florence (Harris) P.; A.A., Coffeyville Jr. Coll., 1940; A.B., Baker U., 1942; m. Geraldine Carr, Feb. 8, 1947; children—Susan Jo, Julie Lynn. With Blue Valley Fed. Savings & Loan Co., Kansas City, Mo., 1946—, successively clk., asst. sec., 1946-52, v.p., 1952-61, dir., 1955—, pres., mng. officer, 1961—; dir. United Mo. Bank Blue Valley, Kansas City. Mem. Independence Bd. of Edn., 1966-72. Trustee, Jackson County 4-H Found.; trustee Baker U., Baldwin City, Kans., Mt. Washington Cemetery; bd. govs. Am. Royal Assn.; bd. dirs. Kansas City Better Bus. Bur. Served with USNR, 1943-46. Hon. life fellow Truman Library Inst.; mem. Am. Savings and Loan Inst. (chpt. pres. 1948), Mo. (v.p. 1964, dir. 1968-69), Kansas City (chpt. pres. 1965-66) savs. and loan leagues, Kansas City C. of C., Independence C. of C. (pres. 1957), Blue Valley Mfrs. and Bus. Mens Assn. (pres. 1966-67), Am. Legion, Delta Tau Delta (Nat. Achievement award 1976). Democrat. Presbyterian (elder). Clubs: Kansas City Chiefs Redcoat, Masons, Rotary (bd. Independence 1970, pres. 1977-78). Home: San Francisco Towers Kansas City MO 64108 Office: 6515 Independence Ave Kansas City MO 64125

PETERS, JUDITH ROCHELLE, educator; b. Phila., July 16, 1951; d. John Bernard and Priscilla Jo (Johnson) P.; B.S. (Senatorial scholar 1970-72), Pa. State U., 1973; M.B.A. (Health Adminstrn. fellow 1973-75), Cornell U., 1975; postgrad. Temple U. Sch. Pharmacy, 1975-77. Supr., Phila. Dept. Recreation, 1971-74; pharmacy intern Needle & Boonin, Zackian Bros., Bell Family Pharmacies, Phila., 1976-79; pharmacy mgr. Adero Pharmacy, Phila., 1980—; tech. asst. Del. Valley Regional Planning Commn., 1973; sci. specialist Phila. Bd. Edn., 1978—. Vol., water safety instr., lifeguard ARC, Phila., 1971—. Mem. Nat. Assn. Health Services Execs., Am. Public Health Assn., Internat. City Mgmt. Assn. Democrat. Presbyterian. Clubs: United Presbyn. Women, United Soul Ensemble. Office: Adero Pharmacy 2267 N 19th St Philadelphia PA 19132

PETERS, ROBERT CARL, distbn. co. exec.; b. Kansas City, Mo., May 17, 1939; s. John Carl and Grace Florine (Campbell) P.; B.S., U. So. Calif., 1961, M.B.A., 1968; m. Kathleen Gallagher, June 2, 1961; children—John, Laura, Daniel, Michael. Project leader info. systems Atlantic Richfield Co., Los Angeles, 1965-67; mgr. info. systems Paramount Pictures Corp., Hollywood, Calif., 1967-69, controller TV div., 1969-70, v.p. fin., 1970-73; pres. non-theatrical div., pres. subs. Paramount Communication, Inc., 1973-80; sr. v.p. Paramount Pictures Corp., 1980—. Served with USMC, 1961-65. Mem. Calif. Motion Picture Council, TV Acad. Arts and Scis. Democrat. Clubs: Cardinal and Gold, Football Alumni, Trojan (U. So. Calif.). Exec. producer film: Man Belongs to the Earth, 1974. Home: 5251 Genesta Ave Encino CA 91316 Office: 5451 Marathon St Hollywood CA 90038

PETERSEN, CONRAD WILLIAM, soap co. exec.; b. Chgo., Mar. 21, 1924; s. William F. and Alma (Schmidt) P.; B.S. cum laude in Mech. Engring., Northwestern U., 1946; m. Kathryn Anne Reebie, Nov. 17, 1951; children—Barbara R., Conrad William. Pres., Petersen Oven Co., Franklin Park, Ill., 1950-58; asst. to pres. and dir. Baker Perkins, Inc., Saginaw, Mich., 1958-62; gen. mgr. indsl. div. Lever Bros. Co., N.Y.C., 1962—. Mem. Representative Town Meeting Greenwich (Conn.); v.p. North East Greenwich Assn., 1980. Served to ensign USNR, 1943-46. Mem. Am. Oil Chemists Soc., Soc. Bakery Engrs., ASME, Tau Beta Pi, Pi Tau Sigma. Clubs: Stanwich (Greenwich); Chemists (N.Y.C.); University (Chgo.). Home: 9 Dingletown Rd Greenwich CT 06830 Office: 390 Park Ave New York NY 10022

PETERSEN, GARY LEE, oil co. exec.; b. Pocatello, Idaho, Jan. 20, 1942; s. Lee Hans and Irma Louise (Ayres) P.; student Idaho State U., 1960-62; B.S., U. Ida., 1964; M.B.A., U. So. Calif., 1973; m. Virginia Sue Mitchell, Dec. 20, 1970; children—Erik Stephen, Dana Kristopher, Heidi Kristine. Tech. service engr. Texaco, Inc., Wilmington, Calif., 1964-73; staff engr. Texaco, Inc., Houston, 1973-75; asst. to pres./v.p. U.S. Oil & Refining Co., Los Angeles, 1975-79, pres., 1979—; dir. Bruin Carbon Dioxide Sales Corp. Mem. Ind. Refiners Assn.'Calif. (dir. 1979—). Presbyterian. Clubs: Jonathan, Petroleum of Los Angeles, U. So. Calif. M.B.A.'s. Home: 4312 Fir Ave Seal Beach CA 90740 Office: 5150 Wilshire Blvd Los Angeles CA 90036

PETERSEN, HAZEL MIRIAM, accountant; b. Oleander, Calif., Oct. 17, 1915; d. Maurice and Lydia (Petersen) Petersen; student Dana Coll., Nebr., 1933, 34, Fresno State Coll., 1934-36. Asst. cashier S.H. Kress & Co., 1936-42; payroll mgr. Valley Express Co., Valley Motor Lines, Inc., 1942-69; claims mgr. Imperial Truck Lines, 1969-70, with accounting dept. Uco Oil Co., Whittier, Calif., 1970—. Pvt. tchr. piano, 1942-60, voice, 1942-62; ch. organist, 1929—, choral dir., 1936—. Mem. Am. Guild Organists, Internat. Platform Assn., Am. Bus. Women's Assn., Choral Condrs. Guild. Clubs: Am. Lutheran Women, Christian Business and Professional Women's. Home: 11846 E Floral Dr Apt 20 Whittier CA 90601 Office: 2100 SE Main Irvine CA 92714

PETERSEN, MARSHALL ARTHUR, mfg. co. exec.; b. Whittier, Calif., June 21, 1938; s. Arthur J. and Ester V. (Jensen) P.; B.S., U. Redlands, 1960; M.B.A. (Danforth fellow), Stanford U., 1962; m. Georgia Lea Higgins, Aug. 21, 1960; children—David M., Steven L., Karen E., Jennifer L. Investor relations mgr. TRW, Inc., Cleve., 1967-69, dir. investor relations, 1969-71, asst. treas., 1971-73, treas., 1973—, v.p., 1976—; treas. Cin. Milacron, Inc., 1977-79; sr. v.p., sec., treas. Am. Microsystems, Inc., 1979—. Mem. Fin. Execs. Inst., Nat. Investor Relations Inst. (past pres.), Omicron Delta Kappa. Home: 19308 Melinda Circle Saratoga CA 95070 Office: 3800 Homestead St Santa Clara CA 95051

PETERSEN, MAUN TYRE, constrn. cons.; b. East Ely, Nev., Apr. 24, 1944; s. Maun Tyre and Gwen (Christiansen) P.; B.S., U. Utah, 1969; m. Margene Winegar. Constrn. auditor Kennecott Copper Corp., N.Y.C., 1970-75; pres., owner Diamond Enterprises, Salt Lake City, 1972—; v.p., dir. Internat. Constrn. Co., Salt Lake City, 1974—; adminstrv. exec. Weyher Constrn. Co., Salt Lake City, 1975-78; v.p., dir. Domgaard Assos., Salt Lake City, 1978-80; partner Elliott-Petersen, Cons., 1980—; chmn. bd. Fox Investment Ltd., Salt Lake City. Del. Utah Democratic party, 1970-72. Mem. Am. Mgmt. Assn., Inst. Internal Auditors. Mormon. Home: 3014 Millcreek Rd Salt Lake City UT 84109 Office: 2040 E 3300 S Suite 3 Salt Lake City UT 84109

PETERSEN, SYDNEY R., oil co. exec.; b. Oakland, Calif., 1930; B.S., U. Calif., Berkeley, 1953; married. With Getty Oil Co., 1955—, group v.p. refining, distbn. and fin., 1974-77, group v.p. fin., 1977-79, pres., chief operating officer, Los Angeles, 1979-80, chmn. bd., chief exec. officer, 1980—, also dir.; dir. Nuclear Fuel Services, Mitsubishi Oil Co. Served with U.S. Army, 1953-55. Office: Getty Oil Co 3810 Wilshire Blvd Los Angeles CA 90010*

PETERSEN, W(ALTER) HAROLD, bus. exec., financeer; b. Council Bluffs, Iowa, Feb. 19, 1928; s. Walter Harry and Emma Elvina (Matthiensen) P.; student UCLA, 1945-48, U. Nebr., Omaha, 1948-49; m. Mary Jacqulyn O'Meara, Apr. 23, 1949; children—Constance Marie, Michael Brian, Mark Stephen, Thomas Robert. Mgr. spl. risks and assn. group depts. Mut. of Omaha, 1948-54; ins. broker, Omaha, 1954-56; supt. agencies Am. United Life, Indpls., 1956-60; exec. v.p., pres. Underwriters Nat. Assurance Co., Indpls., 1960-67; pres., chief exec. officer Petersen Mktg. and Mgmt. Corp., Los Angeles, 1967—; instr. advanced health underwriting seminars Mich. State U., Fla. State U., Purdue U., Tulane U.; pres. Ind. Health Underwriters Assn., 1961-62, Indpls. Health Underwriters Assn., 1960-61; pres., dir. Mass Benefit Corp.; instr. health ins. tng. course and health ins. bus. planning Calif. Soc. Public Employees. Chmn. Council Bluffs (Iowa) ARC, 1954, Community Chest, 1954. Cert. instr. Disability Ins. Tng. Council and Life Underwriters Tng. Council, Health Ins. Tng. Course and Health Ins. in Bus. Planning; registered health underwriter. Mem. Nat. Assn. Life Underwriters, Calif. Assn. Life Underwriters, Los Angeles Assn. Life Underwriters, W. Los Angeles Life Underwriters Assn. (v.p.), Nat. Assn. Health Underwriters, Los Angeles Assn. Health Underwriters, Acad. Ins. and Fin. (pres., dir.). Republican. Clubs: Kiwanis, Mission Lakes Country, Sertoma (pres. Omaha, 1953). Author: The Pilgrim Story, 1978; author, pub. tng. materials in field; contbr. articles to publs. in field; speaker on ins. and fin. Home: 127 S Granville Ave Los Angeles CA 90049 Office: 11661 San Vicente Blvd Los Angeles CA 90049

PETERSON, ARTHUR PAUL, JR., steel co. exec.; b. Chgo., June 20, 1923; s. Arthur Paul and Lillian Susanne (Hummel) P.; B.A., DePauw U., 1946; postgrad Purdue U., 1946-48; m. Idella Felice Fields, July 2, 1944; children—Sheryl Lynn, Arthur Paul, Patricia Sue. Asst. prof. math. Purdue U., 1946-48, asst. prof. naval engring., 1948-50; sales mgr. Alprodco, Inc., Kempton, Ind., 1950-51; with Ingersoll Johnson Steel, New Castel, Ind., 1951—, v.p. sales, 1971—; dir. Pan Am. Bridge Co., New Castle, 1960-61. Committeeman Republican 7th Precinct, New Castle, 1951-53; mem. budget com. United Fund., New Castle, 1974-76; bd. advisors Goodwill Industries, Indpls.; chmn. adminstrv. bd., trustee, vice chmn. fin. commn. First United Methodist Church, New Castle. Served with U.S. Navy, 1943-46; capt. Res. ret. Deocrated Bronze Star with Combat V; recipient Boy Scout Leadership award, 1961. Mem. Naval Res. Assn., Res. Officers Assn., Navy League U.S., U.S. Naval Inst., Am. Mgmt. Assn., Sigma Chi. Clubs: Kiwanis, Westwood Country, Mason, Elks. Home: 1150 Woodlawn Dr New Castle IN 47362 Office: POB 370 W Route 38 New Castle IN 47362

PETERSON, BRUCE ROBERT, bldg. cons.; b. Hutchinson, Minn., Mar. 13, 1947; s. Donald Morris and Margaret Marie (Prieve) P.; student Tex. Lutheran Coll., 1966-68; B.S., Mankato (Minn.) State U., 1969; m. Rebecca Lynn Clapp, May 3, 1980; children—Sonja, Chad, Andy, Mark. Ins. adjuster Hartford Ins. Co., Mpls., 1970-72; sr. claims adjuster Aid Ins. Services, Mpls., 1972-74; bldg. cons. Don Peterson Constrn. Co., Hutchinson, 1974-77; pres. Hutchinson Builders Inc., 1977-79; bldg. cons. Modern Bldg. Systems, Hutchinson, 1979—. Alderman, Hutchinson City Council, 1975—; bd. dirs. Burns Manor, Hutchinson, 1980—; adv. bd. Hutchinson Sr. Citizens, 1976-79; mem. Planning Commn., Hutchinson, 1975-78; mem. Hutchinson Community Edn. Com., 1978—; mem. Hutchinson Park and Recreation Bd., 1978—; mem. Hutchinson Tree Bd., 1980—; council rep. Hutchinson Street Dept., 1975-78; mem. Hutchinson Airport Commn., 1975-78; mem. adv. bd. Hutchinson Area Vocat.-Tech. Sch., 1977-78. Mem. Minn. Recreation and Parks Assn., Minn. Metal Builders Assn., Hutchinson C. of C. Republican. Lutheran. Club: Hutchinson Elks. Office: 1115 W Hwy 7 Hutchinson MN 55350

PETERSON, CORNELIUS RANDALL, computer and energy co. exec.; b. Provo, Utah, Aug. 25, 1947; s. Cornelius Rawlings and Enid (Poulson) P.; B.S. in Acctg. with honors, Brigham Young U., 1972, M.B.A., 1974; m. Sheralyn Strong, June 25, 1975; children—America Jill, Kjirsten Anelalani, Cornelius R. Fin. analyst intern Envirotech Corp., Salt Lake City, summer 1973; bus. mgr. Intermountain Labs., Inc., Midvale, Utah, 1974-75; dir. fin. services Hawaii Campus, Brigham Young U., Laie, 1975-76; loan adminstr. Alexander & Baldwin, Inc., Honolulu, 1976-81; treas. Billings Energy Corp. (Mont.), 1981—; v.p., sec.-treas. Bus. Specialists Internat., Inc.; exec. treas., trustee Enterprise Trust; mng. partner Huiocho; fin. cons. Internat. Mgmt. Specialists; treas. Alexander & Baldwin Employees Fed. and State Polit. Action Coms. Del. Hawaii Constnl. Conv., 1978; sec.-treas. Nuuanu/Punchbowl Neighborhood Bd., 1977-79; active Nat. Taxpayers Union, Citizens for Tax and Spending Limits, Hawaii Right to Life, Hana Pono, Boy Scouts Am. C.P.A.; cert. mgmt. acct. Mem. Am. Inst. C.P.A.'s, Hawaii Soc. C.P.A.'s, Nat. Assn. Accts., Inst. Mgmt. Acctg., Hawaii C. of C., Am. Entrepreneurs Assn., Brigham Young U. Mgmt. Soc. Mormon. Home: 408 E Lakeview Dr Blue Springs MO 64015 Office: 18600 E 37 Terr S Independence MO 64057

PETERSON, CYNTHIA JANE KITTSON, bldg. materials co. exec.; b. Prosser, Wash., Nov. 24, 1948; d. Augustan and Myrna Ann (Nickisch) Kittson; A.A. with honors in Bus. Adminstrn., Columbia Basin Coll., 1975; postgrad. Wash. State U., 1975-77, Central Wash. State U., 1976-77; m. George Charles Peterson, Jan. 13, 1968. Receptionist, St. Luke's Hosp., Marquette, Mich., 1969; dep. treas. Kittitas County Treas.'s Office, Ellensburg, Wash., 1971-73; exec. sec. Frank B. Hall Ins. Co., Portland, Oreg., 1973-74; treas./controller Kennewick (Wash.) Indsl. & Elec. Supply, Inc., 1974—. Bd. dirs. Kennewick-Pasco Community Concert Assn., 1976, vol. membership dr., 1975—. Recipient Outstanding Leadership award Columbia Basin Coll., 1975. Mem. Soc. Cert. Consumer Credit Execs., Tri-Cities Consumer Credit Assn. (dir., sec.; gen. conf. chmn. 1982), Wash. State Consumer Credit Assn., Credit Women-Internat. (pres. Tri-Cities chpt. 1979-80), Internat. Consumer Credit Assn., Tri-Cities C. of C. (legis. com., sub-chmn. usury issue). Roman Catholic. Club: Job's Daus. Home: 4905 W 7th Ave Kennewick WA 99336 Office: 113 E Columbia Dr Kennewick WA 99336

PETERSON, GEORGE ELLSWORTH, JR., financial exec.; b. Bklyn., Apr. 15, 1937; s. George Ellsworth and Marjorie (Day) P.; A.B., U. Calif. at San Francisco State Coll., 1960. Internal auditor, plant controller Crown Zellerbach Corp., San Francisco, Miami, Fla. and Newark, Del., 1963-72; internal auditor, controller, corporate center Planning Research Corp., Los Angeles, 1972-76; controller Casa Blanca Convalescent Homes, San Diego, 1976-78; controller Medevac, Inc., San Diego, 1978-79; cons., 1979—; v.p. fin. Aegean Marble, Inc., San Diego, 1980—. Served with U.S. Army, 1960-62. Mem. Newark C. of C. Episcopalian. Home: 9804 Guisante Terr San Diego CA 92124

PETERSON, HUBERT GERHARD, ins. co. exec.; b. Washington, Apr. 18, 1940; s. Hubert Hooper and Clotilde Ruth (Dinan) P.; student U. Conn., 1958-62; m. Sandra Diane Long, Oct. 1, 1966; children—Kenneth Harmon, Randall Hubert, Allan Douglas. Sr. group rep. Conn. Gen. Ins. Co., N.Y.C., 1962-65; group exec. Am. Mutual Ins. Co., Wethersfield, Conn., 1965-67, field sales mgr., 1967-70; zone mgr. Hartford Ins. Group, Voorhees, N.J., 1970-75, field dir., 1975-77, area dir.-group sales, 1977-80, dir. field sales, group life and health, 1980—; instr., cons. in field. Served with U.S. Army, 1962. Recipient Group Pension award Hartford Ins. Group, 1971, named Mgr. of Year, 1974, 77, Zone Mgr. of Year, 1975, Area of Year, 1979. Mem. Nat. Assn. Security Dealers, U. Conn. Alumni Assn., Chi Phi. Home: 128 Thornhill Rd Cherry Hill NJ 08003 Office: 1201 White Horse Rd Voorhees NJ 08043

PETERSON, J. CHANDLER, fin. planner; b. Swainsboro, Ga., Mar. 28, 1945; s. William James and Lilian (Chandler) P.; A.B., Emory U., 1966, J.D., 1971; m. Barbara Berry, Oct. 29, 1977; children—James Chandler, Thaxton Thrasher. Pres., Victory Farms, Ailey, Ga., 1966—, Ga. Furniture Co., Ailey, 1966—, J. Chandler Peterson/Wealth Mgmt., Atlanta, 1974—; v.p. Ind. Securities Corp., Atlanta, 1969-73; founder, pres. Phoenix Mgmt. Corp., Atlanta, 1977—, Phoenix Petroleum Co., Atlanta, 1977—; dir. Ailey Mfg. Co., Ailey Enterprises Co., Ailey, Inc., Metter Mfg. Co., Embassy Enterprises, Southeastern Oil Co.; admitted to Ga. bar, 1971. Mem. Internat. Assn. Fin. Planners (founding mem., pres. Ga. chpt. 1973-74, nat. pres. 1974-75, nat. chmn. bd. 1975-76). Certified fin. planner Coll. Fin. Planning. Author: Exemptions from Taxation, 1968; contbg. editor Fin. Planner mag., 1973—; pub. The Peterson Report on Wealth Mgmt. newsletter, 1969—; columnist The Peterson Principles, Atlanta mag., 1979—. Office: Cain Tower Suite 700 229 Peachtree St NE Atlanta GA 30303

PETERSON, JAMES EDWARD, econ. devel. cons.; b. Birmingham, Ala., June 5, 1946; s. Isiah and Alberta (Jackson) P.; A.B. in Bus. Adminstrn., Booker T. Washington Bus. Coll., 1967; B.A. in Philosophy and Polit. Sci., U. Calif., Berkeley, 1976; M.A. in Urban Studies and Planning, Antioch U., 1978. Congressional asst. 8th Dist. of Calif., 1970-75; exec. dir. Minority Profession Employment Conf., U. Calif., Berkeley, 1975-76; exec. v.p. Pacific Consultants, Washington, 1976-78; pres. Corp. & Urban Design Assos., Berkeley, Calif., 1978—; lectr. Antioch U. Mem. Alameda County Human Relations Commn., 1975-79; mem. Senate Select Com. of No. Calif., Labor Subcom. on Small Bus., 1980. Mem. Am. Mgmt. Assn., Oakland C. of C., San Francisco Cons. Group. Clubs: Mastermind, Peterson Investment. Author articles in field. Office: Corp & Urban Design Assos 2828 Telegraph Ave Suite 103 Berkeley CA 94705

PETERSON, JAMES HOMER, state ofcl.; b. Galva, Ill., Jan. 9, 1930; s. William James and Grace Ada (Pierce) P.; B.A., Colo. Coll., 1951; postgrad. Tex. Christian U., U. Wis., Ottumwa Heights Coll.; m. Helen Marie Barthell, June 10, 1951; children—Mark Stuart, Sarah Lee, Paige Elizabeth. With Ralston Purina Co., 1952-77, plant mgr., Visalia, Calif., 1962-63, area dir. ops., Fond du Lac, Wis. and Ottumwa, Iowa, 1963-74, v.p., Oklahoma City, 1974-77; dir. purchasing State of Okla., Oklahoma City, 1977—. Asst. treas. Last Frontier council Boy Scouts Am.; trustee Ottumwa Heights Coll.; alumni rep. Colo. Coll. Served with USMC, 1951-53. Mem. U.S. Marine Corps Res. Officers Assn., Oklahoma City C. of C. Presbyterian. Clubs: Oklahoma City Rotary, Masons, Elks. Home: 1421 Mil 1 Creek Rd Edmond OK 73034 Office: State Capitol Oklahoma City OK 73105

PETERSON, JAMES ROBERT, diversified corp. exec.; b. Momence, Ill., Oct. 28, 1927; s. Clyde C. and Pearl P. (Deliere) P.; student St. Thomas Coll., 1945, Iowa State U., 1945-46, U. Colo., 1946, Northwestern U., 1946; B.S. cum laude in Mktg., U. Ill., 1952; postgrad. in bus. Stanford U., 1967; m. Betty Windham, May 12, 1949; children—Richard James, Lynn Ann Peterson Anderson, Susan Kathryn, John Windham. With Pillsbury Co., 1952-76, v.p., gen. mgr. Grocery Products Co., Mpls., 1968-71, group v.p. consumer cos., 1971-73, pres. Pillsbury Co., Mpls., 1973-76, also dir.; exec. v.p. R.J. Reynolds Industries, Inc., Winston-Salem, N.C., 1976—, also dir.; dir. Avon Products, Inc., Dun & Bradstreet Corp., Waste Mgmt., Inc.,

Shedd-Brown, Inc. Bd. regents St. Olaf Coll.; bd. visitors Wake Forest Coll.; trustee Morvaian Music Found., Winston-Salem, Nat. council Boy Scouts Am. Served to lt. USN, 1945-50. Recipient Bronze Table award U. Ill., 1952. Mem. Beta Gamma Sigma (Dirs. Table). Methodist. Club: Old Town (Winston-Salem). Home: 2832 Bartram Rd Winston-Salem NC 27106 Office: RJ Reynolds Industries Inc World Hdqrs Reynolds Blvd Winston-Salem NC 27102

PETERSON, JOHN WESLEY, life underwriter; b. Leonard, Ark., Nov. 1, 1926; s. William W. and Lucy M. (Lewis) P.; student ins. courses So. Meth. U.; m. Laura White, Nov. 15, 1974; children—Manya D. Otis, J. Ross. Successively agt., supr., agy. mgr., agy. dir. John Hancock Mut. Life Ins. Co., 1965; life underwriter estate planning, Tulsa, 1955-65; asso. dir., tchr. So. Meth. U. Inst. Ins.; cons. agy. mgmt. Served with AUS, 1945-46, 50-51. Recipient ins. awards; life mem. Million Dollar Round Table, C.L.U. Mem. Nat. Assn. Life Underwriters (past trustee, sec.), Tulsa Assn. Life Underwriters, Am. Soc. C.L.U.'s, Okla. Leaders' Round Table, Tulsa Estate Planning Forum. Republican. Methodist. Clubs: Cedar Ridge Country, Masons, Shriners. Home: 2477 E 73d Pl Tulsa OK 74136 Office: 4636 S Harvard St Suite G Tulsa OK 74135

PETERSON, PETER G., investment banker; b. Kearney, Nebr., June 5, 1926; s. George and Venetia P.; B.S. summa cum laude, Northwestern U., 1947; M.B.A., U. Chgo., 1951; m. Joan Ganz Cooney, Apr. 26, 1980; children—John, James, David, Holly, Michael. Exec. v.p. Market Facts, Inc., Chgo., 1948-53; dir., asst. to pres. McCann-Erickson, Inc., Chgo., 1953-58; exec. v.p. Bell & Howell Co., Chgo., 1958-61, pres., 1961-68, chmn. bd., 1968-71; asst. to Pres. U.S. for internat. econ. affairs, 1971-73; sec. Commerce, 1972-73; ambassador, personal rep. Pres. U.S., 1973; chmn. bd., dir. Lehman Bros. Kuhn Loeb, Inc., N.Y.C., 1973—; dir. Black & Decker Mfg. Co., Federated Dept. Stores, Inc., Gen. Foods Corp., Minn. Mining & Mfg. Co., Lehman Corp., Cities Service Co., RCA Corp. Bd. dirs. Council on Fgn. Relations; trustee U. Chgo., Com. Econ. Devel., Mus. Modern Art. Named One of Ten Outstanding Young Men in Nation, U.S. Jr. C. Art. C., Bus. Statesman of Year, Harvard Bus. Sch., 1973. Mem. Internat. C. of C. (chmn. U.S. Council). Clubs: Economic (N.Y.C.); Commercial (Chgo.); Links; Maidstone, Augusta Nat. Golf, Blind Brook, Burning Tree, Chicago. Co-author: Marketing: Readings in Market Organization and Price Policies; The U.S. in a Changing World Economy; A Foreign Economic Perspective. Home: 10 Gracie Sq New York NY 10028 Office: One William St New York NY 10004

PETERSON, ROBERT AUSTIN, mower mfg. co. exec.; b. Sioux City, Iowa, July 5, 1925; s. Austen W. and Marie (Mueller) P.; B.S., U. Minn., 1946, B.B.A., 1947; m. Carol May Hudy, May 17, 1952; children—Roberta, Richard, Thomas, Bruce. Credit mgr. New Holland Machine div. Sperry Rand Corp., Mpls., 1952-61; credit mgr. Toro Co., Mpls., 1961-68, treas., 1968-71, v.p., treas., internat. fin., 1971—; pres. Toro Credit Co., 1978—; dir. State Bond & Mortgage Co., New Ulm, Minn., State Bond & Mortgage Life Ins. Co., New Ulm, Norton Corp., Phoenix, Clapper Corp., Boston. Chmn., Central So. Turf Dist., Nashville, Gulf Shore Dist., Pensacola, Fla., Autoturfcare, Darlington, Eng., Prior Lake Spring Lake Watershed Dist., 1970—; chmn., mem. bd. dirs. Prior Lake Bd. Edn., 1965-71; chmn. Scott County Republican Party, 1969-70. Bd. dirs. Scott Carver Mental Health Center, 1969-73, Minn. Watershed Assn., 1972. Served to ensign USNR, 1943-46. Mem. Financial Execs. Inst. Clubs: Prior Lake Yacht; Decathlon Athletic (Mpls.). Home: 14956 Pixie Point Circle SE Prior Lake MN 55372 Office: 8111 Lyndale Ave S Minneapolis MN 55420

PETERSON, ROBERT L., meat processing co. exec.; b. Nebr., July 14, 1932; ed. U. Nebr., 1951; married; children—Mark R., Susan P. With Wilson & Co., Jim Boyle Order Buying Co.; cattle buyer R&C Packing Co., 1956-61; cattle buyer, plant mgr., v.p. carcass prodn. IBP, 1961-69; exec. v.p. ops. Spencer Foods, 1969-71; founder, pres. Madison Foods; 1971-76; pres., dir. Iowa Beef Processors, Inc., Dakota City, Nebr., 1976—. Served with Q.M.C., U.S. Army, 1952-54. Club: Sioux City Country. Office: Iowa Beef Processors Inc Dakota City NE 68731*

PETERSON, ROGER GEORGE, ins. co. exec.; b. New Britain, Conn., Dec. 28, 1925; s. George Edward Eugene and Mildred Amanda (Casperson) P.; A.B., Brown U., 1946; postgrad. U. Conn. Law Sch., 1949-51; m. Jane Rowell Burkle, June 18, 1960; children—Jay Lars, Petter Eric. Budget officer Am. Mut. Co., Boston, 1957-58; treas. N.Am. Assurance Soc., Richmond, Va., 1959-61; prin. mgmt. services div. Joseph Frogatt & Co., N.Y.C., 1962-65; sr. v.p. Nat. Liberty Life Ins. Co., Valley Forge, Pa., 1966-67; pres. Am. Progressive Ins. Co., Mt. Vernon, N.Y., 1968-72; pres., dir. Gerber Life Ins. Co., White Plains, N.Y., 1973—. Served to lt. Supply Corps, USNR, 1946-47, 51-53. Mem. Am. Council Life Ins., Health Ins. Assn. Am., Life Cos. N.Y., Direct Mktg. Advt. Assn., Direct Mktg. Ins. Council. Contbr. articles to profl. jours. Home: 5 Candlelight Pl Greenwich CT 06830 Office: Gerber Life Ins Co 66 Church St White Plains NY 10601

PETERSON, RONALD DEAN, retail exec.; b. Morris, Ill., Nov. 2, 1938; s. Earl William and Ina Doris (Misener) P.; A.B. cum laude, Wheaton (Ill.) Coll., 1961; M.B.A., U. Chgo., 1970; m. Suzanne Ellen Golz, July 8, 1978; children by previous marriage—Kevin, John, Diana; 1 dau., Lauren. Vice pres. mktg. Midwest Stores, 1971, group v.p. sales and mktg., 1971-73, group v.p. dept. ops., 1973-75, exec. v.p., gen. mgr., 1975-76, exec. v.p. mktg., 1976-78; exec. v.p., gen. mgr. Jewel Food Stores, Chgo., 1978—. Chmn. bd. dirs. Gateway Houses Found., 1978-80; trustee Coll. St. Francis; chmn. bldg. com., former pres. Holy Cross Lutheran Ch. Mem. Econs. Club Chgo. Republican. Clubs: Chgo. Golf, Met. (Chgo.). Office: 1955 W North Ave Melrose Park IL 60160

PETERSON, STEVEN JON, broadcasting exec.; b. Fond du Lac, Wis., Jan. 28, 1949; s. Gordon Louis and DeNyse Mary (Parker) P.; grad. Brown Inst., Mpls., 1968; student Columbia Coll., Chgo., 1969; m. Jacquelyn Plaisance, Sept. 18, 1971; children—Shaun, Joshua. Staff announcer Sta. KFIZ, Fond du Lac, 1965-68, news anchorman/talk show host Sta-KFIZ-TV, 1968-71, radio news dir., 1971-75; salesman Sta. KWEB, Rochester, Minn., 1975-76, v.p., gen. mgr. Sta. KWEB-KRCH, 1976-77; pres., gen. mgr. Sta. WPON, WPON Radio, Inc., Pontiac, Mich., 1977—; v.p. PSB Radio Group, Inc., Fond du Lac; pres. Mich. Cablevision & Radio Co., 1980—. Bd. dirs. Oakland County (Mich.) Conv. and Tourism Bur., 1977-78; mem. industry advisory bd. Specs Howard Sch. Broadcast Arts, Southfield, Mich., 1978-79. Served with USAR, 1969-75. Mem. Radio TV News Dirs. Assn., Nat. Assn. Broadcasters, Mich. Broadcasters Assn., North Oakland C. of C. (dir.). Roman Catholic. Club: Elks (Fond du Lac). Home: 2695 Campbellgate Dr Drayton Plains MI 48020 Office: PO Box 1460 Bloomfield Hills MI 48013

PETERSON, THOMAS PARRY, med. clinic adminstr.; b. Ogden, Utah, Dec. 7, 1942; s. Morris Blaine and Mary Lucile (Parry) P.; A.A., Weber State Coll., 1966, B.A., 1968; M.B.A., Harvard, 1970; m. Frances Grambow, Apr. 22, 1966; children—Craig Thomas, Tracy Anne, Kimberly, Jeffrey Blaine, Matthew Joseph, Michael Kevin. Systems analyst Mobil Oil Corp., Boston, 1969-70; dir. Bus. Research Center, Ogden, Utah, 1970-72; instr. Sch. Bus. and Econs., Weber State Coll., Ogden, 1970-72; bus. mgr. Brigham Young U., Laie, Hawaii, 1972-75; exec. dir. Weber County Indsl. Devel. Bur., Ogden, 1975-77; clinic adminstr. Ogden (Utah) Clinic, 1977—. cons. Bonneville Internat. Research Corp., 1970-72; pres. Golden Spike Investment Corp., 1966-72, City Quick Print, Inc.; gen. partner Old Post Rd. Devel. Co., B & T Investments; dir. DVA Mgmt. Cons., Western Factoring and Investment. Mem. Interclub Drug Abuse Com., Ogden, 1971-72; bd. dirs. Kahuku Hosp., 1973-75; state chmn. applicant relation com. Harvard Bus. Sch., 1975—; mem. Utah Fed. Research Com., 1975-78; bd. dirs. Weber Vocat. Workshop, 1975-78; mem. Weber County Merit Council, 1978—; mem. adv. council Utah Dept. Employment Security, 1979—; mem. instl. rev. com. McKay-Dee Hosp. Mem. Am. Mgmt. Assn., Utah Indsl. Execs. Assn. (v.p. 1976-77), Ogden Area C. of C. Med. Group Mgmt. Assn. Democrat. Mem. Ch. of Jesus Christ of Latter-Day Saints. Clubs: Weber, Kiwanis (v.p.), Ogden Racquet and Swim (Ogden). Editor Bus. Spectrum, 1970-72. Home: 2569 E Woodland Dr Ogden UT 84403 Office: Ogden Clinic 4650 Harrison Blvd Ogden UT 84403

PETERY, MARY ANN, wood preserving co. exec.; b. Portland, Oreg.; d. Walter H. and Ida Mae (Hartzell) Bauer; grad. Smaller Co. Mgmt. Program, Harvard U., 1977; children by previous marriage—Melinda, Lorri. Pres., chief exec. officer Selma Pressure Treating Co., Inc. (Calif.), 1977—; corp. officer Selma Leasing Co., Inc., 1971-77; cons. SMBA. Past bd. dirs. Better Bus. Bur. Central Calif.; fund agt. Harvard Bus. Sch., 1979-80; mem. adv. council for forest products dept. to chancellor U. Calif.; mem. Fresno County Pvt. Industry Council; del. White House Conf. Small Bus., 1980; mem. bus. adv. council Calif. State U., Fresno; bd. govs. Am. Wood Preservers Bur.; former ambassador Fresno County C. of C. Mem. Am. Wood Preservers Assn., Nat. Assn. Women Bus. Owners, Nat. Small Bus. Assn., Nat. Fedn. Ind. Bus., Western Wood Preservers Inst. (chmn. Calif. group), C. of C. U.S., Calif. C. of C., Selma C. of C., Harvard Bus. Sch. Assn., Bldg. Industry Assn. (public relations com.), Harvard Club, Fresno County (Calif.) Hist. Soc., Fresno Geneal. Soc., Am. Hist. Soc. of Germans from Russia, Colonial Dames IVII Century, D.A.R., New Eng. Geneol. Soc. Home: PO Box 767 Selma CA 93662 Office: PO Box 40 Selma CA 93662

PETITO, FRANK A., investment banker; b. Trenton, N.J., Sept. 2, 1914; A.B., Princeton, 1936; grad. Babson Inst. Bus. Adminstrn., 1937; m. Laura Haven Flock, Feb. 21, 1941; children—Frank A., David, John. With Morgan Stanley & Co. Inc., and predecessor, N.Y.C., 1937—, partner, 1954—, chmn., 1973-79, adv. dir., 1980—. Trustee, Alfred P. Sloan Found.; bd. dirs. Am.-Italy Soc. Served with AUS, 1940-45. Clubs: River, Univ. (N.Y.C.). Home: 100 Beach Rd Tequesta FL 33458 Office: 1251 Ave of Americas New York NY 10020

PETLAN, GEORGE, mech. engr.; b. Czechoslovakia, Oct. 24, 1927; s. Vojtech and Barbora (Perinova) P.; came to U.S., 1969, naturalized, 1978; diploma mech. engring. State Profl. Sch. Mech. Engring., Czechoslovakia, 1945; m. Helena Smetanova, June 12, 1964. Asst. to prodn. mgr. Sonp Kladno, Czechoslovakia, 1960-68; machinist Z.B. Precision Products, Inc., Woodside, N.Y., 1969-70, Home Care Products, Jamaica, N.Y., 1970-72; mfg. engr. Allomatic Industries, Inc., Woodside, N.Y., 1972-78, sr. mfg. engr., 1978-79, chief mfg. engr., 1979—. Recipient Allomatic ann. presdl. award, 1974. Mem. Soc. Mfg. Engrs., Am. Fedn. Police. Contbr. articles to profl. jour. Home: 32 Sharon Dr New City NY 10956 Office: Allomatic Industries Inc 30-30 60th Wiidsode NY 11377

PETNEL, JOSEPH ANTHONY CESARE, inventor; b. Rome, June 2, 1894; s. Francisco and Matilda (Formato) P.; came to U.S., 1900, naturalized, 1905; student pub. schs., night classes Ford Motor Co., Western Electric Co., Russell Sage Coll., 1925-32; m. Elsa C. Bartels, May 26, 1917; 1 dau., Daphne E. (Mrs. Coulman C. Westcott). Began as newsboy, 1905; apprentice mechanic, 1910; chauffeur, taxi cab driver, 1918-20; with Ford Motor Co., 1925-29, Western Electric Co., 1929-32, dir., 1960; founder, pres. Telephone Dial Finger-Wheel Corp., N.Y.C., 1932; electrician Watervliet Arsenal, 1940-43, recipient award Merit, 1942; atty. pro se merger, 1967; pres. Independent Inventor's Corp. Mem. Internat. Platform Assn., Masonic Vet. Assn. Elk. Patentee in U.S., Gt. Britain, Can.; patents include automobile accessories; metal tape, radiator shutter and cap, auto signal system, electric switches, gauge stencils, armament prodn. improvement, phonograph eccentric, telephone dials, dust shields, silent dial pawl, improved fingerwheels, outside lettering, three-way lamp, other communications and lighting equipment. Home: PO Box 500 598 3d Ave Troy NY 12182

PETOW, ROBERT JACOB, advt. exec.; b. Camp LeJeune, N.C., Apr. 11, 1950; s. John and Gracie Estelle P.; B.S. in Social Sci., U. Oreg., 1971; M.S. in Advt. (Robert W. Sawyer grad. scholar 1979), 1979; m. Sally Johannah Squire, May 13, 1978. Records mgmt. analyst Sec. of State, Salem, Oreg., 1975-78; advt. account exec. Statesman Jour. Newspaper, Salem, 1978—. Served with U.S. Army, 1971-72. Winner Intercollegiate Public Service Campaign Competition, Portland Advt. Fedn., 1979. Mem. Capitol Area Media & Public Relations Orgn., Kappa Tau Alpha. Home: 4760 SE LaCour Milwaukie OR 97222 Office: 280 Church St Salem OR 97301

PETRE, GABRIEL LEWIS, JR., mfg. co. and internat. business exec.; b. Cleve., June 17, 1925; s. Gabriel L. and Julia Rose (Balogh) P.; student Bucknell U., 1943-44, Ohio Wesleyan U., 1944-45, U. Notre Dame, 1945; B.A. in Bus. Adminstrn., George Washington U., 1962; 1 son, Gabriel Lewis III. Joined USN as seaman, 1943, advanced to lt. comdr. AC, 1960, ret., 1964; rep. Eastern region Stewart-Warner Electronics, 1964-65, mgr. Washington ops. Stewart-Warner Corp., 1966-69, export mgr. alemite and instrument divs., 1970-75, dir. export sales Stewart-Warner Internat., Chgo., 1976—. Decorated Air medal (2). Mem. Cleve. Engring. Soc., Chgo. Council Fgn. Relations, Nat. Geographic Soc., Beta Theta Pi. Clubs: Overseas Automotive (N.Y.C.); Internat. Trade (sec., dir.), Auto Exporters (past pres., dir.) (Chgo.); Internat. (Washington); Travelers Century. Office: 1826 Diversey Pkwy Chicago IL 60614

PETROFF, PETER ALBERT, JR., auto repair garage owner; b. Campbell, Ohio, May 16, 1922; s. Peter and Carolyn (Kotlik) P.; student U. St. Louis, 1948; m. Elaine Wedin, Oct. 12, 1946; 1 son, Dennis Lee. Musician, trumpeter, Youngstown, Ohio, 1936-46; head lube dept. Buick Youngstown Co. (Ohio), 1941-42; self-employed in auto trade, Campbell, 1946; automotive metal repairman Park Auto Painting, Newark, 1946-48; automotive metal repairman and refinisher Struthers Auto Service (Ohio), 1948-50; owner, operator Petroff Bros. Auto Body, Campbell, 1950—. Mem. Small Bus. Service Bur., Inc., Columbus, Ohio, Better Bus. Bur. Mahoning County, Inc., Youngstown. Served with USAAF, 1942-46. Mem. Automotive Service Council. Democrat. Methodist. Home: 923 E Philadelphia Ave Youngstown OH 44502 Office: 2765 Wilson Ave Campbell OH 44405

PETROSIAN, TAMARA, bank exec.; b. Salzburg, Austria, Dec. 26, 1945; came to U.S., 1951, naturalized, 1964; d. Gregor and Barbara Varduhi (Malian) P.; B.A. in English, UCLA, 1968, teaching credential, 1969; M.A. with honors in Mgmt. and Adminstrn., Calif. State U., Northridge, 1977. Instr. secondary, adult levels Los Angeles City Schs., 1969-77; dean humanities Santa Ana (Calif.) Coll., 1977-79; asst. v.p., corp. fin. officer World Banking div. Bank of Am., Los Angeles, 1979—; coll. instr. real estate fin., investments, 1977—. Founder, Orange County Music Center, 1978; bd. dirs. Friends of Armenian Music, U. So. Calif., 1979—; bd. govs. Armenian Congress Am., 1980—. Recipient Woman of Year award, 1966. Mem. KCET Bus. and Profl. Council, Orgn. Women Execs., Am. Mgmt. Assn., Assn. Calif. Community Coll. Adminstrs., Los Angeles World Affairs Council, Am. Bus. Women's Assn. (v.p. 1975-76), Armenian Profl. Soc. (treas.) Los Angeles Music Center, Los Angeles C. of C. Mem. Armenian Apostolic Ch. Office: World Banking Div Bank Amerilease Bank of Am 555 S Flower St Los Angeles CA 90071

PETROV, PAUL, fin. exec.; b. Torrington, Conn., June 25, 1943; s. John and Irene Petrov; B.S.M.E., U. Hartford, 1968; M.B.A., U. Pa., 1972. Project engr. Colt Industries, Hartford, Conn., 1965-70; pres., gen. mgr. Flo Tech Corp., Frazer, Pa., 1972-76; v.p. fin. L & K Co., Inc., Shelby, N.C., 1976-78; exec. v.p. fin. Manhattan Industries, Inc., N.Y.C., 1978—; dir. Flo-Tech Corp., VTI, Inc. Mem. Kappa Nu. Home: 220 E 65th St New York NY 10021 Office: 1271 Ave of Americas New York NY 10020

PETRUZATES, ARTHUR PAUL, aircraft co. exec.; b. Rhinelander, Wis., Aug. 12, 1925; s. Peter Paul and Virginia Elsie (Hoffman) P.; B.S., Washington U., St. Louis, 1954; postgrad. St. Louis U., 1955, LL.B., 1962; m. Yvonne Pascal, Aug. 19, 1950; children—Paula Diane, Pamela Lea. Supr., Cerro Industries, Monsanto, Ill., 1952-55; wage and salary supr. Cessna Aircraft Co., Wichita, Kans., 1955-60, personnel mgr., 1960-65, prodn. mgr., 1965—. Served with USNR, 1944-46. Mem. Nat. Assn. Purchasing Mgmt. (certified purchasing mgr.), Wichita C. of C., Wichita Assn. Mgmt. Devel. (past pres.). Republican. Presbyterian. Club: Masons. Home: 1038 Westlink St Wichita KS 67212 Office: Box 1977 Wichita KS 67201

PETRY, GEORGE WAYNE, govt. ofcl.; b. Crowley, La., Feb. 22, 1945; s. Ernest Clinton and Daisy Gladys (Foreman) P.; B.S., U. Southwestern La., 1967; M.S., U. So. Miss., 1968; diploma Stonier Grad. Sch. Banking, Rutgers U., 1979; m. Annelise Arceneaux, June 24, 1972; 1 son, Joshua Wayne. Instr. econs. and fin. U. Southwestern La., Lafayette, 1968-71; asst. nat. bank examiner Office of Controller of Currency, U.S. Treasury, Montgomery, Ala. and New Orleans, 1971-75, nat. bank examiner, Memphis, 1975-77, dep. regional dir. for spl. projects, 1977, regional dir. for spl. surveillance, 1977; bank specialist Banking Cons.'s Am., Memphis, 1977-78; dep. commr. for safety and soundness, bur. fin. instns. Va. State Corp. Commn., Richmond, 1978—. Recipient James Parkerson Property Ins. award U. Southwestern La., 1966; thesis selected for libraries at Rutgers U., Am. Bankers Assn., Howard Grad. Sch. Bus., 1979. Mem. AAUP, La. Tchrs. Assn., So. Econ. Assn., Soc. Fin. Examiners, Internat. Assn. Fin. Planners, Honor Soc. of Coll. of Commerce of U. Southwestern La., Omicron Delta Epsilon, Pi Gamma Mu. Republican. Methodist. Office: 701 E Byrd St Richmond VA 23219

PETRY, JOHN JOSEPH, JR., splty. steel co. exec.; b. Bainbridge, Md., Sept. 8, 1951; s. John Joseph and Dorothy Jane (Plummer) P.; B.S. in Bus. Adminstrn., Pa. State U., 1974; postgrad. Columbia U., 1979; m. Sue Ann Brown, July 28, 1973; 1 son, Joseph Brown. Account exec. Sta. WMAJ, State College, Pa., 1973-74; mgmt. trainee Jones & Laughlin Steel Co., Pitts., 1974, sales corr., Cleve., 1975, salesman N.Y. dist. sales office, 1975-77; sales engr. Sandvik, Inc., Scranton, Pa., 1978, asst. mktg. mgr. Spring div., 1979, distbn. mgr. welding products div., 1980—. Bd. dirs. Allegheny County United Way, 1974; asso. dir. Jr. Achievement of Cleve., 1975; bd. dirs. Wyoming Conf. United Methodist Ch., 1979—. Mem. U.S. C. of C., Am. Mgmt. Assn., Spring Mfrs. Inst., Am. Soc. Bus. Colls. and Univs., Tau Epsilon Phi. Republican. Home: 606 Timber Ln Clarks Summit PA 18411 Office: Box 1220 Scranton PA 18501

PETSCHE, JOSEPH MATTHAIS, ins. co. exec.; b. Cleve., Dec. 31, 1938; s. Harold Frank and Anne Marie (Wauben) P.; student public schs., Willoughby, Ohio; m. Marlene Mae Ostrander; children—Daniel, Jacqueline, Jeffrey. With Jack Shaw Pontiac, Lakewood, Ohio, 1962-66, Jack Shaw Chevrolet, Euclid, Ohio, 1966-72; pres. Joe Petsche Chevrolet-Buick, Inc., Galion, Ohio, 1972-75; salesman, Acceleration Life Ins. Co. (Ohio), Columbus, 1975-76; v.p. Acceleration Life Ins. Co. of Pa., Camp Hill, 1976-79, pres., dir., 1979—; v.p., dir. Keystone Acceleration Corp., 1977—. Mem. ad hoc com. Galion (Ohio) Community Center; mem. fund-raising com. Mansfield Area Boy Scouts Am., 1973-75. Served with USMC, 1956-59. Clubs: Hershey (Pa.) Country, Hershey Italian Lodge. Home: 107 Parkview Rd New Cumberland PA 17070 Office: 209 Senate Ave Suite 670 Camp Hill PA 17011

PETTEGREW, ROBERT L., JR., port exec.; b. Cleve., Oct. 30, 1929; s. Robert L. and Esther P.; B.S. in Econs., Bowling Green State U., 1952; M.B.A., N.Y. U., 1960; m. June Bielke, Nov. 27, 1954; 1 dau., Karen Ann. Mgr. freight transp. planning Port Authority N.Y. and N.J., N.Y.C., 1956-71; exec. dir. S. Jersey Port Corp., Camden, 1971—; mem. N.J. Dist. Export Council, 1979-80. Recipient Commr.'s citation U.S. Customs Service. Mem. Am. Assn. Port Authorities (dir.), N. Atlantic Ports Assn. (dir.). Home: 238 Chittenden Rd Clifton NJ 07013 Office: S Jersey Port Corp 2500 Broadway Camden NJ 08104

PETTERSEN, CHARLES WALDEMAR, electronics co. exec.; b. Akron, Ohio, Jan. 27, 1939; s. Wilbur Eugene and Arvilla (Hosmer) P.; B.S. in Accounting with honors and distinction, San Diego State Coll., 1964; m. Judy Lynn Goodwin, Nov. 26, 1960; children—Weston Waldemar, Carl Wilhelm, Christina Lynn. C.P.A., tax specialist Haskins & Sells, C.P.A.'s, San Diego, 1964-67; v.p. finance Lear Siegler, Inc. Cimron Div., San Diego, 1967-71; asst. sec. Lear Siegler, Inc., Santa Monica, Calif., 1968-71; dir., treas. HM Electronics, Inc., San Diego, 1971-76, exec. v.p., 1976—; sec.-treas. Controlled Water Emission Systems, El Cajon, Calif., 1972-75; v.p. finance Reed Irrigation Systems, El Cajon, 1976. Served with AUS, 1958-60. C.P.A., Calif. Mem. San Diego History Research Center (charter), Mensa, Beta Gamma Sigma, Beta Alpha Psi (v.p. 1964). Clubs: San Diego Track, Stadium Racquetball, San Diego Turtle and Tortoise. Home: 10265 Vista De La Cruz La Mesa CA 92041 Office: 6151 Fairmount Ave San Diego CA 92120

PETTERSSEN, BERNT, film producing co. exec.; b. Boston, Sept. 2, 1940; s. Sverre and Lilian (Bye) P.; student Harvard Coll., 1959, London Sch. Film Technique, 1962-63; B.Sc. summa cum laude, Boston U., m. Donna Voorhees, Sept. 21, 1968; children—Nicholas, Eric. Dir. music therapy Franklin Perkins Sch., Lancaster, Mass., 1960-61; ind. film producer, London, Oslo, 1962-65; founder, pres. Envision Corp., Boston, 1966—; pres. Envision Communications, Inc., Warren, Vt., 1978—. Recipient Blue Ribbon, Am. Film Festival, 1971; 1st award, Nat. Ednl. Film Festival, 1972; 1st award Nat. Visual Communications Festival, 1972; best of category San Francisco Internat. Film Festival, 1977; Gold Camera award U.S. Indsl. Film Festival, 1977; Cine, Golden Eagle, 1978. Mem. Info. Film Producers Am. Internat. Communications Assn., Assn. Ind. Video Filmakers, Ind. Media Producers Assn., Assn. Multi-Image, Harvard Club, Films include: The Shape of a Leaf, 1967, Six Fimmakers in Search of a Wedding, 1969, Pine Tree Camp, 1971, A Stroke of the Pen:

Dimensions of a Presidential Decision, 1975; I See You As A Person, 1977; Energy: Crisis and Challenge, 1979. Home: Brook Rd Warren VT 05674 Office: 51 Sleeper St Boston MA 02210

PETTIGREW, JOHN DAVID, accountant; b. Baldwin County, Ga., July 26, 1950; s. Robert Norris, Sr., and Mary (Overman) P.; B.B.A., Ga. Coll., 1972, M.B.A., 1974; m. Beth Ann Jiles, Apr. 26, 1975; children—John Derek, Mary Alissa. Traffic mgr. Griffin Pipe Products, Milledgeville, Ga., 1972-76; adminstrv. services mgr. fiscal control Ga. Dept. Corrections, Milledgeville, 1976-80; pres. Accurate Acctg. Service, Milledgeville, 1977—. Mem. Nat. Soc. Public Accts., Am. Correctional Assn., Mensa. Baptist. Home: Rural Rt 1 Box 55A Milledgeville GA 31061 Office: 73o N Wayne St Milledgeville GA 31061

PETTIT, KELLY BROOKS, metals recycling furnace mfg. co. exec.; b. Wichita, Kans., Jan. 7, 1953; s. Donald Leroy and Bette Jean P.; student U. Kans., 1971-75; m. Jancy Campbell. Aircraft salesman also commuter pilot Clopine Aircraft Co., Topeka and Lawrence Aviation (Kans.), 1970-75, part-time salesman, pilot United Corp., Topeka, 1970-75, sales mgr., 1975-78, pres., 1978—, also chmn. bd., chief exec. officer. Cert. airline transp. pilot. Mem. Topeka C. of C., Inst. Scrap Iron and Steel, Nat. Assn. Recycling Industries, Delta Upsilon. Republican. Episcopalian. Clubs: Masons, Scottish Rite, Shriners. Home: 7630 Robin Hood Ct Topeka KS 66604 Office: 1947 N Topeka Ave Topeka KS 66608

PETTIT, MARLIN HAZEN, interior design and furnishings co. exec.; b. Oskaloosa, Iowa, Sept. 14, 1942; s. Hazen C. and Rhea Ferne (Schultz) P.; S.B., Mass. Inst. Tech., 1964; postgrad. U. Va. Sch. Law, 1965-66; M.B.A. (Stein, Roe fellow), Harvard U., 1968; m. Maureen Kelly, Aug. 8, 1970; children—Robert Mark, Kelly Nicole. Internat. fin. specialist Chrysler Treas's. Office, Detroit, 1968-69; sr. fin. analyst J. L. Hudson Co., Detroit, 1970, contract div. mgr., 1971-75; pres. Contract Interiors Inc., Detroit, 1975—; exec. v.p., dir. Contract Craftsmen, Inc. Mem. Econ. Club Detroit, Mass. Inst. Tech. Edn. Council. Roman Catholic. Clubs: Detroit Athletic, Renaissance, Rotary (Detroit). Office: 511 Woodward Ave Detroit MI 48226

PETTY, ELIJAH EDWARD, oilseed processing exec.; b. Terre Haute, Ind., June 12, 1920; s. Curtis and Bonnie Belle (Reed) P.; M.E., U. Ariz., 1943; B.S. in Chem. Engring., U. Okla., 1947; m. Nelda Morris, Nov. 8, 1942; children—Montie Curtis, Vicki Ann. Mgr., Anderson Clayton Edible Oil Plant, Sao Paulo, Brazil, 1959-62, Armour Edible Oil Plant, Kankakee, Ill., 1963-66; supt. refineries Archer Daniels Midland Co., Decatur, Ill., 1966-68; v.p. M. Neumonz & Son, N.Y.C., 1968-73; pres. Petco Internat., Mt. Zion, Ill., from 1973, also Chem. Agrl. Processes, Inc., I. & I. Co., Ltd.; chmn. bd. I. & I. Co., Ltd. (Ireland); tech. dir. AGRIMA (Rio de Janeiro); chief exec. officer DIKTIC Inc.; v.p. M&E Engring.; cons. oil seed processing FAO, UN Indsl. Devel. Orgn., Am. Soybean Assn., Fgn. Agr. Service, U.S. Dept. Agr., numerous fgn. cos. and govts. Adv. com. Jacksonville (Ill.) Sch. Bd. Adv. Com.; chmn. Jacksonville Community Chest. Served with AUS, 1943-46. Registered profl. engr., Tex. Mem. Am. Oil Chemists Soc., Am. Inst. Chem. Engrs. Patentee continuous hydrogenation. Home: Rosewood Acres Mount Zion IL 62549 Office: PO Box 309 Mount Zion IL 62549

PETTY, JOHN ROBERT, banker; b. Chgo., Apr. 16, 1930; s. Dewitt Talmage and Beatrice (Worthington) P.; A.B., Brown U., 1951; postgrad. N.Y. U., 1953-54; m. H. Lee Mills, May 11, 1957; children—L. Talmage, Robert D., George M., Victoria L. With Chase Manhattan Bank, N.Y.C., Paris, 1953-66, v.p., 1964-66; dep. asst. sec. for internat. affairs Treasury Dept., Washington, 1966-68, asst. sec. for internat. affairs, 1968-72; partner Lehman Bros., N.Y.C., 1972-76; pres., chmn. exec. com. Marine Midland Bank N.A., N.Y.C., 1976—; dir. RCA, NBC, Hercules Inc., Hongkong and Shanghai Banking Corp. Served with USN, 1951-53. Mem. Council on Fgn. Relations, Fgn. Bondholders Protective Council (pres.). Office: Marine Midland Bank NA 140 Broadway 3d Floor New York NY 10015

PETTY, ORVILLE ANDERSON, II, mfg. co. exec.; b. Phila., Jan. 30, 1915; s. Orlando H. and Priscilla Marcia (Mellersh) P.; B.S. in Econs., U. Pa. Wharton Sch., 1936; m. Jessie Elizabeth Nelms, June 8, 1940; children—O. Anderson III, Gail (Mrs. James S. Riepe). Purchasing agent A.C. Krumm & Son, Phila., 1936-39; sales rep. Container Corp. Am., Phila., 1939-41; sales mgr. Embree Mfg. Co., Elizabeth, N.J., 1945-52; exec. v.p., dir., Schick, Inc., Lancaster, Pa., 1952-59; v.p., dir. Daffin Mfg. Co., Lancaster, 1959-60; sr. group v.p. Lenox, Inc., Trenton, N.J., 1960-79, dir., 1968—. Served from 2d lt. to lt. col. Ordnance Corps, AUS, 1941-45. Mem. Glass Crafts Am. (pres. 1974-75), U. Pa. Wharton Sch. Alumni Soc. (dir.), Phi Delta Theta. Clubs: Trenton; Nassau, The Bedens Brook (Princeton, N.J.). Home: Maple House Bedens Brook Rd Skillman NJ 08558

PEW, GEORGE THOMPSON, JR., rail service co. exec.; b. Bryn Mawr, Pa., Mar. 25, 1942; s. George Thompson and Constance (Clarke) P.; student Yale U., 1965, U. Pitts., 1963-64, U. Pa., 1971; 1 son, George Thompson III. Mgmt. trainee Sun Co., Phila., 1963-64; registered rep. N.Y. Stock Exchange, Butcher & Singer Inc., Phila., 1971—; chief exec. officer, pres. Nat. Rwy. Mgmt. Corp., Villanova, Pa., 1979—; cons. in field; dir. Naramco, Villanova, 1979—; Mem. govt. and founds. com. United Way of Phila., 1973-75; dir. Phila. Charity Ball, 1976—. Served with U.S. Army, 1966-69. Mem. Assn. of M.B.A. Execs. Republican. Episcopalian. Clubs: Union League, Racquet, Rittenhouse, Merion Cricket, The Cts., Bay Head Yacht, St. Elmo. Office: 1 Aldwyn Center Villanova PA 19085 1500 Walnut St Philadelphia PA 19102

PEW, JOHN GLENN, ret. oil co. cons.; b. Beaumont, Tex., May 14, 1902; s. James Edgar and Martha (Layng) P.; student So. Meth. U., 1921, Northeastern U., Cornell U., 1922, Mass. Inst. Tech., 1923-24; m. Roberta Haughton, June 27, 1929; children—John Glenn, Richard Haughton. With Sun Oil Co., Dallas, 1924-67, v.p. charge prodn., 1946-60, sr. v.p., 1960-67, now dir., cons.; former officer, dir. various domestic and fgn. Sun Oil Co. subsidiaries; trustee Glenmede Trust Co., Phila. Mem. nat. com. for edn. center Air Force Acad. Found.; bd. govs. Am. Citizenship Center at Okla. Christian Coll.; nat. trustee Inst. Logopedics; bd. dirs. Boys Clubs Am.; trustee Southwestern Med. Found., Wadley Insts. Molecular Medicine, Dallas Hist. Soc.; trustee, Internat. Oil and Gas Ednl. Center; vice chmn. Inst. Tech., research fellow, mem. adv. bd. Southwestern Legal Found. at So. Meth. U. Mem. Am. Petroleum Inst. (v.p. div. prodn. 1953-54; certificate of appreciation 1954, hon. dir.), Mid-Continent Oil and Gas Assn. (dir. 1936—; distinguished service award Tex. 1942), Tex. Mid-Continent Oil and Gas Assn., Ind. Petroleum Assn. Am., Pioneers Petroleum 25 Year Club (pres. 1965-66), Am. Inst. Mining, Metall. and Petroleum Engrs., Psi Upsilon. Republican. Presbyn. (trustee). Clubs: Dallas Petroleum (pres. 1942), Brook Hollow Golf (Dallas); Phila. Country, Racquet (Phila.); Augusta (Ga.) Nat. Golf; Eisenhower Golf, Broadmoor Golf (Colorado Springs, Colo.). Home: 3525 Turtle Creek Blvd Dallas TX 75219 Office: PO Box 2880 Dallas TX 75221

PEZZUTO, JOSEPH LOUIS, real estate appraiser; b. Bklyn., Sept. 26, 1937; s. Louis Joseph and Evelyn (Riquiere) P.; A.A.S. in Real Estate, Bklyn. Coll., 1960; B.S. (N.Y. State scholar), N.Y. U., 1963; m. Marilyn Trovato, Jan. 18, 1964; children—Joseph, Christopher. Sr. real estate appraiser Greenwich Savs. Bank, N.Y.C., 1967-70, City N.Y. Dept. Real Estate, 1970-73, Franklin Soc. Fed. Savs. and Loan, N.Y.C., 1973-74; prin. real estate appraiser N.Y. State Banking Dept., N.Y.C., 1974—. Mem. Verranzo-Narrows Civic Assn. Served with M.C., U.S. Army, 1960. Mem. N.Y. Council Veterans (dir. pub. relations), Soc. Real Estate Appraisers (exam. com.), Columbia Soc. Real Estate Appraisers, Assn. Fed. Appraisers (program chmn.), Bklyn. Coll. Alumni Assn. (dir. 1974—), Rho Epsilon. Address: 2 World Trade Center New York City NY 10047

PFAFF, GEORGE CHARLES, JR., aerospace co. exec.; b. Balt., Aug. 15, 1918; s. George Charles and Cecelia (Schmitt) P.; B.S., M.I.T., 1939; m. Mary Martha Beckwith, June 14, 1947: children—Carol Ann, Nancy Louise. Structural design engr. Glenn L. Martin Co., Balt., 1939-57; mgr. structures Martin-Orlando (Fla.), 1957-64; structures project engr. Martin-Marietta Corp., Denver, 1964-73, mgr. quality engring., New Orleans, 1973-79, mgr. interdivisional Mx work, 1979—. Mem. Planning and Zoning Commn., Winter Park, Fla., 1960-64. Registered profl. engr., Colo. Fellow Am. Inst. Aero. and Astronautics (asso.); mem. Aerospace Industries Assn. (chmn. aerospace research and testing com. 1962-63), Nat. Acad. Sci. (material adv. bd. 1959-60), Sigma Nu. Club: MIT Alumni (chpt. pres. 1963-64) (Orlando, Fla.). Patentee in field. Home: 323 Landon Dr Slidell LA 70458 Office: PO Box 29304 New Orleans LA 70189

PFANN, JOHN P., corp. exec.; b. Nebraska City, Nebr., May 17, 1929; B.S. in Bus. Adminstrn., U. Nebr.; m. Donna, May 27, 1951; children—Teresa Lee, Joanna Donna. Asst. comptroller ITT, N.Y.C., 1965-71, v.p., 1971—, dep. treas., 1973-76, treas., 1976—, sr. v.p., 1979—. Served with USN, 1945-46. C.P.A. Mem. Am. Inst. C.P.A.'s, Fin. Exec. Inst. Office: ITT 320 Park Ave New York NY 10022*

PFANNSTIEL, CURTIS ALTON, restaurant exec.; b. New Braunfels, Tex., Oct. 26, 1946; s. Benno Rudolph and Clara (Twiefel) P.; student U. Tex., summer 1967, Tex. Luth. Coll., 1965-69; B.A. in Speech, Drama and English; tchrs. cert. St. Mary's U., 1970. Tchr. drama, speech and English, Dept. Edn. V.I., St. Thomas, 1969-70; with Tower of the Ams., Magic Time Machines divs. Frontier Enterprises, 1970—, unit mgr., Austin, Tex., 1975-76, corp. dir. tng. and restaurant design, San Antonio, 1976—. Guest artist and dir. Community Actors Theatre, New Braunfels and Sequin, Tex., 1969—. Recipient Outstanding Young Am. award Rotary Internat., 1966. Mem. San Antonio Restaurant Assn. (dir.), Am. Soc. Tng. and Devel., Am. Mgmt. Assn., Internat. TV Assn., Nat. Restaurant Assn., Alpha Psi Omega (v.p. 1967-69), Omega Tau (pres. 1966-68). Lutheran. Home: 2600 NE Loop 410 San Antonio TX 78217 Office: 8520 Crownhill Blvd San Antonio TX 78209

PFAU, GEORGE HAROLD, JR., broker; b. Milw., May 7, 1924; s. George Harold and Elisabeth C. (Hunter) P.; B.S., Yale, 1948; m. Anne Elizabeth Mayhew; children by former marriage—Mary D., Peter W., Elisabeth C. Salesman A.G. Becker & Co., San Francisco, 1954-55; v.p., sec., dir. Carl W. Stern & Co., San Francisco, 1955-57; with White Weld & Co. Inc., San Francisco, 1957-78, 1st v.p. investment banking and stock brokerage, 1957-78; sr. v.p. Blyth Eastman Paine Webber, San Francisco, 1978—; dir. Monadnock Corp. Bd. dirs. The Guardsmen, 1966-67, Pathfinder Fund, 1974, San Francisco Zool. Soc., 1978-80; trustee Thacher Sch., 1967-76, The Town Sch., 1966-70. Served with C.E., AUS, 1942-44; with Am. Field Service, 1944-45. Mem. Planned Parenthood San Francisco-Alameda (pres. 1968-69, dir. 1965-77), Kappa Beta Phi. Clubs: Calif. Tennis, San Francisco Bond, Pacific Union, Bohemian (San Francisco). Home: 2298 Vallejo St San Francisco CA 94123 Office: Blyth Eastman Paine Webber 555 California St Suite 4300 San Francisco CA 94104

PFEIFER, ARTHUR HERBERT, mfg. co. exec.; b. Bruchsal, Germany, Sept. 20, 1933; came to Can., 1956; s. Arthur and Eva Maria (Bleier) P.; R.I.A., U. Alta. (Can.), 1967, cert. in mgmt. devel., 1972; m. Hedwig E. Bressmer, Apr. 28, 1960; children—Thomas, Nancy, Sandra. Chief cost acct. Can. Phoenix Steel & Pipe Ltd., Edmonton, Alta., 1966-73; chief acct. St. Regis (Alta.) Ltd., Hinton, 1974-76; comptroller Netherlands Overseas Mills Ltd., also Polar Forest Industries Ltd., Prince George, B.C., Can., 1976—. Mem. Can. Tax Found., Soc. Mgmt. Accts., Council Forest Industries. Home: SS3 W Beaverly Rd Prince George BC V2N 2S7 Canada Office: PO Box 789 Prince George BC V2L 4T3 Canada

PFEIFFER, ASTRID ELIZABETH, utility exec.; b. N.Y.C., Nov. 15, 1934; d. Ernest and Alice (Strobel) P.; B.A., Cornell U., 1955; J.D. cum laude, Wayne State U., 1967; grad. exec. program in bus. adminstrn. Columbia U. Grad. Sch. Bus., 1976; m. Edmund Lee Gettier, III, May 28, 1956 (div. 1966); children—Evan Ernest, Elizabeth Lee, Edmund Lee, Sheila Anne, David Brian. Mng. editor Detroit Inst. Arts, 1962-67; admitted to Mich. bar, 1968, N.Y. bar, 1969, Fla. bar, 1975; atty. J.P. Mattimoe, Detroit, 1967-68, Chubb & Son, Inc., N.Y.C., 1969-70, firm Cadwalader, Wickersham & Taft, N.Y.C., 1971-73; corp. sec. Fla. Power & Light Co., Miami, 1973—. Mem. Am. Bar Assn., Fla. Bar Assn., Dade County Bar Assn., Am. Soc. Corp. Secs. (pres. S.E. region). Republican. Roman Catholic. Club: Coral Gables Country. Office: Fla Power & Light Co 9250 W Flagler St PO Box 529100 Miami FL 33152

PFEIFFER, JANE CAHILL, bus. cons., broadcasting exec.; b. Washington, Sept. 29, 1932; d. John Joseph and Helen (Reilly) Cahill; B.A., U. Md., 1954; m. Ralph A. Pfeiffer, Jr., June 3, 1975. With IBM Corp., Armonk, N.Y., 1955-76, sec. mgmt. rev. com., 1970, dir. communications, 1971, v.p. communications and govt. relations, 1972-76; bus. cons., 1976-78; chmn. NBC, 1978—; dir. Chesebrough-Ponds, Inc., Internat. Paper Co., J.C. Penney Co. Participant, White House Fellows program, 1966; mem. Council on Fgn. Relations; mem. Pres.'s Commn. Mil. Compensation, Pres.'s Commn. White House Fellows. Trustee, Rockefeller Found., U. Notre Dame; vis. com. Harvard Med. Sch. and Sch. Dental Medicine; mem. Overseas Devel. Council. Office: NBC 30 Rockefeller Plaza New York NY 10020

PFEIFFER, ROBERT JOHN, bus. exec.; b. Suva, Fiji Islands, Mar. 7, 1920; s. William Albert and Nina (Mac Donald) P.; came to U.S., 1921, naturalized, 1927; grad. high sch., Honolulu, 1937; m. Mary Elizabeth Worts, Nov. 29, 1945; children—Elizabeth Pfeiffer Tumbas, Margaret Pfeiffer Colbrandt, George, Kathleen. With Inter-Island Steam Nav. Co., Ltd. (re-organized to Overseas Terminal, Ltd. 1950, merged into Oahu Ry. and Land Co. 1954), Honolulu, 1937-55, v.p., gen. mgr., 1950-54, mgr. ship agy. dept., 1954-55; v.p., gen. mgr. Pacific Cut Stone and Granite Co., Inc., Alhambra, Calif., 1955-56; v.p., gen. mgr. Matcinal Corp., Alameda, Calif., 1956-58; mgr. div. Pacific Far East Line, Inc., San Francisco, 1958-60; dept. mgr. Matson Nav. Co., San Francisco, 1960—, v.p., 1966-70, sr. v.p., 1970-71, exec. v.p., 1971-73, pres., 1973-79, chmn. bd., chief exec. officer, 1979—; v.p. The Matson Co., San Francisco, 1968-70, pres., 1970—; v.p., gen. mgr. Matson Terminals, Inc., 1960-62, pres., 1962-70, chmn. bd., 1970-79; pres. Matson Services Co., 1970-73, chmn. bd., 1973-79; sr. v.p. The Oceanic S.S. Co., San Francisco, 1970-71, exec. v.p., 1971-73, pres., 1973—; chmn. bd. Matson Agencies, Inc., San Francisco, 1973-78; sr. v.p. Alexander & Baldwin, Inc., Honolulu, 1973-77, dir., exec. v.p., 1977-79, pres., 1979-80, chief exec. officer, 1980, chmn., pres., chief exec. officer, 1980—; dir. Sierra R.R. Co., McBryde Sugar Co., Ltd., A&B Properties, Inc., Wailea Land Corp., Calif. and Hawaiian Sugar Co., others. Past chmn. Maritime Transp. Research Bd., Nat. Acad. Sci.; former mem. commn. sociotech. systems NRC. Trustee Nat. Maritime Mus. Assn. Served to lt. USNR, World War II; comdr. Res. ret. Mem. Nat. Assn. Stevedores (past pres.), Internat. Cargo Handling Coordination Assn. (past pres. U.S. nat. com.), Propeller Club U.S. (past pres. Honolulu), Nat. Def. Transp. Assn. (life), Hawaii, Kauai, Maui, Hawaii Island, Long Beach, Oakland, Los Angeles, San Francisco, Portland, Seattle, Richmond chambers commerce, World Affairs Council No. Calif. (trustee), Am. Bur. Shipping (bd. mgrs.), Aircraft Owners and Pilots Assn. Republican. Clubs: Masons (32 deg.), Shriners, Pacific, Outrigger, Oahu Country (Honolulu); Pacific Union, Bohemian, World Trade (San Francisco). Home: 535 Miner Rd Orinda CA 94563 Office: 822 Bishop St Honolulu HI 96813

PFEIFFER, WARREN GALE, JR., real estate exec.; b. Long Beach, Calif., Nov. 29, 1944; s. Warren Gale and Janet Claire (Thibodeaux) P.; B.B.A., Ga. State U., 1969; m. Mary Kathleen Kramer, Aug. 19, 1965; children—Warren Gale III, John, Laura. With Frost Nat. Bank, San Antonio, 1965-70, Ray Ellison Industries, San Antonio, 1970-76, La Quinta Motor Inns, Inc., San Antonio, 1976-79; mgr., v.p. Wells Fargo Realty Advisors, Inc., San Antonio, 1979. Mem. San Antonio Builders Assn., San Antonio C. of C., S.W. Football Ofcls. Assn. (treas. 1979, 80), San Antonio Mortgage Bankers, Sigma Iota Epsilon. Republican. Roman Catholic. Home: 4218 Ramsgate St San Antonio TX 78230 Office: Wells Fargo Realty Advisors Inc 84 NE Loop 410 Suite 409E San Antonio TX 78216

PFEISTER, RAYMOND LYNN, ins. co. exec.; b. Cape Girardeau, Mo., May 31, 1946; s. Herman Joe and Imogene Elsie (Groseclose) P.; B.S., U. Ill., 1969, M.B.A., 1971; Ph.D., Baruch Coll., City U. N.Y., 1978; m. Susan Jane Selby, July 1, 1969; 1 son, Joseph Robert. Sales analyst Koppers Co., Magnolia, Ark., 1969-70; instr. bus. U. Ill., Urbana, 1971; spl. agt. Prudential Ins. Co. Am., Champaign, Ill., 1971, div. mgr., Balt., 1971-74, mktg. specialist, mgr. group pension, Newark and N.Y.C., 1974; account exec. Alexander & Alexander Inc., N.Y.C., 1974-76, asst. v.p., 1976-78, v.p., 1978-80; v.p. Johnson & Higgins, N.Y.C., 1980—; founder, chmn. bd., chief exec. officer Pfeister Barter Inc., N.Y. Reciprocal Trade Exchange, 1979—; founder, chmn., pres. Pfeister Corp., Wilmington, Del., 1977—; lectr., cons. in field. Pres. Jr. Achievement, Denver, 1963-64; active Boy Scouts Am., 1964—, United Fund, 1973. Named outstanding young man Am., U.S. Jaycees, 1977. Mem. Vernon (Conn.) C. of C., Acad. Mgmt., Am. Psychol. Assn., Nat. Eagle Scout Assn., Soc. Am. Foresters, Forest Products Research Soc., Nat. Life Underwriters Assn., Nat. M.B.A. Assn., U. Ill. Alumni Assn. (life)(v.p. 1974—), Sigma Iota Epsilon. Club: N.Y. Athletic. Author: The Strategic Planning Process for Alexander & Alexander Services, Inc. and Subsidiaries, 1980. Home: 73 Kensington Rd Bronxville NY 10708 Office: Johnson & Higgins 95 Wall St New York NY 10005

PFISTER, DENNIS FRANCIS, office furniture mfg. co. exec.; b. Jasper, Ind., Jan. 2, 1926; s. Amos Francis and Elizabeth (Streicher) P.; student John Carroll U., 1944-45, Ind. U., 1947; B.S. in Edn., Ind. State U., 1950; m. Lelia Jane Jerger, Sept. 3, 1949; children—Joseph, Mary, James. Vice pres., gen. mgr. United Mfg. Co., Jasper, 1954-70, pres., 1970-79, also pres. United Wood Products, Dale Furniture, Globe Furniture, United Chair, United Warehouses, United Woodcrafters, 1970-79; pres., gen. mgr. Pfister Industries, Inc., Jasper, 1979—; v.p., dir. Dorset Corp., Louisville. Served with USN, 1944-45. Mem. Am. Mgmt. Assn., Nat. Office Products Assn., Ind. Mfrs. Assn., Nat. Assn. Furniture Mfrs. Republican. Roman Catholic. Clubs: K.C., Am. Legion. Home: 950 Memorial St Jasper IN 47546 Office: PO Box 664 Jasper IN 47546

PFROMMER, CARL HERMAN, chem. co. exec.; b. Newark, Mar. 17, 1919; s. Herman C. and Agnes (Rampe) P.; B.S., Lafayette Coll., 1940; postgrad. Sch. Bus. U. Kans., 1965; m. Margaret Hartman, Dec. 29, 1942; children—Thomas Carl, Michael Fred. With Mich. Chem. Co., various locations, 1946-61, regional sales mgr., 1955-60, product mgr., 1960-61; with chem. div. Vulcan Materials Co., Newark, 1961—, gen. sales mgr., 1972-73, works mgr., 1974-75, dir. purchasing, Birmingham, Ala., 1975-78, v.p. adminstrn., 1978—. Trustee Perkiomen Sch., Pennsburg, Pa., 1971—. Served with AUS, 1941-45; PTO Mem. N.J. Chemists Club (dir. 1972-75), N.Y. Chemists Club, Am. Chem. Soc. Presbyn. (trustee). Clubs: Green Valley Country (Birmingham); Suburban Golf (Union, N.J.). Home: 3229 Altaloma Dr Birmingham AL 35216 Office: One Metroplex Dr Birmingham AL 35209

PFUND, EDWARD THEODORE, JR., electronics co. exec.; b. Methuen, Mass., Dec. 10, 1923; s. Edwrd Theodore and Mary Elizabeth (Banning) P.; B.S. magna cum laude, Tufts Coll., 1950; postgrad. U. So. Calif., 1950, Columbia U., 1953, UCLA, 1956, 58; m. Marga Emmi Andre, Nov. 10, 1954; children—Angela M., Gloria I., Edward Theodore III. Radio engr., WLAW, Lawrence-Boston, 1942-50; fgn. service staff officer Voice of Am., Tangier, Munich, 1950-54; project mgr., materials specialist United Electrodynamics Inc., Pasadena, Calif., 1956-59; dir. engring., chief engr. Electronics Specialty Co., Los Angeles and Thomaston, Conn., 1959-61; with Hughes Aircraft Co., various locations, 1955, 61—, mgr. Middle East programs and African and S. Am. market devel., Los Angeles, 1971—. Served with AUS, 1942-46. Mem. Phi Beta Kappa, AIAA, Sigma Pi Sigma. Contbr. articles to profl. jours. Home: 25 Silver Saddle Ln Rolling Hills Estates CA 90274 Office: PO Box 92919 Airport Station Los Angeles CA 90009

PFYFFER, ANDRE DE, lawyer; b. Lucerne, Switzerland, Nov. 3, 1928; s. Leodegar and Anna (Carvalho) de P.; Baccalaureat, U. Berne, 1947; postgrad. U. Geneva, 1947-50; M.A. in Law, Columbia, 1954; m. Manon Montrose, Dec. 17, 1954; children—Corinne, Francois. Admitted to Geneva Lawyers Assn., 1952, since practiced in Geneva; partner firm Mes. Hafner & de Pfyffer; dir. Abex Internat. S.A., Automobiles Volvo S.A., Cederroth Internat. S.A., Banque de Paris et des Pays-Bas (Suisse) S.A., Banque Scandinave en Suisse S.A. Mem. Internat. Law Assn., Circle de la Terrasse. Home: 41 Quai Wilson Geneva Switzerland Office: 6 Rue Bellot Geneva Switzerland

PHALEN, WILLIAM RALPH, radio exec.; b. Chgo., Mar. 8, 1943; s. Richard Chambers and Lucile (Pritchard) P.; B.S. in Journalism, U. So. Miss., 1965; m. Judy Lee Jamison, Aug. 3, 1974. Vice pres., dir. KLUC Broadcasting Co., Las Vegas, also KLUC, KMJJ, KZAP, Sacramento, KZZP AM/FM, Phoenix, 1970—; pres., dir. Grabet Inc. parent co. KRQ Radio and KMGX Radio, Tucson, 1973—; mem. adv. bd. ABC Radio Network, 1975—. Bd. dirs. Las Vegas YMCA, 1973, Tucson Jr. Achievement, 1974—; Sec. bd. dirs., v.p. Tucson Tourism Bur., 1974—. Named Outstanding Young Man of Am., Div. of Fuller & Dees, 1972. Mem. Tucson Broadcasters Assn. (pres. 1979). Home: 11616 N Saint Andrews Way Scottsdale AZ 85254 Office: 4513 E Thomas Rd Phoenix AZ 85018

PHARES, ELWOOD WILLIS, chem. co. exec.; b. Elizabeth, N.J., June 1, 1930; s. Eugene E. and Ruth (Royer) P.; B.S. in Chem. Engring. with honors, Rensselaer Poly. Inst., 1951; M.B.A. with distinction, Harvard U., 1955; m. Jacqueline Overturf, Feb. 4, 1956; children—Melissa, Craig. Dir. comml. devel. Velsicol Chem. Co., Chgo., 1955-59; exec. v.p. plastics div. Tenneco Chems., Inc., New Brunswick, N.J., 1959-67; pres. Packaging div. Dart Industries, Inc., Paramus, N.J., 1967-78; chmn., pres. chief exec. officer West Chem. Products Co., Princeton, N.J., 1978—, also dir., chmn. exec. com. Bd. dirs. Princeton Hosp. Served as 1st lt. U.S. Army, 1951-53. Mem. Am. Mgmt. Assn., Am. Chem. Soc., Mfg. Chemists Assn., Tau Beta Pi. Clubs: Harvard (N.Y.C.); Racquet (Chgo.); Coral Beach (Bermuda); Bedens Brook Country, Nassau (Princeton). Home: 94 Rosedale Rd Princeton NJ 08540 Office: 1000 Herrontown Rd Princeton NJ 08540

PHELAN, JAMES BERNARD, ins. co. exec.; b. Akron, Ohio, Sept. 28, 1941; s. Bernard W. and Waneta (Magoteaux) P.; B.A., Kent State U., 1963; married; children—Todd W., Brent J. Ins. agt. Phelan Ins. Agy., Inc., Versailles, Ohio, 1962-72; v.p. Midwestern Ins. Group, Cin., 1972-76; pres. Ins. Mktg. Assos., Versailles, 1976—; tchr. CLU program, Cin. Pres. Versailles Devel. Assn., 1969-70. Chartered property and casualty underwriter; C.L.U. Mem. Profl. Ins. Agts. of Ohio (dir. 1978-81), Ind. Ins. Agts. Assn. of Ohio, Profl. Ins. Agts. of Am., Ind. Ins. Agts. Assn. Am., Western Ohio Trucking Assn., Soc. Chartered Life Underwriters, Soc. Chartered Property and Casualty Underwriters, Soc. Cert. Ins. Counselors. Republican. Roman Catholic. Clubs: Elks, K.C., Eagles, Rotary. Home: 629 E Main St Versailles OH 45380 Office: 617 E Main St Versailles OH 45380

PHELAN, JOHN JOSEPH, JR., stock exchange exec.; b. N.Y.C., May 7, 1931; s. John J. and Edna P.; B.B.A., Adelphi U.; m. Joyce Catherine Campbell, Apr. 3, 1955; children—John, David, Peter. Mem. staff Nash & Co., 1955-57, partner, 1957-62; mng. partner Phelan & Co., 1962-72; became sr. partner Phelan Silver Vesce Barry & Co., 1972; now pres. and chief exec. officer N.Y. Stock Exchange, N.Y.C.; chmn. N.Y. Futures Exchange. Bd. dirs. Mercy Hosp., Heart Fund; bd. advs. Adelphi U.; co-chmn. parents fund Hamilton Coll.; N.Y. Stock Exchange chmn. Catholic Charities; mem. Cardinal's Com. of Laity. Served with USMC; Korea. Decorated knight Sovereign Mil. Order of Malta, knight Holy Sepulchre of Jerusalem; recipient Brotherhood award NCCJ, Nat. Youth Services award B'nai B'rith Found. Mem. Securities Industries Assn. (governing bd. 1978-79, exec. com. 1979-80, dir.), Nat. Market Assn. (chmn. ops. com. 1976-77). Clubs: Creek, Garden City Golf, Cherry Valley Golf, Sewanicka Yacht. Office: 11 Wall St New York NY 10005*

PHELPS, JAMES CARL, petroleum co. exec.; b. Lindsay, Okla., Oct. 14, 1922; s. Thomas and Alma (Thornton) P.; B.S. in Indsl. Engring., Okla. State U., 1949, M.S., 1951; m. Cora Marie Erwin, Apr. 25, 1942; children—Robert R., Ronald C. Refinery engr. Deep Rock Oil Corp., Cushing, Okla., 1950-51; pipeline engr. Service Pipe Line Co., Tulsa, 1951-53; v.p. Continental Pipe Line Co., Ponca City, Okla., 1953-62; v.p. Continental Oil Co., Houston, 1965-66, group v.p., 1966-67, sr. v.p., 1967-70, exec. asst. to pres., 1970-71; pres. Tesoro Petroleum Co., San Antonio, 1971-81; dir. Citizens Nat. Bank. Mem. adv. com. Okla. State U., 1968—; trustee S.W. Tex. Meth. Hosp., 1974—; vice-chmn. bd. San Antonio chpt. Am. Heart Assn.; chmn. United Way San Antonio and Bexar County; chmn. S.W. Tex. Meth. Hosp. Found.; mem. adv. com. U. Tex. at San Antonio, 1978—. Served with USAF, 1943-46. Mem. San Antonio C. of C. (vice-chmn. 1979-80). Methodist (trustee ch.). Office: Tesoro Petroleum Corp 8700 Tesoro Dr San Antonio TX 78286

PHILDIUS, PETER PHILIP, health care exec.; b. Bklyn., Mar. 22, 1930; s. George Philip and Ada (Bunkin) P.; B.B.A., Hofstra Coll., 1957; m. Marlene Drexler, Aug. 28, 1954; children—Cathy, Lisa, Kristi. Pres., Artificial Organs div. Baxter Travenol Labs., Inc., 1973-75, v.p., Chgo., 1975-76, group v.p., 1976-78; pres., chief operating officer Nat. Med. Care, Inc., Boston, 1978—. Served with USN, 1951-55; ETO. Mem. Mass. High Tech. Council, Health Industry Mfrs. Assn. (dir.). Republican. Clubs: Weston Golf, Univ., Algonquin, Greater Boston Running. Home: 81 Westerly Rd Weston MA 02193 Office: 200 Clarendon St Boston MA 02116

PHILIBOSIAN, GEORGE, realtor, real estate and constrn. co. exec.; b. Konia, Turkey, Nov. 15, 1915; s. Haig and Victoria (Huberserian) P.; Degree in Bus. Adminstrn., Constanta U. (Romania), 1933; student Columbia U., 1949; m. Alice Babikian, Oct. 6, 1951; children—Emil H., Alan G., Charles H., Stephen R., Anita Carol. Came to U.S., 1948, naturalized, 1955. Pres., dir. Monarch Realty Corp., 1949—, Glen View Devel. Co., 1955—, Summit Manor, Inc., 1960—, Glen Eaton Inc., 1963—, others; real estate developer, 1949—. Moderator Armenian Evangelical Union N.Am., 1977—; pres. Armenian Missionary Assn. Am., 1971-74, 80—; bd. dirs. Armenian Gen. Benevolent Union Am., 1974—; fellow trustee Armenian Assembly, 1978-79, trustee Englewood (N.J.) Hosp., 1980—; bd. dirs. Armenian Sanatorium Lebanon, 1973—; chmn. Armenian Evangelical World Conf. Master Plan Com., 1978—. Served with Romanian Army, 1930's. Named Man of Year, Knights of Vartan, 1978. Mem. Nat. Assn. Realtors, N.J. Realtors. Republican. Presbyterian (life elder 1962—). Clubs: N.Y. Athletic (N.Y.C.); Knights of Vartan. Home and Office: 420 Deerwood Rd Fort Lee NJ 07024

PHILION, JAMES ROBERT, assn. exec.; b. Glens Falls, N.Y., Jan. 3, 1944; s. Robert Francis and Margery Madeline (Streeter) P.; student Tex. A. & M. U., 1961-63, Arlington State U., 1963-64; m. Sharon Sue McGinness, Dec. 4, 1965; children—Robert Barton, Tami René. Ticket agt./sales rep. Central Airlines, Dallas, 1963-66; account exec. Hertz Corp., Houston, 1966-67; dist. sales mgr. Nat. Car Rental Systems, Inc., 1967-68, Los Angeles, 1968-69, regional sales mgr. western region, Los Angeles, 1969-70, nat. accounts mgr., Mpls., 1970-71, dir. sales, 1971, v.p. sales, 1971-79, corp. v.p., 1978-79; pres., mng. dir., chief exec. officer Airline Passengers Assn., Inc. and treas. Internat. Airline Passengers Assn., Inc., Dallas, 1979—. Mem. Nat. Passenger Traffic Assn. (Account Exec. of Year 1970), Discover Am. Travel Orgn., Traffic Clubs Internat., Am. Soc. Travel Agts., Sales and Mktg. Execs. Home: 2707 Shadow Wood Ct Arlington TX 76011 Office: PO Box 2758 Dallas TX 75221

PHILIPPI, DIETER RUDOLPH, coll. adminstr.; b. Frankfurt, Germany, July 26, 1929; s. Alfred and Ellen Marguerite (Glatzel) P.; B.B.A., Johann Wolfgang Goethe U., 1952; postgrad. Sorbonne, summers 1951, 52; M.B.A., Canadian Inst. Banking, 1953-55; children—Bianca Maria, Christopher Thomas. Came to U.S., 1956, naturalized, 1961. With Toronto-Dominion Bank, Calgary, Edmonton, Alta., Can., 1953-56; chief accountant Baylor U. Coll. Medicine, Houston, 1956-63; controller Wittenberg U., Springfield, Ohio, 1963-68; bus. mgr. Park Coll., Kansas City, Mo., 1968-70; bus. mgr., treas. Lone Mountain Coll., San Francisco, 1970-75; v.p. bus. affairs Findlay (Ohio) Coll., 1975-76; bus. mgr. Bologna (Italy) Center, Johns Hopkins U., 1976-78; dir. bus. and fin. Mt. St. Mary's Coll., Los Angeles, 1978—. Lectr., Laurence U., Santa Barbara, Calif., 1973—; financial cons. various charitable orgns. Pres., German Sch. of East Bay, 1970—; campaign coordinator United Appeals Fund, 1968, recipient Distinguished Service award, 1970; active Boy Scouts, Germany, 1948-52, Can., 1952-56, U.S., 1956—, exec. bd. Tecumseh council, 1967—, recipient Silver Beaver award, Wood badge, 1968. Trustee Cagliada Trust; bd. dirs. Bellaire Gen. Hosp., Greenland Hills Sch. Mem. Am. Accounting Assn., Am., Eastern finance assns., Am. Mgmt. Assn., Am. Assn. U. Adminstrs., Nat., Western assns. coll. and univ. bus. officers, Nat. Assn. Accountants, Am. Assn. Higher Edn., Coll. and Univ. Personnel Assn., San Francisco Consortium, Alpha Phi Omega. Clubs: Rotary; Commonwealth of California (San Francisco); Harbor Heights Country (Punta Gorda, Fla.); Univ. (Kansas City). Home: 2186 N Ecroyd Ave Simi Valley CA 93063 Office: Mount Saint Mary's Coll 12001 Chalon Rd Los Angeles CA 90049

PHILIPS, JOHN NASH, fuel co. exec.; b. Pitts., July 18, 1921; s. Samuel Kniess and Irma Dell (Nash) P.; A.B., Harvard, 1942; LL.B., Boston U., 1949; m. Virginia Lee Shade, Jan. 27, 1946; children—Lisa Graydon (Mrs. Steven Turner), Janice Lee. Admitted to Mass. bar, 1949; with Eastern Gas & Fuel Assos., Boston, 1946—, v.p., 1960-63, sr. v.p., treas., 1963-66, sr. v.p. adminstrn. and fin., 1966-69, exec. v.p., 1969-73, pres., 1973-76, chmn., chmn. bd., 1976—, also trustee; dir. EG&G Inc., Gulfstream Banks, Inc., Gulfstream First Bank and Trust N.A. Trustee, Boca Raton Community Hosp., Boston. Served to capt. F.A., AUS, 1942-46. Clubs: Somerset (Boston); Royal Palm (Boca Raton, Fla.). Home: Boca Raton FL Office: Suite 212 855 S Federal Hwy Boca Raton FL 33432

PHILLIPS, BERT EUGENE, mfg. co. exec.; b. Quincy, Ill., May 8, 1919; s. John Herbert, and Zella Nae (Long) P.; student U. Ill., 1938-39, Quincy Coll., 1940-41; m. Helen Joyce Grummon, Jan. 23, 1943. Aircraft salesman, 1945-47; with Clark Equipment Co., Battle Creek, Mich., 1948—, v.p., gen. mgr. indsl. truck div., 1959-65, group exec. mobile products divs., 1965-66, gen. mgr. constrn. machinery div., 1966-67, exec. v.p., 1967-70, pres. 1970—, also dir.; vice chmn. bd., dir. Clark Leasing Corp., Clark Equipment Credit Corp., Clark Rental Corp., Clark Equipment Overseas Finance Corp.; v.p., dir. Clark Internat. Marketing, S.A., Clark Realty Corp., Clark Equipment Can., Ltd.; dir. Whirlpool Corp., Amsted Industries, Mass. Mut. Life Ins. Co. Trustee Tri-State Coll. Served as flight instr. USAAF, World War II. Mem. Indsl. Truck Assn. (past pres.), Material Handling Inst. (past pres.). Office: Clark Equipment Co Circle Dr Buchanan MI 49107*

PHILLIPS, BETTY JANE, fed. credit union exec.; b. Akron, Mar. 31, 1931; d. Michael and Mary Cecilia (Kucera) Tomanek; student Akron U., 1951, U. Mo., 1977; m. Harvey G. Phillips, June 19, 1965; 1 dau., Ann Marie. Title and mortgage clk. Folk Chevrolet, Inc., Akron, 1949-54; teller BFG Employees Fed. Credit Union, Akron, 1958-60, asst. mgr., 1961-67, mgr., 1968-78, gen. mgr., 1979—. Mem. Credit Union Exec. Soc., Nat. Credit Union Mgmt. Assn. Inc., Nat. Assn. Fed. Credit Unions, Summit County Credit Union Mgrs. Assn., Am. Bus. Women's Assn. (treas.). Home: 5832 Woodward Dr Akron OH 44319 Office: 500 S Main St Akron OH 44318

PHILLIPS, CODY HUNTER, ins. co. exec.; b. Mt. Pleasant, Tex., Aug. 21, 1944; s. Ira Bennett and Grace (Newman) P.; B.A., Baylor U., 1966; J.D., U. Ariz., 1969; postgrad. Harvard Law Sch., 1979, Purdue U., 1978, Southwestern Legal Found., 1978; m. Patricia Edith Whear, May 26, 1974; children—Blake Hunter, Angela Joy. Admitted to Tex. bar, 1969; tax specialist Deloitte, Haskins & Sells, Houston, 1969-70; trust officer First City Nat. Bank of Houston, 1971; regional mktg. dir. Lionel D. Edie & Co., Houston, 1971-73; v.p., sr. trust officer Charles Schreiner Bank, Kerrville, Tex., 1973-75; pvt. practice law, Kerrville, 1975-77; v.p. mktg. and tax research Qualified Plan Cons., Inc., Reno, Nev., 1977-78; v.p., dir. mktg. services Am. Founders Life, Austin, Tex., 1978—; tchr. estate planning Am. Inst. Banking, 1970-72; cons. in estate planning and pensions; lectr. in field. Mem. Am. Bar Assn., Tex. Bar Assn., Travis County Bar Assn., Central Tex. Estate Planning Council, Austin Assn. Life Underwriters, Nat. Assn. Life Underwriters, Am. Soc. C.L.U. Home: 9009 N Plaza Austin TX 78753 Office: PO Box 15427 Austin TX 78761

PHILLIPS, EDWARD EVERETT, III, ins. co. exec.; b. Orange, N.J., Sept. 14, 1927; s. Edward Everett, Jr. and Margaret (Jaffray) P., Jr.; B.A. cum laude, Amherst Coll., 1952; LL.B., Harvard U., 1955. Admitted to Mass. bar, 1955; with firm Mirick, O'Connell, De Mallie & Lougee, Worcester, Mass., 1955-57; with John Hancock Mut. Life Ins. Co., Boston, 1957-69, v.p. agy. dept., 1965-69; with New Eng. Mut. Life Ins. Co., Boston, 1969—, adminstrv. v.p. home office ops., 1971-72, exec. v.p. home office ops., 1972-74, sec., 1969-74, pres., 1974—, chmn. bd., chief exec. officer, 1978—, also dir.; dir. New Eng. Telephone Co., New Eng. Life Equity Services Corp., 1973—. Chmn., dir., mem. exec. com. Mass. Taxpayers Found., Inc.; trustee Amherst Coll., Boston Pvt. Industry Council; past mem. Mass. Bd. Edn.; bd. dirs. Gov.'s Commn. on Property Tax Relief. Served with USMCR, 1945-48. Brookings Inst. pub. affairs fellow, 1965. Mem. Am. Coll. Life Underwriters, Am. Arbitration Assn. (dir.), Health Ins. Assn. Am. (dir.), Mass. Bus. Roundtable (dir.). Office: 501 Boylston St Boston MA 02117

PHILLIPS, EDWIN WILLIAM, concrete, materials supply co. exec.; b. Jersey City, Jan. 26, 1904; s. Edward E. and Elizabeth (Pansing) P.; Litt.B., Rutgers U., 1927; m. Margaret Underhill Alpers, Sept. 12, 1931; children—Adelaide Elizabeth (Mrs. Calvin T. Bull), Kenneth Edwin. Office sales, mgmt. Harrison Supply Co., East Newark, 1927-32, pres., 1948—; mgmt., pres., treas. Concrete Carriers, Inc., 1937-69; exec. v.p., dir. F.F. Phillips, Inc., New Brunswick, N.J.; chmn. bd., chief exec. officer, dir. Phillips Concrete Inc., Hillsborough, N.J.; officer, dir. Mascot Savs. and Loan Assn., Newark, 1954-64, Essential Savs. and Loan Assn., Verona, N.J., 1964-74; Lacrosse coach, 1936-41. Past mem. N.J. Citizens Hwy. Com. Trustee, bd. dirs., past chmn. bd. Boys' Clubs of Newark; trustee Essex County Coll. Found., 1976—. Recipient Man of Year Community Service award Boys' Clubs Newark, 1973. Mem. N.J. Concrete Assn. (dir., past pres.; gen. chmn. 1st Ann. Awards Dinner cosponsored with N.J. chpt. Am. Concrete Inst. 1964, 65, 66), Am. Concrete Inst., Navy League U.S., Circus Saints and Sinners (dir. N.J. tent), Beta Theta Pi. Clubs: Essex, Baltusrol Golf. Home: 144 Lake End Newfoundland NJ 07435 Office: 800 Passaic Ave East Newark NJ 07029

PHILLIPS, ELLIOTT HUNTER, lawyer; b. Birmingham, Mich., Feb. 14, 1919; s. Frank Elliott and Gertrude (Zacharias) P.; A.B. cum laude, Harvard, 1940, J.D., 1947; m. Gail Carolyn Isbey, Apr. 22, 1950; children—Elliott Hunter, Alexandra Robertson. Admitted to Mich. bar, 1948; asso. Hill, Essery, Lewis & Andrews (now Hill, Lewis, Adams, Goodrich & Tait), 1948, partner, 1953—. Pres., sec., dir. Detroit & Can. Tunnel Corp.; pres., dir. Detroit and Windsor Subway Co.; sec., dir. Enterform, Inc. (radio sta. WPHM); sec., dir. Palmer-Shile Co.; pres., trustee McGregor Fund. Trustee Boys Republic, Detroit Inst. for Children; vice chmn. bd. dirs. ARC, Detroit Area council Boy Scouts Am.; mem. overseers com. on univ. resources Harvard U. Served to lt. comdr. USNR, 1941-45. Mem. Detroit, Am. bar assns., State Bar Mich. Episcopalian (sr. warden, vestryman). Clubs: Country, Detroit, Econ., Renaissance, Yondotega, Harvard of Eastern Mich. (pres. 1955-56); Harvard (N.Y.C.). Contbr. legal, accounting jours. Home: 193 Ridge Rd Grosse Pointe Farms MI 48236 Office: 100 Renaissance Center 32d Floor Detroit MI 48243 also 100 E Jefferson Detroit MI 48226

PHILLIPS, FREDERICK PAUL, mortgage banker; b. Mpls., Apr. 18, 1950; s. Paul Richard and Mary Louise (Bakke) P.; B.A. in Econs., St. Olaf Coll., 1972; M.B.A., U. Minn., 1976; m. Merrilyn R. Lindquist, June 17, 1972; 1 dau., Lisa Michelle. Mktg. analyst F&M Savs. Bank, Mpls., 1973-75, securities portfolio specialist, 1975-77, investment officer, 1977-78, mortgage officer, 1978-79, asst. v.p. mortgage adminstrn., 1979—; v.p. planning and adminstrn. F&M Mortgage Corp., Mpls., 1980—. Served with USAF, 1972. Mem. Minn. Mortgage Bankers Assn., Twin Cities Soc. Securities Analysts. Office: 90 S 6th St Minneapolis MN 55402

PHILLIPS, GEORGE CHARLES, JR., health care financing exec.; b. Oklahoma City, Mar. 14, 1932; s. George Charles and Iola (Boatright) P.; B.S., Ohio State U., 1959; M.H.A., Duke U., 1965; student S.D. State Coll., 1949-50, Bowman-Gray Sch. Medicine, Wake Forest Coll., 1960-62, Guilford Coll., 1962-63; m. Joanelle Johnson, Apr. 4, 1956; children—Laurie M., Tiffany N., Melissa D. Adminstrv. asst. Mass. Gen. Hosp., Boston, 1965-68, asst. dir., 1968-72; adminstr. Memorial Med. Center, Springfield, Ill., 1972-74, pres., 1974-76; exec. dir. Illinois Health Facilities Authority, Chgo., 1977—. Chmn. health services div. United Way Campaign, 1974. Served with USMCR, 1953-57. Mem. Am. Hosp. Assn., Ill. Hosp. Assn. (trustee 1974-76), Am. Coll. Hosp. Adminstrs., Am. Mgmt. Soc., Hosp. Fin. Mgmt. Assn., Council Health Financing Authorities. Office: 35 E Wacker Dr Suite 2188 Chicago IL 60601

PHILLIPS, H. HERBERT, hosp. co. exec.; b. Coatesville, Ind., Nov. 5, 1928; s. Olney W. and Hazel M. (Fiel) P.; A.B. in Econs. Ind. U., 1951, postgrad. Law Sch., 1959-62; student FBI Acad., 1952; m. Dorothy L. Krichbaum, Mar. 15, 1953; children—Kenneth N., Matthew S., Michael S. Spl. agt. FBI, Washington, 1952-59, Franklin Life Ins. Co., Indpls., 1959; mgr. indsl. relations Ford Motor Co., Detroit, 1959-70; v.p. indsl. relations Midland Ross Corp., Cleve., 1970-71; v.p. personnel and insdl. relations White Motor Co., Cleve., 1971-76; v.p. adminstrn. No. Telecom Inc., Nashville, 1976-79; v.p. human resources Humana Inc., Louisville, 1979—. Mem. Republican. Methodist. Club: Hunting Creek Country. Home: 6002 Fox Hill Rd Prospect KY 40059 Office: Suite 1800 1st Nat Tower Louisville KY 40201

PHILLIPS, HOLLAND WOODFORD, internat. trade cons.; b. Grand Rapids, Minn., Apr. 30, 1932; s. Holland W. and Irene R. (Johnson) P.; B.B.A., U. Minn., 1955; m. Betty M. O'Neill, Mar. 26, 1955; children—Michael Stephen, Lynn Holly, Ronn Patrick. Partner, pres. Capital Electronics, Inc., St. Paul, 1960-68; v.p. Overseas Mktg. Group, Inc., Balt., 1968-73; dir. internat. div. Leslie Internat., Chgo., 1973-75; founder, pres. Holland W. Phillips & Assos., Ltd., internat. trade cons., Romeoville, Ill., 1975—; lectr. Elmhurst Coll. Vice commodore, bd. dirs. Mpls. Aquatennial, 1966-67. Mem. Chgo. Council Fgn. Relations, Internat. Trade Club Chgo., West Suburban Internat. Trade Club (pres. 1978—). Author: Complete Export Checklist, 1977; contbr. articles on internat. trade and export devel. to profl. jours. Home: 411 Wildwood Ct Romeoville IL 60441

PHILLIPS, JAMES DAVIS, mfg. co. exec.; b. N.Y.C., Nov. 6, 1935; s. Austin Stevenson and Elizabeth Dean (Bennett) P.; B.S., Davis and Elkins Coll., 1957; M.B.A. in Corp. Mgmt., Fairleigh Dickinson U., 1961; m. Helen Haggerty, July 16, 1960; children—William Austin, Kathleen Elizabeth, Ann Bennett. Various fin. positions Lederle div. Am. Cyanamid Co., 1957-69, chief fin. officer pigments div., Wayne, N.J., 1969-71; v.p. fin. Gen. Abrasive Co., 1971-72, v.p. Can. ops., 1972, exec. v.p., 1973-75; pres. Gen. Abrasive div. Dresser Industries, Inc., Niagara Falls, N.Y., 1975—; chmn. bd. Gen. Abrasive Co. Can. Ltd., 1973; mem. adv. bd. Marine Midland Bank. Mem. council Niagara U., 1976—; mem. Mt. View Adv. Bd. of Niagara County, 1977—; mem. bd. Niagara Falls Ind. Edn. Council. Recipient Nat. Comdrs. award DAV, 1978; Disting. Alumni award Davis and Elkins Coll., 1979. Mem. Nat. Assn. Accts., Abrasive Grain Assn. (chmn. bd. 1978-79, dir.), Alpha Sigma Phi, Beta Alpha Beta, Alpha Kappa Psi. Club: Niagara Falls Country. Home: 155 S 5th St Lewiston NY 14092

PHILLIPS, JAMES JOSEPH, furniture mfg. co. exec.; b. Balt., Mar. 30, 1949; s. John Thomas and Mae Catherine (Harper) P.; student Calvert Hall Coll., Miami Dade Jr. Coll., Broward Community Coll., also various specialized courses; m. Susan Miller, Aug. 11, 1967; children—James Joseph, Susan Kelly, Amanda Harper. Systems programmer ITT-Community Devel. Corp., Miami; Fla., 1969-74; sales mgr. S. Atlantic Industries, Ft. Lauderdale, Fla., 1974-76; v.p., dir. Thor Constrn., Inc., Ft. Lauderdale, 1976—; pres., dir. Lord & Beris Furniture Co., Ft. Lauderdale, 1979—; gen. mgr. Mytton Investments Co., Ft. Lauderdale, 1979—. Pres. Lake Areta Civic Assn., 1973. Mem. Ft. Lauderdale C. of C. (dir.), St. Vincent DePaul Soc. Roman Catholic. Club: Pembroke Pines Optimist (coach club little league 1977—). Home: 7365 W 16th Ave Hialeah Lakes FL 33014 Office: 3071 NW 28th St Fort Lauderdale FL 33311

PHILLIPS, JOEL PATRICK, JR., citrus coop. exec.; b. nr. Orlando, Fla., Aug. 23, 1921; s. Joel Patrick and Grace (Horrop) P.; student Maryville Coll., 1940-42, Nat. U. Mexico, 1951, Rollins Coll., 1950; m. Elizabeth A. Bryant, Sept. 1942; children—Robert Patrick, John H., Barbara Grace. Pilot, Fla. Airways, Orlando, 1946-48; citrus grower and trucking, Winter Park, Fla., 1949-57; pub. relations, asst. mgr. Plymouth (Fla.) Citrus Growers Assn., 1957-62, pres., gen. mgr., dir., 1962—; v.p., dir. Plymouth Citrus Products Coop.; dir. State Bank of Apopka, Grower's Loan & Guarantee, Seold-Sweet Growers, Inc., Citrus Central, Inc. Pres. Central Fla. council Boy Scouts Am., 1962—; past mem. nat. adv. council Small Bus. Adminstrn. Del. Republican Nat. Conv., 1960, 64. Served with USAAF, 1944-46. Mem. N.Y. Explorers Club. Home: 450 Mallard Circle Winter Park FL 32789 Office: Plymouth FL 32768

PHILLIPS, JOHN ALAN, bank exec.; b. Corning, N.Y., June 25, 1937; s. Charles John and Maryadina (Mozier) P.; m. Elizabeth Ireland, June 24, 1961; children—Mary Elizabeth, Susan Kathleen. Sec., mng. officer Medford Lakes (N.J.) Savs. & Loan Assn., 1958-59, 62-64; exec. v.p., chief exec. officer Garden State Savs. & Loan Assn., Plainfield, N.J., 1965-68; pres., chief exec. officer Potsdam (N.Y.) Savs. & Loan Assn., 1968-72, North Country Savs. Bank, Ogdensburg, N.Y., 1972—; dir. Savs. Banks Trust Co., SABRO Funding Corp., Thrift Instnl. Servicers, Inc. Chmn. bd. dirs. Assn. for Neighborhood Rehab. Inc.; pres. United Way of St. Lawrence and No. Franklin Counties, 1977-78; bd. dirs. St. Lawrence County Local Devel. Council, 1977—, Pvt. Industry Council, 1979—, St. Lawrence County Econ. Devel. Commn., 1977—, Mater Dei Coll. Served with AUS, U.S. Army, 1959-62. Office: North Country Savs Bank Corner Greene and Caroline Sts Ogdensburg NY 13669

PHILLIPS, JOHN FRANCIS, mgmt. cons. co. exec.; b. N.Y.C., Jan. 25. 1938; s. Frank and Gertrude V. Phillips; B.S., U.S. Mcht. Marine Acad., 1960; M.B.A., St. John's U., 1966; postgrad. in econs. New Sch. for Social Research, 1970—; postgrad. in pub. adminstrn. N.Y. U., 1976—; m. Rita R. McCourt, Sept. 9, 1961; children—Melissa Anne, John William, Heather Lynn. With

Honeywell Co., 1960-65, Control Data Co., 1965-67, United Data Centers, 1967-69, Creative Socio Medics, 1969-74; v.p. Advanced Computer Techniques Co., N.Y.C., 1974—; instr. computers in health Grad. Sch. Pub. Adminstrn., N.Y. U., 1977—. Served with USNR, 1960-64. Mem. Vets. of 7th Regt., Alumni Assn. U.S. Mcht. Marine Acad. Contbr. articles on data processing, systems and automation to profl. publs. Home: 20 Westbrook Rd Kings Point NY 11024 Office: 437 Madison Ave New York City NY 10022

PHILLIPS, JOSEPH, JR., computer cons.; b. Dupont, Pa., June 7, 1933; s. Joseph and Ann (Pilnick) P.; B.S. in Geophysics, Upsala U., 1960; postgrad. Princeton U., 1960; m. Margaret Hassinger, June 6, 1959; children—Patricia, Joseph, Cindy, David, Richard. Program engr. Honeywell, Inc., Boston, 1961-63; data processing mgr. U. So. Calif., Los Angeles, 1965-65; mgr. product planning and long range planning Honeywell, Inc., Boston, 1966-68; founder, v.p. ops. Telefile Computer Corp., Waltham, Mass., 1968-71; pres. Phillips Assos., Inc., Holliston, Mass., 1971—; lectr. U. Mass., U. So. Calif., Advanced Mgmt. Internat.; internat. cons.; computer advisor City of Holliston, 1971-76. Mem. bd. Boy Scouts Am., 1977—; adv. bd. Vocat. Schs. of Framingham (Mass.), 1974—; cons. Cath. Charities of N.Y., 1975—. Mem. IEEE (contbn. award 1977), Data Processing Mgmt. Assn., Codasyl Internat. Office: 770 Washington St Holliston MA 01746

PHILLIPS, MICHAEL, fin. exec.; b. N.Y.C., May 31, 1936; s. Harry and Anne (Kramer) P.; B.Mech. Engring., Cooper Union Sch. Engring., 1957; M.S., M.I.T., 1959. Group leader Cutler-Hammer, Melville, N.Y., 1959-62; econ. engr. Am. Can Co., N.Y.C., 1962-63; mgmt. cons. Dunlap & Assos., N.Y.C., 1963-64; mgmt. scientist Am.-Standard, Inc., N.Y.C., 1964-67; asst. v.p. First Nat. City Bank, N.Y.C., 1967-71; asst. v.p. Security Nat. Bank, Melville, N.Y., 1971-74, v.p., 1974-75; dir. planning and mgmt. scis., card div. Am. Express, N.Y.C., 1975-79, dir. funding and fgn. exchange, 1979-80; v.p. budgets and planning Marsh & McLennan, N.Y.C., 1980—. Mem. Inst. Mgmt. Sci., Ops. Research Soc. Am. Club: M.I.T. Home: 271-29D Grand Central Pkwy Floral Park NY 11005 Office: 1221 Ave of Americas New York NY 10020

PHILLIPS, NICOLAS R. GUTHRIE, mfg. co. exec.; b. Nashville, Sept. 3, 1934; s. Rufus S. and Elizabeth (Guthrie) P.; B.S., U.S. Mcht. Marine Acad., 1956; M.B.A., U. Conn., 1971; m. Bonnie Elizabeth Payer, Feb. 21, 1960; children—Johanna Lea, David Guthrie, Stephen MacLeod, Paul Timothy. Engaged in heavy indsl. mfg., oil exploration, mining and constrn. industries; now gen. mgr. Denver ops. Cooper Industries, Inc.; instr. Vt. State Colls., 1980—. Mem. accreditation com. Tex. SW Coll., 1975-76; mem. pres.'s council Coll. Mt. St. Vincent, 1977—. Served to lt. U.S. Navy, 1956-61. Recipient personal citation from comdr.-in-chief U.S. Atlantic Fleet. Sr. mem. Soc. Mfg. Engrs. Clubs: Off-Soundings, Yachting. Home: PO Box 1020 Denver CO 80201

PHILLIPS, PHILIP KAY, iron and steel products mfg. co. exec.; b. Kansas City, Mo., Jan. 3, 1933; s. Ernest Lloyd and Mildred Blanche (Moser) P.; B.A., Bob Jones U., Greenville, S.C., 1958; postgrad. Central Mo. State U., 1977-78; m. Constance Diana Lucas, June 12, 1955; children—John Allen, David Lee, Stephen Philip, Daniel Paul, Joy Christine. Ordained minister Baptist Ch., 1959; pastor Mt. Moriah Baptist Ch., Clarksburg, Mo. 1958-59; security officer Mo. Dept. Corrections, Jefferson City, Mo., 1959-64; field mgr. office Darby Corp. and Piping Contractors Inc., Kansas City, Kans., 1965-72, safety and security dir. Darby Corp. and Leavenworth Steel Inc., Kansas City, 1972—. Mem. planning com. Kans. Gov.'s Indsl. Safety and Health Conf., 1977-78, chmn. mfg. sect., 1978. Mem. Nat. Safety Mgmt. Soc., Am. Soc. Safety Engrs., Kans. Safety Assn. (v.p., mem. exec. com. 1979). Home: 3205 NE 66th St Gladstone MO 64119 Office: Darby Corp and Leavenworth Steel Inc 1st and Walker Sts Kansas City KS 66110

PHILLIPS, RAYMOND FOY, oil co. exec.; b. Vernon, Tex., July 26, 1935; s. Robert Raymond and Margie Fay (Fowler) P.; B.S. in Chem. Engring., Tex. Tech. U., 1957; m. Maidie Bassett Baldwin, Aug. 28, 1960; children—Maidie Bland, Robert Foy, Fowler Scott. Engaged in new product and new venture marketing research Humble Oil and Refining Co., Baytown, Tex., Houston, and N.Y.C., 1957-63; petroleum product marketing, advt. research Internat. Petroleum, Coral Gables, Fla., Bogota, Colombia, 1963-65; chem. and environmental resources adviser Houston Research Inst., 1965-67; with Pennzoil Co., Houston, 1967-74, dir. land and water resources div., 1970, 71, with new products and new ventures, 1972-74; pres. Mondo Chem. and Supply Co., Houston, 1974-77, R. Foy Phillips & Assos., oil and gas prodn., Houston, 1977—. Mem. N.W. Harris County Pub. Safety Assn. (dir.), Chem. Marketing Research Assn., S.W. Chem. Assn., Soc. Petroleum Engrs. Contbr. articles to profl. jours. Home: 13710 Hambleton Circle Houston TX 77069 Office: Stewart Title Bldg Houston TX 77068

PHILLIPS, RICHARD LEE, ins. co. exec.; b. Newcomerstown, Ohio, May 13, 1926; s. David Rees and Ethel (Rees) P.; B.S. in Bus. Adminstrn., Ohio State U., 1950; m. Virginia Grace Hoewischer, Sept. 17, 1950; children—Douglas Richard, Joy Lynn. With Shelby (Ohio) Mut. Ins. Co., 1950—, spl. agt., 1950-56, asst. sec., 1956-61, sec., 1961-67, v.p. sales, 1967-71, v.p., sec., 1971-76, pres., chmn. bd., chief exec. officer, 1976—, also dir.; pres., chmn. bd., chief exec. officer Shelby Fin. Corp., Shelby Life Ins. Co., IPBS, Inc. instr. Sch. Mut. Ins. Agts. Oberlin Coll., 1967. Chmn., Mansfield campus fund raising drive Ohio State U., 1961; bd. dirs. Mansfield U. Found., 1962; chmn. citizens' adv. bd. Mansfield campus Ohio State U., 1963; pres. Shelby (Ohio) chpt. Am. Field Service, 1965; pres. Shelby Jr. Achievement, 1967; bd. dirs., chmn. Shelby United Fund, 1971; mem. alumni adv. bd. Ohio State U., 1975—; vice chmn. community bldg. fund drive Shelby YMCA, 1976; trustee Richland County Found., Griffith Found. Ins. Edn., Ohio State U. Served with USN, 1943-46. Designated C.P.C.U., Ohio. Mem. Soc. C.P.C.U. (pres. Akron/Canton chpt. 1968), Ohio Ins. Inst. (1st vice-chmn. 1980, sec. 1977), Alliance Am. Insurers (dir.), Ins. Fedn. Ohio (pres. 1980), Kappa Sigma. Republican. Methodist. Home: 58 Louise Dr Shelby OH 44875 Office: 175 Mansfield Ave Shelby OH 44875

PHILLIPS, RICHARD MILES, machine tools co. exec.; b. Akron, Ohio, May 11, 1935; s. Wilmer Miles and Thelma Evelyn (Cooper) P.; student U. Akron, 1957-58, Pierce Coll., 1964-65; m. Merida M. Vough, July 4, 1953; children—Steven Miles, Michael Richard. Pres., chmn. bd. Ward-Riddle Co., Ravenna, Ohio, 1971—, Three/Phase Electronics Corp., Kent, Ohio, 1975—, Phillips Indsl. Properties Inc., Kent, 1974—, Software & Computer Service Inc., Ravenna, 1975—, MSM Leasing & Sales, Stow, Ohio, 1975—, Phillips Precision Drilling Systems, Tallmadge, Ohio, 1979—. Chmn., Republican Party City of Stow, Ohio, 1972-73. Served with AUS, 1952-56. Mem. Stow Jaycees (pres. 1957-58), Am. Soc. Metals, Am. Soc. Tool Mfg. Engrs. Home: 3247 Patty Ann St Stow OH 44224 Office: PO Box 234 239 West Ave Tallmadge OH

PHILLIPS, ROBERT EMMET, banker; b. N.Y.C., July 21, 1933; s. Lawrence E. and Agnes M. (Healy) P.; B.S. in Chem. Engring., U. Notre Dame, 1955; M.B.A. in Fin., Harvard U., 1962. Mgr., Chem. Bank, N.Y.C., 1962-64; v.p. De-Fi Mfg. Co., N.Y.C., 1964-69; v.p. Rinfret Mut. Fund, N.Y.C., 1969-72; asst. v.p. Irving Trust Co., N.Y.C., 1972-75; v.p. Village Savs. Bank, Port Chester, N.Y., 1976-80, sr. v.p., 1980—; cons. Am. Auger Co., 1975-76. Mem. adv. bd., treas. Westchester Community Opportunity Program, 1978—. Served with USAF, 1955-60. Club: Rotary. Home: 210 E 68th St New York NY 10021 Office: 133 N Main St Port Chester NY 10573

PHILLIPS, RUDOLPH MELDON, mfg. co. exec.; b. Oak Park, Ill., Apr. 24, 1941; s. Rudolph Philip and Alice Regina (Lewis) P.; B.S. in Chem. Engring., U. Mo., 1963; M.Chem. Engring., Purdue U., 1965; J.D., Chase Coll., Cin., 1974; m. Bluette Rae Ziebell, Jan. 27, 1962; children—Brock Allen, Blake Wilding. Project engr. Universal Oil Corp., Chgo., 1961, 62; teaching asst. U. Mo., 1962-63, Purdue U., 1963-65; project engr. coffee div. Procter & Gamble, Cin., 1965-67, group leader process devel. mfg. startup, San Francisco, Houston and New Orleans, 1967-68, tech. brand mgr. Folger's Coffee, Cin., 1968-70, tech. brand mgr. Pringles Food div., Cin., 1970-74, sect. mgr. food div., 1974-76; mgr. internal cons. Pet, Inc., St. Louis, 197? 1976-78; group v.p., gen. mgr. flavor and food systems div. PFW div. Hercules, Inc., Middletown, N.Y., 1978—; admitted to Ohio bar, 1974; partner firm Phillips, Bartlett, Junewick & Witte, 1974-76. Mem. adminstrv. bd. Meth. Ch., Cin., 1960-74; dist. commr. Dan Beard council Boy Scouts Am. NSF grantee, 1963-65. Mem. Am. Inst. Chem. Engrs., Engrs. Club St. Louis, Am. Bar Assn., Ohio Bar Assn., Cin. Bar Assn., Nutrition Found., Inc., Inst. Food Tech. Republican. Patentee instant coffee crystals. Office: 33 Sprague Ave Middletown NY 10940

PHILLIPS, SAMUEL JOSEPH, corporate exec.; pres.; b. North Vandergrift, Pa., Sept. 17, 1931; s. Samuel and Margaret (Solomon) P.; B.S., U. Md., 1953; M.B.A., Xavier U., 1960; m. Matina Fidanis, Jan. 28, 1953; children—Diana M., Samuel T., Candice A., Tracy L., Daniel J. With Procter & Gamble Co., Cin., 1956-67, mgr. cost accounting dept., food products div., 1964-65, controller, chief financial officer Folger Coffee Co. div., Kansas City, Mo., 1965-67; controller film div. Polaroid Corp., Waltham, Mass., 1967-69, group controller, Cambridge, Mass., 1969-70; v.p. ops. Healthcare Corp., Boston, 1970; pres. advance surfaces div. and v.p. finance Parkwood Laminates, Lowell, Mass., 1971-72, pres., 1972-74, also dir.; mgmt. cons. Phillips Assos., 1974-75; pres., chmn. Acton Corp. (Mass.), 1975—; dir. Phillips Corp., College Park, Md., Orthodontic Labs, Ky., Covington. Active United Fund, Cin. Trustee, Cin. Summer Opera, 1964-65, N.H. Coll., 1979—, Phillips Found., Annapolis; trustee, chmn. exec. com. Franconia Coll., 1975-77. Served to 1st lt. Arty., AUS, 1953-56. Recipient Kansas City Boy Scout award for community service, 1966. Mem. Financial Exec. Inst. Office: Box 407 Acton MA 01720

PHILLIPS, SHELBY JEAN, health care exec.; b. Huntsville, Ala., Sept. 29, 1938; d. Carl J. and Vedith M. (Guinn) Hill; A.A. in Bus. Mgmt., Alverson Draughn Bus. Coll., Huntsville, 1977; m. Elbert A. Phillips, June 29, 1955 (dec. 1968); children—Sherron, Elbert A., Teresa, Gary, Marsha, Doris. Office mgr., bookkeeper N. Ala. Orthopaedic Center, P.C., Huntsville, 1976—; condr. seminars on med. office mgmt. Address: 401 Lowell Dr Suite 21 Huntsville AL 35801

PHILLIPS, STEPHEN, hotel exec.; b. London, Nov. 11, 1942; s. Alecx and Eleanore P.; ed. Ecole Hoteliere de Lausanne, Switzerland, 1962. Banqueting mgr. Royal Garden Hotel, London, 1967-69; exec. asst. mgr. King David Hotel, Jerusalem, 1969-73; exec. asst. mgr. Dragonara Hotel, Leeds, Eng., 1973-74; gen. mgr. mktg. ops. Four Seasons Hotels Ltd., Toronto, Ont., Can., 1974—; cons. in field. Served with Israel Def. Forces, 1964-66. Mem. Anciens Eleves de l'Ecole Hoteliere de Lausanne, Am. Soc. Travel Agts., Alliance of Can. Travel Assos., Discover Am. Travel Orgn., Am. Soc. Assn. Execs., Can.-U.K. C. of C., France-Can., C. of C. Jewish. Club: Masons. Home: 95 Thorncliffe Park Dr Apt 2103 Toronto ON M4H 1L7 Canada Office: 1100 Eglinton Ave E Don Mills ON M3C 1H8 Canada

PHILLIPS, THOMAS LEONARD, mfg. co. exec.; b. May 2, 1924; B.E.E., Va. Poly. Inst., 1947, M.E.E., 1948; D.B.A. (hon.), Boston Coll., 1974; LL.D., Gordon Coll., 1970; D.Sc., Lowell Technol. Inst., 1970, Northeastern U., 1968; D.C.S., Stonehill Coll., 1968. With Raytheon Co., 1948—, successively designer servo-mechanisms, spl. radar circuits and systems, mgr. missile systems dept., asst. lab. mgr., mgr. and Belford Devel. Labs., v.p., div. gen. mgr., 1948-61, exec. v.p., 1961-64, dir., 1962—, pres., chief operating officer, 1964-75, chief exec. officer, 1968—, chmn. bd., 1975—; dir. John Hancock Mut. Life Ins. Co., State St. Investment Corp., Beech Aircraft Corp. Mem. corp. Mus. Sci., Boston; v.p. Joslin Diabetes Found.; trustee Gordon Coll., Northeastern U., Com. Econ. Devel.; bd. incorporation Diabetes Found., Inc. Recipient Meritorious Public Service award for work on Sparrow III missile system, U.S. Navy. Mem. Nat. Acad. Engring., The Bus. Council, Bus. Roundtable. Office: Raytheon Co 141 Spring St Lexington MA 02173*

PHILLIPS, VIRGINIA GAIL, oil co. exec.; b. Phillipsburg, Kans., Feb. 1, 1952; d. Boyd D. and JoAnn (Larimore) P.; B.A. in Polit. Sci., Okla State U., 1974; M.B.A., Phillips U., 1978; m. A. Calvin Johnson, Aug. 13, 1977 (div.). Social worker HEW, Enid (Okla.) State Sch., 1975-76, coordinator vol. services, 1976; office mgr. Phillips Oil Operating Co., Enid, 1976—; pres. VGP Oil Investments, Enid, 1976—. Contact worker Christian Telephone Ministry, Enid, 1975; worker United Fund Dr., Enid, 1975; mem. aquatics com. YMCA, Enid, 1976. Selected as overseas student in Sweden, Phillips U., 1974, 1st female grad. of M.B.A. program, 1978; Mem. Nat. Polit. Sci. Orgn., Desk and Derrick Nat. Women's Petroleum Industry Assn. (Enid chpt. membership chmn. 1978), Phillips U. Geol. Soc., Phillips U. Masters of Bus. Assn., Alpha Phi (v.p. 1972). Author: Requirements for Small Business Policy manual, 1978. Home: 2406 Sandpiper Enid OK 73701 Office: 702 N Grand Enid OK 73701

PHILLIPS, WARREN HENRY, newspaperman; b. June 28, 1926; s. Abraham and Juliette (Rosenberg) P.; A.B., Queens Coll., 1947; J.D. (hon.), U. Portland, 1973; m. Barbara Anne Thomas, June 16, 1951; children—Lisa, Leslie, Nina. Copyreader, Wall St. Jour., 1947-48, fgn. corr., Germany, 1949-50, chief London bur, 1950-51, fgn. editor, 1951-53, news editor, 1953-54, mng. editor Midwest edit., Chgo., 1954-57, mng. editor, 1957-65; exec. editor Dow Jones & Co., pub. Wall St. Jour., 1965-70, v.p., gen. mgr., 1970-71, editorial dir., 1971—, exec. v.p., 1972, pres., 1972-79, chief exec. officer, 1975—, chmn. bd., 1978—, also dir.; copyreader Stars & Stripes European edit., 1949. Pres., Am. Council Edn. for Journalism, 1971-73; mem. Putlitzer Prizes Bd., 1976—; trustee Columbia U., 1980—. Served with U.S. Army, 1943-45. Named one of 10 Outstanding Young Men in U.S., U.S. Jr. C. of C., 1958. Mem. Am. Newspaper Pubs. Assn. (dir.), Am. Soc. Newspaper Editors (pres. 1975-76). Clubs: Reform (London); River (N.Y.C.); Cosmos (Washington). Author: (with Robert Keatley) China: Behind the Mask, 1973. Office: Dow Jones and Co 22 Cortlandt St New York NY 10007

PHILLIPS, WILLIAM EUGENE, advt. exec.; b. Chgo., Jan. 7, 1930; s. William E. and Alice P.; B.S., Cornell U., 1951; M.B.A., Northwestern Grad. Sch. Commerce, 1955; m. Elizabeth Earl, Aug. 13, 1971; children by previous marriage—Michael, Tom, Sarah. Brand mgr. Procter & Gamble, Cin., 1955-59; with Ogilvy & Mather, Inc., N.Y.C., 1959—, pres., 1974-78, chmn., 1978—; partner Snowbird Ski Area; dir. Bus. Mktg. Corp., N.Y.C., Gen. Housewares Corp. Mem. council Cornell U.; bd. dirs. PAL; trustee Outward Bound, Wells Coll. Served to lt. (j.g.) USNR, 1951-54; Korea. Mem. Am. Assn. Advt. Agys. (dir. Eastern region). Clubs: Murray Hill Racquet; Black Hall Golf; Fenwick. Home: 1 Beekman Pl New York NY 10022 Office: 2 E 48th St New York NY 10017

PHILLIPS, WILLIAM GEORGE, business exec.; b. Cleve., Mar. 3, 1920; s. Edward George and Ina Marie (Cottle) P.; A.B., Antioch Coll., 1942; m. Laverne Anne Evenden, Aug. 7, 1943; children—Karen Anne (Mrs. David F. Berry), Connie Allynette (Mrs. Richard Tressel), Scott William. Pub. accountant Price Waterhouse & Co., Cleve., 1945-48; tax accountant Glidden Co., Cleve., 1948-52, asst. treas., 1952, treas., dir., 1953-67, adminstrv. v.p., 1963-64, pres., 1964-67, chief exec. officer, 1967, pres. Glidden-Durkee div. SCM Corp., 1967-68; pres., chief exec. officer Internat. Multifoods Corp. (formerly Internat. Milling), Mpls., 1968-70, chmn. bd., 1970—; dep. chmn. Mpls. Fed. Res. Bank, 1979—, also dir.; dir. Soo Line R.R. Co., N. Am. Life and Casualty Co., Firestone Tire & Rubber Co., No. States Power Co. Bd. overseers U. Minn. Coll. Bus. Adminstrn.; nat. corp. adv. bd. United Negro Coll. Fund; exec. com. U.S.-Iran Joint Bus. Council; adv. bd. Nat. Alliance Businessmen; bd. dirs. Mpls. Downtown Devel. Corp., Minn. State Council on Econ. Edn.; mem. pres.'s adv. bd. Am. Diabetes Assn.; adv. bd. Inst. Internat. Edn.; trustee Hamline U., 1979—; bd. dirs. Mpls. Found.; trustee Mpls. Soc. Fine Arts, Nat. Jewish Hosp. at Denver, Ednl. Research Council Am. Served to lt., inf. AUS, 1942-45. Mem. Conf. Bd., C. of C. U.S. (dir., mem. U.S.-Can. com.), Ohio Soc. C.P.A.'s, Grocery Mfrs. Am. (dir.), Conf. Bd. Mem. Community Ch. Clubs: Lafayette, Minneapolis (bd. govs.), Woodhill Country. Home: 2610 W Lafayette Rd Excelsior MN 55331 Office: 1200 Multifoods Bldg Minneapolis MN 55402

PHINNEY, MILFORD L., II, tool and die co. exec.; b. Medina, N.Y., Apr. 20, 1950; s. Lewis M. and Grace J. P.; A.B., Colgate U., 1972; M.B.A., State U. N.Y., Buffalo, 1974; J.D., Syracuse U., 1980; m. Antonia duPont Bayard, Nov. 20, 1976. With Phinney Tool & Die Co., Inc., Medina, N.Y., 1973—, v.p., dir., 1975—. Mem. Aircraft Owners and Pilots Assn. Republican Comml., instrument pilot. Office: Phinney Tool & Die Co W Center St Ext Medina NY 14103

PHIPPS, ALLEN MAYHEW, mgmt. cons.; b. Seattle, Oct. 3, 1938; s. Donald Mayhew and Virginia (McGinn) P.; B.A. in Econs., U. Calif., Berkeley, 1961; M.B.A. with honors, Stanford U., 1969; m. Joyce Elisabeth Alberti, Aug. 21, 1971; children—Ramsey Mayhew, Justin Beckwith. Security analyst Morgan Guaranty Trust Co., 1968; with Boston Cons. Group, Inc., 1969—, mgr. 1971-74, mem. sr. team, Calif., 1974-77, corp. v.p., dir., 1975—; mgr. Boston Cons. Group, G.m.b.H., Munich. W. Ger., 1978—. Served to capt. U.S. Army, 1961-67. Decorated Bronze Star, Army Commendation medal with 2 oak leaf clusters. Mem. Alpha Delta Phi. Republican. Presbyterian. Clubs: Brae Burn Country (West Newton, Mass.); Stanford (Calif.) Golf; Univ. (Palo Alto, Calif.). Home: Gerstaecker Strasse 41 8000 Munich 82 Federal Republic of Germany Office: Boston Cons Group GmbH Maximiliansplatz 5 8000 Munich 2 Federal Republic of Germany

PHIPPS, JOHN EDWARD, mgmt. exec.; b. St. Louis, May 15, 1948; s. Charles Edward and Willa Geneva (Dean) P.; B.S., U. Cin., 1970, M.B.A., 1974; m. Christine Dorothea Franke, Aug. 7, 1971; children—Charles Edward, Joshua Owen. Mgmt. trainee Gen. Motors Corp., Norwood, Ohio, 1966-68; indsl. engr. U.S. Shoe Co., Cin., 1969-72, asst. dir. cost control women's div., 1972-74, dir. indsl. engring., Beloit, Wis., 1976-77; sr. footwear applications engr. Camsco, Inc., Richardson, Tex., 1977-78, product mgr., 1978-79, group product mgr., 1979—; cons. in field. Mem. Am. Inst. Indsl. Engrs. (sr.). Home: 2616 Laurel Ln Plano TX 75074 Office: 1200 N Bowser Richardson TX 75081

PHLEGAR, RICHARD ROBERT, sports goods export mgmt. co. exec.; b. N.Y.C., Mar. 16, 1943; s. Francis Carl and Claire Augusta (Plango) P.; student City U. N.Y., 1959-64; m. Linda Jill Brass, Mar. 17, 1964; children—Jeffrey Scott, Russell Alan. With Universal Sports Corp., N.Y.C., 1960—, v.p. finance and spl. projects, 1976—, dir., 1975—; dir. Universal Sports Overseas Corp., Narragansett Mil. Products Corp., Mellor Gym Supply Corp. Mem. Nat. Assn. Export Mgmt. Cos. Democrat. Home: 10 Pal Way Plainview NY 11803 Office: 9 E 40th St New York NY 10016

PIANTI, MARGARET PIACENTINO, corp. planner; b. Christchurch, New Zealand, d. Neil Howard and Margaret Frances (Downs) MacPherson; came to U.S., 1968; C.P.A., U. N.Z.; m. Romano Pianti, Aug. 13, 1962; children—Petite, Hal Robert, Tanya Margaret. Jr. acct. Mitchell & Price, Christchurch, 1958-60; sr. auditor Baker, Sutton & Co., London, 1961; asst. controller Internat. Confedn. of Free Trade Unions, Brussels, 1962-65; controller Sperry Rand Ltd., N.Z., 1965-67; controller Beaumont Assos., Beverly Hills, Calif., 1968-69; mgr. fin. planning and systems The Capital Group, Inc., Los Angeles, 1969-80; corp. planner, 1980—. Mem. N.Z. Soc. Accts., Planning Execs. Inst. (past pres. Los Angeles chpt., regional dir. 1977-80), So. Calif. Corp. Planners (v.p. program 1979), Los Angeles Area C. of C. (chmn. long range planning com. 1978).

PICARD, WILFRED JOSEPH, JR., digital equipment mfg. co. ofcl.; b. Laconia, N.H., Apr. 17, 1935; s. Wilfred Joseph and Rose Aimee (Bolduc) P.; B.S., Northeastern U., 1958; m. Theresa Constance Eccles, Apr. 27, 1968; 1 dau., Pamela Rose. System rep. IBM, Atlanta, 1960-64; mgr. adminstrn. Gulf Am. Corp., Miami, Fla., 1964-68; sr. bus. systems analyst Honeywell Inc., Waltham, Mass., 1968-77; info. resource mgr. U.S. area personnel Digital Equipment Co., Maynard, Mass., 1977—; Speaker 11th Nat. Conf. on Human Resource Mgmt., N.Y.C., 1980. Pres., Charitable Union Mass., 1978—. Served with Signal Corps, U.S. Army, 1958-60. Mem. Data Processing Mgmt. Assn. Club: K.C. (faithful navigator 1973-74, grand knight 1974-75). Home: 18 Westlake Rd Natick MA 01760 Office: Digital Equipment Co Parker St Maynard MA 01754

PICCHIOTTINO, JOHN BERNARD, med. electronics co. exec.; b. Milw., July 11, 1936; s. John Battista and Mary Catherine (Picchiottino) P.; B.S. in Elec. Engring., U. Wis., 1958; M.S. in Elec. Engring. (Hughes Aircraft Co. fellow), U. So. Calif., 1960. Circuit designer Hughes Aircraft Co., Culver City, Calif., 1958-61; design engr. Ball Bros. Research Corp., Boulder, Colo., 1961-65; v.p. Commsult Inc., Boulder, 1965-69; pvt. practice cons., Boulder, 1969-71; pres. Bio Feedback Systems Inc., Boulder, 1971—. Mem. Bio Feedback Soc. Am., Assn. for Advancement of Med. Instrumentation. Club: Colo. Mountain. Patentee in field. Home: 625 Manhattan Circle #209 Boulder CO 80301 Office: 2736 47th St Boulder CO 80301

PICCIONE, JAMES JOSEPH, food co. exec.; b. Columbus, Ohio, Oct. 16, 1938; s. James R. and Rose Marie (Gerardi) P.; student public schs., Columbus; m. Barbara E. Thompson, Mar. 18, 1957; children—Toni Maria, Vicki Lynn, Joseph James, Juli Anne. With Schiffs Shoe Co., Columbus, 1953-57; sales mgr. O.G. Sandbo Co., Columbus, 1957-67; pres., dir. Gage Foods, Melrose Park, Ill., 1967—, Dale Foods, Melrose Park, 1972—; pres. Cap Chem. Co.,

Melrose Park, 1979—; dir. Capitol Food Industries, Chgo. Residence asst. Devonshire Civic Assn., 1961-62. Served with USN, 1956. Mem. Am. Camping Assn., Am. Sch. Food Service Assn., Chgo. C. of C., Round Table Club, 100,000 Club. Republican. Roman Catholic. Office: 1501 N 31st Ave Melrose Park IL 60160

PICIULO, ANTHONY JOSEPH, pharm. co. exec.; b. Buffalo, Feb. 28, 1928; s. Angelo Peter and Marie (Radice) P.; B.S., Niagara U., 1950; postgrad. Canisius Coll., 1952; m. Charlotte B. Ricigliano, May 26, 1951; children—Christine, Annette, Paul, Amy. Sales rep. D.J. Mead Paper Co., 1950, Beechnut Packing Co., 1951-53; terr. mgr. Stuart Pharm. Co., 1953-65; pres., chmn. bd. AVP Pharms., Inc., Clarence, N.Y., 1965—. Served with AUS, 1950-51. Mem. Nat. Ethical Pharm. Assn. Roman Catholic. Office: AVP Pharmaceuticals Inc 9829 Main St Clarence NY 14031

PICKARD, DAVID JANARD, endowment fund exec.; b. Colorado Springs, Colo., Nov. 23, 1933; s. Kenneth Leonard and Ann Ruth (Wemyss) P.; A.B., U. Nebr., 1956; student Berkeley Div. Sch., Yale, 1956-58; children—Laurel Jane, John Mark. Exec. v.p. Tri State Supply, Inc., Scottsbluff, Nebr., 1958-73, Tri State Supply of Sidney, Inc. (Nebr.), 1959-73, v.p. Tri State of Alliance, Inc. (Nebr.), 1965-73, pres. Tri State of Wyoming, Inc., Torrington, 1967-73, exec. v.p. Tri State Warehousing, Inc., Scottsbluff, 1965-73; dir. devel., commr., asst. treas. Kappa Sigma Endowment Fund, Denver, 1973—. Mem. Colo. Yale Assn. Republican. Episcopalian. Clubs: Masons, Star and Crescent, Univ. (Lincoln, Nebr.). Home: 2035 Oriole Ave Colorado Springs CO 80909 Office: PO Box 7715 Colorado Springs CO 80933

PICKARD, RICHARD H., bldg. materials co. exec.; b. Chgo., Feb. 18, 1916; s. Glenn H. and Allene (Clark) P.; B.S. in Chem. Engring., Purdue, 1937; m. Mary Margaret Anderson, Oct. 28, 1939 (div. July 1972); children—Richard H., Susan Elizabeth; m. 2d, Danielle Richy-Dureteste, Oct. 7, 1972. Chem. engr. V.D. Anderson Co., Cleve., 1937-39, Wm. J. Hough Co., Chgo., 1939-41; purchasing agt., U.S. Gypsum Co., Chgo., 1941-66, gen. mgr. minerals div., 1966-70, mng. dir. subsidiary USG Europe, S.A., Ghlin, Belgium, 1970-73, mgr. corporate devel., 1973—. Registered profl. engr., Ill. Mem. Am. Chem. Soc., Assn. Corporate Growth. Presbyn. (deacon, chmn. bd. deacons, 1952-54). Club: Tower (Chgo.). Contbr. articles to sci. publs. Office: 101 S Wacker Dr Chicago IL 60606

PICKERSGILL, JOSEPH ARTHUR, indsl. hygienist; b. Phila., July 30, 1927; s. John Thomas and Elizabeth Josita (McAllister) P.; B.A., Alaska Methodist U., 1962; B.S., Southwestern State Coll., 1967; M.Ed., Our Lady of Lake Coll., 1968; m. Judith Ann Haynes, July 7, 1971; children—James, Bonnie Lee, George, Janet. Served as enlisted man U.S. Navy, 1945-58; sgt. USAF, 1958, advanced through grades to sr. master sgt., 1971; dir. adminstrn. environics br. Air Force Weapons Lab., Kirtland AFB, N.Mex., 1972-74; ret., 1974; dir. tech. studies aeromed. Air Line Pilots Assn., Denver, 1974—; instr. preventive medicine USAF Sch. Aerospace Medicine, Brooks AFB, Tex., 1967-71. Decorated USAF Commendation medal with oak leaf cluster. Mem. Am., Rocky Mountain indsl. hygiene assns., Colo. Golf Assn. (instr. jr. golf program). Clubs: Shriners. Author papers in field. Home: 8331 E Lehigh Dr Denver CO 80237 Office: 12000 E 47th Ave Denver CO 80239

PICKETT, DOYLE C., book wholesaling co. exec.; b. Greencastle, Ind., July 15, 1930; s. Joseph V. and Lora (Phillips) P.; A.B., Wabash Coll., 1952; M.B.A., Ind. U., 1953; m. Dorothy McGinnis; children—Brian Doyle, Marsha Ann. Grad. asst. dept. mgmt. Ind. U. Sch. of Bus., 1952-53; exec. trainee L.S. Ayres & Co., Indpls., 1953-56, employment interviewer, 1956-58, staff asst. to gen. mdse. mgr., 1958-60, office mgr., 1960-62, asst. store mgr., Lafayette, Ind., 1962-64; mgmt. analyst Cummins Engine Co., Inc., Columbus, Ind., 1964-67; adminstrv. asst. to pres. Baker & Taylor Co. div. W.R. Grace & Co., Momence, Ill., 1967-71, mgr. spl. projects, 1971-72, mgr. approval program, Somerville, N.J., 1972-74, mgr. acad. sales N.Am., N.Y.C., 1974-75, dir. program services, Somerville, 1976-80, v.p. mktg., N.Y.C., 1980—. Class agt. Wabash Coll.; adv. bd. 4th Internat. Conf. on Approval Plans/Collection Devel., 1979, nat. profl. newsletter Technicalities, 1980—. Served with AUS, 1953-55. Recipient God and Country award Boy Scouts Am. Mem. Indpls. Zool. Soc. (charter), Spl. Library Assn., Tex. Library Assn., ALA, Soc. Scholarly Pub., Ind. Soc. N.Y., Nat. Trust for Hist. Preservation, Greater Wabash Found., Assn. M.B.A. Execs., Nat. Assn. Wabash Men, Ind. U. Alumni Assn., Delta Tau Delta, Alpha Phi Omega, Pi Delta Epsilon, Blue Key. Mem. Christian Ch. Mason, Kiwanian (charter pres. 1958-60). Co-author: Approval Plans and Academic Libraries, 1977. Contbr. articles to profl. publs. Home: 240 Great Hills Rd Bridgewater NJ 08807 Office: 1515 Broadway 25th Floor New York NY 10036 also 6 Kirby Ave Somerville NJ 08876

PICKETT, FLOYD CARL, ins. co. exec., cons.; b. Des Moines, Sept. 21, 1905; s. William Carl and Barbara (Kronmueller) P.; student public schs., Des Moines; m. Luella C. Peterson, Aug. 1, 1928; children—Barbara Lue, David Floyd. Clerical and claims examiner So. Surety Co., Des Moines, 1922-28, St. Louis, 1928-30, bond claims examiner, N.Y.C., 1930-32; claims examiner liquidation bur. N.Y. State Ins. Dept., N.Y.C., 1932-37; dept. mgr. Home Ins. Co., N.Y.C., 1937-65; v.p. Excel Mortgage Ins. Corp., Bettendorf, Iowa, 1965-74; cons. ins. regulations, Davenport, Iowa, 1974—; 2d v.p. Sovereign Life Ins. Co., Santa Barbara, Calif., 1979—. Mem. Ins. Soc. N.Y., Soc. Fin. Examiners. Presbyterian. Clubs: Hon. Order Blue Goose, Hon. Order Ky. Cols. Contbr. articles to profl. jours. Home and Office: 2501 Jersey Ridge Rd Davenport IA 52803

PICOWER, JEFFRY MARTIN, lawyer, accountant; b. N.Y.C., May 5, 1942; s. Abraham and Gertrude (Phillips) P.; B.S., Pa. State U., 1963; J.D., Bklyn. Law Sch., 1967; M.B.A., Columbia, 1966; LL.M., N.Y. U., 1968: m. Barbara Rubin, Nov. 17, 1968; 1 dau., Gabrielle. Accountant, tax mgr. Homes & Davis, N.Y.C., 1965-70; admitted to N.Y. State bar, 1967; tax mgr. Laventhol and Horwath, N.Y.C., 1970-72; pres. Jeffry M. Picower P.C., N.Y.C., 1972—; lectr. Columbia, 1964—. Mem. Am., N.Y. State bar assns., Am. Inst. C.P.A.'s, N.Y. State Soc. C.P.A.'s. Republican. Jewish religion Club: Atrium. Author: Tax Accounting Techniques to Save Taxes, 1970. Contbg. author, contbr. articles to profl. publs. Home: 207 Gravel Hill Rd Kinnelon NJ 07405 Office: Jeffry M Picower PC 950 3d Ave New York NY 10022

PIECHOCKI, RAYMOND JOSEPH, architect; b. Balt., Mar. 2, 1940; s. Joseph Patrick and Teresa Barbara P.; student Johns Hopkins U., 1963-70; m. Margaret A. Chipman, June 11, 1966; children—Karen Aileen, Alicia Renee. Project mgr. Gaudreau, Inc., Balt., 1961-68, sr. asso., 1971-75; v.p. Mark Beck Assos., Towson, Md., 1968-71; pres. Profl. Design Assos., Balt., 1975-76; project architect Frank Gant Architects, Severna Park, Md., 1976-77, Cochran, Stephenson and Donkervoet, Inc., Balt., 1977-80; with Mark Beck Assos., Inc., Towson, Md., 1980—; also operating dir. Total Bldg. Energy Services; guest lectr. Towson State U. Founder, 1974, thereafter chmn. Timonium Mansion Found.; v.p., dir. Cockeysville-Timonium Jaycees, 1970-75; pres., dir. Pine Valley-Valley Wood Community Assn., 1973-76; bd. dirs. Greater Timonium Bicentennial Com., 1975-77, Lutherville-Timonium Recreation Council, 1977-79; pres. Pinewood Elementary Sch. PTA, 1978-79. Named Jaycee of Year, Cockeysville-Timonium, 1973. Republican. Roman Catholic. Clubs: Md. Sportsmen, Glenmar Sailing Assn., Magothy River Sailing Assn., Bowley Point Yacht. Home: 212 Deep Dale Dr Timonium MD 21093 Office: 925 N Charles St Baltimore MD 21201

PIECUCH, VIRGINIA ANN, bank exec.; b. Chgo., Nov. 22, 1940; d. James John and Helen Catherine (Draus) P.; B.A., Mundelein Coll., 1962. Staff relations officer Beverly Bancorp. Inc., Chgo., 1970-71, mgr. tng. & employee communications, 1971-72; public relations asst. Beverly Bank, Chgo., 1962-65, supr. employee publs., 1962—, staff relations counselor, 1965-68, staff relations officer, 1968-70, personnel mgr., 1972-76, asst. v.p., personnel mgr., 1976-77, v.p. adminstrv. services, 1978—; instr. Chgo. Am. Inst. Banking. Mem. Soc. Personnel Adminstrs. Greater Chgo., Am. Soc. Tng. & Devel., Ill. Tng. Dirs. Assn., Chgo. Bank Personnel Assn., Nat. Assn. Bank Women, Am. Inst. Banking, Am. Soc. Personnel Adminstrn. (accredited). Roman Catholic. Office: 1357 W 103rd St Chicago IL 60643

PIEPER, JAY BROOKS, brewery exec.; b. Atlantic, Iowa, Sept. 11, 1943; s. Elmer Paul and Leona Bertha (Knop) P.; B.A., Cornell Coll., 1965; M.B.A., Washington U., St. Louis, 1967; m. Beverly Jeanne Schultz, Aug. 12, 1967; 1 dau., Cynthia Marie. Staff acct. Pabst Brewing Co., Milw., 1967-69, corp. fin. mgr., 1969-72, treas., 1972—, asst. to pres., 1976-79, v.p. corp. devel., 1979—; dir. P-L Biochemicals, Inc.; instr. Milw. Area Tech. Coll., 1967-69. Mem. Fin. Execs. Inst. Lutheran. Home: 5742 North Bay Ridge Ave Whitefish Bay WI 53217 Office: 917 W Juneau Ave Milwaukee WI 53201

PIERCE, BRUCE J., banker, investment co. exec.; b. Westchester, Pa., Jan. 21, 1938; s. Melvin E. and Sara Elizabeth (Wentzel) P.; B.S. in Econs., U. Pa., 1960; M.B.A., U. Mich., 1963; m. Barbara Ann Woodward, June 25, 1960; children—Lisa Anne, Brian John, Valerie Lee, Andrew MacIntosh. Credit analyst trainee, sr. credit analyst Nat. Bank Detroit, 1960-64; exec. v.p. Bank of N.Mex., Albuquerque, 1964-69, pres., 1970-71, pres., chief exec. officer, dir., 1973-77; pres. Bruce J. Pierce & Assos., Inc., Albuquerque, 1977—; chmn. bd. Funds Mgmt., Inc., Albuquerque, 1978—; gen. partner Rosenwald, Ltd., Albuquerque, 1978—, Auric Partners, Ltd., 1979—. Mem. task force Albuquerque Center, Inc.; mem. adv. council U. N.Mex. Sch. Bus. and Adminstrv. Sci.; bd. dirs. United Way, Neighborhood Housing Services, Albuquerque; chmn. fin. com. St. Joseph Hosp., Albuquerque; sec. Albuquerque Indsl. Devel. Served as officer U.S. Army, 1961. Mem. Robert Morris Assos. (chmn. Rocky Mountain regional adv. council), Fedn. Rocky Mountain States (human resources council), Newcomen Soc. N. Am. Club: Petroleum. Home: 13510 Sunset Canyon Rd NE Albuquerque NM 87111 Office: 320 Central Ave SW Suite 30 Albuquerque NM 87102

PIERCE, BURTON ARMSTRONG, real estate devel. co. exec.; b. Glen Cove, N.Y., Aug. 24, 1929; s. Samuel R. and Hettie (Armstrong) P.; B.S., Cornell U., 1947-51; postgrad. Harvard Bus. Sch., 1955; m. DiAnn F. Kjellsen, June 1, 1968; children—Karen, John, Nina, Michele. With Gen. Foods Corp., White Plains, N.Y., 1957-64; with AMAX, N.Y.C., 1964-68; chief adminstrv. officer Housing and Devel. Adminstrn., N.Y.C., 1968-73; adminstr. Battery Park City Authority, N.Y.C., from 1973; dir., cons. Taw Devel. Corp., Intra-Am. Corp., N.Y.C., 1965-70; pres. Splty. Services, Inc. Bd. dirs., v.p. Riverdale Neighborhood House; bd. dirs., exec. com. Ethical Fieldston Fund; mem. Cornell Assn. Class Officers; bd. dirs. N.Y. Urban League; adminstrv. bd. Cornell U. Council. Served to capt. USAF, 1951-53. Mem. Alpha Phi Alpha. Presbyterian. Club: Harvard (N.Y.C.). Home: 520 Tulfan Terr Riverdale NY 10463 Office: 40 Rector St New York NY 10006

PIERCE, FRANCIS CASIMIR, cons. engr. co. exec.; b. Warren, R.I., May 19, 1924; s. Frank J. and Eva (Soltys) Pierce; student U. Conn., 1943-44; B.S., U. R.I., 1948; M.S., Harvard, 1950; postgrad. Northeastern U., 1951-52; m. Helen Lynette Steinouer, Apr. 24, 1954; children—Paul F., Kenneth J., Nancy L., Karen H., Charles E. Instr. civil engring. U. R.I., Kingston, 1948-49, U. Conn., Storrs, 1950-51; design engr. Praeger-Maguire & Ole Singstad, Boston, 1951-52; chief found. engr. C.A. Maguire & Assos., Providence, 1952-59, asso., 1959-69, v.p., 1969-72; sr. v.p. C.E. Maguire, Inc., 1972-76, officer-in-charge Honolulu office, 1976-78, exec. v.p., corporate dir. ops., 1978—; lectr. found. engring. U. R.I., 1968-69; mem. U.S. com. Internat. Commn. on Large Dams. Vice chmn. Planning Bd. East Providence, R.I., 1960—. Served with AUS, 1942-46. Mem. Am. Soc. C.E. (chpt. past pres., dir.), R.I. Soc. Profl. Engrs. (nat. dir., engr. of year award 1973), Am. Soc. Engring. Edn., Soc. Am. Mil. Engrs., ASTM, Soc. Marine Engrs. and Naval Architects, Am. Soc. Planning Ofcls., Harvard Soc. Engrs., Scientists, Providence Engrs. Soc., R.I. Soc. Planning Agys. (past pres.). Contbr. articles to profl. jours. Home: 156 Barney St Rumford RI 02916 Office: 60 1st Ave Waltham MA 02154

PIERCE, FRANK LAWLER, broker, developer; b. Oakland, Calif., May 11, 1933; s. James Clayton and Edith Helen (Lawler) P.; student Diablo Valley Coll., 1959-61; grad. Real Estate Inst.; m. Claudia Joan Grasse, June 7, 1951; children— Laura Pierce Holt, Carolanne Pierce Simkins, Jennifer Pierce Lawson, Nancy Pierce Gubler. Salesman, gen. mgr. J.C. Pierce Desoto-Plymouth Co., Concord, Calif., 1951-60; realtor, Walnut Creek, Calif., 1960-70, St. George, Utah, 1970—. Bd. dirs. Contra Costa (Calif.) Bd. Realtors, 1969-70; pres. Washington County (Utah) Bd. Realtors, 1973-74. Mem. planning commn. City of St. George, 1970-73; mem. Cherokee Nation of Okla.; Indian student adv. Dixie Coll. Named Outstanding Young Man of Year Walnut Creek Jaycees, 1968. Mem. Nat. Rifle Assn. (life). Clubs: Elks, Masons, Shriners, K.T.; Club: Bloomington Country. Home: 3244 Three Bars Rd Bloomington UT 84770 Office: 720 E St George Blvd St George UT 84770

PIERCE, GILBERT CARROLL, JR., real estate broker; b. Phila., Sept. 12, 1938; s. Gilbert Carroll and Caroline Sophie (Sorber) P.; B.S., Temple U., 1961; m. Eva Marie Whitsel, Oct. 30, 1965; children—Jennifer Ann, Kirsten Carol. With Commonwealth Land Title Ins. Co., Phila., 1963-66; mortgage loan analyst Penn Mut. Life Ins. Co., Phila., 1966-68; with Reed & Stambaugh Co., Phila., 1969—, now sr. v.p. comml. leasing, sales and real estate devel. Trustee Pop Warner Little Scholars, Inc., 1979—. Served with USNR, 1961-63. Mem. Am. Soc. Appraisers, Inst. Real Estate Mgmt., Am. Right of Way Assn., Phila. Bd. Realtors (pres. comml./indsl. 1978). Republican. Clubs: Union League, Urban, Temple U. Downtown (Phila.); Mfrs. Golf and Country (Oreland, Pa.). Office: Reed & Stambaugh Co 4 Penn Center Philadelphia PA 19003

PIERCE, HAROLD JOSEPH, mfg. co. exec.; b. Peabody, Mass., Oct. 7, 1941; s. Ted Ronald and Shirley Elizabeth (Philbrook) P.; A.A. in Bus., Hartnell Coll., 1967; B.S. in Bus. and Indsl. Mgmt., Calif. State U., 1969; postgrad. U. Santa Clara, 1969-72; m. Maria Paulette Moore, Oct. 6, 1964; children—Justene, Christopher, Timothy. Prodn. trainee Dole Pineapple Co., San Jose, Calif., 1959-64; mgr. client services Halcomb Assos., Sunnyvale, Calif., 1969-72; sales mgr. The Southland Corp., Cupertino, Calif., 1972-76; owner, Gen. Bus. Services, Roseville, Calif., 1976—; owner Goal Achievement Assos., Roseville, 1978—; v.p. Orton Enterprises Internat., Sacramento, 1978—; lectr. in field. Scoutmaster Golden Empire Council Boy Scouts Am. Served with USCG, 1963-69. Recipient Wall St. Journal award, 1969, Jr. Achievement citation, 1965, Nat. Wildlife Fedn. Service award, 1974. Mem. Assn. MBA Execs., Nat. Assn. Tax Consultors, Soc. Advancement of Mgmt., Assn. Profl. Mgmt. Cons., Auburn Area C. of C., Latter Day Saints Businessmans Assn. Republican. Mormon. Clubs: Sacramento Area Tip, Elks. Contbr. articles in field. Office: PO Box 1496 Roseville CA 95678

PIERCE, HORACE GREELEY, trade assn. exec.; b. Rochester, N.Y., July 12, 1928; s. Louis S. and Elizabeth (Baybutt) P.; B.A., U. Rochester, 1949, M.S., 1950; m. Phyllis Altman, May 7, 1955; children—Martha Ellen, Mark Evan. With Northeastern Retail Lumbermens Assn., Rochester, 1950—, adminstrv. asst., 1952-56, mng. dir., 1956-60, exec. v.p., 1960—. Fund drive chmn. West Webster Fire Dept., 1955-68. Exec. trustee Northeastern Retail Lumbermens Assn. Group Ins. Trust Fund, 1960—; exec. v.p. Retail Lumber Dealers Found., 1968—. Served with AUS, 1950-52. Mem. Am. Soc. Assn. Execs., Nat. Retail Mchts. Assn., Rochester C. of C., West Webster Vol. Firemens Assn., Am. Mgmt. Assn., Sierra Club, Webster Grange, Am. Soc. Tng. and Devel., Bldg. Material Execs. Assn., Psi Upsilon. Republican. Episcopalian. Clubs: Univ., Oak Hill Country (Rochester); Brae Burn Country (Boston). Editor: Lumber Co-Operator, 1960—. Home: 65 E India Row Boston MA 02110 Office: 339 East Ave Rochester NY 14604 also 65 East India Row Boston MA 02110

PIERCE, JERRY EARL, pub. co. exec.; b. Hinsdale, Ill., Aug. 3, 1941; s. Earl and Adeline A. (Zaranski) P.; B.S., U. Ill., 1964; m. Carol Louise Martin, Aug. 15, 1964; children—Patricia, Barbara, Linda, Bradley. With R.R. Donnelley & Sons, Chgo., 1964-70; with Western Pub. Co., Racine, Wis., 1970—, nat. pubs. sales mgr., 1975—; pres. Pierce Sale Co., Inc.; sec., dir. Sayers Clubs Am., Inc. Served to 1st lt. U.S. Army, 1968-70. Decorated Army Commendation medal. Mem. Printing Industry Am., Sales and Mktg. Execs., N.E. Ohio Restaurant Assn. Republican. Episcopalian. Clubs: Canterbury Country, Cleve. Advt. Home: 22575 Douglas Rd Shaker Heights OH 44122 Office: 24100 Chagrin Blvd Cleveland OH 44122

PIERCE, JOSEPH EDWARD, packaging machinery mfg. co. exec.; b. Allentown, Pa., Mar. 14, 1915; s. Alonza Franklin and Josephine (Lind) P.; student Internat. Corr. Schs., 1943-60; m. Lorene Estella Buchman, Apr. 22, 1939. Supr., L.F. Grammes & Sons, Allentown, 1933-61; plant mgr. Allen Electronics Inc., Bethlehem, Pa., 1961-67; v.p. engring. and prodn. A.E.I. Corp., Bethlehem, 1967-72; prodn. and engring. mgr. Rexcel Packaging Systems, Bethlehem, 1972-74; dir. Packaging Machinery div. Compacting Press Corp., Bethlehem, 1972—. Adv., Bethlehem Vocat. Schs. Democrat. Patentee in packaging field in U.S. and fgn. countries. Home: 1634 N 20th St Allentown PA 18104 Office: 5 Ronca Park Route 191 Bethlehem PA 18017

PIERCE, JOSEPH REED, III, cons. co. exec.; b. McPherson, Kans., Mar. 21, 1942; s. Joseph Reed, Jr. and Maxine Lahoma (Burnside) P.; B.A., U. Kans., 1964, M.B.A., 1966. Project mgr. Boeing Co., Seattle, 1966-70; systems rep. Honeywell, Inc., San Francisco, 1970-71; systems analyst P.I.E., Oakland, Calif., 1972; project mgr. Crown Zellerbach Co., San Francisco, 1972-75; systems planner Fibreboard Co., San Francisco, 1975-76; dist. mgr. Cutler Williams Co., San Francisco, 1976-78; dir. bus. devel. San Francisco Cons. Group, 1978-80; product mktg. mgr. Mathematica, San Francisco, 1980—; instr. computer studies San Francisco Community Coll. Mem. San Francisco Citizens Adv. Bd. Mental Health Services, 1976. Sumerfield grantee, 1965. Mem. Am. Mktg. Assn., Assn. Systems Mgrs. (chmn. tech. seminars com. 1980-81), Psy Chi, Phi Alpha Theta. Clubs: Commonwealth Club Calif., Hold Your Horses. Author: The Little Restaurants of San Francisco, 1973. Home: 477 1/2 Vallejo St San Francisco CA 94133 Office: 1100 Larkspur Landing Circle Suite 200 Larkspur CA 94939

PIERCE, MICHAEL JOSEPH, data services co. exec.; b. Waterbury, Conn., Oct. 6, 1933; s. Michael Joseph and Catherine Teresa (Hallinan) P.; B.A., St. John's U., 1954; M.A. (fellow), U. Notre Dame, 1956; postgrad. (fellow) Ohio State U., 1956-57; m. Rosemary Joan Hagan, Sept. 3, 1955; children—Rosemary, Michael, Thomas, Constance, John. Data processing sales rep. IBM, N.Y.C., 1961-67, distbn. industry edn. coordinator, 1967-69; dir. mktg. Drug Distbn. Data subs. IMS Am., Ltd., Wayne, N.J., 1969-78, group v.p., gen. mgr., 1978—; instr. U. Notre Dame, 1954-56, Ohio State U., 1956-57; tchr. secondary schs., Huntington, N.Y., 1958-61. Mem. Am. Mgmt. Assn., Drug Wholesalers Assn., Nat. Assn. Chain Drug Stores, Nat. Wholesale Druggists Assn. Home: 50 Lookout Rd Mountain Lakes NJ 07046 Office: Drug Distbn Data Wayne Interchange Plaza Wayne NJ 07470

PIERCE, MILT PLOTZ, direct mail cons.; b. N.Y.C., Mar. 21, 1933; s. Louis Plotz and Dinah (Press) P.; B.B.A., Baruch Coll., 1959; M.S., City Coll. N.Y., 1967; m. Deborah Ritter, Dec. 25, 1964; children—Samuel, Esther. Asso. copy chief Hearst Mags., N.Y.C., 1952-56: account exec. Vos & Reichberg, N.Y.C., 1956-58; asst. promotion dir. N.Y. Times, N.Y.C., 1958-59; dean Evening Coll., N.Y. Inst. Tech., 1959-63, asso. prof. mktg., 1970—; pres. Pierce & Assos., N.Y.C., 1964—. Mem. N.Y.C. Planning Bd. No. 5, 1973—, N.Y.C. Mayor's Times Sq. Task Force, 1977-78. Recipient award Direct Mail Mktg. Assn., 1963, 65, 70, 72. Mem. Direct Mail Writer's Guild, Hundred Million Club. Democrat. Jewish. Club: B'nai B'rith. Author: How to Collect Your Unpaid Bills, 1980; Confessions of a Psychic, 1980; Hour Power, 1980; The Money Catalog, 1981; contbr. numerous articles on mktg. and writing to trade jours. Home and office: 162 W 54th St New York NY 10019

PIERCE, RALPH, cons. engr.; b. Chgo., Apr. 14, 1926; s. Charles and Fay (Reznik) P.; B.S. in Elec. Engring., Northwestern U., 1946; m. Adrian; children—Marc Fredrick, Deborah Ann, Elizabeth Allison. Test engr. Am. Elec. Heater Co., Detroit, 1946-47; sr. asso. engr. Detroit Edison Co., 1947-52; sec., chief utility engr. George Wagschal Assos. Detroit, 1952-58; sr. partner Pierce, Yee & Assos., Engrs. and Architects, Detroit, 1958-72; mng. partner Harley Ellington Pierce Yee Assos., Architects, Engrs. and Planners, 1972—. Mem. Dept. Commerce mission to Yugoslavia. Served to ensign USNR, 1944-46; comdr. Res. ret. Registered profl. engr., Mich., Ind., Ill., Ohio, Ky., D.C., N.Y., Fla., Ont.; also nationally certified. Mem. Nat. Soc. Profl. Engrs., Engring. Soc. Detroit, I.E.E.E., Illuminating Engring. Soc., Soc. Coll. and Univ. Planners, Mich. Soc. Architects (profl. affiliate). Works include planning and design of indsl., office, ednl., mcpl., med. and mausoleum facilities; also engaged in energy mgmt. and engring. cons. Home: 5531 Pebbleshire Rd Birmingham MI 48010 Office: 26111 Evergreen Rd Southfield MI 48076

PIERCE, RICHARD ANDREW, banker; b. Key West, Fla., Nov. 13, 1945; s. Joseph Austin and Ruth Amelia (Page) P.; student St. Leo (Fla.) Coll.; m. Jean Marie Alvarez, Dec. 21, 1964; children—Terri Lynn, Troy Coburn. Asst. cashier, asst. v.p., Fla. First Nat. Bank, Key West, 1969-76; v.p., then pres., chmn. bd. Fla. Nat. Bank, Gainesville, 1976-80; pres. Fla. First Nat. Bank Fla. Keys, Key West, 1980—. Bd. dirs. Mental Health Assn., Gainesville, Friends of Five Ednl. TV; adv. bd. Salvation Army, Key West; mem. Fla. Com. 100; Monroe County

(Fla.) campaign chmn., 1980 Recipient Spl. Service award Gainesville chpt. Beta Sigma Phi, 1979. Mem. Southernmost C. of C., Key West C. of C. Office: 422 Front St Key West FL 33040

PIERCE, ROBERT FREDERICK, bus. broker; b. Boston, May 3, 1945; s. Frank Everett and Madeline Mary P.; B.A., Providence Coll., 1967; postgrad. Am. U., 1969; cert. in retailing Suffolk U., 1975; cert. Lowry Nickerson Investment Inst., 1977, Bus. Valuation Inst. Calif., 1979; m. Margaret M. Mulhern, Aug. 23 1974; children—Patricia, Kathleen, Robert, Michael. N.E. mktg. rep. Nat. Instrument Mfg. Co., Sybron, N.Y., 1970-72; sales mgr. Nat. Consumer Products Co., Westfield, Mass., 1973-78; pres. Bus. Brokers Internat. Corp., Braintree, Mass., 1978—; notary public; real estate broker. Served with U.S. Army, 1967-69. Cert. bus. appraiser. Mem. Lowell C. of C., Internat. Bus. Brokerage Assn., Nat. Fedn. Ind. Businessmen, SBA New Eng., Nat. Council Small Business, Nat. Assn. Investment Clubs. Office: 178 Forbes Rd Braintree MA 02184

PIERCE, SAMUEL RILEY, JR., lawyer; b. Glen Cove, N.Y., Sept. 8, 1922; s. Samuel R. and Hettie E. (Armstrong) P.; A.B. with honors, Cornell U., Ithaca, N.Y., 1947, LL.B., 1949; LL.M. in Taxation, N.Y. U., 1952, LL.D., 1972; postgrad. (Ford Found. fellow) Yale Law Sch., 1957-58; m. Barbara Penn Wright, Apr. 1, 1948; 1 dau., Victoria Wright. Admitted to N.Y. bar, 1949, Supreme Ct. bar, 1956; asst. dist. atty. County of N.Y., 1949-53; asst. U.S. atty. for So. Dist. N.Y., 1953-55; asst. to under sec. of labor, Washington, 1955-56; asso. counsel, counsel Judiciary Subcom. on Antitrust, U.S. Ho. Reps., 1956-57; engaged in pvt. practice law, 1957-59, 61-70; judge N.Y. Ct. Gen. Sessions (now part N.Y. State Supreme Ct.), 1959-60; gen. counsel U.S. Treasury, 1970-73; exec. dir., gen. counsel Emergency Loan Guarantee Bd., 1971-73; partner Battle, Fowler, Jaffin, Pierce & Kheel, 1973—; faculty N.Y. U. Sch. Law, 1958—, adj. prof., 1969—; guest speaker colls. and univs.; judge N.Y. Ct. Gen. Sessions, 1959-60; chmn., N.Y. State Minimum Wage Bd. for Hotel Industry, 1961; mem. N.Y. State Banking Bd., 1961-70, N.Y.C. Bd. Edn., 1961; dir. U.S. Industries, Prudential Ins. Co. Am., Gen. Electric Co., Internat. Paper Co., First Nat. Boston Corp., 1st Nat. Bank Boston; bd. govs. Am. Stock Exchange; U.S. del. Conf. on Coops., Georgetown, Brit. Guiana, 1956; mem. panel symposium Mil.-Indsl. Conf. on Atomic Energy, Chgo., 1956; fraternal del. to All-African People's Conf., Accra, Ghana, 1958; mem. Commr. of Internal Revenue's Adv. Group, 1975; mem. Comptroller of Currency's Nat. Adv. Com., 1975—; mem. panel arbitrators Am. Arbitration Assn. and Fed. Mediation and Conciliation Service, 1957—; mem. Nat. Wiretap Commn., 1973-76; mem. Mayor's Com. on Judiciary, N.Y.C. Mem. N.Y. State Republican Campaign Hdqrs. Staff, 1952, 58; gov. N.Y. Young Rep. Club, 1951-53. Trustee Mount Holyoke Coll., 1965-75, Hampton Inst., Cornell U., Howard U., Inst. Internat. Edn., YMCA Greater N.Y. Rand Corp., 1976—, Tax Found., 1977—; bd. dirs. nat. exec. bd. Boy Scouts Am. Served with AUS, 1943-46, as 1st lt. JAGC, 1950-52. Recipient N.Y.C. Jr. C. of C. Annual Distinguished Service award, 1958; Alexander Hamilton award U.S. Treasury Dept., 1973. Mem. Cornell Assn. Class Secs., Telluride Assn., Alumni Cornell U. Alumni Assn. N.Y.C. (gov.), C.I.D. Agts. Assn. (gov.), Am. Bar Assn., Assn. of N.Y.C. Bar, N.Y. County Lawyers Assn., Phi Beta Kappa, Phi Kappa Phi, Alpha Phi Alpha, Alpha Phi Omega. Methodist. Contbr. to profl. jours. Home: 16 W 77th St New York NY 10024 Office: 280 Park Ave New York NY 10017

PIERCE, THOMAS FLOYD, retail trade exec.; b. Bartlett, Tex., Feb. 2, 1916; s. Floyd Nunez and Ellen Gertrude (Wood); student U. Tex., 1934-38; m. 2d, Ethel Michelle Pumphrey, Sept. 1, 1976; 1 son, Thomas Eilers (dec.). Partner, F.N. Pierce & Co., cotton mchts., Taylor, Tex., 1945-52; pres. Delta Constrn. Co., Taylor, 1952-64; partner Williamson County Equipment Co., Inc., retail farm equipment, automobiles, Taylor, 1943-69, chmn. bd., 1969—; dir. City Nat. Bank, Taylor. Mem. Sch. Bd., Taylor, 1964-70. Served with AC, USNR, 1942-45. Decorated D.F.C., Air medal. Presbyterian. Home: 1426 N Main St Taylor TX 76574 Office: 1426 N Main St Taylor TX 76574

PIERCY, GORDON CLAYTON, banker; b. Tacoma Park, Md., Nov. 23, 1944; s. Gordon Clayton and Dorothy Florence (Brummer) P.; B.S., Syracuse U., 1966; M.B.A., Pace U., 1973; m. Susan Jane Eby, July 11, 1970; children—Elizabeth Anne, Kenneth Charles. Mktg. planning asso. Chem. Bank, N.Y.C., 1966-70; sr. market devel. officer Seattle-First Nat. Bank, 1970-74; product expansion adminstr., mktg. planning mgr. Nat. BankAmericard, Inc., San Francisco, 1974-76; v.p., dir. mktg. Wash. Mut. Savs. Bank, Seattle, 1976-80, v.p., dir. mktg. and research, 1981—. Mem. Sales and Mktg. Execs. Internat., Am. Mktg. Assn., Bank Mktg. Assn., Savs. Instn. Mktg. Soc. Am., Seattle Advt. Fedn., Sigma Nu, Alpha Kappa Psi, Delta Mu Delta. Episcopalian. Home: 14108 SE 45th St Bellevue WA 98006 Office: 1101 2d Ave Seattle WA 98111

PIERQUET, CLETUS ARTHUR, service co. exec.; b. Brown County, Wis., Mar. 30, 1923; s. Anton and Laura (Kreicher) P.; student public schs., Green Bay, Wis.; m. Helen Kwaterski, May 28, 1949; children—Richard, Mary, Thomas, Judith, Susan, Laura, Patricia, Louanne, Beckie. With Olson Trailer & Body Co., Green Bay, 1947-59; founder, pres., dir. Truck Equipment, Inc., Green Bay, 1959—, Transport Refrigeration Co., Green Bay, 1959—, K.P. Corp., Green Bay, 1959—; dir. Citizen Am. Bank; mem. adv. bd. Wausau Ins. Co. Served with inf. U.S. Army, 1942-47. Mem. Wis. Motor Carriers Assn. (council safety suprs.), Green Bay Traffic Club, Wis. Motor Safety Council, Am. Legion. Roman Catholic. Clubs: K.C., Lions, Elks. Home: Box 109 Route 2 Denmark WI 54208 Office: PO Box 3280 Green Bay WI 54303

PIERSON, ROBERT DAVID, banker; b. Orange, N.J., Mar. 5, 1935; s. Carleton Wellington and Muriel Browning (Potter) P.; B.A., Lehigh U., 1957; m. Virginia Duncan Knight, Apr. 30, 1960; children—Lisa Duncan, Alexandra Beach, Robert Wellington. Exec. asst. 1st Nat. City Bank N.Y., N.Y.C., 1958-61; asst. to pres. Cooper Labs. Inc., N.Y.C., 1961-65; dir. mktg. services Arbrook div. Johnson & Johnson, Somerville, N.J., 1965-69; v.p. Klemtner Advt. Inc., N.Y.C., 1969-71; v.p., dir. mktg. Bowery Savs. Bank, N.Y.C., 1972—. Pres. conservation com., Morris Twp., N.J., 1968-71; pres. Morristown YMCA, 1969-72; chmn. bd. Morris County Fire and Police Tng. Acad., 1975—; trustee, mem. exec. com. Community Med. Center, Morristown, N.J., 1976. Served with USCG, 1958-59. Recipient Town Crier award N.Y. Fin. Advertisers. Mem. Nat. Assn. Mut. Savs. Banks (mktg. award), Savs. Banks Assn. N.Y. (exec. com. mktg. forum, Silver Baton award), Am. Mktg. Assn., N.Y.C. Bicentennial Corp. (bus. advisory com.), N.Y.C. C. of C. Republican. Presbyterian. Home: Overlook Rd Morristown NJ 07960 Office: 110 E 42d St New York NY 10017

PIERSON, THOMAS FORD, fin. exec.; b. Alamosa, Colo., Feb. 23, 1948; s. Lawrence Height and Dorothe Marie (Glover) P.; B.S., No. Ariz. U., 1970; J.D., U. Denver, 1973; m. Pat J. Benson, Sept. 15, 1968. Jr. exec. Howell's Dept. Stores, 1965-66; pres. Ancilliary Acceptance Corp., 1974-75; v.p. Bank of Woodmoore, 1975, Mahalo Acceptance Corp., 1975; pres. Jagger Leasing, 1976-78; partner Schaefer & Pierson, also pres. Jagger Leasing, Inc., Denver, 1978—; sec./treas., dir. Republic Indsl. Bank, 1st Savs. Indsl. Bank, Bankers Holding Corp., Eagle Mgmt. & Investments, Inc., 1979-80; instr. Nat. Coll. Bus. Mem. Denver C. of C., Beta Gamma Sigma. Republican. Office: 130 E Kiowa Suite 610 Colorado Springs CO 80903

PIGOTT, CHARLES MCGEE, transp. equipment mfg. co. exec.; b. Seattle, Apr. 21, 1929; s. Paul and Theiline (McGee) P.; B.S., Stanford U., 1951; m. Yvonne Flood, Apr. 18, 1953. With PACCAR Inc., Seattle, 1959—, exec. v.p., 1963-65, pres., 1965—; dir. Safeco Corp., Citibank, N.Y.C., Citicorp, Boeing Co., Standard Oil Co. Calif. Mem. The Bus. Council; bd. dirs. SRI Internat. Office: PO Box 1518 Bellevue WA 98009

PIKE, EDWARD CHARLES, ins. exec.; b. Rutland, Vt., Sept. 17, 1942; s. Edward Sanborn and Frances (Mason) P.; B.S.B.A., New Eng. Coll., 1965; children—Heather Frances, Stephanie Ann. Corp. sec. Roger S. Pike, Inc., 1965-68; v.p. Kinney, Pike, Bell & Conner, Inc., 1969-76, exec. v.p., 1976-79, pres., 1979—, also pres. subsidiaries; dir. Proctor Trust Co. Bd. dirs. Vt. YMCA, 1968-71, Rutland Indsl. Devel. Corp., 1978—, Vt. Heart Assn., 1966-69; pres. Rutland Indsl. Devel. Corp., 1979—; mem. Vt. Bd. Public Accountancy, 1979—. Mem. Assurex Internat., New Eng. Surety Assn. (treas. 1971-73), Nat. Assn. Surety and Casualty Agts., Ind. Ins. Agts. Am. (nat. dir.), Ind. Ins. Agts. Vt. (dir., past pres.). Clubs: Ethan Allen, Queeche, Royal Savage Yacht (dir.), Shriners. Home: Killington Gateway Mendon VT 05701 Office: 98 Merchants Row Rutland VT 05701

PIKE, JOHN JACOB, mergers-acquisitions co. exec.; b. Bakersfield, Calif., Mar. 18, 1912; s. Percy M. and Elizabeth P.; A.B. in Economics, Stanford U., 1933; children—Jeffie Pike Wesson, John Jacob, Tyrone F. With Republic Supply Co. of Calif., Los Angeles, 1933-61, pres. and dir., 1939-61; pres., owner J.J. Pike Co., Los Angeles, 1961—; partner William H. Clark Assos., Inc., Los Angeles, 1975-80; dir. Security First Nat. Bank of Los Angeles, 1948-61, So. Counties Gas Co., 1961-72. Dir., Los Angeles Municipal Art Gallery Assos., 1954—; dir. So. Calif. Bldg. Fund, 1948—, pres., 1954—; trustee Claremont Men's Coll., 1948-60. Republican. Episcopalian. Clubs: Calif. (Los Angeles), Los Angeles Country, Bohemian (San Francisco), Alpha Delta Phi. Home: 234 S Figueroa St #1632 Los Angeles CA 90012 Office: Suite 2565 555 S Flower St Los Angeles CA 90071

PILCHIK, RONALD, hosp. supply co. exec.; b. Bklyn., Oct. 28, 1940; s. Irving and Sadie (Eichner) P.; B.S., Bklyn. Coll., 1962; M.S., Fairleigh Dickinson U., 1970, M.B.A., 1974; m. Rochelle Phyllis Turkel, Nov. 4, 1962; children—Evan, Robert, Nancy. Clin. chemist Bellevue Hosp., N.Y.C., 1962-64; supr. gen. diagnostics div. Warner Lambert Co., Morris Plains, N.J., 1964-69; sect. head Roche Diagnostics div. Hoffman-La Roche, Nutley, N.J., 1969-74; mgr. gen. diagnostics internat. div. Warner Lambert Co., Morris, Plains, Dublin, Ireland, 1974-75; v.p. Harleco div. Am. Hosp. Supply Co., Gibbstown, N.J., 1975-78; pres. R. P. Services, 1978-79; v.p., gen. mgr. Nobel Sci. Industries, Alexandria, Va., 1979—; asst. prof. dept. chemistry Fairleigh Dickinson U., 1968-70, grad. sch. bus., 1974—. Chmn. med. device sector Am. Nat. Metric Council. Certified clin. chemist, Nat. Registry in Clin. Chemistry. Mem. Am. Chem. Soc., Am. Assn. for Clin. Chemistry, Health Industries Mfrs. Assn. (chmn. metrication com.). Home: 1816 Lark Ln Cherry Hill NJ 08003 Office: 1423 Leslie Ave Alexandria VA 22301

PILDER, WILLIAM FRANCIS, career counselor; b. Cin., May 28, 1938; s. Frank William and Marie Veronica (Kamp) P.; B.S., U. Dayton, 1960; M.A., Ohio State U., 1965, Ph.D., 1968; m. Leslie Klein, May 25, 1975; children—Heather, Mark, Brendan. Doctoral intern Ohio State U., 1965-68; asst. prof. Ind. U., 1968-72; mgmt. cons., 1972-75; career counselor Mainstream Assos., N.Y.C., 1975-77, prin., 1977-79; pres. Mainstream Access, Inc., career info. services, N.Y.C., 1979—. Dir., author career guides. Office: 21 E 40th St New York NY 10016

PILKO, GEORGE, environ. cons.; b. N.Y.C., Feb. 21, 1949; s. Peter J. and Martha (Tonti) P.; B.S.E. in Chem. Engring., U. Mich., 1971, M.B.A., 1973; m. Susan M. Wasvary, Apr. 28, 1973; 1 son, Brian George. Energy planner, project mgr., coal project Olin Chems., Stamford, Conn., 1973-75, sales rep., indsl. chems., Houston, 1975-77, coll. recruiter, 1974; chem. mktg. cons. Pace Cons. & Engrs., Houston, 1977-78, mgr. environ. mgmt. services, 1978-80; pres. Pilko & Assos., Inc., 1980—. Vice pres. Trailwood Village Community Assn., 1978-79. Recipient Branston prize U. Mich., 1968; Eiseman scholar, 1967-71. Mem. U. Mich. Alumni Club (dir. Houston chpt.). Contbr. article to profl. jour. Home: 2215 Laurel Hill Kingwood TX 77339 Office: 9800 Northwest Freeway Suite 602 Houston TX 77092

PILLAR, EDWARD ANTHONY, elec. mfg. co. exec.; b. Chgo., June 13, 1936; s. Edward Anthony and Mary (Billina) P.; B.S. in Elec. Engring., Ill. Inst. Tech., 1958; m. Kathleen Pydynowski, June 21, 1957; children—Edward, Laura, Michelle. Sales mgr. Fasco Industries, Oak Brook, Ill., 1964-74; gen. mgr. March Mfg. Co., Glenview, Ill., 1972-74; sec.-treas. Hi Tech Inc., Zion, Ill., 1974—, chmn. bd., 1980—. Home: 101 Lakewood Dr Antioch IL 60002 Office: 3600 16th St Zion IL 60099

PILLIOD, CHARLES JULE, JR., rubber co. exec.; b. Cuyahoga Falls, Ohio, Oct. 20, 1918; s. Charles Jule and Julia (Sullivan) P.; student Muskingum Coll., 1937-38, Kent State U., 1938-40; m. Marie Elizabeth Jacobs, June 15, 1946; children—Christine Marie, Charles Jule III, Mark Alan, Stephen Matthew, Renee Elizabeth. With prodn. squadron Goodyear Tire & Rubber Co., 1941; salesman Goodyear Internat. Corp., 1945-47, mgr., dir. Panama, field rep., Costa Rica, 1947-51, field rep., Chile, Bolivia, Peru, 1951-53, asst. sales mgr., Peru, 1953, sales mgr., Colombia, 1954-56, comml. mgr., Brazil, 1956-59, mng. dir., Brazil, 1959-63, sales dir., Eng., 1963-64, mng. dir., Eng., 1964-66, dir. operations, Akron, Ohio, 1966-67, v.p., 1967-71, pres., 1971-72; v.p. Goodyear Tire & Rubber Co., 1971, exec. v.p., dir., 1971-72, pres., 1972-74, pres., chief exec. officer, 1973, chief exec. officer, 1973, chmn. bd., 1974—; dir. CPC Internat., Inc., Mfrs. Hanover Corp., Communications Satellite Corp. Trustee Akron Community Trusts, Com. Econ. Devel., Nat. Urban League; Akron City Hosp.; bd. dirs. Nat. Merit Scholarship Corp., Internat. Road Edn. Found.; trustee U. Akron, Mt. Union Coll., Alliance, Ohio. Served to capt. USAAF, 1942-45. Mem. Rubber Mfrs. Assn. (dir.), U.S.-Mexico C. of C. (dir.); Bus. Roundtable (policy com.), Conf. Bd., Internat. C. of C. (trustee U.S. council). Office: 1144 E Market St Akron OH 44316*

PILLSBURY, JOHN SARGENT, JR., ins. co. exec.; b. Mpls., Oct. 28, 1912; s. John Sargent and Eleanor (Lawler) P.; B.A., Yale U., 1935; LL.B., U. Minn., 1940; m. Katharine Harrison Clark, June 11, 1936; children—John Sargent III, Donaldson C., L. Harrison, Katharine Pillsbury Jose. Employed by Pillsbury Mills, Inc., 1936-37; admitted to Minn. bar, 1940; asso. firm Faegre & Benson, 1940-45, partner, 1946-56; pres., dir. Northwestern Nat. Life Ins. Co., 1956-69, chmn., chief exec. officer, 1969-77, chmn. bd., 1977—; dir. No. Life Ins. Co., North Atlantic Life Ins. Co., Boise Cascade Corp., NW Bell Telephone Co.; trustee Wells Fargo. Trustee, Dunwoody Indsl. Inst.; life dir. Minn. Orch. Assn.; founding trustee Twin Cities Pub. TV. Served from lt. (j.g.) to lt. comdr. Air Combat Intelligence, USNR, 1942-45. Mem. Am., Minn., Hennepin County bar assns., Order of Coif, Phi Delta Phi. Republican. Conglist. Clubs: Minneapolis, Minnetonka Yacht Woodhill Country (Mpls.); Yale (N.Y.C.). Home: 315 Woodhill Rd Wayzata MN 55391 Office: 930 Dain Tower Minneapolis MN 55402

PILZ, ALFRED NORMAN, mfg. co. exec.; b. Evergreen Park, Ill., Oct. 12, 1931; s. Alfred and Erma Louise (Deane) P.; B.S., Ill. Inst. Tech., 1953; M.B.A., Harvard U., 1960; m. Constance Mary Ney, Nov. 29, 1957; children—Kerry, Kurt, Stephen, Matthew. Indsl. engr. Harnischfeffer Corp., Milw., 1956-58; cons. Arthur D. Little, Cambridge, Mass., 1959; asst. to exec. v.p., mgr. prodn. engring. Nat. Forge Co., Irvine, Pa., 1960-62; cons. McKinsey Co., N.Y.C., 1962-64, Cleve., 1964-67; asst. to pres. Cooper Industries, Mt. Vernon, Ohio, 1967; pres., chief exec. officer Ajax Iron Works, Corry, Pa., 1967-72, Swank Refractories Co., Johnstown, Pa., 1972-77, Hyde Park Foundry and Machine Co., Hyde Park, Pa., 1975-78; Shepard Niles Crane and Hoist Co., Montour Falls, N.Y., 1979—; chief exec. officer Chemung Foundry, Elmira, N.Y., 1979—; dir. Carre, Orban & Partner, Geneva, Switzerland, 1979—, Libery Mut. Ins. Co., Erie, Pa. Served with USN, 1953-56; Korea. Club: Merchants and Manufacturers (Montour Falls). Home: Box 244J Route 1 Ligonier PA 15658 Office: RD 1 Genesee St Montour Falls NY 14865

PINA, EDUARDO ISIDORIO, aerospace co. exec.; b. New Bedford, Mass., Oct. 2, 1931; s. Francisco Z. and Maria (Lopes) P.; B.S., U. Mass., 1953, M.A., 1954; postgrad. U. Wash., 1957-58; m. Norma Mae Meggison, Aug. 31, 1953; children—Marcelaine Jean, Eduardo Gary, Matthew Meggison, Jennifer Maria. Instr., U. Mass., 1953-54; lead engr. Boeing Co., Seattle, 1954-55, acting supr., 1955-56, supr., 1956-59, unit chief transport division, Renton, Wash., 1959-64, asst. mgr. computing and analysis airplane div., 1964-66, mgr. ops. and computing tech., comml. airplane div., 1966-67, mgr. div., simulation and operations research, 1967-68, dir. operations research/mgmt., 1968-69, dir. marketing tech. airline analysis, comml. airplane group, 1969-71, dir. sales tech. Boeing Comml. Airplane Co., 1971-79, dir. sales strategy analysis and computing, 1979—. Pres., Sea-Tac, Midway, Des Moines Boys Club, 1969-73; v.p. Seattle and King County Boys' Clubs, 1973-75, 79—, pres., 1976-77, chmn. bd., 1978-79. Mem. Ops. Research Soc. Am., Transp. Research Bd., Soc. Indsl. and Applied Math., Sigma Xi. Republican. Home: PO Box 98085 Zenith WA 98188 Office: PO Box 3707 Renton WA 98128

PINALTO, WILLIAM ALLEN, savs. and loan exec.; b. Upland, Calif., Mar. 24, 1948; s. William Henry and Betty Marguerite (O'Hair) P.; B.B.A., Loyola U., Los Angeles, 1971; M.B.A., Loyola Marymount U., 1979; m. Judith Elaine Kent, July 10, 1971; children—Cynthia Kathleen, William Steven. Fin. mgmt. trainee Home Savs. & Loan Assn., Los Angeles, 1971-72, systems and procedures analyst, 1972-73, fin. analyst, budget coordinator, 1973-74, dir. corp. planning, 1974-79, asst. v.p., 1974-79; treas. Equitable Savs. & Loan Assn., Portland, Oreg., 1979—. Mem. Fin. Mgrs. Soc. of Savs. Instns., Delta Sigma Pi (cert. of recognition 1977), So. Calif. Assn. Philanthropy. Republican. Roman Catholic. Club: Toastmasters. Office: 1300 SW 6th Ave Portland OR 97201

PINCHOFF, ALLAN MARTIN, lawyer; b. Bronx, N.Y., Mar. 3, 1944; s. Joseph E. and Lillian R. (Hershkowitz) P.; B.A., State U. N.Y., 1968, J.D., 1971, M.B.A., 1975; m. Diane Marie Imhof, June 18, 1969; 1 dau., Rebecca Jo. Admitted to D.C. bar, 1975, N.Y. bar, 1976; law clk. Sheinberg, Perla & Parlato, Buffalo, 1969-70; law clk. firm Ilardo, Ilardo & Sheedy, Hamburg, N.Y., 1970-73; accountant Philipps & Co., East Aurora, N.Y., 1975-76; asso. firm D'Amato & Lynch, N.Y.C., 1977-78; mem. firm Augustine, Tronolone, Rosche & Pinchoff, Buffalo, 1978—; gen. counsel Erie County chpt. N.Y. State Assn. Retarded Children; cons. Erie County Office for Aging. Block capt. Am. Cancer Soc., 1975; bd. dirs. Buffalo and Erie County council Girl Scouts U.S.A. Mem. Am., D.C., N.Y. State, Erie County bar assns., N.Y. County Lawyers Assn., Assn. M.B.A. Execs. Republican. Jewish. Home: 267 Linwood Ave Buffalo NY 14209 Office: 470 Franklin St Buffalo NY 14202

PINCUS, THEODORE HENRY, pub. relations exec.; b. Chgo., Sept. 15, 1933; s. Jacob T. and Jeanette E. (Engel) P.; B.S. in Fin., Ind. U., 1955; m. Donna Forman, Mar. 12, 1961; children—Laura, Mark, Susan. Fin. news editor Far East, INS, 1958; sr. asso. Harshe-Rotman & Druck, Inc., 1959; dir. communications Maremont Corp., 1962; chmn. Fin. Relations Bd. Inc., Chgo., 1965—; cons. presdl. campaigns. Mem. nat. exec. bd. Am. Jewish Com. Served to 1st lt. USAF. Mem. Young Presidents Orgn. Author: Giveaway Day, 1975; also articles. Home: 2136 N Cleveland St Chicago IL 60614 Office: 150 E Huron St Chicago IL 60611

PINEAU, JOHN PETER, fin. service co. exec.; b. Fall River, Mass., Aug. 21, 1944; A.M.E., M.I.T., 1964; B.B.A. in Internat. Bus., George Washington U., 1972, M.B.A., 1975; m. Nicole Falchi, July 18, 1970; 1 son, Bernard. Sr. partner Pineau, Krieber Assos., Washington, 1970-74; budget dir. U.S. NRC, Washington, 1974-76; pres. Bus. Fin. Services, Inc. and Bus. Systems, Inc., Arlington, Va., 1976—. Active PTA. Served with inf. U.S. Army, 1965-70. Decorated Silver Star, Bronze Star medal, Cross of Gallantry; recipient Spl. Achievement award U.S. NRC, 1975. Mem. Assn. Program and Budget Analysts. Club: Forest Haven. Home: 609 N Jefferson St Arlington VA 22205 Office: 2425 Wilson Blvd Arlington VA 22201

PINES, HOWARD MARK, lawyer, food co. exec.; b. Stamford, Conn., Oct. 13, 1941; s. Irving H. and Ruth (Drobkin) P.; student Rutgers U., 1959-61; B.S., Western N.Mex. U., 1964; J.D., Seton Hall U., 1970; m. Rochelle Enid Harrowe, Dec. 22, 1966; 1 dau., Kerry Renee. Claims cons. Prudential Ins. Co., Newark, 1964-67; dir. employee relations P. Ballantine & Sons, Newark, 1967-72; dir. employee relations, food div. Standard Brands Inc., N.Y.C., 1972-79, v.p. adminstrn.-consumer products, 1978, sr. v.p. employee relations, 1979—. Mem. Indsl. Relations Soc., Human Relations Planning Soc. Office: 625 Madison Ave New York NY 10022

PINIGIS, EDWIN JAMES, pest control service co. exec.; b. Braddock, Pa., June 19, 1924; s. Donald and Helen (Meskus) P.; B.S. in Chemistry, U. Pitts., 1950; m. Anna Mary Stepien, Sept. 18, 1950; children—Patricia Ann, James D., Cynthia Lynn, Edwin James, Dennis, Charles. Research chemist Pitts. Coke & Chem. Co., 1950-54; tech. service rep. Am. Potash & Chem. Co., 1954-56; tech. supr. Pennwalt Corp., 1956-59; tech. dir. Commonwealth Sanitation Co., 1959-64; tech. dir. J.C. Ehrlich Co., 1964-66; prodn. mgr. Pennzoil Corp., 1966-68; exec. v.p. Dodson Bros., Lynchburg, Va., 1968—; cons. on sanitation and food to heavy and light industry, 1959—. Dist. chem. Boy Scouts Am., 1970-71. Served with U.S. Army, 1943-46. Decorated Purple Heart; recipient cert. of appreciation U. W.Va., 1971. Mem. Am. Chem. Soc., Am. Inst. Chemists, Entomol. Soc. Am., Royal Soc. Health, Assn. Cons. Chemists and Chem. Engrs., Am. Legion, Phi Chi Omega. Episcopalian. Club: Elks. Inventor aquatic weeds control field. Home: 111 Middleboro Pl Lynchburg VA 24502 Office: PO Box 10249 Lynchburg VA 24506

PINKERTON, ROBERT BRUCE, mfg. co. exec.; b. Detroit, Feb. 10, 1941; s. George Fulwell and Janet Lois (Hedke) P.; student M.I.T., 1959-61; B.S. in Mech. Engring., Detroit Inst. Tech., 1965; M.A.E.,

Chrysler Inst. Engring., 1967; J.D., Wayne State U., 1976; m. Barbara Ann Bandfield, Aug. 13, 1966; 1 son, Robert Brent. Various engring. positions Chrysler Engring. Office, Chrysler Corp., Highland Park, Mich., 1967-73, supr. body engring., 1973-76, sr. body engr., 1976-78, emissions and fuel economy planning specialist, 1978-80; dir. engring. Replacement div. TRW, Inc., Cleve., 1980—; mem. Mich. Adv. Com. on Vehicle Inspection and Maintenance, 1979-80. Mem. Soc. Automotive Engrs., Cleve. Engring. Soc. Episcopalian. Club: Western Res. Racquet. Home: 7337 Valerie Ln Hudson OH 44236 Office: 8001 E Pleasant Valley Rd Cleveland OH 44131

PINNELL, WILLIAM GEORGE, univ. ofcl.; b. Clarksburg, W. Va., Sept. 6, 1922; s. George Mason and Anna (Wagner) P.; A.B., W. Va. U., 1950, M.A., 1952; Dr. Bus. Adminstrn., Ind. U., 1954; m. Dortha Elizabeth Graham, June 25, 1946; 1 dau., Georgia Pinnell Stowe. Asst. dean Ind. U. Sch. Bus., 1954-56, became asso. dean, 1956, acting dean, 1959, dean Sch. Bus., 1963-71, v.p., treas., 1971-74, exec. v.p., 1974—; dir. Kroger Co., Central Soya Co., Inc., Public Service Ind.; trustee Am. Fletcher Mortgage Investors. bd. dirs. Ind. U. Found. Served to lt. (j.g.) USNR, 1942-47. Mem. Am., Midwest econ. assns., Am. Finance Assn., Ind. Acad. Social Scis., Internat. Bus. Edn. Assn., Midwest Bus. Adminstrn. Assn., Regional Sci. Assn., Beta Gamma Sigma, Beta Alpha Psi, Sigma Iota Epsilon, Alpha Kappa Psi. Methodist. Author: An Analysis of the Economic Base of Evansville; co-author Case Study of a Depressed Area. Contbr. articles to profl. jours. Home: 2700 Pine Ln-Bittner Woods Bloomington IN 47401

PINNER, DOUGLAS KENNETH, steel co. exec.; b. St. Louis, June 29, 1940; s. Charles William and Esther Ida (Rosenberg) P.; B.S. in Metall. Engring., U. Mo., Rolla, 1963; M.B.A., U. Chgo., 1969; m. Frances Lee Hunter, Sept. 27, 1963; 1 dau., Melissa Lee. Operating engr. U.S. Steel Co., 1966-69; sr. cons. Middlewest Service Co., 1969-70; asst. to chief operating officer Sharon Steel Co., 1970-73; v.p., gen. mgr. Copperweld Steel Co., Warren, Ohio, 1973—; pres. Jessop Steel Co., 1976—; pres., chief exec. officer Guterl Steel Co., Lockport, N.Y., 1978—. Bd. dirs. Trumbull Jr. Achievement. Served to 1st lt. C.E., AUS, 1963-76. Mem. Am. Inst. Mining Engrs., Assn. Iron and Steel Engrs., Am. Iron and Steel Inst., Am. Inst. Metals (nat. fin. com.), Trumbull Mfg. Assn. (dir.), Warren C. of C. (dir.). Republican. Roman Catholic. Club: Trumbull Country. Home: 8516 Hunters Trail Warren OH 44484 Office: 4000 Mahoning Ave Warren OH 44482

PINOLA, JOSEPH J., banker; b. Pittston, Pa., 1925; B.A., Bucknell U., 1949; postgrad. Dartmouth Coll. Grad. Sch. Fin. and Mgmt., Harvard Grad. Sch. Bus. Adminstrn. With Bank of Am., 1951-76, exec. v.p., to 1976; pres., chief operating officer, United Bank Calif., 1976-78; chmn. bd., chief exec. officer, dir. Western Bancorp., Los Angeles, 1978—; dir. United Calif. Bank, First Nat. Bank Ariz., First Nat. Bank Nev. Served with USN. Office: Western Bancorporation 707 Wilshire Blvd Los Angeles CA 90017

PIOT, JOSEPH LEON, consumer products co. exec.; b. East St. Louis, Ill., Sept. 23, 1920; s. Joseph B. and Lucy Elizabeth (Pettersson) P.; B.B.A., Brown Coll., 1939; m. Winifred Clark, Oct. 7, 1950; children—Michelene Marie, Mary Nicolette, Nanette Claire, Cecile Anne. Engr., M.W. Kellogg Co., Woodriver, Ill., 1942-43, Iran, 1944-47, Whiting, Ind., 1947-48; engr. J.C. White Engring. Co., Venezuela, 1949-50; prodn. control supr. U.S. Def. Corp., St. Louis, 1950-55; prodn. material control mgr. Aladdin Industries, Inc., Nashville, 1955-59, export dept. mgr., 1959-73, v.p., 1973—, mng. dir. Aladdin Industries Ltd., Eng., 1975, pres. Aladdin Western Export & EXCO, 1975, v.p., gen. mgr. consumer products div. Aladdin Industries, Nashville, 1976—; dir. Aladdin Industries Ltd. (Eng.), Aladdin Industries Pty. Ltd. (Australia), Aladdin Industries Products of Can., Inc. Mem. Nashville Com. on Fgn. Relations, Ark.-Ten. Dist. Exxort Council (chmn. 1978-79). Clubs: Richland Country, Nashville. Home: 1770 Tyne Blvd Nashville TN 37215 Office: 703 Murfreesboro Rd Nashville TN 37210

PIPER, HENRY GEORGE, mfg. co. exec.; b. Englewood, N.J., Aug. 26, 1922; s. Henry George and Emma Louise Piper; B.S.M.E., Mich. Tech. U., 1948; M.B.A., N.Y. U., 1953; m. Elke Bongardt, June 16, 1973; children—Henry George, Thomas P., Geoffrey I. With Olin Mathieson Chem. Corp., 1948-59; alloy sales mgr. Brush Wellman, Inc., Cleve., 1959-65, v.p. sales, 1965-74, sr. v.p. Beryllium products, 1974-76, pres., chief exec. officer, 1976—, chmn., 1979—. Served with U.S. Army, 1940-45. Named Chief Exec. Officer of Yr., Fin. World, 1979; recipient Silver Medal award Mich. Tech. U. Bd. Control, 1979. Mem. Am. Mgmt. Assn., Soc. Automotive Engrs. Club: Chagrin Valley Country. Office: 17876 Saint Clair Ave Cleveland OH 44110

PIPPEN, JOSEPH FRANKLIN, JR., lawyer, electronics mfg. co. ofcl.; b. Richmond, Va., Jan. 11, 1947; s. Joseph Franklin and Selma(Seay) P., Sr.; B.S. in Econs., Va. Inst. Tech., 1969; J.D., U. Balt., 1975; m. Beverly Price, Dec. 20, 1969; children—Trey, Troy. Mktg. dir. Chesapeake & Potomac Telephone Co. of Md., Washington, 1969; buyer, fin. coordinator Western Electric Co., Balt., 1969-79; admitted to Fla. bar, 1980; gen. mgr. Micro-Plate Co., St. Petersburg, Fla., 1980—; prof. bus. law Anne Arundel Community Coll., 1978-79, St. Petersburg Jr. Coll. Bd. dirs. Ecumenical Ministry Youth; Md. chmn. Hugh O'Brian Youth Found., 1978-79, nat. bd. dirs., 1981. Named Jaycee of Yr., Md. Jaycees, 1979; named an Outstanding Young Man, Md. Jaycees, 1980. Mem. Phi Alpha Delta, Delta Sigma Pi. Republican. Methodist. Club: Hub. Home: 7501 Cumberland Rd Largo FL 33543 Office: 3115 44th Ave N Saint Petersburg FL 33714

PIPPERT, RICHARD HAROLD, pub. co. exec.; b. St. Louis, Nov. 18, 1936; s. Horace B. and Evelyn (Harper) P.; B.S., Washington U., 1958; m. Patricia E. Sheffield, May 14, 1977; children—Nicholas Gregory, Valerie Caroline. Field service rep. D'Arcy Advt. Co., 1958-60, account exec., 1960-62; br. mgr. Coca Cola Co., 1962-65; sr. product mgr. Ralston Purina Co., 1965-69; product mgr. Liggett Group, 1969-70, dir. product mgmt., 1970-74; dir. mktg. Scovill, Inc., N.Y.C., 1974-75; v.p. mktg. CBS, Inc., N.Y.C., 1975-76, v.p. pub. CBS, Inc., N.Y.C., 1979—; v.p. European ops. Holt Saunders, Eng., 1976-79. Republican. Club: Innis Arden. Office: 385 Madison Ave New York NY 10017

PIRATZKY, ALBERT RICHARD, indsl. instrument co. exec.; b. Lyndhurst, N.J., Aug. 20, 1927; s. Albert and Harriet (Schneider) P.; B.S. in Elec. Engring., Newark Coll. Engring. (now N.J. Inst. Tech.), 1961, M.S. in Mgmt. Engring., 1968; m. Josephine J. Gaccione, Sept. 26, 1948; children—Joanne H., Richard J., Thomas J., Roger F. Instrument engr. Pub. Service Electric & Gas Co., Newark, 1944-60; dir. mfg., dir. engring. Electro-Mech Corp. div. Am. Chain & Cable Co. Norwood, N.J., 1960-61, dist. sales mgr. Bristol Co. div., N.Y.C., 1961-68; dir. marketing Intertech Corp., subsidiary Ethyl Corp., Princeton, N.J., 1968-76; gen. mgr. Intertech div. Esterline Angus Instrument Co., Indpls., 1976-79, v.p. mktg., 1979—. Lectr., Am. Mgmt. Assn. Served with USNR, 1945-46. Mem. Instrument Soc. Am. (past pres. N.Y. sect., chmn. symposiums), Sales Execs. Club N.Y., Am. Soc. Testing and Materials. Republican. Home: 3595 Carmel Dr Carmel IN 46032 Office: 1201 Main St Indianapolis IN 46224

PISANO, ANTHONY MARK, restaurant chain exec.; b. Wilkes Barre, Pa., July 2, 1940; s. Joseph S. and Rose Y. (De Romo) P.; B.S., Lehigh U., 1962; M.B.A., N.Y. U., 1964; m. Meryl Gluck. Fin. analyst, IBM, Poughkeepsie, N.Y., 1964-67; fin. cons. Arthur Young & Co., N.Y.C., 1967-70; fin. cons. mgr. Ernst & Ernst, White Plains, N.Y., 1970-75; exec. v.p. fin. and adminstrn. Tombrock Corp., Stamford, Conn., 1975-79, exec. v.p.-fin. and adminstrn., 1979—, also dir. Treas., bd. dirs. Buckingham Condominium; chmn. bus. sector Stamford Clean City Com. Served with USNG, 1965-71. C.P.A., N.Y. Mem. Nat. Restaurant Assn. (chmn. EDP study group), Am. Mgmt. Assn., Stamford Area Commerce and Industry Assn. Nat. Assn. Accountants, Am. Inst. C.P.A.'s. Home: 143 Hoyt St Stamford CT 06905 Office: 580 Main St Stamford CT 06904

PISECCO, PETER ANTHONY, welding equipment co. exec.; b. Camden, N.J., Mar. 29, 1938; s. Anthony and Sarah (Doherty) P.; B.S. in Econs., Villanova U., 1960, postgrad., 1966-67; postgrad. Wharton Sch. Continuing Edn., U. Pa., 1977-78; m. Barbara Elaine Owens, Mar. 2, 1962; children—Peter Anthony, Paul Owen, Pamela Anne. Salesman, Am. Oil Co., Phila., 1961-65; dist. sales mgr. Harris Calorific Co., Boston, 1965-73, Detroit, 1973-75; dist. mgr. Victor Calif. Div., San Francisco, 1975-76; mgr. internat. sales and mktg. Victor Equipment Co., Denton, Tex., 1977-80, dir. mktg. and sales Wingaersheek div., Peabody, Mass., 1980—. Vice-pres. local Republican club, 1970-72, mem. Rep. town com., 1972-73; town chmn. Heart Fund, 1972; treas. PTA, 1974, pres., 1975. Served in U.S. Army, 1960-61. Named Outstanding Jaycee, 1969, an Outstanding Young Man Am., 1970; certificate of exemplary service U.S. Jaycees, 1972, Heart Fund, 1973, Rep. Club, 1973. Mem. Am. Welding Soc. (ednl. staff Detroit sect. 1973-75), U.S. Jaycees (treas. 1969, v.p. 1970), Nat. Welding Supply Assn., Internat. Trade Assn., Center for Internat. Bus. (Dallas). Roman Catholic. Clubs: Elks, K.C. Home: 198 Westford St Chelmsford MA 01824 Office: 2 Dearborn Rd Peabody MA 01960

PISELLI, DONATO, food co. exec.; b. N.Y.C., July 11, 1949; s. Donato and Anna (DeRubeis) P.; A.S., RCA Inst., 1969; B.B.A., Fordham U., 1979; m. Marie Anna Lech, Aug. 14, 1971; children—Jennifer Louise, Jeannine Marie. Supr. computer operations Hearst Publs., N.Y.C., 1968-69; application programmer Diners Club, N.Y.C., 1969-72; mgr. computer operations The Nestle Co., Inc., White Plains, N.Y., 1972-76, tech. support specialist, 1976—; cons. Volt Industries. Mem. Jaycees. Republican. Roman Catholic. Home: Surrey Trail Newtown CT 06482 Office: 100 Bloomingdale Rd White Plains NY 10605

PISTILLI, THOMAS ERNEST, mfg. co. exec.; b. Waterbury, Conn., Oct. 19, 1942; s. Ernest Anthony and Phyllis (Ceddia) P.; B.S. in Bus. Adminstrn., U. Cin., 1964; m. Nancy Giordan, Apr. 23, 1966; children—Todd, Tyler. Accountant, Peat, Marwick & Mitchell & Co., C.P.A.'s, 1964-72; controller Better Packages, Inc., 1972-75, v.p. ops., sales and mktg., 1978-79, pres., 1979—; controller, v.p. leasing div. parent co. Rockaway Corp., 1975-78. C.P.A., Conn. Mem. Am. Inst. C.P.A.'s, Nat. Assn. Accountants, Am. Mgmt. Assn., Conn. Soc. C.P.A.'s. Roman Catholic. Club: Country of Waterbury (Conn.). Home: 64 Hillcrest Ave Watertown CT 06795 Office: 8 Brook St Shelton CT 06484

PISTNER, STEPHEN LAWRENCE, retail co. exec.; b. St. Paul, Mar. 14, 1932; s. Leopold and Prudence Charolette (Selcer) P.; student U. Wash.; B.A., U. Minn., B.S., 1953; m. Jane Evelyn Golden, Sept. 30, 1971; children—Paul David, John Alan, Betsy Ann. Pres., chief exec. officer Target Stores, Inc., Mpls., 1973-76, chmn., chief exec. officer, 1976; exec. v.p. Dayton Hudson Corp., Mpls., 1976-77, pres., chief operating officer, 1976—, also dir.; dir. Northwestern Nat. Bank. Bd. govs. Mt. Sinai Hosp., Mpls.; bd. dirs., mem. exec. com. Minn. Orchestral Assn.; trustee Mpls. Soc. Fine Arts, Sta. KTCA, public TV. Office: Dayton Hudson Corp 777 Nicollet Mall Minneapolis MN 55402

PISTOR, CHARLES HERMAN, JR., banker; b. St. Louis, Aug. 26, 1930; s. Charles Herman and Virginia (Brown) P.; B.B.A., U. Tex., 1952; M.B.A., Harvard U., 1956, So. Meth. U., 1961; grad. Stonier Sch. Banking, Rutgers U., 1964; m. Regina Prikryl, Sept. 20, 1952; children—Lori Ellen, Charles Herman III, Jeffrey Glenn. Pres., dir. Republic Nat. Bank, Dallas, to 1980, chmn., chief exec. officer, 1980—; dir. Republic Financial Services, Inc., Dallas, Republic of Tex. Corp. Trustee, Trinity U.; chmn. SMU Bus. Sch. Found.; mem. Dallas Citizens Council. Served to lt. USNR, 1952-54. Mem. Am. Bankers Assn. (chmn. govt. relations council), Assn. Res. City Bankers. Presbyn. (elder). Club: Dallas Country. Home: 4200 Belclaire St Dallas TX 75205 Office: PO Box 225961 Dallas TX 75265

PISZEK, EDWARD JOHN, mfg. co. exec.; b. Chgo., Oct. 24, 1916; s. Peter and Anna (Sikora) P.; student U. Pa., 1937-43; D. Human Relations (hon.), St. Joseph Coll., 1973; L.H.D. (hon.), Alliance Coll., 1971; hon. doctorate Jagiellonian U., Cracow, Poland, 1974; m. Olga McFadden, Oct. 24, 1937; children—Ann, Edward John, George, Helen, William. Salesman, Campbell Soup Co., Camden, N.J., 1937-42; with Gen. Electric Co., Phila., 1942-46; pres. Mrs. Paul's Kitchens, Phila., 1946—. Bd. dirs. N.Y. Public Library, 1976-80; trustee Germantown Acad.; bd. govs. St. Joseph's Acad. of Food Mktg., 1961-78. Mem. Nat. Fisheries Inst., Grocery Mfrs. Am., Eastern Food Packers Assn., Fgn. Policy Assn., Research Inst. Am. Roman Catholic. Office: 5830 Henry Ave Philadelphia PA 19128

PITBLADO, JOHN M., mfg. co. exec.; b. Mpls., Jan. 25, 1918; s. James M. and Jennie S. (Bark) P.; B.S. in Chem. Engring., U. Minn., 1940; m. Jeanne F. Oistad, Jan. 21, 1942; children—James M., Judy Pitblado Skoglund. Chem. engr. U.S. Steel South Works, Chgo., 1940-41; chem. engr. Mobil Oil Co., Milw., 1941-43; with 3M Co., 1946—, gen. sales and mktg. mgr. coated abrasives and related products div., 1966-68, gen. mgr. bldg. service and cleaning products div., 1968-70, div. v.p., 1970-75, group v.p., 1975-79, pres. U.S. ops., 1979—. Served with USNR, 1943-46. Mem. Chem. Mfrs. Assn. (dir.). Office: 3M Co 3M Center Saint Paul MN 55101*

PITCHER, LINDA RUTH TILLMAN, exec. sec.; b. Orlando, Fla., June 3, 1943; d. Thomas John and Stella Frances (Block) Tillman; student Valencia Community Coll., Orlando, 1973-74, Fla. Jr. Coll., Jacksonville, 1976-77. Exec. sec. to mgr. advance systems engring. Martin Marietta Aerospace Corp., Orlando, 1963-69; exec. sec. to pres., also office mgr., fashion coordinator and writer Act II Jewelry Inc., Orlando, 1969-76; legal asst., sec. Howell, Howell, Liles, Braddock & Milton, Jacksonville, Fla., 1976-78; exec. asst. to owners and developers Regency Sq. Shopping Center, Jacksonville, 1978-80; exec. sec. to sr. v.p. personnel and labor relations Family Lines Rail System, Jacksonville, 1980—. Publicity chmn., v.p. Women of Jacksonville Art Mus., 1977-80; active Women's Guild of Cummer Gallery, Women's Info. Exchange. Mem. Jacksonville Bar Assn. Aux., Nat. Secs. Assn. (asst. treas. 1973-74, sec. 1974-75), LWV, Jacksonville Wine and Food Soc. (sec.-treas.). Republican. Mem. Ch. Religious Sci. Club: Univ. (Jacksonville). Home: 9439 San Jose Blvd Apt 25 Jacksonville FL 32217 Office: 500 Water St Rm 1312 Jacksonville FL 32202

PITCHFORD, LOREN CARL, oil pipeline exec.; b. Tacoma, July 25, 1943; s. Frank John and Louise (Ross) P.; student Yakima Valley Coll., 1962-63, Central Wash. State Coll., 1963-64; B.S., U. Wash., 1967. Exec. trainee U.P. R.R., Omaha, 1968-69, asst. supt. Portland, Oreg., 1969-71; dir. personnel Bumble Bee Seafoods, div. Castle & Cooke Foods, Astoria, Oreg., 1971-74; mgr. compensation and benefits Alyeska Pipeline, Anchorage, 1974—. Campaign chmn. for Omaha, Nat. Alliance Businessmen, 1969, recipient award; pres. Alaska Indsl. Relations Council, 1978-79; v.p. Seattle Jaycees, 1968; mem. Oreg. Gov.'s Ancillary Manpower Planning Bd.; chmn. Clatsop County (Oreg.) Manpower Planning Bd., recipient Outstanding Service award. Recipient speakers award Cosmopolitan Club. Mem. Am. Compensation Assn., Pacific N. W. Personnel Mgmt. Assn., Am. Soc. Personnel Adminstrs. Baptist. Clubs: Rotary, Elks. Author articles in outdoor mags. Home: 6448 Citadel Ln Anchorage AK 99504 Office: 1835 S Bragaw St Anchorage AK 99504

PITFIELD, WARD CHIPMAN, investment co. exec.; b. Montreal, Que., Can., 1925; B.Com., McGill U., 1948. Chmn. bd., pres. Pitfield Mackay Ross Ltd., Toronto, Ont., Can.; dir. CAE Industries Ltd., WCI Can. Ltd., Canadian Gen. Investments Ltd., Toromont Industries Ltd., White Consol. Industries Ltd. Bd. dirs. Hosp for Sick Children. Club: Ont. Jockey (trustee). Office: PO Box 54 Royal Bank Plaza Toronto ON M5K 1H9 Canada

PITLOR, JOEL ROSS, mgmt. cons.; b. Omaha, Oct. 19, 1938; s. Nathan and Molly P.; B.S.M.E., M.I.T., 1962; m. Joan Meltz, June 10, 1962; children—Margot Tara, Nelson Douglas, Heidi Elizabeth. Engr., Union Carbide, Tonawanda, N.Y., 1962-65; mgr. magnetics and cryogenics div. Inc./Magnion, Inc., Burlington, Mass., 1965-72; founder Brucker Magnetics, Burlington, 1972-74; asso. dir. Inst. New Enterprise Devel., Belmont, Mass., also v.p. Venture Founders Corp., Belmont, 1974-79; bus. cons. devel. and fin., Concord, Mass., 1979—; dir. HTC Corp.; mem. faculty Northwestern U. Trustee Boston Children's Theater. Home and Office: 22 Jennie Dugan Rd Concord MA 01742

PITSINOS, PETER NICHOLAS, publisher; b. Athens, Greece, Sept. 5, 1943; came to U.S., 1956, naturalized, 1961; s. Nicholas P. and Athena Pitsinos; B.S., U. Vt., 1966; M.B.A., Syracuse U., 1970; Asst. to budget mgr. Hatco group div. W.R. Grace Co., Fords, N.J., 1970-71; fin. analyst, coordinator internat. mgmt. Internat. Playtex Corp., N.Y.C., 1971-74; fin. analyst Hatco Plastics div. W.R. Grace Co., N.Y.C., 1974-75; with Am. Broadcasting Cos., Inc., N.Y.C., 1975—, dir. adminstrn. publs. div., 1978-79, exec. v.p. R.L. White Co. subs., Louisville, 1980—, also dir. subs. Served to 1st lt. AUS, 1966-68. Office: 1001 W Main St Louisville KY 40202

PITTMAN, G. C., banker; b. Victoria County, Tex., Jan. 22, 1921; s. Edward D. and Willie McCurry Pittman; student Victoria County Jr. Coll., 1938-40, Southwestern Grad. Sch. Banking, So. Meth. U., 1959-61; m. Augusta G. Maurer, Dec. 25, 1942; children—David Jerome, Sharon Ann, Patricia Ann. With Victoria Bank & Trust Co. (Tex.), 1940—, sr. v.p., 1962-69, exec. v.p., 1969-77, pres., mem. exec. com., dir., 1977—; bd. dirs., exec. v.p., gen. adminstr. Victoria Bankshares, Inc.; v.p. Central Computers, Inc., Western States Corp. Bd. trustees Citizens Meml. Hosp., St. Joseph High Sch. Served with AUS, 1942-46. Mem. South Tex. C. of C. (mem. exec. com.), Am. Bankers Assn. Roman Catholic. Club: Serra. Office: PO Box 1698 Victoria TX 77901

PITTMAN, JAMES EUGENE, JR., vermiculturist; b. Long Beach, Calif., May 28, 1948; s. James E. and Lenora Fern (Hunsaker) P.; student in vermiculture and soil husbandry; m. Brenda June Petker, Nov. 12, 1977; children—Kerri Lynn, Michelle N., Olivia Marie. Earthworm grower, owner Templeton (Calif.) Worm Ranch, 1975—; mktg. dir. Jay-Fran Inc., Iowa City, Iowa, 1977—, Invivo Inc., Iowa City, 1977—, Bio-Eco-Systems Inc., Indpls., 1976—; pres. Am. Eco Systems Inc., Templeton, 1977—; mktg. dir. other corps; mem. Calif. Farm Bur., 1975—. Recipient award of appreciation Rotary Internat., 1977, Kiwanis, 1977, Lions, 1976, C. of C. of Atascadero, Calif., 1976, Calif. U.-Calif. Poly. Inst., 1976, Madera Unified Sch. Dist., 1977; certified Los Angeles County Health Dept. Mem. Vermiculturists Trade Assn., Western Organic Growers Assn., Nat. Fedn. Ind. Bus., Nat. SBA. Clubs: Elks, Rotary (dir. local club 1977-78, chmn. world community services local club 1978-79). Home: 149 McKinley St Oceanside CA 92054

PITTS, ALBERT S., fin. planner; b. Phila., Jan. 5, 1933; s. James R. and Christine (Dodds) P.; certificate N.Y. Inst. Finance, 1963, Coll. Financial Planning, Denver, 1973; m. Marian C. Szymanski, Apr. 18, 1953; children—James Albert, Thomas Morton, Christine, Kenneth Daniel. With printing industry, Phila., 1950-60, typographic salesman, 1960-62; mut. fund salesman, part-time 1959-62; v.p. Robinson & Co., Inc., Phila., 1963-70, dir. pension and profit sharing dept., specialist tax-sheltered investments; regional v.p. Putnam Fund Distbrs., Inc., 1970-73; regional v.p. Shareholders Securities Corp., 1974; pres. EDI, Exec. Design Investments, 1974—; regional mgr. Internat. Diamond Corp., 1978—; v.p. R.L. Stevens & Co. Inc., 1976-77. Adv. bd. Villanova U. Coll.; mem. Invest in Am. Nat. Council. Mem. Delaware Valley Assn. Fin. Planners (pres.). Republican. Roman Catholic. Home: 117 Mansion Dr Rose Tree Media PA 19063 Office: Rose Tree Profl Bldg Media PA 19063

PITTS, DON D., telephone co. exec.; b. Little Rock, May 22, 1931; s. James Elmer and Mary Elizabeth (Rexroad) P.; B.S. magna cum laude, Little Rock U., 1964; m. Janice March Hewgley, Feb. 4, 1950; children—Richard William, Walter Gregory. Audit mgr. Arthur Andersen & Co., St. Louis, 1964-69; div. controller Continental Telephone Service Corp., St. Louis, 1969-71, v.p.-subs. accounting, Bakersfield, Calif., 1971-76, controller Continental Telephone Corp., Atlanta, 1976—. Recipient Student Achievement award Wall St. Jour., 1964. Mem. Am. Inst. C.P.A.'s. Office: 56 Perimeter Center E Atlanta GA 30346

PITTS, ELAINE RUTH HALLEAD (MRS. PAUL ELBERT PITTS), premium co. exec.; b. Chgo., June 20, 1917; d. Harry Albert and Ethel Mae (Waring) Hallead; student Ill. Inst. Tech., 1948-49, Art Inst. Chgo., 1947-48; A.A., N.Y. U., 1978; m. Paul Elbert Pitts., Aug. 25, 1945. Packaging engr. Aldens, Inc., Chgo., 1943-46; sr. packaging engr. Spiegel, Inc., Chgo., 1946-52; mgr. package engring. Sperry & Hutchinson Co., Chgo., 1953-59, mgr. consumer relations, N.Y.C., 1959-70, dir. consumer affairs, 1970, v.p. corp. relations, 1970-79; partner Dalton/Pitts Assos., San Mateo, Calif., 1979—; lectr. M.I.T., U. Wis., Purdue U., U. Calif. at Los Angeles, Ill. Inst. Tech., U. Ill. Nat. adv. bd. Distributive Edn. Clubs Am., 1962—, vice chmn., 1964, chmn., 1965; mem. N.Y. State Adv. Council Vocat. Edn. Bd. dirs. S & H Found. Mem. Secs. Guild Chgo. Boys Club (pres. 1963), Bus. and Profl. Women's Club, Soc. Packaging and Handling Engrs. (chpt. pres. 1957, nat. chmn. bd. 1966-67), Soc. Womens Engrs. (nat. exec. com. 1968-69, 77—), U.S. C. of C. (consumer affairs com.), Women Execs. in Pub. Relations (pres. 1977-79), Am. Women Radio and TV (nat. v.p. 1969-70, pres. 1973-74), Pub. Relations Soc. Am. Home: 249 Elm St San Mateo CA 94401 Office: 307 S B St San Mateo CA 94401

PITTS, LARRY KEITH, bank exec.; b. Vincennes, Ind., Apr. 7, 1938; s. Loren A. and Lucille M. (Woodall) P.; B.S., Ind. State U., 1962; grad. Am. Inst. Banking, 1969; m. Lynda Joanne Wolfe; children—Trina Lynn, Michele Janine. With Am. Fletcher Nat. Bank and Trust Co., Indpls., 1962—, v.p., investment officer, 1970-72, sr. v.p., chief trust officer, 1972-79, exec. v.p., chief trust officer, 1979—; exec. v.p. Circle Income Shares, Inc. Chartered fin. analyst. Mem. Inst. Fin. Analysts, Fin. Analyst Fedn., Am. Bankers Assn. (fed. legis. council), Ind. Bankers Assn. (trust chmn. 1975), Indpls. Soc. Fin Analysts (dir., pres. 1974), Econ. Club Indpls. (chmn. lawyers and bankers com. 1980). Republican. Methodist. Clubs: Indpls. Athletic, Columbia, Country Club Indpls., Elks. Home: 1112 Charles Ct Plainfield IN 46168 Office: 101 Monument Cir Indianapolis IN 46277

PIVAN, DAVID BERNARD, mgmt. cons.; b. Chgo., June 30, 1921; s. Herman L. and Leona (Kirchner) P.; student Case Sch. Applied Sci., 1942-43; B.S. in Elec. Engring., Ill. Inst. Tech., 1948; postgrad. Northwestern U., 1950-52; m. Rita Lois Birkner, July 26, 1942; children—Mark, Lynn, Janice. Vice pres., chief engring. Radio Sta. WMOR, Chgo., 1948-50; v.p. Everett Assos., 1950-54; pres., chmn. Pivan Engring. Co., Inc., Chgo., 1954-76; exec. v.p., dir. Hallmark Investment, Inc., Lincolnwood, Ill., 1970-77; exec. v.p., dir. Inmark, Inc., Rockville, Md., 1969-73; exec. v.p., dir. Comtel Corp., Detroit, 1973-76; pres. Pivan Mgmt. Co., Skokie, Ill., 1976—; dir. Corcom, Inc., Libertyville, Ill., Interface Mechanisms, Inc., Seattle. Bd. dirs. Northbrook (Ill.) Public Library, 1979—. Served with U.S. Army, 1944-46. Registered profl. engr., Ill. Mem. Electronic Reps. Assn. (v.p. 1963-69), IEEE, Airplane Owners and Pilots Assn. Contbr. articles to profl. jours.; lectr. Home: 1765 South Ln Northbrook IL 60062 Office: 7840 Lincoln Ave Skokie IL 60077

PIVIROTTO, RICHARD ROY, retail co. exec.; b. Youngstown, Ohio, May 26, 1930; s. Arthur M. and Ruth (Erhardt) P.; B.A., Princeton U., 1952; M.B.A., Harvard U., 1954; m. Mary Patricia Burchfield, June 27, 1953; children—Mary B., Richard Roy, Susan W., Nancy P., David H., Jennifer P. Pres., Joseph Horne Co., Pitts., 1961-70; vice chmn. Asso. Dry Goods Corp., N.Y.C., 1971-72, pres., 1972-76, chmn. bd., 1976—; dir. Chem. Bank, The Gillette Co., Boston, Westinghouse Electric Corp., N.Y. Life Ins. Co., Gen. Am. Investors Co.; charter trustee Princeton U., Bowery Savs. Bank. Trustee, Greenwich Hosp. Assn. Served with U.S. Army, 1955-56. Mem. Am. Retail Fedn. (dir.), Nat. Retail Mchts. Assn. (dir.). Clubs: Union League, Greenwich Country, Princeton of N.Y., Fox Chapel Golf, Duquesne, Rolling Rock, Field (Greenwich). Home: 111 Clapboard Ridge Rd Greenwich CT 06830 Office: 417 Fifth Ave New York NY 10016

PIZOR, LARRY WAYNE, elec. utility exec.; b. New Castle, Pa., Dec. 31, 1945; s. George Ralph and Wanda Mae (Anderson) P.; B.S.E.E., Grove City Coll., 1972; m. Marlene Maxwell, Sept. 8, 1973; children—Robert, Leslie. Jr. engr. Pa. Power Co., Zelienople, 1972-73, asso. engr., 1973-75, dist. engr., 1975-79, supr. transmission and distbn., 1979—. Served with USAF, 1963-67. Republican. Presbyterian. Home: 324 South St Evans City PA 16033 Office: PO Box 40 Zelienople PA 16063

PLACE, JOHN BASSETT MOORE, banking exec.; b. N.Y.C., Nov. 21, 1925; s. Hermann G. and Angela Toland (Moore) P.; student The Citadel, also N.Y. U.; D.Eng. (hon.), Colo. Sch. Mines, 1973; D.S.C. (hon.), Pace U.; m. Katharine Smart, Mar. 22, 1952; children—John Bassett Moore, Marian, Judith. With Chase Manhattan Bank, N.Y.C., 1946—, v.p., 1956-59, sr. v.p., 1959-65, exec. v.p., 1965-68, vice chmn., 1969-71; chmn. bd., pres., chief exec. officer, dir. Anaconda Co., N.Y.C., 1971-78; exec. v.p. Atlantic Richfield Co., 1977-78; pres., dir. Crocker Nat. Corp., San Francisco, 1978—, also prin. subs. Crocker Nat. Bank; dir. Atlantic Richfield Co., Lever Bros. Co., Met. Life Ins. Co. Trustee, Santa Clara Coll. Served to 2d lt. AUS, World War II; ETO. Named Young Man of Year in Banking, N.Y.C., 1960; decorated Gt. Cross Order Civil Merit (Spain). Mem. U.S. C. of C., Council Fgn. Relations, N.Y. C. of C. Clubs: Mining, Union, Links, Hemisphere (N.Y.C.); Millbrook (N.Y.) Golf and Tennis; California (Los Angeles); Internat. Office: Crocker Nat Corp One Montgomery St San Francisco CA 94104

PLANTS, DAVID LEE, fin. exec.; b. Lorain, Ohio, Sept. 22, 1946; s. Robert Lee and Ann Lois (Capehart) P.; B.B.A., Marshall U., 1972; M.B.A., U. Houston, 1978; m. Carolyn Blake, Mar. 4, 1972; children—James Daniel, Leslie Blake. Houston br. mgr. Litton Industries Credit Corp., 1974-78, dist. mgr., 1978-79; leasing officer Bank of Am., Houston, 1979-80; regional mgr. ITT Indsl. Credit Co., Houston, 1980—. Bd. dirs. Marshall U. Artist Series, 1970-72. Served with USN, 1966-69. Mem. Am. Assn. Equip. Lessors, Sigma Alpha Epsilon. Presbyterian. Club: Klein Vol. Fire Dept. Home: 8219 Winding Hill Ln Spring TX 77379 Office: 2900 N Loop W Suite 1095 Houston TX 77092

PLASKETT, THOMAS GEORGE, airline co. exec.; b. Kansas City, Mo., Dec. 24, 1943; s. Warren E. and Frances (Winegar) P.; B.I.E., Gen. Motors Inst., 1966; M.B.A., Harvard, 1968; m. Linda Lee Maxey, June 8, 1968; children—Kimberly Ann, Keith Thomas. Supr. indsl. engring. Chevrolet div. Gen. Motors Corp., Flint, Mich., 1968, supt. indsl. engring., 1969-73, sr. staff asst., treas. staff, N.Y.C., 1973; asst. controller budgets/fin. systems Am. Airlines, Inc., N.Y.C., 1974, v.p. mktg. adminstrn., 1975, sr. v.p. fin., Dallas, 1976—; dir. First United Bancorp., AA Devel. Corp., AA Energy Corp., Americana Hotels, Inc. Mem. Fin. Execs. Inst. (dir.), Am. Mgmt. Assn. Republican. Presbyterian. Club: Las Colinas Country (Irving, Tex.). Home: 3911 Fox Glen Dr Irving TX 75062 Office: PO Box 61616 DFW Airport TX 75261

PLATE, WILLIAM CARL, graphics co. exec.; b. Jennings, La., Dec. 14, 1946; s. Carl Ferdinand and Sara Evelyn (Noland) P.; A.A., Los Angeles Pierce Coll., 1970; B.S., San Jose State U., 1974; m. Nancy Lee Noddings, May 24, 1975 (div. May 1, 1980); 1 dau., Eleanor Lindsey. Founder, pres. Arrow Graphics, San Jose, 1971—, with branches in Woodland Hills, Sacramento and Tustin, Calif., also Phoenix and Dallas. Pres., Naglee Park Homeowners Assn., 1975-77; mem. San Jose Parking Adv. Bd., 1975-77. Mem. Sales and Mktg. Council, Bldg. Industry Assn. Democrat. Home: 1160 Britton Ave San Jose CA 95125 Office: 417 Lano St San Jose CA 95125

PLATT, HAROLD EUGENE, petroleum co. exec.; b. N.Y.C., Sept. 30, 1920; A.B., Duke, 1942; grad. Advanced Mgmt. Program, Harvard, 1967; m. Elizabeth Finlay; children—Donald, Allison, William. With Cities Service Co., Tulsa, 1948—, treas., 1969-72, v.p., 1972—; v.p., dir. Can.-Cities Service Ltd.; pres. Cities Service Found.; dir. Bank of Commerce, Tulsa. Served to lt. comdr. USNR, World War II. Mem. Am. Petroleum Inst., Fin. Execs. Inst., Harvard Advanced Mgmt. Assn., Lambda Chi Alpha. Clubs: Tulsa Country, Summit (Tulsa). Address: Box 300 Tulsa OK 74102

PLATT, ROBERT HOLMES, railway exec.; b. Bklyn., Apr. 1, 1920; s. Foster Holmes and Marie Frances (Quigley) P.; A.B., Colgate U., 1941; LL.D., Ind. Inst. Tech., 1969; m. Colette Gaffney, Sept. 20, 1941; children—J. Garry, Laura Platt Perry, Marion Platt Russotto. Pres., chief exec. officer Magnavox Co., 1968-75; vice chmn. bd., chief adminstrv. officer Lone Star Industries, Inc., 1975-77; exec. v.p. fin. and adminstrn. CONRAIL, Phila., 1977—; dir. Goodyear Tire & Rubber Corp., Lincoln Nat. Corp., U.S. Industries, Inc. Bd. trustees Colgate U. Served with USN, 1943-46. Mem. Econs. Club N.Y. Clubs: Sky, Woodway Country. Home: 345 S 4th St Philadelphia PA 19106 Office: Six Penn Center Plaza Philadelphia PA 19104

PLATTEN, DONALD CAMPBELL, banker; b. N.Y.C., Sept. 19, 1918; s. John Homer and Katherine Campbell (Viele) P.; B.A., Princeton, 1940; grad. Advanced Mgmt. Program, Harvard, 1966; m. Margaret Leslie Wyckoff, June 24, 1940; children—Kathlerine L. (Mrs. Randolph S. Naylor), Peter W., Alison C. (Mrs. Alfred G. Vanderbilt, Jr.). With Chem. Bank N.Y.C., 1940—, sr. v.p., 1964-67, exec. v.p., 1967-70, 1st v.p., 1970-72, pres., 1972-73, chmn. bd., 1973—: chmn. bd. Chem. N.Y. Corp., 1973—; dir. CPC Internat., Inc., Readers Digest Assn. Inc., Asso. Dry Goods Corp., Thomson Newspapers, Inc., Consol. Edison Co. N.Y. Chmn. bd. dirs. Goodwill Industries Greater N.Y.; bd. dirs. United Fund Greater N.Y., Econ. Devel. Council N.Y.; trustee Collegiate Sch., N.Y.C., Am. U. Beirut, United Student Aid Funds; charter trustee Princeton. Served to 1st lt. AUS, 1944-46. Mem. Japan Soc., Council Fgn. Relations, Res. City Bankers Assn. Clubs: Univ., Blind Brook, Links, Pres.'s, Bond (N.Y.C.), Econ. (N.Y.); Laurel Valley Golf (Ligonier, Pa.). Office: Chem NY Corp 20 Pine St New York NY 10005

PLATTS, JOHN, appliance co. exec.; b. Detroit, Nov. 19, 1917; s. Ralph E. and Mary E. (Snyder) P.; student U. Toledo, 1938-39; m. Dorothea M. Sleeper, Nov. 24, 1940; children—Pamela, Polly, Melissa. With Whirlpool Corp., 1941—, dir. purchases laundry plants, St. Joseph, Mich., 1954-55, works mgr. laundry plants, 1955-56, gen. sales mgr., 1956-57, gen. mgr. refrigeration plant, v.p. refrigeration product group, Evansville, Ind., 1957-62, corp. pres., Benton Harbor, Mich., 1962-77 chmn. bd., chief exec. officer, 1971—; dir. Shell Oil Co., Sears Bank & Trust Co., Clark Equipment Co. Mem. adv. council Coll. Engring., U. Notre Dame; mem. nat. execs. com. Nat. Council Crime and Delinquency; sr. mem. Conf. Bd.; trustee Citizens Research Council Mich. Mem. ASHRAE. Clubs: Chgo., Union League, Met. (Chgo.); Point O' Woods Country, Berrien Hills (Benton Harbor, Mich.). Office: Whirlpool Corp Adminstrv Center US 31 N Benton Harbor MI 49022

PLAUT, HAROLD HORST, mining and mfg. co. exec.; b. Phila., Dec. 28, 1927; s. Frederick Leon and Elsa Jeannine (Horst) P.; B.A., Roosevelt U., 1953; M.S., Lake Forest Coll., 1977; m. Elaine Johnson, May 16, 1959. With Internat. Minerals and Chem. Corp., Mundelein, Ill., 1947-69, 69—, sr. traffic research analyst, 1964-69, traffic mgr., 1969-76, gen. traffic mgr.-agr., 1977—. Served with USAF, 1945-47. Registered practitioner ICC. Mem. Assn. ICC Practitioners, Transp. Research Forum, Mensa, Traffic Club Chgo., N. Shore Traffic Club Waukegan. Presbyterian. Home: 201 E Cook Ave Libertyville IL 60048 Office: 421 E Hawley St Mundelein IL 60060

PLAUT, LEWIS G., retail exec.; b. Bklyn., Aug. 27, 1942; s. Jerome and Selma P.; B.A., Columbia Coll., 1965; m. Jane Klamer, July 23, 1967; children—Lauren Gayle, Jodi Rae. Field mgr. Ford Motor Co., 1966-71; with Am. Motors Corp., 1971-74; pres. Decorators Alley Ltd., Roslyn, N.Y., 1978—; dir. Coop. Buying Service, Roslyn. Pres., Suffolk County React, 1976-78. Republican. Home: 64 Granada Circle Mount Sinai NY 11766 Office: 20 Lumber Rd Roslyn NY 11576

PLESKAC, JOHN JOSEPH, JR., indsl. engr.; b. David City, Nebr., Feb. 16, 1942; s. John J. and Marie R. (Sypal) P.; B.S. in Indsl. Engring., U. Nebr., Omaha, 1967; M.S. I.M.S.E., U. Nebr., Lincoln, 1975; m. Marilyn Kay Juranek, June 6, 1964; children—Lisa K., Shari L., John R. Supr. wired equipment mfg. Western Elec. Co., Omaha, 1966-68, supr. prodn. control, 1968-71, supr. tng., 1971-74, indsl. engr., 1974-75, planning engr., 1975-79, sr. planning engr., 1979—. Co-founder, pres. Holling Heights Parent-Tchrs. Orgn., 1970-72; mem. planning com. Millard Sch. Dist., 1974-75, Douglas County 4-H Ice Skating Com., 1975—; active in student career guidance U. Nebr., Omaha, 1975—. Named Outstanding Undergrad. student U. Nebr., Omaha, 1967; registered profl. engr., Nebr. Mem. Am. Inst. Indsl. Engrs. (sr., pres., 1972-73), Nat. Soc. Profl. Engrs., U. Nebr. at Omaha Alumni Assn. (dir. 1981—), Alpha Pi Mu, Gamma Pi Sigma. Office: Western Elec Co PO Box 14000 W Omaha Sta Omaha NE 68114

PLESSET, ERNST HAECKEL, physicist, investor; b. Pitts., Aug. 17, 1913; s. B. M. and Anna (Swartz) P.; B.S., U. Pitts., 1933; A.M., Harvard, 1939, Ph.D., 1941; m. Pauline Riedeburg, May 5, 1959; children—Sarah Jean (Mrs. Daniel Quillen), Julius L., Mark J. Mills, Ann Mills. Physicist, Manhattan Dist., 1942-43; physicist to research mgr. Research Labs., Douglas Aircraft Co., 1943-47; chief physics div. Rand Corp., 1947-56; exec. dir. devel. Westinghouse Electric Co., 1956-57; pres. E.H. Plesset Assos., Inc., 1957-64, chmn. bd., 1957-67; gen. partner Plesset Family Partnership, 1971—; pres. Plesset Family Corp., 1978-79, chmn., sec., 1979—; aerospace cons., 1961-63; pres., chmn. bd. Capital for Tech. Industries, Inc., 1961-67; chmn. Cap Tech., Inc., 1967-78. Mem. sci. adv. bd. USAF, 1957-63, chmn. nuclear panel, 1958-63. Chmn. bd. trustees, overseer Immaculate Heart Coll., 1970-71. Mem. Calif. Motor Vehicle Pollution Control Bd., 1962-67, chmn., 1966-67. Fellow Am. Phys. Soc.; mem. Am. Arbitration Assn. (nat. panel arbitrators). Home: 309 Manuella Ave Woodside CA 94062

PLESSNER, RENÉ, exec. search co. exec.; b. Antwerp, Belgium, June 28, 1938; came to U.S., 1942, naturalized, 1947; s. Henri and Mary P.; B.A., Columbia Coll., 1960. Mktg. staff Helena Rubinstein, Inc., 1961-64, Lehn & Fink, Inc., 1964-65, Faberge, 1966-68, Revlon, N.Y.C., 1968-69; pres. Spectrum Cosmetics, Inc., N.Y.C., 1970-71, René Plessner Assos., Inc., N.Y.C., 1972—. Served with U.S. Army, 1960-61. Office: 450 Park Ave New York NY 10032

PLIMPTON, RODNEY BORLAND, mgmt. cons.; b. Framingham, Mass., Jan. 19, 1939; s. Barton Fiske and Beatrice (Borland) P.; A.B. with honors, Dartmouth Coll., 1963; M.B.A. with high distinction, Amos Tuck Sch. Bus., 1964; Ph.D., Stanford U., 1976; m. Betty Joel Futch, June 15, 1968; children—Laura Nadine, Scott Borland. Mem. corporate mktg. staff Ford Motor Co., 1964-65; pres. PW Research of Pitts., Inc., 1965-66; mgmt. cons. Harbridge House, Inc., Boston, 1966-69; asst. prof. Amos Tuck Sch., Dartmouth Coll., Hanover, N.H., 1973-76; pres. Organizational Cons. Services, Concord, Mass., 1976—; adj. prof. Antioch/New Eng. Coll., Keene, N.H. Trustee, deacon Hanover Center Ch., 1975-77; treas. Hanover Republican Com., 1977. Served with USN, 1959-61. NIMH fellow, 1972-73. Mem. Acad. Mgmt. Clubs: Camden Yacht, Megunticook Golf (Camden, Maine). Home: 111 Old Pickard Rd Concord MA 01742 Office: PO Box 661 Concord MA 01742

PLOEN, ERIC LUDWIG, health care cons. corp. exec.; b. Bronx, N.Y., Sept. 7, 1937; s. Frederick and Elizabeth P.; B.A., City U. N.Y., 1968; m. Linda Mary White, Oct. 2, 1977; 1 son, Bradford Frederick; 1 son by previous marriage, Scott Robert. Asso. program mgr. Kollsman Instrument Corp., Syosset, N.Y., 1960-68; asso. dir. Greater N.Y. Hosp. Assn., N.Y.C., 1968-74; asst. pres. United Hosp. Fund of N.Y., N.Y.C., 1974-76; pres. Affiliated Risk Control Adminstrs., Inc., Great Neck, N.Y., 1976—; guest lectr. Sch. Indsl. and Labor Relations, Cornell U., 1973-74. Mem. Hosp. Fin. Mgmt. Assn., Hosp. Mgmt. Systems Soc., Am. Soc. for Hosp. Risk Mgmt. Clubs: Lake Isle, Masons. Home: 20 Lamesa Ave Eastchester NY 10707 Office: Affiliated Risk Control Adminstrs 55 Northern Blvd Great Neck NY 11021

PLOTKIN, IRVING H(ERMAN), cons. econs.; b. Bklyn., July 19, 1941; s. Samuel H. and Dorothy (Falick) P.; B.S. in Econs., Wharton Sch., U. Pa., 1963; Ph.D. in Math. Econs., Mass. Inst. Tech., 1968; m. Janet V. Bufe, July 26, 1969; children—Aaron Jacob, Joshua Benjamin. Corporate planning analyst Mobil Oil Co., N.Y.C., 1962-63, Mobil Oil Italiana, Genoa, Italy, 1965; ind. cons. econs. and operations research to banks, mut. funds, ins. cos. govt. agys., Cambridge, Mass., 1965-68; sr. economist Arthur D. Little, Inc., Cambridge, 1968—, dir. regulation and econs., 1974—, v.p., 1979—; dir. Arthur D. Little Valuation, Inc., 1980—; instr. finance and computer scis. Mass. Inst. Tech., 1965-68; lectr. maj. univs. U.S. and abroad; expert witness U.S. Senate coms., U.S. Ct. Claims, I.C.C., FTC, Fed. Maritime Commn., other fed. and state govt. agys., 1967—. NASA fellow, 1963-66, NSF fellow, 1967, Am. Bankers Assn. fellow, 1968. Mem. Am. Econ. Assn., Econometric Soc., Am. Finance Assn., Beta Gamma Sigma, Pi Gamma Mu, Tau Delta Phi (chpt. pres. 1962-63). Editorial reviewer Jour. Am. Statis. Assn., 1968, Jour. Indsl. Econs., 1968—; author: Prices and Profits in the Property and Liability Insurance Industry, 1967; The Consequences of Industrial Regulation on Profitability, Risk Taking, and Innovation, 1969; National Policy, Technology, and Economic Forces Affecting the Industrial Organization of Marine Transportation, 1970; Government Regulation of the Air Freight Industry, 1971; The Private Mortgage Insurance Industry, 1975; On The Theory and Practice of Rate Review and Profit Measurement in Title Insurance, 1978; Torrens in the United States, 1978; also numerous articles and papers in profl. jours. Home: 55 Baskin Rd Lexington MA 02173 Office: 35 Acorn Park Cambridge MA 02140

PLOTNICK, BARRY REYMAN (REY BARRY), realtor, pub. relations cons.; b. Stamford, Conn., Feb. 15, 1937; s. Bernard and Selma Jean (Reyman) P.; student U. Va., 1959; m. Virginia Murray Leonard, Feb. 14, 1970; children—Brooke Barney, Apple Tracy. Radio broadcaster, 1957-61; founder Records for Recollectors, Stamford, 1963; sec.-treas., dir. finance and devel. Edn., Inc., Charlottesville, Va., 1972—; owner Rey Barry Assos., Charlottesville, 1972—; founder Univ. Realty, 1976—. Publisher, editor Central Va. Mag., 1964-66; columnist, edn. writer The Daily Progress, Charlottesville, 1966-71; TV producer U. Va., 1973-77; vis. lectr. U. Va. Sch. Continuing Edn., 1970-78. Bd. dirs. Central Va. Civil Liberties Union; bd. dirs. ACLU Va., Edn., Inc., Charlottesville; mem. Albemarle County Democratic Steering Com.; sec. Albemarle County Bd. of Equalization. Recipient Meritorious Service award Civil Air Patrol, 1967. Mem. Asso. Press Mng. Editors Assn., Investigative Reporters and Editors, Reporters Com. for a Free Press. Office: PO Box 312 Charlottesville VA 22902

PLUGGE, WILFRED ROBERT, corp. exec.; b. Hartman, Ark., Apr. 28, 1924; s. John and Marie (Eveld) P.; student Tulsa U., 1946-54; M.M.A., Harvard U., 1957; m. Mary Josephine Scott, Sept. 5, 1946. Dir. fin. analysis Am. Airlines, N.Y.C., 1946-59, asst. v.p. tech. services, 1959-64, v.p. info. services, 1964-70; sr. v.p. info. services ITT-Avis, N.Y.C., 1970-75; exec. dir. SRI Internat., 1975—; dir. Incoterm Corp., Wellington Systems. Served with USAF, 1942-45. Decorated Bronze Star. Mem. Nat. Def. Transp. Assn. Republican. Roman Catholic. Clubs: Sleepy Hollow Country, Cloyd, Indian Springs Country. Home: 17 Davies St Suite 1 London England Office: 12/16 Addiscombe Rd Croydon CRO OXT England

PLUMMER, A. Q., accountant; b. Moran, Tex., Dec. 23, 1921; s. John W. and Mittie (Gill) P.; B.B.A., U. Tex., 1947; m. Betty F. Cantrell, June 4, 1949; children—John Cantrell, Jim Mcclung, Betsy Beal. Accountant, The Tex. Co., Houston, 1947-55; tax accountant Tex. Gulf Producing Co., Houston, 1956-60, chief accountant, 1960—; chief accountant Libyan Am. Oil Co., Houston, 1960—; sec.-treas. Barbers Hill Salt Water Co., Houston, 1960-65; pvt. practice accounting, Brenham, Tex., 1965—. Instr. accounting S. Tex. Coll. 1956-57. Treas., S.W. Houston Cub Scout pack Boy Scouts Am., 1961; bd. dirs. St. Jude Hosp.; bd. dirs., sec. Bohme Meml. Hosp. mem. Brazos Valley Estate Council. Served with the USAAF, 1943-45. C.P.A., Tex. Mem. Tax Exec. Inst., Tex. Soc. C.P.A.'s (sec., treas. Houston; dir. chpt.), Washington County C. of C. Methodist (steward, auditor, sec. stewardship and finance comm.), Am. Inst. C.P.A.'s. Clubs: Lions, Heritage Soc. Home: Route 3 Box 384 Brenham TX 77833 Office: PO Box 671 Plum Hill Rd Brenham TX 77833

PLUMMER, DAVIS WARD, JR., acct., state ofcl.; b. May 8, 1947; s. Davis Ward and Olive Jane (Rogers) P.; B.S., Susquehanna U., 1970. Staff acct. Price Waterhouse & Co., Buffalo, 1970-71; sr. acct. Eichhorn & Weinreber, Buffalo, 1971-73; sr. auditor med. facilities N.Y. State Dept. Health, Bur. Audit and Investigation, Buffalo, 1973-74, asso. med. facilities auditor, 1974-76, prin. med. facilities auditor, 1976—. Price Waterhouse scholar, 1966-67; C.P.A. Mem. Am. Inst. C.P.A.'s, N.Y. State Soc. C.P.A.'s, Theta Chi. Home: 94 Hickory Hill Rd Williamsville NY 14221 Office: NY State Dept Health 584 Delaware Ave Buffalo NY 14202

PLUMMER, PAUL JAMES, telephone co. exec.; b. Scottsbluff, Nebr., Aug. 3, 1946; s. Virgil Frank and Helen Louise (Hultberg) P.; B.A., U. Nebr., 1968; postgrad. Platte Coll., 1974-75; m. Pamela Lee Purdom, June 26, 1976. With Gen. Telephone Co. of the Midwest, 1968—, div. traffic supr., Columbus, Nebr., 1969-75, div. traffic mgr., Columbia, Mo., 1975-78, labor relations adminstr., Grinnell, Iowa, 1978-79, labor relations mgr., 1979—. Active Boy Scouts Am. Mem. Am. Assn. Personnel Adminstrn., Personnel Mgmt. Assn. Columbia (exec. bd. dirs., 1st v.p. 1975-78). Episcopalian. Clubs: Optimist (past pres. Columbus, Nebr., lt. gov. Nebr. 1973-74), Elks. Home: 106 14th Ave Grinnell IA 50112 Office: 11 11th Ave Grinnell IA 50112

PLUNKETT, CHARLES WALTER, ry. exec.; b. Franks, Mo., May 2, 1926; s. Charley Amos and Ethel M. (Rockey) P.; grad. high sch. With Rock Island R.R., Chgo., 1943-58, supr. constrn. signal dept., 1959-62; ops. mgr., sales engr. Matisa Equipment Corp., Chicago Heights, Ill., 1962-67; asst. chief engr. Mo. Pacific R.R., St. Louis, 1967-68; gen. mgr. sales Jackson Vibrators, Inc., Chgo., 1969-70, v.p. r.r. sales, 1970, exec. v.p. r.r. products, 1973; pres. Comml. Quality Feed Center, Inc., Lebanon, Mo., 1973—, Material Cons., Inc., Lebanon, 1975—; pres., bus. mgr., dir. Served with USAAF, 1944-46. Decorated Purple Heart, D.F.C., Air Medal. Mem. Ry. Engring-Maintenance and Supplies Assn. (dir. 1968-71), Ry. Engring. Assn., Roadmasters and Maintenance of Way Assn. Clubs: Union League (Chgo.); Optimists. Home: Washington Apts Lebanon MO 65536 Office: 274 W Pierce St Lebanon MO 65536

PLYLER, BOB LEE, ladder mfg. co. exec.; b. Batesville, Ark., Dec. 20, 1936; s. Lee Roy and Altha Cleo (McSpadden) P.; A.A., Arlington State Coll., 1955; B.A., Tex. A. and M. U., 1957; A.F.D. (hon.), London Inst., 1972; m. Etoile Lanell Favor, July 19, 1957; children—Vonda Lynn, Pamela Lee, Bobby Lee, Joseph Lane. With Lone Star Ladder Co., 1957-66, plant mgr., 1966; founder, pres. Acme Ladders, Inc., Houston, 1966—. Past pres. Gulf Meadows Civic Assn.;

spl. adviser, master of ceremonies Consular Ball of Houston, 1964-76; master of ceremonies Noches Americas Internat. Ball; past protocol rep. Office of Mayor; past v.p. Greater Houston Civic Assn., 1965-67; mem. fund raising com. Nat. Jewish Hosp., Denver, 1970-74. Commr., chmn. Galveston County Drainage Dist. 3, 1973—; bd. dirs. Mayor's Houston Taipia Sister City Com., 1968-71. Served with USAF, 1955-56. Mem. C. of C. Baptist (v.p. 1969-70). Clubs: Masons (master), Shriners. Home: 367 Corinthian Way Corinthian Point TX 77378 Office: Box 26593 Houston TX 77207

PLYLER, WILLIAM OGDEN, restaurant exec.; b. Memphis, July 20, 1948; s. Tracy and Ann Clark (Ogden) P., Jr.; student U. So. Miss., 1966-67, U. Tenn., Knoxville, 1967 69, Columbia Community Coll., 1970-71, Memphis State U., 1971-72; m. Suzanne Claire Overton, Nov. 23, 1971; children—William Ogden II, Clair Overton. Pres., Wendy's of Memphis, 1973-76, Wencal Mgmt., Inc., Memphis, 1976-79; owner, pres. Wenco Mgmt., Inc., Memphis, 1976—; owner, operator Double WW Ranch, Rossville, Tenn., 1977—. Named col. State of Tenn., hon. gov. State of Ohio, hon. exec. asst. to mayor Shelby County. Mem. Am. Hereford Assn., Nat. Cattleman's Assn., Tenn. Livestock Assn., Memphis Restaurant Assn. (dir. 1973-76, dir. sr. achievement 1977—). Republican. Episcopalian. Home: Route 1 Box 123 Rossville TN 38066 Office: 2500 Mt Moriah St Suite 300 Memphis TN 38118

PODANY, ELVIRA CHARLOTTE, cosmetologist; b. Milw., May 17, 1917; d. Frank and Elizabeth Augusta (Willison) Ogrentz; student Cudahy (Wis.) pub. schs.; m. William Podany, Feb. 23, 1946; 1 dau., Julie Ann Podany Bellin. Owner, Central Beauty Shop, Port Washington, Wis., 1936-45, Vera's Style Salon, Port Washington, 1945-55, Beauté by Vera, Cedarburg, Wis., 1943-48, Beauté by Vera, West Bend, Wis., 1955—, Vera's II, West Bend, 1976—, also PCE Enterprises, West Bend; tech. instr. cosmetology and related subjects Wis. Tech. Inst. Recipient 1st Place, State Style Body, 1956. Lic. State Cosmetology instr. Mem. Nat. Hairdressers Assn., Wis., Hairdressers c Assn., Wis. Hair Fashion Com., Bus. and Profl. Women's Club, West Bend C. of C. (dir.). Republican. Club: Moose. Home and office: 446A S Main West Bend WI 53095

PODESTA, MARTIN WILLIAM, advt. agy. exec.; b. San Jose, Calif., Apr. 6, 1947; m. Nancy Jean McMahon, 1969; children—Mark Anthony, Amy Elizabeth, Annemarie. Sales rep. Empire Broadcasting Co., San Jose, 1972-73; account exec. Darien, Russell and Hill Advt., San Jose, 1973-76; pres. Martin Podesta Co., San Jose, 1976—; owner Italian Fishing Co., 1979—. Mem. Consumer Affairs Commn. Santa Clara County, 1978-80, chmn., 1980. Served with U.S. Army, 1966-68. Office: 100 N Winchester Blvd San Jose CA 95128

POEHLMAN, CLARE FRANCIS, automotive parts distbn. co. exec.; b. Windsor, Ont., Can., June 28, 1931; came to U.S. 1970, naturalized, 1975; s. Francis Clare and Jean Helen (Keith) P.; B.B.A., U. Windsor, 1954; m. Patricia Ann, May 16; children—Lee Ann, Keith Clare. Dir. mktg.-aftermarket Can. Kenworth Co., Vancouver, B.C., Can., 1964-70; dir. mktg. and service parts Internat. Harvester Co., Chgo., 1970-77; v.p. sales-indsl. and aftermarket Sheller Globe Corp., Toledo, 1977—. Recipient award Automotive Service Industry Assn. Mem. Pacific N.W. Ski Instrs. Assn. Baptist. Club: Masons. Home: 3857 Millrun Ct Toledo OH 43623 Office: 1505 Jefferson Ave Toledo OH 43624

POEHNER, RAYMOND GLENN, banker; b. Cleve., Oct. 1, 1923; s. Raymond Frank and Winifred (Kirchbaum) P.; student pub. schs., Chgo. and Cleve.; m. Frances E. Dunaway Gillespie, Jan. 4, 1958; children—R. David, Jacquline Diane, Leslie Marie, Jon Anthony, Rebecca Glen; stepchildren—Bruce Gillespie, Tony Gillespie. Enlisted U.S. Navy, 1941, advanced through grades to chief petty officer, 1957, ret., 1965; with Security Pacific Nat. Bank, San Diego, 1966—, loan officer, 1971-74, credit card officer, 1975—81, asst. br. mgr., 1974-81, asst. mgr., 1981—. Mem. U.S. Naval Inst., Am. Security Council, Am. Biog. Soc. Republican. Club: Optimist (dir. 1978). Home: 6674 Water St Gulf Breeze FL 32561 Office: 4144 El Cajon Blvd San Diego CA 92105

POHL, KENNETH ROY, electronics co. exec.; b. Beloit, Wis., Nov. 11, 1941; s. Walter John and Ruth Margret (Wieck) P.; student Wis. State Coll., Whitewater, 1959-60, Milton Coll., 1963-66; A.A. in Liberal Arts; m. Deloris Jean Harris, Sept. 22, 1970. With Beloit Corp., 1960-63; mgr. trainee Faimly Fin. Corp., 1966; with Chrysler Corp., 1966-67; owner, operator bowling alley and lounge, 1967-68; with Automatic Electric Co., Genoa, Ill., 1968-69; buyer Fox Corp., Janesville, Wis., 1969-70; materials mgr. Clinton Electronic Corp., Loves Park, Ill., 1970-72, supr. sales adminstrn., 1972-80, import-export mgr. and corp. gen. traffic mgr., 1980-81, import-export mgr., corp. gen. traffic and distbn. mgr., 1981—; dir. Air Pack Enterprises, Inc., Schaumburg, Ill.; cons. internat. transp.; mem. Midwest Shippers Adv. Fed. Maritime Commn. Founder, exec. dir. Tri-State All Star Bowling Assn. Mem. Am. Prodn. and Inventory Control Soc., Ill. C. of C. Lutheran. Clubs: Lions, Rock River Valley Traffic; World Trade (charter mem., pres. 1980) (Nortren, Ill.). Home: 134 Carey Dr PO Box L Clinton WI 53525 Office: 6701 Clinton Rd Box 2277 Loves Park IL 61131

POHLMANN, WILLIAM ALBERT, trust co. exec.; b. Detroit, Sept. 9, 1939; s. William Kuno and Lillian Augusta Marie Antonio (Muenzmaier) P.; B.B.A. in Fin., U. Wis., Milw., 1962, postgrad. in bus., 1965-72; m. Patty Lou Gooler, June 9, 1962; children—William Andrew, Barry Alan. Security analyst Marine Nat. Exchange Bank Milw., 1962-70; trust investment officer Midland Nat. Bank Milw., 1970-72; chief operating officer East Wis. Trustee Co., Manitowoc, 1972—, chief exec. officer, 1978—, pres., 1979—, also dir.; lectr. Manitowoc Center, U. Wis., 1978—. Pres., Manitowoc United Way, Y's Mens Club; bd. dirs., treas. Manitowoc-Two Rivers YMCA. Mem. Fin. Analysts Fedn., Milw. Investment Analysts Soc., Wis. Trustees Assn., Manitowoc C. of C. (chmn. civic beautification com., pride com.). Club: Manitowoc Rotary. Office: 1000 Franklin St Manitowoc WI 54220

POINDEXTER, EDDIE LLOYD, drug chain exec.; b. Clarksdale, Miss., Oct. 1, 1943; s. Robert and Mary (Arnold) P.; B.S. in Pharmacy, Tex. So. U., 1967; postgrad. Sch. Pharmacy, U. Miss., 1967. With Walgreen Drug Stores, 1967—, mgr. super center, Chgo., 1972-73, dist. mgr. trainee, 1973, dist. mgr. unassigned, 1974-75, central dist. mgr., Chgo., 1975—. Mem. adv. bd. Chgo. Housing Authority Sr. Centers of Englewood, 1973-77; mem. edn. support rev. bd. Dept. Human Services, 1977—; mem. Englewood Shopping Concourse Commn., 1978—. Recipient Leadership award E.T. Browne Co., N.Y.C., 1978; Outstanding and Dedicated Service award Dept. Human Services, 1978; registered pharmacist, Miss., Ill., Ind. Mem. Am., Ill. pharm. assns., Chgo. Pharmacists Assn. (officer), Nat. Pharmacists Assn., Englewood Bus. Men's Assn. (pres.), Omega Psi Phi, Alpha Kappa Mu. Methodist. Home: 8959 S Cregier Ave Chicago IL 60617 Office: 7000 W 111 St Worth IL 60482

POINDEXTER, SHARON FAYE, mgmt. cons. co. exec.; b. Hope, Ark., Feb. 21, 1944; d. Governor and Minnie Maudell (Littrell) Poindexter; B.S. in Edn., Wichita State U., 1969, postgrad. in bus. adminstrn. (fellow), 1972-73. Lectr. English, Wichita (Kans.) State U., 1969-73, dir. tutorial program, 1971-72; dir. tng. Wichita Community Action, 1970-71; communication cons. United Meth. Ministry, 1973-74; pres. Poindexter Assos., consultants, Wichita, 1974—; cons. to fed., state and city govts., nat. bd. YWCA, Nat. council Girl Scouts U.S.A., Nat. Assn. Bank Women, United Meth. Ch.; del. White House Conf. on Small Bus., 1980. Pres., Wichita YWCA; mem. alumni bd. dirs. Wichita State U. Recipient Community Leadership award Wichita State U. Student Leadership Assn., 1979. Mem. Nat. Fedn. Ind. Bus., Nat. Assn. Women Bus. Owners, treas., pres. local chpt.), Am. Soc. Bus. of Mgmt. Consultants, Kans. Assn. Commerce and Industry, Wichita C. of C. (com. chmn.). Mem. Ch. of Religious Sci. Research on small bus., changing work force. Office: 111 W Douglas Ave Suite 509 Wichita KS 67202

POINSETTE, DONALD EUGENE, bus. exec., value mgmt. cons.; b. Fort Wayne, Ind., Aug. 17, 1914; s. Eugene Joseph and Julia Anna (Wyss) P.; student Purdue U., 1934, Ind. U., 1935-37, 64; m. Anne Katherine Farrell, Apr. 15, 1939; children—Donald J., Eugene J., Leo J., Sharon Poinsette Smith, Irene Poinsette Snyder, Cynthia Poinsette West, Maryanne, Philip J. With various cos., 1937-39; metall. research and field sales cons. P.R. Mallory Corp., 1939-49; dist. sales mgr. Derringer Metall. Corp., Chgo., 1949-50; plant engr. Cornell-Dubilier Electric Corp., Indpls., 1950-53; with Jenn-Air Corp., Indpls., 1953-74, purchasing dir., 1953-71, mgr. value engring. and quality control, 1969-74; bus. mgmt. cons. Mays and Assos., Indpls., 1974-76; valve mgmt. cons., Indpls. Named to U.S. Finder's List, Nat. Engrs. Register, 1956. Pres., Marian Coll. Parents Club, Indpls., 1969-70; com. mem. Boy Scouts Am. Nat. trustee Xavier U., 1972-73, Dad's Club, Cin. Mem. Nat. Assn. Purchasing Mgmt., Indpls. Purchasing Mgmt. Assn., Soc. Am. Value Engrs. (certified value specialist; sec.-treas. Central Ind. chpt. 1972-73), Soc. Ret. Execs. Indpls. C. of C., Ind. U., Purdue U. alumni assns., Columbian (pres. 1972-73), Triad choral groups, Internat. Platform Assn., Tau Kappa Epsilon. Club: K.C. (4 deg.). Home: 5760 Susan Dr E Indianapolis IN 46250

POINTER, TOM L., mfg. co. exec.; b. Oklahoma City, May 11, 1949; s. Tom H. and Maxine J. (Duger) P.; B.B.A., U. Okla., 1971; m. Judy M. Hill, June 6, 1970; 1 dau., Christine M. Auditor, Coopers & Lybrand, 1971-72; asst. controller Gaedcke Equip. Co., Houston, 1972-76; controller Weed Eater div. Emerson Electric, Houston, 1976-78; controller BPS div. Baker Internat., Houston, 1978-80; corp. controller Camco, Houston, 1980—; instr. acctg. Houston Community Coll., 1977-78. Active Westbury Civic Club, 1975-80. Served with U.S. Army, 1970-76. C.P.A., Tex. Mem. Houston Jaycees (controller 1977-78), Tex. Soc. C.P.A.'s, Am. Inst. C.P.A.'s, Nat. Assn. Accts., Am. Inst. Corporate Controllers. Clubs: Forum, Atascocita Country. Space City Ski. Office: PO Box 14484 Houston TX 77021

POKORNY, HANS HELLMUT KARL, engring. cons.; b. Berlin-Charlottenburg, Germany, Nov. 27, 1909; arrived Can., 1940, naturalized, 1947; s. Francis Joseph and Erna Louise (Prehn) P.; Ingenieur, Mech. and Elec. Engring., Gauss Inst. Tech., 1932; m. Amy MacGowan, July 17, 1948; children—John Stanley, Louise Evelyn. Prodn. engr. Siemens Works, Berlin, 1932-36; pres. Pokorny Plating Works, Ltd., London, 1936-40; asst. mgr. Machinery Service Ltd., Ville Lasalle, Montreal, Que., Can., 1942-45; pres. Richmond Machine Tool & Die Casting Ltd., v.p. Capitol Industries Ltd., Montreal, 1945-70; pres. Hanson Ltd., cons. to die casting industry, Perth, Ont., 1970—; bd. dirs. Die Casting Research Found. Mcpl. councillor, Perth, 1976—; bd. dirs. Great War Meml. Hosp., 1976—; chmn. North Burgess Library Bd., Perth, 1976—. Mem. Am. Die Casting Inst. (recipient Austin T. Lillegran award 1968, Doehler award 1970), Soc. Die Casting Engrs. (life mem., past pres.), Die Casting Fedn. (gov. 1978-80). Club: Sr. Crafts Fellowship (dir.-in-charge fins. Perth). Author tech. publs. in field. Home and Office: Rural Route 3 Otty Lake Perth ON K7H 3C5 Canada

POLACH, JAROSLAV (JAY) GEORGE, economist, internat. lawyer, govt. ofcl.; b. Ostrava, Czechoslovakia, Apr. 20, 1914; s. Francis and Marie (Pach) P.; came to U.S., 1952, naturalized, 1957; A.B., Tech. Coll., Ostrava, 1933; D. Law, Masaryk U., Brno, Czechoslovakia, 1938; M.A. in Econs., Am. U., Washington, 1958, Ph.D. in Econs., 1962; LL.M., George Washington U., 1959; m. Eva Bozena Mocek, Feb. 8, 1943. Corporate counsellor, mem. bd. adminstrn. Czechoslovakian Metall. Works, Ferromet, 1946-48; internat. analyst, editor U.S. Govt., Washington, 1948-60; staff economist, research asso. Resources for Future Inc., Washington, 1961-70; sr. industry economist/Econ. Adv. group IRS, Washington, 1970-75; sr. advisor energy, internat. economist Office of Sec. Dept. Treasury, Washington, 1975—; lectr. econs. and indsl. orgns., U. Md., 1970—; bd. dirs. Internat. Research Inst., Inc., 1968-69; Served with Czechoslovakian Armed Forces, 1939-43, RAF, 1943-45. Recipient certificate of achievement IRS, 1973. Mem. Czechoslovak Soc. Arts Scis. Am. (chmn., editor), Am. Sokol (exec. com. 1970—), Am. Soc. Internat. Law (standing com. nuclear energy world order 1968-73), Internat. Econs. Soc. Contbr. articles and revs. in field to profl. publs. Home: 225 Panorama Dr Oxon Hill MD 20021

POLAYES, MAURICE BENJAMIN, electronic and indsl. test equipment distbg. co. exec.; b. New Haven, May 9, 1923; s. Abraham N. and Ida (Stern) P.; student Colo. U., 1941-43, Boston U., 1952; spl. degree Harvard U. Grad. Sch. Bus. Adminstrn., 1971; m. Adele Toby Oren, Apr. 22, 1963; children—Andrew, Gregory. Staff engr. Sta. WELI, New Haven, 1943-44, Sta. WSTC, Stamford, Conn., 1944; sr. engr. Sta. WLAW, ABC, Boston, 1944-54; engr. in charge radio Andover Police Dept., 1946-51; sales mgr. N.E. area Philips Indsl. Instrumentation Dealer, 1954-59; pres. Addelco Corp., Needham, Mass., since 1959—; dir. Astro Communications Co.; mgmt. cons., 1955—; adviser on disaster communications, 1954—. Active Boy Scouts Am. Registered profl. engr., Mass. Fellow Am. Soc. for Nondestructive Testing (past chmn. Boston sect.); mem. IEEE, Nat. Soc. Profl. Engrs., Am. Inst. Aeros. and Astronautics, Soc. for Exptl. Stress Analysis, Instrument Soc. Am., Harvard Bus. Sch. Assn. Boston. Clubs: Harvard (Boston), Harvard Faculty, Rotary. Contbr. articles on nondestructive testing, instrumentation and applications, phys. measurement applications, automated electronic testing procedures to profl. publs. Home: 82 Pine Grove St Needham MA 02194 Office: 56 Pickering St Needham MA 02192

POLIAN, HAROLD O., investment banker; b. Omaha, Oct. 14, 1893; s. John A. and Ida Louise (Brandt) P.; LL.B., Creighton U., 1921; m. Gladys L. Fessenden, 1921; children—Virginia Avalon, Maxine Lenore. With Peters Trust Co., Omaha, 1921-26; investment banker Smith Polian & Co., Omaha, 1927—; chmn. finance com. So. Calif. Water Co., Los Angeles; chmn. bd. Edison Sault Electric Co., Sault Ste. Marie, Mich., Kirkpatrick, Pettis, Smith, Polian, Inc., 1966—. Trustee Neb. Meth. Hosp. Mem. Neb. Investment Bankers Assn. (past pres.), Omaha C. of C., Am. Legion. Presbyn. Clubs: Union League (Chgo.); Omaha, Omaha Press, Happy Hollow. Home: 2527 Country Club Ave Omaha NE 68104 Office: 1623 Farnam St Suite 700 Omaha NE 68102

POLICELLA, ANTHONY JAMES, parking system corp. exec.; b. Beacon, N.Y., Sept. 2, 1944; s. Donato Anthony and Mildred Lorraine (Burke) P.; B.A., SUNY, New Paltz, 1971; m. Paulette Resnick, Mar. 3, 1978; 1 dau., Hilary. Dir. operational controls and procedures Meyers Parking Systems, Inc., N.Y.C., 1971-75, v.p., officer, 1977—; contract adminstr. Edison Parking Corp., Newark, 1975-77. Mem. Nat. Parking Assn., Instl. and Mcpl. Parking Congress, Transp. Research Bd., Downtown Research and Devel. Center, Calif. Parking Assn., Met. Garage Bd. Trade, Downtown Council Poughkeepsie (N.Y.). Contbr. articles in field to profl. publs. Home: 226 W Clinton Ave Tenafly NJ 07670 Office: 1441 Broadway New York NY 10018

POLINGER, DAVID HARRIS, broadcasting exec.; b. N.Y.C., Mar. 16, 1927; s. Elliot Hirsch and Raye (Newberger) P.; A.B., Duke U., 1949; M.A., N.Y. U., 1971; grad. Indsl. Coll. Armed Forces, 1965-67; m. Roberta Gilman, Jan. 20, 1952; children—Mark Joseph, Doria Lyn. Free-lance radio and TV producer-dir., N.Y.C., 1950; dir. Latin Am. div. Voice of Am., N.Y.C., 1951-52; v.p., gen. mgr. WKAQ-TV, San Juan, P.R., 1953-54; pres. Inter-Am. Prodns., Inc., San Juan, 1954-56; v.p., gen. mgr. WAPA-TV, San Juan, 1955-57, WNTA AM-FM-TV and NTA Spot Sales, N.Y.C., 1958-59; exec. v.p. Lewis & Polinger Advt. Agy., Washington, 1959-60; pres. broadcast div. Friendly Frost, Inc., Westbury, N.Y., WTFM, N.Y.C., WGLI, Babylon, N.Y., WQMF, Babylon, 1961-70; communications cons. to cable TV operations radio and TV stas., broadcast reps., N.Y., 1961—; pres. Suburban Broadcasting Corp., L.I., 1973-76; v.p. Holmes Protection, Inc., N.Y.C., 1970-73; v.p. ops. Bell Television, Inc., N.Y.C., 1970-73; v.p., asst. to pres. WPIX, Inc., N.Y.C., 1976—; adj. prof. communications N.Y. Inst. Tech., Old Westbury; adj. prof. bus. adminstrn. Dowling Coll., Oakdale, N.Y., Coll. Ins., N.Y.C.; adj. prof. communications CCNY. Pres., Carcinoid Tumor and Seratonin Research Found., 1969—; mem. alumni admissions com. Duke U., N.Y., 1969—; mem. adv. com. Manhattan Narcotics Addition Control Commn., 1970—; trustee Performing Arts Found., Island Symphony Soc.; v.p. Internat. Radio and TV Found., 1979—; mem. council Hofstra U. Served with USNR, 1944-46. Mem. Nat. Def. Exec. Res., Nat. Assn. Broadcasters (chmn. FM com. 1967-68, chmn. com. cable copyright royalties 1979—), Broadcast Pioneers, Nat. Acad. TV Arts and Scis., Internat. Broadcasting Soc., Internat. Radio and TV Soc. (v.p. Internat. Radio and TV Found. 1978—), L.I. Advt. Club, Advt. Club N.Y., Jaycees, Navy League, Alpha Epsilon Rho. Home: 500 E 77th St New York NY 10021 Office: 11 WPIX Plaza New York NY 10017

POLITZINER, NORMAN JAY, ins. and pension cons.; b. New Brunswick, N.J., Oct. 30, 1942; s. Seymour and Ethel (Watkin) P.; B.S., N.Y. U., 1964; M.B.A., Rutgers U., 1966; m. Dorothy Miriam Strauss, Oct. 19, 1968; children—Deborah, Amanda. Mgr. carpet dept. Bloomingdales, N.Y.C., 1967-68; asst. buyer Sears Roebuck & Co., N.Y.C., 1969; v.p. ops. Diamond Supply Co., New Brunswick, N.J., 1969-77; sales cons. Modern Estate Planning, Edison, N.J., 1978—; cons. retail trade. Mem. North Brunswick Com. for Gifted Children, 1977—; mem. fundraising com. North Brunswick Jewish Community Center. Served with AUS, 1966-72. Mem. Nat. Assn. Life Underwriters. Home: 1505 N Indian Pl North Brunswick NJ 08902 Office: 1628 Oak Tree Rd Edison NJ 08817

POLIZZI, NICHOLAS GERALD, constrn. co. exec.; b. Cleve., Dec. 3, 1935; s. Alfred M. and Philomena (Valentino) P.; B. Bldg. Constrn., U. Fla., 1957; m. Mary Ann Palmer, Aug. 4, 1974; children—Michael Christian, Nicole Antoinette, Andrea, Phillip. Vice pres., dir. Thompson-Polizzi Constrn. Co., Coral Gables, Fla., 1957-60; sec., treas., dir. Polizzi Constrn. Co., Coral Gables, 1960-75; pres. Polizzi Constrn. Co., Coral Gables, 1975-80, Nicholas G. Polizzi & Assos., constrn. cons., 1975-80, The Polozzi Cos., 1980—. Active Met. Dade County Unsafe Structures and Minimum Housing Appeals Bd., 1966-70, Met. Dade County Planning Adv. Bd., 1974—; ann. mem. Dade County United Way, 1964—, div. chmn., 1967-71; dir. Dade County March of Dimes, 1969-70; trustee Met. Mus. and Art Center, 1971—, sec. bd., 1977-78; mgmt. trustee to various labor benefit trusts, 1965-75; pres. Progress for Dade County, 1973-79; chmn. bd. trustees Constrn. Industry Advancement Fund, 1961—. Served with USAF Res., 1958-62. Recipient Am. Service Honor medal, Citizens com. Army, Navy, Air Force, 1958. Mem. Asso. Gen. Contractors Am. (chpt. pres. 1971-72; chpt. dir. 1967—), State Council Am. Gen. Contractors (mem. com. 1966), Beta Theta Pi. K.C. (trustee 1964-67). Clubs: Palm Bay, University (Miami, Fla.). Home: 4980 San Amaro Dr Coral Gables FL 33146 Office: 298 Granello Ave Coral Gables FL 33146

POLK, ROBERT CHARLES, public transp. exec.; b. Detroit, Apr. 18, 1938; s. Wardell Alfonso and Josephine Annette (Wheeler) P.; B.A. in Psychology and Edn. (univ. fellow 1961), Dillard U., New Orleans, 1962; m. Ella Kathryn Lewis, July 17, 1961; children—Robert Charles, Renata M., Regene C., Rasha C. Tchr., Detroit Public Schs., 1962-64; trainee Gen. Motors Corp., 1964-65; indsl. relations rep. Ford Motor Co., 1965-68; labor relations supr. LTV-Aero Space Co., Warren, Mich., 1968-72; labor relations mgr. Vernors Inc., Detroit, 1972-74, RC Cola, Houston, 1974-76; asst. dir. staff services St. Luke's Hosp., Tex. Children's Hosp., Tex. Heart Inst., Houston, 1976-79; now labor relations mgr. in field of public transp., Houston. Bd. advs. Detroit YMCA, 1969; precinct del. Tex. Democratic State Conv., 1977. Mem. Am. Arbitration Assn., Am. Public Transit Assn., Am. Soc. Personnel Adminstrn., Houston Personnel Assn., Kappa Alpha Psi (outstanding undergrad. award Southwestern region 1962). Home: 11402 Hillcraft St Houston TX 77035 Office: 6001 Gulf Freeway Houston TX 77023

POLL, ROBERT EUGENE, JR., investment banker; b. Urbana, Ill., Apr. 16, 1948; s. Robert Eugene and Dorothy (Baker) P.; A.B., Kenyon Coll., 1970; M.B.A., Ind. U., 1972; postgrad. Pub. Fin. Inst., U. Mich., 1976; m. Leslie Boutwell Tompkins, Aug. 8, 1970. Asst. treas., portfolio investment banking div. Chase Manhattan Bank, N.Y.C., 1974-76, 2d v.p. treasury div., 1976-77, v.p. treasury div., 1977-78; investment banker Lazard Freres & Co., 1978—. Adviser, Ind. Small Bus. Assistance Program, 1970; adv. bd. U. Mich. Pub. Fin. Inst. Mem. N.Y. Acad. Scis., Am. Mgmt. Assn., Am. Mktg. Assn., Nat. Trust Historic Preservation, Ind. U., Kenyon Coll. alumni assns., Westchester Arts Council, Delta Tau Delta. Republican. Episcopalian. Clubs: Union League, Wharton Bus. (N.Y.C.); Rockaway Hunt; Lawrence Beach; Cedarhurst Yacht. Home: 177 E 77th St Apt 6B New York NY 10017 Office: Lazard Freres & Co One Rockefeller Plaza New York NY 10020

POLLACK, RICHARD MARTIN, banker; b. Bklyn., June 20, 1929; s. Walter and Pauline (Woitovich) P.; B.S. cum laude, N.Y. U., 1960; m. Joan McLinskey, Feb. 14, 1953; children—Karen, Gary, Kenneth, Gwen. Asst. sec. Mfrs. Trust Co., N.Y.C., 1947-59; asst. v.p. Meadowbrook Nat. Bank, West Hempstead, N.Y., 1960-64; with Sears Bank and Trust Co., Chgo., 1964—, exec. v.p. investment div., 1980—. Dir. banking research com. Northwestern U.; chmn. Chgo. div. Jr. Achievement of Chgo., 1979; past mem. coms. Crusade of Mercy, Chgo. Mem. Fin. Execs. Inst., Dealer Bank Assn., Municipal Bond Club. Republican. Roman Catholic. Office: Sears Bank and Trust Co Sears Tower Chicago IL 60606

POLLACK, ROY HOWARD, radio co. exec.; b. New Rochelle, N.Y., 1927; B.S.E.E., M.E., Columbia U.; married. Div. v.p., gen. mgr. Fairchild Camera & Instrument Co., 1971-73; with RCA Corp., 1950-71, 73—, corp. v.p., gen. mgr. consumer electronics div.,

1974-79, corp. group v.p., 1979, exec. v.p., 1979—, also dir. Office: 30 Rockefeller Plaza New York NY 10020*

POLLACK, STEPHEN J., stockbroker; b. N.Y.C., Aug. 25, 1937; s. Harold S. and Gladys H. Pollack; B.S. in Econs., Wharton Sch., U. Pa., 1960. Vice pres. retail sales Drexel Burnham Lambert, N.Y.C., 1960-77; v.p., asst. mgr. Dean Witter Reynolds Inc., N.Y.C., 1977—. Served with USAR, 1966. Mem. Internat. Assn. Fin. Planners, Assn. Investment Bankers (dir.). Jewish. Clubs: Young Men's Philanthropic, Town, Atrium, Schuylkill Country, Wharton Sch., U. Pa., Yale, Fresh Meadow Country. Home: 245 E 40th St Apt 14-E New York NY 10016 Office: Dean Witter Reynolds Inc 919 Third Ave New York NY 10022

POLLAK, NORMAN LEE, accountant; b. Chgo., Aug. 16, 1931; s. Emery and Helen (Solomon) P.; diploma in commerce Northwestern U., 1955; postgrad. Pierce Coll., 1960-63, UCLA Extension; m. Hilda Tea Brower, June 16, 1980; ciildren—Martin Joel, Elise Susan, Rhonda Louise. Jr., sr. accountant David Himmelblau & Co., Chgo., 1952-56; sr. accountant Barrios, Hilliard, Sain & Co., Beverly Hills, Calif., 1957-58; pvt. practice C.P.A., Encino, also Van Nuys, Calif., 1958-62 Sherman Oaks, Calif., 1962—, Westlake Village, Calif., 1971—; pres. Norman L. Pollak Accountancy Corp., 1971—. Guest lectr. U. Calif. at Westwood, also Los Angeles, 1962; speaker, lectr., before various civic and profl. groups. Mem. Valley Estate Planning Council, sec., 1962-63, v.p., 1963-64, pres., 1964-65; v.p. Ventura County Estate Planning Council, 1977-78, pres., 1979. C.P.A., Calif. Mem. Am. Inst. C.P.A.'s, Calif. Soc. C.P.A.'s (com. cooperation credit grantors, securities industry com., chmn. San Fernando Valley tech. discussions group 1960-61), Am. Accounting Assn., Nat. Assn. Accountants Delta Mu Delta, Northwestern Alumni Club. Jewish (past financial sec. temple). Mem. B'nai B'rith (past treas.). Home: 31731 Foxfield Dr Westlake Village CA 91361 Office: 32107 Lindero Canyon Rd Suite 225 Westlake Village CA 91361

POLLAN, STEPHEN MICHAEL, investment co. exec., real estate cons., author; b. N.Y.C., May 19, 1929; s. Robert David and Harriet (Morganstern) P.; student L.I. U., 1947-49, Coll. City N.Y., 1949-51; LL.B., Bklyn. Law Sch., 1951, J.D., 1976; m. Corinne Staller, July 18, 1954; children—Michael, Lori, Traci, Dana. Admitted to N.Y. bar, 1951; founder law firm Pollan, Zimmer, Fishbach & Hertan, N.Y.C. and Melville, L.I., N.Y., 1953—; founder, pres. Country Capital Corp., small bus. investment corp., N.Y.C., 1960-70; pres. Royal Bus. Funds Corp., 1970-76; sr. real estate cons. Nat. Bank N. Am., 1976-78; asso. prof. bus. Marymount Manhattan Coll.; chmn. bd. Precision DeLuxe Film Labs., Inc., N.Y.C.; dir. Holmes Protection, Bell TV, Electro Sound Group Inc.; panelist lectr. venture capital industry; mem. small bus. investment co. adv. council SBA; adviser Pres.'s Com. Small Bus., 1974. Vice chmn. UN Com. for UN Day, 1971-72; organizer Collegiate Forum of Air, N.Y.C., 1948; founder Gay Head Taxpayers Assn.; pres. Gay Head Community Council, 1975; bd. dirs. Nassau County (N.Y.) Cerebral Palsy Assn. Mem. Nat. Assn. Small Bus. Investment Cos. (region pres. 1975, bd. govs., certificate of appreciation). Co-author: The Best on Martha's Vineyard; The Consumers Credit Hand Book. Home: 1095 Park Ave New York NY 10028 also Gay Head Martha's Vineyard MA 02535 Office: 221 E 71st St New York NY 10021

POLLARD, ARNOLD BRUCE, mgmt. cons.; b. Bklyn., Dec. 26, 1942; s. Samuel M. and Helen (Kaufman) P.; B.S. in Engring. Physics, Cornell U., 1964; M.S. in Engring. Sci., Stanford U., 1966, Ph.D. in Mgmt. Sci. (AEC fellow), 1969; m. Renee V. Rudin, Aug. 15, 1965; children—Jill Karen, Lisa Meredith. Mgr. decision analysis group Stanford Research Inst., Menlo Park, Calif., 1968-74; pres. Instl. Data Services, Newburgh, N.Y., 1972-74; pres. Decision Assos., Great Neck, N.Y., 1974—; adj. asst. prof. Columbia U. Grad. Sch. Bus., N.Y.C., 1970-72. Mem. Inst. Mgmt. Sci., Tau Beta Pi, Phi Eta Sigma. Clubs: Univ. (N.Y.C.); Fleetwood.

POLLARD, RICHARD FREDERICK, banker; b. Rockville Centre, N.Y., Feb. 27, 1933; s. Arthur H. and Elsa M. (Pathke) P.; B.B.A. magna cum laude, Hofstra U., 1963; postgrad. N.Y. U., 1964-65; m. Evelyn M. Compton, Nov. 30, 1957; children—Jeffrey, David. Successively dir. manpower planning, personnel dir., sr. lending officer, sr. v.p. Chase Manhattan Bank, N.Y.C., 1950-76; exec. v.p. Baybanks, Inc., also pres. Baybank Boston N.A., 1976—. Mem. N.Y.C. Bd. Edn. Coop. Edn. Bd.; nat. bd. dirs. RIF, Inc.; treas., bd. mgrs. Seamen's Ch. Inst.; mem. Maritime Transp. Bd. of Nat. Research Found. Mem. Robert Morris Assos. Republican. Home: 16 Hammond Circle Sudbury MA 01776 Office: 175 Federal St Boston MA 02110

POLLOCK, ARTHUR JESS, lawyer; b. Jersey City, July 22, 1950; s. Meyer and Selma Pollock; B.A., Fairleigh Dickinson U., 1973; J.D., Western State U., 1977. Mktg. research analyst Analysis Research Ltd., San Diego, 1974-76; pres. Advt. and Devel. Assos., San Diego, 1974; v.p. Original Non-Smoking Ashtray Co., Los Angeles, 1978; admitted to Calif. bar, 1977; practice law, San Diego and Los Angeles; of counsel to firm Levy, Bivona & Cohen, N.Y.C. and Los Angeles, Leon J. Kaye, Solicitors, London. Recipient Found. Press award, 1976; Am. Jurisprudence awards, 1974, 75, 76, 77. Mem. Am., Los Angeles County, Beverly Hills bar assns., Am. Trial Lawyers Assn. Office: 2049 Century Park E Suite 2790 Los Angeles CA 90067

POLLOCK, CLARK, broadcasting co. exec.; b. Van Wert, Ohio, Nov. 28, 1924; s. Cheselden Barrett and Leila (Clark) P.; student Purdue U., 1942-43, 46; m. Elizabeth Louise Good, Mar. 26, 1949; children—Christopher Barrett, Micaela Louise, Roland MacGregor. Technician, Purdue U. Theater, 1946-48, staff announcer Sta. WBAA, 1943-47; announcer, copy writer, newsman Radio Stas. WGL and WOWO, Ft. Wayne, Ind., 1944-45; producer, prodn. mgr., program dir. Sta. WNBF, AM, FM, TV, Binghamton, N.Y., 1949-57; program dir. Sta. KVTV, Sioux City, Iowa, 1957-66; dir., v.p. ops. Nationwide Communications Inc., Columbus, Ohio, 1966-74, v.p., gen. mgr., 1974—. Bd. dirs. Columbus Ballet Met. Recipient Spl. award Sioux City chpt. NCCJ, 1966. Mem. Broadcast Edn. Assn. (dir. 1968-73, sec.-treas. 1974, pres. 1975-76). Republican. Episcopalian. Club: Columbus Athletic. Home: 7494 Gatestone Ln Worthington OH 43085 Office: 1 Nationwide Plaza Columbus OH 43216

POLLOCK, LOUISE, fin. planner; b. Pitts., Apr. 2, 1919; d. Walter Edward and Anna Katherine (Schoenberger) Brickman; student U. Tex., 1936-37; grad. Coll. Fin. Planning, 1975-77; m. Robert Thomas Pollock, Mar. 10, 1968 (dec.); children by previous marriages, John W. Carlisle, Jr., Noel Griffin, Carol Klippenstein. Branch mgr. Fort Worth (Tex.) Savs. and Loan Assn., 1954-63, Trevost Savs. & Loan Assn., Phila., 1963-68; estate planning specialist Ralph S. Wilford Co., La Mesa, Calif., 1970-77; pres., certified fin. planner pvt. ledger Fin. Services, Inc., San Diego, 1977; owner Pollock & Assos., fin. planning, San Diego. Pres. council of aux. Coll. of Emeiti. Mem. Internat. Assn. Fin. Planners, Nat. Alumni Assn. Coll. Fin. Planning, Profl. Women's Center (emeriti counsel), Women in Bus., Bus. and Profl. Clubs San Diego (pres.'s council). Republican. Swedenborgian. Club: Altrusa (pres.). Home: 400 Greenfield Dr Sp 37 El Cajon CA 92021 Office: 2515 Camino del Rio S Suite 204 San Diego CA 92108

POLLOCK, WILLIAM KENNETH, apparel co. exec.; b. Chgo., June 7, 1942; s. Kenneth William and Miriam (Inglis) P.; student Ripon Coll., 1960, Pittsburg State U., 1961; B.A., U. Oreg., 1964; m. Aileen Cheatham, Sept. 6, 1969; children—Penny Paige, Heather Morgan. With Key Industries, Inc., Fort Scott, Kans., 1964-72, corp. sec., office mgr., 1967-72; pres. Allee, Inc., Madisonville, Tex., 1972-80; pres. Key Industries, Inc., Fort Scott, 1980—. Republican. Home: 304 W 9th St Fort Scott KS 66701 Office: PO Box 389 Fort Scott KS 66701

POLOWAY, RICHARD JOEL, mfg. co. exec.; b. Balt., Apr. 28, 1952; s. Robert and Shirley (Stolker) P.; B.A., Oglethorpe U., 1973; M.B.A., Loyola Coll., Balt., 1981. Theatre mgr. Center Stage, Balt., 1969-70, Peachtree Exptl. Theatre, Atlanta, 1971-72, Atlanta Children's Theatre, 1972-73, English Theatre of Israel, Tel Aviv, 1974-75, The Khan Theatre, Jerusalem, 1975-76, Once Upon A Stage, Orlando, Fla., 1976-77, Bolton Hill Dinner Theatre, Balt., 1977; exec. v.p. Bilt-In Wood Products Inc., Balt., 1977—. Cert. pvt. pilot. Mem. Actors Equity Assn., AFTRA, Nat. Assn. Plastic Fabricators, Nat. Kitchen Cabinets Assn., Am. Inst. Kitchen Designers, Md. Homebuilders Assn. Club: Shipmates Motorcycle. Home: 2025 Druid Park Dr Baltimore MD 21211 Office: 3500 Clipper Rd Baltimore MD 21211

POLSKY, BARRY PAUL, public relations exec.; b. Chgo., June 7, 1940; s. Samuel Charles and Reva (Schultz) P.; A.B., U. Ill., 1961; m. Myra Rae Herson, July 2, 1972; children—Anne, Elizabeth. Editor, reporter The Jewish Week, Washington, 1965-68; reporter Chgo. Tribune, 1968-70, Congressional Quarterly, Washington, 1970-74; v.p. Carl Byoir & Assos., Inc., Washington, 1974—. Served with USAR, 1962-64. Mem. Public Relations Soc. Am., Internat. Assn. Bus. Communicators. Co-author: Watergate: Chronology of a Crisis, 1974. Office: 1899 L St NW Washington DC 20036

POLSON, MARLENE ANN, coll. bookstore mgr.; b. Pittsfield, Mass., Sept. 1, 1953; d. Francis Grover and Lucille Theresa (Ruscetta) P.; Asso. in Bus. Careers, Berkshire Community Coll., 1975; basic cert. Am. Inst. Banking, 1976; postgrad. in bus. adminstrn. Rochester (N.Y.) Inst. Tech. With City Savs. Bank Pittsfield, 1974-76; textbook coordinator Bookstore, Rochester Inst. Tech., 1976-77, asst. textbook mgr., 1977, textbook mgr., 1977-79, mgr. Rochester Inst. Tech. Bookstore at Eisenhower Coll., Seneca Falls, N.Y., 1979—. Mem. Nat. Assn. Coll. Stores (seminar cert. 1979), Assn. Am. Pubs. (fin. cert. 1979). Office: Rochester Inst Tech Bookstore at Eisenhower Coll Route 89 Seneca Falls NY 13148

POLT, GEORGE DEWEY, JR., real estate broker and appraiser; b. Hunterdon County, N.J., July 9, 1926; s. George Dewey and Anna Janet (Schafer) P.; ed. pub. schs., Teterboro (N.J.) Sch. Aeros.; m. Margaret Carolyn Coleman, Mar. 15, 1952 (div. 1980); children—Cynthia Ann, Terry Jane, Charles Herbert, George Woodward. Salesman, Gen. Baking Co., Easton, Pa., 1952; repair and maintenance supr. Polt Bus Co., Glen Gardner, N.J., 1952-68; registered rep., securities broker Investment Services, Belvidere, N.J., 1968-71; real estate broker George D. Polt, Jr., Washington, N.J., 1970—. Charter mem. Lebanon Twp. Fire Co.; mem. Lebanon Twp. Bd. Adjustments, 1971, Lebanon Twp. Governing Body, 1972-74; mayor Lebanon Twp., 1974. Served with USAAF, 1944-46. Mem. Warren County (v.p., dir. 1976, pres. 1977), N.J. (dir.) bds. Realtors. Home: 424 Hollow Rd Glen Gardner NJ 08826 Office: 129 E Washington Ave Washington NJ 07882

POLYCHRON, JOHN P., consumer products co. exec.; b. Valley Stream, N.Y., Aug. 9, 1936; s. Harry Robert and Lucille Elizabeth (McLaughlin) P.; B.S. in Economics, U. Pa., 1958; M.B.A., N.Y. U., 1970; m. Adrienne Lecraw, Oct. 8, 1977; children—Leslie Dale, Jason John. Salesman, Procter & Gamble Co., N.Y.C., 1958-62; dir. sales T.J. Lipton, Inc., Englewood Cliffs, N.J., 1962-74; pres., chief exec. officer Popsicle Industries, Englewood, N.J., 1974-79, R. J. Reynolds Tabacosdo Brasil Ltd., Rio de Janeiro, 1979—. Mem. Am. Logistics Assn. Clubs: Knickerbocker Country, Jockey, Gavea Golf and Country. Home: Rua Leoncio Correia 150 Rio de Janeiro Brazil 22450 Office: Caixa Postal 3588 Rio de Janeiro Brazil 20000

POLYDORIS, NICHOLAS G., mfg. co. exec.; b. Chgo., July 7, 1930; s. George and Annetta (Karas) P.; B.S.E.E., Northwestern U., 1954; m. Gloria Lucas, May 28, 1952; children—Stephen, Janet, Lynn, Susan, Nancy. Trainee, Fairbanks Morris Co., 1954-55; dist. mgr. Fasco Industries, Rochester, N.Y., 1955-57; founder, pres., dir. ENM Co., Chgo., 1957—; dir. Gladstone-Norwood Bank. Bd. dirs. Great Hellenic Found., North Shore Mental Health Assn. Recipient Service award Northwestern U., 1965. Mem. Ill., Nat. socs. profl. engrs., Pres. Orgn. Club: Kenilworth, Michigan Shores, John Evans. Home: 327 Leicester Rd Kenilworth IL 60043 Office: 20 N Wacker Dr Chicago IL 60606

POMERANTZ, SHERWIN BERNARD, data processing exec.; b. N.Y.C., Nov. 18, 1939; s. Sidney and Anna (Simons) P.; B.S. in Indsl. Engring., N.Y. U., 1960; M.S. in Mech. Engring. (teaching fellow), U. Ill., 1962; m. Barbara Sue Rashbaum, Jan. 27, 1962; children—Shari, Deborah. Instr. mech. engring. U. Ill., Champaign, 1960-62; instr. engring. drawing Cuyahoga Community Coll., Cleve., 1962-64; controller Masten Corp., Chgo., 1964-1966; pres. founder Controls for Industry Inc., Chgo., 1966—. Pres., Allied Jewish Sch. Bd. Met. Chgo., 1975-78; pres. Maine Twp. Jewish Congregation, Des Plaines, Ill., 1976-78; exec. v.p. bd. Jewish Edn. Met. Chgo., 1978—; pres. Midwest region United Synagogue Am., 1978—, also chmn. council regional presidents; bd. dirs. World Council of Synagogues, 1979—. Served to capt. Signal Corps U.S. Army, 1962-64. Named Man of Yr., Israel Bond Orgn., 1973. Mem. ASME, Chgo. Assn. Commerce and Industry, Mensa, Alpha Epsilon Pi (nat. v.p.). Weekly columnist Chgo. Jewish Post and Opinion, 1975-78; contbr. articles to profl. jours. Home: 8812 Church St Des Plaines IL 60016 Office: 2635 Peterson Ave Chicago IL 60659

POMERANZ, FELIX, accountant; b. Vienna, Austria, Mar. 28, 1926; s. Joseph and Irene (Meninger) P.; B.B.A., Coll. City N.Y., 1948; M.S., Columbia U., 1949; m. Rita Lewin, June 14, 1953; children—Jeffrey Arthur, Andrew Joseph. Audit staff Coopers & Lybrand, C.P.A.'s, N.Y.C., 1949-56, dir. operational auditing, 1966-68, partner, 1968—; mgr. Marks, Grey & Shron (now Kenneth Leventhal & Co.), C.P.A.'s, 1956-58; asst. chief auditor Am.-Standard, N.Y.C., 1958-62; mgr. systems Westvaco Corp., N.Y.C., 1962-66. Mem. adv. com. New Sch. for Social Research; trustee Nat. Center for Automated Info. Retrieval. Served to 1st lt. AUS, 1944-46, 51-52. C.P.A., N.Y., Va., La., N.C. Mem. Am. Inst. C.P.A.'s (chmn. com. on social reporting), N.Y. State Soc. C.P.A.'s, Am. Prodn. and Inventory Control Soc., Assn. Systems Mgmt., Acad. Acctg. Historians (trustee), Assn. Govt. Accts., Intergovtl. Audit Forums, Am. Acctg. Assn., Columbia Bus. Assos., Beta Gamma Sigma. Co-author: Pensions-An Accounting and Management Guide, 1976; Auditing in the Public Sector—Efficiency, Economy, and Program Results, 1976. Contbr. articles to profl. jours. Home: 64-58 213 St Bayside NY 11364 Office: 1251 Ave of Americas New York NY 10020

POMEROY, CHESTER MITCHELL, former chem. and mining co. exec.; b. Gays Mills, Wis., Aug. 26, 1916; s. Harry Ralph and Addie Letucia (Mitchel) P.; student Wis. Inst. Tech., 1940; B.S. in Engring., U. Mo., 1947; m. Marguerite Ethel Muse, June 18, 1944; children—Barbara Gayle Pomeroy Minter, Virginia Cheryl Pomeroy Doxas. With Dupont Co., 1947—, tech. rep., research engr., supt. market devel., Wilmington, Del., 1956-71, mktg. mgr., Phila., N.Y.C., 1971-73, supt. market research, Wilmington, 1973-77, ret., 1977; mktg. cons., 1977—. Area committeeman Republican Com.; elder Presbyterian Ch., Wilmington, 1960—. Served to maj. U.S. Army, 1942-46. Decorated Bronze Star with Oak Leaf Cluster; Breast Order of Yuu Hui (China). Registered profl. engr., Del. Mem. Am. Inst. Mineral Engrs., Soc. Mining Engrs., Chem. Market Research Assn. Republican. Clubs: Masons (33 deg.), Shriners (past potentate), DuPont Country. Patentee in field. Home: 7826 N Pines View Dr McCormick Ranch Scottsdale AZ 85258

POMPAN, JACK MAURICE, mgmt. cons.; b. N.Y.C., Jan. 23, 1926; s. Maurice A. and Helen (Schmidt) P.; B.S. in Indsl. Mgmt., Ga. Inst. Tech., 1948; M.B.A. with distinction, N.Y. U., 1973, advanced profl. certificate, 1978; m. Esther Scharaga, July 4, 1958; children—Neil Charles, Lori Beth. Trainee to budget mgr. Redmond Co., Owosso, Mich., 1948-55; mgmt. cons. Coopers and Lybrand, N.Y.C., 1955-60; controller Hazel Bishop Inc., N.Y.C., 1960-61; treas. Floyds Stores Inc., Valley Stream, N.Y., 1961-66; pres. Farmers Pantry Inc., Mamaroneck, N.Y., 1966-68; v.p. pub. div. Intext, Inc., N.Y.C., 1968-74; prin. Baxter, Pompan & Storr, Mgmt. Cons.'s, Greenwich, Conn., 1974—; adj. prof. Hofstra U., 1977, Roth Grad. Sch. Bus. Adminstrn., C. W. Post Center, L.I. U., 1974-79. Trustee, edn. chmn. Central Synogogue, Rockville Centre, N.Y., 1976—. Served to lt. USNR, 1943-46, 51-53. Mem. Am. Fin. Assn., N.Y. U. Bus. Forum, Nat. Assn. Accts. (cert. of merit 1953), Regional Plan Assn. Bus. and econs. editor Info. Please Almanac, 1978, 79, 80, 81. Home: 389 Raymond St Rockville Centre NY 11570

POMPROWITZ, JOHN JOSEPH, transp. exec. b. Green Bay, Wis., May 7, 1938; s. Joseph and Helen E. (Vander Linden) P.; student Marquette U., 1957; B.S., Tri-State Coll., 1961; m. Mary L. Terp, Oct. 19, 1963; children—Krina A., Joely L., Robin L. With L.C.L. Transit Co., Green Bay, 1961—, pres., 1967—. Pres. Common Carrier Conf.-Irregular Route, 1978; co-chmn. Green Bay Labor Mgmt. Council, 1980. Active YMCA, Boy Scouts Am., YWCA, Diocesan Service Appeal; bd. dirs. Green Bay United Way, 1978—; mem. Brown County Juvenile Adv. Bd., 1979-80. Mem. Green Bay Area C. of C. Republican. Office: PO Box 949 Green Bay WI 54305 Office: PO Box 949 Green Bay WI 54305

POND, BYRON OLIVER, JR., automotive parts mfg. co. exec.; b. Royal Oak, Mich., July 6, 1936; s. Byron Oliver and Irene Alma (Torikka) P.; B.S. in Bus. Adminstrn., Wayne State U., 1961; m. Margaret J. Kenney, Dec. 17, 1960; children—Douglas, David, Byron, Eric. Dist. sales mgr. Fed. Mogul Corp., Cleve., 1965-68; v.p., gen. mgr. nat. accounts Maremont Corp., Chgo., 1974-76, sr. v.p., 1976-78, exec. v.p., dir., 1978, pres., chief exec. officer, 1979—. Served with U.S. Army, 1954-56. Mem. Automotive Parts and Accessories Assn. (dir.). Republican. Office: Maremont Corp 200 Randolph Chicago IL 60601*

POND, CALVIN PARKER, retail co. exec.; b. Mpls., Nov. 6, 1924; s. Clarence Parker and Peggy (Jacobson) P.; student U. Wis., 1946, Grinnell Coll., 1946-48, Mich. State U., 1947; B.A., U. Minn., 1948; M.A., U. Denver, 1950; m. Elizabeth Jeanne Holden, Aug. 26, 1950; children—Shaun Parker, Deborah Jeanne, Berek Martin. With San Antonio Express & News, 1950-51, Statewide Drive-In Theatres, 1951-52; mgr. C. of C., McCook, Neb., 1952-53; exec. dir. Asso. Retailers, Omaha, 1953-54; exec. dir. Denver Retail Mchts. Assn., 1954-58; treas., dir. Magic Mountain Inc., 1956; v.p. Calamac Corp., 1956-58; became pub. relations dir. Denver div. Safeway Stores, Inc., 1967, now v.p., corp. pub. affairs, Oakland, Calif. Mem. Gov.'s Edn!. Adv. Com., 1957-58; exec. com. UN Com. in Colo., 1955-58. Chmn. commerce com. Denver Centennial Commemoration Authority, 1958-59; mem. adv. com. Denver Urban Renewal Authority; bd. dirs. Citizens Mission. exec. com. Mile High United Fund; trustee Colo. Women's Coll., Denver, Booth Meml. Hosp. Served from 2d lt to 1st lt. AUS, 1950-59. ETO. Decorated Bronze Star, Purple Heart; chevalier l'Ordre du Merite Commercial et Industriel (France). Mem. Pub. Relations Soc. Am. (pres. Colo. chpt.), Asso. Colls. Colo. (trustee), Calif. Retail Mchts. Assn., Judo Black Belt Fedn., Colo. C. of C. (dir.), Internat. Downtown Exec. Assn., Am. Retail Assn. Execs., Council Western Retail Assns. (dir.), Denver Retail Mchts. Assn. (dir.), Internat. Platform Assn., Am. Legion, V.F.W. Lion, Elk. Clubs: Commonwealth (San Francisco); University, Nat. Press (Washington). Home: 8073 Hansom Dr Oakland CA Office: Safeway Stores 4th and Jackson Sts Oakland CA 94660

POND, DOUGLAS, banker. Chmn. chief exec. officer Bank of El Paso (Tex.). Office: 5160 Montana Ave El Paso TX 79903*

PONTILLO, GUY JOSEPH, mgmt. cons.; b. N.Y.C., Aug. 14, 1929; s. John and Lena (Pastore) P.; B.B.A., St. John's U., 1952; M.B.A. in Fin., L.I. U., 1980; m. Dorothy Maggipinto, Sept. 20, 1952; children—Donna Maria, Angela, Joanne. Controller, staff asst. Tensolite Insulated Wire Co., Inc., Tarrytown, N.Y., 1956-60; asst. controller Univ. Loudspeakers div. L.T.V., White Plains, N.Y., 1960-63; controller, asst. treas. Superior Mfg. and Instrument Corp., Astoria, N.Y., 1963-69; v.p., chief exec. officer Process Plants Corp., N.Y.C., 1969-77; pres. RM Assos., mgmt. consultants, 1977—. Mem. bd., controller Franciscan Mission Assos.; financial cons. to Order Friars Minor Province Immaculate Conception, 1965—. Served with M.I., AUS, 1952-56. Mem. Am. Inst. Corporate Controllers, Nat. Assn. Accountants, Indsl. Mgmt. Clubs: (pres. zone 4, 1963-64), Delta Psi Upsilon. Roman Catholic (pres. Holy Name Soc., 1961-63). Home and Office: 242 Concord Rd Yonkers NY 10710

POOKRUM, ERIC HEYWOOD, lawyer; b. Detroit, June 28, 1953; s. Max and Evelyn Lucille (Colemen) P.; B.A., Williams Coll., 1975; J.D., Georgetown U., 1979, M.S., 1981; 1 son, Dane D. Admitted to Mich. bar, 1980, D.C. bar, 1980; law clk. Antitrust div. Dept. Justice, Washington, 1976-79; atty.-advisor fin. div. investment mgmt. SEC, Washington, 1979—. Mem. Am. Bar Assn., James Brown Scott Internat. Law Soc., Delta Theta Phi. Home: 1421 Massachusetts Ave #307 Washington DC 20005 Office: 500 N Capitol St Washington DC 20549

POOLE, ARTHUR FRENCH, mfg. co. exec.; b. Bristol, Conn., Jan. 4, 1942; s. Arthur Barnard and Helen (Burdick) P.; B.S., Cornell U., 1964; m. Sayra Babcock, Feb. 17, 1968; 1 dau., Hilary French. Mgmt. cons. Horwath & Horwath, N.Y.C., 1964-65; pres. Colonial Inns, Inc., Torrington, Conn., 1965-66; buyer Torrington Co., 1966-69; mfg. mgr. Mitral Corp., Harwinton, Conn., 1969-72, v.p., 1972—, pres., 1974—; v.p. Yorkshire Ltd., Harwinton, 1974—. Mem. Harwinton Bd. Edn., 1965-73, chmn., 1972-73; mem. Region Dist. 10 Bd. Edn., 1974—, chmn., 1975—; founder, pres. Har-Bur Summer Theatre for Youth, 1969—. Mem. Nat. Tool, Die and Precision Machining Assn. (bd. dirs. Conn. chpt. 1975—), Conn. Bus. and Industry Assn. Club: Harwinton Lions. Home: Burlington Rd Harwinton CT 06790 Office: 1010 County Line Rd Harwinton CT 06790

POOLE, EUGENE HOLCOMBE, mcht., banker; b. Cross Anchor, S.C., Sept. 20, 1907; s. Mark Collier and Kate (Holcombe) P.; B.A., Furman U., 1927; m. Lois Vashti Workman, Oct. 29, 1929; 1 dau., Peggy Lois. Prin., grammar sch., Orangeburg, S.C., 1927-37; founder, mgr. Poole's 5 cents to $1.00 Stores, Holly Hill, S.C., 1937—, also Santee Wholesale Co., Inc., 1947—; chmn., chief exec. officer, dir. Farmers & Mchts. Bank of S.C., 1946—. Past chmn. bd. trustees Orangeburg Regional Hosp.; trustee Furman U., Greenville. Served as lt. USNR, 1944-46. Mem. S.C. Assn. Ind. Banks (dir., past pres.), Am. Legion. Baptist. Clubs: Masons, Lions. Home: Peake St Holly Hill SC 29059 Office: 811 State St Holly Hill SC 29059

POOLE, JOHN W., real estate devel. co. exec. Pres., chief exec. officer Daon Devel. Corp., Vancouver, B.C., Can. Office: 999 W Hastings St Vancouver BC V6C 2W7 Canada*

POOLE, THOMAS CARL, JR., mfg. co. exec.; b. Leeds, Ala., Feb. 19, 1921; s. Thomas Carl and Grace (King) P.; B.S., Auburn U., 1948; postgrad. Coll. Advanced Traffic of Chgo. at Jacksonville State U., 1950-51; m. Mary Louise Miller, Oct. 7, 1960; children—Thomas Carl III, John Preston. Mgr. traffic and shipping planning M & H Valve & Fittings Co. (name now Dresser Mfg. Div.) div. Dresser Industries, Anniston, Ala., 1949—. Traffic cons. various firms, 1960—. Served with USAAF, 1943. Mem. N.E. Ala. Traffic and Transp. Club (gov. 1960), Phi Kappa Tau. Home: Route 5 Box 567 Anniston AL 36201 Office: W 23d St Anniston AL 36201

POOLE, THOMAS MYERS, mgmt. cons.; b. Phila., June 14, 1926; s. Raymond M. and Emma Louise (Myers) P.; B.S. in Econs., Wharton Sch., U. Pa., 1950; postgrad. N.Y. U., 1954-55, Columbia U., 1955-56; m. Jane Pressey, June 25, 1955; children—Joanne Louise, Grace Ellen. Mgr. spl. studies, Richardson-Merrell, N.Y.C., 1950-56; account supr. N.W. Ayer ABH Internat., Phila., N.Y.C., 1956-62; mktg. mgr. Lever Bros. Co., N.Y.C., 1963-72; dir. gen. line mktg., patient care div. Johnson & Johnson, New Brunswick, N.J., 1972-74; v.p., gen. mgr. Airwick Brands div. Ciba-Geigy, Carlstadt, N.J., 1974-75; pres. Thomas M. Poole & Assos., Princeton, N.J., 1975—; cons. in new product devel. mktg. mgmt. and corp. strategy. Mem. Republican County Com., 1976—; chmn. Princeton Wildlife Refuge, 1970-74; mem. U. Pa. Secondary Schs. Com., 1964—; trustee Princeton Unitarian Ch., 1977-80; chmn. Republican Party Orgn., Princeton, 1980—. Served with U.S. Army, 1944-46. Republican. Home: 52 Mason Dr Princeton NJ 08540

POOLEY, ED, chain grocery exec.; b. Tacoma, Jan. 10, 1937; s. William and May E. Pooley; B.B.A. in Mktg., U. Wash., Seattle, 1963, postgrad., 1975; m. Barbara Ann Abbott, Aug. 7, 1959; children—Nora, Lisa, Bill. Salesman, Carnation Milk & Ice Cream Co., Portland, Oreg., 1963-65, Darigold Fresh Milk & Ice Cream Co., Seattle, 1965-66; with Associated Grocers, Inc., 1966—, v.p. wholesale ops., Seattle, 1972-78, sr. v.p. wholesale ops., 1978—. Exec. com. Seattle March of Dimes; pres. council Maple Leaf and Grace Lutheran Chs., Federal Way, Wash., 1978; pres. bd. Federal Way Boys/Girls Club; mem. bus. curriculum adv. com. Federal Way Sch. Dist., 1979. Served with USNR, 1955-57. Named Man of Yr., Seattle March of Dimes, 1979. Clubs: Seattle Rotary; Fircrest Country (Tacoma). Home: 30009 24th Ave SW Federal Way WA 98003 Office: 3301 S Norfolk St PO Box 3763 Seattle WA 98124

POOR, GOLDEN EARL, dept. store exec., mgmt. cons.; b. Herriman, Utah, Aug. 27, 1928; s. Charles Earl and Daisy Lorraine (Miller) P.; B.S., U. Utah, 1951; LL.B., 1956, M.B.A., 1956; m. Olive Edna Atwood, June 22, 1949; children—Terrie, Jackie, Cindy, Lorie, Trent, Kimberly. Indsl. engr. U.S. Steel Corp., Provo, Utah, 1956-59; dir. mgmt. engring. Riches, Research, Inc., Palo Alto, Calif., 1959-62; exec. asst. N. Am. Aviation, Inc., Anaheim, Calif., 1962-65; material handling mgr. Zion's Coop. Merc. Instn., Salt Lake City, 1965-66, asst. mgr. downtown store, 1966-70, div. sales and service mgr., 1970-72, project mgr., 1972-74, service center mgr., 1974—; mgmt. cons. Golden Approach, Salt Lake City, 1966—; owner 3 control centers Espree Cosmetics Corp., Salt Lake City, Provo, Ogden, Utah, 1978—. Served with USAF, 1951-53. Named Control Center Dir. of Year, Espree Cosmetics Corp., 1979. Mem. Am. Inst. Indsl. Engrs., Am. Mgmt. Assn., Utah State Bar. Mormon. Home: 4305 Diana Way Salt Lake City UT 84117 Office: 2200 S 9th W Salt Lake City UT 84110

POOR, JOHN SHEPPARD, bank exec.; b. Bath, N.Y., Aug. 21, 1922; s. Charles Lane and Janet (Sheppard) P.; student Williams Coll., 1940-42; M.B.A., Harvard U., 1947; m. Jordan Lee Avery, July 29, 1943; children—Avery, Penelope, Deborah. Statistician, Morgan Stanley & Co., N.Y.C., 1947-58, partner, 1958-75, mng. dir., 1970-78, adv. dir., 1979; vice chmn., mng. dir. Morgan & Cie Internat., Paris, 1967-69, 1973-75; vice chmn. Morgan Guaranty, Ltd., London, 1980—. Served with U.S. Navy, 1942-45. Clubs: Knickerbocker; N.Y. Yacht; Seawanhaha Corinthian Yacht; Royal Ocean Racing; Royal Corinthian Yacht; Cruising of America. Office: PO Box 124 30 Throgmorton St London EC 2N 2NT England

POORBAUGH, WILLIAM JAMES, grain co. exec.; b. York, Pa., Jan. 31, 1914; s. James Allen and Susan Elnora (Muhlenberg) P.; B.S., Pa. State U., 1935; m. Anna Grove Fishel, June 19, 1938; 1 dau., Margaret Ellen. With Pa. State U. and U. Ky. Agrl. Extension, 1935-37, U.S. Dept. Agr., 1937-47, P.R. Markley Inc., grain mcht., Phila., 1947-53; founder, pres. Poorbaugh Grain, Inc., Lancaster, Pa., 1953—; dir. Commonwealth Nat. Bank, Harrisburg, Pa., ACandS, Lancaster, Lancaster Milling Co., Inc. Sec. bd. trustees Lancaster Gen. Hosp.; sec. bd. dirs. Lancaster Cleft Palate Clinic. Mem. Nat. Grain and Feed Dealers Assn., Lancaster C. of C. Mason, Kiwanian. Club: Hamilton (dir.). Presbyn. (trustee, pres. bd. 1965-71). Home: 2520 Mondamin Farm Rd Lancaster PA 17601 Office: Griest Bldg Lancaster PA 17603

POPE, BRIAN SAMUEL, imported automobile specialist co. exec.; b. England, Dec. 18, 1938; s. Samuel and Gladys (Smith) P.; came to U.S., 1967; diploma London Sch. Printing and Graphic Arts, 1961; divorced; children—Marina, Samuel, Jeremy. Engaged in printing and allied trades, 1954-68; founder, 1968, since pres., owner Mekatron Corp., Berkeley, Calif. Mem. Automotive Service Industries Assn., Concord, Berkeley chambers commerce. Club: Rotary. Home: 72 Camino Encinas Orinda CA 94563 Office: 2655 Shattuck Ave Berkeley CA 94704

POPE, JAMES GLORE, employee benefits cons. co. exec.; b. Niagara Falls, N.Y., Apr. 10, 1942; s. Ernest Purser and Eva (Glore) P.; B.E.E., Ga. Inst. Tech., 1965; m. Rosalie deLissa Hall, June 12, 1965; children—James Brian, Kristen Elizabeth. Engr., then area supr. E.I. DuPont Co., Seaford, Del., 1965-70; asst. to pres. Electronic Data Systems, Dallas, 1970-75; v.p. Hazlehurst & Assos., Inc., Atlanta, 1975-77, pres., dir., 1977; pres., dir. H & A Benefit Systems, Inc., Atlanta, 1979; dir. Blackburn & Co. Mem. Am. Soc. Personnel Adminstrs., So. Pension Conf., Assn. for Corp. Growth, Hollyberry Civic Assn. (com. chmn. 1978-80). Republican. Presbyterian. Office: 235 Peachtree St Atlanta GA 30303

POPE, (JOHN) JOSEPH, banker; b. Gistoux, Belgium, July 27, 1921 (parents Canadian citizens); s. Maurice Arthur and Simonne Marie (du Monceau de Bergendal) P.; student U. Ottawa (Can.), 1939; m. Claudine de Lannoy, June 8, 1953; children—Sybil, Francis, Allan, Lois, Nora, Julian, Michael. With Bank of Montreal, Ottawa, Ont., Can., 1940, Hull, Que., Can., 1941-47, Montreal, Que., 1947-54; dir. Burns Bros. & Denton Ltd., Toronto, Ont., 1954-62; propr. Pope & Co., Toronto, 1962—; mng. partner Scrooge & Marley, real estate mgmt., 1979—; pres., dir. Chaumont Securities Ltd., 1966—, Kamm, Garland & Co., Ltd., 1977—, also Marina Lodge. Bd. dirs. Toronto French Sch., Inc. Served to lt., arty. Canadian Army, 1942-46. Fellow Inst. Canadian Bankers; mem. Investment Dealers Assn., Boston (asso.), Phila. (asso.), Montreal stock exchanges, Winnipeg Commodity Exchange. Mem. Liberal party Can. Roman Catholic. Clubs: Nat., Badminton and Racquet (Toronto). Home: 61 Cluny Dr Toronto ON M4W 2R1 Canada Office: 15 Duncan St Toronto ON M5H 3P9 Canada

POPE, RICHARD LOUIS, wholesale glass co. exec.; b. N.J., Sept. 19, 1939; s. William B. and Dorothy W. (Ulrich) P.; B.S. in Ceramics (State scholar), B.S. in Chemistry (State scholar), Rutgers U., 1962; M.S. in Indsl. Adminstrn., Purdue U., 1963; m. Jacqueline Ann Colacecchi, Oct. 3, 1964; children—Jennifer, Melissa, Brian. Market specialist Corning Glass Works (N.Y.), 1963-65; founder, pres., chmn. bd. Vesta Glass Inc., Corning, 1965—, The Glass Menagerie, 1978—; pres. Kriss Kringle's Christmas Shop, 1980—; adv. bd. Monroe Savs. Bank, 1978—; dir. So. Finger Lakes Devel., Inc., 1980—; guest lectr. Corning Community Coll. Mem. planning bd. Town of Corning, 1975—; bd. dirs., v.p. Spencer Crest Nature Center, 1975—; mem. planning bd. SE Steuben County, 1976—; mem. mktg., mgmt., econs. adv. bd. Corning Community Coll.; bd. dirs. Three Rivers Devel. Found., 1978—. Mem. Greater Corning Area C. of C. (dir. 1977-80, v.p. and pres.-elect 1980-81), Tau Kappa Epsilon. Republican. Club: Corning Rotary (dir. 1980—). Home: Overlook Dr Corning NY 14830 Office: PO Box 1426 Corning NY 14830

POPKIN, PHILIP, fin. co. exec.; b. Salem, Mass., Sept. 26, 1918; s. Samuel and Anna (Boyarski) P.; student Boston U., 1936-38, U. Calif., Berkeley, 1945-46; m. Nancy Eleanor Popkin, June 17, 1951; children—Deborah Faye, Samuel Jeffrey. Asst. advt. mgr. Jewish Adv. Pub. Corp., Boston, 1946-56; account exec. Parsons, Friedman & Central, Inc., 1956-57; sales rep. Investors Diversified Services, Inc., Salem, 1957-79, dist. sales mgr., 1972-76; pres. Tax and Investment Strategies, Salem, 1979—. Pres., Magic Lantern Playhouse of Greater Lynn, Mass., 1963-64. Served with RCAF, 1942-44, USAAF, 1944-45. Mem. Internat. Assn. Fin. Planners, Greater Boston Assn. Fin. Planners (dir. 1974-80). Address: G-1 568 Loring Hills Ave Salem MA 01970

POPOFSKY, DAVID, advt. exec.; b. Bklyn., Feb. 6, 1934; s. Isidore and Gladys (Wlosko) P.; B.A., The Citadel, 1956; M.S., Bklyn. Coll. Pharmacy, 1964; postgrad. N.Y. U. Grad. Sch. Bus., 1965; m. Barbara Rubenstein, Oct. 15, 1959; children—Michael Howard, F. Scott. Sales rep. Pfizer Labs., 1958-61; mktg. mgr. Pharmacraft Co., 1961-62; asst. to pres. Sudler & Hennessey, advt., 1962-64; sr. v.p., dir. client services Rumrill-Hoyt, Inc., 1964-71; pres., chief exec. officer Popfsky Advt., Inc., N.Y.C., 1971—; vis. prof. Bklyn. Coll. Pharmacy, Grad. Sch. L.I. U., Columbia U. Coll. Pharm. Scis. bd. dirs. Nat. Asthma Center, Denver. Served with AUS, 1956-58. Mem. Pharm. Advt. Club, Am. Mktg. Assn., League Advt. Agencies, Assn. Citadel Men, Alumni Assn. Bklyn. Coll. Pharmacy, Am. Jewish Congress, Assn. Welfare of Israeli Soldiers (dir.). Club: Brigadier (The Citadel). Author papers in field. Address: 180 Madison Ave New York NY 10016*

POPOVIC, DEYAN HONEYMAN, investment adviser; b. Morristown, N.J., May 11, 1943; s. Milan Dusan and Fairlie (Honeyman) P.; B.S., Boston U., 1966. Analyst, investment adviser N.Y. Hanseatic, N.Y.C., 1969-70, Walker Laird, Inc., N.Y.C., 1970-74, White, Weld & Co., N.Y.C., 1974-77; pres. Individual Investors, Inc., 1977—; dir. Chemex Corp. Served to 1st. lt. U.S. Army, 1966-69. Mem. N.Y. Soc. Security Analysts. Home: 70 W 87th St New York NY 10024 Office: Individual Investors Inc 115 Broadway Suite 203 New York NY 10006

POPPA, RYAL R., computer co. exec.; b. Wahpeton, N.D., Nov. 7, 1933; s. Ray Edward and Annabelle (Phillips) P.; B.B.A., Claremont Men's Coll., 1957; m. Ruth Ann Curry, June 21, 1952; children—Sheryl Lynn, Kimberly Marie. Sales trainee IBM, 1957-59, sales rep., 1959-62, product marketing rep., 1963, sales mgr., 1964-66; v.p., gen. mgr. Comml. Computers Inc., Los Angeles, 1966-67; v.p. Greyhound Computer Corp., Chgo., 1967-68, pres., chief exec., dir., 1969-70; pres., chief exec. officer, dir., mem. exec. com. Data Processing Fin. and Gen. (N.Y. Stock Exchange), Hartsdale, N.Y., 1970-72; exec. v.p., chief fin. officer, dir., mem. exec. com. Mohawk Data Scis. Corp., N.Y., 1972-73; chmn., pres., chief exec. officer Pertec Computer Corp., Los Angeles, 1973—. Trustee, mem. exec. com., chmn. devel. com. President's Adv. Council; past chmn. Project 80, Los Angeles, Claremont Men's Coll.; charter mem., Friends of Founders of Los Angeles Music Center, Poppa Computer Center; mem. Nat. UN Day Com.; sustaining mem. Los Angeles County Mus. Arts; founder Charles Baggabe Inst. Recipient Community Service award Am. Jewish Com., 1980. Mem. Am. Electronics Assn. (past dir., mem. exec. com., chmn. Los Angeles council), Computer and Communications Industry Assn. (dir., chmn., mem. exec. com., past SW regional chmn.), U. So. Calif. Assos., Cardinal and Gold, Golden Circle Calif., Young Presidents Orgn. Republican. Home: 1533 Via Leon Palos Verdes Estates CA 90274 Office: Pertec Computer Corp 12910 Culver Blvd Los Angeles CA 90066

POPPINGA, EVALENE JACOBS, Realtor; d. Dan and Dora E. (Whitney) Jacobs; student pub. schs., Marshall, Mo.; grad. Realtors Inst. Mo.; m. Cecil W. Poppinga, Nov. 15, 1958; 1 dau., Reva Denne. Sales rep. Swishers Real Estate, Marshall, Mo., 1962-70; broker Poppinga Real Estate, Marshall, 1970—. Mem. Mo. Assn. Realtors (dist. v.p. 1977-80), Realtors Nat. Mktg. Inst., Marshall C. of C., Am. Bus. Women's Assn., Central Mo. Bd. Realtors (pres. 1976), Nat. Assn. Realtors, Women's Council Realtors (v.p. 1980), Am. Quarter Horse Assn., Humane Soc. of Mo. Baptist. Home: Rural Route 3 Marshall MO 65340 Office: 1060 S Odell Marshall MO 65340

PORTELLI, VINCENT GEORGE, bus. cons., corp. exec.; b. Detroit, Jan. 6, 1932; s. Camillo and Mary (Borg) P.; B.S., U. Detroit, 1953, tchr. certificate, 1961; M.A., U. Mich., 1965; postgrad. Harvard Grad. Sch. Bus. Adminstrn., summer 1971; m. Eugenia A. Naruc, Feb. 7, 1959; children—Debra, Mark, David, Anne, James. Mgmt. trainee, cost accountant, cost analyst, sr. internal auditor, sr. cost accountant Ford Motor Co., Dearborn, Mich., 1953-60; tchr. Bedford Sch., Dearborn Heights, Mich., 1960-62; bus. mgr., adminstrv. asst. to dir. Wayne State U. Center For Adult Edn., 1962-64; controller, dir. bus. affairs Mercy Coll. of Detroit, 1964-73; sec.-treas. Am. Sunroof Corp., v.p., corp. sec., 1977—; sec.-treas. Automobile Splty. Corp., Southgate, Mich., 1973—; pres., dir. Servia, Inc., cons. to mgmt., Livonia, Mich., 1980—. Rep. adv. council Livonia Bd. Edn., 1968-71; v.p. Country Homes Estates Civic Assn., 1971—; commr. Econ. Devel. Corp. Mem. Employers Assn. Detroit, Am. Soc. Tng. Dirs., Am. Arbitration Assn. (mem. nat. panel), Delta Sigma Pi, Beta Gamma Sigma. Republican. Roman Catholic. Home: 36790 Ladywood St Livonia MI 48154 Office: PO Box 2447 Livonia MI 48151

PORTER, CLYDE ROBERT, seat recline mechanisms mfg. co. exec.; b. Santa Monica, Calif., Sept. 9, 1926; s. P. L. and Luora (Wallace) P.; student Santa Monica City Coll., 1945-47, U. Calif., Los Angeles, 1947-49; B.S., U. Idaho, 1950; m. Mary Lou Hoff, Oct. 10, 1955; children—Pamela Ann, Nancy Louise. Pres., P.L. Porter Co., Woodland Hills, Calif., 1950—; dir. Haven Hills. Mem. Soc. Automotive Engrs., Am. Production Inventory Control Soc., Nat. Screw Machine Assn., Personnel Indsl. Relations Assn., Los Angeles, Woodland Hills (dir.) chambers commerce. Club: Rotary. Patentee hydro-mech. products. Home: 1737 Roscomare Rd Los Angeles CA 90024 Office: 6355 DeSoto Ave Woodland Hills CA 91367

PORTER, DIXIE LEE, ins. agt.; b. Bountiful, Utah, June 7, 1931; d. John Lloyd and Ida May (Robinson) Mathis; B.S., U. Calif. at Berkeley, 1956, M.B.A., 1957. Personnel aide City of Berkeley (Calif.), 1957-59; employment supr. Kaiser Health Found., Los Angeles, 1959-60; personnel analyst U. Calif. at Los Angeles, 1961-63; personnel mgr. Reuben H. Donnelley, Santa Monica, Calif., 1963-64, Good Samaritan Hosp., San Jose, Calif., 1965-67; fgn. service officer AID, Saigon, Vietnam, 1967-71; gen. agt. Charter Life Ins. Co., Los Angeles, 1972-77; gen. agt. Kennesaw Life Ins. Co., Atlanta, from 1978; now pres. Women's Ins. Enterprises, Ltd.; cons. in field; dir. Aegis Health Corp. Co-chairperson Comprehensive Health Planning Commn. Santa Clara County, Calif., 1973-76; bd. dirs. Samaritan Home Services, Family Care, U. Calif. Sch. Bus. Adminstrn., Berkeley, 1974-76; mem. task force on equal access to econ. power U.S. Nat. Women's Agenda, 1977—. Served with USMC, 1950-52. C.L.U. Mem. C.L.U. Soc., U. Calif. Alumni Assn., U. Calif. Sch. Bus. Adminstrn. Alumni Assn., Life Ins. Underwriters Assn., AAUW, Bus. and Profl. Women, Prytanean Alumni, Beta Gamma Sigma. Republican. Episcopalian. Zonta. Home and Office: PO Box 64 Los Gatos CA 95031

PORTER, DONALD JUDSON, fin. exec.; b. Hartford, Conn., Nov. 6, 1936; s. Donald Truman and Carline (Heath) P.; B.S. in Fin., U. Conn., 1962; m. June 13, 1969; children—Kimberly, Cynthia, Laurie, Bradford, Lisa. Br. mgr. Hartford Soc. for Savs., 1962-67; investment banker, Advest, Hartford, 1967-73; v.p. fin. Nat. Telephone Co., East Hartford, Conn., 1973-75; account v.p. Paine Webber Jackson & Curtis, Inc., Hartford, 1976—. Dir. public relations Greater Hartford Open, 1964. Served with USMC, 1955-58. Home: 10 Drumlin Rd West Simsbury CT 06092 Office: 10 Constitution Plaza Hartford CT 06103

PORTER, DUDLEY, JR., lawyer, found. exec.; b. Paris, Tenn., May 10, 1915; s. Dudley and Mary (Bolling) P.; student Murray State Coll., 1933-34; LL.B., Cumberland U., 1936; m. Mary Rhoda Montague, Oct. 21, 1950. Admitted to Tenn. bar, 1937; asst. atty. gen. State of Tenn., 1937-40; mem. firm Tyne, Peebles, Henry & Tyne, Nashville, 1940-49; mem. law dept. Nat. Life & Accident Ins. Co., Nashville, 1940-49; with Provident Life & Accident Ins. Co., Chattanooga, 1949—, v.p., gen. counsel, sec., dir. 1966-70, sr. v.p., gen. counsel, sec., 1970-72, vice chmn. bd., sr. counsel, 1972-76, now dir.; of counsel law firm Chambliss, Bahner, Crutchfield, Gaston & Irvine, Chattanooga, 1976—; v.p., trustee Maclellan Found.; dir. Coca-Cola Bottling Corp., Cin. Mem. Hamilton County Juvenile Ct. Commn., 1958-64, chmn., 1963-64; mem. Tenn. Hist. Commn., 1976—; trustee Tenn. chpt. The Nature Conservancy. Served with AUS, 1942-46; ETO. Mem. Am., Tenn., Chattanooga bar assns., Assn. Life Ins. Counsel (pres. 1974-75), Am. Life Conv. (chmn. legal sect. 1958), Sigma Alpha Epsilon. Presbyn. Clubs: Mountain City (Chattanooga); Belle Meade (Nashville). Home: Healing Springs Rd Elder Mountain Route 8 Chattanooga TN 37409 Office: 1014 Maclellan Bldg Chattanooga TN 37402

PORTER, GARY LYNN, state ofcl.; b. Bartlesville, Okla., Feb. 18, 1946; s. Leonard Edwin and Rosella Elizabeth Best (Smith) P.; B.S., Southwestern Okla. State U., 1969; M.B.A., Oklahoma City U., 1974; postgrad. U. Okla., 1975—; m. Mary Elizabeth Nicholson, Jan. 23, 1971; 1 son, Martin Edwin. Intern pharmacist VA Hosp., Oklahoma City, 1968; registered pharmacist Wright's Drug Store, Poteau, Okla., 1969-70; instr. pharmacy adminstrn. and pharmaceutics Southwestern State U., Weatherford, Okla., 1970-75, admission counselor, 1970-73, dir. continuing edn., 1973-75; preventive med. cons. Okla. State Dept. Health, Oklahoma City, 1974-75, pharmacy cons., 1975-78, dir. Okla. Poison Info. Center, 1975-78; dir., exec. com. mem. Pharmat, Inc., Lawrence, Kans., 1973-75; pres. RLM, Inc., 1978—, RLM Mgmt. Co., 1979—; adminstr. Hodges Nursing Home, Inc., 1979—. Mem. adminstrv. bd. local Methodist ch., 1979—. Recipient Disting. Alumnus award Southwestern Pharmacy Alumni Assn., 1975. Fellow Am. Coll. Apothecaries; mem. Am. Pharm. Assn., Am. Soc. Hosp. Pharmacists, Nat. Assn. Retail Druggists, Okla. Pharm. Assn., Am. Assn. Colls. Pharmacy, Am. Assn. Poison Control Centers, Okla. County Pharm. Assn., Adult Edn. Assn. U.S.A., Higher Edn. Alumni Council Okla., Okla. Edn. Assn., Okla. Adult and Continuing Edn. Assn., Elk City C. of C. (ambassador 1980—), Phi Delta Chi. Democrat. Clubs: Rotary (dir. 1979-81, v.p. 1981—), Jaycees (Elk City); Weatherford Rotary (treas. 1974-75), Kiwanis (sec. N.W. Oklahoma City 1975-76, pres. 1977-78). Home: PO Box 532 Elk City OK 73648 Office: PO Box 629 Elk City OK 73648

PORTER, JOHN WHEELOCK, airline exec.; b. Rockford, Ill., Dec. 7, 1921; s. Carson Hosmer and Marguerite Elizabeth (Wheelock) P.; B.S., Beloit Coll., 1943; postgrad. Northwestern U., 1947-50; m. Elizabeth Jane Chandler, Mar. 9, 1946; children—Carol Porter Lovelace, Donald Robert, Charles William. Indsl. engr. United Airlines, Chgo., 1946-57, project leader, 1957-66, dir. orgn. planning, 1966-77, v.p. adminstrn. computer div., 1977-80, v.p. ops., computer and communications services div., 1981—; lectr. Ohio State U., Columbus, 1959, Iowa State U., Ames, 1960, Northwestern U., Evanston, Ill., 1961. Treas. Christ Ch., Oak Brook, Ill., 1965—, bd. trustees, 1965—, elder, 1965—. Served with USAAF, 1943-46. Recipient Econ. Planning Adminstrn. award United Airlines 1971. Mem. Orgn. Planning Council Conf. Bd. (chmn. 1977). Republican. Club: La Grange Country. Home: 4 Oak Brook Club Dr G 301 Oak Brook IL 60521 Office: United Airlines PO Box 66100 Chicago IL 60666

PORTER, LANA GARNER, communications co. exec.; b. Salem, Ill., Dec. 31, 1943; d. Marion E. and Belva M. (Hayden) Garner; B.A., Murray State U., 1965, M.A., 1972; M.B.A., Ohio State U., 1980; m. Michael E. Porter, June 7, 1964; 1 dau., Catherine Diane. Tchr. jr. high sch. French, Hopkinsville, Ky., 1964-66; tchr. high sch. English, French and speech, Benton, Ky., 1966-69; instr. Murray (Ky.) State U., 1969-70; ednl. researcher Battelle Meml. Inst., Columbus, Ohio, 1970-73; coordinator of info., research, and devel. Planned Parenthood of Columbus, 1973-76; account exec. Ohio Bell Telephone Co., Columbus, 1976-78, adminstrv. mgr., Cleve., 1978-79, industry mgr., 1979—. Trustee, sec. Cerebral Palsy of Columbus, 1977-78; trustee United Cerebral Palsy of Cuyahoga County, 1979—. Mem. Am. Mgmt. Assn., Am. Soc. Profl. and Exec. Women, Jr. League, Alpha Omicron Pi Alumna. Republican. Presbyterian. Home: 163 Elm Ct Chagrin Falls OH 44022 Office: Ohio Bell Telephone Co 1020 Bolivar St 4th Floor Cleveland OH 44115

PORTER, STUART WILLIAMS, investment co. exec.; b. Detroit, Jan. 11, 1937; s. Stuart Perlee and Alma Bernice (Williams) P.; B.S., U. Mich., 1960; M.B.A. (Am. Acctg. Assn. fellow), U. Chgo., 1967, postgrad., 1967-68; m. Myrna Marlene Denham, June 27, 1964; children—Stuart, Randall. Vice pres., partner, dir. research A.G. Becker & Co., Inc., Chgo., 1969-77; partner Weiss, Peck & Greer, Chgo., 1977—. Chmn., Crusade of Mercy, 1973. Served with USAF, 1961-62. Recipient award for excellence in bus. and acctg. Fin. Exec. Inst., 1966. Mem. Midwest Pension Conf., Investment Analysts Soc. Chgo., Fin. Analysts Fedn., Beta Gamma Sigma. Presbyterian. Clubs: Chgo. Athletic Assn.; Forest Grove Tennis (Arlington, Ill.); Turnberry Country (Crystal Lake, Ill.); Renaissance (Detroit). Home: 130 Wyngate Dr Barrington IL 60010 Office: 30 N La Salle St Chicago IL 60602

PORTER, WILLIAM LANSING, investment advisor; b. Worcester, Mass., Nov. 10, 1947; s. John Armour and Elizabeth (Wynn) P.; B.A. in Econs., Boston U., 1969; student law U. Ga., 1970-72; m. Patricia Lyden, June 12, 1971; children—Ericka Marie Lyden, William Lansing. Pres., Northeastern Fin. Advisors, Worcester, Mass., 1972-77, Southeastern Fin. Advisors, Atlanta, 1977—; real estate salesman Crossroads Realty, Atlanta, 1979—; tax cons. internat. corps. Sec., Mass. Republican. Com., 1969-70. Cert. fin. planner, registered investment advisor. Mem. Internat. Assn. Fin. Planners, Ga. Assn. Fin. Planners, Ducks Unltd. Baptist. Club: Lions. Author: A Return to the Gold Standard—How Likely?; Introductory Financial Planning—A Primer. Office: 3100 Briarcliff Rd Atlanta GA 30329

PORTER, WINSTON SEYMOUR, realty co. exec.; b. Port Maitland, N.S., Can., Sept. 17, 1909; s. Lyndon E. and Lillian D. (Sanders) P.; came to U.S., 1926, naturalized, 1935; student Northwestern U., 1936-38; m. Ruth Lyon, Sept. 29, 1934; children—Robert G., Lynne S. With Estate of Marshall Field, 1934-43, asst. regional rent dir. OPA, Chgo., 1944-46; v.p. Oliver S. Turner & Co. (now Turner, Bailey & Zoll, Inc.), Chgo., 1946-67; v.p. Arthur Rubloff & Co., 1967—. Trustee Deerfield, Ill., 1959-63; chmn. finance com. Deerfield, 1959-63, chmn. Deerfield Plan Commn., 1954-59, N.W. Suburban Planning Commn., 1958; active Boy Scouts Am. Mem. Field Mus. Natural History (asso. life), Art Inst. Chgo., Nat. Assn. Bldg. Mgrs., Chgo. Real Estate Bd., Ill. C. of C., Order of Arrow, Smithsonian Assos., Lambda Alpha (chpt. pres. 1940). Presbyn. Clubs: Builders, Canadian (Chgo.); Northbrook (Ill.) Gun. Home: 24001 Muirlands Blvd Greenbriar 281 El Toro CA 92630

PORTNER, PEER MICHAEL, med. device co. exec.; b. Mombasa, Kenya, Jan. 8, 1940; came to U.S., 1969; s. Walter and Ilse Margarethe (von Rothe) P.; B.Sc., McGill U., Montreal, Que., Can., 1961, M.Sc. (Univ. fellow), 1964, Ph.D., 1968; m. Dorothy Buckland, June 16, 1972; children—Catherine Lynne, Karen Dawn. NRC Can. postdoctoral fellow Oxford (Eng.) U., 1968-69; with Andros Inc., Berkeley, Calif., 1969—, v.p., dir. research and devel., 1973-79, exec. v.p., dir. research, 1979—; cons. asso. prof. cardiovascular surgery Stanford U. Med Center; mem. U.S. del. U.S.-USSR Symposium in Mechanically Assisted Circulation, Tbilisi, USSR, 1979. Vice pres., bd. dirs. East Bay Ballet Theatre, Berkeley, 1978—. Fellow European Soc. Artificial Organs; mem. AAAS, Am. Heart Assn., Am. Phys. Soc., Am. Soc. Artificial Organs, ASTM, Am. Assn. Med Instrumentation, Biomed. Engring. Soc. (sr.), Can. Assn. Physics, IEEE, Internat. Soc. Artificial Organs (editorial bd. 1977—), N.Y. Acad. Scis. Roman Catholic. Contbr. numerous articles to profl. publs.; patentee in field. Office: 2332 4th St Berkeley CA 94710

PORTNOW, NEIL, record co. exec. Pres., Twentieth Century-Fox Records, Inc., Los Angeles. Office: 8544 Sunset Blvd Los Angeles CA 90069

PORTNOY, IRVING LEO, chemist; b. Bklyn., Oct. 4, 1925; s. Jacob and Lillie (Weinstein) P.; B.S., Coll. City N.Y., 1948; M.A., Columbia, 1953; m. Kyla Einstein (dec. 1964); children—Valerie, Edward; m. 2d, Judith Glass, Aug. 14, 1966. Chemist Liquid Conditioning Corp., Linden, N.J., 1948-49; chief chemist Water Service Labs., Inc., N.Y.C., 1950-69; chief chemist Olin Water Services, Olin Corp., 1970-71, dist. sales mgr., 1971-74, bus. mgr., 1974—. Served with AUS, 1944-46. Decorated Bronze Star. Registered profl. engr., Calif. Mem. Am. Chem. Soc., N.Y. Water Pollution Control Assn., Nat. Assn. Corrosion Engrs., ASHRAE. Home: 344 Beverly Rd Douglaston NY 11363 Office: 615 W 131st St New York NY 10027

POSNER, ROY EDWARD, ins., hotel, theatre and tobacco co. exec.; b. Chgo., Aug. 24, 1933; s. Lew and Julia (Cvetan) P.; student U. Ill., 1951-53, Internat. Accountants Soc. Inc., Chgo., 1956-59, Loyola U., 1959, Advanced Mgmt. Program, Harvard, 1976; m. Donna Lea Williams, June 9, 1956; children—Karen Lee, Sheryl Lynn. C.P.A., Frank W. Dibble Co., Chgo., 1956-61; C.P.A., supr. Harris Kerr Forster & Co., Chgo., 1961-66; with Loews Corp., N.Y.C., 1966—, v.p. fin. services, chief fin. officer, 1973—; dir. Gen. Fin. Corp., Evanston, Ill., Bulova Systems and Instruments Corp., N.Y.C. Pres., No. Regional Valley High Sch. Music Parents Assn., 1978-79. Served with AUS, 1953-55. C.P.A., Ill. Mem. Am. Inst. C.P.A.'s, Ill., N.Y. State socs. C.P.A.'s, Financial Execs. Ins., Ins. Accounting and Statis. Assn., Internat. Hospitality Accountants Assn., Am. Hotel and Motel Assn., Delta Tau Delta. Club: Alpine (N.J.) Country. Mem. com. 7th edit. The Uniform System of Accounting for Hotels. Home: 273 Whitman St Haworth NJ 07641 Office: 666 Fifth Ave New York City NY 10019

POSSATI, MARIO, electronic gauge co. exec.; b. Cordoba, Argentina, Apr. 7, 1922; s. Pompeo and Rosa (Badini) P.; B.S. in Mech. Engring., Bologna U., 1946; m. Manfredi Gabriella, June 4, 1947; children—Stefano, Marco, Edoardo, Alberto. Tech. mgr. Officine Macaferri, Bologna, Italy, 1946-48; gen. mgr. Baschieri & Pellagri, 1949-52; founder MARPOSS, Bologna, 1952, pres., 1952—. Served with Italian Air Force, 1943. Mem. Profl. Engrs. Assn. Italy, Soc. Mfg. Engrs. Home: 23 Viale Carducci Bologna I 40125 Italy Office: Finike Italiana Marposs SpA Via Saliceto 13 Bentivoglio (Bologna) 40010 Italy

POSSEHL, JAMES HENRY, fin. exec.; b. Tacoma, Aug. 3, 1944; s. Stanfield Louis and Hollis Reva (Clayton) P.; B.A. in Mktg., U. Wash., 1966; m. Karen Ann Lundin, June 19, 1965; children—Jeff, Bob, Cheryl. With Shell Oil Co., Seattle, 1966-69; incorporator, v.p., dir. Internat. Financing, Inc., Seattle, 1969-71; pres., chmn. bd. Republic Fin. Corp., Denver, 1971—. Pres., Titans, Youth Athletic Team, 1977—; mgr., bd. dirs. Arapahoe Youth League, 1978—. Mem. Am. Assn. Equipment Lessors, Denver C. of C., Denver Exec. Club, Colo. Assn. Lessors, Western Assn. Equipment Lessors, Phi Kappa Psi. Republican. Clubs: Univ. Hills Rotary (dir. 1978—), Denver Barbarian Rugby Football. Home: 10958 E Crestridge Circle Englewood CO 80111 Office: 10651 E Bethany Dr PO Box 22564 Denver CO 80222

POST, ALLEN, lawyer; b. Newnan, Ga., Dec. 3, 1906; s. William Glenn and Rosa Kate (Muse) P.; A.B. summa cum laude, U. Ga., 1927; B.A. in Juris. with first honors (Rhodes scholar), Oxford U., 1929, B.C.L., 1930, M.A., 1933; Ph.D.; m. Mary Chastaine Cook, Dec. 27, 1934; 1 son, Allen W. Jr. Admitted to Ga. bar, 1930; spl. atty. gen. Ga., 1934-35; asst. atty. gen. assigned Ga. Pub. Service Commn., 1934; dep. atty. gen. Ga., 1957; partner firm Moise, Post & Gardner, Atlanta, 1942-61; sr. partner Hansell, Post, Brandon & Dorsey, 1962—, specializing in bus. and corp. law; lectr., writer on legal subjects; hon. dir. First Nat. Bank Atlanta, First Nat. Holding Corp.; dir. Ga. Hwy. Express, Inc., Elmac, Inc., Am. Cast Iron Pipe Co.; dir., exec. com. Atlanta Gas Light Co., Atlantic Am. Corp.; dir. Thomaston Mills, Inc., Beaudry Ford, Inc. Trustee, W N Banks Found., Howell Fund, Ragan and King Charitable Found.; pres. Atlanta Estate Planning Council. Chmn. of Navy Day, Atlanta, 1937-39. Mem. Ga. Democratic Exec. Com. (chmn. com. to rewrite election laws and revise primary rules of Ga. 1956); mem. Gov.'s Staff; mem. State Com. to Revise Income Tax Laws of Ga., 1956; mem. polit. action com. Nat. Democratic Com. Trustee, mem. exec. com. Atlanta Arts Alliance. Served as lt. comdr. USNR, World War II. Fellow Am. Coll. Probate Counsel, Am. Coll. Trial Lawyers; mem. Atlanta (exec. com., pres. 1956), Am., Ga. bar assns., Am. Judicature Soc., Am. Legion (comdr.), Am. Assn. Rhodes Scholars, S.A.R., Sphinx, Phi Beta Kappa, Phi Kappa Phi, Phi Delta Phi, Kappa Alpha. Methodist (chmn. bd. stewards, trustee). Rotarian. Clubs: Old War Horse Lawyers (pres.); Commerce, Capital City, Piedmont Driving, Lawyers (Atlanta). Home: 620 Peachtree Battle Ave NW Atlanta GA 30327 Office: First National Bank Tower Atlanta GA 30303

POST, DAVID A., communications co. exec.; b. N.Y.C., Oct. 20, 1941; s. Emil R. and Ruth (Rosen) P.; student Coll. City N.Y. 1959-61, N.Y. U. 1975-76; m. Arlene Goldbrum, June 10, 1962; children—Randee, Lori, Jill. Partner, Zuckerman, Smith & Co., N.Y.C., 1967-71; v.p., dir. corporate fin. Andresen & Co., N.Y.C., 1971-73; exec. v.p., dir. R.K. Pace Post & Co., investment bankers, N.Y.C., 1973-75; pres., chmn. bd. dirs. Page Am. Communications Inc., N.Y.C., 1975—; cons. to various cos. Mem. Investment Bankers Assn., Investment Assn. N.Y. Author various pieces for TV. Home: 400 E 57th St New York City NY 10022 Office: Page Am 150 E 58th St 22d Floor New York City NY 10022

POST, GARRET WAYNE, temporary help service co. exec.; b. Waterbury, Conn., May 17, 1941; s. Harold Benjamin and Grace (Gailey) P.; student Bates Coll., 1959-61; B.S., N.Y. U., 1964; postgrad. Am. U., 1965-67; m. Sandra Gordon, Sept. 30, 1967; children—Stuart Gordon, Mark Douglas, Sharon Gailey. Mgmt. trainee Manpower Inc., Waterbury, Conn., 1967-69, asst. treas., 1969-71, v.p., 1971-80, gen. mgr., 1973—, pres., 1980—; v.p. Transpersonnel, Inc., Waterbury, 1969-80, pres., 1980—; incorporator Manpower Tech. Services of Conn., 1977, treas., 1977, v.p., treas., 1978. Bd. dirs. United Way of Central Naugatuck Valley, 1976—, v.p., 1980—. Served with USCG, 1964—. Mem. Sales and Mktg. Execs. (pres. 1975). Republican. Congregationalist. Home: 130 Mixville Rd Cheshire CT 06410 Office: 24 Central Ave Waterbury CT 06702

POST, HERSCHEL E., JR., banker; b. Oakland, Calif., Oct. 9, 1939; s. Herschel E. and Marie Estelle (Connelley) P.; A.B., Yale U., 1961; B.A., Oxford (Eng.) U., 1963; LL.B., Harvard U., 1966; m. Peggy Mayne, Aug. 24, 1963; children—Herschel Day, Clarissa Elliott, Eliza. Asso. firm Davis, Polk & Wardwell, N.Y.C., 1966-69; exec. dir. Parks Council of N.Y.C., 1969-72; asst. resident counsel Morgan Guaranty Trust Co. of N.Y., N.Y.C., 1972-73; dep. adminstr. parks, recreation and cultural affairs City of N.Y., 1973; v.p. Morgan Guaranty Trust Co., Brussels, 1974-78, London, 1978—. Democrat. Episcopalian. Home: 31 Hyde Park Gate London England Office: 30 Throgmorton St London ECZ England

POSTICH, GEORGE, univ. adminstr.; b. North Chicago, Ill., Mar. 24, 1930; s. Rade and Minnie (Svilar) P.; B.S., U. Wis., 1952; M.B.A., Harvard U., 1964; postgrad. Bowling Green State U.; m. Margaret Anne Jordan, June 14, 1952; children—Steven, Kevin, Kathryn, Mary, Anne, Shawn, Shane. Commd. ensign, U.S. Navy, 1952, advanced through grades to capt., 1952-75, exec. officer Electronic Supply Office, Great Lakes, Ill., 1972-74; ret., 1975; v.p. ops. Bowling Green State U., 1975—; asst. prof. U. N.Mex., 1954-56. Dept. Def. coordinator Cleve. Nat. Air Show and Air Races, 1971. Mem. Ret. Officers Assn., Inter-Univ. Council Fiscal Officers, Nat. Assn. Coll. and Univ. Bus. Officers, Bowling Green C. of C. (trustee), U. Wis. Alumni Assn., Harvard Bus. Sch. Club, Phi Beta Kappa, Phi Eta Sigma, Phi Kappa Phi. Club: Falcon. Home: 316 Donbar Dr Bowling Green OH 43402 Office: 911 Administration Bldg Bowling Green State U Thurstin St Bowling Green OH 43403

POSTIGO, TITO, life ins. co. exec.; b. Lima, Peru, July 10, 1942; s. Augusto Julio and Georgina Angelica Postigo; came to U.S., 1962; B.S., USAF Acad., 1964; children—Melanie K., Marissa L. Commd. 2d lt. USAF, 1964, advanced through grades to capt., 1970; service in Eng., SE Asia; resigned, 1970; with Equitable Life Assurance Soc. U.S., 1971—, dist. mgr., Santa Barbara, Calif., 1972—. Bd. dirs. Joseph Kennedy's Spl. Olympic Program for Retarded. Decorated D.F.C. (9), Purple Heart (2), Bronze Star; named Mgr. of Year, Hill Agy., Western div. Equitable Life Assurance Soc. U.S., 1976. Mem. Million Dollar Roundtable, Gen. Mgrs. and Agts. Assn. (past chpt. pres.), Nat. Assn. Life Underwriters, Am. Soc. C.L.U.'s. Republican. Roman Catholic. Club: Optimist. Participant Olympic Games, Rome, 1960, Japan, 1964. Office: Suite 200 1333 Camino del Rio S San Diego CA 92108

POSTLEWAITE, WILLIAM MARC, publisher; b. Louisville, Oct. 10, 1944; s. William and Gretchen (Heingardner) P.; student E. Tenn. State U., 1963-65, U. Tenn., 1970-76, Rochester Inst. Tech., summer 1973, Harvard U., 1978; m. Marion Milton, Dec. 27, 1969; children—Brian, Matthew, Andrew. Salesman, Addressograph Multigraph Corp., 1968-69; reporter Knoxville (Tenn.) Jour., 1969-70; editor Sevier County (Tenn.) News-Record, 1970-72; gen. mgr. The Mountain Press, Gatlinburg, Tenn., 1972-75, pres., pub., 1975—. Bd. dirs. Sevier County Animal Shelter. Mem. Nat. Newspaper Assn., Southeastern Pubs. Assn., Tenn. Press Assn. (dir.), Sigma Delta Chi. Republican. Methodist. Clubs: Lions, Rotary, Elks. Home: McCarter Hollow Rd Sevierville TN 37862 Office: Cartertown Rd Gatlinburg TN 37738

POSTON, WILLARD CLIFFORD, JR., gen. contractor: b. Liveoak, Fla., Feb. 7, 1927; s. Willard Clifford and Dorothy (Daniels) P.; B.S., Clemson (S.C.) Coll., 1952; m. Vonnie Poston, June 13, 1953; children—Clifford Culley, Jane Louise. Tchr., S.C., 1952-53; gen. contractor, Lake City, S.C., 1954-60; with A.J. Kellos Constrn. Co., Augusta, Ga., 1961-67, Charles R. Hughes Constrn. Co., Thomson, Ga., 1967-70; pres. Two State Constrn. Co., Inc., Thomson, 1970—. Served with AUS, 1945-47. Baptist. Clubs: Rotary, Masons, Shriners. Home: Belle Meade Country Club Thomson GA 30824 Office: PO Drawer 239 Washington Rd and I 20 Thomson GA 30824

POTE, FRANK ROBERT, SR., editor; b. Medford, Mass., Apr. 8, 1919; s. Frank Walter and Marguerite Edith (Hanna) P.; A.B. in Econs., Tufts U., 1941; postgrad. Harvard Bus. Sch., 1941, Boston U., 1965-68; m. Marjorie Kathryn Emms, May 30, 1943; children—Frank Robert, Laurinda Ellen Pote Clarkson. New Eng. publicity dir. Kemper Ins. Co., 1946-56; nat. advt. mgr. Boston-Old Colony Ins. Cos., Boston, 1956-59; asso. editor The Standard, ins. weekly Standard Pub. Co., Boston, 1959-66, editor The Standard, 1966—, pres., dir., pub., 1968—. Town chmn. Whitman Cub Scouts, 1956-59; chmn. Whitman Cerebral Palsy, 1963. Served to lt. USNR, 1942-46; ETO. Mem. Ins. Advt. Conf., Ins. Library Assn. Boston (trustee), Norwell Hist. Soc. (exec. sec. 1979—), Hist. Soc. of Early Am. Decoration. Delta Upsilon. Republican. Congregationalist. Clubs: Old Colony Harvard, Boston Tufts. Editor: A Practical Approach to Inland Marine Insurance, 1979. Home: 767 Grove St Norwell MA 02061 Office: Standard Pub Co 1073 Hancock St Quincy MA 02169

POTE, GARRY LEE, investment banker; b. Roaring Spring, Pa., Jan. 16, 1941; s. Arthur Paul and Ada M. (Knisely) P.; B.A. with distinction, Juniata Coll., 1968; M.B.A., U. Pa., 1970; m. Jo Anne Bergstresser, July 6, 1963; 1 dau., Nicole Andrea. With Merrill Lynch Pierce Fenner & Smith, N.Y.C., 1970-73; treas. Equimark Corp., Pitts., 1973-75; v.p. Bache Halsey Stuart Shields, Inc., N.Y.C., 1975-77, 1st v.p., 1978; 1st v.p. Loeb Rhoades, Hornblower & Co., N.Y.C., 1978-79; sr. v.p. Shearson Loeb Rhoades, Inc., N.Y.C., 1979—. Mem. alumni council Juniata Coll. Served with USMCR, 1962-66. Mem. Am. Fin. Assn., N.Y. C. of C. and Industry (com. currency and fin.). Republican. Presbyterian. Clubs: Princeton, Pa. (N.Y.C.); Pitts. Home: 383 Michigan Rd New Canaan CT 06840 Office: 14 Wall St New York NY 10005

POTEET, BILLY JAMES, athletic sportswear mfg. co. exec.; b. Abilene, Tex., Mar. 14, 1945; s. Wayne C. and Mary Josephine (Nevins) P.; B.S. in Pharmacy, Southwestern Okla. State U., 1968; m. Rebecca Anne Hedrick, May 17, 1969; children—Christopher James, Phillip Brandon. Self-employed pharmacist, 1968-69, 72-73; sales and mktg. rep. Eli Lilly & Co., 1973-79; pres., chief exec. officer Gulf Coast and Pacific, Inc., Escondido, Calif., 1979—. Served with USN, 1969-72. Mem. Am. Pharm. Assn., Nat. Rifle Assn., Naval Res. Assn., U.S. Naval Inst. Republican. Methodist. Club: Masons. Office: 620-B Venture St Escondido CA 92025

POTRATZ, EUGENE ROBERT, banker; b. Oconomowoc, Wis., Mar. 24, 1936; s. Henry Fredrick and Isabel Marie (Lang) P.; ed. Grad. Sch. Banking, Am. Inst. Banking and U. Wis. extension courses; m. Carol Jean Kraft, Dec. 2, 1961; children—Timothy Eugene, Jill Renata. With 1st Nat. Bank of Oconomowoc, 1954—, exec. v.p., 1974-80, pres., 1980—, dir., 1973—. Former treas. Town of Summit. Served with AUS, 1958-60. Clubs: Oconomowoc Lions (past pres.), Oconomowoc Golf (v.p., dir.). Office: 138 E Wisconsin Ave Oconomowoc WI 53066

POTTER, ALTA CLIFFORD, investment securities account exec. counselor, former state ofcl.; b. Salt Lake City; d. William Ernest and Margaret (McLean) Clifford; grad. bus. adminstrn. U. Calif. at Los Angeles; m. Franklin J. Potter (div.); children—Clifford, Naomi. Owner, mgr. Alta Clifford Beautiful Clothes, Long Beach, Calif.; legislative polit. campaign mgr., 1940, 42, 44, 50; bus. mgmt., pub. relations counselor, 1945-53; vocat. counselor Woodbury U., Los Angeles, 1953-55; dep. dir. planning and ops. Office of Civil Def. of Los Angeles, 1955, chief ednl. activities div., 1956-58; chief and commr. indsl. welfare div. State of Calif. Indsl. Relations Dept., also mem. Gov.'s Personnel Bd., 1958-60; investment securities counselor, 1960—; account exec. Investogenic Services, Inc., Marina del Rey; account exec., investment counselor Internat. Diamond Corp., San Rafael, Calif., 1980—. Invited observer UN Orgn., San Francisco, 1945; mem. Mayor's Community Adv. Com. Elected Republican candidate Calif. Legislature, 1944; mem. Calif. Rep. State Exec. Com., 1944-46; pres. Hollywood Woman's Rep. Club, 1942-44; mem. Rep. Assos.; 1st v.p. So. Calif. Rep. Club, 1955-56. Mem. Nat. Bus. and Profl. Women's Club, Calif. Cancer Research (past chmn. Los Angeles), Los Angeles, Hollywood chambers commerce, Nat. Pub. Relations Forum, A.I.M. (asso.), Assistance League Calif., Nat. Soc. Lit. and Arts, Truman Library Soc., Nat. Trust Historic Preservation, Smithsonian Assos., Internat. Platform Assn., Town and Gown of U. So. Calif., World Affairs Council, Parliamentary Conf., Pals of Sacramento, Calif. Las Companeros. Clubs: Knife and Fork Dinner, Commonwealth Dinner, Ebell (Los Angeles); Beverly Hills. Home: 6720 Hill Park Dr Hollywood CA 90028 Office: 4335 Marina City Dr Marina City Club Marina del Rey CA 90291 also Am Investors Corp 1275 A St Hayward CA 94541

POTTER, CLARKE JAMES, JR., holding co. exec.; b. Dennison, Iowa, May 9, 1944; s. Clarke James and Marie E. (Paustch) P.; B.S. in Bus. Adminstrn., U. Ky., 1967; m. Starr Michel, June 17, 1972; children—Scott, Todd, Greg. Pres., Blue Ribbon Steel Co., Louisville, 1970-76; v.p. mktg. Potter Industries Inc., Louisville, 1976-78; pres. The Trafalgar Co., Louisville, 1979—. Served to 1st lt., arty., U.S. Army, 1967-70. Republican. Methodist. Club: Big Springs Country (Louisville). Home: 205 Gibson Rd Louisville KY 40207 Office: PO Box 43272 Louisville KY 40243

POTTER, GEORGE HARRIS, bank exec.; b. Pitts., Dec. 15, 1936; s. William Sommerville and Katharine (Rockwell) P.; A.B., Colgate U., 1959; m. Nicole Enfield Weir, May 1, 1977; children—Clara Potter Mokher, George Harris, Faris Feland, Jonathan Rockwell, Kristin Enfield Weir, David Bruce Weir, Jr., Jennifer Berkey Weir. Life underwriter Equitable Life Assurance Soc. of U.S., Pitts., 1958-59; with Pitts. Nat. Bank, 1959-64; asst. treas. First Nat. Bank of Miami (Fla.), 1964, asst. v.p., 1964, v.p., 1969-79; v.p. Central Nat. Bank of Cleve., 1979—; dir. Motive Parts Co., Pa., 1962-64, Pitts. Testing Lab., 1973—; mng. partner PTL Assos., 1978—. Mem. adv. bd. Vanguard Sch., Coconut Grove, Fla., 1968-79. Mem. Am. Trucking Assn. (nat. acctg. and fin. council), Nat. Assn. Corp. Dirs., Phi Delta Theta. Republican. Congregationalist. Clubs: Univ. (Pitts.); River Oaks Racquet. Home: 18151 Clifton Rd Lakewood OH 44107 Office: 800 Superior Ave Cleveland OH 44114

POTTER, KEITH R., business exec.; b. Chester, Pa., 1917; B.A., Johns Hopkins U., 1937; LL.B., U. Balt., 1940; married. With Internat. Harvester Co., Chgo., 1947—, asst. treas., 1962-66, treas., 1966-69, v.p. fin., 1969-71, exec. v.p., chief fin. officer, then exec. v.p. fin. and chief fin. officer, now vice chmn., also dir.; dir. Continental Ill. Nat. Bank & Trust Co., Continental Ill. Corp., Ill. Power Co. Chmn. fin. com., trustee Farm Found. Served to capt. USAAC, 1941-47. Mem. Fin. Execs. Inst., Machinery and Allied Products Inst. (fin. council). Office: 401 N Michigan Ave Chicago IL 60611*

POTTER, PARKER BENEDICT, fuel co. exec.; b. East Orange, N.J., Oct. 16, 1926; s. Thomas and Mavis (Benedict) P.; B.A., U. Va., 1952; m. Carol Landis, Jan. 19, 1957; children—Parker Benedict, Suzanne, Thomas M., Marianne. With M.A. Hanna Co., Phila., 1954-60; with Peabody Coal Co., Columbus, Ohio 1960-76, v.p. sales, 1971-72, v.p. internat. sales, 1972-76; pres. Colony Fuel Corp., 1976—. Pres., Bexley Civic Improvement Assn., 1970—; co-chmn. Columbus Pro-Am Charity Golf Tournament, 1973; bd. dirs. Boys Own Youth Shelter, 1972-75. Served with USNR, 1944-46; PTO. Mem. Internat. Platform Assn., U. Va. Alumni Assn. (life), Hun Sch. Alumni Assn. (com. mem. 1976—), Washington Assn. N.J., U.S. Navy League. Republican. Presbyn. Clubs: Columbus Country (trustee), Columbus. Home: 160 S Ardmore Rd Bexley OH 43209 Office: 4150 E Main St Columbus OH 43213

POTTER, ROY WILSON, urban planner; b. Cin., July 9, 1924; s. Elmer Roe and Essie (Jones) P.; B.Arch., Miami U., Ohio, 1947; M. City Planning, U. Calif., Berkeley, 1954; m. Ruth Louise FitzGerald,

Nov. 22, 1955; children—Dirk Wilson (dec.), Steven Roe, Erik Wilson. Dir. advance planning Stanislaus Cities, County Urban Region, Modesto, Calif., 1955-57; dir. planning City of Fremont (Calif.), 1958-66; dir. tech. services, office internat. affairs HUD, Washington, 1966-68; dir. planning Md. Nat. Capitol Park and Planning Commn., Silver Spring, 1968-70; dir. planning San Joaquin County, Stockton, Calif., 1970-71; exec. v.p. San Diegans, Inc., San Diego, 1971—; lectr., cons. in field. Chmn. Land Devel. Adv. Bd., City of San Diego, 1973-77; co-chmn. San Diego Air Transp. Study, 1972-75; bd. dirs. San Diego Urban League. Recipient Disting. Service award San Joaquin County Econ. Devel. Assn., 1971. Mem. Am. Planning Assn., Am. Inst. Cert. Planners, Nat. Assn. Housing and Redevel. Ofcls., Urban Land Inst., Internat. Downtown Execs. (dir.), Internat. Fedn. Housing and Planning, North Shores Amateur Radio Club (v.p.), Lambda Alpha. Club: Rotary. Contbr. articles in field to profl. jours. Home: 801 LaJolla Rancho Rd La Jolla CA 92037 Office: 600 B St Suite 1325 San Deigo CA 92101

POTTS, ROBERT ANTHONY, pub. exec.; b. Chester, Pa., Sept. 11, 1927; s. William James and Sara Louis (Watson) P.; B.A., Pace Coll., 1952; m. Eva Morra, Sept. 8, 1955; children—Mark, Matthew, Amy, Abby. Vice-pres. Cahners Pub. Co., Inc., N.Y.C., 1952-72; vice-pres. Intercontinental Pubs., Stamford, Conn., 1972-75; exec. v.p., pub. Dun's Rev. mag. Dun & Bradstreet Publs., N.Y.C., 1975—. Served with USAAF, 1945-47. Club: Wings Club (N.Y.C.). Contbr. articles on sales and publ. mgmt. to Folio mag. Office: 666 5th Ave New York NY 10019

POULIOT, JEAN ADELARD, broadcasting exec.; b. Quebec City, Can., June 6, 1923; s. Adrien and Laure (Clark) P.; B.A., Seminaire de Que., 1941; B.A.Sc. in E.E., Laval U., 1945; m. Rachel Lebel, Sept. 8, 1945; children—Jean, Vincent, Louis, Adrien, Martin. Research engr. Canadian Signal Research and Devel. Establishment, Ottawa, 1945-49; supt. Canadian Navy Elec. Labs., 1949-52; exec. engr. Famous Players, Toronto, 1952-57; gen. mgr. TV de Que., Ltee., 1957-62, mng. dir., 1962-71; pres., chief exec. officer Tele-Capital, Ltd., Quebec City, 1971-78; pres., chief exec. officer CFCF Inc., Montreal, Que., 1979—; past pres. Tele-Capital Enterprises, Ltd., Broadcast News, Lstad., Sta. CHRC-Am and FM, Cine-Capitale Ltee, Tapis Rouge Aero Service, Inc., Que. Aviation Ltee., Que. Aviation Air Service, Ltee.; v.p. Cinevideo, Inc., Les Productions du Verseau; dir. Tele-Metropole, Inc. (Montreal), TV de la Baie des Chaleurs. Mem. Canadian Assn. Broadcasters (pres. 1965-67). Roman Catholic. Clubs: Garrison, Royal Que. Golf, Royal Montreal Golf, Laval sur le Lac Golf, Miami Lakes Golf, Mount Royal. Home: 99 Gordon Crescent Westmount PQ H3Y 1N1 Canada Office: 405 Ogilvy Ave Montreal PQ H3N 1M4 Canada

POULIOT, LEONARD B., internat. mgmt. cons., lectr., educator; b. Worcester, Mass., Dec. 22, 1923; s. Napoleon and Rose; B.S., U. of Ams., Mexico, 1949; M.A. in Bus., George Washington U., 1962; postgrad. U. Cin., 1972—; m. Marguerite Dormieres, Aug. 25, 1945. Sr. personnel exec. Dept. Def. U.S. Army Civilian Personnel, 1952-62; sr. officer Office of Asst. Sec. State, Washington and 1st sec. diplomatic service U.S. Embassy, Bonn, Germany, 1962-67; dir. personnel and mgmt. Smithsonian Instn., 1968-70; dep. adminstr. for mgmt. Food and Nutrition Service, Agr. Dept., 1970-72; asso. asst. sec. Dept. Labor, 1972-74; asst. adminstr. for mgmt. and adminstrn. Fed. Energy Adminstrn., Washington, 1974-75; v.p. U.S. Industries, Inc., N.Y.C., 1975-76; internat. mgmt. cons., Arlington, Va., 1976—; exec. v.p. Exec. Resource Assos., Inc.; asso. prof. George Washington U. Grad. Sch. Bus., 1963-73; faculty, chmn. exec. devel., mgmt. and supervision Grad. Sch. Dept. Agr., 1963-75, now sr. asso., faculty. Served as aviator USN, 1943-47. Recipient numerous achievement awards, U.S. Govt. Mem. Am. Mgmt. Assn. (sr. faculty), Am. Soc. Pub. Adminstrn. (past v.p. D.C. chpt.), Am. Soc. Tng. and Devel. (past pres. D.C. chpt.). Clubs: Yale (N.Y.C.); Internat. (Washington). Home: Crystal Plaza South 908 2111 Jefferson Davis Hwy Arlington VA 22202

POUNDS, WILLIAM FRANK, educator; b. Fayette County, Pa., Apr. 9, 1928; s. Joseph Frank and Helen (Fry) P.; B.S., Carnegie Inst. Tech., 1950, M.S., 1959, Ph.D., 1964; m. Helen Ann Means, Mar. 6, 1954; children—Thomas McClure, Julia Elizabeth. Indsl. engr. Eastman Kodak Co., 1950-51, 55-57; cons. Pitts. Plate Glass Co., 1958-59, asst. to gen. mgr. Forbes Finishes div., 1960-61; mem. faculty Sloan Sch. Mgmt., M.I.T., 1961—, prof., 1966—, dean, 1966-80; dir. EG&G, Inc., Putnam Funds, Sun Co., Gen. Mills, Inc., Stop & Shop Inc. Served to lt. (j.g.) USNR, 1951-55. Fellow Am. Acad. Arts and Scis.; mem. Inst. Mgmt. Sci. (pres. Boston chpt. 1965-66). Office: 50 Memorial Dr Cambridge MA 02139

POUPARD, JAMES JOSEPH, heavy machinery co. exec.; b. Monroe, Mich., Mar. 21, 1932; s. Edmund Lawrence and Ruth Mary (Soleau) P.; Ph.B. in Econs., U. Detroit, 1964; m. Essie Ruth Gilmer, Aug. 21, 1954; children—Michelle, Brenda, Dennis, Gary. With River Raisin Paper Co., Monroe, 1955, Mercury div. Ford Motor Co., 1956-57; with Chrysler Corp., Detroit, 1957-67, internat. ops. controller Airtemp div., Dayton, Ohio, 1967-72; controller indsl. truck div. Allis-Chalmers Corp., Matteson, Ill., 1972-79, v.p., asst. treas. Allis-Chalmers Export IV, 1974-79; v.p. control and fin. Westinghouse airbrake constrn. and mining group Am. Standard, Inc., Peoria, Ill., 1980—. Active local Little League Baseball, Basketball and Football; coach Jr. Football League, Dunlap, Ill.; treas. Flossmoor (Ill.) Baseball League, Inc.; chmn. football com. athletic bd. Infant Jesus of Prague Parish, also head football coach; mem. priority com. Peoria United Way; pres. Devinwood Homeowners Assn., 1980—. Served with USAF, 1951-55; Korea. Mem. Corporate Controllers Inst., Nat. Assn. Accountants. Flossmoor Hills Civic Assn. Roman Catholic. Club: Dayton Optimist. Home: 11918 Windcrest Ct Dunlap IL 61525 Office: 2301 NE Adams St Peoria IL

POVEY, THOMAS GEORGE, office systems co. exec.; b. Norristown, Pa., Dec. 27, 1920; s. Thomas and Blanche (Groff) P.; B.S., Temple U., 1948; m. Bettina O. Houghton, June 2, 1945; children—Bettina C., Denise E. With Sperry Remington div. Sperry Rand Corp., Phila., also Newark, N.Y.C., 1948—, eastern regional gen. sales mgr., 1960-63, nat. gen. sales mgr., N.Y.C., 1966-67, dir. mktg., Marietta, Ohio, 1968-71, v.p. mktg., 1972-73, v.p. fed. govt. mktg., Washington, 1973-76, pres. Remco Bus. Systems, Inc., Washington, 1976—. Lectr. Newark High Sch., 1954-56, Belleville (N.J.) High Sch., 1956-58, Fairleigh Dickinson Coll., Paterson, N.J., 1957-58, Pace Coll., N.Y.C., 1965—, Georgetown U., 1974, ednl. TV, N.Y.C., 1965—. Dir. Community Fund, Essex Fells, N.J., 1967. Served as 1st lt. with USAF, 1942-45. Decorated Air medal; named Remington Dartnell Salesman of Year, 1950. Mem. Internat. Platform Assn., Smithsonian Assos., Internat. Systems Dealer Assn. (dir. 1977-78), Office Systems Equipment Coop. (pres. 1978-80), Pi Delta Epsilon (pres. 1948). Republican. Methodist. Home: 227 Cape St John Rd Annapolis MD 21401 Office: 8000 Parston Dr Washington DC 20028

POWDRILL, GARY LEO, automotive co. exec.; b. Butte, Mont., Nov. 26, 1945; s. Harold Holmes and Genevieve Marie (Tansey) P.; B.S., Gonzaga U., 1969; M.B.A., U. Detroit, 1973; m. Marsha McKeon, Oct. 6, 1979. Plant layout and design engr. Ford Motor Co., Sterling Heights, Mich., 1969-73, divisional plant engr., chassis div., 1973-74, sect. supr. plant engring., Indpls., 1974-78, mgr. plant engring., Indpls., 1978—. Registered profl. engr., Ind. Mem. Indpls. Soc. Profl. Engrs., Indpls. C. of C. (mayor's tech. adv. com. 1975—). Roman Catholic. Club: Elks. Home: Rural Route 1 Box SC 8 New Palestine IN 46163 Office: 6900 English Ave Indianapolis IN 46219

POWELL, CHARLES G., advt. co. exec.; b. N.Y.C., Oct. 4, 1928; s. Bonney Macoy and Elizabeth (Gould) P.; A.B. Colgate U., 1951; postgrad. U. Hawaii, 1951-52, N.Y.U., 1952-54; m. Norma Antonio, Aug. 11, 1962; children—Elizabeth Antonio, Charlene Kimball. Researcher Young & Rubicam, N.Y.C. 1954-56; acct. exec. Batten, Barton, Durstine & Osborne, N.Y.C., 1956-65; acct. supr. Mendelsohn Advtg., N.Y.C., 1965-68; v.p. advtg. Buchen Advtg., Inc., N.Y.C., 1968-71; writer, dir. marketing Foodgraphics Corps., N.Y.C., 1971-73; creative dir. Instnl. Advt. Assos., Hingham, Mass., 1973-74; supr. foodservice Mandabach & Simms Inc., N.Y.C., 1974—; dir. East of Suez Inc., Wolfeboro, N.H., CPR Corp., Manila, Philippines. Mem. Les Amis d'Escoffier Assn., Am. Culinary Fedn. (sec.). Address: RFD 1 Wolfeboro NH 03894

POWELL, DONALD LEWIS, mgmt. cons.; b. Easley, S.C., May 27, 1937; s. Plumer Marion and Essie Virginia (Freeman) P.; student Mars Hill Coll., 1955-56; B.S. in Pharmacy, (Am. Found. Pharm. Edn. scholar, Kappa Psi scholar), Med. U. S.C., 1959; M.S. in Pharmacy, U. Tex., 1966; m. Barbara Jeannine Russell, Aug. 29, 1964; children—David Douglass, Margaret Bentley. Research asso. U. Tenn. Med. Units, Memphis, 1968-70; sect. supr. quality control Hyland div. Baxter Travenol Labs., Costa Mesa, Calif., 1970-71, mgr. quality control, 1971-72, ops. mgr. quality control, 1972-74, dir. quality control, 1974-78; dir. quality control William Harvey Co. div. C.R. Bard, Inc., 1978-79; v.p. tech. ops. Bowman & Assos., Inc., 1979—. Mem. ann. fund raising com. YMCA, 1975-76; campaigner, state and local govt. candidates; membership chmn. Lido Sands Community Assn., 1973; sr. warden St. James Episcopal Ch., Newport Beach, Calif., 1977-79. Served to lt. comdr. USPHS, 1960-68. Mem. Health Industries Mfrs. Assn. (vice chmn. mfg., engring. Q.A. sect. 1974-79), Pharm. Mfrs. Assn. (biol. sect.), Am. Soc. Quality Control (forum speaker), Mariners Community Assn. Newport Beach, Newport Harbor Art Mus., AAAS, N.Y. Acad. Sci., Rho Chi, Kappa Psi. Democrat. Contbr. articles to profl. jours. Home: 3047 Farmington Ln NW Atlanta GA 30339

POWELL, ERNESTINE BREISCH, lawyer; b. Moundsville, W.Va., Feb. 16, 1906; d. Ernest Elmer and Belle (Wallace) Breisch; student Dayton YMCA Law Sch., 1929; m. Roger K. Powell, Nov. 15, 1935; children—R. Keith (dec.), Diane L.D., Bruce W. Admitted to Ohio bar, 1929; tax analyst tax dept. Wall, Cassell & Groneweg, Dayton, Ohio, 1929-31; practiced law, 1931-40; gen. counsel for Dayton Jobbers and Mfrs. Assn., 1931-41; mem. firm Powell, Powell & Weimer, Columbus, Ohio, 1944—. Ohio chmn. Nat. Woman's Party, Washington, 1950-51, nat. chmn., 1953, hon. nat. chmn. Pres. vol. activities com. Columbus State Sch., 1960-61, mem. bd. trustees, 1957-59. Mem. Nat. Assn. Women Lawyers, Am., Ohio, Columbus bar assns., Nat. Soc. Arts and Letters (pres. Columbus chpt. 1963-64), Nat. Lawyers Club (charter mem.). Co-author: Tax Ideas, 1955; Estate Tax Techniques, 1956—. Editor-in-chief: Women Lawyers Jour., 1943-45. Office: 17 S High St Columbus OH 43215

POWELL, FRANCIS WILSON, mag. editor, freelance writer; b. Northampton, Mass., Dec. 22, 1907; s. Lyman Pierson and Mary Gertrude (Wilson) P.; A.B., N.Y. U., 1929; m. Harriet Kathryn Powell, June 25, 1941; children—Elizabeth Lawrence Powell Mitchell, Marian Eloise Powell Bryant. Asst. buyer to mgr. basement advt. Abraham & Straus, Inc., N.Y.C., 1930-37; advt. mgr. Am. Furniture Co., El Paso, Tex., 1938-39; asst. advt. mgr. Western Auto Supply Co., Los Angeles, 1940-52; advt. mgr. Stauffer System, Los Angeles, 1953-55; various positions several Los Angeles advt. agencies, 1955-62; freelance writer advt. copy, trade paper articles, Los Angeles, 1962—; feature editor Tile & Decorative Surfaces mag., Los Angeles, 1976—. Platoon leader Los Angeles Aux. Police, 1941-45. Served to corporal Army N.G., 1926-28. Democrat. Episcopalian. Home and Office: 10320 Mather Ave Sunland CA 91040

POWELL, GRAHAM JOHN, holding co. exec.; b. Croydon, Eng., May 13, 1936; s. Ernest John and Mary Margaret (Williams) P.; came to U.S., 1971; student Haileybury Coll., Eng.; B.A., Exeter Coll., Oxford (Eng.) U., 1959; M.A., 1971; m. Mary Melinda Cassel, June 24, 1973. Mgmt. trainee Shell-Mex & BP Ltd., London, 1959-63; chief internal auditor BP (W. Africa) Ltd., Nigeria, 1963-67; group fin. controller EMI Ltd., London, 1967-71; v.p. planning Capitol Industries Inc., Hollywood, Calif., 1971-72; pres. Audio Devices Inc., Glenbrook, Conn., 1972-74; asst. mng. dir. EMI Records Ltd., London, 1974-75; chmn. EMI Tech., Inc., Danbury, Conn., 1975—; div. dir. EMI Ltd., London; dir. Threshold Tech. Inc., Delran, N.J. Served to lt. Royal Signal Corp, Brit. Army, 1954-56. Fellow Royal Econ. Soc. Home: Dads Ln Stamford CT 06903 Office: 100 Research Dr Glenbrook CT 06906

POWELL, HAROLD FRYBURG, mfg. co. exec.; b. Corry, Pa., Oct. 18, 1932; s. Harold K. and Freda F. Powell; B.S. in Econs., Wharton Sch., U. Pa.; postgrad. Western Res. U.; m. Jacqueline Williams, May 14, 1955; children—Jeffrey, Stephen. Securities analyst Central Nat. Bank, Cleve., 1955-61; asst. treas. Carling Brewing Co., Cleve., 1961-63, div. controller, St. Louis, 1961-67; mgr. corp. planning, then asst. to pres. Philip Morris Inc., N.Y.C., 1967-71; v.p. Benson & Hedges (Can.) Ltd., Toronto, 1971-74; v.p. fin. Standard Brands Ltd., Montreal, Que., Can., 1974-76, Internat. Standard Brands Inc., N.Y.C., 1976-77; v.p., treas. Standard Brands Inc., N.Y.C., 1977-79, v.p., comptroller, 1979—. Office: Standard Brands Inc 625 Madison Ave New York NY 10022

POWELL, JOHN ERIC, mining engr.; b. Wales, U.K., June 22, 1931; s. William John and Phyllis (Evans) P.; came to U.S., 1977; diploma in elec. engring. Glamorgan Coll. Tech., Treforest, South Wales, 1957, diploma in mining, 1959; m. Beryl Howard, Apr. 9, 1955; children—Katrina, Nicola, Andrian, Darren. Mining engr. U.K. Nat. Coal Bd., 1959-61; group engr. Bengal Coal, India, 1961-65; mining engr. PD Tech. Services, London, 1965-68; sales engr. Mine Equipment Co., Toronto, Ont., Can., 1968-70; sr. mining engr. Wright Engrs., Vancouver, B.C., Can., 1970-71; pres. Delway Engring., Vancouver, 1971-74; projects mgr. Radmark Engring., Vancouver, 1974-77, v.p., Pitts., 1977—; cons. in field. Recipient Dowty prize Glamorgn Coll. Tech., 1957, W.R. Davies prize South Wales Inst. Engrs., 1961; registered profl. engr., Ont.; registered mine mgr., Gt. Brit., India, B.C., Can.; chartered engr., Gt. Brit. Mem. Soc. Mining Engrs., Can. Inst. Mining and Metallurgy, Pa. Soc. Profl. Engrs. Contbr. articles on transp. in coal mines to profl. jours., 1961-78; co-patentee pneumatic ditch backfill concept. Home: 955 Lakemont Dr Pittsburgh PA 15243 Office: PO Box 13267 Pittsburgh PA 15243

POWELL, JOHN ROLFE, accountant; b. Birmingham, Ala., Mar. 23, 1915; s. Bolling Raines and Marie (Arnold) P.; B.Accounts, Wheeler Bus. Coll., Birmingham, 1933; grad. LaSalle Extension U., 1936; m. Sarah Randolph Lacy, Apr. 15, 1939; children—Sarah Lacy Powell Pudner, Medora Braxton Powell Fahnestock, Marie Bolling Powell Walker, John Rolfe. Office mgr. Rawlings & Starke Ins. Agy., Montgomery, Ala., 1934-40; accountant, propr. John Rolfe Powell, Montgomery, Ala., 1941—; co-chmn. 17th Joint Fed. Tax Clinic, U. Ala., 1963, chmn. 18th Clinic, 1964. Chmn. budget and fin. com. Montgomery Child Care Council, 1967-69. C.P.A., Ala. Mem. Ala. Soc. C.P.A.'s (chpt. pres. 1961-62), Ala. Assn. Pub. Accountants (chpt. pres. 1954), Nat. Assn. Accountants (chpt. pres. 1967-68), Am. Inst. C.P.A.'s (regional joint trial bd. 1975-76), Montgomery Estate Planning Council (exec. com. 1979-80). Episcopalian. Club: Rotary. Home: 1345 Glen Grattan Montgomery AL 36111 Office: 507 Executive Bldg Montgomery AL 36104

POWELL, MAX C., packaging co. exec.; b. Findlay, Ohio, Apr. 14, 1919; s. Forrest H. and Merlynn C. P.; A.B., U. Mo., 1941, J.D., 1943; student, Centre D'Etudes Industrielles, Geneva, 1956; m. Jane E. Windsor, Dec. 2, 1945. Admitted to Mo. bar, 1943, Ohio bar, 1946; asso. firm Fuller, Harrington, Seney and Henry, Toledo, 1945-46; with Owens-Ill., 1946—, v.p., gen. mgr. Owens-Ill. Internat., S.A., Geneva, 1960-66, v.p. forest products div. Owens-Ill., Toledo, 1966-72, v.p. internat. div., 1972-73, v.p. corp. mergers and acquisitions, 1973—. Trustee, St. Luke's Hosp., Maumee, Ohio, 1974-78. Served to lt. (j.g.) USN, 1943-45. Club: Inverness (Toledo). Office: PO Box 1035 Toledo OH 43666

POWELL, RALPH EDWIN, mfg. co. exec.; b. Kentfield, Calif., Sept. 22, 1946; s. Ralph Edwin and Essie (Harris) P.; student U. of the South, 1964-65; B.S. in Engring. Mgmt., U.S. Air Force Acad., 1969; postgrad. Tex. A&M U., 1970; m. Wendy Kovac, Dec. 29, 1969; children—Elizabeth, Ralph, Jonathan, Eleanor. Commd. 2d lt. U.S. Air Force, 1969, advanced through grades to capt., 1972; ret., 1974; with Joy Mfg. Co., 1974-78, relocation and constrn. project mgr., Colorado Springs, Colo., 1977-78, elastomers ops. mgr., 1978—. Mem. Polyurethane Mfrs. Assn., Soc. Am. Value Engrs., Adminstrv. Mgmt. Soc. (program chmn. 1977-78), Chi Epsilon Pi. Republican. Presbyterian. Home: 3210 Red Onion Circle Colorado Springs CO 80918 Office: 1170 Ford St Colorado Springs CO 80915

POWELL, RAMON JESSE, cons., lawyer; b. Macon, Mo., Mar. 1, 1935; s. Robert Evan and Blanche Odella (Dry) P.; A.B., U. Mo., 1957; postgrad. (Fulbright scholar) U. Brussels, 1957-58; J.D., Harvard, 1965. Admitted to D.C. bar, 1966, Va. bar, 1975, U.S. Supreme Ct. bar, 1975; atty. adviser Office Gen. Counsel, Office Chief Engr., Dept. Army, Washington, 1965-70; gen. counsel U.S. Water Resources Council, Washington, 1970-74; individual practice law, Washington, 1975-76; pres., gen. counsel Leman Powell Assos., Inc., Alexandria, Va., 1976—. Served as officer USAF, 1958-62. Mem. Va. Trial Lawyers Assn., Bar Assn. D.C., Am., Fed. bar assns., Nat. Lawyers Club, Beta Theta Pi, Phi Beta Kappa, Omicron Delta Kappa, Delta Sigma Rho. Office: 303 Wythe Bldg 515 Wythe St Alexandria VA 22314

POWELL, RAYMOND WILLIAM, fin. planner; b. Waterbury, Conn., June 17, 1944; s. Don C. and Kathryn (Linhard) P.; B.S., So. Conn. State Coll., New Haven, 1966, M.S., 1969; postgrad. U. Bridgeport (Conn.); m. Janet Yasinski, June 24, 1967; 1 son, Raymond Joseph. Pres., R.W. Powell Enterprises, Inc., fin. and tax cons., Watertown, Conn., 1972—; dir.-owner Educators Tax Service, Watertown, 1972—, Powell's Acctg. Service, 1975—, Powell's Fin. Planning Service, 1977—. Vice chmn. Watertown Town Council, 1975-76. Cert. fin. planner. Mem. Nat. Assn. Enrolled Agts., Internat. Assn. Fin. Planners, Am. Soc. Tax Cons., Conn. Assn. Enrolled Agts. Democrat. Author articles in field. Address: 417 Smith Pond Rd Watertown CT 06795

POWELL, ROBERT DOMINICK, lawyer; b. Bklyn., Mar. 30, 1942; s. Ralph and Dorothy Piccola; B.A., U. Pa., 1963; LL.B., St. John's U., 1966; LL.M., Georgetown U., 1978; m. Pamela Van Horn Powell, Aug. 19, 1978. Admitted to N.Y. bar, 1966, D.C. bar, 1967, Md. bar, 1976, also to practice before U.S. Supreme Ct., Circuit Cts. Appeals, D.C. Circuit Ct. Appeals; trial atty. FAA, Washington, 1966-68; asso. firm Welch & Morgan, Washington, 1968-69; partner firm Smith & Pepper, Washington, 1969-72, Powell & Becker, 1972-73, Sanders, Schnabel, Joseph & Powell, Washington, 1978—; gen. counsel Nat. Bus. Aircraft Assn., Nat. Coal and Surface Mining Council, U.S. Coal Conclave. Mem. Internat. Law Soc., Am., Fed., N.Y. State, Md., D.C. bar assns., Am. Trial Lawyers Assn., Am. Judicature Soc. Club: Wings (N.Y.C.). Author: Faint and Low, Soft and Sweet (poetry), 1971. Office: 730 15th St NW Washington DC 20005

POWELL, ROBERT NICHOLAS, ins. co. exec.; b. Detroit, June 14, 1928; s. Nicholas Miles and Helen Katherine (Davis) P.; B.B.A., U. Mich., 1951, M.A., 1952; m. Patricia A. Tashjian, Apr. 18, 1953; children—Pamela R. Powell Freday, Laura J. Powell McGonagle, Lucy A. With Calif.-Western States Life Ins. Co., Sacramento, 1952-69, v.p., actuary, 1962-69, v.p., chief actuary, 1969; v.p. Nationwide Corp., Columbus, Ohio, 1969-79; pres., chief exec. officer West Coast Life/Gulf Atlantic Life, San Francisco, 1980—, also dir. Served with U.S. Army, 1946-47. Fellow Soc. Actuaries; mem. Am. Acad. Actuaries. Republican. Presbyterian. Office: 1275 Market St San Francisco CA 94103

POWELL, WILLIAM COUNCIL, mfg. co. exec.; b. Burlington, N.C., Nov. 5, 1948; s. Thomas Edward and Annabelle (Council) P.; B.S., Va. Mil. Inst., 1971; M.B.A., Wake Forest U., 1974; student Elon Coll., 1971, U. S.C., 1968-70; m. Jacqueline Garrison, July 3, 1976; 1 son, William Council. Vice pres. Bobbitt Labs., Burlington, N.C., 1974-77, pres., 1977—; chmn. bd. Home Entertainment & Decor Systems, Inc., Burlington, 1978—; v.p. Warren Land Co., 1978—; pres. Powell Leasing Co., 1979—; dir. Carolina Biol. Supply Co., Inc. Served to capt. USAR, 1971-79. Real estate broker, N.C. Mem. Soc. Plastics Engrs., NAM. Democrat. Methodist. Club: Ducks Unltd. (steering com.). Home: 1616 Rockwood Ave Burlington NC 27215 Office: 1834 W Davis St Burlington NC 27215

POWELL, WILLIAM WINTERSMITH, consumer products co. exec.; b. Woodbury, N.J., May 18, 1937; s. William and Marcia (Wintersmith) P.; A.B. magna cum laude, Princeton U., 1959; m. Virginia Thais Richards, Feb. 23, 1963. Various mktg. positions Colgate Palmolive Co., N.Y. and Europe, 1959-64, 66-71, mng. dir., Milan, Italy, 1972-73, v.p., gen. mgr. Household Products div., N.Y.C., 1974-75, corporate v.p., 1975—; pres., chief exec. officer Kendall Co., Boston, 1975-78, also dir. various subsidiaries; group v.p. diversified cos. Colgate Palmolive Co., N.Y.C., 1979—; with Ogilvy & Mather, 1964-65. Trustee Children's Hosp., Boston; bd. dirs. Mass. Taxpayers Assn., 1976-78; mem. Mayor's Advisory Bd. Cultural Affairs, Boston. Served with U.S. Army, 1960. Mem. Soap and Detergents Mfrs. Assn. (dir. 1974-75), Am. C. of C. in Italy (dir. 1972-73). Address: 300 Park Ave New York NY 10022

POWER, JOEL RALPH, fin. relations exec.; b. Berwyn, Ill., Sept. 7, 1939; s. Joseph R. and Lois M. (Lindsey) P.; student Colo. Sch. Mines (Pullman Found. scholar) 1957-58; B.A. in English, No. Ill. U., 1963; m. Sharon Mary Newman, June 17, 1961; children—Andrew Baird, Mary Joel. Div. mgr. Sears, Roebuck & Co., Washington, 1965-67; tech. writer IIT Inst., Annapolis, Md., 1967-68; documentation supr. URS Systems Corp., Killeen, Tex., 1968-70; dir. pub. info. McKendree Coll., Lebanon, Ill., 1970-71; pub. relations supr. Standard Oil Co. Ind., Chgo., 1971-72, Eastern pub. relations supr.,

Atlanta, 1972-74, sr. staff advisor, New Orleans, 1974-76; pres. Powerline, Inc., Grand Rapids, Mich., 1977-79, also associated with E.F. Hutton & Co., Keller-Crescent Co., J.I. Scott Co.; mgr. corp. relations Mitchell Energy & Devel. Corp., Houston, 1980—; chmn. pub. info. COST Atlantic and Clean Atlantic Assos., 1976; nat. publicity chmn. Agr. Day, 1979, 80; lectr. various colls. and univs. 1970—. Served with U.S. Army, 1963-65. Cert., N.Y. Stock Exchange, Nat. Assn. Securities Dealers. Mem. Nat. Investor Relations Inst., Petroleum Investor Relations Assn., Alpha Tau Omega. Contbr. articles to profl. publs. Office: Mitchell Energy & Devel Corp 2001 Timberloch Pl Woodlands TX 77380

POWERS, DEMOSTHENES JOHN, fin. group exec.; b. Zeigler, Ill., Nov. 20, 1929; s. John George Antimisaris and Anna (Georgiadis) P.; B.S., Robert Morris Coll., 1951; spl. studies U. Pitts., 1952-58; m. Helene Tousimis, June 26, 1955; children—John D., Alexandros D., Danae M. Founder, pres. Powers Ins. Agy., Inc., Pitts., 1958, Phoenix Credit Corp., Columbus, Ohio, 1970, Phoenix Leasing Co., Pitts., 1974, Travel Corp. Am. Chmn., Pan-Hellenic Congress Western Pa.; pres., founder Periclean Found., Hellenic Cultural Center; mem. council Greek Orthodox Diocese of Pitts. Mem. Ind. Ins. Agts., Credit Assn. U.S. Republican. Clubs: Rotary, Kiwanis, Ahepa. Home: 2293 William Penn Hwy Pittsburgh PA 15235 Office: Seville Sq Suite 1202 4293 Greensburg Pike Pittsburgh PA 15235

POWERS, EARL HERSHEL, diversified co. exec.; b. Tell City, Ind., May 5, 1934; s. Archie E. and Mabel (Hobbs) P.; B.S., Western Ky. U., 1961; m. Sharon A. Grimes, Jan. 15, 1972; children from previous marriage—Allen, Patricia, Kimberly, Lisa Fentress, Jeff Fentress. Account exec., Wolverine World Wide, Rockford, Mich., 1961-67; owner Powers Cos., Inc. bldg. and devel. real estate, Evansville, Ind., 1967—, Newburgh, Ind., 1969—; chmn. First Nat. Mortgage Co., pres. Ky., Ind. Co.; pres. Koal Industries Corp., Inc.; dir. Powers Co. Tenn., Powers Co. Fla. Adv., Council Govts., 1973-75; pres., Zion United Ch. of Christ; bd. dirs. Good Samaritan Home. Served with USNR, 1954-58. Recipient Silver Key award for condominium design U.S. Steel, 1973. Mem. C. of C., Nat. Home Builders Assn. (nat. outstanding achievement award, 1974) Nat. Inst. Real Estate Brokers, Evansville Bd. Realtors, Multiple Listing Service, Phi Delta Kappa, LaSalle Law Alumni Club. Mason (Shriner), Elk. Clubs: Tri State Racquet, Oak Meadow. Office: 5200 Washington Ave Evansville IN 47715

POWERS, JAMES JOSEPH, lawyer, ins. co. exec.; b. N.Y.C., Oct. 25, 1936; s. James Michael and Margaret (Kaley) P.; B.B.A., Iona Coll., 1963; J.D., St. John's U., 1968; m. Mary E. Grifferty, Oct. 17, 1959; children—Stephen, Patricia Ann, Theresa, Kevin, Matthew. With claims dept. N.Y. Central R.R., 1951-58; successively adjuster, claim supr., claim mgr., home office claim supr., various ins. and ins. related cos., 1958-72; regional claim mgr. Foremost Ins. Co., 1972-76; v.p. Worexco Corp., N.Y.C., 1976-77; v.p., sec. Constitution Reins. Co., 1977—. Bd. dirs. Mid-Hudson Soc. Epilepsy, 1977—. Mem. Fedn. Ins. Counsel, Excess and Surplus Lines Claims Assn. Roman Catholic. Club: K.C. (past grand knight). Home: 62 Convent Rd Nanuet NY 10954 Office: 110 William St New York NY 10038

POWERS, JOHN GLENN, JR., mfg. co. exec.; b. Evanston, Ill., Nov. 7, 1930; s. John Glenn and Marjorie (McShane) P.; B.S.M.E., Marquette U., 1952; m. Joan M. Dougherty, June 6, 1974; children by previous marriage—John J., Daniel M., Anne M., William P., James F., Kathleen V.; stepchildren—Paula Aussem, Jack Aussem, Nancy Aussem. With Benjamin Electric Mfg. Co., Des Plaines, Ill., 1954-58; with Signode Corp., Glenview, Ill., 1958—, v.p. mfg., 1976—. Trustee, Goodwill Industries, Chgo., 1979—. Served with U.S. Army, 1952-54. Republican. Roman Catholic. Home: 3980 Gregory Dr Northbrook IL 60062 Office: 3600 W Lake Ave Glenview IL 60025

POWERS, LAWRENCE EDWARD, advt. exec.; b. Waterford, N.Y., Aug. 26, 1946; s. John Joseph and Bertha Mary (Whiting) P.; B.S. in Mktg., New Eng. Coll., 1969; m. Nancy P. Venaziano, Nov. 6, 1970; children—Ellen M., Nancy L., Erin E., Megan A. With Troy Pub. Co. (N.Y.), 1969-75, Capital Newspapers Group, Albany, N.Y., 1975-79; nat. classified advt. mgr. San Francisco Newspaper Agy., 1979—. First pres., charter mem. Waterford Young Rep. Club, 1964. Clubs: San Francisco Press, K.C. Office: 925 Mission St San Francisco CA 94103

POWERS, ODELL EUGENE, business exec.; b. Peoria, Ill., May 2, 1928; s. Clarence O. and Beulah P. (Fernandez) P.; B.A., Bradley U., 1952; m. Elizabeth Marie Johnson, Mar. 12, 1950; children—Mark Daniel, Kristin Lynne, Julianne Lynne, Elizabeth M. Mng. dir. Caterpillar Mitsubishi, Inc., Tokyo, 1963-67; dir. internat. fin. and adminstrn. Honeywell, Inc., Mpls., 1967-69, v.p., Brussels, 1969-71, v.p. parent co., also exec. v.p. Honeywell-Europe, 1971-73; pres., chief exec. officer Turbodyne Corp., Mpls., 1973-76, chmn., chief exec. officer, 1976-78; chmn., chief exec. officer Worthington Compressors Co., Holyoke, Mass., 1976-78; pres., chief operating officer, dir. McGraw-Edison Co., Rolling Meadows, Ill., 1979-80; pres., chief operating officer S.J. Groves & Sons Co., Mpls., 1980—; dir. Internat. Multifoods, Mpls. Trustee, Bradley U., Peoria. Served with AUS, 1946-47. Mem. U.S. C. of C. (internat. trade subcom.). Republican. Presbyterian. Clubs: Minneapolis, Minikahda Country (Mpls); Chicago; Deepdale Golf (N.Y.); Metropolitan (N.Y.C.). Office: PO Box 1267 Minneapolis MN 55440

POWERS, ROBERT A., investment banker; b. Mt. Vernon, N.Y., 1918; ed. Yale, 1940. Chmn., chief exec. officer Smith Barney, Harris Upham & Co., Inc. Address: 1345 Ave of Americas New York NY 10019

POWERS, ROBERT THROOP, chem. co. exec.; b. Brookline, Pa., Mar. 27, 1921; s. Heman T. and Margaret (Reynolds) P.; B.A., Wabash Coll., 1943; m. Helen Bagge, July 31, 1943; children—Elizabeth, Susan, Robert. With Nalco Chem. Co., Chgo., 1946—, exec. v.p., 1965-70, pres., 1970-77, chmn. bd., 1971—, chief exec. officer, 1971-79; dir. Amsted Industries, Bliss & Laughlin Industries, McGraw-Edison Co. Trustee Wabash Coll., George Williams Coll., Glenwood Sch. for Boys. Served with USNR, 1943-46. Mem. Ill. C. of C., Phi Gamma Delta. Presbyn. Clubs: Chicago, Mid-Am., Carlton, Hinsdale Golf, Butler Nat. Golf, Pinnacle Peak Country. Home: 179 Briarwood Loop Oak Brook IL 60521 Office: 2901 Butterfield Rd Oak Brook IL 60521

POWERS, RONALD GEORGE, corp. bank and govtl. mgmt. cons.; b. N.Y.C., July 9, 1934; s. Lee Whitney and R. Anne Powers; m. Elizabeth Braislin McClellan, July 24, 1980. Pres., Ronald Powers, Inc., Westport, Conn., 1971; adviser to banks, corps. and govts. on strategy and mgmt., 1971—. Republican. Episcopalian. Club: La Coquille (Palm Beach, Fla.). Home: 5 Crooked Mile Rd Westport CT 06880 Office: 8 Broad St Westport CT 06880

POWNALL, THOMAS GILMORE, corp. exec.; b. Cumberland, Md., Jan. 20, 1922; B.S.E.E., U.S. Naval Acad., 1946. Pres., chief operating officer, dir. Martin Marietta Corp., Bethesda, Md.; dir. Sundstrand Corp. Office: 6801 Rockledge Dr Bethesda MD 20034

POWNING, MAYNARD WALKER, elec. mfg. co. exec.; b. Boston, Sept. 21, 1931; s. Kimball Colby and Carolyn (Walker) P.; A.B. in Social Relations, Harvard, 1953. With Koehler Mfg. Co., Marlboro, Mass., 1957—, purchasing agt., 1961-64, pres., dir., 1964—; dir. Associated Industries of Mass., Blue Gold Sea Farms Inc. Served to 1st lt. with USAF, 1954-56; Korea. Mem. Smaller Bus. Assn. New Eng., The Newcomen Soc., Young Pres.' Orgn. Club: Somerset, Harvard (Boston). Home: 780 Boylston St Boston MA 02199 Office: 123 Felton St Marlboro MA 01752

POYLE, RICHARD PHILIP, ins. agy. exec.; b. Detroit, Feb. 9, 1946; s. Philip and Ann (Honigman) P.; B.A. in Risk and Ins., Mich. State U., 1967; 1 dau., Erin. Exec. v.p. Poyle Assos., Inc., Birmingham, Mich., 1976, pres., 1976—. Vice chmn. div. Allied Jewish Campaign, 1979-80. Mem. Mich. Surplus Agts. Assn., Engring. Soc. Detroit, Nat. Space Assn., Jacques Cousteau Soc. Republican. Clubs: Econ., Standard (Detroit). Office: Poyle Assos Inc 30200 Telegraph Rd Suite 281 Birmingham MI 48010

PRACHT, IRENA, corp. exec.; b. Council Grove, Kans., Dec. 24, 1927; d. Berend Hiram and Amanda (Anderson) Bicker; B.S. in Bus., Kans. State Coll., Emporia, 1949; student Kans. State Agrl. Coll., Manhattan, 1944-45; m. Harold Ray Pracht, Oct. 23, 1948; children—Rae Ann Pracht Lowery, Gregory Ray, Rena Rochelle Pracht Coby, Glen Fredrick. Bookkeeper, Eby Constrn. Co., Wichita, Kans., 1951-52; partner Bell Sewing Centers, Tex. & N.Mex., 1954-62, Tri-State Sewing Machine Distbrs., Council Grove, 1962-68, Pracht Enterprises, El Paso, Tex., 1975—; acct. Mize, Houser & Reed, C.P.A.'s, Topeka, 1968-69, Tex. Mfg. Co., El Paso, 1969-71; controller Farah Mfg. Co., El Paso, 1971—; sec.-treas. Vernon Investment Corp., El Paso, 1971—. C.P.A., Tex. Mem. Tex. Soc. C.P.A.'s, Theta Sigma Upsilon, Xi Phi. Democrat. Home: 3110 Dundee St El Paso TX 79925 Office: 8889 Gateway W El Paso TX 79925

PRADO, DANIEL HERRERA, fin. cons.; b. San Antonio, May 27, 1949; s. Domingo F. and Juanita H. (Herrera) P.; B.B.A., St. Mary U., 1971, M.B.A., 1974; m. Tamara Jean Little, May 30, 1970; children—Nicole Denise, Danielle Marie. Mktg. analyst Volkswagen of Am., San Antonio, 1971-72, advt. asst., 1972, asst. distbn. mgr., 1972-73, dist. sales mgr., 1973-76; pres. Las Cocinas, Inc., San Antonio, 1976-78; asso. Avante Internat. Systems Corp., San Antonio, 1978—; mem. bus. faculty San Antonio Coll., 1977—. Mem. Am. Mktg. Assn., Assn. M.B.A. Execs., Tex. Real Estate Brokers, San Antonio Realtor Assn. Roman Catholic. Home: 90 Mossey Cup Ln San Antonio TX 78231 Office: 830 NE Loop 410 Suite 303 San Antonio TX 78209

PRADO-RUIZ, ENRIQUE, steel co. exec.; b. El Paso, Tex., Dec. 24, 1914; s. Gilberto and Maria (Ruiz) Prado; Engr. of Mines, Tex. Coll. Mines and Metallurgy, U. Tex., 1939; m. Maria Garza, Apr. 14, 1951; children—Enrique, Maluza, Malena, Guadalupe, Ricardo. Plant supt. Cia Maderera de Ventanas, Durango, Mex., 1946-52; dir. Comision de Fomento Minero, Saltillo, Mex., 1961-68; mine mgr. Masapil Copper Co., Saltillo, 1960-61; mine mgr. Calabaza unit Minera Penoles, S.A., 1952-60; asst. dir. Fundidora Monterrey, S.A. (Mex.), 1968—. Mem. Geol. Soc. Am., Assn. Ingenieros Metalurgistas y Geologos (founding). Roman Catholic. Home: 406-P Guadalquivir Col Del Valle NL Mexico Office: 1000-S Zaragoza Monterrey NL Mexico

PRAGER, H(ILLEL) LEE, sound equipment mfg. co. exec.; b. Bklyn., July 11, 1935; s. Benjamin and Sadye Z. (Newman) P.; B.S., Mass. Inst. Tech., 1957; M.B.A., Xavier U. Ohio, 1963; m. Patricia D. Allan, May 6, 1955; children—Deborah D., Jill P. Sales engr. Goodyear Tire & Rubber Co., Akron, Ohio, 1957-61; field rep. Lightolier, Inc., Cin., 1961-63; market devel. specialist USI Film Products div. Nat. Distillers, Stratford, Conn., 1963-65; product mgr. Extrudo Film Corp. div. Standard Oil N.J., N.Y.C., 1965-68; gen. mgr. wheel products Amerace-Esna Corp., Butler, N.J., 1968-74; v.p., gen. mgr. lawn watering products div. Amerace Corp., Worthington, Ohio, 1974-75; pres. H.B. Sherman Co. div. Citation Cos. Inc., Battle Creek, Mich., 1975-79; 1979—; pres. Prager Land Trust, Interdeck Devel. Co.; v.p., gen. mgr. Atlas Sound Co., Parsippany, N.J. Mem. Soc. Plastic Engrs., Am. Marketing Assn. Club: Chequesset Yacht and Country (Wellfleet, Mass.). Home: 38 Lake Dr Mountain Lakes NJ 07046 Office: 10 Pomeroy Rd Parsippany NJ 07054

PRAGER, HERMAN JOHN, JR., mfg. co. exec.; b. New Orleans, Jan. 14, 1925; s. Herman John and Althea May (Dowty) P.; student La. State U., 1942, Tulane U., 1946; m. Katherine Mary Landry, Sept. 11, 1946; children—Herman John, III, Kurt Francis. With Prager, Inc., gear and machine products, New Orleans, 1946—, now pres., chief exec. officer. Served with USNR, 1942-46. Mem. NAM, Am. Mgmt. Assn., Mfrs. and Repairers Assn., New Orleans C. of C., Am. Legion, U.S. Submarine Vets. World War II (past comdr. La.), Am. Power Boat Assn., New Orleans Power Boat Assn. (past commodore), Internat. Game Fishing Assn. Roman Catholic. Clubs: New Orleans Big Game Fishing (founder, 1960, since pres.), Internat. House, Plimsoll, So. Yacht. Tally-Ho, Pensacola (Fla.) Big Game Fishing, Kona Big Game Fishing, K.C. (3 deg.). Author articles on sports-fishing. Home: 1718 Oriole St New Orleans LA 70122 Office: 472 Howard Ave New Orleans LA 70130

PRASSEL, FREDERICK FRANZ, constrn. co. exec.; b. San Antonio, Nov. 14, 1934; s. Victor, Sr., and Eda Marie (Groos) P.; student U. Tubingen (Germany), Trinity U.; B.A., U. Tex., 1959; postgrad. doctoral program Calif. Western U.; m. Barbara Fry, July 2, 1959; children—Charlotte, Victor B., Edie C. Owner, pres. Prassel Constrn. Co., San Antonio, 1959—; sec.-treas., dir. Pras-Mel Corp.; pub. speaker. Bd. dirs. YMCA; deacon First Presbyterian Ch.; pres. Arthur Gray Jones Choir, 1978-80; mem. Leadership San Antonio Program, 1979-80. Served with U.S. Army, 1957-59. Mem. Am. Mgmt. Assn., Nat. Fedn. Ind. Bus., Builders Exchange of Tex., Constrn. Specifications Inst., Internat. Platform Assn., San Antonio C. of C., San Antonio Mus. Assn. Presbyterian. Clubs: Downtown (pres. 1980), Toastmasters (pres. 1976, gov. 1977-78), Oak Hills Country, Beethoven Maennerchor, Rotary (sec. 1978-79, service chmn. 1979-80, sgt.-at-arms 1980-81). Home: 116 Cardinal Ave San Antonio TX 78209 Office: 1000 S Comal St PO Box 526 San Antonio TX 78292

PRATHER, WILLIAM LEO, coll. adminstr.; b. Donna, Tex., Feb. 5, 1940; s. Leo Claudius and Iris Margaret (Frensley) P.; B.B.A., U. Tex., Austin, 1961; M.Accounting Sci., U. Ill., 1966; postgrad. U. Southwestern La., 1965; postgrad. mgmt. Am. Mgmt. Assn.; m. Judy Abbott, Aug. 23, 1963; children—Kristin Ann, Angela Lynn. Asst. bus. mgr. Amarillo (Tex.) Coll., 1961-64, dir. EDP tech., 1964-65, bus. mgr., 1965—; mem. coordinating bd. pub. community coll. formula adv. com. Tex. Coll. and Univ. System, 1971—, coordinating bd. spl. adv. com. community coll. programs. Treas., state conv. Tex. Library Assn., Amarillo, 1970; bd. dirs. Amarillo Girl Scouts, 1980-82. NSF grantee, 1965. Mem. Nat. (chmn. two-year colls. com. 1979-81), So. (chmn. jr. coll. com. 1976-77) assns. coll. and univ. bus. officers, Delta Sigma Pi. Club: Rotary (dist. treas. 1980-81). Co-author: A Workbook for IBM Machine Operation and Wiring, 1967. Home: 3316 Lombard Rd Amarillo TX 79106 Office: PO Box 447 Amarillo TX 79178

PRATT, CHARLES ALEXANDER, assn. exec.; b. Greensboro, N.C., Sept. 26, 1940; s. Charles Alexander and Evelyn (Kernodle) P.; B.A. in Econs., Guilford Coll., 1962; children—Alicia, Evelyn. Ins. investigator EquiFax, San Diego, Calif., 1963-66; owner, pres. Aquarium Products Internat., San Diego, 1966-79, asst. mgr. Mgmt. Recruiters, San Diego, 1979-80; exec. dir. Soc. Computer Simulation, 1980—. Treas. Sweetwater Valley Civic Assn., 1979; mem. Sweetwater Valley Community Planning Group, 1977-79. Mem. Data Processing Mgmt. Assn. Democrat. Home: 2545 Ridgeway Dr National City CA 92050 Office: 1010 Pearl St LaJolla CA 92032

PRATT, CHARLES HENRY, investor; b. Phoenix, May 15, 1911; s. Charles Henry and Ellen (Baber) P.; A.B. cum laude, Harvard, 1933; postgrad. M.I.T., 1941; postgrad. U.S. Command Gen. Staff Sch., French Army War Coll., U.S. Def. Strategic Intelligence Sch.; m. Charlotte Munn Sumner, Apr. 22, 1943; children—Judith, Sarah, Marie, Thomas. Mem. exec. tng. squad R. H. Macy & Co., N.Y.C., 1933; buyer L. Bamberger & Co., Newark, N.J., 1934; asst. sales mgr. Calif. Milling Corp., Los Angeles, 1935-40, Sheffield Farms Co., N.Y.C., 1941; commd. 2nd lt., U.S. Army, 1942, advanced through grades to col., 1960, ret., 1964; with Flagstaff Indsl. Park, Inc., 1964—, dir., v.p., Phoenix, 1972-80; propr. Kingpin Enterprises; cons. Latin Am. affairs Dept. State, 1964-66. Mem. city council City of Prescott (Ariz.), 1970-74, vice mayor, 1970-74; v.p. Ariz.-Mexico Commn., 1973-74; exec. com. Ariz. League of Cities and Towns, 1973-74; adv. bd. Ariz. Dept. Economic Security, 1974, Ariz. Emergency Services Assn., 1970-74, Ariz. Intergovtl. Personnel Act, 1978—. Decorated Legion of Merit (U.S.), Médaille de la Reconnaissance (France); Abdon Calderon medal (Ecuador). Mem. Ariz. Hist. Soc., Retired Officers Assn., Fine Arts Assn. Prescott, Prescott Corral of Westerners, SHAPE Officers Assn. Republican. Home: 320 Plaza Dr Prescott AZ 86301 also 1737 Montana Vista Lake Havasu City AZ 86403 Office: PO Box 1801 Prescott AZ 86301

PRATT, DONALD HENRY, mfg. co. exec.; b. Hays, Kans., Dec. 2, 1937; s. Donald Edwin and Ida Marjorie (Dreiling) P.; B.S., Wichita State U., 1960; M.B.A., Harvard, 1965; m. George-Ann Hinkle, June 7, 1960; children—Jacqueline, Donald Ashley. Indsl. engr. Proctor & Gamble, Kansas City, Kans., 1960, Butler Mfg. Co., Galesburg, Ill., 1965-67, mgr., Kansas City, Mo., 1967-73, v.p., 1973-78, sr. v.p., 1978—, also dir.; dir. Union Nat. Bank, Wichita, Kans., 1973—. Bd. dirs. Kansas City (Mo.) Art Inst., 1979—. Served to capt., USAF, 1960-63. Mem. Wichita State U. Alumni Assn., Harvard Bus. Sch. Alumni Assn., Friends of the Zoo, Am. Mktg. Assn., Am. Inst. Steel Constrn., Metal Bldg. Mfrs. Assn., Beta Theta Pi. Home: 2303 W 59th St Shawnee Mission KS 66208 Office: PO Box 917 Kansas City MO 64141

PRATT, DOUGLAS MCLAIN, transp. co. exec.; b. 1911. Pres., Balt. Transit Co., 1952-55, Phila. Transit Co., 1955-62; pres. Nat. City Lines, Inc., Denver, 1962-78, chief exec. officer, 1962—, chmn., 1978—; chmn. exec. com., chief exec. officer, div. TIME-DC Inc. Office: 5555 S Denver Technical Center Pkwy Englewood CO 80110*

PRATT, DUDLEY C., JR., electric co. exec.; b. 1927; B.E. in Civil Engring., Yale U., 1950, M.E. in Structural Engring., 1951; M.B.A., U. Hawaii, 1971. Designer, Hawaiian Electric Co. Inc., Honolulu, 1953-56, asst. supt. distbn., 1956-59, asst. mgr. ops., 1959-61, mgr. distbn., 1961-69, asst. to pres., 1969-71, v.p. planning, 1971-80, exec. v.p., 1980—, also dir. Served to maj. U.S. Army. Office: 900 Richards St Honolulu HI 96813*

PRATT, EDMUND TAYLOR, JR., pharm. co. exec.; b. Savannah, Ga., Feb. 22, 1927; s. Edmund Taylor and Rose (Miller) P.; B.S. in Elec. Engring. magna cum laude, Duke U., 1947; M.B.A., U. Pa., 1949; m. Jeanette Louise Carneale, Feb. 10, 1951; children—Randolf Ryland, Keith Taylor. With IBM Corp., 1949-51, 54-57, asst. to exec. v.p., 1956-57; with IBM World Trade Corp., 1957-62, controller, 1958-62; asst. sec. financial mgmt. Dept. Army, 1962-64; controller Pfizer Inc., N.Y.C., 1964-67, v.p. operations internat. subsidiaries, 1967-69, chmn. bd., pres. internat. subsidiaries, 1969-71, exec. v.p. Pfizer Inc., 1970-71, pres., 1971-72, chmn., chief exec. officer, 1972—; also chmn. exec. com.; dir. Chase Manhattan Corp., Internat. Paper Co., Gen. Motors Corp. Trustee Com. for Econ. Devel., U.S. council Internat. C. of C.; bd. dirs. Internat. Exec. Service Corps, Japan Soc.; chmn. Emergency Com. for Am. Trade; trustee Duke U.; bd. overseers Wharton Sch. Commerce and Finance. Served to lt. (j.g.) USNR, 1952-54. Mem. Bus. Council, Bus. Roundtable (policy com.), N.Y. Chamber Commerce and Industry (dir.), N.Y.C. Partnership, Phi Beta Kappa. Office: 235 E 42d St New York NY 10017

PRATT, HARVEY ARTHUR, cons. pharmacist; b. Syracuse, N.Y., Mar. 6, 1939; s. James Arthur and Lavina Charlotte (Harvey) P.; B.S. in Pharmacy, U. Pitts., 1960; m. Ann Louise Rogers, July 31, 1974; children—Linda, Leann, Michelle, Jennine, Arriana. Store mgr., various stores Walgreen Co., Chgo., Gary, Ind., Houston, Baton Rouge and Denver, 1960-67; buyer May D&F, Denver, 1967-69; pres. Drug Fair, Inc., Englewood, Colo., 1969-79; cons., prin. Pratt and Assos., Englewood, 1979—; small bus. rep. Health Care Fin. Adminstrn., adv. to dir. Office Mgmt. and Budget, 1980—; mem. pharmacy faculty U. Colo., 1977—; bd. dirs., sec. Colo. Found. Med. Care, 1978—; chmn. 28th Western States Pharmacy Conf. Chmn., Englewood Holiday Parade, 1976—; vice chmn. Englewood Bd. Adjustments and Appeals; pres.-elect Englewood United Suburban C. of C. Named Pharmacist of Distinction, 1974; recipient Outstanding Service award Englewood C. of C., 1976. Mem. Colo. Pharmacal Assn., Am. Mgmt. Assn., Nat Assn. Retail Druggists, Am. Pharm. Assn. Denver Area Pharmacy Assn., Colo. Retail Liquor Dealers. Republican. Lutheran. Club: Arapahoe County Republican Men's. Office: PO Box B Englewood CO 80150

PRATT, JAMES LELAND, JR., electronics co. exec.; b. Colesville, N.Y., Dec. 17, 1933; s. James Leland and Agnes Carrie (Allen) P.; B.A., Hartwick Coll., 1958; M.S. (Gen. Aniline & Film grantee), Broome Coll., 1962; m. Judith Ann Esposito, June 21, 1974. Mgr., Gen. Aniline & Film, Binghamton, N.Y., 1957-65; prodn. mgr. N.Am. Phillips, Saugerties, N.Y., 1965-67; systems mgr. Control Data Corp., Rockville, Md., 1969-71; mktg. devel. mgr. Bunker Ramo Corp., Chgo., 1971-75; telecommunications mktg. dir. Gulf & Western Elco Corp., Willow Grove, Pa., 1975-77; dir. mktg. GTE Sylvania, Titusville, Pa., 1977—. Bd. dirs. Binghamton Recreation Comm., bd. dirs., pres. Alpha Delta Omega, Phi Sigma Kappa Alumni. Mem. Mil. Electronics and Communications Assn., Soc. Photog. Sci. Engrs., Soc. Phometric Instrumentation Engrs., Internal Electronic Elec. Engrs., U.S. Ind. Telephone Assn.; Electronic Connector Study Group. Patentee in field. Home: 3700 Kinter Hall Rd Edinboro PA 16412 Office: RD 2 Titusville PA 16354

PRATT, ROGER LEE, fiberglass co. exec.; b. Newark, Ohio, Aug. 16, 1927; s. Colburn L. and Sarah Maria (Pratt) Myers; B.A. in Psychology, Coll. Wooster (Ohio), 1949; m. Goldia Marie Eikleberry, June 17, 1950; children—David Lee, Toni Marie, Terry Sue, Howard Arthur. Salesman, Frye Furniture Co., Rittman, Ohio, 1949; asst. store mgr. J.J. Newberry Co., Wooster, Ohio, 1949-50; with Owens Corning Fiberglass Corp., 1950—, sr. economic analyst, 1968-70, mgr. financial analysis and cost control, Toledo, 1970-77, mgr. corporate cost control, 1977-79, dir. cost control and budgeting,

1979—. Asst. scoutmaster Boy Scouts Am., 1950-75. Republican. Club: Masons. Home: 727 Richards Rd Toledo OH 43607 Office: PO Box 901 Fiberglas Tower Toledo OH 43659

PRAVITZ, KENNETH LEROY, mfg. co. exec.; b. Fargo, N.D., June 24, 1927; s. Kenneth L. and Eleanor (Farr) P.; B.S., U. San Francisco, 1954; M.B.A., Ariz. State U., 1962; m. Eleanor J. Corral, Aug. 24, 1952; children—Kenneth B., Nora A. Indsl. engr. Montgomery Ward, Oakland, Calif., 1953-55; plant mgr., Fibreboard Products, San Francisco, 1955-67; asst. gen. mgr. Royal Industries, Pasadena, Calif., 1967-69; pres. F.P. Adams Co., Fullerton, Calif., 1969-71, Ariz. Pallet Co., Phoenix, 1962-71; dir. both cos.; gen. mgr. Stone Container Corp., Chgo., 1971-76; pres., chief exec. officer LD Plastic Molding Co., Santa Ana, Calif., 1976—, also Plating on Plastics, Inc., Anaheim. Served with USNR, 1945-46. Mem. TAPPI, Soc. Plastics Engrs., Soc. Plastics Industry. Home: 40 Cypress Tree Ln Irvine CA 92716 Office: 1305 E Wakeham Ave Santa Ana CA 92702

PRAY, ROBERT WILSON, drying systems mfg. exec.; b. Oakland, Calif., Sept. 6, 1926; s. Philander Wilson and Edith Nan (Swenson) P.; B.S., U.S. Mcht. Marine Acad., 1946; m. Anne Donohue, Mar. 14, 1947; children—Robert Wilson, Noel Anne. Engring. officer with various mcht. ships, 1946-51; with Minn. Mining & Mfg. Co., 1953-67; sales mgr. Thermogenics, Greenwich, Conn., 1967-68, v.p., 1969-70, pres., 1971-76; pres., dir. Flynn Drying Systems, Inc., New Rochelle, N.Y., 1977-80, Thermogenics Corp., Stamford, Conn., 1980—. Republican committeeman, N.Y., 1961-73. Served to lt. USNR, 1951-53. Recipient Environ. award Printing Industries Am., 1973, 75. Mem. Soc. Mfg. Engrs. Club: Lions. Patentee. Home: 40 W Elm St Greenwich CT 06830 Office: 190 Henry St Stamford CT 06902

PREBE, WILLIAM FRANCIS, automotive and truck parts co. exec.; b. Toledo, Aug. 27, 1922; s. Kaiser and Gertrude Mary (Hurley) P.; B.B.A., U. Toledo, 1949; m. Jeanette Marie Burtscher, July 2, 1949; children—Ronald William, Susan Lynette. With Dana Corp., automotive and truck parts mfr., Toledo, 1952—, market research mgr., 1966-68, corp. economist, 1969-76, v.p., economist, 1976—; adj. prof. econs. U. Toledo, 1975—. Served to lt. (j.g.) USNR, 1942-46, 50-52. Mem. Am. Statis Assn., Nat. Assn. Bus. Economists, Automotive Market Research Council (pres. 1980-81), Fourth Dist. Economists Round Table, American Turners, U. Toledo Bus. Alumni Assn. (sec. 1972-73) K.C. Contbr. articles to profl. publs. Home: 3620 Orchard Trail Toledo OH 43613 Office: PO Box 1000 Toledo OH 43697

PREBLE, JAMES JARVIS, banker; b. Waltham, Mass., Oct. 7, 1923; s. James Jarvis and Edwina (Jewett) P.; m. Lenore Ellsworth, July 12, 1945; children—Lenore B. (Mrs. Mark Leonardi), Linda (Mrs. A.S. Deming), Susan (Mrs. James Holtredt). Exec. v.p. United Bank & Trust Co., Hartford, Conn., 1960-63, pres., chief exec. officer, dir., 1963—; pres., chief exec. officer, dir. 1st Conn. Bancorp., Inc., 1970—; dir. Stockpole, Moore Tryon Co., Hartford, Pioneer Credit Corp., Hartford, Raymond Precision Industries, Middletown, Conn., New London County Mut. Ins. Co., Norwich, Conn., New Britain (Conn.) Nat. Bank, Simsbury (Conn.) Bank & Trust Co.; instr. Am. Inst. Banking, Williams Coll. Corporator Hartford Hosp., Mt. Sinai Hosp., Inst. of Living. Home: 88 Belknap Rd West Hartford CT 06117 Office: 101 Pearl St Hartford CT 06103

PREECE, TIMOTHY FRANCIS, aluminum co. exec.; b. Waterloo, Iowa, July 13, 1927; s. Wade Owen and Mary Agnes (Molumby) P.; B.S., Georgetown U. Sch. Fgn. Service, 1951; M.B.A., Harvard, 1953; m. Maryanne Dunn, June 27, 1953; children—Catherine Mary, Sarah, Thomas. Asst. to mgr. banking and credit internat. div. Ford Motor Co., N.Y.C., 1953-55; mgr. internat. office Carborundum Co., N.Y.C., 1955-57; sr. asst. treas. internat. div. planning and ops. Mobil Oil, N.Y., 1958-67; treas. internat. ops. Kaiser Aluminum & Chem. Corp., Oakland, Calif., 1968-69, asst. treas., 1970-71, corporate v.p., dir. planning and control, 1971—; chmn. bd., pres. Kaiser Center Inc., Kaiser Properties. No. Calif. vice chmn. NAACP Legal Def. Fund; bd. dirs. San Ramon Valley Little League. Served with USNR, 1945-47. Roman Catholic. Office: 300 Lakeside Dr Oakland CA 94643

PREEDY, CHARLES EVAN, financial cons.; b. Limon, Colo., Dec. 22, 1942; s. Oscar Roscoe and Helen Musa (Lawrence) P.; B.S., Calif. State U. at Los Angeles, 1969. Chief operating officer Hawaii Profl. Investors, Ltd., Honolulu, 1971-73; exec. v.p. Estate Builders Internat., Newport Beach, Calif., 1973-76; chmn. bd. dirs. Tennis Concepts, Inc., Newport Beach, 1976—; v.p. Trinity Pacific Fin. Group, Inc., 1979—; fin. cons. Sponsor, Children's Hosp. of Orange County (Calif.) Fund Raising Campaign, 1978. Served with USN, 1961-65. Mem. Sigma Nu. Republican. Clubs: John Wayne Tennis, Newport Bayview Yacht. Home: 765 Promontory Dr W Newport Beach CA 92660

PREIKSCHAT, EKHARD, control mfg. exec.; b. Insterburg, Germany; came to U.S., 1958, naturalized, 1968; s. Fritz and Martha P.; B.S., U. Wash., 1964, M.S., 1965; Ph.D., U. Birmingham (Eng.), 1966; m. Rosemary Hacking, Dec. 18, 1968; children—Andrew, Stephen. Research fellow U. Birmingham, 1965-69; research asso. U. Wash., 1969-72; v.p., chief exec. officer F.P. Research Lab., Inc., 1969-79; v.p., chief exec. officer EVR Control Mfg. & Devel. U.S.A., Inc., Bellevue, Wash., 1979—. Mem. IEEE, TAPPI, Am. Phys. Soc., Nat. Fedn. Ind. Bus., Phi Beta Kappa, Delta Phi Alpha, Xi Omega. Contbr. articles to tech. jours. Office: PO Box 1442 Bellevue WA 98005

PREMARAJAN, ADACHIRA N., machine tool mfg. co. exec.; b. India, Nov. 29, 1942; s. Adachira and Neleri V. (Sharada) Gopalan; student engring. and mgmt. I.I.E.T., Madras, India, York U.; m. Paniyan Vanaja, May 23, 1971; 1 son, Michael. Engring. trainee, 1961-64; tool and die maker, Madras, India, 1964-69; with Douglas Aircraft Co., Can., 1972-74, Picker X-Ray Mfg. Co., Can., 1972-74; purchasing and prodn. coordinator Burnside Equipment, Inc., Toronto, from 1974; founder, pres. PREM Industries, Inc., Grand Island, N.Y.; with J & A Keller Tech. Corp. Inc., Buffalo, Grand Island and Toronto. Mem. Nat. Assn. Precision Tool and Die Mfrs. Hindu. Office: Box 550 Grand Island NY 14072

PRENDERGAST, BRIAN, ins. co. exec.; b. Denver, July 26, 1948; s. Edmund T. and Yvonne S. (Saliba) P.; B.S., U.S. Air Force Acad., 1970; M.A., Central Mich. U., 1972; m. Alice Sawaya, Dec. 26, 1970; children—Amy L., Christina M. Ins. agt. Sunset Life, United Fidelity Life, 1976-78; partner, registered prin. Colo. Investor Services, Denver, 1979—; owner Prendergast & Assos., Denver, 1979—; lectr. Sunset Life's Agt. Conf., 1980. Roman Catholic. Clubs: Cedars of Lebanon (pres. 1979-80), Denver Athletic. Author: (with Douglas Nutt) Property Profile, 1978. Home: 11890 E Louisiana Ave Aurora CO 80012 Office: 2730 S Federal St Denver CO 80236

PRENDIVILLE, JOHN FRANCIS, JR., telephone co. exec.; b. Boston, May 26, 1928; s. John Francis and Helen Anne (Erickson) P.; B.S.E.E., Northeastern U., 1948, M.S.E.E., 1959; S.M., M.I.T., 1962; m. Mary Doris Johnson, June 18, 1955; children—Karen, John, Kristen. With New Eng. Telephone Co., 1948—, now v.p. network, Boston. Served with U.S. Army, 1950-54. Sloan fellow, 1961-62. Mem. IEEE, Tau Beta Pi. Roman Catholic. Home: 27 Elm St Acton MA 01720 Office: 185 Franklin St Boston MA 02107

PRENG, DAVID EDWARD, mgmt. cons.; b. Chgo., Sept. 30, 1946; s. Edward M. and Frances (Maras) P.: B.S., Marquette U., 1969; M.B.A., DePaul U., 1973; m. JoAnne Ferzoco, Dec. 6, 1969; children—Mark, Laura, Stephen. Supr., Shell Oil Co., Houston and Chgo., 1969-73; controller Litton Office Products, Houston, 1973-74; v.p. Addington & Assos., Houston, 1974-76; exec. v.p. Mantech S.W., Inc., Houston, 1976-77; sr. asso. Energy div. Korn/Ferry Internat., Houston, 1977-78; v.p. Kors Marlar & Assos., 1978-80; pres. Preng & Assos., 1980—. Vice chmn. parish council St. Albert Catholic Ch., also fin. adv. bd., men's club. Home: 3010 Bucknell Ct Sugar Land TX 77478

PRENSNER, STEVEN RANDOLPH, orgn. exec.; b. Houston, Oct. 19, 1949; s. Steven and Selma Ida (Berger) P.; B.A. (scholar), Howard Payne Coll., 1972; M.B.A., So. Ill. U., 1974. Asst. instr. bus. So. Ill. U., 1972-74; dir. accounting, asst. prof. bus. Trinity Coll. and Div. Sch., Deerfield, Ill., 1974-75, controller, 1975-77, v.p. for fin., treas., 1978-79; treas. The Navigators, Colorado Springs, Colo., 1979—. Mem. Nat. Assn. Coll. and Univ. Bus. Officers, Blue Key, Gamma Beta Phi. Club: Navigators. Home: 1081 Stanton Colorado Springs CO 80907 Office: PO Box 6000 The Navigators Colorado Springs CO 80934

PRENTICE, STEWART WEBSTER, r.r. exec.; b. Cin., May 4, 1919; s. Robert James and Grace Webster (Lombard) P.; student Coll. Advanced Traffic, Chgo., 1938-41, U. Oreg., 1941-43, LaSalle U., 1969-73; foster children—Robert, Carol, Debra, Cindy. Page make-up editor, dispatcher Chgo. Daily News, 1938-40; passenger agt., chief clk. Alton R.R., asst. terminal mgr. Chgo. Union Sta., 1940-46; dispatcher, traffic dir. Chgo. & Western Ind. R.R., 1946—. Mem. Coll. Advanced Traffic Alumni Assn., Internat. Traffic Clubs Assn., Exptl. Aviation Assn., Delta Nu Alpha. Congregationalist. Home: 800 Circle Ave Forest Park IL 60130 Office: 80 E Jackson Blvd Chicago IL 60602

PRESCHLACK, JOHN EDWARD, office equipment co. exec.; b. N.Y.C., May 30, 1933; s. William and Anna M. (Hrubesch) P.; B.S. in Elec. Engring., Mass. Inst. Tech., 1954; M.B.A., Harvard, 1958; m. Lynn A. Stanley, Dec. 29, 1962; children—John E., James S., David C. Sales engr. E.I. DuPont de Nemours Co., Wilmington, Del., 1954; partner McKinsey Co. Inc., N.Y.C., 1958-62, 64-67, London, 1962-64, Dusseldorf, Germany, 1967-72; pres. graphic products div. Itek Corp., Lexington, Mass., 1973-77; pres., chief exec. officer Gen. Binding Corp., Northbrook, Ill., 1977—; dir. House of Vision, Inc., Maytag Co. Served to 1st lt. USAF, 1954-56. Mem. Chgo. Hort. Soc. (dir.), Tau Beta Pi. Republican. Roman Catholic. Club: Onwentsia. Home: 820 E Westminster Rd Lake Forest IL 60045 Office: One GBC Plaza Northbrook IL 60062

PRESCOTT, WILLIAM O'NEAL, savs. and loan exec.; b. N.Y.C., Oct. 2, 1928; s. Cecil Jerome and Rita Gladys (Veal) P.; diploma N. Ga. Coll., 1946; student U. N.C.; B.B.A., U. Ga., Atlanta, 1954; m. Mary Mann, May 15, 1949; children—William O'Neal, Patricia Prescott McClellan, Mary Margaret. File clk. jr. underwriter automobile and Workman's compensation depts. USF & G., Atlanta, 1946-48; sales trainee casualty ins. B.D. Cole, Inc., West Palm Beach, Fla., 1948-50; adminstrv. asst. to James C. Mann, Conyers, Ga., 1950-55; sales rep. Burroughs Corp., Birmingham and Florence, Ala., Atlanta, Asheville, N.C., 1955-74; controller, treas. Asheville Fed. Savs. & Loan Assn. (N.C.), 1974-76, pres., 1976—; mgmt. com. Automated Payments Systems, Inc. Bd. dirs. United Way, ARC, Asheville Revitalization Commn., 1979-80; former mem. diaconate 1st Presbyterian Ch.; bd. dirs. Pisgah council Girl Scouts U.S.A. Mem. U.S. League Savs. Assns., N.C. Savs. and Loan League, Carolinas Fin. Fedn., Asheville C. of C. (dir. 1979-80). Clubs: Asheville Rotary, Downtown City, Biltmore Forest Country. Office: 11 Church St Asheville NC 28801

PRESLEY, BRIAN, corp. exec.; b. Evansville, Ind., Dec. 28, 1941; s. Harry and Ruth P.; B.S. in Bus. Adminstrn., U. Evansville, 1963; M.B.A. Mich. State U., m. Mary Nell Minyard, Aug. 17, 1972; children—Debra, Cynthia, David, Jeffrey, Clark, Gregory, Steven. Market research analyst Stanley Works, New Britain, Conn., 1964-68; tax shelter coordinator F.I. Dupont, Memphis, 1968-73; v.p. Bullington Schas, Memphis, 1973-75; pres., mng. gen. partner Presley Assos., Memphis, 1965—; pres., chief fin. officer CSG, Inc., Memphis, 1975—; gen. partner various real estate and oil and gas partnerships, 1974—. Pres., Gulf Terr. Condominium Assn., 1977-80, Memphis area Alumni Assn. Tau Kappa Epsilon, 1979-80; bd. dirs. Apt. Council Tenn., 1980—. Mem. Tenn. Oil and Gas Assn., Young Realtors (head fin. com.), Real Estate Securities and Syndication Inst., Fin. Analysts Fedn. Presbyterian. Clubs: Summit, Petroleum, Braniff Internat. Council and Elans (life mem.), Admirals (life). Host syndicated radio show for sr. citizens, 1979—. Home: 1491 Vinton Memphis TN 38104 Office: 1032 S Cooper Memphis TN 38104

PRESS, STANLEY, banker; b. New Brunswick, N.J., June 30, 1937; s. Ben and Ann (Stritch) P.; B.S. with honors in Chem. Engring., Clarkson Coll. Tech., 1959, M.S. in Chem. Engring., 1961; M.B.A., Harvard U., 1965; m. Ada Merle Dinerman, June 20, 1965; children—Helene J., Richard A., Rachel H. Process engr. Gen. Electric Co., Waterford, N.Y., 1960-62; prodn. engr. Merck & Co., Rahway, N.J., 1962-63; ops. supr. Monsanto Co., Everett, Mass., 1965-68; asst. to pres. and controller Ace Electronics Co., Somerville, Mass., 1968-69; mgmt. cons. Touche Ross & Co., N.Y.C., 1969-75; v.p. Citibank, N.A., N.Y.C., 1975—. Texaco fellow, 1959-60. Mem. Phalanx, Tau Beta Pi, Omega Chi Epsilon. Home: 383 Oak Ave Cedarhurst NY 11516 Office: Citibank NA 399 Park Ave New York NY 10043

PRESTIA, MICHAEL ANTHONY, accounting exec.; b. S.I., N.Y., Oct. 6, 1931; s. Anthony and Antoinette (Folino) P.; M.B.A., N.Y. U., 1956; B.A., 1953; m. Nancy Ferrandino, July 4, 1959 (div. May 1970); 1 son, Anthony. Sr. accountant Gluckman & Schacht, C.P.A.'s, N.Y.C., 1953-60; chief financial officer Franklin Broadcasting Co., N.Y.C., 1960-63; chief accountant asst. to bus. officer, sec. Cooper Union for Advancement Sci. and Art, N.Y.C., 1963-66; bus. officer Inst. Pub. Adminstrn., N.Y.C., 1966-71, controller, 1971-78, treas., 1978—. Cons. taxation and tax planning, 1959—. Served with AUS, 1953-55. C.P.A., N.Y. Mem. Am. Inst. C.P.A.'s, N.Y. State Soc. C.P.A.'s. Home: 53-06 Francis Lewis Blvd Bayside NY 11364 Office: 55 W 44th St New York NY 10036

PRESTIGIACOMO, SAM LOUIS, mfg. co. exec.; b. Louisville, Oct. 17, 1933; s. Louis Joseph and Kathleen Theresa (Downs) P.; student U. Louisville, 1955; m. Mary Jo Ann Maddux, June 11, 1955; children—Michele, Michael, John, Jennifer. Supr., Nat. Linen Service, Louisville, 1958-69; with Standard Gravure Corp., Louisville, 1969-80; owner Prospector Enterprises, Louisville, 1974—. Served with USN, 1951-54; ETO. Roman Catholic. Home: 2106 Tyler Ln Louisville KY 40205 Office: 2640 Frankfort Ave Louisville KY 40206

PRESTON, DONALD DUWAYNE, ins. broker; b. Los Angeles, Aug. 11, 1948; s. Daniel and Dorothy Fern (Preston) Miller; student Rio Hondo Coll., Whittier, Calif., 1968; m. Gail Holloway, Sept. 6, 1976. Account exec. Employers Ins. Co. Wausau, 1972-74; risk mgr. Sonitrol Security Systems Inc., Anderson, Ind., 1974-76; account mgr. Fred S. James, Chgo., 1976-77; pres. Scripps Agy. Inc., Chgo., 1977—. Served with AUS, 1969-71. Clubs: Exmoor Country, K.P. Address: 236 Glenview Rd Glenview IL 60025

PRESTON, DONALD GENE, banker; b. Danville, Ky., Feb. 3, 1945; s. H.D. and L.C. Preston; A.B. (Wall St. Jour. award fin. 1967, Frankel award econs. 1967-, Centre Coll. Ky., 1967; M.B.A. (grad. fellow 1967-68), U. Ky., 1968; m. Susan S. Schoolfield, Mar. 7, 1981; children—Amy D., Jon A., Andrew M., James A. Ops. analyst Gen. Dynamics Corp., Ft. Worth, 1968-70; with Wachovia Bank & Trust Co., 1970—, v.p. Southeastern corp. banking, Winston-Salem, N.C., 1974—. Mem. Winston-Salem Arts Council; mem. Forsyth County Mental Health Assn. Mem. Am. Econ. Assn., Am. Mgmt. Assn., Foxhall Civic Assn. (treas. 1974—), Beta Gamma Sigma, Omicron Delta Kappa. Presbyterian. Club: Westwood. Home: 1225 Willowlake Ct Winston-Salem NC 27106 Office: PO Box 3099 Winston-Salem NC 27102

PRESTON, JOHN RICHARD, banker, lawyer; b. Cleve., July 1, 1945; s. Stanley Walter and Lillian H. (Nyland) P.; B.A., Bowling Green U., 1967; J.D., Case Western Res. U., 1970; m. Linda Kay Nelson, Aug. 12, 1967; 1 dau., Kate. Admitted to Ohio bar, 1971, Okla. bar, 1978; practice law, Cleve., 1971-73; asst. counsel, asst. sec. Union Commerce Bank and Union Commerce Corp., Cleve., 1973-75; asst. v.p. law Soc. Nat. Bank of Cleve., 1975-77; v.p., gen. counsel First Nat. Bank & Trust Co. of Oklahoma City and First Okla. Bancorp., Inc., 1977-79, sr. v.p., gen. counsel, 1979—, sec. 1980—; dir. various real estate, oil and gas, investment cos. Served with USAR, 1971. Mem. Am., Ohio, Okla., Cleve. bar assns. Clubs: Beacon, Greens Golf and Racquet. Editor-in-chief Case Western Res. Jour. Internat. Law, 1969-70. Office: PO Box 25189 Oklahoma City OK 73125

PRESTON, LEWIS THOMPSON, banker; b. N.Y.C., Aug. 5, 1926; s. Lewis Thompson and Priscilla (Baldwin) P.; grad. Harvard U., 1951; m. Gladys Pulitzer, Apr. 17, 1959; children—Linda Pulitzer Bartlett, Victoria Maria Bartlett, Lucile Baldwin, Lewis Thompson, Priscilla Munn, Electra. With J.P. Morgan & Co. (merged with Guaranty Trust Co., named Morgan Guaranty Trust Co. 1959), 1951—, vice chmn. bd., dir. J.P. Morgan & Co. and Morgan Guaranty Trust Co., N.Y.C., 1976-78, mem. corporate office, mem. exec. com., 1976—, pres. J.P. Morgan and Morgan Guaranty Trust Co., 1978—. Trustee, N.Y. U. Served with USMC, 1944-46. Mem. The Pilgrims, Council Fgn. Relations, Res. City Bankers Assn. Republican. Episcopalian. Clubs: The Brook, The River (N.Y.C.); Bedford Golf and Tennis. Office: 23 Wall St New York NY 10015

PRESTON, RICHARD, bus. found. exec.; b. Brookline, Mass., Mar. 31, 1913; d. Eugene Walter Ong and Bessie (Woodbury) P.; A.B., Harvard, 1937; m. Carolyn Crandall, Feb. 27, 1943; children—Julie-Ann, Patricia Woodbury, Richard Thomas, Christopher, Robert Gutterson, Chmn., Mass. Republican Fin. Com. 1951-52; commr. Commerce Mass., 1953-58; pres. Economic Devel. Assos., Boston, 1958-62; economic devel. cons. Belgium Govt., 1957; exec. dir. N.H. State Planning and Devel. Com., 1960-61; exec. v.p. Am. Indsl. Devel. Council, Boston, 1962-73; pres. Am. Indsl. Devel. Council Ednl. Found., S. Hamilton, Mass., 1973—; lectr. in field, 1956-76. Served with USNR, 1942-46. Recipient Man of Yr. award Northeastern Indsl. Devel. Assn. (1973). Certified indsl. developer. Fellow Am. Indsl. Devel. Council (life mem.); mem. Northeastern Indsl. Devel. Assn. Indsl. Developers Assn. (Canada), Mass., So. indsl. devel. councils, Urban Land Inst., Council Urban Economic Devel., Gt. Lakes Area Devel. Council. Republican. Episcopalian. Clubs: Myopia Hunt, Cruising (Am.); Lodge: John H. Heard. Author: Universe Indsl. Devel. Editor: Principles Indsl. Devel., Indian Indsl. Devel. Manual For & By Native Ams., Indsl. Devel. Concepts & Principles (H.L. Hunker). Home: 454 Bay Rd Hamilton MA 01936 Office: 66 Railroad Ave S Hamilton MA 01982

PRESTON, SEYMOUR STOTLER, III, mfg. co. exec.; b. Media, Pa., Sept. 11, 1933; s. Seymour Stotler and Mary Alicia (Harper) P.; B.A., Williams Coll., 1956; M.B.A., Harvard U., 1958; m. Jean Eller Holman, Sept. 8, 1956; children—Courtney J., Katherine E., Alicia D., Shelley S. With Pennwalt Corp., Phila., 1961—, v.p. chems., 1974-75, exec. v.p. chems. and equipment ops., 1975-77, pres., chief operating officer, 1977—; dir. Phila. Nat. Corp., Phila. Nat. Bank. Trustee Shipley Sch., Bryn Mawr, Pa., 1976—. Served with USAF, 1958-61. Mem. Chem. Mfrs. Assn. (dir. 1978—), Soc. Chem. Industry, Greater Phila. C. of C. (dir. 1979—). Presbyterian. Clubs: Union League, Urban. Office: Three Parkway Philadelphia PA 19102

PRESTON, WILLIAM ALLEN, plastics mfg. co. exec.; b. Colorado Springs, Colo., June 11, 1936; s. William Harold and Alice Eleanor (Allen) P.; M.S., Colo. Sch. Mines, 1958; M.B.A., Stanford U., 1961; m. Janet Louise Johnson, Aug. 31, 1958; children—William Allen, Jean E. Sales rep. Ducommun Inc., 1961-62; mktg. mgr., sales mgr. Super-Temp Corp., 1962-65, Explosive Tech. Inc., 1962-65; gen. mgr. Fansteel, Inc., Los Angeles, 1965-69; pres. APM, Inc., Palo Alto, Calif., 1970—; dir. Pacific Sci. Co., Redlake Corp., Diversified Electronics Co., Oxford Labs., Physics Internat., Univ. Nat. Bank & Trust Co.; lectr. mktg. Stanford U., 1969—. Served to 1st lt. U.S. Army, 1958-59. Recipient Thomas A. Clark award Alpha Tau Omega, 1958. Republican. Episcopalian. Clubs: University, Palo Alto, Elks. Home: 1230 Hamilton Ave Palo Alto CA 94301 Office: 2465 E Bayshore Suite 321 Palo Alto CA 94303

PRESTON, WILLIAM SANFORD, III, retail jeweler; b. Burlington, Vt., Dec. 14, 1946; s. William Sanford, Jr. and Janet (Clark) P.; B.A. in Geography and Polit. Sci., U. Vt., 1969; m. Margaret Allyn Homestead, June 20, 1970; children—Bryan Edward, Melissa White. With F.J. Preston & Son, Inc., Burlington, Vt., 1969—, now pres., dir. Chmn., Downtown Burlington Devel. Assn., 1973-77; bd. dirs. Med. Center Hosp. Vt. Assos., 1975-78, bd. govs., 1977—; bd. dirs. YMCA, Burlington, 1976-77, Sara Holbrook Center for Girls, 1976-77; mem. Shelburne Mus., 1977—; mem. athletic council U. Vt., 1975-76, mem. Vt. council, 1977—; del. White House Conf. on Small Bus., 1980. Registered jeweler, Vt. Mem. Am. Gem Soc., Retail Jewelers Am., Boston Jewelers Club, Fire Jewelers Guild (pres.-elect 1979-80), Lake Champlain Regional C. of C. (dir. and pres. 1978-79), Sigma Alpha Epsilon (state trustee 1971-77). Congregationalist. Clubs: Rotary (past pres.), Ethan Allen. Home: Hills Point Rd Charlotte VT 05445 Office: 17 Church St Burlington VT 05452

PRETZINGER, DONALD LEONARD, ins. co. exec.; b. Los Angeles, Sept. 17, 1923; s. Leonard Kistler and Beatrice Katherine (Haupt) P.; B.S., Oreg. State U., 1948; M.S., U. So. Calif., 1949; C.L.U., Am. Coll. Life Underwriters, 1974; m. Beverly Helen Winnard, Aug. 30, 1946; children—Christine Ann, Kathryn Louise, Kerry Lynn. Tchr., Fillmore and Los Angeles, 1949-51; spl. agt. FBI, Tex., Ark., N.Y., 1951-56; sales mgr. Farmers Group, Inc., 1956-66, regional mgr., Portland, Oreg., 1966-69; v.p., gen. mgr. Farmers New World Life, Mercer Island, Wash., 1969-78; pres. Farmers Ins. Co.

Wash., Seattle, 1969-78; v.p. profl. liability Farmers Group, Inc., Los Angeles, 1978—; dir. Farmers Ins. Co. Wash. Pres., Northridge Townhomes Estates Homeowners Assn., 1978-79. Served with USNR, 1942-46; PTO. Mem. Soc. Chartered Life Underwriters, Naval Aviation Assn., Wash. Ins. Council (dir.). Republican. Episcopalian. Clubs: Northridge Tennis, Masons; Kiwanis (dir. 1970-76) (Mercer Island). Home: 18125 Andrea Circle No 1 Northridge CA 91325 Office: 4680 Wilshire Blvd Los Angeles CA 90010

PREVILLE, GERARD RICHARD, ins. co. exec.; b. N.Y.C., Feb. 9, 1921; s. Sidney L. and Matilda Preville; B.B.A., Pace U., 1949; m. Wanda Duglin, Sept. 30, 1945; children—Barry Gregg, Marian Helene, Lisa Ann. With David Berdon and Co., N.Y.C., 1942, Richlin Advt. Co. Inc., N.Y.C., 1946-57; with N.Y. Life Ins. Co., New Rochelle, N.Y., 1958—, field underwriter, 1980—. Active Estate Planning Council Westchester; pres. Sinai Temple, Mt. Vernon, N.Y., 1972-1973, chmn. bd., 1974-1975. Served with U.S. Army, 1942-1945. Recipient various ins. awards; C.L.U. Mem. Life Underwriters Westchester (bd. dirs.), Nat. Assn. Life Underwriters, Pace U. Alumni Assn. (trustee 1970-1973, v.p. 1971). VFW. Clubs: Leaders of Westchester (pres. 1968), Masons (master Mt. Masada Lodge, 1963). Speaker, contbr. articles to industry related publs. Home: Eastchester NY Office: New York Life Insurance Co 1 Sheraton Plaza New Rochelle NY 10801

PREVOSTI, MARIO VIRGILIO, employment service exec.; b. N.Y.C., July 18, 1923; s. Louis Bortolo and Julia (Mattiotti) P.; student U. Minn., 1953; m. Helene McDonough, Jan. 10, 1957; children—Louis, Helene, Nicholas, Anthony, Mary, Joy. Enlisted U.S. Air Force, 1942, advanced through grades to maj., 1960, ret., 1964; pres., chief exec. officer Snelling & Snelling of S.I., Inc., 1978—, mem. nat. exec. council, 1977-79. Pres., Bard Ave. Homeowners Assn., S.I., 1978—; mem. youth activities council Sacred Heart Ch., S.I., 1965-80. Decorated D.F.C., Air medal with 4 oak leaf clusters, Air Force Commendation medal with oak leaf cluster. Mem. Air Force Assn., Ret. Officers Assn., Res. Officers Assn., S.I. C. of C., Soc. of Asso. Franchisee Execs. Republican. Roman Catholic. Office: 25 Victory Blvd Staten Island NY 10301

PREWETT, DANIEL LESTER, financial cons.; b. Troy, N.Y., Oct. 4, 1950; s. Lester Leon and Edith Mary (DiPace) P.; B.S. in Fin., SUNY, 19—; Ph.D., Pacific Western U., 1978, D.B.A., 1979. Agt., Prudential Ins. Co., Delmar, N.Y., 1973-75, sales mgr., 1975-77; v.p. Suburban Cons., Inc., Albany, N.Y., 1978—; pres. Prewett Agys. Inc., 1975—; gen. partner Empire Mgmt. Cos. I, II, III, IV, 1978—; v.p. Pulsar Realty Inc., Guilderland, N.Y., 1979—; pres. Empire Ambulance, Inc., 1980—, Suburban Cons., Inc., 1981—; speaker, lectr. in field. Pres. N.E. CB Club, Guilderland, N.Y., 1977-80. Served to 2d lt. U.S. Army, 1969-76. Recipient various sales awards, 1973-79; named to Outstanding Young Men Am., U.S. Jaycees, 1980. Mem. Nat. Assn. Life Underwriters, Am. Motorcycle Assn., Albany Assn. Life Underwriters, Pacific Western Alumni Assn., Blue Knights (hon.). Roman Catholic. Clubs: Romers Cycle, Elks. Author: The F.U.D.G.E. Factor, The Federal Undisclosed Deducation Guide for Everyone, 1979; (with C.E. Miller) Guide to Limited Partnerships for Investors, 1980. Home: 6055 Johnston Rd Slingerlands NY 12159 Office: Suburban Cons Inc Exec Park Dr Albany NY 12203

PREY, JOHN HARRY, elec. engr.; b. Kalamazoo, May 9, 1942; s. Richard Norman and Mary Louise (Moore) P.; B.S. in Elec. Engring., U. Mich., 1965; m. Erica Marian Grommeck, Oct. 22, 1977. Mgmt. trainee Chrysler Corp., Detroit, 1965-67; quality control mgr. Chrysler Foundry, Indpls., 1967-74; quality assurance dir. Rockwell Internat., Hopedale, Mass., 1974-76; staff engr. Deere & Co., Moline, Ill., 1976—. Bd. dirs. Trinity Episcopal Ch., Indpls., 1972-74. Mem. Am. Foundrymen's Soc. (dir., mem. sand reclamation com.). Republican. Author paper on energy mgmt., presented at profl. conf. Home: 31 Meadowbrook Dr Geneseo IL 61254 Office: John Deere Rd Moline IL 61265

PREYSZ, LOUIS ROBERT FONSS, JR., business cons.; b. Elkins, W. Va., July 15, 1916; s. Louis Robert Fonss and Lucile (Falardeau) P.; student U. Ky., 1946-47; m. Lucille Parks, Oct. 17, 1941; children—Louis Robert Fonss III, Carole (Mrs. Richard Carmichael), Marsha, James Jay, Lorentz Dreyer. Asst. to pres. North Star Corp., Indian Head Mining Co., Hazard, Ky., 1948-51; controller Meadow River Lumber Co., Rainelle, W. Va., 1951-55; agt. insp. Internal Revenue Service, Cin., 1955; controller Creamery Package Mfg. Co. (merged into St. Regis Paper Co.), Chgo., 1956-64, sec., Toronto, Ont., Can., 1956-64; v.p., treas. Gisholt Machine Co., Madison, Wis., 1964-66, dir. Gisholt Gt. Britain, London, Gisholt-Italia (merged into Giddings & Lewis Inc.), Milan, 1964-70, exec. v.p., 1966-70, v.p. Giddings & Lewis, Inc. (parent co.), Fond du Lac, Wis., 1967-70; corporate cons., 1970—; chmn. exec. com. dir. T and T Tech., Inc., Madison, 1972, chmn. bd., chief exec. officer, 1972-73; fin. cons. to bd. dirs. Meadow River Lumber Co., Rainelle, W. Va. (co. merged into Ga. Pacific Corp.), 1970-72; cons. to bd. dirs. Norland Corp., Ft. Atkinson, Wis., 1971—; cons. Cordis Corp., Miami, Fla., 1972—. Bd. dirs. Madison YMCA, 1967-70. Served to capt. USMCR, 1936-46. C.P.A., Ill., W.Va. Mem. Am. Inst. C.P.A.'s, W.Va. Soc. C.P.A.'s, Berea Coll. Alumni Assn., Ret. Marine Officers Assn., AAU. Episcopalian. Club: Chgo. Athletic Assn. Address: Route 1 Drake Rd Poynette WI 53955

PRICE, BRUCE ALFRED, ins. agt.; b. Grosse Pointe, Mich., Sept. 28, 1941; s. Alfred I. and Luella B. (Ellsworth) P.; diploma San Francisco Coll. Mortuary Sci., 1963; m. Barbara Ann Wilhelm, Sept. 6, 1969; children—Robert Bruce and Casey Wilhelm (twins). Life ins. salesman, 1967—; propr. Bruce A. Price & Assos., employee benefit programs, Detroit, 1972—. Served with U.S. Army, 1959-61. Group study exchangee Rotary Internat., 1972. Mem. Million Dollar Round Table, Detroit Assn. Life Underwriters, Grosse Pointe Mchts. Assn. (pres. 1979-81), Ins. Study Group, Detroit Area Ins. Assn. Club: Masons. Home: 1038 Greentree Bloomfield Hills MI 48013 Office: 18121 E 8 Mile Rd East Detroit MI 48021

PRICE, EARL LAWRENCE, brokerage exec.; b. Laramie, Wyo., Feb. 25, 1946; s. Earl Raymond and Bella (Williams) P.; student U. Wyo., 1963-67; m. Elaine Duncan, Sept. 30, 1978; 1 dau., Julia Elizabeth. Pres., Price Motors, Laramie, 1968-70; pres. Real Estate Investment, Laramie, 1972-76; ind. cons. internat. finance, Zurich, Switzerland, 1972-76; mng. partner Price & Co., Chgo., 1976—, Newcomb Govt. Securities Co., N.Y.C.; chmn. Coherent Systems, Inc.; dir. Imprint Editions, London, Altback, Price Entertainment, Inc., Los Angeles. Bd. dirs. Ft. Collins Symphony. Mem. Internat. Assn. Fin. Planners, Chgo. Assn. Commerce and Industry. Episcopalian. Home: 415 S Howes Apt 1104 Fort Collins CO 80521 Office: 767 5th Ave 34th Floor New York NY 10153

PRICE, EDGAR HILLEARY, JR., public relations co. exec.; b. Jacksonville, Fla., Jan. 1, 1918; s. Edgar Hilleary Price and Mary Williams (Phillips) Price Goodwin; student U. Fla., 1937-38; m. Elise Ingram, June 24, 1947; 1 son, Jerald Steven. Mgr. comml. flower farm, 1945-49; mgr. Fla. Gladiolus Growers Assn., 1949-55; exec. v.p. Tropicana Products, Inc., 1955-72, dir. govt. and industry relations div., 1972—, also dir.; exec. v.p. Indsl. Glass Co., Inc., 1963-72 (all Bradenton, Fla.); pres., chmn. bd. The Price Co., Inc., Bradenton, 1972—, also dir.; dir. First City Fed. Savs. & Loan Assn. Manatee County, Bradenton, Gen. Telephone Co. Fla., Tampa, Fla. Power & Light Co., Miami, Fla. Cypress Gardens, Inc., Winter Haven. Chmn., Manatee County (Fla.) chpt. A.R.C., 1955; chmn. Bradenton Community Chest, 1956; mem. U. Fla. Liason Com., 1959-61; chmn. Manatee County United Appeal, 1961; chmn. charter adv. com. City of Bradenton, 1958; mem. Gov's Com. Rehab. Handicapped, 1958-63, Zoning Adjustment Bd. Sarasota-Bradenton Airport Authority, 1959-63; chmn. spl. commn. study aboliton death penalty, 1963-65; chmn. Fla. Citrus Commn., 1971-74; mem. Fla. Council of 100. Mem. Fla. Senate, 1958-66; del. Dem. Nat. Conv., 1960, dist. del., 1964. Bd. dirs. Fla. State Fair Assn., Fla. Citrus Expn.; trustee Stetson U. Served to 1st lt. USAAF, 1941-45; ETO. Named Boss of Year, Nat. Secs. Assn., 1959, Man of Year for Fla. Agr., Progressive Farmer Mag., 1961; recipient Merit awards Am. Flag Assn., 1962, Gamma Sigma Delta, 1965, Leadership award Fla. Agrl. Extension Service, 1963, Outstanding Senator award Fla. Radio Broadcasters, 1965, Most Valubable Mem. Fla. Legislature, Allen Morris award, 1965; Most Valuable Mem. Fla. Senate award St. Petersburg Times, 1965; Brotherhood award Sarasota chpt. Nat. Council Christians and Jews, 1966, Distinguished Alumni award U. Fla., named Manatee County Outstanding Citizen, 1971. Mem. Am. Legion, V.F.W., Mil. Order World Wars, Fla. (past pres.), Manatee County (past pres.) chambers commerce, N.A.M. (dir. 2 terms), Fla. Hort. Soc. (chmn.), Fla. Flower Assn., Senatoma Internat. (Dist. Service to Mankind award 1976), Blue Key (hon.), Omicron Delta Kappa (hon.), Sigma Alpha Epsilon. Baptist (deacon). Kiwanian (pres. 1955). Home: 3009 Riverview Blvd Bradenton FL 33505 Office: POB 9270 Bradenton FL 33506

PRICE, GEORGE EDWARD, computer phototypesetting co. exec.; b. Chgo., June 20, 1940; s. Edward August and Maxine Leland (Crow) P.; A.A. with honors, Lincoln Coll., 1961; B.S. with honors, Bradley U., 1963. Pres., Graphic Sales, Inc., Chgo., 1968—. Mem. St. Cornelius Sch. Bd., Chgo., 1980—. Served to capt. USAF, 1964-68. Mem. Printing Industry Ill., Chgo. Assn. Commerce and Industry, Printing Industry Am., Ill. Typographical Assn. Republican. Roman Catholic. Home: 5444 N Lotus Ave Chicago IL 60630 Office: 550 W Jackson Blvd Suite 419 Chicago IL 60606

PRICE, HARVEY EARL, banker; b. Johnston County, N.C., Aug. 6, 1920; s. Moses Leon and Lettie (Wall) P.; grad. Sch. Commerce, Atlantic Christian Coll., Wilson, N.C., 1941; Carolinas Sch. Banking, Chapel Hill, N.C., 1946, 58; m. Eleanor Farmer Blow, Feb. 22, 1947; children—Harvey Craig, Stephen Russ. With accounting sect. Post Ordnance Dept., U.S. Army, Ft. Bragg, 1941-42; with First-Citizens Bank & Trust Co., Smithfield, N.C., 1942—, auditor, 1950—, now sr. v.p., gen. auditor; instr. auditing and comml. law Am. Inst. Banking, 1955-56. Pres., Smithfield PTA, 1965-66; dist. committeeman, fin. chmn. Century Club, Boy Scouts Am., 1965—; v.p., membership chmn. N.C. Symphony Soc., 1968-70. Bd. dirs. Johnston County Mental Health Assn., 1962-70. Mem. Bank Adminstrn. Inst., N.C. Bankers Assn. (tax research com.). Democrat. Baptist (sec. bd. deacons 1963-67, chmn. 1970-72, Sunday sch. tchr. 1962—). Club: Rotary (pres. Smithfield 1964-65). Home: 805 Vermont St Smithfield NC 27577 Office: 241 E Market St Smithfield NC 27577

PRICE, JOYCE ELLEN, real estate devel. co. exec.; b. Huntington, W.Va., Sept. 2, 1945; d. James Wallace and Estelle Elizabeth (Pemberton) P.; B.A., Ohio State U., 1968, B.F.A., 1968; Pres., Price, Ltd., Inc., Huntington, 1970—, Wallace Constrn. Co., Huntington, 1976—, The P.C.T. Co. of Huntington, 1977—; v.p., sec. James W. Price, Inc., Huntington, 1976—; partner The Ellenco Corp., Huntington, 1980—. Dir., trustee The Herschel C. Price Ednl. Found., 1976—. Recipient Key to City of Huntington, 1979. Mem. AAUW. Republican. Methodist. Home: 2785 3d Ave Huntington WV 25702 Office: 3035 Merrill Ave Huntington WV 25702

PRICE, LARRY LEE, banker; b. Muscatine, Iowa, Apr. 19, 1936; s. Herman Jasper and Nora Mathilda (Jebens) P.; student Muscatine Jr. Coll., 1955-56; grad. Grad. Sch. Banking, Madison, Wis., 1970; m. Julianne Carol Boldt, June 8, 1956; children—Ronald L., Linda C., Robert C., Janelle E. Dept. mgr. J.C. Penny Co., 1956-62, Bloomington, Ind., 1962; with Bank of Taney County, 1962-73, cashier, 1965-72, exec. v.p., 1972-73; pres. Bank of Kimberling City (Mo.), 1973—, dir., 1973—. Pres. Sr. Citizen's Housing Assn., Forsyth, 1970-72. Mem. Mo., Ind., Am. bankers assns., Kimberling City C. of C. (past pres.). Republican. Lutheran. Clubs: Lions, Elks. Home: 40 Skyline Dr Kimberling City MO 65686 Office: PO Box 948 Kimberling City MO 65686

PRICE, LARRY LEE, dental lab. exec.; b. Waynesboro, Pa., Oct. 13, 1948; s. Paul Lenard and Ruth Estella Lucille Price; student Hagerstown Jr. Coll., 1968, Career Acad. Sch. Dental Tech., 1969; journeyman's degree Pa. Dept. Labor and Industry, 1973; m. Rosalie Ann, Apr. 24, 1971; children—Chad David, Shelley Dawn, Shawn Douglas. Head dept. crown and bridge Barrett Labs., Chambersburg, Pa., 1974; pres., owner, operator Price Dental Labs., Waynesboro, 1974—; sec. Pa. State Dental Lab. Assn. Clinic at Lewisburg State Prison for Inmates Reahab. Chmn. Waynesboro chpt. Am. Heart Assn., 1979-81; supr. Washington Twp. Planning Commn., 1981—. Cert. dental technician. Mem. Pa. Assn. Dental Labs., Nat. Assn. Dental Labs. Mem. Brethren Ch. Clubs: Rotary (chmn. membership 1977), Waynesboro Country (chmn. golf com.) (Waynesboro). Home: 11835 Orchard Ln Waynesboro PA 17268 Office: 416 Cleveland Ave Waynesboro PA 17268

PRICE, MARGARET KATHERINE MCCALL, loan co. exec.; b. Abingdon, Va., July 14, 1922; d. Thomas Ezekiel and Mary Florence (Andrews) McCall; grad. Mary Dalton Frye Pvt. Secretarial Sch., Abingdon, Va., 1941; m. Beecher E. Price, July 5, 1950. With Holston Loan Co., Bristol, Tenn., 1942—, sec., treas., dir., 1978—. Cert. consumer credit exec. Mem. Bus. and Profl. Womens Club, Bristol Credit Granters Assn. Clubs: Twin City Rebekah Lodge, Va. Asher Bus. Womens Bible. Home: 305 Hemlock Rd Bristol TN 37620 Office: 31 6th St Bristol TN 37620

PRICE, MARK MICHAEL, bldg. devel. cons.; b. Cleve., Jan. 20, 1920; s. Mark Michael and Sarah Ann (Moran) P.; ed. U. Detroit, 1939, Cleve. Coll., 1946; m. Ellen Elizabeth Hafford, June 3, 1948; children—Marilyn Michelle, Pamela Susan. With Desk Tops, Inc., Cleve., 1950; dir. Vistron Door Corp., Cleve., 1962; pres., chief exec. officer Bldg. Devel. Counsel Inc., Washington. Mem. Cleve. Mayor's Bus. Men's Civic Com., 1977-78. Mem. Soc. Mktg. Profls., Nat. Press Club. Roman Catholic. Clubs: Army Navy, Nat. Dem., Capital (Washington). Office: 1629 K St NW Suite 400 Washington DC 20006

PRICE, PATRICK HILARY, mortgage banker; b. Coos Bay, Oreg., Feb. 1, 1928; s. Frank Emerson and Genevieve (Helm) P.; student U. Oreg., 1952, Ind. U., 1974; m. Jean Marie Roberts, Oct. 10, 1957; children—Hilary, Cynthia, Bryan, Julie. With San Francisco Fed. Savs. & Loan Assn., 1953—, sr. v.p., chief loan officer, 1968-77, exec. v.p., 1977—, also dir.; dir. Fransican Fin. Corp., San Francisco Aux. Corp. Bd. dirs. Los Amigos de Los Americas, Marin, Calif. 1977. Served with U.S. Navy, 1946-48. Mem. Bay Area Mortgage Assn. (pres. 1964-65, San Francisco Real Estate Bd. (past dir.), Bay Area Real Estate Council (dir. 1977-79, pres. 1979). Club: St. Francis Yacht (San Francisco). Office: 85 Post St San Francisco CA 94104

PRICE, ROBERT, investment banker, lawyer; b. N.Y.C., Aug. 27, 1932; s. Solomon and Frances (Berger) P.; A.B., N.Y. U., 1953; LL.D., Columbia U., 1958; m. Margery Beth Wiener, Dec. 18, 1955; children—Eileen Marcia, Steven. With R. H. Macy & Co., Inc., 1955-58; admitted to N.Y. bar, 1958, also U.S. Dist. Cts., U.S. Ct. Appeals, U.S. Supreme Ct., ICC, FCC, U.S. Internal Revenue Service; practiced in N.Y.C., 1958—; law clk. to judge U.S. Dist. Ct. So. Dist. N.Y., 1958-59; asst. U.S. atty. So. Dist. N.Y., 1959-60; partner Kupferman & Price, 1960-65; chmn. bd., pres. Atlantic States Industries Inc., 1963-66; pres. WNVY, Pensacola, Fla., 1965-66, WLOB, Portland, Maine, 1965-66; dep. mayor, N.Y.C., 1965-66; exec. v.p., dir. Dreyfus Corp., N.Y.C., 1966-69; v.p., investment officer Dreyfus Fund, until 1969; chmn., pres., dir. Price Capital Corp., also Price Mgmt. Corp., N.Y.C., 1969-72; gen. partner, spl. counsel Lazard, Freres & Co., 1972—; adv. com. Bankers Trust Co. N.Y.; dir. Transocean Holding Corp., Lane Bryant, Inc.; lectr. National Indsl. Conf. Bd. Chmn., N.Y.C. Port Authority Negotiating Com. for World Trade Center, 1965-66; mem. N.Y.C. Policy Planning Council, 1966; spl. counsel N.Y. State Joint Legis. Com. on Ct. Reorganization, 1962-63; asst. counsel N.Y. State Joint Legis. Com. on N.Y. Banking Laws, 1961-62; chmn. govt. and civil service div. United Jewish Appeal Greater N.Y., 1966; co-chmn. Met. N.Y. Red Cross Blood Drive, 1966; mem. nat. exec. com. Columbia Law Sch. 16th Ann. Fund Drive, 1966-67. Vice pres. N.Y. Young Republican Club, 1957-58; campaign mgr. John V. Lindsay campaigns for congressman, N.Y.C., 1958, 60, 62, 64; del. N.Y. Republican State Conv., 1962, 66; campaign mgr. Nelson A. Rockefeller, Oreg. Rep. presdl. primary campaign, 1964; campaign mgr. Lindsay campaign for mayor, N.Y.C., 1965; lectr. Rep. Nat. Com., 1966—. Bd. dirs. Am. Friends Hebrew U.; past trustee Columbia U. Sch. Pharm. Scis., Birch Wathen Sch. Served with U.S. Army, 1953-55. Recipient Yeshiva U. Heritage award, 1966. Public Service award Queens Cath. War Vets., 1966, Public Service award Phila. 21 Jewel Sq. Club, 1967, Outstanding Young Man of Yr. award N.Y.C. Jr. C. of C., 1967; named One of America's Ten Outstanding Young Men, U.S. Jr. C. of C., 1967. Mem. Am., N.Y.C. bar assns., N.Y. State Dist. Attys. Assn., Council Fgn. Relations, Columbia Law Sch. Alumni Assn. (dir.), Scribes, Tau Kappa Alpha. Author articles. Home: 25 E 86th St New York NY 10028 Office: Lazard Freres Co One Rockefeller Plaza New York NY 10020

PRICE, RONALD JAMES, elec. products mfg. co. exec.; b. Wellsville, Ohio, Jan. 26, 1933; s. Thomas Pugh and Dorothy Maud (Saltsman) P.; B.A. in Math., Wooster Coll., 1953; B.S. in Mech. Engring., Ohio U., 1955; m. Phyllis Eileen Mangan, Feb. 15, 1958; children—Penny Eileen, Deborah Lynn. Sales engr. Westinghouse Corp., Detroit, 1957-62, dist. mgr., 1962-65, product mgr., standard control div., Beaver, Pa., 1965-68, sales mgr., 1968; v.p., gen. mgr. Fife Fla. Electric Supply, Tampa, Fla., 1968-71; mktg. mgr. Westinghouse Control Products Div., Beaver, 1971-75, engring. mgr., 1975-77, mgr. mktg. and strategic planning Indsl. Control Bus. unit, 1977-78; acting gen. mgr. specialty transformer div., Greenville, Pa., 1976, control equipment group mktg. mgr., 1978-80; gen. mgr. Bryant div. Westinghouse Electric Corp., Bridgeport, Conn., 1980—; vis. lectr. Mich. State U. M.B.A. program. Trustee Beaver County Recreational Authority, 1972—; mem. Council of 100, Tampa, 1969-71; pres. Beaver Civic Assn.; chmn. Ft. McIntosh dist. Boy Scouts Am., Beaver. Served with U.S. Army, 1958. Recipient Bausch & Lombe Sci. award, 1950. Registered profl. engr., Mich., Ohio, Pa. Mem. Nat. Soc. Profl. Engrs., Nat. Elec. Mfrs. Assn. (indsl. control, systems sec., chmn. adv. com. for user needs), Elec. Council of Fla., Nat. Assn. of Elec. Distbrs. (speaker), Nat. Assn. Mfrs. (industry speaker), Am. Mgmt. Assn. (lectr.). Republican. Presbyterian. Home: 252A Agawam Dr Stratford CT 06497 Office: 1421 State St PO Box D Bridgeport CT 06602

PRICE, THOMAS DWIGHT, sales cons.; b. Birmingham, Ala., Aug. 23, 1947; s. William T. and Helen L. Price; B.S. in B.A., Auburn U., 1969. Acct., So. Bell Telephone Co., Jacksonville, Fla., 1970-72; copier specialist Xerox Corp., Atlanta, 1972-74; sales mgr. Qwip Systems, Atlanta, 1974-76; pres. ASCA, Inc., Atlanta, 1976—. Served with USCG, 1969-70. Mem. Sales and Mktg. Execs., Auburn U. Alumni Assn. (pres. 1970-72). Address: 3057 Balearic Dr Marietta GA 30067

PRICE, THOMAS EMILE, export sales, investment, fin. co. exec., sports assn. ofcl.; b. Cin., Nov. 4, 1921; s. Edwin Charles and Lillian Elizabeth (Werk) P.; B.B.A., U. Tex., 1943; postgrad. Harvard U., 1944; m. Lois Margaret Gahr Matthews, Dec. 21, 1970; 1 dau. by previous marriage, Dorothy Elizabeth Wood Price; stepchildren—Bruce Albert, Mark Frederic, Scott Herbert, Eric William Matthews. Co-founder Indsl. Waxes, Inc., 1946, sec., 1946-75, treas., 1946-76, pres., 1975-76; co-founder Climax Products Corp., Cin., 1953, sec., 1957-59, treas., 1956-57, v.p., 1953-57; co-founder Price Y Cia, Inc., Cin., 1946—, sec., 1946-75, treas., 1946—, pres., 1975—, also dir.; co-founder Premium Finishes Sales, Inc., Cin., 1963—, pres., 1975—, also dir.; co-founder Price Paper Products Corp., Cin., 1956, treas., 1956—, pres., 1975—, sec., 1956-75, also dir.; mem. Cin. Regional Export Expansion Com., 1961-63; dir. Central Acceptance Corp., 1954-55; founding mem. and dir. Cin. Royals Basketball Club Co., 1959-73. Referee Tri-State Tennis Championships, 1963-68, Western Tennis Championships, 1969-70, Nat. Father-Son Clay Court Championships, 1974—, Tennis Grand Masters Championships, 1975-77, 80; vol. coach Walnut Hills High Sch. Boys Team, Cin., 1970—; chmn. and coach Greater Cin. Jr. Davis Cup, 1968-78; co-founder Tennis Patrons of Cin., Inc., 1951, trustee, 1951—, pres., 1958-63, 68; co-founder Greater Cin. Tennis Assn., 1979. Participant in fund raising drives Cin. Boys Amateur Baseball Fund; chmn. Greater Cin. YMCA World Service Fund Drive, 1962-64; trustee Cin. World Affairs Inst., 1957-60, gen. chmn., 1959. Served to 1st lt. USAAF, 1943-46; ETO. Elected to Western Hills High Sch. Sport Hall of Honor; hon. mem. Almaden Grand Masters, 1980. Mem. Cin. Fgn. Credit Club, Cin. World Trade Club (pres. 1959), U.S. Trotting Assn., Cin. Hist. Soc., U.S. Lawn Tennis Assn. (trustee 1959-60, 62-64, chmn. Jr. Davis Cup com. 1960-62, mem. jrs. and boys championships com. 1960—, founder of Col. James H. Bishop award 1962), Ohio Valley (trustee 1948—, Gillespie award 1957, Dredge award 1973, pres. 1952-53), Western (trustee 1951—, mem. championships adv. com. 1969—, pres. 1959-60, Melvin R. Bergman Disting. Service award 1979) tennis assns., Cin., Eastern Hills indoor tennis clubs, Phi Gamma Delta. Republican. Presbyterian. Clubs: Cin. Country, Univ., Cin. Tennis (pres. 1957-58, advisory com. 1959—). Nationally ranked boys 15, 1936, jr. tennis player, 1939. History columnist Tennis Talk Greater Cin., 1978-80. Home: 504 Williamsburg Rd Cincinnati OH 45215 Office: Dixie Terminal Bldg Suite 925 Cincinnati OH 45202

PRICE, WALLACE WALTER, assn. exec.; b. East St. Louis, Ill., Mar. 10, 1921; s. Sam P. and Pennie (Johnson) P.; B.Ed., So. Ill. U., 1942; postgrad. Mt. Vernon Sch. Law, 1947-48, U. Md., 1948-49; M.S., Va. State Coll., 1953; postgrad. U. Pa., 1959, Seton Hall Law Sch., 1977-79; m. Hortense M. McWoods, Dec. 1, 1944; children—Sandra D., Wallace Walter II, Catherine A. Inducted as pvt., Q.M.C., U.S. Army, 1943, advanced through grades to lt. col.,

1963; major assignments include chief of logistics U.S. Army Security Agy., Europe, 1960-63; Far Eastern commd., Japan, 1949-51, Korea, 1950-51; dir. tng., asso. prof. mil. sci., tactics dept. Va. State Coll., Petersburg, 1951-53; plans officer U.S. Army Gen. Depot, 1954-57, others; ret., 1964; mgr. of procedures and grant of operating authority, Olin Corp., Stamford, Conn., 1964-71; asst. v.p. of personnel Seatrain Shipbuilding Corp., Bklyn. Navy Yard, 1972; pres. Cons. Adminstrv. Mgmt., Teaneck, N.J., 1972-73; dir. Urban Affairs and Equal Opportunity, Pan Am. World Airways, N.Y.C. 1972-75; pres., co-founder The Edges Group, Inc., N.Y.C., 1969-77, treas., 1979—; corporate mgr. Affirmative Action Programs, Becton Dickinson & Co., Rutherford, N.J., 1976—, cons., 1976—; spl. cons. Gov. of V.I. Planning Group, 1974; now exec. dir. United Cerebral Palsy Assns. N.J., 1978—; chmn. Adv. Bd. for Community Relations, Teaneck, N.J., 1965-77; pres. Urban League for Bergen County (N.J.), 1968-70; council man, Teaneck, 1977-78; chmn. affirmative action com. Bd. Edn., Teaneck, N.J. 1976—; v.p. European Congress of Am. Parents and Tchrs., 1962-63; bd. dirs. Bergen County United Fund, 1972—, Community Chest, 1970—; mem. Affirmative Action com. N.J. Sports and Expn. Authority, 1974. Decorated Air medal; recipient Outstanding Achievement award Urban League of Bergen County, 1972, One of 10 Gt. Men of Bergen County award, 1970; award U.S. Army Northeastern Regional Recruiting Command, 1975. Mem. Nat. Market Developers Assn. (treas. 1965-67), Ret. Officers Assn., Parents of West Point Cadets Assn., Defense Logistical Assn., NAACP (life), Bus. and Profl. Men's Orgn. (pres. 1968-70), Alpha Phi Alpha (Ann. Merit award eastern region 1960), Mu Tau Pi. Democrat. Methodist. Club: Masons. Author: (poems) Sweet and Low, 1955; editor: Atomic Observer, 1946; asso. editor So. Ill. U. newspaper, 1940-42. Home: 585 W Englewood Ave Teaneck NJ 07666

PRICE, WALTER EARL, wholesale candy and tobacco co. exec.; b. Port Arthur, Tex., July 1, 1907; s. John William and Lula Mary (Farris) P.; grad. high sch.; m. Gladys C. Wagner, Mar. 25, 1935; 1 dau., Eddie Mae Niscavits. Asst. chemist Gulf Oil Corp., Port Arthur, 1925-29; pres., gen. mgr. Price & Co., Port Arthur, 1929—; dir. First Nat. Bank, Port Arthur. Served to 1st lt. U.S. Army, 1943-46. Mem. Nat. Assn. Tobacco Distbrs., Tex. Assn. Tobacco Distbrs. (dir., pres.). Democrat. Baptist. Club: Rotary (Port Arthur). Office: Box 190 Port Arthur TX 77640

PRICHARD, MERRILL E., exec.; b. Wheaton, Ill., July 13, 1925; s. Harold C. and Ann F. (Bailey) P.; B.S., U. Ill., 1948; postgrad. U. Chgo., Northwestern U.; m. Betty Ann Tibbits, Sept. 2, 1947; children—Ann (Mrs. James A. Wallace), Sue (Mrs. James O. Hodges III). Sports reporter Wheaton Daily Jour., Chgo. City News Bur., Lombard (Ill.) Spectator, 1940-42; sports editor Glen Ellyn (Ill.) News, summer 1942; asst. editor Mag. of Sigma Chi and Sigma Chi Bull., 1948-49, editor, 1949-55, also exec. dir. Sigma Chi Frat., 1953-55; asst. to pres. C.P. Clare & Co., mfrs., 1956-59, v.p., 1959-66, exec. v.p., 1966-71, also dir., 1961-71; vice chmn. C.P. Clare Internat. N.V., Tongren, Belgium, 1962-71; group v.p. Gen. Instrument Corp., 1968-71; dir. C.P. Clare Can., Ltd., 1957-71; v.p. ops. Cummins-Allison Corp., 1971-73; group v.p., dir. Powers Regulator Co., Skokie, Ill., 1973-77, pres., 1977-78; vice chmn., dir. v.p., dir. Powers Regulator Co., Can. Ltd., Toronto, Ont., 1974-78; v.p., gen. mgr. Pneutronics div. Gardner-Denver Co., Grand Haven, Mich., 1978—; pres. Cooper Electronics div. Cooper Industries, Nashua, N.H., 1980—; dir. Belden-Corp., Asso. Steel Co., Houston, Econergy, Inc., Chgo., Container Technologies Inc., Barrington, Ill. Served as staff sgt. AUS, 1945-46; editor, pub. relations Camp McCoy, Wis. Mem. Sigma Chi (past pres. house corp.), Kappa Tau Alpha, Sigma Delta Chi. Editor 1950, 52, 54 edits. The Norman Shield, also centennial commemorative issue The Mag. of Sigma Chi, 1955. Office: 15 Charron Ave Nashua NH 03063

PRICKETT, GARY JAMES, paper products co. exec.; b. Paul's Valley, Okla., Oct. 21, 1950; s. Loy E. and Robert (Wynn) P.; student Southwestern State U., 1968-69; B.A., So. Oreg. State Coll., 1973; m. Janet L. Haney, Sept. 21, 1971; 1 dau., Pamela Jean. Sales rep. Splevin's Music Corp., Los Angeles, 1973-74; asst. mgr. Thrifty Drug Stores, Inc., Los Angeles, 1974-75; store mgr., student store buyer UCLA, 1975-77; with Recycled Paper Products, Inc., Houston, 1977—, S.W. regional sales mgr., 1978-80, v.p. Western sales div., 1980—, dir., 1980—. Office: PO Box 73612 Houston TX 77090

PRIDDY, ARTHUR PAUL, engring. co. exec.; b. Danville, Ark., Nov. 18, 1913; s. Arthur Buril and Augusta (Ellington) P.; B.S.M.E., U. Ark., 1935; m. Mary Elizabeth Rogers, Aug. 14, 1937; children—Anne, Mary Jane, Thomas Henderson. Engr., Public Service Commn., Little Rock, 1935-37, Ark. Power & Light, Pine Bluff, 1937-42; mech. engr. Ebasco Services, Inc., N.Y.C., 1942-70; mech. engr. Chas. T. Main, Inc., Boston, 1970—, now pres. Fellow Am. Cons. Engrs. Council. Methodist. Office: Chas T Main Inc Prudential Center Boston MA 02199

PRIDEAUX, WILLIAM DON, food broker; b. Schockapee, Minn., June 27, 1940; s. William David Don and Phyllis (Beadle) P.; student Austin (Minn.) pub. schs.; m. Dorothy Mae Lickwar, Nov. 7, 1971; stepchildren—Deborah Ann Barrett, William Lawrence Barrett; children by previous marriage—Sherry Ann, David Joseph. Vice pres., dir. Royal Refreshments and Vending, Fullerton, Calif., 1959-62; exec. v.p. sales, dir. Nat. Packets, Canoga Park, Calif., 1962-66; exec. v.p., dir. Serv-A-Portion, Van Nuys, Calif., 1966-69; pres., dir. Rainbow, Inc. divs. of food brokerage, cold storage and distbn., Honolulu, 1969—. Mem. Nat., Hawaii food brokers assns., Nat. Frozen Food Assn., Honolulu Sales and Mktg. Club, Hawaii Hotel Assn., Hawaii Restaurant Assn., Sales and Mktg. Club Internat. Republican. Jewish religion. Home: 1603 Laukahi St Honolulu HI 96821 Office: 98-715 Kuahao Pl Pearl City HI 96782

PRIESS, FRIEDRICH, banker; b. Bremen, Germany, Oct. 19, 1903; s. Georg P. and Paula (Tonnesmann) P.; ed. U. Freiburg, U. Marburg; m. Maria Buttner, 1931; 4 children. Individual practice law, Bremen, 1929-30; legal adviser Philips Gloeilampenfabrieken, Eindhoven, Netherlands, 1929-30; judge, Bremen, 1930-37, Hamburg, 1937-50; v.p. Landeszentralbank, Hamburg, 1950-56; partner M.M. Warburg-Brinckmann, Wirtz & Co., Hamburg, 1956-73. Office: 75 Ferdinandstrasse D 2000 Hamburg 1 Federal Republic of Germany

PRIEST, JEROME, computer corp. exec.; b. Providence, Oct. 16, 1931; s. Ira Marcus and Mildred Edna P.; A.B., Yale, 1953; M.B.A., Columbia, 1957; m. Christine Lynn, Dec. 16, 1961; children—Julia Marie, Alexander Raphael. In sales mgmt., gen. mgmt. IBM, White Plains, N.Y., 1957-67; pres. Computer Resources Corp., Darien, Conn., 1967—, also dir.; pres. Graphicenter E. Ltd., Darien, 1975—; vis. prof. Norwalk (Conn.) Community Coll.; vis. lectr. Columbia U. Sch. Bus., N.Y.C. Bd. dirs. Nat. Multiple Sclerosis Soc. So. Fairfield County, Opera of New Eng., Arts Council of Norwalk. Served with C.E., U.S. Army, 1953-55. Contbr. articles to mags. Office: 1082 Post Rd Darien CT 06820

PRIGMORE, DONALD GENE, telephone co. exec.; b. Leon, Kans., Sept. 26, 1932; s. Harry Edward and Mary Julia (Doyle) P.; B.S.C.E., Kans. State Coll., 1955; M.B.A., U. Mich., 1958; m. June Mary O'Connell, May 15, 1970; children—Marc, Elizabeth Ann, Mary Kathryn, Christine. Spl. studies engr. Gen. Telephone Co. of Mich., Muskegon, 1958-62, div. mgr., Three Rivers, 1962-69, pres., 1979—; plant dir., service dir. GTE Service Corp., N.Y.C., 1969-72, regional v.p. mktg. and customer services, Irving, Tex., 1978-79; v.p. ops. Gen. Telephone Co. Inc., Ft. Wayne, 1972-76; v.p. ops. Gen. Telephone Co. Southwest, San Angelo, Tex., 1976-77, v.p. mktg. and customer services, 1977-78; dir. Hackley Bank & Trust. Trustee Greater Muskegon Indsl. Fund, 1980. Registered profl. engr., Mich., Ind. Tex. Mem. Am. Mktg. Assn., Nat. Soc. Profl. Engrs. Clubs: Muskegon Country, Century. Office: 455 E Ellis Rd Muskegon MI 49443

PRIGMORE, GEORGE DANIEL, real estate exec.; b. West Springfield, Mass., Mar. 8, 1943; s. William H. and Mildred Johanna (Hausmann) P.; A.B., Union Coll., 1965; M.B.A. with distinction, Harvard U., 1968. Self employed real estate developer, Boston, 1968-76; pres. Hawthorne Constrn. Co., Boston, 1971-73, Hobbs Brook Devel. Corp., Waltham, Mass., 1972-77; pres., dir. Con-Dev Mgmt. Co., Inc., Boston, 1975-78, Accu-Rate, Inc., Boston, 1977—; pres. FMR Properties div. FMR Corp., 1978—; treas., dir. W.C. Vaughan Co., Inc., Boston, 1978—; chmn. real estate dept. Northeastern U., Boston, 1974-76. Certified rev. appraiser. Home: 85 State St Boston MA 02109 Office: 82 Devonshire St Boston MA 02109

PRIMI, DON ALEXIS, advt. and pub. relations exec.; b. N.Y.C., Jan. 14, 1947; s. John Prosper, Sr. and Eileen Mary P.; A. in Advt., State U. N.Y., Farmingdale, 1967; B.S. in Mktg. and Advt., Hofstra U., 1971; advanced astron. studies degree Vanderbilt Mus. and Planetarium, 1976; m. Cheryll Ann Cain, Apr. 26, 1969. Gen. mgr. Recreational Pub. Corp., 1966-68; pres., owner Indsl. Advt. Assos., Inc., Great Neck, N.Y., 1968—, 3 Railmark, Ltd., 1971—, Don Primi & Assos., 1976—, Logo Looms, Ltd., 1978—; cons. to ry. industry, brick and clay products industry; designer corp. identity programs. Recipient awards Printing Industries Met. N.Y., Gold Boli advt. awards, Kimberly-Clark Graphic excellence awards, awards Astron. Assn. Am. Mem. Ry. Progress Inst., Astro-Assn. Am. R.R.'s., R.R. Pub. Relations Assn., Nat. R.R. Assn. Passengers, Sales and Mktg. Execs., Assn. Indsl. Advertisers, N.Y. R.R. Club, Astron. Soc. L.I. (pres., pub. relations dir.), Rail Mktg. Club N.Y. Designs published in periodicals. Office: 185 Main St Port Washington NY 11050

PRIMICH, THEODORE, sheet metal co. exec.; b. Manassas, Va., May 28, 1915; s. John and Mary (Zudock) P.; grad. high sch.; m. Katherine Pollak, Jan. 30, 1938; children—Geraldine Mary (Mrs. John R. Pigott), Katherine Jean (Mrs. Tom Workman). Vice pres. G.W. Berkheimer Co., Gary, Ind., 1936—; pres. Gary Steel Products Corp., 1945—; v.p. Primich Warehouses; pres. Primich Engineered Products. Mem. Air Distbn. Inst., Ind. Mfrs. Assn., Nat., Ind., Gary chambers commerce, NAM, Midwest Indsl. Mgmt. Assn., N.Am. Heating and Air Conditioning Assn. Lion. Club: Gary Country. Patentee in field. Home: 1937 W 61st Pl Merrillville IN 46410 Office: 4400 W 9th Ave Gary IN 46406

PRIMM, RAYMOND, electronic exec.; b. Alix, Ark., July 17, 1933; s. James Preston and Maggie Mae (Birchfield) P.; student Ark. Poly. Inst., 1952-54, Kansas City Jr. Coll., 1958-59, U. N.Mex., 1964-65; m. Virginia L. Schaeffer, Jan. 19, 1957; children—Theresa D., Donna L., Shari D., James P.R. Vice pres. mktg. Data Tech., Inc., 1959-66; engring. mgr. Pan Am. Systems, 1966-68; mfrs. rep., 1968-70; gen. mgr. Lek-Trol, Inc., 1970-72; pres. Innovation Industries, Inc., Roswell, N.Mex., 1972—. Chmn. Albuquerque United Community Fund; fund raising capt. St. Joseph's Hosp., Albuquerque. Served with AUS, 1950-52, USAF, 1954-58. Decorated Bronze Star. Mem. Instrumentation Soc. Am., Am. Soc. Quality Control, Nat. Assn. Elevator Contractors, Nat. Assn. Material Handling. Democrat. Designed and developed electronic instrumentation for 5-year study of Cochiti Dam; crew mem. atomic tests Operation Teapot (Nev.), Operation Redwing (Bikini and Eniwetok Atolls). Home: Route 1 Box 38E Roswell NM 88201 Office: 5012 S Main St PO Box 6681 Roswell NM 88201

PRIMO, MARIE NASH, mgr. shopping centers; b. Clarksburg, W.Va., Dec. 10, 1928; d. Frank and Josephine (DiMaria) Nash; student pub. schs., Clarksburg; m. Joseph C. Primo, Sept. 27, 1953; 1 dau., Joan E. Sec., Nat. Bank Detroit, 1945-46; exec. sec. Cutting Tool Mfrs. Assn., Detroit, 1946-50; adminstrv. asst. Irwin I. Cohn, atty., Detroit, 1950—; mgr. Bloomfield Shopping Plaza, Birmingham, Mich., 1959—, North Hill Center, Avon Twp., Mich., 1957—, Drayton Plains Shopping Center (Mich.), 1958—, South Allen Shopping Center, Allen Park, Mich., 1953-77, Huron-Tel Corner, Pontiac, Mich., 1977—; officer, dir., numerous privately held corps. Mem. steering com., treas. Univ. Liggett Antiques Show, 1971-76, mem. adv. com., 1977—; mem. parents com. Wellesley Coll., 1979—. Mem. Founders Soc. Detroit Inst. Arts, Mich. Humane Soc., Detroit Zool. Soc., Smithsonian Assos., Grosse Pointe War Meml. Assn., Grosse Pointe Pub. Library Assn., Detroit Grand Opera Assn., Women's Econ. Club. Roman Catholic. Home: 1341 N Renaud Rd Grosse Pointe Woods MI 48236 Office: 2290 1st National Bldg Detroit MI 48226

PRIMUS, JOHN LORENZ, banker; b. Vinton, Iowa, Jan. 1, 1938; s. Lorenz R. and Hazel M. (Lockhart) P.; B.S., Iowa State U., 1965; M.B.A., Golden Gate U., 1974; m. Helen L. Sears, Aug. 12, 1962; children—Michael John, Daniel Lorenz. With Bank of Am. Nat. Trust and Savs. Assn., Fresno, Calif., 1965—, now v.p.; lectr. Calif. State U., Chico, 1974—, Fresno, 1979—, Butte Coll., 1974—, Golden Gate U., 1974. Served with Army N.G., 1958-59. Recipient cert. of outstanding accomplishment Golden Gate U.; cert. jr. coll. instr., Calif.; cert. comml. lender Am. Bankers Assn. Mem. Am. Inst. Banking (cert.), Assn. M.B.A. Execs., Mortgage Lenders Assn. Central Calif. (v.p. 1980). Office: 1011 Van Ness Ave Fresno CA 93721

PRINCE, GEORGE BURLING, JR., mfg. co. exec.; b. White Plains, N.Y., June 17, 1934; s. George Burling and Ruth (McCarthy) P.; A.B., Yale U., 1956; m. Leonide Therese Campbell, Oct. 14, 1961; children—George Burling III, Caroline, David, Julie. Salesman, Procter & Gamble Co., Cin., 1958-60; account exec. Aitkin Kynett Co., Phila., 1960-64; new products dir. Colgate-Palmolive Co., N.Y.C., 1964-73; v.p. mktg. Hertz Corp., N.Y.C., 1973-77; v.p. mktg. Whitehall Labs. div. Am. Home Products Corp., N.Y.C., 1977—. Served with U.S. Army, 1956-58. Republican. Roman Catholic. Clubs: Westchester Country (Rye, N.Y.); Yale of N.Y. (N.Y.C.). Home: 96 Londonderry Dr Greenwich CT 06830 Office: 685 3d Ave New York NY 10017

PRINCE, WALTER NEWELL, bldg. maintenance co. exec.; b. Los Angeles, Dec. 6, 1935; s. Haig Marquis and Mary Eileen (Newell) P.; student Los Angeles Bus. Coll., 1953, U. Miami, 1954, U. Md., 1956, U. So. Calif., 1958, U. Utah, 1960, UCLA, 1961, others; 1 son, Haig Marquis. Editor, Rocketdyne div. Rockwell Corp., Canoga Park, Calif., 1962-67; gen. mgr. Pacific Coast Properties, Hollywood, Calif., 1967-69; chmn. bd., pres. Exec.-Suite Services, Inc., Northridge, Calif., 1969—; dir. Consol. Resources, Inc., Con. Served with U.S. Army, 1956-58. Mem. Nat. Assn. Service Contractors, Acad. Polit. and Social Scis., Los Angeles World Affairs Council, UCLA Alumni Assn. Hollywood C. of C., Northridge C. of C., Nat. Assn. Govt. Communicators. Office: 19025 Parthenia St Suite 200 Northridge CA 91324

PRINCE, WARREN VICTOR, mech. engr.; b. Kansas City, Mo., May 21, 1911; s. Charles William and Bertha (Lybarger) P.; student engring. Baker U., 1930-34; m. Edna Skinner Scott, Aug. 31, 1975; children—Charlotte E. (Mrs. Wm. K. Smith), Leslie Warren, Charles Allan, Charlene Diane. Design engr. Hoover Co., North Canton, Ohio, 1934-39; tool and machine design Thompson Products, Inc., Cleve., 1939-41; devel. engr. The Acrotorque Co., 1941-42; asst. chief devel. engr. The Weatherhead Co., 1942-45; pres. Prince Indsl. Plastics Corp., 1945-46; cons. engr., mech., plastics and plant prodn. problems, Kansas City and Los Angeles, 1946-50; project engr. Aerojet Gen. Corp., 1950-64; chief engr. Deposilube Mfg. Co., 1964-65; cons., 1965-66; sr. mech. engr. Avery Label Co., 1966-68; sr. project engr. machine design projects AMF, Inc., 1969-72; mech. cons. engr. as machine and product design specialist, 1972-80; pres. Contour Spltys., Inc., 1980—; evening instr. Mt. San Antonio Coll. Registered mech. engr., Calif. Received Soc. Plastics Engrs. 1948 Nat. award for establishing basic laws of plastic molding process. Mem. Soc. Plastics Engrs., Soc. Plastics Industry, Am. Soc. Tool and Mfg. Engrs., Kappa Sigma. Presbyterian. Mason (Shriner). Club: Rotary. Contbr. articles to profl. jours. Patentee in field. Office: 838 N West St Anaheim CA 92801

PRINDIVILLE, ROBERT A., investment co. exec.; b. Chgo., Aug. 18, 1935; s. James A. and Mary G. (Greening) P.; B.S., Marquette U., 1958; m. Kathleen J. Hardie, Aug. 8, 1959; children—Eleanor, Victoria, Christopher, Charles, Anne Louise, Mary Alice, Genevieve. Sr. v.p., dir. Thomson McKinnon Securities, N.Y.C., 1957—; mem. N.Y. Stock Exchange, 1970-71, Chgo. Bd. Trade, 1966-74; dir. Chgo. Bd. Option Exchange, The Mgmt. Group Inc., Realty World Corp. Roman Catholic. Home: 3 Beechcroft Rd Short Hills NJ 07078 Office: 1 New York Plaza New York NY 10004

PRINDL, ANDREAS ROBERT, banker; b. Decatur, Ill., Nov. 25, 1939; s. Frank Joseph and Vivian (Mitchell) P.; A.B., magna cum laude, Princeton U., 1961; postgrad. London Sch. Econs., 1963-64; Ph.D., U. Ky., 1964; m. Veronica M. Koerber, Sept. 12, 1963; children—Karin A., Christopher A. With Morgan Guaranty Trust Co., N.Y.C., 1964—, asst. treas., Frankfurt, Ger., 1966-70, asst. v.p., London, 1970-72, v.p., 1972-76, v.p., gen. mgr., Tokyo, 1976-80; dir. Kanebo Cadbury Ltd., Tokyo, 1976-80; exec. dir. Saudi Internat. Bank, London, 1980—; dir. Saudi Internat. Bank (Nassau). Trustee Internat. Christian U., Tokyo, 1979-80. Mem. Am. Econ. Assn., Inst. of Bankers, Am. C. of C. in Japan, Am.-Japan Soc. Co-author: International Money Management, 1971; author: Foreign Exchange Risk, 1976. Home: Wings Pl Ditchling Sussex England Office: Saudi Internat Bank 99 Bishopsgate London EC24 3TB England

PRINGLE, FRANK E., JR., mfg. co. exec.; b. Lawrence, Kans., Nov. 8, 1925; s. Frank E. and Ruth (Edgar) P.; student U. Kans., 1946-48, Ill. Inst. Tech., 1948-49, Northwestern U., 1949; m. Mary Ann Pringle, May 1, 1948; 1 dau., Nancy Joan. With Sperry Products, Inc., 1948-56, sales mgr. indsl. div., 1954-56; with Howe Scale Co., Rutland, Vt., 1956-60, gen. sales mgr., 1957-60; with Hayssen Mfg. Co., Sheboygan, Wis., 1960—, v.p. sales mktg., 1960-68, pres., 1968—. Bd. dirs. Sheboygan Meml. Hosp. Served with U.S. Navy, 1943-46. Clubs: Sheboygan Country (v.p.), Sheboygan Econs. (pres.). Patentee in field. Home: 4626 Superior Sheboygan WI 53081 Office: Hy 42 N Sheboygan WI 53081

PRINTUP, JOHN MONROE, ret. advt. and mktg. cons.; b. Oak Park, Ill., Oct. 14, 1919; s. John Monroe and Edna Mae (Hartman) P.; student No. Ill. U., No. Ill. Coll. Optometry; children—Michael, Bonnie, Richard, Susan. Owner-operator clothing store and bowling alley, Hampshire, Ill., 1947-51; So. mgr. Indsl. Publs., New Orleans, 1951-52; pres. John Printup & Assos., Miami, Fla., 1952-64, chmn. bd., Atlanta, 1965-77; cons. Cahners Pub. Co., Inc., Atlanta, 1977-79. Served with USAF, 1941-45. Recipient Eagle Scout award with bronze palm; decorated Meritorious Service award, Am. Def. medal, Victory in Europe medal, World War II medal, others. Mem. Bus. and Profl. Advt. Assn. (chmn. edn. com. 1974—). Republican. Methodist. Clubs: Masons, Shriners. Contbr. articles to profl. jours. Home: 210 Worth Dr NW Atlanta GA 30327

PRIOR, WILLIAM ALLEN, electronics co. exec.; b. Benton Harbor, Mich., Jan. 14, 1927; s. Allen Ames and Madeline Isabel (Taylor) P.; A.B., Harvard U., 1950, M.B.A., 1954; m. Irmgard C.L. Becker-Ehmck, Oct. 30, 1971; children—Stephanie Sayles, Alexandra Taylor, Robert Eames, Eleanor Norton, Michael Becker-Ehmck, Jeffrey Renner. Salesman, IBM Corp., N.Y.C., 1950-52; sales engr. Lincoln Electric Co., Cleve., 1954-57; v.p., dir. Hammond, Kennedy & Co., Inc., N.Y.C., 1957-67; v.p. Singer Co., N.Y.C., 1967-68; pres., dir. Tansitor Electronics, Inc., Bennington, Vt., 1968-71; pres. Aerotron, Inc., Raleigh, N.C., 1971—; dir. Aerotron Barbados Ltd., Occidental Life Ins. Co. N.C., McM Corp., Waycom Internat. Ltd. Served with A.C., AUS, 1945-46. Mem. IEEE. Clubs: River, Harvard (N.Y.C.); Raleigh Racquet, North Ridge Country (Raleigh). Home: 6816 Rainwater Rd Raleigh NC 27609 Office: US Hwy 1 N Raleigh NC 27611

PRITCHARD, JAMES FRANCIS, bicycle transmission co. exec.; b. Clinton, Mass., Sept. 2, 1923; s. Walter and Doris A. (Champney) P.; A.B.A., Nichols Coll., 1947; B.S., U. N.H., 1952; m. Marion Clark Harrington, Feb. 5, 1948; children—Linda, James, Shawn, Jennifer. Dist. mgr. Continental Can Co., St. Louis, 1952-55; regional mgr. Waddell & Read, Inc., Fitchburg, Mass., 1955-60; pres., sole propr. J.F. Pritchard & Co., Fitchburg, 1960-73; pres., treas. Bicycle Transmission Corp. of Am., Leominster, Mass., 1973—, Bicycle Tech. Corp. of Am., 1979—; lectr. in field; cons. in investment banking; liaison officer U.S. Air Force Acad. for congressional dist. Mass., 1961-63. Served with US Army, 1943-45, to capt., USAF, 1950-52. Elected to Hall of Fame, Nichols Coll., Dudley, Mass. Mem. 168th Combat Engring. Assn. (pres. 1958). Patentee in field. Home: 803 Pleasant St Leominster MA 01453 Office: Plains Rd Claremont NH 03473

PRITCHARD, WALTER H., JR., retail exec.; b. Cleve., Dec. 7, 1941; s. Walter H. and Marian (Moore) P.; A.B., Hamilton Coll., 1963; M.B.A., Columbia U., 1969; m. Mary Karen Kenney, Aug. 19, 1973; children—Walter, Jennifer, Melissa. Sr. accountant Peat Marwick Mitchell, Los Angeles, 1969-73; controller Teledyne Post, Des Plaines, Ill., 1974-78; v.p. fin. Western Graphics Corp., Eugene, Oreg., 1979—. Served with U.S. Navy, 1964-68. Mem. Am. Inst. C.P.A.'s. Republican. Home: 889 Lariat Dr Eugene OH 97401 Office: 3535 W 1st Ave Eugene OR 97402

PRITZKER, JAY ARTHUR, lawyer; b. Chgo., Aug. 26, 1922; s. Abraham Nicholas and Fanny (Doppelt) P.; B.Sc., Northwestern U., 1941, J.D., 1947; m. Marian Friend, Aug. 31, 1947; children—Nancy (dec.), Thomas, John, Daniel, Jean. Asst. custodian Alien Property Adminstrn., 1947; admitted to Ill. bar, 1947, since practiced in Chgo.; partner firm Pritzker & Pritzker, 1948—; chmn. bd., pres. Hyatt Internat.; chmn. bd. Hyatt Corp.; Marmon Group, Inc.; dir. Elsinore Corp., Continental Air Lines; partner Chgo. Mill & Lumber Co., Mich.-Calif. Lumber Co. Trustee, U. Chgo. Served as aviator USNR,

World War II. Mem. Am., Chgo. bar assns. Clubs: Standard, Comml., Lake Shore, Mid-Day, Arts, Vince (Chgo.). Office: 2 First Nat Plaza Chicago IL 60603

PRITZKER, ROBERT ALAN, mfg. co. exec.; b. Chgo., June 30, 1926; s. Abram Nicholas and Fanny (Doppelt) P.; B.S. in Indsl. Engring., Ill. Inst. Tech., 1946; postgrad. in bus. adminstrn. U. Ill.; m. Irene Dryburgh, Feb. 15, 1980; children by previous marriage—James Nicholas, Linda, Karen. Engaged in mfg., 1946—; pres., dir. GL Corp., Marmon Group Inc., Chgo.; dir. RegO Group, Inc., Peoples Energy Corp., Hyatt Corp., Hyatt Internat. Corp., Chgo., Salem Corp., Pitts. Vice pres., bd. dirs. Pritzker Found., Chgo.; trustee vice chmn. Ill. Inst. Tech. Office: 39 S LaSalle St Chicago IL 60603

PRITZKER, THOMAS JAY, hotel exec.; b. Chgo., June 6, 1950; s. Jay A. and Marian F. Pritzker; B.A., Claremont (Calif.) Men's Coll., 1971; M.B.A., U. Chgo., 1972, J.D., 1976; m. Margot Lyn Barrow-Sicree, Sept. 4, 1977; 1 son, Jason Nicholas. Admitted to Ill. bar, 1976; asso. firm Katten Muchin Gitles Zavis Pearl & Galler, Chgo., 1976-77; successively asst. gen. counsel, asst. to chmn. bd., exec. v.p. Hyatt Corp., Rosemont, Ill., 1977-80, pres., 1980—, also dir.; dir. Hyatt Hotels Corp.; partner Pritzker & Pritzker, Chgo., 1976—. Bd. dirs. Michael Reese Hosp., Chgo., 1978—. Served with USAFR, 1970-71. Mem. Am. Bar Assn., Ill. Bar Assn., Chgo. Bar Assn. Clubs: Standard, Lake Shore Country. Office: Hyatt Corp One Hyatt Center 9700 W Bryn Mawr Ave Rosemont IL 60018

PROCHNOW, HERBERT VICTOR, former govt. ofcl., banker, author; b. Wilton, Wis., May 19, 1897; s. Adolph and Alvina (Liefke) P.; B.A., U. Wis., 1921, M.A., 1922, LL.D. (hon.), 1956; Ph.D., Northwestern U., 1947, LL.D. (hon.), 1963; hon. Litt.D., Millikin U., 1952; LL.D., Ripon Coll., 1950, Lake Forest U., 1964, Monmouth Coll., 1965, U. N.D., 1966; D.H.L., Thiel Coll., 1965; m. Laura Virginia Stinson, June 12, 1928 (dec. Aug. 11, 1977); 1 son, Herbert Victor. Successively prin. Kendall (Wis.) High Sch., asst. prof. bus. adminstrn. Ind. U., purchasing agt. and advt. mgr. Union Trust Co., Chgo.; various positions 1st Nat. Bank of Chgo., until 1960, exec. v.p., dir., 1960-62, pres., dir., 1962-68, hon. dir., 1968-73; financial columnist Chgo. Sunday Tribune, 1968-70. Sec. fed. adv. council Fed. Res. System, 1945—; pres. Internat. Monetary Conf., 1968, now cons., hon. mem. apptd. spl. cons. to sec. of state, 1955, 57; dep. under sec. of state for econ. affairs, 1955-56; mem. U.S. delegation to Colombo Conf., Singapore, 1955, OECD, Paris, 1956; alternate gov. Internat. Bank and IMF, 1955-56; chmn. U.S. delegation Gen. Agreement on Tariffs and Trade, Geneva, 1956. Former lectr. Loyola U., Ind. U., Northwestern U.; dir. summer Grad. Sch. Banking, U. Wis., 1945—. Treas., Nat. 4-H Clubs, 1962-69. Former trustee McCormick Theol. Sem., Evanston Hosp., 1964-73. Served with AEF, 1918-19. Decorated comdr.'s cross Order Merit (Fed. Republic Germany); Order Vasa (Sweden); recipient Bus. Statesmanship award Harvard Bus. Sch. Assn. Chgo., 1965. Mem. Am. Econ. Assn., Am. Finance Assn., Nat. Assn. Bus. Economists, Chgo. Assn. Commerce and Industry (pres. 1964-65), Chgo. Council on Fgn. Relations (pres. 1966-67), Soc. Midland Authors, Beta Gamma Sigma (nat. honoree). Clubs: Commercial; Glen View; University, Chicago, Rotary, Chicago Sunday Evening (trustee), Union League (Chicago); Executives, Bankers. Co-author: The Next Century is America's, 1938. Practical Bank Credit, 1939, rev. edit., 1963; The Public Speaker's Treasure Chest, 1942, rev. edit. (with Herbert V. Prochnow, Jr.), 1964, 77. Author: Great Stories from Great Lives (an anthology), 1944; Meditations on the Ten Commandments, 1946; The Toastmaster's Handbook, 1949; Term Loans and Theories of Bank Liquidity, 1949; Successful Speakers Handbook, 1951; 1001 Ways to Improve Your Conversations and Speeches, 1952; Meditations on the Beatitudes, 1952; The Speaker's Treasury of Stories for All Occasions, 1953; The Speaker's Handbook of Epigrams and Witticisms, 1955; The Toastmaster's and Speaker's Handbook, 1955; Speakers Treasury for Sunday School Teachers, 1955; A Treasury of Stories Illustrations, Epigrams and Quotations for Ministers and Teachers, 1956; The New Guide for Toastmasters, 1956; Meditations on The Lord's Prayer, 1957; A Family Treasury of Inspiration and Faith, 1958; The New Speaker's Treasury of Wit and Wisdom, 1958; Speaker's Book of Illustrations, 1960; Effective Public Speaking, 1960; The Complete Toastmaster, 1960; 1001 Tips and Quips for Speakers and Toastmasters, 1962; 1400 Ideas for Speakers and Toastmasters, 1964; co-author: (with Herbert V. Prochnow, Jr.) A Dictionary of Wit, Widsom and Satire, 1962, Successful Toastmaster, 1966, A Treasury of Humorous Quotations for Speakers, Writers, and Home Reference, 1969, The Changing World of Banking, 1974; (with Everett M. Dirksen) Quotation Finder, 1971; (with Herbert V. Prochnow, Jr.) Toastmaster's Treasure Chest, 1979. Editor: American Financial Institutions, 1951; Determining the Business Outlook, 1954; The Federal Reserve System, 1960; World Economic Problems and Policies, 1965; The Five-Year Outlook for Interest Rates, 1968; The One-Bank Holding Co., 1969; The Eurodollar, 1970; The Five-Year Outlook for Interest Rates in the United States and Abroad, 1972; Dilemmas Facing the Nation, 1979; Bank Credit, 1981. Home: 2950 Harrison St Evanston IL 60201 Office: One First National Plaza Chicago IL 60670

PROCHNOW, HERBERT VICTOR, JR., banker, lawyer; b. Evanston, Ill., May 26, 1931; s. Herbert V. and Laura (Stinson) P.; A.B., Harvard, 1953, J.D., 1956; A.M., U. Chgo., 1958; m. Lucia Boyden, Aug. 6, 1966; children—Thomas Herbert, Laura Stinson. Admitted to Ill. bar, 1957; with 1st Nat. Bank Chgo., 1958—, asst. atty., 1961-63, atty., 1963-69, sr. atty., 1969-73, counsel, 1973-78, adminstrv. asst. to chmn. bd., 1978—. Mem. Am., Ill., Chgo. (chmn. com. on internat. law 1970-71) bar assns., Am. Soc. Internat. Law, Phi Beta Kappa. Clubs: Chicago; Harvard (N.Y.C.); Economic, Executives, Law, Legal, Onwentsia, University (all Chgo.). Author: (with Herbert V. Prochnow) The Changing World of Banking, 1974; The Public Speaker's Treasure Chest, 1977; also articles in legal publs. Home: 226 Ravine Forest Dr Lake Bluff IL 60044 Office: One First National Plaza Chicago IL 60670

PROCK, MICHAEL JOHN, steel co. exec.; b. Cohoes, N.Y., Aug. 21, 1953; s. John J. and Stacia K. (Wysocki) P.; B.S. in Econs., Siena Coll., 1975; M.B.A., Rensselaer Poly. Inst., 1976. With Colt Industries, 1976—, foreman Fairbanks Morse engine div., Beloit, Wis., 1976-78, mfg. supt. Garlock, Inc., mech. packing div., Palmyra, N.Y., 1978-79, supr. material Crucible Compaction Metals, Oakdale, Pa., 1979—; dir. Vikram Corp. Mem. Republican Com., Cohoes. Recipient service award Jr. Achievement, Beloit, 1976, 77. Mem. Pitts. Purchasing Mgrs. Assn. Republican. Roman Catholic. Home: 930 Margarite Dr Apt B Pittsburgh PA 15216 Office: Crucible Compaction Metals Div Colt Industries McKee and Robb Hill Rd Oakdale PA 15071

PROCKNOW, DONALD EUGENE, business exec.; b. Madison, S.D., May 27, 1923; s. Fred Anthony and Ruth (Trevor) P.; student S.D. Sch. Mines, 1941-43; B.S. in Elec. Engring., U. Wis., 1947; m. Esther J. Ehlert, May 16, 1953; children—Eugene, Charles. With Western Electric Co., 1947—, successively engr., asst. supt. devel., engring. Hawthorne works, Chgo., spl. assignment, N.Y.C., supt. precision apparatus and Waveguide shops, asst. works mgr. N.C. works, asst. engr. mfg., N.Y.C., engr. mfg., gen. mgr. Central region Service div., Chgo., 1947-65, v.p. parent co., 1965-69, exec. v.p., dir., 1969-71, pres., dir., mem. exec. com., 1971—; dir. Teletype Corp., J.P. Morgan Co., Morgan-Guaranty Bank, Bell Telephone Labs., CPC Internat., Ingersoll-Rand Co., Prudential Ins. Co. Pres., Greater N.Y. council Boy Scouts Am., 1975-76, mem. nat. exec. bd., 1979—; trustee Independent Coll. Funds Am.; trustee Clarkson Coll. Tech., Potsdam, N.Y. Served with USNR, 1943-46. Mem. Theta Tau, Sigma Tau, Eta Kappa Nu, Tau Beta Pi. Methodist. Mason (Shriner). Home: 18 Saw Mill Rd Saddle River NJ 07458 Office: 222 Broadway New York NY 10038

PROCTOR, BARBARA GARDNER, advt. agy. exec., writer; b. Asheville, N.C.; d. William and Bernice (Baxter) Gardner; B.A., Talladega (Ala.) Coll., 1954; hon. doctorate So. Meth. U.; m. Carl L. Proctor, July 20, 1961 (div. Nov. 1963); 1 son, Morgan Eugene. Music critic. contbg. editor Down Beat Mag., Chgo., from 1958; internat. dir. Vee Jay Records, Chgo., 1961-63; contbr. to gen. periodicals, 1952—; now chmn. bd., pres., creative dir. Proctor & Gardner Advt., Chgo.; dir. Seway Nat. Bank. Mem. commerce adv. council U. Ill.; mem. Chgo. Urban League, Chgo. Econ. Devel. Corp.; bd. dirs. People United to Save Humanity, Mt. Sinai Hosp., Better Bus. Bur. Cons. pub. relations and promotion, record industry. Recipient Armstrong Creative Writing award, 1954; awards Chgo. Fedn. Advt. Clubs, N.Y. Art Dirs. Club, Woman's Day; Frederick Douglas Humanitarian award, 1975; named Chgo. Advt. Woman of Year, 1974; Headliner award Women in Communication, 1978; Mary M. Bethune Achievement award Nat. Bus. League, 1976; Leader of Year award NAACP. Mem. Chgo. Media Women, Nat. Assn. Radio Arts and Sci., Women's Advt. Club, Cosmopolitan C. of C. (dir.), Female Execs. Assn., Internat. Platform Assn., Smithsonian Instn. Assos., Ill. C. of C. (dir.). Author TV documentary Blues for a Gardenia, 1963. Office: Proctor and Gardner Advt 111 E Wacker Dr Chicago IL 60601

PROFITT, LESLIE M., mfg. co. exec.; b. Winchester, Ky., Sept. 2, 1920; s. James Albin and Samantha Ethel (Shelton) P.; student U. Cin., 1952-60; m. Opal Mae DeHart, Sept. 3, 1943; children—Richard, Douglas, Karen. Asst. chief insp. Aeronca, Inc., Middletown, Ohio, 1940-45; owner food market, Middletown, 1947; foreman Eversharp, Inc., Middletown, 1948-49; with Monsanto Co., Miamisburg, Ohio, 1949-52; with Aeronca, Inc., Middletown, 1952-65; engring. tech. specialist Gen. Electric Co., Cin., 1965-80; owner, pres. Modified Tubular Products, Inc., Middletown, 1977—, InS, Inc., Middletown, 1979—; cons. in field; lectr. in field. Rep. precinct committeeman, 1956. Mem. Nat. Small Bus. Assn., Internat. Entrepreneurs Assn. Republican. Patentee in field. Home: 147 Sunset Ct Monroe OH 45050 Office: 401 N University Blvd Middletown OH 45042

PROGIN, GERARD HENRI, watch and electronic components co. exec.; b. Fribourg, Switzerland, Feb. 3, 1939; s. Gustave and Yvonne (Moret) P.; came to U.S., 1966; M.B.A., Fribourg U., 1962; m. Marie Lisa, Aug. 29, 1968. Export sales mgr. Ciba-Geigy, Summit, N.J., 1967-69; purchasing mgr. Zyma Pharms., Nyon, Switzerland, 1962-64; adminstrv. asst. Ciba SA, Brussels, Belgium, 1965-66; v.p. fin. and adminstrn., treas. Portescap U.S., N.Y.C., 1969—. Served to lt. Swiss Army, 1959-64. Mem. Am. Mgmt. Assn. Clubs: Rotary, 24 Karat. Home: 60 Sutton Pl S New York NY 10022 Office: 730 Fifth Ave New York NY 10019

PRONIN, BURT, ins. exec.; b. Bklyn., Apr. 9, 1930; s. William and Bertha (Kantor) P.; student Los Angeles City Coll., 1948-50; A.A., Calif. State Coll., Los Angeles, 1952; m. Barbara Lenore Markman, May 28, 1967; children—Stacy Michele, Michael Brett. Advt. exec. Sears Roebuck & Co., Los Angeles, 1954-61; actor, Los Angeles, 1961-63; agt. Aetna Life Ins. Co., Los Angeles, 1963-75; asst. gen. agt. Nat. Life Ins. Co., also v.p. Comprehensive Fin. Planning, Inc., Los Angeles, 1975—. Bd. dirs. Hope House for Multiple-Handicapped, Inc., 1970—, Temple Shalom, 1978—. Served with Signal Corps, AUS, 1952-54. Recipient sales awards ins. cos. Mem. Nat., Calif., East San Gabriel Valley assns. life underwriters. Author: A License to Steal-Corporate Split Dollar Life; SEP, The Least Understood Pension. Home: 3117 Sunset Hill Dr West Covina CA 91791 Office: 328 E San Bernardino Rd Covina CA 91723

PROOM, BURT CHANDLER, ins. co. exec.; b. Bklyn., Apr. 23, 1925; s. Robert W. and Erma S. (Stellenwerf) P.; B.A., Dartmouth Coll., 1949; m. Carolyn Harper, Dec. 8, 1950; children—B. Chandler, William, Mary Elizabeth. Bond underwriter Md. Casualty Co., Harrisburg, Pa., 1950-56, asst. resident mgr. Harrisburg br. office, v.p., 1956-59, Phila. br. office, 1959-64, asst. resident mgr., 1964-73; resident v.p. underwriting Midwestern Group, Cin., 1973-74; pres. Am. Nuclear Insurers, Farmington, Conn., 1974—. Served with U.S. Army, 1943-45. Mem. Ins. Soc. Phila. (pres. 1970), Casualty and Property Ins. Mgrs. Assn. Phila., Soc. CPCU's (nat. pres. 1979-80). Republican. Espicopalian. Clubs: City of Hartford, Hartford Canoe, Down Town of Phila.; Country of Farmington. Home: 33 Rocklyn Dr West Simsbury CT 06092 Office: 270 Farmington Ave Suite 245 Farmington CT 06032

PROPECK, TIMOTHY JOSEPH, semicondr. mfg. co. exec.; b. Los Angeles, Oct. 18, 1946; s. John Joseph and Marjorie May (Talley) P.; B.A., Pomona Coll., 1968; M.B.A., U. Minn., 1977; m. Susan, Dec. 22, 1973; children—Kristin, Lynsey. Mktg. engr. Rosemount Inc., Mpls., 1973-75; sales engr. Tex. Instruments Co., Mpls., 1975-77; account mgr. Mostek Co., Mpls., 1977, maj. account mgr., Dallas, 1977-78, mgr. mktg., 1978—. Served with USAF, 1969-73. Decorated D.F.C. with cluster; Phi Kappa Phi scholar, 1976-77. Home: 6008 Timber Creek Dallas TX 75248

PROPER, RICHARD NICHOLS, retail store exec.; b. Jefferson, N.Y., Nov. 5, 1937; s. Clarence Eli and Mabel Cynthia (Nichols) P.; B.A. in Econs., Syracuse U., 1959, B.S., in Indsl. Engring., 1960; m. Sandra Nielsen; children—Michael, Geoffrey, Eric, Lisa. Indsl. engr. Ford Motor Co., Dearborn, Mich., 1960-62; indsl. engr. supr., cons. Kroger Co., Cin., 1962-67; mgr. indsl. engring. Maas Bros., Tampa, Fla., 1967-68, distbn. mgr., 1969-75, v.p. distbn., 1975-79, sr. v.p. control and distbn., 1979—. Mem. Am. Inst. Indsl. Engrs., Tampa C. of Co. Clubs: Mason, Shrine, Cove Cay Country. Home: 2213 Kent Pl Clearwater FL 33516 Office: 4130 Gandy Blvd Tampa FL 33611

PROPES, ALICE IDA, Realtor; b. Gold Beach, Oreg., Aug. 9, 1927; d. Elmer Revis and Helen Violet (Fischer) Costelloe; student pub. schs., Gold Beach; grad. Realtors Inst.; m. Frank Findley Propes, June 17, 1952; children—Sheri Lue, Michael Frank. Chief operator West Coast Telephone Co., Gold Beach, 1945-52; partner Washington Utilities Constrn. Co., 1952-60, sec.-treas., 1960—; partner Mt. Springs Arabian Ranch, 1962—; owner, Realtor, Mt. Springs Realty, Willamina, Oreg., 1973—. Mem. Rock County Planning Commn., 1981—. Mem. Oreg., Portland, Polk County (Realtor of Year 1976, pres. 1978) bds. Realtors, Oreg. Assn. Realtors (dist. v.p. 1980—), Farm and Land Inst. (accredited farm and land mem.), Dallas Area C. of C. Republican. Presbyterian. Home: 225 SE Walnut Dr Dallas OR 97338 Office: 333 South Main St Box 899 Willamina OR 97396

PROPHETER, MICHAEL ROBERT, financial exec.; b. Sterling, Ill., Mar. 2, 1943; s. Robert Aaron and Florence Louise (O'Malley) P.; B.S. in B.A., Northwestern, 1965, M.B.A., 1966; m. Virginia Grennan, Dec. 28, 1963; children—Kevin, David, Douglas, Katherine, Elizabeth. Fin. analyst Burroughs Corp., Rochester, N.Y., 1966-70, mgr. fin. analysis, Detroit, 1970-74; area controller Internat. div. Abbott Labs., North Chicago, Ill., 1974-75; dir. accounting and procedures Continental Can Co., Chgo., 1975-76; dir. financial systems Bendix Corp., Southfield, Mich., 1976-78; v.p. fin. Canton Co. subs. Pacific Holding Corp., Balt., 1978—. Mem. Fin. Execs. Inst., Nat. Assn. Accountants, Systems and Procedures Assn., Phi Gamma Delta. Club: Downtown Racquet. Home: 4 Holly Branch Ct Glen Arm MD 21057 Office: World Trade Center Baltimore MD 21203

PROSISE, ROBERT EDWARD, mfg. co. exec.; b. Napa, Calif., Oct. 28, 1929; s. Harry Theodore and Lena Olive (Attebery) P.; A.A., Napa Jr. Coll., 1949; B.S., U. Calif. at Berkeley, 1951; M.B.A. (scholar) Stanford, 1957; m. Betty Rose Simmons, May 27, 1952; children—Kathleen Rose, Harry Theodore, Pamela Kay, Bonnie Jean, Theodore Orrin. Sales rep. Adolph Blaich, Inc., Burlingame, Calif., 1957-60, div. mgr., 1960-62; asst. to v.p. Browning Arms Co., Morgan, Utah, 1962-68, mgr., 1968-70, mdse. mgr., 1970-74; mktg. mgr. Gerber Legendary Blades, Portland, Oreg., 1974-75; pres., gen. mgr., dir. Jarman Co., Milwaukie, Oreg., 1976—; part-time faculty Portland (Oreg.) State U. Served with USNR, 1952-55. Mem. Sales Mgmt. Execs. Internat., Alpha Gama Sigma. Republican. Presbyterian. Home: 9945 SW Pembrook St Tigard OR 97223 Office: 5675 International Way Milwaukie OR 97222

PROTHRO, GERALD DENNIS, computer co. exec.; b. Atlanta, Sept. 27, 1942; s. Charles Emery and Esther (Jones) P.; B.S., Howard U., 1966, M.S., 1969; postgrad. Harvard Grad. Sch. Bus. Adminstrn., 1975; m. Brenda Jean Bell, Feb. 14, 1976; 1 son, Gerald Dennis. Physicist, NASA, Goddard Space Flight Center, Green Belt, Md., 1965-69; asso. systems analyst IBM, Burlington, Vt., 1969, sr. asso. systems analyst, 1969-71, mgr. process line central engring. systems, 1971, mgr. process line central analysis systems, 1971-73, project mgr. systems facilities and support, 1973-74, mgr. info. systems strategy System Product div., White Plains, N.Y., 1974-75, dir. system assurance, data processing product group, 1975-78, mgr. processors systems data systems div. Poughkeepsie Devel. Lab., 1978-79, mgr. site resourses and bus. planning, 1979—. NDEA fellow, 1967-69; NASA grantee, 1965-69; recipient Black Achievers award YMCA Harlem, 1976; Div. award IBM, 1979. Mem. NAACP, Urban League, Am. Inst. Physics, AAAS, Automatic Computing Machines, Sigma Phi Sigma, Beta Kappa Ki. Presbyn. Club Harvard N.Y.C. Contbr. articles to profl. jours. Home: Stream Ln Pleasant Valley NY 12569 Office: PO Box 390 Poughkeepsie NY 12602

PROTTER, HAROLD EDWIN, TV exec.; b. N.Y.C., Dec. 21, 1941; s. Joseph and Ann (Packer) P.; B.S. in Bus. Adminstrn., U. Conn., 1962, postgrad. Law Sch., 1963; m. Gail Brekke, Dec. 29, 1975; children—Steven, Sabrina. Sales mgr. Telerep, Inc., Detroit, 1970; v.p., gen. sales mgr., then v.p., gen. mgr. sta. WXIX, Cin., 1970-74; v.p., gen. mgr. sta. KPLR-TV, St. Louis, 1974—; exec. v.p., chief operating officer 220 TV, Inc., St. Louis, 1979—; exec. com. Arbitron Adv. Council, 1979-80. Recipient Arbitron Innovator award, 1972. Mem. Assn. Ind. TV Stas. (dir., chmn. new tech. com. 1979-80), Ind. TV News Assn. (charter, dir.), Nat. Acad. TV Arts and Scis. (pres., gov. St. Louis chpt. 1979), Advt. Club Greater St. Louis. Home: 4632 Maryland Ave St Louis MO 63108 Office: 4935 Lindell Blvd St Louis MO 63108

PROUT, PATRICK MICHAEL, banker; b. Trinidad, W.I., July 8, 1941; s. Rupert S. and Iris A. P.; came to U.S., 1954, naturalized, 1955; B.S. in Engring., U.S. Naval Acad., 1964; M.B.A. (Goldman Sachs fellow), Harvard U., 1973; m. Faye A. Whitfield, Apr. 17, 1976; children—Nicole Simone, Danielle Monique. Mktg. rep. IBM, Washington, 1968-71; brand mgr. Miller Brewing Co., Milw., 1973-75; v.p., lending officer Chase Manhattan Bank, N.Y.C., 1975—; dir. Fin. Debt and Counseling Services (Milw.). Mem. membership task force NAACP, 1977—. Served to capt., USMC, 1964-68; Vietnam. Decorated Bronze Star with Combat V. Mem. Am. Mgmt. Assn., Black Urban Bankers Coalition, Nat. Fin. Assn., U.S. Naval Acad., Harvard Bus. Sch. alumni assns. Roman Catholic. Club: Harvard (N.Y.C.). Home: 25 Waterside Plaza New York NY 10010

PROVIDENTI, A. C., petroleum co. exec.; b. N.Y.C., Jan. 28, 1938; s. Charles and Josephine P.; B.B.A. in Accounting, St. Francis Coll., 1967; M.B.A., Fordham U., 1971; m. Frances Celandano, July 25, 1964; children—Karen, Anthony Charles, David, Joy. Comml. lending officer Franklin Nat. Bank, N.Y.C., 1969-70; corp. cons., Port Washington, N.Y., 1970-77; pres. Total Resources Inc. (merged into Northville Industries Corp. 1977), Jericho, N.Y., 1977; sr. v.p. fin. and adminstrn. Northville Industries Corp., Melville, N.Y., 1977—; cons., dir. Petroterminal de Panama S.A. Bd. regents St. Francis Coll.; bd. dirs. L.I. Assn., 1976—, v.p. natural resources, 1975-77; bd. dirs. L.I. Forum for Tech., Action Com. for L.I., Island Philharm. Soc. Served with U.S. Army, 1959-61. Recipient Service award L.I. Assn., 1977, also awards for pub. speaking. Mem. Am. Petroleum Assn., Am. Mgmt. Assn. Roman Catholic. Clubs: Manhasset Bay Sportsmen, Port Washington Yacht, Cornell of N.Y. Contbr. articles on econs. of regional oil transp. and environ. impact to profl. publs. Home: 24 South Ct Port Washington NY 11050 Office: 1 Huntington Quadrangle Melville NY 11747

PROVOST, DAVID EMILE, mail order shoe co. exec.; b. Detroit, Oct. 28, 1949; s. Emile L. and Terese M. (Disnard) P.; B.B.A., Northeastern U., 1975, B.S. in Acctg., 1975; M.B.A., Boston U., 1978; m. Linda S. Shepard, June 20, 1969; children—Emilie Noelle, Natalie Elizabeth. Acct., Romanow Enterprises, Westwood, Mass., 1973; controller Lion Precision Corp., Newton, Mass., 1973-75, Life Support Equipment Corp., Woburn, Mass., 1975-78; clk., treas. Lawson Hill Leather & Shoe Co., Inc., Waltham, Mass., 1978—; controller Profl. Advt. Services, Sanford, Maine, 1979—; gen. partner Provost Agy., Weston, Mass., 1980—, Whats UP? Co., Marlborough, Mass., 1980; dir. White House Corp., Westborough, Mass. Served with Fin. Corps, U.S. Army, 1970-72. Mem. Jr. C. of C. (dir., v.p.). Home: 57 Silver St Norwood MA 02062

PROVOST, DONALD EDGAR, engring. and constrn. co. exec.; b. Denver, Aug. 26, 1912; s. Charles Edgar and Beda Amanda (Rapp) P.; student U. Colo., 1932-33; m. Eldyne Herbst, Dec. 15, 1938; 1 dau., Sheila Kay Provost Meredith. Project engr. Stearns-Roger Corp., Denver, 1937-43, project mgr., 1944-54, mgr. power div., 1955-58, v.p., 1959-63, pres., chmn., 1963—, pres. and chmn. subs.; dir. General Iron Works Co., Mountain Bell, Rio Grande Industries Inc., Denver & Rio Grande Western R.R., First Nat. Bancorp., First Nat. Bank. Bd. dirs. Lutheran Med. Center, Denver, 1968—; trustee U. Denver. Registered profl. engr., Colo. Republican. Congregationalist. Clubs: Cherry Hills Country, Denver Country, Thunderbird Country.

PRUETT, GERTRUDE MOTE, investment research co. exec.; b. Double Springs, Ala., Aug. 2, 1918; d. Thomas J. and Martha Janie (Gray) Mote; student State Tchrs. Coll., Florence, Ala., 1935-38; 1 son, Harold M. Pres., Investors Research Services, Inc., Beverly Hills, Calif., 1975—. Mem. adv. bd. Salvation Army, Anchorage. Mem. Bus. and Profl. Women's Club, Beverly Hills C. of C. Republican. Office: Suite 104 8383 Wilshire Blvd Beverly Hills CA 90211

PRUETT, WILFORD RAY, fin. cons.; b. Plainview, Tex., Dec. 4, 1927; s. Hubert Fred and Sylvia Maude (Wilcox) P.; B.B.A., U. Tex., 1953; diploma Rutgers U., 1962; m. Billye Jean Marshall, Nov. 7, 1948; children—Susan Kay Pruett Stamilio, David Dee, Marshall Ray. Exec. trainee First Nat. Bank, Fort Worth, 1953-56; v.p. City Nat. Bank, Fort Smith, Ark., 1960-64, Corpus Christi (Tex.) Bank, 1964-67; chmn., pres., chief exec. officer Union Bank of Benton (Ark.), 1967—; cons. Fed. Nat. Bank, Shawnee, Okla., 1978—; exec. v.p. Thunderbird Fin. Corp., Shawnee; chmn. bd. Union Affiliate Realty Corp., Benton, 1971-75; justice of peace, Benton, 1969—. Mem. Ark. Mus. and Cultural Commn., 1973—; vice chmn. Goals for Central Ark., 1973; chmn. Saline County (Ark.) Council Econ. Edn., 1971-74; dir. Saline County (Ark.) Fair Assn., 1970—; exec. council Boy Scouts Am., Benton, 1968—; v.p. Ouachita area devel. council, 1972-74; chmn. United Fund drives, Benton, 1967—; chmn. citizens com. for schs., Benton, 1971-73; vice chmn. Central Ark. Resource Conservation and Devel. Area Council, 1974-75; mem. Ouachita River Valley Assn., 1970—, v.p., 1972-74. Bd. dirs. Saline County Library, 1969—, vice-chmn., 1973—; bd. dirs. Ark. Bapt. Found., 1969—; chmn. bd. Saline Choral Soc., 1975. Served with USNR, 1945-48. Named Outstanding Young Man, City of Fort Smith, Ark., 1963; Boss of Year, Jr. C. of C., 1967, Bus. and Profl. Women, 1974. Mem. Ark. Bankers Assn. (mem. savs. and mktg. com. 1972-75, chmn. 1974), Okla. Bankers Assn. (chmn. ops. and EFT com. 1977-78; sr. mgmt. com. 1977-78), Robert Morris Assos. (dir., sec. 1966, chpt. dir. 1972-74, mem. credit div. governing council 1974-75; chmn. small bank services com. 1973-75; Spl. Service award 1977), Ark. C. of C. (dir. 1974—), Heart of Ark. Travel Assn. (v.p., 1972, dir. dir. 1971-74), Nat. Alliance fo for Businessmen (adv. council 1970-73), Saline County C. of C. (pres. 1969-70, dir. 1968-72). Baptist (bd. deacons 1968—, chmn. 1972-73). Rotarian (dir. 1970-71). Clubs: Trace Creek Country; Little Rock. Home: 40 Northridge Shawnee OK 74801 Office: Suite 404 Fed Nat Bank Bldg Shawnee OK 74801

PRULHIERE, WILLIAM ROBERT, ins. agt.; b. Akron, Ohio, May 5, 1925; s. Alfred Henry and Mary Armilda (Brown) P.; student Am. Coll. Life Underwriters, 1965-68; m. Agnes Rose Kurty, Sept. 25, 1943; children—Cheryl Lee, Kathryn Elaine, Robert Alfred, Janice Mary, James William. Vice pres. Tallmadge Furniture & Mfg. Co. (Ohio), 1946-62; agt. to agy. mgr. Equitable Life Assurance Soc. U.S., 1965-75; gen. agt. Central Life Assurance of Iowa, Albuquerque, 1975-80; agy. mgr. Bankers Life of Iowa, Ft. Worth br., 1980—. Pres., Christian Students Activities, 1978—. Served with USNR, 1943-45. Mem. Nat. Assn. Life Underwriters, Chartered Life Underwriters, Gen. Agts. and Mgrs. Conf. Republican. Mem. Ch. of Christ (deacon). Office: 1200 Summit Suite 400 Fort Worth TX 76102

PRUNER, HAROLD, bus. cons.; b. Chickasah, Okla., Feb. 10, 1930; s. Charles Beaver and Cynthia Payne (Anderson) P.; B.S. in Geol. Engring., U. Okla., 1956; m. Billie Ann Stamper, Dec. 21, 1951; children—Ronald Mark, Russell Aaron, David Randall. Sr. engr. Shell Oil Co., Denver, also Houston, 1956-65, mgr., 1965-67; loan officer, mineral appraisal expert Morgan Guaranty Trust Co., N.Y.C., 1967-70; exec. dir. Oil Investment Inst., Greenwich, Conn., also Washington, 1970-71; petroleum and fin. in pvt. practice, Riverside, Conn., 1971—; organizer, condr. seminars on tax sheltered investments; speaker on Indian claims, developed investments for claims awards; claims rep., tribal councilman Delaware Tribe of Western Okla., 1966—; testimony on Indian legis. before Congress, 1968—. Trustee First Congregational Ch., Old Greenwich, Conn., 1977—. Served with USAF, 1948-52. Mem. Soc. Petroleum Engrs., Sigma Gamma Epsilon, Sigma Tau, Tau Beta Pi. Republican. Clubs: Innis Arden Golf (Old Greenwich, Conn.); Landmark (Stamford, Conn.), Petroleum (Tulsa); Bankers (Miami, Fla.). Home: 1 Kernan Pl Old Greenwich CT 06870 Office: 17 Wilmot Ln Riverside CT 06878

PRUPAS, MELVERN IRVING, food co. exec.; b. Montreal, Que., Can., Dec. 16, 1926; s. Harry and Esther (Braunstein) P.; student Sir George Williams U., 1943-45, Montreal Tech. Inst., 1946, Mt. Allison U., 1967, N.Y. State Coll. Agr., Cornell U., 1971, U. Guelph, 1971-72; m. Sheila Ditkofsky, Mar. 21, 1948; children—Michael, Richard, Norman, David, Dianne. Salesman, Crescent Cheese Co., 1947-50, sales mgr., 1951-56, dir., v.p., 1956-72, dir., v.p., sec., 1972-77; v.p., dir. Maycrest Co. Ltd., 1960-77; sec.-treas., dir. Les Produits Laitiers Marieville (Que., Can.) Ltee., 1956-72, v.p., sec., dir., 1972-77; founder En Ville newspaper, 1962; pres., dir. Ambassador Food Sales Ltd., 1964—; sec.-treas., dir. Proops Press Inc., 1967-70 (all Montreal); pres. Dadnaram Ltd. of Edmonton, 1973—. Bd. dirs. YM-YWHA of Montreal, 1954-72, gov., 1956-66, gov.-benefactor, 1967—, met. campaign chmn., 1966; cubmaster Boy Scouts of Can., Mount Royal, 1960-71; chmn. food div. Combined Jewish Appeal, Montreal, 1961-63, trade coordinator, 1964-65, vice chmn. trades. 1969-70, vice chmn. spl. names, 1972-73; bd. dirs. Jewish Nat. Fund Montreal, 1970-72; v.p. Algonquin Home and Sch. Assn., 1971-72. Recipient Scouters Warrant, Boy Scouts of Can. 1963; Chevalier Medal, Chaine des Rotisseurs, 1964; Ida Steinberg Meml. trophy Combined Jewish Appeal, 1969; Golden Gloves Heavyweight Boxing Champion, 1941; mem. Can. Olympic Basketball Team, 1948. Mem. Province of Que. Food Brokers Assn. (dir. 1968-70), Food Service Execs., Assn., Can. Restaurant Assn., Chaine de Rotisseurs in Montreal Baillage, Confrerie Des Vignerons De St. Vincents, Guilde des Fromagers Confrerie de Saint-Uguzon, Montreal Bd. of Trade, Can. C. of C., Comml. Travellers Assn. Can., Food Brokers Assn. Can., Can. Importers Assn., Can-Israel C. of C., Am. Mus. Natural History, Playwrights Workshop, Jewish Theol. Sem. Am., Canadian Council Christians and Jews, Mt. Royal Property Owners Assn. (dir. 1968-70). Jewish religion (dir. Congregation Beth El 1960-65, v.p. 1964-65, sec. 1969-70, v.p. 1971-73, pres. 1973-75). Mem. B'nai B'rith. Clubs: Cedarbrooke Golf and Country (St. Sophie); Montreal Anglers and Hunters, Rotary, Canadian, Amici (pres. 1950-51, 65-66). Address: Suite 707 80 Lakeshore Rd Point Claire PQ H9S 4H6 Canada

PRY, ROBERT HENRY, electronics co. research and devel. exec.; b. Dormont, Pa., Dec. 28, 1923; s. William Henry and Marie Eda (Freeman) P.; student Tex. A&M U., 1941-42, Okla. State U., 1943, U. Manchester (Eng.), 1945; B.S. in Physics, Tex. A&I U., 1947; M.A. in Physics, Rice U., 1949, Ph.D., 1951; m. Claude Marcelle Freyss, Dec. 21, 1947; children—Phillip Paul, Terry Allen, Pamela Lee, Patricia Ann, David Robert. Research asso., research labs. Gen. Electric Co., Schenectady, 1951-60, mgr. alloys studies, 1960-62, mgr. properties studies, 1962-65, mgr. liaison and transition, 1965-67, mgr. corp. research and devel. metallurgy and ceramics lab., 1967-72, mgr. corp. research and devel. materials sci. and engring., 1972-74, mgr. corp. research and devel. electronics sci. and engring., 1974-76; v.p. research and devel. Combustion Engring. Co., Stamford, Conn., 1976-77; v.p. research and devel. Gould Inc., Rolling Meadow, Ill., 1977-79, exec. v.p. research and devel., 1979—. Mem. indsl. panel on sci. and tech. NSF; mem. indsl. adv. council U. Ill., Chgo.; mem. vis. com. U. Pa. Served with Signal Corps, U.S. Army, 1943-46. Fellow AAAS, Am. Soc. Metals; mem. Am. Phys. Soc., Am. Inst. Physics, AIME, IEEE, Am. Mgmt. Assn. (chmn. research and devel. council), Indsl. Research Inst., Nat. Lab. Task Force, Metal Properties Council (dir.). Contbr. articles to profl. publs.; inventor materials, devices. Office: 10 Gould Center Rolling Meadows IL 60008

PRYOR, HUBERT, mag. editor; b. Buenos Aires, Argentina, Mar. 18, 1916; s. John W. and Hilda A. (Cowes) P.; came to U.S., 1940, derivative citizenship; grad. St. George's Coll., Argentina, 1932; student U. London (Eng.), 1934-36; m. Ellen M. Ach, Sept. 25, 1940; children—Alan, Gerald, David; m. 2d, Roberta J. Baughman, Apr. 11, 1959; m. 3d, Luanne W. Van Norden, Oct. 31, 1967; stepchildren—Andrew, Adrienne. Corr. in S.Am. for United Press, 1937-39; pub. relations rep. Pan Am. Airways in Buenos Aires, 1939-40; reporter N.Y. Herald Tribune, 1940-41; writer, dir. short-wave newsroom CBS, 1941-46; asst. mng. editor Knickerbocker Weekly, 1946-47; sr. editor Look mag., 1947-62; creative supr. Wilson, Haight & Welch, advt., 1962-63; editor Science Digest, 1963-67; mng. editor Med. World News, 1967; editor Modern Maturity, NRTA Jour., 1967—; editorial dir. Dynamic Years, 1977—. Served to lt. USNR, 1943-46. Mem. Am. Soc. Mag. Editors. Home: 44 Paloma Ave Long Beach CA 90803 Office: 215 Long Beach Blvd Long Beach CA 90802

PRYOR, WALLACE CYRAL, oil and gas mfg. co. exec.; b. Concord, Ga., Sept. 16, 1922; s. Harry Gwyn and Maude Mae (Johnson) P.; student St. Olaf Coll., Northfield, Minn., 1946; m. Myrtle Nelsen, Nov. 2, 1946 (div. 1967); children—John Wallace, David Nelsen, Paul Richard, Mark Bernard, Peter Gwyn, Joel Phillip, Andrew George; m. 2d, Jeannette Altman. Farmer, Pike County, Ga., 1946-54; civilian electrician Atlanta Army Depot, Forest Park, Ga., 1954-62; electrician and mechanic Spellman Engring., Orlando, Fla., 1962-64; vocat. instr. State of Ga., Atlanta, 1964-66; mechanic, electrician, Atlanta, 1966-68; 1969; pres. Pryor Oil Co. and Pryor Gasohol Co. Inc., Griffin, Ga., 1969—; v.p. U.S. Fuels, Inc., Griffin, Mid-Ga. Gasohol, Inc. Served with USNR, 1942-46. Mem. Ga. Oilmen's Assn., Ga. Ind. Oilmen's Assn., S.E. Gasohol Conf. (co-chmn. 1979). Am. Legion (past comdr.), Ga. Gasahol Commn. (pres. 1979—). DAV, Nat. Gasohol Commn. Democrat. Baptist. Clubs: Masons (past worshipful master), Order Eastern Star (past worthy patron). Home: 715 W Poplar St Griffin GA 30223 Office: Pryor Oil Co 1234 W Taylor St Griffin GA 30223

PSAROUTHAKIS, JOHN, mfg. co. exec.; b. Canea, Crete, Greece, June 29, 1932; s. Michael and Stamatia (Tsikouldani) P.; B.S., Mass. Inst. Tech., 1957, M.S., 1962; Ph.D., U. Md., 1965; Program for Execs., Carnegie-Mellon U., 1968; m. Inga Lundgren, Aug. 1, 1959; children—Michael, Peter. Dept. mgr. Thermo Electron Corp., Waltham, Mass., 1958-62; research dept. mgr., nuclear div. Martin Marietta Corp., Balt., 1962-66; dir. tech. and new product planning Allis Chalmers Corp., Milw., 1966-70; group v.p. internat. operations and internat. corporate devel. Masco Corp., Taylor, Mich., 1970-73, corp. v.p. planning and engring., 1973-77, group v.p. internat. ops. and internat. corp. devel., 1977—; pres. J.P. Industries, Inc., Ann Arbor, Mich.; chmn. Masinco A.G., Switzerland; pres. Mariani SpA, Italy; dir. Century S.p.A., Corp., Italy, Holzer Co. GmbH, Germany. Recipient Distinguished Young Scientist award Md. Acad. Sci., 1965. Mem. Am. Mgmt. Assn., Am. Metals Soc., Bus. Internat., Conf. Bd., Mich. C. of C. Club: Liberty Lawn Tennis (Ann Arbor). Contbr. articles to profl. jours. Patentee in field. Home: 2119 Melrose St Ann Arbor MI 48104 Office: 825 Victors Way Ann Arbor MI 48104

PSIHAS, GEORGE PETER, automotive co. exec.; b. Detroit, Mar. 3, 1927; s. Peter and Anastassia (Moskovus) P.; B.S., U.S. Mil. Acad., 1951; M.B.A., Ind. No. U., 1971, D.B.A., 1974; m. Bessie A. Annas, June 17, 1951; children—Pamela Renia, Xenia Ann. Commd. 2d lt. U.S. Army, 1951, advanced through grades to lt. col., 1972, ret., 1957; asst. mgr. planning and control Missile div. Chrysler Corp., Huntsville, Ala., 1957-61, mgr. govt. relations def. div., 1961-70, dir. mktg. def. group, 1970-76, mgr. adminstrn. electronics div., 1976-80, div. def. planning and adminstrn., 1980, v.p. adminstrn. and mktg. Chrysler Def. Inc., Sterling Heights, Mich., 1980—; adj. prof. mgmt. and adminstrn. Ind. No. Profl. Sch. Mgmt., Marion; lectr. Southeastern Inst. Tech., Webster Coll., Detroit. Trustee Southeastern Inst. Tech., Huntsville; mem. NATO Adv. Indsl. Group, Dept. Def. Decorated D.S.C., Purple Heart. Mem. Am. Def. Preparedness Assn. (past chmn. tank and automotive div.; bronze medallion for tech. chairmanship), Assn. U.S. Army (past adv. bd., past pres. Mich. chpt.), C. of C., West Point Soc. (Tenn. Valley chpt.), Legion of Valor. Democrat. Greek Orthodox. Clubs: Army-Navy Country (D.C.); Huntsville Country. Home: 3003 Cedar Key Dr Lake Orion MI 48035 Office: 6000 E 17 Mile Rd Sterling Heights MI 48078

PUCKETT, CHARLES ELLSWORTH, food co. exec.; b. Harper, Kans., Mar. 21, 1943; s. Charles Ellsworth and Lillie Marie (Barker) P.; B.S. in Bus. Adminstrn., Pittsburg (Kans.) State U., 1965; m. Donna Ruth Henry, Aug. 21, 1965; children—Denise Marie, Darren Eugene. Ter. sales mgr. John Deere Co., Denver, 1964-68; ter. sales mgr. Hunt Wesson Foods, Denver, 1968-70, zone sales mgr., Kansas City, Kans., 1970-71, dist. sales mgr., Denver, 1971-75, Los Angeles, 1975—. Pres. Peppertree Homeowners Assn., Tustin, Calif., 1977; Cub Scout chmn. Orange County council Boy Scouts Am.; mem. Christian Businessmen's Com., Santa Ana, Calif.; sustaining mem. Santa Ana-Tustin YMCA; mem. Fellowship Christian Athletes; bd. deacons Christian Ch., chmn. evangelism com., Sunday sch. tchr.; mgr. Tustin Nat. Little League, 1977—. Named Outstanding Young Alumnus Pittsburg State U., 1977; Dist. Sales Mgr. of Year, Hunt Wesson Foods, 1973-75. Mem. So. Calif., Colo.-Wyo. restaurant assns., Pitts. State U. Alumni Assn. (sec. 1978-79, pres. So. Calif. chpt. 1979-80) Republican. Home: 2301 Caper Tree Dr Tustin CA 92680 Office: 2600 Nutwood Fullerton CA 92631

PUCKETT, HELEN LOUISE, tax cons. co. exec.; b. Ripley, Ohio, Oct. 29, 1934; d. Joseph and Gladys Muriel (Madden) Haney; student Columbus Bus. U., 1971; m. Marvin R. Puckett, May 29, 1953 (dec.); children—Steven W., Thomas J. Bookkeeper, Al-Win Tng., Inc., West Jefferson, Ohio, 1971—, sec.-treas., 1971—, agt., 1977-79; notary public, 1975—. Sunday Sch. tchr. London (Ohio) Ch. of Christ, 1975—, pres. Women's Fellowship, 1979-80. Home: 130 Columbia Ave London OH 43140 Office: 485 Glade Run Rd West Jefferson OH 43162

PUEPPKE, GLENN HOWARD, furniture co. exec., farmer; b. Amenia, N.D., Apr. 12, 1927; s. Howard Monroe and Malinda Wilhelmina (Judisch) P.; student Concordia Coll., 1945-46; m. Letha Pauline Mitchell, Sept. 4, 1948 (dec.); children—Steven, David, Eric, Howard, Clinton; m. 2d, Ruth Bernice Kleinsasser, Sept. 19, 1965. With Macklanborg Supply Co., Oklahoma City, 1947, Collins, Dietz, Morris Co., Oklahoma City, 1948-50; farmer nr. Erie, N.D., 1950—; pres. G & G Transport Co., Erie, 1960-66, Pan African Traders Ltd.; co-founder Arkota Industries, furniture mfg. co., Valley City, N.D., 1971—, vice chmn., 1970—; mem. N.D. Trade Mission to Middle East, 1976; N.D. del. People's Republic of China, 1978; mem. adv. com. CCREC Power Coop. Pres., Erie (N.D.) Sch. Bd., 1965-67, Dakota Sch. Bd., 1970-79; chmn. Cass County 4C's, 1966. Bd. dirs. St. Lukes Hosp., 1958-60. Mem. Nat. Sunflower Growers Assn., Red River Valley Bean Growers Assn., N.D. Farm Bur., Profl. Farmers Am., Internat. Platform Assn., Alpha Epsilon Sigma. Mem. Ch. of God (vice chmn. N.D. mission 1971-73). Republican. Club: Eagles. Home: Erie ND 58029

PUGH, JOHN ROBERT, shipping co. exec.; b. Syracuse, N.Y., Sept. 10, 1947; s. Merton Nils and Muriel Frances (Gibbs) P.; B.S., U. Oreg., 1969. With B&B Fisheries Inc., Kodiak, Alaska, 1974-76; supt. Alaska Pacific Seafoods Co., Kodiak, 1976-78; spl. commodities supr. Sealand Freight Service, Inc., Kodiak, Alaska, 1978—; owner John Pugh Enterprisers, Inc.; instr. Kodiak Community Coll., 1974-75. Mem. Kodiak Island Borough Planning and Zoning Commn., 1976-80, chmn., 1980; mem. Kodiak City Council, 1980—, dep. mayor, 1980—. bd. dirs. Kodiak Island Borough Mental Health Center, 1972-74; bd. dirs. Kodiak Hist. Soc., 1980—, pres., 1977-80; mem. conf. bd. Internat. Pacific Halibut Commn., 1978. Democrat. Lutheran. Home: 410 Cope St Box 685 Kodiak AK 99615 Office: Box 2545 Kodiak AK 99615

PUGH, JULIAN FRANKLIN, home bldg. corp. exec.; b. Houston, Sept. 22, 1938; s. Jack Thomas and Lora Virginia (Smith) P.; student Baylor U., 1957-58, Abilene Christian U., 1957-61, S. Tex. Coll., 1961-64, U. Houston, 1964-68; m. Sharon D. Brasell, Dec. 17, 1966; children—Julian Franklin II, Shawnna D., Steven C. Sr. acctg. clk. Internat. Harvester Corp., 1962-64; sales mgr. Superior Homes, Inc., Houston, 1964-68, v.p. mktg., 1974—; pres. Land Investments of Tex., Inc., Houston, 1967-74. Mem. Tex. Constl. Rev. Com., 1973-74; founder S.H. Ednl. Foundn., 1978, bd. dirs., 1978—; active Am. Cancer Soc., 1975-76, 78-79. Mem. Nat. Assn. Homebuilders (life mem. Million Dollar Circle, Nat. Sales and Mktg. Exec. of Year 1979), Inst. Residential Mktg., Greater Houston Builders Assn., Tex. Assn. Builders, Sales and Mktg. Council, Am. Philatelists and Numismatists, Houston C. of C., Houston Philatelic Soc., Am. Philatelic Soc., Am. Bible Soc., Am. Mktg. Assn. Mem. Ch. of Christ. Office: Superior Homes Inc PO Box 38290 Houston TX 77088

PUGH, MARCUS WILLIAM, govt. ofcl.; b. Washington, Sept. 20, 1937; s. Marcus William and Edna May (Horner) P.; A.B., Duke U., 1959; postgrad. George Washington U., 1961-63, U.S. Dept. Agr. Grad. Sch., 1963-65; m. Patricia Ann Lippart, June 8, 1978; 1 son, David. Acct., Mayflower Hotel, Washington, 1959-60, FDA, Washington, 1960-65, USPHS, Washington, 1965-68; supr. acct., chief fin. services br. Environ. Health Service, Washington, 1969-70; chief acctg. ops. br. EPA, Washington, 1970-74, chief fiscal policies and procedures br., 1974-79, dir. fin. mgmt. div., 1979—; rep. Joint Fin. Mgmt. Improvement Program, 1976—. Recipient Outstanding Achievement award EPA, 1973, 78. Mem. Planning Execs. Inst. (pres. Capital chpt. 1977-78), Assn. Govt. Accts., Nat. Cash Mgmt. Task Force, Theta Chi Alumni Assn. (pres. 1968-72). Office: EPA 401 M St SW Washington DC 20015

PUGLIESE, ROCCO VINCENT, assn. exec.; b. Trenton, N.J., June 16, 1953; s. Joseph and Helen Rose Pugliese; B.A., Gannon Coll., 1975; M.P.A., Pa. State U., 1977. Research aide Pa. State Senate, Harrisburg, 1975-77; research analyst Transp. Com., Pa. Ho. of Reps., 1977-78; exec. dir. Pa. Food Processors Assn., Harrisburg, 1978—. Mem. Pa. State Agrl. Adv. Council. Mem. Am. Soc. Public Adminstrn. Democrat. Roman Catholic. Home: 1304 Chatham Rd Camp Hill PA 17011 Office: 22 S 3d St Harrisburg PA 17101

PUIG, VICENTE PAUL, JR., food importer and distbr.; b. Havana, Cuba, May 4, 1932; s. Vicente and Celia (Goyenechea) P.; came to U.S., 1960, naturalized, 1965; comml. studies Ruston Acad., Havana, 1946-50, N.Y. U. Sch. Bus. and Mgmt., 1970; grad. gen. mgmt. seminar Am. Mgmt. Assn., 1977; m. Virginia D. Rodriguez, Feb. 12, 1956; children—Virginia M., Vincent P., Victoria I. With Vicente Puig, S.A., Havana, 1950-60, v.p., 1960-62; sec. J. M. Rodriguez & Co., Inc., Ft. Lee, N.J., 1962-63; sr. partner Vicente Puig & Co., Inc., Saddle Brook, N.J., 1963—, exec. v.p., 1963—; exec. v.p. V. & P. Import, Inc., Saddle Brook, 1963—, 4 Rosol Ln. Realty Corp., Saddle Brook, 1974—; v.p. Vicente Puig of Fla., Inc., Hialeah Gardens, 1973—, Conservas Nacionales, S.A., Santo Domingo, Dominican Republic, 1979—, Tamar Realty Corp., Hialeah Gardens, 1979—; mem. adv. bd. Banco Popular de P.R., N.Y.C., 1975-80, El Tiempo Newspaper, N.Y.C., 1976-80. Mem. Spain-U.S. C. of C. (dir. 1975, 79-80), Am. Mgmt. Assn. Republican. Roman Catholic. Club: N.Y. Athletic (N.Y.C.). Home: 243 Prospect Ave Park Ridge NJ 07656

PULLEY, ROBERT WOOD, real estate exec; b. Hamilton, Ohio, Jan. 25, 1931; s. Verlin Louis and Corola (Wood) P.; B.S., Miami U., Oxford, Ohio, 1952; m. Doris Maxine Stanfill, June 12, 1952; children—Richard Robert, Jennifer Lynn. Sales mgr. Capitol Dry Cleaning Co., Dayton, Ohio, 1956-62; div. mgr. Theo H. Davies, Honolulu, 1962-64; br. mgr. Walter Carpet Mills, Honolulu, 1964-67; pres. Trans Pacific Devel. Corp., Honolulu, 1967-73, Robt. W. Pulley & Assos., Honolulu, 1973—, Pentagram Corp., Honolulu, 1976—; dir. Hawaiiana Mgmt. Co. Trustee Honolulu Theater for Youth, 1973-75. Served as pilot USN, 1952-56. Mem. Omicron Delta Kappa, Phi Delta Theta, Phi Eta Sigma. Clubs: Plaza, Waialae Country. Home: 1065 Kaimoku Pl Honolulu HI 96821 Office: Suite 1908 Financial Plaza of the Pacific Honolulu HI 96813

PULLING, RICHARD KEILER, mfg. co. exec.; b. Erie, Pa., Sept. 19, 1928; s. Clarence Keiler and Ruth (McLeod) P.; B.S., Pa. State U., 1951; M.B.A., U. Detroit, 1960; grad. Advanced Mgmt. Program, Harvard U., 1969; m. Doris M. Coutier, May 15, 1954; children—Lori, Richard Keiler, Keith, Tracy. Project engr. Dravo Corp., Pitts., 1954-55; various positions Interpace Corp., Parsippany, N.J., 1955-79, including prodn. mgr., sales mgr., v.p. planning and corp. devel., pres. Lock Joint Products div., group v.p., also dir.; pres. Interpace Can., 1973-79; pres., dir. Lock Joint Pipe of P.R., 1970-79, Coloca of Venezuela, 1973-79; pres., dir. R & G Sloane Mfg. Co., Inc., Sun Valley, Calif., 1979—; dir. Canplas of Can., A.C.I. Sloane of Austrailia, Accessorios Para Constrn., Costa Rica, Piezas Plasticas C.A., Dominican Republic. Mem. city council, Kinnelon, N.J., 1967-69; chmn. Kinnelon Zoning Bd., 1964-67; chmn. Allamuchy (N.J.) Planning Bd., 1970—. Served with C.E.C., USN, 1951-54. Registered profl. engr., Ill., N.J. Clubs: Panther Valley Golf and Country (v.p., dir.) (Allamuchy, N.J.); Westlake Yacht (Westlake Village, Calif.). Home: 3939 Freshwind Circle Westlake Village CA 91361 Office: 7606 N Clybourn Sun Valley CA 91352

PUMILIA, RICHARD KENNETH, steel co. exec.; b. Elmhurst, Ill., Aug. 6, 1934; s. Frank C. and Helen M. Pumilia; B.A. with distinction, Northwestern U., 1956; m. Jeanne DuVal Cleborne, June 23, 1956; children—Richard Bryce, Steven Colt, Susan Jeanne. Sales trainee Bethlehem Steel Corp. (Pa.), 1956-57, salesman, St. Paul, 1958-61, product rep., Bethlehem, 1961-68; mgr. sales galvanized products Empire Detroit Steel div. Cyclops Corp., Mansfield, Ohio, 1968-71, mgr. sales rolled steel products, 1971-75; pres. Am. Strip Steel, Inc., Kearny, N.J., 1975—; adv. bd. Eastern Steel Barrel Co., 1977—. Mem. Steel Service Center Inst. (dir. N.Y. chpt. 1978, mem. nat. public relations com. 1980—), Phi Beta Kappa, Zeta Psi. Clubs: Progressive Era Assn. (N.Y.C.); Morris County Golf (Morristown, N.J.); Saucon Valley Country (Bethlehem, Pa.). Contbr. articles to profl. publ. Home: 54 Stone Fence Rd Bernardsville NJ 07924 Office: 55 Passaic Ave Kearny NJ 07032

PUNDSACK, FRED LEIGH, mining and mfg. co. exec.; b. Pinckneyville, Ill., Sept. 14, 1925; s. Fred and Ruby P.; B.S., U. Ill., 1949, Ph.D., 1952; m. Barbara H. Keene, June 11, 1948. With Johns-Manville Corp., Denver, 1952—, chemist, 1952-63, dir.,

1963-69, v.p. research and devel., 1969-76, exec. v.p. ops., 1976, pres., chief operating officer, 1979—; dir. Colo. Nat. Bank, Denver. Trustee Midwest Research Inst., Kansas City, Mo., Colo. Sch. Mines Research Inst. Served with U.S. Army, 1943-46. Decorated Bronze Star, Purple Heart. Mem. Am. Chem. Soc., Indsl. Research Inst., Inc., AAAS. Clubs: Cherry Hills Country, Denver Country (Denver); Union League (N.Y.C.). Author articles, patentee in field. Office: PO Box 5108 Denver CO 80217

PUNTNEY, DOYLE EUGENE, coal co. exec.; b. Mt. Vernon, Ill., Mar. 9, 1945; s. Denzil D. and Leona Mae (Veatch) P.; B.A. in Bus. Adminstrn., Central Meth. Coll., Fayette, Mo., 1968; m. Gayle Elizabeth Cobb, June 15, 1968; children—Kevin Mathew, Kristin Lynn. Jr. accountant Main Lafrentz, St. Louis, 1968-70; mgr. corporate accounting Arch Mineral Corp., St. Louis, 1970-73, mgr. sales accounts and distbn., 1973-74; account mgr. Amax Coal Co., Indpls., 1975-80; regional sales mgr. MAPCO, Inc., 1980—; v.p. sales Circle City Coal Corp., Indpls.; student tchr. acctg. Central Meth. Coll. Methodist. Home: 8339 E 82d St Indianapolis IN 46256

PUNTURERI, ALBERT RICHARD, chem. co. exec.; b. Grove City, Pa., Aug. 24, 1931; s. Joseph S. and Eva (Gallo) P.; B.S. in Chem. Engring., Grove City Coll., 1959; M.S.B.A., Northeastern U., 1967; m. Patricia Lee Clark, Dec. 13, 1960; children—Joseph Scott, Charles Michael, Patricia Leigh, Kristen Ann. Chem. sales Diamond Shamrock Corp., Cleve., N.Y., Boston, 1959-65, sales mgr., Boston, 1965-68; v.p. sales mktg. Interstate Chem. Co., Mercer, Pa., 1968-69, exec. v.p., 1970-71, pres., 1972-76, pres., chmn. bd., 1976—; dir. Interstate Foundry Products Inc., Mercer Internat. Corp., Pitt Energy Corp., Moore Chem. Corp. Bd. dirs., vice chmn. Bashline Meml. Hosp., Grove City, 1976-77; bd. dirs., exec. com. United Community Hosp., Grove City, 1978. Served with U.S. Army, 1952-54. Mem. Cleve., Pitts. chem. assns., Am. Foundrymens' Soc., Chem. Club New Eng. Republican. Roman Catholic. Home: 618 Forest Dr Grove City PA 16127 Office: 2797 Freedland Rd West Middlesex PA 16159

PURCELL, FENTON PETER, cons. engr.; b. Paterson, N.J., Nov. 23, 1942; s. Lee Thomas and Dorothy P.; B.C.E., Rensselaer Poly. Inst., 1965; m. Susan Duggan, Feb. 20, 1971; children—Aimee and Suzie (twins), Jacqueline. Engr., Lee T. Purcell Assos., cons. engrs., Paterson, 1965-66, partner, 1969—; v.p. Fenton Corp., Paterson, 1970—. Bd. dirs. Ramapo Valley chpt. ARC, 1978—, 1st v.p., 1980. Served to capt. Med. Service Corps, U.S. Army, 1966-69. Decorated Army Commendation medal; registered profl. engr., N.J., N.Y. State, Pa., Mass.; lic. profl. planner, N.J. Mem. Am. Water Works Assn., Water Pollution Control Fedn., N.J. Cons. Engrs. Council, Am. Cons. Engrs. Council, Rensselaer Soc. Engrs., N.J. Water Pollution Control Assn., Nat. Soc. Profl. Engrs., N.J. Soc. Profl. Engrs. Home: 4 Highview Terr Upper Saddle River NJ 07458 Office: Lee T Purcell Assos 60 Hamilton St Paterson NJ 07505

PURCELL, JOHN ROPER, publishing exec.; b. Petersburg, Va., Nov. 17, 1931; s. John and Emily (Roper) P.; student Bucknell U. 1949-51; LL.B., U. Va., 1959; m. Ann L. Sundberg, July 24, 1954; children—Kathleen A., John R., Wendy L., Michael B. Accountant, Musselman & Drysdale, Charlottesville, Va., 1956-59; admitted to Va. bar, 1959, D.C. bar, 1959; asso. firm Covington & Burling, Washington, 1959-62; asst. controller United Technologies Corp., Hartford, Conn., 1962-68; sr. v.p., fin. and ops., dir. Gannett Co., Rochester, N.Y., 1968-77; exec. v.p., dir. CBS Inc., N.Y.C., 1977—; dir. Bausch & Lomb, Rochester. Trustee Bucknell U. Served with USN, 1951-55. Decorated Purple Heart. Office: 51 W 52d St New York NY 10019

PURCELL, LEO THOMAS, JR., sanitary engr.; b. Pompton Lakes, N.J., July 28, 1935; s. Leo Thomas and Dorthy (Charette) P.; student St. Lawrence U., 1953-55; B.C.E., Manhattan Coll., 1958; m. Rosemary M. Hewitt, Aug. 23, 1958; children—Leo Thomas III, Cynthia Anne. With Lee T. Purcell, Cons. Engr., Paterson, N.J., 1958, engr., 1962-64; engr. Interstate Sanitation Commn., N.Y.C., 1958-59; partner Lee T. Purcell Assos., Cons. Engrs., Paterson, 1965—; pres. Fenton Corp., 1974—. Served to lt. Med. Service Corps, AUS, 1959-62. Registered profl. engr., N.J., N.Y., Conn., Pa., Fla.; registered profl. planner, N.J.; diplomate Am. Acad. Environ. Engrs. Mem. Am. Soc. C.E., Water Pollution Control Fedn., N.J. Water Pollution Control Assn., N.J. Cons. Engrs. Council, Am. Water Works Assn., N.J. Inst. Bldg. and Constrn., Beta Theta Pi. Home: 7 Seminole Way Chatham NJ 07928 Office: 60 Hamilton St Paterson NJ 07505

PURCELL, PHILIP JAMES, retail chain exec.; b. Salt Lake City, Sept. 5, 1943; s. Philip James and Shirley (Sorensen) P.; B.B.A., U. Notre Dame, 1965; M.Sc., U. London, 1967; M.B.A., U. Chgo., 1967; m. Anne Marie McNamara, Apr. 2, 1964; children—David Philip, Peter Andrew, Mark Edward, Michael James, Paul Martin, Philip Patrick. With McKinsey & Co., Inc., 1967-78, dir./mng. dir. Chgo. office, 1978; v.p. corp. planning Sears, Roebuck and Co., Chgo., 1978—; dir. Homart Devel. Co. Clubs: Econ., Chgo., Mid-Am., North Shore Country. Office: Sears Roebuck and Co Sears Tower Chicago IL 60684

PURCELL, ROGER OWEN, bus. cons.; b. Sheridan, Wyo., May 16, 1938; s. Maurice F. and Opal L. (Rogers) P.; B.S. in Bus. Adminstrn. and Econs., Lewis and Clark U., 1960; postgrad. in bus. adminstrn., U. Alaska, 1978—; m. Louise Marie Pleshnik, Dec. 3, 1959; children—Roger Owen, Dana O. Agt., broker life ins., 1961-65; gen. agt., supt. agencies Am. Trust Life Ins. Co., 1965-69; sec.-treas. to pres. A.I.M., Inc., 1969-75; owner, operator Profl. Bus. Counseling, Anchorage, 1975—. Former bd. dirs. Boys Clubs Alaska. Named Man of Year, Am. Trust Life, 1968. Mem. Am. Mgmt. Assn., Anchorage C. of C. Clubs: Masons, Shriners, DeMolay. Author: How to Invest in Mortgages, 1980. Office: PO Box 4 2877 Anchorage AK 99509

PURCELL, WALTER LAMBUTH, mgmt. cons., economist; b. Shady Dale, Ga., Mar. 26, 1922; s. William E. and Lillie (Neese) P.; A.A., Reinhardt Coll., 1941; B.S., Piedmont Coll., 1942, B.A., 1943; LL.B., Emory U., 1959, LL.M., 1963; m. Dorothy Dimsdale, Jan. 17, 1947; children—Cheryl and Melvyn K. (twins). With Dun & Bradstreet, Inc., Atlanta region, 1947-62; dir. Dept. Community Service DeKalb County, Atlanta, 1962-65; pres. Purcell Cons. Assos., Inc., Decatur, Ga., 1965—; chmn. bd. Exec. Edn., Inc., Bus. Mgmt. Edn. Group. Research asso. Emory U. Grad. Sch. Arts and Scis. Mem. 4th Congl. Dist. Panel on Small Business, Higher Edn., Mental Health, 1965—; pres. DeKalb Community Council, 1964-65; mem. adv. bd. DeKalb Edn. Extension Service, 1962—; mem. Nat. Com. on Support to Pub. Schs., 1965—; bd. dirs. DeKalb adv. chpt. A.R.C., 1957—, Met. Atlanta; bd. dirs. Ga. Heart Assn., Atlanta Assn. for Retarded Children, S.E. Regional YMCA, DeKalb unit Am. Cancer Soc.; chmn. finance com. bd. pensions No. Ga. Conf. United Methodist Ch.; chmn. finance com. Meth. Found. Served with AUS, 1942-45. Certified mgmt. cons. Fellow Am. Park and Recreation Soc.; mem. So. Finance Assn., Atlanta Soc. Financial Analysts, Pub. Relations Soc. Am., Ga. Pub. Relations Soc., Inst. Mgmt. Consultants (regional v.p.), Assn. Mgmt. Consultants (trustee), Atlanta Press Club, Ga. Hosp. Assn., Am., Ga. recreation socs., Ga. Library Assn., Ga. Gerontology Soc., C. of C. (dir.), So. Assn. Inst. Psychol. Services, Delta Theta Phi, Phi Delta Kappa. Methodist (trustee, bd. laity). Clubs: Kiwanis (past lt. gov.), Toastmasters, (past pres.), Druid Hills Golf, Atlanta Commerce, Atlanta Statesman; Decatur Executive. Home: 1099 C N Jamestown Rd Decatur GA 30033 Office: 1st National Bank Bldg Decatur GA 30030

PURDIE, WILLIAM JAMES, III, data processor; b. Atlanta, Oct. 27, 1946; s. William James and Sara Elizabeth (Fries) P.; B.S. in Indsl. Mgmt., Ga. Inst. Tech., 1969; cert. in data processing Inst. for Certification Computer Profls., 1976, cert. in data processing auditing, 1979; m. Ruby West, Apr. 5, 1969; children—Deanna Kay, James Brian. Planner, United Nuclear Corp., New Haven, Conn., 1969-70; tech. cons. Tymshare Inc., Darien, Conn., 1971-73; data processing specialist Mgmt. Con. Services div. Ernst & Ernst, Atlanta, 1974—; lectr. in field. Mem. Data Processing Mgmt. Assn., Soc. Cert. Data Processors, So. Calif. Computer Soc., Alpha Kappa Psi (life). Club: Civitan Internat. (project dir. Cliftondale, Ga. chpt. 1975-76, pres. elect 1978-79 pres. 1979-80). Home: 833 Countryside Ct Marietta GA 30067 Office: 3600 First Nat Tower Atlanta GA 30303

PURNELL, RICHARD INGRAM, ins. broker; b. Balt., July 25, 1918; s. Lyttleton Bowen and Mary D. (Ingram) P.; A.B. with honors, Princeton, 1940; m. Marguerite W. Hillman, July 9, 1958; children—Marguerite W., Peter F. With Johnson & Higgins, 1946—, pres. Johnson & Higgins of Pa., Inc., Phila., 1962-70, dir. Johnson & Higgins, N.Y.C., 1963—, pres., N.Y.C., 1970—, chief exec. officer, 1972—, chmn. bd., 1974—. Bd. dirs. Downtown-Lower Manhattan Assn., 1971—, United Fund Greater N.Y., 1979—; trustee Coll. of Ins., N.Y.C., 1975—, Protestant Theol. Sem., Alexandria, Va., 1976—, Presbyn. Hosp., N.Y.C., 1977—, Cardigan Mountain Sch., 1977, Am. Inst. Property and Liability Underwriters/Ins. Inst. Am., 1977—; pres. Anglo-Am. Ins. Scholarship Found.; vice chmn. council for univ. resources Princeton U. Served with USAAF, 1941-46. Decorated Silver Star medal, Air medal with two oak leaf clusters, Purple Heart. Episcopalian (mem. vestry). Home: Piping Rock Rd Locust Valley NY 11560 Office: 95 Wall St New York NY 10005

PURTILL, FREDERIC LEE, glass co. exec.; b. Watsonville, Calif., Dec. 22, 1926; s. Henry Lee and Olive (Nohrden) P.; A.A., Salinas Jr. Coll., 1948; B.S., U. Nev., 1951; postgrad. Stanford, 1960; m. Adrienne Georgia Hall, Aug. 23, 1952; children—Denise, Elizabeth, Frederic. Sales trainee Owens-Corning Fiberglas Corp., Santa Clara, Calif., 1951, co. sales rep. San Francisco br., 1952, product specialist roofing, Santa Clara, 1953-54, sales industry mgr. bldg. materials, 1954-59, sales div. mgr. bldg. materials, 1959-60, marketing mgr. Pacific coast div., 1960, v.p. marketing Pacific coast div., 1961-68, v.p. marketing home bldg. products, 1968-70, v.p., gen. mgr. Fiberglas Reinforced Plastic Components, 1970-74, v.p., gen. mgr. archtl. products div., 1974-76, v.p., gen. mgr. bldg. products operating div., 1976—, v.p., gen. mgr. roofing products operating div., 1977—. Served with USNR, 1944-46. Mem. Asphalt Roofing Mfrs. Assn. (dir., dir. producers council, mem. exec. com.). Home: 3707 W Bancroft St Toledo OH 43606 Office: Fiberglas Tower Toledo OH 43659

PUSATERI, ANGELO, air charter broker; b. N.Y.C., June 12, 1940; s. Cesare and Phyllis (Albertini) P.; A.A.S., CCNY, 1968; B.B.A., Baruch Coll., 1970, M.B.A., 1976; m. Francine Giambrone, Apr. 17, 1961; children—Richard, Steven, Claudine, Jennifer. Mgr. Eastern region Philippine Airlines, N.Y.C., 1965-66; dir. internat. services REA Express, N.Y.C., 1967-69; v.p. mktg. Expressco, N.Y.C., 1970-74; v.p., gen. mgr. air freight Kuehne & Nagel, Inc., N.Y.C., 1975-79; pres. AirContact, Inc., Lake Success, N.Y., 1979—; dir. Scandinavian Overseas Services, Inc., 1979—. Served with U.S. Army, 1959-60. Mem. N.Y. Metro Traffic League. Republican. Roman Catholic. Clubs: Air Cargo Sale, Wings. Home: 17 Cary Rd Herricks NY 11040 Office: 2001 Marcus Ave Lake Success NY 11042

PUSKARZ, ANTHONY RICHARD, JR., bus. exec.; b. New Britain, Conn., Dec. 30, 1943; s. Anthony Richard and Marian Joanne (Kawecki) P.; B.S., Rochester Inst. Tech., 1965; M.B.A., Boston U., 1967; m. Ann-Mary Sztaba, Aug. 3, 1968; children—Jennifer, Allison, Eric. Pres., treas. Art Press Inc., New Britain, 1967—; dir., corporator Peoples Bank of New Britain; lectr in field. Bd. dirs. New Britain Symphony. Justice of peace, notary pub. Mem. Polish Am. Bus. and Profl. Assn. Republican. Roman Catholic. Clubs: Rotary, Oaks, Polish Falcons, World Series of Hartford. Home: 11 Chamberlain St New Britain CT 06052 Office: 500 Burritt St New Britain CT 06053

PUSKAS, ELEK, parachute mfg. co. exec.; b. Kassa, Hungary, Nov. 29, 1942; came to U.S., 1961, naturalized, 1972; s. Elek and Olga (Derfinyak) P.; m. Lona Lee Zimmerman, Dec. 30, 1972 (dec.). Mechanic, Keystone Motors, Berwyn, Pa., 1962-65; dir. ops. SSE, Inc., Pennsauken, N.J., 1965-76; pres. Para-Flite, Inc., Pennsauken, 1976—; owner, mgr. Ripcord Paracenter, Inc., Lumberton, N.J., 1969-77. Mem. Safe Assn., Franklin Inst., Smithsonian Asso., Costeau Soc., U.S. Parachute Assn., Am. Mgmt. Assn., Airline Passenger Assn., U.S. Hang Gliding Assn., AIAA. Democrat. Patentee in field. Office: 5801 Magnolia Ave Pennsauken NJ 08110

PUTERBAUGH, KATHRYN ELIZABETH, corporate exec.; b. Denver, Mar. 5, 1924; d. Fredric John and Cora (Zoph) Puterbaugh; B.A., U. Colo., 1945. Accountant F.J. Puterbaugh & Co., Denver, 1946-49; sec. to Herbert Bayer, artist, designer, 1950-51; accountant Himel's, New Orleans, 1951-53; asst. controller Berol Pen Co., 1953-54; office mgr., controller Garratt-Callahan Co., Millbrae, Calif., 1955-65, corporate treas., 1966—, also dir. Mem. com. for dedication Millbrae library, 1961; mem. steering com. People-to-People Program, Millbrae, 1962; historian Millbrae Sister City Program, 1962-63; mem. Belmont-San Carlos Human Relations Com., 1968-70; active various community fund drives; judge Bank Am. Youth Achievement Awards, 1973. Mem. Calif. Republicans, NOW (charter mem., chpt. v.p. 1966-68), Nat. Assn. Accountants. Episcopalian. Clubs: Soroptimist Millbrae-San Bruno (pres. 1965-66, various regional offices, coms.); Ski (Bear Valley, Calif.). Home: 3382 Brittan Ave San Carlos CA 94070 Office: 111 Rollins Rd Millbrae CA 94030

PUTNAM, GEORGE, investment co. exec.; b. Manchester, Mass., Aug. 20, 1926; s. George and Katharine (Harte) P.; A.B. magna cum laude, Harvard U., 1949, M.B.A. with distinction, 1951; m. Barbara Weld; children—George III, Barbara Putnam Lyman, Susan Weld. Security analyst Putnam Mgmt. Co., Boston, 1951-61, pres., chief exec. officer, 1961-70, chmn. bd., chief exec. officer, 1970—, trustee Putnam Growth Fund, 1957—, chmn., 1969—, trustee George Putnam Fund of Boston, 1959—, chmn., 1969—; pres., dir. Putnam Income Fund, Inc., Putnam Investors Fund, Inc., Putnam Equities Fund, Inc., Putnam Vista Fund, Inc., Putnam Voyager Fund, Inc., Putnam Duofund, Inc., Putnam Convertible Fund, Inc., Putnam Daily Dividend Trust, Putnam Tax-Exempt Income Fund, Putnam Option Income Trust, Putnam High Yield Trust; chmn. bd. Marsh & McLennar Asset Mgmt. Co., Putnam Mgmt. Co., Inc.; dir. various Putnam subs., including Putnam Adv. Co., Inc., Putnam Capital Mgmt. Inc., Putnam Fund Distbrs., Inc., Putnam Adminstrv. Services Co., Inc.; dir. Am. Mut. Ins. Co., Boston Co. Inc., Boston Safe Deposit and Trust Co., Combustion Engring., Inc., Freeport Minerals Co., Garfinckel, Brooks Bros., Miller & Rhoads, Inc., Mallinckrodt, Inc.; dir., vice chmn. Controlled Risk Ins. Co.; mem. corp. Provident Instn. for Savs.; gov. Investment Co. Inst., chmn., 1972-74. Overseer Harvard U., 1967—, treas., 1973—, mem. Harvard Corp. and Overseers, 1973—; mem. corp. Northeastern U., Beverly Hosp., Beverly, Mass.; trustee, chmn. fin. com. Wellesley Coll.; trustee Mass. Gen. Hosp., Boston, Colonial Williamsburg (Va.) Found., Vincent Meml. Hosp., Boston, New Eng. Aquarium, Boston, Jackson Labs., Bar Harbor, Maine; chmn. bd. McLean Hosp., Belmont, Mass.; chmn. bd. Harvard Mgmt. Co.; dir. various univ. related corps. Office: Putnam Mgmt Co Inc 265 Franklin St Boston MA 02110

PUTNAM, ROBERT SARGENT, metal products mfg. co. exec.; b. Redlands, Calif., Sept. 29, 1915; s. Harold W. and Laura (Sargent) P.; B.A., U. Redlands, 1937, D.B.A., 1975; exchange student U. Hawaii, 1936; credentials in edn. adminstrn. Claremont Coll., 1940; m. Virginia Pearl Demaree, June 12, 1938; children—Janet Rae Putnam Johnson, Barbara Carol Putnam Carpenter. Tchr., adminstr. Redlands Jr. High Sch., 1937-42; field rep. U.S. Civil Service Commn., Los Angeles, 1942; mgr. indsl. relations Solar Aircraft Co., San Diego, 1953-59; mgr. adminstrn. Thiokol Chem. Co. Brigham City, Utah, 1959-61; dir. indsl. relations TRW Semiconductors, Inc., Lawndale, Calif., 1961-64, Sci. Data Systems, Santa Monica, 1964-66; corporate v.p., dir. indsl. relations Norris-Industries, Inc., Los Angeles, 1966—. Speaker before various groups, dir. seminars, 1945—. Trustee U. Redlands, 1977—. Served to lt. comdr. USNR, 1942-48. Mem. So. Calif. Industry-Edn. Council (dir. 1967-72), San Diego Personnel Mgmt. Assn. (pres. 1955), Am. Soc. Personnel Adminstrn. (dir. 1974-76, nat. chmn. employee and labor relations com. 1970-75, mem. chmn.'s adv. council), Am. Compensation Assn., Calif. Mfrs. Assn., Am. Soc. for Pub. Adminstrn. (pres. San Diego 1952), San Diego Fed. Bus. Assn. (pres. 1950), Personnel and Indsl. Relations Assn. Los Angeles, Am. Mgmt. Assn., U. Redlands Alumni Assn. (pres. 1959); Town Hall, Calif. Republican. Congregationalist. Office: One Golden Shore Long Beach CA 90802

PUTNEY, MARK WILLIAM, lawyer, utility co. exec.; b. Marshalltown, Iowa, Jan. 25, 1929; s. Lawrence Charles and Geneva B. (Eldridge) P.; B.A., U. Iowa, 1951, J.D., 1957; m. Ray Ann Bartnek, May 26, 1962; children—Andi Bartnek Falk, William Bradford, Blake Reinhart. Admitted to Iowa bar, 1957, U.S. Supreme Ct. bar, 1960; atty. Iowa Power and Light Co., Des Moines, 1957-61, v.p., gen. counsel, 1972-73, sr. v.p., gen. counsel, 1973-80, exec. v.p., 1980—, also dir.; exec. v.p. Iowa Resources Inc., 1980—, also dir.; partner firm Bradshaw, Fowler, Proctor & Fairgrave, Des Moines, 1961-72; pres., dir. Bradford & Blake Ltd., Des Moines; partner Bradmark Ranch, Des Moines, Gladbrook Farms (Iowa); dir. Iowa-Des Moines Nat. Bank. Civilian aide to Sec. Army for Iowa, 1975-77; chmn. Iowa Com. for Employer Support of Guard and Res., 1979—; bd. dirs. Planned Parenthood Iowa, 1968-70; bd. dirs. Delta Chi Ednl. Found.; Des Moines YMCA, 1976—, Iowa Luth. Hosp., 1977—. Served with USAF, 1951-53. Mem. Polk County (exec. com. 1973-75), Iowa, Am., Fed. Power bar assns., Greater Des Moines C. of C. (dir. 1976-80), Delta Chi, Phi Delta Phi. Republican. Episcopalian. Clubs: Rotary, Masons, Shriners, Des Moines (sec. 1973-76, v.p. 1976, pres. 1977), Wakonda (sec. 1980, v.p. 1981) (Des Moines). Home: 6675 NW Beaver Dr Des Moines IA 50323 Office: Iowa Resources Inc 666 Grand Ave Des Moines IA 50303

PYATT, GRANT EDWARD, investment securities exec.; b. Unity, Wis., Oct. 22, 1906; s. Samuel Christian and Mabel (Binning) P.; student Oreg. State U., 1936-37; m. Dorothy Louise Olson, Dec. 26, 1940; children—Susan Carol Fatzinger, Grant Edward. Self employed food retailer Grant's Market, Pyatt's Fine Meats, Corvallis, Oreg., 1936-48; asst. to investment counselor J. Henry Helser & Co., Portland, Ore., 1948-50; account exec. Camp & Co., Investment Securities, Portland, 1951-54; Willamette Valley mgr. Lind, Somers & Collins, Inc., Portland, 1958-71; v.p., Willamette Valley mgr., dir. Somers, Grove & Co., Inc., 1971—. Pres., Harding Sch. PTA, Corvallis, 1956-57; chmn. sustaining membership Oreg. Trail council Boy Scouts Am., 1956-57; pres. Human Relations Guild, Portland, 1951. Mem. Corvallis City Council, 1947-49, 59-60, 63-69, Corvallis Park and Recreation Bd., 1956-59. Trustee Corvallis Pub. Library; bd. dirs. Corvallis Ambulance Service, 1975-80; mem. Oreg. Found. Served with USMCR, 1942-44. Mem. Corvallis C. of C. (past pres.), Rose Soc. (past pres.), Portland Assn. Financial Planners, Am. Security Council, Albany Area C. of C. Christian Scientist. Clubs: Oreg. State U. Beaver, Marines Meml. Corvallis Civitan (charter pres. 1960-61). Home: 231 SW 9th St Corvallis OR 97330 Office: 310 NW 5th St Corvallis OR 97330

PYE, WILLIAM WATTS, mgmt. cons.; b. Northfield, Minn., Nov. 19, 1938; s. Robert Edward and Genevieve (Miller) P.; B.A., Ripon Coll., 1961; M.B.A., Ind. U., 1963; postgrad. U. Minn., 1966-70; m. Helen Louise Lovestedt, June 22, 1968; children—Erica Lee, Danna Louise, Emily Susanne. With Pillsbury Co., Mpls., 1965-72, mgmt. tng. specialist, 1967-69, dir. personnel, internat., 1969-72; v.p., dir. Hallowell Pye Assos., Inc., Mpls., 1972-78; pres. Mgmt. Systems Cons. Group, Mpls., 1978—; dir., officer State Bank Morristown (Minn.), 1965—, pres., dir., 1976—; pres. State Morristown Agy., Property and Casualty Incorp.; dir. Aladdin Internat. Corp.; officer, dir. Hydra Power Machine Works Inc.; past mem. adv. bd. continuing bus. edn. U. Minn., adv. bd. Coll. Edn.; lectr. U. Minn., Coll. St. Thomas. Mem. Minn. Title IV Council; bd. dirs., past pres. Alfred Adler Inst. Minn.; adv. bd. Exec. Program for Smaller Bus., Stanford U. Served to lt. U.S. Army, 1963-65. Mem. Twin City Personnel Assn., Bank Mktg. Assn., Am. Soc. Tng. and Devel. (pres., dir. So. Minn. chpt., Torch award 1975). Republican. Episcopalian. Home: 27968 Smithtown Rd Excelsior MN 55331 Office: 2401 W 66th St Minneapolis MN 55423

PYLE, HOWARD, III, utility exec.; b. Richmond, Va., Feb. 1, 1940; s. Wilfrid and Anne Woolston (Roller) P.; A.B., Princeton, 1962; LL.B., U. Va., 1967, J.D., 1970; m. Caroline Oglesby Smith, June 18, 1965; children—Elizabeth Roller, Howard. Career trainee CIA, Washington, 1967-69; adminstrv. asst. to Congressman Odin Langen, Washington, 1969-70, Congressman Hastings Keith, Washington, 1971; asst. to sec. Dept. Interior, Washington, 1971-73; Washington rep. Standard Oil Co. of Ind., Washington, 1973-77; mgr. fed. pub. affairs R.J. Reynolds Industries, Inc., Winston-Salem, N.C., 1977-80; dir. fed. relations Houston Light & Power Co., Washington, 1980—. Served with USN, 1962-64. Mem. Am. Bar Assn., D.C. Bar, Va. Bar, Nat. Rifle Assn., Res. Officers Assn., SAR, Delta Theta Phi. Republican. Episcopalian. Clubs: Va. Country, Kenwood Golf and Country. Home and Office: 4930 Quebec St NW Washington DC 20016

PYLE, MICHAEL TERRY, reins. co. exec.; b. Camden, N.J., May 20, 1938; s. William B. and Elizabeth C. (Craig) P.; m. Peggy Barychko, Nov. 25, 1959; children—Laurie, Christina, Kim, Nancy, Andrew. With Royal Globe Ins. Co., 1958-61, Great Am. Ins. Co., 1961-66, Constellation Reins. Co., 1966-68, Guy Carpenter & Co., 1968-69; asst. sec. Gen. Reins. Corp. and Herbert Clough, Inc., 1969-72; asst. v.p. Willcox Baringer Co., 1972-73; sr. v.p. Fin. Reins., Inc. and W.J. Burt & Assos., also sr. v.p. mktg. Ormond Reins. Group, Inc., Ormond Beach, Fla., 1973—. Served with USAF, 1956-60. Mem. Nat. Assn. Ind. Insurers, Fla. Assn. Domestic Ins. Cos. Republican. Presbyterian. Home: 19 Oakmond Circle Ormond Beach FL 32074 Office: 140 S Atlantic Ave Ormond Beach FL 32074

PYLE, ROBERT NOBLE, business and polit. cons.; b. Wilmington, Del., Oct. 23, 1926; s. Joseph Lybrand and La Verne Ruth (Noble) P.; A.B., Dickinson Coll., Carlisle, Pa., 1948; postgrad. Wharton Sch. U. Pa., 1949; m. Edith Ayrault Rose, Feb. 11, 1950; children—Robert Noble, Mark C., Nicholas A., Sarah Livingston. Congl. asst. U.S. Ho. of Reps., also U.S. Senate, 1952-63; campaign cons., 1958—; engaged in constrn. bus., 1963-69; lobbyist, 1969—; pres. Robert N. Pyle & Assos., Inc., cons., Washington, 1969—; dir. Barlow Corp.; Washington rep. various baking, fur, oil and comml. cos. Served with AUS, 1945-46. Mem. Am. Soc. Assn. Execs., Assn. Execs. Club, Phi Kappa Psi. Republican. Presbyterian. Clubs: City Tavern (Washington); Kenwood Golf and Country. Author articles in field. Home: 3255 O St NW Washington DC 20007 Office: 1701 K St NW Suite 1003 Washington DC 20006

PYLE, THOMAS OAKLEY, health care exec.; b. Binghamton, N.Y., Feb. 20, 1940; s. William Henry and Sybil (Tyner) P.; student Mass. Inst. Tech., 1956-57; M.B.A. with distinction, Harvard, 1967; m. Regina Johnstone Schlank, Oct. 6, 1962; Page, NBC, N.Y.C., 1957-58; prodn. asst. Ted Mack Original Amateur Hour, N.Y.C., 1958-59; various positions CBS Television, N.Y.C., 1959-61; account exec. Young and Rubicam, Inc., N.Y.C., 1961-65; asst. to pres., asst. gen. mgr. Elizabeth Arden Sales Corp., N.Y.C., 1967-68; v.p. Beck Industries, N.Y.C., 1969; v.p. Boston Consulting Group, 1970-72; asso. dir. Harvard Community Health Plan, Boston, 1972-74, exec. v.p., 1974-78, pres., 1978—; vis. lectr. Harvard Sch. Pub. Health, 1978; dir. Daniel O'Connell's Sons, Inc., Holyoke, Mass., 1973-78; chmn. Controlled Risk Ins. Co., Ltd., Cayman Islands, 1976—; treas., dir. Group Health Assn. Am.; cons. in field. Served with U.S. Army, 1962. Am. Clubs: Harvard Bus. Sch. Assn., Harvard (Boston). Home: 1905 Beacon St Waban MA 02168 Office: 1 Fenway Plaza Boston MA 02215

PYLES, THOMAS TERRILL, mktg. exec.; b. St. Louis, Aug. 11, 1942; s. Manuel Aaron and Mary Lucille P.; A.A.S., Syracuse U., 1968, A.A.S. (with honors), 1969; B.B.A.(with honors), U. Cincinnati, 1970. Pricing mgr. Gen. Cable Corp., N.Y.C., 1970-71; prod. mgr. major appliances, Westinghouse Internat., N.Y.C., 1971-74; corp. dir. mktg. Bro-Dart Industries, Williamsport, Pa., 1974-75; mgr. mktg. GK Technologies, Greenwich, Conn., 1975-77; v.p., dir. mktg. ATI Inc., Southport, Conn., 1977-79; pres. MARCON Assos., Greenwich, Conn., 1979—; cons. in field; dir. Ken Woodburn, Inc.; adv. council Hardware/Housewares Trade Fair. Served with USAF, 1961-66. Recipient Best New Product Concept award N.J. Design Art Inst., 1976, Clio award for best packaging design, 1977. Mem. Am. Mgmt. Assn., Am. Mktg. Assn., Hardware Trade Assn. (young execs. com.), Beta Gamma Sigma (Phi Beta Kappa), U. Cincinnati Alumni Assn. Clubs: Halloween Yacht (Stamford, Conn.); Southport Racquet; Sales Execs., Automotive Boosters (N.Y.C.); Marina Bay Racquet (Ft. Lauderdale, Fla.). Home: 19B Weavers Hill Greenwich CT 06830

PYNE, EBEN WRIGHT, banker; b. N.Y.C., June 14, 1917; s. Grafton H. and Leta Constance (Wright) P.; grad. Groton Sch., 1935; A.B., Princeton, 1939; m. Hilda Holloway, Dec. 16, 1941; children—Constance Howland Pyne Ranges (dec.), Lillian Stokes (Mrs. Lillian Pyne-Corbin), Mary Alison. Clerk 1st Nat. City Trust Co. (formerly City Bank Farmers Trust Co., 1939, v.p., asst. to pres., 1952-56, exec. v.p., 1956, pres., dir., 1957-61; asst. cashier Nat. City Bank of N.Y., 1946-50, asst. v.p., 1950-52, v.p., 1952-53, sr. v.p., 1960—; dir. GDV, Inc., U.S. Life Ins. Co. City of N.Y., Home Ins. Co., L.I. R.R., City Investing Co., City Home Corp., Gen. Devel. Corp., Long Island Lighting Co., W.R. Grace and Co. Mem. N.Y. State Met. Transp. Authority, 1965-75; commr. N.Y.C. Transit Authority, Triborough Bridge and Tunnel Authority, Manhattan and Bronx Surface Transit Authority, Stewart Airport, S.I. Rapid Transit Operating Authority, all 1965-75; adv. bd. Nassau County council Boy Scouts Am.; bd. dirs. Nassau Hosp.; trustee Juilliard Sch., St. Luke's Hosp., Grace Inst., Grace Found. Served as maj. AUS, 1940-46. Decorated Bronze Star. Mem. Pilgrims of U.S. (exec. com.), Bklyn. Inst. Arts and Scis. (trustee), N.Y. Zool. Soc. (trustee). Clubs: Piping Rock (Locust Valley, L.I.); Bond, Links (gov.), Racquet and Tennis, River (N.Y.C.); Ivy (Princeton, N.J.); Links Golf (North Hills, L.I.). Home: Old Westbury NY 11568 Office: One Citicorp Center New York NY 10043

PYZOW, JOHN ROBERT, auditor; b. N.Y.C., Mar. 26, 1947; s. John Jay and Helen (Kotteck) P.; A.A.S. in Acctg., SUNY, Delhi, 1966. Bookkeeper, Inland Credit Corp., N.Y.C., 1968-70; controller Blackstone Devel. Co., Providence, 1970-73; field auditor comml. fin. Century Industries, Inc., N.Y.C., 1973-77; with public acctg. firms Sam Brecker C.P.A., Brown & Krupp C.P.A.'s, 1977-80; auditor Richard Kim Co. C.P.A.'s, N.Y.C., 1980—; portfolio mgr. Linear Details Co., N.Y.C., 1978—; lectr. double entry system trouble shooting. Mem. Musicians Union. Author: The Physicist and the Bookkeeper, A Brief Course in Rhythmic Security. Home and Office: 505 E 14th St 7B New York NY 10009

QUAAL, WARD LOUIS, broadcasting exec.; b. Ishpeming, Mich., Apr. 7, 1919; s. Sigfred Emil and Alma C. (Larson) Q.; A.B., U. Mich., 1941; LL.D., Mundelein Coll., 1962, No. Mich U., 1967, Lincoln Coll., 1968, Elmhurst Coll., 1967, De Paul U., 1974; m. Dorothy Jane Graham, Mar. 9, 1944; children—Graham, Jennifer. Announcer, writer, sta. WDMJ, Marquette, Mich., 1936-37; announcer, writer, producer WJR, Detroit, 1937-41; spl. events announcer-producer WGN, Chgo., 1941-42, asst. to gen. mgr., 1945-49; dir. Clear Channel Broadcasting Service, Washington, 1949-52; asst. gen. mgr. Crosley Broadcasting Corp., Cin., 1952, v.p., asst. gen. mgr., 1953-56; v.p., gen. mgr., dir. WGN Continental Broadcasting Co., Inc., Chgo., 1956-74, pres., dir., 1961-74; dir. Christine Valmy, Inc.; pres. Ward L. Quaal Co., 1974—; chief exec. officer Clear Channel Broadcasting Service, 1964-74; chmn. exec. com., dir. WLW Radio, Inc., Cin., 1975—; dir. Universal Resources Corp., 1969—. Bd. dirs. Farm Found., MacCormac Jr. Coll., Chgo., 1974—; chmn. exec. com. Council for TV Devel., 1969-72; bd. dirs. Broadcasters Found., Internat. Radio and TV Found., Sears & Roebuck Found., 1970-73; trustee Hillsdale Coll. Served as lt. USNR, 1942-45. Recipient Distinguished Alumnus award U. Mich., 1967, award Freedoms Found., 1969, Loyola U. Key, 1970; named Broadcast Man of Year, 1968, Chgo. Advt. Club Man of Year, 1973, Communicator of Year Jewish United Fund, Ill. Broadcaster of Year, 1973, Distinguished Service award Nat. Assn. Broadcasters, 1973, numerous other awards. Mem. Assn. Maximum Service Telecasters, Inc. (dir.), Chgo. Better Bus. Bur. (chmn. bd., dir. 1964-67), Assn. Better Bus. Burs. Internat. (chmn., gov. 1967-71), Broadcast Pioneers (pres., dir. 1962-63), Delta Tau Delta (disting. service chpt.). Clubs: Kenwood Golf and Country (Washington); Chicago, Exmoor Country, Mid-America; Lakeside Golf (Hollywood, Calif.); El Niguel Country (Laguna Niguel, Calif.); Bankers (San Francisco). Co-author: Broadcast Management, rev. edit., 1975. Home: 1706 Northfield Sq Northfield IL 60093 Office: Suite 370 O'Hare Plaza 5725 E River Rd Chicago IL 60631

QUACKENBUSH, ROBERT DONALD, ins. co. exec.; b. Paterson, N.J., Oct. 2, 1921; s. Joseph Henry and Lydia (Stauss) Q.; student U. Ind., 1944, Washington and Lee U., 1945, N.J. State Tchrs. Coll., 1946-47; m. Audrey Gordon, Apr. 28, 1945; children—Susan Gordon, Kathleen Bette, Lynn Audrey. Exec., Quackenbush & Sons, Inc., 1946-53; mgr. credit ins. Bankers Nat. Life Ins. Co., Montclair, N.J., 1955-56, dir. group sales, 1957, dir. agys., 1958-59, 2d v.p. group sales, 1960-63, v.p. group, 1964-69; pres. Central Nat. Life Ins. Co. Omaha, Morristown, N.J., 1971-77, chmn., chief exec. officer, 1978—; pres. Guaranty Life Ins. Co. Am., Wilmington, Del., 1970-77, chmn., chief exec. officer, 1978—; pres. BFC Agy., Inc., Wilmington, 1978—, BFC Agy. Am., Wilmington, 1978—, BFC Agy. Nev., Wilmington, 1978—; chmn., chief exec. officer Am. Centennial Ins. Co., Morristown, 1978—, Beneficial Internat. Ins. Co., Hamilton, Bermuda, 1978—, Guaranty Life Ins. Co. Am., Wilmington, 1978—, Consol. Marine and Gen. Ins. Co. Ltd., London, 1978—, Northwestern Security Life Ins. Co., Wilkesboro, N.C., 1979—, Beneficial Am. Ins. Co. Ltd., Hamilton, Bermuda, 1979—, Western Nat. Life Ins. Co., Amarillo, Tex., 1979—, Comco Ins. Co., Amarillo, 1979—, Standard Mgmt. Co., Amarillo, 1979—, Service Gen. Ins. Co., Columbus, Ohio, 1979—, Service Mgmt. Corp., Columbus, 1979—, FTS Life Ins. Co., Dallas, 1979—, Benico, Inc., Morristown, 1979—, Guaranteed Equity Life Ins. Co., Chgo., 1980—, Petroleum State Ins. Co., Baton Rouge, 1980—, Consol. Life Assurance Co., London, 1980—, others. Adviser Nat. Assn. Ins. Commrs., 1968-69. Exec. sec. Jersey Com., 1954; chmn. bd. adjustment Frelinghuysen Twp., N.J., 1967—. Served to lt. AUS, 1940-46. Decorated Purple Heart with oak leaf cluster, Bronze Star, French fourragere in colors, Croix de Guerre, Bronze Arrowhead; named Ky. Col. Mem. Holland Soc. N.Y. (pres.), N.J. Jr. C. of C. (pres. retail div. 1950-51), Paterson C. of C. Episcopalian (vestryman). Club: Panther Valley. Home: Box 332 Johnsonburg NJ 07846 Office: 55 Madison Ave Morristown NJ 07960

QUAGLIAROLI, JOHN A., mergers, acquisitions and pvt. placements firm exec.; b. Hartford, Conn., Nov. 17, 1938; s. John and Mary Rose (Salvatore) Q.; B.S.E.E., Worcester Poly. Inst., 1961; M.B.A., Syracuse U., 1965; P.M.D., Harvard Bus. Sch., 1975; m. Judith Fowler, Nov. 15, 1969; children—Peter, James. With data processing div. IBM, 1965-72; product mgmt. and adminstrn. Citicorp, 1972-74; dir. mktg. Multitone Electronics, Springfield, N.J., 1975; v.p. F.L. Mannix & Co., 1975-76; pres. Fowler, Anthony & Co., Wellesley Hills, Mass., 1976—; bd. dirs. 1st Ipswich Corp. Bd. dirs., chmn. spl. gifts com. Italian Home for Children, Jamaica Plain, Mass. Served to 1st lt. U.S. Army, 1961-63. Mem. Harvard Bus. Sch. Assn. Roman Catholic. Club: Harvard (Boston). Home: 41 Edgewater Dr Needham MA 02192 Office: 20 Walnut St Wellesley Hills MA 02181

QUAIN, MITCHELL I., investment co. exec.; b. N.Y.C., Nov. 15, 1951; s. Norman N. and Helen C. Quain; M.B.A. with distinction, Harvard U., 1975; m. Cheryl Flom, Aug. 25, 1974; children—Michael, Rhonda. Vice pres. research Wertheim & Co., N.Y.C., 1979—; tech. adv. panel U.S. Robots Corp. Marion Yebner Nature Conservatory fellow, 1978-80. Mem. N.Y. Soc. Security Analysts, Machinery Analysts N.Y. (treas.), Am. Rd. Builders Assn., Internat. Robot Found., U.S. Tennis Assn. Author: The Agricultural Equipment Industry, 1977; The Pump & Valve Industries, 1980; The Factory of the Future, 1981. Home: Butternut Ln Katonah NY 10536 Office: 200 Park Ave New York NY 10017

QUAKKELAAR, ARNOLD JAY, controls mfg. ofcl.; b. Muskegon, Mich., July 9, 1937; s. Jasper and Cornelia Margaret (Koster) Q.; B.S., Calvin Coll., Grand Rapids, Mich., 1960; m. Norma Elaine Flietstra, Aug. 28, 1959; children—Daniel, David, Douglas, Dale, Dean. Engr., Johnson Controls, Inc., Grand Rapids, 1960-64, br. engring. mgr., 1964-68, installation and engring. mgr., 1968-71, nat. installation and engring. mgr., Milw., 1971-80; nat. mgr. customer support services Allen Bradley Co., Milw., 1980—; lectr., mgmt. cons.; chief U.S. del. to Internat. Standards Orgn., 1976-79. Mem. Community Bldg. Bd., 1977—. Registered profl. engr., Wis. Mem. Nat. Soc. Profl. Engrs., Wis. Soc. Profl. Engrs., ASHRAE, Nat. Fire Protection Assn. (chmn. tech. com. on fire safety symbols). Home: 15150 Red Fox Ln Elm Grove WI 53122 Office: 1201 S 2d St Milwaukee WI 53204

QUAN, DICK, engr.; b. Vancouver, B.C., Can., Nov. 20, 1925; s. Gow and Dar Shee Q.; B. Applied Sci., U. B.C., 1949; M.S., Calif. Inst. Tech., 1952; m. Ida Ing, 1952; children—Gary, Brian. With Hawker Siddeley Can., Inc., Toronto, 1952—, dir. corp. research and devel., 1975—. Mem. ASME, Soc. Automotive Engrs., Assn. Profl. Engrs. Ont., Can. Aeros. and Space Inst., Can. Research Mgmt. Assn. Home: 53 Ashmount Crescent Weston ON M9R 1C9 Canada Office: Box 6001 Toronto AMF ON L5P 1B3 Canada

QUARLES, CHARLES OTIS, constrn. co. exec.: b. Los Angeles, Sept. 11, 1945; s. Eddie and Carrie Pearl (Chandler) Q.: B.S., Calif. State U., 1972; M.B.A., Harvard U., 1974; m. Jo Ann Haywood, July 24, 1966; children—Brickell, Starlett, Quenton. Loan officer United Calif. Bank, Los Angeles, 1974-77; pres. E A C Constrn. Corp., Los Angeles, 1977—; instr. Los Angeles Community Coll. Dist., 1976. Served with U.S. Army, 1966-69. Mem. Harvard Bus. Sch. Club of So. Calif., Nat. Black M.B.A. Assn., Beta Alpha Psi, Beta Gamma Sigma. Home: 5221 Bedford Ave Los Angeles CA 90056 Office: 10124 S Broadway Los Angeles CA 90003

QUARLES, FREDERICK HUNDLEY, III, fin. co. exec.; b. Charlottesville, Va., June 24, 1940; s. Frederick Hundley and Sara Louise (Hunter) Q., Jr.; m. Hollace Ellen Henkel, Apr. 12, 1969; children—Ashley Louise, Ellen Michelle. Real estate investor, 1965-70; pres. Mooney Mite Aircraft Corp., Charlottesville, Va., 1970-78; dir. Commonwealth Capital Corp., 1978—, D.F.F., Inc., Charlottesville; fin. cons. to banks and fed. insured instns.; airline transport pilot, flight instr. in airplanes and instruments; Served with USNR, 1965-67. Mem. U. Va. Alumni Assn., Aircraft Owners and Pilots Assn., Mooney Mite Owners Assn. (exec. dir. 1965-78). Lutheran. Editor Mooney Mite Owners Assn. Bull., 1967—; patentee in field. Office: Box 3999 Charlottesville VA 22903

QUARLES, JOSEPH VERY, business exec.; b. Milw., Jan. 26, 1908; s. Joseph Very and Ethel Julia (Grant) Q.; B.A., Princeton U., 1929; postgrad. Harvard U. Sch. Bus., 1929-30; m. Mary Louise Fronheiser, June 6, 1931; children—Joseph Very III, Julia Grant Quarles Reggi. With Simmons Co., N.Y.C., 1930-75, pres., 1968-75; dir. H.K. Porter Co. Inc., Pitts., Mo. Portland Cement Co., St. Louis, Crane Co., N.Y.C. Republican. Clubs: Round Hill (Greenwich, Conn.); Clove Valley Rod and Gun. Home: 299 Round Hill Rd Greenwich CT 06830

QUARLES, MERVYN, VINCENT, accountant; b. Augusta, Ga., Oct. 8, 1921; s. Oscar Marcellus and Isabella Cecilia (Irving) Q.; student U. Cin., 1940-42, DePaul U., Chgo., eves. 1950-56; m. Margaret Mary Kennedy, Sept. 16, 1948; children—Margaret M., Mervyn Vincent, James M., Janet M., John W. Auditor, Bansley & Kiener, C.P.A.'s, Chgo., 1956-59; sta. accountant Channel Two, CBS, Chgo., 1959-62; internal auditor Central Farmers Fertilizer Co., Chgo., 1963-66; treas. Olson & Bartholomay Inc., 1966-70; pres. Mervyn V. Quarles, P.C., C.P.A., Homewood, Ill., 1970—; dir. Am. Perforator Co. Treas., Village of Hazel Crest (Ill.), 1966-69. Served with AUS, 1942-48. C.P.A., Ill. Mem. Am. Inst. C.P.A.'s, Ill. Soc. C.P.A.'s. Roman Catholic. Home: 17344 Mahoney Pkwy Hazel Crest IL 60429 Office: 2711 W 183d St Homewood IL 60430

QUASHA, WILLIAM HOWARD, lawyer; b. N.Y.C., May 19, 1912; B.S. in Mech. Engring., N.Y. U., 1933, M.A., 1935; LL.B., St. John's U., 1936; m. Phyllis Grant, Apr. 17, 1946; children—Wayne Grant, Alan Grant, Jill. Admitted to N.Y. bar, 1936, Philippine bar, 1945, U.S. Supreme Ct. bar, 1947; practiced in N.Y.C., 1936-42, Manila, Philippines, 1946—; sr. partner Quasha, Asperilla, Ancheta, Valmonte, Peña and Marcos; dir. Marcopper Mining Corp., Manila. Faculty, N.Y. U., 1933-35, Santo Tomas U., Manila, 1946-48; vis. asso. prof. L.I. U., summer 1966; lectr. Harvard Law Sch., summer 1976, U. Philippines Coll. Law, 1979. Mem. nat. exec. bd. Boy Scouts Philippines, 1955-74, mem. exec. bd. Manila council, 1949-74, v.p., treas., 1964-74, hon. life pres., 1970; v.p., legal counsel Acacia Mut. Aid Soc., Inc., Manila, 1963—; mem. exec. bd. Far East council Boy Scouts Am., 1973—, mem. nat. exec. bd., 1977—; pres. bd. trustees St. Luke's Hosp., Manila, 1975—; trustee Jose P. Laurel Meml. Found.; chmn. Republicans Abroad Com., Philippines. Served with AUS, 1942-46; PTO; lt. col. Res. Decorated Bronze Star with oak leaf cluster, Philippine Legion of Honor (officer rank); recipient Silver Tamaraw, Boy Scouts Philippines, 1959, Silver Fir Tree Br., Boy Scouts Austria, 1960; Distinguished Eagle Scout award Boy Scouts Am., 1970, Silver Buffalo award, 1974. Spl. award and citation City of Manila, 1970. Mem. Am., Fed. bar assns., Integrated Bar of Philippines, Law Asia, Internat. Bar Assn., Am. Soc. Internat. Law, Am. C. of C. of Philippines, Philippine Hist. Soc., Navy League U.S. (judge adv., chartermem.), Am. Assn. Philippines, Propeller Club U.S. (past pres., charter mem. Manila chpt.), Philippine Constn. Assn. (life), Philippine Soc. Internat. Law, Ramon Magsaysay Meml. Soc., Knights of Rizal (knight comdr.), Nat. Sojourners (pres. 1959), Am. Legion (dept. comdr. 1954-55), Manila Jr. C. of C. (asso., v.p. 1949), Internat. C. of C. (gov. Philippine council 1964—). Episcopalian (sr. warden, chancellor). Mason (33 deg., grand master 1962-63), Shriner, Elk (bd. dirs. palsy project 1954-69, chmn. 1963-65), Rotarian (past dir. Manila). Clubs: Nat. Lawyers' (Washington); Am. Nat. (Sydney, Australia); Creek (L.I.); University (N.Y.); Army and Navy, Manila Polo, Valle Verde Country; Makati Sports, others. Author: (with Rensis Likert) Revised Minnesota Paper Form Board Test. Home: 22 Molave Pl Makati Metro Manila Philippines Office: Don Pablo Bldg 114 Amorsolo St Legaspi Village Metro Manila Philippines

QUATTLEBAUM, HELEN DRAKE, diversified mfg. and service co. exec.; b. Chattanooga, Apr. 2, 1943; d. Charles Barry and Madelyn Lenis (Garner) Neill; B.A. in Math., Fla. State U., 1966; M.B.A. in Acctg., Ga. State U., 1977; m. John Ray Quattlebaum, May 26, 1978. Acctg. clk. Ga. Dept. State, 1962-66; accountant Modern Foods, Inc., Winter Haven, Fla., 1970-72; mgr. corp. acctg. Nat. Service Industries, Inc., Atlanta, 1972—. C.P.A., Ga. Mem. Am. Inst. C.P.A.'s, Nat. Assn. Accountants (past dir. employment). Republican. Episcopalian. Home: 2701 Cedar Forks Dr Marietta GA 30062 Office: 1180 Peachtree St NE Atlanta GA 30309

QUATTLEBAUM, OWEN MCDERMED, investment counselor; b. Anniston, Ala., Dec. 26, 1935; s. Lester Nowell and Lucy (McDermed) Q.; A.B., U. Ga., 1957; M.A., Fletcher Sch. Law and Diplomacy, Tufts U., 1959; m. Gail Sheldon, Aug. 11, 1979. Asst. sec. Bank N.Y., N.Y.C., 1966, investment officer, 1967-69, v.p., 1969—, v.p., dept. head, investment mgrs. service, 1970—, v.p., investment counsel, 1977-78, v.p., mgr. investment counsel div., 1978—. Vice chmn. bd. mgrs. Bklyn. Central YMCA, recipient Man of Year award, 1973. Served with USCG, 1959-60. Mem. N.Y. Soc. Security Analysts, Inst. Chartered Fin. Analysts, Phi Beta Kappa. Episcopalian. Club: Heights Casino. Home: 170 Columbia Heights Brooklyn NY 11201 Office: 48 Wall St New York NY 10015

QUATTLEBAUM, WALTER EMMETT, JR., telephone co. exec.; b. Midville, Ga., Dec. 22, 1922; s. Walter Emmett and Eva (Bagley) Q.; student Murrey Vocational Sch., Charleston, S.C., 1941, U. Hawaii, 1943; m. Dorothy Evelyn Clewis, Oct. 19, 1946; children—Walter Emmett III, Amalia Ann. Former owner Fla. Telephone Exchange, Sneads, Cottondale, Grand Ridge, Bonifay, Westville, and Seagrove Beach, Quattlebaum Telephone Supply Co., Quattlebaum Investments, also Spanish Trail Motel, Bonifay, Fla.; v.p., dir. Seminole Telephone Co., Donalsonville, Ga.; now investment analyst Quattlebaum Investments and others. City councilman, Sneads, 1950-52, pres. City Council, 1953. Served with AUS, 1944-46. Mem. Fla. Telephone Assn., Telephone Pioneers Am. Methodist. Office: Bonifay FL 32425

QUEALLY, FRANCIS XAVIER, ins. exec.; b. N.Y.C., July 10, 1927; s. Michael J. and Kathleen M. (Ronayne) Q.; B.S., Fordham U., 1950; M.B.A., U. Pa., 1952; m. Claire L. Doyle, Sept. 10, 1955; children—Mary Louise, Francis X., W. Doyle, Joanne, Paul. Agy. mgr. Equitable Life Assurance Soc. U.S., N.Y.C., 1952—; instr. Hofstra U., 1958-59. Bd. dirs. Berkley in Scarsdale Assn., 1972-74. Served with USN, 1945-46; PTO. Mem. Am. Soc. C.L.U.'s, Nat. Assn. Life Underwriters, Gen. Agts. and Mgrs. Assn. (life), Million Dollar Roundtable. Republican. Roman Catholic. Clubs: Wharton Bus. Sch., N.Y. Athletic; Winged Foot Golf (Mamaroneck, N.Y.). Home: 50 Tisdale Rd Scarsdale NY 10583 Office: 1700 Broadway New York NY 10019 also One Communication Plaza Stamford CT 06902

QUEEN, ROBERT ISAAC, public relations exec.; b. N.Y.C., Aug. 12, 1919; s. Joseph and Clara (Rodin) Q.; B.S., Coll. City N.Y., 1942; L.H.D., Am. Coll. Polit. Sci., 1968; m. Bella Arkin, Sept. 2, 1955; children—Alan N., Joseph W., Ann Claire. With U.S. Govt., 1942-55; owner, mgr. Robert I. Queen & Assos., pub. relations, N.Y.C., 1955—; exec. v.p. Print & Broadcast Campaigns, Inc., 1971-74. Teaching cons. Sch. Continuing Profl. Studies, Pratt Inst., 1963-64; N.Y.-N.J. news editor Press Wire Feature Services, 1955-78; pub. relations cons. Pratt Inst., 1963-65, Acad. Aeros., 1965-67, Voorhees Tech. Inst., 1965-68; N.Y. press cons. Congressman Alfred E. Santangelo, 1960-63, 66, 67; dir. pub. relations Bronx County Office Civil Def.; pub. relations counsel N.Y. State Senator John R. Dunne, 1969-71; pub. relations aide to city councilmen, 1971-73; pub. relations counsel Hon. Thomas J. Manton, 1971-73; pub. affairs officer to State Assemblyman Leonard P. Stavisky, 1974-77; pub. relations counsel N.Y. State Senator Jeremiah B. Bloom, 1977-78, N.Y. Assemblyman Saul Wesprin, 1979—. Recipient Nat. Short Story award Delta Sigma Lambda, 1951, also various awards for civic and community service; Presdl. commendation for bravery, 1974, also citations from borough pres., mayor and gov. N.Y., N.Y.C. Police Dept. Served with OSS, AUS, World War II. Mem. Broadcast Pioneers (life), Am. Soc. Hosp. Pub. Relations Dirs., N.Y. Press Club, Newspaper Reporters Assn. N.Y.C., Newspaper Guild N.Y., Pub. Relations Soc. Am., Army-Navy Union (past N.Y. State pub. relations dir.), DAV (past county comdr.), Order Ky. Cols., Sigma Delta Chi. Clubs: N.Y. Press, Overseas Press of Am., Nat. Writers, Silurians. Author: Emigres in Wartime, 1940; Tabloid Tales, 1945; Guilty They Said, 1945; dramatic scripts for The Green Hornet, The Shadow, Suspense, The Web, other shows; Handbook on Public Relations, 1957; Creative PR in Planning Special Events, 1965-67; (with Bella Queen) Elephant Comes to Play, 1965. Polit. campaign cons. and writer for radio and TV. Home and Office: 144-45 35th Ave Flushing NY 11354

QUELLMALZ, HENRY, printing co. exec.; b. Balt., May 18, 1915; s. Frederick and Edith Margaret (Shaw) Q.; B.A., Princeton, 1937; m. Marion Agar Lynch, Aug. 2, 1940; children—Lynn Quellmalz Johnson, Susan Quellmalz Mastan, Jane Quellmalz Carey. Dir. personnel, Macy's Men's Store, 1938-40; asst. mgr. Fowlers Dept. Store, Glens Falls, N.Y., 1940-41; personnel dir. U.S. Army postexchanges, Fort Meade, Md., 1941-44; with Boyd Printing Co., Albany, N.Y., 1944—, pres., 1952—; v.p. Q Corp. U.S. Agt. for WHO publs., 1960—; dir. Bankers Trust Co. Albany. Campaign chmn. ARC, Albany, 1957; bd. dirs. Camelot Home for Boys; bd. govs. Doane Stuart Sch., Albany, 1977-79, treas. bd., 1977-78; vice chmn. Family Service Assn. Am. Salute to Families, 1979, Nat. UN Day Com., 1980; adv. bd. Empire State Found. of Ind. Liberal Arts Colls.; bd. dirs. Am. Assn. World Health. Served with AUS, 1943. Recipient Pres.'s award Am. Assn. Mental Deficiency, 1976. Mem. Albany Area C. of C., Printing Industry Am. Democrat. Episcopalian. Clubs: Princeton, Univ., Fort Orange, Hudson River, Board Room (N.Y.C.). Home: 1 Park Hill Dr Apt 6 Menands NY 12204 Office: 49 Sheridan Ave Albany NY 12210

QUEST, ARTHUR EUGENE, JR., canvas co. exec.; b. Atoka, Okla., Oct. 9, 1914; s. Arthur Eugene and Lula (Moore) Q.; B.S., W. Tex. State Coll., 1939; postgrad. So. Meth. U., 1944; m. Audrey Ann Bell, June 30, 1944; children—Jean Ann, Arthur Eugene, III. With Am. Tel. & Tel., 1941-43; engr. Tex. Health Dept., 1943-45; partner A.E. Quest & Sons Mfg. Co., Lubbock, Tex. 1946—; pres. A.E. Quest & Sons, Inc., 1972—; owner cotton farm, Lorenzo, Tex., 1960—; mem. exec. bd. Snake River Ranch Corp., Idaho, Corps. Great S.W., Dallas, Twin Lakes Corp., Denver; mem. exec. bd., sr. v.p. Great S.W. Life Co., Houston; ind. oilman. Active Boy Scouts Am., recipient Silver Beaver, 1952, trustee Trust Fund; founder A.E. Quest, Jr. Student Loan Endowment Fund, W. Tex. State Coll., 1954; past pres. L.E.A.R.N. student fund; dist. chmn. Masonic Sch. and Old Age Home. Former bd. regents W. Tex. State U. Named Man of Year, Lubbock Jr. C. of C., 1948; recipient Wisdom award Honor. Mem. Canvas Mfrs. Assn. (pres. Tex. and Okla.), W. Tex. Ex-Student Assn. (past. pres.), Oil Mill Machinery Mfrs. and Supply Assn. (past pres.). Methodist (trustee). Clubs: South Plains Shrine (past pres.), Red Raider (Lubbock), Masons (32 deg.), Elks, Lions. Composer songs. Home: 3311 46th St Lubbock TX 79413 Office: 222 E 34th St Lubbock TX 79404

QUIBLE, NORMAN ERNEST, accountant; b. Long Pine, Nebr., Aug. 30, 1924; s. Paul James and Lena (Powell) Q.; B.C.S., Benjamin Franklin U., 1948, M.C.S., 1949; m. Rennie Simpson Gulick, Dec. 27, 1944; children—Kathleen Elaine, Paul Joseph. Asst. treas. Dairy Soc. Internat., Washington, 1951—, Dairy Industries Supply Assn., Washington, 1951-61; prof. accounting Benjamin Franklin U., Washington, 1956-72; practice accounting, Seabrook, Md., 1961—; sec.-treas. Francis Gasch's Sons Funeral Home, 1973—; dir., treas. Radio Position Finding Corp. Treas., Parkway Estates Citizens Assn., 1954-57, v.p., 1957-58; treas. Charles Carroll Jr. High Sch. P.T.A., 1961-62, Gaywood Elementary Sch. P.T.A., 1962-63; 1st v.p. DuVal Sr. High Sch. P.T.A., 1963-64, pres., 1964-65. Asst. treas. Lions Dist. 22C Eye Bank and Research Found., 1973-74, treas., 1974-75, 79—, dir. Camp for Deaf, 1979-82. C.P.A., D.C., Md. Mem. Am., D.C., Md. insts. C.P.A.'s, Nat. Accounting Assn., Nat. Fedn. Ind. Business, Benjamin Franklin U. Alumni Assn. Republican. Methodist (mem. finance commn. 1960-61, ofcl. bd. 1961-68, trustee 1962-68, sec.-treas. bd. trustees 1963-68). Lion (local pres. 1973-74, dist. gov. 1978-79). Club: Green Acres Swim (dir., treas. 1962-68, pres. 1967-68). Home: 6808 96th Pl Seabrook MD 20801 Office: 9470 Annapolis Rd Suite 113 Seabrook MD 20801

QUICK, JOHN BARTON, cons. firm exec.; b. Portland, Oreg., Oct. 19, 1931; s. Alfred L. and Ellen H. (Tichenot) Q.; student U. Denver, 1949-51, 53-54, U. Oreg., 1954-55; U. Colo., 1962-65; Ph.D., Union Grad. Sch., 1973; children—Margaret Ann, James Edward. Mgr. info. services Ball Bros. Research, Boulder, Colo., 1960-66; creative dir. The Interpublic Group of Cos., N.Y.C., 1967-68; mgr. advt., promotion Clin Corp., N.Y.C., 1968-70; sr. cons. Arthur D. Little, Inc., Cambridge, Mass., 1970-79; pres. Lakehill Mgmt. Center, Arlington, Mass., 1979—; tchr. Harvard Univs. Center for Continuing Edn. and Inst. for Ednl. Mgmt., Cambridge, 1975-79. Served with USAF Res., 1951-53. Mem. Co. Mil. Historians, Soc. Motion Picture and TV Engrs., Am. Mktg. Assn. Author: Artists and Illustrator's Encyclopedia, 2d edit., 1978; Small Studio Video Tape Production, 2d edit., 1976; Handbook of Film Production, 1973; Dictionary of Weapons and Military Terms, 1974; A Short Book on the Subject of Speaking, 1978; Cons. editor, contbg. editor Dictionary of Scientific and Technical Terms. Office: 30 Hamilton Rd Arlington MA 02174

QUIGG, RICHARD JOHN, casting co. exec.; b. Bethlehem, Pa., Nov. 12, 1930; s. John Paul and Frances (Gruver) Q.; B.S., Va. Poly. Inst., 1952; M.S., Lehigh U., 1954; Ph.D., Case Inst. Tech., 1959; J.D., Cleve. State U., 1966; m. Joan Clampett, Apr. 7, 1956; children—Richard John, Daniel, Laura. Metallurgist, DuPont de Nemours & Co., Inc., Newport, Del., 1952-53, Rem-Cru Titanium, Inc., Midland, Pa., 1954-56; mgr. materials TRW, Inc., Cleve., 1959-67, mgr. research and devel., 1967-70; exec. v.p., chief operations officer Jetshapes, Inc., Rockleigh, N.J., 1970-73, pres., 1973—. Recipient W.A. Tarr award for achievement in earth scis. Sigma Gamma Epsilon, 1952. Mem. Am. Soc. Metals, Am. Inst. Mining and Metall. Engrs., Am. Soc. Testing Materials. Patentee in high temperature superalloys. Home: 99 Fox Hedge Rd Saddle River NJ 07458 Office: Rockleigh Indsl Park Rockleigh NJ 07647

QUIGLEY, EDWARD THOMAS, JR., computer systems co. exec.; b. Newark, June 6, 1948; s. Edward Thomas and Ann Regina (Hepburn) Q.; student U. Md., 1972-75; m. Denise Bixby, July 31, 1971. Partner, cons. Q&W Assos., 1975-76; v.p., treas. Applied Systems Corp., Bethesda, Md., 1976—, Telecheck Washington, Inc., Bethesda, 1979—. Served with USAF, 1967-71. Mem. Delta Sigma Pi. Roman Catholic. Office: 6935 Wisconsin Ave Bethesda MD 20015

QUIGLEY, JEROME HAROLD, mining and mfg. co. exec.; b. Green Bay, Wis., Apr. 19, 1925; s. Harold D. and Mabel (Hansen) Q.; B.S., St. Norbert Coll., 1951; m. Lorraine A. Rocheleau, May 3, 1947; children—Kathy, Ross, Michael, Daniel, Mary Beth, Andrew, Maureen. Personnel adminstr. Gen. Motors Corp., 1959-64; dir. indsl. relations Raytheon Co., Santa Barbara, Calif., 1964-67; dir. personnel U. Calif., Santa Barbara, 1967-72; corp. dir. indsl. relations Gen. Research Corp., 1972-73; dir. indsl. relations ISS Sperry Univac, 1973-75; corp. dir. indsl. relations Four-Phase Systems, Inc., Cupertino, Calif., 1975; sr. v.p. human resources UNC Resources, Inc., Falls Church, Va., 1975—. Bd. dirs. Jr. Achievement, Washington. Served with U.S. Navy, 1943-47. Mem. Am. Electronics Assn., Am. Soc. Personnel Adminstrs. Republican. Roman Catholic. Club: Regency Racquet. Home: 1800 Old Meadow Rd McLean VA 22102 Office: 7700 Leesburg Pike Falls Church VA 22043

QUILLEN, JEFFREY GLENN, savs. and loan exec.; b. East Chicago, Ind., July 15, 1942; s. Glenn William and Mary (Banas) W.; student West Liberty Coll., 1960-62; m. Judith Ann House, Aug. 10, 1962; children—Tracey, Brian W. Asst. v.p. First Nat. Bank, Steubenville, Ohio, 1965-71; v.p. Maine Nat. Bank, Portland, 1971-74; pres. Resource Mgmt. Co., Lexington, Ky., 1974-76; v.p., controller Nat. Bank Commerce, Charleston, W.Va., 1976-78; mng. officer, sec.-treas. First Steubenville Savs. & Loan, 1978—, also dir. Bd. dirs., v.p. United Way, Jr. Achievement; pres. Youth Soccer League. Served with U.S. Army, 1962-65. Mem. Soc. for Fin. Mgrs., Steubenville C. of C., Am. Legion. Republican. Presbyterian. Clubs: Elks (exalted ruler), Steubenville Country. Home: 124 Hiddenwood Dr Steubenville OH 43925 Office: 100 N 3d St Steubenville OH 43952

QUINLAN, THOMAS STERLING, marketing exec.; b. Cleve., Oct. 24, 1926; s. Thomas Patrick and Irene (Wilmore) Q.; B.S. magna cum laude, Western Res. U., 1948; postgrad. Columbia, 1949-50, N.Y. U., 1973-75, City U. N.Y., 1977—. Project supr. marketing research div. Dun & Bradstreet, Inc., N.Y.C., 1951-53; asst. copy supr., asst. brand mgr. Procter & Gamble, Inc., Cin., 1953-55; advt. brand mgr. Internat. Latex, Inc., N.Y.C., 1955-56; dir. new products marketing Revlon, Inc., N.Y.C., 1956-59, dir. marketing, 1965-66; v.p., account supr. Ted Bates & Co., advt. agy., N.Y.C., 1959-65; sr. v.p., mgmt. supr., creative dir. Lennen & Newell, Inc., N.Y.C., 1967-70; creative dir. Menley & James Labs., Ltd. div. Smith Kline & French, Phila., 1970-71; pres. Quinlan & Assos., N.Y.C., 1971—; mem. grad. faculty Baruch Coll., City U. N.Y., 1978—. Served with AUS, 1944-46. Mem. Acad. of Mgmt., Am. Mktg. Assn., Inst. Mgmt. Sci., Am. Psychol. Assn. (affiliate), Phi Beta Kappa. Office: PO Box 138 Madison Sq New York NY 10010

QUINN, CARROLL THOMAS, lawyer, corp. mgr.; b. Brunswick, Ga., Nov. 14, 1946; s. Thomas G. and Norma L. (Allen) Q.; B.A. in Natural Scis., St. Anselms Coll., Manchester, N.H., 1968; J.D., New Eng. Sch. Law, 1974; m. Pamela A. Miller, July, 1980; children by previous marriage—Todd Michael, Jeffrey Carroll. Sales rep. pharms. Parke, Davis & Co., Lowell, Mass., 1968-72, med. surg. rep., 1973-75, sales trainer, med.-surg. div., 1974-75, sales mgr. N. Central area, 1975-76; nat. sales mgr. Whitestone Products, Piscataway, N.J., 1976-79; gen. mgr. USM Weather-Shield Systems Co., Stanhope, N.J., 1979—; admitted to Mass. bar, 1974; individual practice law, Lowell, 1975; instr. bus. law Lowell U., 1975. Mem. Am., Mass. bar assns. Home: 29 Park Ave Newton NJ 07860 Office: Furnace St Stanhope NJ 07874

QUINN, DONALD EDWARD, satellite communications exec.; b. N.Y.C., Jan. 8, 1932; s. James and Elsie (Busch) Q.; B.S. in Social Sci., Fordham U., 1958; M.A., N.Y. U., 1960; m. Catherine Grant, May 21, 1955; children—Ann, Joan, Donna, Eileen, Robert, Carolyn. Asst. editor Ry. Express Agy., N.Y.C., 1958-59; mgr. mktg. adminstr. Radio Engring. Labs., Long Island City, N.Y., 1959-69; dir. mktg. services Compat Corp., Westbury, N.Y., 1969-70; mgr. public affairs RCA Globcom, N.Y.C., 1972-76; dir. public affairs RCA Am. Communications, Piscataway, N.J., 1976-79, v.p. Alascom relations, 1979—. Pres. Rosedale (N.Y.) Civic Assn., 1974-75. Served with USNR, 1952-56. Mem. N.Y. Assn. Indsl. Communications, (past pres.), Nat. Cable TV Assn., Armed Forces Communications and Electronics Assn. (past sec. N.Y. chpt.), Nat. Assn. Broadcasters, U.S. Ind. Telephone Assn. Office: 400 College Rd E Princeton NJ 08540

QUINN, EDWARD JAMES, banker; b. N.Y.C., Apr. 2, 1911; s. Edward M. and Mary M. (Schneider) Q.; student Hofstra Coll., 1946-52; grad. Am. Inst. Banking, 1932-39, Grad. Sch. Banking at Rutgers, 1955-57; m. Marie A. Stafford, Apr. 22, 1939; children—Mary Ann (Mrs. Mary Ann Brown), James E., Patrick M., Sheila G. Messenger, J.S. Bache & Co., N.Y.C., 1926-27; bookkeeper Nassau-Suffolk Bond & Mortgage Guaranty Co., Mineola, N.Y., 1928; sr. v.p. European-Am. Bank and Trust Co., N.Y.C., 1928—. Chmn. investment com. United Fund L.I., 1968-71; treas. Nassau County Boy Scouts Am., 1936-39, Nassau County March Dimes, 1947-48, Nassau County Easter Seal Appeal, 1948-55, Suffolk County Cancer Soc., 1955-57, Union Free Sch. Dist. 22, Farmingdale, 1948-57; mem. U.S. Savs. Bond Com., Nassau County, 1952-65; bd. regents Royal Arcanum, 1938-39, grand committeeman, 1940-41. Bd. Appeals Village Farmingdale, 1941-56. Served with Med. Detachment AUS, 1943-46. Mem. Municipal Forum N.Y., Municipal Finance Officers Assn. U.S., L.I. Bankers Assn. (chmn. check clearing com. 1955, legislative com. 1965-71), Nat. Assn. Accountants, Am. Legion. Rotarian, Clubs: Brentwood (N.Y.) Country; Gull Haven Golf (Central Islip, N.Y.); Harbor Hills Country (Belle Terre, N.Y.). Home: 383 West Hills Rd Huntington NY 11743

QUINN, FRANCIS XAVIER, labor arbitrator-mediator; b. Dunmore, Pa., June 9, 1932; s. Frank T. and Alice B. (Maher) Q.; A.B., Fordham U., 1956, M.A., 1958; S.T.B., Woodstock Coll., 1964; M.S.I.R., Loyola U., Chgo., 1966; Ph.D. in Indsl. Relations, Calif. Western U., 1976. Joined S.J., Roman Catholic Ch., 1950; ordained priest Roman Cath. Ch., 1963; apptd. to Ry. Emergency Bd., 1975, to Fgn. Service Grievance Bd., 1976, 78, 81. Named Tchr. of Yr., Freedom Found., 1959; recipient Human Relations award City of Phila., 1971, others. Mem. Nat. Acad. Arbitrators (gov.), Indsl. Relations Research Assn., Assn. for Social Econs. (exec. council), Soc. for Dispute Resolution, Am. Arbitration Assn. (arbitrator). Democrat. Editor: The Ethical Aftermath Series, 1962-81. Address: Longport-Seaview 416 Longport NJ 08403

QUINN, JAMES DAVID, bus. exec.; b. Cleve., Oct. 23, 1929; s. Harold Martin and Marion Elizabeth (White) Q.; B.S. in Chem. Engring., W. Va. U., 1953; m. Jeanne Ann Beidler, July 3, 1952; children—Daniel, Stephen, Peter, Jennifer, Carolyn, Adam. Research engr., prodn. engr. Dow Chem. Co., Freeport, Tex., 1953-57; sales engr., project mgr., div. mgr. Haveg Industries, Wilmington, Del., 1957-64; exec. v.p., pres., chmn. bd. Pure Industries, Inc., St. Marys, Pa., 1964—, also dir.; chmn. St. Marys Indsl. Council, 1970-71; dir. Pa. Bank & Trust Co., Penn. Traffic Corp. Vice chmn. bd. trustees Andrew Kaul Meml. Hosp., St. Marys, 1974-78, trustee, 1967—; bd. dirs. Boys Club St. Marys, 1970—; bd. dirs. DuBois (Pa.) Ednl. Found., 1970—, pres., 1980—; pres. St. Marys United Fund, 1969-70. Served with U.S. Army, 1947-49. Mem. Am. Mgmt. Assn., Nat. Elec. Mfrs. Assn., St. Marys C. of C. Club: Elks. Home: 628 Sherry Rd Saint Marys PA 15857 Office: Hall Ave Saint Marys PA 15857

QUINN, JOHN CHARLES, JR., computer cons. co. exec.; b. Mineola, N.Y., Jan. 14, 1921; s. John Charles and Mary Delores (Donlon) Q.; B.S., Fordham U., 1943; postgrad. in Bus., N.Y. U., 1946, 47; m. Jane Veronica Coletti, June 17, 1943; children—Mary, Elizabeth, Patricia, John, Barbara, Milliam, Eileen, Peter. Exec. v.p. Autographic Bus. Forms, Inc., Hackensack, N.J., 1961-63; v.p./gen. mgr. Litton Automated Bus. Services, N.Y.C., 1963-66; pres. Ticketron, Inc., N.Y.C., 1966-72; pres., chief exec. officer Balt. Bus. Forms, Inc., 1972-77; pres., chief exec. officer Graphic Services Mgmt. Inc., 1977-79; v.p. telecommunications div. Internat. Computing Co., 1979—; dir. Peck & Peck. Served with USNR, 1942-45. Mem. Internat. Bus. Forms Assn., Nat. Assn. Cost Accountants, Computer Machinery Assn. Home: 403 Walpole Ct Timonium MD 21093 Office: 7131 Rutherford Rd Baltimore MD 21207

QUINN, MICHAEL DESMOND, mortgage banker; b. Balt., Sept. 4, 1936; s. Michael Joseph and Gladys (Baldwin) Q.; B.A., U. Md., 1970; m. Mary Annette McHenry, Apr. 11, 1961; children—Cailin A., Maureen K., Patricia B., Marianne P. Regional mgr. trainee Household Finance Corp., Chgo., 1958-60; with Weaver Bros., Inc. of Md., Balt., 1960—, investment v.p., corporate dir. Interim Loan dept., 1978—; chmn. bd., pres. Wye Mortgage Corp., 1977—; chmn. Wye Ins. Agy., Inc.; faculty evening coll. Johns Hopkins U., also Essex Community Coll., 1967—. Mem. Mayor's Adv. Com. Community Improvement, 1967—; mem. gov.'s task force Md. Housing Ins. Fund; mem. Md. Health Claims Arbitration Panel; mem. Cath. Commn. on Aged. Bd. dirs. Stella Maris Hospice; dist. adv. council U.S. Small Bus. Adminstrn. Served with USN, 1956-58. Mem. Md. Mortgage Bankers Assn. (pres. bd. govs.), Real Estate Bd. Greater Balt. (dir.), Home Builders Assn. Md., Md. Bankers Assn., Greater Balt. Com., Ancient Order Hibernians, Balt Jr. Assn. Commerce (Richard Troja Meml. award 1967, Outstanding Young Man of Balt. 1969). Home: 8207 Robin 19Hood Ct Baltimore MD 21204 Office: 28 Allegheny Ave Baltimore MD 21204

QUINN, OLIN BYRON, bank exec.; b. Longleaf, La., Sept. 30, 1917; s. Willie W. and Elizabeth Dorcas Q.; B.S., La. State U., 1949; M.S., Sch. Banking of the South, 1965; m. Vellene Sanders, Feb. 1, 1975; children—Laura Quinn Guidry, Julianne I., William S. Compton. With Fed. Intermediate Credit Bank of New Orleans, 1952-59; treas. Fed. Land Bank of New Orleans, 1959-65, v.p., treas., 1965-68, sr. v.p., 1968-69, pres., 1969—. Served with USNR. Mem. U.S. C. of C. (mem. food and agr. com.), New Orleans C. of C. (mem. agribus. com.). Club: Kiwanis. Office: 860 St Charles Ave New Orleans LA 70130

QUINN, ROBERT WESLEY, JR., investment co. exec.; b. Newark, Feb. 22, 1948; s. Robert Wesley and Elizabeth Francis (Campbell) Q.; B.A., Baldwin Wallace Coll., 1970; m. Cynthia Gail MacLeod, Sept. 6, 1969; children—Scott MacLeod, Brian Campbell, Elizabeth Allen. Investment officer Banker Trust Co., N.Y.C., 1971-73; mcpl. specialist Smith Barney & Co., N.Y.C., 1974; investment officer Central Nat. Bank, Cleve., 1974-75; pres., chief ops. officer Gelfand, Quinn & Assos., Inc., Cleve., 1975—. Active Bus. in Action; mem. fundraising com. Cleve. Orch. Served with USN, 1968-71. Mem. Cleve. Soc. Security Analysts, N.E. Ohio Fin. Mgrs. Soc. Republican. Presbyterian. Club: Shaker Hts. Country. Home: 17712 Berwyn Rd Shaker Heights OH 44120 Office: Leader Bldg Cleveland OH

QUINN, THOMAS HOWARD, banker; b. N.Y.C., Aug. 4, 1902; s. Thomas Charles and Frances (Quinn) Q.; LL.B., N.Y.U., 1927; m. Adele G. Pearl, Aug. 28, 1948 (dec.). Founder, pres. USLife Title Ins. Co. N.Y. (formerly Inter-County Title Ins. Co. N.Y.), 1937-74; founder, chmn. First Gen. Resources Co., 1962—; dir. West Side Fed. Savs. and Loan Assn., N.Y.C., Park Electro Chem. Co.; regional dir. Valley Bank L.I., Bank of N.Y., Valley Stream, 1954—; dir. county trust div. Bank of N.Y., White Plains, N.Y., 1949—. Bd. dirs. N.Y.C. Pub. Devel. Corp.; pres., bd. dirs. Caldwell B. Esselstyn Found.; pres. Columbia County Community and Welfare Fund; trustee, pres. Columbia Meml. Hosp., Hudson, N.Y.; trustee, pres. Olana, Hudson. Mem. N.Y. State Land Title Assn. (dir.). Clubs: Old Chatham (N.Y.) Hunt (dir.); Clover Reach Bath and Tennis (West Ghent, N.Y.); Columbia Golf and Country (Hudson, N.Y.); N.Y. Athletic (N.Y.C.). Home: The Alrae 37 E 64th St New York NY 10021 Office: 505 Park Ave New York NY 10022

QUIÑONES, CARLOS RAMÓN, mfg. co. exec.; b. Humacao, P.R., Oct. 9, 1951; s. Carlos Manuel and Thelma Gloria (Aponte) Q.; B.S., Rensselaer Poly. Inst., 1975; M.B.A., Cornell U., 1979; m. Patricia Ann Russom, June 10, 1975; 1 son, Carlos Daniel. Plant engr. Metro. Edison Co., Three Mile Island Nuclear Sta., Middletown, Pa., 1975-76; nuclear safety engr. Westinghouse Electric Corp., Madison, Pa., 1976-77; bus. adv. Exxon Enterprises, Inc., Florham Park, N.J., 1978; corp. planning cons. Emerson Electric Co., St. Louis, 1979-80; asst. to pres., chief operating officer Emerson Electric, St. Louis, 1980—; cons. in field. Alfred P. Sloan Found. fellow, 1977-78; Exxon grad. fellow, 1978-79. Mem. Am. Mktg. Assn., Assn. M.B.A. Execs. Roman Catholic. Club: Cornell. Office: 8100 W Florissant St Saint Louis MO 63136

QUINT, JAMES HERBERT, pub. co. exec.; b. Kenton, Ohio, Mar. 29, 1915; s. Warren Elmer and Dorothy Kathryn (Ziegler) Q.; student Bluffton Coll., 1931-34; children—Polly Duval (Mrs. Roderick Avery,) Barbara Lee (Mrs. J. Rios); m. 2d, Carolyn Jean Morgan, Apr. 14, 1969. Journalist, 1934—; exec. pub., editor Ensign mag., San Mateo, Calif., 1968—; editorial cons. Mem. Internat. Platform Assn., Internat. Oceanographic Found., Boating Writers Internat., U.S. Power Squadrons (past rear comdr.), Sigma Delta Chi. Clubs: Press of San Francisco, Commonwealth (San Francisco). Home: 55 W 40th Ave San Mateo CA 94403 Office: PO Box 5007 San Mateo CA 94402

QUINTANA, MICHAEL ANGEL, mech. engr.; b. Havana, Cuba, Dec. 17, 1935; came to U.S., 1960, naturalized, 1965; m. Miguel Angel and Hada Cleopatra (Otero) Q.; B.S. in Mech. Engring., Villanova U., 1959; M.S. in Mech. Engring., Northeastern U., 1966; m. Maria P. Gonzalez, May 7, 1960; children—Maria P., Isabel C., Miguel A., Francisco A. Mech. engr. standards and quality control dept. Colgate-Palmolive Co., 1960; project engr. Malden Mills Inc., Lawrence, Mass., 1961-66, sr. project engr., 1966-70, sr. corp. engr., 1970-77, engring. mgr. Fur div., 1978—; mem. faculty continuing edn. div. Merrimack Coll., 1966—. Bd. dirs. ARC, 1971-74; treas. Merrimack Valley Cuban Assn. Recipient award Am. Security Council, 1965. Mem. Nat. Rifle Assn., Met. Opera Guild, U.S. Chess Fedn., Mass. Chess Assn. Roman Catholic. Inventor textile package for pile fabrics. Home: 46 Lorenzo Circle Methuen MA 01844 Office: 46 Stafford St Lawrence MA 01841

QUIRK, WILLIAM JOSEPH, publisher; b. Boston, Nov. 28, 1942; s. William and Catherine (Hayes) Q.; B.A., Suffolk U., 1967; postgrad. N.Y. U., 1969, Sch. Visual Arts, 1970; m. Margaret Anne LaFerte, June 29, 1968. Editor, Am. Inst. Physics, N.Y.C., 1969-70; prodn. mgr. Am. Mgmt. Assn., N.Y.C., 1970-73, mgr. planning and control, 1973-75; v.p. Mgmt. Resources, Inc., N.Y.C., 1975-77, exec. v.p., treas., 1977—, also dir. Mem. Am. Mgmt. Assn., Direct Mail Mktg. Assn., Nat. Small Bus. Assn., World Future Soc. Editor: (with Patricia C. Haskell) Executive Guide to Consumer Law, 1978; (with Haskell) Executive Guide to Workers Compensation, 1978; (with Haskell) The Local Union and Its People, 1977; author: (with Peter C. Reid and P.C. Haskell) Managerial Finance for Non-Financial Managers, 1978. Office: 155 E 56th St New York NY 10022

QUIS, HAROLD JOSEPH, mfg. co. exec.; b. Newark, May 6, 1929; s. Harold Joseph and Helen C. (Crealey) Q.; A.A., Union Jr. Coll., 1950; B.A., Fla. So. Coll., 1951; postgrad. Columbia, 1953; m. Marguerite J. Schaul, July 2, 1955; children—Stephanie Anne, Daphne Dianne, Aimee Suzanne. Industry mktg. specialist Market Planning Service, N.Y.C., 1954-56; asst. to dir. planning Celanese Chem. Co., N.Y.C., 1956-58, asst. to controller, supr. sales research and forecasting, 1958-60, mgr. marketing analysis and forecasting, 1960-62, dir. mktg. planning, 1962-64, dir. mktg. services, 1964-65; mgr. chem. industry services N.Y. Central System, 1965-66; mgr. planning Wallace & Tiernan, 1966-70; dir. corp. devel. Union Camp Corp., Wayne, N.J., 1970-72; pres., chmn. bd. Jersey Industries, Inc., 1968-71; pres., dir. X-Rail Systems, Inc., Newark, 1972—. Pres. Young Men's Bd. Trade, N.Y.C., 1962-63, chmn. bd., 1963-64; dir. N.Y. Bd. Trade, 1963-64, Councilman, Borough of Bernardsville, 1971-78, pres., 1976-77; mem. Borough Bernardsville Bd. Adjustment, 1969-71, Planning Bd., 1972-77; bd. dirs. Newark Transp. Council, 1975—. Served with USMCR, 1946, 51. Home: Anderson Hill Rd Bernardsville NJ 07924 Office: 60 Park Pl Newark NJ 07102

QUIST, EVERIL ARNOLD, agri-bus. exec.; b. Litchfield, Minn., Mar. 18, 1930; s. Albert Edwin and Martha Engelina (Carlson) Q.; degree in Agrl. Mktg., U. Minn., 1948; m. Joyce Marie Hendrickson, Aug. 20, 1951; children—Larry, Ronald, James, Randy. Gen. mgr. Associated Farmers Corp., Clinton, Wis., 1963-68; area mktg. mgr. FS Services, Woodstock, Ill., 1969-72; dist. sales mgr. Crows Hybrid Corn Co., Milford, Ill., 1972-74; mktg. and sales cons. Equity Coop., East Troy, Wis., 1974-77; v.p. sales and mktg. Pearson Agri-Systems, Plover, Wis., 1977—, also dir.; owner, pres. Everil A. Quist & Assos., Stevens Point, Wis.; cons. in field. Cubmaster, Boy Scouts Am., 1968-74; trustee Village of Sharon (Wis.), 1972-76; ward chmn. Republican Party, 1972-76. Served with USN, 1951-54. pvt. pilot. Mem. Am. Farm Bur. Fedn., Internat. Silo Assn., Am. Inst. Parliamentarians. Republican. Lutheran. Club: Toastmasters. Home: 432 Verrill St Stevens Point WI 54481 Office: PO Box 288 #51 S Plover WI 54467

QURASHI, MAQBOOL A., communications co. exec.; b. Daska, Pakistan, Sept. 16, 1932; came to U.S., 1960; s. Abdul Hameed and Nazir (Begum) Q.; B.S. in Engring., Drexel U., 1971; m. Reinhild Ruemanap, Mar. 26, 1956; children—Ronnie, Ruby, Michelle. Plant mgr. Crescent Textile, Pakistan, 1956-59; technician, project engr. Jerrold Electronics Corp., Phila., 1962-69; engring. mgr. Magnavox, Syracuse, N.Y., 1969-74; founder AM Cable TV Industries, Inc., Quakertown, Pa., 1974, chief exec. officer, chmn. bd., 1974—. Mem. Soc. Cable TV Engrs. (sr.), Upper Bucks County C. of C. (2d v.p. 1980—, exec. bd.). Republican. Islamic. Club: Rotary (pres. 1980—). Patentee in field. Office: 1110 N West End Blvd Quakertown PA 18951

RABBERS, NORMAN LLOYD, cons. engring. co. exec.; b. Kalamazoo, Dec. 31, 1925; s. Oscar Archibald and Nellie Hertha (Jones) R.; student Oberlin Coll., 1943-44; B.S.E. in Civil Engring., U. Mich., 1946; postgrad. Western Mich. U., 1946, Northwestern U., 1972; m. Jean Von Holten; children by previous marriage, David, Kenneth, Thomas, Vicki. Hwy. engr. Mich. Hwy. Dept., 1946-47; engring. draftsman L. C. Kingscott Co., Kalamazoo, 1947-48; structural designer Sargent & Lundy, Chgo., 1948-50, structural design engr. and structural project engr., 1953-63, systems and standards adminstr., 1974-79; structural design engr. Floyd G. Brown, Marion, Ohio, 1952-53; partner Upper Peninsula Engring. Assos., Chgo., 1963-64; structural project engr. Pioneer Service & Engring. Co., 1964-67; dir. bus. devel., De Leuw, Cather & Co., Chgo., 1967-70; practice civil and structural engring., 1970-71; project mgr. Mark Lovejoy & Assos., Inc., Burr Ridge, Ill., 1971-72; mgr. civil div. The Engr. Collaborative, Chgo., 1972-73; v.p. ops. Ervin Engring. Ill., Oak Brook, 1973-74; power group project engr. Darin & Armstrong, Inc., Southfield, Mich., 1979-80; mgr. power engring. Detroit Black & Veatch, Detroit, 1980—. Mem. nat. exec. com. Y-Indian Guides, YMCA, 1960-69; bd. dirs. B.R. Ryall YMCA, Wheaton, Ill., 1961-70, chmn., 1968-69; vice chmn. DuPage (county, Ill.) Planning Council, 1967-69; mem. Darien (Ill.) Econ. Devel. Commn., 1973-74; mem. planning com. Chgo. Met. Housing and Planning Council, 1977-79. Served to capt. USMCR, 1943-46, 50-52. Registered profl. engr., Ill., Mich., Ohio; registered structural engr., Ill. Fellow ASCE (chmn. urban planning and devel. Ill. sect. 1968-69). Republican. Lutheran. Home: 720 Coachman Dr Apt 4 Troy MI 48084 Office: 200 Renaissance Center Suite 1220 Detroit MI 48243

RABEL, WILLIAM HUITT, ins. co. assn. exec.; b. Brownsville, Tex., May 28, 1941; s. Adolphus B. and Jane (Huitt) R.; B.B.A., Tex. A. and M. U., 1963; M.A., U. Pa., 1970, Ph.D., 1973; m. Judith J. Vananzi, Dec. 17, 1967; children—Nicole M., Danielle K., W. Huitt. Asst. prof. ins. Syracuse (N.Y.) U., 1966-71; dir. chartered life underwriters curriculum devel. Am. Coll. Life Underwriters, 1971-73; econ. affairs officer ins. br. UN Conf. Trade and Devel., Geneva, Switzerland, 1973-75; dean S.S. Huebner Sch. C.L.U. Studies, Am. Coll., Bryn Mawr, Pa., 1975-78; v.p., dir. Life Mgmt. Inst., Life Office Mgmt. Assn., Atlanta, 1978—; adj. prof. ins. Ga. State U., Atlanta, 1978—; cons. Asian Inst. Ins., Gen. Arab Ins. Fedn. Munnerlyn scholar, 1962-63, S.S. Huebner Found. fellow, 1963-66. Mem. Am. Risk and Ins. Assn., Am. Soc. C.L.U., Assn. Internat. da Droit de L'Assurance (sec. U.S. chpt.), Ins. Co. Edn. Dirs. Soc., So. Risk and Ins. Assn., Phi Eta Sigma. Episcopalian. Cons. editor, contbg. author Life and Health Insurance Handbook, 1973; bd. advs. Jour. Accounting, Auditing and Finance, 1977—. Home: 191 Camden Rd NE Atlanta GA 30309 Office: 100 Colony Square Atlanta GA 30309

RABINOWICZ, BERNARD, small bus. cons.; b. London, Jan. 12, 1948; came to U.S., 1948, naturalized, 1952; s. Mechel and Malka R.; student in Computer Sci., Pratt Inst., 1970; student N.Y. U., 1973-75; M.B.A., Adelphi U., 1978; m. Esther Feldman, Apr. 17, 1968; children—Joseph, Chana, Sarah, Rebecca. Cons., Programming Methods, Inc., 1971; programmer analyst Fed. Res. Bank of N.Y., 1972-74; computer analyst Chem. Bank of N.Y., 1974-76; computer specialist Montefiore Hosp., N.Y.C., 1976-78; pres. Micronomics Bus. Systems, Inc., N.Y.C., 1978—. Vice pres. Congregation Beth David, 1972—. Recipient cert. of achievement Program Products, Inc., 1979, IBM, 1980. Mem. Data Processing Mgmt. Assn., Assn. Computing Machinery, AChduth Data Processing Assn. (dir.). Club: M.I.T. Venture Clinic.

RABINOWITZ, STEPHEN LEE, kitchen designer; b. Phila., Nov. 13, 1941; s. Albert A. and Rosalind (Kaisen) R.; student Temple U., 1958-59, Goddard Coll., 1959-62; m. Barbara Halpert, Sept. 9, 1963; children—Eric, Brian, Larry, Seth. Scene designer, asst. dir. Robert Lawrence Studios div. RKO, N.Y.C., 1963-64; v.p. sales Am. Video Corp., Barrington, N.J., 1964—, designer, prin. A.V. Custom Kitchens div., 1965—. Mem. Am. Inst. Kitchen Dealers (exec. v.p. Mid-Atlantic chpt.), Council Certified Kitchen Designers (regional coordinator). Home: 31 Grove St Haddonfield NJ 08033 Office: A V Custom Kitchen div Am Video Corp 222 White Horse Pike Barrington NJ 08007

RABON, WILLIAM JAMES, JR., architect; b. Marion, S.C., Feb. 7, 1931; s. William James and Beatrice (Baker) R.; B.S. in Arch., Clemson (S.C.) Coll., 1951; B.Arch., N.C. State Coll., 1955; M.Arch., Mass. Inst. Tech., 1956. Designer archtl. firms in N.Y.C. and Birmingham, Mich., 1958-61; designer, asso. John Carl Warnecke and Assos., San Francisco, 1961-63, 64-66, Keyes, Lethbridge and Condon, Washington, 1966-68; prin. archtl. partner A.M. Kinney and William J. Rabon Assos., Cin., 1968—; v.p., dir. archtl. design A.M. Kinney, Inc., Cin., 1977—; lectr. U. Calif., Berkeley, 1963-65; asst. prof. archtl. design Catholic U. Am., 1967-68; prin. works include Kaiser Tech. Center, Pleasanton, Calif. (Indsl. Lab. of Year award), 1970; Clermont Nat. Bank, Milford, Ohio, 1971; Pavilion bldg. Children's Hosp. Med. Center, Cin. (AIA Design award), 1973; EG&G, Hydrospace, Inc., Rockville, Md. (AIA Design award), 1970; Mead Johnson Park, Evansville, Ind. (Indsl. Research Lab. of Year hon. mention), 1973; Hamilton County Vocat. Sch., Cin., 1972; hdqrs. lab. EPA, Cin., 1975; Arapahoe Chem. Co. Research Center, Boulder, Colo. (Indsl. Research Lab. of Year award 1976; Concrete Reinforced Steel Inst. Nat. Design award), 1976; NALCO Chem. Co. Research Center, Naperville, Ill., 1980; Proctor & Gamble-Winton Hill Tunnel, Cin. (AIA Design award), 1978. Served to 1st lt. AUS, 1951-53; Korea. Decorated Silver Star, Bronze Star with V device, Purple Heart; M.I.T. Grad. Sch. scholar, 1955-56; Fulbright scholar, Italy, 1957-58. Mem. AIA (Design award 1980). Office: 2900 Vernon Pl Cincinnati OH 45219

RABSTEJNEK, GEORGE JOHN, JR., mgmt. cons.; b. Queens, N.Y., June 14, 1932; s. George John and Rose Anna (Krasa) R.; B. Indsl. Engring., Ga. Inst. Tech., 1954; postgrad. law U. Conn., 1969, bus. adminstrn. N.Y. U., 1965-69, Harvard Bus. Sch., 1975; m. Patsy Kidd, July 17, 1964; 1 dau., Marley Ann. Supr. purchasing Westinghouse Electric Corp., Bridgeport, Conn., 1957-61; project mgr. systems div. IBM, Poughkeepsie, N.Y., 1961-65; dir. material mgmt. services div. Harbridge House mgmt. cons., Boston, 1965-69, v.p., group head, 1969-75, exec. v.p., 1975-76, pres., 1976—, also dir.; chmn. bd. Devel. Sci. Services, Inc., 1978—; dir. Golightly & Co. Internat., Inc., Gellman Research Assos., Inc. Mgr., Cohasset United Fund Com., 1974; mem. parish com. 1st Parish Ch.; mem. advisory bd. Town of Cohasset. Served to comdr. USNR, 1958-75. Mem. Navy League, Naval Res. Assn., Nat. Def. Preparedness Assn., Nat. Security Indsl. Assn., Am. Security Council, Am. Inst. Indsl. Engrs., Aircraft Owners and Pilots Assn., Harvard Bus. Sch. Assn., World Affairs Council, Pan Am. Soc. (bd. govs.), Alpha Pi Mu, Phi Kappa Sigma. Unitarian. Clubs: Harvard (Boston); Union League (N.Y.C.); Cohasset Yacht, Cohasset Tennis and Squash. Contbr. articles to profl. jours. Home: 181 Border St Cohasset MA 02025 Office: 11 Arlington St Boston MA 02116

RACE, PETER KEMPTON, ins. co. exec.; b. West Chester, Pa., Jan. 8, 1931; s. Shirley Kempton and Mary Woods (Ellis) R.; B.A., Bowdoin Coll., 1952; m. Ruth Eldridge, Sept. 19, 1953; children—Robert K., Alan D. Underwriter, Royal Globe Ins. Group, Boston and N.Y.C., 1952-59; research analyst Boit, Dalton & Church, Boston, 1959-60; office mgr. Am. Policyholders Ins. Co., Wakefield, Mass., 1960-62, asst. v.p., underwriting mgr., 1962-74, v.p., field ops. mgr., 1974-76; v.p., underwriting mgr. Electric Mut. Liability Ins. Co., Lynn, Mass., 1976—. Past pres. Boxford (Mass.) Athletic Assn.; mem. troop com. Boy Scouts Am., Boxford; mem. Boxford Sch. Bldg. Com.; mem. Boxford Sch. Com., 1962-71, past chmn.; mem. Mascinomet Regional Dist. Sch. Com., 1971-80, chmn., 1973-74, 79-80. Served with U.S. Army, 1952-54. C.P.C.U. Republican. Unitarian. Club: Boxford Couples (past pres.). Home: 51 Middleton Rd Boxford MA 01921 Office: Electric Mut Liability Ins Co 715 Lynnway St Lynn MA 01905

RACEK, EDWARD WILLIAM, sch. adminstr.; b. Bklyn., Jan. 30, 1922; s. Edward Lee and Anna (Slezak) R.; B.S. in Petroleum Engring., U. Tulsa, 1948; M.A. in Sch. Adminstrn.; m. Mary A. Hall, July 20, 1945; children—Edward L., Donald J., Richard W. Petroleum engr. Acme Well Supply Co., N.Y.C., 1948-67, now cons., Piscataway, N.J.; prin. St. Mary's Sch., Plainfield, N.J., 1971-77; asst. sch. bus. adminstr. Middlesex County Vocat. and Tech. Schs., 1977—. Served with USAAF, 1942-45. Decorated Air medal with three oak leaf clusters, Purple Heart. Mem. Am. Inst. Mining Engrs., Kappa Alpha. Roman Catholic. Home: 218 Old New Brunswick Rd Piscataway NJ 08854

RACETTE, JACQUES, personnel agy. exec.; b. Montreal, Que., Can., Aug. 5, 1933; s. Fernando and Lucile (de Tornancour) R.; grad. Coll. Mont Saint-Louis, 1952; m. Claudette Verreau, June 29, 1957; children—Guy, Line, Diane. With retail credit co., 1955-59; sales rep. Procter & Gamble Co., 1959-63; sales mgr. Cyanamid of Can., 1963-66; with 500 Selection Services, Montreal, 1966—, v.p., 1968—. Registered profl. employment cons. Mem. Assn. Profl. Employment Agys. and Consultants (nat. pres., past pres. Que. chpt.), Sales and Mktg. Club Montreal (past pres.). Roman Catholic. Clubs: Canadien (Montreal); Golf Le Cardinal. Office: 615 Dorchester Blvd W Montreal PQ H3B 1P6 Canada

RACHAL, ELISABETH LYMAN, mgmt. cons.; b. Boston, Nov. 12, 1943; d. Ernest McIntosh and Elisabeth Bemis (Reed) Lyman; B.A., Colby Coll., 1965; M.A., U. Mich., 1966; M.B.A. (fellow 1971-73), Harvard, 1973; m. Paul Hoffman Rachal, June 16, 1973; children—Elisabeth Reed, Lauren Hoffman, Alison Lyman. Univ. adminstr. Radcliffe Coll., Cambridge, Mass., Brandeis U., Waltham, Mass., 1966-71; faculty research asst. Harvard Bus. Sch., Boston, 1973-74; mgmt. cons. Baxter Travenol Labs., Inc., Deerfield, Ill., 1974-76; ind. mgmt. cons., Paris, 1976-79; mgmt. cons. Booz, Allen and Hamilton, Paris, 1979-80. Treas. bd. dirs. Women's Inst. for Continuing Edn., Am. Coll., Paris. Mem. Am. Women's Group in Paris (treas.), Am. C. of C. in France (dir.). Clubs: American, Harvard Bus. Sch. (Paris). Developed and published bus. mgmt. teaching materials. Home: 607 Spruce St Winnetka IL 60093

RACHINSKY, JOSEPH WALTER, ins. co. exec.; b. Bayonne, N.J., June 5, 1946; s. John and Mary Theresa (Dudek) R.; B.A., Seton Hall U., 1968; M.A., Rutgers U., 1969; m. Mary Patricia Gelchion, June 27, 1971; children—Joseph Walter, Merdith Ellen. Various group underwriting positions Mut. Benefit Life Ins. Co., Newark, 1970-76, asst. mgr. group underwriting and issue, 1976-78; sec. group and spl. risk underwriting Reliance Standard Life Ins. Co., Phila., 1978—; instr. Health Ins. Assn. Am., 1974—. Served with inf. U.S. Army, 1969-70; Vietnam. Decorated Army Commendation medal; Vietnam Cross for Gallantry. Mem. Life Office Mgmt. Assn., Health Ins. Assn. Am., Am. Spl. Risk Assn., Am. Soc. C.L.U. Roman Catholic. Office: 4 Penn Center Plaza Philadelphia PA 19103

RACHLIN, AARON MICHAEL, furniture mfg. co. exec.; b. Reading, Pa., Aug. 1, 1945; s. Theodore and Louise (Goldberg) R.; B.S., Pa. State U., 1967; m. Peggy Greiner, July 9, 1965; children—James, Tracy. With Rachlin Furniture Inc., Sinking Springs, Pa., 1965—, treas., 1968—, also dir. Mem. NAM. Republican. Jewish. Clubs: Berks Camera, B'nai B'rith. Office: 628 Columbia Ave Sinking Spring PA 19608

RACHLIN, ROBERT, pension co. exec.; b. N.Y.C., Feb. 6, 1925; s. I. Jack and Jennie (Bezahler) R.; B.B.A., Coll. City N.Y., 1948; M.S.F.S., Am. Coll., 1980; m. Pearl Sherman, June 27, 1948; children—Jeffrey, Amy, Wendy. Accountant, Biller & Snyder, N.Y.C., 1948-49; life ins. agt. Equitable Life Assurance Soc., N.Y.C., 1949-51, Conn. Mut. Life Ins. Co., N.Y.C., 1951-60; propr. Corp. Planning Assos., N.Y.C., 1961-75; chmn. bd. Compensation Planning Corp., N.Y.C., 1976-79; pres. Rachlin Pension Adminstrn. Inc., N.Y.C., 1980—; adj. asso. prof. income taxation Coll. of Ins., N.Y.C., 1972—; adj. tchr. income taxation C.W. Post Coll., L.I. U., 1977-79, N.Y. Center Fin. Studies, N.Y.C., 1980—. Pres. Sleepy Hollow Community Concert Assn., Tarrytown, N.Y., 1960's. Served with U.S. Army, 1943-46. Decorated Combat Inf. badge. C.L.U. Mem. Am. Soc. C.L.U.'s, N.Y. Life Underwriters Assn., Am. Soc. Pension Actuaries, Am. Acad. Actuaries, Million Dollar Round Table, Top of the Table. Home: Gracemere Tarrytown NY 10591 also Whitingham VT Office: 666 Fifth Ave New York NY 10019

RACKMIL, CHARLES IRWIN, JR., valve co. exec.; b. Phila., Apr. 29, 1932; s. Charles Irwin and Anna Marie (Schaeffer) R.; student Drexel Inst. Tech., 1951-52, 55-57; m. Nancy Anne Berwick, June 13, 1953; children—Barbara, Charles Irwin III. Sr. acct. Cuneo Press, Phila., 1950-62; dir. budgets Schick Elec. Co., Lancaster, Pa., 1962-71; div. comptroller ITT Grinnell Valve Co., Inc., Lancaster, 1972—; mem. Data Processing Bd.; tax cons. Chmn. Parent/Tchrs. Orgn., 1955-56. Served with AUS, 1953-55. Cert. Comptrollers Inst. Am. Mem. Nat. Assn. Accts. Democrat. Roman Catholic. Office: 33 Centerville Rd Lancaster PA 17603

RACZKOWSKI, RICK HENRYK, mfg. co. exec.; b. Poznan, Poland, Oct. 29, 1921; immigrated to Can., 1956, naturalized, 1961; s. Wlodzimierz and Edith (Kyak) R.; student U. Poland, 1939; m. Morgan, Nov. 25, 1947; children—Richard, Yvonne. Planner, Philips Electronics, Toronto, Ont., Can., 1956-61; with Croven Ltd., Whitby, Ont., Can., 1961—, purchasing mgr., 1962—. Served with RAF, 1940-49, Pakistan Air Force, 1949-56. Mem. C. of C. (pres. 1980-). Roman Catholic. Clubs: 420 Club, Club of RCAF. Home: 911 Walton Blvd Whitby ON L1N 3G6 Canada Office: 500 Beech St Whitby ON Canada L1N 5S5

RADAKER, BYRON CLAIRE, mfg. co. exec.; b. West Freedom, Pa., Mar. 19, 1934; s. Ralph Jacob and Mary Grace (Kilgore) R.; B.S. in Bus. Adminstrn., Kent State U., 1959; m. Shirley Ann Hotchkiss, Nov. 28, 1953; children—Keith, Kelly, Kirsten, Kyle. Sales rep. Gillette Safety Razor, 1959-61; sales and mktg. ofcl. Allied Chem. Co., 1961-66; sr. mgmt. ofcl. Certain Teed Corp., 1966-72, pres., chief operating officer, 1972-74; exec. v.p. planning Congoleum Corp., Portsmouth, N.H., 1975-76, dep. chmn. bd., chief operating officer, 1976-77, pres., chief exec. officer, 1977-79, chmn. bd., pres., chief exec. officer, 1979-80, chmn. bd., chief exec. officer, 1980—. Served with C.E., AUS, 1954-56. Office: PO Box 4040 Portsmouth NH 03801

RADEN, LOUIS, tape and label corp. exec.; b. Detroit, June 17, 1929; s. Harry M. and Joan (Morris) R.; B.A., Trinity Coll., 1951; postgrad. N.Y. U., 1952; m. Mary K. Knowlton, June 18, 1949; children—Louis III, Pamela, Jacqueline. With Time, Inc., 1951-52; with Quaker Chem. Corp., 1952-63, sales mgr., 1957-63; exec. v.p. Gen. Tape & Supply, Inc., Detroit, 1963-68, pres., chmn. bd., 1969—; pres. Mich. Gun Clubs, 1973-77. Fifth reunion chmn. Trinity Coll., 1956, pres. Mich. alumni, 1965-72; trustee, Mich. Diocese Episcopal Ch. Recipient Key Man award Greater Hartford Jaycees, 1957. Mem. Nat. Rifle Assn. (life), Nat. Skeet Shooting Assn. (life, nat. dir. 1977-79), Greater Detroit Bd. Commerce, Mich. C. of C., C. of C. U.S., Theta Xi (life; Disting. Service award 1957, alumni pres.). Republican. Clubs: University; Detroit Golf, Detroit Gun. Home: 1133 Ivy Glen Circle Bloomfield Hills MI 48013 Office: 7451 W Eight Mile Rd Detroit MI 48221

RADER, DAVID L., ins. co. exec.; b. Columbus, Ohio, Nov. 2, 1946; s. Earl R. and Ruth R.; student Wittenberg U., 1964-66; B.A., Ohio State U., 1968; m. Martha Cardwell, Sept. 9, 1967. Research asso. Ohio Legislature, 1968-70; asso. exec. dir. Ohio Med. Assn., Columbus, 1971-76; v.p., sec. Physicians Ins. Co. Ohio, Columbus, 1976-80; sec. Pico Life Ins. Co., Columbus, 1978-80, pres., 1980—; dir. Ky. Med. Ins. Co. Past mem. Planning Commn. Upper Arlington, Ohio. Clubs: University (Columbus); Moundbuilders Country. Home: 883 Lakeshore Dr E Harbor Hills Hebron OH 43025 Office: PO Box 281 Pickerington OH 43147

RADER, FRANK K., gas transmission co. exec.; b. 1919; B.A., So. Meth. U., 1941; LL.B., Harvard U., 1948; married. With Tex. Gas Transmission Corp., Owensboro, Ky., 1952—, v.p., 1957-61, sr. v.p. regulation, rates, sales, gas supply and corp. planning, 1961-67, exec. v.p., 1967-68, pres., 1968-76, vice chmn. bd., 1976-80, chmn., 1980—, also dir. Office: 3800 Frederica St Owensboro KY 42301*

RADFORD, GARY ALLEN, radio co. exec.; b. Mitchell, S.D., May 2, 1938; s. Floyd L. and Elda C. (Jerke) R.; B.S., S.D. Sch. Mines and Tech., 1960; M.S., Iowa State U., 1972; m. Margo L. Melander, July 18, 1960; children—Mary E., Ronald P. Project elec. engr. Reynolds Elec. & Engring. Co., El Paso, Tex., 1960-68; with Collins Radio Co., Dallas, 1968—, program mgr. for mil. (airborne) avionics systems, 1977—; cons. in field. Leader youth programs YMCA, Cedar Rapids; asst. scoutmaster Boy Scouts Am., Cedar Rapids, 1970-72. Registered profl. engr., Ala., Iowa, Tex. Mem. IEEE, Am. Inst. Plant Engrs., Nat. Soc. Profl. Engrs., Theta Tau. Lutheran. Clubs: Los Rios, Elmcrest Country. Home: 1917 Country Club Dr Plano TX 75074 Office: PO Box 10462 Dallas TX

RADICE, PEARL ROSE, ins. co. personnel exec.; b. Bklyn., Apr. 4, 1935; d. Gerald and Ida Gloria Rose; A.S. in Mgmt.-Devel. cum laude, Miami-Dade Community Coll., 1975; B.S. in Mktg.-Mgmt., Barry Coll., 1977, M.B.A., 1979; m. Gerard Allan Radice, July 30, 1952 (dec. 1970); children—Helen Marie Radice Dube, Patricia Anne Radice Petersen, Gerard Allen. Sec.-bookkeeper Morton Sales Corp., Miami, Fla., 1963; with Am. Title Ins. Co., Miami, 1963—, purchasing agt., 1974-77, human resources officer, 1977—; lectr. in mgmt. Miami-Dade Community Coll. Campaign coordinator United Way, Miami, 1974—; mem. Holy Family Sch. Bd., North Miami, 1977-78; mem. Holy Family Stewardship Program, North Miami, 1979-80; vol. Heart Fund, Community OutReach, ARC; sec. Latin Affairs Com. City of North Miami Beach. Mem. Am. Soc. Personnel Adminstrs., Am. Bus. Women's Assn., Nat. Assn. Purchasing Mgrs., M.B.A. Assn., Big Bros./Big Sisters of Greater Miami (asso.), Phi Lambda Pi. Home: 1311 NE 154th St North Miami Beach FL 33162 Office: 1101 Brickell Ave Miami FL 33131

RADLI, JOHN ANTHONY, securities co. exec.; b. Newark, May 8, 1940; s. John Michael and Louise Mae (Casagrande) R.; student Columbia Coll., 1958-60; B.A., Upsala Coll., East Orange, N.J., 1962; m. Cynthia E. Koch, May 25, 1963; children—John Robert, Cynthia Joyce. Tax accountant Chase Manhattan Bank, 1963; sales exec. trainee, salesman J.B. Hanauer, Newark, 1963-68; exec. v.p., treas., dir. Gibraltar Securities Co., Florham Park, N.J., 1968—. Chmn., Upsala Coll. Venture Fund, 1974; trustee, mem. fin. investment com. Upsala Coll., also mem. Pres.'s Forum/Alumni Fund, 1968—. Mem. Securities Investment Dealers, Greater Newark C. of C., Franklin Mint Soc. Republican. Home: 26 Windsor Pl Essex Fells NJ 07021 also 1 Baltimore Blvd Sea Girt NJ 08750 Office: 10 James St Florham Park NJ 07932

RADSCH, ROBERT WINMILL, investment co. exec.; b. N.Y.C., Dec. 19, 1942; s. Robert Henry and Virginia (Winmill) R.; B.A., Yale U., 1965; M.B.A., Columbia U., 1967; m. Mary Louise Stalter, Dec. 16, 1967. Asst. sec., portfolio mgr. Schroder Trust, N.Y.C., 1969-71; v.p. Davis/Dinsmore Mgmt. Co., N.Y.C., 1971-76, 77—; dir. investor relations Lone Star Industries, N.Y.C., 1976-77; dir. Bull & Bear Group of Funds. Trustee, Holland Lodge Found., 1979—. Chartered fin. analyst. Mem. Fin. Analysts Fedn., N.Y. Soc. Security Analysts (dir.), St. Andrews Soc., New Eng. Soc. Episcopalian. Clubs: Piping Rock; Seattle Tennis; Badminton (N.Y.C.); Masons. Home: 1435 Lexington Ave New York NY 10028 Office: 660 Madison Ave New York NY 10017

RADUNS, EDWARD BERNARD, banker; b. Bklyn., Oct. 1, 1930; s. Solomon and Zena (Walpoff) R.; B.B.A., U. Miami, 1952, M.B.A., 1976; m. Barbara Lifschen, June 14, 1952; children—Kerry, Judy, Cathy. With Crestwood Constrn. Co., Miami, Fla., 1955-57, S.C. Bluh Co., Miami, 1958-60; with Lawyers Mortgage & Title Co., Miami, 1960-61; with So. Mortgage Assos., Miami, 1961—, pres., chief exec. officer, 1967—; dir. First City Bank Dade County. Served with U.S. Army, 1952-55; ETO. Mem. Mortgage Bankers Assn. Miami,

Mortgage Bankers Assn. Am., Mortgage Bankers Assn. Fla., Miami Bd. Realtors, Am. Coll. Real Estate Consultants, Nat. Fee Appraisers, Cert. Rev. Appraisers. Address: 1999 S W 27th Ave Miami FL 33145

RAE, MATTHEW SANDERSON, JR., lawyer; b. Pitts., Sept. 12, 1922; s. Matthew Sanderson and Olive (Waite) R.; A.B., Duke, 1946, LL.B., 1947; postgrad. Stanford, 1951; m. Janet Hettman, May 2, 1953; children—Mary-Anna, Margaret, Janet. Asst. to dean Duke Sch. Law, Durham, N.C., 1947-48; admitted to Md. bar, 1948, Calif. bar, 1951, U.S. Supreme Ct. bar, 1967; asso. firm Karl F. Steinmann, Balt., 1948-49, Guthrie, Darling & Shattuck, Los Angeles, 1953-54; nat. field rep. Phi Alpha Delta Frat., Los Angeles, 1949-51; research atty. Calif. Supreme Ct., San Francisco, 1951-52; partner firm Darling, Rae & Gute, Los Angeles, 1955—; mem. probate law cons. group Calif. Bd. Legal Specialization, 1977—. Vice pres. Los Angeles County Republican Assembly, 1959-64; mem. Los Angeles County Rep. Central Com., 1960-64, 77—, mem. Rep. Exec. Com., 1977—, vice chmn. 17th Congl. Dist., 1960-62, 28th Congl. Dist., 1962-64; chmn. 27th Senatorial Dist., 1977—; chmn. 46th Assembly Dist., 1962-64; mem. Rep. State Central Com., 1966—, mem. exec. com., 1966-67; parliamentarian Calif. Rep. League, 1964-65, exec. v.p., 1965-66, pres., 1966-67; bd. dirs. Rep. Assos., 1979—. Served to 2d lt. USAAF, World War II. Fellow Am. Coll. Probate Counsel; mem. Am., Los Angeles County (chmn. probate and trust law com. 1964-66, exec. com., conf. of dels. 1978—, chmn. legis. com. 1980—), South Bay bar assns., Internat. Acad. Estate and Trust Law (academician, exec. council 1974-78), State Bar Calif. (chmn. jour. com. 1970-71, chmn. probate com. 1974-75, exec. com. estate planning, trust and probate law sect. 1977—), World Affairs Council, Lawyers Club Los Angeles, Town Hall of Calif. (bd. govs. 1970-78, pres. 1975), Internat. Platform Assn., Am. Legion (comdr. Allied post 1969-70), Legion Lex (dir. 1964—, pres. 1969-71), Air Force Assn., Aircraft Owners and Pilots Assn., Phi Beta Kappa, Omicron Delta Kappa, Phi Alpha Delta (supreme justice 1972-74, Disting. Service chpt. 1978), Sigma Nu. Presbyterian. Clubs: Rotary, Chancery, Stock Exchange, Commonwealth. Home: 600 John St Manhattan Beach CA 90266 Office: 523 W 6th St Los Angeles CA 90014

RAELSON, JEFFREY ELLIOTT, wine co. exec., fundraising counselor; b. N.Y.C., Oct. 29, 1942; s. Leo and Gertrude (Hammer) R.; B.S., L.I. U., 1965; M.S., Queens Coll., 1967; M.A., Columbia U., 1969; Dr. Gerontology (hon.), London Inst., 1973; m. Paula Barbara Goldman, May 14, 1972; 1 son, Greg David. Asst. prof. recreation and related community services City U. N.Y., 1965-74; regional mgr. Pieroth Bros, Inc., Chgo., 1975-78; pres., chmn. P.J. Gourmand Inc., 1978—; pres., chmn. Japhco Internat., Inc., P.J. Gourmand, Inc., P.J. Gourmand of Greater Boston, Inc.; wine cons. Recipient cert. of service N.Y. State Legis. Adv. Com., 1969; Adminstrn. on Aging grantee, 1968-70. Mem. Pieroth German Wine Soc., Gourmand Societe de Vin, Les Amis de Vin. Clubs: B'nai Brith (v.p. 1978). Author: Getting to Know German Wines, 1979. Office: P J Gourmand 13911 NW 20th Ct Miami FL 33054

RAETTIG, LUTZ ROGER, banker; b. Berlin, Jan. 27, 1943; s. Gerhard and Sigrune Raettig; diploma V.F.M. in Bus. Adminstrn., Hamburg U., 1967, Dr. Rer. Pol., 1969; m. Christiane Richter, Oct. 16, 1970; 1 son, Jan-Philip. Sci. asst. Hamburg (W. Ger.) U., 1967-79, asst. prof. banking and fin., 1969-70; asst. to bd. Westdeutsche Landesbank, Duesseldorf, W. Ger., 1970-73, head Latin Am. dept., 1975-76, head Asia dept., 1976-78, br. mgr., sr. v.p., N.Y.C., 1978—; exec. dir. Orion Multinat. Services Ltd., London, 1973-75; dir. Orion Bank Ltd., London, Orion Pacific Ltd., Hong Kong, Multinat. Orion Leasing Holding N.V., Amsterdam, Libra Bank, London. Mng. dir. Comite Europeen pour le Progress Economique et Social, Frankfurt, W. Ger., 1970-76. Clubs: Apawamis, Board Room; Zur Vahr (Bremen, W. Ger.). Author: Equity Financings, 1974; contbr. articles to profl. jours. Office: 450 Park Ave New York NY 10022

RAEZER, JOHN, computer software co. exec.; b. N.Y.C., Mar. 21, 1941; s. Ottomer and Anna (Kleinfelder) R.; B.A. magna cum laude, Harvard U., 1963; M.A. in Econs., U. Pa., 1964; m. Carol McFadden, July 1, 1967; children—James, Kara, Lauren. Instr. econs. Villanova U., 1964-66; with Smith Barney, Harris Upham, N.Y.C., 1966-67; asst. v.p. Drexel Burnham Lambert, Phila., 1967-68; pres. Streamlight Corp., King of Prussia, Pa., 1973-77; pres. Finpac Corp., Narberth, Pa., 1968—; dir. N.Am. Lace, Mader Group; lectr. advanced mgmt. program U. Hawaii, 1978, U. Pa., 1967—; founder, dir. Omni Exploration, 1969—, Circle Travel, 1974—. Elder, Newtown Square Presbyterian Ch., 1978—; bd. dirs., chmn. fin. com. Center Internat. Visitors, 1978—. Home: Gradyville Rd Newtown Square PA 19073

RAFALKO, JOHN, banker, lessor; b. Fairfield, Iowa, Sept. 26, 1944; s. Alfonse A. and Margaret (Oliver) R.; B.A., Bradley U., 1970; grad. Stonier Grad. Sch. Banking, Rutgers U., 1980; m. Rebecca A. Gower, Aug. 17, 1968; 1 dau., Ann-Martine. Trust rep. Nat. Comml. Bank & Trust Co., Albany, N.Y., 1970-73; asst. v.p., 1975-79; asst. v.p. First Comml. Banks, Inc., Albany, 1973-75; vice-pres., mgr.-in-charge UBC Leasing of N.Y., Albany, 1979—; dir. Living Resource Corp., Living Resource Devel. Corp. Served with U.S. Army, 1963-66. Mem. Am. Inst. Banking, Assn. Registered Bank Holding Cos. (leasing com.), Am. Assn. Leasing Agts., Am. Assn. Equipment Lessors. Democrat. Roman Catholic. Club: Winding Brook Country.

RAFFERTY, CHRISTOPHER LAWRENCE, investment exec.; b. N.Y.C., May 12, 1948; s. Bernard and Natalie Church (Rice) R.; B.A., Stanford U., 1970; J.D., Georgetown U., 1975. Admitted to Tex. bar, 1975; asso. firm Bracewell & Patterson, Houston, 1975-78; v.p., house counsel Coronado Minerals Co., Houston, 1978-79; investment officer Union Venture Corp., Los Angeles, 1980—. Served to lt. USN, 1970-72. Mem. State Bar Tex., Am. Bar Assn. Office: 445 S Figueroa St Los Angeles CA 90071

RAFTIS, MICHAEL JOSEPH, advt. agy. exec.; b. Waterloo, Iowa, Apr. 12, 1941; s. Harold J. and Coletta M. Raftis; children—Wendy, Connie, Jill, Robin, Lacy, Jennifer. With Sears, Roebuck & Co., Mpls., 1962-64; profl. musician, 1962-68; sales and sta. mgr. Sta. WSMJ, Greenfield, Ind., 1968-70; account exec. Sta. WIFE, Indpls., 1970-72; owner, gen. mgr. Sta. WVTS, Terre Haute, Ind., 1972-77; partner Eisenhardt & Assos., Terre Haute, 1977-78; air personality Sta. WBOW, Terre Haute, 1978—; pres. Raftis: The Agy., Terre Haute, 1980—; owner, pub. TV Facts of Terre Haute, 1980—; partner Pink Flamingo Bar & Restaurant, Terre Haute, 1980—. Bd. dirs. Terre Haute Girls Club, Heart Assn. Served with USN, 1958-62. Mem. Advt. Rev. Council (dir.), Better Bus. Bur. (dir.), Terre Haute Ad Club (past pres.), Am. Legion, VFW. Democrat. Roman Catholic. Elk. Home: 33 S 22d St Terre Haute IN 47807 Office: 68 Ohio St Terre Haute IN 47807

RAGAN, SEABORN BRYANT TIMMONS, businessman; b. Augusta, Ga., Apr. 28, 1929; s. Alexander Timothy and Ela Lucille (Timmons) R.; student Emory U., 1946-49, U. Ga., 1952-53; A.B., Ga. State Coll., 1959; m. Sandra Glyn Farris, Sept. 5, 1958; children—Seaborn Bryant Timmons, Sandra Leigh. With Gulf Oil Co., various locations, 1957—, v.p. Korea Oil mktg. ops., Seoul, Korea, 1967-73, dist. mktg. mgr., Phila., 1973-76, project mgr. new products and new bus. devel., mktg. coordination, Houston, 1976-79, dir. market research Gulf Oil U.S., 1979—. Counselor, USO, Korea, 1972-73. Served with U.S. Army Res., 1948-60. Mem. alumni exec. com. Salisbury Sch., Conn., 1975-76, S.W. field rep., 1976—. Mem. SAR, Audubon Soc., Soc. Archtl. Historians, Nat. Trust for Historic Preservation, Nat. Hist. Soc., Nat. Geog. Soc., Smithsonian Assos., Am. Mus. Natural History Assos., Am. Enterprise Inst. for Public Policy Research (asso.), Nat. Archives Assos., Victorian Soc., Cousteau Soc., Oceanic Soc., Am. Field Service, Internat. Platform Assn., Am. Mktg. Assn., Houston Bd. Realtors. Republican. Episcopalian. Club: Wilchester. Home: 13502 Barryknoll St Houston TX 77079 Office: 2 Houston Center PO Box 1519 Houston TX 77001

RAGAN, WILLIAM ANDREW, health care exec.; b. Homestead Park, Pa., Sept. 22, 1926; s. John David and Susan (Luteran) R.; A.B., Dartmouth Coll., 1947; Ph.D., U. N.D., 1949; postgrad. Ohio State U., 1949-51; m. Mary Irene Howley, Feb. 3, 1951; children—John David, Kathleen, Bridgette, Christine, William Andrew, Maureen. Research mgr. E.I. DuPont De Nemours & Co., Inc., Circleville, Ohio, Buffalo, Florence, S.C., 1951-70; with RCA, Indpls., 1970-72; chief engr. research and devel. Kendall Co., Boston, 1972-76, dir. indsl. product research, 1972-73, v.p. research and devel., 1973-76; v.p. research and devel. Becton-Dickinson, Rutherford, N.J., 1976—. Advisor, Nat. Tech. Info. Service, 1979-80; mem. domestic policy review on innovation Commerce Dept., 1979. Mem. Am. Chem. Soc., AAAS, N.Y. Acad. Sci., Indsl. Research Inst. Home: 121 Oak Dr Upper Saddle River NJ 07458 Office: Rutherford NJ 07070

RAGOT, HENRY WARREN, lawyer, state asst atty. gen.; b. Mt. Kisco, N.Y., June 30, 1921; s. Henry E. and Mabel P. (Mandeville) R.; A.B., Lafayette Coll., 1943; LL.B., U. Pa., 1946; m. Virginia F. Valentine, May 16, 1953; 1 dau., Kathleen E. Admitted to Pa. bar, 1950; individual practice law, Easton, Pa., 1947-60; asst. title officer Commonwealth Land Title Ins. Co., Lancaster, Pa., Phila., 1954-60, title officer City Title Ins. Co., Levittown, Pa., 1960-69; asst. atty. gen. Pa. Gen. State Authority (merged into Pa. Dept. Gen. Services 1975), Harrisburg, 1969—; dir. Consol. Realty Corp., Diversified Real Estate Trust; instr. realty courses. Sec. council St. Mark's Evangelical Luth. Ch., Harrisburg, Pa., 1970-75; del. Central Pa. Synod, 1978, pres. Central Pa. alumni, 1971, 79. Mem. Pa. Bar Assn. Home: 3103 Schoolhouse Ln Harrisburg PA 17109 Office: Pennsylvania Dept General Services 6th Floor North Office Bldg Harrisburg PA 17120

RAHMANI, GHOLAMREZA MOSSAVER, travel bur. exec.; b. Tehran, Iran, Jan. 17, 1912; s. Aliasghar and Khadijeh Rahmani; came to U.S., 1963; B.S., Air Force Cadet Sch., Tehran, 1935; grad. Staff and War Coll., Tehran, 1940; LL.B., U. Tehran, 1943; B.S., Ecole Superieur de Nav. Aerienne, France, 1947; M.B.A., Columbia U., N.Y.C., 1965; m. Pourandokht Amir-Fazli, June 11, 1949; children—Yasmin, Ali, Sohrab, Farhad. Formerly dep. chief of staff edn. and ops. Iranian Air Force, concurrently sec., dir. Air Force Fedn. Ski and Mountaineering Club; prof. tactics and logistics, subsequently chmn. air ops. studies Staff and War Coll., Tehran, 1940-52; Iranian mil. attache in Iraq, Jordan and Syria, 1952-53; mgr. internat. dept. Bank Saderat, Tehran, 1954-59, gen. mgr., Hamburg, 1959-62, Paris and London, 1962-63; pres. Persepolis Travel, Ltd., N.Y.C., 1967—. Served to col. Iranian Air Force, 1935-54. Decorated Merit medal, 2 Sci. medals for publs. in air navigation and missiles. Mem. Alumni Assn. Grad. Sch. Bus. Columbia U. Liberal. Home: 98-05 67th Ave Forest Hills NY 11374 Office: 667 Madison Ave New York NY 10021

RAHN, ALVIN ALBERT, banker; b. St. Paul, Apr. 8, 1925; s. Albert and Manda (Lau) R.; B.B.A., U. Minn., 1949; grad. Stonier Grad. Sch. Banking, 1968; m. Helen B. Lyngen, June 10, 1950; children—Jennifer, Karen, Paul. Sr. v.p., treas. First Bank System, Inc., Mpls., 1975—; dir. FBS Fin. Inc., First System Agys. Served with U.S. Navy, 1943-46. C.P.A., Minn. Mem. Fin. Execs. Inst., Am. Inst. C.P.A.'s, Minn. Soc. C.P.A.'s. Club: Mpls. Athletic. Office: PO Box 522 Minneapolis MN 55480

RAHT, JOHN MILTON, pub. co. exec.; b. Hereford, Tex., June 6, 1928; s. Carlysle Graham and Lula Franklin (Orr) R.; B.A., Ariz. State U., 1955, postgrad., 1959-61; children—Charles William, David Graham. Field rep. textbook dept. Holt, Rinehart & Winston Pub., N.Y.C., 1961-67; editor Glencoe Press subs. Macmillan, Beverly Hills, Calif., 1967-70; v.p. Computer Technology Info. Inc., Newport Beach, Calif., 1970-72; Western mgr. NBC Ednl. Enterprises, Burbank, Calif., 1972-75; founder, mgr. Ednl. Noises & Sounds Pub. Co., San Clemente, Calif., 1975—. Served with U.S. Army, 1950-53; Korea. Decorated Bronze Star, Silver Star. Author: (with B. Raht) Guide to Southern California, 1971; Sound Stories and Sound Library, 1974; (with A. Elwood) Points of View, 1975, Walking Out, 1979. Home and Office: Box 591 San Clemente CA 92672

RAIHALL, DENIS TAYLOR, educator; b. Pitts., Mar. 2, 1941; s. Stephen Francis and Dorothy Jane (Taylor) R.; B.A., Bethany Coll., 1962; M.B.A., U. Pitts., 1963; Ph.D. in Finance, Pa. State U., 1967; m. Sydney Suzanne Stover, Dec. 28, 1963; children—Jeffrey, James, Steven, Douglas. Asst prof. U. Del., Newark, 1966-70; asso. prof. and asso. dean sch. bus. and econs. Calif. State U., Hayward, 1970-73; prof. finance Am. Coll., Bryn Mawr, Pa., 1973—, chmn. finance dept., 1973-74, dean grad. sch. fin. scis., 1974-77, v.p. for academic affairs, 1977-80; prof. acctg. Drexel U., Phila., 1980—. Pres. Sentinel Equity Assn., 1967-73; dir. Calif. Energy Corp.; cons. Nat. Assn. Mutual Savs. Banks, 1968, Bank Adminstrn. Inst., 1977. Recipient Wall St. Jour. award, 1962, Excellence in Teaching award, U. Del., 1969. Mem. Am., Eastern Finance assns., Fin. Mgmt. Assn., Beta Gamma Sigma, Sigma Nu. Author: Family Finance, 1975; Money Managament for the Consumer, 1975. Editor: Savings Bank Financial Management, 1979. Home: 1206 Clearbrook Rd West Chester PA 19380 Office: Coll of Business Drexel U Philadelphia PA 19104

RAINER, DONALD LEEVAN, banker; b. Albia, Iowa, Mar. 19, 1926; s. Herman Lester and Vesta Ida (Meek) R.; B.S., N.E. Mo. State U., 1952; M.B.A., Iowa State U., 1977; m. Josephine Iris McCarty, June 2, 1948; children—Deborah Ann, Randall Lee. Tchr. pub. schs., Edison, Nebr., Winthrop and Newhall, Iowa, 1952-58; sales mgr. North Iowa Hatcheries, Osage, 1958-59; fieldman Farm Bur., Fayette, Iowa, 1959-63; asst. cashier Bank of Fayette, 1963-66, Security State Bank, Pine Island, 1966-68; v.p., loan Adminstr. Decatur County State Bank, Leon, Iowa, 1968-73; with Bankers Trust Co., Des Moines, 1973—, v.p., agr. specialist, 1978—. Mem. Iowa Vocat. Edn. Council; chmn. bd. dirs. Decator County Hosp., 1972-73; chmn. bd. trustees United Meth. Ch., 1971; active Boy Scouts Am. Served with AF, USN, 1944-46. Mem. Iowa Bankers Assn., Farmers Grain and Livestock Assn., Am. Inst. Banking, Assn. M.B.A. Execs. Republican. Home: 702 S 5th St Grimes IA 50111 Office: 110 S Main Grimes IA 50111

RAINER, LOUISE ELAINE, planning tax seminar exec.; b. Indpls., Sept. 25, 1942; d. John Francis and Wynona E. (Thornburg) Byrd; grad. S. Jersey Bus. Machines, 1960; student Purdue U., 1960-61, Cambridge (Ohio) Coll., 1962-63; children—Brenda Louise, Veronica Jean. Pvt. sec. Edmund Sci. Research Co., Barrington, N.J., 1961-62, Radio Corp. Am., Cambridge, Ohio, 1962-64, Prudential Ins. Co., Cheyenne, Wyo., 1964-67, Muncie, Ind., 1967-69, Columbus, Ohio, 1970-72; operator Texaco Service Sta., Winchester, Ind., 1968-70; golden galaxy mgr. Tupperware, Dart Industries, Columbus, 1972-75; with The Merchant Prince (Trading Corp. Am.), Columbus, 1975—, state dir., 1976-79; planning tax seminar exec.; Colorado Springs, Colo., 1979—. Fund raiser chmn. Fire Dept., New Albany, Ohio; chmn. Red Cross, Haddonfield, N.J.; chmn. Heart Fund Dr., Cheyenne; mem. Columbus Schs. PTO; inservice leader and tchr. devel. course dir. Mormon Ch., Columbus. Recipient Lions Club Citizenship award, 1959. Mem. Nat. Assn. Life Underwriters, Postal Commemorative Soc., Powder Room Guns and Ammo Pistol Club. Republican. Home: 1422 Kiowa Box 307 Florissant CO 80816 Office: 2 N Nevada Suite 1420 Colorado Springs CO 80903

RAINES, RONALD BRUCE, accountant; b. Sydney, Australia, Nov. 6, 1929; s. Douglas William and Jean Laurie (Pilcher) R.; diploma Sydney Boys High Sch., 1947; m. Helen Janet Cadwallader, Oct. 21, 1977; children—Ronald Douglas, Fenella Jann, Douglas Antony. Partner, R.A. Irish & Michelmore, Chartered Accountants, Sydney, 1955-65; chmn. bd. Australian Elec. Industries Ltd., 1964-68, New S. Wales State Dockyard, 1968-77; dir. The Greater Union Orgn. Ltd., Kemtron Ltd., Enacon Ltd., Blue Metal Industries Ltd., Nat. Mut. Life Assn. Australasia Ltd., Johnson Matthey Holdings Ltd., P.T. Koba Tin, Citinational Ltd., Kajuara Mining Corp. Ltd., Alex Howden Group (Australia) Ltd., Eastmet Ltd., Nat. Mut. Bldg. Soc. N.S.W., Brambles Crouch Ltd., Found. 41, 600 Machinery Australia Pty. Ltd. Mem. Legis. Council New S. Wales, 1977-78, Met. (Sydney) Waste Disposal Authority. Fellow Chartered Inst. Accountants Australia, Australian Inst. Mgmt., Securities Inst. Australia. Clubs: Australian, Royal Sydney Golf, Australian Jockey, Sydney Turf. Home: Point Piper New South Wales Australia Office: GPO Box 1742 Sydney New South Wales 2001 Australia

RAINEY, NINA GLADYS DULLEN, pub. co. exec.; b. Avis, Pa., Mar. 13, 1935; d. Charles Franklin and Nina Gladys Dullen Stover; student U. Colo.; children—Kathy Eileen Rainey, Brian Matthew. Asst. mgr. Slenderelle Internat., Phila., 1958-59, Singer Sewing Center, Williamsport, Pa., 1960-61; sales exec. Edgerton Realty, Kenmore, Wash., 1966-67; mgr. Inter Mark Inc., Denver, 1970-71; with Barnum Pub. Co., Inc., Denver, 1971—, v.p. bus., dir., 1972—. Publicity chmn. King County Hosp. Number 2 Commn., Bothell, Wash., 1967; pres. King County Hosp. Aux., Bothell, 1967; publicity chmn. S.W. Republicans, Denver, 1973-74; mem. Rep. Nat. Com.; mem. nat. adv. bd. Am. Security Council; adminstrv. asst. to councilman Denver City Council, 1971-75. Mem. Nat. Geog. Soc., Smithsonian Instn., Uptown Bus. and Profl. Women's Club, Internat. Platform Assn. Clubs: Lincoln, U.S. Senatorial. Home: 1290 S Williams St Denver CO 80210

RAISMAN, MYRON STUART, accountant, lawyer; b. Bklyn., Apr. 29, 1935; s. Irving and Mildred (Goldberg) R.; B.B.A. cum laude, CCNY, 1955; LL.B., N.Y. U., 1960; m. Susan Jacobs, June 23, 1957; children—Nancy, Ruth. Accountant, Simonoff, Peyers & Citrin, C.P.A.'s, N.Y.C., 1955-57, Irving Raisman, C.P.A., N.Y.C., 1957-60; admitted to N.Y. bar, 1960; partner firm Raisman & Raisman, C.P.A.'s and attys., N.Y.C., 1960-68; individual practice acctg. and law, Smithtown, N.Y., 1968-69; sr. partner firm Raisman & Spinner, C.P.A.'s, Deer Park, N.Y., 1969—; guest lectr. Columbia U., C.W. Post Coll.; charter mem. Center Banking and Money Mgmt., Adelphia U., Garden City, N.Y.; mem. Tax Inst., C.W. Post Coll. Bd. dirs. Greater N.Y., United Jewish Appeal, 1980, mem. bd. govs., asso. exec. chmn. Eastern L.I., 1980, cash chmn. Eastern L.I., 1978-70; v.p. YM-YWHA Suffolk County, 1979; bd. dirs. Commack (N.Y.) Jewish Center, 1980. C.P.A., N.Y. Mem. N.Y. State Soc. C.P.A.'s, Beta Gamma Sigma. Republican. Jewish. Home: 35 New Mill Rd Smithtown NY 11787 Office: 2100 Deer Park Ave Deer Park NY 11729

RAJPUROHIT, DAVID S., mfg. co. exec.; b. India, June 16, 1945; came to U.S., 1969, naturalized, 1978; s. Kan S. and Yasoda B. Rajpurohit; B.S. with honors in Mech. Engring., U. Jodhpur, 1967; M.S. with honors in Mech. Engring., Indian Inst. Tech., Bombay, 1969; M.S. in Indsl. Engring., Stanford U., 1970; m. Hansa Purohit, Sept. 2, 1957. Mgmt. cons., Palo Alto, Calif., 1970-71; sr. indsl. engr. Maidenform Co., Bayonne, N.J., 1971-74; project mgr. corp. planning Johnson & Johnson, New Brunswick, N.J., 1974-76; mgr. productivity engring. Becton Dickinson & Co., Rutherford, N.J., 1976-79, dir. indsl. engring., 1979—. Nat. Merit scholar, 1962-69; Tata and Mahindra scholar, 1969. Mem. Am. Inst. Indsl. Engrs. (chpt. program chm. 1974), ASME, Am. Mgmt. Assn., Inst. Mgmt. Sci. Hindu. Club: United Runners (Ridgewood). Author, patentee in field. Home: 629 Grove St Ridgewood NJ 07450 Office: Becton Dickinson Co Stanley St Rutherford NJ 07070

RALEIGH, W. JAMES, textile co. exec.; b. Newark, Feb. 28, 1928; s. Walter J. and Eleanor F. (Stevens) R.; B.S., Seton Hall U., 1950; children—Kimberly, Christopher. Gen. sales mgr. Chicopee Mfg. Co., Boston, also Evanston, Ill., Cornelia, Ga., N.Y.C., to 1964; pres. Clinton Mills Sales Corp., N.Y.C., 1965—; instr. Northeastern U., 1956-60. Bd. dirs. N.Y. Found. for Sr. Citizens, 1981—; mem. Mayor's Adv. Council, N.Y.C., 1981—; sr. v.p. N.Y. Bd. Trade, 1981, chmn. textile sect., 1975-77. Served with USCG, 1945-47. Mem. Am. Textile Mfrs. Inst. (chmn. mktg. com. 1980), Anti-Defamation League B'nai B'rith (chmn. 1980). Clubs: University, Bay Head Yacht. Home: 81 Irving Pl New York NY 10003 Office: 111 W 40th St New York NY 10018

RALSTON, CARL CONRAD, constrn. co. exec.; b. Owensboro, Ky., Nov. 1, 1927; s. Carl C. and Elizabeth (Little) R.; Asso. B.B.A., Ky. Bus. Coll., 1949; B.A., Ky. Wesleyan Coll., 1956; m. Patricia Warren, Nov. 12, 1971; children—Pamela Kay, Kelly Michelle. Pub. accountant, 1956; chief accountant, estimator Mills & Jones Constrn. Co., St. Petersburg, Fla., 1957-60, project mgr., 1960-65, v.p., 1965-79, sr. v.p., 1979—. Pres., Cross Bayou Little League, Seminole, Fla., 1959-61; treas. Seminole Lake Civic Assn., Seminole, 1959-62. Trustee Southeastern Ironworkers' Health and Welfare Fund. Served with USAAF, 1945-47. Mem. Am. Mgmt. Assn., Assn. Gen. Contractors (chpt. dir. 1969-70), Am. Inst. Constructors, Am. Soc. Profl. Estimators. Clubs: St. Petersburg Yacht; Feather Sound Country, Seminole Lake Country (gov. 1964-67, chmn. bd. 1967-68) (Seminole), Masons. Home: 1451 Seagull Dr S Pasadena FL 33707 Office: 400 23d St S Saint Petersburg FL 33731

RAMAT, EMIL, bus. exec.; b. Czechoslovakia, Nov. 1, 1922; s. Samuel and Charlotte (Einhorn) Rosenberg; student in Czechoslovakia; m. Hanna Landa, Feb. 10, 1946 (dec.); children—Vera, Charles. Vice-pres., Puro-Ramat Properties, Inc., N.Y.C., 1961; pres. Prel Corp., real estate, N.Y.C., 1961-66, chmn. bd., chief exec. officer, 1969-72; pres. Inter-Coastal Properties, Inc., real estate, Orangeburg, N.Y., 1964-69; partner Graylyn Assos., real estate, N.Y.C., 1964—, Ramat and Landa, Orangeburg, 1965-69; pres. Ramland Properties, Inc., Orangeburg, 1965-69, Lak-How Realty Corp., Orangeburg, 1965—, Ramelle Properties, Inc., Orangeburg, 1965-68, Ramble Properties Corp., Orangeburg, 1965-69; v.p. Arlan Corp., real estate, Orangeburg, 1965—; partner Piermont Realty Corp., Orangeburg, 1965—, Haverstraw Indsl. Park Co., Orangeburg, 1969; pres. Prel Plaza, Inc., Orangeburg, 1966-69; v.p. Lanram Corp., real estate, Orangeburg, 1966—, Colline Properties, Inc., real estate, Orangeburg, 1966—; partner Prel Gardens Co., real estate, Orangeburg, 1967-69, R. L. & W. Property Co., Orangeburg, 1967-69;

pres. Marram Properties, Inc., Orangeburg, 1967—, Sparkill Indl. Park Co., Orangeburg, 1967—; chmn. bd., chief exec. officer Midland Resources Inc., Ft. Lee, N.J.; dir. Bankers Trust Hudson Valley, N.A. Served as capt. Czech Legion; Russia. Decorated Fgn. Disting. Service award. Club: Town of City of N.Y. Office: 1530 Palisade Ave Fort Lee NJ 07024

RAMBERT, GORDON ARTHUR, corp. exec.; b. Rochester, N.Y., Mar. 6, 1922; s. Arthur Frederick and Mildred (Baker) R.; B.S., Lehigh U., 1949; m. Jeanne Audrey Bucher, Dec. 27, 1947; children—Paul A., Cynthia L., Gregory N., Michele M. Personnel mgr. Jamestown Malleable Iron Corp. (N.Y.), 1955-58; mgr. compensation Todd div. Burroughs Corp., Rochester, 1958-64; asst. sec., dir. personnel Consol-Vacuum Corp., Rochester, 1964-66; v.p. indsl. relations Joslyn Mfg. & Supply Co., Chgo., 1966-70; pres. Rambert and Co., Inc., mgmt. cons., Lake Bluff, Ill., 1970—; adv. cons. on exec. compensation Midwest Indsl. Mgmt. Assn. Served with Signal Corps AUS, 1942-46. Mem. Am. Soc. Personnel Adminstrn. (dir. 1968—, treas. 1970, 71), Indsl. Relations Assn., Indsl. Relations Research Assn., N.A.M. (indsl. relations com.), Lambs (dir.). Home: 641 Williams Ct Gurnee IL 60031 Office: 11 N Skokie Hwy Lake Bluff IL 60044

RAMER, LAWRENCE JEROME, business exec.; b. Bayonne, N.J., July 29, 1928; s. Sidney and Anne (Strassman) R.; B.A. in Econs., Lafayette Coll., 1950; M.B.A., Harvard, 1957; m. Ina Lee Brown, June 30, 1957; children—Stephanie Beryl, Susan Meredith, Douglas Strassman. Sales rep. then v.p. United Sheet Metal Co., Bayonne, 1953-55; with Am. Cement Corp., 1957-64, v.p. marketing div. Riverside Cement Co., 1960-62, v.p. marketing parent co., 1962-64; vice chmn. bd., chief exec. officer Clavier Corp., N.Y.C., 1965-66; exec. v.p. Pacific Western Industries, Los Angeles, 1966-68, vice chmn. bd., 1968-70; chmn. bd. Perry-Austen Mfg. Co., N.Y.C., 1970-71; pres. Ramer Corp., Los Angeles, 1971-72; chmn. bd. Luminall Paints, Inc., Los Angeles, 1972—, Somerset Mgmt. Group, Los Angeles, 1975—; pres., chief exec. officer Nat. Portland Cement Co. Fla., 1975—; chmn. bd., chief exec. officer Bruning Paint Co., Balt., 1979—, Pacific Coast Cement Co., Los Angeles, 1979—; chmn. Sutro Partners, Inc., Los Angeles, 1977—. Trustee, Lafayette Coll., Easton, Pa.; exec. bd. Am. Jewish Com., Los Angeles. Office: 1800 Century Park E Los Angeles CA 90067

RAMLOW, DONALD ERIC, mgmt. cons.; b. Toledo, Apr. 13, 1919; s. Albert G. and Anna M. (Bullerdick) R.; student Wittenberg U., 1936-38, U. Toledo, 1938, U. W.Va., 1943-44; m. Helen R. Cousineau, Aug. 16, 1941; children—Patricia Ann, Donald Gilbert, Linna Dell. Indsl. engr. Detroit Harvester Co., Toledo, 1940-42; various exec. positions Owens Corning Fiberglas Corp., Newark, Ohio, 1946-57; asso. A.T. Kearney, Inc., Chgo., 1957-61, prin., 1962-64, v.p., 1965-75, pres., 1975—; dir., chmn. exec. com. RTE Corp.; dir., chmn. nominating and dir. practices committee Koehring Co. Bd. dirs. Family Care Services, 1972; vice chmn. suburban campaign United Way/Crusade of Mercy, 1975, chief crusader, 1976-80; mem. allocations com. United Way, 1976—. Served to capt. AUS, 1942-46. Mem. Assn. Cons. Mgmt. Engrs. (past dir.), Inst. Mgmt. Cons., Ill. C. of C. (chmn. bd. 1978-80), Chgo. Assn. Commerce and Industry. Lutheran. Clubs: Chicago, Park Ridge Country. Co-author: Production Planning and Control, 1967. Home: 931 S Broadway Park Ridge IL 60068 Office: A T Kearney Inc 100 S Wacker St Chicago IL 60606

RAMO, SIMON, engring. exec.; b. Salt Lake City, May 7, 1913; s. Benjamin and Clara (Trestman) R.; B.S., U. Utah, 1933, D.Sc. (hon.), 1961; Ph.D., Calif. Inst. Tech., 1936; D.Eng. (hon.), Case Inst. Tech., 1960, U. Mich., 1966, Poly. Inst. N.Y., 1971; D.Sc. (hon.), Union Coll., 1963, Worcester Poly. Inst., 1968, U. Akron, 1969, Cleve. State U., 1976; LL.D. (hon.), Carnegie Mellon U., 1970, U. So. Calif., 1972; m. Virginia May Smith, July 25, 1937; children—James Brian, Alan Martin. With Gen. Electric Co., 1936-46; v.p., dir. ops. Hughes Aircraft Co., 1946-53; with The Ramo-Wooldridge Corp., Los Angeles, 1953-58; pres. Space Tech. Labs., 1957-58; sci. dir. U.S. intercontinental guided missile program, 1954-58; pres. Bunker-Ramo Corp., 1964-66; dir. TRW Inc., 1954—, chmn. sci. and tech. com., 1978—, exec. v.p., 1958-61, vice chmn. bd., 1961-78, chmn. exec. com., 1969-78, chmn. bd. TRW-Fujitsu Co., 1980—; vis. prof. mgmt. sci. Calif. Inst. Tech., 1978—; chmn. Center for Study of Am. Experience, U. So. Calif., 1978—; faculty fellow J.F. Kennedy Sch. Govt., Harvard U., 1980—; dir. Union Bank, Times Mirror Co.; chmn. Pres.'s Com. on Sci. and Tech., 1976-77; mem. sec.'s adv. council Dept. Commerce, 1976-77; mem. roster of consultants to adminstr. ERDA, 1976-77. Mem. White House Energy Research and Devel. Adv. Council, 1973-75; mem. adv. com. on sci. and fgn. affairs U.S. State Dept., 1973-75. Trustee emeritus Calif. State Univs.; trustee Nat. Symphony Orch. Assn., Calif. Inst. Tech.; bd. visitors UCLA Sch. Medicine, 1980—; bd. govs. Performing Arts Council of Music Center Los Angeles; bd. dirs. Music Center Found., Los Angeles World Affairs Council, Nat. Energy Found. Recipient awards Eta Kappa Nu; Electronic Achievement award IEEE, 1953; Turnbull award I.A.S., 1956; Steinmetz award AIEE, 1959; Schwab award Am. Iron and Steel Inst., 1968; P.T. Johns award Arnold Air Soc., 1960; Am. Acad. Achievement award, 1964; WEMA medal of achievement, 1970; Distinguished Service gold medal AFCEA, 1970; Outstanding Achievement in Bus. Mgmt. award U. So. Calif., 1971; Kayan medal Columbia U., 1972; award of merit Am. Cons. Engrs. Council, 1974; Golden Omega award IEEE-M.E.N.A., 1975; Delmer S. Fahrney medal The Franklin Inst., 1978; Outstanding Achievement award in Engring. Mgmt., U. So. Calif., 1979; Nat. medal of Sci., 1979; Bus. Statesman award Harvard Bus. Sch. Assn., 1979; Founders medal IEEE, 1980. Fellow IEEE, AIAA, Am. Acad. Arts and Scis., Am. Phys. Soc., AAAS; founding mem. Nat. Acad. Engring.; mem. Nat. Acad. Scis., Am. Philos. Soc. Author sci., engring. and mgmt. books. Office: 1 Space Park Redondo Beach CA 90278

RAMOS, ARTHUR LOUIS, mktg. exec.; b. N.Y.C., May 17, 1944; s. Fabian D. and Mary E. (Pallozzi) R.; B.S., N.Y. Inst. Tech., 1969; M.S., Antioch U., 1981; m. Elizabeth E. Earls, July 6, 1973; children—Jennifer, Meredith. Sr. tech. writer Digitronics, Inc., Albertson, N.Y., 1968-70; publs. mgr. Iomec, Inc., Southboro, Mass., 1970-73; publs. mgr. Waters Assos., Milford, Mass., 1973-76, communications mgr., 1976-80, internat. mktg. communications mgr., 1980—. Mem. Am. Mgmt. Assn., Am. Mktg. Assn., Soc. Tech. Communicators. Office: 34 Maple St Milford MA 01757

RAMSEY, DOUGLAS VAUGHN, banker; b. Staunton, Va., Nov. 1, 1947; s. Tully Vaughn and Martha Marie (Bower) R.; student Ky. Wesleyan Coll., 1967, Va. Commonwealth U., 1969-74, Va./Md. Bankers Sch., 1975; grad. Bus. of Banking Sch., 1977; m. Tracy Leigh Baldwin, Nov. 30, 1968; children—Patience Leigh, Michael Vaughn. Mgr. corp. depository services United Va. Bankshares, Inc., Richmond, 1971-73, quality control mgr., 1973-74, sr. ops. officer, 1974-76; v.p. Central Bank & Trust Co., Lexington, Ky., 1976-78; v.p. ops. Am. Security Bank, N.A., Washington, 1979—; instr. Lexington chpt. Am. Inst. Banking. Corp. team capt. United Way, Richmond, 1975-76; adult vol. Reston Youth Soccer; bd. dirs. Reston Community Assn., 1980—; team coach Reston Youth Basketball; hotline counselor Crisis Intervention, Richmond, 1975-76. Mem. Bank Adminstrn. Inst. (chpt. ops. com.), Mid-Atlantic Clearinghouse Assn. (dir.), Met. Area Work Mgmt. Assn., Am. Mgmt. Assn., Am. Bankers Assn. Republican. Baptist. Home: 2214 Golf Course Dr Reston VA 22091 Office: 635 Massachusetts Ave NW Washington DC 20001

RAMSEY, RALPH HEYWARD, JR., lawyer; b. Wedgefield, S.C. Apr. 7, 1900; s. Ralph Heyward and Una Elizabeth (Wells) R.; B.S., U. S.C., 1921, M.A., 1923, LL.B., 1924; m. Mary Dick Alford, Aug. 27, 1926; children—Mary Ann, Ralph Heyward, III, Gayle Edward, Sarah Martha. Admitted to S.C. bar, 1924, N.C., 1926; mem. firm Purdy & Ramsey, Sumter, S.C., 1924-26; practice of law, Hendersonville, N.C., 1926, Brevard, N.C., 1926—; sr. mem. firm Ramsey, Hill, Smart, Ramsey & Hunt, P.A. and predecessor firm, 1961—; city atty. Brevard, 1933-53; county atty. Transylvania County (N.C.), 1939-60, 64-72; dir., sec. Golf Club Estates, Inc., Round Hill Estates, Inc.; sec.-treas., dir. Evergreen Devel. Co.; asst. sec. Sapphire Valley Devel. Corp., Connestee Falls Devel. Corp. Mem. N.C. Sch. Commn., 1941-43, Commn. on Solicitorial and Jud. Dists., 1945-47, N.C. Gen. Statutes Commn., 1946-49, N.C. Medical Care Commn., 1953-56, Western N.C. Regional Planning Commn., 1956-61, N.C. State Bar Council, 1962-75. Mayor, Town of Brevard, 1931-33; mem. N.C. Senate, 1935-37. Trustee Transylvania Community Hosp. (chmn.); chmn. Lyday Meml. Hosp., Brevard, 1933-40; trustee Mars Hill Coll., vice chmn., 1965-66, chmn., 1970-71, 73—. Mem. Internat. Platform Assn., C. of C. (dir. 1935-75), Am. Legion, Brevard Music Found. (trustee 1947-60), N.C. State Bar (2d v.p. 1972, 1st v.p. 1973, pres. 1974), Am., N.C., S.C., 29th Jud. Dist., Transylvania County bar assns., N.C. Jud. Council, Pi Kappa Phi. Democrat. Baptist. Kiwanian (lt. gov. Div. 1, Carolinas Dist. 1965). Club: Lake Toxaway Country. Author booklet and articles. Home: High Meadows Route 4 Box 196 Brevard NC 28712 Office: Legal Bldg Brevard NC 28712

RAMSEY, ROGER ALAN, financial exec.; b. Houston, June 25, 1938; s. Theo Adolph and Madeline Esther (Anderson) R.; B.S. in Commerce cum laude, Tex. Christian U., 1960; m. Gayle Etta Garbs, Jan. 27, 1957; children—Craig, Christopher, Carrie, Curtis. Mgr. tax dept. Arthur Andersen & Co., Houston, 1960-69; v.p., treas. Am. Refuse Systems, Inc., Houston, 1969; v.p. fin. Browning-Ferris Industries, Inc., 1969-76; pres. Criterion Capital Corp., Houston, 1976—; organizer Parkway Nat. Bank; chmn. bd. Criterion Mgmt. Co.; dir. Funds Adv. Co., Houston, Funds, Inc., Consol. Fibres, Inc., San Francisco, Fannin Bank, Houston, The Houstonian, Inc. Mem. Fin. Execs. Inst., Am. Inst. C.P.A.'s, Tex. Soc. C.P.A.'s, Tex. Christian U. Alumni Assn. (v.p., dir. nat. orgn.), Beta Gamma Sigma, Sigma Alpha Epsilon. Methodist. Clubs: Houston Racquet, Houstonian; Les Ambassadeurs (London). Home: 380 Blalock St Houston TX 77024 Office: 111 N Post Oak Ln Houston TX 77024

RAMSEY, WILLIAM DALE, JR., petroleum co. sales exec.; b. Indpls., Apr. 14, 1936; s. William Dale and Laura Jane (Stout) R.; A.B. in Econs. (James Bowdoin scholar), Bowdoin Coll., 1958; m. Mary Alice Ihnet, Aug. 9, 1969; children—Robin, Scott, Kimberly, Jennifer. With Shell Oil Co., 1958—, salesman, Albany, N.Y., 1960, mdsg. rep., Milton, N.Y., 1961-63, real estate and mktg. investments rep., Jacksonville, Fla., 1963-65, dist. sales supr., St. Paul, 1965-67, employee relations rep., Chgo., 1967-69, spl. assignment mktg. staff-adminstrn., N.Y.C., recruitment mgr., Chgo., 1970-72, sales mgr., Chgo., 1973-75, sales mgr., Detroit, 1975-79, dist. mgr. N.J. and Pa., Newark, 1979—; dir. N.Am. Fin. Services, 1971-72; lectr., speaker on energy, radio, TV, appearances, 1972—; guest lectr. on bus. five univs., 1967-72; v.p., dir. Malibu East Corp., 1973-74; mem. Am. Right of Way Assn., 1963-65. Active Chgo. Urban League, 1971-75; mem. program com., bus. adv. council Nat. Republican Congressional Com.; mem. Gov.'s Council on Tourism and Commerce, Minn., 1965-67; mem. Founders Soc., Detroit Inst. Arts. Served to capt. U.S. Army, 1958-60. Mem. Soc. Environ. Econ. Devel., N.J. Petroleum Council (exec. com.), Midwest Coll. Placement Assn., Chem. and Petroleum Employer Com., N.J. C. of C., Met. Detroit Conv. and Visitors Bur. Presbyterian. Clubs: Ponte Vedra, Beechview Racket and Swim, Bowdoin Alumni Club N.Y.C. Author Corp. Recruitment and Employee Relations Organizational Effectiveness Study, 1969. Home: 23 Pepperidge Rd Morristown NJ 07960 Office: PO Box 600 West Orange NJ 07052

RAND, ALONZO CUTTING, JR., tech. services corp. exec.; b. Ispwich, Mass., Nov. 1, 1922; s. Alonzo Cutting and Amy Milton (Dickinson) R.; B.S. in Mech. Engring., Northeastern U., 1947; postgrad. M.I.T., 1947-49, Grad. Sch. Engring., N.Y. U., 1953-56; m. Margaret Chase Hubbard, Dec. 31, 1944; children—Alison Cutting, Elizabeth Rand Keys, Peter Dickinson, John Bradstreet. With particle accelerator project, nuclear engring. dept. M.I.T., Cambridge, 1947-49; engr. Brookhaven (N.Y.) Nat. Lab., 1949-55; mgr. nuclear dept. Marsh and McLennan, N.Y.C., 1956-71, mgr. corp. loss prevention, 1970-71; mgr. M&M Protection Cons.'s, 1971-76, pres., chief exec. officer Clayton Environ. Cons.'s (subs. Marsh & McLennan), 1975—, sr. v.p., head loss control div., 1976-80, head tech. services, 1980—; dir. Marsh & McLennan, Inc.; advisor sponsors Plowshare Ins. Symposium, 1965; cons. So. Interstate Nuclear Bd. for report, 1966; participant, speaker Internat. Atomic Energy Agency Conf., Monaco, 1968, Stockholm, 1972, advisor to panel Experts on Nuclear Ins., Vienna, Austria, 1969; cons. Nuclear Mut. Ltd.; participant Marine (Hull) Ins. Seminar, Casablanca, Morocco, 1975. Founding dir., treas., fin. chmn. Nat. Energy Found.; chmn. fin. com., lic. lay reader Christ Episcopal Ch., Bellport, N.Y., vestryman. Served with U.S. Army, 1943-46. Certified occupational hearing conservationist; lic. profl. engr., N.Y. Mem. Nat., N.Y. State socs. profl. engrs., Am. Nuclear Soc., Nat. Fire Protection Assn., ASME, Safety Execs. N.Y. Club: Hearth. Patentee system for unloading reactors. Home: 51 Munsell Rd East Patchogue NY 11772 Office: 1221 Ave of Americas New York NY 10020

RANDALL, EDWARD, III, investment banker; b. Galveston, Tex., Jan. 11, 1927; s. Edward and Katharine (Risher) R.; B.A., U. Tex., 1949; m. Eliza Lovett, May 3, 1952; children—Martha Lovett Randall Galbraith, Laura Ballinger, Helen Wicks, Edward IV. Asso. with Rotan Mosle Inc., Houston, 1948-55, partner, 1955-66, v.p., 1966-68, chmn. exec. com., 1968-70, pres., 1970—, also chief exec. officer; chmn. bd. Rotan Mosle Fin. Corp., 1977—; dir. Houston Nat. Bank, Tracor, Inc., Am. Nat. Fin. Corp., S.W. Mortgage Realty Trust; mem. bd. dirs. N.Y. Stock Exchange, 1977—. Mem. exec. com. Chancellors Council U. Tex.; sr. council St. Martin's Episcopal Ch.; mem. Rice U. Assos.; bd. dirs. Alley Theatre; trustee Kinkaid Sch. Served with USMCR, 1944-46. Mem. Phi Delta Theta. Home: 5135 Green Tree Rd Houston TX 77056 Office: 1500 South Tower Pennzoil Pl Houston TX 77002*

RANDALL, GERALD ROBERT, music pub. and record co. exec.; b. Summitville, N.Y., May 27, 1936; s. Samuel Jay and Florence Katherine (Boyce) R.; student pub. schs., Ellenville, N.Y. Freelance writer, 1957—; lyricist and composer, 1965—; ind. record producer and personnel mgr. musical group, 1967—; pres. H. & G Randall Pub. Co. and Randall Records, Syracuse, N.Y., 1972—; v.p. P.J. Reilly Funeral Homes, Inc., Middletown, N.Y. Served with AUS, 1959-61. Mem. ASCAP. Republican. Methodist. Home: 29 Elaine Rd Milford CT 06460 Office: 1900 W Genesee St Syracuse NY 13204

RANDALL, JAMES R., business exec.; b. 1924; B.S. in Chem. Engring., U. Wis., 1948; married. Tech. dir. Cargill Inc., 1948-68; v.p. prodn. and engring. Archer-Daniels-Midland Co., 1968-69, exec. v.p., 1969-75, pres., 1975—, also dir. Served with U.S. Army, 1943-46. Office: 4666 Faries Pkwy Decatur IL 62525*

RANDALL, KENNETH ALFRED, orgn. exec.; b. Ogden, Utah, June 22, 1927; s. J. William and Beatrice (Pingree) R.; student Weber Coll., 1945-47; B.S., Brigham Young U., 1949, M.S., 1958; postgrad. Stonier Grad. Sch. Banking, 1960; m. Jeraldine Daynes Smith, Aug. 20, 1952; children—Shelly Marie Randall Millard, Nancy Kay Randall Mackey, Tami Lee. With State Bank of Provo (Utah), 1947-63, pres., 1963; mem. bd. FDIC, Washington, 1964-70, chmn., 1965-70; vice-chmn., dir. United Va. Bankshares Inc., Richmond, 1970-71, pres., chief exec. officer, 1971-75, chmn., chief exec. officer, from 1975; pres. The Conf. Bd., Inc., N.Y.C., 1976—; dir. BBDO Internat., Inc., Consol.-Bathurst, Inc. and subs.'s, Jaguar Rover Triumph Inc., N.E. Bancorp., Inc. and subs. Union Trust Co., Va. Electric and Power Co., Oppenheimer Fund, Inc. and 8 affiliated funds; mem. exec. com. Adv. Council Japan-U.S. Econ. Relations; mem. U.S. sect. European Community-U.S. Businessmen's Council; mem.-at-large USA-BIAC, Bus. and Industry Adv. Com., OECD; mem. adv. council Electric Power Research Inst.; mem. Pres.'s Commn. Fin. Structure and Regulation, 1970-71. Trustee-at-large, mem. exec. com. Ind. Coll. Funds Am., Inc.; trustee Mary Baldwin Coll.; mem. adv. council J. L. Kellogg Grad. Sch. Mgmt., Northwestern U. Republican. Mem. Ch. Jesus Christ of Latter-day Saints. Clubs: Links, River (N.Y.C.). Office: The Conference Bd 845 Third Ave New York NY 10022

RANDALL, PHILLIP MELVIN, telecommunications co. exec.; b. Youngstown, Ohio, Dec. 15, 1946; s. John and Effie R.; B.S., Youngstown State U., 1968; M.A., U. Mich., 1974; postgrad. U. Akron, 1978—; m. Evelyn Tracy, Oct. 3, 1970. Tchr., Youngstown Public Schs., 1968-69; mgr. human resources Ohio Bell Telephone Co., Cleve., 1969—; coordinator retirement edn. Inst. Life-Span Devel. and Gerontology, Akron, 1975—; cons. indsl. gerontology and retirement edn., various corps.; lectr. U. Akron, 1974—. Chmn., Sr. Citizen Commn. City of Akron, 1978-80; trustee Sr. Worker Action Program, 1975-79; mem. adv. bd. Akron YMCA, 1979-80. Mem. Nat. Gerontol. Soc., Nat. Black Caucus on the Aged, Am. Soc. Tng. and Devel., Phi Kappa Phi. Contbr. articles to profl. jours. Office: 2525 State Rd Cuyahoga Falls OH 44223

RANDALL, ROBERT L., bus. economist; b. Aberdeen, S.D., Dec. 28, 1936; s. Harry Eugene and Juanita Alice (Barstow) R.; M.S. in Phys. Chemistry, U. Chgo., 1960, M.B.A., 1963. Market devel. chemist E.I. du Pont de Nemours & Co., Inc., Wilmington, Del., 1963-65; chem. economist Battelle Meml. Inst., Columbus, Ohio, 1965-68; mgr. market and econ. research Kennecott Copper Corp., N.Y.C., 1968-74, economist, 1974—. Mem. A.A.A.S., AIME, Am. Econ. Assn., Am. Statis. Assn., Am. Chem. Soc., Metall. Soc., N.Y. Acad. Scis. Contbr. articles to profl. jours.; contbg. author: Computer Methods for the '80's. Home: 812 Memorial Dr Cambridge MA 02139 Office: 128 Spring St Lexington MA 02173

RANDALL, ROLAND RODROCK, real estate counselor; b. Doylestown, Pa., Oct. 12, 1898; s. William Lacey and Anna Elizabeth (Rodrock) R.; B.S. in Econs., Wharton Sch. U. Pa., 1921; student case study course Am. Inst. Real Estate Appraisers, U. Pa., 1939; m. Marion Burnside Heist, Dec. 5, 1922 (dec. May 1977); children—Roland Rodrock, Sue Randall. Securities salesman, 1921-25; real estate broker, cons., appraiser specializing in indsl., comml., instl., large scale housing and specialty types real estate, Phila., 1925-52; real estate counselor, Phila., 1952—; faculty, lectr. real estate extension, evening sch. U. Pa., 1947—; treas., dir. N.E. Corner Walnut and Juniper Sts., Inc. Vice pres., bd. dirs. Phila. Council on Alcoholism, Inc.; bd. dirs. Delaware Valley area Nat. Council on Alcoholism; trustee will Stephen Girard; mem. adv. com. econ. devel. analysis for indsl. land facilities in Phila., Phila. Devel. Corp. Former chmn. bds. of view for acquisition of land by U.S. War Dept., also U.S. Signal Corps., World War II; cons. expert, mem. speakers bur. War Loan Drives, World War II. Active YMCA; chmn. real estate div. A.R.C., 1945; chmn. real estate com. March of Dimes, 1948; chmn. estate div. United Fund, 1951, vice chmn. real estate div., 1952—; dir., real estate counselor Jr. Achievement Phila. Met. Area, Inc., 1953-65; chmn., mem. Phila. Housing Authority, 1937-47; com. mem. Citizens Council on City Planning, 1954-55; dir. Nat. Com. on Housing, Inc.; chmn. Greater Phila. Com. for Emergency Def. Plant Location, ODM, 1951—; chmn. Phila. County div., mem. exec. com. Greater Phila.-Del.-South Jersey Council; bd. govs. Delaware Valley Council, 1956—; adv. com. Phila. Eastwick Housing Market Analysis; real estate counselor to Dept. Commerce, Phila.; mem. joint exec. com. Improvement and Devel. of Phila. Port Area; chmn. Pa. Real Estate Commn. Mem. bd. corporators, exec. planning council Med. Coll. Pa. and Hosp. Served as 2d lt. U.S. Army, World War I. Recipient Silver award U.S. Treasury Dept., 21st Ward Phila. Community Council award, 1961; Girard Sq. Assn. award, 1964. Mem. Am. Soc. Real Estate Counselors (nat. pres. 1953-55), Soc. Indsl. Realtors (pres. 1949), Am. Inst. Real Estate Appraisers (pres. Phila. 1947), Am. Inst. Real Estate Mgmt., Nat. Assn. Real Estate Bds. (dir., past officer), Pa. Realtor Assn. (pres. 1941), U.S. C. of C. (nat. councillor), Phila. Real Estate Bd. (bd. govs., pres. 1938), Nat. Inst. Real Estate Brokers, Urban Land Inst. (indsl. council, community builders council), Nat. Assn. Housing and Redevel. Ofcls., Greater Phila. C. of C., Internat. Real Estate Fedn. (Am. chpt.), Assessors Assn. Phila., Municipal Assessors Assn. Pa., Property Service, Inc., Saving Fund Soc. Germantown (bd. mgrs. emeritus), Pa. Soc., adv. council Naval Affairs City Phila. (adv. council), Spiritual Frontiers Fellowship (exec. council), Bucks County Hist. Soc., Am. Legion, Underdown-Assembly Artisans, Am. Arbitration Assn. (nat. panel arbitrators), Cruiser Olympia Assn. (dir.), Order St. Luke The Physician, Internat. Frat. of Lambda Alpha (pres. Phila. chpt.), Phi Gamma Delta. Episcopalian (past sr. warden). Mason. Clubs: Racquet (gov.), Church, Alden Park Players (pres. 1948-49) (Phila.). Contbr. articles on real estate. Home: The Dorchester Rittenhouse Sq Philadelphia PA 19103 Office: Jackson-Cross Co 2000 Market St Philadelphia PA 19103

RANDALL, WILLIAM B., mfg. co. exec.; b. Phila., Jan. 8, 1921; s. Albert and Ann (Fine) R.; student Rider Coll., 1940-41; m. Geraldine Kempson, Aug. 10, 1943; children—Robert, Erica Lynn, Lisa. Gen. sales mgr. Lowres Optical Mfg. Co., Newark, 1946-49; pres., founder Rand Sales Co., N.Y.C., 1949-58; gen. mgr. Sea & Ski Co. (formerly Rolley Co.) div. Botany Industries, Inc., Millbrae, Calif., 1958-61, pres., 1961-65; v.p. Botany Industries, Inc., 1961-65; chmn. bd. Renauld Internat., Reading, Pa., 1963-65; pres., dir. Sea & Ski Corp., 1965-66; pres. Renauld, Reno, 1965-67; chmn. bd. Randall Internat., Ltd., 1967-68; pres. Rand Pacific, Burlingame, 1967-68, Exec. Products Internat., Ltd., Santa Monica, Calif., 1969-71, also pres. Group 42, 1969-71; pres. New Product Devel. Center, 1971—, Internat. Concept Center, Inc., 1971—, Sun Research Center, 1974—, La Costa Products Internat., 1975—, Source West Inc., 1976—. Served to 1st lt., navigator, USAAF, 1942-45. Mem. Am. Mgmt. Assn., Nat. Wholesale Druggists Assn., Nat. Assn. Chain Drug Stores, Toiletry Merchandisers Assn., Advt. Club N.Y. Home: 7150 Arenal

Lane Carlsbad CA 92008 Office: 2251 Las Palmas Dr Carlsbad CA 92008

RANDALL, WILLIAM SEYMOUR, water pump and hydraulic systems mfg. co. exec.; b. Champaign, Ill., July 5, 1933; s. Glenn Seymour and Audrey (Honnold) R.; B.S., Ind. State U., 1959; m. Carol Mischler, Aug. 23, 1958; children—Steve, Cathy, Mike, Jennifer. Plant controller Scott Paper Co., Hoboken, N.J., 1963-64; div. controller Sheller Globe Corp., Montpelier, Ind., 1964-67; controller Amana Refrigeration Co. (Iowa), 1967-70; div. controller Trane Co., Clarksville, Tenn., 1970-74, corp. controller, LaCrosse, Wis., 1974-79; v.p., chief fin. officer, sec. Sta-Rite Industries, Milw., 1979—. Bd. dirs. Jr. Achievement, 1972-74, DePaul Hosp., Milw. Served with U.S. Army, 1954-55. Mem. Fin. Execs. Inst., Corp. Controllers Orgn. Republican. Clubs: Univ., Western Racquet. Home: 1780 Brojan Dr Elm Grove WI 53122 Office: 777 E Wisconsin Ave Milwaukee WI 53202

RANDAZZO, GARY WAYNE, pub. co. exec.; b. Georgetown, Tex., Sept. 23, 1947; s. Frank Birchmans and Edna Earle (Forbis) R.; B.B.A., U. Tex., Austin, 1973; M.B.A., Tex. A&I U., Corpus Christi, 1976; m. Joyce Sue McNorton, Oct. 7, 1966; children—Gary Wayne, Vanessa, Jason. Asst. to v.p. research and controls H.E.B. Grocery Co., 1973-74; instr. Del Mar Coll., Corpus Christi, Tex., 1974-76; planning/market research coordinator Caller-Times Pub. Co., Corpus Christi, 1976-77, asst. controller, 1977-78, controller, 1978, bus. mgr., 1979—; mem. Harte-Hanks Long Range Planning Com. Loaned exec. United Way, 1977, mem. allocations com., 1979, co-chmn. spl. projects div., 1979. Nat. Food Brokers Scholar, 1972-73. Mem. Inst. Newspaper Controllers and Fin. Officers, Tex. Jr. Coll. Mgmt. Educators Assn. (past sec.), Corpus Christi C. of C. Baptist. Club: Kiwanis. Author: Effectiveness of an Interest Penalty to Control Cash in Multi-Retail Outlet Organization, 1976. Home: 3814 Dunbrook St Corpus Christi TX 78415 Office: Caller-Times Pub Co 820 N Lower Broadway Corpus Christi TX 78401

RANDLE, WILLIAM MALCOLM, banker; b. Jacksonville, Fla., Dec. 22, 1939; s. William Yancy and Frances Romano (Goff) R.; A.A., Jacksonville U., 1959; B.S. in Bus. Adminstrn. (Schenley Found. scholar), U. Fla., 1962; M.B.A., Loyola U., New Orleans, 1969; m. Judy Mary Mroczek, Dec. 31, 1963; children—William Malcolm, Andrew F. With Atlantic Bancorp., Jacksonville, 1969—, mktg. officer, 1970-72, asst. v.p., 1972-73, v.p., dir. mktg., 1973-80, v.p. mktg. and br. services, 1980—; conf. speaker. Chmn., Jacksonville Area C. of C. Nat. Advt. Task Force, 1977-79. Served from ensign to lt. comdr., USN, 1962-69. Mem. Bank Mktg. Assn., Sales and Mktg. Execs. Jacksonville, Jacksonville Advt. Club, Jacksonville Research Assn. (pres. 1971-72), Beta Gamma Sigma. Democrat. Clubs: Ye Mystic Reveller, University, Park Avenue Racquet. Office: 200 W Forsyth St Gen Mail Center Jacksonville FL 32231

RANELLI, JOHN RAYMOND, fin. exec.; b. New London, Conn., Sept. 25, 1946; s. Frank Robert and Sue Mary (Bongo) R.; A.B. in History, Coll. Holy Cross, 1968; student U. Loyola, Rome, 1966-67; M.B.A., Dartmouth Coll., 1973; m. Paula Jean Contillo, June 8, 1968; children—Carina, Christina, Jennifer. Fin. analyst Gen. Motors Corp., N.Y.C., 1973-74; mgr. fin. adminstrn. No. Telecom, Inc., Nashville, 1975-76, asst. treas., 1976-77, treas., 1977-78, asst. controller, Montreal, Que., Can., 1978-79; treas. ARA Services, Phila., 1979—. Served with USN, 1968-71. Fulbright scholar, 1968. Mem. Fin. Execs. Inst., Fin. Mgrs. Assn. Roman Catholic. Clubs: K.C., Elks. Home: 118 Chartwell Crescent Beaconsfield PQ H9W 1C3 Canada Office: ARA Services Independence Sq W Philadelphia PA 19106

RANELLI, RICHARD JOSEPH, bank exec.; b. New London, Conn., June 16, 1950; s. Frank Robert and Sue Mary (Bongo) R.; B.A. in Math. cum laude, Assumption Coll., 1972; M.S. in Computer Sci., Worcester Poly. Inst., 1975; m. Laurina Ellen Niland, June 6, 1970; children—Jeffrey, Dianna. With Hartford Nat. Bank (Conn.), 1973-79, check processing and fin. systems mgr., 1974-76, trust systems mgr., 1977-78, asst. v.p. trust and corp. systems devel., 1979; dir. data processing Fin. Industry Systems, Lawrence, Mass., 1980—; v.p. data processing Md. Nat. Bank, Balt., 1980—. Coach soccer and basketball Glastonbury (Conn.) and Andover (Mass.) Recreation. Mem. Kappa Mu Epsilon. Home: 1146 Starmount Dr Bel Air MD 21014 Office: 225 N Calvert St Baltimore MD 21203

RANGOS, JOHN G., mfg. co. exec.; b. Steubenville, Ohio, July 27, 1929; s. Gust and Anna (Svokas) R.; student Houston Bus. Coll., 1949-50; m. Patricia A.; children—John G., Alexander W., Janica Anne. Pres., chmn. bd. U.S. Utilities Service Corp., Monroeville, Pa., U.S. Services Corp., Monroeville, Chambers Devel. Co., Inc., Monroeville, 1978—, So. Alleghenies Disposal Services, Hosopple, Pa., 1978—, William H. Martin Inc., Washington, Pa., 1978—, Tri Valley Mcpl. Supply, 1978—, Ran Sales Inc., 1978—, Security Bur., Inc., 1978—. Bd. dirs. Craig House-Technoma, 1974-75, treas., 1975-76; mem. nat. com. UN Assn., 1977—; chmn. fund raising UNICEF, Pitts., 1977; bd. dirs. Holy Cross Sem. Theology, Boston, 1962-63; mem. Clergy Laity Council N.Y.; bd. dirs. Greek Orthodox Ch. Presentation of Christ, Pitts., 1968-70; nat. del. U.S. Olympic Com., 1980. Served with U.S. Army, 1951-54; Korea. Democrat. Clubs: Nat. Football Hall of Fame, Press, Allegheny, Churchvill Valley Country, Masons, Shriners. Pioneer in sewage sludge disposal, disposal sites and resource recovery systems of complex wastes (methane energy). Home: 78 Locksley Dr Pittsburgh PA 15235 Office: 470 Mall Circle Dr Monroeville PA 15146

RANKIN, WILLIAM PARKMAN, publishing co. exec.; b. Boston, Feb. 6, 1917; s. George William and Bertha W. (Clowe) R.; B.S., Syracuse U., 1941; M.B.A., N.Y. U., 1949, Ph.D., 1979; m. Ruth E. Gerard, Sept. 12, 1942; children—Douglas W., Joan W. Sales exec. Redbook mag., N.Y.C., 1945-49; sales exec. This Week mag., N.Y.C., 1949-55, adminstrv. exec., 1955-60, v.p., 1957-60, v.p., bd. dirs. advt. sales, sales devel. dir., 1960-63, exec. v.p., 1963-69; gen. exec. newspaper div. Time, Inc., 1969-70; gen. mgr. feature service Newsweek, Inc., N.Y.C., 1970-72, financial and ins. advt. mgr., 1972—; lectr. Syracuse U., N.Y. U., Berkeley Sch. Mem. adv. council Sch. Journalism, Syracuse U. Mem. Sigma Delta Chi, Alpha Delta Sigma. Clubs: N.Y. Dutch Treat, Met. Adv. Golf Assn., Winged Foot Golf. Author: Selling Retail Advertising, 1944; The Technique of Selling Magazine Advertising, 1949; Business Management of Magazines, 1980. Home: 15 York Rd Larchmont NY 10538 also Bridge Rd Bomoseen VT 05732 Office: 444 Madison Ave New York NY 10022

RANKINE, BAXTER JAMES, valve co. exec.; b. Moncks Corner, S.C., June 30, 1936; s. Baxter Grey and Mary DeLellis (Bradley) R.; B.S. in Engring., UCLA, 1959; m. Joyce Marie Lemery, July 24, 1965; children—David James, Julie Dee. Mfg. mgmt. trainee Gen. Electric Co., 1960-63, indsl. engr., Schenectady, 1963-65; material control mgr. Collins Radio Co., Newport Beach, Calif., 1965-67; v.p. engring. and mfg. Pacific Pumping Co., Oakland, Calif., 1967-73, v.p. mktg., 1973-75; dir. corp. devel. Mark Controls Corp., Evanston, Ill., 1975-77; pres. MCC Center Line, Tulsa, 1977-78; pres. MCC Pacific Valves, Long Beach, Calif., 1978—. Served with USCG, 1959-60. Mem. Kappa Sigma. Republican. Roman Catholic. Home: 30330 Cartier Dr Rancho Palos Verdes CA 90274 Office: MCC Pacific Valves 3201 Walnut Long Beach CA 90807

RANNO, PHILIP GREGORY, metal finishing cons.; b. N.Y.C., Aug. 29, 1914; s. Sebastian and Josephine Marie (Presti) R.; student CCNY, 1932-33, Columbia U., 1933-35; m. Louise E. Voelker, Dec. 30, 1954; children—Gregory, Louise, Nancy, Dianne; children by previous marriage—Philip, Marlene. Partner, gen. mgr. Imperial Plating Co., Bklyn., 1932-53; gen. mgr. for Manhattan Project at Bart Labs., Belleville, N.J., 1942-45; v.p., gen. mgr. Detroit Die Casting Corp., 1955-60; pres. Ranno Electro Plating Corp., Saddle Brook, N.J., 1959-79; cons. Pat Hathaway, Inc., South Hackensack, N.J., 1979—. Mem. Masters Electroplating Assn., Nat. Assn. Metal Finishers, Am. Electroplaters Assn. Republican. Roman Catholic. Office: Pat Hathaway Inc 11 Leuning St South Hackensack NJ 07606

RANSOM, MARY ANN, business exec.; b. Sistersville, W.Va., Jan. 25, 1916; d. Lewis Velton and Florence Elizabeth (Clawson) Ransom; student Ohio U., 1941. Asso. Parkersburg Office Supply Co., 1934—, sec.-treas., dir., 1947—; 1st violinist Parkersburg Symphony Orch., Marietta Coll. Symphony Orch. W.Va. rep. on nat. bd. Woman's Med. Coll. of Pa., Phila.; v.p. Community Concerts, Inc. Bd. dirs. United Fund; trustee Alderson-Broaddus Coll. Mem. D.A.R., P.E.O., Nat. Soc. Arts and Letters. Baptist. Clubs: Parkersburg Country. Home: 601 Tenth and One Half St Parkersburg WV 26101 Office: 326 Fifth St Parkersburg WV 26101

RANSONE, RALPH EDWARD, soft drink co. exec.; b. Richmond, Va., Apr. 22, 1918; s. Ivan Richard and Grace Cecil (Taylor) R.; B.C.S., Benjamin Franklin U., 1947; m. Lorine Jenny Glessner, Sept. 4, 1943; 1 dau., Cheryl Raline. Staff accountant F.L. Worcester & Co., Richmond, Va., 1948-52; plant accountant Continental Can Co., Richmond, 1952-58; controller Pepsi Cola Bottling Co., Richmond, 1958-71; sec.-treas. Coca-Cola Bottling Co., Richmond, 1971—; mgmt. cons.; corporate officer, dir. 13 soft drink corps. Served with USAAF, 1941-45; PTO. Mem. Nat. Assn. Accountants. Republican. Baptist. Club: Masons. Author: The Magic Formula for Mail Order Success, 1972. Home: 911 Kent Rd Apt 4 Richmond VA 23221 Office: 1706 Roseneath Rd Richmond VA 23230

RANT, WALTER FRANCIS, chem. co. exec.; b. N.Y.C., Aug. 4, 1925; s. Francis Walter and Anastazia (Kindrick) R.; B.S., U. Pitts., 1950, M. Lit., 1950; postgrad. Am. Inst. Banking, 1955-57, N.Y. U., 1957-65; m. Evelyn M. Buddy, Oct. 7, 1950; children—Melinda, Nadine, Walter Francis II. Asst. mgr. investment research dept. Walston & Co., N.Y.C., 1951-56, mgr. investment research dept. Cosgrove, Miller & Whitehead, 1956-57, Gregory & Sons, 1957-58; sr. security analyst Lionel D. Edie & Co., 1958-60, Goodbody & Co., 1960-65; v.p. corporate devel. Essex Chem. Corp., Clifton, N.J., 1965—. Served to 1st lt. USAAF, 1943-47; ret. maj. Res. Recipient Morris award Am. Inst. Banking, 1955. Mem. Am. Econ. Assn., N.Y. Soc. Security Analysts, Inst. Chartered Fin. Analysts. Contbr. articles profl. jours. Home: 19 Beresford Rd Allendale NJ 07401 Office: 1401 Broad St Clifton NJ 07015

RANZ, FRANK STEPHEN, machine tool distbg. co. exec.; b. Blue Ash, Ohio, Oct. 31, 1918; s. William R. and Alvina (Snook) R.; E.E., U. Cin., 1940; m. Joan Kreamelmeyer, Apr. 8, 1967. Engr., R.K. LeBlond M.T. Co., 1940-41, Natco, Richmond, Ind., 1941-42; indsl. engr. Yarnall-Waring Co., 1946-47; sales engr. W.K. Mill Holland Machinery Co., 1947-51, French Oil Mill Machinery Co., 1950-51; pres., owner The Frank S. Ranz Co., Cin., 1951—. Served to 2s lt. AUS, 1942-46. Registered profl. engr., Ohio. Republican. Clubs: Kenwood Country (Cin.); Masons. Home and office: 4668 E Galbraith Rd Cincinnati OH 45236

RAO, GOPAL UDIAVAR (GENE), data processing exec.; b. Bombay; came to U.S., 1960; s. Srinivasa U. and Ratnabai M. Shanbhogue; B.A. with honors, U. Bombay, 1958, M.A. in Econs., 1959; M.B.A., U. Chgo., 1962; m. Theresa M. Schmid, June 17, 1965; children—Ashok G., Sheila Y., Chandani R., Anand A. Research asst. Harvard U., 1962-63; ter. mgr. Alcon Labs., Ft. Worth, 1963-65; ins. programmer Equitable Life Assurance Soc., Des Moines, 1965-66; project leader Dial Fin. Corp., Des Moines, 1967-70; v.p., tech. mgr. Beneficial Mgmt. Corp., Morristown, N.J., 1970—; asso. prof. econs. Drake U., 1966-68. Recipient presdl. awards for excellence in fin. tech. system designs, 1971, 77, 78, 79. Mem. Data Processing Mgmt. Assn., Airlines Control Program Users Group (chmn.), IBM Share and Guide Assn., Nat. Consumers Fin. Assn. (tech. and communication subcom.). Clubs: Arrowhead Tennis, Mt. Freedom Racquet. Author: Elephant Baby, Ency. Britannica, 1962. Office: 200 South St Morristown NJ 07960

RAO, VEERESWARA U., chem. co. exec.; b. Ramachandrapuram, India, Mar. 15, 1930; s. Satyanarayana and Annapoorna (Ganti) Upadhyayula; B.Sc. with honors, Andhra U., Visakhapatnam, India, 1950, M.S., 1951; Ph.D., Wayne State U., 1965; M.B.A., Nat. U., San Diego, 1978; m. Harish Rao, Apr. 20, 1969; 1 child. Mgr. research and devel. Matthey Bishop, Inc., Malvern, Pa., 1967-72; pres. metals div. Cladan, Inc., San Diego, 1973-75; gen. mgr., tech. dir. GTI Research and Devel. Center, San Diego, 1975-76; mgr. materials devel. ITW Emcon, San Diego, 1976-78; v.p. Gemini Industries, Santa Ana, Calif., 1978—; adj. prof. LaJolla U.; cons. in field. Mem. Am. Chem. Soc., Internat. Soc. Hybrid Microelectronics, Franklin Inst., N.Y. Acad. Scis., Sigma Xi, Phi Lambda Upsilon. Hindu. Club: Rotary. Contbr. articles to profl. jours. Home: 1 Blue River Irvine CA 92714 Office: 2311 S Pullman St Santa Ana CA 92705

RAPETTI, EDWARD J., business exec.; b. N.Y.C., 1923; B.E.E., Manhattan Coll., 1944. Exec. v.p. Ambac Industries Inc., 1944-79; group v.p. auto group United Technologies Corp., Hartford, Conn., 1979—. Office: United Technologies Bldg Hartford CT 06101*

RAPHAEL, CARL SAMUEL, pharm. co. exec.; b. Kew Gardens, N.Y., Apr. 23, 1943; s. Harold and Ruth R.; B.S., Dalhousie U., 1965; M.A., Queens Coll., 1966; M.B.A., Fordham U., 1974; m. Ellen Gibson Muller, Jan. 15, 1966; children—Larissa, Heather. Pharm. rep. Hoffmann-LaRoche, Nutley, N.J., 1967-70, med. center rep., 1970-71, mktg. research asst., 1971-72, mktg. research analyst, 1972-73, sr. analyst, coordinator health econs., 1973-75; mktg. mgr. Health Application Systems, Inc., Saddle Brook, N.J., 1975-76; sr. mktg. analyst Merck, Sharp & Dohme, West Point, Pa., 1976-78; product research mgr. and mgr. mktg. analysis E.R. Squibb & Sons, Inc., Lawrenceville, N.J., 1978-79; v.p., research dir. Danis Research, Inc., Fairfield, N.J., 1979-80, sr. v.p., 1980—; cons. health care adminstrn. Mem. Union County Consumer Affairs Adv. Com., 1974, vice chmn., 1975-76, chmn., 1976-77; mem. Warrington Ambulance Corps., Bucks County Emergency Health Council; crew chief and pres. Registered Emergency Technicians Assn. Mem. Group Health Assn. Am., Assn. M.B.A. Execs., Pharm. Mfrs. Assn., Am. Mktg. Assn., Pharm. Mktg. Research Group, AAU, Am. Philatelic Assn., Tau Epsilon Phi. Home: 1705 LaRue Ln Warrington PA 18976 Office: 116 Fairfield Rd Fairfield NJ 07006

RAPOPORT, BERNARD, life ins. co. exec.; b. San Antonio, July 17, 1917; s. David and Riva (Feldman) R.; B.A., U. Tex., 1939; m. Adure Jean Newman, Feb. 15, 1942; 1 son, Ronald B. With Zales Jewelry, Austin, Tex., 1936-39, Wichita Falls, Tex., 1943, Kruger Jewelry Co., Austin and Wichita Falls, 1939-40; partner Art's Jewelry Store, Waco, Tex., 1944-49; gen. agt. Pioneer Am. Life Ins. Co., 1950-51; with Am. Income Life Ins. Co., Waco, 1951—, chmn. bd., chief exec. officer; dir. Citizens Nat. Bank. Mem. Democratic Nat. Fin. Com., 1976—, Dem. House and Senate Council, Washington, 1978—, Tex. Dem. Fin. Council, Austin, 1975—; mem. Com. for Public Justice, N.Y.C., 1971—; chmn. United Negro Coll. Fund, Waco, 1979—; mem. Center for Study of Dem. Instns., 1971—; bd. dirs. Mexican-Am. Legal Def. and Ednl. Fund, 1976—; trustee Paul Quinn Coll., Waco, 1963—; mem. Tex. Consumer Assn., Univ. Cancer Found., Nat. Space Inst., Nat. Council Crime and Delinquency, Scientists' Inst. for Public Info., others. Honored by naming of Bernard Rapoport Postgrad. Inst. for Digestive Health and Nutrition, N.Y.C., 1979; recipient Disting. Spl. award Office and Profl. Employees Internat. Union, 1979; Service award B'nai B'rith, 1971; award Am. Digestive Disease Soc., 1979, A. Philip Randolph Inst., 1979. Jewish. Club: B'nai B'rith. Home: 2332 Wendy Ln Waco TX 76710 Office: 1200 Wooded Acres Waco TX 76710

RAPOZA, EDWARD J., med. instrument mfg. co. exec.; b. 1936; B.S. in Engring., Stevens Inst. Tech., 1958; M.S. in Engring., U. Pa., 1960. With RCA, ITT, Kearfott div. Singer Co.; v.p. research and devel. Clay Adams, Parsippany, N.J., 1967-73, pres., 1973—. Office: care Clay Adams 299 Webro Rd Parsippany NJ 07054

RAPP, MELVILLE BENJAMIN, sales and mgmt. exec.; b. N.Y.C., Apr. 16, 1906; s. Harry and Mathilda (Katz) R.; student Coll. City of N.Y., 1923-26; m. Rachel Marx, Mar. 31, 1942; children—Richard T., Robert D. Account exec. Gen. Outdoor Advt. Co., N.Y.C., 1926-33; pres. Keystate Outdoor Advt. Co., 1933-40, C. & S. Labs., Miami, Fla., 1941-47; v.p. Automatic Products Co., N.Y.C., 1947-51; exec. v.p., dir. Apco, Inc., 1951-60, Apco Products Corp., 1951-60, Practical Products Corp., 1951-60, Practical Industries, 1951-60, Apco Internat. Corp., 1951-60, v.p., dir. Continental Vending Machine Corp., Westbury, L.I., N.Y., 1961-63; exec. v.p. Continental-Apco, Inc., 1961-63; sr. cons. The Vendo Co., Kansas City, Mo., 1964-71; pres. Parmel Assos., Inc., Pompano Beach, Fla., 1945—, Parmel Galleries, Pompano Beach, 1967—. Mem. Nat. Automatic Merchandizing Assn. (dir. 1956-64), Nat. Assn. Concessionaires (hon. life dir.), Am. Fedn. Arts, Nat. Assn. Tobacco Distbrs., Am. Mgmt. Assn., Am. Philatelic Soc., Am. Topical Assn., Soc. Philatelic Americans, Am. Numis. Assn., Bur. Issues Assn., Philatelic Found. Clubs: Sales Executive, Variety Internat. (N.Y.C.). Address: PO Box 728 Pompano Beach FL 33061

RARDIN, JOHN ARTHUR, pub. co. exec.; b. Charleston, Ill., Apr. 29, 1930; s. John Briggs and Margaret Fayette (Hopper) R.; B.S., Eastern Ill. U., 1954; M.S., U. Ill., 1961; m. Rosemary Boyd, Jan. 17, 1952; children—Byron, Erin, Jerrine, John A. Newspaper editor Eastern Ill. U., Charleston, 1951; editor, Charleston Daily News, 1952, 1955-57; financial editor Champaign-Urbana (Ill.) Courier, 1959-62; research asst. Ill. Bus. Review, Champaign-Urbana, 1956-59; tchr., Rockford and Des Plaines, Ill., 1963-66; owner Rardin Graphics, Charleston, 1966—; pres., Graphic Creations, Inc., Charleston, 1970—; v.p. G.I.R.E. Internat. & Charleston, 1980—. Served with AUS, 1952-54. Mem. Nat. Pilots Assn., Aircraft Owners and Pilots Assn., Ill. Press Assn., Ill. Pilots Assn., Charleston C. of C., Pi Delta Kappa. Clubs: Rotary, Toastmasters. Home: 1003 Monroe St Charleston IL 61920 Office: 617 18th St Charleston IL 61920

RARIG, EMORY WEBSTER, JR., ednl. adminstr.; b. Catawissa, Pa., Mar. 25, 1926; s. Emory Webster and Nora Bell (Cherrington) R.; B.S. in Bus. Edn., Bloomsburg State Coll., 1951; M.A. in Bus. Edn., Tchrs. Coll., Columbia U., 1963, Ed.D., 1968; m. Mary Elizabeth Johnson, July 3, 1970. Tchr. bus. edn. Mechanicsburg (Pa.) Sr. High Sch., 1951-61; sec., adminstrv. asst., part-time instr. Tchrs. Coll., Columbia U., N.Y.C., 1961-68; dir. bus. edn. Bloomsburg (Pa.) State Coll., 1968-70, dean Sch. Bus., 1970—; evaluator accrediting commn. Assn. Ind. Colls. and Schs., Washington; mem. Pa. Vocat. Edn. Adv. Com., 1973-76, chmn., 1975-76. Trustee, Lackawanna Jr. Coll., Scranton, Pa.; pres. ch. council St. Paul's Luth. Ch., Numidia, Pa. Served with USN, 1944-47. Recipient ten year trustee medal Lackawanna Jr. Coll., 1979. Mem. NEA, Nat. Bus. Edn. Assn., Nat. Assn. Accts., Am. Acctg. Assn., Am. Mgmt. Socs., Am. Assn. Higher Edn., Pa. State Edn. Assn. (local br. pres. 1959-61), AAUP, Am. Assn. Univ. Adminstrs., Pi Omega Pi (faculty advisor Alpha Delta chpt.), Phi Delta Kappa. Republican. Club: Bloomsburg Kiwanis (song leader). Editor: The Community Junior College: An Annotated Bibliography, 1966. Home: 236 W Third St Bloomsburg PA 17815 Office: 108 Waller Hall Bloomsburg State College Bloomsburg PA 17815

RASA, GERALD LYNN, coll. adminstr.; b. Higginsville, Mo., Dec. 3, 1946; s. Clifford and Gladys Louise (Dohrman) R.; B.S., Central Mo. State U., 1968, M.A., 1969; m. Catherine; children—Jason Christopher, Jennifer Lynn. News dir., asst. pub. relations dir. Elmhurst Coll., 1969-74; dir. pub. relations Thiel Coll., 1974-79; pub. info. and editorial services mgr. The Transp. Research Center, U. Tenn., Knoxville, 1979—; profl. cons. communications. Nat. pres. Little People of America, Inc., 1974—, Little People of America Found., 1974—. Mem. Council for Advancement and Support of Edn. Lutheran. Home: 6103 Easton Rd at Butterfly Lake Knoxville TN 37920 Office: U Tenn Knoxville TN 37920

RASBURY, AVERY GUINN, investment firm exec.; b. Fort Worth, Dec. 18, 1923; s. William Avery and Annie Lee (Lynn) R.; student Decatur (Tex.) Bapt. Coll., 1947-48; B.B.A., North Tex. State U., 1950, postgrad., 1950-51; m. Linda Loo Baker, Nov. 19, 1971; 1 dau. by previous marriage, Sandra (Mrs. John Thomas Cleveland, III). Asst. accountant McKesson-Robbins Inc., Houston, 1951; sr. accountant Koshkin & Levingston, C.P.A.'s., Houston, 1951-53; exec. asst., bus. mgr. J. Robert Neal, Houston, 1953-71, 74-79, 81, Las Vegas, Nev., 1971-74, 80—; exec. v.p., dir. West-Jet Aviation Co., Las Vegas, 1971-74; pres., dir. Bonhomme Corp., Houston, Las Vegas, 1967—, Multi-Fab Inc., Houston, 1972-78, G.H. Hart Co., Inc., Houston, 1978—; v.p., dir. Aerostar Nev. Corp., Las Vegas, 1980—; v.p., controller, dir. Process Equipment Engrs., Inc., Houston, 1980—. Served with USMCR, 1941-47; PTO, Phillipines. Mem. Nat. Soc. Pub. Accountants, Civitan Internat. (Civitan of Year 1963, Outstanding Club pres. 1966, lt. gov. dist. 1966-67), Second Marine Div. Assn. (pres. 1958-59, treas. 1964—), Nat. Rifle Assn., Internat. Platform Assn., Houston Livestock Show and Rodeo. Republican. Baptist (deacon). Clubs: Hearthstone Country, Las Vegas Country. Home: 1608 S Gessner Rd Houston TX 77063 Office: 1230 Antoine St Houston TX 77055

RASCH, STANLEY ALVIN, mgmt. cons.; b. N.Y.C., May 15, 1930; s. Joseph and Betty (Mollot) R.; B.A., Coll. City N.Y., 1952; M.I.L.R., Cornell U., 1956; m. Marcia Louise Glatman, Feb. 17, 1980; children—Bruce, Jody, Mark, Stuart. Vice pres. Bache & Co., Inc., N.Y.C., 1960-71; dir. personnel Salomon Bros., N.Y.C., 1971-73; pres. Rasch & Hertz Personnel Inc., N.Y.C., 1973-79, Stanley Rasch & Assos., Ltd., N.Y.C., 1979—. Served with U.S. Army, 1953-55. Mem. Assn. Personnel Cons.'s N.Y. (pres.), Nat. Assn. Personnel Cons.'s, Wall St. Personnel Mgmt. Assn., UN Assn. Democrat. Jewish. Clubs: Benjamin Franklin Reform Democratic, New Dem.

Home: 139 E 35th St New York NY 10016 Office: 2 W 45 St New York NY 10036

RASCHKE, ALFRED CHARLES, pump mfg. co. exec.; b. Chgo., Aug. 4, 1924; s. Alfred Henry and Gladys Merle (Emery) R.; grad. Exec. Devel. Program, U. Mich., 1966, Advanced Mgmt. Program, Harvard U., 1973; m. Loraine Maude Twigg, Aug. 31, 1946; children—Loral Jean, Charles Allen. With Minn. Mining & Mfrs. Co., Chgo., 1942-50, br. office mgr., 1950; pres. Bennett Pump Co., Muskegon, Mich., 1950—, Ind. Pump Co., Muskegon, 1980—; dir. Enterprise Brass Works. Sect. chmn. United Way of Muskegon County; mem. city council City of Whitehall, 1952-58, mayor, 1958. Served with U.S. Army, 1943-46. Mem. Am. Petroleum Inst., Petroleum Equipment Inst. (codir.), Gasoline Pump Mfrs. Assn. (chmn.), Muskegon Mfrs. A (dir.), Harvard Bus. Club Western Mich. Episcopalian. Clubs: Century (bd. govs.) (Muskegon). Office: Bennett Pump Co PO Box 597 Muskegon MI 49443

RASHEDI, T. A., banker; b. Khost, Afghanistan, Mar. 3, 1936; s. Sahibzada Mohammad Tayyib and Deenmana Latif; came to U.S., 1965; F.S.C., T.I. Coll., Lahore, Pakistan, 1951-53; student Queens Coll., 1967-68; M.B.A., Golden Gate U., San Francisco, 1969; children—Mohammad Sharif, Deen Mana, Mohammed Arshad. Controller, USI Mgmt., Vancouver, B.C., Can., 1969-70; v.p. internat. banking United Fin. Group, San Francisco, 1970-73; asst. controller Bank of Am., San Francisco, 1973-75, asst. v.p., mgr. of investments Bank Am. Europe, Middle East and Africa, 1975-77; v.p., mgr. fin. analysis and mgmt. reporting Seattle First Nat. Bank, 1977-78; prin. cons. Cons. div. Boeing Co., Seattle, 1971-79; v.p., mgr. resources mgmt. and planning Old Nat. Bank, Spokane, Wash. and propr. and gen. mgr. MR VEE DUB, Seattle, 1979—; dir. USI Bank of Panama, 1971-72, Kommerzial Bank, Zurich, Switzerland. Pres., Parents Group, Marin County, Calif., 1974; mem. adv. com. for handicapped children Marin County, 1974. Mem. Planning Execs. Inst., C. of C., Boeing Mgmt. Assn. Contbr. articles in field of loan pricing and profitability. Home: 20138 44th Ave NE Seattle WA 98155 Office: 13323 Lake City Way NE Seattle WA 98125

RASMANIS, EGONS, electronics co. exec.; b. Riga, Latvia, July 12, 1924; s. Janis Andrejs and Anna (Smemanis) R.; came to U.S., 1950, naturalized, 1955; B.Sc., Friedrich Alexander U., Erlangen, Ger., 1949; postgrad. Northeastern U., 1955; m. Vita Anita Skulte, June 30, 1956; children—Anita Ilze, Ingrid Inta, Linda Irene. Mgr. devel. engring. CBS Electronics, Lowell, Mass., 1956-60; project mgr., prin. engr. GT & E Sylvania, Waltham, Mass., 1960-64; mgr. microelectronics Amperex Co., Cranston, R.I., 1964-69, mgr. mfg., 1969-72; co-founder, v.p. sales Micro Components Corp., Cranston, 1972-78; v.p. sales Cherry Semicondr. Co., 1978—. Pres. Latvian Acad. Soc. Fraternitas Metropolitana, Boston, 1957-59, 62-64, 75-77, 79—. Mem. Internat. Soc. Hybrid Microelectronics. Lutheran. Patentee in field of semicondrs. and microelectronics. Home: 151 Westwood Dr East Greenwich RI 02818 Office: 99 Bald Hill Rd Cranston RI 02920

RASMUSON, ELMER EDWIN, banker; b. Yakutat, Alaska, Feb. 15, 1909; s. Edward Anton and Jenny (Olson) R.; B.S. magna cum laude, Harvard, 1930, A.M., 1935; student U. Grenoble, 1930; LL.D. (hon.), U. Alaska, 1970; m. Lile Vivian Bernard, Oct. 27, 1939 (dec. 1960); children—Edward Bernard, Lile Muchmore, Judy Ann; m. 2d, Mary Louise Milligan, Nov. 4, 1961. Chief accountant Nat. Investors Corp., N.Y.C., 1933-35; prin. Arthur Andersen & Co., N.Y.C., 1935-43; pres. Nat. Bank of Alaska, 1943-65, chmn., 1965—; dir. Anchorage-Westward Hotel Co. Mayor of Anchorage, 1964-67; civilian aide Alaska to sec. of army, 1959-67; Swedish consul for Alaska, 1955-77. Pres. Alaska council Boy Scouts Am. Mem. city council, Anchorage, 1945, chmn. city planning commn., 1950-53; U.S. commr. Internat. N. Pacific Fisheries Commn., 1969—; mem. Nat. Marine Fisheries Adv. Com., 1974-77, N. Pacific Fishery Mgmt. Council, 1976-77. Trustee, Alaska Permanent Fund, 1980—; sec.-treas., Loussac Found.; bd. dirs. Lincoln Inst. Land Policy, 1980—; chmn. bd. Rasmuson Found.; sec. Rhodes Scholarship Com. for Alaska, 1960-66; regent U. Alaska, 1949-69; trustee King's Lake Camp, Inc., 1944—. Decorated Royal Order Vasa 1st Class, comdr. Royal Order No. Star (Sweden); recipient Outstanding Civilian Service medal; named Alaskan of Yr., 1976. C.P.A., N.Y., Tex., Alaska. Mem. Pioneers Alaska, Alaska Bankers Assn. (past pres.), Phi Beta Kappa. Republican. Presbyterian. Clubs: Masons, Elks, Rotary (past pres. Anchorage); Harvard (N.Y.C. and Boston); Wash. Athletic, Rainier, Seattle Yacht (Seattle); Explorers; Thunderbird (Palm Desert, Calif.); Bohemian (San Francisco). Office: Box 600 Anchorage AK 99510

RASMUSSEN, EDWARD FREDERICK, airline co. exec.; b. Mpls., June 5, 1940; s. Hans Edward and Lois Ruth (Welch) R.; student pub. schs., Hopkins, Minn.; m. Lena K. Clement, May 1981; stepchildren—Greg Carvalho, Heather Carvalho; 1 son by previous marriage, John Edward. Served as enlisted man U.S. Navy, 1959-67, with Western Air Lines, Los Angeles, 1967—, avionics line service foreman, Los Angeles, 1975. Mem. Internat. Platform Assn. Republican. Home: 10488 Apache River Ave Fountain Valley CA 92708 Office: PO Box 92005 World Way Center Los Angeles CA 90009

RASMUSSEN, WILLIAM FRANKLYN, TV exec.; b. Chgo., Oct. 15, 1932; s. William Arnold and Gertrude Ann (O'Conner) R.; B.A., DePauw U., 1954; M.B.A., Rutgers U., 1960; m. Lois Ann McDonnell, June 25, 1955; children—Scott William, Glenn Justin, Lynn Sharon. Advt. asst. Lamp div. Westinghouse Corp., Bloomfield, N.J., 1957-59; v.p., gen. mgr. Ad-Aid, Inc., Newark, 1959-62; sports dir. Sta. WTTT-AM, Amherst, Mass., 1962-64; sports dir. Sta. WWLP-TV, Springfield, Mass., 1965-69, news dir., co-anchor, 1970-74; communications dir. New Eng. Whalers, Hartford, 1974-78; founder, chmn. ESPN, Inc., Bristol, Conn., 1978-80; chmn. Enterprise Radio, Inc., Avon, Conn., 1980—; dir. Rasmussen Enterprises, Inc., Avon. Served with USAF, 1954-56. Edward Rector scholar, 1950-54. Mem. Nat. Cable TV Assn. Pioneer in 24-hour day sports network for TV cable systems. Office: Enterprise Radio 40 Darling Dr Avon CT 06001

RASPA, RALPH FRANK, constrn. co. exec.; b. Rivesville, W.Va., Feb. 26, 1927; s. Frank and Catherine (Scalise) R.; student W.Va. Bus. Coll., 1944-45; B.S. in Journalism, Fairmont State Coll., 1951; m. Edith E. Barth, Nov. 22, 1953; children—Cecilia, Ralph M., Joni. Pres., Mountaineer Homes, Fairmont, W.Va., 1959-65, Community Homes, Fairmont, 1964—, Mt. Vernon Devel. Co., Fairmont, 1970-74, Hallmark Homes, Fairmont, 1976—. Bd. dirs. Marion County 3-A. Served with U.S. Army, 1945-46. Mem. Nat. Home Builders Assn. Democrat. Roman Catholic. Club: Elks. Home: PO Box 1143 Fairmont WV 26554 Office: PO Box 226 Fairmont WV 26554

RASSIEUR, CHARLES LOUIS, mfg. co. exec.; b. St. Louis, July 4, 1931; s. Theodore Edward and Margaret (Kuehn) R.; B.S., Yale U., 1953; m. Roberta Dower Boyd, Dec. 27, 1974. With Central Mine Equipment Co., St. Louis, 1956—, v.p., 1959-66, pres., 1966—; dir. Custom Packaging Corp., Vess Ltd. Served with U.S. Army, 1953-55. Mem. ASTM. Office: 6200 N Broadway Saint Louis MO 63147

RATCLIFFE, MYRON FENWICK, investment mgmt. exec., banker; b. Evanston, Ill.; s. James Lewis and Jean (Gardner) R.; B.S., U. Ill., 1925; m. Margaret Archibald; 1 dau., Elizabeth Robertson (Mrs. Robert W. Heinze). With Goldman, Sachs & Co., 1925-33; adminstr. financial codes NRA, 1934-35; with Lehman Bros., 1936-49; partner Bache & Co., 1949-56; pres., dir. Miami Corp., Chgo., 1956-77, Cutler Oil & Gas Corp., 1956-77; chmn. bd., dir. Nat. Blvd. Bank of Chgo., 1956—; dir. Nat.-Standard Co., Niles, Mich.; gov. Midwest Stock Exchange, 1949-56. Trustee Children's Home and Aid Soc. Ill. Served as lt. col. AUS, 1942-46. Decorated Legion of Merit. Mason. Clubs: Bond, Chicago, Mid-America, Casino (Chgo.); Old Elm, Ft. Sheridan (Ill.); Indian Hill (Winnetka, Ill.); Birnam Wood Golf (Santa Barbara, Calif.). Home: 82 Indian Hill Rd Winnetka IL 60093 Office: 410 N Michigan Ave Chicago IL 60611

RATCLIFFE, SHELIA PANNELL, personnel cons.; b. Batesburg, S.C., July 23, 1953; d. Craig Dennis and Mary Kathleen (Fisher) Pannell; married; B.A., Western Carolina U., 1973, M.A., 1977. Employment supr. Litton Industries, Murphy, N.C., 1974-78; with Dunhill of Knoxville, Inc. (Tenn.), fin. personnel specialists, 1980—; personnel mgmt. cons. Ratcliffe & Co., 1980—; instr. personnel adminstrn. U. Tenn.; indsl. relations mgr. Am. Thread Co., Marble, N.C., 1978—; instr. Tri-County Community Coll.; instr. Mars Hill Coll.; cons. indsl., sch.-sponsored tng. Vice pres. Cherokee County United Fund, 1980. Named Cherokee County Young Career Woman, 1978. Mem. Am. Soc. Tng. and Devel. (past v.p.), Western N.C. Safety Council. Baptist. Clubs: Altrusa (ext. chmn.), Cherokee County Women's Assn. Golf. Home: 556 Lost Tree Ln Knoxville TN 37922 Office: Suite 1317 United Am Plaza Knoxville TN 37929

RATH, JAMES ARTHUR, III, public relations cons.; b. Honolulu, Dec. 30, 1931; s. James Arthur and Ruth (Lyman) R.; B.A., Hamilton Coll., 1953; postgrad. Syracuse U., 1958-62; m. Jenaud Schwartz, Feb. 14, 1976; children by previous marriage—Lani, Scott, Luana, Keone, James Arthur. Advt. mgr. Ottaway Newspapers Radio, N.Y. and Pa., 1953-57; account exec. Spitz Advt., Syracuse, N.Y., 1957-60; v.p. L.M. Harvey, N.Y.C. and Syracuse, 1960-63; partner Rath-Johnston Co., Rochester, N.Y.C. and Syracuse, 1963-65; pres. Rath Orgn., Syracuse, Rochester and N.Y.C., 1965—; adj. prof. Newhouse Sch. Communications, Syracuse U., 1973—; lectr. in field. Bd. dirs. Syracuse Ballet Theatre, 1975-76, Civic Morning Musicals, 1974-76, Planned Parenthood, 1966-68, Priority One, 1969-70, Salt City Playhouse, 1965-75. Recipient award N.Y. Art Dirs., N.Y.C., 1977; named Man of Yr., Am. Mktg. Assn., 1969. Mem. Public Relations Soc. Am. (chpt. pres. 1966-68, chmn. eastern dist. 1966-67, Silver Anvil award 1963, 65, 66, 68), Bank Mktg. Assn. (Gold Coin award 1969), Bus. and Indsl. Communications, Hawaiian Mission Soc. Author: History of Professional Photography, 1977; Marketing Professional Photography, 1978; History of Eastman Kodak Co., 1980; contbr. articles to profl. jours.; columnist. Home: 17 Montgomery St Cherry Valley NY 13320 Office: Rath Orgn Hills Bldg Syracuse NY 13202

RATLIFF, JOHN WESLEY, mgmt. cons.; b. Goree, Tex., Feb. 11, 1934; s. Wellington Harve and Grace (Thornton) R.; student U. Tex., 1951-52; B.B.A., N. Tex. State U., 1955; m. Robbie Harlan, May 31, 1955; children—Robin Anne Ratliff Shivers, John Wesley, Lisa Karen, Kimberly Harlan. Mktg. exec. IBM, Ft. Worth, 1962-67; partner Rausher Pierce Securities Corp., Ft. Worth, 1967-69; pres. Venture Capital Mgmt., Inc., Ft. Worth, 1969-73, chmn. bd., 1969-73; spl. asst. to chief exec. officer and to chmn. bd. Tandy Corp., Ft. Worth, 1973-78; chmn. bd. Lancelot Corp., Ft. Worth, 1970-73; chmn. bd. Am. Time Corp., 1969-72; pres. RCM Corp., Ft. Worth, 1978—. Bd. dirs. First United Meth. Ch., 1968—, Fort Worth Girl's Club, 1976-78. Served to lt. USN, 1956-62. Recipient Sales Mktg. Exec. Victor award, 1965. Mem. Phi Kappa Sigma. Clubs: Shady Oaks Country; Fort Worth. Office: 1201 Fort Worth Club Tower Fort Worth TX 76102

RATONYI, ROBERT, telephone co. exec.; b. Budapest, Hungary, Jan. 11, 1938; B.S. in Mech. Engring., M.I.T., 1963, M.S., 1964; M.S. in Mgmt., Drexel U., 1967; m. Eva Iren Vero, Aug. 18, 1963; children—David, Tina. Research asst. M.I.T., 1963-64; design engr., test. supr. Gen. Electric Co., 1964; bus. analyst corp. planning staff Gilbarco, Inc. div. Exxon Enterprises, 1967-70; sr. bus. devel. analyst Xerox Corp., 1970-72, mgr. forward planning data system div., 1972-76, mgr. bus. strategy planning office systems div., 1976-78; v.p. corp. devel. Continental Telephone Corp., Atlanta, 1978—. Mem. benefits com. Assembly of Engring., Nat. Research Council. Mem. Am. Mgmt. Assn., N.Am. Soc. Corp. Planning. Office: 56 Perimeter Center E Atlanta GA 30346

RAU, ALFRED, forging co. exec.; b. Bamberg, Ger., Dec. 31, 1927; s. Karl Eduard and Annie R.; came to U.S., 1960, naturalized, 1965; student Institito De Segunda Ensenanza Del Vedado, Vedado, Havana, Cuba, 1942-47, St. Tomas U.; m. Albertine Marie Hooijer, Nov. 6, 1955; children—Annette Caroline, Michel George. Partner, Compania Comercial Olympia, S.A., steel mill reps., Havana, Cuba, 1947-56; co-founder, gen. mgr. Metalurgica Basica Nacional, S.A., Havana, 1956-60; mgr. export mktg. Nat. Forge Co., Irvine, Pa., 1960-63, v.p. mktg., 1966-67, v.p., gen. mgr. Irvine and Titusville, Pa., 1967-68, exec. v.p., 1968-79, pres., chief operating officer, 1979—; v.p. Nat. Forge Export Corp., Brussels, Belgium, 1963-66. Mem. bd. dirs. Warren County Sch. Dist., 1976—. Mem. Bus. Internat., Machinery and Allied Products Inst., Internat. Ops. Council. Clubs: Valley Hunt; Conewango Valley Country.

RAU, JOHN EDWARD, banker; b. Milw., June 19, 1948; s. Edward J. and Grace Barbara (Kutschenreuter) R.; B.A., B.S., Boston Coll., 1970; M.B.A., Harvard, 1972. Dir. corporate devel. 1st Chgo. Corp., Chgo., 1973-74, corporate officer finance and treasury, 1975; mgr. planning and adminstrn. 1st Nat. Bank Chgo., 1976-77, v.p., div. mgr., 1977-78, gen. mgr. internat. banking, 1979; exec. v.p. Exchange Nat. Bank Chgo., 1980—; asst. prof. finance Master Program, Chgo. Keller Grad. Sch. Bus. Election judge Project LEAP, 1976; bd. contbrs. Henrotin Hosp., 1975; mem. asso. bd. Chgo. Child Care Soc. Served with U.S. Army, 1970-71. Harvard-Goldman, Sachs Sr. Finance fellow, 1971-72; Finnegan Outstanding Grad. grantee, 1969-70. Mem. Assn. Masters in Bus. Adminstrn., Art Inst. Chgo., Am. Mgmt. Assn. (instr.). Clubs: Harvard Bus. Sch., Harvard, Athletic Assn. (Chgo.); Mid-Town. Author: (with D.J. Vitale) Dividend Policy, The Corporate Treasurers Handbook, 1976. Home: 1310 Ritchie Ct Chicago IL 60610 Office: 130 S LaSalle St Chicago IL 60603

RAUCH, ARTHUR IRVING, pharm. co. exec.; b. N.Y.C., Sept. 18, 1933; s. David and Miriam (Frankel) R.; B.A. magna cum laude (Rufus Choate scholar), Dartmouth, 1954, M.S., Amos Tuck Sch. Bus. Adminstrn., 1955; m. Roxane M. Spiller, Aug. 19, 1962 (div. 1977); children—David S., Janine B. Security analyst Lionel D. Edie & Co., N.Y.C., 1959-64; group dir. research Eastman Dillon, Union Securities & Co., N.Y.C., 1964-68; v.p., sr. analyst Laird, Inc., N.Y.C., 1968-69, dir. research, 1969-71, sr. v.p., 1970-73; partner Oppenheimer & Co., N.Y.C., 1973-77; v.p. corp. devel. Rorer Group Inc., Ft. Washington, Pa., 1977—. Exec. com. Dartmouth Class of 1954, 1968-79. Bd. dirs. Schuster Fund, 1968-69; mem. investment com. Becker Fund, 1969-73. Served to lt. (j.g.) USNR, 1956-59. Chartered financial analyst. Mem. N.Y. Soc. Security Analysts, Financial Analysts Fedn. (corporate information com.), Phi Beta Kappa. Club: Dartmouth College (N.Y.C.). Home: 116 Cheshire Dr Penllyn PA 19422 Office: 500 Virginia Ave Fort Washington PA 19034

RAUSCH, ELDRED ALBERT, retail chain exec.; b. Plain City, Ohio, Feb., 1922; s. Albert and Josephine R.; B.A., Ohio State U., 1943; J.D., DePaul U., 1951; m. 1946. With U.S. Gypsum Co., 1949-51; with Sears, Roebuck and Co., Chgo., 1952—, nat. risk and ins. mgr., 1964—; admitted to Ill. bar, 1951. Served with USNR, 1943-46. Decorated Purple Heart; C.P.C.U. Mem. Am. Mgmt. Assn., Risk and Ins. Mgmt. Soc. Office: Sears Tower Dept 765 Chicago IL 60684

RAUSCH, GEORGE HANS, mfg. co. exec.; b. Vienna, Austria, Apr. 22, 1927; came to U.S., 1939, naturalized, 1945; s. Leopold and Alma (Weissenstein) R.; B.S., N.Y. U., 1952, Ph.D., 1965; M.S., Columbia U., 1956; m. Helen Stern, June 20, 1954; children—Debra Susan, Douglas Jay. With Mason Candies, Inc., Mineola, N.Y., 1957-70, chief exec. officer, pres., 1963-70; chief exec. officer, pres. Didactic Systems, Inc., Westbury, N.Y., 1970-73, Wallace Candies, Elizabeth, N.J., 1974; exec. v.p., chief ops. officer Schrafft Candy Co., Waltham, Mass., 1974-78; chmn. bd., Corporate Growth Resources, Waltham, 1978—; prof. Pace U., N.Y.C., Hofstra U., Hempstead, N.Y., 1964-74. Served with U.S. Army, 1945-46. Mem. Am. Arbitration Assn. (arbitrator 1954—), AAUP, Nat. Assn. Tobacco Disbrs., Nat. Candy Wholesalers, Assn. Mfrs. Chocolate and Confectionery (dir. 1964-78), Mensa. Club: Candy Execs. Contbr. articles to profl. jours. Home: 44 Rawson Rd Brookline MA 02146 Office: 303 Wyman St Waltham MA 02154

RAUSENBERGER, MARTIN LACEY, auto import exec.; b. Hackensack, N.J., Sept. 12, 1939; s. Wilfred Albert and Winifred (Lacey) R.; B.S. in Bus. Adminstrn., The Citadel, Charleston, S.C., 1963; postgrad. Fairleigh Dickinson U.; m. Geraldine Patricia Wolff, Jan. 8, 1966; children—Wendy Jean, Douglas Joseph, Corrin Holley. Warranty analyst Chevrolet Motor div. Gen. Motors Corp., 1964-67; successively warranty auditor, service coordinator, Warranty adminstr., customer relations mgr. World Wide Volkswagen Corp., 1968-74; asst. nat. service mgr. Bricklin Vehicle Corp., 1975-76; regional service-parts tng. instr. Fiat Motors N. Am., 1976-77; nat. customer relations mgr. Subaru Am., Inc., Pennsauken, N.J., 1977—. Pres., Green Pond (N.J.) 1st Aid Squadron, 1966; treas. Kings Grant Civic Assn., Marlton, N.J., 1979—; active local Boy Scouts Am. Recipient various awards Boy Scouts Am. Mem. Internat. Assn. Word Processors, Soc. Consumers Affairs and Profls. Roman Catholic. Clubs: Green Pond Water Ski, Kings Grant Chess. Author manuals. Home: 2 Kirkbridge Ct E Marlton NJ 08053 Office: 7040 Central Pkwy Pennsauken NJ 08109

RAUTH, J. DONALD, bus. exec.; b. Pitman, N.J., Jan. 7, 1918; s. Harry J. and H. Virginia (Kline) R.; B.M.E., Drexel Inst. Tech., 1940, Ph.D. (hon.), 1964; m. Catherine A. Burns, May 1, 1943; children—J. Donald, Kathryn Virginia. With Martin Co. (now Martin Marietta Corp., merged with Am. Marietta Corp. 1961), Balt., 1940—, pres. aerospace group, 1967-69; pres., chief exec. officer Martin-Marietta Aluminum, Inc., 1969-72; pres. Martin-Marietta Corp., 1972-77, chmn. bd., chief exec. officer, 1977—; dir. Am. Security Corp., Am. Security Bank NA, Acacia Mut. Life Ins. Co., Brunswick Corp. Trustee Drexel U. Office: 6801 Rockledge Dr Bethesda MD 20034*

RAVA, JOSEPH JOHN, appraisal co. exec.; b. Pittston, Pa., July 2, 1941; s. Joseph Martin and Anna Irene (Mikitish) R.; B.S. in Math. and Physics, U. Scranton, 1962; m. Diana Judith Wyandt, Oct. 12, 1963; children—Joseph Stephen, Rachael Ann. Computer programmer Pa. R.R., Phila., 1965-66; programmer systems analyst E.D.P. Corp. of Pa., King of Prussia, 1966-67, dir. data processing, 1967-69, v.p., 1969-70; dir. data processing Marshall & Stevens Inc., Phila., 1970-71, area adminstr., 1971-73, area v.p. adminstrn., 1973-78, corp. v.p., gen. mgr., 1978—. Active various civic orgns. Served to capt. U.S. Army, 1963-65. Mem. Data Processing Mgmt. Assn., Hosp. Fin. Mgmt. Assn., Am. Mgmt. Assn., U.S. Jaycees (life senator), Upper Merion Jaycees (dir. 1969), Audubon Oaks Jaycees (pres. 1974, v.p. 1975, state dir. 1976). Democrat. Roman Catholic. Home: 1025 Longspur Rd Audubon PA 19407 Office: 1845 Walnut St Philadelphia PA 19103

RAVESE, JOSEPH JOHN, fin. exec.; b. N.Y.C., Nov. 3, 1921; s. Frank and Mary Frances (Loschiavo) R.; B.S., Columbia U., 1945; m. Theresa G. Quaranta, Oct. 13, 1957; children—Theresa G., Mary Louise. Sr. acct. Ernst & Ernst, N.Y.C., 1939-42; sr. auditor Nat. Parts Mfg. Corp., N.Y.C., 1942-45; asst. controller Mack Mfg. Corp., N.Y.C., 1945-47; asst. controller, asst. sec. Stein, Hall & Co., Inc., N.Y.C., 1947-68; controller Gries Reproducer Co. div. Coats and Clark, Inc., New Rochelle, N.Y., 1969—; cons., lectr. Served with AUS, 1941-43. C.P.A., N.Y. Mem. Nat. Assn. Accts., Nat. Soc. Public Accts., Data Processing Mgmt. Assn., Inst. Internal Auditors. Home: 1065 Clay Ave Pelham Manor NY 10803 Office: 125 Beechwood Ave New Rochelle NY 10802

RAWAL, BHARAT SINGH, research lab. mgr.; b. New Delhi, India, Dec. 4, 1948; came to U.S., 1970, naturalized, 1979; s. Ram S. and Shakuntla (Dhingra) R.; B.S. in Engring., Indian Inst. Tech., Kanpur, 1970; M.S., Case-Western Res. U., Cleve., 1973; Ph.D. (fellow), Rensselaer Poly. Inst., 1976; m. Reeta Pawa, Jan. 18, 1975; 1 dau., Ekta. Research asso. N.C. State U., 1977-78; research scientist AVX Ceramics Corp., Myrtle Beach, S.C., 1978-79, sect. mgr. corp. research lab., 1979—. Army Research Office grantee, 1977-78. Mem. Am. Ceramic Soc., AAAS, ASTM. Contbr. articles to internat. jours. Home: 531 Forestbrook Dr Myrtle Beach SC 29577 Office: PO Box 867 Myrtle Beach SC 29577

RAWLINGS, JAMES WILSON, business exec.; b. Provo, Utah, Oct. 12, 1929; s. Arnold Eber and Corinne (Wilson) R.; B.S., Brigham Young U., 1955; J.D., U. Utah, 1958; m. Joan E. Berkhimer, Mar. 28, 1952; children—Stephen C., Suzanne C., Diane I., Scott D., David B. Admitted to Utah bar, 1958, N.Y. bar, 1959; asso. firm Chadbourne, Parke, Whiteside and Woolf, 1958-60; with Union Carbide Corp., 1960—, v.p. metals div., 1969-78, chmn. bd., pres. Union Carbide So. Africa, Inc., N.Y.C., 1978—. Served with USAF, 1950-54. Mem. Utah Bar Assn., Am. Bar Assn., Order of Coif. Club: University (N.Y.C.). Editor-in-chief Utah Law Rev., 1958. Office: 270 Park Ave New York NY 10017

RAWLINGS, WILLIAM EDWIN, diversified mfg. co. exec.; b. Newport, Ky., Oct. 5, 1931; s. John Thomas and Margaret (Widrig) R.; B.A. cum laude, Washington and Lee U., 1953; M.B.A., Harvard U., 1955; m. Arlene Graham Hunt, June 5, 1961; children—John, Christopher, Susan, Lesley. With Gen. Foods Corp., 1958-73, pres. Pet Foods div., then corp. v.p., until 1973; group v.p. The Gillette Co., Boston, 1974-77; pres., dir. Am. Maize-Products Co., N.Y.C., 1977—; dir. West Chem. Co. Bd. dirs. USN Meml. Found. Served to lt. USN, 1955-58. Mem. Grocery Mfrs. Assn., Corn Refiners Assn. Roman Catholic. Clubs: Harvard of N.Y.C.; Essex County. Home: 489 Silvermine Rd New Canaan CT 06840 Office: 22 Gate House Rd Stamford CT 06902

RAWLINS, RICHARD CALDWELL, banker; b. Borger, Tex., Sept. 18, 1946; s. Carl Elbert and Anne (Caldwell) R.; A.A.S. in Bus., Cooke County Jr. Coll., 1971; B.B.A., N. Tex. State U., 1973; m. Diana Gail Peairs, Dec. 1, 1970; 1 dau., Annot Caryl. Officer trainee Corsicana (Tex.) Nat. Bank, 1973-74, asst. v.p., loan officer, 1974-75, ops. officer, 1975-78, v.p. mortgage loan dept., loan officer, 1978; v.p., controller 1st Nat. Bank of Irving (Tex.), 1978-80; v.p., cashier Kermit (Tex.) State Bank, 1980—. Treas., dir. Community Services, Inc., Corsicana, 1975—; bd. dirs. Am. Cancer Soc., 1973-76, chmn. nominating com., 1974-75; farm mgmt. com. Navarro County (Tex.) Extension Services, 1974-76. Served with USN, 1965-69. Recipient numerous commendations, citations. Mem. Am. Inst. Banking, Bank Adminstrn. Inst. (chpt. dir.), Nat., Tex. rifle assns. Episcopalian. Club: Ducks Unlimited, Lions, Winkler Country Trap and Gun. Home: PO Box 202 Kermit TX 79745 Office: PO Drawer K Kermit TX 79745

RAWLS, WALTER CECIL, JR., lawyer, scientist; b. Richmond, Va., Sept. 13, 1928; s. Walter Cecil and Ella (Freeman) R.; A.B., U. Mo., 1951; J.D., Washington U., St. Louis, 1958; D.Sc. (hon.), Davis Coll. 1973; m. Sheila Daphne Kirsch, June 30, 1954; children—James David, Richard Wayne. Agt. for France, Am. Trust Life Ins. Co., Wichita Falls, Tex., 1953-54; admitted to Fla. bar, 1958, since practiced in Jacksonville, Fla.; mem. firm Ragland, Kurz, Toole, 1958, Marks, Gray, Yates, Conroy, Gibbs, 1959; pvt. practice, 1960-67, 69—; partner Thomas & Rawls, 1963-67, Ogier, Stubbs, & Rawls, 1967-68; treas. Ga.-Fla. Oil & Refining Co., Inc.; v.p., dir. Capital Res. Ltd.; v.p., sec., dir. CANVI-ANDOR; pres. Biomagnetics Internat., Inc.; dir. F.I.D. Internat., Internat. Films Corp.; asso. dir. A.R.D. Research Lab. Mem. adv. com. Washington U. Law Sch. Served with AUS, 1951-53. Fellow Coll. Human Scis.; mem. Am., Jacksonville bar assns., Fla. Bar, Am. Soc. Internat. Law, Am. Legion, S.A.R., S.C.V., AAAS, N.Y. Acad. Scis., English Speaking Union, Am. Trial Lawyers Assn., Am. Arbitration Assn., Am. Philatelic Soc., Phi Delta Theta, Delta Theta Phi. Republican. Clubs: Explorers; Metropolitan Dinner (officer, mem. orgn. com.) (Jacksonville, Fla.). Co-author: Magnetism and Its Effects on the Living System; The Magnetic Effect; The Rainbow in Your Hands; The Magnetic Blueprint of Life. Home: 3584 Beauclerc Rd Jacksonville FL 32217 Office: 2301 Park Ave Orange Park FL 32073

RAWSON, MERLE RICHARD, appliance mfg. co. exec.; b. Chgo., June 9, 1924; s. Richard W. and Flora (Morgan) R.; student U. Ill., 1946-48; B.S., Northwestern U., 1949; m. Jane Armstrong, July 5, 1947; children—David M., Jeffrey M., Laurel J. Asst. to plant controller John Wood Co., 1949-58; asst. controller Easy Laundry Appliances, Chgo.. 1958-61; controller O'Bryan Brothers, Chgo., 1961; budget dir. Hoover Co., North Canton, Ohio, 1961-62, controller, 1962-64, v.p., treas., 1964-69, dir., 1968—, sr. v.p., treas., 1969-75, chmn., chief exec. officer, 1975—; dir. Hoover Indsl. y Comml. S.A. (Colombia), 1967; dir. Hoover Worldwide Corp., 1968, sr. v.p., 1969-71, exec. v.p., 1971-75, chmn., chief exec. officer, 1975—; chmn. Hoover Ltd. (U.K.), 1978—; dir. Hoover Co., Ltd. (Can.), Hoover, Ltd. (U.K.), Hoover Mexicana S.A. de C.V., Hoover Holland B.V., S.A. Hoover (France), Hoover Adminstrv. Services, S.A. (Belgium), Hoover Export Corp., Chemko Comml. Products, Canton, Soc. Corp., Cleve., Harter Bank & Trust Co. Trustee, Eisenhower Exchange Fellowship, Ohio Found. Ind. Colls., Citizens Council for Ohio Schs.; mem. adv. council Pace U.; mem. Aultman Hosp. Assn., Aultman Hosp. Devel. Found. Served with F.A., AUS, 1943-46. Mem. Council Fgn. Relations, Stark County Bluecoats, Brit.-N.Am. Com. Clubs: Union League (N.Y.C.); Capitol Hill; Canton; Congress Lake Country; Rotary (hon.). Office: Hoover Co 101 E Maple St North Canton OH 44720

RAY, GEORGE DAWSON, savs. and loan exec.; b. Mundelein, Ill., Aug. 26, 1914; s. Lloyd Carlysle and Ellen Cecelia (Dawson) R.; S.B. in Aerospace Engring., M.I.T., 1936; postgrad. Inst. Fin. Edn., 1975-79, U. Buffalo, 1941; m. Nancy Campbell Humphrey, Dec. 2, 1944; children—Wendy, Elizabeth, Nancy. Aerospace engr. Douglas Aircraft Co., 1936-40, Curtiss-Wright Co., 1936-41; chief aircraft engr. Bell Aerospace Corp., Niagara Falls, N.Y., 1941-60; sr. project engr. Boeing Co., Seattle, 1960-70; ret., 1970; chief engr. Structural Concepts Co., Chgo., 1970-73; v.p. Mundelein Savs. & Loan Assn., 1973—. Fellow AIAA (asso.). Republican. Roman Catholic. Patentee swimming pool enclosure, aerospace field. Home: 634 Nordic Ct PO Box 55 Libertyville IL 60048 Office: 401 N Seymour Ave PO Box 547 Mundelein IL 60060

RAY, RATHBURN APPLEGATE, real estate investment broker; b. Chattanooga, Apr. 17, 1908; s. George Lee and Mary Elizabeth (Thornton) R.; student Tenn. Wesleyan Coll., 1929; B.S. in Bus. Adminstrn., U. Tenn., 1931; postgrad. Vanderbilt U., 1935; m. Mary Margaret Prophater, Dec. 26, 1934; children—Margaret Suzanne (Mrs. William C. Stanton), Sandra Darlene (Mrs. Herbert R. Sherlin), Mary Elizabeth (Mrs. Frank W. Davis), Rathburn Applegate, Donna Virginia (Mrs. J.E. Moore, Jr.), Ann Carol (Mrs. Ronald H. Kersey), George Lee II, Laura Melissa. Rep. western area TVA, Knoxville, Tenn., 1935-43, supr. prodn. control center Tenn. Eastman Corp., Oak Ridge, 1943-46; owner Rathburn A. Ray Co., Athens, Tenn., 1946—. Chmn., McMinn County Indsl. Devel. Corp., 1955-56. Mem. Athens C. of C., Athens Bd. Realtors (pres. 1969-70, 71-72), Nat. Soc. Exchange Counselors, Nat. Assn. Real Estate Bds. (Medal of Service 1957), Internat. Traders Club (nat. dir. 1962-63), Nat. Office Mgmt. Assn., Nat. Motel Brokers Assn. Am., Omega Tau Rho, Delta Sigma Pi, Phi Pi Phi. Methodist (trustee local ch. 1952-56). Clubs: Elks, Kiwanis, Springbrook Country. Research in real estate. Home: 413 Madison Ave NE Athens TN 37303 Office: 104 Washington Ave NE Athens TN 37303

RAY, VANCE ROBERT, fin. cons.; b. Savannah, Ga., Jan. 8, 1938; s. Vance Robert and Blanche (Aikens) R.; student Armstrong Jr. Coll., 1955-56, U. Ga., 1957-58, N.Y. U., 1959-60. Bus. analyst Phoenix Mut. Ins. Co., Atlanta, 1965-67; treas. Fashion Pillows, Jackson, Ga., 1968-69; v.p. fin. Internat. Modular Industries Co., Atlanta, 1970-72; sr. partner Ray & Scofield, accts. and auditors, Atlanta, 1972-79; pres. F.A.M.E., Inc., Smyrna, Ga., 1979—; chmn. Fin. Warehouse Assn., 1978—. Past pres. Northwoods PTA, Butts County Jr. High PTA; cubmaster, Jackson, Ga. Mem. Internat. Accts. Soc., Nat. Hist. Soc., Nat. Assn. Accts. Club: Optimists (past pres.). Home: 680 Willow Creek Dr Atlanta GA 30328 Office: 1190 Winchester Pkwy Suite 210 Smyrna GA 30080

RAYBOULD, MICHAEL WILLIAM, music educator; b. Montreal, Que., Can., June 18, 1951; s. Henry and Maria Paulina (Onehschkevich) R.; m. Susan Elizabeth Bradley, Dec. 20, 1974; 1 dau., Tammy Theresa. Tchr., bus. mgr. Do-Re-Mi Acad. of Music, Verdun, Que., 1970-74; mus. dir., bus. mgr. Raybould Mus. Enterprises, Ottawa, Ont., Can., 1974—; ofcl. Ont.-Que. Music Festival, Canadian Amateur Music Pageant. Mem. Music Educators Nat. Council, Nat. Guild Piano Tchrs., Am. Fedn. Musicians, Music Tchrs. Nat. Assn., Better Bus. Bur., Canadian C. of C. Author: Just a Little Theory, 1979. Office: 900 Greenbank Rd #212 Nepean ON K2J 1S8 Canada

RAYBURN, B. J., mfg. co. exec.; b. Alvarado, Tex., Aug. 26, 1929; s. G.A. and Sarah A. (Wiggins) R.; B.S. in Mech. Engring., U.S. Air Force Inst., 1955; m. Jane Tymula, Apr. 24, 1964; 1 dau., Kimberly Ann. Gen. supr. quality Gen. Dynamics Co., 1948-60; gen. mgr. AMF, Belfast, No. Ireland, 1967-69; pres., chief exec. officer Campbell Chain Co., 1969-79, now dir.; pres., chief exec. officer Masoneilan Internat. Inc., Houston, 1979—, also dir.; dir. Granite State Mfg. Co., Commonwealth Nat. Bank, Weissenfels-Campbell, Italy. Mem. President's Assn. Republican. Baptist. Clubs: Rotary, Masons. Office: 1776 Woodstead Ct The Woodlands TX 77380

RAYBURN, JOHN KING, retail exec.; b. Mount Pleasant, Tenn., Jan. 14, 1908; s. Elbert Brevard and Alice (McCauley) R.; B.S., U. Tenn., 1932; m. Doris Mason, June 10, 1937; children—John King, James McCauley. Prin., Bodenham High Sch., 1932-35; tchr. Giles County High Sch., 1936-46; owner, mgr. Rayburn Motor Co., Pulaski, Tenn., 1946—. Bd. dirs. Giles County Hosp., 1959-77, chmn. bd., 1972-77; elder, 1st Presbyn. Ch., Pulaski, 1954—; mem. bd. Alderman Pulaski, 1962-77. Mem. Giles County C. of C. (pres. 1955-56, Mid South Farm Equipment Assn., Kappa Alpha. Democrat. Home: 604 W Flower St Pulaski TN 38478 Office: 432 W College St Pulaski TN 38478

RAYMOND, NORMAN H., stock broker; b. Newark, Feb. 2, 1945; s. Morris and Mary Raymond; B.S., Drexel U., 1967; m. Marsha La Poff, July 16, 1967; children—Joshua, Alison. Trainee, Delafield & Delafield, South Orange, N.J., 1968-70; asst. mgr. Janney Montgomery Scott, South Orange, 1970-74; v.p., mgr. Gruntal & Co., South Orange, 1974—; dir. Roysons Inc. Mem. Roseland (N.J.) Bd. Edn.; v.p. Crest Assn. Columnist, Wall St. Close-Up, 1978—. Home: 4 White Oak Rd Roseland NJ 07068 Office: 131 South Orange Ave South Orange NJ 07079

RAYMOND, RICHARD WERNER, ins. co. exec.; b. Evanston, Ill., Oct. 16, 1918; s. Werner Carl and Delia Catherine (Cannon) R.; student Drake U., 1936-37; B.A., Franklin Coll., 1941; m. Kathleen Lisman, Dec. 29, 1941; children—Linda Kathleen, Richard Carl, Philip Warren. Group rep. Washington Nat. Ins. Co., 1941-47, group supr., Richmond, Va., 1947-51, agy. supr., 1951-58, 3d v.p., 1958-63, 2d v.p., 1963-72, v.p., dir. group dept., Evanston, 1972—, also mem. mktg. planning bd., intercorp. mktg. com.; dir. Washington Nat. Equity Co., Washington Nat. Fin. Services Co. Trustee, Franklin Coll., 1977—. Served with USAAF, 1942-46. Mem. Life Ins. Mktg. Research Assn. (group mktg. com.), Health Ins. Assn. Am., Ins. Econs. Soc., Evanston C. of C., Ill. C. of C., Nat. C. of C. Republican. Presbyterian. Club: Kiwanis (Evanston). Home: 437 Highcrest Cr Wilmette IL 60091 Office: 1630 Chicago Ave Evanston IL 60201

RAYNER, ARNO ALFRED, investment exec.; b. San Francisco, Sept. 23, 1928; s. Kurt and Angela (Flasch) R.; A.A., U. Calif. at Berkeley, 1947, B.S., 1949, M.B.A., 1954; m. Kenyon Reid, June 14, 1951; children—Eric, Jill, Neal. Security analyst Bank of Calif., San Francisco, 1950-54; with Indsl. Indemnity Co., San Francisco, 1954-74, sr. v.p., 1972-74; with Bechtel Corp., 1975-76, v.p. Bechtel Internat. Services; investment cons., 1976—; pres., dir. Rayner Assos., Inc., Mill Valley, Calif., 1977—; dir. Invest-In-Am., Beaver Ins. Co., San Francisco. Served with AUS, 1951-52. Mem. San Francisco Security Analysts, San Francisco Bond Club, Inst. Chartered Fin. Analysts, Am. Fin. Assn. Clubs: Kiwanis, Bohemian, World Trade. Home: 275 E Strawberry Dr Mill Valley CA 94941 Office: 655 Redwood Hwy Mill Valley CA 94941

RAYNOLDS, JOHN FISKE, III, acquisition co. exec.; b. Mpls., Sept. 25, 1929; s. John Fiske and Valeria E. (Blunt) R.; B.A. cum laude in English, Williams Coll., 1951; postgrad. Grad. Sch. Bus. Adminstrn., Stanford, 1954; m. J. Sinclair Winton, Sept. 9, 1955; children—William Sinclair, Virginia Crane, Helen Winton. Mng. partner Raynolds Motor Co., Salinas, Calif., 1955-60; economist U.S. Army Staff Group, Dept. Def., Washington, 1961-62; mgr. African commodities M&M Candies, Accra, Ghana, W. Africa, 1962-66, personnel dir., Hackettstown, N.J., 1967; dir. corporate devel. Mars, Inc., Washington, 1968; sr. officer, corporate fin. group Butcher & Sherrerd, Phila., 1969-70; exec. v.p. Heede Internat., Inc., Stamford, Conn., 1971—; pres., dir. Sky Van Systems, Inc., Stamford, 1971—; pres. Heede Industries, Inc., Greenwich, Conn., 1979—. Trustee, Outward Bound, Inc., 1975—; chmn. bd. trustees Congregational Ch., New Canaan, Conn., 1976—, fin. chmn., 1974. Served as lt. j.g. USNR, 1951-54. Mem. Nat. Assn. Elevator Safety Authorities. Republican. Clubs: New Canaan Field, Williams. Contbr. Haiku poetry to mags. Office: 30 Elm St Greenwich CT 06830

RAYS, RICHARD, mfg. co. exec.; b. Jersey City, Jan. 16, 1939; s. Catherine (Kuezmarski) R.; B.S. in Acctg., Rutgers U., 1969; postgrad. Pepperdine U., 1979; m. Carol Ann Dombrowski, Aug. 13, 1966; children—Christine, Cynthia, Scott. Acctg. clk. Atlas Corp., N.Y.C., 1956-59; acct. Gt. Lakes Carbon Corp., N.Y.C., 1959-62; with Computer Diode Corp., Fair Lawn, N.J., 1962-64; asst. controller Am. Express Co., N.Y.C., 1964-69; comptroller, v.p. fin. Electrogas Dynamics, Inc., N.Y.C., 1970-76; controller Vetco Offshore, Inc., Houston, also Ventura, Calif., 1976-79; controller Oncor Corp., Houston, 1979—. Served with USAF, 1956-62. C.P.A., Tex. Club: Kingwood Country. Home: 3606 Ash Park Kingwood TX 77339

RAZVI, AGA MASHALLAH, mfg. co. exec.; b. Hyderabad, India, Aug. 1, 1943; came to U.S., 1969, naturalized, 1978; s. Jaffar Ali and Khanum (Sultan) R.; B.E., Osmania U., India, 1966; M.S., U. Wis., 1970; postgrad. Poly. Inst. N.Y., 1973-75; M.B.A., Pace U., 1977; m. Abida Naqvi, Jan. 18, 1972; children—Amena, Fatema. Engr., Bio-visual Products, India, 1966-67; grad. engr. Bharat Heavy Electricals, India, 1967-69; with Westvaco Corp., Covington, Va. and N.Y.C., 1970—, mech. design supr., 1976-78, asst. mgr. mfg. services group, 1978—. Bd. dirs. Stonewall Jackson Area council, Boy Scouts Am., 1972-74, area chmn. So. Dist., 1973-74. Rotary Club scholar, 1965-66; Mem. TAPPI, Am. Forestry Assn., Forest Products Research Soc. Club: Kiwanis (dir. 1972-73). Home: 36 George St Bloomfield NJ 07003 Office: 299 Park Ave New York NY 10017

READ, BERTRAM, printing and pub. co. exec.; b. Cambridge, Mass., Sept. 4, 1929; s. Richard W. and Clara Read; A.B., Harvard Coll., 1952; m. Clare T. Read; children—William G., Lee Wendell, John H. Noble III. Vice-pres., dir. mktg. and sales Regensteiner Press, Chgo., 1973; exec. v.p. Williams Press, Albany, N.Y., 1973-76; pres. Shiver Mountain Press, Washington Depot, Conn., 1976—; pres. Fairview Printers, Greenwich, Conn.; mem. adv. council First Nat. Bank of Litchfield (Conn.). Area chmn. Harvard Coll. Alumni Schs. Com., 1965—; trustee Wykeham Rise Sch., Washington, Conn. Clubs: Washington, Stanwich, Harvard of N.Y.C., Lions. Home: Washington CT 06793 Office: Washington Depot CT 06794

READE, CHARLES FALKINER, JR., mfg. exec.; b. Evanston, Ill., June 24, 1941; s. Charles Falkiner and Elizabeth (Boomer) R.; B.B.A., U. Miami, 1965; P.M.D., Harvard U., 1971; m. Emily Schroeder, Sept. 9, 1978; 1 dau., Amanda Browning. Salesman, So. Bell Tel. & Tel., 1965-66, Blyth Eastman Dillon & Co. Inc., 1969-73; regional instl. sales mgr. Reynolds Securities Co., 1973-77; dir. metal powder div., gen. mgr. chem. and advt. divs. Reade Mfg. Co., Inc., Lakehurst, N.J., 1977—; lectr. non-ferrous metals. Chmn. Keep Rumson (N.J.) Safe Com.; active United Way, Rumson Vol. Fire Dept.; vol. cons. minority bus.; mem. Republican Nat. Fin. Com.; former nat. chmn. Friends for Reagan Com., Businessmen for Pres. Ford Com. Served to capt. U.S. Army, 1966-69; Vietnam. Decorated Air medal, Bronze Star with two oak leaf clusters. Mem. Iron and Steel Inst., Am. Foundrymen's Soc., ASTM, AMVETS (life), AIME, Am. Def. Preparedness Assn., Am. Powder Metallurgy Inst., Air Force Assn., NAM. Clubs: N.Y. Yacht; Harvard (N.Y.C. and Phila.); Monmouth Boat, Navesink River Rod and Gun, N. Shrewsbury Ice Boat and Yacht. Office: Reade Manufacturing Co Inc Ridgeway Blvd Lakehurst NJ 08733

REAGAN, RICHARD GERALD, moving co. exec.; b. Buffalo, Nov. 20, 1926; s. Gerald N. and Irene P. (Pouthier) R.; B.S., Canisius Coll., 1948; m. Barbara L. McNutt, Jan. 20, 1951; children—Debra Ann, Tamara Louise. Vice pres. Cook Internat. Movers, Inc., Buffalo, 1955-66; pres. Cook Moving Systems, Inc., Buffalo, 1966—, O.J. Glenn Moving & Storage, Inc., Buffalo, 1974—, Tampa Bay Moving Systems, Inc. (Fla.), 1976—; dir. United Van Lines. Served with U.S. Army, 1953-55. Mem. Am. Movers Conf., Nat. Furniture Warehousemans Assn., N.Y. State Movers and Warehousemans Assn., Buffalo C. of C. (chmn. transp. commn. 1973), Cheektowaga C. of C. (dir. 1968-72). Office: 1845 Dale Rd Buffalo NY 14225

REAM, NORMAN J., mgmt. cons., former govt. ofcl.; b. Aurora, Ill., June 20, 1912; s. Edward F. and Margaret E. (Colbert) R.; B.S., U. Ill., 1934; postgrad. Northwestern U., 1940-41; m. Eileen M. Bouvia May 24, 1952; children—Judith Ellen (Mrs. William Miles), Patricia M. (Mrs. Paul Michel), Norma Jane (Mrs. Robert Yamaguchi), John Patrick. Mem. controller's staff Pure Oil Co., Chgo., 1934-41; accountant Touche, Niven & Co., C.P.A.'s, Chgo., 1941-42; sr. cons. George Fry & Assos., Chgo., 1942-47; dir. accounting research IBM, N.Y.C., 1947-50; asst. treas. Lever Bros., N.Y.C., 1950-53; corp. dir. systems planning Lockheed Aircraft Corp., Burbank, Calif., 1953-65; dir. Inst. for Computer Scis. and Tech., Nat. Bur. Standards, Washington, 1965-66; spl. asst. to sec. navy, Washington, also mem. Navy Secretariat, 1966-69; prin. S. D. Leiderdorf & Co., N.Y.C., 1969-71; chmn. Jamerica Cons. Group, San Clemente, Calif., 1971—; guest lectr. Japan Mgmt. Assn., Japan Productivity Center, Tokyo, 1963-69, Japan Acad. Scis., Hiroshima, 1965; mem. U.S. del. UN Conf. on Application Sci. and Tech. for Benefit Less Developed Areas, Geneva, 1963; speaker Internat. Mgmt. Congress CIOS XV, Tokyo, 1969, Constl. Assembly Interam. Center Tax Adminstrn., Panama, 1967, 1st Internat. Conf. on Communications, Tokyo, 1972. Gen. chmn. Incorporation City of Downey, Calif., 1956. Recipient Distinguished Civilian Service medal USN. C.P.A., Calif., Ill., N.Y. Mem. Am. Inst. C.P.A.'s, Calif., N.Y. socs. C.P.A.'s, Am. Accounting Assn. IEEE, Inst. Mgmt. Scis., Am. Mgmt. Assn. (sr. planning council). Contbr. articles to profl. publs. Home: 511 Avenida San Juan San Clemente CA 92672 Office: San Clemente CA

REARDON, DONALD THOMAS, business exec.; b. Irvington, N.J., Sept. 13, 1934; s. Paul and Marie Anne (Tears) R.; B.S. in Bus. Adminstrn., Seton Hall U., 1956; m. Marlene C. Golembeski, Feb. 8, 1958; children—Caryl Lynn, Donald Thomas, Suzanne, Patricia Anne, Jacqueline, Jennifer. Systems analyst Colonial Life Ins. Co., East Orange, N.J., 1958-61; dist. supr. systems reps. Burroughs Corp., N.Y.C., 1961-64; v.p. Bank N.Am., N.Y.C., 1964-67; v.p. Seamen's Bank for Savs., N.Y.C., 1967-73; exec. v.p. Carteret Savs. and Loan Assn., Newark, 1973-76; fin. cons., 1976-77; Eastern regional sales mgr. Datasaab Systems Inc., U.S., N.Y.C., 1977—. Served to lt. comdr. USCGR, 1956-57. Home: 5 Prince Rd East Brunswick NJ 08816 Office: 437 Madison Ave New York NY 10022

REARDON, PAUL ALOYSIUS, assn. exec., economist; b. Knoxville, Tenn., Dec. 25, 1936; s. Paul Aloysius and Martha Elizabeth (Moore) R.; B.S. in Bus. Adminstrn., U. Mo., Columbia, 1963, M.A. in Econs., 1964, Ph.D. in Econs., 1968; m. Patricia Ann Williams, Sept. 2, 1961; 1 son, Paul Brian. Instr. econs. U. Mo., Rolla, 1966-67; asst. prof. econs. Cleve. State U., 1967-71; research asso. econs. analysis and study group C. of C. of U.S., 1972-77, sr. economist, 1977-79, asso. chief economist, adminstrn., surveys, forecasting, 1980—. Pres. Boxwood House Owners Assn., Rehoboth Beach, Del., 1979—. Served with USN, 1954-57. Mem. Am. Econ. Assn., Nat. Economists Club, Nat. Assn. Bus. Economists, Beta Gamma Sigma. Contbr. articles to periodicals. Home: 14008 Rippling Brook Dr Silver Spring MD 20906 Office: 1615 H St Washington DC 20062

REBANKS, LESLIE, architect; b. Cockerham, Eng., Jan. 18, 1927; s. John Thomas and Lily R.; Diploma in Architecture, Oxford U., 1955; m. Wendy Weston, Feb. 26, 1965; children—Tamara, Claudia. Founder, prin. Leslie Rebanks, architects, London, 1963-66, Toronto, Ont., Can., 1966-79; prin. Rebanks/Vagi Architects, Toronto, 1979—; pres. R.D.R. Bldg. Corp., Ltd., Toronto, 1979—; profl. adviser Ont. Masons Relations Council. Served with Brit. Army, 1945-48. Recipient grand prize, 2d prize Am. Inst. Bus. Designers, 1976; World Housing medal Habitation Space Italy, 1980, 81. Mem. Royal Inst. Brit. Architects, Royal Archtl. Inst. Can., Ont. Assn. Architects, Royal Automobile Club U.K., Club: Empire (Toronto). Contbg. editor Can. Interiors mag., 1970-80. Home: 543 Blythwood Rd Toronto ON M4N 2B4 Canada Office: 22 St Clair Ave E Toronto ON M4T 2S3 Canada

REBELO, JOHN G., JR., banker; b. San Diego, July 7, 1940; s. John G. and Mary Ida (Francisco) R.; B.S., U. Calif., Berkeley, 1964; children—John, Jeff, Jenifer, Max David. Br. mgr., various locations So. Calif. First Nat. Bank, 1968-72, v.p., area mgr., 1973, regional v.p., 1974; chmn. bd., pres. Peninsula Bank of San Diego. Bd. dirs. Cabrillo Med. Center; pres. Cabrillo Festival, Inc., 1979, 80. Mem. Calif. Bankers Assn. Office: Peninsula Bank of San Diego 1331 Rosecrans St San Diego CA 92106

REBENSTORF, JOHN CHRISTIAN, III, mining co. exec.; b. Kenosha, Wis., July 11, 1929; s. John Christian and Lucy (Kowalski) R.; ed. trade sch.; m. Dorothy Jean Wodetzki, July 25, 1948; children—John, Bruce, Jane, David, Richard, Thomas, Dorothy J. With Gen. Motors Co., Danville, Ill., 1948-54, LaGrange, Ill., 1954-56; with Dukane Corp., St. Charles, Ill., 1956-60; mgr. indsl. engring. Quincy (Ill.) Speaker Co., 1960-66; asst. to pres. Lakeside Cable Corp., Danville, 1966-70; pres. Goldfield Deep Mines Co. Nev., San Bernardino, Calif., 1970—, also AAA-Fin. Corp. Nev.; cons. mining, metals, geology. Chmn. parents com. U. Redlands. Served with USMC, 1945-48; ATO. U. Redlands fellow, 1976. Mem. Am. Forestry Assn., Western Mining Council, Pub. Land Users Coalition. Seventh Day Adventist. Author: Poems, 1971; Patterns, 1970. Home: 26158 Lynwood Dr Highland CA 92346 Office: 2695 Del Rosa St San Bernardino CA 92404

REBENSTORF, NORMAN E., JR., banker; b. Aurora, Ill., May 17, 1947; s. Norman E. and Elizabeth J. Rebenstorf; student (Aurora Found. scholar) Aurora Coll., 1965-66; student U. Wis. Grad. Sch. Banking, 1978-80; m. Roberta Larson, June 16, 1973. Asst. ops. officer Batavia Bank (Ill.), 1970-73; asst. v.p. Washington Bank & Trust Co., Naperville, Ill., 1973-76; v.p. ops. Naperville Nat. Bank & Trust Co., 1976—; mem. adv. bd. Met. Computer Center Inc., Naperville, 1979—. Served with U.S. Army, 1967-70. Recipient Frank R. Curda award Am. Inst. Banking 1978. Lutheran. Clubs: Naperville Noon Lions (sec.), Moose. Office: 136 S Washington St Naperville IL 60540

RECHTER, HERBERT LESLIE, auto parts co. exec.; b. Bklyn., June 8, 1932; s. Nathan and Flora (Schwartz) R.; B.A., Wayne State U., 1954; m. Yvonne Joan Mayor, Jan. 12, 1958; children—Mitchell, Brenda, Ronald. With Allied Accessories & Auto Parts Co., 1965—, pres., 1972—; pres. Gen. Mouldings, Oak Park, Mich., 1975—; dir. Aerosol Systems. Exec. v.p. City of Hope, 1979—; trustee Temple Israel, 1980—. Served with U.S. Army, 1956-58. Named Automotive Man of Yr., 1979. Mem. Parts and Accessories Assn. (v.p. 1975-77), C. of C. Mich., Ford Motor Adv. Council. Republican. Clubs: Tam O Shanter Country, Renaissance, Rolls Royce Owners. Office: 1551 E Lincoln St Madison Heights MI 48071

RECORR, CHARLES KENNETH, stockbroker; b. Newark, Feb. 4, 1946; s. Kenneth Howard and Doris Evelyn (Rinaldi) ReC.; student Mo. Valley Coll., 1964; asso. degree Thomas A. Edison Coll., 1972; student N.Y. Inst. Fin.; children—Kenneth William, Christopher Charles. Account exec. Merrill Lynch, Pierce, Fenner & Smith, Inc., Newark, 1974-75, corp. cons., N.Y.C., 1976, asst. v.p., corp. services mgr.; account exec. Oppenheimer & Co., N.Y.C., 1975-76; adj. instr. N.Y. Inst. Fin.; bd. dirs. Center for Pension Studies. Served to capt. U.S. Army, 1965-72. Decorated Silver Star, Bronze Star, Air medal, Purple Heart, Vietnamese Congressional Medal of Honor. Mem. Am. Fin. Assn., Am. Stock Exchange Club. Unitarian. Home: 320 E 50th St New York NY 10022 Office: Merrill Lynch Pierce Fenner & Smith Inc 165 Broadway One Liberty Plaza New York NY 10080

RECTOR, ROBERT LEE, public acct., cons.; b. Washington, June 16, 1943; s. Hilden LaVern and Lois Marie (Hickok) R.; B.S., Kent State U., 1965; M.S., State U. N.Y., Albany, 1968; m. Linda Martha Zuschlag, Dec. 19, 1964; children—Courtenay Marie, Drew Alan, Egan Alward. Systems analyst, programmer IBM Corp., Kingston, N.Y., 1965-68; div. mgr. systems Allied Chem. Co., N.Y.C., 1968-70; cons. Booz, Allen and Hamilton, N.Y.C., 1971; pres., founder, Rector's Lemon Tree, landscape firm and nursery, Port Richey, Fla., 1971—; prin., founder Anson Lee Rector & Co., public accts., Tarpon Springs, Fla., 1965—; dir. Homes Internat., Inc., Exec. Tng. Inst.; seminar leader, speaker numerous colls. and univs. in U.S. and Can.; seminar instr. Harvard U. Past mem. Bd. of Appeals and Adjustments, City of New Port Richey, Fla. Mem. Inst. Mgmt. Scientists, Indsl. Mgmt. Soc., Am. Mktg. Assn., Exec. Planning Inst., Am. Inst. Profl. Cons., Acad. Mgmt., Nat. Soc. Public Accts., Clearwater, New Port Richey chambers of commerce. Republican. Author books, fin. tng. manuals, numerous mag. articles. Home: 1122 Jasmin Dr New Port Richey FL 33552 Office: 1410 Lake Tarpon Ave Tarpon Springs FL 33589

REDDEN, HARRAL ARTHUR, JR., ins. agy. exec.; b. Neptune, N.J., Aug. 14, 1936; s. Harral A. and Evelyn (Camp) R.; B.A., Ursinus Coll., 1958; children—Stephen D., Scott H. Partner Redden Agy., Red Bank, N.J., 1958—; instr. Brookdale Community Coll., 1972-80. Pres., Little Silver (N.J.) Community Appeal, 1971—; bd. dirs. Planned Parenthood Monmouth County (N.J.). Served to 1st lt. USAR, 1963-70. Designated CIC. Mem. Monmouth County Ind. Ins. Agts. Assn. (pres. 1966-67), Soc. C.P.C.U.'s (pres. Central Jersey chpt. 1968-69), Ind. Ins. Agts. N.J. (exec. com.). Republican. Methodist. Clubs: Sea Bright Lawn Tennis (Rumson, N.J.); Monmouth Boat, Root Beer & Checker (Red Bank). Home: 100 Seaview Ave Monmouth Beach NJ 07750 Office: 718 River Rd PO Box 262 Fair Haven NJ 07701

REDDEN, ROBERT HARDING, energy/constrn. co. exec.; b. Oklahoma City, Apr. 29, 1943; s. Gene Robert and Jamsie R.; B.A., Northeastern State U., 1965; postgrad. U. Okla. Sch. Law, 1965-66; m. Mary Claire Detjen, June 3, 1965; 1 dau., Michelle Ann. Asst. ins. mgr. Pan Am. Petroleum Corp., 1965-70; asst. ins. mgr. Williams Cos., Tulsa, 1970-77; dir. treasury and ins. Willbros Energy Services Co., Tulsa, 1977—; v.p., dir. Langside Ltd., Hamilton, Bermuda, 1971-77; cons. corp ins. programs, internat. ins. Mem. Risk and Ins. Mgmt. Soc. (sec.-treas. Okla. chpt. 1972-73). Home: 6630 S 218 East Ave Broken Arrow OK 74012 Office: 2530 E 71st St Tulsa OK 74136

REDDING, MAX HERMAN, lingerie co. exec.; b. Cedar Falls, N.C., Feb. 18, 1931; s. Clyde C. and Eunice L. (Wrenn) R.; B.S. in Bus. Adminstrn., U. N.C., 1956; m. Emily Ann Stone, Jan. 21, 1951; children—Shannon S., Bonna W. Acct., Bowman & Blue, C.P.A.'s, High Point, N.C., 1956-58; controller Pinehurst Textiles, Inc., Asheboro, N.C., 1958-70, v.p., controller, 1970-78, sec.-treas., 1978—, pres., 1980—, dir., 1959—; sec.-treas. Pinehurst Sales, Inc., Asheboro, 1978—, dir., 1962—; pres. Tricot, Inc., Asheboro, 1978—, dir., 1963—. Bd. bus. advs. Asheboro Jr. Coll.; mem. budget com., bd. dirs. United Fund. Served with USAF, 1951-53. Mem. Piedmont Personnel Assn., Asheboro Jaycees. Democrat. Methodist. Clubs: Asheboro Country (dir.), Seven Lakes Golf Assn. Home: PO Box 516 W Lexington Rd Asheboro NC 27203 Office: 120 E Pritchard St Asheboro NC 27203

REDDISH, JOHN JOSEPH, mgmt. cons. co. exec.; b. Albany, N.Y., July 23, 1946; s. Leonard Frank and Marion Elizabeth (McElveney) R.; N.Y., 1975-77. Arts, Fordham U., 1968; m. Sharon L. Cloud; 1 son by previous marriage. Pub. relations asst. Civil Service Employees Assn., Albany, 1967-68; asso. editor Edison Electric Inst., N.Y.C., 1968-69; dir. info. services N.Y. State Nurses Assn., Guilderland, 1969-70; pres. RA Group, Inc., Advt. and Pub. Relations, Albany, 1970-77; v.p. The Presidents Assn. div. Am. Mgmt. Assos., N.Y.C., 1977-79; pres., dir. Advent Mgmt. Assos., Ltd., West Chester, Pa., 1979—; cons. mktg. and mgmt. Chmn. bd. Kairos Center for Care and Counseling, Albany, 1974-77; bd. dirs. Focus Chs. of Albany, 1975-76; bd. deacons Emmanuel Bapt. Ch., 1974-77; hon. trustee Nat. French and Indian Wars Mus., Hudson Falls, N.Y., 1975-77. Club: Fordham-Cornell of N.Y. Contbr. articles to profl. jours.

REDENBAUGH, ROBERT EARL, sales exec.; b. Toledo, June 26, 1924; s. Clifford E. and Sylvia (Reynolds) R.; student Yale U., 1943-44; B.S. in Mech. Engring., Washington U., St. Louis, 1949; m. Jacqueline M. McDonald, June 12, 1948; 1 dau., Patricia Ann. With Lincoln-St. Louis div. McNeil Corp., 1942—, product engr., 1946-53, sales mgr. original equipment mfrs. div., St. Louis, 1953—. Served with AUS, 1944-46. Decorated Purple Heart. Mem. Am. Soc. Agrl. Engrs., Am. Def. Preparedness Assn. (life). Home: 1570 St Denis St Florissant MO 63033 Office: 4010 Goodfellow Blvd Saint Louis MO 63120

REDMAN, DONALD ANDREW, electronics co. exec.; b. Chesterton-Porter, Ind., Aug. 12, 1926; s. Donald Alonzo and Evelyn Sophia (Johnson) R.; B.S., Gannon Coll., 1952; M.B.A., UCLA, 1976; m. Katherine Sarah Church, Jan. 18, 1975; children—Chester, Connie, Kenneth, Peggy, Nancy, Frank, Daniel. With GTE Telephone Cos., 1947-78, v.p. controller, 1960-78; v.p. fin. Western regions telephone ops. GTE Service Corp., Los Gatos, Calif., 1978-79, v.p. fin. hdqrs. telephone ops., 1979-80; v.p. budgets and measurements GTE Corp., Stamford, Conn., 1980—. Active Boy Scouts Am. Served with U.S. Army, 1944-46. Mem. Calif. C. of C., Calif. Council Econ. Edn. Republican. Presbyterian. Office: 1 Stamford Forum Stamford CT 06904

REDMAN, ERIC MICHAEL, real estate broker; b. Palouse, Wash., Jan. 26, 1946; s. Bernard F. and Lois J. (Hanson) R.; student (Union Pacific R.R. scholar), Wash. State U., 1964-65; m. Sandra J. Redman, Aug. 9, 1970; children—Ronni, Natalie, Michael. Owner, operator Redman's Resort, Idaho, 1972-74; asso. James S. Black & Co., Coeur d'Alene, Idaho, 1974-75, Kelley Realty, Coeur d'Alene, 1975-76; owner, broker All Star Realty Co., Coeur d'Alene, 1976-78; pres., broker E.M. Redman Co., Spokane, 1978—; owner Parkwood South; chmn. bd. Sales/Redman, Inc.; pres. Pacesetter Builders. Served with USAF, 1965-69. Mem. Bayview C. of C. (pres.). Clubs: Rotary, Inland Empire Exchangors, N. Idaho Exchangors. Office: E M Redman Co Tapio Office Center Suite 207 104 S Freya Spokane WA 99203

REDMON, EDWARD JOHN, aerospace co. exec.; b. Freeport, Ill., Sept. 25, 1914; s. Alexander E. and Mary Mabel (Hines) R.; A.B., UCLA, 1937; M.A., U. So. Calif., 1939; m. Helen Louise Brown, June 1, 1944. Sr. job analyst Lockheed Aircraft, Burbank, Calif., 1940-51, wage and salary adminstr., Marietta, Calif., 1951-53, with Missile Systems Div., 1953-57, mgr. wage and salary adminstrn., head mgmt. compensation, Sunnyvale, Calif., 1957-80; cons. and lectr. in field. Mem. Western Mgmt. Assn., Calif. Personnel Assn., Electronics Salary and Wage Assn., Electronics Industries Assn., Calif. Salary Adminstrs. Assn., Am. Mgmt. Assn. Republican. Methodist. Contbr. articles to profl. jours. Home: 12190 Fallen Leaf Ln Los Altos CA 94022 Office: 1111 Lockheed Way Sunnyvale CA 94086

REDSTONE, SUMNER MURRAY, theatre exec., lawyer; b. Boston, May 27, 1923; s. Michael and Belle (Ostrovsky) R.; B.A., Harvard, 1944, LL.B., 1947; m. Phyllis Gloria Raphael, July 6, 1947; children—Brent Dale, Shari Ellin. Admitted to Mass. bar, 1947, D.C. bar, 1951, also U.S. Supreme Ct.; law sec. U.S. Ct. Appeals for 9th Circuit, 1947-48; instr. U. San Francisco Law Sch. and Labor Mgmt. Sch., 1947; spl. asst. to U.S. atty. gen., 1948-51; partner firm Ford, Bergson, Adams, Borkland & Redstone, Washington, 1951-54; exec. v.p. Northeast Drive-In Theatre Corp., 1954-67; pres. Northeast Theatre Corp.; dir. ACE Prodns. Inc. Chmn., Jimmy Fund, Boston, 1960; met. div. N.E. Combined Jewish Philanthropies, 1963. Trustee Children's Cancer Research Found., Art Lending Library; sponsor Boston Mus. Sci.; bd. dirs. Boston Arts Festival, Will Rogers Meml. Fund; bd. overseers Sidney Farber Cancer Inst.; mem. corp. New Eng. Med. Center; adv. com. Kennedy Center for Performing Arts. Served to 1st lt. AUS, 1943-45. Decorated Army Commendation medal; named one of ten outstanding young men Greater Boston C. of C., 1958; recipient William J. German Human Relations award entertainment and communications div. Am. Jewish Com., 1977. Mem. Am. Congress Exhibitors (exec. com. 1961—), Theatre Owners Am. (asst. pres. 1960-63, pres. 1964-65, chmn. bd. 1966). Mason. Clubs: University, Harvard, Variety New Eng. (Boston). Home: 98 Baldpate Hill Ave Newton MA 02159 Office: 31 St James Ave Boston MA 02116

REECE, SANDRA LYNNE, broadcast co. exec.; b. Niagara Falls, Ont., Can., Aug. 22, 1949; d. Harold H. and Margaret J. (Easto) Dewberry; student public schs., Niagara Falls, Ont.; children—Laurie Lynne, Darrin Michale, Shelly Patricia. Fashion show dir. Sarah Coventry Can. Ltd., Cambridge, Ont., 1973, unit mgr., 1974, br. mgr., 1975, regional mgr., 1976-78; distbn. mgr. Hydroculture Luwasa, St. Catharines, Ont., 1978-80; area devel. mgr. Michele Lynn Can. Ltd., Mississauga, Ont., 1980—; promotions dir. Radio Sta. CJRN, Niagara Falls. Active fund raising Muscular Dystrophy and Cystic Fibrosis, 1975-80. Mem. Niagara Promotions Assn., Stamford Horticulture Soc. Home: 6236 Johnson Dr Niagara Falls ON L2J 3J5 Canada Office: CJRN PO Box 710 Niagara Falls ON L2E 6X7 Canada

REED, CARLYLE, publishing co. exec.; b. Glendale, Ariz., July 9, 1915; s. Henry Clay and Blanche (List) R.; student Ariz. State Coll., 1933-34, Woodbury Bus. Coll., 1934; m. Eleanor Pitkin, Mar. 31, 1962; children—Carolyn Ione Reed Joel, Darlene Ann Reed Harden; stepchildren—Stan Pitkin, David Pitkin. Asst. editor Glendale News, 1934-36, Central Ariz. Light & Power Co., 1936-38; pub. El Cajon Valley News, 1938-53, editor, 1953-54; co-pub. LaMesa Scout, gen. mgr. Intercity Press, 1938-52; pub. relations cons. Carlyle Reed & Assos., 1954-56; spl. rep. of dir. Water Resources, State of Calif., Sacramento, 1956-57; legislative rep. San Diego Union and Tribune, 1956, pub.'s office rep., 1957; legislative rep. Copley Newspapers, Sacramento, 1957; asst. to pub. Union Tribune, 1964-66; pub. Sacramento Union, 1966-75, pub. emeritus, 1975—; cons. Sierra Pub. Co., 1975—; v.p., dir. Copley Newspapers, 1964-75; pres. Carlyle Reed & Assos., 1975. Commodore Port of Sacramento, 1969—; mem., past chmn. Sacramento Host Com.; mem. adv. bd. Golden Empire council Boy Scouts Am. Bd. govs. Mercy Found., Sacramento Symphony Assn., Crocker Art Gallery; adv. bd. Sacramento State U. Named Publisher of Year in Calif., 1974. Mem. Calif. Newspaper Pubs. Assn. (dir., pres. 1977), Calif. Press Assn. (pres. 1979-80, dir.), Navy League, Sigma Delta Chi. Clubs: Sutter; Del Paso Country; Grandfathers of Am. Home: 5094 Keane Dr Carmichael CA 95608

REED, CHARLES EDWARD, oil co. ofcl.; b. McRoberts, Ky., Dec. 14, 1951; s. Julia B. Taylor; B.S. in Psychology, Cumberland Coll., 1975; m. Clara M. Higgins, Dec. 30, 1971; 1 dau., Crystal L. With Bethlehem Mines Corp., Washington, Pa., 1975-80, indsl. relations coordinator, 1976-80, sr. indsl. relations coordinator, 1980; employee relations rep. Atlantic Richfield Corp., Denver, 1980—. Bd. dirs., treas. Lemoyne Community Center, Washington, Pa., 1979—, instr. tennis, 1979; established C.E. Reed track and acad. scholarship, 1979. Home: 6383 S Harlan Way Littleton CO 80123 Office: PO Box 5300 Denver CO 80217

REED, DALE CHARLES, business exec.; b. Bethesda, Md., Aug. 22, 1948; s. Dale Calvin and Barbara Loraine (Thurman) R.; B.A. in Economics, Trinity Coll., Hartford, Conn., 1970; postgrad. Kent State U., 1971, Northwestern U., 1972-73, Bryant Coll., Smithfield, R.I., 1974-75, Ga. State U., 1978-79; m. Gayle Irene Ponto, Feb. 2, 1974; children—Dustin Christopher, Lindsey Diana, Allison Meredith. Fin. analyst of reinforced plastics operation Automotive Products Group, Rockwell Internat. Corp., Ashtabula, Ohio, 1970-71; accountant J & H Internat. Corp., Chgo., 1971-73; div. controller Fiberloys div. Rogers Corp. (Conn.), 1973-76, controller, adminstrv. mgr., group controller Engineered Products Group, Lithonia, Ga., 1976—. Bd. dirs. Friends of Trinity Rowing. Mem. Am. Mgmt. Assn., Nat. Assn. Amateur Oarsmen, Ga. Bus. and Industry Assn., Mensa, Intertel, Alpha Chi Rho. Republican. Episcopalian. Home: 378 William Ivey Rd Lilburn GA 30247 Office: 5259 Minola Dr Lithonia GA 30058

REED, DENNIS KIRK, franchise co. exec.; b. Norwalk, Ohio, July 7, 1944; s. Kenneth Wayne and Helen Mae (Kline) R.; B.S., Ohio State U., 1966; m. Carole Joann Winemiller, Sept. 3, 1966; children—Matthew Thomas, Lisa Renee. Sales rep., Xerox Corp., Columbus, Ohio, 1969-75, duplicator product specialist, 1971-73, sr. sales exec. govt. ednl. med. accts., 1974, sr. microsystems sales rep., 1974-75; mktg. cons. Century 21 So. Ohio, Columbus, 1975-77, mktg. mgr., Century 21 of New Eng., Inc., Burlington, Mass., 1977, dir. sales and mgmt. devel., 1977-78, pres., chief exec. officer, 1978-81, also dir.; pres., chief exec. officer Gold Crest Warranty Corp., 1981—, Uniglobe Travel N.E. Inc., 1981—. Coach, City Youth Athletic League; chmn. Polit. Action Com. on Trademark Infringement, 1978-80. Served to 1st lt. arty. U.S. Army, 1967-69. Mem. Am. Mgmt. Assn., Presidents Assn., Mensa. Mem. sch. bd. Heritage Christian Sch., 1977-79. Home: RFD 2 Pond Rd Derry NH 03038 Office: Century 21 of New Eng Inc 15 New England Exec Park Burlington MA 01803

REED, FRANCIS WILLIAM, telephone co. exec.; b. East Rodman, N.Y., Apr. 20, 1928; s. L.E. and Laura E. Reed; student U. Mich., 1967; m. Florence N. Nohle, June 21, 1952; children—Linda, Brian, Amy. Supr., Gen. Telephone Co. Upstate N.Y., Johnstown, 1955-62, plant dir., 1962-67, div. mgr., 1968-71, v.p. ops., 1971-78; plant dir. Gen. Telephone of Ky., Lexington, 1967-68; pres., div. mgr. Continental Telephone Co. of Upstate N.Y., Johnstown, 1978—; adv. bd. Johnstown Br. State Bank of Albany, 1972—. Served with U.S. Army, 1951-53. Mem. N.Y. State Telephone Assn. (pres. 1978-80, dir. 1971—), Fulton County C. of C. (dir.). Republican. Presbyterian. Club: Rotary. Office: 850 Harrison St Johnston NY 12095

REED, GEORGE FORD, JR., automobile club exec.; b. Hollywood, Calif., Dec. 26, 1946; s. George Ford and Mary Anita Reed; B.A. in Econs. with honors, U. So. Calif., 1969, M.A., 1971. Analyst planning and research Larwin Group, Beverly Hills, Calif., 1971-72; with Automobile Club So. Calif., Los Angeles, 1972—, supr. mgmt. info., research and devel., 1973-74, mgr. fin. and market analysis, 1975—; instr. bus. and econs. Los Angeles Community Coll. Mem. population task force Los Angeles C. of C., 1974—; mem. Gov. Calif. Statewide Econ. Summit Conf., 1974. Served with AUS, 1969. Mem. Assn. Corporate Real Estate Execs., Nat. Assn. Bus. Economists, Western Regional Sci. Assn., Am. Mgmt. Assn., Omicron Delta Epsilon. Home: 1001 S Westgate Ave Los Angeles CA 90049 Office: 2601 S Figueroa St Los Angeles CA 90007

REED, HOWARD A., publisher; b. N.Y.C., Nov. 26, 1925; s. Joseph and Ann (Ollstein) R.; B.A., City U. N.Y., 1948; m. Dolores Josephsohn, Nov. 20, 1949; children—Janet Caryn, Robert Keith. Vice pres. Caldwell-Clements, Inc., N.Y.C., 1953-56; pres. Electronic Techncian, Inc., N.Y.C., 1957-61, U.S. Indsl. Publs., Inc., N.Y.C., 1961-71, Bart Publs., Inc. div. Cox Broadcasting Corp., N.Y.C., 1971—; dir. U.S. Electronic Publs., Inc., Electronic Transmission, Inc. Served with U.S. Army, 1945-46; ETO. Recipient Indsl. Mktg. award; named Man of Yr. in Electronic Service Industry. Mem. Am. Mktg. Assn. Republican. Clubs: Fairview Country (Greenwich, Conn.); Dalton (Ga.) Country. Office: Bart Publs Inc 919 3d Ave New York NY 10022

REED, JAMES A., electric steel co. exec.; b. Burgettstown, Pa., 1927; grad. Washington and Jefferson Coll., 1951. Pres., chief exec. officer, dir. Union Steel Electric Corp., Carnegie, Pa. Office: PO Box 465 Carnegie PA 15106*

REED, JESSE FRANCIS, business exec.; b. Federalsburg, Md., June 6, 1925; s. Homer F. and Lola Irene (Stevens) R.; B.A. in Fine Art, Montclair Coll., 1950; D.D., Gnostic Sem., 1968; m. Mary Grace Mayo, July 9, 1944; 1 son, Gary. Owner, Reed's Frozen Foods, Paterson, N.J., 1950-59; pres. A.E. Inc., N.Y.C., 1959-72, Intercontinental Bus. Research & Devel. Inc., San Francisco, 1959-72, Dallas and Washington, 1972—, Intercontinental Oil & Ore Inc., Carson City, Nev., 1972—; chmn. bd., pres. Cosmo U.S.A., Inc., Dallas and Washington, 1974—, Internat. Fine Art Inc., 1979—; chmn. bd. Gnosis, 1980—. Bd. dirs. Am. Art Alliance, Inc., Internat. Art Exchange, Ltd., Inc., Worldwide Art Exchange, Inc., dirs. Gnostic Ch. Served with USN, 1942-46. Recipient various Art Show awards in Tex., Calif., N.J., N.Y. Mem. Screen Writers Guild, Cattlemen's Assn. Inventor protein converter, system to translate all ednl. disciplines into their pictorial presentations. Office: Box 12488 Dallas TX 75225

REED, JIMMY BURL, SR., auto supply co. exec.; b. Williamson, W.Va., June 30, 1924; s. William Sidney and Mary (Purdy) R.; B.S. in Bus. Adminstrn., U. Palm Beach, 1949; m. Lorene Helen Alderman, Oct. 11, 1947; children—Jimmy Burl, William Michael, Helen Lynn. Retail salesman Goodyear Tire & Rubber Co., Inc., West Palm Beach, Fla., 1949-51, retail store mgr., Miami, Fla., 1951-53, retail store mgr., Tampa, Fla., 1953-59, dist. truck tires sales mgr., Jacksonville, Fla., 1959-62, dist. petroleum sales mgr. State of Ala., 1962-65, regional petroleum sales mgr. So. region, 1965-67; propr., pres. Dublin Auto Supply Co. (Va.), 1967—, Leisure Living Homes, Inc., Dublin, 1973—. Pres. Dublin United Way, 1973-74; chmn. Pulaski County (Va.) United Way, 1975; mem. New River Community Coll. Adv. Bd., 1975—; bd. dirs. Pulaski County Lifesaving, 1974-75. Served with USN, 1943-46; PTO. Mem. Nat. Assn. of Ind. Bus., Pulaski County C. of C. (dir. 1976-77). Club: Lions (dir. 1974-76). Methodist. Home: 7th and Jordan Sts Radford VA 24141 Office: Dublin Auto Supply PO Box 1107 Dublin VA 24084

REED, JOHN CARRE, investment banker, co. exec.; b. Phila., Dec. 29, 1943; s. Frank Carre and Mary Frances (Stoughton) R.; B.A. in Econs., Boston U., 1967; M.B.A., Rutgers U., 1969; m. Marcia Ann Moore, Aug. 26, 1967; children—Amanda Elizabeth, Kristi Carre. Fin. analyst Bache & Co. (now Bache Halsey Stuart Shields), N.Y.C., 1969-73; asst. treas. Chase Manhattan Bank, N.Y.C., 1973-76; v.p. research Ryan, Beck & Co., West Orange, N.J., 1976—; treas., dir. Fayson Lakes Water Co., Fayson Lakes Community, Inc. Republican. Clubs: U.S. Power Squadrons, Lackawanna Squadron, Fayson Lakes Yacht (capt. 1978, commodore 1980). Home: 149 Boonton Ave Kinnelon NJ 07405 Office: 80 Main St West Orange NJ 07052

REED, JOHN GRADY, lawyer; b. Peterborough, Ont., Can., Apr. 5, 1929; s. John Theron and Lilian (Grady) R.; A.B., Harvard U., 1951, LL.B., 1957; m. Miriam Wilkes Bell, May 1, 1954; children—Roberta, Christine, Karen, Laura, Margaret, Abigail, Elisabeth. Admitted to N.Y. bar, 1957, D.C. bar, 1974; asso. firm White & Case, 1957-66, partner, 1967—; dir. The F & M Schaefer Corp., 1968—. Dir., Nat. Sch. Vol. Program, 1977-80. Served with USN, 1951-54. Mem. Am. Bar Assn., N.Y. Bar Assn., D.C. Bar Assn., Assn. Bar City N.Y., Am. Law Inst. Roman Catholic. Clubs: Army-Navy, Down-Town Assn. Home: 8221 Burning Tree Rd Bethesda MD 20034 Office: 1747 Pennsylvania Ave NW Washington DC 20006

REED, JOHN SHEDD, railway exec.; b. Chgo., June 9, 1917; s. Kersey Coates and Helen (Shedd) R.; B.S., Yale U., 1939; m. Marjorie Lindsay, May 4, 1946; children—Ginevra Coates, Lindsay Keith, Helen Shedd, Peter Shedd, John Shedd. With A., T. & S.F. Ry., 1939—, beginning as test dept. asst., Topeka, successively spl. rep. to gen. supt. transp., Chgo., transp. insp., Amarillo, Tex., trainmaster, Slaton, Tex., Pueblo, Colo., 1952, supt. Mo. div., Marceline, Mo., asst. to v.p., Chgo., 1954, exec. asst. to pres., 1957, v.p., finance, 1959-64, v.p. exec. dept., 1964-67, pres., 1967, pres., chief exec. officer, 1968—; pres. Santa Fe Industries, 1968-78, chmn., chief exec. officer, 1973—; dir. No. Trust Co., Dart and Kraft, Inc. Served from ensign to lt. comdr. USNR, 1940-46. Clubs: Chicago, Old Elm Shoreacres, Onwentsia. Home: 301 W Laurel Ave Lake Forest IL 60045 Office: 224 S Michigan Ave Chicago IL 60604

REED, RICHARD WEBSTER, coal co. and distbn. co. exec.; b. New Haven, Mar. 21, 1920; s. Malcolm Willard and Dorothy (Vickery) R.; student Cornell U., 1943; m. Garnet Roberta Gallup, Sept. 23, 1949; children—Nancy, Dorothy, Richard Webster, Robert. Salesman, Montgomery Bros., Seattle, 1947-50, mgr., Seattle,

1950-54, gen. mgr., San Francisco, 1955-57, pres., Burlingame, 1958-68, chmn. bd., 1968—; pres. Environ. Power Ltd., Pitts., 1970-75, chmn. bd., 1975—; chmn. bd. Penn Pocahontas Coal Co., Pitts., 1974-78, now dir. Served as pilot USAAF, 1941-47. Decorated Air medal with nine clusters, D.F.C. Mem. Chi Phi. Clubs: Cornell, Comml. San Francisco, Duquesne, Fox Chapel Golf, Iron City Fishing. Home: 3235 Ralston Ave Hillsborough CA 94010 Office: 1831 Bayshore Hwy Burlingame CA 94010 also 307 4th Ave Pittsburgh PA 15213

REED, ROBERT GEORGE, III, oil co. exec.; b. Cambridge, Mass., Aug. 9, 1927; s. Robert George and Morjorie B. Reed; grad. Phillips Acad., Andover, Mass.; B.A. in Econs., Dartmouth Coll., 1949; A.M.P., Harvard U., 1970; m. Maggie L. Fisher, Mar. 22, 1974; children—Sandra McNickle, Valerie Sloan, Jonathan J., John-Paul. Mktg. mgr. Tidewater Oil subs. Getty Oil, Los Angeles, 1957-64; v.p. mktg. Cities Service Co., Tulsa, 1964-72; exec. v.p. Tesoro Petroleum Corp., San Antonio, 1972-79; chmn. bd., chief exec. officer Clark Oil & Refining Corp., Milw., 1979—; dir. Marine Nat. Exchange Bank, 1st Houston Energy Corp. Bd. dirs. DePaul Hosp. Found., 1979—, Milw. Symphony, 1979—, Greater Milw. Com. Community Devel., 1980—, Public Expenditure Survey Wis., 1980—, Met. Milw. YMCA; mem. adv. council U. Wis., Milw. Sch. Bus. Adminstrn., U. Wis., Milw. Found., Milwaukee County council Boy Scouts Am. Served with USNR, 1945-46. Mem. Nat. Petroleum Refiners Assn. (dir.), Am. Petroleum Inst., Com. Equitable Access to Crude Oil (chmn.). Republican. Clubs: Milw. Athletic, Milw., Milw. Country, Univ. Office: 8530 W National Ave Milwaukee WI 53227

REED, ROLLAND MAURICE, heavy machinery exec.; b. LaCrosse, Wis., July 15, 1927; s. Christen Leiver and Norma Marie (Peterson) R.; B.S. in Econs., U. Wis., 1951; grad. Ind. U. Exec. Program, 1974; m. Irene Ann Sukup, June 16, 1951; children—Christen J., Mark O., Joseph P., John C., Ann C. Ty. mgr. Baker Mfg. Co., 1951-52; with Caterpillar Tractor Co., Peoria, Ill., 1953-69, asst. mgr. Western sales, 1966-69; distbr. sales mgr. Internat. Harvester Co., Melrose Park, Ill., 1969-73, mgr. distbr., dealer br. devel. and adminstrn., 1973-76; v.p. mktg. U.S.-Can., Grove Mfg. Co., Shady Grove, Pa., 1976-78, also dir.; v.p. mktg., partner Long Machinery Co., Missoula, Mont., 1979—; chmn., instr. polit. action course U.S. C. of C.; adviser, grad. asst. Dale Carnegie Course; lectr. U. Ind. Mem. exec. bd., Silver Beaver conferee N.W. Suburban council Boy Scouts Am., also commr. Mason-Dixon council, pres. Western service area Mont., leader Norway World Scout Jamboree, mem. exec. adv. bd. Ind. U. Served with USNR, 1945-47. Mem. Am. Mining Congress, Pacific Logging Congress, Assn. Equipment Distbrs.-Nat. Industry Roundtable, Am. Legion, Beavers. K.C. Clubs: Fountain Head Country, Rogue Valley Country. Contbr. articles to forest industry publs., constrn. and conservation jours. Address: 1740 Cyprus Ct Missoula MT 59801

REED, STUART MARSHALL, rail co. exec.; b. Howell, Mich., July 24, 1925; s. Charles P. and Ora Nokes (Woodin) R.; B.S.E., U. Mich., 1949, M.B.A., 1950; m. Joann Irene Utley, July 2, 1949; children—Paul S., Robert U., Thomas C., Barbara J. With Ford Motor Co., Dearborn, Mich., 1950-59; mgr. quality control Cummins Engine Co., Columbus, Ind., 1959-61; v.p. mfg. C.P. Electronics Co., Columbus, 1961-63; mgr. cost analysis Am. Motors Corp., Detroit, 1963-64, plant mgr., Grand Rapids, Mich., Milw., 1964-68, v.p. mfg., Detroit, 1968-75, group v.p. ops., 1975-79; pres., chief operating officer Consol. Rail Corp., Phila., 1979—; dir. 1st Nat. Bank Kenosha (Wis.). Served with Signal Corps, AUS, 1944-45. Mem. Soc. Automotive Engrs., Am. Inst. Indsl. Engrs., Am. Soc. Quality Control, Engring. Soc. Detroit. Home: 455 Timber Ln Devon PA 19333 Office: 1846 Six Penn Center Plaza Philadelphia PA 19104

REED, THEODORE EVANS, union exec.; b. Boston, May 6, 1932; s. Gerald M., Jr. and Helen E. (Evans) R.; B.A., Northeastern U., 1955; postgrad. McCoy Coll., Johns Hopkins U., 1960, George Washington U., 1963, U. Calif., Berkeley, 1971-76, George Meany Labor Studies Center, Silver Spring, Md., 1976-80; m. Gloria Gobbi, Sept. 14, 1952; children—Geoffrey Mark, Gerald Scott, Suzan Leslie, Sandra Lynn, Russell Steven. Asso. engr. long range advanced design dept. Martin Co., Middle River, Md., 1956-58; ops. analyst Ops. Research Office, Johns Hopkins U., 1959-63; designer, mgr. info. data banks Stanford Research Inst., 1963-65; overseas resident, research dir. future projects Sri-Bonn (Ger.), 1965-70; dir., advisor, sr. cost analyst Stanford Research Inst., Menlo Park, Calif., 1965-71; dir. research and stats. Western Conf. Operating Engrs., 1971-75; asst. dir. research Internat. Union Operating Engrs., Washington, 1976-78, dir. research, 1978—; mem. labor research adv. council Dept. Labor; labor adv. group Multilateral Trade Negotiations; mem. Mayor Rockville (Md.) Com. Urban Renewal; elder St. Andrews United Presbyn. Ch., Rockville, Md. Recipient George Meany award for outstanding service to youth Internat. Union Operating Engrs., AFL-CIO, 1979, Best Ideas award Am. Inst. Plant Engrs., 1975; also various Boy Scout Am. tng. awards. Mem. Ops. Research Soc. Am., Americans for Energy Ind., Am. Inst. Plant Engrs. (chpt. v.p., program chmn. 1974-75), Consumer Fedn. Am., Washington Health Security Action Coalition, Am. Econ. Assn., Indsl. Relations Research Assn. Democrat. Author monographs, papers, reports in field. Home: 9324 Winterset Dr Potomac MD 20854 Office: 1125 17th St NW Washington DC 20036

REED, WILLIAM GUY, restaurant exec.; b. Richmond, Ky., Feb. 6, 1942; s. William S. and Nina (Kanatzar) R.; B.A., Eastern Ky. U., 1963; postgrad. Eastern Ky. U., 1963-64; m. Janice Woods, Feb. 28, 1974; children—Tommy, Guy, Dee Dee. Tchr. Richmond, Ky., 1963-64; asst. mgr. Jerry's Restaurants, Lexington, 1964-65; mgr., v.p. Corbin Restaurant Inc., Lexington, 1965-68, pres., 1968—; pres. Middlesboro Restaurant Inc., Lexington, 1971—; v.p., London Restaurant Inc., Lexington, 1975—; sec.-treas. Sioux Empire Restaurant Inc., Lexington, 1975—. Mem. Corbin, London, Middlesboro (Ky.) chambers commerce, Ky. Cols. Ky. Restaurant Assn. Baptist. Masons, Shriners. Home: 909 Chinoe Rd Lexington KY 40502 Office: 152 E Reynolds Rd Lexington KY 40503

REEDY, CLIFFORD EUGENE, adjustment co. exec.; b. Parsons, Kans., Dec. 2, 1922; s. George and Mary Augusta (Vandegrift) R.; student Parsons Jr. Coll., S.E. Mo. State Coll., 1942-43, Columbia U., 1944; m. Betty Lou Overby, Oct. 27, 1944; children—Clifford Eugene, Carol Lue. Claim agt. Mo.-Kans.-Tex. R.R. Co., Parsons, Kans., 1946-57; casualty adjuster Western Adjustment & Inspection Co., Parsons, 1957-58; regional casualty supr. GAS Bus. Services, Wichita, Kans., Peoria, Ill., 1958-61, dept. casualty mgr., exec. mgr., gen. mgr., Chgo., 1961-71, nat. sales mgr., v.p. products and product devel., exec. v.p., pres., N.Y.C., 1971-77; pres. Am. Internat. Adjustment Co., N.Y.C., 1977—. Served to lt. (j.g.) USNR, 1942-46. Mem. Loss Execs. Assn. Republican. Home: 175 Wentworth Dr Berkeley Heights NJ 07922 Office: 70 Pine St New York NY 10005

REEDY, JAMES WINTON, mfg. co. exec.; b. Rockton, Ill., Oct. 6, 1946; s. Lawrence Winton and Florence Evelyn (Goodsell) R.; student U. Ill., 1964-66; B.S., U. Wis., 1971; postgrad. No. Ill. U., 1971-73; m. Susan Clark, June 22, 1968; children—Jason Winton, Joshua William, Jacob Wade. Sales mktg. coordinator Regal Beloit Corp., South Beloit, Ill., 1973, corp. personnel dir., 1974, chief personnel officer, 1978, v.p. adminstrn., 1979—; dir. Beloit Econ. Devel. Corp., 1980—. Bd. dirs. United Givers Fund, 1975—, pres., 1979; bd. dirs. Family Service Assn., Beloit, 1976—, treas., 1979, 80; mem. Rockton Zoning Bd., 1979; cons. to high sch. vocat. program, 1976—. Served with U.S. Army, 1967-69. Recipient Outstanding Achievement awards United Givers Fund, 1975-79. Mem. Am. Soc. Personnel Adminstrs., Blackhawk Assn. (pres. bd. 1974-77), Blackhawk Personnel (pres. 1977). Republican. Methodist. Contbr. articles to profl. jours. Home: 635 E Franklin St Rockton IL 61072 Office: PO Box 38 Rockton Rd South Beloit IL 61080

REEHER, THOMAS WILLIAM, computer center exec.; b. Ellwood City, Pa., Mar. 28, 1953; s. Perry Lee and Nancy Elizabeth (Litman) R.; B.A., Allegheny Coll., 1975; M.A. in Communications, Pa. State U., 1977. Asst. plant mgr. Silver Maple Foods Inc., New Castle, Pa., 1977-78; mgr. Best Resume Service, Akron, Ohio, 1978-79; communications coordinator Westinghouse Tele-Computer Center, Pitts., 1979—; pres. TWR Enterprises, Pitts. Mem. Internat. Assn. Bus. Communicators, Braddock Area C. of C. Republican. Club: Rotary (v.p. 1980-81). Contbr. articles to mags. Home: 406 Hay St Pittsburgh PA 15221 Office: 1001 Brinton Rd Pittsburgh PA 15221

REEM, HERBERT FELIX, engr., economist; b. Vienna, Austria, Dec. 5, 1921; s. Emil and Roma (Druckman) R.; B.S. in Civil Engring., Internat. Inst. Tech., 1943, C.E., 1949; M.S., Columbia, 1954; Ph.D.; m. Anne Liese Geier, Oct. 27, 1956; 1 dau., Evelyn M. Asst. engr. Municipal Corp., Jerusalem, 1944-48; area engr. Ministry Finance, 1949-50; structural engr. U.S. forces, Austria, 1950-51; civil, structural engr. Tippetts, Abbett, McCarthy, Stratton, Engrs. and Architects, N.Y.C., 1951-56; cons. engr., N.Y.C., 1956-57; chief power sect. C.E., Fed. Power Commn., also research economist, Washington, 1963-65; mgmt. engr. Office Sec. Def., Washington, 1965-73; dir. spl. projects Dept. Energy, 1973—. Del., Engrs. Joint Council on Govt. Com. Served to lt. USNR, 1948-49. Recipient Wallace prize Brit. Commonwealth, 1947. Registered profl. engr., D.C., Del. Chartered engr., U.K. Col., aide de camp to gov. Tenn. Fellow Am. Soc. C.E., Inst. Structural Engrs.; sr. mem. Am. Inst. Indsl. Engrs. (pres. 1964-66); mem. Nat. Soc. Profl. Engrs., Assn. Energy Engrs. (chmn. energy engrs. in govt. council, v.p.). Contbg. author: Mineral Yearbook, 1965. Author: The Impact of Technological Change, 1965; Energy Resource Management; Future of Electric Power Production; others. Home: 6329 Lakeview Dr Falls Church VA 22041 Office: Dept Energy Washington DC

REES, WILLIAM MASON, business exec.; b. Bklyn., Mar. 17, 1916; s. Gomer H. and Pauline M. (Mason) R.; B.A., Yale, 1937; m. Marianna Adair, Nov. 2, 1940. With Chubb & Son, Inc., N.Y.C., 1937—, dir. 1959—, chmn., 1970—; dir. Chubb Corp., 1967—, chmn., 1970—; dir. Fed. Ins. Co., 1964—, chmn., 1970—; dir. Vigilant Ins. Co., 1961—, chmn., 1970—; chmn. bd., pres. Gt. No. Ins. Co., 1966—; dir. Pacific Indemnity Co., Colonial Life Ins. Co. Am., United Life & Accident Ins. Co., Bellemead Devel. Corp. Trustee Markle Found. Served to lt. col. C.E., AUS, 1942-45. Episcopalian. Office: 100 William St New York NY 10038

REESE, ANDREW JOEL, lawyer; b. Los Angeles, May 5, 1945; s. John Henry and Margaret (Smith) R.; student U. So. Calif., 1963-64; B.S. with honors in Econs., Calif. State Poly. U., 1972; J.D., Harvard U., 1975; A.A. in Bus. and Real Estate, Mendocino Coll., 1979; m. Karon K. Wolf, Sept. 1, 1967; 1 dau., Elisabeth K. Admitted to Calif. bar, 1975; asso. firm Pacht, Ross, Warne, Bernhard & Sears, Inc., Los Angeles, 1975-76; dep. dist. atty. Mendocino County Dist. Atty.'s Office, Ukiah, Calif., 1976-79; partner firm Adams, Henderson & Reese, Ukiah, 1979—; instr. law and real estate Mendocino Coll., Ukiah, 1978-80. Sec.-treas., dir. Mendocino County Employees Credit Union, 1979—. Pres., Alcohol Rehab. Corp., 1980—; chmn. interim policy adv. council Mendocino Alcohol Project, 1980—. Served with USAF, 1964-68. Mem. Am. Bar Assn., Calif. Bar Assn. Republican. Club: 20-30 Internat. (Ukiah). Home: 1699 Woodland Terr Ukiah CA 95482 Office: PO Box 998 215 W Standley St Ukiah CA 95482

REESE, JOSEPH HAMMOND, JR., employee benefit cons., ins. and real estate mgmt. exec.; b. Phila., Aug. 29, 1928; s. Joseph Hammond and Ethel (Allen) R.; B.A. in Econs., Washington and Lee U., 1950; postgrad. Wharton Sch., U. Pa., 1950; cert. Am. Coll., 1955; m. Joan Barton, Feb. 7, 1975; children—Daniel, Linda; stepchildren—Anne Harbison, Carol Harbison, Will Harbison. Agt., Penn Mut. Life Ins. Co., Phila., 1950-61, asst. gen. agt., 1958-60; chmn., chief exec. officer Reese & Co. Inc., Abington, Pa., 1961—; chief exec. officer Montgomery Mgmt. Corp., Abington, 1972—; gen. agt. Mass. Mut. Life Ins. Co., Phila., 1961—. Trustee Franklin and Marshall Coll., 1972-77; bd. dirs. Holy Redeemer Hosp., Meadowbrook, Pa. Served to 1st lt. USAF, 1950-53. Mem. Am. Soc. Pension Actuaries, Am. Soc. C.L.U.'s (pres. Phila. chpt. 1960-61), Nat. Assn. Life Underwriters (life and qualifying mem. Million Dollar Round Table 1956—), Young Pres.'s Orgn., Phila. Pres.'s Orgn. Republican. Episcopalian. Clubs: Huntington Valley Country (Abington, Pa.); Union League (Phila.); Seaview Country (Abescon, N.J.); Wilderness Country (Naples, Fla.); Skytop Lodge (Pa.); Ponte Vedra (Fla.). Home: Hidden Glen Meadowbrook PA 19046 Office: PO Box 199 Abington PA 19001

REESE, WILLIAM WILLIS, banker; b. N.Y.C., July 8, 1940; s. Willis Livingston Meiser and Frances Galletin (Stevens) R.; B.A., Trinity Coll., 1963; M.B.A., J.D., Columbia U., 1970; m. Sona Lawrence Van Voorhees. Admitted to N.Y. bar, 1972; research analyst Morgan Guaranty Trust Co., N.Y.C., 1971-73, investment research officer, 1973-77, asst. v.p., 1977—. Bd. dirs. N.Y.C. Ballet, 1975—, Counseling and Human Devel. Center, 1977—, 3d St. Music Sch. Settlement, 1976—; trustee Millbrook Sch., 1972—. Served with USAF, 1963-67. Mem. Am., Inter-Am., N.Y. State (sec. com. on internat. law 1973-76), Dutchess County bar assns., Bank and Fin. Analysts Assn. (dir. 1979—), N.Y. Soc. Security Analysts, Certified Fin. Analysts, Assn. Bar City N.Y. Republican. Episcopalian. Clubs: Union, Racquet and Tennis, Rockaway Hunt, Mt. Holyoke Lodge. Home: Obercreek Farm New Hamburg NY 12560 Office: 9 W 57th St New York NY 10019

REEVE, RONALD CROPPER, JR., mfg. exec.; b. Logan, Utah, Jan. 29, 1943; s. Ronald Cropper and Aldus (Moser) R.; B.Sc. in Physics, Ohio State U., 1967; M.B.A. in Mktg., Xavier U., 1972; m. Deborah Lynn Crooks, Dec. 31, 1976; children—Heather Renee, Michael Scott, Thomas Adam. Successively devel. engr., research engr., product planner Specialty Materials dept. Gen. Electric Co., Worthington, Ohio, 1969-73; successively product mgr., mgr., gen. mgr. Air Products & Chems., Inc., Lancaster, Ohio, 1974-79; founder, pres. Advanced Robotics Corp., Hebron, Ohio, 1979—. Served with USAF, 1968-69. Mem. Am. Welding Soc., Am. Soc. Metals, Soc. Mfg. Engrs., Robot Inst. Am. Club: Hoover Yacht. Patentee diamond crystal structure. Home: 1131 Hempstead Ct Westerville OH 43081 Office: Bldg 8 Newark Indsl Park Hebron OH 43025

REEVES, AIDNEY MONROE, bus. devel. exec.; b. Ruby, Tex., Aug. 23, 1935; s. Monroe S. and Agnes (Hammond) R.; B.S., Hundington Coll., 1960; postgrad. U. Tenn., 1963-64, U. Ala., 1966-67; m. Ruth Weaver, June 8, 1958; children—Francis Elizabeth, Peggy Anne. Dir. mktg. Rust Engring. Co., Birmingham, Ala., 1966-76; v.p. sales Barnard & Burk, Baton Rouge, 1976-77; v.p. sales Davey Powergas, Houston, 1978-80; mgr. bus. devel. Brown & Root, Houston, 1980—. Mem. Millbrook Bd. Health, 1962-63; mem. Mcpl. Adv. Council, 1961-67. Served with USAF, 1953-57. Mem. Am. Inst. Chem. Engrs., TAPPI. Mem. Ch. of Christ. Home: 3515 Oak Lake Dr Kingwood TX 77339 Office: PO Box 3 Houston TX 77001

REEVES, CHARLES MERCER, JR., corp. exec.; b. Sanford, N.C., Feb. 14, 1919; s. Charles Mercer and Suzanne Easten (Purvis) R.; B.S. in Bus. Adminstrn., U. N.C., 1940; m. Sarah Frances Crosby, Oct. 12, 1940; children—Charles Mercer III, David Crosby, Suzanne (Mrs. James Marion Parrott IV), John Mercer II. Pres., 1st Provident Co., Inc., Sanford, 1949-77; chmn. bd. Atlantic & Western Ry. and Atlantic & Western Fin. Corp., Sanford, 1968—; pres., chmn. So. Provident Life Ins. Co., Phoenix; dir. Steel and Pipe Corp., Sanford, S.C. Bank Corp., Columbia, S.C.; partner Rich Mountain Assos., Boone, N.C., Cape Lookout Assos., Morehead City, N.C. Mem. N.C. Banking Commn., 1954-61, 69-73. Mem. N.C. Higher Bd. Edn., 1961-62; bd. govs. Meth. Coll., Fayetteville, N.C.; dist. exec. com. Boy Scouts Am., 1964—. Commr., Lee County, 1953-55. Served with AC USNR, World War II. Mem. Mensa, SAR, Beta Theta Pi. Methodist. Rotarian. Home: Reeves Ridge Farm Sanford NC 27330 Office: 317 Chatham St Sanford NC 27330

REEVES, DAVID LEE, pub. co. exec.; b. Portsmouth, Ohio, July 18, 1915; s. David Lee and Mary Olive (Bridge) R.; B.A., Wittenberg U., 1939; m. Floy Annette Moll, July 31, 1943. Trainee, Gen. Elec. Corp., Schenectady, 1940-43; indsl. engring. dept. supr. Armour & Co., Chgo., 1943-49, sales mgr., 1950-51; cons. to industries and cos., Chgo., 1951-53; dist. sales mgr. Prentice-Hall, Inc., Chgo., 1953-63, ednl. dir., Englewood Cliffs, N.J., 1963-73, pres. Loose Leaf Services div., Englewood Cliffs, 1974—. Mem. Am. Assn. Law Libraries, Am. Soc. Personnel Adminstrn. Office: Route 9W Englewood Cliffs NJ 07632

REEVES, PAUL JOHN, precision sheet metal fabricating co. exec.; b. Cleve., Dec. 3, 1933; s. John Love and Esther Myrtle (Goudy) R.; B.B.A., Cleve. State U., 1960; M.B.A., Case-Western Res. U., 1967; postgrad. Harvard U. Bus. Sch., 1977; m. Kathryn Vadarie Blair, Nov. 3, 1956. Sr. auditor Price Waterhouse & Co., Cleve., 1959-67; mgr. mgmt. audit Cooper Industries, Inc., Houston, 1967-71; pres., chief exec. officer Overly-Hautz Co., Cleve., 1971—. Served with USMC, 1952-55; Korea. C.P.A., Cleve. Mem. Assn. for Mgmt. Excellence (dir.), Fabricating Mfrs. Assn. (dir.), Am. Inst. C.P.A.'s, Ohio Soc. C.P.A.'s. Republican. Baptist. Home: 3981 N Valley Dr Fairview Park OH 44126 Office: 8617 Clinton Rd Cleveland OH 44144

REEVES, WILLIAM RAY, investment banking co. exec.; b. Corbin, Ky., Feb. 8, 1937; s. Leslie Joseph and Phoebe Mae (Hale) R.; B.Chem. Engring., U. Cin., 1959; postgrad. Harvard U., 1960-61; M.B.A., U. Va., 1964; m. Mary Agnes O'Rourke, Dec. 30, 1972; children—Katherine Margaret, David William Joseph, Robert Sean Hale. Cons., Fantus div. Dun & Bradstreet, N.Y.C., 1969-70; pres. Barnett Chem. Products, Inc., Phila., 1970-72; cons. Nat. Center for Resource Recovery, Washington, 1972-73; v.p. Interstate Gen. Corp., St. Charles, Md., San Juan, P.R., 1973-81; pres. New Energy Investment Services, Inc., Washington, 1981—; dir. St. Charles Health Services, Inc., 1977—. Served as capt. U.S. Army, 1960-61. Registered profl. engr., Ohio, Md. Mem. Port Tobacco Restoration Soc. (pres., dir. 1976—), Charles County (Md.) Heart Assn. (chmn. 1976-77), Nat. Energy Resources Orgn., Met. Washington Bd. Trade, Harvard Bus. Sch. Club Washington. Club: Hawthorne Country. Patentee radio controlled fishing boat, 1968. Home: Sunnytop Farm Port Tobacco MD 20677 Office: 336 Post Office Rd St Charles MD 20601

REGAN, DONALD THOMAS, securities exec.; b. Cambridge, Mass., Dec. 21, 1918; B.A., Harvard, 1940; m. Ann G. Buchanan, July 11, 1942; children—Donna, Donald, Richard, Diane. With Merrill Lynch, Pierce, Fenner & Smith, Inc., and predecessor, 1946—, sec., dir. adminstrv. div., 1960-64, exec. v.p., 1964-68, pres., 1968-71, chmn. bd., 1971-80; chmn. bd., chief exec. officer Merrill Lynch & Co., Inc., 1973—; dir. Securities Investor Protection Corp., 1971-73; vice chmn. bd. N.Y. Stock Exchange, 1972-75. Trustee, Charles E. Merrill Trust, Com. Econ. Devel.; chmn. bd. trustees U. Pa., 1974-78; bd. dirs. Beekman Downtown Hosp., 1969-73. Served to lt. col. USMCR, World War II. Mem. Bus. Roundtable (policy com. 1978—), Investment Bankers Assn. Am. (v.p., gov. 1966-67). Clubs: Met., Burning Tree, Army-Navy (Washington); Baltusrol Golf; Bond (gov.), Economic (N.Y.C.). Author: A View from the Street, 1972. Office: One Liberty Plaza 165 Broadway New York NY 10006

REGAN, PETER JOHN, banker; b. Lawrence, Mass., Oct. 10, 1942; s. Walter A. and Mary (Murphy) R.; B.S. in B.A., Boston U., 1965; m. Julie Potter, Dec. 31, 1966; children—John P., Katey M., James P., Kim M. Acct., Haskins & Sells, C.P.A.'s, Boston, 1965-66; account exec. James Talcott Inc., Boston, 1966-69; exec. v.p., treas., dir. Market Masters Industries Inc., Greenwich, Conn., 1969-71; comml. loan dir. Ford Motor Credit Co., Dearborn, Mich., 1971-74; v.p. Shawmut Bank of Boston N.A., 1974—. Lic. real estate broker, Mass. Mem. New Eng. Assn. Credit Execs., Nat. Assn. Mktg. Execs., Nat. Assn. Mfg. Execs. Roman Catholic. Home: 4 Embassy Ln Andover MA Office: Shawmut Bank 1 Federal St Boston MA 02211

REGARDIE, RENAY NADLER, market research co. exec.; b. Bronx, N.Y., May 30, 1942; d. Samuel and Lillian (Wolfson) Nadler; B.S. magna cum laude in Bus. Adminstrn., (mktg. program award 1964), Am. U., 1964; m. William Arthur Regardie, May 29, 1965; children—Robert Jon, Marc Eric. Jr. copywriter Robert Kline Advt., Richmond, Va., 1964-65; research analyst Chesapeake & Potomac Telephone Co., Washington, 1965-68; sr. research analyst Am. Research Bur., Beltsville, Md., 1970-72; pres. Housing Data Reports, Inc., Bethesda, Md., 1976—. Mem. Nat. Assn. Home Builders, D.C. Homebuilders Assn., No. Va. Homebuilders Assn., Suburban Md. Homebuilders Assn., Phi Kappa Phi. Jewish. New homes columnist Real Estate Washington mag.; contbg. columnist Washington Post. Office: 4330 East West Hwy Bethesda MD 20014

REGELBRUGGE, ROGER RAFAEL, steel prodn. and engring. co. exec.; b. Eeklo, Belgium, May 22, 1930; s. Victor and Rachel (Roesbeke) R.; came to U.S., 1957, naturalized, 1961; M.E., State Tech. Coll. (Belgium), 1951; Indsl. Engr., Gen. Motors Inst., 1955; M.S., Mich. State U., 1964; m. Dorcas Merchant; children—Anita, Marc, Laurie, Jon, Craig, Kurt. Chief devel. engr. Hayes-Albion Corp., Jackson, Mich., 1960-62; gen. mgr. Airmaster div., 1962-66; tech. dir. Koehring Internat., Milw., 1966-67; gen. mgr. Menck & Hambrock, Hamburg, Germany, 1967-69; group v.p. internat. operations Koehring Co., Milw., 1969-74; exec. v.p. Korf Industries, Inc., Charlotte, N.C., 1974-77, pres., 1977—, also dir.; chmn. bd. Midrex Corp., 1975—, Georgetown Steel Corp., 1977—, Georgetown Tex. Steel Corp., 1977—; dir. Nachman Corp. Bd. dirs. Internat. Sch., Hamburg, Germany, 1967-69, Am. Iron and Steel Inst. Served to 2d lt. Belgian Army, 1951-53. Mem. ASME, Soc. Automotive Engrs., St. Vincent de Paul Soc. Office: Korf Industries Inc Charlotte NC 28202

REGISTER, MARVIN THOMAS, constrn. co. exec.; b. Jacksonville, Fla., Nov. 16, 1935; s. Thomas Sherman and Agatha Ernestine (Atkinson) R.; B.S. in Bldg. Constrn., U. Fla., 1963; m. Earlene Ruth Gibson, Aug. 6, 1960; children—Glenn Thomas, Pamela Diane, Gavin Andrew. Area engr. constrn. div. E. I. DuPont & Co., Richmond, Va., 1963-64; estimator Burroughs & Preston, Inc., Gen. Contractors, Falls Church, Va., 1964-67, Proefke-Nielsen Constrn. Co., Dunedin, Fla., 1967-68; pres., co-owner Caladesi Constrn. Co., Clearwater, Fla., 1968-69; project mgr. Vernon Burgess & Assos., Constrn. Cons., Clearwater, 1969-70, DFS Constrn. Co., St. Petersburg, Fla., 1970-72, Frank J. Rooney, Inc., Gen. Contractors, Tampa, Fla., 1972-75; pres., operator M.T. Register & Assos., Gen. Contractors and Constrn. Mgmt., Dunedin, 1976—. Chmn., Dunedin City Charter Rev. Com. (cited for outstanding service 1975); past vice chmn. Dunedin Planning and Zoning Bd.; vice chmn. Dunedin Health Facilities; mem. Mease Hosp. Devel. Bd., pres. Mease Hosp. Assn.; past chmn. Dunedin Community Blood Drive; past mem. Pinellas Area Transp. Study Com.; past pres. Dunedin Nat. Little League; past pres. Dunedin Youth Winter Instructional Baseball League. Served to sgt. U.S. Army, 1953-56. Named Dunedin History Maker, Dunedin Hist. Soc., 1978. Registered gen. contractor, Fla. Mem. Am. Inst. Contractors, Associated Builders and Contractors Assn. Republican. Presbyterian. Clubs: Sertoma (past pres.; named Sertoman of Year 1970), Masons; Rotary (Dunedin). Home: 1101 Idlewild Dr South Dunedin FL 33528 Office: MT Register & Assos Gen Contractors 1008 Broadway Dunedin FL 33528

REGNIER, ROBERT DENNIS, banker; b. Kansas City, Kans., Dec. 31, 1948; s. Victor Lemmie and Helen (Benning) R.; B.A., Kans. State U., 1974; M.B.A., U. Mo., 1979; m. Ann McKee, Aug. 13, 1978; 1 dau., Kate Elizabeth. Clk., Boatmen's Bank & Trust, Kansas City, Kans., 1970-71, teller, 1971-72, comml. officer, 1972-74, asst. v.p., 1974-76, v.p., 1976-78, sr. v.p., 1978—. Served with Army. Mem. Mo. Bankers Assn., Bank Adminstrn. Inst., Am. Bankers Assn. Republican. Episcopalian. Clubs: Univ., Carriage. Home: 9218 Cherokee Pl Leawood KS 66206 Office: 1101 Baltimore Kansas City MO 64105

REGUNBERG, JEROME, publisher; b. N.Y.C., Mar. 21, 1923; s. Joseph and Sarah (Belarae) R.; B.A., CCNY, 1943; D.V.M., Brandeis U., 1946; postgrad. Vassar Coll.; m. Bernice F. Morowitz, Aug. 3, 1947; children—Michal A., J. Jonathan, Daron Z. Sr. exec. veterinarian UN Relief and Rehab. Adminstrn., Newport News, Va., 1946-48; v.p. Queen City Co., Inc., Poughkeepsie, N.Y., 1948-60, pres., 1960—; pub. Mid Hudson Leisure, 1972—; exec. scientist Internat. Unifor, 1969—; chmn. bd. Esotechnica Inc., 1978—; cons. Ulster County Community Coll. Del., World Zionist Congress, 1958; artistic dir., founding dir. High Ton Opera Co., 1960; dir. Poughkeepsie Urban Renewal, 1974-76. Mem. Atlantic Ind. Distbrs. Assn., AVMA. Democrat. Jewish. Patentee in field. Home: 136 Parker Ave Poughkeepsie NY 12601

REHFELD, ROBERT WILLIAM, lumber and paper mfg. co. exec.; b. Sheboygan, Wis., Nov. 18, 1917; s. Alvin A. and Hazel R. (Bachman) R.; B.A. in Acctg., U. Wis., 1939; m. Jean Ellen Lentz, Aug. 31, 1945; children—Robert William, James Allen, Thomas Arthur. Sr. acct. Arthur Andersen & Co., Los Angeles, 1945-46, mgr., San Francisco, 1946-51; treas., controller SW Forest Industries, Inc., Phoenix, 1951-61, v.p. fin., treas., 1961—; dir. Ariz. Blue Shield. Bd. dirs. Jr. Achievement, Phoenix; trustee Phoenix Gen. Hosp. Served to lt. (s.g.) USNR, 1942-45. C.P.A., Ariz., Calif. Mem. Am. Inst. C.P.A.'s, Ariz. Soc. C.P.A.'s, Fin. Execs. Inst. Clubs: Phoenix Country, Ariz. (Phoenix); White Mountain Country (Pinetop, Ariz.). Home: 510 W Coronado St Phoenix AZ 85003 Office: PO Box 7548 Phoenix AZ 85011

REHM, JOHN EDWIN, mfg. co. exec.; b. Bucyrus, Ohio, Oct. 20, 1924; s. Lester Carl and Mary O'Dale (Myers) R.; student Heidelberg U., 1942, U. Ala., 1943-44, Ohio State U., 1946-49. Asst. plant engr. Shunk Mfg. Co., Inc., Bucyrus, 1949-53, prodn. mgr., 1951-61, plant mgr., 1961-65, mgr. prodn. services, 1965-68, mgr. customer service dept., 1968-69, ops. mgr., 1969-70, v.p. ops., 1970-71; materials mgr. Oury Engring. Co., Marion, Ohio, 1971-73, W.W. Sly Mfg. Co., Cleve., 1973—; v.p., gen. mgr. Moody Mfg. Co., Inc., Maben, Miss., 1979—. Bd. dirs. Bucyrus United Community Fund, 1969-70. Served with AUS, 1943-46; PTO. Decorated Bronze Star (2). Mem. Am. Soc. Personnel Adminstrn., Bucyrus Area C. of C. (v.p. 1966, pres. 1967). Republican. Clubs: Elks, Rotary. Home: 48 Chickasaw St Starkville MS 39759

REHR, BRUCE ROGER, mut. fund exec.; b. Reading, Pa., June 29, 1928; s. Garrett John and Anna Alma (Fry) R.; B.A. in Econs., Dickinson Coll., Carlisle, Pa., 1950; m. Nancy Lou Bain, July 21, 1951; children—Roger Bruce, Linda Jane Rehr Patton, Garrett Henry, Scott Lambert. Vice pres. J.L. Hain & Co., Reading, 1950-68; pres., chief exec. officer Penn Sq. Mgmt. Corp., Reading, 1968—; chmn. bd. Penn Sq. Mut. Fund, 1968—; dir. Wyomissing New Home Fed. Savs. & Loan Assn. Bd. dirs. Reading Hosp. and Med. Center, 1968—, YMCA Reading and Berks County, 1970—, Hawk Mt. council Boy Scouts Am., 1968—; v.p., trustee Dickinson Coll., 1970—. Served with AUS, 1950-52. Mem. No-Load Mut. Fund Assn. (dir.), Phi Beta Kappa, Omicron Delta Kappa, Sigma Chi. Republican. Lutheran. Clubs: Wyomissing, Iris, Berkshire Country. Home: 92 Grandview Blvd Wyomissing Hills Reading PA 19609 Office: Berkshire Towers 101 N 5th St Reading PA 19601

REICHARDT, CARL EDWIN, banker; b. Houston, July 6, 1931; s. Carl E. and Cora E. (Robichaux) R.; B.A. in Econs., U. So. Calif., 1956; postgrad. Advanced Mgmt. Program, Harvard U., 1975; m. Patricia Longenecker, June 19, 1954; children—Carl, Gretchen, Frederick. Exec. v.p. Union Bank, Los Angeles, 1960-70; pres. Wells Fargo Realty Advisors, San Francisco, 1970-72; pres., trustee Wells Fargo Mortgage Investors, San Francisco, 1970-72; exec. v.p. Wells Fargo & Co., San Francisco, 1973-78, mem. exec. com., 1977-78, pres., 1978—, also dir.; pres. Wells Fargo Bank, N.A., San Francisco, 1978—; dir. Golden West Homes, Hosp. Corp. Am., Newhall Land & Farming Co. Bd. dirs. Mt. Zion Hosp. and Med. Center, San Francisco; bd. dirs. United Way of Bay area, campaign chmn., 1980; trustees San Domenico Sch. Served with USN, 1951-54. Mem. Robert Morris Assos. (dir.), Assn. Res. City Bankers. Clubs: San Francisco Yacht, Pacific Union (San Francisco); Links (N.Y.C.); Meadow.*

REICHERT, JACK FRANK, mfg. co. exec.; b. West Allis, Wis., Sept. 27, 1930; s. Arthur Andrew and Emily Bertha (Wallinger) R.; cert. mktg. U. Wis., Milw., 1957; M.A., Harvard U., 1970; m. Corrine Violet Helf, Apr. 5, 1952; children—Susan Marie, John Arthur. With Gen. Electric Co., 1948-57; with Brunswick Corp., Skokie, Ill., 1957—, pres. Mercury Marine div., 1971-72, corp. v.p., 1974-77, v.p. Marine Power Group, 1974-77, pres., chief operating officer, 1977—; also dir.; dir. Nat. Exchange Bank, Fond du Lac, Wis., Sanshin Industries Co. Ltd., Japan; mem. adminstrv. adv. council U. Wis. Milw. Sch. Bus. Adminstrn. Trustee, Carroll Coll., Waukesha, Ill.; bd. dirs. McCormick Theol. Sem., Chgo.; indsl. chmn. United Fund of Fond du Lac, 1977; trustee lst Presbyterian Ch. of Lake Forest. Served with U.S. Army, 1951-53. Recipient Disting. Alumnus of Yr. award U. Wis., Milw., 1979. Mem. President's Club of Loyola U. Chgo. (hon.), Harvard Bus. Sch. Club Chgo., Beta Gamma Sigma. Club: Knollwood. Office: 1 Brunswick Plaza Skokie IL 70077

REICHERT, NORMAN VERNON, transp. co. exec.; b. Berwyn, Ill., Apr. 17, 1921; s. John G. and Valeria (Hoffman) R.; B.S. in Bus. Adminstrn., Northwestern U., 1943; postgrad. Harvard, 1943-44; m. Wilma Eleanor Catey, Feb. 5, 1944; children—Susan, Norman V. Accountant, Arthur Young & Co., Chgo., 1946-50; central finance staff, controller styling div. Ford Motor Co., Dearborn, Mich., 1950-61; asst. treas. Philco Ford Corp., Phila., 1961-69; asst. treas. United Air Lines, Inc., 1969-72; v.p. finance Trailer Train Co., also Am. Rail Box Car Co. and Railgon, Chgo., 1972—; dir. Hamburg Industries Inc., Augusta, Ga., Calpro, Inc., Riverside, Calif., Acorn Industries, Jacksonville, Fla., Delpro Co., Wilmington, Del. Served to lt. USNR, 1943-46. C.P.A., Ill. Mem. Am. Inst. C.P.A.'s, Financial Exec. Inst., Newcomen Soc., Beta Alpha Psi, Sigma Alpha Epsilon. Clubs: Union League, Knollwood, Exec. Home: 921 Grandview Ln Lake Forest IL 60045 Office: 101 N Wacker Dr Chicago IL 60606

REID, BRUCE WALLACE, JR., fin. exec.; b. Charlotte, N.C., Sept. 29, 1941; s. Bruce Wallace and Virginia W. (Harrison) R.; student U. Tenn., 1961-62; m. Sereda Ann Pasquariello, Aug. 4, 1961; children—Lisa Ann, Bruce Philip, Angela, Andrew Vincent. With UMIC, Inc., Memphis, 1966-76; with Donald Sheldon & Co., Inc., Memphis, 1976—, br. mgr., 1980—. Served with USMCR, 1959-60. Republican. Roman Catholic. Club: K.C. Home: 1204 Chamberlain St Memphis TN 38138 Office: 5575 Poplar St Suite 307 Memphis TN 38117

REID, JOSEPH EDMONDSON, oil co. exec.; b. Meridian, Miss., Mar. 18, 1929; s. Benjamin Franklin and Lottie (James) R.; B.S. in Petroleum Engring., La. State U., 1951; M.B.A., Harvard U., 1956; m. Bobby Jean Ray, Sept. 6, 1955; children—Lisa R., Joseph T., Taylor L., Leslie C., David H. Exploittion engr. Shell Oil Co., 1954; mgr. oil and gas div. Cabot Corp., Pampa, Tex., 1956-67; asst. to chmn. Panhandle Eastern Pipe Line Co., Houston, 1967-68; exec. v.p. Trunkline Gas Co., Houston, 1968-72; pres. Superior Oil Co., Houston, 1972—, also dir.; dir. First City Nat. Bank, Houston, McIntyre Mines, Calgary, Falconbridge Nickel Mines, Toronto, Canadian Superior, Calgary, Western Platinum, Ltd., Johannesburg, South Africa. Trustee Gray County (Tex.) Sch. Bd., 1966-67. Served to 2d lt. U.SAF, 1951-52. Mem. Am. Assn. Petroleum Geologists, AIME, Am. Assn. Petroleum Landmen, Am. Petroleum Inst., Soc. Petroleum Engrs., Ind. Petroleum Assn. Am. Baptist. Clubs: Houston, Ramada, (dir. 1979—), Houston Country, Petroleum. Home: 651 Shady Hollow Houston TX 77056 Office: PO Box 1521 Houston TX 77001

REIFF, DENNIS RAYMOND, ins. broker; b. Yonkers, N.Y., Nov. 4, 1945; s. Harold G. and Helen C. R.; B.A., U. Buffalo, 1969; m. Patricia A. Halliday, June 22, 1974; children—Dylan H., Virginia H. With Factory Mut. System, 1970-72, 73-75, Marsh & McLennan Corp., 1975-76; with Capitol Risk Concepts, N.Y.C, 1976—, dir. mktg. Mem. U. Buffalo Alumni Assn. Home: 41 W 83d St New York NY 10024 Office: Capitol Risk Concepts One Penn Plaza New York NY 10001

REIFF, WILLIAM DAVID, corp. exec.; b. Chgo., Apr. 14, 1930; s. David Lester and Dora Agnes (Deffner) R.; B.B.A., U. Wash., 1951; M.B.A., Northwestern U., 1952; m. Elaine Rottrup, May 23, 1953; children—Lorene Grace, Stephen Dean, Marie Hope. Pres., Acme Internat., Exec. Suite, Employees Credit Corp., Andex Inc., Spokane, 1952—. Served with U.S. Army, 1951-52. Mem. Sales & Mktg. Execs. Internat., Nat. Assn. Personnel Cons., Nat. Assn. Temporary Services. Clubs: Rotary, Spokane. Contbr. articles in field to profl. jours. Office: 12815 E Sprague Spokane WA 99216

REIFSNYDER, CHARLES FRANK, lawyer; b. Ottumwa, Iowa, Sept. 6, 1920; s. Charles L. and Lena (Emery) R.; A.B., George Washington U., 1944, LL.B., 1946; m. Sally Ann Evans, Dec. 27, 1948; children—Daniel Alan, Jeremy Evans; m. 2d, Nancy Lee Laws, Mar. 4, 1960; 1 son, Frank Laws. Admitted to D.C. bar, 1945; sec. to Judge T. Alan Goldsborough, U.S. Dist. Ct., Washington, 1945; law clk. Chief Judge Bolitha J. Laws, U.S. Dist. Ct., 1946-47; asst. U.S. atty., Washington, 1947-51; spl. asst. to Atty. Gen. U.S., 1950-51; asso. firm Hogan & Hartson, Washington, 1951-58, partner, 1959—. Chmn. personnel security rev. bd. ERDA (formerly AEC); trustee Legal Aid Agy. (now Pub. Defender Service), D.C., 1960-67; bd. dirs. Nat. Jud. Coll., Reno, 1968-70. Fellow Inst. Jud. Adminstrn., N.Y.C., 1967-68. Fellow Internat. Soc. Barristers, Am. Bar Found.; mem. Am. (chmn. spl. com. on coordination jud. improvements 1971-74, mem. spl. com. on atomic energy law 1969-73, chmn. div. jud. adminstrn. 1967-68, del. 1968-69), Fed., Fed. Energy (pres. 1981—, chmn. com. natural gas 1967-68), D.C. (dir. 1955-56) bar assns., Am. Arbitration Assn., (nat. panel arbitrators), Am. Judicature Soc. (dir. 1972-76), Am. Law Inst., Phi Delta Phi, Sigma Nu. Episcopalian. Clubs: Metropolitan, Nat. Lawyers, Barristers, Lawyers (Washington); Gibson Island (Md.) Yacht Squadron; Annapolis (Md.) Yacht; Farmington Country (Charlottesville, Va.). Home: Gibson Island MD 21056 Office: 815 Connecticut Ave Washington DC 20006

REIGHARD, M(YRTLE) ELIZABETH, acct., oil and tire service co. exec.; b. Washington, Iowa, Mar. 28, 1937; d. Sherman Luther and Icle Edith (Nelson) Crom; student Kirkwood Community Coll., Cedar Rapids, Iowa, 1976-77; m. Wayne E. Reighard, Jan. 8, 1955; children—Joel Vincent, Jeffrey Phillip (dec.), Brian Douglas. Owner Wayne's Oil and Tire Service, Washington, 1964-75, v.p., sec.-treas. 1975—, also dir. Mem. troop com. Boy Scouts Am., Washington, 1967—, chmn. advancement and troop awards, 1970—; den mother Cub Scouts Am., Washington, 1969-73, com. chmn., 1974-79. Recipient award of merit Boy Scouts Am., 1978. Mem. Iowa Tire Dealers Assn., Digital Equipment Computer Users Soc., Woman's Internat. Bowling Congress, Iowa Women's Bowling Assn. (sec.-treas. Washington-Columbus Junction chpt.), Nat. Thespians Assn. Republican. Baptist. Home: Rural Route 2 Box 32 Washington IA 52353 Office: 220 E Washington St Washington IA 52353

REILEY, HENRY BAKER, JR., publisher; b. Trenton, N.J., May 24, 1908; s. Henry Baker and Naomi (Kessler) R.; A.B., Allegheny Coll., 1937; M.A., Boston U., 1940, S.T.B., 1941; m. Betty Holmes, Sept. 24, 1940; children—Henry Baker III, David Holmes. Mech. supt. Somerset (Pa.) Daily Am., 1929-32, mng. editor, editorial writer, 1958-62, editor, pub., 1962—; sec. Somerset Newspapers, Inc., 1960-62, pres., 1962—, treas., 1962-70; editor Berlin Pa. Record, 1932-34; ordained to ministry Methodist Ch., 1941, minister Central Pa. Conf., 1940-51, Ohio Conf., 1951-58; exchange pastor Meth. Ch. Heswall, Eng., 1957. Pres., Everett P.T.A., Bedford County, 1948-49; mem. Hire the Handicapped Com., 1959—, chmn., 1961; mem. Somerset-Bedford County Mental Health-Mental Retardation Bd., 1967—, chmn., 1967-71, 76. Bd. dirs. Somerset County Health and Welfare Council, 1963-72, Pa. Mental Health, Inc., 1964-70, Somerset County Devel. Council, 1967—; bd. dirs. YMCA, Somerset, 1960—, sec. 1961-70, vice-chmn., 1974, mem. Nat. council from S.W. dist. Pa., 1968-70, chmn. southwest dist. Pa. State YMCA, 1969-73, State bd. dirs., 1970-74, state trustee, 1970-73, chmn. dist. services com., 1977—; bd. dirs. Tableland Community Assn., 1965-68, 70—, chmn., 1965-67; trustee Cresson Center, 1972-79. Mem. C. of C. (dir. 1963-65, pres. bd. 1964), S.A.R. (pres. 1967, pres. Pa. soc. 1978), Somerset County Hist. Soc., Pa. Am. newspaper pubs. assns., Nat. Newspaper Assn., Theta Chi. Republican. Mason (32 deg.), Rotarian. Home: PO Box 613 Somerset PA 15501 Office: 334 W Main St Somerset PA 15501

REILEY, THOMAS PHILLIP, electronics co. mgr.; b. Ft. Lewis, Wash., May 5, 1950; s. Thomas Phillip and Anne Marie (Russick) R.; B.Sc. in Biophysics, Pa. State U., 1973; postgrad. in Bus. Adminstrn., Rutgers U. Inventory supr. Leland Tube Co., S. Plainfield, N.J., 1973-76; prodn. inventory control supr. Bomar Crystal Co., Middlesex, N.J., 1976-79; prodn. control mgr. Codi Semicondr. Inc., Linden, N.J., 1979—. Mem. Am. Inventory and Prodn. Control Soc. (chmn. ednl. com. Raritan Valley chpt.). Republican. Home: 56 Carlton Club Dr Piscataway NJ 08854 Office: 350 Hurst St Linden NJ 07036

REILLY, EDWARD PATRICK, brokerage co. exec.; b. N.Y.C., Apr. 4, 1936; s. Hugh I. and Elizabeth (O'Hara) R.; B.B.A., Iona Coll., 1958; M.B.A., N.Y. U., 1960; m. Roseann Dolan, Sept. 21, 1963; children—Edward Patrick, Patricia Ann, Kevin Séan. With Home Ins. Co., N.Y.C., 1962-64, Clark Dodge, N.Y.C., 1964-68; oil and gas analyst E.F. Hutton, N.Y.C., 1968-72; with Loeb Rhoades, N.Y.C., 1972-76; oil analyst, v.p. Prescott Ball & Turben, N.Y.C., 1976-78; v.p. Fahnestock & Co., N.Y.C., 1978—. Mem. N.Y. Soc. Security Analysts (co-chmn. Oil Group), Nat. Assn. Petroleum Investment Analysts, Am. Petroleum Inst. Republican. Roman Catholic. Home: 31 Eileen Way Edison NJ 08817 Office: 110 Wall St New York City NY 10005

REILLY, FRANCIS JOSEPH, oxygen co. exec.; b. Phila., June 25, 1926; s. Thomas Aloysius and Marie Mercedes (Doyle) R.; B.S., St. Joseph's U., 1948; postgrad. Temple U., 1950-51, Villanova U., 1957-59, U. Mich., 1976, Rutgers U., 1977, U. Pa., 1979; m. Theresa Rose Coyle, Apr. 18, 1953; children—Francis Joseph, Mark T., Sarah A., Terrance J. Tchr., Sch. Dist. of Phila., 1947-60; ter. rep. Liquid Carbonic, Pitts., 1960-66; dist. mgr. Consol. Vacuum Corp., Columbus, Ohio, 1966-70, Wang Labs., Columbus, 1970-73; gen. mgr. Columbus Oxygen Co., 1973—. Founding mem., dir. W. Hempfield (Pa.) Civic Assn., 1967-71; founding mem., dir. NW Columbus Civic Assn., 1971-75. Recipient Service award Mayor's Council Human Rights, Phila., 1956. Mem. Nat. Welding Supply Assn., Am. Welding Soc., Columbus C. of C. Republican. Roman Catholic. Club: Hide-a-Way Hills. Home: Columbus OH 43220 Office: 876 S Front St Columbus OH 43206

REILLY, FRANK KELLY, educator; b. Chgo., Dec. 30, 1935; s. Clarence Raymond and Mary Josephine (Ruckrigel) R.; B.B.A., U. Notre Dame, 1957; M.B.A., Northwestern U., 1961; M.B.A., U. Chgo., 1964, Ph.D., 1968; m. Therese Adele Bourke, Aug. 2, 1958; children—Frank Kelly, III, Clarence Raymond, II, Therese B., Edgar B. Stock and bond trader Goldman, Sachs & Co., Chgo., 1958-59; security analyst Technology Fund, Chgo., 1959-62; asst. prof. U. Kans., 1965-68, asso. prof., 1968-72; prof. bus., asso. dir. Bur. Bus. and Econ. Research, U. Wyo., 1972-75; prof. finance U. Ill., Urbana, 1975—. Served with U.S. Army, 1957. Arthur J. Schmidt Found. fellow, 1962-65, U. Chgo. fellow, 1963-65. Mem. Am., Midwest, Western (exec. com. 1973-75), So., Eastern (exec. com. 1979—) finance assns., Fin. Analysts Fedn., Fin. Mgmt. Assn. (v.p. 1977-78, 79-80), Nat. Bur. Econ. Research, Chgo. Analysts Soc., Inst. Chartered Fin. Analysts, Midwest Bus. Adminstrn. Assn. (pres. 1974-75), Beta Gamma Sigma. Roman Catholic. Author: Investment Analysis and Portfolio Management, 1979. Editor: Readings and Issues in Investments, 1975; asso. editor Fin. Rev., Quar. Rev. Econs. and Bus., Fin. Mgmt. Home: 54 Chestnut Ct Champaign IL 61820 Office: Coll Commerce U Ill Urbana IL 61801

REILLY, JAMES PATRICK, holding co. exec.; b. Vineland, N.J., July 19, 1940; s. Joseph Patrick and Frances Margaret (Brown) R.; B.S. in Acctg., St. Joseph's U., 1962; m. Ann Mary Vastano, Sept. 15, 1962; children—James Patrick, Diane Mary, Michael James, Christine Ann. Accountant, Price Waterhouse & Co., Newark, 1962-69; v.p., treas. Metrocare, Inc., South Amboy, N.J., 1969-75; v.p., treas., controller Hanson Industries, Inc., Iselin, N.J., 1975-78, sr. v.p., 1978—; dir. Hygrade Food Products, Detroit, Interstate United Corp., Chgo., Carisbrook Industries, Inc., Iselin, N.J., Seacoast Products Corp., Port Monmouth, N.J. Mgr., N. Edison Little League; v.p. St. Francis Athletic Assn. C.P.A., N.J. Mem. Am. Inst. C.P.A.'s. Roman Catholic. Club: K.C. Office: 100 Wood Ave S Iselin NJ 08830

REILLY, PETER C., chem. co. exec.; b. Indpls., Jan. 19, 1907; s. Peter C. and Ineva (Gash) R.; A.B., U. Colo., 1929; M.B.A., Harvard, 1931; m. Jeanette Parker, Sept. 15, 1932; children—Marie (Mrs. Jack H. Heed), Sara Jean (Mrs. Clarke Wilhelm), Patricia Ann (Mrs. Michael Davis). With accounting dept. Republic Creosoting Co., Indpls., 1931-32; sales dept. Reilly Tar & Chem. Corp., N.Y.C., 1932-36, v.p., Eastern mgr., 1936-52; v.p. sales, treas. both cos., Indpls., 1952-59, pres., 1959-73, chmn. bd., 1973-75, vice chmn., 1975—; dir., mem. exec. com. Ind. Nat. Corp. Indpls.; dir. Ind. Nat. Bank. Bd. dirs. United Fund Greater Indpls.; bd. govs. Jr. Achievement Indpls. Mem. adv. council U. Notre Dame Sch. Commerce, 1947—. Mem. Chem. Spltys. Mfg. Assn. (treas. 1950-60, past dir.), Mfg. Chemists Assn. (past dir.), Am. Chem. Soc., Soc. Chem. Industry (dir. Am. sect. 1979—). Clubs: Union League, Harvard, Chemist (N.Y.C.); Larchmont (N.Y.) Yacht; Indianapolis Athletic, Pine Valley Golf, Meridian Hills Country, Columbia (Indpls.); One Hundred (dir.). Home: 1015 Stratford Hall Indianapolis IN 46260 Office: 1510 Market Square Center 151 N Delaware St Indianapolis IN 46204

REILLY, RICHARD ANTHONY, conglomerate exec.; b. New Haven, Aug. 11, 1935; s. Andrew J. and Marie A. (Manns) R.; B.A., Washington Coll., 1958; M.B.A., N.Y. U., 1974; m. Ellen Green, June 27, 1959; children—Michael, Maureen. Mgr., Dun & Bradstreet, Inc., San Francisco, 1959-66; cash mgr. Calif. and Hawaiian Sugar Co., San Francisco, 1966-68; dir. cash mgmt. Pepsi Co., Inc., Purchase, N.Y., 1968-75; mgr. treasury ops. Am. Hess Corp., N.Y.C., 1975-77, mgr. supply planning and ship utilization, 1977-80; asst. treas. Norton Simon Inc., N.Y.C., 1980—. Served with U.S. Army, 1958-59. Roman Catholic. Home: 52 Bucyrus Ave RD 1 Carmel NY 10512 Office: 277 Park Ave New York NY 10017

REILLY, ROBERT ARTHUR, newspaper exec.; b. Sharon, Conn., Oct. 2, 1939; s. Harry and Elsa Marie (Swanson) R.; student Ala. Coll., 1961-62, Jacksonville State Coll., 1962-63; B.A., Ariz. State U., 1965; M.A., U. Iowa, 1968; Nat. Endowment Humanities fellow Fletcher Sch. Law and Diplomacy, Tufts U., 1979; postgrad. Stanford U., 1980; m. Diane Beverly Bailey, Aug. 13, 1970. Consumer writer, columnist Phila. Inquirer, 1968-73; So. Ariz. bur. chief, investigative reporter The Ariz. Republic, Phoenix, 1974-78; owner Fourth Estate Publs., Phoenix, 1977—; editor-pub. The Wildcat Sports Jour., Phoenix, 1977-78, Sun Devil News, Phoenix, 1977—; instr. Temple U., Phila., part-time, 1969-72. Mem. Sun Angel Found. Served with U.S. Army, 1958-61. Mem. Profl. Journalism Soc. Tucson, Phoenix Press Clubs, Am. Film Inst., Ariz. State U. Alumni Assn. (dir.), Phi Delta Epsilon, Sigma Delta Chi. Roman Catholic. Club: Tucson Nat.

Golf. Home: 2323 N Central Ave Phoenix AZ 85004 Office: PO Box 309 Phoenix AZ 85001

REIM, ROBERT GEORGE, printing and office equipment mfg. co. exec.; b. St. Louis, Sept. 14, 1920; s. Herman Theodore and Pauline Kathryn (Illig) R.; student Jefferson Coll., St. Louis, 1943; m. Lucille Ruth Neely, Jan. 24, 1944; children—Sandra, Gary, Linda, Robert. Founder, Color-Art, Inc., St. Louis, 1946—, chmn. bd., 1965—; dir. Commerce Bank of Kirkwood, Concordia House of Kirkwood. Vice pres. St. Joseph Hosp., Kirkwood; councilman City of Kirkwood, 1960-64, mayor, 1964-70; bd. dirs. St. Louis County (Mo.) Minimum Municipal Standards Commn. Served with U.S. Navy, 1942-46. Mem. Kirkwood Area C. of C. (pres. 1958), Printing Industries Am., Nat. Office Products Assn., Graphic Arts Inst. Nat. Assn. Printers and Lithographers, Printing Industries St. Louis. Republican. Lutheran. Club: Greenbriar Hills Country. Editor: Hammermill Helps, 1972-80. Home: 8 Lemp Rd Kirkwood MO 63122 Office: 10300 Watson Rd Saint Louis MO 63127

REIM, VICTOR P., banker; b. New Ulm, Minn., Nov., 22, 1939; s. Victor and Marie (Bremer) R.; B.S. with honors cum laude, St. John's U., Minn., 1961; postgrad. U. Minn. Grad. Sch. Bus., Grad. Sch. Banking, U. Wis., Madison, 1968; sr. bank officers seminar Harvard. Grad. Sch. Bus., 1971; children—Ann Marie, Philip, Amy, Erick. With Comml. State Bank, St. Paul, 1963—, dir., 1974—, pres., chief exec. officer, 1975—, chmn. bd., 1976—; v.p. Jacob Schmidt Co., 1976—; mem. exec. com., dir. Am. Bancorp. Inc., 1977—; chmn. bd., pres. London Sq. Bank, Eau Claire, Wis. Div. chmn. United Way, 1979; mem. investment adv. council Minn. State Bd. Investment, 1978-79; bd. dirs. Catholic Charities St. Paul; trustee Convent of the Visitation Sch., St. Mary's Jr. Coll.; mem. steering com. St. Thomas Middle Sch.; vice-chmn. bd. trustees St. Paul Jaycees Found.; mem. adv. com. Hugh O'Brien Minn. Youth Leadership Seminar, 1977-78, 78-79; bd. dirs., mem. steering com. Operation '85; chmn. St. Paul Econ. Adv. Com., 1976-77; mem. Capitol Area Archtl. and Planning Commn., 1970-74; mem. exec. com. Minn. Golf Classic, 1967-68, 69; mem. U.S. Savs. Bond Com., St. Paul Pioneer Hook and Ladder Club, Met. Hwy. Local Consent Adv. Com., St. Paul 100 Club. Mem. Am. Legion, St. Paul Jaycees (v.p. 1968-69). Clubs: K.C. (council), St. Paul Minutemen, Town and Country, Minn., St. Paul Athletic (dir. 1979), Optimists (dist. gov. 1972-73; pres. St. Paul club 1969-70; mem. internat. community service com. 1972-73; v.p. internat. 1975-76). Office: Commercial State Bank 35 W 5th St Saint Paul MN 55102

REINARD, ROY, JR., ins. agt.; b. Phila., May 11, 1930; s. Roy and Dorothy Violet (Krebs) R.; student night classes, U. Pa., 1950-54; m. Ethel Walters, June 28, 1952; children—Roy, Kimberly, Holly. Stock clk. Phoenix London Group, 1949; underwriter Nat. Union Ins. Co., 1949-52; underwriter The Reinard Agy., Inc., Feasterville, Pa., 1952-62, pres., 1962—; mem. agy. council Firemans Fund, Gulf Ins. Co., CNA, Farmers Reliance Co., INA; past pres. Shenandoah Mut. Fire Ins. Co. Active Nat. Tax Limitation Com.; bd. dirs. Bucks County Tourist Commn.; bd. trustees Bucks County Hist. Soc.; active Bucks County Conservancy, Feasterville Businessmen's Assn. Served with USNR, 1949-59. Mem. Profl. Ins. Agts. Assn., Pa. Ind. Ins. Agts. Assn. (dir.), Pennsbury Soc., Agts. and Brokers Assn. Phila. and Suburbs, Nat. Assn. Life Underwriters, Phila. Agts. Assn. (pres.), Bucks County C. of C. (dir.). Clubs: Masons, Odd Fellows, Independence Sq., Somerton Lions (pres.), Ocean City Garden. Home: 87 Crescent Dr Holland PA 18966 Office: 25 Bustleton Ave Feasterville PA 19047

REININGA, JOHN H., JR., real estate developer; b. Toledo, Sept. 24, 1936; s. John H. and Ina Margaret (Chatwin) R.; B.S. in Chem. Engring., U. Colo., 1958; M.B.A., Stanford U., 1960; m. Carlene Harman; children—John H., Robert W., Michelle, Michael M. Dist. sales rep. Continental Oil Co., Houston, 1961-62; project mgr. Draper Cos., San Francisco, 1963-65; project mgr. Desmond MacTavish & Assos., San Francisco, 1965-66; founder, pres. Reininga Corp., San Francisco, 1967—. Served with U.S. Army, 1960-61. Cert. shopping center mgr. Mem. Internat. Council Shopping Centers (trustee), Calif. Bus. Properties Assn. (adv. bd.), Urban Land Inst., Bankers Club San Francisco, Chi Psi. Club: Meadow (Fairfax, Calif.). Office: 425 California St San Francisco CA 94104

REINSCH, JAMES LEONARD, radio and TV exec.; b. Streator, Ill., June 28, 1908; s. Henry Emil and Lillian (Funk) R.; B.S., Northwestern U., 1934; m. Phyllis McGeough, Feb. 1, 1936; children—Penelope Luise Bohn, James Leonard. Began broadcasting career radio sta. WLS, Chgo., 1924; pres. Cox Broadcasting Corp., 1964-74, chmn., 1977-79, also dir.; co-chmn. Warner Annex Cable Co., N.Y.C., 1979—; dir. 1st Nat. Bank Atlanta; radio adviser to White House, 1945-52; mem. Carnegie Commn. on Future Pub. Broadcasting; former mem. adv. com. USIA; former mem. adv. com. Rand Corp. Trustee Ednl. Found. Am. Women in Radio and TV; bd. dirs. Nat. Cancer Bd. Exec. dir. Democratic Nat. Conv., 1960, 64; TV-radio dir. Dem. presdl. campaign, 1960; program coordinator Dem. Nat. Conv., 1968. Recipient D.F. Keller award Northwestern U., Pulse Man of Year, 1974, Gold medal award Internat. Radio and TV Soc., 1973, Distinguished Achievement in Broadcasting award Di Gamma Kappa, 1974, Distinguished Service award Nat. Assn. Broadcasters, 1978, Dir.'s award Am. Women in Radio and TV. Mem. Atlanta Art Assn., Internat. Radio and TV Soc., Sigma Delta Chi, Phi Gamma Kappa. Clubs: Rotary; Pioneers (N.Y.C.); Capital City, Peachtree Golf (Atlanta); Nat. Capital Democratic (Washington). Co-author: Radio Station Management, 1948, rev. edit., 1960. Home: 3671 Northside Dr NW Atlanta GA 30305 Office: 75 Rockefeller Plaza New York NY 10019

REINSDORF, JERRY MICHAEL, bus. exec., lawyer; b. Bklyn., Feb. 25, 1936; s. Max and Marion (Smith) R.; B.A., George Washington U., 1957; J.D., Northwestern U., 1960; m. Martyl F. Rifkin, Dec. 29, 1956; children—David Jason, Susan Janeen, Michael Andrew, Jonathan Milton. Admitted to D.C., Ill. bars, 1960; atty. staff regional counsel IRS, Chgo., 1960-64; asso. law firm Chapman & Cutler, 1964-68; partner law firm Altman, Kurlander & Weiss, 1968-73; of counsel firm Katten, Muchin, Gitles, Zavis, Pearl & Galler, 1974-79; gen. partner Carlyle Real Estate Ltd. Partnership, 1972—, chmn. bd. The Balcor Co., Skokie, Ill., 1973—; mng. partner TBC Films, 1975—; lectr. John Marshall Law Sch., 1966-68; dir. Real Estate Securities and Syndication Inst., 1972-76; also speaker. Co-chmn., Ill. Profls. for Sen. Ralph Smith, 1970; bd. dirs. Ednl. Tape Rec. for Blind, 1979—. C.P.A., Ill.; specialist in real estate securities. Mem. Am., Ill., Chgo., Fed. bar assns., Order of Coif, Omega Tau Rho. Author: (with L. Herbert Schneider) Uses of Life Insurance in Qualified Employee Benefit Plans, 1970. Office: 10024 Skokie Blvd Skokie IL 60077

REIQUAM, ROBERT LEE, bank exec.; b. Choteau, Mont., Apr. 10, 1936; s. William D. and Bessie P. (Crane) R.; B.S. in Agrl. Edn., Mont. State U., 1958; m. Betty L. Thompson, Nov. 26, 1955; children—Carmen, Christopher, Cynthia. Operator-mgr., Reiquam Ranch Co., Dutton, Mont., 1958-63; extension agt. Teton County (Mont.), 1963-65; agrl. rep. First Nat. Bank, Gt. Falls, Mont., 1965-68; agrl. loan officer First Nat. Bank, Miles City, Mont., 1968-70, v.p., 1970-74, pres., chief exec. officer, 1975—; speaker. Mem. Miles City Sch. Bd., chmn., 1976; vice-chmn. Miles City Sch. Community Council; pres. Miles City Area C. of C.; bd. dirs. Mont. 4-H Found.; treas. Custer County (Mont.) Republican Central Com. Named Outstanding 4-H Alumnus, 1974; Boss of Yr., Miles City Jaycees, 1976. Mem. Mont. Bankers Assn. (treas. 1979-80), Am. Bankers Assn., Western Environ. Trade Assn. (dir.). Lutheran. Clubs: Lions (pres. Miles City club, Gt. Falls club), Miles City Town and Country (dir.), Elks. Contbr. numerous articles to banking and agrl. publs. Office: PO Box 1139 Miles City MT 59301

REISNER, ROBERT, electronic co. exec.; b. Poughkeepsie, N.Y., July 9, 1948; B.A. in Bus., Marist Coll., Poughkeepsie, 1971; M.B.A. in Fin., So. Ill. U., 1978; m. Elaine Kearns, May 17, 1970; children—Joshua, Kristina, Megan. Computer systems and mktg. IBM Corp., Poughkeepsie, East Fishkill, N.Y. and Trenton, N.J., 1967-75; bus. planning mgmt. RCA Corp., Cherry Hill, N.J., 1975-79; dir. fin. RCA Corp. Info. Systems and Services, Cherry Hill, 1979—; lectr. in field. Home: 300 Flint Ct N Yardley PA 19067 Office: 204-2 Route 38 Cherry Hill NJ 08358

REISS, ELAINE SERLIN, lawyer; b. N.Y.C., Oct. 27, 1940; d. Morris and Dorothy Miriam (Geyer) Serlin; B.A., N.Y. U., 1961, LL.B., 1964, LL.M., 1973; m. Joel A. Reiss, Sept. 1, 1963; children—Joshua Adam, Naomi. Admitted to N.Y. State bar, 1965; asso. Doyle Dane Bernbach, 1965-68, Ogilvy & Mather, Inc., N.Y.C., 1968-72, v.p., 1972-77, mgr. legal dept., 1972-77, sr. v.p., 1977-79, council of dirs., sr. v.p., mgr. legal dept., 1979—. Mem. Assn. Am. Advt. Agys., Assn. Bar City N.Y. Office: 2 E 48th St New York NY 10017

REISTLE, CARL ERNEST, JR., petroleum engr.; b. Denver, June 26, 1901; s. Carl E. and Leonara I. (McMaster) R.; B.S., U. Okla., 1922; student Harvard Sch. Bus. Adminstrn., 1948; D.Sc., U. Tulsa, 1966; m. Mattie A. Muldrow, June 23, 1922; children—Bette Jean (Mrs. Geo. F. Pierce), Mattie Ann, (Mrs. James Tracy Clark), Nancy L. (Mrs. Wilson Hayes Holliday), Carl Ernest III. Petroleum chemist U.S. Bur. Mines, 1922-29; petroleum engr., 1929-33; chmn. East Texas Engring. Assn., 1933-36; with Humble Oil & Refining Co., 1936-66, successively engr. in charge, chief petroleum engr., gen. supt. prodn., mgr. prodn. dept., dir. mgr. prodn. dept., dir. charge prodn. dept. 1951-55, v.p. charge prodn. dept., 1955-57, exec. v.p., 1957-61, pres., 1961-63, chmn. bd. and chief exec. officer, 1963-66, cons., 1966—; dir. Eltra Corp.; dir., chmn. bd. Olincraft, Inc., 1974-77, chmn. exec. com., 1977-78. Trustee Houston Mus. Natural Sci. Recipient Anthony Lucas medal, 1958; Engr. of Year award Nat. Soc. Profl. Engrs., 1966. Mem. Mining and Metall. Soc. Am., Am. Petroleum Inst. (dir.), Am. Inst. Mining and Metall. Engrs. (pres. 1956), Sigma Xi, Tau Beta Pi, Sigma Tau, Alpha Chi Sigma. Clubs: Petroleum, Ramada, River Oaks Country. Home: 3196 Chevy Chase Houston TX 77019 Office: 1100 Milam Bldg Suite 4601 Houston TX 77002

REITER, SYDNEY HOWARD, energy conservation firm owner; b. Midland, Pa., May 13, 1925; s. Fred Martin and Anna (Schlesinger) R.; B.S., U. Cin., 1947; M.S.E., Pa. State U., 1949; M.A., Princeton U., 1954; m. Constance Rohr, June 6, 1954; children—Marjorie, Richard, Daniel, Paul, David. Research and devel. asso. Air Reduction Co., Murray Hill, N.J., 1962-68; mgr. electrostatic precipitators Mikropul Corp., Summit, N.J., 1968-75; owner, operator Atlantic Engring. Co. Newark, 1975—; lectr. in field. Cubmaster, Boy Scouts Am. Mem. ASME (sect. chmn.), Mech. Engring. Soc., AIAA, ASHRAE, Sigma Xi. Contbr. articles to profl. jours. Home: 3 Clearview Rd Mountainside NJ 07092

REITMEISTER, NOEL WILLIAM, fin. planner, investment, ins. and commodity broker; b. Bklyn., Aug. 12, 1938; s. Morris G. and Anna (Miller) R.; B.A. in Economics, Queens Coll., 1960; M.B.A. in Indsl. Psychology and Bus., CUNY, 1969; diploma N.Y. Inst. Fin., 1969; C.F.P., Coll. Fin. Planning, 1974; m. Elaine Schendelman, Sept. 16, 1961; children—Gregg Allen, Stephen Michael. Account exec. duPont Walston, Chgo., Gary and Merrillville, Ind., 1969-74; sr. investment broker A.G. Edwards & Sons, Merrillville, 1974-79, v.p.-investments, 1979—; partner Ind. Investments; ltd. partner Petro Lewis, Parker Nat. Property Investors, Nora Assos.; vice chmn. bd. Menorah Credit Union, 1979-81, chmn., 1981—; dir. Arctic Exploration, Inc.; guest speaker, lectr. univs.; cons. and lectr. Calumet Coll. (Ind.). Bd. dirs. South Suburban HELP, 1968-69; trustee Temple Anshe Sholom, 1975—; local troop coordinator Boy Scouts Am., 1977-78; mem. Anti-Defamation League Cabinet, 1978—; v.p. Chgo. B'nai B'rith Council. Served with USAR, 1960-66. Cert. fin. planner; cert. fin. examiner; registered rep. N.Y. Stock Exchange, Am. Stock Exchange, Midwest Stock Exchange, Pacific Stock Exchange, Boston Stock Exchange, PBW Exchange, Chgo. Bd. Trade, Chgo. Mercantile Exchange, Comex, NASD, Chgo. Options Exchange; lic. broker, N.Y., N.J., Conn., Mass., Ohio, Fla., Ariz., Okla., Ill., Ind. Mem. Coll. Fin. Planning, Inst. Certified Fin. Planners, Chgo. Assn. Fin. Planners, Internat. Assn. Fin. Planners (charter), Nat. Soc. Registered Reps. Clubs: Masons, Shriners, B'nai B'rith (pres. lodge). Home: 2246 Flossmoor Rd Flossmoor IL 60422 Office: 8300 Mississippi Merrillville IN 46410

REKEY, ANDRAS GEZA, investment co. exec., fin. cons.; b. Budapest, Feb. 23, 1951; came to U.S., 1956, naturalized, 1966; s. Maria (Domotor) Rekey; M.S. magna cum laude in Econs., U. Pa., 1973; M.B.A. cum laude, Harvard U., 1975. Asso. in corp. fin. Lehman Bros. Inc., N.Y.C., 1975-78; pres. Andras G. Rekey Inc., N.Y.C., 1978—; dir. Guerlain Cauthers Rekey Inc., 1065 Park Ave. Corp. Mem. adv. com. Met. Mus. Art, N.Y.C. Mem. Beta Gamma Sigma. Republican. Episcopalian. Clubs: Century (U. Pa.); Harvard (N.Y.C.); Friars Honor Soc. (U. Pa.). Home and Office: 1065 Park Ave New York NY 10028

REMCO, JAN RAYMOND, investment co. exec.; b. Wilkes-Barre, Pa., July 3, 1920; s. Vincent Matthew and Susan (Selesky) R.; M.B.A., Wharton Sch. Bus. Adminstrn., U. Pa., 1946; m. Doris Simpson, Mar. 21, 1960; Pres., Cassware, Inc., Wilkes-Barre, 1955-60, Plaines Security Corp., Asbury Park, N.J., 1961-65; pres., chief exec. officer Raymond Resnhaw Found., Inc., crude oil, refinery ops., shipping, hotels, European housing constrn. and devel., Asbury Park, N.J., 1965—; dir. numerous corps. Republican. Address: PO Box 853 Asbury Park NJ 07712

REMICH, JOHN PATRICK, savs. and loan assn. exec.; b. Pensacola, Fla., Dec. 30, 1930; s. James J. and Margaret E. (McHugh) R.; B.S., Fla. State U., 1959; m. Barbara Toney, July 4, 1960; children—John, Karen, Teresa, Janet, Nancy. With Pensacola Home and Savs. Assn., 1960—, v.p., 1966-69, pres., 1969—. Chmn. Stewardship Commn., Roman Catholic Diocese of Pensacola-Tallahassee, 1979-80; pres. Pensacola Cath. High Sch. Found., 1977-80; pres. United Way of Escambia County (Fla.), 1979-80; mem. adv. bd. Baptist Hosp., Pensacola; mem. Escambia County Appeals Rev. Bd.; mem. exec. bd. Gulf Coast council Boy Scouts Am., Silver Beaver award, 1975. Served with U.S. Army, 1955-57. Mem. Home Builders West Fla., Fla. Savs. and Loan League (dir.). Clubs: Civitan (Pensacola); K.C. Office: 251 W Garden St PO Box 12089 Pensacola FL 32590

REMICK, ROBERT MERRICK, fin. services co. exec.; b. Newton, Mass., May 8, 1924; s. Robert Merrick and Mary Lombard (Moore) R.; B.S., N.Y. U., 1952; children—Lee, Scot, Lynn. Jr. security analyst Moody's Co., N.Y.C., 1947; asst. to pres. Investors Counsel, Inc., N.Y.C., 1947-50; sales supr. New Eng. Life Ins. Co., N.Y.C., 1950-54; ednl. dir. Conn. Mut. Life Ins. Co., N.Y.C., 1954-57; founder, pres. Income Planning Assos., Ltd., N.Y.C., 1957—; gen. agt. Conn. Mut. Life Ins. Co., N.Y.C., 1957-73, regular agt., 1974—; chmn. bd. dirs. Computer Income Planning Corp., N.Y.C., 1967—; instr. econs. and fin. Coll. Ins., N.Y.C., 1967-72. Served with USNR, 1942-45. C.L.U., enrolled actuary. Mem. Million Dollar Round Table (life), Am. Soc. C.L.U.'s, N.Y. Soc. Security Analysts, Nat. Assn. Security Dealers, Am. Acad. Actuaries, Am. Soc. Pension Actuaries, Am. Pension Conf., Nat. Assn. Life Underwriters. Home: 116 Central Park S New York NY 10019 Office: 122 E 42 St New York NY 10168

REMILLARD, LAURENT JOSEPH, mgmt. co. exec.; b. N. Adams, Mass., May 23, 1934; s. Romeo and Edna Ann (Lecyer) R.; B.S. in Fin., Bryant Coll., 1958; m. Ann Crilly Holzemer, May 23, 1959; children—Laurent Joseph, John, Daniel, Thomas. Asst. treas. Owens-Ill., Inc., Toledo, 1958-68, IU Internat., Phila., 1969—; asst. treas. C. Brewer & Co., Ltd.; affiliate of IU Internat., Honolulu, 1969-75, exec. v.p., 1975-78, v.p., controller, 1978—. Served with USN, 1950-53. Republican. Roman Catholic. Home: 1725 Old Gulph Rd Villanova PA 19085 Office: 1500 Walnut St Philadelphia PA 19102

REMMER, JAMES EDWARD, photo equipment co. exec.; b. Rockport, Calif., Mar. 12, 1927; s. Victor Herbert and Ellen (Stahl) R.; teaching credential San Diego State Coll., 1947; m. Denise O. Sours, Aug. 17, 1947; children—James H., Jan A., Jeffrey B.; m. 2d, Luana Jean Warwick, Mar. 1975. Gen. mgr. San Diego Office Equipment Co., 1956-63; subsidiary v.p. A.B. Dick Co., San Diego, 1959-63; zone mgr. Xerox Corp., Los Angeles, 1963-68; v.p., gen. mgr. Houston Fearless Corp., 1968-70; pres. Cintel Corp., Los Angeles, 1970-72; v.p. Falls Land & Devel. Corp., 1972-74; zone dir. Saxon Bus. Products, 1974—; dir. Columbis Mgmt. Scis. Corp., Encino, Calif., 1969—; dir. Gov. Cons., Inc., Washington, 1969—; cons. Technology, Inc., Dayton, Ohio, 1970—; tchr. sales and marketing U. Calif. at Berkeley, 1951—, Arlington Jr. Coll., 1953-54. Bd. dirs. Calif. Mus. Found., 1967—, So. Calif. Industry and Edn. Council, 1966—, Jr. Achievement, 1960—; mem. Port Commn., San Diego, 1959-62; dir. sales and marketing execs. Mayor's Speakers Bur., 1959. Served with USMC, 1945, 50-51. Mem. A.I.M., Pres. Council, Research Inst. Am., Soc. Reproduction Engrs., Sigma Alpha Epsilon, Epsilon Eta. Home: 17232 Cliquot Ct Poway CA 92064 Office: 4420 Hotel Circle Ct Suite 150 San Diego CA 92108

REMPEL, ROBERT HENRY, research and devel. co. exec.; b. Drake, Sask., Can., Apr. 1, 1938; s. Henry I. and Elizabeth (Enns) R.; B.Sc., Oxford Coll. Arts and Scis., 1971; Ph.D., U. Beverly Hills, 1978; m. Sandra Alexandria Cowieson, Oct. 26, 1960; children—Tanya, Evan, Andrea. Technologist, U. Sask., 1958; dir. research Trigon Assos., 1959; gen. mgr. Can. Sci. Research Ltd., 1960-64; pres. Indsl. Control Systems Ltd., Toronto, Ont., Can., 1965-71, Mono Research Labs. Ltd., Shelburne, Ont., 1971—; tech. cons. Payton Assos. Ltd., Toronto. Served as pilot officer RCAF, 1958. Province of Ont. grantee; Nat. Research Council grantee. Mem. Inst. Chartered Engrs. Ont. (pres. 1967-68), IEEE, Can. Med. and Biol. Engring. Soc. Home: Rural Route 4 Shelburne ON LON ISO Canada Office: 1 Industrial Rd Shelburne ON LON ISO Canada

RENDA, DOMINIC PHILLIP, airline co. exec.; b. Steubenville, Ohio, Dec. 25, 1913; s. Joseph J. and Catherine (Roberta) R.; B.S. in Bus. Adminstrn., J.D., Ohio State U., 1938; m. Delores E. Noland, July 12, 1980; children—Dominique Patricia, Dominic Phillip, Patrick Blake. Admitted to Ohio bar, 1938; practice law, Steubenville, 1938-41; adminstrv. asst. to mem. Congress, 1941-42; with Western Air Lines, Inc., Los Angeles, 1946-68, asst. sec., 1947, v.p. legal, 1954-65, sr. v.p. legal, corp. sec., 1958-68; pres. Air Micronesia, Inc., Los Angeles, 1968-73; sr. v.p. internat. and pub. affairs Continental Air Lines, Inc., 1968-73; exec. v.p., dir., mem. exec. com. Western Air Lines, 1973-76, pres., mem. exec. and nominating coms., 1976-79, pres., chief exec. officer, mem. exec., nominating and mgmt. resources and compensation coms., 1979—; dir. Bank of Montreal (Calif.). Mem. bus. adminstrn. adv. council Coll. Adminstrv. Sci., Ohio State U., 1974—, mem. alumni adv. bd., 1976—; bd. councilors Sch. Internat. Relations, U. So. Calif., 1967—; trustee Peace Found., Caroline Islands, 1976—; chmn. devel. com. Marymount High Sch., 1977—. Served to lt. comdr. USNR, 1942-46. Mem. Calif., Ohio state bars, Am., Los Angeles County (past trustee) bar assns., Calif. C. of C. (dir.), Phi Alpha Delta (pres. Los Angeles 1965-66). Clubs: Los Angeles Chancery (pres. 1966-67), Marina City, Bel-Air Country. Home: 101 Udine Way Los Angeles CA 90024 Office: 6060 Avion Dr Los Angeles CA 90045

RENDER, WILLIAM LANE, real estate appraiser; b. Hollywood, Calif., Feb. 26, 1939; s. William Douglas and Rosemary Ruth (Hummel) R.; student U. Oreg., 1957-59, Mexico City Coll., 1958, U. Tex., 1962, San Antonio Coll., 1970-71; m. Paulene Mary Lou, Jan. 5, 1963; children—Renee, Paulette. Pvt. practice real estate appraisal, San Antonio, 1975—. Served with USAF, 1959-63. Mem. Soc. Real Estate Appraisers, Nat. Assn. Review Appraisers. Home: 13039 N Hunters Circle San Antonio TX 78230 Office: 1901 NW Military Hwy Suite 211 San Antonio TX 78213

RENDINE, PAUL, investment banker; b. Connellsville, Pa., Feb. 3, 1944; s. Lawrence Anthony and Margaret Irene (Shaffer) R.; student U. Md., 1962-65, George Washington U., 1970-71; B.S. in Bus. and Econs., Salisbury State Coll., 1974; m. Nancy Jean LeCocq, Jan. 9, 1971; 1 dau., Kristin Elizabeth. Commd. ensign and naval flight officer U.S. Navy, 1965, advanced through grades to lt., 1969; resigned, 1973; v.p. adminstrn. Rysson-Md. Corp., Riverdale, Md., 1973-75; account exec. Dean Witter Reynolds Co., Inc., Salisbury, Md., 1975-80; v.p., br. officer mgr. Wheat First Securities, Inc., Greenville, N.C., 1980—; mem. adj. faculty, bus. and econs. Wor-Wic Tech. Community Coll.; commodity hedging instr. Wor-Wic Tech. Community Coll. and Wicomico County Agrl. Extension Office; adj. faculty mgmt. East Carolina U.; organizer, 1st pres. Salisbury State Coll. Bus. and Econs. Soc., 1973. Organizer, 1st pres. Friends of Salisbury Zoo, 1977-79; v.p. Wicomico County Christian Athletic Assn., 1979-80; chmn. Wicomico County unit Am. Cancer Soc. Crusade, 1977-78, pres., 1978-79; chmn. gen. bus. div. Wicomico County United Way, 1979; v.p. Prince Georges Young Republican Club, 1974-75; awards chmn. Md. Fedn. Young Reps., 1975-76; editor Md. Rep. Party Newspaper, 1975—; mem., vice-chmn. Wicomico County Rep. Central Com., 1976—; communications chmn. Md. Rep. Party, 1976-77, chmn. rules com., 1978-80; chmn. Ch. Maj. Mission Fund, Presbyterian Ch., 1978. Decorated Navy Commendation medal with oak leaf cluster, Air medal with 8 oak leaf clusters; Air Gallantry Cross (Vietnam); recipient Wall St. Jour. award, 1974; Outstanding Young Man of Salisbury award Jaycees, 1977; Disting. Service award, Salisbury, 1977; Achievement award Am. Cancer Soc., 1977. Mem. Am. Assn. Zool. Parks and Aquariums, Salisbury Jr. C. of C. (dir. 1976-78), Greenville C. of C. (congl. action com. 1980—), Delta Upsilon. Home: 109 Williams St Greenville NC 27834 Office: 200 W 3d St Greenville NC 27834

RENDLEMAN, RICHARD JAMES, JR., educator; b. Salisbury, N.C., June 2, 1949; s. Richard James and Patricia DuBois (Proctor) R.; A.B. in Acctg., Duke U., 1971; Ph.D. in Bus. Adminstrn., U. N.C., 1976; m. Nancy Walker Sherwin, Mar. 10, 1974. Teaching asst. U. N.C., Chapel Hill, 1974; instr. investments, Duke U., Durham, N.C., 1975, asso. prof. fin. Grad. Sch. Bus., 1980—; asst. prof. fin. Grad. Sch. Mgmt., Northwestern U., Evanston, Ill., 1976-79; vis. prof. fin. Coll. of Commerce, DePaul U., Chgo., 1979-80; mem., market maker Chgo. Bd. Options Exchange, 1979, mem. securities and new products com.; cons. FCC, 1975, Western Electric, Charlotte, N.C., 1975-76, Chgo. Bd. of Trade, 1977, Chgo. Bd. Options Exchange, 1977, Gen. Dynamics, 1980; participant banking research and fin. workshops. Mem. Am. Fin. Assn., Am. Econ. Assn., Eastern Fin. Assn., Fin. Mgmt. Assn., So. Econ. Assn., So. Fin. Assn., Western Econ. Assn. Republican. Episcopalian. Contbr. articles to profl. jours. Home: 2101 Tyson St Raleigh NC 27612 Office: Grad School of Business Duke U Durham NC 27706

RENEKER, MARYANN ESPOSITO, state ofcl.; b. Easton, Pa., Apr. 7, 1951; d. Anthony Joseph and Angelina Elizabeth (De Pietro) Esposito; B.A., Chestnut Hill Coll., Phila., 1973; M.P.A., Pa. State U., 1978; m. Gary A. Reneker; Elem. sch. tchr., Bethlehem, Pa., 1973-74; jr. coll. instr., Easton, 1974-75; acct. Christmas Club A Corp./Osceola Graphics, Inc., Easton, 1976-77; intern South Central regional planning office Gov. Pa. Justice Commn., Harrisburg, 1977-78; staff asst. Pa. Higher Edn. Assistance Agy., Harrisburg, 1978-79; budget analyst Gov. Pa. Office Budget, Harrisburg, 1979—. Senatorial scholar, 1969-73, 77-78; grantee Pa. Higher Edn. Assistance Agy., 1969-73. Mem. Am. Soc. Public Adminstrn., Jaycettes (service and welfare chairperson). Office: Gov Pa Office of Budget Strawberry Sq Harrisburg PA 17127

RENIER, JAMES J., business exec.; B.S. in Chemistry, Coll. St. Thomas; Ph.D. in Phys. Chemistry, Iowa State U. With U.S. AEC, to 1956; with Honeywell Inc., Mpls., 1956—, corp. v.p., gen. mgr. data systems ops., 1970-74, v.p. aerospace and def. group, 1974-76, group v.p., 1976-78, corp. exec. v.p., 1978-79, pres. control systems, 1979—, also dir. Office: Honeywell Plaza Minneapolis MN 55408*

RENKIS, ALAN ILMARS, plastics formulating co. exec.; b. Preili, Latvia, Apr. 16, 1938; s. Joseph and Malvine (Sturitis) R.; came to U.S., 1950, naturalized, 1956; B.S. in Chem. Engring., Pa. State U., 1960; m. Inara Balodis, July 15, 1961; children—Martin Alan, Laura Alise. With product devel. and tech. service div. Diamond Alkali Co., Painesville, Ohio, 1960-63; tech. dir. G.S. Plastics Co., Cleve., 1963; founder, pres. Thermoclad Co., Erie, Pa., 1963—, also Norwalk, Calif., 1972—. Mem. Young Pres.'s Orgn., Soc. Plastics Engrs., Sigma Pi, Fraternitas Metropolitana (Latvian Student frat.). Clubs: Univ., Erie, Maennerchor, Kahkwa (Erie). Developer comml. PVC resins for formulating fluidized bed coating powders; formulations and compounding techniques. Home: 5109 Watson Rd Erie PA 16505 Office: 4690 Iroquois Ave Erie PA 16511

RENNA, ANTHONY ALFRED, land developing co. exec.; b. Schenectady, Aug. 24, 1920; s. Nicola and Arcangela (Iovino) R.; student pub. schs., Schenectady; m. Rita Helen Beaudry, Feb. 15, 1947; children—Sandra, Alice, Anthony, Anita. Salesman Renna Bros. & Co., wholesale distbrs., Schenectady, 1938-53; pres. Sandy Sales Co., non food merchandisers, Schenectady, 1953—; pres. Renco Enterprises Inc., land developers, Schenectady, 1968—. Served with inf. AUS, 1942-46; PTO. Decorated Purple Heart. Mem. Toiletry Merchandisers Assn. (regional v.p. 1957-58), Service Merchandisers Am. (chmn. coms., officer 1958—). Clubs: Rotary, Sons of Italy. Home: 141 Western Pkwy Schenectady NY 12304 Office: 22 College St PO Box 52 Schenectady NY 12301

RENNER, WILLIAM BEACH, aluminum co. exec.; b. Middletown, Ohio, Sept. 29, 1920; s. L.C. and Pearl (Beach) R.; A.B., Wittenberg U., 1942; m. Elizabeth Anne Kemp, Feb. 5, 1944; children—Richard K., William Beach, Peter A. Vice pres. sales, mill products Aluminum Co. of Am., Pitts., 1973-75, pres., dir., 1975—; dir. Shell Oil Co., Pitts. Nat. Bank, Pitts. Nat. Corp. Mem. citizens sponsoring com. Allegheny Conf. Community Devel.; bd. dirs. Regional Indsl. Devel. Corp. of S.W. Pa.; trustee Shadyside Hosp.; bd. dirs. Wittenberg U. Served with USNR, 1942-45, 50-52. Mem. Aluminum Assn. (chmn.), Am. Soc. Corp. Execs., Greater Pitts. C. of C. Office: 1501 Alcoa Bldg Pittsburgh PA 15219

RENOFF, PAUL VERNON, ret. elec. mfrs. rep.; b. Balt., July 17, 1911; s. Henry John and Mary E. (Snyder) R.; B.E.E., Johns Hopkins, 1932; m. Margaret Hamilton Houghton, June 18, 1937; children—Ronald Hamilton, Lois Ellen (Mrs. Henry Ward Brockett), Cynthia Houghton (Mrs. George A. Taler). Engr., H.R. Houghton, 1933-36; partner Houghton & Renoff, 1936-45, Paul V. Renoff Co., 1945-66; pres. Renoff Assos., Inc. 1966-73; former dir. Edwin L. Wiegand Co., Skan-A-Matic Corp., United Co. Past pres., Roland Ct. Maintenance Corp.; past pres. Arundel Beach Improvement Assn.; mem. Magothy River Assn.; former dir. Roland Park Civic League. Registered profl. engr. Md. Mem. Amigas de Calle del Cristo 255, Engrs. Club, IEEE, U.S. Power Squadron, Md. Hist. Soc. Democrat. Clubs: Johns Hopkins, Chartwell Golf & Country (Severna Park, Md.). Home: 4326 Roland Ct Baltimore MD 21210 also 454 Arundel Beach Rd Severne Park MD 21146 also PO Box 1 Sugar Loaf Shores FL 33044

RENOUD, DOROTHY OWEN, publishing co. exec.; b. Far Rockaway, N.Y., Aug. 11, 1933; d. Herbert William and Elizabeth (Fischer) Owen; ed. pub. schs., bus. courses; m. David F. Renoud, Jan. 18, 1958; children—David, Douglas. File clk. Reinhold Pub. Co., N.Y.C., 1951-59, sales adminstrv. mgr., 1959-61; asst. to circulation mgr. United Tech. Pub. Co., Garden City, N.Y., 1961-63, circulation dir., 1963—. Mem. Subscription Fulfillment Mgrs. Assn., Nat. Bus. Circulation Council Long Beach Fire Dept. Ladies Aux. Home: 527 West Chester St Long Beach NY 11561 Office: 645 Stewart Ave Garden City NY 11530

RENSTROM, PAUL ANTHONY, banker; b. San Francisco, Nov. 6, 1934; s. Conrad Wilhelm and Margaret McCormick (King) R.; B.S., U. Notre Dame, 1956; postgrad. Amos Tuck Sch., Dartmouth Coll., 1973-76; m. Nancy Armitage Langenbahn, June 5, 1956; children—Paul, John, Christopher, Gregory, Peter. Mgmt. trainee Wells Fargo Bank, San Francisco, 1958-61, v.p. internat. credit adminstrn., 1976-81, sr. v.p. credit policy group, 1981—; controller Farnsworth Electronics div. ITT Components, 1961-62; asst. controller frequency and time div. Hewlett Packard, 1962-63. Served with Airborne Inf., U.S. Army, 1956-58. Mem. Am. Petroleum Inst., Nat. Assn. Credit Mgmt. Democrat. Roman Catholic. Clubs: Univ., Serra (San Francisco). Home: 930 Continental Dr Menlo Park CA 94025 Office: 464 California St San Francisco CA 94144

RENTSCHLER, FREDERICK BRANT, consumer products mfg. co. exec.; b. N.Y.C., Aug. 12, 1939; s. George Adam and Rita (Mitchell) R.; B.A. in Econs., Vanderbilt U., 1961; M.B.A., Harvard U., 1968; m. Marguerite E. O'Shaughnessy, Nov. 20, 1971; 1 son, Anthony. Dir. mktg., toiletries and household Armour-Dial Co., Phoenix, 1972-74, v.p. toiletries, 1974-76, v.p. new bus. devel., 1976-77, pres. Armour Internat., 1977-78, pres. Armour-Dial Co., 1978-80; pres. Hunt-Wesson Foods, Inc., 1980—; dir. Charleston Corp. Mem. Pres.'s Commn. on White House Fellows, 1971-72; bd. dirs. Compass IV, 1975, Scottsdale Center for Arts, 1975-76; mem. men's council Heard Mus., 1975—. Served to capt. USMC, 1961-65. Recipient J. Leslie Rawlins award Harvard U. Grad. Sch. Bus., 1968. Mem. Nat. Food Processors Assn. (dir.), Young Presidents' Orgn. Republican. Roman Catholic. Clubs: Links (N.Y.C.); Racquet (Chgo.); Paradise Valley, Arizona (Phoenix). Office: Hunt-Wesson Foods Inc 1645 W Valencia Dr Fullerton CA

REPANICH, NORMAN JOHN, indsl. devel. co. exec.; b. Sacramento, Apr. 19, 1934; s. Peter John and Norma Katherine (Martinovich) R.; A.A., Coll. of Sequoias, 1965; B.A., Calif. State U., Fresno, 1967; m. Janet Elaine Thomas, Aug. 11, 1962; children—Peter, Aynn. With Santa Barbara (Calif.) C. of C., 1967-68; mgr. tourist and conv. Tulare C. of C., 1968-73; dir. Solano Co. Indsl. Devel. Agy., Fairfield, Calif., 1974-78; dir. Econ. Devel., Greenville, S.C., 1978-79; dir. Fairmont (W.Va.) Indsl. and Credit Corp., 1979—. Sec.-treas. Tulare (Calif.) Local Devel. Corp., 1969-73; planning commr. Tulare, 1971-74; chmn. Marion County Vocat. Tech. Adv. Council, 1980—. Served with USN, 1951-55. Mem. Nat. Assn. Indsl. Parks, Am. Indsl. Devel. Council, Sigma Delta Chi. Roman Catholic. Club: Rotary. Home: 11 Park Dr Fairmont WV 26554 Office: Rm 309 Deveny Bldg Fairmont WV 26554

REPIC, EDWARD MICHAEL, mgmt. cons. co. exec.; b. Cleve., June 7, 1935; s. Michael Ray and Anne Margaret Repic; B.Aero. Engring., Ohio State U., 1962; M.S. in Aero. Engring., U. So. Calif., 1964; M.B.A., Pepperdine U., 1975; m. Patricia Raye DeBlass, June 30, 1956; children—Terri Lynn, Raymond Anthony, Toni D'ann, Edward Michael. Mgr. Space div. Rockwell Internat., Downey, Calif., 1962-72, mgr. Saberliner div., Los Angeles, 1972-75, mgr. Admiral div., Chgo., 1975-76, engring. mgr. Missile Systems div., Anaheim, Calif., 1976-79; founder, pres. Effective Mgmt. Resources Corp., Anaheim, 1979—; instr. grad. mgmt. U. So. Calif., 1978—, West Coast U., 1964—; condr. mgmt. seminars throughout U.S. and Europe, 1978—. Mem. Am. Mgmt. Assn., AIAA, ASME, Mensa. Club: Diogenes. Author: Basic Thermodynamics, 1968; Managing Engineers, 1979. Home: 2229 Nyon Ave Anaheim CA 92806 Office: 843 State College Blvd Anaheim CA 92806

REPPERT, ALFRED REED, bank exec.; b. Morgantown, W.Va., Mar. 4, 1919; s. Edmund Hare and Beulah Clare (Getty) R.; B.S.E., Princeton U., 1940; m. Elizabeth Ann Long, Apr. 15, 1944; children—Elizabeth Reed, Anne Clare. With various coal cos., W.Va., 1940-64; v.p. Union Nat. Bank Clarksburg (W.Va.), 1964-72, pres., 1972—; dir. Balt. br. Fed. Res. Bank Richmond, Greer Steel Co., First Nat. Bank of Philippi. Bd. dirs., treas. United Hosp. Center, Clarksburg. Mem. Clarksburg C. of C. Office: Union Nat Bank Clarksburg Clarksburg WV 26301

RERES, ANTHONY PETER, securities co. exec.; b. Bklyn., Apr. 6, 1934; s. Andrew and Jean R.; A.A.S., N.Y. City Community Coll., 1962; cert. Am. Mgmt. Assn., 1964, Assn. Stock Exchange Firms, 1967, Profession Mgmt. Seminars, 1970; Mgmt. cert., Am. Mgmt. Assn., 1972; Helen Mazzarella, Apr. 28, 1956; children—Andrew, Jean, Diane, Anthony, Denise. Ops. troubleshooter Bache & Co., N.Y.C., 1953-59; mgr. stock record dept. Walston & Co., Inc., N.Y.C., 1959-61; asst. to controller Emanuel, Deetjen & Co., N.Y.C., 1961-64; mgr. internal audit dept. Hemphill, Noyes & Co., N.Y.C., 1964-65; asst. to nat. dir. ops. Dempsey-Tegler & Co., Inc., N.Y.C., 1965-66; v.p. Stock Clearing Corp. subs. N.Y. Stock Exchange, N.Y.C., 1966-72; exec. v.p. Pacific Securities Depository div. Pacific Stock Exchange, San Francisco, 1973-74; dir. participant services Depository Trust Co. (formerly Central Cert. Service), N.Y.C., 1973-77; sr. v.p. mktg. Swiss Am. Securities Inc., N.Y.C., 1977—; dir. Solar Engring. Group, Princeton, N.J., 1979-80. Mem. Inst. Internal Auditors, Security Industry Assn. (exec. com. 1971-73), Securities Industry (joint industry com.), Renaissance Homeowners Assn. (pres. 1976-77). Democrat. Club: City Midday. Home: 5 Berkshire Dr East Windsor NJ 08520 Office: 100 Wall St New York NY 10005

RESLEY, GEORGE BOULTER, sales exec.; b. Ft. Stockton, Tex., Nov. 23, 1945; s. Horace Ernest and Annie Jane (Boulter) R.; B.B.A., Tex. A. and M. U., 1969; grad. Dale Carnegie Course, 1976; m. Virginia Beth Hopper, July 22, 1972. Sales rep. for 3-C Corp., Odessa, Tex., 1969-72; mid-continent sales mgr. Vetco 3-C Corp., Tulsa, 1973-74; mid-continent sales mgr. Vetco Services, Inc., Tulsa, 1974-78; regional sales mgr. C-E Vetco Services, Inc., Tulsa, 1979—. Recipient 10 Yr. award C-E Vetco Services, Inc., 1979. Mem. Internat. Assn. Drilling Contractors, Nat. Assn. Corrosion Engrs., Soc. Petroleum Engrs., Tex. Muzzle Loading Rifle Assn., Osage Muzzle Loading Rifle Assn., Nat. Rifle Assn. (life), Can. Assn. Drilling Contractors, Lincoln Continental Owners Club. Republican. Christian Scientist. Clubs: Tex. A. and M. Univ. Century, N. Am. Aerospace Rod and Gun, Westerners. Office: 4343 S 118th East Ave Tulsa OK 74145

RESNIK, SOL LEON, mfg. co. exec.; b. Providence, May 16, 1930; s. Nathan and Fanny (Priest) R.; B.S., U. R.I., 1953; M.B.A., U. Pa., 1954; m. Esther Petersohn, June 20, 1954; children—David, Marcia, Linda. Founder, exec., pres. Emblem & Badge Inc., Providence, 1954—; partner Village Park Realty, 1970—; pres. 859 Realty Co., Providence, 1960-74; partner Diplomat Assos., Providence, 1970—, Eleven-Eleven Assos., Providence, 1974-76; chmn. bd. dirs. Promotion Corp. Am., Providence, 1970-76. Bd. dirs. Providence Hebrew Day Sch., 1960-73; bd. dirs. R.I. Broadway Theatre League, 1965-73, R.I. Jewish Community Center, 1974-76, Jewish Fedn. R.I., 1973-76, 77—, Narragansett Bay Devel. Soc., 1974—, Temple Emanu-El. Mem. Mfg. Jewelers and Silversmiths Am. Mason (Shriner, 32 deg.). Home: 41 Westford Rd Providence RI 02906 Office: 859 N Main St Providence RI 02940

RETHORE, BERNARD GABRIEL, diversified co. exec.; b. Bklyn., May 22, 1941; s. Francis Joseph and Katharine Eunice (MacDwyer) R.; B.A., Yale, 1962; M.B.A., U. Pa., 1967; m. Marilyn Irene Watt, Dec. 1, 1962; children—Bernard Michael, Tara Jean, Kevin Watt, Alexandra Marie, Rebecca Anne. Asso., McKinsey & Co., Inc., Washington, 1967, then sr. asso., 1973; v.p./gen. mgr. Greer div. Microdot, Inc., Darien, Conn., 1973-77, v.p. ops. Connector Group, 1977-78, pres. Bus. Devel. Group, 1978—; cons. U.S. Govt., UN. Mem. dean's adv. bd. Wharton Sch. Bus., U. Pa., 1972—. Served to capt., inf., AUS, 1962-65. Decorated Bronze Star. Mem. Wharton Bus. Sch. Alumni Assn. (dir., pres.), Assn. U.S. Army. Clubs: Yale, Wharton Bus. Sch. (N.Y.C.). Home: 18 Crooked Mile Rd Westport CT 06880 Office: 23 Old Kings Hwy S Darien CT 06820

RETTEW, BONNIE RAY, spices co. exec.; b. Balt., July 12, 1950; d. Horace and Betty (Spiekermann) R.; B.A. magna cum laude, U. Balt., 1977, postgrad., 1977—. Br. adminstrv. mgr. Burrough Corp., Balt., 1972-76; mktg. asst. spices McCormick & Co., Hunt Valley, Md., 1977—. Bd. govs. U. Balt., 1978. Mem. Am. Mktg. Assn. Office: 204 Wight Ave Hunt Valley MD 21031

REUTERSHAN, CHRISTOPHER, banker; b. Southampton, N.Y., June 6, 1952; s. Robert Gordon and Ann Patricia (Cronin) R.; A.B. in Econs., Colgate U., 1974. With Chase Manhattan Bank, N.Y.C., 1975-80, asst. treas. internat. dept., Peru, 1976-78, 2d v.p. internat. dept. commodity fin., 1978-80; mgr. trade and commodity fin. Chase Manhattan Can. Ltd., Toronto, 1981—. Asst. treas. Center Inter-Am. Relations, N.Y.C., 1978-80. Recipient President's award Chase Manhattan Bank, 1978. Club: Univ. (N.Y.C.). Home: 55 Harbour Sq Suite 2914 Toronto ON M5J 2L1 Canada Office: 3605 Commerce Ct W Toronto ON M5L 1G1 Canada

REVZIN, STANLEY ALEXANDER, mfg. co. pres.; b. N.Y.C., Jan. 13, 1924; s. Boris and Fannie (Ellinoff) R.; B.E.E., Coll. City N.Y., 1948; postgrad. Poly. Inst. Bklyn., 1951-53; m. Marcia Korsun, Sept. 3, 1950; children—Marc Warren, Bruce David. Electronic engr. U.S. Army Signal Corps Engring. Labs., Fort Monmouth, N.J., 1948-54; mgr. engring. Lewyt Mfg. Corp., N.Y.C., 1954-60; with Bristol Electronics Inc., New Bedford, Mass., 1960—, v.p., 1961-69, pres., 1969—; dir. Transdyne Corp., New Bedford; pres., Bristol Industries, Inc., New Bedford, 1967—, Bristol Electronics Internat., New Bedford, 1972—. Mem. Town Meeting, Dartmouth, Mass., 1970—. Bd. dirs. Moby Dick council Boy Scouts Am., 1964—, Jewish Welfare Fedn., 1970—. Served to 1st lt. AUS, 1942-46: ETO. Decorated Combat Infantryman Badge, Bronze Star medal. Mem. I.E.E.E., Sigma Kappa Tau, Small Bus. Assn. New England. Mason. Home: 47 Evelyn St North Dartmouth MA 02747 Office: 651 Orchard St New Bedford MA 02744

REX, RAYMOND RUSSELL, JR., fin. cons.; b. Phila., June 24, 1938; s. Raymond Russell and Frances (Mills) R.; B.S., Am. Internat. Coll., 1975; m. Sept. 17, 1960; children—Suellen, Raymond Russell III, Donna. Visual communications specialist Tecnifax Corp., Oklahoma City, 1960-65; sales service mgr., Scott Graphics, South Hadley, Mass., 1965-71; fin. and mgmt. cons., Hadley, Mass., 1971—; corp. clk. Wok Inc., YA How Corp. Inc. Mem. Hampshire County United Fund Budget Com., 1973-74, Hadley Indsl. Devel. Commn., 1976-80. Served with USAF, 1956-60. Roman Catholic. Clubs: Lions (pres. 1980—), Hadley Young Men's, Hadley Men's. Home: 5 Laurel Dr Hadley MA 01035 Office: 8 River Dr Hadley MA 01035

REXING, DAVID JOSEPH, water system ofcl.; b. Evansville, Ind., Sept. 21, 1950; s. Joseph Henry and Anita Marie (Baehl) R.; A.B., U. Evansville, 1972; postgrad. U. Ariz., 1975; M.B.A., U. Nev., 1981; m. Mariann McDuffee, Aug. 6, 1976. Chemist, Evansville (Ind.) Waterworks, 1971-72; research asst. U. Ariz., Tucson, 1972-75; lab. supt. So. Nev. Water System, Boulder City, 1975—. Certified grade IV water treatment operator, Nev. Mem. Am. Inst. Chemists (fellow 1971-72), Am. Waterworks Assn. (standard methods com.), Phi Kappa Phi, Phi Beta Chi, Kappa Mu Epsilon, Blue Key. Contbr. articles in field to publs. Office: 243 Lakeshore Rd Boulder City NV 89005

REYES, JOSE MARIA, trading co. exec.; b. Bogota, Columbia, Dec. 26, 1951, came to U.S., 1977; s. Luis Carlos Reyes and Josefina de Reyes; Law Degree, U. La Gran Colombia, 1976. Mgr., Hacienda Azucarera Chune, Valle del Cauca, Colombia, 1974-76; gen. sec. Ficitec, Bogota, 1976-77; control mgr. Eldorado Trading Co., Miami, Fla., 1977-78, mgr., 1978-79, pres., gen. mgr., 1979—; v.p. Esmeralda Trading Co.; mem. exec. com. Flores Columbiana. Roman Catholic. Clubs: Jockey, Polo (Bogota); Pinos Polo, Mutiny (Miami). Columnist, El Siglo. Office: Eldorado Trading Co Box 523302 Miami FL 33152

REYNDERS, CHARLTON, JR., stock broker; b. N.Y.C., Dec. 1, 1937; s. Charlton and Eliza Ellen (Lemon) R.; grad. St. Paul's Sch., Concord, N.H., 1955; A.B., Princeton, 1959; m. Knowlton Ames, Sept. 23, 1961; children—John V.W. III, Charlton III, Alys Ames. With Harris, Upham & Co., Inc., N.Y.C., 1963-76, v.p., 1968-73, 1st v.p., 1973-76, also dir., mem. exec. com.; 1st v.p., dir. Smith Barney, Harris Upham & Co., Inc., N.Y.C., 1976-79; founder, chmn. Reynders, Gray & Co., Inc., 1979—; exchange ofcl. Am. Stock Exchange, 1974-78. Served to lt. (j.g.) USNR, 1959-62. Republican. Episcopalian. Clubs: Racquet and Tennis, Bedford Golf and Tennis. Home: McLain St Bedford Hills NY 10507 Office: 120 Broadway New York NY 10005

REYNOLDS, DAVID PARHAM, metal products mfg. exec.; b. Bristol, Tenn., June 16, 1915; s. Richard Samuel and Julia Louise (Parham) R.; student Princeton U., 1938; m. Margaret Harrison, Mar. 25, 1944; children—Margaret Allis, Julia Parham, Dorothy Harrison. With Reynolds Metals Co., 1937—, salesman, asst. mgr. aircraft parts, 1937-44, asst. v.p., 1944-46, v.p., 1946-57, exec. v.p., 1958—, gen. mgr., 1969-75, vice chmn. bd., chmn. exec. com., 1975-76, chmn. bd., chief exec. officer, 1976—; chmn. bd., dir. Robertshaw Controls, 1978—; dir. Reynolds Metals Co., Reynolds Aluminum Sales Co., Reynolds Internat., Inc., Reynolds Aluminum Co. Can., Eskimo Pie Corp., United Va. Bankshares, Reynolds Jamaica Mines, Ltd. Founding mem. Nat. Center for Resource Recovery; trustee Lawrenceville Sch. Mem. Aluminum Assn. Presbyterian. Home: 8905 Tresco Rd Richmond VA 23229 Office: 6601 Broad St Rd Richmond VA 23261

REYNOLDS, DORIS KOOI (MRS. JAMES CREW REYNOLDS), banker, former Republican nat. committeewoman; b. Chgo.; d. Peter and Mary Helen (Brown) Kooi; ed. Lewis Inst., Chgo., and The Castle, Miss Mason's Sch., Tarrytown, N.Y.; m. James Crew Reynolds, Oct. 30, 1923; 1 dau., Crewe Kooi (Mrs. Selmer E. Moeller). Republican State committeewoman, Sheridan County, Wyo., 1936-37; pres. meeting to organize Nat. Fedn. Rep. Women's Clubs, 1937; mem. Rep. Nat. Com., 1937-48; organizer State Fedn. Women's Rep. Study Groups and Clubs of Wyo. (charter mem. Nat. Fedn. Women's Rep. Clubs), 1939; promoted passage of 50-50 Law in Wyo., 1939; mem. rules com. Rep. Nat. Conv., 1940, contests com., 1944, arrangements com., 1948. Mem. state com. Nat. War Fund; local radio chmn., United China Relief; mem. exec. com. and chmn. finance com. Sheridan Youth Center; pres. Sheridan Woman's Club, 1953-54; past pres. Bus. and Profl. Women's Club, Sheridan, past state fedn. parliamentarian, chmn. legislative com.; dir. Grand View Addition Co.; former v.p., dir. Sheridan Flouring Mills, Inc.; pres., dir. D and D Hardware Co., Sheridan, Bank Commerce, Sheridan. Mem. Zoning Bd. City of Sheridan, 1946-49; chmn. legis. com. Sheridan Hosp. Constrn. Bd.; mem. aux. Sherman County Meml. Hosp. Adopted mem. Crow Indian Tribe. Mem. Nat. Assn. Bank Women, Am. Legion Aux. (past unit pres., past dist. pres. Dept. Wyo.; past state poppy chmn. and membership chmn.), C. of C. (former chmn. museum com.), VFW Aux., State Hist. Soc., Hist. and Mus. Assn. No. Wyo. and So. Mont. (pres.), P.T.A., Order Eastern Star (past matron, past grand chaplain, past grand marshal), Continental Confedn. Adopted Indians, White Shrine of Jerusalem, Does (charter), Pythian Sisters (past chief), YWCA, YMCA (sustaining Century mem.), Daus. of the Nile (first queen Sahida Temple, Supreme Dep. 1951-52, 55-57; parliamentarian), Wyo. Beekeepers Assn., Social Order of Beauceant (past pres.), Internat. Order Job's Daus. (past grand guardian of Wyo., supreme dep. Nev., 1956-57, supreme jurisprudence com. 1956-59), Mont., Wyo. hist. socs., Community Concert Assn. (dir.), Order of Amaranth (charter), Sigma Tau Epsilon Pi, Phi Delta Sigma. Episcopalian. Rebekah. Clubs: Sheridan Country, Bighorn Executive, Sheridan Garden. Author: Handbook for Republican Party Workers, 1940, 44, 52, 56. Home: 334 W Burrows Box 153 Sheridan WY 82801

REYNOLDS, JAMES, mgmt. cons.; b. Detroit, Mar. 22, 1941; s. Richard James and Esther (Nikander) R.; B.A. in Econs., N.Y. U., 1965, postgrad., 1965-66. Cons. to pres. Rothrock, Reynolds & Reynolds Inc., N.Y.C., 1966-70; sr. v.p. health, med. div. Booz, Allen & Hamilton, N.Y.C., 1970—; dir. Booz, Allen & Hamilton, Inc., 1976-79; chmn. bd. J.X. Reynolds Ltd., dealers fine art; faculty mem. to United Hosp. Fund of N.Y. Mem. Shared Services Com. of Regional Med. Program, N.Y.C.; bd. Salvation Army Children's Day Center, N.Y.C., 1967-70, Salvation Army Women's Lodge, N.Y.C., 1969-70, Health Center Mgmt. Inst. Recipient N.Y. U. Founders award, 1965. Mem. Am. Pub. Health Assn., Am. Mgmt. Assn., Assn. of Am. Med. Colls., Am. Hosp. Assn., Hosp. Mgmt. Systems Soc., Hosp. Fin. Mgmt. Assn., Victorian Soc., Phi Beta Kappa. Episcopalian. Clubs: Mus. Modern Art, Met. Mus. Art, Met. Opera Guild (N.Y.C.). Developer integrated mgmt. system for acad. health centers, 1977, orgn. multi-hosp. systems, 1979. Home: 45 Sutton Pl S New York NY 10022 Office: 245 Park Ave New York NY 10017

REYNOLDS, JOHN CHARLES, communications co. exec.; b. Bklyn., May 12, 1933; s. Patrick and Mary (Keicher) R.; B.B.A., St. John's U., 1954; M.B.A., N.Y. U., 1961; m. Theresa Ellen Donahue, July 6, 1957; children—Thomas, Brian, Catherine, Maureen, Patricia, Kevin. Mgmt. trainee W.R. Grace & Co., 1956-57; with Grace Line, 1957-61; Panama Agys., 1957-58; mgr. Budgetary Controls, N.Y.C., 1958-61; with ITT, 1961—, gen. mgr. Caribbean-P.R., 1967-76, gen. mgr. voice communication cos., N.Y.C., 1977-78, corp. v.p., pres. and group mgr. communications ops. group, 1979—. Mem. adv. com. trustees Dartmouth Inst., Hanover, N.H. mem. organizing com. Pan Am Games, 1978; trustee Daytop Village, 1981, Presbyn. Hosp., San Juan, P.R., 1972-76; 1st v.p. Jr. Achievement P.R., 1974-76. Served in U.S. Army, 1954-56. Named hon. citizen New Orleans, 1980, San Juan, 1975. Mem. Am. Mgmt. Assn., Armed Forces Communications and Electronics Assn., Am. Inst. Mgmt. Roman Catholic. Clubs: Harbor View; Ridgewood Country; Bankers (P.R.). Home: 24 Cambridge Dr Allendale NJ 07401 Office: ITT 67 Broad St New York NY 10004

REYNOLDS, ROBERT FRANKLIN, bldg. contractor; b. Vanatta, Ohio, July 18, 1923; s. James Calvin and Edith May (Hughes) R.; student pub. schs., Vanatta and Newark, Ohio; m. Mary Martha Gleckler, Mar. 9, 1945; 1 dau., Sandra Lynn Miller. Dairy and hog farmer, St. Louisville, Ohio, 1947-56; carpenter Rockwell Mfg. Co., Newark, Ohio, 1955-56; owner, operator R.F. Reynolds Co., Newark, 1957—. Served with U.S. Army, 1943-46; PTO. Mem. Nat., Ohio, Licking County homebuilders assns. Republican. Lutheran. Club: Licking Springs Trout and Golf. Address: 746 Robin Hood Dr Newark OH 43055

REYNOLDS, ROBERT GREGORY, toxicologist; b. Chgo., July 29, 1952; s. Robert G. and Loys Delle (Kever) R.; B.S. in Nutrition and Food Sci., M.I.T., 1973, postgrad. in toxicology, 1973-78; postgrad. in mgmt. Sloan Sch. Mgmt., 1977-78. Mng. editor The Graduate Mag., M.I.T., 1975-78; v.p. Internat. Contact Bur., Ft. Lauderdale, Fla., 1977—; staff toxicologist, asst. to v.p. for mktg. Enviro Control, Inc., Rockville, Md., 1978-79; dir. tech. resources Borriston Research Labs., Inc., Temple Hills, Md., 1979-80; dir. mktg. Northrop Services Inc., Research Triangle Park, N.C., 1980—; toxicological cons. Energy Resources Co., Inc, Cambridge. NSF fellow, 1973. Mem. Am. Acad. Clin. Toxicology, AAAS. Episcopalian. Contbr. chpts. to textbook, lab. manual, sci. jours. and govt. publs. Office: PO Box 12313 Research Triangle Park NC 27709

REYNOLDS, ROBERT HARRISON, export co. exec.; b. Mpls., Sept. 6, 1913; s. Clarence H. and Helen (Doyle) R.; student pub. schs., Vinton, Iowa; m. Gladys Marie Gaster, Apr. 7, 1934; 1 dau., Shirley Anne (Mrs. Frank S. Potestio). Export sales mgr., rolled products sales mgr. Colo. Fuel & Iron Corp., Denver, 1938-46; pres. Rocky Mountain Export Co., Inc., Denver, 1941—, Projects Gen. Am., Denver, 1967—; dir. Electromedics, Inc. Club: Denver. Home: 580 S Clinton St Denver CO 80231 Office: 1860 Lincoln St Denver CO 80203

REYNOLDS, RUSSELL SEAMAN, JR., exec. recruiting cons.; b. Greenwich, Conn., Dec. 14, 1931; s. Russell Seaman and Virginia Dare (Carter) R.; B.A., Yale, 1954; postgrad. N.Y. U., 1958-61; m. Deborah Ann Toll, July 21, 1956; children—Russell Seaman, III, Jeffrey Toll, Deborah Chase. Asst. v.p. nat. div. Morgan Guaranty Trust Co. of N.Y., 1957-66; partner William H. Clark Assos., Inc., 1966-69; pres. Russell Reynolds Assos., Inc., N.Y.C., 1969-71, chmn., 1971—. Past chmn. Campaign for Yale for Greenwich Area; bd. dirs. Greenwich Hist. Soc.; mem. adv. bd. Salvation Army Greater N.Y.; past trustee Westminster Sch., Hotchkiss Sch.; trustee Greenwich Hosp., Hurricane Island Outward Bound Sch. Served as 1st lt., SAC, USAF, 1954-57. Mem. Assn. Exec. Recruiting Cons. Clubs: Round Hill; Indian Harbor Yacht; N.Y. Yacht; Links; Recess; Economic; Yale; Amateur Ski (N.Y.C.); Mill Reef; Calif. Home: 39 Clapboard Ridge Rd Greenwich CT 06830 Office: 245 Park Ave New York NY 10017

REYNOLDS, WILLIAM GLASGOW, lawyer; b. Dover, Tenn., July 15, 1911; s. John Lacey and Harriett Edwina (Glasgow) R.; A.B., Vanderbilt U., 1932, J.D., 1935; m. Nancy Bradford du Pont, May 18, 1940; children—Katherine Glasgow Reynolds Sturges, William Bradford, Mary Parminter Reynolds Savage, Cynthia du Pont Reynolds Farris. Admitted to Tenn. bar, 1935, D.C. bar, 1964, U.S. Supreme Ct. bar, 1945; gen. practice, Nashville, 1934-35; with E.I. du Pont de Nemours & Co., 1935-71, chief counsel advt., pub. relations and central research depts., 1954-71; with firm Morris, Nichols, Arsht & Tunnell, Wilmington, Del., 1972—; dir., mem. exec. com. and trust com. Del. Trust Co., Wilmington, 1972—; resident counsel Remington Arms Co., Bridgeport, Conn., 1940-41; with Office Gen. Counsel, U.S. Navy, 1942-43, Exec. Office Sec. Navy, 1944, Office Asst. Sec. Navy, 1945. Permanent mem. jud. conf. 3d Jud. Circuit U.S., 1955—; rep. chem. industry Water Resources Policy Com., 1950; mem. adv. com. Patent Office, Dept. Commerce, 1954. Mem. Internat. Conf. Indsl. and Municipal Air Pollution, 1949; mem. com. of experts on internat. trademark treaties World Indsl. Property Orgn. Hearings, Geneva, 1969-72, Vienna, 1973, Comecon Congress, Moscow, 1974; mem. Nat. Com. Assay U.S. Mints, 1958, chmn., 1958; mem. chmn. devel. council Vanderbilt Law Sch., 1968-70, mem. visitors com., 1968—. Alt. del. Republican Nat. Conv., 1956; mem. Rep. Nat. Com. Assos., 1956-65; bd. dirs., sec. Rencourt Found. Del., 1955—; bd. dirs. United Community Fund No. Del., 1948-53, exec. com., 1949-51; trustee, chmn. bldg. com. Children's Home, Claymont and Wilmington, 1946-47, pres., 1947-51; bd. dirs., mem. bldg. com. Del. Art Center, 1948-64; bd. dirs. U.S. Tastevin Found., 1977—, pres., 1979-80. Recipient Founders medal Vanderbilt U. Law Sch., 1935, U.S. Navy commendations, 1943, 45. Mem. U.S. Trademark Assn. (chmn. bd., pres. 1964, hon. chmn. 1965, past presidents council 1977—), Mfg. Chemists Assn. (chmn. lawyers adv. com. 1954), Assn. Internationale pour la protection de la Propriété Industrielle, Am. Judicature Soc., Am., Fed., D.C., Del. bar assns., Del., Tenn. trial lawyers assns., Nashville Bar and Library Assn., Navy League U.S., Vanderbilt Law Alumni Assn. (dir. 1961-64, nat. pres. 1970-71), Carolina Plantation Soc. (gov. Wilmington 1976-77), Order of Coif, Phi Kappa Psi. Episcopalian (past warden, vestryman, chmn. bldg. com.). Clubs: Confrerie des Chevaliers du Tastevin (grand officer Wilmington chpt. 1972—, nat. council 1973—, grand intendant 1975—, del. gen. 1976—, chmn. bd., chief exec. officer for N. Am. 1977); Union League (N.Y.C.); Chevy Chase (Md.) Country; Greenville Country (dir. 1962-65), Vicmead Hunt (Greenville, Del.); Wilmington (Del.); Lincoln of Del. (dir. 1968-71). Author: The Law of Water and Water Rights in the Tenn. River Valley, 1934; Local Restrictions on the Pollution of Inland Waters, 1948; Trademark Management-A Guide for Businessmen, 1955; Trademark Selection, 1960; also numerous articles, treatises. Home: Old Kennett Rd Greenville DE 19807 Office: 1702 Am Internat Bldg Wilmington DE 19801

RHEE, CHASE CHONGGWANG, export-import co. exec.; b. Korea, Feb. 26, 1942; s. Jongbae and Moohee Shin R.; B.A. in Fgn. Trade, Seoul Nat. U., 1968; M.A. in Internat. Mgmt., Am. Grad. Sch. Internat. Mgmt., Phoenix, 1970; m. Socorro DeLuna, June 26, 1971; children—Tammie, Jennifer. Mgmt. trainee Samyang Co., Ltd., Seoul, 1968-69; fgn. documentation officer Hongkong Bank of Calif., 1971-72; pres. Ameriko Industries Corp., Pasadena, Calif., 1972—. Served with Korean Army, 1963-66. Mem. Export Mgrs. Assn. Calif. Republican. Presbyterian. Club: Los Angeles Olympic Lions (pres. 1980-81). Home: 3610 Fairmeade Rd Pasadena CA 91107 Office: 750 E Green St Pasadena CA 91101

RHIND, JOHN CHRISTOPHER, assn. exec.; b. Birmingham, Eng., Feb. 19, 1934; s. John Joseph and Helen Florence (Walker) R.; m. Rita Diane Evans, June 21, 1958; children—Oonagh C., Michael J., Christopher J., Sarah C. With Pearl Assurance Co., Can., 1958-59; with Guardian Ins. Co. of Can., 1959-74, claims and adminstrn. mgr., 1972-74; asst. gen. mgr. Ins. Inst. of Can., Toronto, 1974-76, pres., chief exec. officer, 1979—. Mem. adv. bd. Sch. Continuing Studies, U. Toronto, Seneca Coll., George Brown Coll. Served with Brit. Army, 1952-54. Fellow Ins. Inst. Can.; mem. Ins. Inst. Ont., Ont. Ins. Adjusters Assn., Inst. Assn. Execs. (cert. assn. exec.). Roman Catholic. Clubs: Board of Trade (Toronto); Richview Golf. Office: 55 University Ave Toronto M5J 2H7 ON Canada

RHOADS, RUSH LEE, advt. co. exec.; b. Lusk, Wyo., Sept. 30, 1947; s. Frank John and Beatrice Bea McCloskey; student Colo. U., 1965-66, Arapahoe Jr. Coll., 1966-67, Colo. Inst. Art, 1967-68, 70-72. Asst. design dir. Academy Sign Co., Denver, 1973-74; pres., owner, designer Advt. and Design Assos., Ltd., Denver, 1974—. Recipient Grande Alphie, Denver Advt. Fedn., 1975. Mem. Art Dirs. Club Denver, Ad Club Denver, Prodn. Club Denver, Denver C. of C. Methodist. Home and Office: 1724 Vine St #301 Denver CO 80206

RHODES, ANN L(OUISE), constrn. co. exec.; b. Ft. Worth, Oct. 17, 1941; d. Jon Knox and Carol Jane (Greene) R.; student Tex. Christian U., 1960-63. Vice pres. Rhodes Enterprises Inc., Ft. Worth, 1963-77; owner-mgr. Lucky R Ranch, Ft. Worth, 1969—, Ann L. Rhodes Investments, Ft. Worth, 1976—; pres., chmn. bd. ALR Enterprises, Inc., Ft. Worth, 1977—. Bd. dirs. Tarrant Council Alcoholism, 1973-78, hon. bd. dirs., 1978—; bd. dirs. N.W. Tex. council Arthritis Found., 1977—; exec. com. Tarrant County Republican Party, 1964-69. Recipient various service awards. Mem. Am. Mgmt. Assns., Nat. Fedn. Ind. Bus., Am. Horse Council, Kappa Kappa Gamma. Episcopalian. Office: Suite 908 Ridglea Bank Bldg Fort Worth TX 76116

RHODES, DONALD ELLSWORTH, ins. co. exec.; b. New Castle, Pa., Oct. 21, 1915; s. Oscar Ellsworth and Alice R. (Heasley) R.; A.B., Grove City (Pa.) Coll., 1937; LL.B., U. Mich., 1948; postgrad. U. Wis., 1965-66; m. Emily Swanson, June 15, 1940; children—Susan Rhodes Stefanski, Jeffrey E. Draftsman, Bell Telephone Co. Pa., 1937-38, Dept. Hwys., State of Pa., 1938-39; mgr. Retail Credit Co., Johnstown and Beaver, Pa., 1939-41; supr. drafting Curtiss-Wright Corp., Beaver and Caldwell, N.J., 1941-46; with Citizens Ins. Co. Am., Howell, Mich., 1948—, v.p., 1959—, gen. counsel, 1968—, sec., 1964—, also dir.; v.p., gen. counsel Beacon Mut. Indeminity Co., Columbus, Ohio, 1971—, sec., 1976—, also dir.; v.p., gen. counsel, sec. Am. Select Risk Ins. Co., Columbus, 1979—, also dir. Co-chmn. United Fund, Howell, 1969; pres., dir. Lansing (Mich.) Mental Health Clinic, 1956-61. Mem. State Bar Mich., Am. Bar Assn., Fedn. Ins. Counsel, Ins. Fedn. Ohio, Mich. Ins. Lawyers Council, Mich. Assn. Ins. Cos., Pi Gamma Mu. Presbyterian. Clubs: Masons, Shriners, Elks. Home: 1444 Crest Rd Howell MI 48843 Office: 645 W Grand River St Howell MI 48843

RHODES, ERIC FOSTER, editor, pub.; b. Luray, Va., Feb. 5, 1927; s. Wallace Keith and Bertha (Foster) R.; A.A., George Washington U., 1949, A.B., 1950, M.A., 1952, Ed.D., 1967; m. Barbara Ellen Henson, Oct. 19, 1946; children—Roxanne Jane, Laurel Lee; m. 2d, Lorraine Endresen, July 29, 1972; m. 3d, Daisy Chun, May 31, 1980. Tchr. high sch., Arlington, Va., 1950-52; counselor Washington Lee High Sch., Arlington, 1952-53, dir. publs., 1953-54, chmn. dept. English, 1954-55; exec. sec. Arlington Edn. Assn., 1952-53, Montgomery County (Md.) Edn. Assn., 1955-57; lectr. edn. George Washington U., 1955-60; salary cons. N.E.A., Washington, 1957-58, asst. dir. membership div., 1958-60, dir. N.Y. regional office, N.Y.C., 1960-64, ednl. cons. Ednl. Research Services, White Plains, N.Y., 1964-65; pres. Ednl. Service Bur., Inc., Arlington, 1965-72, chmn. bd., 1972-80; pres. Negotiations Consultation Services, Inc., 1969-80, Eastern States Advt. Inc., 1970-79, EFR Corp., 1972—; exec. dir. Assn. Negotiators and Contract Adminstrs., 1981—; dir. Employee Futures Research, 1980—; owner Frederick Foster Galleries, 1974—. Cons. Va. Dept. Community Colls., 1965-77; employee relations ofcl. City of Orlando, 1980—; vice-chancellor Va. Community Coll. System, 1970-71; lectr. edn. Frostburg (Md.) State Coll., 1967. Mem. Civil Rights Commn., Franklin Twp., N.J., 1962-64; mem. Franklin Twp. Bd. Edn., 1964-65; mem. adv. bd. Keep Am. Beautiful, 1964-75, nat. chmn., 1968. Served with AUS, 1945-47. Mem. Am. Assn. Sch. Adminstrs., N.E.A., Edn. Press Assn., Nat. Assn. Ednl. Negotiators (exec. dir. 1971—), Phi Delta Kappa (chpt. pres. 1959-60), Fed. Schoolmen's Club, N.Y. Schoolmasters Club. Club: Lions. Author: Negotiating Salaries; 41 Ways to Cut Budget Costs. Editor: Inside Negotiations, Employee Benefits and Contract Administration. Home: PO Box 272 Orlando FL 32802 Office: 120 S Court St Orlando FL 32801

RHODES, KENT, pub. assn. exec.; b. Bklyn., Feb. 5, 1912; s. Clarence and Louise (Rhodes) Klinck; B.S., Amos Tuck Sch., Dartmouth, 1933; m. Christina Riordan, July 19, 1952; children—David Christian, Jean Louise, Brian Mark. Editor, pub. Dartmouth Pictorial, 1931-33; with Time Inc., 1933-44; with Reader's Digest Assn., Inc., Pleasantville, N.Y., 1944—, dir., 1965—, exec. v.p., 1970-75, pres., 1975-76, chmn. bd. 1976—; pres. Mag. Pubs. Assn., N.Y.C., 1979—; dir. Internat. Exec. Service Corps., 1973—. Bd. dirs. Reader's Digest Found., 1970—, pres., 1974—; trustee Outward Bound, 1966—, pres., 1971-72, chmn. bd., 1973; bd. dirs. Hurricane Island (Maine) Outward Bound Sch., 1971-76, Harvey Sch., Katonah, N.Y., 1966-75, Internat. House, 1977—, Up with People, 1977—; mem. Presdl. Commn. on Postal Service, 1976-77. Recipient William Caxton Human Relations award Am. Jewish Com., 1965. Mem. Mag. Pubs. Assn. (dir. 1956—, chmn. 1960-61), Assn. Publ. Prodn. Mgrs. (founder, 1st pres. 1939—), Nat. Inst. Social Sci., Westchester County Assn. (dir. 1972—, vice chmn. 1975-78, chmn. 1978—), Direct Mail Mktg. Assn. (dir. 1964-72, vice chmn. 1971), Advt. Council (dir. 1979—), Zeta Psi. Clubs: Union League, Univ. (N.Y.C.); Sleepy Hollow (Scarborough, N.Y.); Fishers Island (N.Y.) Country. Home: 860 UN Plaza Apt 19A New York NY 10017 Office: Mag Pubs Assn 575 Lexington Ave New York NY 10022

RHODES, TOM B., business exec.; b. Waco, Tex., 1917; B.A., Stanford U., 1939; LL.B., U. Tex., 1942; married. Admitted to Tex. bar; partner firm Atkinson & Rhodes, Dallas, 1946-59; v.p., gen. counsel Sedco Inc., Dallas, 1960-73, vice chmn. bd., sr. v.p., gen. counsel, 1973-77, chmn. bd., 1977—, also dir. Office: Sedco Inc 1901 N Akard St Dallas TX 75201*

RHUDE, ALBERT LAUREN, coll. pres.; b. Duluth, Minn., July 20, 1929; s. Arthur Louis and Amanda Louise R.; B.A., Augustana Coll., Sioux Falls, S.D., 1953; D.C.S., Ft. Lauderdale (Fla.) Coll., 1970; m. Lila Jean Dullerud, June 7, 1953; children—David, Mark, Kim, Joni, Scott. Vice pres. Nettleton Colls., Sioux City, Iowa, 1959-68; pres. Lear Siegler Career Center, Denver, 1968-72, Chaparral Career Coll., Tucson, 1972—. Mem. Oro Valley Town Council, 1975-78. Served with USMC, 1949-52. Mem. Am. Ind. Colls. and Schs. (pres. 1972, mem. of yr. 1979), Ariz. Pvt. Sch. Assn. Republican. Lutheran. Clubs: Tucson Breakfast, Oro Valley Country (past pres.). Contbr. articles to profl. jours. Home: 225 Oro Valley Dr Oro Valley AZ 85704 Office: 5001 E Speedway St Tucson AZ 95712

RIBAKOFF, CHARLES K., II, automotive mgmt. co. exec.; b. Cleve., Dec. 31, 1947; s. Eugene J. and Corrinne H. (Ascherman) R.; B.A., U. Va., 1969; M.B.A., Boston U., 1972; m. Phyllis Susan Dondis, May 25, 1978. Treas., Car Conditioners, Inc., Natick, Mass., 1971—; mktg. dir. Natick Auto Sales, Inc., 1971-73, gen. mgr., 1973-76, v.p., 1976—; v.p. Harr Lincoln Mercury Inc., Worcester, 1976—, Automotive Mgmt., Inc., Natick, 1977—, Natick Dodge, 1980—; pres. Charles Chevrolet, 1980—, AMI Fleet Group, 1980—, Boston Theatre Projects Inc., 1980—, Next Move Theatre, 1980—; instr. mktg. Boston U., 1973—. Mem. young leadership cabinet United Jewish Appeal; founder, 1st nat. chmn. student coordinating com. Israel Emergency Fund. Jewish. Club: Belmont Country. Office: PO Box 685 Natick MA 01760

RIBOUD, JEAN, oil service and electronics co. exec.; b. Lyon, France, Nov. 15, 1919; s. Camille and Helene (Frachon) R.; grad. Faculte de Droit, Ecoles des Scis. Politiques, Paris, 1939; m. Krishna Roy, Oct. 1, 1949; 1 son, Christophe. Exec. v.p. Schlumberger Ltd., 1963-65, pres., chief exec. officer, 1965—, chmn. bd., 1975—, also dir.; mem. internat. council Morgan Guaranty Trust Co. Clubs: Links, Sky, Links Golf (N.Y.C.); Blind Brook (N.Y.); LaBoulie (Paris); Desert Forest Golf (Carefree, Ariz.); Augusta (Ga.) Nat. Golf. Address: 277 Park Ave New York NY 10017

RICCARDI, JOSEPH ANTHONY, investment banker; b. N.Y.C., Sept. 8, 1929; s. Michael and Julia (Vittore) R.; B.B.A., CCNY, 1951; m. Leah R. Nichols, Oct. 26, 1963; children—Joseph Michael, Ellen Marie. Mgr. fin. analysis Gen. Electric Credit Corp., 1953-66; mgr. fin. analysis Eastern Airlines, 1966-67; treas. U.S. Aerolease Corp., 1967-69; v.p. investment banking div. Goldman Sachs & Co., N.Y.C., 1969—. Bd. dirs. United Way, Ridgewood, N.J., 1973-75. Served with U.S. Army, 1951-53. Mem. Assn. Equipment Lessors. Roman Catholic. Club: Ridgewood Country. Office: 55 Broad St New York NY 10004

RICCARDO, JOHN JOSEPH, automotive co. exec.; b. Little Falls, N.Y., July 2, 1924; s. Peter and Mary (Cirillo) R.; student N.Y. Coll. for Tchrs., 1942; B.A., U. Mich., 1949, M.A., 1950; LL.B. (hon.), No. Mich. U., 1971; Sc.D., Lawrence Inst. Tech., 1972; m. Thelma L. Fife, Aug. 5, 1950; children—Mary Catherine, Teresa Anna, Margaret Lynn, Peter Douglas, John Christopher. Mgr., Touche, Ross, Bailey & Smart, Detroit, 1950-59; financial staff exec. internat. ops. Chrysler Corp., Detroit, 1959-60, gen. mgr. Export-Import div., 1960-61, v.p., ops. mgr. Chrysler Can., 1961-62, exec. v.p. Chrysler Can., 1962-63, gen. sales mgr. Dodge div., 1963-64, asst. gen. mgr. Dodge div., 1964-65, asst. gen. mgr. Chrysler-Plymouth div., 1965-66, v.p. mktg., 1966, group v.p. domestic automotive, 1967, group v.p. U.S. and Can. automotive, 1967-70, pres., 1970-79, chmn., chief exec. officer, 1976-79; dir. Chrysler Fin. Corp.; mem. Nat. Bus. Council for Consumer Affairs; mem. automotive sub-council Nat. Indsl. Pollution Control Council. Lay chmn. Archdiocesan Devel. Fund, Detroit, 1968; gen. chmn. Meadowbrook Music Festival and Theater, Rochester, Mich., 1971; v.p., mem. exec. com. United Found., Detroit. Bd. dirs., mem. devel. council U. Mich. Served with AUS, 1943-45; CBI. C.P.A., Mich. Mem. Am. Inst. C.P.A.'s, Mich. Assn. C.P.A.'s, Motor Vehicle Mfrs. Assn (vice chmn.), Sales and Mktg. execs., Hwy. Users Fedn. (dir.), Phi Beta Kappa. Clubs: Bloomfield Hills Country; Detroit Athletic (pres. 1975), Detroit. Office: 900 Tower Dr Troy MI 48098*

RICE, CHARLES EDWARD, sign co. exec.; b. Independence, Kans., Mar. 18, 1944; s. Edward Forrest and Lilly Ethel (Duncan) R.; A.A., Independence Community Coll., 1974; m. Meredith A. Miller, July 11, 1965; children—Timothy, Paul, Soli, Eric. With Kans. Box & Lumber Co., Independence, 1968, Starcraft Inc., Independence, 1969-70; owner, mgr. Rice Sign Co., Independence, 1970—. Instr. hunter safety, Kans.; v.p. Montgomery County Taxpayers Assn., 1979-80. Served with USAF, 1965-68. Recipient cert. of merit for outstanding dedication to hunter safety edn. in Kans., 1980. Mem. Kans. Assn. Hunter Safety Instrs., Nat. Rifle Assn., Kans. Rifle Assn., Nat. Locksmith Assn., S.E. Kans. Woodcarvers Assn. Mem. Ch. of God. Clubs: Independence Gun; Joplin-Coffeyville Spokesmens. Home: Rural Route 1 Box 247 Neodesha KS 66757 Office: 122 W Main St Independence KS 67301

RICE, CHARLES EDWARD, banker; b. Tenn., Aug. 4, 1935; s. Charles Edward and Louise (Goodson) R.; B.B.A., U. Miami, 1958; M.B.A., Rollins Coll., 1964; grad. Advanced Mgmt. Program, Harvard U., 1975; m. Dianne Tauscher; children—Danny, Celeste, Michelle. Vice pres. Barnett Bank, Winter Park, Fla., 1965-67, pres., 1967-71; exec. v.p. Barnett Banks of Fla., Jacksonville, 1971-73, pres., 1973-79, pres., chief exec. officer, 1979—, also dir. Bd. dirs. St. Vincent Med. Center; trustee Rollins Coll. Club: Jacksonville Country. Office: 100 Laura St Jacksonville FL 32203*

RICE, DAVID FLEMING, corp. officer, real estate investor; b. Hawkinsville, Ga., Aug. 30, 1907; s. Alexander John and Janie (Fleming) R.; B.S. in Civil Engring., Ga. Inst. Tech., 1929; m. Erlyne Lanier, July 22, 1934; children—David Lanier, Robert Fleming; m. 2d, Anagene Bartram, Jan. 29, 1966 (div. 1969). Dept. head Sears Roebuck & Co., Atlanta, 1929-37; owner, operator Ellen Rice Restaurant, 1937-48, Town House Restaurant, 1948-54; officer various corps. Mem. Ga. Bd. Edn., 1961-76, vice chmn., 1970—, also mem. finance com.; area v.p. Nat. Assn. State Bds. Edn., 1966-68; mem. study mission Am. Assn. Sch. Adminstrs., USSR, 1969. Bd. regents U. System Ga., Atlanta, 1954-61. Mem. Nat., Ga. edn. assns., Am., Ga. vocational assns., Navy League U.S., Atlanta Restaurant Assn. (pres. 1945-46, 52), Internat. Platform Assn., Pi Delta Epsilon, Sigma Nu. Episcopalian. Rotarian. Club: Atlanta Athletic. Office: Suite 813 3060 Pharr Ct North NW Atlanta GA 30305

RICE, DENIS TIMLIN, lawyer; b. Milw., July 11, 1932; s. Cyrus Francis and Kathleen (Timlin) R.; A.B., Princeton U., 1954; J.D., U. Mich., 1959; children—James Connelly, Tracy Ellen. Admitted to Calif. bar, 1960; practiced in San Francisco, 1960—; asso. firm Pillsbury, Madison & Sutro, 1959-61, Howard & Prim. 1961-63; officer, dir. firm Howard, Prim, Rice, Nemerovski, Canady & Pollak, 1964—; sec., dir. Gensler & Assos., Inc., San Francisco. Sec., San Francisco Democratic Assn., 1960-61; councilman City of Tiburon, Calif., 1968-72, mayor, 1970-72; supr. Marin County, 1977—, chmn., 1979-80; dir. Marin County Transit Dist., 1970-72, 77—, chmn., 1979-81; mem. Marin Local Agy. Formation Commn., 1975—; del. Assn. Bay Area Govts., 1978—; mem. San Francisco Bay Conservation and Devel. Commn., 1977—, Met. Transp. Commn., 1980—. Served to 1st lt. AUS, 1955-57. Recipient Freedom Found. medal, 1956. Mem. State Bar Calif., Am. (fed. regulation of securities com.), San Francisco bar assns., Princeton Alumni Assn. No. Calif. (pres.), Am. Judicature Soc., Order of Coif, Phi Beta Kappa, Phi Delta Phi. Clubs: Tiburon Penisula, Corinthian Yacht (Tiburon, Calif.); Bankers, Univ., Olympic (San Francisco); Nassau (Princeton, N.J.). Home: 1463 Vistazo W Tiburon CA 94120 Office: 650 California St San Francisco CA 94108

RICE, DOROTHEA MCKIM (MRS. LEON RICE), tech. librarian; b. Worcester, Mass.; d. Paul and Katherine E. (McKim) Coine; A.B., Boston U., 1935, postgrad., 1937-38, Columbia, 1945-46, 52-53; m. Leon Rice, Apr. 20, 1946. Librarian, Boston Pub. Library, 1936-45; reference asst. 1st Nat. City Bank, N.Y.C., 1945-46; librarian Vick Chem. Co., N.Y.C., 1946-48; spl. project cataloger Port of N.Y. Authority, 1949; asst. librarian Nat. Indsl. Conf. Bd., 1949-51; tech. librarian Am. Metal Climax, Inc. (formerly Am. Metal Co., Ltd.), 1951-82. Vol. work various N.Y. hosps. Mem. Spl. Libraries Assn. (editor metals div. News; chmn. auditing com. 1956-58, chmn. nominating com. metals div. 1962-64, tech. div. 1966-67, chmn. pub. relations com. 1964, chmn. goals com. metals div. 1966-67, nat. chmn. non-serials publs. com. 1966-67, chmn. metals div. 1970, exec. bd. of tech.-sci. div. 1971), Am. Soc. Metals, Mus. Modern Art, Wilderness Soc., Delta Delta Delta. Unitarian. Address: 5D Carriage Dr R1 Brewster MA 02631

RICE, HENRY HART, real estate exec.; b. N.Y.C., Mar. 2, 1911; s. Sidney Henry and Maude (Jacobs) R.; student Townsend Harris Prep. Sch., 1924-26, N.Y. U., 1927; m. Grace Hecker, Aug. 9, 1936 (dec.); children—Edward Hart, Eve Hart; m. 2d, Margaret Goldfarb, Apr. 9, 1976. Real estate broker Hanford and Henderson, Inc., 1932-36, Butler & Baldwin, 1936-41; asst. adminstr. rent dept. OPA, tech. adviser Nat. Housing Agy., chief conversion mgmt. div., chief sales div. Fed. Pub. Housing Adminstrn., Washington, 1942-46, chief appraiser N.Y.C. regional office, 1947; v.p. J. Clarence Davies Realty Co., Inc., N.Y.C., 1947-53; v.p. James Felt & Co., Inc., N.Y.C. 1953-69, sr. v.p., 1969-73; exec. v.p. James Felt-Huberth & Huberth, Inc., 1973-75; chmn. bd. James Felt Realty, 1975—; v.p., dir. 480 Park Avenue Corp.; asso. prof. Sch. Continuing Edn. and Extension Services, N.Y. U.; former chmn. sales broker com. Real Estate Bd. N.Y.; bd. dirs. E. Side Assn., Realty Found. N.Y., N.Y.C. Public Devel. Corp.; adv. bd. N.Y. U. Real Estate Inst. Past trustee North Castle Free Library; bd. dirs. N.Y.C. Pub. Devel. Corp. Services, Inc., Recipient Most Ingenious Realtor award, 1957, 69, 79. Mem. N.Y.C. Real Estate Bd. (past gov., dir. brokerage div.), Am. Soc. Real Estate Counselors. Clubs: Nat. Realty, N.Y. U., Faculty. Editorial bd. Real Estate Rev. Home: 210 Hook Rd Katonah NY 10536 also 480 Park Ave New York NY 10028 Office: 488 Madison Ave New York NY 10022

RICE, JON MICHAEL, cutting tool mfg. co. exec.; b. Sturgis, Mich., Dec. 30, 1949; children—Stanley B. and Norma J. (West) R.; B.B.A., Western Mich. U., 1973; m. Cynthia K. Walworth, Aug. 23, 1969; children—Gabriel, Lucas, Kelly. Sales mgr. C.O. Porter Machinery Co., Grand Rapids, Mich., 1974-77; sales mgr. Electrode Dressers, Inc., Byron Center, Mich., 1977-78, v.p., gen. mgr., 1978—, also dir. Office: 7780 Clyde Park SW Byron Center MI 49315

RICE, JOSEPH ALBERT, banker; b. Cranford, N.J., Oct. 11, 1924; s. Louis A. and Elizabeth J. (Michael) R.; B.Aero. Engring., Rensselaer Poly. Inst., 1948; M.Indsl. Engring., N.Y. U., 1952, M.A., 1968; m. Katharine Wolfe, Sept. 11, 1948; children—Walter, Carol, Philip, Alan. With Grumman Aircraft Engring. Corp., 1948-53; with IBM, N.Y.C., 1953-65, mgr. ops., real estate, constrn. divs., 1963-65, dep. group exec. N.Am. Comml. telecommunications group, pres. telecommunications div. ITT Corp., N.Y.C., 1965-67; sr. v.p. Irving Trust Co., N.Y.C., 1967-69, exec. v.p., 1969-72, sr. exec. v.p., 1972-73, vice chmn., 1973-74, pres., 1974; also dir.; exec. v.p. Irving Bank Corp., 1971-74, vice chmn., 1974-75, pres., 1975—, also dir. Bd. dirs., chmn. Greater N.Y. Fund/United Way. Served to 1st lt. C.E., AUS, 1943-46. Mem. Assn. Bank Holding Cos. (dir. 1979). Clubs: Univ. (N.Y.C.); Sleepy Hollow Country (Scarborough, N.Y.). Home: 15 Rose Ln Chappaqua NY 10514 Office: 1 Wall St New York NY 10015

RICE, K(ENNETH) WAYNE, investment advisor; b. Richmond, Va., Feb. 28, 1944; s. R. Martin and Edith Gay Rice; B.S. in Archtl. Engring., Va. Poly. Inst., 1967; m. Sharon Carter Scruggs, Aug. 13, 1966; children—Donni Carter, Trevor Scott. With Wheeling Corrugating Co., 1967-68, 70-72, sales engr., Oakland, Calif., 1970-72; real estate salesman Multi Fin. Corp., Oakland, 1972-73; pres. Investment Research Group, Hayward, Calif., 1973—; chpt. dir. Constrn. Specifications Inst., 1971-72. Served with U.S. Army, 1968-70; Vietnam. Decorated Bronze Star; recipient various certs. appreciation. Mem. Am. Mgmt. Assn., Calif. Assn. Realtors, East Bay Exchange Assn. (dir. 1980), So. Alamadea Apts. Owners Assn. (pres., dir. 1977-79). Methodist. Office: 22634 2d St Suite 200 Hayward CA 94541

RICE, LAWRENCE ROGER, investment co. exec.; b. N.Y.C., July 20, 1946; s. Lewis Henry and Gloria Virginia (Hoffman) R.; B.A. in Econs., U. Calif., Los Angeles, 1967; M.B.A. in Finance, Columbia U., 1969; m. Joan Rathe. Analyst Dupont Walston, Inc., N.Y.C., 1969-74, E. F. Hutton & Co., Inc., 1974; v.p., dir. Bree, Rice & Co., Inc., 1975-76; v.p. Rosenkrantz, Ehrenkrantz, Lyon & Ross, Inc., 1977—. Served in N.Y. N.G., 1969-74. Mem. N.Y. Soc. Security Analysts, Entertainment Analysts Group, U. Calif. at Los Angeles Alumni Assn. Club: Columbia Bus. Sch. Office: 6 E 43d St New York NY 10017

RICE, LESLIE RAY, mfg. co. exec.; b. Johnstown, Pa., Oct. 20, 1932; s. Arthur and LaVerne Esther (Clevanger) R.; B.S. in Elec. Engring., U. Pitts., 1959, postgrad., 1962-63; postgrad. U. Rochester, 1959-60; m. Joan Marie Ozajkowski, Sept. 1, 1956; children—Kevin, Kelly, Shawn, Kristen. Design engr. mil. electronics Gen. Dynamics Co., 1959-62; project mgr. Transmission-Semicondr. div. Westinghouse Electric Co., New Stanton, Pa., 1962-68, reliability mgr. Semicondr. div., Youngwood, Pa., 1968-72; v.p. engring. Mansfield Products Co. (Ohio), 1972—; participant Internat. Meeting on High Voltage DC Transmission, U. Manchester (Eng.), 1966. Active Jr. Achievement, Boy Scouts Am., United Way. Served with U.S. Army, 1953-55. Mem. IEEE, Mansfield C. of C. Club: Elks. Contbr. articles to tech. jours., author 2 handbooks; patentee in field. Home: 1498 Brookpark Dr Mansfield OH 44906 Office: 246 E 4th St Mansfield OH 44902

RICE, MABEL MCCULLOUGH (MRS. CLINTON D. RICE), motor co. exec.; b. Lamoni, Iowa, Jan. 8, 1904; d. Issac and Bertha (Naylor) Bedell; B.Bus. Law, Blackstone Coll., Chgo., 1954-60; m. Guy Leroy McCullough, Aug. 1, 1921; 1 son, Gary; m. 2d, Clinton D. Rice, Aug. 13, 1948; 1 son, Clinton Thane. With McCullough Motor Co., Groundbirch, B.C., Can., 1936—, pres., 1948—, dir., 1936-72; officer Ringduck Corp., Mt. Ayr, Iowa; dir. Mount Ayr Developing Co. Bd. dirs. Ringgold County Hosp. Mem. Bus. and Profl. Women's Club. Republican. Methodist. Club: Order of Eastern Star (worthy matron 1928). Developer of land in Can. Address: 117 E Madison St Mount Ayr IA 50854 Office: Groundbirch BC Canada

RICE, MONTY GREY, marine, recreational vehicle co. exec.; b. Covington, Va., Nov. 11, 1946; s. Cyril Sanderson and Violet Marie (Hepler) R.; student Ferrum Jr. Coll. (Va.), 1965-66; B.S., Oreg. State U., 1970; m. Deborah Ann Janicek, Mar. 21, 1970; children—Joseph Sanderson, Patrick Grey. Mgr. firearms and motorcycle div. Cascade Merc Sports-Marine Inc., Salem, Oreg., 1971-74, v.p., gen. mgr., part-owner, 1977—; partner J & R Land Co., Salem, 1973—; instr. Dale Carnegie course on human relations and effective speaking. Mem. Town of Salem Sub-area Adv. C., 1977-78. Served with U.S. Army, 1970-71. Mem. NW Marine Trade Assn. Roman Catholic. Clubs: Rotary, Sertoma, Elks. Home: 1642 Marigold St NE Salem OR 97303 Office: 4490 River Rd N Salem OR 97303

RICE, RICHARD EDWARD, agribus. and dental products co. exec.; b. Lincoln, Nebr., Sept. 23, 1932; s. William J. and Anna Laura (Merrigan) R.; B.S., U. Nebr., 1957; M.B.A., U. Calif., Berkeley, 1959; m. Madeline M. Gourlay, May 12, 1956; children—William, James, Mary Elizabeth, Nancy. Vice pres. mktg. div. Norden Labs., Smith Kline, Lincoln, 1959-79; exec. v.p. Syntex Agribus. and Dental Products, Des Moines, 1979—. Bd. dirs. YMCA, Lincoln, Nebr., 1976-79, United Way, 1976-79, Animal Health Inst., Washington, 1980-83. Served with USAF, 1951-55. Republican. Roman Catholic. Home: 803 36th St West Des Moines IA 50265 Office: PO Box 863 Des Moines IA 50304

RICE, VICTOR ALBERT, mfg. co. exec.; b. Hitchin, Hertfordshire, Eng., Mar. 7, 1941; s. Albert Edward and Rosina Emmeline (Pallant) R.; m. Sharla C. Waitzman, June 25, 1970; children—Gregg, Kristin, Jonathan. Various fin. positions Ford Motor (U.K.), 1957-64, Cummins Engines (U.K.), 1964-67, Chrysler (U.K.), 1968-70, Perkins Engines Group Ltd. (U.K.), 1970-74; comptroller Massey-Ferguson Ltd., Toronto, Ont., Can., 1975-77, v.p. staff ops., 1977-78, pres., chief operating officer, 1978-80, chmn. bd., chief exec. officer, 1980—. Mem. Farm and Indsl. Equipment Inst. (dir.), Bd. Trade Met. Toronto, Fin. Execs. Inst., Am. Mgmt. Assn. (pres.'s assn.), Brit. Inst. Mktg., Inst. Dirs. Anglican. Clubs: Royal Can. Yacht, Toronto Golf (Toronto); Carlton (London). Office: 200 University Ave Toronto ON M5H 3E4 Canada

RICE, WILLIAM ADAM, indsl. supply co. exec.; b. Charleston, W.Va., July 19, 1919; s. Vaughan Stacey and Margaret Sue (Ryan) R.; A.B., Morris Harvey Coll., 1942; m. Shirley June Rosenbaum, Dec. 19, 1942; children—William Adam, Michael A., Joseph V. With Va. Welding Supply Co., Charleston, 1946—, pres., 1962—; pres. Bimjo Corp., Charleston, 1969—; dir. Bank of W.Va., Charleston. Chmn., Central W.Va. Airport Authority, 1972—; treas. W.Va. Econ. Devel. Authority, 1970—. Trustee, vice chmn. Charleston Area Med. Center, Morris Harvey Coll., 1972—; bd. dirs. Com. 100. Served with USNR, 1944-46. Recipient Morris Harvey Coll. 75th Anniversary Alumni Honor award, 1963. Mem. Am. Welding Soc., Nat. Welding Supply Assn. (pres. 1953-54). Mason (Shriner, Jester), Rotarian. Home: 1411 Connel Rd Charleston WV 25314 Office: One Oregon Charleston WV 25301

RICE, WILLIAM DAVID, advt. agy. exec.; b. Salt Lake City, Jan. 30, 1920; s. William and Elsie (Cohn) R.; B.S. in Chemistry, U. Utah, 1942; m. Adrienne Schwartz, Mar. 3, 1957 (dec. May 1964); m. 2d, JoAnne Twelves, Nov. 9, 1966; children—William E., Robert G., Taylor D., James A. Pres. Advt. Research Assos., Salt Lake City, 1946-47; v.p. Cooper & Crowe Inc., advt., Salt Lake City, 1947-53, pres. Demiris, Rice & Assos., Inc., Salt Lake City, 1953—. Pres., Utah Travelers Aid Soc., 1972-73, Salt Lake Mental Health Assn., 1961-62, Utah Assn. Mental Health, 1964-66; v.p. communications Nat. Assn. Mental Health, 1973-75; chmn. Utah Mental Health Adv. Council, 1978-80; bd. dirs. Hospice of Salt Lake City, 1978—; chmn. com. for severely mentally impaired, Salt Lake City, 1979—. Served to comdr. USNR, 1941-46. Mem. Am. Inst. Mgmt. (pres.'s council 1971, 72), Mensa (Utah proctor 1970—), Utah Assn. Advt. Agencies, Internat. Platform Assn. Clubs: Salt Lake Ad, Univ. Home: 1435 Military Way Salt Lake City UT 84103 Office: Demiris Rice & Assos 429 Atlas Bldg Salt Lake City UT 84101

RICE, WILLIAM THOMAS, railroad exec.; b. Hague, Va., June 13, 1912; s. John and Elizabeth Conway (Snow) R.; B.S. in Civil Engring., Va. Poly. Inst., 1934; LL.D. (hon.), Stetson U., 1959; m. Jaqueline Johnston, Sept. 14, 1935; children—John Thomas, Jaqueline Norma. With Pa. R.R., 1934-42; joined Richmond, Fredericksburg & Potomac R.R., 1946, pres., dir., 1955-57; pres., dir., mem. exec. com. Atlantic Coast Line R.R. Co. (merged into Seaboard Coast Line R.R. 1967), 1957—; now chmn. emeritus, mem. exec. com., dir. Seaboard Coast Line Industries; dir. Seaboard Coast Line R.R., Louisville & Nashville R.R., First and Mchts. Nat. Bank of Richmond, Fla. Nat. Bank of Jacksonville, Graniteville Co., Home Ins. Co., Chem. Bank, Commonwealth Nat. Gas Co., Richmond, Fla. Rock Industries. Trustee Va. Mus. Fine Arts. Served from 1st lt. to lt. col. AUS, 1942-46; maj. gen. Res. ret. Decorated Legion of Merit With 2 oak leaf clusters. Mem. Newcomen Soc., Omicron Delta Kappa, Tau Beta Pi. Episcopalian. Rotarian. Clubs: Sky, Union League (N.Y.C.); Metropolitan (Washington); Country of Va., Commonwealth (Richmond, Va.); River, Timuquana Country (Jacksonville, Fla.); Augusta (Ga.) Nat.; Burning Tree (Md.). Home: 8739 Riverside Dr Richmond VA 23235 Office: Seaboard Coast Line R R Co 3600 W Broad St Richmond VA 23230

RICE, WILLIAM YNGVE, petroleum distbg. co. exec.; b. Tyler, Tex., June 22, 1930; s. John Herbert and Mamie Lucille (Horton) R.; B.B.A. in Mgmt., Baylor U., 1951; m. Rachel Gallenkemp, Jan. 26, 1952; children—William Yngve III, John Robin, Drew. With accounting dept. Tex. Eastman Co., 1951-58; partner in petroleum product sales co. for Cities Service Oil Co., 1958-70; pres., dir. Eastex Oil Co. Inc., Longview, Tex., 1970-79; partner Magnum Corp., 1979—; chmn. Town North Nat. Bank, Longview; dir. Southland Savs. & Loan, Longview, Amectran, Inc., Dallas, Reliable Warehouse, Inc., Longview, Computer Funds Inc., Dallas. Chmn. bd. deacons First Baptist Ch., Longview; city commr. Longview, 1969-80, mayor, 1970-71, 76-77; vice chmn. East Tex. Council Govts., 1970; dir. Sabine River Authority of Tex. Recipient Longview Outstanding Citizen of Yr. award, 1971; Community Achievement award Phillips Petroleum Co., 1975. Mem. Tex. Oil Marketers Assn., Nat. Oil Jobber Council, East Tex., Longview chambers commerce, Delta Sigma Pi. Clubs: Longview Rotary; Dallas-Caddo; Oak Forest Country; Baylor-Longview, Masons. Home: 1308 Inverness St Longview TX 75601 Office: Box 1406 Longview TX 75601

RICH, ERIC, sales exec.; b. Znojmo, Czechoslovakia, Oct. 1, 1921; s. Sandor and Alice (Schifferes) Reich; ed. U. Coll. Wales, Bangor; m. Ilse L. B. Renard, Nov. 14, 1959; children—Susan Frances, Sally Dora, Charles Anthony. Came to U.S., 1955, naturalized, 1962. Export sales mgr. Pilot Radio, Ltd., London, 1945-49; dir. Derwent Exports, Ltd., London, 1949-55; export sales mgr. Am. Molding Powder & Chem. Corp., N.Y.C., 1956-58; with Gering Plastics Co. dept. Monsanto Chem. Co., Kenilworth, N.J., 1958-67; v.p., gen. mgr. Goldmark Plastics Internat., Inc., New Hyde Park, N.Y., 1967—. Served with RAF, 1941-45. Decorated Gallantry medal, 1939-43 Star, Atlantic Star. Home: 111 7th St Garden City NY 11530 Office: Nassau Terminal Rd New Hyde Park NY 11040

RICH, GAIUS BARRETT, IV, banker; b. Lexington, Ky., Aug. 2, 1932; s. Baius Barrett and Ruth Jenkins R.; ed. Yale U.; m. Marguerite Post, Sept. 12, 1959; children—Jonathan, David, Louise. Vice pres. Citibank N.A. Ltd., South Africa. Bd. dirs., treas. Am. Friends of Community Devel. Served with arty., U.S. Army, 1954-56. Mem. Am. Soc. Johannesburg (pres. 1978-79), Am. C. of C. of Johannesburg. Clubs: Yale (N.Y.C.); Wanderers (Johannesburg). Home: 104 Forest Rd Johannesburg 2001 South Africa Office: Citibank NA Ltd PO Box 9773 Johannesburg 2000 South Africa*

RICH, JOHN DANIEL, mgmt. cons.; b. Atlanta, May 29, 1927; s. Les J. and Jonita G. Rich; B.S., U. Pa., 1948; M.A., Sorbonne, 1949; m. Nanette Offray, Jan. 25, 1957; children—Karen, Douglas, Bryan. Vice pres. Dreyfus Ashby, N.Y.C., 1951; dir. mktg. Van Munching Imports, N.Y.C., 1956; nat. sales mgr. credit card div. Am. Express Co., N.Y.C., 1958-60; account supr. Ted Bates, N.Y.C., 1960-62; asso. dir. mktg. Pepsi Cola, N.Y.C., 1962-65; prin. John D. Rich & Partners, N.Y.C., 1965-72; pres. Fry Cons., N.Y.C., 1977—. Mem. Republican Town Com., Wilton, Conn. Mem. Assn. Cons. Mgmt. Engrs. (public relations com.). Republican. Episcopalian. Clubs: Princeton (N.Y.C.); U. Pa. of Fairfield County (pres.) (Conn.); Wilton (Conn.) Riding, Confrerie des Chevaliers des Tastevins. Home: 90 Olmstead Hill Wilton CT 06897 Office: 60 E 42d St New York NY 10017

RICHARDS, ALBERT EDWARD, catalyst mfg. co. exec.; b. Portsmouth, Eng., May 7, 1914; s. Charles Henry and Elizabeth (Hunt) R.; B.Sc. with 1st class honours, London U., 1936; m. Frances Lorraine Milton, May 13, 1939; children—Edward William, Carol Anne, Virginia Frances. With Johnson, Matthey & Co., Ltd., London, Eng., 1933-54; gen. mgr. Universal-Matthey Products, Ltd., Enfield, Eng., 1954-60, mng. dir., 1960-78, dir., 1978—; pres. dir. gen. Universal-Matthey Products (France), S.A., Paris, 1962-79; pres. Universal-Matthey Products (Italia), Rome, 1965—; Geschaftsfuhrer, Universal-Matthey Products (Deutschland), Cologne, Germany, 1959-79; dir. Johnson, Matthey & Co. Fellow Inst. Mining and Metallurgy. Home: 3 The Ave Potters Bar Hertfordshire England Office: 100 High St Southgate North London England

RICHARDS, ANDREW JOHN, III, cocoa mfg. co. exec.; b. Phila., Sept. 29, 1939; s. Andrew John and Alice (Brooks) R.; B.S. in Bus. Adminstrn., Temple U., 1965; m. June 13, 1968; children—Cheryl Lynn, Donna Marie, Karen Ann, Daniel Christopher. Controller Goren Foods Co., Inc., Thorofare, N.J., 1968-72; controller I.C.P. Cocoa Inc., Glassboro, N.J., 1972-80, treas., 1980—, also dir.; dir. ICAM, Inc. Served with U.S. Army, 1956-59. Mem. Nat. Assn. Accts. Office: ICP Cocoa Inc 600 Ellis Rd Glassboro NJ 08028

RICHARDS, CHRISTINE-LOUISE, artist, publishing co. exec.; b. Radnor, Pa., Jan. 11, 1910; d. Joseph Ernest and Catherine (Fletcher) R.; student pvt. schs.; art schs., N.Y.C., Munich, Germany. One-woman shows; Stockbridge, Mass., 1947, 48, 52, 53, Oneonta, N.Y., 1960, 61; exhibited in group shows Stockbridge Art Assn., 1931-32; represented in permanent collections; Calif., Mass., N.Y.; owner, founder, pres. Blue Star Music Pub. Co., Pittsfield, Mass., 1946—, now Morris, N.Y. Mem. Phila. Art Alliance, Am. Fedn. Musicians, Nightingale-Bamford Alumni Assn., Met. Mus. Art, Audubon Soc., Nat. Assn. Am. Composers U.S.A., Emergency Aid of Pa., Pa. Acad. Fine Arts, Accademia Italia della Arti d del Lavora (Gold medal). Club: Peale (Phila.). Author and illustrator: The Blue Star Fairy Book of Stories for Children; The Blue Star Fairy Book of More Stories for Children; The Blue Star Fairy Book of New Stories for Children, 1980. Composer: (song) What Makes Me Dream of You, 1950, others. Contbr. portrait to Artists U.S.A., 1970-71. Address: Blue Star Music PO Box 185 Morris NY 13808

RICHARDS, DAVID LAMONT, metall. engr.; b. New Castle, Pa., Apr. 5, 1947; s. Karl Lamont and Shirley Ruth (Clausen) R.; student Westminster Coll., 1975, Youngstown State U., 1976-77, Kent State U., 1977-79, Metal Engring. Inst., 1977-78. With indsl. sales dept. New Castle Battery Mfg. Co. (Pa.), 1971-74; with quality control dept. Universal Rundle Corp., New Castle, 1974; metallurgist Copperweld Steel Co., Warren, Ohio, 1975—, asst. supr. personnel, 1978-79, asst. supr. employment and benefits, 1979—; adj. instr. Kent State U.; guest lectr. Trumbull County Joint Vocat. Schs. Mem. bus. tech. adv. com. Kent State U.; past div. chmn. indsl. div. United Fund; com. adv. Warren Trumbull Urban League. Served with USAF, 1965. Mem. Am. Soc. for Metals, Am. Inst. Mining, Metall. and Petroleum Engrs., Personnel Assn. Eastern Ohio and Western Pa., Nat. Psychiat. Assn., Smithsonian Nat. Assos. Republican. Presbyterian. Home: care Karl Richards Rd 5 Lakewood Beach New Castle PA 16105 Office: 4085 Mahoning Ave Warren OH 44483

RICHARDS, EDWARD F., graphic arts co. exec., artist; b. Peoria, Ill., Apr. 7, 1939; s. Stephen Jerome and Maureen Alice (O'Grady) R.; B.F.A., U. Ill., Champaign-Urbana, 1959; M.B.A., Loyola U., Chgo., 1961; m. Angela Marie Steffano, June 11, 1960; 1 son, Andre. Comml. artist Terra Arts, Inc., Chgo., 1961-63, creative dir., 1963-66, v.p. prodn., 1966-71; owner, pres. Dezign, Ltd., 1971—, Graphics, Ltd., 1978—; instr. graphic design Northwestern Evening Div., Chgo., 1966—; exhibited in numerous one man and group shows. Democratic precinct capt., 1970—; bd. dirs. D.A. Smythe Found., 1970—. Mem. Am. Assn. Graphic Artists. Roman Catholic. Clubs: K.C., Rotary, Kiwanis, Ill. Athletic. Author: Graphic Design for the Novice, 1972. Home: 1218 Roosevelt Ave Glenview IL 60025

RICHARDS, GARY WALTER, fin. exec.; b. Reno, Nev., Jan. 13, 1941; s. Curtis Franklin and Jewell Dean (Rorie) R.; B.S., Okla. State U., 1962; student law U. Mo. at Kansas City, 1970-72; m. Karen Lee Kirk, May 28, 1964; children—Kirk Richards, Kevin Richards. Dir. univ. program People to People, Inc., Kansas City, Mo., 1962-64; stockbroker Dean Witter & Co., Inc., Kansas City, Mo., 1964-70; trust officer United Mo. Bank, Kansas City, 1970-72; dir. pension services B.C. Christopher & Co., Kansas City, Mo., 1972-73; mgr. employee benefits Peat, Marwick, Mitchell & Co., Kansas City, Mo., 1973-77; pres. Fin. Mgmt. Cons.'s, Inc., Overland Park, Kans., 1977—; asso. Alec Mackenzie & Assoc., Inc., Greenwich, N.Y., 1977—; condr. numerous time mgmt. and fin. planning seminars, U.S., Can., Brazil, Eng., Belgium, Germany, Holland. Bd. govs. Bacchus Cultural & Ednl. Found., 1970-73. Certified fin. planner; lic. instr. personal money mgmt. tng. course. Mem. Guild Friends of Art (pres. 1970-71), Nat. Assn. Pvt. Pension and Welfare Plans (regional chmn. 1977-79),

Am. Mgmt. Assn., Internat. Assn. Fin. Planners, Inst. Certified Fin. Planners (editorial rev. bd. jour. 1979—). Club: Mission Hills. Office: Suite 110 4801 W 110th St Overland Park KS 66211

RICHARDS, GILBERT FRANCIS, mfg. co. exec.; b. Prairieburg, Iowa, Nov. 2, 1915; s. Raymond D. and Theresa (O'Connor) R.; ed. Tilton Acad.; LL.D., Ursinus Coll., 1973; m. Mary Elizabeth Hanchett, May 13, 1959; children—Patricia Richards Roorda, Michael, Sheri Stanton (Mrs. M.D. McManus), Jan Stanton (Mrs. T.E. Johnson), Lauri Stanton (Mrs. C.R. Taylor), James Stanton, Mary Elizabeth. Dist. mgr. Permanente Cement Co., 1944-45; dist. sales mgr. Kaiser Gypsum Co., 1945-48, gen. sales mgr., 1948-52; gen. sales mgr. Kaiser Metal Products, 1952-56; v.p. sales Sharples Corp., 1956-58; with The Budd Co., Phila., 1958—, gen. mgr. sales automotive div., 1958-65, v.p., gen. mgr. automotive div., 1965-68, pres., gen. mgr. automotive div., 1968-71, exec. v.p. automotive products, 1971, pres., chief exec. officer, 1971-74, chmn., chief exec. officer, 1974—, also dir.; dir. Budd Can., Inc., Transport Indemnity, Los Angeles, Fed. Mogul Corp., Thyssen Industrie, W. Ger. Bd. dirs. United Found. of Detroit; gen. chmn. Greater Detroit Torch Drive, 1971. Mem. Western Hwy. Inst. (dir.), Econ. Club Detroit (dir.), Hwy. Users Fedn. Safety and Mobility, Traffic Safety Assn. Mich., Traffic Improvement Assn. Oakland County (dir.), Am. Def. Preparedness Assn., Am. Mfrs. Assn., Soc. Automotive Engrs. Clubs: Detroit, Bloomfield Hills (Mich.) Country; Eldorado Country, Marrakesh Country (Palm Desert, Calif.); Yondotega. Home: 1009 Stratford Ln Bloomfield Hills MI 48013 Office: 3155 W Big Beaver Rd Troy MI 48084

RICHARDS, H. REX, textile chemist, educator; b. Timmins, Ont., Can., Feb. 9, 1926; came to U.S., 1971, naturalized, 1977; s. Ewart and Louise (Trevithick) R.; B.S. in Chemistry, Leeds (Eng.) U., 1949, Ph.D. in Textile Sci. (Courtaulds scholar, Internat. Wool Secretariat fellow), 1954; m. Yvette Shaw, Aug. 6, 1949; children—Carol-Niki, Elaine. Textile chemist Bradford (Eng.) Dyers' Assn., 1954-56; sr. phys. chemist Def. Research Bd., Ottawa, Ont., 1956-62, staff officer, 1962-64; prof., head dept. textiles, clothing and design U. Guelph (Ont.), 1964-71; prof. textiles and clothing Colo. State U., Ft. Collins, 1971—, head dept., 1971—; cons. in field. Recipient Can. Textile Sci. award, 1968; various research grants. Fellow Textile Inst., Plastics and Rubber Inst.; mem. Inst. Textile Sci. (pres. 1965-66), Fiber Soc., Am. Assn. Textile Chemists and Colorists, Sigma Xi. Contbr. articles to profl. jours. Office: 314 Gifford Bldg Colo State U Fort Collins CO 80523

RICHARDS, ROBERT L., business exec.; b. 1927; student Canton Bus. Coll.; married. Vice pres. truck components group Eaton Corp., 1979; pres., chief exec. officer, dir. GF Bus. Equipment Co. Inc., Youngstown, Ohio; dir. Eaton Mfrs. S.A., Mex., Koyo Eaton Co. Ltd., Japan, Eaton Axles Ltd., Warrington, Eng., Peoples BancShares Inc. Office: 416 E Dennick Ave Box 1108 Youngstown OH 44501*

RICHARDS, WILLIAM GEORGE, savs. and loan exec.; b. Lockhart, Tex., Feb. 20, 1920; s. Cyrus F. and Gussie (Baldridge) R.; LL.B., U. Tex., 1948; m. Winnifred Adams, Nov. 23, 1940 (dec. May 1969); children—Bettye Ann (Mrs. Rogers), Mark Andrew; m. 2d, Corrie Marsh, Mar. 29, 1972. Admitted to Tex. bar, 1948; practiced law with father, Lockhart, 1948-55; v.p., atty., dir. Lockhart Savs. & Loan Assn., 1948-55; exec. v.p. Benjamin Franklin Savs. & Loan Assn., 1955-64, pres., 1964-74, vice-chmn. bd., 1974-75; chmn. bd., chief exec. officer Surety Savs. Assn., Houston, 1977-79; trustee Savs. & Loan Found., Inc., 1957-59. Mem. Tex. Ho. of Reps., 1947-50; mayor of Lockhart, 1954-55. Mem. adv. com. Coll. Bus. Adminstrn. U. Houston, 1966-70. Served with USNR, 1942-45. Mem. Nat. League Insured Savs. Assns. (exec. com. 1962-66), Houston C. of C. (dir. 1966, 68-73), Tex. Savs. and Loan League (dir. 1953-63, 63-66; pres. 1967-68), Phi Delta Phi. Democrat. Episcopalian. Clubs: Onion Creek, The Citadel, Austin (Austin). Home: 11007 Pinehurst Dr Austin TX 78747

RICHARDSON, DEAN EUGENE, banker; b. West Branch, Mich., Dec. 27, 1927; s. Robert F. and Helen (Husted) R.; A.B., Mich. State U., 1950; LL.B., U. Mich., 1953; postgrad. Stonier Grad. Sch. Banking, 1965; m. Barbara Trytten, June 14, 1952; children—Ann Elizabeth, John Matthew. With Indsl. Nat. Bank, Detroit, 1953-55; with Mfrs. Nat. Bank, Detroit, 1955—, v.p. adminstrn., 1964-66, sr. v.p., 1966-67, exec. v.p., 1967-69, pres., chief exec., 1969—, also chmn., dir.; chmn. bd. dirs. Mrs.-Detroit Internat. Corp., 1973—; gov. Adela Corp. of Luxembourg, Atlantic Internat. Bank of London; dir. Detroit Edison Co., R.P. Scherer Corp., Tecumseh Products Co. Served with USNR, 1945-46. Mem. Mich., Detroit bar assns., Assn. Res. City Bankers, Am. Inst. Banking, Men's Forum, Robert Morris Assos., Econ. Club Detroit (dir.), Newcomen Soc. N. Am. Episcopalian. Mason (K.T.) Clubs: Detroit Athletic, Detroit, Country of Detroit. Office: Mfrs Nat Corp 100 Renaissance Center Detroit MI 48243*

RICHARDSON, EDDIE PRICE, II, publisher; b. Carrolton, Miss., Mar. 29, 1936; s. Eddie Price and Helen Richardson; student U. Md., 1956-60, McNease State Coll., 1960-63; m. Kathy Shorter, Apr. 5, 1958; children—Karen, Angie. Exec. dir., Lubbock (Tex.) Opportunities Industrialization Center, 1970-74; asst. mgr. Wyatt's Cafeteria, Abilene and Lubbock, 1974-76; co-publisher, mng. editor Lubbock Digest Newspaper, 1977—; cons. Eddie P. Richardson & Assos., Lubbock, 1970—. Served with USAF, 1954-64; Vietnam. Laos. Mem. U.S. Black C. of C. (founder Lubbock chpt.), VFW (dir.), Nat. Bus. League. Democrat. Roman Catholic. Clubs: Merry Makers, Shriners, Masons, others. Mem. Gov's. Council on Children and Youth, 1969, Mayor's Council on Vets, 1970-72; bd. dirs. ACLU, 1969-73. Syndicated columnist My Views, 1969—, Why Not?, 1977—. Home: 5013 57th St Lubbock TX 79414 Office: 510 E 23d St Lubbock TX 79404

RICHARDSON, FRANCIS JOSEPH, III, investment counsel, investment analyst, fin. analyst; b. New Orleans, Mar. 22, 1943; s. Francis J. and Stella M. (Schulze) R.; B.B.A., Tulane U., 1965, postgrad. Tax Insts., 1967-74; M.B.A., Loyola U., New Orleans, 1970; postgrad. Goethe Inst., W. Ger., summer 1966; cert. Am. Inst. Banking, 1972; postgrad. Sch. Banking of South, La. State U., 1975; m. Carolyn Mary Bienvenu, Apr. 17, 1971; children—Caroline LeGardeur, Edward Emile. Jr. mech. engr. Michoud plant, Saturn launch systems br. Boeing Aerospace, New Orleans, 1964-66; various positions IBM Computer Systems Engring., New Orleans, 1966-71; investment service rep. First Nat. Bank of Commerce, New Orleans, 1971-76, v.p. and mgr. trust investment dept., 1976-78, investment counsel, fin. analyst, 1978—; account exec., registered rep. William O'Neil & Co. Inc. of Los Angeles, New Orleans, 1978-79; account exec. retail/instl. Bache, Halsey, Stuart, Shields, New Orleans, 1979—. Mem. Republican State Central Com., 1st Rep. Dist., 1969-70; bd. dirs. Big Bros., 1973-74, Museums Com. Jeuness D'Orleans, 1974-75. Fellow Fin. Analysts Fedn.; mem. Fin. Analysts Soc. New Orleans, Assn. M.B.A. Execs., New Orleans C. of C. (del. 1974-75), Le Debut de Jeunnes Filles Novelle Orleans, Navy League, Am. Econ. Assn., Am. Mgmt. Assn., La. Soc. SAR (state treas. 1973-74), Mil. Order Fgn. Wars, Mil. and Hospitaller Order St. Lazarus of Jerusalem (So. del. editor), Thackeray Soc. New Orleans (founding dir.), Soc. War of 1812 New Orleans, Tulane Assn. Bus. Alumni, Phi Delta Phi (Cert. of Merit 1970), Young Men's Bus. Club Greater New Orleans (dir. 1965-68), Alpha Tau Omega. Roman Catholic. Clubs: Masons, So. Yacht; Calif. Yacht (Marina del Rey); New Orleans Country, New Orleans Athletic, Roundtable of New Orleans (sec. 1972-74); Wailers Ski (Los Angeles); Rotary. Home and Office: PO Drawer 52768 New Orleans LA 70152

RICHARDSON, GEORGE TAYLOR, business exec.; b. Winnipeg, Man., Can., Sept. 22, 1924; s. James A. and Muriel (Sprague) R.; B.Commerce, U. Man., 1946, LL.D., 1969; m. Tannis Maree Thorlakson, Oct. 30, 1948; children—David, Hartley, Karen. With James Richardson & Sons, Ltd., Winnipeg, 1946—, v.p., 1954-66, pres., 1966—; sr. partner Richardson Securities Can., 1947—; dir. Pioneer Grain Co., Ltd., 1946—, pres., 1964-71, chmn. bd., 1971—; dir. Richardson Terminals, Ltd., 1946—, pres., 1964-71, chmn., 1971—; chmn. bd. Richardson Securities, Inc., N.Y.C. and Chgo., 1968—; gov. Hudson's Bay Co., Winnipeg; dir. Hudson's Bay Oil & Gas Co. Ltd., Inco Ltd.; v.p., dir. Can. Imperial Bank Commerce, Toronto; pres. Lombard Pl., Ltd., Winnipeg, 1968; mem. Toronto, Midwest stock exchanges, Chgo. Bd. Trade, Winnipeg Commodity Exchange, Chgo. Merc. Exchange, Commodity Exchange, Inc. Hon. dir. Can. Aviation Hall of Fame. Named hon. col. City of Winnipeg Air Res. Squadron. Home: Briarmeade Lot 197 St Mary's Rd St Germain PO MB R0G 2A0 Canada Office: Richardson Bldg 30th Floor One Lombard Pl Winnipeg MB R3B 0Y1 Canada

RICHARDSON, HERBERT HEATH, mech. engr.; b. Lynn, Mass., Sept. 24, 1930; s. Walter Blake and Isabel Emily (Heath); S.B., S.M. with honors, M.I.T., 1955, Sc.D., 1958; m. Barbara Ellsworth, Oct. 6, 1973. Research asst., research engr. Dynamic Analysis and Control Lab., M.I.T., 1953-57, instr., 1957-58, mem. faculty, 1958—, prof. mech. engring., 1968—, head dept., 1974—; with Ballistics Research Lab., Aberdeen Proving Ground, Md., 1958; chief scientist Dept. Transp., Washington, 1970-72; sr. cons. Foster-Miller Assos. Served as officer U.S. Army, 1968. Recipient medal Am. Ordnance Assn., 1953; Gold medal Pi Tau Sigma, 1963; Meritorious Service award and medal Dept. Transp., 1972; registered profl. engr., Mass. Fellow ASME (Moody award fluids engring. div. 1970); mem. Nat. Acad. Engring., N.Y. Acad. Sci., Am. Soc. Engring. Edn., Advanced Transit Assn., Sigma Xi, Tau Beta Pi. Author: Introduction to System Dynamics, 1971; also articles. Home: 4 Latisquama Rd Southboro MA 01772 Office: Room 3-173 MIT Cambridge MA 02139

RICHARDSON, HERBERT WAYNE, mall adminstr., writer; b. McKeesport, Pa., Oct. 16, 1946; s. George and Lois Irene (Dietz) R.; diploma Famous Writers Sch., 1973; B.S. in Humanities, Calif. State Coll., 1976, M.A. in Communications, 1978; m. Victoria Anna Bielawski, Sept. 26, 1970; 1 son, Richard Wayne. Asst. dept. mgr. Donora Motors Inc. (Pa.), 1971-72; dept. mgr. Leo Hughes Ford Sales, Brownsville, Pa., 1972; asst. dept. mgr. W.T. Grant Co., Belle Vernon, Pa., 1972-75; head student prodns. Cal-Tel Studios, California, Pa., 1974-76; programming and prodn. mgr. Chartiers Valley Cablevision Co., Canonsburg, Pa., 1977; grad. asst. dept. communications California (Pa.) State Coll., 1977-78; communications exec. WaynCo Writing, Arlington, Tex., from 1978; now maintenance mgr. Six Flags Mall, Arlington. Asst. coach baseball YMCA, 1979; football coach Optimists, 1979; active PTA. Mem. Stella Woodall Poetry Soc. Internat., Arlington Gifted and Talented Assn., Pi Delta Epsilon. Clubs: Lions, Optimists. Contbr. poetry to various publs. Home and Office: 2406 Reever Ave Arlington TX 76010

RICHARDSON, JAMES E., hosp. adminstr.; b. Ruston, La., Mar. 23, 1949; s. James and Martha Evelyn (Rives) R.; B.S., La. Tech. U., 1972; postgrad. U. Ala., 1975-76; m. Paula Sue Frisby, May 19, 1973; M.B.A., Pepperdine U., 1980. Auditor, Blue Cross of La., 1972, sr. auditor, 1973; controller Savoy (La.) Meml. Hosp. Found., 1974-76, exec. dir., 1976—; pres. Health Care Fin. Mgmt., Inc., Mamou, 1976—; bd. dirs. Savoy Pharmacy; bd. dirs., sec.-treas. Aquarius Offshore Logistics, Inc. Vice pres. Acadian Acres Assn., 1976—. Mem. Hosp. Fin. Mgmt. Assn., Hosp. Mgmt. Systems Soc., Mid-La. Health Systems Agency. Democrat. Baptist. Club: Rotary (past pres.). Home: 812 Elm St Mamou LA 70554 Office: 801 Poinciana Ave Mamou LA 70554

RICHARDSON, JOSEPH LEONARD, bus. exec.; b. Kansas City, Mo., Apr. 23, 1940; s. Joseph and Genevieve A. R.; B.A. in Sociology, Lincoln U., 1964; m. Jacqueline O. Webb, July 24, 1976; 1 dau., Jolawn. Employment rep. Butler Mfg. Co., Kansas City, 1968-69, div. employee relations mgr., Mpls., 1970-72; cons. John Tschohl & Assos., Mpls., 1972-73; acct. rep. Mgmt. Recruiters, Mpls., 1973-76; tng. mgr. The Toro Co., Bloomington, Minn., 1976-80; pres. J. R. & Assos., Inc., Burnsville, Minn., 1980—. Pres. Pan Hellenic Council, 1977—, Great Circle Factory; bd. dirs. Greater Kansas City Jr. Achievement, 1964, Phyllis Wheatley House, Mpls., 1971-72. Served with M.P., AUS, 1964-68; Vietnam. Decorated Army Commendation medal with oak leaf cluster; named Rookie of Year, Minn. Employment Assn., 1974. Mem. Am. Soc. Tng. and Devel., Twin City Personnel Assn., Am. Soc. Personnel Adminstrs., Alpha Phi Alpha. Clubs: Rotary, Investment (pres. 1971-73). Methodist. Home: 11505 22d Ave S Burnsville MN 55337 Office: 101 W Burnsville Pkwy Burnsville MN 55337

RICHARDSON, LEE, JR., consumer affairs cons.; b. Washington, July 8, 1940; s. Stewart and Margaret Jane (Strachan) R.; B.S., U. Richmond, 1962; M.B.A., Emory U., 1963; D.B.A., U. Colo., 1966; m. Doralee Alice Forsythe, Dec. 23, 1960; children—Lee-Ellen, Stewart, Lauren. Mem. faculty dept. mktg. La. State U., 1966-77, prof., chmn., 1974-77; dir. U.S. Office Consumer Affairs, Washington, 1977-79; consumer affairs cons., Columbia, Md., 1979—. Mem. Consumer Fedn. Am. (pres. 1976-77, dir. 1980—), Am. Nat. Metric Council (dir., chmn. consumer liaison com.). Co-editor Readings in Corporation Finance, 1966; Readings in Marketing, 1967. Editor: Dimensions of Communication, 1969. Office: PO Box 1106 Columbia MD 21044

RICHARDSON, MARION WACHTER, title co. exec.; b. Jamaica, N.Y., Oct. 7, 1947; d. Raymond C. and Marion I (Heid) Dezendorf; student public schs., N.Y.C.; m. Frank K. Richardson, Apr. 6, 1980; 1 son, Eric George Wachter. With U.S. Life Title Ins. Co. and predecessor, 1966—, title examiner and reader, White Plains, N.Y., 1975-77, adminstrv. asst., New City, N.Y., 1977-78, asst. v.p., office mgr., 1978—. Mem. Am. Soc. Profl. and Exec. Women. Office: 20 S Main St New City NY 10956

RICHARDSON, ROBERT A., lawyer; b. Cleve., Feb. 15, 1939; s. Allen B. and Margaret C. (Thomas) R.; B.A., Ohio Wesleyan U., 1961; LL.B., Harvard, 1964; m. Carolyn Eck. Admitted to Ohio bar, 1964; asso. firm Calfee, Halter & Griswold, 1969-72, partner, 1972—; mem. nat. panel Am. Arbitration Assn., 1966—; lectr. securities law, corp. law Cleve. State U., 1972-76. Trustee, Big Bros. Greater Cleve., 1974—, v.p., 1975-76, pres., 1977-78; exec. com. of men's com. Cleve. Playhouse, 1979—, trustee, 1981—; trustee Neighborhood Centers, 1981—. Mem. Am., Ohio State, Cleve. (social chmn. young lawyers sect. 1967, law day chmn. 1968) bar assns., Nat. Assn. Bond Attys., Cleve. Council on World Affairs (chmn. world affairs forum, mem. exec. com., trustee 1973—), English Speaking Union (treas., dir. 1973-75, 78—), Cleve. Philos. Soc., Omicron Delta Kappa, Delta Sigma Rho. Clubs: Cleve. Skating, University. Home: 2870 Plymouth Pepper Pike OH 44124 Office: Central Nat Bank Bldg Cleveland OH

RICHARDSON, ROY, mfg. co. exec.; b. Chgo., Mar. 22, 1931; s. John George and Margaret Beattie (Henderson) R.; B.A. in Psychology, Macalester Coll., 1952; M.A. in Labor and Indsl. Relations, U. Ill., 1953; Ph.D. in Indsl. Relations, U. Minn., 1969; m. Mary C. Westphal, May 16, 1970; children—Beth Allison, Jessica, Adam, Roman, Alexis. With Honeywell, Inc., Mpls., 1956-70, corp. manpower mgr., 1967-70; mgr. Manpower Devel. and Tng. Internat. Harvester, Chgo., 1970-73; dir. personnel U. Minn., 1973-75; v.p. human resources Onan Corp., Mpls., 1975—; pres. Personnel Surveys, Inc., Mpls., 1978-80. Vice pres. Mpls. Urban League, 1962-64. Recipient Disting. Citizens award City of Mpls., 1964. Mem. Am. Soc. Personnel Adminstrs., Am. Compensation Assn., U. Minn. Indsl. Relations Alumni Soc. (dir. 1979—, pres. 1981—). Republican. Episcopalian. Club: Edina Country. Author: Fair Pay and Work, 1971. Home: 5509 Goya Ln Edina MN 55436 Office: 1400 73d Ave NE Minneapolis MN 55432

RICHARDSON, WILLIAM HERBERT, fin. exec.; b. Halifax, N.S., May 22, 1933; s. Cyril B. and Eva Marie (Petrie) R.; student Dalhousie U., 1967-69; m. Constance Lesley Vincent, Oct. 8, 1954; children—Gary, Lee, Lesley, Susan, Robbie, Kelli. Pres., chief exec. officer Balcom Chattick Ltd., Halifax, 1967—; treas. Maritime Theatres Ltd., Halifax, 1969—; pres. Empire Theatres Ltd., Halifax, 1978—; dir. Sobey Leased Properties Ltd., Balcom Chittick Ltd., Halifax Devel. Ltd., Nfld. Drugs Ltd., Lawton's Drug Stores Ltd., Woodlawn Pharmacy Ltd., Maritime Theatres Ltd., Empire Theatres Ltd.; v.p. Empire Co. Ltd. Vice chmn. N.S. Resources Devel. Bd., 1976-80. Mem. Fin. Execs. Inst. (pres. 1975-76), Soc. Mgmt. Accts. of N.S. (v.p./chmn. edn. com. 1979-80), Soc. Mgmt. Accts. of Can. (v.p. 1980-81). Clubs: Halifax, Ashburn Golf and Country (dir. 1976-78), Halifax Bd. Trade (dir. 1978—). Home: 11 Rockmanor Dr Bedford NS B4A 2V3 Canada Office: PO Box 634 Halifax NS B3J 2T4

RICHCREEK, THOMAS DAVID, savs. and loan assn. exec.; b. Ashtabula, Ohio, Aug. 28, 1939; s. Wayne Leory and Lois (Betz) R.; grad. key Grad. Sch. Savs. and Loans, 1973; degree of distinction Inst. Fin. Edn., 1974; m. Phyllis Jane White, Aug. 12, 1961; 1 son, Christopher Jon. With Ashtabula County Savs. & Loan Co., 1960-75, v.p., 1969-75, 1st exec. v.p., 1975; exec. v.p. 1st Fed. Savs. & Loan Assn. Ashtabula, 1975-77, pres., mng. officer, 1977—; Active Ashtabula Jaycees, 1965-75, pres., 1967-68; trustee Ashtabula Area Devel. Assn., 1967—; mem. Ash- tabula City Council, 1969; mem. budget panel United Community Service, Ashtabula County; vice chmn. Ashtabula Twp. Zoning Bd. Appeals, 1974-79; treas. Council on Alcoholism and Drug Abuse, 1975-76, v.p., 1976-79; elder, mem. long range planning com., vice chmn. bd. trustees, Harris Meml. Presbyterian Ch., Ashtabula. Served with USN, 1957-60. Recipient various Jaycee awards including Man of Yr. award 1966, Key-man award 1967, 69. Mem. Ohio League Savs. Assns. (sec. Dist. 8, chmn. edn. com.), U.S. League Savs. Assns., Inst. Fin. Edn. (organizer chpt. 1970, pres. chpt. 1970-72, permanent sec. 1973-76). Democrat. Club: Elks. Office: 4148 Main Ave PO Box 769 Ashtabula OH 44004

RICHEY, LESTER ALAN, computer scientist; b. Vancouver, Wash., July 26, 1941; s. Sterling Glen and Anne Bertha (Lundy) R.; student Cascade Coll., 1959-61, U. Wash., 1962, Seattle Pacific Coll., 1963-64; B.S., Oreg. State U., 1973; m. Karine Kathlene Goehring, Dec. 9, 1961; children—Bruce Alan, Jennifer Diane. Electronic data processing analyst Boeing Co. Airplane Div., Renton, Wash., 1961-66; electronic data processing programmer State Compensation Dept. Oreg., Salem, 1966-67; systems specialist, project leader Oreg. State U. Computer Center, Corvallis, 1967-80; sr. systems analyst Seafirst Computer Services Corp., Seattle, 1980—. Mem. Corvallis Republican Com., 1978; v.p. Highland View Jr. High Sch. PTA, Corvallis, 1975. Home: 20 151st Pl SE Bellevue WA 98007 Office: Seafirst Computer Services Corp Seattle WA 98168

RICHIE, ERNEST CARL, mfg. co. exec.; b. Mannheim, Germany, Aug. 25, 1912; s. Carl and Maria (Aberle) R.; came to U.S., 1954, naturalized, 1959; M.S. in Electronics, Tech. U. Berlin, 1936; m. Gertrude E. Heyartz, Apr. 22, 1948; children—Peter Carl, Patricia Monica, Raymond Ronald. Mgr. electronics factory Gen. Electric Co., Buenos Aires, 1938-54, dir., 1952-54; works mgr. tuner div. Sarkes Tarzian, Inc., Bloomington, Ind., 1954-77; pres. Tuner Service Corp., Bloomington, 1965—; gen. mgr. Sarkes Tarzian Mexicana, 1967-77; exec. v.p. Eastern Electronic Co., Taipei, 1970-77; pres. Cableconverter Service Corp., Bloomington, 1977-78; cons. Tonfunk, Karisruhe, Germany, 1961, Dean Bros., Indpls., 1961-65. Author: Appliances, 1945; Radio Equipment for FM, 1945; contbr. articles to profl. jours. Home: 316 Lakewood Dr Bloomington IN 47401 Office: Tuner Service Corp 537 S Walnut St Bloomington IN 47401

RICHMAN, ANTHONY E., textile rental service co. exec.; b. Los Angeles, Dec. 13, 1941; s. Irving M. and Helen V. (Muchnic) R.; B.S., U. So. Calif., 1964; m. Judy Harriet Richman, Dec. 19, 1964; children—Lisa Michele, Jennifer Beth. With Renta Uniform & Towel Supply Co., Los Angeles, 1964—, service mgr., 1969, sales and service mgr., 1970-73, plant mgr., 1973-75, gen. mgr., dir., 1975-78, chief exec. officer, 1978—, v.p., sec.-treas., 1975—. Bd. dirs. Guild for Children, 1979—, Valley Guild for Cystic Fibrosis, 1974—. Recipient cert. of achievement Linen Supply Assn. Am., 1979. Mem. Textile Rental Services Assn. Am. (past dir.). Office: Renta Uniform & Towel Supply Co 3200 N Figueroa St Los Angeles CA 90065

RICHMAN, BORIS SAMUEL (BOB), data processing exec.; b. Brockton, Mass., Nov. 18, 1931; s. Abraham H. and Rose Richman; A.S. in Acctg., Bentley Coll., 1964; B.S.B.A., Boston U., 1965; exec. program M.I.T., 1976; m. Elaine Rosen, Sept. 1, 1963; children—Sandra, Mark. Mgr., Univac Data Processing Center, Sperry Rand Corp., 1956-64; br. tech. mgr. Burroughs Corp., 1964-69; mgr. corp. tech. services MIS and EDP planning and control United Brands Co., Boston, 1970—. Served with USAF, 1950-53. Cert. in data processing Inst. Cert. Computer Profls. Mem. Data Processing Mgmt. Assn. (past chpt. pres.). Club: Needham-Wellesley Lodge, B'nai B'rith (pres.).

RICHMAN, JOHN MARSHALL, food co. exec.; b. N.Y.C., Nov. 9, 1927; s. Arthur and Madeleine (Marshall) R.; B.A., Yale, 1949; LL.B., Harvard, 1952; m. Priscilla Frary, Sept. 3, 1951; children—Catherine M., Diana H. Admitted to N.Y. State bar, 1953, Ill. bar, 1973; asso. firm Leve, Hecht, Hadfield & McAlpin, N.Y.C., 1952-54; mem. law dept. Kraft, Inc., 1954-63, gen. counsel Sealtest Foods div., 1963-67, asst. gen. counsel, 1967-70, v.p., gen. counsel, 1970-73, sr. v.p., gen. counsel, 1973-75, sr. v.p. adminstrn., gen. counsel, 1975-79, dep. chmn., 1979, chmn. bd., chief exec. officer, 1979-80, chmn. bd., chief exec. officer Dart & Kraft, Inc., 1980—. Congregationalist. Clubs: Executives, Econ., Mid-Am. (Chgo.); Union League (N.Y.C.); Westmoreland Country (Wilmette, Ill.). Office: Kraft Inc Kraft Ct Glenview IL 60025

RICHMAN, MARVIN JORDAN, real estate developer; b. N.Y.C., July 13, 1939; s. Morris and Minnie (Graubart) R.; B.Arch., Mass. Inst. Tech., 1962; M.Urban Planning, N.Y. U., 1966, postgrad.,

1967-69; M.B.A., U. Chgo., 1977; m. Amy Paula Rubin, July 31, 1966; children—Mark Jason, Keith Hayden, Susanne Elizabeth. Architect, planner Skidmore, Owings & Merrill, N.Y.C., 1964, Conklin & Rossant, N.Y.C., 1965-67; partner Vizbaras & Assos., N.Y.C., 1968-69; v.p. Urban Investment and Devel. Co., Chgo., 1969-79, sr. v.p., 1979; pres. First City Devels. Corp., Beverly Hills, Calif., 1979-80, Olympia & York Calif. Equities Corp., 1981—; lectr. N.Y. U., 1967-69. Served with USAF, 1963-64. Licensed architect and real estate broker. Mem. AIA, Am. Planning Assn., Am. Arbitration Assn., Internat. Council Shopping Centers. Home: 3238 Fond Dr Encino CA 91436 Office: 611 W 6th St Los Angeles CA 90017

RICHMOND, CHARLES FREDERICK, mfg. co. exec.; b. New Bedford, Mass., Apr. 12, 1935; s. Albert Irwin and Nellie (Barlow) R.; B.S. in Bus. Adminstrn., Norwich U., 1957; m. Frances Rollins, June 15, 1957; children—Kirk, Scott, Gregg, Dean. Engring. writer Boeing Airplane Co., Seattle, 1957-58; chief contract adminstrn. Avco Corp., Wilmington, Mass., 1958-72; dir. adminstrn. Am. Sci. & Engring. Corp., Cambridge, Mass., 1972-75; dir. contract mgmt. and product support Kollsman Instrument Co., Merrimack, N.H., 1975—. Com. mem. Boy Scouts Am., N. Essex Council, 1965-80; mem. Andover (Mass.) Taxpayers Assn., 1968-72. Served with U.S. Army, 1958-59, to capt., USAR, 1959-67. Mem. Am. Mgmt. Assn., Am. Def. Preparedness Assn. (dir. 1978-81), Nat. Contract Mgmt. Assn., Assn. U.S. Army. Republican. Home: 48 Prospect Rd Andover MA 01810 Office: Daniel Webster Hwy S Merrimack NH 03054

RICHMOND, DONALDSON, bank exec.; b. Detroit, June 8, 1942; student Rochester Inst. Tech., 1975-76, U. Rochester, 1973-74, Kans. State U., 1963; married; 2 children. Asst. kiln operator Detroit Lime Co., 1965-66; asst. br. mgr. City Fin. Corp., Detroit, 1966-67; programmer Nat. Bank of Detroit, 1967-68; programmer analyst Mich. Blue Shield, 1968-69, Hosp. Computer Center, Flint, Mich., 1969-71, Bendix Corp., Southfield, Mich., 1971-73; bus. systems analyst Xerox Corp., Rochester, N.Y., 1973-76; v.p. Crocker Nat. Bank, San Francisco, 1976-79; v.p. Bank of Am., San Francisco, 1979—. Served with U.S. Army, 1959-65.

RICHMOND, HAROLD WAYNE, physician, med. service adminstr.; b. Oakdale, La., July 11, 1925; s. Harold E. and Essie (Seals) R.; B.S., U. Southwestern La., 1946; M.D., La. State U., 1948; m. Frances Alexa Womack, Sept. 30, 1950; 1 son, Mark Kimbrough. Intern, Confederate Meml. Med. Center, Shreveport, La., 1948-49, resident in orthopedics and surgery, 1949-50; pvt. practice medicine specializing in orthopedic surgery, Oakdale, 1950-60; med. dir. Cummins Engine Co., Columbus, Ind., 1960-74, corporate med. dir., 1974—; co-founder, med. dir. Columbus Occupational Health Center, 1970—; mem. staff Bartholomew County Hosp., Columbus. Served to lt. (j.g.), M.C., USNR, 1951-53. Recipient Ind. Good Samaritan award, 1979; diplomate Am. Bd. Family Practice, Am. Bd. Preventive Medicine. Fellow Am. Coll. Preventive Medicine, Am. Acad. Family Practice, Am. Acad. Occupational Medicine; mem. Royal Soc. Medicine (affiliate). Club: Columbia (Indpls.). Home: 3960 Waycross Dr Columbus IN 47201 Office: 605 Cottage Ave Columbus IN 47201

RICHMOND, JOHN, lawyer; b. Oakland, Calif., Dec. 10, 1907; s. Samuel and Sarah (Stein) R.; B.S., U. Calif. at Berkeley, 1928, M.S., 1934; LL.B., Oakland Coll. Law, 1942. Pres., Richmond Enterprises, Berkeley, 1928—; admitted to Calif. bar, 1946, since practiced in Berkeley; pres. Richmond Enterprises. Gen. chmn. Berkeley Meml. Services, 1963. Served with USAAF, 1942-45. Mem. Am., Fed., Alameda County bar assns., State Bar Calif., Pan Xenia, AAAS, Internat. Platform Assn., Supreme Ct. Hist. Soc., Smithsonian Assos. U. Calif. Alumni Assn., V.F.W. Mason (Shriner). Club: Nat. Lawyers. Office: 1611 Bonita Ave Berkeley CA 94709

RICHMOND, JOHN COOPER, airline exec.; b. Birmingham, Ala., July 29, 1934; s. John and Ruby Ethel (Cooper) R.; student Ga. State U., 1952-56; m. Annemarie Strobl, Feb. 21, 1963; children—John Charles, James Douglas, Anglia Ruby Lee, Ruth Helen. Aircraft and power plant mechanic, Atlanta, 1960-67; sales exec. Eastern Airlines, Chgo. and Seattle, 1967-69, cargo sales mgr., Chgo., 1969-70, mgr. cargo sales and service, regional sales mgr., Boston, 1970-79; dir. cargo customer service Braniff, Dallas, 1979-80, staff dir. cargo service program, 1980—. Chmn. budget com. city of Brentwood (N.H.), 1972-77; pres., Commn. on Airport Crime, 1977-78; mem. Brentwood Sch. Bd., 1977-78; moderator Town and Sch. Dist. Meetings, Brentwood, 1978-79; dir. New Eng. Transp. Mus. Bd., 1978-79. Mem. Logan Airport Mgrs. Council, Air Transport Assn. Republican. Roman Catholic. Office: PO Box 61747 DFW Airport TX 75261

RICHMOND, TULLIE TAYLOR, ret. pub. accountant; b. Columbus, Ohio, Oct. 31, 1923; s. Loren M. and Ruth (Shannon) R.; B.S., Ohio State U., 1950; m. Mary Jane Gabriel, July 24, 1943; children—Shera Lynn (Mrs. J. Hunter Skaggs), Dana Gabriel, Mark Loren, Michael Kent. Sr. accountant Lybrand, Ross Bros. & Montgomery, C.P.A.'s, Columbus, 1950-62; pres. Comp-Tool, Inc., Ashtabula, Ohio, 1963-66; partner Adams & Richmond, C.P.A.'s, Ashtabula, 1962-65; partner Adams, Richmond & Moore, C.P.A.'s, Ashtabula, 1965-66; treas. H. W. Satchwell & Co., Columbus, 1962-68; v.p., treas. Turner & Shepard, Inc., Columbus, 1966-78, also dir.; sec., dir. Turner & Shepard Agy., Inc., owner Tullie T. Richmond, C.P.A., Columbus, 1966-78; dir. Shaker Parking Co., Cleve. Mem. Ashtubula Area Devel. Assn., 1965-66, Copyright-Table to Find Transps.; patron Ashtabula Fine Arts Center; adviser to bd. dirs. Bethel Goodwill Industries, Ashtabula. Served with AUS, 1943-46. Mem. Am. Inst. C.P.A.'s, Ohio Soc. C.P.A.'s, Nat. Assn. Accountants, Am. Accounting Assn., Ohio State U. Assn. (life), Assn. for Systems Mgmt. Methodist. Mason (32 deg., Shriner), Lion. Home: 5955 Litchfield Rd Worthington OH 43085

RICHTER, BARRY, stockbroker; b. Bklyn., Sept. 5, 1935; s. Emil and Rose R.; B.A., Bklyn. Coll., 1957; m. Francine Reiner, Jan. 23, 1965; children—Alyse, Lauren, Eric. Asst. trader, sr. v.p. Steiner Rouse & Co., Inc., 1961-74; gen. partner, mgr. Gruntal and Co., N.Y.C., 1974—; investment advisor Jewish Tchrs. Assn. Trustee, Chemotherapy Found., Inc.; bd. dirs. Radio City Synagogue. Mem. DAV (life). Club: K.P. Address: 32 Angler Ln Port Washington NY 11050

RICHTER, JAMES LEO, banker; b. Chgo., Feb. 7, 1934; s. Leo Oswald and Luella (Fischer) R.; B.S.C. in Econs., DePaul U., 1956; postgrad. U. Va., 1957-58; m. Diane E. Harrison, June 25, 1955; children—Suzanne, Thomas, Mary. Loan officer, appraiser Draper & Kramer, Inc., Chgo., 1954-63; with U.S. Dept. Housing and Urban Devel., Chgo., 1963-68; asst. v.p. Percy Wilson Mortgage & Finance Corp., Chgo., 1968-69; v.p. Fed. Home Loan Bank, Chgo., 1969-71; regional v.p. Fed. Home Loan Mortgage Corp., 1970-71; cons. Fed. Home Loan Bank Bd., Washington, 1971-72, dir. Office Fed. Home Loan Banks, 1972-77; exec. v.p. Met. Savs. Assn., Farmington Hills, Mich., 1977-78; pres. Mother Lode Savs. and Loan Assn., Sacramento, 1979—; lectr. urban econs. Chgo. City Coll., 1967-71. Mem. St. John of Cross Parish Council, Western Springs, Ill., 1967-71. Bd. advisers Benedictine Sisters of Sacred Heart, Lisle, Ill., 1969-71. Served with AUS, 1956-58. Mem. Nat. Assn. Housing and Redevel. Ofcls. (speaker 1965-68, exec. com. 1968-72, pres. Chgo. chpt. 1970-71), Chgo. Mortgage Bankers Assn., Mensa. Pi Gamma Mu, Phi Sigma Phi. Roman Catholic. Home: 7480 Greenwich Dr Birmingham MI 48010 Office: 800 L St Sacramento CA 95814

RICHTER, LEAH, dental lab. exec.; b. N.Y.C., Apr. 13, 1933; d. Jack and Sadie (Ungar) Geller; B.A. cum laude, Hunter Coll., 1954; M.A., Columbia U., 1957; m. Norbert Richter, June 24, 1956; children—Jack A., Ronald E. Tchr. public schs., N.Y.C., 1956-59, tchr., chmn. dept. gen. sci., 1960-61; mgr. dental lab. Norbert Richter Dental Studio, Inc., N.Y.C., 1961-75, exec. dir. Norbert Richter Dental Studio and Norco Dental Lab., Inc., 1976—. Mem. United Dental Services (exec. sec. 1967-79, dir. 1967-78), Nat. Assn. Dental Labs., N.Y. State Dental Lab. Assn., Phi Beta Kappa, Phi Sigma. Office: 515 Madison Ave New York NY 10022

RICHTER, MARGARET-ANN, ins. agy. exec.; b. Haddonfield, N.J., Mar. 17, 1947; s. Neil S. and Jean-Rae (Turner) Phillips; student Kean Coll., 1966-69; m. Paul T.A. Richter, Aug. 21, 1967; 1 son, William Roberts. Art instr., docent Newark Mus., 1966-69; office and sales mgr. Joseph M. Sulock, Westmont, N.J., 1969-75; sales rep. Prudentail Life Ins. Co., Cherry Hill, N.J., 1975-76; owner, operator M. Richter Ins. (became div. of Gallagher Assos. Inc. 1978), Westmont, 1976-78; v.p. sales Gallagher Assos. Inc., Haddonfield, 1979—. Home: 58 Cambridge Rd Westmont NJ 08108 Office: Gallagher Assos Inc 118 Ellis St Haddonfield NJ 08033

RICHTER, ROBERT JOHN, tubing and wire co. exec.; b. Chgo., Aug. 18, 1947; s. Irving Bernard and Jean (Feldman) R.; B.S., U. Ariz., 1970; B.S., M.S.I.M., Am. Grad. Sch. Internat. Mgmt., 1971. Asst. buyer, group mgr. The Emproium div. Carter, Hawley, Hale Stores, San Francisco, 1971-73; corp. banking officer Unided Calif. Bank div. Western Bank Corp., Los Angeles, 1973-75; cons. Burning Bar, Inc. and J.J.J. Wire, Inc., Costa Mesa, Calif., 1975-77; sec.-treas. Mister Sirloin, Inc., Chatsworth, Calif., 1977-78; fin. cons., gen. mgr. Pueblo Wire & Tube Co., Inc. (Colo.), 1978—; cons. in field. Mem. Nat. Welding Suppliers Assn., Alpha Epsilon Pi. Office: 60 Greenhorn Dr Pueblo CO 81004

RICKARD, LARRY D., real estate broker; b. Seneca, Mo., June 11, 1943; s. Orval P. and Hettie C. (Ritter) R.; B.B.A., Wichita State U., 1965, M.B.A., 1968. Instr., Golden Gate Coll., San Francisco, 1968-72; owner, broker Continental Real Estate, Wichita, Kans., 1973—; instr. Omni Real Estate Sch., Wichita, 1973—, pres., 1977—; loan officer, chmn. credit com. and bd. dirs. Edwards Fed. Credit Union, 1970-71. Served to capt., USAF, 1968-72. Cert. real estate brokerage mgr. Mem. Wichita Met. Bd. Realtors (dir. 1976-77), Nat. Assn. Realtors, Realtors Nat. Mktg. Inst., Kans. Assn. Realtors. Club: Crestview Country. Home: Box 18552 115 S Rutan St Hillcrest Apt Bldg Wichita KS 67218 Office: Box 18552 3241 E Douglas St Wichita KS 67218

RICKEL, EDGAR JOHN, grain mdsg. and mfg. co. exec.; b. Salina, Kans., July 15, 1925; s. Edgar Leslie and Hazel (Silver) R.; B.S. in Civil Engring., U. Kans., 1948; m. Alice Virginia Peete, Dec. 10, 1955; children—Janet Sue, Elizabeth Ann, Mary Virginia. Vice pres. Rickel, Inc., also Rickel Mfg. Corp., Kansas City, Mo., 1952-69, pres., chmn. bd., 1969—. Mem. Soc. Automotive Engrs., Am. Soc. Agrl. Engrs. Republican. Episcopalian. Club: Indian Hills Country. Devel. high flotation fertilizer application vehicle. Office: 4800 Main St Suite 430 Kansas City MO 64112

RICKELTON, DAVID, cons. engr.; b. Glasgow, Scotland, Nov. 8, 1916; s. John and Catherine (Simpson) R.; student Bklyn. Polytech. Inst., 1940, Pratt Inst., 1942; m. Virginia Thompson, Nov. 29, 1942 (dec.); children—David Kendall, John Thompson; m. 2d, Geneva Y. Brown, June 19, 1968. Came to U.S., 1923, naturalized, 1929. With Aeronca Inc. Environmental Control Group (formerly Buensod-Stacey Corp.), Charlotte, N.C., 1940—, successively draftsman, engr., cons., 1940-65, v.p., 1965-76, gen. mgr., 1975-76; cons. engr., 1976—. Served from pvt. to lt. AUS, 1942, to capt., 1944-46. Registered profl. engr. N.C. Fellow Am. Soc. Heating, Refrigeration and Air Conditioning Engrs. (presdl. mem., pres. 1974-75); mem. Nat. Soc. Profl. Engrs. Mem. Ch. of Christ (elder). Home and office: 3413 Highview Rd Charlotte NC 28210

RICKER, JOHN BOYKIN, JR., fin. holding co. exec.; b. Augusta, Ga., Nov. 20, 1917; s. John B. and Emily Clark (Denny) R.; B.A., Southwestern Coll., 1938. Mgr. Cotton Fire and Marine Underwriters, Memphis, 1955-63; pres., chief exec. officer Marine Office of Am., N.Y.C., 1964-74; chmn. bd., chief exec. officer Continental Corp., N.Y.C., 1976—; dir. Franklin Life Ins. Co., Phoenix Assurance Co. N.Y., Almaden Vineyards, Inc., Mfrs. Hanover Trust Co., Ins. Corp. of Ireland, Ltd., Continental Corp., Continental Ins. Cos. Bd. dirs. Southwestern Coll., 1967-71, United Way of Tri-State; bd. govs. N.Y. Ins. Exchange; mem. Econ. Devel. Council N.Y.C., ARC. Served with USNR, 1942-46. Decorated Bronze Star. Mem. Property Casualty Ins. Council, Am. Inst. Property and Liability Underwriters (trustee), N.Y. C. of C., Am. Inst. Marine Underwriters (past pres.), U.S. Salvage Assn. Republican. Episcopalian. Clubs: Baltusrol Country, India House. Office: Continental Corp 80 Maiden Ln New York NY 10038

RICKERT, EDWIN WEIMER, investment counsel; b. Connersville, Ind., June 17, 1914; s. Edwin and Grace (Weimer) R.; A.B., Columbia U., 1936; m. Ruth Alma Fulcher, July 9, 1942; children—Jean Adelia, Wendy Grace, Allen Edwin. Security analyst, economist Mackubin, Legg & Co., Balt., 1936-40; indsl. analyst Office of Prodn. Mgmt., Washington, 1940-41; supr. commodity econ. research Standard Brnds, Inc., N.Y.C., 1946-53; with Brundage, Story & Rose, N.Y.C., 1953—, partner, 1966—. Trustee, Columbia U. Press, 1977—. Served to capt. U.S. Army, 1941-46; ret. lt. col. Res. Mem. Investment Counsel Assn. Am., N.Y. Soc. Security Analysts. Republican. Presbyterian. Clubs: Broad Street (N.Y.C.); Grachur (Balt.). Home: 56 Dogwood Ln Rockville Centre NY 11570 Office: 90 Broad St New York NY 10004

RICKLEFS, THOMAS RAYMOND, county adminstr., indsl. developer; b. Fond du Lac, Wis., July 6, 1945; s. Raymond Henry and Mary Eleanore (Dana) R.; B.S.B.A., U. Wis., Oshkosh, 1968; indsl. devel. cert. U. Ill., 1978; postgrad. U. Okla., 1979—; grad. Wis. state real estate N. Central Tech. Inst., 1979; m. Sue Ellen Eiring, Aug. 10, 1968; children—Mark T., Jeffrey T., Ellen M. Sales rep. R. J. Reynolds Industries, Eau Claire, Wis., 1968-70, area sales and mktg. rep., Wausau, Wis., 1970-78; sales rep. Pitney-Bowes, Inc., Green Bay, Wis., 1970—; exec. dir. Marathon County (Wis.) Econ. Devel. Council, 1978—; cons. city and county devel. orgns. Chmn., Parish Festival, Wausau, 1976-80; coach, bd. dirs., sec. Wausau Youth Hockey, 1976-80; coach/umpire Little League, Wausau; staff govtl. liaison Marathon County C. of C. Mfg. Council and Indsl. Transp. Com., 1978—; dist. dir. Marathon County United Way, 1979. Recipient econ. devel. cert. Gov. Wis., 1979. Mem. Am. Indsl. Devel. Council, Wis. Econ. Devel. Assn., Gt. Lakes Area Devel. Council, Marathon County Devel. Corp., Wis. Community Devel. Assn., Wausau Area Jaycees (Dir. of Yr. 1975, 76, Econ. Devel. Project of Yr. award for Wis. 1976), Ducks Unltd., Nat. Rifle Assn. Roman Catholic. Clubs: Wausau Skeet and Trap., Parish Men's. Office: 427 Fourth St PO Box 569 Wausau WI 54401

RICKLIN, SAUL, plastics co. exec.; b. N.Y.C., Sept. 5, 1919; s. Isaac and Rose (Brodotsky) R.; B.S., Columbia U., 1939, Chem. Engr., 1940; m. Lois Webster, Jan. 18, 1947; children—Donald R., Leslie Ricklin Wells, Ethan J., Roger D. Chief process engr. Metal & Thermit, Rahway, N.J., 1940-47; asst. prof. Brown U., Providence, 1947-54; owner Ricklin Research Assos., Providence, 1954-59; chmn. bd. Dixon Industries Corp., Bristol, R.I., 1959—; exec. v.p. NTN-Rulon Industries, Japan; dir. Entwistle Co., Hudson, Mass., EFD, East Providence, ACS Industries, Woonsocket, R.I. Vice chmn. Found. for Repertory Theatre, Providence, 1978—; bd. dirs. Bristol YMCA, 1970-78; trustee Rogers Free Library, Bristol, 1967-77. Served with USAF, 1946-47. Recipient U.S. Naval Ordnance Devel. award. Mem. Soc. Plastics Industry (dir.), Am. Chem. Soc., Am. Inst. Chem. Engrs., Am. Soc. Lubricating Engrs. Contbr. articles to profl. jours.; patentee in field. Home: 145 Ferry Rd Bristol RI 02809 Office: 380 Metacom Ave Bristol RI 02809

RICKS, JAMES VERNON, JR., farm equipment dealership exec.; b. Greenwood, Miss., June 15, 1938; s. James Vernon and Myrdice Mae (Bailey) R.; B.S. in Aero. Engring. (Fairchild scholar), Miss. State U., 1960, M.S. in Mech. Engring., 1961; m. Valley Estelle Edwards, Mar. 16, 1962; children—James Vernon III, Michael Matthew. Instr. engring. aero. engring. dept. Miss. State U., 1960-61; research aerodynamicist Boeing Mil. Airplane Co., Wichita, Kans., 1961; owner, operator Ricks Motor Service, Greenwood, Miss., 1961—, H-D Services, Inc., Jackson, Miss., 1973—, Protex, Inc., Greenwood, 1974—, Honda Services, Inc., Greenwood, 1977—, Computer Services, Greenwood, 1979—. Registered profl. engr., Miss.; lic. pilot. Mem. Mid-South Farm Equipment Dealers Assn., Air Force Assn., Aircraft Owners and Pilots Assn., Confederate Air Force, Tau Beta Pi, Phi Kappa Phi, Omicron Delta Kappa. Methodist. Home: 1101 Grand Blvd Greenwood MS 38930 Office: Ricks Motor Service Hwy 82E Greenwood MS 38930

RIDDER, BERNARD HERMAN, JR., newspaper pub.; b. N.Y.C., Dec. 8, 1916; s. Bernard Herman and Nell (Hickey) R.; B.A., Princeton U., 1938; m. Jane Delano, Feb. 24, 1939; children—Laura, Paul A., Peter, Robin, Jill. Advt. dir. Duluth News-Tribune, 1941-42, gen. mgr., 1947-52, pub., 1952-72; pub. St. Paul Dispatch-Pioneer Press, 1959-73; pres. Ridder Publs., Inc., 1969—; chmn. bd. Knight-Ridder Newspapers, 1979—; dir. Asso. Press, 1954-64; chmn. bd. Minn. Vikings Football Club, 1961-77; dir. Seattle Times, Great Lakes Paper Co., Ltd. Sr. v.p. U. Minn. Found. Served from ensign to lt., USNR, 1942-45. Recipient Journalism award U. Minn., also Regents award. Mem. U.S. Golf Assn. (mem. exec. com. 1958-64). Clubs: Royal and Ancient Golf (St. Andrews, Scotland); Burning Tree Golf (Washington); Somerset Country (St. Paul). Office: 55 E 44th St Saint Paul MN 55101

RIDDER, PAUL ANTHONY, newspaper exec.; b. Duluth, Minn., Sept. 22, 1940; s. Bernard H. and Jane (Delano) R.; B.A. in Econs., U. Mich., 1962; m. Constance Louise Meach, Nov. 6, 1960; children—Katherine Lee, Linda Jane, Susan Delano, Paul Anthony. With Aberdeen (S.D.) Am. News, 1962-63, Pasadena (Calif.) Star News, 1963-64; with San Jose (Calif.) Mercury News, 1964—, gen. mgr., 1975-77, pub., 1977—, pres., 1979—. Bd. dirs. San Jose C. of C., 1975; bd. regents U. Santa Clara; mem. pres.'s council and adv. bd. San Jose State U.; chmn. United Way campaign, 1980. Recipient 2d Ann. Disting. Citizen award Santa Clara County council Boy Scouts Am., 1976, Ann. Brotherhood award NCCJ, 1979. Mem. Young Pres.'s Orgn., Santa Clara County Mfg. Group (dir.). Clubs: La Rinconada Country (Los Gatos, Calif.); San Jose Country; Cypress Point (Pebble Beach, Calif.). Office: 750 Ridder Park Dr San Jose CA 95190

RIDDLE, LINDSEY GRANT, broadcasting co. exec.; b. Preston, Mo., Aug. 11, 1910; s. Joseph Grant and Jessie (Lindsey) R.; grad. pub. high sch.; m. Edwina Giles Barthe, Sept. 3, 1951; 1 dau., Martha (Mrs. Gary Bankson). Studio supr. WHB Broadcasting Co., Kansas City, Mo., 1933-46; chief engr. Stephens Broadcasting Service, Inc. (name changed to WDSU Broadcasting Corp., 1950), New Orleans, 1946-48, chief engr., 1949-66, v.p., chief engring. Royal St. Corp., WDSU-TV Inc., New Orleans, 1966—. Mem. tech. adv. com. Delgado Coll., New Orleans, 1970—; chmn. services subcom. La. Industry Adv. Com., 1967—; mem. Lakewood Property Owners Assn. New Orleans, 1961—. Registered profl. engr., La. Mem. Nat. Assn. Broadcasters (tech. com.), Assn. Broadcast Engring. Standards (tech. com.), I.E.E.E. (sr. mem.), Assn. Fedn. Communications Cons. Engrs., Nat. Soc. Profl. Engrs., La. Engring. Soc., Armed Forces Radio Services, New Orleans Engring. Club, New Orleans C. of C., Young Men's Bus. Club New Orleans, Royal Radio Club (pres.), Delta DX Amateur Radio Club (license W5JG), Am. Radio Relay League. Democrat. Methodist. Contbr. articles to profl. jours. Home: 5646 Bellaire Dr New Orleans LA 70124 Office: 520 Royal St New Orleans LA 70130

RIDGELY, HENRY JOHNSON, lawyer; b. Camden, Del., Nov. 17, 1913; s. Charles duPont and Helene Marjorie (Rudolph) R.; A.B., U. Del., 1935; J.D., George Washington U., 1939; m. Mary Lille Berry, Dec. 3, 1938 (dec.); children—Nicholas, Henry duPont; m. 2d, Gloria J. Rogers, Sept. 9, 1967 (div.); 1 son, John Henry; m. 3d, Sandra M. Maybee, Mar. 16, 1974. Admitted to D.C. bar, 1939, U.S. Supreme Ct. bar, 1943, Del. bar, 1940, since practiced in Dover, now sr. partner Ridgely & Ridgely; dep. atty. gen. of Del. for Kent County, 1947-54; atty. Kent County Levy Court, 1947-49; revised Code Commn., 1949-53; dir. Legislative Reference Bur. (chief counsel to gov. and Gen. Assembly), 1957-61; dir. Del. R.R. Co. Spl. atty. to Del. ins. commr., 1964-67, 69; personnel commr. Kent County, 1967-68. Mem. Del. Commn. Shell Fish, 1943, Commn. for Feebleminded, 1955-56; mem. Del. Code Revision Commn., 1957-61, Superior Ct. Jury Study Com., 1963-64; 1st chmn. Del. Pension Fund Trustees, 1970-74; vice chmn. econ. devel. com. Gov.'s Del. Tomorrow Project, 1974-77. Del., Republican Nat. Conv., 1952, 56; asst. gen. counsel Del. State Rep. Com., 1972-74. Bd. dirs. Del. State Ballett, Kent County Arts Council. Served as lt. USNR, 1943-46. Mem. Am., Del. (v.p. 1961-64, 79-80), D.C., Fed., Inter Am., Kent County (pres. 1967-68) bar assns., Am. Judicature Soc., Am. Trial Lawyers Assn., Nat. Assn. R.R. Trial Counsel, English-Speaking Union, hist. socs. Del., Md., and Pa., S.A.R. (Silver Citizenship award 1978), Magna Charter Barons, Air Force Assn., VFW, Am. Legion, Sigma Nu. Episcopalian. Republican. Clubs: Masons (32 deg., Shriner, K.T.), Odd Fellows. Clubs: Church of Del. (pres. 1961-62), Tred Avon Yacht, Chesapeake Bay Yacht Racing Assn., Amateur Radio (W3ZEU). Home: Spruce Haven RD 2 Box 194A Camden DE 19934 also Apt 37 1 Cape Henhopen Dr Lewes DE 19958 Office: 307 S State St PO Drawer C Dover DE 19901

RIDGWAY, SARA RANEY, tobacco co. exec.; b. Jackson, Miss., July 30, 1944; d. Charles Robert and Sara (Raney) R.; B.B.A., U. Miss., 1966; postgrad. Ga. State U., 1966-68. Account exec. Tucker Wayne & Co., Atlanta, 1966-69; account rep. J. Walter Thompson & Co., N.Y.C., 1969-71; account exec. Grey Advt., N.Y.C., 1971-72; account supr. Hicks & Greist, N.Y.C., 1972-74; brand mgr. Lorillard Co., N.Y.C., 1974-77, dir. pub. relations, 1977-80, v.p. public relations. Active, St. Bartholomew's Community Club, 1974—; mem. steering com. YWCA-Tribute to Women in Internat. Industry, 1978, award, 1978. Recipient Outstanding Young People of Atlanta award,

1969. Mem. Nat. Assn. Tobacco Distbrs. (dir. young execs. div.), Women in Communications, Public Relations Soc. Am., Publicity Club N.Y., Advt. Women N.Y. Republican. Methodist. Home: 420 E 55th St New York NY 10022 Office: 666 Fifth Ave New York NY 10103

RIDINGS, PAUL OVERTON, pub. relations agy. exec.; b. Meadville, Mo., May 3, 1917; s. Joseph Willard and Lilly May (Sayers) R.; B.A., Tex. Christian U., 1938; M.A., U. Mo., 1939; m. Freddie Williams, Oct. 21, 1939; children—Ruth Anne Ridings Rayel, Paul Overton. Asst. sports editor Fort Worth Press, 1938; editor Ennis (Tex.) Daily News, 1939-40; dir. pub. relations, chmn. dept. journalism Midland Luth. Coll., Fremont, Neb., 1940-42; dir. pub. relations Ill. Inst. Tech. and affiliates, Armour Research Found., Inst. Gas Tech., Chgo., 1942-44; dir. pub. relations Mpls. office McCann-Ericson, Inc., 1944-45; pres., owner Ridings & Ferris, Inc., Chgo., 1945-48; dir. pub. relations, chmn. dept. journalism Tex. Christian U., Fort Worth, 1948-50; co-owner, co-pres. Witherspoon & Ridings, Inc., Fort Worth, 1950-55; pres., owner Paul Ridings Pub. Relations, Ft. Worth, 1955—; dean, chief exec. officer Northwood Inst. Tex., Cedar Hill (on leave), 1974-75. Founding dir. Granville Walker Scholarship Found., 1966—. Recipient Most Valuable Alumnus award Tex. Christian U., 1954, Royal Purple award, 1971; Meritorious Service award Counselors sect. Pub. Relations Soc. Am., 1972; Quality Dealer Pub. Relations award Time mag., 1972; Golden Wheel award Overseas Motors Corp., 1974. Mem. Tex. Christian U. Alumni Assn. (nat. pres. 1953-54), Pub. Relations Soc. Am. (pres. Chgo. chpt. 1948, nat. dir. 1949, pres. North Tex. chpt. 1968, sec.-treas. S.W. dist. 1969, nat. exec. com. counselors sect. 1969-71, nat. sec.-treas. counselors sect. 1971), Publicity Club Chgo. (dir. 1943-44, 46-48), Kappa Phi Omega (nat. pres. 1937-40, 44-45), Delta Upsilon, Sigma Delta Chi, Pi Delta Epsilon (grand nat. councilman 1940-42, 43-44), Kappa Tau Alpha. Mem. Christian Ch. Mason (Shriner). Clubs: Colonial Country; Fort Worth. Home: 600 Green River Trail Fort Worth TX 76103 Office: 3467 West Freeway Fort Worth TX 76107

RIDLEY, JAMES RUSSELL, ins. co. exec.; b. Atlanta, July 26, 1928; s. Harry William and Ruby (Latham) R.; B.B.A., U. Ga., 1949; m. Nerrell Levoile Long, Aug. 29, 1948; children—James Russell, Jean H. Ridley Hines, Robyn C. Ridley-Johnson. Mgr., Life of Ga., 1950-57; v.p. Universal Am. Life, 1957-60; asst. to pres. United Family Life, 1960-61 (all Atlanta); sr. cons. Life Ins. Mktg. Research Assn., Hartford, Conn., 1961-65; v.p., dir. Standard Life, Jackson, Miss., 1965-69; sr. v.p., dir. ops. ITT Life, Mpls., 1969-76; pres. Integon Life, Winston-Salem, N.C., 1976—, also dir., mem. exec. and fin. cos.; chmn. bd. Integon Mortgage Guaranty Corp.; Winston-Salem dir. N.C. Nat. Bank. Former v.p., now bd. dirs. Winston-Salem Arts Council; bd. dirs. Winston-Salem YMCA; former vestryman, chmn. fin. St. Philip's Episcopal Ch. CLU. Fellow Life Mgmt. Inst.; mem. Am. Council Life Ins. (econ. policy com.), Winston-Salem C. of C. (dir., mem. exec. com.), Am. Soc. CLU's, Nat. Assn. Life Underwriters (Winston-Salem chpt.), Delta Tau Delta. Club: Forsyth Country. Home: 600 Archer Rd Winston-Salem NC 27106 Office: 500 W 5th St Winston-Salem NC 27102

RIEBEL, ROBERT GERARD, mfg. co. exec.; b. Scranton, Pa., July 29, 1929; s. John Joseph and Elizabeth Loretta (Moran) R.; B.S., U. Balt., 1957; m. Florence Marie Magosh, Sept. 3, 1950; children—Robert, Kathleen, Michael, Marion, Joanne. Adminstrv. supr. Social Security Adminstrn., 1950-60; br. mgr. Hertz Corp., Balt., 1960-67; systems analyst Ryder Systems, Balt., 1967-73; controller Howard Uniform Co., Balt., 1973—. Served with AUS, 1951-54; Korea. Democrat. Roman Catholic. Clubs: Moose, Optimist. Home: 1950 Inverton Rd Baltimore MD 21222 Office: 313 W Baltimore St Baltimore MD 21201

RIECK, BLAINE GOMER, cons. co. exec.; b. Lehighton, Pa., Jan. 25, 1923; s. Arlene Grace R.; B.S. in Chemistry, Muhlenberg Coll., 1950; postgrad. Columbia, 1954; m. Shirley Anne Nash, June 21, 1975; children—Elaine Louise, Deborah Anne, Robin Allison, William Christopher. Asst. to v.p. Fisher Sci. Co., N.Y.C., 1950-55; project engr., planning and scheduling mgr., mgr. corp. relations, mgr. internat. planning, mgr. mktg. services, mgr. adminstrn. and planning, dep. div. mgr. Westinghouse Electric, Pitts., 1955-74; project mgr. Bechtel Power Corp., Gaithersburg, Md., 1974-75; v.p. Stiefel Assos., Inc., Tampa, Fla., 1975-78; project mgr. Smith & Gillespie Engrs., Inc., Jacksonville, Fla., 1978-80, Norflor Constrn. Corp., Orlando, Fla., 1980—; mem. tech. rev. com. pyrolysis waste treatment project Kennewick, Wash., 1971-72, trade mission to Middle East, U.S. Dept. Commerce, 1974. Bd. dirs. Southwestern Community Mental Health Assn., 1958-65, pres., 1963-64; borough councilman, pres. and chief exec. officer Pleasant Hills (Pa.), 1967-70; bd. dirs. Kadlec Med. Center Found., Richland, Wash., 1970-72; chmn., pub. relations dir., publicity chmn. Richland Lutheran Ch., 1971-72; choir dir., councilman Grace Luth. Ch., Tampa, 1976-77. Served with U.S. Army, 1943-45. Republican. Mem. Tri-Cities C. of (past dir.). Club: Masons. Home: 316 Coronado Rd Venice FL 33595 Office: 360 Landstreet Rd Orlando FL 32809

RIECKER, JOHN E(RNEST), lawyer, bank exec.; b. Ann Arbor, Mich., Nov. 25, 1930; s. Herman H. and Elizabeth (Wertz) R.; A.B. with distinction, U. Mich., 1952, J.D. with distinction, 1954; m. Margaret Ann Towsley, July 30, 1955; children—John Towsley, Margaret Elizabeth. Admitted to Mich. bar, 1954, Calif. bar, 1955, U.S. Supreme Ct. bar, 1958, U.S. Tax Ct., 1959; asso. law firm Bonisteel & Bonisteel, Ann Arbor, 1954-55; partner Francis, Wetmore & Riecker, Midland, 1958-66, Gillespie & Riecker & George, Midland, 1966-77, Riecker, George & Hartley, 1977—; chmn. bd. First Midland Bank & Trust Co., Midland; dir. various Mich. corps.; mem. N. Am. trade mission to Europe, 1964. Mem. exec. com. Mich. United Fund, 1969-72. Sec. Mich. Found. Advanced Research; mem. Mich. Charter Rev. Com., 1971; trustee, treas. Delta Coll., 1964-66; asst. sec. Towsley Found., Ann Arbor, Herbert H. and Grace A. Dow Found., Midland; mem. State of Mich. Bd. of Ethics; bd. govs. Northwood Inst., 1969-71; bd. dirs. U. Mich. Devel. Council. Served as 1st lt. Judge Adv. Gens. Corps, AUS, 1955-58; Mem. Mich. Bar Assn. (tax council 1973), Midland C. of C. dir., pres. 1971), Phi Beta Kappa, Phi Kappa Phi, Alpha Delta Phi, Phi Delta Phi, Sigma Iota Epsilon. Republican. Espiscopalian (vestryman 1964-70, sr. warden 1966). Clubs: U. Mich. Presidents, U. Mich. Benefactors, Benmark, Midland Country, Saginaw, Saginaw Valley Torch; Detroit Athletic, Renaissance (Detroit). Contbr. articles to law revs. and jours. Asst. editor Mich. Law Rev., 1953-54. Home: 3211 Valley Dr Midland MI 48640 Office: 414 Townsend Midland MI 48640

RIEDEL, ARTHUR ALBERT, diversified co. exec.; b. Portland, Oreg., Dec. 25, 1930; s. Arthur Albert and Ollie Ruth Riedel; student Stanford U., 1950-53; children—James, Christina. With Riedel Internat., Inc., Portland, 1953—, now pres., chmn. bd.; pres., chmn. bd. subsidiaries Environ. Emergency Services Co., Willamette Western Co., Willamette Tug and Barge Co., Western-Marine Brazil Ltd., Western-Pacific Constrn. Materials Co., Western-Pacific Dredging Co., Western Pacific Drilling Co., Western-Pacific Erectors Co., Western-Pacific Founds. Co., Western Pacific Marine Services Co., Western Tug and Barge Co., World Security Services Co.; dir. Sceptre Dredging (Can.). Chmn. Gov.'s Maritime Affairs Commn. of Oreg.; bd. dirs. Columbia Pacific council Boy Scouts Am.; trustee Lewis and Clark Coll.; chmn. Nat. Transp. Week, 1979, Oreg. Transp. Week, 1979. Named Bus. Leader of Year, Asso. Gen. Contractors, 1979. Mem. Assn. Nat. Dredging (dir.), Young Presidents Orgn. Am., Portland C. of C. (dir.), World Dredging Assn. (past pres.), Beavers. Republican. Clubs: Univ., Arlington, Waverly Country, Rotary, Multnomah Athletic (Portland); Rainier (Seattle); World Trade (San Francisco); Masons, Shriners. Office: 4555 N Channel Ave Portland OR 97208

RIEDEL, PAUL SCHREITER, mobile homes co. exec.; b. Minden City, Mich., Oct. 8, 1911; s. Louis Herman and Anna (Schreiter) R.; student Mich. State U., 1928-31, Detroit Bus. U., 1932; m. Dorothy Artha Slack, Oct. 17, 1932; children—Daniel P., Andrea Lynn. Propr., L.H. Riedel Lumber Co., 1941-46, pres. L.H. Riedel Lumber Co., Inc., 1946-53; pres. Marlette Coach Co., mobile homes, Marlette, Mich., 1953-58; pres. Vindale Corp., Dayton, Ohio, 1958-76, hon. chmn. bd., cons., 1976—; dir. emeritus First Nat. Bank Dayton. Mem. Navy League, Naples Council. Presbyterian. Clubs: Masons, Shriners, Dayton Country, Bicycle, Moorings Country; Capitol Hill (Washington). Office: 2150 Gulf Shore Blvd N Apt 401 Naples FL 33940

RIEDER, OTTO EUGEN, distillery exec.; b. Rothenfluh, Switzerland, Feb. 1; s. Hans Ernst and Rosa (Fluhbacher) R.; Dipl. M.E., Kantons Technikum, Zurich, Switzerland, 1951; m. Huguette Marie Labrosse, Sept. 1, 1956; children—Otto, Eric. Came to Can., 1952, naturalized, 1957. Mech. engr. Maschinenfabrik Oerlikon, Zurich, 1951-52; plant mgr. Montebello Metals Ltd. (Que., Can.), 1952-55; plant mgr. Gen. Impact Extrusion Ltd., Toronto, Ont., Can., 1955-62, gen. mgr., exec. v.p., 1962-70; founder, pres. Rieder Distillery Ltd., Toronto, 1970—; dir. Uddeholm Steels Ltd., NEECO Circuit Design Systems Ltd. Served with Swiss Air Force, 1945-52. Recipient Design awards, Am. Soc. Testing Materials, 1965-66. Mem. Swiss Tech. Assn., Swiss-Canadian Businessmen Assn. Patentee in field. Home: 23 Clearside Pl Etobicoke M9C 2G7 ON Canada Office: 297 S Service Rd Grimsby ON L3M 4E9 Canada

RIEDY, JOHN K., business exec.; b. Chgo., June 29, 1916; s. Elmer B. and Evelyn (Marcoe) R.; m. Mary Eileen Grogan, Feb. 8, 1941; children—Robert D., John M., Michael J. Vice pres. Florsheim Shoe Co., Chgo., 1957-66, pres., 1967-70, now chmn. bd.; vice chmn. bd. Interco, Inc., St. Louis; dir. First Nat. Bank St. Louis, Pet Inc., Union Electric Co. Home: 200 S Brentwood Blvd Clayton MO 63105 Office: 10 Broadway Saint Louis MO 63102

RIEG, GEORGE STANLEY, JR., lawyer, accountant; b. Chgo., Nov. 28, 1926; s. George Stanley and Helene (Hermanns) R.; Ph.B., U. Chgo., 1945, M.B.A., 1949, J.D., 1953; m. Helga Hedwig Mattern, Aug. 4, 1962; children—George Stanley Rieg VI, Monica Maria. C.P.A., Arthur Andersen & Co., 1949-51, George S. Rieg, Sr., 1953-54, George S. Rieg, Jr., 1954—; admitted to Ill. bar, 1954, since in pvt. practice; professiorial lectr. in fed. taxation and accounting U. Chgo. Grad. Sch. Bus., 1954—; mgr. ins. dept. Chgo. Bridge & Iron Co., 1956-57. Served from pvt. to pfc. Mil. Police, AUS, 1946-47; capt. Res. Mil. Govt. Co., now col. C.P.A., Ill. Mem. Am., Ill., Chgo. bar assns., U. Chgo. Alumni Assn., Res. Officers Assn., Ill. Soc. C.P.A.'s, Am. Youth Hostels, Chgo. Council Fgn. Relations, Sigma Chi. Roman Catholic. Elk, K.C. Clubs: Germania, Riviera Country, Chicago Catholic University, German of Chicago, City (Chgo.); Turnverein Eiche, d'Lustige Holzhacker Baum. Home: 10449 S Hamilton Ave Chicago IL 60643 Office: 19 S LaSalle St Chicago IL 60603

RIEGGER, GERI MARIANNE, bank exec.; b. N.Y.C., Feb. 23, 1939; d. Arthur and Johanna Lina (Schmidt) R.; B.S., Concordia Tchrs. Coll., River Forest, Ill., 1960; m. Alan L. Krakow, Aug. 22, 1969; 1 son, Jason. Adv. systems engr. IBM, N.Y.C., 1961-69; v.p. computer ops. Mfrs. Hanover Trust, N.Y.C., 1969-73; White House fellow, Washington, 1974-75; asst. to group exec. IBM, White Plains, N.Y., 1973-77; v.p. systems devel. Fed. Res. Bank N.Y., N.Y.C., 1977—. Mem. computerization bd. Multiple Sclerosis Soc., 1971-73; mem. regional bd. White House Fellows, 1978-79. Mem. Computer Execs. Roundtable (exec. com. 1980—), Am. Bankers Assn. (edn. com. 1971-73), Assn. Computing Machinery, Nat. Assn. Bank Women, NOW, Nat. Women's Polit. Caucus, Common Cause. Office: 33 Liberty St New York NY 10045

RIEGLE, ROBERT ROY, meat packing co. exec.; b. Greenville, Ohio, July 30, 1927; s. Alvin N. and Nola M. (Dickey) R.; student Internat. Coll., 1952-53; m. Donna L. Rogers, Nov. 21, 1954; children—Kirk, Karen Riegle Weingart. Accountant, Coopers & Lybrand, Fort Wayne, 1953-67; mgr. corp. accounting Peter Eckrich & Sons, Inc., Fort Wayne, 1967-69; v.p., sec., controller E.W. Kneip, Inc., Forest Park, Ill., 1969—, also dir. Mem. Am. Inst. C.P.A.'s, Ind. Assn. C.P.A.'s, Nat. Inst. Controllers, Nat. Assn. Accountants, Adminstrv. Mgmt. Soc., Am. Mgmt. Assn. Club: Lions (pres. 1975). Home: 3903 Saratoga Ave Downers Grove IL 60515 Office: 7501 Brown Ave Forest Park IL 60130

RIEK, FOREST O., JR., mech. engr.; b. Rhinelander, Wis., Sept. 1, 1928; s. Forest Otto and Dorothea (Maier) R.; B.E., U. So. Calif., 1951; C.T.S., Bloy Episcopal Sch. Theology, 1972; m. Elizabeth Ann Paterson, June 4, 1955; children—Elizabeth, Forest Owen III, Karl. Research technician Lockheed-Calif. Co., Burbank, 1951-52, jr. research engr., 1952-53, research engr., 1953-58, sr. research engr., 1958-66, research specialist, 1966-80, sr. research specialist, 1980—, also dep. program mgr.; cons. engr. West Coast Sound Co.; owner Ecclesia Supply Center. Liturgical authority St. Stephen's Episcopal Ch., Hollywood, Calif.; mem. Bishop's Commn. on Scouting; asst. dist. commr. Hollywood/Wilshire Dist. council Boy Scouts Am.; past flotilla comdr. USCG Aux. Mem. Am. Soc. M.E., Soc. Motion Picture and Television Engrs., Audio Engring. Soc., Lambda Chi Alpha, Alpha Eta Rho. Republican. Mason. Patentee in field. Home: 3722 Effingham Pl Los Angeles CA 90027 Office: PO Box 551 Rye Canyon Research Lab Burbank CA 91503

RIELLY, THOMAS PATRICK, stock market exec.; b. Grand Rapids, Mich., Jan. 3, 1948; s. John R. Rielly and Ruth Ann (Mohr) R.; B.S., U. Tenn., Knoxville, 1971; postgrad. N.Y. Inst. Fin., 1972; m. Jennifer Louise Huppert, June 26, 1972; children—Ashley Grace, Brittany Ann. Brokerage trainee John Hancock br. Shearson Hammill & Co., mems. N.Y. Stock Exchange, 1970-71; mem. regional tax shelter sales staff Shearson Hayden Stone, Inc., mems. N.Y. Stock Exchange, Chgo., 1971-74; pres. T. Rielly, Inc., registered broker/dealer, 1974-78; specialist, market maker Chgo. Bd. Options Exchange, 1975—; cons. Mem. Internat. Entrepreneurs Assn., Phi Sigma Kappa. (past pres.). Democrat. Roman Catholic. Clubs: Wall Street, Young Presidents (pres.) (Chgo.); East Bank. Office: Chgo Bd Options Exchange 141 W Jackson Blvd Chicago IL 60602

RIEVMAN, ALAN CHARLES, info. services co. exec.; b. Bridgeport, Conn., Feb. 5, 1937; s. Harry and Sophie (Levene) R.; B.S., U. Conn., 1957; m. Ellen Ruth Bai, June 7, 1959; children—David, Joshua, Miriam. Accountant, Harry Wunsch, C.P.A., Port Chester, N.Y., 1957-59, John Leask, Jr., C.P.A., Fairfield, Conn., 1959-60; mem. staff, then partner Robinson, Preece and Co., C.P.A.'s, Norwalk, Conn., 1960-69; v.p. fin. Nat. CSS, Inc., Wilton, Conn., 1969—; chmn. com. taxation Assn. Data Processing Service Orgns. Inc., 1977-79. Chmn. ad hoc com. to form Fairfield-Westchester chpt. Nat. Found. Ileitis and Colitis, 1980. C.P.A., Conn. Mem. Fin. Execs. Inst., Conn. Soc. C.P.A.'s (Gold medal 1958). Democrat. Jewish. Home: 1 Tower Ridge Westport CT 06880 Office: 187 Danbury Rd Wilton CT 06897

RIGANO, FRANK ANTHONY, assn. exec.; b. White Plains, N.Y., Feb. 14, 1942; s. Anthony Frank and Angelina (Patane) R.; B.P.S., Pace U., 1975, M.B.A., 1979; m. Rose Marie Sinopoli, Apr. 28, 1963; children—Clifford Allan, Craig Mathew. Mgr. planning and adminstrn. Gen. Adjustment Bus., Inc., N.Y.C., 1970-73; dir. systems cons. Compudat Systems Corp., N.Y.C., 1973-77; dir. systems devel. ABC, N.Y.C., 1977-80; v.p. info. services Am. Mgmt. Assn., N.Y.C., 1980—. Cert. in data processing. Mem. Data Processing Mgmt. Assn. Home: 9 Beverly Dr Rye NY 10580 Office: ABC 1330 Ave of Americas New York NY 10019

RIGGS, ARTHUR J(ORDY), lawyer; b. Nyack, N.Y., Apr. 3, 1916; s. Oscar H. and Adele (Jordy) R.; A.B., Princeton, 1937; LL.B., Harvard, 1940; m. Virginia Holloway, Oct. 15, 1942; children—Arthur James, Emily Adele, Keith Holloway, George Bennett. Admitted to Mass. bar, 1940, Tex. bar, 1943; asso. Warner, Stackpole, Stetson & Bradlee, Boston, 1940-41, Solicitor's Office U.S. Dept. Labor, 1941-42; mem. firm Johnson, Bromberg, Leeds & Riggs. Certified specialist in labor law. Mem. State Bar Tex., Am., Dallas bar assns., Southwestern Legal Found., Phi Beta Kappa. Home: 4116 Amherst St Dallas TX 75225 Office: 4400 Republic Nat Bank Tower Dallas TX 75201

RIGGS, BRUCE JAMES, state fin. ofcl.; b. Troy, N.Y., Mar. 5, 1916; s. Dennie B. and Mary E. (Karnagahan) R.; B.S. in Bus. Adminstrn., Syracuse U., 1939; m. Emily G. Bayly, Apr. 20, 1946; children—Emily Anne, Carol Lyster, Gail Ellen. With mgmt. and sales depts. various cos., 1939-42, 46-48; with coated abrasive and tape divs. (formerly Behr-Manning div.) Norton Co., Troy, 1949-70, gen. traffic mgr., 1970-74; dir. corporate transp. and distbn. Combustion Engring., Inc., Windsor, Conn., 1975-76; dir. transp. service div. and dir. transp. fin. rev. div. N.Y. State Dept. Transp., Office of Regulatory Affairs, 1975— Albany, 1974-76; lectr. phys. distbn. Am. Mgmt. Assn.; lectr. U. Va., Mich. State U., Columbia grad. schs. bus., Am. U. Sch. Bus. Adminstrn. Bd. dirs. Rensselaer County (N.Y.) chpt. ARC. Served to capt. U.S. Army, 1942-46; ETO. Decorated Bronze Star. Mem. Nat. Council Phys. Distbn. Mgmt. (past pres., recipient John Drury Sheahan award 1969), Nat. Indsl. Traffic League (past com. chmn.), Nat. Freight Traffic Assn., Asso. Industries N.Y. State (past gen. chmn. transp. council), Am. Soc. Traffic and Transp. (founding mem.), Internat. Material Mgmt. Soc. (certified), Delta Nu Alpha (named Nat. Transp. Man of Yr. 1969). Clubs: Troy Country (bd. govs.), Troy. Contbr. articles to profl. jours.; mem. editorial bd. Jour. Bus. Logistics, 1976—; mem. editorial com. Transp. and Distbn. Mgmt., 1960-75. Home: East Acres Troy NY 12180 Office: 1220 Washington Ave Albany NY 12232

RIGGS, THOMAS JEFFRIES, JR., metall. engr., corp. exec.; b. Logan, W.Va., June 1, 1916; student Marshall Coll., 1935, Duke U., 1935-36, U.S. Naval Acad., 1936-37; B.S. in Metall. Engring., U. Ill., 1941; grad. Army Gen. Staff and Command Sch., Ft. Leavenworth, Kans., 1943; m. Maxine L. Nickell, Dec. 8, 1939; children—Thomas Jeffries III, Julia Lee; m. 2d, Virginia Griggs Barrett, Nov. 12, 1948; children—Robin Rhys, Geoffrey Godwyn, Rory Balfour, Merry Murray. Became sales engr. Linde Air Products Co., 1941; personnel supr. Ford, Bacon & Davis, Inc., Chgo., 1947-49, bus. rep., N.Y.C., 1949-50; gen. mgr., later v.p., gen. mgr. Tele-Trip Policy Co., Inc., N.Y.C., 1950-53; with F.L. Jacobs Co., Detroit, 1953-56, gen. sales mgr., exec. v.p., pres., 1954-56; exec. v.p., gen. mgr. Gabriel Co., Cleve., 1956-58; pres. Thomas J. Riggs Jr. & Assos., Inc., 1958-59; group v.p. operations Textron Inc., Providence, 1959-72; exec. v.p., dir. Katy Industries, Inc., Elgin, Ill., 1972-75; dir. HMW Industries, Stamford, Conn., 1973-76; pres., chief exec. officer Lawson Hemphill Inc., Central Falls, R.I., 1975—; dir. Internat. Paper Box Machine Co., Nashua, N.H., 1978—, Rawcliffe, Providence, 1979—. Served to lt. col. C.E., U.S. Army, 1941-46; to col. M.I., Office Mil. Attache, Mexico, 1946-47. Decorated Silver Star, Purple Heart; Croix de Guerre (Belgium, France). Mem. N.Y. and R.I. Soc. Mil. and Naval Officers World Wars, Res. Officers Assn., Am. Textile Machinery Assn. (dir., exec. com. 1977—), Smaller Bus. Assn. New Eng. (dir. 1980—), Sigma Chi. Episcopalian (vestryman). Clubs: Army-Navy (Washington); Providence Hope; Agawam; U.S. Seniors Golf Assn. (N.Y.C.). Home: 6 Olive St Providence RI 02906 Office: Lawson-Hemphill Inc PO Box 759 Pawtucket RI 02862

RIGGS, WILLIAM MCKNIGHT, electronic instrument co. exec.; b. Balt., Dec. 15, 1940; s. Lawrence Albert and Thelma Virginia (McKnight) R.; B.S., Coll. of Wooster, 1963; Ph.D., U. Kans., 1967; m. Linda Beth Johnson, Dec. 29, 1963; children—Eric Andrew McKnight, Karin Elizabeth. Research chemist E.I. DuPont de Nemours & Co., Inc., Wilmington, Del., 1967-72, lab. supr., Monrovia, Calif., 1972-73, product mgr., 1973-75; product mgr. Phys. Electronics Industries, Eden Prairie, Minn., 1975-78; gen. mgr. (Europe), surface scis. div. Perkin-Elmer Co., Munich, W. Ger., 1978—; adj. prof. U. Minn., 1976-78. Mem. Am. Chem. Soc., Soc. for Applied Spectroscopy, Fedn. Am. Scientists, Am. Mgmt. Assn., Sigma Xi. Unitarian. Author: Handbook of X-Ray Photoelectron Spectroscopy, 1979. Home: PO Box 805 Wayzata MN 55391 also Parkstrasse 6 8013 Haar Federal Republic of Germany Office: 6509 Flying Cloud Dr Eden Prairie MN 55344 also Perkin-Elmer GmbH Bahuhofstrasse 30 8011 Vaterstetten Federal Republic Germany

RIGSBEE, WILLIAM ALTON, life ins. exec.; b. Durham, N.C., July 10, 1926; s. Coley Leonard and Julia Hill (Hackney) R.; B.A., Duke U., 1950; m. Shirley Reese, Morgan, July 12, 1952; children—William Alton, Steven R., James M. With Home Security Life Ins. Co., Durham, to 1956, Franklin Life Ins. Co., Springfield, Ill., 1956-61; with Midland Nat. Life Ins. Co., Sioux Falls, S.D., 1961—, pres., chmn. bd.; dir. Northwestern Nat. Bank, Sioux Falls, Northwestern Bell Telephone Co., Omaha. Bd. dirs. Downtown Devel. Corp., Sioux Falls. Served with F.A., U.S. Army, 1944-46; ETO. Mem. Am. Council Life Ins. (state v.p.). Office: One Midland Plaza Sioux Falls SD 57193

RIGSBY, JOHN NEWTON, cable TV exec.; b. Easton, Pa., Aug. 18, 1946; s. John M. and Shirley J. R.; A.B., in Polit. Sci., Brown U., 1968; M.B.A., Harvard U., 1976; m. Virginia L. Blackwell, July 11, 1976; 1 son, John Blackwell. Commd. ensign U.S. Navy, 1968, advanced through grades to lt., 1971; selected to Naval Destroyer Sch., Newport, R.I., 1970-71; mgmt. cons. to chief naval ops. Mgmt. Devel. Program, Pearl Harbor, Hawaii, 1973-74; ret., 1974; Western regional mgr. Am. TV and Communications Corp., San Diego, 1976-79, div. mgr. cable ops., Englewood, Colo., 1979—. Decorated Navy Achievement medal, Navy Commendation medal. Mem. Calif. Community TV Assn. (dir.). Republican. Presbyterian. Clubs: Brown U., Harvard Bus. Sch. Home: 2391 Oak Ridge Rd Sedalia CO 80135 Office: 160 Inverness Dr W Englewood CO 80112

RIKLIS, MESHULAM, mfg. exec.; b. Turkey, Dec. 2, 1923; s. Pinhas and Betty (Guberer) R.; grad. high sch., Israel; student U. N.Mex., 1947; B.A., Ohio State U., 1950, M.B.A., 1966; m. Judith Stern, Dec. 17, 1944; children—Simona Ackerman, Marcia, Ira. Came to U.S., 1947, naturalized, 1955. Co-dir. youth activities and mil. tng. Hertzlia High Sch., Tel-Aviv, 1942; tchr. Hebrew, Talmud Torah Sch., Mpls., 1951; with research dept. Piper, Jaffray & Hopwood, 1951-53, sales rep., 1953-56; chmn., chief exec. officer Rapid Electrotype Co., Am. Colortype Co., 1956-57, pres. merged cos., Rapid-Am. Corp., 1957, pres., 1958-80, chmn., 1958—; chief exec. BTL Corp., 1960; chmn. McCrory Corp., 1960-79, pres., 1965-67, chief exec., 1967. Served with Brit. 8th Army, 1942-46. Mem. Pi Mu Epsilon. Jewish. Office: 888 7th Ave New York NY 10019

RILES, GEORGE GRIFFITH, stockbroker; b. Macon, Ga., Dec. 16, 1948; s. Frederick Emerson and Gladys Alice (Griffith) R.; B.S. in Indsl. Mgmt., Ga. Inst. Tech., 1970; M.B.A., Valdosta State Coll., 1977; m. Carolyn Victoria McGarity, Mar. 21, 1970; children—Robert Frederick, Katherine Victoria. Research asso. Fed. Res. Bank, Atlanta, 1970-71; v.p. The Robinson-Humphrey Co., Inc., Albany, Ga., 1973-79; asst. v.p., mgr. Merrill Lynch, Pierce, Fenner & Smith, Inc., Albany, 1979—. Served to capt. U.S. Army, 1971-73; Korea. Decorated Army Commendation medal. Mem. Ga. Inst. Tech. Alumni Assn. (v.p. 1977-78, pres. 1978-79), Phi Kappa Phi, Phi Delta Theta. Presbyterian. Clubs: Doublegate Country, Pine Forest Racquet, Elks. Home: 1709 Lowell Ln Albany GA 31707 Office: PO Box 1609 Albany GA 31702

RILEY, ASTER NEY, labor union ofcl.; b. Crosbyton, Tex., June 28, 1937; s. Olive Wildman and Nannie Pauline (Easter) R.; B.S. in Acctg., Rutgers U., 1976; m. Harriet Alice Nardo, July 12, 1958; children—Denise, Tara, John. Sr. acct. Kearfott div. Singer Co., Little Falls, N.J., 1960-76; acctg. supr. Thompson McKinnon Securities Co., N.Y.C., 1977-78; office mgr., chief acct. Internat. Union of Elec., Radio and Mech. Workers, AFL-CIO Pension and Health Funds, Bloomfield, N.J., 1978—. Treas., All Saints Episcopal Ch., Glen Rock, N.J., 1978—; exempt fireman Glen Rock Fire Dept., 1963-71. Served with USN, 1955-60. Mem. Internat. Found. Employee Benefits Plans. Home: 802 S Maple Ave Glen Rock NJ 07452 Office: 1460 Broad St Bloomfield NJ 07003

RILEY, DONALD CROSBY, mktg. exec.; b. Oklahoma City, Sept. 27, 1925; s. Robert and Leila (Crosby) R.; B.B.A., Ohio State U., 1945; M.B.A., Met. Collegiate Inst. London, 1947; Ph.D., Pacific Northwestern U., 1949; m. Dorothy Donahue, Jan. 10, 1950 (div.). Dir. profl. relations Chas. Pfizer & Co., Inc., Pfizer Labs. div., N.Y.C., 1950-61; N.Y. regional sales mgr. Victoreen Instrument Co., Inc., 1960-66; owner Riley Mktg. Assos., N.Y.C., 1966-72; v.p. sales and mktg. Am. Metering Systems, Inc., N.Y.C., 1972-78; v.p. Cross & Brown Co., N.Y.C., 1978—; bus. asso. Greenwich Research Corp. (Conn.). Commr. of deeds City of N.Y., 1980—. Mem. Sales Execs. Club N.Y., Sales and Mktg. Execs. Internat., Nat. Realty Club, Realty Bd. N.Y. Club: N.Y. Athletic. Home: 40 Central Park S New York NY 10019 Office: 522 Fifth Ave 3d Floor New York NY 10036

RILEY, KATHLEEN ANN, chemist, mgmt. cons., business planner; b. Norfolk, Va., Jan. 30, 1945; d. Edward Miles and Ruth Annette (Powers) Riley; student Sophie Newcomb Coll., 1962-64; B.S. in Chemistry, Coll. of William and Mary, 1967; M.S. in Chemistry, U. Ill., 1970; postgrad. U. Ill. Med. Center, 1970-72; M.B.A., Northwestern U., 1977. Teaching asst. U. Ill., Urbana, 1968-70; pharm. asst. Abbott Labs., North Chicago, Ill., 1970-73, clin. research asso., 1973-75, sr. clin. research asso., 1975-76; cons. Mgmt. Analysis Center, Inc., Northbrook, Ill., 1976-77; sr. bus. planner FMC Corp., Phila., 1977-79, mgr. bus. planning, 1979—. Mem. Am. Mgmt. Assn., N. Am. Soc. Corp. Planners, Planning Execs. Inst., Phila. Women's Network (dir.), Sigma Xi, Iota Sigma Pi. Episcopalian. Contbr. articles on pharmacology to profl. jours. Patentee in pharm. compounds. Home: 1830 Rittenhouse Sq Philadelphia PA 19103 Office: 2000 Market St Philadelphia PA 19103

RILEY, MICHAEL JOSEPH, utility co. exec.; b. Rochester, N.H., Mar. 14, 1943; s. Matthew Howard and Agnes Marie (Redden) R.; B.S., U.S. Naval Acad., 1965; M.B.A., U. So. Calif., 1972; D.B.A., Harvard U., 1977; m. Nancy Sarah Mason, July 25, 1970; children—Shawn, Paul, James, Sarah. Analyst, Office of Institutional Studies U. So. Calif., 1971-72; acct. Teradyne Inc., Boston, 1972-73; research asst., research asso. Harvard U., 1973-76; pvt. practice fin. consulting, Cambridge, Mass., 1973-76; exec. asst. to chief fin. officer and pres. Northeast Utilities, Hartford, Conn., 1976-79, asst. controller, 1979—; lectr. fin. U. Conn., 1977—. Served to lt. (j.g.) USN, 1965-70; Vietnam. Decorated Air medal. Mem. Fin. Execs. Inst. (dir. Hartford chpt. 1980—). Author: (with D.B. Crane) Now Accounts, Strategies for Financial Institutions, 1978. Home: 84 Trinity Ave Glastonbury CT 06033 Office: PO Box 270 Hartford CT 06011

RILEY, RAMON ROBERT, printing co. exec.; b. Madison, Wis., Nov. 12, 1935; s. Robert Daniel and Violet (Thysse) R.; student U. Wis., 1958; m. Eloise Ann Evert, June 1, 1957; children—Robert John, Patrick Sullivan. Sole propr. Riley Printing Co., Madison, 1958-65; printing technician State of Wis., Madison, 1965-72; with Webcrafters, Inc., Palatine, Ill., 1972—, v.p., 1978—; faculty Madison Tech. Coll., 1974, 75. Mem. So. Calif. Bookbuilders (dir. 1972-78), Bookbuilders West (pres. 1975-76), Chgo. Book Clinic (dir. 1980—), Book Mfg. Inst., Printing Industries Am. Republican. Lutheran. Club: Kiwanis (pres. 1963-64). Home: 20364 Meadow Ln Barrington IL 60010 Office: 540 N Court St Palatine IL 60067

RILEY, RICHARD A., rubber co. exec.; b. 1916; B.A., Providence Coll., 1937; married. With Firestone Tire and Rubber Co., 1939—, accountant, Fall River, Mass., 1939-42, comptroller World Bestos div., 1942-56, pres. World Bestos div., 1956-60, pres. Firestone Rubber and Latex Products Co., Fall River, 1960-65, pres. Synthetic Rubber and Latex Co., 1965-68, pres. Firestone Steel Products Co., 1968, v.p. diversified products div. parent co., Akron, Ohio, 1968-71, exec. v.p., 1971-72, pres., 1972-76, chief exec. officer, 1973—, chmn., 1976—, also dir. Office:

RILEY, RICHARD WILLIAM, mfg. co. exec.; b. Orange, N.J., Mar. 19, 1942; s. William Robert and Rhoda Margaret (Richards) R.; B.S., Cornell U., 1963; m. Carol Ann Guarino, June 24, 1964; children—Paul, John, Bryant. Gen. mgr. Manor Country Club, Rockville, Md., 1964-67, Robert Morris Inn, Oxford, Md., 1967-70; v.p., gen. mgr. Compac Corp., Monmouth Junction, N.J. and Fullerton, Calif., 1970-76; pres. Label-Aire, Inc., Fullerton, Calif., 1976—; dir. Textured Products, Inc. Mem. Packaging Machinery Mfrs. Inst., Cornell Soc. Hotelmen, Newport Harbor Area C. of C., Cornell Alumni Assn. So. Calif. Republican. Club: Balboa Bay. Office: 3801 Artesia Blvd Fullerton CA 92633

RILEY, WILLIAM O., steel co. exec.; b. 1921; student Ga. Inst. Tech.; LL.B., Atlanta Law Sch.; married. With Atlantic Steel Co., Atlanta, 1940—, v.p. indsl. relations, 1963-68, v.p. indsl. and public relations, 1968-69, v.p. adminstrn., treas., 1969-71, sr. v.p., 1971-76, exec. v.p., 1976-78, pres., 1978—, also dir.; dir. Atlantic Bldg. Systems Inc. Office: PO Box 1714 Atlanta GA 30301*

RIMER, LAURA PEEPLES, banker; b. Atlanta, Feb. 12, 1921; d. Ralph Woods and Clara Elizabeth (Smith) Peeples; student DeKalb Coll., 1965; postgrad. Sch. Bank Mktg., U. Colo., 1970-71; m. James Roland Rimer, Oct. 6, 1939; children—Ruthanne, James Roland, Laura Rimer Lanza. Woman's editor Decatur-DeKalb News (Ga.), 1958-65; asst. to woman's editor Lynchburg News (Va.), 1965-66; asst. v.p., pub. relations officer Central Fidelity Bank, N.A., Lynchburg, from 1967, now v.p. public relations; pub. relations cons. Holiday Lake 4-H Ednl. Center, Inc. Named Douglas S. Freeman Pub. Relations Profl. of Year, 1978. Bd. dirs., sec. Lynchburg Kaleidoscope, Inc., 1975-78; bd. dirs. Lynchburg Humane Soc., Inc., 1977-80, Jones Meml. Library, Lynchburg Hist. Found., Inc., 1978—; mem. Renewal and Devel. Lynchburg, Inc. Mem. Lynchburg Pub. Relations Assn. (treas. 1975-76), Va. Bankers Assn. (com. pub. info. and mktg. 1975-77), Nat. Assn. Bank Women, Advt. Club Lynchburg (sec. 1968, 69, 70). Episcopalian. Home: 81 N Princeton Circle Lynchburg VA 24503

RIMPAU, EDWARD L., ret. realtor; b. Pasadena, Calif., Nov. 26, 1898; s. Benjamin A. and Clara (Thrall) R.; A.B., Stanford, 1921; m. Helen Burntrager, Nov. 14, 1923; children—Theodore, Edward L. Realtor, Los Angeles, 1922-70. Mem. Los Angeles County Court House Com., 1955-59; bd. dirs. Hosp. Charity Fund, 1960-80; co-incorporator Miracle Mile Assn., 1941, dir. 1941-67, pres., 1947-52; dir. Property Owners Tax Assn., Calif., 1956-80. Served with USNRF, World War I, USNR, World War II; lt. comdr. ret. Mem. Res. Officers Assn. (life), Ret. Officers Assn. (life), Am. Legion (life). Roman Catholic. Home: 2294-D Via Puerta Laguna Hills CA 92653

RINDERKNECHT, HANS ULRICH, lawyer; b. Zurich, Switzerland, May 13, 1920; s. Dr. Hans Jakob and Lina (Moos) R.; student Zurich Jr. Coll., 1933-36; B.A., Zurich Tchrs.'s Coll., 1940; B.L., Zurich, Berne U. Law Schs., 1944. Prin., Rinderknecht & Co. AG, attys., Zurich, 1944—; chmn. bd. DHJ Industries AG, Zug, Switzerland, 1973—, Tropilog AG, Zurich, 1960—, Taurean Investments N.V., Curacao, N.A., 1972—, Taurean Films S.A., Zug, Switzerland, 1972—, Galerie Lopes AG, Zurich, 1976—, MEMCO S.A., Muenchenstein, Switzerland; vice chmn. Allied Chem. S.A., Zug, 1963—; dir. A-T-O, Inc., Cleve., Paradise Island Bridge Co., Ltd., Nassau, Bahamas, Island Investments Ltd., Victoria, Seychelles. Mem. Am. C. of C. Switzerland (dir., treas. 1967-71). Clubs: Metropolitan (N.Y.C.); Baur au Lac, Zurich. Home: 79 Zuercherstrasse Rapperswil Switzerland Office: 7 Beethovenstrasse 8022 Zurich Switzerland

RINEHART, JOHN STAFFORD, mgmt. cons.; b. Chgo., May 16, 1931; s. Joseph Carlin and Esther Stafford R.; student Centre Coll. of Ky., 1949-50; B.S., U. Ky., 1954; m. Mary Margaret Wilmeth, July 7, 1956; children—Mary Margaret, Esther Jane, John Stafford. Indsl. engr., corp. methods coordinator Sonoco Products Co., Hartsville, S.C., 1957-60; v.p. S.J. Fecht & Assos., Chgo., 1961-65; pres., owner Continental Cons., Columbia, S.C., 1966—; partner Fredericksburg Assos., Colonels Creek Assos., Nottingham Assos., Southland Farms, Inc.; v.p. Bus. Devel. and Mgmt. Corp., Charlotte, N.C.; v.p., dir. Retirement and Health Communities, Inc.; trustee J.C. Rinehart Co. Served to capt. USAF, 1955-57. Mem. N.C. Assn. Personnel Services (v.p.), Nat. Assn. Personnel Cons., ASME, Nat. Personnel Assos. Republican. Episcopalian. Club: Forest Lake Country. Home: 16 Woodhill Circle Columbia SC 29209 Office: PO Box 5675 Columbia SC 29250

RING, EDWARD ALFRED, bus. cons.; b. N.Y.C., Dec. 23, 1922; s. Herman Baer and Reva (Goodman) R.; student Stevens Inst. Tech., 1941-42, U.S. Navy Bomb Disposal Sch., 1943, Rider Coll., 1946; m. Geraldine R. Dubin, Nov. 16, 1947; children—William E., Steven E., Ellen L., Leslie D. Pres., The Elec. Co., Pineville, Pa., 1946-50; v.p. Circle F Mfg. Co., Trenton, N.J., 1950-64; pres., chmn. bd. Circle F Industries, Inc., Trenton, 1964-69, chmn. bd., chief exec. officer, 1969-79; now dir.; cons. in bus., Princeton, N.J., 1979—; dir. N.J. Nat. Bank, Stacy Fed. Savs. & Loan Assn., Veedercrest Vineyards, Ringsbridge Vintners, CIRFICO Holdings Corp. Vice chmn. N.J. Council on the Arts, 1967, chmn., 1971-72; v.p. Del. Valley United Fund; pres. N.J. region Am. Jewish Com., 1969-76. Served with USNR, 1942-46; PTO. Recipient grand award Collectors Club, 1964, Indsl. Improvement award, N.Y. Lamp Assn., 1966; named Disting. Citizen of 1967-68, Sales and Mktg. Execs. Central N.J. Mem. Nat. Elec. Mfrs. Assn., Nat. Assn. Corp. Dirs. Republican. Clubs: Nassau, Palm Springs Racquet, Greenacres Country, Los Angeles Founders. Author: Only a President, 1969. Office: 20 Nassau St Suite 10 Princeton NJ 08540

RINGE, RICHARD DUQUETTE, leasing co. exec.; b. Portland, Oreg., Apr. 21, 1923; s. George T. and Edna J. (Duquette) R.; student Oreg. State U., 1941-43, U. Idaho, 1943-44; M.B.A., Harvard, 1947; m. Jean M. Wahlgren, June 10, 1945. Asst. controller to controller indsl. div. Am. Standard, 1958-63; asst. corporate controller Trans Union Corp., 1963-65; controller tank car div. Union Tank Car Co., 1965-70; exec. v.p. Trans Union Fin. Corp., 1970-71, pres., 1971—. Served to lt. (s.g.), USNR; World War II, Korea. C.P.A. Mem. Internat. Health Evaluation Assn. (sec./treas.), Assn. Equipment Lessors, Fin. Execs. Inst., Am. Inst. C.P.A.'s. Presbyterian. Clubs: Harvard Bus. Sch. of No. Calif., Union League; Knollwood (Lake Forest, Ill.). Home: 35 Valencia Ct Portola Valley CA 94025 Office: 1164 Triton Dr Foster City CA 94404

RINGHOFER, JOSEPH FRANK, bus. services co. exec.; b. Chgo., May 15, 1936; s. Joseph Frank and Eleanor (McGee) R.; B.S.I.E., Indsl. Engring. Coll., Chgo., 1964; M.S.I.R., Loyola U., Chgo., 1978; m. Mariana Hall, Apr. 4, 1959; children—Joseph Frank III, Daniel, Jonathan. Indsl. engr. Tuthill Pump Co., Chgo., 1959-65; indsl. engr. Interlake Steel div. Howell Co., St. Charles, Ill., 1965-68, plant engr., 1968-70, supt., 1970-73, mgr. indsl. relations, 1973-76; mgr. employee and community relations Allis Chalmers Corp., Batavia, Ill., 1976—. Exec. bd. Two Rivers council Boy Scouts Am., 1973—; sec. St. Charles (Ill.) Fire Dept., 1968—. Served with USN, 1956-58. Mem. Valley Indsl. Assn., Kane DuPage Personnel Assn., Am. Mgmt. Assn., Am. Soc. Personnel Adminstrn., Indsl. Relations Research Assn., Nat. Safety Council, Jaycees (pres. St. Charles 1968), St. Charles C. of C. (v.p. 1974), Batavia C. of C. (v.p. 1979). Assn. for Ind. Devel. (v.p.). Clubs: Kiwanis (pres. St. Charles 1971-72), Rotary (pres. Batavia 1979—), Moose, St. Charles Hockey. Home: 4N 150 Thornetree Rd Saint Charles IL 60174 Office: 1500 N Raddant Rd Batavia IL 60510

RINGLER, IRA, pharm. mfg. co. exec.; b. Bklyn., Feb. 11, 1928; s. Louis and Bessie (Diamond) R.; B.S., Ohio State U., 1951; M. Nutritional Scis., Cornell U., 1953, Ph.D. in Biochemistry, 1955; m. Nancy Moss, June 6, 1954; children—Susan, Julie, Ralph; m. 2d, Edgra Kessel, Nov. 29, 1969. Dir. exptl. therapeutics and research sect. Lederle Labs. Div., Pearl River, N.Y., 1966-69, dir. research, 1969-75; v.p. research mgmt. and corp. devel. Abbott Labs., North Chicago, Ill., 1975-76, v.p. corp. research and exptl. therapy, 1976, v.p. pharm. products research and devel., 1976—; chmn. sci. adv. com. Pharm. Mfg. Assn. Found., 1974-76. Served with AUS, 1946-48. Mem. Am. Soc. Pharmacology and Exptl. Therapeutics, Endocrine Soc., Am. Soc. Biol. Chemists, Am. Inst. Chemists, Am. Chem. Soc., Internat. Soc. Biochem. Pharmacology, Sigma Xi, Phi Kappa Phi. Home: Plum Tree Rd Barrington Hills IL 60010 Office: Abbott Laboratories 14th and Sheridan Rds North Chicago IL 60064

RINGLER, ROBIN LYNN, chem. mfg. co. exec.; b. Cleve., May 1, 1949; s. Robert Carl and Marion Lynnette (Smith) R.; B.S.M.E., Rensselaer Poly. Inst., 1971; M.B.A., U. Santa Clara, 1976. Engr., Phelps Dodge Copper Products Corp., El Paso, 1971-73; sr. engr. Bechtel Corp., San Francisco, 1973-76; prodn. mgr. Chemelex, Redwood City, Calif., 1976-78; mgr. mfg. Chemelex div. Raychem Corp., Redwood City, 1978-79, bus. mgr. wire and cable div., 1979; pres. Remco Cons., cons. engrs., San Francisco, 1974—. Registered profl. engr. Calif. Mem. Nat. Soc. Profl. Engrs., Am. Prodn. and Inventory Control Soc., Aircraft Owners and Pilots Assn., Porsche Club Am., Lambda Chi Alpha. Republican. Christian Scientist. Patentee in field. Home: 1339 Bonnet Ct San Jose CA 95132 Office: 2201 Bay Rd Redwood City CA 94063

RINGLER, WILLIAM SYLVESTER, bank exec.; b. McKeesport, Pa., Aug. 9, 1939; s. William A. and Ruby B. (Clifton) R.; B.S. in Math., Waynesburg Coll., 1963; M.B.A., U. Pitts., 1977; m. Evelyn L. Yalch, Nov. 26, 1966; children—Diane Leigh, Christine Carrie, Jill Susan, Wendy Louise. Systems analyst Gen. Electric, Co., Pitts., 1969-70; systems and programming exec. Equibank, Pitts., 1970-77, v.p., 1976-77; sr. v.p., mgr. systems and data processing ops. Central Bank, Birmingham, Ala., 1977-79; v.p., data processing mgr. First Nat. Bank of Birmingham, 1979—; instr. U. Ala., Birmingham, 1978-79. Served with Peace Corps, 1963-65. Cert. Data Processor. Mem. Data Processing Mgmt. Assn. Republican. Methodist. Clubs: Green Valley Country, Masons, Shriners. Home: 2308 Ponderosa Circle Vestavia Hills AL 35216 Office: PO Box 11007 Birmingham AL 35288

RINGLEY, ROGER (RICE), mfg. co. exec.; b. Pactola, S.D., Oct. 2, 1925; s. Roy Emery and Virginia Elwilda (Rice) R.; student Ariz. State U., 1950; m. Lova Lee Fowler, June 20, 1958; children—Michael, Phillip, Pauline, Robin, Leslie. With Dresser Industries, 1966—, pres. Dresser Mfg. div., Bradford, Pa., 1971-74, pres. Indsl. Specialties Group, Pitts., 1974—. Trustee Inst. Gas Tech. Served with USN, 1942-46. Mem. Internat. Mgmt. and Devel. Inst. (council). Clubs: Duquesne, Oakmont Country. Home: 212 Highland Rd Pittsburgh PA 15238 Office: 3 Gateway Center Pittsburgh PA 15222

RINGOEN, HOWARD CHARLES, indsl. and fin. cons.; b. Mpls., June 8, 1932; s. Gordon Wayne and Rose Ethel (Hagen) R.; B.A., U. Wash., 1957; postgrad. Def. System Mgmt. Sch., 1971; m. AidaLou M. Stubsjoen, Feb. 17, 1955; children—Howard, Polly, Michael, Kristi, Sonja. With Boeing Aero Space Co., Seattle, 1957-79, fin. mgr. Minuteman program, 1969-72, bus. mgr. SRAM program, 1973-75, program mgr. SRAM program, 1975-77, productivity mgr., 1977-79, dir. MTL, 1978-79, bd. control, treas. Boeing Mgmt. Assn.; pres. H.C. Ringoen Assos., Tukwila, Wash., 1979—. Mem. Am. Def. Preparedness Assn. (chmn. project mgmt. div.). Home: 18911 4th St SW Seattle WA 98166 Office: 675 Strander Blvd Tukwila WA 98188

RINGWOOD, JAMES JOSEPH, JR., magnetic tape mfg. co. exec.; b. N.Y.C., Nov. 21, 1935; s. James Joseph and Letitia (Kiefer) R.; certificate Am. Inst. Banking, 1958; B.S. in Communication Arts, N.Y. U., 1963; m. Maureen T. Regan, May 6, 1967; children—Kimberly Ann, James Joseph. Dist. sales mgr. Reeves Soundcraft Co., N.Y.C., 1963-67; regional sales mgr. Memorex Corp., N.Y.C, Santa Clara, Calif., 1967-71; partner, sales mgr. Karex Inc., Sunnyvale, Calif. and N.Y.C., 1971-76; nat. sales mgr. Maxell Corp. Am., Moonachie, N.J., 1976—. Mem. Indsl. TV Assn., Internat. Tape Assn., Nat. Audio-Visual Assn., Soc. Motion Picture and TV Engrs., N.Y. U. Club. Roman Catholic. Home: 12 West Dr Fairfield NJ 07006 Office: 60 Oxford Dr Moonachie NJ 07074

RINKEMA, HARRY, oil co. exec.; b. South Holland, Ill., Apr. 6, 1922; s. Peter and Minnie (DeRuiter) R.; B.S., U. Iowa, 1946; A.M., Harvard U., 1961; m. Elizabeth Hoekstra, May 12, 1944; children—Marsha Lynn, Robert Alan, Linda Joy. With Standard Oil Co. (Ind.) and its affiliates, 1946—, mktg. mgr., Atlanta, 1961-66, mktg. mgr. internat., N.Y.C., 1966-69, mng. dir., Milan, Italy, 1969-71, regional v.p., Chgo., 1971-75, v.p. marine transp., Chgo., 1975—. Served with USNR, 1943-46. Mem. Fedn. Am. Controlled Shipping, Oil Cos. Inst. Marine Pollution Compensation Ltd., Am. Inst. Merchant Shipping, Am. Petroleum Inst. Republican. Presbyterian. Clubs: Cress Creek Country, Mid-America. Office: 200 E Randolph Dr Chicago IL 60601

RINNE, AUSTIN DEAN, ins. co. exec.; b. Indpls., Aug. 14, 1919; s. Hermann H. and Marie (Knudsen) R.; student Ind. U., 1938-40; grad. ins. marketing Purdue U., 1947; m. Martha Jo Runyan, Dec. 29, 1941; children—Erik Knudsen, Barbara Jane. With Northwestern Mut. Life Milw., 1946—, dist. agt., Indpls., 1956-58, gen. agt. N. Tex., Dallas, 1958—; dir. Bank of Dallas, 1977—, Dallas Bancshares, 1980—; guest lectr. Purdue U., 1956, So. Meth. U., 1961. Mem. adv. council ins. dept. North Tex. State U., 1972—; bd. dirs. Dallas Civic Opera Guild, 1967-73, Park Cities YMCA, 1959-63, Dallas. Served to capt. USAAF, 1941-45; ETO. Decorated Air medal with cluster, Purple Heart, others; charter and life recipient Nat. Mgmt. award Nat. Assn. Life Underwriters. Mem. Am. Legion (comdr. 1967-68), Nat. Assn. Barbed Wire Clubs (pres. 1947-48), Grad. Soc. Insts. Ins. Marketing (pres. 1949-50), Dallas Gen. Agts. and Mgrs. Assn. (dir. 1962-63), Dallas Assn. Life Underwriters (dir. 1960-63), Dallas Estate Planning Council (pres. 1965-66), Mil. Order World Wars, Ind. U. Alumni Assn. Dallas-Ft. Worth (pres. 1966-67), Internat. Platform Assn., English-Speaking Union (dir., v.p. Dallas chpt. 1972—), Phi Kappa Psi Alumni Assn. (pres. 1951-52), Phi Kappa Psi (exec. council 1972-76). Clubs: City, Dallas Country, Knife and Fork, Northshore (Dallas); Sertoma (pres. 1967-68). Home: 4311 Bordeaux St Dallas TX 75205 Office: 3635 Lemmon Ave Dallas TX 75219

RINTOUL, BEECHER, labor, indsl. relations cons.; b. Taft, Calif., Nov. 3, 1917; s. Beecher and Deane (O'Conner) R.; B.S., U. Calif., 1939, M.S., 1941; m. Mary Margaret Brown, May 21, 1946; children—Beecher III, Laurie Deane. Asst. engr. So. Pacific Co., 1938—; labor/indsl. relations cons., 1938—. Gen. chmn. Assn. R.R. Maintenance of Way Suprs., Assn. Ry. Tech. Employes, 1940—. Registered profl. mech. engr., Calif. Mem. Sigma Xi, Tau Beta Pi. Democrat. Presbyn. Home: 614 Creston Rd Berkeley CA 94708 Office: 1 Market St San Francisco CA 94105

RIORDAN, ARTHUR WHELDON, publisher; b. N.Y.C., Dec. 10, 1925; s. Eugene Arthur and Constance Nickerson (Wheldon) R.; B.S.M.E., CCNY, 1949; student mgmt. devel. program Harvard U., 1965; m. Marguerite Donohue, Apr. 10, 1950; children—Vicotria, Arthur, Christopher. With Proctor & Gamble, 1948-50, Syncro Corp., 1950-55, Bramson Pub. Co., 1955-74; pub. Penton Pub. Co., Cleve., 1974—; dir. Ames Corp. Fire commr. Watch Hill, R.I., 1968, 77. Served with USMC, 1943-45. Recipient Jesse Neal Editorial award, 1980. Mem. Am. Production and Inventory Control Soc., Am.

Productivity Council. Republican. Club: Watch Hill Yacht. Office: Penton Plaza Cleveland OH 44114

RIORDAN, PETER JOHN, chem. co. exec.; b. Newark, May 20, 1945; s. James Joseph and Margaret Ann (O'Connor) R.; B.S. in Mgmt., Fairleigh Dickinson U., 1969, M.B.A. in Fin., 1973, postgrad. in accounting, 1977—; m. Rosemary Ann Lynch, Nov. 24, 1973. Programmer analyst E.R. Squibb Co., East Brunswick, N.J., 1969-72; systems analyst Newsweek, Livingston, N.J., 1972-73; sr. systems analyst Wakefern Food Co., Elizabeth, N.J., 1973-76; systems mgr. Rizzioli Publs. Co., N.Y.C., 1976; mgr. data processing Lonza Inc., Fairlawn, N.J., 1977—; adj. instr. Essex County Coll., 1975—, mem. data processing adv. bd., 1976—; pres. Data Processing Mgmt. & Evaluation Group, Inc., Livingston, N.J., 1976—; mem. data communications adv. bd. Data Com Publs., N.Y.C., 1976—. Aux. police officer, Livingston. Mem. Assn. for Systems Mgmt. (treas. No. N.J. chpt. 1977-78, pres. 1979-80, named Systems Man of Yr. 1978), Livingston Jaycees (sec. 1975). Republican. Roman Catholic. Home: 28 Shadowlawn Dr Livingston NJ 07039 Office: 22-10 Route 208 Fairlawn NJ 07410

RIPLEY, KENNETH CLAY, physicist; b. Winchester, Ind., Apr. 17, 1904; s. Giles E. and Harriet L. (Marsh) R.; B.M.E., U. Ark., 1927, M.Sc., U. Pitts., 1932; m. Ellen Kearns, Dec. 28, 1949; 1 dau., Margaret M. Asst. engr. Research Labs., Westinghouse Electric & Mfg. Co., 1927-31; instr. machine design Purdue U., 1935; asst. physicist Naval Research Lab., 1936-39; asst. engr., asso. physicist, physicist, research group Bur. Ships, 1939-49 sr. physicist fluid dynamics sci. sect., 1949-60; staff, comdr. Joint Task Force ONE (Operation Crossroads), 1946; cons. on roll stblzn. ships John J. McMullen Assos., Inc., naval architects, N.Y.C., 1960—; pres. Kenneth C. Ripley Co. Mem. Am. Phys. Soc., Tau Beta Pi. Methodist. Author: (with Dr. O. G. Tietjens) Air Resistance of High-Speed Trains and Interurban Cars. Inventor in field. Home: 3058 Harrison St NW Washington DC 20015

RIPLEY, STUART MCKINNON, real estate cons.; b. St. Louis, July 28, 1930; s. Rob Roy and Nina Pearl (Young) R.; B.A., U. Redlands, 1952; M.B.A., U. Calif., Berkeley, 1959; m. Marilyn Haerr MacDiarmid, Dec. 28, 1964; children—Jill, Bruce, Kent. Vice pres., dir. J.H. Hedrick & Co., Santa Barbara and San Diego, 1958-63; v.p. mktg. Cavanaugh Devel. Co., San Gabriel, Calif., 1963-65; v.p. mktg. dir. Calabasas Park, Bechtel Corp., Calabasas, Calif., 1967-69; v.p. mktg. Avco Community Developers, Inc., La Jolla, Calif., 1969-74; mktg. dir. U.S. Home Corp., Fla. Div., Clearwater, 1974-75; v.p., mktg. dir. Valcas Internat. Corp., San Diego, 1976-77, pres., 1977; pres. Stuart M. Ripley, Inc., 1977—; pres., dir. Howard's Camper Country, Inc., National City, Calif., 1975-77; lectr. U. Calif. at Los Angeles, 1961. Served with USN, 1952-55. U. Redlands fellow, 1960—. Mem. Nat. Assn. Homebuilders, Sales and Mktg. Council, Sales and Mktg. Execs., Pi Chi. Republican. Episcopalian. Club: Elks. Home and Office: 13180 Portofino Dr Del Mar CA 92014

RIPPY, WILLIAM FRANCIS, property and assets mgmt. co. exec.; b. Salem, Ill., Mar. 22, 1944; s. William Byron and Mary Martha (Stevenson) R.; B.S. in Bus. Adminstrn., Greenville Coll., 1965; m. Barbara Gail Olsen, Sept. 25, 1965; children—Steven Todd, Beth Anne, Megan Lynn. Sales rep. IBM, 1965-67; data processing officer Bank of Ill., 1967-69; owner, mgr. Bill Rippy Real Estate, Mt. Vernon, Ill., 1969-72; v.p. mktg. Fin. Computing Corp., St. Louis, 1972-74; v.p. Unicon, designers, builders, Highland, Ill., 1974-76; regional mgr. Linclay Corp., Kansas City, Mo., 1976-79; pres. Cohen Asset Mgmt., Inc., Kansas City, Mo., 1979—. Drive chmn. Jefferson County United Fund, 1970-71; state chmn. polit. action com. Farmers Union, 1971. Mem. Mo. Builders Assn. (chmn. legis. com. 1976). Democrat. Methodist. Home: 2109 Sunvale Dr Olathe KS 66061 Office: 1100 Main St Kansas City MO 64105

RIPS, SERGE, econ. cons.; b. Minsk, Russia, Feb. 28, 1907; s. Jack and Raissa (Muravin) R.; student Royal Athenaeum and high course polit. and econ. sci., Antwerp, Belgium, 1921-27; m. Thea Sacher. Came to U.S., 1941, naturalized, 1944. Asso. with newspaper Neptune and Midi, Belgium, also mgr. ins. co., 1926-40; with U.S. OWI, Bd. Econ. Warfare, Fgn. Econ. Adminstrn., 1942-45; econ. adviser to Greece, Washington, 1945; adviser to Royal Thai Govt., spl. asst. on wartime financial problems to Ministry of Fgn. Affairs of Thailand, 1947-55; spl. asst. to Pres. of Haiti, 1955; econ. cons., Washington, 1946—. Decorated officer Order of Legion of Honor (France); knight comdr. Order of White Elephant (Thailand); knight comdr. Order Sacred Treasure (Japan); knight Isabel the Catholic (Spain); knight Order of Crown (Italy); officer Order of Crown (Rumania); Order of Jade, Order of Golden Ear (China). Mem. Siam Soc. (Bangkok). Home: 4101 Cathedral Ave NW Washington DC 20016

RIS, HOWARD CLINTON, paper co. exec.; b. Bayside, N.Y., Nov. 26, 1915; s. Charles H. and Dorothy (Smyth) R.; A.B., Duke U., 1938; postgrad. U. Maine, 1938; m. Edythe Arenholz, Oct. 23, 1943 (dec. 1975); children—Barbara Ris Walden, Howard Clinton; m. 2d, Patricia Gill Hake, July 23, 1977. Vice pres. Ris Paper Co., N.Y.C., 1946-54, pres., 1954-77, chmn. bd., chief exec. officer, 1977—; pres. Ris Paper Co., Washington, Ris Paper Co. Pa., Ris Paper Co. New Eng., Ris Paper Co. N.Y. Served with U.S. Army, spl. agt. CIC, 1942-46. Mem. Nat. Paper Trade Assn. (bd. dirs.), Paper Mchts. Assn. N.Y. (past pres.). Republican. Episcopalian. Clubs: Garden City Golf, Cherry Valley, Lawrence Beach, Union League, Lake Placid. Office: Ris Paper Co Inc 45-11 33d St Long Island City NY 11101

RISCH, FRANK ALLAN, energy co. exec.; b. Balt., Dec. 16, 1942; s. Herbert H. and Irma B. R.; B.S., Pa. State U., 1964; M.S. in Indsl. Adminstrn., Carnegie Mellon U., 1966; m. Helen E. Winnick, Mar. 22, 1964; children—Jonathan D., Jolene F. Fin. analyst Standard Oil Co. (N.J.) (now Exxon Corp.), N.Y.C., 1966-69, fin. advisor Esso Europe, Inc. London, 1969-73, treas., fin. and planning mgr. Esso Pappas, Athens, Greece, 1973-75, mgr. internat. sales, 1975-76, treas. Exxon Nuclear Co., Bellevue, Wash., 1976-78, treas., fin. and planning mgr., treas., 1978-80, mgr. internat. fin. planning and econs. Exxon Corp., N.Y.C., 1980—. Active, United Way, Boy Scouts Am. Served with U.S. Army, 1961-62. Mem. Fin. Execs. Inst.

RISMILLER, BRUCE ROBERT, mfg. co. exec.; b. Reading, Pa., July 12, 1937; s. Ronald Robert and Ethel T. (Klein) R.; B.A., Lebanon Valley Coll., 1960; M.A., Millersville State Coll., 1964; postgrad. Temple U., 1964-67; m. Janet Lee Blank, May 12, 1958; 1 son, Gregory Ross. Mgr. personnel devel. and communications Xerox Corp., Webster, N.Y., 1967-71, mgr. personnel relations staff, 1971, mgr. coll. relations and employment, Rochester, N.Y., 1971-74, regional personnel mgr., Washington, 1974-77, personnel mgr. U.S. ops., 1977-79, v.p. personnel, 1979—. Pres. bd. dirs. Family Service, Rochester, N.Y., 1974-75, pres. nat. bd. dirs.; mem. allocations com. United Community Chest of Greater Rochester. Mem. Am. Mgmt. Assn., Nat. Assn. Tng. and Devel., Washington Personnel Assn., Nat. C. of C. (mem. manpower com. 1974—). Home: 7136 Van Hook Dr Dallas TX 75248 Office: 1341 W Mockingbird Ln Dallas TX 75246

RISS, ROBERT BAILEY, fin. co. exec.; b. Salida, Colo., May 27, 1927; s. Richard R. and Louise (Roberts) R.; B.S. in Bus. Adminstrn., U. Kans., 1949; children—Edward Stayton, G. Leslie, Laura Bailey, Juliana Warren. Pres., Riss Internat. Corp., Kansas City, Mo., 1950-80, chmn. bd., 1964—; founder, pres., chmn. bd. Republic Industries, Inc., Kansas City, 1969—; pres. Grandview Bank & Trust Co., 1969-80, chmn. bd., 1969—; chmn. bd., treas. Columbia Properties, Inc., Kansas City, 1969—; chmn. bd. Johnson Motor Lines, Inc., Charlotte, N.C., 1979-81; mem. exec. com. ERC Corp., Kansas City, 1979-80, mem. fin. com., 1977-80, dir., 1976-80; adv. dir. United Mo. Bank of Kansas City, 1978-80; pres., chmn. bd. Dominion Banqueshares, Kansas City, 1980—. Pres., Boys Club of Kansas City, Mo., 1956; officer United Fund Campaign, 1952-54; chmn. Muscular Dystrophy Assn. Fund Drive of Greater Kansas City Area, 1955; mem. Kansas City Crime Commn., 1955-56; mem. adv. com. Am. Field Service, 1968-72; bd. dirs. Kansas City Area council Boy Scouts Am., 1971—, Mission Hills Homes Assn., 1973, Downtown, Inc., Kansas City, Mo., 1970—; bd. govs. Agrl. Hall of Fame, 1975—; bd. dirs. American Royal Assn., 1979—, v.p., 1980—; bd. govs. Safety Council, 1952-56; trustee U. Kans. Endowment Assn., 1970—, mem. exec. com., 1974—, vice-chmn., 1980—. Named Most Outstanding Young Man in State of Mo., U.S. Jr. C. of C., 1956; recipient Silver Beaver award Boy Scouts Am., 1972; Fred Ellsworth medallion U. Kans., 1979, Disting. Service citation, 1976. Mem. Kansas U. Alumni Assn. (pres. 1969-70, dir. 1968-74). Clubs: Kansas City (chmn. exec. com., 1st v.p. 1973); Univ.; Olympic; Ponte Vedra; Farmington Country; N.Y. Athletic; Mission Hills Country. Home: 9202 W 71st St Merriam KS 66204 Office: Riss Internat Corp 903 Grand Ave Kansas City MO 64106

RISSLER, MAHLON NOLT, grocery co. exec.; b. Lancaster, Pa., June 24, 1936; s. Daniel Shelly and Lizzie M. Rissler; B.S. in Bus. Adminstrn., Ohio Christian Coll., 1971; postgrad. James Madison U., 1972-76; m. Gloria Grace Weaver, June 6, 1959; children—Jay Clair, Ruth Ann, Debra Joy. Vol. service Eastern Mennonite Bd. Missions, Fla., Washington, 1958-59; office mgr. Keystone Bay & Burlap Co., Lancaster, 1960-61; controller Provident Book Store, Lancaster, 1961-66; dir. computer center Eastern Mennonite Coll., Harrisonburg, Va., 1966-75; mgr. Dutch Foods Farm Market, Inc., Dayton, Va., 1976-78, pres., chmn., 1979—. Sunday Sch. tchr. New Danville Mennonite Ch., 1959-61, asst. Sunday Sch. supt., 1960-65; auditor Philhaven Hosp., 1962-65. Mem. Pa. Grocers Assn., Malone and Hyde Grocery Assn., Gideons Internat. Home: 1311 Greystone St Harrisonburg VA 22801 Office: Box 3A Hwy 42 S Dayton VA 22821

RITCHEY, SAMUEL DONLEY, JR., retail exec.; b. Derry Twp., Pa., July 16, 1933; s. Samuel Donley and Florence Catherine (Litsch) R.; B.S., San Diego State U., 1955, M.S., 1963; postgrad. (Sloan Found. fellow), Stanford, 1964; m. Sharon Marie Anderson, Apr. 6, 1956; children—Michael Donley, Tamara Louise, Shawn Christopher. Store mgr. supermarkets Lucky Stores Inc., San Diego and Phoenix, 1957-61, store supr. Gemco div., 1965-66, dist. mgr. Gemco, 1966-68, nonfood mdse. mgr. parent co., 1968-69, div. mgr. Gemco, v.p. parent co., 1969-72, sr. v.p. Lucky Stores, Inc., Dublin, Calif., 1972-75, exec. v.p., 1975-78, pres., chief operating officer, 1978-80, pres., chief exec. officer, 1980—, also dir.; dir. Crocker Nat. Corp., Crocker Nat. Bank; lectr. mgmt. dept. San Jose State U. Pres., dir. Sloan Alumni Adv. Bd., Stanford U.; bd. dirs. Bay Area Council Boy Scouts Am. Recipient Food Industry Man of Yr. award U. So. Calif., 1979. Mem. Western Assn. Food Chains (pres., dir.), Food Mktg. Inst. (dir.). Republican. Presbyterian. Office: Lucky Stores Inc 6300 Clark Ave Dublin CA 94566

RITCHIE, CEDRIC ELMER, banker; b. Upper Kent, N.B., Can., Aug. 22, 1927; s. E. Thomas and Marion (Henderson) R.; student pub. schs., Bath, N.B.; m. Barbara Binnington, Apr. 20, 1956. With Bank of N.S., Bath, 1945—, chief gen. mgr., Toronto, 1970—, pres., 1972-79, chief exec. officer, 1972—, chmn. bd., 1974—, also dir.; chmn. bd. Bank N.S. Channel Islands Ltd., Bank N.S. Trust Co. Channel Islands Ltd., Bank of N.S. Trust Co. (U.K.) Ltd., Bank of N.S. Trust Co. W.I. Ltd., Empire Realty Co. Ltd., Bank N.S. Trust Co. (Bahamas) Ltd., Bank N.S. Trust Co. (Caribbean) Ltd., BNS Internat. (U.K.) Ltd., Bank of N.S. Internat. Ltd., Bank N.S. Trust Co. (Cayman) Ltd.; pres. Bluenose Investments Ltd., Nova Scotia Corp.; dir. numerous companies; mem. Can. Econ. Policy Com. Bd. govs. Olympic Trust Can. Recipient Human Relations award Can. Council Christians and Jews, 1976. Clubs: Caledon Ski, Canadian, Donalda, Empire, Mt. Royal, Mid Ocean, National, Toronto, York. Office: Bank of NS 44 King St W Toronto ON M5H 1E2 Canada*

RITCHIE, DANIEL LEE, broadcastong exec.; b. Springfield, Ill., Sept. 19, 1931; s. Daniel Felix and Jessie Dee (Binney) R.; B.A., Harvard U., 1954, M.B.A., 1956. Exec. v.p. MCA, Inc., Los Angeles, 1967-70; pres. Archon Pure Products Co., Los Angeles, 1970-73; exec. v.p. Westinghouse Electric Corp., Pitts., 1975-78; pres. corp. staff and strategic planning Westinghouse Broadcasting Co., 1978-79, pres., chief exec. officer, 1979—. Served with U.S. Army, 1956-58. Address: 90 Park Ave New York NY 10016*

RITCHIE, JOHN DUFF, cons.; b. Burnley, Eng., June 6, 1917; s. George Southern and Elizabeth (Duff) R.; student Eton (Eng.) Coll., 1930, Royal Naval Tng. and Royal Naval Schs., 1934-38; m. Elizabeth Louis Sunderland, Nov. 5, 1960; children by previous marriage—Jean Helen (Mrs. David G. Maby), Sarah Elizabeth (Mrs. Robert Wood). Commd. cadet Royal Navy, 1934, advanced through grades to lt. comdr., 1944; retired, 1948; with Royal Dutch Shell Group, 1948-77, assigned various countries, 1948-67, pres. subsidiary Asiatic Petroleum Corp., 1967-77; pres., dir. JDR Consultancy, N.Y.C., 1977—; dir. New Eng. Electric System, McDermott Inc. Decorated D.S.C.; comdr. Order Brit. Empire. Mem. Brit. Inst. Mgmt., Inst. Personnel Mgmt. (asso.). Club: Yale, (N.Y.C.). Home: Leggett Rd Stone Ridge NY 12484

RITCHIE, RONALD JULIAN, electronics mfg. co. exec.; b. Pueblo, Colo., Dec. 29, 1940; s. Julius Carl and Mildred (Shubert) R.; student U.S. Mil. Acad., West Point, N.Y., 1958-60; B.S.E.E. with honors, So. Meth. U., 1963; M.B.A., Stanford U., 1965; m. Sarah Elizabeth Green, May 26, 1962; children—Christopher, Rachael. With Tex. Instruments, Inc., Houston, 1960—, successively co-op engring. student, mfg. engr., br. planning mgr., plant mgr. Tex. Instruments Can., plant mgr. Tex. Instruments Curacao, mng. dir. Tex. Instruments Deutschland, asst. v.p. internat. semicondr. trade operations, v.p. calculator div., v.p. U.S. Consumer Products, v.p. Terminals and Peripherals div., 1980—. Bd. dirs. Tex. Tech. U. Found., South Plains council Boy Scouts Am., United Way, Methodist Hosp. Registered profl. engr., Tex. Mem. Sigma Tau, Eta Kappa Nu. Club: Rotary. Office: PO Box 1444 MS 7707 Houston TX 77001

RITT, PAUL EDWARD, electronics co. exec.; b. Balt., Mar. 3, 1928; s. Paul Edward and Mary (Knight) R.; B.S. in Chemistry, Loyola At Balt., 1950, M.S. in Chemistry, 1952; Ph.D. in Chemistry, Georgetown U., 1954; m. Dorothy Ann Wintz, Dec. 30, 1950; children—Paul Edward, Peter M., John W., James T., Mary Carol, Matthew J. Research asso. Harris Research Lab., Washington, 1950-52; chemist Melpar, Inc., aerospace research, Falls Church, Va., 1952-60, research dir., 1960-62, v.p. research, 1962-65, v.p. research and engring., 1965-67; v.p., gen. mgr. Tng. Corp. Am., 1965-67; pres. applied sci. div., applied tech. div. Litton Industries, Bethesda, Md., 1967-68; v.p., dir. research Gen. Telephone & Electronics Labs., Waltham, Mass., 1968—; instr. U. Va., 1956-58, Am. U., 1959—. Fellow Am. Inst. Chemists; mem. Am. Phys. Soc., Am. Inst. Physics, Am. Chem. Soc. Contbr. articles to profl. jours. Patentee. Home: 36 Sylvan Ln Weston MA 02193 Office: 40 Sylvan Rd Waltham MA 02154

RITTENHOUSE, DAVID RAYMOND, investment co. exec.; b. Griswold, Ill.; s. Edward F. and Mary E. (Griswold) R.; B.A. cum laude, U. Mich., 1933; m. Cornelia Arnos, June 14, 1933; children—Barbara, Linda, Susan, Sally. Vice pres. Securities Inc., Toledo, 1937-46; pres. Rittenhouse Motors, Inc., Toledo, 1946-71, Toledo Discount Co., 1950—. Served with USNR, 1944-46. Mem. Toledo Bd. Edn., also past pres.; mem. Ohio Bd. Edn.; trustee Toledo Mus. Art, 1969—. Mem. Toledo C. of C. (v.p.), Toledo Automobile Club (dir.), Phi Beta Kappa, Phi Kappa Phi, Beta Theta Pi. Mem. First Congl. Ch. Clubs: Rotary (pres. Toledo), Hermits, Belmont Country, Toledo. Home: 10641 Cardiff Rd Perrysburg OH 43551 Office: 309 N Reynolds Rd Toledo OH 43615

RITTERHOFF, C. WILLIAM, steel co. exec.; b. Balt.; B.S. in Mech. Engring., Mass. Inst. Tech., 1947; grad. Advanced Mgmt. Program, Harvard, 1973. Asst. engr. mech. dept. then various supervisory positions Bethlehem Steel Corp., Sparrows Point, Md., 1948-57, asst. supt. Sparrows Point plate mill, 1957-60, asst. chief engr. plant engring. dept., 1960-63, asst. chief engr. Burns Harbor project, 1963, asst. gen. mgr., 1963-67, gen. mgr. Burns Harbor plant, 1967-70, v.p. manufactured products steel operations, 1970-71, v.p. prodn. charge manufactured products and West Coast steel plants, 1971-72, v.p. prodn., steel operations, 1972-74, exec. v.p., dir., 1974-77, vice chmn., 1977—. Mem. Am. Iron and Steel Inst., Assn. Iron and Steel Engrs., Hwy. Users Fedn. (dir.), NAM (dir.). Office: Bethlehem Steel Corp Bethlehem PA 18016

RITTERSPACH, KENNETH CHARLES, photog. equipment mfg. co. exec.; b. Waukegan, Ill., May 13, 1942; s. Blair and Alice Jane (Austin) R.; B.A., Yale U., 1964; M.B.A., Stanford U., 1970, Ph.D., 1972. Peace Corps vol., Venezuela, 1964-66; tchr. math. Barstow Sch., Kansas City, Mo., 1966-68; dep. exec. dir. bus. and adminstrn. N.Y.C. Pub. Sch. System, 1971-78; pres. King Concept Corp., Edina, Minn., 1978—. Home: 5638 Hyland Courts Dr Bloomington MN 55437 Office: King Concept Corp 5190 W 76th St Edina MN 55435

RIVARD, MARCELL ANTOINE, mfg. co. exec.; b. Barre, Vt., Dec. 22, 1930; s. Lucien M. and Lea C. (Roy) R.; B.S., U.S. Mcht. Marine Acad., 1953; children—Steven Mark, Patricia Susan, James Erik. With Carrier Corp., Syracuse, N.Y., 1956—, v.p. service operation, 1973-76, v.p. mfg., 1976—. Bd. dirs. Child and Family Service, Syracuse. Served with U.S. Navy, 1954-56. Mem. Carrier Corp. Mgmt. Assn. Republican. Roman Catholic. Home: 1409 Riverbend Dr Baldwinsville NY 13027

RIVERA-EMMANUELLI, RAFAEL LUIS, banker; b. Guayanilla, P.R., Apr. 11, 1933; s. Rafael and Luisa Maria (Emmanuelli) Rivera-Rivera; B.B.A., Cath. U. P.R., 1960; grad. Bank Adminstrn. Inst., 1965, Am. Inst. Banking, P.R., 1966; m. Maria Maiz de Rivera, Dec. 22, 1955; children—Rafael, Naida, Mayra, Roberto. Asst. auditor Arthur Andersen & Co., San Juan, P.R., 1960; officer trainee Banco Credito Ahorro Ponceno, Ponce, P.R., 1960-61, accountant, 1961-64, asst. comptroller, 1964-67; dir. computer center, San Juan, 1967-68; asst. v.p. trust ops., 1968-69; bank cons. Peat Marwich, Mitchell & Co., San Juan, 1969-70; v.p., controller Banco Economias, San Juan, 1970-72, sr. v.p., 1972-74; bank cons. Rivera Emmanuelli Assos., San Juan, 1974-75; pres. Banco Financiero Ahorro Ponce, 1975-78; exec. v.p. Girod Trust Co., San Juan, 1978—; instr. Am. Inst. Banking (P.R.), Instituto Cultural Comunidad, Cath. U. P.R., 1966. Served with U.S. Army, 1953-55. Mem. Fin. Execs. Inst., Nat. Assn. Accountants, Bank Adminstrn. Inst. P.R. (pres. 1971-72), Club Ponce Mus. Art, Exchange Club Perla del Sur, Phi Sigma Alpha. Roman Catholic. Clubs: El Vigia Rotary; P.R. Bankers; Ponce Yacht and Fishing, Deportivo de Ponce; Atrium (N.Y.C.). Author: Principios de Operaciones Bancarias, 1979. Home: Galvez 302 Borinquen Gardens Rio Piedras PR 00926 Office: Calle Tetuan 355 San Juan PR 00901

RIVIERE, JAMES CHARLES, computer systems co. exec.; b. Monticello, Ark., June 21, 1941; s. James Horace and Elsie Nora (Douglass) R.; student Southwestern at Memphis, 1959-62; B.A., U. Wash., 1966; M.B.A., Am. Grad. U., 1976; children—Jean-marie, William Douglas, Robert Wayne, John Patrick, Joseph Andrew, Louis Richard. With The Boeing Co., Seattle, 1962-63, New Orleans, 1963-67; mcpl. real estate and property mgr. City of Seattle 1970-72; asst. treas. System Devel. Corp., Santa Monica, 1972-73, corp. dir. adminstrn., 1974-75, v.p., gen. mgr. electronic pub. systems div., 1975-76, corp. v.p. ops., 1977—; dir. Frontier, Inc., Houston. Chmn. bd. dirs. St. Raymond's Dominican Council. Recipient award Math. Assn. Am. Mem. Santa Monica C. of C., Nat. Contract Mgmt. Assn., Am. Soc. Mfg. Engrs., Am. Mgmt. Assn., Am. Inst. Indsl. Engrs., Pi Kappa Alpha. Republican. Presbyn. Home: 4541 45th St NW Washington DC 20016 Office: 2500 Colorado St Santa Monica CA 90406

RIVKIN, DAVID HERSHEL, electronics co. exec.; b. Hartford, Conn., Mar. 25, 1927; s. Samuel and Betty (Warschavsky) R.; cert. U. Oslo, 1947; B.S., Trinity Coll., Hartford, 1948; M.B.A., Stanford U., 1950; m. Judith Mathilda Ganz, June 14, 1953; children—Edward Scott, Kenneth Alan, Deborah Ann. Dir. mktg. mil. electronics div. Motorola, Inc., Chgo., 1954-64; pres. Radiochemistry Co., Louisville, 1964-65; mktg. mgr. power electronics div. Louis Allis Co., Greendale, Wis., 1965-66; pres. Courier Communications Co., Los Angeles and Hillside, N.J., 1966-71; v.p. electronics group Gladding Corp., Syracuse, N.Y., 1971-72; chmn. bd., treas. Numark Electronics Corp., Edison, N.J., 1972—. Vice pres. Deerfield (Ill.) Twp. Voters Assn., 1962-64. Served with USNR, 1945-46. Mem. IEEE. Republican. Home: 473 Long Hill Dr Short Hills NJ 07078

RIZZI, JOSEPH VITO, retail exec.; b. Berwyn, Ill., Dec. 5, 1949; s. Joseph and Mary Catherine (Mancini) R.; B.S. in Commerce summa cum laude, DePaul U., 1971; M.B.A., U. Chgo., 1973; J.D. magna cum laude, U. Notre Dame, 1976; m. Candace Kunz, June 24, 1972; 1 dau., Jennifer. Admitted to Ill. bar, 1976; law clk. to judge U.S. Dist. Ct. No. Dist. Ill., 1976-77; exec. v.p. T.B.R. Enterprises, Inc., Downers Grove, Ill., 1977—. Mem. Nat. Retail Merchants Assn., Am. Bar Assn., Ill. Bar Assn., Delta Epsilon Sigma. Roman Catholic. Asso. editor Notre Dame Lawyer, 1975-76; contbr. articles to profl. publs. Home: 6824 Meadowcrest Dr Downers Grove IL 60515 Office: 7323 Lemont Rd Downers Grove IL 60515

ROACH, JAMES EDWARD, wholesale co. exec.; b. Hutchinson, Kans., Oct. 28, 1917; s. Edward Graham and Marguerite Louise (Campbell) R.; B.B.A., U. Tex., Austin, 1939; m. Georgia Patricia Brooks, Apr. 19, 1941; children—James Graham, Stephen Campbell. Trainee, Firestone Tire & Rubber Co., 1939; trainee Esco, Ltd., Corpus Christi, Tex., 1940-41, various sales and mgmt. positions, 1946-55, gen. mgr., 1955—; chmn. bd. dirs. Vol. Purchasing Groups, Inc., Bonham, Tex., 1958—. Treas., John Young for Congress Campaign, 1978—. Served to lt. USNR, 1942-45. Mem. Tex. Seedsmen's Assn. (pres. 1960-61, 77-78), Corpus Christi Grain

Exchange (pres. 1961-62, 80-81), South Tex. County Elevator Assn. (pres.), Phi Kappa Psi. Roman Catholic. Clubs: Corpus Christi Country (pres. 1973-74), Rotary. Home: 5041 Cascade St Corpus Christi TX 78413 Office: PO Box 6467 Corpus Christi TX 78411

ROACH, WILLIAM RANKIN, pipe line co. exec.; b. San Angelo, Tex., Apr. 28, 1946; s. William Thomas and Christine Helen (Glenn) R.; B.B.A., Tex. Christian U., 1968, M.B.A. (univ. grad. fellow), 1970; m. Bobby Jo Woodside, June 7, 1968; children—Gabe William, Glen Robert. Adminstrv. asso., then auditor Sun Co., Dallas, 1970-74; comptroller Reamco, Inc., Lafayette, La., 1974-75; sec.-treas. Sperry Sun, Inc., Sugarland, Tex., 1975-78; mgr. fin. control Sun Pipe Line Co., Tulsa, 1978-80, mgr. acctg. and external reporting, 1980—. Recipient cert. of merit U.S. Jr. C. of C., 1979; C.P.A., Tex. Mem. Nat. Assn. Accountants, Am. Inst. C.P.A.'s, Tex. Soc. C.P.A.'s. Republican. Methodist. Club: Houston Frog (charter). Home: 3795 E 82d St Tulsa OK 74136 Office: PO Box 2039 Tulsa OK 74120

ROBARGE, RONALD WILLIAM, mfg. co. exec.; b. Middlesex County, N.J., May 6, 1938; s. Claude William and Martha (Richards) R.; B.S., N.C. State U., 1960; m. Marilyn Cook, June 11, 1960; children—Karen Lynn, Richard William. Asst. supt. Sonoco Products Co., Hartsville, S.C., 1963-69; plant engr. Fieldcrest Mills, Inc., Stokesdale, N.C., 1969-73; plant mgr. Royal Carolina Corp., Greensboro, N.C., 1973-74; pres. Spartan Mfg. Corp., Kernersville, N.C., 1974—. Served with arty. U.S. Army, 1961-63. Registered profl. engr., N.C. Mem. Internat. San. Supply Assn. Methodist. Home: 1010 Pine Knolls Rd Kernersville NC 27284 Office: Spartan Mfg Corp 1500 Brookford St Kernersville NC 27284

ROBBINS, BOB, electrical service co. exec.; b. Ottawa, Ill., May 8, 1934; s. Chester M. and Helen R.; B.S. in B.A., U. Denver, 1959; A.B.A., Pueblo Jr. Coll., 1961; A.S. in Elec. Engring., Richland Community Coll., 1977; m. Melba James, Feb. 1, 1974; children—James, Malinda, Robert, Terry, Felicia, Halena, Gregory. Vice pres. Space Com Inc., Colorado Springs, Colo., 1961-70; chief engr. Robbins Electric Service Co., Mulberry Grove, Ill., 1970—; instr. basic electricity and safety, civic and med. groups. Served with AUS, 1951-54: Korea. Mem. Am. Inst. Elec. Engrs., Am. Mfrs. Assn. Office: PO Box 11303 Saint Louis MO 63105

ROBBINS, CHARLES D., mining co. exec.; b. New Rochelle, N.Y., Feb. 15, 1923; s. Charles D. and Beulah (Prince) R.; student Bowdoin Coll., 1942-43; m. Lucille Mercier, Aug. 16, 1958; children—Charles D. III, Sarah Jane, James Bruce. Pres., Thunderwood Explorations, Ltd., 1975—, Que. Explorers Corp. Ltd., Gold Hawk Mines Ltd., Gold Reef Resources Ltd. Served to 2d lt. AUS, 1943-46. Mem. Am. Inst. Mining, Metall. and Petroleum Engrs., Canadian Inst. Mining, Zeta Psi. Roman Catholic. Contbr. articles on gold to profl. jours. Developer 1st comml. base metal mine in Maine; discovered iron and gold in So. Que., gold in No. Que. Home: 704 Rue Bonair Beloeil PQ J36 2B5 Canada Office: 130 Brunelle St Beloeil PQ Canada

ROBBINS, DONALD LEE, container mfg. co. exec.; b. Kansas City, Mo., Feb. 6, 1938; s. Efton Carey and Marjorie Maxine (Spain) R.; B.S., M.I.T., 1960; M.B.A., U. Mo., Kansas City, 1969; m. Janet Kathryn Brown, Feb. 12, 1966; children—Scott, Christopher, Kevin. Indsl. engr., prodn. control Burd & Fletcher Co., Kansas City, Mo., 1960-72; indsl. engr. Olinkraft, Kansas City, 1972; with Kansas City Central Paper Box Co., 1972—, v.p., gen. mgr., 1972—, dir., 1977—. Recipient award for excellence Indsl. Editor's Assn. Kansas City, 1967. Mem. Printing Industries Assn. Kansas City (sec., dir.). Club: Printing Execs. (Kansas City). Office: Kansas City Central Paper Box Co 2911 Belleview St Kansas City MO 64108

ROBBINS, HARVEY A., textile co. exec.; b. N.Y.C., Apr. 29, 1922; s. Ira B. and Mildred (Loewy) R.; student U. Mich., 1940-42, Cornell U., 1943, Columbia, 1945; m. Carolyn Edith Goldsmith, June 8, 1947; children—Margaret Ann (Mrs. Jay Jacobson), James Andrew. Vice pres. Silberstein-Goldsmith, N.Y.C., 1946-50, North Advt., Chgo., 1950-59; v.p. M. Lowenstein & Sons, Inc., N.Y.C., also pres. Wamsutta/Pacific Domestic div., 1959-69; pres. Burlington Domestics div. Burlington Industries, N.Y.C., 1969-73; v.p. United Mchts. & Mfrs., N.Y.C., 1973-78; v.p. PRF Corp., 1978-80; exec. v.p. Whisper Soft Mills, N.Y.C., 1980—. Bd. dirs. Fedn. for Handicapped, Ednl. Found. for Fashion Industries; corp. mem. Lesley Coll., Cambridge, Mass. Served with AUS, 1942-45. Decorated Purple Heart, Combat Inf. badge. Mem. Am. Mgmt. Assn., Am. Arbitration Assn., Textile Distbrs. Assn., Sigma Alpha Mu. Clubs: Woodmere Bay Yacht (trustee); U. Mich., Hemisphere (N.Y.C.). Home: 35 Brook Rd Valley Stream NY 11581 Office: 111 W York St New York NY 10018

ROBBINS, JAMES TATE, mfrs. rep. co. exec.; b. Washington, Feb. 12, 1945; s. Frank Mix, Jr. and Margaret (Williams) R.; A.B. in Econs., U. N.C., Chapel Hill, 1967; grad. exec. devel. program U. Tenn., Knoxville, 1979; m. Martha Walker, Sept. 2, 1972; children—John Walker, Margaret Elizabeth. Salesman, Southwestern Co., 1965-67; with Robbins and Bohr, Inc., 1970-80, v.p., Chattanooga, 1975-80, treas., 1977-80, also dir.; pres. Jim Robbins and Assos. Inc., Knoxville, 1980—. Served to 1st lt. U.S. Army, 1967-70. Mem. ASHRAE, Am. Foundrymen's Soc. Republican. Methodist. Clubs: Concord Yacht (Knoxville); Mountain City (Chattanooga). Home: 85 Madrid Ct Knoxville TN 37923 Office: 325 Erin Dr Knoxville TN 37919

ROBERSON, ROBERT STEPHEN, archtl. woodwork mfg. co. exec.; b. Mt. Kisco, N.Y., Nov. 30, 1942; s. Robert H. and Mercedes C. (Stack) R.; B.S., N.Y. U., 1964; M.B.A., Coll. of William and Mary, 1973; m. Barbara Colbert Drane, Oct. 21, 1967; children—Elizabeth deV., Merritt B., Barbara D. Various positions in fin. and bldg. industries, 1964-67; asst. to pres., now treas., exec. v.p., dir. Weaver Bros., Inc., Newport News, Va., 1967—; treas., dir. Drane Lumber Co., Inc., N.Y.C.; past dir. First Peninsula Bank & Trust Co., Hampton, Va. Mem. Newport News Republican City Com.; past bd. dirs. Peninsula unit Am. Cancer Soc., Newport News; past bd. dirs. Heritage council Girl Scouts U.S.A., Hampton; trustee Newport News Pub. Library. Mem. Newcomen Soc. N.Am., Soc. Colonial Wars, SR, Colonial Order of Acorn, Vet. Corps of Arty., Huguenot Soc. of N.J., Sovereign Mil. Order of Temple of Jerusalem, Assn. of Ex-Members of Squadron A, Blue Key, Delta Sigma Xi. Episcopalian. Clubs: Union, St. Nicholas Soc., Church (N.Y.C.); Hay Harbor (Fishers Island, N.Y.); Farmington Country (Charlottesville, Va.); James River Country, Hampton Roads Cotillion, Rotary (Newport News). Home: 58 James Landing Rd Newport News VA 23606 Office: PO Box 806 24th-26th Sts at Terminal Ave Newport News VA 23607

ROBERTS, ALLEN EARL, film producer, author; b. Pawtucket, R.I., Oct. 11, 1917; s. John and Lillian Phillips (Wilson) R.; student public schs., also Internat. Corr. Schs., Armed Forces Inst., T. C. Williams Law Sch.; m. Dorothy Grimes, June 12, 1946; children—Allen E., R. Wayne, Kenneth D., Marcia L., Brian K. With U.S. Govt., 1946-50, Bank of Va., 1950-52, Henrico County (Va.), 1952-54, Capitol City Iron Works, 1954-56, Va. Bur. Correctional Field Units, 1956-72; owner Imagination Unlimited!, Highland Springs, Va., 1969—; producer, author, dir. numerous films including: Saga of the Holy Royal Arch of Freemasonry, 1974; series Leadership Training Films, 1969-75; The Brotherhood of Man, 1975; Challenge O!, 1977; Precious Heritage, 1977; Lonely World, 1980; author: House Undivided, 1961; Freemasonry's Servant, 1969; Key to Freemasonry's Growth, 1969; The Craft and Its Symbols, 1974; G. Washington: Master Mason, 1976; Frontier Cornerstone, 1980; others. Served with USNR, 1942-45. Recipient Masonic awards; Silver award Internat. Film and TV Festival N.Y., 1974, 75, 77, Gold award, 1977. Mem. Acad. Cert. Adminstrv. Mgrs., Info. Film Producers Am., Soc. Motion Picture and TV Producers. Methodist. Club: Masons. Home: 110 Quince Ave Highland Springs VA 23075 Office: 1 A-B South Holly Ave Highland Springs VA 23075

ROBERTS, CALVIN THOMAS, fin. co. exec.; b. Emporia, Kans., Sept. 2, 1937; s. Edward John and Esther Bernice R.; B.S., Emporia State U., 1961; m. Norma Kae Sielert, June 2, 1957; children—Shari, Joani. Ins. adjuster Gen. Adjustment Bur., Kansas City, 1961-64; real estate investment field rep. Travelers Ins. Co., Kansas City, 1964-69; with Travelers Ins. Co., Hartford, Conn., 1969-80, sec. real estate dept., 1975-80, field supr. Prospect Co. subs., 1970-80, v.p. Panther Valley Ltd., subs., 1974-80; pres. Nat. Capital Corp., Hamden, Conn., 1980—; dir. De Matteo Constrn. Co., Hamden. Bd. dirs. Conn. Valley council Girl Scouts U.S.A., 1976-79, v.p. Tolland Corp., Girl Scout camp, 1979—; mem. Tolland (Conn.) Econ. Devel. Commn., 1978—. Served with U.S. Army, 1962. Mem. Nat. Apt. Assn. Council. Republican. Congregationalist. Club: Tolland Booster (dir.). Home: 37 Valleyview Dr Tolland CT 06084 Office: 2911 Dixwell Ave Hamden CT 06518

ROBERTS, CLAYTON JOHN, telephone co. exec.; b. Mpls., May 4, 1948; s. Richard Burt and Martha Marie (Row) R.; B.S. in Engring., U.S. Mil. Acad., 1970; m. Paula J. Ward, June 21, 1980. Adminstrv. asst. Interior Telephone Co., Anchorage, 1975-76, v.p. revenue requirements, 1976; v.p., 1976—. Pres. Alaska hockey adv. bd. Boys Club of Am., 1978-79. Served to capt. U.S. Army, 1970-75. Mem. Armed Forces Communications and Electronics Assn., Alaska Waterfowl Assn. Republican. Lutheran. Office: 508 W 6th Ave Anchorage AK 99501

ROBERTS, CURTIS BUSH, ins. agy. exec.; b. Beaumont, Tex., Aug. 17, 1933; s. Carroll Harry and Dorothy (Barber) R.; B.B.A., U. Tex., Austin, 1954; postgrad. So. Meth. U., 1962; m. Jean Jackson, Nov. 20, 1954; children—William Mason, Kevin Carroll. Spl. agt. Fireman Fund Ins. Group, 1954-56, bond mgr., 1956-62, regional mgr., 1962-64, nationwide mgr., 1964-66; v.p. Highlands Ins. Group, Houston, 1966-70, sr. v.p., 1971-74; sr. v.p. The Mills Co., Dallas, 1974-77, pres., 1977—; dir. Luthur Hill & Assos., Dallas. Mem. curriculum com., constrn. degree program E. Tex. State U. Mem. Nat. Assn. Surety Bond Producers, Associated Builders and Contractors (dir.), Associated Gen. Contractors (dir.), Am. Sub-contractors Assn. (dir.), Nat. Assn. Casualty and Surety Agts., Pan Am. Surety Assn. (founder, charter mem.). Episcopalian. Clubs: City, Plaza Athletic, Cedar Creek Country. Home: 4505 N Versailles St Dallas TX 75205 Office: The Mills Co 800 One Main Pl Dallas TX 75250

ROBERTS, DONNA JOYCE, lawyer; b. Detroit, Jan. 5, 1935; d. Clarence Edward and Marcella Ann (Just) Hawke; LL.B. magna cum laude, U. Detroit, 1964; m. Raymond Roberts, May 22, 1954; children—Michael J., Christopher J.; m. 2nd Donald R. Petersen, Nov. 1, 1979. Admitted to Mich. bar, 1965; law clk. Sugar & Schwartz, Detroit, 1963; atty./investigator Wayne County Friend of the Ct., Detroit, 1965-67, 69-70; atty. Dow Chem. Co., Midland, Mich., 1973-76, dir. product stewardship, 1976-79, asst. gen. counsel environ. law sect., 1979—; bd. dirs. Dow Chem. Employees Credit Union, 1974—, pres., 1977. Mem. Midland Bd. Edn., 1975-79, pres., 1977-79; bd. dirs. United Way of Midland County, 1979—. Recipient Am. Jurisprudence awards, 1962-64; Corpus Juris Secundum awards, 1962-64; Gamma Eta Gamma award, 1962. Mem. Am. Bar Assn., State Bar of Mich., Midland County Bar Assn., Career Women in Industry. Clubs: Zonta, Midland Art Council, Birchwood Farms Estate. Home: 6210 Siebert St Midland MI 48640 Office: 2030 Dow Center Midland MI 48640

ROBERTS, GEOFFREY ARTHUR SEBRY, internat. bus. cons., electronic mfg. co. exec.; b. London, Sept. 25, 1913; s. Arthur Bell and Elizabeth Kate (Sebry) R.; B.Sc. in Elec. Engring., London U., 1937; m. Clara Diana Meruelo, Jan. 22, 1954; children—Diane Elizabeth, Ian Geoffrey. Came to U.S., 1945, naturalized, 1952. With Marconi's Wireless Telegraph Co., London, 1937-40; spl. overseas rep. for Latin Am., RCA, 1945-59; founder OKI Electronics Am., Inc., Ft. Lauderdale, Fla., 1959, chmn. bd., 1959-78, chmn. emeritus, 1978—; founder, past chief exec. officer PEC Industries subs. Reliance Electric of Ohio, Ft. Lauderdale; founder Cosmopol, Inc., Ft. Lauderdale, 1979, pres., 1979—. Mem. Broward Indsl. Bd., Ft. Lauderdale; chmn., bd. dirs. Florida Oaks Sch., Ft. Lauderdale. Served with RAF, 1940-45. Recipient Key to Port Everglades, Fla., 1969. Mem. Aircraft Owners and Pilots Assn., Nat. Pilots Assn. (recipient Safe Pilot award 1970, Flight Proficiency award 1974), Nat. Aero. Assn., Nat. Bus. Aircraft Assn., N.Am. Telephone Assn. (past dir.), Opera Guild (dir. Ft. Lauderdale), Silver Wings Frat., Royal Air Force Ferry Command Assn. (Can.), Royal Air Force Assn. (Gt. Britain), Fla. C. of C., Ft. Lauderdale C. of C. Republican. Roman Catholic. Clubs: Le Club Internat., Lauderdale Yacht, Tower (Ft. Lauderdale). Home: 62 Fiesta Way Fort Lauderdale FL 33301 Office: Cosmopol Inc 1040 Bayview Dr Fort Lauderdale FL 33304

ROBERTS, GEORGE A., metallurgist, metals corp. exec.; b. Uniontown, Pa., Feb. 18, 1919; s. Jacob Earle and Mary M. (Bower) R.; student U.S. Naval Acad., 1935-37; B.Sc., Carnegie Inst. Tech., 1939, M.Sc., 1941, D.Sc., 1942; m. Betty E. Matthewson, May 31, 1941; children—George Thomas, William John, Mary Ellen; m. 2d, Jeanne Marie Polk. Technician, Bell Telephone Labs., N.Y.C., 1938; research dir. Vasco Metals Corp. (formerly Vanadium Alloys Steel Co.), Latrobe, Pa., 1940-45, chief metallurgist, 1945-53, v.p., 1953-61, pres., 1961-66, past chmn. bd., now pres., dir. Teledyne, Inc. (merger with Vasco Metals Corp.), Los Angeles, 1966—; hon. lectr. Société Française de Metallurgie, 1960; pres. Am. Soc. Metals Found. Edn. and Research, 1955-56, trustee, 1954-59, 63-64; trustee Carnegie-Mellon U. Fellow Metall. Soc., Am. Inst. Mining, Metall. and Petroleum Engrs., Am. Soc. Metals (chmn. Pitts. chpt. 1949-50, internat. pres. 1954-55, gold medal 1977); mem. Nat. Acad. Engring., Am. Soc. Metals, Metal Powder Industries Fedn. (dir. 1952-55, pres. 1957-61), Am. Iron and Steel Inst., Soc. Mfg. Engrs., Tau Beta Pi; hon. life mem. several fgn. socs. Methodist. Author: Tool Steels, 1944, 62. Contbr. articles to trade jours. Office: Teledyne Inc Suite 1800 1901 Ave of the Stars Los Angeles CA 90067

ROBERTS, GEORGE CHRISTOPHER, mfg. exec.; b. Ridley Park, Pa., May 27, 1936; s. George H. and Marion C. (Smullen) R.; m. Adriana Toribio, July 19, 1966; children—Tupac A., Capac Y. Sr. engr. ITT, Paramus, N.J., 1960-65; program mgr. Arde Research, Mawah, N.J., 1965-67; Space-Life Sci. program mgr., research div. GATX, 1967-69; dir. research and devel. Monogram Industries, Los Angeles, 1969-71; pres. Environ. Protection Center, Inc., Los Angeles, 1970-76; pres. INCA-One Corp, Los Angeles, 1972—, INCA-Two Corp., 1977—, INCA-Three Corp., 1978—; v.p. Chimu Assos. Advt. Agency, 1977—. Patentee automotive safety and sanitation systems, recreational vehicle equipment. Home: 755 Firth Brentwood CA 90049 Office: 9625 Bellanca Los Angeles CA 90045

ROBERTS, GEORGE OWEN, univ. adminstr., sociologist; b. Bumpe, Sierra Leone, West Africa, Jan. 15, 1928; s. Owen Gordon Price and Neneh Jamintu Fullah; came to U.S., 1947, naturalized, 1957; B.S., Hampton (Va.) Inst., 1952; M.A., Catholic U. Am., 1955, Ph.D., 1961; certificate in ednl. mgmt. Harvard U. Sch. Bus., 1972; m. Michaela Magdalene Balboa-Leigh, June 4, 1977; children by previous marriages—George Owen, Alvita, Neneh, Arthur. Gen. edn. coordinator State U. N.Y., New Paltz, 1964-68; dept. chmn. Hampton Inst., 1968-69; asst. vice chancellor U. Calif., Irvine, 1972-75, spl. asst. to exec. vice chancellor, 1975-79, chmn. comparative culture program, 1979—; ednl. cons. U.S. Office Edn., State Calif. Mem. Orange County (Calif.) Grand Jury, 1971-72, Calif. Criminal Justice Council, 1972-74, Disneyland Community Services Awards Com., 1975-76. Ford Found. fellow, 1955-56; Carnegie Found. fellow, 1957; USPHS fellow, 1957-58; U. Calif. fellow, 1972-73. Mem. African Studies Assn., Middle East Inst., Am. Sociol. Assn., Am. Assn. Higher Edn. Democrat. Episcopalian. Author: Afro-Arab Fraternity, 1980; mem. editorial bd. Jour. Black Studies; contbr. articles to profl. publs. Home: 22152 Pheasant St El Toro CA 92630 Office: Social Science Tower U Calif Irvine CA 92717

ROBERTS, HENRY REGINALD, ins. co. exec.; b. Toronto, Ont., Can., June 2, 1916; s. Alfred Reginald and Mary Margaret (Creighton) R.; B.A. in Math. and Physics, U. Toronto, 1937; L.H.D. (hon.), Clarkson Coll. Tech.; LL.D., Trinity Coll., U. Hartford; m. Margaret Elizabeth Fisher, May 23, 1940; children—Michael Alfred, Barbara Elizabeth, William Henry, Margaret Jane. Come to U.S., 1945, naturalized, 1954. With Mfrs. Life Ins. Co., Toronto, 1937-42; with Conn. Gen. Life Ins. Co., Hartford, 1945—, 2d v.p., 1958-60, exec. v.p., dir., 1960-61, pres., chief exec. officer, 1961-76; chmn. bd. Aetna Ins. Co., affiliate, 1966-76; pres., dir. Conn. Gen. Ins. Corp., 1967-76; chmn. bd. CGIC, 1976—; dir. Gen. Foods Corp., So. New Eng. Telephone Co.; dir. Greater Hartford Corp. Mem. adv. com. on bus. programs Brookings Instn.; corporator Hartford Hosp., Mt. Sinai Hosp., St. Francis Hosp., Conn. Inst. for Blind, Health Planning Council Inc. of Hartford. Former bd. dirs. Am. Council Life Ins., Health Ins. Inst.; bd. dirs. Internat. Exec. Service Corps; trustee Hartford Grad. Center, Conn. Pub. TV, Kingswood-Oxford Sch.; Fellow Soc. Actuaries; mem. Ins. Assn. Conn. (past chmn.), Greater Hartford C. of C. (dir.). Office: Conn Gen Life Ins Co Hartford CT 06152*

ROBERTS, JOE WENDELL, mech. engr.; b. Lubbock, Tex., Oct. 11, 1932; s. J.W. and Wynell S. (Squires) R.; B.S.M.E., U. N.Mex., 1959; m. Janice E. Anderson, Nov. 24, 1955; children—Wynn D., Carol. Engr., Singleton Co., Albuquerque, 1959-62; v.p. Rees Co., Albuquerque, 1962-66; owner, operator Roberts Corp., Albuquerque, 1966-74, Carico Lake Mining Co., Elko, Nev., and Albuquerque, 1974-77; pres. Thermal-Safe Insulation Corp., Albuquerque, 1977—. Served with USN, 1950-54. Mem. ASME, ASHRAE, Cellulose Mfrs. Assn. Home: 3121 Vermont St NE Albuquerque NM 87110 Office: 523 Rankin St NE Albuquerque NM 87107

ROBERTS, KENNETH LEWIS, banker; b. Dunganon, Va., Dec. 12, 1932; s. Clarence E. and Katherine (Osborne) R.; B.A., Vanderbilt U., 1954, LL.B., 1959; m. Anne Foster Cook, Sept. 10, 1955; children—Kenneth Lewis, Patrick Foster. Admitted to Tenn. bar, 1959; asst. prof. law Vanderbilt U., Nashville, 1959-60, lectr., 1960-66; asso. firm Waller, Lansden & Dortch, Nashville, 1960-66; from v.p. to exec. v.p. and dir. Commerce Union Bank, Nashville, 1966-71; pres., chief exec. officer, dir. Central Nat. Bank and Central Nat. Corp., Richmond, Va., 1971-76; pres., chief exec. officer, dir. First Am. Nat. Bank and vice-chmn. First Amtenn Corp., Nashville, 1976-77; pres., chief exec. officer First Am. Bank and First Amtenn Corp., 1977-79, chmn. bd., chief exec. officer, 1979—; dir. Genesco, Inc. Trustee, Vanderbilt U.; chmn. adv. bd. INROADS/Nashville, Inc., 1978; mem. exec. bd. Middle Tenn. council Boy Scouts Am., 1977; bd. dirs. Tenn. Ind. Colls. Fund, Leadership Nashville, Blair Sch. Music. Served as lt., Chem. Corps, U.S. Army, 1955-57. Mem. Assn. Bank Holding Cos. (dir.), Assn. Res. City Bankers, Order of Coif, Nashville Area C. of C. (dir.). Presbyterian. Clubs: Cumberland (Nashville); Belle Meade Country. Home: 3800 Woodlawn Dr Nashville TN 37215 Office: First American Bank First American Center Nashville TN 37237

ROBERTS, LYNN B., computer products mktg. co. exec.; b. Ogden, Utah, Aug. 5, 1933; s. William James and Marguerite Louise (Davis) R.; A.S. in Bus. Adminstrn., Weber Coll., 1953; B.S. in Econs., U. Utah., 1959; m. Diann McEntire. children—David Lynn, Joan Marie, John Daniel, Julia Diann, Richard Douglas. Staff mgr. Mountain Bell Telephone, 1959-64; with Burroughs Corp., 1964-72, account mgr., Salt Lake City, 1971-72; sales engr. Control Data Corp., Salt Lake City, 1972-74; dist. mgr. Data Systems Mktg., Salt Lake City, 1974—; a founder Computer System Dynamics, 1975; pres. ROBOC Corp.; guest speaker in field to sales tng. seminars, univs., civic orgns. Mem. Bountiful (Utah) Citizens Adv. Council, 1965-67; bd. dirs. Utah Jaycees, 1967. Served with inf. U.S. Army, 1953-55. Recipient SPOKE award U.S. Jaycees, 1968. Mem. Data Processing Mgrs. Assn. Club: Kiwanis (Salt Lake City). Office: 940 N 400 E North Salt Lake City UT 84115

ROBERTS, MARK GEORGE, computer co. exec.; b. Springfield, Mass., July 15, 1946; s. Clarence George and Louise Florence (Major) R.; A.B. in Math. and Physics, Holy Cross Coll., 1968; postgrad. mgmt. program Northeastern U., 1974; postgrad. in computer sci. U. N.Mex., 1970-71; postgrad. in bus. adminstrn. Clark U., 1976—; m. Sally May Flanagan, June 10, 1967. Mathematician, group leader Dikewood Corp., Albuquerque, 1968-70; founder, pres. Shire Inc., Albuquerque, 1970-71; with Digital Equipment Corp., 1971—, dist. software services mgr., Albuquerque, 1971, Ramada Inns account mgr., asst. to v.p. spl. projects, Maynard, Mass., 1972, mgr. advanced systems product line, Marlboro, Mass., 1973-74, mgr. comml. systems mktg., 1975-76, product line mktg. mgr., 1976-78, product line mgr., service industries bus., Merrimack, N.H., 1979, product line mgr., service industry mktg. strategy and devel., 1980—. McCarthy scholar, 1964-68; recipient Nugent award for excellence in physics, 1968. Mem. Am. Mgmt. Assn., Am. Computing Professional Assn. (sr.). Home: Osgood Rd Milford NH 03055 Office: Continental Blvd Merrimack NH 03054

ROBERTS, MARTIN, advt. exec., publisher; b. N.Y.C., Oct. 22, 1923; s. Selig and Anna (Ashinoff) R.; B.A., N.Y. U., 1946; student Fordham U., 1943, Columbia U., 1947-48; m. Kitt Pappas, Oct. 29, 1961; 1 son, Jonathan. Producer, dir. Nelson Prodns., Inc., 1948-53; dir. advt., promotion and publicity Nat. Telefilm Assn., 1953-61; pres. Martin Roberts & Assos., Inc., Beverly Hills, Calif., 1961—; pub. Videocassette and CATV Newsletter, 1971—, Satellite Age, 1978—; pres. Tape Books, 1973—; asso. prof. Coll. City N.Y., 1950-53, U. So. Calif., 1977—; guest lectr. univs. Served with Signal Corps and inf., USAAF, 1943-46; ETO. Decorated Purple Heart; recipient Billboard award for best TV promotion, 1956-57, Gold medal of merit Italian Govt., 1973. Mem. Soc. Motion Picture and TV Engrs., Internat. TV Assn. Democrat. Author: Videocassettes—the Systems, the Markets, the Future, 1970. Home: 3314 Scadlock Ln Sherman Oaks CA 91403 Office: 270 N Canon Dr #103 Beverly Hills CA 90210

ROBERTS, RICHARD CHASE, surg. co. exec.; b. N.Y.C., May 1, 1950; s. Richard David and Louise (Chase) R.; B.S., H.H. Lehman Coll., 1972; M.S., City Coll. N.Y., 1977; m. Jane Grace Rifkin, Sept. 2, 1978; children—Adam, Jennifer. Faculty, Bd. of Edn., N.Y.C., part-time 1972-78; with A & O Surg. Co., Inc., Bronx, 1972-78, regional mgr., Houston, 1978—. Nat. Def. grantee, 1968-72. Mem. Am. Surg. Trade Assn. Home: 9010 Railton St Houston TX 77080 Office: Katy Freeway Plaza 9446 Old Katy Rd Suite 104 Houston TX 77055

ROBERTS, RICHARD G., ins. co. exec.; b. Oskaloosa, Ia., June 17, 1941; s. Glen O. and Catherine E. (Geneva) R.; B.A., U. Fla., 1963; C.L.U., Am. Coll. Life Underwriters, 1973, M.S. and Fin. Services, 1980; m. Marilyn, Dec. 22, 1962; children—Adrienne, Melinda. Mgmt. trainee Fed. Res. Bank, San Francisco, 1963-64; ins. agt. Coll. Life Ins. Am., Berkeley, 1964-74; with Roberts & Assocs., Ins. Brokerage Agy., Walnut Creek, Calif., 1974-79; pres. Richard G. Roberts, C.L.U. & Assocs., Inc., Walnut Creek, 1976—. Pres. Estate Planning Council of Diablo Valley, 1979—. C.L.U., Calif. Mem. C.L.U. Assn. Am. (chpt. bd. dirs. 1975-76), Oakland East-Bay Life Underwriters Assn. (dir. 1974-76), Nat. Assn. Life Underwriters, Million Dollar Roundtable, Leading Life Producers Assn. No. Calif. (sec.), Estate Planning Council Diablo Valley (past pres.). Republican. Club: Round Hill Country. Home: 2173 Nelda Way Alamo CA 94507 Office: 1615 Bonanza St Walnut Creek CA 94596

ROBERTS, ROBERT FRANKLIN, oil co. exec.; b. Austin, Tex., Nov. 29, 1924; s. Allen Pinckney and Lillian (Lane) R.; J.D., U. Tex., 1945; m. Leila Crain, Dec. 23, 1951; 1 son, Mark Allen. Admitted to Tex. State bar, 1945; asso. law firm Hamilton, Hamilton, Turner & Hutchison, Dallas, 1945-47; ind. oil producer, La., 1948-63; pres., chmn. bd., chief exec. officer Crystal Oil Co., Shreveport, La., 1963—; dir. La. Bank & Trust Co., Shreveport. Mem. State Bar Tex., Petroleum Club Shreveport. Episcopalian. Clubs: Univ. (bd. govs.), Shreveport Country, Thoroughbred Assn. Am. Office: Crystal Oil Bldg PO Box 21101 Shreveport LA 71120

ROBERTS, STEVEN MICHAEL, petroleum retail and wholesale co. exec.; b. Springfield, Mass., Sept. 26, 1945; s. Abbott S. and Lenore (Furst) R.; B.S. in Psychology, U. Pa., 1967; postgrad. in bus. adminstrn. Boston U., 1967-69; m. Georgianne H. Howell, Mar. 29, 1970; children—Rachel, Lindsay, Jana. With F.L. Roberts & Co., Inc., Springfield, summers 1961-68, exec. v.p., 1969—; pvt. detective Simmons Detective Agy., Boston, 1968-69; incorporator Springfield Inst. for Savs. Bd. dirs. Springfield Central Bus. Dist., Inc., 1978—; mem. Springfield Riverfront Design Com., 1978—. Mem. Springfield C. of C. Jewish. Club: Crestview Country. Office: PO Box 1964 Springfield MA 01101

ROBERTS, WILLIAM LAWRENCE, appraiser, broker, real estate exec.; b. Boston, Jan. 20, 1924; s. James Joseph and Mary Margaret (Galvin) R.; student Northeastern U., 1949-51, Rutgers U., 1952-54; LL.B., Blackstone Sch. Law, 1959; grad. Realtors Inst., 1975; m. Josephine Mary DeLeo, July 22, 1945; children—James Joseph, Linda Marie (Mrs. John Hamilton Glover), William Lawrence. With RCA, Camden, N.J., 1951-58, Midwest regional rep., 1955, N.E. regional rep., 1956; sr. mem. tech. staff Thompson Ramo Wooldridge Co., Redondo Beach, Calif., 1958-60, N.E. regional mgr., 1960-61; mgr. marketing Sperry Rand Research Center, Sudbury, Mass., 1961-62; research and devel. marketing mgr. Litton Industries, Beverly Hills, Calif., 1962-65, dir. data systems, div. aero Service Corp., 1965-66; with Collins Radio Co., Dallas, 1966-74, venture analyst, mgr. sales service div., 1973-74; with Merrill Lynch-Paula Stringer, Inc., Dallas, 1974—, now v.p., mgr.; instr. real estate appraising Real Estate Career Coll. Chmn. cub scouts Fort Stanwix council Boy Scouts Am., 1956-57, asst. dist. commr., 1965-66; pres. Meadowbrook P.T.A., Pennsauken, N.J., 1953-54; capt. fund drive Plano YMCA, 1975. Campaign mgr. Kennedy/Johnson, Rome, N.Y., 1960. Served with USNR, 1942-45: PTO. Recipient Citizens award City Utica (N.Y.), 1963. Mem. Nat. Assn. Realtors, Tex. Assn. Realtors (edn. com.), Collins County Bd. Realtors (pres. 1981—), Soc. Real Estate Appraisers (edn. com. Dallas chpt. 1981—, designated sr. residential appraiser), Nat. Assn. Rev. Appraisers (cert. rev. appraiser), IEEE (sr. mem., nat. exec. com. 1960-64), Am. Rocket Soc., Am. Inst. Aero. and Astronautics, Armed Forces Communications and Electronics Assn. (nat. dir. 1959-67), Am. Angus Assn., Nat. Mktg. Inst. (cert. residential specialist, cert. residential broker). Author: (with Vernon Poehls) Naval Shipboard Communications Building Block Design Handbook, 1952; Test Agenda and Record of Performance of Shipboard Electronic Systems, 1953. Home: 3021 Princeton Dr Plano TX 75074 Office: Merrill Lynch-Paula Stringer Inc 6730 LBJ Freeway Suite 2240 Dallas TX 75240

ROBERTSON, A. JOHN, JR., acctg. cons. and tax co. exec.; b. Mpls., Dec. 25, 1937; s. Alvin J. and Ruth (Whalen) R.; B.S. cum laude, Coll. Holy Cross, Worcester, Mass., 1958; m. Joan Davies Morahan, June 22, 1962; 1 dau., Ellen Meredith. With Peat, Marwick, Mitchell & Co., 1960-65, 68—, partner, 1968—, mng. partner, Rome, 1968-72, partner-in-charge of European tng., Paris, 1972-73, sr. regional partner France, Spain and N. Africa, Paris La Defense, France, 1973-79, mng. partner, St. Louis, 1979—; asst. corp. controller Otis Elevator Co., 1965-68. Mem. Fin. Execs. Inst., Am. Inst. C.P.A's, N.Y. Soc. C.P.A's., Mo. Soc. C.P.A.'s, Ill. Soc. C.P.A.'s, Nat. Assn. Accts. Clubs: Polo de Paris, Maxim's Bus. (Paris); Old Warson Country, St. Louis, Racquet, Noonday, Mo. Athletic (St. Louis). Home: 4 Upper Ladue Rd Saint Louis MO 63124 Office: 720 Olive St Saint Louis MO 63101

ROBERTSON, CLYDE WISE, JR., trucking co. exec.; b. nr. Abilene, Tex., Aug. 27, 1917; s. Clyde Wise and Effie Beulah (Trantham) R.; grad. high sch.; m. Lena Ruth Harris, June 25, 1939; children—Bruce, Susan (Mrs. Stephen Elliott Davis), Jane (Mrs. Don Hall). With Am. Nat. Bank, Amarillo, Tex., 1940-44; office mgr. Hill Lines, Inc., Amarillo, 1944-46, gen. auditor, 1946-52, asst. gen. mgr., 1952-60; gen. mgr. H-M div. Ill.-Calif. Express, Inc., Amarillo, 1960-62, v.p., Amarillo and Dallas, 1962-70, pres., Denver, 1970-76, also dir.; pres. Strickland Transp. Co., Inc., Dallas, 1976-78; pres., dir. Ace Express, Inc., Dallas, 1978—, Ace Leasing Co., Inc., Dallas, 1977-78, Tattered Cover, Inc., Amarillo; dir. Exchange Savs. and Loan Assn., Dallas. Former bd. govs. Regular Common Carrier Conf. Mem. Southwest Operators Assn. (dir.), Western Hwy. Inst. Republican. Baptist. Clubs: Garden of the Gods (Colorado Springs); Las Colinas Country (Dallas). Home: 3727 Princess Ln Dallas TX 75229

ROBERTSON, GERALD LESLIE, foundry co. exec.; b. St. Joseph, Mo., Aug. 8, 1934; s. James Leo and Laura Elizabeth R.; student Gen. Motors Inst., Flint, Mich., 1952-56; grad. Mgmt. Program Harvard, 1974; m. Joan Alice Brock, Aug. 16, 1956; children—Stephen, Christopher, Julianne, Scott. Supr., Central Foundry div. Gen. Motors, Defiance, Ohio, 19S2-58; methods engr. Diamond Nat. Corp., Middleton, Ohio, 1958-60; indsl. engr. Mead Containers, Cin., 1960-62, mgr. dist. mfg., Durham, N.C., 1962-66, mgr. dist. mfg., Chgo., 1966-68; gen. mgr. Xenia Services, Zurich, Switzerland, 1968-72; v.p., gen. mgr. Soil pipe ops. Mead Corp. Anniston, Ala., 1972-74; exec. v.p. Mead Indsl. Products, Birmingham, 1974-75; pres. Lynchburg Foundry Co., (Va.), 1975—; dir. United Va. Bank/First Nat. Vice chmn. United Way Central Va., Lynchburg, 1975, chmn., 1976, pres., 1977—, bd. dirs., 1978; bd. dirs. Jr. Achievement, 1978, pres., 1979; chmn. S.E. region Foundry Edn. Found., 1977-78, trustee-at-large, 1978—; pres. council Randolph-Macon Woman's Coll., Lynchburg, 1979-80. Mem. Am. Foundrymen's Soc., Foundry Edn. Found., Va. Mfrs. Assn. (dir. 1978), Iron Castings Soc., Am. Mgmt. Assn., Lynchburg C. of C. (dir. 1978-79). Home: 3001 Sedgewick Dr Lynchburg VA 24503 Office: PO Box 411 Lynchburg VA 24505

ROBERTSON, JAMES ALLEN, risk mgmt. cons.; b. Burlington, Iowa, Jan. 24, 1948; s. George Allen and Betty Irene (Beck) R.; student Knox Coll., 1965-66; B.A., U. Iowa, 1969; postgrad. San Francisco Theol. Sem./Grad. Theol. Union, 1969-70; M.S.A., Pepperdine U., 1976; m. Stephanie Peacock. Casualty underwriter Hartford Ins. Group, San Francisco, 1970-72, supervising underwriter, 1972-73, Los Angeles, 1973-74; asst. v.p. Tausch Ins. Brokers, Santa Ana, Calif., 1974-75; cons. Warren, McVeigh & Griffin, 1975-76; sr. v.p. Reed Risk Mgmt., San Francisco, 1976-78; pres. James A. Robertson & Assos., Inc., El Paso, Tex., 1978-79; prin. cons., v.p. Warren, McVeigh & Griffin, Newport Beach, Calif., 1979; asso. in risk mgmt. C.P.C.U. Mem. Soc. Chartered Property Casualty Underwriters, Omicron Delta Kappa. Republican. Author: The Umbrella Book, 1979. Office: 1420 Bristol St N Suite 220 Newport Beach CA 92660

ROBERTSON, JAMES EDWARD, tire and motor supply co., investment co. exec.; b. St. Joseph, Mo., Nov. 27, 1931; s. James Leo and Laura E. (Rupp) R.; grad. St. Joseph Jr. Coll., 1951; m. Jolene Ann O'Connor, Sept. 3, 1956; children—Mike, Jina, John, Jan. With Leo Robertson Tire & Motor Supply, Inc., St. Joseph, 1952—, pres., dir., 1959—; partner Robertson Bros., St. Joseph, also RB Partnership, J & J Bros.; pres. Seneca Bancshares, 1972-78, now dir.; chmn., dir. Citizens State Bank, Seneca, 1971-76; sec., dir. Kans. Bancshares, 1971-75. dir. Ameribanc of St. Joseph, 1977. Pres., bd. dirs. J. Leo Robertson Found., 1965—, New Life-Inner City, 1969-74, St. Joseph Hosp., 1973—; chmn. Mayor's Drug Commn., 1970-78; bd. dirs. St. Joseph Public Sch. System, 1968-76, v.p., 1973-75, pres., 1975-76; trustee George Bode Trust, St. Joseph, 1976—; mem. Mo. Sch. Bd., 1978—; Served with USAF, 1951-52. Mem. Nat. Tire Dealers and Retreaders Assn., C. of C. (dir. 1952-55), Am. Mgmt. Assn., Soc. Advancement of Mgmt. Roman Catholic. Home: 35 Stonecrest St St Joseph MO 64506 Office: 1801 Frederick St St Joseph MO 64501

ROBERTSON, SARA STEWART, bank exec.; b. N.Y.C., Feb. 4, 1940; d. John Elliott and Mary Terry Stewart; B.A., Conn. Coll., 1961; M.B.A., Am. U., 1969; m. James Young Robertson, Nov. 29, 1975. Comml. banking trainee The First Nat. Bank of Chgo., 1969-70, asst. v.p. First Chgo. Leasing Corp., 1971-75, v.p., 1975—, head corporate cash mgmt. div., 1975-77, sr. area rep. Continental Europe, 1977-79, group head multinat. corporate banking area, 1979—. Club: Woman's Athletic (Chgo.). Home: 3200 N Lake Shore Dr Chicago IL 60657 Office: 1 First National Plaza Chicago IL 60670

ROBERTSON, THOMAS DONNELL, electronics co. exec.; b. Virginia Beach, Va., May 7, 1952; s. Willie Lee and Gertie Mae Samuel; B.S., U. Md., 1974; B.S., Norfolk State Coll., 1971; m. Gail V. Brown, Mar. 2, 1978; 1 son, Jamell. Police community relations advisor Norfolk (Va.) Police Dept., 1969-71; dir. United Fedn. Youth, 1971-74; exec. dir. Nat. Youth Devel. Assn., 1974-77; gen. mgr. Community Bd. 85, 1979-80; pres., founder D. & E. Electronics, Inc., Bklyn., 1975-80. Mem. Gov.'s Youth Adv. Council; co-chmn. Mayor's Youth Adv. Council. Served to capt. AUS, 1971. Mem. Am. Mgmt. Assn., Nat. Hist. Soc., Nat. Audubon Soc., Smithsonian Instn., Costeau Soc., VFW, Alpha Beta Kappa. Democrat. Baptist. Office: 653 MacDonough St Brooklyn NY 11233

ROBERTSON, WILLIAM EDWARD, mktg. co. exec.; b. Carteret, N.J., Dec. 15, 1916; s. William E. and Beneva (Roy) R.; B.A., Bucknell U., 1938; m. Dorothy Mary Dunn, Sept. 21, 1940 (div.); children—William E. III, Malcolm B., Douglas A.; m. 2d, Regina E. Gallagher, Nov. 24, 1971. Reporter, editorial writer Courier-News, Plainfield, N.J., 1938-42; asst. to pub. Harpers Mag., N.Y.C., 1946-50; asso. pub. dir. U.S. News & World Report, Washington, 1950-69; chmn. bd. Communications Marketing, Inc., Washington, 1970-72; also dir.; chmn. bd., dir. Marketing Concepts, Inc., Washington, 1972-80; dir. Survey Research Center, U. N. Fla., Jacksonville, 1980—. Served to capt. AUS, 1942-46, 51-52. Mem. Am. Marketing Assn., Nat. Economists Club. Republican. Episcopalian. Clubs: International; Washington Golf and Country (Arlington, Va.); Ponte Vedra (Fla.); Profl. Golfers Assn. Players (Sawgrass, Ponte Vedra, Fla.). Home: 218 Pablo Rd Ponte Vedra FL 32082 Office: U N Fla 4567 St John's Bluff Rd S Jacksonville FL 32216

ROBEY, FREDERICK FELIX, investment co. exec.; b. Prague, Czechoslovakia, June 25, 1923; came to U.S., 1939, naturalized, 1943; s. Leopold and Margaret (Fanta) R.; A.B. in Econs., Inst. Montana, Zug, Switzerland, 1946; postgrad. U. Pitts., 1944, N.Y. U., 1946, N.Y. Inst. Fin., 1960; m. Sidney Jean Brown, Dec. 24, 1965. Sales mgr. Baronet Leather Goods, N.Y.C., 1947-59; account exec./stock broker Walston & Co., Inc., N.Y.C., 1960-69, Glore Forgan Staats, N.Y.C., 1969-70; stock broker/br. mgr. A.G. Edwards & Co., St. Louis, 1970-72; v.p. Thomson & Mckinnon Securities, Inc., Morristown, N.J., 1973—. Trustee Allocca Found. Learning Disabilities. Served to capt. M.I., AUS, 1945-46. Clubs: Rockaway River Country (Denville, N.J.); Smoke Rise (N.J.). Home: 500 Pepperidge Tree Terr Smoke Rise Kinnelon NJ 07405 Office: 95 Madison Ave Morristown NJ 07960

ROBICHAUX, JOLYN HOWARD, ice cream co. exec.; b. Cairo, Ill., May 21, 1928; d. Edward C. and Margaret (Love) Howard; A.B., Chgo. State U., 1960; m. Joseph J. Robichaux, June 7, 1952 (dec. Apr. 1971); children—Sheila Veronica, Joseph Howard. Midwest rep. Betty Crocker home service dept. Gen. Mills Co., 1960-65; with Charles A. Davis & Assos., pub. relations, 1965-67; with Baldwin Ice Cream Co., Chgo., 1967—, pres., gen. mgr., 1971—; nutrition cons. State Dept. in Africa, 1956. Mem. Cook County (Ill.) Jury Commn., 1971-72; bd. dirs. P.U.S.H., Chgo. Urban League, Chgo. Community Ventures, Inc. Recipient Community Service award Chgo. Jaycees, 1973; One of Ten Outstanding Black Bus. Persons award, Chgo. Blackbook, 1973; Black Excellence in Bus. award P.U.S.H., 1975; named Cosmopolitan Woman of Yr., 1976. Mem. Iota Phi Lambda. Roman Catholic. Office: 4825 S Indiana Ave Chicago IL 60615

ROBILLARD, RAYMOND ALFRED, univ. adminstr.; b. Holyoke, Mass., Jan. 26, 1923; s. Lucien and Nellie (Robillard) R.; B.B.A. in Accounting, Northeastern U., 1952; postgrad. U. Toledo, 1955; M.B.A. in Fin., U. Mass., 1959; Ph.D. in Polit. Sci., Am. Internat. Open U. (now Clayton U.), 1978; m. Jennifer Karzy, July 30, 1960; children—Phillip Raymond, Paul Francis; stepchildren—John Michael Brodowski, Thomas Peter Brodowski. Costs and budget dir. Holyoke Card & Paper Co., Springfield, Mass., 1946-52; supervisory accountant Springfield Armory, 1952-59; mgr. adminstrn. and fin. control surface communications div. RCA, Camden, N.J., 1959-62; fin. mgr. Martin-Marietta Corp., Balt., 1962-65; controller, asst. treas. AAI Corp., Balt., 1965-67; bus. mgr. Eastern Shore campus U. Md., Princess Anne, 1967—; lectr. Loyola Coll., Balt., 1963-68, Johns Hopkins U., Balt., 1965-70. Controller, Nat. Chicken Festival, Delmarva Poultry Industry, Georgetown, Del., 1970; mem. arts and crafts com. Wye Inst., Queenstown, Md., 1971-78; mem. adv. council Somerset County (Md.) Bd. Edn.; mem. Md. Ednl. TV Planning Council, 1968-78; founder bd. dirs., pres. Eastern Shore Arts and Crafts Center, Princess Anne, 1971—; bd. dirs. Olde Princess Anne Days Historic Trust, 1973—; bd. dirs., asst. treas. Samuel Chase House Restoration Council, Princess Anne, 1975—; fin. advisor, bd. dirs. Somerset County Bicentennial Commn., Princess Anne, 1974-80; cons. Inst. Chesapeake Bay Studies, Wye Mills, Md., 1975—, Inst. Mediterranean Studies, Dubrovnik (Yugoslavia) and Tokyo, 1976—; project evaluator Md. Com. for Humanities, 1979; mem. Acad. Council, Clayton U., St. Louis, 1979—. Served with M.I., U.S. Army, 1942-46. Decorated Croix de Guerre with bronze star (France); recipient Outstanding Boss award Jaycees, Cambridge, Ohio, 1961; Man of Year award Marylander and Herald Newspapers, Princess Anne, 1971; N award Northeastern U., 1951. Mem. Princess Anne Area C. of C. (pres. 1969—), Fin. Execs. Inst., Nat. Assn. Coll. and Univ. Bus. Officers, Internat. Studies Assn., Overseas Devel. Council, Delmarva Indsl. Devel. Assn., Coll. and Univ. Personnel Assn., Am. Legion, Epsilon Phi Sigma, Phi Kappa Phi (life mem.). Republican. Club: Johns Hopkins. Author: Union Financial Accounting and Reporting Practices, 1959; The Place of Capitalism and Morality in a Free Society, 1959; Free Enterprise as a Factor in National Economies: Problems and Perspectives, 1977; Interdependence of Free Enterprise and Governments in the Global Marketplace, 1979; contbr. articles to profl. jours. Home: Hillcreek 1305 Milldam Rd Towson MD 21204 Office: U Md Eastern Shore Princess Anne MD 21853

ROBIN, ARNOLD MARTIN, business service co. exec.; b. New Haven, Oct. 8, 1940; s. Abe and Marie (Zito) R.; B.S. in Bus. Adminstrn., U. Conn., 1963; m. Rochelle Marie Hueso, June 25, 1966; 1 dau., Nichelle Marie. Dir. cost reimbursement Nat. Med. Enterprises, Los Angeles, 1971-74, v.p., 1974—, So. Calif. regional controller, 1974-76, chief hosp. fin. officer, 1976-78; pres. Syndicated Office Systems, Garden Grove, Calif., 1978—. C.P.A., Calif.; cert. Calif. Bur. of Correction and Investigative Services. Mem. Am. Inst. C.P.A.'s, Calif. Soc. C.P.A.'s, Hosp. Fin. Mgmt. Assn. (advanced mem.), Am. Acctg. Assn., Acctg. Research Assn. Home: 3773 Pacific Ave Long Beach CA 90807 Office: 12441 Knott St Suite 104 Garden Grove CA 92641

ROBIN, VINCENT JOSEPH, III, corp. exec.; b. Larose, La., Mar. 4, 1918; s. Vincent Joseph and Edverine (Savoie) R.; student Internat. Corp. Sch., 1943-45. Internat. Corr. Schs., 1965; m. Erline E. Chaisson, June 1, 1935 (div.); children—Joel P., Marian (Mrs. Russell DiMarco), Donald J., Vincent Joseph IV; m. 2d, Linda L. Rostran, Mar. 25, 1975; 1 dau., Alexandra Cristina. Owner, exec. pres. Robin Boat Rental Service, Inc., Robin, Inc., Offshore Crewboats Inc., Marine Taxis, Inc., Marian Ann, Inc., Robin Internat. Marine Towing Corp., Robin Marine Corp., Robin Towing Corp., Robin Crewboat Corp., Harvey, La., 1947—. Rotarian, K.C. Clubs: Krewe of Bacchus, Young Man's Business (New Orleans). Home: 797 Marlene Dr Gretna LA 70053 Office: 440 Pailet St PO Box 526 Harvey LA 70058

ROBINS, GARY BRUCE, beverage co. exec.; b. Columbus, Ohio, June 6, 1946; s. Louis and Sara (Kahn) R.; student Ohio State U., 1964-66; m. Constance Kiefer, Aug. 11, 1967; children—Dean, Chad, Bret, Zach. Salesman, Excello Wine Co., Columbus, 1967-70, v.p., 1971—; pres. Hi-State Beverage Co., Columbus, 1977—, also dir.; v.p. The Robins Beverage Group, 1980—. Active United Jewish Fund, 1970—; bd. dirs. Jewish Family Service, 1975; mem. Columbus Conv. and Visitors Bur.; mem. Columbus Quincentennial Exposition 1992. Mem. Wholesale Beer Assn. Ohio, Nat., Beer Wholesalers Assn., Wine and Spirits Wholesalers Am., Ohio Wholesale Wine Dealers Assn., Columbus Mfrs. Reps. Assn., Columbus C. of C., Ohio C. of C. Clubs: B'nai B'rith, Winding Hollow Country, Columbus Men's ORT. Home: 389 S Merkle Rd Columbus OH 43209 Office: 949 King Ave Columbus OH 43212

ROBINS, KENNETH TURNER, controller; b. Hamilton, Ont., Can., Nov. 27, 1938; s. Carle Ashton and Anne Mary (Beresner) R.; student McMaster U., 1959-62; m. Judith A. Rohmer, Sept. 15, 1964; children—Paul Andrew, Cameron Mathew. With Chagnon, MacGillivray & Co., Chartered Accts., Hamilton, Ont., 1962-67; controller Barringham Plastics Ltd., Clarkson, Ont., 1967-68; budget supr. Procor Ltd., Oakville, Ont., 1968-69, internal acctg. mgr., 1969-70, chief acct., 1971-73, div. controller, 1974-77, group controller, 1978—. Bd. dirs. United Way, Oakville, 1975-78, indsl. campaign chmn., 1976-77, budget and allocations chmn., 1978. Served to lt. Royal Canadian Naval Res., 1960-66. Mem. Inst. Chartered Accts. of Ont., Fin. Execs. Inst., Canadian Inst. Chartered Accts., C. of C. Mem. Conservative Party. Mem. Ch. of Eng. Clubs: Burlington Golf and Country, Burlington Boating and Sailing. Home: 283 Plains Rd W Burlington ON L7T I6I Canada Office: 2001 Speers Rd Oakville ON L6J 5E1 Canada

ROBINS, MIRIAM CLAIR, ins. co. exec.; b. Denver, Sept. 19, 1935; d. H. Rupard and Mildred L. (Opie) Robins; B.A., Colo. Coll., 1957; M.A., U. Denver, 1959. Instr. piano, organ, Denver, 1957-62; v.p., dir. Olinger Life Ins. Co., Denver, 1961-63, exec. v.p., dir., 1963-73, pres., dir., 1973-78, vice chmn. bd., 1978—. Tchr., music arranger for talent competition Miss America, 1958; v.p. Colo. Life Conv., Denver, 1966-67. Mem. Kappa Delta Pi, Mu Phi Epsilon, Kappa Alpha Theta. Republican. Clubs: Denver; Denver Athletic; Century (U. Denver); Cutler (Colo. Coll.). Home: Polo Club N 2552 E Alameda Ave Apt 23 Denver CO 80209 Office: Box 11128 Highlands Sta Denver CO 80211

ROBINSON, BERNARD LEO, lawyer; b. Kalamazoo, Feb. 14, 1924; s. Louis Harvey and Sue Mary (Starr) R.; B.S., U. Ill., 1947, M.S., 1958, postgrad. in structural dynamics, 1959; J.D., U. N.Mex., 1973; m. Betsy Nadell, May 30, 1947; children—Robert Bruce, Patricia Anne, Jean Carol. Research engr. Assn. Am. Railroads, 1947-49; instr. architecture Rensselaer Poly. Inst., 1949-51; commd. 2d lt. Corps Engrs., U.S. Army, 1945, advanced through grades to lt. col., 1965, ret., 1968; engr. Nuclear Def. Research Corp., Albuquerque, 1968-69; exec. v.p. Hi-Z Mining Corp., Albuquerque, 1969-70; exec. v.p. Financial Services, Inc., Albuquerque, 1971-73; admitted to N.Mex. bar; practiced in Albuquerque, 1973—; pres. First Capital of Albuquerque, Inc.; sec. Hi-Z Mining Corp. Dist. commr. Boy Scouts Am., 1960-62. Vice chmn. Republican Dist. Com., 1968-70. Decorated Air medal, Combat Infantryman's Badge, Joint Services Commendation medal. Mem. ASCE, Soc. Am. Mil. Engrs., Am., N.Mex., Albuquerque bar assns., Comml. Law League Am., Ret. Officers Assn., DAV, Assn. U.S. Army. Home: 6024 Vista Campo NE Albuquerque NM 87109 Office: 1200 University NE Albuquerque NM 87106

ROBINSON, CARLETON BRYANT, business exec.; b. Little Falls, N.Y., July 1, 1911; s. George A. and Luvern (Baum) R.; B.S., U. Pa., 1933; children (by previous marriage)—Linda Anne, Nancy Patricia;

m. Mary Gilbert, Mar. 20, 1965. Sales mgr. J. & E. Stevens Co., Cromwell, Conn. 1934-40; v.p. sec. George A. Robinson & Co. Inc., East Rochester, N.Y., 1940, now pres. Mem. Delta Kappa Epsilon. Mason. Clubs: Yale, University (Rochester); Century; Monroe Golf. Home: Brightford Heights Rochester NY 14610 Office: Geo A Robinson & Co Inc East Rochester NY 14445

ROBINSON, CHARLES HALL, cotton yarn mfg. co. exec.; b. Morehead City, N.C., July 24, 1919; s. Charles Oakley and Ivy (Blades) R.; A.B. in Econs., Princeton U., 1941; postgrad. Harvard U. Sch. Bus., 1946-47; m. Margaret Patricia Birch, Feb. 8, 1947; children—Charles Hall, Patricia B. With Robinson Mfg. Co., Elizabeth City, N.C., 1948—, v.p., 1950-68, pres., chief exec. officer, 1968—; dir. First Union Corp., Charlotte, N.C., 1969—; pres. First & Citizens Nat. Bank, Elizabeth City, 1968-69. Pres. Pasquotank United Fund, Elizabeth City, 1969-70; trustee St. Mary's Sch., Raleigh, N.C., 1970-71; chmn. adminstrv. bd. First United Methodist Ch., Elizabeth City. Served to capt. U.S. Army, 1942-46; ETO. Republican. Clubs: Rotary (pres. club 1973-74), Pines Lakes Golf (Elizabeth City); Norfolk (Va.) Yacht and Country, Masons. Home: 1830 Rivershore Rd Elizabeth City NC 27909 Office: Robinson Mfg Co Chestnut St and Hughes Blvd Elizabeth City NC 27909

ROBINSON, CHRISTOPHER JOHN NIELD, ins. brokerage exec.; b. Lancashire, Eng., Oct. 5, 1934; s. John Cuthbert and Marjorie (Winterton) R.; came to U.S., 1977; student pvt. schs., Kent and Surrey, U.K.; m. Penelope Morley, Mar. 30, 1976. With Osler Hammond & Nanton, 1966-68, merged with Reed, Stenhouse Inc., 1968—, formerly v.p. in Can., sr. v.p., N.Y.C., 1977—; bd. dirs. Brit. Am. C. of C. Served with Royal Dragoons, Brit. Army, 1953-56. Clubs: N.Y. Yacht, Royal Can. Yacht, Larchmont (N.Y.) Yacht. Home: 7 E 74th St New York City NY 10021 Office: 88 Pine St New York NY 10005

ROBINSON, GREGORY CHARLES, lawyer, mfg. co. exec.; b. Chgo., Sept. 26, 1946; s. John Charles and Shirley Jane (Arneson) R.; B.S. in Indsl. Mgmt., Purdue U., 1969; M.B.A., Ind. U., 1972, J.D., 1972; m. Christy True Evans, June 17, 1968; children—Hillary True, Taylor Davis. Admitted to Ind. bar, 1972; comml. banking officer Central Nat. Bank, Cleve., 1972-75; v.p., sec., treas. Custom Materials Inc., Chagrin Falls, Ohio, 1975—; pres. CMI Leasing Inc., Chagrin Falls, 1979—; gen. partner CMI Properties Ltd., Chagrin Falls, 1977—; sec., treas. Mfg. Machines Systems Inc., Chagrin Falls, 1980—. Mem. Am. Bar Assn., Assn. Profl. M.B.A.'s, Chagrin Falls Jaycees (pres. 1977-78, dir. 1976-79, Outstanding Jaycee award 1980), Phi Kappa Psi. Home: 442 Walters Rd Chagrin Falls OH 44022 Office: 16865 Park Circle Dr Chagrin Falls OH 44022

ROBINSON, IRWIN JAY, lawyer; b. Bay City, Mich., Oct. 8, 1928; s. Robert R. and Anne (Kaplan) R.; A.B., U. Mich., 1950; LL.B., Columbia, 1953; m. Janet Binder, July 7, 1957; children—Elizabeth Binder, Jonathan Meyer, Eve Kimberly. Admitted to N.Y. bar, 1956; asso. atty. Breed, Abbott & Morgan, N.Y.C., 1955-58; asst. to partners Dreyfus & Co., N.Y.C., 1958-59; asso. firm Greenbaum, Wolff & Ernst, N.Y.C., 1959-65, partner, 1966-76; sr. partner firm Rosenman Colin Freund Lewis & Cohen, N.Y.C., 1976—; treas. Roechling Steel, Inc., N.Y.C.; dir., sec. Townsley Internat. Sales, Ltd., N.Y.C., Empire Holdings, Inc., San Francisco; dir. Gross Cash Registers, Inc., Elk Grove, Ill., Asian Internat. Bank, N.Y.C.; authorized U.S. rep. Marinduque Mining & Indsl. Corp., Manila, Philippines. Bd. dirs., v.p. Henry St. Settlement; bd. dirs., pres. New Fed. Theatre; bd. dirs., Nat. Jewish Welfare Bd. Served with Transp. Corps, AUS, 1953-55. Mem. Am. (mem. com. on commodities), N.Y. State bar assns., Assn. Bar City N.Y., Philippine-Am. C. of C. (v.p., sec., dir.). Home: 4622 Grosvenor Ave Riverdale NY 10471 Office: 575 Madison Ave New York NY 10022

ROBINSON, JAMES D., III, corp. exec.; b. Atlanta, Nov. 19, 1935; B.S., Ga. Inst. Tech., 1957; M.B.A., Harvard U., 1961. Officer various depts. Morgan Guaranty Trust Co. of N.Y., 1961-66, asst. v.p., staff asst. to chmn. bd. and pres., 1967-68; gen. partner corp. fin. dept. White, Weld & Co., 1968-70; exec. v.p. Am. Express Co., N.Y.C., 1970-75, pres., 1975-77, chmn. bd., chief exec. officer, 1977—, dir., 1975—, pres., chief exec. officer Am. Express Internat. Banking Corp., 1971-73, chmn. bd. Am. Express Credit Corp., 1973; dir. Fireman's Fund Am. Ins. Cos., Coca-Cola Co., Union Pacific Corp., Trust Co. of Ga., Bristol-Myers Co.; chmn. N.Y. State Savs. Bond Co., 1980-81. Vice chmn. Meml. Hosp. for Cancer and Allied Diseases; bd. overseers, bd. mgrs. Meml. Sloan-Kettering Cancer Center; mem. Adv. Council on Japan-U.S. Econ. Relations; bd. govs. United Way Am. Served to lt. USNR, 1957-59. Mem. Council Fgn. Relations, Econ. Club N.Y., Bus. Roundtable, Bus. Council, European Community-U.S. Businessmen's Council (U.S. sect.), N.Y. Chamber of Commerce and Industry (dir.), Econ. Devel. Council of N.Y.C., Inc. (dir.), N.Y. Stock Exchange Listed Co. Adv. Com., Rockefeller Univ. Council, Pilgrims of U.S. Club: Links (bd. govs.). Office: Am Express Plaza New York NY 10004

ROBINSON, JAMES WILLIAM, mgmt. cons.; b. Bklyn., Feb. 22, 1919; s. Charles Edward and Adelaide (Reimer) R.; A.B., Cornell U., 1940, LL.B., 1942; m. Dorothy L. Luckow, July 5, 1946; 1 dau., Joan Barbara. Admitted to N.Y. bar, 1942; practice in N.Y.C., 1946—; asso. atty. Whitman, Ransom & Coulson, 1946-57; with W.Va. Pulp & Paper Co. (now Westvaco Corp.), N.Y.C., 1957-69, sec., 1966-69; prin. Georgeson & Co. Inc., cons. and proxy solicitation, 1969—. Served to capt. AUS, 1942-46. Decorated Bronze Star medal. Mem. Am., N.Y. State bar assns., Assn. Bar City N.Y., Am. Soc. Corp. Secs., Stock Transfer Assn., Phi Delta Phi, Lambda Chi Alpha. Club: North Hempstead Country. Editor: Tender Offers Handbook, 1974. Home: 66 Woodedge Rd Plandome NY 11030 Office: Wall St Plaza New York NY 10005

ROBINSON, JOHN FREDERICK, assn. exec.; b. N.Y.C., May 3, 1944; s. George and Ruth (Harris) R.; B.B.A., Baruch Coll., 1972; m. Vilma Pamilla Arthur, Aug. 20, 1977. Supr. office services Cancer Care, Inc., N.Y.C., 1968-76; mgr. adminstrv. services Bedford-Stuyvesant Restoration, Bklyn., 1977-79. Pres., Nat. Minority Bus. Council, Inc., 1979—. Mem. Fed. Exec. Bd., Am. Mgmt. Assn. (pres.), Alliance of Minority Bus. Orgns., Nat. Council for Policy Rev. (dir.), Coalition for Common Sense in Govt. Procurement. Contbr. articles to mgmt. jours. Home: 170-40 Cedarcroft Rd Jamaica Estates NY 11432 Office: 235 E 42d St New York NY 10017

ROBINSON, JOSEPH ANTHONY, retail jeweler; b. Boise, Idaho, Dec. 3, 1925; s. Joseph Anthony and Margaret Maud (McWaters) R.; student U. Idaho, 1943-44; m. Dorothy Lou Taylor, Dec. 27, 1946; 1 dau., Katherine C. With M.G. Sexty's Jewelers, Boise, 1946-56, mgr., 1956-60, partner, 1961-67; owner, pres. Sexty's Jewelers, Inc., Boise, 1968—. Bd. dirs. United Way of Ada County, 1971, Boise Family YMCA, 1974. Served with U.S. Army, 1944-46. Decorated Purple Heart, Bronze Star; recipient Golden Loupe award Am. Gem Soc., 1970. Mem. Boise C. of C., Am. Gem Soc., Internat. Retail Jewelers Assn., Nat. Fedn. Ind. Bus., Jewelers Vigilance Com., Retail Jewelers Am. Republican. Episcopalian. Clubs: Rotary (dir. 1979-80), Arid, Hillcrest Country, DAV, Elks, Masons (32 deg., Shriner), Royal Order Jesters, Internat. Order Cabiri, Low Twelve Fund of Idaho (dir., sec. 1955—). Home: PO Box 40 Idaho City ID 83631 Office: PO Box 2792 Boise ID 83701

ROBINSON, LAURETTA DEBORAH, lawyer, banker; b. Bayside, N.Y., Aug. 18, 1914; d. Henry and Lauretta (Fitz Gerald) Robinson; A.B., Cornell U., 1934, LL.B., 1944; student N.Y. Inst. Finance, 1959-60, Am. Inst. Banking, 1966-67; m. Albert A. Plentl, July 11, 1947 (div. 1957). Admitted to N.Y. bar, 1945; mem. legal staff Shearman & Sterling, attys., N.Y.C., 1944-53; account exec. Sterling Grace & Co., N.Y.C., 1959-61, Hardy & Co., 1961-65; with Citibank, N.A., N.Y.C., 1965—, asst. trust officer, 1966-68, trust officer, 1968-75, asst. v.p., 1976-77, v.p., 1977—. Bd. dirs. Girls Club N.Y., 1962-75, v.p., 1964-67; bd. dir. Girls Clubs Am., 1964-79, asst. treas., 1967-68; exec. com. Womens Aux. N.Y. Hosp., 1964-79. Mem. N.Y. State Bar, Fed. Bar So. Dist. N.Y. Club: Cosmopolitan. Home: 14 Sutton Pl S New York NY 10022 Office: One Citicorp Center New York NY 10022

ROBINSON, MAURICE RICHARD, publisher; b. Wilkinsburg, Pa., Dec. 24, 1895; s. Richard Bradley and Rachel S.C. (Calderwood) R.; A.B., Dartmouth Coll., 1920; m. Florence Liddell, June 2, 1934; children—Richard, Susan, Barbara, Florence, William. Founded Western Pa. Scholastic, 1920, title changed to Scholastic, 1922, Scholastic Mags., Inc., pubs. 27 elementary and secondary sch. classroom periodicals, pubs., distbrs. books, recs., filmstrips to schools, pres., pub., 1922-63, chmn. bd., chief exec. officer, 1963-75, chmn. bd., 1975—. Served from pvt. to 2d lt. U.S. Army, 1917-19. Recipient Pa. award for excellence in edn., 1969; Henry Johnson Fisher award, 1970. Mem. Assn. Am. Pubs. (pres. 1962-63), Delta Tau Delta. United Presbyn. Clubs: Cosmos (Washington); Apawamis (Rye, N.Y.); University (N.Y.C.). Office: Scholastic Mags 50 W 44th St New York NY 10036

ROBINSON, PEGGY ELLAIN, pub. relations exec., real estate broker, writer, cons.; b. Slaton, Tex., June 24, 1928; d. John T. and Gladys B.L. (Olson) Whitesides; B.F.A. in Broadcasting, U. Tex., 1951; postgrad. Sch. Journalism, U. Mo., 1967-68; m. Frank Eugene Robinson, June 4, 1952; 1 dau., Lindley Ellain. Asst. writer of advt. and promotion NBC-TV, N.Y.C., 1951-52; asst. pub. relations exec. Sta. WOAI-TV San Antonio, 1952-53; writer Mithoff Advt. Co., El Paso, Tex., 1954-56; free lance pub. relations exec. Emcee TV show, KELP-TV, KROD-TV, El Paso, 1956-58; editor, propr. Shop Talk mag., Lawton, Okla., 1958-60; owner, pub. relations dir. Town and Country Real Estate Co., Lawton, 1959-62, 1970—; free lance writer feature stories for newspapers, mags., various TV and radio stations, 1953—; columnist Shop Talk, Ideas in Homes, Lawton, 1959—. Bd. dirs. Lawton Heritage Assn. Mem. Women in Communications, Nat., Okla. assns. of realtors, Am. Bus. Women's Assn., AAUW, Lawton Bd. of Realtors, Honolulu Press Club, C. of C. (internat. relations com., tourism and conv. com.), Kappa Tau Alpha, Alpha Delta Pi. Democrat. Methodist. Clubs: Ft. Sill Officers' Wives Club, Lawton Book and Play Rev. Club. Home: 1614 NW 34th St Lawton OK 73501 Office: 626 D Suite 6 Lawton OK 73501

ROBINSON, PETER CLARK, corp. exec.; b. Brighton, Mass., Nov. 16, 1938; s. Richard and Mary Elizabeth (Cooper) R.; B.S. in Fgn. Service, Georgetown U., 1961; M.B.A., Babson Inst., 1963; m. Sylvia Phyllis Petschek, Aug. 26, 1961 (div. 1973); children—Marc Louis, Nicholas Daniel, Andrea Suzanne. Asst. supt. prodn. Mass. Broken Stone Co., Weston, 1961-62, night shift supt., 1962-65, v.p. operations, 1968, v.p., dir., 1969-75; gen. supt. Berlin Stone Co., 1965-67, v.p. operations, 1968, v.p., dir., 1969-75; v.p., dir. Holden Trap Rock Co., to 1975; pres. J.P. Burroughs & Sons, Inc. aggregate div., subsidiary Blount, Inc., Saginaw, Mich., and Montgomery, Ala., 1975-80, v.p. parent co., Montgomery, 1978—. Mem. Nat. Crushed Stone Assn., Am. Mktg. Assn., Planning Execs. Inst., N.Am. Soc. Planning, Engring. Soc. Detroit, Am. Soc. Agrl. Engrs. Clubs: Economic (Detroit); Saginaw (Mich.); Capital City (Montgomery). Home: PO Box 11561 Montgomery AL 36111 Office: PO Box 949 Montgomery AL 36102

ROBINSON, ROBERT ARMSTRONG, pension fund exec.; b. Waterbury, Conn., Sept. 11, 1925; s. Robert and Ethel (Armstrong) R.; A.B. magna cum laude, Brown U., 1950, M.A., 1952; postgrad. U. Ill., 1954-55; Litt.D., Episcopal Theol. Sem. Ky., 1971; D.C.L., U. of South, Tenn.; LL.D. (hon.), Nashotah House, Oconomowoc, Wis., 1980; m. D. Ann Harding, June 7, 1947; 1 dau., Gayllis Robinson Ward. Instr. English, Brown U., 1950-53; instr. English, asst. prof. rhetoric U. Ill., 1953-56; trust officer Colonial Bank & Trust Co., Waterbury, 1956-63, v.p., trust officer, 1963-65, sr. trust officer, 1965-66; v.p., sec. Ch. Pension Fund and Affiliates, Ch. Life Ins. Corp., Ch. Ins. Co., Ch. Hymnal Corp., 1966-67, exec. v.p., 1967-68, pres., dir., 1968—; dir. Morehouse-Barlow Co., Inc. Trustee, Episc. Theol. Sem. Ky., Hillspeak, Eureka Springs, Ark., Nat. Cathedral, Washington; exec. bd. Boy Scouts Am., N.Y.C., Voorhees Coll. Served with inf. AUS, 1943-46. Decorated Purple Heart with oak leaf cluster. Mem. Newcomen Soc., St. Andrew's Soc., Phi Beta Kappa. Episcopalian (vestryman). Clubs: Brown, Union, Church (N.Y.C.); Athenaeum (London); Country of Darien. Home: 251 Laurel Rd New Canaan CT 06840 Office: 800 2d Ave New York NY 10017

ROBINSON, ROBERT PORTER (SKIP), ins. broker; b. Chgo., Nov. 19, 1939; s. Chauncey William and Daisy (Ballard) R.; B.A., U. Ill., 1963; grad. teaching intern U. Calif., Berkeley, 1966; m. Drusilla Norene Sims, Sept. 3, 1961; 1 son, Jon Gabré; m. 2d, Barbara Dell Maynard, Feb. 18, 1969; children—Amy Dell, Sarah Elizabeth. Mem. nat. staff and editor Bull., Nat. Student Assn., Phila., 1961-62; publs. staff Nat. Council Tchrs. English, Champaign, Ill., 1962-63; editorial staffs Nat. Assn. Ednl. Broadcasters, Am. Mktg. Assn., Champaign, 1963-65; tchr. pub. schs., Mt. View, Calif., 1965-66, Danville, Calif., 1966-68, Benicia, Calif., 1968, Merritt Coll., Oakland, Calif., 1968-69; editor Calif. New Careers Assn., Oakland, 1969; tchr. pub. schs., Berkeley, Calif., 1969-70; co-organizer, ednl. therapist Odyssey Sch., Walnut Creek, Calif., 1970-71; cons. Met. Ins., 1971-72, sales mgr., 1972; spl. agt. Bankers of Iowa Ins. Co., 1972-73, broker, 1973—, health and disability broker, 1972—; registered rep. Freeman and Assos., Burlingame, Calif., 1972-73, Howells and Co., Oakland, 1973-76, Planned Investments, Inc., 1976—; solicitor Am. Ind. Agy., Oakland, 1973; v.p. Intravest Centaur Corp., San Rafael, Calif., 1973-76; asso. Pen-Cal, Inc., 1973—, v.p., 1976-77; supr. Home Life of N.Y., 1977—; tchr., 1976—; counselor Saturday guidance program, San Leandro (Calif.) Unified Sch. Dist.; U.S. choral rep. World's Fair, Brussels, Belgium, 1958. Sec. Champaign Democratic Central Com.; del. Calif. Dem. Council; pres. bd. dirs. Synergy Sch., Martinez, Calif., 1979—. Mem. San Francisco Chorale, Oakland Symphony Chorus. Editor: Student Community Involvement, 1961; Calif. Earthquake, 1969, B-63 Report, 1970; A Gambler's Almanac, 1973; Charitable Employee Benefits Design, 1981. Home: 5750 Merriewood Dr Oakland CA 94611 Office: Suite 3220 50 California St San Francisco CA 94111

ROBINSON, ROBERT WILLIAM, realtor; b. Lancaster, S.C., Dec. 1, 1917; s. Redic Earl and Myrtle (Beckham) R.; B.S. in Textile Chemistry, Clemson Coll., 1938; m. Carolyn J. Crews, May 29, 1938; children—Joan C., Robert W. Partner, E. Robinson Laundry, 1938-41, pres., 1946-51; pres. Robinson Realty Co., Columbia, S.C., 1951—; pres. E. Robinson Laundry & Dry Cleaning Co., Inc., Robinson Realty, Inc., Robinson Machinery Co., Inc., 1961—, Robinson Holding Co., Inc., 1961—, E & M, Inc., 1962—, Robinson Apparel master, Inc., 1977—; sec. BACO, Inc., 1972; sec., dir. Continental of S.C., 1972, FS, Inc. Served as capt. USAAF, 1942-46. Baptist. Mem. Friars of Columbia (sec., dir.). Clubs: Lions, Palmetto. Home: 4314 Converse St Columbia SC 29206 Office: 2549 Forest Dr Columbia SC 29204

ROBINSON, RONALD JAMES, petroleum engr.; b. Pueblo, Colo., Mar. 10, 1946; s. James Claude and Doris Loraine Robinson; B.S. in Math. and Physics, So. Colo. State Coll., 1968; M.S. in Physics, Baylor U., Waco, Tex., 1971; Ph.D. in Petroleum Engring., Tex. A. and M. U., 1974; m. Bonnie Lynn Martin, Aug. 31, 1968; children—Kevin James, Kyle Bryant, Kurt David. With Getty Oil Co., 1973-78, dist. reservoir engr., Bakersfield, Calif., 1975-78; mgr. thermal recovery Grace Petroleum Corp., Oklahoma City, 1978-79; sr. cons. INTERCOMP Resource Devel. and Engring., Houston, 1979-80; supr. thermal research Getty Oil Co., Houston, 1980—. NASA fellow, 1968. Mem. Can. Inst. Mining, Soc. Profl. Well Log Analysts, Soc. Petroleum Engrs. (dir.), Scientists Research Soc. N. Am., Sigma Xi. Club: Kiwanis. Author papers in field. Office: PO Box 42214 Houston TX 77042

ROBINSON, WARREN LOWE, utility exec.; b. Logan, Utah, Apr. 11, 1950; s. Floyd Comish and Grace (Lowe) R.; B.S. in Bus. Mgmt., Brigham Young U., 1974; M.B.A., Boise State U., 1976; m. Ann Lee Decker, May 21, 1977; children—Casey and Cody (twins), Stephanie. Div. rep. whole goods project, mem. corp. steering com., J.I. Case Co., Racine, Wis., 1974-75; fin. analyst Intermountain Gas Co., Boise, Idaho, 1976-77, dir. budgets and corp. fin. planning, 1977-79, asst. to pres. for corp. planning, 1980—. Bd. dirs. Young Republicans, Racine, 1975; pres. Ada County chpt. Am. Cancer Soc., chmn. Idaho Div. Crusade Com., 1980-81. Served with N.G., 1968-76. Mem. Assn. M.B.A. Execs. Republican. Mormon. Home: 6175 Sterling Ln Boise ID 83703 Office: 555 S Cole Rd Boise ID 83707

ROBISON, ADOLF C., textile co. exec.; b. N.Y.C., Feb. 24, 1904; s. Louis and Paula (Cohn) R.; A.B., Columbia, 1924; LL.D., Fairleigh Dickinson U., 1966, Kyung Hee U., Korea, 1968; m. Ann Green, Aug. 28, 1927; children—Peter J., Michael D. Pres., Robison Industries, Inc., 1941—; pres. Robison Export Corp.; pres. Israel Speaks publ., 1955-56; chmn. bd. Robison-Anton Textile Co., 1949—; pres. Seaboard Export Co.; dir. P.E.C. Israel Econ. Corp., Peoples Trust Co., United Jersey Bank N.J. Past pres. Teaneck Community Chest; pres. Bergen Philharmonic Soc., Robison Found.; past pres. Teaneck Community Chest; pres. Bergen Philharmonic Soc.; past pres. Teaneck Jewish Community Center; pres. Class of 1924, Columbia Coll., mem. Soc. Class Pres.'s; past councilman Twp. Teaneck, N.J.; past v.p. Am. Israel Cultural Found.; bd. govs. N.Y. Cultural Center, Hackensack (N.J.) Hosp., Grad. Schs. Yeshiva U.; bd. overseers Fairleigh Dickinson U.; bd. dirs. Jerusalem Found., Bergenstage Inc., Center for Israel and Jewish Studies of Columbia U.; trustee William Carlos Williams Center for Performing Arts; mem. nat. bd. govs. Israel Bonds; exec. com. Am. Israel Cultural Exchange Found. Mem. Bergen County C. of C. (dir.). Home: 554 S Forest Dr Teaneck NJ 07666 Office: 175 Bergen Blvd Fairview NJ 07022

ROBISON, ANN GREEN (MRS. ADOLF ROBISON), textile co. exec.; b. N.Y.C., Nov. 19, 1904; d. Boris and Mary (Sugarman) Green; B.A., U. Maine, 1924, L.H.D., 1975; M.A., Columbia, 1936; grad. Women's Inst., Jewish Theol. Sem. Am., also postgrad.; m. Adolf Robison, Aug. 28, 1927; children—Peter Jordan, Michael Douglas. Tchr. French, Mattanawcooh Acad., Lincoln, Maine, 1924-25, New Rochelle, N.Y., 1925-38; v.p. Robison-Textile Co., 1941-59; treas. Robison-Anton Textile Co., 1959—; v.p. Robison Industries, Inc., 1966—. Accredited observer at UN in U.S. and France, 1947-52; lectr. U.S. Delegation in Italy, 1951; mem. state com. Radio Free Europe; mem. adv. com. dept. Hebraic studies, chmn. spl. com. scholarships and grants dept. Hebraica, Rutgers U. Chmn. women's div. Teaneck United Jewish Appeal, also nat. lectr., named Woman of Year, 1964; sr. adviser womens' div. Israel Bonds; mem. UN com. United Synagogue Council Am.; bd. dirs. Bergen Community Mus.; life mem. Hadassah; v.p. Robison Found.; mem. membership, program, interfaith and univ. coms. Am. Israel Cultural Found.; mem. nat. exec. com., sec. Am. Israel Pub. Affairs Com.; mem. membership cabinet Am. Histadrut Cultural Exchange Inst. Mem. bd., chmn. internat. affairs Republican Women's Clubs Bergen County, county rep. state bd. N.J. Mem. bd., exec. com., chmn. pub. affairs com., v.p. Am. Lung Assn. of N.J., named to Hall of Fame, 1980; mem. bd., exec. com., rep. dir. state bd., chmn. bylaws com., coms. on edn., pub. relations and rehab. Bergen Passaic County Lung Assn.; mem. bd., exec. com., co-chmn. adult center for Jewish and related studies YM-YWHA Bergen County; v.p. Nat. Jewish Community Relations Adv. Council, 1971—; mem. bd. Nat. Council Jewish Women Ednl. Research Center, Hebrew U., Israel; v.p., gen. campaign chmn. Jewish Fedn. Community Services Bergen County; mem. pres.'s adv. com. on Bergen in Israel, Bergen Community Coll. Recipient medal of merit Fairleigh Dickinson U. Mem. AAUW (nat. com. on internat. relations, program chmn., chmn. fellowship com., dir.), Internat. Council Jewish Women (v.p., chmn. resolutions com., editor newsletter), Nat. Council Jewish Women (nat. bd., exec. com., chmn. internat. affairs, nat. sub-com. Jewish affairs, vice chmn., rep. to several orgns., mem. numerous coms.), Internat. Relations for Federated Woman's Clubs of N.J. (div. chmn.), Town and Gown Soc., League Women Voters, Brandeis U. Women's Assn. (life), Internat. Platform Assn., Phi Beta Kappa, Phi Kappa Phi. Club: Teaneck College (dir., program chmn., chmn. ways and means com.). Columnist, On the Go, The Jewish Standard. Home: 554 S Forest Dr Teaneck NJ 07666 Office: 175 Bergen Blvd Fairview NJ 07022

ROBLES, RICARDO JULIO, agribus. co. exec.; b. Panama City, Panama, Mar. 21, 1926; s. Rogelio and Sibila (Ramirez) R.; B.S. (Kellogg Found. scholar), Carleton Coll., 1947; m. Johanna Sienko, May 26, 1951; children—Richard, John, Jeffrey, Jane. With Cargill, Inc., various locations, 1947—, asst. v.p., Mpls., 1967—, pres. Cargill Americas Inc., Mpls., 1971—, regional mgr. Latin Am., Mpls., 1971—; chmn. bd. Latin Am. Agribus. Devel. Corp., 1978—; dir. Flagship Banks Inc., Miami, Fla. Republican. Roman Catholic. Home: 17825 6th Ave N Wayzata MN 55447 Office: Cargill Inc Pan Am Div PO Box 9300 Minneapolis MN

ROCCHEGGIANI, GUIDO, paper co. exec.; b. Milan, Italy, June 27, 1934; came to U.S., 1960, naturalized, 1966; s. Edoardo and Antonia (Piatti) R.; Ph.D. in Pure Chemistry, U. Pavia (Italy), 1958; M.B.A., Drexel U., 1966. Research chemist Istituto Ricerche Derivati Vegetali, Milan, 1958-60; research chemist, then sect. head Scott Paper Co., Phila., 1960-69, venture dir., 1972-78, dir. new venture devel., 1978-79, dir. functional planning, 1979—; dir. Bellarte Internat. Inc. Cert. profl. chemist, Italy. Mem. Am. Mgmt. Assn., World Future Soc. Patentee printing fluids. Home: PO Box 251 Bala Cynwyd PA 19004 Office: Scott Plaza 1 Philadelphia PA 19113

ROCHEMONT, MICHAEL STUART, maintenance corp. exec.; b. Plymouth, Montserrat, B.W.I., May 25, 1925; immigrated to Can., 1934, naturalized, 1972; s. Michael Joseph Alexander and Edith Joan (Norton) R.; student McGill U., 1945-47, Sir George Williams Coll., 1950-52; m. Shirley June Thompson, Dec. 9, 1949;

children—Michael, Richard, Wendy, Glenn, Peter, Sharon, Tracy. Purchasing agt. Bristol Myers of Can., Montreal, Que., 1950-55; sales rep. Atlas Printing Co., Montreal, 1956-57; produce mgr. Steinberg's Ltd., Montreal, 1957-61; br. mgr. Empire Maintenance, Inc., Toronto, Ont., 1961—. Served with Royal Canadian Air Force, 1944-45, 48-49. Mem. Bldg. Owners and Mgrs. Assn., Bldg. Maintenance Contractors Assn., Toronto Exec. Assn. Mem. Ch. of Eng. Club: Masons. Office: 2333 Dundas St W #207 Toronto ON M6R 3A6 Canada

ROCHETTO, EVELYN MARIE, assn. exec.; b. Chgo., d. Lucius J. and Clara M. (Jung) Young; Ph.B., Northwestern U., 1952; m. Paul A. Rochetto, June 9, 1937. Profl. musician, 1930-50; membership sec. Internat. Soc. Gen. Semantics, 1950-55, exec. sec., 1955—, dir., 1952—. Mem. AAUW (pres. Chgo. br. 1956, 58, 64—, mem. bd. 1953—), Chgo. Story League (pres. 1970—), Am. Legion (mem. bd.), Friends Mentally Ill (pres. 1958—), Alpha Sigma Lambda (dir.). Club: Woman's University (pres. 1966—). Home: 5240 N Sheridan Rd Chicago IL 60640

ROCHLIS, JAMES JOSEPH, diversified mfg. corp. exec.; b. Phila., Apr. 12, 1916; s. Aaron and Gussie (Pearlene) R.; student public schs.; m. Riva Singer, Mar. 21, 1943; children—Jeffrey A., Susan J. Salesman, Mid-City Tire Co., Phila., 1945-46, gen. mgr., 1946-49; pres. Ram Rubber Co., Phila., 1948-49; rep. Blair & Co., Phila., 1949-61, bus. analyst, 1955-61; dir., chmn. exec. com. Mono-Sol Corp., Gary, Ind., 1959—; pres., chief exec. officer, dir. Baldwin-Montrose Chem. Co., Inc., N.Y.C., 1961-68; v.p. Chris-Craft Industries, Inc., N.Y.C., 1968-69, exec. v.p., 1969—, dir., 1968—, pres. Baldwin-NAFI Industries div., 1968—, pres. Chris-Craft Corp., Pompano Beach, Fla., 1969-71; dir. Montrose Chem. Co. Calif., Torrance and Mex., 1961—; dir. Centlivre Brewing Corp., Fort Wayne, Ind., 1959-61, Baldwin Rubber Co., Inc., Pontiac, Mich., 1959-61, Tusco Products Co., Inc., Cass City, Mich., Huron Rubber Co., Norwalk, Ohio, 1959-62, Gen. Artist Corp., N.Y.C., 1961-68, Cyclamate Corp. Am., 1965-66, Tele-Rep, Inc., N.Y.C., 1968-69, Piper Aircraft Corp., Lock Haven, Pa., 1969—, Chris-Craft Pacific, Inc., 1969—, Argonaut Taiwan Corp., Taipei, 1968—. Mem. AIAA, Fin. Analysts Soc. Phila., Soc. Naval Architects and Marine Engrs., Eastern Cruiser Assn., Antique and Classic Boat Soc., Chris-Craft Antique and Classic Boat Soc. Club: Atrium (N.Y.C.). Office: Chris Craft Industries Inc 600 Madison Ave New York NY 10022

ROCK, GERALD EUGENE, office machines co. exec.; b. St. Libory, Nebr., June 14, 1933; s. Gerald Michael and Agnes Evaline (Gebhart) R.; student Central State Tchrs. Coll., Edmond, Okla., 1952; m. Sandra Lynn Clary, Mar. 5, 1955; children—Kimberly Ann, Kevin Michael, Gerald Garner (dec.), Jennifer Lynn, Matthew Barton. Mgr., Rock Feed Yards, 1955, 60-62; sales rep. Fuller Brush Co., 1956, Am. Chicle Co., 1956-57, Pillsbury Co., 1958-59, 3M Co., 1963-64; founder, pres. Diversified Sales and Service Co. (name Grand Island Copy Machine Co. 1970, Copi R, Inc. 1980, doing bus. as The Copy Co.), Grand Island, Nebr., 1964—, Omaha, 1979—. Asst. packmaster, Webelos leader Boy Scouts Am., 1975-76. Served with USAF, 1951-55; Korea. Mem. Nat. Office Machine Dealers Assn. Democrat. Roman Catholic. Home: Route 3 Box 15A Grand Island NE 68801 Office: 404 W 4th St Grand Island NE 68801 also 10801 Elm St Rockbrook Omaha NE 68144

ROCK, MILTON L., mgmt. cons.; b. Phila., Feb. 25, 1921; s. Maurice and Mary (Lee) R.; B.A., Temple U., 1946, M.A., 1947; Ph.D., U. Rochester, 1949; m. Shirley Cylinder, Aug. 3, 1943; children—Susan Rock Herzog, Robert Henry. With Hay Assos., Phila., 1949—, mng. partner, 1959—. Bd. trustees Temple U., 1979; bd. govs. Temple U. Hosp., 1975—; mem. Pres.'s Nat. Commn. Manpower Policy, 1974-77; chmn. Middle Atlantic Regional Manpower Adv. Com., Dept. Labor, 1972-74; mem. council Phila. Orch., 1979—. Served with AUS, 1942-45. Fellow Am. Psychol. Assn.; mem. Assn. Cons. Mgmt. Engrs. (past pres., dir.), Internat. Assn. Applied Psychology, Inst. Mgmt. Consultants (founding mem.), James Smithson Soc. Clubs: Union League, Philmont Country. Author: (with others) The Executive Percept Analytic Scale, 1963, Development of Bank Management Personnel, 1969; editor: McGraw-Hill Handbook of Wage and Salary Administration, 1972. Office: Hay Associates 229 S 18th St Philadelphia PA 19103

ROCK, STUART, electronics co. exec.; b. Bklyn., Feb. 22, 1935; s. Harry and Sadie (Noss) R.; B.M.E., Poly. Inst. Bklyn., 1957; m. Cynthia Koodin, Nov. 10, 1957; children—Mitchell, Shari. Dir. ops. Republic Electronics Industries Corp., N.Y.C., 1966-72; v.p. planning Seatrain Shipbuilding Corp., N.Y.C., 1973-75; v.p. mfg. Harman Kardon, N.Y.C., 1976-78; pres. Integrated Sound Systems, Inc., N.Y.C., 1978—; cons. in field. Founder, pres. S. Woodbury Taxpayers Assn., 1964-70. Mem. ASME, IEEE, Nat. Assn. Broadcasters. Club: Masons. Home: 20 Shadow Ln Woodbury NY 11797 Office: 29 50 Northern Blvd Long Island City NY 11101

ROCKEFELLER, DAVID, ret. banker; b. N.Y.C., June 12, 1915; s. John Davison, Jr. and Abby Greene (Aldrich) R.; B.S., Harvard, 1936, LL.D. (hon.), 1969; Ph.D., U. Chgo., 1940; LL.D. (hon.), Columbia, 1954, Bowdoin Coll., 1958, Jewish Theol. Sem., 1958, Williams Coll., 1966, Wagner Coll., 1967, Pace Coll., 1970, St. John's U., 1971, U. Liberia, 1979; m. Margaret McGrath, Sept. 7, 1940; children—David, Abby A., Neva, Margaret, Richard Gilder, Eileen McGrath. Sec. to Mayor Fiorello H. LaGuardia, 1940-41; asst. regional dir. Office Def. Health and Welfare Service, 1941-42; 2d v.p. Chase Nat. Bank, 1948-49, v.p., 1949-51, sr. v.p., 1952-55; exec. v.p. Chase Manhattan Bank, 1955-57, vice chmn. bd. dirs., 1957-61, pres., chmn. exec. com., 1961-69, chief exec. officer, 1969-80, chmn., 1980-81, also dir.; dir. Rockefeller Center, Inc., Fed. Res. Bank N.Y., 1973-76; dir. Internat. Exec. Service Corps, chmn., 1964-68; pres. N.Y. Clearing House, 1976-77; Mem. Bus. Council; sr. exec. council Conf. Bd., 1973; mem. bus. adv. council Urban Devel. Corp. N.Y. State, 1968-72; mem. Trilateral Commn. Chmn. bd. Downtown Lower Manhattan Assn., Rockefeller U., Mus. Modern Art, 1962-72, Council Fgn. Relations, Inc., Commn. on White House Fellows, 1964-65; chmn. Rockefeller Bros. Fund, 1980—; hon. trustee Rockefeller Family Fund, John F. Kennedy Library, U. Chgo., 1947-62, Carnegie Endowment Internat. Peace, 1947-60; trustee Council of Ams., chmn., 1965-70; bd. dirs. Center for Inter-Am. Relations, chmn., 1966-70; bd. dirs. Bus. Com. for Arts, Overseas Devel. Council, Internat. House, N.Y.C., 1940-63; bd. dirs. Morningside Heights, 1947-70, pres., 1947-57, chmn., 1957-65; bd. overseers Harvard, 1954-60, 62-68, 73-74, pres., 1966-68. Served to capt. AUS, 1942-45. Decorated Legion of Merit; Legion of Honor (France); Order of Merit (Italy); Order of So. Cross (Brazil); Most Exalted Order of White Elephant (Thailand); Order of Cross of Boyaca (Colombia); Order of Vasco Nunez de Balboa (Panama); Order of Cedars (Lebanon); El Sol del Peru 1821; Humane Order of African Redemption (Liberia); Order of Crown (Belgium); Most Noble Order of Crown (Thailand); Ordre Nationale Ivoire (Ivory Coast); recipient World Brotherhood award Jewish Theol. Sem., 1953; Gold Medal award Nat. Inst. Social Scis., 1967; N.Y.C. Planning medal AIA, 1968; C. Walter Nichols award N.Y. U., 1970; award Regional Plan Assn., 1971. Clubs: Harvard, River, Univ., Century Assn., Links, Knickerbocker (N.Y.C.). Author: Unused Resources and Economic Waste, 1940; Creative Management in Banking, 1964. Office: 1 Chase Manhattan Plaza New York NY 10015

ROCKEFELLER, GODFREY STILLMAN, corp. exec.; b. N.Y.C., May 1, 1899; B.A., Yale U., 1921; m. Helen Gratz; children—Godfrey A., Marion Rockefeller Stone, Audrey Rockefeller Blair, Lucy Rockefeller Stewart, Peter. With Cranston Print Works Co., N.Y.C., 1930—, now chmn. bd., pres.; dir. Freeport Minerals Co., Istel Fund. Served to lt. col. USAAF, 1943-45. Home: Mead Ln Greenwich CT 06830 Office: 1412 Broadway New York NY 10018

ROCKOFF, NEIL F., broadcasting exec.; b. Bayonne, N.J., Mar. 19, 1938; s. Herman C. and Florence (Laden) R.; B.S., U. Vt., 1962; m. Deborah Ray Hoch, July 2, 1967; children—Cherie, Cindy. Research analyst H-R TV, Blair Radio, N.Y.C., 1965-67; dir. mktg. research Christal Co., N.Y.C., 1967-68; account exec. spot sales CBS Radio, N.Y.C., 1968-69; gen. sales mgr. Sta. WEEI, Boston, 1969-70, Sta. WCBS-FM, N.Y.C., 1970; sales mgr. nat. sales CBS-FM, 1971; mgr. Sta. KNX-FM, Los Angeles, 1971-72; v.p., gen. mgr. Sta. WLAK-FM, Chgo., 1972-75; v.p., gen. mgr. Sta. WHN, N.Y.C., 1975-78; v.p. radio div. Storer Broadcasting Co., Miami, Fla., 1978—; pres. Force Communications Investment Corp., 1979—; v.p., gen. mgr. Sta. KHJ Radio, Los Angeles; innovated radio format Mellow Sound. Mem. Country Music Assn. (v.p., treas., dir.), N.Y. Market Radio Broadcasters (chmn. bd.). Home: PO Box 1967 Rancho Santa Fe CA 92067

ROCKWELL, CHARLES STEWART, instrument co. exec.; b. Oneida, N.Y., Jan. 2, 1912; s. Charles W. and Elizabeth (Hatch) R.; B.S., St. Lawrence U., 1936; m. Dorothy Elliott, Sept. 4, 1937; children—Pamela (Mrs. Jack Rathmell), Jill (Mrs. Robert Fransen), Lucinda (Mrs. Donald Scott), Elliott (Mrs. Michael McCulley). In ins. bus., 1937-43; clk. Sperry Gyroscope Co. div. Sperry Rand Corp., 1943-44, shop planning supt. engring. labs., 1944-46, prodn. control supt., 1946, prodn. control mgr., 1947-51; v.p. works mgr. Sperry Farragut Co. div. Sperry Rand Corp., 1951-57, pres. 1957-66; v.p., gen. mgr. Ford Instrument Co. div. Sperry Rand Corp., Long Island City, N.Y., 1957, pres., gen. mgr., 1957-66, v.p. Sperry Gyroscope div., 1966—, v.p., gen. mgr., 1967, pres., 1968-71, pres., Monroe Harbour, Inc., 1971-77; chmn. bd., chief exec. officer Magnetic Head Corp., Hauppage, N.Y., 1972—; mem. adv. bd. Abilities, Inc., Albertson, N.Y. Mem. Am. Ordnance Assn. (past pres. N.Y. post), AIAA, Nat. Security Indsl. Assn., Sigma Alpha Epsilon, Sigma Pi Sigma. Home: 10 Lorraine Ct Roslyn NY Office: Magnetic Head Corp 25 Glen Head Rd Glen Head NY 11545

ROCKWELL, ELIZABETH DENNIS, savs. and loan assn. exec.; b. Houston; d. Robert Richard and Nezzell Alderton (Christie) Dennis; student Rice U., 1939-40, U. Houston, 1938-39, 40-42; divorced. Asst. purchasing agt. Standard Oil Co. Tex., 1942-66; with Heights Savs. Assn., Houston, 1966—, asst. sec., 1967-70, asst. v.p., 1970-75, v.p., mgr. bus. services dept., 1975—; 2d v.p. Desk and Derrick Club Am., 1960-61; instr. Coll. of Mainland, Texas City, Tex.; instr. Downtown Coll. and Continuing Edn. Center, U. Houston, also mem. savs. and loan adv. com. Downtown Coll., mem. adv. com. Coll. Bus. Adminstrn. Named Outstanding Woman of Yr., YWCA. Mem. Am. Savs. and Loan League (state dir. 1973-76, chpt. pres. 1971-72; pres. S.W. regional conf. 1972-73; Leaders award 1972), Savs. Inst. Mktg. Soc. Am. (Key Person award 1974), Inst. Fin. Edn., Fin. Mgrs., Soc. Savs. Instns., U.S. Savs. League, Houston Heights Assn. (charter, dir. 1973-77), Houston North Assn. Author articles. Home: 3617 Yoakum Blvd Houston TX 77006 Office: PO Box 7483 Houston TX 77008

ROCKWELL, NATT LELAND, tool and die co. exec.; b. Nashua, N.H., Apr. 30, 1943; s. Warren Leland and Margarite Caroline (Reynold) R.; student N.H. Tech. Inst., 1962-63; m. Elaine Marie Reale, Dec. 20, 1969; children—Jonathan, Bill, Todd, Michele. Machinist, Nashua Indsl. Machine Co., 1963-65; toolmaker N.H. Ball Bearing, Peterboro, 1967-68; master moldmaker Hy-Ten Die & Devel. Corp., Milford, N.H., 1969-74; pres. Rockwell Tool & Die Corp., New Boston, N.H., 1975—. Served with AUS, 1965-67. Home and Office: Lyndeboro Rd New Boston NH 03070

ROCKWELL, WILLIAM HEARNE, lawyer; b. Taunton, Mass., Oct. 28, 1919; s. Julius and Alice (Hearne) R.; grad. Philips Acad.; A.B., U. Mich., 1941, M.A., 1947; LL.B., Columbia, 1950; m. Elizabeth Virginia Goode, Feb. 3, 1948; children—Enid Rockwell, Karen Rockwell, William Goode Rockwell (dec.). Admitted to N.Y. State bar, 1950; asso. Donovan, Leisure, Newton & Irvine, 1950-51; asst. sec. The Valve Mfrs. Assn., 1951-55; sec. Am. Carpet Inst., Inc., 1956-66, sec., treas., 1966-68; sec. gen. counsel Am. Nat. Standards Inst., N.Y.C., 1969—; gen. counsel Contemporary Dance, Inc., 1962—, Rondo Dance Theatre, Inc., 1970—, Montserrat Found., 1972—, Product Liability Prevention Conf., 1974—. Mem. bd. ethics Town of Pound Ridge, N.Y. Served from pvt. to maj. Transp. Corps, AUS, 1941-46. Mem. Assn. Bar City N.Y., Am. Bar Assn. (mem. anti-trust com.), Am., N.Y. socs. assn. execs., Nat. Safety Council, Nat. Panel Arbitrators, Am. Arbitration Assn., Columbia Law Sch. Alumni Assn. (dir.), Pound Ridge Land Conservancy. Clubs: Belham River Valley Country; Montserrat Yacht; Pound Ridge Tennis; New York Athletic; University (Washington). Home: Pine Brook Rd Pound Ridge NY 10576 Office: 1430 Broadway New York NY 10018

ROCKWOOD, DAVID SPARROW, banker; b. Hollis, N.Y., Feb. 19, 1938; s. Joseph L. and Cam (Rockwood) Hodges; B.S., U. Fla., 1966; LL.B., LaSalle Extension U., 1973; M.S., Am. Coll., 1980; m. Jane Shepard, Aug. 15, 1964; children—Debra, Karen. Asst. to dir. sales Prudential Ins. Co., Jacksonville, Fla., 1966-68; ins. broker Mut. Benefit Life, Jacksonville, 1968-71; trust officer Huntington Nat. Bank, Columbus, Ohio, 1971-73; asst. v.p., investment counselor 1st Nat. Bank Mpls., 1973-76; v.p., head trust officer 1st Nat. Bank Neenah (Wis.), 1976-80; sr. v.p. Sun Bank, Leesburg, Fla., 1980—. Served with USCG, 1957-61. C.L.U. Mem. Appleton Estate Planning Council, Winnebago County Bar Assn., Wis. Trustees Assn., Fox Valley Assn. Life Underwriters, Sigma Chi. Republican. Baptist. Club: Rotary. Home: 2933 La Salida Way Leesburg FL 32748 Office: PO Box 8 Leesburg FL 32748

ROCKWOOD, FREDERICK WHITNEY, mfg. co. exec., lawyer; b. Salt Lake City, Dec. 18, 1947; s. Lewis Frederick and Muriel (Whitney) R.; student U. Utah, 1966-67, 70, Nat. Def. Fgn. Lang. fellow Columbia U., 1970; A.B. with distinction, Stanford U., 1972; J.D., Harvard U., 1975; m. Alyce Jolene Edmunds, Aug. 26, 1970; children—Justin Frederick, Alyce Melissa, Jennifer Jolene. Admitted to Mass. bar, 1975; mgmt. cons. The Boston Cons. Group, Inc., 1975-77, Bain and Co., Boston, 1977; dir. corp. strategy Hillenbrand Industries, Inc., Batesville, Ind., 1977-78, sr. v.p. corp. planning, 1978—; lectr. div. mgmt. edn. Grad. Sch. Bus. Adminstrn., U. Mich., 1980. Vol. rep., asst. to mission pres. So. Far East Mission, Ch. of Jesus Christ of Latter-day Saints, Hong Kong, 1967-69. Mem. Strategic Planning Inst. (council 1978—), Phi Beta Kappa. Mormon. Bd. editors Harvard Internat. Law Jour., 1974-75. Home: 503 W Pearl St Batesville IN 47006 Office: Hillenbrand Industries Inc Hwy 46 Batesville IN 47006

RODDEN, DONNA STRICKLAND, city ofcl.; b. Albion, N.Y., Aug. 10, 1926; d. Burroughs A. and Mildred C. (MacDuffie) S.; B.S., Syracuse (N.Y.) U., 1946; M.S., State U. N.Y., Brockport, 1962; postgrad. N.Y. U. and State U. N.Y., Geneseo; div.; children—Roberta Ann Rodden Tundermann, Ellen Christine Rodden Capurso. Editor, Enterprise, Lyndonville, N.Y., 1947-48, Herald-Tribune, Middleport, N.Y., 1948-49; TV dir. Cayton, Inc., N.Y.C., 1949-56; mayor Village of Albion, 1973—. Pres., bd. dirs. Orleans County Council for Arts, 1975-77; bd. dirs. Cobblestone Soc., 1976-80; mem. N.Y. State Friendship Force, 1977; co-chmn. N.Y. State Concerned Citizens for the Arts, 1978-80; dir. Swan Library. Recipient Distinguished Service award Girl Scouts U.S.A., 1973; Woman in Govt. award League Women Voters, 1975; Presdl. award Albion Jr. C. of C., 1975; Women Who Changed the World award NOW, 1975; Citizenship award Am. Legion, 1976; Kennedy Found. medal, 1975. Mem. Nat. Bus. and Profl. Women's Assn., Internat. Platform Assn., Northwestern Frontier Assn. Village Ofcls. (pres. 1980-81). Republican. Baptist. Clubs: Order Eastern Star (past matron), Abeel Rebekkahs. Home: 327 W Bank St Albion NY 14411 Office: Village Hall E Bank St Albion NY 14411

RODDEY, OTHA CHARLES, engring. exec.; b. Crossett, Ark., Jan. 7, 1924; s. Otha Columbus and Ann Laura (Holland) R.; B.S., La. State U., 1947; S.M., M.I.T., 1951; m. Hilda Blaine, Oct. 7, 1951; children—Leah Ann, Mary Robin. Devel. engr. Esso Standard Oil Co., Baton Rouge, 1949-51; process engr., sales engr., mgr. sales Southwestern Engring. Co., Los Angeles, 1951-58; bus. devel. engr. Ralph M. Parsons Co., Los Angeles, 1961-65, v.p. process ops., 1965-73, sr. v.p. Petroleum-Chem. div., Pasadena, Calif., 1974-78, exec. v.p., 1978, pres., 1979—. Served to capt., AUS, 1943-46. Mem. Am. Inst. Chem. Engrs., The Beavers, Sigma Xi, Phi Eta Sigma, Tau Beta Pi, Phi Lambda Upsilon, Phi Kappa Phi, Omicron Delta Kappa. Republican. Presbyterian. Clubs: Annandale Golf, Seven Lakes Country. Office: 100 W Walnut St Pasadena CA 91124

RODENBAUGH, RALPH LESTER, mfg. co. exec.; b. Pitts., Apr. 21, 1941; s. Ralph F. and Gladys L. (Atkinson) R.; student Marietta Coll., 1959-61, U. Pitts., 1962-66. Lab. technician color div. Ferro Corp., Pitts., 1962-66; with Deco Coatings Corp., Pitts., 1966—, v.p. ops., 1974—, dir., 1977—. Methodist. Patentee in field. Home: 2291 Reis Run Rd Franklin Park PA 15237 Office: 355 Rochester Rd Pittsburgh PA 15237

RODERICK, DAVID MILTON, steel co. exec.; b. Pitts., May 3, 1924; s. Milton S. and Anna R. (Baskin) R.; B.S., U. Pitts., 1956; m. Elizabeth J. Costello, Jan. 31, 1948; children—David Milton, Patricia Ann. Thomas Kevin. With U.S. Steel Corp., Pitts., 1959—, v.p. accounting, 1964-67, chmn. fin. com., 1973-75, pres., dir., 1975-79, chmn., chief exec. officer, 1979—; dir. Aetna Life & Casualty Co., Procter & Gamble Co., Tax Found., Inc., No. Tier Pipeline Co.; mem. internat. council Morgan Guaranty Trust Co. of N.Y. Mem. exec. bd. Allegheny Trails council Boy Scouts Am.; mem. citizens sponsoring com. Allegheny Conf. on Community Devel.; bd. govs. United Way Am.; bd. dirs. United Way of Allegheny County; bd. dirs., pres. Pitts. Symphony Soc.; trustee Carnegie Inst., Mercy Hosp., Carnegie-Mellon U., Shady Side Acad. Served with USMC, World War II. Mem. Am. Iron and Steel Inst., Econ. Club N.Y., Newcomen Soc., Pa. Soc. Clubs: Links (N.Y.C.); Duquesne, Laurel Valley Golf, Fox Chapel Golf, Pitts. Field, Rolling Rock; Pine Valley Golf (N.J.). Office: 600 Grant St Pittsburgh PA 15230*

RODERICKS, CHARLES MANUEL, JR., accountant, tax exec.; b. Allentown, Pa., June 10, 1952; s. Charles Manuel and Rose (Barros) R.; B.S., Bentley Coll., 1974, M.S. in Taxation, 1978; m. Diane Aucoin, Aug. 22, 1975; children—Charles III, Jared. Auditor, Coopers & Lybrand, Boston, 1974-76, tax specialist, 1976-77, tax supr., 1978-79, tax mgr., 1979—. C.P.A., Mass. Mem. Am. Inst. C.P.A.'s, Mass. Soc. C.P.A.'s. Home: 32 Linden St Needham MA 02192 Office: 100 Federal St Coopers & Lybrand Boston MA 02110

RODGERS, FRANCIS RAYMOND, stainless steel equipment mfg. co. exec.; b. Chgo., Oct. 23, 1923; s. Francis Raymond and Elizabeth (Collins) R.; B.A., Yale U., 1950; m. Louise Shine, Oct. 14, 1950; children—Christopher, Stephen, Mary, Catherine. Salesman, Central Steel & Wire Co., Chgo., 1950-54; sales mgr. Krueger Fabricating Co., Madison, Wis., 1954-60; pres. Dec Aviation Inc., Madison, 1960-63; mng. dir. Fabage Ltd., Ellesmere, Eng., 1963-66; v.p. mfg. Dairy Equipment Co., Madison, 1966-69; exec. v.p. Dec Internat., Madison, 1969-75, pres., chief exec. officer, 1975—. Served to lt. (j.g.) USNR, 1942-46. Clubs: Maple Bluff Country, Four Lakes Yacht, Yale of Wis. Office: 1919 S Stoughton Rd Madison WI 53706

RODGERS, JAMES CHESTER, fluid power products mfg. co. exec.; b. Newark, Sept. 4, 1919; s. Chester Howard and Florence (O'Conner) R.; B.S., U. Cin., 1947, M.E., 1947; m. Rosemary V. Koenig, June 6, 1940; children—Rosemary F., Virginia C., Valarie A. Sales engr. to mgr. Ingersoll Rand Co., Chgo., 1947-62; dir. mktg. Scully Jones & Co., Chgo., 1962-63; v.p. Thor Power Tool Co., 1963-65; asst. to exec. v.p. Symington Wayne Corp., Chgo., 1965-69; v.p. API Industries, Inc., Elmhurst, Ill., 1969; v.p., gen. mgr. Tysaman Machine div. Carborundum Corp., Knoxville, Tenn., 1969-71; dir. mktg. BFF div. Whittaker Corp., Berwick, Pa., 1976-77; mgr. mktg. ops. Gen. Contracting Co., Saudi Arabia, 1978; pres. Origa Corp., Elmhurst, 1978—; chief exec. officer MASTA. Served to lt. (j.g.) USN, 1940-43; with USAF, 1943-45. Mem. ASME, Soc. Mfg. Engrs., VFW. Republican. Roman Catholic. Contbr. articles to tech. jours. Office: Origa Corp 928 Oak Lawn Ave Elmhurst IL 60126

RODGERS, JAMES OLIVER, telecommunications exec.; b. Columbus, Ga., Dec. 24, 1948; s. Dennis Oliver and Rachel (Peterson) R.; B.S. in Elec. Engring., Howard U., 1970; M.B.A., U. Ala., Birmingham, 1977; m. Sharon Lynette Dudley, July 6, 1968; children—Adrianne, Nichele, Shana, Shawna. Engr., S. Central Bell Co., Louisville, 1970, 72-74, staff mgr., Birmingham, Ala., 1974-76, dist. staff mgr., 1976—. Chmn. comprehensive subcom. Citizens Adv. Com.-Birmingham Planning Com., 1978—; mem. choirs and adminstrv. coms. Sixth Ave Baptist Ch., Birmingham. Served with U.S. Army, 1970-72. Mem. IEEE, Communications Soc., Assn. of M.B.A. Execs., Assn. for Devel. of Black Mgrs., Birmingham Jaycees (dir.), Howard U. Alumni Assn. (pres.). Democrat. Home: 7120 Pinetree Ln Fairfield AL 35064 Office: S Central Bell Co 600 N 19th St 7th Floor Birmingham AL 35201

RODGERS, JAMES ROBERT, import co. exec.; b. Arcata, Calif., Feb. 20, 1942; s. Robert E. and Barbara Jane (Evans) R.; B.S. in Natural Resource, Oreg. State U., 1966, M.S. in Resource Geography (Crown Zellerbach Corp. fellow), 1967; m. Mary L. Nash, Sept. 15, 1962; children—Michelle Joy, Robert Shawn. Geographer, U.S. Army Corps of Engrs., 1967-73; pres., gen. mgr. J.R. Rodgers, Ltd., Tualatin, Oreg., 1973—; v.p. Wheeler Imports, Kansas City, Mo. Mem. Nat. Assn. Geographers. Republican. Office: PO Box 829 Tualatin OR 97062

RODGERS, NANCY LUCILLE, businesswoman; b. Denver, Aug. 22, 1934; d. Francis Randolf and Irma Lucille (Budy) Baker; student pub. schs.; m. George J. Rodgers, Feb. 18, 1968; children by previous marriage—Kellie Rae, Joy Lynn, Timothy Francis, Thomas Francis. Mgr., Western Telelarm, Inc., 1973-77; pres. Rodgers Police Patrol, Inc., San Diego, 1973—; br. mgr. Honeywell Inc., Protection Services div., San Diego, 1977-79; pres. IMAGE, Inc. and Western Solar Specialties, 1979-80; cons., mem. speakers' bur. MOVE, Profl. Women's Center. Mem. advisory bd. Elect Dr. Geraldine Rickman to

Calif. State Senate, 1977-78; bd. dirs. Central City Assn. Mem. Am. Soc. Indsl. Security, Western, Nat. burglar and fire alarm assns., Calif. Assn. Licensed Investigators, Sales and Mktg. Execs. Internat., Am. Soc. Women Execs., Profl. Women's Assn., Apt. Rental and Owners Assn., Am. Bus. Women's Assn. Republican. Club: Soroptimist. Office: 3780 5th Ave San Diego CA 92103

RODGERS, PETER JAY, real estate exec.; b. Bklyn., Sept. 16, 1939; s. Leonard Sidney and Cecelia Naomi (Koch) R.; B.E.E., Cornell U., 1962; postgrad. San Jose State Coll., 1963-66, Wharton Sch. Fin., 1972-73; children—Karen Lisa, Keith Robert, Jennifer Leah. Project mgr. Lockheed Missiles & Space Co., Sunnyvale, Calif., 1962-67; project mgr. Gen. Electric Co., King of Prussia, Pa., 1967-71; v.p. Capital Investment Devel. Corp., Lionville, Pa., 1971-78; pres. Jalc Real Estate Corp., Lionville, 1978—, RCR Assos., Inc., Lionville, 1975—; v.p. Integrated Industries, Inc., Exton, Pa., 1978—. Pres., dir. No. Chester County Community Concert Assn., 1968-76; treas. Valley Forge Gen. Hosp. Use Study Com., 1973-75; chmn. East Pikeland Twp. Bd. Suprs., 1972-78; pres., mem. exec. com. Chester County Assn. Twp. Ofcls., 1974-78; mem. legis. resolutions com. Pa. Assn. Twp. Suprs., 1977-78. Lic. profl. engr., Pa.; lic. real estate salesman, Pa. Mem. Am. Planning Assn. Republican. Home: Coldstream Rd Phoenixville PA 19460 Office: PO Box 158 110 Pickering Way Lionville PA 19353

RODGERS, RICHARD RANDOLPH, assn. exec.; b. Madison, Ind., July 28, 1948; s. Richard Payne and Marjorie Jean (Bishop) R.; B.S. in Acctg., U. Ky., 1970, postgrad., 1972-73; m. Sharron Kaye Manley, Aug. 15, 1970; 1 child, Leigh Walker. Acct., Sullivan and Clancy, C.P.A.'s, Lexington, Ky., 1969-72; pvt. practice acctg., Lexington, 1972-73; comptroller Council of State Govts., Lexington, 1973-75; dir. adminstrn. and fin. Nat. Gov.'s Assn., Washington, 1975—, sec.-treas., 1977—, treas. Center for Policy Research, 1977—; chmn. bd. State Services Orgn. Pres., Lansdowne Neighborhood Assn., 1972-73; vice chmn. bd. deacons McLean Baptist Ch., 1979-80. Served with Army. N.G., 1970-76. Mem. Washington Soc. Assn. Execs., Greater Washington Bd. of Trade, Ky. Soc. of Washington, U. Ky. Alumni Assn., Phi Gamma Delta. Baptist. Home: 9825 Fosbak Dr Vienna VA 22180 Office: Suite 250 Hall of States 444 N Capitol St NW Washington DC 20001

RODKEY, ELIZABETH S., business exec.; b. nr. Hagerstown, Md.; d. Martin and Martha (Myers) Summers; B.C.S., Columbus U., 1947, M.C.S., 1948; postgrad. George Washington U., Am. U.; m. William Rodkey, Oct. 1942 (div. Oct. 1953). Govt. employee, 1940-50; chief accountant St. Agnes Hosp., Balt., 1950-55; dir. finance Nat. Fedn. Bus. and Profl. Women's Clubs, Inc., 1956-57; C.P.A. on internat. staff Haskins and Sells, C.P.A.'s, 1956-59; comptroller Nat. Fence Mfg. Co., Inc., Bladensburg, Md. 1961-65; chief central acctg. and purchasing office DAC, 1967—, now sr. auditor, acting chief internal revenue div. Bd. dirs. St. Agnes Hosp., Balt. C.P.A., Md. Mem. Am. Soc. Women Accountants (organizer Balt. chpt., charter and first pres.), Am. Woman's Soc. C.P.A.'s, Md. Assn. C.P.A.'s, Inc., Nat. Assn. Accountants, Am. Accounting Assn., Soc. for Advancement Mgmt. Mem. Christian Ch. Writer articles in field. Home: Box 5 Cluster S286 River Meadow Subdiv 6022 Columbia MD 21045 Office: Post Comptrollers Office Fort Meade MD 20755

RODOWSKAS, CHRISTOPHER A., JR., assn. exec.; b. Balt., July 27, 1939; s. Christopher A. and Aldona R.; B.S. in Pharmacy, Fordham U., 1961; M.S. in Pharm. Adminstrn., Purdue U., 1963, Ph.D. in Pharm. Adminstrn.; m. Carolyn; children—Christopher A., Matthew. Asst. prof. U. Conn., 1964-68; asst. prof. Ohio State U., 1968-70, asso. prof. pharmacy, 1970-72; project dir. Manpower Info. Study, Am. Assn. Colls. Pharmacy, Bethesda, Md., 1971-73, dir. Office Ednl. Research and Devel., 1973-75, exec. dir., 1975—; chmn. Council of Govs. Health Manpower Planning Com.; chmn. drug abuse edn. Ohio Dept. Edn.; T. Edward Hicks Meml. lectr. Mass. Coll. Pharmacy; Kauffman Meml. lectr. Ohio State U. Diebold Citation fellow Am. Found. Pharm. Edn.; recipient Disting. Service to Pharmacy award Wayne State U.; Lyman award Am. Assn. Colls. Pharmacy. Mem. Fedn. Assn. Schs. Health Professions, Coalition for Health Funding, Am., Md. Pharm. assns., Acad. Pharm. Scis., Pharm. Scis. Research Com., U.S. Pharmacopeial Conv., Am. Public Health Assn., Am. Soc. Hosp. Pharmacists, AAAS, Am. Inst. History of Pharmacy, Am. Soc. Assn. Execs., Am. Med. Colls., Kappa Psi, Rho Chi, Sigma Xi. Author 6 books; contbr. 200 articles to nat. pharmacy jours. Home: 1103 Meurilee Ln Silver Spring MD 20901 Office: Am Assn Colls Pharmacy 4630 Montgomery Ave Bethesda MD 20014

RODRIGUEZ, EDOUARD, tile mfg. co. exec.; b. Ingrannes, France, Apr. 19, 1943; came to U.S., 1975; s. Pedro and Therese (Perez) R.; student schs., Romorantin, France; m. Dominique Deshrosses, Dec. 5, 1964; children—Fabrice, Alexa. Comml. div. coordinator Briare France, Loiret, 1964, comml. div. mgr., 1964-66, comml. div. mgr., sales adminstr., product mgr., 1970-75, pres. Briare Co., Inc. U.S.A., Baldwin, N.Y., 1975—. Served with French Army, 1962-63. Mem. Am. Soc. Interior Decorators and Designers, AAU. Club: Road Runner (N.Y.C.). Office: Briare Co Inc 775 Brooklyn Ave Baldwin NY 11510

RODRIGUEZ, KAY ALICE, realtor, restauranteur; b. Yankton, S.D., Apr. 28, 1936; d. Charles Thomas and Hilda Ann (Huber) Hocking; children—John, Debra, Janette, Patricia, Charles Joseph. Owner, Bond Realty, Las Vegas, Nev., 1965-72, Bark-K Realty, Las Vegas, 1972—; owner Country Rebel Restaurant and Lounge, Las Vegas, 1980—; chmn. realtor com. Las Vegas Bd. Realtors. Active Clark County Dem. Central Com. Roman Catholic. Home: 4557 El Como Way Las Vegas NC 89121 Office: 530 E St Louis St Las Vegas NC 89104

RODRIGUEZ, SALLIE ANN, mfg. co. ofcl.; b. Highland Park, Mich., May 30, 1947; d. Robert Gilbert and Ruth Mary (Brown) Domke; B.S. in M.E., Marquette U., 1979; B.S. in Bus. Edn., Central Mich. U., 1970; M.B.A., U. Detroit, 1975; m. Reynel Rodriguez, Nov. 7, 1970; children—Holly, Heather. Instr., Detroit Bus. Inst., 1971-75; staff cons. Learson Asso., Detroit, 1975-76; compensation analyst, employment rep. Diamond Shamrock Corp., Cleve., 1976-78; mgr. salary and benefits adminstrn. Babcock & Wilcox, Bloomfield Hills, Mich., 1978—; pres. Glouster Gallery. Mem. Parma Sch. Dist. bus. bd., 1977. Mem. Am. Soc. Personnel Adminstrn., Am. Soc. for Training and Devel., Assn. of MBA Execs. Club: Cleve. Womens City. Home: 33970 Glouster Circle Farmington Hills MI 48018 Office: 2550 S Telegraph Suite 200 Bloomfield Hills MI 48018

RODSTEIN, HENRY, fin. exec.; b. Johnstown, Pa., Sept. 3, 1946; s. Herman and Helen (Fisher) R.; B.S. in Bus. Adminstrn., U. Fla., 1968; M.B.A., Pace U., 1971; m. Roberta M. Herzog, Sept. 26, 1971; 1 dau., T. Kimberly. Asst. sec. Chem. Bank, N.Y.C., 1968-73; mortgage officer Pearce Mayer & Greer Inc., N.Y.C., 1974-75; v.p. Capital Bank, Miami, Fla., 1975-78; pres. Westfield Fin. Corp., Miami, 1978—. Sect. chmn. United Way, Miami, 1976-77; treas. Boy Scouts Am., Miami, 1978. Lic. mortgage broker; lic. real estate salesman. Mem. Comml. Loan officers Assn., Mortgage Brokers Assn. Miami (dir. 1979-81), Pi Lambda Phi. Democrat. Clubs: Bankers, Downtown Athletic, B'nai B'rith (lodge pres. 1976-79). Home: Miami FL Office: PO Box 3397 2800 Simkins Rd Miami FL 33152

RODY, WALTER WILLIAM, shipbldg. co. exec.; b. St. Petersburg, Fla., Aug. 16, 1926; s. Walter and Mary (Fleitas) R.; B.E. in Civil Engring., Tulane U., 1948; M.B.A., La. State U., 1969; m. Joyce Dolores Van Sandt, July 27, 1949; children—Walter Wayne, Wendelyn Wren, Wendell Wesley. Office engr. Mene Grande Oil Co., San Tome, Venezuela, 1948-50; constrn. engr. A.N. Goldberg, New Orleans, 1950-52; prodn. engr. Avondale Shipyards, New Orleans, 1952-53, chief cost engr., 1953-54, chief engr., 1954-58, asst. to pres., 1958-59, prodn. mgr., 1959-65, v.p., 1966-69; dir. prodn. planning and control Ingalls/Litton Shipbldg., Inc., Pascagoula, Miss., 1969-71, dir. shipbldg., 1971-72; marine and indsl. cons., 1972-78; pres. Port Allen Marine Services, Inc., Baton Rouge, 1978—. Chmn. adv. bd. Salvation Army, New Orleans, 1965; pres. Met. Crime Commn. New Orleans, 1965-66. Recipient Disting. Service award New Orleans Jaycees, 1962; Citizen of Yr. award Jefferson Parish Sheriffs Assn., 1966. Mem. Am. Waterway Operators, ASTM (chmn. Gulf Region 1969), Traffic Club Baton Rouge, Tulane Engrs. Club. Methodist. Clubs: Skyline Country, Orange Beach Marina (Mobile, Ala.); Sherwood Forest Country (Baton Rouge); Masons, Shriners, Grand Consistory of La. (knights comdr. ct. of honor) (New Orleans). Contbr. articles to profl. jours. Home: 328 Woodstone Ct Baton Rouge LA 70808 Office: PO Box 108 Port Allen LA 70767

ROE, RICHARD C., mattress mktg. and mfg. co. exec.; b. Des Moines, Jan. 4, 1930; s. Lloyd E. and Mary E. (Nuzum) R.; B.S. in Indsl. Engring., Iowa State U., 1952; m. Sally McGlothlen, May 28, 1932; children—Stephen James, Julie Ann. Indsl. engr. Maytag Co., Newton, Iowa, 1952-56; gen. mgr. mfg. Schnadig Corp., Chgo., 1956-66; group v.p. Sealy, Inc., Chgo., 1966—, pres. Sealy Spring Corp., 1972—, pres. Sealy Furniture Corp., 1978—. Mem. Am. Mgmt. Assn., Nat. Soc. Profl. Engrs., Am. Inst. Indsl. Engrs., Nat. Assn. Bedding Mfrs. (v.p., trustee). Registered profl. engr., Iowa, Ind., Ill. Episcopalian. Clubs: Mchts. and Mfrs. (gov.), Elks. Office: 470 Merchandise Mart Chicago IL 60654

ROE, THOMAS ANDERSON, bldg. material co. exec.; b. Greenville, S.C., May 29, 1927; s. Thomas A. and Leila M. (Cunningham) R.; B.A., Furman U., 1948; m. Bette Verner Bain, Oct. 14, 1950 (div. 1979); children—Elizabeth Overton Roe Mason, Thomas Anderson III, Phillip Stradley, John Verner. Asst. in cancer research program Furman U., Greenville, 1947-48; asst. to pres. Citizens Lumber Co., Greenville, 1948-61, pres., 1961-65; v.p. Am. Holdings, Inc., Dominican Republic, 1964-70; chmn. bd. First Piedmont Corp., Greenville, 1967-74, First Piedmont Bank & Trust Co., Greenville, 1967-74; chmn. bd. Builder Marts of Am., Inc., 1965—; adj. prof. faculty bus. adminstrn. Furman U., 1980—. Mem. Greenville County Redevel. Authority, 1971-75; hon. asst. sgt.-at-arms Republican Nat. Conv., 1960, del.-at-large, 1964; air inspector CAP, 1948-51; bd. dirs. Nat. Found. for Ileitis and Colitis, 1975-76, Greenville United Cerebral Palsy, 1960, ARC, Greenville, 1962-64; trustee Christ Ch. Episcopal Sch., Greenville, 1970-72. Mem. Greenville Home Bldg. Assn. (Builder of Yr. award 1962, v.p. 1961-62), Nat. Assn. of Home Builders (mem. internat. housing com. 1965-66), Greater Greenville C. of C. (pres. 1970), Piedmont Econs. Club (co-founder 1974). Episcopalian. Clubs: Greenville Sertoma (pres. 1960-61, Outstanding Leadership award 1961); Green Valley Country, Poinsett. Address: PO Box 4255 Greenville SC 29608

ROEDER, GEORGE ALBERT, JR., banker; b. Hackensack, N.J., Sept. 28, 1920; s. George Albert and Gertrude (Miller) R.; B.S. in Econs., U. Pa., 1942; M.B.A., Harvard, 1947; m. Anne T. Connor, June 7, 1947; children—Jane Anne, Russell K. With Chase Manhattan Bank, N.Y.C., 1947—, successively trainee, asst. cashier, asst. v.p., v.p., sr. v.p., 1947-61, exec. v.p., 1961-69, vice chmn., dir., 1969—; dir. Allied Stores Corp., Nat. Reins. Corp. Bd. dirs. United Way of N.Y.C. Served from pfc. to maj. USMCR, 1942-45. Decorated Bronze Star. Mem. Phi Delta Theta. Office: 1 Chase Manhattan Plaza New York NY 10081

ROEDIGER, FREDERICK EVERETT, elec. engr.; b. N.Y.C., July 9, 1921; s. T. Frederick and Anna Marie (Linck) R.; B.S. in Physics, Muhlenberg Coll., 1943; M.E.E., Rensselaer Poly. Inst. (Eastman Kodak Grad. fellow 1947-49) 1949; m. Susannah Alice Eastwood, Oct. 14, 1944; children—Barbara Eastwood, Jane Anne, Frank Linck. Instr. physics, elec. engring. Rensselaer Poly. Inst., 1945-49; prof. elec. engring. Ordnance Sch., 1949-51; chief fire control engring. sect. Aberdeen Proving Ground, 1951-53, chief engring. projects br. fire control div., 1953-56; chief test analysis sect. Lincoln Project Office Air Force Cambridge Research Center, 1956-58; tech. asst. to prodn. mgr. Andover plant Raytheon Mfg. Co., 1958; prodn. test mgr. Andover Plant, Raytheon Co., 1958-62, microwave assembly and test mgr., 1962, prodn. mgr. 1962-63, systems engring. mgr. Andover operation, 1963-65; program mgr. anti-submarine warfare systems Sperry Gyroscope div. Sperry Rand Corp., Great Neck, N.Y., 1966-68, program dir. anti-submarine warfare systems Sperry Gyroscope div., 1968—. Mem. anti-submarine warfare adv. com. Dept. Def., 1966—. Vice pres. Nassau County Council Boy Scouts Am., 1974—; pres. Webster Village Devel. Assn., 1952-55. Served as lt. (j.g.), USN, 1943-46; comdr. Res. Mem. A.A.A.S., Am. Inst. Aeros. and Astronautics, I.E.E.E., Am. Soc. Engring. Edn., Am. Soc. Naval Engrs., Nat. Security Indsl. Assn., Am. Ordnance Assn., Sigma Xi, Omicron Delta Kappa. Lutheran (mem. council). Mason. Home: Glenby Ln Brookville NY 11545 Office: Sperry Gyroscope Div Great Neck NY 11020

ROEDING, GEORGE CHRISTIAN, JR., nurseryman; b. Fresno, Calif., Dec. 31, 1901; s. George Christian and Elizabeth (Thorne) R.; student Cornell U., 1921-23, U. Calif., 1924; m. Frances Baldwin, Aug. 10, 1927; children—Bruce, George Christian, Gerald, Diane. Pres., mgr. Calif. Nursery Co., Niles Dist., Fremont, 1926—. Chmn. exec. com. on revival Ala. County Fair, 1940; pres. Washington Twp. Tax Payers Assn., 1932; rep. So. Ala. County dir. East Bay Regional Park, 1962-70. Mem. Pacific Coast Nursery (pres. 1930), Calif. Assn. Nurserymen (pres. 1934), Met. Oakland Area C. of C. (dir.), Chi Psi. Republican. Episcopalian. Clubs: Rotary (Oakland), Athenian Nile, Soc. Calif. Pioneers. Hort. designer, compiler publ.: Gardens of the Expn., World Fair at Treasure Island, San Francisco, 1939. Home: 245 Hillview Dr Fremont CA 94536 Office: PO Box 2278 Fremont CA 94536

ROEHL, FREDERICK CHRISTIAN, food broker; b. Lake Mills, Wis., May 19, 1911; s. Gustave and Anna Marie (Punzel) R.; B.A., Valparaiso U., 1932. Asst. sales mgr. Wis. Canners Exchange, Oconomowoc, 1933-38; pres. F. C. Roehl and Co., Inc., Oconomowoc, Wis., 1938—. Trustee Wis. Luth. Synod, 1966-72, 78—; sec., v.p., dir. Meml. Hosp. at Oconomowoc, 1968—; bd. dirs. Shorehaven/Knollward Homes, 1973—; mem. pres.'s council Valparaiso U. Served with Q.M.C., AUS, 1942-46. Mem. Nat. Food Brokers Assn., Oconomowoc C. of C. (sec. 1947-48). Republican. Clubs: Milw. Athletic, Kiwanis. Home: 35055 W Fairview Rd Oconomowoc WI 53066 Office: PO Box 168 Oconomowoc WI 53066

ROELING, GERARD HENRY, investment co. exec.; b. New Orleans, July 11, 1939; s. William Henry and Gladys Nathalie (Pavlovich) R.; B.A., U. Mich., 1960, M.B.A. with honors, 1961; m. Bette Ann Bichet, Jan. 30, 1960; children—Gerard Patrick, Stewart VanWay, William Jeffrey. Chemist, La. FDA, New Orleans, 1957-59; mem. div. and corp. financial and mktg. staff Ford Motor Co., Dearborn, Mich., 1961-66; mem. mktg. staff Exxon Corp., Houston, 1966-69; dir. research and planning Asso. Credit Burs., Inc., exec. v.p. Credit Services Internat., Inc., Houston, 1969-72; pres., chmn. bd. Am. Forum Corp., Houston, 1972—; dir. M.F. Roeling, Inc.; pres. Associated Bus. Cons.'s, Houston, 1972—. Mem. econ. adv. com. to staff Pres. Nixon, 1970-72. Pres., Brookwood Estates Assn., Livonia, Mich., 1964-66; 1st v.p. Livonia Fedn. Civic Assn., 1965, pres., 1966; chmn. Livonia Civic Affairs Com., 1965; mem. Citizens Adv. Com., 1964-66; pres. Houston Museum Am. History, 1974-78; mem. Capital Improvement and Long Range Planning Com., 1964-66, Sch. Bd. Adv. Com., 1965-66, United Fund, 1966-67, Houston Grand Opera, 1975, Houston Advanced Urban Analysis Com., 1968, Meml. Glen Assn., 1968, 69, Inst. Internat. Edn., 1972—. Bd. dirs. Mus. Am. Architecture and Decorative Arts, Houston chpt. March of Dimes. Mem. Am. Mktg. Assn., Market Research Assn., Advt. Fedn., Nat. Assn. Real Estate Bds., C. of C., Phi Kappa Phi, Alpha Kappa Psi. Author articles. Home: 11910 Clarendon Ln Houston TX 77024 Office: 6300 Richmond Ave Houston TX 77057

ROESCHLAUB, RONALD CURTIS, bus. exec., lawyer; b. Denver, Apr. 16, 1913; s. Harry Morris and Roy (Turner) R.; B.A. in Econs., U. Calif. at Los Angeles, 1935, M.A. in Econs., 1937; LL. B. cum laude, Harvard, 1940; 1 son, Ronald W.; m. 2d, Jean Clinton Davis, Jan. 9, 1965; children—David J. Davis, Diane J. Davis, Bruce C. Davis. Admitted to Calif. bar, 1940, since practiced in Los Angeles; pres. Irontite Products Co., Hellyer Steel Parts Co., Los Angeles; dir. Clinton's Restaurants. Served to lt. USNR, 1942-46. Mem. Am. Bar Assn., Calif. State Bar. Clubs: Los Angeles Athletic, Los Angeles Country (Los Angeles). Home: 5005 Los Feliz Blvd Los Angeles CA 90027 Office: 707 Wilshire Blvd Suite 4810 Los Angeles CA 90017

ROESELER, WOLFGANG GUENTHER, city planner; b. Berlin, Germany, Mar. 30, 1925; s. Karl Ludwig and Therese (Guenther) R.; Ph.D., Philipps State U. of Hesse, Marburg, W. Germany, 1946-49; LL.B., Blackstone Sch. Law, Chgo., 1958; m. Eva Maria Jante, Mar. 12, 1947; children—Marion, Joanie, Karl. Asso. planner Kansas City (Mo.) Planning Commn., 1950-52; city planning dir. City of Palm Springs, Calif., 1952-54; sr. planner city Kansas City, 1954-56; prin. asso. Ladislas Segoe & Assos., Cin., 1956-64; dir. urban and regional planning Howard, Needles, Tammen & Bergendoff, cons. Kansas City, N.Y.C., 1964-68; owner W.G. Roeseler, Cons. City Planner and Transp. Specialist, Bryan, Tex., 1969—; prof., head dept. urban and regional planning Tex. A. and M. U., 1975—. Mem. Am. Inst. Certified Planners, Inst. Transport Engrs., Nat. Acad. Scis., Am. Planning Assn. Contbr. articles to profl. jours. Home: 2508 Broadmoor PO Box 4007 Bryan TX 77801 Office: Tex A and M U College Station TX 77843

ROESS, MARTIN JOHN, savs. and loan exec.; b. Ocala, Fla., Dec. 18, 1907; s. Martin John and Mary R.; A.B., Cornell U., 1930, LL.D., 1931; children—Diane Celeste, Robert Thornton, Martin John, Mary Susan, Morgen Leslie, Sherry Allison. Admitted to Fla. bar, U.S. Supreme Ct.; asso. firm Rogers & Towers, Jacksonville, Fla., 1931-34; chief counsel Rental Housing div. FHA, Washington, 1934-38, dist. dir. Fla., Jacksonville, 1947-48; v.p., gen. counsel A. Lloyd Goode Contracting Co., Washington, 1938-46; pres. Builders Mortgage Corp., St. Petersburg, Fla., 1948-51; chmn. bd., pres. Guaranty Savs. & Loan Assn., St. Petersburg, 1960—; chmn. bd. Am. Bank, St. Petersburg, 1973-74, N.Am. Ins. Agy., 1955—. Bd. dirs. Shelter div. Fed. Civil Def. Adminstrn., Washington; circuit judge 6th Jud. Circuit, St. Petersburg. Former bd. dirs. Fla. Council 100; chmn. Oceanography. Served to lt. USNR, 1943-45. Knickerbocker fellow; Asst. Law Librarian scholar; registered real estate broker, lic. ins. agt., Fla. Mem. Ind. Bankers Fla. (dir.), St. Petersburg Bar Assn., Am. Bar Assn., Fla. Bar Assn., D.C. Bar Assn., Fla. Bankers Assn., Am. Bankers Assn., Mortgage Bankers Assn. Fla., St. Petersburg Bd. Realtors, Fla. Savs. and Loan League, U.S. Savs. and Loan League, Cornell Law Assn., Nat. Savs. and Loan League, Conf. Bd., James Smithson Soc., St. Petersburg C. of C., Commerce Club Pineallas County, Phi Beta Kappa, Phi Delta Phi, Sigma Alpha Epsilon, Phi Delta Psi. Clubs: Univ. (Washington); Cornell (N.Y.C.); River, Univ., Seminole (Jacksonville); St. Petersburg Yacht, Treasure Island, Fla. Yacht and Tennis (St. Petersburg); Univ. (Tampa). Office: 2100 66th St N Saint Petersburg FL 33710

ROETHLE, JOHN DONALD, corp. exec.; b. Milw., Mar. 2, 1933; s. Rueben Henry and Helen Irene R.; B.A. in Econs., Loras Coll., 1958; M.B.A., Northwestern U., 1959; m. Janet Y. Zemlicka, Sept. 10, 1960; children—Elizabeth Ann, John Henry, Christopher Charles. Sales and adminstrv. asst. Rexnord, Milw., 1959-61; gen. mgr., treas. Wis. Capital Corp., Milw., 1961-62; v.p. fin. Romar Filter Corp., Milw., 1962-63; exec. v.p. Anderson/Roethle & Assos., Inc., Milw., 1963-70, pres., 1970—; Instr. fin., Marquette U., Milw., 1959-72; lectr. U. Wis., Madison, U. Wis., Milw., Milw. Sch. Engring., 1964-70. Commr., Milw. County Planning Commn., 1972—; fin. chmn. Milw. Tennis Classic, 1976—; bd. dirs. Sacred Heart Rehab. Hosp., 1979—, Friends of the Mus., 1979—. Mem. Center for Venture Mgmt., Inc. (vice chmn., treas. 1967-75), Inst. Mgmt. Cons. (dir. 1980—), Assn. Mgmt. Cons. (trustee 1979—). Republican. Episcopalian. Clubs: Univ., Rotary (dir. 1976-79, treas. 1978-79). Contbr. articles to profl. publs.; lectr. in field. Home: 6311 N Berkeley Blvd Whitefish Bay WI 53217 Office: 811 E Wisconsin Ave Milwaukee WI 53202

ROETSCHKE, RONALD CLAY, oil pipe co. exec.; b. Clifton, Tex., Mar. 18, 1934; s. August, Jr., and Susana M. (Seljos) R.; B.S., Tex. A. and M. U., 1955; postgrad. Okla. State U., 1957-59; m. Elizabeth Ann McGowen, Aug. 19, 1972; children—Martha Rice, Ramona Lindsey, Drucilla Morren. Range conservationist Soil Conservation Service, U.S. Dept. Agr., Colorado City, Tex., 1955; chemist Phillips Petroleum Co., Pasadena, Tex. and Bartlesville, Okla., 1955-61, office mgr., Pasadena, Calif., Akron, Ohio and Detroit, 1961-66, tech. sales and devel. engr., Atlanta, 1966-68; owner, pres. Coastal Pipe Co. and Coastal Pipe and Supply, Inc., Houston and Midland, Tex., 1968—. Worker Nat. Republican Congl. Com. Mem. Soc. Plastics Engrs., Am. Security Council (nat. adv. bd.). Lutheran. Clubs: Midland A. and M., Century A. and M., Tex. A. and M. Home: 1609 N Garfield St Midland TX 79701 Office: PO Box 4813 Midland TX 79704

ROFFEY, ROBERT CAMERON, JR., ins. co. exec.; b. Gloucester, Mass., Oct. 22, 1935; s. Robert Cameron and Rauni Elizabeth R.; student U. Mass., 1953-54; B.S., Mass. Maritime Acad., 1957, B.S., 1980; m. Roslyn Hancock, June 6, 1958; children—Sharen Lee, Chris Cameron, Curt Farrell, With Comml. Union Assurance Cos., Boston, 1961—, asst. v.p. personnel, 1970-73, v.p. personnel, 1973-75, sr. v.p. adminstrn., 1975-80, 1st sr. v.p., 1980—. Also dir. Bd. dirs. Jr. Achievement Eastern Mass. Served to lt. USN, 1957-61. Mem. Am. Soc. Personnel Adminstrn., Am. Ins. Assn. Home: 126 W Shore Dr Marblehead MA 01945 Office: One Beacon St Boston MA 02108

ROGEN, NEIL ELLIOTT, tech. group exec.; b. N.Y.C., May 1, 1933; s. Harry T. and Sylvia A. (Grayson) R.; B.S., Poly. Inst. N.Y., 1954; M.S., Mass. Inst. Tech., 1956, Met. Engr., 1957; m. Elisabeth Von Krogh, May 28, 1961; children—Stephanie Ingrid Elisabeth, John Harald. Prin. metallurgist Battelle Meml. Inst., Columbus, Ohio, 1954-55; research asst. Mass. Inst. Tech., Cambridge, 1955-60; pres. Ilikon Corp./Cambridge Metal Research, Natick, Mass., 1958-62; fellow Royal Sch. Mines, Imperial Coll., London, 1962-65; chief metals and ceramics AVCO Systems Div., Wilmington, Mass., 1965-67; pres. Polyclon, Inc., Woburn, Mass., 1967-71; pres. Neil E. Rogen Assos., Waltham, Mass., 1971-80; v.p. Nedlog Tech. Group, Arvada, Colo., 1977—; pres. Elektra Energy Corp., Houston, 1979—. Mem. Am. Inst. Metall. Engrs., Am. Soc. Metals, Licensing Execs. Soc., Sigma Xi. Club: Royal Norwegian Yacht (Oslo). Contbr. articles on materials engring. to profl. jours. Holder more than 30 patents in field. Home: 206 Plaza Verde Dr Houston TX 77038 Office: 340 N Belt E Houston TX 77060

ROGERS, ARTHUR MERRIAM, JR., banker; b. Rochester, Minn., Apr. 19, 1941; s. Arthur Merriam and Marguerite (MacCoy) R.; B.A., Yale U., 1963; m. Barbara Whitney, Nov. 27, 1965; children—Arthur III, Alison, Whitney. Joined Morgan Guaranty Trust Co., 1963; asst. mgr. Banca Morgan Vanwiller, Milan, Italy, 1967-73; v.p., ter. head Middle East and African ter. Morgan Guaranty Trust Co., N.Y.C., 1974-76, v.p., asst. gen. mgr. London office, 1976—; gen. mgr. Bank of Kuwait and the Middle East, Kuwait, 1976-78. Trustee Kips Bay Boys Club, N.Y.C., 1966—. Mem. English-Speaking Union. Club: Links (N.Y.C.). Home: 23 Wilton Pl London England Office: 1 Angel Ct London England

ROGERS, EARL JAMES, electronics co. exec.; b. Hays, Kans., Apr. 7, 1935; s. Arthur Marion and Katherine Lois (Rhoades) R.; B.S., Mass. Inst. Tech., 1959, M.S., 1961, Sc.D., 1964; m. Bonnie Alberta Sytsma, Nov. 26, 1955; children—Caryn Lyn, James Bradley. Chief engr. Dynisco, Inc., 1961-64, Micro Systems, Inc., 1964-67; gen. mgr. Life Systems div. Bourns, Inc., 1968-72; pres. Precision Monolithics, Inc., Santa Clara, Calif., 1973—. Mem. ASME, Instrument Soc. Am., Semiconductor Industries Assn. Republican. Mem. United Ch. of Christ. Clubs: Masons, Shriners. Home: 6632 Leyland Park Dr San Jose CA 95120 Office: 1500 Space Park Dr Santa Clara CA 95050

ROGERS, EUGENE LEROY, elec. co. exec.; b. Jackson Center, Ohio, July 6, 1918; s. Orlando Allen and Cecile (Linson) R.; B.S. Ohio No. U., 1940; postgrad. U.S. Naval Service Schs., U.S. Naval Acad., 1942, Harvard, 1942, Mass. Inst. Tech., 1942; J.D., Georgetown U., 1951; m. Eleanor Margaret Moon, June 27, 1943; children—Linda Karin, Charlotte Elaine. Design engr. West Penn Power Co., Pitts., 1940-42; radar design engr. U.S. Navy Bur. Aeros., Washington, 1946-52; sales exec. Dalmo Victor Co., Washington, 1952-55; admitted to Washington bar, 1952, partner firm Bailey & Rogers, Washington, 1955-57; dir. marketing Microwave Tube div. Litton Industries, San Carlus, Calif., 1957-59; dir. marketing Ampex Corp., Instrumentation Product Co., Redwood City, Calif., 1959-61; v.p. marketing, legal counsel Microwave Electronics Corp., Palo Alto, 1961-65; v.p. internat., gen. counsel Memorex Corp., Santa Clara, 1965-69, dir.; v.p. Internat. Plastronics/Perfection Corp.; v.p. corporate planning Data Tech. Corp., 1969-70; v.p., dir. Spectotherm Corp., Santa Clara, Calif., 1972-76; dir. Avantek Corp., 1968-79, Antekna Corp., 1971-79; dir., sec. Caere Corp.; dir. Quantic Corp., Viking Labs., Inc., Datacognition Inc., Luxtrom Corp., Gen. Tech. Corp., Quantex Corp. Served as lt. USNR, 1942-46. Registered profl. engr., D.C. Mem. Am., Fed., D.C. bar assns., Nat. Assn. Contract Adminstr., Sigma Pi, Gamma Eta Gamma. Presbyn. Elk, Clubs: Washington Golf and Country, Nat. Lawyers. Home: 119 Sunkist Ln Los Altos CA 94022 Office: 3040 Olcott St Santa Clara CA 95051

ROGERS, GARDNER SPENCER, r.r. co. exec.; b. Bryn Mawr, Pa., Sept. 16, 1926; s. Gardner Spencer and Frances (Lloyd) R.; student Episcopal Acad., 1940-44, Mass. Inst. Tech., 1944-45; B.S., U. Colo., 1951; m. Margaret Elizabeth Windsor, July 18, 1954; children—Ann Windsor, Barbara Lloyd. With W.P. R.R. Co., San Francisco, 1947-70, engr. costs, valuation, statistics, 1964-69, asst. to gen. mgr. planning, control, 1969, asst. gen. mgr., 1970; gen. mgr. Civil & Mech. Maintenance Pty. Ltd., 1970-77, also dir.; mgr. Western Australian operations Fluor Australia Pty. Ltd., 1971-73, gen. mgr. ry. div., 1973-77; gen. mgr. Pilbara Industries, 1971-73; dir. budgets and control Consol. Rail Corp., 1978-79, sr. dir. budgets, planning and control, 1980—. Mem. spl. adv. team r.r. ofcls. to U.S. Govt., 1962; r.r. adv. com. on r.r. property ICC, 1966-70. Mng. trustee Daniel B. Gardner Trust, Chgo.; alt. trustee Cathedral Sq. Found., Perth; bd. dirs. Ch. of Eng. Schs.' Trust, 1975-77. Registered profl. engr., Calif. Mem. Instn. Engrs. Australia, Am. C. of C. in Australia (dir., v.p., chmn. Western Australian exec. com. 1976-77), Swanleigh (chmn. exec. com. 1974-77, council), Am. Ry. Engr. Assn., Ry. and Locomotive Hist. Soc., Soc. of Cin., Mil. Order Loyal Legion (vice comdr.), Colo. Alumni Assn. No. Calif. (pres. 1951-52), Alpha Tau Omega (high council 1964-68). Republican. Mem. Ch. of Eng. (vestryman 1971-77, mem. synod and provincial synod 1973-77, diocesan council 1974-77). Clubs: Berkeley Tennis, Pacific Railway (San Francisco), Commonwealth Calif.); Australian-Am. (Perth, Australia). Home: 579 Brinton Rd Wayne PA 19087 Office: Six Penn Center Plaza Philadelphia PA 19104

ROGERS, JAMES BEELAND, JR., investment co. exec.; b. Balt., Oct. 19, 1942; s. James Beeland and Ernestine Barbara (Brewer) R.; B.A. cum laude, Yale, 1964; B.A. with honors, M.A. in Politics, Philosophy and Economics, Oxford (Eng.) U., 1966. Investment analyst Bache & Co., N.Y.C., 1968-69, R. Gilder & Co., N.Y.C., 1969-70; asst. to chmn. Neuberger & Berman, N.Y.C., 1970-71; exec. v.p. Soros Fund Mgmt. (formerly Double Eagle Fund), N.Y.C., 1971-80; chmn. bd. Rogers Investments and B. W. Rogers, Inc., 1980—. Served to lt. U.S. Army, 1966-68. Home: 352 Riverside Dr New York NY 10025

ROGERS, JAMES ELVIN, ins. co. ofcl.; b. Hardtner, Kans., Mar. 3, 1953; s. Mac Elvin and Margie Leona R.; A.A., Garden City Community Jr. Coll., 1973; postgrad. Wichita State U., 1975-76; m. Shyrlene Ann Donavan, Aug. 9, 1975 (div. 1979). Service coordinator Sellers Tractor Co., Inc., Wichita, Kans., 1975-76; agt. Penn Mut. Life Ins. Co., Dodge City, Kans., 1976-77, dist. mgr., Springfield, Mo., 1978—; seminar coordinator Mut. Assn. Profl. Services, 1978; founder, prin. Rogers & Assos., fin. service firm, 1979—. Mem. Nat., Mo. Assns. Life Underwriters, Gen. Agts. and Mgrs. Conf., Penn Mut. Pres.'s Club (panel). Democrat. Baptist. Club: Jaycees. Home: 2150 S Ingram Mill Rd Apt 840 Springfield MO 65804 Office: 1736 E Sunshine Suite 305 Springfield MO 65804

ROGERS, JAMES FRANKLIN, JR., bus. machine co. exec.; b. Mankato, Minn., Feb. 15, 1939; s. James Franklin and Marilynn Marie (Fenger) R.; B.S., U. Minn., 1961; m. Mary Pauline Bever, Dec. 10, 1960; children—David James, Steven James, Richard James, Timothy James. Reporter, St. Paul Pioneer Press, 1958-61, AP, Mpls., 1961-64; sr. div. publicist 3M Co., St. Paul, 1964-69; mktg. mgr. Rockwell Internat., Pitts., 1969, nat. sales mgr. Crestliner div., Little Falls, Minn., 1969-73; sr. v.p. Riddell div. Wynn's Internat., Chgo., 1973-77; div. mgr. Craftek div. Exxon Enteprises, Inc., Raleigh, N.C., 1977-79; exec. v.p., gen. mgr. Ace Fastener div. Am. Brands, Inc., Chgo., 1979—. Served with U.S. Army, 1962-64. Decorated Disting. Service Medal. Mem. Nat. Office Products Assn., Wholesale Stationers Assn., Research Inst. Am., Am. Mgmt. Assn., Minn. Alumni Assn. Republican. Methodist. Clubs: U. Minn. M, Admirals, Ionosphere, Red Carpet. Home: 662 W Medford Dr Palatine IL 60067 Office: 4100 W Victoria St Chicago IL 60646

ROGERS, JOHN WILLARD, constrn. co. exec.; b. Oak Park, Ill., Dec. 20, 1908; s. Walter Alexander and Julia Margaret (Cushing) R.; student U. Wis., 1926-29; m. Ruth Woods Stiles, Apr. 16, 1933; 1 dau., Diane Rogers Carroll. With Bates & Rogers Constrn. Corp., 1929—; crane fireman, operator, carpenter, Ohio, 1929-31, civil engr., W.Va., 1931-32, foreman, Azusa, Calif., 1933-36, master mechanic, Dover, Ohio, 1936-37, supt., Villa Park, Ill., 1937-38, estimator, Chgo., 1939, tunnel supt., Chambersburg, Pa., 1939-40, div. supt. Kingsbury (Ind.) Ordinance Plant, 1940-41, project supt., Joliet, Ill., Duluth, Minn., 1941-42, Vicksburg, Miss., 1942, gen. supt. Alcan Hwy., Whitehorse, Yukon Ter., Alaska, 1943-45, dir., 1944—, sec., treas., Chgo., 1946-47, v.p., treas., 1948-61, exec. v.p., treas., 1961-67, pres., treas., 1968-79, chmn., chief exec. officer, 1979—, also dir. Bates & Rogers Found. Pres., trustee Glen Ellyn (Ill.) YMCA, 1937-58; mem. Glen Ellyn Sch. Bd., 1950-53; trustee George Williams Coll., 1956—; bd. dirs. Jr. Achievement Chgo.; mem. adv. bd. B.R. Ryall YMCA. Mem. ASCE, Western Soc. Engrs., Am. Inst. Constructors, Cons. Constructors Council, Ohio Contractors Assn. (Hall of Fame), Associated Gen. Contractors Am. (dir.), Asso. Gen. Contractors Ill. (dir.), Builders Assn. Chgo. (dir.), Ill. Legis. Network (chmn.), Nat. Assn. Gen. Contractors (regional chmn. legis. network), Beavers (founding mem.). Republican. Congregationalist. Clubs: Union League Chgo. (active Civic and Arts Found.), Execs., Econ.; Glen Oak Country (Glen Ellyn); Capitol Hill (Washington); Surf (Surfside, Fla.). Office: 600 W Jackson Blvd Chicago IL 60606

ROGERS, JUSTIN TOWNER, JR., utility exec.; b. Sandusky, Ohio, Aug. 4, 1929; s. Justin Towner and Barbara Eloise (Larkin) R.; A.B. cum laude, Princeton U., 1951; J.D., U. Mich., 1954; m. Virginia Logan Luscombe, May 6, 1955; children—Sarah Luscombe, Anne Larkin, Justin Towner, III. Admitted to Ohio bar, 1954; asso. firm Wright, Harlor, Purpus, Morris & Arnold, Columbus, 1956-58; with Ohio Edison Co., 1958—, exec. v.p., 1978-80, pres., 1980—, dir., 1970—; chmn. bd., dir. Pa. Power Co., New Castle; dir. First Nat. Bank, Akron; bd. dirs. Ohio Electric Utility Inst. Past pres. Akron Community Trusts, Akron Child Guidance Center; past chmn. Akron Asso. Health Agencies; trustee Akron Regional Devel. Bd., Akron Community Trusts, Akron Gen. Med. Center; adv. com. Coll. Arts and Scis., U. Akron. Served with AUS, 1954-56. Mem. Am. Bar Assn., Ohio Bar Assn., Phi Delta Phi, Beta Gamma Sigma. Clubs: City, Portage Country (Akron); Princeton (N.Y.C.); Capitol Hill (Washington). Home: 175 Aurora St Hudson OH 44236 Office: 76 S Main St Akron OH 44308

ROGERS, KELLY WALTER, internat. transp. co. exec.; b. Chgo., July 26, 1930; s. Kelly Howard and Sophie Dolores (Bednarczyk) R.; student Chgo. and Calvert City (Ky.) pub. schs., 1936-48; m. Celeste Fern Mykol, Oct. 4, 1962; children—Derrick, Karla, Blake. Truck driver various firms, 1957-61; regional mgr. northwestern states Republic Van Lines, Seattle, 1961-63; regional mgr., western area Greyhound Van Lines div. Greyhound, Corp., Los Angeles, 1964-71; exec. v.p., gen. mgr. Hawaiian Hauling Service, Honolulu, 1971-74; asst. gen. mgr. Atlas Van Lines Internat., Evansville, Ind., 1974, v.p. and gen. mgr., 1974-76, exec. v.p., 1976, pres., 1976—. Served with U.S. Army, 1948-53. Named Boss of Year, Internat. Secs. Assn., 1976; commd. Ky. Col., 1976. Mem. Nat. Def. Transp. Assn., Household Goods Forwarders Assn. Am., Inc. Republican. Baptist. Club: Oak Meadow Golf & Country. Home: 410 Kings Valley Rd Evansville IN 47711 Office: 1212 St George Rd Evansville IN 47711

ROGERS, KING WALTER, JR., grocery stores exec.; b. Dyersburg, Tenn., Aug. 19, 1912; s. King Walter and Essie (Martin) R.; B.A., U. Tenn., 1934; postgrad. Harvard Bus. Sch., 1934-36; m. Mildred Hampton Moss, May 23, 1943; children—King Walter III, Robert Moss. Exec., Pennel-Edenton Wholesale Grocery, Dyersburg, 1936-39; with K.W. Rogers & Son, Inc., Dyersburg, 1939—, pres., dir., 1943—; pres. Nehi Bottling Co., Dyersburg; Ardmore Tel. Co. (Tenn.); dir. Holiday Inns, Dyersburg, United Tel. Co., Chapel Hills, Tenn., Crockett Tel. Co., Friendship, Tenn., First Citizens Nat. Bank Dyersburg, First Fed. Savs. & Loan Assn., Dyersburg; pres. Tipton County Utilities Inc., Dyersburg. Chmn., U. Tenn. Devel. Council, 1969-70; mem. exec. com. Hosp. for Crippled Adults, Memphis, 1961-70. Bd. dirs. West Tenn. Area council Boy Scouts Am.; bd. mgrs. Meth. Hosp., Memphis, pres. bd. trustees, 1975-79; mem. Dyersburg Electric Bd., 1957—; mem. bd., exec. com. Obion-Forked Deer Basin Authority, 1973—. Served with AUS, 1942-45. Decorated Boy Scouts Silver Beaver award. Mem. Tenn. Retail Mchts. Council (pres. 1967), Nat. Piggly Wiggly Operators Assn. (pres. 1964-65). Methodist (trustee Memphis conf. 1953-56). Rotarian (dist. gov. 1960-61). Home: 950 Troy Ave Dyersburg TN 38024

ROGERS, LEONARD GILBERT, corp. exec.; b. N.Y.C., July 11, 1929; s. Arthur and Julia (Gilbert) R.; student Westminster Coll., 1947-48, Syracuse U., 1948-49; m. Adelle Maureen McClendon, Mar. 21, 1959; children—Julia Lynn, Douglas Arthur, Laura Elizabeth. Pres. Rogers Inc., N.Y.C., 1951-69; v.p. allied products Consol. Cigar Corp., N.Y.C., 1969-70, v.p. internat. and corporate devel., 1970-71, v.p. internat. operations and devel., 1972-73; sr. v.p. consumer div. Gulf & Western Industries, 1973-74; chmn. bd. Todhunter Internat., Inc., West Palm Beach, Fla., 1974—; chmn. bd., pres. Wespac Investors Trust, 1975—, Wespac Financial Corp., 1975-76. Mem. N.Y.C. Mayor's Com. for Youth, 1962. Mem. Nat. Assn. Tobacco Distbrs. (exec. mgmt. div.), Assn. Corporate Growth, Sigma Nu. Clubs: N.Y. Athletic; Beach (Palm Beach). Home: 100 Worth Ave Palm Beach FL 33480 Office: 324 Datura St West Palm Beach FL 33401

ROGERS, LEWIS ADDISON, JR., credit union exec.; b. Anchorage, Nov. 20, 1945; s. Lewis Addison and Ruth (Kimball) R.; A.A., Foothill Coll., 1966; postgrad. Golden Gate U., 1966-70; m. Linnet Karen Trefts, Jan. 24, 1971; children—Brett Addison, Kevin Tarleton. Mgr., Interstate Auto Delivery, San Francisco, 1966-71; office mgr. Friendly Ford, Inc. and Glacier Lincoln Mercury, Inc., Anchorage, 1971-74; ops. mgr. Alaska Mcpl. Employees Fed. Credit Union, Anchorage, 1974-77; gen. mgr. Alaska R.R. Fed. Credit Union, Anchorage, 1977—; dir. Alaska League Services, Inc., 1976-78, Alaska Meml. Services, 1976-79. Bd. dirs. Anchorage Businessmens Assn., 1976—, Anchorage Credit Bur., 1976-79. Mem. Anchorage C. of C., Commonwealth N., Inc., Credit Union Execs. Soc., Nat. Credit Union Youth Involvement Bd. (dir. 1977—), Credit Union Nat. Assn., Jaycees. Republican. Episcopalian. Club: Optimists. Office: 320 W 1st Ave Anchorage AK 99501

ROGERS, N. STEWART, indsl. distbn. co. exec.; b. Seattle, Feb. 23, 1930; s. Nat S. and Marian (Wurzbacher) R.; B.A. in Econs., Stanford U., 1951; m. Jane Steele, Mar. 15, 1952; children—Susan, Mark, Steven. Asst. treas. Van Waters & Rogers Inc., San Mateo, Calif., 1952-56, treas., 1956-66; treas. Univar Corp., Seattle, 1966-71, sr. v.p. fin., 1971—; dir. John Fluke Mfg. Co., Van Waters & Rogers, Ltd., VWR Sci., Inc., Penick & Ford, Ltd., Pacific Resins & Chems. Inc.; pres. Guardsman Ins. Co. Pres., The Arboretum Found., 1973-76; sr. v.p. Seattle Opera, 1979-80. Republican. Clubs: Harbor (pres. 1976-77), Rainier (treas. 1979-80, trustee 1980—), Seattle Yacht, Saralee Country. Office: 1600 Norton Bldg Seattle WA 98104

ROGERS, NATHANIEL SIMS, banker; b. New Albany, Miss., Nov. 17, 1919; s. Arthur L. and Elizabeth (Bouton) R.; A.B., Millsaps Coll., 1941; M.B.A., Harvard, 1947; m. Helen Elizabeth Ricks, July 3, 1942; children—Alice, John, Lewis. With Deposit Guaranty Bank and Trust Co., Jackson, Miss., 1947-69, 1st v.p., 1957-58, pres., dir., 1958-69, chmn. bd. 1st City Nat. Bank Houston, 1969—; pres. 1st City Bancorp. Tex. Inc.; dir. Standard Life Ins. Co., Gulf States Utilities Co., Gt. So. Life Ins. Co., Lomas & Nettleton Fin. Corp. Chmn. Jackson United Givers Fund, 1957, pres., 1959, bd. dirs., 1958-61; pres. Andrew Jackson area council Boy Scouts Am., 1962; trustee Miss. Found. Ind. Colls., 1959-69; past pres., trustee Millsaps Coll.; trustee Methodist Hosp., Houston. Served to lt. (s.g.) USNR, 1942-46. Named Outstanding Young Man of Year, Jackson Jr. C. of C., 1955. Mem. Am. (pres. 1969-70), Miss. (pres. jr. banker sect. 1952-53; pres. 1964-65) bankers assns., Robert Morris Assos. (pres. S.E. chpt. 1954-55, nat. dir. 1959-62), Assn. Res. City Bankers, Jackson C. of C. (pres. 1962), Young Pres.'s Orgn., Millsaps Coll. Alumni Assn. (pres. 1955-56), Newcomen Soc., Omicron Delta Kappa, Kappa Alpha. Methodist (ofcl. bd.). Home: 3631 Meadow Lake Ln Houston TX 77027 Office: PO Box 2557 Houston TX 77001

ROGERS, STUART CLARK, mktg. communications exec.; b. Atlanta, Dec. 19, 1937; s. Berto Cocroft and Margaret Stuart (Clark) R.; student U. N.Mex., 1956-57; B.A., Hofstra U., 1960; m. Polly Childs, Mar. 24, 1962; 1 dau., Alexandra Peyton. Asst. to pres. Creative Plastics Corp., 1957-60; actor, 1960-61; media buyer Benton & Bowles, N.Y.C., 1964-65; account exec., asso. Todd Harris Advt., Webster, N.Y., 1966; advt. coordinator bus. systems markets div. Eastman Kodak Co., Rochester, N.Y., 1966-73, producer presentations and promotions, 1973-78, advt. coordinator-internat., 1978-79, supr. internat. comml./indsl. advt., 1979—; owner, creative dir. S.C. Rogers Advt., Rochester, 1972—. Chmn. adv. council Sta. WGMC-FM, 1973-75. Served with U.S. Army, 1961-63. Mem. Bus./Profl. Advt. Assn. (pres. Rochester chpt. 1977-78, internat. v.p. 1978-79), Internat. Micrographic Congress (public relations com. 1979—), Midgard Guild Rochester (pres.), SAR (pres. Rochester chpt. 1975-78). Republican. Episcopalian. Home: 74 South St Pittsford NY 14534 also Lake Bluff RD3 Wolcott NY 14590 Office: 343 State St Rochester NY 14650

ROGERS, VAN RENSSELAER, exhbn. center exec.; b. nr. Lexington, Ky., Jan. 9, 1914; s. Edgar Alfred and Nellie Estella (Burton) R.; grad. Cleve. Inst. Art, 1937; m. Ruth Charlotte Reichelt, Aug. 3, 1941; 1 son, Peter Van. Commnd. sculptor Walt Disney Enterprises, Hollywood, Calif., 1937-38; co-founder Rogers Bennett Studios, Cleve., 1938; pres., owner Rogers Display Studios div. NESCO, Inc., Cleve., 1959—. Asst. registrar John Huntington Poly. Inst., Cleve., 1938-41. Chmn. Zoning Commn., Russell Twp., Geauga County, Ohio, 1974. Served to lt. comdr. USNR, 1942-46. Mem. Exhibit Designers and Producers Assn. (pres. Ohio Valley chpt. 1967), North and South Skirmish Assn., Nat. Trade Show Exhibitors Assn. (founder), Nat. Muzzle Loading Rifle Assn., Greater Cleve. Growth Assn., Western Reserve Hist. Soc., Geauga County Hist. Soc. (life), Ohio Hist. Soc., Archaeol. Soc. Ohio, Russell Hist. Soc. (founding mem.). Clubs: Masons (32 deg.), K.T., Advertising (Cleve.). Home: 8230 Fairmount Rd Novelty OH 44072 Office: Rogers Displays Inc 26470 Lakeland Blvd Cleveland OH 44132

ROHDE, JAMES VINCENT, telephone equipment mfg. co. exec.; b. O'Neill, Nebr., Jan. 25, 1939; s. Ambrose Vincent and Loretta Cecilia Rohde; B.C.S., Seattle U., 1962; children—Maria L., Sonja C., Daniele T. Exec. account mgr. NCR Co., Los Angeles, 1965-68; sales mgr. Donovan Hershey Corp., Oakland, Calif., 1968-71; sales dir. GCE Telephone Co., Oakland, 1971-74; pres., dir. Applied Telephone Tech. Co., Oakland, 1974-75; v.p. sales and mktg. Automation Sales Co., Inc., Oakland, 1975—. Republican. Roman Catholic. Office: 344 40th St Oakland CA 94609

ROHDE, MARY HOBEN, moving and storage co. exec.; b. Galesburg, Ill., Mar. 10, 1919; d. Anthony and Mary Christina (Lyon) Hoben; A.A., Kearney (Nebr.) State Tchrs. Coll., 1939; postgrad. Laramie (Wyo.) County Commmunity Coll., 1971-75; m. Ted Rohde, May 21, 1942 (dec.); children—Theodore A., Michael J. Office mgr., sec. Aavon Moving & Storage Co., Cheyenne, Wyo., 1949-72, pres., 1972—; elected del. to 1980 White House Conf. on Small Bus. Mem. Am. Trucking Assn., Ind. Bus. Assn. of Wyo., Inc., Exec. Club. Cheyenne, Am. Legion Aux. (state pres. 1964). Roman Catholic. Clubs: Cheyenne Toastmistress (pres. 1969, pres. Council IV, High Plains Region 1979-80), Laramie County Dem. Womens, Zonta Internat. Office: PO Box 503 Cheyenne WY 82001

ROHNER, GERRIT JOHN, telecommunications co. exec.; b. Manchester, N.H., Apr. 24, 1922; s. Bernardus J. and Hendrika (Van Baaren) R.; student RCA Inst., N.Y.C., 1940-42, Northeastern U., Boston, 1942-44; m. Marjorie L. Hollis, Jan. 22, 1944; children—Gerrit J., Bonnie Jean Rohner Sackett, Cheryl Amy. Group v.p. Sperry Rand Corp., 1959-66; v.p., gen. mgr. Magnavox Co., 1966-71; exec. v.p. Schiller Industries, 1971-77; pres., chief exec. officer Capehart Co., Norwich, Conn., 1977-80, also dir.; pres., chief operating officer, dir. TII Industries, Inc., Lindenhurst N.Y., 1980—; dir. Prairie Co. Recipient Silver Knight Mgmt. award NAM, 1970. Mem. Am. Inst. Engring. Edn., IEEE, Am. Mgmt. Assn. Club: Shriners. Home: 851 Vauxhall St Extension Quaker Hill CT 06375 Office: 100 N Strong Ave Lindenhurst NY 11757

ROLL, RICHARD JEFFREY, pub. co. exec.; b. N.Y.C., May 18, 1952; s. Irwin Clifford and Marilyn R.; B.A., Brown U., 1974; M.B.A., Harvard U., 1977; Asst. dir. mktg. Nat. Homes Jour., Lowell, Mass., 1974-75; product mgr. Citibank, N.Y.C., 1977-78; v.p., pub. Today's Communications Inc., N.Y.C., 1978-79; pres. Best Years Resources, Inc., N.Y.C., 1979—, pub. The Best Years Guide, nat. Sunday newspaper supplement, 1980—; cons. Mem. adv. bd. Senior Summary, N.Y. Jr. League publ., 1979—; trustee John T. Lewis Meml. Scholarship Fund, Columbia U., 1979—. Mem. Internat. Soc. Pre-Retirement Planners, Harvard Bus. Sch. Club N.Y. Clubs: Harvard of N.Y.C., Brown U. Co-author (with Hugh Downs) The Best Years Book; (with G. Douglas Young) Getting Yours, 1981. Office: 400 E 54th St New York NY 10022

ROLLAND, BURTON ARTHUR, machine tool co. exec.; b. Rockford, Ill., Nov. 17, 1933; s. Arthur J. and Helen L. (Ledin) R.; B.S. in Mech. Engring., Milw. Sch. Engring., 1962; m. June E. Nelson, May 23, 1959; children—Jeffrey Burton, Denise Ann. Sales engr. Barber-Colman Co., Rockford, Ill., 1962-64; sales and advt. mgr. Hill-Rockford (Ill.) Co., 1964-70; proposal engring. mgr. W. A. Whitney Corp., Rockford, 1970-72; N.C. product sales mgr. W. A. Whitney Corp., 1972-79; product mgr. Hurco Mfg. Co., Inc., Indpls., 1979—; lectr. in field. Served with U.S. Army, 1955-57. Mem. Soc. Mfg. Engrs., Nat. Speakers Assn., Numerical Control Soc. Clubs: Sailing, Racquetball. Inventor automatic riveting machine, 1968; balacing vehicle, 1970; combination CNC punching and plasma-arc cutting machine, 1974; portable door lock, 1979; contbr. articles to profl. jours. Office: 6602 Guion Rd Indianapolis IN 46268

ROLLAND, IAN MCKENZIE, ins. co. exec.; b. Fort Wayne, Ind., June 3, 1933; s. David and Florence (Hunter) R.; B.A., DePauw U., 1955; M.A., U. Mich., 1956; m. Miriam Vee Flickinger, July 3, 1955; children—Cheri Lynn, Lawrence David, Robert Arthur, Carol Ann, Sara Kay. With Lincoln Nat. Life Ins. Co., Fort Wayne, 1956—, sr. v.p., 1973-77, pres., chief exec. officer, 1977—; pres., chief exec. officer Lincoln Nat. Corp., 1975—, dir. affiliate cos.; dir. Central Soya Co., No. Ind. Public Service Co., Gen. Telephone of Ind., Lincoln Fin. Corp. Chmn. citizens bd. St. Francis Coll.; bd. dirs. United Way, Neighborhood Care, Inc., Parkview Meml. Hosp., YMCA, Met. Bd. Mem. Soc. Actuaries (v.p.), Am. Acad. Actuaries, Health Inst. Assn. Am. (dir.), Am. Council Life Ins. (dir.). Methodist. Home: 3825 Dalewood Dr Fort Wayne IN 46805 Office: 1300 S Clinton Fort Wayne IN 46802

ROLLETTE, DONALD LUIS, elec. mfg. co. exec.; b. Balt., Sept. 19, 1930; s. Louis R. and Grace Mildred Rollette; student Leader Tng. Inst., 1970; m. Doris Agnes Fletcher, Jan. 6, 1951; children—Donald L., Richard Paul, Lisa Marie. With Westinghouse Electric Corp., Balt., 1954—, crafts foreman, 1962-74, supr., 1974-77, mgr. maintenance dept., 1977—, instr. maintenance mgmt., 1980—. Served with USMC, 1947-51. Mem. Nat. Rifle Assn. Democrat. Lutheran. Clubs: Moose, Optomist Internat. Home: 111 N Longcrosse Rd Linthicum MD 21090 Office: Westinghouse Defense and Electronics Center Balt-Wash Internat Airport PO Box 1693 MS T100 Baltimore MD 21203

ROLOFSON, JAMES WESLEY, health physicist, govt. ofcl.; b. Rockford, Ill., Mar. 12, 1942; s. Donald Wesley and Fern Anita (Bensen) R.; B.A. (Alumni scholar), Nebr. Wesleyan U., 1964; M.S. (USPHS NIH grad. fellow), N.D. State U., 1966; M.B.A., Am. U., 1973; m. Catherine Ann Packett, June 5, 1965; 1 son, Curt James. Radiation safety officer, x-ray exposure control lab. Bur. Radiol. Health, HEW, Rockville, Md., 1966-69; health physicist div. biol. effects, 1969-70; research health physicist Office Research Monitoring, U.S. EPA, Rockville, 1970-72, staff officer, office radiation programs, Washington, 1972-73; program mgmt. officer Bur. Radiol. Health, FDA, Rockville, 1973-77, chief program support br. div. electronic products, 1977-79, asst. to asso. dir. mgmt. and systems, 1979—; lab. instr. Coll. Pharmacy N.D. State U., 1965; cons. Inst. Resource Mgmt., Inc., Bethesda, Md., 1976. Recipient Commendation medal USPHS, 1975; Service citation Soc. Photo-Optical Instrumentation Engrs., 1975; named Outstanding Young Man Am., 1976. Republican. Methodist. Contbr. articles in field to sci. jours. Home: 16421 Blackrock Rd Germantown MD 20767

ROM, IRVING, amusement and gaming equipment mfg. co. exec.; b. Bklyn., Sept. 25, 1923; s. Samuel and Bertha (Ruvinsky) R.; B.B.A., CCNY, 1949; J.D., N.Y. U., 1954; m. Dorothy Ozeroff, Oct. 16, 1948; 1 dau., Beth Rom-Rymer. Admitted to N.Y. bar, 1954; partner firm Clarence Rainess & Co., N.Y.C., 1961-76; with Bally Mfg. Corp., Chgo., 1976—, exec. v.p. fin., 1976—, also dir., chmn. exec. com.; adj. asso. prof. Pace U., N.Y.C., 1955-65. Served with USAF, 1943-46. C.P.A., N.Y. Mem. Am. Inst. C.P.A.'s, N.Y. State Soc. C.P.A.'s. Home: 1300 N Lake Shore Dr Chicago IL 60610 Office: 2640 W Belmont Ave Chicago IL 60618

ROMA, GEORGE EDWARD, textile mfr.; b. Newark, Aug. 20, 1931; s. Thomas G. and Rose P. (Piegaro) R.; B.S., Seton Hall U., 1955; m. Sandra R. DeBella, Apr. 21, 1957; children—Robert G., Dara M. Sr. accountant Thomas J. Corbett & Co., 1955-61; asst. v.p. James Talcott, Inc., 1961-69; exec. v.p. Sweet-Orr & Co., N.Y.C., 1969—. Mem. Livingston (N.J.) Little League Baseball, Livingston Babe Ruth League. Served with AUS, 1952-53. Mem. Prime Raters (treas.). Home: 11 Marberne Terr Livingston NJ 07039 Office: 1290 Ave of Americas New York NY 10019

ROMA, THOMAS, real estate developer; b. Allentown, Pa., May 28, 1934; s. Dante and Mary Virginia (Faust) R.; student Drexel U., Phila., 1954-56; B.B.A., U. Miami (Fla.), 1957; m. Jean Romayne Brotzman, Oct. 23, 1954; children—Mary Catherine, Stephen Thomas, Elizabeth Ann. Owner, operator Roma Devel. Co., Allentown, 1957—; builder Springhouse Farms (South Whitehall Twp., Pa.); builder, owner Cedar Crest Blvd. Office Center (Lehigh County, Pa.); v.p. CCG Water Co., 1956-59. Life pres. William Allen High Sch. Class of 1952. Licensed real estate broker, Pa. Mem. Lehigh Valley Home Builders Assn. (treas. 1961-62), Nat. Assn. Home Builders. Lutheran. Home: 3958 Lincoln Pkwy W Allentown PA 18104 Office: 1401 Cedar Crest Blvd Allentown PA 18104

ROMAINE, STEPHEN GEORGE, educator; b. Hartford, Conn., Mar. 26, 1927; s. Stephen G. and Florence (Lennon) R.; B.S., Trinity Coll., 1950; M.S., U. Conn., 1956, postgrad., 1967; M.S., Simmons Coll., 1975; m. Nellie Maria Uccello, July 28, 1962. Tchr., Ellsworth Meml. High Sch., S. Windsor, Conn., 1950-59, Conard High Sch., W. Hartford, Conn., 1959-70; tchr. chemistry William H. Hall High Sch., W. Hartford, Conn., 1970—, faculty adviser Med. Careers Club, 1970—. Served with USN, 1945-46. NSF grantee, 1970-74. Mem. NEA, Conn., W. Hartford edn. assns., Nat., Conn. sci. tchrs. assns., New Eng. Chemistry Tchrs. Assn. Republican. Home: 102 Tredeau St Hartford CT 06114 Office: 975 N Main St W Hartford CT 06117

ROMAN, DOUGLAS ERNEST, bus. exec.; b. Winnipeg, Man., Can., Apr. 20, 1946; s. Ernest Rudolph and Miniie (Kuhlman) R.; came to U.S., 1963, naturalized, 1968; student Bob Jones U., 1966, Biola Coll., 1969-70, Cypress Jr. Coll., 1970; m. M. Katherine Miller, Mar. 19, 1977. Asst. to v.p. engring. Ceme Corp., 1969; sr. designer, estimator Hood Corp., 1970; estimator Am. Pipe Co., 1971; mech. engr., exec. Kiemech div. Peter Kewit, 1972; owner Environ. Contractors, 1973; owner, mgr. Cross Prodns. Co., Hollywood, Calif., 1974—; owner, mgr. Cross Prodns. Co., Inc., Cross Trust Co.; dir. Timothy Enterprises, Am. Mktg. Co., Crossroads Mfg. Ltd. (Can.), Crossroads Mfg. U.S.A., Crossroads Prodns. Co., Creative Composition, Album Art. Served with USMC, 1967-68. Decorated Purple Heart. Republican. Baptist. Copyright owner 628 works of mdse. art. Home: 415 N Redrock St Anaheim CA 92807 Office: 1285 N Jefferson Ave Anaheim CA 92807

ROMAN, KENNETH, JR., advt. exec.; b. Boston, Sept. 6, 1930; s. Kenneth and Bernice (Freedman) R.; B.A., Dartmouth Coll., 1952; m. Ellen Fischer, Mar. 27, 1953; 1 son, Neil Kenneth. Asst. advt. mgr. Interchem. Corp., N.Y.C., 1952-54; advt. mgr. Raymond Rosen Co., Phila., 1954-55, Allied Chem. Corp., N.Y.C., 1955-63; various positions Ogilvy & Mather, Inc., N.Y.C., 1963-79, pres., 1979—. Mem. exec. bd. ARC Greater N.Y., community appeal chmn., 1977-80; trustee Am. Place Theatre, 1975-80. Clubs: Univ.; Madison (Conn.) Beach. Author: How to Advertise, 1976; How to Write Better, 1979. Home: 7 Gracie Sq New York NY 10028 Office: 2 E 48 St New York NY 10071

ROMAN, LEE L., direct mktg. co. exec.; b. N.Y.C., Dec. 12, 1953; s. Burt and Evelyn Roberts; B.S., Albany State U., 1975; m. Connie La Londe, May 4, 1974; 1 son, Benjamin. Direct mktg. mgr. Trade Properties, Inc., Farmingdale, N.Y., 1973-75; v.p. Edith Roman Assos., Inc., N.Y.C., 1975—; instr. Hunter Coll., N.Y.C., Bur. Bus. and Tech., N.Y.C. Mem. Direct Mail Mktg. Assn., Direct Mktg. Writer's Guild. Clubs: N.Y. Advt., Moose. Office: Edith Roman Assos Inc 875 Ave of Americas New York NY 10001

ROMAN, MURRAY, telephone mktg. exec.; b. Russia, Mar. 12, 1920; s. Aaron and Elsa; came to U.S., 1923, naturalized, 1927; m. Eva Cseko, Jan. 3, 1966; children—Michael P., Nina, Ernan. Publicist, Am. Cancer Soc., 1945-46, United Artists and 20th Century Fox Corp., 1946-52; nat. publicity dir. United Service for New Ams., 1952-61; West Coast regional dir. Am. Fin. & Devel. Corp. for Israel, 1952-61; exec. v.p. Am. Fund for Israel Instns., 1952-61; cons. Democratic Nat. Com., Republican Nat. Com., 1952-61; pres. Communicator Network, Inc., N.Y.C., also v.p. Gilbert Mktg. Group, 1961-63; cons. R.H. Donnelley Corp., 1963-66; chmn., chief exec. officer M.R.A. Assos. and Campaign Communications Inst. of Am. Inc., N.Y.C., 1967—; designer and condr. workshops and seminars for profl. assns. and univs. Served with USAF, 1942-45. Mem. Com. of Corp. Telephone Users (founding chmn.), Telephone Mktg. Council of the Direct Mail/Mktg. Assn. (chmn. 1975), Am. Mktg. Assn., Direct Mail Mktg. Assn., N.Y. Sales Execs. Club. Clubs: Atrium (N.Y.C.); B'nai B'rith. Author: The Political Marketplace, 1972; Telephone Marketing: How to Build Your Business by Telephone, 1976. Office: 555 W 57th St New York NY 10019

ROMAN, STEPHEN BOLESLAV, mining co. exec.; b. Slovakia, Apr. 17, 1921; s. George and Helen Roman; student Agrl. Coll.; m. Betty Gardon, Oct. 20, 1945; 4 sons, 3 daus. Chmn. bd., chief exec. officer, dir. Denison Mines Ltd., Toronto, Ont., Can., chmn. bd., dir. Roman Corp., Ltd.; dir. Crown Life Ins. Co., Guaranty Trust Co. Can., Pacific Tin Consol. Corp. Hon. bd. dirs. Royal Agrl. Winter Fair Assn. Can.; trustee Toronto Sch. Theology. Served with Canadian Army, World War II. Mem. Canadian Slovak League, Bd. Trade of Met. Toronto. Catholic. Club: Engineers. Office: PO Box 40 Royal Bank Plaza Toronto ON M5J 2K2 Canada

ROMANO, FREDERICK VICTOR, JR., found. exec.; b. N.Y.C., Jan. 11, 1936; s. Frederick Victor and Margaret Agnes (Santelmo) R.; B.A. in Econs., Iona Coll., New Rochelle, N.Y., 1956; M.B.A. in Fin. and Investments, Bernard Baruch Coll., 1967; m. Rosemarie Falcone, Apr. 6, 1958; children—Lisa, Christine, Frederick. Credit analyst Dun & Bradstreet Co., N.Y.C., 1958-61; with Merrill Lynch, Pierce, Fenner & Smith, N.Y.C., 1961-73, investment industry specialist, 1967-73; with Ford Found., 1973—, dir. securities research, 1976-79, dir. adminstrn., fin. div., 1979—; lectr. in field. Pres., California Ridge Civic Assn., 1978-80; chmn. fin. adv. com. Eastchester (N.Y.) Town Bd., 1979; Served with U.S. Army, 1957. Mem. Am. Mgmt. Assn., N.Y. Soc. Security Analysts, Machinery Analysts N.Y. (pres. 1973-74). Republican. Club: Eastchester Kiwanis (past pres.). Home: 36 Forbes Blvd Eastchester NY 10709 Office: 320 E 43d St New York NY 10017

ROMANO, OLGA AMERICA MARIA YACO, acctg. mgr.; b. Chgo., Aug. 30, 1929; d. Vito Anthony and Elizabeth (Mohr) Yaco; student Northwestern U., 1945-47, El Camino Jr. Coll., 1956-58; m. John Vincent Romano, Aug. 17, 1963; children—James, Dale, Gary Robert. Accountant, Motorola, Inc., Chgo., 1948-54; exec. sec., accountant S.L. Abbot Co., Los Angeles, 1954-56, A-1 Food Service, Inc., Hawthorne, Calif., 1958-62; sr. accountant Wheeler & Co., C.P.A., Lancaster, Calif., 1962-63; exec. sec., comptroller Ablestik Adhesive Co., Gardena, Calif., 1963-67, Stor Ad Printers, Inc., San Jose, Calif., 1967-71; accountant J & O Assos., San Jose, 1971-73; corporate sec., dir. Kring Constrn. Co., San Jose, 1973-77; controller Sierra Lithograph, Inc., Sunnyvale, Calif., 1978-79; gen. acctg. mgr. Xynetics, Inc., Santa Clara, Calif., 1979—. Republican. Roman Catholic. Club: Jaguar Asso. Group (treas.). Home: 10380 Scenic Blvd Cupertino CA 95014 Office: 2901 Coronado Dr Santa Clara CA 95051

ROMANO, RONALD ANTHONY, advt. and mktg. cons.; b. June 2, 1953; s. R. John and Vincenza Elaine Romano; student Wheeling Coll., 1971-72; B.S., Fairleigh Dickinson U., 1974; M.A., Columbia U., 1976. With Lockwood Pub. Co., N.Y.C., 1971-73, Vance Pub. Corp., N.Y.C., 1973-74; co-founder Ad Group, Inc., Hackensack, N.J., 1975—; asso. founder Danbury, Thorne & Co., concert producers, 1979; partner HBH Assos., Inc., Park Ridge, N.J., 1979—; v.p. mktg. Conti Advt. Agy., Montvale, N.J., 1979—; advt. cons. Bd. dirs. Classic Ballet Co. N.J. Winner first place indsl. advt. N.J. Advt. Assn., 1978. Republican. Roman Catholic. Research on paper industry. Home: 345 Prospect Ave Hackensack NJ 07601 also 812 Park Ave New York NY 10023

ROMBACH, GEORGE FREDERICK, financial exec., acct.; b. Detroit, Dec. 17, 1944; s. James Charles and Eleanor Joan (Ranes) R.; A.A. in Bus. Adminstrn., Victor Valley Coll., 1966; B.S. in Bus. Adminstrn., Calif. State U., Northridge, 1969; B.S. in Law, Irvine U., 1979; M.S. in Acctg., Pacific Western U., 1980; Sr. staff acct. Elmer Fox Westheimer & Co., C.P.A.'s, Los Angeles, 1968-71; sr. partner Rombach, Martin & Co., C.P.A.'s, Los Angeles and San Francisco, 1971-74; v.p. fin. Aviation Service & Support Corp., Long Beach, Calif., 1974-76; v.p. Orangematic, Inc., Irvine, Calif., 1976-77; v.p. adminstrn. and fin. Sir Speedy, Inc., Newport Beach, Calif., 1977-78; v.p. fin. Dana Industries, Inc., Buena Park, Calif., 1978-80; pres. Spa-Trol, Inc., Newport Beach, 1980—; dir. Regency Aluminum Products, Inc., Orangematic, Inc.; guest lectr. Internat. Entrepreneurs Assn. Served with U.S. Army, 1963-64. Recipient bus. adminstrn. award Bank of Am., 1966; C.P.A., Calif. Mem. Am. Inst. C.P.A.'s, Am. Inst. Corp. Controllers, Am. Mgmt. Assn., Calif. Soc. C.P.A.'s, Ancient Mariners Sailing Soc., Schooner Assn. Am. (pres. 1978), So. Calif. Yachting Assn. (del.), Wooden Hull Owners Assn. (commodore 1977), Alpha Gamma Sigma (life). Republican. Lutheran. Club: Windjammers Yacht (flag officer). Author: The Log of the Don Quixote, 1978; Guide to Race Committee Signals—1977 Rules, 1978; contbg. editor to The Leisure Life, 1978. Home: 2775 Mesa Verde Dr E Apt A-106 Costa Mesa CA 92626 Office: 871-B W 15 St Newport Beach CA 92663

ROME, RICHARD MORRIS, bank service co. exec.; b. Boston, Nov. 17, 1923; s. Ellis and Mildred Rebecca (Field) R.; B.S. in Chem. Engring., Tufts U., 1947; postgrad. Mass. Inst. Tech., 1951; m. Winifred Helen, Oct. 15, 1960; children—Jeffrey Owen, Lawrence Craig. Research chem. engr. Mass. Inst. Tech., 1947-51; mgr. computer applications div. Stone & Webster Engring. Corp., Boston, 1951-72; dir. adminstrn. Consol. Edison N.Y., 1972-74; pres., chief exec. officer Maine Info. Systems, Bangor, 1974—; cons. engr., 1969-72. Mem. Republican Town Com., Hanover, Mass., 1950-54. Served to lt. (j.g.) USN, 1943-46, to capt., 1972. Decorated Navy Commendation medal; registered profl. engr., Mass. Mem. Assn. Computing Machinery, Am. Inst. Chem. Engrs., Navy League, Naval Res. Assn. Clubs: Rotary, Masons. Patentee sulfur burners, sulfur dioxide process; contbr. articles to profl. jours. Home: Battle Ave Castine ME 04421 Office: 99 Washington St Bangor ME 04401

ROMINE, MAURICE GENE, computer co. exec.; b. Nashville, Oct. 18, 1941; s. Ollen Tate and Jewel (Stinnitt) R.; A.A., Fla. Coll., Temple Terrace, 1961; B.E.E., U. Fla., 1963; postgrad. U. Ala., 1965-71; m. Linda Rae Gross, Sept. 3, 1961; children—Maurice Bradley, Jay Brent. System test engr. Honeywell, St. Petersburg, Fla., 1963-65; elec. design engr. Boeing Co., Huntsville, 1965-70; advanced computer design engr. Sperry Co., Huntsville, 1970-71; owner, operator Romine's Carpet & Drapery Center, Inc., Clearwater, Fla., 1971-76; sr. systems engr. M&S Computing, Inc., Huntsville, 1976—, gen. mgr. European ops., 1979—. Mem. Pinellas County (Fla.) Sch. Adv. Bd., 1974-76; co-pres. Skycrest PTA., 1975-76. Mem. IEEE. Republican. Mem. Ch. of Christ. Home: Blankeneser Chaussee 157 C 2000 Schenefeld Federal Republic Germany Office: M&S Computing GmbH Mexicoring 5/17 2000 Hamburg 60 Federal Republic Germany

RONCELLI, BERNEDETTE MARY, tool mfg. co. exec.; b. Detroit, May 1, 1924; d. Carmine and Constance Roncone; student public schs., Detroit; m. Paul Edward Roncelli, July 7, 1944; children—Janet, Sandra, Karen. Founder, pres. Bermar Assos., Inc., 1969—, Birmingham, Mich., 1969-80, Troy, Mich., 1980—. Recipient creative sales display award Cross Fraser, 1974; Employer of Year award, 1980. Mem. Machine Tool Industry Assn., Nat. Assn. Women Bus. Owners, Mich. Businessmen (dir. 1980), Troy C. of C. Club: Detroit Arty. Gun (sec.-treas. 1957-58). Office: Bermar Assos Inc 1155 Rankin St Troy MI 48084

RONDEPIERRE, EDMOND FRANCOIS, ins. co. exec.; b. N.Y.C., Jan. 15, 1930; s. Jules Gilberte and Margaret Murray (Moore) R.; B.S., U.S. Mcht. Marine Acad., 1952; J.D., Temple U., 1959; m. M. Anne Lerch, July 5, 1952; children—Aimee S., Stephen C., Peter E., Anne W. Third mate Nat. Bulk Carriers, 1952-53; with Ins. Co. of N. Am., 1955-70, asst. gen. counsel, 1967-70; gen. counsel INA Corp., 1970-77, dep. chief legal affairs, 1977; v.p., gen. counsel Gen. Reinsurance Corp., Greenwich, Conn., 1977-79, sr. vp., corp. sec., gen. counsel, 1979—; dir. various subs. and affiliated cos.; dir. NYIE Security Fund. Bd. dirs. Voluntary Action Center. Served to lt. USN, 1953-55. C.P.C.U. Mem. Am. Bar Assn., D.C. Bar, Inter Am. Bar, Soc. of Chartered Property and Casualty Underwriters, Internat. Assn. Ins. Counsel (past dir.), Reinsurance Assn. Am. Roman Catholic. Home: 8 Linda Ln Darien CT 06820 Office: Gen Reinsurance Corp 600 Steamboat Rd Greenwich CT 06830

RONEY, HAROLD NELSON, lawyer; b. Madison College, Tenn., Jan. 17, 1939; s. Harold B. and Elsie N.; B.S., David Lipscomb Coll., 1960; J.D., Vanderbilt U., 1963; m. Judith Rose, Feb. 21, 1970. Admitted to Tenn. bar, 1963, U.S. Supreme Ct. bar, 1969; individual practice law, McMinnville, 1963-70; partner firm Camp and Roney, McMinnville, 1971—; owner, gen. mgr. WHNR-FM, McMinnville, 1963-71; asso. editor Sumner County Star, Hendersonville, Tenn., 1955-58; sec., dir. Tenn. Metal Fabricating Corp., McMinnville, 1966—. Mem. Tenn. Ho. of Reps., 1960-64; mem. McMinnville Bd. Aldermen, 1964-67, vice mayor, 1967; pres. United Way, 1967; chmn. Nat. Found. Warren County, 1968; mem. dist. com. Boy Scouts Am., 1972-74; bd. dirs. Sunny Acres Home for Children, 1974—; mem. devel. council Freed-Hardeman Coll., 1976—; mem. devel. council David Lipscomb Coll., 1975—; tchr., mem. worship com. Westwood Ch. of Christ, McMinnville, 1974—, edn. com., 1976—. Mem. Am., Tenn. (ho. of dels. 1972—), McMinnville (pres. 1974-75, dir. 1975—) bar assns., Tenn. Trial Lawyers Assn. (bd. govs. 1973-76), Assn. Trial Lawyers Am., Alpha Kappa Psi, Pi Kappa Delta, Delta Theta Phi. Club: McMinnville Rotary (pres. 1979-80, Paul Harris fellow 1979). Address: Box 590 Profl Bldg 111 West Ct McMinnville TN 37110

RONTY, BRUNO GEORGE, phonograph record mfg. co. exec.; b. Lwow, Poland, June 10, 1922; s. Leon and Hermina (Elsner) R.; student Lwow Lyceum of Humanities, 1938-40; B.A., Conservatory, 1939, M.A., M.F.A., 1941, Ph.D., 1945; m. Wanda von Rudolph, Nov. 3, 1943 (div. 1959); 1 dau., Maria; m. 2nd, Michele van Beveren, June 12, 1962 (div. 1972). Came to U.S., 1946, naturalized, 1955. Tenor, USSR, Poland, Sweden, U.S., 1940-50; pres. Colosseum Records, Inc., N.Y.C., 1950—, Musicart Internat., Ltd., N.Y.C., Wilton, Conn., 1958—; pres. Acropole Corp. Am., N.Y.C., 1972—; producer Bruno Hi-Fi Records; voice instr. N.Y.C.; tenor, gen. dir. cultural exchange program Musica Nostra et Vostra, Nat. Corp. Am., 1973—. Bd. dirs. Ministry Culture, Art, Poland, 1945; pres. Narcolepsy and Cataplexy Found. Am., 1975—, Cultural Exchange Soc. Am., 1976—. Served with Polish Army, 1942-45. Decorated Grunwald Cross; Polonia Restituta. Roman Catholic. Office: Suite 2D 1410 York Ave New York NY 10021

ROOHM, EDWARD BLINN, supermarket exec.; b. Detroit, Apr. 23, 1944; s. Dwight Alden and Estelle Louise (Blinn) R.; B.B.A., Ga. State U., 1967; m. Judith Nell Dusenbury, Jan. 6, 1968; children—Pamela Carol, Matthew Edward, Laura Elizabeth, Katherine Ann. Head grocery buyer Colonial Stores, Atlanta, 1973-75, grocery merchandising mgr., 1976-77, merchandising mgr., Thomasville, Ga., 1978, v.p., gen. mgr., 1979—. Bd. dirs. Metro. Atlanta Boys' Clubs, Inc., 1972—. Served with USN, 1968-71. Mem. Food Mktg. Inst. Episcopalian. Club: Rotary. Home: Route 3 Hiding Pl Thomasville GA 31792 Office: PO Box 500 Thomasville GA 31792

ROOKER, GEORGE SENSABAUGH, petroleum co. exec.; b. Memphis, Dec. 30, 1918; s. Jesse Paul and Mai Platt (Sensabaugh) R.; B.B.A., So. Meth. U., 1943; m. Dorothy Dale Ivy, Oct. 17, 1942; children—Paul George, Andrew Dale, Mark Fitzgerald, David Wayne. Pres., Met. Dallas Corp., 1956—; chmn. Dorchester Gas Producting Co., Dallas, 1960—; chmn. Wynnewood State Bank, Dallas, 1965-68; pres., chief exec. officer Dorchester Gas Corp., Dallas, 1970-80, chmn., chief exec. officer, 1980—; dir. Merc. Nat. Bank, Dallas, Arabian Shield Devel. Co., Del Norte Tech., Inc., Dallas, Monarch Tile Mfg., Inc., San Angelo, Tex. Trustee, C.C. Young Meml. Home, Inc., 1960—. Served with USAAF, 1943-45. Mem. Mid Continent Oil and Gas Assn. (dir.), Tex. Mid-Continent Oil and Gas Assn., Ind. Petroleum Assn. Am. (Dallas wildcat com., dir. com. publicly-owned cos.), Am. Petroleum Inst. Republican. Methodist. Clubs: Northwood, Dallas Petroleum, Engineers (Dallas); Hideaway Lake. Office: 5735 Pineland Dr Dallas TX 75231*

ROONEY, C. PAT, JR., steel co. exec.; b. Pitts., May 16, 1932; s. Charles Patrick and Stella (Dougherty) R.; B.S., U. Notre Dame, 1954; postgrad. U. Pitts., 1962; m. Alice Katherine Moore, June 12, 1954; children—Elizabeth, Susan, Barbara, Patrick, Theresa, Michael, Kevin. Mfg. engr. Atomic Power div. Westinghouse Corp., Pitts., 1956-59; with computer systems U.S. Steel Corp., Homestead, Pa., 1959-62, Gary, Ind., 1962-63, Chgo., 1963-67, with accounting dept., Pitts. hdqrs., 1967-69, South Chicago, Ill., 1969-71, mgr. accounting, Fairless Hills, Pa., 1971—. Bd. dirs. Bucks County Pa. Economy League, 1973—, chmn., 1977—; mem. Gov.'s Com. on Penndot Merit Rev., 1979. Served to lt. (j.g.) USNR, 1954-56. Recipient 1st award Wunsch Found., 1959. Mem. Bucks County C. of C. (dir. 1975-76), Nat. Assn. Accountants. Republican. Roman Catholic. Home: 573 Kings Rd Yardley PA 19067 Office: Fairless Works US Steel Corp Fairless Hills PA 19030

ROOS, LAWRENCE KALTER, banker; b. St. Louis, Feb. 1, 1918; s. Sol and Selma (Kalter) R.; B.A., Yale U., 1940; LL.D., U. Mo., 1974; LL.D., Westminster Coll., Fulton, Mo., 1980; m. Mary Watson, Apr. 30, 1955; children—Lawrence K., Pamela, Jennifer, Mary Ellen. Mem. Mo. Ho. of Reps., 1946-50; pres. Mound City Trust Co., St.

Louis, 1950-62, also chmn. 1st Security Bank, Kirkwood, Mo.; county exec. St. Louis County, 1962-74; exec. v.p., dir. 1st Nat. Bank St. Louis, 1975-76; pres. Fed. Res. Bank St. Louis, 1976—. Republican gubernatorial candidate, Mo., 1968; bd. dirs. St. Louis Jewish Hosp., St. Louis Regional Commerce and Growth Assn., 1976-80, United Way Greater St. Louis, Govt. Research Inst., St. Louis; chmn. Mo. Com. for Re-election of Pres., 1972; del. Rep. Nat. Conv., 1972; Mo. del. Rep. Nat. Com., 1973-74; mem. U.S. Adv. Commn. on Intergovtl. Relations, 1969-74; mem. adv. com. Woodrow Wilson Internat. Center for Scholars, 1974. Served with AUS, 1941-45. Decorated Bronze Star. Named St. Louis Globe Democrat Man of Yr., 1974; recipient Torch of Liberty award Anti-defamation League, 1974. Chmn. bd. East West Gateway Coordinating Com., 1965-67, 73-75; chmn. Mo. Crusade for Freedom, 1954; mem. Pres.'s Commn. on Jobs for Vietnam Vets., 1971; pres. Wesley House Found., St. Louis, 1955-60; bd. dirs. Central Inst. for Deaf, 1975—. Office: PO Box 442 Saint Louis MO 63166

ROOS, MICHAEL, mgmt. info. systems cons.; b. N.Y.C., Nov. 20, 1940; s. Allan J. and Dene S. (Lindau) R.; B.A., San Francisco State Coll., 1964; m. Jane Ellen Mayo, Apr. 17, 1971; 1 dau., Katherine Linda. With Equitable Life Assurance Soc. U.S., N.Y.C., 1969-79, asso. dir. mgmt. sci. div., 1977-79; pres. Michael Roos, Inc., N.Y.C., 1979—; mem. faculty program gifted youth Hunter Coll., 1979-80; adj. faculty New Sch. Social Research, 1980; speaker in field. Served as officer USNR, 1966-69. Mem. Assn. Computing Machinery, Soc. Mgmt. Info. Systems, Inst. Mgmt. Scis., Assn. Ednl. Data Systems. Address: 25 E 86th St New York NY 10028

ROOS, WILLIAM JOSEPH, retail co. exec.; b. Balt., Apr. 7, 1921; s. Isadore and Josephine Millhauser (Katz) R.; B.S., Bucknell U., 1947; m. Paula Sparrow, Nov. 17, 1951; children—Liza Beth, Sigmund Jonas, Joel Isadore. With Katz Bros. Inc., Honesdale, Pa., 1948—, pres., 1970—. Vice chmn. Wayne County (Pa.) Library Assn., 1975—. Served with Signal Corps, U.S. Army, 1943-47. Home: 7 Hillcrest Circle Honesdale PA 18431 Office: 627/641 Main St Honesdale PA 18431

ROOST, (HAROLD) CHARLES, metal forming equipment exec.; b. Lansing, Mich., Aug. 10, 1936; s. Francis W. and Rose M. R.; B.A., Wheaton Coll., 1958; M.A., Mich. State U., 1969, Ph.D., 1974; m. Pamela Lou Miller, Apr. 18, 1980; children—Cindy Jo, Marilee Kay. Dir., Lansing Youth for Christ, 1959-67; div. v.p. Youth for Christ Internat., 1967-71; exec. dir. Camp Barakel, 1971-72; dean of students, v.p. John Wesley Coll., 1972-75, pres., 1975-77; asst. to pres. Nat. Welding of Mich., also gen. mgr. Metalist Internat. div. Nat. Welding, Conroe, Tex., 1977—; pres. Metaform Inc.; dir. Pan Am. Ministries. Mem. ASME, Am. Metal Stamping Assn., Forging Industry Am. Baptist. Home: 8A Lakeside Villa Montgomery TX 77356 Office: 2210 N Frazier St Suite 290 Conroe TX 77302

ROOT, ALAN CHARLES, diversified mfg. co. exec.; b. Essex, Eng., Apr. 11, 1925; s. Charles Stanley and Lillian (Collins) R.; B.A., Oxford U., Eng., 1943; M.A., Cambridge U., Eng., 1951; M.B.A., Stanford, 1953. Research analyst Dow Chem. Co., Midland, Mich., 1954-55; mgr. marketing research Gen. Electric Co., 1955-61; v.p.-bus. planning Mosler Safe Co., Hamilton, Ohio, 1961-70, now only officer; sr. v.p. ops. services Am. Standard, Inc., N.Y.C., 1970—; dir. Mosler de P.R., Amstan Trucking Inc. Served to capt. AUS, 1944-48. Mem. Am. Inst. Chem. Engrs. (asso. producer tv series Chem. Engrs. Midland sect. 1955), Pilgrims U.S., Newcomen Soc. N.Am. Clubs: West Side Tennis (Forest Hills, N.Y.); N.Y. Athletic, University (N.Y.C.). Home: 35 Park Ave New York NY 10016 Office: 40 W 40th St New York NY 10018

ROOTS, PETER CHARLES, data processing co. exec.; b. Munich, W. Ger., Mar. 19, 1921; came to U.S., 1939, naturalized, 1943; s. Josef and Ruth R.; B.S., Sch. Fgn. Service, Georgetown U., 1948, LL.B., J.D., 1952; m. Teruyo Ashihara, Nov. 11, 1970; children—Stephanie E. Roots Karsten, Judith A. Roots-Carver, David H., Catherine E. Admitted to Md. bar, U.S. Tax Ct. bar, 1952; atty. Sperry Corp., N.Y.C., 1952-65; exec. Sperry Rand Corp. fgn. subs., Germany, Japan, 1965-70; pres. Inverdata GMBH, W. Ger., 1970—; dir. MST, Santa Ana, Calif., 1978—. Served with AUS, 1943-46. Mem. Am. Bar Assn. Club: Kronberg Golf & Land (W. Ger.). Author: (with Greene & Thompson) Developing Munitions for War, 1952. Home: Adolph-Kolping Strasse 6078 Neu Isenburg 1 West Germany Office: Inverdata GMBH Adolph-Kolping Str 6078 Neu Isenburg 1 West Germany

ROPER, JOHN LONSDALE, II, shipbuilding co. exec.; b. Norfolk, Va., Sept. 18, 1902; s. George Wisham and Isabelle Place (Hayward) R.; student Princeton U., 1920-21; m. Sarah Engel Dryfoos, Apr. 7, 1926; children—John Lonsdale III, George W. II, Isabel Roper Yates. With Norfolk Shipbuilding & Drydock Corp., 1925—, v.p., 1944, asst. gen. mgr., v.p., 1946, exec. v.p., treas., 1955, pres., gen. mgr., 1956, pres., chief exec. officer, 1968-73, chmn. bd., 1973—; officer, dir. John L. Roper Estate Inc., Lonsdale Bldg. Corp., Botetourt Bldg. Corp.; dir. United Va. Bank/Seaboard Nat., United Va. Bankshares; dir. adv. bd. for State of Va., Liberty Mut. Ins. Co. Commr., Norfolk Redevel. and Housing Authority; trustee Eastern Va. Med. Sch.; trustee, mem. distbn. com. Norfolk Found.; pres., dir. emeritus Norfolk United Fund; chmn. bd. trustees Chrysler Mus., Norfolk; bd. dirs. Urban Coalition of Norfolk. Recipient Marquis award, 1965; Disting. Service medal Cosmopolitan Club of Norfolk, 1969; Disting. Service award Hampton Rds. Maritime Assn., 1973. Mem. Am. Bur. Shipping, Hampton Rds. Maritime Assn. (past pres., dir.), Shipbuilders Council Am. (dir.), Am. Inst. Mgmt. (pres.'s council), Norfolk C. of C., Soc. Naval Architects and Marine Engrs. Episcopalian. Clubs: Propeller of U.S., Capitol Hill (Washington); Commonwealth (Richmond); Whitehall, Princeton (N.Y.C.); Va. (Norfolk); Princess Anne Country (Virginia Beach); Norfolk Yacht and Country. Home: 1336 W Princess Anne Rd Norfolk VA 23507 Office: PO Box 2100 Norfolk VA 23501

ROPER, RAYMOND WARREN, JR., assn. exec.; b. Springfield, Mo., Apr. 26, 1940; s. Raymond Warren and Mary Frances (Hacker) R.; B.A., Benedictine Coll., 1961; postgrad. Drury Coll., 1961-62, U. Ill., 1962; m. Judith Ann Haynes, Jan. 5, 1963; children—Mark, Gregory, Douglas. Asst. dir. mgmt. tng. Frisco Ry., Springfield, 1965-68, minority affairs officer, 1968-69; dir. operations U.S. Jaycees, Tulsa, 1969-71, dir. adminstrn., 1971-72, dir. services, 1972, exec. v.p., 1972-74; exec. v.p. Mo. Assn. Realtors, Columbia, 1974-78; sr. v.p. Nat. Assn. Realtors, Chgo., 1978—. Commr., Mayor's Commn. on Human Rights, Springfield, 1969; mem. Gov.'s Task Force on Med. Malpractice Ins., 1975. Cubmaster, Boy Scouts Am., Tulsa, 1973, chmn. sustaining membership campaign, Columbia, 1975. Trustee, sec. Jaycee War Meml. Fund, 1972-74, U.S. Jaycees Found., 1972-74. Recipient Outstanding Jaycee of Year award, Springfield, Mo., 1967. Mem. Am. Soc. Assn. Execs., Chgo. Soc. Assn. Execs., Nat. Assn. Realtors. Republican. Roman Catholic. Rotarian. Clubs: Carlton, Chgo. Athletic Assn., Mich. Ave. Home: 22 W 5th St Hinsdale IL 60521 Office: 430 N Michigan Ave Chicago IL 60611

ROPER, ROBERT BRIAN, mathematician; b. Pittston, Maine, June 1, 1944; s. Thomas and Ruth (Graffam) R.; S.B., Mass. Inst. Tech., 1965. Applied mathematician Systems Research Labs., Inc., Dayton, Ohio, 1965-69; v.p., dir. research Thomte-Roper, Inc., Boston, 1969-76; mgr. commodities and weather info. service Data Resources, Inc., Lexington, Mass., 1977—, founder, pres. Investment Strategies, Inc. Home: 40 Pondview Rd Arlington MA 02174 Office: 60 State St Suite 3330 Boston MA 02109

RORER, JOHN WHITELEY, publisher; b. Phila., Aug. 4, 1930; s. Ronald Erle and Hazel (Whiteley) R.; B.S., U. Pa., 1952; M.B.A., Drexel U., 1956; m. Beverly Case, June 6, 1953. Credit analyst Phila. Nat. Bank, 1954-56; asst. purchasing dir., comptroller inplant feeding system Curtis Publ. Co., Phila., 1956-68; dir. purchasing Chilton Pub. Co., Phila., 1968-70; founding pres. Focus Bus. Weekly, Bus. News, Inc., Phila., 1970—; fin. and real estate cons. Served to capt. AUS, 1952-54. Mem. Assn. Indsl. Advt., Mktg. and Communications Execs. Assn., Nat. Assn. Area Bus. Publs. (co-founder, dir. 1978—). Republican. Episcopalian. Clubs: Union League, Engrs. (Phila.). Home: 7520 Rogers Ave Upper Darby PA 19082 Office: 1015 Chestnut St Philadelphia PA 19107

RORK, ALLEN WRIGHT, ins. co. exec.; b. Mpls., May 4, 1944; s. Allen Willard and Lorraine (Wright) R.; A.B., Williams Coll., 1966; M.B.A., Harvard U., 1968; m. Marilyn Greene, Aug. 26, 1967; children—Jennifer, Tamara. Fin. analyst, then adminstrv. asst. to comptroller Time Inc., N.Y.C., 1968-71; with Hartford Ins. Group (Conn.), 1971—, asst. treas., then asso. treas., 1975-79, treas., 1979-80, asst. v.p., 1980—; treas. Hartford Fire Ins. Co., also subsidiaries parent co.; chmn. investment com. Indsl. Risk Insurers. Bd. dirs. Child and Family Services Hartford, 1980—; treas. Hartford Citizens Com. Effective Govt., 1979-80; investment adv. com. Simsbury Vis. Nursing Assn., 1980—. Mem. Fin. Analysts Fedn., Hartford Soc. Fin. Analysts, Phi Beta Kappa. Office: Hartford Plaza Hartford CT 06115

RORKE, MARIE MOORE, financial exec.; b. N.Y.C., Oct. 6, 1933; d. William J. and Cleo (Kascpre) Moore; student Hunter Coll., 1951-52; m. Charles Rorke, May 15, 1953; 1 son, C. William. Exec. sec. Avis Car Leasing Co., Plainview, N.Y., 1964-66; bus. office rep. N.Y. Telephone Co., Huntington, 1966-67; corp. sec., asst. treas., controller Geotel, Inc., Amityville, N.Y., 1967—; dir. AFP Industries. Sec., Heatherwood Civic Assn., Huntington, 1965—. Mem. Am. Inst. Corp. Controllers, Am. Soc. Profl. and Exec. Women. Home: 8 Coe Pl Huntington NY 11746 Office: 185 Dixon Ave Amityville NY 11701

ROSA, DOMINICK JOHN, cosmetic co. exec.; b. Flushing, N.Y., July 7, 1949; s. Sebastian John and Frances Theresa (Poveromo) R.; B.S., Manhattan Coll., 1971. Accounting clk. Hearst Corp., 1969-71; jr. accountant George A. Fuller Corp., constrn., 1971-73; sr. accountant Syska & Hennessy, Inc., cons. engrs., N.Y.C., 1973; asst. controller Make-Up Center, Ltd., Moonachie, N.J., 1973-74, controller, 1974-77, controller, dir. EDP, 1977—, fin. cons., 1977—, pres., chief exec. officer Make-Up Center of L.I. Home: 34 S Rodono Rd Upper Saddle River NJ 07458

ROSAEN, LARS OSCAR, flow meter mfg. co. exec.; b. Detroit, Apr. 9, 1953; s. Nils Olav and Edith (Marion) R.; student U. Mich., 1971-72, Eastern Mich. U., 1972-74; m. Leslie J. Bauman, Aug. 24, 1974; children—Alison, Catherine. Head new product design and tooling Universal Filters Inc., Hazel Park, Mich., 1974-76, gen. mgr., 1976-78, pres., chief exec. officer, 1978—, also dir. Mem. Am. Mgmt. Assn., Am. Soc. for Metals, C. of C. U.S., Soc. Mfg. Engrs., Mich. Mfrs. Assn. Republican. Patentee in field. Office: Universal Filters Inc 1755 E Nine Mile St Hazel Park MI 48030

ROSE, ARTHUR MORRIS, wholesale hardware exec.; b. Bklyn., Mar. 7, 1943; s. Lawrence and Lillian (Rosen) R.; B.S., N.Y. U., 1964; M.B.A. with distinction, Adelphi U., 1978; m. Nadine Posner; children—Sharon Elisabeth, Kevin Benjamin, Amy Meredith. Exec. trainee, mgr. boy's dept. Gertz Dept. Stores, Hicksville, N.Y., 1966; registered rep. Loeb Rhoades & Co., N.Y.C., 1967; v.p. L. Rose Hardware Inc., Bklyn., 1968—. Mem. Am. Mgmt. Assn., Inst. Mgmt. Scis., Am. Radio Relay League, Delta Mu Delta. Jewish. Home: 40 Stoner Ave Great Neck NY 11021 Office: care L Rose Hardware Inc 201 Snediker Ave Brooklyn NY 11207

ROSE, CHARLES FREDERICK, mfg. co. exec.; b. Southampton, N.Y., May 19, 1935; s. Harvey S. and Carolyn (Bancroft) R.; B.S.M.E., Lehigh U., 1958; M.B.A., Butler U., 1971; m. Judith F. Yakey, Aug. 8, 1970; children—D. Robbin, Austin F. Jr. engr. Astatic Corp., Conneaut, Ohio, 1958-61; engr. RCA Corp., Indpls., 1961-74; pres. Electronic Products, Inc., Indpls., 1974—, dir., 1974—. Registered profl. engr., Ind. Mem. ASME. Republican. Patentee in field of tape recorder mechanisms and radio electronics. Home: 7765 Zionsville Rd Indianapolis IN 46268 Office: 5741 W 85th St Indianapolis IN 46278

ROSE, HUGH, engine co. exec.; b. Evanston, Ill., Sept. 10, 1926; s. Howard Gray and Catherine (Wilcox) R.; B.S. in Physics, U. Mich., 1951, M.S. in Geophysics, 1952; m. Mary Moore Austin, Oct. 25, 1952; children—Susan, Nancy, Gregory, Matthew, Mary. With mktg. dept. Caterpillar, Inc., Peoria, Ill., 1952-66; v.p., mktg. mgr. Cummins Engine Co., Columbus, Ind., 1966-80; pres. Cummins Northeastern, Inc., 1969-80; pres., chief operating officer Power Systems Assos., Los Angeles, 1980—. Bd. dirs. mem. exec. com. Jordan Hosp. Served with USAAF, World War II. Fellow AAAS; mem. Acacia, Sigma Gamma Epsilon, Beta Beta Beta. Clubs: Algonquin (v.p.), Boston Madison Sq. Garden, Beacon Soc. (pres.), Duxbury Yacht, U. Mich. Clubs: Longwood Cricket. Presbyterian. Home: Governor Wentworth Rd Amherst NH 03031 Office: Box 7044 Los Angeles CA 90022

ROSE, JULES FREED, retail food exec.; b. N.Y.C., Feb. 4, 1936; s. Myles and Selma (Freed) R.; B.A., Dartmouth Coll., 1957; student law and accounting courses Cornell U.; m. Marilyn Judith Sloan, Apr. 10, 1960; children—Patti Renee, Mitchell Brian, Randi Sloan. Exec. trainee Lerner Shops, 1957; with Food City Supermarkets, 1959; with Sloan's Super Markets, N.Y.C., 1960—, exec. v.p., 1969-79, pres., 1979—; chmn. Eastern Frosted Foods Lectr. N.Y. Agrl. Coll., Farmingdale. Nat. trustee NCCJ, 1975-80; bd. dirs. Lido Homes Civic Assn. Served with AUS, 1958-60. Named Supermarket of Year N.Y. State Food Mchts., 1969, Frozen Food Merchandiser of Year Eastern Frosted Foods Assn., 1969—; Man of Yr., Nat. Prepared Frozen Food Assn., 1979. Mem. Food Industry Alliance (pres. 1973-74), Greater N.Y. Food Council (1st v.p. 1978-79), Soc. Personnel Adminstrn., Pub. Personnel Adminstrn. Jewish. Club: B'nai B'rith (trustee, v.p. 1970-75, pres. 1975—). Contbr. articles to publs. Home: 4 Foxwood Rd Kingspoint NY 11024 Office: 2 Bennett Ave New York NY 10033

ROSE, LAWRENCE REILLY, shopping center exec.; b. Toledo, Ohio, June 21, 1927; s. Clifford Lawrence and Elizabeth M. (Reilly) R.; B.Sc., Ohio State U., 1950; postgrad. Mich. State U., U. Ariz.; m. Kathleen Winifred Marmion, Sept. 17, 1955; children—Kevin C., Maureen A., Susan W., Brian M., Colleen E., Sheila M. Exec. dir. Main Place Mall, Buffalo, 1970-73; gen. mgr. Orlando Fashion Square (Fla.), 1973-75; gen. mgr. Lockport (N.Y.) Mall, 1975-78, gen. mgr., 1979—. V.p., gen. mgr. Plaza Carolina, San Juan, P.R., 1978-79. Mem. Zoning Bd. Appeals, Town of Amherst (N.Y.), 1969-73, 76-78; mem. Republican Com., Town of Amherst, 1961-73, 76-78. Served with USN, 1945-46. Mem. Internat. Council Shopping Centers. Republican. Roman Catholic. Clubs: Kiwanis (v.p., Disting. Service award), Kenan Center (trustee) (Lockport). Home: 102 Carriage Circle Williamsville NY 14221

ROSE, MICHAEL DAVID, hotel corp. exec.; b. Akron, Ohio, Mar. 2, 1942; s. William H. and Annabel L. (Kennedy) R.; B.B.A., U. Cin., 1963; LL.B., Harvard U., 1966; m. Regina Marie Franco, Dec. 15, 1973; children—Matthew Derek Franco, Gabrielle Elaine Franco. Admitted to Ohio bar, 1966; lectr. U. Cin., 1966-67; atty. firm Strauss, Troy & Ruehlmann, Cin., 1966-72; exec. v.p. Winegardner Internat., Cin., 1972-74; v.p. hotel group Holiday Inns, Inc., Memphis, 1974-76, pres. hotel group, 1976-78, corp. exec. v.p., 1978-79, pres., 1979—; dir. Commerce Union Bank of Memphis. Bd. dirs. Memphis Arts Council, 1979—, Lausanne Sch., 1978—; mem. Future Memphis, 1979—; mem. nat. adv. com. U. Cin., 1979—. Mem. Ohio Bar Assn., Young Pres.'s Orgn., Memphis C. of C. (fin. com. 1979). Clubs: Econ. Memphis, Racquet of Memphis. Office: Holiday Inns Inc 3742 Lamar Ave Memphis TN 38195*

ROSE, SANFORD SAMUEL, equipment corp. exec.; b. Seattle, Feb. 10, 1938; s. Alec Julius and Brangie (Goodman) R.; B.A. in Mktg., U. Wash., 1960; m. Paula Jean Sussman, Nov. 19, 1963; children—Alisa, Michael, Megan. Salesman, Leed's, Seattle, 1957-58, Iden's Men's Store, Seattle, 1959-60; mgr. Roxbury Furniture, Seattle, 1961-67; pres. Equipment Importers, Inc., Tacoma, Wash., 1967—; dir. Gen. Metals of Tacoma. Bd. dirs. Seattle Symphony, 1970-80, Seattle Art Mus., 1975-80, Jewish Family Service, 1979-80, Bellevue Art Mus., 1978-80; council of ops. Hertzl-Ner Tamid; pres. Sibleywood Assn., 1966. Served to lt. U.S. Army, 1960-61. Mem. Constrn. Industry Mfrs. Assn., Am. Rental Assn., Splty. Tools and Fasteners Distbrs. Assn., Nat. Tire Dealers Retreaders Assn., Asso. Equipment Distbrs., Material Handling Equipment Distbrs. Assn., World Trade Center, Am. Importers Assn., Motor and Equipment Mfrs. Assn., Seattle Symphony Assn., Seattle Art Mus. Jewish. Clubs: Central Park Tennis, Jewish Community Center Health. Office: Equipment Importers Inc 1901 Jefferson St Tacoma WA 98402

ROSE, WALTER EVERETT, conglomerate exec.; b. Defiance, Ohio, Dec. 24, 1942; s. Walter Gaylon and Lurline Gwendolyn (Doenges) R.; B. M.E., U. Fla., 1965; postgrad. in bus. N.Y. U., 1969-71; m. Hendrika Sannigje Kamphuis, Sept. 23, 1977; children—William Everett, Jessica Anne. Project mgr. Rayonier Quebec, Port-Cartier, 1971-74, mill mgr., 1974-75, v.p., chief adminstrv. officer, 1977-79; dir. bus. planning ITT Rayonier Inc., N.Y.C., 1975-77; v.p. ops. Thomas Tilling Inc., N.Y.C., 1979—. Home: 16 Barnstable Ln Greenwich CT 06830 Office: 345 Park Ave New York NY 10022

ROSE, WILLIAM ECKHART, III, automotive supply co. exec.; b. Balt., July 22, 1943; s. William Eckhart and Beatrice Estelle (Cavey) R.; student public schs., Balt.; m. Audrey Carol Henriques, Sept. 24, 1967; children—William Isaac, Joseph Nathan Henriques. Employed in field of interior and design and sign printing, 1960-65; with Crown Automotive, Washington, 1965—, mgr. ops., 1967-68, v.p. sales and ops., 1969—. Leader Boy Scouts Am. Recipient spl. achievement award Md. Jaycees, 1969. Mem. Am. Mgmt. Assn., Md. Jaycees (dir. 1968-69). Democrat. Jewish. Club: Odd Fellows. Office: Crown Automotive 442 N St NW Washington DC 20001

ROSEBERRY, LARRY STEPHEN, fin. cons.; b. Radford, Va., Jan. 24, 1950; s. Lawrence Alexander and Mary Lee R.; student Tenn. Mil. Inst., 1968-69, Middle Tenn. State U., 1969-71; m. Janis Rucker, June 9, 1973; children—Larry Stephen. Systems analyst, Hamilton Nat. Bank, Chattanooga, 1971-73; bus. mgr. Haun Pontiac Cadillac Co., Athens, Tenn., 1973-74; dist. mgr., regional mgr. World Service Life Ins. Co., Fort Worth, 1974-77; pres. Continental Mgmt. Group, St. Louis, 1977—. Active, Big Bros. Am. Mem. Sales and Mktg. Execs. Am., Smithsonian Assos. Methodist. Home: 402 Woodland Hill Ct Manchester MO 63011 Office: CMG PO Box 936 Manchester MO 63011

ROSEMAN, JACK, computer services co. exec.; b. Lynn, Mass., June 13, 1931; s. Abraham and Bessie (Guz) R.; B.A., Boston U., 1954; M.S., U. Mass., 1955; m. Judith Ann Rosenthal, Feb. 21, 1960; children—Laura, Alan, Shari. Instr., U. Mass., 1958-60; dir. info. processing CEIR, Inc., Washington, 1960-66; v.p. KMS Tech. Center, Washington, 1966-70; pres. On-Line Systems, Inc., Pitts., from 1970, also dir.; chmn., pres. United Computing Internat. subs. United Telecommunications, Inc., 1979-80; pvt. investor, cons., propr. JR Enterprises, 1980—. Treas., Democratic ward, 1965. Mem. Am. Fedn. Info. Processing (program chmn. 1964), Assn. Computing Machinery (program chmn.). Republican. Jewish. Club: Wildwood Golf. Home: 117 Doray Dr Pittsburgh PA 15237 Office: 115 Evergreen Heights Dr Pittsburgh PA 15229

ROSEMEYER, KENNETH ALLEN, univ. fin. exec.; b. Cin., Sept. 28, 1949; s. Arnold Joseph and Mary Grace (Tenbrunsel) R.; B.A. in Bus. Adminstrn., Thomas More Coll., 1971; postgrad. in bus. adminstrn. Xavier U., Cin., 1972—; m. Beverle Elizabeth Buttelwerth, May 14, 1975; children—Tara Ellen, Megan Elizabeth. With Cin. Post & Times Star, 1968-73, asst. accounting dept. mgr., 1972-73; accounting supr. Northlich, Stolley, Inc., Cin., 1973-80; asso. dir. payroll and employee records processing services U. Cin., 1980—; speaker career days to high schs., vocat. schs., colls.; dir. Quality Maid Products, Inc., Cin. Mem. Kappa Sigma Upsilon Frat. Alumni, Elder High Sch. Alumni Club. Home: 3350 Felicity Dr Cincinnati OH 45211 Office: 305 Beecher Hall U Cincinnati Cincinnati OH 45241

ROSEN, GERALD ROBERT, editor; b. N.Y.C., Nov. 17, 1930; s. Sol and Essie (Shapiro) R.; B.S., Ind. U., 1951, M.A., 1953; m. Lois Lehrman, May 9, 1958; 1 son, Evan Mark. Civilian intelligence analyst Dept. Def., N.Y.C., 1955-58; asso. editor Challenge mag., N.Y.C., 1959-61, mng. editor 1961-64, 65-66; sr. editor Dun's Rev., N.Y.C., 1964-65, nat. affairs editor, 1967-77, exec. editor, 1977—, personal fin. corr. Westinghouse Broadcasting Co., 1980. Served with AUS, 1953-55. Mem. Soc. Am. Bus. and Econ. Writers, N.Y. Fin. Writers Assn., White House Corr. Assn. Club: Nat. Press (Washington). Office: 666 Fifth Ave New York NY 10019

ROSEN, HOWARD MARK, accountant, lawyer; b. Youngstown, Ohio, Sept. 22, 1950; s. Arnold A. and Sandra Lynn (Glick) R.; B.B.A. (scholarship 1972-73), U. Cin., 1973; J.D., U. Akron (Ohio), 1980; m. Wendy Siegel, June 4, 1972; 1 son, Adam D. Sr. tax acct. Arthur Andersen & Co., C.P.A.'s, Boston, 1973-75; tax mgr. Courier Corp., Lowell, Mass., 1975-78; v.p. fin. RICO Internat., Warren, Ohio, 1978-79, dir., 1978—; tax mgr., head dept. Goddard, Thomas & Co., C.P.A.'s, Youngstown, 1979-80, Heinick, Slavin & Co., C.P.A.'s, Akron, 1980—; dir. Recreational Industries, Inc.; cons. in field. Mem. planning task force U. Cin. Recipient V.I.T.A. Service award, 1981; C.P.A., Ohio. Mem. Tax Inst. Am., Assn. Atty. C.P.A.'s, Ohio Soc. C.P.A.'s. Republican. Office: 1540 W Market St Akron OH 44313

ROSEN, JAY MARTIN, lawyer, communications co. exec.; b. Tarrytown, N.Y., Nov. 18, 1937; s. Louis and Esther (Kaplan) R.; B.A., Bowling Green State U., 1959; LL.B., N.Y. U., 1961, LL.M., 1968; m. Jean E. Saberski, May 25, 1958; children—Bruce, Jeffrey, Daniel. Admitted to N.Y. bar, 1961; atty. FTC, 1961-64, Western

Electric Co., Inc., 1964-68; sr. atty. Gen. Telephone & Electronics Corp., N.Y.C., 1968-69, v.p., gen. counsel GTE Data Services Corp., Tampa, Fla., 1968-69; v.p., gen. counsel GTE Info. Systems Inc., White Plains, N.Y., 1971-76; gen. counsel GTE Communications Products Group, Stamford, Conn., 1976—; dir. GTE Export Corp., GTE Internat. Systems Corp., Sylvania Tech. Systems, Inc. Mem. N.Y. Bar Assn., Am. Bar Assn. Home: 86 Riverbank Dr Stamford CT 06903 Office: GTE Communications Products Group One Stamford Forum Stamford CT 06904

ROSEN, MARC A., cosmetic mfg. co. exec.; b. Paterson, N.J., Sept. 30, 1946; s. Harry Louis and Lillian (Berkowitz) R.; B.F.A., Carnegie Mellon U., 1968; M.S., Pratt Inst., 1970. Packaging dir. Stephan Lion Inc., 1971-73; dir. promotional packaging Revlon Corp., N.Y.C., 1973-76; v.p. corp. design Elizabeth Arden Inc., N.Y.C., 1976—. Office: 1345 Ave of Americas New York NY 10019

ROSEN, MICHAEL HOWARD, real estate exec.; b. N.Y.C., May 22, 1943; s. Irving Edward and Lilyan Ruth (Ruttenberg) R.; A.B., Tufts U., 1965; m. Joni Frances Breckel, Dec. 29, 1978; children by previous marriage—Daniel Matthew, Lenise Gayle; stepchildren—Jeffrey, Kelli, Molli Lynch. Masonry field supt. Morris Brick Masons Corp., N.Y.C., 1965-66; regional mgr. Rosen Properties, Inc., N.Y.C., 1966-68, v.p. real estate ops., 1968-71; exec. v.p. Rosen Orgn. Inc., N.Y.C., 1971-75, dir., 1971-75; v.p. apt. ops. Monumental Properties, Inc., and Monumental Properties Trust, Balt., 1975-79; exec. v.p. Town and Country Mgmt. Corp., Balt., 1979—; housing adv. panel McGraw-Hill, 1979. Chmn., United Way participation Monumental Properties, 1978, Town and Country Mgmt. Corp., 1979; active Wellwood Little League baseball and basketball. Lic. real estate broker, N.Y. State. Mem. Real Estate Bd. N.Y., Bronx Realty Adv. Bd., Bldg. Industry League, Apt. Owners Adv. Council Westchester County, Bldgs. Inst. Westchester and Putnam Counties, Local #16 Bricklayers, Masons and Plasterers Internat. Union Am., Met. Fair Rent Com., Nat. Realty Com., Apl. Owners and Mgrs. Assn. Am., Home Builders Assn. Md., Apt. Builders and Owners Council Md. (dir. 1976-77), Young Man's Leadership Council, Advt. Club Balt. Jewish. Clubs: Suburban Balt. County, Center. Home: 110 Nob Hill Park Dr Reisterstown MD 21136 Office: 25 S Charles St Suite 2121 Baltimore MD 21201

ROSEN, RICHARD HERBERT, energy tech. co. exec.; b. Cambridge, Mass., Apr. 12, 1939; s. Samuel Robert and Marguerite Edith (Garfield) R.; B.S., Boston U., 1963; M.F.S., Harvard U., 1970, Ph.D., 1977; m. Marguerite Alice Piret, Dec. 23, 1970; 1 son, Andrew Lawrence. Ops. analyst Nat. Shawmut Bank, Boston, 1963-64; v.p. Abt Assos., Inc., Cambridge, 1964-68; pres. Urban Systems, Inc., Cambridge, 1969-73; pres., chief scientist Energy Resources Co., Inc., Cambridge, 1974—; dir. Am. Exploration Co., Inc.; cons. in field. Mem. investment policy com. Harvard U., 1980—. Mem. AAAS, Ecol. Soc. Am., Am. Statis. Assn. Contbr. articles on energy and environ. subjects to profl. jours. Office: 185 Alewife Brook Pkwy Cambridge MA 02178

ROSEN, ROBERT LEON, investment co. exec.; b. N.Y.C., Oct. 7, 1946; s. Isadore and Mollie (Frommer) R.; B.A., City U. N.Y., 1968; M.B.A., N.Y. U., 1970; m. Roberta Merker, Apr. 7, 1968; children—Jonathan Adam, Joshua Eric. Lending officer Mfrs. Hanover Trust Co., N.Y.C., 1968-73; v.p., sr. bank analyst Shearson Hayden Stone, N.Y.C., 1973-76, exec. asst. to pres., adminstrv. officer domestic br. system, 1976-79, pres. Shearson Realty Group, 1979—; dir. Landauer Internat., Inc., Western Pacific Fin. Corp. adj. prof. Fordham U. Grad. Sch. Bus., 1969—. Served with USAR, 1968-73. Mem. N.Y. Soc. Security Analysts, Bank and Fin. Analysts Soc., Fin. Analysts Fedn., Mortgage Roundtable. Home: 7 Woody Ln Westport CT 06880 Office: Shearson Hayden Stone Two World Trade Center New York NY 10048

ROSENAU, FREDERICK SUMNER, auto and motorcycle dealer; b. Detroit, May 8, 1942; s. Arthur W. and Elizabeth M. (Sumner) R.; student Southfield (Mich.) public schs.; m. Patricia V. Paul, July 10, 1971; children—Robert Dean, Kathleen Mary; 1 stepdau., Shawn Lorraine Paul. Printer, Safran Printing Co., Detorit, 1960-71; pres. Pete's Custom Cycle Center, Detroit, 1971-75, Parts Galore, Inc., Dearborn, Mich., 1972—, Westwood Motors, Inc., Inkster, Mich., 1979—, Westwood Leasing Co., 1980—, Computer Stuff Inc. Mem. Nat. Auto Dealers Assn., Mich. Auto Dealers Assn., Detroit Auto Dealers Assn., Nat. Assn. Credit Mgrs. Motorcycle Trades Assn. (past dir.), Mich. Motorcycle Dealers Assn. (dir.). Office: 26429 Michigan Ave Inkster MI 48141

ROSENBAUM, ARNOLD MICHAEL, ins. co. exec.; b. N.Y.C., Apr. 12, 1940; s. Nelson and Hattie (Clark) R.; B.S., N.Y. U., 1973; M.B.A., Pace U., 1976; m. Marsha Ruth Smook, Jan. 3, 1971; 1 dau., Nadine Dawn. Agt., Met. Life Ins. Co., N.Y.C., 1966-68; dir. estate planning E.K. Leaton Agy., N.Y.C., 1971—; asst. gen. agt. Guardian Life Ins. Co., N.Y.C., 1968-71; v.p., gen. mgr. Exec. Programs, Inc., 1975—, Analytical Estate Planning Services, Inc., 1979—; adj. asst. prof. Coll. Ins., N.Y.C., 1972-78. Bd. dirs., sec.-treas. Twin Rivers Homeowners Assn., 1977-80; mem. East Windsor (N.J.) Zoning Bd., 1977—. Served with AUS, 1962-63. Mem. Am. Soc. C.L.U., N.Y.C. Life Underwriters Assn., N.Y. U. Tax Soc. (v.p. 1979-80). Home: 174 Hollingston Pl East Windsor NJ 08520 Office: E K Leaton Agency 430 Park Ave New York NY 10022

ROSENBAUM, IRVING MEIR, dept. store chain exec.; b. Dresden, Germany, Apr. 20, 1921; s. Max and Clara (Koerner) R.; B.A. in Econs., New Sch. Social Research, N.Y.C., 1953; M.A., N.Y. U., 1956; m. Hanni Schein, Oct. 15, 1953; children—Eli M., Daniel S., Michael J. With S.E. Nichols, Inc., N.Y.C., 1938—, mdse. mgr., 1957-60, pres., 1960-72, chmn. bd., 1972—; chmn. bd. Schreiber Co., Lititz, Pa., 1972—. Mem. bus. adv. com. Norman Thomas High Sch., N.Y.C., 1976—; exec. v.p. Solomon Schechter Sch. of Nassau and Suffolk Counties, 1974—; bd. dirs. United Jewish Appeal, Fedn. Jewish Philanthropies and Israel Bonds, 1975—. Served in U.S. Army, 1943-45; NATOUSA, ETO. Recipient Prime Minister's medal Israel, 1976. Mem. Nat. Mass Retailing Inst., U.S. C. of C. (govt. and regulatory affairs com. 1977-80, council on adminstrv. law 1981—). Jewish. Club: Lake Mohawk Country (Sparta, N.J.). Home: Great Neck NY 11021 also Sparta NJ 07871 Office: 500 8th Ave New York NY 10018

ROSENBAUM, ROBERT NEIL, mfrs. rep.; b. Bridgeport, Conn., Nov. 20, 1937; s. Maurice and Faye (Dorchinsky) R.; B.S.E.E., U. Conn., 1959; m. Linda A. Kaplan, July 10, 1960; children—Sheryl, Michael. Design engr. Andersen Labs., Bloomfield, Conn., 1962-66, Teledyne, Princeton, N.J., 1966-71; mgr. tech. mktg. pubs. Analogic Corp., Wakefield, Mass., 1972-74; pres. Sturdy/Conn., Guilford, Conn., 1974—. Mem. Electronics Rep. Assn. Address: 32 Horseshoe Rd Guilford CT 06437

ROSENBAUM, ROBERT STEPHEN, fin. printing co. exec.; b. Bklyn., Jan. 16, 1946; s. Max and Fay (Toppel) R.; B.E.E., CCNY, 1968; M.B.A., Fairleigh Dickinson U., 1975; m. Karyn Barshop, June 22, 1968; children—Stacie, Craig. With Sorg Printing Co., N.Y.C., 1971-72; v.p., sales mgr. Ad Press, Ltd., N.Y.C., 1972-79; pres. R.S. Rosenbaum & Co., Inc., N.Y.C., 1979—. Home: 12 Bearbrook Dr Woodcliff Lake NJ 07675 Office: 200 Hudson St New York NY 10013

ROSENBERG, ALLEN LEON, banker; b. Los Angeles, Jan. 28, 1909; s. Morris and Rose R.; student Pomona Coll., 1926-28; m. Rose Rosen, Feb. 16, 1930; 1 son, Robert G. Partner, Belvedere Gardens Drug Co., Los Angeles, 1930-33; pres. Thrifty-Payless Drugs, Inc., Phoenix, 1933-42; chmn. Central Ariz. War Price and Rationing Bd., OPA, 1942-44; sec., treas. Allied Grain Co., Phoenix, 1944-56; pres. Allied Sales Co., Phoenix, 1944-63; Ariz. State mgr. Continental Grain Co., Phoenix, 1959-61; sr. v.p. Guaranty Bank, Phoenix, 1962-64; pres., dir. Bank of Scottsdale, Ariz., 1964-66; pres., dir. Pioneer Bank of Ariz., Phoenix, 1966-69, also chief exec. officer; pres., dir. Great Western Bank & Trust, Phoenix, 1969-74, vice chmn., 1974—; exec. dir. Ariz. Community Found., 1978—. Mem. Phoenix City Council, 1952-53; mem. Ariz. Human Relations Commn., 1964-65; chmn. Phoenix Area Air Service Com., 1962-75; pres. Jr. Achievement of Met. Phoenix, Inc., 1965-67; mem. Ariz. Regional Export Expansion Council, 1967-71; chmn. Phoenix Municipal Aeros. Bd., 1976—, Ariz. Gov.'s Econ. Security Adv. Council, 1978—; mem. nat. bd. dirs. NCCJ, 1961-64; chmn. bd. dirs. Ariz. State U. Found., 1976-78; bd. dirs. Central Ariz. Project Assn., Phoenix Symphony Assn., Phoenix Bus. Devel. Corp., 1978—; bd. dirs., finance chmn. Ariz. Acad. Recipient Nat. Jr. Achievement award, 1967; Sertoma Internat. Service to Mankind award, 1967; Humanitarian award Nat. Jewish Hosp./Nat. Asthma Center, 1979; named Hon. State Farmer, Future Farmers Am. Mem. Am. Soc. Corporate Secs., Ariz. (pres. 1971-72), Am. (governing council 1972-74) bankers assns., Nat. Alliance Businessmen (dir. Phoenix), Western Ind. Bankers (exec. council 1972-76), Phoenix C. of C. (pres. 1964-65), Phoenix Thunderbirds (life), Nu Alpha Phi, Beta Gamma Sigma (hon.). Sigma Tau. Mason (Shriner), Kiwanian (past pres., lt. gov. Valley of Sun club). Clubs: Phoenix Country, Ariz., Kiva. Home: 3600 N 5th Ave Phoenix AZ 85013 Office: PO Box 2012 Phoenix AZ 85001

ROSENBERG, JOEL BARRY, govt. economist; b. Bronx, N.Y., Aug. 14, 1942; s. Benjamin and Miriam Dorothy (Yellin) R.; B.A., Queens Coll., 1964, M.A., 1966; Ph.D., Brown U., 1972; m. Judith Lynne Jackler, Aug. 26, 1965; children—Jeffrey Alan, Marc David. Cons., Commonwealth Services, Washington, 1970-71; asst. prof. econs. SUNY, Geneseo, 1971-75, Case Western Res. U., Cleve., 1975-76; industry economist IRS, Washington, 1976—. NDEA fellow, Brown U., 1966-69. Mem. Am. Econ. Assn., Am. Statis. Assn. Contbr. articles to profl. jours. Home: 13 Glazebrook Ct Gaithersburg MD 20760 Office: 1111 Constitution Ave NW Washington DC 20224

ROSENBERG, LEONARD HERMAN, ins. exec.; b. Balt., Dec. 1, 1912; s. Henry I. and Laura (Hollander) R.; B.S., Carnegie Inst. Tech., 1934; grad. Command and Gen. Staff Sch.; m. Edna Mazer, Nov. 20, 1936; children—Theodore M., Victor L., Laurie H., Leonard H. With Strasco Ins. Agy., Balt., 1935—, successively salesman, underwriter, gen. mgr., v.p. finance, 1948—; dist. mgr. Reliance Life Ins. Co., Pitts., 1935-39; state agt. Columbus Mut. Life Ins. Co., 1939-55; founder, pres. Chesapeake Life Ins. Co., Balt., 1956-73, chmn. bd., 1973—; v.p. Chesapeake Investment Corp., 1963-68, pres., 1968-74; pres. Preferred Equity Ins. Co. Denver, 1968-70, chmn. bd., 1970-71; v.p. Chesapeake Fund, 1963-68, pres., 1968-74; dir. John L. Deaton Med. Nursing Center, Inc., 1968-79, Charles Light Parking, Inc., 1968-79, Bayshore Industries, Inc. (Md.), 1949-61; dir., mem. exec. com., chmn. finance com. Nat. City Bank Md., 1967-70. Instr. math., physics Night Sch., Balt. City Coll., 1935-39; instr. civilian pilot tng. program Johns Hopkins U., 1939-42. Commr., Md. Traffic Safety Commn., 1957-67; mem. Gov.'s Commn. to Revise Md. Ins. Laws, 1960; commr. Md. Pub. Broadcasting Commn., 1967-71, chmn., 1971—; mem. curricula com. Balt. Jr. Coll., 1966-77; mem. Pres. Johnson's Spl. Adv. Council for Vocational Edn., 1967-68, Pres.'s Fed. Financial Aid to Higher Edn. Com., 1969-70; pres. Balt. Community Concert Assn., 1955-56; chmn. Balt. Adv. Council on Vocational Edn., 1970—; mem. Md. Adv. Council on Vocational Edn., 1970-74; mem. Nat. Adv. Commn. on Flammable Fabrics, 1970-73; mem. Md. Commn. to Study Structure and Governance of Edn., 1972-73, chmn., 1973-76; asst. sec., dir. Md. Life & Health Ins. Guaranty Assn., 1972—; dir. Nat. Asso. Life Cos., 1965—, pres., 1968-70. Mem. steering com. Nat. Inst. for Career Edn., 1976-77; bd. advs. Humanities Inst., Inc., 1979—; trustee Carnegie-Mellon U., 1964-70, Sears Scholarship, U. Md., Tau Delta Phi Found., Community Coll. Balt., 1976—; bd. dirs. Ins. Hall of Fame; bd. dir., bd. govs. Internat. Ins. Seminars; bd. govs. Pub. Broadcasting Service, 1972-77, chmn. devel. com., 1974-77. Served from 2d lt. to capt. USAAF, 1942-45; lt. col. Res., ret. Recipient Outstanding Alumni award Carnegie-Mellon U., 1967; William P. White award for outstanding service to the ins. industry, 1967; Outstanding Alumni award Tau Delta Phi, 1967. Mem. Inst. Aero. Sci., Inst. Nav., Nat. Assn. Life Cos. (pres. 1968-70). Jewish. Club: Centre (Balt.). Contbr. articles to ins. jours. Lectr. in field. Home: 22 Bouton Green Village of Cross Keys Baltimore MD 21210 Office: 527 St Paul St Baltimore MD 21202

ROSENBERG, THEODORE MAZER, urban devel. exec.; b. Balt., Dec. 27, 1941; s. Leonard H. and Edna G. (Mazer) R.; student U. Okla., also courses Loyola U., Carnegie Inst. Tech., So. Meth. U. Inst. Ins. Mktg., N.Y. U. Investment Co. Officers Program, Boston U., U. Chgo. Life Officers Investment Program; m. Michele Leslie Kayne, May 7, 1978; children—Elizabeth Ellen, Jacob Henry, Seth Aaron. Restaurant mgr. RGS, Inc., 1963; agt., then dist. agt., gen. agt., new product devel., investment policy and capital planning Chesapeake Life Ins. Co., 1964-78, spl. adviser to chmn. bd., 1974-78; exec. v.p. Chesapeake Investment Corp., 1969-74, also dir.; pres. Chesapeake Equity Sales, Inc., 1969-74, also dir.; controller, treas. Chesapeake Fund, Inc., 1969-74; v.p. Industry Savs. Plans, Inc., 1968-69, 80-81, Fed. Hill Assos., Inc., 1979-80; v.p., treas. Barclay Brent Corp., 1971-73; pres. Twin Oaks Assts., 1978—, Twin Oaks Advisors, 1978—, Wesmarco Enterprises, 1979-80; gen. partner Beatman Joint Venture, 1979—, Bokel Joint Venture, 1980—. Chmn., Balt. Free Fgn. Trade Zone Study, 1967; v.p., treas. Balt. Bus. Opportunity Center, Balt. Small Bus. Devel. Center, 1970-73; 1st v.p., treas. Greater Homewood Community Corp., 1970-73; treas. North Central Balt. Health Corp., 1972; pres. Dickyville Assn., Inc., 1974, Balt. Learning Center, 1974—; adv. bd. Morgan State U. Sch. Bus., 1970-73, North Baltimore Gen. Hosp., 1972-73, Social Sci. Research Inc., 1974—, Rail Preservation Ltd., 1976—; bd. dirs. Balt. United Fellowship, 1975—, Mt. Vernon-Belvedere Improvement Assn., 1977—, Balt.-Jerosulem Theater Project, 1979—, Balt. Chamber Orch. Co., 1980—; mem. Balt. City Neighborhood Preservation Council, 1976—; chmn. Archtl. Rev. Com., Mt. Vernon Hist. Dist., 1979—; scoutmaster troop 97, Boy Scouts Am., 1977; bd. dirs. 5th Dist. New Democratic Coalition, 1976—, campaign treas., 1976-79, pres., 1978-80; mem. Beth Am Downtown Congregation. Recipient plaques Nat. Assn. Life Ins. Cos., Nat. Quality award Nat. Assn. Life Underwriters. Mem. Balt. Stock Traders Assn., Mid-Atlantic Options Soc., Soc. Fin. Examiners, Assn. Computing Machinery Nat. Council Urban Devel., Nat. Trust Hist. Preservation, Balt. Heritage Soc. Democrat. Jewish. Home: 5007 Forest Park Ave Baltimore MD 21207 Office: 521 St Paul Pl Baltimore MD 21203

ROSENBLATT, LEON BERYL, textile co. exec.; b. N.Y.C., Jan. 11, 1930; s. George and Jean L. (Lewis) R.; B.B.A., CCNY, 1949; A.A. in Textiles, Fairleigh Dickinson U., 1950; m. Sandra Stern, June 28, 1959; children—Geri Sue, Steven Philip, Alisa Beth. Pres., Leon B. Rosenblatt Textiles Ltd., N.Y.C., 1954—. Served with Q.M.C., U.S. Army, 1951-55. Mem. Am. Printed Fabric Council (pres. 1979-80), Textile Square Club (dir.). Club: Masons (past master). Home: 532 Cedarwood Dr Cedarhurst NY 11516 Office: 469 7th Ave New York NY 10018

ROSENBLATT, LEONARD, constrn. products exec.; b. N.Y.C., Oct. 20, 1929; s. Max and Mollie (Oberman) R.; ed. CCNY, Harvard Advanced Mgmt. Program; m. Miriam Brautman, Nov. 22, 1956; children—Barton, Helane. With Witco Chem. Co., N.Y.C., 1953-63; exec. v.p. Constrn. Products div. W.R. Grace & Co., Cambridge, Mass., 1963—. Bd. dirs. League Sch. of Boston; mem. Fla. Council 100. Served with USAAF, 1947-48. Mem. Producers Council (dir.). Club: Harvard. Office: 62 Whittemore Ave Cambridge MA 02140

ROSENBLUM, MARC JOSEPH, govt. economist; b. Bklyn., July 27, 1936; s. William and Henrietta (Feld) R.; A.B., City U. N.Y., 1963, M.A., 1964; Ph.D., U. Minn., 1972. Asst. prof. econs. John Jay Coll., City U. N.Y., 1971-76; research scientist Am. Inst. for Research, Washington, 1976-77; staff economist Nat. Commn. on Employment and Unemployment Statistics, Washington, 1977-78; chief economist U.S. Equal Employment Opportunity Commn., Washington, 1979—. Served with U.S. Army, 1958-60. Mem. Indsl. Relations Research Assn. Contbr. articles to profl. jours.; editorial adv. bd. Aging and Work, 1978—. Office: 2401 E St NW Washington DC 20506

ROSENCRANZ, ROBERT, elec. engr.; b. Chgo., July 2, 1926; s. Bernard and Lillian (Greenstein) R.; B.S. in Elec. Engring., U. Ill., 1948; B.S. in Indsl. Engring., Ill. Inst. Tech., 1955, B.S. in Mech. and Aerospace Engring., 1969; M.B.A., Roosevelt U., 1977; m. Judith Diane Levey, June 29, 1952; children—Leslie Joyce, Holly Ann. Chief engr. Standard Stamping & Perforating Co., Chgo., 1948-58, also cons. engr.; research engr. Clearing Machine Corp. div. U.S. Industries, Chgo., 1958-60; sr. elec. engr. U.S. Industries Tech. Center, Pompano Beach, Fla., 1960-61; chief engr. Lumen Electronics div. Esterline Angus Instrument Co., Joliet, Ill., 1961-65, Zenith Electric Co., Chgo., 1965-66; mgr. electronic and optical engring. Sargent-Welch Sci. Co., Skokie, Ill., 1966-73; sr. staff engr. Abbott Labs., North Chicago, Ill., 1973—. Served with USNR, 1944-46. Mem. I.E.E.E., Instrument Soc. Am. (sr.), Soc. Photog. Scientists and Engrs. (pres. Chgo. chpt. 1970-71; Service award 1972), Beta Gamma Sigma, Mason (Shriner). Contbr. articles to profl. jours. Patentee in field. Home: 1762 McCraren Rd Highland Park IL 60035 Office: Abbott Park North Chicago IL 60064

ROSENDALE, GEORGE WILLIAM, aircraft co. exec.; b. Keenan, Okla., Nov. 4, 1933; s. John Webster and Laura Lee (Schawo) R.; student Okla. Baptist U., 1957-58, U. Wichita, 1959-63; B.A. in English, Wichita State U., 1969, M.S. in Adminstrn., 1971; m. Penney Sue Tillotson, Dec. 27, 1964; children—James Christopher, Kathleen Marie, John Charles. Engring. draftsman Skyline Corp., Wichita, Kans., 1952, Boeing Aircraft Co., Wichita, Kans., 1953, O.A. Sutton Corp., Wichita, 1956, engring. checker, 1956-57; dept. clk. Cessna Aircraft Co., Wichita, 1958-59, bench hand, 1959-61, scheduling clk., 1961-62, mfg. scheduler, 1962-67, personnel rep., 1967-69, tng. supr., 1969-73, mgr. employee tng. and devel., 1973—; vocat. instr. evening sch. Wichita pub. schs., 1963. Area comdr. United Fund, Wichita, 1971; sec., Haysville Jr. Football League, Haysville, Kans., 1973-75; study com. chmn. Wichita Community Planning Council, 1972-73; mem. Haysville Planning Commn., 1976—, chmn., 1977-79; exec. com. Kans. State Employment and Tng. Council, 1979—; sch. tchr. Olivet Bapt. Ch., Wichita, 1951-53; children's choir dir. 2d Gen. Hosp. Chapel, Ger., 1955-56; music dir. Southside Bapt. Ch., Wichita, 1956-57; minister music Bapt. Ch., Hominy, Okla., 1957-60, youth dir., 1958-60; asst. music dir. Open Door Bapt. Ch., Haysville, 1971, numerous other ch. positions; bd. dirs. Christian Braile Found., 1971-74, Amigos de SER, Wichita, 1975-77. Am. Cancer Soc., Sedgwick County (Kans.) unit, 1977—, Ark-Valley Jr. Football League, 1974-75. Served with U.S. Army, 1953-56. Recipient Campaign award United Fund of Wichita, 1969, 70, 71, Outstanding Service plaque award Am. Cancer Soc., 1978, 79, Individual Support award, 1979. Mem. Am. Mgmt. Assn., Am. Soc. Personnel Adminstrn. (pres. Wichita chpt. 1973-74, past president's plaque award 1975, tng. and devel. com. 1979), Employee Devel. Assn., Wichita Area C. of C. (mem. manpower resources com. 1974), Psi Chi. Republican. Home: 424 Hollywood Dr Wichita KS 67217 Office: Cessna Wallace Div PO Box 7704 Wichita KS 67277

ROSENE, LEE C., cosmetic co. cons.; b. Chgo., Nov. 5, 1912; s. David and Belle (Baim) R.; student pub. schs.; m. Dorothe Ann Rosen, Dec. 30, 1934; children—Sara Lynn (Mrs. Radell), Alexander. Sales rep. Max Factor & Co., Hollywood, Calif., 1936-46, divisional sales mgr., Chgo., 1946-51, regional sales mgr., 1951-57, dir. U.S. sales, Hollywood, 1957—, v.p., dir. U.S. sales, 1960-68, sr. v.p., 1968—; pres. devel. div., 1970—, cons., 1973-76, ret., 1976; mktg. and sales cons., 1976—; dir. Argo Petroleum Corp. Bd. dirs. Service Corps Ret. Execs. Mem. Am. Mgmt. Assn., Town Hall of Calif., Los Angeles C. of C., Los Angeles World Affairs Council, AIM, Am. Assn. Ret. Persons. Clubs: Beverly Hills (pres. 1960—); Brentwood Country; City of Hope Merchants; Variety Internat. Home: 2222 Ave of Stars Century Towers W Los Angeles CA 90067

ROSENFELD, DONALD ALAN, photographer, bus. exec.; b. Cambridge, Mass., Apr. 20, 1944; s. Jerome M. and Elaine L. (Ackerson) R.; grad. Cheshire Acad. (Conn.), 1962; student Bryant and Stratton, 1964. Research asst. radar meteorology Mass. Inst. Tech., Cambridge, 1965-67; meteorologist radio stas. WREB, WBCN and WERS, Holyoke; Boston, 1965-68; pres. New Eng. News & Photo Co., Boston, 1968—, New Eng. Service Co., Boston, 1969—, Investment Co. of New Eng., Boston, 1970—, New Eng. Electronics Co., 1971—; dir. Jerome Press, Inc., Boston; chief photographer N.E. Legal Photography Co., Boston, 1970—; Mass. Registry of Motor Vehicles, 1974-77. Mem. Nat. Press Photographers Assn., Am. Meterology Soc. (sec., treas. Boston chpt. 1964-67), Evidence Photographers Internat. Council, Internat. Assn. Identification, New Eng. Police Photographers Assn., Mass. Trial Lawyers Assn. Address: PO Box 10 Brookline MA 02146

ROSENFELD, HERBERT ARTHUR, sporting goods co. exec.; b. N.Y.C., June 4, 1941; s. Frederic I. and Etta (Friedman) R.; B.S., U. Miami, 1962; postgrad. Columbia U., 1963; m. Michelle Stone, July 17, 1965; children—Jason, Karen. Controller, Premier Athletic Products Co., Rivervale, N.J., 1963-77; pres. Equilink Corp., N.Y.C., 1977-79; pres. MacGregor Athletic Products Co., East Rutherford, N.J., 1979—. Pres. Bergen County (N.J.) Sports Assn., 1979; v.p. YMHA, Bergen County, 1980. Mem. Sporting Goods Mfg. Assn. Jewish. Office: 25 E Union St East Rutherford NJ 07073

ROSENFELD, JOSEPH, concrete co. exec.; b. Medway, Mass., Dec. 3, 1907; s. Abraham and Annie (Candleman) R.; student pub. schs., Milford, Mass. Mgr., Abraham Rosenfeld Sand & Gravel Co., Milford, 1925-32; owner, operator Rosenfeld Washed Sand & Stone Co., Hopedale, Mass., 1932—, also concrete plants, Dedham,

Plainville, Ashland, Walpole, Mass.; vice chmn., dir. Home Nat. Bank, Milford; dir. Milford Water Co., Milford Indsl. Com., 1966; chmn. Milford Indsl. Devel. Commn., 1966-76. Pres., Milford Combined Charities, 1958-59; mem. gifts com. Milford Hosp., 1961, mem. bd. mgrs., trustee; hon. chmn. Milford Heart Fund; mem. Milford Town Meeting, 1935-73; mem. men's assos. Jewish Meml. Hosp., 1969; chmn. Milford area Mass. Assn. for Mental Health, 1967—; sponsor Nat. Jewish Hosp., 1969, Greater Boston Assn. Retarded Children, Milford and Hopedale Little League, Hopedale Women's Softball League, Babe Ruth League; mem. adv. bd. Algonquin council Boy Scouts Am.; recipient Distinguished Citizen award, 1974; mem. com. Speakers Ann. Charity Ball, 1965-67; mem. Milford Sch. Bldg. Com.; donor bldg. for Rosenfeld Hebrew Sch., Milford; hon. chmn. Milford Area March of Dimes campaign, 1970; Bd. dirs. Worcester chpt. Prevention Cruelty to Children, 1971, Central chpt. Mass. Heart Assn., 1967, Mass. 4-H Found. Recipient citation United Jewish Appeal, 1953, Milford Hebrew Assn., 1958, Milford Kiwanis Club, 1960, Community Service award V.F.W. Post 9373, 1961, citation Trustees Kiwanis-Rotary Pub. Service Trust, Greater Boston Assn. Retarded Children, Inc., Worcester chpt. Milford Heart Fund, 1966; Certificate of appreciation Nat. Found.-March of Dimes, 1968; Community leader of Am. award, 1969; State of Israel award, 1973; other awards. Mem. Asso. Gen. Contractors Am., Mass. Bldg. Congress, Utility Contractors New Eng., Home Builders Assn. Greater Boston, Nat. Assn. Home Builders U.S., Mass. Motor Truck Assn. Inc., Mass. Concrete Inst. (dir.), Milford (dir., mem. exec. bd., Distinguished Service award 1976), Greater Boston chambers commerce, A.I.M. (pres.'s council 1966), Milford Hebrew Assn. (trustee), Art Inst. Boston. Republican. Jewish religion. Lion (charter Milford, pres. 1956-57), Elk; mem. B'nai B'rith (25 year silver honor certificate for humanitarian programs 1961). Clubs: Century; Hopedale Country; Portuguese de Instrucao E Recreio Inc. (Milford) (hon. life mem.; citation 1965); Milford Sons of Italy Dramatic and Sportsman's (hon.); Bungay Brook Sporting (hon.) (Bellingham). Home: 34 Cedar St Milford MA 01757 Office: 75 Plain St Hopedale MA 01747

ROSENFELD, WILLIAM JED, architect, publisher, fin. exec.; b. N.Y.C., Jan. 25, 1943; s. Louis J. and Elizabeth R.; B.Arch. with honors, Pratt Inst., 1966; student (Fulbright scholar) Middle East Tech. U., Ankara, Turkey, 1964-65; m. Serpil Tolga, Dec. 15, 1966; children—Elif, Eren. Architect, 1966—; pub., pres. Diesel Fuel Services, Inc., N.Y.C., 1975—; pres. Salem Capital Corp., N.Y.C., 1972—. Mem. AIA, Nat. Assn. Printers and Lithographers, Nat. Council Archtl. Registration Bds. Office: 415 Lexington Ave New York NY 10017

ROSENFIELD, JAMES RICHARD, direct mktg. exec.; b. Cin., Aug. 25, 1945; s. Herman and Catherine R.; B.A., Columbia Coll., 1967; m. Frederica Maule, May 31, 1969. Promotion mgr. AMS Press, N.Y.C., 1969-71; dir. advt. Matthew Bender & Co., N.Y.C., 1971-76; dir. mktg. Cordura Publs., Inc., La Jolla, Calif., 1976-79; dir. advt. Monex Internat. Ltd., Newport Beach, Calif., 1979-81; dir. Western ops. The D.M. Group, Inc., N.Y.C., 1981—; lectr. on direct mktg. Mem. San Diego Direct Mktg. Club (founder, pres.), Direct Mail Mktg. Assn., Direct Mktg. Club So. Calif. Home: 6841 El Fuerte Carlsbad CA 92008 Office: 3611 5th Ave San Diego CA 92103

ROSENGARTEN, FREDERIC, JR., author, spice prodn. exec., found. exec.; b. Phila., Oct. 4, 1916; s. Frederic and E. Marion (Sims) R.; A.B., Princeton, 1938; m. Miriam B. Osterhoust, June 18, 1941; children—Miriam Suydam (Mrs. Gerrit Lansing), Clara (Mrs. Eric Urbahn), Lynn, Joan Davison. Mgr. v.p. Exptl. Plantations, Inc. (subsidiary Merck & Co.), C.A., 1940-43, in charge of quinine plantations in Guatemala and Costa Rica, 1940-43; self-employed producer coffee, spices, essential oils in Guatemala, 1947-58; pres. Monte de Oro, S.A., Guatemala Corp., Guatemala City, Guatemala, 1958-72; pres. U. of Valley of Guatemala Found. Trustee, Escuela Agrícola Panamericana, El Zamorano, Honduras, Pacific Tropical Bot. Garden. Served from pvt. to 1st lt., AUS, 1944-46. Decorated Order of the Quetzal (Guatemala). Hon. research fellow econ. botany Harvard. Fellow Linnean Soc. London. Episcopalian. Clubs: Guatemala Country (pres. 1957); Seminole Golf (Palm Beach, Fla.); Racquet (Phila.). Developer of Guatemalan cardomon. Author: The Book of Spices, 1969; Freebooters Must Die!, 1976 Home: 247 Jungle Rd Palm Beach FL 33480

ROSENHECK, HERBERT B., mgmt. cons.; b. Los Angeles, Aug. 31, 1929; s. David William and Anne (Rosler) R.; B.C.S., Southwestern U., 1953; m. Marcia Ann Levine, Dec. 24, 1950; children—Robin Lee Kale, Michael David. Dir. corp. systems and data processing Hoffman Electronics, El Monte, Calif., 1960-65; mgr. info. systems TRW Systems, El Segundo, Calif., 1965-69; exec. v.p. Data-Station, Culver City, Calif., 1969-70; v.p., gen. mgr. TRW Info. Services Div., Orange County, Calif., 1970-75; pres. HBR Assos., Mgmt. Cons., Northridge, Calif., 1975—. Served with U.S. Army, 1950-52. Republican. Club: Encino. Address: 18830 Los Alimos St Northridge CA 91326

ROSENMAN, DANIEL, merchandising, marketing co. exec.; b. N.Y.C., Sept. 30, 1924; s. David and Sara (Sharlin) R.; B.B.A., Coll. City N.Y., 1946; M.B.A., Wharton Inst. Finance, 1948; M.A., Fordham U., 1952; Ph.D. in Archeology, U. Mexico, 1958; m. Barbara Klapper, Dec. 30, 1964; children—David, Kelly. Registered rep. Lehman Bros., N.Y.C., 1946-50; pres. Sheldon Picture Tube Corp., div. Allied Electric Products, Inc., Irvington, N.J., 1950-54; pres., dir. Invest-Mex S.A., Mexico City, 1951—; v.p. J.H.I. div. Measured Mktg., Culver City, Calif., 1965—; lectr. major U.S. univs. Recipient Nat. Sales Exec. of Year award, 1951, 53, 56, 60, Humanitarian medal Pres. Lopez Mateos, Mexico, 1960. Mem. IEEE, Producers for Asso. Components for Electronics, Soc. for Advancement Mgmt., Assn. Fgn. Corrs., Nat. Oceanographic Soc. (dir.), Bankers Club Mexico City, Overseas Press Club. Home: PO Box 3067 Beverly Hills CA 90212

ROSENOW, ROBERT JOHN, agribus. exec.; b. Ludington, Mich., Apr. 9, 1949; s. John Hilliard and Iola Mae (Miller) R.; student Ferris State Coll., 1967-69; B.S. with high honors, Mich. State U., 1971, postgrad., 1971-73; postgrad. Saginaw Valley State Coll., 1979; m. LaWana C. Krupinski, Nov. 9, 1969; children—Tricia Caroline, Robert John. Coordinator student programs Coll. Agr. and Natural Resources, Mich. State U., 1971-73; v.p., gen. mgr. Mackinac Land & Cattle Co., Whittemore, Mich., 1973—; mem. extension agrl. adv. com. Mich. State U. Leader 4-H Club, Whittemore. Recipient Outstanding Leadership award Coll. Agr. and Natural Resources, Mich. State U., 1971; named Hon. State Farmer, Future Farmers Am., Mich., 1973, Hon. Chpt. Farmer, Whittemore, 1978. Mem. Mich. Cattlemen's Assn., Mich. Grain and Agrl. Dealers Assn., Cattle Pac (dir.), Nat. Cattlemen's Assn., Mich. Farm Bur., Mich. Farm Mgrs. and Rural Appraisers. Republican. Home: 5703 E Mills Rd Prescott MI 48756 Office: 8805 W Meadow Rd Whittemore MI 48770

ROSENSAFT, MELVIN, mgmt. cons., educator; b. N.Y.C., Jan. 28, 1919; s. Nathan and Yetta (Applebaum) R.; certificate State Tchrs. Coll. at Paterson, N.J., 1938-40; B.S. cum laude, Rider Coll., 1942; M.B.A., Suffolk U., 1978; m. Beatrice Golombek, June 27, 1954; children—David Norman, Lester Jay, Emily Susan. Field dep. U.S. Internal Revenue Service, Newark, 1942-43; office mgr. Gt. Am. Plastics Co., 1944-46, comptroller, 1946-47, works mgr., 1947-48, asst. to pres., 1950-52, v.p. in charge mfg., 1956-62, exec. v.p., gen. mgr., 1962-71; pres., mng. dir. Irwin Products, Toronto, Ont., Can., 1949-50; pres., chief exec. officer Gt. Am. Chem. Corp., Fitchburg, Mass., 1971-76, dir., 1969-77; pres., chief operating officer Artefactos Plásticos, Mexico City, Mexico, 1948-49; mgr. plastics div. Ideal Plastics Co., Hollis, N.Y., 1953-55; exec. v.p. Irwin Corp., N.Y.C., Leominster Plastics Co., Nashua Plastics Co., Fitchburg Realty Corp., Factory St. Realty, Nashua, N.H.; pres., chief exec. officer Melvin Rosensaft & Assos., Leominster, Mass., 1976—; chmn. bd., chief exec. officer Cons. to Mgmt., Inc., 1980—; dir. Lastomerex, Inc., Jefferson, Mass., 1978—; mgmt. cons., 1976—; asso. prof. mgmt. Keene (N.H.) State Coll., 1979—; master lectr. mgmt., mktg. Suffolk U. Grad. Sch. Bus. Adminstrn., Boston; adj. faculty Fitchburg State Coll., Mt. Wachusett Community Coll. Chmn. troop com. Nashoba Valley council Boy Scouts Am.; examiner ARC; pres., bd. dirs., trustee Fitchburg-Leominster Community Center; mem. adv. com. City of Leominster Urban Renewal; adv. com. Mass. Regional Vocat. Tech. Sch.; bd. dirs. Fitchburg Gen. Hosp.; v.p., bd. dirs. F.I.A. Credit Union; adv. econ. and indsl. devel. City of Leominster; mem. Fitchburg Indsl. Devel. Commn.; lobbyist for Mass. industry against passage of proposed flat-rate power cost legislation; fellow Benjamin Franklin Assos., U. Pa., Phila.; fellow Scheie Eye Inst., Presbyn. Hosp., U. Pa., Phila. Served with AUS, 1943-44. Lic. real estate broker, Mass. Mem. Inst. Mgmt. Sci., Inst. of Mgmt. Cons. (cert. mgmt. cons.), Soc. Profl. Mgmt. Cons., Soc. Plastics Engrs. (profl. mem.), AAUP, Am. Mgmt. Assn., C. of C., Soc. Plastics Industry (vinylchloride and polyvinyl chloride producers com.), Chem. Soc. Gt. Britain, Internat. Platform Assn., Delta Mu Delta. Club: Commerce (past pres.). Author various tech. papers including indsl. impact study, indsl. devel. needs assessment. Home and Office: 59 Crescent Rd Leominster MA 01453

ROSENSHINE, ALLEN GILBERT, advt. co. exec.; b. N.Y.C., Mar. 14, 1939; s. Aaron and Anna (Zuckerman) R.; A.B., Columbia Coll., 1960; m. Suzan Weston-Webb, Aug. 31, 1979; children—Andrew, Jonathan. Copywriter, J.B. Rundle, advt., N.Y.C., 1962-65; copywriter Batten, Barton, Durstine & Osborn, N.Y.C., 1965, copy supr., 1967, v.p., 1968, asso. creative dir., 1970, sr. v.p., creative dir., 1975-77, exec. v.p., 1977-80, pres., 1980—, also dir., mem. exec. com.; exec. v.p., dir. BBDO Internat.; lectr. gen. studies Bklyn. Coll., 1961-65. Office: 383 Madison Ave New York NY 10017

ROSENSTEEL, GARY RALPH, EDP auditor; b. Northampton, Eng., Apr. 15, 1946 (father Am. citizen); s. Elmer Ralph Rosensteel, Jr. B.S. in Polit. Sci., Valparaiso U., 1968; M.B.A., U. Pitts., 1973; m. Anita Marie Colamarino; children—Steven Paul, Brian Scott. Systems analyst Westinghouse Tele-Computer, Pitts., 1969-73, Carnegie-Mellon U., 1973-74; sr. systems analyst Allegheny Airlines, 1974-77; mgr. systems devel. County of Allegheny, Pitts., 1977-78; EDP auditor Rockwell Internat., Pitts., 1978-79; pres. Rosensteel Assos., Los Angeles, 1979—. Advanceman of Pres. Ford, 1975-76. Mem. Internat. Computer Cons. Assn., Assn. Systems Mgmt., Tng. Assn. So. Calif., Am. Soc. Tng. and Devel. Address: 3635 Artesia Blvd Torrance CA 90504

ROSENSTEEL, JOHN WILLIAM, ins. co. exec.; b. Chgo., June 4, 1940; s. Harold Eugene and Alice Catherine (Shanahan) R.; B.S., Coll. Holy Cross, 1962; m. Virginia Woulfe, Jan. 20, 1968; children—Elizabeth, Margaret, Jill. Rep. home office group div. Aetna Life & Casualty Co., Chgo., 1967-71, asst. regional dir. splty. mktg. Midwest region Aetna Variable Annuity Life Ins. Co., 1971-72, regional dir. splty. mktg. and deferred compensation sales Aetna Life & Casualty Co., 1972-75, nat. dir. deferred compensation sales, Hartford, Conn., 1975—, tax deferred annuity, 1976—. Served with USNR, 1963-66; Vietnam. C.L.U. Mem. Nat. Assn. Life Underwriters, Nat., Hartford assns. C.L.U.'s. Roman Catholic. Clubs: Beverly Country, St. Ignatius High Sch. Alumni, Coll. Holy Cross Alumni.

ROSENSTEIN, ALLEN BERTRAM, elec. engr., educator; b. Balt., Aug. 25, 1920; s. Morton and Mary (Epstein) R.; B.S., U. Ariz., 1940; M.S., U. Calif. at Los Angeles, 1950, Ph.D., 1958; m. Betty Lebell; children—Jerry Tyler, Lisa Nan, Adam Mark. Elec. engr. Consol. Vultee Aircraft, 1940-41; sr. elec. engr. Lockheed Aircraft Corp., 1941-42; chief plant engr. Utility Fan Corp., 1942-44; prof. engring. U. Calif. at Los Angeles, 1946—; founder, chmn. bd. Inet, Inc., 1947-53; cons. engr., 1954—; chmn. bd. dirs. Pioneer Magnetics, Inc.; dir. Internat. Transformer Co. Inc., Fgn. Resource Services. Cons. ednl. planning UNESCO, Venezuela, 1974-76. Bd. dirs. Vista Hill Psychiat. Found. Served with USN, 1944-46. Mem. Am. Inst. E.E., I.E.E.E., Am. Soc. Engring. Edn., N.Y. Acad. Scis., A.A.A.S., Sigma Xi, Phi Kappa Phi, Delta Phi Sigma, Tau Beta Pi. Contbr. to profl. jours. Patentee. Author: (with others) Engineering Communications, 1965, A Study of a Profession and Professional Education, 1968. Home: 314 S Rockingham Ave Los Angeles CA 90049

ROSENSTEIN, NEIL HOWARD, corp. exec.; b. N.Y.C., Apr. 28, 1926; s. Arnold and Adele (Bersoff) R.; B.B.A, Coll. City N.Y., 1946; m. Miriam Simpson, May 26, 1950; children—Arnold, Carol, Diane. Partner, Rosenstein & Bilger, C.P.A.'s, N.Y.C., 1950-66; pres. Haven Industries, N.Y.C., and Los Angeles, 1966-70; chmn. bd. Nat. Sugar Refining Co, Phila., 1969-71, Am. Cytology Services Corp., North Hollywood, Calif., 1971—; pres. Bristol Silver Mines, Exacta, Inc., 1979—; chmn. Pitts. Condors basketball team, 1969-70. Past mem. adv. bd. Profl. Karate Assn.; past trustee Am. Basketball Assn.; chmn. bd. Los Angeles Ballet Co., 1970-71; bd. dirs. ACLU Found., 1973-76. C.P.A., N.Y. Mem. N.Y. State Soc. C.P.A.'s, Calif. Clin. Lab. Assn., Nat. Acad. TV Arts and Scis. Jewish. Clubs: Racquet of Palm Springs, Pips Internat. Office: 6440 Coldwater Canyon North Hollywood CA 91606

ROSENTHAL, HERBERT M., real estate exec.; b. Chgo., Oct. 1922; s. Nathan and Bess (Jacobson) R.; B.S. in Econs., U. Ill., 1947; m. Kaye L. Kimbro, June 27, 1950; children—Robert N., Richard M., Steven E., James D. Pres. Hyland Builders, 1949-55; pres. Dunbar Corp., Chgo., 1955—, chmn. bd., 1973—. Served in USAAF, 1943-47; ETO. Recipient Builder of Yr. award Home Builders Assn. Chgo., 1966; Recognition award Commonwealth Edison, 1971. Mem. Nat. Assn. Home Builders, Sigma Alpha Mu. Clubs: Mid-Am., Carlton, Plaza. Introduced condominium type dwelling to U.S., 1962. Home: 1353 Westmoor Trail Winnetka IL 60093 Office: 3201 W Devon Ave Chicago IL 60693

ROSENTHAL, HOWARD KANE, printing co. exec.; b. Seattle, Jan. 12, 1933; s. Roy G. and Sadie K. R.; B.A. in Journalism, U. Wash., 1955; m. Jacquelyn Teller, Jan. 9, 1958; children—Scott Alan, Kenneth Lee. With University Printing Co., Seattle, 1957—, v.p., 1961-69, pres., chief exec. officer, 1970—, bd. dirs. Bd. dirs. Univ. Dist. Parking Assos., Wash. Printing Industries Welfare Fund, Bellevue Art Mus.; adv. bd. Factory of Visual Art. Served with U.S. Army, 1955-57. Mem. Printing Industry of Seattle (pres. 1964-65, named printer of yr. 1969-70), Wash./Alaska Printing Industry (dir.), Printing Industry Am. (nat. dir.), Creative Printers Am. (dir., v.p.), Nat. Assn. Printers and Lithographers, Univ. C. of C. (past dir.). Clubs: Supersonics Racquet, Bellevue Athletic. Home: 136 141st Pl NE Bellevue WA 98007 Office: 4133 University Way NE Seattle WA 98105

ROSENTHAL, MILTON FREDERICK, corp. exec.; b. N.Y.C., Nov. 24, 1913; s. Jacob C. and Louise (Berger) R.; B.A., City Coll. N.Y., 1932; LL.B., Columbia, 1935; m. Frieda Bojar, Feb. 28, 1943; 1 dau. Anne Janine. Admitted to N.Y. bar, 1935; research asst. N.Y. State Law Revision Commn. 1935-37; law sec. Fed. Judge William Bondy, 1937-40; asso. atty. Leve, Hecht & Hadfield, 1940-42; sec., treas. Hugo Stinnes Corp., 1946-48, exec. v.p., treas., 1948-49, pres., dir., 1949-64; pres., dir. Minerals and Chems. Philipp Corp., N.Y.C., 1964-67; pres., dir., Engelhard Minerals & Chems. Corp., N.Y.C., 1967-77, chmn., 1977—, pres., 1979—; dir. European-Am. Banking Corp., European-Am. Bank & Trust Co., Schering-Plough Corp., Ferro Corp., Midlantic Banks Inc. Bd. dirs. U.S.-USSR Trade and Econ. Council, Nat. Council U.S.-China Trade; bd. dirs., chmn. Am. sect. Romanian-U.S. Econ. Council. Bd. dirs. United Cerebral Palsy Research and Ednl. Found., Inc., Mt. Sinai Med. Center; trustee Mt. Sinai Hosp. Served to 1st lt., judge adv. gen. dept. U.S. Army, 1942-45. Mem. Assn. Bar City N.Y., Chgo. Bar Assn., Columbia Law Sch. Alumni Assn., Judge Adv. Assn., Fgn. Policy Assn. (dir.), Phi Beta Kappa. Home: Woodlands Rd Harrison NY 10528 Office: 1221 Ave of Americas New York NY 10020

ROSENZWEIG, STAN, telecommunications exec.; b. Bklyn., Jan. 25, 1942; s. William and Esther (Carp) R.; B.A., Bklyn. Coll., 1968; m. Susan Freimer, July 16, 1967. Communications cons. N.Y. Telephone Co., N.Y.C., 1967-72; communications analyst Tel-Plan, Inc., N.Y.C., 1972-73; founder, pres. Nat. Telephone Planning Corp., N.Y.C., Yonkers and Rockville Centre, N.Y., 1973-78; pres. Interconnect Mgmt. Corp., 1978—; dir. Am. Teleconnect Corp., 1979—; lectr. univs. and corps. Bd. dirs. Yonkers unit Am. Cancer Soc., 1976—, crusade chmn., 1977-78, vice-chmn. pub. edn. Westchester div., 1977-78. Mem. Yonkers C. of C. (chmn. state affairs com. 1973-79), Am. Mgmt. Assn., Soc. Telecommunications Cons.'s (founder, officer, dir.), Am. Hotel and Motel Assn., N.Y. State Hotel and Motel Assn. Club: Harlem Yacht. Contbr. articles to profl. jours. Home: 156 Read Ave Crestwood NY 10707 Office: 645 S 3d Ave Mount Vernon NY 10550

ROSETT, RICHARD NATHANIEL, economist; b. Balt., Feb. 29, 1928; s. Walter and Essie (Stofberg) R.; B.A., Columbia U., 1953; M.A., Yale U., 1954, Ph.D., 1957; m. Madelon Louise George, June 24, 1951; children—Claudia Anne, Martha Victoria Rosett Lutz, Joshua George, Sarah Elizabeth, Charles Richard. Instr., Yale U., 1956-58; mem. faculty U. Rochester (N.Y.), 1958-74, chmn. dept. econs., 1966-74, prof., 1967-74; prof. preventive medicine and community health, 1969-74; prof. bus. econs., dean Grad. Sch. Bus., U. Chgo., 1974—; dir. GATX Corp., Marshall Field Co., McGraw Edison Co., Nat. Can Corp., Kemper Ins. Co., Sears Bank & Trust Co., Chgo., Gen. Instrument Corp., N.Y.C. Trustee, Tax Found., 1975—, Chgo. Coll. Osteo. Medicine, 1976—, Nat. Bur. Econ. Research, 1977—. Served with USNR, 1944-45. Mem. Am. Econ. Assn., Econometric Assn., Mont Pelerin Soc., Chgo. Assn. Commerce and Industry (dir. 1980—), Beta Gamma Sigma. Phi Beta Kappa. Clubs: Chgo., Quadrangle, Cosmos, Econ., Plaza. Editor: The Role of Health Insurance in the Health Services Sector, 1976; contbr. articles to profl. jours. Home: 5706 S Woodlawn Ave Chicago IL 60637 Office: Grad Sch Bus U Chgo Chicago IL 60637

ROSIN, MORRIS, mfg. co. exec.; b. San Antonio, Feb. 21, 1924; s. Berco and Leja (Dupchansky) R.; student Tex. A. and M. U., 1942, St. Mary's U., 1941-42, 45-47; m. Ethel Rosenberg, Dec. 15, 1965; children—Susan Rosin Gachman, Charles, Lindsay. Sec.-treas. Bimbi Mfg. Co., 1949-67; pres. Bimbi Shoe Co. div. Athlone Industries, San Antonio, 1970-72; v.p. Athlone Industires, Parsippany, N.J., 1967-72; pres. Adro Pro, San Antonio, 1966-74, Yoakum Bend Corp., San Antonio, 1968—; sec.-treas. R & R Corp., San Antonio, 1970-72. Served with USAAF, 1942-45. Mason (32 deg., Shriner). Home: 6325 B Bandera Dallas TX 75225 Office: POB 12625 Dallas TX 75225

ROSS, ADRIAN E., diamond drilling co. exec.; b. Clintonville, N.Y., Mar. 6, 1912; s. James A. and Bertha (Beardsley) R.; B.S. in Elec. Engring., Mass. Inst. Tech., 1934, M.S. in Elec. Engring., 1935; m. Ruth T. Hill, Mar. 2, 1934; children—James A., Daniel R. Materials engr. USN, 1935-37; devel. engr. Electrolux Corp., 1937-41; chief engr. and asst. to pres. Sprague & Henwood, Inc., Scranton, Pa., 1946-53, dir., 1951—, pres., 1953-74, chmn. bd., 1963—; pres., dir. Sprague & Henwood de Venezuela; dir. Hands Eng. Ltd., Scranton Lackawanna Indsl. Bldg. Co., N.E. Bank of Pa., Wesel Corp., profl. engrs. Past chmn. bd., now trustee Keystone Jr. Coll.; pres., dir. James A. Ross Found., Sprague & Henwood Found.; chmn. bd. trustees Johnson Sch. Tech. Served from lt. to lt. col. Air Communication. USAAF, 1941-46. Profl. engr., Pa. Mem. Diamond Core Drill Mfrs. Assn. (past pres.), Am. Inst. Mining Engrs., Am. Soc. C.E., Soc. Profl Engrs., U.S. Nat. Council Soil Mechanics, Indsl. Diamond Assn. Am. (past pres.), C. of C. Presbyn. Clubs: Mining (N.Y.C.); Scranton, Mass. Institute Technology (Scranton, Pa.). Contbr. articles to Mining Congress Jour., Mining Engring., Engring. and Mining Jour., Diamond Drill Handbook. Home: 5 Overlook Rd Clarks Green PA 18411 Office: 221 West Olive St Scranton PA 18506

ROSS, BETTY GRACE, med. distbg. co. exec.; b. N.Y.C., July 14, 1931; d. Philip and Nancy Anna (Meredith) Boccella; R.N., Presbyn. Hosp., 1952; student Ariz. State U., 1960-62; m. Robert W. Ross, Mar. 1, 1968 (div. July 1976). Sr. operating rm. nurse Roosevelt Hosp., N.Y.C., 1953-58, pvt. surg. nurse, neurosurgery group, 1958-59, orthopedic surgery group, 1960-64; mem. sales staff Zimmer U.S.A., Phoenix, Ariz., 1964-71, owner, distbr. Zimmer Ross Assos., Phoenix, 1971—, Zimmer-Ross Ltd., 1978—; instr. operating room nursing Englewood (N.J.) Hosp., 1960. Mem. Assn. Operating Room Nurses Phoenix (charter mem.), Maricopa Mental Health Assn., Bloomfield Coll. Alumni Assn. Republican. Bd. dirs., chmn. finance com. Gloria Dei Luth. Ch., Paradise Valley, Ariz. Club: Century. Home: 5713 Cattletrack St N Scottsdale AZ 95253 Office: 1232 Missouri St E Phoenix AZ 95014

ROSS, BETTY JEAN, jewelry co. exec.; b. Kansas City, Mo., Aug. 6, 1928; d. George W. and Ida Terry; student Phillips U., 1946-47, LaSalle Extension U., 1954-55, U. N. Mex., 1970-71; m. Bob L. Ross, Feb. 19, 1950; children—Lee Elliot, Elizabeth Jean, Eric William, Eden Amanda. Prodn. and control staff Black Sivalls & Bryson Co., 1946-50; purchasing agt., credit mgr. Maisel Co., Albuquerque, 1956—; credit mgr. Sun Bell Corp., Albuquerque, 1972—. Mem. Am. Mgmt. Assn., Nat. Assn. Credit Mgmt., D & B Credit Roundtable. Republican. Methodist. Home: 1501 Betts St NE Albuquerque NM 87112 Office: 7500 Bluewater Rd Albuquerque NM 87104

ROSS, COLEMAN DEVANE, accountant; b. Greensboro, N.C., Mar. 18, 1943; s. Guy Matthews and Nancy McConnell (Coleman) R.; B.S. in Bus. Adminstrn., U. N.C., 1965; m. Carol Louise Morde, Aug. 26, 1965; children—Coleman, Jonathan, Andrew. With Price Waterhouse & Co., various locations, 1965—, partner, Hartford, Conn., 1977—. Mem. exec. bd., treas. Long Rivers Council, Boy Scouts Am., 1978—; bd. dirs., treas. Family Service Soc. Greater Hartford, 1977-80. Fellow Life Mgmt. Inst.; mem. Am. Inst. C.P.A.'s (mem. reinsurance auditing and acctg. task force 1979—), N.C. Assn.

C.P.A.'s, Conn. Soc. C.P.A.'s, Am. Soc. CLU's. Clubs: Hartford, Hopmeadow Country. Home: 11 Neal Dr Simsbury CT 06070 Office: One Financial Plaza Hartford CT 06103

ROSS, DONALD KEITH, ins. co. exec.; b. Rochester, N.Y., July 1, 1925; s. Alexander L.and Althea G. (Granger) R.; B.E., Yale, 1946; M.B.A., Harvard, 1948; m. Mary F. Fyffe, June 4, 1949; children—Catherine (Mrs. Charles P. Lesher), Susan (Mrs. William Gardner Morris, Jr.), Donald Keith, Deborah Anne. With N.Y. Life Ins. Co., N.Y.C., 1948—, exec. v.p. 1974-80, pres., 1980—; dir. Munich Mgmt. Corp., Munich Am. Reins. Co., Consol. Edison Co. N.Y.; pres. N.Y. Life Fund, Inc. Trustee, Colonial Williamsburg (Va.) Found. Served to ensign USNR. Club: Links. Office: NY Life Ins Co 51 Madison Ave New York NY 10010*

ROSS, ERNEST BRUCE, investment co. exec.; b. Bklyn., Aug. 15, 1942; s. William Henne and Jeanne (Amsterdam) R.; B.S., Pa. State U., 1964; M.B.A., N.Y. U., 1967; m. Tonia Carlene Padova, Oct. 8, 1975; 1 dau., Kristen Jeanne. With Irving Trust Co., N.Y.C., 1969-71; with W.E. Hutton & Co., N.Y.C., 1971-74; v.p. Relsor Corp., White Plains, N.Y., 1974—, also dir. Served with USAF, 1967-69. Mem. Am. Mgmt. Assn. Clubs: Jockey (Miami); Ocean Reef, Sheldrake Yacht. Office: 327 Ridgeway White Plains NY 10605

ROSS, HAROLD LEROY, JR., advt. research co. exec.; b. Trenton, N.J., July 5, 1934; s. Harold Leroy and Lucy Fortch (Zeller) R.; B.S., Rutgers U., 1955; m. Robina Margaret Mould, July 3, 1964; children—Peter Stuart, Brian Alexander, Jennifer Karen. With Gallup & Robinson, 1955-72, v.p., dir., 1965-72; chmn. bd. dirs. Mapes and Ross, Inc., Princeton, N.J., 1972—; dir. Montgomery Nat. Bank; condr. profl. seminars in field, U.S. and Europe. Served with AUS, 1957-59. Mem. Am. Mktg. Assn. Author studies on advt. effectiveness; created syndicated TV and mag. test systems. Home: 3 Cherrybrook Dr Princeton NJ 08540 Office: 1101 State Rd Princeton NJ 08540

ROSS, J(AMES) ROBERT, oil co. exec.; b. Mexia, Tex., June 9, 1924; s. Dudley Warren and Betty (McGilvary) R.; B.B.A. cum laude, So. Meth. U.; m. Betty Jane Fischer, Sept. 11, 1953. With Magnolia Petroleum Co., Dallas, 1941-59, mgr. controllers dept., 1955-59; mgr. controllers dept. Socony Mobil Oil Co., N.Y.C., 1959-60; asst. controller Mobil Chem. Co., N.Y.C., 1960-68; sr. cons. Mobil Oil Corp., N.Y.C., 1968-72, sr. con. fed. reporting Mobil Corp., N.Y.C., 1972—. C.P.A., Tex. Mem. Am. Petroleum Inst., Am. Inst. C.P.A.'s, Tex. Soc. C.P.A.'s, Nat. Accts. Assn., Bus. Adv. Council Fed. Reporting, Am. Mgmt. Assn., Beta Gamma Sigma. Republican. Presbyterian. Clubs: Masons, K.T. Home: Salem Straits Darien CT 06820 Office: 150 E 42d St New York NY 10017

ROSS, JESSE, med. equipment co. exec., inventor; b. Bklyn., Apr. 18, 1921; s. Hyman and Anna (Zeiss) R.; student bus. adminstrn. Butler U., 1940, mech. engring., N.Y. U., 1941, aero. engring., Mass. State Coll., 1943, indsl. mgmt., Coll. City N.Y., 1950; m. Gladys Glasberg, Jan. 26, 1943; children—David, Janet, Daniel. Founder, pres., chmn. bd. Ross Indsl. Service, indsl. mgmt. cons., 1946-57; founder, pres., chmn. bd. Diapulse Corp. of Am., Great Neck, N.Y., 1957—; lectr. on biophys. effects of electromagnetic energy. Served with USAF, 1942-45. Mem. A.A.A.S., Assn. Advancement Med. Instrumentation, N.Y. Acad. Sci. Mason. Contbr. articles to profl. jours. Office: 475 Northern Blvd Great Neck NY 11021

ROSS, KATHLEEN LOUISE, banker; b. Downey, Calif., Oct. 12, 1948; d. Earl Kenneth and Josephine Barbara R.; B.A., Calif. State U., Long Beach, 1969; M.B.A., Pepperdine U., 1980. Credit officer Union Bank, Los Angeles, 1971-75; comml. loan officer Calif. Can. Bank, San Francisco, 1975-77, asst. v.p., regional credit supr., 1977-80; v.p. loans Western Women's Bank, San Francisco, 1977; asst. v.p. corr. banking United Calif. Bank, San Francisco, 1980—; lectr. Am. Inst. Banking, U. Calif. Extension, Golden Gate U. Commr., City of Mountain View (Calif.); bd. dirs. Bay Area Urban League. Mem. Profl. Women's Alliance, Calif. Bankers Assn. Contbr. articles to mags. and newspapers; TV commentator on consumer issues. Office: 405 Montgomery St San Francisco CA 94105

ROSS, KENNETH MALCOLM, JR., banker; b. East Orange, N.J., Apr. 26, 1921; s. Kenneth Malcolm and Anna Helena (Millering) R.; B.A., Rutgers U., 1942; M.B.A, Harvard, 1952; m. Yvonne Violet Pelletier, Feb. 23, 1946; children—Kenneth Malcolm III, Carolyn, Mitchell, Scott, Laurie. Commd. ensign USN, 1943, advanced through grades to lt. comdr., 1952; ret., 1964; economist 1st Nat. Bank Ariz., Phoenix, 1964—, v.p., 1974—; pres. EPI-HAB Inc., 1972-73; faculty asso. Ariz. State U., 1974-77. Mem. Phoenix Housing Commn., 1972-76, Ariz. Treasurers Adv. Com., 1972-74, Ariz. Econ. Estimates Commn., 1978—; mem. adv. com. Joint Legis. Budget Com., 1971—. Mem. Ariz. Acad., Ariz. Econ. Round Table (pres. 1973), Nat. Assn. Bus. Economists, Ariz. Harvard Bus. Sch. Club (chmn. 1973). Republican. Roman Catholic. Club: Arizona. Home: 1145 Concorda Dr Tempe AZ 85282 Office: Box 20551 Phoenix AZ 85036

ROSS, LORRAINE WILCOX (MRS. MALCOLM ALEXANDER ROSS), publicist; b. nr. Watford City, N.D., July 9, 1919; d. Eugene Howard and Inga Gunvalda (Jaeger) Wilcox; grad. Seattle Secretarial Sch., 1939; m. Earl Marion Meyer, Oct. 22, 1939 (div. Mar. 1951); children—Kathleen Adele, Richard Lee, Kristy Ilona; m. Malcolm Alexander Ross, Mar 12, 1951 (dec. 1974); 1 son, Malcolm Alexander. Sec., bookkeeper Rayonier, Inc., Port Angeles, Wash., 1951-54; saleswoman, display advt. Port Angeles Evening News, 1957-59; editor Clallam County Shopping News, Port Angeles, 1961; owner Publicity by Lorraine, Port Angeles, 1960—; pub. Port Angeles This Week, tourist guide, 1960—; owner Lorraine Ross, Realtor, 1968—; mem. area adv. bd. Wash. Dept. Commerce, 1977—. Organizing publicist Wash. Timber Utilization Assn., 1960; publicity coordinator Port Angeles Centennial, 1962. Councilman City Port Angeles, 1969-77, chmn. Greater Port Angeles Community Devel. Study, 1970; chmn. Clallam County Govtl. Council, 1976-77; Republican presdl. elector, 1964; fin. chmn. Clallam County Rep. Central Com., 1977—. Mem. Nat. Assn. Real Estate Bds. (treas. N. Olympic chpt. women's council 1964-67, v.p. 1968—), Port Angeles Bd. Realtors (sec. 1969—), D.A.R. Episcopalian. Author: (with John McCallum) Port Angeles, U.S.A., 1961. Home and Office: 418 E Front St Port Angeles WA 98362

ROSS, MUNRO SACKS, fin. exec.; b. Hackensack, N.J., Apr. 10, 1939; s. Selig J. and Sylvia G. (Sacks) R.; B.S., Boston U., 1960; M.B.A., N.Y. U., 1963; m. Cecile Schoenblum, June 12, 1960; children—Steven, Laura. Fin. analyst Air Reduction Inc., Indsl. Gases div., N.Y.C., 1965-68; fin. mgr. Curtiss-Wright Corp., Design & Build Group, Caldwell, N.J., 1968-70; controller Tamy Inc., Fairfield, N.J., 1970-75; corporate controller Meadox Medicals, Inc., Oakland, N.J., 1975-79; v.p. fin. Strauss Internat. Industries, Inc., N.Y.C., 1980—; adj. prof. bus. adminstrn. Fairleigh Dickinson U., Madison, N.J., 1965-76; lectr. in field. Treas., Temple Beth Tikvah, Wayne, 1977-79. Recipient citation U.S. Dept. Treasury. Mem. Am. Mgmt. Assn., Nat. Assn. Accts., Fin. Execs. Inst., Alpha Epsilon Pi (life). Jewish. K.P. Home: 78 Tall Oaks Dr Wayne NJ 07470

ROSS, MYRON DONALD, cons.; b. Chgo., Sept. 30, 1909; s. Michael J. and Bertha (Krutch) R.; B.S., Northwestern U., 1934; m. Marie V. Manning, June 13, 1935; children—Donald R., Darlene M. With Jewel Cos., Inc., Melrose Park, Ill., 1932-70, as mgr. inventory control, cost accounting depts., mgr. cash, payroll dept., store personnel mgr., office mgr., 1932-45, mgr. cash operating div., 1945-54, mgr. systems div., 1954-63, mgr. electronic data processing div., 1963-66, asst. to controller, 1966-68, asst. to exec. v.p., 1968-70; cons. office adminstrn., 1970—. Recipient Merit Award key Office Mgmt. Assn. Chgo., 1950, Leadership plaque Nat. Office Mgmt. Assn., 1951. Mem. Chgo. Office Mgmt. Assn. (pres. 1949-50), Adminstrv. Mgmt. Soc., Bus. Electronics Round Table (pres. 1964-65). Club: Executives (Chgo.). Home: 10543 Dorchester Rd Westchester IL 60153

ROSS, ROBERT EDWARD, businessman; b. Pratt, Kans., May 3, 1926; s. Amil John and Nellie Ruth (Dunn) R.; B.A., Colo. U., 1950; m. Colleen Runyan, Oct. 12, 1952; children—Kenton Lee, Robyn Scott. Owner, pres. Ross Heating and Plumbing, Dodge City, Kans., until 1977; owner, pres. Rossonian Investments Co., Dodge City, 1977—. Bd. dirs. Dodge City Hosp.; chmn. Dodge City Regional Planning Comm., 1965-75. Served with USN, 1944-46. Mem. Beta Theta Pi. Address: 2011 Hi St Dodge City KS 67801

ROSS, ROBERT HARTSEL, concrete equipment co. exec.; b. Gorman, Tex., Aug. 30, 1920; s. Reuben B. and Madena E. Ross; student Tarleton State Coll., Stephenville, Tex., 1941; B.G.S., Howard Payne U.; m. Joy McAuley, Feb. 14, 1975; children—Bruce M., DiAnn Ross Wristen, Vicki L. Mng. partner Ross & Sons Constrn. Co., Brownwood, Tex., 1946-67; founder, pres., chief exec. officer Ross Co., Brownwood, 1956—; pres. Comml. Janitorial Supplies, Inc., Brownwood; chmn. bd. Century Machinery Co., Inc., Phoenix; chmn. bd., dir. Citizens Nat. Bank Brownwood; adv. dir. Dublin (Tex.) Nat. Bank; dir. Farmers & Mchts. Bank of DeLeon (Tex.). Mem. Brownwood Pub. Sch. Bd., 1952-56; trustee Howard Payne U., Brownwood, 1958—; mem. adv. commn. Tex. Rangers, 1972—. Served to lt. col. USAAF, 1941-46. Named SBA Small Businessman of Year Tex., 1973, Outstanding Soil Conservationist Brown County, 1970; life mem. Tex. Rangers Hall of Fame, 1976; certified law enforcement officer Tex. Mem. Am. Concrete Paving Assn. (dir. 1972—), Nat. Ready Mix Concrete Assn. (dir. 1972—), Concrete Plant Mfrs. Bur. (chmn. 1970-72), Nat. Asso. Equipment Distbrs. Assn. (nat. industry round table com. 1974—), Tex. Ready Mixed Concrete Assn., W. Tex. Fair Assn. (v.p. Abilene 1971-73), Tex. Aggregates and Concrete Assn. (chmn. mfrs. and tech. div.), Constrn. Industry Mfrs. Assn. (dir. 1979—). Baptist. Clubs: Rotary (pres. 1980-81), Masons (32 deg.), Shriners. Home: Route 1 PO Box 265R Lake Brownwood TX 76801 Office: PO Box 70 209 Early Blvd Brownwood TX 76801

ROSS, ROBERTA MAYE, office mgmt. services co. exec.; b. Santa Paula, Calif., Jan. 9, 1928; d. Theodore Arthur and Minnie Thelma Stangland; student Ventura Jr. Coll., 1946, LaVern U., 1971; m. John Paul Ross, June 20, 1959; children—Theodore David, Victoria. Office mgr. S. Port Engring. Co., Los Angeles, 1949-57; controller Trent Meredith, Inc., Oxnard, Calif., 1957-60, Framing Contractors Ltd., Oxnard, 1957-60; owner, operator Roberta Ross Adminstrv. Assts., Oxnard, 1960—; sec., treas. Oxel, Inc., Oxnard, Victoria Land & Co., Inc., Oxnard. Treas. Oxnard-Port Hueneme Youth Employment Service, 1973-77, pres., 1977-78, 2d v.p., 1978—. Recipient Oxnard Bus. and Profl. Women's Community Service and Outstanding Achievement award, 1976. Mem. Nat. Sec. Assn. (named Boss of Yr., Anacapa chpt. 1980), Am. Soc. Women Accountants. Club: Altrusa (Oxnard). Home: 3272 Milligan Dr Camarillo CA 93010 Office: 740 Richmond Ave Oxnard CA 93030

ROSS, RODERIC HENRY, ins. exec.; b. Jamestown, N.Y., July 14, 1930; s. Edwin A. and Mary Elizabeth (Dornberger) R.; A.B., Hobart Coll., Geneva, N.Y., 1952; LL.D. (hon.), Hobart Coll., 1979; m. Patricia Johnson, Aug. 6, 1955; children—Timothy, Amy, Jane, Christopher. With Phila. Life Ins. Co., 1954—, beginning as mem. public relations dept., successively with group dept., field rep., exec. asst. to chmn., 1970-72, sr. v.p. mktg., 1972-73, pres., dir., 1973—; dir. Phila. Life Asset Mgmt. Co., Provident Nat. Bank, Provident Nat. Corp., Hunt Mfg. Co., Million Dollar Round Table Found., Des Plains, Ill., Ins. Fedn. Pa., Inc. (chmn. 1979-80). Former vestryman St. David's Episcopal Ch., Radnor, Pa.; former dir. Upper Main Line YMCA and Community Center, Berwyn, Pa.; dir. Old Phila. Devel. Corp., Better Break '80; vice chmn. bd. trustees Hobert and William Smith Colls., Geneva, Pa. Recipient ins. sales awards; C.L.U. Mem. Nat. Assn. Life Underwriters, Phila. Assn. Life Underwriters, Am. Soc. C.L.U.'s, Million Dollar Round Table (life). Clubs: Union League, Racquet, Orpheus (Phila.); St. David's (Pa.) Golf; Pine Valley Golf (Clementon, N.J.). Office: 111 N Broad St Philadelphia PA 19107

ROSS, STEVEN J., corp. exec.; b. N.Y.C., 1927; B.A., Paul Smith Coll., 1948. Pres., dir. Kinney Services, Inc. (name changed to Warner Communications Inc.), 1961-72, chmn. bd., chief exec. officer, from 1972, now pres., chief exec. officer. Bd. dirs. Lenox Hill Hosp., Inst. Sports Medicine and Athletic Trauma, N.Y. Conv. and Visitors Bur., N.Y.C. Conv. and Exhbn. Center, Com. for Better N.Y.; mem. steering com. N.Y. Urban Coalition. Served with USNR, World War II. Mem. Young Presidents Club. Office: 75 Rockefeller Plaza New York NY 10019*

ROSS, STEVEN SANDER, writer, editor; b. Boston, May 29, 1946; s. Eli Woodrow and Lillian Faye (Arrick) R.; B.S. in Physics, Rensselaer Poly. Inst., 1969; M.S. in Journalism, Columbia U., 1970; m. Nancy Lawrence Bush, June 23, 1970; children—Marion Joyce, Heather Rebecca, Leah Elizabeth. Editor, McGraw-Hill's Air and Water News, 1970-72; asso. editor McGraw-Hill Chem. Engring., 1972; editor New Eng. Mag., MBA Communications, Inc., N.Y.C., 1972-77; editorial dir., 1977-79; mng. editor Boardroom Reports, 1979-80; dir. spl. studies Environ. Info. Center, N.Y.C., 1973—, also editor new product devel. Warren, Gorham & Lamont, N.Y.C., 1980-81; editor-in-chief Direct mag., 1981—; adj. faculty Columbia U., 1974—; mgmt. cons.; dir. Armstrong Found.; frequent lectr. to mgmt.; condr. seminars Am. Mgmt. Assn. Mem. Leonia (N.J.) Environ. Commn., 1976—, Leonia Planning Bd., 1979—; bd. dirs. League Conservation Legislation, N.J., 1977—; v.p. Congregation Adas Emuno, Leonia, 1974—; mem. Citizens for Better Transit, 1977—; chmn. Leonia Master Plan Rev. Com., 1980—. Recipient cert. of appreciation EPA, 1979; named Citizen of Year, N.Y. State Soc. Profl. Engrs., 1978; recipient chmn.'s award pvt. practice div. Nat. Soc. Profl. Engrs., 1975; edited 1st prize articles U. Mo. Bus. Press Competition, 1976, 78. Fellow Am. Inst. Chemists; mem. ASTM, AAAS, Am. Soc. Quality Control, Sigma Delta Chi, Pi Delta Epsilon. Democrat. Editor: (with Fred Price and Robert Davidson) McGraw-Hill's 1972 Report on Business and the Environment, 1972; Land Use Planning Abstracts 1970-1973, 1973; Land Use Planning Abstracts 1974-1975, 1975; Toxic Substances Sourcebook, 1978; Toxic Substances Sourcebook II, 1980; author: Trends in Pollution Control, 1973; Environment Regulation Handbook, 1973; (with John Kolb) Product Safety and Liability: A Desk Reference, 1980; contbr. articles to newspapers, mags. and jours. Home: 120 Irving St PO Box L Leonia NJ 07605

ROSS, STUART TENNENT, surgeon; b. East Hampton, N.Y., Jan. 16, 1907; s. Howard Victor and Grace (Conover) R.; A.B., Columbia Coll., 1927, M.D., 1930; m. Jean Goodman, June 29, 1933; 1 dau., Jane. Intern Meth. Hosp., Bklyn., 1930-31, resident, 1931-32; resident United Hosp., Port Chester, N.Y., 1932-33; individual practice medicine, specializing in colon and rectal surgery, Garden City, N.Y., 1933—; mem. staff Massau Hosp., Mineola, N.Y.; lectr. Polyclinic Med. Sch. and Hosp., N.Y.C., 1942-48; asso. prof. clin. surgery SUNY, Stony Brook, 1979. Mem. Adv. Bd. Med. Specialties, 1951-68; bd. dirs. Nassau div. Am. Cancer Soc., 1960-63; pres. Am. Bd. Colon and Rectal Surgery, 1965. Served to lt. col. U.S. Army, 1943-45. Decorated Legion of Merit; diplomate Am. Bd. Colon and Rectal Surgery, Pan-Pacific Surg. Assn. Fellow Am. Proctologic Soc. (pres. 1955, gold key 1956), N.Y. Soc. Colon and Rectal Surgeons, Pa. Soc. Colon and Rectal Surgery (hon.), N.J., Mex. proctologic socs. (hon.), A.C.S., Internat. Coll. Surgeons, Nassau Surg. Soc. (pres., gold medallion 1960), AMA (ho. of dels. 1957-63); mem. Argentinian (hon.), Brazilian (corr.) proctologic socs., Royal Soc. Medicine, World Med. Assn., Mensa, Pan-Am. Med. Assn., Internat. Soc. Univ. Colon. and Rectal Surgery. Author: Synopsis of Anorectal Diseases, 1959; Proctology, 1954; (with H.E. Bacon) Atlas-Surgery of Anus, Rectum and Colon, 1954. Contbr. articles to med. publs. Office: 520 Franklin Ave Garden City NY 11530

ROSS, WILBUR LOUIS, JR., investment banker; b. Weehawken, N.J., Nov. 28, 1937; s. Wilbur Louis and Agnes Hope (O'Neill) R.; A.B., Yale U., 1959; M.B.A. with distinction, Harvard U., 1961; m. Judith Nodine, 1969; children—Jessica, Amanda. Asso., Wood, Struthers & Winthrop, N.Y.C., 1963-64; v.p. de Vegh Internat. Corp., N.Y.C., 1963-64; gen. partner Faulkner, Dawkins & Sullivan, N.Y.C., 1964—, pres., dir., 1971—; dir. exec. com. Peabody Internat. Corp., Inc., Texstar Corp.; dir. Aileen, Inc., Armada Corp., Land Resources Corp., Mid-Central Properties, Ltd., Hoskins Mfg. Co., Ryan Fin. Services, Inc., New Ct. Securities Corp., Sheldon Petroleum Corp., Investors Ins. Holding Co., New Court Leasing, Inc., Geo Internat. Corp., Govt. Services Savs. & Loan, Inc. Mem. Joint Legis. Commn. on Energy Policy for State N.Y. Treas. N.Y. State Democratic Com.; gov., mem. exec. com. Bklyn. Mus.; trustee Bklyn. Inst. Arts and Scis.; bd. govs. Yale U. Art Gallery. Served as 1st lt. AUS, 1961-63. Chartered financial analyst. Author: (with others) Teaching Machines, 1962; (with others) Applied Programed Instruction, 1962. Home: 1 W 72d St New York NY 10023 Office: 1 Rockefeller Plaza York NY 10020

ROSS, WILLIAM DANIEL, chemist; b. Elmira, N.Y., Nov. 22, 1917; s. Walter P. and Mary (Daly) R.; B.A., Columbia, 1938; B.S., Columbia Engring. Sch., 1939; m. Sophie E. Gebert, 1961; 1 dau., Celia Mary. With pigments dept. E. I. du Pont de Nemours & Co., Inc., Edge Moor, Del., 1939—, research asso., 1962-68, research fellow, 1968—. Mem. A.A.A.S., Am. Chem. Soc., Am. Inst. Chem. Engrs., N.Y. Acad. Scis., Phila. Soc. for Paint Tech., Optical Soc. Am. Patentee in calcination. Home: 36 Ridgewood Circle Ridgewood Wilmington DE 19809 Office: Du Pont Co Pigments Dept Exptl Sta Wilmington DE 19898

ROSSI, ANTHONY JOHN, JR., transmission products mfg. co. exec.; b. Chgo., June 2, 1934; s. Anthony John and Angelina Maria (Rosselli) R.; student public schs., Inglewood, Calif.; m. Elizabeth M. Knoester, Sept. 27, 1969; children—Anthony John III, Angelina M., Michelle L., Michael S., Elizabeth A. With Rossi Industries, Pomona, Calif., 1955-80, Upland, Calif., 1980—, owner, operator, 1958—; cons. in field. Served with Paratroopers, U.S. Army, 1950-55. Named Marine Mfr. of Yr., Vapor Trails Mag., 1975, recipient Marine Engring. and Design of Yr. award 1976. Mem. Ind. Garage Owners Am., Marine Assn. Republican. Roman Catholic. Designer Sterndrive transmission. Office: 1693 W Arrow Hwy B-2 Upland CA 91786

ROSSI, ROBERT JOHN, newspaper mgmt. cons.; b. Pitts., Jan. 5, 1928; s. John Baptist and Carmella Marie (Pastore) R.; B.A., Denison U., 1950; postgrad. 1963; m. Mary Kathryn Rust, June 30, 1951; children—Shannon Elizabeth, Claudia Irene. Advt. dir., bus. mgr. Willoughby (Ohio) News-Herald, 1953-60; advt. dir. Elgin (Ill.) Courier-News, 1960-64; editor and pub. New Albany (Ind.) Tribune and Sunday Ledger, 1964-71; mgmt. cons. Thomson Newspapers, Inc., Chgo., 1971, gen. mgr. So. div., Tampa, Fla., 1972-73; v.p., chief ops. officer Park Newspapers, Inc., Ithaca, N.Y., 1974-79, also dir.; dir. No. N.Y. Pub. Co., Manassas Journal, Warner Robins Daily Sun, Plymouth (Ind.) Pilot-News, Norwich (N.Y.) Evening Sun, Bremen Enquirer, Nappanee Advance-News, Lockport Union Sun Jour., Brooksville Sun Jour., Nebr. City News-Press. Bd. dirs. Ky. Opera Assn., Ky.-Ind. Comprehensive Health Planning Council. Served with U.S. Army, 1946. Mem. Am., So. newspaper pubs. assns. Club: Filson. Republican. Methodist. Home: Turnip Creek Farm Rural Route 1 Box 227-B Brookneal VA 24528 Office: Terrace Hill POB 550 Ithaca NY 14850

ROSSMANN, JOHN FRANCIS, transp. co. exec., author; b. St. Louis, Sept. 27, 1942; s. John Wilford and Bernice Imelda (Graf) R.; B.S., St. Louis U., 1964; M.B.A., Pepperdine U., 1978; m. Lois Gayle Giles, Oct. 26, 1968; children—Erik, Kristin. Dir. employee communications Fluor Corp., Los Angeles, 1970-71; mgr. corporate communications Times Mirror Co., Los Angeles, 1971-74; v.p. Hester Communications, Santa Ana, Calif., 1974-78; pres. Motorized Vehicle div. Sachs Motors U.S.A., Westlake, Ohio, 1978—. Served with Army N.G., 1965-67. Mem. Moped Assn. Am. (dir. 1979-80), Sales and Mktg. Execs. of Greater Cleve. Presbyterian. Author: Mind Masters, 1974; Shamballah, 1975; The Door, 1975; Amazons, 1976; Recycled Souls, 1977. Home: 32692 Redwood St Avon Lake OH 44012 Office: 909 Crocker Rd Westlake OH 44145

ROSSOW, ALFRED WALTER, JR., food co. exec.; b. Buffalo, Mar. 24, 1933; s. Alfred Walter and Loretta H. (Krieger) R.; B.A., Harvard Coll., 1955, M.B.A., 1957; m. Phyllis Ruth Seaman, June 20, 1959; children—Bruce Allen, Christopher Ward. Product mgr., Gen. Foods Corp., White Plains, N.Y., 1960-67; sr. v.p. Harrell Internat, Westport, Conn., 1968-79; v.p. mktg. Aurora Products, Hempstead, N.Y., 1970; v.p. mktg./sales Pepsi-Cola Co., Purchase, N.Y., 1971-74; group v.p. United Brands Co., N.Y.C., 1975—. Trustee, Mid-Fairfield Child Guidance Center, 1973-74. Served with U.S. Army. Mem. Am. Mktg. Assn. Club: Harvard. Office: 1271 Avenue of the Americas New York NY 10020

ROSSWAY, MELVIN WEAVER, r.r. exec.; b. Belle Plaine, Iowa, Sept. 7, 1918; s. Samuel W. and Edna (Weaver) R.; diploma in certified pub. accounting, Internat. Corr. Schs., 1953; m. Marian Ruth Morehead, Oct. 31, 1946; children—Ronald Alan, Rhonda Kay, Rita Jean. Agt. helper C. & N. W. Ry., 1937-38, telegraph, sta. agt., 1938-53, traveling accountant, Chgo., 1953-56; asst. controller, auditor Lake Superior & Ishpeming R.R. Co., Marquette, Mich., 1956-58, treas., controller, 1958-61, v.p., treas., controller, 1961-73, sr. v.p., 1973-79, exec. v.p., sec., treas., 1979—; pres., dir. Lasco Devel. Corp.; dir. 1st Nat. Bank & Trust Co., Mich. Fin. Corp. Treas. Marquette Hosp. Bond Authority. Served with AUS, 1944-46; dist. staff officer USCG Aux. Mem. Tax Execs. (Wis. chpt.), Am. Legion, Marquette Range Engrs., Marquette C. of C. Republican. Lutheran. Clubs: Masons, Lions, Elks. Home: 800 W Magnetic St Marquette MI 49855 Office: 105 E Washington St Marquette MI 49855

ROST, JAMES A., business exec.; b. Red Lion, Pa., 1932; A.B., Gettysburg Coll., 1954; married. Acct., Arthur Andersen & Co., 1957-62; sr. v.p., treas., chief fin. officer, dir. ARA Services Inc., 1962-79; pres., chief exec. officer, dir. Interstate United Corp. Served to 1st lt. USAF, 1954-57. Office: 120 S Riverside Plaza Chicago IL 60606

ROSZEL, STEPHEN SAMUEL, JR., oil co. exec.; b. Middleburg, Va., Sept. 22, 1921; s. Stephen Samuel and Rosa Dulany (Hall) R.; student architecture Va. Poly. Inst., 1939-41, U. Va., 1941-42; m. Susan Katherine Hull, Mar. 5, 1949; children—Susan, Stephen, Thomas. Vice pres. Pan Air Corp., New Orleans, 1947-48, Superior Oil Co., Lafayette, La., 1949-55; gen. sales mgr. Eastman Oil Well Survey Co., Denver, 1955-58; mgr. indsl., pub. relations J. Ray McDermott & Co., Inc., New Orleans, 1959-64; officer, dir. Petroleum Exploration, Inc., 1964-67; sales mgr. Ingram Contractors Australia, 1967-68; sr. v.p. Ingram Internat., S.A., 1969-72; v.p. operations Ingram Far East Pte. Ltd., 1969-72; mgr. Ingram Contractors Indonesia, 1969-72; mgr. sales-Far East, Oceanic Contractors, Inc., McDermott S.E. Asia, 1972-73; pres. Jardine Offshore, Ltd., also Jardine (H.K.) Ltd., Singapore, 1973-77; pres. ETPM-USA, Inc., Houston, 1977—; dir. Malaco Chem. Co., Singapore, Petroleum Cons., Ltd., Hong Kong, Educoin Co., Inc., New Orleans, Plastiflex Corp., Houston. Writer, photographer, producer indsl. films, 1948—. Served in RAF, also to maj. USAAF, World War II. Decorated Allied Service medal. Mem. Quiet Birdmen, Ox-5 Soc. Episcopalian. Mason. Clubs: Corpus Christi Yacht; Univ. (Houston); Singapore Petroleum; Holiday of New Orleans (past pres.); Sugar Creek Country; RACV (Melbourne); Tanglin, American, Singapore Yacht (Singapore). Home: 1917 Country Club Dr Sugarland TX 77478 Office: 1917 Country Club Dr Sugarland TX 77418

ROSZTOCZY, FERENC ERNO, business exec.; b. Szeged, Hungary, Aug. 16, 1932; s. Ferenc Lipot and Edith Jolan (Kunzl) R.; M.S., U. Szeged, 1955; Ph.D., U. Calif. at Berkeley, 1961; m. Diane Elder, Dec. 21, 1963; children—Thomas Ferenc, Robert Anthony, Stephanie Elder. Came to U.S., 1957, naturalized, 1962. Phys. chemist Stanford Research Inst., Menlo Park, Calif., 1961-64; mem. tech. staff Bell Labs., Murray Hill, N.J., 1964-68; mgr. semicondr. materials Bell & Howell, Pasadena, Calif., 1968-69; mgr. semicondr. crystal growth and device engring. Varian Assos., Palo Alto, Calif., 1969-75; dir. Ariz. Machinery Co., Avondale, 1974—, pres., 1975—, chmn. bd., 1976—; dir. Ariz. Indsl. Machinery Co., 1975—. Cons. Siltec Corp., Menlo Park, Calif., 1971-72. Mem. Electrochem. Soc., Sigma Xi. Roman Catholic. Clubs: Rotary, Wigwam Country. Contbr. articles to profl. jours. Patentee in field. Home: PO Box 1486 Litchfield Park AZ 85340 Office: Ariz Machinery Co 11111 W McDowell Rd Avondale AZ 85323

ROTELLA, ANGELINA THERESA, banker; b. Perth Amboy, N.J., Aug. 18, 1931; d. Vincent and Rose (Sirianni) Rotella; B.A., Rutgers Newark Coll. Arts and Scis., 1952. Audit clk. First Bank and Trust Co., Perth Amboy, 1952-64, asst. auditor, 1964-65, auditor, 1965-69; asst. auditor Nat. State Bank, Perth Amboy, N.J., 1969-71; asst. v.p. Nat. State Bank, Elizabeth, N.J., 1971-79, v.p., Linden, N.J., 1979—. Mem. Rutgers Alumni Assn., Nat. Assn. Bank Women, Am. Inst. Banking. Roman Catholic (asst. treas. bldg. fund 1968-79). Home: 365 Prospect St Perth Amboy NJ 08861 Office: 401 Park Ave Linden NJ 07036

ROTH, CARL, financial exec.; b. Frydlandt, Czechoslovakia, Dec. 15, 1946; s. Samuel and Elizabeth (Ehrlich) R.; came to U.S., 1949, naturalized, 1956; B.S., Fairleigh Dickinson U., 1969; m. Geraldine Miller, 1977. Sr. accountant Price Waterhouse & Co., Newark, 1969-72, mgr. internal audit, 1972-73; dir. fin. planning Bonwit Teller, N.Y.C., 1973-74; asst. corp. controller The Duplan Corp., N.Y.C., 1974-77; group controller M. Lowenstein & Sons, Inc., N.Y.C., 1977-78; dir. internal audit Bonwit Teller, N.Y.C., 1978-80; owner, prin. Carl Roth, C.P.A., Hackensack, N.J., 1980—. Mem. Kiwanis community tax aid program, N.Y.C. C.P.A., N.J., N.Y. Mem. Am. Inst. C.P.A.'s, Inst. Internal Auditors, Nat. Assn. Accountants, N.J., N.Y. socs. C.P.A.'s. Home: 235 Prospect Ave Hackensack NJ 07601 Office: 411 Hackensack Ave Hackensack NJ 07601

ROTH, JOANNE EDITH, chem. engr.; b. Newark, Oct. 21, 1945; d. Nicholas R. and Eileen M. (Spaid) Marucci; B.S. in Chem. Engring. (N.J. State scholar 1963-67), Newark Coll. Engring., 1967; m. Robert J. Roth, Aug. 26, 1967; children—Robert Charles, Stephanie Mary. Control systems engr. Colgate Palmolive Co., Jersey City, 1967-71; cost engr. Am. Cyanamid, Wayne, N.J., 1974-76; project engr. Sandoz, Inc., East Hanover, N.J., 1976-79; sr. engr. Hoffmann La Roche, Nutley, N.J., 1979—; participant profl. meetings. Mem. town com. to study disproportionate sch. enrollments, Westfield, N.J., 1977-78. Registered profl. engr., N.J. Mem. Am. Inst. Chem. Engrs., Soc. Woman Engrs. Home: 832 Embree Crescent Westfield NJ 07090 Office: 1200 Wall St West Lyndhurst NJ 07071

ROTH, MARTIN L., metal products co. exec.; b. Newark, N.J., Jan. 25, 1918; s. Abraham and Bella (Lichter) R.; B.S., N.Y. U., 1949; m. Selma R. Rich, Sept. 12, 1954; children—Robert A., Brad R. Sales mgr. South River (N.J.) Metal Products Co., Inc., 1951-60, dir. mktg., Matawan, N.J., 1968—; distbr. sales mgr. Alpha Wire Corp., N.Y.C., 1960-61; sales rep., mktg. cons. Martin L. Roth & Assos., 1961-63; distbr. sales mgr. JFD Electronics Corp., Bklyn., 1963-68. Served with USAAF, 1942-45. Mem. Electronic Industries Assn. (mem. Medallion Club). Jewish. Office: PO Box 394 Matawan NJ 07747

ROTH, MILLARD SHYNE, venture capital co. exec.; b. Toronto, Ont., Can., Oct. 28, 1937; s. Manuel J. and Juanita (Axler) R.; B. Mgmt. Engring., Rensselaer Poly. Inst., 1959; M.S. in Indsl. Mgmt., Purdue U., 1960; m. Sonya Dolly Kaplan, Apr. 12, 1962; children—Andrew, Maxine. Asst. to gen. mgr. prodn. Electric Reduction Co. Can. Ltd., Toronto, 1960-62; corporate controller Levy Industries Ltd., Toronto, 1962-64; partner Hecker Roth & Assos., Toronto, 1964-65; pres. Corporate Growth Assistance Ltd., Toronto, 1965—; pres. Bus. Venture Co. Inc., Toronto, 1979—; dir. Leaserite Corp. Ltd., Inniskillin House Wines Inc. Bd. dirs. Conservatory Cinematographic Art, Montreal, Que., Can., Baycrest Centre for Geriatric Care, Toronto. Mem. Can. Motion Picture Distributors Assn. (mem. exec. com. 1975—), Assn. Profl. Engrs. Province Ont., Inst. Mgmt. Cons. Ont., Inst. Assn. Execs. Progressive Conservative. Club: Oakdale Golf and Country. Home: 14 Berkindale Dr Willowdale ON M2L 1Z2 Canada Office: 22 St Clair Ave E Toronto ON M4T 2S4 Canada

ROTH, RICHARD C., pet supply co. exec.; b. Bklyn., July 26, 1937; s. Carl E. and Rose M. Roth; B.B.A., Manhattan Coll., 1959; m. Barbara A. Swift, June 13, 1959; children—Steven R., Susan E., Kevin R. Account exec. Batten Barton Durstine & Osborn, 1959-62; v.p. new products Block Drug Co., Jersey City, 1962-75; sr. v.p. Metaframe Corp., Elmwood Park, N.J., 1975-77; pres., owner Brookside Products Inc., Allendale, N.J., 1977—; pres. Pet Village Inc., Stroudsburg, Pa., 1980—; lectr. N.Y. U., 1974, 75. Campaign cons. Middlesex County (N.J.) Republican Com., 1966-71, pres. Milltown (N.J.) Rep. Club, 1968-71; fund dr. chmn. Milltown Library Assn., 1973, trustee, 1974-76. Mem. Assn. Nat. Advertisers (founder/chmn. new products mktg. com. 1974-76), Nat. Acad. TV Arts and Scis. Patentee medicinal device. Office: Brookside Products Inc 53 Cottage Pl Allendale NJ 07401

ROTH, ROBERT MERLE, stock broker; b. Milw., Mar. 6, 1930; s. Stanley and Elsie (Erman) R.; B.A., Colby Coll., 1951; m. Helen Harper Palen, Apr. 16, 1955; children—Mark, Karen, Jeffrey. Vice pres. Waddell & Reed, Inc., Miami, Fla., 1955-57, Wilmington, Del., 1957-63, Hartford, Conn., 1963-66; pres. Mark Securities, Inc., West Hartford, Conn., 1966—. Mem. West Hartford Bd. Edn., 1973-77; pres. All-Sports Youth Council, West Hartford, 1979—; bd. dirs. West Hartford WMCA, 1980—. Served to lt. (j.g.) USNR, 1951-55. Mem. Internat. Assn. Financial Planners (dir.), West Hartford Taxpayers Assn. (treas. 1979—), West Hartford C. of C. Club: Conn. Traditional Jazz (dir.). Home: 96 Van Buren Ave West Hartford CT 06107 Office: 1007 Farmington Ave West Hartford CT 06107

ROTH, SYDNEY MARTIN, advt. and mass market planning specialist; b. Jersey City, June 3, 1903; s. Edward M. and Bessie (Kauffman) R.; ed. Ill. Inst. Tech. (formerly Lewis Inst.), U. Chgo.; m. Adele Cashwan, Nov. 24, 1944 (div.). Vice pres. Roth, Schenker & Bernhard, Inc. (formerly Morris Schenker Roth) advt. agy. and mass market devel., Chgo., 1935-39, pres. 1939-43; pres. Roth Brothers & Co. (successors to Roth, Schenker & Bernhard, Inc.), 1943—; a founding dir. Growth Industries Shares, Inc., producers ednl. films and video tapes; wartime cons. U.S. Dept. Agr., Food Distbn. Adminstrn. Served on bus. adv. com. Pres.'s Council Econ. Advisers. Founding pres. Community Child Guidance Centers of Chgo.; adv., founding life mem. Mingei Internat. Mus. World Folk Art. Hon. fellow Truman Library Inst. Mem. Am. Soc. Adlerian Psychology, Mental Health Assn. Chgo., Am. Mktg. Assn., Am. Inst. Graphic Arts, Fgn. Policy Assn., Nat. Planning Assn., Internat. Platform Assn., Chgo. Council on Fgn. Relations, Oreg. Soc. Individual Psychology (hon. life), Individual Psychology Assn. Chgo. (past pres.), Internat. Assn. Individual Psychology (co-chmn. film and video tape prodn. com.), Am. Crafts Council, World Crafts Council, Art Inst. Chgo. (life). Club: City of Chicago. Founder, pub. Am. edit. Internat. Jour. Individual Psychology. Home: 880 N Lake Shore Dr Chicago IL 60611 Office: 1 E Wacker Dr Chicago IL 60601

ROTH, WILLIAM GEORGE, air conditioning mfg. co. exec.; b. Lamberton, Minn., Oct. 3, 1938; s. Euclair Ford and Kathryn (Kluegel) R.; B.S. in Mech. Engring., U. Notre Dame, 1960; M.S. in Indsl. Adminstrn., Purdue U., 1961; m. Patricia E. Gibson, Aug. 27, 1960; children—William, David. With Trane Co., 1961—, v.p., gen. mgr. consumer products, 1973-77, dep. chmn., LaCrosse, Wis., 1977-78, chmn. bd., chief exec. officer, 1978—. Mem. NAM (dir.), Wis. Mfrs. and Commerce Assn. (dir.). Office: 3600 Pammel Creek Rd La Crosse WI 54601

ROTHELL, GEORGE EDWIN, banker; b. Norfolk, Nebr., Dec. 17, 1930; s. Frank Stephen and Margaret Anna (Howorth) R.; B.S. in Bus. Adminstrn., U. Nebr., 1952; m. Elaine Marie Jones; 1 dau., Leslie Elaine. Vice pres. Bank of Am., Los Angeles, 1960-72; mng. dir. Western Am. Bank (Europe) Ltd., London, 1972-77; exec. v.p. United Calif. Bank, Los Angeles, 1977-78, pres., 1978-80, pres. Western Bancorp., 1980—. Served with USMCR, 1952-56. Address: Western Bancorporation 707 Wilshire Blvd Los Angeles CA 90017

ROTHSCHILD, BERNHARD ANDREW, JR., steel co. exec.; b. DeQuincy, La., July 18, 1914; s. Bernhard A. and Esther (Glasson) R.; student Centenary Coll., 1930-32; m. Dorothy Hoskins, May 5, 1942. Field supt. erection Rothschild Boiler & Tank Works, Shreveport, La., 1935-40, v.p. mfg. and constrn., 1945-59, pres., 1959-69, pres., chmn. bd., 1965—; dir. La. Bank; pres. Leets Corp. Pres. Shreveport Indsl. Council, 1960; chmn. Salvation Army, 1969; chmn. Shreveport Boys Club, 1968-69; bd. dirs. Pub. Affairs Research Council, 1970—; trustee Gulf South Research Inst., 1973—. Served with AUS, 1941-46. Mem. Am. Welding Soc., Shreveport C. of C. (dir. 1955-62), Miss. Valley Assn. (dir. 1965-71, v.p. 1972-80), Red River Valley Assn. (dir. 1960-78). Episcopalian (sr. warden, mem. finance com. Diocese of La.). Clubs: Masons, Shriners. Home: 815 Crescent Rd Shreveport LA 71107 Office: PO Box 1663 Shreveport LA 71102

ROTHSCHILD, WILLIAM EDWARD, strategic planner; b. Bklyn., Nov. 28, 1933; s. William Henry and Florence T. (Sharpe) R.; B.S., Fordham U., 1955; postgrad. in psychology Temple U., 1962; m. Alma C. Carey, Dec. 26, 1957; children—Robert, Stephen, Karen, William. With Gen. Electric Co., Fairfield, Conn., 1955—, program mgr. exec. edn., 1965-70, program mgr. strategic planning, 1970-78, mgr. strategy planning integration, 1978-79, mgr. corp. strategy and devel., 1980—; mem. faculty Columbia Exec. Programs, Harvard Bus. Sch.; cons. to industry. Lectr., cons., mem. St. Jerome's Sch. Bd., 1970-72. Served with AUS, 1957-58. Mem. Am. Mgmt. Assn., Corporate Planning Assn., Fordham Alumni Assn. Roman Catholic. Author: The C.A.S.E. Approach—a Valuable Aid to Management Development, 1971; Putting It All Together—a Guide to Strategic Thinking, 1976; Strategic Alternatives—Selection, Development and Implementation, 1979; Competitive Analyses—The Missing Link, 1979; How to Ensure the Continued Growth of Strategic Planning, 1980. Home: 19 Thistle Rd Norwalk CT 06851 Office: 3135 Easton Turnpike Fairfield CT 06431

ROTHSTEIN, STANLEY ROBERT, mgmt. cons.; b. Jersey City, July 19, 1937; s. Sigmund David and Ruth (Weiss) R.; B.Met.E., Rensselaer Poly. Inst., 1960; M.B.A., City U. N.Y., 1962; m. Michael Krown, June 11, 1961; children—Seth Reuben, Miriam Fran. Sales and estimating engr. Arwood Corp., N.Y.C., 1960-62; dir. materials mgmt. Fairchild Semiconductor, South Portland, Maine, 1963-68; chief prodn. planning and control United Tech. Center, Sunnyvale, Calif., 1968-70; founder, pres. Thales Assos., 1970-72; mfg. mgr. Fairchild MOD, 1970-72; mgr. mgmt. cons. services mfg. and distbn. industries div. Coopers & Lybrand, 1972-74; dir. client services and applications G.A. Smith Co., Santa Clara, Calif., 1974-76; founder, mng. partner, sr. cons. PROMAS, Santa Clara, 1976-80; founder, exec. v.p. Axcess Systems Systems Corp., Sunnyvale, 1980—; adj. prof. U. Redlands; lectr. Golden Gate U., U. Phoenix, DeAnza Coll. Trustee, Sunnyvale Sch. Dist., 1977-81. Mem. Am. Prodn. and Inventory Control Soc., Am. Mgmt. Assn., World Futures Soc., Assn. Mgmt. Cons., Am. Inst. Profl. Cons., Innovation Soc. Home: 1136 Sherwood Ct Sunnyvale CA 94087 Office: 1400 Coleman Ave Santa Clara CA 95050

ROTHWELL, RONALD DUKE, publishing co. exec.; b. Phila.; B.A. in Psychology, Villanova U., 1973, M.A. in Polit. Sci., 1974. Research asst. Villanova (Pa.) U., 1973-74; tchr. Phila. Sch. Dist., 1975-77; market specialist Chilton Co., Radnor, Pa., 1977—. Adminstr. legis. liaison Charles Drew Award Com., Phila., 1980—. Recipient community service award North Central Phila. Celebration of Life Festival, 1979. Mem. Am. Mgmt. Assn., Urban League. Office: Chilton Co Chilton Way Radnor PA 19089

ROTMAN, DOUGLAS ALLEN, farm equipment co. exec.; b. Cawker City, Kans., Dec. 24, 1942; s. Antone Allen and Gladys Elizabeth (Deters) R.; B.S. in Engring. Sci., U.S. Air Force Acad., 1964; M.B.A., Harvard U., 1973; m. Nancy Lee Anderson, Apr. 3, 1971; 1 dau., Julie Margie, Planning analyst Machinery Group, FMC Corp., Chgo., 1973-74; gen. mgr. Danuser div. Hesston Corp., Claremore, Okla., 1974-75; product mgr. hydraulic cranes div. FMC Corp., Lexington, Ky., 1976-78; v.p. mktg. Kewanee (Ill.) Machinery div. Chromalloy Am. Corp., 1979—; instr. Claremore Jr. Coll., 1974-75. Served to capt. USAF, 1964-71; Vietnam. Decorated D.F.C. with oak leaf cluster, 11 Air Medals. Mem. Nat. Agrl. Mktg. Assn. Republican. Lutheran. Home: 415 E Prospect St Kewanee IL 61443 Office: 1516 Burlington Ave Kewanee IL 61443

ROTMAN, MORRIS BERNARD, pub. relations cons.; b. Chgo., June 6, 1918; s. Louis and Etta (Harris) R.; student Wright Jr. Coll., 1936-37, Northwestern U., 1937-39; m. Sylvia Sugar, Mar. 1, 1944; children—Betty Ruth, Jesse, Richard. Editor, Times Neighborhood publs., Chgo., 1938-40; asst. editor City News Bur., 1940-42; mng. editor Scott Field Broadcaster, USAAF, 1942-43; publicity dir. Community and War Fund of Met. Chgo., 1943-45; v.p. William R. Harshe Assos., Chgo., 1945-49, pres., 1949-66, chmn. bd., chief exec. officer, 1966—, named changed to Harshe-Rotman & Druck, Inc., 1962. Bd. dirs. Nat. Com. Prevention of Child Abuse, Center for Sports Medicine; chmn. solicitations pub. relations div. Community Fund Chgo., 1948-49, spl. events chmn., 1953; chmn. communications div. Jewish Fedn. Chgo., 1965, Combined Jewish Appeal, 1966; bd. dirs. Rehab. Inst.; trustee Roosevelt U. Recipient Prime Minister Israel medal, 1969. Mem. Pub. Relations Soc. Am. (past dir.), Chgo. Pres.'s Orgn. (pres. 1970-71), Chief Exec. Forum, World Bus. Council, Chgo. Press Vets. Assn., Sigma Delta Chi. Clubs: Mid-Am., Standard, Publicity, Press (Chgo.); Bryn Mawr Country; Hillcrest Country (Los Angeles); Tamarisk Country (Palm Springs); Headline. Home: 400 E Randolph St Chicago IL 60601 Office: 444 N Michigan Ave Chicago IL 60611 also 300 E 44th St New York NY 10017 also 3345 Wilshire Blvd Los Angeles CA 90010 also 27 Albemarle St London England also 1010 Wisconsin Ave NW Washington DC 20007 also 1900 W Loop S Houston TX 77027 also 727 N 1st St Saint Louis MO 63102

ROTOLO, ELIO RICHARD, banker; b. Bklyn., Jan. 2, 1924; s. Rosario and Antoinette Carbonaro; student Bklyn. Coll., 1942; B.S., Lehigh U., 1949; postgrad. Rutgers U., 1953-55, Stevens Inst., 1963-66. Mgr. indsl. engring. Dollin Corp., Irvington, N.J., 1952-60; prin. Arthur Young & Co., N.Y.C., 1960-70; dir. mfg. engring. Internat. Tel.&Tel. Corp., N.Y.C., 1970-75; v.p. Security Pacific Nat. Bank, Los Angeles, 1975—. Republican county committeeman, Union, N.J., 1955-60. Served to 1st lt. AUS, 1942-45. Fellow Am. Inst. Indsl. Engrs. (nat. pres. 1967-68), Engrs. Joint Council. Lion. Contbr. articles to profl. jours. Home: 4369 LaBarca Dr Tarzana CA 91356 Office: 333 S Hope St Los Angeles CA 90071

ROTTENBERG, RALPH, garden supplies co. exec.; b. Providence, July 31, 1939; s. Louis L. and Eleanor C. (Frisch) R.; B.S. in Econs., U. Pa., 1961; m. A. Antonette Parduski, Oct. 20, 1979; children by previous marriage—James Scott, Steven Marc, Julie Beth; stepchildren—Christine Michelle, Wayne Addison, Bradford Anthony. Ops. mgr. Darbco Inc., East Providence, R.I., 1961-71, v.p., 1971-78, pres., 1978—. Trustee, Temple Sinai, 1974—. Served with U.S. Army, 1961, N.G., 1961-68. Mem. Lawn and Garden Distbrs. Assn., N.E. Greenhouse Suppliers Assn. (v.p. 1979). Jewish. Clubs: Lions (pres. 1971), Masons. Address: 7 Wildflower Rd Barrington RI 02806

ROTTER, PAUL TALBOTT, life ins. exec.; b. Parsons, Kans., Feb. 21, 1918; s. J. and LaNora (Talbott) R.; B.S. summa cum laude, Harvard, 1937; m. Virginia Sutherlin Barksdale, July 17, 1943; children—Carolyn Sutherlin, Diane Talbott. Asst. mathematician Prudential Ins. Co. of Am., Newark, 1938-46; with Mut. Benefit Life Ins. Co., 1946—, successively asst. mathematician, asso. mathematician, mathematician, 1946-59, v.p., 1959-69, exec. v.p., 1969-78, now ret. Mem. Madison Bd. Edn., 1958-64, pres., 1959-64. Trustee, mem. budget com. United Campaign of Madison, 1951-55; mem. bd., chmn. advancement com. Robert Treat council Boy Scouts, 1959-64. Fellow Soc. Actuaries (bd. govs. 1965-68, gen. chmn. edn. and exam., com. 1963-66, chmn. adv. com. on edn. and exams. 1969-72); mem. Brit. Inst. Actuaries (asso.), Am. Acad. Actuaries (v.p., 1968-70, bd. dirs., chmn. edn. and exam. com. 1963-66, chmn. rev. and evaluation com. 1968-74), Asso. Harvard Alumni (regional dir. 1965-69), Actuaries Club N.Y. (pres. 1967-68), Harvard Alumni Assn. (v.p. 1964-66), Phi Beta Kappa Assos., Phi Beta Kappa. Clubs: Harvard of N.J. (pres. 1956-57), Harvard of N.Y., Morris County Golf. Office: 520 Broad St Newark NJ 07102

ROTUNDA, DONALD THEODORE, economist; b. Blue Island, Ill., Feb. 14, 1945; s. Nicholas and Frances (Manna) R.; B.A., Georgetown U., 1967; M.A., London Sch. Econs., 1968, Ph.D., 1972. Analyst, NASA, Washington, 1972; lectr. in econs. U. D.C., 1973; legis. asst. Ho. of Reps., Washington, 1974-76, economist budget com., 1977; mgmt. analyst Office Mgmt. and Budget, Washington, 1977—; Mem. Am. Hist. Assn. Roman Catholic. Club: Washington Print. Contbr. numerous articles to Washington Star newspaper, New Republic mag. Home: 3852 Calvert St NW Washington DC 20007 Office: Office of Mgmt and Budget New Exec Office Bldg Washington DC 20503

ROUBOS, GARY LYNN, diversified mfg. exec.; b. Denver, Nov. 7, 1936; s. Dorr and Lillian Margaret R.; B.S. in Chem. Engring. with high honors, U. Colo., 1959; M.B.A. with distinction, Harvard U., 1963; m. Terie Joan Anderson, Feb. 20, 1960; children—Lyndel, Leslie. With Boise Cascade Corp., 1963-71; exec. v.p. Dieterich Standard Corp., Boulder, Colo., 1971-75, pres., 1975-76, merged with Dover Corp., 1975, exec. v.p. Dover Corp., N.Y.C., 1975-76, pres., 1977—. Bd. dirs. Colo. U. Found.; exec. com. Strategic Planning Inst. Served to 1st lt. C.E., AUS, 1959-61. Clubs: Tokeneke (Darien, Conn.); Board Room (N.Y.C.). Office: 277 Park Ave New York NY 10172

ROUDANE, CHARLES, mfg. co. exec.; b. Los Angeles, July 16, 1927; s. Rudolph and Irene (Warner) R.; B.S., Tulane, 1950; m. Orient Fox, Aug. 20, 1948; children—Mark, Matthew. Regional mgr. Master div. Koehring Co., Chgo., 1955-57, gen. mgr., 1957-67; gen. sales mgr. Wilton Corp., Schiller Park, Ill., 1967-70; with Flexonics div. UOP Inc., Bartlett, Ill., 1970—, v.p., gen. mgr., 1973—. Served with AUS, 1945-46. Elected to Inaugural Hall of Fame, Am. Mgmt. Assn. Mem. Am. Mgmt. Assn. Marketing Council, ASME, Newcomen Soc. Office: 300 E Devon Ave Bartlett IL 60103

ROUDYBUSH, FRANKLIN, business exec.; b. Washington, Sept. 17, 1906; s. Col. R. Franklin and Frances (Mahon) R.; student Consular Acad. and U. Vienna, 1925-26; Academie Julian, Paris, Ecole Nationale des Langues Orientales Vivantes, Paris, France, 1926; U. Paris, 1926-28; U. Madrid, 1928, B.F.S., Georgetown U., 1929-30; postgrad. Harvard Bus. Sch., 1930-31; M.A., George Washington U., 1944; Ph.D., U. Strasbourg, 1953; m. Alexandra Brown. Dean, Roudybush Fgn. Service Sch., 1931-42; prof. internat. econ. relations Southeastern U., 1938-45. Dir. Pan-Am. Inst., Roudybush Fgn. Service Sch., U.S., France. Attended sessions Council of Europe, and assembly of Schuman Plan Pool for Iron and Steel. Mem. Am. Soc. Internat. Law, Delta Phi Epsilon. Clubs: Miramar Golf, Oporto, Harvard, Nat. Press, Nat. Yacht, Middletown,

Portmarmock, Fitzwilliam, and Stevens Green; Dunlaughaire Golf (Dublin); Hamilton (London); Royal Aberdeen Golf (Scotland); Harvard Business School (Paris). Author: The Present State of Western Capitalism, 1959. Editor Affairs Mag., 1938-42. Author monographs: An Analysis of the Educational Background and Experience of 828 United States Foreign Service Officers; Evaluative Criteria for Foreign Service Schools and Foreign Service Training; XX Century Diplomacy; Diplomacy and Art; The Twentieth Century; Diplomatic Language; Why the Tragic Collapse of the British Empire; The French Educational System, 1974; Techniques of Diplomacy and Negotiation, 1978; Economic Geography, 1981. Office: 15 Ave du President Wilson Paris 16 France Office: Sauveterre de Rouergue l'Aveyron France also Moledo do Minho Minho Portugal

ROULAC, STEPHEN EARL, fin. cons. firm exec.; b. San Francisco, Aug. 15, 1945; s. Phil Williams and Elizabeth May (Young) R.; B.A., Pomona Coll., 1967; M.B.A., Harvard U., 1970; J.D., Boalt Hall Sch. Law, 1976; Ph.D., Stanford U., 1978; m. Holly Anne Gibson, Nov. 18, 1978; 1 son, Arthur Young. Constrn. supt. Roulac Constrn. Co., Pasadena, Calif., 1963-66; research asst. Econs. Research Assos., Los Angeles, 1966-67; asso. economist Urbanomics Research Assos., Claremont, Calif., 1967; acquisition auditor Litton Industries, 1967-68; tax cons. Coopers and Lybrand, Los Angeles, 1968; planning cons. Owens-Corning Fiberglass Corp., Toledo, Ohio, 1969-70; pres. Questor Assos., San Francisco, 1972—; lectr. bus. adminstrn. Stanford Grad. Sch. Bus., 1971-79; lectr. bus. adminstrn. and architecture U. Calif., 1972-77; adj. prof. Hastings Coll. Law, San Francisco, 1977-78. Mem. real estate adv. com. Calif. Commr. of Corps., 1973. C.P.A. Mem. Am. Econs. Assn., Am. Fin. Assn., Am. Real Estate and Urban Econs. Assn. Clubs: Los Angeles Adventurers, Harvard (N.Y.C.). Author numerous books including: Modern Real Estate Investment, also articles. Office: 115 Sansome St San Francisco CA 94104

ROULEAU, ARMAND GERALD, indsl. engr.; b. Lewiston, Maine, Oct. 31, 1947; s. Armand Joseph and Georgette Pauline (Laurendeau) R.; B.S. in Textile Engring., U. Lowell, 1969; M.B.A. with honors, U. Maine, 1974; m. Barbara Ann Allen, Nov. 28, 1970; children—Christopher, Daniel. Jr. indsl. engr. to spl. project indsl. engr. Bates Mfg. Co., Lewiston, 1970-73, prodn. supt., 1973-74; prodn. supr. Philips Elmet div. N. Am. Philips Co., Lewiston, 1974-78; indsl. engr. B. & M. div. William Underwood Co., Portland, Maine, 1978-79; indsl. engr. Keyes Fibre Co. div. Arcata Co., Waterville, Maine, 1979—; instr. Husson Coll. Mem. Am. Inst. Indsl. Engrs. (chpt. pres.). Roman Catholic. Home: 23 Smiley Ave Winslow ME 04902 Office: Keyes Fibre Co College Ave Waterville ME 04901

ROULETTE, HAROLD CLYDE, ins. co. exec.; b. South Gate, Calif., July 12, 1928; s. Clyde Alexander and Helen Elizabeth R.; student Los Angeles State Coll., U. So. Calif., UCLA; diploma Ins. Inst. Am.; m. Shirley Adlam, May 28, 1948; children—Glenn P., Donna. With Farmers Ins. Group, 1947—, regional mgr., Austin, Tex., 1973-77; exec. v.p. Ohio State Life Ins. Co., Columbus, 1977-78, pres., 1978—, also dir.; vice-chmn. bd. Tex. Auto Assigned Risk Plan, 1973-77, Tex. Catastrophe Property Assn., 1973-77. Trustee, Griffith Found., Columbus, 1978—; chmn. bd. Southwestern Ins. Info. Inst., Inc., 1976-77; bd. dirs. Ohio Ins. Inst., 1980—. Served with USN, 1953-54. Mem. Soc. C.P.C.U.'s, Ins. Inst. Am. Republican. Methodist. Clubs: Rotary, Elks. Office: PO Box 910 Columbus OH 43216

ROUNDS, GEORGE RUSHTON, assn. exec.; b. Providence, Jan. 18, 1934; s. George I. and Irma E. (Rath) R.; B.A., Williams Coll.; m.; children—Heather Shea, George Robinson, Jon Timothy. Reporter, Stamford (Conn.) Adv., 1957-59; tech. editor Boating Industry mag., N.Y.C., 1959-68; asso. editor Skiing Trade News, N.Y.C., 1968-69; account exec. H.A. Bruno & Assos., N.Y.C., 1969-71; sec. Nat. Assn. Engine and Boat Mfrs., N.Y.C., 1971-79; dir. assn. services Nat. Marine Mfrs. Assn., Chgo., 1979—. Recipient editorial achievement award Bus. Pubs. Assn., 1967; Mem. Am. Soc. Assn. Execs. (cert). Office: Nat Marine Mfrs Assn 401 N Michigan Ave Chicago IL 60611

ROUNDY, PAUL VERE, III, internat. projects exec.; b. Long Branch, N.J., Oct. 4, 1941; s. Paul Vere and Jane Norma (Vaughan) R.; B.S., U.S. Naval Acad., 1963; M.B.A., U. New Haven, 1976; m. Patricia Ann Liebhardt, Apr. 5, 1964; children—Paul Vere IV, Jason Benedict, Nathaniel Liebhardt. Project engr. Xerox Corp., Rochester, N.Y., 1969-71; dep. program mgr. electric boat div. Gen. Dynamics, Groton, Conn., 1971-76; mktg. mgr. Pacific Architects & Engrs., Inc., Washington, 1976-80, dir. European ops., Frankfurt, Germany, 1980—. Served with USN, 1963-69. Mem. Soc. Am. Mil. Engrs. Club: Army-Navy (Washington). Home: Old South Rd Masons Island Mystic CT 06355 Office: 6-12 Hungener St 6000 Frankfurt Germany

ROUNTREE, HORACE GENE, retail trade co. exec., religious orgn. ofcl.; b. Pelican, La., Oct. 19, 1931; s. Perry and Ada M. (DeSoto) R.; B.S., S.W. Mo. State Coll., 1959; Ed.M., U. Okla., 1964; postgrad. Washington U., St. Louis, 1966, U. Ark., 1970-75; m. Carol J. Thompson, June 23, 1962; children—William Hunter, Clare Marguerite. Tchr., Johnson Jr. High Sch., Cheyenne, Wyo., 1962-63, Centennial High Sch., Pueblo, Colo., 1959-61; instr. English and reading Meramec Community Coll., St. Louis, 1965-66; counselor Hamsher High Sch., Webster Grove, Mo., 1965-66; personnel and mktg. dir. west central div. Ralston Purina Co., Rogers, Ark., 1966-71; v.p. corp. and public affairs Wal-Mart Stores, Inc., Bentonville, Ark., 1972—; cons. human behavior and communications, Bentonville, 1971—. Chmn. Pres.'s Com. on Employment Handicapped, 1967—; dist. chmn. Beaver Lake Dist. council Boy Scouts Am., 1970-72, v.p. Westark council, 1971-72; mem. Mo. Liturgical Council, Roman Catholic Archdiocese of St. Louis, 1966; bd. dirs. Ozark Guidance Center, pres., 1973—; bd. dirs. Nat. Council of Cath. Laity, pres., 1971-73; bd. dirs. Easter Seal Soc., 1968-75; chmn. Gov.'s Com. Employment of Handicapped, 1967—; del. White House Conf. on Handicapped, 1977. Recipient Distinguished Service award Jr. C. of C., 1969, Nat. citation Muscular Dystrophy Assn. Am., 1959. Mem. Ark. Retail Mchts. Assn. (chmn. bd. 1979—), Mo. Retail Mchts. Assn. (dir. 1977—), Ark. Free Enterprise Assn. (pres. 1969-70), Am. Mgmt. Assn., Am. Soc. Personnel Adminstrs., Mass Retailing Inst. (personnel exec. com. 1974—), Ark. (dir. 1978—), Rogers (dir. 1967-70, mayor's citizens com. 1967-69), U.S. (pub. affairs com. 1974—) chambers commerce, Ark. Found. of Associated Colls. (trustee 1975—), Phi Delta Kappa, Alpha Psi Omega. Roman Catholic. Clubs: Rotary (pres. 1969-70, Am. Citizens award 1970, R.I. gov. Dist. 611, 1980-81), K.C. Author: Thy Will Be Done in All Things, 1962; editor: Eight Hundred Colleges Face the Future (Danforth Found. Commn.), 1966; Church Sponsored Higher Education in the United States (M. Patillo, J. McKenzie); contbr. articles on personnel counseling and edn. to profl. publs. Home: 905 S 15th St Rogers AR 72756 Office: PO Box 116 702 SW 8th St Bentonville AR 72712

ROURKE, MICHAEL JAMES, retail exec.; b. Mpls., Dec. 5, 1934; s. James Vernon and Mary Margurite (Allen) R.; B.B.A. cum laude, U. Minn., 1958; m. Mary Ellen Little, June 20, 1959; children—Patricia Marie, Kathleen Ann, Michael John, Erin Maureen, Daniel Robert. Prodn. promotion mgr. Weyerhaeuser Co., Tacoma, 1960-66; dir. advt. and public relations Boise Cascade Corp., 1966-73; exec. v.p. Davies and Rourke Advt., Boise, 1973-77; v.p. corp. affairs Great Atlantic and Pacific Tea Co., Montvale, N.J., 1977—. Served with USN, 1954-56. Mem. Food Mktg. Inst. Roman Catholic. Club: Apple Ridge Country. Home: 28 Knollwood Rd Upper Saddle River NJ 07658

ROUSCH, RALPH STEPHEN, bus. exec.; b. Bklyn., Oct. 25, 1940; s. David and Martha (Fellner) R.; B.B.A., Hofstra U., 1962; m. Adrienne Buchwald, Mar. 1, 1960; children—Jeffrey, Jaimee. Audit mgr. small bus. Price Waterhouse & Co., N.Y., 1962-69; v.p. finance Davis Computer Systems, N.Y., 1969-70; v.p. HMW Industries, Inc., Stamford, Conn., 1970-80, pres., chief operating officer Handi Man Industries subs. HMW Industries, Newark, 1980—. C.P.A., N.Y. Mem. Nat. Assn. Accountants (sec. N.Y. chpt. 1968), Am. Inst. C.P.A.'s, N.Y. State Soc. C.P.A.'s. Home: 2878 Saddle Ridge Dr Yorktown Heights NY 10598 Office: 191 Fabyan Pl Newark NJ 07112

ROUSSEAU, RAYMOND ADRIEN, utilities co. exec.; b. New Bedford, Mass., June 26, 1932; s. Joseph Adrien and Lorette (Cloutier) R.; B.S.M.E., Southeastern Mass. U., 1954; M.S., Northeastern U., 1964; postgrad. Rutgers U., 1965, U. Mich., 1971; m. Elaine Theresa Emerson, June 16, 1956; children—David Raymond, Marc Christopher, Suzanne Marie, Peter James. Mech. engr. U.S. Naval Sta., Newport, R.I., 1954-55; project engr. Continental Screw Co., New Bedford, Mass., 1955-58, mech. engr. metals and controls, nuclear products div., Attleboro, Mass., 1958-59; with New Bedford Gas & Edison Light Co. (Mass.), 1959—, gen. supt., 1971-78; dir. prodn. services New Eng. Gas & Electric Assn., Sandwich, Mass., 1978—. Registered profl. engr., Mass. Mem. Freetown-Lakeville Regional Sch. Com., 1973-77. Mem. ASME. Roman Catholic. Club: Lions. Home: 25 Rounsevell Dr E Freetown MA 02717 Office: PO Box 527 Freezer Rd Sandwich MA 02563

ROUX, AMBROISE MARIE CASIMIR, elec. co. exec.; b. Piscop, France, June 26, 1921; s. Andre and Cecile (Marcilhacy) R.; student Coll. Stanislas, Paris, France, 1932-40, Ecole Polytechnique, 1940-41, Ecole des Ponts and Chaussees, 1942-44, Ecole Superieure d'Electricite, 1945-46; m. Francoise Marion, June 17, 1946; children—Christian, Veronique. Engr., Dept. Civil Engring. France, 1944-51; exec. dir. Office Sec. States for Industry and Commerce, 1952-55; sr. v.p. Compagnie Generale d'Electricite Paris, 1955-63, pres., 1963—, chmn. bd., 1970—; hon. chmn. Petrofigaz, Afnor; chmn. bd. Compagnie Industrielle des Télécommunications-CIT-Alcatel, 1966—, Compagnie Electro-Financière, Paris, 1969—; chmn. bd. Assn. des Grande Entreprises Françaises faisant appel a l'Epargne, 1976—; v.p. Crédit Commercial de France, 1974—; dir. Cie Financiere de Paris & des Pays-Bas, Ste la Radiotechnique, Alsthom-Atlantique, Credit National, Pechiney Ugine Kuhlmann, La Generale Occidentale, Trocadero Participations. Decorated comdr. Legion of Honor, comdr. Merite Commercial, comdr. de l'Instruction Publique. Mem. Fedn. French Industries (vice chmn. 1966-75, 1st vice chmn. 1975—). Home: 17 Pl des Estats-Unis Paris 75116 France Office: Compagnie Generale d'Electricite Paris 54 Rue la Boetie F75 382 Paris Cedex 08 France

ROUZIER, CARL, bus. services exec.; b. Port-au-Prince, Haiti, Oct. 22, 1936; came to U.S., 1964; s. Daniel and Nina (Berne) R.; A.A., Coll. de Port-au-Prince, 1956; B.Acctg., Ecole de Commerce Julien Craan, Port-au-Prince, 1958; m. Marie Simone Lafontant, Dec. 12, 1959; children—Martine, Carl, Daniel. Acct., Trans World Trading Co., Port-au-Prince, 1958-63; gen. mgr. Mutual Parking Inc., N.Y.C., 1964-70; dir., co-owner Data Bus. Service Co., Kew Gardens, N.Y., 1970-76; pres. Innovative Bus. Services Inc., Jamaica, N.Y., 1976—. Mem. Am. Soc. Bus. and Mgmt. Cons.'s, Nat. Assn. Income Tax Practitioners, Nat. Assn. Tax Consultors, Nat. Small Bus. Assn. Club: Masons. Home: 92-34 173d St Jamaica NY 11433

ROWAN, ROBERT D., bus. exec.; b. Holland, Mich., Mar. 27, 1922; s. Joseph Henry and Mabel Barbara (Streur) R.; student Hope Coll., 1940-41; B.S., Mich. State U., 1947; m. Frieda A. Young, Apr. 2, 1945; children—Richard Paul, Kristin Louise, Ruthann Marie. Audit supr. Touche, Niven, Bailey & Smart, C.P.A.'s, Detroit, 1947-55; with Fruehauf Corp., Detroit, 1955—, v.p., controller, 1962-70, exec. v.p.-fin., 1970-72, pres., chief operating officer, 1972-74, pres., chief exec. officer, dir., 1974—, chmn. bd., chmn. exec. com., 1980—; v.p., dir. Fruehauf Trailer Co. Can. Ltd., Trailer Acceptance Co. Ltd., Fruehauf Distbg. Co., Fruehauf Internat. Ltd.; dir. Fruehauf Fin. Co., Fruehauf France S.A., Decatur Aluminum Co., Jacksonville Shipyards, Inc., others. C.P.A., Mich. Mem. Controllers Inst. Am. (dir. Detroit), Mich. Assn. C.P.A.'s, Clubs: Masons, Renaissance, Detroit Athletic, Detroit; Sky (N.Y.C.); Oakland Hills Country (Birmingham, Mich.). Office: Fruehauf Corp 10900 Harper Ave Detroit MI 48213

ROWE, BARRY MORTON, univ. purchasing adminstr.; b. Worcester, Mass., June 1, 1933; A.A., Boston U., 1953, B.S. in B.A., 1955; postgrad. Navy Officers Candidate Sch., 1956. Mgr. purchasing Charles Stark Draper Lab., Inc., Cambridge, Mass., 1962-78; dir. purchasing and stores M.I.T., Cambridge, 1978—. Served with USN, 1956-59, to comdr., USNR, 1959-76. Mem. Nat. Assn. Ednl. Buyers, Nat. Assn. Purchasing Mgrs. (cert). Office: Mass Inst Tech 77 Massachusetts Ave E18 360 Cambridge MA 02139

ROWE, BONNIE GORDON, music co. exec.; b. Buford, Ga., May 3, 1922; s. Bonnie Gordon and Alma (Poole) R.; student Ga. Evening Coll., 1939-41, U. Wichita, 1948-49, Ga. State Coll., 1949-52; m. Mary Wilburta Shidler; 1 dau., Sharon Lynn; m. 2d, Gloria Lucille Fairfax, Feb. 17, 1962 (div.); 1 dau., Susan Rebecca. Traffic mgr. Bonanza Air Lines, Las Vega, 1946-48; music tchr. 1948-52; owner Rowe Accordion Distbg. Co., Rowe Accordion Center, Atlanta, 1952-56, Atlanta Music Pub. Co., 1956—, B. Rowe Music Co., Atlanta, 1957—; pres.-treas. B.C.R. Corp. Served to lt. col. USAAF, World War II; ETO. Decorated Air medals with three oak leaf clusters. Mem. Southeastern Accordion Assn. (past pres.), Nat. Assn. Music Mchts., Atlanta Fedn. Musicians, Travelers Protective Assn., Atlanta C. of C. Res. Officers Assn., Internat. Platform Assn., Am. Legion, Gamma Delta Phi. Clubs: Sandtown Civitan (past pres., lt. gov., pres. Met. Atlanta Council), Elks. Dobbins AFB Officers. Composer: Accordionique, 1953, Vivolet, 1956, More and More and More, 1964, Dedication, 1964, All I Really See Is You, 1965, I Love Only You, 1965, Predudio Reminisci, 1969. Home: 5085 Erin Rd SW Atlanta GA 30331 Office: 10 Hawthorne Plaza Mableton GA 30059

ROWE, BRIAN HENRY, aircraft engine co. exec.; b. London, May 6, 1931; s. Henry William and Myra Frances (Creed) R.; came to U.S., 1957, naturalized, 1965; B.S. with honors, Kings Coll., Durham U., 1955; m. Jill Penelope Trapp, Dec. 8, 1955; children—Linda, Penny, David. Apprentice to advanced design engr. DeHavilland Engine Co., London, 1947-57; design engr. Gen. Electric Co., Cin., 1957-59, application engr., 1959-62, mgr. mktg. lift fan, Lynn, Mass., 1962-63, mgr. CF700 design, 1963-64, mgr. component engring. CF700/J85, 1964-66, mgr. prodn. engring., 1966-67, gen. mgr. CF6 dept., Cin., 1967-72, v.p., gen. mgr. comml. engine div., 1972-74, mktg. div., 1974-76, aircraft engring. div., 1976—. Mem. Cin. Energy Conservation Com., 1974—; mem. Cin. Airport Bd., also chmn. finance com., 1976—; active United Appeal. Fellow Royal Aero. Soc.; mem. Am. Inst. Aeros. and Astronautics, Conquistadores del Cielo. Club: India Hill Swim and Tennis Club. Patentee in field. Home: 7870 Tecumseh Trail Cincinnati OH 45215 Office: Gen Electric Co 1 Neuman Way Cincinnati OH 45215

ROWE, HARVEY JOHN, mfg. co. exec.; b. Oshkosh, Wis., Jan. 29, 1936; s. Harvey Jackson and Grace Linnea (Anderson) R.; B.A., U. Mo., 1958; m. Marjorie Susan Beckman, Feb. 28, 1959; children—Richard Edward, Renee, Suzanne, Risa Lee. Mgmt. tng. and advt. merchandiser Walgreen Co., Chgo., 1958-63; sales agt. Equitable Life Assurance Co., Chgo., 1963; buyer, asst. purchasing mgr. U.S. Gypsum Co., Chgo., 1963-72, mktg. mgr. Chem. div., 1972-79; gen. mgr. Arrowhead Building Materials, Kansas City, Kans., 1979—. Trustee, Village of Deer Park, Ill., 1975—; past pres., co-founder Barrington Area Hockey League. Served with USN, 1958. Mem. Home Builders Assn. Kansas City, Kansas City Area C. of C., Sigma Phi Epsilon. Republican. Christian Scientist. Club: Hillcrest Country. Home: 10219 Catalina Overland Park KS 66207 Office: 2820 Roe Ln Kansas City KS 66103

ROWE, ROBERT HETSLEY, ins. co. exec.; b. Rockport, Ky., Sept. 1, 1929; s. Hetsley and Bessie Katherine (Acton) R.; B.A., Mich. State U., 1980; m. Leone Ann Wald, Jan. 9, 1960; children—Gregory David, Matthew Owen. With Ohio-Ky. region Internat. Ladies Garment Workers Union, 1954-59; group rep. Nationwide Ins., Columbus, Ohio and Detroit, 1959-61; v.p. League Life Ins. Co., Detroit, 1961-71; chief dep. ins. commr. State of Mich., Lansing, 1971-76; sr. v.p. League Ins. Cos., Detroit, 1976—; interim exec. dir. Health Central Inc., Lansing, 1979. Served with USMC, 1946-48, 51-52. Fellow Fin. Analysts Fedn., Life Office Mgmt. Inst.; mem. Am. Risk and Ins. Assn. Democrat. Home: 640 Kensington St East Lansing MI 48823 Office: 15600 Providence Dr Southfield MI 48075

ROWE, WILLARD C., fastener mfg. co. exec.; b. New Bedford, Mass., Oct. 16, 1929; s. Preston B. and Herma C. Rowe: B.A., Dartmouth Coll., 1951; M.B.A., Northeastern U., 1963; m. Kay Nielsen, July 3, 1979; children—Gail, Bruce. Trainee, Gen. Electric Co., Bridgeport, Conn., 1954-57; chief acct. Small Tube Products Co., Inc., Waterbury, Conn., 1957; asst. controller Toni div. Gillette Co., Chgo., 1957-64; mgmt. cons. Booz, Allen & Hamilton, Inc., Chgo., 1964-66; div. controller George D. Roper Corp., Kankakee, Ill., 1966-67; v.p. Armour-Dial, Inc., Chgo., 1967-72; fastener group pres., corp. v.p. Ill. Tool Works, Chgo., 1972-77; group pres., corp. v.p., dir. The Lamson & Sessions Co., Cleve., 1977—. Active various charity fund drives, local polit. orgns. Served to lt. (j.g.) USN, 1951-54. Mem. Fin. Execs. Inst., also various trade assns. Republican. Club: Chagrin Valley Country. Office: 2000 Bond Court Bldg 1300 E 9th St Cleveland OH 44114

ROWLAND, CLIFFORD VANCE, labor relations exec.; b. New Castle, Pa., Apr. 6, 1930; s. Faunt Mitchell and Mary Elizabeth (Lour) R.; B.S., Cornell U., 1953; m. Jeanette Jane Smith, Aug. 29, 1952; children—Theresa Gayle, Mitchell Vance. Vice-pres. indsl. relations Grace Line Inc., N.Y.C., 1969-71; asst. regional postmaster gen. for employee and labor relations N.E., U.S. Postal Service, N.Y.C., Washington, 1971-75, labor relations exec. N. Jersey dist., 1975—. Chmn. bd. dirs. Student Agencies, Inc., Ithaca, N.Y.; pres. Bd. Edn., Berkeley Heights, N.J., 1962-63. Served with USNR, 1948-49. Mem. Indsl. Relations Research Assn., Cornell U. Sch. Indsl. and Labor Relations Alumni Assn. (dir.). Presbyterian. Clubs: Lions Internat., Kiwanis. Home: 122 Southern Blvd Chatham NJ 07928 Office: Room 201 US Post Office Federal Sq Newark NJ 07102

ROWLAND, JAY MILLER, JR., container co. exec.; b. Boulder, Colo., Feb. 15, 1921; s. Jay Miller and Maude Louise (Eckel) R.; student Tulane U., 1940-43, Kans. State Tchrs. Coll., 1943; LL.B., Tulane U., 1948, J.D., 1969; postgrad. in Bus. Adminstrn., Houston U., 1964; m. Leonora Schwartz, Dec. 9, 1943; 1 son, Jay Miller. Staff adjuster, storm loss supr., br. claims mgr. Gen. Adjustment Bur., Inc., Colo., Wyo., N.Mex., 1948-54; claim examiner, dist. claim office mgr., claim analyst Allstate Ins. Co., Miss. and Ark., 1954-58; home office claims mgr. Delta Fire and Casualty Co., Baton Rouge, La., 1958-59; claims dept. mgr. Pioneer Mut. Casualty Co., Columbus, Ohio, 1959-61; supt. claims, claims sec., asst. v.p. Preferred Ins. Co. of Grand Rapids (Mich.), 1961-62, v.p. subs. S.W. Indeminity Co. of Dallas, 1961-62; investigator-negotiator, asst. dir. indsl. relations Ala. Dry Dock and Shipbldg. Co., Mobile, 1962-67; dist. claim mgr., div. claim tng. adminstr. Am. Mut. Ins. Cos., Bryn Mawr, Pa., 1967-69; personnel dir., mgr. personnel relations U. S.Ala., Med. Center, Mobile, 1969-75; mgr. indsl. relations The Lerio Corp., Mobile, 1975—; part-time freelance photojournalist. Mem. port devel. and legis. coms. C. of C., 1964-67; past mem. bd. dirs. Mobile County Assn. Mental Health, C.A.N. Rehab. Found., 1974-79; mem. Pres.'s Com. Employment Handicapped; chmn. project rev. com. S.W. Health Systems Agy.; chmn. job service improvement com. Ala. Employment Service, Mobile, 1978-80; mem. Ala. Gov.'s Com. Served with USAF, 1942-46; U.S.N.G., 1953-54. Recipient Certificate of Appreciation, Vocat. Rehab. and Crippled Children Services, 1970; Citation for Meritorious Service, Pres. Com. on Employment of the Handicapped, 1972; Outstanding Service award Mobile County Assn. Mental Health, 1973; Certificate of award Internat. Assn. Personnel in Employment Security, 1975; Outstanding Service award Ala. Assn. Mental Health, 1976; cert. appreciation U. South Ala. Med. Center, 1975, Mobile County chpt. Nat. Assn. for Mental Health, 1979; recipient prizes and awards for photography. Mem. Am. Soc. Personnel Adminstrn. Personnel Accreditation Inst. (accredited exec.), Mobile Personnel Assn. (past dir.), Am. Arbitration Assn., Nat. Panel Consumer Arbitrators, Asso. Industries of Ala., Mobile Press Club, Camera South of Mobile (v.p.), Amateur Trapshooting Assn., Bur. of Nat. Affairs, Inc. (personnel policies forum 1977-78). Presbyterian. Clubs: Hole in One, Tulane Alumni T, Masons. Numerous photos and articles published in newspapers and mags. Home: PO Box 113 Spanish Fort AL 36527 Office: PO Box 2084 Mobile AL 36652

ROWLAND, RAYMOND EDGAR, bus. exec.; b. Kansas, Ill., Dec. 8, 1902; s. William and Lula Pearl (Estes) R.; student U. Ill., 1921-23; B.S., U. Wis.; m. Connie Lou Melton, July 30, 1928; children—Raymond Edgar, Eleanor Frances and Doris Elaine (twins). Sales div. Ralston Purina Co., 1926-34, plant mgr., Circleville, Ohio, 1934-40, asst. v.p., St. Louis, 1940-43, v.p., 1943-56, pres., 1956-64, chmn. bd., chief exec. officer, 1964-68, dir., 1951-74; dir. Merc. Trust Co.; chmn. bd. Barnes Hosp., St. Louis, 1968—. Bd. dirs. St. Louis Area council Boy Scouts Am., 1962—; trustee Wis. Alumni Research Assn., 1963—. Mem. Alpha Zeta (hon.), Phi Sigma (hon.). Presbyterian. Clubs: Noonday, Bellerive Country, Bogey, St. Louis, Eldorado Country, Crystal Downs Country, Bohemian. Home: 710 S Hanley Rd Clayton MO 63105 Office: Barnes Hospital Barnes Hospital Plaza St Louis MO 63110

ROWLAND, ROBERT ARTHUR, mfg. co. exec., plant engr.; b. Davenport, Iowa, 1928; s. Ernist Roberts and Nina May (Osborn) R.; B.S., U. Iowa, Iowa City, 1952; m. Virginia May Felt, Sept. 4, 1948; children—Barbara, Deborah, Jennie. Engr., Rock Island Arsenal (Ill.), 1952, Davenport Machine & Foundry Co. (Iowa), 1953-58; plant engr. Dock Foundry, Three Rivers, Mich., 1958-59; maintenance mgr. Wehr Steel Corp., Milw., 1959-63, 1971-72; maintenance mgr.

Brillion Iron Works (Wis.), 1963-71; dir. plant engring. Electron Corp., Littleton, Colo., 1972—; founder, pres. Systems and Control Design Inc., Littleton; speaker on plant engring. throughout U.S. Mem. Am. Foundrymen's Soc. (engring. speaker, chmn. Rocky Mountain chpt., nat. dir. 1979—), Am. Inst. Plant Engrs. (certified engr.). Methodist. Club: Lions. Contbr. articles, tech. reports to Am. Foundrymen's Soc. publs. Home: 5207 Mabre Ct Littleton CO 80123 Office: 5101 S Rio Grande Littleton CO 80120

ROWLAND, RONEY, ins. co. exec.; b. Durham, N.C., July 28, 1932; s. Roney and Helen Hobbs (Smith) R.; student Hampden-Sydney Coll., 1949-51; A.B., U. S.C., 1956; m. Elizabeth Louise McKeithen, Dec. 6, 1958; children—Roney III, Mary Elizabeth, Carol McKeithen. Underwriter, Prudential Ins. Co. Am., Jacksonville, Fla., 1956-58; supr. group issue Life Ins. Co. Va., Richmond, 1958-60, asst. mgr. group ins. adminstrn., 1960-66, mgr. group underwriting, 1966-68, asst. v.p. group sales, 1968-71, 2d. v.p. group sales, 1971-73, v.p. group ins. sales and adminstrn., 1973-80; sr. v.p. Inter-County Hospitalization Plan, Jenkintown, Pa., 1980—. Served with U.S. Army, 1954-55. Methodist. Clubs: Sales and Marketing Execs. (Richmond); Woodfield (South Hill, Va.). Home: PO Box 433 South Hill VA 23970 Office: Inter-County Hospitalization Plan Foxcroft Sq Jenkintown PA 19046

ROWLEY, GEOFFREY HERBERT, mgmt. cons.; b. Harrow, Middlesex, Eng., Nov. 10, 1935; s. Herbert and Muriel Jessie (Nicolls) R.; came to U.S., 1962; B.A., Bristol U. (Eng.), 1958; Certificate of Indsl. Adminstrn., Glasgow U., 1962; M.B.A., Harvard U., 1964. Purchasing officer Pirelli Ltd., London, 1958-61; research asso. Assn. for Internat. Research, Inc., Cambridge, Mass., 1964-68, v.p., dir., 1968—, cons. in expatriate compensation, 1964—; lectr. in field. Served with Royal Navy, 1953-55. Mem. Am. Compensation Assn., Am. Soc. Personnel Adminstrn., Brit. Inst. Mgmt. Club: Harvard. Contbr. articles in field to profl. jours. Home: 11 Berkeley Pl Cambridge MA 02138 Office: 1100 Massachusetts Ave Cambridge MA 02138

ROWLEY, WORTH, lawyer; b. Boston, Aug. 14, 1916; s. Clarence Worth and Catherine Agnes (Foley) F.; J.D., Northeastern U., 1938; m. Jacqueline Magrath, May 4, 1941 (div. 1971); children—Jonathan M., Susannah W., Belinda P., Joshua F.; m. 2d, Jane A. Pedersen, Apr. 1, 1972; children—Clarence W., Eliza Ann. Admitted to Mass. bar, 1938; pvt. practice law, Boston, 1938-41; atty. Office of Price Adminstrn., Washington, 1942; spl. asst. to atty. gen. Antitrust Div., U.S. Dept. Justice, Washington, 1945-58; partner Cummings & Sellers, Washington, 1958-63; partner Rowley & Watts, Washington, 1964—. Served with USN, 1942-45. Mem. Am. Law Inst., Am., Interam., Fed., D.C. bar assns. Democrat. Unitarian. Clubs: Univ., Internat., Nat. Press, Lawyers (Washington); West River Sailing (Galesville, Md.). Home: 2446 Kalorama Rd NW Washington DC 20008 also Mt Vernon Ave Hyannis Port MA 02647 Office: 1990 M St NW Washington DC 20036

ROY, CHARLES PHILLIP, mfg. co. exec.; b. Tulsa, July 16, 1945; s. Eugene W. and Hertha V. (Hulett) R.; student Kansas City Coll. and Bible Coll., 1966; children—Cyndee Lynn, Trina Annette, Phillip Todd. Owner, mgr. Royal Washette, Inc., Huntington, W.Va., 1968-75; with KEI, Chanute, Kans., 1970-78, sales mgr., 1973-75, dir. advt. and promotions, 1975-78; gen. mgr. Baldwin Piano & Organ Co., Chanute, 1979—; dir. R.W. Inc. Charlie Roy Day proclaimed by Nashville and State of Tenn., 1978. Mem. Nat. Assn. Music Mchts., Country Music Assn., Audio Engring. Soc., Adminstrv. Mgmt. Soc. Home: 1314 S 8th St Humboldt KS 66748 Office: 908 W Chestnut St Chanute KS 66720

ROY, DAVID BRUCE, bank exec.; b. Pitts., Nov. 2, 1931; s. John Lester and Clara Agnes (Ruoff) R.; A.B. in Econs., Princeton U., 1954; m. Nancy Lee Knapp, June 24, 1960; children—Dana Kathryn, Scott David, Julie Lynn. Mktg. mgr. data processing div. IBM, Pitts., 1956-69; v.p. Fed. Home Loan Bank Pitts., 1969-74; exec. v.p. Rome Savs. Bank (N.Y.), 1974-75, pres., 1975-78, pres., chief exec. officer, 1978—; dir. Rome Indsl. Devel. Corp., Oneida County Indsl. Devel. Corp. Commr., McCandless Twp. (N.Y.), 1972-74; mem. Town of Kirkland (N.Y.) Planning Bd., 1976—; pres. Rome United Way, 1978, chmn. long range planning com., 1980; bd. dirs. Rome C. of C. Served with Security Agy., U.S. Army, 1954-56. Recipient various wards United Way, 1975-78. Mem. Nat. Assn. Mut. Savs. Banks, Savs. Banks Assn. N.Y. State. Republican. Presbyterian. Clubs: Princeton (N.Y.C.); Teugega Country, Rome, Masons, Shriners. Office: 100 On The Mall PO Box 311 Rome NY 13440

ROY, GERARD THEOPHIL, software service and cons. co. exec.; b. Exeter, N.H., Aug. 30, 1949; s. Achille Theophil and Mary Jane Yvonne (LaRoche) R.; cert. data processing Concord Comml. Coll., 1968-69; student Fitchburg State Coll., 1970-71, Lowell Technol. Inst., 1971, U. N.H., 1971-74; m. Nancy Gail Walwyn, June 7, 1969; children—Jennifer Anne, Aimee Nicole. Sr. computer operator Raytheon Co., Bedford, Mass., 1969-71; supr. computer ops. U. N.H., Durham, 1971-74; ops. mgr. Investors Mortgage Ins. Co., Boston, 1974-76; systems engr. Warren Bros. Co., Cambridge, Mass., 1976; owner, pres. Systems & Consulting Services, Inc., Boston, 1976—. Office: Systems & Consulting Services Inc 20 Kilby St Boston MA 02109

ROY, JACQUES MARCEL, actuary, govt. ofcl.; b. Levis, Que., Can., Aug. 23, 1942; s. Yves and Louise (Boutin) R.; B.Comm., Laval U., 1965; children—Julie, Alain, Marie-Josee. With Sun Life, 1965-69; actuarial asst., asst. underwriting officer Que. Ministere des Consommateurs, 1969—, dir. actuarial services, 1969-74, dep. supt. ins., 1974-77, supr. of ins., 1977—; part-time instr. Laval U. Fellow Soc. Actuaries; mem. Can. Inst. Actuaries. Club: Levis Golf. Home: 1312 Des Seigneurs Ste Foy PQ E1W 3H7 Canada Office: 800 Place D'Youville 803 Quebec PQ G1R 4Y5 Canada

ROY, ROBERT CHADWICK, ins. agy. exec.; b. Washington, Feb. 17, 1927; s. Leonard Cornell and Mary Cooley R.; B.A., George Washington U., 1948; m. Joyce L. Snodgrass, Sept. 5, 1945; children—Sandra Roy Bradshaw, Robert Chadwick, Florence Roy Cox, Jonathan C. Chief underwriter Northwestern Nat. Ins. Co., Washington, 1945-52; pres., dir. Robert C. Roy Agy., Inc., Delray Beach, Fla., 1952—, Roy Am., Inc., Delray Beach, 1962—, Century Ins. Co. of N.Y., 1969-72, Nat. Reins. Underwriters, Inc., Delray Beach, 1969—, Delta Mfg. Corp., Palm Beach, Fla., 1978—, Energy Corp. 1, Virginia, Minn., 1977—, Energy Corp 2, Birmingham, Ala., 1977—, B.L.Q. Inc., Birmingham, 1977—, M.D. Catheter Corp., Birmingham, 1977—, Roy Oil, Gas & Coal Mines, Jamestown, Tenn., 1980—, Roy Energy Corp. of Ky., Corbin, 1979—; dir. Nat. Educators Life Ins. Co. Served to lt. (j.g.) USN, 1944-46. Decorated Silver Star, Purple Heart; named Employer of Yr., State of Fla., 1974, 80. Mem. Nat. Assn. Ins. Agts., Fla. Assn. Ins. Agts., Ins. Agts. Assn. Palm Beach County, U.S. C. of C., Million Dollar Round Table. Republican. Episcopalian. Clubs: Country of Fla.; Delray Dunes Country, Pine Tree Country, Hunters Run Country. Author: Aviation, 1965; Liability Insurance, 1966; patentee. Home: 3900 South Lake Dr Boynton Beach FL 33435 Office: Robert C Roy Agy Inc 600 E Atlantic Ave Delray Beach FL 33444

ROY, SIEGFRIED SHANKAR, tool and die co. exec.; b. Dhanbad, India, Apr. 16, 1928; came to U.S., 1963, naturalized, 1967; s. Shurid K. and Hermine (Steinbrener) R.; B.S. in Mech. Engring., Ill. Inst. Tech., 1949; m. Marty Patricia Grant, Sept. 30, 1955; children—Kiran C., Shawn A. Vice pres., gen. mgr. N. Am. Philips, Inc., N.Y.C., 1967-69; asst. to v.p. plastics mfg. Am. Can Co., Greenwich, Conn., 1969-73; dir. tech. devel. plastic beverage bottle div. Continental Group, Inc., N.Y.C., 1973-79; gen. mgr. Continental Tool & Die, Continental Group, Inc., Merrimack, N.H., 1979—. Mem. Soc. Plastics Engrs. Patentee products and processes in plastics tech. Home: 34 Nathan Lord Rd Amherst NH 03031 Office: Continental Tool & Die Continental Group Inc 12 Continental Blvd Merrimack NH 03054

ROYER, ROBERT LEWIS, utility exec.; b. Louisville, Jan. 2, 1928; s. Carl Brown and Martha Helen (Garrett) B.; B.S.E.E., Rose Hulman Inst. Tech., 1949; m. Carol Jean Pierce, June 24, 1950; children—Jenifer Lea Royer Case, Todd Pierce, Robert Douglas. With Louisville Gas & Electric Co., 1949—, asst. supt. elec. distbn. dept., 1958-61, staff engr., 1961-62, asst. v.p.-ops., 1962-63, asst. v.p. and asst. gen. supt., 1964-65, v.p. and gen. supt., 1964-69, v.p.-ops., 1969-78, exec. v.p., 1978, pres., chief exec. officer, 1978—, dir., 1972—; mem. generation res. panel E. Central Area Reliability Council, 1970-74, mem. coordination rev. com., 1975-78, exec. bd., 1978—; mem. Ky. Energy Resources Commn., 1975-79; mem. energy task force Gov.'s Econ. Devel. Commn., 1976-79; mem. Ky. Energy Research Bd., 1978—; v.p. Ind.-Ky. Electric Corp., 1979—; dir. Ohio Valley Transmission Corp., Citizens Fidelity Corp., Citizens Fidelity Bank & Trust Co. Mem. exec. bd. Old Ky. Home council Boy Scouts Am., 1967, v.p. dist. ops., 1970-75, 79-80, council commr. and rep. to nat. council, 1975—; bd. dirs. East End Boys' Club, 1975-78; trustee Spirit of Louisville Found., 1978—, J. Graham Brown Found., 1980—; bd. mgrs. Rose-Hulman Inst. Tech., 1979—; mem. Louisville Devel. Com., 1979—. Served in U.S. Army, 1953-55. Recipient Silver Beaver award Boy Scouts Am., 1975. Mem. Louisville Automobile Club (dir. 1974, treas. 1978-79, v.p. 1979—), Louisville Area C. of C. (dir. 1978-80), IEEE, Exec. Clubs Louisville. Registered profl. engr., Ky. Methodist. Clubs: Hurstbourne Country, Jefferson, Pendennis, Downtown Optimists (youth work com. 1970-78, dir. 1970-73, 75-78), Louisville Rotary. Home: 4014 Norbourne Blvd Louisville KY 40207 Office: PO Box 32010 Louisville KY 40232

ROYSTER, GEORGE ERWIN, savs. and loan exec.; b. Statesville, N.C., July 10, 1928; s. Ira Gay and Catherine Margaret (Poesy) R.; B.A., U. Tenn., 1955; m. Joy Angeline Inman, Nov. 23, 1968; children—Joy Angeline, Eric Inman, George. Asst. v.p. Integon Corp., Winston-Salem, N.C., 1955-68; v.p. Liberty Life Ins. Co., Greenville, S.C., 1968—; pres. dir. LIBCO, Inc., Greenville, 1970; sr. v.p. mktg. Am. Found. Life Ins. Co., Little Rock, 1971-74, exec. v.p., 1974-75, also dir., mem. exec. com; pres., mng. officer United People's Fed. Savs. & Loan Assn., Ft. Smith, Ark., 1976—. Bd. dirs., treas. Ft. Smith Heritage Found.; trustee St. Edwards Mercy Med. Center; exec. bd. West Ark. Area council Boy Scouts Am.; bd. dirs. Ft. Smith Girls Club. Mem. C. of C. (dir.), Sigma Alpha Epsilon. Episcopalian (lay reader 1962). Clubs: Hardscrabble Country, Town (Ft. Smith). Home: 3508 Old Oaks Ln Fort Smith AR 72903 Office: 17 N 6th St Fort Smith AR 72901

ROZAK, THOMAS, fin. cons.; b. St. Louis, Apr. 5, 1939; s. Anthony George and Regina Rose (Doyle) R.; student St. Louis U., N.Y. Inst. Fin. Registered rep. R.W. Pressprich & Co., mems. N.Y. State Exchange, 1962-64 with Intercontinental Diversified Corp., 1964-78, dir., sec., 1975-78; adminstrv. asst., dir., officer companies of Wallace Groves, founder Freeport, Bahamas, 1978-80; pres. Taino Devel. Co. Ltd., 1978—; dir. various privately held cos. Bd. dirs. Wallace Groves Aquaculture Found. Roman Catholic. Club: Bankers (Miami, Fla.). Home: 405 Fairway Manor PO Box F-5 Freeport Bahamas Office: PO Box 340939 Coral Gables FL 33114

ROZEL, SAMUEL JOSEPH, mfg. co. exec.; b. Louisville, Apr. 22, 1935; s. Sam and Anna (Sessmer) R.; B.S., U. Louisville, 1955, LL.B., 1957; Advanced Mgmt. Program, Harvard U. Bus. Sch., 1979; m. Jeanne Frances Foulkes, July 3, 1965; children—Brooke Jane, John Samuel. Admitted to Ind. bar, 1970, Ky. bar, 1958, D.C. bar, 1962, Minn. bar, 1968; staff atty. Fed. Trade Commn., Washington, 1962-67; sr. atty., antitrust counsel Honeywell, Inc., Mpls., 1967-69; counsel, consumer electronics group Magnavox Co., Fort Wayne, Ind., 1969-71, v.p., gen. counsel, 1971-75, sec., 1973-75; sr. v.p. U.S. Philips Corp., 1975—; sec. to governing com. U.S. Philips Trust, 1977; sec., exec. mgmt. com. N.Am. Phillips Corp. Served to capt. Judge Adv. Gen. Corps, AUS, 1958-62. Mem. Am., Fed., Ind., Ky. bar assns. Clubs: Union League, Harvard (N.Y.C.); Lawyers (Washington). Home: 215 S Bald Hill Rd New Canaan CT 06840 Office: 100 E 42d St New York NY 10017

ROZELLE, FREDERICK CHASE, JR., trust banker; b. Dunmore, Pa., Jan. 14, 1926; s. Fred Chase and Helen Mariel (Waring) R.; B.N.S., Coll. of Holy Cross, 1946; B.S., Yale U., 1948; m. Ruth Conant Anderson, June 21, 1947; children—Anne Boyer, Page Anderson, Frederick Chase III. Agt., Travelers Ins. Co., Portland, Maine, 1948-52, New Eng. Mut. Life Ins. Co., Boston, 1954-58; asst. mgr. John C. Paige & Co., Boston, 1952-54; sr. v.p. Instnl. Investment div. 1st Nat. Bank Boston, 1958—. Chmn. bd. trustees Andover Newton Theol. Sch.; gen. chmn. United Negro Coll. Fund; regional co-chmn. NCCJ. Served with USN, 1943-46. C.L.U. Republican. Mem. United Ch. of Christ. Clubs: Algonquin, Badminton and Tennis. Home: 326 Main St Winchester MA 01890 Office: 100 Federal St Boston MA 02110

ROZIC, JOHN LAWRENCE, die mfg. co. ofcl.; b. Butler, Pa., Dec. 27, 1946; s. Steve Albert and Margaret Julia (Kiselick) R.; Asso. Degree in Indsl. Mgmt. cum laude, Butler County Community Coll., 1977; m. Margaret Ann Dudek, Sept. 2, 1972; children—Jenifer Marie and Nathan John (twins). Salesman, Reliable Furniture Co., Butler, 1964-65; with Oberg Mfg. Co. Inc., Freeport, Pa., 1965—, estimator, 1972-74, quotation supr., 1974-80, market analyst, 1980, mfg. engr., 1980—. Home: 437 Bear Creek Rd Sarver PA 16055 Office: Oberg Mfg Co Inc Silverville Rd Freeport PA 16229

RUBEL, JOHN (HOWARD), rail equipment rental co. exec.; b. Ottumwa, Iowa, July 16, 1948; s. Howard M. and Mary Louise (Herber) R.; A.B., U. Notre Dame, 1970; M.B.A., U. Chgo., 1971; m. Martha Herman, Jan. 8, 1972; 1 son, Paul G. Project dir. Rockwell Internat., Chgo., 1971-77; v.p., controller N. Am. Car Corp., Chgo., 1977-78; pres. Cap-Form, Inc., Chgo., 1978-81; v.p. sales and mktg. Emons Industries, Inc., 1981—. Mem. Am. Assn. Equipment Leasors, Corp. Controllers Soc., Am. Short Line R.R. Assn. Republican. Roman Catholic. Home: 5800 Highland Dr Palatine IL 60067 Office: 327 S LaSalle St Chicago IL 60604

RUBENSTEIN, ALBERT IRWIN, fin. exec.; b. Chgo., Mar. 28, 1927; s. William D. and Regina (Ribaysen) R.; student Herzl City Coll., 1944-46, Roosevelt Coll., 1946-48; LL.B., J.D., John Marshall Law Sch., 1951; m. Joyce Shirley Leeman, June 12, 1954; children—Jeffrey, Lauren, Jan. Admitted to Ill. bar, 1951; individual practice law, Chgo., 1951-64; pres., chief exec. officer Fleetwood Realty Corp., Chgo., 1969—, also dir.; sr. partner Fleetwood Realty Co., Chgo., 1969—; dir. Exec. Bus. Center, Inc., Fleetwood Industries; lectr. in field. Mem. Am. Bar Assn., Ill. Bar Assn., Chgo. Bar Assn., Am. Trial Lawyers Assn., Chgo. Assn. Commerce and Industry, Nat. Real Estate Bd., Chgo. Real Estate Bd. (dir. 1980—), Decalogue Soc. Lawyers, Nat. Realty Com., Inc., Am. Arbitration Soc. Clubs: Covenant of Ill., B'nai B'rith. Contbr. articles in field to profl. jours. Office: 200 W Jackson Chicago IL 60606

RUBENSTEIN, MARTIN, broadcasting exec.; b. Bklyn., Oct. 16, 1935; s. Charles and Evelyn R.; B.A. in Polit. Sci., Bklyn. Coll., 1957; LL.B., Columbia U., 1961; m. Cora Gurien, June 12, 1958; children—Deborah, William. Admitted to N.Y. bar, 1962, D.C. bar, 1980; with ABC, 1961-78, dir. legal and bus. affairs ABC News, N.Y.C., 1966-69, v.p., gen. mgr., N.Y.C., 1969-78; exec. v.p. Mut. Broadcasting System, Inc., Arlington, Va., 1978-79, pres., chief exec. officer, 1979—. Active United Cerebral Palsy Assns., Inc., 1964—, nat. v.p., 1975, chmn. fin. com., 1972. Served with Air N.G., 1957-63. Mem. Radio TV News Dirs. Assn., Internat. Radio and TV Soc., N.Y. State Bar Assn., Radio Advt. Bur. (dir.), Nat. Assn. Broadcasters (mem. radio bd.), Advt. Council (dir.), Fed. City Council (trustee). Jewish.

RUBIN, DAVID JOEL, business exec.; b. N.Y.C., Apr. 3, 1945; s. Reuven and Esther (Davis) R.; B.Sc. summa cum laude, Poly. Inst. Bklyn., 1971; S.M. with honors, Sloan Sch. Mgmt., M.I.T., 1973; m. Carmela Bitter, July 11, 1968; children—Gideon, Michal. Electronic data processing mgr. Dan Hotels Corp., Tel Aviv, Israel, 1973-74; nat. sales mgr. Tamkin Computers Ltd., Tel Aviv, 1974-76; partner, v.p. Elul Technologies Ltd., Tel Aviv, 1976-80; also dir.; owner, pres. Migdar Ltd., Tel Aviv, 1980—. Served with Israeli Army, 1963-67. Mem. Assn. Computing Machinery, Israeli Assn. Data Processing, Israeli Assn. System Analysts, Mensa, Tau Beta Pi. Jewish. Home: 2 Shlomzion Hamalka Herzlia Israel Office: 4 Weizman St PO Box 33601 Tel Aviv 6 1336 Israel

RUBIN, HAROLD TOBY, internat. mineral co. exec.; b. Balt., Sept. 20, 1943; s. Edwin Roland and Ruth (Cohen) Astrachan; B.S. cum laude in Fin., U. Balt., 1969; m. Temma Delores Nelson, June 19, 1966; children—Asher Martin, Dana Elizabeth. Engring. budget adminstr. Westinghouse Def. and Space Center, 1969-71; mgr. cost acctg. and budgets Peterson Howell & Heather, 1971-73; corp. acctg. mgr. ITC Enterprises, Ltd., and subs. ITC, Inc., Internat. Trading Co., Inc. and ITC Japan, Ltd., Towson, Md., 1973-74, corp. comptroller, 1974-77, v.p., 1977—, dir., 1977—, also v.p., dir. Bus. Teaching Aids div. Artistic Typing Hdqrs., Inc., 1972-80, exec. v.p., dir., 1980—; dir. Environ. Control Systems, Inc. Bd. dirs. Baltimore County Gen. Hosp. Found., 1978-79, fin. com., 1979—. Mem. Nat. Assn. Accts., Greater Randallstown Jaycees (dir. 1975, v.p., 1976, legal counsel, 1977, presdl. award of honor, 1976, Chmn. of Yr. 1976). Jewish. Club: Masons. Home: 3921 Zurich Rd Randallstown MD 21133 Office: PO Box 5519 409 Washington Ave Towson MD 21204

RUBIN, ROBERT AVROM, lawyer; b. Queens, N.Y., Nov. 19, 1938; s. Joseph Leonard and Hilda Rubin; B.C.E., Cornell U., 1961; J.D., Columbia U., 1964; m. Charlotte Loewy, June 10, 1962; children—Debra Lynne, Julie Suzanne. Admitted to N.Y. State bar, 1964; now partner Postner & Rubin, N.Y.C.; Lectr. continuing edn. Registered profl. engr., N.Y. Fellow ASCE (past sec. exec. com. constrn. div.); mem. Am. Arbitration Assn. (constrn. industry panel), Moles, Am., N.Y. State bar assns., N.Y. County Lawyers Assn., Chi Epsilon. Jewish. Contbr. to profl. texts and jours. Home: 47 Plaza St Brooklyn NY 11217 Office: 17 Battery Pl New York NY 10004

RUBIN, STEPHEN DAVID, baking co. exec.; b. Milw., May 30, 1939; s. Ephraim I. and Ruth (Grodin) R.; B.B.A., U. Wis., 1961, J.D., 1965; m. Marcia Rubin; children—Wendy Lynn, Michael Allen. Vice pres. Liberman & Gittlen Metal Co., Grand Rapids, Mich., 1965-73; pres. Graver-Dearborn Corp., Chgo., 1966-79, Mercil Plating Co., Chgo., 1968-74, Master Plating Co., Chgo., 1968-74; v.p. P.J. Gould Co., Chgo., 1973-74, Odd Oz Amusements, Chgo., 1974-75; pres. Donnell Co., Chgo., 1974-76, Bake-Rite Baking Co., Stevens Point, Wis., 1976-80, Am. Dynamics Corp., 1978—. Mem. Young Men's Jewish Council (sec., dir.), Young Pres.'s Orgn., Zeta Beta Tau. Home: 7314 Lowell St Lincolnwood IL 60646 Office: 224 N Ada Chicago IL 60607

RUBINBERG, MICHAEL WARREN, mfg. co. exec.; b. Bklyn., Mar. 21, 1941; s. Milton and Sarah R.; B.S. in Chem. Engring., Poly. Inst. Bklyn., 1962, M.S., 1966; J.D., Bklyn. Law Sch., 1969; m. Cynthia Weiss, June 27, 1964; children—Julie, Ilissa, Matthew. Admitted to N.Y. bar, 1970; design engr. Yula Corp., Bronx, 1962-64; asst. chief engr. Doyle & Roth Mfg. Co., N.Y.C., 1964-68; v.p. Lindy Coil div. Fecor Industries, Bronx, 1969-74; pres., founder Rubicon Indsl. Corp., Valley Stream, N.Y., 1974—; pres. Taylor Tank Co., Valley Stream, 1977—. Mem. Am. Inst. Chem. Engrs. Jewish. Home: 39 Angler Ln Port Washington NY 11050 Office: Hook Creek Blvd and 145th Ave Valley Stream NY 11581

RUBINER, RAYMOND KOPEL, investment co. exec.; b. Detroit, Sept. 14, 1918; s. Abram Joseph and Dora (Presman) R.; student Wayne State U., 1934-36, McKinley Coll. Law, 1937-39; B.S., Great Lakes Coll., 1959; m. Elise Julia Cohen, Dec. 11, 1939; children—Lois Elaine, Joan Carol, Audrey Jane. With Cunningham Drug Corp., Detroit, 1933-40; real estate investor, Mich. and Fla., 1946-60; v.p. Hubbard Assos. Real Estate Investment Co., Detroit, 1961-70; pres. Gen. Properties Corp., Birmingham, Mich., 1970—; dir. Glades Hotel Properties, Redington Beach, Fla., Broderick Tower Properties, Detroit; cons. to Amber & Amber Devel. Co.; lectr. Oakland U., Rochester, Mich., 1964-68. Mem. Mayor's Detroit Tomorrow Com., 1952-55. Served with AUS, 1941-46. Mem. Am. Arbitration Assn., Am. Soc. Appraisers, Nat. Assn. Accountants, Nat. Assn. Pub. Accountants, Nat. Assn. Real Estate Bds., Birmingham-Bloomfield Bd. Realtors, Detroit Bd. Realtors. Club: Mason. Home: 2945 Woodward Ave Winter Bldg #88 Bloomfield Hills MI 48013 Office: 280 N Woodward Ave Suite 307 Birmingham MI 48011

RUBINOFF, LARRY, ins. co. exec.; b. Singen, Germany, June 27, 1947; came to U.S., 1950, naturalized, 1957; s. Herman H. and Vera (Mazin) R.; student Syracuse U., 1964-68, Rochester Inst. Tech., 1972-73, Am. Coll. Life Underwriters, 1980—; m. Donna A. Anders, Apr. 3, 1980; 1 son, Jeffrey P.; stepchildren—Debra and Marc Anders. Dist. credit mgr. Westinghouse Elec. Co., 1969-72; pres. Layhill Sounds Unltd., Inc., 1971-72; v.p. Sentry Color Labs., Ltd., 1973-75; sec.-treas. Magnum, Inc., 1975—; pres., chmn. bd. The Rubinoff Co., Balt., 1979—; chmn. bd., pres. The Richmore Co., 1980—. Bd. dirs. Mt. Royal Improvement Assn.; v.p. Citizens on Patrol, Perry Hall Gardens Improvement Assn. Served with U.S. Army, 1966-72. Mem. Nat. Assn. Life Underwriters. Democrat. Office: 300 N Charles St Suite 200 Baltimore MD 21201

RUBINOFF, RONALD S., mfg. co. exec.; b. Syracuse, N.Y., Feb. 9, 1956; s. Herman H. and Vera (Mazin) R.; B.S. in Fin. and Mktg., Syracuse U., 1977; m. T.J. Leah DeLuca. Asst. controller Air Conditioning Distbrs. Inc., Syracuse, 1975-76; asst. controller credit and collections Carrier Distbg. Co., Syracuse, 1976-77; accountant controllers dept. Carrier Air Conditioning Co., Syracuse, 1977, ops. analyst, mem. adminstrv. staff wholesale distbn. network, 1977-79, controller and ops. mgr. Carrier Distbg. Co., Miami, 1979—; cons. SBA. Jewish. Home: 450 N Commodore Dr Plantation FL 33325 Office: 120 NE 179th St North Miami Beach FL 33162

RUBINSKY, GERALD, publishing and mktg. co. exec.; b. Bklyn., June 23, 1929; s. Al and Jessie (Emerling) R.; B.B.A., Bklyn. Coll., 1951; postgrad. Acad. Advanced Traffic, 1952, Nat. Sales Tng. Inst. 1958-59; m. Thelma Ashkenazi, Oct. 7, 1951; children—Rhonda E. Rubinsky Palatiello, Susan M. Rubinsky Brodsky. Mktg. rep. Doubleday Pub. Co., Phila., 1960-61; asst. to v.p. Simon & Schuster, Inc., 1961-62; asst. nat. sales mgr. MacMillan, Inc., N.Y.C., 1962-64; dir. mktg. Am. R.D.M. Corp., N.Y.C., 1964-67, Arco Pub. Co., Inc., N.Y.C., 1967-70; dir. mktg. Times Mirror Corp., N.Y.C., 1970-71; v.p. mktg. Pyramid Communications div. Harcourt Brace Jovanovich Inc., N.Y.C., 1971-76; dir. planning Baker & Taylor div. W.R. Grace & Co., N.Y.C., 1976; pres., pub. Condor Pub. Co., Inc., N.Y.C., 1977-79; pres., chief exec. officer Mktg. Mates of Am., N.Y.C., 1979-80; nat. sales mgr. Internat. Patterns, Inc., Deer Park, N.Y., 1980—. Served with U.S. Army, 1948-50. Mem. Assn. Am. Pubs., Sales Execs. Club N.Y., Bklyn. Coll. Alumni Assn. Home: 3405 NW 48th Ave Lauderdale Lakes FL 33319 Office: 367 Bay Shore Rd Deer Park NY 11729

RUBLE, JOSEPH ROBERT, oil co. exec.; b. Pitts., Nov. 15, 1936; s. Joseph William and Gladys (Pricener) R.; B.S., John Carrol U., 1959; P.M.D., Harvard U., 1976; m. Carolyn T. Spieldenner, June 10, 1961; children—Joey, Theresa, John, Jim, Jeff, Jay. Sales rep. Sun Oil Co., Cleve., 1960-64, merchandising mgr., Pitts., 1964-67, sales mgr., 1967-73, dist. mgr., Tampa, Fla., 1974, Louisville, 1976-78, mgr. CAM2, pvt. label oils and automotive products, Phila., 1959—. Served to capt., U.S. Army, 1960. Mem. Am. Mgmt. Assn., Motor and Equipment Mfrs. Assn., Automotive Warehouse Distbrs. Assn., Automotive Parts and Accessories Assn. Roman Catholic. Home: Rural Route 7 Laurel Dr Vincentown NJ 08088 Office: 1845 Walnut St Philadelphia PA 19103

RUBLE, THOMAS JAMES, mfg. co. exec.; b. Toledo, Nov. 27, 1952; s. Eugene Leonard and Junita Ellen (Ferner) R.; B.M.E., Gen. Motors Inst., 1975; m. Jacquelyn Ann Deppen, Feb. 16, 1974; children—Brian Anthony, Craig Michael, Andrew Thomas. Prodn. engr. Delco Moraine div. Gen. Motors Corp., Dayton, Ohio, 1975-76, prodn. supr., 1976-77, prodn. gen. supr., 1977-79, project mgr., 1979—. Mem. Am. Mgmt. Assn., Soc. Mfg. Engrs., Theta Xi. Office: 1420 Wisconsin Blvd Dayton OH 45401

RUBLOFF, ARTHUR, real estate exec., developer; b. Duluth, Minn.; s. Solomon W. and Mary Rubloff; m. Josephine Sheehan; 1 dau., Mary Hilem Taylor. Engaged in real estate devel.; chmn. bd. Rubloff Devel Corp., rep. real estate interests throughout world; pres., chmn. bd. North Kansas City Devel Corp. (Mo.); developer Carl Sandburg Village, Chgo. Chmn. bd. dirs. United Cerebral Palsy Chgo.; chmn. bd., nat. exec. com. United Cerebral Palsy Assn., N.Y.C.; bd. dirs. Chgo. Heart Assn., Lyric Opera Chgo., Lawson YMCA, Chgo.; bd. dirs., v.p. One Hundred Club Chgo.; charter mem. bd. govs. Med. Research Inst. Michael Reese Hosp.; nat. bd. NCCJ; citizens bd. Loyola U., U. Chgo.; bd. dirs. Rehab. Inst. Chgo., Jr. Achievement of Chgo., Chgo. Boys Clubs, Bergstrom Mus.; trustee Hull House, Chgo. Recipient Columbus Ohio award Am. Planning and Civic Assn., 1954; Horatio Alger award Am. Schs. and Colls. Assn., 1956, Stella Della Solidarieta Italiana award, 1956, Man of Year award Catholic War Vets., 1963, Outstanding Civic Leader Little Fower Sem. Soc., 1969, award Chgo. Heart Assn., 1971, Chicagoan of Year Boys Clubs, 1972, King of Hearts Variety Clubs, 1972, Humanitarian award B'nai B'rith Internat., 1975, others. Fellow Brandeis U.; mem. Greater North Michigan Ave. Assn. (founder, dir., past pres.), State St. Council (dir.), All Chgo. Citizens Com., Chgo. Assn. Commerce and Industry (sec., dir.), Chgo. Better Bus. Bur. (adv. council), Internat. Real Estate Fedn. (Am. chpt.), Civic Fedn., Art Inst. Chgo., Chgo. Council of Girl Scouts, United Negro Coll. Fund. Nat. Assn. Housing and Redevel. Ofcls., Com. Econ., Cultural Devel., Chgo. Bd. Underwriters, Chgo. Real Estate Bd., Nat. Assn. Real Estate Bds., Mayor's Com. on Econ. Devel., Am. Soc. Real Estate Counselors, Lambda Alpha. Clubs: Standard, Execs., Oil Men's (hon.) Mid-Day, Whitehall, Met., Monroe, Mid-Am., Econ., Arts (Chgo.); Harmonie, Doubles, Hemisphere, El Morocco (N.Y.C.); Poinciana (Palm Beach, Fla.); Racquet (Palm Springs, Calif.). Pioneered, sponsored No. Mich. Ave-Magnificent Mile, Fort Dearborn, Old North Town; creator Evergreen Park Shopping Plaza, 1947; creator, developer Southland, Sun Valley and East Ridge. Home: 1040 Lake Shore Dr Chicago IL 60611 Office: 69 W Washington St Chicago IL 60602 also 781 Fifth Ave New York NY 10022

RUBLOFF, BURTON, real estate broker and appraiser; b. Chisholm, Minn., June 1, 1912; s. Solomon W. and Mary Rubloff; grad. Northwestern U., 1940; m. Patricia F. Williams, July 17, 1943; 1 dau., Jenifer. With Arthur Rubloff & Co., Chgo., 1930—, sr. v.p., 1976—. Bd. dirs. Municipal Art League Chgo., Wacker Dr. Assn., West Central Assn. Chgo. Served as sgt. AUS, 1943-46; ETO. Mem. Nat., Ill., Chgo. assns. real estate bds., Bldg. Mgrs. Assn. Chgo., Am. Inst. Real Estate Appraisers (Ill. chpt.), Lambda Alpha. Club: John Evans (Northwestern U.), City of Chgo. (gov.). Home: 633 N Waukegan Rd Lake Forest IL 60045 Office: 69 W Washington St Chicago IL 60602

RUBY, LUCIEN, venture capitalist; b. Knoxville, Tenn., Feb. 9, 1944; s. Clyde and Lorena Virginia (Dempster) R.; B.S.C.E., Duke U., 1966; M.B.A., Harvard U., 1977. Engr., RMK-BRJ, South Vietnam, 1966-67; founder, chief exec. officer Ruby Enterprises, Washington, 1969-75, Combined Supply Group, Ltd., 1971-74; pres. Antal's Restaurant, Inc., 1969-75; mgr. Vt. Investment Capital, Inc., South Royalton, Vt., 1976; partner Ruby Realty Co., Madisonville, Ky., 1967—; partner Kentuckian Assos., 1980, Tennessean Assos., 1980, TAPS Partners, 1980; asso. Strategic Planning Inst., 1977-79; prin. Brentwood Assos., Los Angeles, 1979—. Mem. Harvard Bus. Sch. Assn. (sect. sec.), Sigma Alpha Epsilon. Clubs: Santa Monica Rugby, HBS Old Boys Touring Rugby. Author: Venture Capital Investing, 1977. Office: 11661 San Vicente Blvd Los Angeles CA 90049

RUCCIUS, FREDERICK EDWARD, JR., banker; b. Wyndmoor, Pa., Feb. 29, 1928; s. Frederick Edward and Dorothy Mae (Maust) R.; student Muhlenberg Coll., 1945-46, U. Pa., eves. 1950-56; grad. Stonier Grad. Sch. Banking, Rutgers U., 1962; m. Ruth Louise Lowe, Aug. 13, 1949; children—Frederick Edward III, William L., Ann L., Karen L. Vice pres. Continental Bank, Norristown, Pa., 1948-68; sr. v.p. Bank of Pa., Reading, 1968-74, pres., 1974-77, chmn., chief exec. officer, dir., 1977—; dir. B-O-P Corp., BOP Realty Co. Nat. Bd. dirs., vice chmn. Camp Fire Inc.; bd. dirs. United Way Berks County, Reading Center City Devel. Fund, Greater Berks Devel. Fund, Chit Chat Found., Reading Musical Found., Community Gen. Hosp. Mem. Reading-Berks C. of C. (dir.), Pa. Bankers Assn. Republican. Lutheran. Clubs: Wyomissing, Berkshire, Iris. Home: 1006 Reading Blvd Wyomissing PA 19610 Office: Bank of Pennsylvania 50 N 5th St Reading PA 19603

RUCHABER, LARRY RALPH, mfg. co. exec.; b. Independence, Mo., Mar. 12, 1948; s. Harry F. and Ellen A. (Friend) R.; student Lane Community Coll., 1972-74, U. Oreg., 1974-76; children—Jason, Nichole. Rep., I.D.S., Inc., Jacksonville, Fla., 1971-72; stockbroker Walston & Co., Inc., Eugene, Oreg., 1972-75; stockbroker Foster & Marshall, Eugene, 1975-77, resident mgr., 1977-78; mng. partner L.R. Ruchaber & Assos., Roseburg, Oreg., 1977—; pres., chmn. bd. Orvest Industries, Inc., Roseburg, 1978—, Orteck Labs., Inc., Portland. Mem. council City of Roseburg, 1979—; 1st v.p. Umpqua Valley Homebuilders Assn., Roseburg, 1979—. Served with USN, 1966-70. Mem. Phi Theta Kappa. Republican. Office: 580 SE Oak St Roseburg OR 97470

RUCKSTUHL, KONRAD, resource recovery specialist; b. Basel, Switzerland, Aug. 27, 1920; came to U.S., 1977; s. Konrad Johann and Martha (Attinger) R.; grad. Comml. Inst., Basel, 1939; m. Judy Adair, June 30, 1968; children—Natascha, Tanya. With Swiss Waste Council, 1940; asso. resource recovery firms, 1940—; chmn. SPM Group, Inc., Englewood, Colo., 1977—; cons. Served with Swiss Army, World War II. Mem. Internat. Soc. Sugar Cane Technologists. Inventor, internat. patentee fields of resource recovery and waste processing. Home: 1019 E Easter Way Littleton CO 80122 Office: 14 Inverness Dr E Englewood CO 80112

RUDA, HOWARD, finance co. exec.; b. N.Y.C., Sept. 7, 1932; s. Menahem and Lucy (Gillenson) R.; B.A., Coll. City N.Y., 1954; J.D., Columbia, 1959; m. Leah E. Zeliger, Sept. 22, 1963. Admitted to N.Y. bar, 1959; asso. then partner firm Laporte & Meyers, N.Y.C., 1959-63; with C.I.T. Fin. Corp., N.Y.C., 1963—, asst. gen. counsel, 1968—, gen. counsel, v.p., dir. C.I.T. Corp., C.I.T. Leasing Corp., 1973—. Served with U.S. Army, 1954-56. Mem. Phi Beta Kappa. Jewish. Home: 8 Mirrielees Rd Great Neck NY 11021 Office: 650 Madison Ave New York NY 10022

RUDDY, GLEN DEE, consumer credit exec.; b. Cle Elm, Wash., Apr. 1, 1919; s. Roland Earl and Pearl (Razey) R.; m. Mabel Eileen Mayes, Jan. 22, 1946. Pres. Credit Burs. Tulare County, Visalia, Calif., 1945—, Electronic Bus. Service, Visalia, 1961—; coordinator Automation Research, Inc., 1961—; pres. Glen D. Ruddy Enterprises, Inc., 1968—; sec. A.M. Systems, Inc., Reno, 1967—; pres. Affiliated Comml. Agys., Inc., Visalia, 1976—; v.p. Affiliated Credit Burs. Ontario-Pomona, Ontario, Calif., 1973—; partner Credit Bur. Dinuba-Reedley, Visalia, 1960—, Bonded Collection Services, South Gate, Calif., 1974—. Dean Western Mgmt. Inst., U. Calif., 1964. Served with AUS, 1940-45, 52-53. Hon. fellow Certified Consumer Credit Execs.; mem. Asso. Credit Burs. Pacific S.W. (sec.-treas. 1955-68, chmn. bd. trustees group ins. 1960—), Internat. Consumer Credit Assn., Calif. Assn. Collectors (unit pres. 1976—), Med.-Dental-Hosp. Assn. Am. (nat. (treas.), Internat. Platform Assn., Medallion Mktg. Assn. (pres. 1974—). Home: 811 Linda Vista Visalia CA 93277 Office: 132 N Valley Oaks Dr Visalia CA 93291

RUDE, ALAN JOHN, securities co. exec.; b. Montclair, N.J., Dec. 13, 1938; s. Alan Gregory and Bea Bernadette (Downey) R.; B.A. in Econs. with honors, Cornell U., 1960; M.B.A. in Fin., Harvard U., 1962; m. Eleanor May Stanford, Aug. 19, 1961; children—Catherine Anne, Mary Elizabeth. Asso., Dillon Read & Co. N.Y.C., 1964-65; mgr. planning Celanese Corp., N.Y.C., 1965-68; pres. Globalmart Internat., Inc. Rockville, Md., 1968-71; asst. treas. Am. Home Products, N.Y.C., 1971-73; v.p. 1st Jersey Securities, N.Y.C., 1973-75; v.p. Paine Webber Jackson & Curtis, N.Y.C., 1976-80; partner A.J. Rude & Co., Yardley, Pa., 1980—. Candidate, Morrisville Boro Council, 1977; regional dir. Carter Campaign, 1976; vestryman Episcopalian Ch. of Incarnation, Morrisville, Pa. Served as 1st lt. U.S. Army, 1962-64. Mem. Money Marketeers N.Y. Democrat. Club: Investment of N.Y., Cornell, Park Pl. Squash (N.Y.C.). Home: 451 N Lafayette St Morrisville PA 19067 Office: 10 Penn Valley Dr Yardley PA 19067

RUDEL, THOMAS RYDER, machine tool exec.; b. Montreal, Que., Can., Apr. 20, 1905 (parents Am. citizens); s. Clarence Merrill and Anna (Ryder) R.; A.B., Princeton U., 1929; m. Doris Taylor, July 3, 1934 (dec. Feb. 1970); 1 dau., Barbara Susan (Mrs. John K. Wendt); m. 2d, Margaret Murchison, Apr. 3, 1971. With Eberhard Faber Pencil Co., 1932-52, pres., chmn. bd., 1949-52; founder, chmn. bd. Rudel Machinery Co., Inc., 1941—; with Rudel Machinery Co., Ltd., 1938-60, chmn. bd., 1944-60; founder, chmn. bd. Am. SIP Corp., 1950—; dir., chmn. bd. V. & O. Press Co., Inc.; dir. Baker Bros., Inc., Lynch Corp.; pres., dir. Am. Machine Tool Consortium, Inc.; trustee Lincoln Savs. Bank; asst. dir. machine tool div. NPA, 1951-52. Trustee Lawrenceville Sch., Ethel Walker Sch., Goucher Coll. Mem. U.S. Trade Mark Assn. (dir. 1940-52), Am. Soc. Tool Engrs., Am. Arbitration Assn. (panel arbitrators), Acad. Polit. Sci. (life), Bklyn. C. of C. (dir. 1949-70), Nat. Machine Tool Builders Assn. (treas., dir. 1969-72, chmn. bd. 1977-78), Am. Machine Tool Distbrs. Assn. (dir., pres. 1953-54). Episcopalian. Home: 2 Sutton Pl S New York NY 10022 Office: 100 E 42d St New York NY 10017

RUDER, WILLIAM, pub. relations cons.; b. N.Y.C., Oct. 17, 1921; s. Jacob L. and Rose (Rosenburg) R.; B.S.S., Coll. City N.Y., 1942; m. Helen Finn, Sept. 21, 1945 (div. Jan. 1, 1980); children—Robin, Abby, Brian, Michal Ellen, Eric; m. Betty Cott. May 23, 1980. Dir. exploitation Samuel Goldwyn Prodns., 1946-48; pres. Ruder & Finn, Inc., N.Y.C., 1948—; asst. sec. U.S. Dept. Commerce, 1960-62; with Kelso Bangert & Co., Inc. (investment banking); Tobe lectr. Harvard U. Mem. Harrison (N.Y.) Sch. Bd.; chmn. Harrison Twp. Democratic Com.; exec. com. Bus. Com. for the Arts; bd. govs. UN Assn.; chmn. Manhattanville Coll. Served to capt. USAF, 1941-46. Co-author: The Businessman's Guide to Washington, 1964, rev. edit., 1975. Office: 110 E 59th St New York NY 10022

RUDINE, RUBY LEOTA THAGARD (MRS. WALTER HENRY RUDINE), steel co. exec.; b. Lockney, Tex., Dec. 9, 1908; d. Thomas Warner and Ora J. (Waggoner) Thagard; student pub. schs.; m. Walter Henry Rudine, July 12, 1938. With Santa Fe Ry., Los Angeles, 1925-26; sr. stenographer, clk. Planning Commn., City of Inglewood (Calif.) Bldg. Dept., 1926-48; v.p. Riverside Steel, Santa Fe Springs, Calif., 1952-79, Riverton Indsl. Steel Co., South Gate, Calif., 1966—, Valley Engring., Rialto, Calif., 1956—. Clubs: Los Coyotes Country (Buenos Park, Calif.); Founders (Los Angeles); Friendly Hills Womans (Whittier, Calif.). Home: 9726 La Cima Dr Whittier CA 90603 Office: 11400 Greenstone Santa Fe Springs CA 90670

RUDING, H. ONNO, banker; b. Breda, Netherlands, Aug. 15, 1939; s. Roelof and Annie M. (Fehmers) R.; M.S. in Econs., Erasmus U., Rotterdam, 1964, Ph.D. in Econs. cum laude, 1969; m. Renée V. Hekking, Apr. 24, 1971; 2 children. Head div. internat. monetary affairs Treasury Gen., Netherlands Ministry Fin., The Hague, 1965-70; joint gen. mgr. Amsterdam-Rotterdam Bank NV, 1971-76, mem. bd. mng. dirs., 1981—; exec. dir. IMF, Washington, 1977-80. Served as officer Dutch Army, 1964-65. Office: Herengracht 595 1017 CE Amsterdam Netherlands

RUDMAN, DANIEL STEPHEN, mgmt. cons.; b. Galesburg, Ill., Nov. 15, 1945; s. Mitchell and Rose (Levy) R.; B.S., U. Ill., 1969; m. Susan Meyer, June 22, 1969; children—Debbie, Julie. With Brown Specialty, Galesburg, 1969-75, Doyle Furniture, Galesburg, 1975; owner, mgmt. cons. Rudman & Assos., Galesburg, 1976—. Chmn., Mayor's Com. on Recreation, Galesburg, 1978; treas. Temple Sholom, Galesburg, 1978-80. Named Outstanding Person in Ill., Ill. Jr. C. of C., 1978. Mem. Galesburg Jr. C. of C. (pres. 1975), Galesburg C. of C. (dir. 1975), Ill. Soc. C.P.A.'s, Am. Mgmt. Assn., Am. Soc. Tng. and Devel., Alpha Kappa Psi, Beta Gamma Sigma. Republican. Jewish. Club: B'nai B'rith (pres. 1978—). Author tapes: Winning Attitudes and Actions, 1979; Tax Planning for Small Corporations, 1979; Stress and Relaxation, 1980; Estate Planning is for Everyone, 1980. Home: 1033 Woodbine Circle Galesburg IL 61401 Office: 1320 N Henderson St Galesburg IL 61401

RUDMAN, JACK, publishing co. exec.; b. N.Y.C., Oct. 29, 1912; s. Max and Fannie (Marder) R.; B.A., Coll. City N.Y., 1931, M.S. in Edn., 1933; postgrad. New Sch., 1942-45; m. Frances Zimmerman, Jan. 30, 1943; children—Gerald J., Stephanie R. (Mrs. William K. Joseph), Michael P. Tchr. social studies high schs., N.Y.C., 1935-61; lectr. polit. sci. Queens Coll., Flushing, N.Y., 1948-60; pres., chief exec. officer, editor-in-chief, dir. Nat. Learning Corp., Syosset, N.Y., 1967—; pres., chief exec. officer, editor-in-chief, dir. Coll. Pub. Corp., Bklyn., 1954-66. Served with AUS, World War II. Mem. Assn. Am. Pubs., Com. of Publicly Owned Cos., Com. Econ. Devel., Pres.'s Assn., Nat. Assn. Corp. Dirs. Author, editor over 3000 books, including Passbook Series, Admission Test Series, Merriwell Series, College-Level Examination Series, Career Examination Series. Office: 212 Michael Dr Syosset NY 11791

RUDOLPH, ALLEN MORTON, elec. mfg. co. exec.; b. Cambridge, Mass., Jan. 3, 1932; s. William J. and Bessie C. Rudolph; B.S., Tufts U., 1953; m. Sylvia Sacks, Dec. 14, 1952; children—Deborah Ellen, Helene Paula, Gregory Charles. Partner, Rudolph & Co., Boston, 1953-79; pres. Rudolph & Co., Inc., Boston, 1979—. Chmn. VIP telethon com. United Cerebral Palsy Found., Boston, 1976-80; bd. dirs. United Cerebral Palsy of Met. Boston, 1976. Mem. Nat. Elec. Mfrs. Reps. Assn. (pres. 1978-79, gov., exec. com., Disting. Service award 1980). Clubs: Chesnut Hill Country (v.p. 1977-78), Masons. Developer computer program for elec. mfrs. reps. Home: 75 Woodchester Dr Chestnut Hill MA 02167 Office: 568 E 1st St PO Box 232 Boston MA 02127

RUDOLPH, RONALD EARL, utility exec.; b. Grayville, Ill., Mar. 1, 1903; s. Loren and Grace (Estes) R.; grad. Foot's Bus. Coll., 1919; m. Marian H. Faust, May 22, 1930; 1 dau., Barbara (Mrs. George F. Kachlein III). Sec.-treas., mgr. Wyo. Res. Oil Co., Ellensburg, Wash., 1935—; mgr., pres. Ellensburg Telephone Co., 1937-70, chmn. bd., 1970—; mgr., pres. Selah Telephone Co. (Wash.) (merged with Ellensburg Telephone Co.), 1950-70; clk. Bur. Reclamation, Boise, Idaho, 1919-26, chief accountant, 1926-35, sec.-treas. Kittitas County Reclamation Dist., Ellensburg, 1930-35; personnel dir. Lower Colo. River Authority, Austin, Tex., 1935-37. Pres., YMCA, 1936-44, Community Chest, 1948; bd. dirs. Community Concert Assn., 1944-49, pres., 1946-47; bd. dirs. Boy Scouts Am., 1944-45. Mem. U.S. Ind. Telephone Assn. (dir. 1958-66, pres. 1963-64), Ellensburg C. of C. (pres. 1945). Episcopalian. Clubs: Rotary (past pres.), Elks; Press, Century 21, Ellensburg Golf and Country, Yakima (Wash.) Golf and Country, Seattle Golf, Wash. Athletic (Seattle), Seattle Rainier, Birnam Woods Golf, Balboa (Mexico). Home: 901 E 2d Ave Ellensburg WA 98926 Office: PO Box 308 Ellensburg WA 98926

RUEF, GORDON MICHAEL, fin. exec.; b. Bremerton, Wash., Nov. 29, 1948; s. Gordon L. and Janice A. (Olund) R.; B.A., U. Va., 1973, postgrad., 1973; 1 dau., Erin Danielle. Sales asso. Carriage Realty, Washington, 1973-75, loan officer Steed Mortgage Co., Washington, 1975-76; asst. v.p. mortgage lending Carey Winston Co., Camp Springs, Md., 1977—. Republican. Office: 4710 Auth Pl Suite 530 Camp Springs DC 20031

RUEGSEGGER, LOYAL, JR., elec. co. exec.; b. Canton, Ohio, June 19, 1920; s. Loyal and Dora (Leyman) R.; student Purdue U., 1945-46; B.S. in Elec. Engring., Ohio No. U., 1950; m. L. June Smith, May 20, 1944; children—Carol June, Loyal III. Test engr. Eureka Williams Corp., Bloomington, Ill., 1950-51; system relay engr. Ohio Power Co., Canton, 1951-54; coordinator field engrs. Ohio Valley Electric Corp., Gallipolis, Ohio, 1954-56, system engr. meter supr., Piketon, Ohio, 1956—. Corr. Edison Electric Inst. Judge, Ohio State Jr. Science Fair at Ohio Wesleyan U., Delaware. Served from pvt. to tech. sgt. USAAF, 1941-45. Decorated D.F.C., Air Medal with 10 oak leaf clusters (Army). Mem. Mid-South Metermens Assn. (2d v.p. 1957-58), I.E.E.E. (sr.), Power Engr. Soc. (sr.), Ohio Acad. Sci., Nat., Ky. Socs. profl. engrs., Instrument Soc. Am. (sr. mem.), V.F.W., Am. Legion, AMVETS, Mason (Shriner); mem. Order Eastern Star. Contbr. articles to profl. jours. Home: 1171 SR552 Waverly OH 45690 Office: PO Box 468 Piketon OH 45661

RUF, JACOB FREDERICK, info. systems devel. exec.; b. Kansas City, Mo., Dec. 30, 1936; s. Paul William and Amalia (Maier) R.; Asso. Sci. in Engring., Met. Jr. Coll. Kansas City; B.S. in Chem. Engring., Kans. U., 1959, M.S., 1967; m. Sondra Sue Ramsey, Aug. 30, 1957; children—Kurtis M., Brian A., Eric J., Jacob Frederick II, Sondra Sue II. Research engr. Panhandle Eastern Pipe Line, 1959-61; supr. sci. systems Great Lakes Pipe Line, 1961-63; mgr. systems devel. Black & Sivals & Bryson, Kansas City, Mo., 1963-66; dir. data systems Met. Planning Commn., Kansas City region, 1966-69; pres. Mid-Continent Computing Inc., Kansas City, Mo., 1967-69; exec. v.p. Info. Systems Devel. Inc., Kansas City, 1969-77; v.p. NLT-Computer Services Corp., 1976-77; pres. Ruf Corp., Olathe, Kans., 1976—; chmn. Internat. Users Group, Info. Mgmt. Process Reporting System, 1979—. Mem. accrediting study team Nat. Assn. Trade and Tech. Schs.; math. judge Nat. Sci. Fair, 1973, Kansas City Sci. Fair; mem. adv. bd. Mid-Am. regional council Emergency Med. Systems; mem. Gov. Kans. Adv. Council Info. and Communication Systems, 1968-74, Gov. Mo. Adv. Council Comprehensive Health Planning, 1972-73, Gov. Mo. Adv. Council State Center Health Statistics; mem. Jo. County (Kans.) Mayors Adv. Bd. Transp. Planning, 1971-72; mem. mid-Am. regional council Population Projection Adv. Bd. and econ. devel. adv. com.; mem. Merriam (Kans.) Zoning Bd. Appeals, Jo. County Water Bd., 1970-72; tech. adv. com. Kansas City Heart Assn., 1975—; bd. dirs. Infant Devel. Center, 1979—. Served with USNR, 1954-59. Mem. Assn. Computing Machinery (chmn. Kansas City chpt. 1967), Am. Inst. Chem. Engrs., Mo. Pub. Health Assn., Urban and Regional Info. Systems Assn. Contbr. articles on chem. engring., urban planning, info. systems to tech. jours. Home: 13700 Pflumm Rd Olathe KS 66062 Office: 9726 Pflumm Rd Olathe KS 66061

RUFFI, STEPHEN JOSEPH, multinat. mfg. co. exec.; b. McAdoo, Pa., Oct. 25, 1927; s. Stephen John and Stephanie (Severa) R.; B.A., Columbia U., 1950, M.S., Grad. Sch. Bus., 1951; m. Audree Kuehne, Sept. 12, 1953; children—Andrea, Stephen G., Leslie. Sr. auditor Arthur Andersen & Co., 1951-56; asst. controller Emhart Corp., Farmington, Conn., 1956-61, asst. treas., then treas., 1961-67, v.p. internat., 1967-72, group pres. for spl. machinery, 1972-76, exec. v.p., 1979—, also dir., 1980—, group pres. United Machinery Group, USM Corp. subs., Beverly, Mass., 1976-79; dir. Emhart Industries, Inc., USM Corp., United Shore Machinery Corp. (Internat.), Ltd., USM Spain, AB Sundsvall Verkstader; asso. dir. Conn. Bank & Trust Co. Bd. dirs. Hartford Symphony Orch., 1963—, mem. exec. com., 1973—, v.p., 1973-79, 1st v.p., 1979-80. Served with U.S. Army, 1946-47. C.P.A., N.Y. State. Mem. Am. Inst. C.P.A.'s, Conn. Soc. C.P.A.'s. Home: 93 Westmont St West Hartford CT 06117 Office: 426 Colt Hwy Farmington CT 06032

RUFFLEY, JOSEPH FRANCIS, accountant; b. Hollidaysburg, Pa., June 2, 1913; s. Frank and Anna M. R.; B.S., Strayer Coll., 1939; M.C.S., Columbus U., 1941; B.S., Am. U., 1965; m. Ruth Constance Yingling, 1937; children—Constance Ann Ruffley Locraft, Donald Frank, Joseph Francis. Mem. staff R.G. Rankin & Co., C.P.A.'s, 1939-48; mgr. Washington office, 1945-48; partner Sayre & Stiles, Accountants and Auditors, 1948-50; top supervisory auditor GAO, Washington, 1950-69; dir. audit staff Office of Treas., Dept. Treasury, 1969-74, dir. audit staff Bur. Govt. Fin. Ops., 1974—. C.P.A. Mem. Am. Inst. C.P.A.'s, Am. Accounting Assn., Fed. Govt. Accountants Assn., Am. Soc. Pub. Adminstrn. Roman Catholic. Home: 408 Ethan Allen Ave Takoma Park MD 20012 Office: 1100 Vermone Ave NW Washington DC 20226

RUFFNER, FREDERICK G., JR., publisher; b. Akron, Ohio, Aug. 6, 1926; s. Frederick G. and Olive Mae (Taylor) R.; B.S., Ohio State U., 1950; m. Mary Ann Evans, Oct. 8, 1954; children—Frederick G., Peter Evans. Advt. mgr. Jim Robbins Co., Royal Oak, Mich., 1950-52; research mgr. Gen. Detroit Corp., 1953-55; pres. Gale Research Co., reference book pub., Detroit, 1954—. Mem. exec. bd. Detroit council Boy Scouts Am., 1974—, v.p. council, 1976—; bd. dirs. Friends of Library Ohio State U., Friends of Detroit Pub. Library, 1969—, pres., 1975-76; trustee Bon Secours Hosp., Grosse Pointe, Mich., Etruscan Found., Florence, Italy. Served to 1st lt. AUS, 1944-46. Decorated Bronze Star; recipient Centennial award Ohio State U., 1970, Mem. Am. Antiquarian Soc., Am. Mgmt. Assn., ALA, Info. Industry Assn., Am. Assn. Museums, Bibliog. Soc. Am., Newcomen Soc., Nature Conservancy, Sierra Club, Econ. Club, Archives Am. Art, Am. Name Soc., Early Am. Industries Assn., Hist. Soc. Mich., Pres.'s Assn., Nat. Trust Historic Preservation, Navy League, Am. Land Devel. Assn., Jaguar Soc., Citroen Club, Fairfield Heritage Soc., Pvt. Libraries Assn., Friends Ft. Lauderdale Pub. Library (pres. 1974—), Ohio State U. Club (pres. Detroit chpt. 1958), Tau Kappa Epsilon. Republican. Methodist (mem. bd.). Clubs: Masons, Shriners; Torch, Detroit Athletic, Detroit, Book (dir. 1967-71), Prismatic (Detroit); Scarab; Faculty (Ohio State U.); Marco Polo, Princeton, Salmagundi (N.Y.C.); Le Club Internat. (Ft. Lauderdale, Fla.); Ocean Reef (Key Largo, Fla.); Los Angeles Athletic; Grosse Pointe Yacht. Editor: Ency. of Associations, 1956-68, Code Names Dictionary, 1963, Acronyms and Initialisms Dictionary, 1965. Patentee in field of graphic arts. Home: 221 Lewiston Rd Grosse Pointe Farms MI 48236 also 336 Coral Way Fort Lauderdale FL 33301 Office: Gale Research Co Book Tower Detroit MI 48226 also 1700 E Las Olas Blvd Fort Lauderdale FL 33301

RUGER, WILLIAM BATTERMAN, firearms mfg. co. exec.; b. Bklyn., June 21, 1916; s. Adolph and May R.; student U. N.C., 1936-38; m. Mary Thompson, Aug. 26, 1938; children—William Batterman, Carolyn Amalie Ruger Vogel, James Thompson. Firearms design engr. U.S. Armory, Springfield, Mass., 1939-40; small arms designer Auto Ordnance, Bridgeport, Conn., 1941-45; founder, pres. Ruger Corp., Southport, Conn., 1946-48; co-founder Sturm, Ruger & Co., Inc., Southport, 1948, chmn., pres., treas., Southport, also Newport, N.H., 1948—. Past trustee Salisbury Sch.; past bd. dirs. Nat. Shooting Sports Found. Recipient Handgunner of Yr. award, 1975; Nat. Leadership award Hunting Hall of Fame, 1979. Mem. Nat. Rifle Assn. (past dir.), Sporting Arms and Ammunition Inst. (v.p.), Vintage Sports Car Club Am., Rolls Royce Owners Club, Bentley Driver's Club Ltd., Blue Mountain Forest Assn., Delta Kappa Epsilon. Lutheran. Clubs: Campfire, Pequot Yacht. Contbr. articles on firearms and related subjects to profl. publs.; patentee in field of firearms. Office: Lacey Pl Southport Conn 06490 also Sturm Ruger & Co Inc Guild Rd Newport NH 03773

RUGGLES, RICHARD LEROY, food mfg. corp. exec.; b. Peoria, Ill., July 20, 1936; s. Harold Ira and Edna (McManus) R.; student St. Ambrose Coll., 1955-57; B.S., Bradley U., 1959; postgrad. U. Wis.; m. Veronica Jurkovich, Apr. 4, 1959; children—Michael Joseph, Joseph Patrick, Robert James, Ann Marie, Andrew Richard, Patricia. Documentation clk. Caterpillar Tractor Co., Peoria, 1959-60; with Oscar Mayer & Co., 1960-78, large accounts sales rep., Mpls., 1965-66, dist. sales mgr., Charlotte, N.C., 1966-68, asst. plant sales mgr., Davenport, Iowa, 1968-69, distbn. center mgr., Oklahoma City, 1969-78; gen. mgr. OM Ingredients, Inc., Madison, Wis., 1978—. Mem. Am. Mgmt. Assn., Am. Spice Trade Assn., Potato Chip/Snack Food Assn., Inst. Food Technologists, Pickle Packers Internat., Nat. Food Brokers Assn. Republican. Roman Catholic. Office: OM Ingredients Inc 1910 Roth St Madison WI 53701

RUGGLES, ROBERT THOMAS, fin. exec., investment counselor; b. Waterloo, Ia., Oct. 11, 1931; s. Thomas C. and Georgia (Whitmer) R.; B.S. in Commerce, N.Y.U., 1954, M.B.A., 1956; m. Francine Paré, May 31, 1958; children—Ruth Marie, Anne Catharine. Came to Can., 1964. Asst. economist Savs. Banks Trust Co., N.Y.C., 1957-59; chief statistician Coty, Inc., N.Y.C., 1959-62; corporate economist Internat. Minerals and Chem. Co., Skokie, Ill., 1962-64, Anthes Ltd., St. Catherine's, Ont., Can., 1964-66; with Imasco Ltd., Montreal, Que., Can., 1966-81, mgr. pension fund investments, 1969-71, corporate v.p., 1971-81, also dir.; chmn. and chief exec. officer Ruggles & Crysdale, Inc., investment counseling and pension funds mgmt. co., Toronto, Ont., 1981—; dir. Can. Northwest Land Ltd. Served with USN, 1951-54. Office: Royal Bank Plaza PO Box 84 Toronto ON M5J 2J2 Canada

RUHLMAN, JAMES DOUGLAS, indsl. engr.; b. Warren, Pa., Nov. 3, 1942; s. Herman Cloyd and Virginia Lee (Weimer) R.; student Metals Engring. Inst., 1974; m. Nancy Ellen Lobdell, Nov. 3, 1967; children—Justin Douglas, James David. Final insp. Nat. Forge Co., 1968-69, cost estimator, Irvine, Pa., 1969-76, product engr., 1976-79, supr. product engring., 1979—. Pres., Irvine Elementary Sch. PTA, 1976-77. Served with USMC, 1960-64. Mem. Am. Soc. Metals. Home: RD 1 Box 18 Youngsville PA 16371 Office: Front St Irvine PA 16329

RUIZ, JOSE ALEJANDRO, constrn. co. exec.; b. Lima, Peru, Feb. 20, 1948; s. Pedro Alejandro and Estela Aida (Correa) R.; B. Mech. and Elec. Engring., Universidad Nacional de Ingenieria, Lima, Peru, 1968; B.S. in E.E., Bucknell U., 1970; M.S. in E.E., Stanford U., 1974; m. Teresita Jesus Marquez, June 17, 1971; children—Noe Alfredo, Saul Efrain. Project engr. Amdhal Corp., Sunnyvale, Calif., 1972-74; owner, mgr. Reliable Packaging, San Jose, Calif., 1974-75; land officer Techo Inc., Watsonville, Calif., 1975-77, project devel. officer, 1977-78, chief exec. officer, 1978—; cons. Appropriate Tech. Internat. Cons., Capitola, Calif. Mem. adv. com. on tech. edn. U. Calif., Santa Cruz, 1978; past bd. dirs. El Pajaro Community Devel. Corp.; bd. dirs., sec. Santa Cruz Community Credit Union, Inc., 1979—; bd. dirs., treas. South County Commn. on Alcoholism, 1979-81. Stanford U. fellow, 1970-74. Mem. IEEE, Nat. Soc. Profl. Engrs., Alexander Hamilton Inst., Soc. for Internat. Devel., Nat. Assn. Housing and Redevel. Ofcls., Calif. Coalition for Rural Housing, Internat. Assn. for Housing Sci. Home: PO Box 1133 Watsonville CA 95077 Office: 10 Alexander St Watsonville CA 95076

RULE, ELTON H., communications co. exec.; b. Stockton, Calif.; s. James Elton and Lillian (Hoerl) R.; grad. Sacramento Coll.; m. Betty Louise Bender; children—Cindy Rule Dunne, Christie, James. With KABC-TV, Los Angeles, 1952-68, v.p., gen. mgr., 1961-68; pres. ABC TV Network, 1968-70; group v.p. Am. Broadcasting Cos., Inc., N.Y.C., 1969-70, broadcast div. pres., 1970-72, pres., chief operating officer, mem. exec. com., 1972—, dir., 1970—. Mem. adv. bd. and exec. com. Inst. Sports Medicine and Athletic Trauma, Lenox Hill Hosp., N.Y.C., 1973—; charter mem. bd. visitors UCLA Sch. Medicine, 1980—. Mem. Calif. Broadcasters Assn. (pres. 1966-67). Office: 1330 Ave of the Americas New York NY 10019

RULEMAN, DAVID ARNOLD, broadcasting exec.; b. Vancouver, Wash., Nov. 6, 1946; s. Robert Nelson and Freda Agnes (Hall) R.; student Mesa Coll., San Diego, 1965-67, San Diego State U., 1967-68; Engr. license Wade Sch. Radio and TV, 1968; m. Tracy Jeanne Murray, May 13, 1966; children—Lisa Ann, Anastasia Louise, Monica Marie. Newswriter, Sta. KSDO, San Diego, 1967-68; news dir. KWCO, Chickasha, Okla., 1969-70; news corr. Mid Am. Media, Moline, Ill., 1970-71; broadcaster KSDO News Radio, San Diego, 1971; gen. mgr. Hart Enterprises, Inc., San Diego, 1971-72; sales mgr. KOWN AM & FM, Escondido, Calif., 1973-76, v.p., gen. mgr., 1976—; pres. Wordsworth, Inc., Radio Del Rey Inc., 1978—, Sta. KRKC, 1979—, Thousand Oaks Radio Corp., 1980—, Sta KNJO; guest instr. Palomar Coll. Mem. coordinating com. Combined Fed. Campaign, San Diego, 1976—; community chmn. Escondido United Way/Chad Campaign, 1977; bd. dirs. United Way North County, 1980—; bd. dirs. North County Assn. for Retarded, San Diego, recipient Friendship award, 1975-76; pub. relations coordinator Am. Cancer Soc., Escondido, 1978; bd. dirs. Salvation Army, Escondido. Recipient 11 awards for best story coverage Okla. AP, best news coverage Okla., 1969, best investigative reporting and coverage Iowa Broadcasters and Ill. News Broadcast Assn., 1970, Hon. Okie award Okla. Gov. Dewey Bartlett, 1969, Move the Bell award for fund raising promotion for moving Liberty Bell, 1976. Mem. San Diego Broadcasters Assn., Calif. Advt. Club, Radio and TV News Dirs., Calif. Assn. for Retarded (award for fund raising for spl. olympics 1975), Escondido C. of C. Trade Club. Democrat. Club: Kiwanis (charter pres.) (S. Escondido). Home: 1832 Craigmore Ave Escondido CA 92027 Office: 1523 E Valley Pkwy Escondido CA 92026

RUMELY, EMMET SCOTT, ret. automobile co. exec., co. exec., banker; b. N.Y.C., Feb. 15, 1918; s. Edward A. and Fanny (Scott) R.; B.S., Yale U., 1939; postgrad. U. Mich., 1940-41; m. Elizabeth Hodges, July 5, 1947; children—Virginia H., Elizabeth Scott (Mrs. Charles F. Visser), Scott Hodges. Mgr., Marenisco Farms, La Porte County, Ind., 1939-73; dir. La Porte Hotel Co., Inc., 1938-70, pres., 1965-70; pres., dir. Rumely Corp., 1970—; product planning mgr. tractor ops. Ford Motor Co., Birmingham, Mich., 1961-70, asst. to v.p., gen. mgr., 1970-75; dir. 1st Nat. Bank & Trust Co., La Porte, 1953—. Mem. Detroit Fine Arts Founders Soc., Am. Soc. Agrl. Engrs., Soc. Automotive Engrs., Am. Mktg. Assn., Detroit Hist. Assn. Clubs: Orchard Lake (Mich.) Country; Huron Mountain (Big Bay, Mich.); Otsego Ski (Gaylord, Mich.); Yale (Detroit). Home: 207 Abbey Rd Birmingham MI 48008 Office: 800 Jefferson Ave La Porte IN 46350

RUMMLER, GEARY ALBERT, mgmt. cons.; b. Belding, Mich., Apr. 16, 1937; s. Richard Albert and Josephine Juanita (Crampton) R.; B.B.A., U. Mich., 1959, M.B.A., 1960, Ed.S., 1968, Ph.D., 1971; m. Margaret Mary Tetzlaff, Sept. 8, 1956; children—Christopher, Richard, Matthew. Asst. personnel dir. Office Research Adminstrn., U. Mich., 1960-61, asst. dir. Inst. Behavioral Research and Programmed Instrn., 1961-62, co-founder, dir. Center Programmed Learning for Bus., 1962-69; pres., co-founder Praxis Corp., N.Y.C., 1969-79; pres. Kepner-Tregoe Strategy Group, Princeton, N.J., 1979—; lectr. Harvard U., Catholic U. Am., Fairleigh-Dickinson U. Treas. Watchung Hills (N.J.) Adult Sch., 1976-78. Mem. Nat. Soc. Performance and Instrn. (pres. 1968; Presdl. citation 1972, Life Mem. award 1977), Am. Soc. Tng. and Devel., Tng. Research Forum. Author: Managing the Instructional Programming Effort, 1967, Labor Relations for Supervisors, 1968; also articles, chpt. in handbook. Office: PO Box 704 Research Rd Princeton NJ 08540

RUMPELTIN, FRANK EDWARD, JR., mfg. co. exec.; b. Newark, May 17, 1945; s. Frank Edward and Lillian Veronica (Hallisey) R.; A.B., Lafayette Coll., 1967; M.B.A., Rutgers U., 1969; m. Elizabeth Estelle Wynne, Aug. 2, 1969; children—Frank Edward, Evelyn Wynne, Elizabeth Blair. Product mgr. Am. Cyanamid Co., Wayne, N.J., 1969-73; account exec. Wells, Rich, Green Advt. Agy., N.Y.C., 1973; product mgr. Lehn & Fink Products Co., Montvale, N.J., 1973-75, group product mgr., 1975-77, v.p. mktg., 1977-78, exec. asst. to pres., 1978-79; pres. The d-Con Co., Inc., Montvale, 1979—. Mem. Zeta Psi. Club: Optimists (Chester). Roman Catholic. Home: South Rd Chester NJ 07930 Office: 225 Summit Ave Montvale NJ 07645

RUMPH, HAROLD HENRY, data communications co. exec.; b. Amarillo, Tex., Oct. 3, 1930; s. Clarice P. and Rosalie (Roy) R.; B.S., U.S. Naval Acad., 1953; m. Norma Jean Veglia, Dec. 14, 1976; children—Pierce, Christina, Rhonda, Elizabeth, Margaret, Stephen, Michael. System engr. IBM, 1962-65, system engring. mgr., 1965-69, br. mgr., 1969-70; mgr. large systems RCA, Marlboro, Mass., 1970-71; dir. mktg. Amdahl Corp., Sunnyvale, Calif., 1972-73; regional mgr. Milacron, Cin., 1973-74; mgr. office info. systems planning Xerox Corp., El Segundo, Calif., 1974-75; v.p. mktg. Memorex Corp., Santa Clara, Calif., 1975-76; v.p. mktg. Harris Computer Systems Div., Dallas, 1976-79, Harris Data Communications Div., 1979—. Leader, Cub Scouts Am., 1964-66, Boy Scouts Am., 1967-73; active civic assns., Littleton, Colo., 1966-68, Carmel, Ind., 1969-70. Served to capt. USAF, 1953-62. Recipient Outstanding System Engr. award IBM 1964, Outstanding Contbn. award, 1966, Pres.'s Cup, 1969. Mem. U.S. Naval Acad. Alumni Assn. (life). Republican. Methodist. Home: 6319 Mill Point Circle Dallas TX 75248 Office: Harris Data Communications Div 16001 Dallas Pkwy Dallas TX 75240

RUMSFELD, DONALD, former sec. defense; b. Chgo., July 9, 1932; s. George Donald and Jeannette (Husted) R.; B.A., Princeton U., 1954; hon. degrees Park Coll., Ill. Coll., Lake Forest Coll.; m. Joyce Pierson, Dec. 27, 1954; children—Valerie, Marcy, Nicholas. Adminstrv. asst. U.S. Ho. of Reps., 1958-59; with A.G. Becker Co., Chgo., 1960-62; mem. 88th-91st congresses from 13th Dist. Ill.; dir. OEO, 1969-70; dir. Cost of Living Council, 1971-73; U.S. ambassador to NATO, 1973-74; mem. Cabinet, White House chief of staff, 1974-75; sec. Dept. Def., 1975-77; pres., chief exec. officer G.D. Searle & Co., Skokie, Ill., 1977—; dir. Sears, Roebuck & Co., Rand Corp., Bendix, People's Energy Co. Served with USN, 1954-57. All-Navy wrestling champion, 1956; recipient OIC Exec. Govt. award, 1975; Disting. Eagle Scout award, 1976; Medal of Freedom, 1977. Republican. Office: GD Searle & Co PO Box 1045 Skokie IL 60076

RUND, JOSEPH VICTOR, mfg. co. exec.; b. Chgo., Jan. 17, 1941; s. Joseph Victor and Betty (Potucek) R.; B.S. in Indsl. Mgmt., U. Ill., 1964; m. Patricia Darlene Condon, Feb. 2, 1964; children—Joseph Victor III, James Scott. Asst. salesman Appliance div. Sunbeam Corp., Phila., 1966-67, territorial mgr. Personal Care div., Mpls., 1967-68, dist. sales mgr. Appliance Group, Peoria, Ill., 1968-69, Detroit, 1969-73, market mgr. Sunbeam Appliance Co. div., Chgo., 1973-75, sr. account exec. Product Spltys., Inc. div., Chgo., 1975-77, product mgr. Home Comfort Group, Sunbeam Appliance Co., Chgo., 1977, dir. contract sales Sunbeam Outdoor Co. div., Chgo., 1977-78, v.p. contract sales, 1978—, v.p. contract sales Aircap Mfrs., Inc. div., Tuelo, Miss., 1978—. Mgr., coach Wheaton (Ill.) Little League Baseball, 1974-78, Wheaton Youth Football, 1974-77; treas. Streams Homeowners Property Assn., 1977-78. Served to 1st lt. U.S. Army, 1964-66. Mem. Outdoor Power Equipment Assn., U. Ill. Alumni Assn., Phi Kappa Tau. Republican. Roman Catholic. Home: 1473 Sandy Hook Wheaton IL 60187 Office: 2001 S York Rd Oak Brook IL 60521

RUNDLETT, DONALD HODGMAN, banker; b. New Rochelle, N.Y., July 5, 1935; s. Raymond Crawford and Eunice Wade (Hodgman) R.; B.A., Bowdoin Coll., 1957; m. Mary Jane Keller, Oct. 11, 1958; children—Deborah, Raymond, Elizabeth, Donald Hodgman. Account exec. Mobil Oil Co., Inc., N.Y.C., 1958-62; sr. account exec. Merrill Lynch Pierce, Fenner & Smith, Inc., N.Y.C., 1962-71; sr. v.p. White, Weld & Co., Inc., N.Y.C., 1971-77, also dir.; sr. v.p., head div. pvt. banking Citibank, N.A., N.Y.C., 1977—. Pres. United Fund, Bronxville, Eastchester, Tuckahoe, N.Y., 1974; pres. bd. govs. Lawrence Hosp., Bronxville; elder Gt. Consistory Reformed Ch. Bronxville. Served to capt. armored div. USAR, 1958-64. Recipient Citizenship award Am. Legion, Eastchester, N.Y., 1978. Republican. Clubs: River (N.Y.C.); Siwanoy Country, Bronxville Field (Bronxville); Farmington Country (Charlottesville, Va.); Nat. Golf Links Am. Office: 153 E 53d St New York NY 10043

RUNGLIN, ARNOLD WALTER, mfrs. rep.; b. Roland, Iowa, Sept. 19, 1912; s. Joseph B. and Walnette (Wierson) Rognlien; B.S., Iowa State Coll., 1935; m. Adele Zielger, Feb. 15, 1936; children—Bruce, David, Julie. With Firestone Tire & Rubber Co., Akron, Ohio, 1935-42; founder A. Walt Runglin Co., Inc., Mfrs. Rep., Los Angeles, 1945, pres., 1945-76, chmn., 1977—; pres. Western Icee, Los Angeles, 1966-76, chmn. bd., 1977—; chmn. bd. Cardillo Travel Systems, Los Angeles, 1973—, pres., 1954-73. Mem. Republican Statesmen, Los Angeles, 1976—. Served to lt. (s.g.) USN, 1942-45. Mem. Affiliated Automotive Reps., Mfrs. Agts. Nat. Assn., Automotive Parts and Accessories Assn. Lutheran. Clubs: Bel Air Country (Los Angeles); Springs Country (Rancho Mirage, Calif.); Los Angeles Athletic. Author: America's Newest Profession, 1976. Home: 515 Ocean Ave Santa Monica CA 90402 Office: 5710 Hannum Ave Culver City CA 90230

RUNYAN, TIMOTHY MACK, chem. co. exec.; b. Elwood, Ind., Sept. 23, 1946; s. Curtis Mack and Anita (Van Blair) R.; B.S. in Fin., Ball State U., 1972; 1 dau., Jodi. Plant acct., acctg. supr. Owens Corning Fiberglas Corp., Toledo, 1972-74; sr. internal auditor Westinghouse Credit Corp., Pitts., 1974-75; acctg. supr. Mobay Chem. Corp., Charleston, S.C., 1975-76, acctg. specialist, 1976-77, acctg. systems analyst, 1977-78, sr. fin. analyst, 1978-79, plant acctg. mgr., 1980—. Served with USCG, 1965-69. Mem. Nat. Assn. Accts., Am. Mgmt. Assn., Am. Legion. Republican. Club: Elks. Home: 110 Mulberry Hill Dr Summerville SC 29483 Office: PO Box 10288 Charleston SC 29411

RUOPP, FREDERICK JOHN, investment counselor; b. Chgo., Apr. 15, 1930; s. Frederick Otto and Evelyn Charlotte (Walker) R.; B.S. in Banking and Fin. with honors, U. Ill., 1952; M.B.A. in Fin., Northwestern U., 1957; m. Joyce Marie Bowker, Sept. 15, 1956; children—Frederick John, Christopher James. Trust officer First Nat. Bank Chgo., 1954-61; sr. security analyst Occidental Life Ins. Co., Los Angeles, 1961-69; mgr. family accounts Lehman Bros., N.Y.C., 1969-70; pres. Chelsea Mgmt. Co., Los Angeles, 1970—; mem. fin. com. Century Nat. Ins. Co. Served with arty. U.S. Army, 1952-54. Mem. N.Y. Soc. Security Analysts, Los Angeles Soc. Fin. Analysts, Inst. Chartered Fin. Analysts, Pepperdine Assos. Clubs: Calif.; Stock Exchange (Los Angeles). Home: 16708 Huerta Rd Encino CA 91436 Office: 523 W Sixth St Los Angeles CA 90014

RUPERT, EDWARD THOMAS, business exec.; b. Milw., Mar. 26, 1948; s. Edward J. and Dorothy (Deming) R.; B.S. in Engring. Physics, Colo. Sch. Mines, 1971; M.B.A., Creighton U., 1977; m. Carolyn Hammes, Sept. 16, 1972 (dec.); 1 son, Christopher; m. 2d, Ann Marie Jorgensen, Nov. 30, 1979. Prodn. control mgr. Safeway Stores Inc., Denver, 1970-72, plant supt., Omaha, 1972-78; mktg. statis. analyst Omaha Steaks Internat., 1973-75; v.p., sec.-treas., dir. Interstate Bldg. Services Inc., 1977—; exec. v.p., dir. Applied Behavioral Research, Inc., Omaha, 1979-80; ops. analyst Omaha Public Power Dist., 1979—. Mem. Am. Soc. Metals, MBA Assos. Creighton U. (v.p. alumni affairs), Consortium Group. Democrat. Roman Catholic.

RUPPLE, BRENTON H(ILLS), investment banker; b. Waukesha, Wis., June 3, 1924; s. Ray L. and Murl (Hills) R.; B.S., U. Wis., 1948; m. Betty Anderson, May 31, 1947; children—Martha, Scott, Brenton Hills. Exec. v.p. Robert W. Baird & Co., Milw., 1968-73, pres., 1973—, chief exec. officer, 1975—, chmn. bd., 1978—; mem. Fin. Acctg. Standards Adv. Council, 1978; dir. Securities Investor Protection Corp. Past gov. Am. Stock Exchange. Vice chmn. United Fund; treas. YMCA Greater Milw. Bd. dirs. Milw. chpt. ARC, v.p. Greater Milw. Com.; corp. mem. Columbia Hosp., Milw. Children's Hosp.; past pres. Milwaukee County council Boy Scouts Am.; trustee Milw. Boy Scout Fund, Milw. Symphony Endowment, Carroll Coll.; v.p., mem. exec. com. U. Wis. Found.; bd. dirs. Milw. Better Bus. Bur.; Served with USAAF, 1943-45. Mem. Investment Bankers Assn. (gov.), Milw. Assn. Commerce (dir.), Wis. Mfrs. and Commerce Assn. (dir.), Securities Industry Assn. (vice chmn., mem. exec. com.). Clubs: Milwaukee, Milwaukee Country, Town, University (Milw.). Home: 7830 N River Rd Milwaukee WI 53217 Office: 777 E Wisconsin Ave Milwaukee WI 53201

RUSH, RICHARD HENRY, financier, author, educator, economist; b. N.Y.C., Mar. 6, 1915; s. Henry F. and Bessie (Vreeland) R.; A.B. summa cum laude (Rufus Choate scholar), Dartmouth Coll., 1937, M.C.S., 1938; M.B.A. with highest distinction, Harvard U., 1941; D.C.S., 1942; Littauer fellow, George Baker scholar, 1941-42; m. Julia Halloran, Aug. 15, 1956; 1 dau. by previous marriage, Sallie Haywood. Asst. to chief Div. Regional Economy, U.S. Dept. Commerce, 1942-43; spl. asst. to pres. All Am. Aviation, 1943-45; chief aviation U.S. Bur. Fgn. and Domestic Commerce, Washington, 1945-46; exec. head Supermarket Inst., Boston, 1947-48; exec. asst. J. Paul Getty, financier, mfr., 1951-52; partner Rush and Halloran, financiers, insurers, Washington, 1952-57; pres. Richard H. Rush Enterprises, Washington, 1958—; pres., chmn. bd. N. Am. Acceptance Corp., Washington, 1956-59; prof., dir. fin. program Am. U., Washington, 1967-70, 79—, dir. dept. fin. and bus. instns., 1978; dir. aircraft div. Nat. Security Resources Bd., 1948-51. Trustee Finch Coll., 1968-72, chmn. fin. and devel., 1969-71, chmn. mus. com., 1968-72. Mem. Am. Mktg. Assn. (chmn. aviation com.), Am. Econ. Assn., Am. Platform Assn., AAUP, Phi Beta Kappa, Omicron Delta Kappa, Phi Kappa Phi. Club: Harvard of N.Y. Author: Opportunities for Establishing New Business in Aviation, 1947; Trade Barriers in the Food Industry, 1943; Art as an Investment, 1961; A Strategy of Investing for Higher Return, 1962; The Techniques of Becoming Wealthy, 1963; Antiques as an Investment, 1968; The Wrecking Operation: Phase One, 1972; Investments You Can Live With and Enjoy, 1974, 3d edit., 1976; Techniques of Becoming Wealthy, 1978; Selling Your Collectibles,

1981; Automobiles as an Investment, 1981; contbg. editor, contbr. articles Wall St. Transcript, 1971—, The Art/Antiques Investment Report, 1973—; contbg. editor Wall Street Reports, 1971-74; columnist Diplomatic World, 1971-75; contbr. articles to profl. jours. Speaker on investments, art, antiques as investments. Address: Box 17 Darien CT 06820 also Villa Cornaro Piombino Dese Italy

RUSHTON, WILLIAM JAMES, ins. co. exec.; b. Birmingham, Ala., July 10, 1900; B.S., Washington and Lee U., 1921; H.H.D. (hon.), Southwestern U., 1959; LL.D. (hon.), U. Ala., Birmingham, 1980; m. Elizabeth Perry, 1926 (dec. 1972); children—William James, III, James. Asst. mgr. Birmingham Ice & Cold Storage Co., 1922-27, v.p., 1927-32, pres., 1932-38, vice chmn. bd., sec., 1938-57; dir. Protective Life Ins. Co., Birmingham, 1927—, pres., 1937-67, chmn. bd., 1967-76; chmn. bd. Franklin Coal Mining Co., 1927-42; dir. First Nat. Bank of Birmingham, 1927-73, Ala. Power Co., 1934-70, Investment Co. Am. (Calif.), Gulf, Mobile & Ohio R.R., 1940-72, Ill. Central Gulf R.R., 1972-74, Moore-Handley Hardware Co., 1948-63. Deacon, elder, chmn. bd. trustees, now hon. life elder First Presbyn. Ch. of Birmingham; mem. bd. annuities and relief Presbyn. Ch. U.S., 1959-67; dir. Boy Scout Council, 1925-55, pres., 1927-30; civilian chief Birmingham Ordnance Dist., U.S. Army, 1946-61; dir. Birmingham Community Chest Ann. Appeal for Funds, 1937—, v.p., 1942-43, 48-52, pres., 1954, mem. exec. com., 1945-56; hon. life dir. Nat. Citizens Com. United Community Campaigns of Am., 1961-74; bd. dirs. Salvation Army, YMCA, Birmingham; pres., life trustee So. Research Inst.; trustee Agnes Scott Coll., Decatur, Ga., 1935-45; life trustee Children's Hosp., Birmingham Mus. Art. Served to col. AUS, World War II. Decorated Legion of Merit; elected to Ala. Acad. of Honor, 1975, Ala. Bus. Hall of Fame, 1980. Mem. Nat. Assn. Refrigerated Warehouses (pres. 1933-35), Am. Warehousemen's Assn. (pres. 1935-36), Nat. Assn. Ice Industries (dir. 1928—, pres. 1936-37), Life Ins. Assn. Am. (dir. 1955-61), Health Ins. Assn. Am. (dir. 1964-67), Am. Life Conv. (v.p. Ala.), Inst. Life Ins. (dir. 1963-69), Asso. Industries Ala. (dir. 1956-63), Am. Ordnance Assn. (v.p. 1942-64). Clubs: Rotary (pres. 1952-53), Birmingham Country; Mountain Brook; The Club; Downtown; Redstone. Home: 2848 Balmoral Rd Birmingham AL 35223 Office: Protective Life Ins Co PO Box 2606 Birmingham AL 35202

RUSHTON, WILLIAM JAMES, III, ins. co. exec.; b. Birmingham, Ala., Apr. 23, 1929; s. William James and Elizabeth (Perry) R.; B.A. in Math. magna cum laude, Princeton U., 1951; m. LaVona Price, 1955; children—William James IV, Deakins Ford, Tunstall Perry. With Protective Life Ins. Co., Birmingham, 1954—, v.p., 1962-63, agy. v.p., 1963-67, pres., 1967—, chief exec. officer, 1969—, also dir.; mem. Million Dollar Round Table, 1962; dir. Ala. Power Co., So. Co., First Nat. Bank Birmingham, Southern Co., Avondale Mills, Ala. Bancorp., Economy Co. Bd. visitors Coll. Commerce and Bus. Adminstrn. U. Ala., 1972—; trustee So. Research Inst., Birmingham, 1973—, Children's Hosp., Birmingham, 1964-77, Birmingham So. Coll., 1977—, Bapt. Hosp. Found., Birmingham, 1967-78; chmn. United Way Campaign, Birmingham, 1977; bd. dirs. United Appeal, Birmingham, 1974—; deacon First Presbyterian Ch., Birmingham. Served to capt., arty. U.S. Army, Korea. Decorated Bronze Star; elected to Ala. Acad. of Honor, 1979. Fellow Soc. Actuaries; mem. Am. Council Life Ins. (dir.), Birmingham C. of C. Club: Rotary (dir. local club), Mountain Brook Country, Relay House, Birmingham Country, Redstone. Home: 2900 Cherokee Rd Birmingham AL 35223 Office: Protective Life Ins Co PO Box 2606 Birmingham AL 35202

RUSINKO, FRANK, JR., mfg. co. exec.; b. Nanticoke, Pa., Oct. 12, 1930; s. Frank and Eva (Rudawsky) R.: B.A., Pa. State U., 1952, M.S., 1954, Ph.D., 1958; m. Lucy Geryak, June 1, 1957; children—Nancy, Lawrence. Vice-pres., tech. dir. Airco Speer Carbon Graphite, St. Mary's Pa., 1971-76; pres. Edimax, Inc., Broadview, Ill., 1976-78; pres. Electrotools, Inc., Broadview, 1978—; dir. Houden Systems, Inc. Mem. Am. Chem. Soc., Am. Carbon Soc., N.Y. Acad. Sci., Am. Mgmt. Assn., Sigma Xi. Home: 13 Charleston Rd Hinsdale IL 60521 Office: 2500 S 27th Ave Broadview IL 60153

RUSITZKY, HARRIS HIRSCH, food service co. exec.; b. New Bedford, Mass., Jan. 9, 1935; s. Samuel D. and Sadie (Feinberg) R.; Asso. Applied Sci., Rochester Inst. Tech., 1955, B.S., 1956; postgrad. U. Rochester, 1959-60; m. Joan E. Feinbloom, Jan. 20, 1963; children—William, Lisa, Mark. Dir. food services, men's housing State U. N.Y. at Geneseo, 1958-60; regional ops. mgr. ARA Services Corp., Rochester, N.Y., 1960-65; pres. Serv-Rite Food Service & Cons. Corp., Rochester, 1965—; cons. in field; dir. Varicare Corp., Restaurant-Inn Corp. Chmn. bd. dirs. Jr. Achievement Rochester, 1980—; trustee Rochester Inst. Tech. Served with USMCR, 1956-58. Mem. Rochester C. of C. (trustee 1976—), Nat. Restaurant Assn. (nat. dir. 1978—), N.Y. State Restaurant Assn. (state pres. 1975-76, pres. Rochester chpt. 1973-74). Clubs: Rochester Yacht, U. of Rochester, Rotary (pres. Rochester 1980—). Home: 3493 East Ave Rochester NY 14618 Office: 100 White Spruce Blvd Rochester NY 14623

RUSSELL, DAVID EDWARD, carpet mfg. co. exec.; b. Charlotte, N.C., Oct. 3, 1936; s. Ernest Edward Russell and Margaret Lillian (Gordon) R.; B.S., U. N.C., 1960; M.A., Ga. State U., 1965; m. Glynnis Patricia Sousley, Aug. 23, 1968; children—Robert Kevin, Margaret Lisa, Staci Dawn. Programmer, Douglas Aircraft Co., 1957-60; programming supr. Lockheed Aircraft Co., 1960-64; data processing supr. Sears, Roebuck & Corp., 1964-66; dir. computer systems devel. Trans World Airlines, 1966-70; v.p. data processing So. Airways, Atlanta, 1970-73; v.p. hardware and software devel. Scidata Computer Corp., Atlanta, 1973-75; v.p., dir. mgmt. info. services Galaxy Carpet Mills, Inc., Chatsworth, Ga., 1975—. Mem. curriculum adv. coms. Dalton Jr. Coll., Pickens Tech. Sch.; coach Whitfield County Youth Football Assn., United Girls Softball Assn. Served with USAF, 1954. Recipient spl. meritorious citation Murray County High Sch., 1979. Mem. Data Processing Mgmt. Assn. (nat. speaker numerous chpts.). Baptist. Club: Ruritan. Home: 141 N Hills Dr Cohutta GA 30710 Office: PO Box 800 Chatsworth GA 30705

RUSSELL, EDWARD THOMAS, banker; b. Stamford, Conn., June 15, 1941; s. Thomas B. and Margaret L. (Mead) R.; A.S., Quinnipiac Coll., 1962, B.S. in Accounting, 1964; student Stonier Grad. Sch. Banking, 1977; m. Beverly J. Richards, June 17, 1967; children—David R. and Deborah L. (twins), Kevin C. With Fidelity Trust Co., Stamford, 1964—, asst. v.p. treas.'s dept., 1972-74, v.p., 1974—. Cubmaster, Cub Scout Pack 46, Stamford, 1976-78; bd. dirs. Stamford Youth Soccer League, 1977—, pres., 1979—; treas. Emmanuel Episcopal Ch., 1972-76, jr. warden, 1978-79, vestryman, 1980—. Recipient chpt. leadership award Bank Adminstrn. Inst., 1979, nat. award, 1979; award for service and achievement Stamford Bd. of Recreation, 1979. Mem. Am. Inst. Banking (dir. Stamford chpt. 1977-79, pres. Western Conn. chpt. 1978-79, pres. Bank Adminstrn. Inst., Western Conn. chpt. 1978-79, dir. 1979-80), Nat. Assn. Accts. Club: Hubbard Heights Men's (gov., pres. 1976-79). Office: 129 Atlantic St Stamford CT 06904

RUSSELL, GARDNER HALE, mfg. bldg. exec.; b. Salt Lake City, Aug. 12, 1920; s. Harry James and Agnes (Gardner) R.; student Universidad de Costa Rica, 1942; B.A., Miami U., 1944; postgrad. Stanford, 1946-47; m. Dorothy Annette Richardson, July 24, 1949; children—Sheryl, Kathy, Bryan, Jana Lynn. Missionary, Ch. of Jesus Christ of Latter-day Saints, Argentina, 1941-43, mission sec., 1942; export mgr. Soule Steel Co., San Francisco, 1947-50; gen. mgr. Tim Mfg. Corp., San Juan, P.R., 1951-53; mgr. Pan Am. Plastics, West Indies Plastics, Rio Piedras, P.R., 1953-55; pres. Humphrey Assos., Inc., furniture mfrs., Santurce, P.R., 1954-61, dir., 1957-61; pres., dir. INSA, Inc., 1961—; pres., dir. Rico Plastics, Inc.; cons. Arcadia Corp.; pres. Universal Industries Corp. (formerly Intercore Industries Corp.); pres. Uruguay-Paraguay Mission, Ch. of Jesus Christ of Latter-day Saints, 1970-73; v.p. Penterra Corp., 1973—; dir. F.I.T. Aviation, Inc., 1975—, Univ. Enterprises, Inc., Fla. Inst. Tech., 1975—. Bd. dirs., trustee Presbyn. Hosp., Santurce, P.R., vice chmn. bd. trustees, finance com. Inter-Am. U., San German, P.R. Mem. Steel Allocations Hearings, Washington, 1948; steel export adv. com. Office Internat. Trade, 1947-49. Asst. to mil. attache San Jose, C.R., also Rio de Janeiro, Brazil, 1942-44. Mem. San Juan Alumni Assn. (treas.), Economia y Estadisticas, P.R. Mfrs. Assn. (edn. com.), Internat. Mfrs. Assn., Beta Theta Pi. Mem. Ch. of Jesus Christ of Latter-day Saints (dist. councilman for P.R. 1958-72, pres. Caribbean dist.). Rotarian (Santurce, P.R.). Home: 645 Cinnamon Ct Satellite Beach FL 32937

RUSSELL, JAMES PAUL, chem. co. ofcl.; b. Akron, Ohio, Nov. 6, 1945; s. Paul and Rebecca T. (Bryant) R.; student Kent State U., 1963-66; B.S. in Chem. Engring., Ohio State U., 1972; M.B.A., Ill. Inst. Tech., 1980; m. Janice Arlene Peterson, Nov. 14, 1968; children—Rachel A., Paul B. Chem. operator Goodrich-Gulf Co., Independence, Ohio, 1965-66; process devel. engr. Diamond Shamrock Co., Painesville, Ohio, 1972; tech. service supr. Noury Chem. div. Armak Co., Burt, N.Y., 1972-75, product mgr., 1975-76, area mgr. Armak Co., McCook, Ill., 1976-78, production supt., Morris, Ill., 1978—. Advisor Jr. Hi. Methodist Youth Fellowship, 1976-78; chmn. Ch. Mission and Social Concerns, 1974-75; active Indian Princess program, YMCA, 1976-78; advisor Jr. Achievement, 1975. Served with U.S. Army, 1967-69. Recipient citation Jr. Achievement, 1975; certificate in labor mgmt. disputes, Niagara U., 1976. Mem. Am. Inst. Chem. Engrs., Am. Mgmt. Assn. Club: Ohio State U. Vets. Assn. (v.p., 1970-72). Office: PO Box 310 Morris IL 60450

RUSSELL, MARYELLEN MOYLAN, home care products co. exec.; b. Grand Rapids, Mich., Oct. 20, 1922; d. Thomas James and Helen Griffith (Howe) Moylan; children—Karen, Donald, Kathleen. Regional sales mgr. Home Decorators, Inc., Newark, N.Y., 1940-56; stylist, dir. field edn. Beauty Counselors, Inc., Grosse Pointe, Mich., 1956-72; asst. to v.p. new product devel., internat. div. Stanley Home Products Co., Westfield, Mass., 1977-80; fashion coordinator Amway Corp., Ada, Mich., 1980—; instr. Katharine Gibbs Schs., N.Y. U. Chmn. ways and means Detroit Symphony Orch. Women's Assn.; past capt. Gt. Lakes region CAP; chmn. navigational aids com. Gov.'s Air Service Com. State of N.H. Named Woman of Yr., Wayne State U., 1968. Mem. Fashion Group, Ninety-Nines (past internat. parliamentarian, chpt. chmn., govt. New Eng. sect.). Republican. Club: Westfield Sportsmen's. Office: Amway Corp 7575 Fulton Rd Ada MI 49355

RUSSELL, PAUL GEORGE, lawyer; b. Akron, Ohio, Feb. 23, 1929; s. Paul George and Fern (Winter) R.; A.B. with honors in Polit. Sci., Kenyon Coll., 1950; postgrad. in Bus., Western Res. U., 1956; LL.B., Harvard U., 1957. Admitted to N.Y. bar, 1958; asso. Dewey, Ballantine, Bushby, Palmer & Wood, N.Y.C., 1957-60; asst. to mng. partner E.F. Hutton & Co., then sec. E.F. Hutton & Co., Inc., N.Y.C., 1960-63; asso. LeBoeuf, Lamb, Leiby & MacRae, N.Y.C., 1963-67, partner, 1967-78; partner firm Morgan, Lewis & Bockius, N.Y.C., 1978—. Trustee Emerson Coll. Served to lt. USNR, 1951-54. Mem. Am. (chmn. utility financing com., pub. utility sect. 1976—, mem. council 1977—), N.Y. State, Fed. Power bar assns., Assn. Bar City N.Y., Beta Theta Pi, Tau Kappa Alpha. Clubs: Racquet and Tennis, Down Town Assn. (N.Y.C.); Piping Rock (Locust Valley, N.Y.). Home: 3 E 77th St New York City NY 10021 Office: 9 W 57th St New York City NY 10005

RUSSELL, PETER EDGELL, trust co. exec.; b. N.Y.C., Nov. 9, 1919; s. John E. and Olive J. (Edgell) R.; B.A., Wesleyan U., 1942; m. Amy Allen Alpaugh, May 21, 1948; children—William, John, Maija. With Hawaiian Trust Co. Ltd., Honolulu, 1947—, exec. v.p., 1965-71, pres., 1971-75, pres., chief exec. officer, 1975-80, chmn. bd., chief exec. officer, 1980—; dir. E.E. Black, Ltd., Castle & Cooke, Inc., 1st Ins. Co. of Hawaii, Lanihau Corp., Motor Supply Ltd., Victoria Ward, Ltd.; dir., Aloha United Way; trustee H.K.L. Castle Found., S.N. and Mary Castle Found.; v.p., trustee Bernice P. Bishop Mus.; dir. Oahu Devel. Conf. Served with U.S. Mcht. Marine, 1943-45. Republican. Episcopalian. Clubs: Pacific, Kaneohe Yacht, Outrigger Canoe. Office: 111 S King St Honolulu HI 96813

RUSSELL, PHEBE GALE (MRS. FRANK M. RUSSELL), broadcasting exec.; b. N.Y.C., Dec. 23, 1910; d. George H. and Marian (Hyde) Gale; grad. high sch.; m. Frank M. Russell, Sept. 25, 1940; children—Gale, Morgan N. Publicity dir. NBC, Washington, 1929-39; v.p. radio sta. WICO, Salisbury, Md., 1958-62; pres. Ellensburg TV Cable Corp., Washington, 1961-68, PGR Enterprises, Inc., 1962-71; owner TV Cable Cos. Appalachia, Norton, Big Stone Gap, Va., 1962-77; dir. Delmarva Broadcasting Co., 1958-62. Mem. women's bd. George Washington U. Hosp. Mem. DAR, Mayflower Soc., Huguenot Soc., D.C. Women's Golf Assn. Clubs: Kenwood Garden (pres. 1963-64), Congressional Country (Washington). Address: 5101 River Rd #918 Washington DC 20016

RUSSELL, R. ROBERT, economist; b. Rock Springs, Wyo., Feb. 17, 1938; s. Ralph Cyril and Elizabeth (Russell) Goddard; B.A., U. Calif., 1961; Ph.D., Harvard U., 1964; m. Judith Lynn Honey, Aug. 14, 1959; children—Jeffrey Robert, Kevin Gregory. Teaching fellow Harvard U., 1963-64; asst. prof., then asso. prof. econs. U. Calif., Santa Barbara, 1964-73; vis. asso. prof. U. Calif., San Diego, 1972-73, asso. prof., 1973-74, prof. econs., 1974—; vis. prof. U. Kans., fall 1975; former dir. Council Wage and Price Stability. Democrat. Contbr. articles to profl. publns. Office: Dept Econs U Calif La Jolla CA 92093*

RUSSELL, RICHARD ALAN, boat mfg. co. exec.; b. Erie, Pa., Sept. 8, 1936; s. Reginald Frank and Thelma Johanna (Zimmer) R.; B.A., Pa. State U., 1958; m. Donna Bisbee, July 10, 1965; children—Debra Russell, Cary Russell. With Molded Fiber Glass Boat Co., Union City, Pa., 1963—, sales mgr., 1969-71, v.p. mktg., 1971—. Served with U.S. Army, 1960-62. Mem. Nat. Marine Mfrs. Assn., Pa. Marine Dealers Assn., Outdoor Writers Am. (asso.), Am. Legion. Republican. Methodist. Clubs: Union City Skeet, Moose. Contbr. articles on boating to mags., newspapers, 1970—. Home: 25 W High St Union City PA 16438 Office: 55 4th Ave Union City PA 16438

RUSSELL, RICHARD EVANS, steel co. exec.; b. Boston, Apr. 19, 1920; s. George Edmund and Jean Elizabeth (Keating) R.; S.B., Mass. Inst. Tech., 1942; m. Lillian May Fors, Nov. 2, 1968; children—Jean Penrose, Elizabeth K., Richard Evans. Gen. foreman Chase Bross & Copper, Waterbury, Conn., 1946-60; prodn. mgr. J. Bishop & Co., Malvern, Pa., 1961-63; mng. dir. Fine Tubes, Ltd., Plymouth, Eng., 1966-68; asst. to exec. v.p. Superior Tube, Norristown, Pa., 1963-70, plant mgr., Dunkirk, N.Y., 1971-72; gen. mgr. Mich. Seamless Tube div. Quanex, South Lyon, 1972—; guest lectr. Bath (Eng.) U., 1967. Mem. South Lyon Econ. Devel. Commn., 1977—; adv. bd. Eastern Mich. U. Bus. Sch., 1976—; bd. dirs. Brooks Hosp., 1970-72; town chmn. United Fund, 1956. Served as capt. ordnance USAR, 1942-45. Mem. Am. Soc. Metals, Am. Mgmt. Assn. Republican. Episcopalian. Patentee in field. Home: 3331 Woodlea Dr Ann Arbor MI 48103 Office: 400 McMunn St South Lyon MI 48178

RUSSELL, ROBERT PEYTON, leasing co. exec.; b. St. Louis, Apr. 3, 1938; s. Robert William and Dorothy Herbst R.; B.A. in Psychology and Econs., DePauw U., 1960; m. Gloria Rose Sceehe, Aug. 5, 1967; children—Kathy, George, Russell, Stephen, Karen. Regional mgr. Luber-Finer, 1960-67, Butler Mfg. Co., 1967-69; v.p. fin. Equilease Corp., N.Y.C., 1969-75; regional mgr. Mut. Leasing Co., also Baldwin United Leasing Co., Chgo., 1975-79; regional v.p. Prime Leasing Co., Chgo., 1979—; pres. Custom Leasing Corp., St. Louis, 1976—, Russco Enterprises Co., St. Louis, 1979—; mng. partner M.D. Leasing Co., St. Louis, 1980—. Mem. Am. Assn. Equipment Lessors, Hosp. Fin. Mgmt. Assn. Republican. Roman Catholic. Clubs: Mo. Athletic, Four Seasons Country. Home: 40 Patterson St Saint Louis MO 63141 Office: 711 Old Ballas Rd Saint Louis MO 63141

RUSSELL, THOMAS FRANK, mfg. co. exec.; b. Detroit, Apr. 7, 1924; s. Frank W. and Agnes V. (Kuhn) R.; student engring. Rutgers U., 1943; B.S. in Acctg., U. Detroit, 1948; m. Ruth H. Costello, June 25, 1949; children—R. Brandon, Scott K. With Fed.-Mogul Corp., Detroit, 1942—, controller, 1959-64, v.p. fin., 1964, v.p., group mgr., pres., 1972-75, chmn. bd., chief exec. officer, 1975—. Trustee U. Detroit. Served with AUS, 1943-45; ETO. Office: Federal Mogul Corp PO Box 1966 Detroit MI 48235

RUSSO, EDWARD RAYMOND, bus. exec.; b. Newark, Mar. 16, 1946; s. Michael E. and Antonette (Martino) R.; B.S., Rochester Inst. Tech., 1968; m. Diana I. Forzani, Feb. 10, 1973; children—Edward Joseph, Deanna Marie. Prodn. mgr. Systematic Bus. Forms, Paramus, N.J., 1968-69; plant mgr. Essex Systems, Inc., N.Y.C., 1969-70; v.p. Urban Data Systems, Inc., Newark, 1970—; tchr. advanced photo lithography Manhattan Sch. Printing, N.Y.C., 1970-72; lectr. in field. Judge, Juvenile Ct. Chester (N.J.), 1977—; councilman Chester; pres. Chester Twp. Council, 1981; bd. dirs. Chester (N.J.) Music Soc., 1976—. Mem. Internat. Bus. Forms Industry (govt. liaison com.), Greater Newark C. of C. Republican. Roman Catholic. Club: Lions (v.p. Chester 1978—, pres. 1981-82). Home: F168 Twin Brooks Trail Chester NJ 07930 Office: 850 Frelinghuysen Ave Newark NJ 07114

RUSSO, JOHN ANTHONY, JR., timber co. exec.; b. Baton Rouge, Mar. 31, 1950; s. John Anthony and Beatrice Ann (Churchill) R.; B.S. in Forestry, La. State U., 1972; m. Stephanie T. Young, Aug. 19, 1972; children—Amy Lynn, Matthew Nicholas. Timber marker U.S. Forest Service, 1970; trainee Internat. Paper Co., Pineville, La., 1972; unit procurement forester Continental Forest Industries, Hodge, La., 1973-78, dist. mgr. wood procurement, 1978-80; v.p. ARK-LA-TEX Timber Co., Inc., Bossier City, La., 1980—. Mem. Soc. Am. Foresters, La. Forestry Assn., Forest Farmers Assn., Homer Jaycees (local dir. 1974-75), Xi Sigma Pi, Alpha Zeta. Home: Route 1 Box 234F Ruston LA 71270 Office: 2056 E Texas St Bossier City LA 71111

RUSSO, PETER FRANCIS, fin. co. exec.; b. Brockton, Mass., May 24, 1932; s. Francis George and Mary Alice (Maxwell) R.; B.S., Bryant Coll., 1957; m. Joan Theresa Dolfuss, June 6, 1959; children—Frank John, Paul Robert, Laura Jean. Corp. auditor Am. Standard, Inc., N.Y.C., 1957-59; supr. Spark, Mann & Co., C.P.A.'s, Boston, 1959-66; asst. treas. Stevens Liner Assos., Webster, Mass., 1966-67; dir. corp. acctg. and fin. Rustcraft Greeting Cards, Inc., Dedham, Mass., 1967-70; v.p. fin., treas. Multibank Fin. Corp., Boston, 1970—; dir. Multibank Computer Corp., Multibank Internat. Bd. dirs. Battleship Mass., 1974—, Old Colony Council, Cath. Charities, 1974—. Served with USN, 1950-54. C.P.A., Mass. Mem. Nat. Assn. Accts., Am. Inst. C.P.A.'s, Mass. Soc. C.P.A.'s, Tax Execs. Inst., Bank Adminstrn. Inst., Nat. Assn. Controllers. Home: 86 Tilton Ave Brockton MA 02401 Office: 1400 Hancock St Quincy MA 02169

RUSSO, VINCENT PAUL, JR., food broker; b. Washington, Jan. 3, 1930; s. Vincent Paul and Julia (Escher) R.; B.A., U. Md., 1965; m. Annette Mooney June 23, 1979; children by previous marriage—David M., Steven Paul, Douglas A., Russell W.; stepsons—David Lee, Eric Scott. Photographer, FBI, Washington, 1948-54; salesman McCormick & Co., Balt., 1954-62, W. C. Barnett & Sons, Riverdale, Md., 1962-67; dir. food service Food Enterprises, Inc., Balt., 1967-69; asst. mgr. sales, food service, Harry B. Cook Co., College Park, Md., 1969-72; v.p. food service Craig Brokerage Co., Columbia, Md., 1972—; adv. bd. A.E. Staley Co., 1975—. Cub Scout master Boy Scouts Am., 1964-66; justice of the peace, Prince Georges County, Md., 1965-66. Mem. Internat. Food Service Execs. Assn. (named Purveyor of Yr., Balt. br. 1972, newsletter editor 1975—), Md. Restaurant Assn. Republican. Lutheran. Club: Sons of Italy. Poetry pub. Little Patuxent Rev., 1979. Home: 5263 Brook Way Columbia MD 21044 Office: 9121 Red Branch Rd Columbia MD 21045

RUST, EDWARD BARRY, ins. exec.; b. Bloomington, Ill., Sept. 5, 1918; s. Adlai H. and Florence Fifer) Barry) R.; A.B. cum laude in Econs., Stanford U., 1940; m. Harriet B. Fuller, Aug. 7, 1940; children—Florence M., Harriet H., Edward B. Asst. sec. State Farm Mut. Automobile Ins. Co., 1942; dir. br. offices, 1946-51, v.p., 1951-58, pres., 1958—; also chief exec. officer, dir., exec. com.; pres., dir. State Farm Life Ins. Co.; pres., dir., exec. com. State Farm Fire & Casualty Co.; pres. State Farm Life & Accident Assurance Co., State Farm County Mut. Ins. Co. Tex., State Farm Gen. Inst. Co.; dir. Gen. Telephone Co. Ill. Trustee Ill. Wesleyan U. Served as lt. USNR, 1943-46. Mem. U.S. C. of C. (dir., pres. 1972-73), Phi Beta Kappa. Office: One State Farm Plaza Bloomington IL 61701*

RUSUNEN, ROBERT LEE, marine constrn. co. exec.; b. Missoula, Mont., Mar. 16, 1946; s. John Ruben and Eloise (Kingston) R.; B.S., U. Mont., 1971; M.B.A., Wash. State U., 1977; m. Sherry Martha Hofmann, June 16, 1972; children—Robert James, Billy John. Buyer, mdse. mgr. Hart-Albin Co., Billings, Mont., 1972-75; mgr. trainee Gen. Electric Supply Co., Seattle, 1976-77, mgr. materials, 1977-79; dir. purchasing and office services Riedel Internat. Inc., Portland, Oreg., 1979—. Served with USAF, 1964-68; Vietnam. Decorated Purple Heart. Mem. Nat. Assn. Purchasing Mgmt. (cert. purchasing mgr.), Purchasing Mgmt. Assn. Wash., Purchasing Mgmt. Assn. Oreg., U.S. Jr. C. of C., M.B.A. Grad. Assn., Assn. M.B.A. Execs. Baptist. Home: 5323-A NW Cherry St Vancouver WA 98663 Office: 4555 N Channel Ave Portland OR 97208

RUSYNYK, DENNIS JOHN, indsl. exec.; b. Cleve., May 6, 1948; s. Sam and Victoria (Gluszik) R.; B.B.A., Ohio U., 1970. Laborer, Union Carbide Corp., Cleve., summers 1966-70; press operator Airco Welding Products, Cleve., 1971-73; indsl. engr. Lamson & Sessions Co., Cleve., 1973-75; supr. Gen. Industries, Elyria, Ohio, 1975—. Treas. Little League North, Elyria, 1977-78; advisor Jr. Achievement Assn., Elyria, 1974-75. Greek Catholic. Developer one resin formulations in bulk molding compounds. Home: 327 Canterbury Ct Elyria OH 44035 Office: Gen Industries Co Olive & Taylor Sts Elyria OH 44035

RUTEN, STEPHEN CHARLES, constrn. co. exec.; b. Aurora, Ill., Dec. 30, 1947; s. Leo C.L. and Shirley Elaine (Dudgeon) R.; student in chemistry and math. Tex. Tech. U., 1967-70; m. Ella Ann Hill, Nov. 18, 1967; children—Michelle Elaine, Christopher Stephen Leo. Draftsman, Henry Pratt Co., Aurora, Ill., 1965-66; salesman Jack McQueen Realtors, 1969-70; apprentice carpenter J.C. Penney's Co., Lubbock, Tex., 1970-71, Pharr Constrn. Co., Lubbock, 1971-72; carpenter Brochsteins Inc., Houston, 1972, H.A. Padgett Constrn. Co., Lubbock, 1972-74; project mgr. and estimator Page & Wirtz Constrn. Co., Lubbock, 1974-76; chief estimator Furr's Constrn. Co. Inc., gen. contractors, Lubbock, 1976-77, constrn. mgr., 1977-78, gen. mgr., v.p., 1978-79; pres., gen. mgr., 1979—; bd. dirs. joint apprenticeship local #1884 Carpenters Union. Served with USAF, 1966-69. Mem. Asso. Gen. Contractors Am., Am. Mgmt. Assn., Am. Radio Relay League, Lubbock Computer Club, U.S. Jaycees, Constrn. Specifications Inst. (industry dir. local chpt. 1979-80). Republican. Baptist. Clubs: Masons (32 deg.), Lubbock Amateur Radio. Home: 3513 57th St Lubbock TX 79413 Office: 2223 Ave E PO Box 1650 Lubbock TX 79408

RUTHERFOORD, JOHN PENN, mgmt. and engring. exec.; b. Roanoke, Va., Mar. 26, 1914; s. Julian Hamilton and Willie Edmondson (Penn) R.; B.S. in Engring., U. Va., 1936, B.S. in Elec. Engring., 1937; m. Ann Elizabeth Kincanon, Dec. 26, 1940; children—John Penn, Julia Hamilton, James Kincanon, Charles Thomas. With Gen. Electric Co., 1937-58, mgmt. cons., exec. staff, 1954-58, mgr. advanced mgmt. course, 1957-58; div. gen. mgr. Raytheon Co., Lexington, Mass., 1958-61; pres., dir. Sorenson Co., Norwalk, Conn., 1959-61; v.p., treas., dir. APRA Precipitator Co., N.Y.C., 1959-61; exec. v.p., dir. Internat. Resistance Co., Phila., 1961-64; exec. v.p., dir. Penn Controls, Inc., Goshen, Ind., 1964-67; exec. v.p. Burgess Battery Co., Freeport, Ill., 1967-68; div. gen. mgr. Clevite Corp., Cleve., 1968-69; exec. v.p., dir. Mouldings, Inc., Marion, Va., 1970-72; pres. Rutherfoord Assos., Marion, 1972—. Pres., N. Shore Sales Execs. Club, Lynn, Mass., 1950-51; mem. mayor's adv. council, Freeport, 1967-68; dir. Smyth-Bland Regional Library, 1970-80, chmn., 1973-78. Recipient disting. service award Smyth County Mental Health Assn., 1978. Mem. Assn. Energy Engrs., Air Pollution Control Assn., ASHRAE, Nat. Soc. Profl. Engrs., Va. Soc. Profl. Engrs. (pres. 1979-80; outstanding service award 1975, 80), Marion C. of C. (dir. 1974-77, 1st v.p. 1976-77). Episcopalian. Clubs: Shenandoah (Roanoke), Kiwanis (pres. 1974-75; disting. pres. award Kiwanis Internat. 1975). Contbr. articles on traffic safety, lighting, energy conservation to publs.; developer method of predrying sawmill waste for fuel. Home: 116 Dogwood Dr PO Box 664 Marion VA 24354 Office: Center Bldg PO Box 664 Marion VA 24354

RUTHERFURD, GUY GERARD, JR., investment co. exec.; b. Richmond, Va., Jan. 30, 1940; s. Guy Gerard and Georgette (Whelan) R.; A.B., Princeton U., 1962; M.B.A., Harvard, 1968; m. Marie Seilern-Aspang, Dec. 28, 1973; children—Elizabeth, Christopher. With White Weld & Co. (now div. Merrill Lynch), N.Y.C., 1968—, investment mgr., 1970—. Bd. dirs. Lenox Hill Neighborhood Assn., 1970—, treas., 1975—; bd. dirs. Ripon Soc. Served to lt. USN, 1962-66. Cert. fin. analyst. Mem. N.Y. Soc. Security Analysts. Clubs: Racquet and Tennis, Links. Office: Merrill Lynch White Weld Co 1 Liberty Plaza 34th Floor New York NY 10080

RUTKOSKI, FRANK VIRGIL, ins. co. exec.; b. Minden City, Mich., Oct. 2, 1935; s. Enick and Helen Rutkoski; student ins. Mich. State U., 1967; student acctg. Northeastern Sch. Commerce, Bay City, Mich., 1959; m. Joann Koroleski, Oct. 27, 1962; children—Ann Marie, John M., Paul E., Nancy J., Edward F. Salesman, Gambles, Cass City, Mich., 1946-59; with Bauer Candy Co., Cass City, Mich., 1959-62; mgr. Montgomery Ward Co., Port Huron, Mich., 1962-67; farm estate planner, agy. builder Farm Bur. Ins. Co., Lansing, Mich., 1966-77; dist. sales mgr. Farm Family Life/Mut. Ins. Co., Albany, N.Y., 1977—; farm ins. cons., 1975—; instr. life ins. State of N.Y., 1978—. Rep., Amherst Civic Assn. Named Man of Yr., Owosso Jaycees, 1966, Agy. Mgr. of Yr., Mich. Farm Bur., 1971. Mem. Nat. Assn. Life Underwriters (nat. quality award 1973), N.Y. State Life Underwriters Assn. (del.), Life Underwriters Century Club, Sales and Mktg. Execs. Club, Gen. Agts. and Mfrs. Club, Holy Name Soc. Roman Catholic. Clubs: K.C. (dep. grand knight 1976-77), Polish Falcons. Home: 116 Cheshire Ln East Amherst NY 14051 Office: 3725 Walden Ave Lancaster NY 14086

RUTLEDGE, WILLIAM ALVIN, elec. appliance mfg. co. exec.; b. St. Louis, Aug. 16, 1924; s. Alvin T. and Gladys (Koupal) R.; B.E.E., U.Mo., Rolla, 1946; m. Katherine Veronic Kruta, July 1, 1950; children—William Michael, Robert Kevin, Richard Allen, Kimberly Ann. With General Electric Co., Ft. Wayne, Ind., 1946-74, gen. mgr. gen. purpose motor dept., appliance component div., until 1974; group v.p. Emerson Electric Co., St. Louis, 1974-76, exec. v.p. ops., 1976-77, vice-chmn. bd. dirs., 1977—. Served with AUS. Patentee in field. Office: 8100 W Florissant Ave Saint Louis MO 63136

RUTTENBERG, DERALD H., corp. exec.; b. LaFayette, Ind., Feb. 17, 1916; s. Joseph C. and Hattie Ruttenberg; B.A., U. Wis., 1937; LL.B., Yale U., 1940; I.A., Harvard U., 1943; m. Janet Kadesky, June 16, 1951; children—John Charles, Eric M., Katherine T., Hattie. Chmn. bd. Consol. Foundries and Mfg. Co., 1947-59; chmn. bd., pres. Josam Mfg. Co., 1959-62; chmn. bd. Ill. Iron & Bolt Co. (now Tinicum, Inc.), Chgo., 1961-71, I-T-E Circuit Breaker Co., 1967-68, I-T-E Imperial Corp. (merger I-T-E Circuit Breaker and Imperial Eastman Corp.), 1968-73; pres., chief exec. officer Studebaker-Worthington, Inc., N.Y.C., 1969-71, chmn. bd., chief exec. officer, 1971-80; chmn. bd. Madison Fund, 1980—; dir. McGraw Edison Co., IU Internat. Trustee Mt. Sinai Hosp., N.Y.C. Served with USAAF, 1943-45. Office: One Dag Hammarskjold Plaza New York NY 10017

RUTTER, CHARLES FRANCIS, savs. and loan assn. exec.; b. Waltham, Mass., May 2, 1923; s. Robert P. and Helen L. (Adams) R.; B.A., Tufts U., 1947; m. Priscilla Chapin, Feb. 9, 1946 (dec.); children—Susan Holtham, Anne Shaw, Lynn. Trainee, Waltham Fed. Savs. and Loan Assn., 1950; examiner Fed. Home Loan Bank, 1951-55; treas. Nashua Co-Op. Bank (N.H.), 1955-63, treas., v.p., 1963-69; v.p., mng. officer Nashua Fed. Savs. and Loan Assn., 1969-71, pres., 1971—, dir.; dir. Fed. Home Loan Bank of Boston, 1970-76. Pres., Greater Nashua Community Assn., 1970—; mem. adv. bd. St. Joseph Hosp.; dir. Arts and Sci. Center, Nashua; dir. Boys' Club of Nashua. Served with U.S. Navy, 1943-46. Mem. N.H. Savs. and Loan Coop. Bank League (past pres.), Soc. Fin. Mgrs. (past pres. Boston chpt.), Fed. Savs. League New Eng. (vice chmn. 1977-78, chmn. 1978-79), Inst. Fin. Edn. (past nat. dir.), U.S. League Savs. Assn. Club: Rotary. Office: 157 Main St Nashua NH 03061

RUTZ, ROGER DUANE, economist; b. Greeley, Colo., Nov. 27, 1952; s. Wilbert and Lorraine (Schilling) R.; B.S., U. Nebr., Lincoln, 1974, M.A. (Nebr. Bankers Assn. research fellow), 1976, Ph.D., 1979. Instr., U. Nebr., Lincoln, 1975-78; staff economist Fed. Res. Bd., Washington, 1978—; adj. asst. prof. fin. George Washington U., 1979—. Mem. Fin. Mgmt. Assn., Am. Fin. Assn., Am. Econ. Assn. Republican. Contbr. articles to profl. jours. Home: 2024 Hopewood Dr Falls Church VA 22043 Office: M1156 Fed Res Bd Washington DC 20551

RUTZEN, ARTHUR COOPER, JR., indsl. chem. co. exec.; b. Chgo., Nov. 18, 1947; s. Arthur Cooper and Helen Doyle Rutzen; B.S. in Bus. & Econs., Lehigh U., 1970, M.B.A., 1972; m. Dolores Cornachia, May 26, 1973; children—Sandy, Arthur C., Judy. Account exec. Merrill Lynch Pierce Fenner & Smith, N.Y.C., 1971-75; mgr. bus. analysis and mktg. positions Union Carbide Corp., N.Y.C., N.Y., 1975-77; dir. nat. accounts Liquid Air Corp., San Francisco, 1977—; participant nat. accounts mgmt. study Mktg. Sci. Inst., 1980. Head wrestling coach PAL, Nassau County, L.I., N.Y., 1974. Recipient Spl. Service award Union Carbide, 1976, Meritorious Achievement award, Union Carbide, 1977. Mem. Nat. Accounts Mktg. Assn., Merrill Lynch Exec. Club, Sales and Mktg. Execs. Assn. San Francisco. Protestant. Clubs: Golden Gateway Tennis, Lehigh U. Alumni. Home: 15 Whaleship Plaza San Francisco CA 94111 Office: One Embarcadero Center San Francisco CA 94111

RUUD, EGIL GUSTAV, multi-market co. exec.; b. Oslo, Nov. 20, 1922; s. Sigurd Evenson and Jenny Marie (Bue) R.; came to U.S., 1929, naturalized, 1933; A.B., Hobart Coll., 1949; postgrad. Sales Mgmt. Inst., 1960, U. Ind. Exec. Tng. Course, 1964; m. Suzanne Tamlyn Lawes, Nov. 19, 1949; children—Barbara Tamlyn, Bradford Evenson. Salesman, Shuron Optical Co., St. Louis, 1949-50, br. mgr., 1951-52, mgr. brs., Milw., Cin., 1953-58, field sales mgr., 1959-61, gen. sales mgr., 1962-64, exec. v.p., 1965, pres., 1966-68; group v.p. Textron Inc., Providence, 1969—; dir. Avid Corp., LexiData, Inc. Mem. pres.'s adv. com. Hobart Coll., 1962; active United Fund, 1967-68; bd. dirs. R.I. Philharmonic. Served with USAAF, 1943-45; ETO. Home: 3 Bagy Wrinkle Cove Warren RI 02885 Office: 40 Westminster St Providence RI 02903

RYALS, STANLEY DEE, investment counsel; b. Boise Valley, Idaho, Nov. 23, 1925; s. Oren Franklin and Etta Grace (Gibby) R.; B.A. in Econs., Willamette U., 1949; grad. (fellow) Am. Inst. Econ. Research, 1953, Pacific Coast Banking Sch., U. Wash., 1962; m. Barbara Louise Robinson, May 27, 1949; children—Steven D., Stuart D., Stanton D., Scott D., Spencer D. Trust officer Nat. Bank of Commerce, Seattle, 1955-64; v.p./investment officer Bank of Calif., Los Angeles, 1964-70; vice-chmn., dir. portfolio mgmt. Transam. Investment Mgmt. Co., Los Angeles, 1970-72; v.p./mgr. Western region Standard & Poor's/Intercapital, Los Angeles, 1972-73; exec. v.p., dir. Everett Harris & Co., Los Angeles, 1973-75; pres., dir. Beneficial Standard Investment Mgmt. Corp., Los Angeles, 1975-78, investment counsel, 1978—; instr. U. Wash., Seattle, 1955-60. Trustee, Myrtle L. Atkinson Found., 1973—. Served with U.S. Army, 1943-46. Chartered fin. analyst. Mem. Los Angeles Soc. Fin. Analysts (past pres.), Inst. Chartered Fin. Analysts, Beta Theta Pi, Blue Key; fellow Fin. Analysts Fedn. Republican. Unitarian. Club: Lions (past pres.) (Seattle). Author: How to Invest Wisely, 1954; Investment Trusts and Funds, 1954. Asso. editor C.F.A. Digest, 1973—. Home: 924 Chehalem Rd La Canada CA 91011 Office: 4529 Angeles Crest Hwy La Canada CA 91011

RYAN, DONALD PATRICK, contractor; b. Janesville, Wis., July 13, 1930; s. William H. and Myrtle (Westrick) R.; B.S. in Civil Engring., U. Wis., 1953, B.S. in Naval Sci., 1953; m. Diana Houser, July 17, 1954; children—Patrick, Susannah, Nancy, David, Josephine, Rebecca, Polly, Adam. Partner, Ryan Bros. Co., Janesville, Wis., 1949—; dir. Ryan, Inc., Janesville; pres. Engring. Service Corp., Janesville, 1959—; pres. P. W. Ryan Sons, Inc., Janesville; dir. Mchts. and Savs. Bank, Janesville, MS Bancorp. Bd. dirs. U. Wis. Found. Served with USNR, 1953-55. Registered profl. engr., Wis., Ill. Mem. Nat. Soc. Profl. Engrs., Wis. Meml. Union Bldg. Assn. (trustee), Wis. Rd. Builders Assn. (dir.), U. Wis. Alumni Assn., Chi Epsilon, Phi Delta Theta. Home: 703 St Lawrence Ave Janesville WI 53545 Office: PO Box 1079 Janesville WI 53545

RYAN, EDWARD JOHN, JR., health care co. exec.; b. Warren, Ohio, May 25, 1936; s. Edward and Thelma (Veneman) R.; B.S. in Indsl. Relations, Northeastern U., 1963; m. Dorothy C. Ryan, Oct. 1970. Purchasing agt. Fenwal Co., Framingham, Mass., 1958-63; successively mfg. supr., reference supr., recruiting supr. Dupont Co., Wilmington, Del., 1963-70; v.p. profl. relations Hosp. Corp. Am., Nashville, 1972-77; dir. internat. recruiting Whittaker Corp., Los Angeles, 1977-79; sr. v.p. profl. relations Nat. Med. Enterprises, Los Angeles, 1979—; cons. human resources and recruiting. Served with USAF, 1954-58. Mem. Internat. Personnel Assn., Am. Mgmt. Assn., Soc. for Advancement Mgmt., Am. Assn. Compensation Analysts, World, Am. hosp. assns. Club: Masons. Office: Nat Med Enterprises Inc 11620 Wilshire Blvd Suite 1010 Los Angeles CA 90025

RYAN, FRANK JAMES, investment co. exec.; b. Boston, May 22, 1934; s. James Francis and Edna Anna (Schnaufer) R.; B.Sc., Cornell U., 1955, M.B.A., 1959, M.A., 1959; postgrad. N.Y. U. Sch. Law, 1961-62; m. Catherine Joyce Fujiwara, July 15, 1966; children—Nicole Melia, Todd Thomas, Scott James. With fgn. investment dept. Goodbody & Co., N.Y.C., 1959-61; asst. v.p. fgn. investment Am. Fgn. Ins. Assn., N.Y.C., 1962-66; asst. treas. fgn. investment Am. Life Ins. Co., Bermuda, 1966-69; v.p. fgn. investment C.V. Starr & Co., N.Y.C., 1969-78; v.p. InterSec Research Corp., N.Y.C., 1978-79; investment mgr. Abu Dhabi Investment Authority, Abu Dhabi, United Arab Emirates, 1979—. Served with AUS, 1955, 58-59. Mem. Acad. Polit. Sci., Am. Acad. Polit. and Social Sci., Am. Soc. Internat. Law, Cornell Soc. Engrs., Cornell Soc. Hotelmen, Internat. Studies Assn., N.Y. Soc. Security Analysts, Fgn. Analysts Fedn. Club: N.Y. Athletic. Home: 27 Minute Man Hill Westport CT 06880 Office: PO Box 3600 Abu Dhabi United Arab Emirates

RYAN, GEORGE MARSHALL, computer mfr.; b. Eau Claire, Wis., Mar. 5, 1922; s. Richard Clark and Doris (Fennel) R.; B.B.A. with sr. honors, U. Wis., 1948; m. Beverly Winfred Morarity, Dec. 2, 1942; children—Patrice Louise, Marc Kevin, Meaghan Tara, Stacie Bostwick. With Touche, Ross, Bailey & Smart, 1948-50; v.p., gen. mgr. Benson-Lehner Corp., 1950-53, later pres.; asst. to v.p. Friden Corp., 1953-54; chmn. bd. Intercontinental Systems; asst. to pres. Pertec Corp., 1970-73; chmn. bd., chief exec. officer Cado Systems Corp., Torrance, Calif., 1974—; mem. Lloyds of London, 1971—. Served with AUS, 1940-44. C.P.A. Office: 2771 Toledo St Torrance CA 90503

RYAN, JAMES HERBERT, security and retail services co. exec.; b. Petersburg, Va., Feb. 1, 1931; s. Richard Hillsdon and Mary Orgain (Mann) R.; B.S., U.S. Mil. Acad., 1955; M.A., U. Pa., 1962; M.S., George Washington U., 1972; P.M.D., Harvard U., 1972; m. Patricia Louise Abbott, June 7, 1955; 1 dau., Pamela Louise. Commd. 2d lt. U.S. Army, 1955, advanced through grades to lt. col., 1968, ret., 1972; gen. mgr. U.S. ops. Ryan Enterprises, Washington, 1970-73; pres. Ford Enterprises, Ltd., Mt. Rainier, Md., 1973—; dir. Rydon, Inc., Seahaven, Inc. Advisor to Sec. of Army, 1975; bd. govs. USO, 1977—; chmn. USO hdqrs. relocation com., 1977—. Decorated Legion of Merit, Soldiers medal, Bronze Star, Air medal, Vietnamese Gallantry Cross. Mem. Young Pres.'s Orgn., Am. Mgmt. Assn., Am. Soc. Indsl. Security, Nat. Retail Mchts. Assn., Md. Investigation and Security Assn., Ret. Officers Assn., West Point Soc. D.C. Episcopalian. Club: Capital Yacht. Home: 4501 Beechwood Rd College Park MD 20740 Office: 3241 Rhode Island Ave Mount Rainier MD 20822

RYAN, JOHN THOMAS, JR., mfg. exec.; b. Pitts., Mar. 1, 1912; s. John Thomas and Julia (Brown) R.; B.S., Pa. State Coll., 1934; M.B.A., Harvard U., 1936; D.Sc. (hon.), Duquesne U., 1959; LL.D. (hon.), U. Notre Dame, 1973; m. Mary Irene O'Brien, Aug. 1, 1939; children—Irene Ryan Shaw, John III, Michael, Daniel, Julia Ryan Parker, William. Engr., Mine Safety Appliances Co., 1938-40, gen. mgr., 1940-48, exec. v.p., dir., 1948-53, pres., dir. 1953-63, chmn. bd., 1963—; dir. Allegheny Ludlum Industries, Inc., Internat. Minerals & Chem. Corp., H.J. Heinz Co. Past pres. Hosp. Council W.Pa.; bd. dirs. Thomas Edison Found., Children's Hosp.; vice chmn., mem. exec. com. Regional Indsl. Devel. Corp.; past chmn., mem. exec. com. Allegheny Conf. Community Devel.; chmn. Univ. Health Center Pitts.; trustee U. Notre Dame. Named Knight of Malta. Mem. Am. Inst. Mining and Metall. Engrs., ASME, Council Fgn. Relations, Phi Delta Theta, Tau Beta Pi. Roman Catholic. Clubs: Pitts. Golf, Univ., Duquesne, Fox Chapel, Rolling Rock; Union League, Chgo., N.Y. Yacht (N.Y.C.); Met. (Washington). Home: W Woodland Rd Pittsburgh PA 15232 Office: 600 Penn Center Blvd Pittsburgh PA 15235

RYAN, KEVIN MATTHEW, ins. agy. exec.; b. Boston, Jan. 23, 1939; s. James Joseph and Anne Dorothea (Smith) R.; A.B., Fairfield U., 1960; m. Eileen Reilly, June 10, 1960; children—Edward, Risa, Darian. With Aetna Casualty and Surety Co., Hartford, Conn., 1960-64; actuary Indsl. Indemnity Co., San Francisco, 1964-68; dep. dir. Ins. Dept., State of Ill., Springfield, 1968-72; v.p. Ins. Services Office, Phila., 1972-76; v.p., partner Milliman & Robertson, Inc., Wayne, Pa., 1976-80; pres. Nat. Council on Compensation Ins., 1980—. Fellow Casualty Actuarial Soc., Conf. of Actuaries in Public Practice; mem. Am. Acad. Actuaries (dir., treas., mem. exec. com.). Republican. Roman Catholic. Clubs: Charter Chase (treas. 1975), N.Y. Athletic, Hershey Mill Golf. Office: Nat Council Compensation Insurance One Penn Plaza New York NY 10019

RYAN, LAWRENCE EUGENE, lawyer; b. Boston, Aug. 4, 1913; s. John and Margaret (Fitzgerald) R.; J.D., Boston Coll., 1943. Admitted to Mass. bar, 1943, Mass. Dist. Ct. bar, 1944; law clk. Mass. Supreme Jud. Ct., 1943-46; asst. atty. gen. Commonwealth of Mass., 1946-49; asst. dist. counsel Region 1, OPS, Boston, 1949-50; atty. Mass. Recodification Commn., 1951-53; right-of-way atty. Mass. Turnpike Authority, Boston 1954-66, resident counsel, 1966—; asso. prof. Portia Law Sch., 1945-52; instr. Boston Coll. Law, 1944-45, Northeastern Law Sch., 1945-46. Mem. Internat. Bridge, Tunnel and Turnpike Assn. Democrat. Roman Catholic. Home: 53 Mather St Dorchester MA 02124 Office: Mass Turnpike Authority Prudential Center Suite 3000 Boston MA 02199

RYAN, LEO VINCENT, univ. dean; b. Waukon, Iowa, Apr. 6, 1927; s. John Joseph and Mary Irene (O'Brien) R.; B.S., Marquette U., 1949; M.B.A., DePaul U., 1954; Ph.D., St. Louis U., 1958; postgrad. Catholic U. Am., 1951-52, Bradley U., 1952-54, Northwestern U., 1950. Joined Order Clerics of St. Viator, Roman Catholic Ch., 1950; mem. faculty Marquette U., Milw., 1957-65, dir. continuing edn. summer sessions, coordinator evening divs., 1959-65, prof. indsl. mgmt., 1964; prof. mgmt. Loyola U., Chgo., 1965-66, adj. prof. mgmt., 1967-69; dir. Peace Corps, Lagos, Nigeria, 1966-67, Ibadan, Nigeria, 1967-68; asst. superior gen. and treas. gen. Clerics of St. Viator, Rome, 1968-69, dir. edn. Am. province, Arlington Heights, Ill., 1969-74; pres. St. Viator High Sch., 1972-74; dean Coll. Bus. Adminstrn. U. Notre Dame (Ind.), 1975-80, Coll. Commerce, DePaul U., Chgo., 1980—; dir. Peace Corps tng. program, 1962-65; adj. prof. human devel. St. Mary's Coll., Winona, Minn., 1972-74; mem. sch. bd. Archdiocese Chgo., 1972-75; mem. nat. edn. com. U.S. Cath. Conf., 1971-75, mem. exec. com., 1973-75; mem. nat. adv. bd. Benedictine Sisters of Nauvoo, 1973—; vis. prof. U. Ife, Ibadan, 1967, dir. Vilter Mfg. Co., Filbert Corp., Vilter Sales & Service, Vilter Internat., 1973—, 1st Bank System, Wis. div., 1977—, Haas Co., 1976—, McHugh, Freeman Assos., 1978—. Mem. Pres.'s Com. on Employment Handicapped, 1959-75, Wis. Gov.'s Com. on Employment Handicapped, 1959-65, Wis. Gov.'s Com. on UN, 1961-64; cons. Vatican Sec. of State, Pontifical Commn. on Justice and Peace, 1968-70. Served with inf. U.S. Army, 1945-47. Recipient Freedom award Berlin Commn., 1961; chieftaincy title Asoju Atoaja of Oshogbo, Oba Adenle I, Yorubaland, Nigeria, 1967; Brother Leo V. Ryan award created in his honor Cath. Bus. Edn. Assn., 1962; named Man of Year, Jr. C. of C. Milw., 1959, Marquette U. Bus. Adminstrn. Alumni Man of Year, 1974; recipient B'nai B'rith Interfaith award Milw., 1963; Distinguished Alumnus award DePaul U., 1976; Milw. Bd. Realtors travelling fellow, 1964; Nat. Assn. Purchasing Agts. faculty fellow, 1958. Mem. Nigeria Inst. Mgmt., Cath. Bus. Edn. Assn. (nat. pres. 1960-62, nat. exec. bd. 1960-64), Assn. Sch. Bus. Ofcls. (nat. com. chmn. 1965-67), Am. Assembly Collegiate Schs. Bus. (mem. com. internat. relations, program com.), Am. Fgn. Service Assn., Conf. Religious Dirs. Edn., Nat. Cath. Edn. Assn., Soc. Advancement Mgmt., Nigerian Inst. Mgmt., Pi Gamma Mu, Alpha Sigma Nu, Alpha Kappa Psi, Beta Alpha Psi (named Tchr. of Yr., U. Notre Dame 1980), Delta Mu Delta, Tau Kappa Epsilon, Beta Gamma Sigma (dir. 1978—, chmn. chpt. ops. 1980—). Club: K.C. Author: The Business Management of Central Catholic High School, 1958; Accounting Manual for Catholic Elementary and Secondary School, 1969; also articles. Home: 1212 E Euclid St Arlington Heights IL 60004 Office: Office of Dean Coll Commerce 25 E Jackson Blvd Chicago IL 60604

RYAN, PATRICK MICHAEL, food mfg. co. exec.; b. S.I., N.Y., Feb. 16, 1937; s. Thomas F. and Helen (Kelly) R.; B.A. magna cum laude, St. Francis Coll., 1957; J.D., Villanova U., 1960; m. Judith M. Steelman, July 16, 1977; children—Sarah, Judith, Kathleen, Michael, Courtney. Admitted to N.Y. bar, 1961, Calif. bar, 1965; atty. Antitrust div. U.S. Dept. Justice, Washington, 1960-64; with Hunt Wesson Foods Inc., Fullerton, Calif., 1964—, asst. gen. counsel, 1968-70, sec., v.p., gen. counsel, 1970—; instr. U. So. Calif. Law Sch. Served with USAFR, 1960-71. Mem. Orange County Bar Assn. (chmn. corp. law sect. 1970), Calif. Bar Assn., Am. Bar Assn., Order of Coif. Office: 1645 W Valencia Dr Fullerton CA 93634

RYAN, RALPH JOHN, JR., econ. devel. specialist; b. Calais, Maine, Oct. 21, 1951; s. Ralph John and Marie Rose (McCurdy) R.; student U. Paris, 1972, U. Edinburgh (Scotland), 1972-73; B.A., Bates Coll., Lewiston, Maine, 1970-74; M.A., Kent (Ohio) State U., 1976. Grad. teaching asst. Kent State U., 1974; dir. econ. devel. City of Calais, 1976-79; econ. devel. specialist Franklin County, State of Mass., Greenfield, 1979—. Sec., Econ. Devel. Bd., 1976-79; dir. Washington County Devel. Corp., 1978-79, WGBH-TV. Mem. Montague Zoning Bd. of Appeals; bd. dirs. Franklin County Vocat. Tech. Sch. Mem. Calais Area C. of C. (sec. 1976). Democrat. Episcopalian. Home: 57 Main St Shelburne Falls MA 01370 Office: County Court House Greenfield MA 01301

RYAN, ROBERT S., fin. advisor; b. Morristown, N.J., July 20, 1924; s. Francis J. and Ida May (Keefe) R.; B.S., U. Tulsa, 1952; postgrad. Stanford Sch. Credit, Finan. Mgmt., 1963-66; m. Margie Riehl, Oct. 17, 1953; children—Mary Beth, Robert S., Joseph A., Kate K. Petroleum engr. Pan Am. Petroleum Corp., Tulsa, 1952-59; petroleum engr. Citibank Nat. Assn., N.Y.C., 1959-62, asst. v.p., 1962-69, v.p. metals, mining dept., 1969-76, v.p., head of global project finance dept., 1976-81; fin. advisor to oil, gas and minerals industries, 1981—. Mem. spl. gifts com. United Fund, Madison, N.J., 1969. Served with USN, 1942-48; PTO. Decorated Purple Heart, 7 Asia-PTO stars; registered profl. petroleum engr., Okla. Mem. Am. Inst. Mining Engrs. (dir., v.p. finance, 1972-75, Krumb Fund investment com. 1972-75, Hoover medal bd. award 1977), Soc. Petroleum Engrs., Soc. Mining Engrs., Am. Mining Congress. Home: 15 Academy Rd Madison NJ 07940 Office: 488 Madison Ave New York City NY 10022

RYAN, THOMAS JOSEPH, engring. and constrn. co. exec.; b. Bklyn., Dec. 2, 1930; s. Patrick Joseph and Mary Manion (Cunningham) R.; B.B.A., St. John's U., 1953; M.B.A., N.Y. U., 1963; m. Frances E. Bergen, June 20, 1953; children—Thomas C., Jacqueline, Deirdre B. Dir. taxes M.W. Kellogg Co., N.Y.C., 1964-70; internat. tax specialist Continental Oil Co., Stamford, Conn., 1970-72, v.p. fin. Kellogg Internat. Corp., London, exec. v.p., 1975, pres., 1975-76; sr. v.p. Pullman Kellogg div. Pullman Inc., Houston, 1976-78, pres., 1978—; v.p. Pullman Inc., 1979—. Served with U.S. Army, 1953-55. Roman Catholic. Home: 851 Silvergate Dr Houston TX 77079 Office: 3 Greenway Plaza E Houston TX 77046

RYAN, WILLIAM DESMOND, investment exec.; b. Tulsa, Sept. 12, 1920; s. William Riley and Neva (Cunefare) R.; B.S., U. So. Calif., 1944; m. Gloria Owen, Mar. 7, 1980; children by previous marriages—Dean Lloyd, Kevin William, Patrick Spaulding, Colleen Faries. Founder pub. Campus Mag., 1946-49; asso. pub. Sun Up Mag., San Antonio, 1950; pres. Ryan Advt. Co., 1950; pres. Southwestern Progress Corp., Beverly Hills, Calif., also Progress Bldg. Corp., 1954—, Royal Land Corp., King Corp., Dean Management Corp., 1957—, Royal Hawaiian Mgmt. Corp., 1966—. Mem. Los Angeles-Bombay Sister Cities Com.; founding and charter pres. Sunset Young Republican Club; editor Calif. State Young Rep. Newspaper, 1953; bd. dirs. Am. Bur. Med. Aid Free China; mem. nat. exec. bd. Children's Village, U.S.A.; active Internat. Orphans, Inc. Served from ensign to lt. (j.g.) USNR, 1944-46. Mem. Navy League, So. Calif. Opera Guild, World Affairs Council. Clubs: Balboa Bay, Shadow Mountain, The Beverly Hills; Coral Casino Beach and Cabana (Santa Barbara); La Jolla Beach and Tennis, Coronado Yacht, Kona Kai, Penthouse Executive, Silver Dollar, Cellar, Cave des Roys, Gaslight, Palm Springs Key (gov.), Trojan, Million Miler, Exec. Dinner, Mary and Joseph League, Lifelighters, Masons. Home: 1020 Casiano Rd Bel-Air Los Angeles CA 90049 also Keauhou Beach Box 2352 Kailua-Kona HI 96740 Office: 473 S Robertson Blvd Beverly Hills CA 90211

RYAN, WILLIAM HOWARD, mfg. co. exec.; b. Rochester, N.Y., Mar. 18, 1914; s. Willis James and Amelia Mary (Ginter) R.; student Ill. Inst. Tech., 1938-39; B.S., Boston U., 1955; postgrad. Harvard U., 1964-66; m. Mary Elizabeth Black, Aug. 9, 1941. Equipment engr. Automatic Electric Co., Chgo., 1937-39; research scientist Polaroid Corp., Cambridge, Mass., 1939-65; pres. Polyphor Corp., indsl. coatings, Framingham, Mass., 1970—; research cons. Polaroid Corp., Cambridge, 1965-71. Mem. Soc. Motion Picture and TV Engrs. (del. intersoc. color council 1946-71), Soc. Photog. Scientists and Engrs., Royal Photog. Soc. Gt. Britain, Am. Chem. Soc., Soc. Archtl. Historians Gt. Britain, Soc. Archtl. Historians. Patentee in three-dimensional photography, instant-photography, light polarizers. Author: (with H.T. Kalmus, Jack Warner and others) New Screen Techniques, 1952; (with Desmond Guinness) Irish Houses and Castles, 1971; The White House: An Architectural History, 1980. Office: 4 New York Ave Framingham MA 01701

RYAN, WILLIAM JOSEPH, broadcasting co. exec.; b. Nyack, N.Y., Apr. 14, 1932; s. William Joseph and Elizabeth Mary (Langley) R.; B.A., U. Notre Dame, 1954; m. Jane Householder, June 27, 1970; children—Ashley Allison, William Joseph III. Mem. staff WSBT-WSBT-TV, South Bend, Ind., 1953-55; producer Jules Power Prodns., Chgo., 1955-56; pres., gen. mgr. Radio Naples Inc. (WNOG-WNFM), Naples, Fla., 1956-69; v.p. and gen. mgr. Radio Naples div. Palmer Broadcasting Co. (WNOG-WCVU). 1969—, v.p. and gen. mgr. subsidiary Palmer Cablevision, 1972-81; corp. v.p. for cable TV, Palmer Communications, 1981—; chmn. Cable TV Advt. Bur., 1980—; dir. 1st Nat. Bank and Trust Co. Pres., Collier County unit Am. Cancer Soc., 1972-74; bd. dirs. Naples Community Hosp. Mem. for Collier County, Republican State Com., 1971-72. Served with AUS, 1958-67. Mem. So. (pres. 1978-79), Fla. (pres. 1974-76) cable TV assns., Fla. Assn. Broadcasters (chmn. Fla. State Industry Adv. com. 1963-81), S.W. Fla. Assn. Broadcasters (pres. 1970-71), Naples Area C. of C. (pres. 1969-70), Naples Council Navy League (pres. 1971-72). Clubs: Royal Poinciana Golf and Country, Naples Bath and Tennis, Kiwanis (pres. 1966-67), K C (grand knights). Home: 1312 Murex Dr Naples FL 33940 Office: 333 8th St S Naples FL 33940

RYAN, WILLIAM JOSEPH, investment banker; b. Dublin, Ireland, July 10, 1934; s. William Joseph and Mary R.; B.A., Stanford U., 1968; m. Maria Loreto Freeman, Dec. 15, 1968; children—Eleanor, Robert. Land surveyor, Alaska, 1957-64; with Crocker Nat. Bank, San Francisco, 1971—, v.p., 1974—. Mem. Stanford U. Alumni Assn. Roman Catholic. Clubs: Stanford Golf, San Francisco Bond. Home: 40 Evergreen Kentfield CA 94904 Office: 1 Montgomery San Francisco CA 94104

RYAN, WILLIAM JOSEPH, newspaper publisher; b. N.Y.C., Apr. 25, 1941; s. William Joseph and Marean (Munch) R.; B.B.A., Baruch Coll., City U. N.Y., 1969; m. Joan Leslie Turbity, Oct. 1, 1960; children—Kevin Patrick, Kimberly Ann. Sr. budget analyst CBS, N.Y.C., 1966-69; controller Harper's mag., N.Y.C., 1969-71, N.Y. mag., N.Y.C., 1971-74; v.p. fin. Village Voice, N.Y.C., 1974-77, pres./pub., 1977—; mem. mgmt. com. Museums of N.Y. mag.; Morton Wollman disting. lectr. Baruch Coll., 1978. Adv. bd. dirs. Force 13 Theatre Co., Inc.; mem. ops. bd. Performing Artists Psychotherapy Service, Postgrad. Center for Mental Health; bd. dirs. Com. for Astor Pl. Home: 336 West End Ave New York NY 10023 Office: Village Voice Inc 842 Broadway New York NY 10003

RYDZ, JOHN S., mfg. co. exec.; b. Milw., May 7, 1925; s. John M. and Victoria R.; B.S., M.I.T., 1952; M.S., U. Pa., 1956; m. Clare L. Steinke, May 18, 1946; children—Karen E., John A. Corp. staff RCA, N.Y.C., 1959-61; exec. v.p., dir. Nucor Co., Phoenix, 1961-66; v.p. Diebold Inc., Canton, Ohio, 1966-71; v.p. engring. SPG Singer Co., 1971-78; dir. corp. office innovation Singer Co. Stamford, Conn., 1978—; indsl. adv. bd. on productivity M.I.T.; mem. machine systems group Stevens Inst. Tech. Served with USNR, 1943-46. Author, patentee in field. Home: 8 Briarcliffe Dr Scotch Plains NJ 07076 Office: 276 Eldridge Rd Fairfield NJ 07006

RYKERT, JOHN CHARLES, investment fund exec.; b. London, Eng., Mar. 19, 1930; s. Harold Edmund and Aimee (Gundy) R.; came to Can., 1931; degree bus. adminstrn. with honors, U. Western Ont. (London, Can.), 1953; m. Carol S. Hudson, Aug. 27, 1955; children—Serena, Elizabeth, Pamela, John Charles. With Wood Gundy Ltd., Toronto, Ont., Can., 1954-69, security analyst, 1959-64, registered rep., 1964-69; individual practice as fin. cons., Toronto, 1969-71; v.p., treas., dir. Canadian Gen. Investments Ltd., Toronto, 1971—; v.p., treas., dir. 3d Canadian Gen. Investment Trust, Toronto, 1971—; Trustee, Upper Can. Coll. Found. Clubs: Toronto, York, Badminton and Racquet (all Toronto). Home: 103 Poplar Plains Rd Toronto ON M4V 2N1 Canada Office: 110 Yonge St Suite 1702 Toronto ON M5C 1T4 Canada

RYNDERS, LEO JULIAN, real estate appraiser; b. Ft. Smith, Ark., Mar. 18, 1912; s. Wesley N. and Ella (Brownfield) R.; B.A., B.J., U. Mo., 1934; m. Kathryn Elizabeth Schwartz, Aug. 19, 1939; children—Ray David, Ronald Edward, Carol Ann. With Rynders & Rynders, Ft. Smith, 1934-37; partner Ark. Democrat, Little Rock, 1937; dist. mgr. subscription sales Curtis Pub. Co., Phila., 1937-38; with Am. News Co., Dallas, St. Louis and Abilene, Tex., 1938-55, div. mgr. W. Tex. and Eastern N.Mex., 1941-55; salesman Henley Realty Co., 1955-59; sales mgr., appraiser Dick Lawrence Assos., Realtors and Appraisers, 1959-77; owner Leo J. Rynders, Sr. Residential Appraiser, Abilene, Tex., 1977—; chmn. multiple listing service Abilene Bd. Realtors, 1969, 75. Active Boy Scouts Am. Mem. Soc. Real Estate Appraisers (contbr. article to assn. jour.), Abilene Bd. Realtors, Tex. Assn. Realtors (lt. gov. 1961-62, vice chmn. bd. govs. 1962), Nat. Assn. Realtors (Grad. Realtors Inst. designation), Tex. Profl. Photographers Assn., Photog. Soc. Am. (contbr. articles to jour.), Kappa Tau Alpha, Sigma Delta Chi, Delta Tau Delta. Republican. Methodist. Club: Kiwanis (pres. Key City 1975-76). Exhibited photographs at Abilene Fine Arts Mus., La. Fine Arts Mus., Amy Graves Ryan Fine Arts Mus., Abilene. Home and Office: 2042 Sayles Blvd Abilene TX 79605

RYON, THOMAS S(HIPLEY), tobacco co. exec.; b. Washington, May 29, 1917; s. Norman Eugene and Mary (Shipley) R.; A.B., Duke U., 1938; m. Ruth Elizabeth Green, Apr. 12, 1940; children—Thomas Shipley, David Osmond. Travel and study in Europe and Africa, 1938; real estate and income tax specialist, Washington, 1939; mgr. A.C. Monk Enterprises, 1940-43; comptroller A.C. Monk & Co., Inc., Farmville, N.C., 1943-45, asst. sec., 1945-54, sec., 1954—, v.p., 1971—; pres. Security Savs. & Loan, Farmville, 1960-72; sec., dir. Eastern Tobacco Co.; sr. v.p., dir. First Fed. Savs. & Loan Pitt County, 1972—; v.p. Dixon-Hamilton Tobacco Co., 1971—, Mohenco Corp., Wendell, N.C., 1976—; pres. Farmville Tobacco Bd. Trade, 1966-68. Chmn. Farmville com. Boy Scouts Am., 1957-63; dir. Farmville Little League, 1977—, Farmville Community Chest, Farmville United Fund; vice chmn. Farmville Sch. Bd., 1957, chmn., 1958-63; chmn. Farmville Housing Authority, 1974—. Mem. N.C. World Trade Assn. (dir.), Farmville C. of C. (dir.). Democrat. Episcopalian. Clubs: Wilson Coin; Farmville Coin, Farmville Country (past sec.-treas.). Home: 1007 Fountain Hwy Farmville NC 27828 Office: West Marlboro Rd Farmville NC 27828

RYTTEN, JACK EDWARD, internal security cons., investigator; b. Port Chester, N.Y., Sept. 23, 1914; s. Charles and Anita (Lazarone) R.; grad. Alviene Acad., N.Y.C., 1932; m. Pattie Dize, Feb. 25, 1950; 1 dau., Barbara Ann. Asst. credit mgr. Blum's Dept. Store, Balt., 1938-42; credit mgr.-comptroller Ann Lewis Shops, Balt., 1942-44; indsl. security cons., investigator J.E. Rytten Assos., Balt., 1944—; spl. cons. police-community relations, Balt., 1963—; vis. lectr. Balt. chpt. Am. Inst. Banking, 1965, Nat. Assn. Bank Audit, Control and Operation, 1968, Mt. St. Agnes Coll., Balt., 1968, Engring. Soc. Balt., 1969; spl. cons. consumer credit fraud Equitable Trust Co., Balt., 1951-72; spl. cons. mgmt.-employee problems First Nat. Bank, Balt., 1971—; spl. investigative cons. trust dept. Md. Nat. Bank, 1979—; co-founder Profl. Forum, Balt., pres., 1965-68; mem. adv. bd. Am. Security Council. Chmn. com. on juvenile delinquency control Balt. County Council of PTA's, 1957-59; chmn. sub-com. on law enforcement problems Republican State Central Com. of Md., 1962-64; bd. sponsors Nat. Right to Work Legal Found., 1973—. Recipient Liberty award Congress of Freedom, 1969. Mem. Internat. Assn. for Identification, Am. Soc. Criminology, AAAS, Am. Conservative Union, Ams. Against Union Control of Govt., Mil. Police Assn. (life), Md. Hist. Soc., Police-Law Soc. (Chgo. chpt.), Engring. Soc. Balt. (dir. publicity com. 1977-78). Methodist. Author: Basic Laws on the Admissibility of Confessions, 1961; Judicial Oversights and Punishment, 1965; (with Thomas Clifford) Examination of Private Investigators in Deposition Proceedings, 1968; Re-Affirming Our Roles As Professionals, 1969; An Investigator's View of Crime and Punishment, 1973; An Investigator's View of the Liberal Press, 1974; Private vs. Public Education, 1975; The Community and the Engineering Profession, 1975; The Assault on Competence, 1978; Regulation Man and His Invisible Victims, 1979; The Liberal Mentality and the Malpractice Mess, 1979; Labor Unions in a Free Market, 1979; Correcting the Media, 1979; The Family Circle and America's Future, 1980. Contbg. feature writer: Daily Record Balt., 1970—, Jeffersonian, Towson, Md., 1973—, Courier-Jour., Louisville, 1975; syndicated columnist The Investigator's Notebook, 1978; book rev. editor Balt. Engr., 1979-80. Home: 8415 Bellona Ln Baltimore MD 21204 Office: 315 Ruxton Towers Baltimore MD 21204

SAADE, WILLIAM MAROUN, systems engr.; b. Beirut, Lebanon, Mar. 25, 1945; s. Maroun Joseph and Laurice (Nader) S.; came to U.S., 1968; first prizes Ecole ste Genevieve Versailles, 1963-65; student Preparatory Math Ecole Centrale Paris, 1965-68; M.Ops. Research, Stanford U., 1969, postgrad., 1973—. With IBM, Beirut, Lebanon, 1969-73, mktg. div. Middle East, 77-78, on edn. leave, Palo Alto, Calif., 1973—, with Internat. Decision Analysis Group, Menlo Park, Calif., 1978—; cons.; lectr. engring. econ. system dept. Stanford U. Ednl. Cooperation Foreign Council France fellow. Mem. Stanford Alumni Club for Lebanon (co-founder), Alumni Ecole Centrale De Paris (treas. Lebanese br., 1969-73). Author articles in field. Home: 4189 Cherry Oaks Palo Alto CA 94306 Office: PO Box 8993 Stanford Univ Palo Alto CA 94305

SAAG, EDWARD SWITOW, wholesale elec. co. exec.; b. Louisville, Sept. 21, 1924; s. David and Lela Switow S.; student Ind. U., 1942-43; m. Elaine Koppel, June 1, 1948; children—Terry Saag Herman, Barbara Saag Nefouse, Michael Saag. Builder, developer, Louisville, 1947-68; v.p. M. Switow & Sons, Louisville, 1948-74; owner, operator A-M Electric Co., Louisville, 1974—, pres., 1978—; v.p. Reclu Corp., Louisville, 1979-80; v.p. Crossroad Cinema, Inc., Lexington, Ky., 1977-80; v.p. Indian Forest Enterprises, Louisville, 1965-80. Trustee Jewish Hosp., Louisville; bd. dirs. Adath Israel Temple. Served with C.E., U.S. Army, 1943-45. Decorated Purple Heart. Mem. Nat. Assn. Ind. Lighting Distbrs. Democrat. Jewish. Clubs: Standard Country (past dir.); Lions (Louisville). Home: 4302 Talahi Way Louisville KY 40207 Office: 823 W Main St Louisville KY 40202

SAARI, REYNOLD LEONARD, indsl. exec.; b. Negaunee, Mich., Jan. 13, 1935; s. Leonard Matt and Impi Gustava (Patana) S.; B.E.E. (Lake Shore Engring. scholar), Mich. Tech. U., 1957; M.S. (Hughes Grad. fellow), U. Calif., Los Angeles, 1959; M.B.A., Harvard, 1969; m. Jeanne Alice Donaldson, July 28, 1962. Research engr. Hughes Aircraft Co., Culver City, Calif., 1957-60; lead engr. Boeing Co., Seattle, 1960-67, engring. exec., 1969—; dir. Western States Industries, Trigon Devel. Corp; dir., founder, owner Evergreen State Industries, Inc. Mem. IEEE. Home: 4500 141st Ave SE Bellevue WA 98006

SABATINO, ANTHONY CARMEN, ins. co. exec.; b. Chgo., June 22, 1930; s. Russell Anthony and Isabel Fradinardo S.; B.S. in Accounting, Walton Sch. Commerce, 1968; m. Dolores M. Rito, May 5, 1951; children—Paul, Susan, Pamela. Office mgr. accountant Elgin Gravure Service (Ill.), 1956-57; sr. accountant Edward J. Hutchens, C.P.A., Chgo., 1957-69; treas. Casualty Ins. Co., Chgo., 1969—; treas. CIC Financial Corp., Chgo., 1977—; treas., dir. CIC Acceptance Corp.; dir. Walensa Direct Mail Service, Inc. Served with AUS, 1951-53; ETO. Mem. Am. Accounting Assn., Ins. Accounting and Statis. Assn., Adminstrv. Mgmt. Soc., Am. Mgmt. Assn. Moose. Clubs: North Riverside (Ill.) Sportsman's (pres. 1970-71); Columbian (sec.) (Chgo.). Home: 2225 S Burr Oak Ave North Riverside IL 60546 Office: 222 N Michigan Ave Chicago IL 60601

SABLE, RONALD KEITH, air force officer; b. Farmington, Iowa, May 8, 1941; s. Roy Cecil and Pauline Elizabeth (Ramey) S.; B.S., Iowa Wesleyan Coll., 1963; M.S., So. Ill. U., 1975; m. Sandra Lea Trumbo, May 31, 1963; 1 dau., Ronna Kay. Commd. 2d lt. U.S. Air Force, 1963, advanced through grades to lt. col., 1976, dep. chief staff plans Mil. Airlift Command, chief continental U.S. plans, Scott AFB, Ill., 1973-75, civil air policy analyst, 1975-77, sr. pilot, 1977, advance agt. presdl. travel, Washington, 1974-79, dep. dir. Mil. Airlift Command, asst. for civil air, Scott AFB, 1978-79; chief air ops. Sec. of Air Force Office of Legis. Liaison, 1979—; author and lectr. in field. Active United Fund, Air Force Assistance Fund campaign. Decorated D.F.C., Air medal with 3 clusters, Meritorious Service medal with cluster, Air Force Commendation medal with cluster; recipient George Washington medal and Honor award Valley Forge Freedoms Found., 1974, 76. Mem. Air Force Assn., Am. Assn. Airport Execs., Order Daedalians, Air Force Village Found. (life). Methodist. Office: Sec of Air Force Office of Legis Liaison Washington DC 20330

SABO, WALTER RICHARD, JR., broadcasting exec.; b. Orange, N.J., Sept. 3, 1952; s. Walter Richard and Gloria (Vagon) S.; B.A. in English and Communications cum laude, Syracuse U., 1973. Newsman, Sta. WCRV, Washington, N.J., 1965-70; columnist Worrall Publs., 1968-70; editor, writer Syracuse U. Publs., 1971-74; air personality Sta. WOLF, 1970; air talent, promotion mgr. Sta. WOR-FM, N.Y.C., 1973-74; air personality, promotion mgr. Stas. WNBC/WNWS, N.Y.C., 1974-76; dir. ABC-FM Radio Network, N.Y.C., 1976-78; exec. v.p. FM Radio, radio div. NBC, N.Y.C., 1978—; lectr., alumni adv. Syracuse U.; lectr. N.Y. U.; adv. bd. Alpha Epsilon Rho. Recipient award for broadcast journalism excellence Sigma Delta Chi, 1972, Mktg. award Kodak Co., 1972. Mem. Nat. Assn. Broadcasters (programming bd.). Club: Nat. Arts (N.Y.C.). Home: 241 3d Ave New York NY 10003 Office: 30 Rockefeller Plaza New York NY 10020

SABOE, KARL EDWARD, banker; b. Cleve., Feb. 2, 1941; s. Karl Edward and Ruby (Duncan) S.; A.B., Westminster Coll., 1963; m. Toni Lynn Culver, Feb. 9, 1963; children—Kira, Erin. Vice-pres. Commerce Bank of Kirkwood (Mo.), 1967-69; v.p. Commerce Bank, St. Charles, Mo., 1970; sr. v.p. United Bank of Greeley (Colo.), 1971-77, exec. v.p., 1980—; pres. United Bank of La Salle (Colo.), 1978-79. Served to lt. U.S. Navy, 1963-66. Office: PO Box 1057 Greeley CO 80632

SACHS, ARTHUR GORDON, magazine exec.; b. Mt. Kisco, N.Y., Oct. 21, 1941; s. James Henry and Margery (Fay) S.; A.B., Harvard U., 1963, postgrad. Bus. Sch., 1966-67; m. Mary Allen Hawkins, Apr. 26, 1969; children—Andrew Kimball, Christopher Allen, Timothy Hawkins. Asst. to mng. dir. Economist, London, 1963-64; with sales and mgmt. depts. Sci. Am., N.Y.C., 1964-74; pub. cons., 1974-76; asso. pub. More mag., N.Y.C., 1976; bus. mgr. Natural History mag., N.Y.C., 1976-77; asso. pub. Human Nature mag., 1977-79; bus. mgr. Time mag., N.Y.C., 1979—, Am. Indian Archeol. Inst., Washington, 1980—. Trustee, West Side Montessori Sch., N.Y.C., 1979—. Clubs: Harvard, Coffee House (N.Y.C.). Office: Time-Life Bldg 1271 Ave Americas New York NY 10020

SACHS, JOHN P., business exec.; b. Duesseldorf, Ger., 1926; B.A. in Chem. Engring., Ill. Inst. Tech., 1948, M.A., 1950, Ph.D., 1952; married. With Union Carbide Corp., 1951-66; v.p. ops., later group v.p. Great Lakes Carbon Corp., 1966-78, pres., chief exec. officer, dir., 1978; chmn. bd., dir. Gen. Refractories Co., 1979—. Served with U.S. Army, World War II. Office: 50 Monument Rd Bala Cynwyd PA 19004*

SACHTJEN, WILBUR MANLEY, exec. recruiting cons.; b. Madison, Wis., Oct. 23, 1927; s. Wilbur P. and Kathryn M. Sachtjen; B.B.A., U. Wis., 1950; M.B.A., Harvard U., 1955; m. Nancy O'Neil, Aug. 25, 1956; children—Barry, Brendan, Jeffrey, Todd. With Harris Trust and Savs. Bank, Chgo., 1950-53, Morgan, Stanley & Co., N.Y.C., 1955-57; asso. McKinsey & Co., mgmt. cons., N.Y.C., 1957-64; v.p. Pfizer Internat., N.Y.C., 1964-68; planning dir. Am. Can Co., N.Y.C., 1969-72; v.p. Owen Webb, Inc., N.Y.C., 1972-75; pres. Wilbur M. Sachtjen Assos., Inc., Bronxville, N.Y., 1976—. Bd. govs. Lawrence Hosp., Bronxville, N.Y., 1973—, pres., 1975-76; bd. dirs. United Fund Westchester County, 1970. Served with AUS, 1945-47. Clubs: Harvard, Harvard Bus. Sch. (dir. 1960-63) (N.Y.C.); Siwanoy Country (Bronxville); Lake Waramaug Country (Kent, Conn.). Address: 1 The High Rd Bronxville NY 10708

SACKLOW, STEWART IRWIN, advt. exec.; b. Albany, N.Y., July 29, 1942; s. Jacob David and Freida Ruth (Pearlman) S.; A.A.S., N.Y.C. Community Coll., 1962; B.S., Western Mich. U., 1965; m. Harriette Lynn Cooperman, July 2, 1967; 1 son, Ian Marc. Asst. dist. office Humble Oil & Refining Co., Inc., Albany, 1963-65; dir. advt. and sales promotion Albany Pub. Markets div. Weiss Foods, 1965-68; v.p. advt. and sales promotion Golub Corp., Schenectady, 1968-78; pres., creative dir. Wolkcas Advt., Inc., 1978—. Mem. Dist. Atty.'s readiness team; active Albany County Cerebral Palsy Telethons, 1966-68; mem. fund drive com. WMHT-TV ednl. TV, 1967-74; bd. dirs. Vedio Spirit Upstate Leukemia Assn., Cystic Fibrosis Found.; active Gov. Clinton council Boy Scouts Am. Recipient certificate merit Nat. Research Bur., 1966, Freedoms Found., 1966, Amsterdam Recorder, 1968, Retail Advt. Conf., 1969, 70, Woman's Day Mag., 1971, 70, 73, 74, 75; Grand Nat. award Am. Dairy Assn., 1969, Hunt Wesson Foods, 1970; recipient 4 1st place awards Am. Advt. Fedn., 1972, Crystal Prism award, 1973; Effie award Am. Mgmt. Assn., 1972; Silver medal award Am. Advt. Fed., 1973, Addy award, 1973, 74, 75, 76, 77; award excellence Retail Advt. Conf., 1971, 72, 73; Best 15 Internat. Ads award Internat. Newspaper Advt. Execs., 1972. Mem. Ad Club N.Y. (pres. 1976-77, dir. 1972—), Am. Advt. Fedn. (bd. govs. 1975), Profl. Public Relations Council, N.Y. Art Dirs. Mem. B'nai B'rith. Clubs: Albany Yacht, Schenectady Racquet, K.P. Home: 162 Fairfield Ct Voorheesville NY 12186 Office: 8 Wade Rd Latham NY 12110

SADDLER, GARY LYNN, mfg. co. exec.; b. Colby, Kans., June 17, 1941; s. Guy M. and Berta M. (Strayer) S.; B.S. in Bus. Adminstrn., Ft. Hays (Kans.) State Coll., 1964; m. Nancy Carolyn Howard, Sept. 2, 1967; children—Lara Lyn, Garlyn Beth. Ter. mgr. Burroughs Corp., Denver, 1968-70, systems rep., Englewood, Colo., 1970-72, systems supr., 1972-78, mgr. programs applications, 1978—; cons. in field. Served to lt., USNR, 1964-67. Mem. Phi Mu Alpha. Republican.

Baptist. Home: 2201 S Corona St Denver CO 80210 Office: 5501 S Valley Hwy Englewood CO 80111

SADLER, CARL LEON, mfg. co. exec.; b. Little Rock, Sept. 23, 1916; s. Carl Leon and Lucy Anne (McRae) S.; B.S. in Mech. Engring., Purdue U., D.Eng. (hon.), 1974; m. Priscilla Anne Williamson, Oct. 4, 1973; children—Anne, James Charles. Group engr. Westinghouse Electric Co., 1946-47; chief engr., gen. mgr., pres. and gen. mgr., corp. v.p. Def. Products div., exec. v.p. ops., exec. v.p. and chief ops. officer, pres., chief ops. officer Sundstrand Corp., 1947-77; chmn., chief exec. officer Rohr Industries, Inc., Chula Vista, Calif., 1981—; dir. Aircraft Gear Corp., TIMCO. Pres., Rockford Meml. Hosp., 1978. Served to maj. USAAF, 1940-46. Decorated Legion of Merit. Mem. Ill. Mfrs. Assn. (vice chmn. 1975). Republican. Presbyterian. Office: PO Box 878 Chula Vista CA 92012

SADOWSKI, CHESTER PHILIP, bldg. co. exec.; b. Pensacola, Fla., May 28, 1946; s. Chester Philip and Florence P. (Perry) S.; B.S. in Bus. Adminstrn., U. Fla., 1968; m. Jerriann Gibson Steller, Oct. 4, 1975; 1 dau., Julie Kathryn. With Arthur Andersen & Co., Tampa, Fla., 1969-74; successively audit sr., mgr. audit U.S. Home Corp., Houston, 1974—. Mem. Am. Inst. C.P.A.'s, Fla. Inst. C.P.A.'s, Nat. Assn. Accts. Office: 1177 W Loop S Box 2863 Houston TX 77001

SAEKI, SHINJI, fire protection co. exec.; b. Kanagawa, Japan, Oct. 20, 1933; came to U.S., 1974; s. Keisuke and Fuku (Inoue) S.; student Tokyo U., 1955-59; m. Noriko Kanouchi, Oct. 3, 1960; children—Rika, Chika. Salesman, Nichiei Housing Materials, 1951-55, Okura Trading Co., Ltd., 1959-72; with Nittan Co., Ltd., Tokyo, 1972-74; with Nittan Corp., Des Plaines, Ill., 1974—, exec. v.p., 1974—. Cert. tech. translator German-Japanese, Nat. Transl. Inst. of Sci. and Tech. Mem. Nat. Fire Protection Assn., Japan Tech. Translator Assn. Buddhist. Home: 314 N Home St Park Ridge IL 60068 Office: Nittan Corp 1299 Rand Rd Des Plaines IL 60016

SAETHER, KOLBJORN, structural engr.; b. Trondheim, Norway, July 16, 1925; s. Arne and Beatrice (Thommessen) S.; M.S., Eidgenossische Technische Hochschule (Zurich), 1949; children—Eva, Erik, Linda. With Norwegian Corps Engrs., 1949-50, DeLeuw-Cather & Co., 1951-54, Portland Cement Assn., 1955, Case Found. Co., 1956; pres. Kolbjorn Saether & Assos. Inc., Chgo., 1956—, also Saether Industries, Inc. Served with Norwegian Air Force, 1949-50. Registered structural engr., Ill.; registered profl. engr., Ill., Calif., Wis., Minn., Ind., Mich., Pa., Mo. Mem. ASCE, Norwegian Soc. Civil Engrs., Structural Engrs. Assn. Ill. (v.p.), Prestressed Concrete Inst., Am. Concrete Inst. Author tech. publs. Patentee MCLS Lift-Slab System, Sky-Fork Loading Tool, C-Lock Air Supported Bldgs. Home: 934 Linden Ave Wilmette IL 60091 Office: 221 La Salle St Chicago IL 60601

SAFFORD, ROBERT OWEN, financial exec.; b. Meadville, Pa., Aug. 3, 1934; s. Owen S.; B.S., Cornell U., Ithaca, N.Y., 1956; m. Patricia Hofheins, Dec. 18, 1956; children—Robert Owen, Susan Diane, Thomas Hofheins, Ann Elizabeth. Nat. sales trainer Easterling Co., Chgo., 1958-62; regional dir. Land of Lincoln Life Ins. Co., Springfield, Ill., 1962-63; co-founder, dir., exec. v.p. Alexander Hamilton Life Ins. Co., Farmington, Mich., 1963-71; dir. Nat. Liberty Corp., Valley Forge, Pa., 1972-75; exec. v.p., chief operating officer, dir. Nat. Home Life Assurance Co., Malvern, Pa., 1973-80; pres. Hamilton Fin. Co., Paoli, Pa., 1980—. Active Campus Crusade for Christ, Voice of Christian Youth, Christian Businessmen's Com. Served to 1st lt. USMC, 1956-58. Mem. Sales/Mktg. Execs., Internat. Platform Assn., Nat. Assn. Life Cos. (v.p.), Fellowship of Christian Athletes, Delta Upsilon. Republican. Clubs; Cornell, Waynesborough Country. Home: 403 Margo Ln Berwyn PA 19312 Office: 15 Paoli Plaza Suites H-K Paoli PA 19301

SAGAN, JOHN, automobile co. exec.; b. Youngstown, Ohio, Mar. 9, 1921; s. John and Mary (Jubinsky) S.; B.A. in Econs., Ohio Wesleyan U., 1948; M.A., U. Ill., 1949, Ph.D., 1951; m. Margaret Pickett, July 24, 1948; children—John, Linda, Scott. Fellow, Ohio Wesleyan U., 1946-48; scholar, fellow research U. Ill., 1948-51; with Ford Motor Co., 1951—, treas., 1966-69, v.p., treas., 1969—; dir. Ford Motor Credit Co., Ford Internat. Capital Corp., Ford Motor Land Devel. Corp., Transcon Ins. Ltd., Am. Road Ins. Co.; chmn. Fed. Res. Bank Chgo. Chmn. bd. trustees Ohio Wesleyan U., 1964—; trustee Com. Econ. Devel. U.S.A., Oakwood Hosp., Dearborn, Mich.; mem. council finance and adminstrn. Detroit conf. United Methodist Ch.; trustee YMCA Found. Detroit. Served with USNR, 1943-46. Mem. Am. Econ. Assn., Fin. Analysts Soc., Conf. Bd. (council fin. execs.), Phi Beta Kappa, Phi Kappa Phi, Delta Sigma Rho. Office: Ford Motor Co American Rd Dearborn MI 48121

SAGE, ROBERT, hotel exec.; b. Boston, June 11, 1926; s. Harry and Mollie (Goodsnyder) Saganskу; A.B., Colby Coll., 1949, M.A., 1974; m. Phyllis Sara Caplan, June 5, 1949; children—Marjorie, William, Jane. Mgr., Phillips Drug Co., Boston, 1949-50; treas. Coronet Sales Co., Boston, 1950-58; pres. Fenway Motor Hotels, Boston, 1958—. Chmn., Colby Coll. Alumni Fund, 1968-71; pres. Parker Hill Med. Center, 1968-74; trustee Colby Coll., 1974—, chmn. devel. com., 1975—; v.p. Hebrew Rehab. Center for Aged, 1978—; vice-chmn. Greater Boston Conv. and Tourist Bur., 1978—; bd. dirs., mem. exec. com. Harvard Community Health Plan, 1979—; trustee Beth Israel Hosp. Served with AUS, 1945-47. Recipient Hotel Hall of Fame award Hospitality mag., 1970, Hotelman of Year award New Eng. Hotel Sales Mgmt. Assn., 1965. Mem. Mass. Hotel-Motel Assn. (pres. 1968-70), Am. Hotel and Motel Assn. (dir. 1974-78), Hotel Sales Mgmt. Assn. (chpt. past pres. 1965), New Eng. Inn Keepers Assn. (pres. 1976-78), Greater Boston Hotel and Motel Inn Assn. (pres. 1971-72), Mass. Restaurant Assn. (dir. 1971-77), Colby Coll. Alumni Assn. (pres. 1972-74), Wightman Tennis Center, Tau Delta Phi. Mason. Home: 6 Cynthia Rd Newton MA 02159 Office: 677 Beacon St Boston MA 02215

SAGER, ARTHUR WOODBURY, speech cons.; b. Gardiner, Maine, July 4, 1904; s. George R. and Jennie (Cunningham) S.; B.A., Bates Coll., 1926; m. Frieda Hall, Oct. 20, 1961; children—Jean, Eleanor, Perry. Tchr., coach Gov. Dummer Acad., Byfield, Mass., 1930-72; cons. Morgan Guaranty Trust Co., N.Y.C., 1960—, McGraw-Hill Publs. Co., N.Y.C., 1955—, Comml. Union Assurance Cos., Boston, 1973—, Monsanto Co., St. Louis, 1973—; pres. Arthur Sager Assoc., Inc., Topsfield, Mass., 1950—. Mem. Newcomen Soc. N. Am. Republican. Club: Harvard, New Eng. Olympians (pres. 1977-78). Author: Speech at a Glance, 1974; Speak Your Way to Success, 1968. Address: PO Box 36 Topsfield MA 01983

SAGER, DONALD ALLEN, ins. co. exec.; b. Cleve., Sept. 13, 1930; s. Albert A. and Dolores V. Sager; B.A., U. Md., 1958, postgrad. Law Sch., 1958-60; m. Shirley Thompson, Dec. 23, 1951; children—Donald Allen, David A. Underwriter, Monumental Life Ins. Co., Balt., 1958-60, sr. underwriter, 1960-61, adminstrv. asst., underwriter, 1961-64; sr. underwriter Am. Health and Life Ins. Co., Balt., 1964-69, chief underwriter, individual, 1969-70, sr. systems analyst, 1970-71, mgr. underwriting dept., 1971-72, dir. ins. services, 1972, v.p., ins. services, 1972, bd. dirs., 1972-77, exec. com., 1972-77; asst. v.p. mktg. services Univ. Life Ins. Co., Indpls., 1977-81; v.p. Vulcan Life Ins. Co., 1981—; dir. Am. Health and Life Ins. Co., 1972-77; dir. Hearing and Speech Agy. of Met. Balt., 1974-77. Pres., treas. Essex Recreation Council, 1966-73; treas., player/coach rep. Essex Tackle Football, 1966-73. Served with U.S. Army, 1951-53. Decorated Bronze Star. Recipient home office life underwriting cert., cert. Health Ins. Assn. Am., meritorious award Inst. Home Office Underwriting. Mem. Internat. Assn. Fin. Planners, Phi Alpha Delta. Republican. Lutheran. Clubs: Masons, Shrine, Scottish Rite (Balt.). Home: 1105 Indian Pipe Ln Zionsville IN 46077 Office: PO Box 1886 Birmingham AL 35201

SAIJPAUL, KEWAL KRISHAN, agrl. engr.; b. Hoshiarpur, Punjab, India, July 8, 1945; s. Trilochan Nath and Shkuntla Devi S.; came to U.S., 1969, naturalized, 1975; B.S., Punjab Agrl. U., 1969; M.S., Ohio State U., 1970, Ph.D., 1973. Research/teaching asso., agrl. engring. dept. Ohio State U., 1969-73, research engr., 1976-77; cons. engr. Varo Engrs., Ltd., Columbus, Ohio, 1973-75; cons. engr. asst. to Dr. H.J. Barre, Worthington, Ohio, 1975-76; design engr. Sperry New Holland div. Sperry Rand Corp., New Holland, Pa., 1977-79; devel. engr., corp. advanced harvesting systems Internat. Harvester, Chgo., 1979—. Mem. Council Agrl. Sci. and Tech. Mem. Am. (Paper award 1978), Indian socs. agrl. engrs., Sigma Xi, Alpha Epsilon. Hindu. Contbr. numerous articles to engring. publs. Home: 2021 S Wolf Rd #414 Hillside IL 60162 Office: 4415 W Harrison St Suite 530 Hillside IL 60162

SAINE, LEONARD WATSON, contractor; b. Acworth, Ga., July 1, 1894; s. James Paty and Elizabeth (Watson) S.; student civil engring. Ga. Sch. Tech., 1911-14; student law U. Mich., 1915; LL.B., Atlanta Law Sch., 1916; m. Mary Ruth Hudson, Apr. 17, 1918; 1 dau., Mary Elizabeth (Mrs. Robert Reynolds). Engr., constrn. supt. J. B. McCrary Co., Atlanta, 1917-27; salesman, sales mgr., dir. Central Foundry Co., N.Y.C., 1927-33; sales engr. Walworth Co., N.Y.C., 1935-40; pres., dir. Saine Co., Inc., gen. contractors, 1942—; owner Leonard W. Saine Registered Dealers, municipal and utility supply co., Orlando. Served with C. E. Corps, USN, 1918-19. Registered profl. engr. Mem. Nat. Soc. Profl. Engrs., Fla. Engring. Soc., Beta Theta Pi. Mason. Home: 1555 W Fairbanks Av Winter Park FL 32789

ST. CLAIR, JAMES WYATT, JR., elec. products mfg. co. exec.; b. Aurora, Ill., Oct. 14, 1945; s. James W. and Grace Marie (Ahasic) St.C.; A.B. U. Notre Dame, 1967, B.S. in Mech. Engring., 1968; M.B.A., U. Chgo., 1975; m. Linda Marie Gessner, May 4, 1974. Asst. sales engr. indsl. field sales Westinghouse Electric Corp., Chgo., 1968-70, sales engr. indsl. field sales, 1970, sales engr. constrn. field sales, 1971-75, mktg. rep. constrn. sales support, Pitts., 1975-77, mgr. constrn. planning, 1977-78, staff planning mgr. industry sales support, 1978-79, plant mgr. distbn. equipment div., 1979—. Roman Catholic. Home: 22 Sunset Hill Rd Simsbury CT 06070 Office: 570 Hayden Station Rd Windsor CT 06095

ST. CLAIR, THOMAS MCBRYAR, mfg. co. exec.; b. Wilkinsburg, Pa., Sept. 26, 1935; s. Fred C. and Dorothy E. (Renner) St. C.; A.B., Allegheny Coll., 1957; M.S., M.I.T., 1958; postgrad. Advanced Mgmt. Program, Harvard U.; m. Sarah K. Stewart, Aug. 1, 1959; children—Janet, Susan, Carol. With Koppers Co., Inc., Pitts., 1958—, asst. to gen. mgr. Engring. & Constrn. div., 1966-69, comptroller, asst. treas. parent co., 1969-78, pres. Engineered Metal Products Group, 1978—. Trustee, Allegheny Coll., Meadville, Pa. Mem. Fin. Execs. Inst., Allegheny Coll. Alumni Assn. Presbyterian. Clubs: Duquesne, University. Office: 1550 Koppers Bldg Pittsburgh PA 15219

ST. CLAIR, WILBUR WINGATE, JR., ins. agt.; b. Washington, May 16, 1929; s. Wilbur Wingate and Evelyn Levely (Mattingly) St. C.; student Southeastern U., George Washington U.; m. Adenia Norvell Stearn, June 30, 1951; children—Adenia Maria St. Clair Wockenfuss, Thomas John. Automobile salesman, 1953-57; agt. Mass. Mut. Life Ins. Co., 1957—; dir. Century Nat. Bank, Washington. Recipient various sales awards. Mem. Adv. Assn. Life Underwriters (polit. liaison), Million Dollar Round Table (polit. liaison), Mass. Mut. Life Ins. Co. Agts. Assn. (pres. 1979; Agt. of Year 1979), D.C. Soc. C.L.U.'s (pres. elect 1980). Republican. Baptist. Clubs: Columbia Country, Ocean City Golf and Yacht, Ocean City Marlin. Home: 707 Winhall Way Silver Spring MD 20904 Office: 4201 Connecticut Ave NW Washington DC 20008

ST. GEORGE, NICHOLAS JAMES, lawyer, manufactured housing co. exec.; b. Waltham, Mass., Feb. 11, 1939; s. Louis and Rose (Argonti) St. G.; B.A. in Econs., Coll. William and Mary, 1960, J.D., 1965; m. Lorna Bowen, Dec. 24, 1960; children—Blane Stephen, Nicholas John. Trainee, Gen. Electric Co., Schenectady, 1960; admitted to Va. bar, 1965; trust rep. Va. Nat. Bank, Norfolk, 1965-66; group v.p.-in-charge investment banking dept., dir. Legg Mason-Wood Walker, Washington, 1966-76; v.p. Ferguson Enterprises, Newport News, Va., 1977-78; pres., chief exec. officer Oakwood Homes Corp., Greensboro, N.C., 1979—, also dir.; regional arbitrator Nat. Assn. Security Dealers. Served to 1st lt. U.S. Army, 1960-62. Mem. Manufactured Housing Inst. (dir., fin. chmn.), Am. Mgmt. Assn., Am. Bar Assn., Va. State Bar Assn. Republican. Roman Catholic. Home: 201 W Bessemer Ave Greensboro NC 27401 Office: Oakwood Homes Corp PO Box 7386 Greensboro NC 27407

ST. JOHN, CHARLES RAYMOND, metal processing co. exec.; b. Jackson, Mich., Apr. 1, 1917; s. J.F. and Mary (Ezoa) St. J.; student Jackson Jr. Coll., 1936-37; B.S. in Metall. Engring., U. Mich., 1938-39; m. Dorothy Marie West, Dec. 21, 1939; 1 son—Kenneth. Lab. technician Frost Gear & Forge Co., 1939-41; metallurgist Jackson Comml. Heat Treat Co., 1941-42; owner Indsl. Steel Treating Co., Jackson, 1942—, pres., 1950-70, chmn. bd., 1970—; owner St. John Mfg. Co., Jackson, 1949—; v.p. Jada Mfg. Co., Rives Junction, B. & S. Machine & Tool Co.; pres. Jackson Sports Arena; v.p. Stanton Co., Jackson; pres. S.C. Liquidating Co., Jackson. Past chmn. Social Services Bd., Jackson County, Mich.; past chmn. bd. trustees Jackson Med. Care Facility; mem. Gov.'s Small Bus. Adv. Council. Mem. Jackson Mfg. Assn. (past pres.), Am. Soc. Metals (past chmn.), Am. Soc. Tool and Mfg. Engrs. (past chmn.), Jackson Jr. (nat. dir. 1950, past chmn. regional planning commn. 1971—), Jackson (past dir.) chambers commerce. Lion. Club: Jackson Country. Home: 3776 Maidstone Rd Jackson MI 49203 Office: 613 Carroll St Jackson MI 49202

ST. JOHN, HENRY SEWELL, JR., utility co. exec.; b. Birmingham, Ala., Aug. 18, 1938; s. H. Sewell and Carrie M. (Bond) St. J.; student David Lipscomb Coll., 1956-58, U. Tenn., 1958-59, U. Ala., 1962-64; m. J. Ann Morris, Mar. 7, 1959; children—Sherri Ann, Brian Lee, Teresa Lynn, Cynthia Faye. Engring. aide Ala. Power Co., Enterprise, 1960-62, Birmingham, 1962-66; asst. chief engr. Riviera Utilities, Foley, 1966-71, sec.-treas., gen. mgr., 1971—. Deacon, Foley Ch. of Christ, 1975—; active Am. Cancer Soc., chmn. bd. Baldwin County unit, 1977; bd. dirs. AGAPE of Mobile, 1977—; bd. dirs. South Baldwin Civic Chorus, pres., 1979—. Mem. IEEE., South Ala. Power Distbrs. Assn. (chmn. 1973-74), Ala. Consumer-Owned Power Distbrs. Assn. (chmn. 1974-75, sec.-treas. 1980—), Municipal Electric Utility Assn. Ala. (exec. com., dir. 1971—), South Baldwin C. of C. (pres. 1974, dir. 1981—). Club: Gulf Shores Golf (dir. 1974-75). Rotarian. Home: PO Box 818 Foley AL 36536 Office: PO Box 550 Foley AL 36536

ST. MARTIN, RAOUL, steel co. exec.; b. Ste. Victoire de Sorel, Que., Can., Dec. 12, 1933; s. Rene and Alice (Lavallee) St. Martin; ed. Couvant St. Joseph de Sorel and Coll. Martel, 1941-50; m. Jeanne d'Arc Plouffe, July 16, 1955; children—Diane, Pierre. Clk., Sorel Industries Ltd., St. Joseph de Sorel, Que., 1950-51, invoice audit clk., 1951-55, buyer, 1955-57; sales rep. Val Royal LaSalle, St. Hyacinthe, Que., 1957-59; buyer and cost clk. Crucible Steel of Can. Ltd., St. Joseph de Sorel, 1959-62; purchasing agt. Colt Industries (Can.) Ltd., St. Joseph de Sorel, 1962—. Mem. Can. Assn. Purchasing Agts. Club: K.C. Home: 8690 Croissant d'Auteuil Tracy PQ J3R 4M8 Canada Office: 101 Montcalm St Saint Joseph de Sorel PQ J3R 1B9 Canada

ST. PETER, ALPHONSE FRANCIS, mgmt. and travel cons. co. exec.; b. St. Johnsbury, Vt., Nov. 18, 1914; s. Alphonse Lawrence and Francella (Downing) St. P.; B.S. in Indsl. Relations, Marquette U., 1951; M.B.A., U. Wis., 1954; postgrad. exec. program Columbia U., 1971; m. Margaret E. Whitney, Oct. 6, 1944; children—James W., Fran Daniel. With Mobil Oil Co., 1939-56, staff asst. employee relations, Milw., 1950-56; personnel mgr. Kyle Plant, Line Material Industries, Milw., 1956-59; mgr. indsl. relations Delhi Taylor Oil Co., Dallas, 1959-63; v.p. personnel So. Union Co., Dallas, 1963-79; ret., 1979; pres. ALPEG Inc., mgmt. and travel cons., Dallas, 1980—; instr. Marquette U., 1955-58. Deacon, Highland Park Presbyn. Ch., 1961-71, elder, 1971-77; pres. Mental Health Assn. Dallas, 1976-77; pres.-elect Tex. Mental Health Assn., 1980—. Served with USAAF, 1942-46. Accredited exec. in personnel. Mem. Am. Gas Assn., So. Gas Assn., Am. Mgmt. Assn., Am. Soc. for Personnel Adminstrn., Conf. Bd., Dallas Personnel Assn., Execs. Assn. Columbia U., U. Wis. Alumni Assn., Marquette U. Alumni Assn. Republican. Clubs: Dallas Athletic-Country, Kiwanis (pres. Dallas 1967, lt. gov. Tex.-Okla. dist. 1971). Home and office: 5225 Prestonhaven Dr Dallas TX 75229

SAITY, DAVID AZIZ, art objects and jewelry co. exec.; b. Baghdad, Iraq, Dec. 29, 1930; came to U.S., 1965, naturalized, 1971; s. Itzhak and Nina (Nur-el) S.; student N.Y. U., 1966-68; m. Chaya Polonsky, Dec. 12, 1965. Controller, Constellation Hygeia, Bronx, N.Y., 1965-67; pres. CDS Enterprises Ltd., N.Y.C., 1967—. Mem. Jewelers of Am., Inc., C. of C. of Am. Democrat. Jewish. Office: 239 W 72d St New York NY 10023

SAKATA, GARY NOBUYUKI, mfg. co. exec.; b. Los Angeles, Aug. 18, 1947; s. Yukio and Hisako (Nakamoto) S.; A.S., Los Angeles Trade-Tech. Coll., 1968; B.S., Calif. State U., 1970; m. Janet Yoshiko Yokoyama, Nov. 29, 1979. Prodn. planner Scott & Scott Printers, Santa Monica, Calif., 1975-76; asst. purchasing agt. Western Lithograph, Los Angeles, 1972-78; purchasing agt. Stuart F. Cooper, Los Angeles, 1978-79; purchasing mgr. Jeffries Banknote, Los Angeles, 1979—. Conf. treas. Pacific Coast Japanese Free Meth. Ch., 1978-80. Served with U.S. Army, 1970-72. Mem. Printing Industries Assn. So. Calif., Purchasing Mgrs. Assn. of Los Angeles. Methodist. Office: 1330 W Pico Blvd Los Angeles CA 90015

SAKOVER, RAYMOND PAUL, radiologist; b. Chgo., Oct. 8, 1944; s. Max and Lena (Berardi) S.; B.S. (James scholar), U. Ill., 1965, M.D., 1969; m. Patricia Ellyn Taylor, June 7, 1969; children—Shelley Lynn, Michael Paul. Intern, St. Francis Hosp., Evanston, Ill., 1969-70, resident, 1970-73; practice medicine specializing in radiology, Riverside, Calif., 1975—; staff radiologist Riverside Community Hosp., 1975—; clin. instr. Loma Linda (Calif.) U. Med. Center, 1976—. Bd. dirs. Lung Assn. Riverside, 1978—. Served with USNR, 1973-75. Diplomate Am. Bd. Radiology. Mem. Am. Coll. Radiology, Soc. Nuclear Medicine, AMA, Calif. Med. Soc., N.Am., Calif. radiol. socs., African Lovebird Soc. Roman Catholic. Contbr. articles in field to profl. jours. Office: 6941 Brockton Ave Riverside CA 92506

SAKOWITZ, ROBERT TOBIAS, splty. store exec.; b. Houston, Oct. 13, 1938; s. Bernard and Ann S.; B.A. in History and Econs. cum laude, Harvard U., 1960; 1 son, Robert Tobias. Buyer Young Houstonian jr. dept. Sakowitz, Inc., Houston, 1962-65, mdse. mgr., exec. v.p., 1964-71, gen. mdse. mgr., 1971-75, pres., chief exec. officer, 1975—; dir., mem. audit and compensation coms. Morse Shoe Co., Canton, Mass.; dir., mem. loan and discount com. Galleria Bank. Bd. selectors Am. Inst. Public Service; commr., past chmn. Houston Mcpl. Arts Commn.; nat. bd. dirs., mem. exec. com. High Sch. Performing Arts, Houston, Am. Council for Arts; bd. dirs. Houston Symphony Soc., NCCJ, Houston Festival, Found. for Joffrey Ballet, Inc.; chmn. S.E. del. White House Conf. Small Bus.; trustee chpt. Nat. Found. Ileitis and Colitis. Served with USAF, 1961. Decorated chevalier l'Ordre National de la Merite, France, 1976; recipient award Am. Acad. Achievement, 1973; mem. Internat. Best Dressed List, 1970—; mem. Internat. Best Dressed Hall of Fame, 1975; recipient Ann. Display award Nat. Assn. Display Industries, 1976, Epingle d'Or award French Fashion Fedn., 1972; one of ten Outstanding U.S. Bus. Leaders, Northwood Inst., 1981. Mem. Nat. Retail Mchts. Assn. (dir., internat. com., exec. com.), Young Pres.'s Orgn., Houston C. of C. (dir., freedoms task force com., small bus. com.). Clubs: Knickerbocker, Harvard (N.Y.C.); Houstonian, Met. Racquet (Houston); Fly (Cambridge, Mass.); So. Hills Country (Tulsa). Office: 1111 Main St Houston TX 77002

SAKS, LEANORE PATRICIA, investment co. exec.; b. N.Y.C., Nov. 6, 1929; d. Herman Alexander and Esther Marilyn (Lewis) Sacks; student UCLA, 1949-50, postgrad., 1973-75, U. Miami, 1970-71, Lumbleau Real Estate Sch., 1971, Anthony Schs., 1973, Gemol. Inst. Am., 1977; m. M. Stuart Liquorman, June 24, 1949 (div.); children—Wayne, Jan, Melinda. Founder, pres. Investments Ltd., Los Angeles, 1971—; officer Joseph Clapsaddle Presentations; dir. Westwood Bankcorp.; public speaker, developer, syndicator. Mem. World Affairs Council, Western Los Angeles Regional C. of C., Women in Bus., Nat. Assn. Women Bus. Owners, UCLA Alumni Assn. Clubs: Rolls Royce Owners, Marina City (Los Angeles); Curzon House (London). Contbr. articles to newspapers and mags.

SALANT, RICHARD S., broadcasting co. exec.; b. N.Y.C., Apr. 14, 1914; s. Louis and Florence (Aronson) S.; A.B., Harvard U., 1935, LL.B., 1938. Admitted to N.Y. bar, 1938; atty. U.S. Govt., 1938-43; asso. Rosenman, Goldmark, Colin & Kaye, 1946-48, partner, 1948-52; v.p. CBS, Inc., 1952-61, dir., 1961-68; pres. CBS News, 1961-64, 64-79, v.p. CBS Inc., 1964-66; vice chmn. NBC Inc., 1979—, also dir. Served to lt. comdr., USNR, 1943-46. Office: NBC 30 Rockefeller Plaza New York NY 10020*

SALAZAR, MICHAEL BRIEN, air transp. exec.; b. Kanakanak, Alaska, May 14, 1941; s. Louis A. and Margaret A. (O'Brien) S.; B.S., Seattle U., 1963; m. Barbara Ann Dunn, Nov. 19, 1967; children—Gerald O'Brien, Cassee Ann. Chief pilot Temsco Helicopters, Ketchikan, Alaska, 1969-72; purchasing agt. Ketchikan Pulp Co., 1972-73; pres. Ketchikan Air Service, Inc., 1973—; aviation cons. Mem. Borough of Ketchikan Assembly, 1976—, mem. city council, 1976—. Served with U.S. Army, 1963-69. Decorated D.F.C., Bronze Star (2), Air medals (16), Purple Heart. Recipient Presdl. Vietnam Era Vets. award, 1979. Mem. Alaska Air Carriers (v.p. 1979). Clubs: Elks, Moose, Am. Legion. Home: 520 Washington St Ketchikan AK 99901 Office: Ketchikan Internat Airport Ketchikan AK 99901

SALE, ALVIN THOMAS, fin. exec.; b. Winston-Salem, N.C., Feb. 8, 1947; s. Raymer Martin and Doris Velna (Linville) S.; B.S., U. N.C., 1969; M.B.A., Ga. State U., 1972; postgrad. Stonier Grad. Sch. Banking, 1980; m. Suzanne Clark, Aug. 18, 1968; 1 dau., Allison Ivy. With First Nat. Bank of Atlanta, 1969-73; v.p., mgr. mgmt. acctg. dept. Union Planters Nat. Bank, Memphis, 1974-75, sr. v.p., mgr. consumer lending div., 1976—; pres. Planters Life Ins. Co., Memphis, 1976—, Madison Loan & Trift, Memphis, 1976—. Bd. dirs. Memphis Consumer Credit Counseling Service, 1978—; capt. United Way, Memphis, 1978-80, Cancer Crusade, Memphis, 1979. Mem. Am. Inst. Banking, Planning Execs. Inst., MidSouth Assn. Bus. Economists, Consumer Bankers Assn. (legis. com.), Beta Gamma Sigma. Methodist. Office: 67 Madison Ave Memphis TN 38103

SALEH, JOSEPH, research and devel. co. exec.; b. Tehran, Iran, Dec. 17, 1950; came to U.S., 1973; s. Loghman and Hayat (Harounian) S.; B.S. in Elec. Engring., UCLA, 1972, M.S., 1975, Ph.D. in Computer Sci., 1980. Systems designer NIRT, Tehran, 1972-74; postgrad. research engr. UCLA, 1974-76; dir. decision support systems Perceptronics, Inc., Woodland Hills, Calif., 1976-80; pres. Decision Support Industries, Inc., Encino, Calif., 1980—. Mem. IEEE, Soc. Applied Learning Tech. Home: 22489 Venido Rd Woodland Hills CA 91364 Office: 5107 Gaviota Ave Encino CA 91436

SALEM, HARRY, toxicology lab. exec.; b. Windsor, Ont., Can., Mar. 21, 1929; s. Oscar and Bessie (Pierce) S.; came to U.S., 1959, naturalized, 1965; B.A. in Gen. Sci., U. Western Ont., 1950; B.Sc. in Pharmacy, U. Mich., 1953; M.A. in Pharmacology, U. Toronto, 1955, Ph.D., 1958; m. Florence Rosenbaum, June 30, 1957; 1 son, Jerome Sheldon. Research asst. U. Toronto, 1958-59; pharmacologist Air Shields, Inc., Hatboro, Pa., 1959-62; sr. pharmacologist Smith, Kline & French Labs., Phila., 1962-65; dir. respiratory research labs. Nat. Drug Co., Phila., 1965-70; dir. pharmacology and toxicology Smith, Miller & Patch, Inc., New Brunswick, N.J., 1970-72; dir. pharmacology and toxicology Cooper Labs., Inc., Cedar Knolls, N.J., 1972-76; pres. Cannon Labs., Inc., Reading, Pa., 1977-79; pres. Cosmopolitan Safety Evaluations, Inc., Somerville, N.J., 1979—; instr. pharmacology and toxicology U. Toronto, 1953-58; instr. pharmacology Sch. Medicine, U. Pa., 1960-66, asso. in pharmacology, 1966-68, asst. prof., 1968-75, now asso. prof.; adj. prof. environmental health Coll. Pharmacy, Temple U., 1968—; cons. Med. Documentation Service, Coll. Physicians. Fellow N.Y. Acad. Sci.; mem. Internat. Inflammation Club, Internat. Soc. Biochemical Pharmacology, Acad. Sci. Phila., AAAS, Am. Chem. Soc., Am. Coll. Clin. Pharmacology, Am. Pharm. Assn., Am. Soc. Clin. Pharmacology and Therapeutics, Am. Soc. for Pharmacology and Exptl. Therapeutics, Drug Info. Assn., Reticuloendothelial Soc., Soc. Comparative Ophthalmology (v.p.), Soc. Toxicology, Am. Coll. Toxicology, Pharmacology Soc. Can., Physiol. Soc. Phila. Mem. editorial bd. Drug Information Jour., 1974—, Internat. Ency. of Pharmacology and Therapeutics, 1970—, Pharmacology and Therapeutics, 1970—, Jour. Environ. Pathology and Toxicology, 1979—. Contbr. sci. articles to profl. books and jours. Patentee method of lowering intraocular pressure with antazoline. Home: 918 Rock Ln Elkins Park PA 19117 Office: Cosmopolitan Safety Evaluations Inc 76 4th St Somerville NJ 08876

SALEN, ROGER LEE, housing corp. exec.; b. Washington, Mar. 8, 1938; s. Benjamin and Minnie (Cohen) S.; B.A., U. Md., 1961, LL.B., 1964. Admitted to U.S. Circuit Ct. Appeals bar, 1965, 66; U.S. Dist. Ct. bar, 1965; v.p., sec. Riley Bros., Inc., Silver Spring, Md., 1964-75; dir. multi-family mortgage fin. program Community Devel. Adminstrn., Dept. Econs. and Community Devel., State of Md., Annapolis, 1975-79; regional dir. Nat. Housing Partnership, Washington, 1979—. Mem. Md. Bar Assn., D.C. Bar Assn. Clubs: Amity of Washington, Samuel Gompers Lodge. Home: 121 Lafayette Ave Annapolis MD 21401 Office: 1133 15th St NW Washington DC 20005

SALERNO, VINCENT, engring. and constrn. co. exec.; b. Bellona, Italy, Sept. 28, 1933; s. Pasquale and Mary G. (Carusone) S.; came to U.S., 1946; B.M.E., CCNY, 1957; M.M.E., City U. N.Y., 1963; m. Nancy Quatela, Aug. 21, 1955; children—Robert, Richard, Ronald. With Sci. Design Co., N.Y.C., 1957-68, 69-78, dir. gen. engring., 1974-76, v.p. projects, 1976-77, v.p. ops., 1977-78, v.p., gen. mgr., Houston, 1978—; pres. Sci. Design Constructors, Inc., 1979—; chief mech. engr. Chem Systems Inc., N.Y.C., 1968. Cubmaster Boy Scouts Am., Merrick, N.Y., 1967-69; coach Little League, 1967-68; commr. Merrick Basketball League, 1973-77. Served in C.E., U.S. Army Res., 1957-65. Mem. ASME, Am. Inst. Chem. Engrs., Project Mgmt. Inst., Am. Assn. Cost Engrs., Am. Inst. Indsl. Engrs. Republican. Roman Catholic. Club: Univ. (Houston). Home: 18234 Barbuda Ln Nassau Bay Houston TX 77058 Office: 6750 West Loop S Bellaire TX 77401

SALIBA, JACOB, business co. exec.; b. East Broughton, Que., Can., June 10, 1913 (parents U.S. citizens); s. Said and Nazira (David) S.; B.S., Boston U., 1941; m. Adla Mudarri, May 31, 1942; children—John, Thomas, Barbara. Sr. supervising engr. Thompson and Lichtner Co., Boston, 1944-49; pres. Kingston Dress Co., Boston, 1949-51; pres. Indsl. & Mgmt. Assos., Inc., Boston, 1951-54; pres., dir. Maine Dress Co., Cornish, Me., 1948-61; exec. v.p., mem. exec. com. Cortland Corp., Inc. (formerly Brockway Motor Co., Inc.), N.Y.C., 1954-59, also dir.; exec. v.p. Sawyer-Tower, Inc., Boston, 1955-56, pres., 1956-59, dir., 1955-60; v.p. Farrington Mfg. Co.; exec. v.p. Farrington Packaging Corp., Farrington Instruments Corp., 1959-61; pres. N.E. Industries, Inc., 1961—, Fanny Farmer Candy Shops, Inc., 1963-66, W. F. Schraft & Sons Corp., 1967-68; pres. frozen foods div. W. R. Grace & Co., 1967-68; pres. Katy Industries, Inc., 1969—; dir. A.M. Castle & Co., Mo.-Kan.-Tex. R.R. Co., Bush Universal Inc., HMW Industries, Inc. Spl. cons. Material Command, USAF, Dayton, O., 1942-43, chief air staff USAF, 1952, comdr. air material command USAF, 1952-54; co-chmn. Air Force Spare Study Group, 1953. Mem. corp. Mass. Gen. Hosp., Mus. Sci.; trustee Boston U. Methodist. Clubs: Union League (N.Y.C.); Algonquin, Engineers (Boston); Bridgton Highlands Country (Bridgton, Me.). Home: 151 Rutledge Rd Belmont MA 02178 Office: Prudential Tower Boston MA 02199

SALIBA, THOMAS HABIB, banker, investment adviser; b. Boston, Dec. 18, 1945; s. Jacob and Adla (Mudarri) S.; ed. Belmont Hill Sch.; B.A., Colby Coll., 1967; M.B.A., Columbia, 1969; m. Rita Sharon Eckelkamp, May 31, 1975; children—Nadia Elaine, Leila Barbara. Mgmt. cons. A.T. Kearney & Co., N.Y.C., 1969-71; sr. mgmt. cons. Arthur D. Little Inc., Cambridge, Mass., 1971-75; v.p. Northeast Industries, Inc., Boston, 1971—, also dir.; v.p. 1st Nat. Bank of Chgo., 1975—; v.p., dir. Maple Rock Orchards; dir., mem. exec. com. UBAF Arab Am. Bank; dir. NE Industries, Inc. Aramea, Inc., Saco Valley Cold Storage, Inc., N.E. Properties, Inc., 1st Chgo. Internat.-New Eng. Mem. long term planning task force Cumberland County Civic Center. Mem. U.S. Arab C. of C., Delta Kappa Epsilon. Clubs: Harraseeket Yacht, Union League, Bridgton Highlands Country, Univ. Home: Spar Cove South Freeport ME 04078 Office: The 1st Nat Bank Chgo 200 Clarendon St Boston MA 02166

SALINERO, OMAR DIAZ, cons. business analyst; b. Guines, Cuba, Aug. 25, 1954; came to U.S., 1961, naturalized, 1976; s. Omar Nilo Diaz-Salinero and Elvira Adelina Manaricua; B.B.A., Fla. Internat. U., 1977, grad. Sch. Fin. and Internat. Bus., 1980; postgrad. Syracuse U. Law Sch., 1978. Credit sales mgr. Goodyear Tire & Rubber Co., North Miami, Fla., 1977; credit mgr. Smith, Richardson & Conroy Co., Miami, 1978; mgr. customer accounts Racal-Milgo Info. Systems, Inc., Miami, 1979; cons. bus. analyst, Miami, 1979—. Mem. Am. Mktg. Assn. (chpt. v.p. 1976-78), Fin. Mgmt. Assn., Greater Miami Jaycees (v.p.). Roman Catholic. Club: Kendall Health and Racquet.

SALISBURY, ROBERT ELMORE, financier, industrialist; b. N.Y.C., Apr. 15, 1922; s. Zoll Elmore and Margaret B. (Cameron-Boveda) S.; student N.Y. U., 1940-41; m. Nancy Hoadley Kirkland, Aug. 18, 1972; children by previous marriage—Robert Cameron, Joyce Ellen, Elizabeth Anne, Nancy Jane. Chief operating officer Citibank N.A., Rio de Janeiro, Brazil, 1946-52; dir. Latin Am. pub. Time-Life Internat., N.Y.C., 1952-62; dep. dir. Regional Office C. Am., AID, Guatemala City, 1962-63; pres. Internat. Capital Devel. Ltd., Basel, Switzerland, 1963-67; v.p. Coenen & Co., Inc., N.Y.C., 1968-69; pres. Cameron, Stuart & Co., N.Y.C., 1970—; chmn. Salisbury Energy Group, Ltd., N.Y.C., 1973—. Chmn. bd. dirs. The Space Coalition, N.Y.C., 1980—; dir., v.p. The Greater New York Fund, N.Y.C., 1976—; treas. Am. Sch., Rio de Janeiro, 1948-56; v.p. Am. Benevolent Soc., Mexico City, 1956-59; chmn. bd. trustees French & Polyclinic Med. Sch. and Health Center, N.Y.C., 1975-79; bd. dirs. Girls' Club N.Y., 1977-80, Children of Bellevue, 1977-78; mem. nat. com. Young Republicans Fla., 1960-61; trustee Child Study/Well Met Assn., 1976-78. Served with USAAF, 1941-45. Mem. Ind. Petroleum Assn. Am. (regional dir. 1974-78), Nat. Inst. Social Scis. (v.p., dir. 1978—), Am. C. of C. in Rio de Janeiro (dir. 1952-56). Episcopalian. Clubs: Met., Brook (N.Y.C.); Nat. Golf Links (Southampton, N.Y.). Home: 945 Fifth Ave New York NY 10021 Office: 501 Madison Ave New York NY 10022

SALKO, HENRY S., textile co. exec.; b. N.Y.C., Feb. 24, 1925; s. Max and Louise M. (Ginsberg) S.; B.S. in Econs., Wharton Sch. Fin., U. Pa., 1949; children—Richard Michael, Karen Leslie, Amy Lynn. With Max Salko Corp., N.Y.C., 1949—, v.p., 1958—. Chmn., Citizens for Eisenhower; pres. Young Republicans Larchmont Mamaroneck, 1953; mem. Rep. Town Com., Mamaroneck, 1953-56; trustee Harrison (N.Y.) Jewish Community Center, 1970-73; mem. Public Employees Relations Bd. Harrison, 1970-73. Served with 75th Inf. Div., U.S. Army, 1943-45. Decorated Bronze Star, Purple Heart. Mem. N.Y. Acad. Sci., Retail Assos. Group, Delta Sigma Rho, Alpha Epsilon Pi. Clubs: B'nai B'rith (gov. dist. 1 1979-81), Textile Squre, Wharton, City Athletic. Home: 1 Putnam Green St Greenwich CT 06830 Office: Max Salko Corp 17 W 31st St New York NY 10001

SALLAH, MAJEED JIM, real estate developer; b. Boston, Aug. 5, 1920; s. Herbert K. and Rose (Karem) S.; student Gloucester (Mass.) public schs.; m. Aline C. Powers, Apr. 10, 1970; children—Christopher M., Melissa Rose. Pres., dir. Glo-Bit Fish Co., Gloucester, 1947-48, Live-Pak of Ohio, Inc., 1947-51, Cape Ann Glass Co., Inc., Gloucester, 1950-72, Cape Ann Realty Corp., Gloucester, 1961—, Marias Restaurant, Gloucester, 1960—; pres., treas., dir. Gloucester Hot-Top Constrn. Co., Gloucester, 1967-75; trustee Christopher Investment Trust; dir. Lutsal, Inc. Pres. Lebanese-Am. Bus. Men's Club; treas. Lebanese-Maronite Soc. Served with AUS, 1942-45. Decorated Bronze Star. Mem. Gloucester Assos., Cape Ann Investment Corp., Am. Legion, Amvets, Hon. Order Ky. Cols. Roman Catholic. Clubs: Lions, Elks. Home: 58 Hilltop Rd Gloucester MA 01930 Office: 56 Hilltop Rd Gloucester MA 01930

SALMON, ELIAHU JOHN, pub. health specialist, environmentalist; b. Jerusalem, Dec. 15, 1928; s. Israel and Esther Malka (Toledo) S.; B.Sc. in Civil Engring., Utah State U., 1951; Ph.D. in Pub. Health (Pub. Health Service fellow), U. Mich., 1964; m. Bara Zila Chalfen, Dec. 11, 1956; children—Amir, Gil Israel. Dir. health and waste disposal div. Israeli Atomic Energy Center, Yavneh, 1957-69; cons. in occupational and environ. health to Israeli Ministry of Health, Jerusalem and Tel-Aviv, 1957-69; vis. prof. environ. scis. and continuing med. edn. Tel Aviv U. and Technion, Israel Inst. Tech., 1964-69; sr. scientist WHO, Geneva, 1969-74; sr. staff mem. energy and environment Nat. Acad. Scis., Washington, 1974-77, nat. sr. staff mem., 1978—; pres. Environment, Health, Energy Resources Corp.; sr. staff mem. med. scis., energy Nat. Acad. Scis., 1978—; sr. research asso. Resources for the Future, Washington, 1977-78; adj. prof. mgmt. U. Md. Served with C.E. and Sci. Corps, Israeli Army, 1956-60. Woodrow Wilson scholar, 1948-50. Mem. Am. Chem. Soc., Am. Health Physics Soc. (certified health physicist), Am. Indsl. Hygiene Assn., Am. Pub. Health Assn. Jewish. Club: Tackahoe Recreation. Author numerous articles on energy, health and environment. Home: 7128 Old Dominion Dr McLean VA 22101 Office: Nat Acad Scis 2101 Constitution Ave NW Washington DC 20418

SALO, RALPH WALTER, dept. store exec.; b. N.Y.C., July 13, 1943; s. Alfred D. and Irene M. (Olsen) S.; A.B. with distinction, Ind. U., 1964, M.B.A. in Fin., 1965; m. Lesley Jean Wright, Aug. 21, 1965; children—Kirsten, Katherine, Jill. Fin. analyst Chrysler Corp., Highland Park, Mich., 1965-71; plant controller Amerace Corp., Medora, Ind., 1971-73; v.p., controller Hudsons, Dayton Hudson Corp., Detroit, 1973—. Bd. dirs. Civic Searchlight; mem. allocation com. United Community Services Detroit; mem. fin. com. Luth. Social Services Mich. Served with USN, 1966-70. Mem. N. Am. Soc. Corp. Planners, Retail Fin. Execs. Detroit, Econ. Club Detroit, Phi Beta Kappa, Beta Gamma Sigma. Lutheran. Club: Detroit Athletic. Home: 2417 Wexford Ave Troy MI 48084 Office: 1206 Woodward Ave Detroit MI 48226

SALOMON, J. EUGENE, food industry exec.; b. Gijon, Spain, Sept. 29, 1928; came to U.S., 1960, naturalized, 1965; s. Robert S. and Juana M. (Rugarcia) S.; B.S. in Sugar Tech., U. Havana, 1952, M.S. in Agrl. Engring., 1952; m. Beatrice Porcelli, Dec. 3, 1961; children—J. Eugene, Maria C., Henry R., Robert M. Tchr., Belen Sch., Havana, Cuba, 1948-51; chief chemist, mgr. agrl. ops. Central Fe Sugar Co., Camajuani, Cuba, 1952-56; plant supt., plant mgr. Central Providencia Sugar Co., Güines-Havana, Cuba, 1956-60; successively research chemist, process research engr., asst. to pres., v.p. plant ops. SuCrest Corp., N.Y.C., 1960-75, corp. v.p., div. pres., 1976—. Mem. Inst. Food Technologists, Sugar Industry Technologists, Sugar Club, U.S. Chess Fedn., World Trade Center Assn. Democrat. Roman Catholic. Club: Westfield (N.J.) Chess (dir.). Home: 2 Romeo Ct Old Bridge NJ 08857 Office: 900 Route 9 Woodbridge NJ 07095

SALOMON, RICHARD EDWARD, fin. mgmt. exec.; b. N.Y.C., Dec. 3, 1942; s. Richard Bernard and Edna May (Barnes) S.; B.A. magna cum laude, Yale, 1964; M.B.A., Columbia, 1967; m. Christie Holmes Calder, July 18, 1964; children—David, Christina, Evanne, Jennifer. With credit dept. Time Inc., N.Y.C., 1967-68; staff asso. Rockefeller Bros. Fund, N.Y.C., 1968-70; fin. affairs staff asso. Rockefeller Family & Assos., N.Y.C., 1970—; dir. L'Enfant Plaza Inc., Claymark Inc., Atlanta Investing Inc., DeKalb Inc., Greenrock Corp., Embarcadero Center Inc. Trustee, Greenwich (Conn.) Country Day Sch., 1971—, Hurricane Island Outward Bound Sch., 1972-77, Union Settlement Assn., 1969-72, Choate-Rosemary Hall, 1980—. Mem. Am. Mktg. Assn. (recipient Annual award 1966), Am. Fin. Assn., Phi Beta Kappa, Sigma Tau. Clubs: Greenwich Field (dir. 1978—), Stanwich (dir. 1973-76), Madison Beach (dir. 1978—), Yale of N.Y. Home: 275 Old Church Rd Greenwich CT 06830 Office: Room 5600 30 Rockefeller Plaza New York NY 10112

SALOMON, WILLIAM ROGER, investment banking exec.; b. N.Y.C., Apr. 2, 1914; s. Percy F. and Elsie (Heiman) S.; ed. King Sch., Stamford, Conn., 1933; m. Virginia Foster, Jan. 7, 1937; children—Peter F., Susan Saloman Seiniger. Joined Salomon Bros., N.Y.C., 1933, partner, 1944—, mem. exec. com., 1958, mng. partner, 1963-78, ltd. partner, 1978—; mem. bd. govs. N.Y. Stock Exchange, 1970-72; mem. Downtown Manhattan adv. com. Chase Manhattan Bank, 1969—. Mem. investment policy com. Smithsonian Instn., 1971—; mem. Brit.-N. Am. Com., 1972—, also subcom. on world monetary affairs, U.S. membership com.; mem. gen. com. N.Y. Money Market, Fed. Res. Bank, N.Y., 1972—. Bd. mgrs. Hosp. for Spl. Surgery, N.Y.C., 1979—; trustee, mem. fin. com. N.Y. U., 1971—; trustee Outward Bound, Inc. Served with USAAF, 1945-46. Fellow Albert Gallatin Assos N.Y. U.; mem. Securities Industry Assn. Clubs: Harmonie, Bond (past pres.), Economic (N.Y.C.); Lyford Cay (Bahamas); Coral Beach and Tennis (Bermuda); Nat. Golf Links Am., Meadow (Southampton, N.Y.). Home: 550 Park Ave New York NY 10021 Office: 1 New York Plaza New York NY 10004

SALT, ALBERT ALEXANDER, wood products co. exec.; b. Corona, N.Y., July 14, 1920; s. Albert Edward and Elizabeth (Glass) S.; B.S., U. Ga., 1942; M.F., Yale, 1947; m. Gertrude Essig, June 19, 1947; children—Gary Craig, Alger Dean. Apprentice, Am. Lumber & Treating Co., 1946-47, lab. technician, 1947-49, salesman, 1949-52, dir. quality control, 1952-54; v.p., mgr. Cape Fear Wood Preserving, Inc., Fayetteville, N.C., 1954-57; co-founder pres., mgr. Salt Wood Products, Inc., Cove City, N.C., 1957—; dir. Br. Banking & Trust Co., Trenton, N.C. 4-H adult leader, Cove City and Craven County, N.C., 1959—; organizer Ruritan and Vol. Fire Dept., Cove City, 1959-60; mem. steering com. Craven Tech. Inst., 1960. Served to capt. AUS, 1943-46; ETO. Decorated Bronze Star. Mem. Forest Products Research Soc., Asso. Gen. Contractors Am., Soc. Am. Foresters, Quality Wood Preservers Soc., Am., N.C. (pres. 1972-73) wood preservers assns., U. Ga., Yale alumni assns., 2d Cav. Assn. (life), Blue Key, Xi Sigma Pi, Alpha Zeta. Mason; mem. Order Eastern Star. Clubs: Quaker Neck Golf and Country (membership and fin. com. 1966—). Office: PO Box 68 Cove City NC 28523

SALT, HADDON NORMAN, restaurant exec.; b. Stanfree, Eng., Oct. 18, 1928; s. Charles Haddon and May (London) S.; student Queen Elizabeth Sch. for Boys, Eng.; m. Grace Lawson, Apr. 2, 1949; children—Diana, Barry, John. Mgr. fish and chips shop, Skegness, Eng., 1945-47; partner in hotel and restaurants, 1949-60; propr. fish and chips shops Eng., 1960-64; established H. Salt, Esq. Fish & Chips in U.S. and Can., 1965-69; cons. on pub. relations, San Rafael, Calif., 1969—; land developer in Mexico; quarter-horse breeder. Served with Royal Navy, 1947-49. Ky. col. Paul Harris fellow. Christian Scientist. Rotarian. Clubs: Bohemian, St. Francis Yacht (San Francisco); Marin Yacht. Home: 24737 Arnold Dr Sonoma CA 95476

SALTER, WILLIAM SIDNEY, bank exec.; b. Washington, Oct. 30, 1932; s. William Sidney and Vivian Helen S.; B.S., Georgetown U., 1959; postgrad. exec. mgmt. program Columbia U., 1977; m. Iris Schachter, Jan. 14, 1956; children—Deborah, Kevin, Beth. Comml. lending officer Bank of Am., San Francisco, Hong Kong, 1959-71; sr. v.p., officer-in-charge internat. div. 1st Nat. Bank of St. Louis, 1971—; lectr. local coll. M.B.A. programs. Served with USNR, 1951-55. Mem. Council for Fgn. Affairs (dir.), UN Assn. St. Louis (dir.), Japan Am. Soc. (dir.), Am. Inst. Banking, Bankers Assn. for Fgn. Trade. Unitarian. Office: First Nat Bank of St Louis 515 Olive St Saint Louis MO 63166

SALTZMAN, JACK DAVID, elec. co. exec.; b. N.Y.C., Aug. 4, 1920; s. Morris and Regina (Bauch) S.; B.S. in Elec. Engring., N.Y. U., 1940; m. Margaret Decker, Nov. 4, 1960; children—Mark David, Lisa Rachel, Ira Robert. Engr., Fischbach & Moore, Inc., 1940-48, chief engr., project mgr., 1948; chmn. bd. Tujax Industries, Inc., Del. and Md., Artcraft Elec. Supply Del., Artcraft Elec. Supply Md., Consol. Elec. Supply, Hollywood, Fla., Consol. Elec. Supply, Ft. Myers, Fla., sec. treas. Central Elec. Supply Co., Orlando, Fla., Consol. Elec. Supply, Bradenton, Consol. Elec. Supply Co., Miami, Consol. Elec. Supply, Ft. Lauderdale, Consol. Elec. Supply, Melbourne, Fla., Consol. Elec. Supply, Key West, Fla., Major Elec. Supply Co., Stuart, Fla., Major Elec. Supply, Ft. Pierce; treas. Mid Eastern Funding, Union, Seigler Assos., East Orange, N.J., Mansion Assos., N.Y.C.; v.p. Hwy. Leasing Corp., Jersey City, Hwy. Terminal Corp., Jersey City; pres. M.R. Saltzman, Deal. Chmn., Israel Bond Dr., Deal. Chmn. bd. Hillel Sch., N.J., Monmouth County YW-YMHA; former chmn. bd., v.p. Jewish Hosp. and Rehab. Center N.J.; bd. dirs. Kingsbrook Jewish Med. Center, Bklyn., Salvation Army, Jersey City, Fight for Sight; a founder Technion Inst. Israel; trustee, prin. Saltzman Found.; bd. dirs., v.p. Hillel Sch., Miami; trustee Jewish Fedn. S. Broward (Fla.); v.p. Am. Friends of Hebrew U. Home: 5210 N 35th St Hollywood FL 33021 Office: 3800 NW 31st Ave Miami FL 33021

SALVATORE, JAMES DANIEL, data processing co. exec.; b. Columbus, Ohio, Sept. 20, 1947; s. Dante and Lulu Louise (Kinzelman) S.; B.S., Ohio State U., 1970; postgrad. Mata Coll., 1970; M.B.A., Xavier U., 1975. Data processing mgr. Robershaw Controls Co., Columbus, 1971-75, W.A. Butler Co., Columbus, 1975—. Chmn., Ohio Spl. Olympics for retarded children and adults. Recipient cert. in data processing Inst. for Certification Computer Profls. Mem. Assn. Masters of Bus. Adminstrn. Execs., Data Processing Mgmt. Assn., Assn. for Systems Mgmt. Republican. Roman Catholic. Clubs: Guild Athletic; Ohio State U. Pres.'s. Home: 777 Clubview Blvd Worthington OH 43085 Office: 4140 Fisher Rd Columbus OH 43228

SALVESEN, ARNE RICHTER, specialty valves mfg. co. exec.; b. Wausau, Wis., Apr. 27, 1938; s. Jorgen R. and Gunvor (Eberhardt) S.; B.S. in Mech. Engring., U. Wis., 1961, B.S. in Naval Sci., 1961; M.B.A., Harvard U., 1970; m. Karin Hoffmann, Sept. 1966; children—Nina, Bjorn. Project engr. Zimpro div. Sterling Drug Co., Rothschild, Wis., 1966-68; cons. Arthur D. Little Co., Cambridge, Mass., 1969; dir. corp. devel. Mark Controls Corp., Evanston, Ill., 1970-73, v.p. internat., 1973-78, pres., 1978—, pres. MCC MARPAC unit, 1971—. Mgr., Evanston United Fund. Served to lt. USN, 1961-65. Mem. Evanston C. of C. (dir.), Am. Pipe Fittings Assn., Valve Mfrs. Assn., Sigma Phi. Club: Westmoreland Country. Home: 1378 Ashland St Wilmette IL 60091 Office: 1900 Dempster St Evanston IL 60204

SALVESON, MELVIN ERWIN, business exec., educator; b. Brea, Calif., Jan. 16, 1919; s. John T. and Elizabeth (Green) S.; B.S., U. Calif., Berkeley, 1941; M.S., M.I.T., 1947; Ph.D., U. Chgo., 1952; m. Joan Y. Stipek, Aug. 22, 1944; children—Eric C., Kent Erwin. Cons., McKinsey & Co., N.Y.C., 1948-49; asst. prof., dir. mgmt. sci. research UCLA, 1949-54; mgr. advanced data systems Gen. Electric Co., Louisville and N.Y.C., 1954-57; pres. Mgmt. Scis. Corp., Los Angeles, 1957-67; group v.p. Control Data/CEIR, Inc., 1967-68; pres. Electronic Currency Corp. (formerly U.S. Civil Systems Corp.), 1968—; founder Master Charge System, Los Angeles, 1966; chmn. Corporate Strategies Internat.; prof. bus. Pepperdine U.; adj. prof. U.

So. Calif.; adviser data processing City of Los Angeles, 1962-64; adviser futures forecasting IBM, 1957-61, strategic systems planning USAF, 1961-67, info. systems Calif. Dept. Human Resources, 1972-73, City Los Angeles Automated Urban Data Base, 1962-67; tech. transfer NASA, 1965-70, others. Served to lt. comdr. USNR, 1941-46. Fellow AAAS; mem. Inst. Mgmt. Sci. (founder, past pres.). Republican. Club: Founders (Los Angeles Philharmonic Orch.). Editor: Business Strategy, Planning Rev.; contbr. articles to profl. jours. Home: 1577 N Bundy Dr Los Angeles CA 90049

SALYARD, ROBERT RUSSEL, mfg. co. exec.; b. York, Nebr., Oct. 25, 1926; s. Floyd E. and Thelma M. (Roberts) S.; B.S., Northwestern U., 1947; M.B.A., Harvard U., 1951; m. Ann Biddle Barriger, July 2, 1955; children—Ann Biddle, Elizabeth Thatcher, Margaret Roberts, Robert Russel. Methods engr. Inland Steel Corp., Chgo., 1951-53; prin. Cresap, McCormick & Paget, mgmt. cons., Chgo. and San Francisco, 1963-64; with Am. Cement Corp., 1963-69, sr. v.p., 1969; pres., chief exec. officer Fin. Corp. Ariz., 1969-72, dir., mem. exec. com., 1972-74; exec. v.p., chief ops. officer A.V.C. Corp., Phila., 1975-76, pres., Radnor, Pa., 1976—, also dir. Served to ensign USNR, 1947-49. Mem. Newcomen Soc. N. Am. Clubs: Phila. Country, Harvard Bus. Sch. (Phila.); Calif. (Los Angeles). Office: 2 Radnor Corp Center Radnor PA 19087

SALYER, PAUL HUDSON, coal co. exec.; b. Royalton, Ky., Nov. 29, 1930; s. Ollie and Fannie (Adams) S.; student pub. schs., Salyersville, Ky.; m. Marcella K. Hensley, Aug. 7, 1971; children—Donald P., Joe A. Owner, mgr. Gulf Service Sta., Salyersville, 1957-67, Salyer Excavating Co., 1965-73, Salyer Coal Co., 1974—; pres., owner Coastline Coal Corp., Salyersville, 1973—. Mem. city council City of Salyerville, 1963, mayor, 1964-65. Democrat. Baptist. Clubs: Kiwanis, Sportsman, Shriners. Home: PO Box 433 Salyersville KY 41465

SALZANO, EDWARD P., food co. exec.; b. Bklyn., Apr. 9, 1947; s. Edward F. and Carmela Salzano; B.S. in Indsl. Engring., N.Y. U., 1973; m. Evelyn Mulinaro, June 13, 1970; children—Danielle, Noelle. Salesman, Bulkley Dunton Linde Lathrop Inc., N.Y.C., 1966, asst. dir. splty. products, 1969-70, dir. disposable products, 1970-72; pres., chief exec. officer Bell Beer & Ice Distbrs. Inc., Little Neck, N.Y., 1976-79, Auburndale Beer & Ice Distbrs. Inc., Flushing, N.Y., 1972-79; pres. Francesco Rinaldi Food Co., Bklyn., 1979—; exec. v.p. Omni Continental, Inc., Ft. Lee, N.J., 1979—. Mem. Italian-Am. C. of C. (dir.), Cheese Importers Assn. (dir.), Pres.'s Assn., Am. Mgmt. Assn. Roman Catholic. Clubs: N.Y. U., Paerdegat Racquet. Home: 1327 E 52d St Brooklyn NY 11234 Office: 1605 John St Fort Lee NJ 07024

SALZBERG, LYN, advt. and mktg. exec.; b. Pitts., July 10, 1934; s. Harold K. and Altha C. S.; B.A. in Journalism, Pa. State U., 1956. With Dancer Fitzgerald-Sample, N.Y.C., 1956—, sr. v.p., mgmt. supr., 1976—. Home: 106 Sunrise Hill Rd Norwalk CT 06851 Office: 405 Lexington Ave New York NY 10174

SALZBURG, JOSEPH SHELDON, govt. ofcl.; b. Mayfield, Pa., July 13, 1926; s. Samuel and Anna (Eber) S.; student U. So. Calif., 1945-46; A.B. in Clin. Psychology, U. Miami (Fla.), 1951; postgrad. U. Md., 1960, U. Pitts., 1968, Calif. Western U., 1977-80; m. Carmen A. Albaladejo, Apr. 16, 1978. Field dir. ARC, various locations, 1951-63, exec. dir., Jersey City, 1963-67; fgn. service res. officer Dept. of State/AID, 1967—, project mgr. rural devel., Mali, 1978—. Shelter mgr. Office of Civil Def., Jersey City, 1964-67. Served with AUS, 1947-48. Decorated Purple Heart, Bronze Star; recipient Presdl. Medal of Freedom, 1954, City Plaque for outstanding service, Jersey City, 1967, State Dept. Meritorious Honor award, 1972, Vietnam Presl. Order of Merit 1st class, 1974. Mem. Am. Fgn. Service Assn., Am. Numismatic Assn., Smithsonian Assos., Internat. Platform Assn. Author: (short stories) A Child of Unknown Parents, 1954, The Little Things, 1956; Of Power and Faith, 1967; (essays) Moments of Inspiration, 1961; (poetry) The Joys of Living, 1963, A Thousand Delights, 1970; (philosophy) Reflections Through a Moving Lens, 1980; (fiction) The Dividing Lines, 1965, Evil Be My Good, 1970, No Place of Her Own, 1971, The Dream-Seeker, 1972, The Right Time, The Right Place, 1978; (non-fiction) Tales of Aragon, 1960, Vietnam: Beyond the War, 1975; contbr. articles tech. jours. Home: 2272 Pimmit Run Ln Apt 104 Falls Church VA 22043

SALZMAN, RICHARD WILLIAM, wholesale clothing co. exec.; b. Los Angeles, Nov. 22, 1958; s. Paul and Anne (Myersberg) S.; student public schs., Los Angeles. Stockboy, Marathon Clothing, Los Angeles, 1976-77, salesman, 1977, sales and mgmt. trainee, 1977-78, br. mgr., San Francisco, 1978-80, San Diego, 1980—. Mem. Union of Concerned Scientists, Green Peace, Environ. Def. Fund, Coalition for Non-Nuclear World. ACLU. Democrat. Home: 12548 Everglade St Los Angeles CA 90066 Office: 828 S Wall St Los Angeles CA 90015

SALZMAN, RONALD NORMAN, mfg. co. exec.; b. Amityville, N.Y., Mar. 28, 1943; s. Leo and Shirley (Shapiro) S.; B.S., Columbia U., 1964, M.S., 1965; Ph.D. in Mech. Engring., W.Va. U., 1973; m. Susan Lynn Wurtzman, Aug. 8, 1976; 1 dau., Andrea. Research scientist North American, Downey, Calif., 1965-67; engr., scientist McDonnell-Douglas, Huntington Beach, Calif., 1967-69; cons. Appalachain Lab. for Occupational Respiratory Diseases, Morgantown, W.Va., 1972-74; profl. engr. Hamilton Engrs. P.C., Rochester, N.Y., 1973-74; dir. research and devel. Mixing Equipment Co., Inc., Rochester, 1974—. Chmn. environ. group Democratic Party, Rochester, 1973-75, Rochester Environ. Commn., 1974-77, pres., 1977. Registered profl. engr., N.Y., W.Va. Mem. Nat. Soc. Profl. Engrs., ASME, Am. Inst. Chem. Engrs. Jewish. Author papers in field. Home: 260 Susquehanna Rd Rochester NY 14618 Office: 135 Mount Read Blvd Rochester NY 14611

SAMANIE, DONALD PAUL, JR., oil field equipment co. exec.; b. Big Springs, Tex., Mar. 11, 1944; s. Donald Paul and J. Marie (Long) S.; B.A. in Biology and Psychology (univ. football scholar), Harding U., 1966; M.A. in Psychology (univ. fellow), Okla. State U., 1968; m. Linda C. Johnson, Sept. 6, 1966; children—Julie Rene, Tracie Marie. Vice pres. GOEX, Inc. subs. Pengo Industries Inc., Scranton, Pa., 1973-77, chmn. bd., 1977—, v.p. and group v.p. responsible for multiple cos. and divs., parent co., Ft. Worth, 1977—, chmn. bd. Gen. Tex. Corp. subs. Pengo Industries Inc., 1977—. Deacon, Randol Mill Ch. of Christ, Arlington, Tex. Served to capt. USAF, 1968-73; Vietnam. Mem. Am. Mgmt. Assn., Am. Prodn. and Inventory Control Assn. Republican. Home: 712 Portofino Arlington TX 76012 Office: 1400 Everman Pkwy Fort Worth TX 76142

SAMEK, EDWARD LASKER, mfg. co. exec.; b. N.Y.C., Oct. 26, 1936; s. Richard E. and Jane L. Samek; B.S. in Commerce and Fin., Bucknell U., 1958; M.B.A., Columbia U., 1960; m. Marthann Lauver, June 26, 1960; children—Anne, Margaret, Elizabeth. Brand mgr. Procter & Gamble Co., Cin., 1960-62; dir. New products Johnson & Johnson, New Brunswick, N.J., 1962-67; v.p., gen. mgr. Avon Products Inc., N.Y.C., 1967-75; pres., chief exec. officer Childcraft Edn. Corp., Edison, N.J., 1975-78, also dir.; pres. Hudson Pharm. Corp., W. Caldwell, N.J., 1978—. Pres. bd. trustees Hartridge Sch., Plainfield, N.J., 1969-76; v.p. bd. trustees Wardlaw-Hartridge Sch., Plainfield and Edison, 1975—; trustee Plainfield Symphomy, 1976—. Served with Ordnance Corps, U.S. Army, 1958-59. Mem. Young Pres.'s Orgn. Clubs: Williams, Metuchen (N.J.) Golf and Country. Home: 1717 Woodland Ave Edison NJ 08817

SAMEK, PAUL HERMAN, dept. store exec.; b. New Rochelle, N.Y., May 28, 1923; s. Emil and Sophie (Rich) S.; student U. Wis., 1942; B.A., Dartmouth, 1945; m. Arlene DuBoff; children—Benjamin, Mark, Renee. Actor, Barter Theatre, Abingdon, Va., 1939; radio announcer Sta. WDAE, Tampa, Fla., 1947; newspaper display salesman Tampa Daily Times, 1949; owner, operator women's specialty shop, Winston-Salem, N.C., 1950-57; territorial buyer Sears, Roebuck & Co., Alhambra, Calif., 1957—. Pres., founder Big Bros. Am., Jacksonville, Fla., 1961; pres. apparel industry div. Save A Life, Los Angeles, 1970-76. Served with USNR, 1942-44; PTO. Mem. Dartmouth Club Fla. (sec. 1960). Clubs: Masons, Shriners. Home: 4461 Van Noord St Studio City CA 91604 Office: 900 S Fremont Ave Alhambra CA 91802

SAMLOWSKI, MARTIN A. F., mfg. exec.; b. Apr. 22, 1938; B.Commerce, McGill U. Various exec. positions Henkel Group, Ville d'Anjou, Que., Can., 1963—, pres. and chief exec. officer, 1979—; cons. various mfg. firms. Mem. Canadian-German C. of C. (sr. v.p. 1978—). Office: 9550 Ray-Lawson Ville d'Anjou PQ H1J 1L3 Canada

SAMMETH, PHILIP, mktg. cons.; b. Bklyn., Sept. 15, 1909; s. Henry Peter and Bertha (Fischer) S.; B.A., Ohio State U., 1933; LL.B., St. Lawrence U., 1940; m. Miriam Keller, May 23, 1943; children—Barbara, William. Exec. dir. worldwide, merchandising and pubs. Walt Disney Prodns., Burbank, Calif., 1969-72; v.p. Walt Disney Music Co., Burbank, 1972-75; mktg. cons., Los Angeles, 1972—. Served to capt. U.S. Army, 1942-46. Decorated Army Commendation medal. Mem. Acad. Motion Pictures Arts and Scis., Phi Sigma Delta, Zeta Beta Tau, Iota Theta. Republican. Jewish. Club: Mountaingate Country (Los Angeles). Address: 308 S Westgate Ave Los Angeles CA 90049

SAMMUT, BRUCE ARTHUR, fin. exec.; b. Detroit, Dec. 27, 1937; s. Edward P. and Ruth K. (Wilson) S.; B.S., Miami U., Oxford, Ohio, 1960; m. Nancy Lee Pickartz, Feb. 27, 1960; children—Mark, John. With Marathon div. Am. Can, Neenah, Wis., 1960-61; account mgr. IBM, Syracuse, N.Y., 1961-68; account exec. Merrill Lynch, N.Y.C., 1968-70; regional mgr. Halsey, Stuart & Co., Syracuse, 1970-73, Adams & Peck, Syracuse, 1973-75; chmn. Crawford & Sammut, Syracuse, 1975—. Registered fin. prin. Mem. Nat. Assn. Security Dealers. Roman Catholic. Club: Univ. Home: E Lake Rd Skaneateles NY 13152 Office: 1310 Mony Plaza Syracuse NY 13201

SAMPLES, WILLARD ENOCH, credit union exec.; b. Milnor, N.D., Mar. 9, 1927; s. William J. and Olive Alberta (Tanner) S.; student Pacific Coll., 1945-47, Retail Credit Mgmt. Sch., 1955-58, U. Alaska, 1974, U. Wis., 1975; m. V. Jeanette Ochampaugh, Apr. 17, 1949; 1 son, William J. Accountant, Chase Bag Co., Portland, Oreg., 1947-49; with Retail Credit Co., Inc., 1949-72, asst. mgr., Portland, 1959, mgr. Alaska, 1963-72; gen. mgr. Fed. Alaska Fed. Credit Union, Anchorage, 1972—. Pres., Western Alaska council Boy Scouts Am., 1976-78, nat. bd. rep., 1977—; sec. Charles W. Smith Meml., 1967; trustee First Christian (Disciples of Christ) Ch., Anchorage, 1967—, chmn. bd. elders, Anchorage, 1978—; chmn. Anchorage Mayor's Prayer Breakfast, 1965-66; coach Boys Club Alaska, 1965-72. Served with AUS, 1944-46. Decorated Merit award with oak leaf cluster; recipient Silver Beaver award Boy Scouts Am., 1970. Mem. Credit Union Execs. Soc., Credit Union Nat. Assn. (dir. 1974—), Alaska Credit Union League (dir. 1974-77, chmn. legis. affairs com. 1974-77), Anchorage C. of C. Republican. Clubs: Anchorage Rotary (sec. 1975-76, treas. 1977—), Civ Air (dir. 1974-76, 80—), Christian Businessmen's (dir. 1964—). Author articles in field; editor Thrifty Digest, 1972-79. Home: 2859 Knik Ave Anchorage AK 99503 Office: Pouch 7-505 731 I St Anchorage AK 99510

SAMPSON, HARVEY EARL, electronics and food mktg. corp. exec.; b. Bklyn., Mar. 29, 1929; s. Harvey and Betty (McKenna) S.; B.A., Cornell U., 1951; m. Carolyn M. White, June 23, 1973; children—Shelley E., Holly F., Peter F., Jeffrey F. Sales mgr., v.p. mktg. Harvey Radio Co., N.Y.C., 1953-67; pres. The Harvey Group, Inc., Woodbury, N.Y., 1967—, chmn. bd., 1978—. Bd. dirs. Huntington (N.Y.) Arts Council, 1972—; trustee Cornell U., 1977—; bd. overseers Cornell U. Med. Coll., 1979—. Served to 1st lt. U.S. Army, 1951-53. Mem. Audio Engring. Soc. (gov.). Presbyterian. Club: Nassau Country (dir.). Office: Harvey Group Inc 60 Crossways Park W Woodbury NY 11797

SAMPSON, JOHN EUGENE, mfg. co. exec.; b. Lincoln, Nebr., Feb. 25, 1941; s. Delbert John and Mary Etta (Dodrill) S.; A.B. with distinction, Nebr. Wesleyan U., 1963; M.B.A., Ind. U., 1964; m. Mary Margaret Treanor, Aug. 14, 1965; children—J. Mark, Sharon. Mgmt. asst., exec. trainee Office Sec. Def., Washington, 1963-64; staff mem. Com. Econ. Devel., Washington, 1964-69; coordinator environ. planning Gen. Mills, Inc., Mpls., 1969-72, mgr. devel. planning, 1972-74; dir. corp. planning, chmn. budget com. Central Soya Co., Inc., Ft. Wayne, Ind., 1974-76, v.p. corporate planning, chmn. budget com., 1976-80, v.p. corp. planning and devel., chmn. budget com., 1980—; dir. O's Gold Seed Co., 1977—. Trustee Nebr. Wesleyan U., 1970—; chmn. adminstrv. bd. St. Joseph United Meth. Ch., Ft. Wayne, 1979—; lay mem. North Ind. Annual Conf., United Meth. Ch., 1980. Mem. Ind. U. Sch. Bus. Alumni Assn. (bd. dirs.). Home: 5212 W Arlington Park Blvd Fort Wayne IN 46815 Office: Central Soya Co Inc 1300 Fort Wayne National Bank Building Fort Wayne IN 46802

SAMSIL, DORRIS MCDOWELL, fin. exec.; b. Trigg County, Ky., Aug. 11, 1946; s. Dorris McDowell and Grace Myrle (Gibbs) S.; B.S., Austin Peay State U., 1967; M.S., U. So. Calif., 1974; C.L.U., Am. Coll., 1977; m. Dolores Katheryn Ruff, Sept. 21, 1968; children—Dana Michele, Damon Michael, Sabrina Lynn. Tchr., Montgomery County Sch. System, Clarksville, Tenn., 1967-68, Duval County, Jacksonville, Fla., 1968-69; ins. agt. Lincoln Nat. Life, Daytona Beach, Fla., 1974-77, sales mgr., 1977—. Served with USAF, 1969-74. Decorated Air medal; recipient Nat. Quality award, 1976, 77. Mem. Jr. C. of C., Austin Peay State U. Alumni Assn., U. So. Calif. Alumni Assn., Nat. Assn. Life Underwriters, Gen. Agts. and Mgrs. Assn., Central Fla. C.L.U.'s, Gold Key Soc. of C.L.U.'s, Mensa. Clubs: Citrus, Kiwanis. Home: 251 Banbury Ct Longwood FL 32750 Office: 3319 Maguire Blvd Suite 150 Orlando FL 32803

SAMUELS, JOHN STOCKWELL, III, financier, diversified industry exec.; b. Galveston, Tex., Sept. 15, 1933; s. John Stockwell and Helen Yvonne (Poole) S.; B.A., Tex. A. and M. U., 1954, M.S., 1954; LL.B., Harvard U., 1960; children—Evelyn, John Stockwell, Ainlay, Peter A.H. Chmn. bd. Carbomin Internat. Inc., N.Y.C., 1973—. Chmn. bd. City Center Music and Drama, Inc., N.Y.C., 1975—, N.Y.C. Ballet, 1976—, N.Y.C. Opera, 1976—; bd. dirs. Lincoln Center for Performing Arts. Served with U.S. Army, 1954-57. Clubs: Century; Piping Rock (Locust Valley, L.I.); Meadow (Southampton, L.I.), Southampton Bathing Corp.; Galveston (Tex.) Arty.; Chicago. Office: Carbomin Internat Inc PO Box 581 Lenox Hill Station New York NY 10021

SAMUELSEN, JOHN DAVID, beverage wholesaler; b. Hettinger, N.D., Aug. 30, 1943; s. James Calvin and Shirley Marie (Howell) S.; B.A., Black Hills State Coll., 1967; m. Ruth Ann Duncan, Aug. 24, 1968; 1 son, John Christopher. Ins. adjuster Gen. Adjustment Bur., Bismarck, N.D., 1968-69; gen. mgr. Lakes Bldg. Corp., Rapid City, S.D., 1969-70; sales mgr. Rushmore Homes, Rapid City, 1970-71; salesman Highland Beverage Co., Rapid City, 1971-72, v.p., co-owner, 1972-78, pres., owner, 1978—. Mem. Nat. Beer Wholesalers Assn., S.D. Beer Wholesalers Assn. (dir. 1974—, pres. 1975-76, legis. adv. 1975—), Rocky Mountain Beer Wholesalers (dir. 1972—), Rocky Mountain Conf. Beer Distbrs. Assn. (pres. 1979—), Rapid City C. of C. (dir. 1979), Greater S.D. Assn. Republican. Clubs: Elks; Rapid City Sertoma. Home: 4531 S Glen Pl Rapid City SD 57701 Office: 802 E St Patrick St Rapid City SD 57701

SAMUELSON, PAUL ANTHONY, economist; b. Gary, Ind., May 15, 1915; s. Frank and Ella (Lipton) S.; B.S., U. Chgo., 1935; M.A., Harvard U., 1936, Ph.D. (David A. Wells prize 1941), 1941; hon. degrees: LL.D., U. Chgo., Oberlin Coll., 1961, Boston Coll., 1964, Ind. U., 1966, U. Mich., 1967, Claremont Grad. Sch., 1970, U. N.H., 1971, Keio U., 1971; D.Litt., Ripon Coll., 1962, No. Mich. U., 1973; L.H.D., Seton Hall Coll., 1971, Williams Coll., 1971; D.Sc., East Anglia U., Norwich, Eng., 1966, U. Mass., 1972, U. R.I., 1972; LL.D., Harvard U., 1972, Gustavus Adolphus Coll., 1974, U. So. Calif., 1975, U. Pa., 1976, U. Rochester, 1976, Emmanuel Coll., 1977, Stonehill Coll., 1978; Doctorate Honoris Causa, U. Catholique de Louvain (Belgium), 1976, Cath. U. at Riva Aguero Inst., Lima, Peru, 1980; hon. degree City U. London, 1980; m. Marion Crawford, July 2, 1938 (dec.); children—Jane Kendall, Margaret Wray, William Frank, Robert James, John Crawford, Paul Reid. Prof. econs. M.I.T., 1940—, Inst. prof., 1966, mem. staff Radiation Lab., 1944-45; prof. internat. econ. relations Fletcher Sch. Law and Diplomacy, part-time 1945; cons. Nat. Resources Planning Bd., 1941-43, WPB, 1945, U.S. Treasury, 1945-52, 61—, Bur. Budget, 1952, RAND Corp., 1948-75, Fed. Res. Bd., 1965—, Council Econ. Advisers, 1960—; econ. adviser to Pres. Kennedy; sr. adviser Brookings Panel on Econ. Activity; mem. spl. commn. on social scis. NSF, 1967—; cons. Joint Econ. Council, Congressional Budget Office; Stamp Meml. lectr., London, 1961; Wicksell lectr., Stockholm, 1962; Franklin lectr., Detroit, 1962; Hoyt vis. fellow Calhoun Coll., Yale U., 1962; Carnegie Found. reflective year, 1965-66; John von Neumann lectr. U. Wis., 1971; Gerhard Colm Meml. lectr. New Sch. for Social Research, N.Y.C., 1971; Davidson lectr. U. N.H., 1971; Sultzbacher Meml. lectr. Columbia Law Sch., N.Y.C., 1974; J. Willard Gibbs lectr. Am. Math. Soc., San Francisco, 1974; John Diebold lectr. Harvard U., 1976. Chmn. Pres.'s Task Force Maintaining Am. Prosperity, 1964; mem. Nat. Task Force on Econ. Edn., 1960-61; mem. adv. bd. Nat. Commn. Money and Credit, 1958-60. Hon. fellow London Sch. Econs. and Polit. Sci.; Guggenheim fellow, 1948-49; Ford Found. research fellow, 1958-59; recipient John Bates Clark medal Am. Econ. Assn., 1947; Alfred Nobel Meml. prize in econ. sci., 1970; medal of Honor, U. Evansville (Ill.), 1970; Albert Einstein Commemorative award, 1971; Distinguished Service award Investment Edn. Inst., Nat. Assn. Investment Clubs, 1974. Fellow Brit. Acad. (corr.), Am. Philos. Soc., Econometric Soc. (v.p. 1950, pres. 1951), Am. Econ. Assn. (hon.; pres. 1961); mem. Com. Econ. Devel. (commn. on nat. goals, research adv. bd. 1959-60), Am. Acad. Arts and Scis., Internat. Econ. Assn. (pres. 1966-68, hon. pres.), Nat. Acad. Scis., Phi Beta Kappa, Omicron Delta Kappa (trustee). Author: Foundations of Economic Analysis, 1947; Economics, 1948-80; Readings in Economics, 1955; (with R. Dorfman and R.M. Solow) Linear Programming and Economic Analysis, 1958; Collected Scientific Papers, 4 vols., 1966, 72, 78; co-author numerous other books; contbr. numerous articles to profl. jours.; columnist Newsweek. Home: 75 Clairemont Rd Belmont MA 02178

SANBORN, FREDERICK ARTHUR, real estate exec.; b. Denver, Mar. 15, 1930; s. Frederick William and Dorothy (Gildersleeve) S.; B.A., U. Colo., 1953; children—Kristina, Scott, John. Engaged in life ins., 1956-58, indsl. sales, 1958-62, real estate brokerage with Kendrick, Maurer & Smith, and John Burnham & Co., 1962-70; with Grubb & Ellis Co., 1970-75, regional v.p. in charge San Diego and Los Angeles ops., 1974-75; pres. Bus. Properties Brokerage Co., 1975—. Bd. dirs. Econ. Devel. Corp. San Diego, 1973-74, San Diego Bd. Realtors, 1963—. Served to 1st lt. USAF, 1954-56. Mem. Los Angeles C. of C., San Diegans Inc., San Diego C. of C., Colo. U. Alumni Assn. (chpt. pres. 1956), Beta Theta Pi (v.p. 1952, dir. 1957). Republican. Baptist. Clubs: Lomas Santa Fe Country; Cuyamaca; Kona Kai. Author articles in field. Home: 2728 Bayside Walk San Diego CA 92109 Office: 5353 Mission Center Rd San Diego CA 92108

SANBORN, GEORGE RICHARD, airline co. exec.; b. Youngstown, Ohio, Jan. 29, 1916; s. George Walter and Marguret (Lewis) S.; B.S. in Mech. Engring., Carnegie Inst. Tech., 1937; m. Anabel Barrington Crowell, May 14, 1938; children—George W. II, Virginia Ann. Engring. sales and service Boeing Co., Renton, Wash., 1937-52, dir. orgn. planning, 1952-56, dir. contract adminstrn., 1956-57, dir. comml. sales, 1957-66, dir. marketing, 1966-69; v.p. aircraft sales and services Am. Airlines, Inc., N.Y.C., 1969—. Republican precinct committeeman, 1954-56. Bd. dirs. Japan-Am. Soc.; mem. transp. adv. council Carnegie-Mellon U. Recipient Civilian Outstanding Service award Air Force, World War II. Mem. Kappa Sigma. Episcopalian (vestryman). Clubs: Overlake Golf & Country (Medina, Wash.); Seattle Skeet and Gun; Wings, Regency Whist (N.Y.C.). Home: 6328 Bandera Ave Dallas TX 75225 Office: PO Box 61616 DFW Airport TX 75261

SANCHEZ, FEDERICO FIDENCIO, real estate exec.; b. Havana, Cuba, June 4, 1941; s. Federico P. and Esther C. (Febles) S.; came to U.S., 1958, naturalized, 1968; B.C.E., Rensselaer Poly. Inst., 1962; M.B.A., Harvard, 1968; m. Elisa Ortiz-Brunet, Dec. 19, 1964; children—Federico, Ricardo, Elimari. Civil engr., project mgr. Chgo. Bridge & Iron Co., 1962-66; pres., v.p. various real estate devel. cos., Puerto Rico, 1968-73; partner, dir. Palmas Realty Corp., sr. v.p. devel., dir. Palmas Del Mar Co., Humacao, P.R., 1974-77; pres. FFS Assos., Inc., 1977—, Federico F. Sanchez and Co., Villa Clarita Devel. Corp., URE Corp.; prof. mgmt. U. P.R., 1969-71. Rep. Harvard Bus. Sch.; bd. govs. United Way. Mem. ASCE, Urban Land Inst., Nat. Assn. Realtors, Nat. Assn. Homebuilders (treas., dir.). Roman Catholic. Clubs: Palmas Del Mar, Harvard Bus. Sch. of So. Fla., Caparra Country. Home: 1817 Miosotis Santa Maria Rio Piedras PR 00927 Office: FFS Associates Suite 1812 Banco Popular Center Hato Rey PR 00918

SANDALLS, WILLIAM THOMAS, JR., bank holding co. exec.; b. Newport, R.I., Jan. 7, 1944; s. William Thomas and Marion (Hellman) S.; B.S. cum laude, Yale U., 1966; M.B.A., Harvard U., 1972; M.S. in Taxation, Bentley Coll., Waltham, Mass., 1979; m. Katharine Anne Flood, June 22, 1968; children—William Thomas, III, Benjamin Flood. Sr. accountant Arthur Andersen & Co., C.P.A.'s, Boston, 1972-74; chmn. bd., chief exec. officer BayBanks Data Services, Inc., Waltham, 1980—; asst. controller, asst. treas. BayBanks, Inc., Boston, 1974-75, asst. v.p., 1975-77, treas., 1977—, exec. v.p., 1979—. Served to lt. USN, 1966-70; Vietnam. Decorated Navy Achievement medal; C.P.A., Mass. Mem. Am. Inst. C.P.A.'s, Tax Execs. Inst., Mass. Soc. C.P.A.'s. Episcopalian. Club: Harvard (Boston). Office: 175 Federal St Boston MA 02110

SANDEROFF, LEIGH ALAN, fin. planner; b. Washington, May 19, 1949; s. Colbert and Sylvai Lee (Sherman) S.; B.S., U. Md., 1976; m. Rebecca Sanderoff, July 5, 1971; children—Harry Matthew, Rachel Kara. Agt., Prudential Ins. Co., 1974-75; pres. Sanderoff Assos., Ltd., Damascus, Md., 1976—, Hands Ventures, Inc., 1980—. Cert. fin. planner Coll. Fin. Planning, 1980. Mem. Internat. Assn. Fin. Planners, Sururban Md. Life Underwriters Assn., Jaycees. Jewish. Club: Lions. Home: 19408 Laguna Dr Gaithersburg MD 20760 Office: Sanderoff Assos Ltd 9929-C Main St Damascus MD 20750

SANDERS, BILL GORDON, city planner; b. Stevenson, Ala., Mar. 7, 1939; s. Sam B. and Grace P. (Prince) S.; B.A., U. Chattanooga, 1961; M.S. in City Planning, Ga. Inst. Tech., 1966; m. Pamella Liles, Oct. 8, 1971; children—Curt, Cyndi, Sage, Damon. Chief planner SE Tenn. Area Office, Tenn. State Planning Com., Chattanooga, 1966-67; pres. B.G. Sanders & Assos., Inc., Atlanta 1967—, ADC Constrn. Co., Atlanta, 1967—; gen. partner 40 Ltd. Housing Partnerships, 1967—; chmn. bd. MPS, Inc., Atlanta, 1972—. Served to lt lt., U.S. Army, 1962-63. Recipient Student of Yr. award Am. Inst. Planners, 1966. Mem. Nat. Assn. Housing and Redevel., Task Force on Housing. Club: Atlanta Coit Youth Assn. (pres. 1979, athletic dir. 1980—). Office: 6405 Barfield Rd Atlanta GA 30328

SANDERS, DONN ALAN, tng. and devel. specialist; b. Phila., Apr. 6, 1951; s. Fred and Shirley (Kaplan) S.; B.S., Pa. State U., 1972; M.B.A., Temple U., 1980. Mgmt. tng. and devel. advisor ARA Services, Radnor, Pa., 1974-78, ops. mgmt. cons., sr. advisor, 1978-80; pres. MDS and Assos., Phila., 1980—. Active Society Hill Civic Assn., Fairmount Civic Assn. Mem. Am. Soc. for Tng. and Devel., Am. Soc. for Hosp. Food Service Adminstrs., Am. Soc. for Hosp. Educators and Trainers. Club: Society Hill. Office: 617 Pine St Philadelphia PA 19106

SANDERS, STEPHEN EDWIN, retail store exec.; b. Houston, Jan. 9, 1952; s. R.L. and Dorothy Jean (Martin) S.; B.B.A., Abilene Christian U., 1975; postgrad. Georgetown U., 1976. Mgr. fur boutiques Saks Fifth Ave., N.Y.C., 1976-78; exec. mgr. fur salon I. Magnin, Washington, from 1978, now regional East Coast fur buyer. Mem. U.S. Jr. C. of C., N.Y. Fur Assn. Republican. Mem. Ch. of Christ. Home: 1615 Que St NW Apt 601 Washington DC 20009 Office: I Magnin White Flint Mall Kensington MD 20745

SANDERSON, REGINOLD ROBERT, communications co. mgr.; b. Birmingham, Ala., Apr. 22, 1948; s. Robert Lee and Louise (Glover) S.; B.S., Birmingham So. Coll., 1970; postgrad. in computer and info. scis. U. Ala., Birmingham, 1978, Miles Coll. Sch. Law, 1981; m. Coradean E. Carson, Aug. 8, 1970; 1 son, Reginold Robert. Career postman U.S. Post Office, Birmingham, 1966-70; asst. systems analyst, systems analyst, application programmer, ops. technician, lead systems programmer, sr. systems analyst S. Central Bell Telephone Co., Birmingham, 1970-77, mgr. info. systems, 1977—; cons. in field. Democrat. Roman Catholic. Home: 924 Cherry Ave Birmingham AL 35214 Office: 1876 Data Dr Rm S-310 Birmingham AL 35244

SANDERSON, ROBERT JACKSON, credit union exec.; b. Bonham, Tex., Dec. 23, 1945; s. Andy Ray and Mildred (Ross) S.; B.A. in Polit. Sci. (Sam Rayburn Found. scholar), N. Tex. State U., Denton, 1969; m. Virginia Ruth Amos, Mar. 24, 1967; children—Connie Marie, Holly Michelle. Asst. mgr. Denton (Tex.) C. of C., 1967-69; v.p. Denton Area Tchrs. Credit Union, 1969-76; mgr. Amarillo (Tex.) Pantex Fed. Credit Union, 1976-77; credit union mktg. rep. Service Bur. Co., Dallas, 1977-79; pres. OEA Credit Union, Oklahoma City, 1979—; counselor Denton County Probation dept., 1970-76. Mem. Credit Union Execs. Soc., Oklahoma City Credit Union Mgrs. Assn. Baptist. Home: 13625 Pin Oak Pl Edmond OK 73034 Office: 4031 Lincoln Blvd Oklahoma City OK 73105

SANDLER, HERBERT M., savs. and loan assn. exec.; b. N.Y.C., Nov. 16, 1931; s. William B. and Hilda (Schattan) S.; B.S.S., CCNY, 1951; J.S.D., Columbia U., 1954; m. Marion Osher, Mar. 26, 1961. Admitted to N.Y. bar, 1956; asst. counsel Waterfront Commn. N.Y. Harbor, 1956-59; partner firm Sandler & Sandler, N.Y.C., 1960-62; pres. Golden West Savs. & Loan Assn., Oakland, Calif., 1963-75; chmn. bd., chief exec. officer World Savs. & Loan Assn., Oakland, 1975—; pres. Golden West Fin. Corp., Oakland, 1963-75, chmn. bd., chief exec. officer, 1975—. Served with AUS, 1954-56. Office: 1970 Broadway Oakland CA 94612

SANDLIN, GEORGE WILSON, real estate broker, mortgage banker; b. Glen Rose, Tex., May 13, 1912; s. Walter Algie and Margaret (Parks) S.; student pub. schs., also Schreiner Inst.; m. Ruth Ina Zollinger, Sept. 21, 1941 (dec. 1975); children—George Walter Raoul, Carole Ruth, Sarah Louise, Margaret Ina. Field rep. HOLC, San Antonio, 1934-36; pres. Sandlin Mortgage Corp., Austin, Tex.; owner Sandlin & Co., 1936—; chmn. bd., pres. Internat. Creations, Inc.; pres., dir. Trans-Pacific Resorts, Inc.; pres. Profl. Arts, Inc.; ind. fee appraiser. Chmn., Tex. Real Estate Commn., 1949-55. Mem. Austin City Planning Commn., 1947-52, chmn., 1951-52. Chmn. Tex. Dem. Exec. Com., 1954-56. Pres. chmn. bd. Tex. Found., 1955—. Served as lt. comdr. USNR, World War II; PTO. Recipient silver citizenship medal Vets. Fgn. Wars, 1957. Mem. Tex. Assn. Realtors (dir., pres. 1979), Austin Real Estate Bd. (past pres.), Inst. Real Estate Mgmt., Inst. Real Estate Brokers, Mortgage Bankers Assn., Nat. Assn. Realtors, Am. Legion, V.F.W. Episcopalian. Clubs: Austin Country, Headliners. Home: 1801 Lavaca 7L Austin TX 78701 Office: 308 W 15th St Austin TX 78701

SANDNER, JOHN FRANCIS, lawyer, broker; b. Chgo., Nov. 3, 1941; s. James and Margaret (Elmore) S.; B.A., So. Ill. U., 1965; J.D., U. Notre Dame, 1968; m. Carole Ruth Erhardt, Feb. 14, 1970; children—Kathleen Dyan, Christopher John, Angela Marie, Michael John. Admitted to Ill. bar, 1968; mem. Chgo. Merc. Exchange, 1971—, Internat. Monetary Market, 1973—; pres. John F. Sandner & Assos., Chgo., 1973—, Rufenacht, Bromagen & Hertz, Inc., Chgo., 1978—; chmn. rules com. Chgo. Merc. Exchange, 1977, chmn. floor facilities and ops. com., 1977-79, chmn. arbitration com., 1976-77, bd. govs., 1977—, chmn. bus. conduct com., 1977-79, vice chmn. commodity rep. com., 1978-79, exec. com., 1978-79, chmn. exec. com., 1980—, chmn. bd. govs., 1980—. Recipient Dr. Ruth Jackson award award Law Sci. Acad., 1967; Dean Clarence E. Manion award, A Harold Weber award, 1st prize moot ct. competition U. Notre Dame Law Sch., 1968. Mem. Am. Arbitration Assn., Am., Ill., Chgo. bar assns. Roman Catholic. Clubs: Notre Dame (gov. 1980—), Mid Am. (Chgo.); Metropolitan. Office: 222 S Riverside Plaza Chicago IL 60606

SANDNESS, CLAIRE, food co. exec. Chmn., Land O'Lakes, Inc., Mpls. Address: 614 McKinley Pl Minneapolis MN 55413*

SANDOSKY, FAYE PAGE, data processor; b. Smithville, Tenn., Feb. 25, 1944; d. Charlie Haskell and Hattie Nell (Winnard) Page; B.S. in Math., Middle Tenn. State U., 1964; m. Robert Francis Sandosky, May 6, 1966. With Dept. Def., 1964—, project mgr., Ft. Meade, Md., 1972-78, computer systems br. mgr., 1978—. Mem. Am. Mgmt. Assn., Computer and Info. Scis. Inst., Cryptologic Math. Inst., Woodmark Community Assn. (sec. 1974-75). Home: 12224 Fawnhaven Ct Ellicott City MD 21043 Office: 9800 Savage Rd Fort George Meade MD 20755

SANDOVAL, JULIAN, fin., estate and business cons.; b. Wichita, Kans., Feb. 16, 1924; s. Jose Hipolito and Felicitas (Frausto) S.; B.S. in Bus. Adminstrn., U. Wyo., 1953; m. Angelina Valdéz, Sept. 7, 1947; children—Rosalinda, Mary, Anthony. With Union Pacific R.R., 1942-67; pvt. practice acctg. and tax services, fin. cons., Laramie, Wyo., 1962-72; founder, pres. Mgmt. Cons., Inc., specializing in fin., estate, and bus. cons., Laramie, 1972—. Active local and state polit. campaigns, 1956-60. Served with USMC, 1942-46. Democrat. Roman Catholic. Home: 908 Mitchell St Laramie WY 82070 Office: 1050 N 3d St Unit C Suite H Laramie WY 82070

SANDOW, BERNARD, collection agy. exec.; b. Bronx, N.Y., May 4, 1936; s. David and Ray (Belkin) S.; student N.Y. U., 1953; m. Andrea Eisnitz, Jan. 31, 1973; children—Rai Beth, Stacey Ann. Office mgr. E.J. Korvettes, N.Y.C., 1956-68; store controller Klein's, Yonkers, N.Y., 1969; bus. mgr. Commentary Library, N.Y.C., 1970; pres. Systematic Recovery Service Ltd., N.Y.C., 1971—. Served with USAR, 1960-61. Mem. Am. Collectors Assn. (past unit and regional pres.), Am. Comml. Collectors Assn., Met. Retail Fin. Execs. Assn., Consumer Credit Assn. Met. N.Y. Home: 1 Carter Ln Monsey NY 10952 Office: 1790 Broadway New York NY 10019

SANDS, IRA JAY, lawyer, investment cons.; b. N.Y.C.; B.A., N.Y. U.; J.D. (Harlan Fiske Stone fellow), Columbia; m. Kiti Reiner; children—Nelson, Tiffany, Summer Paige. Admitted N.Y. State bar, 1944, U.S. Supreme Ct. bar; practiced law in N.Y.C.; dir., mgr., partner First Republic Corp., 1957—, chmn. bd., 1958—, sec., 1960—; dir., chmn. First Republic Underwriter, Inc., 1958—; dir., pres. Waltham Mgmt. Inc. (Mass.), 1959—; mng. partner Korvette Bldg. Assos. (N.Y.), 1957, Fairfax Bldg. Assos. (Mo.), 1958, Engring. Bldg. Assos. (Ill.), 1958—, Williamsbridge Assos. (N.Y.), 1958, Waltham Engring. & Research Co., (Mass.), 1958, First Republic Funding Agy. (N.Y.), 1961—, Atlantic Co. (Fla.), 1961, Marchwood Realty Co. (Pa.), 1961, Video Film Center Assos. (N.Y.C.), 1962—, DeMille Theatre Co. (N.Y.C.), 1962—; gen. partner Allstate Ins. Bldg. Co., N.Y.C., 1958, Velvex Mid-City Parking Center, N.Y.C., 1959, Manhattan Parking Assos., N.Y.C., 1959, Imperial Sq. Co. (N.Y.), 1960—, Hempstead Real Estate Enterprises (N.Y.), 1959, Ohio Indsl. Assos., 1961, Cypress Plaza Assos. (Fla.), 1961, Peoria Parking Co. (Ill.), 1961, Gulf Assos. Co. (Fla.), 1961, Pelham Park Assos. (Pa.), 1961; chmn., dir. First Republic Co., Inc., 1957-66, Triple P. Parking Corp. (Ill.), 1960—, Park Circle Apts., Inc. (N.Y.), 1960, Home Circle Apts., Inc. (Pa.), 1961, Beau Rivage Corp. (Fla.), 1961—, Holme Realty Corp., (Pa.), 1962—; gen. agt. Patriot Life Ins. Co. (N.Y.C.), 1959-66, Northeastern Life Ins. Co. Inc. (N.Y.), 1961-65, Citizens Life Ins. Co. (N.Y.C.), 1962—; chmn. bd., chmn. exec. com., sec., dir. First Republic Corp. Am., 1961-66; chmn. exec. com., sec., dir. First Republic Bldg. Corp., 1962-66; chmn. Tri-Mgmt. Co., 1957-66, Nat. Med. Industries, Inc., 1968—, Health Insts. Leasing Corp., 1968—, Am. Med. Computer Corp., 1969—; pres. Med. Contract Supply Corp., 1968—, N.Y. Capital Group Inc., 1976—, Nat. City Capital Corp., 1977—, City Capital Corp., 1978—. dir. Sq. Mgmt. Corp. (Hempstead, N.Y.); real estate cons. pension plans. Trustee Baldwin Sch. (N.Y.), 1975-78. Served to lt. AUS. Mem. Nat. Real Estate Club, Am. (anti-trust sect., litigation sect.), N.Y. State (sect. on banking and corps.), Nassau County (sect. on fed. cts., sect. on corps.) bar assns., Fed. Bar Assn., Fed. Bar Council, N.Y. Real Estate Bd., Columbia Law Sch. Alumni Assn. (class chmn.), Bldg. Owners and Mgrs. Assn. Mason (32 deg., Shriner). Clubs: Atrium, N.Y. University, Touchdown; Channel Yacht (N.J.); Jockey (Fla.). Home: New York NY Office: 515 Madison Ave New York NY 10022 also 14 NE 1st Ave Miami FL 33132

SANDWEISS, HOWARD WAYNE, security service co. exec.; b. Los Angeles, May 26, 1940; s. Melvin and Charlotte (Leiman) S.; B.S., UCLA, 1969, M.S., 1971; M.B.A., Pepperdine U., 1978; children—Richard, Marni, Bryan. With Los Angeles County Sheriffs Dept., 1965-71; sr. project engr. Canoga Electronics, Chatsworth, Calif., 1960-70; founder, pres., chief exec. officer Protectal Corp., Woodland Hills, Calif., 1970—; lectr. on electronics and security. Mem. Internat. Police Congress, Internat. Acad. for Criminology, Nat. Acad. for Criminology, Spl. Agents Assn., Chief of Police Assn., Am. Soc. Indsl. Security. Address: Protectal Corp 22130 Clarendon St Woodland Hills CA 91367

SANDWEISS, LEONARD SAMUEL, lawyer; b. Detroit, July 24, 1931; s. Norman and Sadie Judith (Tilchin) S.; B.A. with distinction and honors in Econs., U. Mich., 1953; postgrad. London Sch. Econs., summer 1953; M.A. in Internat. Relations (Clayton fellow), Fletcher Sch. Law and Diplomacy, Tufts U., 1954; J.D., U. Mich., 1959; m. Varda Gutnik Ecker, 1979; 1 dau., Rachel Lili. Admitted to N.Y. State bar, 1960; asso. firm Curtis, Mallet-Prevost, Colt & Mosle, N.Y.C., 1959-63, Paskus, Gordon & Hyman, N.Y.C., 1963-64; individual practice law, N.Y.C., 1964—; dir. Josiah Wedgwood & Sons, Inc., 1963—; instr. Am. govt. San Antonio Jr. Coll., 1955-56. Mem. Coalition for a Democratic Majority, 1974—, mem. task force on fgn. policy, 1974-76, mem. exec. com., 1979—; mem. com. on legis. Citizens Union, N.Y.C., 1969-71; mem. exec. com. East Side Dem. Club, N.Y.C., 1966-70; mem. com. visitors U. Mich. Law Sch., 1977—; staff mem. com. on exec. br. govt. N.Y. State Constl. Conv., 1967. Served with U.S. Army, 1954-56. Mem. Am., N.Y. State bar assns., Assn. Bar City N.Y., Am. Soc. Internat. Law, Fed. Bar Council, Internat. Assn. Jewish Lawyers and Jurists, U.S. Trademark Assn., Brit.-Am. C. of C., Nat. Wildlife Fedn., Am. Jewish Com. (mem. adv. panel N.Y. chpt. 1977—, exec. com. N.Y. chpt. 1981—), Order Coif, Phi Beta Kappa. Jewish. Home: 435 E 65th St New York NY 10021 Office: 630 Fifth Ave New York NY 10020

SANFORD, EARL STANLEY, investment banker; b. Norfolk, Nebr., June 11, 1927; s. Abraham L. and Grace (Lande) S.; B.B.A., U. Minn., 1953; m. Barbara Flanagan, Dec. 17, 1966; children by previous marriage—Anne L., Melinda J., Albert I. With J.M. Dain & Co., Inc., Mpls., 1953-63; with Kidder, Peabody & Co., Inc., Mpls., 1963—, v.p., 1967—, resident mgr. Mpls. office, 1963—. Mem. exec. com. Mpls. Soc. Fine Arts; bd. dirs. Minn. Orchestral Assn.; trustee Northland Coll., Ashland, Wis.; mem. 5th Dist. Republican Search Com. Served with USN, 1945, U.S. Army, 1950-52. Mem. Securities Industry Assn. (past gov. mid-continent group), Mpls. C. of C. (past dir.), Phoenix Hon. Soc., Minn. Alumni Assn. Clubs: Mpls., Mpls. Athletic, Minn. Alumni, Kiwanis, 6 O'Clock. Home: 1510 Mount Curve Ave Minneapolis MN 55403 Office: Kidder Peabody & Co Inc 1650 IDS Center 80 S 8th St Minneapolis MN 55402

SANFORD, G. FOSTER, III, ins. exec.; b. Can., June 14, 1929; s. G. Foster, Jr., and Alice L. (Laurie) S.; A.B., U. Pa., 1952; m. Cecelia Greene, Jan. 11, 1975; children—G. Foster IV, Laurie Sue, Bruce R., Stricker C., Herbert C. Spl. agt. Atlantic Mut. Ins. Co., N.Y.C., 1952-57; pres. Sanford & Purvis, Inc., Upper Montclair, N.J., 1957—. Bd. dirs. West Essex Rehab. Center; pres. Montclair YMCA, 1978-80; gen. chmn. fund dr. United Way of North Essex, 1975, Montclair ARC, 1978; mem. Montclair Bd. Zoning Adjustment, 1978—; elder Presbyn. Ch. Upper Montclair, 1978—. Served with USNR, 1950-55. Mem. Montclair C. of C. (pres. 1963-64). Republican. Clubs: U. Pa. Alumni of Suburban N.J. (dir.), Montclair Lions (pres. 1964-65), Montclair Golf, Brant Beach Yacht (commodore 1980). Office: Sanford & Purvis Inc 211 Bellevue Ave Upper Montclair NJ 07043

SANDFORT, HORST GERHARD, electronics co. exec.; b. Gronau, Germany, July 9, 1942; came to U.S., 1979; s. Gerhard and Hermanna Gerda (tenVenne) H.; Abitur, Gymnasium Nordhorn, 1964; postgrad. Kaufmann Berufsschule Frankfurt, 1964-66, Industrie Kaufmann, 1966; m. Lieselotte Karoline Wagner, July 10, 1970; children—Anke, Marc. Field sales rep. Hoechst AG, Hamburg, W. Ger., 1966-68; field sales engr. Tex. Instruments, Frankfort, W. Ger., 1968-69, mktg. mgr., 1970-74; gen. mgr. Litronix Central Europe, Frankfort, 1974-75; gen. mgr. Fairchild Camera and Instruments, Garching/Munich, W. Ger., 1975-79, dir. European mktg., Mountain View, Calif., 1979-80, gen. mgr. Central Europe, Garching, 1980—. Office: Daimler Strasse 15 8046 Garching West Germany

SANSON, RUDOLPH JOHN, JR., lawyer; b. Passaic, N.J., Nov. 15, 1937; s. Rudolph John and Edith H. S.; B.S. in Fin., Seton Hall U., 1960, J.D., 1968; LL.M. in Taxation, N.Y. U., 1972; m. Marilyn H. Pavlick, Dec. 30, 1960; children—Jacqueline Carole, Susan Jill. Admitted to N.J. bar, 1968; tax acct. Am. Cyanamid Co., 1963-67, Pepsico, Inc., N.Y.C., 1967-68; asso. tax counsel, asst. to sr. v.p. taxes Gulf & Western Industries, 1968-72, asso. counsel, 1972—. Served with Fin. Corps, AUS, 1961-63. Mem. Am. Bar Assn., N.J. Bar Assn. Home: 40 Brook Terr Wayne NJ 07470 Office: Gulf and Western Industries Inc 1 Gulf and Western Plaza New York NY 10023

SANTNER, HAROLD JAY, mfg. co. exec.; b. Harlan, Kans., Apr. 16, 1921; s. Roy Fleetwood and Mary Jane (Neilson) S.; B.S. in Bus. Adminstrn., Kans. State U., 1942; m. Elsie Louise Freeman, Dec. 22, 1945; children—Steven, Mary, Elizabeth, Michael, Patricia. Various positions in fin. mgmt. Gen. Electric Co., 1946-66; controller utility div. Combustion Engring. Inc., 1966-67; v.p., controller Worcester County Nat. Bank (Mass.), 1968-74; v.p., controller Worcester Bancorp, Inc., 1974-77; v.p., treas. Package Machinery Co., 1977—. Served to lt. USNR, 1942-46. Mem. Fin. Exec. Inst. Club: Masons. Home: 94 Cheshire Dr Longmeadow MA 01106 Office: 330 Chestnut St East Longmeadow MA 01028

SANTRY, ARTHUR JOSEPH, JR., engring. co. exec.; b. Brookline, Mass., Aug. 1, 1918; s. Arthur Joseph and Suzanne (Cawley) S.; B.A., Williams Coll., 1941; LL.B., Harvard, 1948; m. Julia Timmins, June 4, 1955; children—Arthur Joseph III, Suzanne, Peter, Charles, Robert. Admitted to Mass. bar, 1948; partner firm Putnam, Bell, Santry & Ray, Boston, 1948-56; sec. Combustion Engring., Inc., Stamford, Conn., 1956-57, v.p., 1957, vice chmn., 1957, pres., chief exec. officer, vice chmn. exec. com., 1963—, also dir.; dir. AMAX, Inc., Greenwich, Conn., Bristol-Myers Co., N.Y., Jenney Oil Co., Inc., Newton, Mass., N. Am. Reins. Corp., N.Y., N. Am. Reassurance Co., N.Y., Putnam Trust Co. of Greenwich, Conn., Singer Co., N.Y. Served to lt. (s.g.) USNR, 1942-46. Mem. Soc. Naval Architects and Marine Engrs., Navy League U.S., Econ. Club of N.Y. Clubs: Board Room, Links, New York Yacht (N.Y.C.); Seawanhaka Corinthian Yacht (Oyster Bay, N.Y.); Storm Trysail (Larchmont, N.Y.); Country (Brookline, Mass.); Eastern Yacht (Marblehead, Mass.); Indian Harbor Yacht, Field, Round Hill (Greenwich, Conn.); Lyford Cay (Nassau, Bahamas); Royal Bermuda Yacht (Hamilton); Royal Ocean Racing (London, Eng.). Home: 62 Vineyard Ln Greenwich CT 06830 Office: 900 Long Ridge Rd Stamford CT 06902

SAPERSTEIN, MICHAEL, lawyer, investment banking co. exec.; b. N.Y.C., Mar. 14, 1941; s. Herman and Ida Saperstein; B.A., Colgate U., 1962; J.D., Fordham U., 1965; 1 dau., Kim. Admitted to N.Y. State bar, 1965; asst. corp. counsel City of N.Y., 1965-66; asso. dir. div. trading markets SEC, Washington, 1969-73; gen. partner Bear Stearns & Co., N.Y.C., 1973—; lectr. on securities regulations Practicing Law Inst., 1970—. Mem. Am. Bar Assn. Contbr. articles to profl. jours. Home: 215 E 68th St New York NY 10021 Office: 55 Water St New York NY 10041

SAPERSTON, HOWARD TRUMAN, JR., indsl. realtor; b. Buffalo, Oct. 4, 1939; s. Howard Truman and Nan Lucille (Basch) S.; B.A., Franklin Marshall Coll., 1963; m. Mary Barnard Franklin, Sept. 9, 1967; children—Howard Truman III, William Scott. Vice pres. D'Ambrosia, Hogan, Oppenheimer, Saperston & Voit Real Estate Assos., Inc., Buffalo, 1963—. Pres., Buffalo Boys' Club, 1973-75; trustee Nichols Sch., 1975—; bd. dirs. Planned Parenthood of Buffalo, 1966-69, Salvation Army, 1967-81, Multiple Sclerosis Soc., 1968-70, Jr. Achievement, 1969-78; mem. adv. bd. Children's Hosp., 1973-77; bd. dirs. Buffalo Sabre Hockey Team, 1970—, YMCA, 1972-81; chmn. Buffalo Area U.S. Olympic Com., 1972—; chmn. Western N.Y. com. for 1981 Maccabiah Games in Israel; mem. Arthritis Found. Western N.Y., 1981—. Mem. Soc. Indsl. Realtors, Greater Buffalo Bd. Realtors (past dir.), Buffalo Area C. of C. (mem. Indsl. Real Estate Council 1977—). Republican. Jewish. Club: Buffalo. Home: 100 Morris Ave Buffalo NY 14214 Office: D'Ambrosia Hogan Oppenheimer Saperston & Voit Real Estate Assos Inc 560 Delaware Ave Buffalo NY 14202

SAPIENZA, JOHN THOMAS, lawyer; b. South Orange, N.J., Feb. 26, 1913; s. James C. and Rosalie (Giaimo) S.; A.B. summa cum laude, Harvard, 1934, LL.B. magna cum laude, 1937; m. Virginia H. Gignoux, Feb. 12, 1972; children by previous marriage—John Thomas, James K. Admitted to N.Y. bar, 1938, D.C. bar, 1943; law clk. Judge A. N. Hand, N.Y.C., 1937-38, Justice Stanley Reed, Washington, 1938-39; asso. firm Wright, Gordon, Zachry & Parlin, N.Y.C., 1939-41; asso. firm Covington & Burling, Washington, 1941-48, partner, 1949—. Dir. Hiram Walker-Gooderham & Worts Ltd., Hiram Walker & Sons, Inc., Hiram Walker-Consumers Home Ltd., Wyman-Gordon Co., Am. Security Corp., Am. Security Bank N.A. Trustee George Washington U. Served to lt. comdr. USNR, 1943-46. Mem. Am., D.C., Fed., Internat. bar assns., Am. Law Inst., Confrerie des Chevaliers du Tastevin, Phi Beta Kappa. Clubs: Burning Tree, Metropolitan, International (Washington); Farmington (Charlottesville, Va.). Pres., Harvard Law Rev., 1936-37. Home: Apt 204 N Watergate East 2510 Virginia Ave NW Washington DC 20037 Office: 888 16th St NW Washington DC 20006

SAPOCH, JOHN CRIM, JR., mgmt. and planning cons.; b. Allentown, Pa., Feb. 1, 1937; s. John Crim and Dorothy Salome (Rems) S.; B.A. (John Prentice Poe award 1957), Princeton U., 1958; M.B.A., Wharton Sch., U. Pa., 1964; m. Betty Wingert, Aug. 9, 1958; children—John Crim, III, William Martin. Tchr., coach, dean students Kent (Conn.) Sch., 1958-61; asst. to dean admissions U. Pa., 1961-62; sec. for alumni assns. Princeton U., 1962-65, adminstrv. dir. univ. conf., 1965-66; from adminstrv. dir. to exec. v.p. J.P. Cleaver Co. Inc., Princeton, 1966-78; pres. Cleaver-Pacific Co., Los Angeles, 1971-78; chmn. bd., pres., dir. SINC, Princeton, 1978—; pres., dir. Profl. Transp. Services Inc., 1978—; chmn., dir. Princeton Pacific, Inc., 1980—. Pres., Class of 1958, Princeton U., 1958-68; bd. dirs., treas. Princeton Youth Center, 1966-70; a founder, trustee Princeton Youth Fund, 1967-68; a founder, bd. dirs. Pct Midget Football League, 1968-73; bd. dirs. Venture Racing, 1971-72; chmn. Friends Princeton U. Football, 1974-78; a founder, chmn. Friends Princeton High Sch. Athletics, 1978-80. Recipient various football awards, also certs. appreciation. Mem. Princeton U. Alumni Assn., Wharton Grad. Sch. Alumni Assn. Clubs: Princeton (N.Y.C.); Ivy; 200 Mercer County (N.J.). Author manuals, reports in field. Address: 4 Hawthorne Ave Princeton NJ 08540

SAPP, JOHN DAVID, ins. co. exec.; b. Lakeland, Fla., Nov. 9, 1913; s. John Wilson and Mary Alice (Buchan) S.; B.S. in Bus. Adminstrn., U. Fla., 1941; M.Internat. Affairs, George Washington U., 1963; m. Essye Emily Hodge, May 2, 1943; children—Florence R., Catherine E. Commd. 2d lt. U.S. Army, 1941, advanced through grades to col., 1960; ret., 1968; exec. com., v.p., pres. Armed Forces Coop. Insuring Assn., Ft. Leavenworth, Kans., dir. planning, 1969-70, dep. exec. dir., 1970-75, exec. dir., 1975—. Bd. dirs. Jr. Achievement, pres., 1968; pres. Ft. Leavenworth Bd. Edn., 1969—. Decorated Legion of Merit with two oak leaf clusters, Bronze Star, Army Commendation medal with two oak leaf clusters, D.S.M., Republic of Vietnam. Mem. Sigma Nu, Omicron Delta Kappa. Republican. Episcopalian. Clubs: Rotary, Masons, K.T., Elks. Home: 420 Arch St Leavenworth KS 66048 Office: Box G Fort Leavenworth KS 66027

SARANOW, MITCHELL HARRIS, food co. exec.; b. Chgo., Oct. 14, 1945; s. William Leader and Dorothy (Pinsky) S.; B.S.B.A. with high distinction, Northwestern U., 1967; J.D. cum laude, Harvard U., 1971; M.B.A. with distinction (George F. Baker scholar), Harvard U. Bus. Sch., 1971; m. Linda Lee Billig, Sept. 8, 1973; children—Jennifer Wynne, Julie Ann. Admitted to Ill. bar, 1971, Mo. bar, 1976; asso. firm Mayer, Brown & Platt, Chgo., 1971-73; investment banker Becker and Warburg, Paribas Group, Inc., Chgo., 1973-75; v.p. finance and law Sunmark Cos., St. Louis, 1975-79; v.p., treas. CFS Continental, Inc., Chgo., 1979—; cons., dir. Matrix Enterprises, Inc. State Farm Exceptional Student fellow. Mem. standards rev. com. Chgo. United Way. Mem. Fin. Execs. Inst., Am. Bar Assn., Chgo. Bar Assn., Beta Gamma Sigma, Phi Epsilon Pi. Clubs: Econs., Union League, Harvard Bus. Sch. (Chgo.) (dir.); Harvard Bus. Sch. Century. Home: 305 W Fullerton Pkwy Chicago IL 60614 Office: 100 S Wacker Dr Suite 1222 Chicago IL 60606

SARGENT, DEAN WALTER, cons. engr.; b. Pekin, Ill., Sept. 5, 1927; s. Walter Albert and Dora (Beetler) S.; grad. Wentworth Mill. Acad., 1945; m. Henrietta L. Schenning, Oct. 9, 1948; children—Lee, Deann, Beth, Stacey, Michael, Jeffrey. Engr. Catapillar Tractor Co., Peoria, Ill., 1951-53, Stas. WMBD-AM, FM, TV, Peoria, 1953-64; field engr. RCA Services Co., 1964-66; product specialist RCA, Camden, N.J., 1966-67; pres. D.W. Sargent Broadcast Service, Cherry Hill, N.J., 1967—. Served with USAF, 1945-51. Mem. Nat. Assn. Broadcasters, Soc. Motion Picture and TV Engrs., IEEE. Republican. Methodist. Contbr. articles in field to profl. jours. Home and Office: 804 Richard Rd Cherry Hill NJ 08034

SARGENT, JOHN TURNER, publisher; b. Lawrence, N.Y., June 26, 1924; s. Charles and Dagmar (Wetmore) S.; m. Neltje Doubleday, May 16, 1953 (div.); children—Ellen, John Turner. Editor Doubleday & Co., Inc., N.Y.C., 1946-49, v.p., 1950-61, pres., 1961-78, chmn. bd., 1978—, also dir.; trustee East River Savs. Bank; dir. Grumman Corp., Atlantic Mut. Cos. Trustee, Am. Acad. in Rome, N.Y. Zool. Soc., Kips Bay Boys Club, N.Y. Pub. Library. Home: Halsey Ln Watermill NY 11976 Office: 245 Park Ave New York NY 10167

SARGENT, WARREN NICHOLS, JR., cons. co. exec.; b. New London, Conn., Sept. 17, 1946; s. Warren Nichols and Janice Carolyn (Warner) S.; B.S.M.E., U. Conn., 1968, M.S., 1970, M.B.A., 1971; postgrad. U. Tex., Dallas, 1975—. Systems analyst, programmer U. Conn., 1965-71, City of Hartford (Conn.), 1968-71; instr. Univ. Computing Co., Arlington, Tex., 1973, cons., Nashville, 1973-74, mgr. bus. planning, Dallas, 1974-75, bus. devel., 1975-77; gen. mgr. Bonanza Internat., Houston, 1977, dir. franchising, Dallas, 1978; dir. computer services programs INPUT, Palo Alto, Calif., 1979—. Served to lt. USAF, 1971-73. Decorated D.S.M. Mem. Computer Industry Guide, Share, Adapso, Beta Gamma Sigma. Clubs: Sports, Internat. Mgmt. Address: PO Box 50182 Palo Alto CA 94303

SAROSDY, AUREL FRANCIS, forging co. exec.; b. North Hollywood, Calif., May 19, 1924; s. Louis J. and Margaret (Nemeth) S.; B.S. in M.E., Carnegie Inst. Tech., 1944, B.S. in Indsl. Mgmt., 1957; m. Emma Clyde Hodge, II, June 24, 1950; children—Karen Sarosdy Beeghly, Emma Sarosdy Purdy, Mark, Margaret Clyde. With Patterson-Emerson-Comstock, Warren, Ohio, 1947, Blaw-Knox Co., Pitts., 1948-56, Robertshaw-Fulton Controls Co., Youngwood, Pa., 1956-58; pres. Pitts. Forgins Co., Pitts., 1958—. Served to lt., (j.g.), USNR, 1944-46. Registered profl. engr., Pa. Mem. Forging Industry Assn. (pres. 1966-67), Ry. Progress Inst. (exec. com. of governing bd.). Clubs: Duquesne, Univ., Fox Chapel (Pitts.); Rolling Rock, Laurel Valley. Home: PO Box 344 RD 2 Ligonier PA 15658 Office: Pittsburgh Forgins Co Gateway 3 Pittsburgh PA 15222

SARVAY, JOHN THOMAS, indsl. designer, business exec.; b. Weirton, W.Va., Apr. 29, 1937; s. George and Anna (Kasich) S.; B.S. in Design, U. Cin., 1961; postgrad. Case Western Res. U., 1963; m. Beth Ann Ogan, July 15, 1961; children—Margaret Louise, Anna Beth. Plant mgr., dir. design Altech div. Ravens Metals Products, Parkersburg, W.Va., 1960-63; mgr. applied research Ohio Rubber Co. div. Eagle-Pitcher Corp., Willoughby, Ohio, 1963-65; devel. mgr. Standard Products Co., Cleve., 1965-70; dir. tech. info. group Stirling Homex Corp., Avon, N.Y., 1970-72; dir. corporate design and mktg. services Schlegel Corp., Rochester, N.Y., 1972-77; v.p. mktg. Modernfold, an Am. Standard Co., New Castle, Ind., 1977-79; sr. sales rep. Computervision Corp., Bedford, Mass., 1979—; planning cons. Wirt County (W.Va.), 1962-63. Recipient awards for water color paintings. Mem. Am. Inst. Aeros. and Astronautics, ASTM, Soc. Automotive Engrs., Am. Soc. Metals, Aircraft Owners and Pilots Assn., Bldg. Research and Adv. Bd., Indsl. Designers Soc. Am., Brit. Airways Exec. Club. Byzantine Catholic. Club: Kiwanis (Cleve.). Contbr. articles to profl. jours. Patentee in field of archtl. wall and window systems (5). Home: 1200 Ivywood Ct New Castle IN 47362 Office: Box 444 New Castle IN 47362

SARVET, WALTER MORTON, mfg. co. exec.; b. Coatesville, Pa., Aug. 15, 1928; s. Benjamin P. and Betty (Batt) S.; B.S., Temple U., 1953; m. Ruth M. Marcus, Dec. 22, 1957; children—Nancy, Barry. Revenue examiner City of Phila., 1954-56; pub. accountant Ralph M. Fratkin & Co., C.P.A., Phila., 1956-57; accountant J.K. Lasser & Co., N.Y.C., 1957-62; 1st v.p., tax dir. Shearson, Hammill & Co., Inc., N.Y.C., 1962-75; tax mgr. Matsushita Electric Corp. Am., Secaucus, N.J., 1976—. Served with AUS, 1946-49. C.P.A., N.Y., N.J. Mem. Am. Inst. C.P.A.'s, N.Y. State Soc. C.P.A.'s, N.J. Soc. C.P.A.'s, Tax Execs. Inst., Wall St. Tax Assn., Am. Acctg. Assn. Home: 108 Kings Walk Massapequa Park NY 11762 Office: One Panasonic Way Secaucus NJ 07094

SASAKI, Y. TITO, bus. services co. exec.; b. Tokyo, Feb. 6, 1938; s. Yoshinaga and Chiyoko (Imada) S.; came to U.S., 1967; B.S., Chiba U., 1959; postgrad. Royal Coll. Art, London, 1961, U. Oslo, 1962; M.S., Athens Tech. Inst., Greece, 1964; postgrad. U. Calif. at Berkeley, 1969; m. Janet Louise Cline, June 27, 1963; 1 dau., Heather N. Chief designer Aires Camera Industries Co., Tokyo, 1958-59; tech. officer London County Council, 1961-62; researcher Athens Center Ekistics, 1964-66; sr. researcher Battelle Inst., Geneva, 1966-68; project engr. Marin County Transit Dist., San Rafael, Calif., 1968-69; chief planning, research Golden Gate Bridge Dist., San Francisco, 1969-74; pres. Visio Internat. Inc., San Francisco, 1973—; chmn. steering com. Kawada Industries Inc., Tokyo, 1974—. Mem. Republican Nat. Com., Am. Security Council. Mem. Am. Inst. Cert. Planners, World Soc. Ekistics, Brit. Soc. Long Range Planning. Roman Catholic. Office: Visio Internat Inc 360 Post St San Francisco CA 94108

SASLOFSKY, HARRY ISADORE, vending sales exec.; b. Phila., Nov. 14, 1920; s. Hyman and Sophie S.; student U. Pa., 1951-52, St. Joseph's U., 1956-58; m. Blanche Goldberg, Jan. 23, 1942; children—Sandra, Sharon. Owner, operator Wonder Beverages, 1946-58; dist. sales mgr. Gen. Foods Corp., 1958-70; nat. sales mgr. Ellis Importing Co., Phila., 1970-80, v.p. vend products div., 1980—. Judge of elections, 1950-79; Democratic committeeman, 1950-79; chmn. Community Steering Com., 1960-72. Served with AUS, 1942-46. Decorated Bronze Star Medal; recipient Chapel of Four Chaplains award, 1950; 5 Sales Mgrs. awards, award Sales and Mktg. Execs., 1960, 65, 70. Mem. Nat. Automatic Merchandising Assn., Nat. Coffee Service Assn., Nat. Restaurant Assn., Sales and Mktg. Execs. Suburban Phila., Am. Legion. Clubs: Kiwanis, Masons, Variety. Home: 7608 Brentwood Rd Philadelphia PA 19151 Office: 2835 Bridge St Philadelphia PA 19137

SASS, CHARLES EDWARD, paper converting co. exec.; b. Joliet, Ill., Apr. 8, 1925; s. Louis F. and Elizabeth C. (Lauffer) S.; student Joliet Jr. Coll., 1943-45, Walton Sch. Commerce, 1945-47. m. Virginia Louise Morton, Apr. 14, 1946. Div. controller Standard Brands, Inc., Indpls., 1947-53; controller Stonebridge Paper Co., Wilmington, Ill., 1953-60; treas. Cel-Fibe div. Johnson & Johnson Co., Milltown, N.J., 1960-71; v.p. fin. Conso Products div. Consol. Foods Co., Yonkers, N.Y., 1971-74; v.p., gen. mgr. Stirling Converting Co., Inc., Bound Brook, N.J., 1975—, vice chmn., 1978—, also dir. Mem. Am. Paper Inst. (tissue div.), Internat. Assn. Wiping Cloth Mfrs. Republican. Presbyterian. Club: Elks (Somerville, N.J.). Home: 15 Flintlock Dr Warren NJ 07060 Office: PO Box 29 27 E Kearny St Bound Brook NJ 08805

SASS, MARTIN D., investment firm exec.; b. N.Y.C., June 8, 1942; s. Arthur Vernon and Florence Clara S.; B.S., Bklyn. Coll., 1962; postgrad. Coll. City Coll. N.Y., N.Y. U.; m. Barbara Berg, Aug. 31, 1963; children—Lara, Ari. Founder, officer Spl. Situations div. Argus Research, 1963-69; pres. Neuwirth Mgmt. and Research Corp., 1969-72; pres., chmn. M.D. Sass Investors Services, Inc., N.Y.C., 1972—; pres. CCC Advisors, Inc., Am. Mgmt. Enterprises, Inc.; chmn. Corporate Capital Cons., 1974—. Mem. Fin. Analysts Fedn., Internat. Found. Employee Benefit Plans, N.Y. Soc. Security Analysts, Internat. Assn. Fin. Planners. Office: 475 Park Ave S New York NY 10016

SASSON, MAURICE E., retail children's clothing co. exec.; b. Bklyn., July 9, 1940; s. Elie M. and Sarah (Dweck) S.; student public schs., Bklyn.; children—Sarah, Elie. With Sasson's Youth World Inc., Irvington, N.J., 1957—, Bayonne, N.J., 1969—, Orange, N.J., 1971—. Home: 90 Riverside Dr New York NY 10024 Office: 1001 Springfield Ave Irvington NJ 07111

SASSOVER, NATHAN, electronics co. exec.; b. Deggendorf, Germany, July 27, 1948; s. Adolf and Anna S.; student Berklee Coll. Music, 1964, 65, U. Wis., 1966. Ind. composer, producer film, TV and electronic music, N.Y.C., 1969-72; prin. Motion Picture Music Inc., N.Y.C., 1972-78; founder, pres. TMX Inc., mfr. digital coding system for communication; security and control products, N.Y.C., 1972-78, Los Angeles, 1978—; founder, pres. Instar Corp., microelectronics cons., Los Angeles, 1978—; founder TMX Systems Ltd., No. Ireland, 1979; co-founder Unifund Inc., Unifund Venture Group. Mem. Am. Fedn. Musicians. Office: 1100 Glendon Ave Suite 1244 Los Angeles CA 90024

SATMARY, HELEN JOANNE, Realtor; b. Washington, Oct. 22, 1932; d. Earl Clyde and Lena Marie (Polvinale) Coppock; student Am. U., 1952, George Washington U., 1955-56, Grad. Realtors Inst., 1971-72, Fairfield U., 1969; m. Peter Charles Satmary, Oct. 5, 1957, (div.); children—Pamela, Stephen, Mark, Karen, Vincent. Sec., Commerce Dept., analytical asst. Dept. Agr., Washington, 1952-57; sales mgr. Fairfield County Real Estate (Conn.), 1966-68; owner, realtor Joanne Satmary Real Estate, Fairfield, 1969-79; owner Conn. Real Properties Inc., Milford, 1980—; co-owner Fairfield Real Estate Sch. Vol., Providence Hosp., Washington, 1951-57. Mem. Fairfield Bd. Realtors (edn. chmn. 1971, 76, chmn. grievance com. 1973, chmn. round table 1973, dir. 1974—), Nat. Assn. Real Estate Bds., New Haven Bd. Realtors, Bridgeport Bd. Realtors (chmn. grievance com.), Network Homes of New Eng. (sec.), Women's Council, Network of Exec. Women, Nat. Assn. Farm and Land Brokers, Conn. Assn. Real Estate Bds., Nat. Inst. Real Estate Brokers, Fairfield C. of C. (dir. 1976-68, co-chmn. art show 1976-77). Home: 111 Nottingham Ct Meriden CT 06450 Office: 550 New Haven Ave Milford CT 06460

SATTERWHITE, HENRY ALLEN, airline exec., newspaper pub.; b. Fredericksburg, Va., Nov. 1, 1902; s. Charles Emmett and Caroline Thornton (Dommitt) S.; B.M.E., Va. Poly. Inst., 1926; D.C.S. (hon.), St. Bonaventure U., 1965; m. Margaret Hungiville, Feb. 2, 1940; children—John Henry, Mary Ann. Pub., v.p. Bradford Publs., Inc., Pa., 1943—; dir. Allegheny Airlines, Inc., 1952—, chmn. bd., 1956-78, chmn. emeritus, 1978—; pres. Condor Corp., Marion Pub. Co.; dir. Top Line Corp., Daily Am. Pub. Co. Pres. Bradford Indsl. Corp., 1951-62, bd. dirs., 1951—; mem. bd. Bradford City Planning Commn., 1959—; mem. Com. 100, Miami Beach, Fla., 1949—. Chmn. McKean County Democratic Com., 1935-40; mem. Pa. Dem. Com., 1944-59; mem. Pa. Indsl. Devel. Authority, 1974—. Mem. adv. bd. U. Pitts. Bradford Campus, 1962—; asso. trustee St. Bonaventure U., 1963-74. Mem. Pa. Soc., Newcomen Soc., Bradford Area C. of C., Pa., Am. newspaper pubs. assns. Club: Nat. Aviation (Washington). Home: 792 South Ave Bradford PA 16701 Office: 43 Main St Bradford PA 16701

SAUCIER, WILHEMINE EVELYN, energy co. exec.; b. Mankato, Minn., July 31, 1935; d. Durant Alfred and Dorothy Evelyn (Black) LaBrie; student U. Minn., 1962-65; m. Richard Holzinger, 1954 (div. 1963); children—Stephen, Renee, Todd, John; m. 2d, David Owen Saucier, Apr. 11, 1970 (div. 1975). With Mpls. Honeywell Co., 1953, Pillsbury Co., 1955, Gen. Mills, Inc., 1956, U.S. Air Conditioning Co., 1957, Corrick & Dietrich, Mpls., 1958; with urban planning firm Nason, Wehrman, Knight and Chapman, Mpls., 1962; with Medtronic, Inc., med. electronic devices, Mpls., 1965-73, v.p., 1971-73; adminstrv. v.p. Saucier, Inc., Eden Prairie, Minn., 1973-75; bus. cons., 1973-78; v.p. adminstrn. Lund-Martin Co., Mpls., 1978-80; v.p. Starr Engring. Corp., 1980—. Co-chmn. spl. gifts dir. United Way Mpls., 1973—; mem. Minnetonka Planning Commn., 1974—. Mem. Pub. Relations Soc. Am., Assn. Advancement Med. Instrumentation, Minn., Am. water ski assns., Am. Mgmt. Soc., N.Am. Soc. Corp. Planners, Zonta Internat. Club: Tower (gov.). Home: 4647 Ellerdale Rd Minnetonka MN 55343

SAUDER, A. LELAND, petroleum co. exec.; b. Madison, Kans., Jan. 17, 1925; s. Aaron Leland and Bessie (Wiggins) S.; B.S. in Petroleum Engring., U. Kans., 1950; m. Johnnie Marie Waggoner, Nov. 17, 1951; children—Alane Marie, John Waggoner, Suzanne. With Gulf Oil Co., 1950-51; ind. oil operator, Wichita Falls, Tex., 1951—; dir. Moran Drilling Co.; dir. profit sharing trust Sauder Mgmt. Co.; cons. in field; cattle rancher, Wichita and Wise counties. Mem. adv. bd. Geology Assos., U. Kans. Served to ensign USNR, 1944-46. Mem. Am. Assn. Petroleum Geologists (del.), North Tex. Geol. Soc., Ind. Petroleum Assn. Am., Tex. Ind. Producers and Royalty Assn., North Tex. Oil and Gas Assn. (dir.), Kappa Sigma, Tau Beta Pi. Clubs: Wichita, Wichita Falls Country; Chaparral. Home: 2300 Irving Pl Wichita Falls TX 76308 Office: 202 Hamilton Bldg Wichita Falls TX 76301

SAUER, RAY NEAL, corp. exec.; b. Houston, July 30, 1934; s. Ray George and Anna Maria (Johnson) S.; A.B. in Chem. Engring., Rice U., 1956; M.S. in Chem. Engring., U. Tex., 1958; m. Bettie Marian Hickman, Oct. 22, 1969; children—Steven N., Lynn H., Nancy L. Research engr. Marathon Oil Co., Littleton, Colo., 1958-59; sr. systems engr., product mktg. rep., mgr. data acquisition and control systems IBM Corp., Houston and Los Angeles, 1959-69; staff mgr. Transamerica Corp., Los Angeles, 1970-72; region mgr. Cin. Milacron, Houston, 1972-76; pres. AccuraTech, Inc., Houston, 1976—. Usher St. Luke's Methodist Ch., 1973—. Served to lt. U.S. Army, 1957. Recipient IBM Outstanding Contribution award, 1964; registered profl. engr., Tex. Mem. Project Mgmt. Inst., Tau Beta Pi, Sigma Tau, Omega Chi Epsilon, Phi Lambda Upsilon. Developer LESS/TIME and TIMETABLE, computer software for project mgmt. Home: 5422 Chevy Chase Dr Houston TX 77056

SAUL, RALLY, optical co. exec.; b. Houston, Sept. 20, 1930; s. J. H. and Martha S.; B.B.A., U. Houston, 1949, M.B.A., 1950; student The Wharton Sch., U. Pa., 1978; m. Ann Saul, Oct. 19, 1952. Div. v.p. RCA, Cherry Hill, N.J., 1952-58; v.p. sales Hazel Bishop, Inc., N.Y.C. and Newark, 1958-63; exec. v.p. mktg. Aloe Lab., Ft. Lauderdale, Fla., 1963-68; exec. v.p., gen. mgr. Marla Williams, Inc., Houston, 1969-72; mgmt. cons., regional mgr. Optyl Corp., Houston, 1973-75, 75-81; cons. mgmt., mktg. Served to capt. USAF, 1950-52. Decorated D.F.C. with two oak leaf clusters, Air medal with four oak leaf clusters. Mem. Sales and Mktg. Execs. Address: 3103 Rockyridge Houston TX 77063

SAUL, RALPH SOUTHEY, fin. co. exec.; b. Bklyn., May 21, 1922; s. Walter Emerson and Helen Douglas (Coutts) S.; B.A., U. Chgo., 1947; LL.B., Yale U., 1951; LL.D. (hon.), Alfred U.; m. Bette Jane Bertschinger, June 16, 1956; children—Robert Southey, Jane Adams. With Am. embassy, Prague, Czechoslovakia, 1947-48; admitted to D.C. bar, 1951, N.Y. bar, 1952; asso. firm Lyeth & Voorhees, N.Y.C., 1951-52; asst. counsel to Gov. N.Y. State, 1952-54; staff atty. RCA, 1954-58; with SEC, 1958-65, dir. div. trading and markets, 1963-65; v.p. corp. devel. Investors Diversified Services, Inc., Mpls., 1965-66; pres. Am. Stock Exchange, N.Y.C., 1966-71; chmn. mgmt. com. First Boston Corp., 1971-74; vice-chmn. INA Corp., Phila., 1974-75, chmn., chief exec. officer, 1975—; dir. Sun Co., Pennwalt Corp., Compagnie Financiere de Suez. Bd. dirs. Bus. Council Pa.; trustee U. Pa., Com. Econ. Devel. Served with USNR, 1943-46; PTO. Mem. Am. Bar Assn. Clubs: Union League, Phila. (Phila.); Merion Golf; Bond, Econ. (N.Y.C.); Board Room; Links; Commonwealth of Calif. Home: 549 Avonwood Rd Haverford PA 19041 Office: INA Corp 1600 Arch St Philadelphia PA 19101

SAUNDERS, ALBERT HENRY, mfg. co. exec.; b. Logan, Iowa, Feb. 11, 1902; s. Arthur Lumb and Sarah (Hix) S.; grad. high sch.; m. Edith Rhodes, June 7, 1925 (dec. Dec. 1968); 1 son, Joseph Arthur. Operator family ranch, Creston, Mont., 1928; with Remington Rand Typewriter Co., 1928-37, br. mgr., Youngstown, Ohio, 1933-36, spl. rep., 1936-38; eastern sales rep. Acoustor Co., Youngstown, 1938-40; salesman Royal Typewriter Co., supplied div. Maine, N.H., Vt., Portland, Maine, 1942-46; founder, pres. Saunders Mfg. Co., Inc., Winthrop, Maine, 1946—. Home: RD 2 Winthrop ME 04364 Office: Box 243 Winthrop ME 04364

SAUNDERS, CHARLES ALMAR, JR., slate co. exec.; b. Richmond, Va., Sept. 7, 1921; s. Charles Almar and Alma (Strickland) S.; student U. Richmond, 1939-41, U. Hawaii, 1943-44; m. Genevieve Cooke, May 8, 1948. With Buckingham-Va. Slate Corp., Richmond, Va., 1961—, sec., 1970-73, pres., 1973—; with Strickland Foundry & Machinery, Richmond, 1961—, pres., 1970-74, chmn. bd., 1974—. Served with USAF, 1942-45. Mem. Bldg. Stone Inst. (pres. 1976-77), Constrn. Specification Inst. Republican. Baptist. Clubs: Country of Va., Masons. Home: 4708 Grandway Rd Richmond VA 23226 Office: 4110 Fitzhugh Ave Richmond VA 23230

SAUNDERS, HERBERT LEE, lawyer; b. N.Y.C., Nov. 4, 1925; s. Jack and Sadie S.; student Poly. Inst. Bklyn., 1943-44, 46-47; LL.B., Bklyn. Law Sch., 1950; m. Loretta Tymon, Mar. 22, 1958; children—Robert, Jill, Joan. Admitted to N.Y. bar, 1951, U.S. Supreme Ct. bar, 1979; atty. Nat. Prodn. Authority, N.Y.C., 1951-54, N.Y. Ordnance Div., U.S. Army, 1953-54; atty. trial dept. Consol. Mut. Ins. Co., Bklyn., 1954-58; co-founder Leo Tymon & Sons, Inc., N.Y.C., 1959—, sec.-treas., 1959—; individual practice law, N.Y.C., 1959—. Served with USNR, 1944-46. Mem. Queens County Bar Assn., N.Y. Assn. Trial Lawyers, Nat. Assn. Claimants Compensation Attys., Am. Judicature Soc. Office: One Old Country Rd Carle Place NY 11514

SAUNDERS, JOHN RAMSEY, gallery exec.; b. Detroit, Aug. 16, 1949; s. Gordon and Ruth (Ramsey) S.; B.S. in Math., Fla. Presbyn. Coll., 1971; M.B.A., Wharton Sch. Fin., U. Pa., 1973; m. Masako Susukida; children—Robert, Sakura. Fgn. exchange trader Am. Express Internat. Banking Corp., N.Y.C., 1973-74, Manila, Philippines, 1974-75, asst. treas. medium term lending, London, 1975-76; owner, dir. Coin Galleries, London, 1976—; 1st v.p. Financiera Andesita S.A. Mem. Am. Numismatic Soc., Am. Numismatic Assn., Brit. Numismatic Trade Assn., Philippine Numismatic and Antiquarian Soc., Garden State Numismatic Assn., Gt. Eastern Numismatic Assn., Ala. Numismatic Assn., Ky. Numismatic Soc. Presbyterian. Office: 10 The Arches Villiers St London WC 2 England also Suite 132 Mission Viejo Mall Mission Viejo CA 92691

SAUNDERS, JOSEPH ARTHUR, office products mfg. co. exec.; b. Creston, Mont., July 9, 1926; s. Albert Henry and Edith Margaret (Rhodes) S.; ed. pub. schs. Youngstown, Ohio and Winthrop, Maine; m. Lois Evelyn White, June 19, 1948; children—Albert Henry II, Margaret Jean. With Saunders Mfg. Co. Inc., Winthrop, 1947—, exec. v.p., 1967-77, pres., 1977—, chief exec. officer, 1967—; co-founder, sec. Dirigo Bank & Trust Co., Augusta, Maine, 1969—, also dir.; dir. Forms Mfrs. Equipment Co., Orlando, Fla. Served with U.S. Army, 1945-47. Mem. Maine C. of C. (dir. 1976-80), Kennebec Valley C. of C., Soc. Mfg. Engrs. (cert. new product engr.), Internat. Bus. Forms Industries (chmn. assos. 1976-77), Nat. Bus. Forms Assn., Nat. Office Products Assn., Am. Mgmt. Assn., Assn. Systems Mgmt., Fabricating Machinery Assn., Am. Soc. Metals, Binding Industries Am., Printing Industries Am., Am. Legion, other orgns. Clubs: Masons, Shriners. Patentee in field. Home: Touisett Point Readfield ME 04355 Office: Box 243 Winthrop ME 04364

SAUNDERS, RICHARD D., holding co. exec. Pres., chief exec. officer, dir. WTC Inc., Newport Beach, Calif. Office: 1400 Quail St Newport Beach CA 92660*

SAUNDERS, THURMAN C., acctg. exec.; b. Winston Salem, N.C., Nov. 6, 1943; s. Thurman R. and Nadine J. (Creed) S.; B.A. in Bus. Adminstrn. and Acctg., U. N.C., 1970; certificate nuclear power quality control program Westinghouse Electric Corp., 1972; m. Sharon Ann Hicks, Dec. 27, 1970; children—Thurman Jason, Carol Lynn. Staff asst. to elec. dept. mgr. Westinghouse Electric Corp., Buchanan, N.Y., 1970-74; staff accountant Ronder & Ronder, P.C., Kingston, N.Y., 1974-75; v.p./controller corporate planning and fin. mgmt. Black Electric, Inc., Wappingers Falls, N.Y., 1975-79; mgr. cost acctg. Bassick Sack div. Stewart Warner Corp., Winston Salem, N.C., 1979-81; acct. Thurman C. Saunders Acctg., Winston Salem, 1981—. Served with USN, 1961-64. J.A. Jones Constrn. Co. scholar,

1968-70. Club: Masons (past master). Home: 2306 Vincent Rd Winston-Salem NC 27106 Office: 3618 Reynolda Rd Winston Salem NC 27106

SAUNDERS, WILLIAM RALPH, mag. pub.; b. Rosedale, L.I., N.Y., Apr. 6, 1930; s. Mitchell E. and Dorothy A. (Munzer) S.; Asso. B.S., Leicester Jr. Coll., 1954; B.S., U. Bridgeport, 1956; postgrad. N.Y. U., 1957-58; m. Dorothy A. Braun, Aug. 29, 1954; children—Stephen Scott, Scott Stuart, Robert Mitchell; m. 2d, Marie E. Nellis, July 16, 1977. With Mut. Benefit Life Ins. Co., 1956-57; estate planner Mitchell E. Saunders Co., 1956-58; account exec. Diamond Internat. Corp., 1958-60; account mgr. Nations Bus. mag., N.Y.C., 1960-65, Eastern advt. mgr., 1965-68; advt. dir. IEEE Spectrum mag., N.Y.C., 1968-77, asso. pub., 1978—; cons. The William Co., 1974—. Served with USMC, 1948-52; Korea. Decorated Purple Heart. Mem. IEEE, Bus./Profl. Advt. Assn., Soc. Nat. Assn. Publs., Eastern Advt. Golf Assn., N.Y. State Consumer Mag. Club (past pres.), DAV, Theta Sigma. Republican. Roman Catholic. Clubs: Advt. N.Y., Cornell. Home: 145 E 27th St New York NY 10016 also PO Box 254 Mt Washington Rd South Egremont MA 01234 Office: 345 E 47th St New York NY 10017

SAURDIFF, PAUL LEON, JR., automobile dealer; b. Thief River Falls, Minn., Mar. 31, 1942; s. Paul Leon and Selma Amanda (Dalos) S.; B.S., U. Bemidji, 1964; m. Julie Marie Hagen, July 6, 1974; children—Brandi Rachelle, Michael Jeffrey. Tchr. public schs., Minn., Nev., 1965-68; internal audit dept. staff Bemis Co., Inc., Mpls., 1969-74; sec.-treas., bus. mgr. Rydell Chevrolet Co., Grand Forks, N.D., 1975—; sec.-treas. Polar Investments, Inc., 1975—. Served with USAR, 1965-71. Club: Elks. Address: 2700 S Washington St Grand Forks ND 58201

SAUTER, MELVIN H., ins. agy. exec.; b. Prior Lake, Minn., Jan. 20, 1927; s. Henry R. and Mary (Kloempkin) S.; student U. Minn., 1952; m. June 11, 1951; children—James, William, David, Daniel. Agt., Mut. Service Ins., Mpls., 1960-61, Lincoln Nat. Life, St. Paul, 1961-66; owner Mel Sauter Ins. Agy., Prior Lake, 1962—; gen. agt. Jefferson Nat. Life, Prior Lake, 1980—. Mem. Sch. Bd., Prior Lake, 1974—, chmn., 1975, 79, treas., 1976, clk., 1979; chmn. ch. council, 1974. Served with USN, 1944-52. Recipient Nat. Quality award Nat. Life Underwriters Assn., 1977, 78, others. Club: Rotary (sec. 1979, v.p. 1980).

SAVAGE, STANLEY ERNEST, oil field equipment co. exec.; b. Tacoma, Sept. 25, 1933; s. Howard Carlton and Edith Raine (Flaskett) S.; B.S., U. Oreg., 1955; M.B.A., U. Calif., Berkeley, 1961; m. Patricia Hamilton, Apr. 19, 1958; children—Shannon, Shelley, Patrick. Asst. to pres. Hydril Co., Los Angeles, 1970-76; v.p., gen. mgr. TXT div. Vapor Co., Houston, 1976-80; v.p. mktg. Reed Am. div. Baker Internat., Houston, 1980—. Served to capt. USAF, 1955-58. Mem. Petroleum Equipment Supplies Assn., Assn. Oilwell Servicing Contractors, Internat. Assn. Drilling Contractors. Republican. Clubs: The Woodlands Country; Houston: Met. Racquet. Office: PO Box 4383 Houston TX 77210

SAVAGE, WILLIAM EDWARD, ins. exec.; b. Jersey City, Sept. 1, 1940; s. William Francis and Virginia (Howatt) S.; student N.J. Inst. Tech., 1959, Rutgers U., 1964; m. Barbara Ann Fette, Nov. 4, 1961; children—Barbara Karen, William Christopher, Shawn Michael. With Prudential Ins. Co. Am., 1959—, beginning as claims examiner group pensions, Newark, 1959-64, successively underwriter, group pension systems designer, group pension systems adminstr., Los Angeles, 1972-74, group pension systems mgr., Florham Park, N.J., 1974—. Mem. Edn. Bd., 1970-72; exec. dir. Alive, Inc., 1972; soccer coach, 1975-80. Served with C.E., AUS, 1961. C.L.U.; 3 certs. in mgmt. Am. Coll. Roman Catholic. Home: 337 Daniel St Rockaway Township Dover PO NJ 07801 Office: Group Pension Office Prudential Insurance Co of America Florham Park NJ 07932

SAVILLE, MICHAEL LEE, electronics co. exec.; b. Pocatello, Idaho, May 3, 1944; s. Harry Eugene and Marge (Meyer) S.; student U. Md., 1963-66, Idaho State U., 1969-75; m. Susan Rochelle Clark, Mar. 23, 1968; children—Mark, Hope, Christopher. Customer engr. IBM, Pocatello, 1966-75, service planning rep., Rochester, Minn., 1976-79, field mgr., Los Angeles, 1979—. Served with USAF, 1962-66. Recipient various Jaycee awards, including Minn. Jaycees Bronze Key, 1977, Gold Key, 1978, U.S. Jaycees lM. Keith Upson award, 1978, U.S. Jaycees Outstanding Dist. Dir. award, 1978, Outstanding Young Man of Am., 1979, 81. Mem. Amateur Radio Relay League, Calif. Jaycees (regional dir. 1980-81). Lutheran. Office: 3550 Wilshire Blvd Los Angeles CA 90010

SAVIN, RONALD RICHARD, chem. co. exec.; b. Cleve., Oct. 16, 1927; s. Samuel and Ada (Silver) S.; student U. Cin., 1944-46; B.A. in Chemistry and Lit., U. Mich., 1948; postgrad. La Sorbonne, Paris, 1949-50; grad. Air War Coll., 1975; postgrad. Indsl. Coll. Armed Forces, 1975; m. Gloria Ann Hopkins, Apr. 21, 1962; children—Danielle Elizabeth, Andre Lianne. Vice pres. Premium Finishes, Inc., Cin., 1957-58, pres., owner, 1958—. Active Boy Scouts Am.; mem. Malabar Found., 1960. Served with USAF, 1950-55; ETO, Korea; col. Res. Mem. Soc. Mfg. Engrs. (sr.), AIM (pres.'s council), Nat. Assn. Corrosion Engrs., Air Force Assn., Cin. C. of C. Clubs: Clermont, Curzon House (London); Desert Island Country (Palm Springs, Calif.). Mem. mgmt. adv. council Chem. Week Mag.; contbr. articles to profl. jours. Home: 3100 Venetian Villas 4000 Gulf Stream Blvd North Naples FL 33940 also Desert Island 900 Island Dr Rancho Mirage CA 92270 Office: 10448 Chester Rd Cincinnati OH 45215

SAVIO, L. DON, banker; b. Lexington, Mo., June 1, 1931; s. Lawrence and Madeline (Beretta) S.; student Grad. Sch. Banking, U. Wis., 1966; m. Annabelle Cretzmeyer, June 18, 1960; children—Ellen, Donna, Jane. With Comml. Bank, Lexington, 1950—, v.p., 1969-74, exec. v.p., 1974-76, pres., chief exec. officer, 1976—, dir., 1976—. Treas. Lexington Improvement Corp.; sec.-treas. Lexington Indsl. Devel. Authority; sec. Anderson House Found.; treas. Sr. Citizens Adv. Bd.; bd. dirs. United Fund. Served with U.S. Army, 1952-54. Mem. Mo. Bankers Assn., Lexington Turner Soc. (life), Am. Legion (trustee George Thomas Cullom post 1980). Roman Catholic. Club: Elks (past exalted ruler)(Lexington). Office: PO Box 428 Lexington MO 64067

SAVITZ, SAMUEL J., actuarial cons. firm exec.; b. Phila., Dec. 23, 1936; s. Paul and Ann (Gechman) S.; B.S. in Bus. Adminstrn., Temple U., 1958; postgrad. U. Pa., 1960-62, Temple U., 1965; m. Selma Goldberg, June 15, 1958; children—Jacqueline Beverly, Steven Leslie, Michelle Lynn. Pension analyst Provident Mut. Life Ins. Co., Phila., 1958-61; v.p. The Wirkman Co., Phila., 1961-64; pres. Samuel J. Savitz & Assoc., Inc., Phila., 1964—; vis. lectr. U. Pa., Phila., 1960, La. State U., 1972-74; faculty Villanova U., 1971-75; cons. in field. Mem. pension com. Fedn. Jewish Agencies, Phila., 1960. Served with USAR, 1954-62. Mem. Am. Soc. Pension Actuaries (dir. 1969-75), Am. Soc. C.L.U.'s, Assn. Advanced Life Underwriting. Jewish. Contbr. articles in field to profl. jours. Home: 470 Conshohocken State Rd Bala Cynwyd PA 19004 Office: 1845 Walnut St Philadelphia PA 19103

SAVOCA, S. EDWARD, mfg. co. exec., realty co. exec.; b. N.Y.C., Mar. 28, 1928; s. Samuel C. and Catherine A. Savoca; B.S. in Econs., Villanova U., 1950; M.B.A., Temple U., 1952; m. Constance M. Renna, Nov. 21, 1953; children—Cathryn, Samuel, Elizabeth, Karen. Pres., Alsam Shoe Mfg. Co., Lititz, Pa., 1966—; pres. Phoenix Shoe Co., Lancaster, Pa., 1979—; partner Savoca Realty Co., Leola, Pa. Served with U.S. Navy, 1946-48, U.S. Army, 1952-54. Mem. Pa. Shoe and Leather Assn. Roman Catholic. Office: 117 Walnut St Lititz PA 17543

SAWHILL, JOHN CRITTENDEN, mgmt. co. exec.; b. Cleve., June 12, 1936; s. James Mumford and Mary (Gipe) S.; A.B., Princeton U., 1958; Ph.D., N.Y. U., 1963; D.H.L. (hon.), Md. Inst. Coll. Art, Pace U.; LL.D. (hon.), Syracuse U.; m. Isabel Van Devanter, Sept. 13, 1958; 1 son, James Winslow. Sr. v.p. Comml. Credit Co., Balt., 1968-73; asso. dir. Office Mgmt. and Budget, Washington, 1973-74; adminstr. Fed. Energy Adminstrn., Washington, 1974-75; lectr., 1975; pres. N.Y. U., 1975-79; dep. sec. Dept. of Energy, Washington, 1979-80; chmn., chief exec. officer Synthetic Fuels Corp., Washington, 1980-81; sr. partner, dir. McKinsey & Co., Washington, 1981—; dir. RCA, Phillip Morris, Consol. Edison, Crane Corp., Gen. Am. Investors, Am. Internat. Group, Automatic Data Process, N. Am. Coal Co. Mem. N.Y. State Fin. Control Bd.; trustee Urban Inst. Mem. AAAS (dir.). Presbyterian. Clubs: River, Century, Met., Chevy Chase. Author: Energy: Managing the Transitions, 1978; Energy Conservation and Public Policy, 1979. Office: 1700 Pennsylvania Ave NW Washington DC

SAWIN, ROBERT DREW, devel. center exec.; b. Marblehead, Mass., Oct. 14, 1940; s. John Staples and Woneta Dee (Forest) S.; Ph.D. in Internat. Relations, Sangkum Reaster Niyum U. (Cambodia), 1969; LL.D. (hon.), Saigon U., 1970; m. Arnelda L. Lindmark, Nov. 28, 1964; children—Billy, Tom, Robyn, Robert, Rachel. S.E. Asian analyst U.S. Govt., 1959-69; dir. prisoner of war negotiations S.E. Asia, Christian and Missionary Alliance, 1969-73; dir. Congressional relations Western Union Corp., Washington, 1974-75; dir. Nat. Center for Vietnamese Resettlement, Washington, 1975-77; internat. v.p. Incolay Studios, San Fernando, 1977-80; pres. Arid Lands Devel. Center, Los Angeles, 1980—. Served with USMC, 1959-63. Republican. Presbyterian. Clubs: Congressional, Internat. Office: 445 Fox St San Fernando CA 91340

SAWYER, JOHN CHARLES, gas co. exec.; b. Greenville, S.C., Nov. 27, 1935; s. Albert Carroll and Mary Ida (Stevenson) S.; m. Joanne Slade; children—Suzanne, Charlene, John Charles. Pres., Sawyer Gas of Jacksonville, (Fla.) Inc., Sawyer Gas of the Beaches, Inc., Jacksonville Beach, Fla., Sawyer Home Gas, Inc., Lake City, Fla., Sawyer Slade Gas of Starke (Fla.) Inc., Sawyer Deel Gas, Inc., Green Cove Springs, Fla., Sawyer Air Conditioning, Jacksonville. Served with U.S. Army, 1958-59. Recipient Disting. Service award Fla. Liquid Propane Gas Assn., 1972, 74, 75. Mem. C. of C. Bradford County (pres.). Democrat. Methodist. Club: Rotary (Jacksonville). Office: 7162 Phillips Hwy Jacksonville FL 32216

SAWYER, STANLEY FRED, telephone co. exec.; b. Kenmare, N.D., Sept. 20, 1938; s. Bernard Frank and Orpha Willora (Parkinson) S.; student pub. schs., Kenmare; m. Sharon Kay Johnson, Mar. 7, 1959; children—Shelly, Stephanie, Shannon. Installer, Western Electric Co., 1956-59; mem. central office maintenance staff Souris River Telephone Co., Minot, N.D., 1959-64; with Continental Telephone Co., various locations, 1964—, comml. supr., Espanola, N.Mex., 1972-74, dist. mgr., Homedale, Idaho, 1974-75, div. mktg. supr., Phoenix, 1975-77; internat. mktg. mgr. Continental Telephone Internat. Corp., 1977-79, internat. mktg. dir., 1979—. Mem. Ind. Telephone Pioneer Assn. Republican. Home: 215 Thompson Pl Roswell GA 30075 Office: 223 Perimeter Center Pkwy Atlanta GA 30346

SAWYER, THOMAS EDGAR, mgmt. cons. co. exec.; b. Homer, La., July 7, 1932; s. Sidney Edgar and Ruth (Bickman) S.; B.S., UCLA, 1959; M.A., Occidental Coll., 1969; m. Joyce Mezzanatto, Aug. 22, 1954; children—Jeffrey T., Scott A., Robert J., Julie Anne. Project engr. Garrett Corp., Los Angeles, 1954-60; mgr. devel. ops. TRW Systems, Redondo Beach, Calif., 1960-66; spl. asst. to gov. State of Calif., Sacramento, 1967-69; prin., gen. mgr. Planning Research Corp., McLean, Va., 1969-72; dep. dir. OEO, Washington, 1972-74; asso. prof. bus. mgmt. Brigham Young U., 1974-78; pres. Mesa Corp., Provo, 1978—, chmn. bd., 1978—; dir. Insul Chem. Corp., Magus Corp., Farm and Poultry Corp. Chmn. Indian edn. avt. com. Utah State Sch. Bd. Served with USMC, 1950-53. Mem. Am. Mgmt. Assn., Am. Soc. Public Adminstrn. Republican. Mormon. Club: Mason. Author: Assimilation Versus Self-Indentity: A Modern Native American Perspective, 1976. Home: 548 W 630 S Orem UT 84057 Office: 1156 S State St Suite 105 Orem UT 84057

SAXER, CRAIG SANDFORD, fin. exec.; b. Phila., Feb. 26, 1947; s. Lewis Paul and Dorothy (Waite) S.; B.A. in Econs., Haverford Coll., 1969; m. Barbara L. Costello, Apr. 12, 1977; 1 dau., Kristen Carey. Audit staff supr. Coopers & Lybrand, Phila., 1969-74; asst. treas. Norcross, Inc., West Chester, Pa., 1974-76; asst. auditor Provident Nat. Bank, Phila., 1976-78, mgr. corp. cash and analysis, 1978-79, asst. v.p. strategic planning, 1978—. Bd. dirs. Haverford Hosp. Assn., 1976—, sec.-treas., 1977—. Served with USMCR, 1969-75. Mem. Am. Inst. C.P.A.'s, Pa. Inst. C.P.A.'s. Lutheran. Address: 1037 Singer Ln Eagleville PA 19408

SAYAD, HOMER ELISHA, accountant, banker; b. Iran, Aug. 15, 1915; s. Elisha Elija and Najeeba Mar (Joseph) S.; B.S., U. Nottingham (Eng.), 1937; student Northwestern U., 1937-39; came to U.S., 1937; m. Elizabeth Foster Gentry, May 10, 1963; children—Elisha William Gentry, Helene Elizabeth Todd. Mgr. of Deloitte, Plender, Griffiths & Co., Chgo., 1939-52, merger into Haskins & Sells, 1952, partner, 1952—, sr. partner, St. Louis office, 1954-78, cons., 1978-79; sr. v.p. Mark Twain Bancshares, Inc., 1979—; dir. Consol. Grain and Barge Co. Chmn. profl. div. United Fund of Greater St. Louis, 1959-60; past pres. Opera Theatre of St. Louis; pres. Loretto-Hilton Repertory Theatre, 1971-75; mem. Zool. Park and Mus. Dist. Bd., 1972-74. Bd. dirs. St. Louis Symphony Soc., St. Louis Children's Hosp.; past pres. and chmn. bd. dirs. Arts and Edn. Council Greater St. Louis; bd. dirs., trustee William Woods Coll., Fulton, Mo.; mem. 22d Circuit Jud. Commn. Served from pvt. to master sgt. AUS, 1943-46. Mem. Am. Inst. C.P.A.'s, Am. Accounting Assn., Mo. Soc. C.P.A.'s (past pres.), UN Assn. (dir. St. Louis chpt. 1978—). Clubs: Bellerive Country (bd. dirs.), Racquet (past treas., bd. dirs.), Noonday (past treas.), St. Louis. Home: 41 Westmoreland Pl Saint Louis MO 63108 Office: 8820 Ladue Rd Saint Louis MO 63124

SAYER, JOHN SAMUEL, mech. engr.; b. St. Paul, July 27, 1917; s. Arthur and Genevieve (Ollis) S.; B.S., U. Minn., 1940; m. Elizabeth Hughes, June 9, 1940; children—Stephen, Susan, Kathryn, Nancy. Cons. sect. mgr. E. I. duPont de Nemours & Co., Wilmington, Del. to 1960; exec. v.p. Documentation, Inc., Washington, 1960-62; v.p. marketing and corporate planning Auerbach Corp., Phila., 1962-64; v.p. Information Dynamics Corp., Boston, 1964-65; pvt. cons. information systems, Boxford, Mass., 1965—; exec. v.p. Leasco Systems and Research, 1970; pvt. cons., 1971-72; exec. v.p. Leasco Information Products Co., 1973-74; pres. Remac Corp., 1974-80, v.p. research and devel., 1980—. Mem. ASME, Nat. Microfilm Assn., Am. Soc. for Info. Sci., Pi Tau Sigma, Triangle. Address: 13209 Colton Ln Gaithersburg MD 20760

SAYERS, OPAL MARIE KIMBALL (MRS. ROBERT DELL SAYERS), corp. exec.; b. Jacksonville, Fla., Aug. 13, 1940; d. George Sharpe and Thelma (Huckaby) Kimball; student pub. schs.; m. Robert Dell Sayers, Oct. 3, 1958; children—Sheila Marie, Treca Marie. Bookkeeper Perry News-Herald, Perry, Fla., 1959-60, sales rep., 1968—; treas. Aluminum Fabricated Products, Inc., C.S.T. Enterprises, Inc., 1973—; mgr. Perry-Taylor County C. of C., 1961-65. Taylor County rep., Tallahassee Democrat newspaper, 1961-64. Sec. Taylor County's Ann. Pine Tree Festival, 1961-66; sec. Fla. Forest Festival, 1966-67, mem. steering com., 1972, 73, gen. chmn., 1977; chmn. econ. devel. com. Ch. of Nazarene; chmn. bd. trustees Doctors Meml. Hosp., 1979-80. Mem. Perry-Taylor County C. of C. (treas. 1973-74, pres. 1975-76). Democrat. Nazarene. Clubs: Junior Woman's (chmn. conservation natural resources); Perry Woman's (pres., 1st v.p. 1972-75). Office: POB 1107 Perry FL 32347

SAYLOR, ALLEN GENE, biomed. co. exec.; b. Berlin, Pa., Dec. 3, 1933; s. Stewart Cleveland and Rachel Jane (Paul) S.; B.S. in Acctg., Southeastern U., Washington, 1973; m. Faye D. Custer, Aug. 31, 1957; children—Joni, Heidi, Natalie, Shane. Chief acct. Briggs & Co., Landover, Md., 1967-70; acctg. mgr. Gen. Capital Corp., Washington, 1970-71; div. controller T.I. Swartz & Sons, Balt., 1971-73; bus. mgr. Linbro div. Flow Labs. Inc., Hamden, Conn., 1973-81, adminstrv. mgr., Dublin, Va., 1981—. Served with Signal Corps, U.S. Army, 1955-57. Home: 1613 Kennedy Ave Blacksburg VA 24060 Office: PO Box 1065 Rock Rd Dublin VA 24084

SAYRE, LANSING GLENN LYTLE, pub. accountant; b. Cin., July 24, 1901; s. Charles Lansing and Amanda Glenn (Lytle) S.; ed. pvt. tutors; m. Elizabeth Goble, Feb. 14, 1957. Pvt. practice pub. accounting, Los Angeles, 1943—. Mem. S.R. (past pres.), Soc. Colonial Wars (past gov. Calif. soc., life mem. gen. council), Order Founders and Patriots Am. (past gov. gen.), Mil. Order Loyal Legion (past comdr.), Soc. War 1812, Huguenot Soc. Calif. (past v.p.), Mil. Order Crusades, Baronial Order Magna Charta (surity), Order Crown Charlemagne (past v.p. gen.), Nat. Gavel Club, Nat. Soc. Public Accountants, Soc. Calif. Accountants. Mason (32 deg., Shriner), Elk. Home: 901 Cumberland Rd Glendale CA 91202

SAZER, GARY NEIL, lawyer; b. Chgo., July 14, 1946; s. David and Eleanor (Miller) S.; B.A., N.Y. U., 1971; J.D., Hofstra U., 1974; m. Lois Gail Kolen, Aug. 21, 1971; children—Eric Scott, Jonathan Adam. Admitted to N.Y. bar, 1975; acquisitions cons. Empress Internat. Ltd., N.Y.C., 1970-72; asso. firm Windels & Marx, N.Y.C., 1972-76; partner firm Rubinstein & Sazer, N.Y.C., 1976-79; individual practice law, 1979—; comml. arbitrator Am. Arbitration Assn., 1974—; lectr. on comml. law Nassau Bar Assn.; exec. asst. Mayor Gt. Neck Plaza (N.Y.), 1971-73. Mem. Internat. (com. on sale goods), Am., N.Y. State bar assns., Assn. Bar City N.Y., New York County Lawyers Assn., Am. Horse Council, Airplane Owners and Pilots Assn. Republican. Jewish. Mem., pub. Hofstra Law Rev., 1973, 74; research on currency price fluctuation in internat. comml. agreements. Home: 28 Woodland Pl Great Neck NY 11021 Office: 60 Cutter Mill Rd Great Neck NY 11021

SCAFE, LINCOLN ROBERT, JR., air conditioning service co. exec.; b. Cleve., July 28, 1922; s. Lincoln Robert and Charlotte (Hawkins) S.; student Cornell U., 1940-41; m. Mary Anne Wilkinson, Nov. 14, 1945; children—Amanda Katharine, Lincoln Robert. Service mgr. Avery Engring. Co., Cleve., 1946-51; nat. service mgr. Trane Co., LaCrosse, Wis., 1951-57; service and installation mgr. Mech. Equipment Supply Co., Honolulu, 1957-58; chief engr. Sam P. Wallace of Pacific, Honolulu, 1958-62; pres. Air Conditioning Service Co., Inc., Honolulu, 1962—. Served with USNR, 1942-45; PTO. Mem. Am. Soc. Heating, Refrigeration and Air Conditioning Engrs., Hawaii C. of C., Alpha Delta Phi. Clubs: Outrigger Canoe, Cornell Hawaii (past pres.). Republican. Contbr. articles to profl. jours. Address: 314 Anolani St Honolulu HI 96821

SCALETTA, SYLVESTER, II, acct.; b. Johnstown, Pa., May 18, 1946; s. Vito Charles and Eva Marie (Michlena) S.; diploma in higher acctg. Cambria Rowe Bus. Coll., Johnstown, 1967; B.S. in Public Acctg., Dyke Coll., Cleve., 1969; postgrad. in real estate U. Pitts., Johnstown, Am. Inst. C.P.A.'s; m. Edith M. Stutzman, Sept. 13, 1969; 1 son, Brian K. Staff acct. Harry K. Sickler, Jr., C.P.A., 1969-70, Young & Co., C.P.A.'s, Altoona, Pa., 1970-71, Ginsburg & Ondick, C.P.A.s, Johnstown, 1971-73; controller John E. Sroka, real estate and mortgage broker, Johnstown, 1973-77; owner, mgr. Sylvester Scaletta, II, C.P.A., fin. broker, Johnstown, 1977—. Bd. dirs. United Cerebral Palsy So. Alleghenies Region, Inc., 1976—. C.P.A., Pa. Mem. Am. Inst. C.P.A.'s, Pa. Inst. C.P.A.'s, Nat. Assn. Accts. (dir. 1973, 76), Cambria County Bd. Realtors, Greater Johnstown C. of C., Greater Johnstown Jaycees (dir. 1972-73), United Consumers Alleghenies (treas. 1975). Democrat. Roman Catholic. Club: Nat. Exchange. Home and office: 1113 Riffith St Johnstown PA 15902

SCALLON, FRANK JOHN, louver co. exec.; b. Brewster, N.Y., Aug. 29, 1899; s. Francis John and Johanna (Moriarty) S.; student pub. schs., Ridgefield, Conn.; m. Florence Matilda Miller, May 18, 1933. Bellhop, Lake Waccabuc Inn, South Salem, N.Y.; clk. then asst. radio engr. Marconi Wireless Co., N.Y.C.; with Hayden-Stone, brokerage house, N.Y.C., 1918; herdsman A.B. Barnes farm, Wilton, Conn.; inspector Norwalk Tire and Rubber Co. (Conn.), to 1929; ins. agent John Hancock Co., from 1929; owner Scallon Roofing Co., from 1936; now pres. Midget Louver Co., Norwalk. Frank J. Scallow Found. formed, 1978. Roman Catholic. Elk. Patentee. Home: 255 West Rocks Rd Norwalk CT 06852 Office: 800 Main Ave Norwalk CT 06852

SCANNELL, DANIEL ANDREW, found. exec.; b. San Francisco, Mar. 13, 1934; s. Andrew M. and Ann Elizabeth (White) S.; B.A., St. Marys Coll. Calif., 1957; postgrad. San Francisco State U., 1964; m. Maureen Anne O'Brien, Aug. 17, 1957; children—Sheila, Patrick, Sean, Colleen, Daniel J., Kathy. Publs. editor Kaiser Steel Corp., Oakland, Calif., 1957-64, mgr. communications Kaiser Industries Corp., 1964-68; dir. pub. relations, Kaiser Found. Health Plan, 1969—. Mem. Communications Com. No. Calif. Cancer Program, 1977—. Served with U.S. Army, 1953-55. Mem. Public Relations Soc. Am. (exec. com. health sect. 1978—), Am. Soc. Hosp. Pub. Relations, Am. Pub. Health Assn. Home: 4333 Harbord Dr Oakland CA 94618 Office: Kaiser Foundation Health Plan 1924 Broadway Oakland CA 94612

SCANNELL, JOHN CASEY, lawyer; b. Somerville, Mass., Mar. 27, 1943; B.A., Siena Coll., Loudonville, N.Y., 1965; J.D., N.Y. U., 1974. Admitted to N.Y. bar, 1975; asso. firm Townley & Updike, N.Y.C., 1974-76; atty. Combustion Engring. Inc., Windsor, Conn., 1976-78; indsl. relations counsel Diamond Internat. Corp., N.Y.C., 1978—. Served to lt. USN, 1966-69. Mem. N.Y. State Bar Assn., Bar Assn. City N.Y. Office: 733 3d Ave New York NY 10017

SCARFF, WILLIAM JOSEPH, elec. mfg. co. ofcl.; b. Cleve., Feb. 18, 1935; s. Fredrick Joseph and Elizabeth Ann (Wilson) S.; B.E.E., Fenn Coll., 1964; M.S. in Engring. Mgmt., Syracuse U., Northeastern U., 1971; m. Erma Gene Martin, Feb. 4, 1961; children—William Joseph, Stephen David. Research and devel. lamp products Gen. Electric Co., Cleve., 1954-64, with mfg. mgmt. program, various locations, 1964-67, quality control engr. broadcast products, Syracuse, N.Y., 1967-69, mgr. advanced quality control engring., West Lynn, Mass., 1969-71, mgr. advanced mfg. engring., 1971-72, mgr. shop ops. automation systems, 1972-74, mgr. apparatus service shops operation, St. Louis, 1974-79, ter. service mgr., 1979-80, gen. mgr. east central apparatus service dept., Cleve., 1980—; instr. Corporate Mgmt. Devel. Inst.; chmn. Boston chpt. G.E. Elfun Soc., 1974, St. Louis chpt., 1978. Solicitor, Jr. Achievement, 1976. Served with USNR, 1956-58. Registered profl. engr., Ohio, Ind. Mem. Am. Soc. Quality Control (sr.), Ill. Mining Inst., Open Pit Mining Assn., Miner's Elec. Group, Eta Kappa Nu, Pi Mu Epsilon. Presbyterian (elder). Clubs: Engrs. (St. Louis); Southwestern R.R., Masons. Home: 32299 S Woodland Rd Pepper Pike OH 44124 Office: 1000 Lakeside Ave Cleveland OH 44114

SCARLETT, WILLIAM JOHN, III, life ins. co. exec.; b. Kansas City, Mo., Sept. 4, 1936; s. William John and Mable Gertrude (Andress) S.; B.S. in Accounting, Lehigh U., 1958; M.S. in Fin. Services, Am. Coll., Bryn Mawr, Pa., 1980; m. Nancy Fowler, Mar. 24, 1964; children—William John IV, James Hunter. Accountant, Price Waterhouse & Co., 1958-59, 61-62; pres. The Scarlett Agy., Inc., 1963-72; spl. agt. Northwestern Mut. Life Ins. Co., Basking Ridge, N.J., 1974—; chmn. Tennis World Inc., Caldwell, N.J., 1972—; owner Two Shunpike Rd. Co. 1972—. Bd. dirs. Big Bros. of Somerset County, Round Valley Vet. Hosp. Served with U.S. Army, 1959-61. Mem. Nat. Assn. Life Underwriters, Million Dollar Round Table (life), Phi Gamma Delta, Omicron Delta Kappa. N.J. tennis champion, 10 yrs.; former nat. paddle tennis champion. Home: 158 Childs Rd Basking Ridge NJ 07920 Office: Two Shunpike Rd Madison NJ 07940

SCATTERGOOD, JOHN ROBERT, plumbing supply co. exec.; b. Providence, Jan. 1, 1944; s. Hudson Clegg and Rachel (Baldwin) G.; B.S., U. R.I., 1965; m. Marcia Ann Telford, July 16, 1966; children—Carrie Ann, Rebecca Brooke, Jed Andrew. Auditor, Arthur Anderson & Co., N.Y.C., 1965-68; acctg. mgr., cost acctg. budget mgr. Fafnir Bearing Co., New Britain, Conn., 1968-73; gen. plant acctg. mgr. Grinnell Fire Protection Systems, Providence, 1973-76; gen. mgr. Litchfield County Plumbing Supply, Torrington, Conn., 1976—. Treas., officer St. Matthias Episcopal Ch., Coventry, R.I., 1975-76, Trinity Episcopal Ch., Torrington, 1980—. Mem. Plumbing Heating Wholesalers of New Eng. Republican. Club: Greenwoods Country. Home: RFD 2 Winsted CT 06098 Office: Litchfield County Plumbing Supply 261 Oak Ave Torrington CT 06790

SCERBO, FRANCIS BARRY, food service adminstr.; b. Fulton, N.Y., Feb. 3, 1943; s. Francis Albert and Ahleen (Downing) S.; B.A. in Bus. Adminstrn., Hiram Scott Coll., 1971; m. Dorothea Ann Guettler, Aug. 16, 1969; children—Anthony J., Andrew A. Asst. dir. aux. services Hiram Scott Coll., Scottsbluff, Nebr., 1968-71; asst. dir. food service, Univ. Center, U. Mont., Missoula, 1971-72; dir. univ. food services De Paul U., Chgo., 1973-76; exec. dir., dir. dining services Aux. Campus Enterprises, SUNY, Binghamton, Inc., 1976—. Tech. dir. Syracuse Symphony Opera, 1963, 64; dir. Wildcat Hills Pageant, Scottsbluff, 1970, 71; cub master Boy Scouts Am., 1979—. Served with USAF, 1966-68. Mem. Nat. Restaurant Assn., Nat. Assn. Coll. Aux. Services, Nat. Assn. Coll. and Univ. Food Services, N.Y. State Restaurant Assn., SUNY Aux. Services Assn. Democrat. Roman Catholic. Clubs: Optimist, Toastmasters. Home: 2028 Ford Rd Endicott NY 13760 Office: Aux Campus Enterprises SUNY at Binghamton Inc Vestal Parkway E Binghamton NY 13901

SCHACHT, HENRY BREWER, diesel engine mfg. co. exec.; b. Erie, Pa., Oct. 16, 1934; s. Henry Blass and Virginia (Brewer) S.; B.S., Yale U., 1956; M.B.A., Harvard U., 1962; m. Nancy Godfrey, Aug. 27, 1960; children—James, Laura, Jane, Mary. Sales trainee Am. Brake Shoe Co., N.Y.C., 1956-57; investment mgr. Irwin Mgmt. Co., Columbus, Ind., 1962-64; v.p. fin. Cummins Engine Co., Inc., Columbus, 1964-66, v.p., central area mgr. internat., London, Eng., 1966-67, group v.p. internat. and subsidiaries, 1967-69, pres., Columbus, 1969—, chmn., chief exec. officer, 1977—; dir. CBS, Kirloskar-Cummins, Ltd., Poona, India. Trustee Com. Economic Devel., Urban Inst., Rockefeller Found., Brookings Inst.; mem. adv. bd. Yale U. Sch. Orgn. and Mgmt.; mem. Western Hwy. Inst.; mem. Trilateral Commn. Served with USNR, 1957-60. Mem. Conf. Bd. (trustee), Council Fgn. Relations, Mgmt. Execs. Soc., Tau Beta Pi. Republican. Home: 4300 N Riverside Dr Columbus IN 47201 Office: 1000 5th St Columbus IN 47201

SCHAD, THEODORE GEORGE, JR., food co. exec.; b. N.Y.C., Mar. 4, 1927; s. Theodore George and Helen (Tennyson) S.; Student Va. Mil. Inst., 1944-45; B.S., Ill. Inst. Tech., 1950, M.S., 1951; m. Karma Rose Cundell, Mar. 21, 1957 (dec.); children—Roberta, Theodore George, III, Olive (Mrs. Richard L. Smith), Peter. Vice pres. mktg. Gt. Western Savs., Los Angeles, 1961-63; prin., nat. dir. mktg. and econs. Peat, Marwick, Mitchell & Co., Los Angeles and N.Y.C., 1964-71; chmn. bd., pres., chief exec. officer, dir. Lou Ana Foods, Inc., Opelousas, La., 1971—; chmn. bd., pres., chief exec. officer, dir. Lou Ana Industries, Inc.; pres., chief exec. officer, dir. Lou Ana Industries Internat., Inc. Pres., Mamaroneck (N.Y.) Parents of Retarded Children Assn., 1970-71; trustee Va. Mil. Inst. Found., 1978—; bd. dirs. Council for a Better La., 1975—, U.S. Indsl. Council, 1979—. Served to 2d lt., C.E., U.S. Army, 1945-47. Mem. Am. Mktg. Assn. (pres. So. Calif. chpt. 1961-62, dir. 1962-63), Greater Opelousas C. of C. (pres. 1972-73). Club: Sertoma (founding pres. Brentwood chpt. 1963) (Los Angeles). Home: PO Box 591 Opelousas LA 70570 Office: 731 N Railroad Ave Opelousas LA 70570

SCHAEBERLE, ROBERT MARTIN, food co. exec.; b. Newark, Jan. 2, 1923; s. Frederick M. and Bertha M. (Thieleman) S.; A.B., Dartmouth, 1945; m. Barbara J. Slockbower, Aug. 15, 1945. With Nabisco, Inc., 1946—; pres., 1968-73, chmn., 1973—; dir. Prudential Ins. Co. Libbey-Owens-Ford Co. Served to lt. comdr. USNR, World War II. Mem. Financial Execs. Inst., Grocery Mfrs. Assn. (dir.). Office: East Hanover NJ 07936

SCHAEFER, CARL BARRY, r.r. exec.; b. Elizabeth, N.J., Feb. 23, 1939; s. Carl H. and Evelyn G. (Conk) S.; B.S. in Engring., Princeton, 1961; M.S. in Engring., U. Pa., 1962; LL.B., Columbia, 1965; M.B.A., N.Y. U., 1970; m. Carol Ann Craft, July 11, 1970; children—Sara Elizabeth, Susan Craft. Admitted to N.Y. bar, 1965, Nebr. bar, 1972; atty. firm Kelley, Drye, Warren, Clark, Carr & Ellis, N.Y.C., 1966-69; asst. gen. counsel Union Pacific R.R. Co., N.Y.C., 1969-72, Western gen. counsel, Omaha, 1972—, v.p., 1974-77, v.p. law, 1977—; dir. Trailer Train Co., Am. Rail Box Car Corp., Union Pacific Motor Freight Co. Trustee, Brownell-Talbot Sch.; bd. dirs. Children's Meml. Hosp., Omaha Indsl. Found.; mem. adv. council U. Nebr. at Omaha Bus. Sch., 1977—. Mem. Am., Nebr. bar assns., Alumni Fedn. Columbia (dir. 1970-72), Columbia Law Sch. Alumni Assn. (sec. 1968-70, dir. 1970-73), Phi Delta Phi. Clubs: Princeton of N.Y., Rockaway Hunting, Omaha Country, Omaha. Home: 402 George Blvd Omaha NE 68132 Office: 1416 Dodge St Omaha NE 68179

SCHAEFER, CHARLES VALENTINE, JR., mfg. co. exec.; b. N.Y.C., July 7, 1914; s. Charles V. and Louise E. (Emmerich) S.; M.E., Stevens Inst. Tech., 1936, D.Eng. (hon.), 1979; m. Lillian A. Meyer, Oct. 8, 1938; children—Charles Valentine, Lynn Ann. Mgr. main plant DeLaval Steam Turbine Co., Trenton, N.J.; v.p. Friend Mfg. Co., Gasport, N.Y., 1936-50; pres., dir. Bennett Mfg. Co., Alden, N.Y., 1952-55, Aeroil Products Co., Inc., South Hackensack, N.J., 1955—, Muller Machinery Co., Metuchen, N.J., 1957—, Everlasting Valve Co., Cranford, N.J., 1965—; dir. Doyle & Roth Mfg. Co., N.Y.C., Blackwell Burner Co., San Antonio, N.J. Mgrs. Ins. Co. Vice chmn. bd. trustees Stevens Inst. Tech. Registered profl. engr., N.J. Mem. N.J. Bus. and Industry Assn. (trustee), Am. Mgmt. Assn., Am. Assn. Indsl. Mgmt., ASME, Fluid Controls, Inc., N.J. C. of C. (dir., past chmn. No. N.J.), Tau Beta Pi. Presbyterian. Clubs: Ridgewood Country, Lake Mohawk Golf, Boca Raton Hotel and Club. Office: 69 Wesley St South Hackensack NJ 07606

SCHAEFER, JAMES DAVID, constrn. co. exec.; b. Lima, Peru, May 4, 1946 (parents Am. citizens); s. Willard W. and Alice L. Schaefer; B.S. in Fgn. Service, Georgetown U., 1968. Stock record, RW Pressprich, N.Y.C., 1968-70; line supt. Boise Cascade, Lafayette, Colo., 1971-72; pres. Brandt Constrn. Inc., Mill Valley, Calif., 1975—; pres. Fall Creek Enterprises, Mill Valley, 1973—. Mem. Nat. Fedn. Ind. Business, Marin County Builders' Exchange. Office: #219 E Blithedale Mill Valley CA 94941

SCHAEFER, JAMES THEODORE, real estate exec.; b. Evanston, Ill., Aug. 29, 1937; s. Theodore Stanley and Catherine Grace (O'Keefe) S.; B.S.C., DePaul U., 1959; M.B.A., Northwestern U., 1966; m. Mary J. Konrad; children—John Edward, Margaret Elizabeth. Rep., Humble Oil & Refining Co., 1961-67; land acquisition mgr. Material Service div. Gen. Dynamics Corp., 1967-70; corp. real estate mgr. Universal Oil Products Co., 1970-71; v.p. UOP Realty Devel. Co., Des Plaines, Ill., 1971-77, pres., 1977—; dir. Coppertown Devel. Corp. Alderman, Park Ridge, Ill., 1979—; treas. Park Ridge Fine Arts Soc., 1980—. Served with U.S. Army, 1960. Mem. Indsl. Devel. Research Council (treas.), Urban Land Inst., Mich. State C. of C., DePaul U. Alumni Assn. (v.p. 1979—). Republican. Roman Catholic. Clubs: Park Ridge Country, Miscowaubik. Office: 10 UOP Plaza Des Plaines IL 60016

SCHAEFFER, ROBERT FRANÇOIS, printing co. exec.; b. Esch/Alzette, Luxembourg, Nov. 7, 1930; came to U.S., 1953; s. Philippe Jean-Pierre and Marguerite Schaeffer; Diplome, Hautes Etudes Commerciales, Paris, 1953; postgrad. (Fulbright scholar), U. Kans., 1953-54; children—Jeanne M., Edward P. Researcher, Chambre des Métiers, Luxembourg, 1954-56; exec. v.p. Krug Litho Art Co., North Kansas City, Mo., 1956—. Pres., Kansas City Ballet, 1970; trustee Conservatory of Music, U. Mo., 1975—. Decorated chevalier Order of Merit (Luxembourg); recipient Elmer G. Voight award Ednl. Council Graphic Arts, 1969; named hon. consul of Luxembourg. Mem. Printing Industries Am. (Man of Yr. 1980), Nat. Assn. Printers and Lithographers, Nat. Assn. Litho Clubs (pres. 1966-67), Walter Soderstrom Soc. Contbr. articles to profl. jours. Office: 1429 Atlantic St North Kansas City MO 64116

SCHAEVITZ, ABRAHAM ROBERT, industrialist; b. N.Y.C., Dec. 11, 1923; s. Harry Gerson and Anna (Finkle) S.; student Camden (N.J.) pub. schs.; m. Estelle Malerman, Oct. 21, 1944; children—Susan Elaine, Frances Rosanne, Lester Paul. With Super Tire Engring. Co., Pennsauken, N.J., 1941—, v.p., treas., 1941-65, pres., chmn. bd., 1966—; v.p., treas. Supercap Corp., Pennsauken, 1956-65, pres., chmn. bd., 1966—. Active Mus. Assos. of Phila. Mus. Art, Benjamin Franklin Assos. of U. Pa., Franklin Inst., Phila. Orch. Assn.; fellow Sheie Eye Inst. Served with AUS, 1943-44. Mem. Am. Trucking Assn., N.J. (dir.), Pa., N.Y., N.C., S.C. motor truck assns., Nat. Tire Dealers and Retreaders Assn., Am. Retreaders Assn., Antiquarian Horol. Soc. (Eng.), Rolls Royce Owners Club, Rolls Royce Enthusiasts Club (Eng.), Classic Car Club Am., Charles Willson Peale Soc. of Pa. Acad. Fine Arts, World Affairs Council Phila. Clubs: Marco Polo, Atrium (N.Y.C.); Curzon House, LeCercle (London); Vesper, Union League (Phila.), Masons, Variety Clubs Internat. Inventor tire undertread probe. Home: 250 Indian Creek Rd Wynnewood PA 19151 Office: 7255 Crescent Blvd Pennsauken NJ 08110

SCHAFER, CARL WALTER, univ. fin. exec.; b. Chgo., Jan. 16, 1936; s. MacHenry George and Gertrude (Herrick) S.; B.A. with distinction, U. Rochester, 1958; m. June Elizabeth Perry, Feb. 2, 1963; 1 son, MacHenry George II. Budget examiner Bur. Budget, Exec. Office Pres., Washington, 1961-64, legis. analyst, 1964-66, dep. dir. budget preparation, 1966-68, dir. budget preparation, 1968-69; staff asst. U.S. Ho. of Reps. Appropriations Com., Washington, 1969; dir. budget Princeton U., 1969-72, treas., 1972-76, fin. v.p., treas., 1976—, lectr. indsl. adminstrn., 1975; pres., chief exec. officer Palmer Sq., Inc., real estate and hotel co., 1979—; dir. Princeton Bank & Trust Co., 1979—. Trustee, treas. McCarter Theatre Co., Inc., Princeton, 1974-76. Served with USN, 1958-61. Mem. Eastern (exec. com.), Nat. assns. coll. and univ. bus. officers, Consortium Financing Higher Edn., Phi Beta Kappa. Republican. Episcopalian. Home: 44 Lake Ln Princeton NJ 08540 Office: 1 Nassau Hall Princeton Univ Princeton NJ 08544

SCHAFER, EDWARD THOMAS, household products mfg. co. exec.; b. Bismarck, N.D., Aug. 8, 1946; s. Harold Lyle and Marian Margaret (Nelsen) S.; B.S., U. N.D., 1969; M.B.A., U. Denver, 1970; children—Edward Thomas, Ellie Sue. With Gold Seal Co., Summit, N.J., 1971—, v.p., 1974-75, chmn. mgmt. team, 1975-78, pres., 1978—. Mem. Soap and Detergent Assn., Sigma Nu. Episcopalian. Office: 45 River Rd Summit NJ 07901

SCHAFFER, FRANKLIN EDWIN, advt. and pub. relations agy. exec.; b. New Rochelle, N.Y., Jan. 1, 1924; s. Franklin Pierce and Isabel Cornell (Young) S.; A.B. summa cum laude, Princeton, 1945; m. Diane Phyllis Wormser, Mar. 17, 1951; children—Quentin Munro, Darcy Diane, Jocelyn Grant. With Fred Eldean Orgn., 1947-49, G. Munro Hubbard, 1949-53; with Doremus & Co., N.Y.C., 1954—, pres., 1967-73, chmn., chief exec. officer, 1973—; dir. Affiliate Artists, Inc. Bd. dirs. Greenwich Community Chest; trustee Greenwich Library, Greenwich Hosp. Served to 1st lt. AUS, 1942-45. Decorated Army Commendation medal. Mem. Am. Assn. Advt. Agys. (gov. N.Y. council 1973-74, chmn. com. on client services 1975—, nat. dir. 1975—), Pub. Relations Soc. Am., Phi Beta Kappa, Sigma Xi. Republican. Presbyterian. Clubs: Field, Belle Haven (Greenwich); Recess, Brook, Princeton (N.Y.C.). Home: 72 Butternut Hollow Rd Greenwich CT 06830 Office: 120 Broadway New York NY 10005

SCHAFFIR, KURT HERBERT, mgmt. systems cons.; b. Vienna, Austria, July 23, 1925; came to U.S., 1939, naturalized, 1945; s. Leo and Charlotte Lola S.; B.S. in Chem. Engring., Case Western Res. U., 1945; M.S. in Chem. Engring., Columbia U., 1946, D.Engring. Sci., 1962; m. Sandra Nelkin, July 29, 1958; children—Linda Ann, Holly Jo, Jonathan Adam. Prodn. supr. Merck & Co. Inc., Rahway, N.J., 1946-50, project engr., 1950-53, mgr. ops. research, 1953-57; mgr. ops. research Arthur Andersen & Co., N.Y.C., 1957-62, partner cons. div., 1962—; lectr. mgmt. Columbia U., N.Y. U., Pace Coll., Am. Mgmt. Assn.; research asso. Internat. Inst. Applied Scis., Vienna, Austria, 1975-76. Adv. council Sch. of Bus. Manhattan Coll., 1970-72. Served with U.S. Army, 1945-46. Mem. Am. Chem. Soc., Inst. Mgmt. Scis., Ops. Research Soc. Am., Am. Mktg. Assn., Nat. Assn. Accts., Am. Inst. Indsl. Engrs. Author: Marketing Information Systems, 1972; contbr. writings to publs.

SCHAG, ERNEST JOHN, JR., lawyer; b. Los Angeles, Jan. 16, 1933; s. Ernest J. and Dora L. (Jackson) S.; A.B., U. So. Calif., 1954, J.D., 1959; LL.M., N.Y. U., 1960; m. Mary Margaret Hawkins; children—John Barton, Laurie Ann, Tracy Lee. Admitted to Calif. bar, 1960, N.Y. bar, 1960, U.S. Supreme Ct. bar, 1966; atty. Lillick, Geary, McHose, Roethke & Myers, Los Angeles, 1960-62; individual law practice, Beverly Hills, Calif., 1962-64; partner Barnes, Schag, Johnson & Carlson, and predecessor firms, Newport Beach, Calif., 1964-76, Meserve, Mumper & Hughes, Newport Beach, 1978—; lectr. state bar U. Calif.; founder Cablescan, Inc. (subsidiary Thomas & Betts Corp.), Anaheim, Calif. Past pres. Cameo Community Assn.; v.p. Orange County council Boy Scouts Am. Served to lt. USNR, 1954-56. Fellow Am. Coll. Probate Counsel; mem. Am., N.Y., Los Angeles County, Orange County bar assns., State Bar Calif., USC Assos., U. So. Calif. Alumni Assn., Blue Key, Skull and Dagger, Phi Delta Phi, Tau Kappa Epsilon. Clubs: Balboa Bay, Big Canyon Country, Ironwood Country, Newport Harbor Yacht; Tuna (Avalon). Home: 5 Maritime Dr Corona del Mar CA 92625 Office: 5190 Campus Dr Newport Beach CA 92660

SCHAGER, KEES, investment exec.; b. Den Helder, Netherlands, Sept. 14, 1946; came to U.S., 1965; s. Cornelis and Aafje (Broekhuizen) S.; B.A. (Fulbright scholar), SUNY, Plattsburgh, 1967; M.B.A., Columbia U., 1969; m. Anne Lester, June 29, 1969; 1 son, Nicholas. Mem. fin. dept. Am. Can Co., N.Y.C., 1969-70; sr. v.p., dir. fgn. research Arnhold and S. Bleichroeder, Inc., N.Y.C., 1972—. Mem. Fin. Analysts Fedn., N.Y. Soc. Security Analysts, N.Y. Assn. Fgn. Analysts. Clubs: Univ., Netherlands (N.Y.C.). Research on South African gold, platinum and diamond cos., economy and cos. of Malaysia and Singapore. Home: 58 Garden Rd Scarsdale NY 10583 Office: 30 Broad St New York NY 10004

SCHAIBLE, C. DONELDA, ins. co. exec.; b. Ypsilanti, Mich., Mar. 31, 1920; d. Theodore E. and Charlotte (Clark) Schaible; A.B. in Social Work, U. Mich., 1942. Systems service rep. IBM, Detroit, 1942-44, spl. personnel research, N.Y.C., 1944-47; personnel asst. Washington Nat. Ins. Co., Evanston, Ill., 1948, asst. personnel dir., 1948-49, personnel dir., 1949—, 3d v.p., 1980—. Personnel cons. Ill. Shore Girl Scout Council. Mem. adv. com. Evanston Child Care Center Assn., 1967-68; adv. council Evanston Sawyer Coll. Bus., 1969-71. Mem. Am. Personnel and Guidance Assn., Chgo. Guidance and Personnel Assn. (dir. 1952-55, hospitality com. 1958-59), Nat. Vocational Guidance Assn., Ill. (human resources com. 1975-76, labor relations com.), Evanston (chmn. personnel mgrs. group 1970-71) chambers commerce, No. Ill. Indsl. Assn. (personnel practices survey com. 1959-62, vice chmn. 1961), Level/50 Group, Am. Assn. U. Women, Pi Beta Phi. Republican. Methodist (ofcl. bd. 1956-59, 62-65, mem. lay personnel com. 1963-68). Home: 1567 Ridge Ave Evanston IL 60201 Office: 1630 Chicago Ave Evanston IL 60201

SCHALLERT, DONOVAN HOMER, ins. co. exec.; b. Madison, Wis., Aug. 13, 1924; s. William Herbert and Rose Mary (Meyers) S.; B.B.A., U. Wis., 1949; m. Patricia Anne Tolen, Mar. 23, 1973; children—James Britton, Don William, Deborah Sue, Jon Carl, David Lewis. Rate supr. State Farm Ins. Co., Marshall, Mich., 1949-51; state mgr. Kemper Ins. Co., West Bend, Wis., 1951-59; br. mgr. Dairyland Ins. Co., Denver, 1959-69; pres., dir. Guaranty Nat. Ins. Co. and Guaranty Nat. Corp., Denver, 1969—; dir. Cayman Islands Re-ins. Co. Served with U.S. Army, 1943-46; ETO, NATOUSA. Decorated Bronze Star (3), others. Mem. Tex. Surplus Lines Assn. (asso.), Colo. 1752 Club (asso.), Am. Assn. Mng. Gen. Agts. Republican. Club: Optmists (past pres.). Home: 6150 E Briarwood Circle Englewood CO 80112 Office: 100 Inverness Terr E PO Box 3329 Englewood CO 80155

SCHANCK, FRANCIS RABER, investment banker; b. Los Angeles, Oct. 22, 1907; s. Francis Raber and Florence Ethel (Carr) S.; student Stanford, 1926-29; m. Kathryn Sterling Short, June 10, 1933; children—Jordan Thomas, Susan, Peter Carr. Successively with E.A. Pierce & Co., Anderson & Fox Co., also C.F. Childs & Co., 1927-30; office and dept. mgr. First Boston Corp., Portland, Oreg., San Francisco, Los Angeles and Chgo., 1930-42, 46-48; dept. mgr., partner Bacon, Whipple & Co., Chgo., 1948-62, mng. partner, 1962—. Past mem. bds. edn. Community Consol. Sch. Dist. 181 and High Sch. Dist. 86, DuPage-Cook County, Ill. Past trustee Village Hinsdale, Ill. Served to comdr. USNR, World War II; PTO. Mem. Investment Bankers Assn. Am. (chmn. central states group 1962-63, nat. bd. govs. and v.p. 1964-65, 1st v.p. 1966-67, pres. 1967-68), Security Industry Assn. (chmn. governing council 1972), Municipal Bond Club Chgo. (past pres.), Bond Club Chgo. (past pres.), Zeta Psi. Clubs: Chicago, Commercial, Union League, Attic (Chgo.); Hinsdale Golf; Links (N.Y.C.). Home: 537 Pamela Circle Hinsdale IL 60521 Office: 135 S LaSalle St Chicago IL 60603

SCHANCK, JORDAN THOMAS, mfg. co. exec.; b. Portland, Oreg., Feb. 5, 1931; s. Francis R. and Catherine (Short) S.; B.A., Dartmouth, 1952; m. Barbara Burgoyne, Apr. 27, 1957; children—Karen, William, Rebecca. Field engr. Signode Corp, Glenview, Ill., 1954-56, packaging lab. tech., 1957, asst. to v.p. sales, 1958, sales rep., 1959, sales mgr. Paslode div., 1960-65, Eastern div., 1966, asst. to pres., 1967-69, v.p. corporate planning, 1970-71, exec. v.p., 1972, pres., chief operating officer, 1973-75, pres., chief exec. officer, 1975—; dir. Am. Nat. Bank, Maytag Co, Amsted Industries, Lindberg Corp, Signode Corp. Mem. advisory bd. YMCA Metro. Chgo., BUILD Chgo.; bd. govs. United Republican Fund, Soc. for Environ. Awareness, Orchestral Assn. of Chgo. Symphony Orch.; trustee George Williams Coll.; mem. Northwestern U. Assos. Served with U.S. Army, 1952-54. Mem. Ill. Mfrs. Assn., Chgo. Assn. Commerce and Industry. Presbyterian. Clubs: Chgo., Econ. (dir.), Chgo. Commonwealth, Commercial, Mid-Am., Hinsdale Golf. Office: 3600 W Lake Ave Glenview IL 60025

SCHANER, EDUARD RUDOLF, cons. mgmt., investments; b. Trencin, Czechoslovakia, Aug. 3, 1929; s. Karol Rudolf Schaner and Katerina (Zahorai) Horansky; came to U.S., 1958, naturalized, 1964; M.S. in Internat. Trade, Commenius U., Bratislava, Czechoslovakia, 1951; Financial planning and mgmt. parks, recreation services and facilities Bratislava, 1954-57; owner-operator meat products mfg., delicatessen and restaurant facilities San Mateo, Calif., 1964-69; owner, operator, adminstr. retirement home facilities, Palo Alto and Los Altos, Calif., 1970-75; cons. fin. mgmt., pvt. investments, Palo Alto, 1976—; pres. Solar Spectrum Inc., Mountain View, Calif.; pres., treas. Seven Oaks Inc., Los Altos, 1974—, Blue Gables, Inc., Visalia, Calif., 1980—; cons. Mem. Calif. Assn. Residential Care Homes (dir. 1974—). Republican. Roman Catholic. Clubs: Elks, numerous athletic clubs. Home: 3345 La Vida Ave Visalia CA 93277

SCHANTZ, WILLIAM R., JR., soap co. exec.; b. Elizabeth, N.J., May 6, 1928; s. William R. and Marie C. (Eilbacher) S.; B.S., Seton Hall U., 1952; m. Mary Jo Fabian, Feb. 7, 1953; children—Linda, William, Theresa, Thomas. Auditor G. Krueger Brewing Co., Newark, 1952-53; with Colgate-Palmolive Co., N.Y.C., 1953—, payroll supr., 1953-57, sect. head, 1957-61, cashier, 1961-68, treas., asst. sec., 1968—. Mem. adv. bd. Seton Hall U. Bus. Sch. Served with USNR, 1946-48. Recipient Distinguished Alumnus award Seton Hall U. Mem. N.J. C. of C. (dir.), Treasurer's Club N.Y. K.C. Club: Metropolitan. Home: 9 Mulberry Ln Edison NJ 08817 Office: 300 Park Ave New York City NY 10022

SCHAPIRO, JEROME BENTLEY, chems. mfg. co. exec.; b. N.Y.C., Feb. 7, 1930; s. Sol and Claire (Rose) S.; B.Chem. Engring., Syracuse U., 1951; postgrad. Columbia, 1951-52; m. Edith Irene Kravet, Dec. 27, 1953; children—Lois, Robert, Kenneth. Project engr. propellents br. U.S. Naval Air Rocket Test Sta., Lake Denmark, N.J., 1951-52; with Dixo Co., Inc., Rochelle Park, N.J., 1954—, pres., 1966—. Lectr. detergent standards, drycleaning, care labeling, consumers standards, orgns., U.S., 1968—; U.S. del. spokesman on drycleaning Internat. Standards Orgn., Newton, Mass., 1971, Brussels, Belgium, 1972, U.S. del. spokesman on dimensional stability of textiles, Paris, 1975, Ottawa, 1978, chmn. U.S. del. com. on consumer affairs, Geneva, Switzerland, 1974, 75, 76, spokesman U.S. del. on textiles, Paris, 1974, mem. U.S. del. on care labeling of textiles, The Hague, Holland, 1974, U.S. del., chmn. del. council com. on consumer policy, Geneva, 1978, 79, Israel, 1980; fed. govtl. appointee to Industry Functional Adv. Com. on Standards, 1980—. Mem. Montclair (N.J.) Sch. Study Com., 1968-69. Served as 2d lt. USAF, 1952-53. Mem. Am. Inst. Chem. Engrs., Am. Nat. Standards Inst. (dir., chmn. consumer council 1976, 79, 80, mem. steering com. to advise Dept. Commerce on implementation GATT agreements 1976-77, mem. exec. standards council, 1977-79), internat. standards council, chmn. internat. consumer policy adv. com.), Am. Assn. Textile Chemists and Colorists (mem. exec. com. on research 1974-77, chmn. com. on dry cleaning, vice chmn. internat. test methods com.) Am. Chem. Soc., Standards Engring. Soc. (cert.), ASTM (award 1970, chmn. com. D-12, 1974-79, mem. standing com. on internat. standards), Internat. Standards Orgn. (mem. internat. standards steering com. for consumer affairs), Jewish (v.p., treas. temple). Mason. Home: 197 N Mountain Ave Montclair NJ 07042 Office: 158 Central Ave Rochelle Park NJ 07662

SCHAPS, ALLEN JAY, investment properties and corp. relocation co. exec.; b. Milw., Jan. 29, 1932; s. Sidney and Betty (Golin) S.; B.S.C., Roosevelt U., 1954; children—Marci, Scott and Steven (twins), Susan. Buyer, Spiegel Inc., Chgo., 1955-70; new products mgr. Venetianaire Corp., Yonkers, N.Y., 1970-73; v.p. E. Coast sales Unitron Inc., Los Angeles, 1973-74; dir. mktg. Nat. Curtain Corp., N.Y.C., 1974-79; v.p. Bigelow & Schaps Inc., Stamford, Conn., 1980—. Mem. Nat. Bd. Realtors, Conn. Bd. Realtors, Stamford Bd. Realtors, Area Commerce and Industry Assn. Jewish. Home: PO Box 2053 Stamford CT 06906 Office: Bigelow & Schaps Inc 641 Summer St Stamford CT 06901

SCHARF, ROBERT CHARLES, assn. exec.; b. Belleville, N.J., Nov. 9, 1923; s. Nicholas Ambrose and Frances Margaret (Krott) S.; B.A., St. Bonaventure (N.Y.) U., 1946; S.T.B., Holy Name Coll., Washington, 1950; S.T.L., Cath. U. Am., 1958; S.S.L., Pontifical Bibl. Inst., Rome, 1960; A.A. in Acctg., LaSalle U., Chgo., 1979; m. Mary Ann Greco, May 10, 1968; 1 dau., Stacy Ann. Ordained priest Roman Catholic Ch., 1950; resigned, 1968; treas. Sem. of Our Lady of Angels, New Canaan, Conn., 1950-53; asst. treas. gen. curia Franciscan Order, Rome, 1953-55; prof. Bibl. studies Holy Name Coll., 1956-58, St. Bonaventure U., 1960-68; asso. editor Gallagher Report, N.Y.C., 1968-69; exec. dir. Hudson County (N.J.) chpt. ARC, 1969-70, asst. devel. dir. Greater N.Y., 1970-73, dir. devel., 1973—; adj. prof. St. Peter's Coll., Jersey City. Mem. Nat. Soc. Fund Raising Execs., CORPUS. Club: K.C. Co-author teaching manuals. Home: 34 7th St North Arlington NJ 07032 Office: 150 Amsterdam Ave New York NY 10023

SCHARFFENBERGER, GEORGE THOMAS, diversified industry exec.; b. Hollis, N.Y., May 22, 1919; s. George L. and Martha L. (Watson) S.; B.S., Columbia U., 1940; m. Marion Agnes Nelson, July 17, 1948; children—Ann Marie, George Thomas, John Edward, Thomas James, James Nelson, Joan Ellen. With Arthur Andersen & Co., 1940-43; with ITT subs.'s and divs., 1943-59, successively gen. auditor, asst. comptroller, comptroller, asst. to pres., 1943-53, v.p., 1953-55; pres. Kellogg Switchboard & Supply Co. (div.), Chgo., 1955-59, also dir.; pres., dir. Westrex Corp.; v.p. Litton Industries, Inc., 1959-62, sr. v.p., 1962-66, now dir.; exec. v.p. Litton Systems, Inc., 1961-66; chmn., pres., dir. City Investing Co., N.Y.C., 1966—, chief exec. officer, 1966—; dir. Litton Industries, IC Industries, Earle M. Jorgensen Co. Trustee U. So. Calif. Served with AUS, World War II. Mem. Financial Execs. Inst., Met. Mus. Art, Assn. Alumni Columbia Coll. Home: 4 Appaloosa Ln Rolling Hills CA 90274 Office: 767 Fifth Ave New York City NY 10022 also 9100 Wilshire Blvd Beverly Hills CA 90212

SCHARFFENBERGER, WILLIAM J., indsl. co. exec.; b. 1921. Chmn. bd., chief exec. officer Raxham Corp., 1972-74; pres., chief exec. officer Duplan Corp., 1974-77; sr. v.p., chief fin. officer Avnet Inc., 1977-79; pres., dir. Penn-Dixie Industries Inc., N.Y.C., 1979—, also chief exec. officer. Office: 1345 Ave of Americas New York NY 10019*

SCHARWEY, WALDEMAR FRIEDRICH, TV retail exec.; b. Kolberg, Germany, July 21, 1939; immigrated to Can., 1960; s. Waldemar Heinrich and Anneliese (Barzen) S.; B.A., Meml. U. Nfld., 1970. Pres., mng. dir. West End TV Ltd., St. John's, Nfld., 1971—; sec. Martha's Co. Ltd., St. John's, 1977—. Mem. St. John's Bd. of Trade. Office: 3 Blackmarsh Rd St John's NF A1E 3Y3 Canada

SCHATTMAN, HERBERT A., factoring exec.; b. N.Y.C., May 10, 1922; s. Samuel C. and Helen (Peters) S.; B.B.A., N.Y. U., 1948; m. Edna M. Klein, Sept. 15, 1946; children—Nancy Ellen, Richard. With United Factors/Crocker United Factors Co., N.Y.C., 1939-79, sr. v.p., 1970-77, exec. v.p., 1977-79; pres. CBT Factors Corp., N.Y.C., 1979—; pres., dir. Toppers Co. Served with U.S. Army, 1943-46. Mem. Credit and Fin. Mgmt. Assn. (v.p.) Republican. Clubs: Princeton (N.Y.C.); Lone Star Boat, 475. Contbr. articles to profl. jours. Office: 1040 Ave of Americas New York NY 10018

SCHATTNER, ROBERT LEOPOLD, med. supply co. exec.; b. Bklyn., July 17, 1938; s. Louis Lawrence and Rose (Weiss) S.; B.B.A., William and Mary Coll., 1962. Nat. sales mgr. Haemo Sol, Inc., Balt., 1966; founder, pres. Schattner Assos., Inc., Balt., 1966-78; pres. Omnimed, Inc., Maple Shade, N.J., 1978—; partner J.W. Roberts, 1979—. Served with U.S. Army, 1960. Recipient Outstanding Exhibit award Md.-D.C.-Del.-Va. Hosp. Assn., 1972-73; Outstanding Sales and Service award Carstens Health Industries, 1972. Mem. Health Industries Reps. Assn. (founder, pres. 1973; Appreciation award 1973), Am. Soc. Hosp. Pharmacists, Packaging Inst. U.S.A., Mfrs. Agts. Nat. Assn., Nat. I.V. Therapy Assn., N.J. Soc. Hosp. Pharmacy, Am. Surg. Trade Found. (appreciation award 1978), Alpha Kappa Psi. Democrat. Club: N.J. Athletic. Co-inventor I.V. securing device, 1976, chart holder closure, 1976, patient ID Band, 1976. Office: Pine Ave Maple Shade NJ 08052

SCHATZBERG, PAUL LEON, chem. co. exec.; b. N.Y.C., July 16, 1936; B.S. in Acctg., Rider Coll., 1960; M.B.A. in Mgmt., Seton Hall U., 1971. Acctg. mgr. Johnson & Johnson Co., New Brunswick, N.J., 1962-65; regional controller Tenneco, Inc., Garfield, N.J., 1965-68; controller Pantasote Inc., Greenwich, Conn., 1968-73, v.p. fin., 1973-79, exec. v.p., 1979—. Served with U.S. Army, 1954-56. Mem. Am. Mgmt. Assn., Fin. Execs. Inst. Office: PO Box 1800 Greenwich CT 06830

SCHATZMAN, MARVIN JOSEPH, steel co. exec.; b. St. Louis, Feb. 18, 1927; s. Louis and Rose (Babchuck) S.; B.A., St. Louis U., 1949; m. Carol Mary Schroeer, Apr. 15, 1950; children—Caron, Susan, Christopher, Mary, Andrew. Profl. basketball player, 1949-50; exec. v.p. sales Valley Steel Products Co., St. Louis, 1950-62; chmn. bd., pres., chief exec. officer Mid Am. Metals Inc., St. Louis, 1962—; dir., mem. exec. bd. Merc. - Lewis and Clark Bank, St. Louis. Pres. lay bd. DeSmet Jesuit High Sch., also trustee, past div. dir. United Fund, Heart Fund. Served with AUS, 1944-45. Republican. Roman Catholic. Clubs: Media, Greenbriar Hills Country, Goaltenders, Mo. Athletic, Univ., St. Louis, Stadium. Home: 226 Bellington Ln St Louis MO 63141 Office: 4199 Chippewa St St Louis MO 63116

SCHAUB, BENTON HALL, electronics industry exec.; b. Vevay, Ind., Sept. 19, 1917; s. J. Benton and Mary (Hall) S.; B.S., Ill. Wesleyan U., 1939; postgrad. U. Chgo., 1939-41; m. Rosemary duVall Sands, June 7, 1941; children—Benton Hall, Mary duBois. Research physicst Continental Can Co., Chgo., 1939-42; br. engr. Bur. of Ordnance, Navy Dept., Washington, 1945-54; dep. dir. Office of Electronic Research & Engring., Office of Sec. Def., Washington, 1946-49; pres. Kelvin Hughes Am. Corp., Annapolis, Md., 1959-69; v.p. Amecom div. Litton Industries, College Park, Md., 1969-71; pres. Electromech. div. Airtronics, Inc., Washington, 1971-72; v.p. planning and research Vitro Labs., 1972—. Served to lt. USNR, 1942-45. Mem. IEEE (sr.), Am. Ordnance Assn. Episcopalian (sr. warden). Clubs: Indian Landing Boat (past pres.) (Millersville, Md.); Annapolitan, Annapolis Yacht (Annapolis, Md.). Patentee in field. Home: Artois PO Box 28 Gambrills MD 21054 Office: Vitro Labs 14000 Georgia Ave Silver Spring MD 20910

SCHAUER, THOMAS ALFRED, ins. co. exec.; b. Canton, Ohio, Dec. 24, 1927; s. Alfred T. and Marie A. (Luthi) S.; B.Sc., Ohio State U., 1950; m. Joanne Alice Fay, Oct. 30, 1954; children—Alan, David, Susan, William. Ins. agt., Canton, 1951—; with Schauer & Reed Agy., 1951—, Kitzmiller, Tudor & Schauer, 1957—, Webb-Broda & Co., 1971—, Foglesong Agy., 1972—; pres. Ind. Ins. Service Corp. Akron and Canton, Canton, 1964—, Laurenson Agy., 1978—, Wells-Williams, 1978—; dir. Central Trust Co. NE Ohio (N.A.). Chmn., Joint Hosp. Blood Com., 1974; bd. dirs. Better Bus. Bur., Canton, 1970—, chmn., 1979-80; bd. dirs. Dist. YMCA, 1974, v.p., 1975—; bd. dirs. Hosp. Bur. Central Stark City, 1972-78, Aultman Hosp., 1971—, JMS Found., 1968—; bd. dirs. United Way, 1974—, pres., 1976-78; mem. distbn. com. Stark County Found., 1977—; adv. bd. Malone Coll., 1979—; trustee Kent State U., 1980—. Served with USNR, 1946-48. C.L.U., C.P.C.U. Mem. Chartered Ins. Inst. London, Nat. Assn. Mfg., Am. Soc. C.P.C.U.'s, Am. Soc. C.L.U.'s, Am. Mgmt. Assn., Assn. Advanced Life Underwriters, Am. Risk and Ins. Assn., Am. Soc. Pension Actuaries. Clubs: Canton, Brookside Country, Atwood Yacht. Home: 3755 Eaton Dr NW Canton OH 44708 Office: 100 Cleve-Tusc Bldg Canton OH 44702

SCHECHTER, EDWARD R., wholesale grocer; b. Russia, May 14, 1911; came to U.S., 1923, naturalized, 1928; s. Rubin and Pearl (Mintz) S.; student U. Ill.; widower; children—Beverly Schechter Alpern, Howard, Larry. With Southtown Wholesale Grocers, Chgo., 1933—, pres., 1955—, chmn. bd., 1976—; chmn. bd. Wayco Woods Inc., Elk Grove Village, Ill., 1976—; dir. Steel City Nat. Bank. Named Man of Year, City of Hope, 1964. Mem. Ill. Wholesale Grocers Assn. (pres. 1970), Chgo. Wholesale Grocers Assn. (dir.). Jewish. Club: B'nai B'rith. Home: 3505 Lakeview Dr Hazelcrest IL 60429 Office: 929 E 103d St Chicago IL 60628

SCHEDLER, SPENCER JAIME, packaging co. exec.; b. Manila, Philippines, Oct. 23, 1933; s. Edmund W. and Ruth (Spencer) S.; B.S., U. Tulsa, 1955; M.B.A., Harvard, 1962; m. Judy Hamilton, Aug. 30, 1969; children—Ryan Edmund, Spencer Hamilton, Peter Joseph. Petroleum engr., Humble Oil & Refining Co., 1958-60; financial analyst Sinclair Oil Corp., Tulsa, 1963-65, asst. dir. budgets, N.Y.C., 1965-66, mgr. budgets and financial analysis for mfg. and mktg., 1966-67, corporate mgr. budget and analysis, 1968-69; asst. Sec. of Air Force, 1969-73; exec. v.p. Hycel Inc., Houston, 1973-74; gen. mgr., asst. to vice chmn. finance and adminstrn. Continental Can Co., Inc., N.Y.C., 1974-76; gen. mgr. corp. bus. devel. Continental Group, Inc., N.Y.C., 1977—; dir. Myers Group Inc. Served as pilot USAF, 1955-58. Club: Innis Arden Golf. Office: One Harbor Plaza Stamford CT 06902

SCHEER, ARTHUR LESSING, JR., corp. exec.; b. Bklyn., Sept. 10, 1941; s. Arthur Lessing and Gertrude Helen (Jarrach) S.; B.S. in Agr., Mich. State U., 1963; student Pensacola Jr. Coll., 1968-69, Franklin & Marshall Coll., 1972-74; m. Eugenia Pauline Chehansky, Aug. 22, 1964; children—Christine Joy, James Mark, Danielle Stephanie. Material mgr. Redmen Industries, Ephrata, Pa., 1970-74; staff material mgr. Bendix Home Systems, Atlanta, 1974-77, Riverside, Calif., 1977-78; dir. purchasing Wick Bldg. Systems, Arlington, Tex., 1979—. Asst. coach Northside YMCA youth soccer program, 1975-77; mem. Roswell (Ga.) City Fire Com., 1976-77; mem. fin. com. Most Blessed Sacrament Ch., Arlington; counselor, troop leader Longhorn council Boy Scouts Am. Served to capt. USMCR, 1963-69. Decorated Air medal (9), Vietnam Gallantry medal with palm, Vietnam Campaign Ribbon, Vietnam Service Ribbon, Nat. Def. Ribbon, various unit citations. Mem. Marine Corps Res. Officers Assn., Res. Officers Assn., Nat. Forestry Assn., Mich. State U. Alumni Assn. Roman Catholic. Home: 919 Curtis Dr Arlington TX 76012 Office: 1202 Corporate Dr W Arlington TX 76011

SCHEER, MORTON H(ERBERT), mgmt. co. exec.; b. N.Y.C., Feb. 2, 1935; s. Nathan Victor and Gertrude (Koenig) S.; B.S. in Acctg., N.Y. U., 1957; m. Joan S. Weiss, Apr. 12, 1959; children—Amy Deborah, Mark Jeffrey, Neil Nathan. Treas., Allied Concord Fin. Corp., N.Y.C., 1962-64; v.p. Mercantile Fin. Corp., N.Y.C., 1964-66; mgr. comml. financing Gen. Electric Credit Corp., Stamford, Conn., 1966-69; pres., chief exec. officer Service Resources Corp., N.Y.C., 1969—. Served with U.S. Army, 1957-63. Mem. Am. Mgmt. Assn. Republican. Jewish. Club: N.Y. U. Office: 2 Pennsylvania Plaza New York NY 10001

SCHEFTNER, GEROLD, dental equipment mfg. co. exec.; b. Milw., June 1, 1937; s. Arthur Joseph and Alice Agnes (Gregory) S.; student Milw. Bus. Inst., 1953, Great Lakes Naval Acad. Sch. Dental-Med. Surgery, USAF, 1955-56, USAF Inst., 1959, Marquette U., 1959-60; m. Irene; children—Marc A., Margaret L., Mark A., Mary L., Scot P., Michael D. Territorial rep. Mossey-Otto Co., dental retailers, Milw., 1960-63; with Den-Tal-Ez Mfg. Co., dental equipment mfg., Des Moines, 1963—, dir. fgn. affairs, 1969-71, dir. far eastern affairs, 1971-72, exec. dir. internat. sales, mktg., 1973-74, v.p., gen. mgr. internat. ops., 1974—, also dir.; dir. Dentalez (Gt. Britain) Ltd., 1974—; pres. Meridian Corp., Des Moines; mng. dir. Seven Seas Ltd., Bienne, Switzerland; adv./cons. dental div. Gen. Electric Med. Systems, Milw. Mem. Iowa Regional Export Expansion Council, Des Moines, 1969-73; mem. Lake Panorama (Ia.) Devel. Assn., 1972-73; chmn. World Trade Council; dir. U.S. Dept. Commerce Export Council. Mem. advt. bd. St. Charles Boys Home Bldg. Program, Milw., 1963. Served with USAF, 1955-59. Recipient presdl. mgr. of the year award Den-Tal-Ez Co., 1967; Lecture award Faculdade de Odontologia, U. Ribeiro Preto, Brazil, 1974. Mem. Am. Dental Trade Assn., Am. Dental Mfrs. Assn., Greater Des Moines C. of C. (dir.), hon. mem. Hong Kong Dental Trade Assn., Internat. Platform Assn. Republican. Lion. Clubs: TWA Ambassador; International (Frankfurt, Geramny); Iowa World Trade. Research in develop. equipment and apparatus for roentgen dentistry and odontological therapy. Office: Schilfweg 4 2503 Biel/Bienne Switzerland

SCHEIBLE, WILLIAM GUTHRIE, data communications cons.; b. Dayton, Ohio, Feb. 20, 1949; s. Wilbur Roy and Bernice (Myers) S.; B.B.A., Eastern N.Mex. U., 1973; m. Jill Mabe. Sr. analyst Tymshare, Inc., Cupertino, Calif., 1973-78; mgr. network operating systems Tymnet, Inc., Cupertino, 1979; sr. telecommunications cons. Bank of Am., San Francisco, 1979-80; mgr. telecommunications Tymshare Transaction Services, Fremont, Calif., 1980—; instr. Golden Gate U. Mem. Assn. Computing Machinery, Sports Car Club Am., Internat. Motor Sports Assn., Sigma Chi. Republican. Presbyterian. Office: 39100 Liberty Ave Fremont CA 94538

SCHEIBNER, PAUL EDWARD, stock broker; b. Parsons, Kans., Apr. 22, 1917; s. Albert Martin and Ruth (Dearing) S.; student U. N.Mex., 1937-38, Brigham Young U., 1939-40, N.Y. Inst. Finance, 1960; m. Irene Mary Harris, Apr. 1967; children—Paul B., Thomas P. Vice pres. Roberts, Scott & Co., Inc., Palm Springs, Calif., 1966-74, Bateman, Eichler, Hill, Richards, Palm Springs, 1974-75, E.F. Hutton & Co., Palm Springs, 1975—; allied mem. N.Y. Stock Exchange, 1972—; pres. Normandy Mktg. Systems, Ltd., 1978—; fin. mgmt. advisor; contbg. econ. columnist Sand to Sea Publs., Palm Desert, Calif.; cons., lectr. Consumer Conflict in Am. Vice pres., treas., trustee George Randolph Hearst Found.; mem. Com. of 25, Palm Springs. Served with USMCR, 1941-45. Recipient Sales and Marketing Execs. Assn. award, Los Angeles, 1965. Club: Seven Lakes Country (Palm Springs). Home: 1421 N Sunrise Way Villa 37 Palm Springs CA 92262

SCHEID, RANDOLPH LEE, accountant; b. Oakland, Calif., July 4, 1947; s. Leadas Orie and Helen Freida (Befus) S.; B.S., Calif. State U., 1973; A.A., Chabot Coll., 1971; m. Margaret Bennett, Aug. 14, 1971; children—Angela, Danielle. Audit sr. Arthur Young & Co., Oakland, 1973-76; asst. controller Jacuzzi Whirelpool Bath, Inc., Walnut Creek, Calif., 1976-77; owner Randolph L. Scheid, C.P.A. and Randolph L. Scheid, Builder, San Lorenzo, Calif., 1977-79; sr. partner Scheid & Atkinson, C.P.A.'s, Castro Valley, Calif., 1979—; acctg. instr. Chabot Jr. Coll., Hayward, Calif., cons. in field. Served with USN, 1965-69. C.P.A., Calif. Mem. Am. Inst. C.P.A.'s, Calif. Soc. C.P.A.'s, (mem. real estate devel. and contractors com.). Republican. Office: 21646 Redwood Rd Suite B Castro Valley CA 94546

SCHEIHING, GLENN PAUL, mfg. co. exec.; b. Riverdale, Nebr., Aug. 14, 1921; s. Gustav August and Johanna (Tatem) S.; student Nebr. State Coll., 1940-41; m. Frances Mecklenburg, Jan. 6, 1945; children—Carolynn Scheihing McCarthy, Daniel. With Miracle Gas Co., Billings, Mont., 1946-64, pres., 1961-64; dist. mgr. Tuloma Gas Products Co., Billings, 1965-69; chmn. bd., pres. Polar Industries, Inc., Billings, 1969—; dir. Centura Energy Corp. Mem. Midland Empire State Fair Bd., 1964-75, pres., 1968; mem. Yellowstone County Metra Bd., 1975—, pres., 1979—. Served with inf. U.S. Army, 1941-45. Mem. Nat. LP Gas Assn. (state dir. 1956-67), Am. Legion. Republican. Congregationalist. Clubs: Yellowstone Country, Masons, Shriners. Home: 2807 Lyndale Ln Billings MT 59102 Office: 1347 Grand Ave Billings MT 59102

SCHEINMAN, STANLEY BRUCE, diversified co. exec.; b. N.Y.C., Nov. 13, 1933; s. Samuel and Sadie (Seiffer) S.; A.B., Cornell U., 1954; M.B.A., CCNY, 1957; J.D. (Harlan Fiske Stone scholar), Columbia U., 1960; m. Janet L. Donnelly, Dec. 30, 1975; children—Catherine, Anthony. Admitted to N.Y. bar, 1960; asso. firm Cravath, Swaine & Moore, N.Y.C., 1960-62; fgn. aid adminstrv. officer Dept. of State, 1962-63; successively corp. counsel, v.p. fin. and adminstrn. service industries div., internat. gen. counsel Pepsico, Inc., 1964-69; v.p. fin. and adminstrn. U.S.V. Pharm. div. Revlon, Inc., 1970-72; sr. v.p. MCI Communications Corp., 1972-75; pres., chief operating officer, dir. FSC Corp., Pitts., 1976—. Mem. Bar Assn. City N.Y., Fin. Execs. Inst., Internat. Execs. Assn., Am. Bar Assn. Club: Paris-Am. Home: Undermountain Rd Salisbury CT 06068 Office: 1000 RIDC Plaza Pittsburgh PA 15238

SCHELLENGER, JAMES KNOX POLK, investment co. exec.; b. Cape May, N.J., Sept. 14, 1919; s. Henry E. and Edythe (Dellett) S.; B.S. in Econs., U. Pa., 1941, J.D., 1947; m. Ann H. Fussell, Dec. 11, 1948; children—Suzanne F. (Mrs. James G. Williamson), James Knox Polk III, Elizabeth Dellett, Henry Ewen, Georgeann Dock. Admitted to Pa. bar, 1948; practice in Phila., 1948-53; with Delaware Fund, Inc., Phila., 1954—, exec. v.p., 1965-71, pres., 1971-76, chmn. bd., 1977—, also dir.; with Decatur Income Fund, Inc., Phila., 1956—, exec. v.p., 1965-71, pres., 1971-76, chmn. bd., 1977—, also dir.; with Del. Mgmt. Co., Inc., Phila., 1955—, exec. v.p., 1965-71, pres., 1971-76, also dir.; exec. v.p. Delta Trend Fund, Inc., Phila., 1968-71, pres., 1971-76, chmn. bd., 1977—, also dir.; exec. v.p., dir. Delchester Bond Fund, Inc., 1970-71, pres., 1971-76, chmn. bd., 1977—, also dir.; chmn. bd. Del. Investment Advisors, Inc., 1975—; chmn. bd., dir. DMC Tax-Free Income Trust, Pa., 1977—; chmn. bd., dir. Del. Cash Res., 1978—. Trustee, Presbyn.-U. Pa. Med. Center. Served to lt. USNR, 1942-46. Mem. Am., Phila. bar assns., Phila. Financial Analysts Club, U. Pa. Alumni Assn., Navy League, Investment Co. Inst., Nat. Assn. Security Dealers. Clubs: Lawyers, Racquet (Phila.); Varsity (U. Pa.); Waynesboro Country (Paoli, Pa.). Home: 421 Timber Ln Devon PA 19333 Office: 7 Penn Center Plaza Philadelphia PA 19103

SCHELM, ROGER LEONARD, data processing exec.; b. Kingston, N.Y., July 29, 1936; s. Frederick G. and Elizabeth M. (Wojciehowski) S.; B.A. in Polit. Sci., Western Md. Coll., 1958; M.A. in Public Adminstrn., Am. U., 1970; postgrad. U. Md. Law Sch., 1960-62; m. Gloria Mae Dutterer, June 13, 1958; children—Sandra Lee, Theresa Jean, Ginger Lisa. Analytic equipment programmer Nat. Security Agy., Ft. Meade, Md., 1958-60; computer cons. various cons. firms in Balt., Washington area, 1960-68; mgr. Army plans and programs Informatics, Inc., Bethesda, Md., 1968; mgr. def. programs Automation Tech., Inc., Wheaton, Md., 1968-69; dir. advanced planning Genasys Corp., Washington, 1969-71; mgr. info. systems Ins. Co. N.Am., Phila., 1971-72, sect. mgr. computing ops., 1972-74; mgr. tech. services INA Corp., Phila., 1974-75, mgr. spl. tech. projects, 1975-76, asst. dir. tech. services, 1977, asst. dir. spl. tech. projects, 1977-78, asst. dir. adminstrn., 1978-79, asst. dir. resource mgmt., data center design, contingency planning, 1979—; mem. adj. faculty Camden (N.J.) Coll., 1978—; mem. Camden County (N.J.) Coll. Electronic Data Processing Adv. Com., 1980—. Served to capt.

U.S. Army, 1959. Mem. Computer Security Inst. Home: 506 Balsam Rd Cherry Hill NJ 08003 Office: 1600 Arch St Philadelphia PA 19101

SCHEMBERGER, RUTH MARIE, banker; b. Regent, N.D., Nov. 3, 1919; d. John Henry and Fredericka Julianna (Pertner) Monke; grad. high sch.; m. Phillip Schemberger, Dec. 14, 1940; 1 dau., Dianne (Mrs. James Peter Andrew Beneteau). With Citizens State Bank New England (N.D.), 1960—, asst. cashier, 1969—, security officer, 1970-73. Treas. New England Pub. Sch. Dist. 9, 1971-73. Lutheran. Home: New England ND 58647

SCHENCK, ARTHUR CARL, constrn. mgr., cons. engr.; b. Phila., July 31, 1910; s. Rev. Dr. A. Clarence and Hattie Olive (Ritter) S.; B.S., U. Ala., 1934; m. Eloise Elena Williams, July 6, 1934; children—Nancy Elizabeth (Mrs. Robert Edward Smith), Jean Gray (Mrs. Richard G. Rice). Field, resident engr. Stone & Webster Engring. Corp., 1934, 1936-42; insp. U.S. C.E., Phila., 1935-36; v.p. Carpenter Constrn. Co., Inc., Norfolk, Va., 1942-63; prin. A. Carl Schenck and Assos., constrn. mgmt. and engring. cons., Norfolk, 1963—. Mem. Bd. Review Real Estate Assessments; past chmn. lay adv. bd. DePaul Hosp.; adv. council Norfolk Area Med. Center Authority; mem. pub. relations and grad. sch. med. coms. Eastern Va. Med. Authority; mem. Citizens Adv. Com., Norfolk, 1964-65; mem. Va. Airports Authority; bd. dirs. Norfolk-Portsmouth Builders, Contractors Exchange, 1960-63; mem. adv. bd. Tidewater council Boy Scouts Am.; mem. engring. com. Devel. Council, U. Ala., 1958-62; mem. Fire Prevention Adv. Com., Norfolk. Mem. Nat., Va. (past pres.) socs. profl. engrs., Asso. Gen. Contractors Am. (hon. mem., pres. Va. br. 1962), Am. Arbitration Assn. (nat. panel mem.), Tau Beta Pi, Theta Tau, Chi Beta Phi. Lutheran (mem. council 1950—). Clubs: Engineers of Hampton Roads (pres. 1953-54); Kiwanis (pres. 1966) Virginia (Norfolk); Cedar Point Country. Home: 5601 Huntington Pl Norfolk VA 23509 Office: PO Box 7097 Norfolk VA 23509

SCHENDEL, WINFRIED GEORGE, ins. co. exec.; b. Harpstedt, Germany, June 19, 1931; s. Willi Rudolf Max and Anna Margarete (Sassen) S.; came to U.S., 1952, naturalized, 1956; B.S. in Elec. and Indsl. Engring., Hannover-Stadthagen U., Hannover, W. Ger., 1952; m. Joanne Wiiest, Aug. 24, 1953; children—Victor Winfried, Bruce Lawrence, Rachelle Laureen. Elec. draftsman Houston Lighting & Power Co., 1954-57; elec. draftsman, corrosion technician Transcontinental Gas Pipeline Co., Houston, 1957-59; elec. engr. Ken R. White Cons. Engrs., Danver, 1959-61; sales engr. Weco div. Food Machinery & Chem. Corp., various locations, 1961-64; ins. field underwriter N.Y. Life Ins. Co., Denver, 1964-66, asst. mgr., 1966-70, mgmt. asst., 1970-71, gen. mgr., 1971-77, mgr. 1979—; ind. gen. agt., Denver, 1978—. Instl. rep., advancement chmn. Denver Area council Boy scouts Am., Lakewood, Colo., 1968-72; precinct chmn. Republican Party, Jefferson County, Colo., 1976, 78. Recipient Centurion award, 1966; Northwestern Region Leader Manpower Devel. award N.Y. Life Ins. Co., 1968. Mem. Nat. Assn. Life Underwriters, Colo. Assn. Life Underwriters, Gen. Agents and Mgrs. Assn. (recipient Conf. Nat. Mgmt. award 1975), Lakewood C. of C. (pres. people-to-people). Presbyterian (elder). Clubs; Lions, Edelweiss, Internat. Order Rocky Mt. Goats, Masons, Shriners. Home: 13802 W 20th Pl Golden CO 80401 Office: 1385 S Colorado Blvd Suite 704 Denver CO 80222

SCHENK, BOYD FREDERICK, food co. exec.; b. Providence, Utah, July 23, 1922; s. Frederick Lyman and Mabel (Reddish) S.; student U. Utah, 1942, U. Idaho, 1940-43, also exec. program, Columbia U., 1961; m. June Verlee Hansen, Aug. 21, 1942; children—Sandra Lee, Greg F., Brent J., Julie, Peggy. With Pet, Inc., 1947—, pres. frozen foods div., 1963-65, corp. v.p., 1964—, corp. group v.p. 1965—, exec. v.p. ops., 1968—, pres., chief exec. officer, 1969—, chmn. exec. com., 1969-75, chmn. bd., 1975—; dir. 1st Nat. Bank St. Louis, Laclede Gas Co., St. Louis, Ill. Power Co., A.E. Staley Mfg. Co., Decatur, Ill., IC Industries, Inc., Chgo. Mem. exec. bd. St. Louis area council Boy Scouts Am.; mem. Civic Progress, St. Louis; mem. Mo. Cancer Research Center Devel. Council; mem. vis. com. Washington U., St. Louis; bd. assos. Gettysburg (Pa.) Coll. Served with inf. AUS, World War II. Office: PO Box 392 Pet Plaza 400 S 4th St Saint Louis MO 63166

SCHENK, PETER JOSEPH, former telecommunications co. exec.; b. Vienna, Austria, Aug. 10, 1920; s. Joseph and Ilse (Petersen) von Schenk; came to U.S., 1932, naturalized, 1937; A.B. in Physics, Lafayette Coll., 1941; Sc.D. (hon.), Coll. Advanced Sci., Canaan, N.H., 1961; m. Norma B. Otis, Mar. 28, 1941 (div. 1960); children—Peter Joseph, Steven George and Robert Henry (twins); m. 2d, Hazel Regina Holmes, Apr. 8, 1961; 1 dau., Andrea Mary. Instr. physics Lafayette Coll., 1941; product planning mgr. mil. electronic equipment Gen. Electric Co., 1954-55, marketing mgr. def. electronic equipment, 1955-58; asst. to pres. Raytheon Co., 1958-60; exec. v.p. Mitre Corp., 1960-62; mng. partner Peter J. Schenk & Co., Arlington, Va., 1962-64; v.p. govt. communications system dept. Western Union Telegraph Co., 1964-69, v.p. fed. operations, 1969-71, group v.p. pub. services, 1971-73; pres., dir. Telcom, Inc., Vienna, Va., 1973-76, chmn., 1976-78; partner P.J. Schenk & Co., 1978—. Cons. electronics panel Air Force Sci. Adv. Bd., 1956-62. Mem. mil. sci. vis. com. Harvard Coll., 1960-64; mem. Nat. council Boy Scouts Am., 1967—. Trustee Aerospace Edn. Found., 1960—, Coll. Advanced Sci., 1960-63, Air Force Hist. Found., 1959-63, Air Force Acad. Found., 1958-62. Served to lt. col. AUS, USAF, 1941-54; col. Res. Recipient USAF Exceptional Service medal. Sr. mem. I.E.E.E.; mem. Armed Forces Communications and Electronics Assn. (pres. Washington 1962-64), Air Force Assn. (nat. pres. 1957-59, nat. dir. 1955-57, 60). Home: Box 84A Route 1 Jericho VT 05465

SCHENOT, ROBERT DEAN, cons.; b. N.Y.C., May 23, 1949; s. Malcolm Robert and Almeda Elizabeth (Landenslayer) S.; B.A., Hartwick Coll., 1971; M.B.A., U. N.H., 1978. Various positions Boy Scouts Am., N.Y.C., 1971-74, Cape Cod, Mass., 1974-75; programmer, analyst, lead programmer, database designer, project mgr., cons. Computer Applications Support & Devel. Office, Portsmouth, N.H., 1975-79; project leader, cons. Arthur Young & Co., Boston, 1979-80; cons. Corp. Tech. Planning, Portsmouth, 1980—; instr. N.H. Coll., Portsmouth, 1978-79, U. N.H., Durham, 1979-80. Mem. Data Processing Mgmt. Assn., Assn. Computing Machinery, Mensa. Club: Touring of New Eng. Home: PO Box 402 239 Broad St Portsmouth NH 03801 Office: John Hart Mansion The Hill Portsmouth NH 03801

SCHERER, ROGER CLYDE, luminous ceilings co. exec.; b. Norristown, Pa., Apr. 7, 1942; s. Wayne R. and Grace M. (Geiger) S.; B.S., Calif. State Poly. U., Pomona, 1964; M. in Vocat. Edn., Calif. State U., 1975; postgrad. Pepperdine U., 1978—; m. Heather Lorraine Hamren, Nov. 11, 1966; children—Roger Scott, Traci Anne, Wayne Robert II. Br. bank ops. officer Security Pacific Nat. Bank, Riverside, Calif., 1964-66; dept. mgr. Sears Roebuck & Co., Pomona, Calif., 1966-69; production supr. Dolco Packaging Corp., Pico Rivera, Calif., 1969-73, extrusion supt., 1976-78; tchr. Mount San Antonio Coll., Walnut, Calif., 1973-75, 77-78; instr. evening div. Los Angeles Trade Tech. Coll., 1975; asso. prof. indsl. mfg. engring. Calif. State Poly. U., Pomona, 1977—; pres. and gen. mgr. Scherer Enterprises-Suspended Ceiling Systems, Panama, Calif., 1978—; career guidance cons. Tulare (Calif.) County Orgn. for Vocat. Edn., 1975-76. Mem. sch. bd. Pomona Jr. Acad., 1974-75; participant Drive Campaign of United Fund, Pomona, 1967—; deacon Seventh-day Adventist Ch., Claremont, Calif., 1974—. Mem. Soc. of Plastics Engrs. (George Huisman Meml. award 1975), Soc. Mfg. Engrs., Phi Delta Kappa. Republican. Home: 616 E McKinley Ave Pomona CA 91767

SCHERICH, ERWIN THOMAS, engr.; b. Inland, Nebr., Dec. 6, 1918; s. Harry Erwin and Ella (Peterson) S.; student Hastings Coll., 1937-39, N.C. State Coll., 1943-44; B.S., U. Nebr., 1946-48; M.S., U. Colo., 1948-51; m. Jessie Mae Funk, Jan. 1, 1947; children—Janna Rae (Mrs. John R. Thornton), Jerilyn Mae (Mrs. Thomas D. Dobson), Mark Thomas. Civil engr. U.S. Water and Power Resources Service (formerly U.S. Bur. Reclamation), Engring. and Research Center, Denver, 1948—; designing engr. hydraulic structures, chief spillways and outlets sec., div. design, 1974-75, chief dams br. div. design, 1975-78, chief tech. rev. staff, 1978-79, chief tech. rev. div. Dept. Interior, Denver Fed. Center, 1980—. Mem. U.S. Com. on Large Dams. Served as staff sgt. AUS, 1941-45. Profl. engr., Colo., 1952. Mem. ASCE, Nat. Soc. Profl. Engrs. Republican. Methodist. Home: 3915 Balsam St Wheat Ridge CO 80033 Office: Denver Federal Center Denver CO 80225

SCHERLING, RICHARD EDWARD, dept. store exec.; b. Dubuque, Iowa, June 12, 1921; s. Gustav John and Florence (Keller) S.; B.A. in Letters and Bus. Adminstrn., U. Mich., 1942; m. Elizabeth Jeanne Bailie, June 6, 1942; children—Kathryn, Richard Edward, John. With Killian Co., Cedar Rapids, Iowa, 1946—, gen. mdse. mgr., 1950-54, exec. v.p., 1955-66, pres., 1966-71, chmn. bd., 1971-80, chmn. exec. com., 1980, now ret.; dir. Iowa Electric Light & Power, Perpetual Savs. & Loan. Pres., Linn County chpt. ARC, 1960; bd. dirs. St. Lukes Hosp.; trustee Coe Coll., chmn. bd., 1974-77. Served with USNR, 1942-45. Mem. Nat. Retail Mchts. Assn. (chmn. merchandising div. 1966-68), Cedar Rapids C. of C. (pres. 1963), Phi Delta Theta. Republican. Rotarian (pres. Cedar Rapids 1971). Club: Cedar Rapids Country. Home: 2041 Walnut Ct SE Cedar Rapids IA 52403

SCHEUER, RALPH H., lawyer, real estate exec.; b. Albuquerque, Feb. 23, 1946; s. Fritz E. and Doris (Kahn) S.; B.A., U. Colo., 1967; J.D., U. Va., 1970; m. Anne Surath, Mar. 21, 1971; children—Elyse, Stephanie. Admitted to N.M. bar, 1970; atty. firm Sommer Lawler & Scheuer, Santa Fe, 1970—, asso., 1970-72, shareholder, mng. dir., 1972—; organizer, sec. Kesmen Enterprises, Inc., Santa Fe, 1977—; organizer, mng. partner Nemsek Enterprises, Santa Fe, 1978—. Trustee Santa Fe Jewish Temple, 1970—; charter mem. bd. dirs. Orch. Santa Fe, 1976-78; trustee Santa Fe Prep. Sch., 1979—. Mem. Am., N.Mex. bar assns. Home: 1031 Governor Dempsey Dr Santa Fe NM 87501 Office: Sommer Lawler & Scheuer PO Box 1984 Santa Fe NM 87501

SCHEYE, KLAUS GUNTHER, engring. exec.; b. Berlin, Jan. 26, 1923; came to U.S., 1948, naturalized, 1950; s. Eric and Margaret (Simon) S.; B.Sc., Queens U., Ont., 1946; M.B.A., Columbia U., 1950; m. Renate Lachs, Sept. 12, 1948; children—Lilli Margaret, Eric Peter. With Coverdale & Colpitts, Cons. Engrs., 1951-55, W.R. Grace Co., 1955-59; product line mgr. ITT, 1959-66; corp. v.p. W.R. Grace Co., N.Y.C., 1966—; dir. Futter Lumber Co. Treas., bd. trustees Westchester Reform Temple, 1978—. Club: Princeton (N.Y.C.). Office: 1114 Ave of the Americas New York NY 10036

SCHIEFERDECKER, GEORGE PETER, fin. mgmt. co. exec.; b. Bloemendaal, The Netherlands, Feb. 18, 1925; came to U.S., 1958, naturalized, 1969; s. A.A. George and Aaltje (Hesselink) S.; cand. law U. Leiden, 1949; m. Jeannette F.N. van Kleffens, June 30, 1951; children—George, Adriaan, Richard, Janet. Mgr., Jonas & Kruseman, Amsterdam, Holland, 1951-58; sales staff 1st Boston Corp., N.Y.C., 1958-60; analyst Brown Bros., Harriman & Co., N.Y.C., 1960-67; sr. cons. Scudder, Stevens & Clark, N.Y.C., 1967-69; v.p., dir. F. Eberstadt & Co., Inc., N.Y.C., 1969-79, sr. v.p., dir. Eberstadt Asset Mgmt., 1979-81, pres., 1981—. Trustee, chmn. bd. 1st Congregational Ch., Old Greenwich, Conn. Mem. N.Y. Soc. Security Analysts. Republican. Clubs: Riverside Yacht, Downtown Assn. (N.Y.C.). Home: 15 Pilot Rock Ln Riverside CT 06878 Office: 61 Broadway New York NY 10006

SCHIELE, GEORGE WARREN, advt. co. exec.; b. Phila., Aug. 2, 1931; s. Paul Ellsworth and Emma Adele (Gilliam) S.; student Carson Long Inst., 1949; B.S., U. Pa., 1954; m. Joan Ann Burga, Nov. 18, 1961; children—Caroline A., Warren S.C., Erick P.G. Dir. pub. relations Triangle Stas., Phila., 1956-57; advt. mgr. Magness Corp., Wilmington, Del., 1958-59; nat. sales mgr. Broadcast Advertisers Reports, N.Y.C., 1959-61; pres. Broadcast Billing Corp., N.Y.C., 1961-63; gen. mgr. Mailbag Internat., Inc., Stamford, Conn., 1963-64, pres., 1965-80, dir., 1967-80; chmn. 13/21 Corp., Stamford, 1976—; dir. R.H. Carlson Inc., Greenwich, Conn., 1971-77; pres. G.W. Schiele Advt., Greenwich, 1978—; pub., editor-in-chief Once Mag., 1978-80. lectr. N.Y. U., City Coll. N.Y., Am. Mgmt. Assn., Am. Marketing Assn. Dir. Greenwich Transit Dist., 1975-80, Greenwich Community Concert Assn., 1977-79. Served with USAF, 1954-56. Clubs: Pinnacle (N.Y.C.); G.S.C. (Greenwich). Contbr. articles to profl. jours. Home: 19 Hill Rd Greenwich CT 06830 Office: 2777 Summer St Stamford CT 06905

SCHIERHOLZ, WILLIAM FRANCIS, JR., chem. co. exec.; b. St. Louis, Oct. 14, 1921; s. William Francis and Florence Cecelia (Wuensch) S.; B.S. in Engring. Adminstrn., Washington U., St. Louis, 1943; m. Joan Flavin, Sept. 7, 1947; children—Margaret Ann, John W., William F. III. Vice pres., gen. mgr. Fuel Oil of St. Louis, 1949-55; pres. Chemtech Industries, Inc., St. Louis, 1956—; dir. St. Louis Fed. Savs. & Loan Assn. Bd. dirs. Jr. Achievement, St. Louis, Mo. Transp. and Devel. Council; chmn. adv. bd. INROADS. Mo. Served to capt. USAF, 1943-46. Mem. U.S., Mo. (dir., exec. com.), chambers commerce, St. Louis Regional Commerce and Growth Assn. (dir., exec. com.), Am. Assn. Indsl. Mgmt. (pres. 1976), Mfg. Chemists Assn., NAM, Am. Mgmt. Assn. (presidents assn.), Chem. Council Greater St. Louis (pres. 1970), Backstoppers, Affiliated Chem. Group Ltd. (pres. 1966, 79), Beta Theta Pi (pres. alumni assn. 1967, Beta Honor Guest 1977). Clubs: Stadium, Univ., Mo. Athletic, Rotary Round Table, (1st v.p.) (St. Louis); Forest Hills. Home: 1151 Westmoor Pl St Louis MO 63131 Office: 9909 Clayton Rd St Louis MO 63124

SCHIFF, HERBERT HAROLD, shoe co. exec.; b. Columbus, Ohio, Oct. 6, 1916; s. Robert W. and Rebecca (Lurie) S.; grad. Peddie Sch., 1934; B.B.S., U. Pa., 1938; m. Betty Topkis, June 19, 1938; children—Suzanne (Mrs. Murray Gallant), Patricia (Mrs. Richard Hershorin), Jane Ann (Mrs. Douglas J. Fleckner). With SCOA Industries Inc. (formerly Shoe Corp. Am.), Columbus, 1938—, exec. v.p., 1962-65, pres., 1965-68, chmn. bd., chief exec. officer, 1968—, dir., 1955—; dir. Ohio Nat. Bank, Columbus. Mem. exec., adminstrv. coms., bd. dirs. Am. Jewish Joint Distbn. Com.; mem. cabinet United Jewish Appeal; mem. nat. exec. council Am. Jewish Com.; bd dirs. Jewish Center, Heritage House, Hillel Found. Ohio State U., United HIAS, Council Jewish Fedns. and Welfare Funds (vice chmn. legacy and endowment fund com.); bd. dirs., exec. coms., resources devel. com. Am. Jewish Joint Distbn. Com.; trustee, past pres. United Jewish Fund and Council; trustee United Jewish Appeal, United Israel Appeal; fellow, mem. exec. com. Brandeis U.; mem. nat. exec. bd. Am. Jewish Com.; mem. GSA community adv. council for Capital U.; trustee Peddie Sch. Recipient Spirit of Life award City of Hope, 1977; Milton Weill Human Relations award Am. Jewish Com., 1979; Patriots award U.S. Savs. Bonds, 1979; medal Prime Minister of Israel, 1979. Mem. Fgn. Policy Assn. (nat. council), Newcomen Soc. N. Am., Vol. Footwear Retailers Assn. (active hon. dir.), Nat. Footwear Mfg. Assn. (past dir.), Am. Footwear Industries Assn. (dir.), Nat. Retail Mchts. (past dir.), Ohio Retail Mchts. (dir.), Am. Retail Fedn. (dir., vice chmn., mem. exec. com.). Mem. B'nai B'rith. Clubs: Athletic, Winding Hollow Country (Columbus); Standard (Chgo.); Presidents (Ohio State U.); Longboat Key Golf, University (Sarasota, Fla.). Home: 1620 E Broad St Columbus OH 43203 Office: BancOhio Plaza 155 E Broad St Columbus OH 43215

SCHIFF, JOHN JEFFERSON, fin. corp. exec.; b. Cin., Apr. 19, 1916; s. John Jefferson and Marguerite (Cleveland) S.; B.Sc. in Commerce, Ohio State U., 1938; m. Mary Reid, July 26, 1941; children—John Jefferson, Suzanne, Thomas R. Vice chmn. Cin. Ins. Co., 1979—; pres. Cin. Fin. Corp., 1979—; chmn. bd. Inter-Ocean Ins. co., Cin., 1979—; dir. Fifth Third Bancorp. Vice pres. Deaconess Hosp. of Cin., Griffith Found. for Ins. Edn.; trustee Cin. Art Mus. Served to lt. comdr. Supply Corps, USNR, 1942-46. Named Ins. Man of Year in Cin., Cin. Ins. Bd., 1977. Mem. Cin. C. of C. (v.p. 1972). Republican. Methodist. Clubs: Queen City, Western Hills Country. Home: 1926 Beech Grove Dr Cincinnati OH 45238 Office: PO Box 14567 Cincinnati OH 45214

SCHIFF, MILTON A., ins. co. exec.; b. N.Y.C., Feb. 2, 1912; s. David and Rachael (Eisenstadt) S.: m. Adele Berman, Feb. 21, 1934; children—Patricia Estess, Abbey Achs. Exec. v.p. Internat. Life of N.Y., 1960-62; chmn., pres. Madison Life and Asso. Madison Cos., 1962-79; vice chmn. Am. Gen. Life Ins. Co. of N.Y., N.Y.C., 1979—, also dir.; dir. No. Ins. Co. of N.Y., Assurance Co. Am. Mem. Am. Council Life Ins., Life Ins. Cos. of N.Y. Home: 5 Lake Rd Great Neck NY 11020 Office: 845 3d Ave New York NY 10022

SCHIFFER, SPENCER FRANKLIN, mfg. co. exec.; b. N.Y.C., Jan. 30, 1946; s. Gerald and Mae (Itzkowitz) S.; B.S. in Econs., U. Pa., 1967; J.D., St. John's U., 1971; m. Constance Wiener, June 20, 1967; children—Jennifer, Kelly. Admitted to Colo. bar, 1972, N.Y. bar, 1976; partner firm Ware, Unruh & Schiffer, Aspen, Colo., 1971-73, Schiffer & Garfield, Aspen, 1973-75; exec. v.p., chief exec. officer, dir. Eric Scot Sportswear, Inc., N.Y.C., 1975—. Mem. City of Aspen Planning and Zoning Commn., 1973-75, chmn., 1974-75. Served with N.Y. Army N.G., 1968. Mem. Am. Bar Assn., Colo. Bar Assn. Home: 10 St John Pl Port Washington NY 11050 Office: 460 Smith St Farmingdale NY 11735

SCHIFFMAN, STEPHAN, mgmt. cons.; b. N.Y.C., June 14, 1946; s. Walter and Martha S.; B.S., Ithaca Coll., 1968; M.S.W., Cornell U., 1969; postgrad U. Md., 1971-72, Detroit U., 1971-73; m. Anne Feinglass, Aug. 25, 1974; children—Daniele Megan, Jennifer Ruth. Prin. Stephan Schiffman Assos., N.Y.C., 1972—; dir. tng. United Jewish Appeal, N.Y.C., 1975—; practice psychotherapy, N.Y.C., 1976—; dir. DEI Mgmt. Group, N.Y.C., 1979—; mem. faculty Adelphi U., Garden City, N.Y., 1976-80; lectr. N.Y. U., 1977-80, New Sch. Social Research, 1978-80. Mem. Nat. Soc. Fund Raisers (dir.), Am. Mgmt. Assn., TC Acad. Arts and Scis., Assn. Jewish Communal Personnel. Jewish. Club: Cornell. Home: 235 E 87th St New York NY 10028 Office: 1290 Ave of Americas Suite 2900 New York NY 10019 also 888 7th Ave Suite 2800 New York NY 10019

SCHILLING, LOUIS ROBERT, JR., aerospace co. exec.; b. Hackensack, N.J., Nov. 24, 1931; s. Louis Robert and Frances Elizabeth (Loehwing) S.; B.S., Villanova U., 1954; m. Joan Patricia Coughlin, Apr. 21, 1956 (div. 1978); children—Louis Robert III, Lynn Patricia. Staff accountant Shell Chem. Corp., N.Y.C., 1958-61; cost mgr. I.T. & T., Paramus, N.J., 1962-65; accounting mgr. Gen. Foods Corp., White Plains, N.Y., 1965-67; fin. mgr. R.J.R. Foods, Inc., N.Y.C., 1967-69; controller, sec. Henkel Inc. (formerly Standard Chem. Products), Teaneck, N.J., 1969-73; fin. officer Polyester div. W.R. Grace Co., 1973-74; pres. L.R. Schilling & Assos., Montvale, N.J., 1974-76; budget mgr. govt. products div. Pratt and Whitney Aircraft Group United Technologies Corp., 1976—. Served with USNR, 1954-58, 61-62. Mem. Financial Execs. Inst., Assn. Systems Mgmt., N. Am. Yacht Racing Union. Club: Englewood (N.J.) Yacht. Home: 745 Dogwood Rd North Palm Beach FL 33408 Office: PO Box 2691 West Palm Beach FL 33402

SCHILLING, RONALD BARRY, electronics mfg. co. exec.; b. N.Y.C., Jan. 13, 1941; s. Nathan Francis and Ada (Steinhause) S.; B.S. in Elec. Engring., Coll. City N.Y. 1961; M.S. in Elec. Engring., Princeton, 1963; Ph.D., Poly. Inst. N.Y., 1967; m. Marilyn Goldstein, Dec. 25, 1961; children—Karen Robin, Lisa Joy, Robert David. Mem. tech staff RCA Labs., Princeton, N.J., 1961-66, mgr. product engring. Solid State div., Somerville, N.J., 1966-71; mgr. mktg. Solid State div. Motorola Co., Phoenix, 1971-76; with Med. div. Gen. Electric, 1976—, mktg. mgr., Milw., 1976-78, mgr. Far East ops., 1978-80, mgr. strategic planning, 1980-81, gen. mgr., 1981—; adj. lectr. Poly. Inst. Bklyn.; adj. prof. Coll. City N.Y. Vice pres. Colonial Oaks Civic Assn., 1966; pres. Har Zion Congregation, 1975. Mem. IEEE (sr.), Sigma Xi,, Tau Beta Pi, Eta Kappa Nu. Club: K.P. Contbr. articles to profl. jours. and books. Patentee in field. Home: 9515 N Sequoia Dr Bayside WI 53217 Office: Box 414 Milwaukee WI 53201

SCHIMMING, VICTOR MARTIN, retail co. exec.; b. Wichita, Kans., Mar. 5, 1938; s. Martin W. and Meta M. (Brockmeier) S.; student bus. mgmt. and acctg. Wichita State U., 1955-56, 58-60; student Sch. Architecture, U. Kans., 1956-58; m. Sondra L. Wullenweber, Aug. 16, 1959; children—Damon Mark, Derek Martin. Partner, sec.-treas. Snodgrass & Sons Constrn. Co., Inc., Wichita, 1959-68; founder Schimming Vending Service, Wichita, 1965-75, Schimming Coffee Service, Wichita, 1966-75; founder, pres., chmn. bd. Food Specialties, Inc., owners, operators franchised Swiss Colony Cheese Stores in 9 states, Wichita, 1966—; bus. cons. Swiss Colony Stores, Inc., 1972—; pres., chmn. bd. Schimming Corp., Wichita, 1965—, Spl. Touch, Inc., distbrs. splty. foods and equipment, Wichita, 1979—, Tin Pan Galley, Inc., Wichita, 1978—; owner, operator Tin Pan Galley gourmet cookware stores in 3 states. Mem. Nat. Republican Com., 1972—, Kans. Rep. Com., 1972—; bd. dirs. Quivira council, mem. Nat. council Boy Scouts Am.; bd. dirs. Met. Wichita YMCA; bd. advs. St. John's Coll., Winfield, Kans.; bd. dirs. Holy Cross Luth. Ch. and Sch. Recipient various leadership awards Boy Scouts Am. Mem. Internat. Council Shopping Centers, Wichita Area C. of C. (dir., VIP award 1977, 80), Aircraft Owners and Pilots Assn. Clubs: Crestview Country, Wichita Rotary. Home: 205 N Roosevelt St Wichita KS 67208 Office: 353 N Market St PO Box 177 Wichita KS 67201

SCHINAGLE, ALLAN CHARLES, employee benefit cons. firm exec.; b. Cleve., June 7, 1930; s. Elmer William and Mildred (Handlir) S.; B.S. in Bus. Adminstrn., Miami U., Oxford, Ohio, 1953; m. Cynthia Volz Robinson, Apr. 21, 1956; children—Cheryl Lynn, Allan Charles, Holly Anne, Penny Sue. Home office rep. group div. Aetna Life Ins. Co., Cleve. and Louisville, 1953-65, mgr. group div., Cleve., 1965-70;

sr. account exec. Aetna Life & Casualty Co., Cleve., 1970-76; v.p. Rollins Burdick Hunter of Ohio, Inc., Cleve., 1976—; chmn. pres.'s adv. council Central Res. Life Ins. Co. N.Am. Mem. Republican state candidate screening com., 1974; chmn. Rep. exec. and central coms., Geauga County, Ohio, 1970-76; del. to Rep. Nat. Conv., 1976; mem. Geauga County Bd. Elections, 1974-78. Served with USNR, 1948-49. Named Ky. col. Mem. Am. Mgmt. Assn., Internat. Platform Assn., Nat. Life Underwriters Assn., Ohio Life Underwriters Assn. Presbyterian. Clubs: Rotary (dir.), Hunting Creek Country (Louisville), Hillbrook, Chagrin Valley Racquet, Fork and Fiddle. Home: Hillbrook Estate Lane E Hunting Valley OH 44072 Office: 1211 Bond Court Bldg 1300 E 9th St Cleveland OH 44114

SCHINDLER, ERIC H., pharm. co. exec.; b. Cologne, Germany, Mar. 16, 1935; came to Can., naturalized, 1961; s. Hermann T. and Hilde K. S.; B.Commerce with distinction, Sir George Williams U., Montreal, 1968; m. Janine K. Lalonde, Dec. 27, 1957; children—Tanya, Karen, Jennifer-Lee. Acct., Can. Packers Ltd., Montreal, 1957-66; chief fin. officer, gen. mgr. Singer Credit of Can., Ltd., Toronto and Montreal, 1966-71; dir. fin. and administrn. Boehringer Ingelheim Ltd., Montreal, Burlington, Ont., 1972—; dir. Henley Chems. Ltd., PMAC. Mem. Pharm. Mfrs. Assn. Can., Am. Mgmt. Assn. Office: 977 Century Dr Burlington ON L7L 5J8 Canada

SCHINDLER, RUDOLPH LOUIS, retail jewelry co. exec.; b. N.Y.C., Sept. 21, 1915; s. Max and Emma (Lazarus) S.; student U. Iowa, 1933; m. Della Izen, Sept. 18, 1938; children—Ellen, Marvin, Stuart. Salesman, Grand Jewelers, Sioux City, Iowa, 1934-40; pres. Schindler's Jewelers, Sioux City, 1940—; retail cons. for various mfrs., 1948—; co-founder RJO, jewelers buying group, 1965; seminar condr., lectr. retailing, 1948—. Served with U.S. Army, 1943-45. Named Retailer of Yr., Brand Names Found., 1952; recipient cert. of distinction Brand Names Found., 1950, 51. Mem. Retail Jewelers Am., Jewelers Security Alliance, Iowa Jewelers Assn., Sioux City C. of C. Republican. Jewish. Clubs: Kiwanis (dir. 1972-73, pres. 1963), Masons, Shriners, B'nai B'rith. Home: 4004 Hiawatha W Sioux City IA 51104 Office: 502 4th St Sioux City IA 51102

SCHIPKE, PAUL BRIAN, food co. exec.; b. St. Louis, Feb. 23, 1930; s. William Joseph and Christine Auguste (Nickolaus) S.; B.F.A., Washington U., St. Louis, 1954; m. Dorothea Mae Bower, Oct. 16, 1954; children—Janis Carol, Christine Ann. Instr. art Pattonville (Mo.) Consol. Sch. Dist., 1954-55; art dir. Ralston Purina Co., St. Louis, 1957-59; illustrator Aero. Chart and Info. Center, St. Louis, 1955-57; art dir. Wohl Shoe Co., St. Louis, 1959-62; design dir. Roman Co. Advt. Agy., St. Louis, 1962-66; art dir., producer Gardner Advt., St. Louis, 1966-73; asso. dir. Advt. and Publicity Services, Ralston Purina Co., St. Louis, 1973—; instr. drawing Washington U., 1956-70; judge various art and design exhbns. Served with USAF, 1951-53. Recipient Gold medals (2) and other awards ArtsDirts Club St. Louis, Hammermill Graphic Center award, Financial World awards. Lutheran. Clubs: Country Surf, St. Louis County. Designer Busch Gardens family entertainment centers, Tampa, Houston, Los Angeles. Home: 114 W Glenwood Ln Kirkwood MO 63122 Office: Checkerboard Sq Saint Louis MO 63188

SCHISLER, DAVID OWEN, beer co. exec.; b. Calgary, Alta., Can., Dec. 22, 1952; s. Alvin Jesse and Dorothy Ann (Lucas) S.; B.S. (Pres.'s scholar), Colo. State U., 1975. With Adolph Coors Co., Golden, Colo., 1974—, sr. microbiologist, microbiology research and devel., 1977-81, supr. product quality control, microbiology sect., 1981—; in-plant lab. teaching asst., 1976—. Mem. Am. Soc. Brewing Chemists, Am. Soc. for Microbiology, Phi Beta Kappa. Republican. Episcopalian. Clubs: Coors Ski, Coors Trap. Home: 18377 W 58th Dr Golden CO 80401 Office: Adolph Coors Co Mail 300 Golden CO 80401

SCHLAIFER, CHARLES, advt. exec.; b. Omaha, July 1, 1909; s. Abraham S.; privately ed.; Litt.D. (hon.), John F. Kennedy Coll., 1969; m. Evelyn Chaikin, June 10, 1934 (dec. 1978); children—Arlene Lois Schlaifer Silk, Roberta Sandra Schlaifer Semer; m. 2d, Ann Mesavage, July 31, 1980. Newspaper reporter, Omaha, 1926-29; advt. dir. Publix Tri-States Theatres, Nebr., Iowa, 1929-37; mng. dir. United Artists Theatres, San Francisco, 1937-42; nat. advt. cons. United Artists Producers, 1937-42; nat. advt. mgr. 20th Century-Fox Film Corp., N.Y.C., 1942-45, v.p. charge advt. and pub. relations, 1945-49; pres. Charles Schlaifer & Co., Inc., N.Y.C., Los Angeles, 1949—. Vis. prof. N.Y. Sch.; expert witness U.S. Congl. and Senatorial Coms. on mental health, 1949—. Mem. Pres.'s Com. Employment Handicapped, 1960—; co-founder Nat. Assn. Mental Health, 1949; founder, co-chmn. Nat. Mental Health Com., 1949-57; mem. White House Conf. on Children, 1970; mem. nat. mental health adv. council Surgeon Gen. U.S., 1950-54; sec.-treas. Joint Commn. Mental Illness and Health, 1955-61; vice chmn. Found. Child Mental Welfare, 1963. Chmn., trustee N.Y. State Mental Hygiene Facilities Improvement Fund, 1963; chmn. N.Y. State Facilities Devel. Corp., 1969—; mem. adv. council NIMH, 1976—; sec.-treas., bd. dirs. Joint Commn. Mental Health Children; bd. dirs. Hillside Hosp., League Sch. For Seriously Disturbed Children, Menniger Found. Hon. fellow Postgrad. Center for Mental Health. Fellow Am. Psychiat. Assn. (hon.), Am. Orthopsychiat. Assn. (hon.), Brit. Royal Soc. Health (hon.). Co-author: Action for Mental Health, 1961; also articles in psychiat. jours. Home: 150 E 69th St New York NY 10021 Office: 150 E 58th St New York NY 10022 also 6430 Sunset Blvd Los Angeles CA 90028

SCHLAM, MARK HOWARD, internat. mktg. exec.; b. Bklyn., Sept. 24, 1951; s. Murray J. and Sophia (Bonis) S.; B.S., Elec. Engring. (N.Y. State Regents scholar), Poly. Inst. Bklyn., 1972, M.S., 1973. Sales asso. F.W. Madigan Real Estate Co., Flushing, N.Y., 1973-74; sales engr. Dayton T. Brown, Inc., Bohemia, N.Y., 1975-77; mktg., advanced systems Sperry Marine Systems, Gt. Neck, N.Y., 1977—; asso. editor Poly. Press, Bklyn., 1969-76. Mem. Audio Engring. Soc., Acoustical Soc. Am., Am. Inst. Aeros. and Astronautics, Am. Soc. Nondestructive Testing, Am. Soc. Naval Engrs., IEEE, Soc. Tech. Communication, Soc. Automotive Engrs., AAAS, Nat. Pilots Assn., Assn. Old Crows, Nat. Soc. Profl. Engrs., Realtors Nat. Mktg. Inst., Poly. Inst. N.Y. Alumni Assn. (asso. dir. 1973—), Tau Delta Phi. Club: Masons. Asst. editor: Computer Processing in Communications, 1970, Submillimeter Waves, 1971; asso. editor Computers and Automata, 1971, Computer-Communications Networks and Teletraffic, 1972, Optical and Acoustical Micro-Electronics, 1975; Computer Software Engineering, 1976. Home: 25 Chateau Dr Melville NY 11747 Office: Sperry Marine Systems Worldwide Hdqrs Marcus Ave Great Neck NY 11020

SCHLEGEL, JAMES WAYNE, mfg. co. exec.; b. Austin, Tex., Sept. 27, 1943; s. Max William and Thespina (Margos) S.; B.S. in B.A., U. Tex. at Austin, 1965; m. Shirley Ann Kolc, Apr. 19, 1969; 1 dau., Amy Dawn. Sales mgr. Xerox Corp., Kansas City, Mo. and Denver, 1967-75; dist. sales mgr. Compugraphic Corp., Colorado Springs, 1975-78; regional sales mgr. Capp Homes div. Evans Products Co., Bellevue, Wash., 1978—. Served with USAR, 1966-72. Republican. Roman Catholic. Home: 2215 Claremont Rd Carmichael CA 95608 Office: 1300 Ethan Way Sacramento CA 95625

SCHLEIFER, THOMAS CHARLES, mgmt. cons. corp. exec.; b. Newark, Oct. 30, 1942; s. James H. and Mildred S.; student Newark Coll. Engring., 1961-66, Fairleigh Dickinson U., 1972-74, Grad. Sch. Bus., 1975; m. Dolores A. Fischer, Oct. 4, 1961; children—Dolores, Judy, Tom. Project supt. Sudler Constrn. Co., Newark, 1961-63; v.p. S.B.I., Inc., Hanover, N.J., 1963-75, Fogel and Assos., Inc., Edison, N.J., 1974-76; pres. Constrn. Mgmt. Assos., Inc., Morristown, N.J., 1976—; dir., S.B.I., Inc., Constrn. Mgmt. Assos., Inc., CMA Resources, Inc.; instr. Middlesex County Coll., 1974, Bergen Community Coll., 1975; lectr. seminar series Asso. Gen. Contractore Am., 1975, Newark Coll. Engring. Grad. Sch., 1975, 76, N.J. Inst. Tech., 1977, Seton Hall Law Sch.; mgmt. trustee welfare and pension funds, Bricklayers Local 37, 1973-75, Laborers Local 913, 1973-75, Brick-Masons Local 21, 1971-75. Mem. research advisory council U. Tex., Arlington. Recipient Act of Heroism Award, Lions Internat., 1966. Mem. Am. Arbitration Assn. (nat. panel, N.J. Advisory Council; appreciation award 1976), Am. Concrete Inst. (edn. com.), Asso. Gen. Contractors Am. (chmn. continuing edn. com.; mem. joint com. with Surety Assn. Am. 1979—), Am. Inst. Constructors (lectr. nat. forum 1980), Bldg. Contractors Assn. N.J. (chmn. edn. com. 1970-75), Morris Sussex Bldg. Contractors Assn. (pres. 1971-75), N.J. Civil Engring. Tech. Adv. Council, Nat. Inst. Bldg. Scis. (consultative council). Republican. Roman Catholic. Clubs: K.C., Jaycees Am. (1971, 73). Author tng. tape: The Prudent Underwriter, 1978; contbr. articles to profl. publs. Office: 170 E Hanover Ave Morristown NJ 07960

SCHLESS, PHYLLIS ROSS, packaging co. exec.; b. N.Y.C., Apr. 16, 1943; d. Lewis H. and Doris G. Ross; cert. Neighborhood Playhouse Sch. of Theatre, N.Y.C., 1962, N.Y. Sch. Interior Design, 1964; B.A., Wellesley Coll., 1964; M.B.A., Stanford U., 1966; m. Aaron Backer Schless, July 7, 1970; 1 son, Daniel Lewis Ross. Econ. intern J.R. Williston & Beane, 1963; asso. internat. fin. Kuhn Loeb & Co., N.Y.C., 1966-70; cons. fin., 1971-73; sr. fin. analyst TWA, N.Y.C., 1974-75; asso. in corp. fin. specializing in mergers and acquisitions Lazard Freres & Co., N.Y.C., 1976-79; dir. mergers and acquisitions Am. Can Co., Greenwich, Conn., 1979—; mem. dissident slate of dirs. proxy fight So. Conn. Gas Co., 1972-73; fin. adv. Children's Theater, N.Y.C. Parks Dept., 1969. Pres., Greater Bridgeport (Conn.) area Nat. Council Jewish Women, 1972-73, bd. dirs., 1974-75; mem. fin. com. Common Cause, 1973-75; nat. fin. com. Girls Clubs Am., 1978-80, nat. social concerns com., 1981—, bd. dirs., 1979—; bd. dirs. Pauline Koner Dance Co., 1979—, Child Guidance Clinic of Greater Stamford, 1981—. Recipient Bravo award Greenwich YWCA, 1980. Registered rep. N.Y. Stock Exchange. Mem. Fin. Women's Assn., Women'd Econ. Roundtable, ACLU, Audubon Soc., Fortune Soc., Japan Soc. Clubs: Grolier, Stanford Bus. Sch., Wellesley (N.Y.C.). Home: 214 Sunset Hill Rd New Canaan CT 06840 Office: American Ln Greenwich CT 06830

SCHLEY, HERBERT ALLEN, real estate co. exec.; b. Milw., Jan. 28, 1938; s. Herbert Allen and Catharine Luella (Wright) S.; B.B.A., U. Wis., 1959; M.A. in Finance, U. Mich., 1960; m. Gayle Adachi, Oct. 13, 1978; children—Bret, Bart, Billy, Burton, Catharine. Sales, Mut. of N.Y., Denver and Honolulu, 1960-70, MacDonald & Assos. Realty, Inc., Honolulu, 1970-73; pres., dir. Hawaii-Nevada Investment Corp., Honolulu, 1974-79; pres., dir. Real Estate Investment Corp. Am., Honolulu, 1979—, Metroplex Acquisitions, Inc., Dallas, 1979—, Metroplex Investment Corp. Am., Dallas, 1979—, Acquisitions of Am., Inc., 1979—, Am. Comml. Real Estate Securities, Inc., Honolulu, 1979—; cons. comml. and indsl. real estate investments throughout U.S., 1970—. Served with U.S. Army, 1960-62. Mem. Honolulu Bd. Realtors. Republican. Home: 2443 Halekoa Dr Honolulu HI 96821 Office: Suite 2310 Pacific Trade Center Honolulu HI 96813

SCHLICK, ROBERT LEWIS, mktg. exec.; b. Bremerton, Wash., Feb. 26, 1941; s. Danual Franklin and Genevieve Josephine (Strutzel) S.; B.S., Hastings Coll., 1963; M.A.S., U. So. Calif., 1966; m. Ruth Ann Marcellin, July 17, 1965 (dec. Oct. 1977). Teledyne Systems cons. G.S. Rasmussen & Assos., 1964-70; project mgr., sales engr. Lockheed Aircraft Co., 1963-69; dir. mktg. Univ. Computing Co., 1969-74; regional mktg. dir. GTE Data Services, 1974-76; v.p., gen. mgr. Data Magnetics Corp., Torrance, Calif., 1976-78; v.p. mktg. and planning Gloria Marshall, Inc., Downey, Calif., 1978—; dir. CSMC Corp.; mgmt. cons.; lectr. U. So. Calif. Mem. Marina Property Bd. Recipient Scott Wilber award State of Nebr., 1962, Nat. Actuarial award, Nat. Actuarial Assn. Am., 1958, Lockheed Aircraft Pres.'s award, 1969. Mem. Am. Mgmt. Assn., Internat. Mktg. Assn., U. Nebr. Alumni Assn. Clubs: Marina City Yacht, Coral Tree Racket, Barrington, Marina City. Contbr. articles tech. publs. Home: 7929 W 81st St Playa Del Rey CA 90291 Office: 1932 Stonewood Downey CA 90241

SCHLIM, ALBERT WILLIAM, city ofcl.; b. Howard, S.D., Dec. 2, 1930; s. Joseph Francis and Cora Amelia (Erfman) S.; B.S., S.D. State Coll., 1952; M.S., U. Tenn., 1958; m. Pauline Diane Rouvalis, June 1, 1957; children—Tammy Lynn, Joseph Alexander, Commd. 2d. lt., U.S. Army, 1952, advanced through grades to lt. col., 1966; inf. comdr., Korea, 1952-54; assigned Supply Center, France, 1960-64, Pentagon Logistics, Washington, 1964-68; bn. comdr., Vietnam, 1968-69; staff officer, Ft. Monroe, Va., 1969-72; ret. 1972; investment broker Wheat & Co., Newport News, Va., 1972-76; dir. commerce City of Newport News, 1976-79; gen. mgr. Oyster Point Devel. Corp., Newport News, 1979—. Vice-pres. Republican city com., Newport News, 1975—; advisory com. U.S. Rep. Paul Trible, 1978. Decorated D.F.C., Legion of Merit, Air Medal, Meritorious Service Medal, Bronze Star. Mem. So. Indsl. Devel. Council, Am. Indsl. Devel. Council, Va. C. of C., Urban Land Inst., Council Urban Economic Devel., U. Okla. Office Continuing Edn. Republican. Greek Orthodox. Home: 9 Woodlake Circle Newport News VA 23606 Office: 610 Thimble Shoals Blvd Newport News VA 23606

SCHLOERKE, KENNETH WILLIAM, sales and mktg. exec.; b. Milw., Feb. 5, 1920; s. William Fredrick and Elsie Helen (Mueller) S.; student U. Wis.; m. Helen Marie Betz, July 19, 1941; children—Karen, Dennis, Scott. Asst. theatre mgr. Warner-Saxe Theatres, Milw., 1938-40; supr. prodn. control Oilgear Co., Milw., 1940-46; asst. to sales mgr. Baso Products, Milw., 1946-52; sales mgr. McNaulin Incinerators, Inc., Milw., 1953-67, pres., 1967-74; dir. marketing Summit Metal Fabricating and Mfg. Co., Cudahy, 1974, Manierre Corp., Waukesha, Wis., 1974-75; mgr. sales and mktg. Incinerator div. Kelley Co., Milw., 1976—; pres. Ardenott and Assos. Inc., 1976—; dir. M.C.N. Corp., Milw. Trustee Mick A. Naulin Found., Ltd. Served with USMCR, 1944-46. Mem. Incinerator Inst. Am. (pres. 1973). Mason. Club: Milw. Fire Bell. Home: 84O N Andover Ct Mequon WI 53092 Office: 6720 N Teutonia Ave Milwaukee WI 53209

SCHLOSBERG, RICHARD TURNER, III, newspaper exec.; b. Ardmore, Okla., Apr. 6, 1944; s. Richard Turner and Helen M. (Kopff) S.; B.S., U.S. Air Force Acad., 1965; M.B.A., Harvard U., 1972; m. Katharine Jo Carah, Aug. 14, 1965; children—Richard Turner IV, Deborah Sue. Fin. analyst treas.'s dept. E.I. DuPont de Nemours & Co., Wilmington, Del., 1972-74; bus. mgr. Anderson (S.C.) Ind. and Daily Mail, 1975-76; gen. mgr. Corpus Christi (Tex.) Caller-Times, 1976-79, pres., 1979—, v.p. Harte Hanks Communications, Inc., San Antonio, 1979—. Vice pres. United Way of Coastal Bend. Served with USAF, 1965-70. Decorated Air medal with four oak leaf clusters. Mem. Am. Newspaper Pubs. Assn., Corpus Christi C. of C. (exec. com.). Home: 263 Cape Aron Corpus Christi TX 78412 Office: PO Box 9136 Corpus Christi TX 78408

SCHLOSSMAN, MITCHELL LLOYD, chem. corp. exec.; b. Bklyn., Dec. 30, 1935; s. Jack Lewis and Rae (Wernick) S.; B.S., N.Y. U., 1956; postgrad. Bklyn. Coll., 1956-59; m. Barbara Nadell, Dec. 24, 1956; children—David, Edye, Julie. Group leader Revlon Inc., 1957-63; mgr. research and devel. Pfizer Inc., Parsippany, N.J., 1963-69; dir. tech. ops. Paris Cosmetics Inc., Jersey City, 1964-70; exec. v.p. Prince Industries Ltd., Linden, N.J., 1970-74; v.p. Malmstrom Chems. div. Emery Industries, Linden, 1974-78; pres. Tevco, Inc., Carlstadt, N.J., 1978—. Fellow Soc. Cosmetic Chemists (Merit award 1971); mem. Am. Chem. Soc. Club: K.P. Contbr. articles to profl. jours. Patentee in field. Home: 20 Lake Shore Dr Rockaway NJ 07866 Office: Tevco Inc 507 Washington Ave Carlstadt NJ 07072

SCHLUETER, JAMES ARTHUR, computer services co. exec.; b. Oshkosh, Wis., Sept. 22, 1933; s. Arthur Walter and Eleanor Mary (Carmody) S.; student U. Wis., 1951-53, Harvard Bus. Sch., 1973; m. Patricia J. Fogarty, Sept. 8, 1956; children—James, Jennifer, John. Office mgr. Consol. Freightways, Menasha, Wis., 1954-58, office mgr., Mpls., 1958-59, sr. acct., Akron, Ohio, 1959-61, mgr. payroll-mileage, 1961-69, dir. transp., 1969-73, v.p. transp., 1973-78; pres. CF Data Services, Inc., Portland, Oreg., 1978—; dir. Lile Internat. Republican. Episcopalian. Club: Rotary. Home: 12220 SW Walnut St Tigard OR 97223 Office: PO Box 3477 Portland OR 97208

SCHLUSSMAN, GILBERT MARTIN, plastic co. exec.; b. Bklyn., Sept. 2, 1926; s. David and Sarah (Malinsky) S.; B.Chem. Engring., Poly. Inst. Bklyn., 1949; m. Rona June Kotcher, Feb. 16, 1950; children—Peri, Sandford, Stefan. Plant mgr. Formed Container Corp., Orangeburg, N.Y., 1960-63, Union Carbide Corp., Fairlawn, N.J., 1963-69; v.p. Norprint div. No. Petrochem. Co., N.Y.C., 1969-74; v.p. Poly-Tech div. U.S. Industries, Mpls., 1976—. Bd. dirs. Jewish Family and Children's Service Inc., Adath Jeshuran Congregation, Am.-Israel C. of C.; mem. community relations panel Mpls. Fedn. Jewish Services; mem. aging panel Mpls. Fedn. for Jewish Services; mem. adv. bd. Internat. Order of DeMolay. Served with U.S. Army, 1945-46. Mem. Am. Mgmt. Assn. Clubs: Masons, Shriners. Patentee. Office: US Industries 1401 W 94th St Minneapolis MN 55431

SCHLUTER, PETER MUELLER, electronics co. exec.; b. Greenwich, Conn., May 24, 1933; s. Fredric Edward and Charlotte (Mueller) S.; B.M.E., Cornell U., 1956; m. Jaquelin Ambler Lamond, Apr. 18, 1970; children—Jane Randolph, Charlotte Mueller, Anne Ambler. Sr. engr. Thiokol Chem. Corp., Brigham City, Utah, 1958-59; asso. Porter Internat. Co., Washington, 1960-65, v.p., 1965-66, pres., treas., dir., 1966-70; pres., treas. dir. Zito Co., Derry, N.H., 1970-72; internat. bus. cons., Washington, 1972-74; v.p., dir. Buck Engring. Co. Inc., Farmingdale, N.J., 1975, pres., chief exec. officer, dir., 1975—; dir. Keystone Forging Co., Northumberland, Pa. Mem. Republican Inaugural Book and Program Com., 1969; mem. community adv. bd. Monmouth council Girl Scouts U.S.; bd. dirs. United Way of Monmouth County. Mem. Pi Tau Sigma. Clubs: Metropolitan (Washington); Rumson Country. Home: 3 N Cherry Ln Rumson NJ 07760 Office: POB 686 Farmingdale NJ 07727

SCHMALZRIED, MARVIN EUGENE, diversified drug co. exec.; b. Dighton, Kan., Nov. 11, 1924; s. Carl D. and Marie M. (Bahm) S.; B.B.A., Northwestern U., 1949; LL.B., U. Conn., 1955; m. Jean Landino, Nov. 27, 1946; children—Darlene M., Candace, Cynthia, Derek, Valerie, Rebecca. Accountant, Webster, Blanchard & Willard, Hartford, Conn., 1950-55; admitted to Conn. bar, 1955; controller, asst. treas. J.B. Williams Co., Glastonbury, Conn., 1955-57; treas., sec. Curtis 1000, Inc., Atlanta, 1957-61; asst. to pres. Am. Home Products Corp., N.Y.C., 1961-63, comptroller, 1964-67, v.p., 1967-72, sr. v.p., 1972—. Deacon, First Congl. Ch., Darien, Conn. Recipient Gold medal Conn. Soc. C.P.A.'s 1953. C.P.A., Conn. Mem. Am. Inst. C.P.A.'s, Am. Bar Assn., Financial Execs. Inst. Clubs: Darien Country, Old Friday Evening Reading Soc. Home: 10 Duffy's-Lane Darien CT 06820 Office: 685 3d Ave New York City NY 10017

SCHMID, HORST A., govt. ofcl. Can.; b. Bavaria; came to Can., 1952, naturalized, 1958. Agt. for Alta. seed dealer, Europe, 1956-58; partner Boreal Factors Ltd., export co., Edmonton, Alta., Can., 1961-71; mem. Legis. Assembly Alta., Edmonton, 1971—, cabinet minister of culture, youth and recreation, 1971-75, cabinet minister of govt. services and minister responsible for culture, 1975-79, cabinet minister of state for econ. devel.-internat. trade, 1979—. Active civic, provincial, fed. campaigns, 1960—; adv. for preservation ethnocultural heritage of Alta. to leader Progressive Conservative Assn. Alta., 1965-71; bd. govs. Edmonton Opera Assn.; hon. chmn. Commonwealth Arts Assn. Recipient numerous awards from provincial, nat. and internat. cultural orgns.; named Hon. Indian Chief Flying Eagle, 1976. Hon. mem. numerous orgns. Office: 324 Legis Bldg Edmonton AB T5K 2B6 Canada

SCHMID, JAMES FRANCIS, engr.; b. Longbranch, N.J., Aug. 21, 1922; s. Emil and Anna (Lhota) S.; grad. U.S. Mcht. Marine Acad., 1944; B.S.M.E., Poly. Inst. Bklyn., 1972; m. Mary Wohlpart, Jan. 22, 1944; 1 son, James J. Engring. instr. U.S. Mcht. Marine Acad., Kings Point, N.Y., 1944-46; engring. officer U.S. Lines at Sea, 1946-49; maintenance engr. N.Y. Eye and Ear Infirmary, N.Y.C, 1949-51; engr. Hotel New Yorker, N.Y.C., 1951-53; bldg. supt. Chrysler N.Y. Co. div. Chrysler Corp., N.Y.C., 1953-56; chief engr. Nassau Hosp., Mineola, N.Y., 1956-63; dir. engring. Bklyn. Hosp., 1963-78; plant engr. Bush Terminal Assos., Bklyn., 1978—; cons. in field. Mem. Nat. Assn. Power Engrs. (pres. 1975-76), Nat. Inst. for Uniform Licensing of Power Engrs. (dir. 1976—), Am. Soc. Hosp. Engrs., Hosp. Exec. Engrs. Greater N.Y., Greater N.Y. Hosp. Assn. (vice chmn. adv. com. 1977), ASME, Air Pollution Control Assn. (TS2.2 com.), Am. Nat. Standards Inst., Nat. Fire Protection Assn., Kings Point Alumni Soc., U.S. Mcht. Marine Acad. Alumni Assn. (life). Roman Catholic. Home: 63 Mark Dr Manahawkin NJ 08050 also 52 Galewood Dr Matawan NJ 07747 Office: 269 37th St Brooklyn NY 11232

SCHMIDT, A. CARL, mfg. co. exec.; b. Buffalo, Mar. 31, 1916; s. Adolf and Gussie (Sperber) S.; B.S. in Indsl. Engring., Gen. Motors Inst., 1951; B.S., Hillsdale (Mich.) Coll., 1959; m. Doris Rundles, Oct. 18, 1941; children—David, Stephen, Daniel, Joseph. Gen. mgr. Aldrich & Steimle Co., Hillsdale, 1950-63; gen. mgr., v.p. Am. Airmotive Co., Miami, Fla., 1963-65; dir. ops., then v.p. Fairchild Hiller Corp., Miami and St. Petersburg, Fla., 1965-71; v.p., gen. mgr. Friedrich-Climate Master Co., Ft. Lauderdale, Fla., 1970—. Mem. Am. Soc. Heating and Refrigeration Engrs., Aircraft Owners and Pilots Assn., Navy League, Delta Tau Delta. Kiwanis. Episcopalian. Clubs: Kiwanis, U.S. Power Squadron, Coral Ridge Yacht. Patentee in field. Home: 3101 NE 44th St Fort Lauderdale FL 33308 Office: 2000 W Commercial Blvd Fort Lauderdale FL 33309

SCHMIDT, ALBERT DANIEL, utilities co. exec.; b. Alpena, S.D., Nov. 16, 1925; s. Ernest Otto and Dorothea Marie Augusta S.; student Miami U., Oxford, Ohio, 1943-45; B.S. with honors in Elec. Engring., S.D. Sch. Mines and Tech., 1949; m. Joyce Bernice Anderson, Nov.

24, 1946; children—Roxanne Rae Schmidt Eisen, Janet Jaye Schmidt Foss. With Northwestern Public Service Co., 1949—, v.p. ops., Huron, S.D., 1958-65, pres., chief exec. officer, 1965-80, chmn. bd., chief exec. officer, 1980—, also dir.; mem. adv. bd. Huron br. Northwestern Nat. Bank; mem. exec. com., vice-chmn. Mid-Continent Area Power Pool; trustee Nat. Electric Reliability Council; dir. U.S. Indsl. Council, Gas Distbrs. Info. Service. Trustee, Huron Coll., 1970-73. Served to lt. (j.g.) USNR, 1943-46. Named Man of Yr., S.D. Electric Council, 1979; Boss of Yr., Huron Jaycees, 1979. Mem. N. Central Electric Assn. (exec. com., past pres.), Food and Energy Council (dir., chmn.), Nat. Assn. OTC Cos. (adv. council), U.S. Indsl. Council (dir.), Greater S.D. C. of C. (dir.), S.D. Council Econ. Edn. (dir.), Nat. Assn. Electric Cos. (past dir.), Am. Gas Assn. (past dir.), Midwest Gas Assn. (past pres.), S.D. Electric Council, S.D. Engring. Soc., Am. Legion, Huron C. of C. Republican. Lutheran. Clubs: Elks, Masons, Huron Country, Order Eastern Star (past patron). Office: Northwestern Public Service Co Northwestern Nat Bank Bldg Huron SD 57350

SCHMIDT, C. OSCAR, JR., machinery mfg. co. exec.; b. Cin.; s. C. Oscar and Charlotte A. (Fritz) S.; Mech. Engring., U. Cin., also B.S. in Mech. Engring.; M.B.A., Harvard; postgrad. Rutgers U.; L.H.D. (hon.), Sterling Coll.; m. Eugenia Hill Williams, June 29, 1944 (dec. June 22, 1975); children—Carl O., Christoph R., Milton W., Eugene H., Juliann R. Schmidt Hansen; m. 2d, Georgia Lee Schmidt, Aug. 9, 1977. Apprentice, Am. Can Co., Cin.; mem. engring. dept. Cin. Shaper; now with Cin. Butchers' Supply Co., successively asst. to pres., v.p. prodn., v.p., gen. mgr., exec. v.p., now pres., also dir.; dir. Boss Pack Co.; pres., dir. BEC, Inc., Trussville, Ala., Winbco Boss Co., Ottumwa, Iowa; pres. Omeco-Boss Co.; dir. Cin. Refrigerator & Fixture Works, Ky. Chem. Industries, Inc., Meat Packers Equipment, Inc. of Fla., Mille Lacs Products Co.; dir., chmn. bd., treas. LeFiell Co. Active Boy Scouts Am., past chmn. Valley dist.; chmn. finance com. Nat. United Cerebral Palsy Assn.; mem. review com. United Funds Cin. Mem. Pres.'s bd. assos. Rose Hulman Inst. Tech.; trustee, past pres. Hamilton County Soc. for Crippled Children, United Cerebral Palsy of Cin.; trustee Deaconess Hosp., also mem. sch. com. Served to capt. U.S. Army, 1940-45. Recipient Disting. Engring. Alumnus award U. Cin., 1969; Silver Beaver award Boy Scouts Am., also Harman award. Registered profl. engr., Ohio. Mem. Am. Oil Chemists Soc. (life), Am. Ordnance Assn., Engrs. Soc. Cin., Am. Assn. Indsl. Mgmt. (dir.), Air Pollution Soc., Cin. Indsl. Inst., Cin. C. of C., Meat Industry Supply and Equipment Assn. (dir., past co-chmn.), N.A.M. Nat. Metal Trades Assn. (mem. dist. council), Meat Machinery Mfrs. Inst. (past pres.), Acacia (past sec.-treas.), Heroes of '76, Cin. Hist. Soc. (life), Cin. Natural History Mus., Audubon Soc., Ohio Hist. Soc., Nat. Parks Assn., Zool. Soc. Cin., Aircraft Owners and Pilot Assn., U. Cin. Alumni Assn., Cin. Harvard Bus. Sch. Alumni (past sec.-treas.), Harvard Alumni Assn., Harvard Bus. Sch. Assn., Kappa Sigma Pi (dir., nat. sec.). Presbyterian (ruling elder, past pres. adult class, ruling elder commr., mem. eccles. order com.). Mason (Shriner), Clubs: Cincinnati; Wyoming Golf, Rotary (active various coms., rep. internat. meetings Tokyo, Montreal). Contbr. articles in field to profl. jours. Patentee in field. Home: 405 Meadow Lane Cincinnati OH 45215 Office: Box 16098 5601 Helen St Elmwood Pl Cincinnati OH 45216

SCHMIDT, CHAUNCEY EVERETT, banker; b. Oxford, Iowa, June 7, 1931; s. Walter F. and Vilda (Saxton) S.; B.S., U.S. Naval Acad., 1953; M.B.A., Harvard U., 1959; m. Anne Garrett McWilliams, Mar. 3, 1954; children—Carla Anne, Julia Garrett, Chauncey Everett. Vice pres., gen. mgr. London br. 1st Nat. Bank of Chgo., 1965-68, v.p. for Europe, Middle East and Africa, 1968-69, sr. v.p., 1969-72, exec. v.p., 1972, vice chmn. bd., 1973, pres., 1974-75; chmn. bd., pres., chief exec. officer The Bank of Calif., N.A., San Francisco, 1976—; dir. Amfac, Inc.; mem. fed. adv. council FRS; adv. council Japan-U.S. Econ. Relations, Pacific Rim Bankers Program. Bd. dirs. Bay Area Council, Calif. Roundtable; mem. SRI Internat. Council; bd. govs. San Francisco Symphony; exec. bd. San Francisco Bay area council Boy Scouts Am. Served to lt., USAF, 1953-56. Mem. Calif. Bankers Clearing House Assn. (dir.), Assn. Res. City Bankers, Internat. Monetary Conf., Am. Bankers Assn. Clubs: Comml. (Chgo.), Bohemian. Office: Bank of Calif 400 California St San Francisco CA 94104

SCHMIDT, FREDERICK WILLIAM, constrn. co. exec.; b. Greenfield, Mass., Feb. 1, 1940; s. Frederick Conrad and Elizabeth Ann (Weissenborn) S.; student Greenfield Community Coll., 1966; 1 dau. from previous marriage—Sarah Ann. Founder, pres. Pyramid Constrn., Inc., Greenfield, Mass., 1967—, Millbrook Corp., 1980—; owner Candelight Resort Inn. Mem. Greenfield Town Meeting, 1965-68. Mem. Universal Swimming Pool Assn. (pres.). Roman Catholic. Clubs: Greenfield Country, Elks. Office: 1 Wheeler St Greenfield MA 01301

SCHMIDT, GARY EMIL, retail co. exec.; b. Toledo, Oct. 30, 1940; s. Emil August and Edna (Mowery) S.; B.A., Northwestern U., 1962. Bus. editor Calif. Apparel news, weekly newspaper, Los Angeles, 1968-69; feature editor Men's Stylist mag., monthly, Los Angeles, 1970-71; mng. editor Style for Men, weekly, Los Angeles, 1971-72; pres. Am. Century Mktg., Inc., Los Angeles, 1973—, also dir. Served with U.S. Army, 1962-65. Mem. Authors League Am., Authors Guild. Republican. Unitarian. Home: 4000 Coldwater Canyon Ave Studio City CA 91604

SCHMIDT, GENE LILLARD, ednl. adminstr.; b. Louisville, July 29, 1944; s. Lillard August and Grace Elizabeth (Scroggin) S.; B.S., Western Mich. U., 1966, M.A., 1967; Ed.D., U. Ill., 1974; m. Sandra Lea Banik, Aug. 9, 1969; children—Zachary, Casey. Asst. intramural dir., tchr. Western Mich. U., Kalamazoo, 1966-67; tchr., coach, Roselle (Ill.) pub. schs., 1967-70; asst. prin. West Chicago (Ill.) High Sch., 1970-73; asst. adminstr. elementary edn., U. Ill., Urbana, 1973-74; adminstrs. asst. Willowbrook High Sch., Villa Park, Ill., 1974-77; supt. North Boone Dist. 200, Poplar Grove, Ill., 1977-80; supt. schs., Dansville, N.Y., 1980—. Mem. Am., Ill., assn. schl. adminstrs., Am. Assn. Curriculum Devel., No. Ill. Coop. in Edn., Phi Delta Kappa. Contbr. articles to profl. jours. Home: Dansville NY Office: Route 63 Dansville NY 14437

SCHMIDT, HAROLD EUGENE, land co. exec.; b. Cedar Rapids, Iowa, Oct. 12, 1925; s. Alfons W. and Lillie (Schlegel) S.; B.S. in Civil Engring., U. Iowa, 1949; M.S. in San. Engring., Mass. Inst. Tech., 1953; m. Lucy Hermann, Apr. 13, 1957; children—Harold, Sandra. Research and devel. engr. Chgo. Pump Co., 1949-51; engr. A.B. Kononoff, Miami, Fla., 1956-58; with Gen. Devel. Corp., 1958—, v.p. utilities, asst. v.p. ops., 1967-72, v.p., 1972-73, v.p. communities, 1973—; pres. Gen. Devel. Utilities, Inc.; dir. Port Charlotte Bank. Served to capt. USAF, 1951-56. Registered profl. engr., Fla. Mem. Am. Water Works Assn., Water Pollution Control Fedn., Sigma Xi, Chi Epsilon. Home: 641 W 53d St Hialeah FL 33012 Office: 1111 S Bayshore Dr Miami FL 33131

SCHMIDT, JOHN JOSEPH, holding co. exec.; b. Chgo., Jan. 13, 1928; s. William Fred and Mildred C. (Petrone) S.; B.S., DePaul U., 1951; J.D., Loyola U., Chgo., 1955; m. Gail Bormann, Oct. 8, 1955; children—Cathleen M., Karen B., Linda G. Admitted to Ill. bar, 1955; trial atty. The Atchison, Topeka and Santa Fe Ry., Chgo., 1955-69, asst. v.p. exec. dept., 1969-73; v.p. Santa Fe Industries, Inc., Chgo., 1969-73, exec. v.p., 1973-78, pres., 1978—, also dir.; dir. The Atchison, Topeka and Santa Fe Ry., Santa Fe Natural Resources, Inc., Santa Fe Pipelines, Inc., Harris Trust & Savs. Bank, Harris Bankcorp, Inc. Mem. Zoning Bd. Appeals, Planning Commn., Village of Burr Ridge, Ill., 1973—. Served with U.S. Army, 1945-47. Mem. Am., Ill., Chgo. bar assns., Soc. Trial Lawyers (past dir.), Ill. Def. Council (past pres.), Nat. Assn. R.R. Trial Counsel (past pres.). Clubs: Chgo. Athletic, Chgo. Economic. Office: Santa Fe Industries 224 S Michigan Ave Chicago IL 60604*

SCHMIDT, MELBA IRENE (MRS. MARQUIS RIGHTMIRE SCHMIDT), real estate exec.; b. Grand Junction, Colo., Jan. 14, 1908; d. Claud DeNel and Gertrude Beatrice (Cartmel) Smith; student U. Calif., Los Angeles, 1926-27; grad. pianoforte pedagogy, New Eng. Conservatory of Music, 1930; m. Marquis Rightmire Schmidt, Aug. 2, 1932; children—Mark Ronald, Ralph Normand, Beatrice Jane (Mrs. Jerry Roberson). Pvt. tchr. piano and musical readings, Grand Junction, 1930-40; tchr. harmony and music theory Mesa Jr. Coll., Grand Junction, 1943; dir. publicity and pub. relations C.D. Smith Co., drug and sundries wholesalers, Grand Junction, 1951-73, v.p., dir. 1970-73; partner Smith Assos., real estate and investments, 1948—; pres. Sterling Co., real estate, 1976—, also chmn. bd.; dir. Walsh Enterprises, Inc., Anaheim, Calif., Hy Grade Labs., Inc. Gen. chmn., an organizer Mesa County Community Concert Assn., 1944-60. Bd. dirs. Grand Junction Art Center, 1951-54. Mem. Music Assos., of Aspen (regional dir. 1962-66), Nat. Fedn. Music Clubs (chmn. Aspen music sch. scholar 1964—), Colo. Fedn. Music Clubs (pres. 1962-64, state bd. mem. 1959—), P.E.O., Pi Kappa Lambda, Alpha Chi Omega. Republican. Presbyterian. Club: Wednesday Music (pres. 1952-55). Home: 536 N 7th St Grand Junction CO 81501 Office: PO Box 756 Grand Junction CO 81501

SCHMIDT, PETER ROBERT, mgmt. cons.; b. N.Y.C., Dec. 11, 1934; s. Herman Robert and Amelia Helene (Mucha) S.; A.B., Duke U., 1956; m. Anne Rue Parker, June 6, 1956; children—Elizabeth Anne, Robert Charles, Susan Diane. With Bell Telephone Labs., Inc., 1961-69, group supr., 1968-69; search specialist Boyden Assos., Inc., N.Y.C., 1969-70, dir. research, 1970-72, asso., 1972-73, v.p., 1973-74, v.p. ops., 1974-76, sr. v.p. ops., 1976-79, sr. v.p., gen. mgr., Morristown, N.J., 1979—, also dir., asst. corp. sec. Served with USN, 1956-60, now capt. Res. Mem. U.S. Naval Inst., Naval Res. Assn., Navy League, U.S. Republican. Clubs: Pinnacle, Squadron A (N.Y.C.); Springbrook Country (N.J.). Home: 21 Drake Rd Mendham NJ 07945 Office: 55 Madison Ave Morristown NJ 07960

SCHMIDT, ROBERT A., brewery exec.; b. Tumwater, Wash., Mar. 3, 1915; s. Adolph D. and Winnifred (Lang) S.; student Wash. State U., U.S. Brewers Acad.; m. Jeannette Mikkelsen, Nov. 20, 1937; children—Robert A., Jennifer (Mrs. Thomas R. Ingham, Jr.), Frank C. With Olympia Brewing Co. (Wash.), 1934-77, asst. brewmaster, 1938-41, brewmaster, 1941-47, asst. supt., 1947-50, dir., 1950—, supt., 1951-53, v.p. charge prodn., 1953-63, pres., 1963-77, chmn., 1974—, chief exec. officer, 1974-77, 80—; dir. Seattle-1st Nat. Bank, Olympia Fed. Savs. & Loan Assn. Bd. dirs. Olympia-Tumwater Found. Mem. Master Brewers Assn. Am. (past pres. N.W. dist.), Beta Theta Pi. Elk. Address: PO Box 4066 Tumwater WA 98501*

SCHMIDT, STEVEN WILLIAM, business exec.; b. Downers Grove, Ill., Mar. 29, 1952; s. George John and Winifred Clara (Stange) S.; B.S.cum laude, No. Ill. U., 1974. Staff accountant Touche, Ross & Co., Chgo., 1973-75; accounting mgr. Sanger-Harris Federated Dept. Stores, Dallas, 1976; mgr. external financial reporting, mgr. seasonal planning and analysis May Co., St. Louis, 1976-77; dir. audits Fed. Express Corp., Memphis, 1977—. teaching asst. No. Ill. U., 1975-76. C.P.A., Ill. Mem. Am. Inst. C.P.A.'s. Office: Federal Express AMF Box 727 Memphis TN 38194

SCHMIDT, TERRY DEAN, mgmt. cons. co. exec.; b. Sandpoint, Idaho, Aug. 10, 1947; s. William and Florence Theresa (Seeberger) S.; B.S. in Aerospace Engring., U. Wash., 1969; M.B.A. (Norton Clapp fellow 1970), Harvard U., 1971; m. Sinee Panaree, Mar. 29, 1977. Program analyst Office of Sec. of Transp., Washington, 1971-73; mgmt. cons. PCI, Washington, 1973-77; pres. Diversified Concepts Ltd., Washington, 1977—; instr. Mgmt. Fgn. Service Inst., U.S. Dept. of State, Washington, 1980—. Chief fund agt. Harvard Bus. Sch., 1971—. Recipient Charles T. Main award ASME, 1968; Theodore von Karman Trophy AIAA, 1969. Mem. Am. Soc. for Tng. & Devel. Roman Catholic. Club: Toastmasters. Editor: HarBus News, 1970-71; author and lectr. in field. Home: 1803 N Highland Arlington VA 22201 Office: PO Box 3776 Washington DC 20007

SCHMIDT, WILLIAM MAX, conglomerate exec.; b. Danville, Pa., Nov. 23, 1947; s. Frank Wilhelm and Doris Savilla (Maurer) S.; B.S., U. Pa., 1969; M.B.A., Northwestern, 1971; m. Marylea O'Reilly, Sept. 20, 1980. Mktg. specialist Moody's Investors Service, N.Y.C., 1971-72; dir. mktg. research, 1972-73; asso. cons. William E. Hill & Co., Inc., N.Y.C., 1973-75; mgr. mktg. analysis, white papers group Internat. Paper Co., N.Y.C., 1975-77, product supr. carbonizing tissue, white papers group, 1977-79; dir. market analysis U.S. Industries, Inc., N.Y.C., 1979—. Adviser, Jr. Achievement. Mem. U. Pa. Assn. N.Y.C. (dir. 1975-77), Wharton Bus. Sch. Club N.Y., N. Am. Soc. Corp. Planning, Newcomen Soc. N.Am., Internat. Platform Assn., Am. Mktg. Assn., SAR (life), Sigma Chi (life). Republican. Mem. United Ch. of Christ. Clubs: St. Bartholomew Community, University, University Glee of N.Y., Miramar Ski, Knickerbocker Republican, Sandbar Beach. Home: 147 E 82d St New York City NY 10028 Office: 250 Park Ave New York NY 10017

SCHMITT, CHARLES JEFFREY, computer scientist; b. Oak Ridge, June 9, 1947; s. Charles Rudolph and Alma Jean (Peters) S.; B.Engring., Vanderbilt U., 1969, M.S., 1972; m. Barbara Jean Calfee, Jan. 1, 1970; children—Emily Faye, Charles Eric. Asst. prof. computer sci. Towson State U., 1973—; pres. Micro Electronic Data Systems, Inc., Balt., 1977—; cons. Display Data Corp. certified data processor, certified computer programmer Inst. Certification Computer Profls. Mem. Assn. Computing Machinery (faculty adviser Towson State U. student chpt.), Am. Nat. Standards Inst., IEEE Computer Soc., Chesapeake Microcomputer Club (chmn. Balt. chpt. 1977-78), Md. Assn. for Ednl. Use of Computers. Home: 1000 Litchfield Rd Baltimore MD 21239 Office: 6803 York Rd Baltimore MD 21212

SCHMITT, JOHN BERNARD, co. exec.; b. Bklyn., Jan. 21, 1905; s. George F. and Catherine (Jochim) S.; student Fordham U., 1930; m. Mary D. Doherty, Jan. 28, 1930; children—John F., Francis C., Ellen K. Shaw. Asst. chief field dep. U.S. Treasury Dept., Bklyn., 1935-42; adj. prof. accounting and taxes Fordham U., N.Y.C., 1954-68; partner McArdle & McArdle, Accountants, N.Y.C., 1955-71; exec. dir. J.A. Sexauer Inc., White Plains, N.Y. and Louisville, 1970—, also dir., v.p., trustee Sexauer Found., 1970—; adv. com. Bank N.Y. County Trust Region. Mem. Catholic Accountants Guild, Gt. S. Bay Yacht Racing Assn., Beta Alpha Psi. Clubs: Westchester Hills Golf (gov. 1976—), Accountants (N.Y.C.), U.S. Power Squadron, Sayville Yacht (commodore). Westchester Hills Golf. Home: 36 Prescott Ave White Plains NY 10605 Office: Sexauer Inc 10 Hamilton Ave White Plains NY 10601

SCHMITT, RALPH GEORGE, mfg. co. exec.; b. Tarrytown, N.Y., Aug. 8, 1944; s. Alfons George and Otillie Lucie (Mehler) S.; B.S., Mass. Inst. Tech., 1966, M.S., 1967; M.S., U. Calif., 1970; m. Sandra Lee Watt, Feb. 5, 1965; children—Ralph Scott, Carrie Lee, Kurt Ryan. Engr., McDonnell Douglas, Huntington Beach, Calif., 1967-70, Rockwell Internat., Downey, Calif., 1970-72; pres., chmn. bd. TPG Industries, Los Angeles, 1972-74; gen. mgr. Columbia Yacht div. Whittaker Corp., Chesapeake, Va., 1975-76; v.p. ops., dir. R & G Sloane Mfg. Co., Los Angeles, 1976—. Regional vice chmn. M.I.T. Ednl. Council. NSF fellow, 1966-67. Mem. Am. Mgmt. Assn., Tau Beta Pi, Sigma Xi, Sigma Gamma Tau, Sigma Alpha Epsilon. Republican. Home: 25676 Estoril St Valencia CA 91355 Office: 7606 N Clybourn Ave Sun Valley CA 91352

SCHMITZ, EUGENE GERARD, cons. engr.; b. Brackenridge, Pa., Sept. 17, 1929; s. Wienand Gerard and Florence Marie (Grimm) S.; student Phoenix Coll., 1946-47, Ariz. State U., 1959-61; m. Anna May Lee, May 3, 1952; children—Joyce Marie, Michael Paul, Carol Ann, John David, Eugene. Dist. mgr. Field Enterprise Ednl. Corp., Phoenix, 1955-59; designer, engr. Motorola Inc., Scottsdale, Ariz., 1961-67; project engr. space and re-entry systems div. Philco-Ford Co., Palo Alto, Calif., 1967-70; engring. program adminstr. Memorex Equipment Co., Santa Clara, Calif., 1970-71; plant mgr. Tijuama (Mex.) ops. Philco-Ford, 1971-72; engring. cons. FMC Corp., San Jose, Calif., 1972-75; staff cons. engr. Stetter Assos., Inc., Palo Alto, 1975-80, Schmitz Engring. Assos., 1980—; instr. electronic design Middlton Inst., Phoenix, 1965-66. Served with U.S. Army, 1948-55. Registered profl. engr., Calif. Mem. Soc. Mfg. Engrs. (certified). Republican. Roman Catholic. Home: 3061 Vesuvius Ln San Jose CA 95132 Office: 3061 Vesuvius Ln San Jose CA 95132

SCHMITZ-SMITH, KAREN LEE, mfg. co. exec.; b. Warwick, N.Y., Dec. 6, 1946; d. Willard Franklin and May Bernyce (Maconeghy) Schmitz; B.S. magna cum laude, Western Carolina U., 1968; married. Gen. accountant Gen. Telephone Co. S.E., Durham, N.C., 1968, tax accountant, 1968-69, revenue accounting supr., 1969-70, internal auditor, 1970-71, disbursements supr., 1971-72, supr. div. revenue, 1972-73, mgr. revenues and earnings, 1973-77; adminstr. revenue requirements GTE Service Corp., Stamford, Conn., 1977-79, revenue planning mgr., 1979-81, dir. regulatory matters Gen. Telephone Co. Calif., Santa Monica, Calif., 1981—; lectr. in field Named Career Woman, City Durham, 1974. Mem. Nat. Assn. Accountants (chpt. pres. 1972-73, nat. dir. 1975-76), Western Carolina Univ. Alumni Assn., Bus. and Profl. Womens Club, Beta Sigma Phi (v.p. chpt. 1972), Alpha Phi Sigma. Democrat. Roman Catholic. Club: Toastmasters (pres. 1980). Office: Dept Regulatory Matters Gen Telephone Co 100 Wilshire Blvd PO Box 889 Santa Monica CA 90406

SCHMUECKLE, JEAN ZUKOWSKA (MRS. RICHARD A. SCHMUECKLE), advt. agency exec.; b. Phila., Oct. 10, 1913; d. Ludwig and Eva (Kwiadis) Zukowski; student U. Pa., 1935-36, Charles Morris Sch. Advt., 1937-38, Columbia U., 1941; m. Richard A. Schmueckle, Oct. 2, 1942. Dir., Connelly Orgn., direct mail advt., Phila., 1933-38; asst. to pres. Allied Housing Assos., Inc., Langhorne, Pa., 1938-42; with Cahall Advt. Agency, 1942; owner, pres. Jean Z. Schmueckle Advt. Agency, Rushland, Pa., 1943—. Bd. dirs. Bucks County (Pa.) Pro Musica; com. mem. Bucks County Opera; active various orgns. for preservation of historic homes and for humane treatment of animals; past pres. Del. Valley Music Club, New Hope, Pa. Mem. Phila. Club Advt. Women, Women in Communications, Phila. Art Alliance, Phila. Athenaeum, Elfreth's Alley Assn., Nat. Trust for Hist. Preservation, New Hope Hist. Soc., Phillips Mill Community Assn., Bucks County Conservancy, Bucks County Hist. Soc., Pa. Soc. for Prevention Cruelty to Animals, Am. Anti-Vivisection Soc. Home: Overlook Valley Farm Rushland Bucks County PA 18956 Office: Rushland Bucks County PA 18956

SCHMUTZ, JOHN FRANCIS, lawyer; b. Oneida, N.Y., July 24, 1947; s. William L. and Rosemary Schmutz; B.A., Canisius Coll., 1969; J.D., Notre Dame U., 1972; LL.M., George Washington U., 1975; m. H. Marie Roney, June 7, 1969; children—Gretchen, Jonathan, Nathan. Admitted to Ind. bar, 1972, D.C. bar, 1975, U.S. Supreme Ct. bar, 1975; legislation and major projects officer Office of Judge Adv. Gen., 1972-74; appellate atty. U.S. Army Legal Services Agy., 1974-75; asso. firm Ice, Miller, Donadio & Ryan, Indpls., 1976-77; staff atty. Burger Chef Systems, Inc., Indpls., 1977-78, sr. atty., 1979, asst. chief legal counsel, 1978-80, chief legal counsel, 1980—. Bd. dirs., v.p. Bursan Credit Union; bd. dirs. Food Service and Lodging Inst.; v.p. Blahs, Inc. Mem. Am. Bar Assn., Fed. Bar Assn., Ind. Bar Assn., D.C. Bar Assn., Nat. Restaurant Assn., Food Service and Lodging Inst., K.C. Office: PO Box 927 Indianapolis IN 46206

SCHNACK, GAYLE HEMINGWAY JEPSON (MRS. HAROLD CLIFFORD SCHNACK), corp. exec.; b. Mpls., Aug. 14, 1926; d. Jasper Jay and Ursula (Hemingway) Jepson; student U. Hawaii, 1946; m. Harold Clifford Schnack, Mar. 22, 1947; children—Jerrald Jay, Georgina, Roberta, Michael Clifford. Skater Shipstead & Johnson Ice Follies, 1944-46; v.p. Harcliff Corp., Honolulu, 1964—, Schnack Indsl. Corp., Honolulu, 1969—; v.p. Cedar Corp., Nutmeg Corp., Instant Printers Inc.; ltd. partner Koa Corp. Pres., City Council, 1961-62. Mem. Beta Sigma Phi (chpt. pres. 1955-56). Home: 4261 Panini Loop Honolulu HI 96815 also 1282 Riverside Dr Reno NV 89503 Office: PO Box 3077 Honolulu HI 96802 also 63 Keystone Reno NV 89503

SCHNACK, HAROLD CLIFFORD, lawyer; b. Honolulu, Sept. 27, 1918; s. Ferdinand J. H. and Mary (Pearson) S.; B.A., Stanford, 1940, LL.B., 1947; m. Gayle Hemingway Jepson, Mar. 22, 1947; children—Jerrald Jay, Georgina, Roberta, Michael Clifford. Admitted to Hawaii bar, 1947; dep. prosecutor City and County Honolulu, 1947-48; gen. practice with father, F. Schnack, 1948-60; individual practice Honolulu, 1960—; pres. Harcliff Corp., 1961—; treas., dir. Schnack Properties, Ltd., 1957-72; pres. Schnack Indsl. Corp., 1969—, Instant Printers, Inc., 1971—, Global Answer System, Inc., 1973-78. Vice pres. Goodwill Industries of Honolulu, 1958-66, 69-71, pres., 1971-72. Mem. Am., Hawaii bar assns., Phi Alpha Delta, Alpha Sigma Phi. Mason. Clubs: Outrigger Canoe, Pacific. Home: 4261 Panini Loop Honolulu HI 96816 also 1282 Riverside Dr Reno NV 89503 Office: Suite 301 Alii Bishop Bldg PO Box 3077 Honolulu HI 96802

SCHNAKENBERG, WALTER HERMAN, fin. exec.; b. Bklyn., May 30, 1918; s. John Herman and Margarethe (Fayen) S.; B.S., Columbia U., 1939; m. Charlotte Hildur Schwartz, Apr. 18, 1943; 1 son, Eric. Acct., Peat, Marwick Mitchell & Co., N.Y.C., 1946-52; asst. treas. The Pittston Co., Greenwich, Conn., 1952-56, controller 1956-61, treas., 1961-67, v.p. fin., 1967-80, sr. corp. adviser, 1980—. Served to 1st lt., U.S. Army, 1941-46. Home: Wheat Ln Darien CT 06820 Office: 1 Pickwick Plaza Greenwich CT 06830

SCHNALL, HERBERT KENNETH, publishing co. exec.; b. Bklyn., July 28, 1928; s. Maurice and Sadye R. Schnall. Staff accountant S.D. Leiderdorf & Co., N.Y.C., 1951-52; sr. accountant Peat Marwick, Mitchell & Co., N.Y.C., 1954-57; controller Parents Mag. Enterprises, N.Y.C., 1957-67; pres. New Am. Library, N.Y.C., from 1967, chmn. bd., 1981—. Served to 1st lt. USAF, 1952-54. C.P.A.,

N.Y. Mem. Am. Inst. C.P.A.'s, Assn. Am. Publishers (chmn. mass market paperback div. 1974-75). Jewish. Office: 1633 Broadway New York NY 10019*

SCHNAPF, ABRAHAM, astron-electronics scientist; b. N.Y.C., Aug. 1, 1921; s. Meyer and Gussie S.; B.S. in Mech. Engring., City U. N.Y., 1948; M.S. in Mech. Engring., Drexel U., 1953; m. Edna Wilensky, Oct. 24, 1943; children—Donald J., Bruce M. Devel. engr. Goodyear Aircraft Corp., Akron, Ohio, 1948-50; mgr. devel. engring. RCA Airborne Fire Control Dept., Camden, N.J., 1950-58; program mgr. TIROS Satellite System, RCA Astro-Electronics, Princeton, N.J., 1958-70, mgr. satellite programs, 1970-79, prin. scientist, 1980—; lectr. grad. system engring. M.I.T., 1967, Stanford U., 1970. Recipient Am. Soc. Quality Control Ann. award, 1968; NASA Public Service award, 1969; RCA David Sarnoff award, 1970. Served with USAAF, 1943-46. Fellow AIAA; mem. N.Y. Acad. Sci., AAAS, Am. Meteorol. Soc., Am. Astronautical Soc., Space Pioneers. Contbr. papers on meteorol. satellites, space tech., communications satellites to profl. jours. Patentee in field. Home: Box 150 Willingboro NJ 08046 Office: RCA Astro-Electronics PO Box 800 Princeton NJ 08540

SCHNAPP, ROGER HERBERT, lawyer; b. N.Y.C., Mar. 17, 1946; s. Michael Jay and Beatrice Joan (Becker) S.; B.S., Cornell U., 1966; J.D., Harvard U., 1969; m. Candice Jacqueline Larson, Sept. 15, 1979. Admitted to N.Y. bar, 1970, U.S. Supreme Ct. bar, 1974; atty. CAB, Washington, 1969-70; labor atty. Western Electric Co., N.Y.C., 1970-71; mgr. employee relations Am. Airlines, N.Y.C., 1971-74; labor counsel Am. Electric Power Service Corp., N.Y.C., 1974-78, sr. labor counsel, 1978-80; indsl. counsel relations Trans World Airlines, N.Y.C., 1980—. Mem. Internat. (labor law com.), Am. (chmn. subcom. arbitration and ct. injunctions), N.Y. State bar assns. Editor-in-chief Indsl. and Labor Relations Forum, 1964-66, contbr. articles, 1964-65. Home: 420 E 55th St New York NY 10022 Office: Trans World Airlines 605 3d Ave New York NY

SCHNEEMAN, JUSTIN GERHARDT, bus. exec.; b. Leer, Germany, Apr. 28, 1903; student tech. coll., 1920-22; m. Elizabeth Brauman, Feb. 15, 1930. Insp. Hurley Machine Co., Cicero, Ill., 1923-25; chief draftsman, chief insp. asst. to factory mgr., Gen. Electric X-Ray Corp., Chgo., 1926-37; founder, chmn. X-Ray Products Corp., Los Angeles, 1936—; indsl. X-ray diagnostician and cons. on atomic installations, Richland, Wash., 1947-49. Mem. war metallurgy com. NRC. Mem. Am. Soc. Metals, Am. Foundrymen's Assn., Am. Indsl. Radium and X-Ray Soc., Los Angeles C. of C. Lutheran. Author Industrial X-Ray Interpretation, 1968; also tech. articles. Specialist in nuclear physics with particular reference to X-ray. Designer of stereo-Fluoroscope for med. profession as used for Army and Navy Hosp. Home: 10961 Alta View Dr Studio City CA 91604 Office: 7829 Industry Ave Pico Rivera CA 90660

SCHNEEWEIS, BASIL, carpet mfg. co. exec.; b. Bronx, N.Y., Nov. 20, 1923; s. Abraham and Ethel (Solow) S.; B.S. in Textile Engring., Phila. Coll. Textiles and Sci., 1948; m. Phyllis Gordon, June 8, 1947; children—Meryl Schneeweis Leventhal, Laura Schneeweis Schindler. Tech. dir. Firth Carpet Co., Firthcliffe, N.Y., 1948-66; v.p., gen. mgr. Trend Mills Calif., Los Angeles, 1966-72; group v.p. Mohasco Corp., Amsterdam, N.Y., 1972-79; exec. v.p. Gemini Carpet Mills Inc., Los Angeles, 1979—. Served with AUS, 1943-46. Decorated Purple Heart, Bronze Star. Mem. Am. Carpet Inst., Carpet and Rug Inst., ASTM, Am. Assn. Textile Chemists and Colorists, Am. Assn. Textile Technologists, Jewish Community Center, Jewish Community Council, Jewish Fedn. Welfare Fund. Home: 5240 Zelzah Ave Unit 106 Encino CA 91316 Office: 4368 Bandini Blvd Los Angeles CA 90023

SCHNEIDER, ALAN NEIL, mortgage banker; b. Louisville, Sept. 6, 1916; s. Samuel Joseph and Jennie S.; A.B., DePauw U., Greencastle, Ind., 1938; J.D., Harvard, 1942; m. Mabel M. Pedersen, July 4, 1950; 1 dau., Karen Elizabeth. Admitted to Ky. bar, 1947; pub. relations dir. City of Louisville, 1947-48, adminstrv. asst. mayor, also spl. counsel, 1948-49; asst. city atty., 1950-59; pres., chmn. bd. King's Way Mortgage Co., Coral Gables, Fla., 1960—, Veritas Ins. Agy., 1960—, Omega Title Corp., 1960—, Alpha Inc., 1960—; pres. Sigma Devel. Corp.; dir. Greenacre, Inc.; chief counsel Security Finance Agy., Inc., Southeastern Mortgage Co. Pres. Ky. Library Assn., 1957, pres. Am. Assn. Library Trustees, 1958-59, named Outstanding Trustee, 1959, Trustee Louisville Free Pub. Library, Red Cross Hosp., Louisville, Race Found.; bd. dirs. Fla. Soc. Prevention Blindness. Served to lt. comdr. USNR, 1941-45. Mem. Am., Ky., Louisville, Internat. bar assns., Mortgage Bankers Am., Assn. Former Intelligence officers, Phi Beta Kappa, Sigma Chi (Balfour award 1938). Presbyn. Clubs: Coral Gables Athletic. Coral Gables Country; Bankers, Harvard (Miami); Spl. Forces (London). Office: 265 Sevilla Ave PO Box 158 Coral Gables FL 33134

SCHNEIDER, IRVING, roller skating rink exec.; b. Bklyn., Nov. 15, 1933; s. Benjamin and Sarah (Diment) S.; B.A., Bklyn. Coll., 1956; m. Joyce Wrobel, May 2, 1954; children—Howard, Brenda, Scott. Pres. JGS Hall, Inc., Bklyn., 1967—, Revere Roller Rink, Inc. (Mass.), 1980—; v.p. Commack Roller Rink, Inc. (N.Y.), 1977—. Served with AUS, 1952-54. Office: Commack Roller Rink Inc 70 Vets Hwy Commack NY 11725

SCHNEIDER, LLOYD RHYNEHART, lawyer, editor, air force officer; b. Anchorage, Alaska, July 25, 1949; s. Lloyd William and Mary Ellen S.; B.S. in Mech. Engring. with distinction, U. Nebr., 1971; postgrad. grad. sch. engring. mgmt. UCLA, 1975; J.D. with honors, U. So. Calif., 1978; grad. various mil. tng. schs.; m. Katharine Mary Curtis, Jan. 29, 1970; 1 son, Jeremy Scott. Commd. 2d lt. U.S. Air Force, 1971, advanced through grades to capt., 1975; engring. subsystem mgr. MINUTEMAN System Program Office, Norton AFB, Calif., 1971-72, fin. mgr., mech. systems, 1973-74, mgr. shock isolation systems, 1975; admitted to Calif. bar, 1978, Ct. Mil. Appeals bar, 1978; atty., chief, exec. services div. Office Judge Adv. Gen., Washington, 1978—; editor AF JAG Reporter, Washington, 1978—; dir. Worldwide Automated Law Library System; dir. continuing legal edn. USAF. Bd. dirs., pres. Westgate Child Care Center, Inc. Decorated Air Force Commendation medal with oak leaf cluster; recipient Design Excellence award Am. Soc. Engring. Educators, 1968; award for scholastic excellence Am. Legion, 1970, for mil. excellence, 1971; Am. Jurisprudence award for criminal justice U. So. Calif., 1976. Mem. Internat. Law Soc., Am. Bar Assn. (chmn. mil. law service com. div. young lawyers 1978—, Judge Adv. Gen. rep. 1978—), Fed. Bar Assn. (vice chmn. uniform lawyers com. 1972—), Judge Advs. Assn., Assn. Trial Lawyers Am., ASME, Air Force Assn., Order of Coif, Phi Alpha Delta. Note and article editor So. Calif. Law Rev., 1976-78. Home: 1903 Woodgate Ln McLean VA 22101 Office: Hdqrs USAF/JAES Washington DC 20324

SCHNEIDER, LORIN CHARLES, JR., retail co. exec.; b. Manchester, N.H., Sept. 13, 1949; s. Lorin Charles and Victoria Ann (Pawlowski) S.; B.A. cum laude, Boston U., 1971; postgrad. U. N.H., 1972-76; m. Kathleen Ellen McCue, Aug. 5, 1978. Buyer, Lechmere div. Dayton-Hudson, Cambridge, Mass., 1975-77; v.p. mktg. Presage Corp., Nashua, N.H., 1977-78; v.p., mdse. mgr. K & L Sound, Watertown, Mass., 1979—; teaching asst. Boston U., 1972. Named U.S. Pioneer Dealer of Yr., 1976. Mem. Phi Alpha Theta. Home: 564 School St Belmont MA 02178 Office: 75 N Beacon St Watertown MA 02172

SCHNEIDER, PHILIP VANDERBILT, employee productivity cons. co. exec.; b. Cin., July 15, 1934; s. Philip John and Lefreda (Vanderbilt) S.; B.B.A., U. Cin., 1958; m. Susan Mary Avril, June 6, 1958; children—Philip Vanderbilt, George W. Stockbroker, W.E. Hutton & Co., Cin., 1954-60; mgr. Sakrete No. Calif., 1960-64; stockbroker Glore Forgan Staats & Co., Palo Alto, Calif., 1964-70; dir. Fields Grant & Co., Menlo Park, Calif., 1970-74; stockbroker Drexel Burnham, Lambert, Inc., Palo Alto, 1974-77; pres. Mgmt. Regeneration Programs, Inc., also Community Service Programs, Inc., Redwood City, Calif., 1977—; speaker in field. Sec., Menlo Atherton Jr. C. of C., 1966; trustee Sequoia Union High Sch. Dist., 1969-72; pres. San Mateo County Sch. Bds. Assn., 1972. Served with USMCR, 1953-58. Mem. Assn. Labor-Mgmt. Adminstrs. and Cons. on Alcoholism, Occupational Programs Cons. Assn., Nat. Assn. Alcoholism Counselors. Republican. Episcopalian. Clubs: Redwood City Rotary (pres. 1969-70, dist. award of merit 1970), Sequoia (dir.), Menlo Circus. Author papers in field. Home: 410 Santa Rita Ave Menlo Park CA 94025

SCHNEIDERMAN, BARRY ALAN, lawyer; b. Seattle, June 28, 1933; s. Harry and Margaret S.; B.A., U. Wash., Seattle, 1955, J.D., 1957; m. Judith Arron, June 10, 1968; children—Paul L., Leah. Admitted to Wash. bar, 1957; dep. King County Pros. Atty.'s Office, Seattle, 1959-61; partner firm Burns & Schneiderman, Seattle, 1961-67; pres. firm Burns, Schneiderman & Davis, P.S., Seattle, 1977—; dir. Solkover Davidge Advt. Vice chmn. Seattle chpt. Am. Jewish Com.; pres., bd. dirs. Caroline Kline Galland Home Aged, Seattle; trustee Temple DeHirsch Sinai, Seattle. Served as officer AUS, 1957-59; col. JAGC, Res. Decorated Army Commendation medal, Meritorious Service medal. Mem. Am. Bar Assn., Fed. Bar Assn., Wash. Bar Assn., Seattle-King County Bar Assn. Clubs: Wash. Athletic, College (Seattle), Shriners. Home: 5135 NE Latimer Pl Seattle WA 98105 Office: 1410 Bank Calif Center Seattle WA 98164

SCHNITZER, BARBARA LEVIN, fin. investor, cons.; b. N.Y.C.; d. Harold and Denia R. Levin; A.A., Briarcliff Coll., 1951; student Sophie Newcomb Coll., 1952; m. Ralph Schnitzer, Aug. 8, 1953 (div.); children—Lynn, Frank. Owner, operator Candy Tree, Houston, 1960-63; pvt. practice fin. investing, N.Y.C., 1969—; cons. Fugazy Travel Corp., 1980—. Republican. Jewish. Home and Office: 245 E 63d St New York NY 10021

SCHNITZER, HAROLD JULIUS, real estate investment co. exec.; b. Portland, Oreg., June 8, 1923; s. Sam and Rose Schnitzer; B.S., Mass. Inst. Tech., 1944; m. Arlene Director, Sept. 11, 1949; 1 son, Jordan Director. Vice pres. Schnitzer Industries, Portland, 1946-50; pres. Harsh Investment Corp., Portland, 1950—. Trustees, chmn. bldg. com. Jewish Community Center, Portland; trustee NCCJ; mem. Mayor's Com. Performing Arts Center. Served with U.S. Army, 1944-46. Clubs: Univ., Multnomah Athletic. Office: 811 NW 19th Ave Portland OR 97208

SCHNOBRICH, HENRY GEORGE, JR., architect; b. St. Paul, Nov. 2, 1935; s. Henry George and Myrtle Hildegard (Mossberg) S.; B.Arch., U. Ill., 1961; m. Carol Joan Wienecke, Jan. 9, 1960; children—Richard, Michael, Carolyn. Architect, Wm. D. Murphy & Asso., Northfield, Ill., 1961-66, Ganster & Hennighausen, Waukegan, Ill., 1966-71; corporate architect Robin Constrn. Co., Chgo., 1971; owner, founder H.G. Schnobrich Jr. Assos., architects, Lake Bluff, Ill., 1971—; pres. H R Design-Devel. Corp., Lake Bluff, 1977—. Treas. Lake Bluff Park Bd. Caucas, 1969; mem. Lake Bluff Archtl. Rev. Bd., 1969-71, Lake Bluff Bldg. Commn., 1971-77. Served with C.E., U.S. Army, 1959. Recipient design award Chgo. Lighting Inst., 1976; cert. Nat. Council Archtl. Registration Bds. Mem. Soc. Am. Registered Architects, Nat. Trust for Historic Preservation, Lake Bluff-Lake Forest Hist. Soc., Art Inst. Chgo. Roman Catholic. Home and Office: 222 W Washington St Lake Bluff IL 60044

SCHNOES, ROBERT FREDERICK, business exec. Salesman Midwest sales div. Autographic Register Co., Hoboken, N.J., 1949-50; with quality control dept. Fisher Body div. Gen. Motors Corp., Pitts., 1950-51; successively buyer, supervisory buyer, asst. purchasing agt., asst. to surface ship project mgr. Bettis Atomic Power div. Westinghouse Electric Corp., Pitts., 1951-59; dir. material and facilities Am. Standard Mil. Products Div., Norwood, Mass., 1959-62; exec. v.p. Hamill Mfg. Co., Monroeville, Pa., 1962-63; gen. mgr. aero. research instrument dept. Am. Standard Corp., Chgo., 1963-65, pres. controls div., 1965-68; pres. Dresser Indsl. Valve & Instrument div. Dresser Industries, Inc., Stratford, Conn., 1968-70, pres. Indsl. Spltys. group, Stratford, 1970-71, v.p. ops. Dresser Industries, Inc., Dallas, 1971-74, sr. v.p. ops. office of pres., 1975-77; pres., chief operating officer IC Industries, Inc., Chgo., 1977—, also dir.

SCHNURPEL, HELEN MAMIE PERSELL, realtor; b. Omaha, Aug. 25, 1902; d. John Alva and Mamie Ethel (Davis) Persell; student U. Nebr., 1930; certificate in real estate, U. Calif., Los Angeles, 1959; m. Hans Karl Schnurpel, May 10, 1937. Co-owner Lynwood (Calif.) Realty Co. 1945—, Real Estate Sch. So. Calif., Lynwood, 1951—. Mem. Calif. Real Estate Assn. (dir.), Calif. Assn. Realtors (life), Compton-Lynwood Bd. Realtors (sec.-treas. 1966-67, pres. 1970—, dir.), Internat. Platform Assn., Lynwood C. of C. (treas. 1978-80). Republican. Club: Lynwood Womens (pres. 1975-77). Home: 14143 Dunrobin Ave Bellflower CA 90706 Office: 11228 Atlantic Ave Lynwood CA 90262

SCHOBERT, JANICE, bldg. materials co. exec.; b. Woodland, Calif., June 11, 1945; d. Earl Eugene and Lora Louise (Oxley) Schobert; A.A., Cottey Coll., Nevada, Mo., 1965; B.A., U. South Fla., 1967; m. Edmund E. Allen, Nov. 28, 1973 (div. 1981). Research asst. Asso. Credit Burs., 1967-69; asst. to dir. mktg. Variable Annuity Life Ins. Co., Houston, 1969-71; editor Houston Citizens Bank (now First Internat. Bancshares), 1971-73; pub. relations rep. Jim Walter Corp., Tampa, Fla., 1973-78, mgr. pub. relations services, 1978—. Mem. Women in Communications. Home: 2009 Russell's Dr Tampa FL 33618 Office: PO Box 22601 1500 N Dale Mabry Hwy Tampa FL 33622

SCHOCKE, HAROLD EDWIN, chem. co. exec.; b. Frankfort, Ind., Jan. 7, 1937; s. Frank J. and Helen (Hibbard) S.; B.S., Purdue U., 1960; postgrad. in indsl. engring. Ind. U./Purdue U., Indpls., 1975; m. Winona Jean Westbrook, June 28, 1974; 1 dau., Dayna Laurel. Owner, mgr. Schocke Farms, Inc., Frankfort, 1970-74, Schocke Farm Supply Inc., Frankfort, 1970-74; indsl. engr. Nat. R.R. Transp. Corp., Indpls., 1974-76; area mgr. nat. accounts Occidental Chem. Co., Indpls., 1976-78; regional mgr. C.F. Industries, Long Grove, Ill., 1978—. Mem. County Extension exec. bd., 1960-68, County Council, 1964-68; pres. bd. County Fair, 1968-72. Mem. Am. Mgmt. Assn., Fla. Agrl. Research Inst., Ga. Plant Food Ednl. Soc., Nat. Fertilizer Solutions Assn. Republican. Mem. United Pentecostal Ch. Club: Killearn Country. Home: Rural Route 3 Brandywine Rd South Barrington IL 60010 Office: CF Industries Inc Salem Lake Dr Long Grove IL 60047

SCHOELLER, GUNTER H., hosp. adminstr.; b. Germany, Jan. 22, 1939; s. Hans A. and Elsbeth O. (Barthel) S.; B.A., U. Calif., Berkeley, 1962; M.B.A., Calif. State U., Hayward, 1976; D.B.A., Golden Gate U., 1981; 1 son, Mark Barthel. Operating mgr. Regal Apparel, Inc., Port of Oakland, Calif., 1970-73, gen. mgr., 1973-75; chief engr., project dir. Mills Meml. Hosp., San Mateo, Calif., 1976-78, dir. planning services, 1978-80; dir. planning John Muir Meml. Hosp., Walnut Creek, Calif., 1980-81; asso. adminstr. Eden Hosp., Castro Valley, Calif., 1981—; provider mem. East Bay Health Systems Agy., Oakland, 1980. Served with U.S. Army, 1957-60. Named hon. Ky. col., 1978. Mem. Am. Mgmt. Assns., Am., Calif. socs. hosp. engring., Am. Soc. Hosp. Planning, Assn. M.B.A. Execs., Am. Mktg. Assn. Office: Eden Hosp 20103 Lake Chabot Rd Castro Valley CA 94546

SCHOELLHORN, ROBERT ALBERT, pharm. co. exec.; b. Phila., Aug. 29, 1928; grad. Phila. Coll. Textiles and Sci., 1955. With Am. Cyanamid Co., Wayne, N.J., 1947-73, gen. mgr., pres. Lederle div., 1971-73; exec. v.p. hosp. group Abbott Labs., North Chicago, Ill., 1973-76, pres., 1976—, chief operating officer, 1976-79, chief exec. officer, 1979—, also dir.; dir. SCM Corp. Mem. council biol. scis. Pritzker Sch. Medicine, U. Chgo., 1976—; mem. Northwestern U. Assos.; adv. council J.L. Kellog Grad. Sch. Mgmt., Northwestern U., 1979—; bd. dirs. Food and Drug Law Inst., 1977—, Rehab. Inst. Chgo., 1978—. Mem. Am. Chem. Soc., Soc. Chem. Industry, Chgo. Com. Fgn. Relations, Pharm. Mfrs. Assn., Health Industry Mfrs. Assn. (dir., chmn. 1981). Club: Economic (Chgo.). Office: Abbott Labs Abbott Park North Chicago IL 60064

SCHOEN, STEVAN JAY, lawyer; b. N.Y.C., May 19, 1944; s. Adolf and Ann (Spevack) S.; B.S. in Econs., U. Pa., 1966; J.D., Cornell U., 1969; M.Phil. in Law, Cambridge (Eng.) U., 1979; m. Noelle L'Hommedieu, Sept. 2, 1972. Admitted to N.Mex. bar, 1970, N.Y. bar, 1971, U.S. Tax Ct., 1973, U.S. Supreme Ct. bar, 1976; atty. VISTA, OEO, Albuquerque, 1969-70, nat. mgr. VISTA Law Recruitment Project, Washington, 1970-71; supervising atty. main office Legal Aid Soc. Albuquerque, 1972-73; chief atty. N.Mex. Health and Social Services Dept., Albuquerque, 1973-77; spl. asst. atty. gen., 1973-77; spl. asst. dist. atty., 1973-77; partner firm Schoen & Schoen, Albuquerque, 1977—; mem. rules com. Supreme Ct. N.Mex., 1975-77; speaker N.Mex. State Bar Conv., 1975; dir. Deuterium Geothermal Corp., Urban Labs., Inc. Bd. dirs., v.p. Placitas (N.Mex.) Vol. Fire Dept.; del. N.Mex. Democratic Party Conv., 1978. Recipient certificate of appreciation OEO, 1971. Mem. Am., N.Mex., N.Y. bar assns., Cambridge Grad. Lawyers Soc., Cambridge Union Soc. Home: S R Box 327 Placitas NM 87043 Office: 3225 Candelaria NE Albuquerque NM 87107

SCHOENHEIT, RONALD ALLEN, mfg. co. exec.; b. Portland, Oreg., Apr. 27, 1942; s. Robert H. and Joyce (Dierking) S.; B.S., Oreg. State U., 1965; m. Diane Marie Engel, Feb. 5, 1965; children—Timothy Allen, Lisa Marie, Andrew Karl. Plant engr. FMC Corp., Portland, 1965-68; sr. facilities engr. LTV Corp., Dallas, 1968-69; v.p. Pacific Fence & Wire Co., Portland, 1969-76; v.p., gen. mgr., Pacific Fireplace Furnishings, Inc., Tualatin, Oreg., 1976-80, pres., 1980—; corporate sec., partner Portland Beavers Baseball Club, 1979. Pres., sec. Omega of Sigma Pi Found., 1969—. Mem. Wire Assn., Wood Energy Inst., Fireplace Inst., Sales and Mktg. Execs., Internat., Portland C. of C. Democrat. Lutheran. Office: 20210 SW 102d Ave Tualatin OR 97062

SCHOENWALD, ARTHUR ALLEN, financial adv.; b. Bklyn., Mar. 3, 1940; s. Saul Morris and Charlotte (Lipschitz) S.; B.B.A., Baruch Sch. Bus., CCNY, 1961; M.B.A. (Baruch Sch. honor scholar), U. Chgo., 1962; D.B.A. (Arthur Andersen & Co. fellow), Harvard U., 1968; m. Maxine Rapchik, Nov. 4, 1961; children—Scott M., Ellen Beth. Asst. prof. bus. adminstrn. Rutgers U., Newark, 1967-68, asso. prof., 1968-72; exec. dir. N.J. Public Utilities Commn., Newark, 1972-74; mgr. electric utilities group Salomon Bros., N.Y.C., 1974-75; pres. A.A. Schoenwald Assos., Inc., Colonia, N.J., 1975—; lectr. in field. Fin. cons. N.J. Gov.'s Commn. to Evaluate Capital Needs of N.J., 1968; mem. N.J. Gov.'s Commn. on Public Electric Power Authority, 1975, N.J. Gov.'s Econ. Recovery Commn., 1975; treas. Middlesex County (N.J.) Republican Orgn. Recipient Chgo. Control award Controllers Inst. Am., 1962; named Tchr. of Yr., Rutgers U. Grad. Sch. Bus., 1971. Mem. Fin. Mgmt. Assn., Beta Gamma Sigma, Beta Alpha Psi. Jewish. Clubs: Colonia Country, Channel, K.P., Harvard Bus. Sch. of Greater N.Y., U. Chgo. Bus. of N.Y. Home and Office: 26 Cambridge Dr Colonia NJ 07067

SCHOEPHOERSTER, LORIN KEITH, ins. co. exec.; b. Prairie du Sac, Wis., Jan. 10, 1923; s. Edwin C. and Ruth (Preuss) S.; B.S., Marquette U., 1945; M.B.A., U. Wis., 1951; m. Lillian P. McGilvra, June 1944; children—Douglas E., Linda J., Christine A. Underwriter, Farmers Mut. Group, Madison, Wis., 1948-52; dir. edn. and research Nationwide Ins. Group, Columbus, Ohio, 1952-56, supr. agt. tng., 1956-59; dir. edn. and research State Auto Mut. Ins. Co., Columbus, 1959-64, dir. indsl. relations, 1964-66, v.p., 1966—, sr. v.p. Columbus Security Life Ins. Co., 1978—. Pres. local PTA, 1953; treas. Prairie du Sac Bd. Edn., 1953-56; chmn. United Appeal Columbus, 1965; chmn. bd. Griffith Found., 1968-71, Loman Found., 1972-74. Served with USNR, 1943-46. Named Nat. Health Ins. man of year, 1975. Mem. Soc. Ins. Research (founder, dir. 1970—), Internat. Ins. Seminars (chmn. bd. govs. 1976), Ins. Hall of Fame (gen. chmn. 1965-71), Ins. Co. Edn. Dirs. Soc. (dir. 1962—), Ohio Ins. Inst. (treas. 1977-79), Ohio Ins. Guaranty Assn. (sec. 1976—), Ohio Assn. Mut. Ins. Cos. (v.p. 1980), Gamma Iota Sigma (life). Presbyterian. Contbg. editor: Handbook of Property and Liability Insurance, 1965; editor: Insurance Teaching, 1970; Insurance Training and Education, 1975; Guide to Leadership, 1976; exec. editor Edn. Exchange, 1968—; exec. editor Research Rev., 1970—. Office: 518 E Broad St Columbus OH 43216

SCHOFIELD, WILLIAM ALLEN, mfg. co. exec.; b. Weymouth, Mass., Nov. 22, 1939; s. Ralph E. and Florence A. (Mann) S.; B.S. in M.E., U. Mass., 1969; M.S. in M.E., Worcester Poly. Inst., 1973. m. Paula M. Rondeau, June 8, 1968; children—Evan D., Kara M., Darci A. Engr., Gen. Electric Co., Fitchburg, Mass., 1969-74, mgr. devel. engring. mech. dr. turbine products, 1974-78, sr. engr. mech. dr. turbine products, 1978-80, project mgr. indsl. project engring., 1980—. Served with USAF, 1958-63. Registered profl. engr. Mem. ASME. Roman Catholic. Home: 211 Beaman Rd Sterling Junction MA 01565 Office: 166 Boulder Dr Fitchburg MA 01420

SCHOFIELD, WILLIAM GREENOUGH, ret. univ. ofcl., author; b. Providence, June 13, 1909; s. Harry Leon and Elizabeth (Smallman) S.; student Brown U., 1927-30; m. Blanche Mary Hughes, Nov. 21, 1934; children—Michael, Elinor, Peter. Feature writer Providence Jour., 1936-40; columnist Boston Traveler, 1940-52, chief editorial writer, fgn. news analyst, 1952-67; mgr. editorial services Raytheon Co., 1967-70; asso. dir. pub. information Boston U., 1970-74, ret.; news reporter radio and TV, 1946-56. Founder Freedom Trail, Boston. Served to lt. comdr. USNR, 1942-45, now capt. (ret.) U.S. Naval Res. Mem. Am. Newspaper Guild, Boston Press Club, Ret. Officers Assn., Navy League, Alpha Tau Omega. Roman Catholic. Author: Ashes in the Wilderness, 1942; The Cat in the Convoy, 1946; Payoff in Black, 1947; The Deer Cry, 1948; Seek for a Hero, 1956; Sidewalk Statesman, 1958; Destroyer 60 Years, 1962; Treason Trail,

1964; Eastward the Convoys, 1966; Freedom by the Bay, 1974; others. Home: 16 Hunnewell Circle Newton MA 02158

SCHOLL, HANS RUDOLF, watch co. exec.; b. Bienne, Switzerland, Nov. 9, 1941; came to U.S., 1977; s. Arnold and Heidi S.; Engr. in Micromechanics, Tech. Coll., Bienne, 1963. Engr., Bulova Bienne, 1963-65; with M. Guerdat, 1965-67; mgr. systems engring. Omega Bienne, 1967-69, asst. to v.p. product mgmt., 1970-71, mgr. styling and devel. for internat. line, 1972-76; div. dir. Hamilton Watch, Lancaster, Pa., 1977-78; v.p. mng. dir. Omega (U.S.) Corp., Lancaster, 1979—; v.p. product mgmt. Omega Watch Corp., N.Y.C., 1980—. Served to 1st lt. Swiss Army, 1961-77. Office: 941 Wheatland Ave Lancaster PA 17603

SCHONEMAN, JOHN ARNOLD, ins. co. exec.; b. Chgo., July 9, 1928; s. Edwin H. and Florence S.; B.S. in Safety Engring., Ill. Inst. Tech., 1950; M.B.A. in Fin., U. Chgo., 1956; A.M.P., Harvard U., 1974; m. Mary Fairbank, Nov. 4, 1950; children—Judy Schoneman Beirne, Jim, Bob, Carolyn. With Atlantic Mut. Ins. Co., 1955-76; exec. v.p. Wausau Ins. Cos. (Wis.), 1976-77, pres., chief exec. officer, 1977—; dir. Central Wis. Bankshares, Inc., Am. Mut. Re-ins. Co. Active Jr. Achievement of Wausau, Wis. Found. Ind. Colls., Wausau YMCA Found., Inc.; adv. com. U. Wis. Center. Served with ordnance U.S. Army, 1950-53. Mem. Soc. Fire Protection Engrs., Alliance Am. Insurers (exec. com., dir.), Am. Inst. Property and Liability Underwriters, Ins. Inst. Am., Wausau Area C. of C., Mfrs. and Commerce Wis. Lutheran. Clubs: Pinnacle (N.Y.C.); Wausau. Office: 2000 Westwood Dr Wausau WI 54401

SCHONLAND, RODNEY CARL, customs brokerage exec.; b. San Francisco, Jan. 1, 1947; s. Herbert Emery and Claire (Mills) S.; B.A., Norwich U., Northfield, Vt., 1969; M.B.A., Suffolk U., Boston, 1978; m. Ann P. MacGillivary, July 8, 1972; children—Avery, Heidi. Import mgr. J.F. Moran Co., Boston, 1973-78; v.p. A.J. Elliott Inc., Boston, 1978—; tchr. econs. Fisher Jr. Coll., Duxbury, Mass. Mem. Duxbury Republican Town Com. Served with U.S. Army, 1969-73. Decorated D.F.C., Air medal with V, Bronze Star. Lic. U.S. customs house broker. Mem. Air Cargo Club New Eng. (dir. 1974-76), New England Fisheries Inst., Nat. Fisheries Inst., Fgn. Commerce Club New Eng., Am. Radio Relay League, Suffolk U. Alumni Assn. (dir. 1980—). Roman Catholic. Home: 31 Stockade Path Duxbury MA 02332 Office: 4 Alger St Boston MA 02127

SCHONS, JOSEPH JOHN, process design co. exec.; b. Mankato, Minn., Feb. 2, 1931; s. Joseph Raymond and Catherine Ann (Klaseus) S.; B.Chem. Engring. (Coll. scholar), U. Minn., 1955; m. Doris Ann Dilley, June 14, 1955; children—Michael Gordon, Patrishia Catherine. Design engr. N.Am. Aviation Co., Canoga Park, Calif., 1955-57; chem. engr., refinery supt. Am. Ind. Oil Co., Kuwait, 1957-60; process/project engr. Bechtel Corp., San Francisco, 1960-62; sr. process engr. Arabian Am. Oil Co., Dhahran, Saudi Arabia, 1962-68, staff engr., 1968-73; v.p. bus. devel. Wentworth Bros. Inc., Cin., 1973-78; engring. specialist, exec. mgmt. Arabian Am. Oil Co., Dhahran, Saudi Arabia, 1978—. Served with USN, 1949-50, USAF, 1950-59. Republican. Roman Catholic. Patentee process for concurrent handling of gas liquids with methanol. Office: care Aramco Dhahran Saudi Arabia

SCHOOLS, CHARLES HUGHLETTE, banker, bus. exec., lawyer; b. Lansing, Mich., May 24, 1929; s. Robert Thomas and Lillian Pearl (Lawson) S.; B.S., Am. U., 1952, M.A., 1958; J.D., Washington Coll. of Law, 1963; LL.D., Bethune-Cookman U., 1973; m. Rosemarie Sanchez, Nov. 22, 1952; children—Charles, Michael. Dir. phys. plant Am. U., 1952-66; owner, Gen. Maintenance Service Co., Washington, 1957—, Gen. Security Co., Washington, 1969—; pres., chmn. bd. McLean Bank (Va.), 1974—, Instl. Environ. Mgmt. Services; chmn., pres. Community Assos. of Va., Associated Real Estate Mgmt. Services; dir. Computer Data Systems Inc., DAC Devel. Ltd., Am. Indsl. Devel. Corp., Intercoastal of Iran; mem. Met. Bd. Trades. Pres., McLean Boys' Club; bd. dirs. D.C. Spl. Olympics, Nat. Kidney Found.; trustee Bethune Cookman Coll., Western Md. Coll., Randolph Macon Acad. Served with USAAF, 1946-47, USAF, 1947-48. Mem. Va. C. of C., Profl. Businessman's Orgn., Alpha Tau Omega. Democrat. Clubs: Georgetown of Washington, Touchdown of Washington, Univ. of Washington, Washington Golf and Country, Pisces (Washington); Halifax (Daytona Beach, Fla.); Masons. Home: 1320 Darnall Dr McLean VA 22101 Office: The McLean Bank POB 309 McLean VA 22101 also 8027 Leesburg Pike Vienna VA 22101

SCHOOLS, RANDOLPH ROBERT, bus. exec.; b. Balt., Jan. 28, 1945; s. Walter Robert and Evelyn Mildred (Greenstreet) S.; B.S. in Bus., U. Balt.; M.Liberal Studies, Georgetown U., 1977; m. Barbara Anne Mannix. Ops. mgr. Garfinckel's, Washington, 1973-77; gen. mgr. Recreation and Welfare, Inc., Bethesda, Md., 1977—. Bd. dirs. Fed. Interagy. Fitness Council. Served with Army Intelligence, 1967-70. Mem. League Fed. Recreation Assns. (pres.), Sigma Alpha Omicron. Methodist. Home: 9938 Forest View Pl Gaithersburg MD 20760 Office: 9000 Wisconsin Ave Bldg 31A Bethesda MD 20014

SCHOONMAKER, GEORGE RUSSELL, ret. oil co. exec.; b. Chgo., Dec. 1, 1916; s. George Francis and Helen May (Lindenschmidt) S.; B.S., U. Chgo., 1938, postgrad., 1939-40; m. Marguerite Elaine Harse, Apr. 8, 1944; children—David Russell, Jane Blaine. Geologist, Marathon Oil Co., 1950-53, dist. mgr. Can., 1953-55, asst. div. mgr. fgn., v.p., Findlay, Ohio, 1955-62, exporation mgr. U.S. and Can., 1962-64, v.p. exploration, 1964-78, v.p. exploration projects, 1978-80. Bd. dirs. YMCA, 1964-72, pres., 1970-72. Mem. Am. Assn. Petroleum Geologists, AIME, Internat. Oceanographic Assn., Soc. Exploration Geologists, Am. Assn. Petroleum Landmen, Am. Petroleum Inst., Am. Inst. Profl. Geologists, Ohio Geol. Soc. Home: 119 E Edgar St Findlay OH 45840

SCHRAYER, MAX ROBERT, ins. exec.; b. Chgo., Nov. 17, 1902; s. Robert Max and Jennie (Weber) S.; B.S.E., U. Mich., 1923; m. Mildred Mayer, July 3, 1925; children—Helaine (Mrs. A. A. Freeman), Jean (Mrs. Robert L. Adler), Robert Max. Propr., Max Robert Schrayer & Assos., Chgo., 1933-42, now pres.; v.p. Asso. Agys., Inc., 1942-64, pres., 1965-75, chmn. bd., 1975—; dir. Allied Tube & Conduit Co., Irvin Industries. Gen. chmn. Combined Jewish Appeal, 1964-65, pres., 1966; past pres. Bd. dirs. Better Govt. Assn.; vice chmn. bd. trustees Roosevelt U.; bd. dirs. Am. Joint Distbn. Com., Jewish Telegraphic Agy.; Campaign chmn. Jewish United Fund, 1979—. Home: 4950 Chicago Beach Dr Chicago IL 60615 Office: 223 W Jackson Blvd Chicago IL 60606

SCHRECK, GEORGE ROBERT, ins. co. exec.; b. New Haven, Oct. 25, 1917; s. George Edward and Martha M. Schreck; B.S., Trinity Coll., Hartford, Conn., 1939; postgrad. U. Rochester, Rochester Inst. Tech., Siena Coll., Albany, N.Y., Princeton U.; m. Carolyn M. Ackley, May 30, 1943; children—Barbara C., John R., Craig A., Carol A. With Hartford Ins. Group, 1939-42, 47—, gen. mgr. Rochester Regional Office (N.Y.), 1967—; with Taconic Telephone Co., Chatham, N.Y., 1946-47, coms., 1955—; propr. Ins. Career Sch., Albany, N.Y., 1961-67; tchr. ins. courses, 1967-72. Active various sch. coms., United Fund, youth programs. Served to capt. Transp. Corps, U.S. Army, 1942-46. Mem. Ins. Mgrs. Assn. Rochester, Ins. Mgrs. Assn. Albany, Rochester C. of C., Am. Legion (post comdr. 1956-57). Conservative Republican. Methodist. Patentee non-glare automobile headlight, pocket shoe shine travel pack. Home: 3 Ten Eyke Circle Pittsford NY 14534 Office: One Marine Midland Plaza Rochester NY 14604

SCHREIBER, HANS WILLIAM, mining cons. co. exec.; b. Frankfurt am Main, Germany, Feb. 28, 1932; came to U.S., 1932, naturalized, 1948; s. George Willy-Rudolf and Annie (Weiss) S.; B.A., Amherst Coll., 1954; M.A., Columbia U., 1958; m. Mary Stearns Lyman, June 6, 1955; children—Stephen William, Elizabeth Anne, Margaret Mary. Mining geologist Am. Zinc, Lead & Smelting Co., Silver City, N.Mex., Shullsburg, Wis., Knoxville, Tenn., 1959-64; cons. geologist Dewitt Smith & Co., Inc., N.Y.C., 1964-68; mgr. mining investments Cerro Corp., N.Y.C., 1968-72; v.p., gen. mgr. Phelps Dodge Europa, London, 1972-76; pres. Behre Dolbear & Co., Inc., N.Y.C., 1976—; dir. Dunn Geosci., Inc., geologic cons., Latham, N.Y.; lectr. project financing for mining projects AIME, 1978—. Served with USAF, 1955-57. Mem. AIME, Mining and Metall. Soc., Geol. Soc. Am., Am. Inst. Profl. Geologists, Sigma Xi. Home: 8 Tavano Rd Ossining NY 10562 Office: 230 Park Ave New York NY 10169

SCHREIBER, HARRY, JR., mgmt. cons.; b. Columbus, Ohio, Apr. 1, 1934; s. C. Harry and Audrey (Sard) S.; B.S., Mass. Inst. Tech., 1955; M.B.A., Boston U., 1958; m. Margaret Ruth Heinzman, June 12, 1955; children—Margaret Elizabeth, Thomas Edward, Amy Katherine. Accountant truck and coach div. Gen. Motors Corp., Pontiac, Mich., 1955; instr. Mass. Inst. Tech., 1958-62; pres. Data-Service, Inc., Boston, 1961-65; pres. Harry Schreiber Assos., Wellesley, Mass., 1965; mgr., nat. dir. merchandising Peat, Marwick, Mitchell & Co., N.Y.C., 1966-70, partner, Chgo., 1970-75; chmn. bd. Close, Martin, Schreiber & Co., 1975—. Staff, Work Simplification Conf. Lake Placid, N.Y., 1960-61. Served to 1st lt. AUS, 1956-58. Mem. Am. Inst. Indsl. Engrs. (chmn. data-processing div. 1964-66, chpt. v.p. 1961, 65, chmn. retail industries div. 1976-78), Com. Internat. Congress Transp. Confs., Assn. for Computing Machinery, Assn. for Systems Mgmt., Inst. Mgmt. Scis., Retail Research Soc., Retail Fin. Execs., Nat. Retail Mchts. Assn. (retail systems specifications com.), Food Distbn. Research Soc. (dir. 1972—, pres. 1974), Internat. Trade Club, Japan-Am. Soc. Chgo., Chgo. Assn. Commerce and Industry. Republican. Methodist. Clubs: MIT of Washington; Skokie Country; Reston Golf and Country; Army and Navy (Washington); Plaza (Chgo.). Home: 12137 Stirrup Rd Reston VA 22091 Office: Suite 401 1629 K St NW Washington DC 20006

SCHREIBER, OTTO WILLIAM, mfg. co. exec.; b. Greenwood, Wis., July 4, 1922; s. Otto Waldemar and Meta Wilhelmine (Suemnicht) S.; B.S.E.E., U. Wis., Madison, 1944. Electroacoustic scientist Navy Electronics Lab., San Diego, 1946-56; electronics engr., then mgr. electronic engring. dept., ordnance div. Librascope, Sunnyvale, Calif., 1956-65; chief engr. Teledyne Indsl. Electronics Co., San Jose, Calif., 1965-68; exec. v.p. Marcom Corp., San Francisco, 1969; test mgr. MB Assos., San Ramon, Calif., 1970-71; ops. mgr. Am. Service Products, Inc., Newhall, Calif., 1972-75; mfg. mgr. UTI, Inc., Sunnyvale, Calif., 1975-80; dir. mfg. Hi-Shear Ordnance/Electronics, Torrance, Calif., 1980—. Served to lt. (j.g.) USNR, 1944-46. Mem. IEEE, APICS, Eta Kappa Nu, Kappa Eta Kappa. Republican. Lutheran. Home: PO Box 60454 Sunnyvale CA 94088 Office: 2600 Skypark Dr Torrance CA 90509

SCHREINER, KENNETH VINCENT, hosp. adminstr.; b. Toledo, Ohio, June 27, 1941; s. Vincent and Hazel (Kardos) S.; B.A., Marquette U., 1963; M.P.A., (Sloan scholar), Cornell U., 1970; m. Catherine Spellmire, Feb. 13, 1965; children—Julie, Ellen, Matthew. Field epidemiologist USPHS, Kansas City, Mo., 1963-64, public health adviser, Portland, Maine, 1964-66, Augusta, Maine, 1966-68; asst. adminstr. Park Ridge Hosp., Rochester, N.Y., 1970-77; exec. v.p. Holy Family Hosp., Des Plaines, Ill., 1977-79; v.p. St. Francis Hosp., Evanston, Ill., 1979—; bd. dirs. North Suburban Blood Center, Inc., Glenview, Ill., 1981—. Mem. Bd. Health Village of Wilmette, Ill., 1981—. Lic. nursing home adminstr., N.Y. Mem. Chgo. Hosp. Planning Assn., Am. Coll. Hosp. Adminstrs., Am. Hosp. Assn. Chgo. Health Execs. Forum, Alpha Phi Omega. Club: Rolling Green Country (Arlington Heights Ill.). Home: 2128 Washington Ave Wilmette IL 60091 Office: 355 Ridge St Evanston IL 60202

SCHREUR, A. JEFFREY, Realtor; b. Allegan, Mich., July 1, 1947; s. Ammon Earle and Cora G. (Lewis) S.; B.A., Albion Coll., 1969; M.B.A., So. Meth. U., 1970; m. Susan Soderquist, June 30, 1968; children—Amy, Jennifer, Carrie. Vice-pres., Pickitt & Schreur, Inc., Grand Rapids, Mich., 1970-76; Realtor, Realty, Inc., Grand Rapids, 1977-79, pres. AJS Realty Group, Grand Rapids, 1980—. Pres. bd. dirs. Allegan Area United Way, 1975; chmn. Grand Rapids Area United Way, 1977; chmn. benevolence bd. Mayflower Congl. Ch., 1977, deacon, 1979; bd. dirs. SE Family YMCA. Designated G.R.I. Mem. Nat., Mich. assns. Realtors, Real Estate Securities and Syndication Inst. Republican. Clubs: Econ. of Grand Rapids, Cascade Hills Country, E. Hills Tennis. Home: 1800 Mont-Rue SE Grand Rapids MI 49506 Office: 999 Union Bank Grand Rapids MI 49503

SCHREYER, WILLIAM ALLEN, fin. co. exec.; b. Williamsport, Pa., Jan. 13, 1928; s. William L. and Elizabeth (Engel) S.; B.A. in Bus. Adminstrn., Pa. State U., 1948; m. Joan Legg, Oct. 17, 1953; 1 dau., Drue Ann. With Merrill Lynch & Co., Inc., N.Y.C., 1948—, account exec. Buffalo office, 1950-62, mgr. Trenton (N.J.) offices, 1963-65, v.p., 1965, sales dir. met. region, N.Y.C., met. regional dir., 1972-73, chmn., chief exec. officer Merrill Lynch Govt. Securities Inc. subs. Merrill Lynch & Co., 1973-76; exec. v.p. Merrill Lynch P F & S, Inc., N.Y.C., 1976-78, dir., 1976—; pres., chief adminstrv. officer Merrill Lynch, Pierce, Fenner & Smith, N.Y.C., 1978-80, chief exec. officer, 1980—. Trustee, Med. Center Princeton (N.J.), chmn., 1974—. Served to 1st lt. USAF, 1955-56. Mem. Securities Industry Assn. (gov. 1978-81), Am. Mgmt. Assn. (trustee 1979—), Sigma Phi Epsilon Ednl. Found. Roman Catholic. Clubs: Nasaau, Springdale Golf (Princeton); River (N.Y.C.); Saturn (Buffalo). Office: One Liberty Plaza 165 Broadway New York NY 10080

SCHRIEVER, FRED MARTIN, mgmt. cons.; b. N.Y.C., June 5, 1930; s. Samuel and Sara S.; B.M.E., Poly. Inst. N.Y., 1952, M.M.E., 1958; m. Cheri G. Schriever, Feb. 11, 1953; children—Melissa, Elizabeth E. Design engr. Bar Ray Products Inc., N.Y.C., 1954-56; chief engr. Sperry Rand Corp., N.Y.C., 1956-64; v.p. Booz, Allen & Hamilton, Md. and N.Y., 1964-71; pres., chief exec. Reliance Cons. Group, London and N.Y.C., 1971—; v.p. chief exec. Europe, Reliance Group Inc., London and N.Y.C., 1971—; dir. corps. Served with U.S. Army, 1952-54. Registered profl. engr., N.Y. State, D.C.; cert. mgmt. cons. Fellow Inst. of Dirs., Inst. of Mgmt. Consultants. Club: Marks. Home: 58 Harley House London NW1 5HL England Office: 197 Knightsbridge London SW7 1RN England also Reliance Group Inc 919 3d Ave New York NY 10022

SCHRODER, JURGEN RUDOLF, marine terminal and stevedoring exec.; b. Hamburg, Ger., Sept. 14, 1940; came to U.S., 1966, naturalized, 1972; s. Karl and Else (Wedekind) S.; grad. Nautical Acad. Hamburg, 1963; m. Norma Elizabeth Dell, June 16, 1966; 1 dau., Gisela. Apprentice seaman Hamburg (Ger.) Am. Line and Deutsche Africa Linie, 1957-61; nav. officer Ferdinand Laeisz Reederei, 1963-66; stevedore supt. Tex. Transport & Terminal, 1966-69; ops. mgr. Roberts S.S. Agy., also mgr. James Stevedores, Houston, 1970-73, v.p., 1974-77; v.p., gen. mgr. Manchester Terminal Co., also Manchester Stevedoring Co., Houston, 1979—; 1st v.p., dir. Houston Port Bur., 1977—. Sustaining mem. Republican Nat. Com., 1974-80. Mem. Nat. Assn. Stevedores, W. Gulf Maritime Assn., WORLD Trade Assn., U.S. Naval Inst., Houston World Trade Assn. Republican. Lutheran. Clubs: Warwick, World Trade. Home: 6417 Buffalo Speedway Houston TX 77005 Office: 10000 Manchester St Houston TX 77012

SCHROEDER, ROBERT ANTHONY, lawyer; b. Bendena, Kans., May 19, 1912; s. Anthony and Nanon (Bagby) S.; student U. Kans., 1932-37, LL.B. cum laude, 1937; m. Janet Manning, Nov. 21, 1936; 1 son, Robert Breathitt. Admitted to Mo. bar 1937, U.S. Ct. of Claims, 1956; atty. Allstate Ins. Co., Chgo., 1937-38; asso. Madden, Freeman, Madden & Burke, Kansas City, Mo., 1938-48; partner Swofford, Schroeder & Shankland, Kansas City, 1948-59; pvt. practice law, Law offices Robert A. Schroeder, Kansas City, Mo., 1959-67; partner Schroeder & Schroeder, 1967—. Pres., dir. Douglas County Investment Co., Inc.; v.p. Roxbury State Bank 1954-72, pres., 1972-76, chmn. bd., 1976—, also dir.; v.p., dir. ModDev Co., Inc., 1965—; chmn. bd., dir. Hub State Bank, 1974—. Pres. Mo. Bar Found., 1970-73; charter mem. Kansas City Council; mem. 16th Jud. Commn., 1974-79, Circuit Bar Com., 1972—; mem. Appellate-Jud. Commn. Mo., 1980—. Hon. trustee Kansas City Art Inst. Fellow Am. Bar Found., Am. Coll. Probate Counsel, Kans. U. Law Soc. (trustee 1971-74), Harry S Truman Library Inst. (hon.); mem. Kans. U. Law Alumni Assn. (pres. 1963-64), Am. (del. Ho. of Dels. 1966-70, Mo. chmn. standing com. membership 1966-67), Mo. (vice chmn. continuing legal edn. com. 1958-59, chmn. publs. edn. com. 1962-63, vice chmn. Bar and Bench 1968-71, mem. bar and bench com. 1971-78, chmn. cts. and judiciary com. 1971-72), Kansas City (pres. and chmn. exec. com. 1957-58, chmn. jud. recommendation com. 1957-58, 68, chmn. tornado disaster com. 1957-58, chmn. pub. relations com. 1958-60, chmn. medico-legal com. 1961-63, chmn. law day com. 1963-64, chmn. prepaid legal service com. 1975-76, others, Achievement award 1976) bar assns., Mo. Bar (pres. 1965-66, Pres.'s award 1972), Am. Judicature Soc. (dir.), Nat. Legal Aid and Defender Assn., Bar Assn. Kans. (hon. life), Mo. Inst. for Justice (dir.), Delta Tau Delta, Phi Delta Phi, Order of Coif. Mason. Mem. editorial bd. Kans. Bar Jour., 1935-36. Contbr. numerous articles on Mo. cts. system to profl. publs. Office: 700 Lathrop Bldg 1005 Grand Ave Kansas City MO 64106

SCHROEDER, WALTER ALLEN, lawyer; b. San Francisco, July 29, 1954; s. Carl Walter and Mary (Lee) S.; B.S. in Bus. Adminstrn., Georgetown U., 1976; J.D., U. Houston, 1979. Asst. treas. G.U. Fed. Credit Union, Washington, 1976-77; asst. to pres. U.S.E. Credit Union, Houston, 1977-79; analyst Banc Systems, Inc., Houston, 1979; admitted to Tex. bar, 1979, also U.S. Dist. Cts. for No. and So. Dists. Tex.; briefing atty. Tex. Ct. Civil Appeals, Ft. Worth, 1979-80; asst. counsel Am. Ins. Assn., Houston, 1980—. Trustee Found. Amateur Radio, Washington, 1972-76, chmn. audit com., 1975-76; treas. Houston Echo Soc., 1979. Recipient Indsl. Peace award Georgetown U., 1976. Mem. Am. Bar Assn., State Bar Tex. Republican. Lutheran. Author articles in field. Home: 2800 Jeanetta St Apt 804 Houston TX 77063 Office: 2900 N Loop W Suite 640 Houston TX 77092

SCHROM, DAVID ALLEN, mfg. co. exec.; b. York, Pa., June 15, 1918; s. Stuart and Leah Rebecca (Lehman) S.; B.S. in Indsl. Engring., Pa. State U., 1942; m. Helen E. Stapelkamp, Feb. 27, 1942; children—David Allen, Rebecca Ann. Apprentice to works mgr. York Corp. (Pa.), 1938-61; v.p. mfg. and indsl. relations Delaval Separator Co., Poughkeepsie, N.Y., 1961-65; pres. Indsl. Fastener div. Standard Technologies Corp., Jenkintown, Pa., 1965-70, Brubaker Tool Corp., Millersburg, Pa., 1970-74; v.p., pres. textile machinery group Crompton & Knowles Corp., Charlotte, N.C., 1974—, also dir. Pres., Young Republicans York, 1952; mem. Engring. Manpower Commn., 1958-63; bd. dirs. York United Way, also Poughkeepsie and Harrisburg, Pa., 1958-74. Served with USN, 1943-46. Registered profl. engr., Pa.; cert. mfg. engr. Fellow Inst. Prodn. Engrs. (London) (life); mem. Engrs. Joint Council (dir. 1958-63), Soc. Mfg. Engrs. (life; pres. 1962), Mil. Order World Wars. Republican. Lutheran. Clubs: Charlotte Athletic; Carmel Country. Home: 2710 Beretania Circle Charlotte NC 28211 Office: PO Box 240655 Charlotte NC 28224

SCHRUM, JOHN MARTIN, investment co. exec.; b. Woodward, Iowa, Dec. 6, 1932; s. Peter Fredrich and Leone Anita (Warner) S.; B.S., Iowa State U., 1959; M.S., Purdue U., 1961; Agrl. Econs. degree U. No. Iowa, 1964-67; m. Marilyn Jean Lister, Aug. 9, 1975. High sch. tchr. vocat. agr., sci., econs., 1961-68; with brokerage firm R.G. Dickinson, Cedar Falls, Iowa, 1968-71; investment broker A.G. Edwards and predecessor firm, Waterloo, 1972-79, v.p. sales, 1979—; tchr. econs., mktg. Hawkeye Inst. Tech., evenings 1970—. Republican precinct chmn., 1976—, del. various Rep. convs. 1968—. Mem. Lutheran Laymen's League. Club: D.A.N.K. Home: 3703 McClain Dr Cedar Falls IA 50613 Office: A G Edwards & Co 626 Commercial St Waterloo IA 50701

SCHUBACH, CLARK, stockbroker; b. Kingston, N.Y., Feb. 15, 1942; s. Fred and Bella (Hasenfeld) S.; B.A. in Fin., CCNY, 1963; m. Susan Smolin, Nov. 5, 1967; 1 dau., Hillary Jane. Trainee, Lieberbaum & Co., 1964; account exec. Hirsch & Co., 1964-70, duPont, Glore Forgan, 1970-72; v.p. Edwards & Hanly, 1972-76, Loeb Rhoades, 1976-78; partner Bear Stearns, N.Y.C., 1978—. Active Roslyn chpt. United Cerebral Palsy. Served as sgt. USAR, 1963-64. Jewish. Club: Nob Hill Country (pres. 1975-78). Office: Bear Stearns 55 Water St New York NY 10041

SCHUBERT, BLAKE H., investor, lawyer; b. Wheeling, W.Va., Apr. 21, 1939; s. John Arnold and Esther Elizabeth (Masters) S.; B.A., Ohio Wesleyan U., 1961; J.D., U. Chgo., 1964; m. Carol Jean Cramp, Jan. 13, 1962; children—Cheryl Lynn, Charles Bradley, Elisabeth Anne. Admitted to Ill. bar, 1964; atty. Brunswick Corp., Chgo., 1964-68; asst. group counsel FMC Corp., Chgo., 1968-73; gen. counsel Dresser Tool Group, Chgo., 1973-79; chmn. bd. Schubert Securities Corp., Oak Park, Ill., 1979—, Inter-Am. Investments, Inc., Oak Park, 1980—. Past chmn. 1st United Ch. Endowment Fund, Park Forest (Ill.) Coop. Registered broker dealer, SEC. Mem. Chgo. Bd. Options Exchange, Chgo. Bar Assn., Ill. Bar Assn., Am. Bar Assn. Republican. Home and Office: 522 Linden Ave Oak Park IL 60302

SCHUBERT, RICHARD FRANCIS, steel co. exec.; b. Trenton, N.J., Nov. 2, 1936; s. Yaro and Frances Mary (Hustak) S.; B.A. cum laude, Eastern Nazarene Coll., 1958; LL.B., Yale, 1961; m. Sarah Jane Lockington, Aug. 24, 1957; children—Robyn, David. Admitted to Pa. bar, 1962, also U.S. Supreme Ct., 1972; arbitration atty. Bethlehem Steel Corp. (Pa.), 1961-66, asst. mgr. labor relations, 1966-70; exec. asst. to under sec. labor, Washington, 1970, exec. asst. to sec. labor, 1970, solicitor of labor, 1971-73, under sec. labor, 1973-75; asst. to v.p. indsl. relations Bethlehem Steel Corp., 1973, asst. v.p. pub. affairs, 1975-77, v.p. pub. affairs, 1977-79, pres., 1979-80, vice-chmn. bd., 1980—. Trustee, Eastern Nazarene Coll., Quincy, Mass., Lafayette Coll., Easton, Pa., Nat. Safety Council; bd. dirs. Pennsylvanians for Effective Govt.; bd. visitors UCLA; mem. corp. vis. com. dept. materials sci. and engring. M.I.T. Mem. Pa., Northampton County bar assns., Nat. Alliance of Bus. (dir.), Am. Arbitration Assn., Am. Iron and Steel Inst. (past chmn. internat. trade com.), Council Fgn. Relations, The Conf. Bd., Eastern Nazarene Alumni Assn. (pres. 1969-73, dir.), Phi Alpha Delta. Mem. Ch. of Nazarene. Office: Martin Tower Bethlehem PA 18016

SCHUCH, THEODORIS, educator; b. Ft. Collins, Colo., Oct. 12, 1927; d. Leland S. and Frances (Beeler) S.; student U. Denver, 1946-47; B.S. magna cum laude, U. Colo., 1970, M.B.A., 1972; postgrad. No. Ariz. U., 1975-78; children—Alison Noma, Judith Henderson. Med. sec., asst., Denver, 1956-60, 60-64; key order editor C.A. Norgren Co., Littleton, Colo., 1964-68; sec., librarian asst. Boulder (Colo.) Valley Sch. Dist., 1968-70; sec. to deans U. Colo., Boulder, 1970-72; tchr. part time Boulder Valley Sch. Dist., 1971-73; credit analyst 1st Nat. Bank of Denver, 1972-74; founding faculty mem., program specialist, div. chairperson Northland Pioneer Coll., Navajo County Community Coll. Dist., Holbrook, Ariz., 1974-79; customer service adviser Continental Telephone of West, 1979-80; tchr. Agua Fria Union High Sch., Avondale, Ariz., 1980—. Mem. Am. Mgmt. Assn., Nat., Western, Ariz. bus. edn. assns., Am. Vocat. Assn., Ariz. Vocat. Assn., NEA, Ariz. Edn. Assn., NOW, Beta Gamma Sigma, Beta Sigma, Delta Kappa Gamma. Mem. United Ch. Christ. Home: 4662 W Krall St Glendale AZ 85301

SCHUCK, MARJORIE MASSEY (MRS. FRANZ SCHUCK), publisher, editor; b. Winchester, Va., Oct. 9, 1921; d. Carl Frederick and Margaret Harriet (Parmele) Massey; student U. Minn., 1941-43, New Sch., N.Y.C., 1948, N.Y. U., 1952, 54-55; m. Ernest George Metcalfe, Dec. 2, 1943 (div. Oct. 1949); m. Franz Schuck, Nov. 11, 1953 (dec. Jan. 1958). Mem. editorial bd. St. Petersburg Poetry Assn., 1967-68; co-editor, pub. Poetry Venture Mag., St. Petersburg, Fla., 1968-69, editor, pub., 1969-79; pub., editor poetry anthologies, 1972—; founder, owner, pres. Valkyrie Press Inc., 1972—; founder Valkyrie Press Round Table Forum and Workshop for Writers, 1975-80; founder Valkyrie Press Reference Library, 1975—; founder, owner Freedom Press, 1976—. Cons. designs and formats, trade publs., ann. reports, lit. books and pamphlets, 1973—; founder, owner, pres. MS Records, Inc., 1974-79, Marjorie Schuck Pub., Inc., 1974-79; judge poetry and speech contests, 1970—; mem. adminstrv. bd. Suncoast Mgmt. Inst., 1977-78; chmn. Women and Mgmt. Seminars, 1977-78. Corr. rec. sec. Women's Aux. Hosp. for Spl. Surgery, N.Y.C., 1947-59; mem. Pinellas County Arts Council, 1976—, chmn., 1977-78; active St. Petersburg Mus. Fine Arts (charter); St. Petersburg Arts Center Assn. Bd. dirs., pub. relations chmn. Soc. for Prevention Cruelty to Animals, 1968-71. Named Fla. Patriot, Fla. Bicentennial Commn., 1976—. Mem. Acad. Am. Poets, Pinellas Suncoast C of C., Com. of 100 of Pinellas County, Coordinating Council Lit. Mags., A.S.C.A.P., Com. Small Mag. Editors and Pubs. (founding mem. So. region orgn.), Fla. Suncoast Writers Confs. (a founder, co-dir., lectr. 1973—), Nat. Fedn. Press Women, Women in Mgmt., Pi Beta Phi. Democrat. Episcopalian. Author: Speeches and Writings for the Cause of Freedom, 1973. Contbr. poetry to profl. jours.; publisher Angel City (Patrick D. Smith), produced as feature movie CBS-TV, 1980. Home: 8245 26th Ave N St Petersburg FL 33710 Office: 2135-2149 1st Ave S St Petersburg FL 33712

SCHUETZ, JACOB CHICKERING, ins. agt.; b. Yankton, S.D., Nov. 14, 1926; s. Jacob Chickering and Frances Anna (Hohenthaner) S.; B.S., U. Wyo., 1948; m. Sharon L. Nunn, Mar. 2, 1958; children—Susan W. Schuetz Erickson, Gregory D., Debra A., Wendy L. Agt., Midwest Life Ins. Co., Casper, Wyo., 1948-62; owner, mgr. J.C. Schuetz Inc., fire and casualty agy., Casper, 1954-68; gen. agt. Southland Life Ins. Co., Casper, 1962—. Served with USAAF, 1945. C.L.U. Mem. Central Wyo. (pres. 1952-53), Wyo. (pres. 1955-56) life underwriters assns., Izaak Walton League Am. Republican. Mem. Christian Ch. Clubs: Lions, Elks. Home: 333 S Grant St Casper WY 82601 Office: 1445 S Poplar St Casper WY 82601

SCHUH, JACK WILLIAM, aluminum co. exec.; b. Longview, Wash., Aug. 27, 1932; s. John William and Rose (Bombkamp) S.; student U. Portland, 1950-52; B.A. and B.S., U. Wash., 1956; m. Dorothy Jane Harmon, Apr. 30, 1960; children—Robert James, Kathy Jane, Jennifer Lynn. Engr., Kaiser Alum, Spokane, Wash., 1957-58; prodn. supr., Ravenswood, W.Va., 1958-61, India, 1962; prodn. supt. Reynolds Metals, Troutdale, Oreg., 1963-68; prodn. supt. Reynolds Internat.-Alcasa, 1969-71; plant mgr. Reynolds Internat.-Iran, 1972-75, Reynolds Internat.-Venalum, 1975-78; v.p., gen. mgr. Alcasa, 1979—. Pres., Gresham (Oreg.) P.T.A., 1966-68. Decorated Medal of Francisco de Miranda (Venezuela). Mem. AIME. Roman Catholic. Clubs: Nautico, Caroni, Elks, K.C. Home: Calee Ambato 17 Puerto Ordaz Venezuela Office: Alcasa Apt 115 Puerto Ordaz Venezuela

SCHULER, RAYMOND T., assn. exec.; b. Kingston, N.Y.; B.A. in Pub. Adminstrn., Syracuse U., 1952, postgrad. Maxwell Grad. Sch. Citizenship and Pub. Affairs; LL.D., LeMoyne Coll., 1978; m. Patricia Ann Martin; children—Patti, Ellen. Asst. to chief engr. N.Y. State Dept. Pub. Works, 1957-65, asst. dep. supt. pub. works, 1965-67; asst. exec. dep. commr. N.Y. State Dept. Transp., 1967-72, commr., 1972-77; also mem. numerous spl. state coms. and commns., chmn. policy and steering coms. West Side Project N.Y.C.; pres. Asso. Industries of N.Y. State, Inc., Albany, 1977—; chmn. Tri-State Regional Planning Commn., 1975-76; head 17-state coalition for Hwy. Trust Fund; mem. exec. com. Nat. Acad. Sci.; Harry E. Salzberg Meml. lectr. Syracuse U., 1976; dir. Schenectady Savs. Bank. Chmn. Syracuse U. Gift Trust; trustee, Second Century Fund exec. com. and adv. com. Syracuse U.; chmn. 1977 State Employees United Fund Campaign; bd. dirs. United Fund of Albany, Sunnyview Hosp., and Rehab. Center, Schenectady, N.Y., State Canal Mus., Syracuse, Schenectady Art Center Theater, St. Clare's Hosp., Schenectady; bd. dirs. Albany Med. Coll.; mem. adv. council N.Y. State Sch. Indsl. Labor Relations, Cornell U. Served with inf. USMC; Korea. Recipient George Arents Pioneer medal Syracuse U., Salzberg medallion, 1976; citation for dedicated leadership in making Dept. Transp. a model for other states Gov. N.Y., 1977. Mem. Syracuse U. Alumni Assn. (pres. Alumni Class 1952, nat. dir.), Sierra Club. Roman Catholic. Clubs: Syracuse Alumni Men's (organizer, pres.) (Albany) Schenectady County Alumni. Creator N.Y. State Environ. Action Plan for Transp.; instrumental in passage of N.Y. State r.r. preservation legislation. Office: Associated Industries NY State Inc 150 State St Albany NY 12207

SCHULHOF, MICHAEL PETER, office products mfg. co. exec.; b. N.Y.C., Nov. 30, 1942; s. Rudolph B. and Hannelore (Buck) S.; B.A., Grinnell Coll., 1964; M.Sc., Cornell U., 1967; Ph.D. (NSF fellow), Brandeis U., 1970; m. Paola Nissim, Apr. 17, 1969; children—David Kenneth, Jonathan Nissim. Research fellow Brookhaven Nat. Lab., Upton, N.Y., 1969-71; asst. to v.p. mfg. CBS Records, CBS Inc., N.Y.C., 1971-73; gen. mgr. bus. products div. Sony Corp., N.Y.C., 1973-77, v.p., 1977-78, sr. v.p., 1978—; pres. Sony Industries, Inc., 1978—; dir. Sony Corp. Am. Mem. Am. Phys. Soc., Computer and Bus. Equipment Mfrs. Assn., Am. Radio Relay League, Aircraft Owners and Pilots Assn. Club: Fenway Golf. Contbr. articles to profl. jours. Home: 1021 Park Ave New York NY 10028 Office: 9 W 57th St New York NY 10019

SCHULHOF, SAMUEL A., mgmt. exec.; b. McKeesport, Pa., Apr. 23, 1942; s. Sidney and Evelyn C. (Rosen) S.; B.S., C.W. Post Coll., 1964; postgrad. Duquesne U. Law Sch., 1964-65; m. Katrina Schermerhorn Veeder, Feb. 5, 1972. Mgmt. cons., Pitts., 1967-71; asst. to sec. HEW, Washington, 1971-73; dep. spl. asst. to Pres., Washington, 1973-75; prin. Hay Assos., Inc., Washington, 1976-79; pres., chief operating officer Wander Sales, Inc., Pitts., 1979—; dir. Internat. Bus. Assos., The Washington Group, Inc. Bd. dirs. Joint Mid-East Am. Bus. Conf.; mem. Sec. of Commerce's Com. on Econ. Devel., 1976-78. Mem. Young Presidents Orgn. Republican. Jewish. Clubs: Concordia, Capitol Hill, Trout Unlimited, Fedn. Fly Fisherman, Chaine des Rotisseurs, Scottish Rite, Shriners. Home: 1220 Bennington Ave Pittsburgh PA 15217 Office: Jones St West Elizabeth PA 15088

SCHULMAN, RICHARD CHARLES, banker; b. Miami, Fla., Mar. 21, 1934; s. Harry and Lillian S.; B.A., U. Miami, 1956; m. Susan Barber, Oct. 19, 1974; children—Robin, Melissa, Brett. Prodn. asst. WCKT-TV, Miami, 1956-58; sr. v.p. Biscayne Fed. Savs. & Loan Assn., Miami, 1958—, now dir. non-mortgage investments; instr. Inst. Fin. Edn. Fla., 1970—. Mem. Nat. Savs. and Loan League, Savs. and Loan Public Relations Soc. (pres. 1969), Savs. and Loan Mortgage Officer Soc. (charter), U.S. League Savs. and Loan Assns., Fla. League Savs. and Loans Assn. Democrat. Jewish. Clubs: Progress of Miami (treas. 1975), B'nai B'rith (pres. 1968-69). Home: 20300 W Country Club Dr North Miami Beach FL 33180 Office: 1790 Biscayne Blvd Miami FL 33132

SCHULTE, DAVID MICHAEL, corp. exec.; b. N.Y.C., Nov. 12, 1946; s. Irving and Ruth (Stein) S.; B.A., Williams Coll., 1968; postgrad. (Moody Scholar) Oxford (Eng.) U., 1968-69; J.D., Yale U., 1972; m. Nancy Fisher, June 30, 1968; children—Michael Baver, Katherine Felice. Law clk. Justice Stewart, U.S. Supreme Ct., Washington, 1972-73; spl. asst. to pres. NW Industries, Inc., Chgo., 1973-75, v.p. corp. devel., 1975-79, exec. v.p., 1979—; dir. Manpower Demonstration Research Corp. Bd. dirs. Chgo. Child Care Soc.; mem. exec. com. Yale Law Sch. Assn. Mem. Washington Bar. Assn. Clubs: Racquet of Chgo., Saddle & Cycle. Editor-in-chief: Yale Law Jour., 1971-72. Office: 6300 Sears Tower Chicago IL 60606

SCHULTZ, ARTHUR WARREN, advt. exec.; b. N.Y.C., Jan. 13, 1922; s. Milton Warren and Genevieve (Dann) S.; grad. U. Chgo.; m. Elizabeth Carroll Mahan, Apr. 23, 1949; children—Arthur Warren, John Carroll (dec.), Julia Hollingsworth. With Foote, Cone & Belding Communications, Chgo., 1948—, v.p., 1957-63, sr. v.p., dir., 1963-69, gen. mgr., Chgo. office, 1967-71, exec. v.p., 1969-70, chmn. bd., 1970—; dir. Paxall Inc. Pres. Welfare Council Met. Chgo., 1965-67; mem. bus. adv. council Urban League Chgo., 1971—; pres. Cook County Sch. Nursing, 1963-64; bd. dirs. Chgo. Crime Commn., 1965-71, Community Fund Chgo., 1966-67, Lyric Opera Chgo., 1967-77, Better Bus. Bur., 1970-78, Chgo. Public TV, 1978—, Chgo. Central Area Commn., 1978—; trustee Art Inst., 1975—, YWCA, 1962-74, U. Chgo., 1977—, Chgo. Council Fgn. Relations, 1977—, Lakefront Gardens, Inc., 1978—. Served to 1st lt. USAAF, 1943-45. Mem. Am. Assn. Advt. Agys. (dir. 1968-71, 74-76, chmn. Chgo. council 1964-65, chmn. Central region 1970-71), Delta Kappa Epsilon. Clubs: Chicago, Racquet, Econ., Execs., Comml., Commonwealth; Old Elm Country; Barrington Hills Country. Home: Rt 2 Meadow Hill Rd Barrington IL 60010 Office: 401 N Michigan Ave Chicago IL 60611

SCHULTZ, BRUCE RICHARD, mgmt. cons.; b. N.Y.C.; s. Morris and Shirley Schultz; B.A. in Econs., M.A., Bklyn. Coll.; m. Sharon F. Adler, May 28, 1972; children—Jordan M., Daren T. Dir. career and profl. devel. Bus. Mgmt. Inst., Sch. Continuing Edn., N.Y. U., N.Y.C.; adj. lectr. dept. econs. Bklyn. Coll.; mgmt. cons., N.Y.C.; lectr. in field. Mem. Am. Soc. Personnel Adminstrs., Am. Compensation Assn., Am. Soc. Tng. and Devel. Home: 16 Eastlyn Dr Bardonia NY 10954

SCHULTZ, CARL HERBERT, retailer; b. Chgo., Jan. 9, 1925; s. Herbert V. and Olga (Swanson) S.; B.S. in Gen. Engring., Iowa State U., 1948; m. Helen Ann Stevesson, June 6, 1948; children—Mark, Julia Ann. With Schultz Bros. Co., Lake Zurich, Ill., 1948—, mdse. mgr., store planner, Chgo., 1962-68, v.p., Chgo., 1968-72, pres., Chgo., 1972-74, Lake Zurich, Ill., 1974—; pres. co. subsidiaries Iowa Schultz Bros. Co., Wis. Schultz Bros. Co., Ill. Schultz Bros. Co., Ind. Schultz Bros. Co. Sec., Lake Zurich Indsl. Council, 1975; mem. Lake Bluff (Ill.) Zoning Bd. Appeals, 1976—, chmn., 1978—. Served with AUS, 1944-46. Mem. Assn. Gen. Mdse. Chains (dir.). Presbyterian. Club: Bath and Tennis. Office: 800 N Church St Lake Zurich IL 60047

SCHULTZ, GLENN RAYMOND, investment banker; b. St. Louis, Mar. 4, 1927; s. Raymond Augustus and Olga Opal (Tilley) S.; A.B. in Econs., Harvard U., 1949; postgrad. Chgo. Kent Coll. Law, 1957-59, U. Kansas City Sch. Law, 1955-57, U. Wis. Sch. Banking, Madison, 1964-66; m. Jane Louis Snapp, Feb. 18, 1956; children—Karl Gerhardt (dec.), Katherine Louise, Kristina Lynn. Sec.-treas. A.H. Bennett & Co., Inc., Kansas City, Mo., 1950-57; v.p. Continental Ill. Nat. Bank & Trust Co., Chgo., 1957-67; sr. v.p. Stephens Inc., Little Rock, 1967—. Pres., bd. dirs. Central Ark. Radiation Therapy Inst., Inc., Little Rock; bd. dirs., treas. St. Vincent Infirmary, Little Rock; mem. exec. com., mem. bd. dirs. Hospice of Ark., Inc. Served with U.S. Navy, 1951-54. Mem. Municipal Fin. Officers Assn., Securities Industry Assn., Pub. Securities Assn. Methodist. Clubs: Municipal Bond (Chgo.); Little Rock Racquet, Little Rock; Pleasant Valley Country, Westside Tennis. Home: 3007 Painted Valley Dr Little Rock AR 72212 Office: Stephens Inc 114 E Capitol Ave Little Rock AR 72201

SCHULTZ, REX BYRON, farm credit bank exec.; b. East St. Louis, Ill., May 4, 1939; s. Virgil George and Ollie Velma (McElroy) S.; B.S. in Agrl. Bus., La. State U., 1963; m. Etta Sue Robinson, June 17, 1961; children—Gary James, Russell Byron, Cynthia Leanne, Arminda Sue. With Fed. Land Bank of New Orleans, 1963-69; dir. public relations Farm Credit Banks of New Orleans, 1969-71; info. and fgn. tng. officer FCA, Washington, 1971-72; v.p. mktg. and human resources Fed. Intermediate Credit Bank of Omaha, 1972-80, sr. v.p., 1981—. Mem. supt.'s adv. council Millard Public Schs., Omaha, 1977-79; pres. Montclair Sch. Edn. Assn., 1977-79. Mem. Nat. Agri-Mktg. Assn., Nat. Speakers Assn., Nebr. Council on Public Relations for Agr. Democrat. Baptist. Clubs: Kiwanis, Omaha Agribus. (dir.). Home: 13867 Frances St Omaha NE 68144 Office: Farm Credit Bldg 19th and Douglas Sts Omaha NE 68102

SCHULTZ, THOMAS WILLIAM, health services adminstr.; b. Elmhurst, Ill., Oct. 29, 1949; s. William Albert and Marion Frances (Fanning) S.; B.A., Coll. of St. Thomas, St. Paul, 1971; M.H.A., Duke U., 1973. Adminstrv. fellow Mass. Gen. Hosp., Boston, 1973-75, asst. dir. adminstrv. services, 1975-78; cons. Booz, Allen & Hamilton, Inc., N.Y.C., 1978-80; dir. planning Brookwood Health Services, Birmingham, Ala., 1980—. Mem. Am. Coll. Hosp. Adminstrs., Duke U. Alumni Assn. Home: 3716 Forest Run Rd Birmingham AL 35223 Office: 2010 Medical Center Dr Birmingham AL 35209

SCHULZ, RAINER WALTER, computer co. exec.; b. Berlin, Jan. 29, 1942; s. Horst and Marta S.; came to U.S., 1959, naturalized, 1964; B.A. summa cum laude in Math., San Jose State U., 1964; children—Heidi, Kenneth, Kirsten. System devel. asso. IBM, San Jose, Calif., 1964-65, SDS, Santa Monica, Calif., 1965-67, U. Calif., Berkeley, 1967-70; system mgmt. asso. Stanford (Calif.) U., 1970-77; v.p. Computer Curriculum Corp., Palo Alto, Calif., 1973—, dir., sec., 1978—; cons. NSF., 1974-77. Mem. Am. Electronics Assn., Conf. Bd. Republican. Lutheran. Home: 565 Arastradero Apt 113 Palo Alto CA 94306 Office: 1070 Arastradero Palo Alto CA 94303

SCHULZ, WALTER KURT, mfg. co. exec.; b. Hamburg, Germany, Apr. 9, 1940; s. Richard and Karla Adele (Halm) S.; M.B.A., U. Muenster, 1969; M.Accounting, Ohio State U., 1972; m. Beth Anne Edwards, June 24, 1972; children—Alexander, Ella. Audit mgr. Dr. Jur. W. Kaase, Germany, 1964-68; teaching asso. Ohio State U., 1971-72; systems analyst United Airlines, Chgo., 1973-77; chief fin. officer, corporate sec. Eickhoff-Nat. Mine, Pitts., 1977—. Mem. Am. Mgmt. Assn., Assn. M.B.A. Execs., Aircraft Owners and Pilots Assn. Republican. Home: 136 Beacon Hill Dr Coreopolis PA 15108

SCHULZE, RICHARD, fin. exec., music exec.; b. Gary, Ind., Oct. 20, 1928; s. Otto and Eva Marguerite (Yoder) S.; student U. Chgo., Am. Conservatory, Wabash Coll., 1946-52; m. Theodora Economou, Apr. 16, 1950; 1 son, Otto. Music dir. Telemann Soc., N.Y.C., Ft. Lauderdale, Fla., 1955—; chief mech. engr. Fairchild Sound Co., H.H. Scott, Inc., other cos., 1956-68; producer Amphion Record Co., N.Y.C., Ft. Lauderdale, 1962—; pres. Philharmonic Standard Corp., Concord, Mass., 1969-74; v.p. Stanford Mgmt. Corp., Hallandale, Fla.; appeared at Carnegie Hall, Town Hall, N.Y.C., also other cities; condr., producer over 45 recs. for Vox, Nonesuch, Everest, Amphion, other U.S. and fgn. labels, 1959—; mus. dir. Fla. Pops Orch., appeared with Robert Goulet, Leonard Pennario, other major soloists, 1977—. Structured fin. plan to save Carnegie Hall. Developer computer algorithms for investment banking acctg.; recorded compositions. Office: 8416 SW 20th St North Lauderdale FL

SCHUMACHER, ARNOLD CHARLES, economist; b. Hartford City, Ind., June 25, 1916; s. William S. and Olive (Burk) S.; B.S., Ind. U., M.A., 1940; m. Mary Caulk, Oct. 22, 1960. Vice-pres. Chgo. Title and Trust Co., 1957-79; v.p. Lincoln Nat. Corp., Chgo., 1965-79; pres. Money Market Comments, San Diego, Calif., 1979—. Chmn. Mayor's Com. on Technol. Change, Chgo., 1964-67. Mem. Nat. Assn. Bus. Economists, Am. Econ. Assn., Nat. Investment Analysts Soc. Home: 16674 Orilla Dr San Diego CA 92128

SCHUMACHER, FERDINAND MATHIAS, holding co. exec.; b. Kleve, Germany, Mar. 1, 1939; came to U.S., 1963, naturalized, 1968; s. Josef Peter and Maria Schumacher; B.A. in Bus., U. S.Fla., Tampa, 1969; m. Alberta Louise Seldomridge, Dec. 9, 1967. Staff asso. Joseph Schlitz Brewing Co., Milw., 1969-79; v.p. ops., dir. Isoco Ltd., Pewaukee, Wis., 1979—; pres. Global Trading, Milw., 1980—. Adv., Jr. Achievement Milw., 1976; treas. Alliance Française Milw., 1978—. Mem. Am. Water Works Assn. Republican. Roman Catholic. Office: 11515 W Carmen Ave Milwaukee WI 53225

SCHUMACHER, JOHN CHRISTIAN, semicondr. materials and equipment mfg. co. exec.; b. Spring Valley, Ill., Feb. 8, 1935; s. Joseph Charles and Theresa Isobel (Flynn) S.; B.S., Stanford U., 1956; M.S., M.I.T., 1958; Ph.D., Stanford U., 1973; 1 dau., Jennifer Lea. Research engr. Calif. Inst. Tech., 1958-60; research and teaching asst. M.I.T., 1960-62; dept. mgr. Lockheed Missile & Space Co., Sunnyvale, Calif., 1962-64, program mgr., Palo Alto, Calif., 1964-69; research asso., thesis dir. Stanford U., 1969-73; v.p. J. C. Schumacher Co., Oceanside, Calif., 1973-74, pres., 1974-76, pres., chief exec. officer, 1976—. Chmn. Oceanside New Bus. and Industry Commn., 1976-78. Mem. Oceanside C. of C. (dir. 1974-78), Electrochem. Soc., Newcomen Soc., IEEE, AAAS, Phys. Soc. Am., Am. Inst. Chem. Engrs. Republican. Patentee improved semicondr. device processing materials and equipment; low cost silicon; energy efficient photovoltaic solar cell mfg. Home: 4533 Cove Dr Carlsbad CA 92008 Office: 580 Airport Rd Oceanside CA 92054

SCHUMAN, DANIEL GERALD, indsl. co. exec.; b. N.Y.C., Sept. 12, 1916; s. Jacob A. and Bessie (Hyman) S.; B.S. in Engring., Calif. Inst. Tech., 1937; M.B.A. with distinction, Harvard U., 1941; m. Jacquelyne May, Oct. 25, 1942; children—Joel Leslie, Craig Alan, Meredith Ann. Mgr. mgmt. adv. services Price Waterhouse & Co., N.Y.C., 1946-52; v.p., controller Stromberg Carlson Co., Rochester, N.Y., 1952-59; v.p. fin. Bausch & Lomb, Rochester, 1959-67, exec. v.p. fin. and adminstrn., 1967-71, chmn. bd., 1971-78, chmn. bd. and pres., 1978-80, chmn. bd., chief exec. officer, 1980—; dir. Security Trust Co., Roch, N.Y., Utica Mut. Ins. Co. (N.Y.). Served to lt. comdr. USNR, 1942-45. Mem. Am. Mgmt. Assn. Clubs: Genesee Valley, Irondequoit Country (Rochester). Home: 22 Berkeley St Rochester NY 14607 Office: Lincoln First Tower Rochester NY 14602

SCHUMANN, VERNON KENNETH, indsl. investigator; b. Chgo., July 8; s. Edward Charles and Clara (Hansen) S.; B.S., Northwestern U., 1934, postgrad., 1935-36; m. Susan Nerney, Dec. 27, 1969. Copywriter, Lord & Thomas, Chgo., 1935-40; mgr. Sedgewick Advt., Chgo., 1940-42; dir. security U.S. AEC, Richland, Wash., 1946-52; mgr. Fed. Services, Inc., San Francisco, 1952-53; pres. Vernon K. Schumann Investigations, 1953—; cons. AEC, Gen. Dynamics; exec. advisor Aetna Custodial. Served with AUS, 1942-46. Mem. Calif. Assn. Licensed Investigators, Nat. CIC Assn., Internat. Assn. Chiefs of Police, Soc. Am. Mil. Engrs., Stanford U. Alumni Assn., Mensa. Republican. Lutheran. Club: Elks. Editor Mensa Research Jour., 1968-72. Home: 1042 Oakland Ave Menlo Park CA 94025 Office: PO Box 2283 Menlo Park CA 94025

SCHUNK, EDWARD JEROME, accountant; b. Kenmore, N.Y., Nov. 25, 1927; s. George Millard and Edith May (McGuire) S.; B.B.A., Canisius Coll., Buffalo, 1953; m. Leida M. DiSeipo, Sept. 5, 1953; children—Edward A., Pamela M., Diane A., Marise, Christopher. Sr. acct. Lucker, Kennedy & Felmeden, C.P.A.'s, Buffalo, 1953-61; partner Eichhorn, Weinreber & Schunk, C.P.A.'s, Buffalo, 1953-65; sr. partner Schunk & Wilson, C.P.A.'s, Buffalo, 1965—; treas., dir. Kelogg-Mann Corp., 1980—. Treas., bd. dirs. Buffalo Jr. C. of C., 1962-64. Served with AUS, 1945-47, 50-51. C.P.A., N.Y. Mem. Am. Inst. C.P.A.'s, Nat. Assn. Accts., N.Y. State Soc. C.P.A.'s, Amherst C. of C. Club: Williamsville Rotary (treas. 1980). Home: 230 Bellingham Dr Williamsville NY 14221 Office: 3871 Harlem Rd Buffalo NY 14215

SCHUPAK, LESLIE ALLEN, public relations co. exec.; b. Spokane, Wash., Apr. 5, 1945; s. Leo and Henrietta (Neumann) S.; B.S., Boston U., 1967, M.S., 1971; m. Dianne B. Goldin, June 23, 1968; 1 son, Adam Jason. Asst. to pres., account exec. Sperber Assos., Inc., Boston, 1968-69; account supr. Wilcox & Williams, N.Y.C., 1969-70; v.p., mgr. Daniel J. Edelman Inc., N.Y.C., 1970-72; exec. v.p., prin. Kanan, Corbin, Schupak & Aronow, Inc., N.Y.C., 1972—. Mem. Public Relations Soc. Am., Nat. Investor Relations Inst., N.Y. Soc. Assn. Execs., Hosp. Public Relations Soc. N.Y., 7th Regt. Vets. Assn. Clubs: Twin Oaks Tennis, Theodore Gordon Flyfishers. Home: 2 Whippoorwill Close Chappaqua NY 10514 Office: 99 Park Ave New York NY 10016

SCHURR, JAMES ROBERT, fin. exec.; b. Phila., Oct. 25, 1942; s. Harry William and Clare Regina (Cruice) S.; student Temple U., 1960-61; B.S., Murray State U., 1967; m. Marie Eileen Leahan, Apr. 1, 1967; children—Maryann, Jimmy, Stephen. Audit supr. Ernst & Whinney, Phila., 1967-72; treas. Scottish & York Internat. Ins. Group, Princeton, N.J., 1972—. C.P.A., Pa. Mem. Am. C.P.A.'s, Pa. Inst. C.P.A.'s. Home: 814 Hudson Dr Yardley PA 19067 Office: 101 College Rd Princeton NJ 08540

SCHURTER, KENNETH LEE, mktg. exec.; b. Chgo., July 6, 1938; s. Huldreich and Aldenne (Grusy) S.; B.S. in Chemistry, Ill. Inst. Tech., 1960; M.B.A., U. Chgo., 1967; m. Janet Elaine Moore, Dec. 22, 1963; children—Bradley, Valerie. Tech. sales rep. Union Carbide Corp., N.Y.C., 1960-61, Cin., 1961-63, Houston, 1963-65; with Continental Oil Co., 1967-76, product mgr., 1968-69, regional sales mgr., Chgo., 1969-72, bus. area mgr., Saddle Brook, N.J., Houston, 1972-76; dir. mktg. Shintech, Inc., Houston, 1976—; dir. Vinatex, Ltd. (U.K.), 1973-76; lectr. Am. Mgmt. Assn. Mem. Plastic Pipe and Fittings Assn. (bd. dirs.), Nat. Sanitation Found. (industry adv. com.). Home: 5407 Three Oaks Circle Houston TX 77069

SCHUSTERMAN, CHARLES, oil and gas prodn. and exploration co. exec.; b. Tulsa, Sept. 21, 1935; s. Sam and Sarah Schusterman; B.S. in Petroleum Engring., U. Okla., 1958; m. Lynn Nora Josey, June 17, 1962; children—Harold Josey, Stacy Helen, Jerome Reed. Partner, S & S Pipe and Supply Co., Tulsa, 1959-71; partner Schusterman Oil Co., Tulsa, 1961-71; pres. Schusterman Operating Co., Tulsa, 1971-74, Samson Resources Co., Tulsa, 1971—; chmn. bd. Samson Properties, Inc., Tulsa, 1978—; dir. Republic Bank and Trust Co., Tulsa, Republic Bancorp., Tulsa. Bd. dirs. Tulsa Ballet, 1980, NCCJ, 1979, Tulsa Jewish Community Council, 1976—, Temple Israel, 1976-78, Jewish Community Activities Program, 1979; pres. Tulsa chpt. Am. Jewish Com., 1968-72; bd. govs. Am. Friends of Jerusalem Acad. and Conf. Center, 1980—; public affairs com. Nat. Council for Am. Israel. Served with U.S. Army, 1958. Mem. Ind. Petroleum Assn. Am. (dir.), Okla. Ind. Petroleum Assn., Kans. Ind. Oil and Gas Assn. (past dir.), Calif. Ind. Producers Assn. (past dir.), Tau Beta Pi. Jewish. Office: 2700 First Nat Tower Tulsa OK 74103

SCHUYLER, LAMBERT, JR., exec. search cons.; b. Seattle, Aug. 4, 1938; s. Lambert and Nora Patricia S.; B.S. in Bus. Adminstrn., Babson Coll., Wellesley Hills, Mass., 1964; m. Barbara P. Rick, June 10, 1962; children—Stephen Dodds, Bradley Rick. Sr. cons. Arthur Andersen & Co., Phila., 1966-69; controller Whittaker Corp., Lancaster, Pa., 1969-70; sr. cons. Gilbert/Commonwealth, Reading, Pa., 1970-73; v.p. Billington, Fox & Ellis, Inc., Atlanta, 1973-79, Lamalie Assos., Inc., Atlanta, 1979—. Pres. Winding-Vista Recreation, Tucker, Ga., 1979-80. Mem. Assn. Exec. Recruiting Consultants, Atlanta C. of C. (v.p. N.E. Area council 1977-79). Republican. Office: 3340 Peachtree St NE Atlanta GA 30326

SCHWAM, MARVIN ALBERT, foliage systems co. exec.; b. Newark, Apr. 18, 1942; s. Meyer and Fannie (Lerman) S.; B.F.A., Cooper Union, 1964; m. Jeanette Fein, June 13, 1964; children—Frederic, Matthew. Staff artist Doremus & Co., 1964-66; mgr. Flowerental Corp., N.Y.C., 1966-68; pres. M. Schwam Floralart, N.Y.C., 1968-75; exec. v.p., bd. chmn. Florenco Foliage Systems Corp., N.Y.C., 1975—; pres. Am. Christmas Decorating Service Inc., N.Y.C., Marc Shaw Graphics, Inc., N.Y.C. Industry chmn. March of Dimes, 1975-78; bd. dirs. Happi Found. for Autistic People, N.Y.C. Recipient award of merit for service to Gen. Motors Corp., 1978, award for Highlight of Christmas, Citibank/Citicorp Center, 1978. Mem. Mcpl. Art Soc. N.Y., Am. Mus. Natural History, Alumni Assn. Cooper Union. Designer largest artificial Christmas tree in U.S., Radio City Music Hall, N.Y.C., 1979; decorator Pulitzer Fountain, N.Y.C., 1979-80 Christmas season. Home: 7 E 17th St New York NY 10003 Office: 30-28 Starr Ave Long Island City NY 11101

SCHWANHAUSSER, ROBERT ROWLAND, aero. engr.; b. Buffalo, Sept. 15, 1930; s. Edwin Julius and Helen (Rowland) S.; S.B. in Aero. Engring., Mass. Inst. Tech., 1952; m. Mary Lea Hunter, Oct. 17, 1953 (div. June 1978); children—Robert Hunter, Mark Putnam; m. 2d, Beverly Bohn Allemann, Dec. 31, 1979. Project engr. Continental Aviation & Engring., Detroit, 1954; with Teledyne Ryan Aero. Co. subs. Teledyne, Inc., San Diego, 1954-74, successively field service rep., asst. project engr., project engr., program mgr., program dir., chief engr., dir. drones and spl. projects, v.p. aerospace systems, 1966-72, exec. v.p. programs, 1972-73, exec. v.p. internat. programs, 1973-74; pres. Condur Engring. Corp., La Mesa, Calif., 1974—, Condur Aerospace Corp., El Paso, 1976-77; v.p. bus. devel. All Am. Engring. Co., 1977-79; v.p. internat. requirements Teledyne Ryan Aero. Co., 1979—. Bd. dirs. Cornerstone Found. Served to lt. USAF, 1952-54. Asso. fellow AIAA; mem. Am. Ordnance Assn., Assn. U.S. Army, Air Force Assn., Am. Fighter Pilots Assn., Nat. Assn. Remotely Piloted Vehicles (hon. trustee), Soc. Exptl. Test Pilots, Nat. Mgmt. Assn., Navy League, Theta Delta Chi. Club: Greenhead Hunting (founder). Home: Chalet Les Scabieuses 1936 Verbier Switzerland Office: 2701 Harbor Dr San Diego CA 92138

SCHWANINGER, JAMES CRAIG, SR., retail chain ofcl.; b. St. Louis, Aug. 30, 1942; s. Robert Henry and Marjorie Faye (Faber) S.; student S.E. Mo. State U., 1963-65; B.J., U. Mo., 1967; m. Marilyn Faye Grojean, July 3, 1965; children—James Craig, Jeffrey Carl, Joseph Christopher. News dir. Mo. Press Assn., Columbia, 1965-70; dir. pub. relations Columbia Coll., 1970-72; regional pub. relations rep. J.C. Penney Co., Rolling Meadows, Ill., 1972-74, mgr. product info., N.Y.C., 1974-78, asst. dir. corp. responsibility, 1978-81, mgr. corp. contbns. and memberships, 1981—. Bd. dirs. Columbia United Way, 1970-72, Columbia chpt. A.R.C., 1971-72; active Boy Scouts Am., 1976—; chmn. bd. advisers Our Own of Ocean, Inc., 1977—. Served with USMC, 1959-63. Recipient outstanding community service award City of Columbia, 1972; community service award J.C. Penney Co., 1977; service award U.S. Treasury Dept., 1977. Mem. Pub. Relations Soc. Am., U. Mo. Alumni Assn., USMC Combat Corrs. Assn., Columbia Jaycees (dir. 1970-72), Sigma Tau Gamma (dist. gov. 1970-71), Alpha Delta Sigma. Democrat. Roman Catholic. Author: Tooting Your Own Horn, 1978. Home: 10 Buckingham Dr Jackson NJ 08527 Office: 1301 Ave of Americas New York NY 10019

SCHWARTZ, ALAN MARK, packaging corp. exec.; b. Cambridge, Mass., July 19, 1942; s. Irving and Hannah E. (Carlin) S.; grad. Pomfret Sch., 1960; B.S. in Bus. Adminstrn., Babson Coll., 1964; m. Brenda Greenfield, June 21, 1964; children—Sandra Lynn, Neil Douglas. Sales mgr. Allied Container Corp., Dedham, Mass., 1964-74; pres. Bag State Packaging Corp., Newton, Mass., 1974—. Pres., Men's Assos., Beth Israel Hosp., 1975-78; asso. treas. Combined Jewish Philanthropies Greater Boston, 1978—; bd. dirs. Temple Beth Avodah, 1980—. Clubs: Pine Brook Country (bd. govs. 1979—), Masons. Home: 232 Old Farm Rd Newton MA 02159 Office: Bag State Packaging Corp 120 Wells Ave Newton MA 02159

SCHWARTZ, ALLAN ERWIN, communications co. exec.; b. N.Y.C., Feb. 8, 1933; s. Anthony Schwartz and Lee Schwartz Lax; B.S. in Physics, CCNY, 1968; M.B.A., Iona Coll., 1972; m. Claire, Feb. 6, 1954; children—Steven, Ronald, Jane. Dir. ops. Teleprompter Corp., N.Y.C., 1972-74; nat. mktg. mgr. ADT Co., N.Y.C., 1974-78; sr. v.p. GBC CCTV Corp., N.Y.C., 1978-79; exec. v.p. RAIL Mfg. Corp., Tucker, Ga., 1979—; lectr. Internat. Security Conf., 1975-76; adj. lectr. Nat. Crime Prevention Inst., U. Louisville, 1976-77. Mem. Security Equipment Industry Assn., Nat. Retail Mchts. Assn., Delta Mu Delta. Democrat. Clubs: Ardsley Swim, Westchester Indoor Tennis. Author: Management Guide to Closed Circuit Television Security Systems. Patentee in field. Home: 3 Bristol Pl Yonkers NY 10710 Office: RAIL Mfg Corp 4559 Granite Dr Tucker GA 30084

SCHWARTZ, BRIAN ALAN, psychologist, career planning cons. co. exec.; b. N.Y.C., Jan. 13, 1943; s. Hal Jesse and Marcia Matilda (Gershbein) S.; B.S. in Chemistry, Queens Coll., 1964; Ph.D. in Cons. Psychology (NDEA Title IV fellow), N.Y. U., 1975. Caseworker, N.Y.C. Dept. Social Services, 1964-67; resident fellow N.Y. U., N.Y.C., 1965-70; research dir. N.Y.C. Bur. Child Welfare, 1967-68; staff psychologist Queens Coll., N.Y.C., 1968-76; dir. The Career Planning Center, N.Y.C., 1976—; founder, dir. Perspectives, Greenwich, Conn., 1977—; corp. and orgnl. cons., seminar and workshop dir., lectr. Bd. dirs. Somers Community Center, 1974-76. Mem. Am. Psychol. Assn., Am. Soc. for Tng. and Devel., Internat. Assn. for Applied Psychology, Am. Personnel and Guidance Assn. Office: 12 Havemeyer Pl Greenwich CT 06830

SCHWARTZ, CHAUNCEY MARTIN, II, data processing exec.; b. Rapid City, S.D., Aug. 26, 1947; s. Chauncey Martin and Margarete (Trople) S., Sr.; student Met. State Coll., 1971-75, IBM Tech. Sch., 1968-78; m. Sharon Lee Jones, Dec. 9, 1967; children—Chauncey Martin, Michelle Louisa. Applications programmer U.S. Army, Petersburg, Va. and Tacoma, 1968-70, sr. programmer, team chief, Tacoma, 1970-71; applications programmer Blue Cross & Blue Shield, Denver, 1971, systems programmer, 1971-74, mgr. software, 1974, mgr. support services, 1974-76, mgr. tech. support, 1976, mgr. ops., tech. support, 1976-77, mgr. data processing, 1977-79; mgr. adminstrv. systems Storage Tech. Corp., Louisville, Colo., 1979; systems mgr. McGraw-Hill, Inc., 1979-80; sr. systems engr. Amdahl Corp., 1980—; speaker in field. Chmn., Citizens Adv. Team, Denver, 1975-77, pack com. Denver Cub Scouts, 1977-78. Served with U.S. Army, 1966-71. Colo. Scholars award, 1974. Mem. Data Processing Mgmt. Assn., Assn. Computing Machinery. Republican. Lutheran. Club: Elks. Home: 6919 W Quarto Pl Littleton CO 80123 Office: McGraw-Hill Inc 7400 S Alton Ct Englewood CO 80114

SCHWARTZ, DAVID ELLIOT, food service co. exec.; b. N.Y.C., May 11, 1947; s. Ben and Beatrice Schwartz; B.A., Widner U.; M.A. Adelphi U.; m. Oct. 21, 1979; children—Dennis, Jordan. Mgmt. trainee, then ops. mgr. Am. Airlines, JFK Airport, 1970-75; dir. dietary services Marriott In-Flite Services, JFK Airport, 1975-76, Marriott, Inc., N.Y.C., 1976-77; gen. mgr. Canteen Corp., N.Y.C., 1977-79, dist. mgr. Westchester County and State of N.J., 1979—. Mem. Food Service Execs. Home: 40 Florence Dr Chappaqua NY 10514 Office: 3505 Connors St Bronx NY

SCHWARTZ, DONALD, govt. ofcl.; b. Budapest, Hungary, Apr. 13, 1932; naturalized Canadian citizen, 1954; s. Kalman and Rose (Hirchfeld) S.; M.B.A., Sorbonne, Paris, 1952; M.Sc., U. Laval, Montreal, Que., Can., 1972; m. Louise Fontaine, Apr. 25, 1957; children—Barbara, David, Daniel. Vice pres. Bell Electronics Ltd., Quebec, Que., 1953-72; pres. Giguere Electric Ltd., Quebec, 1960-72, Bell Service, Inc., Quebec, 1966-72; policy advisor to sr. asst. dep. minister Ministry of State for Sci. and Tech., Govt. of Can., Ottawa, Ont., 1972-80; dir. The Touraine Group, DETA. Registered profl. engr., Can. Mem. Order of Engrs. of Que. (adminstr., past pres. Hull-Ottawa chpt.), Assn. Sci., Engring. and Technol. Community Can., Inst. Canadian Engrs. Home: 10 Menton Touraine PQ J8T 5MT Canada Office: 270 Albert St Ottawa ON K1A 1A1 Canada

SCHWARTZ, DONALD ARTHUR, commemorative medallion mfg. co. exec.; b. Bklyn., May 19, 1931; s. Arthur and Helen (Krayer) S.; B.S., N.Y. U., 1956; m. Jeanne Cannon, Dec. 17, 1955; children—William Arthur, Karen Anne. With Comml. Pub. Co., N.Y.C., 1956-71, v.p., 1960-62, pres., 1962-71, also dir.; v.p., dir. Medallic Art Co., Danbury, Conn., 1971-76, chmn. bd., pres., 1976—; dir. Gibbs Brower Internat.; asso. dir. State Nat. Bank. Served with USAF, 1951-53. Mem. Silver Users Assn. (dir.), Advt. Splty. Assn., Comml. Law League Am. Clubs: N.Y. Athletic, Silver Spring Country (dir.) (Ridgefield, Conn.). Office: Medallic Art Co Old Ridgebury Rd Danbury CT 06810

SCHWARTZ, FREDERIC N., corp. dir.; b. Springfield, Mass., 1906; s. Michael J. and Regina (Burdick) S.; A.B., Syracuse U., 1931; LL.D., 1963; m. Eleanor Haley, 1935. Formerly chmn., pres., dir. Bristol-Myers Co. Served as lt. col., chief of operations transfusion div. med. dept. U.S. Army, 1942-45. Awarded Legion of Merit, 1945. Mem. Delta Kappa Epsilon. Clubs: River, University (N.Y.C.). Office: 345 Park Ave New York NY 10022

SCHWARTZ, FREDERICK EVAN, banker; b. Fitchburg, Mass., May 23, 1942; s. Sidney and Gertrude (Tater) S.; grad. Phillips Exeter Acad., 1960; B.S.E., Wharton Sch. Fin. and Commerce, U. Pa., 1967; S.E.P., Stanford U., 1980; m. Bari Lynne Hurwitz, Aug. 2, 1964; children—Alec P.S., Alison P. With Bankers Trust Co., N.Y.C., 1967—, asst. treas., 1969-70, asst. v.p., 1970-72, v.p., 1972-79, sr. v.p., 1979—; sr. credit officer internat. dept., group head internat. credit group, dir. B.T. Asia Ltd., Hong Kong. Trustee Montclair Kimberley Acad., Montclair, N.J., 1980—. Served with U.S. Army, 1961-62. Home: 87 Heller Way Upper Montclair NJ 07043 Office: Bankers Trust Co 280 Park Ave New York NY 10017

SCHWARTZ, GERALD, public relations and fund raising agy. exec.; b. N.Y.C., June 22, 1927; s. George and Martha F. S.; student N.C. State U., 1944-45; A.B., U. Miami, 1949, B.S., 1950, postgrad., 1966-67; m. Felice P., June 25, 1950; children—Gary R., Gregg R., Felice P. Staff writer Miami (Fla.) Herald, 1941-44; publicity dir. U.S. Army in Europe, 1946-48; editor Miami Beach Sun, 1950-51; fund raising and public relations counselor, Miami, 1952-58; press sec. to Gov. Nebr., 1959-60; exec. v.p. Bar-Ilan U., Ramat Gan, Israel, Israel, 1960-61; prin. Gerald Schwartz Agy., Miami, Fla., 1962—. Dep. chmn. Democratic Midwest Conf., 1958-60; pres. Am. Zionist Fedn. So. Fla., 1970-73; nat. bd. dirs. Am. Zionist Fedn.; pres. Pres.'s council Zionist Orgn. Am.; bd. dirs. Temple Emanu-El of Greater Miami, Papanicolaou Cancer Research Inst., Miami, Urban League of Greater Miami; vice chmn. City of Miami Beach Planning Bd., 1953-55; chmn. City of Miami Beach Hurricane Def. Com., 1978—. Served with U.S. Army, 1944-46. Recipient Jerusalem Peace award State of Israel Bonds, 1978. Mem. Public Relations Soc. Am. (accredited; treas. So. Fla. chpt. 1962-64), Am. Public Relations Assn. (pres. chpt. 1960-61), Internat. Assn. Bus. Communicators, Am. Mktg. Assn., Nat. Assn. Fund Raising Execs. (pres. chpt. 1977-78), Miami Beach C. of C. (v.p. 1978-80, 81-82), Lead and Ink, Theta Omicron Pi, Omicron Delta Kappa, Alpha Delta Sigma (pres. chpt. 1965-67), Zeta Beta Tau. Club: B'nai B'rith (pres. lodge 1964-66). Home: 7320 SW 123d St Miami FL 33156 Office: 420 Lincoln Rd Bldg Miami Beach FL 33139

SCHWARTZ, HARRY ALBERT, mfr.; b. Montreal, Que., Can., Feb. 10, 1896; s. Philip and Pearl (Frank) S.; student pub. schs.; m. Margaret L. Hill, Oct. 26, 1929 (dec. 1959); m. 2d, Hilda Freed, Apr. 7, 1962; children—Grace, James Hill, Harry Albert. Chief engr. Defiance Machine Works, Defiance, Ohio, 1917-22; work connected with permanent mold casting process 1922-27; pres., dir. The Montpelier Mfg. Co., 1927-61; pres. Schwartz Assos., Inc., Montpelier. Mem. Ohio C. of C., Am. Soc. M.E., Soc. Automotive Engrs., A.I.M. Club: Rotary. Home: PO Box 7652 Phoenix AZ 85011 Office: Schwartz Assos Inc care First Nat Bank Trust Dept Scottsdale AZ 85252

SCHWARTZ, HERBERT FREDERICK, lawyer; b. Bklyn., Aug. 23, 1935; s. Henry and Blanche Theodora (Goldberg) S.; B.S. in Elec. Engring., M.I.T., 1957; postgrad. Wharton Grad. Sch. Bus., U. Pa., 1959-61, M.A. in Econs., 1964, LL.B. cum laude, 1964; m. Gail Ellen Lubets, Jan. 23, 1960; children—Wendy Helene, Karen Anne, Peter Andrew. Supr. mil. computer applications Philco Corp., Phila., 1959-61, cons., 1961-63; admitted to N.Y. State bar, 1964, U.S. Supreme Ct. bar, 1974, U.S. Patent Office, 1965, various Cts. Appeals and Dist. Cts.; asso. firm Fish & Neave, N.Y.C., 1964-70, jr. partner, 1970-71, sr. partner, 1972—, mem. mng. com., 1976-80; lectr. law U. Pa. Law Sch., 1980. Pres., Greenwich Woods North Assn., 1973-78. Served to 2d lt. Signal Corps, U.S. Army, 1957-59. Mem. Am. Patent Law Assn. (various coms. 1965-79), N.Y. Patent Law Assn. (chmn. antitrust com., lic. restrictions and practices, 1970-72, U.S. patent antitrust devels. com. 1977, fgn. antitrust com. 1978), Am. Bar Assn. (various coms. 1965-79), Assn. Bar City N.Y. (trade regulations com. 1975-78), Greenwich Cove Racing Assn. (commodore 1975—, chmn. race com. 1974-, Ensign Class Assn. (regional commodore), Order of Coif. Clubs: Board Room; Riverside Yacht (chmn. jr. sailing program 1979-80). Editor: U. Pa. Law Rev., 1962-64. Home: Indian Point Ln Riverside CT 06878 Office: 277 Park Ave New York NY 10017

SCHWARTZ, JAMES PETER, real estate broker; b. Bridgeport, Conn., Oct. 30, 1919; s. Joseph and Fannie (Tischler) S.; student Coll. Commerce New Haven, 1939-40; m. Natalie Postol, Mar. 12, 1944; 1 son, Joseph William. Reporter, Bridgeport Times-Star, 1940-41; reporter, photographer Bridgeport Post, 1942-43, 45-49; pres. Jay James Inc., Fairfield, Conn., 1949-70; owner James P. Schwartz & Assos., Fairfield, 1970—; dir. Lafayette Bank & Trust Co. Treas. Greater Bridgeport Bd. Realtors, 1974-77, sr. v.p., 1978, pres., 1979. Pres. Barnum Festival Soc., 1975-76; ringmaster Barnum Festival, 1979; justice of peace, 1970—; mem. Easton (Conn.) Zoning Bd. Appeals, 1971-76; police commr., Easton, 1976—; bd. dirs. Bridgeport div. Am. Cancer Soc., 1977—. Bd. assos. U. Bridgeport, 1962—. Served with AUS, 1943-45. Named Man of Year dept. sociology U. Bridgeport, 1962. Mem. Fairfield Bd. Realtors, Conn., Nat. assns. realtors. Mason. Contbg. editor Photog. Trade News, 1960-70. Home: 78 Blanchard Rd Easton CT 06612 Office: 161 Kings Hwy Fairfield CT 06430

SCHWARTZ, JOSEPH WILLIAM, banker; b. Bridgeport, Conn., Dec. 22, 1950; s. James Peter and Natalie (Postol) S.; B.A., Union Coll., Schenectady, 1972; M.B.A., U. Conn., 1980. Planning intern Capital Dist. Regional Planning Agy., Albany, N.Y., 1973; real estate broker James P. Schwartz & Assos., Fairfield, Conn., 1973-77, asst. v.p., 1980—; adj. faculty Sacred Heart U., Bridgeport, 1975-77; corporate banking rep. Conn. Nat. Bank, Bridgeport, 1977—. Justice of peace; Easton, Conn., 1973-75; mem. town com. Democratic party Easton, 1973—; mem. Conn. State Senate, also chmn. elections com., 1975-77; bd. selectmen Town of Easton, 1977—; bd. dirs. Woodfield Family Services, 1978—, S.W. Conn. Health Systems Agy., 1979—; mem. Conn. Statewide Health Coordinating Council, 1980—; chmn. Heart Fund Easton, 1976—. Recipient 3d. Ann. Legis. award Caucus Conn. Dems., 1976. Jewish. Club: Lions. Home: 21 Dogwood Dr Easton CT 06612 Office: 343 Main St Danbury CT 06810

SCHWARTZ, MARVIN BERNARD, collection co. exec.; b. N.Y.C., Mar. 22, 1930; s. Sol and Shirley S.; B.S. in Mktg., N.Y. U., 1956; m. Myra Cohen, June 11, 1961; children—Nancy, Susan. Pres., Ednl. Supplements Corp., N.Y.C., 1961-67; account exec. CBS Records, N.Y.C., 1967-68; pres. The Capital Group, Inc., Hicksville, N.Y., 1969—. Served with USAF, 1952-54. Mem. Am. Comml. Collection Assn. Home: 1 Thrush Ct East Northport NY 11731 Office: 960 Broadway Hicksville NY 11801

SCHWARTZ, MILTON M., aluminum foundry exec.; b. Manitowoc, Wis., Nov. 22, 1923; s. Abe and Martha Schwartz; student U. Wis., 1943-44, 46; m. Bess Luffman, June 22, 1947; children—Sandra, Barbara, Deborah, David, Cynthia. With Wis. Aluminum Foundry Co., Inc., Manitowoc, 1947—, credit mgr., to 1956, treas., 1956—, exec. v.p., 1959-76, chmn. bd., 1976—. Jewish. Clubs: Elks, B'nai B'rith, Masons. Home: 2121 Rheaume Rd Manitowoc WI 54220 Office: 838 S 16th St Manitowoc WI 54220

SCHWARTZ, MORT, automotive distbr.; b. Bklyn., Sept. 16, 1934; s. Harry and Helen (Rehr) S.; B.S. in Indsl. Engring., N.Y.U., 1956, M.S. in Indsl. Engring., 1961; m. Marilyn Carol Spill, Oct. 27, 1956; children—Jay, Richard, Andrew. With Westinghouse Electric Co., Pitts., Columbus, O., Metuchen, N.J., 1956-66, controller WASSCO div., Pitts., 1966-67, v.p. consumer service Westinghouse, Pitts., 1967-68; v.p. Maremont Corp., 1968-75; exec. v.p. Chanslor & Lyon, Chgo., 1968-69, pres., 1969-75, chmn. bd., pres., Brisbane, Calif., 1975—; faculty Rutgers U., 1959-61. Bd. dirs. Nat. Inst. Automotive Service Excellence, 1976—, Pacific Auto Show, 1977; chmn. Calif. Automotive Task Force, 1978-80. Served to capt. C.E., AUS, 1956-57. Mem. Automotive Warehouse Distbrs. Assn. (vice chmn., dir. 1975—), Calif. Automotive Wholesalers Assn. (dir. 1978—), Pacific Coast Wholesalers Assn. (dir., v.p. 1975), Perstare Et Praestare, Zeta Beta Tau. Home: 2505 Rolling Hills Ct Alamo CA 94507 Office: 380 Valley Dr Brisbane CA 94005

SCHWARTZ, NEIL DAVID, fin. planner; b. Bklyn., Jan. 21, 1942; s. Louis and Rose (Kaplan) S.; B.S. in Acctg., Bklyn. Coll., 1963; M.B.A. in Taxation (fellow) City U. N.Y., 1965; m. Gloria Blatt, Jan. 24, 1965; children—Lisa I., Karen J. Auditor, Coopers & Lybrand, N.Y.C., 1965-66; tchr. N.Y.C. Bd. Edn., 1966-67; sr. auditor Price Waterhouse & Co., N.Y.C., 1967-70; divisional controller, sr. fin. analyst ITT World Hdqrs., N.Y.C., 1970-72; sr. v.p. fin. Sun Life Ins. Co. Am., Balt., 1972-77; pres. FPC, Inc., Plantation, Fla., also pres. Fin. Planning Ins. Agy., Inc., Plantation, 1977—. Treas. Jacaranda Lakes Homeowners Assn. C.P.A., N.Y.; C.L.U. Mem. Am. Inst. C.P.A.'s, N.Y. State Soc. C.P.A.'s, Nat. Assn. Life Underwriters, Fin. Execs. Inst., Am. Mgmt. Assn., Assn. Fin. Planners, West Broward C. of C., Beta Gamma Sigma, Beta Alpha Psi. Jewish. Club: B'nai B'rith. Author: Corporate Financial Planning: Profit and Prophet, 1975; Current GAAP Accounting and Actuarial Practices for Life Insurance Companies, 1976; Good Acquisition Accounting Principles for Life Insurance Companies, 1976. Home: 1070 NW 95th Ave Plantation FL 33322 Office: 120 S University Dr Plantation FL 33317

SCHWARTZ, PETER LEONARD, shipping container service co. exec.; b. Bklyn., Sept. 9, 1937; s. Philip and Zelda (Wolkowisky) S.; ed. pvt. schs.; m. Hope Barbara Jablon, Apr. 4, 1965; children—Michael, Scott, Danielle, Gabrielle. Vice pres. Bklyn. Steel Warehouse, Bklyn., 1956-58; exec. v.p. Bowers Constrn., Lake Success, N.Y., 1959-64; v.p. Steel Haulage Corp., 1965-69; pres. Container Master, Jersey City, 1970—; cons. in field. Trustee Rockland Country Day Sch., 1978. Served with USN, 1955-58. Recipient Service award Our Lady of Hope, Queens, N.Y., 1977.

Mem. Am. Pres.'s Assn., Am. Trucking Assn., Containerization Inst. Republican. Jewish. Clubs: Rotary, Rolls Royce Owner's, Masons. Contbr. articles to profl. jours. Home: Snedens Landing Palisades NY 10964 Office: 248 Johnston Ave Jersey City NJ 07302

SCHWARTZ, ROBERT GEORGE, ins. co. exec.; b. Czechoslovakia, Mar. 27, 1928; s. George and Frances (Antoni) S.; came to U.S., 1929, naturalized, 1935; B.A., Pa. State U., 1949; M.B.A., N.Y. U., 1956; m. Caroline Bachurski, Oct. 12, 1952; children—Joanne, Tracy, Robert G. With Met. Life Ins. Co., N.Y.C., 1949—, v.p. securities, 1968-70, v.p., 1970-75, sr. v.p., 1975-78, exec. v.p./1979-80, vice chmn. bd., chmn. fin. com., 1980—, also dir., chmn. and/or dir. various subs.; dir. NL Industries Inc., N.Y.C., Potlatch Corp., San Francisco, Lowe's Cos., Inc., North Wilkesboro, N.C., Kaiser Cement Corp., Oakland, Calif. Chmn. investment adv. com. The Christophers, Inc., 1979—; bd. dirs. N.Y. council Boy Scouts Am. Served with AUS, 1950-52. Recipient Alumni Achievement award Pa. State U. Coll. Bus. Adminstrn., 1979. Mem. Alpha Chi Rho. Clubs: Treasurers, Seaview Country, Springdale Country; Marco Polo (N.Y.C.); Laurel Valley Golf (Ligonier, Pa.). Office: 1 Madison Ave New York NY 10010

SCHWARTZ, ROBERT NASH, pub. relations exec.; b. Chgo., Mar. 6, 1917; s. Jacob and Sarah (Nerush) S.; B.A. magna cum laude, U. Ill., 1940; m. Judith Goldman, June 3, 1940; children—Frances, James. Reporter, Champaign (Ill.) News-Gazette, 1941-42; reporter, editor St. Louis Post-Dispatch, 1942-43; writer, editor N.Y. Times Sunday dept., 1943-46; editorial writer Chgo. Sun, 1946; bur. mgr., sci. editor Internat. News Service, Chgo., 1947-51; with Manning, Selvage & Lee, N.Y.C., 1957—, sr. v.p., 1967-71, vice chmn. bd., 1971-73, pres., chief exec. officer, 1978—; dir. Benton & Bowles. Trustee Nat. Found. for Infectious Disease. Mem. Public Relations Soc. Am., Nat. Assn. Sci. Writers, AAAS, Phi Beta Kappa. Clubs: Univ., Chemists (N.Y.C.). Home: 33 W 93d St New York NY 10025 also Truro MA 02666 Office: 99 Park Ave New York NY 10016

SCHWARTZ, ROBERT WILLIAM, communications co. exec.; b. N.Y.C., Oct. 23, 1944; s. Edward and Bertha R. Schwartz; B.S., Cornell U., 1967; postgrad. in bus. adminstrn. SUNY, Albany, 1970; m. Gail Beth Greenbaum, Mar. 18, 1967; children—Jill, Evan. Asso., IBM, 1967-68; cons. Peat, Marwick, Mitchell & Co., Albany, 1970-71; v.p. Security Gen. Services, Inc., Rochester, N.Y., 1971-73; v.p. fin. and adminstrn. Gardenway Mfg. Co., Troy, N.Y., 1973-77; exec. v.p. United Telecommunications Corp., Latham, N.Y., 1977-79, pres., 1980—, also dir.; dir. Union Nat. Bank, Albany; adj. prof. Rochester Inst. Tech., 1971-73. Bd. dirs. United Cerebral Palsy of Capital Dist., 1973—; trustee Newman Found., Rensselaer Poly. Inst., 1974-78, Gov. Clinton council Boy Scouts Am. Mem. Am. Mgmt. Assn., N.Am. Telephone Assn., Assn. for Systems Mgmt. Republican. Clubs: Ft. Orange; Econ., Cornell (N.Y.C.). Home: 2 Myton Ln Menands NY 12204 Office: United Telecommunications Corp Plaza Seven Latham NY 12210

SCHWARTZ, STANLEY MARSHALL, graphic arts mfg. co. exec.; b. Phila., Mar. 14, 1940; s. Benjamin and Ida (Matkov) S.; B.S., Temple U., 1962; m. Rosalind Schwartz, May 7, 1961; children—Brian, Julie. Vice-pres., Gen. Hobbies Corp., Phila., 1974, Baum Printing House Inc., Phila., 1976; pres. Zenith Enterprises, Huntingdon Valley, Pa., 1977—. Jewish. Mem. B'nai B'rith. Office: Zenith Enterprises Huntingdon Valley PA 19006

SCHWARTZ, STEVEN MARK, elec. appliance mfg. co. exec.; b. Phila., Feb. 26, 1948; s. Edward and Erika (Schneier) S.; A.B. magna cum laude, Bowdoin Coll., 1970; M.F.A., Columbia U., 1973; m. Paula Mae Levine, May 15, 1979; 1 son, Roger; stepsons—Lee, Derek. Writer, account exec. Schneider & Rich Assos., N.Y.C., 1973-76; sr. account exec. Richard Weiner, Inc., N.Y.C., 1976-78; account supr., v.p. Rowland Co., N.Y.C., 1978-79; exec. speechwriter Gen. Electric Co., Fairfield, Conn., 1979—. Recipient Silver medal for documentary script 8th Internat. Film Festival of Ams., 1975. Mem. Phi Beta Kappa. Republican. Jewish. Club: Bowdoin of N.Y. Home: 19 Round Hill Dr Briarcliff Manor NY 10510 Office: Gen Electric Co 3135 Easton Turnpike Fairfield CT 06431

SCHWARTZMAN, RONALD STEPHEN, maintenenace supply co. exec.; b. Balt., Feb. 26, 1944; s. Joseph and Reba (Frame) S.; B.S., U. Md., 1965; grad. Dale Carnegie course, 1974; postgrad. Georgetown U.; m. Patricia Baer, Nov. 24, 1966; children—Carl Andrew, Heather Michelle. Sales account rep. Copier div. SCM Corp., Balt., 1965-67; sales account rep. Baer Supply Co., Balt., 1967-74, mktg. mgr., 1974-75, exec. v.p., 1975—; exec. v.p. Baer Slade Corp., 1975—; pres. Heather on the Hill Enterprise, Stevenson, Md., Carlson Bldg. Systems, Stevenson; treas., dir., mem. exec. com. Standardized Sanitation Systems, Inc., Burlington, Mass.; dir. Baer Supply Co., Baer Slade Corp. Served with USAR, 1966-72. Mem. Stevenson Improvement Assn., Sales and Mktg. Execs. of Balt., Bldg. Owners and Mgrs. Assn. Balt., Internat. San. Supply Assn., Environ. Mgmt. Assn., Advt. Club Balt., Sigma Delta Chi, Tau Mu Epsilon. Democrat. Jewish. Club: Woodholme Country. Address: 8779 Greenwood Pl Savage MD 20863

SCHWARZ, WILLIAM GORDON, sales, mfg. corp. exec.; b. N.Y.C., July 22, 1933; s. Milton Arthur and Irene (Kuhn) S.; B.S., U. Pa., 1955; m. Barbara Helen Krauss, Dec. 30, 1969; children—Julia, Linda, Erick, Patricia, Ellen, Dana. Buyer, J.C. Penney Co., N.Y.C., 1955-66; nat. retail sales mgr. Montgomery Ward & Co., Chgo., 1966-74; partner Knox-Schwarz Assos., Chgo., 1974-77; pres. Schwarz-Markiewicz Assos., Inc., Chgo., 1978—; v.p. merchandising Alpha Omega Gift Corp., Fountain Valley, Calif., 1980—. Served with AUS, 1956-58. Republican. Roman Catholic. Clubs: Chgo. Housewares, Mchts. and Mfrs. (dir. 1966), Internat. Decorative Accessories of Chgo. (dir. 1977). Home: 1032 Whitehall Dr Northbrook IL 60062 Office: Schwarz-Markiewicz Assos Inc 1420 Merchandise Mart Chicago IL 60654

SCHWARZBACH, DONNA J., Realtor; b. Berkeley, Calif., Nov. 18, 1946; d. Robert W. and Paula (De Lap) Brisbon; student Santa Rosa Jr. Coll., 1964-66, Cabrillo Coll., 1968-70, Antohney Real Estate Sch., 1968, Lumbleau Real Estate Sch., 1977-78; m. Eric Schwarzbach, Sept. 24, 1966; 1 son, Hans Edward. Sec., bookkeeper North Bay Plumbing Contractors, Peteluma, Calif., 1965; bookkeeper and collection clk. Beneficial Fin. Co., Santa Rosa, Calif., 1965-66, San Francisco, 1966; sr. clk. N.Y. Life Ins. Co., San Francisco, 1966-68; bookkeeper, sec. to asst. mgr. Dream Inns, Inc., Santa Cruz, Calif., 1968-69; head county bookkeeper Title Ins. & Trust Co., Santa Cruz, 1969-71, 71-72; Realtor, Schwarzbach Assos., Realtors, Ben Lomond, Calif., 1971—; v.p. E.S.S.U., Inc., Ben Lomond, 1978—; owner, operator Ben Lomond Mobil, 1979, instr. Santa Cruz Bd. Realtors, 1978. Sec. to v.p. San Lorenzo Valley Property Owners' Assn., 1977-78. Mem. Santa Cruz Bd. Realtors, Calif. Assn. Realtors, Nat. Real Estate Assn., Ben Lomond Bus. Assn., Boulder Creek Bus. Assn., San Lorenzo Valley C. of C. Office: 9520 Hwy 9 Ben Lomond CA 95005

SCHWEDEL, RENEE HERMAN, real estate broker; b. Youngstown, Ohio, June 2, 1937; d. George and Gail (Greenberg) Herman; student U. Fla., 1955-56; m. Robert M. Schwedel, June 1, 1958; children—Lisa, David, Steven. Asso., Keyes Co. Realtors, Miami Beach, Fla., 1974-79; pres. Louis Sherry Assos., Inc., Miami Beach, 1979—. Mem. Nat. Assn. Realtors, Fla. Assn. Realtors, Miami Beach Bd. Realtors (dir.). Democrat. Jewish. Home: 990 S Shore Dr Miami Beach FL 33141 Office: 1 Lincoln Rd Bldg Room 202 Miami Beach FL 33139

SCHWEIGER, SEYMOUR MORTON, real estate co. exec.; b. Newark, Oct. 11, 1920; s. Joseph and Anna (Bernstein) S.; m. Sahm Schwartz, June 10, 1945; children—Edward, Dona. Vice pres. Morris Schwartz Associates, Inc., N.Y.C., 1945-59, Phoenix, 1959-72; pres. Normandie Constrn. Co., Phoenix, 1959-60; v.p. Ariz. Ranch House Inn, Inc., Phoenix, 1960-61, Ariz. Ranch House Realty, Inc., Phoenix, 1960—, Atlas Mortgage & Trust Co., Inc., Phoenix, 1963—; sec.-treas. Univ. Devel. Corp., Las Vegas, 1979—; mgmt. cons. The David Corp., Las Vegas, Nev., 1974—. Mem. Ariz. Econ. Devel. Mission to Japan, 1973; chmn. City of Phoenix Environ. Quality Commn., 1975-76; mem. City of Phoenix Sign Ordinance Rev. Com., 1975; mem. advisory com. to treas. State of Ariz., 1973-75; chmn. City of Phoenix Adjustment Bd., 1972-73; chmn. adv. com. Maricopa County Skill Center, 1971; mem. adv. com. Ariz. Corp. Commn., 1975-76; bd. dirs. Melvin Jones Lions Found., v.p., 1976. Served with U.S. Army, 1941-45; PTO. Recipient Bus. Man of Day award Retherford Broadcasting Co., 1965, Nat. Performance award Nat. Assn. Life Underwriters, 1964; award Ariz. Manpower Tng. Assn., 1976; FBI-City of Phoenix Police Dept. award, 1976. Mem. Phoenix Bd. of Realtors, Japanese-Am. Citizens League, Ying On Assn., U.S. Naval Inst., Ariz., Phoenix hist. socs., Valley Commerce Assn. (pres. 1980—), Phoenix C. of C. (valley planning com. 1972-73), Internat. Platform Assn., Navy League, Am. Def. Preparedness Assn. Republican. Jewish. Clubs: Masons (32 deg.), Shriners, Trunk and Tusk, Lions (pres. 1969-70). Home: 334 W Medlock Dr Phoenix AZ 85013 Office: 3550 N Central Ave Phoenix AZ 85012

SCHWEIHS, DANIEL JOSEPH, investment banker; b. Elmhurst, Ill., June 29, 1950; s. Donald N. and Veronica A. (Bruen) S.; B.S. in Mech. Engring., Rose Hulman Inst., 1972; postgrad. U. Mo., 1974-75, Rockhurst Coll., 1977; M.B.A., U. Chgo.; m. Melinda McComb, May 21, 1977. With sales dept. Leonard's Store for Men, Elmhurst, Ill., 1966-72, Am. Air Filter, Louisville, 1972-75; regional sales mgr. Standard Havens, Kansas City, Mo., 1975-78; with Dean Witter Reynolds, Chgo., 1980—. Mem. Nat. Soc. Profl. Engrs., ASME. Home: 5416 S Dorchester Chicago IL 60615

SCHWEITZER, PIERRE-PAUL, banker; b. Strasbourg, France, May 29, 1912; s. Paul and Emma (Munch) S.; grad. univs. Strasbourg and Paris, also Ecole Libre des Sciences Politiques; LL.D., Yale, Harvard, 1966, Leeds (Eng.) U., N.Y. U., 1968, George Washington U., 1972, U. Wales, 1972, Williams Coll., 1972; m. Catherine Hatt, Aug. 7, 1941; children—Louis, Juliette. Ofcl. French Treasury, 1936-47; alternate exec. dir. for France, IMF, 1947-48, mng. dir., chmn. exec. bd., 1963-73; sec. gen. Interministerial Com. European Econ. Coop., 1948-49; financial attache embassy, Washington, 1949-53; dir. treasury Ministry Finance, 1953-60; dept. gov. Bank of France, 1960-63; inspecteur general des finances hon.; chmn. Bank Am. Internat., Luxembourg, 1974-77, Banque Petrofigaz, Paris, 1974, Compagnie de Participations et d'Investissements Holding S.A., Luxembourg, 1975, Société Financière Internat. de Participations, Paris, 1976, Compagnie Monégasque de Banque, Monaco, 1978; adv. bd. Unilever N.V. Rotterdam; dir. Robeco Group, Rotterdam, Banque Pétrofigaz, Paris. Decorated grand officier Legion of Honour, Croix de Guerre, Medaille de la Resistance. Home: 19 rue de Valois Paris 75001 France Office: Petrofigaz 49 Ave de l'Opéra Paris 75002 France

SCHWESINGER, EDMUND ARNO, JR., mgmt. cons.; b. Manila, Philippines, June 22, 1939; s. Edmund Arno and Dora Helene (Axthelm) S.; B.A., St. Lawrence U., 1961; M.B.A., Columbia U., 1968; m. Marjorie Grace Daniel, Oct. 19, 1963. Financial analyst Gen. Motors Corp., N.Y.C., 1961-69; mgr. Peat, Marwick, Mitchell & Co., N.Y.C., 1970-79; prin. A.S. Hansen, Inc., N.Y.C., 1979—; dir. 1st Daniel Corp., Corner Locations Corp; asst. prof. State U. N.Y., Stony Brook. Bd. dirs. Encompass Theatre, 1976-79; trustee Jean Cocteau Reportory, 1976—. Served with U.S. Army, 1966-67; Vietnam. Lutheran. Club: Old Greenwich Yacht. Home: 94 Cutler Rd Greenwich CT 06830 Office: 529 Fifth Ave New York NY 10017

SCHWITTERS, DENNIS PAUL, farm equipment importing co. exec.; b. Des Moines, Dec. 7, 1940; s. Paul M. and Fern M. (Dreier) S.; B.B.S. in Mktg. and Econs., U. Iowa, 1962; m. Charleen T. Keulman, Sept. 16, 1961; children—Scott, Michelle. Mgmt. trainee Internat. Harvester Co., Denver, 1962-63, indsl. zone mgr., 1964, farm equipment zone mgr., 1964-67; owner, mgr. Schwitters Equipment Inc., John Deare dealership, Eldridge, Iowa, 1967-70; pres. Vicon Farm Machinery Inc., Chesapeake, Va., 1970—; mem. mgmt. com. Vicon N.V., Holland. Bd. dirs. Tidewater YMCA, 1976—, chmn. membership com., 1979-80. Mem. Farm Equipment Mfrs. Assn. (dir. 1977—), Norfolk and Chesapeake C. of C. Democrat. Presbyterian. Clubs: YMCA Presidents, YMCA Century. Home: 4509 Kelley Ct Virginia Beach VA 23462 Office: 3741 Cook Blvd Chesapeake VA 23323

SCHWOEBEL, WILLIAM SYLVESTER, business exec.; b. Pitts., May 29, 1912; s. William L. and Anna (Cotter) S.; student U. Pitts.; grad. Advanced Mgmt. Program, Harvard; m. Georgina E. Connell, Dec. 25, 1946 (dec.); m. 2d, Martha L. Bremer, Dec. 10, 1955; children—Ann, Mary. Auditor, Nat. Steel Products Co., Houston, 1939-42; asst. comptroller Nat. Steel Corp., Pitts., 1954-56, controller, 1956-64, v.p., controller, 1964-69, v.p. finance, 1969-72, sr. v.p. finance, 1972-78; chmn. bd., chief exec. officer Corp. Ins. & Reins. Co., Ltd., Bermuda, 1978—; vice-chmn. Nat. Underground Storage, Butler, Pa., 1978—. Served to 1st lt. USAAF, 1942-46. Mem. Fin. Execs. Inst., Am. Iron and Steel Inst., Soc. Fin. Analysts, AIM. Republican. Clubs: Duquesne, St. Clair Country, Rolling Rock. Home: 737 Pinoak Rd Pittsburgh PA 15243 Office: 2900 Grant Bldg Pittsburgh PA 15219

SCIARA, JOSEPH FRANK, real estate broker; b. Chgo., Mar. 7, 1920; s. Antonino and Grace S.; B.A., Ill. Coll. Commerce; m. Amanda Sturgill, Dec. 20, 1948. Pub., exec. officer Post-Tribune newspaper, Chgo., 1952-65; pres. Post Tax Service, Chgo., 1965; real estate broker House of Sciara Realty, Niles, Ill., 1979—. Active Little League. Served with U.S. Army, 1942-47; ETO. Mem. Am. Mgmt. Assn., Am. Ind. Businessmen, Ind. Accts. Assn., Fed. Tax Assn., DAV, VFW, Am.-Italian Vets. Roman Catholic. Home: 9222 Courtland Dr Niles IL 60648

SCIESZKA, JERRY FRANK, educator; b. Waterbury, Vt., July 4, 1938; s. Frank A. and Mabel Ayers (Lyman) S.; A.A.S. in Acctg., Bentley Coll., 1958; student U.S. Mil. Acad., 1959-61; B.S. in Bus. Adminstrn., Suffolk U., 1962, M.S. in Bus. Adminstrn., 1964. Fin. analyst Raytheon Co., Lexington, Mass., 1961-64; mktg. officer State Street Bank, Boston, 1964-68; mgmt. devel. program dir. Model Cities program HUD, 1969-70; pres. Andover (Mass.) Jr. Coll., 1971-77, trustee, 1977-78; chmn. mgmt. dept. Central New Eng. Coll., Worcester, Mass., 1978-79; also asst. prof.; Membership chmn. Mass. Dance Ensemble, 1980. Named Outstanding Tchr., Newbury Jr. Coll., 1976, Andover Jr. Coll., 1977. Mem. Public Relations Soc. Am. (accredited: editor PR News, New Eng. chpt.). Home: 531 Main St Worcester MA 01608 Office: 768 Main St Worcester MA 01610

SCIFRES, ROBERT E., corp. exec.; b. Lafayette, Ind., Dec. 5, 1917; s. Clarence Edgar and Bertha Mae (McCord) S.; B.S.E.E., Purdue U., 1938; M.B.A., M.I.T., 1950; m. Claire O'Brien, Sept. 12, 1969; children by previous marriage—Linda, Caryl, Cynthia, Dianne, Robert, Michael. With Nat. Gypsum Co., 1942—, plant mgr., Shoals, Ind., 1954-56, prodn. mgr. coastal Gypsum plants, 1956-64, v.p. mfg. Huron Cement div., 1964-67, gen. mgr. Kansas Army Ammunition plant, 1967-70, v.p., asst. to chmn. bd., Buffalo, 1970-71, dir., corp. group v.p., 1972-77, vice chmn. bd., 1977, chmn., chief exec. officer, 1977—; dir. Republic Nat. Bank of Dallas, Mem. Tex. Research League (dir.), Tex. Assn. Bus., Dallas Citizens Council, Dallas C. of C., Conf. Bd. Office: 4100 1st International Bldg Dallas TX 75270*

SCOFIELD, GARY LEE, banker; b. Brookings, S.D., Dec. 19, 1944; s. Alonzo Emerson and Mabel Josephine (Jensen) S.; B.S., S.D. State U., 1972; student U. S.D., 1962-63, 64-65; m. Susan Lee Chamberlin, July 6, 1967; children—Charles C., Thomas. Agrl. loan officer Nat. Bank S.D., Huron, 1973, v.p. and mng. officer, Sioux Falls, 1981—; asst. cashier Aberdeen (S.D.) Nat. Bank, 1974-76; liaison credit officer 1st Bank System, Inc., Mpls., 1976-78; pres. 1st State Bank Park River (N.D.), 1978-81. Chmn. S.D., Nat. FFA Found., 1976; mem. long range planning com. St. Ansgar's Hosp., Park River, 1979. Served with AUS, 1965-69. Decorated D.F.C. (2), Air medal (22), Combat Medics Badge. Mem. Park River C. of C., Bank Adminstrn. Inst., Am. Bankers Assn., N.D. Bankers Assn., Upper Midwest Council, Greater N.D. Assn., Alpha Tau Omega. Republican. Club: Lions (dir.). Office: 141 N Main Ave Sioux Falls SD 57101

SCOLARO, GIOVANNI NATALE, corrugated box mfg. co. exec.; b. Pozzallo, Italy, Dec. 25, 1929; came to U.S., 1949, naturalized, 1956; s. Frank and Rose (Nacarano) S.; m. Mary Ballaera, Sept. 5, 1953; children—Rosemarie, Frank, Vincent, Giovanni, Peter, Marie, Antoinette. Foreman, East Chipwah Paper Co., South Hackensack, 1955-63; owner, pres. Balsco Corrugated Box Co., Inc., East Rutherford, N.J., 1963—. Served with U.S. Army, 1951-53. Mem. Nat. Fedn. Independent Bus., Nat. Small Bus. Assn., U.S. C. of C. Roman Catholic. Club: Italian-Am. Forum of Lodi (N.J.). Home: 41 Garden Dr Elmwood Park NJ 07407 Office: 132 Union Ave East Rutherford NJ 07073

SCOLETTI, MICHAEL ANTHONY, JR., stock brokerage co. exec.; b. Pitts., Sept. 21, 1944; s. Michael Anthony and Elvira (Palmieri) S.; B.A. in Polit. Sci., Grove City (Pa.) Coll., 1966; m. Diane D. Dudreck, Sept. 16, 1972. With Moore, Leonard & Lynch, Inc., Pitts., 1967-80, v.p., 1974-80, br. mgr., dir., 1976-80; sr. v.p. Paine Webber Inc., 1980—. Bd. dirs. Murrysville (Pa.) Library. Mem. Murrysville C. of C. Roman Catholic. Club: Monroeville (Pa.) Rotary (dir. 1979-80, treas. 1980-81). Home: 3627 Cal-Ken Dr Murrysville PA 15668

SCOLLARD, GARRETT FRANCIS, TV firm exec.; b. Springfield, Mass., Oct. 6, 1930; s. Cornelius and Mona N. (Donahue) S.; B.S. in Polit. Sci., Coll. Holy Cross, 1952; m. Jeannette Reddish, July 4, 1979; children by previous marriage—Susan, Stephen, Caroline. Account exec. John Blair & Co., Detroit and N.Y.C., 1963-71; founder MMT Sales, Inc., N.Y.C., 1971—, chmn. bd., pres., 1974—. Served with U.S. Army, 1952-54. Mem. Nat. Assn. TV Program Broadcasters, Promotion Assn., Nat. Assn. Broadcasters, Ind. TV Assn., Internat. Radio and TV Soc. Clubs: La Costa Country, Marco Polo, Atrium. Office: 630 3d Ave New York NY 10017

SCOTESE, PETER G., textile co. exec.; b. Phila., Mar. 13, 1920; s. Peter and Caroline (Mangino) S.; grad. U. Pa., 1942; postgrad. Harvard U., 1960; m. Mildred Marie Heintz, Jan. 24, 1942; children—Jane (Mrs. Raymond Joseph Carey III), James Peter. Sec., accountant A. Greenfield & Co., Phila., 1937-46; terr. salesman, Eastern regional sales mgr., gen. sales mgr. Indian Head Mills, N.Y.C., 1947-54, v.p., gen. mgr. finished goods div., 1954-63; chmn. bd. Milw. Boston Store div. Federated Dept. Stores, Inc., 1963-69; v.p. Federated Dept. Stores, Inc., 1964-69; pres., dir. Springs Mills, Inc., N.Y.C., 1969—, vice chmn., 1975, chief exec. officer, 1976—; dir. Armstrong Rubber Co., New Haven, Cooper Industries, Inc., Houston, Bell & Howell Co., Chgo. Co-chmn. NAB-JOBS Program, Milw., 1967-68. Trustee Fashion Inst. Tech., N.Y.C.; vice chmn. bus. adv. com. Met. Mus. Art; nat. trustee Boys Clubs Am. Served to 1st lt. AUS, 1942-46. Decorated Bronze Star medal, Purple Heart with oak leaf cluster; recipient Alumni award of merit Girard Coll. High Sch., Phila., 1968, Community Service award Wis. Allied Constrn. Employers Assn., 1968. Mem. Am. Mgmt. Assn. (chmn. exec. com., dir., gen. mgmt. planning council, v.p. at large), Am. Fedn. Art, Mus. Modern Art. Clubs: Nat. Golf Links Am. (Southampton, L.I.); Lyford Cay (Bahamas); N.Y. Yacht, (N.Y.C.); DeVon Yacht (East Hampton, L.I.). Contbr. chpt. to handbook, articles to mags. and profl. jours. Home: 860 United Nations Plaza New York NY 10017 Office: Springs Mills Inc Fort Mill SC 29715

SCOTT, BLAINE WAHAB, III, ins. exec.; b. Phila., Apr. 22, 1927; s. Blaine W., Jr., and Dorothy (Fox) S.; ed. Friends' Central Sch.; m. Mary L. Howe, Nov. 14, 1964; 1 son, Robert P.; children by previous marriage—M. Kathleen, Bruce K., Sharon L., Linda, Blaine Wahab, Carol. Pres., dir. World Life & Health Ins. Co. of Pa.; chmn. bd. World Mut. Health Ins. Co. Pa.; pres., dir. Worlco Inc., also pres., dir. all affiliates and subsidiaries; pres. Upper Merion Investment Corp.; pres., chmn. bd. N.Am. Med. Centers, Inc.; partner Budget Lodge Valley Forge; sec., dir. Bank of King of Prussia (Pa.); dir. Middle Atlantic Gen. Investment Co., Pilgrim Life Ins. Co., Royal Oak Life Ins. Co., Allied Augusta Mut. Ins. Co., Gen. Devices, Inc. Mem. Upper Merion Bd. Suprs., 1960-66, chmn., 1961-66; mem. devel. council Villanova U., 1974—; trustee Temple U., 1969-73, Valley Forge Mil. Acad. and Jr. Coll., 1978—. Served in U.S. Army, World War II, Korea. Named one of 5 outstanding young men of commonwealth, Pa. Jr. C. of C., 1962. Mem. VFW, Nat. Assn. Health Underwriters, Greater Delaware Valley Assn. Health Underwriters (dir.), S.R., Greater Valley Forge C. of C. (dir.), Ins. Fedn. Pa. (dir.). Clubs: Union League (Phila.); Seaview Country (Absecon, N.J.); Ocean City (N.J.) Yacht. Home: 480 General Washington Rd Wayne PA 19087 Office: 550 W DeKalb Pike King of Prussia PA 19406

SCOTT, CHARLES ORLEN, JR., forest products mfg. co. exec.; b. Morgan City, La., Nov. 5, 1934; s. Charles Orlen and Lola (Fuller) S.; student Miss. State U., 1956-60, Nat. Hardwood Inspection Sch., 1961; m. Betty Carol Pair, Aug. 13, 1970; children—Angela Suzette Floyd, Lola Lee Redwine, Michael Gregory, Scott. Forester's aide Hood Lumber Co., 1955; from forester to asst. sales mgr. Chgo. Mill & Lumber Co., 1960-63; plant mgr. J.H. Hamlen & Son, Inc., 1963-65; with Wholesale Lumber div. Coastal Lumber Co., 1965-69; pres. Mullins Pulpwood, Inc., Natchez, Miss., 1969—; exec. v.p., gen. mgr. Ricks Lumber Co., Inc., Natchez, 1969—, Ricks Chips & Adams County Lumber Sales Co., Natchez, 1969—. Served with USN, 1951-55; Korea. Mem. Am. Pulpwood Assn. (dir.), Nat. Hardwood Lumber Assn., So. Hardwood Lumber Mfg. Assn., So. Hardwood Traffic Assn., S.W. Hardwood Mfg. Club (dir.), Aircraft Owners and Pilots Assn., Natchez C. of C. Democrat. Presbyterian. Club: Masons.

Home: PO Box 129 Washington MS 39190 Office: PO Box 1348 Natchez MS 39120

SCOTT, DAVID C., mfg. co. exec.; b. Akron, Ohio, 1915; grad. U. Ky., 1940, D.Sc. (hon.), 1974; LL.D. (hon.), Marquette U., 1980. Owner engring. cons. firm. Inst. Tech. Research, 1940-45; exec. Gen. Electric Co., 1945-63, mgr. power tube plant, Schenectady, 1954-60; v.p., group exec. several subsidiaries Colt Industries Inc., 1963-68, exec. v.p., dir., 1965-68; pres. Allis-Chalmers Corp., Milw., 1968-69, chmn. bd., pres., chief exec. officer, 1969—; dir. First Wis. Corp., First Wis. Nat. Bank Milw., The Travelers Corp., Harris Corp., Humana, Inc., Am. Can Corp., Royal Crown Cola Co. Bd. dirs. Farm and Indsl. Equipment Inst.; founding mem. Rockefeller U. Council; chmn. U.S. sect. Egypt-U.S. Bus. Council; bd. dirs., mem. exec. com. U.S. sect. Czechoslovak-U.S. Econ. Council; mem. U.S. sect. Iran-U.S. Bus. Council; bd. dirs. U.S.-USSR Trade and Econ. Council, Nat. Council for U.S.-China Trade. Office: 1205 S 70th St POB 512 Milwaukee WI 53214

SCOTT, E. WALTER, corp. exec.; b. Chgo., Feb. 28, 1930; s. Ervin Walter and Louise Cleveland (Doss) S.; B.S., U. So. Calif., 1951, postgrad., 1952; postgrad. So. Meth. U., 1954, Harvard U., 1964; m. Gaynel Hirtensteiner, May 10, 1951; children—Steve Randall, Leslie Gaynel, Jeffrey Rawlins. Zone mgr. Time, Inc., Dallas, 1951-54; asst. to pres. Mecom Oil & Gas Co., Houston, 1954-55; promotion mgr. Disneyland, Anaheim, Calif., 1955-57; pres. Met. Realty Corp., Los Angeles, 1957-61, Orange Julius of Am., Los Angeles, 1961-69; chmn. bd., pres. Ranchaire Corp., 1969—; owner W.H. Spurgeon Bldg., Santa Ana, Calif.; pres. Community Hosp. Services Corp., Newport Beach, Calif., 1972-78, Centre Co. Inc., 1979—. Pres. bd. dirs. Hathaway Home for Children, Los Angeles, 1964-66; developer Colorado Springs Community Hosp., 1975. Served with USAF, 1950-51. Lic. real estate broker, Calif.; lic. airline transport pilot, amateur radio operator. Mem. Phi Kappa Psi. Presbyterian. Author: Poison and Burn Prevention Program for Young Children, 1976. Patentee metal panels lock system. Home: 615 Via Lido Soud Newport Beach CA 92663 Office: 206 W 4th St Suite 433 Santa Ana CA 92701

SCOTT, FRANCIS EDWARD, broadcasting co. exec.; b. Omaha, Oct. 5, 1932; s. John Albert and Mildred Vera (Kessler) Schuchart; B.S., U. Nebr., 1954; m. Jean Marie Wilhelmj, May 23, 1962; children—Thomas, Catherine, Cortney, Wendy, Francis, John. Film editor, newsman Sta. KMTV-TV, Omaha, 1951-55; news anchorman Sta. KVOA-TV, Tucson, 1958-60; news dir., program dir., v.p., gen. mgr. Sta. KBON-TV/KLNG-FM, Omaha, 1960-70; v.p., gen. mgr. Sta. KTLK, Denver, 1973-76; gen. mgr. Sta. WRC/WKYS, Washington, 1976-78; v.p., gen. mgr. WRC-AM Radio, 1978—. Bd. dirs. Multiple Sclerosis Soc., March of Dimes. Served to 1st lt. USAF, 1955-57. Mem. Internat. Radio and TV Soc., Nat. Assn. Broadcasters, Broadcast Pioneers Assn., Md./D.C./Del. Broadcasters Assn. (dir. 1978—), Washington Area Broadcasters Assn. (dir. 1978—), Nat., Omaha press clubs, Sigma Delta Chi. Episcopalian. Club: Congressional Country. Home: 7600 Shadywood Rd Bethesda MD 20034 Office: 4001 Nebraska Ave NW Washington DC 20016

SCOTT, FRANK NICHOLAS, fin. cons.; b. N.Y.C., Mar. 4, 1936; s. Frank Nicholas and Charlotte (Whiteside) S.; B.S., Calif. State U., 1961, M.S. with honors, 1962; postgrad. UCLA, 1963, Alexander Hamilton Inst., 1967, Calif. Western U., 1978; Ph.D., Union Grad. Sch., 1977; m. Joan Olsen, July 1, 1956; children—Nancy Ann, David Olsen. Dir. research center Calif. State U., Sacramento, 1968; exec. v.p. El Dorado Hills subs. John Hancock Ins. Corp., Sacramento, 1966; pres. Community Shelter Corp. subs. TRW, Inc., Sacramento, 1971; chmn. bd. Oakland Fin. Group, Aptos, Calif., 1977—; gen. partner numerous oil/gas and real estate cos. in various states. Cert. community coll. instr., adminstr., sr. residential appraiser, rev. appraiser, fin. planner, lic. real estate broker. Mem. Nat. Assn. Accountants, Soc. Real Estate Appraisers, Nat. Assn. Rev. Appraisers, Nat. Fine Arts Appraisers, Am. Soc. Pension Actuaries, NASD (fin. prin., registered investment adv.), Tae Kwon Do Assn. Am., Beta Gamma Sigma. Inventor econometric personal fin. planning systems. Office: 7600 Old Dominion Ct Aptos CA 95003

SCOTT, FREDERICK WILLIAM ELMER, mech. engr.; b. Atlanta, Sept. 17, 1915; s. Earl Francis and Nina Viola (Elmer) S.; B.S. in Mech. Engring., Ga. Inst. Tech., 1938; M.S., Stevens Inst. Tech., Hoboken, N.J., 1940; m. Mary Cromer Walker, Feb. 7, 1945; children—Frederick William Elmer, Mary Emilie, James Walker. Pres. Earl F. Scott Co., Inc., Atlanta, 1940—; cons. engr. Nat. Linen Service, 1940—, Cavalier Industries, 1954—. Registered profl. engr., Ga. Mem. ASME, Ga. Engring. Soc. (charter). Republican. Episcopalian. Club: Atlanta Athletic. Designer linen service and indsl. uniform plants. Home: 948 Wendover Dr Atlanta GA 30319 Office: 3131 Maple Dr Atlanta GA 30305

SCOTT, GEORGE HAHN, metal co. exec.; b. Toronto, Ont., Can., Oct. 23, 1941; s. George and Grace (Hahn) S.; came to U.S., 1965, naturalized, 1971; B.S., Lafayette Coll., 1965; M.B.A., Fairleigh Dickinson U., 1972; m. Sally Jo Sepic, June 22, 1968; children—David Pitchairn, Douglas Cameron, Heather Lynn. Spl. asst. to mng. dir. Engelhard Europe, London, 1972-74; asst. gen. mgr. Engelhard - H.A. Wilson, Div., Union, N.J., 1974; asst. gen. mgr. ops. Engelhard, Plainville, Mass., 1975, gen. mgr., 1976-79; v.p. Engelhard Industries div. Engelhard Minerals & Chems. Corp., 1979—. Mem. Attleboro C. of C. (dir. 1978-79), Am. Soc. Metals. Republican. Presbyterian. Club: R.I. Country. Home: 7 Preston Dr Barrington RI 02806 Office: Route 152 Plainville MA 02762

SCOTT, HOWARD WINFIELD, JR., temporary help service co. exec.; b. Greenwich, Conn., Feb. 24, 1935; s. Howard Winfield and Janet (Lewis) S.; B.S., Northwestern U., 1957; m. Joan Ann MacDonald, Aug. 12, 1961; children—Howard Winfield III, Thomas MacDonald, Ann Elizabeth. With R.H. Donnelly Corp., Chgo., 1958-59; sales rep. Masonite Corp., Chgo. also Madison, Wis., 1959-61; sales rep. Manpower Inc., Chgo., 1961-63, br. mgr., Kansas City, Mo., 1963-65, area mgr., Mo. and Kans., 1964-65, regional mgr. Salespower div., Phila., 1965-66; asst. advt. mgr. soups Campbell Soup Co., Camden, N.J., 1966-68; pres. PARTIME, Inc., Paoli, Pa., 1968-74; dir. marketing Kelly Services Inc., Southfield, Mich., 1974-78; pres. CDI Temporary Services, Inc., 1978—. Served with AUS, 1957-58. Mem. Nat. Assn. Temporary Services (sec. 1970-71, pres. 1971-73), Kappa Sigma. Republican. Episcopalian. Home: PO Box 237 Paoli PA 19301 also 1204 Annapolis Sea Colony East Bethany Beach DE 19930 Office: CDI Corp 5 Penn Center Plaza Philadelphia PA 19103

SCOTT, ISADORE MEYER, energy co. exec.; b. Wilcoe, W.Va., Nov. 21, 1912; s. David and Libby (Roston) S.; A.B., W.Va. U., 1934, M.A., 1938; J.D., Washington and Lee U., 1937; m. Joan Rosenwald, Feb. 14, 1943; children—Betsy Scott Kleeblatt, Peggy, Jonathan D. Admitted to Va. bar, 1937; practiced law, Richmond, Va., 1937-38; v.p. Lee I. Robinson Hosiery Mills, Phila., 1938-42; with Winner Mfg. Co., Inc., Trenton, 1947-61, v.p., 1947-51, pres., 1951-61; chmn. bd. Tri-Instl. Facilities, Inc., Phila., 1962-78; chmn. bd. TOSCO Corp., Los Angeles, 1978—, also dir.; dir. Am. Stores Co., Girard Bank and Co., Sci. Am., Inc., Starwood Corp., Western Sav. Fund Soc. Phila., Univ. City Assos., Inc. Bd. dirs. S.E. Pa. chpt. ARC; dir. Internat. Rescue Com.; bd. dirs., mem. exec. com. Greater Phila. Partnership, Phila. Mus. Art, Univ. City Sci. Center, Phila.; mem. Phila. Com. Fgn. Relations; trustee Washington and Lee U.; asso. trustee U. Pa. Served with inf. U.S. Army, 1942-46; NATOUSA, ETO. Decorated Legion of Merit, Silver Star, Purple Heart, Bronze Star (U.S.); Crown of Italy; medal of merit (Czechoslovakia); Mentioned-in-dispatches (Eng.). Mem. Phila. Com. Fgn. Relations, Phila. Bar Assn., Va. State Bar, Phi Beta Kappa, Omicron Delta Kappa. Republican. Jewish. Clubs: Union League, Phila., Gulph Mills Golf, Philmont Country, Anglers of Phila., Masons, Locust. Office: 3236 PSFS Bldg 12 S 12th St Philadelphia PA 19107

SCOTT, JAMES FRANCIS, real estate appraiser; b. Geneva, N.Y., June 30, 1921; s. Frank Edward and Agatha Ethel (James) S.; student State U. N.Y. Extension Geneva and Rochester, 1939-41, U. Wis., 1969, U. Conn., 1971; m. Arleen Marie Masucci, Apr. 1, 1944 (div.); children—Gary F., Cheryl M., Margaret Mary Scott James. Photo paper prodn. Eastman Kodak Co., Rochester, N.Y., 1948-50; sr. appraiser Gokey & Galion, Ft. Lauderdale, Fla., 1950-53; owner, operator James F. Scott & Assos., realtors, appraisers, Rochester, 1955-63; pres. Scott Appraisal Service, Rochester, also Atlanta, 1963—; cons., lectr. in field. Served to maj. USAAF, 1942-47; PTO. Decorated Silver Star with oak leaf cluster, Air medal with 5 oak leaf clusters. Mem. Soc. Real Estate Appraisers (internat. v.p. 1974), Am. Right of Way Assn. (sr.), Nat. Assn. Corp. Real Estate Execs. (chmn. appraising and taxation com.). Republican. Roman Catholic. Home: 1549-B Holcomb Bridge Rd Atlanta GA 30071 Office: 6695 Peachtree Industrial Blvd Atlanta GA 30360

SCOTT, JONATHAN LAVON, former grocery chain exec.; b. Nampa, Idaho, Feb. 2, 1930; s. Buell Bonnie and Jewel Pearl (Horn) S.; B.A. magna cum laude, Coll. of Idaho, 1951; m. Barbara Jean Albertson, May 28, 1952 (div. Mar. 1962); children—Joseph Buell, Anthony Robert (dec.); m. 2d, Dolores Hormechea, Dec. 21, 1963; children—Richard Teles, Daniel. With Albertson's, Inc., Boise, Idaho, 1953-74, exec. v.p., 1961-66, pres., 1966-72, vice chmn. bd., chief exec. officer, 1972-74, also dir.; vice chmn. bd. Gt. Atlantic & Pacific Tea Co., Inc., Montvale, N.J., 1974, chmn. bd., chief exec. officer, 1975-80, also dir.; dir. Morrison-Knudsen Co., Trus Joist Corp., Bendix Corp. Bd. dirs. United Way of Tri-State; nat. bd. dirs. Boys Clubs Am.; trustee Com. for Econ. Devel., Coll. of Idaho. Served as 1st lt. USAF, 1953-54. Mem. Econ. Club N.Y. Clubs: Harvard; Sky; Arid (World Trade Center). Home: 86 Cider Hill Upper Saddle River NJ 07458*

SCOTT, LEE ALLEN, employee benefit cons.; b. Daniels, W.Va., Oct. 28, 1940; s. Minor Lee and Margaret Allen (Kay) S.; B.S. in Bus. Adminstrn., W.Va. U., 1962; M.B.A., U. Ky., 1967; C.L.U., 1971; m. Myrah Lou Erickson, July 15, 1962; children—Elizabeth Ashley, Stephanie Erickson, Lee Allen. Mgmt. trainee Gen. Telephone & Electronics Co., 1965-66; regional group mgr. Prudential Ins. Co., 1967-76; pres. Scott & Assos., Inc., employee benefit cons., Parkersburg, W.Va., from 1976; now pres., chmn. bd., chief exec. officer Union Trust Nat. Bank. Bd. dirs. Parkersburg YMCA, Wood County Devel. Authority, Parkersburg United Fund. Served with USAR, 1963-65. Decorated Army Commendation medal. Mem. Am. Soc. C.L.U.'s (chmn. continuing edn. com. Mid Ohio Valley chpt. 1979-80), Nat. Assn. Life Underwriters, Am. Mgmt. Assn., Health Ins. Assn. Am. (chmn. health care com. W.Va.), Estate Planning Council, Internat. Assn. Fin. Planners. Methodist. Clubs: Parkersburg Country, Glade Springs Country, Elks. Home: 141 N Hills Dr Parkersburg WV 26101 Office: 410 1/2 Market St Parkersburg WV 26101

SCOTT, MARGARET ANN SIMON, bank exec.; b. Boston, May 12, 1934; d. Frank A. and Margaret Alice (Gotham) Simon; B.A., Wellesley Coll., 1956; M.A., Boston U., 1965; B.S. in Manpower Adminstrn., U. Utah, 1974; m. Walter N. Scott, Nov. 21, 1959; 1 son, Walter David Kimbley. Research asst. Bell Telephone Labs., Whippany, N.J., 1956-58, U. Louisville Med. Sch., 1959-60, Harvard Med. Sch., 1960-64; instr. polit. sci. Trinity U., San Antonio, 1966-67; dir. info. systems Concentrated Employment Program San Antonio, 1967-68; cons. mgmt. info. systems U.S. Dept. Labor, Washington, 1968; dir. manpower planning Human Resources Adminstrn., N.Y.C., 1969-71; asst. cashier, personnel 1st Nat. City Bank, N.Y.C., 1972-74; asst. v.p. operating group Citibank, N.A., N.Y.C., 1975-77, v.p. investment mgmt. group, 1977—. Mem. Jr. League, 1957—, bd. mgrs. N.Y.C., 1972-74; bd. dirs. 1095 Park Ave Corp., 1976—, YWCA of N.Y.C., 1980—. Mem. Am. Polit. Sci. Assn. Clubs: Wellesley (N.Y.C.); Spinsters of Louisville. Home: 1095 Park Ave New York NY 10022 also Calhoun KY 42327 Office: 153 E 53d St New York NY 10043

SCOTT, MARGARET HOFFMAN, purchasing exec.; b. Youngstown, Ohio, May 11, 1941; d. Leonard Frederick and Barbara Jane (Reebel) Hoffman; B.S., Thomas A. Edison Coll., 1978; grad. cert. mgmt. U. Balt., 1978; m. Ben Hill Scott, June 12, 1967; children—Michael, Barbara, Kevin, Brian. Asst. mdse. mgr. J.B. White Co., Augusta, Ga., 1967-71; office mgr. Med. Coll. Ga., Augusta, 1971-72, sr. sci. buyer, 1972-74; sr. buyer Frederick Cancer Research Center, Litton Bionetics (Md.), 1974-75, mgr. purchasing, 1975-79, mgr. purchasing and logistics, 1979—. Mem. Nat. Assn. Purchasing Mgrs., Nat. Contract Mgmt. Assn., Am. Soc. Profl. and Exec. Women, Internat. Mgmt. Council, Mensa. Office: PO Box B Frederick MD 21701

SCOTT, PETER DOUGLAS, mag. advt. sales rep. firm exec.; b. San Francisco, Oct. 24, 1938; s. Duncan Archibald and Olive (Welty) S.; B.S., U. Calif., Berkeley, 1961; m. Nancy Back Oliver, Apr. 6, 1963; children—Kathleen Oliver, Abigail Back, Peter Douglas, Jr. Vice pres., treas. Duncan Scott & Marshall, Inc., San Francisco, 1961-68; asst. advt. dir. Wynterwade Pub. Co., San Francisco, 1968-69; with Scott, Marshall, Sands & McGinley, Inc., San Francisco, 1969—, pres., 1976—, also dir.; chief exec. officer, San Francisco, 1976—. Served with USAF, 1961. Mem. Nat. Assn. Publishers Reps., Internat. Advt. Assn., San Francisco Advt. Club, San Francisco Advt. Golf Assn. Clubs: Bohemian; Claremont Country; San Francisco Grid. Office: 433 California St San Francisco CA 94104

SCOTT, ROBERT CLINTON, banker; b. Bayonne, N.J., Dec. 13, 1932; s. William James and Marion Josephine (White) S.; A.B., U. Miss., 1954; J.D., U. Mich., 1959; m. Josephine W. Garner, May 31, 1954; children—Marion C., Robin W. Admitted to Ill. bar, 1960; pvt. practice law, Chgo., 1959-67; officer Chgo. Title and Trust Co., 1967-70; sr. v.p. Security Nat. Bank, Battle Creek, Mich., 1970-72; group v.p. Mich. Nat. Bank, Detroit, 1972-77, sr. v.p., 1977—; faculty trust and estates John Marshall Law Sch., Chgo., 1963-67. Served with USMC, 1954-57. Mem. Am. Bar Assn., Detroit Estate Planners Assn. Episcopalian. Clubs: Univ., Forest Lake Country. Home: 2640 Amberly Rd Birmingham MI 48010 Office: 1000 W Maple St Troy MI 48099

SCOTT, ROBERT FREDERICK, utility exec.; b. Biddeford, Maine, Aug. 31, 1929; s. Harry Albert and Caroline Gertrude (McCarthy) S.; B.S. in Bus. Adminstrn., U. N.H., 1953; M.B.A., U. Maine, 1969; children—Bradley David, Gregory James, Cynthia Ann, William Alan, John Frederick. With Central Maine Power Co., Augusta, 1953—, asst. v.p., 1972-74, v.p., 1974-77, sr. v.p., 1977—, also dir.; v.p., dir. Central Securities Corp., 1975—, dir. Maine Yankee Atomic Power Co.; Union Water Power Co.; Cumberland Securities Corp., 1975—; corporator First Consumers Savs. Bank, 1979—. Served with U.S. Army, 1947-49. Office: Edison Dr Augusta ME 04336

SCOTT, RONALD CHARLES, investment co. exec., lawyer; b. Greenville, S.C., Jan. 8, 1948; s. Robert Claude and Louise Helen (Tinsley) S.; B.S., The Citadel, 1970; M.B.A., U. S.C., 1972, J.D., M.Acctg., 1976; m. Debra Dianne Whaley, Aug. 11, 1973. Dir. legal residency, office admissions U. S.C., Columbia, 1971-73; dir. research State Senate S.C., Columbia, 1975-76; pres. R.C. Scott & Assos., Columbia, 1974—, Heritage Title Co., Inc., Columbia, 1978—; admitted to S.C. bar; sr. partner firm Scott and Mathews, P.A., Columbia, 1977—; instr. tax law Coll. Bus. Adminstrn., U. S.C.; cons. Master Planning Assos., Inc. Broker in charge S.C. Real Estate Commn.; campaign vol. Am. Cancer Soc., S.C. Heart Assn., Muscular Dystrophy Assn., Easter Seal Soc.; patron Columbia Town Theatre, Women's Symphony Assn.; sustaining mem. S.C. Democratic party. Served to capt. Adj. Gen. Corps, U.S. Army, 1973. Mem. Am., S.C., Richland County bar assns., Am. Mgmt. Assn., Assn. Citadel Men (life), The Citadel Hon. Soc., Columbia C. of C., Palmetto Land Title Assn., Columbia Estate Planning Council, Psi Sigma Epsilon. Clubs: Oristo Racquet, Quail Racquet and Swim, Palmetto, Summit. Home: 4846 Quail Ln Columbia SC 29206 Office: 903 Calhoun St Columbia SC 29201

SCOTT, STANLEY DEFOREST, lithography co. exec.; b. Hudson County, N.J., Nov. 2, 1926; s. Stanley DeForest and Anne Marie (Volk) S.; B.A., U. So. Calif., 1950; m. Mary Elizabeth Hazard, Dec. 30, 1953. Gen. mgr. Alfred Scott Publishers, N.Y.C., 1951-56; chmn., pres. S.D. Scott Printing Co., Inc., N.Y.C., 1956—. Mem. Mayor's Industry Adv. Council. Served with USNR, 1944-46. Mem. Printing Industries N.Y. (dir.), Am. Inst. Graphic Arts, Young Printing Execs., Soc. Mayflower Descs., Soc. Colonial Wars, St. George's Soc., Sons of Revolution (treas. 1972-73, 3d v.p. 1975-77, 2d v.p. 1977-79, chmn. Fraunces Tavern Mus. devel. com. 1973-79), N.Y. Hist. Soc., Met. Mus. Art, Mus. Modern Art, Morgan Library, other rare book libraries. Republican. Episcopalian. Clubs: Knickerbocker, Union, Downtown Athletic, Merchants, Lawrence Beach. Home: 1 Sutton Place S New York NY 10022 Office: 145 Hudson St New York NY 10013

SCOTT, WALTER BRUCE, electronics co. exec.; b. Chgo., Sept. 18, 1915; s. William and Agnes MacKeller (Valentine) S.; B.S., Drake U., 1938; postgrad. Northwestern U., 1939-40; m. Lucile A. Pilmer, 1940 (dec. 1968); children—Walter, Susan, William, Douglas; m. 2d, Beverly E. Lilly, June 14, 1969; 1 son, Kip. Mem. mfg. analysis staff Am. Can Co., Chgo., 1938-41; asst. to v.p. mfg. J.I. Case Co., Racine, Wis., 1941-46; works mgr. Motorola Inc., Schaumburg, Ill., 1946-52, v.p. mfg., 1952-67, asst. to pres., dir., 1967-70, v.p. mfg. and facilities, 1970—, dir., 1952—; dir. Continental Food Service Co., Hach Chem. Co.; trustee Scanlon Plan Assos., 1978—. Trustee Drake U., 1977—, Gottlieb Meml. Hosp., 1962—. Mem. Am. Mgmt. Assn. (trustee 1978—). Presbyterian. Club: Oak Park Country.

SCOTT, WILLIAM CHARLES, health care exec.; b. Gillespie, Ill., Mar 19, 1937; s. Thomas Bane and Grace (Biggam) S.; B.S., DePaul U., Chgo., 1958; m. Patricia Searson, Aug. 16, 1958; children—William, Kathleen, Robert, Thomas, Jennifer, David. Partner, Arthur Andersen & Co., 1958-69; pres. Recrion Corp., 1969-71; sr. v.p. Cordura Corp., Los Angeles, 1971-73; chief exec. officer, pres. Flagg Industries, Inc., Van Nuys, Calif., 1973—; dir. Ormand Industries, Inc. C.P.A., Ill. Mem. Ill. Soc. C.P.A.'s. Roman Catholic. Home: 4505 Woodley Ave Encino CA 91436 Office: PO Box 9022 Van Nuys CA 91409

SCOTT, WILTON ELEGE, petroleum co. exec.; b. Elgin, Tex., Jan. 3, 1913; s. Samuel S. and Clara (Schuerman) S.; B.A. in Geology, U. Tex., 1936; m. Loradean Allen, 1942; children—Sherman, Susan Scott Simons, Sarah Merchant. Geologist, Standard Oil (N.J.) in Venezuela, 1936-38, Cities Service Co., Hobbs, N.Mex., 1938-44; chief geologist Buffalo Oil Co., Dallas, later v.p., Midland, Tex., 1944-55; with Tenneco, Inc., Houston, 1955—, exec. v.p., 1970-73, vice chmn., 1974, pres., chief exec. officer, 1974-78, chmn. bd., pres., chief exec. officer, 1975-78, chmn. bd., chief exec. officer, 1977-78, also dir.; sr. v.p. Tenneco Oil Co., 1960-61, pres., 1961-70; dir. Republic of Tex. Corp. Mem. Am. Assn. Petroleum Geologists, Houston C. of C. (dir.). Home: 107 Glynn Way Dr Houston TX 77056 Office: PO Box 2511 Houston TX 77001

SCOTT, WINFIELD JAMES, mktg. exec.; b. Worcester, Mass., Jan. 4, 1933; s. Gherald Dean and Helen L. S.; B.A., Norwich U., 1955; postgrad. Marquette U., 1961-62; m. Betty Joan Price, June 29, 1957; children—Mary Jo, Susan Elizabeth. With sales dept. Norton Co., Worcester, 1956, sales rep. Chgo. dist., 1957, sales supr. Wis. dist., 1960-71; founder, pres. The Abrasive Group, Wauwatosa, Wis., 1971—; ad hoc prof. mktg. U. Wis. Extension. Mem. Abrasive Engring. Soc. (co-gen. chmn. internat. conf.), Nat. Small Bus. Assn., Wis. Mfrs. and Commerce, Ind. Bus. Assn. Wis., Met. Milw. Assn. Commerce, Nat. Fedn. Ind. Bus. Republican. Episcopalian. Author: Modern Machine Shop, 1967. Home: 11037 W Derby Ave Wauwatosa WI 53225 Office: PO Box 13244 Wauwatosa WI 53213

SCRAPNECK, EDWARD DAVID, pharm. co. exec.; b. Winnipeg, Man., Can., May 4, 1931; s. Demetrius Harry and Mary (Podolas) S.; student U. Man., 1948-50; m. Vivian Helen Froese, Aug. 25, 1956; children—Daniel George, David Edward, James Robert. With Lincoln Electric, Winnipeg, 1950-52; purchasing agt. Fleming Pedlar, Ltd., Winnipeg, 1952-55; pharm. sales rep. William S. Merrel Ltd., Winnipeg, 1955-56, Burroughs Wellcome Co., Ltd., Winnipeg, 1956—; profl. services coordinator Burroughs Wellcome Co., 1974—, Calmic, Ltd., Winnipeg, 1974—; pres. Kenparks Ent., Winnipeg, 1977—, research coordinator, 1978—. Bd. dirs. Mus. of Man and Nature, Winnipeg, 1977-79; chmn. com. local zoo, 1970-73; coach Youth Bowling Congress, Winnipeg, 1969—. Served with Can. Officers Tng. Corps, 1950. Named Salesman of Yr., Man. Pharmacists Assn. and Nat. Drugs Ltd., 1967; recipient Outstanding Pres. award Sales and Advt. Club, 1972. Mem. Man. Zool. Soc. (pres. 1980-81), Progressive Conservative Assn., Accredited Pharm. Mfrs. Reps. Orgn., Sales and Advt. Club Winnipeg (pres. 1970-72). Progressive Conservative. Mem. United Ch. Clubs: Kiwanis (dir. ch. bd.), Kildonan Canoe (comdr. 1979-80), Red River Drug Rangers, Winnipeg All Star Five Pin League, Ind. Order Foresters. Address: 7 Hooper Pl Winnipeg MB R2G 3C8 Canada

SCRIBNER, EDWARD ARTHUR, fin. investment co. exec.; b. Brighton, Mass., Apr. 3, 1946; s. Edward Elbe and Katherine (Kimball) S.; B.B.A., Boston Coll., 1967; M.B.A., Columbia U., 1969; M.Taxation, Bentley Coll., 1979; m. Jean Teresi, Sept. 23, 1969; children—Tara, Mark, Daniel. Accountant, Peat Marwick Mitchell & Co., Boston, 1969-76; gen. partner Edward Scribner & Co., Watertown, Mass., 1976—. Treas. Intercommunity Homemakers Service, 1977—; treas. Chinese Cultural Center Boston, 1976—, also bd. dirs.; bd. dirs. New Eng. Sch. Acupuncture, 1980—; trustee Community Center Sch. Children Spl. Learning Disabilities. C.P.A.

Mem. Am. Inst. C.P.A.'s, Mass. Soc. C.P.A.'s, Alpha Kappa Psi, Beta Gamma Sigma. Club: K.C. Home: 50 Grosvenor Rd Needham MA 02192 Office: 161 Galen St Watertown MA 02172

SCRIBNER, GILBERT HILTON, JR., real estate broker; b. Milw., June 1, 1918; s. Gilbert Hilton and Nancy (Van Dyke) S.; B.S., Yale, 1939; m. Helen Shoemaker, Mar. 22, 1941; children—Helen S. (Mrs. Gregory E. Euston), Nancy S. (Mrs. David W. Clarke, Jr.), William Van Dyke, II. Pres., Scribner and Co., 1962-77, chmn., 1977—; dir. Gen. Electric Co., No. Trust Co., Quaker Oats Co., Nortrust Corp.; trustee Northwestern Mut. Life Mortgage & Realty Investors. Mem. Chgo. Bldg. Commn., 1967-70; pres. Civic Fedn., 1955-57. Bd. dirs. Chgo. chpt. ARC, 1952-57, 67-72. Chmn., Ill. Commn. for Constnl. Revision, 1958-61; chmn. adv. com. Cook County Forest Preserve Commn. Bd. dirs. Northwestern Meml. Hosp.; trustee Northwestern U. Served as lt. comdr. USNR, 1941-45. Republican. Episcopalian. Clubs: Chicago, University, Commercial (Chgo.); Indian Hill (Winnetka); Shoreacres (Lake Bluff, Ill.); Old Elm (Highland Park, Ill.). Home: 17 Meadowview Dr Northfield IL 60093 Office: 1 First National Plaza Chicago IL 60603

SCRIBNER, RICHARD ORESTES, lawyer, stock exchange exec.; b. Muskegon, Mich., Mar. 10, 1936; s. Edward Kenneth and Kathryn (Crowell) S.; A.B., Princeton U., 1958; LL.B., Columbia U., 1963; m. Inez Zagoreos, Aug. 24, 1963; children—Alexandra, Christopher. Admitted to N.Y. State bar, 1963; asso. firm Davies, Hardy & Schenck, N.Y.C., 1963-67, Regan Goldfarb Powell & Quinn, N.Y.C., 1967; gen. counsel Assn. Stock Exchange Firms, N.Y.C., 1967-71, v.p., 1970-71; gen. counsel, sr. v.p. Securities Industry Assn., N.Y.C., 1972-80; exec. v.p. legal and regulatory affairs Am. Stock Exchange, Inc., N.Y.C., 1980—; lectr. in field. Pres. Princeton U. Class of 1958, 1978—. Served with USMCR, 1958-60. Recipient Toppan Prize, 1962. Mem. Phillips Exeter Alumni Assn. Greater N.Y. (pres. 1971-72), N.Y.C., Am. bar assns. Clubs: Seven Bridges Field (Chappaqua, N.Y.); Princeton (N.Y.C.). Home: 178 Seven Bridges Rd Chappaqua NY 10514 Office: Am Stock Exchange Inc 76 Trinity Pl New York NY 10006

SCRIPPS, CHARLES EDWARD, newspaper publisher; b. San Diego, Jan. 27, 1920; s. Robert Paine and Margaret Lou (Culbertson) S.; student Coll. William and Mary, 1938-40, Pomona Coll., 1940-41; m. Louann Copeland, June 28, 1941 (div. July 1947); m. 2d, Lois Anne MacKay, Oct. 14, 1949; children—Charles Edward, Marilyn Joy, Eaton Mackay, Julia Osborne. Reporter Cleve. Press, 1941; successor-trustee Edward W. Scripps Trust, 1945, chmn. bd. trustees, 1948—, v.p., dir. E.W. Scripps Co., 1946—, chmn. bd., 1953—; dir. various Scripps-Howard newspapers and affiliated enterprises, The First Nat. Bank Cin. Pres., Community Improvement Corp. of Cin. Trustee Freedoms Found.; trustee Webb Sch. Enlisted in USCG, 1942, commd. ensign, USCGR, 1944, advanced to lt. (j.g.), 1945; inactive duty, 1946-72. Mem. CAP, Theta Delta Chi. Home: 10 Grandin Ln Cincinnati OH 45208 Office: 1100 Central Trust Tower Cincinnati OH 45202

SCRIPTER, FRANK C., mfg. co. exec.; b. Dansville, Mich., June 21, 1918; s. Edgar and Maggie Alice (Havens) S.; student Warren's Sch. of Cam Design, 1946; m. Dora Maebelle Smalley, Nov. 2, 1940 (dec. Sept. 1945); 1 dau., Karen Scripter Allen; m. 2d, Elvira Elaine Taylor, Aug. 6, 1951; children—James Michael, Mark Lee, Anita Elaine, Warren Arthur, Charles Edward. Apprentice, Lundberg Screw Products Co., 1940-41; set-up man Reo Motors, Inc., 1942-43; night supt. Manning Bros. Metal Products Co., 1943; with McClaren Screw Products Co., 1946-47; partner Dansville Screw Products Co., 1946-54, pres., dir. Scripco Mfg. Co., Laingsburg, Mich., 1954—. Chmn., Citizens Com. Laingsburg, 1956-58; mem. Laingsburg Community Schs. Bd. Edn., 1971-75, sec., 1973-74, pres., 1974-75. Served with USNR, 1944-45. Mem. Nat. Rifle Assn. (life). Republican. Methodist. Patentee in field. Home: 9701 E Round Lake Rd Laingsburg MI 48848 Office: 9805 E Round Lake Rd Laingsburg MI 48848

SCRITSMIER, JEROME LORENZO, lighting fixture mfg. co. exec.; b. Eau Claire, Wis., July 1, 1925; s. Fredrick Lorenzo and Alvera Mary (Schwab) S.; B.S., Northwestern U., 1950; m. Mildred Joan Lloyd, June 27, 1947; children—Dawn, Lloyd, Janet. Salesman, Sylvania Elec. Products, Los Angeles, 1951-69; owner, mgr. Real Properties, 1965—; pres. Environ. Lighting for Architecture Co., Los Angeles, 1973—. Served with USAAF, 1943-46. Mem. Apt. Assn. (pres., dir. Los Angeles County), Covina Valley Bd. Realtors. Republican. Club: Jonathan (Los Angeles). Home: 2454 N Cameron Ave Covina CA 91724 Office: 17891 Arenth Ave City of Industry CA 91748

SCRUGGS, RICHARD T., aluminum co. exec.; b. Birmingham, Ala., Apr. 4, 1915; s. Josiah Hubert and Willye (Turner) S.; student Birmingham So. Coll., 1933-34, U. Ala., 1934-36; m. Marilyn Bade, Sept. 7, 1938; children—Marilyn (Mrs. Charles Tucker), Sarah (Mrs. Jarrell Estes), Richard Turner II, John Hubert. Salesman, So. Culvert Co., Birmingham, 1936-38, v.p., 1938-42; asst. chief aircraft insp. Bechtel McCone Corp., Birmingham, 1942-46; with Vulcan Metal Products, Inc., Birmingham, 1946—, pres., 1956—, dir., 1945—; pres. Scruggs Investment Co., Birmingham, 1954—. Past chmn. Salvation Army Home and Hosp. Adv. Bd.; mem. adv. bd. Birmingham Salvation Army; chmn. Lee assos. Washington and Lee U., 1975-77. Mem. Screen Mfg. Assn. (pres. 1967-68), Sales and Mktg. Exec. Assn., Newcomen Soc., S.A.R., Birmingham C. of C. (dir. 1964—), Alpha Tau Omega, Delta Sigma Pi; hon. mem. Alpha Circle Omicron Delta Kappa. Republican. Clubs: Birmingham Country, Shoal Creek Country, The Club, Downtown. Home: 3524 Victoria Rd Birmingham AL 35223 Office: 1 Irondale Indsl Park Birmingham AL 35210

SCULLEY, JOHN, soft drink co. exec.; b. N.Y.C., Apr. 6, 1939; s. John and Margaret (Blackburn) S.; student R.I. Sch. Design, 1960; B.Arch., Brown U., 1961; M.B.A., U. Pa., 1963; m. Carol Lee Adams, Mar. 7, 1978; children—Margaret Ann, John Blackburn, Laura Lee. Asst. account exec. Marschlk Co., N.Y.C., 1963-64, account exec., 1964-65, account supr., 1965-67; dir. mktg. Pepsi-Cola, Purchase, N.Y., 1967-69, v.p. mktg., 1970-71, sr. v.p. mktg., 1971-74, pres. PepsiCo Foods, 1974-77, pres., chief exec. officer Pepsi-Cola Co., 1977—. Chmn., Wharton Grad. Exec. Bd., 1980; mem. art adv. com. Brown U., 1980; bd. dirs. Nat. Center Resource Recovery, Keep Am. Beautiful. Clubs: Indian Harbor, Stanwich, N.Y. Athletic; Coral Beach (Bermuda); Wharton Bus. Sch. of N.Y. (dir.); Camden (Maine) Yacht. Office: 700 Anderson Hill Rd Purchase NY 10577

SCULLY, VINCENT JOYCE, chargecard co. exec.; b. N.Y.C., May 7, 1927; s. James Edward and Mary Marcella (Scullin) S.; B.S., Coll. Holy Cross, 1949; m. Joan Margaret Cunningham, Dec. 31, 1949; children—Vincent, Kevin, Keith, Joan, Mary, Barbara. Area mgr. Gen. Electric Credit Corp., White Plains, N.Y., 1957-69; sr. v.p., treas. Eastern States Bankcard Assn., Inc., 1969—, Eastern States Monetary Services, Inc., Lake Success, N.Y., 1976—; controller Omniswitch, Lake Success, 1975—. Treas., Pelham Booster Club. Served with USN, 1945-46. Republican. Roman Catholic. Clubs: Huguenot Yacht; Pinehurst Country. Home: 1341 Manor Circle Pelham Manor NY 10803 Office: 4 Ohio Dr New Hyde Park NY 11040

SCURLOCK, THOMAS JASQUE, JR., mfg. co. exec.; b. Mounds, Ill., Aug. 26, 1940; s. Thomas Jasque and Julia Mae (Fuller) S.; B.E.E., Howard U., 1962; m. Connie Mae Pernell, Jan. 2, 1965; children—Thomas, Karen. With Western Electric Co., Inc., 1962—, dept. chief circuit pack mfg., Chgo., 1971-72, mgmt. tng. program, 1972, dept. chief computer ops., Denver, 1972-74, tech. services mgr., 1974-75, material distbn. mgr., 1975-76, engineered systems mgr., Newark, 1976-77, engineered and operation systems mgr., Morristown, 1977-78, mgr. govt. communications systems and comml. sales, Greensboro, N.C., 1978-79; mgr. mktg. and projects—govt. communications, 1979-80; mgr. Quality Assurance-West, Warrenville, Ill., 1980—. Vice pres., bd. dirs. Fanwood Youth Orgn. Ambassador of Mercy, Chgo. Metro Crusade of Mercy, 1970. Served with U.S. Army, 1962-64. Mem. IEEE (sr.), Tau Beta Pi. Club: Optimists. Home: 6367 Hampshire Ct Lisle IL 60532 Office: Western Electric 28W615 Ferry Rd Warrenville IL 60555

SEABROOK, BELFORD LAWRENCE, JR., environ. waste mgmt. exec.; b. Bridgeton, N.J., Jan. 31, 1935; s. Belford Lawrence and Harriet Jane (Eakins) S.; B.A. in Architecture, Princeton U., 1956; postgrad. Rutgers U., Temple U. Grad. Sch. Bus.; m. Patricia S. Black, Feb. 1, 1958; children—David Lawrence, Kathleen Michelle, Hilary Denise, Matthew Eakins. Indsl. engr. Seabrook Farms (N.J.), 1956-57; 1st line supr. Personal Products div. Johnson & Johnson Co., Milltown, N.J., 1960-64; with Internat. Utilities Co., Phila., 1964-71, dir. staff services, 1969-71; pres. G. & W. H. Corson, Inc., Plymouth Meeting, Pa., 1972-75; pres. IU Conversion Systems, Inc., Horsham, Pa., 1976—, IU Tech. Corp., Horsham, 1977—; pres. Am. Pozzolanic Concrete Assn., 1976—, Envirosafe Services Inc., 1979—. Served to lt. (j.g.) Civil Engr. Corps, USNR, 1958-60. Mem. Phila. Soc. Promotion Agr. Club: Union League (Phila.). Home: 1820 Valley Rd Meadowbrook PA 19046 Office: IU Conversion Systems Inc 115 Gibraltor Rd Horsham PA 19044

SEACH, WILLIAM BOWEN, personal fin. planner; b. New London, Conn., Oct. 28, 1944; s. William Bemis and Alva Ruth (Bowen) S.; student U. Okla., 1963-68; m. Rachel Ann Ramsey, June 18, 1966; 1 dau., Ramsey Elizabeth Bowen. Pres. Seach Assos., South Weymouth, Mass., 1973—; partner, sr. v.p. Fin. Coordinators, Inc., Braintree, Mass., 1974-75; partner, v.p. Fin. Resources Group, Ltd., Boston, 1976-77; partner v.p. Numis. Corp. Am., Inc., Boston, 1977—, also dir.; partner, pres. NCA Service Corp., Inc., Boston, 1977—; tchr. Boston Center Adult Edn., 1974-76; tchr. fin. planning Brockton Center Continuing Edn., 1976-77. Served with U.S. Army, 1969-71; Vietnam. Decorated Army Commendation medal; William Bowen Seach Prose award established by Windmill mag. U. Okla., 1969. Mem. Internat., Greater Boston (chmn.) assns. fin. planners. Congregationalist. Contbr. poems to coll. lit. jours., 1967, 78. Home: 875 Tremont St Duxbury MA 02332 Office: PO Box 178 South Weymouth MA 02190

SEACRIST, JOSEPH FRANCIS, ins. co. exec.; b. Bloomington, Ill., Mar. 31, 1942; s. Marlin Joseph and Margaret (Davidson) S.; B.S., Bradley U., 1964, M.S., 1965. Mem. faculty U. Conn., Storrs, 1965-70; sr. manpower cons. Learning Sysemd div., Xerox Corp., Stamford, Conn., 1970-75; dir. agy. devel. Ind. Ins. Agts. Am., N.Y.C., 1975-77; v.p. human resources Devel. Continental Corp., N.Y.C., 1977—. Fund raiser Boy Scouts Am., Stamford. Mem. Am. Soc. Tng. and Devel., Ins. Co. Edn. Dirs. Soc., Sigma Delta Chi, Pi Kappa Delta, Pi Kappa Phi. Office: 80 Maiden Ln New York NY 10038

SEADLER, STEPHEN EDWARD, business cons. exec., behavioral scientist; b. N.Y.C., 1926; s. Silas Frank and Deborah (Gelbin) S.; A.B. in Physics, Columbia, 1947, postgrad., 1947; postgrad. George Washington U., 1948-50; m. Ingrid Linnea Adolfsson, Aug. 7, 1954; children—Einar Austin, Anna Carin. Legal research asst., editor AEC, Washington, 1947-51; electronic engr. Cushing & Nevell, Warner, Inc., N.Y.C., 1951-54; seminar leader, leader trainer Am. Found. for Continuing Edn., N.Y.C. 1955-57; exec. dir. Medimetric Inst., 1957-59; mem. long range planning com., chmn. corporate forecasting com., marketing research mgr. W. A. Sheaffer Pen Co., Ft. Madison, Ia., 1959-65; founder Internat. Dynamics Corp., Ft. Madison and N.Y.C., 1965, pres., 1965-70; orginator DELTA program for prevention and treatment of violence, 1970; founder Ideological Defense Center, Ft. Madison, also N.Y.C., 1968, pres., 1968—; mgmt. cons. in human resources devel. and conflict reduction, N.Y.C., 1970-73; pres. UNICONSULT computer-based mgmt. scis., N.Y.C., 1973—. Instr. polit. sci. Ia. State Penitentiary, 1959-62. Served with AUS, 1944-46. Mem. Am. Phys. Soc., Am. Statis. Assn., Acad. Polit. Sci., Am. Sociol. Assn., I.E.E.E., Am. Mgmt. Assn., Internat. Platform Assn. Club: Princeton of N.Y. Mason (32 deg., Shriner). Unitarian. Contbr. Ideologics sects. to Administrative Decision Making, 1977, Societal Systems, 1978; management Handbook for Pub. Adminstrs., 1978 (all J.W. Sutherland); also articles profl. jours. Testimony on ideological arms control in Part 4 of Senate Fgn. Relations Com. Hearings on Salt II Treaty, 1979. Office: 521 Fifth Ave New York NY 10017

SEALS, HENRY CHAIM, indsl. co. exec.; b. B. Lodz, Poland, Jan. 3, 1924; s. Josef and Leah (Zimmerkorn) Sliski; came to U.S., 1949, naturalized, 1955; B.A., U. Munich, 1949; M.B.A., So. Methodist U., 1958; Ph.D., Am. Internat. U., St. Louis, 1976; m. Elayne Smith, Oct. 27, 1967; 1 son, Jason T. children by previous marriage—Richard J., Laura S. Comptroller, WJB Corp., Dallas, 1951-56; comptroller Linda-Jo Shoe Co., Dallas, Denton, Gainesville, Tex., 1956-59; v.p. fin. N.Am. Mdse. Corp., N.Y.C., Dallas, 1959-63; v.p. fin. adminstrn. Bogart Industries, Inc., Ft. Worth, 1963-80; exec. v.p., dir. Bogart Enterprises, Inc.; pres. Basic Co., Ft. Worth, Seals Realty Co., Ft. Worth, Seals Mgmt. Co., Ft. Worth; dir. Sutherland Realty & Investment Co., Bogamex. Mem. Am. Inst. Mgmt., Nat. Assn. Accountants, Tex. Assn. of Realtors, Ft. Worth B. Realtors, Gainesville Jr. C. of C. (pres., 1957-59). Jewish religion. Clubs: Century II (Ft. Worth), Ridgles Country; Brookhaven Country (Dallas). Home: 4600 Briarhaven Rd Fort Worth TX 76109 Office: 2701 8th Ave Fort Worth TX 76110

SEAMAN, ALFRED J(ARVIS), advt. exec.; b. Hempstead, L.I., N.Y., Sept. 17, 1912; s. Alfred J. and Ellen (Delaney) S.; B.S., Columbia U., 1935; m. Mary M. Schill, Sept. 26, 1937 (dec. June 1975); children—Marilyn (Mrs. John Olen Pickett, Jr.), Susan, Barry, Deborah; m. 2d, Honor S. Mellor, July 16, 1977. Account exec. Fuller & Smith & Ross, Inc., N.Y.C., 1937-41; partner Knight & Gilbert, Inc., Boston, 1941-43; with Compton Advt., Inc., N.Y.C., 1946-59, exec. v.p., creative dir., dir., 1954-59; vice chmn. bd., chmn. exec. com. SSC&B, Inc. (formerly Sullivan, Stauffer, Colwell & Bayles, Inc.), 1959-60, pres., 1960-79, chmn., chief exec. officer, 1979—; dir., mem. exec. com. and devel. council Interpub. Group of Cos., 1979—; trustee, mayor, chmn. planning bd. Village of Upper Brookville, L.I.; co-chmn., mem. exec. com. Samuel Waxman Cancer Research Found. Served as lt. USNR, 1943-45. Mem. Am. Assn. Advt. Agys. (adv. council, pres. Ednl. Found.), Advt. Council (bd. dirs., chmn. campaigns rev. com.). Clubs: Creek (bd. govs.), Piping Rock, Nat. Golf Links Am. (L.I.); Racquet and Tennis, Links, The Brook (N.Y.C.); Mid-Ocean (Bermuda); Jupiter Island, Seminole (Jupiter Island, Fla.). Home: Wolver Hollow Rd Upper Brookville Oyster Bay NY 11771 Office: One Dag Hammarskjold Plaza New York NY 10017

SEARLE, DANIEL CROW, med. and health services co. exec.; b. Evanston, Ill., May 6, 1926; s. John Gideon and Frances (Crow) S.; B.S., Yale, 1950; M.B.A., Harvard, 1952; m. Dain Depew Fuller, Sept. 2, 1950; children—Anne Searle Meers, Daniel Gideon, Michael Dain. Asst. to sr. v.p. G. D. Searle & Co., Chgo., 1952-53, asst. sec., 1953-56, sec., 1956-63, asst. to pres., 1959, v.p., 1961-63, exec. v.p., 1963-66, pres., chief operating officer, 1966-70, pres., chief exec. officer, 1970-72, chmn. exec. com., chief exec. officer, 1972-77, chmn. bd., 1977—; dir. Harris Trust & Savs. Bank, Utilities, Inc., Jim Walter Corp., Maynard Oil Corp. Bd. dirs. Evanston Hosp.; trustee Northwestern U. Served with USNR, World War II. Mem. Com. for Econ. Devel. (trustee). Republican. Episcopalian. Home: 33 Woodley Rd Winnetka IL 60093 Office: Box 1045 Skokie IL 60076

SEARLE, PHILIP F., banker; b. Kansas City, Mo., July 23, 1924; s. Albert Addison and Edith (Thompson) S.; A.B., Cornell U., 1949; grad. Stonier Grad. Sch. Banking, Rutgers U., 1957, 64, sr. bank officers' seminar Harvard U., 1958; m. Jean Adair Hanneman, Nov. 22, 1950; 1 son, Charles Randolph. With Geneva Savs. & Trust Co. (Ohio), 1949-60, pres., 1959-60; pres., sr. trust officer Northeastern Ohio Nat. Bank, Ashtabula, 1960-69, also dir.; chief exec. officer BancOhio Corp., Columbus, 1969-75, also dir.; chmn. bd., chief exec. officer Flagship Banks Inc., Miami, Fla., 1975—, also dir.; dir. Mid-Continent Telephone Corp.; mem. faculty Ohio Sch. Banking, Ohio U., 1959-70, Nat. Trust Sch., Northwestern U., 1965-68; chmn. bd. regents Stonier Grad. Sch. Banking, Rutgers U., 1975-76, mem. faculty, 1959-70. Bd. dirs. Greater Miami Opera Assn., 1976—; mem. South Fla. Coordinating Council; chmn. Fla. Christmas Seals, 1977-78. Served to capt. AUS, 1943-46, 51-52. Decorated Bronze Star; named Outstanding Citizen, Ashtabula County, Ohio, 1965. Mem. Am. Bankers Assn. (governing council 1978-80), Fla. Assn. Registered Bank Holding Cos. (pres. 1979-81), Fla. Council 100, Assn. Bank Holding Co. (dir. 1979-81), Fla. C. of C. (dir. 1978—), Fla. Bankers Assn. (dir. 1979-81), Phi Kappa Tau. Clubs: Miami; Riviera Country (Coral Gables, Fla.). Author: (with Walter Kennedy) The Management of a Trust Department, 1967; editorial adv. bd. Issues in Bank Regulation, 1978—. Office: 777 Brickell Ave Miami FL 33131

SEARLES, JERRY LEE, television exec., fin. cons.; b. Chgo., July 6, 1931; s. Leo Keith and Mary Rosalynne (Pendy) S. Pres., owner Minn. Buyers Service, St. Paul, 1953-60, Progressive Industries, Diversified, St. Paul, 1953—, Midwest Tele-Prodns., Inc., St. Paul, 1958—; creator TV shows Jeopardy, Let's Make a Deal and Treasure Chest, others; cons. vets. affairs, TV programs, creative writing. Bd. dirs. Minn. Handicapped Recreational Assn., Human Rights Commn.; state comdr. Mil. Order Purple Heart, 1976-77, nat. jr. vice comdr., 1978-79, nat. sr. vice comdr., 1979-80, nat. comdr., 1980-81, nat. fin. committeeman, 1977—, chmn. nat. cemetery program, 1977; pres. Meml. Day Assn., 1980-81; rep. Nat. VA Hosp. Vol. Services, 1977-79. Served with AUS, 1951-52; Korea. Decorated Purple Heart, Bronze Star medal; recipient WCCO-Radio Good Neighbor award, Midwest Writers Assn. award; named Internat. Man of Achievement, Cambridge U., 1980-81. Humanitarian award Minn. Handicapped Assn., Employment of Vets. award, Mem. Writers Guild Am., Ind. Producers in Television, Am. Businessmen's Alliance, United Vets. Council, Am. Assn. Parliamentarians, Am. Legion (Outstanding award 1973), VFW, Amvets, DAV, 40 and 8, Cooties, Internat. War Vets. Alliance. Clubs: Masons, Shriners, Athletic, Millionaires, Univ. Author mag. articles, procedural advt. formats, bus. promotions, books. Home: 1704 Maryland Ave Saint Paul MN 55106

SEARS, BRUCE, wallcovering co. exec.; b. Chgo., Dec. 31, 1941; s. Daniel I. and Adeline (Crane) S.; student U. Ill., 1960-63; children—Bradley, Stacey. With I.S. Crane, Inc., Chgo., 1963—, v.p. sales, 1966-68, v.p., gen. mgr., 1968-70, exec. v.p., 1970-71, pres., 1971-75, chief exec. officer, chmn. bd., 1975—, dir., 1971—; dir. Daceb Corp., Bruce Sears, Inc., Sears/Lupel Assos.; cons. Mem. Wall Covering Wholesalers Assn., Wallcovering Mfg. Assn., Nat. Decorating Products Assn., Nat. Wholesalers Assn. Club: B'nai B'rith. Syndicated columnist Chgo. Sun Times, 1979—. Office: I S Crane Inc 2335 W Wabansia St Chicago IL 60647

SEARS, ROBERT WILLIAM, JR., fiberglas co. exec.; b. Bloomington, Ind., Aug. 27, 1940; s. Robert William and Wilma Jean Sears; B.S. in Mgmt., Ind. U., 1963; m. Constance Joe Sweet, Nov. 4, 1960; 1 dau., Susan Michele. With Owens Corning Fiberglas Co., 1963—, process supr., Newark, Ohio, 1963-65, personnel asst., Barrington, N.J., 1965-66, personnel dir., Huntingdon, Pa., 1966-68, personnel dir., Jackson, Tenn., 1968-72, fabrication supt., 1972-73, personnel dir., Barrington, 1973-77, personnel mgr., Toledo, 1977-79, personnel mgr. corp. staff sci. and tech., 1979—. Loaned exec. Toledo United Way, 1978. Named Outstanding Young Man, Jaycees, 1968; hon. Tenn. col., 1972; community service citation City of Jackson, 1971. Mem. Am. Mgmt. Assn., Am. Soc. Personnel Adminstrn. (2d v.p. local chpt. 1970, 1st v.p. 1971, pres. chpt. 1972; regional dir. Tenn. 1973), Toledo Personnel Assn. (social chmn. 1979). Republican. Home: 845 Yargerville Rd Ida MI 48140 Office: Owens Corning Fiberglas Fiberglas Tower Toledo OH 43659

SEATON, ROBERT FINLAYSON, savs. and loan exec.; b. Hancock, Mich., Nov. 28, 1930; s. Donald W. and Mary Lucille (Finlayson) S.; B.S. in Civil Engring., Mich. Technol. U., 1952; M.B.A., Stanford U., 1956; cert. Grad. Sch. Savs. and Loan, Ind. U.; grad. advanced mgmt. program Inst. Fin. Edn., U. So. Calif., 1973; m. Jean Robards, Apr. 18, 1954; children—Scott, Sandy. Vice pres., sec. Fed. Home Loan Bank of Cin., 1963-67; exec. v.p. 2d Fed. Savs. & Loan Assn. of Cleve., 1972-73, pres., chief exec. officer, 1973-74; pres., chief exec. officer Cardinal Fed. Savs. & Loan Assn., Cleve., 1974—. Vice pres. adminstrn. United Way Services, Cleve., 1975—; trustee, treas. Center Human Services, Cleve., 1975—; trustee Better Bus. Bur., Cleve., 1978—. Served with USN, 1952-54. Mem. Ohio League Savs. Assns. (trustee), Northeastern Ohio League Savs. Assns. (1st v.p.). Methodist. Clubs: Union, Country, Athletic (Cleve.); Bankers (Cin.). Home: 16 Pepper Creek Dr Pepper Pike OH 44124 Office: 333 Euclid Ave Cleveland OH 44114

SEATON, WILLIAM RUSSELL, oil co. exec.; b. Ashland, Ky., Jan. 2, 1928; s. Edward William and Virginia (Russell) S.; B.S., Yale, 1949; m. Suzanne Webb, Aug. 9, 1950; children—Katherine Graham Seaton James, Suzanne Elizabeth Seaton Beach, Mildred Webb Seaton Grizzle, Edward William II. Trainee, Ashland Oil, Inc. (Ky.), 1949, trainee personnel dept., 1950, jr. engr. personnel dept., 1950, adminstrv. asst. personnel, 1951-52, asst. ins. mgr., 1953-55, ins. mgr., 1955-60, exec. asst., 1960-67, v.p., 1967, adminstrv. v.p., 1968, dir., 1969—, sr. v.p., chief adminstrv. officer, 1970-72, vice chmn., 1972—. Trustee, Woodberry Forest Sch., 1976—. Mem. 25-Yr. Club of Petroleum Industry, Chi Psi. Home: 409 Country Club Dr Ashland KY 41101 Office: PO Box 391 Ashland KY 41101

SEAWELL, WILLIAM THOMAS, airline co. exec.; b. Pine Bluff, Ark., Jan. 27, 1918; s. George Marion and Harriet (Aldridge) S.; B.S., U.S. Mil. Acad., 1941; J.D., Harvard, 1949; m. Judith Alexander, June 12, 1941; children—Alexander Brooke, Anne Seawell Robinson.

Commd. 2d lt. U.S. Army, 1941, advanced through grades to brig. gen. USAF, 1959; comdr. 401st Bombardment Group, ETO, World War II; staff hdqrs. USAF, 1945-46; comdr. 11th Bomb Wing SAC, 1953-54; dep. comdr. 7th Air Div., 1954-55; mil. asst. to sec. air force, 1958-59; mil. asst. to dep. sec. def., 1959-61; comdt. cadets U.S. Air Force Acad., 1961-63; v.p. ops. and engring. Air Transport Assn. Am., Washington, 1963-65; sr. v.p. ops. Am. Airlines, 1965-68; pres. Rolls Royce Aero Engines Inc. U.S. subs. Rolls Royce, Ltd., 1968-71; pres., chief operating officer Pan Am. World Airways Inc., N.Y.C., 1971-72, chmn. bd., pres., chief exec. officer, 1972-75, chmn. bd., chief exec. officer, 1976—, also dir.; dir. Cluett, Peabody & Co., Inc., Lehman Corp., J. Ray McDermott & Co., Inc., McGraw Hill, Inc. Decorated Silver Star, D.F.C. with three oak leaf clusters, Air medal with three oak leaf clusters; Croix de Guerre with palm (France). Clubs: Chevy Chase, Met. (Washington); River, Sky, Wings, Links (N.Y.C.). Office: Pan Am World Airways 200 Park Ave New York NY 10166

SEAY, GERALD ROBERT, risk fin. exec.; b. Dallas, July 29, 1947; s. Robert Lincoln and Rita (Vaughn) S.; B.S.B.A., U. Denver, 1970; B.I.M., Am. Grad. Sch. Internat. Mgmt., 1971, M.S.I.M., 1972; Advanced Mgmt. Program, U. Tex., 1979. European rep. Am. Internat. Group, Madrid, 1972-74; internat. rep. Continental Ins. Co., N.Y.C., 1974-75; risk analysis mgr. Cities Service Co., Tulsa, 1975-77; asst. v.p., risk analysis mgr. Marsh & McLennan, Inc., Tulsa, 1977-79, v.p., head of office, 1979—. Cons. Project Bus. of Jr. Achievement; bd. dirs. Tulsa Ballet Theatre; asso. Hillcrest Med. Center. Mem. Met. Tulsa C. of C. Republican. Roman Catholic. Clubs: So. Hills Country, Tulsa Tennis, Tulsa So. Tennis, Tulsa. Home: 2300 Riverside Dr Tulsa OK 74114 Office: 1579 E 21st St Tulsa OK 74114

SEBASTIAN, EDWARD JOHN, comml. banker, mortgage banker; b. Lebanon, Pa., Sept. 2, 1946; s. Stephen George and Helen Agnes (Smith) S.; B.S., Pa. State U., 1968; m. Susan Renee Snypes, May 3, 1969; children—Ashley, Rosalind. Sr. accountant Price Waterhouse & Co., N.Y.C., 1968-73, Charlotte, N.C., 1973, acting mgr., Columbia, S.C., 1973-74; v.p., controller Bankers Trust of S.C., Columbia, 1974-77, sr. v.p. and controller, 1977-79, sr. v.p., controller, asst. sec., dir., 1979-80, vice chmn., sec., cashier, 1980—; sec., treas. B.T. Bldg. Corp., 1978-80, pres., 1980—; pres., chief exec. officer Aiken Speir Inc. (now Bankers Mortgage Corp.), 1979—; tchr. Price Waterhouse Accountant's Continuing Edn. courses Central Piedmont Community Coll., Charlotte, 1973. Chmn., Price Waterhouse United Fund, 1973; past trustee, vice chmn., treas. Wildewood Sch. C.P.A., S.C. Mem. Nat. Assn. Accountants, Am. Inst. C.P.A.'s, Am. Accounting Assn., Bank Adminstrn. Inst. (past dir. chpt.), Nat. Assn. Rev. Appraisers (sr.), Internat. Platform Assn., Am. Inst. Indsl. Engrs., Inst. Mgmt. Sci., Am. Soc. Corp. Secs., Pa. State U. Alumni Assn., Phi Kappa Psi. Democrat. Roman Catholic. Home: 6137 Hampton Ridge Rd Columbia SC 29209 Office: Bankers Trust of SC Bankers Trust Tower Columbia SC 29202

SEBASTIAN, JAMES JOSEPH, real estate devel. co. exec.; b. Warren, Ohio, Apr. 20, 1947; s. James V. and Julie M. S.; B.S., Ohio State U., 1969; M.B.A., Western Colo. U., 1977; m. Molly M. Moline, June 14, 1975. Mgr. sales/engring. Werner Constrn. Co., Columbus, Ohio, 1971-77; dir. adminstrv. services Red Roof Inns, Columbus, Ohio, 1977-78; pres. James J. Sebastian & Co., Inc., real estate developers, cons. and brokers, Columbus, 1978—. Mem. Nat. Republican Com. Mem. Am. Mgmt. Assn., Assn. M.B.A. Execs., Columbus Builders Exchange. Clubs: Columbus Athletic; Little Turtle Country; Amateur Radio Relay League. Home: 103 Nob Hill Dr Gahanna OH 43230 Office: Borden Bldg PO Box 30245 Columbus OH 43230

SEBIRE, JEAN PIERRE, bank exec.; b. Paris, Feb. 29, 1928; came to U.S., 1978; s. Paul A. and Jeanne E. (Le Moutier) S.; law degree, U. Paris, 1949; postgrad. Paris Inst. d'Etudes Politiques, 1952. With Soc. Générale, 1954—, dept. br. mgr., London, 1964-69, gen. br. mgr., London, 1972-78, N.Y.C., 1979—. Served with French Army, 1952-53. Roman Catholic. Home: 870 Fifth Ave New York NY 10021 Office: Soc Générale 50 Rockefeller Plaza New York NY 10020

SECCURRA, SUSAN, mfg. co. exec.; b. Rome, N.Y., Apr. 1, 1954; d. Armando Anthony and Rose Barbara (Franco) S.; B.S. in Econs., Russell Sage Coll., 1976; M.B.A. in Mktg., U. Rochester, 1980. Credit analyst Burroughs Corp., Rochester, 1976, sr. credit analyst, 1976-77, fin. analyst Office Supplies div., 1977-79, mgr. credit and collections Bus. Forms div., 1979-80, mgr. fin. analysis Bus. Forms div., 1980—. Mem. Nat. Assn. Credit Mgrs., Nat. Assn. Female Execs., Phi Kappa Phi. Office: 1150 University Ave Rochester NY 14603

SECUNDA, EUGENE, advt. agy. exec.; b. Bklyn., June 15, 1934; s. Sholom and Betty (Almer) S.; comml. degree N.Y. Inst. Photography, 1955; B.S., N.Y. U., 1956; M.S., Boston U., 1962; m. Shirley Carol Frummer, Sept. 23, 1961; children—Ruthanne, Andrew. News editor Sta. WBMS, 1956-57; reporter New London Daily Day, 1958-59; publicist Universal Pictures, 1959-60, various Broadway shows, 1960-62; sr. publicist 20th Century Fox, N.Y.C., 1962-65; advt. and public relations account supr. J. Walter Thompson, N.Y.C., 1965-73, sr. v.p., dir. corp. and public affairs, 1974-78, sr. v.p., dir. JWT/Entertainment div., 1978-80; sr. v.p., dir. communications services N.W. Ayer ABH Internat., N.Y.C., 1980—; asso. prof. advt. N.Y. U. Sch. Bus. and Adminstrn., 1972—; guest lectr. FBI Acad. Mem. Mcpl. Art Soc. N.Y., Fortune Soc. (adv. council), Sales Execs. Club, Broadway Assos. Office: 1345 Ave of Americas New York NY 10036

SEDER, LAWRENCE RICHARD, leasing and comml. finance exec.; b. Worcester, Mass., Mar. 2, 1935; s. David Jerome and Sylvia (Beizer) S.; B.B.A., U. Mich., 1957, M.B.A., 1958; m. Lesley Crossman, July 20, 1969; children—Robin, Lynn. With Gen. Discount Corp., Boston, 1958, now pres.; pres. CBT Leasing Corp. Instr. finance Boston U., 1959-61. Served with USAF, 1961-62. Mem. Pi Lambda Phi. Club: Belmont Country. Home: 135 Willard Rd Brookline MA 02146 Office: 60 State St Boston MA 02109

SEDGELEY, CARLTON STANLEY, lecture agy. exec.; b. Lewiston, Maine, Dec. 1, 1939; s. Nelson Stanley and Marion Caroline (Giguire) S.; B.S., Springfield Coll., 1963; m. Lucille Lepage, Aug. 8, 1964. Sales trainee Bridgeport Brass, Cambridge, Mass., 1964-65; profl. lectr. Lee Inst., Brookline, Mass., 1965-67; lecture agt. Harry Walker, Inc., Boston, 1966-67; asst. to pres. Northwood Inst., Midland, Mich., 1968-69; pres. Royce Carlton, Inc., N.Y.C., 1969—; acting dir. Jose Greco Found. for Hispanic Dance, Inc., N.Y.C., 1971—. Mem. gala concert com. at Carnegie Hall for Symphonicum Europae Found., Ltd., 1979. Served with U.S. Army, 1963-64. Mem. Nat. Entertainment and Campus Activities Assn., Assn. Am. Dance Cos., Internat. Platform Assn. Contbr. articles to talent mags. Home: 429 E 52d St New York NY 10022 Office: 866 UN Plaza New York NY 10017

SEEDLOCK, ROBERT FRANCIS, engring. and constrn. exec.; b. Newark, Feb. 6, 1913; s. Frank Andrew and Mary Elizabeth (Prosner) S.; student Case Inst. Tech., 1931-33; B.S., U.S. Mil. Acad., 1937; M.S. in Civil Engring., Mass. Inst. Tech., 1940; grad. Armed Forces Staff Coll., 1948, Nat. War Coll., 1958; m. Hortense Orcutt Norton, Sept. 1, 1937; children—Robert Francis, Elizabeth Munsell (Mrs. Norman H. Morrissette), Walter Norton, Mary Marion. Commd. 2d lt. U.S. Army, 1937, advanced through grades to maj. gen., 1963; asst. to dist. engr., Pitts., 1937-39, Tulsa Aircraft Assembly Plant, 1941; regtl. exec. battalion comdr. EUTC, Camp Claiborne, La., 1942; asst. theatre engr., CBI, also comdr. Burma Rd. engrs., and chief engr. Shanghai Base Command, 1943-47; mem. gen. staff U.S. Army, mem. Am. delegation Far Eastern Commn., 1948-49; aide to chief staff U.S. Army, 1949, 54; mem. U.S. del. NATO Ministerial Conf., 1952-53; dep. div. engr. Mediterranean div., 1954-57; mil. asst. to asst. sec. def. pub. affairs, 1958-62; div. engr. Missouri River, Omaha, 1962-63; sr. mem. UN Mil. Armistice Commn., Korea, 1963-64; dir. mil. personnel ODCSPER, Dept. Army, 1964-66; dir. mil. constrn. Office Chief of Engrs., 1966; comdg. gen. U.S. Army Engr. Center and Ft. Belvoir, Va. and comdt. U.S. Army Engr. Sch. Ft. Belvoir, 1966-68; ret. 1968; pres. Yuba Industries, 1968-69, v.p. Standard Prudential Corp. (merger with Yuba Industries), 1969-70; v.p., dir. Petro-Chme. Devel. Co., Inc., N.Y.C., 1968-70, Petchem Constrn. Co., N.Y.C., 1968-70, Petrochem Isoflow Furnaces, Ltd. (Can.), 1968-70; dir. constrn. and devel. Port Authority of Allegheny County, Pitts., 1970-73; asso. Parsons, Brinckerhoff, Quade & Douglas, N.Y.C., 1973—, mgr. So. region, 1975—; dep. project dir. Parsons, Brinckerhoff-Tudor-Bechtel, Atlanta, 1973-76; program dir. Ralph M. Parsons Co., 1977—. Bd. dirs. Army and Air Force Exchange and Motion Picture Service, 1964; mem. Miss. River Commn., 1962-63, Bd. Engrs. Rivers and Harbors, 1962-63, Def. Adv. Commn. Edn., 1964; chmn. Mo. Basin Inter-Agy. Com., 1962-63; fed. rep., chmn. Big Blue River Compact Commn., 1962-63; mem. U.S. Com. on Large Dams, 1962—; exec. bd. Nat. Capital Area council Boy Scouts Am., 1967-68, Atlanta Area council, 1975—. Decorated D.S.M., Legion of Merit with oak leaf cluster; chevalier Legion of Honor (France); 1st class, grade A medal army, navy, air force, also spl. breast Order Yun Hui (China); named Engr. of Year, Met. Atlanta Engring. Soc., 1976; Ga. Engr. of Year in Govt., Ga. Soc. Profl. Engrs., 1976; recipient Silver Beaver award Boy Scouts Am. Registered profl. engr. Fellow Soc. Am. Mil. Engrs. (nat. dir.); mem. ASCE (hon.), Assn. U.S. Army, West Point Soc. N.Y. (life), West Point Soc. Atlanta (pres. 1976), Sigma Xi, Tau Beta Pi. Roman Catholic. Clubs: Army-Navy Country (sec. chmn. bd. govs. 1952-54, 61-62) (Arlington, Va.); Massachusetts Institute of Technology (pres. Shanghai 1946); Metropolitan (N.Y.C.); Oglethorpe (Savannah, Ga.); Ansley Golf (Atlanta, Ga.). Contbr. mil. and engring. jours. Home: 181 S Marengo Pasadena CA 91101 Office: 100 W Walnut Pasadena CA 91124

SEEGAL, HERBERT LEONARD, dept. store exec.; b. Brookline, Mass., Aug. 13, 1915; s. Morris and Rose (Beerman) S.; A.B., U. Mich., 1937; m. Dorothy Goldstein, June 27, 1941 (div. June 1954); children—Jane Laura, Norma Ann. With R.H. White's, Boston, 1937-41, Thalhimer's, Richmond, Va., 1941-53, v.p. charge gen. merchandising, 1949-53; sr. v.p. merchandising, dir. Macy's, N.Y.C., 1953-62; pres. Bamberger's N.J., Newark, 1962-71; dir. R.H. Macy & Co., Inc., N.Y.C., 1965—, vice chmn. bd., 1971-72, pres., 1972-80; cons., 1980—; dir. Midatlantic Nat. Bank and Holding Co., Midatlantic Banks, Inc., N.J. Bell Telephone Co., Lenox, Inc., Jonathan Logan, Inc. Mem. N.J. Econ. Stblzn. Bd.; mem. econ. stblzn. com. regional office Fed. Emergency Mgmt. Agy.; mem. mchts. council N.Y. U. Clubs: City Athletic, Princeton (N.Y.C.); Century Country (Purchase, N.Y.); Two Hundred of Newark (trustee). Office: 220 E 42 St Suite 2802 New York NY 10017

SEEGER, DONALD THOMAS, fin. cons.; b. Shattuck, Okla., Dec. 8, 1942; s. George Joseph and Edna Marie (Terbush) S.; ed. Nebr. State Coll., 1962; grad. Colo. Securities Coll., 1975, Jones Real Estate Coll., 1978; m. Kay Lorraine Koshio, Apr. 25, 1965; children—Joseph Conrad, Gordon Scott. Acct., asst. terminal mgr. Frontier Refining Co., 1964-66; fin. cons. Barden Investment Mgmt. Corp., 1966-68; owner, dir., cert. fin. cons. Seeger & Assos., Colorado Springs, Colo., 1968—; pres. Diversified Services Corp., Fin. Systems, Inc., Seeger Investments; instr. fin. seminars; pub. monthly newsletter The Seeger Summary. Cert. fin. cons.; registered ins. broker, Colo.; registered fin. cons. Am. Credit Exchange. Mem. Nat. Assn. Realtors (cert. realtor-broker), Colorado Springs Assn. Realtors, Nat. Assn. Security Dealers (registered rep.), Nat. Assn. Fin. Consultants, Nat. Assn. Tax Consultors (cert.), Am. Soc. Cert. Fin. Consultants (co-founder, pres.), Colorado Springs C. of C. Republican. Mormon. Club: Rampart Sertoma. Author: Caveat Emptor, 1981; composer. Office: 6170 Lehman Dr Suite 102 Colorado Springs CO 80907

SEEL, MARTIN ANTHONY, banker; b. Jersey City, Mar. 3, 1933; s. Martin and Mildred (Dileo) S.; B.S., Bucknell U., 1955; M.B.A., N.Y. U., 1961; m. Marilyn Kaye Schwartz, Sept. 25, 1955; children—Martin A., Robin Ann, Ellen Mildred, Catherine Elizabeth. Asst. v.p., mgr. Wall St. office Bank Leumi Trust Co., N.Y.C., 1964-71; v.p., mgr. domestic credit dept. Republic Bank N.Y., N.Y.C., 1971-79, supervising loan officer, 1979—; tchr. Am. Inst. Banking, Clifton, N.J., 1962-72. Mem. vestry, chmn. stewardship com. Christ Ch., Bloomfield/Glen Ridge, N.J., 1976-79, treas., 1979—; pres. Glen Ridge Music Parents Assn., 1977-79. Mem. Robert Morris Assos., Bank Credit Assos. N.Y. (bd. govs. 1979-80, sec. 1980—). Episcopalian. Home: 19 Woodland Ave Glen Ridge NJ 07028 Office: 452 Fifth Ave New York NY 10018

SEELIG, GERARD LEO, diversified co. exec.; b. Schluchtern, Germany, June 15, 1926; s. Herman and Bella (Bach) S.; came to U.S., 1934, naturalized, 1943; B.E.E., Ohio State U., 1948; M.S. in Indsl. Mgmt., N.Y. U., 1954; m. Lorraine Peters, June 28, 1953; children—Tina Lynn, Robert Mark and Carol Ann (twins). Electronics engr. Martin Corp., Balt., 1948-50; sr. engr. Fairchild Aircraft Co., Farmingdale, N.Y., 1950-54; program mgr. RCA, Moorestown, N.J., 1954-59, Van Nuys, Calif., 1959-61; div. mgr. Missile & Space Co. div. Lockheed Aircraft Corp., Van Nuys, 1961-63, v.p., gen. mgr. Lockheed Electronics div., Los Angeles, 1963-68; exec. v.p. Lockheed Electronics Co., Inc., Plainfield, N.J., 1968-69, pres., 1969-71; group exec., exec. asst. to office of pres. ITT, N.Y.C., 1971-72, corporate v.p., 1972-79, sr. v.p., 1979—; mem. Ohio Bd. Profl. Engrs. and Surveyors, 1953—. Served with AUS, 1944-46. Registered profl. engr., Ohio. Fellow AIAA (asso.); mem. Western Electronics Mfrs. Assn. (dir.), Electronic Industries Assn. (bd. govs. 1976—), Am. Mgmt. Assn., IEEE (sr.). Office: 320 Park Ave New York NY 10022

SEELIG, M(AURICE) DONALD, planning, design and constrn. co. exec.; b. Ballston Spa, N.Y., Sept. 22, 1930; s. Russell L. and Emily (Davidson) S.; B.E. in Indsl. Engring., Johns Hopkins U., 1954; M.B.A., Northeastern U., 1960; m. Joyce Boudreau, Aug. 30, 1958; children—Kimberley, Avis. Engr., Standard Oil Co. Ohio, Cleve., 1954-56; sr. indsl. engr. plant layout supr. Raytheon Co., Lowell, Mass., 1956-60; mgr. facilities programs Gen. Electric Co., Valley Forge, Pa., 1961-65; purchasing agt. J.I. Case Co., Racine, Wis., 1965-67; sr. cons. R. Muther & Assos., Kansas City, Mo., 1967-71; corporate dir. facilities G.D. Searle Co., Skokie, Ill., 1972-76; mgr. facilities Massey-Ferguson Inc., Racine, 1976-79; chief indsl. engring. H.K. Ferguson Co., San Francisco, 1980—; lectr. adult edn. programs. Mem. Indsl. Devel. Research Council, Nat. Assn. Real Estate Execs., Am. Prodn. Inventory Control Soc. (sr.), Am. Inst. Indsl. Engrs. (sr.), Internat. Materials Mgmt. Soc., Johns Hopkins Alumni Assn. Republican. Episcopalian. Home: 279 Firestone Dr Walnut Creek CA 94598 Office: 140 Howard St San Francisco CA 94105

SEELY, JOHN CONOR, JR., agrl. co. exec.; b. Pittsfield, Mass., May 6, 1939; s. John Conor and Clarice Virginia (Fredenburg) S.; student U. Vt., 1959-62; B.A., U. Mass., 1964, M.B.A., 1965; m. Pamela Marie Blewitt, Aug. 24, 1968. Faculty U. Mass., Amherst, 1965-66; marketing specialist Gen. Electric Co., N.Y.C., 1966-67; pres. Consumer Cons. Corp., Pittsfield, Mass., 1967-69; chmn. bd. Lawn Medic, Inc., Rochester, N.Y., 1969—; dir. Pre-Germ Seeding Corp., Bergen, N.Y., 1972—, F.M. Mills Co., Inc., Bergen, 1972—, Creative Prospects, Inc., Rochester, N.Y., 1972—, Helix Marketing Corp., N.Y.C., 1974—, Resort Accomodations, Inc., West Bridgewater, Vt.; cons. to numerous corps. and instns. Trustee Real Estate Equity Diversification Trust. U. Mass. faculty fellow, 1963-64. Mem. Am. Marketing Assn., C. of C., Beta Gamma Sigma. Clubs: Burdy Hollow Ski (Rochester, N.Y.); Brighton (N.Y.) Tennis. Home: 188 Pitts Colony Dr Rochester NY 14623 Office: 1024 Sibley Tower 25 North St Rochester NY 14604

SEELYE, ALFRED L(EE), educator, bus. exec.; b. Syracuse, N.Y., Feb. 20, 1913; s. F. Alfred D. and Mildred (Lee) S.; B.S., Syracuse U., 1937, M.S., 1939; D.B.A., Ind. U., 1950; m. Kathryn L. Fehr, July 10, 1940. Mem. sales promotion dept. radio sta. WNEW, N.Y.C., 1937-38; instr. mktg., econs. U. Kans., 1939-42, asst. prof. mktg., 1946-47; state price economist Bur. Labor Statistics, Dallas, 1942; regional price economist regional office OPA, Dallas, 1942-46; lectr. marketing Ind. U., 1947-48; asso. prof. marketing U. Tex., 1948-50, prof., chmn. dept. marketing resources, transp. internat. trade, 1950-57; became dean Coll. Bus., Mich. State U., 1957, also dean Grad. Sch. Bus. Adminstrn., 1960-69; chmn., pres. Wolverine World Wide, Inc., 1969-72, dir., 1967-73; prof. bus. adminstrn. U. Akron, 1973-77; distinguished vis. prof. Fla. Atlantic U., 1978—; regional dir. OPS, Dallas, 1951-52 (on leave from Univ.); asst. in establishing Istituto Di Alti Studi Per L'Organizzazione Aziendale, Turin, Italy, also bus. cons. several Italian industrial cos., 1953; cons. marketing problems bus. firms. Mem. Am. Marketing Assn., Am. Econ. Assn., Am. Assn. U. Profs., Mich. State C. of C. (dir.), Beta Gamma Sigma, Psi Upsilon, Alpha Kappa Psi, Alpha Delta Sigma. Author: Fluid Milk Price Control in the Southwest During World War II, 1951; monograph (with J. Hudnall, Jr.) Compensation of Retail Dept. Stores and Splty. Store Salespeople in Major Tex. Cities, 1957; Marketing in Transition, 1958; monograph (with F. M. Bass) Sales Compensation Methods and Policies; also govt. monograph. Contbr. profl. jours. Home: 200 Granger Rd Medina OH 44256 also 3535 Broken Woods Dr Coral Springs FL 33065

SEEMAN, BERNARD, publisher, author; b. N.Y.C., Oct. 19, 1911; s. William J. and Lena (Kerner) S.; student pub. schs.; m. Geraldine Adele Micallef, Jan. 19, 1933. Free lance writer Ken mag., 1938-39; mil. writer, Far East specialist Friday mag., 1939-40; Latin Am. corr. Click mag., 1940-41; war corr. Far East Theatre, 1945 for Readers Scope, Internat. Digest; asso. editor Mag. Digest, also med. and sci. editor, Hillman Publs., 1946-54; exec. v.p. Sci. & Medicine Pub. Co., 1976-78; editor, spl. editorial cons. Science & Medicine Pub. Co., 1978—; exec. editor Internist Observer, Inc., 1958-76. Spl. cons. on Japan OWI, 1944. Mem. Nat. Assn. of Science Writers, Acad. Polit. Sci., Fedn. Am. Scientists, Nat. Acad. Rec. Arts and Scis., Authors League Am., Authors Guild, A.A.A.S., Mus. Modern Art, Astron. Soc. Pacific, Leakey Found. Author: Enemy Japan, 1945; The River of Life, 1961 (winner Howard W. Blakeslee award Am. Heart Assn.); Man Against Pain, 1962; The Story of Electricity and Magnetism, 1962; (with Lawrence Salisbury) Cross-Currents in the Philippines, Inst. of Pacific Relations, 1946; (With Dr. Henry Dolger) How to Live with Diabetes, 1958, 4th edit., 1977; Your Sight, 1968. Office: 372 Central Park W New York NY 10025 Office: One Obtuse Rocks Rd Brookfield Center CT 06805

SEGAL, DANIEL S., mortgage and fin. broker; b. N.Y.C., Aug. 4, 1929; s. Paul and Esther Segal; B.S.S., CCNY, 1949; LL.B., Bklyn. Law Sch., 1951; m. Roberta Segal, Dec. 25, 1960; children—Dawn, Scott, Lisa. Admitted to N.Y. State bar, 1951; practiced in N.Y.C., 1951-68; real estate investor, Fla., 1968—; mortgage broker, Fla., 1970-80; pres. Sage Capital Corp., Miami, Fla., N.Y.C., Denver, San Diego and London, 1979—; cons. to various corps., 1951—. Mem. N.Y. Bar Assn. Republican. Jewish. Clubs: MYY. Mayors, K.P. Author: (novel) Croesus Affair, 1979. Office: 420 Lexington Ave New York NY 10017

SEGAL, JACOB, investment cons.; b. Iasi, Romania, Aug. 11, 1946; s. Rubin and Tova S.; came to U.S., 1973, naturalized, 1977; B.A. in Econs. and Statistics, Hebrew U., 1972, postgrad., 1972-73; M.B.A., U. Calif., Los Angeles, 1976; m. Geri Slobin, Sept. 20, 1972. Computer operator Computer Center, Hebrew U., Jerusalem, 1969-72, programmer, 1972-73; research asst. dept. fin. U. Calif., Los Angeles, 1975, teaching asst., 1975; economist Home Savs. & Loan Assn., Los Angeles, 1976-78, sr. research analyst, 1978—; real estate cons. Wagner/Jacobson Co., 1978—; instr. econs. Inst. Fin. Edn., Los Angeles, 1977-78. Mem. Am. Mgmt. Assn., U. Calif. Los Angeles Alumni Assn. Home: 3318 Coolidge Ave Los Angeles CA 90066 Office: 433 N Camden Dr Suite 400 Beverly Hills CA 90210

SEGAL, JEFFRY MARK, petroleum co. exec.; b. Phila., Aug. 3, 1943; s. Morris and Edith (Pikus) S.; B.S. in Acctg., U. Ariz., 1965, B.S. in Area Devel., 1966, M.B.A. in Acctg., 1969; m. Marianne G. Solomon, Aug. 16, 1970; children—Jonathan Barret, Daniel Jason. Mem. staff Seidman & Seidman, 1967-69; audit sr. Hurdman & Cranstoun, Los Angeles, 1969-70; asso. Irwin, Silberman & Assos., Economists, New Hyde Park, N.Y., 1971-72; audit sr. McMillan, Inc., N.Y.C., 1972-74; controller Chappell Music Co., N.Y.C., 1974-75; controller Chgo. Tribune-N.Y. News Syndicate, Inc., N.Y.C., 1976-79; controller Colvac Internat. Corp., 1980—; dir. Magna Paper Co., N.Y.C.; asst. prof. Queensborough Community Coll. C.P.A., N.Y., Calif. Mem. Am. Inst. C.P.A.'s, N.Y. State, Calif. socs. C.P.A.'s, Am. Acctg. Assn., C.W. Post Coll. Tax Inst. Home: 9 Waydale Dr Dix Hills NY 11746 Office: 420 Lexington Ave New York NY 10170

SEGAL, RICHARD JOEL, fin. co. exec.; b. Newark, June 13, 1939; s. Philip and Pearl (Schneck) S.; B.S. in Bus. Adminstrn., Seton Hall U., South Orange, N.J., 1960; J.D., Southwestern U., Los Angeles, 1967; m. Judith Ann Otrando, Feb. 25, 1977; children—Jason, Jennifer. With Lerner Schuhalter Co., C.P.A.'s, Newark, 1958-62; field agt. IRS, 1962-68; admitted to Calif. bar, 1968; v.p. fin. Daylin, Inc., Los Angeles, 1968-75; propr. Richard J. Segal, Atty.-C.P.A., Los Angeles, 1975-77; v.p. Danmar Fin. Corp., Los Angeles, 1977—; partner firm Kove & Segal, Los Angeles, 1977—. C.P.A., Calif. Mem. Beverly Hill Bar Assn. Republican. Home: 330 Chino Dr Palm Springs CA 92262 Office: 11340 W Olympic Blvd Los Angeles CA 90064

SEGALL, MAURICE, retail co. exec.; b. Joliette, Que., Can., May 16, 1929; s. Jacob and Adela S.; B.A., McGill U., 1950; M.A., Columbia U., 1952; postgrad. (Hudson Bay Co. fellow) London Sch. Econs., 1953-54; m. Sarah Ostrovsky, Nov. 25, 1951; children—Elizabeth, Eric, Peter. Economist, Can. Govt., Ottawa, 1951-55; exec. asst. to pres. Steinberg's, Montreal, Que., Can., 1955-62; with J.C. Penney, N.Y.C., 1962-71, dir. Treasury Stores div., 1970-71; sr. v.p., gen. mgr. card div. Am. Express, N.Y.C., 1971-74, pres. card div., 1974-78, corp. exec. v.p. strategic program devel., 1978; pres., chief exec. officer Zayre Corp., Framingham, Mass., 1978—. Mem. Mass. Bus. Roundtable. Office: Zayre Corp Framingham MA 01701

SEGARD, HAROLD GLEN, mfg. co. exec.; b. Omaha, Feb. 17, 1921; s. Nels and Jessie (Short) S.; student Washington U., 1948; m. C. Dorine Dunton, June 16, 1947; children—Daniel Dean, Timothy Richard. Mgr., Bargain Sq., Famous-Barr, St. Louis, 1948-51; catalog compiler Blackwell-Wielandy, St. Louis, 1951-55; advt. mgr. A.C. McClurg & Co., Chgo., 1955-65; lit. writer, mgr. Helene Curtiss Industries, Chgo., 1966-68; advt. mgr. J.A. Baldwin Mfg. Co., Kearney, Nebr., 1968—. Bd. dirs. Boys Clubs, 1945-75. Served with U.S. Army, 1942-45. Home: 3308 11th Ave Kearney NE 68847 Office: Box 610 Kearney NE 68847

SEGEL, J. NORMAN, garment mfg. co. exec.; b. Toledo, Aug. 1, 1939; s. Sam S. and Dorothy (Gross) S.; B.B.A., Western Res. U., 1961; M.B.A., Adelphi U., 1980; m. Sheila Benkovitz, Jan. 14, 1961; children—Scott Jonathan, David Seth, and Hope Deborah. Accountant, Bobbie Brooks, Cleve., 1961-62; controller Stacy Ames, Long Island City, N.Y., 1962-65, dir. finance, 1965-66, sec.-treas., 1966-70, exec. asst. to pres., 1968-70; v.p. Fairfield-Noble, Inc., N.Y.C., 1970-77; treas. Levin & Hecht Inc., N.Y.C., 1977-79; v.p. fin. Parsons Place Apparel Co. Ltd., N.Y.C., 1979—. Mem. alumni admission bd. Case Western Res. U.; v.p., bd. dirs. Hewlett East Rockaway Jewish Center. Mem. Adminstrn. Mgmt. Soc., Nat. Assn. Accountants, Am. Apparel Mfrs. Assn., Am. Arbitration Assn., Am. Assn. Corporate Controllers, Delta Sigma Pi, Sigma Alpha Mu, Alpha Phi Gamma. Home: 3447 5th St Oceanside NY 11572 Office: 1407 Broadway New York NY 10018

SEGLIN, LEONARD, consulting co. exec.; b. Albany, N.Y., Apr. 4, 1917; s. George Maxwell and Dora S.; B. Chem. Engring., N.Y. U., 1938; M.A., Harvard U., 1939; m. Ruth A. Gardiner, Sept. 20, 1940; children—Michael Owen, Gayle Dee Seglin Lerner. Process engr. Malletane Corp. of N.J., 1939-40; process engr. Ethyl Corp., 1940-46; process engr. FMC Corp., Princeton, N.J., 1946-51, supr., 1951-58, mgr. engring., 1958-61, dir. process research and devel., 1961-73; prin. engr. Bechtel Corp., N.Y.C., 1973-76; pres. Intercontinental Econergy Assos., Inc., N.Y.C., 1976—; adj. prof. chem. engring. Manhattan Coll., 1976—. Fellow Am. Inst. Chem. Engrs.; mem. Am. Chem. Soc. Club: Harvard of N.Y.C. Contbr. articles to profl. jours.; patentee in field. Home: 23 Washington Sq N New York NY 10011 Office: 799 Broadway New York NY 10003

SEGREST, ROSS ALTON, utility cons.; b. Hamlin, Tex., Jan. 20, 1910; s. William Noah and Sarah (McBrayer) S.; B.A. summa cum laude, Baylor U., 1931; m. Hazel Lorene Tiner, Sept, 7, 1946; children—Sara Linda, Melissa Caroline. Sr. accountant A.C. Upleger & Co., C.P.A.'s, Waco, Tex., 1931-36, partner, 1936-42; auditor, adminstrv. asst. Brown Ship-bldg. Co., Houston, 1942-45; comptroller Nat. Instrument Corp., Houston, 1945-49; formerly comptroller, exec. mgr. Brazos Electric Power Coop., Inc., Waco, then exec. v.p., ret., 1977; now utility cons.; dir. Lake Air Nat. Bank; tchr. accounting night sch. Baylor U., Waco, 1951-52. Active Am. Cancer Soc., A.R.C., Camp Fire, United Way of Waco and McLennan County, Waco Civic Theater, Econ. Opportunities Advancement Corp. C.P.A., Tex. Mem. Am. Inst. C.P.A.'s, Tex. Soc. C.P.A.'s (dir., past pres. Central Tex. chpt.), Tex. Electric Coop.'s Accounting Assn. (past pres.), Nat. G. and T. Coops. Mgrs. Assn. (past pres.), Mid-West Power Accounting Assn. (past pres.). Democrat. Baptist. Mason (Shriner). Clubs: Woodland West Country (past pres.), Ridgewood Country. Contbr. articles to profl. publs. Home: 4517 Westchester Waco TX 76710

SEGUIN, SERGE DENIS, wholesale trade co. exec.; b. Vernon, France, May 19, 1947; s. Denis R. and Marie-Madeleine S. (Blanchet) S.; came to U.S., 1970; M.A. with honors in Fin., Ecole Superieure de Commerce, France, 1970; M.B.A., U. Fla., 1972; m. Christine Melingue, June 22, 1974; children—Aldric, Shawn. Grad. research asst. mktg. U. Fla., Gainesville, 1971-72; prof. mgmt. mktg. French army Peace Corps program Laval U., Quebec City, Can., 1972-73; cons. to Motobecane France, 1973-74; v.p. mktg. and sales Motobecane Am., Ltd., Hackensack, N.J., 1975-76, exec. v.p., 1977-78, pres., 1979—, also dir.; chmn., dir. Alsh, Inc., Woodcliff Lake, N.J., 1980—. Mem. Am. Mgmt. Assn., Moped Assn. Am. (founder 1974, chmn. 1974—), French-Am. C. of C. (councillor 1977—). Contbr. articles on mgmt. and mopeds to various mags. and newspapers in U.S. and France; developed legislation, introduced mktg. of mopeds in U.S. Home: 25 Old Farms Rd Woodcliff Lake NJ 07675 Office: 86 Orchard St Hackensack NJ 07601

SEIBERT, DONALD VINCENT, retail chain exec.; b. Hamilton, Ohio, Aug. 17, 1923; s. Carl F. and Minnie L. (Wells) S.; student U. Cin., 1942, D.C.S. (hon.), 1975; LL.D., Nyack Coll., 1974; m. Verna S. Stone, Aug. 24, 1945; children—Donna Jeanne Seibert Daller, Diane Loree Seibert Schiffer, Robert Donald. Exec., J.C. Penney Co., Inc., N.Y.C., 1947-56, store mgr., 1957-58, dist. mgr., 1959-62, corporate exec., 1963-73, chmn., chief exec. officer, 1974—; dir. The Continental Group, Inc.; dir. Citicorp/Citibank, Sperry Corp. Trustee Nyack Coll.; hon. trustee U. Cin.; bd. dirs. Econ. Devel. Council N.Y.C., Nat. Minority Purchasing Council, United Way Am.; chmn. bd. advisers to dean Coll. Bus. Adminstrn., U. Cin. Served with USAAF, 1943-46. Mem. Nat. Retail Mchts. Assn. (dir., past chmn.), N.Y. Chamber Commerce and Industry (dir.), Catalyst, Bus. Roundtable (policy com.). Mem. Christian and Missionary Alliance. Office: 1301 Ave of Americas New York NY 10019

SEIDEL, LEON EDWARD, editor; b. Phila., May 30, 1922; s. Frank and Frances (Fink) S.; B.S. in Textile Engring., Phila. Coll. Textiles and Sci., 1947. Instr., Phila. Coll. Textiles and Sci., 1947-48; plants mgr. Frank Assos., N.Y.C., 1948-56; tech. servicer Dobeckman Co., Cleve., 1956-61; sales mgr. Dow Chem. Co., N.Y.C., 1961-66; v.p. mktg. Metlon Corp., N.Y.C., 1966-69; sr. editor Textile Industries mag. W.R.C. Smith Pub. Co., Atlanta, 1969—. Served with U.S. Army, 1943-45; ETO. Decorated Purple Heart. Mem. Am. Assn. Textile Chemists and Colorists, Am. Assn. Textile Technologists, Textured Yarn Assn. Am. Democrat. Jewish. Author: Applied Textile Marketing, 1970. Address: 209 N Hanover Ave Margate NJ 08402

SEIDEN, HENRY, advt. agy. exec.; b. Bklyn., Sept. 6, 1928; s. Jack S. and Shirley (Berkowitz) S.; B.A., Bklyn. Coll., 1949; M.B.A., CCNY, 1951-54; m. Helena Ruth Zaldin, Sept. 10, 1949; children—Laurie Ann, Matthew Ian. Trainee, Ben Sackheim Advt. Agy., 1949-51; nat. promotion mgr. N.Y. Post Corp., 1951-53; promotion mgr. Crowell-Collier Pub. Co., Inc., 1953-54; copy group head Batten, Barton, Durstine & Osborn, Inc., 1954-60; v.p., creative dir. Keyes, Madden & Jones, 1960-61; v.p., asso. creative dir. McCann-Marschalk, Inc., 1961-65, chmn. plans bd., sr. v.p., 1964-65; sr. v.p., creative dir., dir., prin. Hicks & Greist, Inc., 1965-74, exec. v.p., 1974— (all N.Y.C.). Guest lectr. Bernard M. Baruch Sch. Bus. and Pub. Adminstrn., CCNY, 1962—; guest lectr. New Sch. for Social Scis., Fashion Inst. Tech., SUNY, Lehman Coll. of City U. N.Y., Ohio U.; cons. pub. relations and communications to mayor of New Rochelle, 1959-61; cons. marketing dept. Ohio State U.; spl. cons. to Postmaster Gen. U.S.; communications cons. police commn., N.Y.C.; cons. to the pres. of city council, N.Y.C., 1972-73. Bd. dirs. Police Reserve Assn. N.Y.C.; exec. v.p., bd. dirs. N.Y. Finest Found., 1976—. Recipient award Four Freedoms Found., 1959, Printers Ink, 1960, promotion award Editor and Pub., 1955, Am. TV Commls. Festival award, 1963, 64, 65, 66, 67, 68, 69, Man of Year award Graphic Arts Lodge B'nai B'rith, 1971, numerous other awards. Mem. A.I.M. (asso.), Nat. Acad. Television Arts and Scis., Am. Inst. Graphic Arts (award 1963), Advt. Club N.Y. (exec. judge Andy awards), Advt. Writers Assn. N.Y. (gold key award for best newspaper advt. of year 1962, 63, 64), Am. Marketing Assn. (award Best Mag. Ad, Best TV Comml. 1969), Alpha Phi Omega. Author: Advertising Pure and Simple, 1976. Contbg. editor Madison Avenue mag.; contbg. columnist N.Y. Times. Home: 12 Winchcombe Way Scarsdale NY 10583 Office: 522 Fifth Ave New York NY 10036

SEIDER, HAROLD, music pub. co. exec.; b. Bklyn., July 20, 1933; s. David and Anna S.; A.B., Columbia U., 1955, LL.B., 1955. Exec. v.p. ABKCO Industries, N.Y.C., 1967-71; v.p. bus. affairs United Artists Music and Records Group, Los Angeles, 1972-76, pres. internat. div., 1976-78, pres. United Artists Music Co., Inc., 1978—. Served with U.S. Army, 1959-60. Mem. N.Y. County Law Assn., Columbia U. Law Sch. Alumni Assn. Office: 6753 Hollywood Blvd Los Angeles CA 90028

SEIDMAN, BERT, labor union exec.; b. N.Y.C., Sept. 22, 1919; s. Nathan H. and Jeannette S. (Kaplan) S.; B.A., U. Wis., 1938, M.A., 1941; m. Annabel Henry, Apr. 16, 1948; children—Margaret, Joan, Elizabeth. Economist, research dept. AFL-CIO, Washington, from 1948, European econ. rep., 1962-66, dir. social security dept., Washington, 1966—; mem. U.S. Worker del. ILO, 1958-76; bd. govs. ILO, 1972-75; mem. Fed. Adv. Council Employment Security, 1969-71, Adv. Council on Social Security, 1969-71, 78-79, Health Ins. Benefits Adv. Council, 1970-76, Nat. Commn. on Unemployment Compensation, 1978-80; mem. adv. council Employee Retirement Income Security Act of 1974, 1975. Mem. Indsl. Relations Research Assn. (trustee 1970-73), Nat. Consumers League (v.p. 1979). Home: 6200 Wilson Blvd Apt 1010 Falls Church VA 22044 Office: 815 16th St NW Washington DC 20006

SEIDMAN, HARVEY STANFORD, business exec.; b. Boston, Aug. 20, 1929; s. Maurice Henry and Lillian S.; m. Marilyn Wilensky, Mar. 18, 1952; children—Susan, Rhonda, Amy. Salesman, Ross Motor Parts, Boston, 1950-61; owner Bay State Automotive Supply, Watertown, Mass., 1962-72; pres. Automotive Warehouse Co., Boston, 1972—. Served with U.S. Army, 1946-48. Mem. Watertown C. of C. (past v.p.), Automotive Wholesalers of N.E., Automotive Service Industry Assn., Mass. State Dealers Assn. Jewish. Clubs: Masons, B'nai B'rith. Office: 6 Dexter Ave Watertown MA 02172

SEIDMAN, PAUL JOSEPH, lawyer, govt. ofcl.; b. Phila., Sept. 5, 1948; s. Isadore and Edith (Selditch) S.; B.B.A., Temple U., 1970; J.D., Georgetown U., 1973; m. Jayne I. Levin, May 28, 1972; children—Linda Stacey, David Jeremy. Admitted to D.C. bar, 1973, Pa. bar, 1973, U.S. Ct. Claims bar, 1973, U.S. Tax Ct. bar, 1973; law clk. to Judge Philip Nichols, Jr., U.S. Ct. Claims, Washington, 1973-74; asst. counsel claims and litigation support Naval Sea Systems Command, Office Gen. Counsel, Dept. Navy, Washington, 1974-76; atty. Machinery and Allied Products Inst., Washington, 1976-78; acting dir. Freedom of Info. and Privacy Acts, Office Chief Counsel for Advocacy, SBA, Washington, 1978-79, asst. chief counsel for procurement Office Chief Counsel for Advocacy, 1979—; mem. staff White House Conf. on Small Bus., 1980. Mem. Am. Bar Assn., Fed. Bar Assn. (asst. editor Govt. Contracts Newsletter 1980—). Editorial asst. Tax Lawyer, 1972-73; contbr. articles to profl. jours. Home: 8300 Beech Tree Rd Bethesda MD 20034 Office: 1441 L St NW Washington DC 20416

SEIFERT, RALPH HAMMOND, ins. co. exec.; b. Balt., Mar. 27, 1928; s. Ralph Edwin and Ferole (Hammond) S.; B.A., Brown U., 1950; m. Cynthia Ruder, June 14, 1950 (div. 1978); children—Mitchel Grant, Susan Leslie, Arthur Bradford, Melissa Louise; m. 2d, Sandra Charles, Oct. 6, 1979. Salesman, Liberty Mut. Ins. Co., Phila., 1950-51, S.B. Goddard & Son Co., Woburn, Mass., 1951-54; sales mgr. W.S. Attridge Co., Boston, 1954-57; partner Herbert E. King Agy., Mansfield, Mass., 1957-70; pres. New Eng. Security Ins. Agy., Inc., Mansfield, 1970—, Fin. Security Corp., Mansfield, 1970—; trustee Attleboro Savs. Bank (Mass.). Chmn. Mansfield Indsl. Devel. Commn., 1970—; moderator Town of Mansfield, 1970-73; mem. Downtown Devel. Com., 1975—; chmn. bldg. com. Orthodox Congregational Ch., Mansfield, 1968-70. Served to lt. comdr. USNR, 1950-70. Mem. Ind. Ins. Agts. Mass., Ind. Mut. Agts. New Eng. (past pres.), Mansfield Assn. Ins. Agts. (past pres.), Bristol Norfolk Ind. Ins. Agts. (past pres.). Clubs: Rotary (pres. 1962-63), Masons, Shriners. Contbr. articles to trade jours. Home: Old Maple St Mansfield MA 02048 Office: PO Box 260 100 N Main St Mansfield MA 02048

SEIGFRIED, RAYMOND JOSEPH, hosp. exec.; b. Phila., Aug. 23, 1950; s. Frederick Dale and Anna Victoria (Muni) S.; B.A., Bloomsburg (Pa.) State Coll., 1972; M.A., Antioch U., Yellow Springs, Ohio, 1979; m. Mary Murphy, Aug. 16, 1975. Acad. house counselor Pa. Sch. Deaf, Phila., 1972-74; mgr. Med. Coll. and Hosp., Phila., 1974-78; dir. materials mgmt. Parkview Hosp., Phila., 1978-79, Allentown (Pa.) and Sacred Heart Hosp. Center, 1979—; mem. purchasing adv. com. Hosp. Purchasing Service, Phila. Vice pres. 151st Democratic Com., Phila., 1974. Mem. Am. Soc. Hosp. Materials Mgmt. Roman Catholic. Home: 727 S Muhlenberg St Allentown PA 18103 Office: ASH 1200 S Cedar Crest Blvd Allentown PA 18105

SEINSHELMER, J(OSEPH) F(ELLMAN), JR., ins. exec.; b. Galveston, Tex., Aug. 25, 1913; s. J.F. and Irma (Kraus) S.; B.B.A., Tulane U., 1936; m. Jessie Lee Gould, July 19, 1938; children—Joseph Fellman III, Virginia Lee, Robert Louis. Salesman, Seinsheimer Ins. Agy., 1936-41; with Am. Indemnity Group, 1941—, successively agy. mgr., asst. sec., sec., v.p., 1941-51, pres., dir., 1951—; pres., dir. Am. Indemnity Financial Corp., Am. Indemnity Co., Am. Fire & Indemnity Co., Am. Computing Co., Tex. Gen. Indemnity Co., Am. Finance Co., Galveston, U.S. Securities Corp.; dir. Galveston Corp., Tex. Fibreglas Products, Inc., U.S. Nat. Bancshares, Inc., U.S. Nat. Bank, Galveston. Clubs: Artillery, Galveston. Home: 4809 Woodrow St Galveston TX 77550 Office: One American Indemnity Plaza Galveston TX 77550

SELBY, EDWARD BURFORD, JR., educator; b. Balt., Nov. 12, 1938; B.S. in Indsl. Mgmt., Clemson U., 1962; M.B.A., U. S.C., 1963; Ph.D. in Econs., La. State U., 1967. Asst. prof. econs. N.E. La. U., Monroe, 1966-68; asst. prof. fin. U. Ga., Athens, 1968-72, asso. prof., 1972—, dir. undergrad. studies Coll. Bus. Adminstrn., 1970-75; organizer, dir. Athens Bank & Trust, 1976-80. Mem. Am., So. econ. assns., Am. Fin. Assn., So. Fin. Assn., Beta Gamma Sigma (chpt. pres. 1972-73), Omicron Delta Epsilon. Club: Kiwanis. Author: Money and Banking, 1972; Instructor's Manual for Money and Banking, 1973; contbr. articles to profl. jours. Office: Dept Banking and Finance Coll Bus Adminstrn U Ga Athens GA 30602 also PO Box 2342 Ga Univ Station Athens GA 30602

SELBY, JOHN DOUGLAS, utility exec.; b. Odebolt, Iowa, Oct. 12, 1921; s. John Hanna and Della Anna (Nelson) S.; B.S. in Gen. Engring., Iowa State U., 1946; postgrad. in advanced mgmt. Harvard U. Bus. Sch., 1971. Mem. staff light mil. electronics dept. Gen. Electric Co., Utica, N.Y., 1965-67, aerospace electronics dept., 1967-71, nuclear energy dept., San Jose, Calif., 1971-75; pres., chief exec. officer Consumers Power Co., Jackson, Mich., 1975-79, chmn. bd., pres., 1979—, also dir.; dir. No. Mich. Exploration Co., Plateau Resources Ltd.; dir., officer Mich. Gas Storage Co. Bd. dirs. Atomic Indsl. Forum, 1979—, Inst. Nuclear Power Ops. Served with USN 1942-46. Mem. ASME, Am. Nuclear Soc., Profl. Engrs. Assn., Edison Electric Inst. (dir., mem. com. on nuclear power), Detroit Econs. Club, Mich., Greater Jackson chambers of commerce. Republican. Clubs: Jackson Country, Jackson Town. Office: 212 W Michigan Ave Jackson MI 49201

SELEPEC, JOHN JOSEPH, engring. and constrn. co. fin. exec.; b. North Braddock, Pa., Mar. 18, 1939; s. Charles and Veronica (Sabo) S.; B.B.A., U. Pitts., 1965; m. Eleanor Uhler, Nov. 26, 1960; children—John Joseph, Steven, Thomas, James, Kelly. Cost analyst Mobay Chem. Corp., Pitts., 1962-66; fin. analyst Crucible Steel div. Colt Industries 1966-69; mgmt. cons. Price, Waterhouse & Co., Pitts., 1969-71; v.p. fin. Pullman Swindell, Pitts., 1971—, also dir. various subs.'s. Mem. Fin. Execs. Inst., Internat. Bus. Forum. Clubs: Pitts. Press, Hidden Valley Country. Office: 441 Smithfield St Pittsburgh PA 15222

SELIGMAN, DANIEL, editor; b. N.Y.C., Sept. 25, 1924; s. Irving and Clare (O'Brien) S.; student Rutgers U., 1941-42; A.B., N.Y. U., 1946; m. Mary Gale Sherburn, May 23, 1953; children—Nora, William Paul. Editorial asst. New Leader, 1946; asst. editor Am. Mercury, 1946-50; asso. editor Fortune, 1950-59, editorial bd., 1959-66, asst. mng. editor, 1966-69, exec. editor, 1970-77, asso. mng. editor, 1977—; sr. staff editor all Time, Inc., Publs., 1969-70. Home: 190 E 72d St New York NY 10021 Office: Time and Life Bldg New York NY 10020

SELIGMAN, MOISE BENJAMIN, JR., business exec.; b. Jacksonville, Tenn., Oct. 8, 1918; s. Moise B. and Lucille Delila (Flynn) S.; B.A., Ouachita Bapt. U., 1941; postgrad. U.S. Army War Coll., 1968; m. Mary Elizabeth Strong, Apr. 5, 1942; children—Susan, Moise Benjamin III (dec.), Mary Elizabeth. Sales staff Ark. Paper Co., Little Rock, 1947-50, mgr. specialty dept., 1950-55, asst. div. mgr., 1955-58, v.p., 1958-60, pres., 1960-80, corp. v.p., 1965-80; v.p. IBI Leasing Co., 1960—, Elms Realty, 1960—, Selco Realty, 1960— (all Shreveport); sr. v.p. Consol. Mktg. Inc., Shreveport, 1965-80; owner, pres. Ambassador Travel Agy., Little Rock, 1978—; dir., mem. exec. com. CMI Co., Little Rock, 1965—; chmn. Pate Energy Systems Inc., Little Rock, 1980—; mem. adv. council Nekoosa Paper Co., 1971-75, Scott Paper Co., 1978—. Bd. dirs. Met. YMCA, Little Rock, 1962-66, NCCJ, 1974—; mem. devel. council Ouachita Bapt. U. Served with inf. U.S. Army, 1941-45; maj. gen. Res. (ret.). Decorated Legion of Merit; named Disting. Alumnus, Ouachita Bapt. U., 1978. Mem. Nat. Paper Trade Assn., Res. Officers Assn., Sr. Res. Officers Assn., Little Rock C. of C. (dir. 1963-70, sec.-treas. 1969). Baptist. Clubs: Little Rock, Capital, Masons, Shriners, Kiwanis (pres. Little Rock 1968). Home: 4 Cedar Hill Rd Little Rock AR 72202 Office: 3700 Old Cantrell Rd Little Rock AR 72202

SELLERS, FRED COURT, accountant; b. Ft. Worth, Jan. 19, 1924; s. James Henry and Etta (Court) S.; student U. Houston, 1940-43; m. Ray Vina Aucoin, Oct. 24, 1942; children—Fred Court, Sharon Ann. Accountant, United Gas Corp., Houston, 1941-59; self-employed, Houston, 1959—; sec. Positive Feed, Inc., Northwest Assos., Inc. Past pres. Harris County Youth Scholarship Found. Served with USAAF, 1943-46. Recipient Key Man award Jr. C. of C., 1948. Mem. Am. Inst. C.P.A.'s, Tex. Soc. C.P.A.'s (past chmn. Houston chpt. speakers bur.). Baptist (deacon). Clubs: Optimist (v.p., dir. 1959-65), Rotary. Home: 11601 Green Oaks St Houston TX 77024 Office: 2323 S Voss 630 77057

SELLERS, MICHAEL STUART, data processing exec.; b. Fullerton, Calif., Aug. 25, 1941; s. Melvin Bernard and Virginia Louise (Moffitt) S.; B.S., Calif. State U., 1970; m. Janet LaRae Petit, June 22, 1963; children—Matthew Joseph, Mark Damian, Patrick Michael. Quality control engr. Gen. Dynamics Corp., Pomona, Calif., 1963-74; computer systems analyst Bulk Mail, U.S. Postal Service, Los Angeles, 1974-79; mgr. data processing Stationers Corp., Los Angeles, 1979—. Active Boy Scouts Am., 1972-77. Democrat. Roman Catholic. Home: 7724 Vicky Ave Canoga Park CA 91304 Office: 525 S Spring St Los Angeles CA 90013

SELLERS, ROBERT VERNON, oil co. exec.; b. Bartlesville, Okla., Mar. 26, 1927; s. C. Vernon and Helen (Weeks) S.; B.S. in Mech. Engring., U. Kans., 1948; grad. Advanced Mgmt. Program, Harvard; m. Anna Marie Hughes, Feb. 11, 1950; children—Barbara S. Bredemeier, Patricia S. Wheeler, Scott, John. Service engr. Dowell, Inc., 1949-50; various positions in transp., supply, corporate planning, finance Cities Service Co., 1951-69, v.p. finance, 1969-71, dir., mem. exec. com., 1969—, vice chmn. bd., 1971-72, chmn. bd., chief exec. officer, chmn. exec. com., 1972—, chmn. finance com., 1973—; dir. First Nat. Bank & Trust Co. Tulsa, John Hancock Mut. Life Ins. Co. Asst. to dir. prodn. div. Petroleum Adminstrn. for Def., 1951-52. Bd. dirs., mem. exec. com. Am. Petroleum Inst.; mem. nat. adv. council Salvation Army; mem. adv. bd. U. Kans. Sch. Bus.; trustee Com. Econ. Devel., U. Tulsa, Kans. U. Endowment Assn.; bd. dirs. So. Growth Policies Bd. Served with USNR, 1945-46. Mem. Financial Execs. Inst., Nat. Petroleum Council, Conf. Bd., Council Fgn. Relations, Internat. (trustee U.S. council), Met. Tulsa (dir.) chambers commerce, Sigma Chi, Tau Beta Pi. Clubs: Nat. Golf Links Am., Board Room, Economic (N.Y.C.); The Summit, Tulsa, Southern Hills Country (Tulsa); Internat. (Washington); Pipe Liners. Home: 2131 E 29th St Tulsa OK 74114 Office: Box 300 Tulsa OK 74102

SELLINGER, FRANCIS JOHN, brewing co. exec.; b. Phila., July 8, 1914; s. Frank and L. Caroline (Wiseman) S.; B.S. in Biochemistry St. Joseph's Coll., Phila., 1936; postgrad. Drexel Inst., 1936-37, E.A. Siebel Inst. Tech., Chgo., 1938; m. Helen Brown, Feb. 22, 1941; children—Frank, Mary, Joseph, Helen, Dorothy, John, Patricia, Elizabeth, James. Chief chemist, asst. brewmaster Esslinger Brewing Co., Phila., 1936-41; chief chemist, purchasing agt., Hudepohl Brewing Co., Cin., 1941-46; asst. to gen. mgr. August Wagner Breweries, Columbus, Ohio, 1946-50; owner, pres. Hi-State Beverage Co., 1950-52; supr. packaging and purchasing agt. Burger Brewing Co., 1952, v.p., gen. mgr., 1956-64; asst. to pres. and v.p. and gen. mgr. Anheuser-Busch Inc., St. Louis, 1964, tech. dir. ops., 1964-66, v.p. engring., 1966-74, group v.p., 1974-76, exec. v.p. mgmt. and industry affairs, 1976-77; pres. Jos. Schlitz Brewing Co., Milw., 1977—, vice chmn., chief exec. officer, 1980—, dir., 1979—; dir. Marine Nat. Exchange Bank, Milw. Mem. Master Brewers Assn. Am. Clubs: Milw. Athletic, Milw. Country. Office: Jos Schlitz Brewing Co 235 W Galena St Milwaukee WI 53201

SELVEN, EUGENE RONALD, mgmt. cons. co. exec.; b. Chgo., Oct. 1, 1932; s. Rudolph David and Helen Mae (Schuster) S.; B.S. in Elec. Engring., U. Ill., 1954; M.B.A., So. Meth. U., 1963; children—Kimberly, Karen. Sales rep. IBM Corp., 1954-58; sales engr., regional sales mgr., product marketing mgr. integrated circuits Tex. Instruments, 1958-70; dir. product marketing Fairchild Semiconductors, 1970-71; dir. marketing semiconductor div. Raytheon Co., Mountain View, Calif., 1971-76; founder Selven & Assos., mgmt. consultants, 1976—, Electronic Trend Publs., 1978—, Jenwolf Instruments, Inc., 1980—. Served with AUS, 1954-56. Mem. Peninsula Marketing Assn. Lutheran (dir. edn.). Office: 10080 N Wolfe Rd Suite 372 Cupertino CA 95014

SELVERNE, LEE J., publ. co. exec.; b. N.Y.C., July 15, 1932; s. Harry and Nettie (Schwart) S.; B.S., L.I. U., 1958; M.S., N.Y. U., 1960; m. Linda Nancy Himel, May 26, 1972; 1 son by previous marriage, Michael. Jr. statistician L. Sonneborne & Sons, N.Y.C., 1958-59; research dir. bus. publs. Hearst Corp., N.Y.C., 1959-60; mem. exec. staff Publ. Distbg. Co., N.Y.C., 1960-65; chmn. bd., dir. Worldwide Media Service, N.Y.C., 1968—; pres. Worldwide Spanex Corp., 1978—. Served with U.S. Army, 1950-52. Recipient Small Bus. Mgmt. award L.I. U., 1958. Mem. Internat. Newsstands Circulation Execs. Assn. Club: Alpine Country. Home: 200 E 64th St New York NY 10021 Office: Worldwide Media Service 386 Park Ave S New York NY 10016

SEMANS, GARY ARTHUR, lumber co. exec.; b. Reno, Jan. 28, 1943; s. Arthur W. and Olive C. Semans; A.B., San Francisco State U., 1965, M.B.A., 1966; postgrad. in econs. U. Calif., Berkeley, 1966—; m. Cheryl Ann Fury, Oct. 25, 1975; 1 son, Tippon. Lectr., San Francisco State U., 1966, U. Calif., Berkeley, 1966-69; sec.-treas. Semans Moulding Co., Inc., Sacramento, 1969—; dir. Western Wood Moulding Co. Democrat. Presbyterian. Clubs: St. Francis Yacht, Sutter. Author: Economic Forecasting—The Pine Producer, 1967. Home: 1230 Brewster Dr El Cerrito CA 94530 Office: PO Box 20213 Sacramento CA 95820

SEMLER, BERNARD HENRY, health care co. exec.; b. Winona, Minn., Apr. 20, 1917; s. Henry John and Helen Catherine (Schneider) S.; B.S. summa cum laude, St. Mary's Coll., Winona, 1938; m. Mary Ann Fitzgerald, Mar. 30, 1940; children—Sharon Ann, Thomas B., Bruce E. With Scovell Wellington & Co., C.P.A.'s, Chgo., 1941-49; asst. controller Johnson & Johnson, 1949-55; successively gen. controller, v.p. and controller, exec. v.p. Freeman Shoe Corp., Beloit, Wis., 1955-60; v.p. fin. Hunt Foods and Industries, Inc., Fullerton, Calif., 1960-68; v.p., treas. Norton Simon, Inc., 1968-69; v.p. fin. Abbott Labs., North Chicago, Ill., 1969-74, exec. v.p. fin., 1974—, also dir.; dir. First Nat. Bank Lake Forest (Ill.), Allied Tube & Conduit Corp. Bd. dirs. Lake Forest Hosp. C.P.A., Ill. Mem. Nat. Assn. Accountants (nat. v.p. 1959-60, 1st pres. Raritan Valley chpt. 1955), Am. Mgmt. Assn., Am. Inst. C.P.A.'s (mem., past chmn. steering com. fin. sect.), Pharm. Mfrs. Assn. Clubs: Knollwood, Forge. Home: 125 Blackthorn Ln Lake Forest IL 60045 Office: Abbott Park North Chicago IL 60064

SEMPLE, CECIL SNOWDON, elec. co. exec.; b. Assam, India, Aug. 12, 1917; s. Fordyce B. and Anne (Munro) S.; brought to U.S., 1927, naturalized, 1948; B.A., Colgate U., 1939. Buyer, div. supt. R. H. Macy & Co., 1939-48; buyer Montgomery Ward, 1948-50; v.p. Nachman Corp., Chgo., 1950-55; mgr. radio receiver dept. sales Gen. Electric Co., Bridgeport, Conn., 1955-60, marketing cons., merchandising, N.Y.C., 1966-67, gen. mgr. audio products dept., 1967-68, dep. div. gen. mgr. housewares div., 1968-69, gen. mgr. housewares div., 1969, v.p., 1969-71, comml. v.p., 1971—; v.p. Rich's, Inc., Atlanta, 1960-62, sr. v.p., 1962-66, also mem. exec. com., dir.; dir. Electric Mut. Liability Co., Electric Ins. Co.; trustee People's Savings Bank, Bridgeport. Gen. chmn. Atlanta United Appeal campaign, 1965; chmn. bd. Jr. Achievement Greater Atlanta, 1962-66; bd. dirs. Bridgeport Hosp.; mem. exec. com. Ga. State Coll. Found., 1963-66; vice chmn. bd. trustees Colgate U.; adv. com. Emory U. Sch. Bus. Served to maj. USAAF, 1942-46. Mem. Assn. Home Appliance Mfrs. (dir.), Soc. Advancement Mgmt. (pres. Ga. chpt.), Am. Mgmt. Assn., Atlanta Retail Mchts., Assn. (pres. 1964-66), U.S. C. of C. (mfr.-domestic distbn. com.), Atlanta C. of C (dir.), Bridgeport C. of C., Atlanta Better Bus. Bur. (v.p. 1964-66), Atlanta Conv. Bur. (dir.), St. Andrews Soc. State N.Y. (chmn. bd. mgrs. 1971-72), Lenox Square Mchts. Assn. (dir.), Colgate U. Alumni Assn. (pres.), Delta Kappa Epsilon. Republican. Clubs: Brooklawn Country, Country of Fairfield (Conn.). Home: 25 Cartright St Bridgeport CT 06604 Office: Fairfield CT 06431

SEMPLE, ROBERT JOSEPH, air transport co. exec.; b. N.Y.C., Aug. 1, 1945; s. Robert Joseph and Helen (Kennedy) S.; B.S. in Acctg., Fairleigh Dickinson U., 1967; M.S. in Systems Mgmt., U. So. Calif., 1972; M.B.A. in Fin., Pace U., 1980; m. Margaret Ann Morahan, Jan. 20, 1979; children—Christine Deanne. Acct., Ford Motor Co., Newark, 1973-74; supr. passenger revenue Pan Am. World Airways, Rockleigh, N.J., 1974-75, revenue system analyst, 1975-77, mgr. revenue systems devel., 1977-80, dir. acctg. controls and statis. analysis, 1980—. Served with USAF, 1968-72. Office: King Rd Rockleigh NJ 07647

SENFT, MICHAEL M., investment exec.; b. N.Y.C., Dec. 14, 1939; s. Ben and Mollie S.; B.A. in Econs., Bklyn. Coll., 1961; postgrad. in investments N.Y. U., 1962-64; m. Jennifer Senft, Dec. 15, 1966. Instnl. research analyst N.Y. Stock Exchange mem. firms, 1964-74; gen. partner, dir. research Andresen & Co., N.Y.C., 1973-74; pres. M.M. Senft & Co. Inc., N.Y.C., 1975-77; mng. partner Sentinel Fin. Instruments, N.Y.C., 1978—, Sentinel Govt. Securities, N.Y.C., 1980—; past guest lectr. N.Y. U. Grad Sch. Bus. Adminstrn., New Sch. Social Research, Mem. N.Y. Soc. Security Analysts, N.Y. Acad. Scis. Clubs: Atrium (N.Y.C.); Met., Monroe (Chgo.). Office: 100 Wall St New York NY 10005

SENG, LEO SIMON, recreational vehicle agy. exec.; b. Galesburg, Ill., May 13, 1930; s. Leo Simon and Grace Genivieve (Mulvihill) S.; student public schs., Elwood, Iowa, 1936-48; m. Cynthia Joan Hartvigsen, Sept. 2, 1950; 1 son, David Paul. Owner, operator farm nr. Maquoketa, Iowa, 1946-73; owner, pres. Seng, Inc., Sarasota, Fla., 1975—. Mem. Fla. Mobile Home and Recreational Vehicle Dealers Assn., Fla. Manufactured Housing Assn., Family Motor Coach Assn. Roman Catholic. Club: Elks (Sarasota). Home: 5255 Calle Menorca Sarasota FL 33581 Office: Seng Inc 7707 S Tamiami Trail Sarasota FL 33581

SENG, ROBERT EMMETT, wholesale and retail oil co. exec.; b. St. Louis, Sept. 10, 1923; s. George Killian and Elizabeth (Phillips) S.; B.A., U. Tenn., 1953; m. Emily Ann Musso, July 30, 1949; children—Lizabeth Ann, Laurie Lynn, Robert Anthony. Rep., Nat. Cash Register Co., St. Louis, 1948-49; rep. Shell Oil Co., Wood River, Ill., 1949-51, rep. real estate, Memphis, 1951-52, Birmingham, Ala., 1952-56, dist. supr. Nashville, 1956-58, dist. mgr., Columbia, S.C., 1958-60, Syracuse, N.Y., 1960-65, mgr. market devel., Scarsdale, N.Y., 1965-67; gen. mgr. Reinhardt Oil Corp., Oneonta, N.Y., 1967-68, v.p., 1968-69, pres., 1969—; dir. Corner Food Stores Inc., Reese Marshall Co., Paul Oil Co; lectr. in field; partner Mgmt. Advisors, cons. co., Oneonta, 1967—. Mem. Oneonta Capital Budget and Planning Commn., 1975—; bd. dirs. Otsego County Devel. Co. Served with U.S. Army, 1943-46; PTO. Mem. Empire State Petroleum Assn., Nat. Oil Jobbers Assn., Nat. Assn. Convenience Stores, Sales Execs. Assn. Republican. Episcopalian. Clubs: Rotary (pres. Oneonta 1975-76), Cooperstown Country, Oneonta Country, Oneonta Tennis, Masons, Elks. Author: Economic and Demographic Study of Broome County, N.Y., 1966. Home: 57 Dietz St Oneonta NY 13820 Office: PO Box B Main St West Oneonta NY 13861

SENIOR, RICHARD JOHN LANE, textile rental services exec.; b. Datchet, Eng., July 6, 1940; came to U.S., 1972, naturalized, 1977; s. Harold Denis and Jane Lane Dorothy (Chadwick) S.; B.A., Oxford U., 1962; M.I.A., Yale U., 1964; m. Diana Morgan, Dec. 19, 1966; children—Alden, Alicia, Amanda. Mgmt. cons. McKinsey & Co., Inc., London and Chgo., 1967-74; pres., chief exec. officer Morgan Services, Inc., Chgo., 1974—. Pres. bd. trustees Latin Sch., Chgo. Mem. Textile Rental Services Assn. Am. (pres.-elect, dir., mem. exec. com.). Clubs: Racquet, Chicago, Glen View, Econ. Home: 1420 Lake Shore Dr Chicago IL 60610 Office: Morgan Services Inc 222 N Michigan Ave Chicago IL 60601

SENIOR, WALTER EMANUEL, film distbr., theater, vending, ice cream retail co. exec.; b. N.Y.C., Apr. 30, 1944; s. Solomon Edgar and Ruth Louise (Emanuel) S.; B.A., Rutgers U., 1964; m. Tanya Denise Wilson, June 30, 1973; one son, Jason Emanuel. Trainee, asst. gen. mgr. various Latin Am. territories Paramount Pictures, Hollywood, 1964-67; asst. to v.p. film buying, Wometco Enterprises, Miami, 1967-68, pres. Wometco de P.R., Santurce, 1970—, Hemisphere Film Distbn., 1978—, Wometco Interam. Film Dist., 1980—; dir. Latin Am. film ops. Wometco Ent.; dir. Gometco, Operadora Filmica, Wometco de P.R., Borinquen Enterprises, Wometco Sunny Isle, Wometco Ltd., ADWO. Trustee, bd. dirs. Presbyn. Hosp., San Juan, chmn. fund raising, 1975—; bd. advisers Salvation Army; bd. govs. United Fund San Juan, fund raising chmn., 1977-78, pres. bd. govs., 1978—; pres. bd. dirs. P.R. Center for Fine Arts, 1981—; active Cancer League, Heart Assn. Served with M.C., U.S. Army, 1968-69. Mem. San Juan C. of C., Nat. Assn. Theater Owners. Clubs: Rotary, Lions, Variety P.R. (founder, pres. 1975-76). Home: 71 Washington St Santurce PR 00907 Office: PO Box 9044 Santurce PR 00908

SENNE, STEPHEN MICHAEL, fin. planner; b. Pasadena, Calif., July 5, 1944; s. Delmar Vincent and Penelope Ann (Hahn) S.; A.A., Riverside City Coll., 1972; postgrad. U. Redlands, 1976-81; m. Ingrid J. Asst. supr. SSP Products, Burbank, Calif., 1965-70; life field underwriter, supr., John Hancock Ins., Whittier, Calif., 1970-76; casualty field underwriter Sentry Ins., Ontario, Calif., 1976-79; pres., dir. Stephen Michael Senne, A. Fin. Planner, Inc., Ontario, 1977—; dir., treas. Karate Sch. of Oyama, Inc., Leopard Karate Sch., Inc. Chmn. nuclear radiol. health and safety course Am. Soc. Non-Destructive Testings, 1970-81. Winner first place as editor of mgmt. newspaper nat. competition, 1969; named sportsman of month, Sportsman's Mag., Nov. 1970; winner numerous sales and karate awards; C.L.U. Mem. Internat. Assn. Fin. Planners, Am. Soc. C.L.U., Nat. Assn. Life Underwriters, Nat. Advisory Bd., Am. Police Acad. Republican. Lutheran. Clubs: Calif., Am. Sportsman, South Coast Gun, Glendale Elks. Full karate master (7th degree black belt). Author: The Jungle Detective; Your Financial Report Card. Home and Office: PO Box 1655 Hesperia CA 92345

SENTER, ROGER CAMPBELL, hotel co. exec.; b. Manchester, N.H., Apr. 21, 1932; s. Kenneth Lee and Beatrice (Campbell) S.; B.A., Boston U., 1954, LL.B., 1956. Grad. student tng. program Westinghouse, Pitts., 1956-59; asst. mgr. recruiting Semi-Condr. div. Raytheon, Boston, 1959-61; founder McGovern, Senter & Assos., Inc., Boston, 1961, v.p., 1961-65; dir. recruiting ITT World Hdqrs., N.Y.C., 1965-70; v.p., dir. personnel Sheraton Corp. Am., Boston, 1970-76, sr. v.p., dir. adminstrn., 1976—. Bd. dirs. Mass. Mental Health Assn. Mem. Am. Hotel and Motel Assn., Hotel Sales Mgmt. Assn., Nat. Assn. for Corp. and Profl. Recruiters (pres.). Club: Corinthian Yacht. Home: Roundy's Hill Marblehead MA 01945 Office: 60 State St Boston MA 02210

SENTURIA, RICHARD HARRY, fin. planning co. exec.; b. West Frankfort, Ill., Aug. 14, 1938; s. Irwin J. and Frances (Persow) S.; student So. Ill. U., 1956-57; student Bus. Sch., Washington U., St. Louis, 1957-59, 60-61, Law Sch., 1959-60; m. Ilene M. Bluestein, Dec. 24, 1961; children—Beth, Philip, Laura. From registered rep. to asst. mgr. Dempsey-Tegeler & Co., Inc., St. Louis, 1961-70; asst. mgr. E.F. Hutton & Co., Inc., St. Louis, 1970; sales promotion, research analyst Stix & Co., St. Louis, 1970-74; v.p. in charge sales promotion, tng., seminars, product acquisition, br. mktg. for tax shelter dept. R. Rowland & Co., St. Louis, 1976-79; pres., chief exec. officer Investment Capital Assos., Creve Coeur, Mo., 1979—; structuring and mktg. cons. to Meridian Co., Equity Programs Investment Corp., Cardinal Resources, Bishop Investments, Weinrich, Zitzman & Whitehead, JEV Income Fund, Inc., 1979—; mem. faculty continuing edn. seminar U. Kansas City Dental Sch., 1978; gen. partner Downtown Devel. Assos., Ltd., 1980—, Riverside Granada Royale Partners, Ltd.; v.p. Riverside Devel. Co., Riverside Parking Venture, Inc.; tchr. numerous adult evening schs., St. Louis area, 1961—. Founding mem., dir. Traditional Congregation of Creve Coeur, 1964-72; bd. dirs. Forsyth Sch., 1977—, B'nai Amoona Congregation, 1980; Served with U.S. Army, 1961-62. Mem. Internat. Assn. Fin. Planners, Am. Assn. Registered Reps. Home: 425 Shadybrook Dr Creve Coeur MO 63141 Office: Suite 200 707 N 2d St Saint Louis MO 63102

SEPPA, TAPANI ONNI, engr.; b. Lapua, Finland, Dec. 29, 1938; s. Onni August and Kerttu Aino (Kalkkinen) S.; M.S. in Elec. Engring., Helsinki (Finland) Tech U., 1961; m. Esther Happo, June 10, 1961; 1 son, Timo E. Research engr. Imatra Power Co., Finland, 1961-69; research engr. Reynolds Metals Co., Richmond, Va., 1969-70; various engring. mgmt. positions Burndy Corp., Norwalk, Conn., 1971-76; dir. bus. devel. Lapp div. Interpace Corp., Leroy, N.Y., 1976-77, v.p. and gen. mgr. Pulsafeeder Products div., Rochester, N.Y., 1977-79, v.p. and dir. mktg. Lapp div., LeRoy, N.Y., 1979—; cons. in field. Mem. IEEE (sr.). Contbr. articles to profl. jours. Home: 1 Woodward Dr Le Roy NY 14482 Office: 77 Ridgeland Rd Rochester NY 14623

SEPPI, FRED LLOYD, phys. metallurgist; b. Ogden, Utah, Apr. 9, 1930; s. Fred and Mary (Maccani) S.; B.S. in Physics, Northwestern U., 1951; M.S., U. Detroit, 1963; B.S. in Materials Engring., U. Utah, 1975. Metallurgist, Lindberg Steel Co., Chgo., 1951-55, Detroit Arsenal, Warren, Mich., 1954-64, Ogden (Utah) Air Logistics Center, 1964—. Mem. Am. Soc. Metals (chmn. Bonneville chpt. 1977-78), Soc. Materials Processing, Soc. Applied Spectroscopy, Am. Inst. Indsl. Engring. Roman Catholic. Researcher failure analysis, residual stress X-ray diffraction. Home: 3173 Tyler Ave Ogden UT 84403 Office: MANCM Ogden Air Logistics Center Hill AFB UT 84406

SERAPIGLIA, LOUIS ALFRED, JR., trucking co. exec.; b. Louisville, July 30, 1946; s. Louis Alfred and Ruby Emma (Yaeger) S.; B.E.E., U. Louisville, 1969; m. Mary Catherine Jenne, June 6, 1970; 1 son, Steven L. Electronics engr. Naval Ordnance Sta., Louisville, 1967-69, 69-71; pres. C&L Trucking Co., Inc., Louisville, 1971—, also pres., mgr. C&L Services Industries, Louisville; electronic and hydraulic system designer. Ky. Col. Mem. IEEE. Democrat. Roman Catholic. Home: 5411 Old Heady Rd Louisville KY 40299 Office: 733 Grade Ln Louisville KY 40213

SERFASS, WILLIAM DAVID, JR., corporate exec.; b. Allentown, Pa., Aug. 6, 1930; s. William David and Hermie (Heintzelman) S.; B.S., Temple U., 1952; m. Jessie Anne Joseph Rutledge, Feb. 23, 1957; 1 dau., Jessie Anne. Mgr. Price Waterhouse & Co., C.P.A.'s, N.Y.C., 1952-67; v.p. Laird Industries, Inc., also Laird Corporate Devel., Inc., 1967-70; v.p. Am. European Assos. Inc., N.Y.C., 1970-71; exec. v.p. HMW Industries, Inc. (formerly Hamilton Watch Co.), Stamford, Conn., 1971—, also dir.; dir. Echo Lake Devel. Co., Inc., Hamilton Tech., Inc., Wallace Silversmiths, Inc., Waldom Electronics, Inc., Handi-Man Industries, Inc. C.P.A., N.Y. State, 1958. Mem. Am. Inst. C.P.A.'s, N.Y. State, Conn. socs. C.P.A.'s, Temple U. Assos. (Phila.), Delta Sigma Pi. Clubs: Innis Arden Golf, Temple University Alumni of N.Y. (past pres.). Contbr. articles in field to profl. jours. Home: Woodley Ln Stamford CT 06903 Office: High Ridge Park Stamford CT 06905

SERGESKETTER, BERNARD FRANCIS, telephone co. exec.; b. Balt., July 14, 1936; s. Martin Bernard and Marie Agnes (Hubbuch) S.; B.S. in Elec. Engring., Purdue U., 1958; m. Mary Annette Hull, Sept. 22, 1962; children—Theresa, Stephen, Amy. With AT&T, and affiliates, 1959—; v.p. state region Ill. Bell Telephone Co., Chgo., 1978, v.p. bus. mktg., 1978—. Bd. dirs. Youth Guidance Agy., Chgo., 1979—. Served with AUS, 1959. Mem. Ill. C. of C. (dir.). Office: 225 W Randolph St Chicago IL 60606

SERIANNI, ALBERT T., dental products mfg. co. exec.; b. Phila., Nov. 5, 1928; s. Dominic and Anna (Prince) S.; grad. in bus. adminstrn. Drexel Inst., 1952; postgrad. Columbia U. Sch. Bus., 1968, advanced mgmt. program Harvard U., 1974; m. Phyllis Ann Kremer, Aug. 27, 1948; children—Donna Leigh, A. David, Mark K., J. Kristina. With Kendall Co., 1955-70, mktg. mgr. U.K., Kendall Co. (U.K.) Ltd., London, 1963-65, European dir. mktg., Boston and London, 1965-70; bus. mgr. Dow Lepetit, Milan, Italy, 1970-76; gen. mgr. Kerr div. Sybron Europe AG, Basel, Switzerland, 1976—; dir. Sybron (Europe) AG, Sybron SA France. Mem. adv. bd. Town of Mahant (Mass.), 1961-64. Served with U.S. N.G., 1948-50. Mem. Swiss-Am. C. of C., European Dental Mfrs. Assn., Fedn. Dental Internat. Club: Casino (Basel). Home: St Alban-Ring 151 Basel 40-52 Switzerland Office: 10 Aeschengraben Basel 40-52 Switzerland

SEROKA, JOSEPH STANLEY, mktg. co. exec.; b. Bklyn., Feb. 26, 1926; s. Nicholas and Stella Alexandria (Kozial) S.; B.S., N.Y. U. Sch. of Commerce, 1949; m. Marie Elizabeth Calvert, July 20, 1956; children—Paul, Nancy, Peter. Art dir., acct. exec. W.B. Doner Advt. Agy., N.Y.C., 1949-51; nat. sales promotion mgr. Benrus Watch Co., N.Y.C., 1951-60; dir. The Seroka Group, N.Y.C., Mamaroneck, N.Y., 1960—; cons. in field; participant 45th Joint Civilian Orientation Conf. Mem. nat. com. Keep Am. Beautiful Nat. Conservation Effort, Boy Scouts of Am., 1972, 73 (Save Our Am. Resources award); mem. Central Bus. Dist. Com., Mamaroneck, 1976-79; mem. Pres.'s Adv. Council, Coll. New Rochelle. Served with USMC, 1944-46, USNR, 1950-60. Decorated presdl. unit citation; recipient Certificate of Pub. Service, Gov. of N.Y., 1958. Mem. Am. Legion, Def. Orientation Conf. Assn., 4th Marine Div. Assn. Clubs: Sales, Mktg. Club Westchester (pres. 1975-78, chmn. bd. 1978-79), N.Y. Caledonian Curling (v.p. 1975-77), Sales Execs. of N.Y. Roman Catholic. Home: 314 Delancey Ave Mamaroneck NY 10543 Office: 640 W Boston Post Rd Mamaroneck NY 10543

SERSEN, HOWARD HARRY, interior design with cabinetry cons.; b. Chgo., Apr. 20, 1929; s. Harry S. and Bertha A. S.; B.F.A., Sch. Art Inst. Chgo., 1956; m. Judith Ann Nelson, Sept. 22, 1956; children—Mark Howard, Diane Lynn, Karen Judith, Amy Louise. Engaged in store planning, merchandising display and furniture design concepts Paul MacAlister and Assos., Lake Bluff, Ill., 1952-55, Silvestri Art, Chgo., 1955-56, Montgomery Ward & Co., Chgo., 1956-60, Riebold Co., Chgo., 1960-61, Sears, Roebuck & Co., Chgo., 1961-68; custom cabinet and kitchen design Reynolds Enterprises, Inc., River Grove, Ill., 1967-76; prin. Howard Sersen-Design, Park Ridge, Ill., 1976—; design and planning cons. for kitchens and related storage cabinetry for homes, offices; mfr., distbr. showrooms; visual merchandising display cons. to small retail stores. Art dir. Park Ridge Party, 1964. Served with U.S. Army, 1952-54. Recipient 1st pl. award Bicentennial Kitchen Design Contest, Wood-Mode Cabinets, 1975; Design award Wood Office Furniture Inst. Design Competition, 1952; award Design in Hardwoods Competition, 1958; certified kitchen designer Council Certified Kitchen Designers. Mem. Am. Inst. Kitchen Dealers (sec. Chgo.-Midwest chpt. 1974-75, bd. councillors 1977—, gov. 1978—, recipient Kitchen Design award 1972), Park Ridge Jaycees. Clubs: Park Ridge Univ., Masons, Order De Molay. Kitchen editor Qualified Remodeler mag.; contbr. articles to display, home improvement and kitchen mags.; custom cabinets and kitchen designs featured in several books, also Chgo. Tribune. Home and Office: 1608 S Courtland Ave Park Ridge IL 60068

SERVICE, RICHARD MONTGOMERY, JR., restauranteur; b. Tsingtao, China, Sept. 20, 1947; s. Richard M. and Helen (Gardes) S.; B.A., Pomona Coll., Claremont, Calif., 1970; m. Patricia Delgado, Sept. 23, 1973; 1 dau., Shannon Lee. Environ. planner City of Palm Springs (Calif.), 1971-75; dir. ops. Las Casuelas Nuevas, Inc., 1975-79; pres. Las Casuelas Terraza, Inc., Palm Springs, 1979—. Commr., Housing Authority Riverside County, 1975-78; mem. Palm Springs Planning Commn., 1978—; mem. govt. housing com. Coachella Valley Assn., 1978. Recipient 1st place award Instns. Food Service Design, 1979; Golden Palm award City of Palm Springs, 1980. Mem. Nat. Restaurant Assn., Calif. Restaurant Assn. Office: 222 S Palm Canyon Dr Palm Springs CA 92262

SERWATKA, WALTER DENNIS, pub. co. exec.; b. Irvington, N.J., July 19, 1937; s. Walter F. and Grace Ruth (Sheehan) S.; B.B.A., Upsala Coll., 1959; M.B.A., Fairleigh Dickinson U., 1966; m. Beverly M. Farrell, Aug. 10, 1963; children—David, Nora, Nancy. Fin. analyst U.S. Gypsum Co., 1960-64; plant controller W.Va. Pulp and Paper Co., 1964-68; dir. fin. services Random House, Inc., N.Y.C., 1968-72; with McGraw-Hill Inc., N.Y.C., 1972—, sr. v.p., controller, group v.p., 1979—. Served with U.S. Army, 1959-60. Mem. Planning Execs. Inst., Fin. Execs. Inst., Nat. Assn. Accts. Home: 15 Hamilton Ave Arlington NJ 07032

SETSER, HERSCHEL ALTON, mfg. co. exec.; b. Corbin, Ky., Aug. 15, 1919; s. William Simmie and Ollie Mae (Eldridge) S.; B.S. in Aero. Engring., Aero. U., Chgo., 1948; postgrad. mech. engring. Ill. Inst. Tech., evenings 1951-55; m. Betty Jane Zimmermann, Oct. 9, 1948 (dec. 1975); children—Joan Marie (Mrs. Mark Delaney), Paul Thomas, Judy Terese. Engr., Motorola, Inc., Chgo., 1948-52; sr. engr. Buick Motor div., Willow Springs, Ill., 1952-55, engring. supr., AC Spark Plug div., Milw., 1955-65, AC Electronics div., Milw., 1965-69; mgr. engring. Milw. Electric Tool Corp., Brookfield, Wis., 1969-73, v.p. engring. and quality control, 1973—. Mem. Deaconess Hosp. Soc., Milw., 1963—. Served with A.C., AUS, 1940-45: PTO. Mem. Am. Soc. Metals, Soc. Automotive Engrs., Am. Legion. Mem. United Ch. of Christ. Home: 4265 N 163d St Brookfield WI 53005 Office: 13135 W Lisbon Rd Brookfield WI 53005

SEVERINGHAUS, NELSON, JR., mining co. exec.; b. Gainesville, Ga., Aug. 27, 1929; s. Nelson and Josephine (Thompson) S.; student Ga. Inst. Tech., 1946-48; B.S. in Mining Engring., U. Ariz., 1951; m.

Virginia Terry, Aug. 31, 1952; 1 dau., Virginia Jo. Mining engr. Cities Service, Ducktown, Tenn., 1954-55; from mining engr. to pres. Ga. Marble Co., Atlanta, 1955-76; pres. Franklin Limestone Co., Nashville, 1976—, Franklin Brick Co., Nashville, 1979—; dir. Franklin Industries. Served with C.E., U.S. Army, 1951-54. Mem. Soc. Mining Engrs. of AIME (pres. 1980), Ga. Assn. Mineral Producing Industries (dir. 1974-76), Ga. State C. of C., Theta Tau, Pi Delta Epsilon. Methodist. Club: Atlanta Athletic. Contbr. articles to profl. jours. Home: 6 Foxhall Close Nashville TN 37215 Office: 612 10th Ave N Nashville TN 37203

SEWARD, GEORGE CHESTER, lawyer; b. Omaha, Aug. 4, 1910; s. George Francis and Ada Leona (Rugh) S.; B.A., U. Va., 1933, LL.B., 1936; m. Carroll Frances McKay, Dec. 12, 1936; children—Gordon Day, Patricia McKay (Mrs. Dryden G. Liddle), James Pickett, Deborah Carroll. Admitted to Va. bar, 1935, N.Y. bar, 1937, Ky. bar, 1947, D.C. bar, 1977, also U.S. Supreme Ct., other fed. cts. and agencies; with firm Shearman & Sterling, N.Y.C., 1936-53, Seward & Kissel, N.Y.C., 1953—. Trustee Edwin Gould Found. for Children. Fellow Am. Bar Found. (chmn. spl. com. on model corp. acts 1956-65); mem. Am. Bar Assn. (chmn. sect. corporate banking bus. law 1958-59, chmn. com. corp. law 1952-58, chmn. com. banking 1960-61, rep. from sect. to ho. of dels. 1959-60, 63-74), Internat. Bar Assn. (Am. Bar Assn. rep. on com. monopolies and restrictive trade practices 1960-68, chmn. com. 1965-68, founder, chmn. sect. bus. law 1970-74, hon. life pres. sect., life mem. council), Am. Law Inst. (joint com. with Am. Bar Assn. on continuing legal edn. 1965-74), Phi Beta Kappa, Phi Beta Kappa Assos. (pres. 1969-75), Theta Chi, Delta Sigma Rho, Raven Soc., Cum Laude Soc., Order of Coif. Clubs: Met. (Washington); Univ. (Chgo.); N.Y. Yacht, Down Town Assn., Knickerbocker (N.Y.C.); Scarsdale (N.Y.) Golf; Shelter Island (N.Y.) Yacht. Author: Basic Corporate Practice, 1977; co-author Model Business Corporation Act Annotated. Home: 48 Greenacres Ave Scarsdale NY 10583 Office: Wall St Plaza New York NY 10005

SEWARD, JOHN EDWARD, JR., ins. co. exec.; b. Kirksville, Mo., June 12, 1943; s. John Edward and Ruth Carol (Connell) S.; B.S. in Fin., St. Joseph's Coll., 1968; children—Mitch, J.J. Mgr. acctg. services Guarantee Res. Life Ins. Co., Hammond, Ind., 1964-69; asst. controller Gambles Ins. Group, Mpls., 1969-71, N. Am. Cos., Chgo., 1971-73; pres. Home & Auto. Ins. Co., Chgo., 1975—, also v.p. fin., dir. Bd. dirs. Calumet Council, Boy Scouts Am., 1979—, Teddy Bear Club for Shriners Hosp., 1979—. Designated C.L.U., 1976, Chartered Property and Casualty Underwriter, 1979. Fellow Life Mgmt. Inst. Home: 1240 Camellia Dr Munster IN 46321 Office: 111 W Jackson Blvd Chicago IL 60604

SEWELL, ERIC GEORGE, resort holding and mgmt. co. exec.; b. N.Y.C., July 9, 1935; s. Ernold George and Benajamina Louise S.; B.S., N.Y. U., 1958; M.S. (scholar), Columbia U., 1961; M.B.A., Calif. Western U., 1977; m. Oct. 2, 1971. Dir. Equal Employment Opportunity, U.S. Dept. Labor, Washington, 1967; prof. planning and mgmt. Howard U., Washington, 1969; pres. Travel Way Corp., Washington, 1970; founder, chmn., chief exec. officer, dir. T.W.D. Co., Washington, 1974—; founder, dir. Tourism Found., Washington, Tours Unltd., Washington; pres. Western Service Corp. Active United Way, United Way Trustees Assembly, SW Neighborhood House. Mem. Am. Mgmt. Assn., AAUP, Nat. Soc. Lit. and Arts, Am. Soc. Travel Agts., Internat. Platform Assn., Assn. M.B.A. Execs. Democrat. Episcopalian. Club: Internat. Contbr. articles to profl. jours. Office: Washington DC

SEXTON, DAVID FARRINGTON, lawyer; b. Montclair, N.J., Aug. 20, 1943; s. Dorrance and Marjorie (McComb) S.; A.B., Princeton U., 1966; J.D., U. Pa., 1972; m. Ann Hemelright, Feb. 27, 1971; children—James P., Ashley E., Christopher W. Admitted to N.Y. State bar, 1973; asso. firm Sullivan & Cromwell, N.Y.C., 1972-77; v.p. legal First Boston Corp., N.Y.C., 1977-79, v.p., gen. counsel, 1980—. Mem. Am. Bar Assn., Assn. Bar City N.Y., Japan Soc. (sec. 1976—). Republican. Office: First Boston Corp 20 Exchange Pl New York NY 10005

SEXTON, RICHARD, lawyer, bus. exec.; b. Madison, Wis., May 9, 1929; s. Joseph Cantwell and Eleanor Carr (Kenny) S.; B.S., U. Wis., 1951; LL.B., Yale, 1958; m. Joan Fleming, Feb. 23, 1957; children—Mary, Joseph, Lucy, Michael, Ann, Kate. Admitted to N.Y. State bar, 1959; asso. firm Sullivan & Cromwell, N.Y.C., 1958-64; asst. counsel SCM Corp., N.Y.C., 1964-67, v.p., gen. counsel Smith-Corona Marchant Div., 1967-72, v.p., gen. counsel, sec., 1972—. Served to lt. j.g. USN, 1951-55. Mem. Assn. Bar City N.Y., Am. Bar Assn., U.S. C. of C. (com. antitrust policy). Club: Yale (N.Y.C.). Home: 532 Third St Brooklyn NY 11215 Office: SCM Corp 299 Park Ave New York NY 10017

SEYMORE, WILLIAM ANDREWARTHA, finance co. exec.; b. Greensburg, Pa., Jan. 16, 1943; s. Francis Gerald and Rosehannah (Andrewartha) S.; student Duffs Bus. Sch., 1960-62, U. Hawaii, 1967-68, U. Calif., Los Angeles, 1969-71; m. Elizabeth A. Waters, Feb. 20, 1971; children—Mary Elizabeth, David Matthew, Joshua William. Staff accountant Davies & Mulvihill, Pitts., 1962-65; mgr. Haskins & Sells, Honolulu, 1968-69, Los Angeles, 1969-74; exec. v.p. Calif. Life Corp., Los Angeles, 1974-79, also dir.; treas., controller Allianz Ins. Co., Los Angeles, 1979—. Served with USNR, 1966-67. C.P.A., Pa. Mem. Am. Inst. C.P.A.'s. Republican. Episcopalian. Club: Jonathan (Los Angeles). Home: 2353 E Burnside St Simi CA 93065 Office: 6435 Wilshire Blvd Los Angeles CA 90048

SEYMOUR, EDWARD STANLEY, retail exec.; b. Albany, June 24, 1933; s. Edward F. and Alice (Ingalls) S.; student public schs., Albany; m. Jerri Smith, June 29, 1956; 1 son, Edward Michael. Mgr. sales and ops. Montgomery Ward Co., Albany, 1956-68; nat. sales mgr. Arlans Dept. Stores, N.Y.C., 1968-72; pres. Kelly & Cohen Co., Pitts., 1972-80, Forest City Home Centers, Cleve., 1980—. Served with U.S. Army, 1953-56. Mem. Nat. Appliance and TV Merchandisers (dir.). Club: Order of Ky Cols. Home: 27283 Pineview Dr Westlake OH 44145 Office: 10800 Brookpark Rd Cleveland OH 44130

SEYMOUR, STEPHEN DANA, broadcasting co. exec.; b. N.Y.C., Jan. 6, 1942; s. Dan and E. Louise (Scharff) S.; A.B., Rutgers U., 1964; M.B.A., Columbia U., 1965; m. Sharon Lynn Rose, June 27, 1965; children—Scott, Cregg, Lisa. Salesman, local sales mgr. KDKA-TV, Pitts., 1967-69; sales mgr. WJZ-TV, Balt., 1969-70, gen. mgr., 1972-74; gen. sales mgr. WBZ-TV, Boston, 1971-72; pres. TV Advt. Reps., N.Y.C., 1974-77; v.p. corp. TV sales Group W., N.Y.C., 1976—. Mem. Pres.'s Com. on Alcoholic Abuse, HEW, 1972; mem. regional bd. dirs. New Eng. chpt. Leukemia Assn., 1971-72, Balt. chpt. Urban League, 1972-74; bd. dirs. Metro chpt. YPO, 1974-77. Mem. Nat. Sales Adv. Assn., TV Advt. Bur., Internat. Radio and TV Soc. Home: 56 Whiffle Tree New Canaan CT 06840 Office: TVAR 90 Park Ave New York NY 10016

SEYMOUR, WHITNEY NORTH, lawyer; b. Chgo., Jan. 4, 1901; s. Charles Walton and Margaret (Rugg) S.; A.B., U. Wis., 1920, LL.D., 1962; LL.B., Columbia, 1923, LL.D., 1960; LL.D., Dartmouth, 1960, Duke, 1961, U. Akron, 1961, U. Man., 1961, Trinity Coll., 1964; D.C.L., N.Y.U., 1971; m. Lola V. Vickers, June 17, 1922 (dec. 1975); children—Whitney North, Thaddeus. Admitted to N.Y. bar, 1924; asso. Simpson, Thacher & Bartlett, N.Y.C., 1923-29, partner, 1929-31, 33—; part time lectr. N.Y.U., 1924-31; asst. solicitor gen. U.S., 1931-33; lectr. Law Sch., Yale 1935-45. Mem. N.Y. Temporary Commn. on Cts., 1953-58; mem. atty. gen's. com. antitrust laws, spl. asst. atty. gen. N.Y. waterfront controversy, 1954. Pres. Legal Aid Soc., N.Y., 1945-50, now dir., chmn. bd. sponsors; trustee emeritus Practicing Law Inst.; chmn. bd. Freedom House, 1954-59, 64-65, now hon. chmn.; distbn. com. N.Y. Community Trust; chmn. bd. trustees Carnegie Endowment, 1958-70; trustee Cathedral St. John the Divine; chmn. Joint Conf. Legal Edn., Council Library Resources, Council for Legal Edn. in Profl. Responsibility; mem. mayor's Com. on Judiciary, 1965-77; v.p. Fund for Free Jurists; trustee, chmn. William Nelson Cromwell Found.; trustee N.Y. U. Law Center. Named Episcopal Man of Yr., Bard Coll., 1976. Fellow Am. Bar Found. (pres. 1960-64); mem. Am. Coll. Trial Lawyers (pres. 1963-64), Bar Assn. City N.Y. (pres. 1950-52), N.Y. County Lawyer's Assn., Am. (pres. 1960-61, recipient Gold medal 1971), N.Y. State bar assns., Inst. Jud. Adminstrn. (past pres.), Supreme Ct. Hist. Soc. (v.p.), Am. Arbitration Assn. (pres. 1953-55, former chmn.), Municipal Art Soc. (pres. 1956-58, President's medal 1976), Law Soc. Eng. (hon.), Lincoln's Inn (hon. bencher), N.Y.C. of C. (past mem. exec. com.), Order of Coif, Phi Gamma Delta; hon. mem. Canadian, Wis., Minn., Miss., Tenn., Hawaii, N.H., Fed., Ga. bar assns. Republican. Episcopalian (sr. warden). Clubs: Century, Players, Pilgrims, Down Town, Recess, Salmagundi, Merchants (N.Y.C.); Metropolitan (Washington). Home: 40 Fifth Ave New York NY 10011 Office: 1 Battery Park Plaza New York NY 10004

SHABLESKY, MARTHA PONTIUS (MRS. PETER PAUL SHABLESKY), real estate investment co. exec.; b. Orrville, Ohio, June 29, 1918; d. Howard Taggart and Nova (Mead) Pontius; B.S., Miami U., Oxford, Ohio, 1940; m. Peter Paul Shablesky, Nov. 1, 1947; Exec. dir. Temple Israel, Dayton, Ohio, 1953-58; accountant-adminstr. Anchor Rubber Co., Dayton, 1958-63; controller-gen. mgr. Jos. Patterson & Assos., Dayton, 1963—; sec., asst. treas., dir. Wabash Plaza, Inc., Barlo, Inc., Haa-Guar, Inc., Augusta Plaza, Inc., Anderson Southdale, Inc., Bedford Plaza, Inc., Noblesville Shopping Center, Inc., Richmond Shopping Center, Inc. Asst. treas. Montgomery County chpt. Nat. Arthritis Found., 1970-71. C.P.S. Mem. Internat. Council Shopping Centers, Alpha Omicron Pi. Presbyn. Home: 3660 Briar Pl Dayton OH 45405 Office: 1959 Riverside Dr Dayton OH 45405

SHACHMUT, KENNETH MICHAEL, mgmt. cons.; b. Rockville Centre, N.Y., July 5, 1948; s. William Conrad and Mary (Kierych) S.; B.S.E., Princeton U., 1970; postgrad. Columbia U., 1970-71; M.B.A., Stanford U., 1976; m. Barbara Elizabeth Hulbert, July 20, 1974. Masters fellow Grumman Aerospace Corp., Bethpage, N.Y., 1970-71; asso. McKinsey & Co., Inc., San Francisco, London, Amsterdam, 1976-79; cons. Edgar, Dunn & Conover, Inc., San Francisco, 1979—. Served to lt. (j.g.), USN, 1971-74. Republican. Episcopalian. Clubs: Commonwealth of Calif., Princeton of N.Y. and No. Calif. Author: (with R.S. Brown) Economic Analysis Handbook, 1974; (with C.S. Weinberg) Arts Plan: A Model-Based System for Use in Planning of Performing Arts Series, 1978. Home: 60 Valdez Ave San Francisco CA 94112 Office: 1 Market Plaza San Francisco CA 94105

SHACKELFORD, BARTON WARREN, utility exec.; b. San Francisco, Oct. 12, 1920; s. Frank Harris and Amelia Louise (Schilling) S.; B.S. in Civil Engring., U. Calif., Berkeley, 1941; m. Charlaine Mae Livingston, July 24, 1949; children—Frank, Joan, Linda, Ann. Jr. engr. Todd-Calif. Shipbldg. Corp., 1941-44; with Pacific Gas & Electric Co., 1946—, sr. v.p., then exec. v.p., San Francisco, 1976-79, pres., chief operating officer, 1979—, also dir. Office: Pacific Gas & Electric 77 Beale St San Francisco CA 94106*

SHACKELFORD, JOHN HILARY, JR., diamond co. exec.; b. Murray, Ky., Aug. 4, 1939; s. John Hilary and Alice (Bell) S.; B.S., Murray State U., 1961; M.B.A., U. Md., 1968; m. June Pierce, Sept. 26, 1964; children—Millicent, Hillary, Alison. Asst. prof. mgmt. and mktg. U. Balt., 1968-71; founder, pres., owner SMA Diamond Importers, Inc., N.Y.C., 1968—; mktg. research and mgmt. cons. for bus. and govt. Mem. Am. Mktg. Assn. Office: Suite 1080 II Penn Plaza New York NY 10001

SHADER, MELVIN AARON, electronics co. exec.; b. Orlando, Fla., Apr. 22, 1925; s. Myer and Beatrice E. S.; B.S.E.E., U. Fla., 1945, M.A. in Math., 1948; Ph.D. in Math., Syracuse U., 1954; postdoctoral Columbia U., 1963; m. Florence Harris, June 17, 1955; children—Meryl A., Diane H., Daniel J. Mem. faculty U. Fla., Syracuse U. and Stanford U., 1947-54; with IBM Corp. and IBM World Trade Corp., 1954-68; dir. planning and product mgmt. Info. Network div. Computer Scis., 1969-71; v.p. planning and devel. TRW, Inc., Los Angeles, 1971—; dir. Computer and Communications Tech. Corp. County commiteeman Democratic Party, Westchester, N.Y., 1965-68. Served to lt. (j.g.), USNR, 1945-46. Mem. Assn. Computing Machinery, Internat. Fedn. Info. Processing Socs., Am. Math. Soc., Math. Soc. Am. Office: 10880 Wilshire Blvd Suite 1700 Los Angeles CA 90024

SHAFER, PAULINE MARIE, land devel. co. exec.; b. Saxton, Pa., Mar. 21, 1925; d. Elvin Paul and Ethel Mae (Carbaugh) Dilling; B.S., Ind. U. of Pa., 1945; m. Oscar F. Shafer, May 27, 1955; children—Bonita Marie, Byron Douglas. Payroll supr. Armstrong Cork Co., Lancaster, Pa., 1945-46; office mgr. Eastern Overall Co., Phila., 1946-48; owner, operator Mercury Acctg. Service, Harrisburg, Pa., 1948-55; sec./comptroller Oscar F. Shafer, Inc., Marysville, Pa., 1955-72; treas./comptroller Cumberland Constrn. Co., Dillsburg, Pa., 1965-72; sec./comptroller P & S Devel. Inc., Mechanicsburg, Pa., 1959-76, pres., 1976—, dir., 1959—; corp. dir. Oscar F. Shafer, Inc., 1955—. Pres., Marysville Civic Club, 1970-72; mem. curriculum lay com. Cumberland Valley Sch. Dist., 1976-78, 80—; sec. Assn. for Children with Learning Disabilities, 1979—, parliamentarian, state assn., 1980—; pres. Birthright of Central Pa., 1979—. C.P.A., Pa. Mem. Internat. Platform Assn., Home Builders Assn. Aux. (life mem., pres. 1956-64, 77, state pres. 1962-63, nat. exec. bd. 1959—, nat. pres. 1964), LWV. Presbyterian. Republican. Clubs: United Presbyn. Women's Assn., Service for Others, Silver Spring Women's (pres. 1976-78). Editor: Raport, 1964, 68. Address: 43 Green Ridge Rd Mechanicsburg PA 17055

SHAFER, SETH BYERS, indsl. engring. technician; b. Chambersburg, Pa., Jan. 3, 1928; s. Jacob William and Emma Jane (Byers) S.; A.A., Pa. State U., 1974, certificate in bus. mgmt., 1969; m. Ruth Louise Baker, Aug. 20, 1949; children—Kay Louise, Carol Ann. Indsl. engring. analyst Mack Trucks, Hagerstown, Md., 1966; machine shop foreman Ammunition Peculiar Equipment, Chambersburg, 1967; shop foreman recoil mechanisms Letterkenny Army Depot, Chambersburg, 1968-72, machine shop foreman, 1972-73, indsl. engring. technician, 1973-79, chief recoil br., 1979—. Served with F.A., U.S. Army, 1946-47. Mem. Armed Forces Mgmt. Assn. (treas. 1969-71). Democrat. Methodist. Club: Masons. Home: 2521 Scotland Rd Chambersburg PA 17201 Office: Letterkenny Army Depot Chambersburg PA 17201

SHAFFER, FRANK NEIL, banker; b. Sharon, Pa., Apr. 13, 1946; s. Fred Norman and Grace Muzette (Ray) S.; B.S. in Fin., Duquesne U., Pitts., 1978; m. Sandra Clare Heim, Aug. 1, 1970; children—Frank Neil, Brian Keith, Kevin Charles. Adminstrv. asst. Union Nat. Bank, Pitts., 1971-73; from collector to internat. mgmt. trainee Mellon Bank N.A., Pitts., 1973-77; asst. mgr. comml. loans and mortgages Nat. Bank of Commonwealth, Indiana, Pa., 1977-80; asst. v.p., head comml. banking div. Laurel Nat. Bank, Ebensburg, Pa., 1980—; fin. cons. to small bus. Mem. Republican Nat. Com. Served with USMCR, 1965-69. Mem. Robert Morris Assos., Econs. Club Pitts., Indsl. Mgmt. Club Indiana (treas. 1978—), United Comml. Travelers (sr. councilor 1976). Lutheran. Clubs: Kiwanis, Masons. Home: RD 2 Muller Rd Indiana PA 15701 Office: 111 W High St Ebensburg PA 15931

SHAFFER, JOHN RICHARD, ins. co. exec.; b. Harrisburg, Pa., Dec. 9, 1937; s. Raymond L. and Lillian C. (Alexander) S.; student Grove City Coll., 1956-57, Pa. State U., 1962, Polk Community Coll., 1978; m. Mona Jean Focht, Sept. 16, 1961; children—John Richard, Thomas. Trainee, Pa. Nat. Mut. Casualty Co., Harrisburg, 1960-61, underwriter, 1962-70; underwriter Americana Life Ins. Co., Columbus, Ohio, 1971-73; sec., underwriter United Sun Life Ins. Co., Lakeland, Fla., 1974-77, pres., chief exec. officer, 1977—, also dir. Bd. dirs. Nat. Found. March of Dimes. Served with USN, 1956-60. Mem. Lakeland Area C. of C., Nat. Assn. Life Cos., Ins. Acct. and Stat. Assn. Lutheran. Clubs: Imperial Kaes Country, Masons (past master), Shriners, Cornplanter Tribe #61, Improved Order Redman (past Sachem). Office: 5725 Imperia Lakes Blvd Mulberry FL 33860

SHAFFER, ROBERT CLARENCE, aeros. materials co. exec.; b. Kalamazoo, Oct. 4, 1918; s. Clarence Daniel and Grace Virginia (Garlick) S.; B.A. in Chemistry, Western State Coll., 1939; postgrad. Wayne U., 1943-44; m. Delores Rita Burns, Nov. 22, 1943; children—Rita Ann (Mrs. Ronald Joseph Buchholtz), Mary Kay (Mrs. Donald Earl Hackett, Jr.). Chemist, Ford Motor Research, Dearborn, Mich., 1940-42; head dept. chem. research Bendix Aviation Central Research, Detroit, 1942-49; supr. high polymer research lab. Ford Motor Sci. Center, Dearborn, 1949-53; research engr. N. Am. Aviation, Los Angeles, 1953-56; dir. research Adhesive Engring., San Carlos, Calif., 1956-60; dir. research Westech Plastics, Menlo Park, Calif., 1960-65; mgr. materials research and devel. HITCO Materials Sci. Center, Gardena, Calif., 1965-72, staff asst. to v.p. research and engring. Hitco Def. products div., 1972—. Cons. developed, planned and supervised research programs for def. contractors in fields of missile re-entry materials, 1960-65. Mem. Soc. Materials and Process Engrs. (treas. chpt. 1961-62). Patentee in field. Home: 8040 W 83d St Playa Del Rey CA 90291 Office: 1600 W 135th St Gardena CA 90249

SHAFFER, SHIRLEY JEAN ANDERSON, mfg. co. ofcl.; b. Chgo., Sept. 23, 1925; d. Edwin W. and Marie G. (Nelson) A.; student Pan Am. U., 1943; gen. bus. diploma Durhams Jr. Bus. Coll., 1944; student Northwestern U., 1946-49; m. Lester E. Shaffer, Nov. 5, 1949 (div. 1964); children—Bonnie, Larry, Steven, Scott, Leslie. Owner, operator Grefan Kennels, Norridge, Ill., 1955-64; editorial asst. Peacock Bus. Press, Park Ridge, Ill., 1963-67; sales/service coordinator Goodyear Chem. div. Goodyear Co., Elk Grove, Ill., 1967-68; dir. sales rep., various companies, 1968-73; v.p. Mid Am. Investments, Dallas, 1973-74; credit and collection mgr. Hycel, Inc., Houston, 1974-80, mgr. corp. purchasing (name now Boehringer Mannheim Diagnostics, Inc.), 1980—. Mem. Nat. Conservative Polit. Action Com., The Conservative Caucus; mem. state adv. bd. Presdl. candidate Congressman Phillip M. Crane, 1979—. Mem. Nat. Health Care Credit Group, Nat. Assn. Credit Mgmt., Houston Assn. Credit Mgmt., Am. Kennel Club, Phi Gamma Nu. Republican. Methodist. Home: 6001 Reims Rd #309 Houston TX 77036 Office: 7920 Westpark St PO Box 36329 Houston TX 77036

SHAGAN, MORRIS LEONARD, real estate devel. co. exec.; b. Appalachia, Va., Aug. 23, 1928; s. Aaron and Rose (Abrams) S.; B.S., U. Tenn., 1953; m. Barbara Jean Rosenbloom, July 29, 1962; children—Artie Jay, Robert Brent. Owner, Clinton Shoe Store (Tenn.), 1950-52; pres. Nat. Novelty Co., Knoxville, Tenn., 1956-59; pres. Morris Homes Corp., Atlantic Lumber Co., Leonard Investment Corp., Morris Ins. Services, 1958-63; broker Comml. Realty Co., Knoxville, 1963—; pres. Dalco Rentals, Inc., Knoxville, 1979—. Served as lt. U.S. Army, 1953-55. Clubs: Knox Racquet, U.T. Century, Masons, Shriners. Home: Westborough Subdivision Knoxville TN 37919 Office: 8301 Kingston Pike Knoxville TN 37919

SHAH, BIPIN CHANDRA, banker; b. Patan, India, July 23, 1938; s. Manilal Mohanlal and Kashar (Bhandari) S.; came to U.S., 1958, naturalized, 1967; B.A., Baldwin-Wallace Coll., 1962; M.A., U. Pa., 1965; m. Fay Janet Goldie, Aug. 18, 1962; children—Neile; 1 step-son—Kyle Ober. Info. retrieval specialist Xerox Corp., Rochester, N.Y., 1966; mgr. systems Gen. Electric Co., Valley Forge, Pa., 1966-68; dir. info. div. Mauchley Assos., Phila., 1969-70; pres. Vertex Systems, Inc., King of Prussia, Pa., 1970-74, dir., 1973-74; v.p., sr. officer Fed. Res. Bank of Phila., 1974-78; sr. v.p. Am. Express, 1979-80; exec. v.p. Phila. Nat. Bank, 1980—; lectr. Wharton Sch. Bus., U. Pa., Phila., 1967-68. Recipient Am. Mgmt. Assn. award, 1967. Mem. Am. Mgmt. Assn., Nat. Hon. Philos. Soc. (pres. 1961-62). Democrat. Author: Information Retrieval: State-of-the Art, 1966. Home: 143 Woodside Rd Ardmore PA 19003 Office: PO Box 7618 Philadelphia PA 19101

SHAH, JALIL JOE, exporter; b. Ghoshpuker, India, Aug. 31, 1938; s. Nabi M. and Amina S.; B.A., St. Xaviers Coll., Calcutta, 1959; m. Padma Chatlani, Sept. 13, 1971; children—Vinita, Jimmy. Mng. dir. J & F Reptile Traders, Calcutta, India, 1968-70; travel agt. Unitours, Los Angeles, 1973-74; pres. Intercontinental Traders, Los Angeles, 1975—. Sec., India Am. Soc., 1976. Mem. Los Angeles World Affairs Council, Los Angeles Area C. of C. Islam. Home: 239 S Kingsley Dr Los Angeles CA 90004 Office: PO Box 74744 Los Angeles CA 90004

SHAH, NIRANJAN SHAMALBHAI, engring. co. exec.; b. Pratapnagar, India, Dec. 13, 1944; s. Shamalbhai R. and Aglyarsi S. (Agrawal) S.; M.C.E., U. Miss., 1971; m. Pratima Agrawal, Nov. 29, 1969; children—Smita, Ashish. Field engr. Wickmoor Constrn. Co., Chgo., 1972; structural design engr. Sargent & Lundy, Chgo., 1973-76; chmn. bd. Globetrotters Engring. Co., Chgo., 1976—. Registered profl. engr., Ill., Ind., Wis. Mem. ASCE, Am. Water Works Assn., Assn. Indians in Am. (chmn. engring. council 1977-78). Democrat. Hindu. Office: 1020 S Wabash Ave Suite 802 Chicago IL 60605

SHAH, PRAKASH AMRITLAL, fin. co. exec.; b. Bombay, June 8, 1945; came to U.S., 1967; s. Amritlal J. and Ashrumati A. (Desai) S.; B.S. in Mech. Engring., Baroda U., 1967; M.S. in Mgmt. Sci., Stevens Inst. Tech., Hoboken, N.J., 1969; Ph.D., N.Y. U., 1974; m. Rajul Jhaveri, Dec. 7, 1974; 1 dau., Kaajal. Systems analyst Foster Wheeler Corp., Livingston, N.J., 1968-69; ops. research analyst Nabisco, N.Y.C., 1969; sr. mgmt. scientist Avon Products Co., N.Y.C., 1970-73; dir. mgmt. scis. Time Sharing Resources Co., N.Y.C., 1973-77; v.p., dir. bus. and strategic planning and mgmt. info. systems dept. Am. Express, N.Y.C., 1977—; pres., dir. Amex-Birla Internat. S.A.; mem. program com. INFO '76-'79, conf. and exhbns., 1976-79.

Exec. dir. Indian C. of C. Am., 1978—; pres. India Devel. Service, N.Y.C., 1978—; bd. dirs. Fedn. Indian Assns., 1979—, v.p. Nat. Council of Asian Indians in N. Am. Mem. Nat. Assn. Bus. Economists, Inst. Mgmt. Scis., N. Am. Soc. Corp. Planners, Future Soc. Home: 99-11 60th Ave Apt 6H Rego Park NY 11368 Office: American Express Plaza New York NY 10004

SHAH, VIPUL CHINUBHAI, securities trading corp. exec.; b. Ahmedabad, India, Dec. 22, 1950; came to U.S., 1968, naturalized, 1977; s. Chinubhai Chimanlal and Kusum Chinubahi S.; B.A., U. Wis., Milw., 1971, M.A., 1973; m. Harsha Pandya, Dec. 9, 1978. Fgn. exchange, Euro-currency trader Chem. Bank N.Y., N.Y.C., 1974-76, Westduetche Landesbank, N.Y.C., 1976-77; asst. v.p. Maduff & Sons, Chgo., 1978—; asso. editor Internat. Reports, N.Y.C., 1976—; mem. Internat. Monetary Market, Chgo., 1977—, N.Y. Futures Exchange, N.Y.C., 1980—. Office: Maduff & Sons 222 S Riverside Plaza Chicago IL 60606

SHAHADI, FREDERICK F., govt. comptroller; b. Narbeth, Pa., Feb. 25, 1922; s. Assad G., Sr., and Mae (Sarkes) S.; B.S. in Bus. Adminstrn., Pa. Mil. Coll., 1949; student Villanova U., 1941, U. Pa., 1956, Temple U., 1958; m. Dolly Koury; children—Frederick F., Christina, Amy, Christopher. Tax. cons. to pvt. industry, 1949-53; successively systems acct., head systems acctg. br., head internal rev. div., head gen. acctg. br., head cost acctg. br. Phila. Naval Shipyard, 1953-67; acctg. officer Naval Air Engring. Center, Lakehurst, N.J., 1967-71, dep. comptroller, 1971-78, comptroller, 1978—. Trustee Widener Coll., 1972-75. Served with USNR, World War II; PTO, ETO. Recipient Alumni Service award Pa. Mil. Coll., 1973; Outstanding Alumnus award Widener Coll., 1979. Mem. Am. Soc. Mil. Comptrollers (Navy v.p. Greater Phila. chpt.), Naval Civilian Adminstrs. Assn., Res. Officers Assn., U.S. Naval Inst., Pa. Mil. Coll. Alumni Assn. (nat. pres. 1972-75). Roman Catholic. Club: Sub 'n' Surface Toastmasters (past pres.). Home: 318 Highland Ave Wallingford PA 19086 Office: Comptroller Dept HQ Bldg 26 Naval Air Engineering Center Lakehurst NJ 08783

SHAHEEN, SHOUKY AZEEZ, real estate developer; b. Chgo., July 17, 1929; s. Azeez and Saleemeh Balluteen S.; A.B., U. Chgo., 1950, M.B.A., 1952; m. Doris Bradshaw, May 28, 1961; children—William, Gay. Treas. Katherine Rug Mills, Dalton, Ga., 1953-58; pres. Standard Textile Mills, Cartersville, Ga., 1959-65; owner, Shaheen and Co., Atlanta, 1966—; pres. Phoenix Investments, Inc., Atlantic Warehouse Corp. Former mem. bd. sponsors Atlanta Symphony Orch. Home: 3792 Dumbarton Rd NW Atlanta GA 30327 Office: 3715 Northside Pkwy NW Atlanta GA 30327

SHAINBERG, ABE MICHAEL, trade assn. exec.; b. N.Y.C., May 12, 1953; s. Nuta Meyer and Rachel (Schwartzman) S.; grad. Rabbi Jacob Joseph Sch., 1974; B.A. in Polit. Sci., Bklyn. Coll., City U. N.Y., 1974; J.D., St. John's U., 1977; m. Miryl Fink, Mar. 9, 1976; 1 dau., Debra Sher. Law clk. Hon. J. Arthur Goldberg, N.Y.C., 1974-77; admitted to N.Y. bar, 1978; atty. firm Herschcopf, Graham, Sloane & Block, N.Y.C., 1977-78; asst. exec. dir. Diamond Dealers Club, Inc., N.Y.C., 1978-79, exec. dir., counsel, 1980—. N.Y. State Regents' scholar, 1970-74. Mem. N.Y. State Bar Assn., N.Y. County Lawyers Assn., Bklyn. Bar Assn. Mem. Agvdath Israel of Am. Mng. editor bi-monthly industry newspaper Diamond Club News, 1979—. Office: 30 W 47th St New York NY 10036

SHALHOUP, JUDY LYNN, corp. exec.; b. Charleston, W.Va., Oct. 25, 1940; s. George Ferris and Mary Margaret (Moses) S.; B.A., Morris Harvey Coll., Charleston, 1967; M.S., W.Va. U., 1970. With Union Carbide Corp., 1960—, publicity mgr. plastics, N.Y.C., 1971-73, coatings materials div. advt. mgr., 1973—; v.p., gen. mgr. Fruit Bowl, Charleston, 1975-78. Recipient Bestteller award Bus. Profl. Advt. Assn., 1978, 79; Objectives and Results Advt. award Am. Bus. Press, 1978; Clio Advt. Recognition award, 1978, 79; Art Dirs. Show award, 1979. Mem. Telefood Assn., Fedn. Socs. Coatings Tech. Office: Old Ridgebury Rd Danbury CT 06817

SHALIT, SOL, economist, educator; b. Tel Aviv, Feb. 27, 1936; came to U.S., 1962, naturalized, 1970; s. Abraham Jacob and Mina (Blumrosen) S.; B.A. in Econs. and Stats., Hebrew U., Jerusalem, 1958; M.B.A. in Fin., U. Chgo., 1965, Ph.D. in Bus., 1970; m. Elizabeth Ann Wormser, Sept. 28, 1969; children—Ruthie, Mina, Wendy. Auditor, Kesselman & Kesselman, C.P.A.'s, Jerusalem, 1958-61; asst. prof. econs U. Ill., Chgo. Circle, 1968-74; asso. prof. fin. U. Wis. Sch. Bus., Milw., 1976—; cons., lectr. in field. Bd. dirs. Wis. Forum, Wis. State Council Econ. Edn. Mem. Am. Econ. Assn., Am. Fin. Assn., Wis. Econ. Assn. Jewish. Contbr. articles to profl. jours. Home: 2951 N Lake Dr Milwaukee WI 53211 Office: U Wis Sch Bus PO Box 413 Milwaukee WI 53201

SHALLECK, ALAN BENNETT, energy control equipment co. exec.; b. N.Y.C., Nov. 14, 1938; s. Milton and Rosalyn (Baron) S.; B.S., Mass. Inst. Tech., 1960; M.B.A., Harvard U., 1963. Bus. mgr. ASW programs Grumman Corp., N.Y.C., 1963-66; sr. cons. planning and fin. Diebold Group, N.Y.C., 1966-68; asst. v.p. corporate planning Reliance Group, Inc., N.Y.C., 1968-70; pres. Princeton (N.J.) Labs., Inc., 1970-75; v.p. corporate devel. Carter Wallace Inc., N.Y.C., 1975-77; pres. Aegis Group, Inc., Pennington, N.J., 1977—, Aegis Energy Systems, Inc., Doylestown, Pa., 1977—; dir. Bioassay Systems, Inc., Cambridge, Mass. Served with Signal Corps, U.S. Army, 1960. Mem. IEEE, Solar Energy Industry, N.Y. Acad. Scis. Democrat. Clubs: Harvard, Mass. Inst. Tech. Home: 5 Park Ave Pennington NJ 08534 Office: 607 Airport Blvd Doylestown PA 18901

SHANABERGER, MARK EDWARD, mgmt. cons.; b. Buckhannon, W.Va., Jan. 27, 1902; s. Otterbine Baxter and Flora May (Lewis) S.; m. Sarah Beatric Ramsey, Sept. 2, 1920; children—Elizabeth, Mark, Joan, Richard, Robert. Office mgr. Terminal Storage Co., Washington, 1921-28; div. sales mgr. W. Pa. Power Co., 1928-34; exec. v.p. Keystone Corp., Harrisburg, Pa., 1934-41; orders officer War Prodn. Bd., 1941-44; mktg. and prodn. cons. N.W. Ayer & Sons, Phila., 1944-53; with Barrington & Co., Barrington Internat., N.Y.C., 1953-64, pres., 1956-64, chmn., 1960-64, dir., 1965—; mgmt. cons. spl. problems nationwide, Clearwater, Fla., 1980—. Mem. Assn. Cons. Mgmt. Engrs., Nat. Indsl. Conf. Bd., Am. Mktg. Assn. Republican. Lutheran. Clubs: Canadian (N.Y.C.); Masons. Address: 1001 Willow Branch Ave Clearwater FL 33516

SHANAHAN, EDMOND MICHAEL, savs. and loan exec.; b. Omaha, Oct. 20, 1926; s. Jeremiah and Agnes (Corcoran) S.; B.Econs., St. Mary's Coll., Winona, Minn., 1949; M.A., M.B.A., U. Chgo., 1965; m. Elizabeth Rover, Apr. 26, 1952; children—Michael, Mary Elizabeth, Thomas, Terrence, Robert, Julie Marie. Customer relations and employee tng. Peoples Gas Light & Coke Co., Chgo., 1949-59; instr. DePaul U. Evening Sch., Chgo., 1957-59; pres., dir. Bell Fed. Savs. & Loan Assn., Chgo., 1959—. Served in USN, 1944-46. Clubs: Econ., Chgo. Athletic Assn. Home: 527 S Fernandez Arlington Heights IL 60005 Office: 79 W Monroe St Chicago IL 60603

SHANAHAN, LADY MABEL TERESA BALOCCHI, housing and mktg. exec.; b. Buenas Aires, Argentina, Sept. 15, 1936; came to U.S., 1955, naturalized, 1962; d. Joseph G. and Angela (Rebottaro) Balocchi; B.A., The French Lycee, 1954; postgrad. The Design Center, Calif., 1964; now postgrad. in bus. U. Calif., Irvine; m. Norman G. Shanahan, Dec. 7, 1967; children—Elizabeth Erin, Kathleen Olivia. Jewelry designer Tepper Enterprises, Santa Monica, Calif., 1956-65; asst. mgr. Toy Mart, Beverly Hills, Calif., 1961-67; fashion display coordinator Am. Fashion Products, Westwood, Calif., 1966-73; propr., dir. Terry's Antiques, Los Angeles, 1968-75, v.p. sales and mktg. Shanahan Homes, Inc., Palm Springs, Calif., 1974—; asst. mgr. adminstrn. Desert View Homes, Desert Hot Springs, Calif., 1975-76; land purchasing exec. Cahuilla, Inc., Palm Springs and Newport Beach, 1976—, now pres.; 1st v.p. Caligo, Inc., 1978-79; costume designer Palm Springs Dance Co., 1975-78. Founder, active Music Center of Los Angeles, 1960—; pres. Maarave Group of Hadassah, 1960; mem. adv. bd. Centro Pastoral Guadalupe, Santa Ana, Calif., 1977—. Recipient City of Hope award Mayor of Palermo (Sicily), 1964; Housing award Rural Council of U.S., 1978-79. Mem. Los Angeles C. of C., Calif. Escrow Assn., Sales-Mktg. Council of Orange County, Japanese Pioneer Assn. of Los Angeles, NOW, Palm Springs Hist. Soc., World Affairs Council of the Desert, Palm Springs Opera Guild, N.Y. Opera Guild, Nat. Notary Assn. Clubs: Palm Springs Tennis; Balboa Bay. Home: #3 Palomino Palm Springs CA 92262 Office: PO Box 2737 247 E Tahquitz-McCallum Way Palm Springs CA 92262

SHANK, KENNETH EARL, mfg. co. exec.; b. Priest River, Idaho, Feb. 24, 1929; s. Robert Phillip and Audra Ester (Eckley) S.; LL.B., LaSalle Coll., 1959; B.S. in Bus. Adminstrn., Northeastern U., 1969; certificate in Indsl. Relations, U. Calif., 1969; m. Bonnie Lee Snapp, Feb. 19, 1954. Supervisory engr., tech. advisor U.S. Air Force, Colorado Springs, Colo., 1958-64; mgr. ops. research Raytheon Co., Sudbury, Mass., 1965-71; pres. NHA and Applied Electronics Co., Andover, Mass., 1972-76; pres. Internat. Pammcorp., East Boston, Mass., 1977-78; v.p., dir. Nat. Radio Co., Inc., Melrose, Mass., 1979—; pres. Orion Assos., Inc., 1979—. Served with U.S. Army, 1949-52. Mem. IEEE. Home: 3 Briarwood Rd Framingham MA 01701 Office: 89 Washington St Melrose MA 02176

SHANKLIN, WILLIAM LESLIE, educator, business cons.; b. Louisville, Jan. 22, 1941; s. Howard Lowell and Ava Douglas (Griffen) S.; B.S., Western Ky. U., 1967; M.B.A., U. Ky., 1969; D.B.A. (fellow), U. Md., 1972; m. Joan Willa Sagabiel, June 10, 1967; children—Andrea Leslie, Courtney Kathleen. Indsl. salesman Ga.-Pacific Corp., Louisville, 1967-68; instr. U. Md., College Park, 1970-72; asso. prof. Western Ky. U., Bowling Green, 1972-77; prof. Coll. Bus. Adminstrn., Kent (Ohio) State U., 1977—, chmn. dept. mktg. and transp., 1977—; cons. to numerous bus. orgns., 1972—; mktg. cons. to numerous polit. candidates, 1972—. Served with U.S. Army, 1963-64. Mem. Sales and Mktg. Execs. Internat., Am. Mktg. Assn., Acad. Mgmt., Acad. Mktg. Sci., Alpha Kappa Psi, Beta Gamma Sigma, Phi Eta Sigma. Republican. Roman Catholic. Contbr. numerous articles to profl. jours. Home: 1565 S Lincoln St Kent OH 44240 Office: Dept Mktg and Transp Kent State U Kent OH 44242

SHANNON, CYRIL GEORGE, JR., newspaper exec.; b. Evanston, Ill., Aug. 7, 1926; s. Cyril George and Ann (Van Arsdale) S.; B.S. in Bus. Adminstrn., Northwestern U., 1949; m. Margaret Priscilla Elg, Aug. 6, 1949; children—Margaret Ann, Gregory George, Jeffrey Cort. With Lorenzen & Thompson Inc., Chgo., 1949-50; with Shannon & Assos., Inc., Chgo., 1950-65, v.p., 1954-60, pres., 1960-65, Shannon & Cullen, Inc., Chgo., 1965-69; sr. v.p. Mathews, Shannon & Cullen, Inc., Chgo., 1969-76, Landon Assos., Inc., Chgo., 1976—; dir. Pubs. Assos., Shannon-Whitehead Co. Adv. com. cardiac resuscitation Boy Scouts Am.; active Community Chest, Western Springs Republican Com. Served with USN, 1944-46. Mem. Inland Daily Press Assn., Internat. Newspaper Advt. Execs., Suburban Press-Suburban Newspapers Am. Clubs: University (Chgo.); La Grange (Ill.) Country. Office: 435 N Michigan Ave Chicago IL 60611

SHANNON, MARYLN MAY, automobile dealership exec.; b. McMinnville, Oreg., Apr. 18, 1935; d. Fred John and Fleda Mae (Taylor) Froeschle; student acctg. Portland Bus. Coll., 1953, Gen. Motors Corp. Sch., 1974; student Reynolds and Reynolds Computer Sch., 1974, 75, 79; m. Robert E. Shannon, Aug. 8, 1953; children—Charles F., Kathaleen G., Robert L., Randolph A. Office mgr. Towne Fin. Co., Portland, Oreg., 1962-66; asst. office mgr., asst. lease mgr. Buchanan Chevrolet, Spokane, Wash., 1966-70; bus. mgr., lease mgr. DeNooyer Chevrolet, Inc., Albany, N.Y., 1970—. Mem. Chevrolet-Gen. Motors Council Bus. Mgrs. Home: RD 1 Box 134 A-14 Mechanicville NY 12118 Office: 127 Wolf Rd Albany NY 12205

SHANNON, MELVIN LEROY, ins. co. exec.; b. Fort Morgan, Colo., June 15, 1925; s. Oren and Lodoska (McElhiney) S.; student U. Colo., 1948-53; m. Mary Ellen Palm, Nov. 15, 1946; children—John Edward, Ronald David, Randall James, Russell Dean, Jerold Paul. Asst. casualty actuary Nat. Farmers Union Property & Casualty Co., Denver, 1955-62; with Occidental Fire & Casualty Co. N.C., Denver, 1962—, v.p., treas., 1969-73, pres., dir., 1973—. Active local multiple sclerosis soc. Served with USAAF, 1943-46; PTO. Mem. Ins. Accounting and Statis. Assn. (past sec.-treas., past v.p. Rocky Mountain chpt.), Nat. Assn. Ind. Insurers (governing bd. statis. service 1972-75, dir. assn. 1975—), Denver C. of C. Presbyterian (ruling elder). Home: 9050 E Big Canon Pl Englewood CO 80111 Office: 5670 S Syracuse Circle Suite 500 Englewood CO 80111

SHANTON, JOHN LYNN, mgmt. cons.; b. Kingsburg, Calif., Jan. 7, 1935; s. Lynn Clyde and Myrtle (Peterson) S.; B.S., Western Ky. U., 1957; postgrad. U. Louisville, 1962-64, Capital U. Law Sch., 1970-71; M.B.A., Ohio State U., 1973; m. Shirley Ann Begeman, June 2, 1957; children—John Lynn, Kimberly Ann, Steven Louis. Research chemist Am. Synthetic Rubber Corp., 1960-65; asst. dir. nutritional products info. and asso. scientist Mead Johnson Research Center, Evansville, Ind., 1965-68; advt., promotion mgr. Mead Johnson Labs. and Ross Labs., Evansville, Ind. and Columbus, Ohio, 1968-70; mgr. corp. research and planning dept. Ohio Med. Indemnity, Columbus, 1970-71; dir. mktg. Northeastern Ohio Health Care Found., Youngstown, 1971-73; analyst Mahoning Shenango Area Health Edn. Network, Youngstown, 1973-75; mgr. Nat. Cancer Inst. project, Capital Systems Group, Rockville, Md., 1975-77; dir. devel. Block, McGibony & Assos., Silver Spring, Md., 1977; pres. Health Services Assos., 1977—; cons. in health orgns. mgmt., public health and clin. studies; writer and editor in field. Vice pres. Ind. Public Health Found.; chmn. Health Resource Devel. Com., Health Systems Agy. of Western Md. Served with USN, 1957-60, comdr., USNR. Mem. Am. Public Health Assn., Md. Public Health Assn., Western Md. Tennis Patrons (v.p. 1979-81). Lutheran. Club: Tuscarora Tennis. Home: 2997 Summit Dr Ijamsville MD 21754 Office: PO Box 70 Monrovia MD 21770

SHAPELL, NATHAN, fin. co. exec.; b. Poland, Mar. 6, 1922; s. Benjamin and Hela Shapell; student public schs.; m. Lilly Szenes, June 17, 1946; children—Vera Shapell Guerin, Benjamin. Co-founder Shapell Industries, Inc., Beverly Hills, Calif., 1955, chmn. bd., chief exec. officer; mem. adv. bd. Union Bank, Beverly Hills; cons. to govtl. agys., fin. instns., indsl. firms. Commr., Commn. on Calif. Govt. Orgn. and Economy, 1969—, chmn., 1975—; mem. Calif. Atty. Gen.'s Adv. Council; mem. residential bldgs. adv. com. State Energy Resources Conservation and Devel. Commn.; trustee U. Santa Clara (Calif.), 1976—. Recipient Fin. World award, 1977. Mem. Am. Acad. Achievement (pres. 1975—, Golden Plate award 1974). Jewish. Cllub: Hillcrest Country (Los Angeles). Author: Witness to the Truth, 1974. Office: Shapell Industries 8383 Wilshire Blvd Suite 700 Beverly Hills CA 90211*

SHAPIRO, GEORGE M., lawyer; b. N.Y.C., Dec. 7, 1919; s. Samuel N. and Sarah (Milstein) S.; B.S. cum laude, L.I. U., 1939; LL.B. (Kent scholar), Columbia, 1942; m. Rita V. Lubin, Mar. 29, 1942; children—Karen Shapiro Spector, Sanford. Admitted to N.Y. bar, 1942; staff gov. N.Y., 1945-51; counsel to gov. N.Y., 1951-54; partner Proskauer Rose Goetz & Mendelsohn, 1955—; dir. Bank of Calif., Israel Discount Bank N.Y., Overseas Shipholding Group, La Compagnie Financiere, France. Counsel N.Y. Constl. Revision Commn., 1960-61. Counsel, majority leader N.Y. Senate, 1955-59. Mem. Gov.'s Com. on Reapportionment, 1964, Mayor's Com. on Jud. Appointments, 1966-69. Mem. program com. Rep. Nat. Com., 1959. Pres. Edmond de Rothschild Found.; chmn. council State U. Coll. Medicine; 1954-71. Mem. Council Fgn. Relations. Republican. Clubs: Harmonie, Metropolis. Home: 1160 Park Ave New York NY 10028 Office: 300 Park Ave New York NY 10022

SHAPIRO, IRVING SAUL, lawyer, former mfg. co. exec.; b. Mpls., July 15, 1916; s. Sam I. and Freda (Lane) S.; B.S., U. Minn., 1939, LL.B., 1941; m. Charlotte Farsht, Mar. 1, 1942; children—Stuart Lane, Elizabeth Irene. Admitted to Minn. bar, 1941, Del. bar, 1958, U.S. Supreme Ct. bar, 1944; atty. criminal div. Dept. Justice, 1943-51; with E.I. duPont de Nemours & Co., Inc., 1951-81, v.p., 1970-73, vice chmn. bd., 1973, chmn., chief exec. officer, 1974-81, also dir., chmn. exec. com., chmn. pub. affairs com.; partner firm Skadden, Arps, Slate, Meagher & Flom, N.Y.C., 1981—; dir. Bank of Del., Citicorp, Citibank, IBM, Continental Am. Ins. Co.; mem. Bus. Council, Bus. Roundtable. Bd. dirs. Greater Wilmington Devel. Council; trustee Ford Found., U. Pa. Office: Skadden Arps Slate Meagher & Flom 919 3d Ave New York NY 10003

SHAPIRO, PHILIP, grocery exec.; b. Augusta, Ga., Jan. 4, 1931; s. Harry and Sadie (Rabinowitz) S.; B.A., U. Ga., 1953; m. Sandra Greenburg, Mar. 27, 1960; children—Julie Lyn, Harry, Steven Louis. Bus. mgr., Camp Gordon Rambler weekly, Augusta, Ga., 1955; buyer frozen food Setzers Food Stores, Jacksonville, 1956-61; grocery buyer Setzer div. Food Fair Stores, Inc. Jacksonville, 1961-71, head grocery merchandiser, head grocery buyer Pantry Pride div., 1971—. Mem. Ga. govs. staffs Bushbee, Carter, Mattox, Sanders, Vandiver; bd. dirs. Jacksonville Ice Hockey Team, 1964-65; trustee Etz Chaim Synagogue. Served with U.S. Army, 1953-55; Korea. Mem. Di Gamma Kappa. Democrat. Clubs: University, Bulldog, Island Flyers, Masons, Shriners. Home: 2912 Caballero Dr N Jacksonville FL 32217 Office: 5233 Commonwealth Ave Jacksonville FL 32203

SHAPIRO, RICHARD G., retail exec.; b. N.Y.C., Apr. 4, 1924; s. David and Sophie (Hayflich) S.; B.A., U. Mich., 1946; M.B.A., Harvard U., 1948; m. Lila Eig, July 27, 1951; children—Judith, Amy, Donald. With Lord & Taylor, then chmn. Filene's of Boston; chief exec. officer, pres. Gimbel Brothers Inc., N.Y.C., then v.p. W.R. Grace & Co., N.Y.C., now pres. Specialty Stores div. Served with U.S. Army, 1943-46. Office: WR Grace Co 1114 Ave of Americas New York NY 10036

SHAPLEIGH, WARREN MCKINNEY, food mfg. co. exec.; b. St. Louis, Oct. 27, 1920; s. Alexander Wessel and Lois (McKinney) S.; B.A. in Econs., Yale U., 1942; m. Jane Howard Smith, Sept. 10, 1945; children—Jane Howard, Christine. Vice pres. Shapleigh Hardware Co., St. Louis, 1946-56. Sterling Aluminum Products, St. Louis, 1959-61; pres. Hipolite Co., St. Louis, 1956-59; mgr. diversification planning Ralston Purina Co., St. Louis, 1961-63, v.p. consumer products div., 1963-68, exec. v.p., 1968-70, pres. consumer products group, 1970-72, pres. co., 1972-79, also dir.; chmn. Gard Research Corp., St. Louis; dir. Tidewater Inc., New Orleans, Midland Container Co., Brown Group, Inc., St. Louis, First Nat. Bank, St. Louis Union Trust, Mo. Pacific Corp., Mo. Pacific R.R. Co., J.P. Morgan & Co., Morgan Guaranty Trust Co., Barry Wehmiller Corp., St. Louis. Trustee Jefferson Nat. Expansion Meml. Assn., St. Louis Symphony Soc., Mo. Bot. Garden, Washington U., St. Louis, St. Louis Area council Boy Scouts Am., Brookings Instn. Served to lt. USNR, 1942-46. Clubs: St. Louis Country (pres., gov. 1959-61), Noonday (St. Louis). Home: 1310 Mason Rd Saint Louis MO 63131 Office: 1313 W Essex Saint Louis MO 63122

SHARAK, ERROL WILLIAM, coll. ofcl., energy co. exec.; b. Milw., Sept. 8, 1944; s. George Edward and Ethel Magdeline (Marki) S.; student U. So. Calif., 1962-63, U. Hawaii, 1963-64, Manpower Bus. Tng. Inst., 1967, Rice U., 1979; m. Carol Pauline Enea, May 6, 1966; children—Michael Steven, Jacqueline Marie. With Computer Ops. div. Mueller Climatrol Corp., 1967-70; with Patrick Cudahy Co., Inc., 1970; exec. v.p. Universe Mineral Co. Mont., 1970-72; computer ops. specialist Milw. Area Tech. Coll., 1971—; with H&R Block, Milw., 1972-75, Personalized Income Tax Service, Milw., 1974-79; pres. Tungstun Mining Ltd., Butte, Mont., 1974—; sr. partner Over-the-Road Motor Homes Rental Co., Milw., 1976-78; pres. Errol Energy Co., Inc., Houston, 1980—. Served with USMC, 1962-66; Vietnam. Mem. United Ch. of Christ. Home and Office: 18775 W Observatory Rd New Berlin WI 53151

SHARBAUGH, WILLIAM JAMES, plastics co. exec.; b. Pitts., Apr. 13, 1914; s. Oliver M. and Sadie (Wingenroth) S.; B.S., Carnegie Inst. Tech., 1935; m. Eileen Carey, May 14, 1938; children—William James Eileen (Mrs. W. A. Pinkerton, Jr.), Susan (Mrs. Kenneth A. Cote). Plastics engr. Mil. Products div. Mine Safety Appliances Co., Pitts., 1935-48; pres. Enpro Plastics, St. Louis, 1948-58; mgr. plastics div. Vulcanized Rubber & Plastics Co., Morrisville, Pa., 1958-60; pres. Plastics Assos., consultants, Yardley, Pa., 1960-63; v.p. sales and engring. Robroy Plastics div., Robroy Industries, Morrisville, 1964-66; v.p. mfg. and engring. FESCO div. Cities Service Co., Pitts., 1966-69; exec. v.p. Alladin Plastics div. Crown Zellerbach, Inc., San Francisco, 1972-74, dir. devel. and tech., 1974-78; pres. Plastics Assos., 1978—; founder, chief exec. officer Isobet USA, Inc.; founder, pres. Plastics Closures and Containers Corp.; dir. Plastx, Inc. Instr. plastics engring. Pa. State U., 1943-44. Mem. Soc. Plastics Industry, Am. Mgmt. Assn., Soc. Plastics Engrs. (1st pres. 1945-46), Soc. Plastics Industry, Am. Mgmt. Assn., Tau Beta Pi. Club: Newport Beach Tennis. Home: 1516 Seacrest Dr Corona Del Mar CA 92625 Office: 110 Newport Center Dr 200 Newport Beach CA 92660

SHARBROUGH, STEVEN JAMES, retail chain exec.; b. Monterey Park, Calif., June 2, 1946; s. John and Phyllis S.; B.A., UCLA, 1968, M.A., 1970, Ph.D., 1977; m. Kaye Couerston, Oct. 1, 1965; 1 son, Charles. Teaching fellow UCLA, 1976, instr., 1978; dir. ops. Original Cookie Co., retail chain, Los Angeles, 1976-77; v.p. Creation of Ireland, Beverly Hills, Calif., 1978—. Mem. Beverly Hills C. of C. Democrat. Home: 11336 Waterford St Los Angeles CA 90049 Office: 9534 Brighton Way Beverly Hills CA 90210

SHARP, DAN CECIL, refrigeration supply co. exec.; b. Robertsville, Tenn., July 31, 1940; s. Luther Clyde and Frankie Marie (Smith) S.; A.A., Mt. San Antonio Coll., Walnut, Calif., 1978; m. Kazue Iha, Dec.

17, 1965; 1 son, Michael Wayne. Store mgr. Henry M. Sweeney Corp., Washington, 1969-70, Victor Distbg. Co., Merrifield, Va., 1970-75; partner Authorized Supply Corp., Los Angeles, 1975—; adv. com. Mt. San Antonio Coll., La Puente (Calif.) Vocat. Sch. Active Republican campaigns. Served with USMC, 1958-68. Mem. Research Inst. Am., Refrigeration Service and Engrs. Soc., N.Am. Heating and Air-conditioning Wholesalers Assn., Am. Security Council, Alpha Gamma Sigma. Baptist. Club: Masons. Home: 2509 Woodlark Dr Ontario CA 91761 Office: 12357 E Rush St South El Monte CA 91733

SHARP, HAROLD GENE, marketing exec.; b. Mason City, Iowa, Jan. 23, 1942; s. Harold F. and Mary F. (Yanoski) S.; B.B.A., U. Iowa, 1965; m. Constance J. Corless, Sept. 8, 1962; children—Susan, Michelle, Russel. Dir. merchandising Red Owl Store, 1965-75; dir. controlled brands Super Valu Store, Mpls., 1975-77; sr. v.p. mktg. Am. Community Stores, Omaha, 1977—. Mem. fund bd. Creighton U. Served with U.S. Army, 1966-68. Recipient Disting. award Nat. Food Distbrs., 1978. Mem. Food Mktg. Inst., Sales and Mktg. Execs. Midlands (bd. dirs.). Republican. Methodist. Club: Shriners. Home: 9931 Essex St Omaha NE 68114 Office: 4206 S 108th St Omaha NE 68137

SHARP, HENRY FRANKLIN, investments co. exec.; b. York, Pa., June 21, 1919; s. Charles Claude and Elsie May (Reel) S.; student Inst. Drugless Therapy, 1953; D.A., Okla. Coll. Audiometry, 1955; m. Doris Ethel Klinger, Oct. 4, 1941; 1 son, Henry Franklin. Entertainer clubs and theatres, 1938-41; sales service mgr., personnel mgr. Ga. Pacific Corp., Reading, Pa., 1945-61; zone mgr. I.D.S. Corp., Pa., 1961-63; divisional mgr. Channing Corp., Reading, 1963-69; div. mgr. CNA Investors, Pa., 1969-70; pres., chmn. bd. Century Investments, Inc., Camp Hill, Pa., 1970—; dir. ins. plans and services Consumers Life Ins. Co., Camp Hill; mem. ednl. council Lincoln Coll. Naturopathic Physicians Surgeons. Served to lt. comdr. Am. Coast Patrol, 1938-42. Certified fin. planner. Mem. Nat. Assn. Securities Dealers, Assn. Fin. Planners, Am. Writers Assn., Nat. Assn. Personnel Mgrs. Mormon. Author articles on sales techniques and personnel mgmt. Home: 104 Greenwood Dr Temple PA 19560 Office: 1004 Fernwood Dr Camp Hill PA 17011

SHARP, J. FRANKLIN, communications exec.; b. Johnson County, Ill., Sept. 29, 1938; s. James Albert and Edna Mae (Slack) S.; student So. Ill. U., 1954-56; B.S.I.E., U. Ill., 1959; M.S., Purdue U., 1961, Ph.D., 1966. Asst. prof. economics and indsl. engring. Rutgers U., New Brunswick, N.J., 1964-67; asso. prof. bus. N.Y. U. Grad. Sch. Bus., 1967-71; prof. fin. and acctg. Pace U. Grad. Sch. Bus., 1975—; supr. bus. research AT&T, 1974-77, dist. mgr. corp. planning, 1977—; cons. sharp math. models; lectr. in field. Chartered fin. analyst. Mem. Am. Accounting Assn., Am. Fin. Assn., Fin. Analysts Fedn., Inst. Mgmt. Sci. (chpt. v.p.-acad. 1973, chpt. v.p.-program 1974-75, chpt. v.p.-membership 1975, chpt. pres. 1976-77), N.Am. Soc. Corp. Planning (treas. 1976-77, dir.-at-large 1977-78, chpt. dir. 1975-78), Ops. Research Soc. Am. (pres. corp. planning group 1976—), Internat. Affiliation of Planning Socs. (council 1978—), Theta Xi. Republican. Contbr. articles to profl. publs.; fin. editor Planning Rev., 1975-78, bus. mgr., 1977-78. Home: 315 E 86th St New York NY 10028 Office: AT&T 195 Broadway New York NY 10007

SHARPE, DICK RONALD, merchandising co. exec.; b. Alston, Ga., Feb. 20, 1930; s. Hiram Chestly and Nell (Sharpe) S.; student U. Miami, 1954-58; A.B.M., Miami-Dade Jr. Coll., 1970; m. Elizabeth J. McNamee, Aug. 14, 1949; children—Richard Ronald, Thomas Wayne, Lynda. Salesman, Sunshine Biscuit Co., Miami, Fla., 1952-61; dist. sales mgr. S.C. Johnson & Son, Miami, 1961-75; sales mgr. Fla. Wholesale Drug, Miami, 1975-76; pres. Biscayne Merchandising Co., Miami, 1976—, Acme Sales Co., Inc., Jacksonville, 1979—. Chmn. fin. com., sr. warden and pres. men's club St. Margaret's Episcopal Ch., 1958-78; mem. charter rev. bd. City of Hialeah (Fla.), 1963-64. Served with USN, 1946-52. Recipient Recognition of Service award St. Margaret's Episcopal Ch., 1977. Mem. Hialeah-Miami Springs Realtors, Fla. Real Estate Brokers. Democrat. Episcopalian. Clubs: Optimist, Masons. Home: 5628 SW 103 Ave Cooper City FL 33328 Office: 7250 NW 36 Ave Miami FL 33147

SHARPE, JAMES RALPH, civil engr.; b. Columbus, Ohio, Apr. 15, 1929; s. Leslie P. and Marion F. (Hall) S.; B.S.C.E., Ohio State U., 1951; m. Sally Knorr, Apr. 8, 1961; 1 son, James Douglas. Construct and project engr. Panhandle Eastern Pipeline, 1954-57; field, project and sales engr. Dravo Corp., Pitts., 1957-63, sales mgr., 1963-66, project mgr., 1966-68; gen. sales mgr. Engring. Constrn. div., 1968-70, gen. mgr., 1970-71, v.p., gen. mgr., 1971-74, group v.p. process, constrn. and engring. group, 1974-76, sr. v.p. mktg., 1976-80, sr. v.p. mktg. and internat., 1978-79; pres. Dravo Engrs. and Constructors, Pitts., 1979—. Served to lt. (j.g.), USNR, 1951-54. Mem. Am. Iron and Steel Inst., Am. Mining Congress. Clubs: Duquesne, Laurel Valley Golf. Office: 1 Oliver Plaza Pittsburgh PA 15222

SHARPE, ROBERT EDWARD, found. exec.; b. Jamaica, West Indies, Oct. 17, 1929; s. Christopher Columbus and Mary Ella Sharpe; B.B.A., Golden Gate U., 1966; M.B.A., Sussex Coll. Tech., 1968; 1 son, David Robert. Employment officer, personnel analyst, asso. dean students U. Calif., Irvine, 1968-71; personnel officer Charles Drew Postgrad. Med. Sch., Los Angeles, 1971-73; asst. dir. employee relations St. Joseph Med. Center, Burbank, Calif., 1973-76; adminstr. environ. health program Pub. Health Found. Los Angeles County, Los Angeles, 1976—; tchr., tng. environ. control technicians, 1976—; cons. environ. health, 1976—; instr., fencing master. Mem. sub-area council Health Systems Agy., Los Angeles, 1977—; bd. dirs. Los Los Angeles Friends of Library. Served with USN, 1950-55. Recipient City of Los Angeles Pub. Service award, 1978. Mem. Am., So. Calif. pub. health assns., Soc. for Advancement Mgmt., Nat. Assn. Pub. Health Adminstrs., Internat. Law Soc., Hosp. Personnel Mgrs. Assn., Nat. Assn. Coll. and Univ. Personnel Adminstrs., Nat. Assn. Fin. Aid Adminstrs., Recreation Soc. Calif., Shakespearian Actors Assn Eng. and Am., Los Angeles Black Health Assos., Golden Gate U. Alumni Assn., Kappa Alpha Psi. Democrat. Episcopalian.

SHATTUCK, JOSEPH BOARDMAN, JR., ins. co. exec.; b. Damariscotta, Maine, Aug. 2, 1925; s. Joseph Boardman and Marcia Vivian (Parker) S.; B.A., U. Maine, 1949; m. Marie David Blaney; children—Henry, June, Pamela, Patricia, William. With Liberty Mut. Ins. Co., 1949—, insp., N.Y.C., 1949-51, engr., Phila., 1951-52, dist. engr., Buffalo, 1953-55, div. engr., Newcastle, Pa., 1955-57, sect. engr., Boston, 1957-62, mgr., 1962-69, div. service mgr. fire protection, 1969—, tech. dir., 1977—. Mem. Salisbury (Mass.) Fin. Bd., 1964-65, Salisbury Planning Bd., 1965-71. Served with USAAF, 1943-45. Registered profl. engr., Mass.; certified safety profl.; cert. master level hazard control mgr. Mem. Soc. Fire Protection Engrs., Am. Soc. Safety Engrs., Ins. Loss Control Assn., Am. Legion. Republican. Baptist. Clubs: Masons, Shriners. Home: 109 Folly Mill Rd Salisbury MA 01950 Office: 13 Riverside Rd Weston MA 02193

SHAUB, HAROLD ARTHUR, food processing co. exec.; b. Lancster, Pa., Nov. 28, 1915; s. Arthur and Clara (Cramer) S.; student Drexel Inst. Tech., 1939, B.A., Temple U., 1942, B.S. in Commerce; m. Eileen B. Bair, Aug. 6, 1939; children—John A., Carole Sue (Mrs. Clifford Hoffman), Lynn E. (Mrs. Bill Benton). Indsl. engr. Talon, Inc., Meadville, Pa., 1941-42; with Campbell Soup Co., Camden, N.J., 1942-49, Chgo., 1949-57, asst. plant mgr., 1953-57; v.p., gen. mgr. Campbell Soup Co. Ltd., Toronto, Ont., Can., 1957-61, pres., 1961-66; pres. Pepperidge Farm, Inc., 1966-68; sr. v.p. Campbell Soup Co., 1968-69, exec. v.p., 1969-72, pres., chief exec. officer, 1972-80, dir., 1970—; dir. Scott Paper, Phila., N.J. Bell Telephone Co., Newark, Exxon Corp., N.Y.C., R.H. Macy & Co., N.Y.C.; internat. adv. council Can. Imperial Bank of Commerce, Toronto, 1976—. Trustee, Drexel U.; bd. mgrs. Franklin Inst. Home: 1250 Country Club Rd Gladwyne PA 19035

SHAUGHNESSY, JOHN WILLIAM, JR., labor union ofcl.; b. East Hartford, Conn., May 1, 1925; s. John William and Catherine (Fitzgerald) S.; m. Elizabeth J. Heffron, May 15, 1948; children—Michael, Brian. Pres., Conn. Union Telephone Workers, 1959—; pres. Telecommunications Internat. Union, 1962—; exec. v.p. Nat. Fedn. Ind. Union, 1963—; v.p. Nat. Ind. Union Council, 1960-63. Mem. Human Relations Council, New Haven, Conn.; mem. U. Conn. Labor Edn. Adv. Commn.; bd. dirs. United Way; mayor, East Hartford, 1965-67; chmn. Town Plan Commn., Bldg. Commn., 1954-59; pres. East Hartford Democratic Town Club, 1967-70; chmn. East Hartford Charter Rev. Commn., 1980. Served with USAAF, 1944-46. Recipient Outstanding Service Award Kidney Found. Conn., 1974, vol. service award Nat. Kidney Found., 1975. Democrat. Roman Catholic. Office: 3055 Dixwell Ave Hamden CT 06518

SHAW, GARY EVERETT, pulp mfg. co. exec.; b. Devils Lake, N.D., Jan. 28, 1941; s. Everett L. and Jeanette V. (Guttu) S.; B.A., U. Portland (Oreg.), 1963; student Conn. Inst. of Internat. Traffic, 1973-74; grad. Civil Affairs Officers Advanced Course, 1979; student Command and Gen. Staff Coll., 1980-81; m. Susan Ruth Suthergreen, Aug. 20, 1977; stepchildren—John N., Susan N.; children by previous marriage—Heidi, Tiffany. Tchr. of English, Hudson's Bay High Sch., Vancouver, Wash., 1963-64, Columbia River High Sch., 1964-65; mgmt. trainee pulp and paper div. of Georgia-Pacific Corp., Portland, 1966-69, W. Coast pulp sales and internat. coordinator, 1969-71, E. Coast pulp sales and statis. analyst trainee, Stamford, Conn., 1972-73, mgr. customer services for domestic pulp and newsprint, 1974-77, mgr. adminstrn. of pulp, paper and board sales, Portland, 1977-78, regional mgr. west coast pulp sales, Portland, 1978-81; mgr. adminstrn., statis. analysis and pulp and container board sales planning Georgia-Pacific Internat., Portland, 1978-81. Chmn. Georgia-Pacific's Explorer Scout Career Program, 1969-71. Served to capt. USAR, 1965-81. Mem. Am. Paper Inst. (vice chmn. pulp and raw materials stats. com. 1977-79, chmn. 1979-81, chmn. internat. stats. com. 1978-79), Paper Bag Inst., Civil Affairs Officers Assn., Res. Officers Assn., Sigma Tau Omega. Republican. Lutheran (deacon 1978-80, trustee 1981). Club: Elks. Editor: Wood Pulp and Fiber Statistics, 1974-76. Home: 9208 NW 15th Ave Vancouver WA 98665 Office: Georgia-Pacific Corp 900 SW 5th Ave Portland OR 97204

SHAW, JOHN GARY, franchise co. exec.; b. North Bay, Ont., Can., Mar. 29, 1934; s. John Louden and Edith (Webber) S.; came to U.S., 1977; B.A. with honours in Bus. Adminstrn., U. Western Ont., 1958; chartered accountant Inst. Chartered Accountants, Ont., 1967; m. Beatrice Arden Louise Lemick, Feb. 2, 1957; children—Andrew, Clyde, Thomas. Audit staff Clarkson Gordon & Co., London, Ont., 1964-67; controller Cuddy Foods, Ltd., Strathroy, Ont., 1967-69; exec. v.p. Pop Shoppes Internat., Toronto, 1969-76; pres. Pop Shoppes of Am., Inc., Denver, 1976-77, Grandma Lee's of Am., Inc., Mpls., 1977-79; pres., dir. Franchise Research Ltd., Cayman Islands, 1979—, Grandma Lee's Internat. Ltd., Cayman Islands, 1979—, Transphere Investments Ltd., Cayman Islands, 1979—; dir. Grandma Lee's Inc. Mem. Inst. Chartered Accountants of Ont. Conservative. Home: PO Box 1575 Grand Cayman Cayman Islands BWI Office: 3258 Wharton Way Toronto ON L4X 2C4 Canada

SHAW, MILTON EUGENE, engring. and contracting co. exec.; b. Macy, Ind., Dec. 2, 1925; s. Bernard Oliver and Mabel Marie (Dawald) S.; B.S. with distinction, Manchester Coll., 1949; M.B.A., Ind. U., 1950, D.B.A., 1969; m. Martha Lou Madeford, May 15, 1948; children—Valerie Elaine Shaw Brown. With Mason & Hanger-Silas Mason Co. Inc., various locations, 1951—, asst. sec., Lexington, 1964-73, v.p. adminstrn., 1973—; also dir.; Mem. Dean's Assos. Ind. U., 1974—. Mem. Am. Def. Preparedness Assn., Blue Grass Personnel Assn., Beta Gamma Sigma, Delta Pi Epsilon, Phi Delta Kappa. Home: 101 S Hanover St Lexington KY 40502 Office: 200 W Vine St Suite 7-A Lexington KY 40507

SHAW, PAUL FRANKLIN, mgmt. cons.; b. Lakewood, Ohio, Dec 18, 1913; m. Fereniki Shaw; children—Robert, Barbara. With Cleve. Graphite Bronze div. Clevite Corp., 1942-52, Am. Safety Razor Corp., Bklyn., 1952-53, Republic Aviation Corp., Farmingdale, L.I., N.Y., 1953-57, NAM, N.Y.C., 1957-59, Commerce and Industry Assn. N.Y., 1959-65; v.p. personnel planning Chase Manhattan Bank, N.Y.C., 1965-72, v.p., dir. employee relations, 1972-76, v.p., dir. corp. labor relations, 1976-77, ret., 1977; cons. employee and internat. labor relations Internat. Mgmt. Advisors, Inc., N.Y.C., 1977—. Served with AUS, 1942-45; ETO. Decorated Bronze Star Medal. Mem. N.Y. Personnel Mgmt. Assn. (past pres.), Indsl. Relations Soc. (past pres.), Indsl. Relations Research Assn. (past pres.), Internat. Indsl. Relations Assn. Home: 240 Broad St Williston Park NY 11596 Office: 485 Lexington Ave Suite 2700 New York NY 10017

SHAW, RALPH HERBERT, II, bank exec.; b. Middletown, Conn., Sept. 11, 1929; s. Ralph Herbert and Ida May (Morgan) S.; B.A., Wesleyan U., Middletown, Conn., 1951: M.B.A., U. Hartford, 1966; m. Jean Shirley Adams, Dec. 27, 1952; children—Deborah, Jeffrey Adams. Personnel asst. Idaho ops. Am. Cyanamid, 1951-52; v.p. Shaw Belting Co., Middletown, 1954-63, pres., treas., 1963-77; pres., treas., chief exec. officer City Savs. Bank Middletown, 1977—; lectr. Middlesex Community Coll., 1967-70. Bd. dirs., vice chmn. Middlesex Meml. Hosp.; bd. dirs., campaign chmn. United Way, Middlesex County; past mem. Middletown Republican Town Com.; active in local planning, inland wetlands agys. Served with CIC, U.S. Army, 1952-54. Mem. Am. Inst. Banking, Conn. Savs. Bank Assn., Nat. Savs. Bank Assn. Episcopalian. Club: Rotary (pres. club 1963) (Middletown). Indsl. inventor. Office: 211 S Main St Middletown CT 06457

SHAW, RAY, pub. co. exec.; b. 1934; ed. Tex. Western U., U. Okla.; married. Mng. editor AP-Dow Jones, Dow Jones & Co., N.Y.C., 1966-71, asst. gen. mgr., 1971-72, dir. devel., 1972-73, v.p. devel., 1973-77, exec. v.p., now pres., chief exec. officer, dir. Office: 22 Cortlandt St New York NY 10007*

SHAW, ROBERT JOSEPH, ins. co. exec.; b. Vienna, Austria, Nov. 21, 1931; came to U.S., 1940, naturalized, 1945; s. Sigmund and Alice S.; B.S., U. Ill., 1953; M.B.A., Wharton Sch., U. Pa., 1958; m. Sharon Reva Walner, Oct. 20, 1973; children—Leonora, Jonathan, Leslie, Nicole. Audit mgr. Arthur Young & Co., Chgo., 1958-67; asst. treas. Combined Ins. Co. of Am., Chgo., 1967-78; v.p., controller National-Ben Franklin LIfe Ins. Corp., Chgo., 1978—. Served with U.S. Army, 1953-55. C.P.A., Ill. Fellow Life Mgmt. Inst.; mem. Planning Execs. Inst. (pres. Chgo. chpt. 1979-80), Ins. Acctg. and Statis. Assn. (dir. Chgo. chpt.), Am. Inst. C.P.A.'s, Am. Mgmt. Assn. Jewish. Office: 360 W Jackson Blvd Chicago IL 60606

SHAW, ROBERT REED, advt. agy. exec.; b. Wilkinson, Ind., Sept. 1, 1922; s. Clyde J. and Effie J. (Reed) S.; grad. high sch.; m. Shirley Riha, July 13, 1972; children—Robert Reed, Nona Jane. With advt. div. Sportservice Corp., 1947-50; dir. advt. S.E. U.S., Midwest Advt. Co., Kansas City, Mo., 1950-54; v.p., account exec. Litman, Stevens & Margolis Advt., Kansas City, 1954-55; exec. v.p., account exec. Christenson, Barclay & Shaw, Inc., Kansas City, 1955—; v.p. Musical Prodns. Inc.; v.p., treas. Broadway Enterprises, Broadway Prodns.; pres. Met. Bank, 1967-70. Pres. Civic Safety Assn., 1960-64; bd. dirs. CB & S Profit Sharing Trust. Served with USNR, 1940-44. Decorated Purple Heart. Mem. Advt. and Exec. Club, United Theatre Owners Assn., Nat. Agrl. Advt. and Mktg. Assn., Internat. Platform Assn. Mason. Clubs: Kansas Century (Topeka); Lake Ozark (Mo.) Yacht Assn. (mem. election bd. 1963-70). Home: 11004 W 96th Terr Overland Park KS 66214 Office: 3130 Broadway Kansas City MO 64111

SHAY, JOHN BERNARD, banker; b. S.I., N.Y., Sept. 24, 1933; s. John A. and Eleanor W. (Elwood) S.; ed. St. Peters Coll., 1956, N.Y. U., 1968-70; m. Dorothy Schöenstein, Jan. 11, 1958; children—Deirdre Aileen, John Christopher, James David. With Chase Nat. Bank (name changed to Chase Manhattan Bank 1955), N.Y.C., 1951—, 2d v.p., 1969—, v.p., 1970—, also mgr. cash mgmt. sales and service depts., 1974—; pres. Chase Manhattan Club, 1964-65, mem. adv. com., 1973—. Served with U.S. Army, 1956-58. Mem. Aircraft Owners and Pilots Assn., Sales Execs. Club N.Y. Home: 78 Windermere Rd New York NY 10305 Office: 1 Chase Manhattan Plaza New York NY 10015

SHEA, DANIEL WILLIAM, mgmt. cons.; b. Arlington, Mass., Nov. 13, 1935; s. Daniel William and Marjorie (Ward) S.; A.B., St. John's U., Brighton, Mass., 1957; J.D., Boston Coll., 1962; m. Marjorie Ann Dever, Sept. 21, 1963; children—Catherine Ann, Carolyn Marie, Susan Elizabeth. Admitted to Mass. bar, 1962, Pa. bar, 1967; labor relations mgr. Sun Shipbldg., Chester, Pa., 1965-68, Indsl. Chem. Group, W.R. Grace & Co., Cambridge, Mass., 1968-72; labor relations atty. Singer Co., N.Y.C., 1972-74; corp. dir. labor relations and EEO, W.R. Grace & Co., 1974-78, v.p. personnel Retail Group, 1978-79; mgmt. cons. specializing in employee relations, Darien, Conn., 1979—. Mem. Darien Planning and Zoning Commn., 1979—. Served to lt., USNR, 1962-65; Vietnam. Mem. Am. Bar Assn., Indsl. Relations Soc. N.Y., Indsl. Relations Research Assn. Democrat. Roman Catholic. Clubs: Noroton Yacht (Darien); Princeton (N.Y.C.). Contbr. to The Labor Law of Canada, 1977. Home: 40 Gardiner St Darien CT 06820 Office: PO Box 2031 Darien CT 06820

SHEA, EDWARD EMMET, chem. co. exec.; b. Detroit, May 29, 1932; s. Edward Francis and Margaret Katherine (Downey) S.; A.B., U. Detroit, 1954; LL.B., U. Mich., 1957; m. Ann Marie Conley, Aug. 28, 1957; children—Michael, Maura, Ellen. Admitted to Mich. bar, 1957, N.Y. bar, 1961; asso. firms Simpson Thacher & Bartlett, N.Y.C., 1960-63, Dykema, Wheat, Spencer, Goodnow & Trigg, Detroit, 1963-69, Cadwalader, Wickersham & Taft, N.Y.C., 1969-71; v.p., dir., gen. counsel Reichhold Chems., Inc., White Plains, N.Y., 1971—, chmn. bd., 1972—; officer, dir. Bluebeard's Castle, Inc. (V.I.), Reichhold Quimica de Mexico, S.A., Reichhold Chem. del Caribe, Inc., Reichhold Energy Corp., Henry Reichhold Found., 1972—; adj. prof. comml. law U. Detroit, 1965-69. Served to 1st lt. SAC, USAF, 1957-60. Mem. Phi Alpha Delta. Roman Catholic. Contbr. articles to profl. jours. Office: 525 N Broadway White Plains NY 10603

SHEA, JOHN JOSEPH, mgmt. cons.; b. Memphis, Nov. 19, 1933; s. John Joseph and Geraldine (Foster) S.; B.S., Memphis State U., 1956; postgrad. Harvard U., 1958-59; m. Virginia Ann Schwartz, Sept. 8, 1962; children—Thomas John, Stephen Michael, Eileen Elizabeth. Project planner, ops. mgr. U.S. Post Office and U.S. Air Force, Memphis, 1952-55; systems engr., account mgr. industry program adminstr. IBM Corp., White Plains, N.Y., 1955-68; mgr. new bus. and acquisition Computer Tech., Inc., Chgo., 1968-70; v.p. Firemen's Fund Am. Ins. Cos., San Francisco, 1973-74; ind. mgmt. cons., Los Altos, Calif., 1970—. Served with U.S. Army, 1956-58. Mem. IEEE. Republican. Roman Catholic. Clubs: Commonwealth of Calif., Fremont Hills Country.

SHEA, RICHARD JAMES, chem. co. exec.; b. Melrose, Mass., Dec. 28, 1936; s. James J. and Margaret Mary (Leary) S.; B.S.in Bus. Adminstrn., Boston Coll., 1958; m. Barbara B. Beaudoin, Apr. 26, 1959; children—Michael, Patricia, Stephen, Brian, Catherine. Public acct. Nat. Polychems. Inc., Wilmington Mass., 1963; acct. exec. Sobin Chem. Co., Boston, 1964; pres. T.H. Glennon Co. Inc., Lawrence, Mass., 1964—. Bd. dirs. YMCA. Served to capt. U.S. Army, Mem. New Eng. Chem. Club. Roman Catholic. Clubs: Bellevue Golf, Oyster Harbors. Home: 90 Orchard Ln Melrose MA 02176 Office: 109 Methuen St Lawrence MA 01840

SHEA, STEPHEN WILLIAM, JR., mfg. co. exec.; b. N.Y.C., Sept. 10, 1941; s. Stephen William and Helen F. (Hannigan) S.; B.S., Holy Cross Coll., 1963; postgrad. U. Grenoble (France), 1966-67; M.B.A., Columbia U., 1969; m. Gail Lilleberg, Aug. 26, 1970; children—Serge, Christian. Mgr. fin. reporting The Singer Co., N.Y.C. and Hanan, Ger.; with Am. Can Co. and subs., dir. employee info. systems, 1976-78, v.p. human resources, 1978-80, v.p. lignin chem. group, 1980—. Served with USMC, 1963-66. Office: Greenwich Office Park Bldg 8 Greenwich CT 06830

SHEAHAN, CLAIRE MATHER, ins. co. exec.; b. Bridgeport, Conn., May 9, 1942; d. Robert Elston and Ruth Evelyn (Allen) S.; B.A., Vassar Coll., 1964. Copy editor Yale U. Press, New Haven, 1964-65; advt. press relations Tchrs. Ins. & Annuity Assn.-Coll. Retirement Equities Fund, N.Y.C., 1965-70, editor employee communications, 1970-72, communications specialist, 1972-78, corp. communications adminstr., 1978-80, asst. publs. officer, 1980—. Mem. Life Advertisers Assn., N.Y. Women in Communications, Pub. Relations Soc. Am., N.Y. Fin. Writers Assn., Internat. Assn. Bus. Communicators, N.Y. Bus. Communicators, Nat. Investor Relations Inst., Am. Mgmt. Assn. Episcopalian. Home: 401 E 65th St New York NY 10021 Office: 730 3d Ave New York NY 10017

SHEARER, ANGUS T., JR., real estate investment co. exec.; b. Tulsa, Apr. 1, 1936; s. Angus T. and Annabelle (Kramer) S.; B.S. in Petroleum Engring., U. Tulsa, 1959; M.B.A., U. Utah, 1973; m. Marilyn Oehmich, June 12, 1958; children—Michael Angus, David Harold. Engr., Dow Chem. Co., N.Mex., Utah, 1959-62; engring. mgr. Litton Industries, Salt Lake City, 1962-70; pres. Wallace Assos., Salt Lake City, 1970—; dir. Wallace Assos., Community Bank, Pioneer Bank. Adj. prof. finance U. Utah. Dowell div. Dow Chem. Co. fellow, 1958. Mem. Bldg. Owners and Mgrs. Assn. (recipient award 1977). Episcopalian. Research in real estate investment analysis. Home: 3700 Gilroy Rd Salt Lake City UT 84109 Office: 1518 Walker Bank Bldg Salt Lake City UT 84111

SHEARER, CHARLES EDWARD, JR., lawyer, financial planner; b. Kokomo, Ind., Sept. 2, 1922; s. Charles Edward and Helen Lorene (Kidder) S.; A.S., Kokomo Jr. Coll., 1943; A.B., Ind. U., 1947, J.D., 1953; m. Ruth Mae Nicholson, June 26, 1948; children—Kay Ellen Gardiner, Beth Ann. Indsl. relations cons. Internat. Harvester Co., Indpls., 1947-51; employee relations dir. Indpls. Rys., 1951-53; mgr.

Shelbyville (Ind.) C. of C., 1953-55; partner firm Fink & Shearer Attys., Shelbyville, 1955-57; agy. supr. L. W. McDougall & Assos., Cleve., 1958-63; div. sales mgr. Coll. Life Ins., Indpls., also prin. Charles E. Shearer, Jr. & Assos. Life Ins. Agy., Indpls., 1964-70; sr. v.p. planning and export expansion Export-Import Bank U.S., Washington, 1970-72; v.p. Nat. Funding Analysts, Inc., Washington, 1972—; individual practice law, Washington, 1972—; dir. life and bus. benefits div. Cook, Treadwell & Harry, Inc., Springfield, Va. Mem. Met. Washington YMCA; trustee U.S. Jaycee Found., Tulsa. Served with inf. U.S. Army, 1943-46. Named 1 of 3 Outstanding Young Men of Ind., Ind. Jaycees, 1957. Mem. Fed., Indpls., D.C. bar assns., Nat. Assn. Life Underwriters, C.L.U.'s. of D.C., Am. Legion, Sigma Pi, Phi Delta Phi. Republican. Episcopalian. Home: 4839 Yorktown Blvd Arlington VA 22207 Office: 1700 Pennsylvania Ave NW Suite 270 Washington DC 20006 also 6501 Loisdale Ct Springfield VA 22150

SHEAROUSE, JOSEPH BAYNARD, JR., banker; b. Savannah, Ga., Oct. 23, 1923; s. Joseph Baynard and Martha (Johnston) S.; B.S., U. Fla., 1947; m. Daphne Connelly, Apr. 7, 1951; children—Joseph Baynard, Lee C., William S. Banking positions, 1947—; v.p. Fidelity Federal Savs. & Loan Assn., West Palm Beach, Fla., 1955-67, exec. v.p., 1967-74, pres., 1974—, mng. officer, 1979—. Served with USAAF, 1942-45. Pres., Heart Assn. Palm Beach County, 1966-68, chmn. bd., 1969; bd. dirs. Fla. affiliate Am. Heart Assn., 1965-76, chmn. bd., 1974-76; pres. Legal Aid Soc. Palm Beach County, 1967. Recipient awards Am. Heart Assn., including Disting. Service award, 1976, Spl. Service award Fla. affiliate, 1975. Mem. Inst. Fin. Edn. (chpt. pres. 1957-58), Palm Beach County Loan Officers Soc. (pres. 1964-65), Fla. Savs. and Loan League (dir. state legis. chmn. 1978-80, chmn. dist. I, 1979-80). Democrat. Episcopalian. Clubs: Mayacoo Lakes Country, Palm Beach Yacht, Sailfish of Fla., Tuscawailla, Rotary (dir. 1964, pres. 1968). Office: 218 Datura St West Palm Beach FL 33401

SHEEHAN, DENNIS WILLIAM, lawyer; b. Springfield, Mass., Jan. 2, 1934; s. Timothy A. and H. Marjorie (Kelsey) S.; B.S., U. Md., 1957; J.D., Georgetown U., 1960, LL.M., 1962; m. Elizabeth M. Hellyer, July 27, 1957; children—Dennis William, Catherine Elizabeth, John Edward. Admitted to D.C. bar, 1960, Md. bar, 1960, Mo. bar, 1976, Ohio bar, 1977; legal asst. to chmn. NLRB, Washington, 1960-61; trial atty. U.S. SEC, Washington, 1962-63; corporate atty. Martin-Marietta, Balt., N.Y.C., 1963-64; v.p., gen. counsel, sec. Bunker Ramo Corp., Oak Brook, Ill., 1964-73; exec. v.p., gen. counsel Diversified Industries, Inc., St. Louis, 1973-75, also dir.; v.p., gen. counsel, dir. N-Ren Corp., Cin., 1975-77; v.p., sec., gen. counsel Bliss & Laughlin, Oak Brook, Ill., 1977—; dir. Ames Taping Tools of Can. Ltd., Ont., Jensen Tools, Inc., Phoenix, Compagnie Fischbein S.A., Brussels, BLK Steel, Chgo. Served with AUS, 1954-56. Mem. Am., Fed., Cin., Mo. bar assns., Am. Soc. Corp. Secs., Licensing Execs. Soc., Phi Delta Phi, Pi Sigma Alpha, Delta Sigma Phi. Republican. Clubs: Nat. Lawyers, Metropolitan (Washington); St. Louis; Bankers (Cin.); Economic (Chgo.). Home: 450 Lexington Dr Lake Forest IL 60045 Office: 122 W 22d St Oak Brook IL 60521

SHEEHAN, KENNETH EDWARD, shipping bur. exec.; b. N.Y.C., Aug. 12, 1946; s. William Arvis and Anne Veronica S.; B.S.B.A. in Fin., Georgetown U., 1968; J.D., Fordham U., 1972; children—Megan, Kristen, Elaine. Admitted to N.Y. bar, 1973; law clk., then atty. firm Kirlin, Campbell & Keating, N.Y.C., 1969-76; counsel Am. Bur. Shipping, N.Y.C., 1976—, v.p., 1978—; dir. ABS Group Cos., Inc., ABS Properties, Inc., Am. Bur. Shipping (Hong Kong) Ltd. Founding trustee Mus. Arts N.J. Mem. Soc. Naval Architects and Marine Engrs., Am. Bar Assn., Maritime Law Assn. U.S., N.Y. State Bar Assn., N.J. Bar Assn., Essex County Bar Assn. Roman Catholic. Clubs: Essex Fells Country, Whitehall Lunch. Home: 14 Cypress Ave North Caldwell NJ 07006 Office: 65 Broadway New York NY 10006

SHEEHAN, ROBERT THOMAS, cosmetic co. exec.; b. Bklyn., Mar. 15, 1937; s. Andrew Thomas and Eleanor Frances (Garrett) S.; B.B.A., CCNY, 1958; M.A., N.Y. U., 1959; m. Elizabeth Ellen Jones, Sept. 12, 1964; children—Kerith Leah, Robert Vaughan, Jonathan Lindsay. Fin. analyst Ford Motor Co., Dearborn, Mich., 1961-62; mgr. customer surveys AT&T, N.Y.C., 1962-67; product mgr. Schering Labs., Union, N.J., 1967-69; dir. mktg. Avon Products Inc., London and N.Y.C., 1969-79; pres. Vis-A-Vis, Inc., N.Y.C., 1979—, also dir. Served with U.S. Army, 1958-60. Mem. Direct Selling Assn., Cosmetic, Fragrance and Toiletries Assn., Princeton Soccer Assn. (dir.), Am. Mktg. Assn. Republican. Episcopalian. Clubs: N.Y. Athletic. Home: 660 Pretty Brook Rd Princeton NJ 08540

SHEERIN, HARRY JOHN, paper co. exec.; b. Menasha, Wis., Feb. 4, 1918; s. Harry S. and Julia (Malina) S.; student Lawrence U., 1938-39; m. Jeanne E. Shand, May 28, 1949; 1 dau., Kathleen. With Kimberly Clark Corp., 1940—, mng. dir. Kimberly Clark of Australia, Sydney, 1963-65, v.p., gen. mgr. consumer products div. parent corp., 1965-70, exec. v.p. ops., 1970-71, exec. v.p., 1971-72, pres. Kimberly-Clark Corp., 1972-78, also dir. Served with USAAF, 1941-45. Republican. Roman Catholic. Clubs: Optimist, Elks (Neenah). Home: 218 Congress St Neenah WI 54956 Office: Kimberly Clark Corp N Lake St Neenah WI 54956

SHEETS, FRANK THOMAS, JR., cement co. exec.; b. Springfield, Ill., Feb. 5, 1916; s. Frank Thomas and Naomi Gault (Launder) S.; B.S.C.E., Purdue U., 1938; m. Frances Converse Deal, Nov. 5, 1938; children—Joan, Elizabeth Converse Sheets Richter, Frank Thomas III. With Southwestern Portland Cement Co., 1938—, beginning as sales rep. and engr., successively with ops. and engring., dir. engring. and mfg., v.p., exec. v.p. and gen. mgr., 1938-71, pres., Los Angeles, 1971—, also dir.; dir. Southdown, Inc. Served to lt. USNR, 1942-46. Mem. ASCE, Portland Cement Assn., Sigma Xi, Phi Kappa Psi, Chi Epsilon. Clubs: Jonathan, San Gabriel Country, Valley Hunt. Office: 3055 Wilshire Blvd Los Angeles CA 90010

SHEFF, TINA YU HENG TENG LI, art co. exec.; b. Nanking, China, Nov. 22, 1939; d. Chieh and C.H. (Tai) Teng; M.S.W., N.Y. U., 1961; student Art Students League, Fashion Inst. Tech., 1969-71; m. Donald Sheff, June 21, 1978. Supr. psychiat. social work dept. Meyer Psychiat. Hosp., N.Y.C., 1961-71; pres. Yu Heng Art Co., N.Y.C., 1971—; exhibited one-person shows: China Art Atelier, N.Y.C., 1969. The Way Gallery, N.Y.C., 1970, Jordan March, Miami, 1971. Mem. Nat. Assn. Social Workers, Acad. Cert. Social Workers, Met. Mus. Art, Mus. Modern Art, Am. Ballet Theater Guild. Home: 303 E 57th St New York NY 10022 Office: 880 3d Ave New York NY 10022

SHEFFERT, MARK WARREN, JR., ins. co. exec.; b. Lincoln, Nebr., May 17, 1947; s. Mark Warren and Neneen Marcell (Maxey) S.; grad. U. Minn., 1969, grad. Exec. Program, Grad. Sch. Bus.; LL.B., LeSalle U., 1972; m. Danya Ann Spencer, Apr. 23, 1973; children—Mark Warren, Christopher Douglas. Various mgmt. positions Prudential Life Ins. Co., Mpls. and Detroit, 1970-77; div. v.p. N.Central Life Ins. Co., St. Paul, 1977-78, sr. v.p. mktg., 1978-79, exec. v.p., chief mktg. officer, 1979-80, sr. exec. v.p., chief operating officer, dir., 1980—. Active, Republican Party, YMCA; chmn. Needy Children's Christmas Party, St. Paul, 1979; mem. Fellowship of Christian Athletes, St. Paul. Recipient nat. mgrs. award Gen. Agts. and Mgrs. Assn., 1976, various industry and co. awards. Mem. Nat. Assn. Life Underwriters, S. Oakland County Life Underwriters (pres. 1973), Coll. Life Underwriters, Gold Key Soc. Lutheran. Club: St. Paul Athletic, Normandale Tennis. Home: 309 Brandywine Dr Burnsville MN 55337 Office: 275 E 4th St Saint Paul MN 55101

SHEFFIELD, LARRY AUGUSTUS, telephone co. exec.; b. Troy, N.Y., Jan. 8, 1944; s. Britt Richard and Elise Elizabeth S.; B.A. in Fin. and Bus. Econs., U. Notre Dame, 1965; postgrad. N.Y. U., 1969-70; m. Juanita Williams, June 25, 1965; children—Yolanda Elise, Gretchen Nicole. Asst. to treas. Assos. Investment, South Bend, Ind., 1965-67; accountant and fin. systems cons. Arthur Andersen & Co., N.Y.C., 1967-69; internal audit mgr. Thomson & McKinnon Auchincloss Kohlmeyer, Inc., N.Y.C., 1969-73; supr. internal auditing AT&T, N.Y.C., 1973-74, mgr. internal auditing, 1974-75, dir. cost acctg. classification, 1975-76, mgr. accounting principles, 1976-78, mgr. corporate accounting, 1978, dir. functional acctg. gen. depts., 1978-79, dir. acctg. classification, 1979-80, dir. fin. matters, 1981—; chief statistician N.J. Bell Telephone Co., Newark, 1975-76; vis. prof. Black Exec. Exchange Program, Urban League, 1972—. Chmn., Leadership Inst. N.J., 1977; chmn. sustaining membership enrollment Boy Scouts Am., 1975-76; chmn. allocations com. United Way of Essex and West Hudson, 1975-77; mem. adv. council Black Achievers, Harlem YMCA, 1979—; bd. dirs. Push Operation, N.J., Harlem YMCA, 1979—, Harlem Dowling Children's Service, 1980—. Named N.J. Jaycee of Year, 1974; C.P.A., Ind. Mem. Am. Inst. C.P.A.'s, Nat. Assn. Black Accountants, Inst. Internal Auditors. Home: 185 Christopher St Montclair NJ 07042 Office: 195 Broadway New York NY 10007

SHEFTEL, ROGER TERRY, cons. and investment banking exec.; b. Denver, Sept. 10, 1941; s. Edward and Dorothy (Barnett) S.; B.S. in Econs., U. Pa., 1963; m. Phoebe A. Sherman, Sept. 7, 1968; children—Tisha B., Ryan B. Comml. lending officer Provident Nat. Bank, Phila., 1963-65; asst. to pres. Continental Finance Corp., Denver, 1965-68; v.p. Eastern Indsl. Leasing Corp., Phila., 1968-71, exec. v.p., dir., 1971-73; exec. v.p., dir. HBE Leasing Corp., Phila., 1971-73; pres., dir. Zebley & Strouse, Inc., Phila., 1973-75; dir. Kooly Kupp, Inc., Boyertown, Pa., 1974-77, pres., dir., 1977; prin. Trivest, Phila., 1973-77; pres. Trivest, Inc., Phila., 1977-78, 1670 Corp., mgmt. cons.'s, 1978—, Howard Research Assos., 1980—; prin. Braewood Assos., 1975—, Westchester Pike Assos., Ltd., 1975-78, CVS Assos., 1976-77. Mem. bd. organized classes, exec. com. U. Pa. Mem. Archaeol. Inst. Am., Kite and Key Soc. Clubs: Nantucket Yacht; Friars. Home: 414 Barclay Rd Rosemont PA 19010 Office: One Daylesford Sta 1273 Lancaster Ave Berwyn PA 19312

SHEFTON, JOHN HERBERT, info. systems officer; b. Phila., Jan. 8, 1948; s. Herbert E. and Ethel L. (Drew) S.; B.S., St. Josephs Coll., 1969; M.B.A., U. Pa., 1975; m. Marcia Y. Hamilton, Nov. 12, 1977; 1 son, John. Mgmt. trainee, 1st Pa. Bank, Phila., 1968-69; data preparation mgr. Phila. Nat. Bank, 1972-76, mgr. quality control, 1976—. Pres., Phila. Fin. Basketball League. Served with AUS, 1969-72. Mem. Am. Soc. Quality Control (vice chmn. banking com.). Democrat. Episcopalian. Home: 395 Hillside Rd King of Prussia PA 19406 Office: Three Girard Plaza Philadelphia PA 19106

SHEHAN, THOMAS PATRICK, pension and ins. co. exec.; b. Balt., Apr. 24, 1935; s. John Brooke and Margaret Irene (Anderson) S.; A.B. cum laude, U. Notre Dame, 1957; m. Patricia A. Mullikin, Apr. 26, 1958; children—Jennifer B., Thomas Patrick II, Katherine W., James C. With Conn. Gen. Life Ins. Co., Pitts., 1960—, mgr., 1967—; founder, pres. Shehan-Day & Assos. Inc., pension actuaries and consultants, Pitts., 1976—. Bd. advisers Carlow Coll., Pitts.; v.p. Western Pa. Leukemia Soc. Served to capt. U.S. Army, 1958-60. C.L.U. Mem. Am. Soc. Pension Actuaries, Gen. Agts. and Mgrs. Assn., Soc. C.L.U.'s. Clubs: Duquesne, Pitts. Field, Fox Chapel Racquet (dir.). Home: 442 Dorseyville Rd Pittsburgh PA 15215 Office: 1260 Kossman Bldg Pittsburgh PA 15222

SHEINBERG, SIDNEY JAY, motion picture co. exec.; b. Corpus Christi, Jan. 14, 1935; s. Harry and Tillie (Grossman) S.; A.B., Columbia Coll., 1955; LL.B., Columbia U., 1958; m. Lorraine Gottfried, Aug. 19, 1956; children—Jonathan J., William David. Admitted to Calif. bar, 1958; asso. in law U. Calif. Sch. Law, Los Angeles, 1958-59; with MCA, Inc., Universal City, Calif., 1959—, pres. TV div., 1971-74, exec. v.p. parent co., 1969-73, pres. parent co., 1973—. Mem. Assn. Motion Picture and TV Producers (chmn. bd.). Office: MCA Inc 100 Universal City Plaza Universal City CA 91608*

SHELATO, ORVILLE, contractor; b. Humerick, Ill., Oct. 6, 1900; s. Frank and Chova (Adams) S.; grad. high sch.; m. Florence B. Linck, Apr. 2, 1921; children—Robert, Helen, Jack. Timekeeper, supt., partner McCalman Constrn. Co., Danville, Ill., 1919—. Served with AC, U.S. Army, 1917-18. Mem. Asso. Gen. Contractors Ill. (dir. 1950-52, pres. 1953), Asso. Gen. Contractors Am., Ind. Hwy. Constructors. Mason (32 deg.), Elk. Club: Danville Country. Home: 10 Shorewood Dr S Danville IL 61832 Office: 649 Section St Danville IL 61832

SHELBURNE, C. DANIEL, banker; b. Green Bay, Va., Mar. 31, 1915; s. Thomas Pettus and Mabel (Daniel) S.; B.S., Hampden-Sydney Coll., 1936; M.B.A., U. Pa., 1939-40; postgrad. Stonier Grad. Sch. Banking, 1946-49; m. Edith McDaniel, Dec. 27, 1941; children—John Daniel, Edward McDanel, Thomas Maynard. Sr. bank examiner Fed. Res. Bank, Richmond, Va., 1945-50; with Wachovia Bank & Trust Co., N.A., Winston-Salem, N.C., and Raleigh, N.C., 1950-80, v.p. in charge loan adminstrn. dept., Raleigh, 1955-69, sr. v.p. in charge corp. loan adminstrn. dept., 1969-80; sr. v.p.-treas. N.C. Savs. Guaranty Corp., Raleigh, 1980—; dir. Bus. Devel. Corp. N.C., 1974-80; instr. Grad. Sch. Consumer Banking, U. Va., 1961-78, trustee, 1972-75. Bd. dirs. Wake Tech. Inst. Found.; active Salvation Army, Boy Scouts Am.; past pres. Mental Health Bd. Wake County, Raleigh. Served with Supply Corps, USNR, 1941-45; lt. comdr., ret. Recipient Silver Beaver award Boy Scouts Am., 1969. Mem. C. of C., Robert Morris Assos., Sigma Chi. Episcopalian. Clubs: Carolina Country, Execs. (Raleigh). Home: 2551 Wake Dr Raleigh NC 27608 Office: PO Box 2688 Raleigh NC 27602

SHELDON, DONALD ROCKWELL, ins. broker; b. East Orange, N.J., June 10, 1912; s. John Guyon and Emma May (Sherwood) S.; student Princeton U., 1929-33; A.B., Air U., 1947; m. Miriam I. Kelly, Nov., 1951. With Crum & Forster, 1933-42; with Gen. Fire and Casualty Co., 1955-60, sec., 1960-71; with Consol. Ins. Cos., Bklyn., 1960-71, v.p., 1972; owner, chief exec. officer Allamuchy Agy., Sparta, N.J., 1972—. Founder, 1st pres. Boys Clubs of Newark, Inc. Served with USAAF, 1942-46. Decorated Bronze Star; recipient Bronze Keystone, Boys Clubs Am., 1955. Mem. Ind. Ins. Agents Assn. Republican. Presbyterian. Clubs: Princeton (N.Y.C.); Nassau (Princeton); Lehigh Valley (Allentown, Pa.); Lake Mohawk Country, Masons, Shriners, K.T. Home: 7 E Shore Trail Sparta NJ 07871 Office: 46 Main St Sparta NJ 07871

SHELDON, NANCY W., mgmt. cons.; b. Bryn Mawr, Pa., Nov. 10, 1944; d. John Harold and Elizabeth Sample (Hoff) Way; B.A., Wellesley Coll., 1966; M.A., Columbia U., 1968, M.Phil., 1972; m. Robert Charles Sheldon, June 15, 1968. Mgmt. cons. ABT Assos., Cambridge, Mass., 1969-70; mgmt. cons., v.p. Harbridge House, Inc., Boston, N.Y.C., Los Angeles, 1970-79; pres. Resource Assessment, Inc., Los Angeles, 1979—; partner Resource Devel. Assos., Los Angeles, 1980—, Anubis Group, Ltd., Los Angeles, 1980—. Registered pvt. investigator, Calif. Mem. AAAS, Am. Public Transit Assn., Los Angeles C. of C. Club: Wellesley (Los Angeles). Author: The Economic and Social Benefits of Public Transit, 1973. Contbr. articles to profl. jours. Office: 2261 Stradella Rd Los Angeles CA 90024

SHELDON, ROGER ALPHA, printing and pub. co. exec.; b. Baton Rouge, May 12, 1922; s. William Hannaman and Arta (Sims) S.; B.A., La. State U., 1942, postgrad., 1946; m. Suzanne R. Eaton, Jan. 30, 1972; children by previous marriage—Mark, Elizabeth (Mrs. Alan Danneman), Bonnie (Mrs. Craig Eaton), Paul, David, Patricia. Dep. information officer Houston regional office WAA, 1946-47; account exec. George Kirksey & Assos., Houston, 1947-49; pub. relations counsel Tex. div., Am. Cancer Soc., Houston, 1949-51; editor-writer Merkle Press, Inc., Washington, 1951-61, v.p., editorial dir., 1962-71, v.p. spl. projects, 1971—; information officer Pres.'s Commn. on Status of Women, Washington, 1962. Troop committeeman Nat. Capitol Area council Boy Scouts Am., 1968-76; community relations chmn. Allied Civic Group, Montgomery County, Md., 1955-56. Democratic precinct chmn., Montgomery County, 1968-70. Served with USAAF, World War II. Decorated Air medal; recipient Service certificate Boy Scouts Am., 1960. Mem. Internat. Platform Assn. Unitarian. Club: Nat. Press. Author: Opportunities in Carpentry Careers; This Is Your Washington. Home: 6113 Massachusetts Ave Bethesda MD 20016 Office: 101 Constitution Ave NE Washington DC 20001

SHELL, ROBERT JAMES, contractor; b. Honolulu, Oct. 16, 1930; s. Roscoe and Gladys Rose (Callahan) S.; student Little Rock U., 1947-48; m. Virginia Louise Brooks, Apr. 7, 1973; children—Linda (Mrs. Mark Squires), Vickie, Scott, Cathy, Allison. With Baldwin Co., Little Rock, 1950—, sec., 1961—, treas., 1963-79, v.p.-treas., 1979—, also dir.; sec.-treas., dir. River City Investment Co.; pres. Builders Investment Co. Chmn., Little Rock Censor Bd., 1969—; mem. Little Rock Bd. Adjustment; bd. dirs. Broadmoor Property Owners Assn., 1972-73. Mem. Associated Gen. Contractors Ark. (pres.). Baptist (deacon). Home: 30 St Andrews St Little Rock AR 72207 Office: 322 Gaines St Little Rock AR 72203

SHELLEY, FLORENCE DUBROFF, author, editor, lectr.; b. Balt., Jan. 21, 1921; d. Nathan and Charlotte (Weisman) Dubroff; A.B., Barnard Coll., 1940; M.S., Columbia U., 1941; m. Edwin F. Shelley, Aug. 29, 1941; children—Carolyn Jane, William Edson. Writer, editor public relations dept. J. Walter Thompson Co., N.Y.C., 1941-47; free-lance editor, public relations cons., New Rochelle, N.Y., 1959—; editorial and edn. cons., dir. E.F. Shelley & Co., N.Y.C., 1965-75; cons. Nat. Commn. on Resources for Youth, 1971-75, Nat. Program Ednl. Leadership, 1972-74; pub. Edn.-Tng. Market Report, 1970-73. Pres. New Rochelle Council PTA's, 1964-66, Inwood Community Sch., N.Y.C., 1951-52; mem. adv. com. New Rochelle Community Action Program; bd. dirs. N.Y. State Citizens Council, Universal Solar Systems, New Rochelle. Mem. Am. Acad. Polit. Sci., Am. Ednl. Research Assn., Edn. Writers Assn., Nat. Soc. Study Edn. Charter League (dir.), Nat. Council on Aging. Author: (with Jane Otten) When Your Parents Grow Old, 1976. Office: 339 Oxford Rd New Rochelle NY 10804

SHELLEY, ROGER, pub. relations co. exec.; b. Kew Gardens, N.Y., Sept. 21, 1942; s. Robert and Audrey Jane (Rich) S.; B.A., Miami U., Oxford, Ohio, 1964. Dir. pub. info. Coll. Physicians and Surgeons, Columbia U., N.Y.C., 1966-67; dir. office sci. and med. pub. relations Rutgers U., New Brunswick, N.J., 1968-69; v.p., account exec. Ruder & Finn Inc., N.Y.C., 1969-76; dir. investor relations Revlon Inc., 1976-80, v.p. investor relations, 1980, v.p. corp. affairs and investor relations, pres. Revlon Found., 1980—; instr. pub. relations N.Y.U. Served with U.S. Army, 1965, 68-69. Recipient Paul B. Zucker award. Mem. Nat. Investor Relations Inst., Pub. Relations Soc. Am. Home: 301 E 62d St New York NY 10021 Office: 767 Fifth Ave New York NY 10022

SHELLOW, ROBERT, mgmt. cons. firm exec.; b. Milw., Sept. 22, 1929; s. Henry G. and Sadie Rae (Myers) S.; B.A., Reed Coll., 1951; M.A., U. Mich., 1952, Ph.D., 1955; m. Dorothea Laadt, Aug. 30, 1963; children—Sarah Katherine, Leslie Suzzane. Chief spl. projects sect. NIMH, USPHS, 1955-68; research dir. Nat. Adv. Commn. on Civil Disorders, 1967-68; dir. pilot police dist. Dept. Public Safety, D.C. Govt., 1968-70; prof. Carnegie-Mellon U., Pitts., 1970-75; mgmt. cons., Washington, 1975-78; v.p. Blackstone Assos., Washington, 1977-78; pres. Imar Corp., Washington, 1978—. Served with USAF, 1949-50. Recipient award Fed. Exec. Bd., 1972; USPHS fellow, 1953-54. Mem. Am. Psychol. Assn., Soc. Study Social Problems, Sigma Xi. Author: (with M. Bard) Issues in Law Enforcement, 1976; contbr. articles to profl. jours. Office: 1120 Nat Press Bldg Washington DC 20045

SHELNUTT, ROBERT CURTIS, mfg. co. exec.; b. Shawmut, Ala., Sept. 2, 1928; s. Curtis Lee and Odell (Campbell) S.; B.S. in Chemistry, U. Ga., 1954; M.B.A., Pepperdine U., 1981; m. Faye Mahan; children—Robert Curtis, Susan Elaine. With Am. Enka Co., Lowland, Tenn., 1954-79, gen. tech. supr. chem., spinning and finishing depts., 1969-71, tech. mgr. rayon filament plant, 1971-75, tech. mgr. rayon staple plant, 1975-76, energy and devel. mgr. rayon staple plant, 1976-77, energy and devel., mgr. Tenn. ops., 1977-79; gen. mgr. chem. ops. Chatsworth div. Organon Teknika Corp., Chatsworth, Calif., 1979-81, dir. mfg. and chem. engring. research and devel., Oklahoma City, 1981—. Served with USAF, 1946-49. Mem. Am. Mgmt. Assn. Republican. Home: 9105 Pebble Ln Oklahoma City OK 73132 Office: 5300 S Portland Oklahoma City OK 73119

SHELTON, DAVID HOWARD, bus. educator, univ. adminstr.; b. Winona, Miss., Nov. 30, 1928; s. Tuttle Moses and Kate (Moss) S.; B.A., Millsaps Coll., 1951; M.A., Ohio State U., 1952, Ph.D., 1958; m. Margaret Murff Shelton, Feb. 4, 1951; children—David Keith, Sarah Katherine, Susan Esther. Market analyst Nationwide Ins. Cos., Columbus, Ohio, 1954-56; mem. faculty U. Del., Newark, 1958-65, asso. prof., 1963-65; prof. U. N.C., Greensboro, 1965—, dean Sch. Bus. and Econs., 1970—; pres. N.C. Council on Econ. Edn., 1972—. Served with USNR, 1946-48. Mem. Omicron Delta Kappa, Beta Gamma Sigma. Episcopalian. Office: 401 Bus and Econs Bldg Univ of NC Greensboro NC 27412

SHELTON, HORACE P., JR., lawyer; b. Knoxville, Tenn., June 28, 1916; s. Horace Preston and Mary Elizabeth (Anderson) S.; student U. Tenn., 1935-36; J.D., St. Mary's U., 1940, 46-47; m. Dorothy Adele Fresenius, Dec. 29, 1948; children—Preston F., Elizabeth Adele. Announcer, prodn., radio sta. WNOX, Knoxville, 1933-36, KTSA, San Antonio, 1936-37, KMAC, 1937-40; admitted to Tex. bar, 1947, Tenn., 1975, practiced in San Antonio; asso. Moursund, Ball, Moursund & Bergstrom, 1947-49, Hoyo Wideman & Shelton, 1949-54, Hoyo, Shelton & Haight, 1954-62; individual practice, 1962-76; legal cons., 1976—. Served from 2d lt. to lt. col., AUS, 1940-46; mem. Res. Mem. San Antonio, Williamson County bar assns., Tex. State Bar, Am. Legion, Res. Officers Assn., Mil. Order

World Wars, Sojourners. Episcopalian. Mason (32 deg., Shriner, Jester). Home: 110 Springdale Dr Franklin TN 37064

SHELTON, JAMES ROBERT, banker; b. Fort Worth, July 16, 1942; s. Floyd Odell and Violet Anita (Senter) S.; B.B.A., Tex. Christian U., 1965; grad. Southwestern Grad. Sch. Banking, So. Methodist U., 1974, Am. Inst. Banking, Midland, Tex., 1975; m. Leslie Ann Cohn Foor, Mar. 7, 1981; children by previous marriage—James Craig, Ron David, Wade Travis. Trust officer Fort Worth Nat. Bank, 1965-73; v.p., trust officer Midland Nat. Bank (Tex.), 1973-78; sr. v.p., trust officer City Nat. Bank of Austin (Tex.), 1978—. Pres., chmn. bd. dirs. Midland County chpt. March of Dimes, 1974-78, mem. Travis County chpt., 1978—; dir. Midland chpt. Am. Cancer Soc., 1975-78; former bd. dirs., 1st v.p. Permian Civic Ballet Assn., 1977-78. Mem. Am. Inst. Banking, Tex. Bankers Assn. (profl. relations com. 1978-79, legis. com. 1979-81), Estate Planning Council of Central Tex. (dir. 1981-82), Phi Delta Theta. Republican. Methodist. Clubs: Citadel of Austin, Country of Austin. Home: 11104 Santa Cruz Austin TX 78759 Office: 9th at Congress Austin TX 78701

SHELTON, JOHN BANNER, broadcasting exec.; b. Mayodan, N.C., July 5, 1916; s. Walter Roscoe and Minetti (Fulton) S.; A.A., Mars Hill Coll., 1939; m. Mary Helen Carter, Nov. 15, 1941. Order clk. Gem Dandy, Inc., Madison, N.C., 1939-40, asst. supt., 1940-48; founder, pres., dir. Mayo Broadcasting Corp., Madison, 1948—; chmn. bd. dirs. Bank of Eden (N.C.), 1973—. Chmn., Republican Party 5th Dist. N.C., 1958—. Trustee Morehead Meml. Hosp. Mem. Rockingham County Fine Arts Festival Assn. (membership chmn. 1958-60, pres. 1960-62), Mars Hill Bus. Club Alumni Assn. (pres. 1939-40, 63-64). AIM (fellow pres.'s council). Baptist. Rotarian. Club: Deep Springs Country (Madison). Home: Rural Route 1 Stoneville NC 27048 Office: POB 311 Madison NC 27025

SHENK, JOHN HENRY, engring. co. exec.; b. Junction City, Kans., Dec. 19, 1939; s. Henry Arthur and Katherine Phobe (Frick) S.; B.S.B.A., U. Kans., 1963, B.S.C.E., 1963. Constrn. engr. Dupont Corp., Seaford, Del., 1963; engring. supt. Tumpane Co., Sinop, Turkey, 1965-67; with Pacific Architects and Engrs., Inc. and subs., 1967—, v.p. PAE, Bangkok, Thailand, 1971-72, v.p. S.E. Asia, Pacific Architects and Engrs., Inc., Bangkok, 1972-80, sr. v.p. Pacific Architects and Engrs., Inc., 1980—; dir. PAE Internat., PAE (Thailand) Co. Ltd., Pacific Architects and Engrs. Co., Ltd., Pacific Services Co. Ltd., Pacarchs Services Co. Ltd., Maenning Corp., Syalin PAE/RMI Sdn. Bhd., Service Systems PTE Ltd.; mng. dir. Equipment Logistics Ltd., PAE & RMI Ltd. Served to 1st lt. C.E., U.S. Army, 1963-65. Decorated Army Commendation medal, Army Commendation medal with oak leaf cluster (U.S.); for pub. service (Thailand). Mem. ASCE, Soc. Am. Mil. Engrs., Delta Upsilon (Man of Yr. 1961). Home: 39 Pongsrichan Sapenkwai Suthisarn Bangkok Thailand Office: 5th Floor Jardines Bldg 1032/1-5 Rama IV Road Bangkok Thailand

SHENKUS, ROBERT DENNIS, ins. co. exec.; b. Woodbury, N.J., Dec. 31, 1947; s. Edward Vincent and Mary Frances (O'Brien) S.; B.S. in Mgmt.-Mktg., St. Joseph's Coll., Phila., 1970; C.L.U., 1978; m. Alison Keach, Dec. 5, 1970; children—Jennifer Leigh, Kristen Anne. With Lincoln Nat. Life Ins. Co., Ft. Wayne, Ind., 1970—, group and pension mgr., Balt., 1971-74, regional group and pension mgr., Camp Hill, Pa., 1975—; speaker, lectr. in field. Mem. Nat. Assn. Life Underwriters, Soc. C.L.U.'s, Harrisburg Assn. Life Underwriters (exec. bd. dirs.), Life Underwriter Tng. Council (chmn.), Pinebrook Civic Assn., W. Shore C. of C. (dir. council govt.), Delta Sigma Pi. Republican. Episcopalian. Home: 3811 Bellows Dr Camp Hill PA 17011 Office: 209 Senate Ave Camp Hill PA 17011

SHENNUM, ROBERT HERMAN, telephone co. exec.; b. Scobey, Mont., Apr. 12, 1922; s. Joseph M. and Nellie M. (Robinson) S.; B.S. in Elec. Engring., Mont. State Coll., 1944, M.S., 1948, D. Engring. (hon.), 1963; Ph.D., Calif. Inst. Tech., 1954; m. Doris Postlewait, Mar. 16, 1947; children—Sharon, Keith, Marsha. Instr. elec. engring. Mont. State Coll., 1946-50, Calif. Inst. Tech., Pasadena, 1950-54; cons. Kelman Electric Co., Los Angeles, 1954; elec. engr. transmission and electronic devel. Bell Telephone Labs., Whippany, N.J., 1954—, planner, supr., tech. dir. bldg. TELSTAR satellite, 1966—. Served to 1st. lt., Signal Corp., U.S. Army, 1944-46; ETO. Mem. IEEE (sr.), Sigma Xi. Republican. Methodist. Contbr. articles to profl. publs., patentee signalling Pulse Code Modulation transmission system. Home: 110 Highland Ave Chatham Twp NJ 07928 Office: Bell Labs Whippany Rd Whippany NJ 07981

SHEPARD, CHARLES VIRGIL, human resource exec.; b. Springfield, Ill., Nov. 14, 1940; s. Charles Woodrow and Catherine Elizabeth (Vlakovich) S.; B.A. in Bus. Adminstrn. and Econs., 1962; postgrad. U. Ill. at Urbana, 1966-72; M.B.A., Sangamon State U., 1972; m. Judy A. Wells; children—Cynthia Lynn, Kimberly Lynn. With Allis-Chalmers Corp., Springfield, 1962-73, supr. employee benefits, 1962-67, adminstrv. asst., 1967-68, mgr. personnel services, 1968-70, mgr. orgn. planning and devel., 1970-72, mgr. indsl. relations, 1972-73; mem. corp. indsl. relations staff Rockwell Internat. Corp., Dallas, 1973, dir. indsl. relations, 1973-74, group dir. personnel, 1974-76, v.p. personnel, 1976-77, staff v.p. electronics personnel, 1977-78, corp. staff v.p. employee relations, 1978—, v.p. human resources Gen. Industries, 1980—. Mem. Adv. Council Amigos de Ser, 1976—; mem. adv. bd. Richland Coll., 1975-76; bd. dirs. Jr. Achievement, Dallas Theater Center, Pitts. Public Theatre, 1979—. Mem. Electronic Industries Assn. (indsl. relations council), Am. Soc. Personnel Adminstrn., Dallas C. of C. (dir. 1974-76). Republican. Methodist. Club: Masons. Home: 307 Butternut Ct Fox Chapel PA 15238 Office: Rockwell Internat Pittsburgh PA 15208

SHEPARD, CLARENCE DAY, oil co. exec.; b. Winnipeg, Man., Can., July 31, 1914; s. Clarence Day and May S. (Merrill) S.; ed. McGill U., Montreal, 1931-33; LL.B., U. Man., 1937; m. Caroline Faith Spring, Apr. 23, 1938; children—Clarence Day, Caroline Shepard Nagle, Merrill, Sarah. Called to bar, 1938; internal solicitor Grain Ins. and Guarantee Co., Winnipeg, 1937-39; Western supr. Phoenix Ins. of Hartford Group, Winnipeg, 1939-40; partner firm Thompson, Shepard, Dilts, Jones & Hall., Winnipeg, 1945-57; lectr. Man. Law Sch., 1949-53; chief commr. Bd. Transp. Commrs., Ottawa, 1957-58; acting chmn. Air Transp. Bd., Ottawa, 1958-59; with Gulf Can., 1959-79, chmn. bd., dir., 1964—, chief exec. officer, 1976-80; dir. Toronto Dominion Bank. Chmn., Winnipeg Civic Election Com., 1950-53; trustee Hosp. Sick Children, Toronto; mem. Ont. Alcoholism and Drug Addiction Research Found. Served to capt. Canadian Army, 1940-45. Fellow Ins. Inst. Am.; mem. Bd. Trade Met. Toronto, law socs. Man., Upper Can. Anglican. Clubs: York, Toronto, Canadian, Empire, Donalda Golf and Country, Rideau Country. Office: 130 Adelaide St W Toronto ON M5H 3R6 Canada*

SHEPARD, THOMAS ROCKWELL, JR., orgn. exec.; b. N.Y.C., Aug. 22, 1918; s. Thomas R. and Marie (Dickinson) S.; B.A., Amherst Coll., 1940; m. Nancy Kruidenier, Sept. 20, 1941; children—Sue (Mrs. R. Gerald Mould), Molly (Mrs. Karl Lunkenheimer), Amy K., Thomas R. III. Sales trainee to asst. promotion mgr. Vick Chem. Co., 1940-42; with Look Mag., 1946—, salesman various offices, West Coast mgr., 1947-49, promotion dir., 1955, N.Y. mgr., Eastern ad mgr., 1956, asst. ad mgr., 1957, ad sales mgr., 1961-64, ad dir., 1964-67, pub., 1967-72; cons. Cowles Communications Inc., Outdoor Advt. Assn. Am., 1972-74; pres. Inst. Outdoor Advt., 1974-77. pres. Advt. Council, Rehab. Internat. Pres., chmn. Greenwich Community Chest, 1964, 65; dir. Greenwich Boy's Club, 1960-66; Town Rep., 1961-62; pres. local P.T.A., 1956; chmn. Robert A. Taft Inst. Govt., 1978—. Recipient George Washington Medal award Freedoms Found., 1970, 73. Served as lt. comdr. USNR, 1942-46. Home: 44 Lismore Ln Greenwich CT 06830

SHEPELL, WARREN EDWARD JAMES, indsl. psychologist; b. Winnipeg, Man., Can.; s. Stanley and Anne (Schreyer) S.; B.A., U. Man. United Coll., 1965; M.A.Sc., U. Waterloo (Ont., Can.), 1968; Ph.D., U. Pa., 1974. Staff psychologist Man. Penitentiary, Stony Mountain, 1965-66; personnel researcher Ont. Hydro, Toronto, 1967; staff psychologist Canadian Imperial Bank of Commerce, 1968-71, 74-75; lectr. psychol. services U. Pa., 1971-74; human resources lectr. U. Toronto, 1974—; cons. psychologist Stevenson & Kellogg, Ltd., Toronto, 1975-77; cons. psychologist, founding partner Beech Shepell & Partners Ltd., Toronto, 1977-79; indsl. psychologist Ennis Shepell Indsl. Psychologists, Toronto, 1979—; vol. cons. CUSO, Frontier Coll.; speaker in field. Recipient Wesley award United Coll. U. Man., 1965. Mem. Am. Psychol. Assn., Canadian Psychol. Assn., Ont. Psychol. Assn. (council Bd. Edn. and Tng.), Ont. Amateur Softball Assn. Club: Bloor Park. Home: 47 Spruce St Toronto ON M5A 2H8 Canada Office: 2 Bloor St E Toronto ON M4W 1A8 Canada

SHEPHERD, DAVID H., mgmt. cons. co. exec.; b. Indpls., June 13, 1943; s. Mary C. Shepherd; B.B.A., U. Cin., 1966; M.B.A., Butler U., 1969; m. Jonnie L. Sandlin, Aug. 31, 1974; children—Kellie, Mary Martha. Systems analyst Link Belt div. FMC, Indpls., 1966-68, supr. standard cost acctg., 1968-69; with Touche Ross Co., Detroit, 1970-79, Cleve., 1979—, partner, 1976—. Trustee, Bus. Edn. Alliance, Detroit. Bd. dirs. Town of Westchester (Mich.), 1977-78. Cert. mgmt. cons. Mem. Inst. Mgmt. Consultants, Am. Prodn. and Inventory Control Soc., Am. Mgmt. Assn., Fin. Execs. Inst., Nat. Assn. Accts. Clubs: Detroit Athletic (fin. com.), Oakland Hills Country, Shaker Heights Country. Office: 1801 E 9th St Suite 800 Cleveland OH 44114

SHEPHERD, MARK, JR., electronics co. exec.; b. Dallas, Jan. 18, 1923; s. Mark and Louisa Florence (Daniell) S.; B.S. in Elec. Engring., So. Meth. U., 1942; M.S. in Elec. Engring., U. Ill., Urbana, 1947; m. Mary Alice Murchland, Dec. 21, 1945; children—Debra Aline (Mrs. Rowland K. Robinson), MaryKay Theresa, Marc Blaine. Engr., Gen. Electric Co., 1942-43, Farnsworth TV and Radio Corp., 1947-48; with Tex. Instruments Inc., Dallas, 1948—, asst. v.p. semicondr.-components div., 1954-55, v.p., gen. mgr. semicondr.-components div., 1955-61, exec. v.p., chief operating officer, 1961-66, dir., 1963—, pres., 1967-76, chief exec. officer, 1969—, chmn. bd., 1976—; dir. Rep. Nat. Bank Dallas, U.S. Steel Corp., Republic of Tex. Corp.; mem. internat. council Morgan Guaranty Trust Co. Mem. Adv. Council on Japan-U.S. Econ. Relations; mem. European Community-U.S. Businessmen's Council; mem. adv. council Am. Ditchley Found.; bd. dirs. So. Meth. U. Found. for Sci. and Engring., also trustee, bd. govs. So. Meth. U.; trustee Com. for Econ. Devel.; trustee Am. Enterprise Inst. for Pub. Policy Research; mem. internat. council on future of bus. Center for Strategic and Internat. Studies; mem. Trilateral Commn.; nat. bd. Com. on Present Danger. Served to lt. (j.g.) USNR, 1943-46. Registered profl. engr., Tex. Fellow IEEE; mem. Newcomen Soc., Soc. Exploration Geophysicists, Conf. Bd. (chmn.), Dallas Citizens Council, Bus. Council, Nat. Acad. Engring., Council on Fgn. Relations, Internat. C. of C. (trustee U.S. council), Sigma Xi, Eta Kappa Nu. Home: 5006 Middlegate Rd Dallas TX 75229 Office: Texas Instruments Inc PO Box 225474 MS 236 Dallas TX 75265

SHEPHERD, NORMAN HAROLD, fin. services co. exec.; b. San Bernardino, Calif., Feb. 2, 1944; s. Jess Harold and Ruth Lorraine (Teague) S.; A.A., Glendale Coll., 1965; B.S., Calif. State U., San Jose, 1968; M.B.A., U. So. Calif., 1970; m. Jennifer Joyce Keim, Aug. 30, 1968; children—Gregory Paul, Julie Christine. Logistical planner Singer-Gen. Precision, Glendale, Calif., 1968-69; cons. services mgr. Arthur Young & Co., Dallas, 1970-76; regional controller Hertz Corp., Dallas, 1976-78; gen. mgr. data center First Data Resources, San Mateo, Calif., 1978—. Served with USNR, 1962-64. C.P.A., Calif. Mem. Am. Inst. C.P.A.'s. Presbyterian.

SHEPHERD, RICHARD BUTLER HOOKE, civil engr.; b. Pond, Miss., Feb. 10, 1905; s. Arthur Merson and Louise Maria (Hider) S.; student Cornell U., 1922-23, Miss. State U., 1924, U. Mo., 1925-27, U. Tenn., 1945. Insp., C.E., Vicksburg, Miss., 1928-31, Memphis, 1931-32, civil engr., Memphis, 1932-47; geod. engr. 29th Engring. Bn. Base Topo, Manila P.I., 1948-54; cartographer U.S. Army Map Service, Far East, Tokyo, Japan, 1954-60; ret. 1960; vol. ednl. therapy VA Hosp., Memphis, 1961-63, 69—; registered rep. White and Co., Memphis, 1964-69. Extension instr. U. Tenn., 1942-46, U. Ark., 1944. Pres., Travellers Aid, Memphis. Fellow Am. Congress Surveying and Mapping (life), ASCE (life); mem. Memphis Engrs. Club (life), Soc. Am. Mil. Engrs. (life), Cornell Soc. Engrs., Pi Tau Sigma. Episcopalian. Clubs: Memphis Civitan, Memphis University; Tokyo Lawn Tennis. Home: 1380 Lamar Ave Memphis TN 38104

SHEPHERD, RONALD WILLIAM, soft drink co. exec.; b. Dallas, July 14, 1947; s. James Clarence and Betty Joyce (Stockard) S.; B.A., U. Tex., 1967; B.A. (Econs. fellow), So. Meth. U., 1969; M.S., U. Dallas, 1971; m. Kathryn Kramer, July 28, 1969; children—Patricia Lyn, Kathryn Kristine. Vice pres., treas. Astro Pub. Co., Dallas, 1968-70; zone mgr. Ford Motor Co., Dallas, 1970-73; new products mgr. Pepsi Cola Co., Purchase, N.Y., 1973-77, chief operating officer, exec. v.p. Pepsi Cola Schenectady Bottling Corp., Pepsi Cola Albany Bottling Co., Inc., 1978—; mktg. mgr. Coca Cola, N.Y.C., 1977-78; dir. Am. Colegiate Press, Shepherd Printing. Bd. dirs. Albany dist. Am. Leukemia Soc., 1980—. Mem. Sigma Iota Epsilon, Omega Delta Epsilon. Republican. Christian Scientist. Clubs: Brookings Country, Schyler Meadows Country (Loudonville, N.Y.); Mohawk (Schenectady). Home: 8 Loudon Heights N Loudonville NY 12211 Office: Pepsi Cola Schenectady Bottling Corp Freemans Bridge Rd Schenectady NY 12302

SHEPHERD, THOMAS RINGGOLD, consumer electronics co. exec.; b. Washington, Dec. 28, 1929; s. Henry and Elizabeth Temple (Green) S.; B.A., Washington and Lee U., 1952; M.S., Cornell U., 1956; m. Nancy Lair Hamilton, Aug. 15, 1953; children—Katharine, Ruth, Elizabeth, Thomas. Vice-pres., gen. mgr. GTE Sylvania of Can., Montreal, 1977-78; v.p., gen. sales mgr. Consumer Electronics Co., Batavia, N.Y., 1978; pres., 1978-79; sr. v.p., gen. mgr. GTE Products Corp., Batavia, N.Y., 1979—. Chmn., Stow (Mass.) Spring Festival, 1969-73; bd. dirs. Genesee Meml. Hosp., Batavia, N.Y. Served with USNR, 1952-54. Mem. Electronic Industries Assn. (dir. consumer electronics group). Episcopalian (vestryman, sr. warden 1969-71). Club: Stafford Country, Batavia. Office: 700 Ellicott St Batavia NY 14020

SHEPPARD, ROBERT BLAIR, ins. co. exec.; b. San Francisco, Sept. 11, 1922; s. Robert Boone and Joy Winifred (Sivers) S.; A.B., U. Calif. at Berkeley, 1943; m. June Wayne Phillips, Dec. 13, 1944; children—Stephen Robert, James Mark. Sales mgr. Calif. State Auto Asso., Walnut Creek, 1946-53; with Allstate Ins. Co., Northbrook, Ill., 1953—, exec. v.p., 1971—, pres., 1972—. Dir. Council Better Bus. Burs. Bd. dirs. Advt. Council, Inc., Chgo. Urban League, Coll. of Ins. Served to capt. USMCR, 1942-46. Named Sales and Mktg. Exec. of Year, Sales and Mktg. Execs. Assn. Chgo., 1974. Clubs: Skokie Country (Glencoe, Ill.); Bay Hill (Orlando, Fla.); Carmel Valley Golf (Carmel, Calif.). Office: Allstate Ins Co Allstate Plaza Northbrook IL 60062*

SHEPPARD, WILLIAM ALAN, aerospace co. exec.; b. Pitts., Apr. 1, 1916; s. Walter L. and Helen (Munn) S.; B.S., Lehigh U., 1938; M.S., U. Calif. at Berkeley, 1946; Ph.D., Mass. Inst. Tech., 1961; m. Helen Maxine Johnson, Dec. 5, 1943; children—Alan Huff, Elizabeth A. Engr., Pitts. Coal Co., 1938, U.S. Bur. Mines, Tuscaloosa, Ala., 1939; commd. 2d lt. USAF, 1939, advanced through grades to col., 1951; ret., 1959; gen. mgr. West Coast div. Itek Corp., Palo Alto, Calif., 1959-63; mech. engr. exec., dir. Spl. Systems, Lockheed Missiles & Space Co., Sunnyvale, Calif., 1963—. Bd. dirs. Community Psychiat. Centers, San Francisco. Mem. Phi Delta Theta. Episcopalian. Home: 70 Crescent Dr Palo Alto CA 94301 Office: 1111 Lockheed Way Sunnyvale CA 94088

SHER, PHIL ALLAN, fin. exec.; b. St. Louis, Aug. 24, 1944; s. Abe and Jenny Sher; student St. Louis U., 1962-64; B.S. in Bus. Adminstrn., Washington U., St. Louis, 1966; M.B.A., Am. U., 1970; m. Nina Rae Shenberg, Sept. 5, 1965; children—Kimberly Joy, Colleen Nicole. Systems accountant U.S. Govt., to 1972; sr. systems analyst Am. Investment Co., St. Louis, 1972-74; from budget mgr. to credit scoring mgr. Citicorp-Nationwide Fin. Corp., St. Louis, 1974-76; dir. ops. St. Louis Music Supply Co. Inc., 1976-78; v.p. portfolio mgmt. Citicorp Person to Person Fin. Services Inc., Denver, 1978-80; v.p. credit policy Citicorp Person to Person Inc., Creve Coeur, Mo., 1980—; co-founder Amerel Inc. Served with U.S. Army, 1966-70. Decorated Army Commendation medal. Mem. Am. Mgmt. Assn., Am. Entrepreneurs Assn. Office: 11475 Olde Cabin Rd Creve Coeur MO 63141

SHERAR, JOSEPH WILLIAM, ins. broker, investor; b. Fresno, Calif., Sept. 27, 1930; s. Joseph William Garland and Verna Irene (Kneeland) S.; B.S., U.S. Naval Acad., 1952; J.D., Loyola U., New Orleans, 1965; m. Nancy Barr Gooch, Nov. 6, 1954; children—Deirdra Clarisse, William Gooch, David Kneeland, Lynne Fox. Commd. ensign U.S. Navy, 1952, advanced through grades to lt., 1958; destoyer officer, 1952-53; naval aviator, 1954; landing signal officer, 1956-57; aide to Vice Adm. James Thatch, Com Huk Lant, 1958; flight instr. Saufley Naval Air Sta., Pensacola, Fla., 1958; ret., 1965; trainee Marine Office Am., 1958-59; marine broker Hardin and Ferguson, 1959-61; radar instr. U.S. Maritime Adminstrn., New Orleans, 1961-62; chmn. Ingram-Armistead & Co. SPA, Milan, Italy, 1976-78, Corroon & Black, Inc., New Orleans, 1979; pres. Sherar, Cook & Gardner, Inc., Metairie, La., 1979-80, Sailing Sales Inc., New Orleans, 1972-80; lectr. and seminar chmn. in field; underwriting mem. Lloyd's of London. Edn. chmn. YPO, Rio de Janeiro, Brazil; trustee U.S. Naval Acad. Sailing Found. Inc.; chmn. Fales adv. com. U.S. Naval Acad.; chmn. aviation com. C. of C. New Orleans, 1975-79. Mem. Young Pres.'s Orgn. (chmn. La. chpt. 1978-79), U.S. Naval Acad. Alumni Assn. (pres. New Orleans chpt. 1963), SAR, Delta Theta Phi (life mem.). Clubs: Cruising Am., Royal Ocean Racing London (life), Storm Trysail, N.Y. Yacht, So. Yacht, Colonial Wars Soc. La., Essex (pres. 1971-72), Bienville. Contbr. articles to profl. jours. Office: 2325 Severn Ave Suite 5 Metairie LA 70001

SHERIDAN, KIM ALAN, computer software co. exec.; b. Lima, Ohio, Jan. 24, 1948; s. Charles Joseph and Jayn Elizabeth (Kassner) S.; B.S. in Mktg., U. Ariz., 1970; M.B.A. in Quantitative Analysis, U. Cin., 1971; m. Mary Margaret Gray, July 17, 1970; children—Nathan, Ben, Siovhan, Otto, Stephanie. Salesman, Sears, Roebuck and Co., 1969-70; mem. customer service staff Sheridan Assos., Cin., 1970-73, div. v.p., 1973-76; pres. Interactive Info. Systems Inc., Cin., 1976—. Bd. dirs. Catholic Big Bros., 1973-79. Mem. Am. Inst. Decision Scis., Assn. Data Processing Services Orgn. Roman Catholic. Home: 9475 Fallson Ct Cincinnati OH 45242 Office: IIS Inc 10 Knollcrest Dr Cincinnati OH 45237

SHERIDAN, LEO JOHN, JR., real estate broker; b. Evanston, Ill., Feb. 17, 1935; s. Leo John and Irene Sarah (Leader) S.; B.S., Georgetown U., 1957; m. Olive Mary Fox, June 22, 1957; children—Julie M., Leo John III, Tim P., Mary Helen, Kathleen Susan. Real estate broker L.J. Sheridan & Co., Chgo., 1960-79; partner Butler & Sheridan Real Estate, Winnetka, Ill.; dir. 1st Nat. Bank, Highland Park, Ill., 1971—. Active Chgo. Heart Assn., Crusade of Mercy; chmn. real estate group Am. Cancer Soc., 1968. Bd. dirs. St. Alexious Hosp., Elk Grove Village, Ill., 1962-63. Served with USAF, 1958-60. Mem. Ill. Assn. Realtors (treas. 1979, 2d v.p. 1980), Chgo. Real Estate Bd. (pres. 1974-75), Evanston N. Shore Bd. Realtors (dir.). Lambda Alpha. Clubs: Knollwood Country; Forty (treas. 1969); Dairymen's Country (dir. 1974—) (Boulder Junction, Wis.). Home: 211 Summerfield Northbrook IL 60062 Office: 60 Green Bay Rd Winnetka IL 60093

SHERIDAN, PATRICK MICHAEL, ins. co. exec.; b. Grosse Pointe, Mich., Apr. 13, 1940; s. Paul Phillip and Frances Mary (Rohan) S.; B.B.A., U. Notre Dame, 1962; M.B.A., U. Detroit, 1975; m. Jane Louise Hansinger, May 30, 1962; children—Mary, Patrick, Kelly, Kevin, James. C.P.A., Peat, Marwick, Mitchell & Co., Detroit, 1962-72, audit mgr., 1969-72; exec. v.p. finance Alexander Hamilton Life Ins. Co., Farmington, Mich., 1973-76; exec. v.p. Sun Life Ins. Co. Am., Balt., 1976-78, now dir.; pres. Sun Ins. Services, Inc., Atlanta, 1978—; dir. Coastal States Life Ins. Co., Universal Guaranty Life Ins. Co. Republican candidate for U.S. Congress, 1972. Trustee Met. Fund; bd. dirs. Regional Citizens, 1969-72. Served to capt. AUS, 1963-65. Recipient various Jaycee awards. Mem. Am. Inst. C.P.A.'s, Mich., Md., Ga. assns. C.P.A.'s, U.S. (treas. 1973-74), Mich. (pres. 1971-72), Detroit (pres. 1968-69) jaycees. Home: 175 Spalding Mill Dr Atlanta GA 30338 Office: 260 Peachtree St NW Atlanta GA 30303

SHERIDAN, RICHARD CHAMPLIN, printer and publisher; b. Balt., Feb. 22, 1930; s. Richard Champlin and Jeannette (Kidd) S.; B.S., Johns Hopkins U., 1952; divorced; children—Sally Wright, Barrett Cathell, Richard Champlin, III. Sec., Schneidereith & Sons, Balt., 1954-61; gen. mgr. Everybodys Press Inc., Hanover, Pa., 1961-67, pres., 1967—; pres. Vest Pockets Inc., Balt., 1971—, Communications Graphics Inc., Balt., 1979—; dir. Oles Envelopes Co., Balt., Robinson Graphics Inc., Washington. Served with AUS, 1952-54. Mem. Printing Industries Md., Graphic Arts Assn. Del. Valley (dir.). Republican. Episcopalian. Clubs: Hanover Rotary (pres. 1967-68), Hanover Country, Johns Hopkins. Home: 22 Laurel Woods Ln Hanover PA 17331 Office: Everybodys Press Fame Ave Hanover PA 17331

SHERIDAN, ROBERT HOWARD, JR., investment banker; b. Mpls., July 17, 1933; s. Robert Howard and Nora L. (McIntyre) S.; B.A., Rice U., 1954; postgrad. U. Tex., 1954-55; grad. Investment Bankers Assn. course Wharton Sch. Fin., U. Pa., 1968; m. Mary Ellen Woodruff, Jan. 27, 1962 (div. Nov. 1971); children—Robert Howard, Phillip Douglas. Vice pres. investments Tex. Nat. Bank of Commerce,

Houston, 1955-64; sr. v.p., dir. Moroney Beissner & Co., Inc., 1964-74, Moroney, Beissner Mortgage Co., Inc., Houston, 1966-74, Rotan Mosle Mortgage Co., Houston, 1974-77; v.p. Rotan Mosle Inc., Houston, 1974-76, dir., 1st v.p., 1977—; dir. Rotan Mosle Realty Investments, 1975—. Mem. Houston Soc. Fin. Analysts, Nat. Assn. Securities Dealers, Securities Industry Assn. Clubs: River Oaks Country, Houston (Houston). Home: 265 Chimney Rock Houston TX 77024 Office: 1500 S Tower Pennzoil Pl Houston TX 77002

SHERIFF, FRANCIS JOSEPH, cons.; b. Putnam, Conn., Sept. 8, 1928; s. Memet and Elisima Mary (Trudeau) S.; B.S., U.S. Mil. Acad., 1951; M.B.A., Harvard U., 1957; m. Doris Lorraine Allard, June 9, 1951; children—David F., Robert W., Kenneth R. Commd. cadet U.S. Army, 1947, advanced through grades to col., 1970, ret., 1972; exec. v.p. adminstrn. S. M. Hyman Co., Balt., 1972—, dir., 1974—; dir. Bobby Boyd's Hooligan's Inc., Towson, Md., Hub Enterprises, Inc., Towson. Vice pres. Charles St. Assn., 1976-78; treas. Outpost Community Assn., 1977-78; mem. retail adv. com. Greater Balt. Com., 1976-78. Served with U.S. Army, 1947-72. Decorated Bronze Star (3), Legion of Merit (2). Mem. Adminstrv. Mgmt. Soc., Am. Soc. Personnel Adminstrs. Club: Center. Home: 12706 Ponderosa Ln Glen Arm MD 21057 Office: FJ Sheriff Co Inc 2-A W Pennsylvania Ave Towson MD 21204

SHERIKJIAN, JOSEPH PAUL, broadcasting exec.; b. Jersey City, June 4, 1943; s. Joseph and Carol (Albecker) S.; B.S., St. Peter's Coll., Jersey City, 1965; M.B.A., Fairleigh Dickinson U., 1968; m. Linda Angela Candeloro, June 19, 1965; children—Alison Marie, Joseph, Michele. Salesman, Shaw-Walker Co., 1965-68; mgr. budgets NBC, 1968-70; dir. acctg. radio and TV, RKO Gen. Inc., 1970-72; bus. mgr. sta. WABC-TV, N.Y.C., 1972-73; planning analyst ABC Radio, N.Y.C., 1973-75, dir. fin. and adminstrn., 1975—; tchr. night sch., 1965-70. Past officer Emerson (N.J.) Little League; coach Emerson Baseball, Basketball and Softball. Mem. Am. Mgmt. Assn., Fin. Mgrs. Assn. Roman Catholic. Home: 110 Park Ave Emerson NJ 07630 Office: 1330 6th Ave New York NY 10019

SHERIN, EDWIN ELI, credit card/fin. co. exec.; b. Elmira, N.Y., July 11, 1938; s. Arthur and Carrie Ardaline (Arnold) S.; B.S., Rutgers U., 1961; children—Barry, Troy, Derek. With Am. Express Co., 1968—, v.p. Eastern region, 1977-80, v.p. So. region, Ft. Lauderdale, Fla., 1980—. Bd. dirs. United Way of Broward County (Fla.); bd. dirs. Inverrary Golf Classic. trustee Ft. Lauderdale Mus. Art; mem. S. Fla. Coordinating Com. Served to capt. Intelligence Corps, U.S. Army, 1961-68; ETO. Office: 777 American Expressway Fort Lauderdale FL 33317

SHERMAN, CARLTON JOHN, JR., paper co. exec.; b. Natick, Mass., May 21, 1954; s. Carlton John and Vasiliki (Kounanis) S.; B.S. in Chem. Engring., U. Maine, 1976; cert. Pulp and Paper Tech., 1977; m. Barbara Lynn Schafer, May 13, 1978. Process engr. Procter & Gamble Paper Products Co., Mehoopany, Pa., 1977, team mgr., 1978, process mgr., 1979, area mgr., 1979—, chmn. plant mgrs. safety com., 1980—, mgr. chem. engring. dept., 1980—. Advancement chmn. Boy Scouts Am., Tunkhannock, Pa., 1978—, dist. vice chmn. Penn Mountain council, 1980—; Little League baseball coach, 1979—; 5th and 6th grade basketball coach, Tunkhannock, 1978-79. Product Research grantee Royce Chem. Co., 1976-77. Mem. Paper Industry Mgmt. Assn., TAPPI, Am. Inst. Chem. Engrs., U. Maine at Orono Pulp and Paper Found. Congregationalist. Contbr. articles to profl. jours. Home: RD 6 Tunkhannock PA 18657

SHERMAN, EARL HARVEY, ins. co. exec.; b. Cleve., May 13, 1945; s. Allen and Faye (Salkin) S.; A.A., Santa Monica Coll., 1966; B.B.A., Nat. U., San Diego, 1976, M.B.A., 1977; postgrad. Western State U. Coll. Law, 1973-75; m. Sandra Sue Goff, Sept. 5, 1970; children—Douglas Eric, Amy Nicole. Asst. mgr. Drug King Inc., Santa Monica, 1963-66; sr. claims examiner Argonaut Ins. Co., Los Angeles, 1968-72; claims supr. Firemans Fund Ins. Cos., San Diego, 1972-78; home office claim mgr. Mission Ins. Group, Los Angeles, 1978-80, dir. edn. and tng., 1980—; faculty mem. Ins. Edn. Assn.; guest lectr. Calif. Western Sch. Law, 1976-77, Western Info. Ins. Service, 1973-74. Served with USNR, 1966-68. Mem. Am. Mgmt. Assn., Am. Soc. Tng. and Devel., Ins. Co. Edn. Dirs. Soc. Club: Toastmasters (sec. 1972). Office: 2601 Wilshire Blvd Los Angeles CA 90059

SHERMAN, IRA ALLAN, record co. exec.; b. N.Y.C., Dec. 18, 1946; s. Joseph and Joan (Kokotoff) S.; student Bklyn. Coll., 1964; Asso. degree, Kingsborough Community Coll., 1966; B.A., L.I. U., 1971. Mgr. artist relations/devel. Columbia Records, CBS, N.Y.C., 1971-74, product mgr. Epic Portrait Associated, 1974-77, asso. dir. product mgmt., 1977-78, dir. east coast product mgmt., 1978-79; dir. product mgmt. Infinity Records, Inc. div. MCA/Universal, N.Y.C., 1979—; pres. I.A.S. Mgmt. Inc., N.Y.C., 1980—; performer, writer original music. Recipient platinum record awards.

SHERMAN, JOHN CARTER, investment co. exec.; b. N.Y.C., June 27, 1932; s. S. Dillow and Elizabeth Hazard (Snow) S.; B.A. cum laude, Amherst Coll., 1954; M.B.A., Harvard U., 1959; m. Elinor M. Hafstad, June 15, 1957; children—Kenneth, Tinka, Kristy, Tod. Securities analyst Security Pacific Nat. Bank, Los Angeles, 1959-60; econ. analyst Union Oil Co. Calif., Los Angeles, 1960-62; 2d v.p. investments Occidental Life Ins. Co. Calif., Los Angeles, 1962-70; pres. Transam. Investment Research Inc., Los Angeles, 1970—. Served to 1st lt. USAF, 1954-57. Mem. Los Angeles Soc. Fin. Analysts (pres., bd. govs.), Nat. Assn. Petroleum Investment Analysts, Phi Beta Kappa. Office: Occidental Center Los Angeles CA 90015

SHERMAN, JOSEPH VINCENT, cons. economist, writer; b. Beacon, N.Y., Dec. 18, 1905; s. Joseph Francis and Catherine Adele (Killeen) S.; A.B., Columbia Coll., 1928; m. Viola Signe Maria Lidfeldt, Nov. 18, 1944. Mgr. investment dept. Nat. Newark & Essex Banking Co., Newark, 1929-36; statistician Case, Pomeroy & Co., N.Y.C., 1936-38; v.p. Econ. Analysts, Inc., N.Y., 1938-42; asso. Herbert R. Simonds, cons. engr., 1943-45. Served with AUS, 1942-43. Mem. AAAS, Am. Econ. Assn., Am. Statis. Assn. Author: Research as a Growth Factor in Industry, 1940; The New Plastics, 1945; Plastics Business, 1946; The New Fibers, 1946. Contbr. to Barron's Nat. Business and Financial Weekly and various other pubs., 1939—. Home: 160 Columbia Heights Brooklyn NY 11201 Office: 280 Broadway New York NY 10007

SHERMAN, MARY KENNEDY, business exec.; b. Chgo., June 17, 1919; d. Robert Thomas and Mary Cecelia (Hammond) Kennedy; A.A., Los Angeles Valley Coll., 1966; B.S., Pepperdine U., 1973; M.B.A., 1974; m. Lloyd McBean Sherman, Dec. 1, 1967; children—Tom D. Akins, Mary Patricia Kraakevik. Indsl. relations supr. Douglas Aircraft Co., Inc., Santa Monica, Calif., 1942-61; dir. personnel Helene Curtis Industries, Studio Girl, Glendale, Calif., 1961-65; dir. personnel Semtech Corp., Newbury Park, Calif., 1965-73, v.p., 1973—; lectr., cons. in field. Mem. Am. Mgmt. Assn., Internat. Assn. for Personnel Women, Am. Soc. for Personnel Adminstrn., Personnel and Indsl. Relations Assn., Am. Bus. Women's Assn., Personnel Women of Los Angeles. Republican. Roman Catholic. Club: Zonta Internat. Office: 652 Mitchell Rd Newbury Park CA 91320

SHERMAN, MICHAEL STUART, assn. exec.; b. Norfolk, Va., Dec. 4, 1947; s. Herbert and Helen (Brener) S.; B.S. in Math., Va. Poly. Inst. and State U., 1969; M.A. in Econs., U. Pitts., 1972, Ph.D., 1974; m. Rose Florence Reingold, Aug. 23, 1970; children—David Matthew, Adam Richard. Teaching fellow U. Pitts., 1972-74; staff economist Nat. Assn. Furniture Mfrs., Washington, 1974-75, dir. econ. and market research, 1975—; exec. dir. Summer and Casual Furniture Mfrs. Assn., Washington, 1976—; cons. to furniture mfrs.; guest lectr. for Profile V Furniture Industry Research Project; mem. industry sector adv. com. U.S. Dept. Commerce. Mem. Am. Soc. Assn. Execs. (1st Pl. award Idea Fair 1976, 78), Am. Econ. Assn., Am. Statis. Assn., Nat. Assn. Bus. Economists, World Future Soc. Home: 2506 Lindley Terr Rockville MD 20850 Office: 8401 Connecticut Ave Suite 911 Washington DC 20015

SHERMAN, NORMAN FREDERIC, mktg. exec.; b. Boston, Nov. 22, 1926; s. Samuel Richard and Ceclia M. Sherman; B.S., U.S. Mcht. Marine Acad., 1946; B.J., U. Mo., 1950, B.A., 1950; m. Barbara Ruth Agruss, June 1, 1948; children—Carole Ann, Barry Keith, Marti Isabelle, Suzy Gail. With advt. sales dept. St. Louis Post Dispatch, 1950-54; dir. men's casual footwear Interco Inc., St. Louis, 1954-58; founder, v.p. Direct Mail Corp. Am., St. Louis, 1958-64; founder Sales Communications Corp., St. Louis, 1964-68; dir. U.S. mktg. Howmark of Can., Toronto, Ont., 1969-78; U.S. trustee Universal Entertainment Ltd., Nassau, Bahamas, 1976—; mng. dir. Video Enterprises Worldwide, Waltham, Mass., 1976—; partner Howmark U.S., Newton, Mass., 1977—; pres. The Marketeers, Framingham, Mass., 1979—, Excalibur Internat., Framingham, 1979—; cons. various corps. Served with USNR, 1944-48. Named Man of Yr., St. Louis Direct Mail Club, 1965; recipient award of merit Mem. Direct Mail Advt. Assn., 1966. Mem. U. Mo. Alumni Assn., Aircraft Owners and Pilots Assn., Pilots Internat. Assn., 210 Nat. Found., Alpha Delta Sigma. Clubs: Jefferson (U. Mo.); Quarterback, Masons, Shriners (St. Louis). Home: 5 Merrymount Dr Swampscott MA 01907 Office: 10 Queensway Ct Suite 4 Framingham MA 01701

SHERMAN, OTTO MARTIN, ins. co. exec.; b. N.Y.C., Apr. 7, 1910; s. Martin and Eva (Roth) S.; student N.Y.U., 1930; LL.B., Bklyn. Law Sch., 1931; m. Edna Rosen, May 29, 1936; children—Gail (Mrs. David Banker), James Paul. Admitted to N.Y. State bar, 1931; regional atty. OPA, N.Y. regional office, 1944-45; practiced law, 1945-49; with Equitable Life Ins. U.S., 1949—, asst. mgr., 1951-52; gen. agt. U.S. Life Ins. Co., 1952-59, pres., chmn. bd. Constn. Agy., Inc., 1952-59; asso. dir. agys. Eastern Life Ins. Co. N.Y., 1959-60; exec. v.p., dir. Employers Planning Corp., 1960-63; v.p., dir. agys. Standard Security Life Ins. Co., 1960-62; pres., chmn. bd., chmn. exec. com. Pension Life Ins. Co. Am., 1963-66; pres., chmn. bd. Ben Franklin Life Ins. Co., 1964-73; chmn. bd. Am. Commonwealth Corp., 1964; pres., chmn. bd. Duo-Fund Plan Corp., 1969—; sr. fin. services exec. Fred S. James & Co. N.J., 1979—; adv. bd. U.S. Trust Fund. Mem. Internat. Assn. Health Underwriters (v.p., dir. N.Y. chpt.), Nat. Assn. Life Underwriters, Assn. Advanced Life Underwriters, Passaic-Bergen Life Underwriters Assn. (past pres.), Am. Acad. Polit. and Social Sci., Am., Eastern pension confs., Am. Soc. Pension Actuaries, Am. Risk and Ins. Assn., Am. Mus. Natural History Assn. Home: 1275 15th St Fort Lee NJ 07024 Office: 2083 Center Ave Fort Lee NJ 07024

SHERMAN, ROBERT FRED, mfg. co. exec.; b. Chgo., Dec. 7, 1934; s. Fred A. and Ruth L. (Brown) S.; student Stanford, 1952-53; B.S. in Elec. Engring., U. Wash., 1957, B.S. in Indsl. Engring., 1957; M.S. in Indsl. Mgmt., Mass. Inst. Tech., 1959; m. M. Jill Jones, Nov. 28, 1975; children—Caroline, Jennifer, Kirsten. Instr., Mass. Inst. Tech., 1960; asst. dir. marketing Nat. Forge Co., Warren, Pa., 1960-61; v.p. Booz, Allen & Hamilton, N.Y.C., 1962-70; v.p., dir. Aegis Corp., Coral Gables, Fla., 1970—; chmn., dir. Savannah Machine & Shipyard Co. (Ga.); bd. dirs. Am. com. Lloyd's Register of Shipping, Am. Bur. Shipping. Ford Found. fellow, 1959-60. Mem. Soc. Naval Architects and Marine Engrs., Alpha Delta Phi. Lutheran. Clubs: Union League (N.Y.C.); New York Yacht; Savannah Yacht; Coral Reef Yacht; Chatham. Home: 840 S Alhambra Circle Coral Gables FL 33146 Office: Aegis Corp 250 Catalonia Ave Coral Gables FL 33134

SHERN, DAVID AJER, bank exec.; b. Menomonie, Wis., July 31, 1926; s. Christian A. and Esther Mildred (Ajer) S.; B.A., St. Olaf Coll., 1950; student Stonier Grad. Sch. Banking, Rutgers U., 1961-63; m. Martha Baskin, Sept. 7, 1948; children—Andrew T., Fredric D. Vice-pres. First Nat. Bank of St. Paul, 1950-68; pres. Mid-America Bancorporation, Inc., Mpls., 1968-76; pres. First Trust and Savs. Bank, Davenport, Iowa, 1977—. Bd. dirs. Downtown Davenport Devel. Corp.; treas., bd. dirs. Illowa chpt. ARC. Served with USNR, 1944-46. Mem. Davenport C. of C. (dir. 1978—), Am. Bankers Assn., Iowa Bankers Assn. Republican. Lutheran. Office: 3d and Brady Sts Davenport IA 52805

SHERRERD, JOHN J. F., bus. exec.; b. Phila., Mar. 9, 1930; s. William D. and Isabel F. (Foulkrod) S.; A.B., Princeton U., 1952; M.B.A., Wharton Grad. Sch. U. Pa., 1956; m. Kathleen Compton, Feb. 11, 1956; children—Anne C., John J.F., Susan M. Mgr. instl. research dept. Drexel Harriman Ripley Inc., 1956-1969, partner, 1963-69; co-founder, partner Miller Anderson & Sherrerd, 1969—; dir. Provident Mutual Life Ins. Co. Trustee, The Shipley Sch., Lower Merion Police Pension Fund, Princeton U., 1979—; chmn. investment com. Smith Coll.; mem. investment com. The Hill Sch. Served to lt. U.S. Army, 1952-54. Mem. Phila. Analysts Soc. Republican. Presbyterian. Clubs: Princeton of N.Y.; Merion Golf, Merion Cricket. Home: 833 Muirfield Bryn Mawr PA 19010 Office: 2 Bala-Cyawyd Plaza Bala Cynwyd PA 19004

SHERRILL, HUGH VIRGIL, investment banker; b. Long Beach, Calif., 1920; ed. Yale U. Pres. Bache Halsey Stuart Shields Inc., 1977—, also dir.; dir. Alberto-Culver Co. Trustee Meml. Hosp., N.Y.C., Boys' Club N.Y.C. Mem. Securities Industry Assn. (dir.). Office: 100 Gold St New York NY 10038

SHERRILL, STEPHEN MCHUGH, real estate developer, chem. cons.; b. Mooresville, N.C., Jan. 30, 1940; s. Hugh McLean and Della Louvene (Perkins) S.; student St. John's U., 1961-62, U. Mass., 1967. Bacteriologist, Harvard U. Health Services, Cambridge, Mass., 1963-67; tech. supr. neurochemistry dept. Found. Research on the Nervous System, 1967-69; supr. radioassay dept. Clin-Chem Labs., Boston, 1969-74; research asst. Harvard U. Med. Sch., Boston, 1974-76; nuclear medicine cons. VA, Boston, 1975-76; quality control and prodn. supr. Ria Products, Inc., Waltham, Mass., 1976-77; sr. research asso. Clin. Assays div. Baxter-Travenol, Cambridge, Mass., 1977-80; treas., clk. Manataug Devel. Corp., Marblehead, Mass., also cons. Clin. Assays div. Baxter-Travenol, 1980—; supr. L.I. Hosp. Rehab. Program, Boston, 1968—; Democrat. Patentee method of measuring thyroid hormone. Home: 6 Manataug Trail Marblehead MA 01945 Office: Long Island Hospital Rehabilitation Program Boston MA 02169 also 98 Chestnut St Boston MA 02108

SHERWOOD, DAVID J., ins. co. exec.; b. 1922; ed. Rutgers U., Boston U., Stanford U.; married. Vice pres. Fireman's Fund Am. Ins. Cos., 1946-70; with Prudential Ins. Co. Am., Newark, 1970—, exec. v.p., 1977-78, pres., 1978—, also dir. Served with U.S. Army, 1942-46. Office: Prudential Plaza Newark NJ 07101*

SHERWOOD, JAMES EDWARD, banker; b. Donaldson, Ark., Jan. 3, 1919; s. Crawford Daniel and Rose Etta (Crow) S.; grad. with honors So. Meth. U. Grad. Sch. Banking, 1967; m. Josephine Reed, Dec. 20, 1943; children—Karen Louetta Sherwood Cory, Donald James, Ronald Thomas. With Malvern Nat. Bank (Ark.), 1939-40; asst. cashier Bank of Brinkley (Ark.), 1940-46; with Citizens Nat. Bank & Trust Co., Goose Creek, Tex., 1946-63, sr. v.p., 1960-63; exec. v.p. Republic Nat. Bank Houston, 1963-64; pres., truste officer Bay City Bank & Trust Co. (Tex.), 1964-75; chmn., chief exec. officer Cleburne Nat. Bank (Tex.), 1975—. Served with USAF, 1942-46. Mem. Am. Bankers Assn. (certified comml. lender), Tex. Bankers Assn. (chmn. edn. com. 1974-76), Nat. Real Estate Bd., Tex. Real Estate Bd., Nat. Assn. Real Estate Appraisers, Am. Legion, DAV (life). Methodist. Clubs: Rotary, Masons, Shriners, Christian Businessmen's (founder). Home: 7045 Lakeshore Dr Cleburne TX 76031 Office: 1 N Main St Cleburne TX 76031

SHETTERLY, ROBERT BROWNE, food mfg. co. exec.; b. Corning, N.Y., May 28, 1915; s. Fred F. and Izora A. (Burns) S.; B.A., U. Rochester, 1936; m. Phyllis E. Galloway, June 20, 1942; children—John A., Robert Browne, Thomas H. With Procter & Gamble Co., Cin., 1936—, in advt. dept., 1936-55, advt. mgr. Food Products div., 1955-60, asso. mgr. div., 1960-61, mgr., 1961-65, v.p., gen. mgr. subsidiary Clorox Co., Oakland, Calif., 1965-68, pres., 1968-78, chmn., 1979—; dir. Crocker Nat. Corp. Mem. New Oakland Com.; mem. exec. com. Bay Area Council; trustee Mills Coll., Oakland; pres. Econ. Devel. Corp. Oakland; adv. bd. Jr. Achievement Bay Area. Served from pvt. to capt., USAAF, 1942-46. Mem. NAM (dir.), Psi Upsilon. Republican. Episcopalian. Clubs: Claremont Country (Oakland); Pacific Union (San Francisco). Home: Claremont Country Club 5295 Broadway Terr Oakland CA 94618 Office: 1221 Broadway Oakland CA 94612

SHETTLE, THOMAS BERNARD, mfrs. rep.; b. Balt., May 28, 1936; s. Bernard Thomas and Miriam Mae (Lausch) S.; J.D., U. Balt., 1963; m. Phyllis Eliska Patton, Nov. 26, 1959; children—Daphne, Stewart, Heather. Ins. sales, 1963-73; mfrs. rep., Mt. Carmel, Ind., 1973—; mem. part time faculty bus. dept. Community Coll. Balt., 1965—. Leader handicapped pack Boy Scouts Am.; tchr. Balt. City Jail; coach Lacrosse; chmn., treas., usher Episcopal Ch. Served with Army N.G., 1954-62. Address: 4340 Mount Carmel Rd Upperco MD 21155

SHETTY, SHANKARA RAMA, food packaging co. exec.; b. India, Nov. 19, 1941; s. Rama Chandu and Seetha Rama S.; B.Sc., U. Bombay, 1963, M.Sc. Tech., 1968; M.B.A., Bloomsburg State Coll., 1978; m. Sulochana Shetty, May 15, 1972; 1 child, Ameet. Asst. dir. research and devel. Indian Inst. Packaging, Bombay, 1968-75; packaging specialist Wise Foods div. Borden Inc., Berwick, Pa., 1975-78; packaging and promotion coordinator Drake Bakeries, Wayne, N.J., 1978-80; nat. mgr. packaging quality control Frito-Lay, Inc., Dallas, 1980—. Mem. Inst. Food Technologists, Packaging Inst., Am. Inst. Indsl. Engrs. Contbr. articles to profl. jours. Home: 2617 Carmel Circle Carrollton TX 75006 Office: Suite 813 4747 Leston St Dallas TX 75247

SHEVLIN, MATTHEW JOSEPH, JR., mfg. co. exec.; b. San Francisco, Mar. 23, 1926; s. Matthew Joseph and Virginia Boyd (Willis) S.; student UCLA, 1947, Claremont Men's Coll., 1947-49; m. Barbara Anne Gabel, Apr. 7, 1951; 1 dau., Barbara Victoria. With United Calif. Bank, Los Angeles, 1949-70, v.p. nat. div., 1965-70; v.p. fin. Avco Corp., Greenwich, Conn., 1970-74, treas., 1970-75, sr. v.p. fin., 1974-76, exec. v.p., 1976—; dir. Adams-Campbell Co., Ltd., Paul Revere Investors, Paul Revere Life Ins. Co., Avco Fin. Services. Served with USN, 1944-46, 50-54. Mem. Treasurers Club (N.Y.C.). Clubs: Stanwich (dir.) (Greenwich); Los Angeles Country. Office: Avco Corp 1275 King St Greenwich CT 06830

SHIDLER, JAY HAROLD, II, fin. exec.; b. Pasadena, Calif., Apr. 20, 1946; s. Robert Wharton and Geneveive (Ankrum) S.; B.B.A., U. Hawaii, 1968; m. Wallette Sue Amoy, Feb. 14, 1970; 1 dau., Summer Lei. With Mike McCormack Realtor, Honolulu, 1965-67; appraiser Philip W. Won Co., Honolulu, 1967-69; pres. Real Estate Research Group, Inc., Honolulu, 1969—; partner Shidler & Petty, Honolulu and Seattle, 1971-76; owner, prin. Shidler & Co., Honolulu & Seattle, 1976—; prin. Polynesian Investment Co., Honolulu, 1971—, CDC Investment Co., Honolulu, 1973—, Kapalama Shopping Center Co., Honolulu, 1977—, Waipahu Profl. Center Co., Honolulu, 1978—, Waipouli Investment Co., Honolulu, 1977, Waikiki Market Pl. Investment Co., Honolulu, 1977, Shidler & Shidler, San Francisco, 1978—, Meringoff & Shidler, N.Y.C., 1979—; pres. Islander Inns, Inc., Honolulu, 1979—, Park Ave. Investment Co., N.Y.C., 1979—, McDade & Shidler, Los Angeles, 1980—, So. Grand Investment Co., 1980—. Served to lt., C.E., U.S. Army, 1969-71. Clubs: Pacific, Outrigger, Hawaii Polo. Office: 707 Wilshire Blvd Suite 4370 Los Angeles CA 90017 733 Bishop St 27th Floor Honolulu HI 96813 also Four Embarcadero Center #1630 San Francisco CA 94111 also 375 Park Ave New York NY 10152

SHIELDS, H(ENRY) RICHARD, bus. exec., tax cons.; A.B., Bklyn. Coll.; J.D., N.Y. U.; M.B.A., Harvard U.; m. Frances Augenstein; 1 dau., Eileen. Corporate practice law, 1940-60; sec.-treas. Forbes Realty Corp., 1960—; exec. v.p. Am. Diversified Industries Corp., 1964-66, pres., chmn. bd., 1966—; exec. v.p. Forbes Industries, Ltd., 1965—, also Daily Mirror, Sunday Mirror, N.Y.C.; chmn., chief exec. officer, dir. TTC Industries and subs. Armstrong Glass Mfg. Corp., Erwin, Tenn., 1970—; pres., dir. Euro Industries, Ltd. and dir. subs. Town Formal Wear and Lady B. Fashions Co., 1971—; pres., dir., chief exec. officer Dairene Industries, Ltd., 1971—; dir. Blue Ribbon Mktg. Corp.; govt. appeal agt. SSS; cons. Franklin Cons., Ltd., Gt. Neck, N.Y.; referee, arbitrator Civil Ct. N.Y.C. Mem. N.Y. State Com. on Human Rights. Served to maj. USAF, 1942-46; CBI. Decorated Air Force Commendation medal, Legion of Merit. Mem. Am. Inst. Mgmt. (pres.'s council), Nat. Assn. Accountants, Nat. Tax Assn. (com. on fed. taxation), Tax Inst. Am., Assn. Bar City N.Y. (legis. com.). Club: Harvard. Home: Great Neck NY 11021 Office: 98 Cutter Mill Rd Great Neck NY 11021

SHIELDS, MICHAEL ROY, computer co. exec.; b. Newark, Ohio, Feb. 4, 1947; s. Roy L. and Laura Geraldine (Swart) S.; B.S. in Bus. Adminstrn., Bluffton Coll., 1969; m. Janelle Kay Erskine, Jan. 15, 1977; 1 dau., Jessica Nicole. Tchr., Buckeye Valley Local Schs., Delaware, Ohio, 1969-71; with Burroughs Corp., Columbus, Ohio, 1971-76, Indpls., 1976-79, dist. prodn. mgr., 1976—, industry mktg. coordinator, Detroit, 1979—, mem. exec. adv. council, 1975-76. Decorated Burroughs Corp. Legion Honor. Mem. Data Processing Mgrs. Assn. Methodist. Clubs: Carmel Racquet, Elks. Home: 5591 Kingsfield Dr West Bloomfield MI 48033 Office: Burroughs Pl Detroit MI 48232

SHIFLEY, RALPH LOUIS, mgmt. services co. exec., former naval officer; b. Mounds, Ill., Oct. 26, 1910; s. Marion Monroe and Elizabeth Alice (Hawkins) S.; student U. Ill., 1928; B.S., U.S. Naval Acad., 1933; m. Frances Ellen Norman, Sept. 8, 1936; 1 dau., Susan Elizabeth. Commd. ensign U.S. Navy, 1933, advanced through grades to vice adm., 1967; comdg. officer in U.S.S. Franklin D. Roosevelt, 1958-59; asst. dir., then dir. aviation plans div., staff chief naval ops., Washington, 1959-62; comdr. Carrier Div. 7, 1962-63; vice chief naval materiel, Washington, 1963-67, dep. chief naval ops. (logistics), 1967-71; ret., 1971; exec. v.p., treas. Stanwick Corp., Arlington, Va., 1971-78, pres., 1978—. Decorated Navy Cross, Legion of Merit, D.F.C. with three gold stars, D.S.M., Air medal with two gold stars. Clubs: Army and Navy (Washington); N.Y. Yacht; Army-Navy Country (Arlington); Pinehurst (N.C.) Country. Home: 4738 Tilden St NW Washington DC 20016 Office: Stanwick Corp PO Box 9184 Rosslyn Station Arlington VA 22209

SHILLING, A. GARY, econ. cons.; b. Fremont, Ohio, May 25, 1937; s. A. Vaughn and Lettie E. (O'Narrow) S.; A.B. magna cum laude, Amherst Coll., 1960; M.A., Stanford U., 1962, Ph.D., 1965; m. Margaret E. Bloete, Dec. 22, 1962; children—Geoffrey, Andrew, Stephen, Jennifer. Economist, Standard Oil Co. (N.J.), 1963-67; chief economist Merrill, Lynch, Pierce, Fenner and Smith, 1967-71; research dir. Estabrook & Co., 1971-72; sr. v.p., chief economist White, Weld & Co., 1972-78; pres. A. Gary Shilling & Co., N.Y.C., 1978—; dir. Am. Republic Ins. Co., N.Y.C. Vestryman, Christ Episcopal Ch., Short Hills, N.J., 1978—. Named Wall St. Top Economist, Instn. Investor mag., 1975, 76. Mem. Nat. Assn. Bus. Economists, N.Y. Soc. Security Analysts. Republican. Clubs: Short Hills; City Mid-day (N.Y.C.). Author articles in field. Office: 111 Broadway New York NY 10006

SHIMKIN, LEON, book publisher; b. Bklyn., Apr. 7, 1907; s. Max and Fannie (Nickelsberg) S.; B.C.S., N.Y. U., 1926; m. Rebecca Rabinowitz, Aug. 17, 1930; children—Emily, Michael. Began career as an accountant; later bus. mgr., treas., and dir. various book pub. enterprises; became pres. and dir. Simon & Schuster, Inc., N.Y.C., 1924, now chmn. bd. emeritus; co-founder Pocket Books, Inc., 1939, pres., 1950—. Trustee Com. Econ. Devel.; trustee N.Y. U., N.Y.C. Home: 8 East Dr Larchmont NY 10538 Office: 630 5th Ave New York NY 10020

SHIMKUS, BEATRICE HELEN, banker; b. Mahanoy City, Pa., Sept. 8, 1925; d. John and Elizabeth (Tirva) S.; student public schs., Mahanoy City. Insp., Mahanoy City Shirt Co., 1943-50; with Western Savs. Bank, Phila., 1950—, adminstrv. asst., 1973-74, banking officer, 1974-77, sr. banking officer, 1977—. Mem. Nat. Assn. Bank Women. Office: Western Savs Bank Broad and Chestnut Sts Philadelphia PA 19103

SHIMP, WILLIAM LEE, food franchise co. exec.; b. Miami, Fla., Feb. 26, 1946; s. William C. and Margaret Lee (Helms) S.; B.S., Fla. State U., 1969, M.B.A., 1971; m. Mary Constantino, June 26, 1971; children—William C., Paul V. Asst. night mgr. Burger King, Miami, 1971, restaurant mgr., 1971-74, dist. mgr., 1974-77, operating partner franchise, Lakeland, Fla., 1977—, Winter Haven, Fla., 1977—. Named Outstanding Young Man of Am., U.S. Jaycees, 1979. Roman Catholic. Home: 2115 Kingswood Ct Lakeland FL 33803 Office: Fla Fast Food Service 0402 S Kentucky Ave Lakeland FL 33801

SHIMURA, HIKARU PAUL, mfg. co. exec.; b. Tokyo, Sept. 5, 1948; came to U.S., 1978; s. Yoshihiro John and Aiko (Onodera) S.; B.S., M.I.T., 1972; m. Toni Yolanda Miyahara, May 12, 1973. Pres., Rigaku Corp. and Rigaku Indsl. Corp., Japan, 1972—; pres., chmn. Rigaku/U.S.A., Inc., Danvers, Mass., 1978—. Mem. Japan Jaycees, Sigma Xi. Home: 101 Mount Vernon St Boston MA 02108 Office: 3 Electronics Ave Danvers MA 01923

SHINEMAN, EDWARD THOMPSON, pub. co. exec.; b. Albany, N.Y., Aug. 23, 1943; s. Edward William and Helen Doris (Thompson) S.; B.A., Cornell U., 1966; m. Anne Shepard Collyer, Apr. 1, 1967; children—Carrie, Katryn, Weylon. Copywriter, Cunningham & Walsh Advt., N.Y.C., 1966-68; with Bozell & Jacobs Advt., N.Y.C., 1968-71; sr. copywriter Dancer Fitzgerald & Sample Advt., N.Y.C., 1971-73; with Xerox Learning Systems, Greenwich, Conn., 1973—, product mgr. direct response, mgr. mktg. communications, 1975-79, pub./bus. sector mgr., 1979—. Mem. Direct Mail Mktg. Assn., Am. Soc. Tng. Dirs., Jr. C. of C. Republican. Congregationalist. Home: 525 Ethan Allen Hwy Ridgefield CT 06877 Office: One Pickwick Plaza Greenwich CT 06830

SHINGLETON, WILLIAM EARL, ins. co. exec.; b. Fairmont, W.Va., Dec. 26, 1923; s. Loxley Oliver and Florence (Snodgrass) S.; B.S., W.Va. U., 1947; m. Willa J. Jenkins, July 16, 1949; children—Robert E., Sally Ann. Appraiser, mortgage loan dept. Prudential Ins. Co., 1947-49; treas. Shingleton Bros. Co., Clarksburg, W.Va., 1949-56; v.p. Henry & Hardesty, Inc., Fairmont, 1956-62, pres., 1962—; pres. First Nat. Bank Fairmont, 1980—, also dir.; mem. W.Va. Legislature, 1971—, chmn. legis. rule making rev. com. Ho. of Dels., 1977—, chmn. banking com., 1977-79. Served with AUS, 1943-46. Mem Marion County C. of C., Conf. Ins. Legislators (exec. bd.). Democrat. Presbyterian. Clubs: Kiwanis, Moose, Elks. Home: 803 Henry Dr Fairmont WV 26554 Office: 517 Fairmont Ave Fairmont WV 26554

SHINN, GEORGE LATIMER, investment banker; b. Newark, Ohio, Mar. 12, 1923; s. Leon Powell and Bertha Florence (Latimer) S.; A.B., Amherst Coll., 1948; LL.D., Denison U., 1975; m. Clara LeBaron Sampson, May 21, 1949; children—Deborah, Amy, Martha, Sarah, Andrew. Trainee, Merrill Lynch, Pierce, Fenner & Beane (now Merrill Lynch, Pierce, Fenner & Smith Inc.), 1948-49, account exec., Boston, 1949-57, office mgr., Boston, 1957-60, v.p., office mgr., Phila. 1960-70, exec. v.p., 1969, vice chmn., 1970-73, pres., 1973—; pres. Goodbody & Co., Inc., 1970—, Merrill Lynch & Co., Inc., 1974-75; chmn. bd. 1st Boston Corp., 1975—; dir. N.Y. Times Co.; trustee Greenwich Savs. Bank, N.Y.C., 1976—; dir. N.Y. Stock Exchange, 1977. bd. govs. Am. Stock Exchange, 1970-74. Gen. chmn. United Hosp. Fund, N.Y.C., 1973-74; trustee Internat. House, Phila., 1961-64, Hahneman Med Coll. and Hosp., Phila., 1960-64, Kent Pl. Sch., Summit, N.J., 1966-73, Carnegie Found. for Advancement of Teaching, 1976, Pingry Sch., 1976; chmn. bd. trustees Amherst Coll., 1973—; adv. council Grad. Sch. Bus. U. Chgo., 1969-79; bd. dirs. Research Corp., 1975—, Wildcat Service Corp., 1973—; trustee Morristown (N.J.) Meml Hosp., 1972—, Morris Museum Arts and Scis., Morristown, 1973—. Served to capt. USMCR, 1943-46. Home: Spring Valley Rd Morristown NJ 07960 Office: 20 Exchange Pl New York NY 10005

SHINN, JAMES PATRICK, econ. analyst; b. Charleston, W.Va., Aug. 6, 1943; s. John Perry and Alice Jane (Smith) S.; B.S. in Econs., U. Pa., 1967; M.B.A. in Fin., N.Y. U., 1975; postgrad. in stats. and computer sci. Columbia U., 1979—. Fin. analyst Dun & Bradstreet, N.Y.C., 1967-69; analyst Paine, Webber, Jackson & Curtis, N.Y.C., 1969-70, Standard & Poor's Corp., N.Y.C., 1970-74, Sawyer-Smith Securities, N.Y.C., 1975-78; econ. analyst N.Y. Stock Exchange, 1978—. Treas., Westhampton Improvement Assn.; v.p. Young Republican Club N.Y.C.; active Manhattan Social Orgn. Registered rep., investment adv. Mem. Fin. Analysts Fedn., N.Y. Soc. Security Analysts, Am. Econ. Assn., Am. Statis. Assn., Am. Inst. Banking. Republican. Methodist. Clubs: Manhattan, Westhampton Athletic, Quogue Tennis. Contbr. articles to trade publs. Office: 11 Wall St New York NY 10005

SHINN, RICHARD RANDOLPH, life ins. co. exec.; b. Lakewood, N.J., Jan. 7, 1918; s. Clayton Randolph and Carrie (McGravey) S.; B.S., Rider Coll., 1938; m. Mary Helen Shea, Nov. 8, 1941; children—Kathleen, Patricia, John. With Met. Life Ins. Co., 1939—, 2d v.p., 1959-63, v.p., 1963-64, sr. v.p., 1964-65, adminstrv. v.p., 1965-66, exec. v.p., 1966-68, sr. exec. v.p., 1968-69, pres., dir., 1969—, chief exec. officer, 1973-80, chmn., chief exec. officer, 1980—, chmn., 1980—; dir. Allied Chem. Corp., Chase Manhattan Bank, May Co., Norton Simon, Inc., Sperry, Putnam Trust. Mem. Mayor's Mgmt. Adv. Com., N.Y. C. of C. and Industry; active Bus. Mktg. Corp., N.Y.C., Greenwich (Conn.) Hosp. Assn., United Way of Tri-State. C.L.U. Mem. Health Ins. Assn. Am. (chmn.), Am. Council Life Ins., Am. Coll. Life Underwriters, Bus. Roundtable, Mgmt. Execs. Soc. Clubs: Stanwich (Greenwich, Conn.); Riverside (Conn.) Yacht; Links (N.Y.C.); Blind Brook (Port Chester N.Y.); Knights of Malta. Home: 31 Lindsay Dr Greenwich CT 06830 Office: 1 Madison Ave New York NY 10010

SHIPP, MAURINE SARAH HARSTON (MRS. LEVI ARNOLD SHIPP), realtor; b. Holiday, Mo., Mar. 6, 1913; d. Paul Edward and Sarah Jane (Mitchell) Harston; grad. Ill. Bus. Coll., 1945; student real estate Springfield Jr. Coll., 1962; student law LaSalle Extension U., 1959-62; m. Levi Arnold Shipp, Jan. 30, 1941; children—Jerome Reynolds, Patricia (Mrs. Rodney W. England). With Ill. Dept. Agr., Springfield, 1941-65, supr. livestock industry Brucellosis sect.; saleswoman Morgan-Hamilton Real Estate Co., Springfield, 1962-64; owner, mgr. Shipp Real Estate Agy., Springfield, 1965—. Prin. appraiser urban renewal HUD, 1971-72. Bd. dirs. Springfield Travelers Aid, 1971—, housing com. Community Action; mem. Springfield Pub. Bldg. Commn., 1975-81. Mem. Springfield Bd. Realtors, Nat., Ill. assns. real estate bds., NAACP, Urban League, Iota Phi Lambda. Episcopalian. Mem. Order Eastern Star. Club: Bridge. Home: 31 Bellerive Rd Springfield IL 62704 Office: 2200 E Cook St Springfield IL 62703

SHIPP, VICTOR RAY, ret. typographer; b. Oklahoma City, Nov. 22, 1921; s. Ray and Pauline (Ballensky) S.; student pub. schs.; m. Wilma Fay Scott, Sept. 27, 1948. Owner, Victor R. Shipp Co., Printers of Distinction, Oklahoma City, 1945-49; sales engr. Am. Typefounders Co., 1949; prodn. engr. So. Calif. Newspaper Prodn. Com., 1950-54; gen. mgr. Southwestern Press, Ft. Smith, Ark., 1954-59; mgmt. cons. engr., Greenville, S.C., then Wichita Falls, Tex., 1959-61; pres. Vic Shipp Typography, Inc., Oklahoma City, 1961-73; ret., 1973; former sec. Creative Printers Am.; former pub. Ad Galley. Mem. nat. adv. bd. Am. Security Council; mem. Second Amendment Found., The Conservative Caucus. Served to capt. USAAF, 1942-45. Decorated Air medal, D.F.C. Republican. Club: U.S. Senatorial. Home: 625 NW 19th St Oklahoma City OK 73103

SHIRCLIFF, JAMES VANDERBURGH, broadcasting exec.; b. Vincennes, Ind., Dec. 11, 1938; s. Thomas Maxwell and Martha Bayard (Somes) S.; A.B., Brown U., 1961; postgrad. U. Va., 1963-64; m. Sally Anne Hoing, June 20, 1964; children—Thomas, Susan, Anne, Catherine, Caroline. Asst. gen. mgr. Pepsi Cola Allied Bottlers, Inc., Lynchburg, Va., 1964-65; gen. mgr. First Colony Canners, Inc., Lynchburg, 1965-66; v.p., divisional coordinator Pepsi Cola Allied Bottlers, Inc., Lynchburg, 1966-68, v.p., dir. personnel, 1968-70; v.p., gen. mgr. GCC Beverages, Inc., Lynchburg, 1970-74, group v.p. Va., 1974-75; corporate v.p. Gen. Cinema Corp., Beverage Div., Lynchburg, 1976-77; owner/mgr. WLLL-AM, WGOL-FM, Lynchburg, 1977—; pres. Jamarbo Corp., 1977— presdl. interchange exec., 1975-76; exec. dir. Nat. Indsl. Energy Council, Dept. Commerce, Washington, 1975-76; dir. Bank of Va., Lynchburg, 1971-75. Vice pres. JOBS, Lynchburg, 1970; dir. Central Va. Health Planning Council, 1974-75; mem. Govs. Indsl. Energy Adv. Council, 1976—; dir. Piedmont council, Boy Scouts Am., 1972-73; mem. City of Lynchburg Keep Lynchburg Beautiful Commn., 1974-75, chmn. emergency planning bd., 1974-75, chmn. overall econ. planning council, 1977—; bd. dirs. Lynchburg Broadway Theatre, 1973-75, Acad. Music, 1973-74, United Fund, Lynchburg, 1966-67, Central Va. Industries, 1971-72; chmn. Citizens for a Clean Lynchburg. Served to lt. (j.g.), USN, 1961-63. Recipient Cloyd Meml. award for outstanding service, Greater Lynchburg C. of C., 1975; Va. Soft Drink Assn. citation, 1970, 73, 74; Public Service award Radio-TV Commn. of So. Bapt. Conv. Mem. Va. C. of C. (dir. 1976-79), Greater Lynchburg C. of C. (dir., v.p. 1973-74, chmn. community appearance task force 1977-79), Va. Soft Drink Assn. (pres. 1973-74), Va. Pepsi Cola Bottlers Assn. (pres. 1970-73), Nat., Va. (dir. 1974) assns. broadcasters, Lynchburg Advt. Club (v.p.), Va. AP Broadcasters (dir.), Lynchburg Fine Arts Center (pres.). Roman Catholic. Clubs: Mensa (N.Y.); Commonwealth (Richmond, Va.); Farmington Country (Charlottesville, Va.); Army-Navy (Washington); Oakwood Country (Lynchburg); Piedmont (Lynchburg); Navy League, Galliard, Rotary (pres.). Home: 3525 Otterview Pl Lynchburg VA 24503

SHIREK, JOHN RICHARD, savs. and loan exec.; b. Bismarck, N.D., Feb. 5, 1926; s. James Max and Anna Agatha (Lala) S.; student U. Minn., 1944-46; B.S. with honors, Rollins Coll., 1978; m. Ruth Martha Lietz, Sept. 22, 1950; children—Barbara Jo Shirek Fowler, Jon Richard, Kenneth Edward. Sports editor Bismarck (N.D.) Tribune, 1943-44; with Gate City Savs. and Loan Assn., Fargo, N.D., 1947-65, v.p., dir., 1960-65; exec. v.p., dir. 1st Fed. Savs. and Loan Assn., Melbourne, Fla., 1966-70; pres., dir. 1st Fed. Savs. and Loan Assn., Cocoa, Fla., 1970—; trustee Savs. & Loan Found., Inc., 1980. Chmn., dir. United Fund, Fargo, N.D., 1962-65; dir., exec. bd. mem. Boy Scouts Am., 1960-70; bd. assos. Fla. Inst. Tech., pres., 1968; moderator St. Johns Presbytery, 1979, chmn. coordinating council, 1980; mem. adv. bd. Brevard Art Center and Mus., 1980. Served to lt. (j.g.) USN, World War II. Mem. Fla. Savs. and Loan League (past dir.), Fla. Savs. and Loan Services (dir.), Savs. and Loan Found. (state membership chmn. 1976), Fla. Savs. and Loan Polit. Action Com. (dir. 1976—), U.S. Savs. and Loan League (chmn. advt. and pub. relations com. 1969-70), Downtown Melbourne Assn. (past pres.), Beta Theta Pi, Omicron Delta Epsilon. Republican. Clubs: Citrus (Orlando, Fla.), Suntree Country (Fla.), Masons, Shriners, Elks, Cocoa Rotary (pres. 1979). Office: 505 Brevard Ave Cocoa FL 32922

SHIREY, DAVID THOMAS, clothing co. exec.; b. Greenville, Tex., Aug. 4, 1932; s. Ferrell E. and Mary A. (Breedlove) S.; B.B.A., Baylor U., 1953; M.B.A., Pepperdine U., 1980; m. Johanna Griffin, Nov. 29, 1952; children—Sheilia Ann, David Thomas, Jr., Stewart Conibear. Prodn. mgr. Shirey Co., Inc., Greenville, 1956-69, pres., 1969—; dir. Sempco, Inc., Greenville; bd. govs. Apparel Mart, Dallas, 1967-73; adv. com. on flammability U.S. Consumer Safety Commn., 1978—. Pres. bd. trustees Greenville Ind. Sch. Dist., 1969-72; chmn. bd. trustees Dallas Bapt. Coll., 1967-72; bd. dirs. Dallas Corp. Higher Edn.; mem. Tex. gov.'s workmen's compensation adv. com. Recipient Worthy Citizen award Greenville C. of C., 1971. Mem. Tex. Assn. Bus. (state chmn. 1976, chmn. exec. com.), Am. Apparel Mfrs. Assn. (dir. 1976—, chmn. Children's Sleepwear div. 1977—, v.p. 1980—), Am. Mfrs. Assn. (dir., chmn. apparel products flamability com.). Baptist (chmn. bd. deacons 1961, 69, 71, 74, 76—). Home: 2207 Stanford St Greenville TX 75401 Office: 1917 Stanford St Greenville TX 75401

SHIRILLA, ROBERT MICHAEL, food co. exec.; b. Youngstown, Ohio, Mar. 21, 1949; s. Michael and Jayne S.; B.A. magna cum laude, UCLA, 1971; M.B.A. with honors (Corning fellow), Harvard U., 1975. Asst. product mgr., Gen. Foods Corp., White Plains, N.Y., 1975-77; mktg. mgr. Hunt Wesson Foods Inc., Fullerton, Calif., 1977—. Bd. dirs. Hugh O'Brian Youth Found., State of Calif., 1977—, March of Dimes. Served to 1st lt. U.S. Army, 1971-73. Mem. Los Angeles World Affairs Council, Acad. Polit. Sci., Commerce Assos., Harvard Bus. Sch. Assn. Southern Calif., Town Hall, Los Angeles Jr. C. of C. (chmn. commerce com. bus. sch. 1978—), Internat. Platform Assn., Theta Chi, Alpha Kappa Psi, Beta Gamma Sigma, Phi Alpha Theta, Omicron Delta Epsilon, Pi Mu Epsilon, Pi Sigma Alpha, Pi Gamma Mu, Phi Eta Sigma, Psi Chi, Beta Alpha Psi. Clubs: Harvard (N.Y.C.); Harvard (So. Calif.). Home: 11088 Ophir Dr Los Angeles CA 90024 Office: 1645 W Valencia Dr Fullerton CA 92634

SHIRK, PERRY WILLIAM, logistics engr.; b. Clark, S.D., Aug. 21, 1930; s. John Irvin and Alice Ruth (Palmquist) S.; B.S., Ariz. State U., 1959; M.S. in Personnel Adminstrn., George Washington U., 1967; m. Jean Marie Wentsel, Dec. 20, 1961; children—Steven, Glenn. Commd. 2d lt. U.S. Air Force, advanced through grades to lt. col., 1970; ret., 1973; civil def. coordinator, Culpeper County, Va., 1975-76; security officer Nat. Geographic Soc., Darnestown, Md., 1976-77; constrn. supt. Dart Drug Corp., Landover, Md., 1978-79; mgr. integrated logistics support Research Analysis Mgmt. Corp., Rockville, Md., 1979; mgmt. analyst Info. Spectrum Inc., Arlington, Va., 1979-80; program mgr. Finkelstein Assos., Inc., Gaithersburg, Md., 1980—. Decorated air medal with 9 oak leaf clusters. Mem. Soc. Logistics Engrs., Am. Def. Preparedness Assn., AIAA. Presbyterian. Clubs: Masons, Shriners. Home: 8944 Centerway Rd Gaithersburg MD 20760

SHIVE, ROY ALLEN, chem. cons.; b. York, Pa., Feb. 6, 1901; s. Jacob Allen and Lizzie (Conley) S.; B.S., Pa. State U., 1921; M.S., U. Ill., 1922, Ph.D., 1924; m. Mary Elizabeth Thompson, Sept. 19, 1925 (dec. 1973); children—Roy Allen Jr., Richard Byron. Research chemist Liberty Yeast Corp., Peking, Ill., 1923-24, U.S. Rubber Co., N.Y.C., 1924-26, E.I. duPont de Nemours & Co., Inc., Wilmington, Del., 1926-32; mgr. devel. and prodn. Arco Co., Cleve., 1932-34; mgr. pigment devel. Am. Cyanamid Co., Bound Brook, N.J., 1932-56; internat. cons. to chem. industry, 1956-80. Head chem. manufacture for synthetic rubber war-time program U.S. Govt., 1942-45. Recipient Modern Pioneer award, Nat. Assn. Mfrs., 1940. Mem. Am. Chem. Soc., Am. Inst. Chemists, Comml. Chem. Devel. Assn., Sigma Xi, Phi Lambda Upsilon. Club: Chemists (N.Y.C.). Address: 1786 Middlebrook Rd Bound Brook NJ 08805

SHIVERS, ALLAN, JR., investment exec.; b. San Antonio, Jan. 21, 1946; s. Allan and Marialice (Shary) S.; diploma U. Tex. at Austin, 1964-68; married. Self-employed in investments, Austin, 1969—; dir. Am. Nat. Bank Austin, Thermal Systems Inc. Bd. dirs., v.p. Easter Seal Soc. for Crippled Children and Adults in Tex.; trustee Tex. Inst. Rehab. and Research, St. Edwards U., Tex. Lyceum Assn. Served with USCG, 1969-69. Mem. Sigma Alpha Epsilon. Office: 920 American Bank Tower Austin TX 78701

SHOCKLEY, PAUL NORRIS, JR., banker; b. Greenville, S.C., May 22, 1941; s. Paul Norris and Esther Sue (Alexander) S.; B.A., Furman U., 1963; M.B.A., U. S.C., 1967; m. Jan Lanier Meadows, Aug. 21, 1964; children—Janell Lanier, Paul Norris III. Staff accountant U.S. Gen. Accounting Office, Atlanta and Washington, 1963-64; mgr. mgmt. reporting Wachovia Bank & Trust Co., Winston-Salem, N.C., 1967-72; v.p., treas. So. Bankshares Inc., Richmond, Va., 1972-79; v.p. Jefferson Bankshares, Inc., Charlottesville, Va., 1979—. Served with U.S. Army, 1964-66. Mem. Nat. Assn. Accountants, Am. Inst. Banking, Res. Officers Assn., Blue Ridge Assn., Fin. Execs. Inst., Tau Kappa Epsilon. Republican. Baptist. Club: Farmington Country. Home: 2643 Cardinal Ridge Rd Charlottesville VA 22901 Office: 123 E Main St Charlottesville VA 22901

SHOECRAFT, TIM HENRY, fin. cons., ins. and stock broker; b. Syracuse, N.Y., June 27, 1949; s. Byron H. and Frances G. (Whipple) S.; student Rochester Inst. Tech., 1967-68, 71-72; B.A., State U. N.Y., Oswego, 1973; postgrad. in fin. scis., fin. planning, pension cons. programs. Legal intern Amdursky & Hurlbutt, Oswego, 1973-74; estate analyst Conn. Gen. Life, Syracuse, 1974-76; pres. Shoecraft & Assos. Bus. Cons. Corp., 1976—; v.p. Compensation Analysis, Inc., 1980—. Leader, adviser Hiawatha council Boy Scouts Am., 1969—; active campaign United Way, Oswego, 1975-76; former mem. Oswego County Democratic Com. Served with Intelligence Corps, U.S. Army, 1968-71. Recipient numerous awards Boy Scouts Am., 1969-73; Pres's. Hon. award Conn. Mut. Life, 1977; named to Million Dollar Roundtable, annually, 1977-81; named Agency Leader, Conn. Mut. Life, Syracuse, 1976 annually-79. Mem. Nat., Westchester assns. life underwriters, Nat. Fedn. Ind. Businessmen. Democrat. Methodist. Club: Rotary (dir.) (Oswego). Office: 44 S Broadway Suite 1545 White Plains NY 10601

SHOEMAKER, WILLIAM EDWARD, resort exec.; b. Charleston, W.Va., Sept. 17, 1945; s. Robert Edward and Janet Elizabeth (Hoglund) S.; B.B.A., U. Notre Dame, 1967. Asso. buyer Proctor & Gamble, Cin., 1971-72; gen. mgr. Eastwind, Inc., Anchorage, 1972-73; pres. Golden Horn Lodge, Inc., Anchorage, 1973-79; pres. Hamano & Shoemaker, Inc., 1979—; dir. Cemco, Inc.; treas., dir. Coronado Mining Corp., C.C. Hawley & Assos., Inc. Bd. dirs. Friends of River, Japan. Served with USN, 1967-71. Mem. Alaska Visitors Assn., Game Conservation Internat. Republican. Home: 4811 Bishop Way Anchorage AK 99504 Office: PO Box 546 Anchorage AK 99510

SHOEN, LEONARD SAMUEL, bus. exec.; b. McGrath, Minn., Feb. 29, 1916; s. Samuel J. and Sophia B. (Appert) S.; grad. Moler Barber Coll., 1936; B.A., Oreg. State U., 1941; LL.B., Northwestern U., 1955; m. Anna Mary Carty, 1944 (dec. 1957); m. 2d, Suzanne Gilbaugh, 1958 (div. 1977); m. 3d, Suzanne Whitmore, 1978 (div. 1978). Founder, 1945, then pres. U-Haul Rental System; pres. U-Haul Internat., Inc., from 1952; founder, 1969, thereafter chmn. bd. and pres. Amerco Co., Phoenix. Served with USNR, 1944-45. Author: (autobiography) You and Me, 1980. Office: PO Box 21502 Phoenix AZ 85036

SHOFFNER, MYRON ALLEN, coal co. exec.; b. Dora, Pa., Aug. 28, 1921; s. Charles Myron and Mildred Velma (Tyger) S.; B.S., E.E., Mass. Inst. Tech., 1943; m. Beverly Fairweather Smith, May 21, 1944 (div. 1964); children—Freya A., Kyra J. Engr., Internat. Resistence Corp., Phila., 1946-49; with Ringgold Corp., Kittanning, Pa., 1949-; pres., 1955—; pres. Ringgold Coal Mining Co., Kittanning, 1970—. Served as lt. CAC, AUS, 1943-46. Home: 105 N 6th Ave Butler PA 16001 Office: Ringgold Coal Mining Co Keystone Bldg Kittanning PA 16201

SHONK, ALBERT DAVENPORT, JR., publishers rep.; b. Los Angeles, May 23, 1932; s. Albert Davenport and Jean Spence (Stannard) S.; B.S. in Bus. Adminstrn., U. So. Calif., 1954. Field rep. Los Angeles Examiner, 1954-55, asst. mgr. mktg. div. 1955-56, mgr., 1956-57; account exec. Hearst Advt. Service, Los Angeles, 1957-59; account exec., mgr. San Francisco area Keith H. Evans & Assos., 1959-65; owner, pres. Albert D. Shonk Co., Los Angeles, 1965—; pres., dir. Signet Circle Corp., Inc. Bd. dirs., sec., exec. v.p. Florence Crittenton Services of Los Angeles. Recipient Medallion of Merit Phi Sigma Kappa, 1976. Founders award, 1961. Mem. Advt. Club Los Angeles, Bus. and Profl. Advt. Assn., Publishers Rep. Assn. (regional v.p. 1981—), Peninsula Mktg. Assn., Jr. Advt. Club Los Angeles (dir., treas., hon. life, 1st v.p.), Los Angeles Jr. C. of C., Trojan Club, Inter-Greek Soc. (life dir.), Commerce Assos., Inter-Greek Soc. (co-founder, v.p., dir.), Phi Sigma Kappa (dir. grand council, grand pres. 1979—), Alpha Kappa Psi. Home: 3460 W 7th St Los Angeles CA 90005 Office: 3156 Wilshire Blvd Los Angeles CA 90010

SHONT, ESTHER MAY, trust co. exec.; b. N.Y.C., Nov. 23, 1916; d. Levon Sarkis and Lillian Katherine (Blume) Shont; B.A., Hunter Coll., 1937; M.B.A., N.Y. U., 1949; postgrad. N.Y. Law Sch., 1950-51, N.Y. U. Sch. Law, 1951-53; certificate Bank Adminstrn. Inst. Sch. of Banking U. Wis., 1963-65. With Bankers Trust Co., N.Y.C. 1943—, dep. auditor 1965-68, v.p. securities operations, 1969—, group head, computer systems devel. dept., 1971-73, mgr. mktg. nat. banking dept., 1973—; tchr. Am. Inst. Banking; guest lectr. FBI Acad., Quantico Bay. Past pres. service aux. Beekman Downtown Hosp. Mem. Bank Adminstrn. Inst. (nat. trust commn., 1968-69, nominating com. 1972, chmn. by laws com. N.Y.C. chpt. 1971—, dist. dir. 1972—), Nat. Assn. Banking Women. Home: Brooklyn NY Office: Bankers Trust Co 280 Park Ave New York NY 10017

SHOOK, DIANNE LEE, Realtor; b. Duluth, Minn., Dec. 21, 1936; d. Joseph Frank and Melville Elaine (Munslow) Proff; student Southeastern State U., Durant, Okla., 1958-59, Nat. Assn. Realtors, Comml. Real Estate, 1975; grad. Real Estate Inst., 1976; m. Wendell E. Shook, Nov. 27, 1954; children—Warren Edward, Aimee Michaelle, Jonathan Everett, Lisa Dianne. Loan processor Durant (Okla.) Bank and Trust Co., 1968-71; real estate agt., mgr. comml. real estate div. Pride Real Estate, Oklahoma City, 1971-76; owner, pres. Century 21, Dianne Shook Co., Oklahoma City, 1976—, sales mgr. SW 59th St. office. Vestry mem., ch. treas. St. James Episcopal Ch., Oklahoma City, 1976-77, mem. bishop's growth com. Episcopal Diocese Okla. Cert. real estate broker, cert. residential specialist. Mem. Oklahoma City Metro Bd. Realtors, Women's Council Realtors (dir.), S. Oklahoma City Bd. Realtors (sec., dir. 1977), Oklahoma City Sales and Mktg. Execs. Club, Oklahoma City Met., S. Oklahoma City chambers commerce. Republican. Clubs: Capitol Hill Bus. and Profl. Women's, Beta Sigma Phi (sec. Eta Xi chpt.). Home: 6300 S Broadway Dr Oklahoma City OK 73139 Office: 222 SW 74th St Oklahoma City OK 73159

SHOOK, HERBERT MORRIS, sales and image cons., writer; b. Pitts., May 23, 1912; s. Louis and Anna Ella (Sandler) S.; B.A., Duquesne U., 1933; m. Belle Slutsky, Oct. 21, 1934; children—Lois, Robert L., Richard R., Nancy Joan. Propr., Herber's Jewelry Co., 1939-57; owner Herbert M. Shook Co., 1949-57; mgr., partner Pitts. regional office Markus Assos., 1957-61; pres. Shook Assos. Corp., Pitts., 1961—, Am. Exec. Life Ins. Co., 1961-78; owner Herbert M. Shook Co. Sales Consultants, Discount Hot-Line, Inc. Com. chmn. United Fund; bd. dirs. United Jewish Fund, 1974-78, chmn. ins. div., 1978; bd. dirs. Rodef Shalom Men's Club; mem. Republican Com. Allegheny County, Duquesne U. Alumni. Clubs: Press, Kiwanis. Author: (with Robert L. Shook) How to Be the Complete Professional Salesman, 1974, How to Become a Sales-Marketing Specialist, 1979; Building Sales Confidence Through Sales Knowledge, 1980. Home: 540 N Nevill St Apt 505 Pittsburgh PA 15213 Office: 160 N Craig St Pittsburgh PA 15213

SHOPEY, ROBERT JOHN, mfg. co. exec.; b. Bristol, Conn., June 8, 1939; s. Dennis and Jennie (Sarajak) S.; student Gilbert Sch., 1953-56; children—Robert John II, Linda M. With Pratt & Whitney Aircraft Co., E. Hartford, Conn., 1960-69; shop supt. William Tell Corp., Thomaston, Conn., 1969-71; quality control mgr. Egan Machine Corp., Bristol, Conn., 1971—. Vice pres. Winsted Safety Council, 1960—; chmn., commr. Winchester Housing Authority, 1973—; commr. Econ. Devel. Commn., 1974—; mem. Winsted Fire Dept., 1969—; commr. Housing Bd. Code of Appeals, 1973—; mem. Republican Town com., 1977—; mem. bd. Christian edn. 1st Ch. of Winsted; mem. Community Devel. Action Plan, 1970-71, Public Safety Task Force, 1970-71. Served with USAF, 1956-60. Recipient award Nat. Vehicle Safety Check, 1968; award for distinction State of Conn., 1976. Mem. Am. Soc. Quality Control, Conn. Assn. Mcpl. Devel. Conn. Orgn. Econ. Devel., Indls. Mgmt. Club. Clubs: Redmens, Masons, Elks. Home: 52 Maloney Ct Winsted CT Office: 135 Center St Bristol CT 06098

SHORE, BARRY FREDERIC, diamond co. exec.; b. Boston, Dec. 2, 1948; s. Bernard and Frances Shore; B.A. in History, U. Mass., 1974; internat. degree in history Frei U. (Netherlands), 1972; m. Poradee Kompiranond, Sept. 21, 1977. Owner, mgr. Fred Boutique, Boston, 1972-74; partner Gemma Corp., Los Angeles, 1977-80; pres. Univ. Gems Inc., Los Angeles, 1980—; cons. in field. Jewish. Contbr. Precious Stones Newsletter, 1978-80. Office: 707 Wilshire Blvd 4760 Los Angeles CA 90017

SHORE, SIDNEY X., pub., lectr.; b. N.Y.C., Apr. 7, 1916; s. Morris M. and Dinah M. S.; B.S. in Physics, CCNY, 1938; m. Gabrielle Arie, Jan. 14, 1939; children—Peter, Eric. Physicist, N.Y.C. Dept. Hosps., 1939; radio engr. N.Y.C. Fire Dept., 1941; sr. engr. N. Am. Philips Co., 1942-45; pres. Leshore Corp., 1946-56, Shore Mfg. Corp., 1956-60; v.p. research and devel. Cole Nat. Corp., 1960-63; pub. Creativity in Action, Sharon, Conn., 1972—; pres. Shorex, Cons. Firm, Sharon, 1972—. Mem. Am. Soc. Tng. and Devel., Internat. Solar Energy Soc., Creative Edn. Found., Photog. Soc. Am. Address: Sharon Valley Rd Sharon CT 06069

SHORT, FRANCIS JAMES, automobile co. exec.; b. Gloucester, N.J., Sept. 4, 1927; s. Albert E. and Mary Esther (King) S.; B.S., Rider Coll., Trenton, N.J., 1953; student U. Chgo., 1962; m. Joan C. Chamberlin, May 5, 1951; children—Michael, Cathryn, Margaret, Thomas, Robert. With personnel dept. RCA Service Co., Camden, N.J., 1947-50; adminstr. wages and salary Capchart-Farnsworth div. ITT, Fort Wayne, Ind., 1950-56; personnel cons. Booz, Allen & Hamilton, Chgo., 1956-60; v.p. personnel Globe-Union, Inc., Milw., 1960-70; v.p. personnel Philip Morris Indsl., Milw., 1970-75; v.p. employee relations Allegheny-Ludlum's True Temper Div., Cleve., 1975-77; v.p. personnel and indsl. relations Volkswagen of Am., Inc., Warren, Mich., 1977—. Served with USNR, 1945-46. Mem. Am. Soc. Personnel Adminstrs. (pres.'s council), Indsl. Relations Assn. Wis. (past pres., dir.). Clubs: Cleve. Athletic, Rochester Hills Tennis. Office: 27621 Parkview Blvd Warren MI 48092

SHORT, JAMES LAUGHLIN, steel co. exec.; b. Phila., Apr. 25, 1937; s. Vyval Clarence and Matilda Louise (Elliott) S.; B.S. in Indsl. Engring., Pa. State U., 1959; postgrad. in Bus. Adminstrn., U. Chgo., 1963-65; m. LaVerne Lou Cowan, Nov. 26, 1960; children—Kelly Anne, Holly Lyndell. With Nat. Steel Corp., various locations, 1959—, sr. sales rep., Chgo., 1968-73, sales mgr. Auto Sales div., Detroit, 1973-77, mgr. market planning and forecasting, 1977-79, asst. gen. sales mgr. Auto Sales div., Southfield, Mich., 1979—. Mem. Am. Iron and Steel Inst., Soc. Auto Engrs., Sigma Chi. Republican. Roman Catholic. Clubs: Recess (Detroit); Pine Lake Country (Orchard Lake, Mich.). Home: 1966 Squirrel Valley Dr Bloomfield Hills MI 48013 Office: 4000 Town Center Southfield MI 48075

SHORT, STEVE EUGENE, engr.; b. Crockett, Calif., Oct. 17, 1938; s. Roger Milton and Ida Mae (Mills) S.; B.S. in Gen. Engring. with honors, U. Hawaii, 1972, M.B.A., 1973; M.S. in Meteorology, U. Md., 1980; m. Yumie Sedaka, Feb. 2, 1962; children—Anne Yumie, Justine Yumie, Katherine Yumie. With Nat. Weather Service, NOAA, 1964—, engring. mgr., Silver Spring, Md., 1974-81, automation program mgr., 1980—; mgmt. cons. SBA. Served with USMC, 1956-60. Registered profl. engr., Hawaii. Mem. Am. Meteorol. Soc., Japan-Am. Soc., Am. Soc. Public Adminstrn. Home: 3307 Rolling Rd Chevy Chase MD 20015 Office: Nat Weather Service 8060 13th St Silver Spring MD 20910

SHOSTAK, MARJORIE M., lawyer; b. Lincoln, Nebr., Nov. 14, 1914; d. Samuel Louis and Esther (Orloff) S.; A.B., U. Nebr., 1935. Admitted to Calif. bar, 1945, bar U.S. Customs Ct., U.S. Ct. Customs and Patent Appeals, U.S. Supreme Ct.; admitted to practice before U.S. Treasury Dept.; law clk. with lawyer, Los Angeles, 1935-37, office mgr., 1937-45; partner law firm Philip Stein, 1946-55; sr. partner Stein and Shostak, 1955-76; pres. Stein, Shostak, Shostak & O'Hara, Inc., 1976—; asst. instr. U. So. Calif., 1946-53. Mem. industry adv. com. Los Angeles Customs Dist., 1967-68; mem. Industry Functional Adv. Com. on Customs Valuation, 1980—. Mem. Am., Los Angeles County (chmn. customs law com. 1970-72, mem. customs law com. 1973—) bar assns., Am. Judicature Soc., Nat. Assn. Women Lawyers, Am. Importers Assn. (mem. custom com. 1965-76, mem. importers rights com. 1977—), Assn. Customs Bar (mem. com. on discipline 1967-69, dir. 1967-68, mem. com. on practice, procedure and legis. 1974-77), State Bar Calif., Fgn. Trade Assn. So. Calif. (hon.; dir. 1957-62, chmn. bd. dirs. 1961, sec. 1958, v.p. 1959-60, chmn. com. on sect. 592), Women Lawyers Assn., Los Angeles Area C. of C. (chmn. import legis. com. 1955-70, 76—, world trade exec. com. 1963-75, internat. commerce com., internat. commerce exec. com. 1976—, recipient bronze plaque for outstanding contbn. to cause and advancement internat. trade 1963, gen. chmn. World Trade Week 1972, vice chmn. world trade com. 1970-75), Nat. Lawyers Club, AAUW, Phi Beta Kappa, Alpha Lambda Delta. Club: Internat. (bd. govs.). Office: 3435 Wilshire Blvd Los Angeles CA 90010

SHOWALTER, DAVID HADLEY, computer service bur. exec.; b. Cleve., Dec. 26, 1949; s. Royce Lewis and Paula Kathlene (Moschell) S.; B.S. in Zoology, Ohio State U., 1975; m. Patricia Louise McMullen, Apr. 9, 1976; 1 dau., Kristina Kathlene. Gen. mgr. Heck's Cafe Systems, Cleve., 1977-78; computer operator Computerized Payrolls, Cleve., 1978-79, dir. ops., chief operating officer, 1979—. Served with U.S. Army, 1969-70. Mem. Bus. Adv. Council, Euclid Jaycees, Alpha Phi Omega (life). Office: 714 E 200th St Cleveland OH 44119

SHRADER, TERRELL S., ret. airline exec.; b. Chattanooga, Aug. 4, 1917; s. Terrell and Helen (Spear) S.; LL.D., U. Miami, 1950; m. Janet Seerth, Aug. 9, 1942; children—Terrell S., Janelle (Mrs. Richard L. Smith), Darrell, Michelle. With Eastern Airlines, 1945-59, asst. to the v.p. indsl. and personnel relations, 1950-53, indsl. relations adminstr., 1953-59; dir. indsl. relations Western Air Lines, Los Angeles, 1959-63, asst. v.p. indsl. relations, 1963-65, v.p. indsl. relations, 1965-68; v.p. personnel and labor relations Braniff Airways, Inc., 1968-75, sr. v.p., 1975-80; dir. 1st Nat. Bank, Euless, Tex., 1977—. Served to 1st lt. USAAF, 1942-45. Mem. Fla. Bar Assn., Los Angeles C. of C., Pi Kappa Alpha, Phi Alpha Delta. Rotarian. Home: 16024 Chalfont Circle Dallas TX 75248

SHREIBMAN, S. JUNE SNYDER, public acct.; b. Asbury Park, N.J.; d. Herman and Anna (Flaxer) Snyder; student CCNY, N.Y. U., Temple U.; m. Oscar Shreibman (dec.); 1 son, Henry Maynard. Ind. public acct., cost acct., N.Y.C.; cost acct. with various firms; public acct., asso. Shreibman, Baron & Schwartz, Phila., div. small bus. div., 1960-67; ind. public acct. estate planning, mgmt., Phila., 1967—; public acct., fin. cons. to women in professions, cons. personal fin., estate planning, mgmt., 1972—; vol. cons. Small Bus. Opportunities Corp., Phila., 1967; designer workshops in fin. mgmt., fin. thanatology, course in personal fin. Inst. Awareness, Phila., 1972-76; lectr. in field; 1st woman mem. Pa. Bd. Examiners Public Accts., 1977—; mem. legis. com. Penjerdel Corp.; sec. Pa. C.P.A. Bd., 1980-81. Bd. dirs., project designer, developer Women for Bicentennial (Pa. Corp.), 1974-77; mem. sch. bd. Germantown Jewish Center, Phila.; treas. Eastern Pa. Women's Polit. Caucus, 1969-71; mem. Hadassah, Phila., chmn. public relations and nat. affairs, 1956-59; bd. dirs. Zionist Orgn. Am., Phila., 1970-76, mem. audit com., 1975-76; v.p. Women for Greater Phila., 1978-81. Honoree, inscribed in Women's Hall of Fame (Seneca Falls, N.Y.), Bus. and Profl. Women Phila., 1979. Mem. Nat. Assn. State Bds. Accountancy, Nat. Soc. Public Accts. (accredited; public accts. on state accountancy bds. com.; com. legis. 1979—), Pa. Soc. Public Accts. (chmn. Phila. chpt. 1970-72, chpt. dir. 1961—, state dir. 1965—, mem. IRS liaison com. 1970-72, assistance com. 1969-74, publs. and public relations com. 1961-74), Assn. Tng. and Devel., Greater Phila. C. of C. (tax coms.). Address: Suite 512 1900 John F Kennedy Blvd Philadelphia PA 19103

SHRIER, ADAM LOUIS, energy co. exec.; b. Warsaw, Poland, Mar. 26, 1938; s. Henry Leon and Mathilda June (Czamanska) S.; came to U.S., 1943, naturalized, 1949; B.S., Columbia, 1959; M.S. (Whitney fellow), Mass. Inst. Tech., 1960; D.Eng. and Applied Sci. (NSF fellow), Yale, 1965; postdoctoral visitor U. Cambridge (Eng.), 1965-66; J.D., Fordham U., 1976; m. Diane Kesler, June 10, 1961; children—Jonathan, Lydia, Catherine, David. With Esso Research & Engring. Co., Florham Park and Linden, N.J., 1963-65, 66-72, head environ. scis. research area, 1969-72; coordinator pollution abatement activities, tanker dept. Exxon Internat. Co., N.Y.C., 1972-74; project mgr., energy systems Exxon Enterprises, Inc., N.Y.C., 1974-75, mgr. solar energy projects, 1975-77, gen. mgr. solar heating and cooling div., 1977-78, pres. solar thermal systems div., 1979—; dir. Solar Power Corp., Daystar Corp.; adj. lectr. chem. engring. Columbia, N.Y.C., 1967-68, 68-69. Mem. Am. Inst. Chem. Engrs., Am. Chem. Soc., AAAS, N.Y. Acad. Scis., Internat. Solar Energy Soc., Am. Bar Assn. Contbr. articles to profl. jours. Patentee in field. Home: 543 Park St Upper Montclair NJ 07043 Office: Exxon Corp 1251 Ave of Americas New York NY 10020

SHRIER, STEFAN, applied mathematician; b. Mexico City, Nov. 7, 1942; came to U.S., 1943, naturalized, 1949; s. Henry Leon and Mathilda June (Czamanska) S.; B.S., Columbia U., 1964, M.S., 1966; Ph.D. (NDEA fellow), Brown U., 1977. Research asst. Brown U., 1966-71, 75-77, teaching fellow applied math., 1971-72; chmn. computer sci. program, dir. acad. computing services Wellesley Coll., 1972-75; sr. engr. Booz, Allen & Hamilton, Bethesda, Md., 1977-79; dir. Latin Am. ops. Softech, Inc., Springfield, Va., 1979-80; mem. research staff System Planning Corp., Arlington, Va., 1980—. Mem. AAAS, Am. Math. Soc., IEEE, Math. Assn. Am., Sigma Xi, Tau Beta Pi. Contbr. articles profl. jours. Office: 1500 Wilson Blvd Arlington VA 22209

SHRIVER, DON ALBERT, banker; b. Nashville, Aug. 25, 1943; s. Thomas Abraham and Attie Eugenia (Humphreys) S.; B.A., Vanderbilt U., 1964, postgrad. 1964-66; cert., Nat. Trust Sch., Northwestern U., 1969; grad. Stonier Grad. Sch. Banking, Rutgers U., 1979; m. Bertie Foster, Aug. 14, 1965; children—Dee Vernon. Trust officer First Am. Nat. Bank, Nashville, 1966-73; with Third Nat. Bank, Nashville, 1974—, v.p., central territorial mgr., 1977—. Bd. dirs. Am. Cancer Soc., 1970-77, 80—, treas. 1975-76; chmn. Pub. Info. Com., 1980—, mem. exec. com., 1980-81; bd. dirs. Cystic Fibrosis, 1979—; mem. vestry Christ Episcopal Ch., 1970-74, 76-79, chmn. Christian edn. com., 1978-79. Served with U.S. Army, 1967-73. Mem. Fin. Mgrs. Assn. Nashville (bd. dirs. 1976-79), Am. Bankers Assn. Republican. Episcopalian. Clubs: Belle Meade Country, Exchange, Vanderbilt Alumni (bd. dirs. 1972-76). Home: 3909 Trimble Rd Nashville TN 37215 Office: 201 4th Ave N Nashville TN 37244

SHRIVER, EDGAR LOUIS, psychologist, research and devel. co. exec.; b. Canton, Ohio, Apr. 1, 1927; s. Elmer George and Clara (Kellogg) S.; B.A., Washington and Jefferson Coll., 1950; M.A., U. Rochester, 1951; Ph.D., U. Pitts., 1953; m. Beatrice Meirowitz, 1951 (div. 1961); 1 son, John Adam; m. 2d, Sara Baker Eden, Aug. 15, 1961; children—Katherine Louise, Craig Edgar, Paul Kellogg. Research psychologist Am. Inst. for Research, Pitts., 1951-52; sr. staff scientist Human Resources Research Office, Washington, 1953-68; v.p., dir. Matrix Corp., Alexandria, Va.; pres. Tech. Tng. Corp., Washington, 1961-73; pres. Alexandria Community Sch., 1972-73; pres., chmn. bd. Kinton, Inc., Alexandria, 1973—; cons. Westinghouse Corp., AT&T. Served with USNR, 1945-46. Fellow Am. Psychol. Assn.; mem. AAAS, Eastern Psychol. Assn., D.C. Psychol. Assn., Phi Kappa Sigma. Presbyterian. Office: Suite 205 1500 N Beauregard Alexandria VA 22311

SHRUM, SAMUEL HOPKINS, constrn. co. exec.; b. Dayton, Va., June 19, 1912; s. George Edgar and Annie (Rolston) S.; B.S., Va. Poly. Inst., 1933; postgrad. Westminster Choir Coll., 1938; m. Evelyn L. Vaughan, June 14, 1941; children—Edgar Vaughan, Marilyn Ann. Partner, George E. Shrum & Son, masonry contractors, 1933-42; prodn. engr. Newport News Shipbldg. & Drydock Co., 1942-45; exec. v.p., gen. mgr. treas., dir. Nielsen Constrn. Co., Harrisonburg, Va., 1945-61, pres., 1961-73, chmn. bd., chief exec. officer, 1974-75; dir. Rockingham Nat. Bank; dir., exec. v.p. Alexandria Prestressed Concrete Co., Inc. 1961; exec. v.p., gen. mgr. Shen Valley, Inc. 1964-67, also dir.; sec.-treas., gen. mgr. of Valley Developers, Inc., 1964-70, also dir. Chmn. Capitol Stock Com., vice-chmn. bldg. com.; mem. Rockingham Devel. Corp.; mem. steering com., publicity chmn. Bridgewater Coll. Crusade for Excellence; mem. com. on nominations Presbytery of Lexington; pres. Sunnyside Presbyn. Home, 1967-71, 72—; mem. Nat. Right of work Com., Washington; mem. state adv. council for vocational edn. Commonwealth of Va., 1971-74. Trustee, asst. treas. Sunnyside Presbyn. Home, 1952, bd. dirs., chmn. finances; bd. dirs. Va. Found. Archtl. Edn., Inc.; trustee v.p. Massanetta Springs Bible Conf., 1953-58; mem. Harrisonburg Downtown Devel. Com., 1975—; mem. Indsl. Devel. Authority Rockingham County (Va.); chmn., Westminster Fellowship, Campus Christian Life Com., 1959-65; chmn. coordinating com. Homes for Aging, Synod of Va., 1968-70. Trustee Presbyn. Nursing Homes, Inc.; adv. council Sch. Bus., James Madison U., Harrisonburg, 1978—. Named Va. Constrn. Man of Year, 1970; recipient Nations 1st Nat. Bus. Day award, Bus. Man of Year award, 1975. Mem. Engrs. Soc., Nat. Small Bus. Men's Assn., Nat. Labor-Mgmt. Found., Harrisonburg-Rockingham, Va. chambers commerce, Vocational Indsl. Clubs Am. (hon. life mem.), Shenandoah Valley, Inc., Asso. Gen. Contractors (v.p., dir. Va., mem. nat. com. emergency planning, pres. Va. br. 1969-70, nat. membership com. 1968—, nat. manpower com. 1969—. Presbyn. (past deacon, mem. of session, 1946—). Mason, Rotarian (pres. 1967-68, dir. Harrisonburg). Home: Sunnyside Village Harrisonburg VA 22801 Office: Sunnyside Village Harrisonburg VA 22801

SHUGRUE, MARTIN ROGER, JR., airline exec.; b. Providence, Aug. 31, 1940; s. Martin Roger and Dorothy Elizabeth (Campbell) S.; B.A. in Econs., Providence Coll., 1962; m. Marianne Zaalbert van Zelst, Mar. 9, 1979; children—Catherine, Michael, Marijke. Pilot, flight engr. Pan Am. World Airways, N.Y.C., 1968-70, dir. performance measurements, 1970-72, dir. orgn. planning, 1972-74, staff v.p. corp. personnel, 1974-78, mng. dir. U.K. and Western Europe, London, 1978-80, v.p. personnel, N.Y.C., 1980—. Served with USN, 1962-68. Mem. Airline Orgn. Planning and Adminstrn. Assn. (founding), Res. Officers Assn., Assn. for Naval Aviation, Navy League, U.S. C. of C., Westminster C. of C. Clubs: Wings (N.Y.C.); Am. (London). Home: 26 Berndale Dr Westport CT 06880 Office: 200 Park Ave New York NY 10166

SHULMAN, ANDREW JOSEPH, appliance mfg. co. exec.; b. Cambridge, Mass., July 6, 1941; s. Joseph and Rose Shulman; B.B.A., U. Mass., 1963; M.B.A., Columbia U., 1965; m. Patricia Brenner, Sept. 10, 1967; children—Roberta, David. Salesman, Allied Chem. Coatings Co., Saco, Maine, 1965-66; with ordnance dept. Gen. Electric Co., Pittsfield, Mass., 1966-69, with mktg. mgmt. program lamp dept., Cleve., 1969, product planner splty. materials dept., Columbus, Ohio, 1969-75, cons. corp. cons. services, Bridgeport, Conn., 1975-78, mgr. strategic planning product service dept. Louisville, 1978—. Mem. Elfun Mgmt. Assn., Assn. M.B.A. Execs. Jewish. Author: Steel Grinding: Past, Present, Future, 1970. Home: 7116 Springdale Rd Louisville KY 40222 Office: 315 Watterson City E Louisville KY 40225

SHULTZ, FREDERICK ALAN, data processing exec.; b. Dayton, Ohio, Oct. 17, 1942; s. Frederick Arthur and Imogene (Brown) S.; B.S., Bowling Green State U., 1964; postgrad. Ohio State U., 1964; m. Sandra Lee Werner, June 20, 1964; children—Jody Lynn, Susan Renee. With Nat. Cash Register Co., Dayton, 1964-73, mgr. online retail devel., 1970-72, mgr. online fin. devel., 1972-73; v.p. data processing 1st Fed. Savs. & Loan of Broward, Ft. Lauderdale, Fla., 1973-77; v.p. data processing Peoples Savs. Co., Toledo, 1977—. Bd. dirs. Lucas County Fair Bd. Served with USMC, 1963. Mem. Fin. Mgrs. Soc., Data Processing Mgrs. Assn., Savs. and Loan Inst., Fin. Users Group., Phi Kappa Psi. Republican. Methodist. Clubs: Kiwanis, Masons, Shriners. Home: 1905 Somerville Maumee OH 43537 Office: Caller #10011 Toledo OH 43699

SHUMAKER, MAURICE CALVIN, bank exec.; b. Spokane, Wash., Jan. 13, 1921; s. John Calvin and Alice Mabel (Henderickson) S.; B.A. in Fin., U. Wash., 1947; postgrad. Pacific Coast Banking Sch., 1961; cert. comml. lender U. Okla., 1974; postgrad. Exec. Mgmt. Acad., U. Mich., 1978; m. Beth Ramsey Harius, Apr. 29, 1944; children—Margaret Ann, John William, Mary Beth, David Calvin. With Rainier Bank, Spokane, 1946—, v.p., 1964-76, sr. v.p., mgr. main office, 1976—; mem. adv. bd. Small Bus. Devel. Center, Wash. State U. Pres., Twin Harbors council Boy Scouts Am., 1971-74, v.p. Inland Empire council, 1976-80. Served with USAAF, 1943-45; ETO. Decorated D.F.C., Air medal with 3 oak leaf clusters. Recipient Silver Beaver award Boy Scouts Am., 1970. Mem. Am. Inst. Banking, Wash. Bankers Assn., Robert Morris Assos. Presbyterian. Clubs: Manito

Golf, Spokane City, Wash. Athletic (bd. govs. 1967-69), Elks. Home: E1503 Woodcliff Rd Spokane WA 99203 Office: PO Box 366 Spokane WA 99210

SHUMAN, STANLEY SAXE, investment banker; b. Cambridge, Mass., June 22, 1935; s. Saul Aaron and Sarah Lillian (Saxe) S.; grad. Phillips Acad., Andover, Mass., 1952; B.A., Harvard, 1956, J.D., 1959, M.B.A., 1961; m. Ruth Helen Lande, Nov. 19, 1967; children—David Lande, Michael Adam. Admitted to Mass. bar, 1959; with Allen & Co. Inc., N.Y.C., 1961—, exec. v.p., 1970—, also dir., mem. exec. com.; dir. N.Y. Post Corp., N.Y. Mag., News Am. Pub. Inc. Bd. dirs. Wiltwyck Sch., pres., 1971-78; trustee, v.p. exec. com. Dalton Sch.; v.p., bd. dirs., mem. exec. com. Jewish Guild for the Blind; chmn. Nat. Economic Devel. and Law Center; mem. Gov. Hugh Carey's Task Force on Umemployment; mem. Fin. Control Bd. N.Y.C. Mem. Am. Bar Assn. (comml. arbitration com.). Club: City Athletic, Harvard of Boston, Harvard of N.Y.C., Quaker Ridge Golf, East Hampton Tennis. Home: 17 E 73d St New York NY 10021 Office: 711 Fifth Ave New York NY 10004

SHUMATE, DAN, mobile home co. exec.; b. Little Rock, June 10, 1945; s. John Daniel and Sadie Juanita (Finch) S.; student public schs., Jacksonville, Ark.; m. Linda Kay Russell, Sept. 12, 1969; children—Scott, Stuart, Spencer. Sales mgr., Green Acres Mobile Home Sales, Jacksonville, 1968-72; dist. mgr. retail sales Indon Industries, Ark., 1973-76; owner, pres. Shelter Homes of Ark., Jacksonville, 1973—. Served with U.S. Army, 1963-66. Mem. Ark. Manufactured Housing Assn. (dir. 1977-80, pres. 1981), Jacksonville C. of C., Jacksonville Jaycees (dir. 1968). Democrat. Baptist. Club: Jacksonville Rotary. Home: Route 1 Box 49-A Cabot AR 72023 Office: PO Box 864 Jacksonville AR 72023

SHUMATE, JOHN LEWIS, JR., mobile home dealer; b. Greenwood, S.C., Nov. 24, 1935; s. John Lewis and Mary N. (House) S.; grad. Greenwood High Sch., 1953, Weaver Sch. Real Estate, Kansas City, Mo., 1972; m. Hiroko (Kay) Ito, 1955. Served with U.S. Air Force, 1953-73; mgr. So. Fountain Mobile Homes, Charleston, S.C., 1973-75, Shelter Homes, Charleston, 1975; owner, pres. Silver Key Homes, Inc., Charleston, 1976—. Active Democratic Party S.C. Mem. Manufactured Housing Inst. S.C., Am. Legion. Baptist. Home: 5917 Commonwealth Circle Hanahan SC 29406 Office: 6100 Rivers Ave North Charleston SC 29405

SHUMWAY, DEVAN LAKE, publisher; b. Blanding, Utah, Sept. 22, 1930; s. Lee and Mary (Lake) S.; degree in polit. sci. U. Utah, 1952; m. Barbara Burgoyne, Feb. 3, 1979; children—Mary, DeVan, David, Craig, Lisa, Chris, Graham Thurston; stepchildren—Andrew Ugalde, Janine Ugalde. Reporter and editor UPI, Utah, Mont., Calif., 1950-69; dir. communications Murphy re-election campaign, 1969; asst. dir. communications The White House, 1970-71; dir. public relations Com. to Re-Elect the Pres., 1972; editor The Journal, Springfield, Ill., 1973-74; exec. asst. to chmn. Commodity Futures Trading Commn., 1975-77; pub. Oil Daily, Washington, 1978—, v.p., pub. Coal Industry News, Washington, 1981—. Served with USMCR, 1950-52. Republican. Mormon. Home: 1343 Macbeth St McLean VA 22102 Office: 337 Nat Press Bldg Washington DC 20045

SHUMWAY, FORREST NELSON, business exec., lawyer; b. Skowhegan, Maine, Mar. 21, 1927; s. Sherman Nelson and Agnes Brooks (Mosher) S.; student Deerfield (Mass.) Acad., 1943-45; A.B., Stanford, 1950; LL.B., 1952; LL.D., U. So. Calif., 1974, Pepperdine U., 1978; m. Patricia Ann Kelly, Aug. 12, 1950; children—Sandra Brooks, Garrett Patrick. Admitted to Calif. bar, 1952; staff Office County Counsel, Los Angeles, 1953-57; sec. Signal Cos., Inc., Los Angeles, 1959-61, gen. counsel, 1961, group v.p. ops., 1963, pres., 1964-80, chmn. chief exec. officer, 1980—, also dir.; dir. Transam. Corp., UOP Inc., Garrett Corp., United Calif. Bank, Mack Trucks, Inc., Natomas Co., Wickes Cos., Inc., Golden West Broadcasters. Trustee U. So. Calif., Deerfield Acad. Served to 1st lt. USMCR, 1945-46, 49-55. Mem. Am. Bar Assn., State Bar Calif., Phi Delta Theta. Mason (Shriner). Clubs: Los Angeles Country, California (Los Angeles); Cypress Point (Pebble Beach, Calif.); Bohemian (San Franciso); Newport Harbour Yacht; La Jolla (Calif.) Country; Tuna (Avalon). Office: 11255 N Torrey Pines Rd La Jolla CA 92037

SHUMWAY, RODEN GRANT, savs. and loan assn. exec.; b. Kanab, Utah, Nov. 6, 1921; s. Merlan Grant and Ruth (Glazier) S.; student Northwestern Sch. Mortgage Banking, 1957, Utah State U., 1961; grad. Am. Inst. Banking, 1961, Grad. Sch. Savs., Ind. U., 1977; m. Naomi Maxfield, Mar. 8, 1945; children—Sharene, Jana Lee, Roger. Asst. v.p. Walker Bank & Trust Co., 1946-61; exec. v.p. Pioneer Savs. & Loan Assn., 1961-73, also dir.; pres., chief exec. officer State Savs. & Loan Assn., Salt Lake City, 1973—, also dir.; mem. faculty U. Utah Extension Div., Am. Inst. Banking. Mem. Utah Power Commn., 1960-64; pres. Salt Lake City C. of C., 1966; mem. Salt Lake City City Council, 1970-74; del. Utah Republican Conv., 1972-76. Served with USAAF, 1943-46. Recipient Alumni Merit citation Utah State U., 1977. Mem. Utah Mortgage Banking Assn. (pres. 1979), Utah Home Builders Assn., Utah Savs. and Loan League (officer, trustee). Mormon. Clubs: Univ., Sertoma (pres. club 1967). Office: 125 S Main St Salt Lake City UT 84111

SHUSMAN, EUGENE LOUIS, pharmacies exec.; b. Phila., Mar. 23, 1942; s. Morris P. and Mae F. (Weiss) S.; B.Sc., Temple U. Sch. Pharmacy, 1963; m. Frances Ilene Silver, June 26, 1965; children—Bradford Chandler, Binnie Samantha, Chad Winthrop. Pres., Gene Pharmacy NE, Inc., Phila., 1966—, Gene Rx Abington, Inc., Abing, Pa., 1973—; Sec. bd. dirs. Pinehill Rehab. Center, 1968—; bd. dirs. Community Living Mgmt., Am. Cancer Soc., Israeli Bond New Leadership Group, Am. Friends of Hebrew U.; trustee Jewish Youth Center; mem. PHARMPAC and Am.-Israel Polit. Action Com., Mogen David of Am., Herut. Recipient Merit plaques Merck, Sharp & Dohme, Squibb, Eli Lilly, Upjohn, Schering, Pfizer, Parke-Davis Cos. Mem. Nat., Phila. assns. retail druggists, Am., Pa. assns. retarded citizens, Am., Pa. pharm. assns., C. of C. Republican. Jewish religion. Clubs: Mill Creek Racquet, Prime Ministers, Masons, Shriners, B'rith Sholom, Lions. Home: 1550 Cherry Ln Rydal PA 19046 Office: 7260 Castor Ave Philadelphia PA 19149

SHWIRTZ, DRORA D., telecommunication cons.; b. Israel, Feb. 13, 1944; d. Zvi and Channa Klein; came to U.S., 1962, naturalized, 1968; ed. F.I.T., N.Y.C.; children—Joseph, Jacob. Owner, Com-Con, N.Y.C., 1976—. Office: 310 Madison Ave New York NY 10017

SHYMAN, MARK LINCOLN, indsl. equipment mfg. co. exec.; b. Bklyn., Jan. 5, 1943; s. Seymour Joseph and Sue (Tobias) S.; B.A. in Arts, Lafayette Coll., 1963; M.B.A. in Mktg., City U. N.Y., 1971; m. Judith Margot Zaves, Sept. 30, 1964; children—Bonnie Hope, Jeffrey Lewis. Applications engr. Pall Corp., Glen Cove, N.Y., 1966-69; dist. sales mgr. Jamesbury Corp., Worcester, Mass., 1969-71; v.p., product mgr. Aquanetics, Inc., Plainview, N.Y., 1971-76; mgr. mktg. and sales Cavitron Ultrasonics, Long Island City, N.Y., 1977—. Chmn. pack com. Cub Scouts, 1976-79. Mem. Soc. Plastics Industry, Lafayette Coll. Alumni Assn., Alpha Chi Rho. Jewish. Patentee. Home: 142 Boxwood Dr Kings Park NY 11754 Office: Cavitron Ultrasonics 11-40 Borden Ave Long Island City NY 11101

SIBAL, FRANCISCO RODRIGUEZ, retail and wholesale book co. exec.; b. Manila, Dec. 11, 1951; s. Ernesto Yap and Alegria Yutuc (Rodriguez) S.; B.S. in Econs., Sophia U., Tokyo, 1972; M.Bus.Mgmt., Asian Inst. Mgmt., 1974; m. Aleli La'o, Dec. 12, 1978. Cons. Radiola-Toshiba, Philippines, 1973-74; prof., chmn. dept. bus. St. Joseph Coll., Philippines, 1975-77; v.p. fin. Alemar's Philippines, Manila, 1975-79; exec. v.p. fin. treas. Alemar's Am. Inc., N.Y.C., 1979—; dir. Sibal Found., Inc., Manila. Mem. Fin. Execs. Inst. of Philippines. Home: 1 Acacia St Valle Verde III Pasig Philippines Office: Suite 606 11 Broadway New York NY 10004

SIBBALD, JOHN RISTOW, mgmt. cons.; b. Lincoln, Nebr., June 20, 1936; s. Garth E.W. and Rachel (Wright) S.; B.A., U. Nev., 1958; M.A., U. Ill., 1964; m. Mary Jo Mixon, Feb. 21, 1959; children—Allison, John. Office mgr. Hewitt Assos., Libertyville, Ill., 1964-66; coll. relations mgr. Pfizer Inc., N.Y.C., 1966-69; pres., chief exec. officer Re-Con Systems, N.Y.C., 1969-70; v.p. Booz, Allen & Hamilton, N.Y.C., 1970-73, Chgo., 1973-75; pres., founder John Sibbald Assos., Inc., Chgo., 1975—. Served to capt. AUS, 1958-64. Episcopalian. Home: 804 Lincoln Ave Winnetka IL 60093 Office: 5335 Sears Tower Chicago IL 60606

SIBOLSKI, JOHN ALFRED, JR., pub. co. exec.; b. Pittsfield, Mass., Nov. 4, 1946; s. John A. and Isabelle Barcaster S.; A.A. in Data Processing, Andover Inst. of Bus., 1966; B.S. in Tech. of Mgmt., Am. U., 1967, cert. in data processing, 1974, grad. cert. in data processing, 1978; m. Elizabeth Gallup, Aug. 15, 1970. With Automated Systems Corp., Washington, 1969-71, KMS Tech. Center, Arlington, Va., 1971-72; ind. cons., 1972-73, 74-76; with Law Enforcement Assistance Adminstrn., Dept. Justice, Washington, 1973-74, D.A. Lewis, Assos., Clinton, Md., 1974; with Bur. of Nat. Affairs, Inc., Washington, 1976—, mgr. editorial systems. Recipient spl. achievement award Dept. Justice, 1974. Mem. Data Processing Mgmt. Assn., Am. Soc. for Info. Sci. Home: 565 Wayward Dr Annapolis MD 21401 Office: Bur Nat Affairs Inc 1231 25th St NW Washington DC 20037

SICHER, JOHN DAVID, JR., lawyer; b. N.Y.C., May 26, 1945; s. John David and Dorothy Epstein (Roberts) S.; B.A. cum laude, Harvard U., 1967; J.D., Boston Coll., 1970; 1 dau., Carolyn B. Admitted to N.Y. bar, 1971; asso. firm Paul, Weiss, Rifkind, Wharton & Garrison, N.Y.C., 1972-77; v.p., gen. counsel, dir. Unimax Corp., N.Y.C., 1977—; v.p., gen. counsel N.Y. Fin. Co., 1978—. Bd. govs. N.Y. Boys Athletic League, 1971-73. Clubs: Harvard (N.Y.C.); Century Country. Office: 425 Park Ave New York NY 10022

SICILIANO, FRANK ANTHONY, commodities future exchange co. exec.; b. N.Y.C., July 29, 1947; s. Frank A. and Rose (Buse) S.; B.A., Pace U., 1972, M.A., 1974. Instr. econs. Pace U., 1974; adminstrv. asst. Commodity Exchange, Inc., N.Y.C., 1975-76, asst. to pres., 1976-77, v.p., 1977-79, sr. v.p., 1979—. Recipient award for econs. Wall St. Jour., 1972. Mem. Futures Industry Assn. Home: 56 W 11th St New York NY 10011 Office: 4 World Trade Center New York NY 10048

SICILIANO, ROCCO CARMINE, fin. sers. co. exec.; b. Salt Lake City, Mar. 4, 1922; s. Joseph Vincent and Mary (Arnone) S.; B.A. with honors, U. Utah, 1944; LL.B., Georgetown U., 1948; m. Marion Stiebel, Nov. 8, 1947; children—Loretta, A. Vincent, Fred R., John, Maria. Admitted to D.C. bar, 1949; legal asst. to bd. mem. Nat. Labor Relations Bd., Washington, 1948-50; asst. sec.-treas. Procon Inc., Des Plaines, Ill., 1950-53; asst. sec. labor charge employment and manpower Dept. Labor, Washington, 1953-57; spl. asst. to Eisenhower for personnel mgmt., until 1959; partner Wilkinson, Cragun & Barker, 1959-69; pres. Pacific Maritime Assn., San Francisco, 1965-69; under sec. of commerce, Washington, 1969-71; chmn. bd., Chief exec. officer Ticor, Los Angeles, 1971—, also dir.; dir. So. Pacific Co., Pacific Lighting Corp.; mem. Pay Bd., 1971-73. Mem. Calif. Commn. on Govt. Reform, 1978-79, Calif. Roundtable; mem. nat. adv. council U. Utah; bd. visitors Grad. Sch. Mgmt., U. Calif. at Los Angeles; pres. Los Angeles Philharmonic Assn.; mem. adv. council Grad. Sch. Bus., Stanford U.; vice chmn. com. for Econ. Devel. Served with AUS, 1943-46. Decorated Bronze Star; Order of Merit (Italy). Mem. Am. Bar Assn., Nat. Acad. Public Adminstrn. Clubs: Met. (Washington); Family (San Francisco); Los Angeles. Home: 612 N Rodeo Dr Beverly Hills CA 90210 Office: 6300 Wilshire Blvd Los Angeles CA 90048

SICK, WILLIAM NORMAN, JR., electronics co. exec.; b. Houston, Apr. 20, 1935; s. William Norman and Gladys Phylena (Armstrong) S.; B.A., Rice U., 1957, B.S.E.E., 1958; m. Stephanie Anne Williams, Sept. 14, 1963; children—Jill Melanie, David Louis. With Tex. Instruments, Inc., Dallas, Washington and Phila., 1958-70; pres. Tex. Instruments Asia Ltd., Tokyo, 1971-74; asst. v.p. strategic devel., gen. mgr. metals and controls Europe, Tex. Instruments, Inc., Dallas, 1974-77; pres. Tex. Instruments Internat. Trade Corp., Dallas, 1977; v.p., group mgr. materials and elec. products Tex. Instruments, Inc., Attleboro, Mass., 1977-80, v.p., group mgr. consumer products, Lubbock, Tex., 1980—; guest lectr. Sophia U., Tokyo, 1973; dir. Tex. Instruments Holland B.V. Chmn. bd. Fairhill Sch., Dallas. Recipient Francis award Rice U., 1956. Mem. Japan Am. Soc., IEEE, Sigma Xi, Tau Beta Pi, Sigma Tau. Episcopalian. Clubs: Bent Tree, Milton Hoosic. Contbr. articles in field to profl. jours. Home: 4513 8th St Lubbock TX 79416 Office: 2300 N University Lubbock TX 79408

SIDAR, ALEXANDER GEORGE, JR., assn. exec.; b. Elizabeth, N.J., Feb. 23, 1922; s. Alexander George and Katherine Rose (Juran) S.; B.S., Rutgers U., 1946, M.Ed., 1947; m. Jean Thomas Wilson, Feb. 12, 1944; children—Alexander George, Elizabeth Thomas, Thomas Wilson. Instr., asst. prof., asso. dir. admissions Rutgers U., 1947-63; dean Waynesburg (Pa) Coll., 1963-67, Somerset County Coll., Somerville, N.J., 1967-68; exec. dir. Coll. Scholarship Service, Coll. Bd., N.Y.C., 1968-78; pres. N.J. Assn. Colls. and Univs., East Orange, 1978—; mem. Nat. Task Force for Coordination of Student Fin. Aid, 1976-77; mem. Middle States Accrediting Evaluation Team, 1968. Chmn. recreation commn. City of Somerset, 1959-63; bd. dirs. N.J. Ednl. Opportunity Fund, 1968—, Basking Ridge (N.J.) Library, 1974-77. Served with AC, U.S. Army, 1943-45. Sloan Found. grantee, 1969; Exxon Found. grantee, 1978. Fellow Soc. Advancement Fin. Aid in Higher Edn.; mem. Student Fin. Aid Adminstrs. (nat. council), Am. Assn. Higher Edn., Pa. Dean's Assn., Nat. Assn. Coll. Adminstrs., Nat. Assn. Student Personnel Adminstrs., Eastern Assn. Deans and Advs. Students, Nat. Assn. Coll. Admissions Counselors, Alpha Sigma Phi (pres. Beta Theta chpt. 1954-57). Presbyterian. Office: 564 Springdale Ave East Orange NJ 07017*

SIDDIQI, MOHAMMED SHAHID, accountant; b. Hyderabad, India, Jan. 18, 1942; s. Mohammed Masood and Majeedunissa S.; B.Comm., Osmania U., 1963; m. Azra Sultana, Oct. 18, 1968; children—Rubina, Zarina, Razeena, Majid. Acct., William Offenbach Ltd., London, 1965-66; chief acct. Aronstead Ltd., London, 1966-68; controller M. Loeb Ltd., Ottawa, 1968-74; public acct. A-1 Income Tax Co., Ottawa, 1974-78; controller Top Rank Enterprises, Inc., Ottawa, 1980—. Chaderghat Coll. scholar, 1959. Mem. Brit. Inst. Mgmt., Brit. Soc. Commerce, Assn. Indsl. and Comml. Accts., Nat. Soc. Public Accts., Nat. Soc. Accts. for Coops., Nat. Assn. Accts., Am. Mgmt. Assn., Can. Inst. Mgmt., Am. Acctg. Assn., Am. Chartered Inst. of Fin. Controllers and Adminstrs. Home: 86 Florence St Ottawa ON K1R 5N2 Canada Office: 131 Rank St Ottawa ON K1P 5N7 Canada

SIDEREWICZ, WILLIAM, energy co. exec.; b. New London, Conn., July 7, 1950; s. Anton M. and Gladys T. (Sadowski) S.; B.S.C.E. cum laude, Merrimack Coll., 1972; M.S. (U.S. EPA trainee 1973), Cornell U., 1974; M.B.A. in Fin., Northeastern U.; m. Christine M. Kinney, Sept. 9, 1972. Project engr. Chester Engrs., Coraopolis, Pa., 1974-75; sr. project engr. Calgon Corp., Pitts., 1975-77; sr. tech. staff Mitre Corp., Bedford, Mass., 1977-78; sr. asso. CSI Resource Systems, Boston, 1978-80; project mgr. Wheelabrator-Frye, Hampton, N.H., 1980—. Served with USNR, 1972-77. Recipient N. E. Waterworks award, 1971; ASTM Student award, 1971. Mem. ASCE, Am. Soc. Chem. Engrs., Water Pollution Control Fedn., Water Pollution Control Assn. N.Y., Mu Chi Epsilon. Home: 15 Oak St Marblehead MA 01945 Office: Liberty Ln Hampton NH 03842

SIDHU, JAY SINGH, banker; b. Jullundur, India, Aug. 8, 1951; came to U.S., 1971, naturalized, 1975; s. Bhag Singh and Dhanwant (Grewal) S.; B.B.A., Banaras Hindu U., 1971; M.B.A. (grad. research fellow), Wilkes Coll., 1973; postgrad. Dartmouth Coll., 1976, Wharton Sch., U. Pa., 1977; m. Sherry Athwal, Apr. 9, 1978. Market research officer 1st Valley Bank, Bethlehem, Pa., 1973-74; corp. planning officer 1st Valley Corp., Bethlehem, 1974-75, asst. v.p. corp. planning, 1975-76, v.p. corp. planning and mktg., 1976-79; v.p., dir. mktg. Am. Nat. Bank, Morristown, N.J., 1979—; asso. prof. mgmt. Fairleigh Dickinson U., Madison, N.J., 1979—. Mem. Am. Mktg. Assn., Bank Mktg. Assn. (dir. N.Y. chpt., regional dir.), Planning Execs. Inst. (1st v.p. Lehigh Valley chpt.), Morris County C. of C. Club: Morristown Rotary. Home: 66 Burnham Pkwy Morristown NJ 07960 Office: 225 South St Morristown NJ 07960

SIDNEY, WILLIAM WRIGHT, aerospace co. exec.; b. Anaconda, Mont., Dec. 31, 1929; s. Paul and Lily Maud (Wright) S.; student U. Calif., Berkeley, 1953-56; div.; children—Kay Elise, Paul Daniel. Prodn. supr. Kaiser Aerospace, San Leandro, Calif., 1953-57, project engr., 1957-67, chief engr., 1967-69, gen. mgr., 1969-77; pres. Kaiser Aerotech, San Leandro, Calif., 1977—. Served with USN, 1948-52. Mem. Calif. Alumni Assn., Smithsonian Assos., Nat. Audubon Soc., Am. Mus. Natural History. Home: 18788 E Cavendish Dr Castro Valley CA 94546 Office: 880 Doolittle Dr San Leandro CA 94577

SIECKER, BRUCE RAY, pharm. assn. exec.; b. Gary, Ind., Feb. 13, 1944; s. Albert B. and Mary L. Siecker; B.S. magna cum laude, Purdue U., 1966, M.S. summa cum laude, 1970; Ph.D. summa cum laude, Ohio State U., 197

SIEFF, JOHN PHILIP, hardware distbn. co. exec.; b. Mpls., Mar. 17, 1928; s. Philip and Wilhelmina (Olson) S.; B.A., Cornell Coll., Mt. Vernon, Iowa, 1950; m. Elizabeth Jane Lund, Feb. 18, 1950; children—Christine, Lisa, Martha, Philip, Peter. With S&M Co., Mpls., 1950—, pres., 1971—; pres. Summit Tire Corp., 1978—; pres. Lyndale Hardware Co., Mpls., 1970—. Mem. Sales and Mktg. Execs. Mpls. (past pres.). Republican. Methodist. Clubs: Golden Valley Country (pres. 1976-77), Mpls. Athletic (dir.). Home: 4623 Wooddale Edina MN 55424 Office: 2101 Kennedy St NE Minneapolis MN 55413

SIEGEL, ALAN MICHAEL, communications and design cons.; b. N.Y.C., Aug. 26, 1938; s. Eugene and Ruth (Singer) S.; B.S., Cornell U., 1960; student N.Y. U. Sch. Law, 1960-61; m. Gloria Fern Mendel, Nov. 6, 1965; 1 dau., Stacey Ruth. Sr. account exec. Batten, Barton, Durstine & Osborn, N.Y.C., 1962-65; sr. account exec. Ruder & Finn, N.Y.C., 1966-67; sr. account exec. Sandgren & Murtha, N.Y.C., 1967-68; pres. Siegel and Gale, Inc., N.Y.C., 1968—; adj. asso. prof. Fordham U. Sch. Law; adj. asso. prof., co-dir. Communications Design Center, Carnegie-Mellon U. Bd. dirs. Plain Talk, Inc.; mem. exec. com. Document Design Project, Nat. Inst. Edn. Served with U.S. Army, 1961-62. Mem. Soc. Consumer Affairs Profls., Internat. Assn. Bus. Communicators, Am. Bus. Communication Assn., N.Y. Chamber Commerce and Industry, Communications Industry Council. Club: N.Y. Athletic. Co-author: Simplified Consumer Credit Forms, 1978; columnist Nat. Law Jour., others. Home: 211 Central Park W New York NY 10024 Office: 445 Park Ave New York NY 10022

SIEGEL, ARTHUR, corp. exec.; b. N.Y.C., July 4, 1908; s. Louis and Helena (Kaufman) S.; B.S., N.Y.U., 1930; m. Mirian Bierman, Sept. 3, 1939; children—Barbara Joan (Mrs. Robert Frankfort), Louise Susan (Mrs. Eugene Riordan). Vice pres. Congress Financial Corp., N.Y.C., 1963-68; v.p., dir. Commonwealth United Corp., Chgo., 1969-72; pres., dir. Williams Electronics Inc., Chgo., 1969—; sr. v.p., dir. Seeburg Corp., Chgo., 1968-72; sr. v.p., dir. Inland Credit Corp., N.Y.C., 1953-63; v.p., dir. Indsl. Equipment Credit Corp., N.Y., 1948-53. Home: 437 Golden Isles Dr Hallandale FL 33009 Office: 3401 N California Ave Chicago IL 60618

SIEGEL, BERNARD LEE, mfg. co. exec.; b. Balt., Aug. 7, 1920; s. Mac and Mary (Polokoff) S.; B.A., Johns Hopkins U., 1942; m. Ruth Benjamin, Dec. 26, 1941; children—Miriam Spector, Roslyn Landy, Deborah Kedem, David. Pres., chief exec. officer Colonial Jewelers Inc., Elkton and Chestertown, Md., Harrisburg and Carlisle, Pa., 1945—; pres. Cecil Fed. Savings & Loan Assn., Elkton, Md., 1973—; sec.-treas., chmn. exec. com. Plasticoid Mfg. Co., Elkton, 1955—; chmn. exec. com., dir. Allnation Life Ins. Co. of Del., 1970—. Mem. adv. com. Cecil Community Coll., 1978—; founder, bd. dirs. YMCA of Cecil County, 1950—; pres. Jewish Fedn. Del., 1975-77. Served with U.S. Army, 1943-45. Recipient Youth Services award YMCA, 1974. Mem. Md. Retail Mchts. Assn. (treas.), Elkton C. of C. (pres. 1960-62). Club: Lions. Address: 116 E Main St Elkton MD 21921

SIEGEL, E. LESTER, public relations cons.; b. Chgo., May 9, 1919; s. Emanuel and Bessie (Bass) S.; student U. Ill., 1937-41, Northwestern U., 1946-47; children—Paul, Steven. With Ruder & Finn, N.Y.C., 1951-61; dir. bus. devel. Martin E. Janis, Chgo., 1962-69; freelance bus. and public relations cons., Chgo., 1946—; cons. to Golda Meir, 1952, 73-74. Served with USAAF, 1943-45. Mem. No. Ill. Indsl. Assn., Greater O'Hare Assn., Sales-Mktg. Execs. Club, Nat. Automatic Merchandising Assn. Clubs: Lake Point Tower Duplicate Bridge, B'nai B'rith. Home and Office: 5225 N Kenmore Chicago IL 60640

SIEGEL, HERBERT JAY, mfg. exec.; b. Phila., May 7, 1928; s. Jacob and Fritzi (Stern) S.; B.A., Lehigh U., 1950; m. Ann F. Levy, June 29, 1950; children—John C., William D. Sec., dir. Ofcl. Films, Inc., N.Y.C., 1950-55; v.p., dir. Bev-Rich Products, Inc., Phila., 1955-56, Westley Industries, Inc., Cleve., 1955-58, Phila. Ice Hockey Club, Inc., 1955-60; chmn. bd. Fort Pitt Industries, Inc., Pitts., 1956-58, The Seeburg Corp., 1958-60, Centlivre Brewing Corp. (Ft. Wayne, Ind.), 1959-61, Baldwin-Montrose Chem. Co., Inc., 1961-68; chmn. bd. Gen. Artists Corp., 1960-63, pres., 1963-65; chmn. bd., pres. Chris-Craft Industries, 1967—. Bd. dirs. Phoenix House, 1978—; adv. bd. Vets. Bedside Network, 1980—; v.p. Friars Nat. Assn. Found., 1980—. Club: Friars (N.Y.C.). Home: 190 E 72nd St New York NY 10021 Office: 600 Madison Ave New York NY 10022

SIEGEL, MAURICE MATTHEW, ops. exec.; b. N.Y.C., Mar. 27, 1948; s. Abraham and Rachel (David) S.; student U. Okla., 1965-68, in Bus. Adminstrn., Fordham U., 1975—; m. Hedy L. Cooperman, Sept. 3, 1972; children—Amy Florence, David Stephen. Supr. data input 1969 Books In Print, R.R. Bowker Co., N.Y.C., 1968-69; asst. mgr. royalties Holt, Rinehart & Winston Co. N.Y.C., 1970-73; mgr. inventory control all subs. Random House, Inc., N.Y.C., 1973-77; mgr. warehousing, distbn. New Am. Library, Bergenfield, N.J., 1977—; pres., founder Associated Editors Cons. Firm, 1970—. Served with USAR, 1969. Mem. Assn. Am. Pubs. Jewish. Co-author (with Maria DiValentin) Encyclopedia of Crafts, 1970. Home: 49 Hazelwood Ln Stamford CT 06905 Office: 120 Woodbine St Bergenfield NJ 07621

SIEGEL, MELVYN HARRY, accountant; b. Bronx, N.Y., Oct. 19, 1944; s. Herbert and Minnie S.; B.B.A., CCNY, 1965; M.B.A., U. Chgo., 1974. Asst. prof. bus. and econs. Calumet Coll., East Chicago, Ind., 1967-71; self-employed mgmt. cons., 1971-75; mgr. mgmt. adv. service Naron, Wagner, Voslow, C.P.A.'s, Balt., 1975-77; self-employed mgmt. cons., Balt., 1977-79; pres. Melvyn H. Siegel & Assos., Ltd., Consultants to Mgmt., 1980—. Bd. dirs. Pro Musica Rara, Balt., 1978—. C.P.A., Ill. Mem. Am. Econ. Assn., Am. Inst. C.P.A.'s, Ill. C.P.A. Soc., Md. Assn. C.P.A.'s. Home: 2510 Stone Mill Rd Baltimore MD 21208 Office: 36 S Charles St Suite 910 Baltimore MD 21201

SIEGEL, ROBERT JULES, media research exec.; b. N.Y.C., Dec. 24, 1942; s. David Israel and Dolly Genevieve (Bertine) S.; B.S., Queens Coll., 1966; M.S., Yeshiva U., 1967; m. Phyllis Ann Grossman, Feb. 11, 1968; 1 dau., Amber Lee. Internal cons. for procedures and design Young & Rubicam Internat., N.Y.C., 1969-77; officer of tech. support Nat. State Bank, Elizabeth, N.J., 1977-79; chief applications analyst Interactive Market Systems, N.Y.C., 1979-80; adminstr. research systems NBC, N.Y.C., 1980—. Cert. in data processing. Mem. Data Processing Mgmt. Assn. Club: Viola da Gamba Soc. Am. Home: 401 4th St Park Slope NY 11215 Office: 30 Rockefeller Plaza New York NY 10020

SIEGFRIED, JAMES DAVID, stockbroker; b. Keokuk, Iowa, May 16, 1946; s. Alvin David and Frances J. Seigfried; B.A. in Bus., MacMurray Coll., 1968; m. Cynthia K. Zahm, June 15, 1968; children—Nicole Joy, Tara Noelle, Ashleigh Margaret. Tchr., coach Mid County Sch. System, Lacon, Ill., 1968-72; ins. agt. Aid Assn. for Lutherans, Appleton, Wis., 1972-73; stockbroker Shearson Loeb Rhoades Inc., 1973—, account exec., sr. v.p. investments, Peoria, Ill., 1979-80, v.p., resident mgr., Memphis, 1980—. Mem. Sch. Bd., Mid County Sch. Systems. Republican. Lutheran. Clubs: Creve Coeur, Chiefs (Bradley U.), Lacon Country. Home: 2811 Hunter's Horn S Germantown TN 38138 Office: 5100 Poplar Ave Suite 101 Clark Tower Memphis TN 38137

SIEGFRIED, ROBERT EDWIN, engring. and constrn. co. exec.; b. Allentown, Pa., Jan. 16, 1922; s. Harold Edwin and Bessie (Davies) S.; B.S. in Chem. Engring., Lehigh U., 1943; S.M., Mass. Inst. Tech., 1947; postgrad. Center for Mgmt. Devel., Northeastern U., 1960; m. Blanche Worth, Aug. 17, 1945; children—Martha (Mrs. Frederick M. Fritz), Jay Worth. Process engring. supr. Stone & Webster Engring. Co., London, Eng., 1951-52; process engr. E.B. Badger & Sons Co., Boston, 1947-51; process engring. supr. Badger Co., Cambridge, Mass., 1952-54, project mgr., 1954-56, project and engring. coordinator, 1956-59, asst. engring. mgr., 1959-60, engring. mgr., 1960-65, dir., 1963—, v.p., engring. mgr., 1965-68, pres., 1968, chief exec. officer, 1971—, chmn. bd., 1977—; dir. State Street Boston Corp., State Street Bank and Trust Co.; trustee New Eng. Gas and Electric Assn. Mem. corp., trustee, v.p. Boston Mus. Sci.; mem. corp. Northeastern U. Served with AUS, 1943-46. Registered profl. engr., Mass., Ky., La. Mem. Am. Inst. Chem. Engrs., Fla. Engring. Soc., Nat. Soc. Profl. Engrs., Sigma Xi, Tau Beta Pi. Patentee desalination of sea water. Office: 1 Broadway Cambridge MA 02142

SIEMS, CHRISTA MARTHA, steel co. exec.; b. Uelzen, Germany, June 18, 1934; d. Erich and Else (Lilje) Siems; ed. schs. in Germany. Came to U.S., 1963, naturalized, 1970. Apprentice, Schuhhaus Hoeber, Uelzen, 1950-54; trainee Schuh Schulze, Bueckeburg, Germany, 1954-55; buyer Carl Deckert Co., Goslar/Harz, Germany, 1955-58, Eng., 58-60; sec. Hammer Dental Depot, Goettingen, Germany, 1960-61, Farbwerke Hoechst AG, Hoechst, Germany, 1961-63; with Oetiker, Inc., Livingston, N.J., 1963—, treas., 1969—, also dir.; treas. Oetiker Ltd., Alliston, Ont., Can. Mem. Nat. Right to Work, Amnesty Internat., Animal Protection Inst. Home: 121 River Rd East Hanover NJ 07936 Office: 71-77 Okner Pkwy Livingston NJ 07039

SIENKIEWICZ, JOHN CASIMIR, ins. co. exec.; b. Doylestown, Pa., Oct. 8, 1933; s. Casimir A. and Jane (Patton) S.; B.A., Princeton U., 1955; m. Patricia Davis, May 12, 1956; children—Mark Patton, Peter Casimir. Partner, Hutchinson Rivinus & Co., Phila., 1957-69; managing v.p. Alexander & Alexander, Inc., Phila., 1969-76, sr. v.p., dir. internat., 1974—; dir. Alexander & Alexander Services, Inc. Served to lt. U.S. Navy, 1955-57. Mem. Nat. Assn. Ins. Broker. Presbyterian. Clubs: Racquet, Princeton (Phila., N.Y.C.); Bedens Brook (Princeton, N.J.); Pine Valley (Clemonton, N.J.); Gulph Mills (King of Prussia, Pa.). Home: 55 Winfield Rd Princeton NJ 08540 Office: 1211 Ave of Americas New York NY 10036

SIEWERS, DEAN CHARLES, mktg. cons., educator; b. Marietta, Ohio, July 19, 1927; s. Augustin Y. and Gail L. (Volkwein) S.; B.S., Marietta Coll., 1948; postgrad. U. Md., 1948-51; M.B.A., Duke U., 1974; Ph.D., U. N.C., 1979; m. Waltraud H.H. Edelhoff, Jan. 5, 1974; children—Mark J., Jay A., Robin Gail. Sr. physicist Nat. Bur. Standards, Washington, 1948-65; staff physicist HRB-Singer, Inc., State College, Pa., 1965-70; staff engr. Electric Boat Co.-Gen. Dynamics, Groton, Conn., 1971-72; asst. prof. Rochester Inst. Tech., 1976—, dir. grad. programs in bus., 1978—; cons. in field. Served with U.S. Navy, 1945-46. Mem. Am. Mktg. Assn., Ops. Research Soc., IEEE. Home: 667 Edgewood Ave Rochester NY 14618 Office: Rochester Inst Tech Rochester NY 14623

SIGAL, MICHAEL STEPHEN, system specialist; b. Hartford, Conn., May 16, 1953; s. Abraham Sidney and Marion Blanche (Greenblatt) S.; B.A., Drew U., 1975; cert. in nursing home adminstrn., U. Conn., 1976; cert. in computer programming, Computer Processing Inst., 1977. System specialist Aetna Life & Casualty Ins. Co., Hartford, Conn., 1977—. Mem. Am. Mgmt. Assn. Democrat. Jewish. Home: 27 Seacrest Rd Old Saybrook CT 06475 Office: 151 Farmington Ave Hartford CT 06156

SIGEL, MARSHALL ELLIOT, cons.; b. Hartford, Conn., Nov. 25, 1941; s. Paul and Bessie (Somer) S.; B.S. in Econs., U. Pa., 1963. Exec. v.p. Advo-System div. KMS Industries, Inc., Hartford, 1963-69, pres., 1969-72; now fin. cons.; pres. Ad-Type Corp., Hartford, 1963-69, Ad-Lists, Inc., Hartford, 1963-69. Pres., Class of 63 Alumni, U. Pa.; bd. dirs. Hebrew Acad. of Hartford, Hebrew Home for Aged. Mem. Direct Mail Advt. Assn. (mem. legis. com. 1966-71), Young Pres.'s Orgn., Republican. Clubs: U. Pa. Hartford Alumni (mem. secondary sch. com.), 100 of Conn.; Standard, 200 (Miami); Grove Isle. Home: 600 NE 36th St Apt 922 Miami FL 33137

SIGEL, SIDNEY ZAID, beverage co. exec.; b. Dallas, Feb. 18, 1914; s. Harry and Rae (Wolfe) S.; student So. Meth. U., 1931, 33-34, U. Tex., 1932; m. Myrtle Elizabeth Poag, Jan. 27, 1946; children—David William, Shirley Ann. With Sigel Wholesale Liquor, Shreveport, La., 1934-36; founder Sigel Liquor Stores, Dallas, 1936—, now pres., chief exec. officer. Pres., Dallas Metro Crime Council, 1974-77; bd. dirs. Sky Ranch for Boys, 1978—, Tex. Tourist Council, 1978—. Mem. Tex. Package Store Assn. (pres. 1951-53), Nat. Liquor Stores Assn. (pres. 1977-80, dir. 1956—). Jewish. Clubs: Cipango, Ocean Reef, Masons, Shriners, B'nai B'rith. Office: 2960 Anode Ln Dallas TX 75220

SIGETY, CHARLES EDWARD, lawyer, health care exec.; b. N.Y.C., Oct. 10, 1922; s. Charles and Anna (Toth) S.; B.S., Columbia, 1944; M.B.A. (Baker scholar), Harvard, 1947; LL.B., Yale, 1951; m. Katharine K. Snell, July 17, 1948; children—Charles, Katharine, Robert, Cornelius, Elizabeth Sigety. With Bankers Trust Co., 1939-42; instr. Pratt Inst., 1948; instr. econs. Yale, 1948-50; vis. lectr. accounting Sch. Gen. Studies, Columbia, 1948-50, 52; admitted to N.Y. State bar, 1952, D.C. bar, 1958; rapporteur com. fed. taxation for U.S. council Internat. C. of C., 1952-53; asst. to com. fed. taxation Am. Inst. Accountants, 1950-53; vis. lectr. law Yale, 1952; law practice, N.Y.C. 1952-67; pres., dir. Video Vittles, Inc., 1953-67. Dep. commr. FHA, 1955-57; 1st asst. atty. gen. N.Y., 1958-59; housing cons. Govt. Peru, S.A., 1956; lectr. urban renewal Practising Law Inst., N.Y.C., 1962-66; exec. dir. N.Y. State Housing Finance Agy., 1962-63; Professorial lectr. Pratt Inst., Bklyn., 1962-66; lectr. Sch. Pub. Health Adminstrn., Columbia, 1967-69. Dir., mem. exec. com. Gotham Bank, N.Y.C., 1961-62. Pres., dir. Florence Nightingale Nursing Home, N.Y.C., 1965—; bd. dirs., sec., v.p. Nat. Council Health Care Services, 1969—; chmn. council to Improve Long Term Care, N.Y.C., 1974—; bd. dirs. Am. Hungarian Found., 1974-76. Internat. housing cons., visitor over 40 countries. Served as lt. (j.g.) USNR, 1943-47. Mem. N.Y. County Lawyers Assn., Am. Bar Assn., Harvard Bus. Sch. Assn. (council, 1965-69, area chmn. 1967-69), Am. Coll. Nursing Home Adminstrs., Guild of N.Y. Nursing Homes (pres. 1968-72), Alpha Kappa Psi, Phi Delta Phi. Presbyn. Clubs: Yale, Harvard Business School of N.Y. (pres. 1964-65, chmn. 1965-66), Harvard (N.Y.C.); Metropolitan (Washington). Office: 175 E 96th St New York NY 10028

SIGLER, ANDREW CLARK, forest products industry exec.; b. Bklyn., Sept. 25, 1931; s. Andrew J. and Eleanor (Nicholas) S.; A.B. in Govt., Dartmouth Coll., 1953, M.B.A. in Mktg., Amos Tuck Sch., 1956; m. Margaret Romefelt, June 16, 1956; children—Andrew Clark, Patricia, Elizabeth. With Champion Internat. Corp., Stamford, Conn., 1956—, pres. paper div., 1972, pres. paper and allied products, exec. v.p., pres. paper div., 1972-74, chmn., chief exec. officer, 1974—, also dir.; dir. AMF Inc., Cabot Corp., Chem. N.Y. Corp., RCA. Served from 2d lt. to 1st lt. USMC, 1953-55. Office: 1 Landmark Sq Stamford CT 06921

SIGLER, LEROY WALTER, lawyer, banker, bus. exec.; b. Racine, Wis., Aug. 3, 1926; s. LeRoy I. and Ruth Ann (Wacynski) S.; B.B.A., U. Wis., 1952, LL.B., J.D., 1952; m. Sylvia L. Schmidt, Sept. 20, 1969; children—Suzanne Sigler Storer, Cynthia Sigler Idczak, Lee Scott, Robb Nash, Paul Grant. Admitted to Wis. bar, 1952, Ohio bar, 1967; corp. counsel, asst. sec. J.W. Butler Paper Co. and Butler Paper Co., Chgo., 1952-66; asst. mgr. law dept. Nekoosa Edwards Paper Co., Port Edwards, Wis., 1952-66; asst. sec., gen. counsel Seilon, Inc., Toledo, 1966-68, v.p., sec., gen. counsel, 1968-70, pres. gen. counsel, dir., 1970-79; pres., gen. counsel, dir. Bancorp. Leasing, 1973-79, Thomson Internat. Co., 1971-79, Thomson-Poole, Inc., 1977-79; pres., dir. Thomson Veracruz, S.A., Inmobilaria Elda S.A., 1971-79; v.p., sec., gen. counsel, dir. First Bancorp.; pres., sec., gen. counsel, dir. Air-Way Sanitizor, Inc.; gen. counsel, dir. Nev. Nat. Leasing Co., Inc.; sec., gen. counsel Lamb Enterprises, Inc., Lamb Communications Inc.; various positions including vice chmn., pres., gen. adminstr., sec., gen. counsel, dir. Nev. Nat. Bank; chmn., dir. Greenwood's Bancorp., Inc., 1976—, Nekoosa Port Edwards Bancorp., Inc., 1979—; pres., dir. Nekoosa Port Edwards State Bank, 1980—. Chmn. fund dr. South Wood County (Wis.) United Fund; co-chmn. 5 Commn. Planning Commn.; pres. Village of Port Edwards (Wis.); chmn. South Wood County Airport Commn.; pres. Tri-City Airways, Port Edwards Water Utility. Served with U.S. Army, 1945-47. Recipient Spl. Citizen award City Wisconsin Rapids (Wis.) C. of C., 1964. Mem. Tri-City Bar Assn. (pres.), 7th Circuit Bar Assn. (v.p.), Wisconsin Rapids C. of C. (dir.), Phi Delta Phi. Clubs: Toastmasters (v.p.), Elks (exalted ruler, trustee). Home: 341 Wood Ave Nekoosa WI 54457 Office: 405 Market St Nekoosa WI 54457

SIGMON, JACKSON MARCUS, lawyer; b. Bethlehem, Pa., Apr. 15, 1918; s. William Louis and Jeanette (Marcus) S.; A.B., U. Pitts., 1938; M.A., Fletcher Sch. Internat. Law and Diplomacy, 1939; LL.B., Duke, 1942; student Balliol Coll., Oxford U., Eng., 1945; m. Ruth Friedman, Aug. 22, 1948; children—Mark, Hilary, Jill, Jan, William, Erica. Admitted to Pa. bar, 1943; partner Sigmon & Ross and predecessors, Bethlehem, 1946—; spl. dep. atty. gen. Pa., 1951-55, 63-72, asst. City of Bethlehem, city solicitor of Bethlehem, 1962-65; City of Bethlehem rep., adv. bd. Northampton County com., Republican party, 1956—; counsel Northampton County Rep. Com., 1957—; Rep. state committeeman, 1958-72; mem. disciplinary bd. Supreme Ct. Pa., 1974-80. Served from pvt. to 1st lt. AUS, 1942-46. Decorated Bronze Star medal, Croix de Guerre; recipient Community Leader of Am. commendation, 1969, 72, 75, 76; Disting. Citizen award Marine Corps League, 1980. Mem. Am. Judicature Soc., Am., Pa. (state bd. censors, ho. dels., gov., exec. grievance com.) bar assns., Am., Pa. trial lawyers assns., Def. Research Inst., Pa. Soc. Am. Legion, DAV, Brith Sholom Community Center, Zionist Orgn. Am., Pi Lambda Phi, Pi Sigma Alpha, Sigma Kappa Phi. Mason (32 deg.), B'nai B'rith. Clubs: Union League of Philadelphia, Moselem Springs Golf. Home: 3464 Mountainview Circle Bethlehem PA 18017 Office: 146 E Broad St Bethlehem PA 18018

SIKORA, EUGENE STANLEY, profl. engr.; b. Duquesne, Pa., July 21, 1924; s. Adam Joseph and Helen (Pietrowska) S.; student Okla. Bapt. U., 1943-44; B.S. in Indsl. Engring., U. Pitts., 1949; C.E., Carnegie Inst. Tech., 1951; m. Corinne Mary Coliane, Sept. 7, 1946; children—Karyn Ann, Leslie Ann. Bridge design engr. Gannett, Fleming Corddry & Carpenter, Pitts., 1949-50; structural designer Rust Engring. Co., Pitts., 1950-51, chief field engr., 1951-52, asst. project engr.; project engr. Frank E. Murphy & Assos., Bartow, Fla., 1952-55; v.p. Wellman-Lord Engring. Co., Lakeland, Fla., 1955-61; pres. Gulf Design Co., Lakeland, Fla., 1961-74, v.p. Badger Co., Inc. Subsidiary Raytheon, 1968-74; v.p., dir. Coal Mgmt. Group, Waltham, Mass., 1977—; chmn. Pine Lake Chem., Lakeland, 1974—; chmn., chief exec. officer Basic Resources Corp., Lakeland, 1974—; dir. Am. Bank, Lakeland; chmn. Sikora & Co., Lakeland; pres. Witcher Creek Coal Co., Belle, W.Va., 1979—. Served with USAAF, 1943-45. Mem. Nat. Soc. Profl. Engrs., Am. Inst. Indsl. Engrs., Am. Inst. Chem. Engrs., Am. Inst. Mining, Metall. and Petroleum Engrs., Fla. Engring. Soc., Lakeland C. of C. (bd. mem.). Clubs: Lakeland Yacht (bd. govs.); Lone Palm Golf. Democrat. Roman Catholic. Home: 1400 Seville Lakeland FL 33803 Office: One Lone Palm Pl Lakeland FL 33801

SIKORSKI, NICHOLAS GERALD, consumer products mktg. exec.; b. Montreal, Que., Can., Feb. 19, 1945; s. Gerald and Julie (Baran) S.; B.Sc. in Biochemistry, Loyola U. Montreal, 1968; diploma in mktg. McGill U., 1975; m. Louise Marie Jolicoeur, May 31, 1969; 1 dau., Kimberly Joy. Sr. hosp. rep. Schering Corp., Montreal, 1968-72; ops. mgr. Canadian Lab. Supplies Ltd., Montreal, 1972-73; product mgr. Smith Kline Corp., Montreal, 1973-75; product mgr. Abbott Labs., Montreal, 1975-77, group product mgr. consumer products, 1978—; partner Pearch-Sikorski & Assos. Ltd., Montreal, 1977-78. Active, St. Genevieve PTA, 1979—. Recipient President's award Abbott Labs., 1979. Mem. Am. Mgmt. Assn., Loyola U./Alumni Assn. Liberal. Roman Catholic. Home: 197 Lacharite St LaSalle PQ H8P 2B7 Canada Office: 5400 Cote de Liesse Rd Montreal PQ H4P 1A5 Canada

SILAS, CECIL JESSE, petroleum co. exec.; b. Miami, Fla., Apr. 15, 1932; s. David Edward and Hilda Videll (Carver) S.; B.S. in Chem. Engring., Ga. Inst. Tech., 1954; m. Theodosea Hejda, Nov. 27, 1965; children—Karla, Peter, Michael, James. Gen. mgr. Phillips Petroleum Internat. France, 1962-65; mgr. chem. products and plastics, internat. dept. Phillips Petroleum Co., N.Y.C., 1965-67, devel. dir., 1967-68, pres. Phillips Petroleum Co. Europe/Africa, Brussels, 1968-74; mng. dir. NRG Europe/Africa, London, 1974-76, v.p. NRG Gas and Gas Liquids, Bartlesville, Okla., 1976-78, sr. v.p. NRG, from 1978, now exec. v.p.; dir. Gardner Cryogenics. Mem. adv. bd. Ga. Inst. Tech. Served to 1st lt. Chem. Corps, U.S. Army, 1954-56. Decorated comdr. St. Olva's Order (Norway). Mem. Am. Mgmt. Assn., Nat. Gas Men Okla. Club: Rotary (Bartlesville). Office: 18 Phillips Bldg Bartlesville OK 74004

SILBAUGH, PRESTON NORWOOD, lawyer, savs. and loan assn. exec.; b. Stockton, Calif., Jan. 15, 1918; s. Herbert A. and Della Mae (Masten) S.; A.B. in Philosophy, U. Wash., 1940; J.D., Stanford, 1953; m. Maria Sarah Arriola; children—Judith Ann Silbaugh Freed, Gloria Silbaugh Lethers, Ximena Silbaugh Bräun, Carol Lee Silbaugh Morgan. Personnel asst., group head Lockheed Aircraft Corp., also Lockheed Overseas Corp., 1941-44; traffic rep. Naval Air Transport Service, Pan Am. World Airways, Inc., Honolulu, 1944; employee relations officer Hdqrs. Central Pacific Base Command, War Dept. Office Civilian Personnel, Honolulu, 1944-45; ins., and real estate broker, Palo Alto and Red Bluff, Calif., 1945-54; faculty Law Sch., Stanford, 1954-59, asso. prof. law, 1956-59, asst. dean, 1954-56, asso. dean, 1956-59; chief dep. savs. and loan commr. State of Calif., Los Angeles, 1959-61; bus. and commerce adminstr., dir. investment, savs. and loan commr., 1961-63; of counsel firm Miller, Boyko & Bell, San Diego; dir. Beverly-Hawaiian, Inc., Cie. Européenne de Reassurance Internationale, Belgium, others; dir. Chile Calif. Aid Program, Sacramento and Santiago, Chile, 1963-65; chmn. bd. Beverly Hills Savs. & Loan Assn. (Calif.), 1965—; chmn., dir. Southland Co., Service Corp. of Beverly Hills. Chmn. bd., pres. Simon Bolivar Fund, Beverly Hills; real estate adv. com. U. Calif. Served with USMCR, 1942-43. Mem. Soc. for Internat. Devel., U.S., Nat., Calif. savs. and loan leagues, State Bar of Calif., Am., Beverly Hills, San Diego County bar assns., Am. Judicature Soc., Nat. League Insured Savs. Assns. (internat. com. 1966—), Stanford Alumni Assn., Calif. Aggies Alumni Assn., Alumni Assn. U. Wash., Los Angeles World Affairs Council, Town Hall, Order Coif, Phi Alpha Delta. Democrat. Clubs: Commonwealth of Calif. (San Francisco). Author: The Economics of Personnel Insurance, 1956, also articles. Home: 344 N Palm Dr Beverly Hills CA 90210 Office: 9401 Wilshire Blvd Beverly Hills CA 90212 also 110 Juniper St San Diego CA 92101

SILBER, ALLAN BRUCE, non-ferrous smelting co. exec.; b. Nashua, N.H., Sept. 12, 1943; s. Max I. and Edith K. Silber; B.S. in Bus. Adminstrn., Boston U., 1966; m. Dorothy G. Andler, Dec. 20, 1964; children—Shari Jan, Kenneth Barry, Andrew Marc. Prodn. mgr., spectrochemist N. Kamenske & Co., Inc., Nashua, 1966-72, exec. v.p., from 1974, now v.p., asst. treas.; asst. controller, ops. mgr. Indian Head Millwork Corp., Nashua, 1972-73; No. New Eng. coordinator Andler Sales & Salvage Co., Boston, 1973; pres. On the Move, real estate referral agy.; v.p. Double-oh-Seven, advt. splty. distbrs.; guest lectr. River Coll. Sch. Bus., 1979. Alderman, City of Nashua, 1972-75, spl. asst. to mayor, 1977, mem. park-recreation commn., 1968-72, chmn. commn., 1970-71, chmn. growth study commn., 1978-79; exec. bd. Daniel Webster council Boy Scouts Am., 1976—, chmn. advancement com., 1976—; bd. dirs. Boys Club Nashua, 1972—, Nashua chpt. ARC, 1972-75; bd. dirs. Temple Beth Abraham, 1971-77, treas., 1976-77. Licensed real estate broker, N.H. Mem. Assn. Brass and Bronze Ingot Mfrs. (dir., chmn. research and tech. com.), So. N.H. Assn. Commerce and Industry (dir. 1976-79), Am. Soc. Metals, Soc. Applied Spectroscopy, Nashua C. of C. (dir. 1978—, pres. 1980-81). Republican. Jewish. Club: Rotary Nashua West. Home: 19 Fairhaven Rd Nashua NH 03060 Office: PO Box 724 5 Otterson Ct Nashua NH 03061

SILBERFARB, MARK P., ins. co. exec.; b. Bronx, N.Y., July 13, 1941; s. Leo B. and Bessie S.; B.A., Fairleigh Dickinson U., 1963; m. Susan Harrison, Nov. 22, 1970; children—Andrew Craig, Michael David. Sales mgmt. trainee Lever Bros., N.Y.C., 1963-65; sales asst. Mut. N.Y., N.Y.C., 1965-67, field underwriter agency, 1967-69, asst. agency mgr., 1969-73; ind. gen. agt., N.Y.C., 1973-75; asso. mgr. N.Y. Wein Agency, Mut. N.Y., N.Y.C., 1975-77, mgmt. asso. home office Mut. N.Y., 1978—, agency mgr., 1978—; pres. Pro Med Planning Co. Inc., N.Y.C., 1968—, Am. North Star Group Inc., N.Y.C., 1969—. Trustee, N.Y.C. Kiwanis Found.; mem. men's div. Children's Med. Center N.Y. div. L.I. Jewish Med. Center; devel. adv. bd. Franklin Gen. Hosp., Valley Stream, N.Y.; advisor, bd. dirs. Vols. of Am. Recipient Nat. Quality award Nat. Assn. Life Underwriters, 1977; C.L.U. Mem. Gen. Agts. and Mgrs. Assn. (recipient nat. mgmt. award), Life Underwriters Assn. N.Y.C., Am. Soc. C.L.U.'s, Internat. Assn. Fin. Planners, Nat. Assn. Charitable Estate Planners, Am. Mgmt. Assn., Million Dollar Round Table. Jewish. Club: Kiwanis (immediate past pres.). (N.Y.C.). Home: 705 Peninsula Blvd Woodmere NY 11598 Office: 150 E 58th St New York NY 10155

SILBERMAN, H. LEE, pub. relations exec.; b. Newark, Apr. 26, 1919; s. Louis and Anna (Horel) S.; B.A., U. Wis., 1940; m. Ruth Irene Rapp, June 5, 1948; children—Richard Lyle, Gregory Alan, Todd Walter. Radio continuity writer Sta. WTAQ, Green Bay, Wis., 1940-41; reporter Bayonne (N.J.) Times, 1941-42; sales exec. War Assets Adminstrn., Chgo., 1946-47; copy editor Acme Newspictures, Chgo., 1947; reporter, editorial writer Witchita (Kans.) Eagle, 1948-55; reporter Wall St. Jour., N.Y.C., 1955-57, banking editor, 1957-68; 1st v.p., dir. corporate relations Shearson-Hammill & Co., N.Y.C., 1968-74; editor-in-chief Finance mag., N.Y.C., 1974-76, dir. financial services group Carl Byoir & Assos., Inc., N.Y.C., 1976—, sr. v.p., 1978—; N.Y. corr. Economist of London, 1966-72. Served to capt. C.E., AUS, 1942-46. Recipient Loeb Mag. award U. Conn., 1965, Loeb Achievement award for distinguished writing on finance Gerald M. Loeb Found., 1968. Mem. N.Y. Financial Writers Assn., Soc. Profl. Journalists, Sigma Delta Chi, Am. Soc. Bus. Writers, Am. Soc. Bus. Press Editors, Artus, Phi Kappa Phi, Zeta Beta Tau, Phi Sigma Delta. Republican. Clubs: Overseas Press, Deadline (exec. council). Contbg. editor Finance mag., 1970-74. Contbr. articles to profl. jours. Home: 80 Miller Rd Morristown NJ 07960 Office: 380 Madison Ave New York NY 10017

SILBERMANN, MARVIN HOWARD, appliance mfg. co. exec.; b. Indpls., Mar. 22, 1934; s. William E. and Esther (Feldman) S.; B.A., Ind. U., 1951-53; m. Lynne Regenstreif, Feb. 23, 1958; children—Andrew, Amy, Joe. With Design & Mfg. Corp., Connersville, 1963—, asst. to chmn., 1974-76, vice chmn. bd. dirs. for ops., 1976—. Bd. dirs. Regenstrief Found., Indpls.; pres. Fayette County (Ind.) Bd. Sch. Trustees. Served with U.S. Army, 1954-56. Jewish. Club: Indpls. Athletic. Home: 1725 Country Club Rd Connersville IN 47331 Office: 2000 Illinois St Connersville IN 47331

SILBERT, ARTHUR FREDERICK, financier; b. N.Y.C., Sept. 17, 1928; s. Theodore Herzl and Esther (Itzkowitz) S.; B.S. in Bus. Adminstrn., U. Okla., 1950; m. Roberta Onigman, Aug. 14, 1964; children—Michael L., Scott J., Laurie A., Benjamin O., Theodore Herzl II, Elyssa B. With Sterling Bancorp., N.Y.C., 1966—, exec. v.p., 1971—; exec. v.p. Sterling Nat. Bank, N.Y.C., 1971—, Standard Fin. Corp., N.Y.C., 1950—; pres. Universal Fin. Corp., 1971. Pres. Pilgrim Rd Assn., Ryen, N.Y., 1978—; bd. dirs. Mid-Westchester YM-YWHA, 1980. Served with U.S. Army, 1951-54. Clubs: Old Oaks Country, Harmonie, Standard. Home: Pilgrim Rd Rye NY 10580 Office: Standard Fin Corp 540 Madison Ave New York NY 10022

SILBERT, JACQUELINE, real estate co. exec.; b. Bklyn., Dec. 15, 1921; d. Leon and Mary (Gittell) C.; B.A. with honors in Edn., Hunter Coll., 1942; children—Laurence, Amy Silbert Block. Co-founder, treas. MacClean Service Co. Inc. (multi-state orgn.), Bellerose, N.Y., 1953—; maintenance and constrn. interior design, real estate, mgmt. Vice pres. bd. dirs. Lighthouse; pres. St. John's U. Aux.; bd. dirs. Forest Hills Jewish Center Aux., Temple Emanuel Jewish Inst., R.I.; mem. R.I. State Bd. Edn.; mem. Providence Sch. Bd. Mem. NCCJ (honoree), Hunter Coll. Alumni Assn. (former editor newspaper). Contbr. articles to profl. jours. Office: 249-12 Jericho Turnpike Bellerose NY 11426

SILBERT, MICHAEL THEODORE, apparel mfg. co. exec.; b. Warsaw, Poland, Feb. 10, 1922; s. Stanislaw and Ina (Krausz) S.; came to U.S., 1950, naturalized, 1956; student Polytechnico de Milano (Italy), 1945-46, U. London (Eng.), 1946-47; m. Vera Gutman, Feb. 20, 1953; children—Kenneth, Jeffrey. Asst. designer, prodn. control Gardiner & Sons Textile Mills, Scotland, 1950-51; pres. Fine Wollen Co., N.Y.C., 1951-55; v.p. Scotch Mist Corp., N.Y.C., 1955-56; pres. United Knitwear Co., N.Y.C., 1956—; v.p. Scotch Craft Corp., N.Y.C., 1956—. Served to lt. Brit. Army, 1942-45. Decorated Africa Star, Italy Star, Brit. Def. medal, Brit. War medal. Mem. Ski Industries Am., Am. Assn. Textile Tech., Inc., Am. Assn. Textile Chemists and Colorists. Republican. Clubs: John Foster Dulles Republican; Renaissance Country. Home: 49-70 175th Pl Fresh Meadows NY 11365 Office: 1384 Broadway New York NY 10018

SILCOCK, FRANK ADRIAN, cons. engr.; b. San Antonio, Sept. 24, 1939; s. Frank Holley and Ruth (Caroline Jameton) S.; B.S. in C.E., Tex. A. and M. U., 1963; m. Muriel E. Marshall, Oct. 21, 1961; children—Stephen Spencer, Laurel Kathleen. Cons., constrn. and industry assignments, Houston, 1963-76; founder, pres. Silcock Engring., Houston and San Antonio, 1977—. Cubmaster, Boy Scouts Am., 1977-80, troop com. chmn., 1980—; pres. Klein Pub. Utility Dist., 1977-80; bd. mgrs. Westland YMCA, 1980—; jr. warden St. Patricks Episcopal Ch., 1981—. Mem. Tex. Soc. Profl. Engrs. (pres. San Jacinto chpt. 1980—). Home: 11007 Renwick St Houston TX 77096 Office: 5326 W Bellfort St Houston TX 77035

SILCOX, GORDON BRUCE, recruiting cons. co. exec.; b. Takoma Park, Md., May 11, 1938; s. Walter Bruce and Ruth May (Davis) S.; A.B., Princeton U., 1960; M.B.A., U. Pa., 1965; m. Judith Andrea Smith, Mar. 3, 1970; children—Andrea Davis, Jessica Lyn. Trust investment officer Am. Security Bank, Washington, 1965-69; v.p., trust investment officer, head trust investment div. First Am. Bank of Washington, 1969-77; v.p., prin. Paul Stafford Assos., Ltd., Washington, 1977—; instr. Am. Inst. Banking. Treas., Princeton Class of 1960, 1975-80, v.p., 1980—. Served to lt. (j.g.) USN, 1960-63. Methodist. Clubs: Wharton Sch. (sec. 1980-81), Univ. (Washington); Princeton (treas. Washington 1972-74) (Washington and N.Y.C.); Montclair (Va.) Country. Home: 3811 Dalebrook Dr Dumfries VA 22026 Office: Paul Stafford Assos Ltd 888 17th St NW Washington DC 20006

SILHA, OTTO ADELBERT, pub. exec.; b. Chgo., Jan. 15, 1919; s. Emil Albert and Alice Lucille (Lindstrom) S.; B.A. magna cum laude, U. Minn., 1940; m. Helen Elizabeth Fitch, Sept. 4, 1942; children—Stephen Fitch, David William (dec.), Alice Barbara, Mark Albert. Copyreader, Mpls. Star, 1940-41; promotion dir. Mpls. Star and Tribune, 1947-51, promotion and personnel dir., 1951-54, dir., 1954—, bus. mgr., 1954-65, gen. mgr., 1965-68, v.p., 1956-68, exec. v.p., publisher, 1968-73, pres., 1973-79, chmn. bd., 1979—; dir. Newspaper Advt. Bur., 1970-73, vice-chmn., 1974-76, chmn., 1976-78; dir. Harper & Row, Pubs., Inc., AP, N.W. Bancorp., Northwestern Nat. Bank. Mem. Gov. Minn.'s Adv. Com. Dept. Bus. Devel., 1955-63, chmn., 1957-59. Pres. Mpls. Aquatennial Assn., 1956; v.p., dir. North Star Research Inst., 1963-75; chmn. steering com. Minn. Exptl. City Project, 1966—. Bd. regents U. Minn., 1961-69; bd. dirs. Tyrone Guthrie Theatre Found., 1960-62, Minn. Theatre Co. Found., 1962-72; trustee Mpls. Soc. Fine Arts, 1966-74, 75-76, Midwest Research Inst., 1975—, U. Minn. Found. 1974—; bd. dirs. United Way Mpls., 1961-72; bd. dirs., v.p. Mpls. Area Devel. Corp., 1956-61; vice-chmn. City Venture Corp., 1978—; bd. dirs. Greater Mpls. Met. Housing Corp., 1971—. Served from pvt. to maj. USAAF, 1942-46. Named one of 100 outstanding young men, Mpls., 1953, Boss of Year, Mpls. Jaycees, 1971; recipient Silver medal award Am. Advt. Fedn., 1972; Outstanding Achievement award U. Minn., 1974; Minn. award for Outstanding Service in Journalism, 1978. Mem. Internat. Newspaper Promotion Assn. (pres. 1953-54), Am. Newspaper Pubs. Assn. (dir. Research Inst. 1960-69, pres. 1967-69), Mpls. C. of C. (dir., v.p.), U. Minn. Alumni Assn. (dir. 1959-63), Phi Beta Kappa, Delta Tau Delta (regional v.p. 1947-52), Sigma Delta Chi. Clubs: Mpls. (bd. govs. 1968-73), Advt. Minn., Mpls. Athletic, Minn. Minikahda, 5:55 (pres. 1956-57)(Mpls.); (St. Paul). Author newspaper series USSR Visit, 1970, Far East Report, 1974, Report on South America, 1977, Rare Visit to Tibet, 1979. Home: 6708 Point Dr Minneapolis MN 55435 Office: IDS Tower 6th Floor Minneapolis MN 55402

SILL, ALEXIS MATTOS, data processing co. exec.; b. Rio de Janeiro, Brazil, Apr. 15, 1949; s. Bev Arthur and Gigi Lino (Mattos) S.; came to U.S., 1956, naturalized, 1960; student Golden Gate U., San Francisco; m. Sandra Sarah Ann Heaslip, Aug. 24, 1974; 1 dau., Courtney Jane. Sales mgr. United Calif. Bank, San Francisco, 1971-77; sales exec. Automatic Data Processing, Inc., San Francisco, 1977—. Served with USMCR, 1969-71. Republican. Home: 40 Hillside Ave San Rafael CA 94901 Office: 625 3d St San Francisco CA 94107

SILL, GERALD DE SCHRENCK, hotel corp. exec.; b. Czechoslovakia, Dec. 11, 1917; s. Edward and Margaret (Baroness von Schrenck-Notzing) S.; B.S., Budapest Tech. U., 1942; m. Maria Countess Draskovich, May 11, 1946; children—Susan, Gabrielle. Came to U.S., 1948, naturalized, 1953. With econs. div. U.S. Hdqrs., Vienna, Austria, 1945-48; exec. hotel positions N.Y.C., 1948-52; managerial positions with Hilton Hotel Corp., 1953-61; exec. v.p. Houston Internat. Hotels, Inc., 1961-72, pres., chief exec. officer, 1972—; v.p. Warwick Hotel, Inc., 1980; chmn. overseas com. Preferred Hotels Assn. U.S., Can., Western Europe and S.Am. dir. Tex. Commerce Med. Bank, Houston. Clubs: Warwick (pres.), River Oaks Country (Houston); Marco Polo (N.Y.C.). Home: 2227 Pelham Dr Houston TX 77019 Office: The Warwick 5701 Main St Houston TX 77005

SILLIN, LELAN FLOR, JR., utility exec.; b. Tampa, Fla., Apr. 19, 1918; s. Lelan Flor and Ruth (Berry) S.; A.B. with distinction, U. Mich., 1940, LL.B., 1942; m. Joan Quthwaite, Sept. 26, 1942; children—Lelan Flor, John Outhwaite, Andrew Borden, William Berry. Admitted to N.Y. State bar, 1946; with firm Gould & Wilkie, N.Y.C., 1945-51; with Central Hudson Gas & Electric Corp., Poughkeepsie, N.Y., 1951-68, v.p., asst. gen. mgr., 1955-60, pres., 1960-68, also chief exec. officer, dir.; pres., trustee N.E. Utilities, Hartford, Conn., 1968—, chief exec., 1969—, chmn., 1970—; pres. Conn. Yankee Atomic Power Co., 1968-70, chmn., 1970—; chmn. Northeast Nuclear Energy Co., 1970—; trustee No. Energy Corp.; dir. Hartford Steam Boiler & Inspection Co., Helium Breeder Assos., Irving Bank, Arthur D. Little, Inc.; mem. com. Commn. Natural Resources, NRC. Mem. steering com. Nat. Urban Coalition; past mem. Pres.'s Adv. Com. Environ. Quality; bd. dirs. Elderhostel, Nat. Office Social Responsibility; trustee Edwin Gould Found. for Children, Wesleyan U., Westminster Sch., Hartford Grad. Center; adv. trustee Woodrow Wilson Nat. Fellowship Found.; mem. adv. com. White House Conf. on Balanced Nat. Growth and Econ. Devel.; mem. Public Com. on Mental Health. Served to capt. USMCR, 1942-45. Mem. Am. Arbitration Assn., Atomic Indsl. Forum (dir.), Electric Power Research Inst. (dir.), Am., N.Y. State, Dutchess County bar assns., U.S. C. of C., Soc. Gas Lighting, The Conf. Bd., Am. Judicature Soc. Clubs: Dauntless (Essex, Conn.); Century Assn., Econ., Univ. (N.Y.C.); Hartford. Home: RD 2 Route 156 Lyme CT 06371 Office: NE Utilities PO Box 270 Hartford CT 06101

SILLS, STANLEY S., publishing co. exec.; b. N.Y.C., Nov. 3, 1925; s. Morris N. and Shirley (Bahn) S.; B.S., State U. N.Y., 1950; M.A., Columbia U., 1951; m. Shirley Dieter, Nov. 20, 1951; children—Michael N., David C. From salesman to mktg. mgr. Sci. Research Assos., Chgo., 1955-65; v.p. Am. Book Co., N.Y.C., 1965-68; product line mgr. ITT, N.Y.C., 1968-71; pres. Howard W. Sams & Co. subs. ITT, Inpls., 1971-80, also dir.; gen. mgr. ITT Pub. Co. until 1980; sr. v.p. Filmways and pres. Filmways Pub. Group, 1980; pres. Grosset and Dunlap, N.Y.C., 1980—. Served to 2d lt. USAAF, 1943-46; ETO. Decorated Presdl. citation, five battle stars. Office: Grosset and Dunlap 51 Madison Ave New York NY 10010

SILLS, THOMAS DAVID, contracting exec.; b. Epps, La., Jan. 23, 1934; s. Shelby Sidney and Grace Dora (Post) S.; student La. State U., Baton Rouge, 1951-53; m. Mary Ann Hall, July 3, 1953; children—David Hall, Derek Wayne, Julie Ann. Tradesman to supr. Precision Insulation, Houston, 1954-61; v.p. Johnson Insulation Co., Inc., Cedar Falls, Iowa, 1961-64; v.p. Win-Way, Inc., Freeport, Tex., 1964—. Mem. apprenticeship program Brazosport Jr. Coll., Clute, Tex.; active United Fund, polit. campaigns. Mem. Brazosport C. of C., Assos. Builders and Contractors Tex. Gulf Coast. Baptist. Home: 327 Live Oak St Lake Jackson TX 77566 Office: PO Drawer GG Freeport TX 77541

SILLS, WILLIAM HENRY, III, investment banker; b. Chgo., Jan. 2, 1936; s. William Henry, II and Mary Dorothy (Trude) S.; A.B., Darmouth Coll., 1958; M.A., Northwestern U., 1961; m. Ellen Henriette Gervais, Apr. 24, 1971; children—William Henry, David Andrew Henry. Stockbroker, Bache & Co., Chgo., 1961-65; investment banker Chgo. Corp., Chgo., 1965-79; chmn. bd. Rail Fund Corp., Chgo., 1979—; dir. S&S S.S. Lines, Inc., GSW Corp. Chmn., Geneva Lake (Wis.) Area Joint Transit Commn., 1974-78, Com. to Amend Wis. Constn. for Transp., 1977; mem. Walworth County (Wis.) Overall Econ. Devel. Planning Com., 1977-78, Walworth County Transp. Planning Com., 1975—; pres. Wis. Coalition for Balanced Transp., 1976—; chmn. exec. com. Republican Party Wis., 1978—. Served with USMCR, 1956-59. Mem. Am. Soc. Traffic and Transp., Am. Short Line R.R. Assn., Am. Soc. Equipment Lessors, Am. Public Transit Assn., Ill. Public Transit Assn., Delta Kappa Epsilon. Episcopalian. Clubs: Lake Geneva Country, Lake Geneva Yacht, Skeeter Ice Boat, Delavan Sportsman. Author papers in field. Office: 134 S LaSalle St Suite 1000 Chicago IL 60604

SILTANEN, JOHN CARL, indsl. engr.; b. Kings County, N.Y., May 21, 1913; s. Karl and Fanny (Jusenius) S.; B.Sc. in Engring., N.Y. U., 1938; M.S., Calif. Inst. Tech., 1946; LL.B., LaSalle U., 1952, M. Indsl. Engring., 1958; diploma Air War Coll., 1963; m. Elinor Van Kan, May 30, 1942. Group engr. Brewster Aircraft Co., N.Y.C., 1939-41; asst. chief design engr. Vertol Aircraft Co., Morton, Pa., 1950-53; asst. quality mgr. Curtiss Wright Corp., Woodridge, N.J., 1953-54; engring. project field mgr. Bendix Aviation Corp., Teterboro, N.J., 1954-56, Hollywood, Calif., 1956-60; product mgr. advanced systems ITT, Nutley, N.J., 1960-67; v.p. Yucair Transport, Inc.; dir. devel. Caribbean Transport Ltd., 1967-69; gen. mgr. John Siltanen Assos., 1969—. Served to sgt. Finnish Air Force, 1933-34; served from 2d lt. to col. USAAF, 1941-50. Asso. fellow Inst. Aerospace Scis.; mem. IEEE, Archeol. Inst. Am., Soc. Am. Archaeology, Am. Helicopter Soc., Tau Beta Pi, Psi Upsilon. Republican. Lutheran. Home: 101 Prospect Ave Hackensack NJ 07601

SILVER, CHARLES HINTON, JR., real estate broker; b. Ft. Sill, Okla., Dec. 3, 1945; s. Charles Hinton and Betty Winston (Wales) S.; B.A. in Polit. Sci., U. N.C., 1968; M.B.A., Chapman Coll., 1978; m. Katherine Taylor Lumsden, Dec. 21, 1968; children—Anne Cameron, Charles Hinton, Jonas Johnston Carr. Real estate salesman Valley Realty, Irvine, Calif., 1973-76; real estate sales trainee Ind. Tng. Systems, Mission Viejo, Calif., 1976-80; instr. real estate econs. Orange Coast Coll., Costa Mesa, Calif., 1975-80, mem. adv. com. real estate curriculum, 1975—; real estate broker, investment counselor, Newport Beach, Calif., 1976-80; mem. adv. com., dir. Irvine Savs. & Loan Assn.; self-employed investor, 1974—. Served to capt. USMC, 1968-73; Vietnam. Decorated Air medal, Purple Heart. Mem. Nat. Assn. Realtors, Calif. Assn. Realtors (syndication div.), Calif. Assn. Real Estate Tchrs., Grad. Realtors Inst., Real Estate Cert. Inst. Author: Real Estate Economics, 1980. Home and office: Midway Plantation Route 12 Box 137 Raleigh NC 27610

SILVER, JACQUELYN TIMMES, data processing mgr.; b. San Diego, Dec. 28, 1945; d. Francis Xavier and Dorothy Ann (Wellington) Timmes; B.A. in English Lit., Rockford (Ill.) Coll., 1967; M.A., U. Calif., Berkeley, 1973, postgrad. English lit., 1973-75; m. Charles Silver, July 15, 1966 (div.). Programmer, Pacific Telephone Co., San Francisco, 1967-69; teaching asst. U. Calif., Berkeley, 1973-74; systems engr. Electronic Data Systems, San Francisco, 1975-76, systems mgr. devel., San Francisco, 1977-79, Dallas, 1979-80; with Levi Strauss, San Francisco, 1980—. Mem. curriculum com., dept. English, U. Calif., 1973-74. Mem. Nat. Retail Mchts. Assn., U. Calif. Alumni Assn., Phi Beta Kappa. Democrat. Roman Catholic. Club: San Francisco Bay. Home: 2346 Paloma Ct Pinole CA 94564 Office: 55 Francisco St San Francisco CA 94111

SILVER, JEFFREY NATHAN, mfg. co. exec.; b. Racine, Wis., Sept. 15, 1942; s. Irving M. and Sydneye (Blitstein) S.; B.S. in Mech. Engring., U. Wis., 1966; M.B.A., Eastern Mich. U., 1973; m. M. Audrey Gratz, Sept. 25, 1964; children—Sara Courtney, Rhett Wainright. From jr. engr. to staff project engr. Gen. Motors Corp. Proving Ground, Milford, Mich., 1966-73; with automotive service equipment div. Applied Power, Inc., Milw., 1973—, v.p., engring. mgr., 1977-79, v.p. bus. devel., 1979—. Mem. Equipment and Tool Inst. (dir.), Soc. Automotive Engrs. Author papers in field. Office: 11333 W National Ave Milwaukee WI 53227

SILVER, PHILIP ALFRED, data processing co. exec.; b. Stockton, Calif., Feb. 14, 1932; s. Alfred Frank and Edna Verna (Nunn) S.; A.A., Stockton Coll., 1954; B.A., Sacramento State Coll., 1956; m. Yvonne Mathews, May 21, 1960; children—Philip Alfred, Dana Yvonne. Police officer City of North Sacramento (Calif.), 1955-56, City of Newark (Calif.), 1956-57; police adminstr. City of Garden Grove (Calif.), 1957-64, comdr. services div., 1959-60, 63-64; comdr. detective div., 1958-59, 62, patrol div., 1961; mktg. rep., sales team leader IBM, Los Angeles County, 1964-69; staff instr. IBM Edn. Center, Washington, 1969-70; criminal justice program adminstr., data processing div. hdqrs. IBM, Bethesda, Md., 1970-77, sr. mktg. support adminstr. Edn. Center, San Jose, Calif., 1977—; instr. Orange Coast Jr. Coll., 1963-64. Criminal justice commr. Montgomery County (Md.), 1974-77; mem. Data Security and Confidentiality Commn., Santa Clara County, Calif., 1978-80. Served with USAF, 1949-52. Mem. Nat. Trial Ct. Adminstrs., Am. Judicature Soc. Internat. Assn. Chiefs Police, U.S. Naval Acad. Found., Calif. State, Orange County peace officers assns., Republican. Office: 5600 Cottle Rd San Jose CA 95193

SILVER, RALPH DAVID, distilling co. exec.; b. Chgo., Apr. 19, 1924; s. Morris J. and Amelia (Abrams) S.: B.S., U. Chgo., 1943; postgrad. Northwestern U., 1946-48; J.D., DePaul U., 1952; m. Lois Reich, Feb. 4, 1951; children—Jay, Cappy. Staff acct. David Himmelblau & Co., C.P.A.'s, 1946-48; internal revenue agt. U.S. Dept. Treasury, 1948-51; admitted to Ill. bar, 1952; practice law, Chgo., 1952-55; atty. Lawrence J. West, 1952-55; chief fin. exec. Barton Brands, Ltd., Chgo., 1955—. Bd. dirs., pres. Silver Found., 1968—. Served to lt. (j.g.) USNR, 1943-46. Mem. Am. Bar Assn., Chgo. Bar Assn., Am. Inst. C.P.A.'s. Clubs: Green Acres Country; University (Chgo.). Office: Barton Brands Ltd 55 E Monroe St Chicago IL 60603

SILVER, RICHARD GORDON, retail store exec.; b. Cleve., Apr. 8, 1941; s. Morris and Rose (Gordon) S.; B.A., Ohio State U., 1963; m. Arlene Rubin, Aug. 25, 1963; children—Jody Ellen, Brian Robert. Buyer, Higbee Co., Cleve., 1963-69, mdse. coordinator, 1969-71, store mgr., 1971-75, mdse. v.p., 1975-76; gen. mgr. Saks Fifth Ave., Boston, 1976-80; divisional mdse. mgr. Bloomingdale's, Chestnut Hill, Mass., 1980—. Bd. dirs. Chamberlain Sch. Retailing, Boston, 1976—, Better Bus. Bur. Massachusetts Bay, Boston, Congregation Beth El of Sudbury. Mem. Midway Mall Mchts. Assn. (pres. 1971-72), Parmatown Mchts. Assn. (pres. 1972-73), Westgate Mchts. Assn. (dir. 1974-75), Prudential Center Mchts. Assn., Boston C. of C. Clubs: B'nai B'rith, Rotary. Home: 15 Minuteman Ln Sudbury MA 01776

SILVER, RICHARD LUDWIG, chem. co. exec.; b. Cleve., June 26, 1920; s. Joseph Robinson and Elida (Ludwig) S.; A.B., Dartmouth Coll., 1942, M.C.S., 1946; m. Betsy Rogers Andrus, May 10, 1947; children—Walton Andrus, Elida Robinson, Sally Wilcox, William Holbrook, Richard Ludwig. Mem. staff Am. Cyanamid Co., 1946-47; with Akron (Ohio) Chem. Co., 1947—, pres., chief exec. officer, dir., 1963—; v.p., dir. Revlis Corp. Served with USNR, 1942-46. Mem. Rubber Div. of Am. Chem. Soc., Akron Rubber Group, Boston Rubber Group, Akron C. of C. (past pres.). Episcopalian. Clubs: West Akron Kiwanis (past pres.), Dartmouth of N.E. Ohio (past pres.), Akron City (past sec.). Office: 255 Fountain St Akron OH 44304

SILVERA, AMERICO, mktg. and tech. cons. co. exec. b. David, Republic of Panama, Oct. 12, 1912; s. Didacio and Asuncion (Mojica) S.; B.Sc., Instituto Nacional (Panama), 1932; B.Sc. in Architecture, Rensselaer Poly. Inst., 1937; m. Hildegard Else Seelig, June 18, 1937 (div. 1974); children—Robert K., Ronald E., Ricardo R.; m. 2d, Emma M. Morales, 1975; 1 son, Roger A.; 1 adopted son, Edwin. Came to U.S., 1933, naturalized, 1950. With Carrier Corp., from 1937, v.p., regional mgr. Africa/Middle East, Carrier Internat. Corp. subsidiary, N.Y.C., 1964-69, v.p. export sales, from 1969; now pres. Amersil Overseas, Inc., internat. mktg. and tech. cons. firm, Stony Point, N.Y. Mem. fed. adv. com. multilateral trade negotiations Dept. Commerce. Fellow Am. Soc. Heating, Refrigeration and Air Conditioning (chmn. internat. relations com. 1961-64, Distinguished Service award 1964); mem. Air Conditioning and Refrigeration Inst. (mem. internat. trade com. 1972—), Internat. Execs. Assn., Pan-Am. Soc. of U.S.A., Soc. for Internat. Devel., UN Assn. of U.S.A. Contbr. tech. articles to trade jours. Patentee airblast freezing tunnel. Office: 1 Rosewood Dr Stony Point NY 10980

SILVERMAN, BARRY STEVEN, data processing exec.; b. Bklyn., June 17, 1947; s. Sol and Adele S (Gaslow) S.; B.B.A., Pace U., 1969; m. Mimi Salomon, Oct. 11, 1969; children—Nichole, A.J. Staff auditor Haskens & Sells, N.Y.C., 1969-70, sr. edp auditor, 1970-73; sr. internal auditor Gulf & Western Industries, N.Y.C., 1973-74, supr. EDP, 1974-75, asst. mgr., 1975-76, mgr., 1976-78, mgr. data processing planning and tech. services, 1978—. Bd. dirs. N.Y. Met. chpt. Internat. EDP Auditors Assn. Home: 3 Melrose Ln West Nyack NY 10994 Office: Gulf & Western Industries 1 Gulf & Western Plaza New York NY 10023

SILVERMAN, FRED, broadcasting exec.; b. N.Y.C., Sept. 1937; grad. Syracuse U.; M. in TV and Theatre Arts, Ohio State U. With WGN-TV, Chgo.; exec. position WPIX-TV, N.Y.C.; dir. daytime programs CBS-TV, N.Y.C., v.p.-programs, 1970-75; pres. ABC Entertainment, 1975-78; pres. NBC-TV, 1978—. Office: NBC-TV 30 Rockefeller Plaza New York NY 10020*

SILVERSTEIN, NORMAN BERNARD, citrus fruit co. exec.; b. N.Y.C., Sept. 13, 1934; s. Irving and Lillian (Schieren) S.; B.S. in Bus. Mgmt., L.I. U., 1960; m. Diane Bergman, May 30, 1956; children—Lee, Lois, Marjorie. Mgr. adminstrn. Litton Industries, Washington, N.Y.C., 1965-69; v.p., dir. personnel Union Fidelity Corp., Phila., 1969-72; v.p. adminstrn. Am. Agronomics Corp., Arcadia, Fla., 1972-78; pres. Golden Grove Mgmt. Corp., Arcadia, 1978—. Bd. dirs. Asolo Opera Guild, Sarasota, Fla., 1979—; bd. dirs., v.p. Temple Beth Sholom, Sarasota; mem. Long Beach (N.Y.) Urban Renewal Commn., 1967-68. Served with U.S. Army, 1954-56. Mem. Presidents Assn. (Am. Mgmt. Assn.), Fla. Citrus Mut. Office: PO Box 1860 Arcadia FL 33821

SILVERSTEIN, STEPHEN HOWARD, fin. exec.; b. Lowell, Mass., July 5, 1948; s. Jerry L. and Gertrude S.; B.B.A. in Econs., U. Mass., 1970; M.B.A., U. Chgo., 1972; m. Linda Gerhardt, Aug. 16, 1970; children—David, Daniel. Asso., J. Lloyd Johnson Assos., Northbrook, Ill., 1972-75; v.p. finance Car-X Service Systems, Chgo., 1975-77; v.p., treas. Playboy Enterprises, Inc., Chgo., 1977-80, sr. v.p. fin. ops., 1980—. Served as 2d lt. USAF, 1970-72. Mem. Am. Mgmt.

Assn., Soc. Internat. Treas., Beta Gamma Sigma. Home: 1780 Robinwood Ln Riverwoods IL 60015 Office: 919 N Michigan Ave Chicago IL 60611

SILVESTROV, ROLF MICHAEL, civil engr.; b. Gevelsburg, Germany, July 6, 1950; s. Ivan and Hildegard S.; student Gen. Motors Inst., 1968-70, Mercer County Coll., 1970-72, Drexel U., 1972-74; m. Faith Ann Telencio, May 27, 1972. Engr. trainee Gen. Motors Corp., Trenton, N.J., 1968-70; project engr. N.J. Dept. Transp., Trenton, from 1970, now project engr. and dep. bur. chief Aeros. div. Ind. supporting mem. Transp. Research Bd., Washington. Mem. Washington Twp. Planning Bd.; mem. Mercer County Juvenile Conf. Com. Licensed real estate salesman, pvt. pilot. Mem. Nat., N.J., Mercer County assns. Realtors, Aircraft Owners and Pilots Assn., Nat. Assn. State Aviation Ofcls. (airport devel. com.). Clubs: Beechcraft Aero., Engrs. of Trenton. Home: 336-D Gordon Rd Robbinsville NJ 08691 Office: 1035 Parkway Ave Trenton NJ 08629

SILVIN, RICHARD RENÉ, med. co. exec.; b. N.Y.C., May 16, 1948; s. John L. and Nancy T. (Torraco) S.; B.S., Georgetown U., 1969; M.B.A. in Hosp. Adminstrn., Cornell U., 1971; 1 dau., Alexi N. Cons. various med. centers, U.S., Can., France and Germany, 1971-73; dir. planning Am. Hosp. of Paris, 1973-74; pres. Friesen Internat. Inc., Washington, 1974-77; v.p. internat. devel. Am. Med. Internat., Inc., Beverly Hills, Calif., 1978—; dir. survey, mgmt. studies for hosp., health care regulatory agys., U.S. and Europe. Mem. Acad. Health Care Consultants (pres., dir.), Internat. Hosp. Fedn., Am. Pub. Health Assn., Fedn. Am. Hosps., Sloan Program in Health Adminstrn. Alumni Assn., Faith and Hope (v.p., dir.). Contbr. numerous articles to profl. jours. Address: 45 Awixa Ave Bay Shore NY 11706

SILVIOUS, OWEN FRANKLIN, music pub., record mfg., mail order co. exec.; b. Luray, Va., Jan. 15, 1939; s. Omey F. and Effie (Jewell) S.; student pub. schls.; m. Nancy A. Gochenour, Aug. 12, 1961 (div. Apr. 1972); children—Owen F. II, Eugene F. Pres., Luray Music Co., 1966—, East-West Res. Bank Ltd., Nassau; U.S. rep. Travelers Bank and Trust Co. Ltd., Cayman Islands, 1976—, World Wide Trading Co., 1976—; internat. investment cons.; songwriter, Broadcast Music, Inc., N.Y.C. and Nashville, 1967—. Served with AUS, 1956-65. Mem. Nat. Songwriters Guild. Office: PO Box 62 Luray VA 22835

SIM, RAYMOND WILLIAM, woodworking co. exec.; b. Scranton, Pa., Feb. 15, 1907; s. William Mollisom and Rose Mary (Mercer) S.; student George Washington U.; m. Catherine Mary Grieb, Nov. 6, 1937; children—Jane, Michael, Susan, Mary Beth, Deborah Ann. With Washington Woodworking Co., Landover, Md., 1924—, inc., 1930, sec., to 1942, pres., 1942—; partner Beaver Rd. Enterprises, Grapal & Walray. Awarded Key to City, City of Washington, 1960. Mem. Nat. Small Bus. Assn. (pres. 1972-74), Archtl. Woodwork Inst. (nat. treas. 1970-72), Washington Bldg. Congress (pres. 1959-60), Washington Lumbermans Club (pres.), Washington Exec. Assn. (pres. 1953). Republican. Roman Catholic. Clubs: Hoo-Hoo, Columbia Country, Washington Kiwanis, Silver Spring (Md.) Lions (pres. 1954-55). Home: 3720 Cardiff Rd Chevy Chase MD 20015 Office: 2010 Beaver Rd Landover MD 20785

SIME, DAVID, chem. co. exec.; b. Bklyn., Mar. 1, 1931; s. David and Maybelle Ottilie (Mader) S.; B.A., Wesleyan U., Middletown, Conn., 1953; student U. Edinburgh (Scotland), 1952; M.B.A., Babson Coll., 1960; m. Joann Pacino, Feb. 4, 1963; children—Debra Ann, Pamela Jeanne, Dana Evelyn. With Mfrs. Hanover Trust Co., N.Y.C., 1960-74, asst. v.p., 1968-72, v.p., 1972-74; v.p. fin. Universal Natural Resources, Ltd., Beirut, Lebanon, 1974-76; asso. First Fla. Holding Corp., Pompano Beach, 1977; dir. corp. devel. Thiokol Corp., Newtown, Pa., 1977—; chmn. bd. Tigerville Service, Inc., 1966—. Active Garden City (N.Y.) Community Fund, 1966-77. Served with U.S. Army, 1954-58. Recipient Brotherhood award N.Y.C. Black Chs., 1973. Mem. Newcomen Soc. N.Am., Assn. Corp. Growth (sec. N.Y. 1976-77). Republican. Editor: Directory of Business Opportunities, 1968-71. Home: Bailey Dr Buckland Valley Farms Washington Crossing PA 18977 Office: PO Box 1000 Route 332 Newtown PA 18940

SIMMONS, GARY MARVIN, auto supply distbn. co. exec.; b. Adel, Ga., Nov. 11, 1949; s. John Marvin and Sara (Jewell) S.; student Abraham Baldwin Agrl. Coll., 1967-69; m. Mary Anne Wright, Apr. 22, 1976; 1 dau., Mary Kathryn. Salesman, Tifton Air Service (Ga.), 1967, sales mgr., 1968-69; salesman Jones VW, Inc., Tifton, 1970-72; salesman, sales mgr. Prince Chevrolet & Oldsmobile Co., Tifton, 1972-76; gen. mgr., owner Tifton Toyota, Inc., 1976-78; pres. Garma Enterprises, Inc., Tifton, 1978—; cons. distbrs. for auto related cos., 1978—; founder Compu-Car, 1979. Mem. Aircraft Owners and Pilots Assn. Clubs: Springhill Country, Elks, Tifton Sertoma (dir.). Home: 1015 Forrest Ave Tifton GA 31794

SIMMONS, GORDON ROY TIMOTHY, internat. bus. cons.; b. El Paso, Tex., May 26, 1923; s. Benjamin Franklin and Bernice (Scott) S.; B.A., Salem (W.Va.) Coll., 1950; Ph.D., Kyoto (Japan) U., 1958, Duke U., 1962; M.A., U. Va., 1960; m. Yukiyo Numao, Aug. 12, 1971. Enlisted in U.S. Army, commd. officer, 1940, advanced through grades to col., 1951; service in Philippines, Australia, S.W. Pacific, China-Burma, India, Japan, Korea; ret., 1971; dir. Ombudsman Inc., and predecessor, Los Angeles, 1972-78, pres., 1978—. Decorated D.S.C., Bronze Star, Silver Star, Purple Heart. Republican. Buddhist. Author army manuals. Office: 1310 Wilshire Blvd Los Angeles CA 90017

SIMMONS, JAMES BOYD, commodity broker-trader; b. Leavenworth, Kans., Oct. 2, 1944; s. James Louis and Louise (Boyd) S.; B.A. in Bus. and Polit. Sci., William Jewell Coll., 1966; m. Mary Susan Bauman, Oct. 4, 1969; children—Erin Michelle, James Bauman. Vice pres. Andco, Inc., Chgo., 1969-71 (merged with Heinold Commodities 1971); commodity broker and trader, mem. Chgo. Mercantile Exchange, 1971—; cons. Heinold Commodities; group leader Commodity Futures Polit. Fund; mem. faculty Ariz. State U., Tempe, also mem. agrl. adv. com. Republican. Mem. United Chs. of Christ. Club: Masons. Home and Office: 4841 E Marston Dr Paradise Valley AZ 85253

SIMMONS, JOHN DEREK, economist, investment research co. exec.; b. Essex, Eng., July 17, 1931; s. Simon Leonard and Eve (Smart) S.; B.S., Columbia, 1956; M.B.A., Rutgers U., 1959; postgrad. N.Y.U., 1959-62; m. Rosalind Wellish, Mar. 5, 1961; children—Peter Lawrence, Sharon Leslie. Came to U.S., 1952. Chief cost accountant Airborne Accessories, Hillside, N.J., 1952-57; sr. cost analyst Curtiss-Wright Corp., Wood Ridge, N.J., 1957; sr. financial analyst internat. group Ford Motor Co., Jersey City, N.J., 1958-60; research asso. Nat. Assn. Accountants, N.Y.C., 1960-64; asst. to v.p. finance Air Reduction Co., Inc., 1965-67; mgr. corporate planning Anaconda Wire & Cable Co., N.Y.C., 1968; ind. financial cons., 1968-71; asso. cons. Rogers, Slade and Hill, Inc., N.Y.C., 1969-71; security analyst, economist Moore & Schley, Cameron & Co. (name now changed to Fourteen Research Corp.), 1972—. Lectr. econs., mgmt., polit. sci. Rutgers U., 1957-64. Served to 1st lt. Brit. Army, 1950-52. Mem. Am. Econ. Assn., Royal Econ. Soc., N.Y. Soc. Security Analysts. Contbr. articles on econs. of underdeveloped nations, polit. sci., mgmt., finance to U.S. and fgn. profl. and sci. jours. Home: 360 E 72d St New York NY 10021 Office: 201 E 42d St New York NY 10017

SIMMONS, KENNETH ROLAND, constrn. exec.; b. Tulia, Tex., Feb. 14, 1918; s. Clarence and Lelia Ann (Putman) S.; student Texarkana Jr. Coll., 1936-37, U. Ark., 1937-39; m. Mary Marie Allen, Sept. 20, 1941; children—Kenneth Oran, Eugene Carl. With Robert E. McKee, Inc., El Paso, 1939—, gen. supt., 1963—, v.p., 1965—. Mem. Disciples of Christ Ch. Supr. numerous constrn. projects including Grady Gammage Meml. Auditorium, Ariz. State U., Tempe, 1942, Francisco Grande Guest Tower, Casa Grande, Ariz., 1957, L.E.M. Test Facilities, White Sands (N.Mex.) Missile Range, 1965; USAF Acad., nr. Colorado Springs, Colo., 1956-59, William Beaumont Army Hosp., El Paso, 1970, U. Tex. Engring. Sci. Complex, 1974; gen. supr. Ground Transp. Center addition San Francisco Airport, 1976; project mgr., additions SW Portland Cement Plant, Odessa, Tex., 1977, El Paso Natural Gas Kaiser Center Bldg., El Paso, 1979-81. Home: 9824 Trinidad St El Paso TX 79925 Office: 1918 Texas Ave El Paso TX 79998

SIMMONS, MICHAEL, computer corp. exec.; b. Scottsburg, Ind., Mar. 29, 1939; s. Atlas Macom and Marion Cecelia (Dooley) S.; B.S., Ind. State U., 1964; postgrad. Ind. U., 1965-67; m. Sally Lou Montgomery, Aug. 31, 1973. Biology tchr. Arsenal Tech. High Sch., Indpls., 1964-67; instr. data processing Ind. Vocat. Tech. Coll., 1966-67; systems engr. IBM Corp., 1967-70, mktg. rep., 1970-73, adv. finance Industry rep. finance, corporate hdqrs. staff, Princeton, N.J., 1973-75, mktg. mgr. finance, comml. office, Houston, 1975-77, instruction mgr. mktg. tng. center, Dallas, 1977-79, adminstrv. asst. to dir. data processing div. edn. dept. IBM, 1979—. Mem. exec. fin. com. Indpls. Mus. Art, 1971-73. Named an Outstanding Young Man Am., 1972; recipient IBM Corp. Golden Circle mktg. award, 1972. Mem. Data Processing Mgmt. Assn., Ind. Soc. of Chgo., Ind. State U. Alumni Assn. (Indpls. pres. 1966-67), Tau Kappa Epsilon. Roman Catholic. Clubs: Sports Car of Am., Porsche of Am., Kiwanis. Home: 6023 Canyon Springs Rd Dallas TX 75248 Office: 225 Carpenter Freeway E 16th Floor Irving TX 75062

SIMON, ARTHUR JAMES, plastic co. exec.; b. Bklyn., Feb. 12, 1927; s. Harry and Helen (Cline) S.; B.A., U. Ala., 1947; postgrad. Oxford U., 1948; M.B.A., U. Pa., 1949; m. Barbara Colby, July 11, 1955; children—Casey, Meri. Vice pres. Closure Research Assn., Rutherford, N.J., 1950-62; dir. StaZon Fastener, Inc., N.Y.C., 1962-65; pres. Tho-Ro Products, Inc., Carlstadt, N.J., 1965—, F-A-C-T, Inc., Wilmington, Del., 1976—, Eagle Button Co., Inc., Carlstadt, N.J., 1957—; v.p. Sir Steve Mfg. Corp, Rutherford; dir. Vistas in Plastics, Ltd., St. Thomas, V.I., Eagle Closure Corp., Calba Corp.; cons. Forum for Advanced Closure Tech. Vice pres. Riverdale Community Council, 1968-69; mem. Philanthropic 50 Assn., Riverdale Little League. Served with AUS, 1945-48. Decorated Bronze Star; recipient certificate of appreciation City of N.Y., 1962. Mem. AIM (exec. council 1977—), Pres.'s Assn. Am. Mgmt. Assn., Adminstrv. Mgmt. Soc., League Presidents, Factory Adv. Panel, Soc. Plastics Industry, Phi Beta Kappa, Phi Eta Sigma, Sigma Alpha Mu. Club: B and T (New Rochelle, N.Y.). Home: 89 Andrea Ln Westwood NJ 07675 Office: 415 14th St Carlstadt NJ 07072

SIMON, CHARLES KENNETH, corp. exec.; b. N.Y.C., Apr. 7, 1918; s. Herbert M. and Belle J. (Simon) S.; B.S., U. Pa., 1939; postgrad. N.Y. U., Pratt Inst.; m. Liane Nau, July 30, 1966; children—Charles Kenneth, Eric Nau, Lilia Nau. Exec., Brewster Aircraft, 1940-41, York Aircraft Co., 1941-43, Aerojet Gen. Corp., 1959-62; designer, creater Advanced Decision Data System, 1957—; mgmt. scientist, pres. Mgmt. Methods Corp., Sacramento and San Diego, 1962—; pres., mng. dir. Mgmt. Research Found., San Francisco and Coronado, Calif., 1975—; pres., chmn. bd. Cal-Columbian Mining Co.; chmn. bd. Computer Mgmt. Corp., Salt Lake City, 1970—; bd. dirs. Automated Ct. Systems, San Diego, 1976—; cons. Dept. Def., aerospace industry, 1943—; mem. teaching staff U. Calif., 1960-62. Served with USNR, 1944-46. Decorated Bronze Star. Mem. Ops. Research Soc., Inst. Mgmt. Sci., Am. Ordnance Soc., Air Force Assn., Am. Mgmt. Assn. Home: 1720 Avenida Del Mundo Coronado Shores Coronado CA 92118 Office: 44 Montgomery St Suite 500 San Francisco CA 94104 also 1224 10th St Coronado CA 92118

SIMON, CHERYL ANN HAUSLYAK, pharm. co. adminstr.; b. Pottsville, Pa., Dec. 23, 1950; d. Andrew George and Eleanor Helen (Pomian) Hauslyak; student Union County Coll. (N.J.), 1976—; m. Leo Simon, Dec. 11, 1971; 1 dau., Eleanor Louise. Sr. stenographer Bell Labs., Cranford, N.J., 1969-70; with Merck & Co., Inc., Rahway, N.J., 1970—, sec. med. affairs area internat., 1970-76, supr. Word Processing/Communications Center, regulatory affairs, internat., 1976—; speaker to local high schs. Certified profl. sec. Mem. Nat. Secs. Assn. Internat., N.J. Word Processing Info. Exchange, Ladies Aux. of N.J. Air N.G. Home: 1009 Fanny St Elizabeth NJ 07201 Office: PO Box 2000 Rahway NJ 07065

SIMON, DON VERNER, forest products co. exec.; b. Portland, Oreg., Apr. 12, 1932; s. John D. and Esther B. S.; B.S., U. Oreg., 1955; m. Kendall L. Goggans, Dec. 7, 1957; children—Stephen, Janet, Gretchen. With Texaco, Inc., Portland, 1958-60; sales mgr. plywood Oreg. Pacific Industries, Portland, 1960-65, Continental Forest Products, Lake Oswego, Oreg., 1965-71, Willamette Industries, Albany, Oreg., 1971-74, Am. Internat. Forest Products, Beaverton, Oreg., 1974-76; pres. Simon, Crabtree & Ryan, Inc., Lake Grove, Oreg., 1976—. Served with USAF, 1955-57. Mem. Oreg. Assn. Credit Mgmt. Republican. Episcopalian. Club: Multnomah Athletic, Home: 1653 SW Devon Ln Lake Oswego OR 97034 Office: 16325 SW Boones Ferry Rd Lake Grove OR 97034

SIMON, DONALD CAMILLUS, aircraft mfg. co. exec.; b. St. Charles, Mo., Sept. 21, 1922; s. Camillus Edward and Cecilia Theresa (Blaeser) S.; B.S. Aero. Engring. cum laude, Miss. State U., 1944; m. Lucille Katherine Klotzer, Apr. 24, 1948; children—Nancy, Donna, Suzanne. With Cessna Aircraft Co., Wichita, 1945—, asst. chief insp., 1954-57, chief service engring., 1957-69, adminstr. mil. programs, 1969—; tchr. adult edn. Served as ensign USNR, 1944. Mem. Quiet Birdmen, OX-5 Aviation Pioneers, Air Force Assn., Army Aviation Assn., C. of C., Tau Beta Pi. Republican. Roman Catholic. Home: 1000 S Woodlawn #1407 Wichita KS 67218 Office: PO Box 7704 Wichita KS 67277

SIMON, H(UEY) PAUL, lawyer; b. Lafayette, La., Oct. 19, 1923; s. Jules and Ida (Rogers) S.; B.S., U. Southwestern La., 1943, J.D., Tulane U., 1947; m. Carolyn Perkins, Aug. 6, 1949; 1 son, John Clark. Admitted to La. bar, 1947, since practiced in New Orleans; asst. prof. advanced acctg. U. Southwestern La., 1944-45; prin. Haskins & Sells, C.P.A.'s, New Orleans, 1945-57; partner law firm Deutsch, Kerrigan & Stiles, New Orleans, 1957-79; sr. partner law firm Simon, Pexagine, Smith & Redfearn, 1979—; Co-chmn. N.Y. U. Tax Conf., New Orleans, 1976. C.P.A., La., Miss. Mem. Am. Judicature Soc., Internat. (mem. com. on securities issues and trading 1970—), Inter-Am., Am., (mem. com. ct. procedure and bar activities 1958—), La. (com. on legislation and adminstrv. practice), New Orleans bar assns., Am. Inst. C.P.A.'s, Tulane Alumni Assn., Am. Assn. Atty-C.P.A.'s, Soc. La. C.P.A.'s, New Orleans Assn. Notaries, New Orleans C. of C. (council 1952-66), New Orleans Met. Area Com., Council for Better La., Tulane Tax Inst. (program com. 1960—), La. Tax Conf. (program com. 1968-72), Bur. Govtl. Research, Met. Crime Commn., Phi Delta Phi (past pres. New Orleans chpt.), Sigma Pi Alpha. Roman Catholic. Clubs: Young Men's Business (legislation com.), Petroleum, Press, Toastmasters Internat., New Orleans Country (New Orleans); International House (dir. 1976—); Paul Morphy Chess; Lamplighter; Pendennis. Author: Louisiana Income Tax Law, 1956; Changes Effected by the Louisiana Trust Code, 1965; Gifts to Minors and the Parent's Obligation of Support, 1968; Deductions—Business or Hobby, 1975; Role of Attorney in IRS Tax Return Examination, 1978. Asso. editor: The Louisiana C.P.A., 1956-60. Bd. editors Tulane Law Rev., 1945-46. Home: 6075 Canal Blvd New Orleans LA 70124 Office: One Shell Sq Suite 4300 New Orleans LA 70139

SIMON, PETER KLAUS, mfg. co. exec.; b. Frankfurt, Germany, Jan. 16, 1926; s. Maximilian and Charlotte (Liechtenstein) S.; B.Sc., U. London, 1951; m. Berthe Tremblay, Feb. 19, 1955; 1 dau., Danielle Ann. With Raymond Internat., Inc., Houston, 1958-74, group v.p., 1972-74; v.p. Tecon Corp., Dallas, 1975—; pres. Am. Seamless Tubing Inc., Balt., 1976-77, Arlo Systems, Inc., Dallas, 1975—; chief exec. officer Isolite Corp., Los Angeles, 1976-77; dir., partner Randall Ridley Inc., Cons., N.Y.C., 1974-78; dir. constrn. Aircraft Group Northrop Corp., Hawthorne, Calif., 1978-79; cons. constrn. mgmt. and engring. Saudi Arabian Devel. Co., 1979—; v.p. constrn. Shobokshi-SADC, Rolling Hills Estates, Calif., 1979—; cons. Engring. and Mgmt., Houston, 1974-75. Served with Civil Def., London, Eng., 1941-45. Mem. Edison Elec. Inst., Am. Mgmt. Assn. Methodist. Clubs: Dirs. (London); Royal Oak Country (Dallas). Office: 608 Silver Spur Rd Rolling Hills Estates CA 90274

SIMON, ROBERT HENRY, health care co. exec.; b. N.Y.C., July 31, 1931; s. Clarence Kaufman and Ruth G. (Goldwater) S.; B.S. in Chemistry, Purdue U., 1953; grad. Sr. Mgmt. Program, Harvard U., 1975; m. Angela de Mendonca Lima, Mar. 30, 1972; children—Erika, Susan, Alexandra, Adriana. With Miles Labs., Inc., 1970—, area v.p. Far East, Hong Kong, 1973-78, exec. v.p. Ames div., Elkhart, Ind., 1978-80, pres. div., 1980—; dir. Miles-Sankyo K.K., Tokyo. Served with AUS, 1953-55. Mem. Am. Chem. Soc., Am. Soc. Med. Tech. Clubs: Am. (Japan and Hong Kong); Press (asso.), Lawn Tennis (Tokyo). Office: 1127 Myrtle St PO Box 70 Elkhart IN 46515

SIMON, RONALD ISAAC, fin. and real estate cons.; b. Cairo, United Arab Republic, Nov. 4, 1938; s. David and Helene (Zilkha) S.; came to U.S., 1942, naturalized, 1949; B.A., Harvard, 1960; M.A., Columbia, 1962, Ph.D. (Ford Found. fellow), 1968; m. Anne Faith Hartman, June 19, 1960; children—Cheryl Lynne, Eric Lewis, Daniel Jay. Vice pres. Harpers Internat. Inc., N.Y.C., 1959-62; financial analyst Amerace Corp., N.Y.C., 1965-66; v.p. Am. Foresight Inc., Phila., 1966-67; asst. to pres. Avco Corp., N.Y.C., 1967-70, exec. v.p., treas., Avco Community Developers Inc., 1970-73, dir. Avco Community Developers Inc., 1969-73; pres. Ronald I. Simon Inc., La Jolla, Calif., 1973—; dir. Avant-Garde Computing, Inc., Geothermal Devel. Group, Inc., Power Alcohol, Inc. lectr. corp. and real estate financing. Recipient award Nat. Comml. Finance Conf., 1963. Club: University (N.Y.C.). Author articles in field. Home: 1740 El Camino del Teatro La Jolla CA 92037

SIMONDS, ROBERT BRUCE, automobile dealer; b. Seattle, Mar. 30, 1939; s. William, Jr. and Charlotte Mary (Jewell) S.; student Long Beach (Calif.) City Coll., 1957-59, Long Beach State Coll., 1959-61; m. Loretta Frances Fota, Nov. 18, 1961; children—Robert Bruce, Cynthia Suzanne, Christina Michelle. Engr. adminstr. N. Am. Rockwell, Inc., Downey, Calif., 1962-65; dealer, gen. mgr. Mike Salta Pontiac, Inc., Honolulu 1966-74; dealer, gen. mgr. Westward Pontiac, Inc. (now Bob Simonds Pontiac, Inc.), Phoenix, 1974-79, pres., owner, 1979—; dir. Hawaii Automobile Dealers Assn., 1972-74. Bd. dirs. Hawaii Found. Lupus Research, 1972-73. Served as officer inf., USAR, 1964-68. Decorated Medal for Valor with pendant; recipient numerous letters appreciations, service awards. Mem. Ariz. Automobile Dealers Assn., Ariz. C. of C., Better Bus. Bur. Ariz., Sigma Alpha Epsilon. Republican. Roman Catholic. Clubs: Phoenix Country; Waialae Country (Honolulu). Home: 4545 E Oregon Ave Phoenix AZ 85018 Office: 4635 N 7th St Phoenix AZ 85014

SIMPICH, GEORGE CARY, investment banker; b. Washington, June 25, 1923; s. Frederick and Margaret (Edwards) S.; 1 dau., Juliet Elizabeth. Mem. advt. staff Washington Post, 1945-47, Nat. Geog. Mag., 1947-49; with Young & Rubicam Advt. Agy., 1949-51; with Davidson & Co., 1951-56; div. mgr. Fin. Programs, Inc., Washington, 1956-61; investment cons. O'Boyle, Hearne & Fowler, Ltd., Washington, 1961-66; mem. Butcher & Singer Investment Co., and predecessors, Washington, 1966-75; bus. devel. White, Weld & Co., Inc., Washington, 1975-76; v.p. sales Johnston, Lemon & Co., Inc., Bethesda, Md., 1976-77; v.p., prin., resident mgr. Butcher & Singer, Inc., 1977—. Served as pilot USAAC, 1943-45. Mem. Nat. Economists Club, Municipal Fin. Forum, Bond Club. Clubs: Del Ray, Nat. Press. Republican. Episcopalian (vestryman). Home: 23 Wellesley Circle Glen Echo MD 20768 Office: Suite 406 11484 Washington Plaza W Reston VA 22090

SIMPKINS, JOSEPH ALBERT, mfg. co. exec.; b. St. Louis, Sept. 15, 1905; s. Leo and Ella (Friedkin) S.; grad. high sch.; m. Florence Putnam, Oct. 2, 1978; 1 dau. by previous marriage, Linda (Mrs. Farrell Kahn). Self-employed auto dealer, St. Louis, 1929-47; chmn. bd., pres. Tiffany Industries, St. Louis, 1968—; owner Joe Simpkins Oil Co., 1944—. Vice pres. Herbert Hoover Boys Club, 1969—. Bd. dirs. Jewish Hosp., Child Center Our Lady of Grace, Dismes House. Mem. Independent Men's Assn. Club: Variety (pres. 1969-71) (St. Louis). Home: 2220 Warson Rd St Louis MO 63124 Office: 1055 Corporate Square Dr Saint Louis MO 63132

SIMPKINS, ROBERT ALLYN, communications exec.; b. Pasadena, Calif., Apr. 5, 1945; s. Lloyd Garland and Virginia Lee (Reynolds) S.; B.A., Los Angeles State U., 1969; m. Linda Lee Fugate, June 25, 1966; 1 son, Erik Allyn. Mgr. material handling May Co. So. Calif., Arcadia, 1970-71; sales mgr. Accurate Formprint, Inc., South El Monte, Calif., 1972-76, v.p., 1976-77, pres., gen. mgr., 1977-78; pres. gen. mgr. Marina Media, graphic arts cons., Huntington Beach, Calif., 1978-79; mktg. cons. Pacific Telephone, Buena Park, Calif., 1979—. Scoutmaster, Cub Scouts Am.; mgr. Little League; coach Am. Youth Soccer Orgn.; mem. coms. PTA. Recipient internat. award Dynamic Graphics, 1977, 78. Mem. Printing Industries Am., Am. Mgmt. Assn., Smithsonian Instn. (asso.). Unitarian. Home and Office: 16721 Barefoot Circle Huntington Beach CA 92649

SIMPKINS, WILLIAM JAMES, JR., ins. co. exec.; b. Atlanta, Dec. 7, 1918; s. William James and Myrtle L. S.; m. June 13, 1941; children—William John, Sara Joan. Salesman, Franklin Life Ins. Co., Columbus, Ga., 1945-48, gen. agent, 1948-63, regional sales mgr., 1963—. Past pres. United Cerebral Palsy, Columbus; past campaign dir. Muscogee County (Ga.) March of Dimes; bd. dirs. United Givers, Columbus, Little League, Columbus; active Boy Scouts Am., Columbus. Served with USAF, 1941-46. Mem. Nat. Assn. Life Underwriters, Million Dollar Round Table (life), Columbus C. of C. (life). Democrat. Methodist. Contbr. articles to profl. jours. Home: 12

Summit Pl Columbus GA 31906 Office: 211 Wynnton Bldg Columbus GA 31906

SIMPSON, ALLAN BOYD, real estate co. exec.; b. Lakeland, Fla., Nov. 24, 1948; s. Alfred Forsythe and Ruth Jeanette (Coker) S.; B.Indsl. Engring., Ga. Inst. Tech., 1970; M.B.A., U. Pa., 1972; m. Susan June McEwen, Apr. 30, 1976; 1 dau., Lauren Leigh. Dir. mortgage banking Ackerman & Co., Atlanta, 1972-73; v.p. B.F. Saul Co., Atlanta, 1973-79; pres. comml. div. Hooker/Barnes, Atlanta, 1979—, also dir. Bd. dirs. Midtown Bus. Assn., 1979—, treas. bd. dirs., 1979—. Cert. rev. appraiser; lic. realtor, Ga. Mem. Am. Inst. Indsl. Engrs., M.B.A. Execs. Assn., Bldg. Owners and Mgrs. Assn., Nat. Assn. Realtors, U.S. C. of C., Atlanta C. of C. Democrat. Methodist. Club: Atlanta City. Home: 1140 Rosedale Rd Atlanta GA 30306 Office: Hooker/Barnes 2175 Parklake Dr Atlanta GA 30345

SIMPSON, DAVID E., investment banker; b. Chgo., June 13, 1927; s. George H. and Mildred (McElfresh) S.; student Williams Coll., 1946-49; B.S., Northwestern U., 1950, postgrad. in law, 1951-52. With banking, trust depts. No. Trust Co., Chgo., 1952-55; with H.M. Byllesby & Co., Inc., Chgo., 1955-60, asst. v.p., 1957-59, v.p., 1959-60, also pres., dir. subs. Maloney-Crawford Mfg. Co., Tulsa, 1957-59; with McKinsey & Co., Inc., 1960-61; with Paine, Webber, Jackson & Curtis, Inc., N.Y.C., 1961-76, gen. partner, 1967-71, v.p., 1971-76; v.p. Bache, Halsey, Stuart, Shields, 1976—; pres., dir. 11 E. 87th St Corp., 1974—. Life mem. Chgo. Hist. Soc., New Eng. Soc. N.Y.; trustee Lambda Found., N.Y.C. Clubs: Bond, Racquet and Tennis, Leash, City Midday, St. Anthony (gov. 1967-76); Quogue Field, Quoque Beach; Racquet of Chgo. Home: 11 E 87th St New York NY 10028 also Ocean Ave Quogue NY 11959 Office: 100 Gold St New York NY 10038

SIMPSON, DONALD BRUCE, research center exec.; b. Ithaca, N.Y., Dec. 13, 1942; s. Francis Alfred and Drusilla Lucille (Dickson) S.; B.A., Alfred U., 1964; M.S. in Library Sci., Syracuse U., 1970; postgrad. in pub. adminstrn. Ohio State U., 1971-74; m. Lupe M. Rodriguez, Nov. 10, 1977; 1 son, Michael John. Asst. librarian Keuka Coll., 1970-71; head catalog center State Library of Ohio, Columbus, 1971-75; exec. dir. Bibliog. Center for Research, Rocky Mountain Region, Inc., Denver, 1975-80; pres. Center for Research Libraries, Inc., Chgo., 1980—; cons. in field; v.p., mem. exec. com., chmn. fin. com., users council Ohio Coll. Library Center, 1978-80, SALINET Bd., 1976-77; mem. network adv. com. Library of Congress, 1978-80; chmn. legislation com. Council Computerized Library Networks, 1979-80. Served to capt. USAF, 1965-69. Decorated Air Force Commendation medal. Mem. Assn. State Library Agencies (pres. 1977-78), ALA (councilor-at-large 1979—), Am. Mgmt. Assn., Am. Soc. Info. Sci., Spl. Libraries Assn. Club: Quadrangle (Chgo.). Editor: State Library Agencies, 1973-79; contbr. articles to profl. jours. Office: 5721 Cottage Grove Ave Chicago IL 60637

SIMPSON, DOUGLAS W., JR., investment cons.; b. Corning, N.Y., June 17, 1943; s. Douglas W. and Betsy L. (Ross) S.; student in ins. Onondaga Coll., 1974; m. Babs C. Riett, Feb. 8, 1963; children—Tina Lynn, Tonya Lee. Mgr., Hartford Ins. Group, Syracuse, N.Y., 1972-74; gen. mgr., gen. partner Taurus Realty, Corning, N.Y., 1972—; owner Investment Adv. Service, 1972—; pres. 1st Center Assos., Inc., 1974—; sr. employee benefit cons. Aldrich & Cox Inc., Buffalo, 1979—; trustee various pension plans. Bd. dirs. YMCA, Corning, Vol. Clearing House. Served with N.Y. N.G., 1964-68. Mem. Am. Soc. Pension Actuaries (asso.), Internat. Assn. Fin. Planners. Home: 230 Chemung St Corning NY 14830 Office: Aldrich & Cox Inc 274 Delaware Ave Buffalo NY 14202

SIMPSON, HENRY CLAY, JR., electronic banking services mgmt.; b. Lexington, Ky., Nov. 7, 1938; s. Henry Clay and Louisiana (Wood) S.; A.B., U. N.C., 1960; M.B.A., Columbia U., 1962; m. Katherine H. Meyer, July 8, 1967; children—Katherine H., Anne C., Josephine C. Asst. v.p., corporate banking group officer Citibank, N.Y.C., 1962-68, 70-72; research asso. Amos Tuck Sch., Dartmouth Coll., Hanover, N.H., 1968-69; v.p., dir. mktg. TMI Systems Corp., N.Y.C., 1972-78; v.p., mgr. internat. cash mgmt. services, world banking div. Bank of Am., N.Y.C., 1978—. Trustee, sec. The Kentuckians, 1974—; chmn. alumni fund, council world mems. Internat. House 1977—. Served with USAF. Clubs: Univ. (N.Y.C.); Baltusrol Golf (Springfield). Home: 37 Greenbriar Dr Summit NJ 07901 Office: 41 Broad St New York NY 10004

SIMPSON, JAMES LEE, banker; b. Rehoboth, N.Mex., Aug. 28, 1936; s. Lester and Ozella (Wofford) S.; B.G.S. in History and Polit. Sci., U. Nebr., 1973; m. Karen Allene Smith, Sept. 1, 1956; children—Janet Allene, Alan Dale, James Austin. Enlisted man U.S. Air Force, 1953-61; commd. 2d lt., 1961, advanced through grades to maj., 1973; trained in electronic warfare; flew 215 missions in S.E. Asia; ret., 1974; sales mgr. Ek Products, 1974-76; pres. N.Am. Model Enterprises, Inc., Ft. Worth, 1977-79; asst. v.p. mktg. Citizens Nat. Bank, Denton, Tex., 1979-80; v.p. First Nat. Bank, Sanger, Tex., 1980—. Active fund drives United Fund, AF Aid Soc., U.S. Savs. Bonds. Decorated D.F.C., Air Medal with 7 oak leaf clusters. Mem. Acad. Model Aeros. (certified adminstrv. leader), Soaring Soc. Am., Nat. Soaring Soc., League Silent Flight, Fedn. Aeronautique Internationale, Southwest Modelers Show (bd. dirs.). Mormon. Columnist, asso. editor RC Modeler Mag., 1966-77; columnist RC Sportsman, 1977-80; Miniature aircraft designer; designed remote controlled weather research air vehicle for Sch. Atmospheric Research. Home: 206 Diane Sanger TX 76266 Office: PO Box 128 Sanger TX 76266

SIMPSON, JOHN WISTAR, energy cons.; b. Glenn Springs, S.C., Sept. 25, 1914; s. Richard Caspar and Mary (Berkeley) S.; student Wofford Coll., 1932-33, D.Sc., 1972; B.S., U.S. Naval Acad., 1937; M.S., U. Pitts., 1941; D.Sc. (hon.), Seton Hill Coll., 1970; m. Esther Slattery, Jan. 17, 1948; children—John Wistar, Carter B., Patricia A., Barbara J. With Westinghouse Electric Corp., 1937-77, mgr. Navy and Marine switchboard engring., switchgear div., on leave as mgr. nuclear engring. Daniels pile group, Oak Ridge, Nat. Lab., successively asst. engring. mgr. tech. dir. mgr. (Shippingport) project Bettis Atomic Power Lab., 1949-55, v.p. Westinghouse Electric Corp., gen. mgr. Bettis atomic power lab., 1955-59, v.p., gen. mgr. atomic power divs., 1959-62, v.p. engring. and research 1962-63, v.p. electric utility group, 1963-69, pres. power systems, exec. v.p., 1969-74, dir.-officer, chmn. energy com., 1974-78; pres. Simpson Bus. Services, Inc., 1980—; dir. Westinghouse, S.A., Madrid, Off Shore Power Systems; mem. Naval Tech. Mission to Japan, 1945; del. 1st Internat. Conf. on Peaceful Uses Atomic Energy, Geneva, 1955, 2d Internat. Conf., 1958; chmn. Atomic Indsl. Forum, 1974-76; mem. sci. adv. bd. Notre Dame. Trustee, Point Park Coll., Wofford Coll.; mem. governing bd. Nat. Council Chs. Recipient Gold medal for advancement of research Am. Soc. Metals. Fellow IEEE (Edison medal 1971), ASME (hon., George Westinghouse medal 1974), Am. Nuclear Soc. (pres.); mem. Newcomen Soc., Am. Ordnance Assn., Soc. Naval Architects and Marine Engrs., Nat. Acad. Engring., Franklin Inst. (Newcomen Gold medal), Navy League. Clubs: St. Clair Country, Duquesne (Pitts.); Rolling Rock, Laurel Valley Golf (Ligonier, Pa.); Farmington Country (Charlottesville, Va.); Plantation, Bear Creek Golf (Hilton Head, S.C.); Amelia Plantation Golf (Amelia Island, Fla.). Office: 36 E Beach Lagoon Dr Hilton Head Island SC 29928

SIMPSON, LEROY EDWARD, turbine mfg. co. exec.; b. Iowa Falls, Iowa, Nov. 15, 1926; s. Fay and Leona (Tresemer) S.; student Ellsworth Jr. Coll., 1946-47; B.S. in Elec. Engring., Iowa State U., 1950; m. Edith Eleanor Mullen, Oct. 7, 1951; children—Edith Eleanor, LeRoy Edward. Various fin. mgmt. positions Gen. Electric Co., 1950-74; controller gas turbine div. Turbodyne Corp., St. Cloud, Minn., 1974-77; v.p. fin. and adminstrn., sec.-treas. Brown Boveri Turbomachinery, Inc., St. Cloud, 1977—. Served with adj. gen.'s dept. U.S. Army, 1945-46. Mem. Nat. Assn. Accts. (past pres. Albany chpt., past pres. Central Minn. chpt.), Stuart Cameron McLeod Soc. (nat. dir.), Nat. Rifle Assn. (life), Amateur Trapshooting Assn. Clubs: Central Minn. Rifle (past pres., dir.), Central Minn. Gun. Home: 508 Brookwood Ln Sartell MN 56377 Office: Brown Boveri Turbomachinery Inc 711 Anderson Ave N Saint Cloud MN 56301

SIMS, EUGENE RALPH, JR., indsl. engr.; b. N.Y.C., Oct. 12, 1920; s. Eugene Ralph and Rose (Simmons) S.; B. Adminstrv. Engring., N.Y. U., 1947; M.B.A., Ohio U.; m. Ethel Jane Smith, June 8, 1945; children—Pamela Jeanne, Gary Wardner, Phyllis Anne. Tool and instrument maker Sperry Gyroscope Co., N.Y.C., 1939-43; research test engr. N.Y. U., 1947; cons. indsl. engr. Drake, Startzman, Sheahan, Barclay, Inc., N.Y.C., 1947-49; plant mgr. Lit Bros. Warehouse & Furniture Plant, Phila., 1949-50; project indsl. engr. Jeffrey Mfg. Co., Columbus, Ohio, 1950-51; prin. indsl. engr., mgmt. ops. research Battelle Meml. Inst., Columbus, 1951-54; corp. materials handling engr. Anchor Hocking Glass Corp., Lancaster, Ohio, 1954-56; chief indsl. engr., asso. Alden E. Stilson & Assos. Ltd., Columbus, 1956-58; pres. E. Ralph Sims, Jr. & Assos., Inc., Lancaster, 1958—, Fairhill Devel. Corp., Lancaster, 1959—. Dist. commr. Central Ohio council Boy Scouts Am., 1954-56; past mem. adv. council Ohio Tech. Services Program; past mem. Bd. Zoning Appeals Lancaster; sr. pilot/capt. CAP. Served as 1st lt. USAAF, 1943-46. Registered profl. engr., Ohio, Wis., N.Y., Pa., Calif.; chartered engr., U.K. Mem. ASME, Am. Inst. Indsl. Engrs., Inst. Mgmt. Cons.'s (founding mem., dir.), Assn. Mgmt. Cons.'s (pres. 1975-76), Brit. Inst. M.E., Nat. Soc. Profl. Engrs., Am. Mgmt. Assn., Nat. Council Phys. Distbn. Mgmt., Air Force Assn. (charter mem.), Psi Upsilon. Clubs: N.Y. U., Minn. Press, Masons (32 deg.), Shriners. Author: Euphonious Coding, 1967; Planning and Management of Material Flow, 1968; Contemporary Comment in Retrospect, 1973; contbg. editor: Production Handbook, 1958; Materials Handling Handbook, 1958; Handbook of Business Adminstrn., 1967; Ency. Profl. Mgmt., 1978; contbr. articles to trade jours. Home: 114 Luther Ln Lancaster OH 43130 Office: 919 E Fair Ave Lancaster OH 43130

SIMS, ROBERT THOMAS, pharm. mfg. co. exec.; b. Bklyn., July 8, 1936; s. Ambrose Thomas and Marie Ann Sims; B.B.A., Hofstra U., 1960, M.B.A., 1967; m. Yvonne Pansini, May 20, 1961; children—Robert D., Diane M., James W. Sales rep. Pfizer Labs., N.Y.C., 1960-68; market research analyst-mgr. Merck, Sharp & Dohme, West Point, Pa., 1968-74; product mgr. Merck Sharp & Dohme Internat., Rahway, N.J., 1974-76, mktg. dir., 1976-78, exec. dir. mktg., 1978—. Chmn., Montgomery Twp. Planning Commn., 1973-74. Served with U.S. Army, 1956-58. Mem. Am. Mgmt. Assn., Mu Gamma Tau. Republican. Roman Catholic. Home: 546 Glen Ridge Dr S Bridgewater NJ 08807 Office: PO Box 2000 Rahway NJ 07065

SIMS, STEPHEN DOUGLAS, life ins. co. ofcl.; b. Corsicana, Tex., Sept. 13, 1950; s. Robert Quincy and Sara Eugenia (Stubbs) S.; B.B.A., So. Meth. U., 1973; m. Diane Katherine Hinckley, May 25, 1974; 1 son, Christopher Lawrence. Sales asso. Hershel Forester & Co., comml. real estate brokers, Dallas, 1974-75; sales mgr. Dallas-Ellis agy. Mut. of N.Y., 1975—. Mem. Nat. Assn. Life Underwriters, Tex. Assn. Life Underwriters, Dallas Assn. Life Underwriters, Million Dollar Round Table, Mut. of N.Y. Pres.'s Council, Gen. Agts. and Mgrs. Assn., So. Meth. U. Alumni Assn. (dir. 1980—, exec. com.), Phi Gamma Delta. Clubs: So. Meth. U. Mustang, So. Meth. U. Letterman's. Home: 9611 Crestedge Dr Dallas TX 75238 Office: 4525 Lemmon Ave Dallas TX 75219

SIMS, WILBERT NORMAN, equipment mfg. co. exec.; b. Bridgeville, Pa., Sept. 12, 1922; s. Wilbert Leroy and Margaret Belle (Gordon) S.; B.S. in Fuel Tech., Pa. State U., 1949; A.M.P., Harvard U., 1966; m. Martha Lois McClelland, Oct. 18, 1952; 1 son, Scott McClelland. Miner, Pitts. Coal Co., 1940-42; fuel engr. Phila. Coal & Iron Co., 1949-52; gen. purchasing agt. Am. Cyanamid Co., 1952-62; v.p., gen. mgr. indsl. chems. Kaiser Aluminium & Chem. Co., 1962-71; v.p., gen. mgr. Marconaflo Inc., 1971-78, Macronaflo div. McNally Group, Oakland, Calif., 1978—. Pres., E. Bay Area Trails Council, 1978-79, San Ramon Valley Horsemen, 1970, 80; chmn. charitable trusts Calif. Horsemen's Assn., 1979—; equine chmn. for Calif., Morris Animal Found., 1978—; adv. adv. Danville Jr. Horsemen, 1964-80. Served with USAAF, 1943-46. Mem. AIME, Newcomen Soc. N. Am., Phi Delta Theta. Republican. Methodist. Club: Stock Exchange. Author, patentee in field. Home: 10424 Dimple Dell Rd Sandy UT 84092 Office: PO Box 7660 Salt Lake City UT 84107

SIMUNEK, NICHOLAS, investment banker; b. London, Jan. 30, 1939; s. George and Alison (Laird-Cook) S.; came to U.S., 1963; student Sorbonne U., Paris, 1956, McGill U., Montreal, Que., Can., 1961. Pres., Simko Equities Internat. Inc., N.Y.C., 1970—; dir. Randolph Pub. Co., N.Y.C., Peconic Corp., N.Y.C., Champlain Foods, Vt., Cambrian Pub., Toronto, Ont., Can., Middle East Engring., London. Served with Brit. Coldstream Guards, 1956-59. Author: Mergers and Acquisitions—An Art, 1971; International Merger Strategy, 1972. Office: 952 Fifth Ave New York NY 10021

SINCLAIR, IAN DAVID, r.r. co. ofcl.; b. Winnipeg, Man., Can., Dec. 27, 1913; s. John David and Lillian (Matheson) S.; B.A. in Econs., Wesley Coll., U. Man., 1937, LL.D., 1967; LL.B., U. Man. Law Faculty, 1941; m. Ruth Beatrice Drennan, July 17, 1942; children—Ian R., Susan L., Christine R., Donald L. Barrister, Guy, Chappell & Co., Winnipeg, 1937-41; called to Man. bar, 1941, apptd. Queen's counsel, 1961; lectr. torts U. Man., 1942-43; with Canadian Pacific Ltd., 1942—, asst. solicitor, 1942, solicitor, Montreal, Que., Can., 1946, asst. to gen. counsel, 1951; gen. solicitor, 1953, v.p., gen. counsel, 1960, v.p. law, 1960-61, v.p., 1961-66, mem. exec. com., dir., 1961—, pres., 1966-72, chief exec. officer, 1969—, chmn. bd., 1972—; dir., exec. officer Canadian Pacific Air Lines, Ltd., Midland Simcoe Elevator Co., Ltd., Canadian Pacific Enterprises, Ltd.; v.p., dir. Pan Canadian Petroleum Ltd., Cominco Ltd., Royal Bank of Can.; dir. subs.'s Canadian Pacific Steamships Ltd., Canadian Pacific (Bermuda) Ltd., Pacific Logging Co. Ltd., Marathon Realty Co. Ltd., Soo Line RR Co., Great Lakes Forest Products Ltd.; dir. AMCA Internat. Corp., Canadian Investment Fund, Union Carbide Corp., Union Carbide Can. Ltd., Canadian Fund Inc., Can. Marconi Co., Sun Life Assurance Can. Ltd., Seagram Co. Ltd., Dominion Bridge Co., Ltd.; mem. internat. adv. com. Chase Manhattan Corp. Mem. The Conf. Bd. N.Y., Canadian C. of C., Chambre de Commerce (Montreal), Montreal Bd. Trade. Clubs: Canadian Ry., Canadian, Mount Royal (Montreal); Rideau (Ottawa, Ont.). Office: Canadian Pacific Ltd PO Box 6042 Sta A Montreal PQ H3C 3E4 Canada

SINDLER, PHILIP STEVEN, specialty telecommunications co. exec.; b. Miami Beach, Fla., May 11, 1948; s. Bernard and Iris (Sondra) S.; B.S.B.A. in Fin., U. Md., 1973; m. Janice Linda Katz, Nov. 12, 1972. Investment specialist Bache & Co., San Diego, 1974-76, Sutro & Co., La Jolla, Calif., 1976-77; pres., chmn. bd., chief exec. officer Specialized Systems, Inc., San Diego, 1977—. Fund raiser for deaf related polit. action groups, coms. Mem. Electronics Industry Assn., Nat. Assn. Deaf. Office: 11558 Sorrento Valley Rd Bldg 7 San Diego CA 92121

SINGER, CRAIG, fin. services co. exec.; b. N.Y.C., Aug. 13, 1947; s. Albert and Dorothy (Blackman) S.; B.S., Cornell U., 1969; J.D. (Harlan Fiske Stone scholar), Columbia U., 1972; m. Ellen Rappaport, Aug. 31, 1969. Exec., Continental Wingate Co., Inc., N.Y.C., 1972-74; sr. v.p. Integrated Resources, Inc., N.Y.C., 1974—; admitted to N.Y. State bar, 1973; exec. v.p., dir. Assn. Govt. Assisted Housing, Inc., 1976—; mem. exec. com. Coalition for Low and Moderate Income Housing. Home: 60 Riverside Dr New York NY 10024 Office: 666 3d Ave New York NY 10017

SINGER, JOHN DONALD, farm equipment mfg. co. exec.; b. Mpls., Jan. 25, 1927; s. John and Dorothy M. (Cullum) S.; m. Phyllis Jean Wheeler, July 19, 1949; children—Pamela Singer Lambert, Julie Singer Terrell. Designer, Collins Radio, Cedar Rapids, Iowa, 1946-48; designer John Deere Co., Waterloo, Iowa, 1948-73, mgr. office services, 1973—. Mem. Community Devel. Adv. Bd., Waterloo, 1975—; pres. Waterloo Community Playhouse, 1962-77; v.p. Iowa Community Theatre Assn., 1972-74; mem. Recreation Commn., 1974—, N.E. Iowa Area Crime Commn., 1977-80; mem. Iowa Arts Council, 1977—, chmn., 1980; bd. dirs. Affiliated State Arts Agys. of Upper Midwest, 1980—; mem. Nat. Assembly State Art Agys.; mem. Downtown Redevel. Authority, 1980—. Served with USNR, 1944-46, 50-52. Mem. Nat. Microfilm Assn., Am. Records Mgmt. Assn., Word Processing Soc. Republican. Baptist. Clubs: Lions, Elks. Home: 320 Lillian Ln Waterloo IA 50704 Office: Box 270 Waterloo IA 50704

SINGER, JOHN STEPHEN, textile co. exec., real estate co. exec.; b. N.Y.C., Dec. 26, 1938; s. Sam Cook and Leah Rose (Schwarz) S.; student Colo. Coll., 1956-57; B.S., N.C. State U., 1963; m. Madeleine Elaine Zaft, Jan. 14, 1967; children—Leslie Allison, Lisa Christine. Vice pres. Lavitt Industries, N.Y.C., 1967-72; pres. J.S. Singer & Co., Inc., N.Y.C., 1972—, Louis Lavitt Co., Inc., Hickory, 1972—, Northgate Corp., Newton, N.C., 1975—, Hickory Paper Box Co., Inc., 1976—, Westover Devel. Corp., Hickory, 1976—; dir. 1st Nat. Bank of Catawba County, Hickory. Bd. dirs. United Jewish Fedn., 1977-80, Temple Beth-El, 1977-80, Stamford Jewish Center, 1976-79. Mem. Textile Distbrs. Assn., Young Pres.'s Orgn., Textile Salesmen's Assn., Carolina Yarn Assn., Mensa. Republican. Clubs: Palm Beach Country; Harmonie, Rockrimmon Country, Lake Hickory Country. Home: Bayberrie Dr Westover Park Stamford CT 06902 Office: PO Drawer 3425 Hickory NC 28601 also 350 Fifth Ave New York NY 10118

SINGER, MARSHALL RICHARD, chem. cons.; b. Scranton, Pa., Aug. 5, 1916; s. Marshall Monroe and Ethel Sara (Dailey) S.; B.S., Pa. State U., 1938; m. Sara Emma Eppihimer, Apr. 12, 1941. Chemist, supr. Allied Chem. Corp., Claymont, Del., 1938-43, tech. supt., Edgewater, N.J., 1943-49, tech. mgr. operations, N.Y.C., 1949-62, dir. application research labs. and adminstrn., Morristown, N.J., 1963-73; cons. in chem. processing, 1973-76; mgr. engring. specifications Lummus Co., Bloomfield, N.J., 1976—. Mem. plastic adv. group Lowell Tech. Inst., 1969-72. Mem. Am. Chem. Soc., Nat. Wildlife Fedn., Mfg. Chemists Assn. (chmn. packaging com. 1961, 62). Methodist (chmn. bd. trustees 1960-61). Mason (master 1962). Club: Puddingstone Community (Parsippany-Troy Hills, N.J.). Patentee in field. Home: 12 Long Ridge Rd RD 3 Dover NJ 07801 Office: 1515 Broad St Bloomfield NJ 07003

SINGER, MICHAEL NORMAN, systems and risk mgmt. cons.; b. Manhattan, N.Y., July 28, 1946; s. Irving Frederick and Miriam Norma (Wolf) S.; B.S., Cornell U., 1968; Ph.D., U. Rochester, 1976; m. Janet T. Cohn, June 9, 1968; children—Deborah, Sarah. Engr., Anaconda Wire & Cable Co., Hastings on Hudson, N.Y., 1966-68; research asst. U. Rochester (N.Y.), 1968-74; guest scientist Brookhaven Nat. Lab., Upton, L.I., N.Y., 1974-77; sr. systems analyst KLD Assos., Huntington, N.Y., 1977-78; sr. systems cons. Anistics, N.Y.C., 1978-80; mgr. systems and programming Landart Systems, Inc., N.Y.C., 1980—; cons. Mem. Am. Phys. Soc. Home: 14 Upper Dr Huntington NY 11743 Office: 140 Cedar St New York NY 10006

SINGER, THOMAS KENYON, aluminum co. exec.; b. Wilson, N.Y., Jan. 30, 1932; s. Harold T. and Grace I. (Kenyon) S.; B.S. in Econs., U. Pa., 1954; m. Jacqueline G. Moulin, June 8, 1957; children—Marc Andre, Vivianne Grace, Claire Anne, Michele Moulin, Gail Kenyon. Sales trainee Kaiser Aluminum Corp., 1954, export rep., N.Y.C., 1957-59, gen. mgr. Forgings and Rod, Bar and Wire div., 1973-75, v.p., gen. mgr. Washington ops., 1975-76, corporate v.p. govt. and public affairs, 1976—; sales dir. Kaiser Aluminum, Ltd., London, 1959-61, dir. mktg. European region, 1965-66; sales dir. James Booth Aluminum Co., Ltd., Birmingham, Eng., 1961-65; mng. dir. Kaiser Aluminum France, Paris, 1966-67; v.p., gen. mgr. Kaiser/Le Nickel Corp., 1967-73. Served to capt. USAF, 1955-57. Mem. Am. Aluminum Assn., Am. Mining Congress, Mfg. Chemists Assn. Clubs: Internat. (Washington); Commonwealth of Calif. Office: 900 17th St NW Suite 1000 Washington DC 20006

SINGH, MANJIT, hosp. adminstr.; b. Gujranwala, India, Mar. 21, 1946; s. Sardar and Sant (Kaur) S.; B.S., S.R. Coll. of Commerce, 1965; M.B.A., L.I. U., 1975; m. Renu Singh, Feb. 18, 1976; 1 son, Kabir. Chief fin. officer Nat. Chem. Industries, India, 1968-71; acct. Emsar Bradford P.C., C.P.A., N.Y.C., 1972-74; acctg. mgr., controller Provident Hosp., Inc., Balt., 1974-78, v.p. fin., 1978—. Chartered acct., India; C.P.A., New Delhi. Mem. Am. Inst. C.P.A.'s, Hosp. Fin. Mgmt. Assn., Inst. Chartered Accts. India, Md. Assn. C.P.A.'s. Home: 10549 Gateridge Rd Cockeysville MD 21030 Office: Provident Hosp Inc 2600 Liberty Heights Ave Baltimore MD 21215

SINGLETON, EUSTACE BYRON, lawyer; b. Lufkin, Tex., Oct. 3, 1909; s. James Madison and Carolyn Elizabeth (Haygood) S.; A.B., U. Tex., 1933, J.D., 1933; m. Elsie Adeline Bell, May 16, 1936; children—Eustace Byron, Savannah Adeline. Admitted to Tex. bar, 1933, U.S. Supreme Ct. bar, 1941, U.S. Ct. Claims bar, 1952, U.S. Ct. Customs and Patent Appeals bar, 1956, others; mem. firm Underwood, Strickland & Singleton, Amarillo, Tex., 1933-38, Monning & Singleton, Amarillo, 1939-49, Singleton & Trulove, Amarillo, 1950-60; individual practice law, Amarillo, 1961—; corp. counsel City of Amarillo, 1941-48; at various times gen. counsel, dir., exec. mgr. BC & M Drilling, Inc., Mesa, Draughon's Bus. Colls., Amarillo and Lubbock, Inc., Beef Industries, Inc., Amarillo Industries, Inc., Ark. Valley Feed Yard, Lamar, TransEra Research of Dallas, Inc., Am. Grain & Cattle Mgmt., San Antonio, Soweco, Inc., Continental Dynamics Ltd. of Las Vegas, Venture Assos. Mgmt. Corp., Gems Internat., Santa Barbara. Exec. committman Young Dems. of Tex., 1935-46; finance committeeman Amarillo Dem. Com., 1936-40. Chmn. Amarillo chpt. A.R.C., 1938-46; dep. dir. War Savs. Staff, Austin, Tex., 1939-43; nat. committeeman War Finance Com., Dallas, 1943-46. Bd. dirs. Edna Gladney Home; bd. govs. Nat.

Arthritis Found. Mem. Am., Fed., Amarillo bar assns., State Bar Tex., Am. Judicature Soc. Home: 2405 Lipscomb St Amarillo TX 79109 Office: 1408 Am Nat Bank Bldg Box 12055 Amarillo TX 79101

SINGLETON, HENRY EARL, industrialist; b. Haslet, Tex., Nov. 27, 1916; s. John Bartholomew and Victoria (Flores) S.; B.S., M.S., Mass. Inst. Tech., 1940, Sc.D., 1950; m. Caroline A. Wood, Nov. 30, 1942; children—Christina, John, William, James, Diana. Vice pres. Litton Industries, Inc., Beverly Hills, Calif., 1954-60; chmn. bd., chief exec. officer Teledyne, Inc., Los Angeles, 1960—. Home: 384 Delfern Dr Los Angeles CA 90024 Office: 1901 Ave of Stars Los Angeles CA 90067

SINGLETON, KENT JOHN, property mgmt. and engring. co. exec., cons. engr.; b. South Ogden, Utah; s. Clarence Lyman and Lenna Estella (Read) S.; M.S. in Psychology, Utah State U., 1958, D.D. (hon.), 1961; M.S. in Chem.-Mech. Engring., U. Chgo., 1972; m. Joan Nielson, May 23, 1950; children—John, Saul, Kimla, Jenna, Jona, Portia. Refrigeration engr. Asael Farr & Sons Co., 1946-52, dist. mgr., 1952-56; dist. mgr., ednl. dir. Coop. Life Am., 1956-58; ednl. dir., asst. v.p. Ideal Nat. Ins. Co., 1958-60; dist. mgr. DuBois Chems., 1960-72; cons. engr. Dearborn Chems. subs. W.R. Grace & Co., 1972-75; gen. mgr. Gurries Mgmt., Carmel, Calif., 1974—; prin. Singleton Consulting Services, Monterey Peninsula, Calif., 1974—; dir. Cal-Sin Assos., S. & G., Inc., Bergie Mfg. and Fin., Big Valley News, Ideal Nat., Country Mut. Life, Mem. ASHRAE, Profl. Mgrs. Assn., Million Dollar Round Table, Profl. Cons. Assn., Am. Soc. Corrosian Engrs., Profl. Dialogue Engrs. Republican. Mormon. Clubs: Elks, Knife and Fork. Contbr. articles in field to profl. jours. and instructional manuals. Home: 221 Peter Pan Rd Carmel CA 93923 Office: PO Box 22125 Carmel CA 93922

SINGLETON, MARVIN AYERS, physician, real estate broker, bus. exec., rancher; b. Baytown, Tex., Oct. 7, 1939; s. Henry Marvin and Mary Ruth (Mitchell) S.; B.A., U. of the South, 1962; M.D., U. Tenn., 1966; m. Anita; children—Mitchell, Catherine. Intern, City of Memphis Hosps., 1966-67; resident in surgery Highland Alameda City Hosp., Oakland, Calif., 1967-68, resident in otolaryngology U. Tenn. Hosp., Memphis, 1968-71; Am. Acad. Otolaryngology and Ophthalmology fellow in otolaryngic pathology Armed Forces Inst. Pathology, Washington, 1971; fellow in otologic surgery U. Colo. at Gallup (N.Mex.) Indian Med. Center, 1972; practice medicine specializing in otolaryngology and allergies, Joplin, Mo., 1972—; founder, operator Home and Farm Investments, Joplin, 1975—, Video Systems, Joplin, 1977—; staff mem. Freeman Hosp., St. John's Hosp., Joplin; cons. in otolaryngology Parsons (Kans.) State Hosp. and Tng. Center, Mo. Crippled Children's Service, Santa Fe R.R.; pres. Ozark Mfg. Co., Inc., Joplin. Served with USNG, 1966-72. Diplomate Am. Bd. Otolaryngology, Am. Bd. Otorhinolaryngology. Fellow A.C.S., Am. Acad. Otolaryngology and Ophthalmology, Am. Acad. Ophthalmologic and Otolaryngologic Allergy, Am. Coll. Otorhinolaryngologists, Am. Assn. Clin. Immunology and Allergy; mem. AMA (del.), Mo. State, So., Jasper County med. assns., Council of Otolaryngology, Mo. State Allergy Assn., Ear, Nose and Throat Soc. Mo. (past pres.), Joplin C. of C., Sigma Alpha Epsilon, Phi Theta Kappa, Phi Chi. Episcopalian. Club: Elks. Contbr. articles to profl. jours. Home: Five Mile Ranch Route 2 Box 138 Seneca MO 64856 Office: 114 W 32d St Joplin MO 64801

SINGLETON, RAYMOND LEVON, bank and office supply co. exec.; b. Rosedale, Okla., Oct. 26, 1927; s. James William and Ruby Mae (Robison) S.; student Okla. A&M U., 1946; m. Anna Lou Bates, Apr. 2, 1946; children—Sherrie Lurea, Gayla Jean. Dist. mgr. sales Okla. Office & Bank Supply Co., Shawnee, 1948-51; partner Nat. Office & Bank Supply Co., Enid, Okla., 1951-53; v.p., sales mgr. Southwestern Stationery & Bank Supply Co., Lawton, Okla., 1954—, also dir. Served with USN, 1946-47. Mem. Nat. Office Products Assn., Data Processing Mgmt. Assn., C. of C., VFW, Am. Legion. Democrat. Mem. Ch. of Christ. Club: Lawton Country (pres.). Home: 2115 Atlanta St Lawton OK 73505 Office: Southwestern Stationery & Bank Supply Co 309 SW 11th St Lawton OK 73502

SINGMAN, JULIAN HOWARD, lawyer; b. Washington, Mar. 23, 1928; s. Samuel Aaron and Anna (Dick) S.; B.A., George Washington U., 1950; certificate Oxford U., 1950; LL.B., Harvard U., 1953. Admitted to D.C. bar, 1953; all subsequent positions in Washington; law clk. to chief judge U.S. Ct. Appeals, 1953-54; civil appeals atty. U.S. Dept. Justice, 1954-56; asso. chief counsel antitrust subcom. Com. on Judiciary, U.S. Ho. of Reps., 1956-61; dep. adminstr. Maritime Adminstrn., U.S. Dept. Commerce, 1961-62; partner firm Landis, Cohen, Singman and Rauh, 1962—; legal cons. intergovtl. com. on European migration, 1962-66, seafarers' sect. Internat. Transport Workers' Fedn., 1973-78; chmn. drafting com. Internat. Conf. on Standards of Tng., Cert. and Watch Keeping for Seafarers, 1979; pres. Maritime Inst. for Research and Indsl. Devel., Washington, 1980—. Served with Adj. Gen.'s Dept., U.S. Army, 1946-47. Mem. D.C., Va. State bars, Am., Fed., D.C. bar assns., Am. Judicature Soc., Phi Beta Kappa. Clubs: Nat. Democratic, Internat., Georgetown. Home: 10612 Belmont Blvd Lorton VA 22079 Office: 1019 19th St NW Suite 500 Washington DC 20036

SINN, ROBERT SAMUEL, electronic co. exec., pharm. co. exec.; b. Phila., Mar. 9, 1930; s. Charles M. and Dorothea (Koenig) S.; A.B., U. Pa., 1952, M.S., 1957; m. Pamela Gaye; children—Nina A., Robert M. Engr. RCA, Camden, N.J., 1952-60; chmn. bd. Elkins-Sinn Corp., 1967-76; chmn. bd. Microwave Semiconductor Corp., 1968-79; pres. Ultronic Systems Corp., 1960-70, dir., 1960-73; chmn. Wall Street Venture Capital Corp., 1969—; chmn. bd. Klineman Assos., Inc., 1972—; chmn. Robert S. Sinn Securities, Inc., 1976—. Mem. IEEE, Young Pres.'s Orgn., Engrs. Club Phila., N.Y. Acad. Sci., Operations Research Soc. Am. Club: Wall Street. Patentee in field. Home: Rosebud Farms Jobstown NJ 08041

SINNETTE, CLARENCE EASTWOOD, mining co. exec.; b. Vivian, W.Va., Nov. 18, 1911; s. Clarence Patrick and Hilda (Herring) S.; grad. high sch.; m. Virginia Lee Keener, June 10, 1942; children—James Edward, John Clarence. Clk., Island Creek Stores, Holden, W.Va., 1931-36; asst. store mgr. Mallory Stores (W.Va.), 1937-40; cost accountant Mallory Coal Co., 1941-53; cost accountant Powellton Coal Co., Mallory, 1941-53, auditor, 1954-67; chief mine acct. Princess Coals, Inc., 1961-67; sec., treas., fin. v.p. Princess Coal Sales Co. and Sycamore Coal Co., 1967-72; pres. Green Brook Coal Co., Inc., 1970-80, Universal Fuel Sales, Inc., Huntington, W.Va., 1979—. Mem. Am. Mgmt. Assn., Ohio Valley Accts. Assn. (past pres.). Democrat. Methodist. Home: 115 Elwood Ave Huntington WV 25705 Office: Universal Fuel Sales PO Box 573 Huntington WV 25710

SINNINGER, DWIGHT VIRGIL, research engr.; b. Bourbon, Ind., Dec. 29, 1901; s. Norman E. and Myra (Huff) S.; student Armour Inst., 1928, U. Chgo., 1942, Northwestern, 1943; m. Coyla Annetta Annis, Mar. 1, 1929. Electronics research engr. Johnson Labs., Chgo., 1935-42; chief engr. Pathfinder Radio Corp., 1943-44, Rowe Engring. Corp., 1945-48; Hupp Electronics Co. div. Hupp Corp., 1948-61; dir. research Pioneer Electric & Research Corp., Forest Park, Ill., 1961-65, Senn Custom, Inc., Forest Park and San Antonio, 1967—; dir. Rowe Engring. Corp. Registered profl. engr., Ill. Mem. IEEE, Instrument Soc. Am., Armed Forces Communications Assn. Holder several U.S. patents. Address: PO Box 40113 San Antonio TX 78229

SINSHEIMER, WARREN JACK, electronics equipment co. exec., lawyer; b. N.Y.C., May 22, 1927; s. Jerome William and Elizabeth (Berch) S.; student Ind. U., 1943-46; J.D., N.Y. Law Sch., 1950; LL.M., N.Y. U., 1955; M.Phil., Columbia U., 1977; m. Florence Dubin, Mar. 30, 1950; children—Linda, Ralph, Alan, Michael. Admitted to N.Y. bar, 1950; partner firm Sinsheimer, Sinsheimer and Dubin, N.Y.C., 1950-78, Sattalee & Stevens, 1978—; pres., chief exec. officer Plessey, Inc., N.Y.C., 1956-70, chmn. bd., exec. officer, 1970—; dep. chief exec., dir. Plessey Co. Ltd., Ilford, Eng.; dir. Eagle Star Ins. Co. Am. Mem. Westchester Republican County Com., 1955-74; chmn. Nat. Scranton for Pres. Com., 1964; mem. N.Y. State Assembly, 1965-66; chmn. Scarsdale Rep. Town Com., 1971-74; bd. dirs. Friends of Scarsdale Library, Westchester Jewish Community Services, 1976—; bd. visitors Wassaic State Sch., 1961-64. Served with USNR, 1944-45; to 1st lt. USAF, 1950-52. Mem. Inst. Dirs., Assn. Bar City N.Y., Am. Bar Assn., Zeta Beta Tau. Clubs: Beach Point (Mamaronek, N.Y.); Harmonie (N.Y.C.); Town (Scarsdale). Home: 22 Murray Hill Rd Scarsdale NY 10583 Office: 277 Park Ave New York NY 10017

SIPES, JOHN DENNIS, chem. co. exec.; b. Wamego, Kans., Jan. 6, 1936; s. Frank Allen and Winefride (Fanell) S.; B.S., U.S. Naval Acad., 1957; M.B.A., Harvard U., 1964; m. Andrea Murphy, July 6, 1968. With Litton Industries, 1964-72; controller bakery div. ITT, 1972-73; asst. corp. controller Pacific Lighting Corp., 1973-75; v.p. fin. Hooker Chem. Co., Houston, 1976—. Served with USNR, 1957-62. Clubs: University, Memorial Drive Country. Office: 1980 S Post Oak Houston TX 77210

SIRACUSA, ANGELO JOHN, assn. exec.; b. San Francisco, Mar. 26, 1930; s. Louis and Grace Giansiracusa; B.A. in Polit. Sci., U. Santa Clara; B.S. in Bus. Adminstrn., U. Calif., Berkeley. Asst. mgr. San Mateo County (Calif.) Devel. Assn., 1958-61; gen. mgr. Fremont (Calif.) C. of C., 1962-65; v.p. Bay Area Council, San Francisco, 1966-72, pres., 1972—; dir. Am. Ind. Devel. Council, 1971-74; v.p., dir. Calif. Ind. Devel. Exec. Assn., 1968-74; dir. Real Estate Research Council No. Calif., 1968-70, Environ. Info. Clearinghouse, 1972-73, Reel/Grobman Assos., 1980—, Decisions Info. and Analysis, 1980—; mem. steering com. St. Mary's Coll. Exec. Symposium, 1973—, chmn., 1975-76; mem. Gov. Calif.'s Manpower Policy Task Force, 1972-73; mem. adv. com. Calif. Office of Bus. and Ind. Devel., 1980—; mem. San Francisco Mayor's Econ. Adv. Council, 1978—; community adv. Jr. League San Francisco, 1976-80; mem. regional planning com. Assn. Bay Area Govts., 1978—, chmn. econ. devel. adv. com., 1979—, mem. environ. mgmt. task force, 1977-78, mem. ind. siting task force, 1977-78; mem. steering com. San Francisco Forum, 1977-78; mem. exec. group on devel. practices and policies Urban Land Inst., 1979—; mem. Calif. States Urban Small Bus. Employment Project, 1980—; mem. steering com. Bay Area and the World. Trustee, Am. Ind. Devel. Council Edn. Found., 1968-69; mem. adv. council U. San Francisco Sch. Bus. Adminstrn., 1973-77; bd. dirs. Santa Clara U. Alumni Council, 1973-76, San Francisco Devel. Fund, 1979—, Coro Found., 1979—, Big Sisters, Inc., San Francisco, 1980—; mem. planning div. com. United Way of Bay Area. Served with USAF, 1953-57. Mem. Soc. Ind. Realtors, Calif. Assn. C. of C. Execs., No. Calif. Soc. Assn. Execs., Calif. Roundtable, Bay Area Public Affairs Council, LWV, Planning and Conservative League, Conservation Found., Sierra Club, Calif. Tomorrow, San Francisco Planning and Urban Research Assn., Western Govtl. Research Assn., Newcomen Soc. N.Am., Lambda Alpha. Republican. Clubs: Marin Tennis; San Francisco Tennis, Telegraph Hill Racquetball, World Trade, Commonwealth (San Francisco); Beefeaters. Home: 110 Lincoln Dr Sausalito CA 94965 Office: 348 World Trade Center San Francisco CA 94111

SIROTA, RICHARD JAY, graphic arts co. exec.; b. N.Y.C., July 16, 1952; s. Daniel and Lenore Sirota; B.S. (Clem Miller scholar), Cornell U., 1974. Vice pres. Kwik Offset Plate Service, Inc., 1974; pres. Media Color, Inc., 1978—; exec. v.p. Kwik Internat. Color, Ltd., 1976—; graphic arts fin. cons., 1976—; guest columnist N.Y. Times, 1976—, Forbes mag., 1976—. Mem. Nassau County Democratic Com., 1973—; nat. pres. Coll. Young Dems., 1973-74; mem. campaign staff John Lindsey, 1972, George McGovern, 1972; active numerous polit. campaigns. Mem. Printing Industries Am., Young Printing Execs. N.Y. Office: 110 W 32d St New York NY 10001

SISK, ALBERT FLETCHER, JR., ins. agt.; b. Easton, Md., Nov. 25, 1928; s. Albert Fletcher and Helen (Marvel) S.; student Mercersburg Acad., 1945-46, Washington and Lee U., 1946-49; m. Mary Douglass Tweedy, Jan. 8, 1955; children—Douglass Fletcher, Geoffrey Price. With Albert W. Sisk & Son, Preston, Md., 1950-66; ins. agt. Conn. Gen. Life Ins. Co., 1968—; pres. Farrell & Sisk, Inc.; v.p. Atlantic Pension Planners, Inc.; dir. Preston Trucking Co., Inc., Provident State Bank, Preston. Trustee Meml. Hosp., Easton, Md., 1965-71, mem. Sch. Nursing com.; mem. Delmarva Estate Planning Council. Served with USN, 1952-54. C.L.U. Mem. Nat. Assn. Life Underwriters, Nat. Rifle Assn., Am. Soc. C.L.U., Balt. Life Underwriters Assn. Clubs: Lions (past pres.) (Preston); Chesapeake Bay Yacht. Home: Gilpin's Point Route 1 Box 209A Preston MD 21655 Office: One Mill Pl Suite 104 PO Box 179 Easton MD 21601

SISK, JOHN KELLY, newspaper and broadcast exec.; b. Cookeville, Tenn., Mar. 3, 1913; s. Thurman Kelly and Martha Jane (Sewell) S.; B.S., U. Ala., 1934; m. Isbell Lane, Sept. 30, 1936; children—John Kelly, Isbell Lane (Mrs. Lawton Irick, Jr.). Staff mem. S. D. Leidesdorf & Co., N.Y.C., C.P.A's, 1934-39; partner J. Kelly Sisk and Co., C.P.A.'s, Greenville, S.C., 1939-48; treas., bus. mgr. The Greenville News-Piedmont Co., 1948-58, v.p., gen. mgr., 1958-59, pres., 1959-73, chmn. bd., 1963-80, pub., 1966-80; pres. Multimedia, Inc., 1968-73, chief exec. officer, 1973-79, chmn., 1973-80; dir. S.C. Nat. Bank, Liberty Life Ins. Co. Past mem. bd. dirs. YMCA; past chmn. Greenville County Planning and Devel. Bd.; past chmn. Greenville County chpt. A.R.C., Greenville Gen. Hosp.; trustee Converse Coll., Duke Endowment; adv. trustee Furman U. C.P.A., N.Y., S.C. Mem. Downtown Greenville Assn. (dir. 1957), So. Newspaper Pubs. Assn. (pres. 1963, chmn. 1964), S.C. Press Assn. (pres. 1962), Greater Greenville C. of C. (pres. 1953), Am. Newspaper Pubs. Assn., Phi Gamma Delta. Methodist. Clubs: Nat. Press; Poinsett, Greenville Country, Green Valley Country, Cotillion (Greenville); Biltmore (N.C.) Forest Country; Mountain City (Asheville, N.C.); Country of N.C. (Pinehurst); Plantation (Hilton Head Island, S.C.). Home: 20 Southland Ave Greenville SC 29601 Office: 305 S Main St Greenville SC 29601 Died Nov. 6, 1980.

SISSON, EVERETT ARNOLD, diversified corp. exec.; b. Chgo., Oct. 24, 1920; s. Emmett B. and Norma (Merbitz) S.; A.B., Valparaiso U., 1942; m. Roberta E. Blauman, Mar. 20, 1943; children—Nancy Lee Genz, Elizabeth Anne Levy. Sales mgr. Ferrotherm Co., Cleve., 1946-51, Osborn Mfg. Co., Cleve., 1951-56; dir. sales Patterson Foundry & Machine Co., East Liverpool, Ohio, 1956-58; mgr. Sonic Energy Products, Bendix Corp., Davenport, Iowa, 1958-60; pres. Lamb Industries, Inc., Toledo, 1960-65, Edward Lamb Enterprises, 1963-65, Gibraltar Enterprises, Inc., 1963-65, Lehigh Valley Industries, Inc., 1965-66, Am. Growth Industries, Inc., Chgo., 1966—, Protectu Bank Note Corp., 1966-69, Workman Mfg. Co., 1966-69, Amgro Properties, Inc., 1966-69, Am. Growth Devel. Corp., Chgo., 1968—, Oak Brook Club Co. (Ill.), 1969—; chmn. bd., dir., mem. exec. com. Lutheran Mut. Life Ins. Co., Waverly, Iowa, 1965—; chmn. bd., chief exec. officer Hausske-Harlen Furniture Mfg. Co., Peru, Ind., 1976—; dir. Libco Corp., Chgo., Telco Mktg. Services, Inc., Chgo.; trustee Wis. Realty Investment Trust, Milw., 1980—. Pres. council Mayfield Heights (Ohio), 1952-57. Adviser bd. trustees Valparaiso U.; bd. regents Calif. Luth. Coll. Served to capt. USAAF, 1943-46. Mem. Am. Mgmt. Assn., Cleve. Engring. Soc., Am. Mktg. Assn. President's Assn. Home: 1405 Burr Ridge Club Burr Ridge IL 60521 Office: 1550 Spring Rd Oak Brook IL 60521

SIT, EUGENE C., investment co. exec.; b. Canton, China, Aug. 8, 1938; s. Hom Yuen and Sue (Eng) S.; B.S., DePaul U., 1960, postgrad. Grad. Sch. Bus., 1962-65; m. Gail V. Chin, Sept. 14, 1958; children—Ronald, Debra, Roger, Raymond, Robert, Richard. Financial analyst Commonwealth Edison, Chgo., 1960-66, financial asst. to chmn. finance com., 1966-68; asso. portfolio mgr. investors stock fund Investors Diversified Services, Mpls., 1968-69; portfolio mgr. IDS New Dimensions Fund, Mpls., 1969, v.p., portfolio mgr., 1970-72; v.p., sr. portfolio mgr. IDS New Dimensions, IDS Growth Fund, Mpls., 1972-76; pres. IDS Adv., 1976-77, pres., chief exec. officer, 1977—; chief exec. officer IDS Trust Co., 1979—; v.p., dir. South Pacific Restaurant Corp., Chgo., 1960—. Bd. dirs., treas. Loring-Nicollet Bethlehem Community Centers; bd. deacons Christ Presbyn. Ch., Edina, Minn. C.P.A., Ill.; chartered fin. analyst. Mem. Am. Inst. C.P.A.'s, Inst. Chartered Fin. Analysts, Fin. Analysts Fedn., Twin Cities Soc. Security Analysts, Investment Analysts Soc. Chgo. Clubs: Univ., Chgo., Mpls. Home: 6216 Braeburn Circle Edina MN 55435 Office: IDS Tower Minneapolis MN 55402

SITES, HOWARD FRED, fin. exec.; b. Lafayette, Ind., Sept. 4, 1938; s. G. Fred and Valeria P. (Doty) S.; B.S., Ind. U., 1960, M.B.A., 1965; m. Marilyn Ann Gates, June 13, 1964; children—Todd Howard, Timothy Fred. Communications cons. Ind. Bell Telephone Co., Indpls., 1963-64; corporate staff asst. Westinghouse Electric Co., Pitts., 1967-70, div. controller, Richmond, Va., 1970-74; v.p. finance and adminstrn., sec., treas., dir. Infilco Degremont, Inc., Richmond, Va., 1974—; sec.-treas., dir. Degremont Interam. Corp., N.Y.C., Aquamust, Inc., Phoenix; sec.-treas. Infiko Degremont Ltd. (Can.). Served with Signal Corps, U.S. Army, 1961-63. Mem. Am. Mgmt. Assn., French-Am. C. of C., Va. State C. of C., Metro Richmond C. of C. Home: 3449 Cedar Grove Rd Richmond VA 23235 Office: Koger Exec Center Box K7 Richmond VA 23288

SITTENFELD, CURTIS JOSEPH, engring. cons. firm exec.; b. Gleiwitz, Germany, Sept. 16, 1931; came to U.S., 1947, naturalized, 1953; s. Max O. and Lucy (Rosen) S.; B.S., U. Pa., 1953; m. Anita Paula Shaw, Mar. 3, 1953; children—Linda, Vicki, Miriam, Betty. Engr., Nat. Filter Corp., N.Y.C., 1953-60; with NFC Industries, Inc., Mt. Vernon, N.Y., 1960-70, pres., 1967-70; pres., chief exec. officer I.R.A.S. Devel. Corp., White Plains, N.Y., 1970—; dir. Ethanol of Fla., Inc. Served with U.S. Army, 1953-55. Mem. Am. Chem. Soc., Am. Soc. Agrl. Engrs. Clubs: Princeton-Pa. (N.Y.C.); Milbrook (Greenwich, Conn.). Home: 38 Woodside Dr Greenwich CT 06830 Office: 34 S Broadway White Plains NY 10601

SIX, ROBERT FORMAN, airline co. exec.; b. Stockton, Calif., June 25, 1907; s. Clarence Logan and Genevieve (Peters) S.; student public schs., Stockton; D.Sc. (hon.), Colo. U.; m. Audrey Meadows, Aug. 1961. Instr. Stockton and Frisco, Stockton, 1929-33; dist. circulation mgr., San Francisco Chronicle, 1933-35; owner Mouton & Six, 1935-37; pres., dir. Continental Airlines, Inc., Los Angeles, 1938-75, chmn. bd., chief exec. officer, 1975-80, chmn. bd., 1980—; chmn. bd., pres. Continental Air Services, 1966-75; dir. United Bank Denver, Mut. Computer Services. Mem. bd. nominations Nat. Aviation Hall Fame; mem. Los Angeles Conv. Bur.; adv. com. Wright Bros. Hall of Fame Com., USAF Acad. Found., Inc.; mem. Air Quality Adv. Bd. Served as lt. col. USAF, 1942-44; air base comdr. Decorated Army Commendation medal; recipient Tony Jannus award for contbns. to scheduled airline industry, 1977. Mem. Air Transport Assn. Am. (dir.), Wings Club of Am., Conquistadores del Cielo, Nat. Aeros. Assn., Am. Soc. Traffic and Transp., Newcomen Soc. Clubs: Mt. Kenya Safari, Nat. Aviation, El Morocco Internat., Golden Bear, Kansas City, Mid-America, Sky, Vallejo Gun, Rocky Mountain Food and Wine Soc.; Brook (N.Y.C.); Burlingame (Calif.) Country; Denver, Denver Country; Racquet (Palm Springs, Calif.); Travellers (Paris); Chevaliers du Tastevin; Confrerie de la Chaine des Rotisseurs; Mile High (Denver); Am. Sportsman's. Office: Continental Airlines Inc Los Angeles Internat Airport 7300 World Way W Los Angeles CA 90009

SIZEMORE, RICHARD ELLSWORTH, bldg. materials co. exec.; b. Miami, Ariz., Sept. 9, 1936; s. Melvin Ivan and Esther Mildred (Simmons) S.; student pub. schs.; m. Lois Faye Holloway, Aug. 7, 1954; children—Patricia Ann, Penny Lynn. Pay sta. collector, asst. supr. Mountain States Telephone Co., Phoenix, 1955-57; mgr. Sprouse-Reitz Co., Inc., Sandpoint, Idaho, 1957-60; owner, mgr. Hunter Service Center, S&V Sales Co., Mesa, Ariz., 1960-67; asst. mgr. Payless Cashway Lumber Co., Tempe, Ariz., 1967-72; mgr. Babbitts Lumber Div., Holbrook, Ariz., 1972—. Head indsl. devel. Town of Holbrook, 1975—. Mem. Ariz. Lumber and Builders Supply Assn., Am. Quarter Horse Assn., Ariz. Barm Bur. Republican. Baptist. Clubs: Elks, Masons, Order of Eastern Star. Home: Box 547 Holbrook AZ 86025 Office: Box 909 Holbrook AZ 86025

SIZER, PHILLIP SPELMAN, oil field service co. exec.; b. Whittier, Calif., Apr. 11, 1926; s. Frank Milton and Helen Louise (Saylor) S.; B.M.E., So. Meth. U., 1948; m. Evelyn Sue Jones, Aug. 16, 1952; children—Phillip Spelman, Ves W. With Otis Engring. Corp., Dallas, 1948—, project engr., 1958-62, chief devel. engr., 1962-70, v.p. research and devel., 1970-73, v.p. engring. and research, 1973-77, sr. v.p., tech. dir., 1977—, dir., 1975—, dir. thrust hydraulic products and services; dir. Sun Contractors, 1979—; Registered profl. engr., Tex., Okla., Can. Fellow ASME (named Engr. of Yr., North Tex. sect. 1971, chmn. exec. com. petroleum div. 1974-75; exec. com. offshore tech. conf. 1976-79, mem.-at-large); mem. Soc. Petroleum Engrs., Marine Bd. (Nat. Research Council, Assembly of Engring., mem. com. for assessment of safety of outer continental shelf activities 1979-80), Kappa Sigma, Kappa Mu Epsilon, Sigma Tau, Tau Beta Pi, Petroleum Engrs. Club: Dallas. Patentee in field. Home: 14127 Tanglewood Dr Dallas TX 75234 Office: PO Box 34380 Dallas TX 75234

SJOSTROM, GEORGE WILLIAM, newspaper exec.; b. Mpls., Oct. 19, 1924; s. George and Ester (Olson) S.; student U. Nebr., 1943, U. Minn., 1947; B.S. in Advt., U. So. Calif., 1954; m. Joan Kjarstad, June 4, 1949; children—Gregory Stevens, Geoffrey Charles. Advt. dept. Mpls. Star-Tribune, 1947-48; with Los Angeles Examiner, 1948-62, asst. advt. dir., 1959-62; with Los Angeles Herald-Examiner, 1962—, asst. bus. mgr., 1962-65, bus. mgr., 1965-67, gen. mgr., 1967-77; pres. Cal Graphics div. Hearst Corp., 1977—. Bd. dirs. Rancho Simi Recreational Park Dist., 1980; mem. adv. com. Santa Monica Mountain Conservancy. Served with inf. AUS, 1943-46; ETO. Mem. Beta Gamma Sigma. Club: Jonathan (Los Angeles). Home: 815 Tierra Rejada Rd Simi Valley CA 93065 Office: 6370 Altura Blvd Buena Park CA 90620

SKAGGS, L. S., retail co. exec.; b. 1922; married. With Am. Stores Co., 1945—, chmn. bd., chief exec. officer, from 1966, now chmn. bd., pres., chief exec. officer, dir. Served with USAAF, 1942-45. Office: 709 East South Temple Salt Lake City UT 84127*

SKALA, HUBERT Y., tech. services co. exec.; b. Minatitlan, Veracruz, Mex., Nov. 2, 1922; s. Vaclav and Emily (Wagner) S.; B.S. in Petroleum Engring., U. Okla., 1943, B.S. in Geol. Engring., 1944; M.A. in Mining Engring., Stanford, 1945; m. Linda Calles, Sept. 4, 1954; children—Linda Margarita, Nora Maria, Ana Emilia. Geologist, Petroleos Mexicanos, 1944; engr. Shell Oil Co., Calif., also Ecuador, 1946-48; from well-site geologist to asst. gen. mgr. Mexican-Am. Ind. Co., 1949-57; asst. to rep. for Latin Am., Petrofina, S.A., 1958-59; gen. mgr. Maya Petrol, S.A., 1960-61, v.p., 1960-62; gen. mgr. Mueller Brass de Mexico, S.A., Toluca, Mex., 1962-65, Imperial Eastman de Mexico, Toluca, 1966-67, Troquelados y Carrocerias, S.A., 1968-69; partner Servicios Tecnicos Industriales, S.A., 1969—. Registered profl. engr., Tex., Okla. Mem. Am. Inst. Mining Metall. and Petroleum Engrs.,' Asociacion Mexicana de Geologos Petroleros, Asocacion de Ingenieros Petroleros de Mexico. Home: Lafontaine 50 Mexico 5 DF Mexico

SKALKU, ROBERT JOHN, sales and mktg. exec.; b. East Chicago, Ind., Apr. 23, 1939; s. John E. and Rose M. Skalku; student Ind. U., 1957-62, Valparaiso U., 1968-72, Elmhurst Coll., 1980-81; B.A. in Mktg., Drury Coll., 1961; m. Pamela F. Gardner, May 6, 1966; children—G. Brady, Bryan G., Jon R. Hosp. products mgr. Chris Craft Industries, Gary, Ind., 1967-74; dental products mgr. Dental div. Litten Industries, Fort Lauderdale, Fla., 1974-75; pres., chmn. bd. Frontier Steaks, Valparaiso, Ind., 1975-77; div. mgr. Gerber Health Care div. Gerber Products, Fremont, Mich., 1977-80; South regional mgr. Koss Corp., Milw., 1981—; tchr. seminars; cons. new ventures. Founder Corp. Leaders of Am. Served with M.C., U.S. Army, 1962-64. Mem. Am. Mgmt. Assn., Nat. Sales Execs. Mormon. Contbr. articles to trade mags. Home: 204 E 250 S Valparaiso IN 46383 Office: PO Box 486 Valparaiso IN 46383

SKALLE, MAVIS SCHUBERT, corp. exec.; b. Milw., May 6, 1924; d. Gilbert J. and Gertrude S. (Miller) Schubert; B.B.A. summa cum laude, Marquette U., 1945; m. Hans J. Skalle, May 29, 1954; children—Hans J., Heidi Mavis. Vice pres., treas. Foundry Supply Corp., Milw., 1950-54; asst. sec., treas. Ebaloy, Inc., Rockton, Ill., 1951-54; treas., asst. sec. Foundry Equipment Corp., Chgo., 1950-54; asst. sec., treas. Iowa-Mich. Corp., Chgo. and The Whitehall Co., Chgo., 1953-54; exec. sec. Interlachen Country Club, Mpls., 1955-65; v.p., sec. Camelot, Inc., Bloomington, Minn., 1965-80, Skalco Corp., Bloomington, 1975—. Recipient Ivy award, 1975. Mem. Am. Bus. Women's Assn., P.E.O., AAUW, Bus. Adminstrn. Alumni Assn. Marquette U. (steering com. 1955), Phi Chi Theta (nat. advisor 1954-56, nat. pres. 1952-54, nat. v.p. 1950-52), Beta Gamma Sigma, Gamma Pi Eta. Lutheran. Clubs: Edina Woman's (treas. 1966-67, pres. 1968-69), Woman's of Mpls. Home: 5021 Ridge Rd Edina MN 55436

SKELTON, HOWARD CLIFTON, public relations co. exec.; b. Birmingham, Ala., Mar. 6, 1932; s. Howard C. and Sarah Ethel (Holmes) S., Sr.; B.S., Auburn U., 1955; m. Winifred Harriet Karger, May 19, 1962; 1 dau., Susan Lynn. Copywriter Rich's, Inc., Atlanta, 1955-59; copywriter Ga. Power Co., Atlanta, 1959-61; dir. advt. and sales promotion Callaway Mills, Inc. LaGrange, Ga., 1961-65; dir. advt. and sales promotion Thomasville Furniture Industries (N.C.), 1965-66; v.p. in charge of fashion and textiles Gaynor & Ducas, N.Y.C., 1966-70; dir. communications Collins & Aikman, N.Y.C., 1970-73; v.p. Marketplace, Atlanta, 1973-74; v.p. communications and mktg. Internat. City Corp. Atlanta, 1974-75; pres. Howard Skelton Assos., Atlanta, 1976—. Served with Signal Corps, AUS, 1956-58. Recipient Danforth Found. award, 1950. Mem. Omicron Delta Kappa, Lambda Chi Alpha, Sigma Delta Chi. Home: 725 Edgewater Trail NW Atlanta GA 30328 Office: 130 W Wieuca Rd NE Suite 106 Atlanta GA 30342

SKELTON, ROBERT ALEXANDER, univ. exec.; b. Meridian, Miss., Nov. 11, 1936; s. Horace McLemore and Ludie Octavia (Winstead) S.; B.B.A., U. Ga., 1958; m. Gypsy Rose Haygood, Oct. 18, 1959; children—Elizabeth Ann, Shari Diane, Robert Alexander. Chief accountant Mercer U., Macon, Ga., 1961-68, comptroller, 1968-72, bus. mgr., 1973—, comptroller, 1973-75, treas., 1975-80, v.p. fin., treas., 1980—, instr. accounting, 1968-80. Served to 1st lt. USAF, 1958-61. Mem. Nat. Assn. Coll. and Univ. Bus. Officers (mem. accounting principles com. 1970—), Am. Accounting Assn., So. Assn. Coll. and Univ. Bus. Officers, Nat. Assn. Accountants, Alpha Kappa Psi. Home: 1540 Mercer Terr Macon GA 31201 Office: Mercer Univ 1400 Coleman Ave Macon GA 31207

SKIDMORE, FRANCIS JOSEPH, JR., securities co. exec.; b. Newark, June 4, 1943; s. Francis Joseph and Gertrude Elizabeth (Auth) S.; stepson Patricia Ann (Jaekel) Skidmore; student U. Md., 1961-63; B.S. in Econs., Duquesne U., 1968; m. Catherine Ann Stepanek, Mar. 27, 1971; children—Francis Joseph, Patrick Edward, Melissa Catherine. Trust adminstr. Chase Manhattan Bank N.A., N.Y.C., 1968-71, asst. v.p. corp. adv., 1971-74; asst. v.p. sales Lombard Wall Co., N.Y.C., 1974-75; v.p., sales mgr. Foxton Securities Co., N.Y.C., 1975-77; v.p., salesman Cantor Fitzgerald Securities Corp., N.Y.C., 1977—. Mem. Berkeley Heights (N.J.) Drainage Com., 1976-79; pres. Republican Club of Berkeley Heights, 1977-79; chmn. Berkeley Heights Corp. Devel. Com., 1977-79; active United Fund, 1975-77; pres. Chester Ridge Property Owners Assn.; asst. coach Mendham Soccer Club; mem. YMCA Indian Guide Program; active Roman Catholic Ch. Mem. Jaycees, N.Y.C. Am. Legion. Home: 3 Cromwell Dr RD 2 Mendham NJ 07945 Office: Cantor Fitzgerald Securities Inc 1345 Ave of Americas New York NY 10019

SKIDMORE, JAMES ALBERT, JR., mgmt. and engring. cons. co. exec.; b. Newark, June 30, 1932; s. James A. and Frances W. (Barker) S.; B.A., Muhlenburg Coll., 1954; m. Peggy Ann Young, July 10, 1954; children—Jacqueline Sue, James Albert III. Customer sales rep. N.J. Bell Telephone Co., Newark, 1957-65, then dist. sales mgr., div. mktg. mgr.; asst. to pres. for pub. affairs Pepsico Co., Inc., N.Y.C., 1966-69; asst. to Pres. of U.S., 1968-69; v.p. Handy Assos., N.Y.C., 1969-72, pres., 1971-72, chief exec. officer, 1972-78; pres., chief exec. officer Sci. Mgmt. Corp., Moorestown, N.J., 1972-78, chmn. bd., 1975—; dir. Coca Cola Bottling Co., N.Y.C., Franklin State Bank, Somerset, N.J.; lectr. U. Amsterdam (The Netherlands), 1967, U. Toronto (Ont., Can.), U. Helsinki (Finland), 1967, Tokyo U. Mem. Nat. Council on Crime and Delinquency, 1965-66; mem. Advisory Commn. on Youth Employment, 1966-67; state chmn. N.J. Nat. Found. March of Dimes, 1966-73; mem. exec. bd. Watchung Area council Boy Scouts Am., 1972-77; mem. Citizen's Advisory Bd. on Youth Opportunity 1969-75; state chmn. United Citizens for Nixon-Agnew, N.J., 1968; bd. govs. Alpha Tau Omega Found. Fund, 1973; trustee Brick Twp. Hosp., Inc., Brick Town, N.J., 1976—; bd. dirs. Am. Christmas Trains and Trucks, chmn., 1966; pres. Project Concern, San Diego. Served to capt. USMC, 1954-57. Decorated Order of St. John (Eng.); recipient Internat. Understanding award, Brussels, Belgium, 1966, Distinguished Service award, St. Paul, Minn., 1966, Freedom Found.'s George Washington Medal of Honor award, 1965, Outstanding Achievement in Life award Muhlenberg Coll. Alumni, 1966, Ambassador award U.S. Jaycees, 1977, Trinidad and Tobago award Prime Minister of Ireland, 1970. Mem. Young Presidents Orgn., Muhlenburg Coll. Alumni Assn., Alpha Tau Omega. Clubs: Atrium; Capital Hill, Baltusrol Golf, Fiddler's Elbow Country. Guest columnist Rotary Internat. mag., 1966-68, Kiwanis mag., 1966-68, Japan Times on Community Responsibility and Leadership, 1965-67. Home: 641 Ocean Ave Sea Girt NJ 08750 Office: 1011 Route 22 PO Box 6800 Bridgewater NJ 08807

SKIE, GARY OSCAR, fin. services co. exec.; b. Canton, S.D., Feb. 26, 1943; s. Oscar Bernard and Marie Elizabeth (Molvik) S.; student Augustana Coll., 1962-64, U. S.D., 1964-65. Asst. mgr. Skie Oil Co., 1965-68; securities registered rep., 1968-71; public relations account exec. J.H. Adams & Assos., 1971-72; v.p. Investment Research Co., Roseville, Minn., 1972-74; pres. Galen, Inc., Roseville, 1974-78, Fin. Econs., Inc., Roseville, 1978—, MMIR, Inc., Roseville, 1974—; v.p., dir. Planners Fin. Services, Inc., Roseville, 1977—; cons., bd. dirs. Am. Real Estate Schs., Inc., 1979—. Registered investment adv. SEC. Mem. Internat. Assn. Fin. Planners, Nat. Assn. Securities Dealers (securities registered prin., registered rep.). Republican. Lutheran. Club: Optimists (pres.) (Roseville). Home: 1127 Benton Way Arden Hills MN 55112 Office: 2233 Hamline Ave N Roseville MN 55113

SKIFF, RUSSELL ALTON, plastics co. exec.; b. Waterford, Pa., Feb. 26, 1927; s. Albert Alton and Leah Gladys (Allen) S.; B.S. in Chemistry and Math., U. Pitts., 1950; m. Dolores Theresa Molnar, June 25, 1950; children—Russell James, Sandra Lee, Eric Alan, Rebecca Lynn. Metall. chemist Jones & Laughlin Steel Co., Alliquippa, Pa., 1950-51; research and devel. chemist Gen. Electric Co., Erie, Pa., 1951-57; mgr. tech. sales and plant operation Hysol Corp. of Calif., El Monte, 1957-60; sr. research engr. Autonetics div. N. Am. Aviation Co., Downey, Calif., 1960-62; pres., dir. Delta Plastics Co., Visalia, Calif., 1962—; cons. in field of epoxy resin tech. Served with USAAF, 1944-46. Mem. Constrn. Specifications Inst., C. of C. Republican. Presbyterian. Club: Lions (dir.). Contbr. articles on epoxy resin tech. to profl. publs.; patentee in field epoxy polymeric chemistry. Home: 26525 Mulanax Dr Visalia CA 93277 Office: 7449 Ave 304 Visalia CA 93277

SKILLMAN, ERNEST EDWARD, JR., real estate sales and mgmt. exec.; b. New Orleans, Oct. 3, 1937; s. Ernest Edward and Helen Cecilia (Klein) S.; B.A., La. State U., 1960, postgrad. in law, 1960-61; postgrad. Southeastern La. U., 1973. Engaged in real estate mgmt., Baton Rouge, 1964—, sales, 1969—. Active Inter-Civic Club, Baton Rouge; sustaining mem. Republican Nat. Com., 1976—, mem. congressional com., 1978—; mem. pres.'s club Democratic Nat. Com., 1979—. Served with USN, 1961-64; Vietnam. Mem. Aviation Mus. Assn. (charter life), Feliciana C. of C., Am. Def. Preparedness Assn., Baton Rouge Cath. Alumni Club, Ams. Against Union Control, Res. Officers Assn. (life), Acad. Polit. Sci., Mil. Order World Wars (life), Am. Contract Bridge League (sr. master), Naval Res. Assn., U.S. Naval Inst., Am. Security Council (dir.), Air Force Assn., Navy League U.S., Am. Legion, Smithsonian Assos., Submarine Force Library and Mus. Assn. (life), Sigma Chi. Roman Catholic. Clubs: Army and Navy (Washington); Camelot (Baton Rouge). Office: 142 McGehee Dr Baton Rouge LA 70815

SKINNER, PEGGY PELTIER, office and sales mgr.; b. New Iberia, La., Feb. 21, 1942; d. Clay Paul and Viola Theresa (Courrege) Peltier; spl. courses U. S.W. La., 1977; children—Todd, Robin, Darrin, Stephanie, Michele. Credit reporter, collector Iberia Credit Bur., New Iberia, 1960-63; credit reporter Bridgeport (Conn.) Credit Bur., 1963-65; cashier to head cashier and bookkeper Beneficial Fin., New Iberia, 1965-68; sales sec. LeBlanc & Broussard Ford City, New Iberia, 1968-69; head cashier, bookkeeper Coburn, Fin., New Iberia, 1969-71; sales sec. Mobile Home Brokers, Inc., New Iberia, 1971-73; sec., sales rep. to gen. mgr. and sec.-treas. F. & M. Mobile Homes, New Iberia, 1974—. Mem. Iberia Parish Republican Exec. Com., Iberia Assn. Retarded Citizens; former pres. Am. Bus. Women's Assn.; former pres. New Iberia Sr. High Sch. Band Boosters Club. Recipient award Nat. Assn. Retarded Children, 1976. Mem. La. Bd. Realtors, Nat. Assn. Female Execs. Roman Catholic. Office: Route 2 Box 40 New Iberia LA 70560

SKLAR, ALEXANDER, electric co. exec., educator; b. N.Y.C., May 18, 1915; s. David and Bessie (Wolf) S.; student Cooper Union, N.Y.C., 1932-35; M.B.A., Fla. Atlantic U., 1976; m. Hilda Rae Gevarter, Oct. 27, 1940; 1 dau., Carolyn Mae (Mrs. Louis M. Taff). Chief engr. Aerovox Corp., New Bedford, Mass., 1933-39; mgr. mfg., engring. Indsl. Condenser Corp., Chgo., 1939-44; owner Capacitron, Inc., 1944-48; v.p. mfg. Jefferson Electric Co., Bellwood, Ill., 1948-65; v.p., gen. mgr. electro-mech. div. Essex Internat., Detroit, 1965-67; adviser, dir. various corp., 1968—; vis. prof. mgmt. Fla. Atlantic U., Boca Raton, 1971; lectr. profl. mgmt. U. Calif. at Los Angeles, Harvard Grad. Sch. Bus. Adminstrn., U. Ill. Mem. Acad. Internat. Bus., Soc. Automotive Engrs. Address: 4100 Galt Ocean Dr Fort Lauderdale FL 33308

SKODA, CHARLES PAUL, law firm adminstr.; b. Kenya Colony, Brit. East Africa, Dec. 4, 1936; s. Charles J. and Florence Evelyn (Mentzer) S.; B.A., Moorhead State Coll., 1965; m. Adele Louise Halland, Aug. 4, 1965; children—Evelyn Adele, Charles Pomeroy, Fredrick Paul. Reporter, Chgo. Daily News, 1955-56, N.Y. Times, 1956-57; claims supr. Aetna Life & Casualty, 1966-74; adminstr. Archbald & Spray, Santa Barbara, Calif., 1975—. Founding pres. Ops. Kids, Inc., 1970—. Served with U.S. Army, 1960-62. Mem. Assn. Legal Adminstrs.

SKOLNIK, ALVIN DAVID, archtl. firm exec.; b. Bklyn., Mar. 30, 1929; s. Leon and Ethel (Dauer) S.; student State U. N.Y., 1949-51, Bklyn. Coll., 1947-49, 53-55; m. Marilyn Katz, June 12, 1955; 1 son, David. Archtl. draftsman Martyn & Don Weston, Architects, Bklyn., 1953-58, Keally & Patterson, Architects, N.Y.C., 1958-60; project mgr., constrn. supr., specifications writer Chapman, Evans & Delehanty, Architects and Engrs., N.Y.C., 1960-64; dir. research and specifications Skidmore, Owings & Merrill, Architects and Engrs., N.Y.C., 1964—, asso. partner, 1978—; writer and lectr. in field. Active Boy Scouts Am. Served with C.E., U.S. Army, 1951-53. Fellow Constrn. Specifications Inst. (past v.p. N.Y.C. chpt.); mem. ASTM, Am. Concrete Inst., Constrn. Research Council. Office: 400 Park Ave New York City NY 10022

SKORY, DAVID, lawyer; b. Marion, Ind., Oct. 13, 1922; s. Sinour and Shama (Shama) S.; B.A. cum laude, U. Notre Dame, 1947, J.D. cum laude, 1948; m. Frances E. Shultz, Sept. 9, 1950; children—David, Elizabeth, Michael, Sulaf, Carol, John. Admitted to Ind. bar, 1948, N.Y., bar, 1956, U.S. Supreme Ct. bar, 1961, Tex. bar, 1978; mem. firm Jones, Obenchain & Butler, S. Bend, Ind., 1948-49; staff dept. law Trans Arabian Pipe Line Co., Beirut, Lebanon, 1949-55; legal adv. to corporate exploration and prodn. dept. Mobil Oil Corp., N.Y.C., 1955-58; gen. counsel, dep. gen. mgr. Mobil Oil Corp., Tripoli, Libya, 1958-60; legal cons. Bautzer & Skory, Rome, Italy, 1960-77; practice law, Houston, 1978—. Chmn., Republicans for Nixon, Rome, 1966-68; vestry and chancellor St. Paul's Episcopal Ch., Rome, 1961-71; mem. Am. Embassy Com. on Narcotics, Rome, 1969-71; founder, chmn. Oil Co. Sch., Tripoli, Libya, 1958-60; spl. personal and secret liaison between Pres. J.F. Kennedy and the then Crown Prince Faisal of Saudi Arabia, 1961-63. Served with USN, 1942-45. Decorated Commandatori del Lavro, Italian Govt., 1965. Mem. Am. Bar Assn., Tex. Bar Assn., Internat. Law Assn., Italian Am. C. of C. (exec. com. 1963-66). Episcopalian. Clubs: Am. Men's of Italy (exec. com. 1961-66); Petroleum (founder, pres. 1958-60) (Libya); Elks, Masons (Shriner). Office: 2200 S Post Oak Rd Suite 609 Houston TX 77056

SKOUSEN, MARK ANDREW, econ. and fin. writer; b. San Diego, Oct. 19, 1947; s. Leroy B. and Helen L. (McCarty) S.; B.A., Brigham Young U., 1971, M.S., 1972; Ph.D. in Econs., George Washington U., 1977; m. Jo Ann Foster, Apr. 19, 1973; children—Valerie, Timothy, Leslie Ann. Economist, CIA, 1972-74; editor in chief Personal Fin., 1974-79; editor in chief Forecasts & Strategies, Washington, 1980—, also cons. editor Personal Fin. and Tax Angles, 1979—; fin. cons.; speaker fin. and econ. confs.; books include: Playing the Price Controls Game, 1977; The Insider's Banking and Credit Almanac, 1977-80; Mark Skousen's Complete Guide to Financial Privacy, 1979; the 100% Gold Standard, 1978; New Profits from Your Insurance Policy, 1980; High Finance on a Low Budget, 1981. Mem. Am. Econ. Assn. Mormon. Office: PO Box 611 Merrifield CA 22116

SKRIBA, STEPHEN JOSEPH, III, savs. and loan exec.; b. Chgo., Aug. 7, 1947; s. Stephen J. and Evelyn S.; B.A., U. Ill., 1969; M.A., Roosevelt U., 1976; grad. Sch. Savs. and Loan, Ind. U., 1980; m. Andrea Lynn LeCompte, Feb. 14, 1970; children—Brian J., Bryce J. With Clyde Fed. Savs. & Loan Assn., North Riverside, Ill., 1972—, personnel mgr., 1974-75, asst. v.p., 1975-78, v.p., personnel mgr., 1979—. Served with AUS, 1969-70; Vietnam. Mem. Am. Soc. Personnel Adminstrn., Inst. Fin. Edn. (sec.-treas; pres. chpt.). Republican. Roman Catholic. Office: 7222 W Cermak Rd North Riverside IL 60546

SKWERES, THOMAS WALTER, marketing exec.; b. Chgo., May 11, 1929; s. Marion John and Sophie (Rataiczyk) S.; student Wright City Coll., 1947-49, Northwestern U., 1949-55; m. Charmaine Liska, Oct. 28, 1950; children—Thomas Allan, Pamela Charmaine, Patricia Ann. Prodn. mgr. Reincke Meyer & Finn, 1953-55; v.p., account exec. Hanson & Stevens, 1955-62; v.p. sales Ross & White Co., 1962—. Served with AUS, 1951-53. Mem. Wheeling C. of C., Eta Iota Psi. Home: 5613 Snowdrop Ln Lisle IL 60532 Office: 50 W Dundee Rd Wheeling IL 60090

SLACK, GEORGE HENRY, ins. co. exec.; b. Boston, July 9, 1926; s. George Henry and Geraldine Mary (Judge) S.; A.A., Suffolk U., 1950, J.D., 1959; grad. Exec. Program, Ind. U. Grad. Sch. Bus., 1964; m. Virginia Ann Lane, Oct. 30, 1954; children—Elizabeth Ann, Katherine Mary, Christopher Lee, Kevin Michael. Home office claims examiner Employers of Wausau, 1950-61; group mgr. br. ops. Am. States Ins. Co., 1961-64; claims mgr. Forum Ins. Co., 1964-66; asst. sec. Reins. Corp. N.Y., 1966-69; 2d v.p. Covenant Group, Hartford, Conn., 1969-70, v.p. ops., 1970-76; v.p. Security Group, 1976-79, sr. v.p. Security Group, 1979—. Co. chmn. United Fund, 1971-72; mem. fund raising com. YMCA, 1972-74; mem. fin. com. West Hartford Youth Hockey Assn., 1971—. Served with USAAF, 1943-46; PTO; with USAF, 1951-53; Korea. Recipient United Fund award, 1971-72. Mem. Ins. Assn. Conn., Am. Ins. Assn. Claim Exec. Council, Fedn. Ins. Counsel, New Eng. Claim Exec. Assn., Loss Exec. Assn., Am. Mgmt. Assn., Surplus Lines Assn., AIM. Republican. Roman Catholic. Clubs: Univ. of Hartford, Shennecossett Yacht, Pocasset Country, Lions. Home: 53 Wardwell Rd West Hartford CT 06107 Office: 1000 Asylum Ave Hartford CT 06101

SLADE, HORACE EUGENE, univ. adminstr.; b. Rockaway, N.J., Sept. 20, 1919; s. Eugene Leland and Mary Veronica (Parcell) S.; B.S., U. Idaho, 1942, postgrad., 1948-54; postgrad. U. Nebr., 1955; m. Norma Marie Headrick, Aug. 11, 1940; children—Bruce Eugene, James Bradley, Jo Ann Schermerhorn. Asst. accountant to bus. mgr., investment officer U. Idaho, Moscow, from 1942, now emeritus, investment cons. Pres. Western Assos., Inc., Underwater Salvage; past pres., treas. Schermerhorn Investments; chmn. Slade Fin., Ltd.; dir. Idaho State Bank. Sec., treas., trustee Idaho Ad Club Meml. Sch. Fund. Fellow Internat. Oceanographic Found., Idaho Acad. Sci., Oceanic Soc., Library Assos., Inc.; mem. U. Idaho Found., Moscow C. of C., Yellow Dogs. Mason (Shriner); mem. Order Eastern Star, Elk, Moose, Lion. Home: 815 Nez Perce St Moscow ID 83843 Office: Office Financial Affairs U Idaho Moscow ID 83843

SLADE, JOHN H., stockbroker; b. Frankfurt/Main, Germany, May 30, 1908; came to U.S., 1936, naturalized, 1942; s. Paul and Alice (Schmidt) Schlesinger; student public schs., Frankfurt/Main; m. Marianne Rosenbaum, Aug. 10, 1977; children—Barbara Slade Boelsterli, Nicole Slade Weinberg. With Bear Stearns & Co., N.Y.C., 1936—, founder internat. dept., 1948, partner, 1951—, sr. partner in charge internat. dept., 1948—. Served with U.S. Army, 1942-45. Decorated Bronze Star. Club: Harmonie (N.Y.C.). Mem. Am. Olympic Field Hockey Team, 1948. Office: 55 Water St New York NY 10041

SLAGER, RONALD DALE, wholesale-retail co. exec.; b. Kalamazoo, Oct. 16, 1952; s. Robert Peter and Ruth M. Slager; student Western Mich. U., 1970, Mich. State U., 1971; m. Janeen K. Walters, May 4, 1974. Sales rep. Investors Diversified Services, Mpls., 1971-73; sales rep., sales mgr. Dykema Office Supply, Kalamazoo, 1973-77; owner, mgr. Stage Lighting Distbrs., Kalamazoo, 1974-75; co-founder The Hearing Aid Center of Kalamazoo, 1976-78; vice-pres. Hearing Aid Centers of Am., Inc., Kalamazoo, 1978—; v.p., dir. MLR Inc., Kalamazoo, 1980—. Bd. dirs. Kalamazoo Youth for Christ, 1973; adv. Jr. Achievement Kalamazoo, 1978-79; bd. dirs. Youth Opportunities Unltd. Kalamazoo, Inc., 1980—. Mem. Ad Club Kalamazoo, Sales and Mktg. Execs., Kalamazoo C. of C., Ind. Businessmen Assn., A.G. Bell Assn. for Deaf. Reformed Ch. Club: Sertoma (pres. 1976-77, chmn. 1977-78, dist. gov. N.W. Ohio-Mich. dist. 1978-79). Home: 6481 East S Ave Scotts MI 49088 Office: 3130 Portage Rd Kalamazoo MI 49003

SLAGLE, JERRY LOU, banker; b. Grant, Nebr., Nov. 20, 1934; s. John O. and Myrtle E. (Makinster) S.; B.A., Doane Coll., 1956; m. Nancy J. Shearer, Aug. 28, 1955; children—Michael Alan, Steven Douglas, Brian Everett. Claims investigator Liberty Mut. Ins. Co., Indpls., 1956-57, Wichita, Kans., 1958-59, Denver, 1959-60; ins. agt., asst. cashier First Nat. Bank of Julesburg (Colo.), 1960-68; v.p., cashier First Nat. Bank of Holyoke (Colo.), 1968—, also dir.; owner, partner Nat. Ins. Agy., Holyoke, Colo., 1968—; pres., dir. First Nat. Bank Strasburg (Colo.), 1976—. Treas. Holyoke PTA, 1970-71; mem. Phillips County (Colo.) Centennial-Bicentennial Com., 1974—, Town of Holyoke Centennial-Bicentennial Com., 1974—; sec. accountability com. dist. REIJ, Holyoke Sch. Bd., 1974—. Bd. dirs. Will Heginbotham Med. Clinic; bd. dirs. Colo. Rural Health Care Assn., Denver, 1975—, v.p., 1977-78, pres., 1978—. Served with AUS, 1957-58. Recipient service award Jr. C. of C., 1961. Sec.-treas. Phillips County Republican Central Com., 1970—. Mem. Bankers Adminstrs. Inst. (dir. 1963-64). Methodist (mem. commn. on finance 1962-66). Clubs: Lions (dir. 1969—), Elks, Strasburg Service (pres.). Home: Box 386 1665 Longbranch Strasburg CO 80136 Office: First Nat Bank PO Box 97 Strasburg CO 80136

SLATEN, HUBERT EDWIN, JR., real estate appraiser; b. Dumas, Ark., June 15, 1935; s. Hubert Edwin and Emma Jean (Parks) S.; B.S. in Natural Sci. and Mathematics, U. Ark., Monticello, 1957; m. Anna Topaz Williams, Apr. 18, 1956; children—Renee Suzanne, Lori Elise. Pub. sch. adminstr., tchr., Grady, Ark., 1957-58; chief dep. tax assessor Jefferson County, Ark., 1958-63; staff appraiser First Fed. Savs. Assn., Pine Bluff, Ark., 1963-68; owner, operator Slaten Appraisal Co., Pine Bluff, 1968—; dir. Trinity Village Inc., 1979-80. Bd. dirs. Jefferson County United Way, 1973-74; elder Central Presbyterian Ch., Pine Bluff. Mem. Soc. Real Estate Appraisers (pres. Central Ark. chpt. 1973-74, vice gov. dist. 10 1977-78, 81, dir. 1971-73; sr. residential appraiser; sr. real property appraiser), Am. Inst. Real Estate Appraisers (pres. Ark. chpt. 1980), Jefferson Wildlife Assn. (charter), Nat. Rifle Assn., Ducks Unltd. (life). Democrat. Clubs: Masons, Shriners, Rotary (pres. local club 1974). Address: 11 Smugglers Ln Pine Bluff AR 71603

SLATER, DORIS ERNESTINE WILKE, business exec.; b. Oakes, N.D.; d. Arthur Waldemar and Anna Mary (Dill) Wilke; grad. high sch.; m. Lawrence Bert Slater, June 4, 1930 (dec., 1960). Sec. to circulation mgr. Mpls. Daily Star, 1928-30; promotion activities Lions Internat. in U.S., Can., Cuba, 1930-48; exec. sec. parade and spl. events com. Inaugural Com., 1948-49; exec. sec. Nat. Capital Sesquicentennial Commn., 1949-50, Capitol Hill Assos., Inc., 1951, Pres.'s Cup Regatta, 1951; adminstrv. asst. Nat. Assn. Food Chains, 1951-60; v.p., sec.-treas. John A. Logan Assos., Inc., Washington, 1960—; v.p., sec.-treas. Logan, Seaman, Slater, Inc., 1962—; mng. dir. Western Hemisphere, Internat. Assn. Chain Stores, 1964—. With pub. relations div. Boston Met. chpt. ARC, 1941-42; mem. Nat. Cherry Blossom Festival Com., 1949—; mem. Inaugural Ball Com., 1953, 57, 65. Methodist. Lion. Home and Office: 2500 Wisconsin Ave Washington DC 20007

SLATER, GEORGE RICHARD, bank exec.; b. Indpls., Feb. 13, 1924; s. George Greenleaf and Chloe (Shoemaker) S.; B.S., Purdue U., 1946, M.S., 1957, Ph.D., 1963; m. Helen Goodwill, July 1, 1945; children—George Greenleaf, Kathleen Slater Hamar, John Goodwill, Frederick Richard. Chief economist Allis-Chalmers Mfg. Co., Milw., 1957-60; v.p. Citizens Nat. Bank of Decatur (Ill.), 1960-64; sr. v.p., group exec. Harris Trust & Savings Bank, Chgo., 1964-76; pres., chief exec. officer Marine Nat. Exchange Bank, Milw., 1976—, The Marine Corp., Milw., 1978—. Mem. exec. bd. Milw. council Boy Scouts Am., 1976—; trustee Milw. Art Center, 1977—, Marquette U.; bd. dirs. Froedtert Meml. Hosp., Milw., 1977—; mem. Greater Milw. Com., 1977—; bd. visitors U. Wis., Milw., 1978—; bd. dirs. United Performing Arts Fund, 1978—; mem. president's council Purdue U., 1976—, mem. dean's adv. council Krannert Grad. Sch. Mgmt., 1977—; mem. adv. bd. Sch. Bus., U. Wis., Madison, 1977—. Served with U.S. Army, 1943-46; PTO. Mem. Assn. Res. City Bankers. Episcopalian. Clubs: Chgo., Milw., Econ. of Chgo., Milw. Country. Home: 5125 N Palisades Rd Milwaukee WI 53217 Office: 111 E Wisconsin Ave Milwaukee WI 53202

SLATER, MANNING, broadcasting exec.; b. Springfield, Mass., Aug. 29, 1917; s. Ely and Sarah Deenah (Hurwitz) Slotnick; student Rider Coll., 1935-36, U. Fla., 1936-37; B.A., Am. Internat. Coll., 1939; m. Bernice Garson, Aug. 8, 1953 (div.); children—Gary Edward, Richard Stuart; m. 2d, Anita N. Slater. Pres., Indian Orchard Community Market, Inc., 1937-46; v.p., treas. Bridgeport Broadcasting Co., 1947-59; pres., chmn. bd. Hercules Broadcasting Co., Sacramento, 1959—; pres. Slater Broadcasting Co., 1978—; sports writer and broadcaster; broadcast cons., 1961-69. Bd. dirs. Mercy Hosps., Sacramento. Mem. Nat. Assn. Broadcasters, Nat. Radio Broadcasters Assn., Sacramento, Seattle chambers commerce. Jewish. Clubs: Northridge Country (Fair Oaks, Calif.); Comstock (Sacramento). Home: 660 Lake Wilhaggin Dr Sacramento CA 95825 Office: 1337 Howe Ave Sacramento CA 95825

SLATER, ROBERT JOSEPH, steel co. exec.; b. Buffalo, May 13, 1937; s. John Joseph and Anna Mae (McMoil) S.; B.S., Canisius Coll., 1959; m. Patricia Ann Brennan, Oct. 8, 1960; children—Diane, Cynthia. Various positions N.Y. Central R.R., N.Y.C., 1959-70; pres. C&W Ry., Pueblo, Colo., 1971; with CF&I Steel Corp., Pueblo, 1972—, v.p., 1972-76, pres., 1976-80, chmn. bd., 1980—; pres. Crane Co., N.Y.C., 1980—; dir. Medusa Corp., Huttig Sash & Door, St. Louis. Served with AUS, 1960-62. Mem. Am. Iron and Steel Engrs., Am. Iron and Steel Inst. (dir. 1976—), Mensa, Alpha Kappa Psi. Republican. Roman Catholic. Club: Garden of Gods (Colorado Springs, Colo.). Home: 415 Starlite Dr Pueblo CO 81005 Office: 300 Park Ave New York NY 10022

SLATER, SIDNEY DONALD, investment banker; b. N.Y.C., Apr. 8, 1927; s. Moses and Rose (Warshaw) S.; B.A. cum laude, Syracuse U., 1949; M.A., Columbia, 1951, postgrad., 1955; m. Eve Munzer, Mar. 7, 1953; children—Donald, Julia. Investment cons. Standard & Poor's Corp., N.Y.C., 1951-53; lectr. econs. U. Conn., lectr. accounting and finance Upsala Coll., 1954-55; investment banking and dir. research Shields & Co., N.Y.C., 1955-58; investment banking and research Blyth Eastman Dillon & Co., N.Y.C., 1958-61, E.F. Hutton & Co., N.Y.C., 1962-64; pres. Good Rds. Machinery Corp., pres. MainTek, Inc., Canton, Ohio, 1965-67; pres. Amadon Corp., Boston, 1964—; asst. prof. fin. Bentley Coll., Waltham, Mass. Served with USNR, 1945-46. Mem. N.Y. Soc. Security Analysts, Boston Investment Club, Boston C. of C. (Exec. Club), New Eng. Council, Tabard, Pi Sigma Rho, Pi Gamma Mu, Theta Beta Phi. Unitarian (chmn. finance com.). Club: Brae Burn Country. Author: The Strategy of Cash: A liquidity approach to maximizing the company's profits, 1974. Home: 21 Alden Rd Wellesley Hills MA 02181 Office: Amadon Corp 31 Milk St Boston MA 02109

SLAUGHTER, ELMER CUNNINGHAM, mfg. exec.; b. Houston, Sept. 12, 1920; s. Elmer Carlton and Margaret (Cunningham) S.; student N. Tex. State U., 1936-37; E.E., U. Cin., 1942; m. Jeannette Kearney, June 27, 1942; children—Jean Slaughter Johnson, Susan Slaughter Sachs, Dorothy Slaughter Ashmead, Edward, Mary Slaughter McGraw, John, Richard, Michael Doris Slaughter Rea, Rebecca, Nancy Slaughter Salyer, Janet. Established test lab. Lear, Inc., Piqua, Ohio, 1942-45, chief design engr., 1945-46, chief engr., Grand Rapids, Mich., 1946-47; chief engr. Piqua Machine & Mfg. Co., 1948-54; pres. E-M Corp., Fletcher, Ohio, 1947-48, Slaughter Co., Ardmore, Okla., 1954—; cons. Lear, Inc., Grand Rapids, 1947-48, Polo Pump Co., Ill., 1947-49, Safa Alarm Co., Orrville, Ohio, 1948-50; chmn. Mayor's Indsl. Adv. Com., 1971-72. Commr., Piqua Boys' Baseball Assn., 1958-61; chmn. Ardmore Edn. Council, 1970-74; pres. Ardmore Sch. Bd., 1977; pres. bd. dirs. Ardmore Sheltered Workshop, 1970-72. Mem. IEEE, AAAS, Ardmore C. of C. (pres., dir. 1972-75, named Outstanding Citizen 1975), Tau Beta Pi, Eta Kappa Nu, Sigma Xi. Office: Moore and Hailey Sts Ardmore OK 73401

SLAVEN, W(ILLIAM) CHARLES, bus. cons., educator; b. Oneida, Tenn., Aug. 17, 1950; s. Charles Linden and Phyllis Doren (Foster) S.; B.S., Miami U., Oxford, Ohio, 1972, M.B.A., 1974; m. Diana Jean Herth, Sept. 2, 1972; children—Kevin, Brian Charles. Fin. aid counselor Miami U., 1973-74; staff auditor Arthur Young & Co., Cin., 1974-75, computer auditor, 1975-78, computer audit mgr., mgmt. cons., 1978-79; dir. planning and corp. devel. Pizza Hut of Ohio, 1979-80, internal cons., part-time 1980—; vis. lectr. quantitative methods Ohio U., Athens, 1980—. C.P.A., Ohio. Mem. Am. Inst. C.P.A.'s, Ohio Soc. C.P.A.'s, Nat. Accountants Assn., Am. Mgmt. Assn., Data Processing Mgmt. Assn., Soc. Advancement of Mgmt. (past dir.). Mem. Disciples of Christ Ch. Home: 18 Cable Ln Athens OH 45701 Office: Ohio U Athens OH 45701

SLAYDEN, KAY WILSON, mfg. co. exec.; b. Lyons, Ga., Dec. 1, 1934; s. Herbert L. and Marion S. (Lilliott) S.; B.S. in Engring., Auburn (Ala.) U., 1956; m. Nancy Murray, Aug. 11, 1957; children—Kevin, Stephen. Vice pres. ops. Teledyne Brown Engring. Co., Huntsville, Ala., 1960-70; v.p. ops. Fugua Industries Inc., Atlanta, 1970-73, exec. v.p., 1975-80, pres., chief operating officer, 1980—, also dir.; pres. McDonough Power Equipment Co. (Ga.), 1973-75; dir. Norell Southeastern Corp. Served to capt. USAF, 1957-60. Registered profl. engr., Ga. Baptist. Office: 3800 First Nat Tower Atlanta GA 30383*

SLENES, JOHN FREEMAN, real estate broker; b. Fairbanks, Alaska, Sept. 25, 1947; s. Johan Clarence and Fern Hanke (Darling) S.; student Alaska Meth. U., 1965-67; B. Univ. Studies, U. N.Mex., 1970, postgrad., 1979—; m. Dee Elaine Emig, Jan. 25, 1969; children—Shawn Freeman, Chad Johan. Asso., Skyway Realty, Anchorage, 1968, Gineris/Huckabee, Albuquerque, 1969; pres., broker, owner Century 21, Realty Cons., Inc., Albuquerque, 1970—; partner Skinner-Slenes Properties, Albuquerque, 1973-75; owner Slenes Investments, N.Mex., 1970—; instr. Hall Inst. Real Estate, 1975. Mem. Nat. Assn. Realtors, Realtor Assn. N.Mex., Albuquerque Bd. Realtors (chmn. computer com. 1980), U. Century 21 Comml. Investment Soc., N.Mex. Young Republicans (chmn. 1968), Phi Sigma Kappa (pres. 1969). Republican. Lutheran. Clubs: Sports Car Am., Calif. Assn. Tiger Owners, Albuquerque Sports Car (pres. 1976), Shelby Am. Automobile. Home: 8403 Aztec Rd NE Albuquerque NM 87111 Office: 8301 Menaul Blvd NE Albuquerque NM 87110

SLENN, JOHN RAYMOND, elec. equipment co. exec.; b. Phila., Apr. 29, 1933; s. Samuel and Nancy (Sharpe) S.; B.S., Temple U., 1954, postgrad. in Bus. Adminstrn., 1957; m. Elizabeth J. Berry, June 8, 1957; children—Kurt J., Lisa A. Exec. trainee State Farm Ins. Co., 1956-57; employment supr. I-T-E Circuit Breaker Co., Phila., 1957-64, sales application engr., 1964-65; advt. mgr. I-T-E Imperial Corp., Phila., 1965-69, personnel mgr., 1969-76; mgr. employee relations Gould Inc., Phila., 1976—. Served with U.S. Army, 1954-56. Accredited personnel exec. Mem. ey, Indsl. Relations Assn. of Phila., Phila. Survey Group, Am. Mgmt. Assn., Mensa Internat. Home: 719 Stockton Circle Ridley Park PA 19078 Office: 601 E Erie Ave Philadelphia PA 19134

SLEPPY, DAVID LEROY, credit union exec.; b. Reading, Pa., Dec. 20, 1937; s. Blair Marburg and Nellie Mae (Kirkpatrick) S.; student Pa. State Credit Union Inst., 1974, U. Wis. Credit Union Nat. Assn. Sch., 1976; m. Patricia Ann Monahan, Mar. 30, 1963; children—Patrick, Christine. Salesman life ins. co., 1960-66; welder steel mill, 1966-77; founder, sec.-treas., gen. mgr. CTCE Fed. Credit Union, Reading, 1970—. Mem. Credit Union Execs. Soc., Pa. Credit Union League (dir. 1980—). Home: 3246 Harrison Ave Muhlenberg Park Reading PA 19605 Office: PO Box 662 125 Exeter St Reading PA 19603

SLETAGER, JANICE RAE, communications exec.; b. Hastings, Nebr., Jan. 7, 1933; d. Julius Marion and Laura Mae (Foote) Scherbacher; student Whitman Coll., 1950-51; B.A. summa cum laude, Eastern Wash. U., 1966, M.A. summa cum laude, 1972; m. Clyde I. Sletager, June 6, 1953 (div. Mar. 1968); children—Gregory Neil, Chris Andrew. Accounting clk. Ebasco Services, Inc., Clark Fork, Idaho, 1951-53; geology lab. instr. Eastern Wash. U., Cheney, 1965-66, geology research asst., 1966, teaching fellow English, 1966-67, instr. English, 1967; tech. editor Battelle-Northwest, Richland, Wash., 1967-69, sr. tech. editor, 1970, supr. tech. writing, 1971, tech. editing/writing mgr., 1972-78, mgr. communications dept., 1978—. Advt. chmn. Tri-Cities Conv. Bur., 1973-75, mem. exec. bd. 1974-76, trustee, 1973-78. Mem. Am. Mgmt. Assn., Soc. Tech. Communication, MLA, Internat. Platform Assn., Geol. Soc. Am., Kappa Delta Pi, Delta Gamma. Home: 1902 Mahan Ave Richland WA 99352 Office: Battelle-Northwest Battelle Blvd Richland WA 99352

SLICKO, THOMAS MICHAEL, retail exec.; b. Highland, Ind., Apr. 19, 1951; s. Ancietas Frank and Ruth Ann S.; B.S. in Indsl. Mgmt., Purdue U., 1973, M.S. in Mgmt., 1979; m. Marlene Ann Sklanka, Aug. 12, 1972. Salesman, dept. mgr. J.C. Penney Co., Hammond, Ind. and Harvey, Ill., 1971-73; raw materials mgr. Rand McNally Co., Hammond, 1974; gen. mgr. Hyland Corp., Highland, Ind., 1974-75; mgr. sales adminstrn. Dreis & Krump Mfg. Co., Chgo., 1975-78; dir. adminstrv. ops. Maremont Corp., Chgo., 1976-78; v.p. adminstrn., sec.-treas. Lee Enterprises, Inc., Prospect Heights, Ill., 1978-79; dist. mgr. Southland Corp., Hammond, 1979—. Mem. Amateur Golfers Assn., Highland Jr. C. of C. (founder, pres.), Purdue Alumni Assn., Phi Sigma Kappa, Alpha Mu Omega. Home: 7415 McCook St Hammond IN 46323 Office: 3700 179th St Hammond IN 46323

SLINKMAN, ROGER W., electronics co. exec.; b. Joplin, Mo., Aug. 5, 1922; s. William H. and Lois (White) S.; B.S. in Elec. Engring., Kans. State Coll., 1943; m. Loisjean Angstead, Dec. 5, 1943; children—Craig, Kerry Lou, Kevin. Engr., Sylvania, Emporium, Pa., 1943-56, engring. mgr. Emporium, Pa. and Seneca Falls, N.Y., 1956-70, plant mgr., Ottawa, Ohio, 1970-72, v.p. ops. electronic tube div., Seneca Falls, 1972-76, sr. v.p. electronic components group GTE Consumer Electronics, GTE Products Corp., Seneca Falls; chmn. bd. Union Electronics Co.; dir. State Bank of Seneca Falls. Past chmn. Seneca Falls chpt. Am. Field Service; bd. dirs. Taylor-Brown Meml. Hosp., Waterloo, N.Y. Mem. Electronic Industries Assn., IEEE. Club: Seneca Falls Country. Patentee. Home: 23 Leland Dr Seneca Falls NY 13148 Office: GTE Products Corp Johnston St Seneca Falls NY 13148

SLINN, RONALD JOHN ST. LEGER, forest economist; b. Sydney, Australia, Nov. 23, 1928; came to U.S., 1967, naturalized, 1975; s. Herbert Frederick and Lillias E. Beth (McLeod) S.; B.Sc. in Forestry, Sydney U., 1950, diploma in forestry, 1950; M.S. in Forestry, Melbourne U., 1965; Ph.D. (fellow), Duke U., 1970; m. Edith Jean Watts, Jan. 19, 1952; children—Peter J. (dec.), Jennifer E., Barbara P., Ronald P. (dec.), Margaret A. Officer in charge forest mgmt. research Australian Forest Research Inst., 1965-69; asso. prof. forest econs. Duke U., Durham, N.C., 1969-70; v.p. pulp, materials and tech. group Am. Paper Inst., N.Y.C., 1970—. Mem. local environ. commn. Australian Commonwealth scholar, 1946-50. Mem. Soc. Am. Foresters, TAPPI, Paper Industry Mgmt. Assn., Sigma Xi. Republican. Presbyterian. Club: Sky (N.Y.C.). Home: 17 Fieldston Rd Princeton NJ 08540 Office: Am Paper Inst 260 Madison Ave New York NY 10016

SLOAN, ELMER WESTON, furniture mfg. co. exec.; b. Corydon, Iowa, Feb. 15, 1922; s. David Lewis and Jessie Alice (Mitchell) S.; B.C.S., Drake U., 1950; m. Mary Agnes Delles, Aug. 19, 1950; children—Mark Weston, Craig Paul, Timothy Dale, Kathryn Suanne, Jennifer Lynn, Brian Alan. Office mgr. Goodyear Tire & Rubber Co., Clinton, Iowa, 1952-54; indsl. engr. Maytag Co., Newton, Iowa, 1954-56; v.p. mfg. Schnadig Corp., Rushville, Ind., 1956—; dir. Rushville Nat. Bank, 1980—. Cubmaster, Richmond (Ind.) council Boy Scouts Am., 1959-60; mem. Rush County (Ind.) Aviation Bd., 1969; pres. Babe Ruth League, Rushville, 1969; chmn. fund-raising drive St. Mary's Catholic Ch., 1971. Served with USN, 1942-46, 50-52. Mem. Indsl. Mgmt. Soc., Nat. Assn. Furniture Mfrs., Am. Legion, VFW, 45th Naval Seabee Assn. Democrat. Roman Catholic. Clubs: K.C., Elks. Home: RFD 3 Box 266 Rushville IN 46173 Office: PO Box 397 Rushville IN 46173

SLOAN, MACEO ARCHIBALD, ins. co. exec.; b. Newport, Ark., Aug. 10, 1913; s. Cleveland Eugene and Sammie (Patterson) S.; A.B., Prairie View State Coll., 1937; LL.D., Livingstone Coll., 1977; m. Charlotte Alicia Kennedy, Dec. 27, 1943; children—Sylvia M. (Mrs. Frederick Black), Maceo Kennedy. With N.C. Mut. Life Ins. Co., Durham, 1938—, v.p., asso. agy. dir., 1962-64, v.p. home office ops., 1964-69, sr. v.p., 1969-73, exec. v.p., 1973—; chmn., dir. Fed. Res. Bank of Richmond; dir. Duke Power Co. Former trustee Nat. Assembly for Social Policy and Devel.; bd. dirs. N.C. United Way, Durham United Fund; bd. govs. U. N.C.; mem. nat. adv. council, former chmn. adv. bd. Salvation Army; past bd. dirs. N.C. Zool. Soc. Recipient Alumni Achievement award Prairie View State Coll., 1955. C.L.U. Mem. Nat. Ins. Assn. (past pres.), Alpha Phi Alpha, Sigma Pi Phi. Mason. Office: 411 W Chapel Hill St Durham NC 27701

SLOAN, STEPHEN, real estate exec.; b. N.Y.C., June 21, 1932; B.A., Washington and Lee U., 1954; m. Nannette Barkin, Feb. 24, 1956. Partner, Milton Barkin Mgmt. Co., N.Y.C., 1958-70; pres. Lehman Realty Corp., N.Y.C., 1970-74; pres. World-Wide Realty Corp., N.Y.C., 1978—, Stephen Sloan Realty Corp., N.Y.C., 1979—; dir. Realty Found. N.Y., Pacific Design Center, Aquirre Corp. Chmn. urban fishing council N.Y. State Dept. Conservation; trustee Horace Mann Sch. Mem. Am. League Anglers (dir. 1972—), Nat. Coalition Marine Conservation. Republican. Clubs: Explorers, Deep Sea, City Athletic, Chubb Cay. Home: 510 Park Ave New York NY 10022 Office: 230 Park Ave New York NY 10017

SLOAN, WILLIAM PATRICK, printing co. exec.; b. Oak Park, Ill., Nov. 2, 1934; s. Frank A. and Thyra (Bartell) S.; B.S., U. Ill., 1957; m. Karen Mix, Jan. 31, 1980. Mgr. composition R.R. Donnelley & Sons Co., Chgo., 1957-68, group mgr. Electronic Graphics div., 1968-73, regional sales mgr., 1973-78; pres., asst. sec., dir. Sorg Printing Co. of Calif., San Francisco, 1979—. Served with U.S. Army, 1956-57. Mem. Printing Industries No. Calif. (dir. 1980—), Am. Soc. Corporate Secs., Western Stock Transfer Assn., Sigma Iota Epsilon. Club: Bankers (San Francisco). Home: 30B Circle Dr Tiburon CA 94920 Office: 346 1st St San Francisco CA 94105

SLOANE, CHARLES CLIFFORD, III, electronics distbn. co. exec.; b. Plattsburgh, N.Y., Feb. 7, 1928; s. Charles Clifford and Emma Nichols S.; student St. Lawrence U., 1944-45; U.S. Mil. Acad., 1945-50; B.S., U. Mich., 1952, B.A., 1952, M.S., 1952; m. Jody Behrens, Dec. 29, 1951; children—Catherine, Jody, Cynthia. Partner, pres. Angus-Sloane, Inc., Moorestown, N.J., 1956-64; dir. mktg. Powell Electronics Co., Phila., 1964-67; nat. sales mgr. ELCO Corp., Willow Grove, Pa., 1967-70; dir. mktg. ITT Cannon Co., Santa Ana, Calif., 1970-75; gen. mgr. Time Electronics Co. div. Avnet Inc., Mountain View, Calif., 1975—; lectr. in field. Served to 1st lt. U.S. Army, 1952-54. Mem. IEEE, Nat. Electronic Distbrs. Assn., Electronic Reps. Assn. Republican. Presbyterian. Contbr. articles to electronic jours. Home: 22 Mansion Ct Menlo Park CA 94075 Office: 1339 Moffet Park Blvd Sunnyvale CA 94086

SLOVER, WILLIAM GODFREY, educator, city ofcl.; b. Trenton, N.J., June 15, 1938; s. H. Edwin and Marian B. (Beans) Stockwell; B.S. in Edn., Miami U., Oxford, Ohio, 1967, M.Ed., 1970; grad. Inst. Ednl. Mgmt., Harvard U., 1977. Clk., Johnson and Johnson, 1960-61; mgmt. trainee Morgan Guaranty Trust Co., 1961-65; asst. registrar Miami U., Oxford, Ohio, 1967-69, sec. of univ., 1969—, affirmative action officer. Mem. CSC Oxford, 1974—, chmn., 1975, 76, vice chmn., 1977, 78; mem. Tax Equalization Bd. Oxford, 1973-75. Served with USMCR, 1959-64. Mem. Am. Assn. Higher Edn., Newcomen Soc. N.Am., Beta Gamma Sigma, Omicron Delta Kappa, Beta Theta Pi, Phi Delta Kappa. Presbyterian. Home: 505 Brookview Ct Oxford OH 45056 Office: 204 Roudebush Hall Miami U Oxford OH 45056

SLOWITSKY, RICHARD PETER, fin. co. exec.; b. N.Y.C., Jan. 17, 1943; s. Peter and Margaret (Carbone) S.; A.B., U. Mich., 1964; M.B.A., N.Y. U., 1969; m. Joy R. Libretto, Nov. 28, 1964; children—Kera Jean, Laura Ann. Sales mgr. N.Y. Telephone Co., N.Y.C., 1964-69; line mgmt. positions Met. Life Ins. Co., N.Y.C., 1969-73; supt. agys. Home Life Ins. Co. N.Y., N.Y.C., 1973-75; ops. mgr. Equitable Life Assurance Soc. of U.S., N.Y.C., 1975-79; asst. v.p. Citibank, N.Y.C., 1979-80; mgr. edn. and tng. G.E. Credit Corp., 1980—. Mem. Nat. Soc. Performance and Instrn., Am. Soc. Chartered Life Underwriters. Republican. Roman Catholic. Home: 28 Lincoln Dr New Canaan CT 06840 Office: 260 Long Ridge Rd Stamford CT 06902

SLUCHEVSKY, VLADIMIR NICHOLAS, mech. engr.; b. Tzarskoje Sselo, Russia, Feb. 24, 1915; s. Nicolas K. and Ludmila A. (Von Ekse) S.; came to U.S., 1948, naturalized, 1954; Dipl. Ing., U. Belgrade (Yugoslavia), 1941; m. Katherine Von Bock, Feb. 27, 1948; 1 son, Nicholas; 1 stepson, Herman Von Rennenkampff. Plant engr. Carl Walter Co., mining equipment, Salzburg, Austria, 1944-48; plant maintenance engr. Columbia-Geneva Steel Co., Pittsburg, Calif., 1951-56; mech. engr. Kaiser Engrs., Oakland, Calif., 1956-62; group supr. Arthur G. McKee Co., San Mateo, Calif., 1962-80; cons. materials handling, dust and fume control, gen. plant design. Mem. Verein Deutscher Ingenieure. Clubs: Aero (Yugoslavia); Humboldt (Germany). Home: 9850 River Rd Forestville CA 95436

SLUDIKOFF, STANLEY ROBERT, publisher; b. Bronx, N.Y., July 17, 1935; s. Harry and Lillie (Elberger) S.; B.Arch., Pratt Inst., 1957; postgrad. U. So. Calif., 1960-62; m. Ann Paula Blumberg, June 30, 1972; children—Lisa Beth, Jaime Dawn. Project planner Robert E. Alexander, F.A.I.A. & Assos., Los Angeles, 1965-66, Daniel, Mann, Johnson & Mendenhall, City & Regional Planning Consultants, Los Angeles, 1967-70; pres. SRS Enterprises, Inc., also Gambling Times, Inc., Am. Casino Promotions, Inc., Two Worlds Mgmt., Inc., Los Angeles, 1971—; pres. Las Vegas TV Weekly, also Postal West, Las Vegas, 1975—; instr. city and regional planning program U. So. Cal., 1960-63. Mem. Destination 90 Forum, Citizens Planning Group, San Fernando Valley, Calif., 1966-67. Lt. col. U.S. Army Res. Recipient commendation from mayor Los Angeles for work on model cities funding, 1968. Licensed architect, real estate broker. Mem. AIA, Am. Inst. Cert. Planners, Res. Officers Assn., Mensa. Author: (under pen name Stanley Roberts) Winning Blackjack, 1971; How to Win at Weekend Blackjack, 1973. Office: 1018 N Cole Ave Hollywood CA 90038

SLUSSER, EUGENE ALVIN, electronics mfg. co. exec.; b. Denver, Mar. 13, 1922; s. Jesse Alvin and Grace (Carter) S.; B.S. in Physics, U. Denver, 1947; m. Anne L. Longley, Oct. 2, 1943; children—Robert, Jon, Carolyn. Staff mem. Mass. Inst. Tech. Radiation Lab., Cambridge, 1942-45; project engr. Heiland Research

Co., Denver, 1945-47; cons. Gen. Telephone System, N.Y.C., 1947-51; project engr. Airborne Inst. Lab., Mineola, N.Y., 1951-53; v.p. N.E. Electronics Corp., Concord, N.H., 1953-58; pres. Aerotronic Assos., Inc., Contoocook, N.H., 1958—; pres. N.H. Automatic Equipment Corp., Concord, 1962—; chmn., chief exec. officer Aerotronic West, Inc., Contoocook, 1976—; dir. Indianhead Nat. Bank, Concord. Chmn., Hopkinton (N.H.) Water Bd., 1962-69, Hopkinton Planning Bd., 1971-77, Hopkinton Precinct Bd. Adjustment, 1977. Registered profl. engr., N.H. Mem. Aircraft Owners and Pilots Assn. Mason (32 deg.). Patentee electronics field. Home: RFD 1 Concord NH 03301 Office: Riverside Dr Contoocook NH 03229

SLUSSER, ROBERT WYMAN, aerospace co. exec.; b. Mineola, N.Y., May 10, 1938; s. John Leonard and Margaret McKenzie (Wyman) S.; B.S., Mass. Inst. Tech., 1960; M.B.A., U. Pa., 1962; m. Linda Killeas, Aug. 3, 1968; children—Jonathan, Adam, Robert, Patricia. Asso. adminstr.'s staff NASA Hdqrs., Washington, 1962-65; adminstr. mktg. and planning dept., space labs. Northrop Corp., Hawthorne, Calif., 1965-67, mgr. bus. and fin. Warnecke Electron Tubes Co. div., Chgo., 1968-71, controller Cobra program Aircraft div., Hawthorne, 1971-72, mgr. bus. adminstrn. YF-17 Program, 1972-75, mgr. adminstrn. F-18/Cobra programs, also mgr. F-18 Design to cost program, 1975-78, mgr. adminstrn. F-18L program, 1978-79, mgr. engring. adminstrn., 1980—. Grumman Aircraft Engring. scholar, 1956-60. Mem. AIAA. Home: 27604 Alvesta Pl San Pedro CA 90732 Office: 3901 W Broadway Hawthorne CA 90250

SLUSSER, WILLIAM PETER, investment banker; b. Oakland, Calif., June 20, 1929; s. Eugene and Thelma (Donovan) S.; B.A. cum laude, Stanford, 1951; M.B.A., Harvard, 1953; m. Joanne Eleanor Briggs, June 20, 1953; children—Kathleen E., Martin E., Wendelin M., Caroline E., Sarah A. Mgr. spl. situations dept. Dean Witter & Co., N.Y.C., 1955-60; mgr. indsl. dept. Shields Model Roland Securities Inc., 1960-61, partner, sr. v.p. in charge corporate finance dept., 1961-75, also dir, mem. exec. com.; co-mgr. investment banking div., sr. v.p. Paine Webber, Inc., 1975-80; mng. dir. Blyth Eastman Paine Webber, Inc., N.Y.C., 1980—; underwriter or financial cons. Square D. Co., Times Mirror Co., Ashland Oil, Inc., Niagara Frontier Services, Inc., TRW, Inc., SCA Services, Inc., Downey Savs. & Loan, Golden West Fin. Corp., Booth Newspapers, Inc., Holly Hill Lumber Co., Knudsen Corp., States Marine Corp., Superior Coach Corp., Santee Portland Cement Co., Grow Chem. Corp., Dr. Pepper Co. of So. Calif., Gemini Computer Systems, London, Eng., VNU Inc., Haarlem, Netherlands, Reading & Bates Offshore Drilling Co., Houghton Mifflin Co., Pic n Pay Stores; founder original Stockholder Asso. Mortgage Cos. subsidiary First Pa. Corp. Lectr. to profl. assns. Trustee Chol Chol Found.; mem. bd. fin. advisors Columbia U. Bus. Sch. Served to 1st lt. USAF, 1953-55. Mem. Investment Assn. N.Y., Soc. Calif. Pioneers, Alpha Delta Phi (exec. council 1956-62, treas. 1961). Clubs: Knickerbocker, Downtown, Stanford Assos., Harvard (N.Y.C.); Lawrence Beach, Stanford of N.Y. Author numerous articles. Home: 901 Lexington Ave New York NY 10029 also Slusser Ranch Windsor CA 95492 Office: 1221 Ave of Americas New York NY 10020

SMALE, JOHN GRAY, diversified co. exec.; b. Listowel, Ont., Can., Aug. 1, 1927; s. Peter John and Vera Gladys (Gray) S.; B.S. in Bus., Miami U., Oxford, Ohio, 1949, LL.D., 1979; LL.D., Kenyon Coll., 1974; m. Phyllis Anne Weaver, Sept. 2, 1950; children—John Gray, Catherine Anne Smale Caldemeyer, Lisa Beth, Peter McKee. With Vick Chem. Co., 1949-50, Bio-Research, Inc., 1951; with Procter & Gamble Co., Cin., 1952—, pres., 1974—, also dir.; dir. Eastman Kodak Co. Chmn. bd. trustees Kenyon Coll.; mem. Council for Fin. Aid to Edn.; bd. dirs. Cin. Area chpt. ARC, United Negro Coll. Fund, Cin. Mus. Assn. Served with USNR, 1945-46. Mem. Grocery Mfrs. Am. Clubs: Comml., Commonwealth, Cin. Country, Queen City (Cin.). Office: PO Box 599 Cincinnati OH 45201

SMALL, ALBERT HARRISON, engring. corp. exec.; b. Washington, Oct. 15, 1925; s. Albert and Lillian S.; B.Ch.E., U. Va., 1946; student George Washington U. Law Sch., 1947-48, Am. U. Grad. Sch. Bus. Adminstrn., 1949-51; m. Shirley Schwalb, Sept. 14, 1952; children—Susan Carol, Albert H., James H. Founder, So. Engring. Corp., Washington, 1952—, pres., chief exec. officer, 1968—. Served with USNR, 1943-46. Mem. Nat. Assn. Real Estate Bds., Nat. Assn. Home Builders, Urban Land Inst. Republican. Jewish. Clubs: Army-Navy, Internat. Home: 7116 Glenbrook Rd Bethesda MD 20014 Office: 1025 Connecticut Ave NW Suite 307 Washington DC 20036

SMALL, FRANK HERBERT, banker; b. Washington, Aug. 4, 1946; s. Frank Herbert and Kathleen Elizabeth (Ploor) S.; B.A., U. Md., 1970; m. Dora Jean King, Oct. 23, 1973; children—Louisa, Debra, Wayne, Jeff. With Clinton Bank (Md.), 1970-72, asst. v.p., 1971-72; with Equitable Trust Co., Clinton, Md., 1972—, v.p., area supr. Mem. Prince Georges County C. of C. Office: 8901 Woodyard Rd Clinton MD 20735

SMALL, RICHARD DONALD, travel co. exec.; b. West Orange, N.J., May 24, 1929; s. Joseph George and Elizabeth (McGarry) S.; A.B. cum laude, U. Notre Dame, 1951; m. Arlene P. Small; children—Colleen P., Richard Donald, Joseph W., Mark G., Brian P. With Union-Camp Corp., N.Y.C., Chgo., 1952-62; pres. Alumni Holidays, Inc., Studentaire Travel, Inc., Chgo., 1962—, AHI Internat. Corp., Chgo. Mem. Chgo. Assn. Commerce and Industry (edn., visitors bur., transp. coms.). Club: University (Chgo.). Home: 17 Park Ln Park Ridge IL 60068 also 1111 Crandon Blvd Apt B-905 Key Biscayne FL 33149 Office: First Nat Bank Bldg 701 Lee St Des Plaines IL 60016

SMALLEY, ARTHUR LOUIS, JR., engring. and constrn. co. exec.; b. Houston, Jan. 25, 1921; s. Arthur I. and Ebby (Curry) S.; B.S. in Chem. Engring., U. Tex., Austin, 1942; m. Ruth Evelyn Britton, Mar. 18, 1946; children—Arthur Louis III, Tom Edward. Dir. engring. Celanese Chem. Co., Houston, 1964-72; mktg. exec. Fish Engring. Co., Houston, 1972-74; pres. Matthew Hall & Co., Inc., Houston, 1974—; dir. S.A. Scott & Co., Denver, Matthew Hall Internat. Ltd., London. Recipient Silver Beaver award Boy Scouts Am., 1963; registered profl. engr., Tex. Mem. Am. Inst. Chem. Engrs., Am. Petroleum Inst., Petroleum Club Houston. Republican. Episcopalian. Clubs: Rotary, Chemists of N.Y., Oriental (London), Houston. Home: 438 Hunterwood Dr Houston TX 77024 Office: 1200 Milam St #3428 Houston TX 77002

SMART, JACKSON WYMAN, JR., banker; b. Chgo., Aug. 27, 1930; s. Jackson Wyman and Dorothy (Brynes) S.; B.B.A., U. Mich., 1952; M.B.A., Harvard U., 1954; m. Suzanne Tobey, July 6, 1957; children—Jackson Wyman III, Alison Tobey. Asst. v.p. 1st Nat. Bank Chgo., 1956-64; exec. v.p. comml. banking Bank of Commonwealth, Detroit, 1964-69; pres., dir. MSP Industries Corp. (subs. W.R. Grace & Co. 1972), Center Line, Mich., 1969-71, pres., chief exec. officer, 1971-75; chmn., pres., treas., dir. The Delos Internat. Group, Inc. subs. Automatic Data Processing Inc., Princeton, N.J., 1975-77; pres., chief exec. officer, dir. Central Nat. Bank, Chgo., 1977—, chmn., 1978—; chmn. fin. com., dir. Fed. Express Corp., Memphis, 1977—; dir. Thomas Industries, Inc., Louisville, Gulf Resources & Chem. Corp., Houston, John Blair & Co., N.Y.C. Bd. dirs. Evanston (Ill.) Hosp. Served to 1st lt. AUS, 1954-56. Mem. Young Presidents Orgn., Assn. Res. City Bankers, Psi Upsilon. Republican. Presbyterian. Clubs: Birmingham (Mich.) Athletic; Economic, University, Hundred of Cook County, Mid-Day, Chicago (Chgo.); Indian Hill (Winnetka); Coral Beach and Tennis (Bermuda). Office: 120 S LaSalle St Chicago IL 60603

SMART, L(OUIS) EDWIN, business exec.; b. Columbus, Ohio, Nov. 17, 1923; s. Louis Edwin and Esther (Guthery) S.; A.B. magna cum laude, Harvard U., 1947, J.D. magna cum laude, 1949; m. Virginia Alice Knouff, Mar. 1, 1944 (div. 1958); children—Cynthia Stephanie, Douglas Edwin; m. 2d, Jeanie Alberta Milone, Aug. 29, 1964; 1 son, Dana Gregory Milone. Admitted to N.Y. bar, 1950; asso. firm Hughes, Hubbard, & Ewing, N.Y.C., 1949-56; partner firm Hughes, Hubbard, & Reed, N.Y.C., 1957-64; pres. Bendix Internat., N.Y.C., 1964-67; dir. Bendix Corp. and fgn. subsidiaries, 1964-67; sr. v.p. external affairs Trans World Airlines, Inc., 1967-71, dir. exec., fin. coms., 1967—, sr. v.p. corporate affairs, 1971-75, vice chmn., 1976, chmn. bd., chief exec. officer, 1977-78, chmn. bd., 1979—; chmn. bd., pres., chief exec. officer Trans World Corp., 1978—; chmn. exec. com., dir. Hilton Internat. Co., 1967—, Canteen Corp., 1973—, Spartan Food Systems, Inc., 1979; chmn. bd. Hilton Internat. Co., 1980—; dir. ACF Industries, Inc., So. Natural Gas Co., So. Natural Resources, Inc., Continental Corp.; exec. com. Internat. Air Transport Assn.; BIPAC, 1977—; trustee Com. for Econ. Devel., 1977—, Conf. Bd., 1977—. Served to lt. USNR, 1943-46. Mem. Am. Bar Assn., N.Y. County Lawyers Assn., Am. Soc. Travel Agts., Econ. Club N.Y., Phi Beta Kappa, Sigma Alpha Epsilon. Clubs: Presidents, Sky (N.Y.C.). Home: 535 E 86th St New York NY 10028 also Coakley Bay St Croix VI 00820 Office: 605 3d Ave New York NY 10158

SMART, STEPHEN BRUCE, JR., indsl. exec.; b. N.Y.C., Feb. 7, 1923; s. Stephen Bruce and Beatrice (Cobb) S.; student Milton Acad.; A.B. cum laude, Harvard, 1945; M.S., Mass. Inst. Tech., 1947; m. Edith Minturn Merrill, Sept. 10, 1949; children—Edith M. Smart Moore, William Candler, Charlotte M. Smart Rogan, Priscilla. Sales engr. Permutit Co., N.Y., 1947-51; various sales, gen. mgmt. positions Continental Group, Inc. (formerly Continental Can Co.), N.Y.C., 1953—, v.p. Central metal div., 1962-65, v.p. marketing and corporate planning, 1965-67, v.p., asst. gen. mgr. paper operations, 1967-69, group v.p. paper operations, 1969-71, exec. v.p. paper operations, 1971-73, vice chmn. bd., 1973-75, pres., 1975-80, chief exec. officer, 1980—, chmn., 1981—; dir. Rexnord Inc., Chase Manhattan Corp., Chase Manhattan Bank, Life Ins. Co. Va., Celanese Corp. Vice-chmn. bd. trustees Smith Coll.; mem. adv. bd. Columbia U. Sch. Bus. Served to 1st lt. AUS, 1943-46, C.E., 1951-53. Mem. Council Fgn. Relations, Conf. Bd., Sigma Xi. Clubs: Country of Fairfield (Conn.); Pequot Yacht; Blind Brook, River (N.Y.C.); Clove Valley Rod and Gun. Office: care Continental Group Inc 633 3d Ave New York NY 10017

SMEDVIG, MAGNE, real estate developer; b. Stavanger, Norway, Feb. 24, 1920; s. Erling and Henny (Ness) S.; student Seattle U., 1945-49, U. Minn., 1951; postgrad. So. Meth. U., 1959; m. Esther W. Tralnes, Oct. 24, 1942; children—Erling S., Mark S. Suburban agt. Seattle Post-Intelligencer, 1934-42; chief exec. officer Internat. Sons of Norway, Mpls., 1949-75; real estate developer, 1975—. Past bd. dirs., exec. com. Nat. Fraternal Congress Am.; founder S/N Found. Served with USAAF, 1942-45; ETO. Decorated by King Olav V Norway for promotion of cultural relations and arts between U.S., Can. and Norway, 1966. Home: 7200 Wooddale Ave Edina MN 55435 Office: 3910 W 50th St Edina MN 55424

SMELLER, PAUL JOSEPH, ins. co. exec.; b. Barberton, Ohio, Aug. 31, 1941; s. Lloyd F. and Magdalene (Juszli) S.; B.A., Purdue U., 1964; m. Ellen Weidner, Feb. 2, 1963; children—Carl Patrick, Christina Marie, Matthew Christopher Michael. Agt., sales mgr. Met. Life Ins. Co., Akron, Ohio, 1964-70; br. mgr. Montgomery Ward Life Ins. Co., Akron, 1970-71; sales mgr. Union Central Life Ins. Co., Akron, 1971-72, Met. Life Ins., 1972-76; gen. agt. Am. United Life Ins. Co., Akron, 1976-80, Central Res. Life, Akron, 1978-80, Westfield Life, Akron, 1978-80; asst. v.p., mgr. life mktg. Westfield Life Ins. Co., Westfield Center, Ohio, 1980—; instr. bus. ins. Life Underwriters Tng. Council, 1972—; instr. Am. Coll., Bryn Mawr, Pa. and Akron. Treas., Great Trails council Boy Scouts Am., 1972-74; basketball coach Cath Youth Orgn., 1965—. C.L.U. Mem. Nat. Assn. Life Underwriters (com. chmn., 7 nat. quality awards), Am. Soc. C.L.U.'s (com. chmn., v.p. 1980), Gen. Agts. and Mgrs. Assn., Akron Estate Planning Council, Phi Sigma Kappa. Roman Catholic. Home: 383 Allen Dr Wadsworth OH 44281 Office: 341 White Pond Dr Akron OH 44320 also 1 West Park Circle Westfield Center OH 44251

SMETTER, MARTIN, plastics mfg. co. exec.; b. Bklyn., Mar. 2, 1941; s. Fred and Cele (Rosenthal) S.; M.B.A., Pepperdine U., 1972; m. Mary O'Neill, Jan. 18, 1970; 1 son, Michael Anthony. Sales rep. Mohawk Data Scis., Los Angeles, 1971-73; pres. Smetter Real Estate Co., Santa Monica, Calif., 1973-75, Western Case Inc., Tustin, Calif., 1978—; dir. corp. devel. Tax Corp. Am., Burbank, Calif., 1975-78. Served with USN, 1959-64. Mem. Am. Mgmt. Assn. Home: 1507 Mariners Dr Newport Beach CA 92660 Office: 14351 Chambers Rd Tustin CA 92680

SMILES, RONALD, steel fabrication co. exec.; b. Sunderland, Eng., June 15, 1933; s. Andrew and Margaret (Turns) S.; came to U.S., 1957, naturalized, 1974; B.A., U. Pa., 1968; B.S., Phila. Coll. Textiles and Sci., 1969; M.A., Calif. Western U., 1975, Ph.D., 1977; m. Evelyn Lorraine Webster, Apr. 12, 1959; children—Tracy Lynn, Scott Webster, Wendy Louise. Vice pres. Liquid Dynamics Corp., Southampton, Pa., 1968-71; pres., gen. mgr. Internat. Election Systems Corp., Burlington, N.J., 1971-76; plant mgr. Rack Engring. Co., Connellsville, Pa., 1977-80; v.p. Ft. Worth (Tex.) Houdaille, 1980—. Mem. Burlington County (N.J.) Selective Service Bd., 1974-76. Served with Royal Arty., 1951-53. Recipient Class of 1954 Adminstrv. award Wharton Sch., U. Pa. Mem. Greater Connellsville C. of C. (v.p. 1979-80), Night Watch Honor Soc., Sigma Kappa Phi, Alpha Delta Epsilon (award 1968). Club: Rotary Internat. Author: Impact on Legislation of Competition in the Voting Machine Industry, 1978. Home: 4716 Brandingshire Pl Fort Worth TX 76133 Office: Ft Worth Houdaille Fort Worth TX 76101

SMILEY, DONALD B(URDETTE), lawyer; b. Albany, Ill., Apr. 6, 1915; s. Ralph and Etta (Stafford) S.; B.A., Augustana Coll., 1936; J.D., Northwestern U., 1940; m. Dick Cutter, Apr. 10, 1942; children—Margot (Mrs. Alex Humphrey), Sandra (Mrs. George Weiksner), Stafford, Daryl. Admitted to N.Y. bar, 1940, U.S. Supreme Ct. bar, 1945; asso. firm Breed, Abbott & Morgan, N.Y.C., 1940-42; with R.H. Macy & Co., Inc., N.Y.C., 1945—, became sec. and gen. atty., 1953, v.p., treas., 1956-65, vice chmn., treas., 1965-69, chmn., 1969—, also chief exec. officer, dir.; dir. Texasgulf, Inc., Ralston Purina Co., Irving Bank Corp., RCA Corp., NBC, Met. Life Ins. Co., Fidelity Union Bancorp., U.S. Steel Corp., N.Y. Stock Exchange. Trustee Com. for Econ. Devel. Served as lt. USNR, World War II. Mem. Bar Assn. City N.Y., Order of Coif. Clubs: Union League, University (N.Y.C.); Blind Brook (ArmonK, N.Y.); Indian Harbor Yacht, Round Hill (Greenwich, Conn.). Home: 1 Putnam Hill Greenwich CT 06830 Office: 151 W 34th St New York NY 10001

SMILLIE, WILLIAM STONE, county utility exec.; b. Monrovia, Calif., Mar. 22, 1948; s. Roy L. and Bettie L. S.; A.A. in Bus. Adminstrn., Victor Valley Jr. Coll., 1974; children—William Stone, Shelley Ann. Engring. trainee Desert Engring. Co., Apple Valley, Calif., 1966-72; maintenance supr. Boise Cascade Co., Apple Valley, 1972-74; water facilities mgr. County San Bernardino (Calif.), 1974—. Vice pres. Hesperia (Calif.) Mobile Estates, 1974, pres., mem. governing bd., 1976, men. governing com., 1978-79. Cert. water treatment operator, cert. waste water treatment operator, Calif. Mem. Am. Water Works Assn. (cert. water distbn. operator), Nat. Water Well Assn., Calif. Water Pollution Control Assn., Nat. Rifle Assn. (life). Republican. Home: PO Box 1148 Apple Valley CA 92307 Office: 13325 Spring Valley Pkwy Victorville CA 92392

SMILOW, JOEL EMANUEL, consumer package goods co. exec.; b. Washington, Apr. 29, 1933; s. Leo and Anna (Kass) S.; B.A., Yale, 1954; M.B.A., Harvard, 1958; m. Joan Helene Lipman, June 13, 1954; children—Richard James, William Scott, Susan Deborah. Brand mgr. Procter & Gamble Co., Cin., 1958-65; exec. v.p., dir. Glendinning Cos., Inc., Westport, Conn., 1965-69; pres., chief exec. officer Internat. Playtex Inc., Stamford, Conn., 1969—; dir. Recreation Products Retailing Inc., Reeves Communications, Inc. Chmn., Westport-Weston-Wilton United Jewish Appeal Campaign, 1969; bd. dirs. Madison Sq. Boys Club; adv. bd. Big Bros./Big Sisters Am.; mem. 1954 class council Yale, chmn. campaign industry group, 1975-76; active Am. Cancer Soc. Served to lt. (j.g.) USNR, 1954-56. Named Man of Yr., Conn. Digestive Disease Soc., 1974. Mem. Young Presidents Orgn. (treas. chpt. 1974-75), Assn. Yale Alumni (bd. govs., com. chmn.). Jewish (past trustee temple). Clubs: Harvard Bus. Sch. (dir.), Yale (N.Y.C.); Aspetuck Valley Country (Weston, Conn.); 29; Yale of Eastern Fairfield County (dir.). Home: 185 North Ave Westport CT 06880 Office: 700 Fairfield Ave Stamford CT 06902

SMITH, ADELL EDDIE, mgmt. tng. cons. co. exec.; b. Memphis, May 14, 1945; s. Dan Edward and Annie Bell (Slayton) S.; B.A. in Psychology, U. Mo., 1974; m. Bertha Jean Newman, Sept. 8, 1963; 1 dau., Toni Michele. Teaching asst. U. Mo., St. Louis, 1970-74; mgmt. tng. supr. APC Skills Co., Palm Beach, Fla., 1975-77; pres. A. Edward Smith and Assos., St. Louis, 1977—; cons. on upward mobility tng. for women and minorities to bus. and industry, 1977—. Pres. consumer products and services Northwoods-1st Ward Civic Assn., 1980; chmn. edn. and tng. com. Minority Bus. Forum Assn., 1980, pres., 1981; treas. Youth Employment Coalition; mem. St. Louis EEO Group. Served with USAF, 1963-67. Recipient Outstanding Community Service award St. Louis Agy. on Tng. and Employment, 1980, St. Louis Leadership Program Participant award Danforth Found., 1980. Mem. Am. Soc. for Tng. and Devel., Ind. Cons. Am., Am. Inst. Profl. Cons., Am. Entrepreneurs Assn., Community C. of C., St. Louis Black Leadership Roundtable, Christian Athletic Assn. (pres.). Home: 4435 Crestland Dr Saint Louis MO 63121 Office: 3466 Bridgeland Dr Bridgeton MO 63044

SMITH, ALBERT EUGENE, banker; b. Camden, N.J., May 20, 1945; s. Albert Harvey and Marguerite Eleanor (Canfield) S.; B.S., Rutgers U., 1972; m. Meral Kelleher, July 21, 1978. Adminstrv. asst. Bank of N.J., Camden, 1965-71; comptroller, v.p., sr. v.p., treas. Fidelity Bank & Trust Co. of N.J., Pennsauken, 1971—; partner Lutz, Smith & Co., C.P.A.'s, Marlton, N.J., 1973—. Served with USMCR, 1965-71. C.P.A., N.J. Mem. Nat. Assn. Accountants, Am. Soc. C.P.A.'s, N.J. Soc. C.P.A.'s, Am. Inst. Banking, Bank Adminstrn. Inst. Phila., Bank Adminstrn. Inst. South Jersey. Mason. Home: 104 Covered Bridge Rd Cherry Hill NJ 08034 Office: 4900 Route 70 Pennsauken NJ 08105

SMITH, ALEXANDER FORBES, engring. and cons. co. exec.; b. Reading, Pa., Feb. 7, 1929; s. Alexander Forbes and Ethyl Mohn (Wahl) S.; B.S.M.E., Lehigh U., 1950, M.S.M.E., 1951; m. Mary Louise Taylor, Dec. 29, 1970; children—Sandra, Robin, Douglas, Steven. Marine engr. U.S. Naval Boiler and Turbine Lab., Phila., 1951-54; mech. engr. Gilbert Assos., Inc., Reading, Pa., 1955-62, asst. to chief engr., 1962-68, project mgr., 1963-68, v.p.-ops., 1968-70, v.p. and gen. mgr., 1970-73, exec. v.p., 1973-77, group v.p. and chief operating officer, 1977-78, pres. and chief operating officer, 1979, pres., chief exec. officer, 1980—; pres. Commonwealth Assos., Inc.; chmn. bd. GAI-Tronics, Inc.; dir. Gilbert/Commonwealth Cos. Past chmn. adv. bd. Berks campus Pa. State U.; past chmn. Berks County Bd. Assistance; trustee YMCA Reading and Berks County. Mem. C. of C. Reading and Berks County (past dir.), ASME, Pa. Soc. Profl. Engrs. Republican. Episcopalian. Patentee condenser steam space divider; thermometer well for pipes. Home: Cricket Springs Box 308 Geigertown PA 19523 Office: PO Box 1498 Reading PA 19603

SMITH, ARLYN GENE, mgmt. cons.; b. Rozel, Kans., Feb. 12, 1926; s. Glee Sidney and Bernice Mildred (Augustine) S.; B.S., U. Kans., 1949; m. Jacqueline Jane Houdyshell, Mar. 25, 1948; children—Arlyn G., Dana Gaye and Denise Kaye (twins). Editor, Larned Chronoscope, Larned, Kans., 1949-50; partner, chief operating officer cattle and farming operation, Kans., 1950-68; mgmt. cons., Larned, 1968—; dir. Glee Smith Cattle Co., Inc., 1970—. Mem. Kans. Com. on Govtl. Ethics, 1971-73; mem. Rozel (Kans.) City Council, 1950's; dist. fin. chmn. Boy Scouts Am., 1950's; council fin. chmn. Girl Scouts U.S.A., 1960's; mem. adv. council Kans. Geol. Survey; vice chmn. Burning Bush Soc. of Kans. Sch. Religion; mem. Menninger Found.; trustee Jordan Meml. Library; mem. exec. bd. Republican Central Com., Larned; mem. Pima County Rep. Com. Served with USNR, 1943-46, 51-53. Mem. Kans. Livestock Assn., Am. Nat. Cattlemen's Assn., Tucson Execs. Assn., Smithsonian Assos., Larned C. of C. (dir. 1969-71), Am. Legion (comdr. 1966-67), V.F.W., Kans. C. of C. (indsl. research and devel. council), Tucson C. of C. (legis. action com.), Alpha Delta Sigma, Delta Tau Delta. Presbyterian. Clubs: Lions (charter pres.), Masons, Rotary (pres. 1967-68). Author: Agriculture: The Dynamic Years Ahead, contbr. articles in field to profl. jours., newspapers. Home: 5697 N Camino del Sol Tucson AZ 85718 Office: 5055 E Broadway Suite C-214 Tucson AZ 85711

SMITH, ARTHUR HENRY, business cons.; b. Milw., Mar. 11, 1912; s. Charles Arthur and Margaret (Duckart) S.; B.A., U. Wis., 1936; grad. Advanced Mgmt. Program Harvard, 1952; m. Isabelle Marie Skarolid, June 1, 1940; children—Gary Arthur, Virginia Isabelle, Judy Anne. With Gen. Mills, Inc., 1936-60, dir. mgmt. analysis, 1954-60; v.p., dir. Midwest Tech. Devel. Corp., Mpls., 1960-63; pres., dir. Turbomatic, Inc., Mpls., 1962-63; controller Hunt Foods & Industries, Inc., dir. finance Hunt-Wesson foods div., 1963-65; mgmt. cons. Price Waterhouse & Co., 1965-66; v.p., controller Libby, McNeill & Libby, 1966-67; financial v.p., treas., dir. Internat. Industries, Inc., 1967-72; pres. A. Smith & Assos., bus. cons., 1972—; fin. v.p. Herlihy Mgmt. Co., 1977-78. Pres., Asso. Found., Inc., 1977-78. C.P.A., Wis. Mem. Am. Inst. C.P.A.'s, Calif., Minn. socs. C.P.A.'s, Nat. Assn. Accountants (past pres. Mpls. chpt., past nat. dir. and v.p.), Harvard Bus. Sch. Assn. (past mem. nat. exec. council), Stuart Cameron McLeod Soc. (past nat. treas.), Phi Beta Kappa. Contbr. articles to profl. jours. Home: 3735 Argonaut Ave Rocklin CA 95677

SMITH, BEATRICE MYRTLE WARNER, bus. exec.; b. Danbury, Conn., Oct. 14, 1921; d. Llewellyn Steven and Minnie Edna (Benham) Warner; B.S., Western Conn. State Coll., 1943; M.B.A., Pepperdine U., 1976; m. T. Leon Smith, July 29, 1943; children—Patricia Ann Smith Johnson, Thomas Leon. Advt. mgr. Sears Roebuck & Co., Danbury, 1953-57; engring. asso. research Rocketdyne Corp., Canoga Park, Calif., 1958-67; quality assurance engr. Xerox Corp., Hayward, Calif., 1967—; dir. Sabrina Creative Industries, Inc., Office Furniture Restoring, Inc. Recipient Suggestion award Rocketdyne, 1964. Mem. Am. Soc. Quality Control, Am. Mgmt. Assn., Xerox-Diablo Mgmt. Assn. (v.p., dir.). Republican. Roman Catholic. Clubs: Met. Yacht, Jack London Sq. (Oakland, Calif.). Home: 937 New England Village Dr Hayward CA 94544 Office: 26460 Corporate Ave Hayward CA 94545

SMITH, BERNARD JOSEPH, cons. engr.; b. Liverpool, Eng., Aug. 29, 1900; s. Thomas Joseph and Sarah Anne (Crum) S.; B.Engring. with honors, U. Liverpool, 1923, M.Engring., 1926; m. Julia Susan Connolly, June 4, 1929; children—Bernard Joseph Connolly, Sarah Anne Kathleen (Mrs. C.E. Schaffer), Maureen Sheila (Mrs. William J. Gallagher, Jr.), Una Eileen, Aislin Therese Crum (Mrs. William McMahon Nickey, Jr.), Thomas Eugene Malachy, Joan Pauline (Mrs. Edwin H. McClintock), John Phillip Michael. Came to U.S., 1912, naturalized, 1930. Pvt. tutor math., 1923-24; resident engr. Underpinning & Found. Co., N.Y.C., Phila., 1924; insp., underground conduit engr. N.Y. & N.J. Telephone Co. and Ohio Bell Telephone Co., 1924-26; asst. engr. Alexander Potter, cons. engr., 1926-30; pvt. research in hydrology and hydraulics, 1930; design engr. Humble Oil & Refining Co., 1930-32; city engr. Baytown, Tex., 1931-33, city mgr., 1932-33, cons. engr., 1931-34; engr. insp. PWA, Ft. Worth, 1934-35, engr. examiner, 1935-37; pvt. cons. engr., 1937-38; dir. research and personnel City Ft. Worth, 1938-41; lectr. personnel adminstrn., town culture, nat. def. Tex. Christian U., 1940-43; state planning engr. and acting state dir. Tex. Pub. Work Res., 1941-42; asst. regional rep., regional economist Nat. Housing Agy., Dallas, 1942-47; lectr. econs., bus. adminstrn. and engring. So. Meth. U., 1947-53; cons. engr., Dallas, 1947—; chief San Francisco Bay devel. C.E., San Francisco dist., 1957-66; spl. cons. San Francisco Bay Conservation and Devel. Commn., 1966-67; water commr. Santa Cruz County, Calif. Registered profl. engr., Tex., N.J.; registered engr., Calif., N.J., Tex. Fellow ASCE; mem. San Francisco Irish Lit. and Hist. Soc. (pres. 1961-63), Am. Waterworks Assn., Am. Econ. Assn., Soc. Evolutionary Econs., History of Econs. Soc., Tex. Soc. Profl. Engrs., County Louth Archaeol. Soc., Internat. Solar Energy Soc. Mem. Third Order St. Francis. Clubs: Serra (Dallas); Commonwealth of Calif. Author: Town Building, 1939; El Paso Housing Market, 1945; Elements of Housing Marketing Analysis, 1945; The International Scene, 1946; Review and Analysis of EIR for Peripheral Canal, California, 1973. Contbr. articles to U.S., fgn. mags., jours. Address: PO Box 663 Aptos CA 95003

SMITH, BERNARD JOSEPH CONNOLLY, civil engr.; b. Elizabeth, N.J., Mar. 11, 1930; s. Bernard Joseph and Julia Susan (Connolly) S.; B.S., U. Notre Dame, 1951; B.S.C.E., Tex. A. and M. U., 1957; M.B.A., U. Calif. at Berkeley, 1976; m. Margaret Josephine Kerley, Dec. 20, 1971; children—Julia Susan Alice, Teresa Mary Josephine, Anne Marie Kathleen. Civil-hydraulic engr. U.S. Army Corps Engrs., San Francisco, St. Paul, Minn., Kansas City, Mo., Sacramento, 1957-65; civil engr. Fed. Energy Regulatory Commn., San Francisco, 1965—. Served with AUS, 1952-54. Registered Profl. Engr., Calif., Mo. Mem. Am. Soc. Civil Engrs., Am. Economic Assn., Res. Officers Assn. (pres. Calif. chpt. 90, 1973), Catholic Alumni Assn. San Francisco (pres. 1968). Club: Commonwealth of Calif. Home: 247 28th Ave San Francisco CA 94121 Office: 333 Market St San Francisco CA 94105

SMITH, BETTYE L. SEBREE, bus. coll. pres.; b. Owensmouth, Calif., Feb. 25, 1926; d. Roy Albert and Thelma Hattie (Alexander) Sebree; student Brigham Young U., 1944-45, Links Sch. Bus., Boise, Idaho, 1946, Nampa (Idaho) Bus. Coll. 1956; B.A., Alaska Meth. U., 1972; children—Jerye Lou, Marie Louise. Office mgr. Intermountain Surg. Supply Co., Boise, 1945-48; sec., payroll, cost accountant Morrison-Knudsen Co., Fairbanks, Alaska, Boise, 1948-52; payroll, cost accountant Lytle, Green, Birch Contractors, Fairbanks, 1952-54; owner Fairbanks Secretarial Sch., 1957-58, Anchorage Secretarial Sch., 1958-59; pres. Alaska Bus. Coll., Inc., Anchorage, 1959—; owner City Employment Center, Anchorage, 1962-68, Alaska Employment Agy., 1970-72; pres. Arctic Tech. Industries, 1972-75; asso. Manpower, Inc., Anchorage, 1969-72, Kavir, Inc., Sebree, Inc.; franchise holder Western Girl, Inc., 1962-68, Speedwriting Shorthand, 1957-77, Nancy Taylor Finishing Sch., 1960-77, Weaver Sch. Real Estate, 1959-72, ITT-Nat. Data Processing, 1968-77, Taylor Airline Careers, 1968-77, Taylor Hotel-Motel Mgmt., 1972-77 (all Anchorage); pres. Horizons Unltd. Mem. Manpower Planning Council; mem. Anchorage Parking and Traffic Commn., 1972—; bd. dirs. Jr. Achievement; mem. instl. authorization com. Alaska Postsecondary Commn. Cert. adminstrv. mgr., accredited personnel diplomate. Mem. Am. Soc. Personnel Adminstrn., Anchorage C. of C., Nat. Secs. Assn. (chpt. v.p. 1962, seminar chmn. 1961, 67, 73-77), Credit Women Internat., Internat. Platform Assn. Office: 5159 Old Seward Hwy Anchorage AK 99503

SMITH, BRUCE, communications exec.; b. Chgo., May 21, 1942; s. James Bruce and Jane (Ericsson) S.; B.A. in Journalism, U. Calif. at Los Angeles, 1962. Editor, Chgo. FM Guide, 1962-64; feature editor Instns., Chgo., 1964-65; editor Food Service Marketing, Madison, Wis., 1966-73, v.p. editorial devel., Chgo., 1973, editorial dir. Food Service Chain Exec., Food Service Distbn. News, 1974—; editor, pub. Mktg. Decisions for the Food Service Industry, 1976-78; pres. Bruce Smith Public Relations/Mktg. Communications, 1978—; mktg. communications cons. to food and equipment cos.; pres. Internat. Food Editorial Council, 1971—. Recipient Editorial award Nat. Fisheries Inst., 1967, 68, Editorial award Nat. Assn. Coll. and Univ. Food Service Dirs., 1972. Mem. Internat. Food Service Mfrs. Assn., Internat. Wine and Food Soc., Soc. for Advancement Foodservice Research, Newberry Library Assos., English Speaking Union, Art Inst., Field Museum Natural History, Chgo. Press Club. Clubs: Caxton, Whitehall (Chgo.). Author: A Directory of Systems Capability, 1972. Contbr. articles to profl. jours. Home: 205 W Eugenie Chicago IL 60614

SMITH, BRUCE HENRY, accountant, co. exec.; b. Sydney, Australia, Aug. 3, 1925; s. Basil Oswald and Ruth (Symonds) S.; Chartered Accountant, Inst. Chartered Accountants, 1949; m. Olive Hazel Green, Sept. 23, 1949; children—Timothy Peter, Adrienne Denise. Co-founder, B.O. Smith & Son, Sydney, 1955, sr. partner, 1961—; chmn. bd. Cemac Associated Ltd., 1956—, United Australian Industries Ltd., 1960-63, Tangible Securities Ltd., 1965-70, Vokes Australia Pty. Ltd., 1965-71, Project Devel. Corp. Ltd., 1966-69, Project Mining Corp. Ltd., 1968-69, Stott Datagraphics Ltd., 1969-72, Forest Devels. Australia Ltd., 1969-72, MCN Australasia Pty. Ltd., 1972—, Instep Pty. Ltd., 1972-76, Suncoast Group Cos., 1972—, Smith's Gen. Contracting Pty. Ltd., 1972—, Epstein & Co. Ltd., 1973—, Perkins Shipping & Mining Corp. Pty. Ltd., 1973-79, Arnhem Transport Services Pty. Ltd., 1973—; dep. chmn. Buckle Investments Ltd., 1961-64, W.P. Martin Pty. Ltd., 1969-73; dir. Pacific Mining Ltd.; provisional liquidator Surveys & Mining Ltd., 1971, Westron NL, 1973. Scheme trustee Vam Ltd., 1973—; receiver Winns Ltd., 1978—. Ofcl. liquidator New S. Wales, 1963—, Queensland, 1971—, Victoria, 1972—, No. Ter., 1971—, S. Australia, 1973—. Served with Royal Australian Air Force, 1946. Fellow Chartered Inst. Accountants Australia. Clubs: New South Wales, Tattersalls, Sydney Turf, Royal Automobile, Roseville Golf, Australian Jockey, Am. Home: 32 N Arm Rd Middle Cove Sydney New South Wales 2068 Australia Office: 68 Pitt St Sydney New South Wales 2000 Australia

SMITH, C(HARLES) CARNEY, trade assns. exec.; b. Kalamazoo, Nov. 17, 1912; s. Henry and Helen (Carney) S.; student Kalamazoo Coll., 1929-31; A.B., Western Mich. U., 1933; M.A., U. Mich., 1938; LL.D., Alma (Mich.) Coll., 1972; postgrad. Northwestern U., 1940; m. Mildred Krohne, June 18, 1934; children—Patricia Marie (Mrs. M. Kent Barker), Clark Krohne. With City Welfare Dept., Kalamazoo, 1933-35; head dept. speech and dir. forensics No. High Sch., Flint, Mich., 1935-38; chmn. dept. speech Alma Coll., 1938-42; regional dir. Eastern area A.R.C., Washington, 1942-46; mgmt. tng. program dir. Mut. Benefit Life Ins. Co., Newark, 1946-48; gen. agt., Washington, 1948-63; exec. v.p. Nat. Assn. Life Underwriters, Washington, 1963-78, cons., 1979—. Mem. exec. com. People-to-People Internat. Recipient John Newton Russell Meml. award, 1970; Distinguished Alumnus award Western Mich. U., 1972. Chmn. Gen. Agts. and Mgrs. Conf., 1962-63. Bd. dirs. D.C. chpt. A.R.C. Recipient Man of Yr. award Ins. Field mag. 1971. Mem. U.S., D.C. chambers commerce, Tau Kappa Alpha. Republican. Conglist. Clubs: Capitol Hill, University; (Washington); Congressional (Potomac, Md.). Contbr. articles to profl. jours. Home: 809 Vassar Rd Alexandria VA 22314 Office: 1922 F St NW Washington DC 20006

SMITH, CAMERON OUTCALT, oil and gas co. exec.; b. Calgary, Alta., Can., July 29, 1950 (parents Am. citizens); s. William F. II and Jane (Buckley) S.; B.A. summa cum laude, Princeton U., 1972; M.S. in Geology, Pa. State U., 1975; m. Liza Vann, Oct. 10, 1976. Master of English, Hotchkiss Sch., Lakeville, Conn., 1972-73; geologist United Canso Oil & Gas, Ltd., Calgary, 1975-76; asst. to chmn. Catawba Corp., N.Y.C., 1976-78, exec. v.p., dir., 1978—; pres., dir. Taconic Petroleum Corp., 1979—. Bd. dirs. Indian Mountain Sch., Lakeville, 1976-80, treas., 1977-80. Mem. Am. Assn. Petroleum Geologists, Soc. Petroleum Engrs., Can. Soc. Petroleum Geologists, Petroleum Exploration Soc. N.Y., Tulsa Geol. Soc., Phi Beta Kappa. Conservative Republican. Clubs: Union League of N.Y. (dir.); Tulsa, Petroleum (Tulsa). Author: Charles Asbee: An Endeavor in Two Kinds of Failure, 1972; Hydrocarbon Exploration in the North Sea and Adjacent Basins, 1975. Office: 103 E 37th St New York NY 10016

SMITH, CHRISTOPHER JAMES, accountant; b. Belturbet, Ireland, Apr. 1, 1947; s. Christopher and Kathleen Monica S.; B.Com., Univ. Coll. Dublin, 1969; m. Monica McGuckian, Sept. 25, 1976. Acct., Thomas McLintock & Co., London, 1969-74, Thorne Riddell & Co., Calgary, 1975-76; div. controller Petro-Can., Calgary, 1976—. Fellow Inst. Chartered Accts. Eng. and Wales. Home: 7323 Bow Crescent NW Calgary AB T3B 2C9 Canada Office: PO Box 2844 Calgary AB T2P 2M7 Canada

SMITH, DAN CURTIS, constrn. and real estate co. exec.; b. Cedar Creek, Tex., Oct. 27, 1923; s. Hiram Clinton and Sophia Inez (Voss) S.; C.E., U. Tex., 1941; m. Janis Roberts, Sept. 21, 1946; children—Dana Catherine, Christine. With Ramada Inns Inc., 1966-77, constrn. mgr., Phoenix, 1977; pres. Danmont Internat. Corp., 1977—, Dan C. Smith Real Estate, 1977—, Dan C. Smith Constrn., 1977—, Glenn-Smith Internat. Corp., 1981—. Served with USNR, 1943-46. Home: 3214 N 63d Pl Scottsdale AZ 85251 Office: 4835 E Indian School Rd Phoenix AZ 85018

SMITH, DARWIN EATNA, paper co. exec.; b. Garrett, Ind., Apr. 16, 1926; s. Kay B. and Hazel Ruby (Sherman) S.; B.S. in Bus. with distinction, Ind. U., 1950; LL.B. cum laude, Harvard, 1955; m. Lois Claire Archbold, Aug. 19, 1950; children—Steven and Pamela (twins), Valerie, Blair. Admitted to bar; mem. firm Sidley & Austin, Chgo., 1955-58; with Kimberly-Clark Corp., Neenah, Wis., 1958—, gen. atty., 1959-62, v.p., 1962-69, exec. v.p., 1969-70, pres., 1970-71, chmn. bd., chief exec. officer, 1971—; dir. Citibank, Citicorp., Am. Natural Resources Co., United Techs. Corp. Trustee Marquette U. Served with AUS, 1944-46; ETO. Home: Route 1 Box 211 Menasha WI 54952 Office: Kimberly-Clark Corp Neenah WI 54956

SMITH, DAVID PAUL, automotive parts franchisor; b. Billings, Mont., Apr. 23, 1945; s. William G. and Lou Mae (Clement) S.; student bus. adminstrn., Kinman Bus. Sch., 1963-64; m. Paula Lauren Brewster, Aug. 11, 1973; 1 dau., Lauren Bethany. Exec. sec. Watchtower Soc., Bklyn., 1965-72; controller Mighty Distbg. System Am., Inc., Norcross, Ga., 1972-77, exec. v.p., sec.-treas., 1976—. Home: 8060 River Circle Dunwoody GA 30338 Office: 50 Technology Park Atlanta Norcross GA 30092

SMITH, DAVID THOMAS, real estate devel. co. exec.; b. Valley Forge, Pa., May 3, 1949; s. Robert Channel and Mary Elizabeth (Harris) S.; B. Bldg. Constrn., U. Fla., 1972; m. Barbara Jean Katz, Mar. 15, 1975; 1 dau., Lindsey Rose. Dir. Resource Planning and Scheduling dept. Sea Pines Co., Hilton Head Island, S.C., 1972-73; v.p. residential devel., v.p. design and constrn. The Landmarks Group, Inc., Atlanta, 1973-80; v.p. The Wilson Co., Tampa, Fla., 1980—. Mem. Archtl. Rev. Bd., Abington Subdiv., Marietta, Ga., 1976-78. Licensed gen. contractor, Fla. Mem. Am. Inst. Constructors, Fla. Alumni Assn., Lambda Chi Alpha. Republican. Methodist. Home: 10549 Parkcrest Dr Tampa FL 33624 Office: Suite 170 5100 W Kennedy Blvd Tampa FL

SMITH, DAVID WILLIAM, constrn./devel. exec.; b. Dryden, Mich., Dec. 28, 1942; s. Orville Ray and Bertha June (Haynes) S.; grad. high sch.; m. Rosalie Scutari, Dec. 29, 1974; children—Glenn, Debra, Pamela, Steven. Prin., David Smith, Custom Builders, Lapeer, Mich., 1964-69; project mgr. U.S. Homes Corp., Clearwater, Fla., 1970-71; prodn. mgr. Labanque, Inc., Holiday, Fla., 1971-74; pres. West Coast Communities of Fla., Port Richey, 1974—, also Style Craft Homes, Port Richey, Earth Excavating, Port Richey, Pine Ridge Devel. Corp.; chmn. Parade of Homes, Pasco Co., 1980. Served with U.S. Army, 1961-64. Mem. Pasco County Builders Assn. (exec. v.p. 1980). Democrat. Baptist. Club: Masons. Office: 327 1/2 Jasmine Blvd Port Richey FL 33568

SMITH, DEBORAH ARMELDIA, banker; b. Kentwood, La., Feb. 8, 1934; d. Rochelle Melvin and Audrey Juanita (Thomas) Buckhalter; A.A., Wilson Jr. Coll., 1969; Equal Employment Opportunity studies certificate Cornell U., 1978; m. Albert D. Smith, Nov. 28, 1964; 1 dau., Audrey Eleanor Carter. Coding clk. also supr. 5th Army, Chgo., 1955-57; credit investigator Martin Clothing Co., Chgo., 1958-62, Arthur Finance Co., Chgo., 1962-65; asst. mgr. Litt Jewelers, Chgo., 1965; tchr. spl. reading St. Clare Sch., Chgo., 1966-67; methods analyst, purchasing analyst, trust staff asst., jobs tng. analyst, trust operating rep., trust mgr. supr. Continental Ill. Bank, Chgo., 1968-76; mgmt. engr., analyst mgr. Old Stone Bank, Providence, 1976-77, affirmative action officer, 1977-79, asst. treas., corp. affirmative action officer, 1979-80, asst. v.p. personnel, 1980—; dir. Justice Resource Corp., 1979-81. Bd. advisers Univ. Without Walls, Providence, 1978—; dir. membership Women's Assn. Chgo. Jaycees, 1973. Mem. Urban Bankers Assn. R.I. (treas. 1979, dir. public relations 1980), Julia A. Thomas Soc. of Nat. Urban League. Office: 150 S Main St Providence RI 02901

SMITH, DEE, supermarket chain exec.; b. Brigham City, Utah, Sept. 30, 1925; s. Lorenzo J. and Seretha (Iverson) S.; student public schs.; m. Ida Woodyatt, May 5, 1944; children—Fred L., Jeffery P., Richard Dee. Engaged in grocery store bus., 1945—; pres., chief exec. officer Smith's Mgmt. Corp., Salt Lake City, 1945—; dir. First Security Corp.; mem. round table Utah State U.; adv. bd. Weber State U. Bus. Sch. Trustee Cottonwood Hosp. Served with AUS, 1943-45. Recipient Disting. Service award; Golden Plate award Am. Acad. Achievement, 1979. Mem. Food Mktg. Inst. (dir.), Western Assn. Food Chains (past pres.), Utah Retail Grocers Assn. (past pres.). Republican. Mormon. Clubs: Salt Lake City Country; Eldorado Country (Indian Wells, Calif.); Elks, 20-30 (past pres.). Office: 1550 S Redwood Rd Salt Lake City UT 84104

SMITH, DENNIS IVAN, electronics design engr.; b. Great Falls, Mont., Mar. 12, 1952; s. Ivan Herbert and Shirley Jean (Erickson) S.; B.S.E.E., Mont. State U., 1974, M.S.E.E., 1975; m. Suzanne Elizabeth Brown, May 21, 1976; 1 son, Aaron G. Electronics design engr. Tektronix, Beaverton, Oreg., 1974—. Clubs: Road Runner Sq. Dance, Hayloft Rounders Round Dance. Home: 2220 SE Maple St Hillsboro OR 97123 Office: PO Box 500 Beaverton OR 97077

SMITH, DONALD WILLIAM, paint co. exec.; b. Lockport, N.Y., Dec. 31, 1938; s. Elmer Francis (stepfather) and Anna Elizabeth (Keller) Hufnagel; student Canisius Coll., 1956-58; A.A.S. in Chemistry, Erie Community Coll., 1961; m. Kathryn Alice Duffy, May 27, 1967; children—Donald William III, Allison Marie, Erica Ann. Staff asst. Sandia Corp., Albuquerque, 1961-65; technologist Union Carbide Corp., Tonawanda, N.Y., 1966-67; safety engr. Bell Aerospace, Niagara Falls, N.Y., 1968-69; corporate indsl. hygienist Carborundum Co., Niagara Falls, 1970-71; mgr. safety and environ. affairs Pratt & Lambert, Inc., Buffalo, 1972—; mem. hazardous materials transp. com. City of Buffalo Common Council. Vice pres. North Tonawanda Am. Little League; bd. dirs. Western N.Y. Safety Conf. Recipient George Baugh Heckel award Nat. Paint and Coatings Assn., 1980; registered profl. engr., Calif.; cert. safety profl. Mem. Am. Soc. Safety Engrs. (pres. Niagara Frontier chpt.), Nat. Fire Protection Assn., Adhesives and Sealants Council (govt. relations com.), Am. Soc. Indsl. Security, Am. Indsl. Hygiene Assn. (pres. sect. 1970-71), Nat. Safety Mgmt. Soc., Nat. Paint and Coatings Assn. (chmn. occupational health task force), Can. Paint and Coatings Assn. (occupational health and safety com.), Bus. Council N.Y. State (occupational safety and health com.). Home: 509 Meadowbrook Dr North Tonawanda NY 14120 Office: 75 Tonawanda St Buffalo NY 14207

SMITH, DOUGLAS LARUE, mgmt. cons.; b. Madison, Minn., July 25, 1917; s. Julius Waldo and Blanche (LaRue) S.; B.A., U. Minn., 1948; m. Dorothy Jean Hefty, Feb. 8, 1941; children—Pamela Jean Smith Graham, Gregory Douglas. Sales supr. U.S. Gypsum, Chgo., Mpls., 1939-42; account exec. Melamed Hobbs, Mpls., 1946-50; brand mgr. Swift & Co., Chgo., 1950-53; account exec. Batten Barton Burstine, N.Y.C., 1953-55; v.p. mktg. Johnson Wax Co., Racine, Wis., 1955-65; exec. v.p. Lennen and Newell, N.Y.C., 1965-69; sr. v.p. Planmetrics, Inc., N.Y.C., 1969—. Served to maj. U.S. Army, 1942-46. Decorated Bronze Star. Mem. Am. Assn. Advt. Agys. (gov. Eastern region), Assn. Nat. Advertisers (chmn. bd.). Presbyterian. Clubs: Univ., Winged Foot Golf (Mamaroneck, N.Y.); Univ. (Chgo.). Home: 249 E 48th St New York NY 10017 Office: 666 Fifth Ave New York NY 10019

SMITH, EARL JAY, accountant; b. Hagerstown, Md.; s. Frank L. and Leila C. (Beard) S.; ed. LaSalle Extension U., Balt. Coll. Commerce, edn. seminars; m. Viola Garland, Apr. 7, 1946; children—Earlene Marie Smith Johnson, Dennis Garland. Pvt. practice acctg., 1953-62; county auditor Washington County, Md., 1962-74; partner Smith Elliott & Co., 1962-70, inc., 1970, pres., 1970-75; fin. cons., Hagerstown, Md., 1975—; dir. Hagerstown Trust Co. Chairperson, Study Group for Home Rule of Washington County, 1975-76; trustee Washington County Hosp., 1976—; chairperson council fin. and adminstrn. Balt. United Methodist Conf. Served with USAAF, 1943-46; PTO. Mem. Am. Inst. C.P.A.'s, Md. Assn. C.P.A.'s (past pres. Western Md., past dir. Md.), Pa. Inst. C.P.A's, Md. Assn. Public Fin. Officers, Am. Legion, Hagerstown C. of C. Republican. Clubs: Elks, Masons, Shriners, Tall Cedars of Lebanon, Rotary (past dist. gov. internat., Paul Harris fellow). Research on practical uses and applications of solar energy. Home: 11 N Colonial Dr Hagerstown MD 21740 Office: 17 N Colonial Dr Hagerstown MD 21740

SMITH, EARL WILLIAM, mktg. and mgmt. cons.; b. Santa Ana, Calif., Apr. 25, 1921; s. Earl William and Clara Delight (Rounds) S.; student Jr. Coll. Santa Ana, 1939-40; m. Virginia M. Richardi, May 7, 1966; children—Sheri L. Smith Partridge, Cathy M. Smith Russo, Pamela C. Smith Doheney. With Safeway Stores, Inc., 1939—, dist. mgr., 1953-60, retail ops. mgr., Los Angeles, 1960-63, div. mgr., San Diego, 1963-65, div. mgr. So. Calif. div., 1965-72, corporate v.p., 1967-75, S.W. regional mgr., 1972-73, N.W. region, Bellevue, Wash., 1973-75; chmn. bd., chief exec. officer Allied Supermarkets Inc., Detroit, 1975-80, ret., 1980; now dir. and cons.; dir. Pay 'N Save Corp., Seattle. Vice pres. Boy Scouts Am., Los Angeles, 1967-72, v.p. Seattle council, 1974, bd. dirs., 1981—; bd. dirs. Better Bus. Bur. Los Angeles County, 1968-72; mem. council Los Angeles Orthopedic Hosp., 1970-73. Served with AUS, 1944-45. Named Citizen of Year, Stockton, Calif., 1955; recipient Silver Beaver award Boy Scouts Am., 1973. Mem. Food Mktg. Inst. (dir. 1975-80), Food Employers Council So. Calif. (trustee, past dir., v.p.), Seattle C. of C. Clubs: Elks, Rotary; Pauma Valley (Calif.) Country; Seattle Golf; Wash. Athletic. Home: 8542 NE 13th St Bellevue WA 98004

SMITH, EDWARD BYRON, JR., bank exec.; b. Washington, Oct. 1, 1944; s. Edward Byron and Louise de Marigny (Dewey) S.; B.A. in History, Yale, 1966; M.B.A. in Fin., Columbia, 1969, M.Internat. Affairs, 1970; M.B.A. in Econs., N.Y. U., 1974; m. Maureen Dwyer, June 22, 1974; children—Edward Byron, Peter Byron. With No. Trust Co., Chgo., 1970—, v.p., 1976—. Trustee Art Inst. Chgo.; governing mem. Brookfield (Ill.) Zoo, Field Mus., Chgo.; bd. dirs. Lincoln Park Zoo, Chgo., Chgo. Council Fine Arts; mem. assos. bd. Presbyterian-St. Lukes Hosp., Chgo.; trustee Chgo. Home for Incurables. Mem. Modern Poetry Assn. (trustee), Better Govt. Assn., Econ. Club Chgo., Chgo. Bd. Trade. Clubs: Onwentsia, Racquet (Chgo.). Office: 50 S LaSalle St Chicago IL 60675

SMITH, EDWIN, entertainment mgmt. exec.; b. Providence, May 9, 1941; s. Wilbur H.E. and Ethel Lucille S.; Cert. of design, Parson's Sch. Design, 1963; m. Alicia Margaret Caesar, July 17, 1977; stepchildren—Steven, Stacey. Asst. br. mgr. 1st Jersey Nat. Bank, Newark, 1966-69; loan officer U.S. Small Bus. Adminstrn., Newark, 1969-70; bus. opportunity and devel. specialist Medic, Inc., Newark, 1970-74; dir. franchise opportunities clearinghouse Meric, Inc., N.Y.C., 1974-76; acct. exec. Southwestern Bell Telephone Co., Dallas, 1976-81; founder, pres. Vision Mgmt., Inc., performing artist devel. and mgmt., Dallas, 1981—; staff asso. Found. Metaphys. Studies, Dallas. Bd. dirs. Park S. YMCA, Dallas. Served with NG U.S. Army, 1963-69. Mem. Am. Soc. Tng. and Devel., Dallas Black C. of C., Assn. Profl. Color Labs, Photo Mktg. Assn., Profl. Photographers Assn. Office: One Turtle Creek Village Suite 800 Dallas TX 75219

SMITH, ELLISON WARD, univ. adminstr.; b. N.Y.C., Nov. 15, 1922; s. Worthington Ward and Alma (Ellison) S.; student Princeton U., 1941-42; B.A., U. Va., 1948; postgrad. Birmingham Sch. Law, 1958-59; m. Marian Ruth Hart, July 30, 1949; children—Peter Worthington, Anthony Hart. Roving editor corp. publs. IBM, N.Y.C., 1953-55, speechwriter, office of pres., 1956-57; staff writer Birmingham News, 1958-59; natural sci. writer N.Y. Herald Tribune, 1959-62; editor Reports on Research, M.I.T., 1963-68; exec. speechwriter Honeywell Corp., 1968-69; asst. to dean engring. Purdue U., West Lafayette, Ind., 1969—; cons. Ohio State U., 1977-79, Engrs. Council for Profl. Devel., 1973, Arthur D. Little Corp., 1965-67; ednl. cons. Union Carbide Corp., 1975-77. Served with USNR, 1943-46. Recipient Council for Advancement and Support of Edn. nat. communication awards, 1972, 73; Creativity award U.S. TV Commls. Festival, 1975. Mem. Am. Soc. for Engring. Edn., Cin. Soc. Republican. Episcopalian. Club: Princeton of N.Y. Contbr. numerous articles in ednl. field to newspapers, mags.; producer documentary films, TV public service spots. Home: 2004 N Salisbury St West Lafayette IN 47906 Office: Room 101 ENAD Dean's Office Purdue U West Lafayette IN 47907

SMITH, ERIC CRAIG, constrn. co. exec.; b. Washington, Nov. 27, 1945; s. Craig Champney and Mary Elizabeth (Leinen) S.; B.A., Brown U., 1967; M.B.A., Wharton Sch., U. Pa., 1971; m. Nancy Mercer Bishop, Feb. 10, 1973; children—Jordan, Ian. Acct., Arthur Young & Co., C.P.A.'s, N.Y.C., 1971-74; partner, cons. Fails & Assos., Ltd., Raleigh, N.C., 1974-79; v.p., dir. Fishel Co., Columbus, Ohio, 1979—; dir. V.O.G., Inc.; instr. Fails Mgmt. Inst., Raleigh. Served with USN, 1967-70; Vietnam. C.P.A., N.Y. State. Mem. Am. Inst. C.P.A.'s, N.Y. State Soc. C.P.A.'s, Builders Exchange Columbus. Republican. Clubs: Swim and Racquet (Columbus); Brown. Editor, contbr. Contractor's Digest, 1974-79. Home: 2636 Berwyn Rd Columbus OH 43221 Office: 1170 Kinnear Rd Columbus OH 43212

SMITH, ESTHER HAY, banker; b. Hickman County, Tenn., Sept. 18, 1935; d. Ernest and Ola (Deason) Hay; B.A., U. Tenn., Nashville, 1958; student Vanderbilt U. Banking Sch., 1968, Am. Inst. Banking La. State U. Grad. Banking Sch., 1975; m. W. T. Smith, Jr., Apr. 2, 1966; 1 son, Charles Wayne. With Commerce Union Bank, Nashville, 1953—, asst. to pres., 1970-72, asst. v.p., 1972-74, v.p. corr. banking, 1974—, asst. sec. Tenn. Valley Bancorp, holding co. for Commerce Union Bank, 1972—, sec. bd. govs., 1974—; mem. Tenn. Bankers Pub. Relations Com., 1973, 74; spokesperson for banking Am. Bankers Assn., 1976—; mem. citizens advisory com. for vocat. edn. Met. Nashville Public Schs., 1976—; instr. La. State U. Grad. Banking Sch., 1976—. Chmn. spl. gifts Middle Tenn. Heart Fund; chmn. fundraising Cumberland Valley council Girl Scouts U.S.A., 1979; chmn. Wilson County (Tenn.) March of Dimes, 1980. Recipient award of Achievement Nat. Women Execs., 1971, Golden Eagle award Sale Corp. Am., 1971. Mem. Nat. Assn. Bank Women (regional v.p. 1973-74, nat. sec. 1975-76, chmn. quad regional conf. 1977, nat. v.p. 1977-78, nat. pres. 1978-79), Davidson County (Tenn.) Bus., Profl. Women (Woman of Year 1973), Nat. Secs. Assn. (treas. 1967-68), Nashville Area C. of C. (speakers bur.). Mem. Chs. of Christ. Contbr. articles to banking jours. Home: 1717 Cook Dr Lebanon TN 37087 Office: 120 W Main St Lebanon TN 37087

SMITH, EUGENE VALENTINE, chem. co. exec.; b. Ossian, Ind., Jan. 7, 1924; s. Keith R. and Clona M. (Valentine) S.; B.S. in Mech. Engring., Purdue U., 1948; m. Maxine Louise Byerly, May 19, 1945; children—Penelope Ann Smith Scheidt, Rebecca Jo Smith Schinderle. Mech. engr., plant engr. Stanolind Oil and Gas Co., Midwest, Wyo., 1948-54; sr. project engr. Amoco Chems. Corp., Brownsville, Tex., 1954-57, asst. chief plant engr., Texas City, Tex., 1957-61, ops. supr., 1961-65, supt. ops., Joliet, Ill., 1965-71, tech. dir., 1972—. Trustee Jesse Walker United Meth. Ch., 1968—, pres. Trustees, 1972-74, v.p. bd., 1978—; mem. Will-Grundy Mfg. Environ. Control Commn., 1965—; dir. Homeowners Assn., 1971-74. Served with USAAF, 1943-45. Mem. ASME (past pres. Texas City chpt.), Am. Inst. Chem. Engrs. (dir. Joliet sect. 1976—), Three Rivers Mfg. Assn., Joliet C. of C., Pi Tau Sigma, Tau Beta Pi. Republican. Home: 2504 Chevy Chase Dr Joliet IL 60435 Office: PO Box 941 Joliet IL 60434

SMITH, F. ALAN, automobile mfg. co. exec.; b. Springfield, Mass., Apr. 21, 1931; s. Farquhar Wells and Edith Jane (Best) S.; B.A., Dartmouth Coll., 1952, M.B.A., 1953; m. Barbara Eanes, Sept. 29, 1956; 1 son, Christopher Alan. Various positions Gen. Motors Corp., Detroit, 1956-70, asst. treas., 1970-73, gen. asst. treas., 1973, treas., 1973-75, v.p. fin., 1975-80, pres., gen. mgr. Gen. Motors Can., Ltd., Oshawa, Ont., 1980—. Served with USN, 1953-56. Mem. Fin. Execs. Inst., Tax Found., Fin. Execs. Research Found. Clubs: Bloomfield Hills (Mich.) Country; Knickerbocker Country, Met. (N.Y.C.). Office: Gen Motors Can Ltd William St E Oshawa ON L1G 1K7 Canada*

SMITH, FRANCIS EUGENE, consumer products co. exec.; b. Radnor, Ohio, Feb. 17, 1935; s. Ernest Vincent and Eva Ruth (Ewing) S.; B.Chem. Engring., Ohio State U., 1959; m. Roberta Jeanne Fry, June 6, 1964; 1 dau., Kyla Iolene. Engr., Pitts. Plate Glass Co., Mount Vernon, Ohio, 1959-64; engr. Indsl. Gas div. Airco Inc., Union, N.J., 1964-67, engr. Welding products div., 1967-71, engring. mgr. Jackson Products Co. Airco Welding Products div., Warren, Mich., 1971-77; mgr. product engring. Gateway Safety Products Co., Brooklyn Heights, Ohio, 1977-78; sr. engr. Kirby div. Scott and Fetzer Co., Cleve., 1978-80, project mgr., 1980—. Served with U.S. Army, 1959. Mem. Am. Welding Soc., Indsl. Safety Equipment Assn. (chmn. head protection group, 1975). Patentee in gas proportioner. Home: 63 Morningside Dr Chagrin Falls OH 44022 Office: Kirby Tech Center 871 Bassett Rd Westlake OH 44145

SMITH, FRANCIS NICHOLAS, social worker; b. Albany, N.Y., Dec. 27, 1943; s. George N. and Dorothy M. (Wagner) S.; B.A., Siena Coll., 1966; M.S.W., Syracuse U., 1968; M.P.A., SUNY, 1981; m. Mary Frances Plager, June 24, 1967; 1 son, Christopher Francis. Probation program cons. N.Y. State Div. Probation, Albany, 1969-75, asst. practices rev. officer, 1975-77, project dir. Juvenile Intake Project, 1977-79, program adminstr. Juvenile Justice unit, 1979—; pvt. practice marriage and family counselor, Albany, 1972-77; adj. instr. Sch. Social Welfare, SUNY, Albany, 1978—. Served to maj., Med. Service Corps, USAR, 1968—. N.Y. State Probation scholar, 1966-68; named Outstanding Profl. in Human Services, Am. Acad. Human Services, 1974-75, Outstanding Young Man of Am., U.S. Jaycees, 1979; Past Pres.'s award Colonie Jaycees, 1979; cert. social worker, N.Y. Mem. Acad. Cert. Social Workers, Colonie Jaycees (pres. 1978-79, chmn. bd. 1979-80), Am. Probation and Parole Assn., Am. Soc. Public Adminstrn., Nat. Council Crime and Delinquency, Nat. Council Family Relations, Nat. Assn. Social Workers, N.Y. State Soc. Clin. Social Work Psychotherapists, N.Y. State Probation Officers Assn., Res. Officers Assn. U.S., N.Y. State Jaycees, U.S. Jaycees, Middle Atlantic States Correctional Assn., Siena Coll. Alumni Assn., Syracuse U. Alumni Assn., Albany Acad. Fathers Assn. Roman Catholic. Home: 115 Ball Ct Menands NY 12204 Office: 22d Floor Tower Bldg Empire State Plaza Albany NY 12223

SMITH, FREDRIC MARSHALL, adhesives mfg. co. exec.; b. Boston, Aug. 11, 1936; s. Henry and Ida Rose (Selig) S.; B.S., U. Mass., 1957; M.B.A., Columbia U., 1959; m. Sara Ellen Shinberg, Apr. 3, 1960; children—Deborah Sue, Faith Joy. Sales engr. Union Carbide Corp., Chgo., 1960-65, Clifton, N.J., 1965-67; eastern regional sales mgr. Firestone Plastics Co., West Caldwell, N.J., 1967-70; asst. div. mktg. mgr. Hooker Chem.-Ruco div., Burlington, N.J., 1970-72; owner, operator Fadesa Sales Co., Livington, N.J., 1972-74; sales rep. Roman Adhesives Inc., Bloomfield, N.J., 1974-78, v.p. sales, 1978—; guest speaker various profl. meetings. Served with U.S. Army, 1959. Mem. Nat. Decorating Products Assn. Club: Masons. Home: 3 Tabor Ct Livingston NJ 07039 Office: Roman Adhesives Inc 5 Lawrence St Bloomfield NJ 07003

SMITH, GEOFFREY F. N., ins. co. exec.; b. Surrey, Eng., Mar. 11, 1926; s. Sydney A. and Phyllis I. (Elworthy) S.; B.A., U. Toronto, 1947; m. Marguerite H. Scaife, Sept. 25, 1954; children—Geoffrey L., Craig, Gail B. With Can. Life, Toronto, Ont., 1947-53; v.p., actuary Sovereign Life Ins., 1953-63; v.p., actuary Am. Mut. Life Ins. Co., Des Moines, 1963-67, pres., 1967—, chief exec. officer, 1969—. Gen. capital fund chmn. Campfire Girls, 1978-79. Fellow Soc. Actuaries, Can. Inst. Actuaries; mem. Am. Assn. Actuaries. Republican. Episcopalian. Clubs: Des Moines, Des Moines Golf and Country. Office: American Mutual Life Ins Co 418 6th Ave Des Moines IA 50307

SMITH, GEORGE DEE, tobacco co. exec.; b. Winston-Salem, N.C., Nov. 23, 1929; s. George Franklin and Vera (Hilton) S.; A.B., U. N.C., 1951; m. Jeannine Rose Meacham, May 23, 1953; 1 dau., Dee Ann. With R.J. Reynolds Tobacco Co., Winston-Salem, 1955—, asst. to chmn. bd., 1980, sr. v.p., 1980—, also dir.; pres. subs. R.J. Reynolds Tobacco Internat., 1976-80; dir. First Union Nat. Bank, Winston-Salem; trustee Old Salem, Inc.; mem. adv. council Western Carolina U.; pres. Piedmont chpt. Nat. Assn. Accountants, 1969. Chmn. budget com. Winston-Salem United Fund, 1966, treas., 1967; bd. dirs. Winston-Salem Goodwill Industries, 1967, Winston-Salem C. of C., 1981—; trustee Forsyth County Hosp. Authority, 1981—, Moravian Home, Inc., U. N.C., Greensboro; co-chmn. United Negro Coll. Fund, 1980. Served to lt. USNR, 1951-55. Mem. Stuart Cameron McLeod Soc. Mem. Moravian Ch. Club: Winston-Salem Rotary. Office: RJ Reynolds Tobacco Co 4th and Main Sts Winston-Salem NC 27102

SMITH, GEORGE SEVERN, lawyer; b. Van Wert, Ohio, Jan. 31, 1901; s. Harvey C. and Nella (Severn) S.; LL.B., Nat. U., 1928; m. Thelma Gertrude Horst, Jan. 12, 1935; 1 son, George Severn. Admitted to D.C. bar, 1931; chief license div. Fed. Radio Commn., 1929-32; asso. with Paul M. Segal, 1932-41; partner Segal, Smith & Hennessey, attys., Washington, 1942-57. Smith, Hennessey & McDonald, Washington, 1958-62; legal adv. to commr. FCC, Washington, 1962-66, chief Broadcast Bur., 1967-70; counsel to Marmet & Webster, 1971-74. Del. Fed. Communications Bar Assn. to ho. of dels. Am. Bar Assn., 1958-59. Served as pvt. Med. Dept., U.S. Army, 1918-19. Mem. Am. Bar Assn., Fed. Communications Bar Assn. (Washington pres. 1957), Bar Assn. of D.C. Address: 1308 Larry St Van Wert OH 45891

SMITH, GERALD ALVIN, data processing services co. exec.; b. Paso Robles, Calif., Mar. 31, 1939; s. Clark Murson and Eunice Deloris (Nicklas) S.; B.S. in Math., Calif. Poly. U., 1961; m. Patricia Fuhs, Jan. 26, 1963; children—Lisa Marie, Shauna Rae. Mgr. systems Saga Co., Menlo Park, Calif., 1964-66; v.p. Applied Cybernetics Corp., Sunnyvale, Calif., 1966-70; salesman Tenent Co., Sunnyvale, 1970-71; pres. G.A. Smith Co., Santa Clara, Calif., 1972—; founder, v.p. Applied Cybernetics Corp., Sunnyvale, 1965—. Mem. Data Processing Mgmt. Assn. Home: 14081 Sobey Meadows Ct Saratoga CA 95070 Office: 1075 Comstock St Santa Clara CA 95050

SMITH, GLEN ALDEN, mgmt. cons.; b. San Jose, Calif., Sept. 12, 1929; s. Lundy Earl and Edith Ada (Bond) S.; B.A., Stanford U., 1952, M.B.A. (Lane fellow 1953-54), 1954, Ph.D. (Hoover fellow 1957-58, Ford fellow 1958-59), 1959; postgrad. Ocean U. Sch. Law, Los Angeles, 1979-80, Rutgers U. Law Sch., 1980; m. Marilyn Jeanne Dassell, Aug. 26, 1977; children—Susan E. Hall, Kari J. Smith, James M. Hall, Michael G. Smith. Fgn. trade and investment adv. U.S. Fgn. Service, Beirut, 1954-57; asst. prof. internat. mgmt. San Francisco State U., 1959-61; with CIA, 1961; asst. v.p. Kaiser Aluminum Co., 1961-70; prof. mgmt., chmn. bus. dept. Calif. State U., San Bernardino, 1970-72; v.p. Internat. Mill Service Co., 1972-75; pres. Dossell-Smith Assos., mgmt. cons., Hillsborough, N.J., 1975—. Mem. Civic Arts Commn., Walnut Creek, Calif., 1965-66; precinct capt. Walnut Creek Republican Party, 1965-66; pres. Beekman Village Condominium Assn., 1977-80. Served as officer USAF, 1946-49, lt. col. Res. ret. Mem. N. Am. Soc. Corp. Planning, Inst. Mgmt. Scis. (v.p.), Phi Beta Kappa. Methodist. Author: Soviet Foreign Trade, 1973. Address: 115 Devonshire Ct Hillsborough NJ 08876

SMITH, GLENN WILLIAM, pub. accountant; b. Major County, Okla., Dec. 10, 1908; s. Frank Henry and Pearl V. (Brown) S.; student Oklahoma City U., Hills U., 1927-30, Internat. Accounting Soc., 1930; grad. accounting U. Kans., 1948; m. Billie Jeanne Redman, Apr. 2, 1944; children—Richard G., Timothy W. Jr. accountant Bonicamp & Young, Enid, Okla., 1930-33; treas., chief accountant Central Appliance Co., also controller Midwest Maytag Co., Enid, 1933-35; sr. accountant John P. Bonicamp, Wichita, 1935-42; civilian chief accountant USAAF, Air Transport Command, 1942-45; gen. partner Bonicamp, Keolling & Smith, C.P.A.'s, Wichita, 1945-63, Bonicamp, Koelling, Smith & Farrow, 1964-69; partner Peat Marwick Mitchell & Co., 1969-71; pvt. practice accounting, 1971-78, 79—; partner Smith & Russell, 1973-79. Chmn., Wichita Cancer Campaign Com., 1956-58; treas., chmn. Cloudridge Community Center, 1956-66; chmn. explorer post Boy Scouts Am., 1957-58; treas. K-9 patrol Wichita Police Dept., 1956-69; treas. Wichita Crime Commn., 1969-72; mem. Tony Manhardt Inst. Speech Tng.; mem. awards jury Freedoms Found., Valley Forge, 1961. C.P.A., Kans.; hon. adm. Nebr. Navy, 1961; hon. citizen Tex., 1961; hon. mayor San Antonio, Ft. Worth, 1961; recipient Cosmopolitan Club awards, 1951, 63; others. Mem. Kans. Soc. C.P.A.'s (dir. 1957-59, pres. 1960-61, chmn. bd. 1962-64, chmn. nominating com. 1963-64, co-chmn. audit procedures com. 1969-70), Am. Inst. C.P.A.'s (mem. council 1961-62, auditing procedures com. 1965-66), Am. Assn. Oil Well Drilling Contractors, Am. Inst. Accountants (mem. council), Wichita Tennis Assn. (past treas.), C. of C., Kans., Ind., Mid-Continent oil and gas assns., Am. Accounting Assn. Methodist (auditor 1948-79). Clubs: Petroleum, Toastmasters (chpt. sec.-treas. 1958, pres. 1959—), Crest View Country, Cosmopolitan Internat. (gov. Mo.-Kans. fedn. 1956-57, internat. pres. 1960-61, chmn. bd. 1962-63, chmn. past pres.'s council 1962-64); Air Capitol Cosmopolitan (past hon. pres.). Contbr. articles to profl. mags. Home: 8234 Limerick St Wichita KS 67206 Office: 1425 Vickers Kans B&T Bldg Wichita KS 67202

SMITH, GOFF, mfg. co. exec.; b. Jackson, Tenn., Oct. 7, 1916; s. Fred Thomas and Mabel (Goff) S.; B.S. in Engring., U. Mich., 1938, M.B.A., 1939; M.S., M.I.T., 1953; m. Nancy Dall, Nov. 28, 1942 (dec.); children—Goff Thomas, Susan Smith Schmidt; m. 2d, Harriet Oliver, June 23, 1973. With Amsted Industries Inc., 1946—, exec. v.p., then pres., Chgo., 1966-74, pres., chief exec. officer, 1974-80, chmn. bd., chief exec. officer, 1980-81, chmn., 1981—, also dir.; dir. LaSalle Nat. Bank, Chgo., Nalco Chem. Co., Central Ill. Public Service Co., GATX Corp., Clark Equipment Co. Served to maj. AUS, 1941-46. Address: 3700 Prudential Plaza Chicago IL 60601

SMITH, GUERDON DIMMICK, investment banker; b. Toledo, Oct. 5, 1916; s. Frederick William and Alice (Winzenried) S.; student U. Pa., Wharton Sch. Finance, 1934-36, U. Toledo, 1937-38, N.Y. Inst. Finance, 1945; m. Jane Shoemaker, 1946 (dec. 1949); m. 2d, Eleanor Mae McUmber, Jan. 28, 1950 (dec. 1977); children—Kristin Ann, Guerdon Dimmick, Frederick William II. Exec. trainee Libbey-Owens Ford Glass Co., Toledo, 1938-40; mgr. investment dept. Clark, Dodge & Co., Toledo, 1945-51, Dean Witter & Co., J. Barth & Co., Los Angeles, 1951-56; v.p., sec. Bigelow, Smith & Co., Pasadena, 1957-58; sr. partner Guerdon Smith & Co., Santa Barbara, Calif., 1958-65; chmn. Intercontinental Ins. Assos., 1959—; v.p., dir. ins. and fin. research Blyth & Co. Inc., 1965-70; v.p. corp. finance, dir. Shelby Cullom Davis & Co., 1970-71; v.p. Wertheim & Co. Inc., 1971-73; mng. partner Guerdon Smith & Co., 1973—, Kidder, Peabody & Co. Inc., 1976—; dir. Mansion House Center, Southeastern Life Ins. Co., Selico Inc., Kawainui Devel. Corp., N.Y. Stock Exchange, Am. Stock Exchange, Investment Bankers Assn. Am., Firemens Fund Am. Life Ins. Co. N.Y.; pvt. trustee, financial cons., investment mgr., dir. various closed corps. Active Boy Scouts Am., YMCA; bd. dirs. Round Hill Community Ch., Greenwich, Conn. Served with AUS, 1941-45. Mem. Los Angeles Soc. Financial Analysts, Nat. Assn. Securities Dealers, Nat. Fedn. Financial Analysts, U. Pa. Alumni Soc., N.Y. Soc. Security Analysts, Ins., Financial Analysts Assn. N.Y., Sigma Chi. Republican. Presbyn. Clubs: Indian Harbor Yacht; Rotary, Union League (N.Y.C.); Channel City (Calif.), Hope Ranch Park (Santa Barbara); California (Los Angeles); Wharton Bus. Sch. (N.Y.C.). Home: Box 4119 Greenwich CT 06830 Office: 522 Fifth Ave New York NY 10036

SMITH, H. ALLEN, retail co. exec.; b. Oxnard, Calif., Jan. 10, 1947; s. Howard Allen and Bette Jane (Mayes) S.; student U. Hawaii, 1968-70; m. Shawn Kuualoha Lemson, Feb. 12, 1977; 1 son, Cary Keola. Chief engr. Telepromter Cable TV of Hawaii, 1970-73; gen. mgr. Century Cable TV, Redondo Beach, Calif., 1973-74; gen. mgr. Teleprompter Cable TV of Hawaii, Honolulu, 1974-79; chief exec. officer Nifty Moves, Ltd., Honolulu, 1979—, pres. Coffee, Etc. subs., 1979—; instr. Honolulu Community Coll., 1977-78. Served with USN, 1966-69: Vietnam. Mem. Hawaii Cable TV Assn. (dir. 1975—), Soc. Cable TV Engrs. Democrat. Lutheran. Home: 47-028E Hui Iwa Pl Kahaluu HI 96744 Office: Manoa Marketplace Honolulu HI 96822

SMITH, HAROLD PHILIP, chem. and energy purchasing mgr.; b. New Haven, Mar. 14, 1929; s. Philip Augustus and Mabel Elizabeth (Quinn) S.; B. Chem. Engring., Yale U., 1950; m. Marceline Anne Frey, June 26, 1954; children—Kevin Erwin, Marie Michele, Brenda Jean, Deborah Anne. Project engr. Vitro Corp. Am., N.Y.C. and Anniston, Ala., 1950-52; mktg., tech. and mfg. positions with Uniroyal, Inc., Middlebury, Conn., 1955—, corp. purchasing mgr. chems. and energy, 1977—; former instr. U. New Haven, Waterbury State Tech. Coll. Served as destroyer officer USN, 1952-55; Korea. Registered profl. engr., Conn. Mem. Racemics of N.Y.C., Conn. Chem. Club, Sigma Xi, Tau Beta Pi, Alpha Chi Sigma. Republican. Roman Catholic. Contbr. (with P.A. DePaolo) to Advances in Chemistry Series 85, 1968. Home: 23 Nathan Ct Waterbury CT 06708 Office: Uniroyal Inc World Hdqrs Middlebury CT 06749

SMITH, HAROLD WARREN, banker; b. Bklyn., June 7, 1923; s. Harry Warren and Rose Marie (Schlegel) S.; B.S., Rutgers U., 1954; M.B.A., N.Y. U., 1959; m. Teresa Catherine Conley, July 30, 1941; children—Nancy Smith Polleri, Patricia Smith Degree, Margaret Smith Peluso. With Mfrs. Trust Co., N.Y.C., 1941-42, 45—75, organizer, sr. v.p., dir., mgr. Edge Act subs. Mfrs. Hanover Bank Internat., Los Angeles, 1973-74, v.p., regional mgr. charge Japan, Korea, Taiwan, Philippines, Australia, N.Z. and Oceania for parent bank, N.Y.C., 1974-75; v.p., group head charge Asia/Pacific region Fidelity Bank, Phila., 1975-78; organizer, 1978, since pres., chief exec. officer, dir. Asian Internat. Bank, N.Y.C.; vice chmn. Am.-Asian Trade Council. Served with USNR, 1942-45. Mem. Philippine Am. C. of C. (pres., chmn. exec. com., dir.), Philippines-Am. Soc. (treas.), Nat. Fgn. Trade Council, Old Asian Hands, Am. Legion, Rutgers U. Alumni Assn. Republican. Club: World Trade Center. Office: 1 World Trade Center Suite 8935 New York NY 10048

SMITH, HAROLD WEBSTER, savs. and loan exec.; b. Waterbury, Conn., July 23, 1911; s. James Emile and Margaret Loretta (Dunn) S.; A.B. cum laude, Dartmouth Coll., 1933; m. Elizabeth Grant Copenhaver, Nov. 10, 1945; children—Harold Webster, Robert, James, Margaret Smith Smith, Ann. Asst. to dir. mint Treasury Dept., Washington, 1933-35; sec.-treas. First Fed. Savs. and Loan Assn. of Waterbury, 1935-45, pres., dir., 1946—; dir. So. New Eng. Telephone Co., Baldwin-United Corp. Buell Industries. Corporator United Way Greater Waterbury, 1952—, dir., 1951-70; trustee Post Coll., Waterbury Found.; corporator Waterbury Hosp., 1949—, pres., 1961-63, trustee, 1952-70. Served to lt. comdr. USNR, 1942-46. Mem. Savs. and Loan League of Conn. (pres. 1953-54), U.S. League Savs. Assn., Phi Beta Kappa, Alpha Delta Phi. Democrat. Roman Catholic. Clubs: Waterbury, Country of Waterbury, Conn. State Srs. Golf Assn. Home: 22-B Heritage Circle Southbury CT 06488 Office: First Fed Plaza Box 191 Waterbury CT 06720

SMITH, HARTMAN WILLIAM, supermarket exec.; b. Corpus Christi, Tex., June 18, 1944; s. Laban Conrad and Margaret (Hayes) S.; B.S., Ind. U., 1966; m. Nancy Marie Foster, June 6, 1964; children—Kelly Lynn, Christopher Brock, Megan Marie. Research and devel. adminstr., then tax auditor Ind. Dept. Revenue, 1964-66; audit mgr. Arthur Andersen & Co., Indpls., 1966-74; v.p. fin., sec.-treas. Marsh Supermarkets, Inc., Yorktown, Ind., 1974—; asso. mem. faculty acctg. dept. Ind. U.-Purdue U., Indpls., 1972-73. Named Sagamore of Wabash, 1967. C.P.A., Ind. Mem. Am. Inst. C.P.A.'s, Ind. Assn. C.P.A.'s, Soc. Corp. Secs., Fin. Execs. Inst. Home: 4112 W Riverside Ave Muncie IN 47304 Office: Marsh Supermarkets Inc Depot St Yorktown IN 47396

SMITH, HOMER GROVE, ret. banker; b. Washington, Nov. 26, 1909; s. Homer Amos Arthur and Hazel (Grove) S., student Am. Inst. Banking, 1927-29; B.C.S., Benjamin Franklin U., 1931; summer study Pa. State U., 1933; m. Elsa Mildred Tavenner, Aug. 27, 1938; children—Linda, Carla (Mrs. Moxon), Greta (Mrs. Kotler), Martin. With Commn. Nat. Bank, Washington, 1927-30; installations Burroughs Adding Machine Co., 1930-31; staff accountant Haskins & Sells, Balt., 1931-34; land bank examiner FCA, Washington, 1934-36, various adminstrv. positions to asst. dep. prodn. Credit Commr., 1944, asst. dept. dir. Short Term Credit Services, 1953; dep. gov., dir. coop. Bank Service, 1954; pres. Central Bank for Coops., Washington, 1956-72, Denver, 1972-74. Mem. fiscal agy. com. Farm Credit Banks, 1964, 68-70, chmn., 1970. Presbyterian (elder). Club: Rotary. Author: The 13th Bank, A History of the Central Bank for Cooperatives, 1976. Home: 4814 Wellington Dr Chevy Chase MD 20015

SMITH, JAMES DOUGLAS, architect; b. Chgo., May 14, 1943; s. Lyman Douglas and Hallie Marie (Sanders) S.; B.Arch. with honors, U. Ill., 1968; certificate with honors Ecole des Beaux Arts (France), 1967; m. Anita Louise Metzger, June 24, 1967; 1 dau., Elisa Marie. Planner, Northeastern Ill. Planning Commn., Chgo., 1966—, Dept. Devel. and Planning, Chgo., 1968-69; archtl. designer A. Epstein & Sons, Chgo., 1969-72; architect, partner Smith-Kureghian & Assos., Chgo., 1972-77; urban planning cons.; asso. Nathan-Barnes & Assos., Chgo., 1971-77; city architect City of Gary (Ind.), 1977-79; v.p. H. Seay Cantrell Assos. Inc., Gary, 1979—; instr. architecture Am. Inst. Drafting, Chgo., 1974-76. Precinct del. 44th Ward Assembly, Chgo., 1972—, chmn. services com., 1973-74, chmn. steering com., 1974-76, campaign area chmn., 1974; planning dir. Indsl. Council/NW. Community, 1972. Named Outstanding Young Man Am., 1974. Deeter-Ritchey-Sipple fellow, 1967—; A. Epstein Meml. scholar, 1967-68; Allerton traveling fellow (alternate), 1967—. Registered architect, Ill., Mich., Mo., Ind.; lic. real estate broker, Ind. Mem. Gargoyle Soc., Chgo. Assn. Commerce and Industry, A.I.A., Prestressed Concrete Inst., Nat. Council Archtl. Registration Bds., Sigma Tau, Scarab. Co-author Chgo. residential bldg. security ordinance; maj. products include downtown devel. coordinator, Gary, Ind., Sheraton Hotel, Gary, comml. rehab, Louisville and Kansas City, Mo.; co-designer Regency Hyatt House, Chgo. Home: 1215 W Wellington St Chicago IL 60657 Office: 522 Broadway Suite 212 Gary IN 46402

SMITH, JAMES FRANCIS, utilities exec.; b. Saugus, Mass., May 15, 1936; s. James Gregory and Marion Irene (Huckins) S.; A.B., Bentley Coll., 1956; m. Margaret Ellen Frame, Nov. 30, 1963; children—Ellen Hawley, James Gregory. Security analyst Boston Safe Deposit & Trust Co., 1956-58; pub. accountant Robert C. O'Connell, C.P.A., Boston, 1958-60; controller Precision Microwave Co., Saugus, 1960-65; with Orange and Rockland Utilities, Inc., 1965—, v.p., 1969-75, exec. v.p. fin. 1975-78, vice chmn., chmn. exec. com., 1978—, chmn. bd., chief exec. officer, dir., 1979—; affiliated Bay State Gas Co., Concord Electric Co., Exeter & Hampton Electric Co., Fitchburg Gas and Electric Light Co., Boston, 1965-75. Trustee, treas. Tuxedo Meml. Hosp. Served with AUS, 1958-61. Mem. Am. Gas Assn., Edison Electric Inst., Fin. Execs. Inst. Clubs: Tuxedo (gov., treas.)(Tuxedo Park, N.Y.); Met. (N.Y.C.); Rockland Country (Sparkill, N.Y.); Capitol Hill (Washington); Ft. Orange (Albany, N.Y.). Home: Club House Rd Tuxedo Park NY 10987 Office: 1 Blue Hill Plaza Pearl River NY 10965

SMITH, JAMES MONTGOMERY, JR., savs. and loan exec.; b. Greenwood, S.C., May 23, 1918; s. James Montgomery and Mattie Glasgow S.; B.S. in Bus. Adminstrn., Newberry Coll., 1947; m. Harriet Harmon, Aug. 30, 1946; children—Martha Jean Smith Hampshire, James Montgomery. Bookkeeper, Newberry Fed. Savs. & Loan Assn. (S.C.), 1946-48, asst. sec. and treas., 1948-68, sr. v.p., treas., 1968—. Past treas., past bd. dirs. United Fund; past chmn. pack com. Cub Scouts; ruling elder Aveleigh Presbyterian Ch., Newberry; treas. Aveleigh Presbyn. Sunday Sch.; past deacon, past Sunday sch. tchr., past chmn. session's witness com. Aveleigh Presbyn. Ch.; mem. annuities and relief com., mem. audits com. S.C. presbytery Presbyn. Ch. in U.S.; treas. Aveleigh Kindergarten. Served with USN, 1942-45; PTO. Recipient longevity services certs. S.C. Savs. and Loan Assn.; Confederate Cross, Calvin Crozier chpt. U.D.C., 1959. Mem. Fin. Mgrs. Soc. for Savs. Instns., Am. Legion. Club: Masons. Home: 1235 Calhoun St Newberry SC 29108 Office: Newberry Fed Savs & Loan Assn 1330 College St Newberry SC 29108

SMITH, JAMES NELSON, food and vending exec.; b. Georgetown, Ky., July 12, 1924; s. Charles S., Sr., and Lelia C. (Robinson) S.; student Georgetown Coll., 1945-47, Brescia Coll., 1950-51; m. Lida R. Hamilton, June 10, 1947; children—Tom P., Steven H., Sherrie E. Office worker Mallard Pencil Co., Georgetown, 1947-48; grocery canteen routeman, Owensboro, Ky., 1950-51, canteen supr., 1952-53, canteen mgr., 1954-56; nat. supr. Canteen Corp., Chgo., 1957-59; v.p. Canteen of Dixie, Inc., Greenville, S.C., 1959-67, exec. v.p., 1967-77, pres., 1977—. Served with USNR, 1942. Mem. S.C. Automatic Merchandising Assn., S.C. Vending Assn. (past pres.), Greenville C. of C., Greenwood C. of C., Columbia C. of C., Union C. of C., S.C. C. of C., Toccoa (Ga.) C. of C., Clayton (Ga.) C. of C. Democrat. Baptist. Office: PO Box 8416 Greenville SC 29604

SMITH, JEROME BURTON, investment mgmt. co. exec.; b. Chgo., May 4, 1930; s. Paul S. Smith and Della A. Smith Gross; B.S., Iowa State Coll., 1953; m. Ruth Grace Bell, May 29, 1954; children—SaraLee Grace, Bradley Lawrence. Pres., Arboreal Tree Service, Park Ridge, Ill., 1947-52; visual info. supr. Weyerhaeuser Co., Tacoma, 1956-65; pres. Acad. Communicative Arts and Scis., Inc., Tacoma, 1962-69, Congress of Internat. Logging Championships, Inc., Tacoma, 1967-69; exec. v.p. Greenacres, Inc., Seattle, 1967-68; pres. Investors Inst. Inc., Tacoma, 1971-77, Inversionismo S.A., Mexico City, 1973-78, Transworld Trade Tech., Inc., Tacoma, 1976—; dir. Alpental Ski Inc., Snoqualmie, Wash., 1968-77, Bahia Del Rincon, S.A. de C.V., Mexico City, 1967-78, Broadwalk Properties, Inc., Tacoma, 1968-77. Exec. mgr. United Citizens for Sound City Govt., Tacoma, 1958. Served to capt. USAF, 1955. Recipient Outstanding Service award Soc. Am. Foresters-Seattle World's Fair, 1963. Mem. Soc. Am. Foresters, Western Forestry and Conservation Assn., Order of Hoo Hoo, Izaak Walton League. Independent Republican. Presbyterian. Clubs: Tacoma Horse Polo, Mexico City Horse Polo; Woodbrook Hunt (dir.); Alpental Ski; Tacoma Businessmen's, Sunset Beach Boathouse, Univ. Pl. Boosters. Home: 4351-B 67th St Tacoma WA 98466 Office: PO Box 2121 Tacoma WA 98401

SMITH, JOHN JULIUS, fin. analyst; b. Englewood, N.J., May 28, 1941; s. Julius Freeman and Lottie Winfred S.; B.S., U. Ariz., 1969; M.S., Temple U., 1973; Ph.D., Southeastern U., New Orleans, 1981; postgrad. Lehigh U., Coll. William and Mary, U. Pa., U. Wis. Tchr., Tucson, 1966-69; with NASA, Hampton, Va., 1969-73; aero-space technologist Pa. Dept. Environ. Resources, Norristown, 1973-75; with Office of Environ. Analysis, N.J. Dept. Environ. Protection, Trenton, 1979—; faculty Temple U., Phila., 1975—; fin. analyst. Served with U.S. Army, 1964-66. NSF grantee, 1961-62. Mem. Math. Soc. Am., Am. Fedn. Scientists, Soc. Indsl. Applied Math., Can. Math. Congress, Am. Phys. Soc., Am. Assn. Physics Tchrs., AAAS, Math. Assn. Am., Am. Legion, DAV. Club: Masons. Author: The Financial Wizard, 1965; The Broad Spectrum of Financial Analysis, 1968; Aspects of Business Forecast, 1971; Study of Financial Analysis, 1974. Home and Office: 679 Cedar Hill Dr Allentown PA 18103

SMITH, JOHN KEVIN, accountant; b. Benton, Ark., Apr. 28, 1949; s. John and Vera Jane (Murray) S.; computer program certificate San Diego Coll. Bus., 1972; B.S., San Diego State U., 1978. Auditor, Atlas Corp., San Diego, 1976, Sheraton Corp., San Diego, 1976-77, Hyatt Corp., San Diego, 1977-78; accountant Hawthorne Machinery Co., San Diego, 1978-79; accountant Presto Food Products, Los Angeles, 1979—. Active fund-raising Republican party. Served with U.S. Army, 1967-71; Vietnam. Mem. Nat. Assn. Accountants, Am. Mgmt. Assn. Republican. Baptist. Clubs: Masons, Rotary. Office: 929 E 14th St Los Angeles CA 90021

SMITH, JOHN ROLAND, educator; b. Bartlett, N.H., July 17, 1922; s. John and Mabel (Baldwin) S.; student Fla. State U.; m. Patricia Randolph, Feb. 7, 1971; 1 dau., Marilyn. With Falmouth Pub. Co. (Mass.), 1941-42, Kendall Printing Co. (Mass.), 1945-48, St. Petersburg Printing Co. (Fla.), 1948-51; tchr. Tomlinson (Fla.) Vocat. High Sch., 1952-60, Dixie Hollins High Sch., St. Petersburg, 1960-66; dir. trade and indsl. edn. Daytona Beach (Fla.) Community Coll., 1966—; cons. in field. Served with USNR, 1942-45, 51-52. Life mem. Internat. Assn. Printing House Craftsmen (gov. 1965-66), Iota Lambda Sigma; mem. Am. Vocat. Assn., Nat. Assn. Vocat. Adminstrs., Nat. Indsl. Edn. Assn., Fla. Vocat. Assn., Fla. Indsl. Edn. Assn., Fla. Assn. Community Colls. Club: Kiwanis. Home: 1622 S Riverside Dr New Smyrna Beach FL 32069 Office: PO Box 1111 Daytona Beach FL 32015

SMITH, JOSEPH ALAND, constrn. and diversified co. exec.; b. Caldwell, Idaho, Mar. 26, 1930; s. Collis Romer and Verda (Aland) S.; B.A., Coll. Idaho, 1952; M.B.A., Harvard U., 1956; m. Joanne C. Goul, Aug. 11, 1950; children—Mark B., Eric M., Stephanie A. Mem. systems group TRW, Inc., Los Angeles, 1956-58; 1st v.p., dir. Bank Bldg. Corp., St. Louis, 1968-69, exec. v.p., dir., 1969-73, pres., chief exec. officer, dir., 1973-76, chmn. bd. dirs., chief exec. officer, 1976—. Mem. exec. com. Mo. Bapt. Hosp., St. Louis; chmn. mem. President's Council St. Louis U.; trustee Mo. Bapt. Coll.; bd. dirs. YMCA of Greater St. Louis; bd. dirs. Jr. Achievement of Mississippi Valley Inc. Served with USNR, 1952-54. Baptist (mem. personnel com.). Clubs: Stadium, St. Louis, Harvard Bus. Sch., Pacesetters (dir.), Backstoppers of St. Louis, Mo. Athletic. Office: 1130 Hampton Ave Saint Louis MO 63139

SMITH, K(ERMIT) WAYNE, mgmt. cons.; b. Newton, N.C., Sept. 15, 1938; s. Harold Robert and Hazel K. (Smith) S.; B.A., Wake Forest U., 1960; M.A. (Danforth fellow, Woodrow Wilson fellow), Princeton, 1962, Ph.D., 1964; postgrad. U. So. Calif., 1965; m. Audrey M. Kennedy, Dec. 19, 1958; 1 son, Stuart W. Instr., Princeton, 1963; asst. prof. econs., polit. sci. U.S. Mil. Acad., 1963-66; spl. asst. to asst. sec. def. for systems analysis, Washington, 1966-69; program mgr. def. studies RAND Corp., Santa Monica, Calif., 1969-70; dir. program analysis Nat. Security Council, Washington, 1970-72; group v.p. planning Dart Industries, Los Angeles, 1972-73, pres. resort devel. group, 1973-76; exec. v.p. fin. and adminstrn. Washington Group, Inc., Winston-Salem, N.C., 1976-77; mng. partner Coopers & Lybrand, Washington, 1977-80, group mng. partner, 1980—. Mem. vis. com. Brookings Instn., Washington, 1971—; bd. visitors Wake Forest U., Winston-Salem, N.C., 1972—, vice chmn., 1975-76, chmn., 1976-78; mem. fed. govt. exec. com. Am. Inst. C.P.A.'s, 1979—. Served to capt. AUS, 1963-66. Mem. Am. Polit. Sci. Assn., Am. Econ. Assn., Am. Mgmt. Assn., Council Fgn. Relations, Internat. Inst. Strategic Studies, UN Assn., Phi Beta Kappa, Omicron Delta Kappa, Kappa Sigma. Methodist. Clubs: Internat., Capitol Hill, Washington Golf and Country (Washington). Author: How Much is Enough? Shaping the Defense Program, 1961-69, 1971. Contbr. articles to profl. jours. Home: 1004 Woburn Ct McLean VA 22102 Office: 1800 M St NW Washington DC 20036

SMITH, KEVIN WILLIAM, fin. exec.; b. Bayonne, N.J., Oct. 7, 1943; s. Martin and Marie A. (Lonergan) S.; A.B., Seton Hall U., 1965; m. Amy Chapman; children—Sean, Courtenay Chapman. Salesman, Greenwood Mills, Inc., N.Y.C., 1965-66, Investors Planning Corp., East Orange, N.J., 1966-69; v.p. Value Line Securities, N.Y.C., 1969-72; fin. cons. oil, gas, coal, N.Y.C., 1972-80; pres. Arens Petroleum, N.Y.C., 1980—. Clubs: Canadian, Metro. Home: 70 Edgewood Ave West Orange NJ 07052 Office: 11 Broadway New York NY 10004

SMITH, KINGSLEY JOHN, savs. and loan exec.; b. Bklyn., Jan. 28, 1923; s. Stanley G. and Clara Adrienne (Moss) Gay; student U. Ga., 1953, U. Hawaii, 1956-59, U. Kans., 1959, U. Okla., 1960-61; B.S., U. Omaha, 1962; div.; children—Kimberly June, Kingsley John, Lisa Gay. Commd. 2d lt., U.S. Army, 1945, advanced through grades to maj., 1960; ret., 1964; pres., dir. First Fed. Savs. & Loan Assn., Davenport, Iowa, 1964—. Pres., bd. dirs. Jr. Achievement Quad Cities, 1970-73; treas. River Bend council Girl Scouts Am., 1971-73, bd. dirs. Mississippi Valley council, 1973—; bd. dirs. YM/YWCA, 1970-71; bd. dirs. St. Ambrose Inst. Mgmt. Devel. Decorated Bronze Star, Purple Heart. Club: Davenport. Office: 131 W 3d St Davenport IA 52801

SMITH, LAURENCE MARK, radio sta. exec.; b. Manchester, N.H., May 26, 1950; s. Mark Irving and Rena Ellen (Travis) S.; B.Broadcast Mgmt. and Engring., Elkins Inst., 1970; m. Carolyn Joan Dix, Apr. 20, 1974; children—David Andrew, Matthew Christopher, James Michael. Staff announcer Sta. WKNE, Keene, N.H., 1967, Sta. WKBK, Keene, 1968; asst. gen. mgr. Sta. WTSA-WMMJ-FM, Brattleboro, Vt., 1975—; chmn. industry adv. com. FCC, 1975—; mem. New Eng. broadcast adv. com. UPI, 1979—. Vice pres. Brattleboro Winter Carnival, 1970-77; rep. Brattleboro Town Meeting, 1971—; mem. Brattleboro Town Dem. Com., 1973—. Recipient Disting. Service award Brattleboro Jr. C. of C., 1975; Cert. of Recognition, Brattleboro C. of C., 1976. Mem. Radio-TV News Dirs. Assn. Democrat. Home: 33 Lexington Ave Brattleboro VT 05301 Office: PO Box 819 Brattleboro VT 05301

SMITH, LAWRENCE EUGENE, JR., real estate fin. exec.; b. Cleve., June 18, 1935; s. Lawrence Eugene and Margaret Vandaveer (Barber) S.; B.S. in Fin., U. Colo., 1957; m. Gretchen Gay VanScoy, June 20, 1959; children—Sarah Graham, Lisa Ann. Mortgage loan rep. Travelers Ins. Co., Detroit, 1959-60, Mercantile Mortgage Co., St. Louis, 1960-62; dist. supr. Nat. Life Vt., Montpelier and St. Louis, 1962-69; dir. fin. Multicon Properties, Columbus, Ohio, 1969-70, v.p. Roosevelt Fed. Savs. and Loan, St. Louis, 1970-72; sr. v.p. Boatman's Nat. Bank and pres.-dir. Mo. Mortgage & Investment Co. subs. Boatmen's Bancshares, St. Louis, 1972—; v.p., dir. Lawrence E. Smith & Co., Inc., St. Louis, 1965—, also dir. Served to lt. j.g., USN, 1957-59. Mem. St. Louis, Nat. mortgage bankers assns. Republican. Disciples of Christ. Clubs: Media, Corey Lake Yacht. Home: 9381 Sonora Ave Brentwood MO 63144 Office: 100 N Broadway Saint Louis MO 63102

SMITH, LELAND FLOYD, devel. economist; b. Manchester, Conn., Jan. 13, 1939; s. Prevost Floyd and Elizabeth Marie (DeOlde) S.; B.A., U. Oreg., 1964; M.A., Portland State U., 1974; m. Shirley Ann Cramer, Nov. 9, 1968; 1. Kevin Wayne. Econ. devel. rep. Pacific Power & Light Co., Portland, Oreg., 1964-69; mgr. indsl. devel. Portland C. of C., 1969-72; dir. Colorado Springs Indsl. Found. (Colo.), 1972-75; pres. Devel. Mktg. Assos., Tucson and Seattle, 1975—; pvt. practice econ. cons. Mem. Nat. Assn. Bus. Economists, Urban Land Inst., Am. Indsl. Devel. Council, Indsl. Devel. Research Council. Republican. Episcopalian. Club: Washington Athletic. Contbr. articles to profl. jours. Home: 6720 N Columbus Blvd Tucson AZ 85718 Office: PO Box 35580 Tucson AZ 85740

SMITH, LEONARD, constrn. cons. co. exec.; b. Lincoln, Eng., Apr. 2, 1936; came to U.S., 1967; s. Frank and Lillian S.; Chartered Quantity Surveyor, Grantham Coll., 1963; m. Margaret Florence Skelton, Jan. 1960; children—Paul Richard, Stuart Ian, Sarah Louise. Chartered surveyor, Eng., 1953-66; sr. cost engr. Fraser-Brace Engring., Montreal, Ont., Can., 1966-67, Bechtel Corp., Gaithersburg, Md., 1967-70; mng. partner Monk Dunstone Assos., Alexandria, Va., 1970—; dir. Comptec Inc., Gaithersburg. Fellow Royal Instn. Chartered Surveyors (U.K.); mem. Soc. Am. Value Engrs., Am. Assn. Cost Engrs., Constrn. Specifications Inst. Club: Washington Golf and Country. Home: 7419 Exmore St Springfield VA 22150 Office: Monk Dunstone Assos 699 Prince St Alexandria VA 22314 also 55 E Monroe St Chicago IL 60603

SMITH, MARCIA JEAN, acct., tax specialist; b. Kansas City, Mo., Oct. 19, 1947; d. Eugene Hubert and Marcella Juanita (Greene) S.; student U. Nebr., 1965-67; B.A. (Coll. Ednl. Opportunity grantee), Jersey City State Coll., 1971; M.B.A. in Taxation, Golden Gate U., 1976, postgrad., 1976-77; postgrad. in Accounting Pace U., 1977. Legal intern Port Authority N.Y., N.J., N.Y.C., 1972; legis. aide to Harrison A. Williams, U.S. Senator, Washington, 1973; tax accountant Bechtel Corp., San Francisco, 1974-77; sr. tax accountant Equitable Life Assurance Soc. U.S., N.Y.C., 1977; asst. sec. Equitable Life Holding Corp., N.Y.C., 1977-79, Equico Lessors, Inc., Mpls., 1978-79, Equitable Gen. Ins. Group, Ft. Worth, 1977-79, Heritage Life Assurance Co., Toronto, Ont., Can., 1978-79, Informatics, Inc., Los Angeles, 1978-79; sec. Equico Capital Corp., N.Y.C., 1977-79, Equico Personal Credit, Inc., Colorado Springs, Colo., 1978-79, Equico Securities, Inc., N.Y.C., 1977-79, Equitable Environ. Health, Inc., Woodbury, N.Y., 1977-79; tax sr. Arthur Andersen & Co., N.Y.C., 1979—; tax cons.; real estate salesperson. Human rights chmn. YWCA, Lincoln, Nebr., 1966-67. Recipient Certificate of Recognition, Central Mo. State Coll., 1965, Unicameral award State Neb., 1967, Mary McLeod Bethune award Jersey City State Coll., 1971. Mem. Am. Mgmt. Assn., Internat. Tax Inst., Am. Econs. Assn., Internat. Platform Assn., U.S. Senatorial Club. Home: 300 Mercer St 23C New York NY 10003

SMITH, MARLENE ANN, mfg. co. exec.; b. St. Paul, Oct. 6, 1935; d. Edgar Leander and Luella Johanna (Rahn) Johnson; children—Rick, Debora, Ronald, Lori, Carlson. Bookkeeper Jeans Implement Co., Forest Lake, Minn., 1952-53, part-time bookkeeper, 1953-57; head bookkeeper Great Plains Supply, St. Paul, 1960-62; bookkeeper Plastic Products Co., Inc., Lindstrom, Minn., 1962-75, pres., chief exec. officer, 1975—. Bookkeeper, Trinity Lutheran Ch., Lindstrom, 1976—. Mem. Nat. Assn. Women Bus. Owners, Soc. Plastic Engrs. Home: 28940 Olinda Trail Lindstrom MN 55045 Office: 30355 Akerson St Lindstrom MN 55045

SMITH, MARSHALL FRANCIS, diversified co. exec.; b. Chgo., Apr. 30, 1929; s. Marshall E. and Suzanne (Vernia) S.; B.S. in Accounting, U. Ill., 1951; postgrad. U. Chgo., 1954, Northwestern U., 1955; m. Catherine A. Kerin, Sept. 9, 1955; children—Thomas, Kathryn, Suzanne, Elizabeth. Div. controller U.S. Steel Corp., N.Y.C., 1966-67; asst. controller Indian Head, Inc., N.Y.C., 1967-68; v.p., asst. gen. mgr. Wayne Corp. div. Indian Head Co., Richmond, Ind., 1969; v.p., controller Indian Head, Inc., N.Y.C., 1969-72, exec. v.p., 1972-74, pres., chief exec. officer, dir., 1974—; dir. Madera Glass Co., Hapad, Inc. Mem. Psi Upsilon. Home: 571 River Rd Yardley PA 19067 Office: 1211 Blvd of Americas New York NY 10018

SMITH, MAURICE LEO, consultant; b. Bklyn., Dec. 25, 1926; s. Maurice L. and Loretta H. Smith; B.S. in Mettallurgy, U. Notre Dame, 1949; m. Patricia Shea, June 1, 1957; children—Terence, Riley, Erin, Kelly. With metall. products dept. Gen. Electric Co., Detroit, 1949-65, mgr. mktg. staff Chase Brass & Copper Co., Inc., Cleve., 1965-68; corp. dir. bus. planning, v.p. and gen. mgr. Gen. Service Equipment div. Applied Power Inc., Milw., 1968-74; pres. Neptune Water Meter Co., Atlanta, 1974-77; v.p. mktg. Am. Meter div. Singer Co., Phila., 1977-80; pres. MBS Group, Phila., 1980—; dir. T. D. Shea Mfg., Inc. Served to as lt. USMC, 1951-53. Mem. Assn. Indsl. Advertisers (dir. 1963, Bestseller award 1964), Planning Execs. Inst., Am. Mktg. Assn., N. Am. Soc. Corp. Planning. Clubs: Whitemarsh Valley Country, Atlanta Country. Office: 9220 Germantown Ave Philadelphia PA 19118

SMITH, MICHAEL ROLAND, SR., lab. exec.; b. Grantsburg, Wis., Oct. 23, 1938; s. Charles D. and Berneice Ann (Hjort) S.; B.A., U. Minn., 1960; m. Joyce Lee Blaho, Aug. 12, 1969; children—Michelle, Michael Roland. Dist. mgr. sales Rose Chem. Products Co., Columbus, Ohio, 1965-66; co-founder Chardon Labs. Inc., Columbus, 1966—, pres., 1975—, also dir.; co-founder Weatherator Engring. Co., Columbus, 1976, also pres. Mem. Nat. Conservative Caucus; active Jr. Achievement. Served with USCGR, 1960-64. Mem. Columbus C. of C., Chem. Splty. Mfrs. Assn., Internat. San. Supply Assn., Aircraft Owners and Pilots Assn., Hideaway Hills Assn., Pi Sigma Epsilon. Republican. Lutheran. Clubs: Masons, Shriners, Ky. Cols., Highlands Country, Sales Execs. (dir. 1977—). Home: 8948 Chevington Chase Pickerington OH 43147 Office: 539 Stimmel Rd Columbus OH 43216

SMITH, MORTON, ins. exec.; b. Providence, June 4, 1916; s. Jospeh and Sarah (Finkle) S.; B.A., Brown U., 1937; m. Doris T. King, June 15, 1940; 1 dau., Susan Smith Levin. Pres., Morton Smith, Inc., Providence, 1950—, also subs. Medway Marine Corp., 1950—, Medway Ins. Corp., 1950—. Life trustee Miriam Hosp.; hon. trustee United Way, Providence; bd. dirs. Providence Preservation Soc., R.I. Arts Found. at Newport, Musical Arts Found., R.I. Philharmonic Orch., Butler Hosp. Named Aetna Casualty and Surety Co. Man of Yr., 1966. Mem. Ind. Ins. Agts. of R.I., Ind. Ins. Agts. Am., Profl. Ins. Agts. New Eng. Republican. Clubs: Turks Head, Squantum, Newport Country, Hope, Bailey's Beach, Sr. Chopin of R.I. (past pres.). Office: 245 Waterman St Providence RI 02906

SMITH, NEALE ERICSON, mfg. co. exec.; b. Douglas, Ariz., Nov. 6, 1932; s. Roy Ellsworth and Beatrice (Neale) S.; B.S., Calif. Inst. Tech., 1954; M.E.E., Ariz. State U., 1966, M.S. in Physics, 1967; m. Ana Elva Cornejo Gardner, Nov. 21, 1969; children—Neale Ricardo, Eric David, Odin Alonso. Radar devel. engr. Goodyear Aerospace, Litchfield Park, Ariz., 1963-66; physicist, info. theory Lawrence Radiation Lab., Livermore, Calif., 1968; tech. dir. Macromex, S.A., Agua Prieta, Sonora, Mex., 1968—. Served with USMCR, 1954-56. Mem. IEEE, Eta Kappa Nu. Home: 1099 Calle 3ra Agua Prieta Sonora Mexico Office: 1075 Calle 3 Agua Prieta Sonora Mexico

SMITH, NEWMAN DONALD, financial exec.; b. Chesterville, Ont., Can., Dec. 26, 1936; s. Clarke Harold and Ethelwyn Irene (Cross) S.; chartered acct., 1961; registered indsl. acct., 1966; m. Mary Elizabeth Murdoch, June 27, 1964; children—Clarke Murdoch, Brian Newman. With Coopers & Lybrand Inc., Ottawa, Ont., 1955-62; sec.-treas. Deloro Smelting & Refining Co. Ltd., Ottawa, 1963-69, M.J. O'Brien Ltd., Ottawa, 1963-69; v.p., sec. Andres Wines Ltd. and subs., Winona, Ont., 1969—, also dir.; dir. Les Vins Andres du Quebec Ltee. Pres., Hamilton Arthritis Soc. Mem. Fin. Exec. Inst. (dir. Hamilton chpt.), Hamilton Chartered Accts., Hamilton Mgmt. Accts., Chartered Inst. Secs. Clubs: Hamilton Golf and Country, Hamilton. Home: 39 Robinhood Dr Dundas ON L9H 4G2 Canada Office: PO Box 550 Winona ON L0R 2L0 Canada

SMITH, ORIN ROBERT, metals co. exec.; b. Newark, Aug. 13, 1935; s. Sydney R. and Gladys (DeGroff) S.; B.A. in Econs., Brown U., 1957; M.B.A. in Mgmt., Seton Hall U., 1962; m. Ann Raymond, July 11, 1964; children—Lindsay, Robin. Various sales and mktg.

mgmt. positions Allied Chem. Corp., Morristown, N.J., 1960-70; dir. sales and mktg. Richardson-Merrell, Phillipsburg, N.J., 1970-72; with M&T Chems., Greenwich, Conn., 1972-77, pres., 1974-77; with Engelhard Minerals & Chems. Corp., Menlo Park and Edison, N.J., 1977—, sr. corp. v.p., pres. minerals and chems. div., 1978—, dir., 1979—, also pres. and dir. various U.S. subs. of minerals and chems. div. Trustee Ind. Coll. Fund. N.J. Served to lt. (j.g.) USN, 1957-60. Mem. Chem. Mfrs. Assn. (dir.). Clubs: Econ., Union League (N.Y.C.); Essex Hunt (Peapack, N.J.); Fiddler's Elbow Country (Far Hills, N.J.). Author books in field of econometrics and price theory. Home: Holland Rd Far Hills NJ 07931 Office: Engelhard Minerals & Chems Corp Menlo Park Edison NJ 08837

SMITH, PETER LANG, aviation co. exec.; b. Paterson, N.J., Mar 25, 1930; s. Peter and Louise (Lang) S.; B.Ed. with honors U. Nebr., 1965; M.S., U. So. Calif., 1968; m. Vera Marie Elkins, Nov. 2, 1954; 1 son, Dana Lang. Enlisted U.S. Air Force, 1951, commd. 2d lt., 1953, advanced through grades to col., 1974; ret., 1979; aircraft comdr. SAC KC-97 and KC-135, Castle AFB, Calif., 1962-63, instr. SAC combat crew tng. crew, 1963-70, ops. officer, also comdr. rescue helicopter unit Korea, 1971-72; comdr. SAC air refueling squadron, Westover AFB, 1972-73; dep. comdr. ops. 384th Air Refueling Wing, McConnell AFB, Kans., 1973-79; v.p., gen. mgr. Midwest Piper Flight, Inc., Wichita, 1979—. Decorated Air medal. Mem. Am. Mgmt. Assn., Am. Def. Preparedness Assn., Mensa. Clubs: Masons, Shriners. Home: 2483 N Belmont St Wichita KS 67220 Office: PO Box 8067 Munger Sta Wichita KS 67208

SMITH, PETER WALKER, instrument mfg. co. exec.; b. Syracuse, N.Y., May 19, 1923; s. Stanley S. and Elizabeth W. (Young) S.; B.Chem. Engring., Rensselaer Poly. Inst., 1947; M.B.A. cum laude, Harvard U., 1948; J.D. cum laude, Cleve. Marshall Law Sch., 1955; m. Lucile E. Edson, June 22, 1946; children—Andrew, Laurie Smith Falzone, Pamela Smith Schweppe, Stanley. Admitted to Ohio bar, 1955; div. controller Raytheon Co., Lexington, Mass., 1958-66; v.p. fin. indsl. systems group Litton Industries, Stamford, Conn., 1966-70; v.p. fin., treas. Copeland Corp., Sidney, Ohio, 1970-74; v.p. fin., treas., dir. Instrumentation Lab., Inc., Lexington, 1974-78; treas. Ionics, Inc., 1978—; v.p. fin., treas. Data Printer Corp., Malden, Mass., 1980—. Served with AUS, 1943-46, 50-52. Registered profl. engr., Ohio. Mem. Fin. Execs. Inst., Sigma Xi, Tau Beta Pi. Congregationalist. Home: 155 Monument St Concord MA 01742 Office: 65 Grove St Watertown MA 02172

SMITH, PETER WILLIAM, fin. exec.; b. Portland, Maine, Feb. 23, 1936; s. Walt S. and Harriet S. (Hawkins) S.; M.B.A., Syracuse U., 1959; m. Janet S. Langenfeld, Sept. 20, 1958; children—Linda M., William M., David A. Congressional asst. U.S. Ho. of Reps., Washington, 1960-62; asso. exec. dir. Assn. Am. Publishers, Inc., N.Y.C., 1963-69; sr. v.p. Field Enterprises, Inc., Chgo., 1969-80; pres. Fin. Analysis Corp., Chgo., 1976—, Energy and Mineral Exploration Corp., Denver, 1978—, Peter W. Smith & Co., Inc., Chgo., 1980—; dir. Field Italia, Inc., Rome. Asso. bd. mem. Rush Presbyn. St. Luke's Med. Center, Chgo., 1976—; investment com. Met. YMCA Council, Chgo., 1976—; chmn. coll. Young Rep. div. Rep. Nat. Com. Club: Mid-Day (Chgo.). Home: 596 E Cherokee Rd Lake Forest IL 60645 Office: 401 N Wabash Ave Chicago IL 60611

SMITH, PHILIP MEEK, govt. ofcl.; b. Springfield, Ohio, May 18, 1932; s. Clarence Mitchell Smith and Lois Ellen Smith Dudley; B.S., Ohio State U., 1954, M.A., 1955. Staff, U.S. Nat. Com. for IGY, Nat. Acad. Scis. and Arctic Inst., 1957-58, Antarctic logistic and field ops. specialist, 1959-62; acting dir. Antarctic field ops. NSF, 1963-64, dir. Antarctic field ops., 1965-69, dep. head Office Polar Programs, 1969-73, spl. asst. to dir., 1974-76; br. chief energy and sci. div. Office Mgmt. and Budget, 1973-74; exec. sec. Pres.'s Com. on Nat. Medal of Sci., 1974-76; asst. dir. Office Sci. and Tech. Policy, Exec. Office of The Pres., from 1976; now coordinator White House Activities in Indsl. Innovation and Univ.-Industry Relations and Research Budgets. Served to lt. AUS, 1955-57. Recipient Meritorious Service award NSF, 1972. Fellow Nat. Speological Soc.; mem. AAAS, Am. Mgmt. Assn., Antarctican Soc., Fed. Exec. Inst. Alumni Assn. Club: Am. Alpine. Author: (with Henry S. Francis, Jr.) Defrosting Antarctic Secrets, 1962; also articles on speleological research, conservation and park mgmt., also polar research and logistics; contbg. author: Advances in Space Science and Technology, 1969. Spl. editor: Antarctica Since the IGY, Bull. Atomic Scientists, 1970. Home: 464 M St SW Washington DC 20024 Office: Office Sci and Tech Policy Executive Office President White House Washington DC 20500

SMITH, PHILLIP HARTLEY, steel co. exec.; b. Sydney, Australia, Jan. 26, 1927; s. Norman Edward and Elizabeth (Williams) S.; B.Engring. with 1st class honors in Mining and Metallurgy (Nuffield scholar 1949), U. Sydney, 1950; Metall. Engr., Mass. Inst. Tech., 1952; diploma in indsl. relations U. Chgo., 1958; LL.D., Grove City Coll., 1975; m. Martha Frances Dittrich, June 4, 1955; children—Elizabeth, Thomas, Johanna, Alice, Margaret, Sarah. Came to U.S., 1950, naturalized, 1960. Successively trainee, metallurgist, foreman Inland Steel Co., Indiana Harbor, Ind., 1952-55; successively trainee, metallurgist, dir. purchasing and planning La Salle Steel Co., Hammond, Ind., 1956-64; with Copperweld Corp., Pitts., 1964-77, pres., 1968-77, chmn., 1973-77; pres., chief exec. officer, dir. Bekaert Steel Wire Corp., Bekaert N.A., Pitts., 1978—. Trustee, Grove City Coll., Berea (Ky.) Coll., Bell of Pa., Presbyn. Ministers Fund, Presbyn. Lay Com.; chmn. Inroads, Inc. Served as cadet officer Australian Mcht. Marine, 1942-43, Royal Australian Fleet Aux., 1943. Recipient Nat. Open Hearth Steelmaking award, 1955. Presbyterian (ruling elder). Clubs: University (Chgo.); Duquesne (Pitts.); Rolling Rock (Ligonier, Pa.). Editor: Am. Inst. M.E. Handbook, Mechanical Working of Steel, 1961. Patentee in field. Home: 102 Haverford Rd Pittsburgh PA 15238

SMITH, RALPH, TV production exec.; b. N.Y.C., Apr. 12, 1921; s. Louis J. and Blanche (Mallay) S.; student Jr. Coll. Conn., Bridgeport, 1939-40; m. Jeanne Kamberg, Aug. 30, 1942; children—Jeffrey P., Donald E., Barbara L. Regional sales mgr. Dictograph Products, Jamaica, L.I., 1953-55; with Life Assos., Inc., Stratford, Conn., 1955-78, exec. v.p., 1961-78; exec. v.p., sec. Metro. Productions Inc., Hollywood, Calif., 1978—; East coast regional mgr. Beneficial Standard Life Ins. Co., 1965-67, asst. v.p., dir. east coast agencies 1967-69; pres., chmn. bd. Alliance Med. Inns, Inc.; pres. Trafalgar Acceptance Co., Asset Capital & Mgmt.; dir. Comml. Bank Calif. Served with AUS, World War II. Mem. Nat. Assn. TV Program Execs.; Internat. Assn. Tax Cons., Jewish War Vets. Jewish. Clubs: B'nai B'rith; Masons, Shriners. Office: 280 S Beverly Dr Beverly Hills CA 90212

SMITH, RICHARD CRAIG, coop. exec.; b. Niagara Falls., N.Y., Aug. 19, 1947; s. Dudley Phelp and Lillian (Pappas) S.; B.S., Rider Coll., 1970; A.A., Niagara County Community Coll., 1969; m. Judy Ellen Barrons, June 7, 1969; children—Richard James, Denise Christine, Scott Michael, Jason Christopher. Traffic and customer service mgr. Standard Corp./Standard Plastics, Washington, N.J. and Fogelsville, Pa., 1971-77; distbn. supr. Lehigh Valley Coop. Farmers Dairy, Allentown, Pa., 1977, distbn. mgr., 1977-78, dir. fleet ops., 1978—; cons. in field. Fin. officer Boy Scouts Am., Germansville, Pa., 1979—, com. mem. cub scout pact 588, 1978—; mem. Goodwill Fire Co., 1977—, Northwestern Youth Athletic Assn., 1977—. Cert. inspection mechanic, Pa. Mem. Pa. Motor Truck Assn., Pvt. Truck Council Am. Republican. Methodist. Club: Lions. Patentee in field. Home: 1404 Glen Dr Germansville PA 18053 Office: 1000 N 7th St Allentown PA 18001

SMITH, RICHARD LOUIS, JR., ins. co. exec.; b. St. Inigoes, Md., July 20, 1930; s. Richard Louis and Mary Edna (Taylor) S.; student Mt. St. Mary's Coll., 1948-49; m. Mary Regina Mueller, Dec. 2, 1950; children—Elaine Smith Nollet, Janet Smith Brazell, Richard, Dennis, Regina Smith Stanziale. Agt., Peoples Life Ins. Co., Washington, 1951—, v.p. mktg., 1970-74, sr. v.p. mktg., 1974-76, exec. v.p. mktg., 1976—, dir., 1972—; exec. v.p. mktg., dir. Home Life Ins. Co. Am. subs., 1977—. Past pres. PTA; chmn. Essex County (Va.) unit Am. Cancer Soc., 1964. Mem. Life Ins. Mktg. and Research Assn. (dir. 1976—), Am. Soc. C.L.U.'s (dir. 1976-79), Nat. Assn. Life Underwriters, Life Insurers Conf., D.C. C. of C., Hon. Order Ky. Cols. Roman Catholic. Clubs: Ruritan Nat., K.C. Home: 146 Mary's Mount Rd Harwood MD 20776 Office: 601 New Hampshire Ave NW Washington DC 20048

SMITH, RICHARD MILLER, steel co. exec.; b. Bethlehem, Pa., Aug. 29, 1925; s. Herman Percy and Bessie Mary (Miller) S.; B.S. in Indsl. Engring., Lehigh U., 1948; Advanced Mgmt. Program, Harvard U., 1972; m. Shirley Ann Druckenmiller, July 9, 1955; children—Leslie Susan, Gregory Miller, Laurie Elizabeth. With Bethlehem Steel Corp. (Pa.), 1948—, treas., 1972-74, exec. v.p., 1974-77, vice-chmn. bd., 1977—, dir., 1974—; dir. Girard Bank, The Girard Co., BRINCO Ltd. Trustee, Lehigh U., Com. for Econ. Devel.; bd. dirs. Hist. Bethlehem, Inc. Served in USN, 1943-45. Mem. Tau Beta Pi, Alpha Pi Mu, Pi Tau Sigma. Office: Bethlehem Steel Corp Martin Tower Bethlehem PA 18016

SMITH, RICHARD STOWERS, investment banker, rancher; b. San Antonio, Tex., July 20, 1934; s. Luther Stevens and Hazel (Stowers) S.; B.A., Yale, 1955; m. Josephine McRae Powell, Jan. 13, 1962; children—Elliott Stowers, Quincy McRae. Asso. investment banking Lazard Freres Co., N.Y.C., 1958-63; v.p., dir. Russ Co., San Antonio, 1964, N.Y. Securities Co. Inc., 1965-72; sr. v.p., dir. Rotan Mosle Inc., Houston, 1973—; mng. partner Stowers Ranch Co., 1967—; former dir. Mesa Petroleum Co., Chesapeake Industries, Stowers Furniture Co., David M. Lea, Chesterfield Land & Timber Corp., Thomson Industries Ltd.; dir. Verna Corp. Formerly trustee Houston Ballet; bd. dirs., pres. Houston Child Guidance Center. Mem. Investment Assn. (N.Y.). Republican. Episcopalian. Clubs: River, Union, The Recess (N.Y.C.); Hay Harbor, Fishers Island Country (Fishers Island, N.Y.); Argyle (San Antonio); Coronado (Houston); Port Bay Hunting (Rockport); Tex. Corinthian Yacht (Kema). Home: 2233 Troon Rd Houston TX 77019 Office: 1600 S Tower Pennzoil Pl Houston TX 77002

SMITH, ROBERT ADRIAN, packaging mfg. co. exec.; b. Chgo., Oct. 13, 1941; s. Virgil A. and Mildred (McClintick) S.; student U. Ill., 1959-60; B.S., So. Ill. U., 1963; m. Nancy L. Niess; children—Jeffrey, Michael. With Owens-Ill., Inc., Alton, Ill., 1963-67, personnel staff asst., Toledo, 1967-68, indsl. relations dir., Atlanta, 1968-72, indsl. relations dir., adminstrv. mgr., Streator, Ill., 1972-76, plant mgr., Toledo, 1976-78, Lakeland, Fla., 1978—. Mem. grievance panel State of Ill., 1972-76; campaign chmn. United Way, Streator, 1976—. Recipient Distinguished Service award Streator Jr. C. of C., 1975; named Outstanding Citizen Ill., Jaycees, 1975. Club: Rotary (pres. 1976). Office: PO Box 850 Lakeland FL 33802

SMITH, ROBERT DRAKE, transp. co. exec.; b. Ft. Worth, Oct. 26, 1944; s. Kermit Rudebeck and Lynne Grace (Harris) S.; B.A. with honors in Econs., U. Puget Sound, 1966; M.B.A., U. Pa., 1968. Planning analyst C.&N.W. Transp. Co., Chgo., 1968, supr. program planning, 1969, mgr. program planning, 1970-73, corp. sec., 1973—; dir. Western R.R. Properties, Inc., Des Moines & Central Iowa Ry., Ft. Dodge, Des Moines & So. Ry., Mpls. Indsl. Ry., Northwestern Communications Co., Ry. Transfer Mpls., Oshkosh Transp. Co. Vol., Cook County Juvenile Ct., 1970-78; mem. jr. gov. bd. Chgo. Symphony. Mem. Am. Soc. Corp. Secs., Assn. Am. R.R.'s, Nat. Investor Relations Inst., Wharton Sch. Alumni Assn. Clubs: Union League, Barclay, Bd. Room (N.Y.C.). Home: 535 N Michigan Ave #3208 Chicago IL 60611 Office: C&N W Transp Co 400 W Madison St Room 616 Chicago IL 60606

SMITH, ROBERT GENE, paper co. exec.; b. Madison, Mo., May 17, 1927; s. Victor B. and Gladys P. S.; B.S. in Edn., U. Mo., 1951; m. Jean L. Keller, Jan. 21, 1978; children by previous marriage—Sarah Ann, Robert R., J. Paul. Sales rep. J.A. Folger Co., Kansas City, Mo., 1952-54, Wabash Fibre Box Co., Terre Haute, Ind., 1954-68; pres., chief exec. officer, dir. Decatur Container Corp., Oreana, Ill., 1968—; del. White House Conf. on Small Bus., 1980. Mem. Ill. C. of C. (exec. com.), Decatur C. of C. (dir. 1975-78), Assn. Ind. Corrugated Converters, Ill. Mfg. Assn., NAM, Nat. Fedn. Ind. Bus. Served with USMC, 1944-46. Republican. Clubs: Terre Haute Country (pres. 1967-68), Country of Decatur. Home: 54 Green Oak Dr Decatur IL 62526 Office: Rt 48 N Oreana IL 62554

SMITH, ROBERT GRAHAM, bldg. and loan exec.; b. Whiteland, Ind., Sept. 30, 1927; s. Robert and Frances L. (Graham) Smith; A.B., Franklin Coll., 1950; m. Rosejane H. Pruitt, Aug. 6, 1950; children—Carol Jane, Constance Ellen, Robert Graham II. Automobile sales mgr., 1950-51; asst. cashier Johnson County Nat. Bank, Franklin, Ind., 1951-63; pres. Mut. Bldg. & Loan Assn., Franklin, 1963—, also dir. Mem. City Council, Franklin, 1954-62; trustee Johnson County Meml. Hosp., 1975-77. Served with AUS, 1946-47. Recipient Outstanding Citizen award Franklin, 1958. Mem. Franklin C. of C. (Disting. Citizen award 1977), Ind. Heart Found., Franklin Coll. Alumni Council (pres. 1980). Republican. Presbyterian. Clubs: Rotary, Hillview Country. Home: 1090 W Jefferson St Franklin IN 46131 Office: 80 E Jefferson St Franklin IN 46131

SMITH, ROBERT GRANT, JR., hotel exec.; b. Harrisburg, Pa., July 22, 1932; s. Robert Grant and Helen C. (Rice) S.; grad. high sch.; Ph.D. (hon.), Universal Ch., 1967. Pres., Hooks, Inc., Allentown, Pa., 1956—; pres. Sheraton Inn-Allentown, Robert G. Smith, Inc.; former chmn. bd. Parliament Life Ins. Co.; chmn. advisory bd. Met. Savs. & Loan Assn. Chmn., Republican Campaign, Allentown, 1973-74, Pa.-Allentown Watch Dog Com. for Rep. Party, 1974—; chmn. Pres. Ford Com. Lehigh County; past chmn. Allentown Housing Rev. Bd.; bd. dirs. Jr. Achievement, Lehigh County Bicentennial Com.; bd. assos. Cedar Crest Coll.; pres. Allentown Center City Assn.; mem. Allentown Mayor's Econ. Devel. Adv. Com.; councilman, Allentown, 1978-80, v.p., 1979-80, also chmn. ops. com.; treas. City of Allentown, 1980; chmn. bd. Lehigh-Northampton County Arthritis Found. Served with U.S. Army, 1950-54. Mem. Nat. (Silver Spoon award), Pa. (dir.) restaurant assns., Am. Hotel Assn., Pa. Hotel-Motor Inn Assn. Mason. Clubs: Capital Hill (Washington); Tuesday (Harrisburg); Livingston, Lehigh Valley (Allentown). Address: 400 Hamilton St Allentown PA 18105

SMITH, ROBERT HAROLD, communications co. exec.; b. East Orange, N.J., Aug. 17, 1927; s. Harold Taylor and Una (French) S.; B.Sc., Rutgers U., 1948, M.A., 1949; Ph.D., Syracuse U., 1954; m. Ruth Schiela Hatton, Aug. 14, 1966. Lectr. econs. U. Pa., Phila., 1956-58; economist Pa. R.R., Phila., 1956-58; mgmt. cons., 1959-66; v.p. finance and adminstrn., treas., dir. Helme Products, N.Y.C., 1966-67; asst. to mng. partner Wertheim & Co., N.Y.C., 1967-68; sr. v.p., exec. asst. to chmn. ITT, N.Y.C., 1969—.

SMITH, ROBERT I., utility co. exec.; b. 1918; B.S.E., Brown U.; married. With Public Service Electric and Gas Co., 1940—, chief engr., 1965-67, gen. mgr. engring., 1967-68, v.p. electric ops., 1968-71, exec. v.p., 1971-73, pres., 1973-77, chief exec. officer, 1975—, chmn. bd., 1977—, also dir. Office: Public Service Electric and Gas Co 80 Park Pl Newark NJ 07101

SMITH, ROBERT JAMES, utility co. exec.; b. Punxsutawney, Pa., May 13, 1936; s. James A. and Emma Jane (Moyer) S.; B.S., Pa. State U., 1958; B.S. in Mech. Engring., Johns Hopkins U., 1971; M.B.A., U. Balt., 1978; m. Joan Carol Hardesty, June 10, 1961; 1 son, Timothy Robert. Indsl. sales engr. Phila. Gas Works, 1961-63; indsl. sales engr. Balt. Gas & Electric Co., 1963-73, sr. real estate planner, 1973-74, supr. real estate, 1974—. Pres. trustees Central Presbyterian Ch., 1978-79. Served with AUS, 1958-60. Mem. Am. Right of Way Assn. (chem. utilities com. 1978, 80), Greater Balt. Bd. Realtors, Southeastern Electric Exchange. Home: 535 Dunkirk Rd Baltimore MD 21212 Office: PO Box 1475 Baltimore MD 21203

SMITH, ROBERT JAMES, pharm. co. exec.; b. Plattsburgh, N.Y., Apr. 15, 1952; s. Robert Vernon and Margaret Elizabeth (Curran) S.; B.S. in Chem. Engring., Clarkson Coll. Tech., Potsdam, N.Y., 1974. Environ. technician Ayerst Labs., Rouses Point, N.Y., 1974-77, prodn. supr. process control, 1977—. Mem. Am. Mgmt. Assn. Republican. Roman Catholic. Home: 41 Hamilton St Plattsburgh NY 12901 Office: 64 Maple St Rouses Point NY 12979

SMITH, ROBERT WALTER, telecommunications co. exec.; b. Chewsville, Md., Aug. 6, 1940; s. Harry William and Catherine Elizabeth (Leather) S.; B.S. in Bus., U. Md., 1963, postgrad. Law Sch., 1963-64; postgrad. Am. U., 1964-66; m. Ruth P. Phillips, July 27, 1968; children—Robert Walter, Sean Alexander. With Xerox Corp., Balt., Washington, Louisville, Rochester, N.Y., Austin, Tex., Hartford, Conn., 1964-75, br. mgr., Austin, Hartford, 1972-75; v.p., gen. mgr. Eutectic Corp., Flushing, N.Y., 1975; v.p. sales and mktg. Tele/Resources, Inc., Armonk, N.Y., 1976-79; v.p. sales/mktg. ITT Corp., Harrisburg, Pa., 1979—. Home: 841 Kiehl Dr Lemoyne PA 17043 Office: 300 E Park Dr Harrisburg PA 17111

SMITH, ROGER BONHAM, automotive mfg. co. exec.; b. Columbus, Ohio, July 12, 1925; s. Emmet Quimby and Bess (Obetz) S.; student U. Mich., 1942-44, B.B.A., 1947, M.B.A., 1949; m. Barbara Ann Rasch, June 7, 1954; children—Roger Bonham, Jennifer Anne, Victoria Belle, Drew Johnston. With Gen. Motors, Detroit, 1949—, asst. treas., N.Y.C., 1967-68, gen. asst. comptroller, Detroit, 1968, gen. asst. treas., 1968-70, treas., 1970-71, v.p. charge fin. staff, 1971-73; v.p., group exec. in charge of non-automotive and def. group, 1973-74, exec. v.p., 1974—, vice chmn. fin. com., 1975—. Mem. adv. bd. Acctg. Center, U. Mich. Grad. Sch. Bus. Adminstrn.; mem. dean's adv. council Purdue U. Sch. Humanities, Social Sci. and Edn.; trustee Cranbrook Schs., Bloomfield Hills, Mich., Mich. Colls. Found., Detroit; trustee, treas. Automotive Safety Found.; bd. dirs., mem. exec. com., treas. Hwy. Users Fedn. Served with USNR, 1944-46. Mem. Fin. Execs. Inst., Motor Vehicle Mfrs. Assn. (dir., exec. com.). Clubs: Detroit, Detroit Athletic; Orchard Lake (Mich.) Country; Bloomfield Hills Country; Links (N.Y.C.). Home: 3770 Brookfield Dr Bloomfield Hills MI 48013 Office: 3044 W Grand Blvd Detroit MI 48202

SMITH, ROGER CRICHTON, mfg. co. exec.; b. San Francisco, Nov. 3, 1937; s. Junius Penny and Isabel Scott (Crichton) S.; B.A., Colgate U., 1959; M.B.A., Dartmouth, 1964; m. Stephanie Sheldon Thrall, June 15, 1963; children—Gardner Thrall, Prescott Fay, Cameron Goodell. With Revere Copper & Brass, Inc., N.Y.C., 1959-61, Becton-Dickinson, Inc., Rutherford, N.J., 1961-62; domestic sales mgr. Cone Automatic Machine Co., Windsor, Vt., 1964-67; pres. Sinclair Machine Products, Inc., Claremont, N.H., 1967—, Airport Machine Products, Inc. Claremont, 1972—, Garrison Stove Works, Inc., Claremont, 1978—; chmn. bd., treas. Custom Gear, Inc., Andover, Mass.; treas. Garrison Stove Works of Oreg., Inc., 1979—, Garrison Stove Works of Ind. Inc., 1980—. Chmn., Bd. of Selectmen, Woodstock, Vt., 1972-79. Mem. Nat. Screw Machine Products Assn. (trustee 1972-75). Home: Biscuit Hill Farm Woodstock VT 05091 Office: Airport Rd Claremont NH 03743

SMITH, RONALD WARREN, computer co. exec.; b. Jersey City, June 19, 1929; s. Edward T. and Charlotte (Franck) S.; B.S., Fairleigh Dickinson U., 1961; m. Dolores Wynkoop, Aug. 24, 1952; children—Douglas, Michael, Geoffrey, Charlotte, Jennifer. Mgr., Globe Engring. Service, Hoboken, N.J., 1947-50; Devenco, Inc., N.Y.C., 1950-51; customer engr. IBM, Jersey City, 1954-61, field mgr., 1961-64, spl. equipment engr., N.Y.C., 1964-67, mktg. rep., 1967-72, mktg. nat. account mgr., 1972-73, mktg. advisor, 1974-75, program mgr., White Plains, 1976-78, litigation mgr., 1979—. Served with U.S. Army, 1951-53. Mem. IBM Pres. Class, Harvard Grad. Sch. Bus. Adminstrn. Clubs: Masons (past master), Tall Cedars of Lebanon, Order Eastern Star (past patron). Home: 13 Balmoral Dr Spring Valley NY 10977 Office: 445 Hamilton Ave White Plains NY 10977

SMITH, RUSSELL FRANCIS, fin. planning and policies cons.; b. Washington, Mar. 26, 1944; s. Raymond Francis and Elma Gloria (Daugherty) S.; student East Carolina U., 1964, N.C. State U., 1964-65; B.S. with honors, U. Md., 1970, M.B.A., 1976. Exec. asst. mgr. Hotel Corp. Am., Washington, 1966-68; sr. venture capital cons. Initiative Investing Corp., Washington, 1968-69; pres., gen. mgr. Asso. Trades Corp., Washington, 1970-74; cons. in fin., Greenbelt, Md., 1974-76; mng. cons. Bradford Nat. Corp., Washington, 1976-79; v.p. OAO Corp., Washington, 1979—. Chmn. com. on wildlife Prince George's Humane Soc., Hyattsville, Md., 1968-71, Soc. for Prevention of Cruelty of Animals, Hyattsville, 1971-75. Served with U.S. Army, 1963-66. Decorated Silver Star medal, Bronze Star medal with V device, Purple Heart. Mem. Am. Fin. Assn., Ops Research Soc. Am., Am. Acctg. Assn., N. Am. Soc. Corp. Planners, Internat. Assn. Math. Modeling, Assn. M.B.A. Execs., Beta Gamma Sigma, Beta Alpha Psi. Republican. Home: 5921 Cherrywood Terr Greenbelt MD 20770 Office: OAO Corp 1200 New Hampshire Ave NW Washington DC 20036

SMITH, RUSSELL WESLEY, mgmt. cons.; b. Penn Yan, N.Y., Jan. 23, 1947; s. Wesley Sanford and Gladys Klothe S.; A.A.S., SUNY, 1973; B.S. cum laude, N.H. Coll., 1975. With Smith Klothe Asso., Bluff Point, N.Y.; asso. Resource Assos., Inc., Newmarket, N.H., 1979—. Served with Signal Corps, U.S. Army, 1966-68. Methodist.

SMITH, SHERWOOD JOSEPH, office supplies co. exec.; b. Ashtabula, Ohio, Dec. 25, 1923; s. John James and Josephine Julia (Vistejn) S.; B.S.C., Ohio U., 1948; m. JoAnn Cordelia Parker, May 8, 1948 (dec. Nov. 1979); children—Sherwood Joseph, II, Sharon Jo, David John, Scott J. Accountant, Arthur Andersen & Co., C.P.A.'s, N.Y.C. and Cleve., 1948-50; asst. treas. Clyde Porcelain Steel Corp.

(Ohio), 1950-52; with Whirlpool Corp., 1952-68, dir. service, 1960-62, v.p., 1962-68; now chmn., pres. Guthries Office Supply Co. Inc., Evansville, Ind.; controller Henry Fligeltaub Co.; dir. Fed. Res. Bank St. Louis, 1966-72. Served with inf. AUS, 1943-46. Mem. Evansville C. of C., LaPorte Mfg. Assn. (pres. 1957-61). Clubs: Evansville Country, Evansville Kennel, Evansville Petroleum; LaPorte Yacht; Oak Meadows Country (McCutchensville, Ind.). Home: 802 College Hwy Evansville IN 47714

SMITH, STANLEY VLADIMIR, investment banker; b. Rhinelander, Wis., Nov. 16, 1946; s. Valy Zdenek and Sylvia (Cohen) S.; B.S., Cornell U., 1968; M.B.A., U. Chgo., 1972; m. Diane Sue Green, Aug. 8, 1979. Lectr. econs. U. Chgo., 1972; bd. govs. Fed. Res. System intern FRS, Washington, 1972; asst. to pres. First Nat. Bank Chgo., 1974-75; investment banking asso. December Group, Chgo., 1975-77; co-founder, 1977, since dir., treas., v.p. fin. and adminstrn. Seaquest Internat., Ltd.; dir. Seaquest Internat., Inc., 1977—; co. sponsored expdn. to locate and salvage ancient sunken Spanish treasure galleon La Concepcion, 1977. Allied Chem. Co. fellow, 1967; John McMullen fellow, 1969. Mem. Am. Mgmt. Assn., Alpha Delta Phi. Republican. Home: 70 E Scott St Suite 505 Chicago IL 60610 Office: 8 S Michigan Ave Suite 707 Chicago IL 60603

SMITH, STEPHEN ROBERT, remote computing services co. exec.; b. Elgin, Ill., Aug. 25, 1943; s. Robert Homer and Lucille S.; B.S.E.E., Iowa State U., 1965; M.B.A. candidate U. Chgo., 1975-76; m. Valerie J. Crittenton, July 7, 1977; children—Matthew, Amy. Mgmt. trainee U.S. Steel, Lorain, Ohio, 1965-66; sales rep. IBM, San Francisco, 1966-69, mktg. mgr., 1970-71; mgr. mktg. plans Tymshare, Cupertino, Calif., 1971-73, Central region mgr., 1973-74, Midwest area mgr., Chgo., 1974-76, Eastern region mgr., 1976-78, v.p. Eastern region, Darien, Conn., 1978-79, v.p. sales comml. services, 1979—. Clubs: Rotary, Elks. Office: 36 Old Kings Hwy S Darien CT 06820

SMITH, STEWART RUSSELL, investment co. exec.; b. Los Angeles, Aug. 29, 1946; s. Howard Russell and Jeanne Rogers S.; B.A. magna cum laude, Pomona Coll., 1968; J.D. cum laude, Harvard U., 1971; m. Patricia Ann Heydt, Mar. 11, 1972; children—Cameron Stewart, Graham Russell. Admitted to Calif. bar, 1972; trial atty. Dept. Justice, Washington, 1971-73; asso. firm Paul, Hastings, Janofsky & Walker, Los Angeles, 1973-77; individual practice law, San Marino, Calif., 1977-79; pres., dir. Kinsmith Fin. Corp., San Marino, 1979—. Mem. Am. Bar Assn., Los Angeles County Bar Assn., Phi Beta Kappa. Republican. Presbyterian. Clubs: Jonathan (Los Angeles); Annandale Golf (Pasadena, Calif.). Office: 2600 Mission St Suite 201 San Marino CA 91108

SMITH, TAD RANDOLPH, lawyer; b. El Paso, July 20, 1928; s. Eugene Rufus and Dorothy (Derrick) S.; B.B.A., U. Tex., 1952, LL.B., 1951; m. JoAnn Wilson, Aug. 24, 1949; children—Laura, Derrick, Cameron Ann. Admitted to Tex. bar, 1951; asso. firm Kemp, Smith, White, Duncan & Hammond, El Paso, 1951, partner, 1952—; dir. El Paso Electric Co., Panat. Group Inc., State Nat. Bank El Paso, Property Trust Am. Active United Way of El Paso, NCCJ. Mem. Am. Bar Assn., State Bar Tex., El Paso Bar Assn. (pres. 1971-72), El Paso C. of C. (dir. 1979—). Republican. Methodist. Home: 1202 Thunderbird El Paso TX 79912 Office: 2000 State Nat Plaza El Paso TX 79901

SMITH, THEODORE CHARLES, electronics co. exec.; b. Port Huron, Mich., Jan. 21, 1933; s. Clarence George and Lucy Agatha (Lewandowski) S.; B.Econs., U. Detroit, 1957; M.B.A., Syracuse U., 1974; m. Jane Guze, Nov. 13, 1971; children—Kent A., Keith A., L. David, Laura J. Sales mgr. Pegasus Labs. Inc., Troy, Mich., 1958-61, Renwell Industries, South Hadley Falls, Mass., 1961-65; mktg. mgr. Ferrand Industries, Valhalla, N.Y., 1965-71, Umac div. Sperry Rand Corp., Burlington, Vt., 1971-76; exec. v.p. Gen. Numeric Corp., Elk Grove Village, Ill., 1976-80; pres. Yasnac Am., Bensenville, Ill., 1981—; mem. numerically controlled machine tools tech. adv. com. Bur. East West Trade, Dept. Commerce, 1974-76. Served with 11th airborne div. U.S. Army, 1954-56. Mem. Numerical Control Soc., Computer and Automated Systems Assn., Soc. Mfg. Engrs. Clubs: Ethan Allen (Burlington, Vt.); Lake Point Tower (Chgo.); Itasca (Ill.) Country; Lake Forest (Ill.). Contbr. articles to profl. and trade jours. Office: 390 Kent Ave Elk Grove Village IL 60007

SMITH, THOMAS EUGENE, banker; b. Brown's Summit, N.C., Aug. 23, 1930; s. Howard Cleveland and Annie May (Warren) S.; student George Washington U., 1948-50, Am. U., various times; m. Joan Cretcher Hopkins, Sept. 22, 1948; 1 dau., Vicki Joan. Developer, pres. The Potomac Corp., T. Eugene Smith, Inc., 1950—; pres. Nat. Bank of Fairfax (Va.), 1975—, dir., 1964—. Bd. dirs. Wolf Trap Found., chmn. exec. com.; trustee Greater Washington Ednl. TV Assn.; mem. Nat. Capital Planning Commn.; former mem. Fairfax County Bd. Zoning Appeals; former chmn. Fairfax County Planning Commn. Democrat. Episcopalian. Clubs: Georgetown, City Tavern (Washington). Office: National Bank of Fairfax Fairfax VA 22030

SMITH, THOMAS HARRY FRANCIS, chem. co. exec.; b. Paterson, N.J., Feb. 15, 1928; s. Harry H. and Marie C. (Handbridge) S.; B.S., Fordham U., 1947; M.Sc., Phila. Coll. Pharmacy Sci., 1956, Ph.D., 1961; m. Anne P. Malatesta, Nov. 17, 1951; 1 dau., Monica Anne. Pharmacologist, Hoffman LaRoche, Nutley, N.J., 1948-50, Wallace Labs., New Brunswick, N.J., 1950-51; asst. to bus. mgr. Phila. Coll. Pharmacy Sci., 1956-60; lectr. basic scis. U. Pa. Sch. Nursing, 1956-60; sr. toxicologist Wyeth Labs., Radnor, Pa., 1960-63; coordinator, tech. info., Avon Products, Suffern, N.Y., 1963-67; dir. sci. services Lehn & Fink, Montvale, N.J., 1967-71; dir. product quality Lanvin-Charles of Ritz, Holmdel, N.J., 1972-76; corp. dir. product integrity Norda, Inc., 1977-80; dir. Environ. Resources Group, IMS Am. Ltd., 1980—; corp. toxicologist IBM, 1981—. Served with Chem. Corps, AUS, 1952-54. Contbr. articles in toxicology and pharmacology to profl. publs. Home: 392 Holly Dr Wyckoff NJ 07481

SMITH, THOMAS JEFFERSON, III, wholesale hardware co. exec.; b. Dublin, Ga., Oct. 12, 1930; s. Thomas Jefferson and Lucile (Kennebrew) S.; B.A. in Econs., U. Va., 1952; m. Anne Shearouse, Mar. 10, 1957; children—Thomas Jefferson IV, Lucile, Laura, Meda. Salesman, T.J. Smith Wholesale Hardware, McRae, Ga., 1954-57, buyer, 1957-63, pres., chief exec. officer, 1963—; commd. agt. Chevron U.S.A., Inc., 1966-79, jobber, 1979—; pres. Telfair Auto Service, McRae, Ga., 1974—, Sellers of Ga., Inc., McRae, 1978—; chmn. bd. De Soto (Ga.) Nut House, 1979—. Treas., S. Ga. conf. United Methodist Ch., 1974—; chmn. bd. Ocmulgee Acad., 1976-79; pres. Central Ga. council Boy Scouts Am., 1978, rep. nat. council, 1978—. Served with USN, 1952-54; Korea. Recipient Silver Beaver award Boy Scouts Am., 1963. Mem. Nat. Wholesale Hardware Assn., So. Wholesale Hardware Assn., Nat. Assn. Wholesalers, Chevron Agts. Assn., Ga. Agribus. Council, Am. Legion (comdr. 1980). Clubs: Dublin Country; Capital City (Atlanta); Farmington Country (Charlottesville, Va.); Rotary (pres. 1963) (McRae, Ga.). Home: 306 W Graham St McRae GA 31055 Office: T J Smith Wholesale Hardware 120 Scotland Ave McRae GA 31055

SMITH, TIMOTHY DAVID, banker; b. Somerville, Mass., July 10, 1950; s. William and Arlene Sarah (Quill) S.; student State Coll. at Salem (Mass.), 1968-71; m. Stephanie Marie Poor, Dec. 5, 1971; children—Timothy David, Jessica Arlene. Asst. service mgr. Commonwealth Chevrolet, Boston, 1971-72; examiner Commr. Banks Office, Commonwealth of Mass., Boston, 1972-77; ops. officer East Cambridge Savs. Bank, Cambridge, Mass., 1977-79, dir. ops., asst. v.p., 1979—. Bd. dirs. East End Union. Recipient Mass. Bay award United Way, 1978, Achievement award, 1979. Mem. Middlesex B Group Forum, Somerville C. of C., Cambridge C. of C., Somerville Local Devel. Corp., Collegiate Basketball Ofcls. Assn., Internat. Assn. Approved Basketball Ofcls., Eastern New Eng. Baseball Umpires Assn. Office: 292 Cambridge St Cambridge MA 02141

SMITH, VALENTINE JOY (MRS. ROSS JOHN PRIMEAUX), arts and antiquities co. exec.; b. Monette, Mo., Aug. 12, 1929; d. Ira B. and Pauline Goldie (Pyle) Haag; grad. Iola (Kans.) High Sch., 1946; 1 son, Jeffrey Clyde Austin. News and sports reporter Iola Register, 1941-46; sec., dir. pub. relations Fox West Coast Theaters, San Francisco, 1947-50; sec., bookkeeper Desert Inn Hotel, Las Vegas, 1953-54, Thunderbird Hotel, Las Vegas, 1955; stenographer, bookkeeper Electr-Optical Systems, Inc., Pasadena, Calif., 1957-58; exec. sec. Lummus Co., Bloomfield, N.J., 1968-69; loan specialist Trans-West Mortgage Co., Mill Valley, Calif., 1963-65; cons. J. F. Pritchard Constrn. Co., Kansas City, Mo., 1973-74; visual arts cons. Gibson Girls, Tonkawa, Okla., 1974—; pres., founder Liberty Orgn. for Vital Emergencies of the Internat. Newborn Cosmos, 1975—; profl. appraiser arts and antiquities. Vol. Help Line, Inc., Ponca City, 1975—. Mem. Ponca City Art Assn. (Blue Ribbon award 1971). Contbr. articles to publs. Home and office: PO Drawer 33 Tonkawa OK 74653

SMITH, WARD, mfg. co. exec., lawyer; b. Buffalo, Sept. 13, 1930; s. Andrew Leslie and Georgia (Ward) S.; student Georgetown U., 1948-49; A.B., Harvard U., 1952; J.D., U. Buffalo, 1955; m. Gretchen Keller Diefendorf, Oct. 29, 1960; children—Jennifer Hood, Meredith Ward, Jonathan Andrew, Sarah Katherine. Admitted to N.Y. bar, 1955, Mass. bar, 1962, Ohio bar, 1977; asso. firm Lawler & Rockwood, N.Y.C., 1959-62; sec., counsel Whitin Machine Works, Whitinsville, Mass., 1962-66, sec., corp. gen. counsel, 1966-68, v.p., 1968—; sr. v.p. White Consol. Industries, Inc., Cleve., 1969-72, exec. v.p., dir., 1972-79, pres., chief adminstrv. officer, 1979—; dir. N.Am. Coal Corp., Contran Corp. Trustee, Cleve. Orch., Case Western Res. U., Univ. Hosps. of Cleve.; bd. advisers Notre Dame Coll., Cleve. Served to lt. USNR, 1955-59. Mem. Am., N.Y. State bar assns. Clubs: Country (Pepper Pike, Ohio); Pepper Pike, Tavern Union (Cleve.). Home: 19701 N Park Blvd Shaker Heights OH 44122 Office: 11770 Berea Rd Cleveland OH 44111

SMITH, WARREN ALLEN, rec. studio corp. exec.; b. Minburn, Iowa, Oct. 27, 1921; s. Harry Clark and Ruth Marion (Miles) S.; B.A., U. No. Iowa, 1948; M.A., Columbia, 1949. Chmn. dept. English, Bentley Sch., N.Y.C., 1949-54, New Canaan (Conn.) High Sch., 1954—; pres., chmn. bd. Variety Sound Corp., N.Y.C., 1961—; instr. Columbia, 1961-62. Pres., Taursa Fund, 1971-73. Served with AUS, 1940-44. Mem. Mensa, Internat. Press Inst., Am. Unitarian Assn., Brit. Humanist Assn., Humanist Book Club (pres. 1957-62), Bertrand Russell Soc. (v.p. 1977-80), Mensa Investment Club (chmn. 1967, 73—). Book rev. editor The Humanist, 1953-58; contbr. book revs. Library Jour. Author syndicated column Manhattan Scene in W.I. newspapers. Home: 1435 Bedford St Apt 10-A Stamford CT 06905 Office: 130 W 42d St Room 551 New York NY 10036

SMITH, WAVERLY GRAVES, ins. co. exec.; b. Durham, N.C., Jan. 21, 1924; s. George W. and Lyla (Graves) S.; m. Anne Kathleen Williamson, July 30, 1943; children—Cheryl, Allen, Carolyn. With St. Paul Fire & Marine Ins. Co., 1949—, head mktg. div., 1966-69, exec. v.p., 1969-73, pres., 1973-77; pres., chief operating officer St. Paul Cos., Inc., 1978—; dir. Gen. Mills. Mpls. Trustee, chmn. KTCA-TV; bd. dirs. Bush Found. Served with USMCR, 1943-46. Home: 11 Evergreen Rd Saint Paul MN 55110 Office: St Paul Cos Inc 385 Washington St Saint Paul MN 55102

SMITH, WAYNE LAVELLE, banker; b. Roanoke, Va.; s. Jack Marion and Lethia Elsie (LaVelle) S.; B.A., Bridgewater Coll., 1951; M.A., James Madison U., 1968; postgrad. Stonier Grad. Sch. Banking, Rutgers U., 1970; m. Mary Lou Offutt, Aug. 8, 1959; children—Stephen Wayne, Stacey Anne. Cashier 1st Nat. Bank, Harrisonburg, Va., 1960-70; pres. The Planters Bank, Bridgewater, Va., 1970-74; sr. v.p. The Exchange Bank of Polk County, Winter Haven, Fla., 1974—, also dir.; instr. banking Blue Ridge Community Coll., part-time, 1970-73; instr. Polk Community Coll., Winter Haven, 1974-78. Served with USNR, 1953-60. Mem. Winter Haven C. of C. (treas.), Robert Morris Assos. Republican. Presbyn. Office: Exchange Nat Bank 250 Magnolia Ave SW Winter Haven FL 33880

SMITH, WILLARD MONTGOMERY, JR., oil jobber; b. Kingsport, Tenn., May 5, 1924; s. Willard Montgomery and Willie Dare (Patterson) S.; student Va. Poly. Inst., 1941-42, 46-47, 49; m. Ruby Huddle, Nov. 27, 1946; children—Caroline Jane, Jennifer Ann. Mgr., Huddle's Feed & Produce Store, Wytheville, Va., 1949-55; sec.-treas., dir. Farmers Mut. Fire Ins. Assn. Wythe County, Inc., Wytheville, 1954—; pres., dir. Smith Oil Corp., Wytheville, 1955—; organizer, sec., dir. Mountain Security Savs. & Loan Assn., Wytheville, 1973—; dir. Patcon Corp., Wytheville. Mem. Wythe County Bd. Suprs., 1976—; elder Wytheville Presbyterian Ch., 1968—. Served with USAAF, 1942-46. Decorated Air medal. Mem. Wytheville-Wythe County C. of C. (sec., dir. 1968-73), Nat. Oil Jobbers Assn., Va. Petroleum Jobbers Assn., Va. Assn. Mut. Ins. Cos., Va. Savs. and Loan League. Democrat. Club: Wytheville Rotary (pres. 1971-72). Home: 375 S 8th St Wytheville VA 24382 Office: 1005 N 4th St Wytheville VA 24382

SMITH, WILLIAM BENNETT, ins. exec.; b. Pantego, N.C., June 20, 1931; s. Jesse Lee and Dora Venters (Hudson) S.; B.A. magna cum laude, U. N.C., 1954. Engaged in ins. business, 1957—; pres. William B. Smith Agy., N.Y.C., 1967-80; pres. Guaranteed Issue Corp., Ft. Lauderdale, Fla., 1980—. Served with AUS, 1954-57. Mem. Life Office Mgmt. Assn., Life Mgrs. Assn., Life Underwriters Assn., Home Office Underwriters Assn., Phi Beta Kappa (past chpt. sec.). Republican. Clubs: Marco Polo, Business Men's Athletic, Manhattan. Author articles substandard ins. Home: 3003 Terramar Fort Lauderdale FL 33304 Office: Guaranteed Issue Corp Suite 620 1150 N Federal Hwy Fort Lauderdale FL 33304

SMITH, WILLIAM JOHN, packaging co. exec.; b. Cranford, N.J., June 27, 1926; s. William J. and Caroline S. (Gaffney) S.; B.M.E., Syracuse U., 1950; grad. Advanced Mgmt. Program, Harvard U., 1967; m. Dolores A. Masson, Nov. 14, 1953; children—Karen, Judith, William J., John, Steven. With Am. Can Co., 1950—, v.p., gen. mgr. gen. packaging Greenwich, Conn., 1971-72, v.p., gen. mgr. ops. tech., 1973-74, sr. v.p. tech. research and devel. and engring., 1975-79, sr. v.p. tech. sector exec., 1979—, chmn. operating com., 1980—. Mem. vis. com. M.I.T. Served with USN, 1943-46. Mem. Inst. Paper Chemistry, N.J. C. of C. (dir.), Pi Kappa Alpha, Theta Tau. Republican. Roman Catholic. Home: 90 Chatham Rd Stamford CT 06903 Office: Am Can Co American Ln Greenwich CT 06830

SMITH, WILLIAM KENDALL, food co. exec.; b. Oakland, Calif., Apr. 21, 1922; s. Earl B. and Lois (Loeffler) S.; B.B.A, U. Minn., 1947; postgrad. Stanford, 1966-67, Harvard, 1969; m. Jean L. Taylor, May 23, 1949; children—Gregory, Lindsay, Christopher, Vincent. With Gen. Mills Inc., Mpls., v.p., 1968—; dir. Consol. Rail Corp., 1976, Lehigh Coal & Navigation Co., 1972-74. Bd. dirs. Family and Children Services, Mpls. Served with U.S. Army, 1942-45. Decorated Purple Heart. Recipient Salzberg award Syracuse U., 1977. Mem. Nat. Indsl. Traffic League (v.p.), Transp. Research Bd. NRC, (exec. com.), Transp. Assn. Am. (dir.), Transp. Data Coordinating Com. (dir., past chmn.), Traffic Clubs Internat. (past pres.; chmn.; man of year, 1975), U.S. Ry. Assn. (chmn. bd., dir.). Roman Catholic. Clubs: Capitol Hill (Washington); Hazeltine Nat. Golf (Chaska, Minn.). Home: 2439 Shewood Hills Rd Minnetonka MN 55343 Office: PO Box 1113 Minneapolis MN 55440

SMITH, WILLIAM ROBERT, utility co. exec.; b. Mount Clemens, Mich., Nov. 11, 1916; s. Robert L. and Elsie (Chamberlain) S.; B.S., Detroit Inst. Tech., 1947; postgrad. Detroit Coll. Law, U. Mich. Grad. Sch. Bus. Adminstrn.; m. Ann Sheridan; children—William R., Laura A. Indsl. engr. Detroit Edison Co., 1934-60; mgr. econ. devel. East Ohio Gas Co., Cleve., 1960-80; mgr. nat. accounts Consol. Natural Gas Co., Cleve., 1980—; pres. T.S.T. Corp. Councilman, City of Pepper Pike (Ohio); bd. dirs. No. Ohio Research Info. Center; mem. trustees devel. council St. Luke's Hosp.; v.p. Cleve. Ballet, Citizens League Greater Cleve.; bd. dirs. Animal Protective League. Served with USAAF, 1942-45. Registered profl. engr., Mich., Ohio. Fellow Am. Indsl. Devel. Council; mem. Ohio, Cleve. chambers commerce, Cleve. Engring. Soc., Soc. Indsl. Realtors, Nat. Assn. Corp. Real Estate Execs., Assn. Ohio Commodores, Delta Theta Tau. Presbyterian. Clubs: Mid-Day; Shaker Heights (Ohio) Country. Home: 27750 Fairmount Blvd Pepper Pike OH 44124 Office: 1717 E 9th St Cleveland OH 44114

SMITH, WILLIAM SPENCER, oil co. exec.; b. Eagle Grove, Iowa, Oct. 5, 1950; s. Spencer Barker and Gerene Ethel S.; B.A. in Bus., U. No. Iowa, 1973; m. Luann E. Peterson, July 29, 1977. Mktg. rep. IBM, Denver, 1973-76; v.p. ENI Corp., Denver, 1976-80, Knight Royalty Corp., Denver, 1980—; pres. Knight Securities Corp. Mem. youth activities bd. YMCA, 1978—; mem. Nat. Republican Senatorial Com., 1980; trustee, chmn. Rockland Community Ch., 1978—. Republican. Mem. United Ch. of Christ. Club: U. No. Iowa Alumni Athletic. Home: 1506 Shooting Star Dr Golden CO 80401 Office: 1675 Broadway Suite 1910 Denver CO 80202

SMITHBURG, WILLIAM DEAN, diversified mfg. co. exec.; b. Chgo., July 9, 1938; s. Pearl L. and Margaret L. (Savage) S.; B.S.C., DePaul U., 1960; M.B.A., Northwestern U., 1961; m. Alberta Hap, May 25, 1963; children—Susan, Thomas. With Leo Burnett, Chgo., 1961-63, McCann Erickson, 1963-65; with Quaker Oats Co., Chgo., 1966—, now pres., chief operating officer; dir. No. Trust Corp. Trustee, Nutrition Found.; mem. Chgo. Com. Served with USAR, 1959-60. Roman Catholic. Clubs: Econ. (Chgo.); Onwentsia; Union League. Office: 345 Merchandise Mart Plaza Chicago IL 60654

SMITHERS, JOHN ABRAM, business exec.; b. Middletown, N.Y., June 20, 1915; s. Francis Sydney and Eleanor (Boak) S.; grad. high sch.; m. Margaret McClure, Mar. 6, 1947 (div. May 1964); children—Margaret H., John Abram and Eleanor B. (twins), James P.; m. 2d, Jane Braitmayer Howell, June 13, 1964; stepchildren—Kathleen Howell, William D. Howell, Marian B. Howell. Customer and systems engr. IBM, 1935-47; partner Red Hook Apple Industries, 1947-52; chmn. bd., treas., dir., founder STAMP, Inc. (formerly Smithers Tools and Machine Products, Inc.), Rhinebeck, N.Y., 1948—; founder, owner Sawkill Indsl. Park, Rhinebeck. Served as 2d lt., inf., AUS, 1942-46. Mem. Council Industry Southeastern N.Y., Am. Def. Preparedness Assn., Am. Metal Stamping Assn. Clubs: Sippican, Beverly Yacht (Marion, Mass.). Home: RD 2 Box 151 Red Hook NY 12571 Office: Box 391 Rhinebeck NY 12572

SMITHSON, ORLA DALE, oil co. exec.; b. Flint, Mich., Nov. 24, 1921; s. Orla C. and Mable (Downey) S.; student public schs., Clio, Mich.; m. Beverly J. Morse, Mar. 11, 1967; children—Debra Lee (dec.), Jeannine; stepchildren—James, Michael, Helen, Edward, Christopher, Mary Ann, Jeanette. With Smithson Petroleum Co., Clio, 1957-68, pres., 1962-66; founder, pres. Crest Petroleum Co., Flint, 1968, Time Gulf Inc., Lansing, Mich., 1972-74; founder, pres. ODS Energy, Inc., Flint, 1974—. Served with AUS, 1942-46. Mem. Genesee County Power House Assn. (v.p. 1978-79), Ky. Coal Assn., Detroit Coal and Oil Assn. Roman Catholic. Clubs: Elks (Elk of Yr. 1970), U. Mich., 100 of Flint (Mich.). Home: 5510 Broadmoor St Grand Blanc MI 48439 Office: 3425 W Pierson Rd Flint MI 48504

SMOLENYAK, BARBARA ELIZABETH, govt. acct.; b. Newark, Jan. 16, 1945; d. Patsy Paul and Daisy Lee (Starkey) Palmiere; B.S., Monmouth Coll., 1967, M.B.A., 1973; m. George Carl Smolenyak, May 7, 1974; 1 son, Sean Winston. Nat. bank examiner Comptroller of the Currency, N.Y.C., 1967-73; auditor Def. Contract Audit Agy., Alexandria, Va., 1975-76; audit mgr. U.S. Treasury, Washington, 1976—. Mem. Assn. Govt. Accts., D.C. Inst. C.P.A.'s. Republican. Roman Catholic. Office: 1100 Vermont Ave Washington DC 20226

SMOLLEN, LEONARD ELLIOTT, mgmt. and fin. cons.; b. N.Y.C., Jan. 1, 1930; s. Abner Charles and Madeleine (Ehrlich) S.; B.S., Carnegie Inst. Tech., 1951; M.S., Columbia U., 1952; M.E., Mass. Inst. Tech., 1962; m. Mindelle Deborah Hershberg, July 6, 1958; children—Rachel Anne, Jonathan Adam. Sr. engr. Sikorsky Aircraft, Bridgeport, Conn., 1953-57; engring. mgr. Allied Research Assos., Boston, 1957-61; tech. cons. Mitre Corp., Bedford, Mass., 1962-63; chief mech. engr. EG&G, Bedford, 1963-67, program mgr., 1967-69, dir. custom products and program mgmt., 1969-70; exec. v.p. Inst. for New Enterprise Devel., Belmont, Mass., 1971-77, Venture Founders Corp., Waltham, Mass., 1976—; dir. Creare Inc.; lectr. Grad. Sch. Bus. Adminstrn., Northeastern U.; research asso. Sloan Sch. Mgmt., M.I.T., 1970-71. Higgins fellow, 1952; Whitney fellow, 1960. Registered profl. engr., Conn., Mass. Mem. ASME. Clubs: Skating of Boston, Boston Yacht; Winchester Boat. Author: New Venture Creation: A Guide to Small Business Development, 1977; Source Guide for Borrowing Capital, 1977. Home: 10 Central St Winchester MA 01890 Office: 3 Prospect Hill Executive Park 101 4th Ave Waltham MA 02154

SMOLLEN, WILLIAM JOHN, mfg. co. exec.; b. N.Y.C.; s. Hugh Joseph and Alice Elizabeth (Scribner) S.; B.S., Columbia U.; m. Helen Arutunian, Mar. 31, 1951. Mem. profl. staff Hurdman and Cranstoun, C.P.A.'s, N.Y.C., 1945-47; fin. exec. Ebasco Services, N.Y.C., 1947-51; regional fin. exec., v.p. fin. Latin Am. subsidiaries Ford Motor Co., 1951-62; asst. treas. Rockwell Internat., Los Angeles, 1963-80; lectr. profl. seminars. Mem. gen. adminstrn. and fin. com., regional dir. United Way, 1971—; trustee Centinela Hosp., 1974—. Fellow Planning Execs. Inst.; mem. N.Y. Soc. C.P.A.'s, Calif. C.P.A.'s Soc., Fin. Execs. Inst. (dir.), Assn. Pvt. Pension and Welfare Plans (dir.), Nat. Mgmt. Assn., Nat. Assn. Accountants, Newcomen Soc.,

Western Pension Conf., Lake Hollywood Assn. (dir.), C. of C. Contbr. articles to fin. publs. Roman Catholic. Home: 3044 Arrowhead Dr Los Angeles CA 90068

SMUCKLER, HARVEY GLASGOW, bus. exec.; b. Sturgeon Bay, Wis., Aug. 4, 1924; s. Joseph Max and Ruth Mary (Glasgow) S.; B.B.A., U. Wis., 1949; m. Harriet Carol Victor, June 28, 1949; children—Alan Lee, David Todd, Joel Jay. Agt., Mut. of N.Y., Chgo., 1955, asst. mgr., 1957-59; gen. agt. Continental Assurance Co., Milw., 1959-64; pres. Mayflower Life of Wis., Milw., 1964-67; agy. v.p. Bankers Security Life Ins. Soc., Washington, 1967-70, sr. v.p., 1970-74; exec. v.p. Occidental Life Ins. Co. N.C., Raleigh, 1974, pres., 1975-79; pres., chief exec. officer Lincoln Am. Life Ins. Co., Memphis, 1979-80; pres. Ultimate, Ltd., Memphis, 1980—. Active Am. Cancer Soc. Served with USAAF, World War II. C.L.U. Mem. N.C., Raleigh assns. life underwriters, Econ. Club Memphis, Am. Coll. C.L.U., Scabbard and Blade, Phi Epsilon Pi. Mason (32 deg., Shriner). Home: 6357 Shadowood Ln Memphis TN 38119 Office: PO Box 28649 Memphis TN 38128

SNADER, JACK ROSS, cons. co. exec.; b. Athens, Ohio, Feb. 25, 1938; s. Daniel Webster and Mae Estella (Miller) S.; B.S. in Psychology, U. Ill., 1959; m. Sharon Perschnick, Apr. 4, 1959; children—Susan, Brian. Sales promotion mgr. William S. Merrell Co., Cin., 1959-65; product mktg. mgr. Xerox Corp., N.Y.C., 1965-67; gen. mgr. Profl. Communications Assn., Chgo., 1967-69; pres. Systema Corp., cons. in sales and mktg. mgmt, specializing in fin. learning systems, Chgo., 1969—; cons. Nat. Soc. Performance and Instn., Gen. Agts. and Mgrs. Assn. Mem. Chgo. Crime Commn. Mem. Instructional Systems Assn. (founding), Chgo. Assn. Commerce and Industry, Soc. Applied Learning Tech., Midwest Pharm. Advt. Club, Am. Soc. Tng. and Devel., Assn. Mgmt. Clubs: Tower, Exmoor Country, Rotary (Chgo.). Home: 647 Ambleside Dr Deerfield IL 60015 Office: 150 N Wacker Dr Chicago IL 60606

SNEADE, DANIEL CARSON, assn. exec.; b. Sept. 5, 1948; B.S., Va. State Coll., 1977; m. Nancy Jeanne Kolb; 1 dau., Amy Elizabeth. Magistrate, Supreme Ct. Va., Richmond, 1972-75; legal asst. Humphries and Laney, Colonial Heights, Va., 1975-76; campaign coordinator Miller for Gov. campaign, Richmond, Va., 1976-77; asst. to county adminstr. Prince George County (Va.), 1977-78; asst. exec. sec. Va. Gasoline Retailers Assn., Richmond, 1978—. Bd. dirs. Southside Area chpt. ARC; chmn. Colonial Heights Bloodmobile; mem. Colonial Heights Sch. Bd., 1978—; mem. Colonial Heights City Council, 1980—; bus. chmn. Am. Cancer Soc., Am. Heart Assn.; chmn. 36th House Legis. Dist. Democratic Com., Colonial Heights Dem. Com. Mem. Va. Soc. Assn. Execs., Va. Sch. Bds. Assn., Internat. City Mgmt. Assn., Internat. Personnel Mgmt. Assn., Council Va.'s Travel Industries. Office: 1701 E Parham Rd Richmond VA 23228

SNEATH, WILLIAM SCOTT, mfg. co. exec.; b. Buffalo, Mar. 29, 1926; s. William Henry and Cyrena (Kean) S.; B.A., Williams Coll., 1947; M.B.A., Harvard, 1950. With Union Carbide Corp., 1950—, pres., 1971—, dir., 1969—, chmn. bd., 1977—. Office: 270 Park Ave New York NY 10017

SNELLING, DONALD EVERETT, energy co. exec.; b. Mass., June 23, 1940; s. Samuel William and Beatrice (Bamforth) S.; B.A. with honors, U. of South, 1962; M.B.A. in Fin., U. Tulsa, 1968; m. Georganne Cox, Mar. 30, 1963; children—M. Gail, David, Meredith. Cash mgr. Cities Service Oil Co., Tulsa, 1966-68; sr. fin. adv. Esso Eastern, Inc., N.Y.C., 1968; chief fin. officer Vietnam/Cambodia br. Esso Eastern, Saigon, Vietnam, 1969-72; dep. controller Esso Sekiyu K.K., Tokyo, Japan, 1973-75; dir. Esso Asia, Inc., Singapore, 1975-77; controller Esso Australia Ltd., Sydney, 1977-79; exec. v.p. Good Hope Industries Inc., New Orleans, 1979; sr. v.p., chief fin. officer corp., pres. energy and mineral divs., UNC Resources, Inc., Falls Church, Va., 1979—. Served to 1st lt. USAF, 1962-65. C.P.A., Tex. Mem. Tex. Soc. C.P.A.'s, Am. Inst. C.P.A.'s, Phi Gamma Delta. Republican. Episcopalian. Home: 640 Springvale Rd Great Falls VA 22066 Office: UNC Crescent Plaza 7700 Leesburg Pike Falls Church VA 22043

SNIBBE, ELLEN LANSDELL, investment banking co. exec.; b. N.Y.C., Jan. 6, 1950; d. Robert McCawley and Ellen Hienz (Heavey) S.; B.A. cum laude, Briarcliff Coll., 1972; M.B.A., N.Y. U., 1978. Registered rep., mcpl. bond analyst White Weld & Co., N.Y.C., 1972-74; banker Chem. Bank, N.Y.C., 1974-76; mcpl. bond analyst Shearson, Hayden Stone, N.Y.C., 1976-77; asso. in pub. fin. E.F. Hutton Co., N.Y.C., 1977-80, sr. asso. public fin., 1980—; cons. to W.Va. state treas., 1977—. Mem. Helpline, Mayor's Office at City Hall, 1977—, Community Law Office, Harlem, 1977-78; fund raising, fin. coms. N.Y. Jr. League, 1978—. Mem. Nat. Assn. Security Dealers, Investment Assn. N.Y. Republican. Club: Mcpl. Bond Women's of N.Y. Home: 301 E 64th St New York NY 10021 Office: EF Hutton Co 1 Battery Park Plaza New York NY 10005

SNIDER, JAMES RHODES, radiologist; b. Pawnee, Okla., May 16, 1931; s. John Henry and Gladys Opal (Rhodes) S.; B.S., U. Okla., 1953, M.D., 1956; m. Lynadell Vivion, Dec. 27, 1954; children—Jon, Jan. Intern, Edward Meyer Meml. Hosp., Buffalo, 1956-57; resident radiology U. Okla. Med. Center, 1959-62; radiologist Holt-Krock Clinic and Sparks Regional Med. Center, Ft. Smith, Ark., 1962—; cons. USPHS Hosp., Talihina, Okla., 1962—. Dir. Fairfield Community Land Co., Little Rock, 1968—. Mem. Ark. Bd. Pub. Welfare, 1969-71. Bd. dirs. U. Okla. Assn., 1967-70, U. Okla. Alumni Devel. Fund, 1970—; bd. visitors U. Okla. Served to lt. comdr. USNR, 1957-62. Mem. Am. Coll. Radiology, Radiol. Soc. N.Am., Am. Roentgen Ray Soc., AMA, Phi Beta Kappa, Beta Theta Pi (trustee corp.), Alpha Epsilon Delta. Asso. editor Computerized Tomography, 1976—. Home: 5814 Cliff Dr Fort Smith AR 72903 Office: 1500 Dodson St Fort Smith AR 72901

SNINSKI, MARY M., adminstrv. med. technologist; b. Pottsville, Pa., Feb. 24, 1928; d. Nicholas Frank and Concetta I. Macario; A.S., Pa. State Coll., 1948; grad. Pottsville Hosp. Sch. Med. Tech., 1949; student Muhlenberg Coll., 1978; B.S. in Med. Tech., Thomas Jefferson U., 1981; m. Michael John Sninski, Nov. 22, 1951; 1 dau., Jeanne. Adminstrv. med. technologist Pottsville Hosp., 1953—, ednl. coordinator, sch. med. tech., 1953-76, asst. coordinator neonatal monitoring program, 1978—, mem. com. on lab purchasing, 1978—. Pres. Am. Cancer Soc., Pottsville, 1977-79, v.p., 1976-77; pres. Women's Club of Nativity High Sch., Pottsville, 1968-70; lector Our Lady of Mt. Carmel Ch., Minersville, 1978; bd. dirs. county unit ARC, 1979—, NE Pa. Regional Red Cross Blood Service, 1979—. Mem. Registry Med. Technologists of Am. Soc. Clin. Pathologists, Pa. Soc. Cytology (v.p. 1974-75), Am. Soc. Cytology, Internat. Acad. Cytotechnologists. Republican. Roman Catholic. Home: 15 Lewis St Minersville PA 17954 Office: 420 S Jackson St Pottsville PA 17901

SNOOK, JOHN MCCLURE, telephone co. exec.; b. Toledo, May 31, 1917; s. Ward H. and Grace (McClure) S.; student Ohio State U., 1936-43. Instr. history, fine arts and scis. Ohio State U., Columbus; exec. v.p. Gulf Telephone Co., Foley, Ala., 1955-71, pres., 1971—. Chmn., Baldwin Sesquicentennial, 1969; mem. Baldwin County Bicentennial Commn.; pageant chmn., dir. Ft. Morgan Bicentennial Program, 1976; mem. hon. staff Gov. Ala., 1967—; past pres. Friends of Library Assn.; asso. sponsor Gulf Shores Mardi Gras Assn. Hon. a.d.c. lt. col. Ala.; hon. Ala. state trooper; recipient Citizen of Year award Gulf Shores, 1956-57. Mem. Ala.-Miss. Ind. Telephone Assn. (past pres.), Nat. Rifle Assn. (life), Am. Ordnance Assn., South Baldwin C. of C., Delaware County, Baldwin County hist. assns., Defiance and Williams' Hist. Soc., Am. Mus. Nat. History Assn., Nat. Hist. Soc., Nat. Wildlife Fedn., Clan McLeod Soc., Smithsonian Assn., Am. Heritage Soc., Nat. Fedn. Blind, Ohio State Alumni Assn., Ala. Ind. Telephone Assn., Telephone Pioneers, Ind. Pioneers. Clubs: Lions (past pres.), Kiwanis (past pres.; asst. chmn. ann. Christmas Party and Parade). Office: Gulf Telephone Co Box 670 Foley AL 36535

SNOWDEN, LILLIAN RUTH, accountant; b. Monroe, La., Dec. 8, 1941; s. Elijah and Ruth Laura Johnson; student Am. U., 1975-76; B.S. in Bus. Adminstrn., Southeastern U., 1980; m. Ron Snowden, Aug. 30, 1974; children—Jacquelyn, Stephanie, Tio-Carmalita, Demetrius. Fin. sec. Walter Reed Army Med Center, Washington, 1973-77; adminstrv. specialist D.C. N.G., Washington, 1975-76, personnel specialist, 1976-79; cons. Snowden Cons.'s, Washington, 1979-80; accountant/property specialist GSA, Washington, 1980—. Bd. dirs. W Street Ensemble. Decorated Army Commendation medal. Mem. Nat. Council Negro Women, NAACP, D.C. N.G. Assn. (sec. 1975-76, v.p. 1976-77), Delta Sigma Theta (sec. Eastern conf. 1979-80). Democrat. Baptist. Home: 4228 Military Rd NW Washington DC 20015 Office: GSA 7th and D St Washington DC 20407

SNYDER, CHARLES AARON, steel co. exec.; b. Nashville, Feb. 15, 1920; s. Charles Aaron and Lucille (Hill) S.; B.S., U. Tenn., 1947; m. Rosalee Turner, May 31, 1942; 1 dau., Sharon Snyder Pilsch. Project engr. Monsanto Chem. Co., 1947-53; gen. mgr. Snyder Tank Corp., Birmingham, Ala., 1953-54; pres. Dixie Steel & Supply Co., Inc., Tuscaloosa, Ala., 1954—; sec.-treas. Gulf Tank & Fabricating Co., Panama City, Fla., 1958—; pres. Sylacauga Tank Corp. (Ala.), 1961—; sec.-treas. Atmore Tank Corp. (Ala.), 1961—; sec.-treas. So. Heat Exchanger Corp., 1963-73; sec.-treas. Tuscaloosa Warehouse Corp., 1965—; pres. So. Resins, Inc., Moundville, Ala., 1968-76; pres. Dexol, Inc., Tuscaloosa, 1969—; pres. Cherokee Machinery Corp., 1973—, Coral Industries, 1971—; v.p. So. Tank Lining, 1976—; dir. 1st Nat. Bank Tuskaloosa, New Southland Ins. Co., Security Fed. Savs. and Loan Assn. Trustee Druid City Hosp.; bd. dirs., bd. visitors U. Ala., 1975—; commr. Park and Recreation Authority of Tuscaloosa County, 1972—; pres. Druid City Hosp. Meml. Found., 1974, Tuscaloosa Rotary Meml. Found. Mem. Greater Tuscaloosa C. of C. (past pres.), Asso. Industries of Ala. (pres. 1974-75). Clubs: Rotary, Indian Hills Country (past pres.), North River Yacht (dir.). Home: 2715 Cherokee Rd Tuscaloosa AL 35404 Office: Box A Tuscaloosa AL 35404

SNYDER, CHAUNCEY LEROY, govt. ofcl., real estate appraiser; b. Elyria, Ohio, Aug. 16, 1941; s. William McKinley and Marion Floyd (Davis) Ingersoll; student Am. River Coll., 1967-68, San Diego City Coll., 1970, Bakersfield Coll., 1972; m. Lupe Mary Santos, Aug. 5, 1960; children—Lupe Mary, Chauncey Leroy, Naomi Esther, Abdi Zurishaddai, Israel David. Fair chance apprentice HUD-FHA, Sacramento, 1968-69, housing aid, Los Angeles, 1969-70, appraiser trainee, San Diego, 1970-71, field appraiser, Los Angeles, 1971-74, multifamily housing rep., 1974, commitment appraiser, 1974-76, subdiv. appraiser, 1976, commitment appraiser, instr., 1977, supervisory appraiser real estate, 1977—. Served with U.S. Army, 1956-57. Mem. Urban Appraisers Soc. Democrat. Mem. Ch. Name Lord Jesus Christ. Home: 925 S Idaho St La Habra CA 90631 Office: 2500 Wilshire Blvd Los Angeles CA 90057

SNYDER, DAVID RAY, contracting co. exec.; b. Enid, Okla., Dec. 21, 1950; s. Leonard David and Beatrice Mae (Strom) S.; student Okla. State U., 1969-72, U. Tex., Arlington, 1972-74; B.S. in Mech. Engring., So. Methodist U., 1975; m. Janet Le Elmblad, Aug. 17, 1974; 1 dau., Ashley Renée. Draftsman, URS-Forrest & Cotton, Dallas, 1972-73; engr. Clarence Gilmore & Assos., Dallas, cons. engrs., 1973-74; estimater Acoustex Co., Ft. Worth, 1974-76; pres. Integrated Interiors, Ft. Worth, 1976—, ACD, Inc.; owner Snyder Enterprises; partner D&D Supply Co.; accoustical cons. Mem. Nat., Am., Tex. socs. profl. engrs., Fellowship Christian Athletes, Metal Bldg. Dealers Assn. (asso.), Sigma Alpha Epsilon. Republican. Baptist. Club: Masons. Researcher deoxidation water, heat loss due to bldg. orientation. Home: 912 Ridge Dr Bedford TX 76021 Office: 2509 E Weaver St Fort Worth TX 76117

SNYDER, JAMES WILLIAM, JR., bus. exec.; b. South Bend, Ind., Mar. 16, 1948; s. James William and Marjorie Jane (Blakeman) S.; B.B.A., Northwood Inst., 1970; m. Sharon Ann Wallace, Aug. 22, 1970; children—Erin Elizabeth, Stephanie Wallace. Sales mktg. rep. Jim Snyder Sales Co., Grosse Pointe Woods, Mich., 1970-72, v.p., 1972-75, sr. v.p., treas., 1975—, dir., 1972—; mem. bd. Northwood Inst. Alum. active St. John Men's Hosp. Guild, 1971—, Grosse Pointe Woods Police and Fire Aux., 1971—. Mem. Am. Mgmt. Assn., Soc. Advanced Mgmt., Soc. Plastic Engrs., Founders Soc. Detroit Inst. Arts, Automotive Old Timers. Republican. Roman Catholic. Clubs: Detroit Athletic, Detroit Golf, Grosse Pointe Yacht, Grosse Pointe Crisis, The Players; White Hall (Chgo.); Recess. Home: 896 Lochmoor Blvd Grosse Pointe Woods MI 48236 Office: 22811 Mack Ave Suite 105 Saint Clair Shores MI 48080

SNYDER, JOSEPH JULIEN, business exec.; b. Findlay, Ohio, Oct. 29, 1907; s. Paul Julien and Mabel Sarah (Bair) S.; B.S., Carnegie Inst. Tech., 1931; M.B.A., Harvard, 1934; postgrad. Mass. Inst. Tech., 1943-44; m. Helen Torrance Colburn, April 3, 1937; children—Clinton Lytle, Joseph MacGeorge, Susanne Colburn. Vice pres. Colonial Fund, Inc., 1954-75, dir., 1954-77; v.p., dir. Colonial Mgmt. Assos., Inc., Boston, 1945-74; chmn. bd. Quanex Corp. (formerly Mich. Seamless Tube Co.), Houston, 1942-53, dir. 1940—; dir. Transcontinental Gas Pipe Line Corp., Houston, 1951-78, Transco Cos., Inc., 1973-78; trustee Boston Five Cents Savs. Bank, 1950-79; dir. Arthur D. Little, Inc., 1958-77, Liberty Mut. Ins. Cos.; trustee Montagu Boston Investment Trust Ltd., London; mem. staff Radiation Lab. Mass. Inst. Tech., 1944-45, asst. treas., 1946-50, treas., mem. corp., exec. com., 1950-75, life mem. corp., treas. emeritus, fin. cons., 1975—, mem. investment com., 1950—, v.p., 1951-73. Recipient Army-Navy Certificate Appreciation, 1946. Mem. Am. Inst. Chem. Engrs., Am. Acad. Arts and Scis., Harvard Bus. Sch. Alumni Assn. (pres. 1943-44), Beta Theta Pi. Clubs: Detroit; DownTown, St. Botolph (Boston); University (N.Y.C.). Home: 100 Memorial Dr Cambridge MA 02142 Office: 77 Massachusetts Ave Cambridge MA 02139

SNYDER, JULIAN MAXWELL, editor, pub. fin. advisor; b. Boston, Mar. 25, 1928; s. Julian Maxwell and Marian (Bush) S.; B.A. in Philosophy, Ohio U. Reporter, UPI; v.p. AT&T; founder fin. cons. firm, Calif.; fgn. exchange trader, Switzerland; pres., prin. shareholder Moneyline Trading, Inc., N.Y.C.; editor, pub. Internat. Moneyline; lectr. Author: Rules for Financial Survival in the 1980's, 1980; contbr. articles to OPEC Rev., N.Y. Times, Harvard Bus. Rev., others. Office: Internat Moneyline 25 Broad St New York NY 10004

SNYDER, MARK EVAN, mgmt. cons.; b. Wichita, Kans., Jan. 23, 1951; s. Alan Howard and Dorothea (Jones) S.; B.S., U. Tex. at Arlington, 1974, M.S., 1977. Planning analyst Fed. Res. Bank Dallas, 1974-77; asst. to v.p. sales Qwip Systems, Dallas, 1977; electronic funds transfer dir. Tex. Credit Union League, Dallas, 1977-79; v.p. ops. and devel. Real Save Inc., Dallas, 1979—; with Lifson, Herrmann, Blackmarr & Harris Mgmt. Consultants, Dallas, 1979—. Mem. Am. Inst. Indsl. Engrs., Am. Prodn. and Inventory Control Soc., Life Office Mgmt. Assn., Planning Execs. Inst., Soc. Ins. Research, Epsilon Nu Gamma, Alpha Pi Mu. Republican. Presbyterian. Home: 1304 Laurel St Arlington TX 76012 Office: One Turtle Creek Plaza Suite 606 Dallas TX 75219

SNYDER, MICHAEL DENNIS, mgmt. co. exec.; b. Iowa City, Iowa, Nov. 9, 1942; s. Dennis George and Catherine Irene (Brown) O'Brien; B.S. magna cum laude in Math. and Polit. Sci., Mankato State U., 1970; m. Rose Marie Kasper, May 17, 1969; 1 son, Patrick Michael. Acctg. clk. Peavey Co., Omaha, 1965-66, programmer, Mpls., 1966-67; tech. tech. cons. data processing Jostens Inc., Owatonna, Minn., 1967-71, systems mgr. corp. fin., 1971-76, group systems mgr., 1977-78; v.p., chief operating officer Key Mgmt. Inc., Mpls., 1978—, also dir. Cons., Nat. Indian Edn. Assn., 1970-73; ordained deacon Episcopal Ch., 1976. Served with USAF, 1961-65. Mem. Minn. Honeywell User Group (dir. 1973-76, pres. 1974-75). Republican. Home: 1550 E 83d St Bloomington MN 55420 Office: 5201 Eden Circle Edina MN 55436

SNYDER, NATALIE JOYCE, florist; b. Elberfeld, Ind., Feb. 14, 1929; d. Elmer F. and Lydia L. (Ahrens) Thene; student Lockyear's Bus. Coll., 1949; m. James P. Snyder, Apr. 8, 1951; children—James Phillip, James David. With Jim Snyder Florist Greenhouses, Princeton, Ind., 1953—, partner, 1953, sole prop., 1961—. Recipient Florists Transworld Delivery Assn. Disting. award, 1979. Mem. Florists Transworld Delivery Assn., Florafax Internat., Soc. Am. Florists, State Florists Assn. Ind., Ohio Florists Assn., Ky. Florists Assn. Jehovah's Witnesses. Home: 619 S Gibson St Princeton IN 47670

SNYDER, RALPH HOWARD, automotive repair co. exec.; b. Manly, Iowa, July 16, 1923; s. Ralph Harnden and Gertrude Francis (Wendt) S.; student Iowa State U., 1941-43, 46; Brigham Young U., 1943-44; m. Opal Dorothy Peterson, Jan. 19, 1947; children—Donald Carleton, Douglas Eugene, Steven Leroy (dec.). Shop foreman Olds-Cadillac Agy., Estherville, Iowa, 1946-50; exptl. engr. Boeing Aircraft Co., Wichita, Kans., 1950-53; founder Snyder's Garage, Wichita, 1953—. Cons. with instrs. of local auto vocational classes in various high schs. Active Boy Scouts Am., 1959-68. Chmn. Democratic precinct com., 1969-71. Served with USAAF, 1943-46. Mem. Automotive Service Council. Presbyn. (trustee 1971-74). Clubs: Mason, Shrine, Lion, Moose, Bella Vista (Ark.) Country. Home: Route 3 Box K147 Augusta KS 67010 Office: 3419 E Harry St Wichita KS 67218

SNYDER, RICHARD ELLIOT, publishing exec.; b. N.Y.C., Apr. 6, 1933; s. Jack and Molly (Rothman) S.; B.A., Tufts U., 1955; m. Joni Evans, May 19, 1978; children—Jacqueline, Matthew. Asst. mktg. dir. Doubleday & Co., N.Y.C., 1958-60; with Simon & Schuster, N.Y.C., 1960—, publisher, exec. v.p., 1969-75, pres., 1975-79, pres., chief exec. officer, 1979—, also dir. Bd. dirs. Ave. of the Ams. Assn., 1977-78; chmn. pub. com. Lincoln Center corp. fund drive, 1976—; mem. men's spl. gifts com. Am. Cancer Soc., 1976, 78, 79, 80; mem. men's com. The Lighthouse, N.Y. Assn. Blind, 1976—. Served with AUS, 1956-58. Mem. Assn. Am. Pubs. (dir.). Contbr. articles to profl. jours. Home: The Linden Farm Cross River NY 10518 Office: 1230 Ave of the Americas New York NY 10020

SNYDER, RICHARD PERRIN, liquor and wine wholesale exec.; b. N.Y.C., Mar. 12, 1943; s. Perrin Brown and Nancy (Graves) S.; student Pasadena City Coll., 1960-61; m. Sylvia Casanova, May 11, 1968; 1 son, Perrin Richard. Sales rep. Frederick Wildman & Sons, N.Y.C., 1968-70, Julius Wile Sons & Co., N.Y.C., 1970-71; N.J. mgr. Crosse & Blackwell Vintage Cellars, N.Y.C., 1971-75; asst. gen. wine mgr. Knickerbocker Liquors, Syosset, N.Y., 1975-77; gen. wine mgr. Standard Wine & Liquor Co., Woodside, N.Y., 1977—; wine cons. Pres., Little Neck Bay Civic Assn., 1975-77. Mem. Sommelier Soc. Am., Commanderie de Bordeaux, La Confrerie Saint-Etienne-Alsace, La Confrerie des Comités de Nice et de Provence, Confrerie de la Chaine des Rotisseurs, Knights of Vine, Vintners Club San Francisco. Clubs: Larchmont Yacht, Assn. Ex-mems. Squadron A. Office: 26 15 Brooklyn Queens Expwy Woodside NY 11377

SNYDER, ROBERT A., real estate developer; b. Evanston, Ill., Jan. 26, 1945; s. Robert A. and Catherine B. S.; B.A., U. Vt., 1968; m. Patricia Daley, Sept. 28, 1968; children—Sarah M., Christopher R. Pres., dir. Green Mountain Meadows, Inc., Burlington, Vt., 1970-76; owner, pres. The Snyder Co., Inc., Essex Junction, Vt., 1976—. Licensed real estate broker, Vt. Mem. Home Owners Warranty Council Vt., Lake Champlain Regional C. of C., Nat. Assn. Home Builders (dir.), Home Builders Assn. No. Vt. (dir.), Home Builders Assn. Vt. (dir.). Home: 19 Maplewood Ln Essex Junction VT 05452 Office: Main St Essex Junction VT 05452

SNYDER, ROBERT E., mfg. co. exec.; b. Washington, May 22, 1941; s. Harold V. and Floreine L. Snyder; B.S., Marshal U., 1965; m. Patricia Diane Marushi, Apr. 10, 1965; children—Dawn Rene, Robert Shawn. Terr. rep. Kauffman-Latimer Co., 1965-67; with Rubbermaid Comml. Products Co., 1968—, gen. products mgr., 1972-74, nat. sales mgr., 1974-77, v.p. mktg., Winchester, Va., 1977—. Active Big Bros. Served with USMC, 1960. Mem. Sales and Mktg. Assn., Nat. Assn. food Service Mfg., Nat. Office Products Assn. Presbyterian. Office: 3124 Valley Ave Winchester VA 22601

SNYDER, RONALD WARREN, mktg. research and devel. co. exec.; b. Phila., Feb. 6, 1947; s. Ronald Clark and Bertha Elizabeth S.; A.A.S., Gloucester County Coll., Sewell, N.J., 1972. Owner, operator Eagle Advt., Inc., Springfield, Mo., 1973-74; profl. adventurer, 1974-78; chmn. bd., chief exec. officer Overseas Research & Devel. Inc., Springfield, 1978—; Mo. coordinator Vietnam Vets. in Bus., 1979-80; mem. U.S. Senatorial Bus. Adv. Bd. Served with USAR, 1966-69; Vietnam. Decorated Purple Heart, Combat Inf. badge. Mem. Am. Mgmt. Assns., Solar Lobby, Am. Assn. Small Research Cos., Internat. Shooters Devel. Fund, Nat. Rifle Assn., Springfield Area C. of C. Republican. Lutheran. Editor Vanguard mag., 1971-72. Office: Box 267 Jewell Sta Springfield MO 65801

SNYDER, WENDELL LLOYD, JR., hosp. fin. dir.; b. Fairborn, Ohio, Oct. 16, 1945; s. Wendell Lloyd and Mary Louise (Bockstege) S.; B.S., U. Md., 1971; postgrad. George Washington U., 1972-73, U. Calif. at Los Angeles, 1974-75. Data processing mgr. Ringling Bros. Barnum & Bailey Combined Shows, Washington, 1970-72; credit mgr. Stanford Applied Engring., Santa Clara, Calif., 1972-73; asst. controller Meml. Hosp., Gardena, Calif., 1973-75; dir. fin. Los Medanos Community Hosp. Dist., Pittsburg, Calif., 1976—. Mem. data and liaison coms. Health Service Area; active citizens adv. groups, Pittsburg, 1977—. Mem. Nat. Assn. Accountants, Hosp. Fin. Mgmt. Assn., Health Care Execs. of No. Calif. Clubs: Diablo Valley Sailing, Alameda Yacht, Met. Yacht of Oakland (Calif.). Home: 144

Manor Dr West Pittsburg CA 94565 Office: 2311 Loveridge Rd Pittsburg CA 94565

SNYDER, WILLIAM LLOYD, III, fin. cons., paper mfg. co. exec.; b. Lancaster, Pa., Mar. 24, 1944; s. William Lloyd and Elizabeth (Colby) S.; B.A., Amherst Coll., 1966; M.B.A., Harvard U., 1968; m. Deirdre Jane Rhoads, Aug. 20, 1966; children—Alexandra Dugan, Megan Colby, Andrew Rhoads. Partner, Butcher & Sherrerd, Investment Bankers, Phila., 1968-73; owner, operator Snyder and Co., Phila., 1973—; chmn. Intermodal Transp. Systems, Inc., 1973-76; chmn., chief exec. officer, owner Huff Paper Co., 1977—; pres., owner Wynne Bolt & Screw Co., 1979—; owner, chmn. United Paper Co., 1979—. Served to 2d lt. U.S. Army, 1969. Republican. Mem. United Ch. of Christ. Clubs: Phila. Country, Racquet (Phila.); Little Egg Harbor Yacht (Beach Haven, N.J.). Home: 147 Rose Ln Haverford PA 19041 Office: 1529 Walnut St 4th Floor Philadelphia PA 19102

SOARD, RAYMOND, telephone co. exec.; b. Lexington, Ky., Feb. 12, 1922; s. Raymond J. and Betty (Lowry) S.; student Bklyn. Poly. Inst., 1943-44; B.S. in Elec. Engring., U. Ky., 1949; postgrad. U. Ga., 1956, Harvard U., 1958, Mich. State U., 1959, U. Nev., 1963, 76-77, U. Kans., 1976; m. Faye LaVerne Jacobs, May 2, 1942; children—Jane Rae (Mrs. D.E. Dionisio), Raymond Randolph, Suzanne (Mrs. C.C. Curtin), William Thomas. Central office repairman Gen. Telephone Co. Ky., Lexington, 1946-49, plant foreman, 1949-52, gen. traffic engr., 1952-54, gen. traffic mgr., 1954-58, chief engr., 1958-62; engring. mgr. Central Telephone Co., Las Vegas, Nev., 1962-78, gen. mgr., 1978—. Vice chmn. Nev. State Industry Advisory Com., 1965; exec. com. Nev. Drug Abuse Council, 1976-78, pres., 1978—; mem. Las Vegas Bd. Elec. Examiners, 1965-77; committeeman Boulder Dam council Boy Scouts Am., 1962-66; chmn. Clark County (Nev.) Utilities Com., 1970; mem. Emergengy Resources Mgmt. Bd., Civil Defense, 1967. Served with Signal Corps, AUS, 1942-46; PTO. Decorated Bronze Star medal with 2 oak leaf clusters; registered profl. engr., Ky., Nev. Mem. Nat. Soc. Profl. Engrs. (award 1968), Telephone Pioneers Am., Ind. Telephone Pioneer Assn., Armed Forces Communications and Electronics Assn. (pres. 1959), Lexington Ky. Civic Club (pres. 1961), Las Vegas Exchange Club (dir. 1965-68, 77, pres. 1980—). Home: 2112 Burnham Ave Las Vegas NV 89104 Office: 125 Las Vegas Blvd S Las Vegas NV 89101

SOCARRAS-COBIAN, YOHEL, telephone co. ofcl., indsl. engr.; b. Cuba, May 29, 1947; s. Yohel and Haydee (Cobian-Causa) Socarras-Blancard; B.S. Liceo De La Salle, Bogota, Colombia, 1964; B.S. in Indsl. Engring., U. P.R., 1970; m. Sonia Figueroa-Sanchez, May 30, 1971; children—Sonymarie, Yomarie, Sylmarie, Yanmarie. Sta. performance analyst Caribbean div. Eastern Airlines, Inc., San Juan, P.R., 1970-74; manpower and adminstrn. mgr. ITT Caribbean Mfg., Inc., Rio Piedras, P.R., 1974-75; dir. human resources P.R. Telephone Co., Caparra, 1975—. Mem. Am. Inst. Indsl. Engrs. Roman Catholic. Home: Calle 5 #SG-22 Urb Parana Rio Piedras PR 00926 Office: PRTC Hdqrs 1500 Roosevelt Ave Caparra PR 00920

SOCOL, SHELDON ELEAZER, univ. ofcl.; b. N.Y.C., July 10, 1936; s. Irving and Helen (Tuchman) S.; B.A., Yeshiva U., 1958; J.D., N.Y.U., 1963; m. Genia Ruth Prager, Dec. 26, 1959; children—Jeffrey, Steven, Sharon. Asst. bursar Yeshiva U., N.Y.C., 1958-60, asso. bursar, 1960-62, dir. student finances, 1962-70, sec., 1970—, chief fiscal officer, 1971-72, v.p. bus. affairs, 1972—. Mem. N.Y. State Adv. Council on Financial Assistance to Coll. Students, 1969—; asst. dir. Tng. Inst. for Financial Aid Officers, Hunter Coll., City U. N.Y., 1970-71; mem. N.Y.C. Regional Plan for Higher Edn. Regents Adv. Task Force, 1971-72. Pres., Minyon Park Estates, Inc. Mem. Nat. Assn. Coll. and Univ. Attys., NEA, N.Y. State, Met. N.Y.C. financial aid adminstrs. assns., Eastern Assn. Student Financial Aid Officers, Am. Mgmt. Assn., Am. Assn. for Higher Edn., Nat. Assn. Coll. and Univ. Bus. Officers. Home: 136-18 71st Rd Kew Gardens Hills NY 11367 Office: Yeshiva University 500 W 185th St New York NY 10033

SOGNEFEST, PETER WILLIAM, mfg. co. exec.; b. Melrose Park, Ill., Feb. 4, 1941; s. Peter and Alvera E. Sognefest; B.S. in E.E., U. Ill., 1964, M.S., in E.E., 1967; m. Margaret Brunkow, Aug. 15, 1964; children—Scott, Brian, Jennifer. Elec. engr. Magnavox Corp., Urbana, Ill., 1964-67; sr. fellow, mgr. research, United Techs. fellow Mellon Inst., Pitts., 1967-71; gen. mgr. for semicondr. ops. United Techs., Pitts., 1971-77; v.p. instruments and controls bus. unit Motorola Inc., Schaumburg, Ill., 1977—; dir. Two-Six Inc. Mem. IEEE. Republican. Presbyterian. Clubs: Univ., Longue Vue, Forest Grove Tennis. Patentee in field. Home: 4 Back Bay Rd Barrington IL 60010 Office: 1299 E Algonquin Rd Schaumburg IL 60196

SOGOR, BETTIE VAN DYKE, research co. exec.; b. Henderson, N.C., May 15, 1944; s. David Lewis and Ora Loreen (Strum) Van Dyke; B.S., N.C. State U., 1966; M.S. (fellow), Case Western Res. U., 1971, Ph.D. (NIH trainee), 1973; m. Laszlo Sogor, Jan. 9, 1971. Jr. chemist ERDA Labs., Ames, Iowa, 1971; instr. chemistry U. Cin., 1973-74; research chemist Diamond Shamrock Corp., Painesville, Ohio, 1974-76, sr. research chemist, 1976-79, research supr., 1979-80, sr. market research specialist, 1980—; internal cons. Creativity Com. Mem. AAAS, Iota Sigma Pi. Home: 1229 Croyden Rd Lyndhurst OH 44124 Office: 7528 Auburn Rd Painesville OH 44077

SOHIGIAN, HARRY JAMES, stockbroker; b. Cambridge, Mass., Apr. 5, 1938; s. Harry James and Sylvia (Yaghjian) S.; student Northeastern U., 1956-58; B.S. in Bus. Adminstrn., Wayne State U., 1961; cert. N.Y. Inst. Fin., 1971; m. Emily N. Yagoobian, Apr. 30, 1966; children—James Paul, Tina Ann. Sales mgr. Lansing (Mich.) Candy & Cigar Co., 1961-71; salesman 1st Investor's Corp., N.Y.C., 1969-71; registered rep. William C. Roney & Co., Detroit, 1971-77; br. mgr., partner Manley, Bennett, McDonald & Co., Lansing, 1977—; coordinator seminars in field of fin. Mem. Lansing Community Band, 1969-73; active membership drives Lansing YMCA. Mem. Internat. Assn. Fin. Planners, Nat. Assn. Registered Reps. Republican. Mem. Armenian Apostolic Ch. Clubs: Masons, Knights of Vartan. Office: Bus & Trade Center 200 N Washington Sq Lansing MI 48933

SOKOL, MARSHALL DEAN, fin. mktg., systems and services cons.; b. Kansas City, Mo., June 13, 1940; s. Ralph R. and Selma S. (Star) S.; B.A. (Coll. scholar 1958-62, Regents scholar 1958-62), Columbia U., 1962, M.Ph. (NDEA scholar 1963-65, Grad. Faculties scholar 1962-65), Sch. Bus., 1968; m. Phyllis K. Sokol, Nov. 10, 1960; children—Scott, Bruce, Eric. Asso. economist Am. Bankers Assn., 1968-69; sr. fin. economist Conf. Bd., 1970; client services mgr. and sr. asso. Diebold Group, Inc., 1971-72; pres. Marshall D. Sokol Assos. Inc., White Plains, N.Y., 1972—; mem. faculty Hunter Coll., 1963-66, Lehman Coll., 1964-67, Hofstra U., 1967, Pace U., 1972; judge 16th Ann. Town Crier Awards, 1975. Commr. of appraisal Supreme Ct. of N.Y. State, Westchester County, 1974—. Recipient Ford Found. award, 1963-64; Franklin Nat. Bank, Franklin fellow, 1967. Mem. Assn. Govt. Accts., Am. Econ. Assn., Am. Fin. Assn., Nat. Assn. Bus. Economists. Author: Increasing Profits Through Computerized Cash Management System, 1972; Recent Developments in Cash Management Systems, 1977; Corporate Cash Management Practices, 1977; The Systems Approach to Cash Management, 1979. Office: 445 Hamilton Ave White Plains NY 10601

SOKOL, WALTER STANLEY, food industry exec.; b. Jersey City, Jan. 6, 1931; B.S., St. Peter's Coll., 1952; M.B.A., N.Y. U., 1956. Mktg. analyst Maxwell House div. Gen. Foods Corp., Hoboken, N.J., 1952-60; dir. electronic data processing F&M Schaeffer Brewing Co., Bklyn., 1960-67; mgmt. cons. Touche, Ross, Bailey & Smart, N.Y.C., 1967-68, S.D. Leidesdorf & Co., N.Y.C., 1968-69; group controller Internat. Paper Co., N.Y.C., 1970; v.p. fin., sec.-treas., dir. S.B. Thomas, Inc., Specialty Bakers, Totowa, N.J., 1971; instr., mem. adv. bd. Ramapo Coll.; lectr. in field. Mem. Fin. Execs. Inst., Nat. Assn. Accts. Home: 579 Herrick Dr Dover NJ 07081 Office: 930 N Riverview Dr Totowa NJ 07512

SOKOLOFF, KIRIL, editor, writer; b. Lakeland, Fla., Nov. 9, 1947; s. Boris Theodore and Alice St. John (Hunt) S.; B.A. in English, Georgetown U., 1969; m. Catherine Miller, Jan. 24, 1976; 1 son, Kiril St. John. Loan officer Citibank, 1969-71; investment banker G.H. Walker & Co., N.Y.C., 1971-73; mng. editor Personal Fin. Letter, McGraw-Hill Pubs. Co., N.Y.C., 1973-77; sr. editor fin. and investment books McGraw-Hill Book Co., N.Y.C., 1978—; contbg. editor Boardroom Reports, Delta Sky mag., Powell Monetary Analyst, Barron's mag., Bottom Line, Cash Flow mag. Clubs: Racquet and Tennis, Adirondack League. Author: The Thinking Investor's Guide to the Stock Market, 1978; Paine Webber's Handbook of Stock and Bond Analysis, 1979. Home: Mount Holly Rd Katonah NY 10536 Office: 1221 Ave of Americas New York NY 10020

SOLBERG, NORMAN ROBERT, lawyer; b. Toledo, Aug. 28, 1939; s. Archie Norman and Margaret Jane (Olsen) S.; B.A., Columbia Coll., 1961; LL.B., Columbia U., 1964; postgrad. Parker Sch. Fgn. and Comparative Law, 1969; m. Susan Radcliffe Riley, Oct. 7, 1961; children—Eric Norman, Anne Olsen. Admitted to N.Y. bar, 1964, Mass. bar, 1973, Mo. bar, 1978; asso. firm Wickes, Riddell, Bloomer, Jacobi & McGuire, N.Y.C., 1964-69; sr. atty. The Gillette Co., Boston, 1969-75; asst. internat. counsel Monsanto Co., St. Louis, 1975-79; sr. staff counsel Household Fin. Corp., Prospect Heights, Ill., 1979—. Mem. Am. Bar Assn., Assn. Bar Met. St. Louis, Boston Bar Assn., Ill. Bar Assn., Am. Judicature Soc. Republican. Lutheran. Home: 803 Bluff St Glencoe IL 60022 Office: 2700 Sanders Rd Prospect Heights IL 60070

SOLENBERGER, IRA DALE, accountant; b. Douglas, N.D., Mar. 21, 1918; s. Harry Hale and Ragnhildt (Knudtsen) S.; B.B.A., U. Minn., 1947; m. Emma I. Peterson, July 8, 1944; 1 son, David R. With Ernst & Whinney, Kansas City, Mo., 1951—, mgr. tax dept. Treas., Homes Assn., Prairie Village, Kans., 1977—. Treas., Greater Kansas City People to People Council. Served with U.S. Army, 1943-46. C.P.A., Mo. Mem. Am. Inst. C.P.A.'s, Mo. Soc. C.P.A.'s, Estate Planning Council Kansas City. Republican. Congregationalist. Clubs: Kansas City, Blue Hills Country. Home: 7933 Roe Ave Prairie Village KS 66208 Office: 2000 City Center Sq Kansas City MO 64105

SOLIDUM, JAMES, finance and ins. counselor; b. Honolulu, Mar. 12, 1925; s. Narciso and Sergia (Yabo) S.; student U. Hawaii, 1949-50; B.A., U. Oreg., 1953; m. Vickie Mayo, Aug. 14, 1954; children—Arlin James, Nathan Francis, Tobi John, Kamomi Teresa. Promotional salesman Tongg Pub. Co., 1953-54; editor Fil-Am. Tribune, 1954-55; master planning technician Fed. Civil Service, 1955-57; publs. editor Hawaii Sugar Planters Assn., 1957; field agt. Grand Pacific Life Ins. Co., 1957-59, home office asst., 1959-60, supr., 1960-62, asst. v.p., 1962-64; propr. J. Solidum & Assos., Honolulu, 1964—; pres. Fin. Devel. Inst., 1967—; trustee Grand Pacific Life Pension Trust, 1975—. Mem. adv. com. Honolulu dist. SBA, 1971-77, Philippine Consulate in Hawaii, 1959. Pres., Keolu Elementary P.T.A., 1960-62; mem. satisfaction com. Hawaii Visitors Bur., 1963-66; chmn. budget and rev. panel IV, Aloha United Fund, 1966-72, bd. dirs., 1971-77, mem. mgmt. services com., 1977, mem. central com., 1977—; chmn. Kamehameha Dist. finance com. Aloha council Boy Scouts Am., 1966; vice chmn. Businessmen's Cancer Crusade, 1965; chmn. Operation Bayanihan, Hawaii Immigration Task Force, 1970; participant Oahu Housing Workshop, State of Hawaii, Hawaii chpt. HUD, 1970; mem. task force on housing and transp. Alternative Econ. Futures for Hawaii, 1973; chmn. Bicentennial Filipiniana, 1976; chmn. SBA Bicentennial Com., 1976; campaign chmn. State Rep. Rudolph Pacarro, 1964-68; mem. exec. com. Campaign for Reelection U.S. Senator Hiram L. Fong, 1970, Gov. William Quinn for U.S. Senate, 1976; Republican candidate for Hawaii Ho. of Reps., 1972; mem. Rep. Citizens Task Force on Housing, 1973; trustee St. Louis Alumni Found.; trustee Palama Settlement, 1975—, v.p., 1976, treas., 1980; bd. mgrs. Windward YMCA, 1964-67; bd. advisers St. Louis High Sch., 1963-64; bd. govs. Goodwill Industries; bd. dirs. Children's Center, Inc., 1975-77, bd. dirs. Hawaii Multi-Cultural Center, 1977—, treas., 1979; fin. chmn. St. Stephen's Parish Council, 1974—. Served with AUS, 1945-47. C.L.U. Recipient Man of Year award Filipino C. of C., 1965; cert. of merit Aloha United Fund, 1971; Wisdom mag. honor award, 1974; Outstanding Alumnus honor medal St. Louis High Sch., 1976. Mem. C. of C. Hawaii (past v.p., dir.), Filipino C. of C. (past pres., com. chmn.), Am. Soc. C.L.U.'s, Honolulu Assn. Life Underwriters (past com. chmn., dir.), Hawaii Estate Planning Council, Hawaii Plantation Indsl. Editors Assn. (sec.-treas. 1957), St. Louis Alumni Assn. (pres. 1976, dir. 1964—), Phi Kappa Sigma. Republican. Roman Catholic. Home: 2622 Waolani Ave Honolulu HI 96817 Office: 1110 University Ave Honolulu HI 96826

SOLKOFF, JEROME IRA, lawyer; b. Rochester, N.Y., Feb. 15, 1939; s. Samuel and Dorothy (Krovetz) S.; B.S. (Wall St. Jour. scholar), Cornell U., 1961; LL.B., J.D. (Participating Fund scholar), U. Buffalo, 1964; m. Doreen Hurwitz, Aug. 11, 1963; children—Scott Michael, Anne Lynn. Admitted to N.Y. bar, 1965, Fla. bar, 1974; asso. firm Nusbaum, Tarricone, Bilgore, Weltman & Silver, Rochester, 1964-66, Martin Dutcher, Cooke, Mousaw & Vigdor, Rochester, 1966-70; individual practice law, Rochester, 1970-73; sr. municipal atty. Rochester Urban Renewal Agy., 1970-73; house counsel, asst. sec. Arlen Realty Mgmt., Inc. and subs., Miami, 1973-75; atty. Ruden, Barnett, McClosky, Schuster & Schmerer, Ft. Lauderdale, Fla., 1975; counsel Mondex, Inc., Miami, 1975-76; chief legal counsel First Mortgage Investors, Miami Beach, Fla., 1976-79; partner firm Marwin S. Cassel, Miami, 1979—; cons. real estate. Bd. dirs. Hollywood (Fla.) Jewish Community Center, Temple Solal, Hollywood. Mem. Am. Bar Assn., Fla. Bar., Corp. Counsel Assn. Dade County. Republican. Jewish. Club: Masons (Rochester). Home: 3881 N 50th Ave Hollywood FL 33021 Office: Suite 1011 New World Tower 100 N Biscayne Blvd Miami FL 33132

SOLL, GEORGE LAWRENCE, wine and spirits importing co. exec.; b. N.Y.C., Apr. 26, 1922; s. Murray and Dorothy Bertha Soll; B.S. in Econs., U. Pa., 1947; m. Arleen Diane Rosenberg, Dec. 24, 1949; 1 dau., Patricia. Asst. mgr. Eastern div. Browne Vinters Co. div. Seagram Distillers Co., N.Y.C., 1947-62; v.p., gen. mgr. Westminster Importing Co., N.Y.C., 1962-65; v.p., nat. sales mgr. Four Roses Distillers div. Joseph E. Seagram Co., N.Y.C., 1965-73; v.p. govt. and industry relations Monsieur Henri Wines Ltd., White Plains, N.Y., 1973—; wine and spirits writer, cons. Westchester Illustrated mag. Served with USAAF, 1942-45. Decorated D.F.C., Air medal with 6 oak leaf clusters. Trustee, bd. dirs. Big Bros. Mem. Distilled Spirits Council U.S. (French table wine com., rioja wine council). Jewish. Office: 707 Westchester Ave White Plains NY 10604

SOLLENNE, PETER RONALD, ins. co. exec.; b. Lyons, N.Y., July 18, 1948; s. Peter A. and Josephine A. Sollenne; B.S., Boston Coll., 1970; m. Patricia D. Gravino, Aug. 23, 1969. With Arthur Andersen & Co., C.P.A.'s, Boston, 1970-74, PepsiCo Leasing Corp., Lexington, Mass., 1974-75, First Nat. Bank Boston, 1975-77; with Comml. Union Assurance Co., Boston, 1977—, asst. treas., 1977—. C.P.A., Mass. Mem. Am. Inst. C.P.A.'s, Mass. Soc. C.P.A.'s. Home: 71 Ford Rd Sudbury MA 01776 Office: 1 Beacon St Boston MA 02108

SOLOMON, MORTON BERNARD, accountant; b. Freeport, N.Y., Dec. 28, 1929; s. David and Tillie (Rathsprecher) S.; B.S. in Commerce, Washington and Lee U., 1951; M.B.A., U. Pa., 1956; m. Marilyn Lee Zahm, Sept. 4, 1955; children—Laurie, Karen, Joyce. Staff accountant Peat, Marwick, Mitchell & Co., N.Y.C., 1956-61; controller, dir. H.L. Klion, Inc., Westbury, N.Y., 1961-65; exec. asst. dept. stock list N.Y. Stock Exchange, N.Y.C., 1965-68; partner, nat. dir. profl. standards, mem. policy bd. Main Hurdsman & Cranstoun, N.Y.C., 1968—. Served to lt. USNR, 1952-55. C.P.A., N.Y. Mem. Am. Inst. C.P.A.'s (former mem. com. SEC regulation, task forces revenue recognition when right of return exists, interim reporting; mem. FASB advisory com. disclosure criteria), Nat. Assn. Accountants. Contbr. articles to profl. jours. Office: 2 Park Plaza New York NY 10017

SOLOW, ROBERT MERTON, economist, educator; b. Bklyn., Aug. 23, 1924; s. Milton Henry and Hannah Gertrude (Sarney) S.; B.A., Harvard U., 1947, M.A., 1949, Ph.D., 1951; LL.D., U. Chgo., 1967, Brown U., 1972, U. Warwick, 1976; D.Litt., Williams Coll., 1974, Lehigh U., 1977; Dr. honoris causa, U. Paris, 1975; m. Barbara Lewis, Aug. 19, 1945; children—John Lewis, Andrew Robert, Katherine. Mem. faculty Mass. Inst. Tech., 1949—, prof. econs., 1958—, Inst. prof., 1973—; sr. economist Council Econ. Advisers, 1961-62, cons., 1962-68; cons. RAND Corp., 1952-64; Marshall lectr., fellow commoner Peterhouse, U. Cambridge (Eng.), 1963-64; Eastman vis. prof. Oxford U., 1968-69; sr. fellow Soc. Fellows Harvard U., 1975—; dir. Boston Fed. Res. Bank, chmn., 1979-80; mem. Pres.'s Commn. on Income Maintenance, 1968-70, Pres.'s Com. on Tech., Automation and Econ. Progress, 1964-65. Bd. dirs., mem. exec. com. Nat. Bur. Econ. Research; trustee Inst. for Advanced Study, Princeton U., 1972-78. Served with AUS, 1942-45. Fellow Center Advanced Study Behavioral Scis., 1957-58; recipient David A. Wells prize Harvard U., 1951. Fellow Am. Acad. Arts and Scis., Brit. Acad. (corr.), Am. Philos. Soc.; mem. AAAS (v.p. 1970), Nat. Acad. Scis. (council), Am. Econs. Soc. (exec. com. 1964-66; John Bates Clark medal 1961, v.p. 1968, pres. 1979), Econometric Soc. (pres. 1964, mem. exec. com.). Author: Linear Programming and Economic Analysis, 1958; Capital Theory and the Rate of Return, 1963; The Sources of Unemployment in the United States, 1964; Growth Theory, 1970; Price Expectations and the Behavior of the Price Level, 1970. Office: Dept Econs Mass Inst Tech Cambridge MA 02139

SOLTERO, EUGENE ANDRE, oil and gas co. exec.; b. Tarrytown, N.Y., Mar. 17, 1943; s. Albert Vincent and Helen Paula (Stein) S.; B.Engring., Cooper Union, 1964; M.S., M.I.T., 1966; m. Elizabeth Anne Richards, Aug. 23, 1969; children—Karen Elizabeth, Wendy Anne. Econs. and ops. research analyst Sinclair Oil Corp., N.Y.C., 1966-69; mgr. econs. and planning, asst. to pres. Tex. Internat. Petroleum Corp., Oklahoma City, 1969-70; petroleum economist DeGolyer and MacNaughton, Dallas, 1970-72; v.p., gen. mgr. Moore McCormack Energy, Inc., Dallas, 1972—, dir., pres., chief operating officer, 1978—. Sinclair Found. fellow, 1965-66; registered profl. engr., Tex. Fellow AAAS; mem. AIME, Am. Petroleum Inst., Humanist Soc., Ind. Petroleum Assn. Am., Mid-Continent Oil and Gas Assn., Tex. Ind. Producers and Royalty Owners, U.S. Yacht Racing Union. Republican. Presbyterian. Clubs: Dallas Economists, Dallas Petroleum, Royal Oaks Country, White Rock Sailing. Contbr. articles to profl. jours. Office: 6440 N Central Expressway Dallas TX 75206

SOMERS, IRA I., trade assn. exec.; b. Garland, Utah, June 28, 1916; s. George and Linda (Sorensen) S.; B.S., Utah State Agrl. Coll., 1938; Ph.D., Rutgers U., 1939; m. Edna McGavin, June 19, 1946; children—Rebecca, Kevin, Janine, David. With Nat. Food Processors Assn., 1943—, asst. dir. lab. Western Research Lab., Berkeley, Calif., 1952-55, asso. dir., 1955-57, dir. research labs., Berkeley and Seattle, 1957-72, exec. v.p., chief operating officer, 1972—; dir. Food Processors Inst.; pres. Tech S Corp. Mem. Am. Chem. Soc., Inst. Food Technologists, Republican. Mormon. Club: Internat. (Washington). Office: 1333 20th St Washington DC 20036

SOMERVILLE, JOHN GRAHAME, constrn. co. exec.; b. Grand Rapids, Mich., June 8, 1950; s. Robert Bruce and Marie (Fishback) S.; student Ferris State Coll., 1967-68, U. Ariz., 1968-69; m. Lynette Marie Berry, Jan. 5, 1975; children—John Grahame, Chad Lenard. With Somerville Constrn. Co., Palatine, Ill., 1969—, pres., 1976—; dir. Somerville Ill., Tech. Services, Grand Rapids, Mich., 1978—. Mem. Distbn. Contractors Assn., Midwest Gas Assn. Republican. United Ch. of Christ. Office: 433 Wanda Ln Palatine IL 60067

SOMERVILLE, JOSEPH CHARLES, JR., bus. cons.; b. Jacksonville, Fla., July 23, 1953; s. Joseph Charles and Ann V. Somerville; B.A., U. North Fla., 1976, cert. Am. studies, 1976, postgrad. bus. adminstrn., 1976-77; m. Genevieve B. Repper, June 17, 1972. Mgmt. trainee Conn. Gen. Life Ins. Co., 1976-77; rep. Oscar Mayer & Co., 1977-79; mktg. mgr. Midwest, Polaroid Corp., 1979-80; self-employed bus. cons., Dunwoody, Ga., 1979—. Served with USCG, 1970-74. Republican. Club: Toastmasters. Home: 4983 Gunners Run Roswell GA 30075 Office: Box 88173 Dunwoody GA 30338

SOMMER, LAURA JANE WELLENS, stock broker; b. N.Y.C., Apr. 6, 1948; d. Philip L. and Portia (Pomerantz) Wellens; student Columbia U., 1965. Stockbroker, Bache & Co., N.Y.C., 1968-70, E.F. Hutton & Co., Inc., N.Y.C., 1970-75; v.p. Lexer Group Ltd., N.Y.C., 1975—. Active Republican Club, 1973—. Recipient Silver Merit award E.F. Hutton, 1972. Mem. Women's Stockbroker Assn. Home: 181 Skunks Misery Rd Lattingtown NY 11560 Office: 280 Park Ave New York NY 10017

SOMMERS, PATRICK CHARLES, mktg. exec.; b. Cape Girardeau, Mo., May 9, 1947; s. Sidney Samual and Nina Marie (Young) S.; B.S., S.E. Mo. U., 1969; m. Constance Sue Adams, Apr. 3, 1971; 1 dau., Whitney Karma. With Dun & Bradstreet, Inc., various locations, 1971—, v.p., gen. mgr. Mktg. Services div., Toronto, 1974-76, v.p. corp. mktg., 1976—. Served with USAR, 1969-70. Mem. Sales and Mktg. Execs. Internat., Am. Mgmt. Assn., Can. Direct Mailing Assn. Clubs: Rotary, Glen Abbey Country. Home: 6772 Barrisdale Dr Mississauga ON L5N 2H4 Canada Office: 84 Carlton St Toronto ON M5B 1L6 Canada

SOMNOLET, MICHEL PIERRE, fin. exec.; b. Chateaurenault, France, Feb. 6, 1940; came to U.S., 1969; s. Raoul Guillaume and Marthe Somnolet; B.Law, Paris Law Sch., 1963; M.B.A., Hautes Etudes Commerciales, Paris, 1964; m. Ghislaine Elizabeth Tenaille,

Dec. 15, 1961; children—Marc, Karine, Eric. With L'Oreal, France, 1964-74, controller, 1969-74; v.p., treas. Cosmair, Inc.-U.S. Licensee of L'Oreal, Clark, N.J., 1974, sr. v.p. fin. and adminstrn., dir., 1975—; dir. Fleury Corp. Served to capt., armed forces, 1964-66. Mem. French C. of C. in N.Y., French Res. Officers in U.S.A. (sec. 1978). Club: Paris-Am. Home: 824 Standish Ave Westfield NJ 07090 Office: 30 Terminal Ave Clark NJ 07066

SONN, HAROLD WILLIS, utility exec.; b. Trenton, 1921; B.S., Rutgers U., 1943; postgrad. U. Nancy (France), N.Y. U.; married. With Public Service Electric and Gas Co., Newark, 1946—, v.p. services, 1970-74, sr. v.p. adminstrn., 1974-77, sr. v.p., 1977—; pres., chief operating officer PSE&G Research Corp., 1980—; dir. Fidelity Union Trust Co. Served with U.S. Army, 1943-45. Office: 80 Park Pl Newark NJ 07101*

SONTAG, FREDERICK H., public affairs and research cons.; b. Breslau, Germany, Apr. 29, 1924; s. Hugo and Lotte (Laband) S.; came to U.S., 1937, naturalized, 1943; A.B., Colby Coll., Waterville, Maine, 1946; postgrad. Columbia U., 1947-48; m. Edith Virginia Sweeney, Feb. 8, 1958. Asso., Earl Newsom & Co., N.Y.C., 1947-48; public relations, advt. cons. Mchts. Nat. Bank, Syracuse, N.Y., 1948-51; central N.Y. corr. Business Week mag. and other McGraw Hill publs., 1950-51, dir. public relations Business Week mag., 1951-55; manuscript cons. McGraw-Hill Book Co., N.Y.C., 1951-60; asso. Anna M. Rosenberg Assos., N.Y.C., 1957-60; cons. Civic Service, Inc., St. Louis, Washington, 1957—, Winter Olympics, San Francisco, 1960, First Caribbean Mainland Capital Co., N.Y.C., San Juan, P.R., 1962; cons. to Edwin J. Putzell, gen. counsel, sec., v.p. Monsanto Co., St. Louis, 1962-77; cons. to Edwin J. Putzell, Coburn, Croft, Shepherd, Herzog & Putzell, St. Louis and Naples, Fla., 1977—; cons. sec. labor, Washington, 1954-61, Pres.'s Com. on Govt. Employment Policy, 1955-60, U.S. Congressman Thomas B. Curtis, Washington, St. Louis, 1957-69; exec. dir. Com. for Increased Minority Staffing, U.S. Ho. of Reps., 1961-69; cons. Office of Sec., HEW, 1969, 72; dir. Study of Am. Polit. Parties, South Orange, N.J., Cambridge, Mass., 1973—; cons. chmn./commr. U.S. Internat. Trade Commn., 1975-77; legis. cons. N.J. Sen. James H. Wallwork, 1968-79, N.J. Assemblyman Charles L. Hardwick, 1979—, Essex County (N.J.) Freeholder-at-large Lincoln Turner, 1979—; radio and TV analyst, commentator, reporter Maine Public Broadcasting Network, 1973-75, Suburban Cablevision TV3, no. N.J., 1977-79; cons. to bishop Episcopal Diocese, Springfield, Ill., 1947-72; dir. Citizens Found., Syracuse, 1948-50; program planning asso. Nat. Council Episcopal Ch., N.Y.C., 1956-61; cons. United Methodist Ch., Washington, 1965-71; mem. editorial adv. bd. Electoral Studies Yearbook, Sage Pub. Co., Beverly Hills; lectr., discussion leader Inst. Politics, Harvard U., Brookings Instn., Woodrow Wilson Internat. Center of Scholars, Washington, Am. Assembly, Columbia U.; vis. lectr. Colby Coll., Waterville, Maine, 1975. Trustee Husson Coll., Bangor, Maine. Recipient certificate of achievement Am. Pub. Relations Assn., 1952, 54, Silver Anvil award, 1953, Spl. Achievement award U.S. Internat. Trade Commn., 1976. Mem. Pub. Relations Soc. Am. (accredited), Am. Assn. Polit. Consultants (charter), Am. Polit. Sci. Assn., Overseas Press Club Am., N.J. Conf. on Promotion Better Govt., Phi Gamma Mu, Phi Delta Theta. Anglo-Catholic. Author: (with Dr. John S. Saloma III) Parties: The Real Opportunity for Effective Citizen Politics, 1972, softcover, 1973. Contbr. Op Ed pages N.Y. Times, Los Angeles Times, N.J. and Maine newspapers; contbg. writer and reviewer Worrall Newspapers, No. N.J.; nat./regional corr. Am. Church News, The Witness, The Living Church, The Scroll. Office: 764 Scotland Rd Suite 45 South Orange NJ 07079 also PO Box 207 Seal Harbor ME 04675

SOOKNE, HERMAN SOLOMON, real estate exec.; b. Far Rockaway, N.Y., June 30, 1932; s. Harry Martin and Sarah (Kopolov) S.; student Georgetown U., 1951; B.S. in Econs., N.Y. U., 1953; m. Polly Henry, Mar. 21, 1972; children—Charles, David, Susan. Div. mgr. Boise Cascade Bldg. Co., Freehold, N.J., 1968-70; dir. engring. Amprop, Inc., Miami, Fla., 1970-73; v.p. marketing Champion Realty Co., Dallas, 1973-76; loan officer Civic Savs. & Loan Assn., Irving, Tex., 1976-79; pres., chief exec. officer Boman Property Investors, Inc., Houston, 1977-79, also Maintenance Surveys, Inc.; v.p., gen. mgr. Fidinam (U.S.A.) Inc., real estate developer, Houston, 1979—; cons. to cosmetic and pub. bus. Served with AUS, 1953-55. Lic. real estate broker, N.Y. Mem. Am. Inst. Constructors, ASHRAE, Dallas Mus. Fine Arts. Democrat. Mem. Unity Ch. Home: 4655 Wild Indigo #84 Houston TX 77024

SOPER, ROBERT LEE, machinery mfg. co. exec.; b. Eldora, Iowa, Aug. 10, 1921; s. William Henry and Leola (Cox) S.; student Carleton Coll., 1939-41; B.A., U. Mich., 1946; M.B.A. with distinction, Harvard U., 1948; grad. Army Command and Gen. Staff Sch.; m. Nancy Kenealy, Aug. 12, 1972; children—William Lee, Margaret Deane, Julie Elizabeth. Asst. credit mgr., mgr. data processing Black & Decker Mfg. Co., Towson, Md., 1948-49; with Calif. Pellet Mill Co., San Francisco, 1950—, treas., 1960-71, exec. v.p., 1971-74, pres., 1974—; dir. El Morro Industries Calif. Pellet Mill Ltd., CPM/Europe V.B., CPM/Europe S.A., Zeig Sheet Metal Co., CPM/Pacific Ltd. Served with USAAF, 1942-45; CBI, Decorated Air medal, D.F.C. Mem. Calif. C. of C., Calif. Mfrs. Assn., San Francisco C. of C., Calif. Metal Trades Assn. (dir.), World Affairs Council. Clubs: Bankers, Presidio, Commonwealth of Calif. (San Francisco). Home: 2264 Hyde St San Francisco CA 94109 Office: 1800 Folsom St San Francisco CA 94103

SORENSEN, ROBERT HOLM, business exec.; b. Racine, Wis., 1921; B.S. in Elec. Engring., Northwestern U., 1947; married. With Engring. Research Assos. Inc., 1947-51; with Sperry Rand Corp. (formerly Remington Rand Inc.), 1952-59; with Perkin-Elmer Corp., 1959—, v.p., gen. mgr. electro-optical div., 1961-65, v.p. optical group, 1965-66, sr. v.p., 1966-73, pres., chief operating officer, 1973-77, pres., chief exec. officer, 1977-80, chmn. bd., chief exec. officer, 1980—, also dir.; dir. Olin Corp., Phoenix Mut. Life Ins. Co., So. New Eng. Telephone Co. Office: Main Ave Norwalk CT 06856

SORG, HARRY HUDSON, bank exec.; b. Joplin, Mo., Sept. 25, 1946; s. Harry Hudson and Virginia Christine (Dean) S.; student Mo. So. State Coll., 1971-78; m. Susan Elise Anderson, June 6, 1969; children—Lisa Marie, Adam Douglas. Asst. cashier, br. mgr. First Nat. Bank and Trust Co., Joplin, 1967-75; pres., chief exec. officer, trust officer, dir. United Mo. Bank of Joplin, 1976—. Served with U.S. Army, 1969-71. Mem. Mo. Bankers Assn., Joplin Bd. Realtors, Am. Inst. Banking. Clubs: Twin Hills Golf and Country, Kiwanis (chmn. internat. relations com. 1979—). Office: 2300 E 7th St Joplin MO 64801

SORIANO, JOSE M., investor; b. Manila, Philippines, Feb. 6, 1925; s. Andres and Carmen (de Montemar y Martinez) Soriano y Roxas; B.A., Harvard U., 1950; m. Liliane Pingoud, Apr. 6, 1953; children—Jose M., Carmen Paz, Peter. Chmn., A. Soriano Corp., Makati, Rizal, Philippines, 1965-79; chmn., pres., Atlas Mining and Devel. Corp.; sr. exec. v.p., treas. San Miguel Corp., Makati; dir. several cos., Philippines and Hong Kong. Chmn. bd. trustees Andres Soriano Cancer Research Fund, U.S. and Philippines. Served with USNR, 1943-46. Decorated Knight Magistral Grace Sovereign Mil. Order Malta; chevalier Legion of Honor (France); Encomiendade Numero de la Orden de Isabela la Catolica (Spain); ambassador extraordinary Order St. John of Jerusalem of Rhodes and Malta, until 1979. Home: 6 Close Rd Greenwich CT 06830 Office: 1351 Washington Blvd Stamford CT 06902

SORIANO Y DE MONTEMAR, ANDRES, industrialist; b. May 3, 1926; s. Andres Soriano y Roxas and Carmen de Montemar y Martinez; B.S. in Econs., Wharton Sch., U. Pa., 1950; D.Econs. (hon.), U. San Carlos, Cebu City, Philippines, 1968; m. Maria Natividad Loinaz; children—Andres III, Cristina Soriano Illerrera, Eduardo, Carlos Theodore Miguel. Chmn. bd. dirs. Papers Industries Corp. Philippines; chmn. bd., chief exec. officer San Miguel Corp., Philippines; chmn. bd. Ansor Corp., Stamford, Conn., San Miguel Brewery, Ltd., Hong Kong, San Miguel & Swan Holdings Ltd., Papua New Guinea, Papua New Guinea Brewery Pty., Ltd.; chmn. bd., v.p. SDC Internat. Ltd., Can.; pres., dir. A. Soriano Corp., Nin Bay Mining Co. (both Philippines), P.T. Miguel Brewery, Indonesia; sr. v.p., dir. Atlas Consol. Mining and Devel. Corp., Philippines; v.p., dir. Anscor Container Corp., Atlas Fertilizer Corp., Philippine Oil Devel. Co., Inc. (all Philippines); gen. partner Am. Internat. Hardwood Co.; dir. Phelps Dodge Phillippines, Inc., W. Palawan Consol. Nickel Mines, Inc., Herald Publs., Inc., Davao Insular Hotel, Inc., Philippine Match Co., Ltd. (all Philippines), Kapunda Devel. Co., Pty., Ltd., Australia, San Miguel, Fabricas de Cerveza y Malta, S.A., Spain; governing dir. Neptunia Corp., Ltd., Hong Kong; dep. governing dir. Wood Products Internat., Ltd. Pres., trustee Andres Soriano Cancer Research Found., Andres Soriano Found., Inc., chmn., trustee Tondo Youth Found.; trustee Andres Soraino Meml. Found., Cultural Center Philippines, Philippine Bus. Social Progress, Andrea Soriano Cancer Research Fund. Decorated Encomienda con Placa de la Orden del Merito Civil (Spain); comdr. with silver plaque Order St. Gregory Gt. (Vatican); named Bus. Exec. of Yr., 1963, Hon. Alumnus, U. Philippines Coll. Agr., 1975. Clubs: Polo (Paris); American (Hong Kong); Baguio Country, Filipino, University, Valley Golf, Wack Wack Golf and Country (Philippines); Manila, Manila Golf and Country, Manilo Polo, Manila Yacht; U. Pa.; Marco Polo (N.Y.C.); University, Mission Hills Country (Kansas City, Mo.). Home: Office: 8776 Paseo de Roxas Makati Metro Manila Philippines

SORRELL, RONALD GLENN, fin. planner; b. Vancouver, Wash., May 10, 1932; s. Victor G. and Doris M. (Dodson) S.; B.A., Purdue U., 1956; grad. N.Y. Inst. Fin., 1960; m. Marilu Luisa Ciattei, June 2, 1979; children by previous marriage—Tamra Wainani, Todd Glenn. Estate planner Gen. Am. Life, 1957, Schwabacher & Co., 1959-64; mgr. Walston & Co., 1964-70; v.p. Internal Securities Corp., 1970-74; mgr. Am. Pacific Securities Corp., Honolulu and v.p. Nat. Assn. Employee Benefit, 1974—; tchr. stock exchange courses, 1961-74; radio and TV reporter stock market news, 1961-78. Mem. U.S. Olympic Team, 1956; 4 times U.S. volleyball All-Am.; commr. Internat. Profl. Surfers Assn., 1969-71. Served with AUS, 1952-54; Korea. Registered rep. N.Y. Stock Exchange; named most listened to stock broker Honolulu Star Bull., 1967. Mem. Nat. Assn. Securities Dealers (prin.), Internat. Assn. Fin. Planners. Club: Outrigger Canoe (dir. 1975-79, pres. 1979-80). Home: 475 Atkinson Dr Apt 1703 Honolulu HI 96815 Office: 925 Bethel St Suite 311 Honolulu HI 96813

SORRELLS, J. GORDON, banker; b. Dallas, Oct. 8, 1943; s. James Craven and Irene (Bentley) S.; B.S. in Geology, Tex. Christian U., 1967, M.B.A., 1969; postgrad. N.Y. U., 1971; m. Sarah Patrice Prior, Apr. 19, 1980. Asst. treas. Bankers Trust Co., N.Y.C., 1969-73; v.p. 1st City Nat. Bank, Houston, 1973-76, v.p., group mgr. petroleum and minerals dept., 1976-80; sr. v.p., mgr. energy dept. 1st City Bank of Dallas, 1980—; tchr. course in fin. analysis Good Counsel Coll., White Plains, N.Y., 1971. Active Heart Fund, Houston Banks Urban Affairs Com.; bd. dirs. Houston Bus. Growth Corp., MESBIC Fin. Corp. Recipient citation for leadership in Tandy Challenge for Tex. Christian U., 1975. Mem. Am. Inst. Banking, Am. Bankers Assn. (minority lending com.), Nat. Ocean Industries Assn. (fin. com.), Houston Area Alumni Assn. Tex. Christian U. (pres.). Republican. Mem. Christian Ch. (Disciples of Christ). Home: 5315 Waneta Dallas TX 75209 Office: One Main Pl Box 50688 Dallas TX 75250

SOSNA, ROBERT WILLIAM, ins. co. exec.; b. Phila., Nov. 18, 1941; s. Robert William and Catharine Anna (McGowan) S.; B.A., LaSalle Coll., 1963; postgrad. U. Mich., 1975, Xavier U.; m. Lyn T. Sulock, Oct. 24, 1964; children—Jackie, Kate, Kristen. Account underwriter Allstate Ins. Co., Valley Forge, Pa., 1964-70; sr. underwriter Fireman's Fund Ins. Cos., Phila., 1970-71, asso. office mgr., 1971-73, personal lines mgr., 1973-75, sales mgr., 1975-77, adminstrv. exec., San Francisco, 1977-79, gen. mgr., resident v.p., Cin., 1979-80; ops. v.p. CG/Aetna Ins. Co., 1980—; mem. governing com. Ohio Automobile Ins. Plan, 1979-80; instr. Pa. State U., 1974-77. Mem. Ohio Automobile Ins. Plan, Cin. Ins. Execs., Montgomery Bus. Men's Assn. Republican. Roman Catholic. Clubs: Manufacturers Golf and Tennis; Pa.; Cincinnati; University (Hartford, Conn.). Home: 4 Harding Dr Simsbury CT Office: 55 Elm St Hartford CT 06115

SOSS, NEAL MARTIN, economist; b. N.Y.C., Feb. 6, 1949; s. Samuel Louis and Bella (Wexler) S.; B.A., Williams Coll., 1970; Ph.D., Princeton U., 1974; m. Sarah Spitzer, Mar. 26, 1969. Asst. instr. dept. econs. Princeton U., 1972-73; staff economist N.Y. State Div. Budget, Albany, 1973-74; chief economist Office of Sec. to Gov., Albany, 1975-77; dep. supt. banks N.Y. State Banking Dept., N.Y.C., 1977-78, 1st dep. supt. banks, 1978-79; dir. banking research and econ. analysis Office of Controller of Currency, Washington, 1979—; cons. Ednl. Testing Service, Princeton, N.J. Mem. Am. Econ. Assn., Phi Beta Kappa. Club: Williams. Contbr. articles to Jour. History of Ideas, 1973, Jour. Polit. Economy, 1974, Planning for Higher Edn., 1974, Transp. Research, 1976. Home: 78 Seaview Ave New Rochelle NY 10801 Office: 490 L'Enfant Plaza Washington DC 20219

SOTER, NICHOLAS GREGORY, advt. exec.; b. Gt. Falls, Mont., Apr. 26, 1947; s. Sam Nicholas and Bernice (Bennett) S.; B.A. in Communications, Brigham Young U., Provo, Utah, 1971; m. Kathleen Lyman, Feb. 20, 1970; children—Nichole, Erin, Samuel Scott, Kara, Stephen Andrew. With McLean Assos., Provo, 1970-75, chmn. bd., pres., chief exec. officer Soter Assos., Inc., Provo, 1975—; instr. advt. Utah Tech. Coll., Provo. Recipient various advt. awards for creativity, design and writing excellence. Mem. Communications Assn. Utah Valley (pres.), Provo C. of C. Republican. Mem. Ch. Jesus Christ of Latter-day Saints. Author articles in field; co-pub. Jour. of Joseph, 1979, Jour. of Brigham, 1980, LaVell Edwards, 1980. Home: 1728 South 290 East Orem UT 84057 Office: 209 North 400 West Provo UT 84601

SOTTILE, JAMES, III, mining co. exec.; b. Miami, Fla., Aug. 3, 1940; s. James and Ethel (Hooks) S.; B.S. cum laude, U. Fla., 1962; m. Judith Horne, Dec. 5, 1959; children—James IV, Michael, Scott, Thomas, Jennifer. Vice pres. Goldfield Corp., Melbourne, Fla., 1970-71, pres., dir., 1971—; v.p., dir. Canaveral Indian River Groves, Inc., Micco, Fla., 1964-70, Brevard-Indian River Groves, Inc., Micco, 1964-69, Indian River Shores Groves, Inc., 1962-64; pres., dir. Indian Mound Corp., Micco, 1963-69, Original 51 Corp., Micco, 1966-69; v.p. Lake Byrd Citrus Packings Co., Micco, 1963-71, pres., 1971—, also dir.; v.p. Indian River Orange Groves, Inc., Micco, 1963-69, pres., 1969-74, also dir.; pres., dir. Citrus Growers of Fla., Inc., Melbourne, 1970—; v.p., dir. No. Goldfield Investment Ltd., Melbourne, Fla., 1971-79, pres., 1979—, Mamba Engring Co., Inc., Titusville, Fla., 1972—; pres. dir. Black Range Mining Corp., Albuquerque, 1972—, San Pedro Mining Corp., Albuquerque, 1972—, Goldfield Consol. Mines Co., Albuquerque, 1972—; pres. Harlan (Ky.) Fuel Co., 1975—; v.p., dir. Valencia Center, Inc., Coral Gables, Fla., 1964—. Trustee San Sebastian Drainage Dist., Melbourne, 1965-78. Mem. Fla. C. of C. (dir. 1972-76), Young Presidents Orgn. Democrat. Roman Catholic. Clubs: Eau Gallie Yacht (Melbourne); Cat Cay (Bahamas). Home: PO Box 1899 Melbourne FL 32901 Office: 65 E NASA Blvd Melbourne FL 32901

SOUERS, LOREN EATON, lawyer; b. Canton, Ohio, Jan. 29, 1916; s. Loren Edmunds and Ilka (Gaskell) S.; A.B., Denison U., 1937; J.D., Case Western Res. U., 1940, postgrad., 1954-55; m. Mildred Mae McCollum, June 21, 1941; children—Mary Sue James, Loren Eaton. Admitted to Ohio bar, 1940, U.S. Supreme Ct. bar, 1960; asso. firm Black, McCuskey, Souers & Arbaugh, Canton, 1940—, partner, 1946—; dir. Harter Bank & Trust Co., Continental Steel Corp., Kokomo, Ind., Phoenix Mfg. Co., Joliet, Ill. Cons., Ohio Supreme Ct. Continuing Com. Admissions, 1957-59; mem. Ohio Bd. Bar Examiners, 1959-64. Pres., McKinley Area council Boy Scouts Am., 1954-57, mem. nat. council, 1954-71; mem. trust com., sec. Hoover Found.; mem. Canton City Council, 1948-49, mem. Ohio Bd. Edn., 1956-60, v.p., 1958-60; mem. Canton City Bd. Edn., 1961-72, pres., 1965, 68, 71, Canton City Planning Commn., 1972-78; mem. vis. com. Case Western Res. U. Law Sch. Del. Republican Nat. Conv., 1948; Rep. city campaign mgr., 1951, 53. Trustee Denison U., 1967—. Served from pvt. to capt., inf. AUS, 1942-45; ETO. Decorated Fourragere (Belgium). Recipient research prize in econs. Denison U., 1937; Distinguished Service award Canton Jr. C. of C., 1950; Silver Beaver award Boy Scouts Am., 1957. Fellow Am., Ohio (trustee), bar founds.; mem. Internat., Am., Stark County (pres.), Ohio (exec. com. 1976-79, pres. 1980-81) bar assns., Stark County Law Library Assn. (trustee 1946-76 pres. 1972-76), Soc. Benchers, Canton C. of C. (v.p. 1959-60), Phi Delta Theta, Phi Delta Phi, Omicron Delta Kappa, Tau Kappa Alpha, Pi Delta Epsilon. Baptist (chmn. bds. deacons and trustees). Mason (32 deg.). Clubs: Canton, Brookside, Oakwood Country (Canton); Univ. (Columbus). Contbr. to legal publs. Lectr. on legal subjects. Home: 135 195h St NW Canton OH 44709 Office: 1200 Harter Bank Bldg Canton OH 44702

SOULAK, JOSEPH HAROLD, publisher; b. Adams, Wis., Mar. 25, 1932; s. Harold Joseph and Mary I. (Turski) S.; A.B., Providence Coll., 1960; postgrad. Boston U., 1960, Roosevelt U., 1969; m. Leanora Galante, Sept. 1, 1956 (div. Oct. 1971); 1 dau., Deborah; m. 2d, Judith A. Sharpe, Oct. 16, 1975. Sports editor Lakeland Pubs., Grayslake, Ill., 1960-62, news editor, 1962-64, mng. editor, 1964-65; news editor Pawtuxet Valley Times, West Warwick, R.I., 1964; mgr. pub. relations Bastian-Blessing Co., Chgo., 1965-68; publs. mgr. Ryerson Steel, Chgo., 1969; dir. news services Ency. Brit., Inc., Chgo., 1969-75; pub., editor Quality Newspapers/Suburban Publs., Milw., 1975—; columnist/writer Waukegan News-Sun, 1969-75. Mgr. public relations for Ill. Senator, 1964-75. Served with USN, 1952-56; PTO. Mem. Pub. Relations Soc. Am., Ill. C. of C., S. Milw. Assn. Commerce (dir. 1975-76, pres. 1976—), Wis. Press Assn., Suburban Press Found., Nat. Editorial Assn. Club: Chicago Press. Author booklet. Home: 1332 Manitoba Ave S Milwaukee WI 53172 Office: 723 Milwaukee Ave S Milwaukee WI 53172

SOUTH, RONALD LEE, acct., constrn. co. exec.; b. Cullman, Ala., July 19, 1947; s. Robert L. and Johanna T. (Paulisek) S.; B.A. in Acctg., St. Bernard Coll., 1969; M.B.A., U. Tenn., Chattanooga, 1980; children—Traci Michelle, Kathryn Deneise. Staff acct. Moses & Son, C.P.A.'s, Birmingham, Ala., 1969; fin. analyst Moore Handley, Inc., Birmingham, 1972-73; revenue agt. IRS, Chattanooga, 1973-74; office mgr., asst. sec.-treas. Raines Bros., Inc., Chattanooga, 1974—. Served with U.S. Army, 1969-72. Decorated Army Commendation medal, Joint Service Commendation medal. Office: 209 Minor St Chattanooga TN 37405

SOUTHARD, LELAND WAYNE, agrl. economist; b. Salem, Ark., May 3, 1941; s. Wiley Wayne and Mary Leola (Blair) S.; B.S.A., Ark. State U., 1963; M.S., La. State U., 1966; postgrad. U. Md., 1970-75; m. Judith Helen Tyson, June 25, 1977. Grad. asst. La. State U., Baton Rouge, 1963-65, instr., 1966-67; agrl. economist U.S. Dept. Agr., Washington, 1967—; mem. World Food and Agr. Outlook and Situation Bd. for Clearance of monthly Agr. Outlook, 1976—. Recipient Superior Service award U.S. Dept. Agr., 1973. Mem. Orgn. Profl. Employees Dept. Agr., Am. Agrl. Econs. Assn., Western Agrl. Econs. Assn. Mem. Christian Ch. Office: 500 12th St SW Washington DC 20250

SOUTHERLAND, JEROME KEE, farmer, banker; b. Banner, Ark., Sept. 22, 1903; s. James Walter and Melita (Kee) S.; A.A. (hon.), So. Bapt. Coll., 1972; m. Cleo Ferguson, June 2, 1928; children—Virginia Southerland Henry, Carolyn Southerland Shell, Kaye Southerland Bruce. Farmer, poultryman, Floral, Ark., 1928—; founder, pres. J.K. Southerland Poultry Co., Batesville, Ark., 1948-69; a founder Citizens Bank, Batesville, 1953, chmn. bd., 1978—. Deacon, 1st Bapt. Ch., Batesville; trustee So. Bapt. Coll., Walnut Ridge, Ark., 1959—, pres. bd. trustees; v.p. White River Med. Center; chmn. Ark. Livestock and Poultry Commn., 1964-79. Recipient Citizen of Yr. award Kiwanis Club, 1963, Community Devel. award Ark. C. of C., 1975, Ark. Poultry Improvement award, 1978. Mem. Ark. Poultry Fedn. (past pres.), Ark. Cattlemen Assn., Batesville C. of C. (pres. 1975-76, mem. indsl. com., exec. com.). Democrat. Clubs: Masons, Rotary (past pres.). Office: Citizens Bank 3d and College Sts Batesville AR 72501

SOUTHERN, ARLEN DUANE, corp. public relations exec.; b. Liberal, Kans., Apr. 11, 1933; s. N. Leo and Lydia S.; student Panhandle State Coll., 1951-53; B.A. in Journalism, U. Okla., 1956, postgrad. in public relations and advt., 1956; m. Beth Louise Rapp, Sept. 22, 1956; children—Randal David, Stanford Leo. With AP, Oklahoma City, 1954-56; editorial asst. Thompson Products, Cleve., 1956-57; mgr. communications Tapco Group, Cleve., 1959-63; asst. dir. public relations and advt. TRW Inc., Cleve., 1964-68, dir. public relations and advt., 1968-72; v.p. corp. affairs IU Internat. Corp., Phila., 1972—; v.p., dir. Nat. Investor Relations Inst., Washington; pres., dir., past pres. Investor Relations Assn., N.Y.C. Vice chmn. maj. bus. group Phila. United Way, 1978. Served with U.S. Army, 1957-59. Mem. Public Relations Soc. Am., Sigma Delta Chi, Omicron Delta Kappa. Republican. Writer, speaker profl., ednl., indsl. orgns. Home: 407 Chickadee Ln Westtown Twp West Chester PA 19380 Office: 1500 Walnut St Philadelphia PA 19102

SOUTHWOOD, JOHN EUGENE, banker; b. Evansville, Ind., Nov. 7, 1929; s. Walter H. and Vera M. S.; B.A., Vanderbilt U., 1952; student Stonier Grad. Sch. Banking, Rutgers U., Ind. U.; m. Myrna McClain, Dec. 24, 1960; children—Deborah Lynn Southwood Love, John Eugene. With Third Nat. Bank, Nashville, 1952—, asst. cashier, 1957-63, asst. v.p., 1963-68, v.p., 1968-72, exec. v.p., 1976-79, vice chmn., 1979—; pres. Third Nat. Corp.; asso. Owen Sch. Mgmt., Vanderbilt U., Nashville; del. ECOSOC, Geneva, 1978. Mem. Am. Inst. Banking, Bank Adminstrn. Inst., Robert Morris Assos., C. of C. Baptist. Clubs: Richland Country, Temple Hills Country, Exchange,

Quarterback. Home: 7975 Hwy 100 Nashville TN 37221 Office: Third Nat Bank Nashville TN 37244

SOUVEROFF, VERNON WILLIAM, JR., electronics co. exec.; b. Los Angeles, Aug. 12, 1934; s. Vernon William and Aileen Souveroff; B.S. in Elec. Engring., Stanford U., 1957; children—Gail Kathleen, Michael William. With Litton Industries, Los Angeles, 1960-75; with ITT Gilfillan, Van Nuys, Calif., 1975—, pres., 1979—. Served with USAF, 1957-60. Mem. IEEE, Nat. Contracts Mgmt. Assn., Soc. Logistics Engrs., Stanford U. Alumni Assn. Presbyterian. Office: 7821 Orion Ave Van Nuys CA 91409

SOUYOUL, RICHARD, real estate devel. co. exec.; b. Little Rock, Sept. 26, 1945; s. Thomas J. and Genevieve D. S.; B.B.A., Loyola U., Chgo., 1968; M.B.A., L.I. U., 1970; m. Sandra Hatfield, Apr. 16, 1977; 1 dau., Samantha. With John Nuveen & Co., Chgo., 1971-72; prin. Eastdil Realty, N.Y.C., 1972-76; with Rubloff Devel. Corp., Chgo., 1977—, sr. v.p., 81; pres. Walker Souyoul Interests; dir. Devel. Co. of Topeka. Served to capt. U.S. Army, 1970-71. Office: 69 W Washington St Chicago IL 60602

SOWERWINE, ELBERT ORLA, JR., cons. engring. planning and mgmt.; b. Tooele, Utah, Mar. 15, 1915; s. Elbert Orla and Margaret Alice (Evans) S.; B. Chemistry, Cornell U., 1937, Chem. Engr., 1938; children—Sue-Ann Sowerwine Jacobson, Sandra Sowerwine Montgomery, Elbert Orla 3d, John Frederick, Avril Ruth, Albaro Francisco, Octavio Evans, Zaida Margaret. Analytical chemist Raritan Copper Works, Perth Amboy, N.J., summers 1936, 37; research chem. engr. Socony-Vacuum Oil Co., Paulsboro, N.J., 1938-43; prodn. supr. Merck & Co., Elkton, Va., 1943-45; asst. plant mgr. U.S. Indsl. Chems. Co., Newark, 1945-48; project engr. and research dir. Wigton-Abbott Corp., Newark, 1948-50, Cody, Wyo., 1950-55; cons. engring., planning, indsl. and community devel., resource evaluation and mgmt. Wepiti, Wyo., also C.Am. Republics, 1955—. Commr. N.J., Boy Scouts Am., 1938-43; mem. Wapiti and Park County (Wyo.) Sch. Bds., 1954-58; dir. Mont. State Planning Bd., 1959-61; exec. bd. Mo. Basin Research and Devel. Council, 1959-61. Fellow Am. Inst. Chemists; mem. Am. Inst. Chem. Engrs., Am. Planning Assn., Nicaraguan Assn. Engrs. and Architects. Libertarian. Researcher desulfurization of petroleum products, process control; patentee in petroleum and chem. processes and equipment. Home: Broken H Ranch Wapiti WY 82450 Office: Sowerwine Cons Wapiti WY 82450

SOYUGENC, RAHMI, mfg. co. exec.; b. Pazarcik, Turkey, May 5, 1931; s. Ismail and Ayse S.; came to U.S., 1954, naturalized, 1965; B.S. in Indsl. Engring., U. Evansville, 1959; M.S. in Indsl. Engring., Ill. Inst., 1964; m. Marjori Zurstadt, Sept. 10, 1960; children—Altay Yakup, Perihan Ayla. Systems analyst Am. Nat. Bank & Trust Co., Chgo., 1960-63; chief of ops. Chgo. Bd. Health, 1963-70; pres. Evansville Metal Products Co. (Ind.), 1970—, Keller St Corp., Evansville, 1973—. Founder, dir. The Chicago Mosque. Recipient Meritorious Service award Chgo. Heart Assn., 1963, 66. Mem. Ops. Research Soc. Am., Am. Soc. Quality Control (chpt. pres.), Tri-State Council for Sci. and Engring. (region pres.), Turkish Am. Cultural Alliance (charter). Moslem. Clubs: Petroleum, Evansville Country. Home: 119 LaDonna St Evansville IN 47711 Office: Keller St Corp 2100 N 6th Ave Evansville IN 47710

SPADAFINA, JOSEPH MICHAEL, electronics mfg. co. exec.; b. N.Y.C., Apr. 5, 1941; s. Joseph and Lucia Spadafina; B.S.E.E. (Wyman scholar), Pa. Mil. Coll., 1962; M.E.E., U. Del., 1965; postgrad. in contract adminstrn. Hofstra U.; postgrad. in mgmt. Rollins Coll.; children—Donna, Joseph, Lisa. Research fellow U. Del., 1962-64; mktg. program mgr. Hydrosystems, Inc., Melville, N.Y.; mktg. mgr. Peripheral Data Machines, Inc., Hicksville, N.Y.; pres. Bardon Tech. Services, Inc., West Hempstead, N.Y.; v.p., gen. mgr. Revenue Systems, Inc., mfrs. toll collection equipment, Plainview, N.Y.; pres. Autotronic Products Inc., mfr. automated electronic products, Oceanside, N.Y. Served to capt. U.S. Army, 1964-66. Decorated Army Commendation medal; named Distinguished Mil. Grad., Pa. Mil. Coll. Mem. IEEE, Tau Beta Pi. Office: 3300 Lawson Blvd Oceanside NY 11582

SPAIN, RICHARD COLBY, lawyer; b. Evanston, Ill., Nov. 17, 1950; s. Richard Francis and Anne Louise (Brinckerhoff) S.; B.A. cum laude, Lawrence U., 1972; J.D., Case Western Res. U., 1975; m. Nancy Linn Mavec, Aug. 3, 1974; children—Catherine Day, Sarah Colby. Admitted to Ohio bar, 1975; account rep. Arnold Graphics Industries, Uniontown, Ohio, 1975-76; partner firm Spain and Spain, Attys., Cleve., 1976—. Chmn. Young Audiences of Greater Cleve., Inc., 1978—; chmn. fin. com. Fairmount Theatre of Deaf, Inc., Cleve., 1979—; trustee No. Ohio Children's Performing Music Found., Inc., 1980—. Mem. Cleve. Bar Assn., Ohio Bar Assn., Am. Bar Assn. Episcopalian. Home: 3355 North Park Blvd Cleveland Heights OH 44118 Office: 760 Leader Bldg Cleveland OH 44114

SPAMAN, WILLIAM CADWELL, computer services co. exec.; b. Grand Rapids, Mich., Oct. 21, 1941; s. Robert Franklin and Maxine C. (Glaza) S.; student in Indsl. Engring., U. Toledo, 1959-65; m. Carol Sue McKnight, Jan. 21, 1960; children—Robert, Carrie Lyn, Kimberley. Accounts mgr. Continental Brokerage Co., Detroit, 1961-65; mgr. Caltec Inc., Toledo, 1965-69, v.p., 1969-72, pres., 1972—; instr. computer sci. U. Toledo, 1969-71. Mem. curriculum adv. bd. Owens Tech. Coll. Mem. Nat. Assn. Accountants, Data Processing Mgrs. Assn. Episcopalian. Club: Rotary. Home: 2833 Sherbrook Rd Toledo OH 43606 Office: 5415 Secor Rd Toledo OH 43623

SPANGENBERG, J. BRAND, exec. recruitment cons.; b. Milw., May 11, 1939; s. Gilbert F. and Marcella Spangenberg; B.S., Marquette U., 1961; m. Barbara Werner, Aug. 31, 1963; children—Jill, Marie, Beth Ann. Personnel mgr. Allis-Chalmers, Milw., 1962-68; personnel mgr. Cutler-Hammer, Inc., Milw., 1968-73; asso. Conley Assos., Inc., Chgo., 1973-74; pres. The Brand Co., Inc., Mequon, Wis., 1974—; dir. Great Midwest Savs. and Loan Assn., Milw. Served with U.S. Army, 1961. Mem. Assn. Exec. Recruiting Cons., Am. Soc. Personnel Adminstrn., Ind. Bus. Assn. Wis., Metro Milw. Assn. Commerce, Wis. Mfrs. and Commerce, Delta Sigma Pi. Club: Kiwanis. Home: 3003 W Woodland Ct Mequon WI 53092 Office: 12740 N River Rd Mequon WI 53092

SPANGLE, CLARENCE WILBUR, computer co. exec.; b. Wilkinsburg, Pa., Feb. 16, 1925; s. Carl C. and Blanche E. S.; B.S.M.E., Yale U., 1945; J.D., George Washington U., 1952; m. Virginia Galliher, Aug. 11, 1951; 1 son, Henry Bryan. With Honeywell Inc., Mpls., 1947-80, sr. v.p., 1970-71, exec. v.p., 1971-74, pres. Honeywell Info. Systems, Inc., Mpls., 1974-80, also dir. Honeywell Inc.; chmn. Memorex Corp., Santa Clara, Calif., 1980—; admitted to Minn. bar, 1952; dir. Gelco Corp., 1st Bank System, Inc., Mpls. Bd. dirs. Guthrie Theater, Mpls. Served with USNR, 1942-46. Methodist. Office: Memorex Corp San Tomas and Central Expressway Santa Clara CA 95052

SPANGLER, EARL JONES, chocolate co. exec.; b. Campbelltown, Pa., Dec. 15, 1922; s. Abner C. and Beulah M. (Jones) S.; B.S., Lebanon Valley Coll., 1948; m. Edna Reid, Sept. 25, 1948; children—Stephanie Sue, Susan Beth. With Hershey Chocolate Co. (Pa.), 1950—, dir. distbn., 1970-72, div. v.p., 1972-76, pres., 1976—; dir. Hershey Foods Corp.; chmn. bd. Y&S Candies Inc. Served with USNR, 1943-46. Chmn., Dauphin County Hosp. Authority. Mem. Harrisburg C. of C. Clubs: Rotary (past pres.), Masons. Office: 19 E Chocolate Ave Hershey PA 17033

SPANGLER, PAUL LEON, chemist; b. Garnett, Kans., Jan. 5, 1941; s. Don James and Elma (Pinneo) S.; B.A., Kans. State Coll., Pittsburg, 1963, M.S., 1965; m. Mary Jon Hall, June 6, 1965; children—Jennifer Anne, Jeffery Noel. Chemist, Chemagro Corp., Kansas City, Mo., 1965-68; chemist, Mallinckrodt Inc., St. Louis, 1968-74; pres., chief exec. officer Pathfinder Labs., Inc., St. Louis, 1974—. Mem. Am. Chem. Soc. Methodist. Office: 11542 Fort Mims Dr St Louis MO 63141

SPANGLER, RONALD LEROY, television exec., aircraft distbr.; b. York, Pa., Mar. 5, 1937; s. Ivan L. and Sevilla (Senft) S.; student U. Miami (Fla.), 1955-59; m. Patricia Spangler; children—Kathleen, Ronald, Beth Anne. Radio announcer Sta. WSBA, York, 1955-57; TV producer-dir. Sta. WBAL-TV, Balt., 1959-65; pres., chmn. bd. LewRon Television, N.Y.C., 1965-74; pres., chmn. bd. Spanair Inc., distbr. Rockwell Comdr. aircraft, Forest Hill, Md. Mem. Video Tape Producers Assn. N.Y., Rolls Royce Owners Club, Ferrari Clubs Am. Home: 2305 Warfield Dr Forest Hill MD 21050 Office: Forest Hill Industrial Park Forest Hill MD 21050

SPARKS, BILLY SCHLEY, lawyer; b. Marshall, Mo., Oct. 1, 1923; s. John and Clarinda (Schley) S.; A.B., Harvard, 1945, LL.B., 1949; student Mass. Inst. Tech., 1943-44; m. Dorothy O. Stone, May 14, 1946; children—Stephen Stone, Susan Lee, John David. Admitted to Mo. bar, 1949; partner Langworthy, Matz & Linde, Kansas City, Mo., 1949-62, firm Linde, Thomson, Fairchild, Langworthy & Kohn, 1962—. Mem. Mission Planning Council, 1954-63; mem. Dist. 110 Sch. Bd., Johnson County, Kans., 1964-69, pres., 1967-69; mem. Dist. 512 Sch. Bd., Johnson County, 1970-74, pres., 1971-73; mem. Kans. Civil Service Commn., 1975—. Candidate for U.S. Rep., 10th Dist., Kans., 1960, 3rd dist., 1962; treas. Johnson County (Kans.) Democratic Central com., 1958-63; del. to Dem. Nat. Conv., 1964. Served to lt. USAAF, 1944-46. Mem. Kansas City C. of C. (legislative com. 1956-72), Am., Kansas City bar assns., Mo. Bar, Law Assn. of Kansas City, Harvard Law Sch. Assn. Mo. (past dir.), St. Andrews Soc. Mem. Christian Ch. (trustee). Clubs: Harvard (v.p. 1953-54) (Kansas City, Mo.); Tomahawk Hills Country (dir. 1965-69); Milburn Golf and Country. Home: 8517 W 90th Terr Shawnee Mission KS 66212 Office: City Center Square Kansas City MO 64196

SPARKS, GEORGE POWELL, mfg. co. exec.; b. Indpls., Jan. 6, 1943; s. Robert Kennard and Mary Frances (Fink) S.; B.S., Union Coll., 1964; m. Elizabeth Ann Adolphus, Aug. 22, 1965; children—James Kennard, Suzanne Mary. With plastics div. Mobil Chem. Co., 1971-75, group controller, Canadaigua, N.Y., 1974, regional controller, Macedon, N.Y., 1975; controller plastics div. Carborundum Co., Bethel, Vt., 1976-78, gen. mgr. plastics molding, 1978—; instr. fin. Yuba Community Coll., 1970. Com. chmn. Youth Hockey, Buffalo. Served to capt. USAF, 1965-70. Mem. Soc. Plastic Engrs., Soc. Plastics Industry. Home: 10 Pine Dr Hanover NH 03755 Office: GW Plastics Bethel VT 05032

SPARKS, MEREDITH PLEASANT (MRS. WILLIAM J. SPARKS), patent lawyer; b. Palestine, Ill.; d. John L. and Laura (Bicknell) Pleasant; A.B. with distinction, Ind. U., 1927, A.M., 1928; Ph.D., U. Ill., 1936; J.D., Rutgers U., 1958; m. William J. Sparks, Dec. 31, 1930 (dec.); children—Ruth (Mrs. James W. Foster), Katherine (Mrs. Richard L. Albrecht), Charles, John. Tchr. chemistry Rochester (Ind.) High Sch., 1928-29; chemist DuPont Co., Niagara Falls, N.Y., 1929-34, Northam Warren Co., N.Y.C., 1939, Am. Cyanamid Co., Bound Brook, N.J., 1941-46; admitted to Fla. bar, 1958, U.S. Customs and Patent Appeals Ct., U.S. Ct. Claims, U.S. Supreme Ct.; patent agt., 1946-58; patent atty., 1958—. Mem. nat. bd. Med. Coll. Pa. Mem. Assn. Ind. U. Chemists (pres. 1950-51), Internat., Am., Fla., Coral Gables bar assns., Am., N.J., Internat. patent and trademark assns., Am. Chem. Soc., Nat. Assn. Univ. Women (pres.-elect), Fla. Assn. Women Lawyers, Phi Beta Kappa, Sigma Xi, Iota Sigma Pi, Kappa Delta. Club: Zonta. Contbr. articles to profl. jours. Patentee in field. Home: 5129 Granada Blvd Coral Gables FL 33146 Office: The Law Center 370 Minorca Ave Coral Gables FL 33134

SPARKS, ROBERT WILSON, gas co. exec.; b. Amarillo, Tex., Oct. 9, 1918; ed. Tex. Tech. U.; 2 sons. Vice pres. Texaco Can. Ltd., 1973, now chmn., chief exec. officer; exec. v.p., dir. Federated Pipelines Ltd.; chmn. Texaco Can. Resources Ltd. Mem. Can. Petroleum Assn. (gov. Alta. div.). Office: 90 Wynford Dr Donn Mills ON M3C 1K5 Canada*

SPARKS, WILLIAM EARL, developer, builder, Realtor; b. Danville, Va., Dec. 13, 1945; s. Dewey C. and Irene J. (Lewis) S.; B.B.A., U. Ga., 1974; m. Elizabeth Bellamy Lattimore, June 18, 1971; children—Catherine Ashley, William Earl, Robert Lattimore. Vice pres. Lattimore Land Corp., Savannah, Ga., 1974—; exec. v.p. Intercoastal Assos., Inc., Savannah, 1975—; pres. Heritage Ventures, Inc., Savannah, 1976—; pres. Lattimore & Sparks, Inc., Savannah, 1977—; also dir. all above corps. Sec., bd. dirs. St. Andrews on Marsh; bd. dirs. Islands YMCA; chmn. Coastal Ga. Goals Com. Served to capt. U.S. Army, 1967-72. Decorated D.F.C., Bronze Star, Air medal; Cameron Brown Mortgage Bankers scholar, 1971-72. Mem. Nat., Ga., Savannah homebuilders assns., Nat., Ga., Savannah assns. realtors, Asso. Gen. Contractors Am., Alpha Kappa Psi, Phi Kappa Phi. Democrat. Episcopalian. Clubs: Savannah Yacht, Debtors, Wilmington Island Lions (1st v.p.), Oglethorpe, Savannah Inn and Country, Civitan. Home: 111 N Millward Ct Savannah GA 31410 Office: PO Box 3775 Savannah GA 31404

SPATARO, ROBERT PETER, real estate broker; b. Waterbury, Conn., Aug. 4, 1943; s. Paul and Frances S.; B.S., Belknap Coll., 1968; J.D., Atlanta Law Sch., 1976, LL.M., 1977. Owner, mgr. Spataro Realty, Waterbury, 1968—; legal aide Corp. Counsel's Office, City of Waterbury. Mem. Ga. Trial Lawyers Assn., Mensa, Delta Theta Phi (recipient award 1974, dep. state chancellor Ga. 1975, dep. marshall nat. orgn. 1976). Roman Catholic. Address: 7 Plainfield Dr Waterbury CT 06708

SPAUR, ROBERT BREWER, fin. exec.; b. Kansas City, Mo., Apr. 3, 1948; s. Lloyd Robert and Lora Louise (Brewer) S.; student UCLA, 1966-70; B.A., U. Mo., 1971, M.A., 1975. Economist, Franklin Assos., Prairie Village, Kan., 1976-77; pres., investment advisor, economist Capital Mgmt., Mission, Kan., 1977—; econ. cons. Mem. Am. Econs. Assn., U. Mo. Kansas City Alumni Assn., Sigma Nu. Omicron Delta Epsilon. Contbr. articles to profl. jours. Address: 5800 Martway Mission KS 66202

SPEAR, ROBERT JAMES, co. exec.; b. Indpls., Aug. 8, 1922; s. Paul Millard and Audrey Pearl (Stotts) S.; M.E., Purdue U., 1949; m. Barbara Jean McGee, July 23, 1949; children—David Lee, Deborah Dee, Denise Ann. Field service rep. Cummins Engine Co., Inc., service engr., service mgr. So. div., sales mgr. So. div.; v.p. ops. Cummins Ala., Inc., Birmingham, exec. v.p. Served with USN; PTO. Mem. Asso. Equipment Distbrs., Am. Truck Hist. Soc., Ala. Trucking Assn., Ala. Rd. Builders Assn., Ala. Surface Mining Reclamation Council. Republican. Roman Catholic. Clubs: Chase Lake Country, The Club, Bienville. Home: 2647 Chandalar Ln Pelham AL 35124 Office: PO Box 1147 Birmingham AL 35201

SPEAS, ROBERT DIXON, JR., telecommunications co. exec.; b. St. Joseph, Mo., Nov. 16, 1946; s. Robert Dixon and Manette (Hollingsworth) S.; B.S., Stanford U., 1970, M.S., 1970, M.B.A., 1975; m. Bonnie Speas, June 13, 1973. Supr. mgmt. services Ernst & Whinney, San Francisco, 1975-79; prodn. mgr. Rolm Corp., Santa Clara, Calif., 1979—. Bd. dirs. Support Center. Served with USPHS, 1970-72. USPHS fellow, 1972-75. Mem. Ops. Research Soc. Am., Phi Beta Kappa. Co-editor: Operations Research In Health Care, 1975. Home: 4231 Dake Ave Palo Alto CA 94306 Office: Rolm Corp 4900 Old Ironsides Dr Santa Clara CA 95050

SPECHT, FREDERICK LOUIS, lawyer, ins. co. exec.; b. Chgo., Jan. 27, 1939; s. Fred R. and Ida P. (Marini) S.; B.B.A. in Acctg., Loyola U., Chgo., 1962; postgrad. in acctg. U. Ill., 1963; J.D., John Marshall Law Sch., 1968; m. Signe M. Bellande, Sept. 10, 1960; children—Suzanne M., Lisa, Frederick Matthew. Tax acct. J.H. Gilby & Co., Chgo., 1961-63, Interlake Inc., Chgo., 1963-65; tax mgr. Union Spl. Corp., Chgo., 1965-69, AB Dick Co., Chgo., 1972-74; admitted to Ill. bar, 1968; asso. firm Moses, Gibbons, Abramson & Fox, Chgo., 1969-72; mgr. internat. taxes FMC Corp., Chgo., 1974-75; dir. corp. tax Gould Inc., Rolling Meadow, Ill., 1975-78, v.p. taxes, 1978-79; v.p. fin. and adminstrn. Gould-Brown Boveri, Rolling Meadows, 1979-80; v.p. fin. Arthur J. Gallagher & Co., 1980—; spl. asst. atty. gen. State of Ill., 1969-73; teaching asst. John Marshall Law Sch., Chgo., 1972-73. Pres., Edgewater Community Council, 1971-72. C.P.A., Ill. Mem. Am. Bar Assn., Chgo. Bar Assn., Am. Inst. C.P.A.'s, Ill. Inst. C.P.A.'s, Tax Execs. Inst., Chgo. Assn. Commerce and Industry. Home: 113 Rose Terr Tower Lakes Barrington IL 60010

SPECIAN, ROSEMARIE THERESE, mfg. co. exec.; b. Somerville, N.J., Nov. 4, 1944; d. William Michael and Maryann (Dudek) S.; B.S. in Home Econs., Albright Coll., 1966; M.S. in Human Behavior and Devel., Drexel U., 1971; M.B.A., Loyola-Marymount U., 1980. Sales rep. Atlas Crown Brokerage, Los Angeles, 1973-75; regional rep. Reynolds Metals Co., Los Angeles, 1975-77; mktg. mgr. nat. accounts Glass Containers Corp., Anaheim, Calif., 1977-79; sr. package developer Lederle Labs., Pearl River, N.Y., 1980—. Bd. dirs. Student MBA Assn., Loyola-Marymount U., Los Angeles, 1976-77. Mem. Am. Mktg. Assn., N.J. Mktg. Assn., Packaging Inst., N.J. Packaging Assn. Home: 604 Bergen Blvd Ridgefield NJ 07657 Office: N Middletown Rd Pearl River NY 10965

SPECK, RALPH M., purchasing exec.; b. Rockport, Mass., July 24, 1923; s. Reinhard S. and Gertrude M. (Marshall) S.; student public schs., Rockport, Mass.; m. Betty Lou Welding, Jan. 10, 1946; children—Kenneth, Carol, Richard, John, Donna. With Wigman Co., Sioux City, Iowa, 1946—, treas. purchasing, 1960—, treas. bd. dirs., 1969—. Served with USAAF, 1942-46. Office: Wigman Co Box 1018 Sioux City IA 51102

SPECTOR, MARTIN WILSON, retail record and tape chain exec.; b. Norfolk, Va., June 18, 1905; s. William and Rebecca S.; student Manch Sch. Music, Staunton, Va., 1922; B.A., Washington and Lee U., 1925; LL.B., U. Va., 1928; m. Dorothy J. Miller, Mar. 1, 1943; children—Michael, Rosalind, Ann, Bayard. Admitted to Va. bar, 1928, N.Y. bar, 1929; head of talent Universal Pictures, N.Y.C., 1945-47; pres. Specs Music Inc., Miami, Fla., 1948—. Served with U.S. Army, 1942-45. Mem. Fla. Record Retailers (pres. 1955), Soc. Record Dealers Am. (pres. 1960), Friends of Chamber Music Miami, Robert E. Lee Assos., Zeta Beta Tau. Jewish. Clubs: Colonnades, Standard of Miami, Coral Gables (Fla.) Country. Home: 6900 Barquera St Coral Gables FL 33146 Office: 4786SW 72d Ave Miami FL 33155

SPECTOR, REUBEN MICHAEL, chem. co. exec.; b. Montreal, Que., Can., Feb. 25, 1938; s. Alex and Yetta (Stein) S.; B.Sc., Sir George Williams U., 1964; m. Shirley Roslyn Green, Oct. 22, 1961; children—Ilana Paige, Patrice Ellen, Floryssa Beth. With Union Carbide Can. Ltd., Lachine, Que., 1956—, tech. sales rep., 1964-69, sales mgr. polyolefins, 1969—. Mem. Montreal Bd. Trade. Mem. Soc. Plastic Engrs., Soc. Plastic Industry. Home: 5605 Castlewood Ave Montreal PQ H4W 1V1 Canada Office: Union Carbide Can Ltd 2525 JB Deschamps St Lachine PQ H8T 1C6 Canada

SPEECE, GLENN ALFRED, banker; b. Lewistown, Pa., June 21, 1928; s. Edward Johnson and Mary (Hampton) S.; student U. Pitts., 1949-50; diploma Stonier Grad. Sch. Banking, 1965; m. Marjorie Ellen Hopkins, Aug. 14, 1947 (div. Mar. 1969); 1 dau., Sherry; m. 2d, Lorraine Kay Mottillo, Oct. 5, 1970; children—Susan Lorraine, Karen Lorraine. Office mgr. Comml. Credit Corp., Butler, Pa., 1950-52; installment loan mgr. Mellon Nat. Bank N/A, Kittanning, Pa., 1953-58, asst. br. mgr., 1958-61, apptd. asst. v.p., br. mgr., 1961, now v.p., zone mgr.; dir. Kittanning Telephone Co., 1969-70. Pres., Armstrong County (Pa.) Credit Exchange, 1957—, Middle Armstrong County Area Devel. Orgn., 1963-67; asst. treas. Pa. Economy League, 1968-69; mem. Citizens Adv. Bd., Armstrong Sch. Dist., 1968—. Bd. dirs. Suburban Water Authority. Served with USAAF, 1945-47. Presbyn. Elk. Clubs: Kittanning Country (pres. 1967-68); Bankers (dir. Pitts.). Home: 2513 Creekedge Dr Pittsburgh PA 15235 Office: 2008 Mellon Sq Pittsburgh PA 15230

SPEER, PAUL DEE, mcpl. fin. cons.; b. Chgo., May 2, 1902; s. William Walter and May Josephine (Donnelly) S.; student U. Mich., 1920-23; B.S. in Law, Northwestern U., 1925; LL.B., Chgo. Kent Coll. Law, 1926, J.D., 1969; m. Helen A. Carr, June 21, 1930 (dec.); children—Paul Dee, Michael Carr (dec.). Underwriter, A. C. Allyn & Co., Inc., Chgo., 1948-54; mcpl. fin. cons., Chgo., 1954-63; pres. Paul D. Speer & Assos., Inc., Chgo., 1963-80; chmn. bd. Duff and Phelps, Speer & Co., Chgo., 1980—. Pres., bd. dirs. 3550 Lake Shore Dr. Condominium Assn., Chgo., 1978-79. Served with AC, USN, 1942-45. Mem. Am. Bar Assn., Ill. Bar Assn., Bond Club Chgo., Mpcl. Bond Club Chgo., Mcpl. Forum N.Y.C. Roman Catholic. Clubs: Chgo. Athletic (life), Mid-Day (Chgo.); Bob O'Link Golf (Highland Park, Ill.); Thunderbird Country (Palm Springs, Calif.). Office: 55 E Monroe St Suite 4510 Chicago IL 60603

SPEIR, KENNETH GUINTY, lawyer; b. Peabody, Kans., June 22, 1908; s. John and Bessie (Guinty) S.; student Colo. Coll., 1926-28; LL.B., Kans. U., 1931; m. Shirley Whittemore; children—Helen Ann, Patricia Jane, Elizabeth Eve. Admitted to Kans. bar, 1931, N.Mex. bar, 1932, U.S. Supreme Ct. bar, 1943; practice law, Albuquerque, 1932-34, Newton, Kans., 1934—, county atty. Harvey County (Kans.), 1939-41; judge 9th Jud. Dist. Kans., 1941-44; gen. counsel Excel Industries, Inc., Legg Co., Inc., Central Securities, Inc., Acra-Plant, Inc., 1st Fed. Savs. & Loan Assn., Newton. Mem. Kans. State Bd. Health, 1950-51. Served as maj. USMCR, 1942-46. Mem. Am., Kans. State, N.Mex., Harvey County bar assns., Am. Legion, VFW. Republican. Lutheran. Home: 1411 Hillcrest Newton KS 67114 Office: 809 Main St Newton KS 67114

SPEISER, STUART MARSHALL, lawyer; b. N.Y.C., June 4, 1923; s. Joseph and Anne (Jonath) S.; student U. Pa., 1939-42; LL.B., Columbia U., 1948; m. Mary J. McCormick, Feb. 12, 1950; 1 son, James Joseph. Admitted to N.Y. bar, 1948, since practiced in N.Y.C.; mem. Speiser & Krause, 1957—; chmn. bd., chief exec. officer Aerial Application Corp., 1968-71, Hydrophilics Internat., Inc., 1969-76; hon. atty.-gen., La., 1958—. Served with USAAF, 1943-46. Recipient James Smithson medal Smithsonian Instn., 1979. Fellow Internat. Soc. Barristers; mem. Am. Bar Assn., N.Y. County Lawyers Assn. (chmn. subcom. law outer space 1958—), Am. Trial Lawyers Assn. (chmn. aviation law 1955-65), Am. Inst. Aeros. and Astronautics (asso.). Author: Preparation Manual for Aviation Negligence Cases, 1958; Death in the Air, 1957; Liability Problems in Airline Crash Cases, 1957; Private Airplane Accidents, 1958; Speiser's Negligence Jury Charges, 1960; Speiser's Aviation Law Guide, 1962; Lawyers Aviation Handbook, 1964; Recovery for Wrongful Death, 1966, 2d edit., 1975; The Big Negligence Case, 1968; Lawyers Economic Handbook, 1970, 2d edit., 1979; Attorneys' Fees, 1972; Res Ipsa Loquitur, 1973; A Piece of the Action, 1977; Aviation Tort Law, 1978. Editorial bd. Jour. Post Keynesian Economics, 1977—. Home: Westover Ln Stamford CT 06902 Office: Pan Am Bldg 200 Park Ave New York City NY 10017

SPELL, FRANK EDWIN, ins. agy. exec.; b. Jackson, Miss., Nov. 19, 1941; s. O.L. and Ruby E. (Knight) S.; B.A., U. Ala., 1963; m. Bell S. Spell, Aug. 24, 1963; children—Frances E., Frank Edwin. Mem. retail mgmt. staff Sears, Roebuck and Co., Montgomery, Ala., 1963-65; mem. mktg. staff First Nat. Bank, Montgomery, 1965-68; owner Snelling & Snelling, personnel agy., Tuscaloosa, Ala., 1968-69; pres. Frank E. Spell & Assos., Inc., Tuscaloosa, 1969—. Active fund drives, various community orgns. C.L.U. Mem. Life Underwriters Assn. (dir.), Nat. Assn. Life Underwriters, Am. Soc. Pension Actuaries (asso.), Am. Soc. C.L.U.'s, Gen. Agts. and Mgrs. Assn., Million Dollar Round Table. Methodist. Club: North River Yacht, Indian Hills Country, Sertoma (past pres., dir.). Home: 9-D Northwood St Northport AL 35476 Office: 1395 McFarland Blvd E Tuscaloosa AL 35405

SPELLER, MAXINE ELLIOTT WATKINS (MRS. ROBERT E.B. SPELLER), book publisher; b. Roseboro, N.C., Oct. 25, 1906; d. Daniel Anderson and Margaret Louise (Patterson) Watkins; student Louisburg Jr. Coll., 1926; A.B., Duke, 1932; m. Robert E. B. Speller, 1935; children—Robert E. B., Jon Patterson. Designer, Fashion Form Mfg. Corp., 1938-55; sec.-treas. Robert Speller & Sons, pub., Inc., 1955—; treas. East Europe Pub. Co., 1970-75. Trustee Hough's Ency. of Am. Woods Found. Patentee in field of design. Home: 115 E 9th St New York NY 10003 Office: 30 E 23d St New York NY 10010

SPELLER, ROBERT ERNEST BLAKEFIELD, book pub.; b. Chgo., Jan. 19, 1908; s. John Ernest and Florence (Larson) S.; student Columbia, 1929; m. Maxine Elliott Watkins; children—Robert Ernest Blakefield, Jon Patterson. Mng. editor Fgn. Press Service, 1930-31; pres. Mohawk Press, 1931-32, Robert Speller Pub. Corp., 1934-52, Record Concerts Corp., 1940-53, Robert Speller & Sons, Pubs., Inc., 1955—, Norellyn Press, Inc., 1960—, Transglobal News Service, Inc., 1960—; pub. Hough's Ency. Am. Woods, 1957—; chmn. bd., pres., chief exec. officer Nat. Resources Publs., Inc., 1968—; pub. East Europe Mag., 1970—; sec., dir. Encoder Research & Devel. Corp., 1971—, Pecos Internat., Inc., 1974-77; v.p., dir. Pecos Western Corp. of Del., 1973—; dir. Gen. Research Corp., Fashion Form Mfg. Corp. Mem. founding bd. U.S.O. Trustee Philippa Schuyler Meml. Found. Served with Signal Corps, AUS, 1944-45. Founder Gourmet Soc. Clubs: Columbia University (N.Y.C.). Office: 30 E 23d St New York NY 10010

SPELLMAN, DOUGLAS TOBY, media cons.; b. Bronx, May 12, 1942; s. Sydney M. and Leah B. (Rosenberg) S.; B.S., Fairleigh Dickinson U., 1964; m. Ronni I. Epstein, Jan. 16, 1966; children—Laurel Nicole, Daren Scott. Media buyer Doyle, Dane, Bernbach, Inc., N.Y.C., 1965-67; media supr. Ogilvy & Mather, Inc., N.Y.C., 1967-69, media dir., Los Angeles, 1969-75; pres., chmn. bd. Douglas T. Spellman, Inc., Los Angeles, 1976—; guest lectr. sch. bus. UCLA, 1975, U. So. Calif., 1976. Served with U.S. Army Res. N.G., 1964-69. Mem. Aircraft Owners and Pilots Assn. Jewish. Clubs: Rolls Royce Owners, Mercedes Benz Am.

SPENCE, EDWARD RUTLEDGE, plastics mfg. co. exec.; b. Bonne Terre, Mo., Apr. 14, 1926; s. John Harold and Virginia (Marbury) S.; B.S. in Econs. and Law, Washington U., St. Louis, 1949; m. Shirley Doris Fabricius, July 4, 1968; children—Carol, Becky, David. Salesman, Graham Paper Co., St. Louis, 1950-52; sales mgr. Reed Rubber Co., St. Louis, 1952-56; pres. Edward R. Spence Co., Inc., St. Louis, 1956—; dir. Landmark Bank of Ladue. Served with USAAF, 1944-46. Fellow Am. Mgmt. Assn.; mem. Soc. Plastic Engrs., Young Pres.'s Orgn. (chmn. 1974), A.I.M., Am. Assn. Indsl. Mgmt., Regional Commerce and Growth Assn., World Bus. Council, Chief Exec. Forum, Sr. Exec. Orgn. (chmn.), Friends of Zoo (v.p.), Art Mus. Assn., Mo. Bot. Gardens Assn., Mus. Sci. and Industry, Mo., Met. St. Louis chambers commerce, Theta Xi. Clubs: St. Louis Ambassadors, Columns of U. Mo., Century of Washington U., Univ., Frontenac Racquet, Creve Coeur Racket (St. Louis); Old Warson Country. Home: 12315 Boothbay Ct St Louis MO 63141 Office: 10315 Page Industrial Blvd St Louis MO 63132

SPENCE, HOWARD TEE DEVON, lawyer, state regulatory ofcl.; b. Corinth, Miss., Sept. 29, 1949; s. Tee P. and Dorothy M. (Bowers) S.; B.A., Mich. State U., 1970, M.S., 1975, M.L.I.R., 1980; J.D., U. Mich., 1976, M.P.A., 1977; m. Diane Earl; children—Derek, Tina, Steven. Admitted to Mich. bar, 1976, U.S. Supreme Ct. bar, 1980; personnel adminstr. Mich. Dept. Commerce, 1976-77; asst. dir. for policy Mich. Public Service Commn., 1977-78; asst. commr. ins. State of Mich., Lansing, 1978—; pres. Spence and Assos., mgmt. cons.; adj. prof. law Thomas M. Cooley Law Sch., Lansing; dir. Econ. Devel. Corp., Lansing, 1980—. Mem. Am. Mgmt. Assn., Am. Bar Assn., Wolverine Bar Assn., Indsl. Relations Research Assn., Am. Arbitration Assn. (community disputes panel), Am. Soc. Public Adminstrn., Assn. Am. Law Schs., Am. Soc. Personnel Adminstrs., Greater Lansing Regional C. of C., NAACP, Alpha Phi Alpha. Clubs: Econ., Renaissance (Detroit). Home: 4462 Seneca Dr Okemus MI 48864 Office: 1048 Pierpont Ave Lansing MI 48909

SPENCER, DEAN GAYLORD, life ins. co. exec.; b. Yale, Mich., July 11, 1943; s. Clare W. and Helen E. (Dean) S.; A.A., St. Clair Community Coll., 1963; postgrad. Wayne State U., 1963-64; B.A., John Wesley Coll., 1975; m. Joanne E. Reid, Dec. 19, 1964; children—Michelle, Shannon K. and Sheri (twins). With Alexander Hamilton Life, Farmington Hills, Mich., 1965—, agt., 1965-66, state sales trainer, Indpls., 1966-70, regional dir., Southfield, Mich., 1970-72, zone v.p. mktg. Farmington Hills, 1972-74, v.p. mktg. research product devel., 1974-76, v.p. mktg. services, 1976-77, sr. v.p., chief mktg. officer, 1977—, dir., 1979—; dir. Security Trust Life, Farmington Hills, 1974-77. Bd. dirs. Teen Challenge, Inc., 1975—, Graphic Truth, 1979—; Recipient Nat. Quality award Nat. Assn. Life Underwriters, annually, 1966-72. C.L.U. Mem. Detroit Assn. Life Underwriters, Am. Mgmt. Assn., Mensa. Republican. Author: God Never Said We'd Be Leading at the Half; contbr. articles to various publs. Home: 32881 Robinhood Dr Birmingham MI 48010 Office: 33045 Hamilton Blvd Farmington Hills MI 48018

SPENCER, EDSON WHITE, mfg. co. exec.; b. Chgo., June 4, 1926; s. William M. and Gertrude (White) S.; student Princeton, 1943, Northwestern U., U. Mich., 1944; B.A., Williams Coll., 1948; B.A., Oxford (Eng.) U., 1950, M.A., 1950. With Sears, Roebuck & Co., 1951-54, Venezuela and Mpls., 1954; with Honeywell, Inc., 1954—, dir. exports, 1964-65, v.p. fgn. ops., 1965-69, exec. v.p., 1970-74, pres., 1974-78, chief exec. officer, 1974—, chmn. bd., chmn. exec. com., 1978—, also dir. Mem. Mpls. C. of C., St. Paul Com. Fgn. Relations, Mpls. Citizens League, Phi Beta Kappa. Office: 2701 4th Ave S Minneapolis MN 55408*

SPENCER, JAMES ROBERT, film and TV prodn. co. exec.; b. Glendale, Calif., Feb. 8, 1947; s. Roy B. and Margaret A. (Fisher) S.; B.S., San Diego State U., 1968, M.A. in Communications, 1972; M.B.A., Pepperdine U., 1976. Production mgr. Ward/Davis Assos., Pasadena, Calif., 1968-72; market devel. mgr. videocassette Sony Corp., Los Angeles, 1972-74; pres. AMVID Communication Services Inc., Manhattan Beach, Calif., 1974—; founder, pres. Home Entertainment Emporium, 1977—; instr. Los Angeles City Coll. Recipient Indsl. Film award Info. Film Producers Am., 1976; Audio Visual Edn. Assn. Film Research grantee, 1972. Mem. Nat. Acad. TV Arts and Scis., Indsl. TV Assn., Soc. Motion Picture and TV Engrs., Am. Soc. Tng. and Devel., Sigma Pi. Democrat. Roman Catholic. Home: 2307 Poinsettia Ave Manhattan Beach CA 90266 Office: 2100 Sepulveda Blvd Manhattan Beach CA 90266

SPENCER, JOHN RICHARD, lawyer, city ofcl.; b. Kansas City, Mo., Apr. 11, 1940; s. Paul Ripley and Teressa (Wagner) S.; B.B.A., U. Tex., 1964, LL.B., 1965; m. Joyce Ann Rhodenbaugh, Dec. 19, 1961; children—Stephen Myles, Kelly Lynn. Admitted to Tex. bar, 1965, Alaska bar, 1971, U.S. Supreme Ct. bar; asso. Jarrard Cammack & Assos., Pasadena, Tex., 1965-66; post judge adv. Ft. Richardson, Alaska, 1967-70; city atty. City of Anchorage, 1971-75, exec. mgr., chief exec. officer municipality utilities, 1977—; v.p., gen. counsel RCA Alascom, Anchorage, 1975-77; pres. Anchorage Tire Center; trustee Alaska Elec. Health and Welfare and Pension Trust. Vice pres. Anchorage Retarded Childrens Assn.; active Little League Baseball; pres. Rehab. Industries Anchorage; mem. Anchorage Police and Fire Retirement Bd.; chmn. energy com. Alaska Mcpl. League; treas. Susitna Power Now, Inc.; chmn. bd. Olympics '92, Inc.; state chmn. U.S. Olympic Com. Served with AUS, 1966-67; maj. Res. Decorated Army Commendation medal, Legion of Merit. Mem. Fed. (pres. Alaska chpt.), Am., Alaska, Tex. bar assns., Pacific N.W. Waterways Assn. (dir., state v.p.), Anchorage Petroleum Club. Republican. Presbyterian. Clubs: Rotary, Anchorage Racquet. Contbr. articles to profl. jours. Home: 8410 Pioneer St Anchorage AK 99504 Office: Pouch 6-650 Anchorage AK 99502

SPENCER, JOSEPH STEWART, mfg. co. exec.; b. Kilbirnie, Scotland, Apr. 26, 1922; s. Hugh Morrison and Mary (MacInnes) S.; A.B., Harvard, 1948; M.B.A., Columbia, 1950. Tax accountant, asst. to treas., asst. treas., sec.-treas. Union Spl. Corp., 1950-78, v.p., sec., 1978—. Served with AUS, 1942-45. Mem. Am. Soc. Corp. Secs., Ill. C. of C., Ill. St. Andrew Soc., Chgo. Assn. Commerce and Industry. Presbyn. Home: 1450 Astor St Chicago IL 60610 Office: 400 N Franklin St Chicago IL 60610

SPENCER, SHERWOOD, lawyer; b. Ashland, Ky., Jan. 23, 1913; s. Holmes A. and Mary (Baker) S.; B.B.A., U. Fla., 1933, J.D., 1936; LL.D., Nova U., 1975; m. Jean Rowe, Dec. 15, 1940; children—William Sherwood, Carol Ann. Admitted to Fla. bar, 1936, U.S. Supreme Ct. bar, 1963; practice law, Hollywood, Fla., 1939—; city atty. Hollywood, 1949-53; dir. Southeast Bank Broward; dir. Hollywood Fed. Savs. & Loan Assn. Mem. grievance com. 15th Jud. Circuit, 1950-55; chmn. Com. of 100. Mem. Broward Co. (pres. 1949), Fla. State (mem. bd. govs. 1953-63), Am. (com. on unauthorized law practice) bar assns., Fla. Title Assn. (chmn. title examiners' div. 1950-51). Clubs: Rotary (pres. 1948), Yacht (vice commodore 1948), Lauderdale Yacht, Emerald Hills Country. Home: 1600 Rodman St Hollywood FL 33020 Office: Hollywood Fed Bldg Hollywood FL 33021

SPENCER, WILLIAM EDWIN, telephone co. exec.; b. Kansas City, Mo., Mar. 22, 1926; s. Irwin B. and Edith Marie (Peterson) S.; student U. Kansas City, 1942; A.S., Kansas City Jr. Coll., 1945; B.S. in E.E., U. Mo., 1948; postgrad. Iowa State U., 1969; m. Ferne Arlene Nieder, Nov. 14, 1952; children—Elizabeth Ann, Gary William, James Richard, Cathy Sue. With Southwestern Bell Telephone Co., Kansas City, Mo., 1948-50, Topeka, 1952-61, sr. engr., 1966-69, equipment maintenance engr., 1969-76, engring. ops. mgr., 1976-79, dist. mgr., 1979—; mem. tech. staff Bell Telephone Labs., N.Y.C., 1961-62, Holmdel, N.J., 1962-66. Served with AUS, 1950-52. Recipient Best Kans. Idea award Southwestern Bell Telephone Co., 1972. Mem. Kans. Engring. Soc., Nat. Soc. Profl. Engrs., IEEE, Topeka Engrs. Club. Registered profl. engr., Kans. Republican. Patentee in field. Home: 3201 MacVicar Ct Topeka KS 66611 Office: 220 E 6th St Topeka KS 66603

SPENCER, WILLIAM I., banker; b. Grand Junction, Colo., 1917; B.A., Colo. Coll., 1939. With Chem. Bank & Trust Co., 1939-51; with First Nat. City Bank N.Y. (name now Citibank), 1951—, exec. v.p., 1965-70, pres., 1970—, pres. Citicorp, 1970—; dir. Transp. Assn. Am., Bedford Stuyvesant Devel. & Service, Depository Trust Co., Asia Pacific Capial Capital Corp., Ltd., Sears, Roebuck & Co., United Technologies, Inc., Capital Cities Communications Inc. Trustee N.Y. U. Med. Center, Colo. Coll.; pres. First Nat. City Found. Mem. U.S.-Korea Econ. Council, Nat. Adv. Commn. on Banking Policies and Practices. Office: Citicorp 399 Park Ave New York NY 10022*

SPENGLER, WILLIAM FREDERICK, JR., packaging co. exec.; b. Columbus, Ohio, Sept. 22, 1928; s. William Frederick and Louise Esther (Arehart) S.; B.S. in Bus. Adminstrn., Ohio State U., 1950, M.B.A., 1951; m. Sarah Madeline Burd, Aug. 25, 1951; children—William Frederick III, Mary L., John D., Carolyn S. With Owens-Illinois Inc., Toledo, 1951—, comptroller, 1961-63, v.p. div. glass containers, 1963-66, v.p. corp. planning, 1966-68, mng. dir. United Glass Ltd., Eng., 1968-71, asst. gen. mgr. internat. div. Owens-Ill., Toledo, 1971-73, pres. Internat. group, 1973-74, dir. div., 1974-75, exec. v.p. div., 1975-76, pres., chief operating officer internat. ops., 1976-79, domestic ops., 1979—, also mem. exec. com., dir.; dir. Nat. Petro Chems. Corp., N.Y.C.; dir., mem. audit com. Questor Corp., Toledo. Bd. dirs. United Way, Boys' Club Toledo; mem. sr. adv. group Coll. Bus. Adminstrn., Ohio State U.; trustee Bowling Green State U.; mem. adv. council Grad. Sch. Indsl. Adminstrn., Carnegie-Mellon U.; mem. Ohio State Litter Control and Recycling Adv. Council. Served to 1st lt. USAF, 1952-54. Mem. Conf. Bd. (internat. council), Internat. Econ. Policy Assn. (dir.), Nat. Planning Assn. (commn. on changing internat. realities), Internat. C. of C. (exec. com., trustee of U.S. council). Republican. Roman Catholic. Clubs: Toledo Country, Inverness, Toledo; Muirfield Village Golf and Country, Tournament Players (Columbus). Office: PO Box 1035 Toledo OH 43666

SPENLINHAUER, GEORGIA MYRNA, printing co. exec.; b. Cheyenne, Wyo., June 12, 1909; d. Leonard and Rose Mangiaracine; grad. Boston State Coll., 1931; m. John Edward Spenlinhauer, June 30, 1938 (dec.); children—Robert, Stephen, John. Tchr. elementary sch., 1931-33; asst. buyer photog. equipment R.H. White Philately, Boston, 1934-35, buyer, 1935-37; sales promotion asst. Cedric Chase Photo Finishers, Waltham, Mass., 1937-45; co-founder with husband Spencer Press, Inc., Hingham, Mass., 1942, pres., 1945—, chmn. bd., 1972—. Chmn., St. Sebastian's Country Day Sch., Newton, Mass., 1959-61, pres. 1961-62; bd. dirs. Matre Dei Guild for Blind, Newton, 1962-64, Big Brother Assn. Boston, 1977—. Mem. Internat. Platform Assn. Home: 878 Sea View Ave Osterville MA 02655 Office: 90 Industrial Park Rd Hingham MA 02043

SPERLINE, ELIZABETH STARR, corporate exec.; b. La Mesa, Tex., Dec. 16; d. Horace Homer and Hazel (Starr) Van Meter; A.A., Cerritos Coll., Norwalk, Calif., 1968; M.B.A., Pepperdine U., Los Angeles, 1973; m. Vergil A. Sperline, Jr., May 2, 1953 (div. 1973); children—Donald Arthur, Jean Marie, Victoria Elizabeth, Marcella Kathleen. Treas., Coast and Sperline, Inc., Los Angeles, 1966-73; pres. Internat. Product Mgmt. Corp., Newport Beach, Calif., 1972-73, Sperline & Assos., Fullerton, Calif., 1973—, Resources Tech. Corp., Phoenix, 1975—, Am. Indian Bancshares Corp., Phoenix, 1976—, Ampersand Printing Co., Phoenix, Bus. Tech. Corp.; sec. Para-Dynamics Corp., Phoenix; rancher, Utah; pres. Southwestern Rehab. and Counseling, Inc., Phoenix, 1976—; lectr. in field. Mem. Pres.'s Commn. Personnel Interchange, 1974-76; pres. Calif. Young Republicans, 1972-73; advisory bd. Exec. Sch. Bus., U. So. Calif. Mem. Am. Soc. Bus. and Mgmt. Cons., Rep. Women's Club. Club: Village Tennis. Author: Cooking with the Forty-Niners. Home: 6840 E Sunnyvale Rd Paradise Valley AZ 85253 Office: 3550 N Central Ave Suite 808 Phoenix AZ 85012

SPIEGEL, EDWIN JOHN, JR., paper co. exec.; b. St. Louis, Oct. 30, 1920; s. Edwin John and Ruth (Hall) S.; A.B., Dartmouth Coll., 1942; m. Doris Dee Naylor, Jan. 30, 1943; children—Carol Ann (Mrs. C.E. Ramey), Edwin John III. Asst. plant mgr. Gaylord Container Corp., Greenville, S.C., 1946-49, mgr. Folding Carton div., St. Louis, 1949-55; asst. v.p., regional mgr. Gaylord Container div. Crown Zellerbach Corp., St. Louis, 1955-65; v.p. Alton (Ill.) Box Board Co., 1965-68, pres., 1968-79, chief exec. officer, 1969-79, chmn. bd., 1975—; dir. Boatmen's Nat. Bank (St. Louis), 1st Nat. Bank & Trust Co. of Alton, Laclede Steel Co. Bd. dirs. St. Luke's Hosps., St. Louis; active Jr. Achievement Miss. Valley, St. Louis Mcpl. Opera, Civic Progress of St. Louis. Served to lt. USNR, 1942-45. Mem. Dartmouth Alumni Assn., C. of C. Met. St. Louis. Clubs: Bogey, Mo. Athletic, Old Warson Country (St. Louis), St. Louis. Office: 401 Alton St Alton IL 62002

SPIEGEL, JOHN WILLIAM, fin. exec.; b. Indpls., Mar. 14, 1941; s. William S. and Elizabeth (Hall) S.; B.A., Wabash Coll., 1963; M.B.A., Emory U., 1965; m. Nancy S. Welty, June 21, 1963; children—William R., John F., Bradly H. Research asso. IMEDE, Lausanne, Switzerland, 1965-66; credit trainee, bond portfolio mgr. Trust Co. Ga., Atlanta, 1965-72, mgr. data processing, 1973-78, controller, 1975-78, exec. v.p., treas., 1976—, officer, dir. subs. corps., 1976—. Treas., trustee, mem. exec. com. Atlanta Arts Alliance, 1976—; exec. vice chmn. bd. trustees Holy Innocents Episcopal Sch., 1976-79. Recipient Outstanding Grad. award Emory U., 1965. Mem. Am. Bankers Assn., Ga. Bankers Assn., Fin. Execs. Inst. Clubs: Leadership Atlanta, Cherokee Town and Country. Home: 510 Clipper Trail Atlanta GA 30328 Office: PO Box 4418 Atlanta GA 30302

SPIEGEL, SIEGMUND, architect, profl. planner; b. Gera, Germany, Nov. 13, 1919; s. Jakob and Sara (Precker) S.; ed. Coll. City N.Y., 1939-40, Columbia, 1945-50; m. Ruth Josias, Apr. 13, 1945; children—Sandra Renee, Deborah Joan. Came to U.S., 1938, naturalized, 1941. Draftsman, Mayer & Whittlesey, architects, N.Y.C., 1941-47, office mgr., 1947-55; pvt. practice architecture, East Meadow, N.Y., 1956—. Served with AUS, 1941-45; ETO. Decorated Purple Heart, Bronze Star, Croix de Guerre with palme (Belgium); recipient grand prize for instnl. bldgs. (for Syosset Hosp.), L.I. Assn., 1963; grand prize Human Resources Sch., 1966; grand prize Stony Brook Profl. Bldg., 1966; Beautification award, Town Hempstead, N.Y., 1969; Archi award for Harbour Club Apts., L.I. Assn., 1970, for Birchwood Blue Ridge Condominiums, 1974. Fellow Acad. Marketing Sci., L.I.U., 1971. Registered architect, N.Y., N.J., Mass., Md., Va., Pa., Conn., Ga., Vt., Tenn., N.H., Fla. Mem. AIA, N.Y. State Assn. Architects, East Meadow C. of C. (pres. 1966). Club: Kiwanis. Author: The Spiegel Plan. Contbr. articles to Progressive Architecture. Prin. works include: Syosset (N.Y.) Hosp., 1962; Villa Victor Motel, Syosset, 1958; Klein Residence, Balt., 1959; Cameo House apts., Hempstead, N.Y., 1960; Capitol House, East Rockaway, N.Y., 1961; Reliance Fed. Savs. and Loan Assn. Bank, Queens, N.Y., 1961; Louden Hall Psychiat. Hosp., 1963; Human Resources Sch., Albertson, N.Y., 1964; Nassau Center for Emotionally Disturbed Children, 1968; Harbor Club Apt., Babylon, N.Y., 1968; Reliance Fed. Bank, Albertson, 1967; North Isle Club and Apt. Community, Coram, N.Y., 1972; County Fed. Savs. & Loan Assn., Commack, N.Y., 1972; Birchwood Glen Apt. Community, Holtsville, N.Y., 1972; Bayside Fed. Savs. & Loan Bank Plaza, Patchogue, N.Y., 1973; L.E. Woodward Sch. for Emotionally Disturbed Children, Freeport, N.Y., 1974. Home: 1508 Hayes Ct East Meadow NY 11554 Office: 2035 Hempstead Turnpike East Meadow NY 11554

SPIEGELHALDER, OSCAR A., chem. co. exec.; b. Triberg, Germany, June 9, 1906; s. August and Josephine (Reiner) S.; came to U.S., 1927, naturalized, 1933; grad. Siebel Inst. Tech., 1934; student St. John's U., 1932-36, D.C.L. honoris causa, 1980, D.C.S., 1980; postgrad. rubber tech. course Am. Chem. Soc., 1957-58; m. Josefa W. Lechner, May 11, 1929. Apprentice, various other positions in food industry, Germany, 1922-27; rep. faculty house St. John's U., 1932-36; tech. sales Nat. Sugar Refining Co., 1937-44, dept. head, 1941-44; founder, pres., dir. Sunhill Products Co., Inc., N.Y.C., 1944-60; pres., treas., dir. Holloway Sucro-Chems. Corp., N.Y.C., 1946-68; exec. v.p., dir. Kenrich Corp., N.Y.C., 1948-65; chmn. bd. Kenrich Petrochems., Inc., 1965-; pres. Kenrich Internat. div. Holloway Sucro-Chems. Corp.; dir. S.W. Metals, Inc., Phoenix, 1963-64. Treas. Ospieg Relief Fund, N.Y.C., 1946-60. Served with N.Y. Mil. Forces, 1951-53. Recipient Pres.'s Gold medal St. John's U., 1977. Fellow Am. Inst. Chemists; mem. Am. Chem. Soc. (rubber div.), Am. Soc. Baking Engrs. (emeritus), Bayonne C. of C. (dir.), Inst. Food Technologists (charter, emeritus), N.Y., Phila., Los Angeles, Boston rubber groups, Soc. Plastics Engrs., So. Soc. Paint Tech., Ex-Mems. Squadron A-101 Cav. (gov. 1956-61). Rotarian (pres. Bayonne Club 1969-70). Clubs: Squadron A, Chemists (N.Y.C.). Home: Boulevard Towers Bayonne NJ 07002 Office: Foot of E 22d St Bayonne NJ 07002

SPIGAI, DANIEL JOHN, cons. engr.; b. Bronx, N.Y., Mar. 4, 1933; s. James and Victoria (Abbate) S.; B.S., Manhattan Coll., 1954; m. Jacqueline Elizabeth Parisi, Jan. 18, 1958; children—Lisa, Victoria, David, Daniela. Engr. trainee N.Y. Central R.R., Weekauken, N.J., 1954; with Howard, Needles, Tammen & Bergendoff, N.Y. and N.J., 1957-70, project mgr., to 1970; asso. Howard, Needles, Tammen & Bergendoff, Fairfield, N.J. and Alexandria, Va., 1971-73, partner, 1974—. Mem. planning bd. Borough of Oakland (N.J.), 1967. Served with U.S. Army, 1955-57. Registered profl. engr., N.Y., N.J., Pa., Conn., Del., Va., Ga., Maine, Vt., Fla., Mass., N.H.; registered profl. planner, N.J. Mem. ASCE, Nat. Soc. Profl. Engrs., Airport Operators Council Internat., Am. Assn. Airport Execs., Am. Rd. and Transp. Builders Assn. Office: 1500 N Beauregard St Alexandria VA 22311

SPILLANE, LEO JEROME, asphalt co. exec.; b. New Richland, Minn., Aug. 23, 1916; s. John Jerome and Anastasia (Gossman) S.; B.S., St. Thomas Coll., 1937; M.S., U. Minn., 1940, Ph.D., 1942; m. Kathryn F. Grady, June 16, 1946; children—Stacia, Margaret, Leo Jerome, Kathleen, Janet, John, James. Group leader research Allied Chem. Corp., Morristown, N.J., 1942-49; chief chemist Reaction Motors, Inc., Rockaway, N.J., 1949-51; mgr. organic research Lion Oil Co., El Dorado, Ark., 1951-61; mgr. research Monsanto Co., St. Louis, 1961-69; exec. v.p. Gulf States Asphalt Co., Houston, 1969-70, pres., 1970—. Mem. Am. Chem. Soc., Am. Inst. Chem. Engrs., Petroleum Club Houston. Roman Catholic. Author: Refining Petroleum for Chemicals, 1970. Contbr. articles to profl. jours. Patentee in field. Home: 13134 Kimberley Ln Houston TX 77079 Office: Dresser Bldg Suite 535 Houston TX 77002

SPILLER, PETER, steamship co. exec.; b. N.Y.C., Mar. 25, 1945; s. Clifford and Geraldine (Stanneck) S.; B.A. with honors, Wesleyan U., 1966; M.I.A., Columbia U., 1968, postgrad. exec. program for internat. mgrs., 1978; m. Dorothy Elizabeth Barnes, Sept. 7, 1968; children—Alexander, Peter. Asst. to pres. Moller S.S. Co., Inc., N.Y.C., 1970-71, fleet devel. A.P. Moller-Maersk Line, Copenhagen, 1971-73, project mgr., N.Y.C., 1973-75, regional mgr. Maersk Line Agy., Phila., 1976-80, gen. mgr. N.E. region, N.Y.C., 1980—; mgr. space allocation Moller Steamship Co., Inc., 1979-80; interim instr. econs. U. Fla., 1968-69. Nat. Def. Fgn. Lang. fellow, 1967-68. Mem. World Trade Assn. Phila. (dir. 1977-79, chmn. transp. com. 1977-78), Internat. Trade Devel. Assn., Fgn. Policy Assn., Fgn. Commerce Club, Camden Traffic Club, Port of Phila., Maritime Soc., Traffic Club Wilmington (Del.). Clubs: Outdoor S. Jersey, Downtown Athletic, World Trade Center. Asso. editor Jour. Internat. Affairs, 1967-68. Home: Apgar Way RD2 Tewksbury Twp Lebanon NJ 08833 Office: Suite 3527 One World Trade Center New York NY 10048

SPINELLA, ARMANDO SANTO, banker; b. Messina, Italy, Oct. 13, 1936; came to U.S., 1974; s. Giovanni Francesco and Angela (Moschella) S.; ed. in Italy; m. Sylvia M. Davies, June 13, 1964; children—Giovanni, Angela. Mgr. corp. relations Orion Banking Group, London, 1972-74; v.p. in charge corr. banks in U.S. and Can., Credito Italiano, N.Y.C., 1974-81; v.p. rep. in Italy, Security Pacific Nat. Bank, Los Angeles, 1981—. Home: Viale Mazzini 25 Rome Italy

SPINELLI, PHILIP VINCENT, commodity broker; b. Yonkers, N.Y., May 8, 1955; s. Vincent Arthur and Rita Ann (Fuimara) S.; B.S. in Mktg. and Acctg., Fordham U., 1977. Commodity broker, analyst Drexel Burnham Lambert Inc., N.Y.C., 1978—. Mem. Republican Nat. Com. Registered, SEC, Commodity Futures Trading Commn. Mem. Futures Industry Assn. (instr., research group), Phi Eta Pi. Roman Catholic. Author: Cocoa Price Outlook, 1978, 79. Office: 60 Broad St New York NY 10004

SPIRA, S. FRANKLIN, photog. supplies co. exec.; b. Vienna, Austria, Aug. 7, 1924; came to U.S., 1940, naturalized, 1945; s. Hans and Paula (Back) S.; student CCNY, 1943-45; m. Marilyn Hacker, Sept. 3, 1959; children—Jonathan Bruce, Greg Andrew. Pres., Spiratone, Inc., Flushing, N.Y., 1942—. Mem. vis. com. Internat. Mus. Photography, Rochester, N.Y. Mem. Soc. Motion Picture and TV Engrs., Photog. Hist. Soc. N.Y., Photog. Hist. Soc. New Eng., Photog. Hist. Soc. Calif. Jewish. Contbr. articles on photographica collecting to various publs. Home: 158-17 Riverside Dr Whitestone NY 11357 Office: Spiratone Inc 135-06 Northern Blvd Flushing NY 11354

SPIRIDON, CHARLES MICHAEL, bank exec.; b. Bklyn., Mar. 25, 1942; s. Edward Francis and Mary Helena (Jowdy) S.; B.A. in Econs., Bklyn. Coll., 1964; M.B.A., Harvard, 1973; m. Barbara Russi, July 2, 1966. Asst. cashier Halden & Co., N.Y.C., 1964-65; asst. to dir. research Hay Fales & Co., N.Y.C., 1970-71; v.p. Citibank N.A., Citicorp Leasing, Inc., 1973-80, dir. consumer banking bus. Citibank, Taiwan, 1980—; v.p., dir. Citicorp Indsl. Credit, Inc., N.Y.C., until 1980; dir. Taiwan 1st Investment & Trust Co. Ltd. Served to capt. USAF, 1965-70. Mem. Am. Mgmt. Assn., Assn. M.B.A.s. Roman Catholic. Club: Harvard of N.Y.C. Home: 20 Little Farms Rd Larchmont NY 10538 Office: Citibank NA 742 Min Sheng E Rd PO Box 3343 Taipei Taiwan Republic of China

SPITTLER, BETTY JANE, motel mgr.; b. Terre Haute, Ind., Nov. 12, 1922; d. John Thomas and Nellie (Brough) Jones; grad. high sch.; m. Fenton Eugene Spittler, Feb. 19, 1942 (div. July 1968); children—Robert Eugene, Karen Lynn. Mgr., Terrace Inn and Restaurant, Terre Haute, 1964-65, Hickory Manor Hotel. Crystal Lake, Ill., 1965; mgr., buyer St. Mary's Motel, Evansville, Ind., 1965-72; mgr. Donna Ct. Motel, Evansville, 1972—; owner Riverboat Motor Inn, Evansville, 1974—. Mem. Evansville C. of C. (com. mem. 1969—). Republican. Lutheran (ch. council 1962-65, mem. parish bd. 1951-65, supt. Sunday sch. 1950-65). Address: Riverboat Motor Inn 2804 S Kentucky Ave Evansville IN 47714

SPITTLER, JOHN JOSEPH, lawyer; b. Ewing, Nebr., Nov. 11, 1918; s. John B. and Dessie H. (Huston) S.; B.S. in Bus. Adminstrn., U. Nebr., 1940; J.D., Ohio State U., 1948; m. Mary Jane Brannon, June 6, 1943; children—Mary Jane, John Joseph, Cozette, James. Admitted to Ohio bar, 1948; with Frank Gates Service Co., reps. employers in adminstrv. law, Columbus, Ohio, 1947—, sr. v.p., 1977—; dir. Columbus Gen. Fin. Co., Licking Laundry Co., Plungers, Inc. Pres., Ohio Fellowship Christian Athletes, 1968-72. Served with USNR, 1942-45. Decorated Bronze Star, Commendation medal; recipient various service awards. Mem. Am. Bar Assn., Am. Enterprise Inst., Am. Security Council, Navy League (nat. pres. 1979-81), Ohio C. of C. Republican. Lutheran. Clubs: Columbus Athletic, Rotary, Isle of Sandelfoot, Lago Mar, Def. Constrn. Supply Officers. Home: 2435 Coventry Rd Columbus OH 43221 Office: 40 S 3d St Columbus OH 43215

SPITZER, ALLAN THOMAS, retail shoe co. exec.; b. Honolulu, Aug. 31, 1955; s. Arthur Hoerman and Blanche Helen (van Oort) S.; B.A., U. Portland, 1977. With Standard Shoe Store Ltd., Honolulu, 1971—, v.p., sec., gen. mgr., 1977—, also dir. Mem. U.S. C. of C., Hawaii C. of C., Nat. Fedn. Ind. Bus., Hawaii Visitors Bur., Hawaii Employers Council. Republican. Roman Catholic. Clubs: Outrigger Canoe, Pacific, Red Carpet. Home: 1422 Nanaloko Pl Kailua HI 96734 Office: Standard Shoe Store Ltd 2213 Ala Moana Center Honolulu HI 96814

SPITZER, ARTHUR, oil co. exec.; b. Czernowitz, Austria, Aug. 3, 1912; came to U.S., 1951, naturalized, 1957; s. Mendel and Maria (Klier) Tokar; Dr.Law, (hon.), Pepperdine U., 1977; children—Violet, Travis. Owner, Digas Co., Beverly Hills, Calif., 1954-70, pres., 1971-77; chmn. bd. Tesoro Gasoline Mktg., Beverly Hills, 1977—. Mem. Commn. of Califs., Sacramento, 1979—; bd. dirs. Com. for the Caribbeans, Washington, 1978—, Internat. Student Center, UCLA, 1976—, Founders Music Center, Los Angeles, 1978—, Univ. Bd., Pepperdine U., 1977—. Recipient Grand Decoration of Honor for Service to Republic of Austria, 1977. Clubs: Beach and Tennis (La Jolla, Calif.); Racquet (Palm Springs, Calif.). Home: 1011 N Crescent Dr Beverly Hills CA 90210 Office: 9201 W Olympic Blvd Beverly Hills CA 90212

SPITZER, LESTER SYDNEY, stockbroker; b. Boston, Jan. 11, 1911; s. Alexander and Lillian (Daniels) S.; C.B.A., Boston U., 1931; m. Selma Saxe, Nov. 25, 1945; children—Kenneth Curtis, Allison Brook. Sr. v.p. Draper, Sears & Co., Boston, 1968; v.p. E. F. Hutton Co., Inc., Boston, 1969—. Mem. Newcomen Soc., Navy League. Clubs: Belmont Hill, Masons (Shriner). Home: 178 Rutledge Rd Belmont MA 02178 Office: 1 Boston Pl Boston MA 02108

SPITZER, MATTHEW L., retail store exec.; b. Pitts., June 20, 1929; s. Martin and Ruth G. S.; student U. Buffalo, 1948-50; children—Mark, Edward, Eric, Joseph. Product line mgr. Gen. Dynamics, Rochester, N.Y., 1962-67; dir. contracts Friden div. Singer, San Leandro, Calif., 1968-69; asst. v.p. Talcott Computer Leasing, San Francisco, 1970-71; pres. Spitzer Music Co., Inc., Hayward, Calif., 1972—. Clubs: Masons, Mensa. Office: 943 B St Hayward CA 94541

SPITZNAGEL, WILLIAM F., transp. co. exec.; b. Fairfield, Ala., July 15, 1926; B.A., Auburn U., 1949. With Roadway Express, Inc., Akron, Ohio, 1950—, now pres., chmn. bd. Office: Roadway Express Inc 1077 Gorge Blvd Akron OH 44309

SPIVACK, HENRY ARCHER, life ins. co. exec.; b. Bklyn., Apr. 15, 1919; s. Jacob and Pauline (Schwartz) S.; student CCNY, 1936-42; B.B.A., Am. Coll., Bryn Mawr, Pa., 1965; m. Sadie Babe Meiseles, Jan. 1, 1941; children—Ian Jeffrey, Paula Janis. Comptroller, Daniel Jones, Inc., N.Y.C., 1947-59; field underwriter Union Central Life Ins. Co., N.Y.C., 1959—, mgr. programming dept., 1966-69, asso. mgr., 1977-79; pension dir. Bleichroeder, Bing & Co., N.Y.C., 1975-77, confidence agy. div. RBL Group, 1979—; pension dir., employee benefit plan cons., instr. N.Y. State Ins. Dept., C.W. Post Coll., L.I. U., N.Y. Center for Fin. Studies. Served with USN, 1943-46. C.L.U. Mem. Life Underwriters Assn. N.Y., Am. Soc. C.L.U.'s (chmn. N.Y. chpt. pension sect., chmn. profl. liaison com.), Am. Soc. Pension Actuaries, Pensioneers at C.W. Post Coll., C.W. Post Coll. Tax Inst. and Fin. Planning Inst., Practising Law Inst., Internat. Platform Assn., Greater N.Y. Brokers Assn. Club: K.P. (life; past dep. grand chancellor N.Y. state). Contbr. articles to publs.; also lectr., moderator. Office: 2 Park Ave Suite 1000 New York NY 10016

SPIVAK, GLORIA HELENE, corp. exec.; b. N.Y.C., Nov. 17, 1935; B.A., Hunter Coll., N.Y.C., 1956; postgrad. Harvard Grad. Sch. Bus., 1975; M.B.A., Pace U., N.Y.C., 1978; participant Aspen Inst. Humanistic Studies, 1980. Sch. tchr. N.Y.C. Public Schs., 1956-63; tech. analyst J. Dines & Co., N.Y.C., 1963-66; from jr. analyst to portfolio mgr., investment dept. Boise Cascade Corp., N.Y.C., 1967—; mem. bus. research adv. council Bur. Labor Stats., U.S. Dept. Labor, 1977—; cons. Vol. Urban Cons. Group, Inc.; lectr. Adelphi U., Duke U., Harvard Grad. Sch. Bus. Trustee, mem. fin. com. China Med. Bd. N.Y., 1979—. Mem. N.Y. Soc. Security Analysts, Fin. Women's Assn. (past mem. exec. bd., dir. civic affairs com.), N.Y. Asn. Fgn. Analysts, Fgn. Policy Assn., Econ. Club N.Y., Nat. Assn. Bus. Economists. Office: Boise Cascade Corp 437 Madison Ave New York NY 10022

SPIVEY, CURRIE BYRD, JR., constrn. co. exec.; b. Athens, Greece, Mar. 28, 1936; s. Currie Byrd and Elizabeth (Young) S.; (parents Am. citizens); B.S. in Indsl. Mgmt., Clemson U., 1958; postgrad. Emory U., 1968, Harvard U., 1978; m. Harriett Johnson, Dec. 28, 1958; children—Elizabeth A., James C. With Daniel Constrn. Co., Greenville, S.C., 1963—, v.p. sales, 1970-74, group v.p. sales and sr. mgmt. com., 1974-77, pres., chief operating officer, 1977—, also corp. v.p., dir., mem. compensation and benefits and profl. devel. rev. coms. Daniel Internat.; dir. C & S Bank. Mem. adminstrv. bd., fin. com. Methodist Ch., 1977-78; mem. council Wofford Assos. Served to capt. U.S. Army, 1958-62. Mem. Greater Greenville C. of C. (dir.). Clubs: Greenville Country; Poinsett. Office: Daniel Bldg Main St Greenville SC 29602

SPIVEY, JAMES SHERWOOD, exporter; b. Lufkin, Tex., Mar. 2, 1915; s. Madden Calender and Lillie (Hennington) S.; B.S., Tex. A. and M. U., 1937; m. Marilyn Patterson, Nov. 4, 1939; children—Susan, Peter. Mgr., Terrell (Tex.) C. of C., 1939-42; pres., chief exec. officer James S. Spivey, Inc., Washington, 1946—; pres. Am. Commerce Internat., Inc., Washington, 1950—. Served to lt. col. AUS, 1942-46. Decorated Silver Star, Purple Heart, Bronze Star medal with oak leaf cluster (U.S.); Croix de Guerre (France). Mem. Am. Ordnance Assn., Ind. Telephone Pioneer Assn., 90th Div. Assn. Presbyterian (elder). Rotarian (past pres. Washington Club). Club: Congressional Country (Washington). Home: 10828 Alloway Dr Potomac MD 20854 Office: PO Box 34609 Washington DC 20034

SPOHN, PEGGY WEEKS, banking regulatory agy. ofcl.; b. Kingston, Pa., Aug. 23, 1944; d. Edwin Rice and Maudie Milton (Hewitt) Weeks; B.A., Le Moyne Coll., 1966; M.A. in Sociology, Fordham U., 1967; spl. student in sociology Syracuse U., 1965-66, in cross cultural community devel. Cornell U. Coll. Agr., 1964. Program analyst Concentrated Employment Program, Bronx, N.Y., 1967-68; group work supr. Self Help Enterprises, Inc., Modesto, Calif., 1968-69; research analyst Orgn. for Social and Tech. Innovation, Cambridge, Mass., 1969-70; sr. analyst Abt Assos., Cambridge, also research asso. The Urban Inst., Washington, 1970-74; corp. sec. and dep. dir. The Housing Allowance Office, South Bend, Ind., 1974-76; mgr. D.C. office Contract Research Corp., 1976-78; co-founder, corp. officer Network for Housing Research, Inc., Washington, 1968—; dir. programs div., Office of Community Investment, Fed. Home Loan Bank Bd., Washington, 1978-80, dep. dir. Office of Community Investment, 1980—; mem. Nat. Housing Conf., 1976. Vol./team leader community devel. effort Internat. House, LeMoyne Coll., Mex., 1962-66; vol. devel. of Hope Village, a Coop. Community, Inc., 1968—. Office: Fed Home Loan Bank Bd 1700 G St NW Washington DC 20552

SPOONER, RICHARD CODY, machine tool co. exec.; b. Middletown, Conn., July 27, 1944; s. Edward P. and Catherine Angela (Cody) S.; student (Mark A. Porter scholar), Porter Sch. Engring. Design, 1963-65, Conn. State Tech. Coll., 1966, Central Conn. State Coll., 1966; m. Anna Mae Zdanowicz, Apr. 18, 1970; children—R. Chadwick, Stephen John. Design engr. PowerHold Products Co., Rockfall, Conn., 1965-67, sales and service engr., 1967-68, chief engr., 1969-70, design cons., 1974-75, sales mgr., 1975-76, v.p. sales and engring., 1976-79, pres., chief exec. officer, 1979—, dir., 1980—; dir. Dan-Tex Tool Co., Southfield, Mich. Mem. Durham Republican Town Com., 1977-79, chmn. Ways and Means Com., 1978. Mem. Soc. Mfg. Engrs. (chmn. Hartford chpt. 7, 1976-77, Outstanding Service award 1969), Nat. Fedn. Ind. Businessmen, U.S. Power Squadron, Alumni Assn. Porter Sch. of Design (past chmn.). Roman Catholic. Home: Buckboard Rd Durham CT 06422

SPOOR, WILLIAM HOWARD, food co. exec.; b. Pueblo, Colo. Jan. 16, 1923; s. Charles Hinchman and Doris Field (Slaughter) S.; A.B., Dartmouth Coll., 1949; student Denver U., 1949, Stanford U., 1965; m. Janet Spain, Sept. 23, 1950; children—Melanie G., Cynthia F., William Lincoln. With Pillsbury Co., 1949—, v.p. overseas div., 1962, gen. mgr. internat. ops., 1968, now chmn. bd., chief exec. officer; dir. Dayton Hudson Corp., Honeywell, Inc. Bd. dirs. United Negro Coll. Fund, Found. for Mgmt. Edn. in Central Am. Served to 2d lt., inf., AUS, 1943-46. Mem. Minn. Orchestral Assn. (v.p., dir.), Minn. Bus. Partnership. Clubs: Univ., River (N.Y.C.); Woodhill Country; Mpls. Office: Pillsbury Bldg 608 2d Ave S Minneapolis MN 55402*

SPRADLEY, DON DELOY, real estate broker; b. Kern County, Calif., Dec. 8, 1934; s. Clyde Anderson Spradley and Veda Latan (Ellis) Spradley Quade; B.S., Kans. State COll., 1961; postgrad. La Salle Extension U., 1965-68. With Farmers Ins. Group, 1962-65, MFA Mut. Ins. Cos., Columbia, Mo., 1965-72, Medallion Ins. Co., Kansas City, Mo., 1972-74. Owner, pres., broker Olive Branch Realty, Arlington, Tex., 1975—. Lic. real estate broker, lic. ins. adjuster, Tex. Mem. Nat. Assn. Realtors, Tex. Claims Assn., Tex. Assn. Realtors, Arlington Bd. Realtors. Democrat. Baptist. Club: Kiwanis (pres.) (Arlington). Home: 1411 Waggoner Dr Arlington TX 76013 Office: 2417 W Park Row Suite 204 Arlington TX 76013

SPRAGGINS, STEWART, mfg. co. exec.; b. Pheba, Miss., May 17, 1936; s. Sherman Johnson and Lithia (Spencer) S.; A.A., Mary Holmes Coll., 1959; B.A., Knoxville Coll., 1962; M.Ed., Fairfield U., 1971; m. Georgene Caldwell, Apr. 30, 1966; 1 dau., Renee Ericka. Asst. phys. dir. Greater Bridgeport (Conn.) YMCA, 1962-63, phys. dir., 1963-66, exec. of phys. edn. and membership depts., 1966-70; Met. Outreach exec. Greater Oklahoma City YMCA, 1970-72; exec. dir. YMCAs of the Oranges, Central Br., Orange, N.J., 1972-74; exec. dir. Harlem br. Greater N.Y. YMCA's, Rio de Janeiro, Argentina, 1967; mem. Nat. Black YMCA Task Force, 1975, Fedn. Concerned YMCA Assns., 1967-71; chmn. YMCA Tri-State Spl. Program Planning Com., 1970; YMCA commr. for Basketball, N.E. Region, 1970-71; chmn. drug abuse com. Greater Bridgeport Council Chs., 1970-71; adviser Greater Bridgeport Inter-Faith Council, 1974-76; corp. mgr. urban/community affairs J.P. Stevens & Co., Inc., N.Y.C., 1976—. Bd. dirs. James Varick Center, Deux Found.; chmn. Nat. Black Task Force. Served with AUS, 1974. Mem. Assn. Profl. Dirs., Conn. (pres. 1968-69, N.E. (v.p. 1969-70) phys. dirs. socs., Nat. YMCA Phys. Edn. Soc., Nat. YMCA Adminstrn. Soc., Council Concerned Black Execs., Nat. Urban Affairs Council, EDGES, Inc., Bridgeport Umpires Assn., Phi Beta Sigma. Presbyterian. Club: 1800 (Bridgeport). Home: 18 Maplewood Ave Maplewood NJ 07040 Office: JP Stevens & Co Inc 1185 Ave of Americas New York NY 10036

SPRAGUE, IRVINE HENRY, govt. ofcl.; b. San Francisco, July 4, 1921; s. Irvine Henry and Claire Dolores (Kelly) S.; B.A., U. Pacific, 1947; student Stockton Coll., 1940-41, U. Ind., 1943; postgrad. George Washington Law Sch., 1957; grad. Advanced Mgmt. Program, Harvard, 1972; m. Margery Eleanor Craw, Nov. 3, 1940; children—Michael Irvine, Terry Earl, Kristine Ann. Reporter, Stockton (Calif.) Record, 1938-56; adminstrv. asst. to congressman, 1957-62; dep. dir. finance State of Calif., 1963-66; asst. to Pres. Lyndon B. Johnson, White House, Washington, 1967-68; dir. FDIC, Washington, 1969-72; adminstrv. asst. U.S. Ho. of Reps. Majority Whip, 1973-76; exec. dir. Ho. of Reps. Steering and Policy Com., 1977-78; chmn. FDIC, 1979—. Del. Nat. Dem. Conv., 1964. Served to 1st lt. AUS, 1943-46; Res., 1946-70, lt. col., ret. Decorated Bronze Star with cluster, Purple Heart, Combat Inf. Badge. Mem. DAV. Office: 550 17th St Washington DC 20429

SPRENG, JOSEPH FRANCIS, railroad exec.; b. Phila., Aug. 14, 1921; s. Joseph Francis and Beatrice Elizabeth (Pitt) S.; B.A. in Fine Arts, Roger Williams Coll., 1969; m. Katharine Celeste Lynch, July 15, 1944; children—Katharine, Dianne, Michael, Kevin. Various positions, operating dept. Pa. R.R., 1940-67, div. supt., Altoona, 1967-69; div. supt. Penn Central, New Haven, 1969-70, gen. supt. transp., N.Y.C., 1970-74, asst. gen. mgr., Phila., 1974-76; asst. gen. mgr. Consol. R.R. Corp., Pitts., 1976-80, gen. mgr. met. region, N.Y.C., 1980—. Mem. Roselle Park (N.J.) Sch. Bd., 1960-62. Served with RCAF, 1941-42, USMCR, 1942-45, U.S. Army, US, 1950-52. Decorated D.F.C., Air medal with 4 oak leaf clusters, Naval Commendation medal, Purple Heart with oak leaf cluster; recipient 25-Yr. Vet.'s award Boy Scouts Am., 1960. Mem. Am. Assn. R.R. Supts., Ry. Fuel and Operating Officers Assn., Brotherhood Locomotive Engrs., Pitts. Traffic Club. Republican. Roman Catholic. Club: Pitts. Press. Exhibited ink, pastel, water color and lithograph works in various galleris throughout U.S. Home: 2 Lounsbury Rd Croton on Hudson NY 10520 Office: 347 Madison Ave New York NY 10017

SPRIGGS, ROBERT DEAN, mgmt. cons. co. exec.; b. Villa Grove, Ill., Sept. 10, 1929; B.S., U. Ill., 1955, J.D., 1957; m. Judith Hucko, June 28, 1958; children—Jennifer Anne, Jay Robert. Staff asst. labor relations Caterpillar Tractor Co., 1957-58; div. mgr. salaried employment Brunswick Corp., 1958-59; corporate dir. indsl. relations Robertshaw Controls Co., 1959-62; cons. McKinsey & Co. Inc., Chgo., 1962-63; v.p. Johnson & Assos., Chgo., 1963-67; pres. Spriggs & Co. Inc., Chgo., 1967—. Clubs: Saddle and Cycle, Univ., Whitehall, Carleton. Home: 529 W Wrightwood St Chicago IL 60614 Office: 875 N Michigan Ave Chicago IL 60611

SPRINGBORN, ROBERT CARL, research and devel. co. exec.; b. Geneva, Ill., Oct. 19, 1929; s. Carl Frederick and Mable Nellie S.; B.S. in Chemistry, U. Ill., 1951; Ph.D. in Organic Chemistry, 1954; m. Carolyn Jean Kluesing, Sept. 2, 1951; children—Robert J., Deborah Lynn. Chemist, Monsanto Chem. Soc., 1954-58; tech. dir. Marbon Chem. div. Borg-Warner Corp., 1958-63; v.p., tech. dir. Ohio Rubber Co., 1963-65; gen. mgr. Ionics, Inc., 1965-67; v.p. chem. group W.R. Grace & Co., N.Y.C., 1967-69; chmn., pres. Gen. Econs. Corp., Boston, 1969-71; chmn., pres., chief exec. officer Springborn Group, Inc., Enfield, Conn., 1972—. Nat. co-chmn. Com. for Small Bus. Innovation; bd. dirs. YMCA, Parkersburg, W.Va., 1962-63, Am. Te League, Wood County, W.Va. and Lake County, Ohio, 1961-63. Mem. Am. Chem. Soc., AAAS, Plastics Inst. Am. (past chmn.), Nat. Assn. Life Sci. Industries, Soc. Plastics Engrs., Soc. Plastics Industry. Club: Longmeadow (Mass.) Country. Home: 95 Colton Rd Somers CT 06071 Office: Springborn Group Inc One Springborn Center Enfield CT 06082

SPRINGBORN, ROSEMARY KELLY, publ. co. exec.; b. South Bend Ind., June 2, 1932; d. Edward Joseph and Hazel Jeannette (Thompson) Kelly; B.S., Purdue U., 1953; postgrad Northwestern U., 1958-59, U. Mich., 1960; m. Bruce Alan Springborn, Dec. 19, 1964. Mng. editor, Brewer's Digest, Siebel Publ. Co., Chgo., 1955-58; sr. tech. writer Bendix Corp., Ann Arbor, Mich., 1960-63; editor in chief books div. Soc. Mfg. Engrs., Dearborn, Mich., 1965-69; dir. contracts, copyrights and subs. rights Harper & Row Publishers, Inc., Evanston, Ill., 1969-73; mng. editor research and devel. Tech. Publ. Co., Barrington, Ill., 1973-75, editor in chief TPC Tng. Systems, 1975-78; pres. Kelly-Springborn Assos., Inc., Lakeland, Fla., 1978—. Mem. Am. Inst. Plant Engrs., Soc. Mfg. Engrs., Soc. Women Engrs., Am. Soc. Tng. and Devel. (exec. bd. tech. and skills tng. div.), Ill. Tng. Dirs.

Assn., Am. Assn. Higher Edn., Nat. Soc. Performance an Instrn., Am. Tech. Edn. Assn., Am. Vocat. Assn., Am. Assn. Higher Edn. Internat. Visual Literacy Assn. Roman Catholic. Editorial advisory bd. Training mag. Home and Office: 2834 Elizabeth Pl Lakeland FL 33803

SPRINGER, BERL M., electric co. exec.; b. 1921; B.S., Tex. Tech. U., 1943; married. Jr. engr. Wright Aero Corp., 1943-44; with Southwestern Public Service Co., Amarillo, Tex., 1946—, mgr. rates and budget dept., 1967-69, v.p. rates and budget, 1969-72, exec. v.p., 1972-76, pres., chief operating officer, 1976—, also dir. Served to 1st lt. U.S. Army, 1944-46. Office: SPS Tower 6th and Tyler Sts Amarillo TX 79170*

SPRINGER, JACK HENDERSON, city ofcl.; b. Sistersville, W.Va., Apr. 22, 1917; s. A.G. and Joberta (Henderson) S.; B.S., W.Va. U., 1941, M.S., 1949; m. Wanda Attice Davis, June 7, 1952; children—Jack Henderson, Marjo Springer Poole. Coach, commandant Fishburne Mil. Sch., Waynesboro, Va., 1946-48; coach Manchester (Va.) High Sch. and Galax (Va.) High Sch., 1949-54; dir. recreation Statesville (N.C.) Recreation Dept., 1954—. Past nat. bd. dirs. Babe Ruth Baseball Inc.; past pres. Iredell County Cancer Assn. Served to maj. U.S. Army, 1941-46; ETO. Decorated Bronze Star, Army Commendation medal. Mem. Nat. Recreation and Park Assn., N.C. Recreation and Park Soc. (past v.p., fellow award), Am. Assn. Ret. Persons, Nat. Horseshoe Pitchers Assn. (sec.-treas. N.C. 1979-80, spl. award plaque 1979), Am. Legion (Va. vice comdr.), 40 and 8, VFW, DAV (life), Sigma Chi (life). Democrat. Baptist. Clubs: Masons, Shriners, Moose. Home: 925 Henkel Rd Statesville NC 28677 Office: Statesville Recreation Dept 432 W Bell St Statesville NC 28677

SPRINGER, ROBERT P., lawyer; b. Bklyn., Nov. 5, 1928; s. Leo J. and Anna K. (Kasen) S.; student N.Y. U., 1945; B.A., U. Mich., 1948; J.D., Harvard U., 1951; m. Nesha E. Bass, Sept. 23, 1951; children—Nancy, Mark, Carrie, Stephen. Admitted to N.Y. bar, 1951, U.S. Ct. Mil. Appeals, 1952, U.S. Supreme Ct., 1978; partner firm Silk & Pringer, and successors, Boston, 1955-69; pres., gen. counsel Gt. No. Land Corp., Boston, 1969-72; partner firm Linsky, Springer & Finnegan, Boston, 1973-78; sr. partner Springer, Havey & Ziemian, 1978—; chmn. bd. dirs. Space Sciences, Inc., Waltham, Mass., 1967-69; personal counsel to gov. Mass., 1956-60, 62-64; gen. partner KSS Realty Co., Boston, 1968—. Bd. dirs. Mass. Bay Transp. Authority, 1964-69; mem. Natick (Mass.) Town Meeting, 1954-69, 73-74; trustee council Leonard Morse Hosp., Natick. Served with JAGC, U.S. Army, 1951-54. Mem. Am. Bar Assn., Mass. Bar Assn., Boston Bar Assn., Mass. Acad. Trial Lawyers. Jewish. Home: 28 Russell Circle Natick MA 01760 Office: Springer Havey & Ziemian 185 Devonshire St Boston MA 02110

SPRINGSTEEN, DAVID FOLGER, fin. cons.; b. N.Y.C., Mar. 29, 1932; s. Nelson J. and Gwendolyn (Folger) S.; B.S., Mass. Inst. Tech., 1954; M.B.A., Harvard U., 1958; m. Nancy Neller, Oct. 22, 1955; children—Susan F., Linda P. Aero. research scientist Lewis Flight Propulsion Lab. NASA, Cleve., 1955-57; with Chase Manhattan Bank, N.Y.C., 1958-71, asst. treas., 1961-64, 2d v.p., 1964-68, v.p. Energy div., 1969-71; v.p. corp. fin. Stone & Webster Securities Corp., 1971-74; v.p. corp. fin. E.F. Huttons & Co., Inc., N.Y.C., 1974-78; fin. cons., corp. fin. David F. Springsteen Co., Greenwich, Conn., 1978—. Served to lt. USAF, 1955-57. Mem. Holland Soc. Club: Larchmont Yacht. Home: 205 Shore Rd Greenwich CT 06830 Office: 205 Shore Rd Greenwich CT 06830

SPROWL, CHARLES RIGGS, lawyer; b. Lansing, Mich., Aug. 22, 1910; s. Charles Orr and Hazel (Allen) S.; A.B., U. Mich., 1932, J.D. with distinction, 1934; m. Virginia Lee Graham, Jan. 15, 1938; children—Charles R., Robert A., Susan G., Sandra D. Admitted to Ill. bar, 1935, pvt. practice, 1934—; sr. partner Taylor, Miller, Magner, Sprowl & Hutchings; dir. Paul F. Beich Co., Busch & Schmitt, Inc., A.H. Ross & Sons Co., Petersen Aluminum Corp. Mem. bd. edn. New Trier Twp. High Sch., 1959-65, pres., 1963-65; mem. Glencoe Zoning Bd. Appeals, 1956-76, chmn., 1966-76; bd. dirs. Glencoe Pub. Library, 1953-65, pres., 1955-56; bd. dirs. Cradle Soc.; trustee Highland Park Hosp., 1959-69. Mem. Chgo. (bd. mgrs. 1949-51), Ill., Am. bar assns., Juvenile Protective Assn. (dir. 1943-53), Northwestern U. Settlement Assn. (pres. 1963-70), Am. Coll. Trial Lawyers, Soc. Trial Lawyers, Delta Theta Phi, Alpha Chi Rho. Presbyn. Clubs: Law (pres. 1969-70), Legal (pres. 1953-54), University, Monroe, Skokie Country. Home: 558 Washington Ave Glencoe IL 60022 Office: 120 S LaSalle St Chicago IL 60603

SPRUCE, FRANCES BLYTHE, ins. co. exec.; b. Washington, May 4, 1927; d. Samuel Stewart and Nell Trabue (Anderson) Spruce; A.A., Mt. Vernon Jr. Coll., 1947; B.A., George Washington U., 1950; postgrad. Cath. U., 1953. With Group Hospitalization, Inc., Washington, 1950—, field rep., 1958-72, jr. enrollment field rep., 1972, small group coordinator, 1972-74, mgr. mktg. services, 1974—, also hospitalization account exec. Past v.p. Montgomery Players. Mem. Washington Theater Alliance (past pres.), Pi Beta Phi. Democrat. Club: Arts. Home: 4518 Drummond Ave Chevy Chase MD 20015

SPUNT, SHEPARD ARMIN, mgmt. and financial cons.; b. Cambridge, Mass., Feb. 3, 1931; s. Harry and Naomi (Drooker) S.; B.S., U. Pa., 1952, M.B.A., 1956; m. Joan Murray Fooshee, Aug. 6, 1961 (dec. June 1969); children—Erica Frieda and Andrew Murray (twins). Owner, Colonial Realty Co., Brookline, Mass., 1953—, Cambridge, 1960—; sr. asso. Gen. Solids Assos., 1956—; chmn. bd. Gen. Solids Systems Corp., 1971-74; trustee Union Capital Trust, Boston; incorporator Liberty Bank & Trust Co., Boston. Chmn., Com. for Fair Urban Renewal Laws, Mass., 1965—; treas. Ten Men of Mass., 1973—. Pres., New Eng. Council of Young Republicans, 1964-67, 69-71; vice chmn. Young Rep. Nat. Fedn., 1967-69, dir. region I, 1964-67, 69-71; mem. Brookline Republican Town Com., 1960—; del. Atlantic Conf. Young Polit. Leaders, Brussels, 1973. Bd. dirs. Brookline Taxpayers Assn., 1964—, v.p., 1971-72, pres., 1972—. Registered profl. engr., Mass. Mem. Nat. Soc. Profl. Engrs., Rental Housing Assn., Greater Boston Real Estate Bd., Navy League, Boston Athenaeum, Copley Soc. Boston. Club: Masons. Author: (with others) A Business Data Processing Service for Small Business Practitioners, 1956; A Business Data Processing Service for Medical Practitioners, 1956, rev. edit., 1959. Author, sponsor consumer protection and election law legislation Mass. Gen. Ct., 1969—. Patentee in field of automation, lasers, dielectric bonding. Home: 177 Reservoir Rd Chestnut Hill MA 02167 Office: 21 Elmer St Cambridge MA 02138

SPURGEON, EDWARD VAN RENSSELAER, elec. co. ofcl.; b. Santa Barbara, Calif., May 21, 1931; s. Robert Henry and Elizabeth (Delafield) S.; B.A., Dartmouth Coll., 1953, M.S., 1954; m. Patricia Ankeny Trebien Flynn, June 19, 1954; children—Edward van Rensselaer, Elizabeth D. With Gen. Elec. Co., 1966—, mgr. mfg. ops. indsl. controls, Salem, Va., mgr. mfg. kitchen systems operation, Kissimmee, Fla., sr. corp. cons., Fairfield, Conn., 1966-80, projects mgr. corp. cons. services, Bridgeport, Conn., 1980—. Pres., Roanoke (Va.) Childrens Home Soc., 1968; v.p. Roanoke Council Community Services, 1972; bd. dirs. Darien (Conn.) Arts Council, 1979. Served to lt., USNR, 1954-57. Mem. Am. Mgmt. Assn. Republican. Episcopalian. Clubs: Wee Burn Country, Noroton Yacht. Home: 35 Raiders Ln Darien CT 06820 Office: 1285 Boston Ave Bridgeport CT 06602

SPURLOCK, JAMES AUGUSTUS, entertainment exec.; b. Houston, Dec. 15, 1932; s. J.B. and Jon Augusta (Pruit) S.; student U. Houston, 1950-55; children—Mimi, Randy, Ronny, Kyle. Mgr. estimating Tex. Pipe Bending Co., Houston, 1969—; partner Jim Alan Prodns., Houston, 1979—; state dir. Mrs. Tex. Am. Pageant; area dir. Miss Houston-USA Pageant; freelance fin. mgr. Exec. com. Republican Party, 1953-54; sec. bd. deacons Berachah Ch., Houston. Club: Houstonian. Home: 4525 Hummingbird St Houston TX 77035 Office: 2500 Galveston Rd Houston TX 77012

SPURLOCK, LASSENA CLARK, realtor; b. Canton, N.C., Dec. 12, 1912; d. Edward E. and Lucinda C. (Childers) Clark; student U. N.C., Greensboro, 1930-32; grad. Realtor's Inst., U. N.C., Chapel Hill, 1968; m. Albert Thomas Spurlock, Feb. 23, 1946; children—Clark Guin, Lassena Jan. Propr., Lassena C. Spurlock, Realtor, Hickory, N.C., 1974—. Recipient Top Salesman award Multiple Listing Service, 1975. Mem. Hickory, Catawba Valley bds. realtors. Mem. United Ch. of Christ. Home: 567 1st St NW Hickory NC 28601 Office: 27 1st Ave NE Hickory NC 28601

SPURWAY, HAROLD R., retail exec.; b. 1918; A.B., U. Mich., 1940; married. With Mich. Bell Telephone Co., 1940-41; with Carson Pirie Scott and Co., Chgo., 1945—, successively salesman, asst. dept. mgr., dept. mgr., mdse. mgr., asst. to gen. mdse. mgr., asst. to exec. v.p., asst. to chmn. bd., div. v.p., 1945-69, exec. v.p., dir. real estate, 1969-71, exec. v.p., 1971-72, pres., dir., from 1972, now chmn. bd., chief exec. officer; dir. First Fed. Savings and Loan Assn. Wilmette, Edens Plaza State Bank; pres., dir. Randhurst Corp.; trustee Baird & Warner Realty and Mgmt. Investors. Served with USNR, 1941-45. Address: Carson Pirie Scott 1 S State St Chicago IL 60603*

SQUILLACE, ALEXANDER PAUL, investment adviser; b. Missoula, Mont., Feb. 25, 1945; s. Dominick Paul and Kathleen Marie S.; B.S. in Bus. Adminstrn., Ohio State U., 1967; m. Miriam Palmer Patterson, June 17, 1967; children—Sandra, Scott, Brian, Susan. Investment analyst Nationwide Ins. Cos., Columbus, Ohio, 1967-69; instl. bond rep. Hornblower & Weeks-Hemphill, Noyes, Columbus, 1969-71, mgr. fixed income securities, Indpls., 1971-74; v.p. United Nat. Bank-United Nat. Corp., Sioux Falls, S.D., 1974-79; pres. Investment Mgmt. Group, Sioux Falls, S.D., 1979—, Farmers State Bank, Stickney, S.D., 1979—, Bormann Ins. Agy., Stickney, 1979—; vice chmn. S.D. Investment Council; instr. Am. Inst. Banking. Named hon. citizen of Indpls., 1974; chartered fin. analyst. Fellow Fin. Analysts Fedn.; mem. Am. Inst. Banking, S.D. Bankers Assn., S.D. Investment Soc., Twin Cities Soc. Security Analysts, Ohio State Alumni Assn. Home: 2009 E 52d St Sioux Falls SD 57103 Office: 301 S Garfield St Suite 6 Sioux Falls SD 57104

SRINIVASAN, MANDAYAM PARAMEKANTHI, software services exec.; b. Mysore City, India, July 1, 1940; s. Appalacharya Paramekanthi and Singamma Budugan; came to U.S., 1970; B.S., U. Mysore, 1959, B.E. in Mech. Engring., 1963; M.S. in Ops. Research, Poly. Inst. N.Y., 1974; m. Ranganayaki Srirangapatnam, June 18, 1967. Costing engr. Heavy Engring. Corp., Ranchi, Bihar, India, 1963-70; inventory analyst Ideal Corp., Bklyn., 1970-75; systems analyst Electronic Calculus, Inc., N.Y.C., 1975-76; cons. in software Computer Horizons Corp., N.Y.C., 1976—, tchr., cons. in-house tng. Founding mem. governing council Vishwa Hindu Parishad of U.S.A., 1973—, pres. N.Y. State chpt., 1977—. Mem. Assn. for Computing Machinery, Inst. Engrs. (India). Democrat. Hindu. Office: Computer Horizons Corp 747 3d Ave New York NY 10017

STABILE, RONALD LEWIS, chem. engr.; b. N.Y.C., Jan. 22, 1935; s. Arthur U. and Anna M. (Verrastro) S.; B.Chem. Engring., CCNY, 1957; M.S. in Chem. Engring., N.J. Inst. Tech., 1964; m. Anna Vardzal, July 30, 1966; children—Annette J., Nancy M. Chem. engr. U.S. Govt., N.J., N.Y., 1957-63; process engr. Singmaster & Breyer, N.Y.C., 1964; instrumentation application engr. Merck & Co., Inc., Rahway, N.J., 1965-67; process-project engr. Chem. div. Borden, Inc., Leominster, Mass., 1967-69; chem. engr. for cost engring.-process plants U.S. Dept. Agr., Phila., 1969—. Served with U.S. Army, 1960. Mem. Am. Assn. Cost Engrs. (cert.; founding pres. Eastern Pa. sect. 1972-73, chmn. operating-mfg. costs com. 1978—), Am. Assn. Indsl. Engrs., Am. Inst. Chem. Engrs., Nat. Soc. Profl. Engrs., Order Sons Italy in Am., Order of Engrs. Club: Moose. Contbr. articles on econ. studies for chem. process devel. to tech. publs. Office: US Dept Agr 600 E Mermaid Ln Philadelphia PA 19118

STABILE, ROSE TOWNE (MRS. FRED STABILE), bldg. mgmt. cons.; b. Sunderland, Eng.; d. Stephen and Amelia Bergen; student English schs., Tchrs. Coll., Columbia; m. Wilfred Kermode (dec.); m. 2d, Arthur Whittlesey Towne (dec.); m. 3d, G. Norbert Le Vellie (div.); m. 4th, Fred Stabile, May 30, 1970. Formerly auditor Brit. War Office, Whitehall, London; activities and membership dir. N.Y. League of Girls Clubs, N.Y.C.; later real estate exec., also bldg. mgr. State Tower Bldg., Syracuse, N.Y., now cons. and public relations, 1974—; office designer and decorator; lectr. bldg. mgmt. Syracuse U. An initiator Syracuse Peace Council; mem. area sponsoring com. Assn. for Crippled Children and Adults. Mem. Syracuse Real Estate Board, English Speaking Union, Nat., N.Y. assns. real estate bds., Nat. Assn. Bldg. Owners and Mgrs., N.Y. Soc. Real Estate Appraisers, Syracuse C. of C., LWV, Friends of Music-Amherst Coll., Assn. UN, Syracuse Symphony, Internat. Center, Everson Mus., Mus. Modern Art, Women of Rotary, Bus. and Profl. Women's Clubs, Syracuse Library Friends of Reading. Unitarian (chmn. service com. 1956-57). Club: Corinthian. Home: 304 Malverne Dr Syracuse NY 13208 Office: State Tower Bldg Syracuse NY 13202

STACK, AMOS MOREHEAD, steel co. exec.; b. Buie, N.C., Dec. 8, 1926; s. Amos Morehead and Hannah Nash (McNeill) S.; student The Citadel, 1943-44; A.B. in Am. History, U. N.C., 1949; m. Gillian Rose Scaturro, 1963; children—Elizabeth McNeill, Jane Rachel. Truck driver, exec. trainee, employment mgr. McLean Trucking Co., Winston-Salem, N.C., 1949-54; founder, pres., chmn. bd. Hercules Steel Co. Inc., Fayetteville, N.C., 1954—; dir. Capital Asso. Industries, Raleigh, N.C. Del., Nat. Republican Conv., 1964, 68; active state and county Rep. coms. Served with USN, 1944-46; ETO; CBI. Mem. Am. Inst. Steel Constrn., NAM, U.S. C. of C., Steel Joist Inst. (dir.). Presbyterian. Office: 950 Country Club Rd Fayetteville NC 28303

STACK, J. WILLIAM, JR., mgmt. cons.; b. Lansing, Mich., July 13, 1918; s. Joseph William and Helen (Dodge) S.; A.B., Yale, 1940; m. Wolcott Rorick, Sept. 25, 1948; children—Christopher D., Nathan S., Joseph William III, David R., Peter S. Dist. mgr. Oldsmobile div. Gen. Motors Corp., Maine and N.H., 1945-47, Bklyn. and Queens, 1947-48, asst. zone mgr., N.Y.C., 1948-50, zone mgr., Boston, 1950-54, San Francisco, 1954-55, advt. mgr. AC Spark Plug div., 1955-57, dir. sales and contracts Electronic div., 1957-58; v.p. Kurth Malting Co., Milw., 1958-61; gen. sales mgr. Massey Ferguson, Inc., Toronto, Ont., Can., 1962-63; pres. Stancor Ltd., Toronto, 1964-67; pres. William Stack Assos., Inc., N.Y.C., 1968—. Served as lt. comdr. USNR, 1940-45. Episcopalian. Clubs: Milwaukee; N.Y. Yale, Sky, Links; New Canaan (Conn.) Country; Madison Square Garden (N.Y.C.); Blind Brook (Purchase, N.Y.). Home: 1082 West Rd New Canaan CT 06840 Office: 230 Park Ave New York NY 10017

STADDEN, WARREN CARL, architect, civil engr., city planner; b. Watertown, N.Y., June 30, 1922; s. David Irland and Annabel Grace (Clark) S.; B.S., Bucknell U., 1947; student Princeton, 1943-44, Inst. Design and Constrn., 1953-54; m. Jean Marie Russo, Aug. 31, 1946; children—Arlene, Robert, Barbara. Archtl., structural bldg. designer, 1948—; pvt. practice, Roselle, N.J., 1955—; borough engr., bldg. insp., Florham Park, N.J., 1958-60. Fallout shelter analyst U.S. Dept. Def.; tchr. Rutgers U., 1954-59; Mem. planning bd. Borough of Roselle. Mayor, Roselle, 1964-65. Served with AUS, 1943-46. Registered engr., N.J., N.Y., Pa., Mass., Hawaii; registered architect, N.J., Pa., Hawaii. Mem. Nat. (chmn.), N.J. (treas.), Union County (pres.) socs. profl. engrs., N.J. Soc. Architects, N.J. Soc. Profl. Planners, N.J. Conf. Mayors (asso.), A.I.A., Bldg. Ofcls. Assn., Internat. Platform Assn., N.J. Cons. Engrs., Soc. Am. Value Engrs., Pi Mu Epsilon, Phi Eta Sigma, Tau Beta Pi. Presbyn. (elder). Lion (pres. Roselle). Office: 315 E 5th Ave Roselle NJ 07203

STADECK, ROBERT EDWARD, bus. cons.; b. Elizabeth, N.J., Jan. 24, 1947; s. Alois John and Helen (Wills) S.; B.S., Tufts U., 1969; M.A., Kean Coll., 1973; Ph.D./A.B.D., Stevens Inst. Tech., 1975—; m. Mary Dent Chenault, Aug. 9, 1975. Supr., Hewlett-Packard Electronics, Rockaway, N.J., 1969-74; cons. N.J. Med. Sch., Newark, 1975-78; pres. Applied Indsl. Concepts, Summit, N.J., 1977—; faculty Kean Coll., 1974-75, Middlesex County Coll., 1976-78. Cert. sch. psychologist, N.J. Mem. N.J. Assn. Cons. and Edn. Personnel (pres. 1979), Metro. N.Y. Assn. Applied Psychology, Psi Chi. Address: 182 Ashland Rd Summit NJ 07901

STADLER, JOHN WILLIAM, real estate exec.; b. Miami, Fla., Sept. 10, 1946; s. John B. and Lucille R. Stadler; B.S. with honors in Bus. Adminstrn., U. Fla., 1969; m. DeAnne Wilkerson, June 22, 1968; children—John Christopher, Allison, Jennifer. Engaged in real estate and comml. devel., 1971—; pres., broker, dir. Stadler Assos., Inc., Coral Gables, Fla., 1972—; pres., chief exec. officer, dir. affiliated Fla. Corp., including numerous subs. Founder, mem. Players State Theatre. Fellow Internat. Oceanographic Found.; mem. Farm and Land Inst., Miami Bd. Realtors, Coral Gables Bd. Realtors (dir. 1974-75, 78-80, pres. 1976), Kendall-Perrine Bd. Realtors, Homestead-S. Dade Bd. Realtors, Real Estate Securities and Syndication Inst., Nat. Inst. Real Estate Brokers, Fla. Assn. Realtors (dir. 1973-79), Realtor Polit. Action Com. (life), Nat. Assn. Rev. Appraisers (sr.), Coral Gables C. of C., Greater Miami C. of C., Key Biscayne C. of C., S. Dade C. of C., S. Miami C. of C., Econ. Soc. S. Fla., Hist. Soc. S. Fla. (life), Met. Mus. and Art Center. Republican. Presbyterian. Clubs: Two Hundred, Bath, Riviera Country, Generation, Key Biscayne Yacht, Vizcayans. Home: 7310 Mindello St Coral Gables FL 33134 Office: 95 Merrick Way Coral Gables FL 33134

STAFFORD, ERNEST KAY, JR., retail food co. exec.; b. Dublin, Ga., Dec. 31, 1946; s. Ernest Kay and Grace (Keen) S.; student The Citadel, 1964-66; B.B.A., U. Ga., 1968, J.D., 1975; M.B.A., U. So. Calif., 1969; m. Virginia Ann Smith, Aug. 5, 1972; children—Audrey Leigh, Morgan Kay. Admitted to Ga. bar, 1975; with Piggly Wiggly So., Inc., Vidalia, Ga., 1968—, v.p., gen. counsel, 1975—. Trustee Ohoopee Regional Library, 1978—. Served to 1st lt. U.S. Army, 1969-71; Vietnam. Decorated Purple Heart; Sperry-Hutcheson grantee, 1968-69; alumnus Leadership of Ga., Ga. C. of C., 1976. Mem. Am. Bar Assn., State Bar Ga., Food Mktg. Inst. (lawyers and economists com.), C. of C. Vidalia (dir. 1977—), Scabbard and Blade, Phi Kappa Phi. Presbyterian. Club: Kiwanis (Vidalia). Home: 110 Barron St Vidalia GA 30474 Office: PO Drawer 569 Vidalia GA 30474

STAFFORD, PAUL TUTT, mgmt. cons.; b. Liberty, Mo., Sept. 16, 1905; s. Thomas Polhill and Anna Gardner (Tutt) S.; A.B., U. Mo., 1926, A.M., 1930; Ph.D., Princeton U., 1933; m. Helen Elizabeth Thomson, Dec. 14, 1951; children—Paul T., Timothy A., Mark T., Todd L.; 1 dau. by previous marriage, Lucile S. Stafford Proctor. Instr. politics Princeton U., 1933-36, asst. prof., 1936-42, asso. prof., 1942-48; exec. dir. N.J. State Civil Service Commn., 1948-50; exec. sec. to gov. N.J., 1951; asst. to dir. personnel and community relations Internat. Shoe Co., St. Louis, 1952-53; prin., dir. Ashton Dunn Assos., N.Y.C., 1955-59; founder, chmn. Paul Stafford Assos., Ltd., Mgmt. Cons. in Exec. Recruiting, N.Y.C., Chgo., Washington, 1959—. Served with intelligence USNR, 1942-46; comdr. (ret.). Republican. Presbyterian. Clubs: Nassau (Princeton, N.J.); Apawamis (Rye, N.Y.); Coral Beach (Bermuda); Hillsboro (Pompano Beach, Fla.); Princeton (N.Y.C.). Author: Government and the Needy: A Study of Public Assistance in New Jersey, 1941. Home: 30 Russell Rd Princeton NJ 08540 Office: 45 Rockefeller Plaza New York NY 10020

STAFFORD, THOMAS JOHN, govt. ofcl.; b. Brookfield, Ohio, Jan. 28, 1940; s. Thomas Joseph and Ruth Virginia (Koerber) S.; B.S. in Bus. Adminstrn. cum laude, Youngstown State U., 1963; M.B.A., Kent State U., 1968. Commd. 2d lt. U.S. Air Force, 1964, advanced through grades to capt., 1968, resigned, 1974; contracting officer AID, Rosslyn, Va., 1974-75; contracting officer U.S. Fish and Wildlife Service, Washington, 1975-77, chief of contracting, 1977-81, chief div. contracting and gen. services, 1981—; instr. U. West Coast, Pensacola, Fla., 1969. Bd. dirs. Jaycees, Klamath Falls, Oreg., 1965. Named outstanding Air Force procurement officer, 1969; certified profl. contract mgr. Mem. Nat. Contract Mgmt. Assn. Republican. Home: 4242 East-West Hwy Chevy Chase MD 20015 Office: US Fish and Wildlife Service 18th and C Streets NW Washington DC 20240

STAHEL, RUDOLF SHEPHEARD, corporate mktg. exec.; b. New Orleans, Mar. 17, 1938; s. Rudolf and Lucia Quin (Epley) S.; B.B.A., Tulane U., 1959; m. Joe Ann Elizabeth Womack, Sept. 15, 1961; children—Shepheard Womack, Elizabeth, Anne. Mktg. rep. IBM, Baton Rouge, La., 1963-70, instr. mktg. and finance IBM Edn. Center, Princeton, N.J., 1970-73, IBM mktg. mgr., large accounts, Buffalo/Rochester, 1973-77, sr. program mgr. univ. mktg. IBM Gen. Systems Div., Atlanta, 1978—. Served with USN, 1959-63. Home: 3840 Ranch Estates Dr Plano TX 75074

STAHL, LOUIS EDMUND, ret. food co. exec.; b. Boston, June 20, 1914; s. Harry G. and Esther S.; B.S., M.I.T., 1936; m. Dorothy Judith Tishler, Dec. 17, 1939; children—Lesley, Jeffrey. Tech. dir., pres. Stahl Finish Co., Peabody, Mass., 1936-65; pres. Stahl Finish div. Beatrice Foods, Inc., Wilmington, Mass., 1965-70, group mgr. chem. group, 1970-72, pres. Beatrice Chem. div., 1972-78, v.p. Beatrice Foods, Chgo., 1976-79; dir. Shawmut Mchts. Bank, Salem, Mass. Mem. Corp. devel. com. M.I.T.; pres. Rehab. Center for Aged, Swampscott, 1968—. Mem. Am. Chem. Soc., Am. Leather Chemists Assn. Office: 730 Main St Wilmington MA 01887

STAHL, NORBERT, mgmt. cons.; b. Vienna, Austria, Apr. 2, 1923; s. Aaron and Elsa (Paziek) S.; came to U.S., 1939, naturalized, 1944; B.A. in Chemistry, Bklyn. Coll., 1945; M.B.A., N.Y. U., 1962; m. Erika E. Elias, Dec. 20, 1968. With Control Instrument Co. div. Burroughs Corp., Bklyn., 1952-60, group leader, 1956-59, asst. dir. quality control, 1959-60; project supr. UNIVAC div. Remington

Rand Corp., Norwalk-Darien, Conn., 1960-62; project dir. The Emerson Consultants, Inc., N.Y.C., 1962-64, dir. mgmt. info. systems, 1964-66; sr. mgmt. cons. Union Carbide Corp., N.Y.C., 1966-71; pres., chief exec. officer Alpha Metals, Inc., Jersey City, 1972-74, Sublime Products, Inc., Keene, N.H., 1978—; pres. firm Norbert Stahl & Assos., Inc., bus. cons., N.Y.C., 1971—. Mem. Nat. Microfilm Assn. (founder, past state pres.), Am. Mgmt. Assn., ASME, Engrs. Joint Council, N.Y. U., Bklyn. Coll. alumni assns., Tech. Writers, Pubs. Assn., Am. Soc. Reproduction Engrs., Data Processing Mgmt. Assn., Mu Gamma Tau. Contbr. articles bus. and tech. to jours. Home: Black Mountain Rd Dummerston VT 05301 Office: 400 E 56th St 35N New York NY 10022

STAHL, RAYMOND EARL, research chemist; b. Chgo., Feb. 21, 1936; s. Arthur Daniel and Gladys Hazel (Lockwood) S.; Ph.B., Northwestern U., 1971. Technician-coatings formulator DeSoto Inc., Chgo., 1956-62, sr. chemist, research chemist, sr. research chemist, research asso., 1967-73; group leader metal finishes Adcote div. Morton Chem. Co., Chgo., 1962-66; tech. dir., cons. Am. Indsl. Finishes Co., Chgo., 1966-67; staff scientist, research asso. Dexter-Midland Co., Waukegan, Ill., 1973—. Served with U.S. Army, 1954-56; PTO. Fellow Am. Inst. Chemists; mem. Société de Chimie Industrielle, Am. Chem. Soc., Am. Inst. Physics, Am. Phys. Soc., AAAS, Ill. Acad. Sci., Am. Statis. Assn., Am. Math. Assn., Fedn. Socs. Paint Tech., Am. Mgmt. Assn., Am. Platform Assn., Nat., Ill. rifle assns. Republican. Inventor chem. coatings. Home: 2207 Rolling Ridge Ln Lindenhurst IL 60046 Office: Dexter-Midland Co E Water St Waukegan IL 60085

STAINMAKER, ARMAND C., banker. Chmn., Fed. Res. agt. Fed. Res. Bank of St. Louis, also dir. Office: PO Box 442 Saint Louis MO 63166*

STAKOR, DAVID ROBERT MARK, cash flow mgmt. cons.; b. Trafford, Pa., May 12, 1945; s. Miller Howard and Mark Teresa S.; B.A., Mich. State U., 1967; m. Bonnie Jean McLellan, Nov. 2, 1968; 1 son, Christian David McLellan. Account exec. Aetna Life and Casualty Co., Detroit, 1969-79; pres. D.R.M. Stakor & Assos., Inc., Dearborn, Mich., 1979—. Chmn. adv. bd. Lafayette Clinic, Wayne State U., Detroit. Republican. Episcopalian. Home: 1321 E Horseshoe Bend Rochester MI 48063 Office: D R M Stakor & Assos Inc 15350 Commerce Dr N Dearborn MI 48120

STALEY, ARTHUR FRANCIS, health care exec.; b. Toronto, Ont., Can., May 8, 1924; s. Edwin John and Helen Mary (Spellman) S.; came to U.S., 1947, naturalized, 1953; B.A., U. Toronto, 1947; postgrad. Harvard U., 1963; m. Michaeline Stinson, Sept. 11, 1950; children—Marilyn Ann, Kevin Joseph, Michele Marie, Karen Louise, Maureen Alma, Kristine Stinson. Various positions Continental Can Co., 1947-63, nat. mktg. mgr., N.Y.C., 1964-68, gen. mgr. Bond Crown div., 1969-72; pres. Safety Products div. Am. Optical Corp. div. Warner-Lambert, Southbridge, Mass., 1972-75; exec. v.p. Portex, Inc. subs. Smiths Industries Ltd., Wilmington, Mass., 1975—; dir. Allegheny Beverage Co., Smith Industries N.Am. Mem. Am. Mgmt. Assn., Conf. Bd. Republican. Clubs: Union League (N.Y.C.); Wellesley (Mass.) Country; Ponte Vedra (Jacksonville, Fla.). Home: 101 Royalston Rd Wellesley Hills MA 02181 Office: 42 Industrial Way Wilmington MA 01887

STALEY, KENNETH EUGENE, automobile mfg. co. exec.; b. Western, Nebr., Nov. 26, 1904; s. Ernest Grant and Ruby (Steven) S.; student U. Nebr., 1922-24, Armed Forces Indsl. Coll., 1947-48; m. Nell Dowd, Oct. 23, 1928. With Gen. Motors Corp., various locations, 1929-66, gen. sales mgr., Detroit, 1959-62, v.p. distbn., mktg., 1962-66, ret., 1966, mem. Gen. Motors Speakers Bur., 1966—; dir. First Fed. Savs. & Loan, Lake Worth, Fla. Sec. treas., mem. bd. govs. Nat. Hwy. User Conf., Washington, 1962-66; Bd. dirs. Auto Industry Hwy. Safety Com., 1962-66; trustee Fla. Atlantic U. Found., Boca Raton, (Fla.) Community Hosp.; gov. U. Miami (Fla.); mem. bd. regents Gen. Motors Inst., 1962-66. Served to col. AUS, 1941-45; ETO. Decorated Bronze Star, Purple Heart, Presdl. citation; Croix de Guerre (Belgium), others. Mem. Soc. Univ. Founders. Automotive Orgn. Team, Soc. Benefactors Inter-Oceanographic Found., Lambda Chi Alpha. Republican. Roman Catholic. Clubs: Royal Palm Yacht and Country, 100 (Boca Raton); D.A.C. (Detroit). Home: 1200 S Ocean Blvd Boca Raton FL 33432 Office: Gen Motors Bldg Grand Blvd Detroit MI 48202

STALLARD, WAYNE REX, mfr.; b. Lawrence, Kans., Nov. 17, 1926; s. Clarence N. and Nora E. (Herd) S.; B.S. in Bus., U. Kans., 1948; m. Florence A. Schutte, Sept. 6, 1952; children—Rebecca Anne, Melanie Kay, Jennifer Elaine. Acct., Haskins & Sells, 1948-55; v.p., controller to pres. Pitman Mfg. Co., 1955-67; v.p., treas. A.B. Chance Co., 1967-70; pres. Stelco, Inc., Kansas City, Kans., 1970—. Treas., City of Westwood Hills (Kans.); v.p., bd. dirs. Westwood View Sch. Dist. Served to 2d lt. USAAF, 1944-45. C.P.A., Kans. Mem. Farm Indsl. Equipment Inst. (dir.), Nat. Fedn. Ind. Bus. Methodist. Clubs: Carriage, Masons, Shriners. Home: 6107 W 64th Terr Mission KS 66202 Office: 5500 Kansas Ave Kansas City KS 66106

STALLINGS, M(ARION) RONALD, computer co. exec.; b. Sikeston, Mo., Jan. 14, 1944; s. Marion Walter and Myrtle Nadine (Walters) S.; student U. Mo., 1961-63, Semo U., 1965-66, U. Hawaii, 1968-69; m. Karen Sue Cox, Nov. 7, 1975; 1 dau., Shannon Deon. Dist. mgr. Allis Chalmers Corp., Hattiesburg, Miss., Fremont and Scottsbluff, Nebr., 1966-72; pres., chmn. bd. Ag Machinery Inc., Brush, Colo., 1972—; founder Brush Banner newspaper; founder Sure Date Systems, 1979; co-owner Brush Machinery Auction Co.; dir. RSV Enterprises, Inc.; dist. mem. Allis Chalmers dealer communication panel. Past bd. dirs. Morgan County United Way. Served with Intelligence Corps, U.S. Army, 1968-70; Cinpac. Mem. Sigma Phi Epsilon. Clubs: Masons, Elks, Rotary (Brush), Bunker Hill Country (past dir.). Home: 2327 19th Ave Greeley CO 80631 Office: 1309 9th St Greeley CO 80631

STALLINGS, STEVEN LEE ANTHONY, mgmt. cons. co. exec.; b. San Diego, May 12, 1951; s. Learnold and Betty Jean (Constantino) S.; B.S. in Mgmt., Calif. State U., Long Beach, 1977; M.B.A., U. So. Calif., 1980; m. Betty Jo Buffalohead, Jan. 19, 1972; children—Debra Kay, Joyce Alicia. Staff cons. AIFT Inc., San Diego, 1971-74; ind. cons. public adminstrn., San Francisco, 1974-76; exec. dir. region IX, AIC, San Francisco, 1974-76; pres. United Indian Devel. Assn., Los Angeles, 1976—; apptd. to Los Angeles Tng. and Job Devel. Bd., 1980, White House Conf. on Small Bus., 1980. Am. Indian fellow in Bus., U.S. Dept. Edn., 1975, fellow Consortium for Grad. Study in Mgmt., U. So. Calif., 1978. Mem. Fifth Internat. Symposium on Small Bus. (session chmn. 1978). Democrat. Roman Catholic. Club: Lion Host (Los Angeles). Lectr. profl. seminars. Home: 17916 Holmes Cerritos CA 90701 Office: 1541 Wilshire Blvd Suite 307 Los Angeles CA 90017

STALOFF, ARNOLD FRED, securities exec.; b. Dover, N.J., Dec. 12, 1944; s. William and Ida (Greenberg) S.; B.B.A., U. Miami, 1967; m. Sharon Teplitsky, June 10, 1967; children—Kimberly, Lindsay. Statistician, U.S. Census Bur., Washington, 1967-68; fin. analyst U.S. S.E.C., Washington, 1968-71; sr. v.p. Phila. Stock Exchange, 1971-78; mem. bd. Options Price Reporting Authority, 1973-78, Options Clearing Corp., 1976-78; chmn. ops. com. Composite Tape Assn., 1973-78; v.p. Securities Industry Automation Corp.; pres. Fin. Automation Corp., Phila.; instr. stock market Temple U., 1974-78. Republican. Jewish. Home: 1605 Mayflower Ln Cherry Hill NJ 08003 Office: 55 Water St New York NY 10041

STAMBERG, LOUIS MANN, cement co. exec.; b. Ukraine, June 14, 1902; came to U.S., 1904, naturalized, 1906; B.S.C.E., U. Pa., 1924; LL.B., Temple U., 1929; m. Marjorie Salinger Bing, June 25, 1952; children—Louis Collins, Catherine Bing Lipkin. Admitted to Pa. bar, 1929; individual practice law, Allentown, Pa., 1931—; chmn. bd. Coplay Cement Co., Nazareth, Pa., 1971—; dir. Rodale Press, Inc. Chmn., Allentown Zoning Bd., 1951-56; counsel, mem. exec. com. Lehigh County United Way. Mem. Am. Bar Assn., Pa. Bar Assn., Engrs. Club. Lehigh Valley, Allentown C. of C. (dir., exec. com.). Republican. Office: 534 Turner St Allentown PA 18102

STAMP, JAMES ALLEN, fin. cons.; b. Salem, Ohio, Nov. 3, 1942; s. Elmer Richard and Fae L. (Andre) S.; B.Acctg., Mt. Union Coll., 1966; postgrad. U. Akron, 1966-67; m. Margaret J. Boski, June 19, 1966; children—Shawn R., Heather L., Eric L. Telegrapher, CB & Q R.R., Chgo., 1960-62; draftsman Sterling-Salem Corp., Salem, 1962-63; credit mgr. Sears, Roebuck & Co., Alliance, Ohio, 1964-66; acct. Ernst & Ernst, Akron, Ohio, 1966-70; area sales coordinator Bestline Products, Chgo., 1970-73; budget dir. Timken Mercy Hosp., Canton, Ohio, 1973-76; dir. fin. Green Cross Gen. Hosp., Cuyahoga Falls, Ohio, 1977-78; pvt. practice pub. acctg., Norton, Ohio, 1978—; dir. Community World Inc., Agriworld Inc., Mac R & D Inc., Ashtabula Fish & Chips, Inc., No. Fish Co., Inc. Founder, Boardroom Exchange Assn., Norton, 1979; sponsor, coach Little League Baseball, Norton, 1979-80, dir., 1978-79. Mem. Nat. Assn. Accts. (Mem. of Yr. 1980), Ohio Soc. C.P.A.'s, Internat. Platform Assn., Hosp. Fin. Mgmt. Assn., Am. Mortgage Brokers Assn. Republican. Methodist. Home: 3405 Mark Ln Norton OH 44203 Office: PO Box 1216 Norton OH 44203

STAMP, R. J., investor; b. Oklahoma City, Apr. 21, 1937; s. John L. and Mary Stamp; B.A. in Fin., U. Okla.; Ph.D. in Fin., Westerland Coll., Vina, Calif., 1961; m. Carol Baines, Jan. 3, 1958; 3 children. Bus. mgr. Askins, Inc., Oklahoma City, 1962-68; investment mgr. C.B.O.C., Inc., 1968-69; real estate and bus. investor, also cons., Oklahoma City, 1969—. Mem. Internat. Fin. Assn. (past pres.), Universal Life Service Assn. (pres. 1980), Oklahoma City West Assn. (past pres.). Democrat. Methodist. Clubs: Elks, Moose, Lions (past pres. Oklahoma City). Author: Money Finders Directory, 1976. Address: PO Box 75032 Oklahoma City OK 73147

STAMPER, MALCOLM THEODORE, aerospace co. exec.; b. Detroit, Apr. 4, 1925; s. Fred Theodore and Lucille (Cayce) S.; student U. Richmond (Va.), 1943-44; B.E.E., Ga. Inst. Tech., 1946; postgrad. U. Mich., 1946-49; m. Marion Philbin Guinan, Feb. 25, 1946; children—Geoffrey, Kevin, Jamie, David, Mary, Anne. With Gen. Motors Corp., 1949-62; with Boeing Co., Seattle, 1962—, mgr. electronics ops., v.p., gen. mgr. turbine div., 1964-66, v.p., gen. mgr. 747 Airplane program, 1966-69, v.p., gen. mgr. comml. airplane group, 1969-71, corp. sr. v.p. ops., 1971-72, pres. Boeing Co., 1972—; dir. Fed. Res. Bank San Francisco, Nordstrom Co. Chmn. Wash. State U.S. Treasury Savs. Bond Campaign, Boy Scouts Am. Devel. Fund State of Wash., Variety Club Handicapped Children Telethon; candidate U.S. Ho. of Reps., Detroit, 1952; trustee Seattle Art Mus., Seattle Repertory Theatre. Served to ensign USNR, 1943-46. Named Industrialist of Year, 1967; recipient Educator's Golden Key award, 1970. Mem. Nat. Alliance Businessmen, Phi Gamma Delta. Office: Boeing Co 7755 E Marginal Way Seattle WA 98124*

STANAT, RUTH ELLEN, paper co. ofcl.; b. Washington, Nov. 4, 1947; d. James Frances and Wylma Ellen Corrigan; B.S. in Edn. cum laude (acad. scholar), Ohio U., 1969; M.A. in Psychology, N.Y. U., 1973, M.B.A. in Fin., 1977; m. Jon Stanat, June 24, 1972; 1 son, Scott. Regional coordinator quality control div. indsl. engring. United Airlines, 1969-74; sr. analyst market research Springs Mills, Inc., 1974-75; with Internat. Paper Co., N.Y.C., 1975—, sr. analyst market research, product coordinator reprodn. papers, product supr. electrostatic papers, product mgr. spl. markets, 1975-78, mgr. strategic planning splty. packaging group, 1979—. Fund raiser Am. Cancer Soc. Recipient award of merit United Airlines, 1973. Mem. Fin. Women's Assn., Women in Paper, N.Y. U. Bus. Forum, Woman's Econ. Roundtable, Beta Gamma Sigma. Pi Gamma Mu. Lutheran. Home: 875 Fifth Ave Apt 5D New York NY 10021 Office: 220 E 42d St New York NY 10017

STANDLEY, MARVIN MORRIS, telephone co. mgr.; b. Kansas City, Mo., Mar. 15, 1939; s. Lee E. and Nellie E. (Smith) S.; B.S., Central Mo. State U., 1961; M.S., St. Louis U., 1968; m. Suzanne Jane Wedler, July 31, 1970; children—Todd, Scott, Craig. Comml. staff asst. Southwestern Bell Telephone Co., St. Louis, 1961-63, mgr., Fulton, Mo., 1963-64, unit mgr., 1964-66, exchange rate engr., 1966-68, rate engr., 1968-69, supr. personnel devel., 1969-71, dist. mgr., 1971-80, Ferguson, Mo., 1971-80, div. staff mgr., seminar dir., 1980—. Pres., St. Louis County League of C. of C., 1976; chmn. St. Louis County Planning Commn., 1978—; pres. Florissant Fine Arts Council, 1974-77; v.p. Am. Cancer Soc., 1978; bd. mgrs. YMCA, 1976—. Recipient Disting. Service award St. Louis County League chambers commerce, Florissant Valley Jaycees, 1975, 76. Mem. Florissant (Mo.) C. of C. (pres. 1974). Clubs: Rotary (pres. Ferguson 1976-77, dist. gov. elect), Mo. Athletic, Norwood Hills Country. Home: 6630 Lakeside Hills Dr Florissant MO 63033

STANDRIDGE, RONALD L., fin. exec.; b. Rodeo, Calif., June 27, 1939; s. William A. and Delora A. Standridge; B.A. in Acctg., U. Okla., 1965; m. Barbara Standridge, June 14, 1980; children—Cynthia Ann, Heather Lynn. With Arthur Young & Co., 1965-69; fin. v.p., sec. Marion Corp., Mobile, Ala., 1969—. Mem. Am. Inst. C.P.A.'s. Office: One Marion Ave Daphne AL 36652*

STANFILL, DENNIS CAROTHERS, business exec.; b. Centerville, Tenn., Apr. 1, 1927; s. Sam Broome and Hattie (Carothers) S.; B.S., U.S. Naval Acad., 1949; M.A. (Rhodes scholar), Oxford U., 1953; m. Therese Olivieri, June 29, 1951; children—Francesca, Michaela, Dennis Carothers. Corporate fin. specialist Lehman Bros., N.Y.C., 1959-65; v.p. fin. Times Mirror Co., Los Angeles, 1965-69, treas., 1968-69; exec. v.p. 20th Century-Fox Film Corp., 1969-71, chmn. bd., chief exec. officer, 1971—. Served to lt. USN, 1949-59, politicomil. policy div. Office Chief Naval Ops., 1956-59. Office: Box 900 Beverly Hills CA 90213

STANFORD, BILLY P., door-milling mfg. co. exec.; b. Temple, Tex., Oct. 6, 1941; s. Joe B. and Pauline Stanford; student Temple Jr. Coll., 1960-63, U. Tex., 1963-64; m. Diana Blight, Sept. 19, 1964; children—Lisa, Paula, Suzanne. Store dir. H.E. Butt Grocery Co., Corpus Christi, Tex., 1958-74; ops. officer Texas Bank, Temple, 1974; sales mgr. Frito-Lay, Inc., Temple, 1974-75; indsl. relations dir. Rockwool Industries, Inc., Belton, Tex., 1975-80; personnel mgr. Gould Inc., Temple, 1980; personnel dir. Temple Products, Inc., 1980—. Trustee, Belton Ind. Sch. Dist., 1980—; bd. dirs. fin. com. Bell County Republican party; bd. dirs. Belton United Fund, 1972-75, Blue Bonnet council Girl Scouts U.S., 1978-80; bd. dirs. Heart of Tex. council Boy Scouts Am., 1975-77. Served with U.S. Army, 1964-69. Mem. Am. Soc. Personnel Adminstrs., Temple Personnel Assn., Tex. Safety Assn., Ind. Businessmen Am., Tex. Assn. Businessmen, U.S. Jaycees (pres. Belton 1972-73), United Methodist Men. Methodist. Club: Rotary (pres. 1971-72). Home: 621 Estate Dr Belton TX 76513 Office: 2101 Baker Blvd Temple TX 76501

STANFORD, JOHN DAVID, food processing equipment mfg. co. exec.; b. Salem, Ill., Sept. 12, 1946; s. William Thomas and Melba (Hagar) S.; B.S., Georgetown Coll., 1969; m. Donna Maxine Green, Aug. 14, 1971; 1 son, Shane. With Bettendorf Stanford Co., Salem, 1969—, pres., 1970—, owner, 1973—; dir. Best Sales Co., Let's Travel Co. Trustee Kaskaskia Coll. Mem. Georgetown Coll. Assos., Am. Soc. Bakery Engrs., Bakery Equipment Mfg. Assn. Democrat. Baptist. Clubs: Mo. Athletic, Rotary. Office: PO Box 90 Salem IL 62881

STANFORD, MELVIN JOSEPH, educator, mgmt. cons.; b. Logan, Utah, June 13, 1932; s. Joseph Sedley and Ida Pearl (Ivie) S.; B.S. (First Security Found. scholar), Utah State U., 1957; M.B.A. (Donald Kirk David fellow), Harvard U., 1963; Ph.D., U. Ill., 1968; m. Linda Barney, Sept. 2, 1960; children—Connie, Cheryl, Joseph, Theodore, Emily, Charlotte, Charles, Sarah. Asst. audit supr. Utah Tax Commn., Salt Lake City, 1958-61; accountant Haskins & Sells, Boston, 1961-62; accounting staff analyst Arabian Am. Oil Co., Dhahran, Saudi Arabia, 1963-66; teaching and research asst. U. Ill., Urbana, 1966-68; asst. prof. Brigham Young U., Provo, Utah, 1968-69, asso. prof., 1969-74, prof. bus. mgmt., 1974—; vis. prof. mgmt. European grad. programs Boston U., Heidelberg, Germany, 1975-76; mgmt. and fin. cons. Served with USAF, 1951-55. Mem. Acad. Mgmt., Am. Inst. Decision Scis., SAR (pres. Utah Soc. 1978-79, nat. trustee 1979), Alpha Kappa Psi, Phi Kappa Phi. Republican. Mem. Ch. Jesus Christ of Latter-day Saints. Author: New Enterprise Management, 1975; Management Policy, 1979; contbr. cases to textbooks, articles to profl. jours. Home: 1163 E 820 N Provo UT 84601 Office: 203 JKB Brigham Young U Provo UT 84602

STANGER, JOHN WILLIAM, credit co. exec.; b. Boston, Jan. 24, 1923; s. John Sawyer and Leonora (Leo) S.; student Boston U., 1941-43; A.B., Harvard, 1947; m. Valerie Gudel, Apr. 14, 1951; 1 dau., Pamela Beth. With Gen. Electric Credit Corp. subsidiary Gen. Electric Co., 1947—, gen. mgr. comml. and indsl. financing, 1960-62, v.p., gen. mgr. comml., indsl. financing, 1962-75, pres., chief exec. officer, dir., 1975—; chmn. bd. dirs. Puritan Life Ins. Co., Puritan Ins. Co. Served to capt. USAAF, 1943-45, 51-53. Decorated D.F.C. Mem. Southwestern Area Commerce and Industry Assn. (chmn. bd. dirs. 1975—). Republican. Clubs: Harvard Lower Fairfield; Greenwich Country; Union League; Landmark. Home: 72 Perkins Rd Greenwich CT 06830 Office: PO Box 8300 260 Long Ridge Rd Stamford CT 06904

STANLEY, C. MAXWELL, cons. engr.; b. Corning, Iowa, June 16, 1904; s. Claude Maxwell and Laura Esther (Stephenson) S.; B.S., U. Iowa, 1926, M.S., 1930; L.H.D., Iowa Wesleyan Coll., 1961, Augustana Coll., 1978; H.H.D. honoris causa, U. Manila, 1970; m. Elizabeth M. Holthues, Nov. 11, 1927; children—David M., Richard H., Jane S. Buckles. Structural designer Byllesby Engring. & Mgmt. Corp., Chgo., 1926-27; dept. grounds and bldgs. U. Iowa, 1927-28; hydraulic engr. Mgmt. & Engring. Corp., Dubuque, Iowa and Chgo., 1928-32; cons. engr. Young & Stanley, Inc., 1932-39; partner, pres. Stanley Engring. Co., Muscatine, Iowa, 1939-66; pres. Stanley Consultants, Inc., 1966-71, chmn. bd., 1971—; pres. HON Industries, Muscatine, 1944-64, chmn. bd., 1964—; pres. Stanley Cons., Ltd., Liberia, 1959-71, now dir.; mng. dir. Stanley Cons. Ltd., Nigeria, 1960-67, now dir.; pres. World Press Rev., 1975—. Trustee, Iowa Wesleyan Coll., 1951—, chmn., 1963-65; pres. The Stanley Found., 1956—; chmn. Strategy for Peace Confs., 1962—, Confs. on UN of Next Decade, 1965—; bd. dirs. U. Iowa Found., 1966—, pres., 1971-75; mem. President's Commn. on Personnel Interchange, 1976. Recipient John Dunlap prize Iowa Engring. Soc., 1943, Marston award, 1947, Disting. Service award, 1962, Herbert Hoover Humanitarian award, 1979, named hon. mem., 1975; Disting. Service award U. Iowa, 1967; Hancher-Finkbine medallion, 1971. Fellow ASCE (Alfred Nobel prize 1933, Collingwood prize 1935), IEEE, ASME, Am. Cons. Engrs. Council; mem. Nat. Soc. Profl. Engrs. (award for outstanding service 1965, PEPP award 1975), World Federalists U.S.A. (pres. 1954-56, 64-66, council 1947—), World Assn. World Federalists (chmn. council 1958-65), Nat. Planning Assn., New Directions (dir. 1976—). Republican. Methodist. Club: Rotary (Paul Harris award 1976). Author: Waging Peace, 1956; The Consulting Engineer, 1961; Managing Global Problems, 1979; contbr. articles to profl. jours. Home: 115 Sunset Dr Muscatine IA 52761 Office: Stanley Bldg Muscatine IA 52761

STANLEY, DARROL JAMES, investment banker; b. Berkeley, Calif., Dec. 26, 1944; s. Charles J. and Maxine (Phillips) S.; B.S., U. Calif., Berkeley, 1966; M.B.A., U. So. Calif., 1968, D.B.A., 1973; m. Carole Tait, Feb. 3, 1968. Lectr. fin. U. So. Calif., 1968-71; asst. prof. fin. Calif. State U., Northridge, 1971-73; asso. prof. fin. Pepperdine U., Los Angeles, 1973—; mgr. corp. fin. and research Wagenseller & Durst, Inc., Los Angeles, 1972-76; pres. D.J. Stanley & Co., Inc., Los Angeles, 1976—; chmn. Century Gen. Corp., 1973-79. Mem. Am. Soc. Appraisers, Am. Econ. Assn., Am. Fin. Assn., Los Angeles World Affairs Council. Republican. Presbyterian. Home: 10825 Savona Rd Los Angeles CA 90024

STANLEY, JOAN GLORIA, mktg. and sales exec.; b. Hoboken, N.J., June 14, 1939; d. Alexander John and Elfrieda Katherina (Matula) S.; student New Sch. Social Research, 1959-60, N.Y. U., 1960-63. Vice pres. N.Y. Apt. Exchange, N.Y.C., 1965-70; dir. sales promotions Zsa Zsa Internat., N.Y.C., 1970-72; dir. spl. projects Nat. Audubon Soc., N.Y.C., 1972-80, v.p. mktg., 1980—; cons. Mem. Nat. Soc. Fund Raising Execs., Licensing Industry Assn. (v.p.), Mail Mktg. Assn. (dir.), Direct Mail Fundraisers Assn. Home: 35 E 35th St New York NY 10016 Office: National Audubon Soc 950 3d Ave New York NY 10022

STANLEY, LOWELL, business exec.; b. Long Beach, Calif., Aug. 10, 1906; s. George Tatum and Clara (Graves) S.; A.B., U. Calif. at Los Angeles, 1928; m. Helene Archer, Nov. 21, 1934. With Jergins Oil Co., and predecessor, 1933-52, pres., 1950-51, chmn. bd., 1951-52; chmn. bd., chmn. exec. com. successor, Monterey Oil Co., 1952-55; dir. Petrolane Inc., 1943—, chmn. bd., 1961-71, chmn. exec. com., 1971—; dir. Beckman Instruments, Inc., Beckman Instruments Ltd. (Scotland), Beneficial Standard Corp., Great Western Fin. Corp., Gt. Western Savs. & Loan Assn.; panelist fed. tax policy for econ. growth and stability, joint econ. com. U.S. Senate-Ho. Reps., 1955. C.P.A., Calif. Mem. Ind. Petroleum Assn. Am. (past dir.), Am. Inst. C.P.A.'s. Clubs: Calif. (Los Angeles). Office: 1600 E Hill St Signal Hill CA 90806

STANSELL, RONALD BRUCE, investment banker; b. Hammond, Ind., Apr. 9, 1945; s. Herman Bruce and Helen Rose S.; B.A., Wittenberg U., 1967; M.A., Miami U., Oxford, Ohio, 1969; m. Kathie Van Atta, Oct. 2, 1976; 1 dau., Kelsey. Investment officer First Nat. Bank, Chgo., 1969-73; mgr. investments Chrysler Corp., Detroit, 1973; asst. v.p. A.G. Becker, Chgo., 1973-76; v.p. Blyth Eastman Dillon, Chgo., 1976-79; v.p. Dean Witter Reynolds Inc., Chgo.,

1979—. Mem. Mettawa (Ill.) Zoning Bd., 1978—. Served with USMCR, 1968-69. Named to Pres.'s Club, Blyth Eastman Dillon, 1977, 78, 79. Mem. Bond Club Chgo., Investment Analyst Soc., Fixed Income Group. Club: Exmoor Country. Home: Route #1 Box 49 Old School Rd Mettawa IL 60048

STANTON, ROBERT JOHN, JR., investment banker; b. Tulsa, Mar. 1, 1941; s. Robert John and Mary Louise (Locke) S.; B.A. in Econs., Rice U., Houston, 1962; M.B.A., Harvard U., 1965; m. Katherine Whitelaw, Nov. 26, 1966; children—Mary Whitelaw, Robert Locke. From asso. to sr. v.p. E.F. Hutton & Co. Inc., N.Y.C., 1965-77; exec. v.p., dir., mem. exec. com. Rotan Mosle Inc. and Rotan Mosle Fin. Corp., Houston, 1977—; chmn. bd. Alpine Water Co.; dir. Browning-Ferris Industries, Inc., Rio Grande Drilling Co., Bank of Tulsa. Served with USAR, 1962-63. Mem. Securities Industry Assn. (chmn. corp. fin. com. 1981). Clubs: Houston Athletic, Bond of N.Y., Houstonian. Home: 740 Marchmont St Houston TX 77024 Office: 1500 S Tower St Pennzoil Pl Houston TX 77002

STANTON, ROBERT MYTINGER, comml. real estate exec.; b. Portsmouth, Va., Apr. 27, 1938; s. Charles Morgan and Margaret Avis (Austin) S.; student U. N.C., Chapel Hill, 1956-59; B.A. in Banking and Fin., Coll. William and Mary, 1961; 1 dau., Frances Allison. With Goodman Segar Hogan, Inc., Norfolk, Va., 1966—, pres., 1975—. Bd. dirs. Norfolk Acad., Gen. Hosp. of Virginia Beach; devel. com. Eastern Va. Med. Found.; pres. Old Dominion U. Edn. Found. Named First Citizen of Virginia Beach, 1976; cert. property mgr. Inst. Real Estate Mgmt.; cert. shopping center mgr. Internat. Council Shopping Centers. Mem. Internat. Council Shopping Centers (trustee). Episcopalian. Clubs: Princess Anne Country, Harbor, Ocean Reef. Author: (with others) The Valuation of Shopping Centers, 1976; chmn. 1980 edition Dollars and Cents of Shopping Centers. Home: 4004 Oceanfront St Virginia Beach VA 23451 Office: 1 Commercial Pl Suite 1100 Norfolk VA 23510

STANTON, ROGER, editor, publisher, sports broadcaster; b. Mpls., Dec. 31, 1928; s. M. E. and Pearl (Lind) S.; B.A., U. Mich., 1951; m. Pamela Kornmeier, Dec. 19, 1970. With advt. pub. relations dept. Fed. Dept. Stores, Detroit, 1951-54; sales promotion mgr. Wolf Detroit Envelope Co., 1954-56; with Bank Detroit, 1956-64, coordinator employee recreation program, 1957-64; pres., editor, pub. Football News, Detroit, 1962—; sports dir. radio sta. WWWW, Detroit, 1963-70; WXON-TV, 1968-70; pub. Basketball Weekly, 1967—, Big 10 Report, 1972-76, Inside Today's Sports, 1975—. Instr. writing, pub. relations YMCA, Detroit, 1960-62; news corr. radio sta. WLAV, Grand Rapids, Mich., 1962-64; chmn. indsl publs. for Mich. Week, 1958-63. Mem. speakers bur. United Found. Active in pub. relations work, del. Mich. Republican party. Mem. Nat. Sportswriters and Sports Broadcasters Assn., AFTRA, Am. Inst. Banking (pres. forensic club 1960-62), Football Writers Assn. Am., Coll. Sports Dirs., Fellowship Christian Athletes, Pro Football Writers Assn., Detroit Sports Broadcasters Assn., Sigma Delta Chi. Republican. Clubs: Adcraft (publicity chmn.), University Mich. (gov.), Notre Dame (hon.), Economic (publicity com.), Press (Detroit); Palm Bay (Miami Beach); Carleton (Chgo.). Home: 7 Stratford Pl Grosse Pointe MI 48230 Office: 17820 E Warren Detroit MI 48224

STANTON, WALTER OLIVER, electronics co. exec.; b. Canton, Ohio, Sept. 29, 1914; s. Bela Hayden and Edna (Keckeley) S.; E.E., Wayne State U., 1939; m. Mary Ann Wilcox, Apr. 18, 1942; children—Sharon (Mrs. R. Russell), Diana (Mrs. A.G. Thornbrough), Pamela (Mrs. J. O'Donnell). Pres. Pickering & Co., Inc., Plainview, L.I., 1950—, Stanton Magnetics, Inc., 1966—; pres. Pickering Impex S.A., Switzerland, Stanton Impex S.A., Switzerland; dir. Servo Corp. Am. Fellow Audio Engring. Soc. (pres. 1957), Inst. High Fidelity (pres. 1963-67, dir., treas.). Patentee in field. Home: Laurel Hollow Rd Laurel Hollow NY 11791 Office: Sunnyside Blvd Plainview NY 11803

STANZIANO, ARTHUR JOSEPH, electronics co. exec.; b. N.Y.C., Mar. 28, 1920; s. Angelo Benedict and Jeanette Edith (Fonzo) S.; B.S., Columbia, 1941; M.B.A., George Washington U., 1964; m. Margaret Mary Stewart, Feb. 26, 1949; children—Michael, Angela. Commd. ensign, U.S. Navy, 1941, advanced through grades to capt., 1960, ret., 1967; v.p. Hazeltine Corp., Braintree, Mass., 1967-71, Arlington, Va., 1972—. Decorated Medal for Aeronautics (France). Mem. IEEE (Sr.), Am. Mgmt. Assn., Tau Beta Pi. Roman Catholic. Clubs: Internat. (Washington); Fort Meyer Officer, Pentagon Athletic (Arlington, Va.). Home: 3111 Valley Ln Falls Church VA 22044 Office: 2001 Jefferson Davis Hwy Arlington VA 22202

STAPLES, CHARLES OXNARD, computer services exec.; b. Winchester, Mass., Dec. 28, 1937; s. Elton Earle and Miriam (Oxnard) S.; B.S., M.I.T., 1959; M.B.A., Harvard U., 1961; m. Katherine Maclaurin, Aug. 27, 1960; children—Richard, Nancy, Charles. Sr. planner Martin Co., Orlando, Fla., 1961-64; sr. market research specialist U.S. Steel, Pitts., 1964-66; sr. cons. Peat Marwick Mitchell, Boston, 1966-69; dir. corp. services Multicomp Inc., Wellesley, Mass., 1969-71; from v.p. to exec. v.p. Standard Info. Systems, Wellesley, 1971-76; v.p. gen. mgr. Boston ops. United Computing Systems Inc., Wellesley, 1978—; founder, dir. Am. Alarm & Communications, Inc., Winchester, Logos Devel. Corp., Middletown, N.Y. Mem. exec. com. M.I.T. Venture Forum, 1978—. Club: Campton Hollow Ski. Home: 38 Greenwood Rd Wellesley Hills MA 02181 Office: United Computing Systems 300 2d Ave Waltham MA 02154

STAPLES, JOHN ALLAN, aerospace mfg. co. exec.; b. Breckenridge, Minn., July 12, 1922; s. Isel Eugene and Inga Marie (Rekstad) S.; B.S.C., U. N.D., 1943, J.D., 1949; m. Shirley Ann Ness, Apr. 18, 1947; children—Diane K., Terri A. Admitted to N.D. bar, 1949; instr. to asso. prof. Sch. Bus., U. N.D., 1949-56; asst. to comptroller E.J. & E. Ry. Co., 1956-58; various positions DMIR Ry. Co., 1958-63, comptroller, 1964-66; v.p. fin. Premier Indsl. Corp., Cleve., 1966-68; adminstrv. v.p., treas. Cole Nat. Corp., Cleve., 1968-70; v.p. fin. planning Pneumo Corp., Boston, 1971—. Served with U.S. Army, 1943-46. Decorated Bronze Star; C.P.A., N.D. Mem. Am. Inst. C.P.A.'s. Methodist. Clubs: Woodland Golf (Auburndale, Mass.); Cleve. Athletic; Kitchi Gammi (Duluth, Minn.). Office: Pneumo Corp 4800 Prudential Tower Boston MA 02199

STAPLES, LAURANCE STARR, JR., mfg. co. exec.; b. Kansas City, Mo., Jan. 31, 1931; s. Laurance Starr and Bertha Marie (Schaefer) S.; B.S. in Gen. Engring., U. Ill., 1956; m. Barbara Ruth Hazard, Oct. 5, 1957; children—Laurance Starr, III, Mary Ruth. Mgr. applied products Marley Co., Kansas City, Mo., 1957-69; dir. customer service Tempmaster Corp., Kansas City, 1969-71; sales rep. Kansas City Equipment Co., Kansas City, 1971; sales mgr. Havens Cooling Towers div. Havens Steel Co., Kansas City, 1971-73; with L.S. Staples Co., Kansas City, 1974—, pres., 1974—; cons. Butler Mfg. Co., Kansas City, 1971. Supervisor walk chmn. safety and communications March of Dimes, Kansas City, Mo., 1972—, mem. gen. bd., 1977, 79; bd. dirs. Heart of Am. Radio Club, Kansas City, 1978-80; Master of servers St. Paul's Episcopal Ch., Kansas City, 1959-65, vestryman, 1967-73, treas., 1975—; stewardship officer Episc. Diocese W. Mo., 1980—. Served with U.S. Army, 1953-55. Mem. ASHRAE (chpt. pres. 1980—), Am. Inst. Plant Engrs., Am. Soc. Plumbing Engrs., Am. Soc. Mech. Engrs., Kansas City Engrs. Club, Refrigeration Engring. and Tech. Assn., Tau Kappa Epsilon. Episcopalian. Clubs: Heart of America Radio; Kansas City Association for Blind Amateur Radio; MoKan Repeater; Kansas City (pres. 1961-62, corp. agt., trustee). Home: 425 W 49th Terr Kansas City MO 64112 Office: 4643 Wyandotte St Kansas City MO 64112

STAPLES, NORMAN APPLETON, banker; b. St. Croix, V.I., Dec. 12, 1919; s. Appleton H. and Johanne (Svitzer) S.; B.S., U. N.C., 1946; student Am. Inst. Fgn. Trade, Phoenix, 1947; m. Dec. 18, 1944 (div. 1975); 2 sons, 3 daus. With Merrill Lynch, Pierce, Fenner & Smith, Stamford, Conn., 1948-50; with Chem. Bank N.Y. Trust Co. (name changed to Chem. Bank), N.Y.C., 1951—, v.p., 1965—. Served as pilot USNR, 1942-45. Mem. St. Anthony Hall, Naval Aviation Commandery. Clubs: Univ. (N.Y.C.); Turf and Field, Pilgrims (N.Y.); Bath, Royal Automobile (London). Office: Chem Bank Secretariat Bldg UN New York NY 10017

STAPLETON, CRAIG ROBERTS, real estate exec.; b. Kansas City, Mo., Apr. 17, 1945; s. Benjamin Franklin and Katharine Hall S.; A.B. magna cum laude, Harvard U., 1967, M.B.A., 1970; m. Dorothy Walker, Oct. 16, 1971; children—Walker R., Wendy W. Asst. to chmn. Nat. Corp. for Housing Partnerships, Washington, 1970-72; pvt. cons. to Ford Found., HUD, Dept. Treasury, Nat. Commn. Productivity, Washington, 1972-76; pres. IDR Mgmt., Inc., Mpls., 1976-80; pres., trustee IDS Realty Trust, Mpls., 1978-80; pres., dir. Boothe Fin. Corp., San Francisco, 1980—; dir. Devel. Services, Inc., Washington, Oliver Realty, Inc., Pitts., Marsh & McLennan Real Estate Advisors, Inc.; Mem. HUD task force on housing mgmt., 1971, task force to improve fed. programs, 1973; chmn. com. to nominate overseers and dirs. of Harvard U., 1978. Served with USAR, 1967-70. Mem. Young Pres.'s Orgn., Urban Land Inst. Democrat. Clubs: Links (N.Y.C.); Field (Greenwich, Conn.). Home: 12 Park Ave Greenwich CT 06830 Office: 7 Lincoln Ave Greenwich CT 06830

STAPLETON, ROBERT J., devel. co. exec.; b. Ft. Wayne, Ind., Jan. 9, 1922; s. Clarence Albert and Eva Elizabeth (Grashoff) S.; A.B., Valparaiso U., 1946; M.S., U. Wis., 1947; postgrad. U. Mich., 1943, Columbia U., 1943; m. Marilyn Jeane Stinchfield, Sept. 7, 1946; children—Jan Elizabeth, Jill Leigh, Robert Guy. Indsl. devel. rep. Commonwealth Edison Co., Chgo., 1947-55; mng. dir., sec. Clinton Devel. Co. (Iowa), 1955-63; mgr. Cordova (Ill.) Indsl. Park, No. Natural Gas Co., 1963-69; exec. dir. Elgin (Ill.) Econ. Devel. Com., 1969-71; exec. dir. Jobs div. IVAC, LaSalle, Ill., 1971-77; pres. Scioto Econ. Devel. Corp., Portsmouth, Ohio, 1977—; pvt. practice as indsl. devel. cons., Clinton, 1955—. Served to lt. (j.g.) USNR, 1942-46; capt. Res. Mem. Ill. Devel. Council (past pres.), Ret., Res. officers assns., Naval Res. Assn., Urban Land Inst., Nat. Assn. Corp. Real Estate Execs., Council Urban Econ. Devel., Indsl. Devel. Research Council, Am. Soc. Planning Ofcls., Am., Gt. Lakes Area indsl. devel. councils, Portsmouth C. of C., Valparaiso U. Lettermen's Assn. Republican. Lutheran. Clubs: Rotary; Clinton Country (past pres., dir.); Elk's Country. Home: 3219 Old Post Rd Portsmouth OH 45662 Office: 6th and Court Sts Portsmouth OH 45662

STAPP, CHRISTOPHER DENNISON, mfg. co. exec.; b. Orange, Calif., Dec. 12, 1943; s. Olin Herman and Opal Ann (Nicholson) S.; B.S. in Bus. Adminstrn., Woodbury U., 1970; m. Shirley Ann; children—Christopher Joel, Kevin Dennison. Co. credit mgr. Air-Vent Aluminum Awning Co., Chino, Calif., 1962-64, br. mgr., 1964-66, v.p., sec., 1968-74, co-chmn. bd. dirs., 1975—, pres., chmn. bd. dirs., 1975-76; pres., chmn. bd. dirs. Licon Engring., Hayward; exec. sales dir. West Coast Wire Rope, Oakland, Calif., 1978—. Served with AUS, 1966-68. Mem. Am. Mktg. Assn., Woodbury U. Alumni Assn., Western Awning Assn. (sec.-treas. No. Calif. chpt. 1972-74, v.p. 1975-76), Nat. Awning Assn. (dir., v.p. 1977-78, pres. 1978—), Phi Gamma Kappa. Club: Jonathan (Los Angeles). Home: 3381 Pine Wood Ct Hayward CA 94542 Office: 1500 W Winton Ave Hayward CA 94545 also 13247 5th St Chino CA 91710 also 597 85th Ave Oakland CA 94621

STARK, BETTY WALKER, mktg. exec.; b. Manitowoc, Wis., Sept. 18, 1940; d. Woodrow Nelson and Mary Ann (Sieracki) Walker; B.A., U. Wis., 1962, M.S.W., 1971; m. Richard Paul Stark, Apr. 20, 1974. Social worker, pub. info. officer Dane County (Wis.) Social Services, Madison, 1962-72; sales asso. and mgr., cons. Stark Co., Madison, 1972-75; account exec., media dir., v.p. operations Stephan & Brady Advt., Madison, 1975-78; pres. B.W. Stark Consulting, Madison, 1978—; prin. Sahr Seminars Inc., 1978—; v.p. Condominium Ventures, Inc., Madison, 1980—. Bd. dirs. Wis. Arthritis Found.; bd. dirs. Jonah House, Madison, 1974—. Licensed salesperson, Wis. Real Estate Bd. Mem. Meeting Planners Internat., Nat. Assn. Female Execs., Nat. Assn. Social Workers, Wis. Pub. Welfare Assn., Madison Advt. Fedn. (chairperson 1978 Addys awards). Home: 12 Blue Spruce Trail Madison WI 53717 Office: 122 N Hamilton St Madison WI 53703

STARK, EVERETT WALLACE, ins. brokerage co. exec.; b. Vallejo, Calif., June 27, 1906; s. John and Isabella (Young) S.; B.S. in Structural Engring., U. Pacific, 1929; postgrad. Golden Gate Law Coll., 1932-34, Golden Gate Ins. Coll., 1934-36; m. Ann Agnes Turner, Feb. 15, 1931; children—Jeanne (Mrs. Roger Lee Redig), James Everett. With Gt. Am. Ins. Co., San Francisco, 1929-41, regional mgr., 1937-41; partner Carmichael-Stark and Co., 1941-43; propr. Everett W. Stark and Co., San Francisco, 1943-61; pres. Everett W. Stark and Co., Inc., San Francisco, 1961-77, chmn., treas., 1977—; pres. Gilroy Investment Co., 1965—. Mem. founders com. Agr. Bus. Coll., U. Pacific, 1961, mem. fund raising com. Bd. dirs. Tri-cities YMCA. Mem. Nat. Assn. Ins. Brokers, Nat. Soc. Surety Bond Producers, Soc. Ins. Brokers, Asso. Gen. Contractors, Am. Ordnance Assn., Mechanics and Mchts. Inst., Soc. Ins. Brokers Calif. (v.p. 1948-49, exec. com. 1976-77, gov. 1976-77), San Francisco Ins. Forum, Calif. San Francisco chambers commerce, U. Pacific Alumni Assn. (pres. 1934-35), Lick-Wilmerding Alumni Assn. (dir. 1978—), Delta Upsilon. Republican. United Methodist (trustee, finance com., ofcl. bd.). Elk. Clubs: San Francisco Commercial, Commonwealth of Calif. (San Francisco); Progressors (pres.) (Burlingame, Calif.). Home: 1436 Vancouver Ave Burlingame CA 94010 Office: 333 Market St Suite 800 San Francisco CA 94105

STARK, FRANKLIN CULVER, lawyer; b. Unityville, S.D., Apr. 16, 1915; s. Fred H. and Catherine (Culver) S.; J.D., Northwestern U., 1940; A.B., Dakota Wesleyan U., 1937, LL.D., 1939; m. Alice C. Churchill, Sept. 16, 1941 (dec. May 1975); children—Margaret C., Wallace C., Judith C., Franklin C.; m. 2d, Carlyn Kaiser Saxton, July 18, 1976. Admitted to Ill. bar, 1940, Calif. bar, 1946; asso. Sidley, McPherson, Austin & Burgess, Chgo., 1940-41, Fitzgerald, Abbott & Beardsley, Oakland, Calif., 1946-47; sr. mem. firm Stark & Champlin (now Stark, Stewart & Simon), Oakland, 1947—; lectr. comml. law U. Calif. Sch. Bus., 1946-66; staff Office Gen. Counsel, OPA, Washington, 1941-42. Bd. dirs. Sch. Theology at Claremont, Peralta Hosp. Found., Dakota Wesleyan U., Fred Finch Youth Center, Calif.-Nev. United Meth. Found., 1974-80, Oakland Meth. Found.; chmn. bd. trustees Calif.-Nev. Meth. Homes, 1966-73; pres. Oakland Council of Chs., 1954-56; nat. vice-chmn. Campaign for UN Reform. Served with USNR, 1942-45; now comdr. Res. ret. Mem. Am., Calif., Alameda County bar assns., Am. Trial Lawyers Assn., Oakland C. of C., Am. Legion, World Peace Through Law Center (charter), Order of Coif, Phi Kappa Phi, Pi Kappa Delta, Phi Alpha Delta, Methodist. Clubs: Masons, Shriners, Elks; Athenian Nile; Commonwealth (San Francisco). Editor Ill. Law Rev., 1939-40; contbr. articles to legal publs. Home: 333 Wayne Ave Oakland CA 94606 Office: Financial Center Bldg Oakland CA 94612

STARK, JEFFREY MICHAEL, consumer products co. exec.; b. N.Y.C., Jan. 3, 1943; s. Nathan and Ruth (Derman) S.; A.B. in Econs., Lafayette Coll., 1963; M. in Indsl. and Labor Relations, Cornell U., 1965; m. Patricia Joan Birnbaum, June 21, 1964; children—David Alan, Robert Jay, Rachel Lynne. Profl. placement specialist Am.-Standard, Inc., N.Y.C., 1965-67, personnel supr. church products dept., Monson, Mass., 1967-68; tng. supr. Continental Can. Co. Inc., Pitts., 1968-70, indsl. relations staff rep. Eastern Metal div., N.Y.C., 1970-71; Eastern region employee relations mgr. Metal div. N.L. Industries, Inc., Perth Amboy, N.J., 1971-73, mgr. mgmt. devel. MBJ group, N.Y.C., 1973-74, dir. employee relations indsl. chems. div. NL Industries, Inc., Hightstown, N.J., 1974-79; dir. employee relations Consumer Products div. SCM Corp., N.Y.C., 1979—; ind. cons. on orgn., employee relations. Served as sgt. USAR, 1967-73. Named Jaycee of the Quarter, 1972. Mem. Am. Soc. Personnel Adminstrn., Lafayette Coll., Cornell Indsl. Labor Relations alumni assns., Smithsonian Instn. (asso.), Friends of East Brunswick Library, Franklin Twp. Jaycees (dir. 1973), Alpha Chi Rho. Jewish. Author: (with R. Duino) Annotated Bibliography, Selected Readings on Shift Systems, 1964. Home: 6 Plymouth Ln East Brunswick NJ 08816 Office: 299 Park Ave New York NY 10171

STARK, MARTIN JOEL, performing artists mgmt. co. exec.; b. N.Y.C., May 29, 1941; s. Nathan and Lola (Belmont) S.; B.A., Calif. State U., 1966; postgrad. San Fernando Valley Coll. Law, 1966-69; m. Shigemi E. Matsumoto. Systems analyst Industrial Electronic Engrs., Van Nuys, Calif., 1969-71; sales mgr., 1971-73; sales rep. Columbia Artists Mgmt., Inc., N.Y.C., 1973-78, sales mgr., 1978-79, v.p. bus. affairs, mgr. data processing, 1979—; cons. in field. Mem. Am. Symphony Orch. League, Assn. Coll., Univ. and Community Arts Adminstrs., Internat. Soc. Performing Arts Adminstrs., Delta Upsilon. Presbyterian. Home: 60 Riverside Dr Apt 1D New York NY 10024 Office: 165 W 57th St New York NY 10019

STARK, ROBERT JAMES, JR., packing co. exec.; b. N.Y.C., Apr. 11, 1920; s. Robert James and Lucia (Rhyne) S.; B.A., Amherst Coll., 1941; m. Martha K. Lamb, Aug. 5, 1944 (dec. Mar. 1976); children—Martha Louise Stark Clifford, Lucia Burnham Stark Scott, Polly Robertson Stark Manning, Robert Bruce; m. 2d, Stella X. Gilbert, Feb. 5, 1977. Salesman, Graybar Electric Co., N.Y.C., 1941, 45-50; with Crane Packing Co., Morton Grove, Ill., 1952—, asst. sales mgr. seal div., 1952-57, asst. to pres., 1954-57, sales mgr. seal div., 1957-63, asst. v.p. seal sales, 1963-65, v.p. mktg., 1965—, dir., 1968—; v.p. Crane Packing Ltd., Hamilton, Ont., Can., 1956—, also dir.; dir. John Crane Caribe. Active Northbrook (Ill.) United Fund, 1955-60, pres., 1959; mem. Dist. 28 Sch. Bd. Northbrook, 1961-68. Served to lt. USNR, 1941-45; lt. comdr., 1950-52; PTO. Mem. Am. Mgmt. Assn., Research Inst. Am., Ill. C. of C., No. Ill. Indsl. Assn. (pres. 1973), Phi Kappa Psi. Republican. Episcopalian. Clubs: Sunset Ridge Country (Northfield, Ill.), Marshwood at the Landings (Savannah, Ga.). Home: 1854 Somerset Ln Northbrook IL 60062 Office: 6400 W Oakton St Morton Grove IL 60053

STARK, WALTER FRANK, ins. agt.; b. Bklyn., Mar. 26, 1935; s. Frank and Sylvia (Stark) Finberg; B.A., Union Coll., Schenectady, 1955; diploma Ins. Inst., Wakefield, Mass., 1960; m. Jane Goldberg, Sept. 24, 1959; children—Jodi Lynne, Lisa Ellen. Sr. accounts adv. Am. Mut. Liability Ins. Co., 1960-61; v.p. Martin M. Goldberg Co. Inc., N.Y.C., 1961-67, Walter Kaye Assos. Inc., N.Y.C., 1967-71; pres. Stark Ins. Services, also Stark Cons. Group, New City, N.Y., 1971—; cons. in field. Chmn. com. sr. citizen housing Rockland County (N.Y.) Urban Devel. Council 1975. Served with AUS, 1957. Mem. Ind. Ins. Agts., Profl. Ins. Agts. Jewish. Clubs: Su-Mah Camera, Dellwood Country, Masons. Home: 61 Westview Rd Spring Valley NY 10977 Office: 61 S Main St New City NY 10956

STAUB, E. NORMAN, banker; b. Newark, Mar. 13, 1916; s. Walter Adolph and Ida (Flury) S.: A.B., Princeton U., 1937; M.B.A., Harvard U., 1939; m. Mary Ann Dilley, Dec. 28, 1940; children—Susan D. Staub Leofanti, Sandra Staub Bradbury, Stephen R. Jr. acct. Lybrand Ross Bros. & Montgomery, Boston, 1939-41; treas. Nat. Research Co., Cambridge, Mass., 1941-53; with No. Trust Co., Chgo., 1953—, pres., from 1972, chmn., chief exec. officer, 1978—, also No. Trust Corp.; dir. U.S. Gypsum Co. Bd. dirs. Chgo. Central Area Com., Chgo. Council Fgn. Relations; trustee Rush-Presbyn.-St. Luke's Med. Center, Orchestral Assn. Chgo. Symphony Orch., Northwestern U., Better Govt. assn., Mus. Sci. and Industry, also chmn. fin. com.; treas. Chapin Hall, Comml. Club Chgo. Mem. Am. Inst. Banking, Assn. Res. City Bankers (chmn. Chgo. clearing house com.). Republican. Clubs: Econs., Chgo., Old Elm, Indian Hill. Office: 50 S LaSalle St Chicago IL 60675

STAUBER, ERWIN ANTHONY, fin. exec.; b. Milw., Jan. 30, 1924; s. Anthony Peter and Irene Marie (Doettlinger) S.; student Parochial schs., Milw.; m. Apr. 15, 1950. With Old Line Life Ins. Co. Am., Milw., 1942—, asst. treas., 1965—; condr. class Milw. Postal Customer Council, 1974-80, pres., 1977-80. Served with USCGR, 1944-46. Mem. Graphics Mgmt. Assn. Milw. (program chmn. 1980-81). Roman Catholic. Clubs: Milw. Serra, K.C., St. Vincent De Paul Soc. Home: 2943 S 51st St Milwaukee WI 53219 Office: 707 N 11th St PO Box 401 Milwaukee WI 53201

STAUBLIN, JUDITH ANN, computer co. exec.; b. Anderson, Ind., Jan. 17, 1936; d. Leslie Fred and Esta Virginia (Ringo) Wiley; student Ball State U., 1954-55, 69-70, Savs. and Loan Inst., 1962-67, U. Ga., 1974, Wright State U., 1975; children—Juli Jackson, Scott Jackson. Teller, Anderson Fed. Savs. and Loan Assn., Anderson, 1962-64, data processing mgr., 1965-70, loan officer, 1970-72, v.p. systems, 1972-74, fin. systems mktg., 1974-76; fin. dist. mgr. data centers div. NCR Corp., Atlanta, 1977—. Active United Way. Mem. Am. Savs. and Loan Inst., Fin. Mgrs. Soc., Ga. Exec. Women's Network, Am. Soc. Profl. and Exec. Women, Anderson C. of C. Home: 3640 Peachtree Corners West No 1303 Norcross GA 30092 Office: 130 Technology Park Norcross GA 30092

STAUFFACHER, CHARLES B., fin. cons.; b. Karuizawa, Japan, July 13, 1916; s. Albert Daniel and Anna Dorothy (Marty) S.; brought to U.S., 1916; A.B., Pomona Coll., 1937; student Lignan U., Canton, China, 1935-36; A.M., Am. U., 1938; A.M., Harvard, 1940; m. Lillian Frances Moss, Dec. 27, 1941; children—Charles D., Lillian S. Gillies. Research asst. Brookings Instn., 1940-41; with Bur. of Budget, Washington, 1941-52, exec. asst. dir. of bur., 1950-52, on leave as asst. to Dir. Def. Mblzn., 1951-52; lectr. George Washington U., 1949-52; control officer Continental Can Co., 1952-54, v.p. fin., 1954-58, exec. v.p. fin. and adminstrn., 1958; exec. v.p. paper products ops. group, 1959-65, exec. v.p. fin. and adminstrn., 1966-68, sr. exec. v.p., 1969-71, vice chmn., chief adminstrv. and fin. officer, 1971-74, dir., 1960-74; pres., chief exec. officer Field Enterprises, Inc., Chgo., 1974-80; fin. cons. Universe Tankships, N.Y.C., 1980—; dir. FMC Corp., Kemper Co., Lumbermens Mut. Ins. Co., Am. Mfrs. Mut. Ins.

Co., Charter N.Y. Corp., U.S. Gypsum, Trustee Pomona Coll., Com. Econ. Devel. Served as lt. USNR, 1943-46. Mem. Am. Mgmt. Assn., Nat. Acad. Pub. Adminstrn., Council on Fgn. Relations, Phi Beta Kappa. Clubs: Greenwich (Conn.) Country; Chicago; Augusta Nat. Golf; Jupiter Hills Golf; Lost Tree Country; Econ. (N.Y.); Old Elm. Home: 54 N Stanwich Rd Greenwich CT 06830 Office: Burlington Bldg Ave of Americas and 54th St New York NY also 12049 Lost Tree Way Lost Tree Village North Palm Beach FL 33408

STAUNTON, MARSHALL ALFRED, lawyer; b. Milw., Dec. 17, 1928; s. Frederic James and Mildred (Marshall) S.; A.B., Brown U., 1951; J.D., Stanford, 1957; children by previous marriage—Susan M., Julia S.; m. 2d, Ruby Bonn Scudder; children—Melissa A., Jocelyn. Admitted to Calif. bar, 1957, U.S. Ct. Claims; law clk. to asso. justice Calif. Supreme Ct., 1957-59; asso. firm Johnson & Stanton, San Francisco, 1959-74; with Bechtel-Trans Alaska Pipeline Project, 1974-75; counsel for Europe-Africa, Bechtel Internat. Ltd., London, Eng., 1975-78; counsel Bechtel Corp., San Francisco, 1978-79; counsel Bechtel Power Corp., 1979, spl. counsel, 1980-81, counsel litigation, 1981—; spl. counsel San Francisco Inst. for Criminal Justice. Guardsman chmn. Boys Welfare Com., 1965-66. Pres. Menlo Atherton chpt. Calif. Young Republicans, 1965-67, gen. counsel, 1967-68. Served to capt. USMCR, 1951-54. Mem. Am. (pub. contract law sect.), San Francisco (chmn. juvenile ct. com. 1970—) bar assns., State Bar Calif., Legal Aid Soc., Psi Upsilon. Episcopalian (mem. parish sch. bd. 1964-70, vestryman 1965-68, sr. warden 1967, pres. San Mateo deanery 1969-71). Clubs: Family, French, Commonwealth of Calif., Brown U. Home: 1890 Vallejo San Francisco CA 94123 Office: 50 Beale St San Francisco CA 94105

STAVRAKAS, DEAN, textile service co. exec.; b. Chgo., Dec. 6, 1943; s. Sam Gus and Helene (Lazaris) S.; B.A., MacMurray Coll., 1964; grad. Supervisory Devel. Inst., Purdue U., 1976; m. Joanne Stavrakas, Jan. 11, 1970; 1 son, Symeon Dean. With Cosmopolitan Textile Rental Service, Inc., Chgo., 1964—, v.p., gen. mgr., 1970—, mgr. semi-profl. baseball, Chgo. Mem. Ill. Commn. for Bus. and Econ. Devel., 1976-77. Mem. Am. Mgmt. Assn., Textile Rental Services Assn. Am., Textile Maintenance Inst. (dir.), Chgo. Conv. and Tourism Bur., Am. Hellenic Ednl. Progressive Assn. (past dist. govt.), Order of Ahepa (officer). Greek Orthodox. Club: Union League (Chgo). Home: 2961 W Gregory St Chicago IL 60625 Office: Cosmopolitan Textile Rental Service Inc 5730 S Halsted St Chicago IL 60621

STAVROLAKIS, JAMES ALEXANDER, san. products co. exec.; b. Storrs, Utah, Oct. 1, 1921; s. Alexander and Crystal (Haniotis) S.; B.S., Rutgers U., 1943; Sc.D., M.I.T., 1949; postgrad. Columbia U., 1963; m. Rachel Gallup, Feb. 24, 1951; children—Kristalia, Alexander, Marianthe, Stacy Ann, Andrew. Engr., Gen. Electric Co., Oak Ridge, 1949-52; supr. Armour Research Found., Chgo., 1952-55; asst. mgr. Mallinckrodt Chem. Works, St. Louis, 1955-56; devel. mgr. Crucible Steel Co. Am., Pitts., 1956-61; v.p. Am. Standard, Inc., Louisville, 1961-67, gen. mgr., 1967-70; pres. Glasrock Products, Inc., Atlanta, 1970-73, StanBest, Inc., Atlanta, 1974-78; gen. mgr. Gerber San. Products Co., Chgo., 1978—. Served with USAAF, 1942-46. Clubs: N.Y. Engrs.; Big Spring Country (Louisville); Cherokee Town and Country (Atlanta). Home: 2879 Rivermeade Dr Atlanta GA 30327 Office: Gerber San Products Co 4656 W Touhy St Chicago IL 60646

STAVROPOULOS, D(IONYSOS) JOHN, banker; b. Vicksburg, Miss., Jan. 19, 1933; s. John D. and Olga J. (Balodemos) S.; student Millsaps Coll., 1949-50; B.S. cum laude, Miss. State U., 1955; M.B.A., Northwestern U., 1956; m. Alexandra Gatzoyanni, Jan. 10, 1976; children—John, Theodore, Mark, Olga, Katerina. Vice-pres. trust investments First Nat. Bank of Chgo., 1956-69; dir. investment research Bache & Co., N.Y.C., 1969-70; gen. mgr. Athens (Greece) br. First Nat. Bank of Chgo., 1970-73, mgr. marine fin. group, London, 1973-74, sr. v.p., also area head Latin Am., São Paulo, Brazil, 1975-76, head real estate dept., 1976-78, exec. v.p., head comml. banking dept., 1979-80, chmn. credit policy com., 1981—; dir. Central Ill. Public Service Co., 1979—; instr. fin. dept., evening div. Northwestern U., 1962-68. Served with U.S. Army, 1951-53. Chartered fin. analyst. Mem. Investment Analysts Soc. Chgo., Assn. Res. City Bankers, Mortgage Bankers Assn., Chgo. Com., Real Estate Adv. Council. Democrat. Greek Orthodox. Office: First Nat Bank of Chgo 1 First Nat Plaza Chicago IL 60670

STEAD, JAMES JOSEPH, JR., investment banker; b. Chgo., Sept. 13, 1930; s. James Joseph and Irene (Jennings) S.; B.S., DePaul U., 1955, M.B.A., 1957; m. Edith Pearson, Feb. 13, 1954; children—James, Diane, Robert, Caroline. Asst. sec. C. F. Childs & Co., Chgo., 1955-62; exec. v.p., sec. Koenig, Keating & Stead, Inc., Chgo., 1962-66; 2d v.p. Hayden, Stone Inc., Chgo., 1966-69; sr. v.p., nat. sales mgr. Ill. Co., Inc., Chgo., 1969-70; instnl. sales mgr. Reynolds Securities, Inc., 1970-72, v.p., regional instnl. sales mgr., 1976—; resident partner Edwards & Hanly, 1972-74; v.p., instl. sales mgr. Paine, Webber, Jackson's Cuotis, Chgo., 1974-76; v.p., regional sales mgr. Oppenheimer & Co., Inc., Chgo., 1978—; instr. Municipal Bond Sch., Chgo., 1967—. Served with AUS, 1951-53. Mem. Am. Mgmt. Assn., Municipal Finance Forum Washington, Nat. Securities Traders Assn. Clubs: Wall Street (N.Y.C.); Union League, Bond, Municipal Bond, Executives (Chgo.); Olympia Fields (Ill.) Country. Home: 20721 Brookwood Dr Olympia Fields IL 60461 Office: 208 S La Salle St Chicago IL 60604

STEARN, DANIEL RICHARD, assn. exec.; b. Pitts., Apr. 9, 1923; s. Joseph Anthony and Mary Katherine S.; B.A. in Journalism, Duquesne U., Pitts., 1950; m. Margaret Theresa Wagner, Aug. 5, 1950; children—Mary Margaret, Susan Marie. Staff corr. UPI, Pitts., 1950-56; mem. pub. relations staff Crucible Steel Co., Pitts., 1957-58; pub. relations account exec. Lando Inc., Pitts., 1958-61; mgr. pub. relations Instrument Soc. Am., Pitts., 1961-71; mgr. mktg. services Air Pollution Control Assn., Pitts., 1972—; sr. scientist Carnegie-Mellon Inst. Research, 1972—; cons. in field, 1966—. Served with USAAF, 1942-45. Mem. Am. Soc. Assn. Execs., Council Engring. and Sci. Soc. Execs., Nat. Assn. Expn. Mgrs. Democrat. Roman Catholic. Home: 219 Haugh Dr Pittsburgh PA 15237 Office: PO Box 2861 Pittsburgh PA 15230

STEARNS, MILTON SPRAGUE, JR., financial cons. co. exec.; b. N.Y.C., June 3, 1923; s. Milton Sprague and Katherine (Stieglitz) S.; B.S. cum laude, Harvard U., 1946, M.B.A., 1948; m. Virginia McCormick; children—Virginia Stearns King, John Brackett, Barbara Ellison, Kathryn Stearns Sergio, Elizabeth Sprague (dec.). With Fidelity Bank, Phila., 1948-72, group v.p. in charge nat. lending div., 1960-72; pres. Charter Fin. Co., Phila., 1972—; chmn. bd. Judson Infrared, Inc.; dir. Nat. Valve & Mfg. Co., Pitts., West Co., Phoenixville, Pa.; mem. Pa. adv. bd. Am. Mut. Liability Ins. Co. Served with USNR, World War II; lt. (j.g.) Res. ret. Mem. Robert Morris Assos. (pres. Phila. chpt. 1961-62). Clubs: Spee, Merion Golf, Waynesborough Country, Seaview Country, Phila. Skating and Humane Soc., Racquet, Union League (Phila.); Board Room (N.Y.C.); Delray Beach, Delray Beach Yacht, Delray Dunes Golf and Country; Pine Tree Golf. Home: 43 Righters Mill Rd Gladwyne PA 19035 Office: Suite 2700 1700 Market St Philadelphia PA 19103

STEBBINS, RODNEY JEROME, epoxy mfg. co. exec.; b. Klamath Falls, Oreg., July 2, 1936; s. Lester Seral and Volna Grace S.; B.S. in Constrn. Mgmt. and Engring., S.D. Sch. Mines and Tech., 1975; m. Kyong Suk Kim, Nov. 25, 1978; 1 son, Rodney Jerome. Contract adminstr. Premier Waterproofing Co., Denver, 1973-75; project mgr. Harrison Western Corp., Denver, 1975; program mgr. Foster-Miller & Assos., Waltham, Mass., 1978; v.p. adminstrn. Grain Spouting & Elevators of Kans., Inc., Hutchingson, 1979; v.p. Splty. Applications Corp., Reston, Va., 1980-81, Thermal-Chem, Inc., Elk Grove Village, Ill., 1981—; research coms. Urban and Mass Transp. Authority, Washington, 1977-78; cons., speaker, lectr., author in field. Served with USMC, 1953-56; Korea. Named to Hon. Order Ky. Cols., 1978. Mem. Am. Concrete Inst. (coms.), Transp. Research Bd. (coms.). Republican. Club: Rotary. Home: 1596 Manchester Rd Hoffman Estates IL 60195 Office: 1400 Louis Ave Elk Grove Village IL 60007

STEBBINS, WILLIAM MORROW, ins. broker; b. Portland, Oreg., June 30, 1925; s. Liston Ash and Myra M. (Morrow) S.; student Linfield Coll., 1946-47, U. Oreg., 1947-48; B.S., Lewis and Clark Coll., 1949; m. Gloria Mae Russell, June 13, 1947; children—Janice Maureen (Mrs. D. Paul Zundel), Ronald William, Wendy Louise. Broker, rep. Northwestern Nat. Life Ins. Co., Portland, 1947—; pres. Bus. Ins. Service Corp., 1964—; part time faculty Portland State U., 1971—; fin. cons. for bus. and industry. Coach, Little League Baseball, 1964-66. Alumni dir. Lewis and Clark Coll. Fund Raising, 1961-62. Served with USNR, 1943-46, 50-52. Decorated Bronze Star medal with two oak leaf clusters; named Life Ins. Agt. of Year State of Oreg., 1965. Mem. Nat., Portland (past pres.) assns. life underwriters, Am. Soc. C.L.U.'s (chmn. continuing edn. Portland chpt. 1980), Am. Coll. Life Underwriters (past dir.), Million Dollar Round Table (life). Mem. Ch. of Jesus Christ of Latter-day Saints. Clubs: Portland Agenda (past pres.), Masons, Lions (1st v.p.). Contbr. articles to profl. jours. Home: 13273 SW Bull Mountain Rd Tigard OR 97223 Office: Boise Cascade Bldg Portland OR 97201

STEDMAN, ERVIN FRANK, info. processing cons. co. exec.; b. St. Louis, July 27, 1937; s. E. Frank and Lydia Ella (Vogt) S.; A.A., Harris Tchrs. Coll., 1958; B.S., U. Mo., 1972; m. Patricia Sue Williams, Aug. 23, 1958; children—Beth, David, Daniel, Dean. With Maritz Motivation Co. div. Maritz Inc., Fenton, Mo., 1963-80, asst. mgr., 1965-66, mgr., 1967-69, dir., 1969-72, v.p. adminstrn., 1972-75, v.p. ops., 1975-78, corp. v.p., 1978-80; pres. Erv Stedman & Assos., info. processing cons., Chesterfield, Mo., 1980—; dir. Glenn Meadows Ltd. Served with U.S. Army, 1960-63. Mem. Adminstrv. Mgmt. Soc. (dir. systems), Internat. Word Processing Assn. (pres. St. Louis chpt. 1977, internat. dir. 1976, 77, internat. pres. 1978), U. Mo. St. Louis Alumni Assn., Creve Coeur Khoury League. Office: 15438 Harrisburg Ct Chesterfield MO 63017

STEED, HAROLD COOK, bank exec.; b. Clearfield, Utah, June 5, 1920; s. Walter W. and Elma (Cook) S.; B.S., Utah State U., 1942; student Harvard U., 1943; m. Grace Minson, July 19, 1943; children—Pamela, Deborah, John H., Sally. Asst. cashier Clearfield State Bank, 1952-65, cashier, 1965-69, pres., 1969—. Mem. City Council, 1958-63; trustee Davis Meml. Med. Center, 1976—; mem. instl. council Weber State Coll., 1969-77, 79—. Served to capt. U.S. Army, 1942-46; ret. lt. col. USAR, 1963. Recipient Bus. Man of Yr. award Clearfield C. of C., 1979. Mem. Clearfield C. of C. (pres. 1967). Club: Kiwanis. Office: PO Box 308 Clearfield UT 84015

STEED, PINCKNEY FRANKLIN, JR., accountant; b. San Antonio, July 21, 1935; s. Frank and Yeola (Stitt) S.; student Baylor U., 1953-55; B.B.A., U. Tex., 1958; m. Sabra Anne Stratton, Dec. 5, 1964; children—Scott, Mark. Staff acct. Carneiro Chumney & Co., San Antonio, 1959-62; staff acct. T.W. Mohle & Co., Houston, 1963-64, Harris Kerr Forster & Co., Houston, 1964-65; partner Stone & Steed, Houston, 1965-79, owner, 1979—. Treas., Nottingforest Civic Club, 1967, pres., 1968; sec. Turkey Creek Mcpl. Utility Dist., 1968, pres., 1969-70; treas. Nottingham Forest Elem. PTA, 1973, pres., 1976; treas. Harris County Republican Party, 1979-81. Served to 2d lt. U.S. Army, 1959, capt. USAR, 1963-65. C.P.A., Tex. Mem. Tex. Soc. C.P.A.'s, Am. Inst. C.P.A.'s, Beta Theta Pi. Republican. Methodist. Clubs: Toastmasters, Republican Victory (treas. 1968), Meml. Exchange (treas. 1972). Office: 11777 Katy Freeway #240 Houston TX 77079

STEEG, GEORGE FREDERICK, electronics co. exec.; b. N.Y.C., Dec. 21, 1928; s. Frederick William and Frieda (Heuchel) S.; B.E.E., Rensselaer Poly. Inst., 1954, M.E.E. (Gen. Ry. Signal Co. fellow), 1955; M.B.A., George Washington U., 1975; m. Constance Rogers, Oct. 4, 1949. Sr. engr., heavy mil. electronics dept. Gen. Electric Co., Syracuse, N.Y., 1955-58; tech. dir. electronics countermeasures div. Sanders Asso. Inc., Nashua, N.H., 1958-68; cons. engr. Nat. Security Agy., Frankfort, Germany, 1968-71, office chief, Fort Meade, Md., 1971-72; dir. electronic intelligence programs Office of Asst. Sec. Def., Washington, 1972-73, dir. reconnaissance and surveillance, 1973-75, dir. intelligence mgmt., 1975-76; dir. radar div. AIL div. Cutler-Hammer, Inc., L.I., N.Y., 1976-79; v.p. plans and bus. devel. AIL div. Eaton Corp., Arlington, Va., 1979—. Served with USN, 1946-49. Registered profl. engr., Va., Md., N.H.; recipient Sec. Def. Meritorious Civilian Service medal, 1976. Mem. IEEE (sr.), Aerospace and Electronics Systems Soc., Nat. Soc. Profl. Engrs., Assn. U.S. Army, Assn. Old Crows, Sigma Xi, Tau Beta Pi, Eta Kappa Nu. Contbr. articles to profl. jours. Home: 412 Pitt Mews Alexandria VA 22314 Office: AIL Div of Eaton Corp 1725 Jefferson Davis Hwy Arlington VA 22202

STEELE, CHARLES GLEN, accountant; b. Faulkton, S.D., July 24, 1925; s. Clifford D. and Emily O. (Hanson) S.; B.B.A., Golden Gate U., San Francisco, 1951, M.B.A., 1962; m. Shirley June Ferguson, Nov. 9, 1947; children—Richard Alan (dec.), Deborah Ann Steele Most. With Deloitte Haskins & Sells, 1951—, partner, 1963—, partner charge Chgo. office, 1973-76, partner charge personnel and adminstrn., N.Y.C., 1976-78, mng. partner, 1978—; instr. evening program Golden Gate U., 1952-58. Served with USNR, 1943-48. Recipient Elijah Watts Sells Gold medal for highest grade in U.S. for C.P.A. exam., 1951. Mem. Am. Inst. C.P.A.'s, N.Y. State Soc. C.P.A.'s, Am. Accounting Assn., Newcomen Soc. Clubs: Greenwich Country, Princeton, Blind Brook, Links, Board Room. Office: 1114 Ave of Americas New York NY 10036

STEELE, ERNEST CLYDE, ins. co. exec.; b. Corbin, Ky., May 11, 1925; s. J. Fred and Leona (McFarland) S.; B.S. with honors, U. Ky., 1948, M.S., 1950; m. Cora Jones, June 17, 1944; children—Gerald R., David P. Asst. actuary Peninsular Life Ins. Co., Jacksonville, Fla., 1950-54; actuary Pioneer Life & Casualty Co., Gadsden, Ala., 1955; v.p., actuary Guaranty Savs. Life Ins. Co., Montgomery, Ala., 1956-57; exec. v.p., actuary Am. Investment Life Ins. Co., Nashville, 1958-59; pres., actuary Appalachian Nat. Life Ins. Co., Knoxville, 1959-67; sr. v.p., chief investment officer and ops. analyst Coastal States Life Ins. Co., 1968-71, exec. v.p., dir., 1971-74, pres., dir., 1974-79; pres., dir. Occidental Life Ins. Co. N.C., Raleigh, 1979—; dir. Occidental Fire & Casualty Co. Mem. exec. bd. Occoneechee council Boy Scouts Am.; bd. dirs. Ednl. Found., Inc.; mem. devel. council U. Ky. Served to 2d lt. AUS, 1943-45. Fellow Life Mgmt. Inst.; mem. Life Office Mgmt. Assn. (past chmn. bd.), U. Ky. Alumni Assn. (past dir.), Am. Acad. Actuaries, Pi Mu Epsilon. Republican. Baptist (deacon). Home: 3616 Alamance Dr Raleigh NC 27609 Office: 1001 Wade Ave Raleigh NC 27605

STEELE, GEORGE, agrl. co. exec.; b. Pocopson, Pa., Oct. 22, 1918; s. Hugh Exton and Katherine (Stevens) S.; student Pa. State U., 1936-37; m. R. Eleanor Brown, Oct. 18, 1941; children—George B., James R., Richard H. Pres. George Steele and Sons, Inc., dairy farm, 1969—; dir. Pa. Farm Bureau Coop. Assn., 1954-65, v.p., 1963-65; dir. Agway, Inc., Syracuse, N.Y., 1965—, vice chmn., 1970-71, chmn. bd., 1971—, also pres.; dir. Internat. Life, Buffalo, 1971-73, Farm Credit Banks, Balt. Dist., Md., 1963—, Farmers and World Affairs, Inc., 1961-71. Overseer Pa. Grange; trustee Am. Inst. Coop., 1967—. Mem. Sigma Phi Alpha. Mem. Soc. of Friends. Office: Box 4933 Syracuse NY 13221*

STEELE, GEORGE PEABODY, marine transp. exec.; b. San Francisco, July 27, 1924; s. James Mortimer and Erma (Garrett) S.; B.S., U.S. Naval Acad., 1944; m. Elizabeth Yates Fahrion, July 11, 1944; children—Jane Yates Steele Mitchell, James Fahrion. Commd. ensign USN, 1944, advanced through grades to vice adm., 1973; service aboard submarines in Pacific, World War II; comdr. U.S.S. Hardhead, 1955-56; comdr. nuclear powered U.S.S. Seadragon (made 1st NW passage under ice to North Pole), 1959-61; comdr. Polaris missile sub U.S.S. Daniel Boone, 1963-66; head politico-mil. policy div. Europe/NATO br. Office Chief Naval Ops., 1966-68; comdr. Naval Forces, Korea, chief Naval adv. group, Korean Navy, comdr. Naval Component UN Command, 1968-70; comdr. Anti-Submarine Warfare Group 4, 1970-72; dep. asst. chief of staff Supreme Allied Comdr., Europe, SHAPE, Belgium, 1972-73; comdr. U.S. 7th Fleet, 1973-75; ret., 1975; pres., chief exec. officer Interocean Mgmt. Corp., Phila., 1976—. Chmn. bd. dirs. Fgn. Policy Research Inst.; vice-chmn. adv. bd. Eastern Pa. dist. Salvation Army. Decorated D.S.M., Legion of Merit with 4 gold stars; Navy Cross (Peru), Order of Rising Sun (Japan); Cloud and Banner (Republic China); Order Nat. Security of Merit (Republic Korea). Mem. Am. Bur. Shipping, Soc. Naval Architects and Marine Engrs., U.S. Naval Inst. Episcopalian. Clubs: Univ., N.Y. Yacht, India House (N.Y.C.); Union League (Phila.); Army-Navy, Army-Navy Country (Washington). Author: Seadragon, Northwest Under the Ice, 1962; (with H. Gimpel) Nuclear Submarine Skippers and What They Do, 1962; Vengeance in the Depths, 1963. Contbr. articles to profl. publs. and newspapers. Home: 112 Pine St Philadelphia PA 19106 Office: Three Parkway Suite 1300 Philadelphia PA 19102

STEELE, HOWARD EVANS, ins. co. exec.; b. Evanston, Ill., Apr. 2, 1930; s. Clay E. and Hazel (Benedict) S.; B.A. in Polit. Sci. and Econs., DePauw U., 1952; m. Marilyn Smith, Aug. 9, 1952; children—Barbara L., Todd H. Regional group mgr. Lincoln Nat. Life Ins., Co., Ft. Wayne, Ind., 1952-64, dir. group field services, 1964-66, asst. v.p., 1966-67, 2d v.p., 1967-68, v.p., 1968-73, now dir.; sr. v.p. Lincoln Nat. Sales Corp., 1973-74, pres., 1974—; dir. Am. States Ins. Cos. Mem. Life Ins. Mktg. Research Assn. (chmn. bd.), Sigma Alpha Epsilon. Clubs: Fort Wayne Country; Union League (Chgo.). Home: 10510 Vermilyea Pass Fort Wayne IN 46804 Office: 1300 S Clinton St Fort Wayne IN 46801

STEELE, JAMES ARTHUR, stock broker; b. Nampa, Idaho, July 16, 1934; s. Arthur Alexander and Gladys Ione (Miller) S.; B.S., U. Idaho, 1956; m. Janet Kay Headley, Nov. 4, 1961; children—Lisa Ann, Jennifer Rene, James Arthur. Account exec. Merrill Lynch, Pierce, Fenner & Smith, Denver, 1960-67, asst. mgr., 1968-70, resident v.p., br. mgr., Palo Alto, Calif., 1970-77, regional v.p., br. mgr., Boise, Idaho, 1977—; faculty U. Denver, 1964-69, Foothill Coll., 1970-71. Chmn., Palo Alto 73, 1973—. Bd. dirs. United Fund, 1971-73, Univ. and Crescent Park Assn., 1973-75; bd. dirs. Denver YMCA, 1966-70, sec., 1970; trustee Palo Alto Unified Sch. Dist., 1975-77. Served to capt. USAF, 1956-59. Named Man of Year, Denver YMCA, 1969, Boss of Year, Palo Alto Jr. C. of C., 1973. Mem. Rocky Mountain Investment Bankers (edn. chmn. 1966), Palo Alto C. of C. (dir. 1971-75, pres. 1974-75). Clubs: Columbine Country (dir. 1967-69, pres. 1969); Foothill Tennis; Palo Alto; Arid; Crane Creek Country. Author: Merrill Lynch Investment Course, 1966. Home: 1701 Ridgecliff Ln Boise ID 83702 Office: One Capital Center 999 Main St Boise ID 83702

STEELE, OLIVER LEON, seed co. exec.; b. Ill., Apr. 8, 1915; s. Blondee Wood and Mary (Eagle) S.; student Ill. State Normal U., 1934-35; B.S., Ill. Wesleyan U., 1940, Sc.D., 1967; postgrad. U. Ill., 1945-48; m. Ruth Marie Holbert, June 21, 1941; children—David, Dennis, Nancy. Research asso. Michael-Leonard Seed Co., 1936-40; mgr. research dept. Funk Seeds Internat., Inc., 1940-52, asso. research dir., 1952-57, research dir., 1957-63, v.p. research div., 1963-78, research cons., 1979—. Mem. AAAS, Soc. Agronomy, Bot. Soc., Genetics Soc., Genetic Assn. Presbyterian (elder). Club: Rotary. Home: 804 Broadway St Normal IL 61761 Office: 1300 W Washington St Bloomington IL 61701

STEELE, RICHARD ALLEN, utilities co. exec.; b. Indpls., Jan. 8, 1927; s. Harry A. and Helen A. (Kaiser) S.; B.S. in Bus. Adminstrn. cum laude, Butler U., 1950; m. Jean Porteous, Mar. 14, 1951; children—Richard A., William H., Carol Elizabeth. Acct., Citizens Gas and Coke Utility, Indpls., 1950-55, internal auditor, 1955-59, data processing mgr., 1959-63, dir. systems and audit, 1963-64, controller, 1964-67, asst. gen. mgr., 1967-73, pres., chief exec. officer, 1973—; dir. Indpls. Life Ins. Co., Ind. Nat. Corp., Mayflower Corp. Bd. dirs. Greater Indpls. Progress Com., v.p., 1973—; bd. dirs. Arthur Jordan Found., 1979—, Indpls. area chpt. ARC, 1971-80, United Way, 1973—, Day Nursery Found., 1973—, Ind. Symphony Soc., Inc., Park-Tudor Sch.; trustee Butler U., 1974—, Community Hosp., 1974—; bd. dirs., v.p. Jr. Achievement Central Ind. Served with USN, 1944-46, 50-52. C.P.A., Ind. Mem. Am. Gas Assn. (dir. 1975-79), Ind. Gas Assn. (dir. 1968-79, pres. 1971), Am. Coke and Coal Chems. Inst. (dir. 1973—, v.p. 1977-79), Nat. Alliance Businessmen, (chmn. Indpls. Met. area 1976-77), Indpls. C. of C. (vice chmn., mem. exec. com. 1973—), Sigma Chi. Republican. Presbyterian. Club: Meridian Hills Country. Home: 8068 Bayberry Ct Indianapolis IN 46250 Office: 2020 N Meridian St Indianapolis IN 46202

STEELE, RICHARD J., mgmt. cons.; b. Elkhart, Ind., Sept. 27, 1925; s. Cornelius and Harriet (Poel) S.; S.B., Mass. Inst. Tech., 1946; M.B.A., Ind. U., 1949; m. Martha Jean Micko, July 8, 1950; children—Barbara, Cheryl, Patricia, Thomas, Richard J., Marjorie, Gregory, Susan, Kathleen. Vice pres., dir. Fry Consultants, 1950-70; pres. Richard Steele & Partners, Inc., N.Y.C., 1970-71; group v.p. Macro Systems, Inc., Silver Spring, Md., 1971-76; pres. Richard Steele Consultants, Inc., New Canaan, Conn., 1976-78; v.p. Birch & Davis Assos., Inc., Silver Spring, 1978—. Trustee Village of Riverwoods (Ill.), 1967-68. Served with USNR, 1943-47, 52-54; Korea. Certified mgmt. cons.; recipient award of merit Am. Heart Assn., 1974. Mem. Nat. Health Council (v.p.), AAAS, Am. Inst. Indsl. Engrs., Am. Public Health Assn., Internat. Transactional Analysis Assn., Nat. League Nursing, Navy League U.S., Newcomen Soc. N. Am., OD Network, U.S. Naval Inst., World Future Soc. Republican. Unitarian. Author: (with others) McGraw-Hill's Guide to Health Grants and Contracts, 1978; An Introduction to Grants and Contracts in Major HEW Health Agencies, 1976. Home: 5122

Durham Rd E Columbia MD 21044 Office: 1112 Spring St Silver Spring MD 20910

STEELE, RICHARD OATES, chem. co. exec.; b. Charlotte, N.C., Sept. 6, 1921; s. Francis Orlander and Maude (Oates) S.; B.S., U. N.C., 1942; M.A., Princeton U., 1948, Ph.D., 1949; m. Virginia Keene Miller, Aug. 26, 1949; children—Caroline, Ann. Sect. head Textile Research Inst., Princeton, N.J., 1949-53; lab. head Rohm & Haas Co., Phila., 1953-65; with Celanese Corp., 1965—, v.p. fibers mktg., N.Y.C., 1965-73, v.p. fibers mfg., Charlotte, 1973-76, v.p. internat. mfg., N.Y.C., 1976-79, pres. fibers internat., 1979-80, exec. v.p. internat. ops., 1980—; dir., mem. exec. com. Celanese Can., Ltd., 1979—, Celanese Mexicana S.A., 1979—. Bd. dirs. Nat. Fgn. Trade Council, 1980—. Recipient DeWitt Smith award ASTM, 1978. Fellow Fiber Soc. Textile Inst., AAAS; mem. Am. Chem. Soc., Am. Assn. Textile Chemists and Colorists (Olney medal 1963), Textile Research Inst. (chmn. bd. dirs.). Democrat. Presbyn. Club: Princeton of New York. Home: 440 E 56th St New York NY 10022 Office: 1211 Ave of the Americas New York NY 10036

STEELE, THOMAS LEO, mfg. co. exec.; b. Cleve., Mar. 24, 1924; s. Thomas L. and Mary E. (Heusel) S.; A.B., Colgate U., 1946; practitioners license ICC, 1949; student Seton Hall U., 1941-42; m. Patricia M. Hinman, Oct. 22, 1949; children—Kathleen, Thomas, Deborah, Marguerite, Patricia, Therese, Geoffrey. With Nabisco Inc., 1946—, rate clk. to mgr. rate div., N.Y.C., 1946-63, dir. traffic and distbn. Spl. Products div., 1963-77, dir. traffic Biscuit div., East Hanover, N.J., v.p. traffic and distbn. Biscuit div., 1979—; instr. Acad. Advanced Traffic, 1960-65. Served with USMC, 1943-46, 50-52. Decorated Bronze Star. Mem. Grocery Mfrs. Am. Roman Catholic. Club: Traffic. Home: 23 Hunters Ct Hillsdale NJ 07642 Office: Nabisco Inc East Hanover NJ 07936

STEELEY, CHARLES BEAUMONT, toy mfg. co. exec.; b. Phila., Dec. 18, 1931; s. George Tindall and Florence Ruth S.; B.A., Pa. State U., 1953; m. Mary Ann Simon, July 9, 1955; children—Susan Christine, William Charles. Sales and mktg. mgr. Solar Products Corp., 1955-66; nat. sales mgr. Dialogue Mktg., Inc. subs. Time, Inc., 1967-72; v.p. mktg. Athena Communications Corp., 1972-74; gen. mgr. Skilcraft div. Western Pub. Co., Inc., Racine, Wis., 1974—. Served with AUS, 1953-55. Club: Llanerch Country (Havertown, Pa.). Home: 4340 Lighthouse Dr Racine WI 53402 Office: PO Box 705 Racine WI 53404

STEEN, HUGH FLEMING, gas co. exec.; b. Eula, Tex., Mar. 28, 1911; s. Preston C. and Maude C. (Fleming) S.; student La. State U., 1931-32; LL.D. (hon.), N.Mex. State U., 1973; m. Mary Marshall, Aug. 10, 1937; 1 son, Stanley H. With El Paso Natural Gas Co. (Tex.), 1932-78, foreman, supt. field, transmission supt., asst. gen. supt., v.p., gen. supt., 1932-57, v.p., mgr. pipeline ops., 1957-65, vice chmn., chief exec. officer, 1976-78, dir., 1953-78; pres., chief exec. officer The El Paso Co., 1974-78, now adv. dir.; ret., 1978; dir. Vallen Co., Standard Bank, Geosource Inc., El Paso Products Co. Mem. Interstate Natural, Ind., Am., So. and Pacific Coast (past pres.) gas assns. Club: River Oaks Country. Office: PO Box 2185 Houston TX 77001

STEERE, BRUCE MIDDLETON, truck line exec.; b. Evanston, Ill., Dec. 25, 1918; s. Kenneth David and Grace (Duffield) S.; B.A., Yale U., 1942; student indsl. adminstrn. Harvard Bus. Sch., 1943; m. Anne MacCuen Bullivant, July 5, 1968; children—Lucy Duffield, Grace McLaurin, Mrs. Douglas E. Kliever, Richard M. H. Harper III, Patricia B. Harper, Stuart L. Harper. Indsl. engr. Chance Vought Aircraft, Bridgeport, Conn., 1943-45; pres. Steere Tank Lines, Dallas, 1946—; pres., dir. So. Ins. Co., Dallas, 1952—; dir. Republic Fin. Services, Inc., Vanguard Ins. Co., Allied Fin. Co., Indsl. Life Ins. Co. (all Dallas). Mem. Tex. Tank Truck Carriers Assn. (past pres.), Tex. Motor Transp. Assn. (past pres.), Beta Theta Pi. Democrat. Mem. Christian Ch. Clubs: Brook Hollow Golf (Dallas); Koon Kreek (Athens, Tex.); N.Y. Yacht, Cruising of Am. (N.Y.C.); Stone Horse Yacht (Harwich Port, Mass.). Home: 4412 N Versailles St Dallas TX 75209 Office: 2727 Turtle Creek Dallas TX 75219

STEERE, DAVID DUFFIELD, fin. co. exec.; b. Evanston, Ill., Dec. 10, 1913; s. Kenneth David and Grace (Duffield) S.; B.A., Yale U., 1937; M.B.A., Harvard U., 1939; m. Cherrie Perkins Watson, May 25, 1977; children by previous marriage—Catherine, Shirley, Kenneth, Anne. With Allied Fin. Co., Dallas, 1939-42, 46—, chmn. bd., pres., 1950—; with Aluminum Co. of Am., Pitts., 1942-46; chmn. exec. and fin. com., dir. Republic Fin. Services, Inc., 1946—; chmn. bd. Steere Tank Lines, Inc., 1946—; dir. Merc. Nat. Bank. Pres., Dallas Speech and Hearing Center, 1963-64; 1st pres. Callier Center for Communication Disorders, 1965; bd. dirs. Salvation Army, 1970-76, S.W. Outward Bound, 1974—, U.S. Coast Guard Acad. Found., 1975-78; trustee Selwyn Sch., Denton, Tex., 1976—; Mem. Nat. Consumer Fin. Assn., Tex. Consumer Fin. Assn., La. Consumer Fin. Assn., Miss. Consumer Fin. Assn., Tenn. Consumer Fin. Assn., U.S. C. of C., E. Tex. C. of C. Episcopalian. Clubs: N.Y. Yacht, Yale, Stone Horse Yacht, Eastward Ho Country, Everglades, Bath and Tennis, Dallas Athletic, Dallas Gun, Brook Hollow Country, Willow Bend Polo and Hunt, Idlewild, Terpsichorean. Home: 31 Royal Way Dallas TX 75229 Office: 2727 Turtle Creek Blvd Dallas TX 75219

STEFAN, JOSEPH, banker; b. N.Y.C.; s. Alfred and Elsie (Puer) S.: student N.Y.U., 1938-40, Am. Inst. Banking, 1946-48; m. Gloria Virginia Uher; children—Geoffrey Lance, Lorene Claire, Janyce Lynne. With coll. tng. program 1st Nat. City Bank N.Y., 1946-49, officer, 1950-59; mem. exec. mgmt. group as asst. to group exec., v.p. RCA, N.Y.C., 1959-63, v.p. record div., 1963-66, v.p., gen. mgr. Magnetic Products Div., 1967-71; chmn. bd., mng. dir. RCA Ltd., London, Eng., 1968-71; exec. v.p., chief adminstrv. officer, Security Nat. Bank N.Y., N.Y.C., 1972-75; chmn., pres. Miami Nat. Bank, 1975-79, Modernage Furniture Co., 1976-79; pres. Essay on U.S.A., Inc., 1979—; dir. RCA Ltd., Great Britain. Bd. dirs. United Fund L.I.; bd. govs., mem. com. overseers Sch. Banking and Money Mgmt., Adelphi U., Dade County Pillars Club. Served from pvt. to lt. col. C.E. AUS, 1941-46; col. Res. Decorated Bronze Star with oak leaf cluster, Purple Heart, Croix de Guerre (France); recipient United Way award, City of Hope award, Eleanor Roosevelt Humanities award State of Israel, 1976. Mem. Dade County C. of C. Clubs: Sleepy Hollow Country (Scarborough-on-Hudson, N.Y.); Belfry (London); St. Pierre Golf and Country (Chepstow, Eng.); Palm Bay, Jockey, Cricket (Miami); La Gorce Country (Miami Beach). Home: 11111 Biscayne Blvd Miami FL 33161

STEFFEN, JOHN FREDERICK, cons. engr.; b. Cuba, Mo., Jan. 18, 1936; s. William E. and Blanche A. (Licklider) S.; student Washington U., St. Louis, 1953-58; m. Carolyn A. Hardy, Jan. 31, 1958; children—Nancy, Mary, John, William, James. Elec. designer Smith, Hanlon, Zurheide & Levy, 1953-58; elec. engr. Londe, 1958-66; partner Londe, Gordon, Parker, Steffen, 1966-68; pres. John F. Steffen Assos., Inc., St. Louis, 1968—; mem. faculty Washington U. Mem. Am. Cons. Engrs. Council, Cons. Engrs. Council, Flying Engring. Assn., Illuminating Engring. Soc., ASHRAE. Republican. Presbyterian. Office: 2333 Grissom Saint Louis MO 63141*

STEIGROD, ALAN AUGUST, pharm. mfg. co. exec.; b. Phila., June 19, 1937; s. Harry A. and Flora G. Steigrod; B.S. in Pharmacy, Temple U., Phila., 1959; postgrad. Wharton Sch., U. Pa., 1963; m. Dolores Jacobs, Sept. 12, 1965; children—Hope, Adam. With Eli Lilly & Co., 1961-77, nat. mktg. mgr., Mex., 1969-72, regional sales mgr. Eastern U.S., 1973-77; nat. dir. sales Boehringer Ingelheim Ltd., Ridgefield, Conn., 1977—; dir. RonDel Industries, 1965-67. Served with USAR, 1960-61. Mem. Nat. Assn. Retail Druggists, Nat. Wholesale Druggists Assn., Am. Mgmt. Assn. Home: 113 Charter Oak Dr Wilton CT 06897 Office: 90 E Ridge St Ridgefield CT 06877

STEIN, DAVID JEROME, fin. co. exec., fin. cons.; b. Fairbury, Ill., Aug. 10, 1934; s. Frank F. and Doris Eleanor (Elliott) S.; B.S. in Agrl. Econs., U. Ill., 1959; grad. degree in credit and fin. mgmt. Dartmouth Coll., 1968; m. Roberta Frieda Riecks, June 5, 1955; children—Cheryl Ann, Dennis Ray, David Jay, Cindy Lou, Sandra Sue. Field credit mgr. Internat. Harvester Credit Corp., Dixon, Ill., 1959-61, credit supr., Lansing, Mich., 1961-64; retail credit dir. F.S. Services, Inc., Bloomington, Ill., 1964-67; regional fin. services mgr. Monsanto Co., St. Louis, 1967-69, dist. sales mgr., Kansas City, 1969-71; asst. regional mgr. farm mortgages Mut. of N.Y. Life Ins. Co., Kansas City, Mo., 1971-72, asst. to v.p., N.Y.C., 1972-74; fin. cons. and comml. mortgage broker, Peoria, Ill., 1974—; pres. Med. Condominiums, Inc., Peoria, 1975—; propr., mgr. Karmelkorn Shoppe, Peoria, 1975—, Galesburg, Ill., 1975-78; pres. Stein Enterprises, Inc., 1978—; propr. D & R Mktg., 1981—; propr., mgr. 8 Swiss Colony stores, 2 Karmelkorn stores; trustee Doris Stein Land Trust, 1976—; exec. v.p., gen. mgr. Roy Demanes Industries, Inc., Peoria, 1977-78; sec. Ill. Valley Savs. & Loan Assn., 1977-78; pres. Med. Park Physician's Center Condominium Assn., 1975; Elder of ch. council First English Lutheran Ch., Peoria, 1974—, chmn. evangelism and worship com., 1974-78, tchr. adult edn., 1973-77, ch. treas., 1978-81, v.p., 1981—. Served with U.S. Army, 1953-55. Recipient Exec. award Grad. Sch. fin. Mmgt., 1968. Republican. Club: Willow Knolls Country. Home: 906 W Kensington Dr Peoria IL 61614 Office: 906 W Kensington Dr Peoria IL 61614

STEIN, DONALD EUGENE, mfg. co. exec.; b. Upper Gwynedd, Pa., Mar. 31, 1932; s. Albert M. and Esther N. (Sweigert) S.; B.S. in Mech. Engring., U. Ariz., 1957; m. Germaine M. Krauss, Jan. 7, 1956; children—Jeffrey E., Wendelin A., Dorlissa J. Project mgr. Honeywell Co., Pottstown, Pa., 1958-62; mgr. engring. Compudyne Corp., Hatboro, Pa., 1962-65; pres. K-Tron Internat., Scottsdale, Ariz., 1965—. Nat. dir. Big Bros. and Big Sisters Am.; chmn. bd. Mgmt. Inst., Glassboro State Coll., 1977-78. Mem. Assn. Corporate Growth (pres.'s assn.), Delta Sigma Phi. Republican. Club: Masons (Lansdale, Pa.). Patentee in field. Office: 7975 N Hayden Rd Scottsdale AZ 85258

STEIN, HOWARD, mut. fund exec.; b. 1926; student Julliard Sch. Music, 1944-46. With Seaporcel Metal Inc., 1950-53, Bache & Co., 1953-55; asst., dir. Dreyfus Investment Mgmt. of Dreyfus and Co., also gen. partner, 1955-61; v.p. Dreyfus Fund Inc., 1961-65, pres., chmn. bd., 1965—; pres., dir. Dreyfus Corp., 1965-70, chmn. bd., chief exec. officer, 1970—, pres., 1980—; pres., dir. Dreyfus Corp. Can., 1965—. Office: Dreyfus Corp 767 Fifth Ave New York NY 10153

STEIN, JESS, publisher, editor; b. N.Y.C., June 23, 1914; s. Elias and Regina (Goldenberg) S.; A.B., Wayne State U., 1933; M.A., U. Chgo., 1934, postgrad., 1934-36; m. Dorothy Gerner, Mar. 7, 1943; children—Regina (Mrs. Bruce H. Wilson), Eric. Editor, Scott, Foresman & Co., 1934-42; chief reference and rev. units Office of Censorship, Washington, 1942-45; editor Random House, Inc., 1945-50, head coll., reference depts., 1950-59, v.p., 1959-80, also dir.; v.p. Alfred A. Knopf, Inc., 1967-74; mng. editor Am. Coll. Dictionary, 1947-80; editor Am. Everyday Dictionary, 1949-80, Am. Vest Pocket Dictionary, 1951, Vest Pocket Rhyming Dictionary, 1951, Basic Everyday Ency., 1954—; editorial dir. Random House Ency., 1977-80; editor-in-chief Random House Dictionary of English Lang., 1966-80, Random House Coll. Dictionary, rev., 1975; editor-in-chief emeritus Random House reference books, 1980—; pres. Bookmark Pub. Assos., Ltd., 1980—, Jess Stein Assos., 1973—; dir. L.W. Singer, Inc., Random House of Can., Ltd.; mem. Govt. Adv. Com. on Internat. Book Programs, 1964-67. Democratic county committeeman, 1956-58, city com., 1954-58; adv. bd. Hall of Fame, Jerusalem. Mem. Am. Textbook Pubs. Inst. (vice chmn. 1961-62, dir. 1962-65), Coll. Pubs. Group (chmn. 1960-61), MLA, Linguistic Soc., Dialect Soc., Speech Assn., Dictionary Soc. Am., Coll. English Assn., Nat. Council Tchrs. English, NAACP, ACLU, Urban League. Club: Dutch Treat (N.Y.C.). Author: (with R.N. Linscott) Why You Do What You Do, 1956; editor, translator (pseudonym Isai Kamen): Tolstoy's The Kreutzer Sonata, 1957, Great Russian Stories, 1959; editor: Irving's Life of George Washington, 1975; adv. rev. com. U. Mass. Press; cons. Internat. Reading Assn. Home and Office: 11 Sherman Ave White Plains NY 10605

STEIN, MARTIN MATTHEW, economist, research dir.; b. Bad Gastein, Austria, Feb. 21, 1946; s. Leon and Bess (Kicis) S.; came to U.S., 1949, naturalized, 1956; B.S. with high honors in Econs., U. Md., 1967, M.A. in Econs., 1975; D.E.S. avec la mention trés bien in Ops. Research and Applied Math., U. Paris, 1976, D.Sc., 1978; children—Stephen, William, Joshua. Economist, U.S. Dept. Commerce and U.S. Dept. Transp., Washington, 1967-73, U.S. Dept. Interior, Washington, 1973; mgr. socio-econ. group Md. Dept. Transp., Balt., 1973—; dir. transp. research Abt Assos., Inc., Cambridge, Mass.; sr. economist cons. Booz-Allen Hamilton; asst. prof. econs. Sch. Bus., U. Balt.; lectr. Johns Hopkins, Balt.; v.p. Internat. Policy Inst., Washington; sr. tech. adv. energy and transport UN Dept. Tech. Cooperation and Devel., N.Y.C. and UNCTAD, Geneva; adv. com. Def. Econ. Analysis Council, U.S. Dept. Def. Mem. retail trade study exec. com. Greater Balt. Com., 1976, Econ. Devel. Council, Regional Planning Council, 1977-78. Fellow Internat. Inst. Social Econs.; mem. Soc. Govt. Economists (award 1972; founder, pres., chmn. bd.), Nat. Council Assns. for Policy Scis. (co-founder, v.p.), Balt. Econ. Soc. (founder, pres.), Am. Econ. Assn., Internat. Assn. Energy Economists, John Marshall Soc., U.S. C. of C. (coordinator coll. bus. symposium 1966), Transp. Research Bd., Transp. Research Forum, U. Md. Alumni Assn. (council, chpt. v.p., pres. 1973-77, Omicron Delta Epsilon, Delta Sigma Pi, Delta Nu Alpha. Research in transp. and automotive investment, pub. energy policy, socio-econ. impacts of tech. change, safety policy evaluation. Editor: Economic Development, The State and Local Government Perspective, 1976; contbr. articles to profl. jours. Home: 73 Noanett Rd Needham MA 02194 Office: 55 Wheeler St Cambridge MA 02138

STEIN, MICHAEL JOHN, health care cons.; b. Chgo., Mar. 26, 1942; s. James R. and Helen E. (Waterhouse) S.; B.A. in Math., DePaul U., 1964; M.S. in Mgmt., Northwestern U., 1976. Chief mgmt. research sect. Def. Atomic Support Agy., Albuquerque, 1966-67, dir. edn. and tng. programs, 1967-68; mgr. med. assistance program Cook County, Chgo., 1969-72; dir. med. services program No. Cook County, 1972-73; dir. med. services City of Chgo. Programs, 1973-74; spl. cons. for health care Ill. State Legislature, Markham, Ill., 1974-79; dir. health programs Ill. Legis. Adv. Com., 1980—; cons. in mgmt. Recipient Disting. Service award for uncovering fraud in fed. med. care programs Chgo. Assn. Commerce and Industry, 1977. Mem. Am. Hosp. Assn., Grad. Mgmt. Assn., Northwestern U., DePaul U. alumni assns., Chgo. Council Fgn. Relations, Beta Alpha Psi. Home: 3044 W Addison St Chicago IL 60618 Office: 160 N LaSalle St Chicago IL 60601

STEIN, MILTON ASHER, furniture mfg. co. exec.; b. Pottstown, Pa., Mar. 10, 1922; s. Hyman and Rose S.; m. Frankie Goodman, Feb. 7, 1980; children—Jonathan, Soryl, Michael, Diane, Lisa. Partner, C&M Produce Co., Pottstown, Pa., 1939-41; owner Bar B Q Pit Restaurant, Pottstown, 1948-59, Chuck Wagon Restaurant, Wilmington, Del., 1951-59; sales mgr. S.W. Headboards, Inc., Houston, 1960—; partner Gerald Stein Co., Inc., Pitts., 1960—, Lake West Point Estates, Atlanta, 1979—, Gerald Stein Co of Ga., Atlanta, 1971—. Served with U.S. Army, 1941-45. Mem. Nat. Assn. Bedding Mfrs., Nat. Assn. Home Furnishings. Jewish. Clubs: Masons, Shriners. Office: 1633 W North Ave Pittsburgh PA 15233

STEIN, SYDNEY, JR., investment counsellor; b. Chgo., Oct. 24, 1901; s. Sydney and Clara (Meyer) S.; Ph.B., U. Chgo., 1923; m. Jeannette Shembaugh, Jan. 7, 1936 (div. 1972); children—Nancy Capps Stein Seasholes, Susan Shambaugh Stein Elmendorf, Edith Carol. With A.G. Becker & Co., investment bankers, 1923-32; co-founder Sydney Stein, Jr. & Assos., Chgo., investment counsel, 1932 (now Stein Roe & Farnham); cons. Fed. Bur. Budget, Washington, 1941-45; chmn. bd., treas. Leich Electric Co., Genoa, Ill., 1945-50; dir. Stein Roe & Farnham Balanced Fund, Inc., 1948-76, Stein Roe & Farnham Capital Opportunities Fund, Inc., 1954-76, Stein Roe & Farnham Stock Fund, Inc., 1963-76; cons. to pres., dir. Bur. Budget, 1961-67. Mem. Adv. Com. Pvt. Enterprise in Fgn. Aid, 1964-65; mem. Pres.'s Spl. Panel Fed. Salaries, 1965; mem. Randall Adv. Panel on Fed. Pay Systems, 1961-63. Life trustee U. Chgo.; trustee Brookings Instn., Washington, 1960—, vice chmn. bd., 1967-71. Mem. Phi Beta Kappa. Clubs: Tavern, Quadrangle, Attic, Standard, Mid-America, Comml., Arts, Chicago. Home: 1700 E 56th St Chicago IL 60637 Office: 150 S Wacker Dr Chicago IL 60606

STEIN, WILLIAM H., packaging co. exec.; b. Bklyn., Mar. 29, 1935; s. Sam and Madeline (Lucas) S.; B.S., Lehigh U., 1957; postgrad. U. Miami, 1958; m. Dolores Suenderhauf, Aug. 24, 1957; children—Linda Joan, William Martin. Plant engr. Oneida Packaging Products, Inc. subs. Reed-Deeron Corp., Clifton, N.J., 1958-67, asst. v.p., 1967-69, v.p. mfg., 1969—, exec. v.p., asst. sec., 1974—, pres., chief exec. officer, dir., 1975—; v.p. Reed-Deeron Corp., Wellesley, Mass., 1975—; dir. Plastic Piping Systems Inc., Plainfield, N.J. Employer trustee health and welfare trust fund United Paperworkers Internat. Union. Mem. TAPPI, Am. Mgmt. Assn. Patentee in field; comml. pilot. Home: 38 Maria Dr Hillsdale NJ 07642 Office: 10 Clifton Blvd Clifton NJ 07015

STEINBACK, THOMAS R., audio-electronics co. mgr.; b. Evansville, Ind., May 17, 1950; s. Edward Oscar and Thelma Jean (Ellison) S.; B.A., Ambassador Coll., Eng., 1972; postgrad. Miss. State U., 1974-75; M.B.A., Syracuse U., 1980; m. Charla Denny, July 1, 1973. Exec. trainee Ambascol Corp., Eng., 1970-72; asso. office mgr. Ambassador Coll., Pasadena, Calif., 1972-77; fin. loan counselor Syracuse (N.Y.) U., 1978-79; employee relations intern Gen. Electric Co., Syracuse, 1979, mgr. employee relations, Utica, 1979—. Trustee ARC, Utica, 1980—. Recipient Grad. Alumni award Syracuse U., 1980. Mem. Ambassador Internat. Cultural Found., Am. Soc. Personnel Adminstrs., Assn. Grad. Bus. Students, Assn. M.B.A. Execs. Office: 1900 Bleeker St Utica NY 13501

STEINBERG, ALAN WOLFE, investment mgr.; b. Bklyn., Oct. 26, 1927; s. Benjamin F. and Gertrude (Wolfe) S.; A.B. with honors and spl. distinction in Math., Columbia U., 1947, M.S., 1950, postgrad., 1957-59; postgrad. N.Y. U., 1955-56; m. Suzanne Nichols, Oct. 12, 1958; children—Carol, Laura, Benjamin T. Engr., U.S. Dept. Agr., 1948-50; internal computer cons. Port N.Y. Authority, 1954-56; asst. prof. indsl. engring., ops. research N.Y. U., 1956-62; pres. Am. Computing Centers, 1962-66; v.p., dir. TBS Computer Centers Corp., N.Y.C., 1967-76; dir. R-T-W Computer Network Corp., N.Y.C.; gen. partner Alan W. Steinberg Partnership, South Miami, Fla., 1968—; chmn. bd. Midland Capital Corp., N.Y.C.; dir. Interpoint Corp., Chgo. Nat. adviser automation United Jewish Appeal, 1966—; bd. dirs. Herbert O. Wolfe Found., Barrett Sch. Served with AUS, 1950-53. Mem. Assn. Computing Machinery, AAUP, Inst. Mgmt. Scis., N.Y. Acad. Scis., Tropical Audubon Soc. (dir.; co-chmn. fin. com. 1979—), Phi Beta Kappa, Alpha Pi Mu. Author: The Case for a Wealth Tax, 1973; contbr. articles to profl. jours. Home: 11097 Paradela Ave Coral Gables FL 33156 Office: 7800 Red Rd Suite 203 South Miami FL 33143

STEINBERG, JOSEPH SAUL, fin. co. exec.; b. Chgo., Feb. 5, 1944; s. Paul S. and Sylvia (Neikrug) S.; A.B., N.Y. U., 1966; M.B.A., Harvard U., 1970; 1 dau., Sarah Aliza. With U.S. Peace Corps, Jamaica, W.I., 1966-68; pres. Tri City Broadcasting Corp., Lebanon, N.H., 1969-73; v.p. Carl Marks & Co. Inc., N.Y.C., 1970-78; pres., dir. Leucadia Nat. Corp. (formerly Talcott Nat. Corp.), N.Y.C., 1979—; dir. Roberts Consol. Industries, Inc., Stern & Stern Textiles, Inc., Atlantic Research Corp., Am. Investment Co., Charter Nat. Life Ins. Co. Club: Harvard (N.Y.C.). Home: 35 Garden Pl Brooklyn Heights NY 11201 also 645 Circle Dr Solana Beach CA 92075 Office: 1290 Ave of Americas New York NY 10019

STEINBERG, SAUL PHILLIP, holding co. exec.; b. N.Y.C., Aug. 13, 1939; s. Julius and Anne (Cohen) S.; B.S. in Econs., Wharton Sch., U. Pa., 1959; m. Barbara Herzog, May 28, 1961 (div. 1977); children—Laura, Jonathan, Nicholas; m. 2d, Laura Sconocchia, Dec. 20, 1978; 1 son, Julian. Founder, Leasco Corp., N.Y.C., 1961, chmn. bd., pres., chief exec. officer Reliance Group, Inc., N.Y.C., 1962—; chmn. exec. and fin. coms., dir. Reliance Ins. Co., 1968—; dir. Imperial Corp. Am., Rothschild Investment Trust. Trustee, L.I. Jewish Hosp., Saul Steinberg Found.; bd. dirs. Circle in Sq., Juvenile Diabetes Found., United Cerebral Palsy Found.; mem. vis. com. Mass. Inst. Tech.; asso. trustee U. Pa., overseer Wharton Grad. Sch. Fine Arts. Recipient Humanitarian award Am. Jewish Com., 1973. Mem. Am. Mgmt. Assn., Young Pres.'s Orgn. Office: 919 3d Ave New York NY 10022

STEINER, IVAN, JR., property and liability ins. exec.; b. Ossining, N.Y., Jan. 1, 1912; s. Ivan and Merle (Holter) S.; B.A., Coll. Wooster, 1933; m. Lillian C. Gisinger, Dec. 27, 1939; children—Amy L. Steiner Pryor, Michael S., Sara A. Steiner Marks, Deborah J. Steiner Weber, Jeffrey A., Andrew R. With W.C. Myers & Co., gen. ins. agy., Wooster, Ohio, 1936-70; successively solicitor, jr. partner, mng. partner, pres. Whitaker-Myers Ins. Agy. Inc. (merged firms of W.C. Myers & Co. and Whitaker Ins. Agy.), 1970-77, chmn. bd., 1977; ret., 1977, now ins. cons.; dir. Central Trust Co. of Wayne County; v.p., dir. Wayne Recreation, Inc. Instr. ins. Community Coll., U. Akron, 1956-57; vice chmn. all industry com. for revision agt. licensing manual Ohio Ins. Dept., 1960-61; v.p. Gisinger Chevrolet Co., 1958-60. Trustee, YMCA, Wooster, chmn. bd. trustees, 1963-64. Mem. Gov.'s Ins. Advisory Com., 1959, Wooster Civil Service Commn., 1967-73; trustee Greater Wayne County Found., Inc. Served with U.S. Army, 1943-46; ETO. Recipient Red Triangle award YMCA, 1978. C.P.C.U., 1955. Mem. Ins. Inst. Am. (diploma asso. in risk mgmt. 1968), Wooster C. of C. (pres. 1954-55), Ind. Ins. Agts. Assn. Ohio (Paul Revere award 1965, trustee, pres. 1959, chmn. legis.

policy com. 1960, 61, chmn. edn. com. 1965, chmn. long range planning team 1973-74), Wayne County Ind. Agts. Assn. (pres. 1957, co-founder), Ind. Ins. Agts. Assn. Am. (chmn. spl. acquisition cost allowance com. 1959-60), Nat. Soc. C.P.C.U.'s (nat. profl. and trade liaison com. 1959-60, mem. seminar bd. 1964, pres. Akron-Canton chpt. 1965-66, nat. dir. North Central dist. 1966-67, regional v.p. 1968, chmn. bylaws revision com. 1968-69, mem. long range planning bd. 1970-73, chmn. 1973-74), Am. Risk and Ins. Assn., Ins. Soc. Phila., Internat. Platform Assn., SAR, Izaak Walton League Am., Am. Legion, V.F.W. Democrat. Lutheran (ch. council 1946-66, chmn. endowment com., trustee). Mason (32 deg., Shriner), Elk, Rotarian (pres. 1968-69). Clubs: Century, Julie Fe Country. Contbr. articles to trade jours.; co-editor Project 73. Home: 257 W Henrietta St Wooster OH 44691

STEINER, PAUL ANDREW, ins. co. exec.; b. Woodburn, Ind., Feb. 17, 1929; s. Eli G. and Emma M. Steiner; A.B. in Psychology, Taylor U., Upland, Ind., 1950; postgrad. Bluffton (Ohio) Coll.; m. Ruth E. Henry, Sept. 1, 1950; children—Mark, Nancy, Jonathan, David. Social worker Grant County (Ind.), 1950-51; engaged in feed, grain, lumber and constrn. bus., 1951-64; with Brotherhood Mut. Ins. Co., 1964—, v.p., treas., Ft. Wayne, Ind., 1968-71, pres., 1971—, chmn. bd., 1974—. Mem. Bluffton Bd. Edn., 1962-64; bd. dirs. Ft. Wayne Better Bus. Bur., 1979—; vice chmn. bd. Ft. Wayne Bible Coll., 1978—. C.P.C.U., 1972. Mem. Nat. Assn. Mut. Ins. Cos. (dir., Merit award 1973), Soc. C.P.C.U.'s, Conf. Casualty Ins. Cos. (dir., past pres.), Mut. Ins. Cos. Assn. Ind. (dir., past pres.), Greater Ft. Wayne C. of C., Nat. Assn. Evangelicals (treas., Layman of Year award 1977), Am. Bible Soc. (dir.), Christian Bus. Men's Com. Republican. Mem. Evang. Protestant Christian Ch. Club: Rotary. Office: PO Box 2227 Fort Wayne IN 46801

STEINFELD, MANFRED, furniture mfg. co. exec.; b. Josbach, Germany, Apr. 29, 1924; s. Abraham and Paula (Katten) S.; student U. Ill., 1942; B.S. in Commerce, Roosevelt U., 1948; m. Fern Goldman, Nov. 13, 1949; children—Michael, Paul, Jill. Research analyst State of Ill., 1948-50; v.p. Shelby Williams Industries, Inc., Chgo., 1954-63, pres., 1964-72; chmn. bd., 1973—; dir. Amalgamated Trust & Savs. Bank; dir. Albany Trust & Savs. Bank, Met. Bank of Addison (Ill.). Trustee Roosevelt U., Chgo.; pres. Roosevelt U. Bus. Sch. Alumni Council. Served to 1st lt. AUS, 1942-45, 50-52. Decorated Bronze Star, Purple Heart; named Small Bus. Man of Year Central Region, 1967. Mem. Beta Gamma Sigma. Clubs: Standard, Bryn Mawr Country. Home: 1300 Lake Shore Dr Apt 34D Chicago IL 60610 Office: Mdse Mart Room 1348 Chicago IL 60654

STEINHAUSER, JOHN WILLIAM, lawyer, energy exec.; b. Akron, Ohio, June 25, 1924; s. John Hugo and Francis Lillian (Pearson) S.; B.Sc. in Bus. Adminstrn., Ohio State U., 1949; J.D., U. Mich., 1950; m. Patricia E. Mooney, Dec. 1, 1956; children—John, Christian, Mark, Sharon. Admitted to Colo. bar, 1972, Mich. bar, 1950; with Chrysler Corp., 1950—, beginning as atty., successively dir. Latin Am., dir. export sales, gen. mgr. Africa-Far East, dir. Chrysler Internat., Geneva, dir. Africa-Far East, 1950-71, corp. atty., Denver, 1971—; founder, pres. Pearson Energy Corp., 1977, Sharon Energy, Ltd., Denver, 1980, also dir., 1971—. Sponsor Platte Valley Pony Club, Denver Symphony; active Colo. Republican Party. Served with USNR, 1943-46. Mem. Colo. Bar Assn., Mich. Bar Assn., Am. Bar Assn., Soc. Internat. Law, Rocky Mountain Mineral Law Found. Clubs: Cherry Hills, Club de Santiago. Home: 4210 S Dahlia St Englewood CO 80110 Office: Suite 2400 718 17th St Denver CO 80202

STEINMAN, JERRY, newsletter publisher; b. N.Y.C., Feb. 9, 1924; s. Abraham and Celia (Leventhal) S.; B.A. with honors, Ohio State U., 1943; M.A., Columbia U., 1948, postgrad., 1949-50; postgrad. Fordham U., 1953-54; m. Irene Dynenson, Nov. 5, 1951; children—Benjamin Seth, Glen Aaron. Editorial asso. Practising Law Inst., N.Y.C., 1951-55; mng. dir. Nationwide Trade News, Inc., N.Y.C., 1957-62; pres. Steinman Assos., Nanuet, N.Y., 1962-69; pub., pres. Beer Marketer's Insights, Inc., West Nyack, N.Y., 1970—. Bd. dirs. West Nyack Free Library, 1974-76. Served with U.S. Army, 1943-46. Hon. Ky. col. Mem. Newsletter Assn. Am., Brewers Assn. Am. Jewish. Author: (with Wilbur Cross) Service Imperative, 1969; contbr. articles to bus. jours.; asso. editor Jour. Taxation, 1955-57. Home: 16 Aberdeen Dr West Nyack NY 10994 Office: 55 Virginia Ave West Nyack NY 10994

STEINMETZ, LEONARD ARYEH, systems analyst; b. Reghin, Romania, Apr. 1, 1951; s. Joseph and Charlotte (Guttman) Krausz, came to U.S., 1963, naturalized, 1963; B.A. in Econs., Bklyn. Coll., 1972; M.B.A. in Fin. cum laude, Pace U., 1977; m. Rosemary Krausz, Oct. 1, 1977. Program research analyst Human Resources Adminstrn., 1973-76; sr. analyst, project mgr. Kraft div. St. Regis Paper Co., 1976-78; sr. analyst, staff cons. Computer Horizons Corp., N.Y.C., 1978—, also regional mgr. software services; lectr. in field. Mem. AAAS, Assn. Computing Machinery, Delta Mu Delta. Office: 747 3d Ave New York NY 10017

STEINMETZ, MANNING LOUIS, III, fin. co. exec.; b. Glasgow, Mo., Aug. 17, 1942; s. Manning Louis and Stella Marie (Fehling) S.; B.S., N.E. Mo. State U., 1964; m. Karen Suzanne Cockriel, July 18, 1970; children—Melissa Leigh, Suzanne Monique. Casualty ins. underwriter MFA Ins. Co., Columbia, Mo., 1965-67, systems analyst, 1967-70; systems analyst Kirksville (Mo.) Coll. Osteo. Medicine, 1970-72, dir. personnel, 1972-73, dir. devel., 1973-75; broker Edward D. Jones & Co., Maryland Heights, Mo., 1975-78, partner, 1978—; allied mem. N.Y. Stock Exchange. Mem. Mo. Council Public Higher Edn. Served with U.S. Army, 1964-65. Mem. Nat. Assn. Security Dealers, Sigma Tau Gamma. Democrat. Roman Catholic. Clubs: Masons, Shriners, Kiwanis. Home: 2928 W Adams St Saint Charles MO 63301 Office: Edward D Jones & Co 201 Progress Pkwy Maryland Heights MO 63043

STELL, JAMES L., bus. exec.; b. 1924; student U. Fla., U. Miami, Calif. Coll. Commerce. Acct., Jacob G. Efron Co., C.P.A.'s, 1946-51; with Lucky Stores Inc., Dublin, Calif., v.p., 1963-68, sr. v.p., 1968-71, exec. v.p., 1971-74, pres., 1974, now vice chmn., also dir. Office: Lucky Stores Inc 6300 Clark Ave Dublin CA 94566*

STELTMANN, HARRY FREDERICK, automotive co. exec.; b. Elizabeth, N.J., Jan. 11, 1943; s. Harry Frederick and Alverna Ruth (Smithman) S.; B.B.A., Hofstra U., 1964; M.B.A., Eastern Mich. U., 1974; m. Mary Jo Pfeiffer, Dec. 23, 1967; children—Joan, Michael, Andrew, Daniel. Plant fin. analyst Ford Motor Co., Saline, Mich., 1969-72, sr. fin. analyst, Rawsonville, Mich., 1972-73; capital investment mgr. Rockwell Internat. Corp., Troy, Mich., 1973-74, plant controller, Allegan, Mich., 1974-76, div. controller suspenion systems, Troy, 1976-77, div. controller, dir. bus. planning plastics, 1977-78, dir. mktg. and bus. planning plastics, 1978-79, group dir. ops. axle group, 1979—. Active Boy Scouts Am., Troy Youth Polo, mgr., coach Troy Baseball Boosters, 1976—. Served with AUS, 1964-69. Decorated Bronze Star, Purple Heart. Mem. AMA, Am. Inst. Corp. Controllers, Soc. Automotive Engrs., Engring. Soc. Detroit. Presbyterian. Home: 3683 Balfour St Troy MI 48084 Office: 2135 W Maple St Troy MI 48084

STELZER, IRWIN MARK, economist; b. N.Y.C., May 22, 1932; s. Abraham and Fanny (Dolgins) S.; B.A. cum laude, N.Y. U., 1951, M.A., 1952; Ph.D., Cornell U., 1954; m. Elaine Waldman, June 18, 1950 (div. 1964); 1 son, Adam David; m. Agnes Sasaki, Aug. 30, 1966 (div. 1976). Fin. analyst Econometric Inst., 1952; teaching fellow Cornell U., 1953-54; instr. U. Conn., 1954-55; researcher Twentieth Century Fund, 1953-55; economist W. J. Levy, Inc., 1955-56; sr. cons., v.p. Boni, Watkins, Jason and Co., Inc., 1956-61; pres. Nat. Econ. Research Assos., Inc., N.Y.C., 1961—. Lectr. N.Y. U., 1955-56, Coll. City N.Y., 1957-58; researcher Brookings Instn., 1956-57; mem. adv. com. revision of rules of practice and procedure Fed. Energy Regulatory Commn.; mem. energy fin. adv. com. FEA; adv. council Electric Power Research Inst.; Mem. Cornell Univ. Council; mem. Pres.'s Econ. Adv. Panel to Nat. Commn. for Rev. Antitrust Laws; mem. N.Y.C. Mayor's Energy Policy Adv. Group; chmn. tech. adv. com. on impact inadequate electric power supply for Nat. Power Survey, FPC; mem. exec. com., also bd. dirs. Pub. Utility Research Center U. Fla. Bd. dirs. U.S. Nat. Com. World Energy Conf.; mem. bd. governing trustees Am. Ballet Theater. Mem. Am., So. econ. assns., Am. Statis. Assn., Nat. Assn. Bus. Economists, Phi Beta Kappa. Clubs: Cornell, Harbor View, The Wall St., City Athletic, Met. Author: Selected Antitrust Cases: Landmark Decisions; also articles in field. Econs. editor Antitrust Bull. Home: 31 E 79th St New York NY 10021 Office: 5 World Trade Center New York NY 10048

STELZER, ROBERT MORTON, mktg. exec.; b. Yonkers, N.Y., May 28, 1923; s. Louis Elton and Anna (Miller) S.; B.S. in Journalism cum laude, U. Ill., 1947; m. Kyra Higham, Jan. 17, 1976; children by previous marriage-Lance, Cara, Kerry, Tracey, Peter. Mktg. cons. various nat. mfg. cos., 1950-70; dir. Kelly Mktg. div. Kelly Services, Inc., N.Y.C., 1970-73; v.p. Merchandising & Promotion Assos., Inc., N.Y.C., 1973-75; v.p. Budget Rent a Car Corp., Chgo., 1975-80; chief exec. officer Sears Rent a Car div. Budget Rent a Car, Chgo., 1976-80; pres. Marketforce, Inc., Los Angeles, 1980—; exec. v.p. Concessions Mktg., Inc., Los Angeles, 1980—, also dir.; lectr., cons. in field. Served with USAAF, 1942-45; PTO. Decorated Bronze Battle Star. Mem. Am. Mktg. Assn. Contbr. articles to mktg. publs. Home: 5400 Lindley Ave Encino CA 91316

STEM, CARL HERBERT, educator; b. Eagleville, Tenn., Jan. 30, 1935; s. Marion Ogilvie and Sara Elizabeth (Jones) S.; B.A., Vanderbilt U., 1957; Fulbright scholar U. Reading (U.K.), 1957-58; A.M. (Woodrow Wilson fellow, Harvard scholar), Harvard U., 1960, Ph.D., 1969; m. Linda Marlene Wheeler, Dec. 28, 1963; children—Anna Elizabeth, Susan Kathleen, John Carl, David Leslie. Internat. fin. economist, bd. govs. Fed. Res. System, Washington, 1963-70; prof. internat. fin., adminstr. grad. programs, asso. dean, dean Coll. Bus. Adminstrn., prof. econs. Tex. Tech U., Lubbock, 1970—; sr. econ. adviser Office Fgn. Direct Investments, U.S. Dept. Commerce, Washington, 1973-74; cons. U.S. Dept. Treasury, 1974-75; mem. faculty Grad. Sch. Credit and Fin. Mgmt., Lake Success, N.Y., 1974—; adj. scholar Am. Enterprise Inst. Pub. Policy Research, Washington, 1974—; dir. Furr's Cafeterias, Inc., Lubbock, Tex. Served to capt. Security Agy., AUS, 1961-62. Sec.-treas. Mission Jour., Inc., 1969—. Mem. Am. Econ. Assn., Nat. Assn. Bus. Economists, Fin. Mgmt. Assn., Lubbock Econs. Council (pres. 1973), Phi Beta Kappa, Omicron Delta Kappa, Phi Kappa Phi, Beta Gamma Sigma. Mem. Ch. of Christ. Contbr. articles to profl. jours. Home: 6218 Louisville Dr Lubbock TX 79413

STEMPEL, ERNEST EDWARD, ins. exec.; b. N.Y.C., May 10, 1916; s. Frederick Christian and Leah Lillian S.; A.B., Manhattan Coll., 1938; LL.B., Fordham U., 1946; LL.M., N.Y. U., 1949, D.J.S., 1951; m. Phyllis Brooks; children—Diana Brooks, Calvin Pinkcomb, Neil Frederick, Robert Russell. Admitted to N.Y. bar, 1946; with Am. Internat. Underwriters Corp., N.Y.C., 1938-53; v.p., dir. Am. Internat. Co., Ltd., Hamilton, Bermuda, 1953-63, chmn. bd., 1963—; pres., dir. Am. Internat. Assurance Co. (Bermuda) Ltd., Am. Internat. Reins. Co., Ltd., Bermuda; exec. v.p., mem. exec. com., dir. Am. Internat. Group, Inc.; pres., dir. Am. Internat. Comml. Co., Bermuda; dir. C.V. Starr & Co., Inc., N.Y.C., Starr Internat. Co., Inc., Am. Life Ins. Co., Wilmington, Del., Am. Internat. Life Ins. Co. P.R., Am. Internat. Underwriters Overseas, Ltd., Bermuda, Am. Internat. Underwriters (Latin Am.), Inc., Bermuda, Am. Internat. Underwriters Mediterranean, Inc., Bermuda, Mt. Mansfield Co., Inc., Stowe, Vt., Seguros Venezuela, C.A., Caracas, Underwriters Adjustment Co., Panama, Australian Am. Assurance Co., Ltd., Malaysian Am. Assurance Co.; chmn., dir. Am. Internat. Assurance Co., Ltd., Hong Kong, Philippine Am. Ins. Cos., Manila. Served to lt. (s.g.) USNR, 1942-46. Mem. Am. Bar Assn., N.Y. State Bar. Clubs: Marco Polo, Lawyers (N.Y.C.); Royal Bermuda Yacht, Mid-Ocean, Coral Beach (Bermuda). Home: Caliban Cove Fairylands Pembroke Bermuda Office: Am Internat Co Ltd PO Box 152 Hamilton 5 Bermuda

STEMPLER, DAVID SHEPHERD, lawyer, air line exec.; b. N.Y.C., Nov. 24, 1947; s. Jack and Minerva (Rapoport) S.; B.A., Hobart Coll., Geneva, N.Y., 1969; J.D., Georgetown U., 1972; m. Dale Carolyn Meltzer, Oct. 27, 1974. Admitted to N.Y. bar, 1973, D.C. bar, 1974; practice in N.Y.C., 1972-74, Washington, 1974—; individual practice, 1976—; pres., chmn. bd. Florida Airlines, Inc.; chmn. govt. affairs com. of bd. dirs. Airline Passengers Assn., 1979-80. Mem. Am. Bar Assn., Bar Assn. D.C. Club: Aero (Washington). Home: 4201 Cathedral Ave NW Apt 814W Washington DC 20016 Office: 1919 Pennsylvania Ave NW Suite 300 Washington DC 20006

STENSETH, DAVID LOMEN, indsl. devel. found. exec.; b. Crookston, Minn., Dec. 22, 1936; s. Adolph Karl and Oral Blache (Lomen) S.; B.A. in Econs., St. Olaf Coll., 1958; postgrad. U. Okla., 1971-74; m. Shirley Ann Stolz, Sept. 6, 1958; children—Lynne, Maren, David. Adminstrv. asst. to Congressman Odin Langen, Washington, 1958-61; dir. fin. Minn. Republican Com., Mpls., 1961-64; dir. devel. Augustana Coll., Sioux Falls, S.D., 1964-70, acting v.p. for devel., 1968-70; exec. v.p. Sioux Falls Devel. Found., 1970—; dir., treas. S.D. Alcohol Fuels Assos.; dir. Earth Resources Obs., Inc., Brookings Internat. Life Ins. Co. (S.D.), N.Am. Nat. Corp., Columbus, Ohio, Pvt. Industries Council. Active Sioux council Boy Scouts Am., 1975—; mem. S.D. Gov.'s Com. for Juvenile Delinquency, 1969-70; bd. dirs. S.E. Area Vocat. Sch., 1970-74, Parkview Nursing Home, 1968—; bd. dirs. Vis. Nurses Assn., pres., 1974-76; bd. dirs. Sioux Falls Boys Club, v.p., 1970-76; mem. SECOG Economic Devel. Com.; vice chmn. Com. Economic Growth; pres., dir. fellows Augustana Coll.; bd. regents Ind. Devel. Inst.-U. Okla. Mem. Nat. Alliance Bus. (dir. 1974—), S.D. Mfrs. and Processors Assn. (dir. 1977), Am. Indsl. Devel. Council, Nat. Assn. Indsl. Parks, Nordland Heritage Assn. (dir.). Republican. Lutheran. Clubs: Elks, Westward Ho Country (dir. 1970-74). Home: 2308 Wayland Ct Sioux Falls SD 57105 Office: 131 W 10th St Sioux Falls SD 57102

STEPHAN, ROBERT JOSEPH, ins. sales exec.; b. Chico, Calif., May 5, 1924; s. Joseph and Phoebe Julia (Groves) S.; student pub. schs., Santa Monica, Calif.; m. Doris L. Deese, Sept. 15, 1946; children—Robert Joseph, Gregory Porter, Clarke Wilson. With Nat. Producers Life Ins. Co. (acquired by Farm and Home Life Ins. Co. 1980), Phoenix, 1967—, service agt., dir. tng., agy. supr., policy service mgr., 1967-70, agy. dir., 1970-80, exec., 1980—. Served to sgt. USAAF, 1942-46. Mem. Nat. Assn. Life Cos. (agy. v.p.). Republican. Methodist. Clubs: Masons (32 deg.), Shriners. Home: PO Box 32097 Phoenix AZ 85064 Office: PO Box 16294 Phoenix AZ 85011

STEPHENS, CHESTER MARVIN, JR., mgmt. cons.; b. Paducah, Ky., July 25, 1922; s. Chester Marvin and Harriet E. (Williams) S.; student Murray State Coll., 1940-41, U. Louisville, 1946-47; B.S. in Indsl. Adminstrn., U. Ky., 1950; m. Dorothy C. Gatlin, Sept. 27, 1947; children—James Craig, Marsha Louise, Amy Claire, Stephanie Ann. With Ocal Operators Casualty Co., 1950-51; regional office mgr. F.H. McGraw & Co., Hartford, Conn., 1951-59, 65-69; credit coordinator Olin Metals Co., 1961-65; equipment adminstr. C.W. Blakeslee & Sons Inc., New Haven, 1969-75: project adminstr. spl. projects constrn. group Cebor/Westinghouse Corp., Laurel, Md., 1975—. Pres., New Martinsville (W.Va.) Little League, 1962-64; adv. Explorer Scouts, 1963-64. Served with Signal Corps, U.S. Army, 1943-46. Mem. East Shore Bowling Assn. (pres. 1970-75). Democrat. Congregationalist. Home: 10 Ninety Rod Rd Clinton CT 06413 Office: Montpelier Profl Bldg 9811 Mallard Dr Suite 201 Laurel MD 20811

STEPHENS, DOUGLAS CONRAD, broadcasting exec.; b. Kansas City, Mo., Aug. 31, 1937; s. Bernon Lee and Elizabeth Ellen S.; B.A., U. Wichita, 1961; m. Judith Ann Sutera, Sept. 8, 1963; children—Jeffrey Douglas, Jennifer Dawn. Account exec. Goldberg Advt., Denver, 1961-62; sales exec. KIMN Broadcasting, Denver, 1962-70; sales mgr. KDEN Broadcasting Co., Denver, 1971, chmn. bd., pres., Denver, 1971—; chmn. bd., pres. N. Am. Broadcasting, 1971—. Vice chmn. Planning and Zoning Commn. Greenwood Village (Colo.), 1975-79; publicity chmn. Arapaho County Republican Party, 1978-79. Served with USAFR, 1961. Decorated Am. Spirit Honor medal. Mem. Colo. Broadcasters Assn. (pres. 1980), Nat. Assn. Broadcasters, Denver C. of C., Denver Advt. Fedn. Mem. Christian Ch. Clubs: Columbine Country, Perry Park Country, Echo Hills. Office: 5660 S Syracuse Circle Englewood CO 80111

STEPHENS, ERNEST LESLIE, business exec.; b. Whitfield County, Ga., Sept. 13, 1902; s. Charlie Henry and Ellie West (Young) S., B.S., Ga. Inst. Tech., 1927; m. J. Louise Thurman, June 26, 1937; children—Leslie Stephens Nason, George Charles. Student engr. Texaco, Inc., Port Arthur, Tex., 1927-28, mech. engr., N.Y.C., 1928-29, mech. engr. refining dept., engring. div., N.Y.C., 1929-30, spl. rep. sales dept., New Orleans, 1930-31, salesman sales dept., Atlanta, 1931-32, power engr. nat. sales div., Chgo., 1932-34, mech. engr. refining dept., Port Arthur, 1934-40, project engr. engring dept., N.Y.C., 1940-60, asst. chief power engr., Houston, 1960-63, chief power engr., 1963-68; cons. engr. Dow Chem. Co., 1968-70; v.p. engring dept., dir. Interstate Comml. Equipment Inc., Houston, 1970-75; prin., engr. Stephens & Son, 1975—; real estate broker Oldham Real Estate, Wimberley, 1975-77, Woolsey Realty Co., Wimberley, 1977—; treas. de Raat Stephens, Inc., Houston, 1978—. Mem. Sanitation Bd., Pleasantville, N.Y., 1951-57, mem. Zoning Bd. Appeals, 1957-60. Registered profl. engr., Tex. Mem. ASME, Nat., Tex. socs. profl. engrs., Am. Petroleum Inst., Hays County Recreation Assn. (charter). Presbyterian (elder, treas. Chapel-in-the-Hills). Patentee. Home: PO Box 123 Wimberley TX 78676 Office: Woolsey Real Estate Box 102 Wimberley TX 78676

STEPHENS, JACKSON THOMAS, investment exec.; b. Prattsville, Ark., Aug. 9, 1923; s. Albert Jackson and Ethel Rebecca (Pumphrey) S.; grad. Columbia Mil. Acad., Tenn., 1941; student U. Ark., 1941-43; B.S., U.S. Naval Acad., 1946. Pres., Stephens, Inc., Little Rock, Stephens Prodn. Co.; chmn. bd. Union Life Ins. Co., Little Rock; dir. Wal Mart Stores. Trustee U. Ark., 1948-57. Home: Little Rock AR Office: Stephens Bldg Little Rock AR 72201

STEPHENS, JAMES ALLEN, mfg. co. exec.; b. Washington, Feb. 15, 1945; s. Heber James and Eunice Marie (Arth) S.; B.S.B., U. Minn., 1967; postgrad. U. San Diego Law Sch., 1970-71; M.B.A., Am. Grad. U., 1980; m. Kathryn K. Short, June 21, 1980; 1 stepdau., Kristine. Sr. auditor, mgr. acctg. and adminstrn. Westinghouse Electric Corp., Balt. and San Diego, 1967-71; sr. auditor Am. Hoist & Derrick, Mpls., 1971-72; ind. cons., 1972-73; bus. mgr. Honeywell, Inc., Mpls., 1974-77; corp. controller Consol. Transp. Services Corp., Mpls., 1977-79; program mgr. Phoenix Missile program Control Data Corp., Bloomington, Minn., 1979—; ind. cons. to small businesses. Squadron comdr. CAP, 1968-70; scoutmaster Boy Scouts Am., 1967-69. Mem. Am. Mgmt. Assn. Lutheran. Home: 1400 Muir Ln Burnsville MN 55337 Office: 3101 E 80th St Bloomington MN 55440

STEPHENS, JOSEPH VIVIAN, engring. co. exec.; b. Malta, George Cross, Sept. 3, 1925; s. Percy Victor and Maria Stella (Salafia) S.; E.E. diploma City and Guilds of London Inst., 1944; ed. Admiralty Tech. Coll., 1940-44, N.Y. U., 1961-73; m. Anna Luise Katharina Tschanun, Mar. 14, 1953; children—Gabriele Ingwelde, Maria Stella. Engr., naval apprentice Admiralty, London and Malta, 1940-46; elec. fitter, 1946-47; engr. officer Royal Mail Lines Ltd., London, 1948-50; sr. designer draftsman D. Napier & Son Ltd., London, 1950-53; sta. engr. Air Ministry, London, 1953-55; elec. design engr. H.K. Ferguson Co., London, 1955-57; elec. designer Gibbs & Hill, N.Y.C., 1957-58; elec. engr. Vitro Corp. Am., N.Y.C., 1958-61; sr. elec. engr. EBASCO Services, N.Y.C., 1961-66, Bechtel Corp., San Francisco, 1966-67; supervising elec. engr. Gibbs & Hill, N.Y.C., 1967-73; sr. staff mgr. Brown & Root, Houston, 1973-79; dept. mgr. elec. engring. Gilbert/Commonwealth, Jackson, Mich., 1980—. Served with Royal Fleet Aux. Service, 1947-48. At Malta sta., World War II, mass civilian award of George Cross for heroism King George VI, 1942. Registered engr. Engrs. Registration Bd. London, Wis., Conn., Calif. Fellow Elec. and Electronics Technician Engrs. London; mem. IEEE (sr.), ASME, Nat. Soc. Profl. Engrs., Inst. of Exec. Engrs. and Officers, Assn. Supervisory and Exec. Engrs. Gt. Britain. Roman Catholic. Contbr. articles on nuclear safety to profl. jours. Home: 10547 Idlebrook Dr Houston TX 77070

STEPHENS, MICHAEL JON, automobile mfg. co. exec.; b. Alpena, Mich., Aug. 30, 1948; s. Byron L. and Jeanne E. (Hackett) S.; B.S. in Indsl. Engring., Gen. Motors Inst., 1972; M.B.A., Wayne State U., Detroit, 1976. With Gen. Motors Corp., 1967-77, 79—, sr. quality control analyst/engr., Detroit, 1973-77, sr. staff asst. corp. mktg. staff, 1979—; market planning analyst Toyota Motor Sales Co., Torrance, Calif., 1977-78; nat. market and product mgr. Brit. Leyland Inc., Leonia, N.J., 1978-79; adj. prof. bus. Bergen (N.J.) Community Coll., 1978-79. Home: PO Box 1304 Troy MI 48099 Office: GM Bldg Room 9-230 Detroit MI 48202

STEPHENS, NORVAL BLAIR, JR., advt. agy. exec.; b. Chgo., Nov. 20, 1928; s. Norval Blair and Ethel Margaret (Lewis) S.; B.A., DePauw U., 1951; M.B.A., U. Chgo., 1959; m. Diane Forst, Sept. 29, 1951; children—Jill Elizabeth, John Gregory, Sandra Jean (dec.), Katherine Blair, James Norval. Asst. to v.p. ops. Walgreen Drug Co., Chgo., 1953-56; with Needham, Harper & Steers, Inc., N.Y.C., 1956—, sr. v.p., 1970-72, exec. v.p. internat., 1972-74, exec. v.p., dir. N.Y. div., 1974-76, exec. v.p. Chgo. div., 1976—, dir., 1967—; dir. Needham, Harper & Steers Internat., Inc. Commr., chmn. Plan Commn., Arlington Heights, Ill., 1965-67; mem. Pelham (N.Y.) Schs. Bd. Edn., 1972-75; trustee Village of Arlington Heights, 1961-65, Meml. Library, Arlington Heights, 1966-67, Arlington Heights United Fund, 1963-67; bd. dirs. N.W. Community Hosp. Found.,

1976—; bd. dirs. Harper Community Coll. Found., 1977—, pres., 1980—; bd. dirs. Barrington Area Devel. Council, 1978—, DePauw U. Alumni Bd., 1979—; bd. visitors DePauw U., 1979—. Served with USMCR, 1951-53. Named Young Man of Year, Arlington Heights Jr. C. of C., 1964; recipient Rector Scholar 25th Anniversary Class Achievement award DePauw U., 1976. Mem. Internat. Advt. Assn., DePauw U. Chgo. Alumni Assn. (pres. 1977-79), Phi Beta Kappa, Delta Tau Delta. Presbyterian (elder). Clubs: Larchmont Yacht, Mid-Am. Home: 107 Fox Hunt Trail Barrington IL 60010 Office: 303 E Wacker Dr Chicago IL 60601

STEPHENS, RICHARD BERNARD, energy and land co. exec.; b. Cambridge, Mass., Dec. 24, 1934; s. Theron W. and Emma M. (Bernard) S.; B.A. in Econs., Rice U., 1956; postgrad. exec. program in bus. adminstrn. Columbia U., 1974; m. Anne Monique Devant, Oct. 18, 1958; children—Ann, Claire, Jennifer. With Tenneco Oil Co., Lafayette, La. and Oklahoma City, 1960-65; with La. Land & Exploration Co., New Orleans, 1965—, v.p., mgr. land and fee property, 1970—; exec. v.p. Jacintoport Corp., 1974—, v.p. exploration Gulf Coast region and offshore, 1976-79, v.p. prodn. mid-continent and Alaska region, 1979—; pres. Kaluakoi Corp., 1978—, Freeport Oil Co., 1980—. Vice chmn. Greater New Orleans Area United Fund, 1976-77; fund council rep. Rice U., 1977; trustee St. Martins Protestant Episcopal Sch., 1977, Mercy Hosp. New Orleans, 1977—. Served to 1st lt. AUS, 1956-60. Mem. Am. Assn. Petroleum Landmen, Mid Continent Oil and Gas Assn., Am. Petroleum Inst., Ind. Petroleum Assn. Am., Petroleum Club New Orleans (v.p., dir. 1974), Fla. Petroleum Council (exec. com. 1973-74), La. Ind. Producers and Royalty Owners (v.p., dir. 1977-78), Nat. Assn. Indsl. Parks, Soc. Indsl. Realtors. Roman Catholic. Clubs: Beach (officer, dir. 1967-70), Internat. House, Plimsoll, Metairie Country. Home: 4724 Haring Ct Metairie LA 70002 Office: Ten O'One Howard Ave New Orleans LA 70161

STEPHENS, ROGER BRUCE, fin. co. exec.; b. Cedar Rapids, Iowa, Mar. 16, 1940; s. Amos Russell and Marjorie Adell (Pipkin) S.; B.A., U. Oreg., 1962; Ph.D. in Neuroanatomy, Stanford U., 1967, M.D., 1968; postgrad. Wharton Sch. Bus., U. Pa., 1977-78, Stanford Grad. Sch. Bus., 1978-80; m. Jacqueline C. West, Oct. 3, 1964; children—Cynthia, Amy, Bradley. Intern, resident Sacramento Med. Center, 1968-72; practice medicine specializing in anesthesiology, Sacramento, 1972-77; owner Roger B. Stephens Trust Deeds, Sacramento, 1975-77; pres. Granite Home Loans Ltd., Stephens & Stone, Sacramento, 1977-79; pres. Granite Fin. Corp., Sacramento, 1979—. Mem. Sacramento Bd. Realtors, Calif. Assn. Realtors, Calif. Ind. Mortgage Brokers Assn., Nat. Assn. Securities Dealers. Clubs: El Macero Country, Elks. Office: 1500 21st St Suite 200 Sacramento CA 95814

STEPHENS, STEVE, public relations exec.; b. Newport, Ark., Apr. 22, 1930; s. Owen and Allie Mae (Rozzell) S.; student U. Little Rock, 1948; B.S. in Bus. Adminstrn., U. Ark., 1951; postgrad. U. Miss., 1954-55; D.Hum., Southwest Coll., Oklahoma City; m. Ellen Beede, Apr. 21, 1957; children—Stanton, Steele. With CBS-TV, Little Rock, 1957-65; spl. asst. to U.S. Senator John L. McClellan, Washington, 1965-68; corporate v.p. pub. relations and advt. Nat. Investors Life Ins. Co., Little Rock, 1968-69; pres., chmn. bd., chief exec. officer Stephens Investments, Inc., Stephens Internat., Ltd., Little Rock, 1969—; founder Stephens Internat. Travel, Ltd., 1973—; dir. Bolivian Internat. Devel., Sociedad Anomina; adviser Ingenue Mag., 1960-65. State adviser Nat. Found., 1960-64; mem. exec. com. Radio Free Europe, 1961-62; state chmn. Arthritis Found., 1969; state adviser Youth Leadership Council, 1961-65; chmn. Little Rock City Beautiful Commn., 1961-62; mem. Pulaski County Health and Welfare Council, 1961-62; del. Inter-Am. Partners Alliance for Progress Conf., Lima, Peru, 1968, Partners of Alliance Hemisphere Conf., San Jose, Costa Rica; chmn. publicity United Fund campaign, 1968, bd. dirs., 1969-73; publicity chmn., dist. vice chmn. Pioneer dist. Boy Scouts Am., 1969-71; regional chmn., mem. nat. adv. com. March of Dimes, 1974—; bd. dirs. Internat. Services for Blind, Internat. Direct Relief Fund; bd. visitors Army and Navy Acad. Named Bolivian Counsel for Ark., Bolivian Pres., 1969. Served with USMC, 1951-54. Mem. Pub. Relations Soc. Am., Little Rock C. of C., Brit. Inst. Pub. Relations (overseas asso.), Sales and Mktg. Execs. (dir.). Clubs: Masons (32 deg.), Shriners; Little Rock, Pleasant Valley Country, Bahama Sound Beach, Racquet, West Side Tennis. Home: 2823 Painted Valley Dr Little Rock AR 72212 Office: Pleasant Valley Pl Little Rock AR 72212

STEPHENS, WARREN CLAYTON, JR., fin. co. exec.; b. Mobile, Ala., Apr. 6, 1942; s. Warren Clayton and Ellen Story (Fretz) S.; B.A., Notre Dame U., 1964; M.B.A., Stanford U., 1966; m. Millicent A. Wynne, Dec. 28, 1963; children—Warren Clayton III, Brent Christopher, Craig Gordon, Keith Wynne. Second v.p. Chase Manhattan Bank, N.Y.C., 1966-69; corp. v.p., div. pres. Genway Corp., Chgo., 1969-72; v.p., treas. Wheelabrator Frye, Inc., Hampton, N.H., 1972—, also pres. subs. Trailmobile Fin. Co., San Francisco. Nat. alumni sec. U. Notre Dame, 1964-74. Mem. Bus. and Industry Assn. N.H. (chmn. taxation com. 1976-78, dir. 1977—), Notre Dame Alumni Assn., Stanford Bus. Sch. Assn. Roman Catholic. Contbr. articles to profl. jours. Home: 2704 Rollo Rd Santa Rosa CA 95404 Office: 211 Sutter St Suite 309 San Francisco CA 94108

STEPHENS, WILLIAM THEODORE, lawyer, business exec.; b. Balt., Mar. 31, 1922; s. William A. and Mildred (Griffin) S.; student Balt. City Coll., 1939-41, U. Md., 1946-47; A.B., J.D., George Washington U., 1950, postgrad., 1951; m. Arlene Alice Lestl, June 2, 1958; children—William Theodore, Renée Adena. Admitted to Md. bar, 1950, D.C. bar, 1951, Va. bar, 1959; mem. firm J.L. Green, Washington, 1950-51, J.M. Cooper, Washington, 1952-54; own law firm William T. Stephens, Washington, 1955—; sec., gen. counsel, dir. Exotech, Inc., Gaithersburg, Md., KHI Corp., Fairfax, Va.; dir., prin. owner BARBCO, Inc. (Nev.), Fairfax Racquet Club, Inc., Fairfax; mem. adv. bd. Central Fidelity Bank & Trust Co. Mem. exec. com. Nat. Com. on Uniform Traffic Laws and Ordinances, 1967—; speaker Internat. Road Fedn., Tokyo, 1964, London, 1966. Trustee Ophthalmic Research Found., Washington, Fairfax-Brewster Sch., Falls Church, Va., Am. Bikeways Found., Washington. Served to 1st lt. U.S. Army, 1941-45. Mem. Bar Assn. D.C. (sec. taxation 1959-68), Am. (sec. taxation 1959—, sec. corps., banking and bus. law 1960—), D.C., Md., Va. bar assns., XVI Corps Assn. (pres. 1967), Kappa Alpha Order, Delta Theta Phi. Clubs: Commonwealth (Calif.); Univ., Capitol Hill (Washington); Jockey, Racquet Club Internat. (Miami, Fla.); Regency Racquet (McLean, Va.); Army-Navy Country (Arlington, Va.). Home: PO Box 1096 McLean VA 22101 also 881 Ocean Dr Key Biscayne FL 33149 Office: 1828 L St NW Washington DC 20036 also 1800 Old Meadow Rd PO Box 1096 McLean VA 22101

STEPHENSON, ARTHUR EMMET, JR., investment co. exec., banker; b. Bastrop, La., Aug. 29, 1945; s. Arthur Emmet and Edith Louise (Mock) S.; B.S. in Fin. magna cum laude, La. State U., 1967; M.B.A. (Ralph Thomas Sayles fellow), Harvard U., 1969; m. Toni Lyn Edwards, June 17, 1967. Adminstrv. aide to U.S. Sen. Russell Long of La., Washington, 1966; security analyst Fidelity Funds, Boston, 1968; founder, sr. partner Stephenson & Co., Denver, 1969—, Stephenson Mcht. Banking; co-founder, chmn. bd. Charter Bank & Trust; pres. Pennant Oilfield, Inc.; underwriting mem. Lloyd's of London; chmn. bd., pres. Gen. Communications, Inc., Stephenson Internat., Inc.; sr. partner Stoneacre Co., Stephenson, Stephenson Resources, Stephenson Properties; dir. Ins. Systems of Am., Inc., Circle Energy Inc., Pennant Service Co., Brooks Exploration, Inc., Sunergy Communities, Inc., Martin Oil Co., Pioneer Drilling Co.; Del., White House Conf. on Small Bus.; mem. exec. com. Colo. Small Bus. Council. Chartered Chartered fin. analyst. Mem. Denver Soc. Security Analysts (bd. dirs. 1975-77), Colo. Investment Advisers Assn. (treas., bd. dirs. 1975-78), Nat. Assn. Corporate Dirs., Colo. Press Assn., Newcomen Soc., Omicron Delta Kappa, Phi Kappa Phi, Beta Gamma Sigma, Kappa Sigma, Delta Sigma Pi (Leadership Denver 1978-79). Clubs: Petroleum of Denver, Metro Denver Exec. (pres., bd. dirs.), Denver Press, Harvard Bus. Sch. (pres. Colo. 1979, chmn. 1980), Annabel's of London, Harvard Bus. Sch. of N.Y., Harvard of N.Y. Pub. Denver Bus. World, Vail Scene Mag., Devel. Sales Info. Catalogue. Home: 11102 E Harvard Dr Aurora CO 80014 Office: 899 Logan St Denver CO 80203

STEPHENSON, ROBERT ALLAN, bldg. contractor; b. Orange, N.J., June 4, 1934; s. John F. and Mabelle V. (Eckert) S.; student Rutgers U., 1952-54; m. Eleanor M. Metzler, Oct. 17, 1964; children—Kevin John, Robert Allan. Asst. prodn. engr. Stauid Engring., Plainfield, N.J., 1955-57; supt. Nordling Dean & Co., Summit, N.J., 1957-69; pres. Stephenson Assos., Inc., Bridgewater, N.J., 1969—; dir. Sentry Electric Co., H & E-lectric Co. Mem. Tewksbury Twp. (N.J.) Bd. Edn., 1969-72; mem. Pottersville (N.J.) Vol. Fire Co. Served with U.S. Army, 1953-55. Recipient Outstanding Service award Somerset County 4-H Assn., 1974; Sales Achievement award Armco Steel, 1977; Disting. Service award Hunterdon County YMCA, 1978. Mem. NE Indsl. Devel. Assn., Armco Steel Indsl. Devel. Assn. (legis. council), Internat. Mgmt. Council, Hunterdon County (N.J.) C. of C. Republican. Clubs: Rotary, Somerset and Hunterdon 200 Clubs, Masons. Home: 14 McCann Mill Rd Pottersville NJ 07979 Office: 336 Grove St Bridgewater NJ 08807

STERGIOU, EMANUEL JAMES, actuary; b. N.Y.C., Aug. 24, 1949; s. William and Anita (Christakis) S.; B.S. in Math. (Tremaine fellow 1968-71), CCNY, 1971; m. Roseanne Chiara, Feb. 18, 1973; children—William Vincent, Andrew Elias. Actuary, then actuarial supr. Ins. Services Office, N.Y.C., 1970-72; asso. actuary N. Am; Re-ins. Corp., N.Y.C., 1972-74; v.p. Woodward & Fondiller, Inc., Cons. Actuaries, N.Y.C., 1974—; pres. E. James Stergiou Risk Cons., N.Y.C., 1980—; lectr. Am. Mgmt. Assn. workshops, 1979-80. Fellow Casualty Actuarial Soc.; mem. Am. Acad. Actuaries, Internat. Actuarial Assn., Actuarial Studies in Non-Life Ins. Democrat. Greek Orthodox. Contbr. articles to profl. jours. Home: 784 Columbus Ave Apt 9-0 New York NY 10025 Office: 130 E 59th St New York NY 10022

STERLING, DONALD C., bldg. materials mfg. co. exec.; b. Abington, Pa., Mar. 9, 1941; s. Harry M. and Emily L. (Sneed) S.; B.B.A., Oglethorpe U., Atlanta, 1974; M.B.A., Suffolk U., Boston, 1976; m. Mariann A. DeFazio, Oct. 8, 1960; children—Donald G., Douglas M., Daphne. Dist. sales mgr. Homasote Co., Trenton, N.J., 1962-68, regional sales mgr., 1968-72, exec. asst. to v.p. mktg., 1972-78; v.p. sales and mktg. Dacor, Inc., Worcester, Mass., 1978-79; sales mgr. Automated Bldg. Components, Inc., Miami, Fla., 1979—; prof. bus. adminstrn. Mass. Bay Coll. Sec., Pace Acad., Atlanta, 1970-71. Mem. Assn. M.B.A.'s. Club: Charles River Skating (pres.). Home: 4355 SE Fort King St Ocala FL 32670 Office: 7525 NW 37th Ave Miami FL 33159

STERLING, JOHN FRANCIS, textbook publisher; b. Rochester, N.Y., Nov. 1, 1920; s. Frank Bertram and Oliette Catherine (DeNeve) S.; B.B.A., U. Buffalo, 1942; M.Ed., N.Y. U., 1952; LL.D. (hon.), N.H. Coll., 1979; m. Carolyn Virginia Evans, Sept. 4, 1943; children—John Francis, Scott Evans, Alan DeNeve. Vets. counselor U. Buffalo, 1946-46; tchr. bus. edn. Perry (N.Y.) High Sch., 1946-47; instr. econs. and accounting Quinnipiac Coll., New Haven, 1947-49, dir. placement, 1949; pubs. rep. South Western Pub. Co., N.Y., 1949-60, asst. Eastern dist. mgr., 1960-62, Eastern dist. mgr., 1963-67, regional v.p., Pelham Manor, N.Y., 1967—; vis. lectr. schs. and colls.; frequent commencement speaker; curriculum cons. schs. and colls.; mem. adv. bd. Westchester Bus. Inst., White Plains, N.Y. Served to lt. USNR, 1942-45; PTO. Recipient Clinton A. Reed award Bus. Tchrs. Assn. N.Y. State, 1975; Friend of Bus. Edn. citation Bus. Edn. Assn. Met. N.Y., 1977. Mem. Am. Vocat. Assn., Nat. Bus. Edn. Assn., Bus. Tchrs. Assn. N.Y. State (life), N.Y. State Profl. Bookmen's Assn. (pres. 1961), Adminstrv. Mgmt. Soc., Assn. Ednl. Salesmen N.Y. State (pres. 1962), Delta Pi Epsilon. Republican. Home: 428 Wolfs Ln Pelham Manor NY 10803 Office: 925 Spring Rd Pelham Manor NY 10803

STERLING, OLIVER JAMES, oil and gas drilling co. exec.; b. N.Y.C., Nov. 13, 1936; s. Oliver James and Virginia Lee (Boyce) S.; B.S. in Physics, U. Houston, 1959; M.B.A., Columbia U., 1965; m. Miriam Kotler, Dec. 27, 1967; children—James, Vanessa. Pres., chief operating officer Sterling Drilling and Prodn. Co., Inc., N.Y.C., 1978—; pres. Sterling Gas Mgmt., Inc., Natural Gas Mgmt. Ltd.; exec. v.p. Platte River Oil Co.; mng. partner, gen. partner other oil and gas drilling partnerships.; exec. com., bd. dirs. Nat. Com. Am. Fgn. Policy; pres., chmn. bd. Am. Bus. Council of Middle East. Served as officer USAR, 1960-62. Mem. Ind. Oil and Gas Assn. W.Va., Petroleum Exploration Soc. Clubs: Univ., N.Y. Athletic, Pinnacle (N.Y.C.); Meadow, Bathing Corp. (Southampton, N.Y.). Home: 1030 Fifth Ave New York NY 10028 Office: 622 3d Ave New York NY 10017

STERLING, ROBERT LEE, JR., investment co. exec.; b. Cleve., June 12, 1933; s. Robert Lee and Kathryn (Durell) S.; student U. Edinburgh (Scotland), 1955; B.A., Brown U., 1956; M.B.A., Columbia U., 1962; m. Deborah Platt, May 16, 1964; children—Robert Livingston, William Lee, Cameron Platt. Corp. research analyst Morgan Guaranty Trust, N.Y.C., 1962-63; asst. comptroller Western Hemisphere CPC Internat., N.Y.C., 1963-66; v.p. White, Weld & Co., Inc., N.Y.C., 1966-78, Merrill Lynch Asset Mgmt., 1978-80, Wood, Struthers & Winthrop Mgmt. Corp., N.Y.C., 1980—. Trustee, Lenox Hill Hosp., N.Y.C.; bd. dirs. Inst. Sports Medicine and Athletic Trauma. Served to lt. USNR, 1956-60. Mem. New Eng. Soc. (pres.), Nat. Trust Scotland (Edinburgh), St. Andrews Soc., St. Nicholas Soc., Pilgrims, Soc. Cincinnati, Alpha Delta Phi, Alpha Kappa Psi. Clubs: Round Hill (Conn.); Downtown, Univ. (N.Y.C.); Edgartown (Mass.) Yacht. Home: 16 Pheasant Ln Greenwich CT 06830 Office: 120 Broadway New York NY 10271

STERLING, WALTER GAGE, mfg. co. exec.; b. Anahuac, Tex., May 20, 1901; s. Ross Shaw and Maude (Gage) S.; LL.B., U. Tex., 1925; m. Ruth Dermody, Jan. 30, 1941. Admitted to Tex. bar, 1925; with Royalty Properties, Houston, 1927—, v.p., 1946—; pres. Sterling Oil & Refinery 1935-50, Richmond Mfg. Co., 1951—; with Richmond Sales, 1952—; dir. Citizens Nat. Bank & Trust Co., Baytown, Living Bank, Houston; trustee Mortgage & Trust Investors. Trustee Hermann Hosp. Estate, 1950—, pres. bd. trustees, 1965—; trustee Sch. of Ozarks, Point Lookout, Mo., 1973—; regent U. Tex. System, 1975-81; bd. dirs. Tex. Med. Center. Served to capt. USAAF, 1941-44. Mem. Inst. Hemotherapy, S.A.R. (pres. gen. 1968-69), Delta Kappa Epsilon. Clubs: Lakeside Country (past pres.), Petroleum (past pres.) (Houston). Home: 1600 Holcombe Blvd Penthouse A Houston TX 77030 Office: PO Box 289 Houston TX 77001

STERMER, JOHN JOSEPH, funeral dir.; b. Cin., Sept. 28, 1916; s. John and Josephine (Thinnes) S.; Ph.B., Xavier U., Cin., 1938; m. Jeanette Klosterman, Apr. 19, 1941; children—J. Jay, Jenifer. Dir., Vitt & Stermer, Inc., Cin., 1941—, pres., gen. mgr., 1944—; pres., dir. Tannery Savs. & Loan Co., Cin., 1943—. Trustee, Cin. Coll. Mortuary Sci. Found.; pres. South Fairmount Improvement Assn., 1945. Mem. Nat. Funeral Dirs. Assn., Ohio Funeral Dirs. Assn., Greater Cin. Funeral Dirs. Assn., Fairmount Bus. Men's Club (pres. 1951), Cheviot Civic and Bus. Club. Club: Cheviot-Westwood Kiwanis (pres. 1946, 35-Yr. Legion of Honor award 1980). Home: 2984 Westbrook Dr Cincinnati OH 45238 Office: 1824 Westwood Ave Cincinnati OH 45214

STERN, GARY HILTON, economist; b. San Luis Obispo, Calif., Nov. 3, 1944; s. Robert Earl and Joy Merdis (Shimon) S.; A.B. magna cum laude (Univ. Scholar), Washington U., St. Louis, 1967; M.A. (Univ. Scholar), Ph.D., Rice U., 1970; m. Mary Katherine Nelson, Aug. 17, 1969; children—Matthew Stuart, Meredith Faulkner. Mgr. domestic research dept. Fed. Res. Bank of N.Y., N.Y.C., 1973-77; mgr. fixed income research Loeb Rhoades, Hornblower & Co., N.Y.C., 1977-78; sr. economist A. Gary Shilling & Co., N.Y.C., 1978—; adj. prof. Columbia U. Grad. Sch. Bus., N.Y. U. Trustee West Side Montessori Sch., 1978-79. NDEA Scholar, 1967-70; Bache & Co. scholar, 1963-67. Club: Downtown Athletic. Author: In The Name of Money: A Professional's Guide to the Federal Reserve, 1980. Home: 180 Riverside Dr New York NY 10024 Office: A Gary Shilling & Co Inc 111 Broadway New York NY 10006

STERN, GENE, mfg. co. exec.; b. N.Y.C., Jan. 6, 1933; s. Moe and Anna (Polansky) S.; B.A. (scholar), U. Rochester, 1955; M.B.A., Hofstra U., 1970; children—Dianne, Susan, Michael, Sandra. Program adminstr. Hazeltine Corp., Little Neck, N.Y., 1959-63; program planning and control mgr. Grumman Corp., Bethpage, N.Y., 1964-70; financial analyst-internal cons. J. Walter Thompson Co., N.Y.C., 1970-72; dir. finance, v.p. Internat. Corp. Enterprises (name formerly DCI Co.), Dallas, 1972-75; controller, treas. Royal Park, Inc., Dallas, 1975-78, Victor Costa, Inc., Dallas, 1978-79, Prophecy Corp., Dallas, 1979—. Served with USAF, 1956-59. Mem. Nat. Assn. Accountants. Clubs: Lancers, Brookhaven. Author: Commanlity in Planning, 1970. Contbr. articles to profl. jours. Home: 4446 Mill Creek Dallas TX 75234 Office: 1122 Jackson St Dallas TX 75202

STERN, LESLIE WARREN, mgmt. cons.; b. N.Y.C., July 3, 1938; s. Herman and Lillian Bella (Rosenbloom) S.; B.S., Cornell U., 1960; M.B.A., Tulane U., 1967; m. Madeline Carol Kuttner, Jan. 23, 1966; children—Derek Alexandre, Cory Jay. Catering mgr. Irish Internat. Airlines, N.Y.C., 1960-61; dir. mgmt. services Plaza Hotel, Hotel Corp. Am., N.Y.C., 1961-68; pres. L. W. Stern Assos., Inc., N.Y.C., 1968—. Chmn., Cornell Com. on Alumni Trustee Nominations, mem. Cornell U. Council, 1979—. Mem. Am. Mgmt. Assn., N. Am. Soc. Corp. Planning, Assn. Systems Mgmt. (pres. N.Y. chpt. 1970-71), Tulane Grad. Sch. Bus. Alumni (pres. N.Y. chpt. 1973-74), Tulane Alumni Club (pres. Met. N.Y. chpt. 1974-75), Tulane Alumni Assn. (dir.), Cornell U. Alumni Assn. (chmn. communications com., pres. 1980—). Home: 75 East End Ave Apt 6-A New York NY 10028 Office: 120 E 56th St Suite 430 New York NY 10022

STERN, WALTER PHILLIPS, investment exec.; b. N.Y.C., Sept. 26, 1928; s. Leo and Marjorie (Phillips) S.; A.B., Williams Coll., 1950; M.B.A., Harvard U., 1952; m. Elizabeth May, Feb. 12, 1957; children—Sarah May, William May, David May. With Lazard Freres & Co., N.Y.C., 1953-54; asso. Drexel, Burnham Lambert Group, Inc., N.Y.C., 1954-60, partner, 1960-71, sr. exec. v.p., dir., 1972-73; vice-chmn., dir. Capital Research Co., Los Angeles, 1979—, sr. v.p., mng. dir. Eastern ops., 1973-79; chmn. bd. New Perspective Fund, Inc., 1973—, Fundamental Investors, 1978—, Anchor Growth Fund, Inc., 1978—; pres. Capital Guardian Mgmt. Co.; dir. Capital Group, Inc., Income Fund Am., Capital Research Co. S.A., Geneva; pres., chief exec. officer Capital Strategic Services, Inc., 1973—; dir. Growth Fund Am., 1974—, Temple Industries, Diboll, Tex., 1970-73, May Corp., Nashville, Wayne-Gossard Corp., 1973-78; instr. N.Y. U., 1956-62. Chmn. fin. com. Hadassah; bd. dirs. Westchester chpt. Am. Jewish Com.; trustee Fin. Accounting Found., treas., 1975—; adv. bd. Ams. for Energy Independence, 1979—; trustee, vice chmn. Hudson Inst., 1973—, Tel Aviv U., 1976—; v.p., treas., mem. exec. com. Am. Friends of Tel Aviv U., 1976—; treas., v.p., trustee Fin. Analysts Research Found., 1979—; pres., bd. dirs. Research Project on Energy and Econ. Policy, 1974—. Served as 1st lt. USAF, 1952-53. Mem. N.Y. Soc. Security Analysts (former dir.), Fin. Analysts Fedn. (pres. 1971-72, Disting. Service award 1974), Inst. Chartered Fin. Analysts (pres. 1976-77, former trustee), Phi Beta Kappa. Jewish. Clubs: Harvard, Econ., Board Room, Williams (N.Y.C.); Calif. (Los Angeles); Sunningdale Country (Scarsdale, N.Y.). Contbr. articles to profl. pubis. Home: 450 Ft Hill Rd Scarsdale NY 10583 Office: 280 Park Ave New York NY 10017

STERNBERG, HERBERT BERNARD, reference co. exec.; b. N.Y.C., May 20, 1917; s. Max and Henrietta (Geringer) S.; student Columbia U., 1936-40; m. Judith L. Harris; 1 dau. (by previous marriage), Steffani. Real estate mgmt., 1935-38; with U.S. C.E., N.Y.C., 1938, 47; pres. Nationwide Products Corp., N.Y.C., 1947-54; cons. systems engr., 1954-60; with Auto Facto Systems, N.Y.C., 1960-65; chmn. bd. Automated Reference Corp., N.Y.C., 1965—. Served with AUS, 1940-45. Patentee in field. Office: 200 Central Park S New York City NY 10019

STERNE, SUSAN MAINS, fin. exec.; b. N.Y.C., Feb. 28, 1946; d. William Donald and Florence (Sachse) Mains; B.B.A., U. Iowa, 1968; postgrad. N.Y. U., 1969; m. Lawrence Jon Sterne, Apr. 17, 1976; children—Christopher William Southern, Melissa Anne Southern, Marjorie Mains. Asst. economist Goldman Sachs & Co., N.Y.C., 1969-71; economist Cyrus S. Lawrence, Inc., N.Y.C., 1972-75, Faulkner Dawkins & Sullivan, N.Y.C., 1974-76; v.p., economist Salomon Bros., N.Y.C., 1976-79; pres. Econ. Analysis Assos., Cos Cob, Conn., 1979—; lectr. U. Mich. Annual Outlook Conf., 1979; lectr. New Sch., 1978; mem. econ. adv. bd. U.S. Dept. Commerce, 1978-79. Mem. Bus. Econ. Issue Council, Nat. Assn. Bus. Economists, Fin. Analyst Fedn., N.Y. Assn. Bus. Economists, N.Y. Soc. Security Analysts. Contbr. articles to profl. jours. Office: PO Box 1100 Cos Cob CT 06807

STERNLICHT, BENO, research and devel. co. exec.; b. Nowy Sacz, Poland; s. Hugo Charles and Helena (Anisfeld) S.; B.S., Union Coll., 1950; M.S., Columbia U., 1951, Ph.D., 1954, D.Sc. (hon.), 1970; children—Mark David, Eric Alan, Joshua Hugh. Staff engr. Thermal Power Systems Gen. Engring. Lab., Gen. Electric, 1951-54, specialist-applied mechanics Gen. Engring. Lab., 1954-58, cons. engr. Gen. Electric, Schenectady, 1958-61; tech. dir., chmn. bd., co-founder Mech. Tech., Inc., Latham, N.Y., 1961—; pres. 97 Fort Washington Corp., N.Y.C., 1961—, Huben Assos., Corp., N.Y.C., 1959—, Ameast Distbrs. Corp., N.Y.C., 1959—, Starlight Holding Corp., N.Y.C., 1959—, 172 E. 4th St. Corp., N.Y.C., 1956—; dir. Small Diesels Ltd., India, New Eastern India Ltd.; mem. Pres.'s Council Indsl. Innovation, 1979. Pres., VITA (Vols. for Internat. Tech. Assistance),

1965-71, chmn. bd., 1971-73; chmn. NASA Com. on Energy Tech. and Space Propulsion; mem. NASA Research and Tech. Adv. Council, 1970—. Fellow ASME (Machine Design award 1966); mem. AIAA, Nat. Acad. Sci., Am. Soc. Lubrication Engrs., Sigma Xi, Tau Beta Pi., Navy League U.S. Author articles on energy conservation and conversion. Patentee in field. Home: 2520 Whamer Ln Schenectady NY 12309 Office: 968 Albany-Shaker Rd Latham NY 12110

STERNLIGHT, DAVID, economist; b. N.Y.C., Feb. 9, 1933; s. Murry and Geraldine (Lerner) S.; S.B., Mass. Inst. Tech., 1960; Ph.D., London (Eng.) Sch. Econs., 1962; m. Debora Gersten Field, June 19, 1960 (div. 1978); children—Samuel Marc, Alan Lewis, Daniel Jon, Judith Lynn. Mathematician, Rand Corp., 1956-58, IBM Corp., 1958-60; cons. UN, N.Y.C., 1959-60, UNESCO, Paris, France, 1960-62; dir. econ. planning Litton Industries, Inc., Beverly Hills, Calif., 1962-72; presdl. exchange exec., dep. dir. Office Policy Devel., Office Sec. Commerce, Washington, 1972-73; chief economist Atlantic Richfield Co., Inc., Los Angeles, 1973—. Cons. White House Task Force on Urban Employment Opportunities, 1967; mem. Ford/Nat. Acad. Sci./U. Calif. at Los Angeles Task Force on Nat. Engring. Econs. Edn., 1969; Distinguished lectr. U. Calif., 1970; asso. Mass. Inst. Tech. Workshop on Alternative Energy Strategies, 1974—. Served to 1st lt. AUS, 1954-56. Mem. Council Fgn. Relations, UN Assn. (econ. policy council 1977—), Council Sci. and Tech. for Devel., Inst. Mgmt. Scis. (chmn. Washington chpt. 1965-66, council mem. Coll. on Logistics 1965—), Am. Econ. Assn., Nat. Assn. Bus. Economists. Home: PO Box 71665 Los Angeles CA 90071 Office: 515 S Flower St Los Angeles CA 90071

STERTMEYER, RANDALL LEE, insulation corp. exec.; b. Cin., Dec. 10, 1942; s. Harold Henry and Paula Charlotta (Theobald) S.; B.S. in Edn., Miami U., Oxford, Ohio, 1964; M.A., Xavier U., Cin., 1976; postgrad. Sch. Bus., U. Cin., 1977-78; m. Gail Lynn Murphy, Apr. 4, 1968; children—Scott Christopher, Allison Paige. Social worker Hamilton County (Ohio) Welfare Dept., 1965-68; diagnostic social worker Cin. Bd. Edn., 1968-70; pres. Lyran Homes, Inc., Cin., 1970-73; Cin. br. mgr. Mooney and Moses of Ohio, Inc., 1973-77, v.p., Cin., 1977—. Ward chmn. Dem. Com. City of Madeira, Ohio, 1973-78; candidate for city councilman, Madeira, 1975; del. State of Ohio Dem. State Conv., 1975. Served with USAR, 1965-71. Named citizen of the day Sta. WLW, 1978; mem. Tribe Miami, Miami U., 1964. Mem. Nat. Home Builders Assn., Ohio Home Builders Assn., Greater Cin. Home Builders Assn., No. Ky. Home Builders Assn., Greater Cin. Insulation Contractors Assn. (founding chmn. 1978). Home: 9577 Loveland-Maderia Rd Loveland OH 45140 Office: 207 Donald Dr Fairfield OH 45014

STEUBER, DIANE WEIDEL, office coffee service exec.; b. Altoona, Pa., July 4, 1940; d. Edgar Albin and Marjorie Kathleen (Guyer) Weidel; B.A., U. Calif., San Jose, 1962; m. Harold A. Steuber, Jr., Dec. 18, 1960; children—Thomas W., April Rose. Tchr. pub. schs., Cupertino, Calif., 1963-64; head start tchr. Redlands (Calif.) Sch. Dist., 1967-68; v.p., sec.-treas. Associated Services/Royalty Coffee Co., Emeryville, Calif., 1970—. Mem. No. Calif. Coffee Service Assn. (pres. 1977-78), Jr. League Oakland E. Bay (Calif.), Delta Gamma. Republican. Presbyterian. Office: 8210 Capwell Dr Oakland CA 94621

STEVENS, CLYDE BENJAMIN, JR., owner apt. bldgs.; b. Denver, Oct. 10, 1908; s. Clyde Benjamin and Maybelle Olive (Boot) S.; B.S., U.S. Naval Acad., 1930; m. Lucile Lillian-Louise Kip, May 5, 1933; children—Jane Stevens White, Donald K., Patricia S. Schley. Commd. ensign U.S. Navy, 1930, advanced through ranks to rear admiral, 1959, ret., 1959; product planner TRW, Inc., Cleve., 1959-65; research group supr. Boeing Corp., Seattle, 1965-74; sec.-treas. Keshti Corp., Seattle, 1975-77; cons. Goodyear Aerospace Corp., 1965, TRW, Inc., 1967, Nat. Security Indsl. Assn., 1961-76. Decorated Navy Cross, Silver Star (2); registered profl. engr., Wash. Mem. Seattle Apt. Operators Assn. (trustee 1967-76), Nat. Security Indsl. Assn., Nat. Def. Preparedness Assn., Am. Soc. Naval Engrs., U.S. Naval Inst. Clubs: Army and Navy (Washington); Rainier (Seattle). Patentee in field. Home: 2339 Franklin Ave E Seattle WA 98102

STEVENS, DAVID CHRISTOPHER, paper mfg. co. exec.; b. Sundridge, Kent, Eng., Aug. 11, 1934; s. Charles Bridges and Beatrice Maude (Jarratt) S.; came to U.S., 1955, naturalized, 1975; B.S. in Commerce, De Paul U., 1970; M.B.A., U. Chgo., 1976; m. Kathleen Mary Stobart, Nov. 14, 1959; children—Elizabeth Anne, Pamela Jane, Mark Andrew. With Internat. Paper Co., 1955-78; v.p. Mead Containers, 1978-79, v.p. Mead Packaging Internat., Atlanta, 1979—. Served with Brit. Army, 1953-55. Mem. English Speaking Union. Republican. Episcopalian. Clubs: Masons, Wellington, Belfry (London). Home: 30 Cliffside Crossing Atlanta GA 30338 Office: 950 W Marietta St NW Atlanta GA 30302

STEVENS, FORREST WAYNE, metal fabrication co. exec.; b. Portsmouth, Ohio, Apr. 3, 1928; s. Alvin Morton and Naomi (Maggard) S.; B.S. magna cum laude, Cedarville Coll., 1951; grad. Am. Mgmt. Assn. Mgmt. Devel. Program, 1975; m. Betty Joan Boling, Dec. 20, 1947; children—Cathy Ann, Patricia Elaine, Douglas Michael. Vice pres. Western ops. Buckeye Incubator Co., Springfield, Ohio, 1951-62; exec. v.p. LaTorre Farms, Inc., Watsonville, Calif., 962-63; pres. Better Egg Co., Watsonville, 1963-65; pres. Valmont Pacific, Inc., 1964-70; v.p., gen. mgr. Sales Fin. div. Valmont Industries, 1970-77, v.p. mktg. Irrigation div., 1977-79, corp. v.p. and treas., Valley, Nebr., 1979—; pres., dir. Valmont Fin. Corp., Valley, 1975—. Mem. adv. com. Omaha Airport Authority, 1980; adv. U. Nebr. Found. Served with USN, 1945-47. Mem. Am. Assn. Equipment Lessors, Am. Mgmt. Assn., Aircraft Owners and Pilots Assn., Am. Bonanza Soc. Republican. Presbyterian. Clubs: Highland Country, Omaha Press. Home: 22822 Rifle Ridge Terr Elkhorn NE 68022 Office: Valmont Industries Inc Valley NE 68064

STEVENS, ROBERT GENE, bank holding co. exec.; b. Marion, Ill., Jan. 4, 1930; s. Robert B. and Mae (Isaacs) S.; B.S., So. Ill. U., 1951; M.S., U. Ill., 1954, Ph.D., 1958; m. Susan Ann Krejci, Aug. 6, 1955; children—David, Craig, Brian. Instr. accounting U. Ill., Urbana, 1955-58; partner Touche, Ross, N.Y.C., 1958-68; v.p. Citibank, N.Y.C., 1968-70; pres. Old Stone Bank, Providence, 1970-75; chmn., pres., chief exec. officer BancOhio Corp., Columbus, 1976—; chmn., chief exec. officer BancOhio Nat. Bank, Columbus, 1979—. Mng. trustee Old Stone Mortgage and Realty Trust, 1971-75. Served with USAF, 1951-53. Office: 155 E Broad St Columbus OH 43265

STEVENS, ROBERT IVAN, bus. exec.; b. N.Y.C., Feb. 17, 1916; s. Adolph and Beatrice (Freeman) S.; certificate bus. adminstrn. Union Coll., 1937; B.A. in Econs., Rutgers U., 1941; postgrad. N.Y. U., 1946-51, grad. Coll. Engring. Roundtable, 1955; grad. USAF Staff and Command Coll., 1963, Indsl. Coll. Armed Forces, 1964; m. Rosemarie Palm, June 7, 1947; children—Robert Francis, Bruce Palm. Mgr. product planning and systems programming adminstrn. Univac div. Sperry Rand Co., 1959-63; internal cons. NBC, N.Y.C., 1963-67; dir. orgn. adminstrn. ITT Corp., N.Y.C., 1967—. Chmn., Troop 181 Boy Scouts Am., 1965-67, chmn. mgmt. info. systems com. of nat. adv. bd. Served to capt. USAAF, 1941-46, maj. USAF, 1951-52, lt. col. Res. (ret.). Mem. Rutgers Alumni Assn. (pres. NAS Coll. 1970-71), Assn. Systems Mgmt. (pres. N.Y. chpt. 1973-74, outstanding chpt. member award 1969, 74, internat. disting. service award 1974), Air Force Assn. (comdr. Mitchel squadron 1954). Republican. Lutheran. Mem. editorial bd. Jour. for Systems Mgmt. Contbr. articles to profl. jours. Home: 3551 Carrollton Ave Wantagh NY 11793 Office: ITT Corp 320 Park Ave New York NY 10022

STEVENS, THADDEUS KENT, real estate broker; b. Washington, July 2, 1945; s. Roger Babington and Jane (Diddel) S.; A.A.S. in Forestry, Paul Smith's Coll., 1965. Real estate salesman, 1969-72; sales mgr. Stevens, Realtors, Gaines, Pa., 1972-75, co-owner, 1972-75; v.p. Stevens Homestead, Inc., Gaines, 1975-79; pres. Stevens Assos., Inc., Gaines, 1979—; instr. Pa. State U. Served with USCG, 1965-69. Grad. Realtors Inst. Mem. Nat. Assn. Realtors, Realtor's Nat. Mktg. Inst., Farm and Land Inst., Pa. Assn. Realtors (sec. 1981, dir.; chmn. legis. com. 1981), N. Central Pa. Bd. Realtors (past pres., Realtor of Yr. 1976), C. of C., VFW. Republican. Home: 12 Walnut St Wellsboro PA 16901

STEVENS, WHITNEY, textile co. exec.; b. Plainfield, N.J., Nov. 26, 1926; s. Robert TenBroeck and Dorothy Goodwin (Whitney) S.; student Phillips Acad., 1940-44; B.A., Princeton U., 1947; m. 2d, Helene Baldi, Nov. 1, 1961; children—Mark W., David W., Joan. With J.P. Stevens & Co., Inc., N.Y.C., 1948—, v.p., 1958-64, exec. v.p., 1964-69, pres., 1969-79, chmn., chief exec. officer, 1980—, also dir., mem. exec. com.; adv. bd. Chem. Bank, N.Y.C. Vice chmn. bd. trustees St. Luke's/Roosevelt Hosp., N.Y.C., trustee Citizens' Budget Commn., N.Y.C. Served with USNR, 1944-46. Mem. Am. Textile Mfrs. Assn. (internat. trade com.). Clubs: Links (N.Y.C.); Princeton (N.Y.). Office: 1185 Ave of Americas New York NY 10036

STEVENS, WILLIAM DOLLARD, corp. exec.; b. Bayonne, N.J., Aug. 4, 1918; s. William B. and Beatrice (Dollard) S.; B.Mech. Engring., Rensselaer Poly. Inst., 1940; postgrad. Case Inst. Tech., 1958; m. Mary E. King, Oct. 12, 1940; children—Sandra A. (Mrs. Jeffrey N. Melin), Barbara E. (Mrs. Dennis Gallagher), William K. Various engring. and mgmt. positions Babcock & Wilcox Co., N.Y.C., 1940-62; v.p. equipment div. Foster Wheeler Corp., Livingston, N.J., 1962-73, sr. v.p., 1972-74, exec. v.p., 1974-78, chmn. bd., 1978—, also dir.; dir. Forney Engring. Co., Glitsch, Inc., Belco Pollution Control, Inc.; tchr. Pratt Inst., 1946-47. Chmn. fund drive A.R.C., Hackensack, N.J., 1956; planning commr. Hackensack, 1955-58. Trustee Bergen County Mental Health Consultation Center, 1955-58; bd. dirs. Metals Properties Council, 1972-78, chmn., 1981—; bd. overseers N.J. Inst. Tech., 1978—. Served to lt. USNR, 1943-45. Mem. ASME, Sigma Xi, Tau Beta Pi, Phi Kappa Tau. Methodist. Contbr. articles to profl. jours. Patentee in field. Office: 110 S Orange Ave Livingston NJ 07039

STEVENS, WILLIAM JOHN, assn. exec.; b. Dusseldorf, Germany, Aug. 23, 1915; s. Peter and Margaret (Kaumanns) S.; brought to U.S., 1923, naturalized, 1931; student McCall Sch. Printing, 1933; student assn. mgmt. Northwestern U., 1947; m. Dorothy V. Santangini, Feb. 14, 1937. With Ruttle, Shaw & Wetherill, Phila., 1931-34; partner New Era Printing Co., Phila., 1934-37; plant mgr. plant Marcus & Co., Phila., 1937-41; supt. Edward Stern & Co., Phila., 1941-46; exec. sec. Nat. Assn. Photo-Lithographers, N.Y.C., 1946-50, exec. v.p., 1961-64, pres., 1964-71; pres. NPEA Exhibits, Inc., 1971—; v.p. Nat. Printing Equipment Assn.; owner Dorval Co., pub.; exec. sec. Met. Lithographers Assn., N.Y.C., 1946-50; asst. to v.p. Miehle Co., N.Y.C., 1950-56, mgr. Phila. dist., 1956-61; cons. Sales Devel. Inst., Phila., 1960—; mem. Am. Bd. Arbitration, 1962—; chmn. adv. commn. on graphic arts N.Y.C. Community Coll., 1972—; mem. N.J. Motion Picture and Devel. Commn., 1978—. Named Industry Man of Year, Nat. Assn. Photo-Lithographers, 1954, Man of Year, N.Y. Litho Guild, 1962; recipient B'nai B'rith award, 1968; N.Y. Navigators award, 1969; laureate N.Y. Printers Hall of Fame, 1980. Mem. Am., N.Y. socs. assn. execs., Graphic Arts Assn. Execs. (pres. 1969), Tech. Assn. Graphic Arts, Nat. Assn. Litho Clubs (founder, pres. 1947, Industry award 1947, 79, sec. 1964-71), N.Y. Club Printing House Craftsmen. Clubs: Phila. Litho (pres. 1945); N.Y. Litho (N.Y.C.). Author: How to Prepare Copy for Offset Lithography, 1948; Building Construction and Floor Plans for Installing Web Offset Presses; contbr. articles to trade publs. Inventor Hiky-Picker, Quik-Match Color File for selection paint color samples. Home and Office: 431 Lakeview Dr Oradell NJ 07649

STEVENS, WILLIE GEORGE, men's clothing store exec.; b. Woodruff, S.C., May 11, 1952; s. Joe and Loree Virginia (Green) S.; A.A., Spartanburg Methodist Coll., 1972; B.A., Wofford Coll., 1974; m. Sharon L. Westberry, June 4, 1977; children—Sharina, Lakisha, Joseph. Field coordinator Neighborhood Youth Corp., Spartanburg, S.C., 1972-74; lab. technician Union Caribe Corp., Simpsonville, S.C., 1974-75; mgr., menswear buyer The Real Thing, Winston-Salem, N.C., 1975-77; mgr., buyer J. Henry Mens Fashion, Winston-Salem, 1977—; tchr. public schs., Spartanburg County, S.C., 1970-72. Mem. Bus. Action League, Greater Winston Salem C. of C., Omega Psi Phi. Democrat. Home: 308 E Polo Rd Winston-Salem NC 27105 Office: 546 N Trade St Winston-Salem NC 27101

STEVENSON, EUGENE ANTHONY, mfg. co. exec.; b. Niagara Falls, N.Y., Nov. 26, 1947; s. Anthony and Eugenia Anna Maria (Pavan) de Stefano; B.A., Canisius Coll., 1969; M.A., Ind. U., 1971; m. Cheryl Marie Dawson, Dec. 1, 1967; children—Gregory Dawson, Kathryn Dawson. Pub. affairs asst. Allstate Ins. Co., Northbrook, Ill., 1972-74; dir. pub. affairs Motorcycle Safety Found., Washington, 1974-76; mgr. pub. relations Textron Inc., Providence, 1976-78; dir. external relations Continental Group, Inc., Stamford, Conn., 1978-80; dir. fin. communications R. J. Reynolds Industries, Inc., Winston-Salem, N.C., 1980—. Mem. public info. com. internat./intercultural programs Am. Field Service; bd. dirs. Nat. Safety Council. Mem. Pub. Relations Soc. Am., Nat. Investor Relations Inst., Nat. Press Club. Office: R J Reynolds Industries World Hdqrs Winston-Salem NC 27102

STEVENSON, MARK JOSEPH, computer mfg. co. exec.; b. Dubuque, Iowa, Sept. 8, 1938; s. Frank Joseph and Helen M. (Delaney) S.; B.A., U. Iowa, 1960; m. Maureen Ann McDermott, June 23, 1963; children—Elizabeth, Ann, Jennifer. With IBM Corp., 1963-71, br. mgr., Moline, Ill., 1969-71; eastern regional mgr. ITEL Corp., Washington, 1971, dir. mktg., San Francisco, 1971-72; mgr. field mktg. Xerox Corp., Rochester, N.Y., 1972-74, nat. sales mgr., Dallas, 1974-75; v.p. mktg. NBI, Inc., Boulder, Colo., 1976—. Mem. Am. Mgmt. Assn., Internat. Word Processing Assn., Sigma Alpha Epsilon. Republican. Roman Catholic. Home: 7242 Old Post Dr Boulder CO 80301 Office: 1695 38th St Boulder CO 80301

STEVENSON, ROBERT EDWIN, fin. and accounting cons.; b. Iowa City, Jan. 5, 1917; s. Russell A. and Edna Lorraine (Kampenga) S.; B.B.A., U. Minn., 1939; M.B.A., N.Y. U., 1954; grad. Exec. Devel. Program, Stanford U., 1958; m. Pauline Louise McCracken, Sept. 1, 1939 (dec. Oct. 31, 1980); children—Jean Stevenson Simpson, Robert Harold. With Mut. Implement and Hardware Co., Owatonna, Minn., 1939-43, Aero. div. Mpls.-Honeywell Regulator Co., Mpls., 1943-44; with Exxon Corp. and affiliated cos., 1944-77; sr. tax accountant Esso Standard Oil Co., Baton Rouge, 1944-48; head, div. deptl. adminstrn. Standard Oil Co. (N.J.), N.Y.C., 1948-59; asst. controller Carter div. Humble Oil & Refining Co., Tulsa, 1960-64, accounting research coordinator, Houston, 1964-72; coordinator accounting research Exxon Corp., N.Y.C., 1972-77; fin. and accounting cons., New Canaan, Conn., 1977—; advisor Accounting Prins. Bd., 1964-71. Recipient certificate of appreciation Am. Petroleum Inst., 1967. Mem. Am. Accounting Assn. (nat. v.p. 1970-71), Fin. Execs. Inst., Am. Petroleum Inst., Nat. Assn. Accountants, Beta Alpha Psi (nat. adv. bd. 1975—). Republican. Presbyterian. Club: Masons. Contbr. articles to profl. jours. Home: 38 Heritage Hill Rd New Canaan CT 06840

STEVENSON, ROY SATYR, JR., indsl. and constrn. machinery mfg. co. exec.; b. Humboldt, Iowa, June 11, 1938; s. Roy Satyr and Audrey Virginia (Russell) S.; B.S. in Indsl. Engring., Iowa State U., 1961; m. Sandra Joyce Helmich, Nov. 29, 1959; 1 son, Eric Russell Stevenson. With Ingersoll Rand and subs., 1961—, sales engr., Bombay, 1965-67, dir. internat. mktg. air compressor div., Rijwijk, Holland, 1971-75, mng. dir. Swedish Co. and Scandinavian Bromma, 1975-78, dir. Middle East/North African Ops., Athens, Greece, 1979—. Served to capt. U.S. Army, 1962-64; Korea. Lutheran. Club: Toastmasters (pres. Elmira chpt. 1969-70). Home: Herodotoull Politia Greece Office: Athens Tower 17th Floor Messogian 2-4 Athens 610 Greece

STEVENSON, SCOTT L., steel mill service co. exec.; b. Butler, Pa., Nov. 12, 1953; s. Charles E. and Naomi N. (Nicklas) S.; A.A.S. in Acctg., Butler County Community Coll., 1974; B.S. magna cum laude in Bus. Adminstrn., Robert Morris Coll., 1979. Estimator trainee Heckett div. Harsco Corp., Butler, Pa., 1974, estimator, 1974-79, supr. estimating, 1979—. Mem. Nat. Assn. Accts. Home: PO Box 204 Connoquenessing PA 16027 Office: Heckett Div Harsco Corp 612 N Main St Butler PA 16001

STEWART, ARLINGTON KENNETH, machine tool co. exec.; b. Gardner, Mass., Mar. 13, 1926; s. Arlington Kenneth and Edith Nina (Fletcher) S.; B.S. in Elec. Engring., Worcester Poly. Inst., 1950, M.S. in Elec. Engring., 1952; m. Margaret Ruth Blackler, Aug. 5, 1950; children—Nancy, James, Keith, Judith, Matthew. Engr., ITT, Clinton, Mass., 1950-52; engr. Raytheon, Lowell, Mass., 1952-58, ops. mgr., 1958-67; gen. mgr. Bendix, Sturbridge, Mass., 1968-71, div. mgr., Jackson, Mich., 1971-73; pres. Teledyne Pines, Aurora, Ill., 1974—; instr. Worcester Poly. Inst., 1950-51, Lowell Tech. Inst., 1954-56. Chmn. United Fund campaign, 1965, pres. Greater Lowell United Fund, 1966-68; pres. Lowell Family Service, 1964-66. Served with USNR, 1944-46. Mem. Fabricating Mfrs. Assn. (pres. 1976), Sigma Xi, Tau Beta Pi, Eta Kappa Nu. Republican. Congregationalist. Home: 16 Hathaway Crescent Aurora IL 60504 Office: 601 W New York St Aurora IL 60506

STEWART, CHARLIE HAINES, JR., fin. exec.; b. Cairo, Ga., June 3, 1931; s. Charlie Haines and Olee (Voyles) S.; B.B.A., U. Ga., 1958; m. Joan Ethel Chastain, June 10, 1956; children—Charles, Joni. Accountant, McCollum & Simmons, Thomasville, Ga., 1958-60, Wells, Laney, Ehrlich, Baer & Meyer, Orlando, Fla., 1960-69; v.p. Tupperware Internat., Orlando, 1969—, v.p. fin. reporting, 1977—. Active Boy Scouts Am., 1964-70. Served with USN, 1950-53. Mem. Nat. Assn. Accountants (nat. dir. 1978-80). Democrat. Home: 3512 Shamrock Ct Orlando FL 32806 Office: PO Box 1805 Orlando FL 32802

STEWART, EDWARD NICHOLSON, JR., investment mgmt. exec.; b. Bronxville, N.Y., Sept. 28, 1940; s. Edward Nicholson and Helen (Davis) S.; student Hamilton Coll., 1959-62; B.A., New Sch. Social Research, 1965; m. Mary Patricia Hunter, Aug. 8, 1964; children—Pamela Fowler, Wendy Hunter. Dir. membership Investment Co. Inst., N.Y.C., 1968; v.p. Lord, Abbett & Co., N.Y.C., 1969-74; pres. Trevor Stewart Burton & Jacobsen, Inc., N.Y.C., 1974—. Trustee Hackley Sch., 1971—, treas., 1972—, v.p., 1980—; pres. Hackley Alumni Assn., Inc., 1967-69. Mem. Am. Soc. Pension Actuaries (asso.), Investment Assn. N.Y., U.S. Navy League, Delta Kappa Epsilon. Republican. Clubs: Union League (N.Y.C.); Sleepy Hollow Country (Scarborough, N.Y.). Co-founder, editor Hackley Rev., 1963-68. Home: 102 Crest Dr Tarrytown NY 10591 Office: 54 Park Ave New York NY 10016

STEWART, HELEN PREBLE, journalist, oil co. exec.; b. Alexandria, Va., Nov. 15, 1943; d. Eugene Wilford and Dorothy Louise (Donaldson) Preble; B.A. in Journalism, So. Meth. U., 1965; m. Alan Crawford Stewart, Mar. 23, 1968. Successively asst. editor, editor Facets mag. Zale Corp., Dallas, 1966-68; editor The Mustang mag. So. Meth. U. Alumni Center, Dallas, 1968-69; asst. editor The Producing Spark Atlantic Richfield Co., Dallas, 1969-72, editor The Houston Spark, 1971-72, sr. editor ARCO Spark, S.W. mgr. employee communications, 1972-80, Midwest mgr. employee communications, 1980—. Mem. exec. bd. Dallas/Plano Affirmative Action Com., 1980. Recipient several awards Dallas Press Club. Mem. Internat. Assn. Bus. Communicators (chmn. speakers bur., dist. del.; chmn. public relations com., editor Image 1979-80; numerous awards), Theta Sigma Phi. Democrat. Episcopalian. Editor Take 5, 1975. Home: 192 Lookout Mountain Circle Golden CO 80401 Office: Atlantic Richfield Co 555 17th St Denver CO 80217

STEWART, IRELAND JOSEPH, automotive parts mfg. co. exec.; b. Belfast, No. Ireland, Dec. 7, 1934; s. Ireland and Margaret J. (Browne) S.; came to U.S., 1966, naturalized, 1976; B.S., Queen's U. (Ireland), 1963; diploma mgmt. studies with distinction U. Chgo., 1966, M.B.A., 1968. Sr. tech. staff James Mackie & Sons, Ltd., Belfast, 1956-66; asst. dean students U. Chgo. Grad. Sch. Bus., 1968-69; mgmt. cons. Boston Cons. Group, 1969-72; fin. staff cons. Maremont Corp., Chgo., 1972-75, dir. mktg. research and devel., 1973-74, v.p. internat. and corporate officer, 1974-76, sr. v.p., 1978-80, exec. v.p., 1980—; dir. Gabriel India Ltd., Bombay, India, Gabriel Europe, Van Der Hout & Assos., Toronto, Ont., Can., Gabriel of Mex.; dir., chmn. bd. Gabriel S. Africa, 1974-76. Recipient spl. award for Dedication in Advancing Sci. of Automotive Market Forecasting, Automotive Market Research Council, 1976; U. Chgo. Grad. Sch. Bus. scholar, 1968, fellow, 1969. Mem. Am. Mgmt. Assn., Brit. Inst. Mgmt., Midwest Planning Assn., Council Fgn. Relations, Automotive Market Research Council, Internat. Trade Com. of Chgo. Assn. Commerce and Industry. Contbr. articles in field to profl. jours. Home: 235 Willow Ave Deerfield IL 60015 Office: 200 E Randolph Dr Chicago IL 60601

STEWART, JAMES THOMPSON, incentive co./catalog showroom exec.; b. St. Louis, Apr. 2, 1921; s. Freddie and Bertha (Golike) S.; B.S. in Aero. Engring., U. Mich., 1948; grad. Indsl. Coll. Armed Forces, 1960; M.B.A., George Washington U., 1963; m. Georgia M. Schwepker, June 28, 1944; children—James Thompson, Kellie Anne. Commd. 2d lt. USAF, 1942, advanced through grades to lt. gen., 1970; squadron comdr., World War II; comdr. aero. systems div., Wright-Patterson AFB, 1970-76; ret., 1976; corp. v.p. E. F. MacDonald Co., Dayton, Ohio, 1977—, pres. MacDonald Sales Centers, 1978—. Bd. dirs. Dayton Children's Med. Center, 1975-76; com. chmn. United Way, 1978. Decorated D.S.M., Legion of Merit, D.F.C., numerous others; recipient awards AF Assn. Fellow AIAA (dir. 1972-75); mem. Aviation Hall of Fame, AF Assn., Ret. Officers Assn., Am. Legion. Club: Dayton Racquet. Author: Airpower: The

Decisive Force in Korea, 1957. Office: 129 S Ludlow St Dayton OH 45402

STEWART, JOHN CAMERON, chem. co. exec.; b. Warren, Pa., June 16, 1942; s. John Harvey and Dorothy (Hand) S.; B.S. in Chemistry, Pa. State U., 1964; M.S. in Chemistry, Stevens Inst. Tech., 1967; M.B.A. in Fin., Drexel U., 1972; 1 dau., Melinda MacDonald. Sr. research chemist, reaction motors div. Thiokol Chem. Co., Denville, N.J., 1964-67; project mgr. new venture devel., mem. economic fin. planning staff Sun Oil Co., Phila., 1967-72; mgr. fin. planning Far East div. Fuji Xerox, Xerox Corp., Stamford, Conn., 1972-76; mgr. planning, mergers and acquisitions Tenneco Chems., Inc., Saddle Brook, N.J., 1976-78; dir. corp. planning and devel. Sandoz, Inc., East Hanover, N.J., 1978—. Mem. Assn. M.B.A. Execs., Am. Chem. Soc. Republican. Episcopalian. Office: Sandoz Inc Route 10 East Hanover NJ 07936

STEWART, JOHN FORBES, investment counselor; b. San Francisco, Apr. 8, 1929; s. John Loftus and Katherine (Forbes) S.; B.A., Lake Forest Coll., 1951; postgrad. San Jose State Coll. Sch. Bus., 1957; m. Ann Churchman, June 20, 1953; children—Douglas Churchman, Derek Forbes. Registered rep. Dean Witter & Co., Palo Alto, Calif., 1957-65; prin. John F. Stewart Investments, Palo Alto, 1965-67, Los Altos, Calif., 1970—; portfolio mgr. Wells Fargo Bank, San Francisco, 1967-68; instl. rep. research Glore, Forgan, Staats, Inc., San Francisco, 1968-70; cons. Fin. Research & Systems, Menlo Park, Calif., 1975-76. Served to 1st lt. USAF, 1952-55. Mem. Newcomen Soc. N. Am., Aircraft Owners and Pilots Assn. Republican. Christian Scientist. Clubs: Rotary (dir., Los Altos, 1978-80), Commonwealth of Calif. Home: 13075 Alta Ln S Los Altos Hills CA 94022 Office: Suite B 444 1st St Los Altos CA 94022

STEWART, JOSEPH TURNER, JR., diversified co. exec.; b. N.Y.C., Apr. 30, 1929; s. Joseph Turner and Edna (Pride) S.; S.B. with honors, U.S. Mcht. Marine Acad., 1951; M.B.A., Harvard U., 1954; m. Carol Graham, Aug. 7, 1954; children—Lisa D., Alison D. Systems analyst Warner Lambert Co., Morris Plains, N.J., 1954-56, budget supr. internat., 1956-60, asst. div. controller consumer products group, 1960-62, div. controller group, 1962-66, dir. adminstrn. and fin., proprietary drug div., 1966, dir. Lactona products div., 1967; controller Beech-Nut subs. Squibb Corp., N.Y.C., 1968, v.p. fin., 1968-71, v.p. planning, corporate staff parent corp., 1971-79, v.p. fin. and planning, 1979—; vis. prof. BEEP program Nat. Urban League, 1974—; dir., mem. investment com. Minority Equity Capital Corp. Pres. exec. council Harvard Bus. Sch. Assn., 1971—, mem. vis. com. Bus. Sch., 1976—. John Hay Whitney Opportunity fellow, 1952-54; recipient Alumni Outstanding Profl. Achievement award U.S. Mcht. Marine Acad., 1971. Club: Harvard (N.Y.C.). Home: 7 Alden Rd Glen Ridge NJ 07028 Office: 40 W 57th St New York NY 10019

STEWART, MARCUS CROWDER, utilities exec.; b. Whiteville, Tenn., Dec. 14, 1907; s. Marcus Jefferson and Mattie Sue (Crowder) S.; B.S., U. Tenn., 1929, postgrad., 1953, 61; m. Mattie Reeves Patton, June 18, 1936; 1 son, Marcus Crowder. Local mgr. Tenn. Electric Power Co., 1929-39; property recorder TVA, 1939-40; mgr. Sand Mountain Electric Coop., Ft. Payne, Ala., 1940-71, mgr. emeritus, 1971-73, mgmt. cons., 1973—. Engring. mgmt. cons. Sand Mountain Water Authority; co-organizer Farmers Telephone Coop. and Water Systems; signup coordinator N.E. Ala. Water, Sewer and Fire Protection Dist., 1975—. Bd. dirs. Choccolocco council Boy Scouts Am., United Givers Fund DeKalb County. Served to 1st lt. Officers Res. Corp, 1929-46. Recipient Max Howard award for outstanding community achievement, 1975; registered profl. engr., Ala. Mem. Am. Inst. Mgmt. (asso.), North Ala. Pub. Power Distbrs. (chmn. coms.; Outstanding Mgr. grantee 1972), North Ala. Indsl. Devel. Assn. (pres., dir.), Tenn. Valley Pub. Power Assn. (pres., treas., dir.), Ala. Rural Electric Assn. Coops. (pres., dir.), Nat. Rural Elec. Coops. Assn. (pub. relations com. chmn.), Ft. Payne (dir. 1951-54), Rainsville (dir. 1965-68) chambers commerce. Democrat. Methodist (adminstrv. bd., past chmn.). Mason; mem. Order Eastern Star (past worthy patron), Gideons. Author: Crowder Family History, 1981. Home: 206 Forrest Ave S Fort Payne AL 35967 Office: PO Box 581 Fort Payne AL 35967

STEWART, MICHAEL OSBORNE, univ. adminstr.; b. Sacramento, Aug. 25, 1938; s. Morris Albion and Marjorie Cathryn (McFarlin) S.; B.A., U. Calif. at Berkeley, 1960, M.A., 1961; Ph.D. (Grad. fellow), Kans. State U., 1972; m. Lucille Arnette Cooper, June 11, 1961; children—Heather Anne, Blaine Andrew. Asst. dean students San Jose (Calif.) State U., 1965-66; asso. dean students Ft. Hays (Kans.) State U., 1966-71; asst. v.p. acad. affairs, also dir. institutional research, 1971-74; v.p. adminstrn. Peru (Nebr.) State Coll., 1974-79, U. S.D., Vermillion, 1979—. Active Youth Care Inc., Hays, Kans., 1969-74. Served with U.S. Army, 1961-65; lt. col. Res. Decorated Army Commendation medal; NDEA fellow, 1967-68. Mem. Nat., Central assns. coll. and univ. bus. officers, Assn. Instl. Research, Am. Assn. Higher Edn., Am. Assn. Univ. Adminstrs., Kans. Assn. Student Personnel Adminstrs. (pres. 1970-71), Theta Chi (nat. sec. 1978-80), Phi Delta Kappa, Phi Eta Sigma. Democrat. Episcopalian. Club: Elks. Contbr. articles to profl. jours. Home: 1711 E Main St Vermillion SD 57069 Office: U SD Vermillion SD 57069

STEWART, MURRAY EDGAR, business exec.; b. Brandon, Man., Can., Sept. 30, 1926; s. William Murray and Mary Elizabeth (Williams) S.; B.Sc. in Civil Engring., U. Alta. (Can.), 1947; M.Commerce in Bus. Adminstrn., U. Toronto (Can.), 1949; m. Muriel Allison Young, Dec. 28, 1949; children—Janet, Arden, Joan, Karen. Asst. engr. Northwestern Utilities, Ltd., Edmonton, Alta., 1949, gen. mgr. 1956-60, dir. 1960-72; v.p., dir. Northwestern, Can. Western Natural Gas Co., Ltd., Calgary, Alta., 1963-65, pres., 1965-68; pres. Gen. Waterworks Corp., Phila., 1968-71; dir., 1968-72; group v.p. IU Internat. Corp., Phila., 1969-70, sr. v.p., 1970-72; pres., dir. C. Brewer & Co. Ltd., Honolulu, 1972-75; exec. v.p. Alexander & Baldwin Inc., 1975-78; exec. v.p., dir. Foothills Pipe Lines (Yukon) Ltd., Calgary, 1978—. Clubs: Seaview Country (Absecon, N.J.); Mayfair Golf and Country (pres. Edmonton 1967-68); Ranchmens (Calgary); Oahu Golf and Country, Waialae Golf and Country (Honolulu). Home: 4427 Britannia Dr SW Calgary AB T2S 1J4 Canada Office: 1600-205 5th Ave SW Calgary AB T2P 2V7 Canada

STEWART, ROBERT H., III, banker; b. Dallas, Dec. 3, 1925; s. Robert H. Stewart; B.B.A. in Banking, So. Meth. U., 1949; children—Cynthia Caroline, Alice Partee. With Empire State Bank, Dallas, 1949-50; with First Nat. Bank, Dallas, 1951—, v.p., 1953-59, sr. v.p., 1959-60, pres., 1960-65, chmn. bd., 1965-72; chmn. bd. First Internat. Bancshares, Inc., 1972-80, now chmn. exec. com.; dir. Southwestern Life Corp., Southwestern Life Ins. Co., Braniff Internat. Corp., Campbell-Taggart, Inc., PepsiCo, Inc., NCH Corp. Bd. dirs. Dallas Citizens Council. Served to 1st lt. inf. AUS, 1944-46; also Korea. Club: Brook Hollow Golf (Dallas). Office: 1201 Elm St Dallas TX 75270*

STEWART, STEPHEN KNAUL, exec. search cons.; b. Trenton, N.J., Apr. 6, 1933; s. Stephen Knaul and Florence Theresa (Schroeder) S.; B.A. in Psychology, U. Dayton, 1955; m. Jeanne M. Graul, Aug. 24, 1957; children—Elizabeth, Stephen, Jennifer, Christopher. Profl. recruiter Nat. Cash Register Co., Dayton, Ohio, 1960-65; mgr. profl. recruiting Gen. Electric Co., Phoenix, 1965-67, mgr. exec. selection, 1967-68; pres. S.K. Stewart & Assos., Cin., 1968—. Photographer for various orgns. for retarded people, 1978—. Mem. Assn. Exec. Recruiting Cons. Roman Catholic. Office: SK Stewart & Assos The Exec Bldg PO Box 40110 Cincinnati OH 45240

STEYER, ROY HENRY, lawyer; b. Bklyn., July 1, 1918; s. Herman and Augusta (Simon) S.; A.B., Cornell U., 1938; LL.B. cum laude, Yale U., 1941; m. Margaret Fahr, Feb. 21, 1953; children—Hume R., James P., Thomas F. Admitted to N.Y. bar, 1941; pvt. practice, N.Y.C., 1941—; partner Sullivan & Cromwell, 1953—. Chmn., Yale Law Sch. Fund, 1957-59; trustee N.Y.C. Sch. Vol. Program, Inc., 1974-78. Served from ensign to lt. USNR, 1943-46. Mem. Internat., Am., N.Y. State, N.Y.C., N.Y. County (dir. 1972-78) bar assns., Am. Coll. Trial Lawyers, Am. Judicature Soc., N.Y. Law Inst., Yale Law Sch. Alumni Assn. (exec. com., v.p. 1957-67), Order of Coif, Phi Beta Kappa, Phi Kappa Phi. Clubs: Broad St., Yale of N.Y. Home: 112 E 74th St New York NY 10021 Office: 125 Broad St New York NY 10004

STICHT, J. PAUL, fin. co. exec.; b. Clairton, Pa., 1917; B.A., Grove City Coll., 1939; postgrad. U. Pitts. With U.S. Steel Corp., 1939-44; personnel dir. Trans World Airlines, 1944-48; v.p. Campbell Soup Co., 1948-60, pres. internat., 1948-60; pres. Federated Dept. Stores, Inc., 1960-72; chmn. exec. com. R. J. Reynolds Industries, Inc., Winston-Salem, N.C., 1972-73, pres., 1973-79, chief operating officer, 1973-78, chief exec. officer, 1978—, chmn., 1979—; dir. Celanese Corp., Wachovia Corp., Foremost-McKesson, Inc., S.C. Johnson & Son, Inc. Trustee Grove City Coll., Old Salem, Inc., Rockefeller U.; mem. bd. visitors Bowman Gray Sch. Medicine, U. Pitts. Grad. Sch. Bus. Adminstrn., Duke U. Grad. Sch. Bus. Adminstrn. Office: Winston-Salem NC 27102*

STICKLER, JOHN COBB, jour. publisher; b. Washington, July 18, 1937; s. Joseph Harding and Virginia (Cobb) S.; B.A. with honors in Sociology, Yale U., 1959; m. Lucy Han, 1964; children—Stephen Han, Alexander Han. Founder, pres. S/K Internat. Advt. Corp., Seoul, Korea, 1966-76, also stringer CBS News, Seoul, 1967-76; pub., owner Jour. Applied Mgmt., Walnut Creek, Calif.; editor and pub. The Asia Mag., N.Y. Times, Pacific Travel News, Media. Served with U.S. Army, 1962-64. Finalist, Clio awards, 1974. Mem. Internat. Advt. Assn. (founder Korea chpt.), Am. Soc. Journalists and Authors, Bus. Profl. Advt. Assn., Mag. Pub. Assn., East Bay Advt. and Mktg. Club (dir.). Democrat. Club: Yale of No. Calif. Freelance contbr. articles to profl. jours. and newspapers. Office: 1700 Ygnacio Valley Rd Walnut Creek CA 94598

STICKNEY, ALBERT III, banker; b. N.Y.C., Oct. 29, 1944; s. Albert and Eleanor Elizabeth (Herrick) S.; B.A., Harvard U., 1967; m. Susan Kent King, Apr. 27, 1974; children—Katharine Kent, Anna Noyes. Asst. treas. Chase Manhattan Bank, N.Y.C., 1973-75, 2d v.p., 1975-77; asst. v.p. Irving Trust Co., 1977, v.p., 1977—. Served to lt. USNR, 1967-70. Clubs: Harvard (N.Y.C.); Bedford Golf and Tennis, The Leash, Fishers Island Country, Hammonasset Fishing, Ducks Unltd. Home: West Ln Pound Ridge NY 10576 Office: 1 Wall St New York NY 10015

STIEFEL, PAUL, electronic engr.; b. Fuerth, Germany, Feb. 9, 1923; came to U.S., 1938, naturalized, 1943; s. Arthur and Molly (Greenhut) S.; B.S., Ill. Inst. Tech., 1951; M.B.A., U. Chgo., 1971; m. Senta Metzger, July 11, 1948; children—Ronald, Lynne, Michael. Engr., Glenn L. Martin Co., Balt., 1951-52; project engr. Webcor, Inc., Chgo., 1953-55; sr. electronic engr. Indsl. Research Products, Inc., Franklin Park, Ill., 1955-59; mgr. engring. adminstrn. Hammond Organ Co., Chgo., 1958-75; chief engr. Midwest Electronics, Chgo., 1975-78; chief engr. Fideliton, Inc., Arlington Heights, Ill., 1978—. Pres. Bd. Edn. Elem. Sch. Dist. 73, chmn. fin. com., 1964—; chmn. bd. Oakton Community Coll. Dist. 535, chmn. fin. com., 1977—; active Boy Scouts Am. Served with AUS, 1943-46. Registered profl. engr., Ill. Mem. Ill. Soc. Profl. Engrs. (v.p.), IEEE. Patentee in field. Office: 2915 N Western Ave Chicago IL 60618

STIGLICH, NICHOLAS MATTHEW, engring. co. exec.; b. West New York, N.J., July 2, 1918; s. Serafin and Francis (Morin) S.; B.M.E., Bklyn. Poly. Inst., 1950, M.S., 1965; m. Anna Karamian, Jan. 22, 1949; 1 dau., Vivian. Naval architect G.G. Sharp, N.Y.C., 1941-53, partner engr., 1953-64; self-employed as cons., Cresskill, N.J., 1964; pres. Eness Research & Devel. Corp., Westwood, N.J., 1966—. Treas., Community Sch. of Tenafly (N.J.), 1958-62, vice chmn., 1962-66. Registered profl. engr., N.Y., N.J. Mem. Soc. Profl. Engrs., Soc. Naval Architects and Marine Engrs., Internat. Cargo Handling Coordination Assn., Instrument Soc. Am., Internat. Materials Mgmt. Soc., ASTM (chmn. F25.03 com.), Marine Tech. Soc. Patentee in field. Home: 215 8th St Cresskill NJ 07626 Office: 75 Carver Ave Westwood NJ 07675

STIKA, ELAINE ANN, advt. exec.; b. Kenosha, Wis., July 3, 1924; d. Alexander and Paulina L. (Janota) S.; student Kenosha Coll. Commerce, 1943, Mgmt. Center Marquette U., 1960, U. Wis. Kenosha Center, 1963, De Paul U., 1963, Kenosha Tech. Inst., 1970. Asst. to mgr. market list div. sales dept. Macwhyte Wire Rope Co. (now subs. Amsted Industries, Inc.), Kenosha, 1943-49, asst. to advt., sales promotion, pub. relations, mktg. mgr., 1949-65, advt. and sales services adminstr., 1966-73, mktg. services adminstr., 1974—. Sec., treas. Kenosha Civic Council, 1955—; mem. Kenosha County Health Planning Commn., 1969—; mem. bd. adv. bd. Wis. Tb and Respiratory Disease Assn., 1970-79; bd. dirs. Kenosha County council Girl Scouts U.S.A., 1962-68; bd. dirs. Kenosha County Blood Bank, 1964—, pres., 1971-74; bd. dirs. Kenosha County United Fund, 1966-72. Mem. Milw. Assn. Indsl. Advertisers, Constrn. Equipment Advertisers, Kenosha Bradford Alumni Assn. (dir., pres. 1971-73), Kenosha County Hist. Soc., Sigma Alpha Sigma (dir., v.p. 1960-62, pres. 1962-64). Club: Kenosha Advt. (dir. 1959-69, pres. 1963-64). Home: 926 48th St Kenosha WI 53140 Office: 2906 14th Ave Kenosha WI 53141

STILLMAN, FRANCIS DUANE, JR., utility co. exec.; b. Cornwall, N.Y., Mar. 20, 1935; s. Francis Duane and Alice Almira (Jones) S.; B.S. in E.E., Bucknell U., 1960; m. Mary Katherine Hauck, Aug. 31, 1957; children—Frank Kenneth, Kay Evelyn. Planning engr. W. Penn Power Co., Bellefonte, Pa., 1960-61, rate analyst, Greensburg, Pa., 1961-69, supr. rates, 1969-70, mgr. rates, 1971-74; mgr. load research Allegheny Power Service Co., Greensburg, 1974—. Cubmaster, Westmoreland-Fayette council Boy Scouts Am., Greensburg, 1967-70, scoutmaster, 1970-74, chmn. dist. com., 1974—; active Westmoreland County United Way. Served with U.S. Navy, 1954-56. Named Mr. Jaycee, 1965; recipient Silver Beaver, Boy Scouts Am., 1978, Wood Badge award, 1974, Service to Boyhood award, 1974, Dist. award of Merit, 1975, Vigil Honor, 1976. Mem. IEEE, Edison Electric Inst. (rate research com.), Pa. Electric Assn. (rate com.), Westmoreland County Symphony Soc., Greensburg Jaycees. Republican. Methodist. Club: Masons. Home: 15 Waverly Dr Greensburg PA 15601 Office: 800 Cabin Hill Dr Greensburg PA 15601

STILLMAN, ROGER EDWARD, investment co. exec.; b. Lewiston, Idaho, Nov. 19, 1943; s. Carl William and Mildred Eleene (Rogers) S.; B.A. in Communications, Pacific Luth. U., 1966. News dir. Grayson Enterprises, Inc., Honolulu, 1970-72; gen. mgr. Koko Marina Shopping Center, Honolulu, 1972-73; advt.-promotion mgr. Dillingham Corp., Kaahumanu Center, Maui, Hawaii, 1974-76; gen. mgr. Kaahumanu Center, also Lahaina Square, Kahului, Hawaii, 1976-79; dir. property mgmt. Dillingham Investments, Pasadena, Calif., 1980—. Mem. exec. com., spl. events Maui United Way, 1975, 76. Served with USNR, 1966-70; Vietnam. Mem. Internat. Council Shopping Centers, Maui C. of C. (dir. 1977-79). Club: Rotary (Kahului). Office: 221 E Walnut St Pasadena CA 91101

STINE, ORRIN BURR, optical mfg. co. exec.; b. Chgo., Nov. 17, 1925; s. Max A. and Lillian R. (Leviton) S.; Ph.B., U. Chgo., 1944, M.B.A., 1952; B.S., U. Ill., 1948; m. Rachel Eva Goldring, Sept. 6, 1977; 1 dau., Marueen Stine Sadoff. Vice pres. mktg. Stineway Drug Co., 1947-54; pres. Enoz Corp., Chgo., 1956-64; dir. mktg. Borden Chem. Co., N.Y.C., 1965-68, gen. mgr., 1968-71; pres. Wesley Jessen Inc., Chgo., 1971—. Mem. Pres.'s Com. for the Handicapped, 1961-63; bd. dirs. Nat. Eye Research Found., Chgo., 1971-73; trustee Corrective Eye Care Found., Chgo., 1975-78, Am. Com. for Prevention of Suicide, 1978—. Served with U.S. Army, 1943-46. Decorated Silver Star, Bronze Star, Purple Heart. Club: Ill. Athletic. Office: 37 S Wabash Ave Chicago IL 60603

STINEMAN, JOHN A., banker; b. Washington, Oct. 17, 1951; s. Robert G. and Patricia L. (Kenny) S.; A.B. in Govt., Georgetown U., 1973; M.B.A., U. Chgo., 1977. Scholar trainee 1st Nat. Bank Chgo., 1973-75, officer money market dept., 1975-77, asst. v.p. fgn. exchange dept., N.Y.C., 1977-78; asst. v.p. money market Bankers Trust Co., N.Y.C., 1978-79, v.p. money market, 1979—. Mem. Fgn. Exchange Assn. N. Am. Roman Catholic. Club: Downtown Athletic (N.Y.C.). Home: 55 Liberty St New York NY 10005

STINSON, DEANE BRIAN, auditor; b. Ottawa, Ont., Can., Nov. 12, 1930; s. Earl Minto and Clara Edna (Acres) S.; chartered acct. Inst. Chartered Accts. Ont., 1954; m. Patricia Ann Paynter, Aug. 25, 1956; children—Steven Wayne, Brian Richard, Andrew Alan. With Arthur A. Crawley & Co., Ottawa, 1949-54; staff chartered acct. Thorne Riddell, Sault Ste. Marie, Ont., 1958-59, audit partner, 1959-80, mng. partner, 1980—; mem. Ont. Regional Mgmt. Council, 1979—; adv. bd. Guaranty Trust Co., 1975—. Adv. indsl. devel. com. Sault Ste. Marie, 1978—; mem. cultural task force Sault Ste. Marie, 1977-79. Mem. Can. Inst. Chartered Accts. (pres. chpt. 1965), Can. Tax Found. Progressive Conservative. Anglican. Clubs: Rotary (pres. 1978), Sault Ste. Marie Curling. Home: 15 Atlas Ave Sault Ste Marie ON P6A 4Z2 Canada Office: PO Box 578 Sault Ste Marie ON P6A 5M6 Canada

STINSON, GEORGE ARTHUR, lawyer, steel co. exec.; b. Camden, Ark., Feb. 11, 1915; s. John McCollum and Alice (Loving) S.; A.B., Northwestern U., 1936; J.D., Columbia, 1939; LL.D., U. W.Va., Bethany Coll., Theil Coll., Salem Coll.; m. Betty Millsop, May 31, 1947; children—Thomas, Lauretta, Peter, Joel. Admitted to N.Y. bar, 1939; partner firm Cleary, Gottlieb, Friendly & Hamilton, N.Y.C., 1946-61; spl. asst. to atty. gen., acting asst. atty. gen. tax div. Dept. Justice, 1947-48; v.p., sec. Nat. Steel Corp., Pitts., 1961-63, pres., 1963-75, dir., 1963—, chief exec. officer, 1966-80, chmn., 1972-81; dir. Iron Ore Co., Can., Hanna Mining Co., Ralston Purina Co.; trustee Mut. Life Ins. Co. N.Y. Bd. regents Northwestern U.; trustee emeritus U. Pitts.; mem. Presdl. Commn. on Internat. Trade and Investment Policy, 1970-71; chmn. U.S. Indsl. Payroll Savs. Com., 1976. Served to lt. col. USAAF, 1941-45. Decorated Legion of Merit. Mem. Am. Iron and Steel Inst. (chmn. bd. 1969-71), Internat. Iron and Steel Inst. (dir., chmn. 1975-77), Am. Law Inst., Bus. Council, Phi Beta Kappa. Clubs: Links, City Midday, Cloud, Blind Brook (N.Y.C.); Duquesne, Laurel Valley Golf (Pitts.); Gulfstream Golf (Delray, Fla.). Office: Grant Bldg Pittsburgh PA 15219

STIREWALT, JOHN NEWMAN, coal co. exec.; b. Springfield, Ill., July 14, 1931; s. Newman Claude and Genevieve (Henton) S.; A.B., U. Miami, 1953; grad. execs. program Carnegie-Mellon U. Grad. Sch. Indsl. Adminstrn., 1978; m. Joan Marie McCarthy, Dec. 26, 1957; children—Genevieve, Janice, James, Christopher. Salesman, Kaiser Aluminum, Indpls., 1957-63; dist. sales mgr. Consol. Coal, Detroit, 1963-67, Cleve., 1967-73, gen. sales mgr., Detroit, 1973-76, asst. v.p., 1976-79; v.p. mktg. Youghiogheny and Ohio Coal Co., St. Clairsville, Ohio, 1979—; exec. reservist U.S. Interior Dept. emergency solid fuels adminstrn., 1971. Council chmn. Cub Scouts, Highland, Mich., 1976; mem. Mich. Energy Task Force, 1966. Served in U.S. Army, 1954-56. Mem. Ill. Mining Inst., Mich. Coal and Rail, Sigma Chi. Presbyterian. Club: Wheeling Country. Home: Glenwood Rd Wheeling WV 26003 Office: PO Box 1000 Saint Clairsville OH 43935

STIRLING, RAYMOND MARTIN, import and distbn. co. exec.; b. Winnipeg, Man., Can., May 9, 1949; came to U.S., 1952, naturalized, 1959; s. Charles Karl and Zenaides Mary (Klaponski) S.; B.A., Calif. State U., Long Beach, 1971; m. Candace Lynn Shand, Nov. 18, 1979; children—Melissa Lee, Trevor Allen. Dept. mgr. Gemco, Luck Stores, Inc., Santa Ana, Calif., 1968-72; field supr. Rothco Distbrs., Los Angeles, 1972-75; founder, pres. R S Distbrs., Brea, Calif., 1975—; cons. buying and retail orgn. Mem. Assn. Am. Geographers, Am. Quarter Horse Assn., Housewares Club So. Calif. Republican. Roman Catholic. Club: Huntington Seacliff. Office: R S Distbrs 3051 Enterprise St Brea CA 92621

STITLEY, JAMES WALTER, JR., food mfg. exec.; b. York, Pa., May 23, 1944; s. James Walter and Geraldine Salome (Horn) S.; B.S. in Chemistry, Millersville State Coll., 1970; m. Nancy Jane Miller, Dec. 29, 1972. Med. technician York Hosp., 1962-66; research biochemist Carter-Wallace, Inc., Cranbury, N.J., 1970-75; mgr. Ward Labs. div. Ward Foods, East Orange, N.J., 1975-77; mgr. tech. services Pepperidge Farm, Inc., Norwalk, Conn., 1977—; cons. biochemistry and toxicology. Asst. scoutmaster Boy Scouts Am. Mem. Am. Chem. Soc., Am. Mgmt. Assn., Am. Assn. Cereal Chemists, Am. Inst. Baking (ednl. adv. com. 1978—), Instrument Soc. Am. (asso. dir.-food industry liaison), AAAS, Am. Astron. Research Group, York Astron. Soc. (v.p. 1960). Contbr. articles to profl. jours. Patentee in field. Home: Short Woods Rd Rural Route 3 Box 409 New Fairfield CT 06810 Office: Westport Ave Norwalk CT 06856

STOCK, V. N., packing co. exec. Pres., chief exec. officer Can. Packers, Inc. (formerly Can. Packers Ltd.), also dir. Office: 95 St Clair Ave W Toronto ON M4V 1P2 Canada*

STOCKER, NORMAN ROBERT, II, exec. search firm exec.; b. Detroit, Mar. 14, 1945; s. Norman Robert and Verna May (O'Rourke) S.; B.A., Columbia U., 1967; m. Janet Dearinger, Dec. 13, 1975; children—Katherine Ashley, David O'Rourke. Commd. 2d lt. U.S. Marine Corps, 1967, ret., 1974; advanced to maj. U.S. Marine Corps Res., 1978; sales rep. Fla. Steel Drum Co., Pensacola, 1975-77; sr. tech. recruiter Mgmt. Recruiters, Pensacola, 1977-78; pres. SFS Mgmt. Cons., Inc., Pensacola, 1978—. Decorated D.F.C. Mem. Marine Corps Res. Officers Assn., Marine Corps Aviation Assn., Republican. Roman Catholic. Home: 138 Siguenza Dr Pensacola Beach FL 32561 Office: 308 E Government St Pensacola FL 32501

STOCKMAN, ROBERT JOHN, chem. engr.; b. Manitowoc, Wis., Sept. 18, 1928; s. Robert William and Thelma Blanche (Swatsley) S.; B.S., U. Wis., 1951; m. Iona Helen Jewell, June 16, 1951; children—Robert E., John W., James K. Trainee, Union Carbide Corp., Bound Brook, N.J., 1951-52, quality control engr., 1952-67, group leader plastics research and devel., 1967-71, devel. scientist, 1971-75, mgr. planning and contract control patents and licensing dept., 1975-77, mgr. export and licensing services Chems. and Plastics div., 1978-79, mgr. export services ethylene oxide derivatives div., 1979—. Chmn. troop com. Bernardsville (N.J.) Boy Scouts Am., 1965-70. Served with inf., AUS, 1946-47; Korea. Named Distinguished Lutheran Layman, 1967. Mem. Licensing Execs. Soc. Am. Patentee in field. Home: 8 Hillandale Rd E Brookfield CT 06804 Office: Old Ridgebury Rd Danbury CT 06817

STOCKMEYER, CHRIS BOYD, JR., chem. co. exec.; b. Detroit, Jan. 26, 1938; s. C. Boyd and Barbara L. (Tibbitts) S.; B.B.A., U. Mich., 1960, M.B.A., 1963; m. Judith K. Ewaid, July 1, 1965; children—Jennifer, Chris. Mgr., acct. Ernst & Ernst, Detroit, 1962-70; pres. Jed Products Co., Detroit, 1970-75; v.p., treas. Detrex Chem. Industries, Inc., Detroit, 1976—; dir. Wico Metal Products, Inc., J & S Mfg. Co., Wayne Chem. Co., Fabri-Matic, Inc. Mem. Fin. Execs. Inst. Clubs: Oakland Hills Country, Detroit Athletic, Recess, Renaissance. Home: 5574 Fox Hunt Ln West Bloomfield MI 48033 Office: PO Box 501 Detroit MI 48232

STOCKTON, RODNEY MAURICE, cosmetic co. exec.; b. St. Louis, Feb. 3, 1913; s. Rodney M. and Martha Julia (Harkins) S.; student Asbury Coll., 1930-33; D.Sc. (hon.), Ft. Lauderdale Coll., 1978; m. Joan Denise Barnes, Feb. 15, 1963; 1 dau., Denise Twinkle. Indsl. sales engr. Sylvania Indsl. Corp., Chgo., 1937-41, L. Sonneborn & Sons, Chgo., 1941-47; founder, pres., chief exec. officer, chmn. bd. Aloe Creme Labs., Inc., Ft. Lauderdale, Fla., 1953-76; pres. Stockton Enterprises, 1980—. Mem. Ft. Lauderdale Coll. Adv. Bd. of 100, Pres.'s Com. on Employment of Handicapped. Named Ky. Col.; recipient Wisdom award, 1970; Achievement award and Gold medal from Congressman J. Herbert Burke, Gold Key to City, Mayor of Miami Beach, Fla., 1972 Gold Key for med. research from Met. Dade County (Fla.), 1974. Fellow AIM (pres. council); mem. Sales and Mktg. Execs. Assn., Cosmetic, Toiletry and Fragrance Assn., Fla. C. of C. (dir. 1965-71) Ft. Lauderdale C. of C., Aerospace Med. Assn., Franklin Mint Collectors Soc., Smithsonian Assn. (nat.), Internat. Platform Assn. (nat. adv. bd.), Fla. Sheriff Assn. (hon.). Research in use of aloe vera plant in medications and cosmetics. Home: 750 NW 38th St Fort Lauderdale FL 33309

STODDARD, LEON DEE, contracting, engring. and developing co. exec.; b. Grace, Idaho, July 24, 1927; s. Elias Rufus and Mary Leda (Whitehead) S.; student Idaho State U., 1943; m. Donna M. Hansen, Sept. 12, 1948; children—Beverly Dee Stoddard Chipman, Jeffry Leon, Eric Paul. With Morrison-Knudsen Co., Inc., 1949—, v.p., Boise, Idaho, 1971-78, group v.p. mfg. splty. group, 1978—, group v.p. parent co., 1978—, also officer, dir. subsidiaries. Mem. Nat. Republican Congressional Com. Served with U.S. Mcht. Marines, 1943-46. Mem. Am. Inst. Constructors, Soc. Am. Mil. Engrs., Pacific NW Waterways Assn. (dir., state pres.), U.S. Coast Guard Aux., Presidents Assn. Clubs: Ivory 500, Indian Lakes Country, U.S. Senatorial. Office: PO Box 7808 400 Broadway Boise ID 83729

STODDARD, NATHANIEL CLARK, mfg. co. exec.; b. Hartford, Conn., Jan. 22, 1945; s. Nathaniel Styles and Kathryn Roberta (Clark) S.; B.A. with honors, Denison U., 1966; M.B.A. (grad. scholar 1970-72), U. Denver, 1972; m. Kathryn Mallery Headley, Sept. 17, 1966; children—Kimberly Headley, John Clark. Coordinator bus. planning and devel. Samsonite Corp., Denver, 1972-74; dir. planning consumer products div., Beatrice Foods Co., Chgo., 1974-75, v.p. mktg. services Charmglow Products div., Bristol, Wis., 1975-76; v.p. mktg. Universal-Gerwin div. Leigh Products, Inc., Saranac, Mich., 1976-80; dir. mktg. consumer products div. Black & Decker (U.S.) Inc., Easton, Md., 1980—. Asst. coach Youth Football and YMCA Basketball, (U.S.), 1978-80; sustaining mem. Republican Nat. Com., 1979-80. Served with USAF, 1966-70; pilot. Decorated Air Force Commendation medal. Mem. Am. Hardware Mfrs. Assn. (v.p. young execs. 1979—, membership com., packaging com.), Hardware Mktg. Council, Am. Mktg. Assn., Alpha Kappa Delta, Sigma Iota Epsilon, Beta Gamma Sigma. Club: Talbot County Country. Contbr. articles to profl. and sports jours. Office: 515 Glebe Rd Easton MD 21601

STODDART, ALFRED, finance exec.; b. Bellefonte, Pa., Nov. 4, 1941; s. Harold Colburn and Agnes (Benson) S.; B.S. in Accounting, Pa. State U., 1963; m. Catherine Bernabeo, Nov. 23, 1963; children—Paul Benson, Mark Adam. Sr. staff accountant Price Waterhouse & Co., N.Y.C., 1963-69; asst. controller Gen. Host Corp., N.Y.C., 1969-70; exec. v.p., treas., dir. The Harvey Group, Inc., Woodbury, N.Y., 1970—. Served with USAR, 1965-71. C.P.A., N.Y. Mem. Am. Inst. C.P.A.'s, N.Y. State Soc. C.P.A.'s. Methodist. Club: Huntington Crescent. Office: 60 Crossways Park W Woodbury NY 11797

STOECKMANN, KENNETH PAUL, rancher, farmer, land co. exec.; b. Reedsburg, Wis., Mar. 26, 1919; s. Paul Truman and Laura Vivian (Lamont) S.; student Sacramento Jr. Coll., 1939, also vocat. schs.; m. Ethel Dolores Infantas, Sept. 16, 1944; children—Francis P. Priest, Kenneth Paul, William R., Robert W. Capt., All Am. Air Export, Miami, Fla., 1946-54; founder, owner, pres., chmn. bd. Stoeckmann Ranches Inc., Red Bluff, Calif., 1976—; founder, owner, chmn. bd. Stoeckmann Land Co. Inc., Baudette, Minn., 1972—, Stoeckmann Farm Inc., Pecos, Tex., 1977—. Served with USAAF, 1943-45. Decorated Air medal, D.F.C. Home: 1518 Iowa St Pecos TX 79772 Office: Route 2 Box 24 Red Bluff CA 96080

STOETZNER, ERIC WOLDEMAR, newspaper exec.; b. Leipzig, Germany, Mar. 11, 1901; s. Woldemar and Emma (Wolf) S.; student U. Leipzig, 1922; Dr. Econ. Sci., Frankfurt am Main, 1925; m. Fridel Henning-Gronau, Dec. 20, 1927 (dec. Sept. 1967); 1 dau., Renee. Came to U.S., 1938, naturalized, 1944. Advt. dir., bus. mgr., mem. bd. Frankfurter Zeitung, Germany, 1930-38; bus. mgr. mag. of Schurz Found., Phila., 1939-43; research analyst of pub. N.Y. Times, 1944-45, dir. fgn. bus. promotion, 1945-50, dir. fgn. advt., 1950-70, internat. cons., 1970—. Bd. dirs. Stamford Forum World Affairs; citizen adv. The Ferguson Library, Stamford. Decorated Chevalier de l'ordre du Merite Commercial de la France; Officer's Cross, German Order of Merit, 1953; recipient hon. plaque City of Frankfurt, 1979. Mem. Internat. Advt. Assn. (hon. life; v.p. 1956-59), Confrerie des Chevaliers du Tastevin. Quaker. Club: Rotary (N.Y.). Home: 376 Westover Rd Stamford CT 06902

STOGA, EDWIN ANTHONY, motor transp. co. exec.; b. Chgo., Oct. 20, 1928; s. Stephen J. and Rose M. (Golda) S.; student Coll. Advanced Traffic, 1946-47, Roosevelt Coll., 1948-49, Northwestern U., 1948-49; m. Beatrice C. Kerwin, Apr. 24, 1945; children—Leslie Rose (Mrs. Dennis L. Belcher), Alan J., Nancy Kay, Judith Evelyn. Asst. regional traffic mgr. Montgomery Ward & Co., Chgo.-Detroit, 1943-51; motor carrier sales rep. Roadway Transit Co., Detroit, 1951-52; gen. traffic mgr. Fedway Stores, N.Y.C., 1952-53; div. mgr. Motor Carrier, Truck Transport Co., Chgo., 1954-58; asst. v.p. sales Jones Motor Co., Chgo., 1958-66; sr. v.p. sales and mktg. Interstate Motor Freight System, Grand Rapids, 1966-79; pres. Sales and Transp. Cons.'s Co., Grand Rapids, 1979—; v.p. Equity Transp. Co., 1979—; instr. Coll. Advanced Traffic, Chgo., 1950-71. Mem. Am. Soc. Traffic and Transp., Am. Mgmt. Assn., Am. Mktg. Assn., Nat. Council Phys. Distbn. Mgmt., ICC Practitioners Assn., Am. Bus. Club, Internat. Platform Assn., Coll. Advanced Traffic Alumni Assn., Am. Trucking Assn. (pres. sales and marketing council). Roman Catholic. Clubs: Peninsular (Grand Rapids); Traffic (Chgo.). Home: 306 Edgehill Grand Rapids MI 49506 Office: 134 Grandville Ave Grand Rapids MI 49502

STOHL, MILTON ROBERT, mgmt. cons.; b. N.Y.C., July 12, 1917; s. Morris and Rose (Gurewich) S.; student Cooper Union, 1934-35; B.S. in Edn., N.Y. U., 1939; LL.B., LaSalle Extension U., 1968; m. Muriel Rita Buckley, Apr. 25, 1941; children—Ellen Jane (Mrs. Dreman Cook), Suzanne Carol (Mrs. James Larsen), Kathleen (Mrs. Robert Trainor), Robert Buckley. Pres., Vernon Chem. Co., 1953-54; v.p. sales Tech. Tape Corp., 1954-61; v.p. sales and mktg. Mystik Tape div. Borden, Inc., Northfield, Ill., 1961-65; gen. mgr. Borden, Inc./Chem./Consumer Products, 1965-67, v.p., 1967-71, sr. v.p., 1971; pres. Waring Products div. Dynamics Corp. Am., New Hartford, Conn., 1972-75; pres. Milton R. Stohl Assocs., Avon, Conn., 1975—. Trustee Manhattan Coll. Served to 1st lt. AUS, 1943-46. Recipient Distinguished Mktg. Service award N.Y. Sales Execs. Club, 1966. Mem. N.Y. Sales Exec. Club (dir.), Conn. Bus. and Industry Assn. (dir. emeritus). Club: Farmington Woods Country. Patentee in field. Home: 29 Canterbury Ln Farmington Woods CT 06085

STOIK, JOHN LENTIS, oil co. exec.; b. N. Battleford, Sask., Can., Mar. 5, 1920; s. Mike and Barbara (Hoffmann) S.; B.S. in Chem. Engring., U. Sask., 1947; m. Margaret Mary Marshall, Aug. 23, 1943; children—John H., Gary L. With Gulf Can. Ltd., and predecessor and affiliates, 1947—, sr. v.p., 1974-76, pres., chief operating officer, dir., 1976—, chief exec. officer, 1979—; exec. v.p., chief exec. officer Korea Oil Corp., Seoul, 1970-74; mem. bus. and industry adv. com. energy and raw materials OECD, 1975—. bd. dirs. Canadian Exec. Service Overseas; dir. Toronto-Dominion Bank. Bd. dirs. Toronto Symphony. Served as flight instr. RCAF, 1942-45. Mem. Engring. Inst. Can., Am. Petroleum Inst. Mem. Progressive Conservative Party. Mem. United Ch. Can. Clubs: Granite, Engineers, Toronto, Canadian, St. George's Golf and Country (Toronto); Rideau (Ottawa); Masons. Home: 79 Rebecca Ct Rural Route 2 Maple ON L0J 1E0 Canada Office: 130 Adelaide St W Toronto ON M5H 3R6 Canada

STOJANOV, EVGENI (EUGENE) VALENTIN, engring. co. exec.; b. Sofia, Bulgaria, Mar. 31, 1946; came to Can., 1971, naturalized, 1977; s. Valentin Hristov and Maria Jekova (Stancheva) S.; B.A. Sci., U. Waterloo, 1975; m. Boel Marianne Stenstrom, July 19, 1976; children—Gina, Nicole, Dane. Designer, Austin Co. Ltd., Toronto, Ont., Can., 1973-74; chief engr. Brandzel Cons. Ltd., Toronto, 1974-77; pres., cons. engr. Bremel Co. Ltd., Toronto, 1977—. Mem. Assn. Profl. Engrs. Ont., Cons. Engrs. Ont., Engring. Inst. Can., Can. Soc. Civil Engrs. Club: Argonaut Rowing. Office: 278 Ave Rd Suite 101 Toronto ON M4V 2G7 Canada

STOKELY, ALFRED JEHU, canning co. exec.; b. Newport, Tenn., Mar. 26, 1916; s. James R. and Janie May (Jones) S.; A.B., Princeton U., 1938; m. Elizabeth Home, Feb. 24, 1940 (dec. Sept. 5, 1952); children—Alfred J., Randolph H., Barbara Elizabeth; m. 2d, Jeanette Tarkington Danner, Mar. 11, 1953; 1 dau., Martha. Sales statistician Stokely-Van Camp, Inc., 1938-40, prodn. supr., 1940-43, adminstrv. asst., 1943-45, became asst. to pres., 1945, v.p., 1954, exec. v.p., 1956-60, became pres., 1960, chief exec. officer, 1965—, now chmn., also dir.; v.p. Stokely Van Camp Can., Ltd.; dir. Am. Fletcher Nat. Bank and Trust Co., Indpls., Ind. Bell Telephone Co., Indpls., Indpls. Power & Light Co., Am. United Life Ins. Co., Indpls., Hobart Corp. Mem. Phi Beta Kappa. Clubs: Woodstock, Univ. Home: 8198 N Pennsylvania St Indianapolis IN 46240 Office: 941 N Meridian St Indianapolis IN 46204

STOKES, JONE CLIFTON, mgmt. communications cons.; b. Charlotte, N.C., Apr. 18, 1915; s. Ernest Clifton and Nancy Elizabeth (Jones) S.; student George Washington U., 1935-39, U. So. Calif., 1955-57; m. Dorothy Eads Jewell, Nov. 15, 1941; 1 son, Kenneth Blair. Visual info. officer The White House, Washington, 1947-51; commd. U.S. Air Force, 1951, advanced through grades to lt. col., 1965, ret., 1973; staff telecommunications cons. Exec. Office of the Pres., Washington, 1973-78; v.p. Teletrac Systems Corp., 1974-79; pres. Televisual Systems Corp., Washington, 1977—; pres. Fed. Design Council, 1970-72. Served to capt., USAAF, 1942-46. Decorated Legion of Merit, Armed Forces Meritorious Service medal, Air Force Commendation medal with 3 oak leaf clusters. Mem. Info. Film Producers Assn. (bd. govs. 1968-75), Public Mems. Assn. of the Fgn. Service (v.p. 1979—), Am. Fgn. Service Assn., Air Force Assn., Ret. Officers Assn., AIAA. Club: Nat. Space. Home: 7119 Westchester Dr Washington DC 20031

STOLL, ERIC D., mfg. co. exec.; b. N.Y.C., Nov. 15, 1938; s. Duane C. and Bessie (Mosley) S.; B.E.E. magna cum laude, CCNY, 1961; M.E.E., N.Y.U., 1963, Ph.D. with honors, 1966, M.B.A., 1974. Mem. tech. staff Bell Telephone Labs., Murray Hill and Holmdel, N.J., 1961-68; program mgr. Bendix Corp. Nav. and Control Div., Teterboro, N.J., 1968-73; mgr. spl. programs ADT Security Systems Corp., N.Y.C., 1973-79; dir. engring. advanced tech. systems div. Austin Co., Fair Lawn, N.J., 1979—. Recipient Sandor I. Oesterreicher award Elec. Engring. Excellence, 1961, Founders Day award for outstanding scholarship N.Y. U., 1967. Mem. IEEE, Am. Mgmt. Assn., Am. Statis. Assn., Inst. Mgmt. Scis. (pres. Met. N.Y. chpt. 1978-79, v.p. programs 1977-78), Tau Beta Pi, Eta Kappa Nu. Contbr. articles to profl. jours. Home: 117 Hillside Ave Teaneck NJ 07666

STOLL, JAMES ARTHUR, supermarket exec.; b. Canton, Ohio, Mar. 8, 1940; s. Otis Chester and Betty May (Mericle) S.; student Mt. Union Coll., 1959-60, Internat. Accountants Soc., 1962-64; m. Cynthia Louise Ross, Aug. 30, 1959; children—Vickie Lynn, Teresa Joy, Lisa Ann, Sharon Leann, Elizabeth Ann. Asst. mgr. White Cottage Food Center, Inc., Canton, 1955-65, v.p., gen. mgr., 1965-71; founder Stoll's Food, Inc., New Philadelphia, Ohio, 1972, pres., chmn. bd., 1972—. Active United Way. Mem. Asso. Grocers Inc. (bd. dirs. 1972—, chmn. bd. 1975-77, Meritorious Service award 1977), Nat. Assn. Retail Grocers U.S. (bd. dirs. 1977—, chmn. nat. conv. 1980, chmn.-elect 1980), Twin Cities United Retail Mchts. (bd. dirs. 1973), East Central Ohio Food Dealers Assn. (bd. dirs., pres. 1970-72), Ohio Retail Food Dealers Assn. (Grocers Spotlight award 1980), East Canton Jaycees, Tuscarawas County C. of C. Republican. Methodist. Club: Elks. Home: 5355 Woodlynn NE East Canton OH 44730 Office: 504 Bowers Ave NW New Philadelphia OH 44663

STOLLE, THOMAS JOSEPH, constrn. co. exec.; b. Columbus, Ohio, June 15, 1928; s. Edward Joseph and Dorothy Agnes (Hayes) S.; B.S., U.S. Naval Acad., 1952; M.B.A., U. Ark., 1972; m. Sheila Mary Collins, July 19, 1952; children—Michael, Maureen Shawn, Kevin, Patrick, Manuel. Commd. pilot, lt. USAF, 1952, ret., 1975; corp. tng. mgr. human resource devel. Brown & Root, Inc., Houston, 1975—. Mem. Am. Soc. Tng. and Devel., Naval Acad. Alumni Assn., Planning Execs. Inst., Air Force Assn., Ret. Officers Assn. Roman Catholic. Club: K.C. Home: 6015 Craigway Spring TX 77379 Office: PO Box 3 Houston TX 77001

STOLLER, ERIC CHESTER, ins. co. exec.; b. Balt., Oct. 29, 1943; s. Philip and Mollie S. (Estner) S.; B.B.A. magna cum laude, U. Miami, 1964; LL.B., Harvard U., 1967; m. Phyllis Rosenstein, July 23, 1967; children—Nicholas Allen, Matthew Nathaniel. Admitted to N.Y. bar, 1967, Fla. bar, 1980; with Exxon Co., 1967-70; with Am. Bankers Life Assurance Co., Miami, Fla., 1970—, dir. internat. devel., sr. v.p. fin., 1980—; with Fin. Assurance Co., Ltd., Enfield, Eng., 1972—, mng. dir., 1972—. Mem. N.Y. Bar Assn., Fla. Bar Assn. Office: Am Bankers Life Assurance 600 Brickell Ave Miami FL 33131

STOLTE, HENRY FRED, advt. and mktg. exec.; b. N.Y.C., Nov. 12, 1922; s. Fred H. and Elizabeth (Hopper) S.; B.S., Hofstra U., 1949, M.B.A., 1955; m. Helen Tracy Porter, Dec. 1, 1955; 1 son, James Patterson. Marine designer Columbian Bronze Corp., Freeport, N.Y., 1945-49; sales rep. Swift & Co., N.Y.C., 1950-54; sales service mgr. Pfizer, Inc., N.Y.C., 1954-60, budget coordinator, controllers div., 1960-66, marketing and advt. mgr., minerals, pigments and metals div., 1966—. Served with USNR, 1942-45. Mem. Soc. Motion Picture and TV Engrs., Nat. Visual Communications Assn., Aircraft Owners and Pilots Assn. Home: 1728 Sycamore Ave Merrick NY 11566 Office: 235 E 42d St New York City NY 10017

STOLTE, LARRY GENE, computer processing co. exec.; b. Cedar Rapids, Iowa, Sept. 17, 1945; s. Ed August and Emma Wilhelmena (Tank) S.; B.B.A. with highest distinction (FS Services scholar), U. Iowa, 1971; m. Rebecca Jane Tappmeyer, June 13, 1970; children—Scott Edward, Ryan Gene. Tax and auditing acct. McGladrey Hendrickson & Co., Cedar Rapids, 1971-73; v.p. TLS Co., Cedar Rapids, 1973—, also dir. Served to sgt. USMC, 1964-67. C.P.A., Iowa, Ill., Mo., Minn., Wis.; cert. mgmt. acct. Mem. Nat. Assn. Computerized Tax Processors (pres.), Nat. Assn. Accts., Am. Inst. C.P.A.'s, Am. Mgmt. Assn. Republican. Methodist. Home: Rural Route 4 Box 215-E Solon IA 52333 Office: TLS Co 810 1st Ave NE PO Box 1686 Cedar Rapids IA 52406

STOLZ, OTTO GEORGE, textile co. exec.; b. Jn. 23, 1942; s. Otto and Johanna Stolz; B.Engring., Inst. Tech. N.Y., 1963; J.D., U. Va., 1966; diploma Grad. Inst. Internat. Studies, Geneva; m. Jill Viemeister Stolz, Aug. 1964; children—Whitney, Heather. Admitted to Calif. bar, N.C. bar; atty. firm Latham & Watkins, Los Angeles, 1967-71; mem. faculty Duke U. Law Sch., 1972-77; gen. counsel, sr. v.p. Cannon Mills Co., Kannapolis, N.C., 1977-78, exec. v.p., gen. counsel, 1978-79, pres., 1979—, also dir.; dir. Cabarrus Bank & Trust Co., Cannon Found. Mem. Am. Bar Assn., D.C. Bar Assn., N.C. Bar Assn., State Bar Calif. Author: Revenue Sharing: A Legal and Policy Analysis, 1974; also articles. Office: 1 Lakeside Dr Kannapolis NC 28081

STONE, AL, hotel exec.; b. Fort Anne, N.Y., Dec. 30, 1927; s. Ercelle Carrol and Geraldine (Bradway) S.; grad. Profl. Sch. Bus., 1973; m. Joan Frances Hotaling, May 28, 1949; 1 son, Bradley H. Asst. mgr. Hotel McAlpin, N.Y.C., 1948-52; mgr. Woodstock Hotel, N.Y.C., 1952-55; mgr. motor hotels Marriott Industries, Washington, 1955-61; gen. mgr. Summit (N.J.) Suburban Hotel, 1961-72, pres., gen. mgr., 1972—, also dir.; dir. ops. Sheraton Northlake Inn, Atlanta. Served with USMCR, 1944-46. Recipient community service award Summit Kiwanis Club, 1974. Mem. N.J. Hotel and Motel Assn. (dir. 1973—, v.p. 1976—, pres.'s club award 1974-76, presdl. meritorious achievement award 1978). Club: Masons. Home: 54 Robbins Ave Berkeley Heights NJ 07922 Office: 570 Springfield Ave Summit NJ 07901

STONE, ALAN JOHN, mfg. co. exec.; b. Dansville, N.Y., Sept. 9, 1940; s. Guthrie Boyd and Doris Irene (Wolfanger) S.; B.S. in Mech. Engring., Rochester Inst. Tech., 1963; M.B.A., U. Pitts., 1964; m. Sandra Barber, Aug. 22, 1964; children—Teri, Timothy, Michael. Engring. aide Xerox Corp., Webster, N.Y., 1960-63; gen. mgr. plastic component div. Stone Conveyor Co., Inc., Honeoye, N.Y., 1964-67, v.p. sales, 1968; co-founder, pres. dir. Stone Constrn. Equipment Inc., Honeoye, 1969—; founder, pres., dir. Canandaigua Apts. Inc. (N.Y.), 1968—; v.p., dir. Baker Rental Service, Inc., 1973-76; dir. Accu Systems, Inc. Mem. Town of Richmond (N.Y.) Planning Bd., 1970-75, chmn., 1970-71; mem. Honeoye Central Sch. Bd. Edn., 1971-76, pres., 1973-74; com. chmn. pack 10 Boy Scouts Am., 1975-77; mem. Ontario County Overall Econ. Devel. Com., 1976—. Mem. Assn. M.B.A. Execs., Honeoye (chmn. indsl. com. 1974—), Rochester chambers commerce, Constrn. Industry Mfrs. Assn. (exec. mem. new bus. challenges council 1980—). Mem. Ch. of Christ. Patentee in field. Home: Egypt Valley Rd Honeoye NY 14471 Office: 32 E Main St Honeoye NY 14471

STONE, ALLAN GRAYSON, licensing rep.; b. Bklyn., Jan. 5, 1926; s. Frank and Bertha (Lenner) S.; student Hamilton Coll., 1941-45, Adelphi Coll., 1944-48; m. Barbara Betsy Shore, 1948; children—Michael Sanford, Peter Lyle, Robert Adam. Vice-pres. Kagran Corp., N.Y.C., 1948-55; pres. Stone Assos., N.Y.C., 1955-60; pres. Licensing Corp. Am., N.Y.C., 1960-70; pres. Hamilton Projects, Inc., N.Y.C., 1971—; dir. Herald Tribune Radio Network, Inc., Gateway Industries Inc., Def. Electronic Industries, Inc. Served with USNR, 1942-47. Clubs: Yale (N.Y.C.); Shelter Rock Tennis (Manhasset, N.Y.), Boca West Golf (Boca Raton, Fla.). Home: 13 Grenfell Dr Great Neck NY 11020 Office: Olympic Tower 645 Fifth Ave New York NY 10020

STONE, CARL HENRY, computer co. exec.; b. Yankton, S.D., July 2, 1924; s. Carl B. and Ruth L. (Fernald) S.; B.A., Miami U., Oxford, Ohio, 1949; B.Arch., U. Tex., 1950, M.S., 1960; m. Viviane Bomanji, 1945; children—Claudia Anne, Douglas Fernald. Engr., mgr. Union Carbide Nuclear Co., Oak Ridge, 1952-62; mgr. bus. sci., fin. div. Gen. Electric Co., Lynn, Mass., 1965-67; dir. info. processing Bull-Gen. Electric Co., Paris, 1967-70; fin. advisor Honeywell-Bull Corp., Paris, 1970-75, bus. planning N.Am. ops. Honeywell Corp., Waltham, Mass., 1976-77; product mgr. Digital Equipment Corp., Maynard, Mass., 1977—; dir. Firepro, Inc., Wellesley, Mass., 1975—; cons. in field. Mem. Am. Mgmt. Assn., Assn. Computing Machinery, Soc. Mfg. Engrs., Am. Inst. Indsl. Engrs., SAR. Clubs: Cercle Interallie (Paris); Wellesley, Brae Burn Country. Home: 81 Albion Rd Wellesley Hills MA 02181 Office: Digital Equipment Corp Main St Maynard MA 01754

STONE, ELLIOT J., dept. store exec.; b. Boston, Jan. 13, 1921; s. Maurice A. and Ann (Scovell) S.; grad. Clark U., Worcester, Mass., 1943; m. Marion E. Goldberg, Jan. 31, 1943; children—Marcia Stone Finsterwald), Diane. Buyer, R.H. White's, Boston, 1946-52; buyer-mdse. mgr. Gimbels, Pitts., 1952-70; exec. v.p. Maas Bros., Ft. Myers, Fla., 1970-71; exec. v.p. Jordan Marsh Co., Boston, 1972-75, pres., chief exec. officer, dir., 1980—; pres. Gimbels Inc., N.Y.C., 1975—. Served with AUS, World War II; ETO. Decorated Bronze Star. Mem. Nat. Retail Mchts. Assn. Club: Spring Valley Country. Home: 22 Clements Rd Newton MA 02158 also 900 Park Ave New York NY Office: 450 Washington St Boston MA 02158*

STONE, FRED MICHAEL, lawyer, stock exchange exec.; b. Bklyn., Jan. 20, 1943; s. Nathan and Rose (Silverman) S.; A.B. cum laude, Bklyn. Coll., 1964; J.D., Harvard U., 1967; LL.M., N.Y. U., 1971; m. Bonnie B. Dobkin, Aug. 14, 1965; children—Jonathan, Jennifer. Admitted to N.Y. State bar, 1968, U.S. Ct. Claims bar, 1968, ICC bar, 1968; asso. firm. Cadwalader, Wickersham & Taft, N.Y.C., 1967-69; asst. gen. counsel Standard & Poor's/Intercapital, Inc. (now Dean Witter/Intercapital Inc.), N.Y.C., 1969-71; v.p., gen. counsel Neuwirth Mgmt. & Research Corp., Middletown, N.J., 1971-73; v.p., gen. counsel Mocatta Metals Corp., N.Y.C., 1973-76; sr. v.p. legal and regulatory policy div. Am. Stock Exchange, Inc., N.Y.C., 1976—; chmn. exec. com., gov. Amex Commodities Exchange, Inc., N.Y.C., 1980—; lectr. Practising Law Inst. Vice chmn. Township of Manalapan (N.J.) Zoning Bd. Adjustment. Mem. Harvard Law Sch. Assn., Assn. Bar City N.Y. Democrat. Jewish. Office: 86 Trinity Pl New York NY 10006

STONE, HAZEL LUCY ROTH (MRS. NORREL L. STONE), purchasing exec.; b. Des Moines; d. William and Verne Fessler Roth; student U. Iowa, 1937-39, Drake U., 1939-41, U. Kansas City Sch. Law, 1941-43; m. Norrel L. Stone, Jan. 8, 1954. Buyer regional office Montgomery Ward, 1941-43; citrus grower, Haines City, Fla., 1943-48; buyer Maas Bros., St. Petersburg, Fla., 1950—. Instr. marketing Jr. Coll., St. Petersburg, evenings 1950-55; prof. econs., English, money and banking Am. Inst. Banking, St. Petersburg, evenings 1956—. Mem. women's com. Republican Party, Winter Haven, Fla., 1945-46; active various community fund drives; state adviser distributive edn., 1949-75; mem. ombudsman TRY. Named Outstanding Bus. and Profl. Woman of Year, 1956. Mem. Am. Inst. Banking, Internat. Platform Assn., Fla. League Arts, Mus. Fine Arts, Common Cause, Smithsonian Instn., Sirosis Club (pres. 1976-78), Kappa Alpha Theta. Clubs: Republican Congressional, Bath, Contbg. author to textbooks; speaker on metric system, environ. problems. Home: One Beach Dr Apt 1608 Saint Petersburg FL 33701

STONE, HUBERT DEAN, journalist; b. Maryville, Tenn., Sept. 23, 1924; s. Archie Hubert and Annie (Cupp) S.; student Maryville Coll., 1942-43; B.A., U. Okla., 1949; m. Agnes Shirley, Sept. 12, 1953 (dec. Mar. 1973); 1 son, Neal Anson. Sunday editor Maryville-Alcoa Daily Times, 1949; mng. editor Maryville-Alcoa Times, 1949-78, editor, 1978—; v.p. Maryville-Alcoa Newspapers, Inc., 1960—; pres. Stonecraft, 1954—. Mem. mayor's adv. com. City of Maryville; mem. air service adv. com. Knoxville Met. Airport Authority; bd. dirs. United Fund of Blount County, 1961-63, 74-76, vice chmn. campaign, 1971-72, chmn. campaign, 1973, v.p., 1974, pres., 1975; bd. dirs. Maryville Utilities Bd., Blount County Hist. Trust, Nat. Hillbilly Homecoming Assn., Friendsville Acad., 1968-73, Alkiwan Crafts, Inc., 1970-73, Middle E.Tenn. Regional Tourism Group; treas., trustee Smoky Mountains Passion Play Assn.; mem. adv. bd. Harrison-Chilhowee Bapt. Acad. Served from pvt. to staff sgt. AUS, 1943-45. Decorated Bronze Star; named Outstanding Sr. Man of Blount County, 1970, 77. Mem. Profl. Photographers of Am., Internat. Post Card Distbrs. Assn., Great Smoky Mountains Natural History Assn., Ft. Loudoun Assn., Tenn. Jaycees (editor 1954-55, sec.-treas. 1955-56), Jr. Chamber Internat. (senator) Maryville-Alcoa Jaycees (life mem., pres. 1953-54), Blount County (v.p. 1971, 76, pres. 1977), Townsend (dir. 1969-71) chambers commerce, Tenn. Associated Press News Execs. Assn. (v.p. 1973, pres. 1974), Asso. Press Mng. Editors Assn., Tenn. Profl. Photographers Assn., Am. Legion, V.F.W., Chilhowee Bapt. Assn. (chmn. history com.) U. Okla. Alumni Assn. (life mem., pres. East Tenn. chpt. 1954-55), Sigma Delta Chi (life, dir. E. Tenn. chpt.). Baptist (trustee, pres. bd. trustees, deacon, chmn. evangelism, finance, personnel coms.). Mason, Kiwanian (pres. Alcoa 1969-70). Club: Green Meadow Country. Contbr. articles to profl. publs. Home: 1510 Scenic Dr Maryville TN 37801 Office: 307 E Harper Ave Maryville TN 37801

STONE, JAMES HIRAM, oil co. exec.; b. N.Y.C., Dec. 20, 1925; s. Jacob Chauncey and Isabel (Green) S.; B.A., Williams Coll.; postgrad. in geology Tex. A & M U., 1950; children—Suzanne, Andrew, Thomas, Margaret. Owner, operator Stone Oil Co., Cin., 1951—, chmn. bd., chief exec. officer, 1975—; dir. ITI Am. Exchange Corp., Westone Corp.; underwriting mem. Lloyds of London. Bd. dirs. New Orleans Crime Commn., 1976—; mem. Pres.'s Council Tulane U. Served to capt. U.S. Marine Corp, 1943-46. Mem. Ind. Petroleum Assn. Am., New Orleans, Lafayette geol. socs., Ducks United (life). Republican. Episcopalian. Clubs: Los Angeles Rams Football (dir.), Cin. Country, Queen City (Cin.); Lake Placid (N.Y.); Cricuet, Palm Bay (Miami, Fla.); Keenland (Lexington, Ky.); Petroleum, Plimsoli, New Orleans Country (New Orleans). Home: 711 Bienville St New Orleans LA 70130 Office: Stone Oil Corp Pan Am Life Center Suite 2660 601 Poydras St New Orleans LA 70130

STONE, JAMES M., govt. ofcl.; b. N.Y.C., Nov. 12, 1947; s. Henry and Babette (Rosmond) S.; B.A. with highest honors in Econs., Harvard U., 1969, M.A., 1970, Ph.D., 1973. Lectr. econs. Harvard U., Cambridge, Mass., 1973-75; commr. ins. Commonwealth of Mass., 1975-79; chmn. Commodity Futures Trading Commn., Washington, 1979—. Democrat. Author: One Way for Wall Street, 1975; also articles. Home: 1325 18th St NW Washington DC 20036 Office: 2033 K St NW Washington DC 20581

STONE, JAMES MADISON, aerospace co. exec.; b. Bristol, Va., Nov. 19, 1918; s. Claud H. and Hattie (Carmack) S.; student Dallas Sch. Law and Bus., 1937-38, So. Meth. U., 1941-42; D.Sc., Utah State U., 1972; m. Margaret Grace, Oct. 15, 1941; children—James Madison, Donald Lee. Mgr. prodn. and purchasing Am. Type Founders Inc., Elizabeth, N.J., 1950-55; mgr. planning and control Crane Co., Chgo., 1955-56; gen. mgr. Solar Aircraft Co., Des Moines, 1956-60; mgr. material Wasatch div. Thiokol Chem. Corp., Brigham City, Utah, 1960-65, dir. adminstrn., 1965-67, gen. mgr., 1967-69, v.p., gen. mgr., 1969-74, group v.p. govt. systems, 1974—; mem. adv. bd. Box Elder chpt. A.R.C., 1967—; Utah Safety Council, 1968—. Served with USNR, 1944-46. Mem. AIAA, Am. Mgmt. Assn., Am. Def. Preparedness Assn. (past chmn. bd.), Air Force Assn., Assn. U.S. Army, C. of C. Mason, Rotarian. Home: 1187 Michelle Dr Brigham City UT 84302 Office: PO Box 9258 Ogden UT 84409

STONE, LARRY JAY, civil engr., corp. exec.; b. Nashville, Ark., Nov. 16, 1947; s. Harriman Pete and Ruffie Lee (Copeland) S.; student So. State Coll., 1965-67; B.S. in Agrl. Engring., U. Ark., 1970, M.S. in Civil Engring., 1971; postgrad. in Civil Engring., U. Houston, 1971-73; m. Patricia Ann Hardin, Jan. 28, 1972; children—Jeremy Jay, John Matthew. Engring. asst. R.J. Sewell, P.E., Dallas, 1971-72; teaching fellow U. Houston, 1972-73; staff environ. engr. San Jacinto River Authority, Conroe, Tex., 1973; project mgr. Properties Internat., Inc., Houston, 1973-74; project engr. Roy F. Weston, Houston, 1974-75; v.p. Hart Engring. Co., Longview, Tex., 1975-78; exec. v.p. Kindle, Stone & Assos., Inc., Longview, 1978—; cons. in field. Hon. grad. U. Ark., 1970. Mem. ASCE, Tex. Soc. Profl. Engrs. (Young Engr. of Yr., E.Tex. chpt. 1978), E.Tex. Water Utilities Assn., Nat. Soc. Profl. Engrs., Am. Water Works Assn., Am. Water Resources Assn. Mem. Church of Christ. Club: Daybreak Kiwanis. Contbr. writings to publs. in field. Home: 2704 Fleetwood Dr Longview TX 75601 Office: 3218 N Fourth St Longview TX 75601

STONE, ROBERT EDWARD, farm credit co. exec.; b. Prospect, Ohio, Nov. 24, 1934; s. Raymond Lester and Lucille Moore (Thomas) S.; B.S. in Agrl. Econs., Purdue U., 1953-57; m. Sarah Inez Roy, May 31, 1959; children—Dawn, Bradley, James. With credit dept. Central Soya, Inc., Gibson City, Ill., 1957-60, Des Moines, 1960-61, Ft. Wayne, Ind., 1961-65; various mgmt. positions Hancock, Lucas and Auglaize counties Landmark, Inc., Columbus, Ohio, 1965-73; pres. Lebanon (Ohio) Prodn. Credit Assn. 1974—. Mem. Warren County Farm Bur. Republican. Methodist. Clubs: Lebanon Rotary, Masons. Home: 1002 Stanwood Dr Lebanon OH 45036 Office: 420 E Main St Lebanon OH 45036

STONE, ROBERT RYDER, exec. search cons.; b. Mpls., May 19, 1948; s. Robert Allan and Missie Ryder S.; A.B. in Polit. Sci., Williams Coll., 1970; m. Mary Glennon, Sept. 29, 1979. With State Street Bank, Boston, 1970-72; group sales rep. Prudential Ins. Co., N.Y.C., 1972-74; mktg. rep. Fidelity Fin. Corp., Boston, 1974-75; exec. v.p. Olney Corp., N.Y.C., 1975-79; v.p. Eastman & Beauding, N.Y.C., 1979—. Mem. Assn. Exec. Recruiting Cons.'s. Republican. Presbyterian. Clubs: Union (N.Y.C.); Union Boat (Boston). Office: 437 Madison Ave New York NY 10022

STONE, RONALD NORMAN, mfg. co. exec.; b. N.Y.C., Feb. 6, 1944; s. Adolphus and Theresa (Kunze) S.; B.S., U. So. Calif., 1967; m. Lori Kahan, Sept. 13, 1967; children—Tiffany, Brian. Vice pres. fin. Norton Triump Corp., Duarte, Calif., 1973-75; div. controller Fleetwood Enterprises, Riverside, Calif., 1971-73; with Arthur Andersen & Co., Los Angeles, 1967-71; v.p. fin. Pioneer Electronics Am., Long Beach, Calif., 1975—. Served with U.S. Army, 1962-63. C.P.A., Calif. Mem. Assn. Electronic Importers (pres., treas., dir.), Sycamore Park Home Owners Assn. (dir., treas.), Sycamore Park Tennis Assn. (treas., dir.), Fin. Execs. Inst., Am. Inst. C.P.A.'s, Nat. Assn. Accts. Office: 1925 E Dominguez St Long Beach CA 90810

STONE, THOMAS JENNINGS, JR., real estate exec., promoter and developer; b. Sandersville, Ga., Nov. 20, 1914; s. Thomas J. and Ruby (Stanly) S.; student public schs.; m. Mary Linnie Harden, Sept. 28, 1944; 1 dau., Joanne H. In various clerical, auditing, acctg. positions, 1933-36; with W.L. Florence, promoter-developer, Athens, Ga., 1935-41, gen. mgr., sec-treas. various affiliated cos., 1936-41; chief acct. Brunswick Marine Constrn. Corp. (Ga.), 1941-42; practice acctg., auditing, Augusta, Ga., 1946-49; salesman, promoter J.C. Bible, Jr., real estate, Augusta, 1949-51; owner, operator Tom Stone Real Estate, broker, developer, contractor, Augusta, 1951—; developer Town of Martinez (Ga.), 1953-55; owner, developer Meml. Gardens Cemetary, Lincoln Meml. Gardens, 1965--. Served with AUS, 1942-46. Mem. Internat. Platform Assn., Am. Legion. Baptist. Clubs: Masons, Shriners. Office: RFD #1 Box 275 Hwy 56 CSRA Bldg Augusta GA 30906

STONE, WILLIAM ROBERT, mgmt. cons.; b. Smith Center, Kans., July 28, 1921; s. Edward VanBuren and Daisy (Achenbach) S.; S.B., Harvard U., 1943; postgrad. Harvard-Mass. Inst. Tech. Radar Sch., 1944, N.Y. U., 1947-48, Bklyn. Poly. Inst., 1948-51; m. Vivian Adele Dowie, Jan. 31, 1948; children—Pamela Gail, Linda Janise, Wendy Carol. Engr., sect. mgr. Hazeltine Corp., N.Y.C., 1946-56; project controller Gen. Electric Co., 1956-58, specialist mgmt. sci., 1958-60, orgn. cons., 1960-63; gen. mgr., dir. Hunt Electronics, Dallas, 1963-65; cons. mgmt. systems IBM Armonk, N.Y., 1967-69; v.p. A.B. Dick Co., Chgo., 1969-74; exec. v.p. E.F. Johnson Co., Waseca, Minn., 1974-76; partner Brown/Ferrisco, Mgmt. Cons.'s, Wayzata, Minn., 1977-79; pres. Stone, Howard, Nowill & Kouwenhoven, Inc., 1979—; mem. Nat. TV Systems Com., 1951-53; mgmt. cons., 1965-66; cons. U.S. Dept. Commerce, 1973—. Served to lt., Signal Corps, U.S. Army, 1943-46. Mem. IEEE. Republican. Clubs: Radio, Electronic-VIP, Harvard of N.Y., Harvard of Minn. Home: 1009 E Elm Ave Waseca MN 56093 Office: 250 N Central Ave Wayzata MN 55391

STONECIPHER, HARLAND CECIL, ins. co. exec.; b. Ashland, Okla., June 4, 1938; s. Allen Clinton and Viola Vessie S.; B.A., E. Central State U., Ada, Okla., 1960; m. Shirley Ann Thompson, Aug. 22, 1958; children—Allen Clinton, Harland Brent. Tchr. speech, debate coach schs. in Okla., 1961-67; dist. mgr. Nat. Found. Life Ins. Co., Oklahoma City, 1967-69; v.p. Paramount Life Ins. Co., Little Rock, 1969-73; pres., chmn. bd. Pre-Paid Legal Services, Inc., Ada, Okla., 1973—, Profl. Motor Service Club, Inc., 1973—; chmn. bd. Pre-Paid Legal Casualty, Inc., 1973—, Nat. Pre-Paid Legal Services, Inc., 1979—, Career Guidance Systems, Inc., 1980—. Democrat. Baptist. Home: Route 1 Centrahoma OK 74534 Office: PO Box 145 Ada OK 74820

STONER, EDMUND CURTIS, JR., cons. engr.; b. Riverside, Calif., Oct. 20, 1903; s. Edmund Curtis and Margaret (Copley) S.; student Lafayette Coll., 1921-22; B.S. in Elec. Engring., Yale, 1926; m. Margaret Dorman Hamilton, June 23, 1926 (dec. 1958); 1 dau., Margaret Hamilton (Mrs. John N. Schofield, Jr.); m. 2d, Mary J. Garcia, 1960. Chief engr. Internat. Tel. & Tel. Corp., Peru, Cuba and Spain, 1933-41; asst. v.p. Fed. Telephone & Radio, 1945-48; cons. engr. to minister of communications Govt. of Turkey, Ankara, 1948-51; chief engr. Gen. Telephone & Electronics Corp., Muskegon, Mich., 1954-58, chief engr., Tampa, Fla., 1958-65; engr. planning dir. Gen. Telephone Co. Fla., 1965-68; cons. engr., 1969—. Served to lt. col. USAAF, World War II (col. Res. ret.). Decorated Bronze Star; Mil. Order Brit. Empire. Mem. I.E.E.E., Rochester, Muskegon, Tampa chambers commerce, Order of Daedalians, OX-5 Aviation Pioneers, Phi Kappa Psi. Presbyn. Clubs: University (Tampa, Fla.); Yale (N.Y.C.). Home: 310 S Burlingame Ave Temple Terrace FL 33617

STONER, RICHARD BURKETT, mfg. co. exec.; b. Ladoga, Ind., May 15, 1920; s. Edward Norris and Florence May (Burkett) S.; B.S., Ind. U., 1941; J.D., Harvard U., 1947; LL.D., Butler U., 1975; m. Virginia B. Austin, Feb. 22, 1942; children—Pamela T., Richard Burkett, Benjamin Austin, Janet Elizabeth, Rebecca Lee, Joanne Jeannea. Admitted to Ind. bar, 1947; with Cummins Engine Co., Inc., Columbus, Ind., 1947—; vice chmn. bd. dirs.; dir. Kirloskar Cummins Ltd., Poona, India, Am. Fletcher Corp., Am. Fletcher Bank Suisse, Am. Fletcher Nat. Bank & Trust Co., Am. United Life Ins. Co., Public Service Ind. Vice-chmn. Cummins Engine Found.; pres. bd. trustees Ind. U. Served to capt. AUS, 1942-46. Mem. Machinery and Allied Products Inst. (exec. com.), Ind. State C. of C. Democrat. Mem. Disciples of Christ Ch. Club: Indpls. Athletic. Office: 432 Washington St Columbus IN 47201

STOOKEY, JOHN HOYT, chem. co. exec.; b. N.Y.C., Jan. 29, 1930; s. Byron and Helen Phelps (Hoyt) S.; ed. Amherst Coll., 1952, Columbia, 1955; m. Katherine Elizabeth Emory, Sept. 3, 1954; children—Helen Hoyt, Laura Emory, Hunt Emory, Anson Greene Phelps. Asst. v.p. S.Am. Gold & Platinum Co., N.Y.C., 1956-59; officer, dir. various pvt. corps. for Investor Syndicate, 1959-69; U.S. rep. Financiera Metropolitana S.A., N.Y.C., 1962-75, Pub. Works Bank of Mexican Fed. Govt., N.Y.C., 1964-75; pres. Wallace Clark, Inc., N.Y.C., 1970-75, dir., 1962—; pres. Nat. Distillers & Chem. Corp., N.Y.C., 1975—, dir., 1970—; dir. Riegel Textile Corp., 1960—, Rexham Corp., 1979—. Trustee, Boston Symphony Orch., 1969—, Northfield-Mt. Hermon Schs., 1974-79, James Weldon Johnson Community Center, Inc., 1965-70, Oratorio Soc. N.Y., 1965-75, Kodaly Musical Tng. Inst., 1973-75, Council of Ams., 1977—, Bio-Energy Council, 1978—; founder, pres. Berkshire Boy Choir, Inc., 1967—; trustee Coll. Human Services, 1964—, treas., 1964-75; trustee Stowe Sch., Inc., 1960-76, pres., 1960-73; mem. adv. bd. Grosvenor Neighborhood House, 1970—; chmn. health manpower com. United Hosp. Fund, 1966-71; mem. exec. com. Assn. for Better N.Y., 1976—; mem. adv. bd. Music in Deerfield, 1977—; trustee Phelps Stokes Fund, 1980—. Mem. Council Fgn. Relations, Alpha Pi Mu, Delta Kappa Epsilon. Clubs: Union, Down Town Assn., Met. Opera, Pequot Yacht, Center Harbor Yacht, Lenox, Weston Gun, Pinnacle, Century Assn. Home: Sasco Hill Rd Southport CT 06490 Office: 99 Park Ave New York NY 10016

STOOLMAN, HERBERT LEONARD, pub. relations co. exec.; b. Newark, Apr. 6, 1917; s. Abe C. and Ida H. (Sinar) S.; A.B., Catawba Coll., 1937; B.S., Temple U., 1939; postgrad. Harvard, 1938; m. Sarah Janice Cutler, Apr. 6, 1944; children—Cathy Lynn (Mrs. Richard Schwartz), Robert Henry. Pub., East Camden Newspapers, 1941-57; pres. Stoolman Assos., Camden, N.J., 1946—; dir. pub. relations Camden County, N.J., 1953—. Mem. Camden County Econ. Devel. Commn., 1963—, Camden County Cultural and Heritage Commn., 1973—. Served with USAF, 1942-46. Recipient Nat. award Nat. Assn. Counties, 1969, 72, 78, 79; Nat. award Am. Indsl. Devel. Council, 1963. Mem. Am., N.J. hosps. pub. relations assns., S. Jersey, Phila. pub. relations assns., Am. Assn. County Pub. Relations Officers, N.J. Press Assn. Club: Lions (dir. pub. relations). Home: 811 Redman Ave Haddonfield NJ 08033 Office: 315 Cooper St Camden NJ 08102

STOORZA, GAIL, mktg. communications exec.; b. Yoakum, Tex., Aug. 23, 1943; d. Roy Blankenship and Pauline Ray; student N. Tex. State U., 1962. Account exec. Phillips-Ramsey, Inc., 1965-68; dir. advt. and pub. relations Rancho Bernardo, 1968-71; corporate dir. communications Avco Community Developers, Inc., 1971-74; founder, pres. The Gail Stoorza Co., San Diego, 1974—; dir. Sun Savs. & Loan; speaker on mktg. and pub. relations. Citizens adv. council San Diego Community Colls. Named Outstanding Young Citizen San Diego, 1979. Mem. Pub. Relations Soc. Am. (accredited), Nat. Assn. Home Builders, Pacific Coast Builders Conf. (program chmn.), Real Estate Editors and Tennis Writers Assn., San Diego C. of C. (dir.). Club: San Diego City. Home: 6243 Caminito Andreta San Diego CA 92111 Office: 225 Broadway Suite 1309 San Diego CA 92101

STORER, TODD CLEMENT, petroleum engr.; b. Peublo, Colo., Nov. 9, 1922; s. Todd C. and Esther Mathilda (Olson) S.; grad. in Petroleum Engring., Colo. Sch. Mines, 1947; m. Jessie Hope Dean, Oct. 24, 1944 (div. June 1979); children—Todd C., Nancy Storer Yang, Vivian Storer Shields; m. 2d, Doris M. McKinney Perry; 1 stepson, James N. Perry. With Amoco Prodn. Co. and predecessors, Chgo., 1947—, now prodn. systems mgr. Served with C.E., U.S. Army, 1943-46. Mem. Data Processing Mgmt. Assn., Soc. Petroleum Engrs. of AIME. Republican. Episcopalian. Contbr. articles to profl. jours. Home: 140 Center Plaza Tulsa OK 74119 Office: Box 591 Tulsa OK 74102

STORM, ROSWELL HAROLD, security systems co. exec.; b. London, Ky., Jan. 27, 1925; s. Roswell Clarence and Rusa (Taylor) S.; B.S., Union Coll., Ky., 1953; M.A., Eastern Ky. State U., 1958, postgrad., 1967-70; postgrad. U. Ky., 1959-62; m. Mildred Owens, June 1, 1947; children—Gail, James Harold, John Philip, Robert C., Richard D. Tchr., Laurel County Sch. System, London, 1940-49, tchr., coach, 1950-60, counselor, coach, 1960-66, high sch. prin., 1966-76; exec. v.p. Storm Security Systems, Inc., London, 1976—; pres. Republic Energy Co., London, 1975—, Bar Creek Coal Co., London, 1979—. Served with USMC, 1942-45. Decorated Bronze Star with two oak leaf clusters; NDEA grantee, 1959, 68; lic. detective, Ky., Ind., Conn. Mem. Nat. Ret. Tchrs. Assn., Ky. Ret. Tchrs. Assn., World Assn. Detectives, Hon. Order Ky. Cols., VFW. Republican. Baptist. Club: London Rotary (sec. 1952-55). Home: Route 5 Box 438 London KY 40741 Office: 216 E 4th St London KY 40741

STORM, WILLIAM JOHN, restaurant chain exec.; b. Chgo., Feb. 13, 1925; s. Josef and Rose (Steirer) Somogyi; B.S.M.E., U. Ill., 1947; M.B.A., U. Chgo., 1953; m. Barbara L. Larson, June 13, 1953; children—Michael, David, Cynthia, Caroline, Julie, Matthew, Sara. Engr., Western Electric Co., Chgo., 1950-53, U.S. Army C.E., Chgo., 1953-54; cons. engring., New Orleans, 1954-68; partner Alexander Grant & Co., New Orleans, 1968-78; sr. v.p. Church's Fried Chicken, San Antonio, 1978—; mem. faculty Tulane U., Loyola U., 1955-65. Registered profl. engr., La. Mem. Nat. Soc. Profl. Engrs. Republican. Presbyterian. Contbr. articles to profl. jours. Home: 7619 Susan Elaine San Antonio TX 78240 Office: 355 Spencer Ln San Antonio TX 78284

STORMONT, RICHARD MANSFIELD, hotel exec.; b. Chgo., Apr. 4, 1936; s. Daniel Lytle and E. Mildred (Milligan) S.; B.S., Cornell U., 1958; m. Virginia Louellen Walters, Nov. 21, 1959; children—Stacy Lee, Richard Mansfield, John Frederick. Food cost analyst, sales rep. Edgewater Beach Hotel, Chgo., 1957-58, asst. sales mgr. Marriott Motor Hotels, Inc., Washington, 1962-64; dir. sales Marriott Motor Hotel, Atlanta, 1964-68, resident mgr., 1969-71, gen. mgr., Dallas, 1971-73, Phila., 1973-74, Marriott Hotel, Atlanta, 1974-79; pres. Hardin Mgmt. Co., hotel devel., 1979—; v.p. Marriott Hotels, Washington, 1980—; dir. Fred J. Walters & Co., cons. to mgmt. Pres., Atlanta Conv. and Visitors Bur., 1975, chmn. bd., 1976-77; mem. exec. com. Central Atlanta Progress, Inc., 1979—; mem. exec. bd. Boy Scouts Am.; bd. dirs. Better Bus. Bur. Served to lt. (j.g.) USNR, 1959-62. Recipient Distinguished Salesman of Year award Marriott, 1967. Mem. Sales and Mktg. Execs. (pres. Atlanta 1970-71), Pa. (dir. 1974), Dallas (dir.), Atlanta (pres. 1977) hotel-motel assns., Atlanta C. of C. (dir., v.p.), Ga. Bus. and Industry Assn. (dir.), Hotel Sales Mgmt. Assn. (past chpt. pres.), Cornell Soc. Hotelmen (pres. Ga. chpt. 1976), Nat. Alliance Businessmen (vice chmn. pvt. industry council 1978—), Pi Sigma Epsilon, Phi Kappa Psi. Rotarian. Home: 1216 Mottrom Dr McLean VA 22101 Office: Marriott Corp Washington DC 20058

STORRS, THOMAS IRWIN, banker; b. Nashville, Aug. 25, 1918; s. Robert Williamson, Jr., and Addie Sue (Payne) S.; B.A., U. Va., 1940; M.A., Harvard U., 1950, Ph.D., 1955; LL.D. (hon.), U. N.C., Greensboro, 1969; m. Kitty Bird, July 19, 1948; children—Tom, Margaret. Vice pres. Fed. Res. Bank, Richmond, Va., 1934-37, 40-41, 45-60; exec. v.p. N.C. Nat. Bank, Charlotte, 1960-69, pres., 1969-73, chief exec. officer, 1973—; chmn. bd., chief exec. officer NCNB Corp. and N.C. Nat. Bank, 1974; dir. Black & Decker Mfg. Co. Trustee, Davidson Coll., 1980, U. N.C., Charlotte, 1978—; bd. visitors Grad. Sch. Bus. Adminstrn., Duke U., 1974—; trustee Colgate Darden Grad. Bus. Sch. Sponsors, U. Va., 1971-80; bd. dirs. Charlotte Symphony Orch. Soc., United Community Services, pres., 1976-77. Served to comdr. USNR, 1941-45, 51-52. Mem. Am. Bankers Assn., Assn. Res. City Bankers (dir., pres. 1980-81), Internat. Monetary Conf. (dir.). Episcopalian. Office: Charlotte NC 28255

STOTT, MICHAEL ANTHONY, investment co. exec.; b. Patterson, N.J., Nov. 30, 1936; s. William Ross and Irene (Kearns) S.; student Villanova U., 1954-58; m. Alison Walker, June 3, 1961;

children—Michael Anthony, Timothy, Amy, David, Gregory, Thomas. With Blyth Eastman Dillon (merged with Paine Webber Jackson Curtis 1980), 1963—, br. mgr., Newark, 1963-68, v.p. sales, N.Y.C., 1969-76, sr. v.p. sales, 1976-79, sr. v.p. investments, 1979—; cons. D'Jinni Industries, Dayton, Ohio. Mem. Village of Ridgewood (N.J.) Planning Bd., 1968. Clubs: Arcola Country (Paramus, N.J.); High Mountain Golf (Franklin Lakes, N.J.); Upper Ridgwood Tennis; Wall St. (N.Y.C.). Office: 1221 Ave of the Americas Suite 1300 New York NY 10020

STOUDT, JAMES R., cons. co. exec. Formerly pres. Gilbert Commonwealth Cos. (now Gilbert Assos., Inc.), now chmn. Registered profl. engr., Pa. Mem. ASME. Office: 525 Lancaster Ave Reading PA 19603

STOUT, ALBERT WESLEY, transp. co. exec.; b. Denver, Feb. 8, 1926; s. Albert W. and Henrietta (Rabjohn) S.; student Ind. State U., 1951; m. Elsie Hernandez, Nov. 26, 1976; children—Robert W., Shirley Ann. Vice pres., treas. Eastern Express, Inc., Terre Haute, Ind., 1947-71; pres. Motor Freight Corp., Terre Haute, 1968-71; pres. Specialized Transp. div. Ryder System, Inc., Miami, Fla., 1971-79, Atlantic Express, Inc., Atlanta, 1979—. Served to 1st lt. USAR, 1943-46. Mem. Nat. Assn. Shipper Motor Carrier Conf. (pres., chmn. bd.), Am. Soc. Traffic Transp. (dir.), Central States Motor Freight Bur. (dir.), Nat. Motor Freight Traffic Assn. (chmn. bd. dirs.), Ind. Motor Truck Assn. (dir.), ICC Practitioners Assn., Delta Nu Alpha (pres.). Home: 8145 Ball Mill Rd Atlanta GA 30338 Office: 1530 Dunwoody Pkwy Suite 204 Atlanta GA 30338

STOUT, DONALD EVERETT, real estate developer, appraiser; b. Dayton, Ohio, Mar. 16, 1926; s. Thorne Franklin and Lovella Marie (Sweeney) S.; B.S., Miami U., 1950; m. Gloria B. McCormick, Apr. 10, 1948; children—Holly Sue, Scott Kenneth. Mgr. comml.-indsl. div. G. P. Huffman Realty, Dayton, 1954-58; leasing agt., mgr. Forest Park Plaza, Dayton, 1959-71; developer 1st transp. center for trucking in Ohio; pres. devel. cos. for Sunderland Falls Estate, Wright Gate Indsl. Mall, Edglo Land Recycle and Grande Tierra Corp., Dayton, Eastwood Lake Lodge and Marina real estate investment; appraiser FHA, Dept. Transp., utility cos.; pres. Donald E. Stout Inc., Dayton. Served with AUS, 1944-45, USN, 1945-56. Named Outstanding Real Estate Salesman of Ohio, Ohio Bd. Realtors, 1961; licensed real estate broker, Ohio, V.I. Mem. Dayton Area Bd. Realtors (co-founder, 1st pres. salesman div. 1959, exec. adv. com. 1959-60, Outstanding Real Estate Salesman 1961), Nat. Assn. Real Estate Bds., Soc. Real Estate Appraisers (sr. real estate analyst, dir. 1959-60, sec. 1961, pres. 1964), Appraisal Inst., Dayton C. of C., Naval Res. Officers Assn., Phi Delta Theta. Clubs: Trans World Airlines Ambassadors, United Air Lines Half Million Mile, Flying Colonel of Delta Fleet, Exhausted Roosters, Dayton Racquet, Mason (32 deg. Shriner). Contbr. articles to profl. jours. Home: 759 Plantation Ln Dayton OH 45419 Office: 1340 Woodman Dr Dayton OH 45432

STOVALL, JERRY COLEMAN, ins. co. exec.; b. Houston, July 31, 1936; s. Clifford Coleman and Maxine (Lands) S.; B.B.A., U. Houston, 1968; m. Elsie Hostetter, June 20, 1959; 1 son, Brent Allen. Home office adminstr. Am. Gen. Life, Houston, 1955-63, agt., agy. mgr., 1963-66, agy. mgr., regional dir. agencies, regional v.p., 1969-74; sr. brokerage cons. Conn. Gen. Life, Houston, 1966-69; sr. v.p., dir. mktg. Capitol Life Ins. Co., Denver, 1974-78; v.p., dir. mktg. Integon Life Ins. Corp., Winston-Salem, N.C., 1978—. Vice chmn. major gifts drive United Way, Winston-Salem; vice chmn. precinct Rep. Party, Davie County, N.C.; mem. nat. adv. bd. Internat. Assn. Fin. Planners, 1977-78. Served with U.S. Army, 1955-57. C.L.U. Mem. Nat. Assn. Life Underwriters, Am. Soc. C.L.U.'s, Am. Soc. Pension Actuaries (asso.). Baptist. Club: Bermuda Run Country. Home: Box 747 Bermuda Run Advance NC 27006 Office: 500 W 5th St Winston-Salem NC 27102

STOVER, JAMES R., business exec.; b. Marion, Ind., 1927; B.M.E., Cath. U., 1950; LL.B., George Washington U., 1955; married. Project engr. Eisenhauer Mfg. Co., 1950-51; patent examiner U.S. Patent Office, 1951-55; with Eaton Corp., 1955—, group v.p. indsl. and security products, 1974-77, corp. exec. v.p. ops., 1977-78, vice chmn., chief operating officer, transp. products, 1978-79, pres., chief operating officer, 1979—, also dir.; dir. Nat. City Corp., Nat. City Bank, White Consol. Industries. Office: 100 Erieview Plaza Cleveland OH 44114*

STOVER, WILLIAM RUFFNER, ins. co. exec.; b. Washington, Aug. 31, 1922; s. Daniel I. and Carrie E. (Brubaker) S.; grad. Northwestern U., 1945; m. Carolyn McKean, July 19, 1947; children—Deborah Ann Stover Bowgren, Wendi Lee Stover Mirretti, Sherree Kay Stover Bloss. Sales rep. Old Republic Life Ins. Co., Chgo., 1945-49, v.p., 1949-60, sr. v.p., 1960-68, pres., 1968—, also dir.; pres. Old Republic Internat. Corp., Chgo., 1969—, also chief exec. officer; officer, dir. Old Republic Life Ins. Co. N.Y., Old Republic Ins. Co., Pa., Home Owners Life Ins. Co., Chgo., Motorists Beneficial Ins. Co., Old Republic Life Ins. Co. Tex.; dir. Minn. Title Ins. Co., Miss. Valley Title Ins. Co., RMIC Corp., Founders Title Group Inc., Marina Bank, Homac-Barnes, Inc. Office: 307 N Michigan Ave Chicago IL 60601

STOWE, JAMES NORMAN, broadcasting exec.; b. Denver, Aug. 16, 1937; s. John Appolis and Annabelle (Cowen) S.; B.S., U. Nebr., Omaha, 1963; m. Janet Louise Clawson, Nov. 16, 1956; children—Michael, Robert, Christopher. Sales mgr. Stoner Broadcasting Co., Des Moines, 1966-69; gen. mgr. Sta. WGNT, Huntington, W.Va., 1969-71; pres. Music Unlimited, Yuma, Ariz., 1971—; owner, gen. mgr. Magnamedia, Inc., Yuma, 1971—; mem. Ariz. adv. bd. Mountain Bell Telephone, 1980—. Chmn. Yuma United Fund, 1974. Mem. Ariz. Broadcasters Assn. (dir. 1980—), Yuma County C. of C. (chmn. bd. 1975-76), Caballeros De Yuma. Republican. Methodist. Club: Yuma Rotary. Home: 1358 Hettema St Yuma AZ 85364 Office: Box 228 669 Ave B Yuma AZ 85364

STOWHAS, MARGARITA CLARA, lang. sch. and transl. service exec.; b. Santiago, Chile, Nov. 18, 1937; d. A. Raul and Graciela (Sanchez) S.; came to U.S., 1971; Ph.D., Univ. de Chile, 1961; div.; 1 son, Chris M. Cantin. Tchr., Escuela San Patricio, Santiago, 1959; prof. Spanish, Universidad Catolica, Santiago, 1960-64; head social dept. Corporacion de la Vivienda, 1964-71; laborer Childress Canvas, Dallas, 1971; order filler Paradise Corp., Dallas, 1972; mem. office staff Franklin Stores Corp., Dallas, 1972-73; night sch. tchr. Dallas Ind. Sch. Dist., 1973-75; tchr., translator, Dallas, 1973-77; lang. instr. Eastfield Coll., Dallas, 1975-77; exec. dir. Dallas Internat. Lang. Center, 1975—. Mem. Am. Translators Assn., L'Alliance Francaise, North Dallas C. of C. Mem. Ch. Jesus Christ of Latter-day Saints. Office: 1450 Preston Forest Sq Dallas TX 75230

STRAETZ, ROBERT P., business exec.; b. Hillside, N.J., 1921; s. Arthur and Eugenia (Will) S.; grad. U. Chgo.; student Advanced Mgmt. Program at Harvard U.; m. Elizabeth Shimmin, Feb. 5, 1943; children—Robert P., Kathryn. Research chemist Manhattan Project, until 1946; with Textron Inc., 1946—, successively v.p., exec. v.p., pres. Homelite div., until 1974, corp. group v.p., 1974-78, pres., chief operating officer, 1978-79, chmn. bd., chief exec. officer, 1979—, also dir.; dir. Indsl. Nat. Corp. Bd. dirs. Nat. Jr. Achievement, R.I. Port Authority and Econ. Devel. Council. Mem. Providence C. of C. (dir.). Club: Dunes (Narragansett, R.I.). Office: Textron Inc 40 Westminster St Providence RI 02903

STRAHAN, WILLIAM RICHARD, retail franchise exec.; b. Detroit, July 20, 1927; s. Gordon William and Esther Bertha (Hintz) S.; Ph.B., U. Detroit, 1950; m. Sybil E. Wallace, June 6, 1953; children—Patricia A., Kathleen E. Salesman, Radio Distbg. Co., Detroit, 1950-52; with DeSoto div. Chrysler Corp., Detroit, 1952-53, dist. mgr., Boston, 1953-56, new car mgr., 1956-58, used car mgr., bus. mgmt. mgr., 1958-59, nat. used car mgr., 1959-61, nat. used car mgr., Detroit, 1961-65, zone mgr., Los Angeles, 1965-68, gen. mgr. co. distbn., 1968-72; gen. mgr. franchise Midal Internat. Corp., Chgo., 1972-75, v.p. sales, 1975—. Served with USN, 1945. Club: Plum Grove (v.p., dir. 1973-76). Office: 222 S Riverside Plaza Chicago IL 60606

STRAIN, DAVID LEROY, banker; b. Washington, N.C., Feb. 23, 1921; s. David Leroy and Ethel Lois S.; student U. N.C., Chapel Hill, 1940-42, LL.B., 1952; grad. Rutgers U. Grad. Sch. Banking, 1958; m. Marian Lance, May 7, 1955; children—Karen J., Susan M. Successively trust rep., asst. trusteofficer, comml. bank officer, v.p. charge corr. banking and out-of-town accounts Nat. Bank of Commerce, Norfolk, Va., 1952-60; sr. v.p. credit Branch Banking & Trust Co., Wilson, N.C., 1961-62; pres. Charles F. Cates & Sons, Inc., Faison, N.C., 1962-64; exec. v.p. 1st Nat. Bank of Norfolk, 1965-70; exec. v.p. Peoples Nat. Bank, Greenville, S.C., 1970-73; pres., dir. So. Bank & Trust Co., Greenville, 1973—; dir. So. Bancorp., Inc., Charles F. Cates & Sons, Inc., Cates Pickle Sales, Inc., Asso. Distbrs., Inc. Bd. dirs. St. Francis Community Hosp., Greenville Airport Commn.; bd. dirs., former pres. Greenville Jr. Achievement, Inc., Goodwin Industries of Upper S.C., Inc. Served with USAAF, 1942-46. Mem. Newcomen Soc. N. Am., Fin. Execs. Inst. Presbyterian. Club: Greenville Rotary. Office: PO Box 1329 Greenville SC 29602

STRAIT, CHARLES EDWARD, door co. exec.; b. Los Angeles, Aug. 15, 1948; s. Charles Elmer and Emily Silveria (Moses) S.; B.B.A., Loyola U., Los Angeles, 1970; m. Patricia Lynn Bohache, July 11, 1970; 1 son, Randolph Charles. Asst. gen. mgr. Strait Door and Plywood Corp., South El Monte, Calif., 1970, exec. v.p., 1974-76, pres., Chino, Calif., 1977—; v.p. adminstrn. Bellwood Co., Orange, Calif., 1971; v.p. Wall Panel Mfg. Co., 1972-73. Mem. Woodwork Inst. Calif. Democrat. Roman Catholic. Home: 373 Havana Ave Long Beach CA 90814 Office: 13951 Monte Vista Ave Chino CA 91710

STRANAHAN, ROBERT PAUL, JR., lawyer; b. Louisville, Oct. 29, 1929; s. Robert Paul and Anna May (Payne) S.; A.B., Princeton, 1951; J.D., Harvard, 1954; m. Louise Perry, May 12, 1956; children—Susan Dial, Robert Paul III, Carol Payne. Admitted to D.C. bar, 1954, Md. bar, 1964; practiced in Washington, 1957—; asso. firm Wilmer & Broun, 1957-62; partner Wilmer, Cutler & Pickering, 1963-79, Wilmer & Pickering, 1979—; professorial lectr. in law Nat. Law Center, George Washington U., 1969-72. Served to 1st lt. USMCR, 1954-57. Mem. Am., Fed., D.C. bar assns. Clubs: Princeton, Metropolitan, Gridiron (Washington); Chevy Chase (Md.). Home: 5316 Cardinal Ct Bethesda MD 20016 Office: 1666 K St NW Washington DC 20006

STRANBERG, NORMAN CALVIN, aerospace co. exec.; b. Jamestown, N.Y., Oct. 26, 1930; s. Reynold M. and Mary V. (Simcox) S.; student E. Tenn. State U., 1949-50; B.M.E., U. Tenn., 1956; M.M.E., So. Meth. U., 1962; postgrad. in Math., Tex. Christian U., 1963; m. Ladye Melba Stinson, June 15, 1957; children—Ladye Ann, Peter Stinson. Flight test engr. Gen. Dynamics Corp., Ft. Worth, 1956-61, project engr. 1961-67, div. rep., Dayton, Ohio, 1967-68, exec. asst., Ft. Worth, 1968-69, program dir., 1969-71, dir. sales, 1971-73, dir. domestic and internat. mktg., 1973-78, v.p. Europe, 1978—; tchr. math. U. Wis. Extension, Tokyo, 1951-53. Precinct chmn. Republican party, 1959-61; mem. Ft. Worth Air Power Council, 1972—. Served in USAF, 1950-53. Mem. Am. Inst. Aeros. and Astronautics, Am. Def. Preparedness Assn., Nat. Mgmt. Assn., Dallas/Ft. Worth Tenn. Alumni Assn. (pres. 1961-63), So. Meth. U. Alumni Assn. Clubs: Shady Oaks Country, Royal Waterloo Golf, Am. of Brussels, Am. of London, Chateau Sainte Anne. Home: 3 Domaine du Beausant Rosieres 1331 Belgium Office: 7 Lloyd George Brussels 1050 Belgium

STRAND, CURT ROBERT, hotel exec.; b. Vienna, Austria, Nov. 13, 1920; s. Victor and Enit (Zerner) S.; came to U.S., 1937, naturalized, 1943; B.S., Cornell U., 1943; m. Fleur Lillian Emanuel, June 14, 1946; 1 dau., Karen. Supt. service Plaza, N.Y.C., 1947-49; asst. to v.p. Hilton Hotels Corp., 1949-53; v.p. Hilton Internat. Co., N.Y.C., 1953-64, exec. v.p., 1964-67, pres., 1967—; sr. v.p., dir. Trans World Airlines, Inc.; vice chmn. Hilton Service Corp. Lectr., Cornell U. Sch. Hotel Adminstrn. Served with M.I., AUS, 1943-46. Mem. Cornell Soc. Hotelmen. Office: Waldorf Astoria Park Ave New York NY 10022*

STRANG, CHARLES D., mfg. co. exec.; b. Bklyn., Apr. 12, 1921; s. Charles D. and Anna E. (Endner) S.; B.M.E., Poly. Inst. Bklyn., 1943. Mem. mech. engring. staff M.I.T., 1947-51; v.p. engring., then exec. v.p. Kiekhaefer Corp., Fond du Lac, Wis., 1951-64; v.p. marine engring., then exec. v.p. Outboard Marine Corp., Waukegan, Ill., 1966-74, pres., chief exec. officer, 1974—, also dir. Trustee, Poly. Inst. N.Y. Mem. Am. Power Boat Assn. (past pres.), Soc. Automotive Engrs., Union Internat. Motorboating (v.p.), Am. Boat and Yacht Council, Sigma Xi. Club: Waukegan Yacht. Author, patentee in field. Office: 100 Sea Horse Dr Waukegan IL 60085

STRANGE, BOOTH BARRINGTON, petroleum exploration co. exec.; b. Kingston, Okla., Oct. 2, 1913; s. Oscar Alloway and Callie Ruth (Barrington) S.; B.S. in Engring., U. Okla., 1936; m. Laura Wicklund, Feb. 19, 1966; children—Amelia Marie, Eric Thorsen, Carl Thorsen, Booth Barrington, Margaret Laura. With Western Geophys. Co. of Cam., Am., Houston, 1936—, pres., 1965-79, chmn. bd., 1979—; v.p. Litton Industries, 1967—; chief exec. Litton Resources Group, 1974—. Mem. devel. council Tex. Christian U., 1960-66; mem. adv. council Sch. Geology and Geophysics, U. Okla.; bd. dirs. S. Tex., Jr. Achievement. Mem. Soc. Exploration Geophysicists, Am. Assn. Petroleum Geologists, Am. Petroleum Inst. Republican. Clubs: Los Angeles Country; Houston Racquet, Lakeside Country, Houston Petroleum (Houston). Patentee in field of geophys. exploration for oil. Office: PO Box 2469 Houston TX 77001

STRANK, GALE BENJAMIN, market research exec.; b. Middletown, Mo., Jan. 28, 1918; s. Milton B. and Lillian (Gibson) S.; B.S., Mo. U., 1949; postgrad. Columbia U., 1968; m. Margie Delene Admire, Jan. 1, 1944; children—Gale B. II, Melinda Ann. Market analyst Deere & Co., Moline, Ill., 1949-54, corp. mgr. market research, 1959—; mgr. market research John Deere Ltd., Winnipeg, Man., Can., 1955-58. Served to 1st lt. USAAF, 1942-46. Decorated D.F.C., Air medal. Mem. Am. Mktg. Assn., Conf. Bd. (market research council), Delta Sigma Pi. Lutheran. Club: Outing (dir., officer) (Davenport). Home: 244 Hillcrest Ave Davenport IA 52803 Office: John Deere Rd Moline IL 61265

STRATTON, JEANETTE LEE, antique dealer; b. Brush, Colo., July 5, 1942; d. Harvey John and Helen Marjorie Waite; diploma Norfolk (Va.) Bus. Sch., 1961; m. Thomas G. Stratton, Jr., June 26, 1971. Adminstrv. asst., exec. sec. Def. Contract Audit Agy., Electric Boat div. Gen. Dynamics Corp., Groton, Conn., 1968-74; antique dealer and appraiser, 1975—; propr. Stone of Scone Antiques, Canterbury, Conn., 1975—. Recipient Outstanding Performance award Def. Contract Audit Agy., 1972, Sustained Superior Performance award, 1974. Mem. Early Am. Soc., Conn. Citizens Action Group, Canterbury Hist. Soc. Roman Catholic. Address: RFD 1 Box 262 Bingham Rd Canterbury CT 06331

STRATTON, JOHN CARYL, realtor; b. Chgo., July 11, 1920; s. John Frederick Otto and Dorothy Marjorie (Young) S.; B.S. cum laude, Princeton, 1949; M.B.A., U. New Haven, 1980; m. Lucille Waterhouse Hall, Mar. 13, 1974; children by previous marriage—Caryl Stratton Killing, John Caryl II, Susan Hall Levy, Evelyn Hall Brenton, Kenneth Hall. Chief liaison engr., Avco Mfg. Co., Stratford, Conn., 1950-55; pres. Yankee Engring. Service, Newtown, Conn., 1955-65; pres. Stratton Realty, Roxbury, Conn., 1965—; dir. Auto Swage Products Inc.; lectr. U. Conn., 1968-74, Western Conn. State Coll., 1975—. Chmn. Zoning Commn. Newtown, 1971-77. Served with USAF, 1942-46. Decorated D.F.C., Air medal with oak leaf cluster. Mem. Am. Inst. Aeros. and Astronautics, Internat. Real Estate Fedn., Nat. Real Estate Exchange, Newtown Bd. Realtors (pres. 1974, dir. 1975-79), New Milford Bd. Realtors, Conn., Nat. assns. realtors, Internat. Real Estate Fedn., Realtors Nat. Mktg. Inst. (cert. real estate salesman, cert. real estate broker), Nat. Assn. Real Estate Appraisers, Soc. Real Estate Appraisers, Am. Right of Way Assn., Comml. Investment Divs. Greater Stamford (Conn.), Nat. Inst. Farm and Land Brokers, Nat. Assn. Real Estate Counselors, Nat. Assn. Rev. Appraisers (cert. real estate appraiser), Sigma Xi. Republican. Congregationalist. Clubs: N.Y. Athletic, Princeton. Address: Squire Rd Roxbury CT 06783

STRATTON, JOHN ROBERT, mfg. co. exec.; b. Hillsboro, Ohio, Nov. 4, 1928; s. Ronald Robert and Hazel (Duncan) S.; student Case Sch. Applied Sci., 1948-50; m. Margaret Longsdorf, Jan. 17, 1971; children—Kimberly E., Sarah L.; stepchildren—Joseph B., Cherylann. Div. exec. Cleve. Trencher, constrn. equipment, 1967-69; div. mgr. Long Mfg. Co., Tarboro, N.C., 1969-72; v.p. Capacity, Inc., Dallas, 1972—. Served with USMC, 1946-48. Mem. Fluid Power Soc., Am. Trucking Assn. (mem. maintenance com. 1972—, mem. operations council 1972—), Am. Soc. Metals, Soc. Automotive Engrs., Soc. Mining Engrs. of AIME. Address: 6735 Churchill Way Dallas TX 75230

STRAUS, MICHAEL JOSEPH, investment banker; b. Cin., Dec. 25, 1942; s. Abe and Faye V. Straus; B.B.A. in Fin., U. Cin., 1964; student Salmon P. Chase Sch. Law, 1965-66. Claims div. Allstate Ins. Co., 1966-67; trader iron and steel brokerage David J. Joseph Co., 1967-70; comml. real estate div. J.I. Kislak Realty Corp., 1970-73; v.p., dir. Eaton Dental Lab., Inc., 1973—, Tri County Dental Lab., Inc., 1974—; v.p., dir. Envirosystems Corp., 1975—, Venture Investment Corp., 1975—, U.S. Country Club Assos., Inc., 1976—, Soc. Devel. Human Resources, Inc., 1976—, Bryn-Mawr Equity Investors, Inc., 1977—; pres., dir. Radnor Computer Assos., Inc., 1977—; owner, operator Michael J. Straus, Real Estate Co., Bryn Mawr, Pa., 1977—. Cert. real estate broker, Pa.; registered investment advisor. Mem. Phila. Dental Lab. Assn. (pres. 1980—), Sigma Alpha Mu. Republican. Jewish. Clubs: Dutch Hollow Country (Owasco, N.Y.); Golden Slipper Charities. Home: 600 Lewis Rd King of Prussia PA 19406 Office: 890 County Line Rd Bryn Mawr PA 19010

STRAUSS, ALBERT JAMES, cons. paper industry; b. Washington, Dec. 23, 1910; s. Albert A. and Lydia (Thompson) S.; A.B., George Washington U., 1935; m. Violet R. Haney, Nov. 27, 1935. Central purchasing agt. Hecht Co., Washington, 1947-49; purchasing agt. E.F. Drew, Boonton, N.J., 1949-52; v.p. purchasing and transp. Riegel Paper Corp., N.Y.C., 1952-72; v.p., dir. Riegel Products Corp., Milford, N.J., 1972-76; cons. to paper industry, 1976—. Mem. Am. Paper and Pulp Assn. (chmn. materials com. 1960-62), Lehigh Valley Purchasing Assn. (dir. 1958-59), Am. Mgmt. Assn., Nat. Assn. Purchasing Mgrs., Pulp Consumers Assn. (dir.). Contbr. articles to profl. jours. Clubs: Antique Automobile of Am., Williams, Rotary. Home: 930 Bobwhite Pl Harrisonburg VA 22801

STRAUSS, ALFRED CARMICHAEL, cement co. exec.; b. N.Y.C., Oct. 13, 1932; s. Alfred Amiel and Lorraine (Carmichael) S.; B.S., U. N.C., 1954; J.D., U. Mich. Law Sch., 1959; m. Barbara Elizabeth Scully, Apr. 12, 1958; children—Patricia, Michael, Christopher. With Lehigh Portland Cement Co., 1959—, v.p. adminstrn., 1969-71, v.p. N. Central region, Mpls., 1971—. Bd. dirs. Indsl. Devel. Corp. Lehigh Valley. Served with USMCR, 1954-56. Mem. N.Y. State Bar Assn., Pi Kappa Phi, Delta Theta Phi. Presbyn. Home: 1566 Rhode Island St Golden Valley MN 55427 Office: 12300 DuPont Ave S Burnsville MN 55337

STRAUSS, JON CALVERT, univ. adminstr.; b. Chgo., Jan. 17, 1940; s. Charles Earl and Alice Calvert (Woods) S.; B.S. in Elec. Engring., U. Wis., 1959; M.S. in Physics, U. Pitts., 1962; Ph.D. in Systems and Communication Scis., Carnegie Inst. Tech., 1965; m. Joan Helen Bailey, Sept. 19, 1959; children—Susan Lynn, Stephanie Lee. Scientist, Westinghouse, Bettis, Pitts., 1959-60; applied scientist IBM, Pitts., 1960-65; asso. prof. Carnegie Mellon U., Pitts., 1966-70; prof., dir. computer center U. Trondheim (Norway), 1971; dir. computer center, asso. prof. Washington U., St. Louis, 1971-74; v.p. budget and fin. U. Pa., Phila., 1975—; dir. Uni-Coll, Wharton Econometric Forecasting Assos.; cons. in field. Ford Found. fellow, 1962-63. Mem. Assn. for Computing Machinery, Sigma Xi. Patentee. Home: 2031 Naudain St Philadelphia PA 19146 Office: U Pa 3451 Walnut St Room 731 Philadelphia PA 19104

STRAUSS, MARTIN HEINZ, mfg. co. exec.; b. Hoechheim, Germany, May 21, 1927; s. Ben and Rose (Sommer) S.; grad. high sch.; m. Ellen Lindauer, Oct. 27, 1951; children—Gary, Joanne. Came to U.S., 1939, naturalized, 1944. With Kahn & Feldman, Inc., N.Y.C., 1945-57, export mgr., 1950-57; with Plicose Mfg. Corp. div. Diamond Shamrock, N.Y.C., 1957-68; traffic mgr., exec. v.p. Dura Commodities Corp., Harrison, N.Y., 1968—. Served with USNR, 1944-45. Vice pres., chmn. bd. trustees Jewish Community Center, Harrison, N.Y., 1963—. Honored by Jewish Theol. Sem., 1970. Mem. B'nai B'rith (pres.). Home: 515 Harrison Ave Harrison NY 10528 Office: 111 Calvert St Harrison NY 10528

STRAUSS, PETER, distbn. co. exec.; b. Stuttgart, Ger., Aug. 27, 1932; came to U.S., 1936, naturalized, 1943; s. Julius and Eva (Kops) S.; B.A., Harvard U., 1954, M.B.A., 1958; m. Laura Ginsburg, Sept. 23, 1962; children—Carolyn Louise, Diana Kathryn. Trainee, Gen. Cigar Co., Inc., 1958-62, exec. v.p. ops., 1976-78; pres. Met. Distbn. Services, Inc., N.Y.C., 1978—. Mem. N.Y. State adv. com. to U.S. Civil Rights Commn., 1977-80; chmn. Scarsdale (N.Y.) Adv. Council on Human Relations, 1977-80; chmn. Harvard Schs. Com. N.Y.C., 1965—; bd. dirs. Scarsdale Adult Sch., 1979. Served with U.S. Army, 1954-56. Recipient Brotherhood award NCCJ, 1980. Mem. Jamaican-Am. C. of C. (pres. 1975—), Nat. Assn. Tobacco Distbrs. (trustee), Am. Jewish Com. (pres. chpt. 1973-75, mem. nat. exec. com.). Jewish. Home: 156 Brite Ave Scarsdale NY 10583 Office: 45-19 32d Pl Long Island City NY 11101

STRAUSS, WILLIS ADDISON, gas co. exec.; b. Omaha, Apr. 15, 1922; s. Edward M. and Wilhelmina (Hausmann) S.; B.S., Iowa State U., 1947; D.B.A. (hon.), Dakota Wesleyan U., m. Janet Schaefer, Aug. 8, 1946; children—Elizabeth Ann, Susan. With No. Natural Gas Co. (now Internorth, Inc.), Omaha, 1948—, adminstrv. v.p., 1957-59, exec. v.p., 1959-60, pres., 1960-66, pres., chmn. bd., chief exec. officer, 1966-76, chmn. bd., chief exec. officer, 1976-80, chmn. bd., chief policy officer, 1980—, dir. Omaha Nat. Bank, Omaha Nat. Corp., Northwestern Bell Telephone Co., First Bank System, Inc. Mem. Treasury Dept. U.S. Payroll Savs. Com., U.S. Savs. Bond drive, 1967—. Past pres. Omaha Indsl. Found. Bd. dirs. Upper Midwest Research and Devel. Council, Iowa State U. Found. U. Nebr. Found., Boys Clubs Omaha, YMCA, United Community Services, NCCJ; trustee 4-H Club Found.; bd. govs. Knights of Ak-Sar-Ben; bd. dirs. Clarkson Hosp., Creighton U.; mem. adv. bd. Mpls. Area Devel. Corp.; mem. Nat. Center for Voluntary Action; vice chmn. Nat. Energy Study Com.; bus. com. arts Laymen's Nat. Bible Com. Served to 1st lt. AUS, 1942-46. Recipient Nebr. Builders award, 1962; B'nai B'rith Am. citation Henry Monsky lodge Omaha, 1967; Luth. Brotherhood Liberty Bell award, 1967; Iowa State Alumni award, 1967; Omaha YMCA Highest award, 1967; Nat. Brotherhood award NCCJ. Mem. Am. Gas Assn. (exec. com.), Ind. Natural Gas Gas Assn. (exec. com., past pres.), Omaha C. of C. (v.p.), Young Presidents Orgn., Delta Upsilon. Republican. Presbyn. Clubs: Omaha Country; Mpls., Omaha. Office: 2223 Dodge St Omaha NE 68102*

STREETER, EARL LOUIS, lawyer, mgmt. cons. co. exec.; b. Chgo., July 1, 1935; s. Everett William and Grace Louise (Whitney) S.; B.A., Whittier Coll., 1957; M.B.A., U. Calif., Los Angeles, 1965, J.D. (dean's council), 1967; m. Patricia Ellen Hare, June 20, 1958; 1 dau., Michelle Lynn. Research and teaching asst. behavioral sci. U. Calif. at Los Angeles Grad. Sch. Mgmt., 1962-65, adminstrv. analyst and counselor, 1967-69; admitted to Calif. bar, 1968; dir. personnel and mgmt. cons. K. Leventhal Co. C.P.A.'s, Los Angeles, 1969-73; cons. mgmt. adv. services Haskins & Sells C.P.A.'s, Los Angeles, Houston, 1973-75; partner, cons. mgmt. adv. services Streeter-Fricke Assos., Los Angeles and N.Y.C., 1975—; mgmt. cons. Pacific Missile Range, USN, 1975. Cons., Republican Central Com. Los Angeles County, 1976. Served as naval flight officer USNR, 1957-61; lt. comdr. Naval Air Res. Author: A Behavioral Analysis of Executive Recruiting, 1975; The Executive Search Process, 1976. Office: 3250 Wilshire Blvd Suite 900 Los Angeles CA 90010

STREETER, THOMAS WINTHROP, stockbroker; b. N.Y.C., Feb. 23, 1922; s. Thomas W. and Ruth (Cheney) S.; A.B., Dartmouth Coll., 1947, M.S., 1948; m. Barbara Brown, Sept. 7, 1946; children—Mary, Thomas Winthrop, Deborah. Trainee, Am. Optical Co., Southbridge, Mass., 1948-50; sales engr. Diehl Mfg. Co., Somerville, N.J., 1950-57; v.p. Meyer & Depew Co., Inc., Union, N.J., 1957-59; asso. Neville Rodie & Co., N.Y.C., 1959-63; partner G.C. Haas & Co., N.Y.C., 1963-66; chmn. Haas Securities Corp., N.Y.C., 1966-67, Spaulding Securities Corp., N.Y.C., 1977-78; broker Bear, Stearns & Co., N.Y.C., 1978-80; exec. v.p. Seligmann, Harris & Co., Inc., N.Y.C., 1980—. Served with AUS, 1942-45; CBI. Club: Downtown Assn. (N.Y.C.). Home: 253 W 101st St New York NY 10025 Office: 55 Water St 49th Floor New York NY 10041

STREIBICH, RONALD LELAND, coll. adminstr.; b. Peoria, Ill., May 5, 1936; s. Leland Roy and Evelyn (Moffatt) S.; B.A., Knox Coll., 1958; m. Pamela McClure, Apr. 5, 1980; children—John, James. Mem. pub. relations mgmt. staff Gen. Electric Co., Schnectady, 1959-65; dir. devel. Northwestern U., Evanston, Ill., 1965-74, chief fund-raising officer Northwestern Med. Center, Chgo., 1974-76; chief exec. officer Meth. Med. Center Found., Peoria, 1976-79; v.p., sec. Knox Coll., Galesburg, Ill., 1979—. Chmn., Evanston United Fund, 1972-73; Club: Soangetaha Country. Home: 436 S Soangetaha Rd Galesburg IL 61401 Office: Knox College Galesburg IL 61401

STRIBLING, CHARLES BRADFORD, advt. and public relations agy. exec.; b. Oklahoma City, Nov. 29, 1954; s. Philip Morris and Carolyn Amos Stribling; B.J., U. Tex., 1978; m. Robin Leslie Yeager, May 31, 1980. Account exec. Kerss, Chapman, Bua & Norsworthy, Dallas, 1978-79; account exec. Tracy-Locke Advt. and Public Relations, Dallas, 1979—. Mem. Dallas Advt. League, Tex. Public Relations Assn., Internat. Assn. Bus. Communicators, Public Relations Soc. Am., U. Tex. Ex-Students Assn. (life). Democrat. Home: PO Box 140282 Dallas TX 75214 Office: PO Box 50129 Dallas TX 75250

STRICHMAN, GEORGE A., corp. exec.; b. Schenectady, 1916; B. Chem. Engring., Rensselaer Poly. Inst., 1937. Engr., mfg. exec., 1937-48; various exec. positions Gen. Electric Co., 1948-58; dir. mfg. Raytheon Co., 1959; pres. ITT Kellogg div. ITT, 1959-62; pres., chief exec. officer, dir. Fairbanks Whitney Corp. (now Colt Industries Inc), 1962, chmn. bd., pres., 1963-68, chmn. bd., chief exec. officer, 1968—. Trustee, Rensselaer Poly. Inst. Office: 430 Park Ave New York NY 10022

STRICKLAND, ALBERT LEA, mfg. co. exec.; b. Blountsville, Ala., Sept. 4, 1935; s. Albert Newton and Iva Lea Strickland; student Berea Coll., 1953-54, Henry Ford Community Coll., Dearborn, Mich., 1954-57, U. Tenn., Knoxville, 1960-64; m. Gladys Ann Creech, Sept. 3, 1954; children—Danny Keith, Lisa Ann. Toolmaker, Ford Motor Co., 1954-57; missile engr. Hayes Internat., 1958-60; nuclear weapons engr. Union Carbide Nuclear Co., Oak Ridge, 1960-65, mgr. Stellite div., Kokomo, Ind., 1965-73; v.p. Gen. Indicator div. Compudyne Corp., Kokomo, 1973-75; plant mgr. Hydril Co., Houston, 1975-78; pres., dir. Landell Mfg. Inc., The Woodlands, Tex., 1978—; co-partner Landell Services, The Woodlands, 1979—; v.p., dir. C and M Mfg. Inc., The Woodlands, 1979—; pres. Landell Internat. Co., 1980—. Republican. Methodist. Home: 5415 Theall St Houston TX 77066 Office: 2408 Timberloch Pl The Woodlands TX 77380

STRICKLAND, GEORGE HENRY, JR., banker; b. Boston, Nov. 16, 1924; s. George Henry and Ann (Lane) S.; student Denison U., 1945-48; J.D., Ohio State U., 1951; m. Margery Wood, July 31, 1948; children—Ann, George Henry. Admitted to Ohio bar, 1952; asso. firm Estabrook Finn & McKee, Dayton, Ohio, 1952-58; partner firm Young Pryor Lynn Strickland & Falke, Dayton, 1958-71; sr. v.p., head trust dept. Bank of Beaufort, Hilton Head Island and Beaufort, S.C., 1971—. Served with AUS, 1943-45. Mem. Ohio Bar Assn., Dayton Bar Assn., Hilton Head Island C. of C. (dir.). Clubs: Dayton Country (pres.), Rotary (dir.). Home: 24 Willow Oak Ct Hilton Head Island SC 29928 Office: Bank of Beaufort PO Box 5069 Hilton Head Island SC 29928

STRICKLAND, HAROLD ALLISON, JR., mfg. co. exec.; b. Detroit, Feb. 5, 1915; s. Harold A. and Mary (Pugh) S.; B.S. in Mech. Engring., B.S. in Elec. Engring., U. Mich., 1936; M.B.A., Harvard, 1938; m. Ruth Voigt, May 29, 1940; children—Stephanie Mellon (Mrs. Donald Pfaff), Leslie Crandall, Harold Allison III. Exec. engr. Budd Wheel Co., also Budd Co., 1938-50; v.p. Gen. Electric Co., 1950-64; pres. Gen. Signal Corp., Stamford, Conn., 1964-80, exec. cons., 1980—; dir. Cross & Trecker Corp., Bloomfield Hills, Mich., Prime Computer, Inc., Wellesley Hills, Mass. Mem. IEEE, Soc. Automotive Engrs., Machinery and Allied Products Inst., Delta Upsilon. Republican. Conglist. Clubs: University, The Board Room (N.Y.C.); Indian Harbor Yacht. Patentee in field. Home: 70 Oneida Dr Greenwich CT 06830 Office: High Ridge Park Stamford CT 06904

STRICKLAND, HUGH LYNN, petroleum engring. cons. co. exec.; b. Dallas, Oct. 8, 1944; s. Rufe Arthur and Gladys Annelle (Odom) Killgore; B.B.A. in Acctg., Baylor U., 1966; m. Dana Elizabeth Lind, Mar. 11, 1978; children—Laura Lind, William Lucas. Auditor, Arthur Andersen & Co., C.P.A.'s, Dallas, 1969-72; acctg. officer Republic Nat. Bank, Dallas, 1972-76; sr. v.p. North Park Nat. Bank, Dallas, 1976-77; v.p. fin. Gruy Enterprises, Inc., Irving, Tex., 1977—. Served to lt. (j.g.) USNR, 1967-69. C.P.A., Tex. Mem. Am. Inst. C.P.A.'s, Tex. Soc. C.P.A.'s. Republican. Presbyterian. Home: 514 Woodhurst Dr Coppell TX 75019 Office: 150 W Carpenter Freeway Irving TX 75062

STRICKLAND, ROBERT, banking exec.; b. Atlanta, May 20, 1927; s. Robert M. and Jessie (Dickey) S.; B.S. in Econs., Davidson Coll., 1948; LL.B., Atlanta Law Sch., 1953; m. Telside Matthews, July 24, 1953; children—Robert Marion, Douglas Watson, William Logan, Walter Dickey. With Trust Co. Ga., Atlanta, 1948—, pres., 1973-74, 76-78, chmn. bd., 1978—, mem. exec. com., 1974—, chmn. bd. Trust Co. Bank, Atlanta, 1974-76, mem. exec. com., 1973—, also dir. bank and holding co.; dir. Trust Co. Mortgage; 6th dist. rep. Fed. Adv. Council; dir., chmn. audit com. Equifax, Inc., Life Ins. Co. Ga., Ga. U.S. Corp., Ga. Power Co. Chmn., Atlanta Arts Alliance, 1974-77, now trustee, mem. exec. com.; pres. United Way Met. Atlanta, 1975; v.p. bd. trustees, chmn. fin. com. Piedmont Hosp., Atlanta; chmn. bd. trustees Emory U. Served with U.S. Army, 1950-52. Mem. Ga. Bankers Assn. (pres. 1967), Am. Bankers Assn. (Ga. pres. 1969-70), Assn. Res. City Bankers. Methodist. Clubs: Augusta Nat. Golf, Piedmont Driving, Capital City, Commerce, Peachtree Golf, Nine O'Clocks. Office: 1 Park Pl NE Atlanta GA 30303

STRICKLAND, ROBERT LOUIS, corporate exec.; b. Florence, S.C., Mar. 3, 1931; s. Frank M. and Hazel (Eaddy) S.; A.B., U. N.C., 1952; M.B.A. with distinction, Harvard, 1957; m. Elizabeth Ann Miller, Feb. 2, 1952; children—Cynthia Anne, Robert Edson. Advt. mgr. Lowe's Cos., Inc., North Wilkesboro, N.C., 1957-58, operations mgr., 1958-60, marketing mgr., 1960-61, dir. marketing, 1961-69, sr. v.p., 1970-76, exec. v.p., 1976-78, mem. exec. com. Office of Pres., 1970-78, chmn. bd., 1978—, also dir.; v.p., mem. adminstrv. com. Lowe's Profit-Sharing Trust, 1961—, chmn. operations com., 1972-78; mgmt. com. Lowe's Employee Stock Ownership Plan, 1977—; dir. Revelstoke Cos. Ltd., Calgary, Ont. Mem. N.C. Ho. of Reps., 1962-64; mem. Republican exec. com. N.C., 1963-73; speaker, panelist in field. Trustee, sec. bd. Wilkes Community Coll., 1964-73; bd. dirs., v.p. Nat. Home Improvement Council, 1972-76; bd. dirs. N.C. Sch. of Arts Found., 1975-78, ESOP Assn. Am., 1980—, N.C. Bd. Natural and Econ. Resources, 1975-76, Home Center Inst., 1976—, Nat. Council Better Bus. Burs., 1980—. Served with USN, 1952-55, lt., 1955-62. Named Wilkes County Young Man of Year, Wilkes Jr. C. of C., 1962; recipient Gold Oscar, Industry award Financial World, 1972, Distinguished Mcht. award Brand Names Found., 1972, others. Mem. Nat. Assn. Over-The-Counter Cos. (bd. advisers 1973-78), Newcomen Soc., Scabbard and Blade, Phi Beta Kappa, Pi Kappa Alpha. Clubs: Roaring Gap (N.C.); Hound Ears (N.C.); Twin City, Forsyth Country (Winston-Salem, N.C.). Author: Lowe's Cybernetwork, 1969; Lowe's a Living Legend, 1970; Ten Years of Growth, 1971; The Growth Continues, 1972; The Scoreboard, 1978. Contbr. articles to profl. jours. Home: 226 N Stratford Rd Winston-Salem NC 27104 Office: Box 1111 North Wilkesboro NC 28659

STRINGFIELD, HEZZ, JR., chem. co. exec.; b. Heiskell, Tenn., Oct. 4, 1921; s. Hezz and Cecil Willie (Williams) S.; grad. bus. adminstrn. Draughon Coll., 1939; student fin. and bus. U. Tenn.; m. Helen Louise Hinton, Mar. 20, 1939; children—Carolyn Mae Joyce (Mrs. James M. Corum), Don Wayne, Gail Louise (Mrs. John D. Gamble), Debra June (Mrs. Patrick T. Cassidy). Fin. and bus. adminstrn. exec. Clinton Engr. Works, E.I. duPont de Nemours & Co., 1943-44, Manhattan Dist. metall. project, U. Chgo., 1944-45, Monsanto Chem. Co., 1945-48; dir. fin. nuclear div. Union Carbide Corp., Oak Ridge Nat. Lab., 1948-77; ind. bldg. contractor, real estate developer, 1946—; cons. gen. bus., real estate financing, 1946—; pres., dir. FBF, Inc., 1977—. Participant Central Treaty Orgn.-U.S. AID mission to Middle East, 1965. Bd. dirs. Found. Mgmt. Edn., Advancement Mgmt. Corp.; mem. Adv. Council Univs. and Colls. Comdr., USCG Aux., 1962-63. Registered pub. accountant, Tenn. Fellow Soc. Advancement Mgmt. (Profl. Mgr. citation 1963, v.p. 1958-62, exec. v.p. 1962-63, pres. 1963-64, chmn. bd. 1964); mem. Am. Mgmt. Assn., Am. Inst. Accountants, Council for Internat. Progress in Mgmt. (dir. 1964-67), Found. for Internat. Progress in Mgmt. (dir. 1964-67), Advanced Mgmt. Council (dir. 1963-68). Methodist. Home: 5000 Trent Ln Knoxville TN 37922 Office: FBF Inc 1201 Hilton Rd Knoxville TN 37901

STROBECK, CHARLES LEROY, real estate exec.; b. Chgo., June 27, 1928; s. Roy Alfred and Alice Rebecca (Stenberg) S.; A.B., Wheaton Coll., 1949; m. Janet Louise Halverson, June 2, 1951; children—Carol, Nancy, Beth, Jane, Jean. Asso., Sudler & Co., real estate, Chgo., 1949-63, partner, 1959-63; pres. Strobeck, Reiss & Co., real estate, Chgo., 1964—. Pres., South Loop Devel. Co., 1970-75. Trustee, Wheaton Christian High Sch., 1968—, pres. bd., 1970-78; bd. dirs., pres. Chgo. Youth Centers; trustee, pres. Wheaton San. Dist., 1975—. Served with AUS, 1950-51. Mem. Inst. Real Estate Mgmt. (chpt. pres. 1969) nat. pres. 1970), Am. Soc. Real Estate Counselors, Chgo. Real Estate Bd. (1st v.p. 1966, chmn. admissions com. 1969-71), Nat. Assn. Christians Schs. (dir., treas. 1970-79), Union League Club Chgo. (dir. 1968-71, treas. 1972-73, 2d v.p. 1973-74, 1st v.p. 1974-75, pres. 1975-76), Chgo. Bldg. Owners and Mgrs. Assn. (past dir.), Lambda Alpha. Mem. Coll. Ch. Wheaton (chmn. bd. elders 1971-72, elder 1979—). Clubs: Chicago Golf, Mid-America, Union League, Realtors Forty, Realty. Home: Hawthorne Ln Wheaton IL 60187 Office: 134 S La Salle St Chicago IL 60603

STROBLE, FRANCIS ANTHONY, chem. mfg. co. exec.; b. St. Louis, Aug. 20, 1930; s. Frank J. and Loraine L. (Michel) S.; B.S. in Commerce, St. Louis U., 1952, M.S. magna cum laude in Commerce, 1960; postgrad. in mgmt. Northwestern U., 1968; m. Ruth Marie O'Neill, Feb. 14, 1953; children—Deborah, Mark, Susan, Matthew, Karen. Auditor, Hochschield, Bloom & Co., St. Louis, 1954-56; with controllership dept. Monsanto Co., St. Louis, 1956-73, dir. data processing, 1973-75, v.p., controller, 1975-79, v.p. fin., 1979—; dir. Mfrs. Bank & Trust. Mem. profl. adv. bd. U. Ill., 1978-80; lay adv. bd. St. Mary's Health Center, 1975—. Served to 1st lt. USAF, 1952-54. Mem. Fin. Execs. Inst., Am. Inst. C.P.A.'s. Office: 800 N Lindbergh Blvd Saint Louis MO 63166

STROGOFF, ALFRED, food service corp. exec.; b. Chelsea, Mass., Mar. 15, 1928; s. Hyman and Ruth Constance (Brush) S.; B.S. in Mech. Engring., Worcester Poly. Inst., 1949; m. Elaine Harriet Kaplan, Oct. 22, 1950; children—Jody, Nancy, Michael, Lauren, James. Exec. v.p. Adler Electronics Co., New Rochelle, N.Y., 1949-63; group pres. Amecon div. and endl. group Litton Industries, White Plains, N.Y., 1968-70; exec. v.p. corp. services and ops. Sun Chem. Corp., N.Y.C., 1970-76; pres., chief exec. officer Internat. Foodservice Corp., Carson, Calif., 1976—; exec. v.p., dir. Acton Corp., 1980—; pres. Acton Foodservices Corp., 1980—. Recipient Goddard award Worcester Poly. Inst., 1979. Club: Balboa Bay (Calif.). Office: 1065 E Walnut St Carson CA 90746

STROHM, RAYMOND WILLIAM, lab. equipment mfg. co. exec.; b. Elgin, Ill., Sept. 14, 1924; s. Raympnd H. and Norma (Riggs) S.; B.S. in Bus. Adminstrn., Northwestern U., 1948; m. Frances D. Plath, Sept. 1, 1946; children—Phillip A., David N., Meredith L., Ellen K. Pres., Pelam, Inc., Hinsdale, Ill., 1966-70, Gelman Instrument Co., Ann Arbor, Mich., 1971-74, Barnstead div. Sybron, Boston, 1974-78; group v.p. Sybron Corp., Rochester, N.Y., 1978—. Served with USAAC, 1942-46. Mem. Assn. for Advancement of Med. Instrumentation, Sci. Apparatus Makers Assn., Am. Soc. Microbiology, Parenteral Drug Assn., Northwestern Mgmt. Alumni Assn. Club: University (Rochester, N.Y.). Office: 1100 Midtown Tower Rochester NY 14604

STROM, GRACE SAX, land and bus. investor, restaurant and lounge exec.; b. Bridgeport, Wash., Sept. 28, 1928; d. Alfred James and Agnes (Hancock) S.; student Wash. State U., 1946-48; m. Richard J. Strom, July 27, 1949 (dec. 1968); children—Nancy Sax, Larry Fancher, Sally Kim. Sec. various firms, 1948-63; sales agt. Cutler Realty, Depoe Bay, Oreg., 1979—; owner Tuccaway Inn Restaurant & Bar, Hebo, Oreg., 1968-72; pres., mgr. Sea Hag Restaurant & Lounge, Inc., Depoe Bay, 1963—; partner The Wharf, Depoe Bay, Surfside Motels Ltd., Depoe Bay, Sloop John B Tavern, Depoe Bay. Commr., Depoe Bay Sanitary Dist., 1975-79. Mem. Oreg. Restaurant and Bar Assn. (dir. 1978—), Lincoln County Restaurant and Bar Assn., Republican Women of Lincoln County, Depoe Bay C. of C. Republican. Roman Catholic. Home: PO Box 278 Depoe Bay OR 97341 Office: 5858 Hwy 101 Depoe Bay OR 97341

STROM, MILTON G., lawyer; b. Rochester, N.Y., Dec. 5, 1942; s. Harold and Dolly Strom; B.S., U. Pa., 1964; J.D., Cornell U., 1967; m. Barbara Ann Simon, Jan. 18, 1975; children—Carolyn Helene, Michael Edward, Jonathan Brett. Admitted to N.Y. State bar, 1968, U.S. Supreme Ct. bar, 1972; atty., adviser SEC, Washington, 1968-71; mem. firm Skadden, Arps, Slate, Meagher & Flom, N.Y.C., 1971—, partner, 1977—. Served with USCG, 1967-68. Mem. Assn. Bar City N.Y., Am., N.Y. State bar assns. Club: Atrium (N.Y.C.). Home: 20 Kensington Rd Scarsdale NY 10583 Office: 919 3d Ave New York NY 10022

STRONG, ALAN KRAM, computer services co. exec.; b. N.Y.C., Aug. 4, 1936; s. Herman Kram and Ethel Ceil (Goldfinger) S.; student CCNY, 1954-57, UCLA, 1957-59; m. Marjorie Ann Chudner, Jan. 10, 1960; children—Mark Lenard, Derek Adam. Project mgr. Auto Club So. Calif., 1957-60; data processing mgr. Universal Data Processing, 1963-64. exec. v.p. Electronic Systems Personnel, 1964-69; chmn. bd. Career Data Personnel Co., Los Angeles, 1969—; v.p. Info. Industries, Inc., Los Angeles, 1973-78; pres. Contract Personnel Services Co., Los Angeles, 1978—; tchr. Computer Learning Inst., 1964—. Pres., Western Boys Baseball Assn., 1974-76; bd. dirs. Los Angeles Jr. Symphony Assn., 1979—; co-chmn. Hollywood Redevel. Project, 1980. Served with U.S. Army, 1959. Cert. in data processing, in employment consulting. Mem. Data Processing Mgmt. Assn., Sales and Mktg. Execs. Assn., Calif. Employment Assn., Los Angeles C. of C. Republican. Clubs: Los Angeles Athletic Braemar Country. Home: 15428 Runnymede St Van Nuys CA 91406 Office: 3400 W 6th St Suite 209 Los Angeles CA 90020

STRONG, GARY DUANE, bank exec.; b. St. Louis, Apr. 20, 1944; s. Murray Duane and Margaret Jane (Wagoner) S.; A.B., U. Mo., Columbia, 1968. Asst. dir. automated patient history acquisition system Mo. Regional Med. Program, Columbia, 1967-68; asst. advt. dir. C.V. Mosby Pub. Co., St. Louis, 1971-72; dir. advt. ITT Aetna Corp., St. Louis, 1972-75; dir. mktg., advt. and pub. relations Carondelet Savs. & Loan Assn., St. Louis, 1975-79, v.p., 1976—; v.p. Citicorp Homeowners, Inc., St. Louis, 1980—; mktg. cons. Advt. cons. various local polit. campaigns, St. Louis County. Served with U.S. Army, 1968-71. Recipient Flair award Advt. Women Greater St. Louis, 1975, 76, 77, 78; Gold Key award Incentive Mktg. Reps. Am., 1979. Mem. Savs. Inst. Mktg. Soc. Am., Am. Bankers Assn., St. Louis Mktg. Mgrs., Delta Tau Delta. Republican. Mormon. Home: 16606 Dresser Hill Dr Chesterfield MO 63017 Office: 1000 Des Peres Rd Saint Louis MO 63131

STRONG, HERBERT WILLIAM, JR., fin. co. exec.; b. Cleve., Apr. 26, 1925; s. Herbert W. and Gladys (Mosher) S.; B.S., Cal. Inst. Tech., 1946; m. Marion B. Peck, Aug. 30, 1947; children—David W., Herbert W. III (dec.), Claudia B. With engring., sales depts. Harshaw Chem. Co., Cleve., 1947-52; operation mgr., v.p. operations Air Reduction Chem. Co. (and predecessor co.), Cleve., 1953-62; pres. Basic Chems. div. Basic, Inc., Cleve., 1963-79; exec. v.p. DNA Fin., Inc., 1979-80; pres. Strong Fin., Inc., 1980—. Mem. City Council Shaker Heights, 1959-67. Trustee, pres. Beech Brook Childrens Home, Cleve., 1964-71; trustee, v.p. Cleve. Mus. Natural History, 1971—; trustee, pres. Hathaway Brown Sch. Cleve., 1971—. Mem. Am. Chem. Soc. Republican. Episcopalian (vestryman). Clubs: Union, Tavern, Kirtland Country. Home: 18540 Shelburne Rd Shaker Heights OH 44118 Office: Hanna Bldg Cleveland OH 44115

STRONG, JOHN DAVID, ins. co. exec.; b. Cortland, N.Y., Apr. 12, 1936; s. Harold A. and Helen (Horton) S.; B.S., Syracuse (N.Y.) U., 1957; m. Carolyn Margaret Dimmick, Sept. 27, 1958; children—John D., Suzanne E. With Kemper Group, 1957—, exec. v.p. Fed. Kemper Ins. Co., Decatur, Ill., 1974-79, pres., 1979—. Pres., bd. dirs. United Way Decatur and Macon County, 1979-81; pres. United Way Ill., 1980—. Served with USAR, 1957-68. Mem. Alpha Kappa Psi. Clubs: Country of Decatur, Decatur. Office: 2001 E Mound Rd Decatur IL 62526

STRONG, MAURICE FREDERICK, resource co. exec.; b. Oak Lake, Man., Can., Apr. 29, 1929; s. Frederick Milton and Mary (Fyfe) S.; hon. degrees: U. Toronto, 1972, Acad. U., 1972, LaSalle Coll., 1972, U. Alta., 1973, Brandon U., 1973, Springfield Coll., 1973, Yale U., 1973, others; m. Hanne Marstrand, 1980; children by previous marriage—Frederick Maurice, Maureen Louise, Mary Anne, Kenneth Martin. Fin. analyst James Richardson & Sons, Winnipeg, Man. and Calgary, Alta., Can., 1948-51, asst. to pres., 1951-52; mktg. asst. Caltex (Africa) Ltd., Nairobi, Kenya, 1953-54; v.p., treas. Dome Petroleum Ltd., Calgary, 1955-59; pres. Can. Indsl. Gas Ltd., Calgary, 1959-64; Power Corp. Can., Montreal, Que., 1962-66, Can. Internat. Devel. Agy., Ottawa, Ont., 1966-70; exec. dir. environ. program UN, also sec.-gen. UN Conf. Human Environ., N.Y.C., 1971-75; chmn. bd. Petro-Can., Calgary, Alta., 1975-78, AZL Resources, Inc., Phoenix, 1978—, Internat. Energy Devel. Corp., Geneva, Switzerland, 1979—; chmn. Internat. Devel. Research Centre, Ottawa, Ont., Can., 1977-78; vis. prof. York U., 1969; Montague Burton prof. U. Edinburgh (Scotland), 1973. Chmn., Internat. Union Conservation of Nature and Natural Resources, 1977-80; exec. com. Internat. Found. for Developing Alternatives; adv. bd. Inst. Ecology, Padjadjaran U., Bandung, Indonesia; mem. internat. hon. commn. Dag Hammarskjold Found., Sweden; v.p. World Wildlife Fund Internat.; trustee Aspen Inst.; adv. com. Centre for Internat. Environ. Info., N.Y.C. Recipient Tyler Ecology award, 1974; Nat. Audubon Soc. award, 1975; Mellon award, 1975; Freedom Festival award, 1975; First Internat. Pahlavi

Environ. prize, 1976; decorated Order of Can., 1976, Henri Pittier Order, 1977, Order of Golden Ark, 1979. Clubs: Century Assn.; Denver Petroleum; Century, Yale, Metropolitan. Office: PO Box 29008 Phoenix AZ 85038

STRONG, WILLIAM LEE, mfg. co. exec.; b. Jacksonville, Fla., Sept. 17, 1919; s. William M. and Hedwig C. (Ulm) S.; A.B. in Econs., Occidental Coll., 1942; M.B.A. with distinction, Harvard, 1947; m. Betty Jean Stream, Dec. 13, 1941; children—William Lee, Thomas B., Robin E. Budget dir. Byron Jackson div. Borg-Warner Corp.; 1954-56, controller, 1956-57; budget dir. Consol. Freightways, Inc., Menlo Park, Calif., 1957-60, treas., chief financial officer, 1960-62; v.p. finance, treas., dir. Packard Bell Electronics Corp., Los Angeles, 1962-65, treas. Allis-Chalmers Mfg. Co., Milw., 1965-68; v.p., treas. Continental Can Co. (now Continental Group, Inc.), N.Y.C., 1968-75; sr. v.p., chief fin. officer Firestone Tire & Rubber Co., Akron, Ohio, 1976-77, exec. v.p., dir., 1978—; dir. USLife Corp., Transatlantic Fund; mem. adv. bd. Mfrs. Hanover Trust Co., N.Y. Guest lectr. various grad. bus. schs., other groups. Trustee Fin. Execs. Research Found. Served to lt. comdr. USN, 1942-54; PTO; to capt. USNR. Mem. Am. Mgmt. Assn. (financial planning council), Financial Execs. Inst., Treasurers Club N.Y., Conf. Bd. (Council of Fin. Execs.), Phi Gamma Delta. Clubs: Harvard Bus. Sch., Portage Country (Akron). Home: 1033 Bunker Dr Akron OH 44313 Office: 1200 Firestone Pkwy Akron OH 44317

STROOPE, FREDRICK SANFORD, mfg. co. exec.; b. Smackover, Ark., Sept. 6, 1946; s. Fredrick Sanford and Judith (Marshall) S.; student Hendrix Coll., 1964-66; B.B.A., State Coll. of Ark., 1970; m. Judith Ann Morris, Feb. 5, 1965; children—Robert Maurice, Barbara Ellen. Foreman, Fleming & Sons, Inc., Conway, Ark., 1968-69; student asst. accounting dept. State Coll. Ark., Conway, 1969-70; asst. storeroom supr. Ga. Pacific Corp., Crossett, Ark., 1970-73, divisional constrn. purchasing agt. Crossett div., 1973-74; pres. Woodyard Equipment Co., Inc., Zachary, La., 1974-77, Prodn. Castings, Inc., Zachary, 1977—; sec. Prodn. Machine Inc., Zachary, 1977—; sec.-treas. Impeller Repair Service, Inc., 1977—. Pres., treas. Crossett Assn. Retarded Citizens, Crossett, 1973-74. Bd. dirs. Carousel Sch. for Retarded Children, 1973-74, treas., 1973-74. Mem. Nat. Assn. Purchasing Mgrs., U.S. (treas. 1972-73, dir. 1973-74), Crossett (pres. 1972), Zachary (pres. 1976) jaycees. Lion, Rotarian. Club: Corssett Little Theatre. Home: 6444 Fenwood Dr Zachary LA 70791 Office: PO Box 1 Zachary LA 70791

STROTHER, LESTER JAMES, publisher; b. Elizabeth, La., Mar. 9, 1924; s. Theodore H. and Ella (Laird) S.; B.J., U. Mo., 1950; m. Dora Jean Dougherty, Nov. 23, 1966; children—David Lester, Grant Douglas. Night editor El Dorado (Ark.) Daily News, 1950-51; news editor Lake Charles (La.) Am. Press, 1951-52; staff corr. U.P.I., Dallas, 1952-57; free lance writer, Dallas and Forth Worth, 1957-64; asst. city editor Ft. Worth Star Telegram, 1959-63; asso. dir. pub. relations, asso. editor Ft. Worth Mag., 1963-65; pres., chmn. bd., chief exec. officer Tex. Met. Publs. Inc., 1965—, pub. Tex. Metro Mag., Arlington, 1965—, The Strother (Feature) Syndicate, 1977—, Strother & Assos., 1977—, The Strother Letter, 1978—; lectr. in field; tchr. mass communications Tarrant County Jr. Coll., Ft. Worth, 1976—. Mem. Postal Commn., Arlington, 1968—; mem. communication adv. bd. U. Dallas, 1969—; mem. North Tex. region adv. council SBA, 1974—, also chmn. outreach com.; mem. adv. council United Fund, Fort Worth, 1974—; mem. art and advt. adv. council Tex. State Tech. Coll., Waco, 1974—; chmn. heritage com. Richland Hills Bicentennial Commn. Del. Tarrant County (Tex.) Democratic conv., 1968, 72. Bd. dirs. Haltom-Richland (Tex.) unit Am. Cancer Soc., 1975—, Bishop Mason Retreat and Conf. Center, Dallas, 1974—. Served with USNR, 1943-46; comdt. Dallas/Fort Worth Metroplex Sta., Tex. Navy, 1970—. Mem. Ft. Worth (mem. Trinity River devel. com. 1971—), Dallas, Haltom Richland Area (dir. 1968—), Grand Prairie, Arlington chambers commerce, Aviation/Space Writers Assn., Indsl. Editors Assn. (v.p. 1965-66), Dallas Sales and Marketing Exec., Mag. Pubs. Assn., Tex. Mag. Advt. Network (organizer; dir. 1974—), Dallas Advt. League, Soc. for Preservation and Encouragement Barber Shop Quartet Singing in Am., Sigma Delta Chi, Sigma Phi Epsilon, Kappa Alpha Mu. Episcopalian (del. diocesan conv. 1971). Mason (32 deg.); mem. Scottish Clans N. Tex. Clubs: Fort Worth Advt., Fort Worth Knife and Fork, Fort Worth Press; Dallas Press. Home: 3616 Landy Ln Fort Worth TX 76118 Office: PO Box 13405 Fort Worth TX 76118

STROTZ, ROBERT HENRY, univ. pres.; b. Aurora, Ill., Sept. 26, 1922; s. John Marc and Olga (Koerfer) S.; student Duke, 1939-41; B.A., U. Chgo., 1942, Ph.D., 1951; LL.D. (hon.), Ill. Wesleyan U., 1976; LL.D., Millikin U., 1979; children—Vicki, Michael, Frances, Ellen, Ann; m. Margaret L. Hanley. Mem. faculty Northwestern U., Evanston, Ill., 1947—, prof. econs., 1958—, dean Coll. Arts and Scis., 1966-70, pres. univ., 1970—; past dir., chmn. Fed. Res. Bank Chgo.; dir. First Nat. Bank & Trust Co. Evanston, Ill. Tool Works, Inc., Norfolk and Western Ry. Co., Peoples Energy Corp., U.S. Gypsum Co., Mark Controls Corp. Bd. dirs., vice chmn. Nat. Merit Scholarship Corp.; bd. dirs. McGaw Med. Center Northwestern U., Northwestern Meml. Hosp.; trustee Field Mus. Natural History, Mus. Sci. and Industry. Served with AUS, 1943-45. Fellow Econometric Soc.; mem. Am. Econ. Assn., Econometric Soc. (mem. council 1961-67), Royal Econ. Soc. Clubs: Comml., Economic, Execs., Univ., Standard, Tavern, Chgo. (Chgo.); Old Elm (Ft. Sheridan, Ill.); Glen View (Glenview, Ill.); Bohemian (San Francisco). Mng. editor Econometrica, 1953-68; econometrics editor Internat. Ency. Social Scis., 1962-68; editor Contributions to Economic Analysis, 1955-70. Home: 639 Central St Evanston IL 60201 Office: 633 Clark St Evanston IL 60201

STROUD, ROBERT EDWARD, lawyer; b. Chester, S.C., July 24, 1934; s. Coy Franklin and Leila (Caldwell) S.; A.B., Washington and Lee U., 1956, LL.B., 1959; m. Katherine E. Clark Apr. 8, 1961; children—Robert Gordon, Margaret Lathan. Admitted to Va. bar, 1959; asso. McGuire, Woods & Battle, Charlottesville, 1959-64, partner, 1964—; lectr. Washington and Lee U., 1957-59; lectr. in bus. taxation Grad. Sch. Bus. Adminstrn., U. Va., 1969—; lectr. various continuing legal edn. insts. Pres., Charlottesville Housing Found., 1968-73; trustee Presbyn. Found., 1972-73; mem. exec. bd. Presbyn. Ch. U.S., 1972-73; mem. council Presbyn. Synod of Virginias, moderator, 1977-78; mem. council Montreat (N.C.) Mgmt. Council, 1974-77; mem. Washington and Lee Law Council, 1975-80. Served to 2d lt. AUS, 1957. Mem. Am., Va. bar assns., Tax Inst. Am., Am. Judicature Soc., Washington and Lee Law Sch. Assn. (pres. 1979-80), Phi Eta Sigma, Omicron Delta Kappa, Phi Delta Phi. Co-author: Buying, Selling and Merging Businesses, 1975; editor-in-chief Washington and Lee Law Rev., 1959; editor: Advising Small Business Clients, Vol. I, 1978, Vol. II, 1980. Home: 104 Woodstock Dr Charlottesville VA 22901 Office: PO Box 1191 Charlottesville VA 22902

STROUGO, ROBERT, lawyer; b. N.Y.C., May 23, 1943; s. Victor and Mary S.; B.A., City Coll. N.Y., 1960; J.D., N.Y. U., 1970; m. Barbara Lieb, June 27, 1976; 1 dau., Debra. Admitted to N.Y. State bar, 1971; individual practice law, N.Y.C.; asso. dir., 1st v.p. Democracy for Stockholders, Inc.; investment and fin. advisor, fin. planner; lic. real estate broker. Mem. Fed., N.Y., Kings County bar assns., N.Y. Trial Lawyers Assn., N.Y. State Defenders Bar Assn. Home: 505 E 79th St New York NY 10021 Office: 420 Lexington Ave New York NY 10017

STRUBE, WILLIAM CURTIS, educator; b. St. Louis, Sept. 9, 1940; s. William Henry and Irene Louise Strube; B.A. in Econs., Monmouth (Ill.) Coll., 1962; M.B.A., U. Ariz., 1965; Ph.D. in Bus. Adminstrn., U. Ark., 1972; m. Janet Grace Hoetker, June 18, 1966; children—Kim Janette, Randall William. Part-time instr. U. Ark., 1968-69; mem. faculty Drury Coll., Springfield, Mo., 1969-70, asst. dean coll., then dean students, 1973-75, prof., dir. Breech Sch. Bus. Adminstrn., 1975—; v.p. Mergers-Acquisitions, Inc., Springfield, 1979; cons. in field. Bd. dirs. Springfield Boys Club, Springfield Girl Scouts; mem. Springfield Transit Task Force Com., Greene County Community Planning Council, Child Health Task Force of Child Advocacy Council. Mem. Acad. Mgmt., S.W. Fedn. Adminstrv. Disciplines, Assn. Pvt. Enterprise Edn., Ozark Econ. Assn., Midwest Bus. Adminstrn. Assn., Midwest Econs. Assn., Omicron Delta Kappa, Phi Eta Sigma, Theta Chi. Mem. United Ch. Christ. Author papers in field. Home: 3709 Sugar Hill Springfield MO 65804 Office: Breech Sch Drury Coll Springfield MO 65802

STRUBEL, RICHARD PERRY, corp. exec.; b. Evanston, Ill., Aug. 10, 1939; s. Arthur Raymond and Martha (Smith) S.; B.A., Williams Coll., 1962; M.B.A., Harvard U., 1964; m. Linda Jane Freeman, Aug. 25, 1961 (div. 1974); children—Douglas Arthur, Craig Tollerton; m. 2d, Ella Doyle G'sell, Oct. 23, 1976. Asso., Fry Cons., Chgo., 1964-66, managing prin., 1966-68; dir. operational planning N.W. Industries, Inc., Chgo., 1968-69, v.p. corp. devel., 1969-73; chmn. bd., pres. Buckingham Corp., Chgo., 1972-73, group v.p., 1973-79, exec. v.p., 1979—. Bd. dirs. Better Govt. Assn. Presbyterian. Clubs: Chicago, Racquet, Mid-Day, Met. (Chgo.). Office: 6300 Sears Tower Chicago IL 60606

STRUBLE, ROBERT STANLEY, steel co. exec.; b. Morristown, N.J., Aug. 4, 1923; s. Ernest A. and Adele (Hall) S.; B.S. in Commerce, Rider Coll., 1948; m. Lamond Doig, Apr. 21, 1946; children—L. Lynn, Janet D., Meg M., Kim M. Staff accountant Haskins & Sells, 1948-49; control accountant cyclone fence div. U.S. Steel Corp., Newark, 1949-54, supr. cost analysis Am. Steel & Wire div. Waukegan, Ill., 1955-60, sr. systems designer Chgo., 1961-65, supr., sr. cost analyst supply div., Chgo., 1965, mgr. cost and statistics, 1966-71, dist. mgr. U.S. Steel Supply div., Conshohocken, Pa., 1971-74; mgr. operations, comptroller Charles F. Guyon, Inc., Harrison, N.J., 1974-77, v.p. ops., comptroller, 1977—. Chmn., Waukegan Republican Com., 1962-66; vice chmn. Lake County (Ill.) Rep. Party, 1964-66; mem. Andover Twp. Planning Bd., 1979—, councilman, 1979—. Served with USAAF, 1942-45. Decorated D.F.C., Air medal with silver oak leaf cluster. Mem. Am. Legion, V.F.W., Nat. Assn. Accountants, Nat. Assn. Corp. Dirs., Am. Mgmt. Assn. Clubs: Masons; Rotary; Newton (N.J.) Country); Lake Lenape (Andover, N.J.). Home: RD 1 Box 703 Newton NJ 07860 Office: 900 S 4th St Harrison NJ 07029

STRUBY, (CHESTER AL)BERT, newspaper pub.; b. Macon, Ga., Jan. 19, 1917; s. Chester Albert and Julia (Riley) S.; A.B. magna cum laude in Journalism, Mercer U., 1938; m. Jane Whitfield Spearman, May 24, 1947; children—Cynthia Jane Struby Thelen, Neil Albert. Reporter, Macon Telegraph, 1938-40, state editor, 1940-41; state editor, asst. city editor Macon News, 1946-47; exec. editor Macon Telegraph, also Macon News, 1947-57; editor The Telegraph, 1954-57; exec. v.p. and gen. mgr. Macon Telegraph Pub. Co., 1958-76; pres., pub. Macon Telegraph and Macon News, 1977—; chmn. bd. trustees So. Ednl. Reporting Service, 1962-64. Trustee, Sen. Richard Russell Found., 1970—; pres. Ga. State Fair Assn., 1975, Forward Macon, 1977, Macon United Way, 1979; chmn. Macon Housing Authority, 1976-77; chmn. bd. trustees Mercer U., 1978—; v.p. SE Area, Boy Scouts Am., 1980—. Served to lt. comdr. USNR, 1941-46. Decorated Mil. Service Cross; recipient citation Anti-Defamation League B'nai Brith, 1951; Silver Beaver and Virgil honor awards Boy Scouts Am.; named Kiwanis Layman of Yr., 1971. Mem. So. Newspaper Pubs. Assn. (pres. 1966-67), So. Newspaper Pubs. Assn. Found. (chmn. bd. trustees 1967-69), Ga. AP (chmn. 1963-64), Am. Newspaper Pubs. Assn., Ga. Press Assn., Navy League, Air Force Assn., N.C. Soc. of Cincinnati, Greater Macon C. of C. (pres. 1974), Phi Delta Theta. Democrat. Baptist. Clubs: Rotary, Idle Hour Golf, River North Country, Elks. Developed new camellia registered with Am. Camellia Soc. Office: PO Box 4167 Macon GA 31213

STRUWING, MARTIN GEORGE, bank exec.; b. Elgin, Ill., Sept. 2, 1941; s. Milton W. and Alice M. (Shaver) S.; B.A., Iowa Wesleyan Coll., 1963; student U. Wis. Sch. Bank Adminstrn., 1975-77; m. Barbara Goodin, Nov. 30, 1963; children—Daniel, David, Paula. Bank examiner Commr. of Bank & Trust Cos., State of Ill., Chgo., 1963-68; asst. cashier Bartlett State Bank (Ill.) (name changed to Barllett Bank & Trust Co.), 1968-69, cashier, 1970-76, v.p., 1972-78, exec. v.p., 1979, pres., 1979—. Trustee, Village of Streamwood (Ill.), 1973-76; mem. Bartlett Ambulance Commn., 1978—. Mem. Bank Adminstrn. Inst. (pres. DuPage chpt.), Am. Bankers Assn., Ind. Comml. Banks Ill., Independence Bankers. Lutheran. Club: Rotary. Office: 335 S Main St Bartlett IL 60103

STUART, DWIGHT LYMAN, food co. exec.; b. Seattle, Sept. 27, 1924; s. Elbridge Hadley and Nan (Fullerton) S.; student U. Wash., 1947; children by former marriage—Dwight Lyman, William W., Bruce F.; m. 2d, Kathleen Gallant, Oct. 27, 1958; children—Douglas F., Gregory M. With Carnation Co., 1947-48, 50—, asst. v.p., 1957-64, v.p., after 1964, exec. v.p., until 1973, pres., 1973—; self employed as mfrs. rep., 1948-50; dir. E. A. Stuart Co. Served to lt. (j.g.) USNR, 1943-46. Mem. Phi Delta Theta. Club: Los Angeles. Office: Carnation Co 5045 Wilshire Blvd Los Angeles CA 90036*

STUART, EDWARD, JR., forest engr.; b. Boston, June 15, 1917; s. Edward and Helen (Fox) S.; B.S. in Forestry, U. Maine, 1937; F.E. (hon.), Biltmore Forest Sch., Weisbaden, Germany, 1946; children—Edward, Diane, Bruce. Forester, Maine and Can., 1937; with U.S. Forest Service, Mass., Colo., S.D. and Wyo., 1938-42; cons., practicing forester, Va., N.C., S.C., Md. and W.Va., 1946-56; pres., chmn. bd. Eastern Forestry, Inc., Hampton, Va., 1956—; cons., practicing forester, real estate appraiser; guest lectr. forestry U. Maine, U. Nev., Stephen F. Austin State U., U. N.B., U. Wash.; named Va.'s forest conservationist, 1976. Mem. Nat. Def. Exec. Res. Served from lt. to capt. USAF, 1942-46; mil govt. forestry officer, Great Hesse, Germany, 1945-46. Decorated Commendation medal Croix Militaire (Belgium); Conservationist award Va., 1976. Mem. Nat. Assn. Cons. Foresters (pres. 1948-50; exec. council 1950-60, exec. dir. 1960—, editor Cons.), Nat. Council Forestry Assn. Execs., Am. Soc. Appraisers, Am. Forestry Assn. (forest progress adv. council 1950-51), Soc. Am. Foresters (chmn. Rappahannock sect. 1960), Mil. Govt. Assn., Va. Forestry Council, Gloucester, Mathews, Middlesex Realty Bd. (dir.), Nat. Assn. Real Estate Bds., Va. Real Estate Assn., Practicing Foresters Inst. (dir.), S.A.R., Am. Legion. Club: Explorers. Contbr. numerous tech. articles to profl. jours. Contbg. author: Ency. Real Estate Appraising. Home: Box 12 Hayes VA 23072 Office: PO Box 369 Yorktown VA 23690

STUART, GERARD WILLIAM, JR., business exec.; b. Yuba City, Calif., July 28, 1939; s. Gerard William and Geneva Bernice (Stuke) S.; student Yuba Jr. Coll., 1957-59, Chico State Coll., 1959-60; A.B., U. Calif., Davis, 1962; M.L.S., U. Calif., Berkeley, 1963; m. Lenore Francis Loroña, 1981. Rare book librarian Cornell U., 1964-68; bibliographer of scholarly collections Huntington Library, San Marino, Calif., 1968-73, head acquisitions librarian, 1973-75. Sec.-treas., Ravenstree Corp., 1969-81, pres., 1981—, dir., 1969—. Lilly fellow Ind. U., 1963-64. Mem. Bibliog. Soc. Am., Phi Beta Kappa, Alpha Gamma Sigma, Phi Kappa Phi. Clubs: Rolls-Royce Owners, Grolier (N.Y.C.); Zamorano (Los Angeles). Home: Tor Haven Route 1 Box 28 Wellton AZ 85356

STUART, JOHN M., lawyer; b. N.Y.C., Apr. 3, 1927; s. Winchester and Maude (Marberger) S.; B.A., Columbia, 1948, J.D., 1951; m. Marjorie Louise Browne, Dec. 11, 1954; children—Jane, Alice, Richard. Admitted to N.Y. bar, 1951, since practiced in N.Y.C.; asso. Reid & Priest, 1951-64, partner, 1965—. Asst. sec. Minn. Power & Light Co., 1951-64. Producer play Make Me Disappear, N.Y.C. Recipient Internat. Brotherhood Magicians award, 1958, 60, First prize sci. fiction Phila. Writers Conf., 1958. Mem. Am., N.Y. County bar assns., S.R. (legal com.). Republican. Methodist. Author (with Marjorie L. Stuart) You Don't Have To Slay A Dragon, 1976. Contbr. articles to mags. Magician, W. German TV magic spl., 1965; appeared in Spy at the Magic Show benefit for Project Hope, Manhasset, N.Y., 1967. Home: 31 Westgate Blvd Plandome NY 11030 Office: 40 Wall St New York NY 10005

STUART, ROBERT, metal container mfg. exec.; b. Oak Park, Ill., Aug. 3, 1921; s. Robert S. and Marie (Vavra) Solinsky; B.S., U. Ill., 1943; m. Lillian Constance Kondelik, Dec. 5, 1962 (dec. May 1978). Sec.-treas., gen. mgr. Warren Metal Decorating Co., 1947-49; asst. to gen. mgr. Cans, Inc., 1950-52; asst. to v.p. Nat. Can Corp., 1953-59, sr. v.p., 1959-62, exec. v.p., 1962-63, pres., 1963-69, pres., chief exec. officer, 1966-69, chmn. bd., chief exec. officer, 1969-73, chmn. bd., 1973—, chmn. fin. com., also dir.; dir. Chgo. Community Ventures, Inc., LaSalle Nat. Bank, Chgo. Mem. The Conf. Bd.; mem., past 1st chmn. businessman's adv. council for Coll. Bus., U. Ill. Chgo. Circle; bd. dirs. Protestant Found. Chgo.; trustee, mem. devel. council, chmn. major gifts com. Elmhurst Coll.; mem. citizens bd. U. Chgo., also vis. com. Div. Sch.; dir., 1st chmn. Nat. Minority Purchasing Council; mem. Corp. Responsibility Group Greater Chgo., Chinese-Am. Civic Council; mem. bus. adv. council Chgo. Urban League; trustee Ill. Masonic Med. Center, Freedoms Found. at Valley Forge, Provident Hosp.; citizens bd. Loyola U., Chgo.; mem., asso. Rehab. Inst. Chgo.; mem. grand council Am. Indian Center Chgo.; mem., founder adv. bd. Broader Urban Involvement and Leadership Devel.; past pres., dir. Chgo. Crime Commn.; vice chmn. nat. affairs Nat. Council Crime and Delinquency; dir. U. Ill. Found. and mem. Pres.'s council; bd. dirs., v.p. Lloyd Morey Scholarship Fund; trustee, past pres. Central Ch. Chgo.; v.p., bd. dirs. United Republican Fund Ill.; chmn. World Federalists Assn.; trustee emeritus Nat. Jewish Hosp. at Denver; bd. sponsors Evang. Hosp. Assn.; pres. One/Fourth, Inc.; bd. dirs. Ill. Cancer Council, Center for Citizenship Edn. Served from sgt. to capt. AUS, 1943-46. Mem. Can Mfrs. Inst. (past chmn.), Newcomen Soc. N.Am. (chmn. Chgo. area), Alpha Kappa Lambda (past nat. pres. mem. nat. exec. council). Republican. Congregationalist (past pres. ch.). Clubs: Masons (32 deg.), K.T., Rotary (past pres. original club, past commodore internat. yachting fellowship; past dist. gov.); Chgo., Chgo. Yacht, Comml., Econ., Met. (Chgo.); Capitol Hill (Washington). Home: 400 E Randolph St Chicago IL 60601 Office: 8101 W Higgins Rd Chicago IL 60631

STUART, ROBERT DOUGLAS, JR., food co. exec.; b. Hubbard Woods, Ill., Apr. 26, 1916; s. Robert Douglas and Harriet (McClure) S.; B.A., Princeton U., 1937; J.D., Yale U., 1946; m. Barbara McMath Edwards, May 21, 1938; children—Robert Douglas III, James McClure, Marian McClure Stuart Pillsbury, Alexander Douglas. With Quaker Oats Co., Chgo., 1947—, now chmn., chief exec. officer, dir.; dir. UAL, Inc., First Chgo. Corp., Deere & Co., United Air Lines, 1st Nat. Bank Chgo. Mem. adv. bd. Chgo. Urban League; Republican nat. committeeman from Ill., 1964-72; bd. dirs. Grocery Mfrs. Am., Chgo. Area council Boy Scouts Am.; trustee Tax Found., Inc., Princeton U. Served to maj. AUS, 1942-45. Mem. Bus. Council. Home: 1601 Conway Rd Lake Forest IL 60045 Office: Quaker Oats Co Merchandise Mart Chicago IL 60654

STUART, ROBERT WILLARD, stockbroker; b. New Rochelle, N.Y., Apr. 27, 1948; s. Mark James and Kathleen (Cornell) S.; B.S. in Bus. Adminstrn., Georgetown U., 1971; m. Virginia McSweeney, Sept. 16, 1972; children—Leigh Nolan, Kathleen Marie. Partner, Trubee Collins & Co., Buffalo, 1973-76, Fahnestock & Co., N.Y.C., 1976-80; mem. N.Y. Stock Exchange, 1973—. Served with U.S. Army, 1970-71. Clubs: Winged Foot Golf, Madison Square Garden, N.Y. Stock Exchange Luncheon. Home: 28 Pasadena Rd Bronxville NY 10708 Office: 11 Wall St New York NY 10005

STUART, WALTER STANLEY, JR., mfg. co. exec.; b. St. Louis, Sept. 18, 1939; s. Walter Stanley and Barbara (Osborne) S.; student Beloit Coll., 1957-59; B.S., Ind. U., 1962, M.B.A. with honors, 1965; m. Judith M. Anderson, May 18, 1963; children—Michael Carl, Matthew David, Mark Stephen. Product mgmt. staff Gen. Foods Corp., White Plains, N.Y., 1965-67; project dir. advanced methods group N.W. Ayer Co., Phila., 1968-69, v.p., mgmt. supr., Chgo., 1970-73; v.p. corp. mktg. devel. Ball Corp., Muncie, Ind., 1973-74, v.p., gen. mgr. consumer products div., 1974-78; v.p. mktg. services U.S. Gypsum Co., 1978—, pres. Marstrat, Inc. subs., 1978-79, dir., 1978—; instr. mktg. Roosevelt U., Chgo., 1968, Rutgers U., 1969, Northwestern U. Grad. Sch. Mgmt., 1979. Pres., Indian Guide program YMCA, Delaware County, Ind., 1974-75; bd. dirs. Delaware County Jr. Achievement, 1976-78; mem. legis. council Ind. U. Alumni Assn., 1975-78; mem. dean's assos. devel. cabinet Ind. U., 1978—, nat. chmn., 1979—; treas., bd. dirs. Lincolnshire Community Christian Ch., 1979—. Mem. Am. Mktg. Assn. (nat. v.p. 1979), Ind. U. Sch. Bus. Alumni Assn. (past pres., exec. council 1973-78), Assn. Nat. Advertisers (advt. mgmt. policy com. 1978—), Ill. St. Andrew Soc., Ind. Soc. Chgo., Western Adv. Golfer Assn. (bd. govs. 1979—), Art Inst. Chgo., Beta Gamma Sigma, Delta Sigma Pi, Phi Delta Theta, Alpha Delta Sigma. Clubs: Exec. (dir. 1979—, vice-chmn. 1980—), Rotary, Univ., Sales and Mktg., Arts, Tavern (Chgo.); Sales Exec. (N.Y.).); Delaware Country, Muncie (Muncie); Columbia (Indpls.). Author: Guidelines for Successful New Product Test Marketing, 1976. Home: 40 Fox Trail Deerfield IL 60015 Office: 101 S Wacker Dr Chicago IL 60606

STUBBS, GORDON EUGENE, mgmt. analyst; b. Austin, Tex., July 21, 1926; s. Homer Albert and Emily Violet (Armstrong) S.; student U. Ala., 1943-44, San Antonio Coll., 1949-51, U. Puget Sound, 1962-64; B.G.S., Chaminade Coll., 1969; postgrad. U. So. Calif., 1969-70; M.S., U. Hawaii, 1971, Ph.D., 1972; M.A., Central Mich. U., 1974; m. Ruby Mae Durham, Feb. 28, 1946 (div. 1971); 2 sons, Lester Eugene, Gordon William. Prodn. mgr. Dept. Defense, San Antonio, 1950-51; recalled to active duty with U.S. Air Force, 1951, served as aircraft maintenance mgr., San Antonio, 1952-58, chief flight engr., Europe, 1958-61, records mgr., Tacoma, Wash., 1961-64, mgmt. analyst advisor, Riverside, Calif., 1964-66, chief performance engr., Honolulu, 1966-68, adminstrn. mgr., Honolulu, 1968-69, ret. 1969; br.

mgr. Profl. Tax Service, Waipahu, Hawaii, 1970-71; lead indsl. engr. technician, Dept. Defense, Honolulu, 1972-74; lead computer programmer FDA, USPHS, HEW, Washington, 1974-76; mgmt. analyst, Office Asst. Sec. Health, USPHS, HEW, Rockville, Md., 1976—; propr. Stubbs Profl. Enterprises, Honolulu and Washington, 1971—. Served with USAF, 1943-46. Recipient flying safety award, 1965, outstanding achievement award, Pacific Air Force, 1973. Mem. Bus. Forms Mgmt. Assn. Baptist. Clubs: Masons, Shriners. Author: The Development of Human Resources, 1969; Developing Responsive Personalities for Interactive Computer Systems, 1972; An Automated Central Supervisory System, 1974; developer computer systems areas of fin. bus. mgmt., operational controls, taxes, edn., medicine, health care, 1969-78; developed automated standard adminstrv. code system, automated forms mgmt. system. Home: 5414 Juliet St Springfield VA 22151 Office: 5600 Fishers Ln Room 18A-54 Rockville MD 20857

STUDER, DALE FREDERICK, coal co. exec.; b. nr. New Philadelphia, Ohio, Oct. 2, 1921; s. John W. and Louise (Finzer) S.; grad. high sch.; grad. Dale Carnagie course, 1973; m. Kathryn L. Andreas, Aug. 25, 1946; children—Paula Gay, Deborah Elaine. Prin. owner Walden's Ridge Coal Co., 1953—, Tri-State Coal Sales, Chattanooga, 1957—, Pioneer Coal Co., Chattanooga, 1974—, Sequatchie Valley Coal Corp., 1975—, Mid-South Treatment Systems, 1975—, Pine Tree Farms, Dale F. Studer & Assos. Republican Central committeeman, Sugarcreek, Ohio, 1946-49; adv. Tenn. State Legis., 1966-67; adv. SE Tenn. Devel. Dist., 1977; bd. dirs. Tenn. Energy Authority, 1980—; mem. nat. finance council Nat. Dem. Com., 1979—, Reclamation Review Bd. Tenn., 1978—; prin. stockholder, bd. dirs. Chattanooga Choo-Choo, 1975—. Served with USAAF, 1942-46; ATO; ETO. Mem. hon. staff Gov. Tenn. State Coal Operators Assn. (pres. 1975-76, dir. 1974-80), Inst. Explosive Engrs., Inst. Mining Engrs., Am. Legion (comdr. post 1946-49), Nat. Coal Assn., Mining and Reclamation Council Am. (dir. 1978—), Am. Security Council, Internat. Platform Assn. Methodist (dir. 1955-58). Home: 952 Runyan Dr Chattanooga TN 37405 Office: 5519 Hwy 153 Suite 16 Hixson TN 37343

STUDIER, RICHARD JOHN, exterminating co. exec.; b. Cleve., Mar. 17, 1944; s. Harry Edwin and Olive Mae (Bletcher) S.; B.A. in Mgmt., Vincennes U., 1966; B.A. with distinction in Econs., Ohio No. U., 1968; postgrad. Urbana Coll., 1971; m. Pamela Jo Hopper, Aug. 31, 1968; children—Matthew Jason, Christopher James. Pres., mgr. Guarantee Exterminating Co., Cleve., 1963—; pres. Wyco Internat., chem. spltys.; tchr. bus. econs. and acctg. W. Liberty-Salem Schs., 1968-72. Mem. Nat., Ohio, Cleve. pest control assns., Cleve. Sales and Mktg. Execs., Nat. Sales and Mktg. Execs. Club, Cleve. World Trade Assn., Assn. Operative Millers, Am. Inst. Baking, Greater Cleve. Growth Assn., U.S. C. of C., Sigma Pi. Club: Cleve. Exchange. Home: 6212 Meldon Dr Mentor OH 44060 Office: 4811 Carnegie Ave Cleveland OH 44103

STUERMER, EMIL FRANK, advt. and pub. relations agy. exec.; b. Chgo., June 11, 1935; s. Emil Joseph and Frances Madeline (Kochanski) S.; B.A., Coll. St. Thomas, 1957; m. Mary Jo Strauel, June 16, 1956; children—Mary, Scott, Kathy, Patty, Janet, Teresa, Tom. Salesman, Monarch Matrix, Chgo., 1957-60, sales mgr., 1960-65; pres., Ad Systems, Inc., Chgo., 1965—, owner, 1967—; pres., owner Spl. Corr., pub. relations, Chgo., 1968—. Active Boy Scouts Am.; v.p. sch. bd., Glenview, Ill., 1972—. Mem. Printing Platemakers Assn., Printing Industry Ill., Pres. Assn., Am. Mgmt. Assn. Home: 2126 Larkdale Dr Glenview IL 60025 Office: 723 S Wells St Chicago IL 60607

STUHR, ROBERT LEWIS, bus. assn. exec.; b. Tabor, Iowa, Oct. 10, 1917; s. John R. and Elsa J. Stuhr; A.B., Drake U., 1939; M.A., U. Iowa, 1940; Ph.D., Northwestern U., 1961; m. Ruth P. Jones, Sept. 21, 1946; children—John J., Margaret D. Dir. public relations and devel. Drake U., 1947-59; asso. dir. Econ. Club Chgo., 1959-68, exec. dir., 1968—; partner Gonser Gerber Tinker Stuhr, Chgo., 1959—. Served to capt. U.S. Army, 1941-46. Decorated Bronze Star. Mem. Council for Advancement and Support Edn., Internat. Public Relations Assn., Public Relations Soc. Am., Phi Beta Kappa, Omicron Delta Kappa, Sigma Alpha Epsilon. Mem. United Ch. of Christ. Clubs: Univ. (Chgo.); Westmoreland. Editor Bull. on Public Relations and Devel. for Colls., Bull. on Public Relations and Devel. for Ind. Schs., Bull. on Public Relations and Devel. for Hosps. Office: 105 W Madison St Chicago IL 60602

STULTS, ALLEN PARKER, banker; b. Chgo., June 13, 1913; s. Elmer E. and Minnie (Parker) S.; student U. Ill., 1931-32; diploma Northwestern U., 1941; student Loyola U., 1941-42; certificate Rutgers Grad. Sch. Banking, 1945; m. Elizabeth Van Horne, Aug. 19, 1939; children—Laurence, Shirley, John, James. With Fed. Res. Bank, 1933; asst. cashier Am. Nat. Bank & Trust Co., Chgo., 1942-45, asst. v.p., 1946-48, v.p., 1949-56, exec. v.p., 1956-63, pres., 1963-69, chmn. bd., 1969-79, dir., 1957—, hon. chmn. bd., 1980—; dir. McDonald's Corp., Health-Mor, Inc., Verson Allsteel Press Co. Public adviser Midwest Stock Exchange, 1964-65. Mem. adv. council Chgo. Area council, Nat. council Boy Scouts Am.; bus. adv. council Chgo. Urban League; exec. com. Gateway Houses Found.; chmn. bd. Businessman's Council NCCJ; nat. corp. gifts com. United Negro Coll. Fund; mem. U. Ill. Found.; adv. bd. YMCA; bd. dirs. Leadership Council Met. Open Communities; trustee Alice Lloyd Coll. Mem. Am. (pres. 1971-72), Ill. (past pres.) bankers assns., Chgo. Assn. Commerce and Industry (dir.), Ill. C. of C., Phi Gamma Delta, Skull and Crescent. Congregationalist. Clubs: Bankers, Chicago, Economic, Robert Morris Assos. (pres. 1952-53), Comml., Mid-Am.; Sunset Ridge Country (pres. 1956-57) (Winnetka, Ill.); Tucson Nat. Golf. Home: 1420 Sheridan Rd Wilmette IL 60091 Office: 33 N LaSalle St Chicago IL 60690

STULTS, DELWIN CONRAD, drilling co. exec.; b. Lubbock, Tex., June 15, 1930; s. Arthur Carl and Ruth Celestine (Rampy) S.; B.S. in Petroleum Engring., Tex. Tech. U., 1953; m. Sharon Kidd, Dec. 8, 1962; children—Flint Carson, Karina. Area petroleum engr. Honolulu Oil Corp., 1955-60; div. mgr. Harold Brown Co., 1960-63; with Dresser Industries, 1963-74, dist. mgr., Houston, 1963-65, pres. Dresser Atlas Argentina, 1968-72; with Tex. Internat. Co., Houston, 1974-79, exec. v.p., 1977-79, now dir.; pres., chmn. bd. Glendel Drilling Co., Houston, 1979—; dir. Phoenix Resources Co. Active Houston Livestock Show, Boy Scouts Am. Served with USN, 1953-55. Registered profl. engr., Tex. Mem. Assn. Oilwell Servicing Contractors, Internat. Assn. Drilling Contractors, Nomads. Republican. Methodist. Club: Woodlands Country. Office: 4801 Woodway Suite 400E Houston TX 77056

STULTZ, LOUIS CAMERON, pet supply co. exec.; b. Dallas, Jan. 19, 1928; s. Sydnor Marshall and Susie Mae (Cameron) S.; B.B.A., So. Meth. U., 1950; m. Sammye Appleton, Sept. 22, 1956; children—Tracy Melinda, Lisa Michelle. Regional sales mgr. Schick Electric Shaver Co., Lancaster, Pa., 1952-62, The d-Con Co., Inc., N.Y.C., 1963-77; sales mgr. Hartz Mountain Corp., Harrison, N.J., 1977-80; v.p. sales Handy Andy Broom Co., Lindsay, Okla., 1980—. Served with U.S. Army, 1945-49. Mem. So. Meth. U. Alumni Assn., VFW. Republican. Episcopalian. Club: Masons. Home: 3105 Westador Dr Arlington TX 76015

STUMM, DAVID ARTHUR, mgmt. and profl. devel. cons.; b. Aurora, Ill., Mar. 27, 1926; s. Francis Arthur and Edith Cecelia (Johns) S.; B.S.M.E., Marquette U., 1950; M.B.A. in Mktg. and Econs., Xavier U., 1958; postgrad. U. Pitts., 1961-64; m. Jeanette Edith Kammer, May 28, 1949; children—Michael, Gregory, Lisa, Karen. Indsl. sales engr. Westinghouse Corp., 1950-60, mgr. mktg. and personnel devel., 1960-65, div. mktg. mgr., 1965-70; exec. v.p. Radioear Corp., Pitts., 1970-73; mgr. diagnostic equipment div. Mallinckrodt Chem. Co., St. Louis, 1973-74; dir. mktg. Unirad Corp., Denver, 1974-76; v.p., partner, co-founder Barnes McHugh Co., Oak Brook, Ill., 1976—; instr. mktg. Joliet Jr. Coll. Served with arty., AUS, 1944-46. Mem. Am. Mgmt. Assn., Am. Assn. Indsl. Mgmt. (leadership and service award 1976, 77), Sales-Mktg. Execs. Internat., Am. Legion. Clubs: Cress Creek Country, K.C. Author: Introduction to Sales Engineering, 1962; Advanced Industrial Selling, 1981; Personal and Job Effectiveness, 1979. Home: 1525 Wedgefield Circle Naperville IL 60540 Office: Box 1144 Oak Brook IL 60521

STUMM, JOSEPH HANS, ins. co. exec.; b. Aurora, Ill., July 13, 1950; s. Robert J. and Dolores R. S.; A.B., Dartmouth Coll., 1972; M.B.A., Harvard U., 1975; m. Priscilla Wohlforth, Aug. 24, 1974; children—Alexandra, Amanda. With Phoenix Cos., Boston, 1975—, sales mgr., 1978—. C.L.U. Mem. Boston Life Underwriters (dir.), Million Dollar Round Table. Republican. Roman Catholic. Club: Harvard (Boston). Office: Phoenix Cos RKO Bldg Govt Center Boston MA 02114

STUMPE, WARREN ROBERT, mfg. co. exec.; b. Bronx, N.Y., July 15, 1925; s. William A. and Emma J. (Mann) S.; B.S., U.S. Mil. Acad., 1945; M.S., Cornell U., 1949; M. Indsl. Engring., N.Y. U., 1965; m. Jean Marie Mannion, June 5, 1952; children—Jeffrey R., Kathy A., William E. Dep. gen. mgr. AMF's gen. engring. div., Greenwich, Conn., 1954-63; exec. v.p. Dortech, Inc., Stamford, Conn., 1963-69; dir. systems mgmt. group, Mathews conveyor div. REX, Darien, Conn., 1969-71; dir. research and devel. Rexnord Milw., 1971-73; v.p. corporate research and tech. Rexnord, Inc., Milw., 1973—. Founder, pres. No. Little League, Stamford, 1965-69; pres. Turn of River Jr. High Sch. PTA, Stamford, 1967-68; mem. Nat. Com. Employer Support of Guard and Res.; bd. regents Milw. Sch. Engring. Served to capt. C.E., U.S. Army, 1945-54; col. Res. Registered prof. engr., N.Y., Fla., Wis. Mem. Am. Mgmt. Assn., Am. Soc. Mil. Engrs., Process Equipment Mfg. Assn., Indsl. Research Inst., Water Pollution Control Fedn., Tau Beta Pi. Clubs: Wis., Ozaukee Country (Milw.). Home: 2555 W Hemlock Rd Glendale WI 53209 Office: PO Box 2022 Milwaukee WI 53201

STUMPF, ERWIN B., plating co. exec.; b. Newark, Mar. 9, 1917; s. William and Marie (Staiert) S.; student N.Y. U., 1941, Pace Coll., 1947; m. Dorothea L. Seibel, May 11, 1940; children—Erwin B., Christine. Accounting supr. Merck & Co., Rahway, N.J., 1945-60; asst. treas. Community State Bank & Trust Co., Linden, N.J., 1960-61; treas. bus. mgr. dir. Bloomfield (N.J.) Coll., 1961-63 treas., asst. sec. Alloy Steel Products Co., Linden, 1963-67; controller Ampeg Co., Linden, 1967-72; vice-chmn. bd., Controller Grammer Guitar Co., Nashville, 1967-72; v.p., treas., controller Gen. Magnaplate Corp., Linden, 1972—, Ventura, Calif., 1980—; v.p., treas. Am. Magnaplate Tex., Inc., Grand Prairie, 1973—. Elder, trustee Linden Presbyterian Ch.; bd. advisers Linden Tech. High Sch. Served with USAAF, 1942-45. Mem. Am. Assn. Corporate Controllers. Home: 707 Erudo St Linden NJ 07036 also Highland Lakes Rd Highland Lakes NJ 07422

STUNTZ, ROBERT PAUL, engring. exec.; b. El Dorado, Kans., Sept. 13, 1918; s. Ross Maxwell and Anna Laura (Lotz) S.; A.A., Okla. Mil. Acad., 1937; B.S. in M.E., Ga. Inst. Tech., 1940; m. Elizabeth Melmond Schley, Jan. 8, 1942; children—Robert Paul, Anna Laura. With Babcock & Wilcox Co., 1940—, beginning as plant engr., Augusta, Ga., successively sales engr., Chgo., dist. sales mgr., asst. sales mgr., N.Y.C., mgr. field sales, gen. sales mgr., Augusta, gen. mgr. div., 1940-70, v.p., gen. mgr. Refractories div., 1970—; dir. Ceramic Fibres, Ltd., Babcock & Wilcox Refractories, Ltd., Holmes Insulations, Ltd., Productos de Caolin, Inc., Fibras Ceramicas, Inc., Isolite Babcock Refractories Co., Ltd., Gastleberry's Food Co., 1st Nat. Bank & Trust Co. Past bd. dirs. United Way; bd. dirs., pres. Jr. Achievement of Augusta; bd. dirs., met. chmn. Nat. Alliance Businessmen. Served with USNR, 1942-46. Registered profl. engr., Ill. Mem. Am. Iron and Steel Inst., Am. Ceramic Soc., Am. Iron and Steel Engring., Refractories Inst. (dir.), C. of C. Greater Augusta. Episcopalian. Clubs: Friday Friars, N.Y. Yacht, Augusta Country, Pinnacle. Home: 754 McClure Dr Augusta GA 30909 Office: PO Box 923 Augusta GA 30903

STURGES, JOHN SIEBRAND, bank exec.; b. Greenwich, Conn., Feb. 12, 1939; s. Harry Wilton and Elizabeth Helen (Niewenhous) S.; A.B., Harvard, 1960; M.B.A., U. So. Calif., 1965; certificate EDP, N.Y. U., 1972; certificate Life office Mgmt. Assn., 1967; m. Anastasia Daphne Bakalis, May 6, 1967; children—Christina Aurora, Elizabeth Athena. With Equitable Life Assurance Soc. U.S., N.Y.C., 1965-79, mgr. systems devel., 1965-70, mgr. adminstrv. services, 1970-71, dir. compensation, 1971-75, asst. v.p., personnel and adminstrv. services, 1975-77, v.p. adminstrv. and devel. resources, 1977-79; sr. v.p. personnel Nat. Bank of N.Am., N.Y.C., 1979—. Lay reader St. Peters Episcopal Ch., Freehold, N.J., 1972—, vestryman, 1974-79, corporate sec., 1976-79, warden, 1979-80; bd. dirs., sec. Hospice, Freehold Area Hosp., 1979—. Served to lt. USNR, 1960-65. Mem. Commerce Assn., Life Office Mgmt. Assn. (salary adminstrn. com. 1972-75), N.Y. Personnel Mgmt. Assn. (chmn. tng. and devel. com. 1972-77), Am. Soc. Personnel Adminstrn. (dir. N.Y. 1979—), Am. Compensation Assn., Health Ins. Assn. Am. (personnel com. 1972-79), Beta Gamma Sigma (dir., sec. N.Y. 1978—), Phi Kappa Phi. Republican. Home: 8 Winnipeg Ct Morganville NJ 07751 Office: 44 Wall St New York NY 10005

STUTTS, CLYDE LIVINGSTON, banker; b. Scotland County, N.C., Aug. 6, 1912; s. Simon Strauss and Roberta (Livingston) S.; B.S., U. N.C., 1937; m. Ina Rufus Edwards, May 1, 1954; children—Carol (Mrs. P.C. Hammond Jr.), Clyde Livingston, Helen Elizabeth (Mrs. Oscar Greene, III), Rufus Edwards (dec.). With Comml. State Bank, Laurinburg, N.C., 1937-59, exec. v.p., dir., 1946-59; v.p., dir. Citizens State Bank, Bennettsville, S.C., 1954-59; pres. Union Trust Co., Shelby, N.C., 1959-76, also dir.; chmn. bd. Independence Nat. Bank, 1976—; dir. Allied Fin. Services, Inc., 1971—, chmn. bd., 1974—; pres. Carolina Leasing Corp., 1960-76. Pres., chmn. Piedmont Area Devel. Assn., Charlotte, N.C., 1962; council pres., mem. regional exec. com. Cape Fear council Boy Scouts Am., 1953-56; treas. Salvation Army, Shelby, 1966—. Mem. adv. bd. United Fund, 1963—, Gardner-Webb Coll., 1963-75; trustee Brevard Coll., 1976—, Coll. Found., Inc., 1975—. Served to lt. (j.g.) USNR, 1944-46. Recipient Silver Beaver award Boy Scouts Am., 1953. Mem. Am. (treas. 1968-70), N.C. (pres. 1965-66) bankers assns. Mason, Elk, Rotarian. Clubs: Charlotte City; Raleigh (N.C.) City; Cleveland Country, North Lake Country (Shelby). Home: 131 Westfield Rd Shelby NC 28150 Office: 7-9 E Marion St Shelby NC 28150

STUTZMAN, DWAYNE HAROLD, ins. co. exec.; b. Wood River, Nebr., Apr. 4, 1936; s. Willard W. and Mattie (Schweitor) S.; student Goshen (Ind.) Coll., 1954-56, Messiah Coll., Grantham, Pa., 1957; m. Norma L. Minter, Dec. 29, 1956; children—J. Thomas, Curtis D., Scott D., Peggy L. Mgr., Shepherdstown Greeting Cards, Inc., 1958-61, owner, 1967-72; claims adjuster Goodville Mut. Casualty Co., New Holland, Pa., 1961-62, underwriting mgr., 1962-67, v.p., 1967-72, exec. v.p., 1972-79, pres., dir., 1979—; pres., dir. Earl Mut. Ins Co., 1975—; dir. Mennonite Mut. Ins. Co. Sec., Atlantic Conf. Brethren in Christ, Elizabethtown, Pa., 1978-80. Mem. Pa. Assn. Mut. Ins. Cos. (dir. 1974-80, pres. 1980-81). Republican. Office: 625 W Main St New Holland PA 17557

SUAREZ DEL CAMPO, RAUL A., architect; b. Cardenas, Cuba, Mar. 3, 1947; s. Ramon and Rayda (Fernandez) Suarez; came to U.S., 1960, naturalized, 1972; B.A. in Architecture, Washington U., St. Louis, 1970, M.Arch., 1972; m. Lourdes Tirado, June 7, 1969; children—Raul, Michael, Jeannette, Lisa. Architect with archtl. firms in Fla. and P.R., 1969-74; propr. Raul A. Suarez-Del Campo, architect, Miami, Fla., 1974—; inspecting architect Totalbank, All-Am. Nat. Bank; pres. CONSTAD Corp.; instr. Community Design Workshop, Washington U.; prin. works include Divine Providence Ch., Sweetwater, Fla., Good Shepherd Ch., Miami, St. Cecilia Ch., Hialeah, Fla., Shopping Center, Miami, Pet Complex, Davie, Fla., Vet. Hosp., Crystal Lake, Fla., Sinco Townhouses, Miami, Montessori Sch., Pembroke Park, Divine Providence Sch., Miami, Med. and Dental Center, Hialeah, Adminstrn. Bldg., Doe Valley, Ky., Swim and Tennis Club, Sam Rayburn, Tex., residential communities: Libano Ranches, Miami, Woodscape, Miami, Avanti, Sweetwater, Fla., Brandymeadows, Lauderhill, Fla., Battah Residence, Miami, Dominguez Residence, Miami. Roman Catholic. Address: 2515 SW 101 Ct Miami FL 33165

SUDARSKY, JERRY M., industrialist; b. Nhizni Novgorod, Russia, June 12, 1918; s. Selig and Sara (Ars) S.; came to U.S., 1927, naturalized, 1934; student U. Iowa, 1936-39; B.S., Poly. Inst. Bklyn., 1942; Sc.D., Poly. Inst. N.Y., 1976; m. Mildred Axelrod, Aug. 31, 1947; children—Deborah, Donna. Founder, chief exec. officer Bioferm Corp., Wasco, Calif., 1946-66; indsl. cons. United Nations, 1967; founder, chmn. bd. dirs. Israel Chems. Ltd., Tel Aviv, Israel, 1967-70; chmn. bd. IC Internat. Consu., Tel Aviv, 1970-72; vice chmn. Daylin Inc., Los Angeles, 1973-77; pres. JMS Assos., Los Angeles, 1977—; dir. Unico Investment Co., Unico Bank, Tel Aviv. Chmn. bd. dirs. Bezalel Art Acad. Jerusalem; bd. dirs. U. of Judaism, Los Angeles; bd. govs., mem. exec. com. Hebrew U., Jerusalem; trustee Poly. Inst. N.Y. Served with USNR, 1943-46. Mem. Am. Chem. Soc., Sigma Xi. Clubs: Brentwood Country, Canyon Country, Caesaria Country (Israel). Home: 2220 Ave of Stars Los Angeles CA 90067 Office: 10889 Wilshire Blvd Los Angeles CA 90024

SUFANA, RONALD JOHN, fin. and tax planner; b. East Chicago, Ind., Mar. 23, 1939; s. John, Jr., and Helen (Ulieriu) S.; B.A., U. Tulsa, 1963; student law Western State U., 1975; M.B.A. in Fin., Nat. U., 1979; m. Colleen Watts, Mar. 16, 1968; children—Ronald John, Melissa Anne, Christopher David. Commd. ensign U.S. Navy, 1963, advanced through grades to lt., 1973; served with various ships, duty stas., Vietnam, 1964-73, ret., 1973; with Ray Watt Industries, San Diego, 1973-75; pres. Westridge Fin. Services, Inc., San Diego, 1975—; tchr. taxation, fin. planning, estate planning. Decorated Purple Heart, 2 Armed Forces Expeditionary medals (U.S.), Gallantry Cross (Vietnam); certified fin. planner; lic. real estate broker; lic. ins. agt. Mem. Internat. Assn. Fin. Planners (sec. San Diego chpt. 1978-79, v.p. tng. 1979-80), Nat. Assn. Security Dealers (lic.), Nat. Rifle Assn. (life), DAV (life). Republican. Eastern Orthodox. Clubs: Univ. (San Diego), Masons, Lions. Home: 14985 Amso St Poway CA 92064 Office: 3511 Camino del Rio S #210E San Diego CA 92108

SUGRUE, TERRANCE BRIAN, drilling co. exec.; b. Holyoke, Mass., June 23, 1939; s. Roger F. and Anne Marie (Ryan) S.; student N.Y. U., 1958-59, Holyoke Community Coll., 1961-62; m. Gertrude E. McKenna, Sept. 26, 1959; children—Terrance Brian, Timothy D., Leslie A. Mgr. systems and programming Worthington Corp., Holyoke, Mass., 1963-69; mgr. data processing Moore Co., Springfield, Mass., 1969-74; dir. mgmt. info. systems Smith & Wesson Co., Springfield, 1974-76; pres., treas. Precise Industries, South Hadley, Mass., 1976—, also dir.; mem. adv. council Center Econ. Devel., U. Mass., Amherst. Mem. Nat. Fedn. Ind. Bus., S. Hadley C. of C. Club: Palmer (Mass.) Rotary. Home: 7 Bombardier St South Hadley MA 01075 Office: 650 New Ludlow Rd South Hadley MA 01075

SUHR, GEORGE RASMUS, former hotel exec.; b. Sulhamstead, Eng., July 15, 1920; s. Frederik John and Beatrice Mary (Leake) S.; M.B.A., Royal Comml. Coll., Copenhagen, 1941; diploma Social Sci., London U. Poly., 1949; m. Ruth Andersen, Dec. 26, 1942; children—Hannah (Mrs. William G. Stewart Jr.), George-Henrik, John. Came to U.S., 1957. With Autourist Rent-a-Car, Copenhagen, 1950-61, exec. v.p., 1957-61; exec. v.p. Kemwel Group, N.Y.C., 1961-68; v.p. Arthur Frommer Orgn., N.Y.C., 1968-69; pres. Hotel Rep., Inc., N.Y.C., 1969-76, chmn. bd., 1971-76; chmn., pres. Hotelworld Mgmt. Group Inc., 1976-78; dir. mktg. Bahamas Ministry of Tourism, 1979—; dir. Auto-Europe Inc., N.Y.C., Selected European Travel, Inc., N.Y.C. Lectr., Cornell Sch. Hotel Adminstrn., 1971—. World jamboree adminstr., scoutmaster Morris-Sussex council Boy Scouts Am., Chatham, N.J., 1964-69. Served with Intelligence Corps, Brit. Army, 1943-49. Fellow Tourism Soc., Inst. Cert. Travel Agts.; mem. Am. Soc. Assn. Execs. (adv. com. 1972-75), Assn. Group Travel Execs. (v.p. 1970-76), Am. Soc. Travel Agts. (adv. com. 1964-66), Hotel Sales Mgmt. Assn., French C. of C. (councillor 1973-78), Chevalier du Tastevin, Newcomen Soc., Spanish Am. C. of C. Lutheran (mem. ch. council 1958-69). Clubs: Skal, Rotary (N.Y.C.); Royal So. Yacht (Hamble, Eng.); Royal Danish Yacht (Copenhagen). Co-author: The Great Hotels of the World. Contbr. articles to profl. jours. Home: Harbour Mews #33 Cable Beach Nassau Bahamas

SUITER, WILLIAM ORAN, JR., chem. co. exec.; b. Greensboro, N.C., June 17, 1936; s. William Oran and Anna Lois (Mathis) S.; B.S., Duke U., 1958; postgrad. Rice Inst., 1958-59, La. State U., 1960-62; M.B.A. (univ. fellow), U. Del., 1965; m. Larilee Baty, Aug. 28, 1959; children—William Daniel, Kari Elizabeth. Teaching assistantship Rice Inst., Houston, 1958-59; tech. service chemist Copolymer Rubber & Chem. Corp., Baton Rouge, 1959-62; market devel. and customer service specialist film dept. E.I. duPont de Nemours & Co., Inc., Wilmington, Del., 1962-64; sr. marketing research analyst Smith Kline & French Labs., Phila., 1965-67; sr. marketing research analyst Atlas Chem. Industries, Inc. (name changed to ICI Ams. Inc. 1974), Wilmington, 1967—. Active Boy Scouts Am.; chmn. area Alumni admissions adv. com. Duke U., 1968-71; loaned exec. United Fund No. Del., 1970. Mem. Am. Chem. Soc., Chem. Marketing Research Assn. Unitarian (active music, youth work, theater arts, finance). Home: 12 Majestic Court Wilmington DE 19810 Office: ICI Ams Inc Wilmington DE 19897

SUKUP, EUGENE GEORGE, mfg. co. exec.; b. Venus, Nebr., May 11, 1929; s. Louis and Dorothy Amelia (Buerkley) S.; grad. pub. high sch., 1946; m. Mary Elizabeth Bielefeld, Feb. 24, 1952; children—Charles Eugene, Steven Eugene. Farming, Hampton, Iowa, 1946-51; owner and farm mgr., Dougherty, Iowa, 1951—; pres. Sukup Mfg. Co., Sheffield, Iowa, 1963—; pres. Sukup Enterprises, Inc.,

Sheffield, 1968—. Com. mem. Franklin County 4-H, 1958-64; com. mem. North Iowa Area Dist. Mem. Sheffield-Chapin Community Sch. Bd., 1967-79; mem. Franklin County Extension council, 1962-65; bd. regents Waldorf Coll., Forest City, Iowa. Recipient Outstanding Young Farmer award Jr. C. of C., 1962, 4-H Alumni award, 1964. Mem. Farm Bur., Iowa Mfrs. Assn. Republican. Lutheran (ch. council 1960-62, 70-72, pres. 1962, 71). Club: Sheffield Community. Patentee in field. Home: Rural Route Dougherty IA 50433 Office: PO Box 220 North Rd Sheffield IA 50475

SULARZ, FRANK DONALD, mfg. co. exec.; b. Thompson Falls, Mont., Mar. 4, 1934; s. Frank Joseph and Agnes Marie (Bafija) S.; B.S.M.E., Ind. Inst. Tech., 1959; postgrad. Seattle U., 1959-60; postgrad. in law Denver U., 1960-61; diploma exec. devel. program Grad. Sch. Bus., 1961; U. N.Mex., 1971-73; m. Patricia Ann Puphal, Oct. 20, 1956; children—Lisa Ann, Jeffrey David. Mktg. mgr. Envirco div. Becton Dickinson & Co., Albuquerque, 1968-69, gen. mgr., 1969-73; pres. Environ. Systems div. Bio-Dynamics, Inc., Albuquerque, 1973-76, also corp. v.p.; pres., chief exec. officer Exidyne, Inc., Colorado Springs, Colo., 1976—; mem. Colo. Gov.'s Small Bus. Council, 1980—; chmn. N.Mex. State World Trade Commn., 1976-77; chmn. N.Mex. Dist. Export Council, Dept. Commerce, 1974-76. Served with U.S. Army, 1954-56. Recipient Am. Legion Leadership award, 1952. Mem. Water Pollution Control Fedn. Republican. Lutheran. Club: Rotary. Office: Suite 2114 Location 1 Bldg 2 2860 S Circle Dr Colorado Springs CO 80906

SULIER, CORNELIUS WILLIAM, savs. and loan exec.; b. Temperance, Mich., Mar. 12, 1899; s. Frank Henry and Christine Elizabeth (Masserant) S.; student Davis Bus. Coll., 1915-16, Alexander Hamilton Inst., 1923-25, Toledo U., 1918-19; m. Irene Dorner, Jan. 23, 1937; children—Cornelius William, Karolyn Irene (Mrs. Robert W. Buck). Co-owner, operator service sta., 1921-22; salesman, regional supr. Willys Overland Co., 1922-26; pres., gen. mgr. Byron-Sulier Motor Co., Inc., Lexington, Ky., 1926-29; life ins. agt., 1929-32; gen. agt. Fidelity Mut. Life Ins. Co., 1932-39; pres. Sulier Ins. Agy., Inc., Lexington, 1939-74; pres. Reilus Realty Corp.; dir., v.p., pres., chmn. bd. Lexington Fed. Savs. & Loan Assn.; dir. Excelsior Ins. Co. of N.Y.; owner cattle and tobacco farm, 1941-75. Operator, Good Turn Club, 1927-78. Co-founder, pres. Blue Grass Found.; bd. dirs. Community Chest, YMCA, Boy Scouts Am., Girl Scouts Am., Youth Symphony Orch. of Central Ky., Humane Soc., Salvation Army, 1978—; finance chmn., mem. adv. bd. Opportunity Workshop of Lexington. Recipient Outstanding Citizen award Optimist Club, 1941, Silver Beaver award Boy Scouts Am., 1942; named Ky. Col. Mem. Lexington C. of C. (pres.), Lexington Automobile Dealers Assn. (pres.), Lexington Life Underwriters Assn. (pres.), Newcomen Soc., Ky. Aberdeen Angus Assn. (sec.-treas.). Republican. Roman Catholic (trustee). Clubs: Lexington Optimist (pres.), Lexington, Lexington Country, Lafayette. Home: Apt 9A Hanover Towers 101 S Hanover Ave Lexington KY 40502 Office: 1713 Nicholasville Rd Lexington KY 40503

SULLIVAN, BARBARA MARIE, banker; b. Pitts., Apr. 4, 1948; d. John G. and Esther E. (Gallagher) S.; A.B., Trinity Coll., Washington, 1970; M., U. Pitts., 1971; postgrad. Law Sch., Duquesne U., 1974-75; m. Thomas P. Benic, July 9, 1977. Multifamily housing rep. Dept. HUD, Pitts., 1973-75; asst. corp. officer Forest City Dillon, Inc., Cleve., 1975-78; v.p. Mellon Mortgage, Inc. affiliate Mellon Bank, Pitts., 1978—; bd. dirs. Nat. Housing Conf., Washington. Mem. Mayor's Task Force on Downtown Revitalization City of Pitts. Mem. Mortgage Bankers Assn., Nat. Assn. Home Builders, Nat. Assn. Housing and Redevel. Ofcls., Nat. Leased Housing Assn., Women in Housing and Community Devel. Office: 444 Union Trust Bldg Pittsburgh PA 15219

SULLIVAN, CLARENCE EDWARD, JR., comml. banker; b. Vancouver, Wash., Feb. 16, 1925; s. Clarence Edward and Chloe (Rockhill) S.; B.S., U. Mont., 1956; m. Alice Marjorie Stanley, Aug. 30, 1953; children—Marjean Chloe, Clay Rockhill. Constrn. supr. CAA, 1945-55; with Union Bank and Trust Co., Helena, Mont., 1956-66, v.p., 1959-66; v.p. Iowa Des Moines Nat. Bank, 1966-70; v.p. in charge real estate dept. 1st Nat. Bank, Albuquerque, 1970-73; sr. v.p. in charge real estate dept. Bank of N.Mex., Albuquerque, 1973-78; owner, prin. Sullivan & Assos., real estate and fin. cons., Albuquerque, 1978—. Served with USN, 1942-45. Republican. Christian Scientist. Home: 8500 Evangeline NE Albuquerque NM 87111 Office: 48 First Plaza NW Albuquerque NM 87102

SULLIVAN, DENNIS MICHAEL, lawyer; b. San Francisco, Jan. 6, 1945; s. Albert Gifford and Eileen Winona (Ganshirt) S.; B.S.C., U. Santa Clara, 1966; postgrad. Internat. Sch. Law, The Hague, Netherlands, 1967; J.D., Hastings Coll. Law, U. Calif., San Francisco, 1969; m. Evie Ellen Rankin, Oct. 26, 1971; children—Dennis, Ethan, Jennifer, Meghan. Sr. acct. Boitano & Sargent, Santa Clara, Calif., 1963-66; admitted to Calif. bar, 1970, U.S. Supreme Ct. bar, 1978; dep. dist. atty. Alameda County (Calif.), 1971-74; partner firm Sullivan Nakahara Dubois Hove, Oakland, Calif., 1974-80; individual practice law, Oakland, 1980—; gen. counsel, dir., chief fin. officer various small corps.; spl. cons. to Consulate Gen., Fed. Republic Germany, San Francisco; judge pro tem Oakland-Piedmont Mcpl. Ct., 1978—; ct. commr. pro tem various cts. Fed. Republic Germany. Served with U.S. Army, 1970-71. Decorated Army Commendation medal. Recipient Editorial award Hastings Law Jour., 1968. Mem. Alameda County Bar Assn., Am. Bar Assn. Democrat. Roman Catholic. Mem. Editorial bd. Hastings Law Jour., 1968-69. Home: 124 Waldo Ave Piedmont CA 94611 Office: One Kaiser Plaza Suite 1115 Oakland CA 94612

SULLIVAN, DOROTHY ANN GIBBONS, real estate exec.; b. Boston, Nov. 29, 1925; d. Cornelius Patrick and Grace Elizabeth (Murray) Gibbons; A.B., Regis Coll., 1947; spl. studies Mass. Inst. Tech., 1945; m. John F. Sullivan, June 25, 1949; children—Lorraine, Kathleen, John F. III, Carolyn, Christopher. Blood chemist Lahey Clinic, Boston, 1947; stewardess Am. Airlines, 1948; tchr. high sch., Boston, 1948-50; instr. biology Regis Coll., Weston, Mass., 1958, social dir., 1958; Realtor, H.G.M. Realty, Cleve., 1967-70; pres., dir. Country House Realty, Holmdel, N.J., 1973—; dir. Confex, Inc., Mgmt. Basics, Inc. Bd. dirs. Found. for Edn. in Human Relations; active Children's Psychiat. Center. Named Cath. Clubwoman of Year, Jr. Cath. Woman's Club, Reading, Pa., 1956. Mem. Realtors Nat. Mktg. Inst., Fedn. Internationale des Professions Immobilieres, Nat. Assn. Realtors, AAUW, Monmouth County Bd. Realtors, Regis Coll. Alumnae Assn. (pres. N.J. chpt.). Home: 12 Fox Hunt Rd Holmdel NJ 07733 Office: 22 S Holmdel Rd Holmdel NJ 07733

SULLIVAN, EDWARD JOSEPH, electrotype co. exec.; b. Concord, N.H., May 17, 1915; s. Edward J. and Ida (Packard) S.; student St. Anslem's Coll., 1935-36; m. Dorothea M. Ash, Sept. 30, 1944; children—James Ash, Maureen Packard. Treas., Merrimack Electrotyping Corp., 1950-55, pres., 1955—; treas. Sheraton Properties Corp., 1961—; exec. v.p. Blanchard Press Corp., 1968-69; pres. Tridel Housing Devels., 1970—, Ho-Tei Corp., St. Thomas, V.I.; dir. Concord Fed. Savs. Bank; pres. Allied Photo Engraving Corp., 1964. Mem. Concord Hosp. Corp., U.S. Commn. on Civil Rights; chmn. bldg. fund Carmelite Monastery, Concord, 1950, St. Peters Ch. for Bishop Brady High Sch. Bldg. Fund, 1961; citizens com. Concord Housing Authority; commr. Concord Urban Renewal Assn.; v.p., bd. dirs. Diocesan Bur. Housing, Inc., Manchester, N.H., 1975—; bd. dirs. Carpenter Center, Inc., Manchester, N.H., Concord chpt. ARC, Concord Hosp. Served with USNR, 1942-46. Mem. Internat. Assn. Electrotypers and Stereotypers Union, Internat. Assn. Electrotypers and Stereotypers, Inc., Am. Legion, Aircraft Owners and Pilots Assn., Printing Inst. Am., One Hundred Club N.H. Elk. Republican. Roman Catholic. Club: Serra (v.p.). Kiwanian, K.C. Home: 99 Manor Rd Concord NH 03301 Office: 99 Manor Rd Concord NH 03301

SULLIVAN, EDWARD ROBERT, mag. editor; b. Chgo., Mar. 23, 1923; s. Edward Francis and Marie Elizabeth S.; B.A., St. Thomas Coll., Oak Park, Ill., 1950; Ph.B. in Theology, St. Rose Coll., Dubuque, Iowa, 1954; postgrad. in English, DePaul U., Chgo., 1956-57; m. Patricia Ann O'Leary, Feb. 18, 1972. Tchr., Fenwick High Sch., Oak Park, 1954-57; prof. St. Teresa Coll., Winona, Minn., summers 1956-61; mgmt. positions The Boeing Co., Seattle and Renton, Wash., 1958-69; creative dir., dir. Gorin & Holmes Advt. & Public Relations, Seattle, 1969-70; v.p./officer Trans-West Co., Seattle, 1970-71; mgr., editor Seattle Bus. Mag., 1971—; instr. adult edn.; editorial cons.; public speaker. Mem. Bellevue Playbarn Co., 1963-71. Served in inf., U.S. Army, 1943-45, 45-46; Korea. Mem. Am. Soc. Bus. Press Editors. Office: 215 Columbia St Seattle WA 98104

SULLIVAN, EUGENE JOHN JOSEPH, mfg. exec.; b. N.Y.C., Nov. 28, 1920; s. Cornelius and Margaret (Smith) S.; B.S., St. John's U., 1942, D.Commerce, 1973; M.B.A., N.Y. U., 1948; m. Gloria Roesch, Aug. 25, 1943; children—Eugene John Joseph, Edward J., Robert C., Elizabeth Ann. With chem. div. Borden, Inc., N.Y.C., 1946—, beginning as salesman, successively asst. sales, 1957-58, exec. v.p., 1958-64, pres. Borden Chem. Co. div. Borden, Inc., 1964-67; v.p. Borden, Inc., 1964-67, exec. v.p., 1967-73, pres., 1973—, chmn. bd., chief exec. officer, 1979—, also dir.; dir. Borden Co. Ltd. of Eng., Borden Chem. Co. of Can., Bank of N.Y., Atlantic Cos.; trustee Emigrant Savs. Bank; adj. prof. St. John's U. Chmn. bd. St. Francis Hosp., Roslyn, N.Y.; trustee St. John's U.; apptd. by Gov. Hugh Carey as chmn. Gov.'s Council on Internat. Bus., N.Y. State, 1980. Served as lt. USNR, 1942-46; lt. Res. Mem. Grocery Mfrs. Am. (dir.). Clubs: Univ., Sky, Plandome Country, Manhasset Bay Yacht. Office: Borden Inc 277 Park Ave New York NY 10007

SULLIVAN, FRANK E., life ins. co. exec.; b. Lowell, Mass., Aug. 17, 1923; s. William H. and Vera Sullivan; B.S., Notre Dame U., 1945. Adminstrv. asst. to football coach Notre Dame U., 1946-52; gen. agt. Am. United Life Ins. Co., Indpls., 1953-74; pres. Mut. Benefit Life Ins. Co. N.J., 1977—; dir. St. Joseph Bank & Trust Co., South Bend; pres. Million Dollar Round Table, 1967; panelist, lectr. in field. Past pres. South Bend United Fund, United Community Services South Bend, Health Found. No. Ind., St. Joseph County (Ind.) Urban Coalition. Served with USNR, World War II. C.L.U. Author: Delling Life Insurance for Deferred Compensation, 1962; Setting Goals for Million Dollar Production, 1968; The Critical Path to Sales Success, 1970. Past chmn. bd. editors C.L.U. Jour. Office: 520 Broad St Newark NJ 07101*

SULLIVAN, FRED R., diversified mfg. co. exec.; b. Ft. Wayne, Ind., 1914; B.S., Rutgers U., 1938; M.B.A., N.Y. U., 1942; LL.D. (hon.), Washington and Jefferson Coll., 1974; m. Judith Omanoff; children—Nancy, Judith, Fred A. With Monroe Calculating Machine Co., 1934-61, pres., 1953-61; co. merged with Litton Industries, 1958, sr. v.p. Litton Industries, 1961-64; pres., chief exec. officer Walter Kidde & Co., Inc., Clifton, N.J., 1964-66, chmn. bd., chief exec. officer, 1966—; dir. Royal Crown Cos., Inc., Sun Chem. Corp., N.Y.C., Supermarkets Gen. Corp., Woodbridge, N.J., West Orange, N.J., Midatlantic Nat. Bank, Newark, Chromalloy Am. Corp., Context Industries Inc., Technicolor, Inc., Los Angeles, Mass. Mut. Corp. Investors, Inc., Springfield, City Investing Co., N.Y.C., Becton, Dickinson & Co., Paramus, N.J., Dry Dock Savs. Bank, N.Y.C. Bd. overseers Rutgers U. Found.; trustee Found. Coll. Medicine and Dentistry N.J., Newark Museum, Lenox Hill Hosp., N.Y.C., Fordham U., Bronx; bd. dirs. Found. for Children with Learning Disabilities, N.Y.C.; mem. N.Y. Gov.'s Council on Internat. Bus.; mem. adv. bd. and policy com. Coalition of Northeastern Govs. Mem. N.J. C. of C. (dir.). Address: 9 Brighton Rd Clifton NJ 07015

SULLIVAN, GEORGE WILLIAM, JR., communications co. exec.; b. Medford, Mass., Sept. 22, 1932; s. George William and Helen (Dixon) S.; B.B.A., Boston U., 1954; m. Sylvia Anne Caron, July 2, 1955; children—Tracy Anne, Susan Elizabeth, Michael Joseph. With Collins-Rockwell Internat., 1959-79, pres. comml. telecommunications group, 1974-79; exec. v.p. No. Telecom, Inc., Nashville, 1979—; dir. Commerce Union Bank, Nashville. Bd. dirs. Dallas Symphony, 1975-79, So. Methodist U. Found. for Bus. Adminstrn. Served to 1st lt. U.S. Army, 1955-59. Mem. Electronic Industries Assn., Nat. Alliance Bus. (met. Dallas chmn. 1975-77, nat. dir. 1977-79). Club: Nashville City. Office: International Plaza Nashville TN 37217

SULLIVAN, GERALD JAMES, ins. co. exec.; b. Olympia, Wash., Sept. 30, 1937; s. John F. and Elizabeth J. (Yater) S.; B.B.A., U. Wash., 1959; M.B.A., Wharton Sch. U. Pa., 1966; m. Martha A. Kuehlthau, June 12, 1959; children—Gerald James, Thomas, Katheleen, Shannon. Security analyst Hartford Ins. Group (Conn.), 1966-67; chief dep. ins. commr. State of Wash., Olympia, 1967-68; sec. John F. Sullivan Co., Seattle, 1968-71; pres. Walker Sullivan Co., Los Angeles, 1971-80, chmn., 1979; chmn. bd., pres. Gerald J. Sullivan & Assos., Inc., ins. brokers, 1980—; mem. exec. com., chmn. security com. Calif. Surplus Lines Assns., San Francisco, 1974—; dir. New World Mut. Fund, Los Angeles. Served to capt. USAF, 1959-64. C.P.C.U., C.L.U. Roman Catholic. Clubs: Wilshire Country, Pauma Valley Country, Jonathan, Calif., Stock Exchange, K.C. Author: Trends in International Reinsurance Affecting American Reinsurers, 1966. Office: 800 W 6th St Los Angeles CA 90017

SULLIVAN, JAMES MICHAEL, hotel and theme park exec.; b. Cambridge, Mass., July 15, 1943; s. Benjamin Robert and Edith Frances (Downing) S.; B.B.A., Boston Coll., 1965; M.B.A., U. Conn., 1974; m. Joan Gertrude Tynan, Sept. 10, 1966; children—Patricia, James Michael, Kathleen, Brian. Sr. auditor Arthur Andersen & Co., Boston and Hartford, 1965-71; mgr. corp. acctg., dir. internal audit, controller food service and franchising group Heublein, Inc., Farmington, Conn., 1971-78; asst. to pres. Holiday Inns, Inc., Memphis, 1978-79, sr. v.p. fin. gaming group, 1979-80; v.p. fin. of restaurant group and theme park group Marriott Corp., Bethesda, Md., 1980—. Trustee, City of Winding Falls (Ky.), 1975-78; trustee Jefferson County (Ky.) Council for Retarded Citizens, 1975-78; bd. dirs. Memphis-Shelby County Assn. for Retarded Citizens, 1978-79. Served with U.S. Army, 1966. C.P.A., Mass. Mem. Conn. Soc. C.P.A.'s, Am. Inst. C.P.A.'s, Planning Execs. Inst. Roman Catholic. Office: One Marriott Dr Washington DC 20058

SULLIVAN, JOHN J(OSEPH), JR., banker; b. Kansas City, Mo., Apr. 16, 1918; s. John J. and Laura J. (Diviney) S.; A.B. in Econs., Rockhurst Coll., 1939; LL.B., U. Mo., Kansas City, 1950. Salesman, Borden Milk Co., 1939-42; fin. systems specialist Burroughs Corp., Kansas City, Mo., 1946-59; pres. MidAmerican Bank and Trust Co., Shawnee Mission, Kans., 1959—, chmn. bd., 1980—; dir. Life Ins. Co., Kansas, Crested Butte Mountain Resort, Inc., MidAm. Automated Clearing House, Greater Kansas City Clearing House; mem. exec. com. Kans. Devel. Credit Corp. Served with USN, 1942-46. Mem. Am. Bankers Assn. (v.p. Kans.), Kans. Bankers Assn. (past v.p., dir.), Nat. Automated Clearing House Assn., Kans. Assn. Commerce and Industry. Clubs: Blue Hills Country (past pres., dir.), Carriage (dir.). Office: PO Box 2947 Shawnee Mission KS 66201

SULLIVAN, JOHN LEO, computer firm exec.; b. Jersey City, N.J., May 25, 1947; s. Arthur Phillip and Margaret (Griffin) S.; B.A. summa cum laude, Fordham U., 1975, M.S., 1976; m. Catherine J. Atchison, Feb. 20, 1971; children—Christine, Beth, Laura. Owner, Trelex Corp., Yonkers, N.Y., 1969-75; tchr., pvt. tutor Fordham U., 1974-75; data processing faculty Taylor Bus. Inc., N.Y.C., 1976-77; programmer, system analyst ISSS, Inc., N.Y.C., 1975-76, sr. v.p., 1977—; ednl. cons. Taylor Bus. Inst., 1978—. Mem. CCD bd., Christian Edn. Center, Dobbs Ferry, N.Y., 1973-75; mem. curriculum com. Fordham U., 1974. Served with U.S. Army, 1967-69. Decorated Purple Heart, Army Commendation medal. Mem. Am. Mgmt. Assn., Alpha Sigma Lambda. Roman Catholic. Office: 225 Old Newbrunswick Rd Piscataway NJ 08852

SULLIVAN, JOSEPH MICHAEL, life ins. co. exec.; b. Phila., Jan. 12, 1925; s. Denis T. and Catherine G. (Cavanaugh) S.; B.S., St. Joseph's Coll., 1951; postgrad. Temple U. Sch. Law, 1951-52, Am. Coll. Life Underwriters, 1969; m. Maureen A. Crowe, Aug. 8, 1953; children—Sharon Anne, Mary Eileen, Joseph Michael, Brian Alexander, Robert Denis, Matthew Judge, Mary Kristine. Spl. Investigator Retail Credit Co., 1949-52; spl. agt. Lincoln Nat. Life Ins. Co., 1952-55; asst. mgr. Bankers Life Co. Des Moines, 1955-60; regional mgr. Pacific Mut. Life Ins. Co., Phila., 1960-69; pres. Sullivan & Co., Phila., 1969—; adv. Council Pacific Mut. Life Ins. Co., Newport Beach, Calif.; dir. McGettigans Travel Bur., Inc., Phila., Walsh & Walsh, N.Y.C., Nat. Assos., Inc., Cape May, N.J. Pres., Council Civic Assns. Springfield (Pa.), 1957-59; asso. capt. Malvern Weekend Retreat League, Phila. 1964-65; mem. ins. com. Cath. Charities Dr., Phila., 1959-65; bd. govs. St. Joseph's Coll., Phila. Committeeman, Republican party Springfield Twp., 1955-58. Mem. coll. council St. Joseph's Coll. Served with AUS, 1943-46. Recipient Order of Arrow award Boy Scouts Am., 1943. C.L.U. Mem. Phila. Assn. Life Underwriters, Nat. Def. Exec. Res., Order of Arrow (asso. mem.), Cath. Guild for Blind, St. Joseph's Coll. Alumni (treas., v.p. evening div. 1953-54), Am. Legion, V.F.W., Greater Phila. C. of C. (mem. tax, manpower resources coms. 1966-67, mem. com. on higher edn. 1969-70), U.S. Naval Inst., Nat. Assn. Security Dealers, Phila. Estate Planning Council, Million Dollar Round Table. Home: 37 W Golf View Rd Merion Golf Manor Havertown PA 19083 Office: 116 Strafford Bldg Wayne PA 19087 also 127 John St New York NY

SULLIVAN, LAWRENCE WILLIAM, ins. exec.; b. Boston, Dec. 3, 1930; s. James Jordan and Mary Elizabeth (Killeen) S.; A.B., Boston Coll., 1952, J.D., 1958; m. Ruth M. Nagle, May 4, 1955; children—Lauren J., Kendra J., Marcia J., Christopher J. Adjuster Travelers Ins. Co., Boston, 1955-59; admitted to Mass. bar, 1958; claims mgr. Nat. Union Ins. Co., Albany, N.Y., 1959-62; claims supr. Hartford Accident & Indemnity Co., Boston, 1962-63; atty., risk mgr. H.P. Hood Inc., Boston, 1963-76; v.p. Corroon & Black of Mass., Inc., Boston, 1976-81, pres., chief exec. officer, 1981—; teaching staff Ins. Inst. Am.; participant ednl. seminars in field. Served to 1st lt. USMC, 1952-54. Lic. ins. broker, ins. adv., atty. Mass. and fed. cts. Mem. Mass. Bar Assn., Boston Bar Assn., Risk & Ins. Mgmt. Soc. Mass. (pres. 1970-71). Roman Catholic. Office: Corroon & Black of Mass Inc 99 High St Boston MA 02110

SULLIVAN, MARK DAVID, communications co. exec., producer; b. Chgo., Dec. 2, 1934; s. John Martin and Amelia Marie (Stauder) S.; B.A., Northwestern U., 1958. Various exec. positions Jack Morton Prodns., Inc., producers, Dallas and Chgo., 1959-64; v.p., gen. mgr., producer Michael John Assos., Inc., N.Y.C., 1965-66; ind. producer, cons., Dallas and N.Y.C., 1962-71; exec. producer Wilding div. Bell and Howell Co., Detroit, 1971-75, Sandy Corp., Detroit, 1975-78, Jack Morton Prodns., Inc., N.Y.C., 1978-80; pres., producer Mark D. Sullivan, Inc., N.Y.C., 1980—. Served with AUS, 1954-57. Named Alumnus of Year, Phi Kappa Psi N.Y. Alumni Assn., 1971. Mem. Actors Equity Assn., Hotel Sales Mgmt. Assn., Meeting Planners Internat., Phi Kappa Psi (nat. pres. 1972-74, Quarter Century Commn. 1975-78; North Tex. pres. 1960-61, 63-65; N.Y. chmn. bd. 1970-71, pres. 1968-70 alumni assns.). Club: N.Y. Athletic. Home: 123 E 54th St New York NY 10022

SULLIVAN, MICHAEL EVAN, investment and mgmt. co. exec.; b. Phila., Dec. 30, 1940; s. Albert and Ruth (Liebert) S.; B.S., N.Mex. State U., 1966, M.A. (Ednl. Research Tng. Program fellow), 1967; B.S., U. Tex., 1969; M.B.A., U. Houston, 1974; M.S., U. So. Calif., 1976, M.P.A., 1977, postgrad., 1980—; B.S. in Acctg., U. La Verne, 1981; m. Marilyn Billimek, Dec. 15, 1974. Sr. analyst Houston Lighting & Power Co., 1969-74; electronics engr. U.S. Govt., Point Mugu, Calif., 1974-77; mem. tech. staff Hughes Aircraft Co., El Segundo, Calif., 1977-78; staff program adminstr. Ventura div. Northrop Corp., Newbury Park, Calif., 1978-79; div. head engring. div. Navastrogru Co., Point Mugu, 1979—; pres., chmn. bd. Diversified Mgmt. Systems, Inc., Camarillo, Calif., 1978—. Served with U.S. Army, 1958-62. Ednl. Research Info. Clearing House fellow, 1965-67. Mem. Am. Math. Soc., Math. Assn. Am., Am. Statis. Assn., Am. Soc. Public Adminstrn., Math. Assn. Am., Am. Personnel and Guidance Assn., Mcpl. Mgmt. Assts. So. Calif., Phi Kappa Phi, Pi Gamma Mu. Home: PO Box 273 Port Hueneme CA 93041 Office: Navastrogru Co Point Mugu CA 93042

SULLIVAN, PAUL DAVID, mktg. and mgmt. cons.; b. Boston, Dec. 26, 1932; s. John Joseph and Margaret Elizabeth (Tobin) S.; B.S. in Bus. Adminstrn., Boston Coll., 1954; M.B.A., 1964; m. Thomasina P. McKeon, June 11, 1960; children—Neal, Gregory, Paula, Stephen, Maura, Christine. Sales mgr. New Eng. Indsl. Chem., Inc., Watertown, Mass., 1956-59; product mgr. Nat. Radio Co. div. Nat. Co., Melrose, Mass., 1959-67; mktg. mgr. Metal Bellows Co. div. Zurn Industries, Sharon, Mass., 1967-75; pres. New Eng. Research & Mktg., Inc., Wellesley, Mass., 1975—; dir. John R. Hess & Sons, Inc., Cranston, R.I.; condr. indsl. mktg. seminars President's Assn. div. Am. Mgmt. Assn. Served with U.S. Army, 1954-56. Mem. Am. Mktg. Assn. (lectr. indsl. products group 1979—), Instrument Soc. Am., Semiconductor Equipment and Materials Inst., Inc. Home: 28 Grandhill Dr Dover MA 02030 Office: 40 Grove St Wellesley MA 02181

SULLIVAN, PHILIP JAMES, JR., newspaper advt. exec.; b. Manchester, Conn., June 28, 1947; s. Philip James and Ann Sullivan; B.S. in Mktg., U. Conn., 1969; m. Marilyn Welch, Oct. 8, 1977; 1 dau., Erin Margaret. Advt. account exec. Hartford (Conn.) Courant, 1970-75, travel promotion mgr., 1975-78, nat. advt. mgr., 1978-79, retail advt. mgr., 1979—. Mem. Nat. Retail Mchts. Assn., Advt. Club Greater Hartford. Democrat. Roman Catholic. Office: 285 Broad St Hartford CT 06115

SULLIVAN, RAYMOND CHARLES, banker; b. Bklyn., Jan. 9, 1947; s. Francis Xavier and Herminia (Montero) S.; B.A., St. Francis Coll., Bklyn., 1968; M.S., CCNY, 1975; M.B.A., Fordham U., 1978;

C.A.G.S., Pace U., 1980; m. Pilar Punsoda, May 27, 1973; 1 son, Charles Alexander. Ops. officer Banco Popular, N.Y.C., 1972-74; br. mgr. United Americas Bank, N.Y.C., 1974-76; asst. treas. East River Savs. Bank, N.Y.C., 1976—. Active local Boy Scouts Am. Served as officer USN, 1969-72; lt. comdr. Res. Recipient Franciscan Spirit award St. Francis Coll., 1968. Mem. N.Y. State Soc. C.P.A. Candidates, Naval Res. Assn., Res. Officers Assn. Home: 24 Regent Circle Staten Island NY 10312 Office: 26 Cortlandt St New York NY 10007

SULLIVAN, THOMAS CHRISTOPHER, coatings mfg. co. exec.; b. Cleve., July 8, 1937; s. Frank Charles and Margaret Mary (Wilhelmy) S.; B.S., Miami U., Oxford, Ohio, 1959; m. Sandra Simmons, Mar. 12, 1960; children—Frank, Sean, Tommy, Danny, Kathleen, Julie. Divisional sales mgr. Republic Powdered Metals Co., Cleve., 1961-65, exec. v.p., 1965-70; chmn. bd. RPM, Inc., Medina, Ohio, 1971—, pres., 1971-78, also dir.; dir. Overly-Hautz Co., Cleve., Gen. Telephone of Ohio. Bd. dirs. Culver Ednl. Found. Served to lt. (j.g.) USNR, 1959-61. Mem. Nat. Paint and Coatings Assn. (dir.), Young Presidents Orgn., Nat. Assn. Securities Dealers (adv. com.), Culver Legion (pres. 1975). Roman Catholic. Home: 18897 N Valley Dr Fairview Park OH 44126 Office: RPM Inc 2628 Pearl Rd Medina OH 44256

SULLIVAN, WARREN GERALD, diversified industry exec.; b. Chgo., Sept. 8, 1923; s. Gerald Joseph and Marie (Fairrington) S.; A.B., U. Ill., 1947; student U. Wis., 1943; J.D., Northwestern U., 1950; m. Helen Ruth Young, Aug. 21, 1948 (div. May 1974); children—Janet Marie, Warren Douglas, William Carroll; m. 2d, H. Louise Curtis, July 27, 1974. Admitted to Ill. bar, 1950, Conn. bar, 1971; lawyer Ill. Dept. Revenue, Chgo., 1950-52; mem. firm Naphin, Sullivan & Banta, Chgo., 1952-69; asst. gen. counsel labor, v.p. adminstrn. and personnel Avco Corp., Greenwich, Conn., 1969-75; v.p. indsl. relations Gen. Dynamics Corp., St. Louis, 1975—; dir. Asbestos Corp. Ltd., Montreal, Que., Can., Stromberg-Carlson Corp., Tampa, Fla. lectr. Chgo. Bar Assn., 1956-69, U. Wis. Mgmt. Inst., 1964-65. Bd. dirs. YMCA, United Way. Served with AUS, Mil. Intelligence Service, 1942-45; ETO. Mem. Am., Conn., Chgo. (vice chmn. labor law com. 1964-65, chmn. 1966-69) bar assns., Am. Judicature Soc., Indsl. Relations Soc., NAM (chmn. exec. adv. com. 1978), Am. Soc. Personnel Adminstrs., Econ. Club Chgo., Delta Tau Delta, Phi Delta Phi. Clubs: St. Louis; Bellerive Country. Contbr. articles to profl. jours. Home: Rt 1 2482 Indian Tree Run Glencoe MO 63038 Office: Pierre Laclede Center Saint Louis MO 63105

SULLY, BRUCE ALLENBY, road machinery mfr.; b. Winnipeg, Man., Can., Mar. 21, 1926; s. John Alfred and Elodie (Milks) S.; student pvt. sch.; m. Isabel Jean Marshall, Mar. 19, 1976; children—Robin Lynn, Mark Allenby, Michael Alexander; stepchildren—Keith John Hopkinson, Anne Janette Tafeit, Jane Ruth Sager. With Champion Road Machinery Ltd., 1946—, v.p., 1967-68, pres., 1968-79, chmn. bd., 1979—, also dir.; with Champion Road Machinery Sales Ltd., 1946—, sales mgr., 1953-59, v.p., 1960-61, chmn. bd., 1979—, pres., 1962-79; chmn. bd., chief exec. officer Champion Road Machinery Group Ltd.; pres. Rosny Corp. Ltd., Bus. Air Services Ltd., Champion Road Machinery Internat. Corp.; chmn. bd. GEARCO Ltd., Comdr. Air Charter Ltd.; dir. C & C Yachts Ltd. Regional dir. London Symphony Orch.; hon. bd. dirs. Huron Country Playhouse; town councillor, Goderich, Ont., 1958; bd. govs., regional pres. Dominion Drama Festival; bd. dirs. Shaw Festival Found. Served with RCAF, 1943-45, Canadian Army, 1945-46. Mem. Ont. C. of C. (dir.). Home: 5 Cobourg St Goderich ON Canada Office: Maitland Rd Goderich ON Canada

SULZBERGER, ARTHUR OCHS, newspaper exec.; b. N.Y.C., Feb. 5, 1926; s. Arthur Hays and Iphigene (Ochs) S.; B.A., Columbia, 1951; m. Barbara Grant, July 2, 1948 (div. 1956); children—Arthur Ochs, Karen Alden; m. 2d, Carol Fox, Dec. 19, 1956; children—Cynthia Fox, Cathy Jean (adopted). With N.Y. Times Co., N.Y.C, 1951—, now chmn., chief exec. officer and pub., also dir.; chmn. bd. Golf Digest; dir. Times Printing Co., Chattanooga, Gaspesia Pulp & Paper Co., Ltd., Toronto, Ont., Can. Life trustee Columbia U.; trustee Met. Mus. Art; bd. dirs. N.Y. Conv. and Visitors Bur., Center for Inter-Am. Relations. Served to capt. USMCR World War II; Korea. Mem. S.A.R. Clubs: Overseas Press, Explorers (N.Y.C.); Metropolitan (Washington): Century Country (Purchase, N.Y.). Office: 229 W 43d St New York NY 10036

SULZBY, JAMES FREDERICK, JR., realty co. exec.; b. Birmingham, Ala., Dec. 24, 1905; s. James Frederick and Annie (Dobbins) S.; student Howard Coll., Birmingham, 1925-26; A.B., Birmingham-So. Coll., 1928; grad. Am. Inst. Banking, 1934; Litt.D., Athens Coll.; m. Martha Belle Hilton, Nov. 9, 1935; children—James Frederick III, Martha Hilton (Mrs. Robert J.B. Clark). In trust dept. First Nat. Bank of Birmingham, 1929-43; pres. Sulzby Realty Co., 1943—; dir. Home Fed. Savs. and Loan Assn. Dir. Birmingham Area Bd. Realtors, 1948-49, sec., treas., 1948-49, v.p., 1951-52, pres., 1953; past pres. Ala. Bd. Realtors; dir. Nat. Assn. Real Estate Bds., 1952-56. Mem. adv. com. Athens Coll. Chmn., Birmingham Planning Commn., 1948-52; pres. Norwood Gardens, Inc., housing project; mem. Jefferson County Area Planning and Devel. Adv. Bd.; mem. Jefferson County Hist. Commn.; treas. Birmingham Area Ednl. TV, Inc.; mem. Jefferson County Personnel Bd., 1953-56; dir. Ala. Bapt. publ., 1945—; deacon, treas. Southside Bapt. Ch.; historian 75th Anniversary celebration for Birmingham, 1946; pres. Ala. Bapt. Young Peoples Union, 1932-33; trustee Rushton Lectures; bd. govs. Civic Theatre of Birmingham, 1946-48; chmn. Edn. Com., C. of C., 1949-53; mem. humanities advising council Auburn U. Recipient Lit. award Ala. Library Assn., 1962. Mem. Newcomen Soc. N.Am., Ala. Hist. Assn. (pres. 1947-49, sec., 1950—), Ala. Bapt. Hist. Soc., Birmingham Sunday Sch. Council (pres. 1960-61, chmn. exec. com. 1962-64), Birmingham Hist. Soc. (sec. 1940-50, trustee 1950—), Birmingham Civic Symphony Assn. (trustee), Ala. Acad. Sci. (past chmn. bd. trustees, pres. 1965-66), Jefferson County Nat. Found. Infantile Paralysis (chmn. 1951-53), Am. Planning and Civic Assn. (dir.), Ala. Writers Conclave (v.p. 1949, pres. 1950-51), Phi Beta Kappa, Phi Alpha Theta, Delta Sigma Phi, Omicron Delta Kappa. Author: Birmingham As It Was in Jackson County, 1944; Birmingham Sketches, 1945; Annals of the Southside Baptist Church, 1947; Historic Alabama Hotels and Resorts, 1960; Arthur W. Smith, A Birmingham Pioneer, 1855-1944. Democrat. Baptist. Home: 3121 Carlisle Rd Birmingham AL 35213 Office: 1019 Massey Bldg Birmingham AL 35203

SUMMER, VIRGIL CLIFTON, utility exec.; b. Spartanburg, S.C., Aug. 21, 1920; s. Virgil and Lula Maude (Tiner) S.; student mech. engring. and mgmt. Internat. Corr. Sch., 1949; M.S. in Engring., U. S.C., 1968; LL.D. (hon.), Newberry Coll., 1978; m. Vera Ellen Boland, Nov. 2, 1944; children—Brenda Summer Nunamaker, Michael, Kenneth. With S.C. Electric & Gas Co., Columbia, 1937—, asst. plant supt., 1953-55, supt. hydro Saluda Dam, 1955-58, plant supt., 1958-60, supt. prodn., 1960-62, mgr. prodn. ops., 1962-66, v.p. elec. ops. and engring., 1966-67, sr. v.p. ops., 1967-77, pres., chief operating officer, 1977-79, pres., chief exec. officer, 1979—, also dir.; dir. S.C. Nat. Bank, Southeastern Elec. Exchange. Vice-pres., United Way of Midlands; past chmn. Richland-Lexington Counties Commn. Tech. Edn.; bd. dirs. Columbia Urban League, Lexington County Hosp. Edn. Found. Served with USN, 1944-46. S.C. Electric & Gas Co. nuclear sta. named in his honor. Mem. ASME, Nat. Soc. Profl. Engrs. Lutheran. Clubs: Mid-Carolina, Palmetto, Summit, Masons. Home: 122 Holly Ridge Ln West Columbia SC 29169 Office: 320 Main St Columbia SC 29218

SUMMERLIN, GLENN WOOD, advt. agy. exec.; b. Dallas, Ga., Apr. 1, 1934; s. Glenn Wood and Flora (Barrett) S.; student Ga. Inst. Tech., 1951-52; B.B.A., Ga. State U., 1956, M.B.A., 1967; m. Anne Valley, Oct. 16, 1971; children—Glenn Wood III, Edward Lee, Wade Hampton. Prodn. mgr. Fred Worrill Advt., Atlanta, 1956-65; v.p. sales Grizzard Advt., Atlanta, 1965-74, pres., 1974—. Vice chmn. Polaris dist. Boy Scouts Am., 1967. Vice chmn. Ga. State U. Found., 1974; chmn. distributive edn. adv. com. DeKalb Coll., 1974-76; bd. founders Geo. M. Sparks Scholarship Fund; bd. dirs. Atlanta Humane Soc., 1971—, treas., 1973, 80. Recipient C.S. Bolen award So. Council Indsl. Editors, 1967; named Outstanding Young Man in DeKalb County, DeKalb Jaycees, 1967, Alumnus of Year, Ga. State U., 1973. Mem. Direct Mail Mktg. Assn. (Direct Mail Spokesman award 1973), Mail Advt. Service Assn. (pres. N.Ga. chpt. 1959-60), Ga. Assn. Bus. Communicators (pres. 1966-67), Am. Mktg. Assn. (pres. Atlanta chpt. 1973-74), Ga. State U. Alumni Assn. (pres. 1971-72, dir. 1966-78), Sales and Mktg. Execs. Atlanta (dir. 1969-71), Ga. Bus. and Industry Assn. (bd. govs. 1974-76), Asso. Mail Advt. Agys. (pres. 1975-77), Southeastern Arms Collectors Assn., Ga. Arms Collectors Assn. (dir. 1974-76, Pres.'s award 1973), Tenn. Gun Collectors Assn., Tex. Gun Collectors Assn., Assn. Am. Sword Collectors (charter), Mensa, Co. of Mil. Historians, Confederate Hist. Assn. Belgium, Civil War Round Table, Council Abandoned Mil. Outposts, Omicron Delta Kappa. Home: 1133 Ragley Hall Rd NE Atlanta GA 30319 Office: 1144 Mailing Ave SE Atlanta GA 30315

SUMMERS, CHRISTINE MARY, fin. exec.; b. Chgo., Nov. 28, 1951; d. John T. and Helen W. (Ambrozik) Soch; B.S.C., DePaul U., 1973, M.B.A., 1975; m. Patrick J. Summers, June 3, 1979. Staff acct. Continental Ill. Nat. Bank, Chgo., 1973, sr. corporate acct., 1975, sr. acct., 1976, acctg. officer, 1977, mgr. corp. reporting, 1979—, mem. acctg. policy com., interviewer Coll. Relations Bd., 1978-79. Mem. Nat. Assn. Bank Women, Am. Soc. Women Accts. (pres.). Home: 647 Bryan St Elmhurst IL 60126 Office: 231 S LaSalle St Chicago IL 60693

SUMMERS, RICHARD GRANVILLE, real estate broker; b. St. Louis, Sept. 2, 1931; B.S., Princeton, 1952; M. Aero Engring., Cornell U., 1953; m. Patricia Carol Wilmes, June 17, 1952; children—Richard, Jr., Barbara Diane, Carolyn Downey, David Christopher. Sr. engr. Chance Vought Aircraft, Dallas, 1953-54; project engr. Temco Aircraft Corp., Dallas, 1956-58; program engr. Martin Marietta Corp., Denver, 1958-68, mgr., Washington, 1968-74; real estate broker James A. Barker & Assos., Washington, 1974-77; owner, real estate broker R.G. Summers & Co., Washington, 1978—; instr. N.M. A. & M., Las Cruces, 1956. Com. chmn. Boy Scouts Am., Littleton, Colo., 1967-68. Served with AUS, 1954-56. Mem. Sigma Xi. Club: Princeton (N.J.) Quadrangle. Home: 5249 Strathmore Ave Kensington MD 20850 Office: 8150 Leesburg Pike Suite 600 Vienna VA 22180

SUMMERSON, GEORGE WILLIAM, hotel exec.; b. Richmond, Va., Nov. 18, 1903; s. George Ralph and Eula Mead (Ford) S.; B.S., Washington and Lee U., 1927; m. Champe Grant, Dec. 24, 1932; children—Champe (Mrs. Don Hyatt), Sue (Mrs. Irvin Wells III), George William. Gen. auditor Robert E. Lee Hotel, Winston-Salem, N.C., 1929-35; mgr. Washington Duke Hotel, Durham, N.C., 1935-39; gen. mgr. Hotel Gen. Shelby, Hotel Bristol (Va.), 1939-56; pres., gen. mgr. Martha Washington Inn, Abingdon, Va., 1956-80. Pres. Bristol Community Chest, 1950-51, Washington County United Fund, 1964-65; mem. state adv. com. Salvation Army, 1972—, vice chmn. divisional adv. bd., 1973-75. Mayor, mem. City Council, Bristol, 1951-57; vice mayor, mem. Town Council, Abingdon, Va., 1968-70, 71—, mayor, 1972-78. Bd. visitors Sullins Coll., Bristol, Va., 1972-76; bd. dirs., exec. com. Mt. Rogers Planning Commn., 1969—, chmn., 1973-74; mem. Va. Statewide Health Coordinating Council, 1977-81. Recipient Bristol's Outstanding Citizen award V.F.W., 1953; City of Bristol Pub. Service Recognition award, 1954-56; Bristol Centennial Celebration award, 1956; Distinguished Service award Hotel-Motel Greeters, 1969, Va. Hotel-Motel Assn., 1971. Mem. Am. Hotel and Motel Assn. (trustee ednl. inst. 1958-78, pres. inst. 1967-69), Am. (dir. 1949), Va. (pres. 1948), So. (pres. 1952) hotel assns., Hotel Greeters (chpt. pres. 1932), Bristol C. of C. (pres. 1952), Va. Travel Council (pres. 1950-51, outstanding service citation 1952), Abingdon C. of C. (pres. 1959-60), Va. State C. of C. (certificate appreciation 1961, v.p. 1969-71, dir. 1960, 62, 67, 69, 70). Methodist (chmn. adminstrv. bd. 1966-69, lay leader 1970-72). Mason (Shriner), Kiwanian. Club: Glenrochie Country (pres. 1961) (Abingdon). Home: 286 Arlington Ave Bristol VA 24201

SUMNER, GEORGE CLAIBORNE, mfg. co. exec.; b. Potosi, Tex., Oct. 6, 1921; s. Charles L. and Emmie (Harris) S.; B.S., Tex. A. and M. U., 1942; M.S., M.I.T., 1949; M.B.A., Tex. Christian U., 1973; Ph.D., U. Tex., 1979; m. Sue White, Jan. 6, 1963; children—Patrick, Evelyn, Nancy, Stephanie. Research staff Mass. Inst. Tech., 1947-50; mgr. support systems Gen. Dynamics Corp., Fort Worth, 1950—. Served with U.S. Army, 1942-46. Registered profl. engr., Tex.; C.P.A., Tex. Mem. IEEE, Nat. Mgmt. Assn. (chpt. pres. 1975-76), Aerospace Electronics Systems Soc. (bd. govs. 1975—, nat. sec. 1975-76, v.p. 1977-78), Sigma Xi, Beta Gamma Sigma. Methodist. Home: 4000 Harlanwood Dr Fort Worth TX 76109 Office: Box 749 Fort Worth TX 76102

SUMNER, GEORGE WILSON, JR., investment banker; b. Honolulu, May 7, 1927; s. George Wilson and Eva (Focke) S.; B.S., U.S. Naval Acad., 1949; m. Bebe Moody, Aug. 29, 1952; children—Elizabeth Hyde, George Wilson, III. Dir. personnel AMFAC, Honolulu, 1962; account exec. Dean Witter, Honolulu, 1962-67; v.p. Blyth & Co., Honolulu, 1967-71; asst. v.p. E. F. Hutton & Co., Honolulu, 1972—. Bd. dirs. Hawaii Visitors Bur., 1960-62; pres. Bishop Museum Assn., Honolulu, 1969-70, Kaui Keolani Children's Hosp., Honolulu, 1973-76; dir. at large, exec. com. Am. Cancer Soc., N.Y.C., 1977—. Served with USN, 1945-52. Recipient Distinguished Service award Am. Cancer Soc., 1974. Mem. Investment Soc. Hawaii (pres. 1971-72). Episcopalian. Clubs: Oahu Country, Waialae Country, Plaza Court, Honolulu. Home: 3805 Old Pali Rd Honolulu HI 96817 Office: 700 Bishop St Suite 100 Honolulu HI 96813

SUMNERS, WILLIAM GLENN, JR., lawyer; b. Pueblo, Colo., Feb. 23, 1928; s. William Glenn and Ruth (Carmody) S.; B.A., U. Colo., 1952; M.A., Colo. Sch. Mines, 1953; LL.B., U. Denver, 1954; m. Phyllis Aileen Long, June 10, 1961; 1 son, William Glenn. Admitted to Colo. bar, 1954, since practiced in Denver; instr. U. Denver, 1963; dir. various corps.; judge City and County of Denver, 1961-62. Trustee, Rocky Mt. Mineral Law Inst., 1963—. Served with U.S. Army, 1944-47. Mem. Colo. Mining Assn. (pres. 1977), Internat. Bar Assn., Am. Bar Assn., Colo. Bar Assn., Denver Bar Assn., Rocky Mountain Oil and Gas Assn., Rocky Mountain Assn. Geologists, Internat. Assn. Ins. Counsel. Republican. Episcopalian. Home: 612 Race Denver CO 80206 Office: 1600 Broadway Denver CO 80202

SUMNICHT, FRANCIS HENRY, learning innovation center exec.; b. Appleton, Wis., Dec. 25, 1921; s. Henry August and Rose Marie (Honeck) S.; B.S., Marquette U., 1948; m. Patricia Beth Gambsky, Feb. 4, 1964; children—Nancy Lee, Vern, Christopher, Shawn, Eric, Heidi. Advt. and display mgr. Sears Roebuck, Appleton, 1948-51; sec., founder Advance Industries Inc., electronics, Appleton, 1951-70; postmaster, Appleton, 1956-72; sec., founder A-1 Builders, Inc., Appleton, 1954—; partner Sumnicht Supply Co., Appleton, 1951-71; pres., dir. Children's Learning Innovation Center, Inc., Appleton, 1973—; Amway direct distbr. Mem. East Central Wis. Regional Planning Commn., 1974-75; treas. History Alive Inc., hist. mus. found., 1973—; co-founder nat. Pray for Peace movement, 1948. Sec., Outagamie County Republican Com., 1951-55; Wis. chmn. Young Republicans, 1952. Bd. dirs. Sumnicht Charitable Found., 1968—, Outagamie County Hist. Soc., 1948—. Served with USCGR, 1942-46. Mem. Am. Mgmt. Assn., Soc. Advancement Mgmt. (regional v.p. 1971-74), Am. Soc. Personnel Adminstrn., VFW, Am. Legion, Catholic War Vets. Clubs: K.C.; Butte des Morts Country. Home: 325 W Michigan St Appleton WI 54911 Office: 319 W Michigan St Appleton WI 54911

SUMPTER, CURTIS ALVAH, lawyer, banker; b. Floyd, Va., Apr. 9, 1908; s. James Hardee, Sr., and Addie (Harman) S.; B.S., Roanoke Coll., 1929; LL.B., U. Va., 1948. Admitted to Va. bar, 1948; Commonwealth's atty. Floyd County, Va., 1952-75, also counsel Bank of Floyd, 1958—, pres., 1970—. Served with USAAF, 1942-46. Home: Floyd VA 24091 Office: PO Box 85 Floyd VA 24091

SUMRELL, GENE, research chemist; b. Apache, Ariz., Oct. 7, 1919; s. Joe B. and Dixie (Hughes) S.; B.A., Eastern N.Mex. U., 1942; B.S., U. N.Mex., 1947, M.S., 1948; Ph.D., U. Calif. at Berkeley, 1951. Asst. prof. chemistry Eastern N.Mex. U., 1951-53; sr. research chemist J. T. Baker Chem. Co., Phillipsburg, N.J., 1953-58; sr. organic chemist Southwest Research Inst., San Antonio, 1958-59; project leader Food Machinery & Chem. Corp., Balt., 1959-61; research sect. leader El Paso Natural Gas Products Co. (Tex.), 1961-64; project leader So. utilization research and devel. div. U.S. Dept. Agr., New Orleans, 1964-67, investigations head, 1967-73, research leader Oil Seed and Food Lab., So. Regional Research Center, 1973—. Served from pvt. to staff sgt. AUS, 1942-46. Mem. Am. Chem. Soc., A.A.A.S., N.Y. Acad. Scis., Am. Inst. Chemists, Am. Oil Chemists Soc., Am. Assn. Textile Chemists and Colorists, Research Soc. Am., Phi Kappa Phi, Sigma Xi. Home: PO Box 24037 New Orleans LA 70184 Office: 1100 Robert E Lee Blvd New Orleans LA 70179

SUNDERLAND, DAVID KENDALL, real estate developer; b. Detroit, Mar. 25, 1930; s. Maurice Briggs and Helen (Bell) S.; B.A., Dartmouth Coll., 1952; postgrad. U. Mich. Sch. Bus. Adminstrn., 1956-58, Gen. Motors Inst., 1955-56; m. Brooke Williams, Sept. 13, 1975; children—Mark, Caryn, Matthew, Tracy. Fin. analyst Chevrolet div. Gen. Motors Corp., Detroit, 1955-58; budget mgr. Raytheon Co., Andover/Bedford, Mass., 1958-61, div. controller, Oxnard, Calif., 1961-64; v.p. Janss Corp., Los Angeles, 1964-68; pres. Gates Land Co., Colorado Springs, Colo., 1968—. Bd. regents U. Colo., 1978—; bd. dirs. St. Francis Hosp., Colorado Springs, 1973-78. Served in USN, 1952-55. Named Colorado Springs Builder of Yr., 1975; recipient Colo. Builders Disting. Service award, 1977. Mem. Colorado Springs C. of C. (dir. 1974-77), Nat. Assn. Home Builders, Urban Land Inst. Republican. Club: Country of Colo. Office: 155 W Lake Ave Colorado Springs CO 80906

SUNG, C.B., multi-industry co. exec.; b. Shanghai, China, Feb. 1, 1925; s. Tsing-Ching and Hsu-Ying (Ma) S.; B.S., Chiao-Tung U., China, 1945; M.S., Mass. Inst. Tech., 1948; M.B.A., Harvard, 1950; m. Beulah C.H. Kwok, June 4, 1953; children—Dean, Wingate. Came to U.S., 1947; naturalized, 1954. From engr. to dept. chief Nanking-Shanghai Ry. Systems Adminstrn., China, 1945-47; devel. engr. instrumentation Ruge-de Forest, Inc., 1950-52; engr. research labs. Bendix Corp., 1952-62, asst. gen. mgr., 1962-64, gen. mgr., dir., 1964-67, corporate v.p. engring. and research, Detroit, 1967-69, v.p., group exec. advanced tech. group, Southfield, Mich., 1969-72, v.p., group exec. advanced concepts group, 1972-74; pres., chief exec. officer CMA Inc., Cleve., 1974-78; chmn. bd. Airborne Mfg. Co., Elyria, Ohio, 1975-79; chief exec. officer Etec Corp., Hayward, Calif., 1977-79; pres., chief exec. officer E-S Pacific Corp., San Bruno, Calif.; chmn. bd. Cleve. Controls, Inc., 1978—, Tronco, Inc., 1979—, Am. Semicondr., Inc., 1979—; dir. Codata Corp., Varo, Inc., Unison Internat.; cons. in field. Mem. vis. com. Engring. Coll. U. Mich., Carnegie-Mellon U., Oakland U. Mem. Am. Mgmt. Assn., Soc. Automotive Engrs., Sigma Xi. Patentee in field. Home: 2 Bratenahl Pl Cleveland OH 44108 Office: 1200 Bayhill Dr Suite 220 San Bruno CA 94066

SURDAM, ROBERT MCCLELLAN, banker; b. Albany, N.Y., Oct. 28, 1917; s. I. Burke and LeMoyne (McClellan) S.; B.A. cum laude, Williams Coll., 1939; m. Mary Caroline Buhl, July 8, 1946; children—Peter Buhl, Robert McClellan, Mary Caroline. With Nat. Bank of Detroit, 1947—, v.p., 1954-60, sr. v.p., 1960-64, exec. v.p., 1964-66, pres., chief exec. officer, dir., 1966-72, chmn., chief exec. officer, 1972—; dir. Bundy Corp., Burroughs Corp., Internat. Bank Detroit, Bank Tokyo Internat. Ltd. Mem. Assn. Res. City Bankers. Home: 396 Provencal Rd Grosse Pointe Farms MI 48236 Office: PO Box 116 RPA Detroit MI 48232

SURDOVAL, DONALD JAMES, financial exec.; b. N.Y.C., Aug. 26, 1932; s. Donald J. and Catherine A. (Slevin) S.; B.B.A., Manhattan Coll., 1954; m. Patricia Fitzpatrick, May 28, 1955; children—Donald, Lisa, John, Catherine, Brian. Mgr., Touche Ross & Co., 1956-63; treas. Mohican Corp., 1963-65; asst. controller, then v.p., controller Litton Industries, 1965-68; v.p., controller Norton Simon Inc., 1968—; dir. Fuller O'Brien Paint Co. Bd. dirs. Calvary Hosp., N.Y.C. Served to 1st lt. USMCR, 1954-56. C.P.A., N.Y. Mem. Financial Execs. Inst. Club: Hackensack Golf. Home: 87 Winding Way Woodcliff Lake NJ 07675 Office: 277 Park Ave New York NY 10017

SURDOVAL, LAWRENCE ANTHONY, JR., consulting co. exec.; b. Pitts., Sept. 10, 1930; s. Lawrence A. and Pearl E. Surdoval; B.S. in Accounting, Robert Morris Coll., 1954; B.S. in Econs., Duquesne U., 1962; M.P.E., U. Pitts., 1964; children—Nancy Jo, Robert James, Wayne Alan. Sec., Richard King Mellon Found., Pitts., 1959-71; treas. Allegheny Found., Pitts., 1959-68; adminstrv. officer, treas. Sarah Mellon Scaife Found., Pitts., 1971-76; pres. Philanthropic Consultants, Inc., Pitts., 1977—, Nemacolin Inc., 1979—; lectr. on exempt orgns. Vice pres. Family and Children's Service, 1958-76; sec. Whitehall Planning Commn., 1960-79; bd. visitors Sch. Social Work, U. Pitts., 1976—. Served with USMC, 1952-54. Recipient Civic Service award Allegheny County, 1968. Mem. Nat. Assn. Bus. Economists, Internat. Food and Wine Assn., Pitts. Econs. Club, Am. Legion (past post comdr.). Methodist. Clubs: South Hills Country, Duquesne, Press, U.S. Army Officers. Home: 4613 Rolling Hills Rd Pittsburgh PA 15236 Office: Suite Six East Three Gateway Center Pittsburgh PA 15222

SURVAL, HENRY, advt. exec.; b. N.Y.C., Aug. 11, 1929; s. Morris S. and Celia (Karlin) S.; B.S., N.Y. U., 1951, M.A., 1954; m. Claire Abramson, July 1, 1951; children—Miriam Ann, Marcia Diane. Faculty asst. econs. N.Y. U., 1951-52; economist Boni, Watkin,

Mounteer & Co., N.Y.C., 1952-55; with William Esty Advt. Co., N.Y.C., 1955—, v.p., dir. mktg. info. dept., 1971-79, sr. v.p., dir. mktg. and research info. services, 1980—. Bd. dirs. L.I. Cons. Center, 1978—; trustee L.I. Inst. Mental Health, 1980—. Mem. Am. Mktg. Assn., Futures Soc., Chautauqua Soc. Club: K.P. Home: 3424 82d St New York NY 11372 Office: 100 E 42d St New York NY 10017

SUSSKIND, SIEGFRIED, elec. mfg. co. exec.; b. Nuremberg, Gemany, Nov. 27, 1919; s. Maurice and Frieda (Schmal) S.; B.S., Lycele Janson de Sailly, Paris, 1936; E.E., Ecole superieur d'electricite, Paris, 1938; m. Gisela Baer, July 6, 1941; children—M. Roy, Joyce Renee (Mrs. James R. Hancock). Vice pres. Waldorf Instrument Corp., Huntington, N.Y., 1952-59; pres. Intruments Systems Corp., Westbury, N.Y., 1959-63; pres. Omnivend Corp. (merged with Matrix), Hicksville, N.Y., 1964-65, Matrix Research & Devel. Corp. (merged with Eastern Air Devices), Nashua, N.H., 1965-69; pres., chief exec. officer Electro Audio Dynamics, Inc. (formerly Eastern Air Devices, Inc.), Dover, N.H. and Great Neck, N.Y., 1966—; also dir.; chmn. bd., dir. Infinity. Systems, Inc.; dir. Peerless Fabrikkerne, Copenhagen, Denmark, Etablissements Bretton, Cluses, France. Home: Feeks Ln Locust Valley NY 11560 Office: 98 Cutter Mill Rd Great Neck NY 11021

SUSSMAN, SALLY BRAGINSKY, contractor; b. Copenhagen, Denmark, May 21, 1911; d. Max and Esther (Bunenova) Braginsky; came to U.S., 1917, naturalized, 1942; student N.Y. U., 1953, Queens Coll., 1964, Cooper Union Coll., 1967; m. Max Sussman, Feb. 21, 1932 (dec. 1952); children—Marvin, Gerald, Stephen. Pres. Greater N.Y. York Air Conditioning Co., Inc., 1950; pres. Greater N.Y. Mech. Contractors, Inc., N.Y.C., 1967—. Recipient award for achievement Gen. Electric Inst., 1955, Recognition award Carrier Co., 1965. Mem. Soc. Women Engrs. (life), L.I. Bldg. Congress, Mech. Contractors N.Y., Bldg. Trades Employers' Assn. N.Y., Syossit Bus. and Profl. Womens Club L.I. (pres. 1968), Hicksville C. of C. (treas. 1966-69), L.I. Assn. Commerce and Industry. Home: 58-59 206th St Bayside NY 11364

SUSSMAN, STANLEY, cosmetic co. exec.; b. N.Y.C., June 4, 1922; s. Jacob and Fanny (Merrin) S.; B.B.A., CCNY, 1943; m. Gloria Danciger, Oct. 1, 1949; children—Stacey, Jill. Acct. exec. Reiss Advt., N.Y.C., 1945-50; mktg. dir. Revlon, Inc., N.Y.C., 1950-68; v.p. mktg. Helena Rubinstein, N.Y.C., 1968-71; pres. Product Merchandising Corp., N.Y.C., 1971-73; pres. Eylure of London, N.Y.C., 1973—. Served with OSS, 1943-45. Club: Lake Success Golf. Home: 15 Ursula Dr Roslyn NY 11576 Office: 410 Eastern Pkwy Farmingdale NY 11735

SUTCLIFFE, ERIC, lawyer; b. Calif., Jan. 10, 1909; s. Thomas and Annie (Beare) S.; A.B., U. Calif., Berkeley, 1929, J.D., 1932; m. Joan Basche, Aug. 7, 1937; children—Victoria, Marcia, Thomas; m. 2d, Marie Cunningham Paige, Nov. 1, 1975. Admitted to Calif. bar, 1932; mem. firm Orrick, Herrington & Sutcliffe, San Francisco, 1943—; past dir. Hongkong Bank Calif. Trustee, San Francisco Law Library. Fellow Am. Bar Found.; mem. Am., San Francisco bar assns., State Bar of Calif., San Francisco C. of C. (treas. 1960-62, dir. 1968-70), Order of Coif, Phi Gamma Delta, Phi Delta Phi. Clubs: Pacific Union, Bohemian, Commonwealth (San Francisco). Home: 260 King Ave Piedmont CA 94610 Office: 600 Montgomery St San Francisco CA 94111

SUTCLIFFE, WAYNE ALAN, banker; b. Lawrence, Mass., Dec. 27, 1940; s. Arnold and Lillian F. (McCarthy) S.; B.B.A. magna cum laude, U. Mass., 1967, M.B.A., 1969; m. Katherine Doherty, July 27, 1966; children—Karen, Wayne, Kristen. With New Eng. Mchts. Nat. Bank, Boston, 1967-79, v.p. until 1979; pres. First Chgo. Credit Corp. subs. First Chgo. Corp., Chgo., 1979—; former instr. Northeastern U. Served with USAF, 1959-63. Mem. Am. Bankers Assn., Robert Morris Assos. Home: 942 Tim Tam Circle Naperville IL 60540 Office: Two First Nat Plaza Chicago IL

SUTHERLAND, DONALD JAMES, finance co. exec., mfg. co. exec.; b. Teaneck, N.J., Jan. 2, 1931; s. Conrad James and Lavinia Marie (Peters) S.; A.B., Princeton U., 1953; M.B.A., Harvard U., 1958; children—Paige, Donald, Shelley, Julie. Regional sales mgr. Dahlstrom Corp., Jamestown, N.Y., 1958-60; asso. McKinsey & Co., N.Y.C., 1961-64; v.p. Laird, Inc., N.Y.C., 1965-67, New Court Securities Corp., N.Y.C., 1968-70; pres. Quincy Assos., Inc., N.Y.C., 1970-75; pres., corp. gen. partner Quincy Partners, N.Y.C., 1975—; dir. Mark Controls Corp., 1969—, Hager, Inc., 1975—, PBA, Inc., 1977—; chmn. bd. Am. Spring & Wire Splty. Co., Inc., 1977—, Muehlhausen Bros. Spring & Mfg. Co., Inc., 1977—, Publix Shirt Corp., 1979—, Lewis Spring & Mfg. Co., Inc., 1979—, Quincy Spring Group, Inc., 1979—. Mem. Nassau County (N.Y.) Planning Commn., 1965-68; trustee St. Michael's Coll., 1972-81, Sheltering Arms Children's Service, 1973-75. Served to lt. (j.g.) USN, 1953-56. Democrat. Roman Catholic. Clubs: The Creek, Twenty-Nine. Contbr. articles on mgmt. and finance to profl. jours. Home: High Farms Rd Glen Head NY 11545 Office: PO Box 154 Glen Head NY 11545

SUTHERLAND, GEORGE LESLIE, chem. co. exec.; b. Dallas, Aug. 13, 1922; s. Leslie and Madge Alice (Henderson) S.; B.A., U. Tex. at Austin, 1943, M.A., 1947, Ph.D., 1950; m. Mary Gail Hamilton, Sept. 9, 1961; children—Janet Leslie, Gail Irene, Elizabeth Hamilton. With Am. Cyanamid Co., various locations, 1951—, asst. dir. research and devel., Princeton, N.J., 1969-70, dir. research and devel., agr. div., Princeton, 1970-73, v.p. med. research and devel., Pearl River, N.Y., 1973—, dir. med. research div., 1978—, dir. chem. research div., 1980—. Served with USN, 1944-46. Mem. Assn. Research Dirs. (pres. 1975-76), AAAS, Am. Chem. Soc., Chem. Soc. London. Home: 42 Sky Meadow Rd Suffern NY 10901 Office: Middletown Rd Pearl River NY 10965

SUTHERLAND, JOHN ELLIOTT, writer, producer, educator; b. Williston, N.D., Sept. 11, 1910; s. Ronald and Adelaide Mae (Elliott) S.; student U. N.D., 1929-30; B.A., U. Calif. at Los Angeles, 1937; m. Lysiane Wagner, 1952; children—Ronald, Eric, Diane; 1 son by previous marriage, John. Grad. dir. dramatics and debate U. Calif. at Los Angeles, 1938; prodn. mgr., writer, dialogue dir. Walt Disney Prodns., 1939-40; free-lance screenplay writer, Hollywood, 1941; writer-producer-dir. U.S. Army Signal Corps, other govtl. agys., 1941-45; pres. John Sutherland Prodns., Los Angeles, 1946—, also Sutherland Learning Assos. Mem. edn. group Nat. Arthritis Commn., 1975; bd. visitors Grad. Sch. Edn. U. Calif., Los Angeles, 1974. Recipient 250 awards for creative excellence in documentary and ednl. films from domestic and internat. film festivals, 1950—; Sesquicentennial award for creative contbns. ednl. films U. Mich., 1967. Co-author: (feature film) Flight Command, 1941; (hist. novel) The Valiant, 1955. Conceived and produced 1st multi-media learning systems in continuing med. edn. for nurses, in bilingual edn for Mexican Am. Children, 1969-75; producer, pub. Patient Care Audit Multi-Media Learning Systems. Home: 14654 Oxnald St Van Nuys CA 91411

SUTHERLAND, JOHN ELMER, JR., mfg. co. exec.; b. N.Y.C., Dec. 12, 1937; s. John Elmer and Irene (Hoffman) S.; B.S., Fordham U., 1959; postgrad. 1969-71; m. Joan W. Quadrino, Nov. 1961; children—John Elmer, Ann Elizabeth, Patricia Joan, David Christopher. Sr. auditor Price, Waterhouse & Co., Stamford, Conn., 1961-64; mgr. internat. capital planning Gen. Foods Corp., White Plains, N.Y., 1964-67; ops. asst. Schlumberger Ltd., N.Y.C., 1967-69; acting controller Revlon Internat., N.Y.C., 1969-72; v.p., treas. Carnation Internat., Los Angeles, 1972-79, exec. v.p. fin., 1979—. Served to 1st lt. U.S. Army, 1959-61. Mem. Internat. Fiscal Assn., Fin. Execs. Inst., Internat. Tax Inst. Office: 5045 Wilshire Blvd Los Angeles CA 90036

SUTHERLAND, JOHN PEARY, hotel chain exec.; b. Beaumont, Tex., Oct. 27, 1922; s. John Harold and Chiltipin (Born) S.; B.B.A., Mexico City Coll., 1948; m. Joy Willeford, Apr. 12, 1945; children—Joy Elizabeth, Kay Born, Ann Perry. Gen. mgr. Hotel del Prado, Barranquilla, Colombia, 1953-55, Hotel Carrera, Santiago, Chile, 1955-59; gen. mgr. San Juan (P.R.) Inter-Continental Hotel, 1959-61; dir. for Far East and Pacific Inter-Continental Hotels, also gen. mgr. So. Cross Hotel, Melbourne, Australia, 1961-63; v.p. ops. Latin Am., Inter-Continental Hotels, also gen. mgr. Hotel Tamanaco, Caracas, Venezuela, 1963-67; sr. v.p. ops. Inter-Continental Hotels Corp., N.Y.C., 1967-70, pres. Americas div., 1970—. Served as maj. USMCR, World War II. Decorated Air medal (2), D.F.C., Silver Star; Orden del Merito (Chile). Mem. Am. Soc. Travel Agts., Pan Am. Mgmt. Club, Hotel Sales Mgmt. Assn., Confrerie de la Chaine des Rotisseurs, 200 Club Greater Miami (Fla.). Republican. Episcopalian. Clubs: Miami, Riviera Country, So. Cross; Marco Polo (N.Y.C.). Office: 999 S Bayshore Dr Suite 901 Miami FL 33131

SUTNAR, RADOSLAV LADISLAV, real estate devel. co. exec.; b. Prague, Czechoslovakia, July 25, 1929; s. Ladislav and Iska (Kubs) S.; came to U.S., 1946, naturalized, 1951; student State U. N.Y., 1950; B.Arch., Pratt Inst., 1955. M.Arch., 1956; M.City Planning, Harvard U., 1958; Asso. Applied Sci. N.Y.C. Community Coll., 1964; m. Elaine Ford, Nov. 10, 1972. Planner, architect various instns., N.Y.C., 1953-56, 63-64, Boston, 1956-63, Los Angeles, 1964-66; asso. researcher UCLA, 1966-68; exec. dir. environ. goals com. Los Angeles Goals Project, 1966-68; dir. planning, mgr. land devel. Albert C. Martin and Assos., Los Angeles, 1969-73; asso. gen. mgr. real estate investment dept. Prudential Ins. Co. Am., Westlake Village, Project, Calif., 1973-77; v.p. Shapell Industries of Ventura, Inc., Beverly Hills, Calif., 1977—; cons., lectr. in field. Mem. Conejo Valley Bicentennial-Centennial Commn., 1975—, chmn. fin. com., 1975-77; mem. citizens adv. com. Malibu/Santa Monica Mountains 1976—, Comprehensive Planning Commn., 1977-79; mem. adv. com. Mayor of Thousand Oaks (Calif.), 1976. Served from pvt. to capt. N.Y. N.G., 1948-56. Registered architect, Mass. Mem. Am. Inst. Planners, AIA, Am. Soc. Cert. Planners, Urban Land Inst. Club: Harvard So. Calif. Home: 810 N Orlando Ave Los Angeles CA 90069 Office: 8383 Wilshire Blvd Suite 700 Beverly Hills CA 90211

SUTRO, FREDERICK CHARLES, JR., chem. co. exec.; b. Basking Ridge, N.J., June 21, 1920; s. Frederick Charles and Elizabeth Tallman (Winne) S.; student U. Ariz., 1939-40; B.S. in Indsl. Engring., Yale U., 1943; m. Sheila Kelley, Nov. 6, 1943; children—Tracy (Mrs. Charles Horter), Tina Tallman (Mrs. Richard Marsh). Tech. rep. N.Y. area Bakelite Co. div. Union Carbide Corp., 1944-51; mgr. comml. research and devel. PM Industries, Inc., Stamford, Conn., 1951-54; sales supr. plastics Spencer Chem. Co., Kansas City, Mo., 1954-57, mgr. tech. service, 1957-58, product mgr., 1959-60; marketing mgr. Cabot Corp., Boston, 1960-64, asst. to v.p. devel., 1964-66; gen. mgr. plastics dept. USS Chems. div. U.S. Steel Corp., Pitts., 1966-77, asst. to v.p., 1977—; v.p., gen. mgr. Tex/USS Polyolefins Co.; dir. Koro Corp., Hudson, Mass. Served as 2d lt. USAAF, 1943-44. Mem. Soc. Plastics Engrs. (nat. council 1955-61, v.p. 1958, pres. 1959), Plastics Pioneers Assn., Soc. Plastics Industry (dir. 1973-78, exec. com. 1974-78, chmn. pub. affairs com. 1974-76, treas. 1976-78), Yale Engring. Assn. (sec. 1946-49), Phi Gamma Delta. Clubs: Chatham Beach and Tennis; Yale (N.Y.C.); Harvard-Yale-Princeton (Pitts.); Allegheny Country (Sewickley, Pa.). Home: 647 Grove St Sewickley PA 15143 Office: US Steel Corp 600 Grant St Pittsburgh PA 15230

SUTTLES, WILLARD CALVIN, engring. co. exec.; b. Conneaut, Ohio, Jan. 5, 1921; s. Harold Dale and Ann (Eckley) S.; B.S. in Mech. Engring., U. Ala., 1951; m. Mary Lucile James, Apr. 28, 1945; children—Patricia Ann, Willard Calvin. Regional sales rep. B & P Co., Chgo., 1952-63; v.p. Glidewell Foundry Co., Birmingham, Ala., 1963-65; pres. Unexcelled Mfg. Co., Attalla, Ala., 1965-67; owner W.C. Suttles & Assos., Gadsen, Ala., 1967-69; v.p. sales AMS, Inc., Erie, Pa., 1970-72; chief engr., sales mgr. George Fischer Co., Holly, Mich., 1972-78; mgr. systems Jervis B. Webb Co., Farmington Hills, Mich., 1979—; Indsl. cons. Served with USAAF, 1941-45. Mem. Am. Foundrymens Soc., ASME, Am. Soc. Metals. Presbyn. Clubs: Fairlane (Dearborn, Mich.); The Club (Birmingham); Masons (Shriner). Home: 6623 Andersonville Rd Waterford MI 48095 Office: 1 Webb Dr Farmington Hills MI 48018

SUTTON, ERNEST SHAW, aerospace co. exec.; b. Burlington, N.J., May 22, 1922; s. Ernest Shaw, and Elizabeth Bauer (Sholl) S.; B.S., Chem. Engring., U. Pa., 1943; m. Janet Ann Gilbertson, July 1, 1950 (dec.); children—Jane M., Douglas S., Andrea L.; m. 2d. Lois Williams Young, June 12, 1975. Chemist, Nat. Synthetic Rubber Corp., Louisville, 1943-44; Hewitt Robins Rubber Co., Buffalo, 1946-48; head plastics lab. Hamilton Standard div. United Tech. Corp., East Hartford, Conn., 1948-50; chief latex chemist Thermoid Rubber Co., Trenton, 1950-53; head research lab. Elkton (Md.) div. Thiokol Corp., 1953—; pres. Brantwood Corp., 1980—. Served with U.S. Army, 1944-46. Mem. AAAS, Am. Chem. Soc. Republican. Episcopalian. Patentee numerous items. Home: Box 209 RD 1 Landenberg PA 19350 Office: Thiokol Corp Elkton MD 21921

SUTTON, FREDERICK ISLER, JR., realtor; b. Greensboro, N.C., Sept. 13, 1916; s. Fred I. and Annie (Fry) S.; grad. Culver (Ind.) Mil. Acad., 1934; A.B., U. N.C., 1939, student Law Sch., 1939-41; grad. Realtor's Inst., 1956, student Grad. Sch., 1957; m. Helen Sykes Morrison, Mar. 18, 1941; children—Fred I. III, Frank Morrison. Propr., Fred I. Sutton, Jr., realtor, Kinston, N.C., 1946—. Chmn. Kinston Parking Authority; chmn. Kinston Water Resources; pres. Lenoir County United Fund, 1969, 70. Trustee, dean U. N.C. Realtors Inst.; trustee Florence Crittenton Services; v.p. N.C. Real Estate Edn. Found. Served from ensign to lt. comdr. USNR, 1941-46. Named Kinston Realtor of Year, 1963; cert. property mgr. Mem. Kinston (pres.), N.C. (v.p., 1957) bds. realtors, N.C. Assn. Realtors (regional v.p., chmn. ednl. com., dir. Realtors Ednl. Found.), N.C. Assn. Real Estate Bds. (dir., v.p. 1958-60, 61, 63), Newcomen Soc., Am. Power Boat Assn. (region 4 champion 1976, 78, 79, 80), U.S. Power Squadron (navigator; Kinston edn. officer), C. of C. (v.p.), S.R. Presbyn. (deacon). Kiwanian (pres., dir. Kinston), Mason (32 deg., Shriner), Elk. Home: 1101 N Queen St Kinston NC 28501 Office: Sutton Bldg PO Drawer 3309 Kinston NC 28501

SUTTON, GEORGE HILLS, III, mgmt. cons.; b. New Rochelle, N.Y., July 29, 1929; s. George H. and Lillian A. (Watkins) S.; B.S., U. Bridgeport, 1951; m. Nancy A. Tufts, May 3, 1968; children—Catherine, Carol Sue, George Hills IV, Sherry. With AT&T, 1952-59, service engr., 1954-56, comml. rep., 1957-59; corp. mgr. communications and utilities North Am. Aviation Co., El Segundo, Calif., 1959-63; with Litton Industries, Washington, 1964-65, Los Angeles, 1963-64, 65-67, mgr. adminstrv. services, 1963-64, sr. mem. tech. staff, 1965-67; group mgr. Coopers & Lybrand, N.Y.C., 1967-73; pres. Ruxton Assos., Sherman, Conn., 1973—; mem. faculty N.Y. Inst. Finance. Nat. chmn. Telecommunicators for Nixon, 1972; finance dir. Belmont for Senate, Fairfield County (Conn.), 1976; treas. Boughton for Mayor, Danbury, Conn., 1977; park and recreation commr. City of Sherman, 1979-81. Served with USAF, 1951-52. Mem. Inst. Mgmt. Cons. (certified), Am. Arbitration Assn., TeleCommunications Assn. (pres. 1961-62), Am. Hosp. Assn. Clubs: Masons, Shriners, Rotary Internat. Author: Telecommunications, Stock Market Handbook, 1970. Home: Orchard Rest Rd Sherman CT 06784 Office: PO Box L Sherman CT 06784

SUTTON, JOSEPH ANDREW, corporate purchasing (dir.); b. Toronto, Ont., Can., Nov. 10, 1925; s. Joseph Albert and Lena (Franklin) S.; came to U.S., 1966, naturalized, 1973; ed. in bus. adminstrn. Ryerson Inst., Toronto, 1945; m. Ingrid Patricia Foreman, Aug. 31, 1945; children—Judith, Valerie, Naomi. Dir. purchasing Glidden Co. Can., Toronto, 1954-62; mgr. material control Cryovac div. W.R. Grace & Co., Mississauga, Ont., 1962-66, dir. purchasing, Duncan, S.C., 1966—; mem. S.C. Gov's. Mgmt. Rev. Commn., 1972; adj. prof. U. S.C., 1979-80. Served with RCAF, 1943-45. Named Boss of Year Spartanburg PBX Club, 1972. Mem. Purchasing Mgmt. Assn. Carolinas Va. (pres. 1972-73, Thomas award 1974), Nat. Assn. Purchasing Mgmt. (v.p. 1976-77, pres. 1978-79). Republican. Baptist. Home: 20 Hillsborough Dr Greenville SC 29615 Office: Box 464 Duncan SC 29334

SUTTON, NATHAN LEROY, fin. and ins. co. exec.; b. Clarksville, Tenn., June 8, 1927; s. Albert Slayton and Louise Christina (Barnhouse) S.; cert. U. Md., 1967, U. Houston, 1974; m. Evelyn Florence Berry, June 16, 1951; children—Patricia Lee, Janice Norine. With Comml. Credit Corp., Los Angeles and San Mateo, 1948-73, area dir., 1966-73, v.p., 1958-73; sr. v.p. Amfac Credit Corp., also Amfac Thrift & Loan Co., Los Angeles, 1973-75; regional dir. Am. Bankers Ins. Group, Miami, 1975—; cons. fin. instns., Irvine, Calif., 1975—; pres. Calif. Thrift & Loan Assn., 1970-71, 74-75; founding chmn. Thrift Guaranty Corp. Calif., San Francisco, 1971, pres. 1974-75. Served with USNR, 1945-46. Republican. Baptist. Home: 24682 Via De Rio El Toro CA 92630 Office: 2192 Dupont Dr Suite 102 Irvine CA 92715

SUVALLE, MICHAEL RALPH, mfg. co. exec.; b. Cambridge, Mass., May 1, 1945; s. Harold Louis and Harriet Sylvia (Gurwitz) S.; B.A. cum laude, Bowdoin Coll., 1967; M.B.A., Columbia U., 1969; m. Ellen Sue Goldenberg, Nov. 29, 1970; children—Richard, Marjorie. Statis. cons. Holt, Rinehart & Winston, N.Y.C., 1968-69; sr. mktg. research analyst Polaroid Corp., Cambridge, 1969-70, mgr. sales planning and forecasting, 1970-74, film product mgr., 1974-77, sr. mktg. mgr., 1977-80, mgr. Comml. Battery div., 1980—. Club: Masons. Home: 48 Aqueduct Rd Wayland MA 01778 Office: 784 Memorial Dr Cambridge MA 02139

SUZUKI, YASUHIKO, motor co. exec.; b. Mishima, Japan, Sept. 6, 1936; came to U.S., 1968, naturalized, 1978; s. Heiji and Hiro Suzuki; LL.D., Chuo U. Sch. Law, 1960; m. Kyoko Teraizumi, May 14, 1961; children—Iori, Anri, Claude. With Overseas Economic and Tech. Assn., Tokyo, 1960-61; rep. Northwest Orient Airlines, Osaka, Japan, 1961-68; dir. chief rep. Nisshin Chem. Co., N.Y.C., 1968-70; v.p. Nissan Motor Corp. in U.S.A., Washington, 1970—. Mem. Automobile Importers Am. (exec. com., dir.), U.S. C. of C. (internat. investment com.). Buddhist. Club: University (Washington). Office: 1919 Pennsylvania Ave NW Washington DC 20006

SVEC, FREDERICK JOSEPH, appliance mfg. co. exec.; b. Traverse City, Mich., Apr. 6, 1937; s. Joseph Frederick and Jean Grace (Skinner) S.; A.A., Northwestern Mich. U., 1956; B.A., Mich. State U., 1958; m. Sally Ann Van Vorst, Feb. 25, 1955; children—Sue Ann, Toni Jo. With Haskins & Sells, 1958-68, prin., 1966-68; asst. controller The Bendix Corp., Southfield, Mich., 1968-70, controller, 1970-72, v.p., controller, 1972-77, sr. v.p., chief fin. officer, 1977-79, exec. v.p., chief fin. officer, 1979—. Mem. Am. Inst. C.P.A.'s, Fin. Execs. Inst., Soc. Automotive Engrs., Economic Club Detroit. Club: The Renaissance. Office: Bendix Center Southfield MI 48037

SVERDRUP, NILS M., cons. mech. and elec. engr.; b. Halsingborg, Sweden, Feb. 2, 1901; s. Magnus and Mathilda (Asp) S.; M.E. in Elec. Engring., Hassleholm Coll. Tech.; Sweden, 1921; m. Orpha Edna Smith, Aug. 12, 1939. Mech. engr. Baker Raulang Co., Cleve., 1940-43; aircraft and turbine devel. engr. Northrop Aircraft, Inc. Hawthorne, Calif., 1943-48; research and devel. engr. AiResearch Mfg. Co., Los Angeles, 1948-49; mech. elec. engr. Hoffman Radio Corp., 1949-50; tech. analyst, devel. rocket propulsion motors Aerojet-General Corp. (formerly Aerojet Engineering Corp.). Azusa, Calif., 1950-56, tech. specialist, 1956-62; tech. specialist research and devel. spacecrafts and rocket propulsion systems Space-Gen. Corp., El Monte, Calif., 1962-66; cons. engr., 1966—. Registered profl. mech. and elec. engr., Calif. Mem. Brunler Research Found. Author: Accurate Solution for Disc Clutch Torque Capacity, 1949; Hydraulic Flow Phenomena, 1951; Mechanics of Viscosity, 1951; Calculating the Energy Losses in Hydraulic Systems, 1951; Energy Losses in Orifice Flow, 1952; Vibration Phenomena, 1952; Pressure Surges in Hydraulic Circuits, 1953; Theory of Hydraulic Flow Control, 1955. Home: 443 Myrtlewood St West Covina CA 91791

SWAIN, PHILIP RAYMOND, publishing co. exec.; b. Meriden, Conn., Nov. 30, 1929; s. Raymond Francis and Angela Catherine (Maslow) S.; A.B. cum laude, Harvard U., 1950. Tchr. Latin, Greek, pvt. schs., Cambridge and Still River, Mass., 1950-55; editor Ravengate Press, Cambridge, 1955-65, pres., 1965—. Mem. bd. advisers St. Benedict Acad., Still River. Mem. Book Builders of Boston. Roman Catholic. Club: Harvard. Author (as Philip Douglas): Saint of Philadelphia, The Life of Bishop John Neumann, 1977. Home: 56 Carpenter Ave Meriden CT 06450 Office: PO Box 103 Cambridge MA 02138

SWALES, WILLIAM EDWARD, geologist, oil co. exec.; b. Parkersburg, W.Va., May 15, 1925; s. John Richard and Ellen (South) S.; B.A. in Geology, W.Va. U., 1949, M.S. in Geology, 1951; grad. advanced mgmt. program Stanford U., 1968; m. Lydia Eugena Mills, Dec. 26, 1948; children—Joseph V., Susan Eugena, David Lee. With Marathon Oil Co., 1954—, advanced geologist, Evansville, Ind., 1956-57, various positions, Guatemala, Ireland, Eng. and Australia, 1957-66, mgr. Western Hemisphere and Australia div., Findlay, Ohio, 1967-70, exec. v.p. Oasis Oil Co. of Libya, Inc., 1970-72, pres., 1972-74, spl. asst. to sr. v.p. prodn. internat., Findlay, Ohio, 1974, v.p. prodn. internat., 1974-77, dir., 1975—, sr. v.p. prodn. internat., 1977—. Served with USNR, 1943-45. Mem. Am. Petroleum Inst., Am. Assn. Petroleum Geologists, Soc. Petroleum Engrs., Am. Geol. Inst. Clubs: Findlay Country, Muirfield Village Golf. Office: 539 S Main St Findlay OH 45840

SWAN, ALFRED WHITE, JR., banker; b. Miami Beach, Fla., May 15, 1942; s. Alfred White and Evelyn (Leonard) S.; B.S. in Bus. Adminstrn., Va. Poly. Inst., 1963; M.B.A. in Indsl. Mgmt., Fla. State U., 1970; postgrad. Nat. Comml. Lending Grad. Sch., U. Okla., 1976; m. Sherrill Parrish, 1979; children by previous marriage—Heather,

Matthew. With First Union Nat. Bank N.C., 1970—, asst. v.p. N.Y. service office, 1971-73, v.p., head nat. div., 1974-79, sr. v.p., 1979—; mem. faculty Stonier Grad. Sch. Banking, Rutgers U., 1980. Bd. regents Nat. Comml. Lending Grad. Sch., U. Okla., 1978-79. Served to capt. U.S. Army, 1963-68. Decorated Bronze Star with 2 oak leaf clusters, Army Commendation medal, Air medal. Certified comml. lender. Mem. Beta Gamma Sigma (hon.), Sigma Iota Epsilon (hon.). Home: 520 Lakeshore Rd N Denver NC 28037 Office: First Union National Bank Charlotte NC 28288

SWAN, CARL W., oil co. exec.; b. Bolcklow, Mo., Sept. 29, 1925; s. O. C. and Lottie S.; student Coffeyville Jr. Coll., 1947-49; B.A., U. N.Mex., 1951; m. Nona E. Holt, May 1, 1948; 1 son, Mark Edward. Mud engr. Gross Drilling Co., 1951-52; asst. regional mgr. Magnet Cove Barium Corp., 1952-64; pres., owner Basin Petroleum Corp., 1964-76; pres. Res. Oil Inc., 1976; pres., owner Swan Petroleum Corp., 1976—; chmn. bd. Longhorn Oil & Gas Co., Inc., Am. Gypsum Corp.; mem. Congressional Adv. Com. on Energy, 1977-80. Mem. Nat. Republican Senatorial Com., 1977-80. Served with USAAF, 1943-46. Recipient Public Service award Oklahoma City Police Dept., 1979. Mem. Ind. Petroleum Assn. Am. (v.p. fin. com.), Soc. Petroleum Engrs., Okla. Ind. Petroleum Assn., Petroleum Club. Club: Quail Creek Golf and Country. Office: 2601 Northwest Expy #1101 Oil Center W Oklahoma City OK 73112

SWAN, GEORGE SAMUEL, ind. oil producer; b. Balt., Aug. 9, 1914; s. William R. and Carolyn E. (Lamp) S.; grad. McDonogh (Md.) Sch., 1932; student U. Md., Johns Hopkins, U. Va.; m. Pauline E. Womack, 1937; children—Nancy (Mrs. David Williams), Patricia (Mrs. Van Sandstrom), Susan (Mrs. Andrew R. Spence), George Samuel. Asst. office mgr., plant cashier Chevrolet Motor Co., 1932-36; oil scout Tex-Jersey Oil 36, Tyler, Tex., 1937-39; now ind. oil producer, Saginaw, Mich. Past dir. Saginaw A.R.C.; dir. Cancer Soc. Mem. Mich. Oil and Gas Assn. (dir.), Ind. Petroleum Assn. Am. (pub. information com.), Pi Kappa Alpha. Episcopalian (past sr. warden, vestryman). Clubs: Kiwanis (past pres.), Saginaw (past pres.); Lost Tree (North Palm Beach, Fla.); Everglades (Palm Beach); Detroit, Economic (Detroit); Otsego Ski (Gaylord, Mich.). Home: Cottage Grove Roscommon MI 48653 also 11701 Turtle Beach Rd Lost Tree Village North Palm Beach FL 33403 Office: Second Nat Bank Bldg Saginaw MI 48607

SWAN, HERBERT SIEGFRIED, communications co. exec.; b. Montclair, N.J., Jan. 2, 1928; s. Herbert S. and Alma (Oswald) S.; grad. Phillips Exeter Acad., 1945; A.B. in Econs. and Bus. Adminstrn., Lafayette Coll., 1949; m. Roberta J. Whitmire, July 2, 1960; 1 dau., Roberta Allyson. Advt. supr. TV receiver dept. Gen. Electric Co., Syracuse, N.Y., 1954-55; copywriter Bresnick Co. advt. agy., Boston, 1955-58; sr. copywriter J.T. Chirurg Advt. Agy., Boston, 1958-59; advt. mgr. agrl. chems., indsl. minerals div. Internat. Minerals & Chem. Corp., Skokie, Ill., 1958-60; editor Motorola Newsgram, direct mail advt. mgr. Motorola, Chgo., 1962-68; dir. pub. information Motorola Communications & Electronics, Schaumburg, Ill., 1968-70, mgr. indsl. advt. and sales promotion, 1970-73, mgr. field merchandising, 1973—. Served with USAF, 1950-54. Mem. Community Radio Watch (nat. coordinator 1967-68). Home: 48 Little Cahill Rd Cary IL 60013 Office: 1301 E Algonquin Rd Schaumburg IL 60172

SWAN, ROBY SCOTT, food chain exec.; b. Houston, Mar. 3, 1948; s. William Asa and Alice Mae (Ayres) S.; B.A., U. Wyo., 1970; B.Internat. Mgmt., Am. Grad. Sch. Internat. Mgmt., 1971, M.Internat. Mgmt., 1971; m. Barbara Ann Hulpiau, June 22, 1968; children—Gabirella, Jordan. Mng. dir. Pizza Hut del Distrito, S.A. de C.V., Mexico City, 1972-75; sr. mng. dir. Pizza Hut (U.K.) Ltd., Lonodn, 1975—. Mem. Brit. Franchise Assn., Mgmt. Centre Europe, Anglo Am. C. of C., Sail Tng. Assn. Office: Pizza Hut (UK) Ltd 149 Earl's Court Rd London SW 5 England

SWANKE, ALBERT HOMER, architect; b. Thomasville, Ga., Nov. 22, 1909; s. John Christian and Stella (Williams) Schwencke; B.S. in Architecture, Ga. Inst. Tech., Atlanta, 1930; postgrad. Beaux Arts Inst. Design, N.Y.C., 1931; m. Margaret Anne Twaddell, 1936 (dec.); 1 son Albert Homer; m. 2d Dorothy Pratt Williams, 1969. Trainee various archtl. offices, N.Y.C., 1931-35; architect dept. ins. State of N.Y., 1936-42; joined Alfred Easton Poor, 1946, partner, 1952-71; asso. Walker & Poor, Architects, 1947-52; partner Poor and Swanke & Partners, 1972-75; mng. partner Poor, Swanke, Hayden & Connell, 1975-79; sr. partner Swanke Hayden Connell & Partners, 1979—; mem. bd. design Extension of Capitol Project, Washington, 1956-79; panelist Am. Arbitration Assn., 1971-80; dir. 565 Park Ave. Corp. Trustee N.Y. Med. Coll.-Flower & Fifth Ave Hosps., 1963-79, vice chmn., 1968, mem. exec. com., 1965-74, chmn. hosp. com., 1969-72, chmn. planning, devel. and fund raising com., 1973-74; mem. devel. bd. Westchester Med. Center, 1969-73; mem. archtl. bd. rev. Village of Larchmont (N.Y.), 1963-69, chmn., 1968-69; trustee Historic Savannah (Ga.) Found., Inc., 1979—, chmn. archtl. rev. bd., 1978—. Served with USNR. Fellow AIA (treas. conv. 1965), Am. Soc. Registered Architects; mem. NAD, N.Y. Soc. Architects, N.Y. Bldg Congress, Soc. Archtl. Historians, Navy League U.S., Phi Sigma Kappa, Pi Delta Epsilon. Clubs: Century Assn. (N.Y.C.); Boston (New Orleans); Met., Capitol Hills (Washington). Archtl. works include: Extension East Front U.S. Capitol, James Madison Meml. Library Congress Bldg. (Washington); NATO Air Bases (Dreux and Evreux, France); Queens County (N.Y.) Courthouse and Prison. Office: 400 Park Ave New York NY 10022 or 1333 New Hampshire Ave NW Washington DC 20036 or #2 Illinois Center Chicago IL 60601*

SWANKE, ALBERT HOMER, JR., ins. co. exec.; b. New Rochelle, N.Y., May 3, 1942; s. Albert Homer and Margaret Ann (Twaddell) S.; B.A., Yale U., 1964; M.B.A., Columbia U., 1966; m. Valda Inta Abols, May 6, 1967; children—Christian Robert, Elizabeth Indra, Victoria Inta. Fin. analyst IBM World Trade Corp., N.Y.C., 1966-69; fgn. investment mgr. Am. Internat. Group, N.Y.C., 1969-74; asst. v.p., investment officer Am. Life Ins. Co., Wilmington, Del., 1972-74; v.p. Am. Express Internat. Banking Corp., N.Y.C., 1974-76; v.p., treas. INA Internat. Corp., Phila., 1976—; pres. INA Internat. Investors, Ltd., 1979—; dir. Meadowlands Nat. Bank, North Bergen, N.J. Served with USMCR, 1966-72. Mem. Alpha Kappa Psi. Republican. Presbyterian. Clubs: University (N.Y.C.); Racquet (Phila.); Larchmont Yacht. Home: 5 Wallingford Dr Princeton NJ 08540 Office: 1600 Arch St Philadelphia PA 19101

SWANN, RICHARD HILL MCRAE, lawyer; b. Cairo, Ga., Aug. 16, 1923; s. Joseph Paul and Flora Mae (Shiver) S.; LL.B., U. Miami, 1950, D.D.S., 1950; m. Norma Pinder, Aug. 12, 1947; children—Cheryl Swann Babcock, Lynette Swann Sibley. Admitted to Fla. bar, 1950; sr. partner firm Holladay & Swann, Miami, 1951-61; judge City of Miami, 1954-56, 3d Dist. Ct. Appeal, Miami, 1965-72; sr. partner firm Swann & Glass, Coral Gables, Fla., 1972-75, firm Hall & Swann, Coral Gables, 1975-79, firm Gaston Snow Ely Bartlett Hall Swann, Miami, 1979—; hon. consul. gen. of Japan, 1974—. Mem. citizens bd. U. Miami, Fla. Bd. Devel. Mem. Am. Judicature Soc., U.S. Japan Assn., Phi Alpha Delta, Pi Kappa Alpha. Baptist. Clubs: Miami, Riviera Country, Vizcayans. Home: 6328 San Vicente St Coral Gables FL 33146 Office: Gaston Snow Ely Bartlett Hall Swann 2801 Ponce de Leon Blvd Coral Gables FL 33134

SWANSON, DAVID H(ENRY), economist; b. Anoka, Minn., Nov. 1, 1930; s. Henry Otto and Louise Isabell (Holiday) S.; B.A., St. Cloud State Coll., 1953; M.A., U. Minn., 1955; m. Suzanne Nash, Jan. 19, 1952; children—Matthew David, Christopher James. Economist area devel. dept. No. States Power Co., Mpls., 1955-56, staff asst., v.p. sales, 1956-57, economist indsl. devel. dept., 1957-63; dir. area devel. dept. Iowa So. Utilities Co., Centerville, 1963-67, dir. econ. devel. and research, 1967-70; dir. New Orleans Econ. Devel. Council, 1970-72; div. mgr. Kaiser Aetna Texas, New Orleans, 1972-73; dir. corporate research United Services Automobile Assn., San Antonio, 1973-76; pres. Lantern Corp., 1974-79; adminstr. bus. devel. State of Wis., Madison, 1976-78; dir. Center Indsl. Research and Service, Iowa State U., Ames, 1978—, mem. mktg. faculty Sch. of Bus. Adminstrn., 1979—. Vice chmn. Planning Commn. Roseville (Minn.), 1961; mem. Iowa Airport Planning Council, 1968-70; mem. adv. council office Comprehensive Health Planning, 1967-70; mem. adv. com. Center for Indsl. Research and Service, 1967-70, New Orleans Met. Area Com., 1972-73; mem. Dist. Export Council, 1978—; mem. region 7 adv. council SBA, 1978—; dir. Mid-Continent Research and Devel. Council, 1980—; chmn. Iowa del. White House Conf. on Small Bus., 1980. adv. com. U. New Orleans. County finance chmn. Republican Party, 1966-67; bd. dirs. Greater New Orleans Urban League, 1970-73. Served with USAF, 1951-52. C.P.C.U. Mem. Small Bus. Inst. Assn., Soc. Ins. Research, Iowa Profl. Developers, Nat. Assn. Mgmt. Tng. Adv. Centers. Republican. Episcopalian. Clubs: Rotary, Toastmasters (past pres.). Home: 1007 Kennedy Dr Ames IA 50010 Office: Iowa State U Ames IA 50011

SWANSON, JAMES LEE, housewares sales exec.; b. Little Falls, Minn., Jan. 26, 1939; s. Emil John and Hattie E. (Briggs) S.; student St. Cloud (Minn.) State Coll., 1958; m. Dorothy Jane Jackson, Oct. 17, 1959; children—Carrie, Jamie, Steven, Barbara, Sean, Shane. Owner, Compact Assos., Sioux City, Iowa, 1959-62; ind. distbr. Nat. Housewares, Omaha, 1962-69, dist. supr., Central States, 1969-71, area v.p., 1971-75, sr. v.p. and sales dir., 1976-77; pres. Anthony James Internat. Inc., retail chain, 1977—; owner, operator Swanson Thoroughbred Farms. Democrat. Roman Catholic. Home: 1256 Peterson Dr Omaha NE 68130

SWANSON, JOHN JOSEPH, handwriting analyst; b. Boston, May 14, 1918; s. Carl G. and Cecilia (Shea) S.; M. in Graphoanalysis, USAF Command Staff Sch., 1950; m. Mary-Pat Sacco, July 27, 1972. Joined U.S. Air Force, 1941, ret. as master sgt., 1964; assigned Mass. Inst. Tech., 1951-54, NATO Hdqrs., Paris, 1954-57; tchr. forgery detection and handwriting identification Am. Inst. Banking, Boston, 1973-75; owner, mgr. Profl. Assos., East Weymouth, Mass., 1978—. Decorated Legion of Merit. Mem. Internat. Graphoanalysis Soc. Roman Catholic. Author: Handwriting Analysis #1, 1976; Forgery Detection and Handwriting Identification, 1978; The Four-Point System of Handwriting Identification and Forgery Detection, 1978. Office: 49 Lakehurst Ave East Weymouth MA 02189

SWANSON, MARCIA STOFMAN, engring. software co. exec.; b. Atlantic City, N.J., Sept. 30, 1939; d. William J. and Elizabeth Mae (Wax) Stofman; B.S. in Biochemistry, Cornell U., 1961; M.Ed., U. Pitts., 1978; m. John A. Swanson, Feb. 1, 1960; children—Daniel Scott, Andrew Craig, Eric Henry. Lab. technician Dept. Animal Husbandry, Cornell U., Ithaca, N.Y., 1961-63; with Kelly Services, Pitts., 1965-67; corp. sec.-treas., co-founder Swanson Analysis Systems, Inc., Houston, Pa., 1969—, Swanson Engring. Assos. Corp., McMurray, Pa., 1974—; pres. Suburban Air Services, Inc., Morgan, Pa., 1979—. Sec., Woman's Center and Shelter of Pitts., 1975-76, S. Hills interfaith Ministries, 1978—. Mem. Am. Mgmt. Assn., Aircraft Owners and Pilots Assn. Jewish. Home: 1093 Tidewood Dr Bethel Park PA 15102 Office: PO Box 65 Johnson Rd Houston PA 15342

SWANSON, PAUL JOHN, JR., educator; b. Crawfordsville, Ind., May 10, 1934; s. Paul John and Helen (Bath) S.; student DePauw U., 1952; B.S. in Accountancy, U. Ill., 1959, B.S. in Economics and Finance, 1960, M.S. in Finance, 1962, Ph.D., 1966. Grad. teaching asst. U. Ill., 1960-65, grad. research asst. office of provost, 1964-65; asst. prof. finance U. Cin., 1965-67, asso. prof., 1967—, prof.-in-charge dept. quantitative analysis, 1967-68; vis. prof. dept. econs. Yale, 1969, vis. lectr. econ. growth center, 1970; vis. asso. prof. dept. psychol. scis. Purdue U., 1974. Served with AUS, 1956-58. Mem. Inst. Chartered Financial Analysts, Inst. Mgmt. Sci. (pres. Miami Valley chpt. 1970-71), Am. Statis. Assn., Operations Research Soc. Am., Am. Finance Assn., Cin. Soc. Financial Analysts, Nat. Def. Exec. Res., Delta Sigma Pi, Delta Chi, Omicron Delta Gamma, Phi Kappa Phi. Author: (with R.J. Graham) Proceedings of the 1974 Winter Simulation Conference, A Simulation of a Constrained Securities Market, 1974. Home: 3441 Telford St Cincinnati OH 45220

SWANSON, RICHARD JOEL, ins. exec.; b. Chgo., May 18, 1943; s. Carl Eugene and Adeline Swanson; student Valparaiso U., M.B.A., Northwestern U., 1968; m. Penney K. Russell, May 31, 1966; children—Matthew, Amy, Kristopher, Kyle. With Swanson Lumber & Box Co., 1967-68; systems analyst No. Trust Bank, Chgo., 1968; mgr. Touche Ross & Co., Chgo., 1968—76; v.p. adminstrv. dept. CNA Ins., Chgo., 1976—. C.P.A., Ill.; cert. mgmt. cons. Lutheran. Club: Chgo. Athletic Assn. Office: CNA Plaza Chicago IL 60685

SWANSON, ROBERT LINDSEY, JR., mgmt. cons. co. exec.; b. Winchester, Mass., Apr. 3, 1952; s. Edward Chickering and Anne (Cusack) Parkhurst; B.S. in Civil Engring., Cornell U., 1974; M.B.A., Stanford U., 1978; m. Merily Ober, Sept. 13, 1975. Asst. planning engr. Stone & Webster Engring. Corp., Boston, 1974-75; planning engr., 1976; intern Coopers & Lybrand, Boston, 1977; asso. cons. Pittiglio, Rabin, Todd & McGrath, Burlington, Mass., 1978-79, mgr., 1980—; lectr. investment analysis seminars. Mem. edn1. adv. bd. Small Bus. Assn. New Eng.; mem. Cornell Secondary Schs. Admissions Com. Cert. mgmt. accountant. Mem. Nat. Assn. Accts., Stanford Bus. Sch. Alumni Assn. Clubs: Cornell of Boston, Stanford of Boston. Home: 38 Jefferson Rd Winchester MA 01890 Office: 50 Mall Rd Burlington MA 01803

SWANSTROM, KATHRYN RAYMOND (MRS. LUTHER D. SWANSTROM), corp. exec.; b. Milw., Sept. 5, 1907; d. William Hyland and Jessie V. (Bliss) Raymond; student Bryant and Stratton Bus. Coll., 1927-28; m. Luther D. Swanstrom, Aug. 27, 1937; 1 son, William Hyland Raymond. Caterer, Racine, Wis., 1926; dir., sec. Diesel-Ritter Corp., 1942-46; asst. mgr., field rep. Master Reporting Co., 1936-52; pres. Kay C. Raymond Assos., 1952—; v.p., treas. Kenneth G. Mackenzie Assos. Asst. sec. nat. com. U.S.A., Third World Petroleum Congress; sec. Ridge Civic Council, 1943-63; mem. Police Traffic Safety Com., 1943—; mem. Mayor's Com. for Keeping Chgo. Clean. Mem. ASTM, Internat. Platform Assn., Soc. Mayflower Descs., A.I.M., D.A.R., Anti-Cruelty Soc., Pi Omicron (past nat. pres.). Episcopalian. Mem. Eastern Star, Ladies Oriental Shrine of N. Am. Clubs: Beverly Hills Woman's, Nat. Republican Women's, Crescendo Musical. Home: 9027 S Damen Ave Chicago IL 60620 Office: Chicago and 3 Old Hill Farms Rd Westport CT 06880

SWARTZ, JAMES RICHARD, investment co. exec.; b. Pitts., Oct. 4, 1942; s. Frank Thomas and Mary Elizabeth (Roth) S.; A.B., Harvard, 1964; M.S. in Indsl. Adminstrn., Carnegie-Mellon U., 1966; m. Susan Lee Shallcross, June 18, 1966; children—James Scott, Karin Lynn, Kristin Lee. Asst. to v.p. mfg. Campbell Soup Co., Camden, N.J., 1966-68; sr. asso. Cresap, McCormick & Paget, N.Y.C., 1968-72; asst. v.p. G.H. Walker, Laird Inc., N.Y.C., 1972-74; v.p. Citicorp Venture Capital Ltd., N.Y.C., 1974-78; gen. partner VENAD Assos., N.Y.C., 1978—; chmn. bd. Amdax Corp.; dir. Daisy Systems Corp., Loehmann's, Inc., Phys. Acoustics Corp., Control Automation Inc., Lexidata Corp., Ungermann-Bass, Inc., Transatlantic Venture Capital Ltd.; pres. N.Y. Venture Forum, 1977-78. Mem. West Windsor Twp. Conservation Com., 1973-74. Mem. Nat. Venture Capital Assn., Assn. for Corporate Growth, Carnegie-Mellon U. Grad. Sch. Indsl. Adminstrn. Alumni Assn. (dir.). Republican. Episcopalian. Clubs: Harvard (N.Y.C.) (N.J.); Board Room, Racquet and Tennis (N.Y.C.); Nassau (N.J.). Home: 15 Hibben Rd Princeton NJ 08540 Office: 280 Park Ave New York NY 10017

SWEARINGEN, EDWARD JAMES, aircraft co. exec.; b. Lockhart, Tex., Sept. 12, 1925; s. Edward James and Ruby Ima (Williams) S.; student public schs., Lockhart; m. Janice Marie Sweeney Raine, Mar. 7, 1975; children by previous marriage—Frances Swearingen McDaniel, Edward Alan. With Continental Airlines, Howard-Aero, Inc., Lear, Inc., 1941-48; founder Swearingen Co. (name changed to Swearingen Aviation Corp.), San Antonio, 1959, chmn. bd.; founder Jetcrafters, Inc., 1973, pres., chief exec. officer. Recipient award for meritorious service to aviation Nat. Bus. Aircraft Assn.; aviation mechanic safety award FAA; Gov.'s Indsl. Expansion award State of Tex.; Indsl. Expansion award San Antonio C. of C. Patentee various devices for aircraft. Home: 3903 Crestridge St San Antonio TX 78229 Office: PO Box 32622 San Antonio TX 78216*

SWEARINGEN, JOHN ELDRED, oil exec.; b. Columbia, S.C., Sept. 7, 1918; s. John Eldred and Mary (Hough) S.; B.S., U. S.C., 1938; M.S., Carnegie Mellon U., 1939; Eng.D., S.D. Sch. Mines and Tech., Mont. Coll. Mining Sci. and Tech.; LL.D., Knox Coll., DePauw U., U. S.C., Butler U., Ill. Coll., Samford U., Calumet Coll.; D.L.H., Nat. Coll. Edn.; D.Bus. Mgmt., Ind. Inst. Tech.; m. Bonnie L. Bolding, May 18, 1969; children by previous marriage—Marcia Lynn (Mrs. Pfleeger), Sarah Kathryn (Mrs. Origer), Linda Sue. Chem. engr. research dept. Standard Oil Co. (Ind.), Whiting, 1939-47; various positions Amoco Prodn. Co., 1947-51; gen. mgr. prodn. Standard Oil Co. (Ind.), 1951, dir., 1952, v.p. prodn., 1954-56, exec. v.p., 1956-58, pres., 1958-65, chief exec. officer, 1960—, chmn. bd., 1965—; dir. Lockheed Corp., Chase Manhattan Corp. Trustee, Carnegie Mellon U., DePauw U.; bd. dirs. Hwy. Users Conf. for Safety and Mobility, 1969-75, Northwestern Meml. Hosp., Max McGraw Wildlife Found., 1964-75; bd. dirs. Automotive Safety Found., 1959-69, chmn., 1962-64; trustee Orchestral Assn., Chgo., 1973-79; mem. adv. bd. Hoover Instn. on War, Revolution and Peace. Decorated Order of Taj (Iran); comdr. Order of Italian Republic; named Sigma Nu Alumnus of Year, 1978. Fellow Am. Inst. Chem. Engrs.; mem. Conf. Bd. (sr.), Am. Petroleum Inst. (dir.; chmn. 1978-79), AIME, Am. Chem. Soc., Nat. Petroleum Council (chmn. 1974-76), Nat. Acad. Engring., Phi Beta Kappa, Sigma Xi, Tau Beta Pi, Omicron Delta Kappa. Clubs: Glen View; Old Elm (Lake Forest, Ill.); Comml., Chicago, Racquet, Mid-Am., Econ. (Chgo.); Links (N.Y.C.); Bohemian (San Francisco); Eldorado (Palm Springs, Calif.). Home: 1420 Lake Shore Dr Chicago IL 60610 Office: 200 E Randolph Dr Chicago IL 60601

SWEARINGEN, LAWSON LEWIS, ins. co. exec.; b. Tex., Dec. 22, 1919; s. Henry Declouit and Annie Marie (Estlinbaum) S.; B.S. in Bus. Adminstrn., La. Tech. U., 1947; m. Jean Cadwallader, Feb. 2, 1940; children—Carolyn, Sharon, Lawson Lewis. Vice pres. William A. Marbury & Co., Ruston, La., 1947-63; with Comml. Union Ins. Co., Boston, 1963—, sr. v.p., 1973-75, pres., chief exec. officer, 1975-80, chmn. bd., chief exec. officer, 1980—. Bd. dirs. La. North-South Expy. Com., 1967, Nat. Council Crime and Delinquency, 1980—, Gordon Coll., Wenham, Mass., 1974—; mem. La. Polit. Edn. Com., 1968-72. Served as officer AUS, 1944-46, 50-51. Named Outstanding Alumnus of Year, La. Tech. U., 1973. Mem. Ins. Inst. Am., Nat. Bd. Fire Underwriters. Baptist. Address: 1 Beacon St Boston MA 02108

SWEARINGEN, WAYNE ELWYN, mgmt. consulting co. exec.; b. Grant, Nebr., Oct. 30, 1924; s. Laurel Brooks and Edna Ruth (Frank) S.; B.S. in Petroleum Engring., U. Okla., 1948; grad. advanced mgmt. program Harvard U., 1965; m. Dorothy Lorene Wilde, June 7, 1946; children—Scott, Lynn, Brett. Petroleum engr. Stanolind Oil and Gas Co. (now Amoco Petroleum Co.), Okalhoma City, 1948-54; engr. and mgmt. cons. Livingston Oil Co. (now LVO Corp.), Tulsa, 1954-60, exec. v.p., 1961-66, pres., chief exec. officer, 1966-74; pres. Swearingen Mgmt. Assos., Tulsa, 1974—; dir. Western Nat. Bank, Tulsa, Bank of the Lakes, Langley, Okla. Served with USAAF, 1942-45. Mem. Okla. Independent Petroleum Assn. Am. (dir. 1960-80, pres. 1971), Am. Assn. Petroleum Geologists, Independent Petroleum Assn. Am., Pi Epsilon Tau. Republican. Lutheran. Clubs: So. Hills Country, Tulsa, Petroleum of Tulsa. Home: 2526 E 31st St Tulsa OK 74105 Office: 320 S Boston St Suite 1104 Tulsa OK 74103

SWEAT, JAMES EARL, tooling planner; b. Dallas, Jan. 9, 1951; s. Elmer and Mary Frances (Fisher) S.; B.S. in Indsl. Arts, N. Tex. State U., 1973; M.Ed. in Indsl. Tech., E. Tex. State U., 1975; m. Sharon Gwennette Brown, July 18, 1975. Salesman, Sears, Roebuck and Co., 1970; owner, operator Sweat's Furniture, Irving, Tex., 1980—; group tech. analyst, tooling planner Otis Engring. Co., Dallas, 1972-80; instr. mech. tech. Tarrant County Jr. Coll., Ft. Worth. Vice pres. West Irving Improvement Assn., 1980—; scoutmaster Boy Scouts Am., 1977-79. Mem. Soc. Mfg. Engrs., Am. Indsl. Arts Assn., Furniture Stylist Guild. Mem. Churches of Christ. Home: 3905 Clay Ave Irving TX 75061 Office: PO Box 34380 Dallas TX 75431

SWEEN, EARL A., food co. exec.; b. Mpls., Jan. 4, 1921; s. August E. and Florence E. Sween; student U. Minn., 1938-42; m. Shirley Ann Ogin, Feb. 14, 1942; children—Deborah Ann, Thomas Earl. Gen. mgr. Sween Bros. Dairy Farms, Inc., Chanhassen and Wayzata, Minn., 1938-53; route supr. Franklin Dairy Co., Mpls., 1953-55; propr., mgr. Stewart Sandwiches, Eden Prairie, Minn., 1955—, chmn. bd. dirs., 1978—; pres. Nat. Stewart Infrared Assn., Fontana, Wis., 1965-66. Mem. Republican Nat. Com.; sustaining mem. Boy Scouts Am. Republican. Mem. Wayzata Community Ch. Clubs: Lafayette Country, Decathlon Athletic, Port Royal, Masons, Shriners. Home: 2440 Old Beach Rd Wayzata MN 55391 Office: 16101 W 78th St Eden Prairie MN 55344

SWEENEY, ALAN, communications systems co. exec.; b. Peckville, Pa., Feb. 12, 1953; s. Thomas Joseph and Delores Elizabeth (Rodway) S.; student Brandywine Coll., 1976, Center for Degree Studies, 1978, Marywood Coll., 1980. Purchasing agt. Sybran Corp., Wilmington, Del., 1976-78; adminstrv. dir. fed. programs Internat. Corr. Schs., Scranton, Pa., 1978-79; mgr. mktg. service sect. Intext Communications Systems, Scranton, 1979—; cons. Consumer Lawyer Publs., 1978-80. Trustee Blakely Ch. Mem. Am. Soc. Tng. and Devel., Am. Vocat. Assn., Friends of Everhart Mus., Lackawanna County Hist. Soc., Friends of Scranton Public Library (dir. 1979-80). Baptist. Clubs: Masons, Purple (U. Scranton). Co-author: Legal Register of

Attorneys in Service to the Elderly, 1980. Home: 314 Hill St Peckville PA 18452 Office: Oak and Pawnee Sts Scranton PA 18515

SWEENEY, CLAYTON ANTHONY, mfg. co. exec.; b. Pitts., Oct. 20, 1931; s. Denis Regis and Grace Francis (Roche) S.; B.S., Duquesne U., Pitts., 1957, LL.B., 1962; m. Sally Dimond, Oct. 4, 1958; children—Sharon, Lorrie, Maureen, Clayton Anthony, Tara, Megan. Supr. transp. claims H. J. Heinz Co., Pitts., 1955-57; mgr. market research Murray Corp. Am., Pitts., 1957-62; admitted to Pa. bar, 1962; partner firm Buchanan, Ingersoll, Rodewald, Kyle and Buerger, Pitts., 1962-78; sr. v.p. Allegheny Ludlum Industries, Inc., Pitts., 1978—, also dir.; dir. Wilkinson Match, Ltd., Second Fed. Savs. & Loan Assn., Pitts.; adj. prof. law Duquesne U. Law Sch. Bd. dirs. Met. Pitts. Public Broadcasting, Pitts. Roman Cath. Diocesan Sch. Bd., Toner Inst., Christian Assos. Southwestern Pa., Golden Triangle YMCA, Pitts.; mem. sch. bd. St. Thomas More Sch., Bethel Park, Pa. Served with U.S. Army, 1953-55. Named to Century Club, Duquesne U., 1978. Mem. Acad. Trial Lawyers Allegheny County, Am. Bar Assn., Pa. Bar Assn., Allegheny County Bar Assn., St. Thomas More Soc. Office: 2 Oliver Plaza Pittsburgh PA 15222

SWEENEY, GLEN RANDOLPH, investment advisor; b. Charleston, S.C., Mar. 10, 1945; s. Glen Leon and Gertrude Claire (Walton) S.; B.S., Oreg. State U., 1973, M.B.A., 1975; m. Carol Ellen Haggard, June 1, 1969; children—Belle Annette, Sonia Kathleen. Advisor, instr. Sch. Bus., Oreg. State U., Corvallis, 1974-80; investment advisor investors Research Inst., Inc., Corvallis, 1977-80, pres., 1980—. Served with USAF, 1964. Registered investment advisor, Oreg. Mem. Beta Gamma Sigma, Phi Sigma Epsilon. Republican. Presbyterian. Club: Corvallis Country. Author: Capital Budgeting: An Individualized Curriculum, 1977. Home: 444 NW 35th St Corvallis OR 97330 Office: 761 NW Harrison Corvallis OR 97330

SWEENEY, JAMES LEE, govt. def. supply center ofcl.; b. Rocky River, Ohio, Mar. 23, 1930; s. John H. and Mary J. (Walkinshaw) S.; B.B.A., Case-Western Reserve, 1959; m. Marion J. Ridley, Oct. 4, 1958; children—John A., James L. Cost accountant AFB, Dayton, Ohio, 1959-62; accountant Defense Electronics Supply Center, Dayton, 1962-64, budget analyst, 1964-67, budget officer, 1967—; dir. Ohio Valley Broadcasting Corp.; pres. 3001 Hoover Inc. Mem. tax adv. com. Dayton-Montgomery County, 1967-70; bd. dirs. Dayton Human Relations Commn., 1970-74, Model Cities Housing Corp., 1972-74. Served with U.S. Army, 1952-54. Recipient Pub. Service award Def. Electronics Supply Center, 1972. Mem. Alpha Phi Alpha. Episcopalian. Producer, daily commentator Spl. Community Report, Sta. WHIO-TV, 1970—; co-producer 5 half-hour specials, Sta. WHIO-TV, 1974-77. Home: 743 Argonne Dr Dayton OH 45408 Office: DESC-CBO Dayton OH 45444

SWEENEY, JAMES RUSSELL, realtor; b. Indpls., July 2, 1929; s. Russell Thomas and Mildred (McCardle) S.; student Hanover Coll., 1947-48; B.S., Butler U., 1956; m. Rita A. McCann, 1958; children—Kathleen, James, Terrance, Kevin. Founder, owner Sweeney Realty Co., Indpls., 1956—, Sweeney Ins. Agy., Indpls., 1956—. Served with USAF, 1951-54. Mem. Nat. Assn. Real Estate Bds., Ind. Real Estate Assn., Indpls. Real Estate Bd., Profl. Ins. Agts. of Am., Am. Legion, D.A.V. Roman Catholic. Clubs: Highland Country, Indpls. Athletic, Econ. of Indpls. Home: 444 Spring Mill Ln Indianapolis IN 46260 Office: 836 E 64 St Indianapolis IN 46220

SWEENEY, JOHN CHARLES, economist; b. Phila., Oct. 7, 1944; s. James Francis and Helen Marie (Christensen) S.; B.S., St. Joseph's Coll., 1968; M.A., Coll. of William and Mary, 1972; postgrad. N.C. State U., 1976-77; m. Catherine Greenwood, Sept. 4, 1971; 1 son, John Douglas. Securities investment analyst Integon Corp., Winston-Salem, 1972-75; chief economist Social Systems, Inc., Chapel Hill, N.C., 1977-78; asso. Booz, Allen & Hamilton, Bethesda, Md., 1978-79; dir. econ. and fin. analysis and systems Marriott Corp., Washington, 1979-80; v.p., treas. McM Corp., Raleigh, N.C., 1980—; guest lectr. Duke U., Durham, N.C., 1977-78, U. N.C., 1976; lectr. Montgomery Coll., Germantown, Md., 1980. Mem. budget com. United Fund of N.C., 1972-75; del. State Dem. Conv., N.C., 1974. Hagley Found. fellow, 1968; L.P. Evans Fellow in adminstrn., 1970. Mem. Nat. Assn. Bus. Economists, Eastern Fin. Assn., N.C. Soc. Fin. Analysts. Democrat. Roman Catholic. Contbr. articles to profl. jours. Home: 3412 Elvin Ct Raleigh NC 27607 Office: Box 12317 Raleigh NC 27605

SWEENEY, JOHN J., labor union exec.; b. N.Y.C., May 5, 1934; s. James and Agnes (McMorrow) S.; B.A., Iona Coll., 1956; m. Maureen Power, July 21, 1962; children—John Jude, Patricia Maureen. Research asso. Internat. Ladies Garment Workers Union, N.Y.C., 1957-60; contract dir. local 32B, Service Employees Internat. Union, N.Y.C., 1961-76, pres. local 32B-32J, 1976—; sec.-treas. Service Employees Internat. Union, AFL-CIO, Washington, 1979-80, pres., 1980—. Trustee, Iona Coll., New Rochelle, N.Y.; bd. dirs. Cath. Youth Orgn.; vice chmn. Yonkers Community Action Program, 1965-69; mem. N.Y.C. Emergency Aid Commn. Mem. Am. Arbitration Assn. (dir.). Office: 1 E 35th St New York NY 10016 also 2020 K St NW Washington DC 20006

SWEENEY, ROBERT J., oil co. exec.; b. Montpelier, Vt., 1927; B.S., Auburn U., 1948; M.S., La. Tech. U.; postgrad. Grad. Sch. Bus. Adminstrn., Harvard U.; married. With Murphy Oil Corp., El Dorado, Ark., 1952—, pres., chief operating officer, 1972—. Office: 200 Jefferson Ave El Dorado AR 71730

SWEENEY, TIMOTHY JAMES, accountant; b. Hempstead, N.Y., Jan. 14, 1948; s. Gerald Arthur and Sophie (Harasymczuk) S.; A.A.S., Nassau Community Coll., 1968; B.B.A., Hofstra U., 1970; m. Geraldine F. Figliuolo, Jan. 31, 1969; children—Timothy James, Matthew. Controller, Community Hosp. of Schoharie County, Inc., Cobleskill, N.Y., 1972-76; chief fiscal analyst N.Y. State Health Dept., Albany, 1976-77; individual practice acctg., Cobleskill, 1977—; mem. faculty SUNY, Cobleskill, 1976-78. Mem. bus. adv. com. Cobleskill Central Schs., 1975; active Cobleskill Little League, 1978-79, Spl. Olympics, 1978. C.P.A., N.Y. Fellow Hosp. Fin. Mgmt. Assn.; mem. Am. Inst. C.P.A.'s, N.Y. State Soc. C.P.A.'s, N.Y. State Assn. Accts. for Public Interest (health care com. 1980), Cobleskill Area C. of C. (dir., treas.), Hofstra Alumni Assn. Home and Office: 48 North St Cobleskill NY 12043

SWEENEY, WILLIAM JOHN, banker; b. Sunnyside, N.Y., Aug. 3, 1929; s. William Joseph and Mae Margaret (Sullivan) S.; student Mt. St. Michael Acad., 1943-47, Fordham U., 1947-50; B.S., C.W. Post Coll., 1966; children—William, Robert, James. With Textile Banking Co., Inc., N.Y.C., 1950—, v.p., dir. credit, 1976—; dir. N.Y. Credit and Fin. Mgmt. Assn., N.Y. Credit Men's Adjustment Bur., Inc. Fund raiser Catholic Charities Archdiocese N.Y.; mem. Cardinal's Com. Laity Boy Scouts Am., N.Y.C. Recipient N.Y. Inst. Credit Asso. award, 1960; Delta Mu Delta Award, 1965. Mem. Am. Arbitration Assn. Clubs: 475, Toppers Credit (dir.), Town Timers Credit, Capital Credit, Uptown Credit Group (dir.), Titan. Office: 51 Madison Ave New York NY 10010

SWEET, BERNARD, airline exec.; b. Cin., Dec. 6, 1923; s. William B. and Elizabeth (Krent) S.; B.A., U. Wis., 1947; m. Betty Sweet, May 29, 1946; 1 dau., Laurie. Chief accountant Madison (Wis.) VA Hosp., 1948; with Republic Airlines, Inc., Mpls., 1948—, exec. v.p., 1967-69, pres., dir., 1969—, chief exec. officer, 1976—, vice-chmn. bd., 1980—; dir. G & K Services, Inc., S.E. Rykoff & Co., Los Angeles. Served with USAAF, 1943-46. Recipient State of Wis. Aerospace Man of Year award, 1972. Mem. Air Transport Assn. Am. (dir.), Assn. Local Transport Airlines (chmn.). Office: 7500 Airline Dr Minneapolis MN 55450

SWEET, MARC STEVEN, food co. exec.; b. Bklyn., Aug. 15, 1945; s. Edward I. and Bess G. (Freiman) S.; B.B.A. (trustees scholar), Pace Coll., 1967; postgrad. Columbia Sch. Bus., 1967-68; m. Naomi Charna Fishbein, Aug. 22, 1971; children—Erica Rebekah, Miriam Shoshana. Sr. staff auditor Arthur Young & Co., 1969-71; asst. corp. controller Liberty Fabrics of N.Y., Inc., 1971-72; corp. accounting mgr. Tetley Inc., 1972-75, corp. budget mgr., 1975—. Asst. scoutmaster Boy Scouts Am., 1963-66, mem. Flatbush dist. com., 1965-67, Eagle Scout, recipient Gold palm. C.P.A., N.Y. Texaco Co. scholar. Mem. Am. Inst. C.P.A.'s, N.Y. State Soc. C.P.A.'s, Planning Execs. Inst. Home: 1282 E 29th St Brooklyn NY 11210

SWEET, PHILIP W. K., JR., bank exec.; b. Mt. Vernon, N.Y., Dec. 31, 1927; s. Philip W.K. and Katharine (Buhl) S.; A.B., Harvard U., 1950; M.B.A., U. Chgo., 1957; m. Nancy Frederick, July 23, 1950; children—Sandra H., Philip W.K., David A.F. Asst. mgr. No. Trust Co., Chgo., 1957-60, 2d v.p., 1960-63, v.p., 1963-68. sr. v.p., 1968-74, exec. v.p., 1974-75, pres., dir., 1975—; pres., dir. No. Trust Corp., 1975—. Bd. dirs. Johnston R. Bowman Health Center for the Elderly, Lake Forest Hosp., Protestant Found., United Way of Met. Chgo.; vice chmn. Ill. Com. of United Negro Coll. Fund; treas., trustee Chgo. Sunday Evening Club; trustee Lake Forest Improvement Trust, Council of the Americas (N.Y.); mem. council Grad. Sch. Bus., U. Chgo. Served with USN, 1950-53. Mem. Assn. of Res. City Bankers, Bankers Club of Chgo., Econ. Club of Chgo., Bond Club of Chgo. Office: 50 S LaSalle St Chicago IL 60675

SWEET, ROBERT THOMAS, banker; b. Hartford, Conn., June 18, 1938; s. Howard Francis and Catherine Elizabeth (Chesanek) S.; B.A., Trinity Coll., 1960; LL.B., U. Balt., 1966; M.A., Cath. U., 1973; m. Bonita Neumeister, June 29, 1963. Asst. dir. research, asst. v.p. Dean Witter, Investment Bankers, N.Y.C., 1969-71; v.p., trust investment officer Riggs Nat. Bank of Washington, 1971—; lectr. investments George Washington U., Am. U.; adviser Singapore Stock Exchange, Seoul (Korea) Stock Exchange, Venezuelan govt., 1978, Chilean banks. Mem. Community Planning Bd., N.Y.C., 1970; active Washington chpt. ARC; bd. dirs. Vol. Clearinghouse D.C. Served with AUS, 1962. Mem. Washington Soc. Investment Analysts (dir. 1972-73, pres., chmn. bd. 1974-75), N.Y. Soc. Security Analysts, Fin. Analysts Fedn. (internat. analysts com.), Am. Fin. Assn., Nat. Economists Club, Pi Gamma Mu. Clubs: International, Metropolitan (Washington); Hyannis (Mass.) Yacht. Contbr. articles to profl. jours. Home: 4934 Western Ave Chevy Chase MD 20016 Office: 4340 Connecticut Ave Washington DC 20008

SWEET, ROSS BENNETT, ins. co. exec.; b. Solvay, N.Y., May 31, 1917; s. Wallace and Vella E. (Bennett) S.; student Cornell U., 1947-48, Beloit Coll., 1961-63; m. Alice E. Lisdell, Dec. 26, 1942; children—R. Brickley, Erick W., Mary Beth. Asst. cashier First Nat. Bank, Dryden, N.Y., 1945-56; exec. v.p., cashier Unadilla Nat. Bank (N.Y.), 1956-59; sec., treas. Farmers & Traders Life Ins. Co., Syracuse, N.Y., 1959-69, fin. v.p., treas., 1969—, also mem. fin. com., dir.; mem. sponsoring com. N.Y. FFA Leadership Tng. Found., Inc., 1975—. Chmn. corp. SODAC. Served to capt. AUS, 1939-45. Republican. Methodist. Clubs: Masons (32 deg.), Rotary. Home: 2 W Lake St Skaneateles NY 13152 Office: 960 James St Syracuse NY 13201

SWEGEL, DOROTHY, personnel service corp. exec.; b. Forest City, Pa., Dec. 23, 1932; d. John J. and Anna T. (Loush) Swegel; student Chestnut Hill Coll., Phila., 1950-51. Periodicals librarian Charles M. Schwab Meml. Library, Bethlehem (Pa.) Steel Co., 1952-55; with spl. sales Nat. Airlines, Miami, Fla., 1955-58; sr. supr. TWA Ambassadors Club, Kennedy Airport, Jamaica, N.Y., 1959-66; owner, pres. CoverTemp Inc., and Gateway Careers, Inc., White Plains, N.Y., 1969—. Personnel council White Plains Regional C. of C.; mem. New Rochelle C. of C., Westchester County Assn. Mem. Adminstrv. Mgmt. Soc. (pres. 1981—), Sales and Mktg. Execs. of Westchester/Fairfield (dir.), Soroptimist Internat. (v.p. Central Westchester). Republican. Roman Catholic. Office: 235 Main St White Plains NY 10601

SWEITZER, ROBERT LEWIS, banker; b. Olean, N.Y., May 4, 1933; s. Raymond Henry and Della June (Koehler) S.; student Ball State U. Ind. Bankers Sch., 1968; grad. N.Y. State Bankers Consumer Credit and Exec. Devel. Schs., 1971; m. Gail Louise Pepperdine, Sept. 28, 1957; children—Patrick R., Susan J.,Lynn A. With Olean Trust Co., 1951—, asst. v.p., 1967-70, v.p.,1970—, mgr., 1975—; mem. banking adv. com. Alfred U. Treas., Olean C. of C.; mem. Olean Town Council; co-chmn. Hosp. Ball of Roses, Olean; mem. adv. bd. Olean Bus. Inst. Served with USN, 1952-56. Recipient Outstanding Service award Olean Youth Athletics Assn., 1975; notary public, State of N.Y. Mem. Olean High Sch. Alumni Assn. (pres. 1976-77, Outstanding Service award 1979), Am. Legion, Cattaraugus County Bankers Assn. (pres. 1965-66). Republican. Roman Catholic. Clubs: Olean City, Bartlett Country. Home: 23 McCann Rd Olean NY 14760 Office: 129 N Union St Olean NY 14760

SWENSON, ARTHUR WILLIAM, JR., terrazzo mfg. co. exec.; b. St. Louis, Nov. 29, 1925; s. Arthur William and Ruth Marjorie (DeHoog) S.; B.B.A., Washington U., St. Louis, 1949; m. Eloise Grace Green, Sept. 14, 1946; children—Kim, Peter, Krista. Dist. mgr. Eljer Co., Kansas City, Mo., 1950-56; owner Swenson Co. Mfrs. Rep., Shawnee Mission, Kans., 1956—; pres. Stern-Williams Co., Inc., Shawnee Mission, 1962—. Served with inf. U.S. Army, 1943-46. Mem. Am. Soc. Plumbing Engrs., Carthage (Mo.) C. of C., Phi Delta Theta. Republican. Lutheran. Clubs: Homestead Country, Broadview Country. Home: 5411 W 79th Terr Prairie Village KS 66208 Office: 5452 Antioch Rd Shawnee Mission KS 66202

SWENSON, HAROLD FRANCIS, home products mfg. co. exec.; b. N.Y.C., Apr. 28, 1915; s. Charles Henry and Ethel Marie (Igoe) S.; A.B., Manhattan Coll., 1938; student Fordham U. Law Sch., 1938-41; m. Mildred Chandler, Dec. 31, 1943; 1 dau., Sally. Mem. law firm Root, Clark, Buckner & Ballantine, N.Y.C., 1938-41; spl. agt. FBI, 1941-47; indsl. relations exec. Gulf Oil, San Tome, Venezuela, 1947-52; employee relations and security exec. Sears, Roebuck & Co., Chgo., 1953-54; with State Dept., Washington, 1955-65, Def. Dept., Washington, 1965-68; pres., chief exec. officer, dir. Bishop's Service Inc., N.Y.C., 1969-73; v.p. surveys, mktg. and fgn. ops. Intertel Inc., Washington, 1974-78; with law dept., security exec. Chesebrough-Pond's Inc., Greenwich, Conn., 1978—. Polit. attache U.S. Embassy, Buenos Aires, Argentina, 1956-62. Served with USMCR, 1944-46. Mem. Soc. Former FBI Agts., Internat. Assn. Chiefs of Police, Beta Sigma. Clubs: Chantilly Golf and Country (Centerville, Va.); Army-Navy (Washington); Silvermine Golf (Nowalk, Conn.); Downtown Athletic (N.Y.C.). Home: Greenwich CT 06830 Office: 33 Benedict Pl Greenwich CT 06830

SWEPSTON, WILSEY WISE (SWEP), life ins. co. exec.; b. Pine Bluff, Ark., Mar. 1, 1922; s. Addison Blue and Thelma Jean (Fain) S.; student Henderson State Tchrs. Coll., Arkadelphia, Ark., 1941-43, East State Tchrs. Coll., Commerce, Tex., 1943; m. Doris Courtney, Nov. 1947; children—Martha Swepston Cooper, Mary Swepston Crumb. Debit agt. Met. Life Ins. Co., Pine Bluff, 1946-49; salesman Jefferson Supply Co., Pine Bluff, 1949-53; sales mgr. Tupelo (Miss.) Refrigerator Co., 1953-57; agt. Empire Life Ins. Co., Little Rock, 1957-58; dir. mgr. Christian Found. Life IHs. Co., Little Rock, 1958, state mgr., 1960-64, v.p., 1964-68; pres. Lincoln Life & Casualty Co., Lincoln, Nebr., 1969-80, chmn. bd., 1980—, also dir.; dir. Fin. Security Life Ins. Co., Moline, Ill.: former instr. Dale Carnegie; public speaker. Mem. adv. bd. dirs. Salvation Army, chmn. emergency disaster com.; past bd. dirs. N. Central region Boy Scouts Am., 1976-77, past v.p. Old West Trails Area, 1975-77; team leader United Way of Lincoln, 1977-79; mem. The Lincoln Found., community trust, 1978. Served with Combat Engrs., U.S. Army, World War II; ETO. Mem. Nat. Assn. Life Underwriters (past Nebr. chmn. edn. and tng.), Lincoln C. of C. (past chmn. local industry com; mem. speakers bur.), Ins. Fedn. Nebr., Internat. Platform Assn., Internat. Footprint Assn., Ins. Inst. Nebr., Newcomen Soc. N. Am., Nat. Assn. Life Cos. (past dir., state legis. com.), Am. Legion. Republican. Methodist. Clubs: Sertoma, Exec. (past pres., dir.) (Lincoln); Masons, Shriners; Order Eastern Star (Worthy Patron 1980); Hiram; Elks; Univ.; Rebounders; Touchdown; Saturday Night (past pres., dir.). Office: 124 N 11 St Lincoln NE 68501

SWIERCZNSKI, S. THEODORE, farmer, city ofcl.; b. Gaines, N.Y., May 30, 1932; s. Stanley M. and Edna B. (Balcerzak) S.; cert. in labor-mgmt. relations Cornell U., 1967, cert. mgmt. skills, 1971; m. Mary Geraldine Palmer, Oct. 27, 1956; children—Maureen, Tod, Eileen, Colleen, Christeen, Cathleen, Patrick. Owner, operator farm, Albion, N.Y., 1953—; mem. Agrl. Resources Commn. N.Y. State; mem. exec. com farm Bur. of Orleans County (N.Y.); mem. Coop. Extension; bd. dirs. Orleans County Soil and Water Dist., 1970-78, chmn. bd. dirs., 1972-74, vice-chmn. bd. dirs., 1974-78. Mem. Orleans County Legis. Body, 1970-79; supr., chief exec. Town of Gaines, 1970-81; committeeman Lewiston Trail council Boy Scouts Am. Served with USAF, 1950-52. Recipient Friend of Extension award Coop. Extension Orleans County, 1970. Mem. Orleans County Town Suprs. Assn., Assn. Towns N.Y. State. Democrat. Roman Catholic. Clubs: Lions, Am. Legion, K.C., Elks. Author Regional Water Quality Plan for Region # 8 (N.Y. State Dept. Conservation cert. appreciation 1979). Home and Office: 13773 Albion Eagle Harbor Rd Albion NY 14411

SWIFT, A. DEAN, retail trade exec.; b. 1918; B.A., U. Ill., 1940; married. With Sears, Roebuck & Co., 1940—, store mgr., 1949-64, product mgr., 1964-69, v.p. so. territory, 1969-73, pres., 1973-80, now dir.; dir. Commonwealth Edison Co., First Chgo. Corp., Sears Roebuck Acceptance Corp., Allstate Ins. Co., Homart Devel. Co. Address: Sears Roebuck & Co Sears Tower Chicago IL 60684*

SWIFT, GEORGE LEE, lawyer; b. Austin, Tex., Jan. 25, 1936; s. Roy Lee and Anna Jane (Henson) S.; A.B., Johns Hopkins U., 1957; J.D., U. Tex., 1960; 1 son, Justin Lee. Admitted to Tex. bar, 1960, D.C. bar, 1971, U.S. Tax Ct. and Customs Ct. bar; individual practice law, San Marcos, Tex., 1961-63; atty. U.S. Dept. Treasury, Washington, 1963-67; legis. cons. U.S. Post Office, 1967; dir. Office of Fed. Projects, U. Tex. System, 1968-70; pvt. law practice, Washington and Austin, 1971—; pres. The Lander Co., Austin, Washington Investment Properties. Alderman, City of San Marcos, 1962-63; mem. fin. com. Nat. Democratic Com., 1971—. Mem. Am. Soc. Internat. Law, Nat. Assn. Immigration and Nationality Lawyers, D.C., Inter-Am., Tex., Travis County bar assns. Home: 1600 Foxhall Rd NW Washington DC 20007 and 1837 W Lake Dr Austin TX 78741 Office: 1100 17th St NW Washington DC 20036 and 1444 American Bank Tower Austin TX 78701

SWIGERT, SUE ANTHONE, mgmt. and fin. cons.; b. Monmouth, Ill., Mar. 28, 1947; d. Vernon D. and Wilma F. Pilger; B.S. in Human Devel., Pa. State U., 1969; M.B.A., U. Ill., 1974; m. Thomas C. Swigert, May 26, 1974. Sr. cons. Swigert & Assos., Evanston, Ill., 1975—. Served to 1st lt. WAC, 1969-71. Decorated Army Commendation medal. Mem. DAR, P.E.O. (chpt. pres. 1977-80, champlain round table 1980), M.B.A. Assn. (chmn. community affairs com.), Mortar Board Young Women's Aux. of Women's Club of Evanston, Phi Upsilon Omicron. Home: 1567 Ridge Ave Evanston IL 60201 Office: 1603 Orrington Ave Suite 1200 Evanston IL 60201

SWIGERT, THOMAS CRESAP, mgmt. cons.; b. Evanston, Ill., Apr. 17, 1948; s. Verne Wilson and Marjorie (Helm) S.; B.A. in History, U. Ill., 1970, M.B.A., 1975; m. Sue Anthone Pilger, May 26, 1974. Partner, fin. officer S.T. & W., Ltd., Urbana, Ill., 1970-74; gen. bus. cons. Swigert Enterprises, Urbana, 1970-75; mgr. and credit analyst, credit dept. Lake View Trust & Savs. Bank, Chgo., 1975-77; mgmt. cons. Deloitte, Haskins & Sells, C.P.A.'s, Chgo., 1977-78; sr. asso. Swigert & Assos., mgmt. cons., Evanston, 1978—; instr. Am. Inst. Banking, 1978—. Mem. Inst. Mgmt. Cons.'s, U. Ill. Alumni Assn. (life), U. Ill. Commerce Coll. Alumni Assn., S.A.R. (bd. mgrs. Ill. soc.), Sigma Iota Epsilon (treas. 1971). Clubs: Univ. (Evanston); Union League (Chgo.). Home: 1567 Ridge Ave Evanston IL 60201 Office: One American Plaza Suite 312 Evanston IL 60201

SWIHART, JOHN MARION, aircraft mfg. corp. exec.; b. New Winchester, Ohio, Dec. 27, 1923; s. Harry Miron and Fay I. (Cress) S.; B.S. in Physics, Bowling Green State U., 1947; B.S. in Aero. Engring., Ga. Inst. Tech., 1949, postgrad., 1951-53; m. Gloria Ann Stocker, June 15, 1947; children—Vicki Ann, John Richard, Thomas Marion, Mark Andrew. Asst. group leader propulsion group NASA, 1956-58, group leader spl. projects, 1958-59, head advanced configurations group aircraft, 1959-62, chief large supersonic tunnels br., 1962-62; with Boeing Co., 1962—, dir. internat. sales for Far East, Boeing Comml. Airplane Co., Renton, Wash., 1971-74, v.p. Japan, Boeing Internat. Corp., Tokyo, 1973-74, dep. dir. internat. sales, Renton, 1974-75, 7x7 program mgr., Kent, Wash., 1975-76, dir. new airplane product devel., sales, mktg., Seattle, 1976-78, dir. product devel, sales, mktg., 1978-79, v.p. U.S., Can. sales, 1979—. Served to 1st lt. USAAF, 1943-45. Decorated D.F.C., Air medal with 3 oak leaf clusters. Fellow AIAA (chmn. aircraft design com. 1970-72, chmn. Pacific N.W. sec. 1969-70, gen. chmn. aircraft systems and design meeting 1977); mem. Am. Ordnance Assn., Japan-Am. Soc. (pres. 1978-79). Contbr. numerous papers to profl. lit. Office: Boeing Comml Airplane Co PO Box 3707 Seattle WA 98124

SWIMMER, ROSS OWEN, banker; b. Oklahoma City, Oct. 26, 1943; s. Robert Otis and Virginia Marie (Pounder) S.; B.A., U. Okla., 1965, J.D., 1967; m. Margaret Ann McConnell, June 30, 1965; children—Joseph Ross, Michael David. Admitted to Okla. bar; partner firm Hanson, Peterson, Thompkins, Oklahoma City, 1967-72; counsel for Cherokee Nation, Tahlequah, Okla., 1972-74, prin. chief, 1975—; exec. v.p. First Nat. Bank, Tahlequah, 1974, pres., 1975—. Bd. dirs. Five Civilized Tribes Found., Inc.; mem. Inter-tribal Council of Five Civilized Tribes; mem. Okla. Indsl. Devel. Commn.; chmn.

Tahlequah Planning and Zoning Commn.; mem. Tahlequah Area Arts and Humanities Council; vestry St. Basil's Episcopal Ch.; mem. state com. on Indian work Epis. Ch.; mem. exec. com. Eastern Okla. council Boy Scouts Am.; trustee Northeastern State U. Ednl. Found. Mem. Am. Bar Assn., Okla. Bar Assn., Cherokee County Bar Assn., Okla. Bankers Assn., Okla. Hist. Soc., Cherokee Nat. Hist. Soc. (pres. 1979-80), Tahlequah C. of C. (Outstanding Bus. Person 1977). Republican. Home: PO Box 393 Tahlequah OK 74464 Office: PO Box 59 Tahlequah OK 74464

SWINDELL, ROBERT BRASS, mgmt. service co. exec.; b. Pitts., Apr. 24, 1930; s. James A. and Elizabeth (Brass) S.; student U. Pitts., 1948; m. Phyllis J. Sutton, Jan. 1949; children—Robert H., Gary S., Dale M., Robin A. Founder, owner, pres. Dell Fastener Corp., Pitts., 1961-67, Bldg. Fastener Corp., Pitts., 1967-68, Bldg. Fastener Corp., Phila., 1968-72, Exell Toll & Supply Co., Columbus, Ohio, 1972—; pres. Mgmt. Service Corp., Pitts., 1973—, Robert B. Swindell, Inc.; dir. Logos Book Stores. Chmn. devel. com., mem. exec. com., bd. dirs. St. Clair Meml. Hosp.; ofcl. Mt. Lebanon United Presbyn. Ch.; trustee Eutychus Found.; founder, trustee Robert H. Swindell Charitable Trust. Served with USMCR, 1948-50. Mem. Nat. Fastener Distbr. Assn. Republican. Clubs: Pitts. Athletic Assn., Chartiers Country, Ocean Reef.

SWINDELLS, WILLIAM, JR., mfg. co. exec.; b. Oakland, Calif., Sept. 16, 1930; s. William and Irene (Gerlinger) S.; student Amherst Coll., 1948-50; B.S. in Indsl. Engring., Stanford U., 1953; postgrad. Harvard U. Sch. Bus. Adminstrn., 1960; m. Ann Johnston, Mar. 12, 1955; children—William, Jean, Leslie, Charles. With Williamette Industries, Inc., Portland, Oreg., 1953—, exec. v.p., 1974—, pres. bldg. materials group, 1974—; dir. Omark Industries. Bd. dirs. Oreg. Symphony; trustee Willamette U. Served to 2d lt. USAF, 1953. Mem. Oreg. Hist. Soc. (dir.). Clubs: Multnomah, Waverley Country, Arlington. Office: Willamette Industries 1300 SW 5th Ave Portland OR 97201*

SWINTON, BRIAN CHEEVER, real estate co. exec.; b. Salt Lake City, Nov. 8, 1944; s. Elden G. and Venice (Cheever) Miller; B.S. with distinction, U. Utah, 1969; M.B.A. with distinction, Harvard, 1977; m. Sue Annette Stayner, Dec. 27, 1968; children—Cori Sue, Staci Annette, Sonni Leah, Brian Burns, Stayner. Pres., chmn. bd. Western Am. Mgmt., Inc., 1970—, Sweetwater Condoshare and predecessors, 1970—, Sweetwater Park, 1972—; pres. Sweetwater Properties, 1973—; chmn. bd. Resort Systems, Inc., 1974—; pres. First Western Security, 1976—; broker, pres. Sweetwater Realty, 1976—; guest lectr. Harvard U. Past pres. U. Utah Century Club; mem. adv. council Utah State U. Coll. Bus.; pres. United Way, Salt Lake Met. area, 1981; campaign chmn. for U.S. Ho. of Reps. candidate, 1974; chmn. alumni awards com. U. Utah. Served with U.S. Army Res., 1964-70. Recipient Outstanding Cadet award; named One of 13 Outstanding Young Utah Citizens, Utah Holiday Mag., Exec. of Month, Comml. Break Publ. Mem. Urban Land Inst., Am. Land Developers Assn. (dir.), Nat., Utah homebuilders assns., Nat., Utah, Salt Lake realtors assns., U. Utah Alumni Assn. (dir.), Salt Lake City Jaycees (Distinguished Service award), Skull and Bones, Owl and Key, Beehive, Pi Kappa Alpha (nat. v.p.), Delta Sigma Pi (dist. pres.). Mormon (stake pres.). Clubs: Rotary (Salt Lake). Home: 789 North View Dr Salt Lake City UT 84130 Office: 200 N Main Salt Lake City UT 84103

SWOPE, JAMES SIDNEY, cosmetic co. exec.; b. Killeen, Tex., July 8, 1921; s. Charles Walker and Eva (Rodgers) S.; B.S. in Govt. and Politics, U. Md.; postgrad. Naval War Coll., 1954-55, Armed Forces Indsl. Coll., 1960-61; m. Bobbye Sue McGill, Mar. 22, 1945; children—James Sidney, Jeffrey G., Shannon. Commd. ensign U.S. Navy, 1941, advanced through grades to capt., 1960; served with various fighter squadrons, Japan, Philippines, Taiwan and Vietnam; comdg. officer naval base, Fla.; ret., 1971; with CIC Cosmetics Internat. Corp., Dallas, 1971—, v.p. sales, 1973-74, pres., chief exec. officer, 1974—; chmn. bd. Jaison of Dallas, 1977—. Decorated D.S.M., D.F.C. (2), Air medal (7). Mem. Fighter Aces Assn., Assn. Naval Aviators, Tailhook Assn. Methodist. Home: 8615 Inwood Rd Dallas TX 75209 Office: 1414 Round Table St Dallas TX 75247

SYED, SHAFI MOHAMED, mfg. co. exec.; b. Mysore, India, Feb. 10, 1939; came to Can., 1969, naturalized, 1973; s. Bashir Abdul and Rahmat Khanun (Hyder) S.; B.A. with honors, U. Mysore, 1962, D.S.S., 1966; diploma engring. Technische Hochschule, Aachen, W. Ger., 1968, diploma Wirtschaft, 1969; m. Elisabeth Logister, Dec. 23, 1969. Research asst. Dynamit Nobel A.G., Troisdorf, W. Ger., 1966-68; purchasing mgr. Olsonite Corp., Windsor, Ont., Can., 1969-75; purchasing mgr. Bendix Corp., Windsor, 1976-80, mgr. purchasing worldwide, supercharger program center, Southfield, Mich., 1980—, chmn. N. Am. Bendix Chem. Coordination, 1977-79. Mem. Soc. Plastic Engrs., Purchasing Mgmt. Assn. Can. Home: 1 Dolphin Rd Windsor ON N8W 2B1 Canada Office: 945 Prince Rd Windsor ON N8Y 4S3 Canada

SYFERT, ROBERT KENDALL, ins. exec.; b. Columbus, Ohio, Dec. 15, 1917; s. Jacob Ross and Rachel H. (Perry) S.; student Ohio State U., Franklin U.; m. Gwendolyn T. Kemnitzer, Nov. 9, 1940; children—Steven T., Cynthia Jo. Exec. asst. Nationwide Mut. Ins. Cos., Columbus, 1947-57; chief rating sect. Ohio Ins. Dept., Columbus, 1957-59; v.p. Ins. Co. N. Am., Phila., 1959-74; pres. Bankers Standard Ins. Co., Wilmington, Del., 1974—; dir. Nat. Urban Ins. Co.; bd. electors Ins. Hall of Fame. Trustee, Griffith Found. Served to sgt., USAAF, 1943-46. Mem. Soc. Ins. Research. Club: Univ. and Whist (Wilmington). Office: 3531 Silverside Rd Bedford Bldg Wilmington DE 19810

SYLAK, CHARLES JOHN, JR., steel processing co. exec.; b. Rochester, Pa., May 15, 1950; s. Charles John and Josephine Lucille (Shutey) S.; B.A. in Journalism and Mktg. Communications, Duquesne U., 1972. Pub. relations intern Magee-Women's Hosp., Univ. Health Center Pitts., 1971-72; personnel adminstr., elevator div. Westinghouse Electric Corp., Gettysburg, Pa., 1972-75, personnel staff asst., Buffalo divs., 1975-77; mgr. personnel and adminstrn. Shasta, Inc., Coraopolis, Pa., 1977—, sec.-treas., 1978—; dir. Shutey Assos., Inc.; cons. communications J&J Forging Co. Publicity chmn. United Way Adams County (Pa.), 1973; asst. campaign chmn. Easter Seal Soc. Adams County, 1974, campaign chmn., 1975; mem. personnel policies survey panel Bur. Nat. Affairs. Recipient Project PICA award United Way Buffalo and Erie County, 1977. Mem. Pitts. Personnel Assn., Am. Mgmt. Assn., Smaller Mfrs. Council Western Pa., Urban League C. of C. Democrat. Roman Catholic. Clubs: Bear Rocks Community, Seven Oaks Country. Home: 511 Midway Dr Beaver PA 15009 Office: Lewis Ave Coraopolis PA 15108

SYLVESTER, ANGELO, mfg. co. exec.; b. N.Y.C., July 31, 1928; s. Angel and Blanche (Nessanovich) S.; B.S., CCNY, 1955; m. Mary Vasconi, June 29, 1948; children—David, Melodie. Clk., then jr. accountant Big 3 Music Corp., N.Y.C., 1942-55; auditor, then cost mgr. Royal Dutch Oil Shell Group, S.A. and W.I., 1955-61; controller Bimini Run, Ltd., W.I., Bahamas, 1961-64; corporate audit coordinator Talley Industries, Inc., N.Y.C., 1964-73, v.p., asst. treas., asst. sec., controller subs. Sherayne Mfg. Co., N.Y.C., 1973-80, mng. asso. subs. Industrias Manufactureras El Salvador, S.A.; internat. audit mgr. St. Regis Paper Co., 1980—. Recipient El Salvadorean Inst. award of bus. achievement, 1974-76; mgmt. scholar Standard Oil N.J., 1953. Certified internal auditor. Mem. N.Y. Credit and Financial Mgmt. Assn., Inst. Internal Auditors. Author: Stakanovism, 1958. Home: 613 New Norwalk Rd New Canaan CT 06840

SYLVESTER, RICHARD RUSSELL, fin. cons. co. exec.; b. Newton, Iowa, Jan. 10, 1938; s. Leslie Gardner and Effie (Williams) S.; M.B.A., U. So. Calif., 1962; Ph.D., U. Calif., Los Angeles, 1970, postdoctoral scholar in Engring., 1971-73; postdoctoral scholar in Law, Loyola U., 1977-81; m. Irene Elizabeth Lehman, Apr. 17, 1976; children—Bonnie Ann, Vicky Ellis, Juliesta Elaine. Designer corp. offices Gen. Motors Corp., Warren, Mich., 1958; sr. analyst Lockheed Aircraft Corp., Burbank, Calif., 1962-66; sr. planner corporate offices Hughes Aircraft Co., Culver City, Calif., 1966-68; sr. staff economist, staff mgr. TRW, Inc., Redondo Beach, Calif., 1969-70; asst. prof. Calif. State U., 1970-73; mgr. corporate planning Studebaker-Worthington/Celesco, Costa Mesa, Calif., 1973-75; mgmt. cons., owner Sylvester Assos., Los Angeles, 1970—, Ph.D. Pub. Co., Sylvester Appraisal Co., Culver City, 1977—, also Sylvester Advt. Agy., Def. Research Co.; lectr. Northrop U., U. Calif., U. So. Calif., Loyola U., La Verne U., 1961—; asst. prof. Calif. State U., 1970-73; asso. prof. Pepperdine U., 1975-76; co-founder Theta Cable TV, Los Angeles, 1966-67; pres. U.S. Electropower Controls Corp., 1970-71. Gen. Motors Corp. scholar, 1953-57; Ford Found. grantee, 1965; U.S. Fed. Govt. research grantee, 1967-70; U. Calif. postdoctoral scholar in systems engring., 1970-73. Mem. Beta Gamma Sigma, Alpha Kappa Psi. Author: Management Concepts, 1972; The Impending Crisis, 1979; Tax Planning, 4th edit., 1980; Investment Economics, 1980; contbr. tech. reports to profl. lit. Patentee in field. Home: 10860 Arizona Ave Culver City CA 90230

SYLVESTER, TERRY LEE, real estate devel. exec.; b. Cin., June 12, 1949; s. Wilbert Fairbanks and Jewell S.; B.S. in Bus. Accounting, Miami U., Oxford, Ohio, 1972; m. Janet Lynn Brigger, Nov. 29, 1975; children—Carisa, Laura, Jason. Staff accountant Alexander Grant & Co., C.P.A.'s, Cin., 1972; treas., controller Imperial Community Developers, Inc., Cin., subs. of Chelsea Moore Devel. Corp., 1972—; controller home bldg. div. Chelsea Moore Devel. Corp., 1978—; controller, chief fin. officer Armstrong Cos., apt. mgmt., 1978-79, Dorger Investments, Cin., 1979—. Home: 31 Woodmont Ct Fairfield OH 45014 Office: 3660 Hauck Rd Cincinnati OH 45241

SYMONDS, BRUCE KNIGHT, mgmt. cons. services co. exec.; b. Contoocook, N.H., Mar. 20, 1923; s. Arthur George and Winnifred (Chase) S.; A.B. cum laude, Dartmouth Coll., 1950; m. Jane Balderston Cadbury, June 15, 1950; children—William C., Ann F., Robert B. With Ralston Purina Co., St. Louis, 1950-68, dir. market devel. Ralston Purina Internat., 1963-68; dir. mktg. Hubbard Milling Co., Mankato, Minn., 1968-74; v.p. mktg. Murphy Products Co., Burlington, Wis., 1974-75; pres. Bruce K. Symonds & Co., Waukesha, Wis., 1975—; dir. Doane Agrl. Services, Inc. Served with U.S. Army, 1948-50. Mem. Am. Mktg. Assn., Nat. Agri-Marketing Assn., Am. Feed Mfrs. Assn., Nat Feed Ingredients Assn. Methodist. Contbr. articles to profl. jours. Office: W288 S5023 Rockwood Trail Waukesha WI 53186

SYMONDS, H. N. MURRAY, aircraft and aerospace components and systems co. exec.; b. Oklahoma City, Dec. 11, 1930; s. Charles A. and Helen (Rummel) S.; B.S., Okla. State U., 1953; B.A., Okla. U., 1957. Area mgr. Sinclair Oil Co., Okla., 1957; area sales mgr. Macklanberg-Duncan Co., Wichita, Kans., 1958-61; regional sales mgr. Talley Corp., Wichita, 1961-65; v.p. CTR, Inc., Arlington, Tex., 1965-76, chmn. bd., pres., 1976—; v.p., dir. Sota Corp., Los Angeles, 1980—. Served with Counter-Intelligence, AUS, 1953-56. Mem. Kappa Alpha (pres. Okla. State U. 1951-53).

SYM SMITH, ALISTAIR, food co. exec.; b. Buenos Aires, Argentina, June 2, 1933; s. Claude and Stella (Norris) Sym S.; B.B.A., 1961; m. Maria Jankowski, Aug. 31, 1965; children—Sheila, Diego, Martin. With Gillette Co., 1949-74, gen. mgr. Latin Am. group, to 1974; pres. internat. div. Swift & Co., Chgo., 1974—. Served with Argentine Navy, 1954. Club: Saddle and Cycle (Chgo.). Office: Swift Co 115 W Jackson Chicago IL 60604

SZCZEPANSKI, FRANK EDWARD, fin. analyst; b. Chgo., Oct. 10, 1950; s. Edward A. and Dorothy M. (Balon) S.; B.S. with honors, Purdue U., 1973, M.S., 1973; m. Carol A. Budny, May 18, 1974. Fin. analyst Burroughs Corp., Detroit, 1973-75, sr. fin. analyst Latin Am. area, 1975-76, Americas-Pacific div., 1976-77, corp. staff analyst, 1977-78, mgr. fin. analysis, Piscataway, N.J., 1978-79, mgr. acctg., 1979-80, mgr. fin. systems Computer Systems Group, Detroit, 1980-81, mgr. indsl. engring., Piscataway, N.J., 1981—. Mem. Assn. M.B.A. Execs., Internat. Platform Assn., Phi Kappa Phi. Roman Catholic. Office: 330 S Randolphville Rd Piscataway NJ 08854

SZEKELY, DEBORAH SHAINMAN, health and beauty resort exec.; b. N.Y.C., May 3, 1922; d. Harry and Rebecca (Seidman) Shainman; student pub. schs., U.S.A., Tahiti, Mexico; Litt.D. (hon.), Calif. Sch. Profl. Psychology, 1978; m. Edmond Bordeaux Szekely, Dec. 26, 1939 (div. Dec. 1969); children—Livia Soledad, Alexandre Odin; m. Vincent E. Mazzanti, June 16, 1971 (div. 1978). Co-founder, dir. Rancho La Puerta, Tecate, Baja Calif., Mexico, 1940; founder, pres., dir. Golden Door, Inc., Escondido, Calif., 1959—; pres. Golden Door Cosmetics, San Diego. Creator, past dir. Children to Children program, 1960-63; nat. sponsor Save the Children Fedn., 1965—; bd. dirs. Srs. in Philantrophic Services, Inc., 1961, vice chmn., 1963; bd. dirs. San Diego Opera; mem. Pres. Nixon's Conf. Phys. Fitness and Sports, 1968, Pres. Ford's Council Phys. Fitness and Sports, 1975-76; founder, dir. Free Family Fitness and Fun Centers, San Diego; founder, bd. dirs., v.p. Combined Arts and Edn. Council San Diego; bd. dirs. Theatre and Arts Found., Inc.; bd. dirs. Sch. Medicine, U. Calif., San Diego, mem. Chancellor's Club, chmn. bd. overseers, 1976-78; mem. bd. Sch. Bus. Adminstrn., U. San Diego, 1976—; bd. dirs., exec. com. San Diego council Boy Scouts Am., 1976—; mem. adv. council San Diego County Women's chpt. Freedom Found. at Valley Forge, 1976—; chmn. bd. govs. San Diego Stadium Authority, 1976-77; trustee Calif. Sch. Profl. Psychology, 1980—; exec. com., vice chmn. clin. services Menninger Found., 1978—. Named Calif. Small Bus. Person of Year, SBA, 1976; Vol. of Year, S.D. chpt. Fund-Raiser Execs., 1979. Author: The Golden Door Book of Health and Beauty, 1961; Secrets of the Golden Door, 1977. Office: 3085 Renard Way San Diego CA 92103

SZILASI, WILLIAM JOSEPH, securities co. exec.; b. Passaic, N.J., Dec. 23, 1942; s. William James and Erma (Straub) S.; B.S., Rutgers U., 1971; postgrad. N.Y. Law Sch., 1977—; m. Rosemarie Ricciardi, July 26, 1964; 1 son, William James. Accountant, N.J. Bank, Paterson, 1963-65, Nabisco, Fair Lawn, N.J., 1965-67, Rayfield, Albano & Leaf, C.P.A.'s, Newark, 1967-69; v.p. Mitchell, Hutchins Inc., N.Y.C., 1969-77; v.p. compliance Paine Webber Jackson & Curtis, Inc., N.Y.C., 1977-80, v.p. legal, 1980—; allied mem. N.Y. Stock Exchange. Served with USMCR, 1960-63. Mem. Nat. Assn. Securities Dealers, Securities Industry Assn., Futures Industry Assn. Republican. Roman Catholic. Club: Ocean Acres Country. Home: 6 9th St Barnegat NJ 08005 Office: 140 Broadway New York NY 10005

TABACCHI, FRED LAWRENCE, appliance mfg. co. exec.; b. Kelly, N.Mex., Aug. 10, 1917; s. Carl. F. and Dora M. (Katzenstein) T.; student in Bus. Adminstrn., Alexander Hamilton Inst., 1950-51; m. Laura Mae Doebbeling, Dec. 23, 1944; children—Loretta Johndrow, Larry, Terri Beth Gardner. With Hoover Co., 1937—, salesman, Colorado Springs, Colo., 1937-38, dist. mgr., St. Joseph, Mo., 1945-55, br. mgr., Omaha, 1955-57, div. mgr., Cleve., 1959-61, gen. sales mgr., 1962-63, sr. v.p. U.S.-Can. ops., 1964-66, exec. v.p. Hoover Group, 1966-75, pres., chief operating officer Hoover Co., N. Canton, Ohio, 1975—; vice chmn. Hoover Worldwide Corp., pres. Hoover Can., Inc., Hoover Mexicana S.A. de C.V., Hoover Industrial y Comercial S.A., Colombia; dir. Hoover Co., Hoover Worldwide Corp., Hoover Ltd. (U.K.), Hoover Can., Inc., Hoover Industrial y Comercial, S.A., Hoover Mexicana, S.A. de C.A., Chemko Comml. Products (Hoover div.). Chmn., United Negro Coll. Fund, 1971; bd. dirs. Mt. Union Coll.; campaign chmn. Jr. Achievement Program, 1980. Mem. Vacuum Cleaner Assn. Am. (pres. 1973-75), U.S.-Mexico C. of C. (pres., chmn. 1977-79, dir., exec. com. 1979—). Club: Brookside Country (Canton). Office: 101 E Maple St North Canton OH 44220

TABAR, WILLIAM JOHN, recreational products mfg. co. exec.; b. Cleve., Feb. 24, 1931; s. John and Katherine T.; B.S. in Chem. Engring., Pa. State U., 1953; M.S. in Chem. Engring., W.Va. U., 1961; m. Bertha A. Sadlon, July 12, 1952; children—Susan L., Sharon L., Sandra L., William John. With Union Carbide Co., N.Y.C., 1953-69; v.p. mfg. Rochester Button Co., Rochester, N.Y., 1969-74; pres. AMF Head Div., Boulder, Colo., 1974-79; exec. v.p., chief operating officer Scott U.S.A., Clearfield, Utah, 1979—. Pres., Tennis Found. N.A.; mem. Mfrs. Council, Boulder. Served to 1st lt. USMC, 1953-55. Mem. Am. Inst. Chem. Engrs., U.S. Ski Mfrs. Assn. (pres.). Clubs: Boulder Country, Rochester, Elks. Home: 4185 Beus Dr Ogden UT 84403 Office: Freeport Center Bldg D-11 Box 1478 Clearfield UT 84016

TABAT, RONALD JAMES, health industries mfg. co. exec.; b. Waukesha, Wis., May 27, 1945; s. Ralph John and Elaine Pearl (Morrow) T.; Stepson Henry H. Schnitger; B.B.A., U. Wis., Whitewater, 1968, postgrad., 1974-76; m. Bonnie Ruth Garrett, June 10, 1967; children—Jeremy Kim, Rebecca Ja. Asst. mgr. trainee F.W. Woolworth Co., Rockford, Ill., 1968; spl. agt. Northwestern Mut. Life Ins. Co., Balt., 1970-72; sales rep. Siekert & Baum, Inc., Milw., 1972-74; sales rep. Phoenix Products Co., Inc., Milw., 1974-75, sales mgr., 1975-80; sales mgr. splty. packaging Fordem Co., Madison, Wis., 1980—. Served with U.S. Army, 1968-70. Named Top Salesman, Siekert & Baum, Inc., 1973. Mem. Health Industries Mfrs. Assn., Sales and Mktg. Execs. Milw., Keep Am. Beautiful Soc., Nat. Pocket Billiards Assn., Waukesha Billiard Assn. Lutheran. Home: S 36 W 34875 Hwy G Dousman WI 53118 Office: 4715 N 27th St Milwaukee WI 53209

TABENKEN, SAMUEL, beverage and wine distbg. co. exec.; b. Portland, Maine, May 1, 1906; s. Harry and Leah (Marcus) T.; student Portland U., 1924-26; D.B.A. (hon.), Hawthorne Coll., 1978; m. Sally Saklad, Sept. 26, 1954; step-children—James Lee Kaplan, Beth Margot (Mrs. Samuel Metzger). Pres., H. Tabenken Co., Inc., Bangor and Caribou, Maine, 1933—; chmn. bd. Kennebec Trading Co., Inc., 1973—, Wine Mktg. Internat., Inc., San Mateo, Calif., 1974—; treas. Tablease, Inc., Bangor, 1955—. Financial cons. Camp Pinecrest for Girls, Naples, Maine, 1954-59; bd. dirs. SBA; patron arts U. Maine Mem. Maine (pres. 1953-55, dir. 1955-65), Nat. beer wholesalers assns., Maine Trucking Assn., Asso. Industries Maine, Bangor C. of C. Mason (32 deg., Shriner). Club: Penobscot Valley Country (Orono, Maine). Home: 187 Clyde Rd Bangor ME 04401 Office: School St Veazie ME 04401

TABER, BENJAMIN CHATFIELD, mfg. co. exec.; b. Cleve., Oct. 4, 1942; s. Benjamin Charles and Elizabeth (Chatfield) T.; grad. Kent State U., 1964. In nat. sales NBC-TV, Cleve., 1964-67; gen. mgr. Boston div. Lamson & Sessions Co., Cleve., 1967-75; pres. B.C. Taber Co., Inc., Worcester, Mass., 1975—, also dir.; dir. Hygrade Fastener Corp., MANA Inc. Mem. Westborough Bus. and Indsl. Commn. Served as navigator USN, 1960-62. Mem. New Eng. Fastener Assn., New Eng. Iron and Hardware Assn., Mfrs. and Agts. Nat. Assn. Clubs: Plaza, University, Pleasant Valley Country. Contbr. articles to nat. trade publs.; patentee fastener field. Office: 115 Green St Worcester MA 01604

TABOR, STANLEY VASLETT, food co. exec.; b. Southampton, N.Y., Mar. 5, 1931; s. Stanley E. and Dorothy (Fegan) T.; B.S. cum laude, U.S. Mcht. Marine Acad., 1952; LL.B., Fordham U., 1957; LL.M., N.Y. U., 1962; m. Rhoda Edwards Morris, Aug. 25, 1956; children—Peter, Paul. Admitted to N.Y. bar, 1957; asso. firm Thacher, Proffitt, Prizer, Crawley & Wood, N.Y.C., 1957-60; atty. Melville Realty Co., N.Y.C., 1960-61, J.C. Penney Co., N.Y.C., 1961-68; pres. Melville Realty Co. subs. Melville Shoe Co., N.Y.C., 1968-69; v.p. real estate and property Gen. Mills, Inc., Mpls., 1969—. Served to lt. (j.g.), USNR, 1952-54. Mem. Am. Bar Assn., Assn. Bar City N.Y., Nat. Assn. Corporate Real Estate Execs. (chmn. bd.), Minn. Assn. Commerce and Industry (dir.), Bldg. Owner and Mgrs. Assn. Mpls. Republican. Episcopalian. Home: 5709 DeVille Dr Edina MN 55436 Office: 9200 Wayzata Blvd Minneapolis MN 55440

TACKETT, CHARLES WILLIAM, govt. ofcl.; b. Olive Hill, Ky., Mar. 18, 1929; s. Douglas and Opal (McKenzie) T.; Commerce degree, Morehead State U., 1951; M.B.A., U. Md., 1963; m. Lou Rae Heldreth, June 24, 1961; children—Douglas, Jeffrey. With Gentile Air Force Depot, Dayton, Ohio, 1951-54, Air Force Air Materiel Command, Dayton, 1954-57, Army Mil. Traffic Mgmt. Command, Baileys Crossroads, Va., 1957-75; traffic mgr. Drug Enforcement Adminstrn., Washington, 1975—. Pres. Canterbury Woods Civic Assn., 1974. Mem. Nat. Def. Transp. Assn., Am. Fedn. Govt. Employees (pres. local 909, 1972-74), Dayton, D.C. traffic clubs, Delta Nu Alpha. Baptist. Clubs: Toastmasters (pres. 1974). Home: 5113 Southampton Dr Annandale VA 22003 Office: 1405 I St NW Washington DC 20537

TADDEI, ROMANO, electronics co. exec.; b. Guastalla, Italy, June 6, 1934; s. Zeffiro and Dina (Franzoni) T.; came to U.S., 1973; B.S. in Engring., Witwatersrand U., 1956; M.S.E.E., Columbia U., 1979; m. Licia Peluffo, Apr. 5, 1959; children—Laura, Silvana, Marco. Research and devel. mgr. Fuchs Elec. Industries, Alberton, South Africa, 1959-62; nat. field service mgr. Olivetti Africa, Ltd., Johannesburg, South Africa, 1962-66; product design group leader engring. div. Olivetti & Co., Ivrea, Italy, 1966-73, spl. assignment from home office to U.S., 1973—, mgr. East Coast Tech. Center div., N.Y.C., 1977-80, dir. engring. and devel. Olivetti Peripheral Equipment, 1980—. Mem. IEEE, Assn. Computing Machinery, Soc. Info. Display, Am. Mgmt. Assn. Roman Catholic. Patentee in field. Home: 62 Carlton Ln Harrington Park NJ 07640 Office: 525 Executive Blvd Elmsford NY 10523

TAECKENS, DOUGLAS RICHARD, plastics mfg. co. exec.; b. Flint, Mich., May 9, 1950; s. Richard Ernst and Shirley Joanne (Currie) H.; B.A., U. Mich., 1972; m. Lynn Darlene Morey, July 31, 1970; children—James Douglas, April Lynn. With Helmac Products Corp., Flint, Mich., 1972—, nat. sales mgr., 1977-79, v.p. sales and mktg., 1979—. Mem. Am. Mgmt. Assn., Flint Area Sales and Mktg.

Execs., U. Mich. Bus. Adminstrn. Alumni Assn. Republican. Presbyterian. Home: 6047 Blvd Corners Four Grand Blanc MI 48439 Office: PO Box 73 Flint MI 48501

TAFEL, RALPH EDWARD, JR., money mgmt. co. exec.; b. Pitts., Sept. 28, 1933; s. Ralph E. and Donna Elizabeth (Bard) T.; B.S., Allegheny Coll., 1956; m. Sallie Robinson Torrey, Dec. 24, 1967; children—Ralph Edward, III, Troy B., David H.; stepchildren—William A. Torrey, Richard L. Torrey, Peter R. Torrey. Prodn. devel. metallurgist Allegheny Ludlum Steel Co., Albany, N.Y., 1956-58; life ins. salesman Conn. Mut. Co., Pitts., 1958-68; account exec. Babb, Inc., Pitts., 1968-69; pres. Masterplan Funding, Inc., Pitts., 1969-79, chmn. bd., 1979—; dir. Masterplan, Inc. Republican finance chmn. Hampton Twp. (Pa.) for Election Ho. Rep. H. John Heinz, III, 1972; mem. Rep. Nat. Com. Mem. Pitts. Life Underwriters, Pitts. Securities Traders Assn., Nat. Assn. Life Underwriters. Episcopalian. Clubs: Fox Chapel Golf, Masons, Shriners. Office: Four Gateway Center Suite 1515 Pittsburgh PA 15222

TAGGART, DOROTHY HARRIS, investment co. exec.; b. Hartford, Conn., June 5, 1927; d. Lester Lee and Hester Barber Harris; B.A., Wellesley Coll., 1949; M.A., Columbia U., 1966; children—Rush, Alison, Stewart. Tchr. history Public Schs. Weston (Conn.), 1967-68; with Scudder, Stevens & Clark, N.Y.C., 1969—, now asst. v.p. investments; mem. Nat. Com. U.S.-China Relations. Mem. N.Y. Soc. Security Analysts (chmn. edn. and seminar com.), Fin. Women's Assn. Republican. Episcopalian. Clubs: Wellesley (N.Y.C.) (pres.); Cosmopolitan, Canterbury Choral Soc. Office: Scudder Stevens & Clark 345 Park Ave New York NY 10022

TAGGART, SONDRA, publishing co. exec.; b. N.Y.C., July 22, 1934; d. Louis and Rose (Birnbaum) Hamov; B.A., Hunter Coll., 1955; children—Eric, Karen. Founder, dir. Copyright Service Bur., Ltd., N.Y.C., 1957-69; dir., officer Maclen Music, Inc., N.Y.C., 1964-69; pres. Westshore, Inc., pub. internat. bus. materials, Mill Valley, Calif., 1965—; cons. to direct mktg. pub. materials cos. Active, Diane Feinstein for Mayor Campaign, San Francisco, Ronald Reagan for Pres. Campaign. Mem. Advt. Club San Francisco, Women's Polit. Caucus, San Francisco Art Inst., Bus. and Profl. Women's Club. Republican. Club: Commonwealth. Editor: The Red Tapes: Commentaries on Doing Business With The Russians and East Europeans, 1978. Home: 2155 Centro E Tiburon CA 94920

TAGLIAFERRI, LEE GENE, investment banker; b. Mahanoy City, Pa., Aug. 14, 1931; s. Charles and Adele (Cirilli) T.; B.S., U. Pa., 1957; M.B.A., U. Chgo., 1958; m. Maryellen Stanton, Apr. 29, 1962; children—Mark, John, Maryann. Div. comptroller Campbell Soup Co., Camden, N.J., 1958-60; securities analyst Merrill, Lynch, Pierce, Fenner & Smith, Inc., N.Y.C., 1960-62; asst. v.p. U.S. Trust Co. of N.Y., 1962-71; v.p. corporate finance div. Laidlaw & Co., Inc., N.Y.C., 1972-73; pres. Everest Corp., N.Y.C., 1973—; dir. Fairfield Communities Land Co., UEC, Inc., LRA, Inc., Industrialized Bldg. Systems, Inc. Past pres. West Windsor Community Assn. Trustee Schuyler Hall, Columbia, Madison Sq. Boys Club. Served with AUS, 1953-55. K.C. Clubs: University of Pa., Princeton (N.Y.C.). Home: 77 Lillie St Princeton Junction NJ 08550 Office: One Penn Plaza New York NY 10001

TAGUE, BARRY ELWERT, stock broker; b. Phila., June 17, 1938; s. Edward James, Jr. and Eleanor May (Elwert) T.; student Bucknell U., 1956-59; m. Dorothy Elizabeth Beausang, May 14, 1960; children—Kimberly, Nancy, Barry Elwert, Edward James III. Partner, E.J. Tague & Co., Phila., 1959-68; partner Barry E. Tague & Co., Bryn Mawr, Pa., 1968—; exec. v.p., vice chmn. Raymond, James & Assos., Inc., Phila., 1968-76; pres. Tague Securities Corp., Bryn Mawr, Pa., 1976—; chmn. bd. Bryn Mawr Corp., 1976—, Bryn Mawr Group, 1976—; gov. Phila.-Balt.-Washington Stock Exchange, Inc., 1967-77, vice chmn. bd., 1973-74, chmn. bd., 1974-76, also trustee, 1973-76; dir. Stock Clearing Corp. Phila., 1973-76. Active Little League Baseball, 1961-65, 76—; pres. Ithan Sch. PTA, 1971-72. Served with USMCR, 1959-65. Named Man of Year, Raymond, James & Assos., Inc., 1970. Mem. Kappa Sigma. Republican. Episcopalian. Club: Waynesborough Country (Paoli, Pa.). Office: Haverford Plaza 931 Haverford Rd Bryn Mawr PA 19010

TAICLET, RON NELSON, editor, publisher; b. Sharon, Pa., June 30, 1936; s. Richard Nelson and Marjorie Belle (Alderman) T.; B.S., Kent State U., 1958; m. Dorothy Wilch, Feb. 25, 1961; children—Jeffrey, Eric. Mng. editor Wapakoneta Daily News, 1960-61; mng. editor Babcox Automotive Publs., Akron, Ohio, 1961-65; creative copywriter Goodyear Tire & Rubber Co., 1965-68; founder, editor, pub. Tallmadge (Ohio) Circle, also Norton Pride, 1971-74; owner RonTac Publs., Tallmadge, 1974—. Served as capt. U.S. Army, 1959-60. Mem. Internat. Assn. Bus. Communicators. Lutheran. Home: 1689 Northeast Ave Tallmadge OH 44278 Office: 14 Whitehall Dr Tallmadge OH 44278

TAISHOFF, SOL JOSEPH, editor, pub. exec.; b. Minsk, Russia, Oct. 8, 1904; s. Joseph and Rose (Order) T.; ed. pub. schs., Washington; m. Betty Tash, Mar. 6, 1927 (dec. Nov. 1977); children—Joanne Taishoff Cowan (dec.), Lawrence Bruce. Copy person Washington bur. AP, 1920-21, successively dictationist, telegraph operator, reporter, 1922-26; reporter U.S. Daily (now U.S. News and World Report), Washington, 1926-31; radio editor Consol. Press (pen name Robert Mack), 1927-34; mng. editor, co-founder Broadcasting Pub., Inc., 1931-33, editor, 1933—; v.p., treas. Broadcasting mag., 1931-34, pres., editor, pub., 1944-71, chmn., editor, 1971—; v.p., dir. Telecommunications Reports, Inc.; gen. partner Jolar Assos.; past nat. pres. Broadcast Pioneers. Bd. dirs. Washington Journalism Center. Recipient Disting. Service in Journalism award U. Mo., 1953; Disting. Service award Nat. Assn. Broadcasters, 1966. Mem. IEEE (sr.), Soc. Profl. Journalists, Sigma Delta Chi (nat. pres. 1956-57; journalism fellow 1964), Nat. Press Club, Overseas Writers Club. Clubs: Woodmont Country, Nat. Broadcasters (Washington). Home: 4200 Massachusetts Ave NW Washington DC 20016 Office: 1735 DeSales St Washington DC 20036

TAIT, JAMES M., corp. exec.; b. 1920; married. With Butler Bros., 1938-60; with City Products Corp., 1960—, pres. Ben Franklin Stores div., 1967-70, exec. v.p., 1970, pres., chief operating officer, 1971, pres., chief exec. officer, 1971—; dir. Household Finance Corp., Snap-On Tools Corp. Office: City Products Corp 1700 S Wolf Rd Des Plaines IL 60018

TAKEDA, YUKIMATSU, electronics mfg. co. exec.; b. Yamagata, Japan, Apr. 24, 1911; s. Saburo and Kiku (Abiko) T.; B.Engring., Ryojun Inst. Tech., 1934, D.Engring., 1944; m. Michiko Hara, Mar. 19, 1939; children—Yasuko, Masatoshi. Prof., Ryojun Inst. Tech., Kantoshu, Japan, 1940-45; mgr. semiconductor research sect. Nippon Tel. & Tel. Pub. Corp., Japan, 1955-57; gen. mgr. semiconductor div. Nippon Electric Co. Ltd., Tokyo, 1957-65; v.p. engring. Nippon Electric Co., 1966-71, adv. to pres., 1980—; pres. NEC Systems Lab., Inc., Lexington, Mass., 1972-80. Fellow IEEE; mem. Inst. Electronics and Telecommunications Engrs. Japan, Inst. Television Engrs. Japan, Japan Soc. Boston. Home: 24-2 Seijo 5-Chome Setagaya-ku Tokyo 157 Japan Office: Nippon Electric Co 33-1 Shiba 5-Chome Minato-ku Tokyo 108 Japan

TALBOT, MATTHEW JOSEPH, oil co. exec., rancher; b. Mt. Vernon, N.Y., Sept. 4, 1937; s. Matthew J. and Margaret (Green) T.; B.B.A., Iona Coll., 1959-63; m. Maureen Donlan, June 3, 1958; children—Maureen, Kathleen, Matthew. Accountant, S.D. Leidesdorf & Co., N.Y.C., 1961-67; sr. analyst Gen. Foods Corp., White Plains, N.Y., 1967-68; exec. v.p. Tosco Corp., Los Angeles, 1968—, dir., 1973—. Trustee, Craft and Folk Art Mus. Los Angeles County, 1976—; bd. dirs. Center Theatre Group of Los Angeles, 1980—. C.P.A., N.Y. Mem. Am. Inst. C.P.A.'s, N.Y. State Soc. C.P.A.'s, Nat. Assn. Accountants, Calif. Almond Growers Exchange, Sunkist Growers, Inc. Office: 10100 Santa Monica Bldg Los Angeles CA 90067

TALBOT, SAMUEL SPRING, investment advisor; b. Boston, Sept. 20, 1947; s. Dudley and Hope (Halsey) T.; A.B., Harvard U., 1969. Fin. analyst Resource Mgmt. Assos., Boston, 1974-76; pres. Asso. Wholesalers, Inc., West Peabody, Mass., 1977—, Growth Stock Services, Inc., Waltham, Mass., 1980—. Trustee, treas. Fuller Found., Inc. Served with USAF, 1969-73. Mem. World Affairs Council, Am. Electronics Assn. (asso.). Clubs: Cambridge Boat, Harvard Varsity. Address: 5304 Stearns Hill Rd Waltham MA 02154

TALBOTT, THOMAS HOWARD, mfg. co. exec.; b. Kansas City, Mo., Mar. 4, 1940; s. William B. and June K. (Boyce) T.; B.A. in Econs., U. Mo., Kansas City, 1963, M.B.A. (fellow), 1965; m. Linda E. Hood, Mar. 5, 1965. With Mobil Oil Corp., 1965-73, staff analyst, N.Y., 1967-68, asst. to div. controller, Boston, 1968-69, div. supr. systems and indsl. engring., 1969, div. mgr. planning, systems and controls, Kansas City, Mo., 1969-73; project mgr. bus. planning and devel. C.J. Patterson Co., Kansas City, Mo., 1973-74, dir. fine food ops., 1974-75, asst. to pres., 1975-76, v.p. adminstrn., 1976—, dir., 1977—. Hon. fellow Harry S. Truman Library Inst., 1976; active United Fund, 1969, Friends of Art, Univ. Assos., Philharmonic Assos.; adviser Jr. Achievement, 1973. Victor Wilson Scholar, 1958-62. Mem. U. Mo. Kansas City Alumni Assn., Omicron Delta Kappa, Phi Kappa Phi, Tau Kappa Epsilon. Presbyterian. Clubs: Univ., Woodside Racquet. Home: 411 W 60th Terr Kansas City MO 64113 Office: 3947 Broadway Kansas City MO 64111

TALLEY, DALLAS L., mgmt. cons.; b. Pontiac, Mich., Jan. 1, 1933; s. C. Bliss and Elba L. (Barber) T.; B.S. in Personnel Mgmt., So. Ill. U., 1957; m. Elizabeth Brooks, Apr. 9, 1966; children—Rhett, Brooks. Vice pres. mktg. Redcor Corp., Woodland Hills, Calif., 1968-72, Gen. Computer Systems Co., Dallas, 1972-74; pres. Photophysics Corp., Mountain View, Calif., 1974-75, Mktg. Internat., Half Moon Bay, Calif., 1976—; sr. v.p. Qantel Corp., Hayward, Calif., 1980—; chmn. industry adv. bd. Nat. Computer Conf. Mem. Am. Fedn. Info. Processing Socs. Contbr. articles to profl. publs. Office: PO Box 83 Half Moon Bay CA 94019

TALLEY, JERRY LEALAND, bank exec.; b. Kerens, Tex., Sept. 1, 1928; s. Milton E. and Gertrude Marie (Newsom) T.; A.A., Arlington State Coll., 1948; grad. Southwestern Grad. Sch. Banking, So. Methodist U., 1960; m. Rita Evelyn Pierce, July 17, 1950; children—Jan Ell Talley Stewart, Jerri Kay. Farm dir. Sta. KFDX-TV, Wichita Falls, Tex., 1954-56; retail store sales mgr., Gainesville, Tex., 1956-58; asst. v.p. Grayson County State Bank, Sherman, Tex., 1958-59, v.p., 1959-60, exec. v.p., 1960-62, pres., trust officer, 1964—; organizer, pres., chmn. bd. Texoma Savs. Assn., Sherman, 1962-64, now dir.; dir. Day Mfg. Co., Pylon Farms; dir., v.p. Recovery Co.; dir., treas. Grayson Computer Service. Vice chmn. bd. trustees Austin Coll., Sherman; bd. dirs. Med. Plaza Hosp., Sherman; mem. steering com. Jr. Achievement of Grayson County. Served with USAF, 1950-52. Named Outstanding Young Man of Sherman, C. of C., 1959; recipient Silver Beaver award Boy Scouts Am., 1976. Democrat. Presbyterian. Club: Rotary (pres. club 1972-73). Office: PO Box 430 Sherman TX 75090

TALLEY, WILLIAM GILES, JR., container mfg. co. exec.; b. Adel, Ga., Sept. 25, 1939; s. William Giles and Mary (McGlamry) T.; B.S. in Bus. Adminstrn., U. S.C., 1961; m. Jacqueline Vickery, Apr. 14, 1962; children—William Giles, John Lindsey, Bronwyn Ashley. Mgmt. trainee Talley Veneer & Crate Co., Inc., Adel, 1961-62, plant mgr., salesman, Waynesboro, Ga., 1965-67; with Talley's Box Co., Leesburg, Fla., 1962-69, plant mgr., partner, 1967-69; gen. mgr. Growers Container Corp. Inc., Leesburg, 1969—; pres. Talley Acres, 1979—; dir. Sunfirst Nat. Bank Lake County. Bd. dirs. Leesburg Hosp. Assn. Served with USAAF, 1961. Mem. Leesburg C. of C. (dir.), Fla. Forestry Assn. (dir. 1977—), Sigma Alpha Epsilon. Democrat. Methodist. Clubs: Elks, Kiwanis. Home: Lake Griffin Leesburg FL 32748 Office: PO Box 817 Leesburg FL 32748

TALMAGE, KENNETH KELLOGG, mgmt. cons.; b. Morristown, N.J., Jan. 16, 1946; s. Edward Taylor Hunt and Dorathy (Rogers) T.; B.A., Claremont Men's Coll., 1968; M.B.A., Boston U., Brussels, 1976; m. Julie Hume Sprague, May 28, 1973. Asso., Hon. Leonard K. Firestone, Los Angeles, 1973-74; attache Am. Embassy, Brussels, 1974-77; mgmt. cons. strategic planning and fin. Arthur D. Little, Inc., Cambridge, Mass., 1977—; dir. Blackpoint Corp., Sprague Corp. Trustee Humes Found., Hurricane Island Outward Bound Sch., Maine. Served with USNR, 1968-69. Clubs: Country of Brookline (Mass.); Somerset (Boston); Royal Golf (Belgium). Home: Ram Island Farm Cape Elizabeth ME 04107 Office: Arthur D Little Inc Acorn Park Cambridge MA 02140

TALSKY, GENE R., mktg. corp. exec.; b. Los Angeles, Sept. 6, 1936; s. Samuel M. and Helen L. (Neiman) T.; student UCLA, 1954-55; B.A., Goddard Coll., 1971; children—Philip F., Justine L. Ops. trainee United Air Lines, 1955-56; prodn. coordinator IBM Corp., 1956-59; co-founder, gen. mgr. Data-Pak Corp., 1960-62; co-founder, v.p. Republic Service Bur., Los Angeles, 1962-68; bus. devel. mgr. Computer Sci. Corp., Los Angeles and N.Y.C., 1968-71; mgr. plans and programs Informatics, Inc., Fairfield, N.J., 1971-73; exec. v.p. Datair Systems Corp., Chgo., 1973-76, pres. Datair Services, Inc., 1976-77; v.p. mktg. DTSS Inc., Hanover, N.H., 1977-78; founder, pres. Profl. Mktg. Mgmt., Inc., Hanover, 1978—; chmn. bus. plans devel. session, speaker pricing strategy COMDEX, 1979. Recipient ICP Million Dollar Sales award, 1976. Contbr. article on pricing to profl. newsletter. Office: Box 333 Gales Ferry CT 06335

TAMARELLI, ALAN WAYNE, chem. co. exec.; b. Wilkinsburg, Pa., Aug. 13, 1941; s. John Adam and Florence Eleanor (Heacock) T.; B.S., Carnegie Mellon U., 1963, M.S. (NSF fellow), 1965, Ph.D., 1966; M.B.A., N.Y. U., 1972; m. Carol Ann Crawford, Aug. 3, 1963; children—Robin Carol, Alan Wayne. Engr., Exxon Corp., Linden, N.J., 1966, project leader, 1968-70; corp. planner Engelhard Minerals & Chem. Corp., Newark, 1970-71, asst. to exec. v.p., 1971-74, gen. mgr., 1974-77, v.p., 1977-79, group v.p., 1979—. Served to capt. U.S. Army, 1966-68. Mem. Comml. Devel. Assn., N.Am. Soc. Corp. Planning, Am. Inst. Chem. Engrs., Chem. Industry Council N.J. (exec. com.), N.J. Energy Research Inst. (founding trustee), Am. Mgmt. Assn., Am. Chem. Soc., Greater Newark C. of C. (sec., dir.), Sigma Xi, Scabbard and Blade, Tau Beta Pi, Phi Kappa Phi, Omicron Delta Kappa. Home: 49 Wexford Way Basking Ridge NJ 07920 Office: 429 Delancey St Newark NJ 07105

TAMBOLI, AKBAR RASUL, cons. engr.; b. India, July 20, 1942; s. Rasul M. and Chandbi C.; came to U.S., 1965, naturalized, 1968; B.S.E., U. Poona, India, 1964; M.S., Stanford U., 1967; m. Rounkbi G., May 20, 1969; children—Tahira, Ajim. Sr. engr. Miller Assos., Pottsville, Pa., 1967-69; asso. Edwards and Hjorth, N.Y.C., 1970-76; sr. partner, cons. engr. A.R. Tamboli & Assos., Verona, N.J., 1976—. Active Cancer Fund Dr., 1976-77. Mem. ASCE (mem. monograph com., earthquake loading, response), Am. Concrete Inst., Am. Inst. Steel Constrn. Publisher: Analysis and Design of Wind Loads for Tall Buildings, 1974, Structural Vibrations Produced by Ground Motion, 1964. Home and Office: 96 Elmwood Dr Verona NJ 07044

TAMKIN, CURTIS SLOANE, real estate devel. co. exec.; b. Boston, Sept. 21, 1936; s. Hayward and Etta (Goldfarb) T.; B.A. in Econs., Stanford U., 1958; m. Priscilla Martin, Oct. 18, 1975; 1 son, Curtis Sloane. Vice pres., treas., dir. Hayward Tamkin & Co., Inc., mortgage bankers, Los Angeles, 1963-70; mng. partner Property Devel. Co., Los Angeles, 1970—. Bd. govs. Music Center Los Angeles, 1974—; pres. Los Angeles Master Chorale Assn., 1974-78. Served to lt. (j.g.) USNR, 1960-63. Mem. Los Angeles Jr. C. of C. (dir. 1968-69). Republican. Clubs: Burlingame Country, Los Angeles, University. Office: 3600 Wilshire Blvd Los Angeles CA 90010

TAMMANY, ALBERT SQUIRE, III, banker; b. Paget, Bermuda, Aug. 21, 1946; s. Albert Squire Jr. and Marion Genevieve (Galloway) T.; B.A., Stanford U., 1968; M.B.A. (Woodrow Wilson fellow), U. Pa., 1973; m. Teresa Reznor, Sept. 8, 1973. Budget and planning officer Tuskegee Inst., Ala., 1973-74; budget analyst controllers dept. Chase Manhattan Bank, N.Y.C., 1974-75; v.p., div. controller Wells Fargo Bank, San Francisco, 1975-78, v.p., retail group controller, 1978-79; v.p., controller Imperial Bank, Los Angeles, 1979—, v.p. fin., 1980—; cons. Inst. for Services to Edn., Inc., 1973-74. Served with USMC, 1968-71. Wharton Pub. Policy fellow, 1972. Mem. Am. Bankers Assn. (trust ops. com.). Episcopalian. Clubs: Wharton, Stanford (Los Angeles). Office: 9920 La Cienega Blvd Inglewood CA 90301

TAMMERA, FRANK, tech. co. exec.; b. Newark, Feb. 1, 1923; s. Roberto and Maria Grazia (Mazzocchi) T.; ed. schs., Rome, 1930-37; m. Elvira A. Cottone, Sept. 16, 1950; children—Robert, Frank, Michael, Linda. Operator, Ditta Tammaro Roberto & Figli, Rome, 1932-47; insp. Victory Optical Co., Newark, 1947-53; owner Merit Gas Sta., Kearney, N.J. and Gulf Gas Sta., Clifon, N.J., 1953-55, Ever-Fresh Poultry Co., Montclair, N.J., 1955-59, IGA Supermarket, Newark, 1959-69; founder, pres. Pure Tech. Industries Inc., Pine Brook, N.J., 1970—. Mem. Screen Printing Assn. Internat., Soc. Glass Decorators. Roman Catholic. Inventor, designer mech.-chem. processes to reclaim plastic bottles, polyester and aluminum cans, polyester beverage bottles. Home: 177 E McClellan Ave Livingston NJ 07039 Office: 4 Barnet Rd Pine Brook NJ 07058

TAMPONE, DOMINIC, retail store exec.; b. Italy, May 9, 1914; s. Gabriel and Constance (Pierro) T.; came to U.S., 1920, naturalized, 1937; student bus. adminstrn. Alexander Hamilton Inst., electronics and physics RCA Inst. With Hammacher Schlemmer, N.Y.C., 1929—, pres., 1958—; also pres. Invento Products Corp., N.Y.C., 1960—, Three New Yorkers Mfg. Co., 1962—, Plummer McCutcheon, N.Y.C. Served with AUS, 1943-46; ETO. Decorated knight Order of Merit of Italian Republic. Home: 36 Sutton Pl S New York NY 10022 Office: 147 E 57th St New York NY 10022

TAMRAZ, WILLIAM HOWARD, elevator co. exec.; b. Yonkers, N.Y., Dec. 16, 1942; s. William Howard and Anne (Kinn) T.; B.A. in Bus. Adminstrn., Westchester Community Coll., 1962; student Am. Inst. Banking, 1962-65, DeVry Tech. Inst., 1968-72; m. Barbara Ann Wichman, Sept. 11, 1965; children—Dana, Lisa, Nicole. Outside rep. Gramatan Nat. Bank, Bronxville, N.Y., 1962-65; mgr. Gen. Electric Credit Corp., 1965-71; v.p., gen. mgr. Herk Elevator Co., Inc., Bronx, N.Y., 1972—. Adv. com. Yonkers Community Devel., Yonkers Environ. Impact Commn.; pres. Hudson River Fishermen's Assn. Published poet. Office: 670 Grand Concourse Bronx NY 10451

TAMSETT, STEPHEN JAMES, hosp. products co. exec.; b. Herkimer, N.Y., May 31, 1946; s. Stephen Samuel and Josephine Marie (Servello) T.; A.B. in Biology, SUNY, 1966; B.S. in Microbiology, U. Ga., 1968; m. Susan Ott; children—Anne, Jay, Alison. Plant quality assurance mgr. C.R. Bard Inc., Covington, Ga., 1972-74, central quality assurance mgr., Murry Hill, N.J., 1974-76; corp. quality engr. Millipure Corp., Bedford, Mass., 1976-79; corp. central quality assurance mgr. med. devices Kendall Co., Boston, 1979—. Mem. Am. Soc. Microbiology, Am. Soc. Quality Control, Am. Assn. Med. Instrumentation, Health Industry Mfrs. Assn. (G.M.P. tng. task force). Republican. Roman Catholic. Clubs: K.C., Lions. Office: Kendall Co 1 Federal St Boston MA 02101

TANABE, HARUTO, accountant; b. Lahaina, Maui, Hawaii, Apr. 1, 1920; s. Tokuichi and Fusayo (Fukuba) T.; student U. Hawaii, 1948; m. Setsuko Tanaka, July 9, 1944; children—Andrew T., Timothy M., Alvin T. Pub. accountant, Honolulu, 1945—; chief accountant Wahiawa Gen. Hosp., Wahiawa, Hawaii, 1947-52; comptroller Cyprus Hawaiian Cement Corp., Honolulu, 1960-79; dir., sec. Alii Plumbing, Inc., 1969-78. Treas. Pearl City (Hawaii) Community Assn., 1970-71. Dist. councilman Democratic party, 1968, 70, 74, 76, 78. Trustee, sec.-treas. Pub. Employees Health and Welfare Fund of the State of Hawaii, 1974-79. Mem. Nat. Assn. Accts., Nat. Soc. Pub. Accts. (gov. 1979—), Hawaii Assn. Pub. Accountants (v.p. 1972-74, pres. 1974-75), Inst. Corporate Controllers, Honolulu Japanese C. of C. Democrat. Buddhist. Mason (Shriner, 32 deg.), Rotarian. Home: 1657 Paaaina Pl Pearl City HI 96782 Office: 94-889 Waipahu St Suite 202 Waipahu HI 96797

TANAKA, TOGO W(ILLIAM), financial exec.; b. Portland, Oreg., Jan. 7, 1916; s. Masaharu and Katsu (Iwatate) T.; A.B. cum laude, U. Calif. at Los Angeles, 1936; m. Jean Miho Wada, Nov. 14, 1940; children—Jeannine, Christine, Wesley. Editor Los Angeles Japanese Daily News, 1936-41; documentary historian War Relocation Authority, 1942; staff mem. Am. Friends Service Com., Chgo., 1943-45; editor to head publs. div. Am. Tech. Soc., 1945-52; pub. Chgo. Pub. Corp., 1952-56; pub. School-Indsl. Press, Inc., Los Angeles, 1956-60; pres. Gramercy Enterprises, Inc., Los Angeles, Gramercy Mgmt. Co. City commr. Community Redevel. Agy., Los Angeles, 1973-75; dir. Los Angeles Wholesale Produce Market Devel. Corp., Los Angeles br. Fed. Res. Bank, San Francisco; mem. adv. bd. Calif. First Bank, Los Angeles, 1976-78. Mem. citizens mgmt. rev. com. Los Angeles Unified Sch. Dist., 1976-77; adv. consultant to assessor Los Angeles County; bd. govs. Goodwill Industries; trustee Wilshire United Methodist Ch., 1976-78, Calif. Acad. Decathlon; bd. dirs. Meth. Hosp. So. Calif., Crippled Children's Soc., ARC. Recipient merit award Soc. Advancement Mgmt., 1950, mag. award Inst. Graphic Arts, 1953, 1st award Internat. Council Indsl. Editors, 1955. Mem. Los Angeles Area C. of C. (dir. 1974-76), Japan-Am. Soc. So. Calif. (council), Phi Beta Kappa, Pi Sigma Alpha, Pi Gamma Mu. Clubs: Masons, Shriners, Rotary (dir. Los Angeles chpt.), Stock Exchange. Author: (with Frank K. Levin) English Composition and Rhetoric, 1948; (with Dr. Jean Bordeaux) How to Talk More

Effectively, 1948; (with Alma Meland) Easy Pathways in English. Home: 949 Malcolm Ave Los Angeles CA 90024 Office: 445 S Figueroa Los Angeles CA 90071

TANDEN, TEJ BAHADUR, mfg. exec.; b. India, Oct. 21, 1931; s. Raj B. and Saraswati D. T.; came to U.S., 1953, naturalized, 1965; B.S., Banaras Hindu U., 1950; LL.B. with honors, Banaras U., 1952; LL.M., Harvard U., 1954. Systems designer RCA, Camden, N.J., 1957; mgr. computer dept. H. Flynn Mfg. Co., Phila., 1958-59; owner, operator Internat. Trade & Investment Corp., Phila., 1959-63; mgr. tech. services eastern region Univac Co., Blue Bell, Pa., 1964-68; dir. new business Info. Mgmt. Inc., Bedford, Mass., 1969-70; pres., organizer Pacer Corp., Waltham, Mass., 1971-74, Revol Vees, Inc., Chelmsford, Mass., 1974-78; pres. Impex Industries, Inc., North Billerica, Mass., 1978—. Pres., India Assn., Phila., 1956-57. Republican. Hindu. Club: Rotary. Home: 5 University Ln Billerica MA 01821 Office: 239 Rangeway Rd North Billerica MA 01862

TANDY, RUSSELL HAVILAND, JR., banker; b. Rahway, N.J., Dec. 9, 1918; s. Russell Haviland and Jessie M. (Kennedy) T.; A.B., Columbia, 1940; J.D., Fordham U., 1948; m. Mildred N. Ficken, Feb. 14, 1942; children—Russell H. III, Spencer A., David W. Admitted to N.Y. bar, 1948; with U.S. Guarantee Co., 1940-50, asst. sec., Chgo., 1948-50; fin. v.p., dir. Flynn, Harrison & Conroy, Inc., N.Y.C., 1950-67; sr. v.p. Marsh & McLennan, N.Y.C., 1967-79; v.p. Bankers Trust Co., N.Y.C., 1979—; dir. Lincoln Fed. Savs. (N.J.); mem. Lloyds of London. Trustee Gen. Theol. Sem., N.Y.C. Served to maj. AUS, 1942-46. Mem. Am. Bar Assn., S.A.R., Delta Phi. Republican. Episcopalian. Clubs: Down Town; University (N.Y.C.), Island (Hobe Sound, Fla.), Baltusrol Golf (Springfield, N.J.). Home: 7 Isle Ridge W Hobe Sound FL 33455 Office: 250 Royal Palm Way Palm Beach FL 33480

TANG, DAMON, chem. co. exec.; b. Vietnam, July 2, 1944; came to U.S., 1966, naturalized, 1974; s. Chi and Que (Luu) T.; B.S., Cheng Kung U., Taiwan, 1965; M.S., Miss. State U., 1969; m. Pamela H. Sung, Oct. 10, 1969; children—Jennifer, Calvin. Research chemist, plant engr. H & S Chem. Co., Inc., Wallington, N.J., 1969-73, plant mgr., 1973-78, v.p., partner, 1978—. Mem. Am. Inst. Chem. Engrs. Club: Passaic Rotary. Home: 33 Ackerman St Nutley NJ 07110 Office: 52 64 Van Dyk St Wallington NJ 07057

TANG, EDWARD YIU-YAN, semicondr. mfg. co. exec.; b. Shanghai, China, Oct. 10, 1939; came to U.S., 1958, naturalized, 1971; s. William Sai-Tsien Tang and Ling-Van Chang; B.E.E., Cornell U., 1963; M.S., Columbia U., 1965; m. Florence Chen, Mar. 21, 1964. Sr. design engr. NCR, Dayton, Ohio, 1965-66; supr. metal oxide semicondr. circuit devel. Microelectronics div. Philco-Ford Co., Santa Clara, Calif., Blue Bell, Pa., 1966-69; dir. engring. Intersil Inc., Cupertino, Calif., 1969-71; v.p. engring., founder, dir. Eurosil GmbH, Munich, W. Ger., 1971-74; v.p. research and devel. Micro Power Systems Inc., Santa Clara, 1974-78; exec. v.p., chief operating officer Nitron Inc., Cupertino, 1979—, also dir. Mem. IEEE, Am. Electronics Assn. Republican. Contbr. articles to mags.; patentee in field. Home: 1628 Belvoir Dr Los Altos CA 94022 Office: Nitron Inc 10420 Bubb Rd Cupertino CA 95014

TANG, MAN-CHUNG, constrn. exec.; b. Canton, China, Feb. 22, 1938; s. Fay-Pown and Jing-Tze (Ho) T.; B.S.C., Chu Hai Coll., 1959; Diploma Engring., Tech. U., Darmstadt, 1963, Dr.-Eng., 1965; m. Yee-Yun-Fung, Aug. 26, 1966; children—Chin-Chung, Chin-Ning. Bridge engr. Gutehoffnungshutte, West Germany, 1965-68; sr. structural engr. Severud-Perrone-Sturm-Conlin-Bandel, N.Y.C., 1968-70; v.p., chief engr. Dyckerhoff & Widmann, constrn., N.Y.C., 1970-78; pres., dir. DRC Cons.'s, Inc., 1978—; structural cons. Mem. ASCE, Internat. Assn. Bridge and Structural Engring., Nat. Soc. Profl. Engrs., Prestressed Concrete Inst., Am. Concrete Inst. Author publs. in stability theory of structures, long-span bridges, concrete design. Home: 83-23 Midland Pkwy Jamaica Estates NY 11432 Office: 529 Fifth Ave New York NY 10017

TANIGUCHI, RICHARD RYUZO, wholesale bldg. supplies exec.; b. Eleele, Hawaii, Oct. 21, 1913; s. Tokuichi and Sana (Omaye) T.; B.A., U. Hawaii, 1936; m. Sumako Matsul, July 22, 1939; children—Grace Fujiyoshi, Susan Penisten. Accounting clk. Bank of Hawaii, 1935-36; treas., gen. mgr. Hawaii Planing Mill, 1944-54; pres., gen. mgr. Hawaii Hardware Co., Ltd., Hilo, 1954—; pres., dir. Enterprises Hilo; v.p., dir. Hawaii Funeral Home. Chmn. Hawaii County CSC, 1950-56; vice chmn. Hawaii County Tidal Wave Adv. Com., 1961-68; vice chmn. Hawaii Council Tb and Health Assn., 1965; pres. Am. Cancer Soc., 1969-72, state bd. dirs., 1970-78; pres. Hilo Hongwanji Mission 1968-70, sr. adviser, 1972—; v.p. Hawaii Hongwanji Mission, 1969—; mem. Hawaii Comprehensive Health Planning Com., 1970-72. Named Hawaii Vol. of Year, Am. Cancer Soc., 1973, recipient Nat. award Am. Cancer Soc., 1978. Mem. Am. Supply Assn., Nat. Plumbing Wholesalers Assn., Japanese C. of C. and Industry of Hawaii (pres. 1957), Hawaii (dir. 1958-59), Japanese (hon. dir.) chambers commerce, Phi Kappa Phi, Pi Gamma Mu. Home: 572 Iwalani St Hilo HI 96720 Office: 550 Kilauea Ave Hilo HI 96720

TANKER, PAUL A., pension cons.; b. Phila., July 9, 1926; s. Albert and Dora T.; B.A., Pa. State U., 1948; children—Mark, Joanne, Scott, Richard. Pvt. practice acctg., 1948-53; with IRS, 1953-56, pension trust reviewer, 1954-56; with various pension cons. firms, Phila., 1956-59; founder, pres. Paul A. Tanker & Assos., Phila., 1959—; lectr. in field. Trustee Moss Rehab. Hosp. Served with USN, 1943-46. Mem. Am. Soc. Pension Actuaries (dir. 1969-75), Am. Pension Conf., Profit Sharing Council Am., World Affairs Council. Clubs: Vester, Golden Slipper (Phila.); Center (Balt.); Masons, Shriners, B'nai B'rith (pres. 1955-56). Contbr. articles to various profl. jours. Office: Paul A Tanker & Assos 1521 Locust St Philadelphia PA 19102

TANKOOS, BRADLEY JOSEPH, real estate developer; b. N.Y.C., Mar. 7, 1952; s. S. Joseph and Marryrita (Crofton) T., Jr.; B.S. in Bus. Adminstrn., U. Denver, 1974. Second v.p. real estate fin. dept. Chase Manhattan Bank, N.Y.C., 1974-77; owner, mgr. Tankoos & Co., Denver, 1977—. Mem. Internat. Council Shopping Centers, Real Estate Bd. N.Y., Nat. Realty Club, Young Mortgage Bankers Assn. Republican. Roman Catholic. Clubs: Economic, N.Y. Athletic, University (N.Y.C.). Home: 95 Emerson St Denver CO 80218 Office: 6445 E Ohio Ave Denver CO 80224

TANKUS, HARRY, mfg. co. exec.; b. Bialystok, Poland, Aug. 23, 1921; s. Isador and Sima (Siegal) T.; diploma engring., Armour Tech., 1942; student U. Ill., 1946-47; grad. mgmt. course U. Chgo., 1966; m. Lila Beverly Lee, Sept. 9, 1947; children—Rolana, Ilyce. Came to U.S., 1929, naturalized 1929. Insp. dept. head Buick div. Gen. Motors, Melrose Park, Ill., 1942-44; specification engr. Crane Packing Co., Chgo., 1947-53, chief engr., 1953-62, asst. v.p. engring., Morton Grove, 1962-64, asst. v.p. seals sales and engring. cons., mgr. Seal div., 1964-71, v.p. product sales, 1971-76, pres., 1976—, also dir. Bd. dirs. Oakton Community Coll. Ednl. Found., 1977—, pres., 1979—; bd. dirs. Inst. for Indsl. Innovation through Tribology, 1980—; asso. mem. Chgo. Natural History Mus. Served with U.S. Army, 1944-46; ETO. Decorated Purple Heart. Registered profl. engr. Mem. Soc. Automotive Engrs. (chmn. aerospace program seal com. 1965), ASME, Am. Soc. Metals (certificate recognition for design 1965), Western Soc. Engrs., Am. Soc. Lubrication Engrs. (chmn. nat. program com. 1968-69, chmn. indsl. mems. task force 1970 dir./sponsor industry relations com. 1970-74, pres. 1975-76), Nat. Assn. Corrosion Engrs., Am. Soc. Tool and Mfg. Engrs., AAAS, Am. Ordnance Assn., Nat. Conf. on Fluid Power (asso. dir. 1969, dir. 1970, gov. 1971—), Am. Soc. Testing and Materials (chmn. sub-com. carbon-graphite 1965, exec. com. 1962-66). Mason (Shriner), Moose. Contbr. articles in field to tech. jours. Patentee in field. Home: 415 Sunset Dr Wilmette IL 60091 Office: 6400 Oakton Morton Grove IL 60053

TANNE, SOL, fin. cons.; b. N.Y.C., May 30, 1923; s. Louis and Esther (Weiss) T.; B.E.E., Cooper Union, 1947; postgrad. Sch. Bus. Adminstrn. N.Y. U., 1950-52; m. Janice Hopkins, Nov. 2, 1968. Co-founder, exec. v.p. Dasol Corp., N.Y.C., 1954-64; mng. dir. Tanne Thomsen Assos., Rotterdam, Holland, 1964-70; pres. Sol Tanne Assos., Inc., N.Y.C., 1964-79; dir. corp. devel. Purvis Systems Inc., Syosset, N.Y., 1973—; gen. partner Material Resources Investors N.Y., N.Y.C., 1973—; vice chmn. N.Y. Mercantile Exchange, 1977; dir. Purvis Systems Inc. Served with USN, 1944-46; CBI. Mem. Am. Artists Profl. League, Knickerbocker Artists. Patentee package loading and unloading installation. Home: 251 Central Park W New York NY 10024

TANNEN, CHARLES IAN, publishing exec.; b. Bklyn., Aug. 18, 1941; s. Louis and Natalie T.; M.S. in Mktg., Rider Coll., 1963; m. Joan J. Persily, Oct. 18, 1969. Reporter, L.I. Press, 1965-68; asso. editor McGraw-Hill Pub. Co., N.Y.C., 1968-70; editor Enterprise mag., N.Y.C., 1970-72; editor Folio mag., New Canaan, Conn., 1972-75, pub. dir., 1977-80, editor, 1977—, pub., 1980—; pub. New York Bus. mag., 1975-77; editor pub. text for Random House, Inc., 1975; dir. Campaign mag., New York Bus. Pub. Co.; mag. cons., speaker. Dir. press relations N.Y.C. Youth Bd., 1965; pub. industry chmn. March of Dimes, 1976; campaign coordinator N.Y. dep. mayor Timothy Costello, 1964. Served with USAF, 1964. Recipient Jesse Neal certificates of excellence Am. Bus. Press, 1973, 74, 75, Gold medals Soc. Publ. Designers, 1973, 74, 75, certificate of appreciation Profl. div. N.Y. U., 1975. Mem. Am. Soc. Mag. Editors. Home: 35 Quails Trail Stamford CT 06903 Office: Folio Mag 125 Elm St New Canaan CT 06840

TANNEN, STEPHEN DANIEL, mfg. co. exec.; b. Bklyn., July 24, 1946; s. Henry W. and Natalie (Fleischer) T.; B.S., Cornell U., 1968; M.B.A., Columbia U., 1970; m. Ann Beverly Koeppel, Oct. 18, 1970; children—Heather Dawn, Scott Jeffrey. Editor-in-chief, Indsl. and Labor Relations Forum, 1967-68; mem. new product devel. staff Colgate Palmolive Co., N.Y.C., 1970-74, sr. product mgr. Curity first aid products, 1974-76, group product mgr., personal care products div., 1976-78, dir. mktg. sports and recreation div., 1979-80; pres. Etonic Inc., Brockton, Mass., 1980—; lectr. Fashion Inst. Tech. Mem. Rubber Mfrs. Assn. (exec. com. footwear div. 1980—). Republican. Clubs: Inwood Beach, Masons. Home: 163 Hampshire Rd Wellesley MA 02181 Office: 147 Centre St Brockton MA 02403

TANNENBERG, DIETER ERNST ADOLF, bus. equipment co. exec.; b. Chevy Chase, Md., Nov. 24, 1932; s. Wilhelm and Margarete (Mundhenk) T.; B.S. in Mech. Engring., Northwestern U., 1959; m. Ruth Hansen, Feb. 6, 1956; 1 dau., Diana. Supervising engr. Flexonics div. Calumet & Hecla, Inc., Chgo., 1959-61, chief engr., 1961-63, program mgr. advanced space systems, 1963-65, dir. mfg. services, 1965-67; dir. mfg. engring. Smith-Corona, Cortland, N.Y., 1967-69; tech. dir. internat. Singer Co., N.Y.C., 1969-71; v.p. tech., internat. Addressograph-Multigraph Corp., Cleve., 1971-74; mng. dir. Addressograph Multigraph GmbH, Frankfurt/M., Germany, 1974-78; v.p., gen. mgr. Europe, Middle East and Africa, AM Internat., Inc., Chgo., 1978-79, pres. AM Bruning div., 1979—; dir. Mathias Bauerle GmbH, St. Georgen, Germany, 1972-75. Served with M.I., U.S. Army, 1953-56. Registered profl. engr., Ill., N.Y., N.J., Conn., Ohio, Wis., Ind. Mem. ASME, Nat. Soc. Profl. Engrs., Assn. Reprodn. Materials Mfrs. (v.p., dir. 1979—), Pi Tau Sigma. Contbr. chpt. to Handbook of Modern Manufacturing Management, 1970. Patentee in field. Office: AM Internat Inc 1834 Walden Office Sq Schaumburg IL 60196

TANNER, BILLY CHARLES, real estate and holding co. exec.; b. Hartselle, Ala., July 27, 1935; s. Orville Wright and Mabel Nettie (Landers) T.; B.S., U. Ala., 1958; m. Frances Leah Puckett, Jan. 26, 1961; children—Terry Charles, Billy Renea. Developer, builder homes and shopping centers Circle T Devel. Inc., Hartselle, 1959—; builder Han-D-Way Markets, chain convenience stores, 1964—; pres. Tanner Cos., holding co., Hartselle, 1975—. Coordinator North Ala. for Gov. George Wallace, 1964-68; county chmn. Bill Baxley gubernatorial campaign, 1978. Served with AUS, 1957-58. Mem. Commerce Execs. Soc. of U. Ala., Rolls Royce Owners Club Am. Baptist. Clubs: Masons, Rotary (pres. 1978-80). Home: 303 Crescent Dr Hartselle AL 35640 Office: Tanner Heights Plaza Hartselle AL 35640

TANNER, H. C., bus. mgr.; b. Thatcher, Ariz., June 28, 1930; s. Carlos Henry and Carol (Baker) T.; B.S., U.S. Mil. Acad., 1954; M.B.A., U. Chgo., 1963; M.A., U. So. Calif., 1978; m. Mary Ann Swank, Aug. 27, 1960; children—Helen Carol, Hugh Carlos. Commd. 2d lt. U.S. Air Force, 1954, advanced through grades to lt. col., 1969, served as pilot, aircraft comdr. SAC, 1954-60, aide to comdr. Ballistic Systems div., 1960-62, div. chief vulnerability and hardware div. Advanced Ballistic Re-entry Systems, 1963-67; pilot, aircraft comdr. S.E. Asia, 1968-69, mem. strategic study group Office Joint Chiefs of Staff, 1969-73, div. chief vulnerability and hardness div., dep. dir. engring. ICBM Program Office, Norton AFB, Calif., 1973-77, ret., 1977; asst. supt. bus. services Chino (Calif.) Unified Sch. Dist., 1977—. Decorated D.F.C., Air medal with two oak leaf clusters. Mem. Calif. Assn. Sch. Bus. Ofcls. (mem. mgmt. techniques com. So. sect., sec.-treas. San Bernardino chpt.). Home: 2333 E Skyline Dr Brea CA 92621 Office: 5130 Riverside Dr Chino CA 91710

TANNER, HAROLD, investment banker; b. N.Y.C., May 7, 1932; s. Irving and Pauline (Steinlauf) T.; B.S., Cornell U., 1952; M.B.A., Harvard U., 1956; m. Estelle Newman, July 6, 1957; children—David Allen, James Michael, Karen Elizabeth. Vice pres., dir. Blyth & Co., Inc., N.Y.C., 1956-69; exec. v.p., dir. New Court Securities Corp., 1969-76; exec. v.p. Blyth Eastman Dillon & Co., N.Y.C., 1977-80, chmn. operating com., 1979-80; partner Salomen Bros., 1980—. Served to lt. (jg.), USNR, 1952-54. Mem. Vol. Urban Consulting Group (co-founder), Council Fgn. Relations. Clubs: Bond, Recess Century Country. Home: 18 Kensington Rd Scarsdale NY 10583 Office: 1221 Ave of Americas New York NY 10020

TANNER, JOHN PAUL, cons. engr.; b. Cleve., Sept. 22, 1927; s. William and Lucille (McKenney) T.; B.B.A., U. Miami, 1951, B.S. in Indsl. Engring., 1954; M.B.A., Rollins Coll., 1966; m. Mary Magdalen Johnson, Nov. 6, 1948; children—Timothy, Thomas, Christina, John, Roy, William, Joseph, Julia, Daniel, David, Mary Ellen. Engr., Chemstrand Corp., Pensacola, Fla., then sr. engr. Bendix Corp., South Bend, Ind., 1951-58; supr. prodn. engring. Radiation Inc., Melbourne, Fla., 1958-64; chief plans and programs LTV Aerospace Corp., Kennedy Space Center, Fla., 1964-67; dir. indsl. and prodn. engring. Electronic Communications Inc., St. Petersburg, Fla., 1967-74; mgr. mfg. engring. Scott Electronics Corp., Orlando, Fla., 1974-76, McDonnell Douglas Astronautics Co., Titusville, Fla., 1976-78; dir. mfg. Applied Devices Corp., Kissimmee, Fla., 1978-80; pres. John P. Tanner & Assos., cons. engrs., Orlando, Fla., 1969—; lectr. engring. tech. St. Petersburg Jr. Coll., 1968-70, Valencia Community Coll., 1973-75; adj. prof. U. Central Fla., 1975—. Served to lt. USNR, 1951-53; Korea. Registered profl. engr., Fla., Ga. Mem. Am. Inst. Indsl. Engrs. (sr.). Democrat. Roman Catholic. Office: 1410 Pinar Dr Orlando FL 32817

TANOUS, PETER JOSEPH, investment banker; b. N.Y.C., May 21, 1938; s. Joseph Carrington and Rose Marie (Mokarzel) T.; B.A. in Econs., Georgetown U., 1960; m. Barbara Ann MacConnell, Aug. 18, 1962; children—Christopher, Helene, William. With Smith, Barney & Co., Inc. (now Smith Barney, Harris Upham & Co., Inc.), N.Y.C., 1963-78, 2d v.p., mgr. Paris office, 1967, v.p., 1968-78, resident European sales mgr., Paris, 1969-71, internat. sales mgr., N.Y.C., 1971-78, 1st v.p., 1975-78; chmn. bd. Petra Capital Corp., N.Y.C., 1978—. Served to 1st lt. AUS, 1961-63. Mem. Georgetown U. Alumni Assn. (gov. 1968-71), Georgetown Club France (pres. 1968-71). Roman Catholic. Clubs: Met. (N.Y.C.); Automobile de France (Paris). Co-author: The Petrodollar Takeover, 1975; The Wheat Killing, 1979; author: The Earhart Mission, 1979. Home: 136 E 64th St New York NY 10021 Office: 200 Park Ave New York NY 10166

TANTON, JOAN ELIZABETH, mfg. co. exec.; b. Winnipeg, Man., Can., Dec. 28, 1942; d. Kingsley Leverne and Doris Emily (Gilbey) T.; student Royal Coll. Music, 1964-65. With B.C. Telephone Co., Vancouver, 1962-64, 65-66; with Austin Glove Mfg. Co., Sherbrooke, Que., 1968—, v.p., 1972—; cons. theatre and music groups. Bd. dirs. Sherbrooke Hosp., 1978; co-chmn. fin. Internat. Soc. Music Edn. (Can.), 1978. Conservative. Anglican. Home: 77 Acadmey St Lennoxville PQ J1M 1R5 Canada Office: 1140 Panneton St Sherbrooke PQ J1K 2B4 Canada

TANZER, JED SAMUEL, lawyer, fin. cons.; b. Arverne, N.Y., Nov. 16, 1947; s. David and Mildred (Bondy) T.; B.S. with honors in Social Sci., SUNY, Oneonta, 1970; J.D. cum laude, Syracuse U., 1978, M.B.A., 1979; m. Sally Jane Ketcham, July 10, 1971. Tchr., union grievance chmn. Central Sch. Dist., Windsor, N.Y., 1970-75; research asst. Sch. Mgmt., Syracuse (N.Y.) U., 1977-78; admitted to N.Y. State bar, 1979, Fed. Dist. Ct. bar, 1979, U.S. Tax Ct. bar, 1979; sr. atty. Ayco Corp., Albany, N.Y., 1978—; fin. cons., 1978—. Permanent teaching cert. N.Y. State. Mem. Am. Bar Assn., N.Y. State Bar Assn., Justinian Law Soc., Beta Gamma Sigma, Kappa Delta Pi. Home: 127 Jordan Blvd Delmar NY 12054 Office: 12 Metro Park Rd Albany NY 12205

TAPER, S. MARK, financial corp. exec.; b. 1901. Real estate agt., builder and developer, London, Eng., 1920-39; land developer, Calif., 1941-55; with First Charter Financial Corp., 1955—, chmn. bd., pres., chief exec. officer, 1956-62, 66-70, chmn. bd., 1962-66, chmn. bd., chief exec. officer, 1970—, pres., 1980—, also dir. Office: 9465 Wilshire Blvd Beverly Hills CA 90212*

TAPPAN, DAVID S., JR., engring. and constrn. co. exec.; b. China, 1922; B.A., Swarthmore Coll., 1943; M.B.A., Stanford U., 1948; married. With Fluor Corp., Los Angeles, 1952—, v.p. domestic sales, 1959-68, sr. v.p., gen. mgr. engring. and constrn. div., 1968-72, vice chmn., 1976—, also mem. exec. com., dir.; pres. Fluor Engrs. & Constrn., Inc., 1972-76. Served to lt. (j.g.) USNR, 1943-46. Office: 3333 Michelson Dr Irvine CA 92730

TAPPAN, WILLIAM RICHARD, ret. appliance mfg. co. exec.; b. Mansfield, Ohio, Nov. 7, 1914; s. Paul R. and Heloise (Hedges) T.; A.B., Denison U., 1936; M.B.A., Harvard U., 1938; m. Virginia Starkey, Nov. 11, 1938 (dec. Oct. 1974); children—Margaret, Thomas. With Tappan Co., Mansfield, 1938—, salesman, asst. to sales mgr., mgr. war product devel., mgr. new product devel., exec. v.p., 1938-58, pres., 1958-76, chmn., chief exec. officer, 1976-79; dir. Ohio Edison Co., Akron. Home: 3500 Gulf Shore Blvd N Naples FL 33940

TAPPIN, ANTHONY GERALD, mfg. co. exec.; b. London, July 17, 1925; s. Edward Laurence Charles and Cecilia Mary (Seymour) T.; came to U.S., 1940, naturalized, 1944; A.B., Cornell U., 1949; postgrad. Harvard Bus. Sch., 1968; m. Nancy C. Harper, May 17, 1952; children—Cynthia Marie, Amy Elizabeth. Asst. product mgr., chem. div. FMC Corp., N.Y.C., 1950, rep. Washington, 1950-52, dist. sales mgr., Cin., 1952-58, gen. sales mgr., 1958-67, dir. mktg.-asst. div. mgr., 1967-70, dir. purchases, 1970-77, regional v.p., corp. exec. mktg., 1977—. Active United Fund, Crippled Children's Assn. (both N.Y.C.). Served with inf. U.S. Army, 1943-46. Decorated Bronze Star medal, Combat Inf. Badge. Mem. Nat. Petroleum Refiners Assn. (dir. 1977—), Nat. Assn. Purchasing Mgmt. (certified purchasing mgr.), Nat. Accounts Mgrs. Assn. (dir.), Synthetic Organic Chem. Mfrs. Assn., Racemics, Phi Gamma Delta. Republican. Roman Catholic. Clubs: Cornell Fairfield County (Conn.) (pres. 1972-73); Cornell of Phila., Harvard Bus. Sch. Phila., Union League Phila.; Pinnacle (N.Y.C.); Aronimink Golf (Newtown Square, Pa.); Country Darien (Conn.); Capilano Golf and Country (Vancouver, B.C., Can.). Office: FMC Corp 2000 Market St Philadelphia PA 19103

TARASI, LOUIS MICHAEL, JR., lawyer; b. Cheswick, Pa., Sept. 9, 1931; s. Louis M. and Ruth (Records) T.; B.A., Miami U., Oxford, Ohio, 1954; J.D., U. Pa., 1959; m. Patricia R. Finley, June 19, 1954; children—Susan Louise, Louis Michael III, Elizabeth Marie, Brian R., Patricia A., Matthew John. Admitted to Pa. bar, 1960, U.S. Supreme Ct. bar, 1969; asso. firm Burgwin, Ruffin, Perry, Pohl & Springer, Pitts., 1959-65, became partner, 1965; partner Conte, Courtney, & Tarasi, Pitts., 1968-78, Tarasi & Tighe, 1978—; cons.; lectr.; research asst. U. Pa. Law Sch., 1958-59. Mem. St. Vincent de Paul Penal Com., Pitts., 1961—; sec., v.p. St. Thomas More Soc. Pitts., 1963—, also mem. bd. govs. Served with AUS, 1954-56. Mem. Am., Pa., Allegheny County bar assns., Am., Pa. (asso. editor, sec. 1976—, pres. 1979-80), Western Pa. (gov., editor Parliamentarian, pres. 1975-78) trial lawyers assns., Allegheny County Acad. Trial Lawyers. Roman Catholic. Clubs: Allegheny, Lewis Law, Edgeworth, Pittsburgh. Home: 940 Beaver St Sewickley PA 15143 Office: Tarasi & Tighe Bldg Pittsburgh PA 15219

TARBET, GLEN F., writer; b. Salt Lake City, Sept. 30, 1931; s. David E. and Carol (Cornia) Haskell; B.A., Brigham Young U., 1956; student Utah State U., 1949-50; postgrad. U. Utah, 1970-79, Westminster Coll., 1980-81; m. Betty Bennion Brown, Oct. 26, 1966; children—Lauris, Linda, Alan, Jan, Scott, Jami, Carrie, David, Steven, Penny, Victor. Office mgr. Nu Day Elec. Corp., Provo, Utah, 1954-56; specification engr. Radioplane Co., Van Nuys, Calif., 1956-57; reports writer Marquardt Co., Ogden, Utah, 1957-58; asso. engr. Thiokol Corp., Brigham City, Utah, 1958-60; prin. publ. engr., publs. mgr. Sperry Univac, Salt Lake City, 1960-71; editor Brigham Young U. Press, 1972; tech. writing services editor Brigham Young U. Computer Services, Provo, 1973; tech. writing services editor U. Utah Computer Center, 1974-75; sr. tech. writer N.W. Pipeline Co. and N.W. Alaskan Pipeline Co., Salt Lake City, 1975—. Served with USN, 1950-54. Mem. Soc. Tech. Communications (sr.; past chmn. Intermountain chpt.). Republican. Mormon (high priest). Home: 1967

Lambourne Ave Salt Lake City UT 84106 Office: N W Pipeline Corp PO Box 1526 Salt Lake City UT 84110

TARBOX, FRANK KOLBE, ins. co. exec.; b. Mineola, N.Y., Feb. 27, 1923; s. John Preston and Mary (Kolbe) T.; student Swarthmore Coll., 1940-42; A.B., U. Pa., 1947, LL.B., 1950; m. Eleanor Borden, May 1, 1948; children—John Borden, Kathryn Ann. Pvt. practice law, 1950-53, 55-60; asst. U.S. atty. Eastern Dist. Pa., 1953-55; v.p. adminstrn. Penn Mut. Life Ins. Co., Phila., 1960-71, pres., 1971-78, chmn. bd., 1979—, also chief exec. officer; dir. Phila. Nat. Bank, PNB Corp. Trustee United Fund Phila., Dickinson Coll., Carlisle, Pa.; bd. dirs. Phila. Food Distbn. Center, Phila. Urban Coalition, Old Phila. Devel. Corp.; trustee, chmn. bd. S.S. Huebner Found.; asso. trustee U. Pa., also mem. bd. overseers Law Sch. Served with USNR, 1942-46. Mem. Ins. Fedn. Pa. Methodist. Home: 520 Jarden Rd Philadelphia PA 19118 Office: Independence Sq Philadelphia PA 19172

TARGAN, ROBERT SCOTT, neurophysiologist, pharmacist, health co. exec.; b. Phila., Dec. 1, 1938; s. Samuel H. and Sarah (Greenspan) T.; B.S., Registered Pharmacist, Phila. Coll. Pharmacy, 1960; postgrad. U. Del., 1963-64, Temple U., 1965-67, Hebrew U., 1980-81; m. Myra Wolf, Mar. 19, 1961; children—Michele Kayla, Eric David. Partner, Stolker & Targan Pharmacy and Bus. Brokerage, Phila., 1960-63; dir. hosp. and govt. sales and mktg. Armour Pharm. Co., Chgo., 1965-68; pres. Whitehall Pharmacy & Surg., Inc., Phila., 1968-80; pres., chmn. bd. PAC Enterprises Inc., Phila., 1969—; pres. Whitehall Surg. Inc., Phila., 1970—, Universal Profl. Cons.'s, Phila., 1971-72, Surg. Fitting Services, Phila., 1971—, Targan Surg. Assos., 1980—; pres. Surg. Appliance Assos., 1977—; faculty Phila. Coll. Pharmacy; lectr. Hadassah Hebrew U. Med. Center, Jerusalem, 1980-81; cons., lectr. in field. Bd. mgrs. N.J. div. Am. Cancer Soc.; bd. dirs. Jewish Fedn. So. N.J., Jewish Community Relations Council, Jewish Community Center, Harry B. Kellman Hebrew Acad., Jewish Congregation Beth El, Cherry Hill, N.J., Congregation Beth Sholom, Haddon Hts., N.J. Served to lt. USAF, 1962-65. Recipient Lunsford Richardson Pharmacy award, 1959; Kahaner Found. Med. fellow, 1960-61; certified drug distbr. Pa.; licensed pharmacist Pa., N.J., Del., real estate broker, Pa. Mem. Am., Pa. pharm. assns., Am. Orthotic and Prosthetic Assn., Phila. Assn. Retail Druggists, New Eng. Surg. Trade Assn., Phila. Coll. Pharmacy and Sci. Alumni Assn., Am. Soc. Hosp. Pharmacists, Am. Speech and Hearing Assn., Am. Assn. Safety Engr., Assn. Mil. Surgeons U.S. Jewish religion. Clubs: Netanya Aleph Israel Investment (pres. 1975—), Brith Sholom, Gourmet Cherry Hill. Home: 1016 Tampa Ave Cherry Hill NJ 08034 Office: 496 Kings Hwy N Suite 231 Cherry Hill NJ 08034

TARNAY, ROBERT STEVENS, lawyer; b. N.Y.C., May 13, 1913; s. Victor William and Irma (Stevens) T.; A.B., U. Mich., 1934; J.D. with distinction, George Washington U., 1938; m. Anne Marie Larson, Sept. 5, 1936; 1 dau., Alice Anne. Admitted to D.C. bar, 1938, Conn. bar, 1938; spl. asst. to atty. gen. Dept. Justice, Washington, Phila., Calif. and Hawaii, 1938-45; corp. adminstrv. law practice, Washington, 1945—; pres., chmn. bd. Tarsh Co., Washington; pres., dir. Gen. Pub. Co.; exec. v.p., chief exec. officer Cashier and Restaurant Tng. Sch., Inc.; exec. v.p., gen. counsel Mini Rhea, Designer, Inc.; v.p., chmn. bd., pub. Washington Banktrends, Inc.; pres. Mechtronics, Inc.; operating trustee Schiavone Popcorn Devices, Inc., Washington. Active local, state juvenile delinquency work, 1940—; fin. chmn. local chpt. Girl Scouts of Am. 1954-56; chmn. Alexandria (Va.) area Community Chest Budget, 1957—; mem. PTA Council, Family and Welfare Council. Mem. Am., Conn. bar assns., Bar Assn. D.C., Order of Coif, Phi Alpha Delta, Kappa Sigma Phi, Phi Kappa Tau. Congregationalist. Author numerous articles, related econ. works. Home: Route 1 Box 88F Newburg MD 20664

TARNOFF, JEFFREY, investment cons.; b. N.Y.C., June 11, 1947; s. Edwin Max and Betty Fertig T.; B.S., Lehigh U., 1969; M.B.A., U. Chgo., 1971; m. Diane Winifred Seaman, Mar. 15, 1975; 1 dau., Sarah W. Securities analyst Equitable Life Assurance Soc. U.S., N.Y.C., 1971-73; investment officer Chase Investors Mgmt. Corp. N.Y., N.Y.C., 1973-76; v.p. Mfrs. Hanover Trust Co., N.Y.C., 1976-79; investment adv. Weiss, Peck & Greer, N.Y.C., 1979; exec. v.p., dir. ADV Fund Inc., N.Y.C., 1979-81; v.p. Verus Capital, 1981—; v.p. Arnhold & S. Bleichroeder, 1981—; dir. Apex Inc. Mem. class gifts com., ann. giving fund class agt. Lehigh U.; bd. dirs., treas. 470 West End Corp. Mem. Fin. Analysts Fedn., N.Y.C. Soc. Security Analysts. Home: 470 West End Ave New York NY 10024 Office: Verus Capital 30 Broad St New York NY 10004

TAROSKY, ROBERT EUGENE, cons. engr.; b. New Kensington, Pa., Apr. 29, 1942; s. Frank John and Mary Wanda (Bartos) T.; B.S. in Mech. and Aerospace Engring., Ill. Inst. Tech., 1970; m. Verna May Lucci, Feb. 1, 1964 (dec. 1976); m. 2d, Diane Carol Baran, Feb. 25, 1978; children—Michele Lynn, Renata Elizabeth. With Tuthill Pump Co., Alsip, Ill., 1963-68; with Gen. Environments Corp., Morton Grove, Ill., 1970-75, staff engr., 1970-75, cons. engr., 1975-79; with Hazard Engring. Inc., Morton Grove, 1975—, v.p., 1979—. Registered profl. engr., Ill. Mem. Nat. Soc. Profl. Engrs., Ill. Soc. Profl. Engrs., Soc. Automotive Engrs. Home: 818 N Kennicott Ave Arlington Heights IL 60004 Office: Hazard Engring Inc 6208 Lincoln Ave Morton Grove IL 60053

TARR, JAMES LEE, paper co. exec.; b. Red Oak, Iowa, Mar. 22, 1931; s. Glenn and Opal Rosenblatt (Essman) T.; student Kansas City Art Inst., 1954, 55; m. Jayne Carol Jochim, June 13, 1952; children—Deborah Jane, Chad Michael. Artist, photographer, platemaker Henry McGrew Printing Co., Kansas City, Mo., 1955-59; artist, cameraman, color technician Gordon Printing Co., Davenport, Iowa, 1959-65; art dir., coordinator graphic arts, envelope div. Boise Cascade Co., Addison, Ill., 1965—. Served with USN Nat. Security Agy., 1949-54. Home: 721 S 11th Ave Saint Charles IL 60174 Office: 313 Rohlwing Rd Addison IL 60101

TARRANT, ROBERT FRANCIS, glove mfg. exec.; b. Milw., Dec. 22, 1927; s. George Francis and Henrietta Agnes T.; student Milw. public schs.; m. Barbara Bilsky, June 23, 1967. Pres., P & M Distbrs., Westbury, N.Y., 1961-72; v.p. sales Ski div. Aris Gloves, N.Y.C., 1973—. Pres. Deer Park Public Library, Deer Park Civic Assn. Served with USMC, 1946-48. Mem. Ski Industries Am. (1st v.p.). Roman Catholic. Home: 662 W Hill Rd Stamford CT 06902 Office: 417 Fifth Ave New York NY 10016

TARRANT, RONALD WILLIAM, mfg. co. exec.; b. Saginaw, Mich., May 25, 1937; s. William Edward and Lena Henrietta (Bremmer) T.; B.A., Asbury Coll., 1959; postgrad. U. Ky. at Lexington, 1959-61; m. Peggy Jane Carlson; children—Gregory, Bradley, Kurt, John, David. With Square D Co., Lexington, Ky., 1960-64; sales engr. Cutler Hamner, Detroit, 1964-68; owner Russco, Detroit, 1968-70; with Bindicator Co., Port Huron, Mich., 1970-76, sales mgr., 1972-76, gen. mgr., 1974-76; nat. sales mgr. Aero-Go Inc., Seattle, 1976-78; partner Sanneno-Simmons-Tarrant Inc., Seattle, 1978—. Mem. Instrument Soc. Am., Am. Foundrymen's Assn., Soc. Plastics Engrs., B.P.A.A. Assn. Congregationalist. Home: 4479 141st St SE Belleville WA 98006 Office: 2610 1/2 3d Ave Seattle WA 98121

TARRISH, JOSEPH CROMAN, investment bank exec.; b. New Haven, Jan. 1, 1917; s. Abraham and Sonia (Croman) T.; student U. So. Calif., 1935-36, Southwestern U., 1937; m. Pearl Richman, Jan. 31, 1944; children—Sonia, Barbara, Laura. Partner, Tarrish & Shapiro, 1940-46; owner J.C. Tarrish Co., 1947-51; partner Auster-Tarrish Co., 1951-55; owner Melrose Co., 1956-65; pres., chief stockholder J.C. Tarrish Co., Inc., Phoenix, 1967—. Served to adj. gen. Q.M.C. Corps, AUS, 1942-46. Mem. Assn. for Corp. Growth. Office: J C Tarrish Co Inc Suite 1000 3225 N Central Ave Phoenix AZ 85016

TARTAGLIA, JOHN ANGELO, broaching machines mfg. co. exec.; b. Waterbury, Conn., Sept. 29, 1918; s. Angelo M. and Incornata Tartaglia; student public schs., Waterbury: m. Mary L. Pace, Apr. 25, 1953; 1 son, John Michael. Toolmaking apprentice, 1936-44; owner, mgr. tool jobbing co., 1944-48; mgr. tool job shops, 1948-50; pres., treas., founder Bond Tool & Mfg. Co., Inc., Waterbury, 1950—. Mem. Conn. Bus. and Industry Assn., Waterbury Smaller Mfrs. Assn. Patentee in lock hardware and med. instrument fields. Office: Bond Tool & Mfg Co Inc 101 Pierpont Rd Waterbury CT 06705

TASCHEREAU, PIERRE, airline exec.; b. Quebec City, Que., Can., Jan. 13, 1920; s. Edouard and Juliette (Carroll) T.; B.A., Garnier Coll., 1938; LL.L., Laval U., 1941; postgrad. U. Western Ont., 1952; m. Yseult Beaudry, Aug. 13, 1945; children—Paule Taschereau Bernier), Laurent, Francois. Admitted to Que. bar, 1941, created Queen's counsel, 1955; atty. Canadian Nat. R.R. Co., Montreal, 1946-63, v.p. law, 1971-72, exec. v.p. corp. affairs, 1972-74, chmn. bd., 1974-77; dir. Air Can., 1974, chmn. bd., 1976-79, 80—; dir. Royal Trust Co. sr. mem. firm Geoffrion & Prud'homme, Barr, & Solicitors, Montreal, 1963-67. Vice pres. Canadian Transp. Commn., 1967-71. Gov. Hosp. Marie Enfant, Montreal. Served to capt. Canadian Army, 1942-46. Mem. Canadian, Quebec bar assns. Roman Catholic. Club: Mt. Royal (Montreal). Home: 3788 Grey Ave Montreal PQ H4A 3N7 Canada Office: 1 Pl Ville-Marie Montreal PQ H3B 3P7 Canada

TASH, MARTIN ELIAS, publishing co. exec.; b. U.S., Jan. 24, 1941; s. David and Esther T.; B.B.A., Baruch Sch., CCNY, 1962; m. Arlene Sue Klein, June 23, 1962; children—Nat, Faye, Jill. Staff acct. S.D. Leidesdorf & Co., N.Y.C., 1962-66; v.p. fin. LMC Data Inc., N.Y.C., 1966-71, also dir.; v.p., treas. Plenum Pub. Corp., N.Y.C., 1971-77, chmn. bd., pres., 1977—. C.P.A., N.Y. State. Mem. Am. Inst. C.P.A.'s, Beta Alpha Psi. Office: 227 W 17th St New York NY 10011

TASHIRO, NOBORU, investment co. exec.; b. Rocky Ford, Colo., Nov. 18, 1920; s. Suehiko and Sunao (Tanaka) T.; grad. Colo. Sch. Mines, 1941; postgrad. in meteorology, N.Y. U., 1944; LL.B., Westminster Law Sch., Denver, 1952; m. Mary Jane Yamato, Apr. 21, 1949; children—Nancy Louise Tashiro Castillo, Floyd Thomas. Various engring. positions, 1941-52; chief engr. Roberts & Schaeffer Co., Chgo. and N.Y.C., 1952-56; asst. to pres. Gammino Constrn. Co., Providence, 1956-58; v.p. J.F. White Contracting Co., Westwood, Mass., 1958-59; mgmt. cons., Los Angeles, 1959-71; chmn. bd. Titus Investment Co., Monterey Park, Calif., 1971—, Titus Japan Co., Inc., Tokyo, 1974—, House of Lono, Inc., Honolulu, Broad Rec. Studio Inc., Honolulu. Served in USAF, 1943-46. Registered profl. engr., Colo. Mem. Am. Bar Assn., Sigma Gamma Epsilon. Club: Calif. Country. Office: 500 N Garfield Ave Suite 205 Monterey Park CA 91754

TASSEL, SAMUEL BERNARD, ins. agy. exec.; b. Lynn, Mass., Feb. 1, 1923; s. Abraham and Sarah (Clickstein) T.; student Northeastern U., 1942; A.B., Dartmouth Coll., 1947; m. Ruth Berkett, June 4, 1961; children—Lawrence, Nadine. Owner, mgr. Samuel B. Tassel Ins. Agy., Boston, 1948-63; pres., treas. Admiral Ins. Agy. Inc., Lynn, 1963—; dir. W/R Systems Inc., Warner-Am. Express of Essex, Inc.; treas., dir. Am. Title Ins. Agy. Inc.; trustee Admiral Realty Trust. Chmn., Lynn Mayor's Downtown Task Force, 1972-74, 76-80. Served to lt. USNR, 1942-46. C.L.U.; C.P.C.U.; cert. ins. councillor. Mem. Ind. Ins. Agts., Profl. Ins. Agts., North Shore Ins. Agts., Profl. Ins. Agts. New Eng. (dir.), Ind. Ins. Agts. Mass. Democrat. Jewish. Clubs: Volunteer Yacht, Masons, Shriners, Odd Fellows. Home: 400 Paradise Rd Swampscott MA 01907 Office: 20 State St Lynn MA 01901

TATE, MICHAEL ROY, holding co. and ins. co. exec.; b. West Frankfort, Ill., Sept. 29, 1944; s. Roy and Lucille T.; student in accounting So. Ill. U., 1963-66; m. Beverly J. Parton, Jan. 29, 1966; children—M. Scott, M. Shawn. Regional v.p. Modern Income Life Ins. Co., Decatur, Ill., 1971-72, dist. mgr., 1972-73, v.p., 1969-71; tax accountant Chgo. Title & Trust Co., 1969-71; exec. v.p., sec., dir. United Empire Life Ins. Co., Indpls., 1973-76; co-founder, pres., treas., dir. Life of Ind. Corp. and Life of Ind. Ins. Co., Indpls., 1976—. Chmn. bd. Ind. Baptist Found. Served to sgt. U.S. Army, 1966. Decorated Bronze Star. Mem. Ind. Assn. Life Ins. Cos. (founder). Baptist. Office: 911 E 86th St Indianapolis IN 46240

TATE, RUSSELL SAGE, JR., market research exec.; b. Newark, Sept. 5, 1916; s. Russell Sage and Edith (McIver) T.; B.A., U. Richmond, 1937; M.A., Duke, 1939; m. Marian W. Tate, Apr. 29, 1944 (div.); 1 son, Russell Sage III (dec.); m. 2d, Lorraine T. Tate, May 1, 1971. Mgr. soap dept. Armour & Co., Chgo., 1945-48; v.p. Continental Milk Co., Chgo., 1948-51; sales mgr. Greyhound Lines, Chgo., 1951-52; v.p. Market Research Corp. Am., Chgo., 1952-61; pres., chief exec. officer, N.Y.C., 1962-68; pres. market research div. Computer Applications Inc., 1968-71; v.p. Computer Applications Inc., 1968-71; pres. Home Testing Inst./TV-Q, Inc., Manhasset, L.I., N.Y., 1970-71; pres. Mktg. Info. Center, Reuben H. Donnelley Corp., 1972—; pres. Tate Teaching Systems, Inc., N.Y.C., 1970—. Served with USAAF, World War II. Decorated Air medal with 4 oak leaf clusters, D.F.C. with oak leaf cluster; named Man of Conn., 1962. Mem. Am. Mktg. Assn., Omicron Delta Kappa, Tau Kappa Alpha, Pi Delta Epsilon. Clubs: Indian Harbor Yacht, Winged Foot, Lost Tree Golf, Edgewood Valley Country. Research and publs. in field. Home: 1 Strawberry Hill Ave Stamford CT 06902 also 400 Beach Rd Tequesta FL 33458 Office: 1515 Summer St Stamford CT 06905

TATE, STANLEY GRAHAM, real estate developer, city ofcl.; b. Miami, Fla., Apr. 25, 1928; s. J.A. and Anne B. (Behren) Tatelman; B.S., U. Fla., 1948, postgrad., 1949; postgrad. Columbia, 1949; m. Joanne Greenwood, Sept. 11, 1949; children—John Kenneth, Linda Sue, James David. Pres., propr. Stanley Tate Builders, Inc., Miami, 1954—; partner Haft-Gaines Building Corp., Ft. Lauderdale, Fla., 1961-64; partner Investments Diversified Ltd., 1965—; pres. High Point Builders, Inc., 1966—, High Point of Delray Builders, Inc., 1966—, Ryerson & Haynes Realty, Inc., Miami, 1971-76; chmn. bd. Ryerson & Haynes, Inc., Miami, 1971-76; chief exec. officer Associated Mortgage Investors, 1974—; chmn. bd. Envirocivil Engring. Corp.; dir. Pan Am. Bank, N.A., Southeastern Home Mortgage Co., New Line Cinema. Past chmn. United Way of Dade County (Fla.), 1975—; mem. adv. exec. com. YWCA of Miami, 1973—; past v.p. Family and Children's Services of Miami, 1970-77; mayor Town of Bay Harbor Islands, 1971-74, mem. City Council, 1954-77; past bd. dirs., treas. Children's Service Bur., Miami; past bd. dirs. Children's Cardiac Hosp., v.p., 1971; bd. dirs. Miami Heart Inst., 1981—. Recipient Ben-Gurion award State of Israel, 1973, Shalom award, 1971. Mem. Nat. Assn. Home Builders, Asso. Gen. Contractors Am. Jewish (v.p. temple 1972—). Clubs: Westview Country (dir. 1973); Hound Ears, Cricket, Jockey. Home: 1301 100th St Bay Harbor Islands FL 33154 Office: 1175 NE 125th St North Miami FL 33161

TATLOW, RICHARD HENRY, IV, archtl.-engring. co. exec.; b. Washington, June 30, 1939; s. Richard Henry and Annette Victoria (Hart) T.; B.C.E., Cornell U., 1962; M.B.A., U. Va., 1964; m. Anne Rodes Nelson, Nov. 14, 1964; children—Leslie Hart, Richard Henry. With Boeing Co., Chester, Pa., 1964-67; structural engr. Abbott Merkt & Co., Inc., N.Y.C., 1967-68, project mgr., 1968-70, asst. v.p., project mgr., 1970-71, v.p. prodn., 1971-74, pres., 1974—; pres. Abbott Merkt Internat., Inc.; dir. Abbott Merkt Architects, Inc., Penntech Papers, Inc., Mem. Scarsdale Archtl. Rev. Bd., 1971-75; mem. Scarsdale Planning Commn., 1976-79. Served to capt. U.S. Army, 1964-66. Mem. ASCE, Soc. Am. Mil. Engrs., Newcomen Soc. Republican. Presbyterian. Clubs: Shenorock Shore, Fox Meadow Tennis, Army Navy (Washington). Home: 4 Rodney Rd Scarsdale NY 10583 Office: 10 E 40th St Suite 3400 New York NY 10016

TATRO, PAUL EDWARD, r.r. exec.; b. Winthrop, Mass., Oct. 23, 1938; s. Carl Joseph and Margaret Mary (McCann) T.; B.A., Baldwin Wallace Coll., 1960; M.B.A., Case Western Res. U., 1965; Advanced Mgmt. Program, Harvard U., 1978, 79; m. Janet L. Duncan, Aug. 29, 1959; children—Christopher, Geoffrey, Jennifer, Thomas. With Central Nat. Bank of Cleve., 1965-68; acct. Chessie R.R., 1968-72; controller Grand Truck Western R.R. Co., Detroit, 1972-74, v.p. fin., 1974—, also dir.; dir. Grank Trunk Radio Communications, Chgo. & Western Ind. R.R. Co. Served to lt. USCG, 1962-65. Mem. AAR. Clubs: Detroit, Forest Lake Country. Office: 131 W Lafayette Blvd Detroit MI 48226

TATUM, DONALD EDWARDS, fin. services exec.; b. Clover, S.C., Jan. 1, 1924; s. William Otis and Elizabeth (Mayo) T.; student La. State U., 1940-42; C.L.U., Am. Coll. Life Underwriters, 1955, C.L.U.M., 1958; m. Sally J. Marsteller, Mar. 13, 1964; children—William Otis IV, Timothy B., Elizabeth E., Donald Edwards. With Conn. Gen. Life, Hartford, Conn., 1946-62, mgr., Pitts., 1956-62; v.p. Nat. Union Ins. Cos., 1962-67; pres., dir. South Coast Life Ins. Co., Houston, Gt. Nat. Life Ins. Co., Grenat Corp.; sr. v.p. U.S. Life Corp., N.Y.C., 1967-70; pres. Peninsular Life Ins. Co., George Washington Life Ins. Co.; v.p., dir. George Washington Corp., 1970-74; pres., dir. Lincoln Am. Life, 1974-79; account exec. A. Duncan Williams, Inc., 1979—; dir. Lincoln Am. Corp., Tenn. Asso. Life Cos. Active United Fund. Served to lt. USNR, 1943-46. C.L.U. Mem. Assn. Life Underwriters (chpt. dir. 1960-62), Newcomen Soc., Am. Mgmt. Assn., Ark. Racking Horse Assn., Tenn. Walking Horse Breeders and Exhibitors Assn. Presbyterian. Clubs: Rotary (Chagrin Falls, pres. 1955-56); Petroleum, Summit, Tenn., Meadowbrook. Contbr. in field to publs. Home: RD 2 Box 95 Hughes AR 72348 Office: 5100 Poplar Ave Memphis TN 38137

TATUM, THOMAS WALTER, cement mfg. co. exec.; b. Manila, Philippines, Mar. 28, 1937; s. Thomas Brooke and Louise Donovan (Hegwer) T.; B.S., Okla. State U., 1961, M.B.A., 1962; m. Mary Loy, Dec. 27, 1960; children—Bryan T., Lauren L. Sales mgr. Am. Telephone & Telegraph, long lines dept., Dallas, 1962-66, labor relations supr., N.Y.C., 1966-67, ops. supr., St. Louis, 1967-68; div. personnel mgr. Gen. Portland Inc., Dallas, 1968-70, corporate labor relations mgr., 1970-74, corporate dir. employee relations, 1974—. Served with USAFR, 1960-66. Mem. Indsl. Relations Research Assn., Dallas Personnel Assn., Cement Employers Assn., So. Calif. Cement Employers Assn. Republican. Methodist. Clubs: Los Rios Country, Lancers. Home: 6722 Barkworth Dallas TX 75248 Office: PO Box 324 Dallas TX 75221

TATUM, TOBY WAYNE, restaurant chain exec.; b. Yuma, Ariz., Mar. 19, 1945; s. Cecil Wayne and Harriet Virginia (Carlson) T.; A.A., Santa Rosa Jr. Coll., 1968; B.A., Sonoma State U., 1972; M.B.A., San Francisco State U., 1973; m. Mary Ann Krause, Dec. 4, 1976; 1 dau. by previous marriage, Tiffany. Vice pres. fin. Tatum Enterprises, Santa Rosa, Calif., 1973—; asso. prof. mgmt. Sonoma State U., 1975-76; dir. Sonoma State Enterprises, Inc., 1978-80; trustee Sizzler Family Steakhouse Nat. Franchise Assn. Served with U.S. Army, 1968-72. Decorated Bronze Star. Mem. Santa Rosa C. of C. Office: 320 College Ave Santa Rosa CA 95404

TAUBER, ALFRED SEYMOUR, info. systems co. exec.; b. N.Y.C., Aug. 16, 1923; s. Abraham and Mollie (Bertcher) T.; B.M.E., Coll. City N.Y., 1949; M.S. in Indsl. Engring., Columbia and U. Calif., Los Angeles, 1958; m. Florence Holstein, Mar. 15, 1953; 1 son, Andrew Lee. Indsl. engr. Williamsburg Pub. Co., N.Y.C., 1950-56; sr. systems analyst product devel. NCR, Hawthorne, Calif., 1957-62; v.p. advanced devel. and system devel. Image Systems, Los Angeles, 1962-70; cons. info. storage and retrieval, Los Angeles, 1970-72; dir. market devel. Zytron Corp., Menlo Park, Calif., 1972-79; founder, pres. Find-It, info. retrieval co., Info. Architects Inc., 1980—; tchr. document storage and retrieval systems analysis and design U. Calif., Los Angeles. Served to sgt. AUS, 1943-46. Fellow Nat. Micrographics Assn.; mem. Am. Soc. Info. Sci. (chmn. Los Angeles chpt.). Author: Automatic Document Storage and Retrieval, a Market Emerges, 1972. Co-inventor coded character sensing apparatus. Home: 582 Sand Hill Circle Menlo Park CA 94025 Office: 582 Sand Hill Circle Menlo Park CA 94025

TAUBERT, BEVERLY KIRCHER, automotive products mfg. co. exec.; b. Mt. Vernon, N.Y., July 10; d. Herbert C. and Mabel (Eichel) Kircher; grad. Bekeley Bus. Sch., N.Y.C., 1945; m. George G. Taubert, Oct. 2, 1954. Exec. sec. to mayor Mt. Vernon (N.Y.) 1946-52; exec. asst. Metro N.Y. sales Schenley Industries, N.Y.C., 1952-67; sec. H.D.T., Co. Factors, Inc., White Plains, N.Y., 1968-76, pres., 1976—; v.p. Taubert Studios, Inc., Mt. Vernon. Sec., Mt. Vernon Republican Club. Mem. Automotive Service Industries Assn., Automotive Parts and Accessories Assn. Lutheran. Home: 32 Doris Ln Mamaroneck NY 10543 Office: 27 Holland Ave White Plains NY 10603

TAVEL, ROBERT FREDERICK, real estate and ins. broker; b. Johnston City, Ill., June 7, 1943; s. James Robert and Vivian Lee (Brown) T.; m. Lillie Faye Moffett; children—Phillip Jeffery, Sherry Michelle. Salesman, Brockman's Dept. Store, Angleton, Tex., 1963, shoe mgr., Lake Jackson, Tex., 1964, asst. mgr., Alvin, Tex., 1965, mgr., West Columbia, Tex., 1966-71, Deer Park, Tex., 1971-73; gen. mgr. Deer Park Realty, 1973-74; owner, mgr. Tavel Ins. Agy., 1973—; mng. partner Holder-Tavel Realty, 1975-77; owner, mgr. So. Realty, 1978-79; co-owner, mgr. Union Realty, 1979—; sec. Deer Park Met. Listing Assn., 1974-75, pres., 1976; instr. real estate fin. San Jacinto Coll. Charter chmn. West Columbia Library Bd., 1968-71; chmn. West Columbia Beautification Assn., 1970; div. chmn. Brazoria County United Fund Communities, 1971; chmn. Sch. Dist. Drug Edn. Bd., 1970-71; mem. dist. com. Bay Area council Boy Scouts Am., 1969-70; Sunday Sch. supt. Baptist Ch., 1966-71; mem. Deer Park City Council, 1977—. Named West Columbia's Outstanding Young Man, Jr. C. of C., 1970, Deer Park Outstanding Young Man of Yr., 1974; recipient First Outstanding Service award West Columbia City Council, 1971, citation Tex. Gov. Preston for service to Tex. Indsl. Commn., 1970. Mem. Tex. Geneal. Assn., Tex. C. of C. (pres. West

Columbia 1968, Deer Park 1974), Gulf Coast Heritage Soc. (pres. 1975-78, charter), Jaycees (sec.-treas. 1977-78, dir. 1979, Silver Tongue award 1978). Clubs: Masons, Rotary (pres. 1970-71, gov. rep. 1972-74). Home: 2601 Georgia St Deer Park TX 77536 Office: 2201 Center St Deer Park TX 77536

TAVOULAREAS, WILLIAM PETER, oil co. exec.; b. Bklyn., Nov. 9, 1919; s. Peter William and Mary (Palisi) T.; B.B.A., St. John's U., 1941, J.D., 1948; m. Adele Maciejewska, Aug. 13, 1941; children—Peter, Patrice, William. Admitted to N.Y. bar, 1948; with Mobil Oil Corp. 1947—, v.p. plans and programs Mobil Internat. Oil Co., 1961-63, v.p. charge supply and distbn. and internat. sales parent co., 1963-65, sr. v.p., dir., mem. exec. com., 1965-67, v.p. charge supply, transport and Middle East and Indonesian affairs, pres. N.Am. div., 1967-69, corp. pres., 1969—, vice chmn. exec. com., dir.; pres., vice chmn. exec. com., dir. Mobil Corp., 1976—; dir. Gen. Foods Corp., Bankers Trust Co., Bankers Trust N.Y. Corp. Trustee St. John's U., Athens Coll., St. Paul's Sch.; dir. Near East Coll. Assn.; bd. govs. Soc. of N.Y. Hosp. Served with AUS, World War II. Mem. Harbor Acres Assn., Beta Gamma Sigma. Knights of Malta. Clubs: Pinnacle, North Hempstead Country. Office: Mobil Oil Corp 150 E 42d St New York NY 10017

TAWASHA, IBRAHIM YACOUB, business exec.; b. Ramallah, Palestine, Dec. 13, 1924; came to U.S., 1947, naturalized, 1954; s. Y'coub Ghnaim and Jaleeleh S. (Rafeedy) T.; student Jerusalem Law Classes, 1941-45; J.D., King's Coll., London U., 1947; m. Leila T. Kash-shou, Oct. 12, 1958; children—Carolyn J., Jack I., Joseph G. Admitted to Temple bar, 1947; with Brit. Govt., Palestine Mandate, 1939-45, Saudi Embassy, 1947-50; self-employed businessman, 1953-68; dir. Western Region, Arab Info. Center, League of Arab States, San Francisco, 1969-74; pres. Arab-Am. Ventures, Inc., San Francisco, 1974—, chief exec. officer, 1974—; cons. to non-profit orgns.; lectr. on Arab history, culture and politics City Coll. San Francisco. Mem. exec. com. Republican Party of City and County of San Francisco, 1964-68; chmn. Arab-Am. Com., Finche for Senate Com., 1976, Arab-Am. Com., George Cory For Congress, 1976; trustee St. Nicholas Orthodox Ch., San Francisco. Served with U.S. Army, 1950-52. Named Hon. Citizen, State of Tenn., 1975, Ky. Col., 1976; recipient commendation Calif. Senate Rules Com., 1979. Mem. U.S.-Arab C. of C., Joint Mideast Bus. Conf. (adv. bd.), Nat. Assn. Arab Ams. (dir.), World Affairs Council No. Calif. Republican. Club: Commonwealth. Contbr. numerous articles on Arab-Israeli conflict to newspapers, mags. Home: 1990 18th Ave San Francisco CA 94116 Office: 155 Montgomery San Francisco CA 94104

TAWIL, RONALD, footwear importing exec.; exec.; b. Bklyn., Apr. 30, 1946; s. Ralph C. and Pauline (Roffe) T.; student Bklyn. Coll., 1962-64; B.S., City Coll. N.Y., 1967, B.Arch., 1968; m. Rochelle Esses, Mar. 5, 1969; 3 children. With Cowell, Radenhausen & Geffert, architects and engrs., 1968-69; asst. sec. Soundesign Corp., Jersey City, 1969-77, v.p., 1977, v.p. Winthrop Audio Systems div., 1972-75; with E.S. Originals, Inc., N.Y.C., 1978—, dir. Kandu Industries div., 1978—. Founder Spl. Services Deal (N.J.) Synagogue, asst. treas. Shaare Zion Congregation, Bklyn., also mem. exec. com. Office: 20 W 33d St New York NY 10001

TAWNEY, MELVIN LEE, mgmt. cons.; b. Wakeeney, Kans., Aug. 5, 1934; s. J. Warren and Letha M. (Doane) T.; B.S. in Bus. Adminstrn., Kans. State U., 1958; divorced; children—Sandra Jo, Lisa Ann. Acct., Brelsford, Gifford, Hardesty & Bratz, C.P.A.'s, Topeka, 1958-59; controller C.H. Leavall & Co., El Paso, Tex., also exec. v.p. data processing subs., 1959-67; comptroller Oshman's Inc., Houston, 1967-68; mgmt. cons. Peat, Marwick, Mitchell & Co., C.P.A.'s, Houston, 1968-71; pres., chief exec. officer Vicon Instrument Co., Colorado Springs, Colo., 1971-75; treas. Coastal, Inc., Abbeville, La., 1975-76; prin. Waggett-Tawney Assos., mgmt. cons., Houston, 1976-80, M.L. Tawney & Assos., 1980—. Served with AUS, 1954-56. C.P.A., Tex. Mem. Am. Inst. C.P.A.'s, Tex. Soc. C.P.A.'s (chmn. mgmt. services com., dir. Houston chpt.), Houston C. of C. Methodist. Home: 6402 Del Monte St #17 Houston TX 77057 Office: 1800 Saint James Pl Suite 216 Houston TX 77056

TAXELIUS, THOMAS GRAHAM, engring. cons.; b. Spokane, Wash., Jan. 24, 1928; s. Claude William and Bess Maude (Graham) T.; B.S.M.E., Wash. State Coll., 1949; m. Joanne Kelly Trimble, Apr. 18, 1954; children—Robert, Teri. Sr. engring. writer Westinghouse Bettis Atomic Power Lab., Pitts. and Idaho Falls, Idaho, 1956-62; pub. mgr. Kaman Nuclear, Colorado Springs, Colo., 1962-65; chief tech. pubs. Aerojet Nuclear Co., Idaho Falls, 1965-72; pres., chief exec. officer Stafco, Inc., Portland, Oreg., 1972—; cons. in field. Mem. Am. Mgmt. Assn., Am. Nuclear Assn. Republican. Methodist. Clubs: Aero of Portland, Masons, Shriners, K.T. Home: 2030 SW Pheasant Dr Aloha OR 97006 Office: 621 SW Morrison St Portland OR 97205

TAYLOR, ALAN JAMES, publisher, film producer; b. Milo, Maine, Sept. 24, 1949; s. James Stanley and Genieve (Olson) T.; grad. Broadcasting Radio and TV Acad., 1968. Pres. Classic Film Mus. Inc., Dover-Foxcroft, Maine, 1973—, Classic Internat. TV Co., 1973—; mgr. stas. WTOS-FM, WSKW-AM; tchr. Career Acad., Boston, 1969; staff announcer Eternal Word radio program, 1976—; distbr. Ray Harryhausen Fantasy Collection; host TV series Classic Showcase, 1969, Science-Fiction Fantastic, 1974. Mem. Writers Guild Am. East, Dover-Foxcroft Jaycees (award 1974). Democrat. Baptist. Club: Kiwanis. Author: Making a Monster, make-up and costume guide, 1976; (with Sue Roy) A Film Portfolio of Sherlock Holmes, 1976; A Film Portfolio of Shirley Temple, 1976; (with Bill Hume) 50 Years of Sci-Fi and Horror, 1981; (screenplays) (with Bill Hume) Maggie, Snowman, No Greater Love; Earth radio format; articles in Starlog, Fangoria, Fantastic Films and Cinefantastique mags. Address: Taylor Film Prodns 1/3 Union St Dover-Foxcroft ME 04426

TAYLOR, ARTHUR ROBERT, corp. exec.; b. Elizabeth, N.J., July 6, 1935; s. Arthur E. and Marion (Scott) T.; A.B. magna cum laude, Brown U., 1957, M.A., 1961; H.H.D., Bucknell U., 1975; L.H.D., Rensselaer Polytech Inst., 1975, Simmons Coll., 1975; Asst. dir. admissions Brown U., resident fellow, 1957-60, asst. dept. polit. sci., 1959; with First Boston Corp., N.Y.C., 1961-70, v.p. underwriting dept., 1966-70, dir., 1970; v.p. fin. Internat. Paper Co., 1970-71, exec. v.p., 1971-72, also dir., mem. exec. com., 1971-72; pres. CBS Inc., N.Y.C., 1972-76, also dir.; gen. partner Arthur Taylor & Co., N.Y.C., 1977—; dir. Travelers Corp., Rockefeller Center, Inc., DCL, Inc., Am. Friends of Bilderberg, First Boston, Inc.; trustee Franklin Savs. Bank. Trustee Brown U., N.Y. Hosp., William H. Donner Found.; commr. Trilateral Commn. Mem. Council Fgn. Relations, Nat. Com. on Am. Fgn. Policy, Center for Inter-Am. Relations, Jajean Soc., Phi Beta Kappa. Clubs: Century, Brook (N.Y.C.); California (Los Angeles). Office: 30 Rockefeller Plaza Suite 4300 New York NY 10112

TAYLOR, CAROLE ANN, bus. services co. exec.; b. Harrisburg, Pa., Jan. 25, 1940; d. Charles Ross and Sara Isabella (Mullen) Boyer; grad. Dale Carnegie, 1974. Exec. sec. Brunswick Corp., Harrisburg, Pa., 1957-65; office div. mgr. Manpower, Inc., Harrisburg, 1965-69, gen. mgr., 1971—; office mgr. Covenco, Inc., Harrisburg, 1969-71. Bd. dirs. Opportunities Indsl. Center, 1973-74, Wheels, Inc., 1979-81, A.C.E.S., 1979—; div. chmn. United Way, 1976-80; bd. dirs. Harrisburg C. of C., 1973-76 comml. div. chmn., 1976; bd. dirs. ARC, 1978-80, sec., 1978-81. Mem. Adminstrv. Mgmt. Soc. (merit award 1975-76, diamond merit award, 1976-77, top membership producer award 1976-77, sec., v.p. membership, 1st v.p., pres., asst. area dir.), Exec. Women Internat. (founder, pres.). Republican. Contbr. articles to profl. publs. Home: 4835 Sweetbriar Terr Harrisburg PA 17111 Office: 2929 N Front St Harrisburg PA 17110

TAYLOR, CLAUDE IVAN, airline exec.; b. Salisbury, N.B., Can., May 20, 1925; D.C.L. (hon.), U. N.B., 1980; married; 2 children. With Air Can., Montreal, Que., 1949—, v.p. strategic devel., 1970-71, v.p. govt. and industry affairs, 1971-73, v.p. transp. services, 1972-73, v.p. public affairs, 1973-76, pres., chief exec. officer, 1976—; dir. Guinness Peat Aviation; hon. dir. Aviation Hall of Fame Can. Hon. bd. dirs. Can. Nat. Exhbn., Boy Scouts Can.; bd. govs. Montreal Gen. Hosp. Decorated comdr. Order of St. John; recipient Gordon R. McGregor Meml. trophy RCAF Assn., 1980. Mem. Can. C. of C. (exec. council), Internat. Assn. Students Econs. Commerce (bd. advs.), Travel Industry Assn. Can. (past pres.), Air Transport Assn. Can. (past pres.), Internat. Air Transport Assn. (pres. 1979-80), Profl. Corp. Indsl. Accts. Que. Clubs: Mt. Stephen, Mt. Royal, Forest and Stream (Montreal); Rideau (Ottawa); Wings (N.Y.C.). Office: Air Canada Place Ville Marie Montreal PQ H3B 3P7 Canada

TAYLOR, (MARY) CONSTANCE, comml. fisherman, editor; b. Berkeley, Calif., Jan. 9, 1942; d. Archer and Hasseltine (Byrd) T.; grad. Heald Bus. Coll., Oakland, Calif., 1961; student Napa (Calif.) Jr. Coll., 1962-63. Bookkeeper, Acco-Western Wholesale Hardware, Oakland, 1961-62; with Retail Clks. Union, Anchorage, 1964-65; mem. comml. fishing crews, 1966-69; owner, skipper F/V Thetis, Cordova, Alaska, 1969—; pres. Fathom Pub. Co., 1979—; columnist Cordova Times, 1976—. Mem. Cordova City Council, 1977-80; bd. dirs. Alaska Fisheries Devel. Found., 1978-80; sec. Copper River-Price William Sound Adv. Com., 1978—; bd. dirs. Price William Sound Aquaculture Corp., 1979—, sec.-treas., 1980—. Mem. Cordova Aquatic Mktg. Assn. (dir.), Cordova Dist. Fishermen's Union, United Fishermen Alaska, Cordova C. of C. (dir.). Republican. Baptist. Editor Alaska Fisheries Devel. Found. Newsletter, 1978-80, Price William Sound Aquaculture News, 1979—. Home: Box 969 Cordova AK 99574 Office: Box 821 Cordova AK 99574

TAYLOR, CRAWFORD LOGAN, JR., brokerage co. exec.; b. Anniston, Ala., Feb. 17, 1941; s. C. Logan and Catherine J. Taylor; B.A., Birmingham-So. Coll., 1962; M.A. (Mary Taylor Williams fellow), U. N.C., 1970; m. Marlene Smyth, Aug. 24, 1962; children—C. Logan, Merryl Hope. Program coordinator extension div. U. N.C., Chapel Hill, 1966-68, asst. dir. evening coll., 1968-69; account exec. Merrill Lynch, Pierce, Fenner & Smith, Birmingham, Ala., 1969—, v.p., sr. account exec., 1978—. Recipient Disting. Service award Birmingham-So. Coll. Alumni Assn, 1976. Mem. Ala. Security Dealers Assn. (pres. 1977), Newcomen Soc. N. Am., Alpha Tau Omega. Republican. Baptist. Clubs: Vestavia Country, Young Men's Bus. (pres. 1980), Birmingham, Merrill Lynch Chmn.'s. Home: 336 Vesclub Dr Birmingham AL 35216 Office: 1000 FN-SN Bldg Birmingham AL 35203

TAYLOR, DANIEL WHEELER, securities co. exec.; b. Plainfield, N.J., June 8, 1933; s. George Edward and Ida May (Wheeler) T.; A.B. in Econs., Harvard U., 1955, M.B.A., 1960; m. Judith Reed Garnett, Sept. 10, 1960; children—Mark Philip, Amanda Wheeler, Brooks Garnett. Banker's acceptance trader First Boston Corp., N.Y.C., 1961-64, securities salesman, 1964-68, sales mgr. U.S. govt. securities and fed. agencies, 1969-76, mem. sales mgmt. group, 1976-77, securities salesman, v.p. internat. mktg. group, 1977—. Served with USAF, 1955-58. Recipient award United Way of Tri-State, 1976, 77. Republican. Clubs: Noe Pond, Broad St., Money Market Luncheon, Treasury Securities Luncheon Group. Home: 49 East Ln Madison NJ 07940 Office: First Boston Corp 20 Exchange Pl New York NY 10005

TAYLOR, DAVID, banker; b. Derby, Iowa, July 10, 1928; s. Carl E. and Erma Zoe (McMains) T.; B.S.C., State U. Iowa, 1950; m. Ruth Grody, Aug. 5, 1956; children—Cynthia, John, Jeffrey. Sr. auditor Ernst & Ernst, 1952-59; exec. positions Stephens Industries, Inc., and affiliated cos., 1959-63; pres. 1st Fed. State Bank, Des Moines, 1963-74, Hawkeye Bancorp. Investment Mgmt., Inc., 1974-76, Iowa Trust & Savs. Bank, Centerville, Iowa, 1976—; treas., dir. Iowa Student Loan Liquidity Corp. Former pres. Polk County Easter Seal Soc.; bd. dirs. St. Joseph Mercy Hosp. Served with U.S. Army, 1950-52. C.P.A. Mem. Centerville C. of C. (past pres.), Iowa Bankers Assn., Ind. Bankers Assn. Republican. Methodist. Clubs: Des Moines Golf and Country, Des Moines, Appanoose Country, Elks. Office: PO Box 490 Centerville IA 52544

TAYLOR, DAVID MICHAEL, computer services cons.; b. Winnipeg, Man., Can., Aug. 8, 1953; came to U.S., 1964, naturalized, 1973; s. Albert George and Kathleen Rose (Westman) T.; A.S. in Bus., Southwestern Jr. Coll., 1974; B.S. in Bus. Info. Systems, San Diego State U., 1976; m. Buena Flo West, July 26, 1973; children—Eric David, Tanya Jennifer. Systems analyst San Diego County, Calif., 1973-76; chief bus. computer systems Pacific S.W. Airlines, San Diego, 1976-79; computer services cons., San Diego, 1979—. Mem. Data Processing Mgmt. Assn., U.S. Chess Fedn., Internat. Platform Assn., Baja Calif. and Imperial County Chess Confedn. (pres.). Home and Office: 4228 Seri St San Diego CA 92117

TAYLOR, DENNIS, non-ferrous metal sales co. exec.; b. Croydon, Surrey, Eng., May 3, 1924; s. William Michael and Laura Lilian (Lyon) T.; came to U.S., 1966; grad. Officer Tng. Sch., Belgaum, India, 1944; m. Hazel Frances Conyngham, June 12, 1948; children—Deirdre Elizabeth, Linda Caroline, Susan Penelope, Cynthia Joan. Cocoa trader United Africa Co. Ltd., London, 1950-53, 54-56; attached to Cie Niger Francais, Paris, 1953-54; commodity trader H. Lawton Co. Ltd. Toronto, Ont., Can., 1956-58; mgr. commodity trading Drew Brown Ltd., Toronto, 1958-66; trader C. Tennant Sons & Co., N.Y.C., 1966-71, asst. v.p., 1971-73, v.p., 1973-75; pres., dir. EZ Am. Ltd., Stamford, Conn., 1976—. Active fund raising drives United Fund, ARC, Cancer Soc.; vestryman Christ Holy Trinity Episcopal Ch., Westport, Conn. Served with Brit. Army, 1942-44, to capt. Indian Army 1944-47. Mem. Zinc Inst. (dir.), Soc. Die Casting Engrs. (asso.), Copper Club, Am. Inst. Mining Engrs. (asso.), Am. Mgmt. Assn., Smithsonian Instn. Clubs: Mining (N.Y.C.); Landmark, Midtown (Stamford); Pequot Yacht (Southport). Contbr. articles on lead and zinc to Am. Metal Market. Home: 19 Burr Farms Rd Westport CT 06880 Office: EZ Am Ltd 111 Prospect St Stamford CT 06901

TAYLOR, DONALD, diversified capital goods mfg. co. exec.; b. Worcester, Mass., June 2, 1927; s. John A.B. and Alice M. (Weaver) T.; B.S. in Mech. Engring., Worcester Poly. Inst., 1949; grad. Mgmt. Devel. Program, Northeastern U., 1962, Advanced Mgmt. Program, Harvard U., 1979; m. Ruth L. Partridge, June 2, 1950; children—Linda Taylor Robertson, Donald, Mark, John. Various managerial positions Geo. J. Meyer Mfg. Co., 1951-69; pres. Geo. J. Meyer Mfg. div. A-T-O Inc., 1969; exec. v.p. Nordberg div. Rex Chainbelt, Inc., 1969-73; v.p. ops. Rexnord Inc., 1973-78, pres. Nordberg machinery group, 1973-78, pres., chief operating officer, 1978—; dir. Harnischfeger Corp., Johnson Controls Inc., Marine Corp., Marine Nat. Exchange Bank. Mem. adv. bd. Center for Mgmt. Devel., Northeastern U.; trustee St. Francis Hosp.; bd. dirs., vice chmn. Met. Milw. YMCA; mem. Nat. Council YMCA's; bd. dirs. Milw. Symphony Orch.; div. chmn. Milw. United Way Campaign, 1971, unit chmn., 1972; campaign co-chmn. United Performing Arts Fund, 1976. Served with USNR, 1945-46, 50-54. Registered profl. engr., Mass. Mem. ASME. Clubs: Milw. Country, Milw. Athletic, Town, Univ. (Milw.). Office: Rexnord Inc 3500 First Wisconsin Center 777 E Wisconsin Ave Milwaukee WI 53202

TAYLOR, GEORGE ARTHUR, economist; b. King George, Va., May 6, 1942; s. Raymond Arthur and Dorthey Anne (Hooper) T.; B.A., Ohio State U., 1966, M.A., 1970; Ph.D., George Washington U., 1975; married. Economic adviser Commonwealth of Ky., Frankfort, 1971; economist Am. Iron and Steel Inst., Washington, 1972-75; staff economist Internat. Iron and Steel Inst., Brussels, Belgium, 1976-77; mgr. research and planning Bur. of Nat. Affairs Inc., Washington, 1977—; tchr. economics George Washington U., 1974-75. Republican youth chmn. County of Lucas, Ohio, 1969-70. Served with USAF, 1960-63, 68-69. Mem. So. Economic Assn., Nat. Assn. Bus. Economists, Am. Mktg. Assn. Republican. Episcopalian. Club: Foresters. Home: Lake of the Woods Box 318 Locust Grove VA 22508 Office: 1231 25th St NW Washington DC 20037

TAYLOR, GLENN CURTIS, hosp. supply co. mgr.; b. St. Paul, Nov. 26, 1951; s. James L. and Harriet Janeabelle T.; B.A. in Econs., St. Olaf Coll., 1973; M.B.A., U. Minn., 1974; m. Myretta W. Taylor, Sept. 14, 1973; children—Jeffrey, Jason. Comml. loan officer Midland Nat. Bank, Mpls., 1973-76; with Am. Hosp. Supply Co., 1976—, ops. mgr., Norfolk, Va., 1977, area ops. mgr., Columbia, Md., 1977-80, regional sales mgr., Miami, Fla., 1980—; cons. Drs. Supplies, Inc., 1977-79, Am. Internat. Med., Inc., 1980. Mgr., Columbia Youth Assn., 1978—. Office: 1910 NW 97th Ave Miami FL 33172

TAYLOR, HOMER ESTIL, JR., supply co. exec.; b. Charleston, W.Va., Mar. 3, 1942; s. Homer E. and Martha V. (Black) T.; B.S.E.E., W.Va. Inst. Tech., 1970, B.S. in Bus. Mgmt., 1973; m. Donna M. Thompson, Mar. 7, 1960; children—David, Douglas, Beth. Prodn. and engring. mgr. Charleston newspapers, 1961-73; asst. group prodn. and engring. dir. Scripps-Howard Newspapers, 1973-76; pres., gen. mgr. Scripps-Howard Supply Co., Cin., 1977—. Mem. Am. Newspaper Pubs. Assn., Alpha Chi. Republican. Methodist. Office: 1100 Central Trust Tower Cincinnati OH 45202

TAYLOR, IRVING HENRY, oil co. exec.; b. Detroit, Aug. 18, 1922; s. Irving Henry and Lavinia (Startzman) T.; student Swarthmore Coll., 1940-41; B.A., George Washington U., 1949; M.A., Columbia, 1951; m. Katherine Louise Needham, Feb. 6, 1943; 1 dau., Leslie Ann. Fin. analyst Standard Oil Co. (N.J.), N.Y.C., 1952-55, mgr. Western Hemisphere and internat. finance div., 1966; fin. advisor Internat. Petroleum Co., Ltd., Bogota, Colombia, 1956-57, treas., Lima, Peru, 1957-59, treas., Coral Gables, Fla., 1966—, also dir.; asst. treas. Esso Internat., Inc., N.Y.C., 1959-63, mgr. fgn. sales, 1963-64, asst. gen. sales mgr. 1964-66; treas. Esso Inter-Am., Inc., 1966—; dir. Esso Standard Oil S.A. Ltd. Served with USAAF, 1942-46. Mem. Coral Gables C. of C., Artus, Phi Beta Kappa, Pi Gamma Mu, Phi Sigma Kappa. Presbyterian. Club: Riviera Country. Home: 12751 Old Cutler Rd Coral Gables FL 33156 Office: 396 Alhambra Circle Coral Gables FL 33134

TAYLOR, JACK DONALD, chem. co. exec.; b. Los Angeles, Feb. 4, 1946; s. Wallace Cadet and Jean Ann Taylor; B.A., U. Puget Sound, 1968, M.B.A., 1969; diploma in internat. studies Netherlands Sch. Bus., 1968; B.I.M., Am. Grad. Sch. Internat. Mgmt., Phoenix, 1971; m. Myra Susan Hannaby, July 3, 1976. Internat. mktg. trainee Colgate-Palmolive Internat., N.Y.C., 1971; product mgr. Colgate-Palmolive Ltd., Johannesburg, South Africa, 1971-73; mng. dir. Colgate-Palmolive (East Africa) Ltd., Nairobi, Kenya, 1974-75; mng. dir. Diversey East Africa Ltd., Nairobi, 1975-76; U.K. sales and mktg. dir. Diversey Ltd., Northampton, Eng., 1976-80; v.p. mktg. Diversey Corp., Northbrook, Ill., 1980—. Served as lt. (j.g.) USNR, 1969-70. Mem. Alpha Kappa Psi, Sigma Alpha Epsilon. Republican. Presbyterian. Clubs: Muthaiga Country (Nairobi); Mission Hills Country (Northbrook). Office: 2215 Sanders Rd Northbrook IL 60062

TAYLOR, JAMES ARNOLD, assn. exec.; b. Miami, Fla., Aug. 8, 1949; s. Alvin and Elizabeth Taylor; B.A., N.Y. U., 1971, M.S., 1975; m. Christiana Lelester Manuel, June 21, 1969. Programmer/analyst N.Y. U., 1973-75; sr. programmer Bellvue Hosp., N.Y.C., 1975-76; systems programmer Mocatta Metals, N.Y.C., 1976-78; mgr. info. processing IEEE, N.Y.C., 1978—; data processing cons. Mem. Assn. for Computing Machinery, IEEE. Home: 88 Bleecker St 1G New York NY 10012 Office: 345 E 47th St New York NY 10017

TAYLOR, JAMES BOYD, business exec.; b. Owensboro, Ky., May 30, 1919; s. James Hays and Marie Bruce (Boyd) T.; student pub. schs. N.Y.C., Louisville and Owensboro; m. Anna Frances McCandless, May 24, 1943. With IRS, 1943-47; with Glenmore Distilleries Co., Owensboro, 1933-43, 47—, asst. v.p., 1955-64, v.p., gen. mgr., 1964-78; installation mgr. A.P.C. Skills Co., Palm Beach, Fla., 1978-80; dep. sec. public protection and regulation cabinet Commonwealth of Ky., 1980—; dir. Citizens State Bank, Owensboro. Mem. Adv. Council on Naval Affairs; mem. Louisville dist. adv. com. SBA. Trustee Brescia Coll., 1974-76; chmn. bd. Owensboro Daviess County Hosp., 1968-75, Tri State Health Council, 1972-75; mem. Green River Area Health Council, 1972-75. Chosen by U.S. Pres. to receive Loyalty award VFW, 1972. Mem. Owensboro Daviess County (dir. 1967-69), Ky. chambers commerce, Distilled Spirits Inst. Presbyterian. Clubs: Pendennis (Louisville); Petroleum (Evansville); Campbell (Owensboro). Pioneer bulk gauging distilled spirits. Home: 1515 Dean Ave Owensboro KY 42301

TAYLOR, JAMES WESLEY, JR., tree surgeon; b. Middletown, N.Y., Nov. 21, 1947; s. James W. and Jane F. (Hicks) T.; student Montgomery (N.Y.) Public Schs.; m. Dorothy L. Testa, Dec. 8, 1968; children—James Wesley III, Hans Edward, Tonya Lynn. With J.W. Taylor Tree Surgery, Inc., Walden, N.Y., 1970—, pres., treas., 1979—. Served to staff sgt., arty., U.S. Army, 1967-70. Mem. Nat. Arborist Assn., Internat. Soc. Arboriculture, N.Y. State chpt. Internat. Soc. Arboriculture (treas. Arborist chpt.), N.Y. State Nurserymen's Assn. Republican. Methodist. Research on vegative mgmt. for uitlity rights of way. Home: 240C Plains Rd Walden NY 12586 Office: 240B Plains Rd Walden NY 12586

TAYLOR, JOHN PAUL, publisher; b. Valparaiso, Ind., June 24, 1918; s. Paul Rollin and Edna (Gubransen) T.; B.S. in Mech. Engring., Purdue U., 1939; m. Catherine Dorothea Justin, Oct. 28, 1939 (dec.); children—Jessica, Mrs. James Cahoon; m. 2d, Mary Elizabeth Timm, Feb. 1, 1964; children—Paul Adam, Karen. Asso. editor Maujer Publishing Co., 1939-41; founder, pres. John Paul Taylor Pub. Co., St. Joseph, Mich., 1941—; exec. dir. Indsl. Marketing Assos., Inc., St. Joseph, 1946—, Materials Mktg. Assos., Inc., 1963—, Profl. Mfrs. Agts. Inc., 1969—, Mass Merchandising Distbrs. Assn., Inc., 1972—, Heavy Duty Reps. Assn., Inc., 1979—; co-founder Proebsting-Taylor Inc., 1948-55; pres. Sanitane Co., 1978—; partner Kankakee Mfg. Co., 1977—; v.p., pub. Putman Pub. Co., Chgo., 1956-57. Mem. adv. bd. YWCA, St. Joseph, 1952-56, pres., 1979—; pres. Pub. Library Bd. St.

Joseph, 1965—; mem. Berrien County Hist. Commn.; bd. dirs. Twin Cities Symphony, 1967-79. Served to 2d lt., C.E., AUS, 1944-46. Mem. ASME, Instrument Soc. Am., Acacia, Fort Miami Heritage Soc. Mich. (pres. 1965-67, 78-80), Tau Beta Pi, Pi Tau Sigma, Sigma Delta Chi. Episcopalian. Clubs: Econ. of Southwestern Michigan (exec. v.p. 1952-54, pres. 1955—); Rotary; Berrien Hills Country (Benton Harbor, Mich.). Home: 2618 Lakeview Ave Saint Joseph MI 49085 Office: 520 Pleasant St Saint Joseph MI 49085

TAYLOR, KENT DALLAS, real estate co. exec.; b. Winnipeg, Man., Can., Apr. 17, 1936; s. Cecil H. and Thelma M. T.; B.A. in Bus. Adminstrn. and Polit. Sci., Concordia Coll., Moorhead, Minn., 1960; m. Diane M. Smith, Sept. 23, 1961; children—Susan Daphne, Robert David. Real estate analyst Great West Life Assurance Co., Winnipeg, 1960-68, asst. mgr. investments, Toronto, Ont., Can., 1968-69; asst. retail sales mgr. Midland Doherty Securities, Toronto, 1969-70; v.p. Edgecombe Investment Services Ltd., Toronto, 1970-77, pres., 1978—, also dir.; asst. treas. North Am. Life Assurance Co., Toronto, 1970-72; pres. Edgecombe Properties Ltd., Toronto, 1978—. Mem. Internat. Council Shopping Centers, Ont. Mortgage Brokers Assn. Anglican. Club: Blvd of Toronto, Skyline Health, Mimico Cruising, Caledon Ski. Home: 2 Hartfield Ct Toronto ON M9A 3E3 Canada Office: 196 Adelaide St W Toronto ON M5H 1W7 Canada

TAYLOR, LAURIE ANNE, mfg. co. exec.; b. Lake Forest, Ill., May 23, 1952; d. Lewis T. and Virginia Dean (Steele) T.; B.S. cum laude in Econs. (Univ. scholar 1970-74), U. Pa., 1974, M.B.A., 1975; m. Aug. 31, 1975 (div. 1979). Asst. to internat. v.p. Tower, Perrin, Forester, & Crosby, Phila., 1972-74; asst. account exec. Benton & Bowles, N.Y.C., 1975; asst. product mgr. women's fashions and sports eyewear Warner-Lambert, Boston, 1976-77; mktg. mgr. Marine Optical Inc., Boston, 1978—. Rotary Internat. exchange student to Argentina, 1969; Regional Transp. grantee, Parma, Italy, 1972. Mem. Association Internationale des Etudes Economique et Comercial (pres. 1974-75), Am. Mktg. Assn., AAUW, D.A.R. Episcopalian. Clubs: Wharton Grad. Bus., St. Bartholemew Community, Internat. Council Visitors, Jr. League. Address: 3 Andorra Ln Hingham MA 02043

TAYLOR, MARY JOAN (MRS. EDWARD MCKINLEY TAYLOR, JR.), lawyer; b. Kenton, Ohio, Dec. 24, 1926; d. Maurice A. and Martina (Dolan) McMahon; student St. Mary Springs Coll., 1944-45; Asso. Degree in Bus. Adminstrn., Franklin U., 1946-49; J.D., with high distinction, Ohio No. U., 1951; postgrad. U. Wyo., 1954-56; m. Edward McKinley Taylor, Jr., Apr. 23, 1952; 1 dau., Mary Margaret. Admitted to Ohio bar, 1951; gen. practice law, Kenton, 1951-52, Wichita Falls, Tex., 1953—; mem. firm Taylor and Taylor,, Dayton, Ohio, 1957—; law librarian Franklin U., 1948-49. Mem. Ohio Bar Assn., Montgomery County Law Library Assn., Ohio No. U. Alumni Assn. (sec. Miami Valley 1958-60), Kappa Beta Pi, Iota Tau Lambda. Club: Soroptimist. Office: 7417 N Main St Dayton OH 45415

TAYLOR, MAX TOURNER, surgeon, real estate developer; b. Bloomington, Ind., Oct. 2, 1928; s. Forest Edward and Bernice (Kern) T.; B.A. in Chemistry and Agr., Andrews U., 1950; M.D., Loma Linda U., 1955; children—Nina Denise, Larisa Lynn, Maxwell Brent, Todd Bradley. Intern, Marion County Gen. Hosp., Ind. U., Indpls., 1955-56, resident in surgery, 1956-60; practice medicine specializing in gen. and thoracic surgery, Phoenix, 1962-68; pres. Surg. Clinics of Ariz., Ltd., Phoenix, 1968—, Double Circle Ranch Inc., Eagle Creek, Ariz., 1966—, Scottsdale Investment Partnership (Ariz.), 1968—, Taylor-Sherrow Devel. Co., Phoenix, 1976—; partner Addland Devel. Co., San Diego, 1973—; gen. partner Max Taylor & Co., Phoenix, 1978—. Bd. dirs. Camelhead Devel. Corp., Phoenix; mem. Maricopa County Crime Commn., 1969—; consumer adv. ethics com. Ariz. Automobile Dealers Assn., 1980. Served with M.C., U.S. Army, 1960-62. Diplomate Am. Bd. Surgery; lic. real estate broker, Ariz., mortgage broker, Ariz. Fellow A.C.S., Am. Coll. Chest Physicians, Southwestern Surg. Assn., Pan-Pacific Surg. Soc. Republican. Contbr. articles to surg. jours. Home: 5725 E Camelback Rd Phoenix AZ 85018 Office: 525 N 18th St Suite 8 Phoenix AZ 85006

TAYLOR, RALPH ORIEN, JR., developer, builder, investor; b. Kansas City, Mo., Jan. 6, 1919; s. Ralph Orien and Genevieve (Sturgeon) T.; student U. Kansas City, 1936-38; B.S., U. Mo., 1940; m. Betty Boswell, Dec. 7, 1940 (dec. 1959); children—Bradley, Nancy. Partner, Sturgeon & Taylor, 1940-42; owner Sturgeon & Taylor, Inc., 1942—, chmn. bd., 1959—; pres. Sturgeon & Taylor Investment Co., Inc., 1949—, chmn. bd., 1959—; pres. Sturgeon & Taylor Devel. Co., Inc., 1950—, chmn. bd., 1959—; chmn. bd. Sturgeon-Taylor Realty Co., Inc., 1955—; pres., chmn. bd. Tiger Constrn. Co., Inc., Bengal Homes, Inc., Westbrooke Hotels, Inc., Sturgeon & Taylor Co., Joint Venture; exec. com., dir. Patrons State Bank & Trust, Olathe, Kans. Mem. adv. council U. Mo. Sch. Forestry. Served as lt. comdr. USNR, World War II. Decorated Bronze Star medal. Mem. Home Builders Assn. Greater Kansas City (dir., pres.), Johnson County (Kans.), Kansas City (Mo.) real estate bds., Nat. Assn. Home Builders (life dir.), Phi Delta Theta. Clubs: Indian Hills Country; Lauderdale Yacht, Ft. Lauderdale. Home: 3505 W 71st St Prairie Village KS 66208 Office: 6909 Nall Ave Prairie Village KS 66208

TAYLOR, RICHARD JOHN, broadcasting exec.; b. Pittsfield, Mass., Oct. 12, 1952; s. Charles William and Ernestine Emma Taylor; B.A. magna cum laude in Physics, North Adams (Mass.) State Coll., 1974; M.S. summa cum laude in Ednl. Communications, SUNY, Albany, 1975; m. Cathy Theresa Gaudette, June 30, 1979. Announcer, Sta. WQRB, Pittsfield, 1968-70; news reporter, announcer Sta. WBRK AM/FM, Pittsfield, 1970-72, stas. WBEC and WQRB, Pittsfield, 1972-74; TV coordinator North Adams State Coll. TV Center, 1974-75; program mgr. stas. WBEC and WQRB, 1975-79; account exec. stas. WUPE and WUHN, Pittsfield, 1979-80, sales mgr., 1980—; mgmt. adv. Jr. Achievement Radio Co. Bd. dirs. Berkshire County chpt. March of Dimes; media dir. food drive Salvation Army; dir. radiothon Leukemia Soc. Cert. radio mktg. cons. Radio Advt. Bur. Mem. Am. Fedn. Musicians (past pres.), Alpha Chi. Club: So-Ed Ballroom Dance (past officer). Home 7 Marian Ave Pittsfield MA 01201 Office: 501 East St Pittsfield MA 01201

TAYLOR, RICHARD LAVERN, computer co. exec.; b. Dayton, Ohio, Mar. 8, 1950; s. William Edward and Beatrice (Long) T.; B.S. (Ill. State scholar), No. Ill. U., 1972; M.B.A., U. Cin., 1973; m. Jacqueline Madigan, Aug. 19, 1972; children—Kristen Nicole, John William. Sr. staff coordinator Muscular Dystrophy Assn., Chgo., 1968-71; asst. buyer fashionwear McAlpins Co., Cin., 1972-73; internat. sales engr. Honeywell Inc., Mpls., 1973-75, mktg. rep., Boston, 1975-77; chief product devel. analyst Ford Motor Corp., Dearborn, Mich., 1977-80; sr. cons., dir. industry mktg. Control Data Corp., Mpls., 1980—; dir. Choha, Inc.; cons. Minn. Minority Bus. League; lectr. Hennepin Coll. Asso. adviser explorers council Boy Scouts Am.; mem. Hennepin County (Minn.) CETA Adv. Council, 1980. Danforth fellow U. Cin., 1972-73. Mem. Engring. Soc. Detroit, Soc. Automotive Engrs., Am. Mgmt. Assn., Am. Mktg. Assn., Assn. MBA Execs., Delta Sigma Pi, Phi Beta Lambda. Democrat. Roman Catholic. Club: Ski Bums Inc. Home: 8241 Oregon Rd Bloomington MN 55438 Office: 8100 34th Ave S Minneapolis MN 55440

TAYLOR, RICHARD POWELL, lawyer; b. Phila., Sept. 13, 1928; s. Earl Howard and Helen (Martin) T.; student Cornell U., 1946-48; B.A., U. Va., 1950, J.D., 1952; m. Barbara Jo Anne Harris, Dec. 19, 1959; 1 son, Douglas Howard Martin. Admitted to Va. bar, 1952, D.C. bar, 1956; law clk. Judge Armistead M. Dobie, U.S. Ct. Appeals 4th Circuit, 1952-53; practiced in Washington, 1956—; asso. firm Steptoe and Johnson, 1956-61; partner, 1962—, chmn. transp. dept., 1978—; sec., corp. counsel Slick Corp., 1963-69, asst. sec., 1969-72, dir., 1965-68; sec., corp. counsel Slick Indsl. Co., 1963-72; sec., dir. Slick Indsl. Co. Can. Ltd., 1966-72; sec., gen. counsel, dir. Intercontinental Forwarders, Inc., 1969—; gen. counsel Am. Opera Scholarship Soc., 1973—. Nat. v.p. Reagan for Pres. Com., 1979-80. Served to lt. (j.g.) Air Intelligence, USNR, 1953-56. Mem. Am. (vice chmn. aviation com. 1974, chmn. 1975—), Fed., Fed. Power, D.C., Va. bar assns., Am. Judicature Soc., Order of Coif, Raven Soc., Internat. Platform Assn., Chi Phi, Delta Theta Phi. Republican. Episcopalian (vestryman). Clubs: Internat., Capitol Hill, Congl. Country, Nat. Aviation, Potomac Polo. Home: 8801 Belmart Rd Potomac MD 20854 Office: 1250 Connecticut Ave NW Washington DC 20036

TAYLOR, ROBERT CALVIN, mfg. exec.; b. Rocky Mount, N.C., Oct. 5, 1947; s. Robert Calvin and Frances (Proctor) T.; B.A. in English, N.C. State U., 1969; m. Margaret Alene Cashatt, Apr. 27, 1974. Accountant, Coastal Plain Life Ins. Co., Rocky Mount, 1969, programmer trainee, 1970, programmer, 1971, programmer/analyst, 1972-74, systems analyst, 1974-76; systems analyst N.C. Bapt. Hosp., Winston-Salem, 1976, project mgr., 1977-79, mgr. new systems, 1979-80; project mgr. Best Products Co., Richmond, Va., 1980—; computer cons. Pfeiffer Coll., 1978-79. Dist. sec. N.C. Fedn. Young Republicans, 1978. Mem. Rocky Mount Jaycees (sec. 1971, dir. 1972-73), N.C. Jaycees (editor state mag. 1973). Baptist. Contbr. poetry to mags. Home: PO Box 2102 Ashland VA 23005 Office: PO Box 26303 Richmond VA 23260

TAYLOR, ROBERT ELMER, chem. co. exec.; b. Durango, Colo., Aug. 21, 1935; s. Lloyd B. and Helen Golda (McGee) T.; B.S. in Mktg., Brigham Young U., 1957; m. Dorene Smith, June 20, 1956; children—Shereen, Bryan, David, Dean. Economic analyst, distbn. mgr., mktg. services mgr. El Paso Products Co., 1957-68; dir. diversification No. Natural Gas Co., 1968-69; mktg. mgr. No. Petrochem. Co., Des Plaines, Ill., 1970-73, v.p. petrochems. div., 1974—; dir. Calcasieu Chem. Corp., Lake Charles, La.; tchr. evening sch. U. Tex., El Paso, 1960-64, Odessa (Tex.) Coll., 1965-68. Mem. Nat. Petroleum Refiners Assn. (bd. dirs., petrochem. com.), Am. Inst. Chem. Engrs., S.W. Chem. Assn. Republican. Mormon. Home: 1559 Elm Northbrook IL 60062 Office: 2350 E Devon Ave Des Plaines IL 60018

TAYLOR, ROBERT LEWIS, mgmt. scientist, economist, educator; b. Pitts., Dec. 10, 1939; s. Robert William and Elinor Anna (Miller) T.; A.B., Allegheny Coll., 1961; M.B.A., Ohio State U., 1966; D.B.A., Ind. U., 1972; m. Agnes Tartara, June 5, 1961; children—Robert, Michael. Commd. 2d. lt., USAF, 1961, advanced through grades to lt. col., 1977; prof., head dept. mgmt., also dir. procurement research office USAF Acad. Colo., 1972-76; adj. prof. mgmt. U. No. Colo., 1974-77; vis. instr. mgmt. U. Colo., 1975-79; cons., lectr. in field. Chmn. Colo. Sch. Dist. 20 Sounding Bd., 1975-77; commr. Cub Scout programs USAF Acad., 1974-77; chmn. edn. com. Citizens Goals for Colorado Springs; pres. Pine Valley Parent-Tchr. Orgn., 1975; bd. dirs. Pikes Peak region USO, 1978-79. Recipient Nat. U. Extension Assn. Faculty Service award, 1976; decorated Air Force Meritorious Service medal, Air Force Commendation medal with oak leaf cluster. Mem. Acad. Mgmt., Soc. Logistics Engrs. (prize paper award 1973), Inst. Mgmt. Scis., Air Force Assn., Sigma Xi, Pi Gamma Mu, Sigma Iota Epsilon, Beta Gamma Sigma. Eastern Orthodox. Clubs: Kiwanis (treas. club 1974-77). Contbr. articles to profl. publs. Home: 2001 N Cascade Ave Colorado Springs CO 80907 Office: DFEGM USAF Acad CO 80840

TAYLOR, RUSSEL REID, mfg. co. exec., educator; b. Gananoque, Ont., Can., Sept. 9, 1917; s. Howard William and Clara Helen (Reid) T.; B.Commerce, U. Toronto, 1938; D.B.A., Western Colo. U., 1978; m. Kathleen Tierney, Aug. 30, 1963; children—Deborah Reid Souki, Cynthia Rowan Kane. Came to U.S., 1938, naturalized, 1951. Pres., Annis Furs, Inc., Detroit, 1955-61; chmn. Russel Taylor, Inc. div. Consol. Foods Corp., N.Y.C., 1961-78; dir. Minnetonka Labs., Inc., Chaska, Minn., 1975—; adj. asst. prof. Fairleigh Dickinson U. Sch. Bus., 1971-78; asso. prof. Coll. New Rochelle (N.Y.), 1978—; dir. Am. Liquid Fund, Boston. Chmn. coat and suit industry N.Y. Cancer Fund, 1970—. Bd. dirs. Jr. Achievement, Greenwich, Conn., 1974—. Served to lt. comdr. Royal Canadian Navy, 1943-46. Mem. Am. Arbitration Assn., (panel 1956—), Delta Upsilon. Clubs: Union League (N.Y.C.). Home: 71 Byram Shore Rd Byram CT 10573 Office: 512 7th Ave New York NY 10018

TAYLOR, THOMAS HUDSON, JR., import co. exec.; b. Somerville, Mass., June 8, 1920; s. Thomas Hudson and Virginia Gwendolyn (Wilson) T.; B.S. in Econs., Wharton Sch. Fin. and Commerce, U. Pa., 1947; m. Mary Jane Potter, Dec. 1, 1943; children—Thomas Hudson, III, James R., Jane, John E., Virginia. Acctg. exec. Collins & Aikman Corp., Phila., 1947-55, divisional controller automotive div., Albemarle, N.C., 1956-59, asst. dir. purchases, 1960-64; exec. v.p. Carolina Floral Imports, Inc., Gastonia, N.C., 1965-67, pres., treas., 1968—. County commr. Stanly County, Albemarle, N.C., 1962-66. Served to capt. USAAF, 1941-45. Decorated Air medal. Republican. Methodist. Club: Princeton. Home: 1239 Queensgate St Gastonia NC 28052 Office: Box 2201 Gastonia NC 28052

TAYLOR, WILLIAM JAMES, transp. co. exec.; b. Eddystone, Pa., July 29, 1926; s. William J. and Clara Ella (Harris) T.; A.B., Dickinson Coll., 1949; J.D., U. Pa., 1952; m. Jane Currie, Oct. 18, 1958; children—Deborah Ann, Timothy J., Jeffrey Harris. Admitted to Pa. bar, 1953, N.Y. bar, 1961, also U.S. Supreme Ct.; law clk. to chief justice Supreme Ct. Pa., 1952-53; mem. legal dept. Pa. R.R., 1953-61; mem. law dept. REA Express, 1961-62, gen. counsel, 1962-65, v.p., gen. counsel, 1965-66, exec. v.p., gen. counsel, 1966, pres., chief exec. officer, 1966-68, chmn., 1968-69; v.p. Ill. Central R.R., 1969-74; v.p. govtl. affairs Ill. Central Industries, 1969-74, v.p. legal affairs, 1974-76; pres. Ill. Central Gulf R.R., chief operating officer, 1976-78, chief exec. officer, 1978—, also dir.; legis. counsel to trustees Penn Central R.R., 1971-74. Trustee Dickinson Coll. Served with USNR, 1944-46. Mem. Am. Bar Assn., Assn. ICC Practitioners, C. of C., Newcomen Soc. N.Am., Sigma Chi, Omicron Delta Kappa. Clubs: Congressional Country, Internat. (Washington); Barrington Hills (Ill.). Home: 364 Ridge Rd Barrington Hills IL 60010 Office: 233 N Michigan Ave Chicago IL 60601

TAYLOR, WILLIAM O., newspaper exec.; b. Boston, July 19, 1932; s. William Davis and Mary (Hammond) T.; B.A., Harvard U., 1954; m. Sally Coxe, June 20, 1959; children—William Davis II, Edmund C., Augustus R. With Globe Newspaper Co., Boston, 1956—, treas., 1963—, bus. mgr., 1965-69, gen. mgr., 1969-79, also pres.; pres. Affiliated Publs., Inc., 1980—; dir. Million Market Newspapers, Met. Sunday Newspapers. Pres., Indsl. Sch. Crippled Children, 1973—; bd. overseers Boys' Clubs Boston; bd. dirs., United Way of Mass. Bay, Mass. Soc. Prevention Cruelty to Animals, Bur. Advt.; trustee Boston Zool. Soc., New Eng. Aquarium, Fessenden Sch. Mem. Am. Press Inst. (dir.). Served with AUS, 1954-56. Office: 135 William T Morrissey Blvd Boston MA 02125

TAZELAAR, EDWIN JOSEPH, II, ins. co. exec.; b. Chgo., June 16, 1947; s. Edwin Joseph and Nancy Annette (DeStevens) T.; grad. N.W. Police Acad., 1971; student Harper Coll., 1974-76; children—Bradley James, Marcus Thomas, Edwin Joseph III. Police officer Village of Hoffman Estates (Ill.), 1971-77; asso. Am. Family Life Assurance Co. of Columbus, Ga., 1977, dist. mgr., 1978, regional mgr., Palatine, Ill., 1979—; store mgr. Robert Hall Clothes, Chgo., 1968-71. Served with U.S. Army, 1966-68. Recipient Patrol Achievement award Village of Hoffman Estates, 1973; Fireball award Am. Family Life Assurance Co., 1977, co. awards, 1977, 78, named to President's Club, 1978. Mem. Am. Mgrs. Assn., Am. Family Polit. Action Com. Roman Catholic. Home and Office: 730 N Hicks St Suite 600 Palatine IL 60067

TEAGUE, JOSEPH GRANT, med. equipment mfg. co. exec.; b. Providence, Ky., Sept. 27, 1933; s. Carroll Hoyt and Ruth (Thompson) T.; B.S. in Mech. Engring., U. Ky., 1956, M.S., 1958; postgrad. Case Western Res. U.; m. Suzanne Wallace, June 4, 1955; 1 son, Mark Wallace. Test engr. Pratt & Whitney Aircraft Co., 1956; devel. engr. Sandia Corp., Albuquerque, 1958-63; program mgr. TRW Inc., Los Angeles and Cleve., 1962-68; mgmt. cons. McKinsey & Co., Cleve., 1968-70; pres. Ohio-Nuclear Inc., 1970-78; pres. Technicare Corp., Solon, Ohio, 1978—, chief operating officer, 1980—. Mem. Nat. Elec. Mfrs. Assn. (dir. diagnostic imaging sect., chmn. med. instruments sect.), Phi Delta Theta. Republican. Methodist. Office: Technicare Corp 29100 Aurora Blvd Solon OH 44139

TEAMER, CHARLES CARL, SR., univ. adminstr.; b. Shelby, N.C., May 20, 1933; s. Boyd and Mary (Wilkins) T.; B.A., Clark Coll., 1954; postgrad. U. Omaha, 1962-63, Tulane U., 1965-66; m. Mary Alice Dixon, Aug. 3, 1957; children—Charles Carl, Roderic F., Cheryl R. Acct., S.C. State Coll., Orangebury, 1955-56; asst. bus. mgr. Tenn. State U., Nashville, 1958-62; bus. mgr. Wiley Coll., Marshall, Tex., 1962-65; v.p. fiscal affairs Dillard U., New Orleans, 1965—; dir. New Orleans Public Service Co. Bd. dirs. Common Fund; v.p. United Way, New Orleans; v.p. bd. dirs. New Orleans Area Council; treas. M and T Area Com., Lafon Protestant Home; bd. dirs. Ochner Med. Found., Children's Hosp. Served with U.S. Army, 1956-58. Recipient Silver Beaver award Boy Scouts Am., 1968; named one of 10 Outstanding Citizens of New Orleans, 1979. Mem. Nat. Assn. Coll. and Univ. Bus. Officers (past dir.), So. Assn. Coll. and Univ. Bus. Officers (pres.), C. of C. New Orleans, Alpha Phi Alpha (life mem., nat. comptroller). Methodist. Clubs: Masons, Shriners. Office: Dillard U 2601 Gentilly Blvd New Orleans LA 70122

TEASLEY, JERRY MAC, bank exec.; b. Elberton, Ga., Apr. 5, 1951; s. John Martin and Edna Earl (ALmond) T.; student Young Harris (Ga.) Coll., 1969-71; student C and S Consumer Banking Sch., 1974, C and S Comml. Banking Sch., 1975; cert. Ball State U., 1976; B.B.A., U. Ga., 1976, grad. Ga. Banking Sch., 1979; m. Debra Carol DePalma, June 26, 1971; children—John Victor, Benjamin Jerry. With Granite City Bank, Elberton, 1969—, br. mgr., loan officer, 1974-77, asst. v.p., 1977—. Mem. adminstrv. bd. First United Methodist Ch., Elberton, founder Sunday sch. class; chmn. March of Dimes, Elberton; chmn. drive St. Jude's Childrens Hosp., Elberton; treas. Downtown Revitalization Com., Elberton. Mem. Ga. Bankers Assn., Bank Adminstrn. Inst. Clubs: Optimist, Elks.

TEASLEY, LARKIN, ins. co. exec.; b. Cleve., Sept. 23, 1936; s. Ruth R. Wright; B.A., Fisk U., 1957; student Occidental Coll., 1958-59; exec. program UCLA, 1970-71; m. Violet M. Williams, Nov. 26, 1959; children—Lisa, Erica, Laura. Actuarial trainee Golden State Mut. Life Ins. Co., 1958-59; aerospace engr. Gen. Motors Corp., 1960-62; actuarial asst. G.S.M. Life, 1962-63; actuary N.C. Mut. Life Ins. Co., 1963-69; actuary, v.p. Golden State Mut. Life Ins. Co., Los Angeles, 1970-79, pres., 1980—, also dir.; dir. Broadway Fed. Savs. & Loan. Bd. dirs. United Way, Boy Scouts Am., G.S. Minority Found.; mem. Los Angeles County Economy and Efficiency Commn., Calif. State Tchrs. Retirement Bd. Fellow Soc. Actuaries; mem. Am. Acad. Actuaries, Nat. Assn. Bus. Economists, Phi Beta Kappa, Beta Kappa Phi. Office: 1999 W Adams Blvd Los Angeles CA 90019

TEBET, DAVID WILLIAM, TV exec.; b. Phila., Dec. 27, 1920; s. Joshua and Edith (Dechowits) T.; student Temple U., 1941. Public relations ofcl. legitimate theatre prodns. for John C. Wilson, Theatre Guild, others; pub. relations Max Leibman Prodns., 1950—; gen. program exec. NBC-TV, N.Y.C., 1950—; v.p. talent NBC-TV, 1959-79, sr. v.p. NBC, 1975-79; v.p. talent Marble Arch Prodns., Studio City, Calif., 1979—. Adv. bd. Stevens Coll. Named Man of Yr., Conf. Personal Mgrs. West, 1977. Club: Friars (bd. govs., chmn. spl. events com., exec. chmn. ann. testimonial dinners) (N.Y.C.). Home: Beverly Hills Hotel Beverly Hills CA 90210 Office: Marble Arch Prodns 2024 Radford Ave Studio City CA 91604

TECHMAN, JOHN FREDERICK, indsl. parts co. exec.; b. Watertown, N.Y., July 22, 1947; s. Julius Michael and Ruth Veronica (Morford) T.; B.A. in Econs., Union Coll., 1969; m. Jeryl Ann Leahy, July 8, 1972; children—Jonna Michelle, Lauren Kathleen. Sales rep. Lawson Products, Inc., Fresno, Calif., 1975-76, zone mgr., 1976-80, dist. sales mgr., 1980—; pres. T.A.L.K. Indsl. Services, Las Vegas, Nev., 1978-80. Served to capt. USAF, 1969-74. Decorated Air medal, Viet Nam Service medal, others; recipient Rookie Salesman of Yr. award Lawson Products, 1975, Lawson Milestone award, Lawson Silver Anniversary award, 1977, Lawson Encore award, 1979. Mem. Aircraft Owners and Pilots Assn., Beta Theta Pi. Republican. Club: Masons. Contbr. articles to profl. publs. Home and Office: 6466 E Butler Ave Fresno CA 93727

TECOZ, HENRI FRANCOIS, banker; b. Lausanne, Switzerland, June 23, 1919; s. Henri Emile and Helene (Stussy) T.; M.A. in Econs., Paris Ecole des scis. pol., 1938; M.S. in Psychology, U. Geneva, 1939; Ph.D., U. Paris, 1947; m. Ingeborg Vis, Oct. 1, 1943 (div. 1958); children—Henri Patrick, Muriel France; m. 2d, Joselyne Fressel, Dec. 22, 1962; 1 son, Marc Henri. Vice-pres. Utrecht Jaarbeurs (Netherlands), 1948-52; v.p. A.B.M., Amsterdam, Netherlands, 1952-54; v.p. La Concorde Ins. Co., Paris, France, 1954-64; chmn. Consultants Services Asso., Geneva, 1969—; chmn. bd. Investment Bank Zurich (Switzerland), 1966—; dir. Johnson Wax, Caviezel Ins. Ltd., Diamonds Investors and Mfrs. Inc. Chmn. bd. dirs. Devel. Com. La Cote; chmn. bd. dirs. Interphil, Internat. Standing Conf. on Philanthropy. Home: Le Riau 1164 Buchillon Switzerland also 72 rue Ampere Paris 17 France

TEICH, RALPH DONALD, printing co. exec.; b. Chgo., May 24, 1925; s. Curt and Anna (Neither) T.; grad. Lake Forest Acad., 1943; B.S., Northwestern U., 1949; m. Joan Martha Laurine (div. Sept. 1965); children—Deborah, Lawrence, Cheryl, Fred Teich Anderson; m. 2d, Elizabeth Perrizo, Jan. 20, 1968. Pres., R-Dit Enterprises, Inc. Past fund raising area chmn. A.R.C., Glencoe, Ill., Community Chest, Glenview, Ill., N. Shore Country Day Sch., Winnetka, Ill.; active Art Inst., Lyric Opera; past bd. dirs. Chgo. Ballet, Curt Teich Found.; past bd. dirs., v.p., pres. Mid-Am. Ballet Found. of Ill., past dir. Interstate Bd. Mem. Am. Friends Austria (dir. 1965-72), Chgo. Hist. Soc. (life),

Power Squadron, Field Mus. Natural History (life), Chgo. Art Inst. (life), Lake Forest Property Owners Assn. (v.p.), Balzekas Mus. Lithuanian Art, Lake Forest Hist. Soc., Gleassner House, English Speaking Union. Lutheran (deacon, v.p. 1966-73). Mason (32 deg., Shriner). Clubs: Executives, University, Michigan Shores (Chgo.); Waukegan Yacht, Waukegan Swedish Glee. Home: 700 S Ridge Rd Lake Forest IL 60045 Office: PO Box 169 Lake Forest IL 60045

TEICHBERG, IGNATIUS, brokerage co. exec.; b. Poland, Apr. 15, 1923; came to U.S., 1952, naturalized, 1957; s. Benzion H. and Frieda Teichberg; student Krakow U. (Poland); m. Charlotte Hanft, Mar. 2, 1969; 1 son, Benzion. Film dir. Astoria Film, Berlin, 1949-52; dir., owner r.r. co., Oppenheimer, N.Y., 1962-70; head research D.H. Blair Co., N.Y.C., 1970-74, also v.p.; v.p. instl. dept. Gruntal & Co., N.Y.C., 1975—. Jewish. Office: Gruntal & Co 14 Wall St New York NY 10005

TEICHHOLTZ, NATHAN A., computer co. exec.; b. N.Y.C., Jan. 22, 1945; s. Myran and Edna (Janoff) T.; S.B., M.I.T., 1967; P.M.D., Harvard Bus. Sch., 1976; m. Johnetta Mae Artemis, Feb. 10, 1980; children—Colin Hugh, Holly Ann. Developer time sharing systems for PDP-8 and PDP-11 computers Digital Equipment Corp., Maynard, Mass., 1968-73, asst. to engring. v.p., 1974, sr. product mgr. communications products, 1974-78; mgr. communications programs Prime Computer, Inc., Framingham, Mass., 1978-79, dir. software planning, 1979-81, dir. software devel., 1981—; dir. ESP Computer Resources, Hollis, N.H.; lectr. in field. Mem. curriculum adv. bd. Burdett Sch., Boston, 1981—. Office: 500 Old Connecticut Path Framingham MA 01701

TEITLER, SAMUEL L., lawyer, electronics co. exec.; b. N.Y.C., Apr. 26, 1906; s. Julius and Sarah Teitler; LL.B., St. Lawrence U., 1927; m. Beatrice Ostroleng, Mar. 29, 1931; children—Michael, Robert, Ann T. (Mrs. Ozer). Admitted to N.Y. State bar, 1929; mem. law firm Teitler & Teitler, N.Y.C., 1964—; pres. Lepel Corp., Maspeth, N.Y., 1942-46, chmn. bd., 1946—; vice chmn. bd., dir., gen. counsel World Airways, Inc. Oakland, Calif.; sec., gen. counsel, dir., vice chmn. bd., Worldamerica Investors Corp., Oakland, 1968—, also vice chmn. exec. com. Pres., Kew Gardens Community Council, 1954-57. Mem. Am. Soc. Mfg. Engrs., Am. Soc. for Metals, Soc. Plastics Industry, N.Y. County Lawyers Assn., Am. Bar Assn. Jewish religion (pres. temple 1955-56). Club: Lawyers (N.Y.C.). Home: 82-04 141st St Jamaica NY 11435 Office: Lepel High Frequency Labs Inc 59-21 Queens Midtown Expressway Maspeth NY 11378

TEITSWORTH, ROBERT A., petroleum co. exec.; b. 1930; B.S., Stanford, 1952, M.S. in Petroleum Engring., 1953. Geol. engr. Amerada Petroleum Corp., until 1959; with Occidental Petroleum Corp., 1959—, v.p., mgr. N. Am. oil and gas exploration, 1966-71, exec. v.p., mgr. oil and gas exploration, exploration and prodn. div. fgn. and domestic, 1971—, dir., 1979—; pres. Occidental Exploration and Prodn. Co., 1973-77, chmn., chief exec. officer, 1977—; chmn. bd., chief exec. officer Occidental Oil and Gas Corp., 1975—; chmn. bd. Canadian Occidental Petroleum, Ltd., 1970-78, dir., 1978—. Office: 5000 Stockdale Hwy Bakersfield CA 93309

TEKLENBURG, JOHN ARNOLD, internat. mktg. co. exec.; b. Tilburg, The Netherlands; s. Herman G. and Jo (Smulders) T.; M.B.A., No. Ill. U., 1977; D., Tilburg U., 1978; m. Nora Van Erve, Sept. 15, 1973. Credit/fin. specialist PACCAR Internat., Inc., Bellevue, Wash., 1977-78, sr. credit/fin. specialist, 1978, region fin. mgr., 1978, fin. mgr. Wagner div., 1979-81, dist. mgr. Peru, Wagner div., 1981—. Tilburg U. fellow No. Ill. U., 1975-77. Address: care Sermac Casilla 5141 Ave Diagonal 550 Oficina 601 Miraflores Lima 18 Peru

TELEKI, MARGOT WHITESON, communications co. exec.; b. Cleve., May 24, 1935; d. Milton D. and Ilon (Sarkany) Whiteson; grad. New Eng. Conservatory Music, 1952; student Radcliffe Coll., 1950-51, Harvard Extension U., 1950-51, Hunter Coll., 1951-52. Time buyer J. Walter Thompson Co., N.Y.C., 1958-60; head broadcast buyer Reach McClinton & Co., Inc., N.Y.C., 1960-62, media research mgr., 1962; research dir. Sta. WNEW Radio, N.Y.C., 1963-64; sr. research analyst Young & Rubicam, N.Y.C., 1964-65; media buyer, market planner N.W. Ayer & Son, Inc., Phila., 1965-68; sr. editor Media-Scope Mag., N.Y.C., 1968-70, also columnist, 1969—; pres. Teleki Assos., Ltd., N.Y.C., 1970—. Mem. Internat. Richard Wagner Soc. (v.p., dir. 1977—). Club: Yale (N.Y.C.). Contbr. feature articles to various mags. and publs. Address: 37 E 64th St New York NY 10021

TELLING, EDWARD RIGGS, retail exec.; b. Danville, Ill., Apr. 1, 1919; s. Edward Riggs and Margaret Katherine (Matthews) T.; Ph.B., Ill. Wesleyan U., 1942, LL.D., 1978; m. Nancy Hawkins, Dec. 29, 1942; children—Edward R. III, Pamela Telling Grimes, Kathryn Telling Bentley, Nancy Telling O'Shaughnessy, Thomas Cole. With Sears, Roebuck & Co., 1946—, store mgr., 1954-59, zone mgr., 1960-64, mgr. met. N.Y.C. area ops., 1965-67, adminstrv. asst. to v.p. Eastern ter., Phila., 1968, v.p. Eastern ter., 1969-74, exec. v.p. Midwestern ter., Chgo., 1974-75, sr. exec. v.p. field, Chgo., 1976-77, chmn., chief exec. officer, 1978—, also dir.; dir. Allstate Ins. Co., Homart Devel. Co., Kraft, Inc., Sears Roebuck Acceptance Corp., Sears Internat. Fin. Co., Simpsons-Sears Ltd. Bd. dirs. Sears-Roebuck Found.; trustee Savs. and Profit Sharing Fund of Sears Employees, Field Mus. Natural History; mem. Bus. Council, policy com. Bus. Roundtable. Served to lt. USN, 1941-45. Clubs: Chicago, Shoreacres, Old Elm, Commercial. Office: Sears Roebuck & Co Sears Tower Chicago IL 60684*

TEMERLIN, JULIUS LIENER, advt. exec.; b. Ardmore, Okla., Mar. 27, 1928; s. Pincus and Julie (Kahn) T.; B.A., U. Okla., 1950; m. Karla Samuelsohn, Mar. 23, 1950; children—Dana Michelle, Lisa Babette, Sanford Gottesman. Editor Sponsor Mag., N.Y.C., 1950-51; with Glenn Advt. Inc., Dallas, 1952-74, creative dir., chief operating officer, 1970-74; pres. Glenn, Bozell & Jacobs, Inc., 1974-79, chmn. bd. Bozell & Jacobs Internat., 1979—. Bd. dirs. United Way Met. Dallas; mem. adv. com. St. Paul Hosp., Dallas, U. Tex. at Dallas; trustee Timberlawn Psychiat. Research Found., Jas. K. Wilson Scholarship Fund; bd. dirs. Dallas Community Coll. Dist. Found., Tex. Research League; mem. Dallas Citizens Council; active NCCJ. Served to 1st lt., arty. AUS, 1951-52; Korea. Decorated Bronze Star. Mem. Am. Assn. Advt. Agys. (chmn. S.W. council 1969-70), Dallas Advt. League. Clubs: Dallas, Las Colinas Country, Chaparral, Columbian Country. Jewish. Office: PO Box 61200 Dallas/Fort Worth Airport TX 75261

TEMKIN, ROBERT HARVEY, accountant; b. Boston, Oct. 21, 1943; s. Max and Lillian (Giller) T.; B.B.A., U. Mass., 1964; m. Ellen Phyllis Band, Sept. 25, 1966; children—Aron, Rachel, Joshua. With Arthur Young & Co., C.P.A.'s, 1964-72, 73—, audit prin., 1973-75, partner, 1975—, nat. dir. auditing standards, 1980—; controller SCA Services, Inc., Boston, 1972-73; staff dir. Commn. on Auditors Responsibilities, Am. Inst. C.P.A.'s, 1976-78, mem. task force on auditor's report, 1978—. Chmn. ad hoc com low/moderate housing Town of Natick (Mass.), 1972-73, mem. by-law revision com., 1972-73; mem. young leadership United Jewish Appeal, 1976-80, bd. dirs., asst. treas., vice chmn. fin. com. Jewish Home for Elderly of Fairfield County, 1979—; trustee, treas. Congregation Beth El, Norwalk, Conn.; bd. dirs. Jr. Achievement Stamford Area, 1978-80, spl. adv. nat. conf., 1967. C.P.A., Mass., N.Y., Conn. Mem. Am. Inst. C.P.A.'s, Mass. (Silver medal 1964), N.Y. State, Conn. socs. C.P.A.'s. Jewish. Clubs: Landmark (Stamford); Bd. Rm. (N.Y.C.); Birchwood Country (Westport, Conn.). Home: 246 Georgetown Rd Weston CT 06883 Office: 1011 High Ridge Rd Stamford CT 06905 also 277 Park Ave New York NY

TEMPLE, JOHN EDWARD, med. care corp. exec.; b. Cornwall, N.Y., Jan. 1, 1944; B.S., U. Vt., 1971; m. Lorely Eastman, Jan. 24, 1966; children—Ginnah, Alyssa. Mgr., Charles River Labs., 1971; salesman Cordis Corp., 1971-73, asst. dir. mktg., 1973-75; corp. pres., dir. Vermedco, Inc., Suffield, Conn., 1975—. Corporator, Renbrook Sch., 1979. Served with USMC, 1963-67. Decorated Purple Heart (2). Republican. Office: Suffield Village Suffield CT 06078

TEMPLE, JOSEPH GEORGE, JR., chem. co. exec.; b. Bklyn., Aug. 29, 1929; s. Joseph George and Helen Frances (Beney) T.; B.S. in Chem. Engring., Purdue U., 1951; m. Ann Elizabeth McFerran, June 21, 1952; children—Linda Jo James, John. With research and tech. depts., Dow Chem. Co., 1951-54, successively field salesman plastics mktg., Boston, products sales mgr., Midland, Mich., plastics dist. sales mgr., Camden, N.J., 1954-64, product group sales mgr., Midland, 1964-65, bus. mgr. polyolefins, Midland, 1965-67, sales mgr. plastics dept., Midland, 1967-70, gen. mgr., 1970-73, gen. mgr. Mich. div., 1973-76, v.p. mktg., Midland, 1976-78, pres. Dow Chem. Latin Am., Coral Gables, Fla., 1978—, dir., 1979—; dir. Flagship Banks, Inc. Recipient Silver Knight award; Disting. Engr. Alumni award Purdue U. Mem. Soc. Plastics Industry, Mfg. Chemists Assn., Am. Inst. Chem. Engrs., Mich. Mfrs. Assn., Nat. Mgmt. Assn., Citizens Research Council of Mich., Solar Energy Research Corp. Mich. Episcopalian. Office: 2801 Ponce de Leon Blvd Coral Gables FL 33134

TEMPLE, PAUL NATHANIEL, lawyer, investor; b. Cin., Mar. 19, 1923; s. Paul Nathaniel and Alice Marie (White) T.; A.B., Princeton U., 1944; J.D., Harvard U., 1948; m. Karen Borgstrom Aug. 3, 1944; children—Pamela Temple Abell, Lise Temple Greenberg, Robin Elinor, Thomas D. Admitted to Calif. bar, 1948, D.C. bar, 1950; asso. firm Pillsbury, Madison and Sutro, San Francisco, Washington, 1948-51; atty., exec. Celanese Corp., N.Y.C., 1952-54; internat. concessions negotiator Standard Oil N.J., N.Y.C., 1954-60; pres. Esso Affiliates, Spain, 1961-65; exec. v.p. Gas Natural S.A., Barcelona, 1965-69; pres., co-founder Weeks Natural Resources, Ltd., Westport, Conn., Hamilton, Bermuda, 1970-76; pres., dir. Energy Capital Resources, Inc., Rosslyn, Va., 1977—, Energy Capital Ltd., London; dir. NCC Energy Ltd., London; also investor petroleum exploration. Served to ensign USNR, 1944-45. Recipient Civil Merit decoration, Spain, 1969. Mem. Am. C. of C. (pres. Spain 1969), State Bar Calif., Bar Assn. D.C., Inst. Noetic Scis. (co-founder, dir.). Episcopalian. Clubs: Congl. Country (Potomac, Md.); Mid-Ocean (Bermuda); Puerta de Hierro Golf (Madrid, Spain); Royal Prat Golf (Barcelona, Spain). Asso. producer film Born Again, 1977-78. Home: 2700 Calvert St NW Washington DC 20008 Office: Suite 1300 1300 17 St Rosslyn VA 22209

TEMPLETON, JOHN ALEXANDER, II, coal co. exec.; b. Chgo., Mar. 31, 1927; s. Philip Henry and Florence (Moore) T.; B.S., Ind. U., 1950; m. Norma Frazier, Aug. 10, 1949; children—Lori, Linda, Leslie, Sally. Agt., Conn. Mut. Life Ins. Co., Terre Haute, Ind., 1949-51; partner Miller, Templeton, Scott Ins. Agy., Terre Haute, 1951-64; exec. v.p. Templeton Coal Co., Inc., Terre Haute, 1964-72, pres., 1972—, also dir.; pres. Sherwood Templeton Coal Co., Inc., Indpls., 1968—, also dir.; chmn. bd., dir. Plumb Supply Co., Des Moines, 1965—, dir. Mchts. Nat. Bank of Terre Haute, Calvert & Youngblood Coal Co., Inc. Chmn., Vigo County Goldwater for Pres. Com., 1964; trustee, Union Hosp., 1968-80, v.p., 1975; bd. dirs. Ind. State U. Found., 1970—; trustee U. Evansville, 1974-77; bd. of assos. Rose-Hulman Inst. Tech., 1977; v.p., trustee Ind. Asbury Towers, Greencastle, Ind., 1980. Served with U.S. Army, 1946-48. Mem. Ind. Assn. Ins. Agts. (pres. 1959-60), Ind. Coal Assn. (dir.), Lynch Coal Ops. Reciprocal Assn., Interstate Coal Conf. Republican. Methodist. Clubs: Masons, Elks, Scottish Rite.

TENDICK, DONALD LEE, govt. exec.; b. Springfield, Ill., May 10, 1942; s. Eugene Kenneth and Mildred Dorothy (Hahn) T.; B.S. in Agrl. Industries, U. Ill., 1964; M.B.A., U. Chgo., 1972; m. Corrine J. Kagol, Apr. 30, 1966; 1 dau., Eileen Kay. With Dept. Agr., 1964-75, dep. dir. Chgo. Office Commodity Exchange Authority, 1970-75; exec. dir. Commodity Futures Trading Commn., Washington, 1975—. Recipient cert. of merit and award Dept. Agr., 1966, 69. Mem. Am. Bar Assn. (asso.). Lutheran. Office: 2033 K St NW Washington DC 20581

TENDICK, DONALD WILLIAM, oil lamp mfg. co. exec.; b. Milw., Aug. 15, 1927; s. Harry Arthur and Mildred Dillman (Gretsinger) T.; student Emory and Henry Coll., 1945, U. Wis., 1946; m. Rosemary Mastopietro, Nov. 27, 1948; children—Donald William, John Michael. With North Shore Buick, Milw., 1949-54; with Tenoco Oil Co., Milw., 1954-60; retail mktg. dir. Murphy Oil Co., Evanston, Ill., 1960-61; founder, pres. Lamplight Farms, Inc., Brookfield, Wis., 1964—; chmn. Lamplight Farms, Ltd., Llantrisant, Wales. Served with USNR, 1945-46. Founder, 1st tournament dir. Vince Lombardi Meml. Golf Classis, 1971. Episcopalian. Clubs: Rotary (Brookfield); North Hills Country, Bluemound Golf and Country, Masons. Office: Lamplight Farms Inc 21125 W Enterprise Ave Brookfield WI 53005

TENHULZEN, KENNETH DEAN, ins. co. exec.; b. Lincoln, Nebr., Mar. 7, 1941; s. Richard Earl and Florence (TeSelle) TenHulzen; B.S., U. Nebr., 1963; m. Elizabeth Ellen Cherry, Jan. 27, 1962; children—Michael, Jean, Richard. Agt., Security Mut. Life, Nebr., 1962-71; dir. ins. Lincoln Liberty Life, Lincoln, 1971-77; pres. First Nat. Life of the U.S.A., Lincoln, 1977—, also dir. Pres., Nat. Assn. Parents of the Deaf, 1975-79; mem. Lincoln Supts. Adv. Council on Spl. Edn., 1978—. Mem. Nat. Assn. Life Underwriters, Am. Mgmt. Assn., Nebr. Life Underwriters, Am. Mktg. Assn. Presbyterian. Clubs: Lincoln Optimists, Elks. Office: 3600 S 48th St Lincoln NE 68506

TENNANT, HARRY LARENZE, editor; b. Seymour, Iowa, Aug. 17, 1909; s. Frank E. and Myrtle (Tennant) Rouse; B.A., State U. Iowa, 1933; postgrad. U. Calif. at Berkeley, 1936; m. Margaret Alice Free, Feb. 14, 1942. Reporter, S.W. Newspress, Los Angeles, 1934; pub. relations Shuberts Theatrical Co., Los Angeles, San Francisco, 1935-38; writer U.P.I., Omaha, Lincoln, Nebr., Phila., 1940; city editor Ames (Iowa) Daily Tribune, 1941; corr. Chgo.-N.Y. Jours. of Commerce, Washington, 1945-50, Vision Mag., 1961-65; editor Watson Publs., Washington, 1952-65; U.S. editorial dir. Interavia Pubs., Geneva, 1955-69; editor Cahners Publs., Washington, 1965-80, editor Biomed. News, 1971-74, mng. editor Emergency Dept. News, also Oncology Times, 1978-80. Recipient Pioneer Space Writers' award, 1968, Jesse H. Neal Editorial Achievement award, 1975, 76, 77; 1st prize Nat. Composition Assn. award typog. excellence, 1972. Served with AUS, 1942-45. Mem. Nat. Press Club, Nat. Space Club, White House, State Dept. corrs. assns., Aviation and Space Writers Assn., Nat. Space Writers Assn., Aero Club. Contbr. articles to profl. jours. Home: PO Box 499 Mendocino CA 95460

TERASKIEWICZ, EDWARD ARNOLD, internat. money broker; b. Bklyn., June 9, 1946; d. Edward A. and Anna A. (Romeo) T.; cert. Am. Inst. Banking, 1970; m. Geraldine Lucchesi, May 7, 1966; children—Marie Elena, Lisa. Money desk trader Citibank, N.Y.C., 1964-71; gen. partner Mabon Nugent & Co., N.Y.C., 1971—. Served with U.S. Army, 1965-68. Home: 114 Tillman St Staten Island NY 10314 Office: 115 Broadway New York NY 10006

TERKHORN, ROBERT EUGENE, banking exec.; b. Brownstown, Ind., Aug. 1, 1936; s. Robert Frederick and Gladys Marie (Fountain) T.; B.A., Wesleyan U., Conn., 1958; J.D., U. Mich., 1962; M.A., Sch. Advanced Internat. Studies, Johns Hopkins U., 1964; m. Kay West, June 3, 1961; children—Susan Catherine, Robert Charles. Mgr., Citbank, N.A., Beirut, Lebanon, Riyadh, Saudi Arabia and Manama, Bahrain, 1967-71; asst. gen. mgr. Banque Internationale pour l'Afrique Occidental, Paris, 1971-74; v.p. Citbank N.A., N.Y.C., 1974-79; pres., chmn. Citicorp Homeowners, Inc., St. Louis, 1979—, also dir.; dir. 1st Mortgage Corp., St. Louis. Mem. fin. bd. Am. Ch. of Paris, 1972-74; mem. devel. bd. St. Louis Children's Hosp.; class agt. Wesleyan U., 1979-80. Lutheran. Clubs: Sprite Island Yacht (Westport, Conn.); St. Louis (Clayton, Mo.). Office: 1000 Des Peres Rd Des Peres MO 63131

TERNER, EMANUEL M., container mfr.; b. N.Y.C., May 2, 1909; s. Louis and Ida (Katz) T.; student N.Y. U. Sch. Commerce, 1930; H.H.D. (hon.), L.I. U.; m. Mathilda Weisenfeld, June 14, 1931; children—Nancy, Elaine, Carol. Various positions glass container industry, 1929—; with Metro Glass Bottle Co., 1935-66, sec.-treas., 1935-49, pres., 1949-66, now Metro Glass div. Nat. Diary Products Corp.; founder Midland Glass Co., 1968, pres., chmn., chief exec. officer, dir.; dir. Nat. Dairy Products Corp., 1955-66. Trustee Village of South Orange, 1958, Rutgers U., 1979-84; mem. dean's adv. council N.Y. U.; mem. pres.'s council Coll. of Holy Cross, Marquette U. Recipient Madden Meml. award N.Y. U., 1979. Mem. U.S. Brewers Assn. (former trustee), Beta Gamma Sigma (hon.). Club: Tower of Cornell U. Office: Midland Glass Co 277 Park Ave New York NY 10017 also Cliffwood Ave Cliffwood NJ 07721*

TERPANJIAN, SETRAK, indsl. engr.; b. Lice, Diyarbakir, Turkey, Aug. 15, 1946; came to U.S., 1965, naturalized, 1975; s. Nishan and Hayganush (Kalayciyan) T.; B.S. in Indsl. Engring., Fairleigh Dickinson U., 1971. With Revlon Inc., Editon, N.J., 1973—, divisional prodn. supt., 1976-78, mgr. indsl. engring., 1978-80, mgr. indsl. engring. Revlon Internat. Corp., 1980—. Mem. Am. Inst. Indsl. Engrs. (sr.). Club: Knights of Vartan. Home: 24 Poplar Ave North Bruswick NJ 08902 Office: Revlon Internat Corp 767 Fifth Ave New York NY 10022

TERRA, DANIEL JAMES, chem. co. exec.; b. Phila., June 8, 1911; s. Louis J. and Mary (DeLuca) T.; B.S., Penn State U., 1931; m. Adeline Evans Richards, Aug. 7, 1937; children—Penny Jane (dec.), James D. Founder, Lawter Chems., Inc., Chgo., 1940, chmn., chief exec. officer, 1964—, also dir.; dir. McLouth Steel Corp., 1st Nat. Bank & Trust Co., Evanston, Ill., Stewart-Warner Corp., Chgo. Bd. dirs. Chgo. Crime Commn.; past pres. United Republican Fund of Ill.; bd. dirs. Evanston (Ill.) Hosp. Assn., Easter Seal Soc. Met. Chgo., Lyric Opera Chgo.; nat. fin. chmn. Reagan for Pres. Com.; trustee Chgo. Symphony Assn., Dickinson Coll., Roycemore Sch., Evanston, Ravinia Festival Assn.; trustee Ill. Inst. Tech., mem. exec. com. Research Inst.; mem. Chgo. Community Trust; bd. govs. United Republican Fund; mem. com. earlier paintings Art Inst. Chgo., also com. Am. arts; mem. assos. Northwestern U., mem. adv. council Grad. Sch. Mgmt.; mem. Am. Indian Center Chgo.; mem. citizens bd. U. Chgo.; mem. council Pa. State U.; mem. pres.'s council Nat. Coll. Edn.; mem. pres.'s club Loyola U., Chgo.; founder, pres. Terra Mus. Am. Art; ambassador-at-large for cultural affairs U.S. Dept. State. Recipient Winthrop-Sears medal Chem. Industry Assn., 1972; Distinguished Alumnus medal Pa. State U., 1976. Mem. Ill. Mfrs. Assn. (dir.). Clubs: Lauderdale Yacht (Ft. Lauderdale, Fla.); Kenilworth (Ill.); Chicago, Casino, Mid-Am., Commercial, Metropolitan (Chgo.); Westmoreland Country; Capitol Hill (Washington); Links, National Arts (N.Y.C.). Home: 528 Roslyn Rd Kenilworth IL 60043 Office: 990 Skokie Blvd Northbrook IL 60062

TERRELL, CHARLES JOSEPH, aluminum casting foundry exec.; b. Tipton, Ind., Jan. 14, 1908; s. Benjiman Joseph and Hazel (Ogle) T.; student Ball State U., 1926-27; m. Harriet Elizabeth Johnson, Dec. 24, 1928; children—Joanne (Mrs. John Lyons), Joyce (Mrs. Chester Timmons), Jane (Mrs. John Thompson). Lab. technician Gen. Motors Corp., Anderson, Ind., 1941-43; supt. Apex Elec. Mfg. Foundry, Cleve., 1943-45; asst. supt. Nat. Bronze & Aluminum Foundry, Cleve., 1945-46; owner Washington Aluminum Castings Co., Washington Court House, Ohio, 1946—, pres., 1955—. Mem. nat. adv. bd. Am. Security Council, 1971—; mem. Liberty Lobby Bd. Policy, 1972—. Mem. Bass Fisherman Sportsman Soc., Fishing Club Am., Nat. Travel Club. Republican. Baptist. Patentee flower urn. Home: 740 Van Deman St Washington Court House OH 43160 Office: 1011 Mead St Washington Court House OH 43160

TERRELL, W(INSTON) BRUCE, real estate exec.; b. Pasadena, Calif., May 4, 1927; s. Wilfrid Hall and Helen Terry (Brockett) T.; student U. So. Calif., 1946-49; cert. in real estate UCLA, 1955; m. Miriam L. Chapman, Aug. 31, 1946; children—W. Bruce, Trudy Terrell McCabe, Scott Edmund (dec.), Michael Stuart. Vice pres. McLellan Investment Co., Inc., Pasadena, 1955-66, pres., 1966-68; v.p., mgr. real estate devel. Bank of Calif., Los Angeles, 1968-72; sr. v.p., chief operating officer BanCal Mortgage Co., Los Angeles, 1972-76; dir. real estate Fluor Corp., Irvine, Calif., 1977—. Chmn. bd. South Pasadena-San Marino YMCA, 1966-67; pres. San Marino Young Republican Club, 1952. Served with USNR, 1945-46. Mem. Soc. Real Estate Appraisers (certified sr. residential appraiser), Real Estate Certificate Inst., Am. Arbitration Assn. (panel mem.), Nat., Calif. real estate assns., Nat., Calif. mortgage bankers assns. Republican. Episcopalian. Inventor Pickett real estate slide rule, 1957. Home: 27056 Mill Pond W Capistrano Beach CA 92624 Office: 3333 Michelson Dr Irvine CA 92730

TERRY, DIAN LEE, public relations exec.; b. Dallas, July 9, 1946; d. Jack Bryan and Mary Lee (Edwards) T.; A.A., Lon Morris Coll., 1966; B.F.A., U. Tex., 1969. Sr. asso. Lobsenz-Stevens, Inc., N.Y.C., 1970-73; public info. dir. NOW, 1973-74; press sec. N.Y. State ERA Campaign, N.Y.C., 1975; account exec. Rubenstein, Wolfson & Co., N.Y.C., 1976-78; nat. dir. public relations Main Hurdman & Cranston, N.Y.C., 1978—; guest lectr. women's groups, 1978—. Mem. Public Relations Soc. Am., NOW (v.p. N.Y. chpt. 1975-76, exec. v.p. 1977), Am. Enterprise Inst. Contbr. articles to profl. jours.; contbr. World Book Ency., 1976. Office: 140 Broadway New York NY 10005

TERRY, JOSEPH A., banker; b. Bismarck, Ark., Feb. 24, 1936; s. William A. and Virgie Mae (Stinnett) T.; student Henderson State U., 1959-63; m. Frankie Lou Whitley, Nov. 9, 1955; children—Rocky Joe, Mark Stephen, Philip Kyle. Bank examiner Comptroller of Currency, 1963-67; bank examiner State of Ark., 1967-69, asst. bank commr., 1969-72; v.p. Ark. Bank & Trust Co., Hot Springs, 1972-77; pres. 1st Nat. Bank, Paris, Ark., 1977-79; exec. v.p. Citizens Bank & Trust Co., Van Buren, Ark., 1979—. Bd. dirs. Garland County Mental

Health Assn. Served with U.S. Army, 1955-57. Mem. Paris (Ark.) C. of C. (pres. 1978). Baptist. Club: Elks. Office: 3110 Alma Hwy Van Buren AR 72956

TERRY, RONALD, holding co. exec.; b. Memphis, Dec. 5, 1930; B.S., Memphis State U., 1952; postgrad. in Banking, So. Meth. U., 1961; grad. Advanced Mgmt. Program, Harvard Bus. Sch., 1970; m. Beth Howard; children—Natalie Carol, Cynthia Leigh. With First Tenn. Bank N.A., Memphis, from 1957, chmn., chief exec. officer, 1979—; pres. First Tenn. Nat. Corp., 1971, chmn., chief exec. officer, 1973—; dir. Holiday Inns Inc. Chmn., Memphis Jobs Conf., 1980—; bd. dirs., chmn. legis. com. Future Memphis; bd. dirs., past pres. Boys' Clubs Memphis, Arts Appreciation Found.; trustee Memphis State U. Found. Served to lt. USN, 1953-57. Mem. Am. Bankers Assn. (past chmn. govt. relations council, govt. borrowing com.), Assn. Res. City Bankers (dir.; past chmn. govt. relations com.), Assn. Bank Holding Cos. (legis. policy com.). Club: Econ. Memphis (past pres.). Office: 165 Madison Ave Memphis TN 38101

TERWOORD, JAMES ANTHONY, fin. exec.; b. Berea, Ohio, Mar. 6, 1947; s. Anthony Francis and Adeline Blanche (Yanke) T.; B.B.A., Ohio U., 1969; M.B.A., Youngstown State U., 1978; m. Cher Waldeck, June 1, 1974. Acct., Arthur Andersen & Co., Cleve., 1973-75; controller Youngstown Coca-Cola Bottling Co. (Ohio), 1975-79; v.p. fin. Agy. Rent-A-Car, Cleve., 1979—; instr. Youngstown State U., 1978-79. Group chmn. United Appeal of Youngstown, 1977-78. Served with USMC, 1970-73. Mem. Am. Inst. C.P.A.'s, Ohio Soc. C.P.A.'s, Nat. Assn. Accts., Am. Mgmt. Assn. Home: 5557 Landover Ct Parma OH 44134 Office: 466 Northfield Rd Bedford OH 44146

TERZIC, VELIMIR, welding apparatus co. exec.; b. Yugoslavia, Aug. 27, 1912; s. Miloje and Radosava (Vasovic) T.; came to U.S., 1951, naturalized, 1956; B.A. in Accounting, Walton Sch. Commerce, 1961; m. Katarina Mokran, Aug. 10, 1957; 1 son, Brant. Riveter, J.T. Ryerson & Son, Inc., Chgo., 1951-54; accountant Wells Orgns., Inc., Chgo., 1954-60; with Welding Apparatus Co., Chgo., 1961—, pres., 1978—. Mem. Ill. Mfrs. Assn., Nat. Small Bus. Assn. Office: 1668 N Ada St Chicago IL 60622

TESSIER, GASTON ANTHONY, bus. and venture devel., investment and real estate exec.; b. Swanton, Vt., Nov. 30, 1922; s. Joseph A. and Marguerite (Trahan) T.; B.S., St. Michael's Coll., 1943; postgrad. Stevens Inst. Tech., 1943-44; m. Gloria J. McIver, Aug. 12, 1943; children—Michael John, Gaston Anthony, Mary Therese, Jacquelyn Renee. Plant mgr. Maxwell House div. Gen. Foods Corp., San Leandro, Calif., 1953-55, prodn. mgr., Hoboken, N.J., 1955-57, ops. mgr. Birds Eye div., White Plains, N.Y., 1957-60; gen. mgr. subsidiary Calif. Vegetable Concentrates, Inc., Modesto, 1962-65; asst. to pres. Basic Vegetable Products, Inc., San Francisco, 1965, v.p. corporate devel., 1966-67, v.p. mktg. and corporate devel., 1967-70; chmn. bd., chief exec. officer, treas. Healthco, Inc., Boston, 1971-72, Healthcare Nursing Centers, Inc., 1971-72; exec. dir., chief exec. officer Univ. Health Center Inc., Burlington, Vt., 1972-75; pres., chief exec. officer Ventess, Inc., 1973—; partner P.A.R. Assos., 1971—; asso. prof. health care mgmt. U. Vt., 1972-75. Co-founder Jr. Achievement, San Leandro, 1963. Bd. dirs. Nat. Safety Council, East Bay chpt., Oakland; past pres. and dir. Greater Burlington Indsl. Corp.; asso. trustee St. Michael's Coll.; bd. visitors Grad. Sch. Bus., Boston U.; bd. dirs., past pres. Burlington Ecumenical Action Ministry. Mem. Inst. Food Technologists, San Leandro C. of C. (past dir.), Am. Inst. Chem. Engrs. Club: Ethan Allen. Address: 116 S Cove Rd Burlington VT 05401

TESSLER, J. LEONARD, jewelry distbn. co. exec.; b. Phila., Jan. 13, 1923; s. Harry and Bessie (Rubenstein) T.; student pub. schs., Phila.; m. Mildred Price, Mar. 1, 1942; children—A. Robert, Dennis J., Cindy Ruda. Salesman, Albert E. Price Inc., Phila., 1939-43; founder, owner, operator, pres. J. Leonard Tessler Inc., Phila., 1946—; founder, owner, operator Dennis Time Co., Phila., 1972—, chmn. bd., 1976—. Pres. Temple Adath Israel, Merion, Pa., 1969-71; chmn. jeweler div. United Jewish Appeal, Phila., 1975-77; v.p. Solomon Schecter Day Sch., Phila., 1973—; bd. govs. Jewish Theol. Sem. Served with USAAF, 1943-46. Recipient Humanitarian award Chapel Four Chaplains, 1972, City of Jerusalem award State of Israel, 1971. Mem. Nat. Wholesale Jewelers Assn. (dir.). Clubs: Locust, Masons, B'nai B'rith. Home: 1830 Rittenhouse Sq Philadelphia PA 19103 Office: 722 Chestnut St Philadelphia PA 19106

TEU, SANFJORD BROGDYNE, III, banker; b. Washington, Oct. 28, 1943; s. Sanfjord Brogdyne and Margaret Faye (O'Brien) T.; B.A., U. Va., 1966; M.B.A., Coll. William and Mary, 1967; m. Barbara White Myers, Aug. 27, 1966 (div. 1976); children—Michael D., Karen E.; m. 2d, Mary Nevina Shepherd, Mar. 10, 1978. Instr. econs. Va. Commonwealth U., 1967-68; portfolio mgr. Wachovia Bank & Trust Co., Winston-Salem, N.C., 1970-72; portfolio mgr. Fidelity Nat. Bank, Lynchburg, Va., 1972-74, investment div. exec., 1974-79; sr. v.p. Park Nat. Bank, Knoxville, Tenn., 1979—. Served with AUS, 1968-70. Home: 519 Mellen Rd Knoxville TN 37919 Office: 505 S Gay St Knoxville TN 37901

THAGARD, WARREN THOMAS, III, pipeline co. exec.; b. Greenville, Ala., Aug. 7, 1912; s. Warren Thomas and Berta (Canady) T.; B.S., Rice U., 1934; m. Alice W. Epke, May 26, 1956; 1 dau. by previous marriage, Rebecca Thagard Hughes. Indsl. gas sales engr. Atlanta Gas Light Co., 1935-38, mgr. Newnan (Ga.) div., 1938-41; v.p. N.C. Gas Corp., 1946; rate cons. Ebasco Services, Inc., N.Y.C., 1946-47; adminstrv. engr. Tex. Eastern Transmission Corp., Shreveport, La. and Houston, 1947-55, dir. plans and econ. research, 1955-58, mgr. coordinating and planning dept., 1958-60, v.p., 1960-71, sr. v.p., 1971-74, exec. v.p., 1974-75, vice chmn. bd. dirs., 1975-78, also dir. Served to lt. col. AUS, World War II; ETO. Decorated Medaille de La Reconnaissance (France). Registered profl. engr., Ga. Mem. Am., Ind. natural gas assns. Republican. Episcopalian. Clubs: Lakeside Country, Ramada. Home: 2014 Stonewalk Dr Houston TX 77056 Office: PO Box 2521 Houston TX 77001

THAL, LAWRENCE STAMER, optometrist; b. Oakland, Calif., Jan. 28, 1946; s. Bernhardt N. and Betty S. Thal; B.S., U.S. Air Force Acad., 1967; B.S., U. Calif., Berkeley, 1973, 74, O.D., 1975; M.B.A., Golden Gate U., San Francisco, 1978; m. Esther Gordon, Dec. 22, 1968. Commd. 2d lt. USAF, 1967, advanced through grades to maj., 1971; Vietnam; resigned, 1971; pvt. practice optometry, Kensington, Calif., 1975—; clin. instr. neuro-optometry U. Calif. Sch. Optometry, 1978-79, clin. instr. gen. clinic, 1979—; lectr. Grad. Sch. Banking and Fin., Golden Gate U., 1978—; pres. Farallon Devel. Corp., 1980—. Bd. dirs. Kensington Community Service and Police Dists., pres., 1981; bd. dirs. Kensington Improvement Club. Decorated Meritorious Service medal, Air Medal with oak leaf cluster, Commendation medal with 2 oak leaf clusters; Vietnam Cross of Gallantry with palm. Mem. Am. Optometric Assn., Council Sports Vision, Vision Conservation Inst., Calif. Optometric Assn., Alameda-Contra Costa Counties Optometric Soc. (dir. public health), Kensington Bus. and Profl. Assn. (pres. 1979-81), Beta Sigma Kappa. Republican. Club: Lions. Home: 216 Amherst Ave Kensington CA 94708 Office: 291 Arlington Ave Kensington CA 94707

THALER, GEORGE WINSHIP, oil co. exec.; b. McHenry, N.D., Aug. 26, 1919; s. George and Ruby Ann (Starke) Schretenthaler; B.S., U. Eau Claire (Wis.) 1942; postgrad. U. Minn. Sch. Bus., 1946; m. Ferne Elain Larsen, Aug. 4, 1943; children—George, Pamela, Steven, John. Pres., Outdoor Movie Enterprises, Chippewa Falls, Wis., 1947-61, Thaler Oil Co., Chippewa Falls, Wis., 1955—; Wis. dir. Nat. Oil Jobber Council, 1975-78. Mem. Chippewa Falls Planning Commn., 1974—. Served to lt., naval aviator USNR, 1942-45. Mem. Wis. Petroleum Assn. (state pres. 1972), Am. Legion, VFW. Republican. Roman Catholic. Clubs: Elks, Moose, K.C. Home: 1401 Loffler Ct Chippewa Falls WI 54729 Office: 310 S Main St Chippewa Falls WI 54729

THAMM, TOM BROBECK, engring. co. exec.; b. Bradford, Pa., July 26, 1929; s. John Kenneth and Edna Elizabeth (Brobeck) T.; B.S., U.S. Naval Acad., 1952; M.S., Rensselaer Poly. Inst., 1969; m. Sally Ann Snyder, June 11, 1952; children—Mark, Marijke, Michael, Marta, Kenneth, Katherine. Commd. ensign U.S. Navy, 1952, advanced through grades to capt., 1971; dir. field activities mgmt. Naval Sea Systems Command, 1971-72; dep. supr. shipbldg., Newport News, Va., 1973-75; ret., 1975; dir. cost engring. Burns & Roe, Inc., Oradell, N.J., 1975—. Mem. Am. Soc. Naval Engrs. (1st chmn.), Am. Assn. Cost Engrs. (dir.), Am. Inst. Indsl. Engrs., U.S. Naval Inst., Am. Mgmt. Assn., U.S. Naval Acad. Alumni. Assn. Republican. Episcopalian. Contbr. articles to profl. jours; officer, U.S.S. Triton, during first submerged circumnavigation of globe, 1960. Office: 800 Kinderkamack Rd Oradell NJ 07649

THARP, MICHAEL FRANKLIN, food service co. exec.; b. Dallas, Jan. 23, 1939; s. Marcus F. and Dorothy L. Tharp; student in engring. So. Meth. U., 1957-60; B.S. in Psychology, North Tex. State U., 1966; M.B.A., Mercer U., 1975; m. Anita Louise Richards, Sept. 26, 1970; children—Kenneth O., Meredith Lee, Michael F., Monica Aran. Personnel dir. Redman Industries Inc., Dallas, 1971-73; v.p. Blue Cross-Blus Shield, Atlanta, 1973-76; owner, mgr. Tharp & Assos., Atlanta, Dallas, 1976-77; group v.p. Pizza Inn, Inc., Dallas, 1977—; panelist Multi Unit Food Service Operators. Coach boys baseball, Atlanta, 1973-76; active PTA, 1978-79. Served with USAF, 1961-67. Mem. Am. Soc. Personnel Adminstrs., Nat. Restaurant Assn., Am. Mgmt. Assn., Food Service Industry Consortium on Labor Relations. Home: 1413 Flintwood Richardson TX 75081 Office: 2930 Stemmons Freeway Dallas TX 75247

THATCHER, MILTON WINTHROP, paint and wallcovering co. exec.; b. Balt., Mar. 6, 1931; s. Edward and Lillian Elizabeth (Bruce) T.; B.S., U. Balt., 1952; Th.B., Midwestern U., 1956, Th.D., 1958; m. Diane Elizabeth Clouser, July 28, 1975; children—Steven Glenn, Richard Milton, Mark Douglas, Paul Stewart. Ordained minister So. Baptist Conv., 1958, home missionary Canton Mission, Balt., 1958, pastor Gunpowder Baptist Ch., Freeland, Md., 1958-60; dist. sales mgr. Sapolin Paints Inc., Miami, 1961-68, nat. sales mgr., 1968-70, v.p., 1970-74, group v.p., 1974; pres. subs. Kimberly Chems. Inc., 1974-77; v.p. sales, mem. exec. com. Con/Chem Inc., Los Angeles, 1977-79; v.p. wallcovering div. Frazee Industries, San Diego, 1979—. Mem. Am. Mgmt. Assn., Christian Bus. Men's Assn. Republican. Baptist. Club: Masons. Home: 7411 Carlina St Carlsbad CA 92008

THAU, HAROLD ADRIAN, fin. cons.; b. N.Y.C., Sept. 4, 1934; s. Morris and Shirley (Fisbein) T.; B.B.A., CCNY, 1956; M.S., Columbia U., 1958; m. Dorothy Golden, Aug. 4; children—Michael, Amy. Partner, Rosenblum, Rubin, Burn & Thau, C.P.A.'s, N.Y.C., 1962-72; pres. Spectrum Mgmt. Corp. (name formerly Royalty Controls Corp.), N.Y.C. and Stamford, Conn., 1972—, also dir.; sec., dir. John Denver Concerts, Inc., 1973—; sec., treas. Royal Gen. Corp., 1974—; chief fin. officer, dir. Windstar Found., Aspen, Colo., 1976—; sec. John Denver Enterprises, Inc., N.Y.C., 1976—; partner Windstar Prodns., Aspen, 1976—; pres. Windsong Records, Inc., N.Y.C., 1976-80. C.P.A., N.Y. Home: 19 Saugatuck River Rd Weston CT 06883 Office: 1234 Summer St Suite 500 Stamford CT 06905 also 211 E 51 St Suite 8E New York NY 10022

THAYER, PAUL, diversified co. exec.; b. Henryetta, Okla., Nov. 23, 1919; s. Paul Ernest and Opal Marie (Ashenhurst) T.; student U. Wichita, 1937-38, U. Kans., 1939-41; m. Margery Schwartz, Feb. 14, 1947; 1 dau., Brynn. Pilot, Trans World Airlines, 1945-47; chief exptl. test pilot Chance Vought Corp., 1948-50, sales mgr., 1951, sales and service mgr., 1952-54, v.p. sales and service, 1954-58, v.p. Washington ops., 1958-59, v.p., gen. mgr. Vought Aeros. div., 1959-63, pres., 1963; chief flight test Northrop Aircraft Co., 1950-51; sr. v.p. Ling-Temco-Vought, Inc. (name now LTV Corp.), Dallas, 1963, exec. v.p., 1964, chmn. bd., chief exec. officer, 1970—; chmn. bd. chief exec. officer LTV Aerospace Corp., Dallas, 1965-70. Served from ensign to lt. comdr. USNR, 1941-45. Decorated D.F.C., Air medal with nine oak leaf clusters. Recipient Distinguished Service award sec. navy, 1962. Mem. Soc. Exptl. Test Pilots (chmn. membership com.), Phi Gamma Delta. Home: 10200 Hollow Way Dallas TX 75229 Office: PO Box 225003 Dallas TX 75265

THAYER, RUSSELL, airline exec.; b. Phila., Dec. 5, 1922; s. Russell and Shelby Wentworth (Johnson) T.; A.B., Princeton U., 1949; m. Elizabeth Wright Mifflin, June 12, 1947; children—Elizabeth, Dixon, Shelby, Samuel, David. Mgmt. trainee Eastern Air Lines, 1949-52; mgr. cargo sales and service Am. Airlines, Los Angeles, 1952-63; v.p. mktg. Seaboard World Airlines, N.Y.C., 1963-70; sr. v.p. Braniff Airways, Inc., Dallas, 1970-72, exec. v.p., 1972-77, pres., chief operating officer, 1977—, dir., 1971—. Mem. Trinity Ch. Ushers Guild, Princeton, N.J., 1968—. Served with USAAF, 1942-45. Decorated D.F.C. Air medal with 11 oak leaf clusters. Mem. Am. Aviation Hist. Soc., Air Force Assn., Delta Psi. Clubs: Ivy, Pretty Brook Tennis (Princeton); Princeton (N.Y.C.); Phila.; Bay Head (N.J.) Yacht. Office: Braniff International Box 61747 W31A Dallas Forth Worth Airport TX 75261

THAYER, WALTER NELSON, lawyer, investment and communications co. exec.; b. Dannemora, N.Y., Apr. 24, 1910; s. Walter Nelson and Adelaide Helen (McDonell) T.; A.B., Colgate U., 1931; LL.B., Yale U., 1935; m. Jeanne Cooley Greeley, Dec. 27, 1945; children—Ann Thayer O'Shaughnessy, Susan, Gail Thayer Esquibel, Thomas. Admitted to N.Y. bar, 1935; spl. asst. atty. gen. State of N.Y., N.Y.C., 1935-36; asso. firm Donovan, Leisure, Newton & Lumbard, N.Y.C., 1935-37, 38-40; asst. U.S. atty. So. Dist. N.Y., N.Y.C., 1937-38; atty. Lend-Lease Adminstrn., Washington, 1941-42; mem. Harriman Mission, London, 1942-45; gen. counsel Fgn. Econ. Adminstrn., Washington, 1945; partner firm Thayer & Gilbert, N.Y.C., 1946-55; partner firm J.H. Whitney & Co., N.Y.C., 1955-59; pres. N.Y. Herald Tribune, 1961-66, Whitney Communications Corp., 1960—; partner Whitcom Investment Co., N.Y.C., 1967—; pres., dir. Internat. Herald Tribune, 1973—; dir. Bankers Trust Co., Mem. Pres.'s Commn. on Campaign Costs, 1961-62; spl. cons. to Pres., 1969-71; mem. Pres.'s Adv. Council on Exec. Orgn., 1969-71. Chmn. bd. dirs. Vocat. Found., 1937—; trustee Com. Econ. Devel., Mus. Modern Art, 1968—. Republican. Episcopalian. Clubs: Univ. (N.Y.C.); Augusta Nat. Golf., Links, Lyford Cay, Racquet and Tennis. Office: Whitney Communications Corp 110 W 51st St New York NY 10020

THEBAULT, LOUIS PHILIP, graphic communication exec.; b. Madison, N.J., Dec. 14, 1921; s. William Louis and Margaret (Ryan) T.; B.S., Seton Hall Coll., 1943; m. Dorsey Young, Sept. 10, 1944; children—Jeanne, Philip, Brian, Suzette. Advt. mgr. Morristown (N.J.) Daily Record, 1946-54; owner, pres. L.P. Thebault Co., Parsippany, N.J., 1955—; dir. SRI Corp., Crestmont Savs. Assn. Chmn. United Way campaign, 1975-76. Served to 2d lt. USAAF, World War II. Mem. Printing Industry Am., Aircraft Owners and Pilots Assn. Republican. Roman Catholic. Clubs: Univ., Morris County Golf, Dorset Field, Baltusrol Golf, Seaview. Office: PO Box 169 Pomeroy Rd Parsippany NJ 07054

THEROUX, PAUL RICHARD, ins. exec.; b. Ithaca, N.Y., Dec. 15, 1922; s. Frank R. and Louise M. (Sprencel) T.; B.S. in Chem. Engring., Mich. State U., 1947; m. Marjorie E. Withrow, June 28, 1947; children—David, Gary, Linda. Asst. regional mgr. Factory Mutuals, N.Y.C., 1947-60; underwriting mgr. Improved Risk Mutuals, White Plains, N.Y., 1960-66; asst. v.p. State Farm Fire, Bloomington, Ill., 1966-73; asst. v.p. Argonaut Ins., Menlo Park, Calif., 1973-76; v.p. Warner Ins. Group, Chgo., 1976—; v.p. Canners Exchange, 1976—; v.p. Warner Reciprocal, 1976—, Underwriters Ins. Co., 1976—, Lansing B. Warner Co., 1976—. Served to 1st lt. USAF, 1943-46. Mem. Soc. Fire Protection Engrs. Home: 908 S Hillcrest Clearwater FL 33516

THERRIEN, JOSEPH ALEXANDER, JR., real estate co. exec.; b. Hartford, Conn., Jan. 15, 1936; s. Joseph Alexander and Mary Maher (Clancy) T.; B.S., Trinity Coll., 1957; M.A., U. Conn., 1960; M.B.A. with distinction, Harvard U., 1962; m. Catherine Anna Michalik, June 3, 1961; children—Joseph Alexander, Jeffrey Jon, Jill. Accountant, Price Waterhouse & Co., Hartford, 1962-64; dir. planning Mead Corp., South Lee, Mass., 1964-67; v.p. Boise Cascade Corp., N.Y.C., Atlanta, Palo Alto, Calif., Chgo., 1967-72; v.p. Heizer Corp., Chgo., 1972-73; pres., chief exec. officer Round Valley, Inc. subs. IU Internat. Corp., Phila., 1973-78; founder, pres. Amwell Real Estate Corp., 1978—; dir. Safari Systems, Inc. Mem. Gov.'s Council on Housing, 1971; mem. Hunterdon County Transp. Com., 1974—; mem. East Amwell Twp. Planning Bd., 1978—. Mem. Nat. Assn. Home Builders (com. on land use), Urban Land Inst. Democrat. Clubs: Chgo. Athletic; Harvard (N.Y.C.); Beaver Brook, Amwell Valley Hounds Hunt. Office: PO Box 62 Hopewell NJ 08551

THIRUVENGADAM, ALAGU PILLAI, mfg. co. exec.; b. Madurai, India, Aug. 16, 1935; came to U.S., 1962, naturalized, 1972; s. Alagu P. and Kali A. Thiruvengadam; B.Engring., U. Madras, 1957; M.Sc., Ph.D., Indian Inst. Sci., 1961; m. Soundara Valli, Nov. 23, 1961; children—Rama, Raj, Selvy. Chmn. bd., chief exec. officer Daedalean Assos., Inc., Woodbine, Md., 1972—; chmn. Comser Corp., Woodbine, 1976—; sr. partner Compro Co., Marlowe Heights, Md., 1978—, Cooksville Land Devel. Co. (Md.), 1972—; faculty mech. engring. Catholic U. Am., Washington, 1969-75. Pres., Dearborn Center, 1972. Recipient Outstanding Engr. award Washington Engring. and Archtl. Soc., 1964. Mem. ASME (Hess award 1963), ASTM (Merit award 1975). Author: Cavitation Handbook, 1975; contbr. numerous articles to profl. jours. Patentee in field. Home: 10509 William Tell Ln Columbia MD 21044 Office: Daedalean Assos Inc 15110 Frederich Rd Woodbine MD 21797

THOBURN, DAVID MILLS, shipbldg. co. exec.; b. Cleve., Jan. 31, 1930; s. Theodore and Frances (Goff) T.; B.A., Allegheny Coll., 1951; children—David Mills Jr., Mark V. Loan teller Cleve. Trust Co., 1954-61, asst. treas., 1961-65, asst. v.p., 1965-67, v.p., 1967-69, sr. v.p., 1969-78; exec. v.p. Am. Ship Bldg. Co., Cleve., 1978-80; pres., chief exec. officer, dir. Nat. Fitness Centers Inc., 1980—; dir. Am. Automatic Vending Corp., Bowden Mfg. Co. Served with AUS, 1951-54. Mem. Phi Gamma Delta (Cleve. grad. chpt.). Clubs: Mid Day (Cleve.), Union, Kirtland Country. Home: 21210 Colby Rd Shaker Heights OH 44122 Office: 68 Olive St Chagrin Falls OH 44022

THODE, STEPHEN FREDERICK, fin. analyst; b. Bangor, Maine, May 14, 1951; s. Edward Frederick and Mary Isobel (Zoeller) T.; B.A. in Econs., Coe Coll., 1973; M.B.A. in Fin., Ind. U., 1979, D.B.A. in Fin. (doctoral fellow), 1980; m. Julie Ellen Meyer, July 16, 1976. Asso. instr. fin. Ind. U., Bloomington, 1977-80, lectr. fin., 1980; mem. tech. staff corp. econs. dept. Bell Labs., Murray Hill, N.J., 1980—. Election insp. Monroe County (Ind.) Republican Party, 1978-80. Served to 1st lt., USAF, 1973-77. Mem. Am. Fin. Assn., Fin. Mgmt. Assn., Omicron Delta Epsilon, Beta Gamma Sigma. Republican. Episcopalian. Home: 28 Woodland Terr High Bridge NJ 08829 Office: 600 Mountain Ave Murray Hill NJ 07974

THOMAN, GEORGE MICHAEL, garage door co. exec.; b. Aurora, Ill., Nov. 17, 1926; s. George M. and Christine M. (Fidler) T.; A.B., Ripon Coll., 1949; postgrad. Purdue U., 1949-50; m. Adele McClellan, May 28, 1955; children—Nancy, John. Asst. dist. mgr. Stauffer Chem. Co., Chgo., 1953-59; regional sales mgr. chem. div. Vulcan Materials Co., Chgo., 1959-66; v.p. chem. mktg. metals div., Sandusky, Ohio, 1966-79; pres. Action Garage Doors, Inc., Tempe, Ariz., 1979—. Served with U.S. Army, 1944-46. Mem. Am. Chem. Soc. Republican. Roman Catholic. Home: 3816 S Siesta Ln Tempe AZ 85282 Office: 1324 E 8th St Tempe AZ 85281

THOMAS, ALAN, candy co. exec.; b. Evansburg, Pa., Jan. 1, 1923; s. William Roberts and Letta (Garrett) T.; student Rutgers U., 1941-42, 46-47; B.S., Pa. State U., 1949; M.S., U. Minn., 1950, Ph.D., 1954; m. Marguerite Atria, July 1, 1972; children—Garrett Lee, Michael Alan, Randall Stephen, Brett Eliot. Instr., Temple U., Phila., 1950-51, U. Minn., St. Paul, 1951-54; research asst. Bowman Dairy Co., Chgo., 1954-56; research project mgr. M&M Candies div. Mars, Inc., Hackettstown, N.J., 1956-60, product devel. mgr., 1961-64, chocolate research dir. 1964; v.p. research and devel. Mars Candies, Chgo., 1964-67; v.p. research and devel. M&M/Mars Div., Hackettstown, 1967-77, v.p. sci. affairs, 1977-78; gen. mgr. Ethel M, Las Vegas, 1978—. Chmn. industry council of industry liaison panel Food and Nutrition Bd., Nat. Acad. Scis./NRC, 1972-73. Served to 1st lt. inf. AUS, 1942-46. Recipient research award Nat. Confectioners Assn. U.S., 1971. Mem. A.A.A.S., Am. Dairy Sci. Assn., Am. Assn. Cereal Chemists, Inst. Food Technologists, N.Y. Acad. Sci., Am. Assn. Candy Technologists, Gamma Sigma Delta, Phi Kappa Phi. Home: 1625 Westwood Dr Las Vegas NV 89102 Office: Ethel M 3783 E Desert Inn Rd Las Vegas NV 89121

THOMAS, ALAN TOY, chem. engr.; b. Louisville, May 15, 1921; s. M(oses) A(lan) and Ruth (Lacefield) T.; B. Chem. Engring., U. Louisville, 1943, M. Chem. Engring., 1947, Ph.D., 1964; m. Joycelyn Jane Markert, Mar. 18, 1945; children—Thomas Douglas, Tucker Craig. With Brown-Forman Distillers Corp., 1943—, successively apprentice supr., tech. supr., research engr. and statistician, research asso., project and devel. engr., asst. to v.p. dir. prodn., 1943-64, asst. dir. prodn., 1964-72, asst. v.p., 1973-78, v.p., 1978—, dir. prodn., 1973-79, tech. dir., 1979—; v.p. Canadian Mist Distillers Ltd., 1974—; lectr. math. U. Louisville, 1957-59, lectr. bus. mgmt., 1964-76, adj. asst. prof. liberal studies, 1976—. Registered profl. engr., Ind. Fellow AAAS; mem. Fin. Mgmt. Assn., Am. Mgmt. Assn., Assn. Canadian Distillers, Am. Math. Soc., Ops. Research Soc. Am., Distillers Feed Research Council (dir.), Inst. Mgmt. Sci., Am. Soc.

Quality Control, Inst. Math. Statistics, N.Y. Acad. Sci., Phi Lambda Upsilon, Sigma Xi Sigma. Presbyterian. Contbr. articles to profl. jours. Home: 708 Arbor Dr Anchorage KY 40223 Office: PO Box 1080 Louisville KY 40201

THOMAS, ANTHONY REGINALD, journalist; b. Bulawayo, Rhodesia, July 19, 1940; s. Reginald Frank and Eileen Mabel (Kamp) T.; came to U.S., 1976; student pub. schs., Gwelo, Rhodesia. Clk., Rhodesia Rwys., 1958; reporter Bulawayo Chronicle, 1958-60, The Yorkshire Post, London, 1961-64; commonwealth corr. The Scotsman, London, 1965-68; banking corr. London Times, 1968-69, U.S. econs. corr., 1970-73; Brussels corr. The Economist, 1974-75, Am. bus. editor, 1976-80, bus. editor, 1980—. Mem. Nat. Union Journalists. Office: The Economist 75 Rockefeller Plaza New York City NY 10019

THOMAS, BARBARA N., ednl. adminstr.; b. Morgantown, W.Va., Sept. 8, 1936; d. Martin Joseph and Helen Ruth (Klanduch) Nemcosky; B.S., W.Va. U., 1959; div.; children—Cynthia Dawn, Charles Danser III. Tchr., Monogalia County (W.Va.) Schs., 1959-73; supr. W.Va. U., 1963-73; tchr., coordinator Hopkinton (Mass.) Public Schs., 1973-77; exec. dir. W.Va. Career Colls., Morgantown, 1977-79; pres., dir. Allentown (Pa.) Bus. Sch., 1979—; profl. cons. for secretaries. Active as vol. for hosps. and public sch. system. Mem. NEA, Nat. Bus. Edn. Assn., Am. Mgmt. Assn., Assn. Female Execs., Sales and Mktg. Execs., Pa. Bus. Edn. Assn., Pa. Assn. Pvt. Sch. Adminstrs., Bus. and Profl. Women. Republican. Roman Catholic. Clubs: Soroptimist, Zonta. Editor coll. brochures, catalogs, newsletters; contbr. articles to profl. jours. Home: 1701 W Congress St Allentown PA 18104 Office: 801 Hamilton Mall Allentown PA 18101

THOMAS, BERT L., food store exec.; b. Malad, Idaho, 1918; grad. Utah State U., 1939. With Winn-Dixie Stores, Inc., Jacksonville, Fla., 1946—, v.p. mfg., warehousing and delivery, 1952-65, pres., 1965—, chmn. exec. com., 1976—, also dir.; dir. Barnett Banks of Fla. Trustee Jacksonville U.; bd. dirs. Supermarket Inst. Mem. Nat. Assn. Food Chains (dir.). Office: 5050 Edgewood Ct Jacksonville FL 32203*

THOMAS, BIDE L., utility co. exec.; b. Mason City, Iowa, Aug. 14, 1935; s. Brice Lakin and Jane (Duffield) T.; B.S. in Indsl. Adminstrn., Yale U., 1957; M.B.A., Harvard U., 1959; children—Brice, Lorraine, Carolyn. With Commonwealth Edison Co., Chgo., 1959—, various positions sales, statis. research, purchasing depts., 1959-62, dist. mgr., 1963-66, div. comml. mgr., 1966-70, div. v.p., 1970-73, gen. div. mgr., 1973-75, v.p. div. ops., 1975-76, v.p. indsl. relations, 1976-80, exec. v.p., 1980—. Bd. dirs. Ravenswood Hosp. Med. Center, chmn., 1973-77; bd. mgrs. YMCA of Met. Chgo., vice chmn., 1978—; bd. dirs. United Way of Suburban Chgo., v.p., 1979—; bd. dirs. Central DuPage Health Care Found.; bus. adv. council Coll. of Bus. Adminstrn. U. Ill., Chgo., chmn., 1977-79. Mem. Elec. Assn., Econ. Club, Northwestern U. Assos. Club: Chgo. Office: PO Box 767 Chicago IL 60690

THOMAS, BILLY RAY, export co. exec.; b. Elliotville, Ky., June 8, 1948; s. Verna Thomas and Raymond T.; A.A., Miami-Dade Jr. Coll., 1969; B.A., U. West Fla., 1971; m. Elaine Pucko, June 13, 1970; children—Shane Edward, Jason Martin. Sales mgr. Tex. Supply, Inc., 1971-74; dist. sales mgr. Miracle Maid Corp., West Bend, Wis., 1975-78; gen. mgr. Tex. Supply, Inc., Miami, 1979—. Democrat. Methodist. Home: 13731 SW 42d Terr Miami FL 33175 Office: 1010 NE 2d Ave Miami FL 33132

THOMAS, BROOKS, pub. co. exec.; b. Phila., Nov. 28, 1931; s. Walter Horstman and Ruth Sterling (Boomer) T.; B.A., Yale, 1953, LL.B., 1956; grad. Advanced Mgmt. Program, Harvard, 1973; m. Galen Pinckard Clark, Apr. 15, 1969 (div. 1973). Admitted to Pa. bar, 1957, N.Y. bar, 1960; with law firm Winthrop, Stimson, Putnam & Roberts, N.Y.C., 1960-68; sec., gen. counsel Harper & Row, Pubs., Inc., N.Y.C., 1968-69, v.p., gen. counsel, 1969-73, exec. v.p., 1973-79, chief operating officer, 1977—, pres., 1979—, also dir.; chmn. bd. Harper & Row, Ltd., London, 1973—; dir. Harper & Row, Pty. Ltd., Australia, Harla S.A. de C.V., Mex., Harper & Row do Brasil Ltda., Sao Paulo, PM Life Ins. Co. (N.Y.). Pres., bd. dirs. Butterfield House, 1968-72; bd. dirs. Young Audiences, Inc., 1977—; trustee Outward Bound, Inc., 1980—. Served to lt. (j.g.) USNR, 1956-59. Mem. Am. Bar Assn., Assn. Bar City of N.Y., Assn. Am. Pubs. (dir. 1980—). Clubs: Merion Cricket (Phila.); Yale, Univ., Century, N.Y. Yacht (N.Y.C.). Home: 37 W 12th St New York NY 10011 also Essex CT 06426 Office: 10 E 53d St New York NY 10022

THOMAS, CAROL LOUISE JOSEPH (MRS. CHARLES RAYMOND THOMAS), community planning co. exec.; b. Poughkeepsie, N.Y., Aug. 29, 1923; d. Harold Kritzman and Charlotte Carolyn (Freiberg) Joseph; student Vassar Coll., 1941-43, Boston U., 1943, 49; A.B. cum laude, Syracuse U., 1948; M.A., U. Conn., 1950; postgrad. Mass. Inst. Tech., 1950; m. Charles Raymond Thomas, Mar. 21, 1943; children—Charles Joseph, Katharine Louise. Free-lance community planner, 1950-58; partner Sonthoff & Thomas, community planners, 1958-61; pres., treas. Thomas Assos., community planners, 1961-69; dir. Thomas Assos. div. Universal Engring. Corp., Boston, 1969-78; pres. Thomas Planning Services. Dir. Summer Inst. in Community Planning for Minority Groups, HUD, 1969; faculty U. R.I. Grad. Curriculum in Community Planning and Area Devel., 1964—; guest lectr. various colls., 1967—; faculty Grad. Sch. Design, Harvard U., 1974—. Active various community drives; mem. Gov.'s Adv. Com. on Planning, 1963-68, Gov.'s Adv. Com. on CD, 1968-72, Wayland (Mass.) Town Govt. Com., 1958-72; chmn. scholarship awarding com. P.T.A., Wayland, 1965-72; active local Republican Party. Mem. Am. Planning Assn. (pres. N.E. chpt.), Am. Inst. Cert. Planners (pres. New Eng. chpt. 1965-67, chmn. jury of awards 1969-71, mem. bd. examiners 1968-77, nominating com. 1978—), AAUP, Mass. Conf. Planning Dirs., Mass. Fedn. Planning Bds. Republican. Unitarian (mem. parish com. 1958-60). Home: 151 Tremont St Apt 23P Boston MA 02111 Office: 419 Boylston St Boston MA 02116

THOMAS, CHARLES CARROLL, investment counsel; b. N.Y.C., Feb. 15, 1930; s. Charles Carroll and Miriam (Smith) T.; grad. Deerfield Acad., 1947; B.A., Yale U., 1951; m. Carolyn Rose Hirchert, June 16, 1951; children—Charles Carroll, Anne Hatheway, Megan Lloyd. Div. retail programs mgr. Mobil Oil Corp., Boston, 1953-63; exec. v.p. Lionel D. Edie & Co., N.Y.C., 1963-72; exec. v.p. New England Mchts. Co., Boston, 1972-76; v.p., dir. mktg. Loomis, Sayles & Co., Boston, 1976—. Trustee, Deerfield Acad., 1975-78; trustee Babson Coll., 1976—; trustee Cambridge Sch. of Weston (Mass.), 1976—. Served with USAF, 1951-53. Mem. Internat. Found. Health, Welfare and Benefit Plans, Mcpl. Fin. Officers Assn., Assn. of Investment Mgmt. Sales Execs. (pres. 1980—), Air Force Assn. Republican. Congregationalist. Clubs: Yale of N.Y.C., Harvard of Boston. Home: 170 Barnes Hill Rd Concord MA 01742 Office: 225 Franklin St Boston MA 02110

THOMAS, DAVID, mfg. co. exec.; b. N.Y.C., Dec. 8, 1930; s. Max Henry and Edith Caroline (Bott) T.; student Bethany Coll., 1947-48; A.B. summa cum laude, N.Y. U., 1958; M.B.A. with distinction, 1963; m. Joyce Buchanan, Dec. 6, 1958; 1 son, David Buchanan. Adminstrv. officer N.Y. U. extension, 1958-59; with Standard Oil Co. (N.J.), 1959-69, tng. dir. Esso Research, Linden N.J., 1959-61; mgr. Employment and tng. Enjay Chem. Co. div., N.Y.C., 1961-63; mgr. mktg. services, 1964-66, regional sales mgr., 1966-67, mktg. mgr. Esso Chem. S.A., Brussels, Belgium, 1967-68, mgr. capital investment dept. Enjay Chem. Co. div., N.Y.C., 1968-69; mktg. mgr. Internat. Paper Co., N.Y.C., 1969-71; v.p. mktg. Columbia Precision Corp., Hudson, N.Y. and N.Y.C., 1971-72; v.p. mktg. Huyck Corp., Wake Forest, N.C., 1972-73, v.p. fluid control products, 1973-75, v.p. mktg. and new bus. devel., 1975-78; chmn. subs. Chronister Valve Co., Houston, 1973-75; dir. N.C. Internat. Trade Center, 1978—; chmn. bd., dir. Export Fundamentals, Inc.; lectr. N.Y. U., 1958-59, N.C. State U.; mem. U.S. Dept. Commerce Dist. Export Council; participant profl. seminars and confs. Served with AUS, 1948-54. Recipient Alumni Achievement award N.Y. U., 1963. Mem. Am. Mgmt. Assn. (mktg. council 1972-78), Am. Soc. Tng. and Devel., Am. Mktg. Assn., N.C. World Trade Assn. (dir.). Episcopalian. Author: (with P.W. Maloney) Interviewing the Professional Employee, 1961. Home: 5018 Shamrock Dr Raleigh NC 27612 Office: PO Box 5546 Raleigh NC 27650

THOMAS, DAVID WALTER, JR., mfg. co. exec.; b. Asheville, N.C., May 19, 1938; s. David Walter and Francis (Warren) T., Sr.; B.S. in Mech. Engring., N.C. State U., 1962; M.S. in Indsl. Mgmt., U. Tenn., 1974; m. Mary Ruth Gordon, June 10, 1961; children—David, Anne. Field service engr. Huyck Corp., Tenn. and N.C., 1962-63, sales engr., 1963-64, product mgr., 1964-66, mgr. product mgmt., 1966-68, project mgr., 1969-70, mgr. mfg. services, 1968-69, constrn. mgr., 1970-71, start-up engr., 1971, plant mgr., 1971-72, mfg. mgr., 1972-74, v.p., gen. mgr. div., 1974-79, corp. dir. planning, Wake Forest, N.C., 1979—. Dist. chmn. Boy Scouts Am., 1977-78, exec. com. East Tenn. council, 1976-78; mem. budget com. United Way, 1977-78; chmn. personnel com. 1st Bapt. Ch., Greeneville, 1975-77, adult discussion leader, 1970-79. Served with U.S. Army, 1960-61. Elected pres. of class U. Tenn. Exec. Devel. Program, 1974, Issues Speaker, 1977; recipient various hon. coll. leadership awards. Mem. Paper Industry Mgmt. Assn., Golden Chain, Blue Key, Beta Gamma Sigma. Baptist. Clubs: Lions, Exchange. Contbr. research paper, articles to profl. jours. Home: 14204 Crosscreek Rd Raleigh NC 27614 Office: Huyck Corp Wake Forest NC 27612

THOMAS, DEROY CLINTON, ins. exec.; b. Utica, N.Y., Feb. 16, 1926; s. DeRoy Clinton and Katherine T. (Welsh) T.; B.A., Iona Coll., 1949; LL.B., Fordham U., 1952; m. Emily Clark, Feb. 7, 1953; children—Peter, Patricia, Katherine, Elizabeth. Admitted to Conn. bar; counsel Hartford Fire Ins. Co., 1964-65, asst. gen. counsel, 1965-66, gen. counsel, 1966-68, v.p., gen. counsel, 1968-69, sr. v.p., gen. counsel, 1969-73, dir., 1970—, exec. v.p., 1973-76, exec. v.p., 1973-76, pres., chief operating officer, 1976-78, pres., chief exec. officer, 1978-79, chmn. bd., pres., 1979—, also mem. exec., fin. coms.; counsel Hartford Accident & Indemnity Co., 1964-65, asst. gen. counsel, 1965-66, gen. counsel, 1966-68, v.p., gen. counsel, 1968-69, sr. v.p., gen. counsel, 1969-73, dir., 1970—, exec. v.p., 1973-76, pres., chief operating officer, 1976-78, pres., chief exec. officer, 1978-79, chmn. bd., pres., 1979—, chmn. exec. com., 1979—; with Hartford Casualty Ins. Co., 1964—, dir., 1968—, pres., chief operating officer, 1976-78, pres., chief exec. officer, 1978-79, chmn. bd., pres., chmn. exec. com., 1979—; with Hartford Life & Accident Ins. Co., 1967—, dir., 1968—, v.p., 1972-76, pres., 1976—, chief exec. officer, 1978—, chmn. bd., 1979—, also mem. exec. and fin. coms.; with Hartford Life Ins. Co., 1967—, pres., dir., 1976—, chief exec. officer, 1978—, chmn. bd., 1979—, also mem. exec. and fin coms.; pres., dir. Hartford Mgmt. Services Co., 1976—; pres. Hartford Variable Annuity Life Ins. Co., 1976—, chmn. bd., 1979—, also mem. exec. and fin. coms.; with N.Y. Underwriters Ins. Co., 1964—, dir., 1968—, exec. v.p., 1974-76, pres., 1976—, chmn. bd., 1979—, also mem. exec. and fin. coms.; dir. Pacific Ins. Co., Ltd., 1976—, chmn. bd., chief exec. officer, 1978—; dir. Sentinel Ins. Co., Ltd., 1976—, chmn. bd., chief exec. officer, chmn. exec. com., 1978—; pres. Terry Assos., Inc., 1977—; with Twin City Fire Ins. Co., 1964—, dir., 1968—, pres., chief operating officer, 1976-78, pres., chief exec. officer, 1978-79, chmn. bd., pres., 1979—, chmn. exec. com., 1979—; pres., chmn. bd., dir., chmn. exec. com. Hartford Ins. Co. Ala. and Hartford Ins. Co. Ill., 1979—; dir. ITT Hartford Europe, ITT Life Ins. Corp., London-Can. Ins. Co., New Eng. Reins. Co., One Hundred Edgewood Ave., Inc., One Hundred S. Wacker Dr., Inc., Hartford Real Estate Co., Cameron & Colby, First State Ins. Co., Four Thirty Seven Land Co., Inc., Gt. Eastern Ins. Co., Hartex, Inc., Conn. Natural Gas Corp.; chmn. bd. Ins. Info. Inst.; dir. Ins. Services Office; mem. adv. council U.S. Aviation Ins. Group. Bd. dirs. Hartford Ins. Group Found., 1969—, pres., 1979—; bd. dirs. Coordinating Council for Founds., Inc., Jr. Achievement No. Central Conn., United Way Greater Hartford; bd. dirs., pres. Greater Hartford Arts Council; bd. dirs., mem. exec. com. Hartford Hosp.; trustee Wadsworth Atheneum, Iona Coll., Wheelock Coll., Kingswood-Oxford Sch.; corporator St. Francis Hosp., Inst. of Living. Served in USAF, 1944-46. Mem. Greater Hartford C. of C. (dir.), Conn. Bus. and Industry Assn. (dir.), Am. Bar Assn., Am. Fgn. Ins. Assn. (vice-chmn. bd. trustees), Am. Ins. Assn. (dir.), Ins. Assn. Conn. (dir., exec. com.), Ins. Co.-Supported Orgns. Pension Trust (trustee), Property-Casualty Ins. Council. Clubs: Amelia Island Plantation; Hartford Golf, Hartford; Block Island. Office: Hartford Plaza Hartford CT 06115

THOMAS, DONALD LLEWELLYN, bank exec.; b. Niagara Falls, N.Y., Mar. 5, 1917; s. Philip Charles and Dora T. (Redpath) T.; B.S.B.A. magna cum laude, Niagara U., 1948; grad. Stonier Sch. Banking, Rutgers U.; m. Barbara Mae Williams, May 20, 1942; children—Donald Llewellyn, Rhys E. Treas., Niagara County Savs. Bank, N.Y., 1946-58; v.p. No. Trust Co., Chgo., 1958-66; chmn., chief exec. officer Anchor Savs. Bank, Bklyn., 1966—; dir. Central Industry Fund, Thrift Publs., Inc., Drayton Corp., Ltd., Ban Ser; mem. adv. bd. Mfrs. Hanover Trust Co. Bd. dirs. Lutheran Med. Center, Bklyn. C. of C., Community Preservation Corp., N.Y.C., Bklyn. Philharmonia; chmn. Found. Human Ecology. Served to capt. U.S. Army, 1942-46. Named Man of Yr., Bklyn. Sunday Sch. Union, Bklyn. Council Chs., Montauk Club, Bklyn., Indsl. Home for Blind. Mem. Nat. Assn. Mut. Savs. Banks (dir.), Savs. Banks Trust Co. (dir.), Nat. Assn. Bus. Economists. Clubs: Cherry Valley, Garden City, Met., Manhattan, Econ. N.Y., Bklyn., Montauk. Author: (with others) Commercial Bankers Handbook. Office: 5323 Fifth Ave Brooklyn NY 11220

THOMAS, EDGAR WATSON, life ins. co. ofcl.; b. Macon, N.C., May 5, 1939; s. Edgar T. and Lucille T. (Watson) T.; B.S. in Biology Edn. Agrl. and Tech. State U. N.C., 1968; m. Johnsie Williams, Dec. 27, 1962; children—Demetria, Adrienne. Caseworker, N.Y.C. Dept. Social Work, 1968-69; field underwriter N.Y. Life Ins. Co., N.Y.C., 1970-71, asst. mgr., 1971-74, gen. mgr., 1975—. Trustee, Abyssinian Bapt. Ch., N.Y.C., 1971—, pres. usher bd., 1970—. Served with USMC, 1962-66. Recipient Black Achiever in Industry award Harlem YMCA, 1975. Mem. Nat. Assn. Life Underwriters (Gen. Agts. and Mgrs. Conf.). Democrat. Clubs: Kiwanis, Masons. Home: 2600 Netherland Ave Bronx NY 10463 Office: 55 W 125th St New York NY 10027

THOMAS, FARRELL SIDNEY, airline exec.; b. Columbus, Ga., Mar. 9, 1937; s. Autry Lee and Helen (Conover) T.; student W. Ga. Coll., 1954-55, Ca. State Coll., 1956-57; m. Trudy Butler, June 29, 1957; 1 son, Timothy Farrell. Supr. data processing dept. United Family Life Ins. Co., Atlanta, 1956-63; sales rep. Nat. Life & Accident Ins. Co., Atlanta, 1963-66; pres. All Am. Trophies, Inc., Forest Park, Ga., 1967-77, Pioneer Airlines, Inc., Atlanta, 1978—. Mem. Forest Park Jaycees (pres. 1969-70), Atlanta Area Football Offcls. Assn. (pres. 1973-74), Forest Park Sr. High Quaterback Club (pres. 1975-76), Aircraft Owners and Pilots Assn., Nat. Air Transport Assn. Democrat. Baptist. Home: 1435 Dauset Dr Griffin GA 30223 Office: Griffin-Spalding County Airport Griffin GA 30223

THOMAS, FRANCIS DARRELL, oil compounder exec.; b. Palestine, Ill., Feb. 11, 1928; s. Odin F. and Dorothy (Carrol) T.; B.S., Butler U., 1951; children—Steven, Bruce, Gail. Regional mgr. Sun Oil Co., Cin., 1955-72; pres. Keenan Oil Co., Cin., 1972-74; gen. mgr. Weatherator Engring. Co., Columbus, Ohio, 1975-76; pres. Nat. Oil and Chem. Co., Hamilton, Ohio, 1976—. Served with USMC, 1946-47. Mem. Ind. Oil Compounders Assn., Assn. Petroleum Re-refiners (past mem. nat. exec. com.), Am. Soc. Lubrication Engrs. (past chmn. Cin. sect.). Republican. Clubs: Clovernook Country, Masons, Shriners. Office: 1000 Forest Ave Hamilton OH 45015

THOMAS, GARY BRUCE, banker; b. Clearwater, S.C., Mar. 14, 1942; s. Gilbert Jacob and Irma Vera (Busbee) T.; B.S. with honors in Acctg. (Price Waterhouse scholar), U. N.C., Charlotte, 1971; m. Anne Soliday, Nov. 25, 1961; children—Eric Christopher, Angela Dee. Trust dept. Wachovia Bank & Trust Co., Charlotte, 1963-69; tax acct. Ernst & Ernst, Charlotte, 1969-71; audit mgr. Price Waterhouse & Co., Columbia, S.C., Charlotte, 1971-77; v.p., asst. controller Bankers Trust of S.C., Columbia, 1977-80, sr. v.p., controller, 1980—. Bd. visitors Harbison Campus, Midlands Tech. Coll., Columbia. C.P.A., N.C. Mem. Am. Inst. C.P.A.'s, N.C. Assn. C.P.A.'s, S.C. Assn. C.P.A.'s, Nat. Assn. Accts., Nat. Consumer Fin. Assn., Am. Inst. Bankers, U. N.C.-Charlotte Alumni Assn. Club: Dutch Fork Civitan (treas. 1976-78, pres.-elect 1978-79, pres. 1979-80). Home: 343 Lockshire Rd Columbia SC 29210 Office: PO Box 448 Columbia SC 29202

THOMAS, GENE, consultant; b. Oregon, Ill., Aug. 18, 1931; s. Franklin C. and Lois I. (Lichty) T.; B.S. in Engring., Iowa State U., 1954; m. Barbara Trelfa, June 25, 1955; children—Greg, Kevin, Wendy, Glenn. Mktg. and devel. ofcl. IBM, 1956-66, br. mgr., Balt., 1968-69, mfg. industry mgr., 1966-80; founder Thomas, Laguban & Assos., Inc., Barrington, Ill., 1969—. Mem. Barrington Sch. Bd. Served with USAFR, 1954-56. Mem. Am. Prodn. and Inventory Control Soc. (past pres. Balt.), Soc. Mfg. Engrs., Am. Inst. Indsl. Engrs. Inventor computer software; first installer of capacity (finite) planning in U.S. Home: 749 Orchard Dr Barrington IL 60010 Office: 16535 Bluemound Rd Brookfield WI 53005

THOMAS, HERBERT LEON, JR., life ins. co. exec.; b. Little Rock, Jan. 8, 1921; s. Herbert Leon and Ruby (Collier) T.; B.S. in Econs., Wharton Sch. of U. Pa., 1942; postgrad. Harvard U.; m. Rayma Jean Pickens, June 7, 1947; children—Gray Rodriques-Barbera, Clare Pickens, Herbert Leon, III. With First Pyramid Life Ins. Co., Little Rock, 1946—, exec. v.p., agy. dir., 1958-59, exec. v.p., 1959-60, pres., 1960-80, chmn. bd., pres., 1980—; chmn. bd. City Nat. Bank, Ft. Smith, Ark., Citizens Bank, Booneville, Ark.; dir. First Nat. Bank, Little Rock. Past pres., bd. dirs. Little Rock Boys' Club; bd. dirs. Little Rock United Way, YMCA. Served with USNR, World War II. C.L.U. Mem. Am. Assn. C.L.U.'s, Nat. Assn. Life Cos., Am. Mgmt. Assn. (president's assn.), U. Ark. Wild Hogs, Ark. Tennis Patrons Found. Clubs: Little Rock Country, Eden Isle Country. Home: 1709 N Spruce St Little Rock AR 72207 Office: 650 Shackleford Rd Little Rock AR 72211

THOMAS, JESSE CALVIN, employment cons.; b. Chgo., Jan. 2, 1945; s. Ollie Temolian and Jessie Lee (Bailey) T.; student Electronics Tech., 1963-65, William L. Dawson Free Sch. Bus., 1968; m. Sharon Somerville, May 13, 1978; children—Paul Calvin, Jeru Anderson, Erika Shadik Somerville. Test equipment technician Zenith Radio Corp., Chgo., 1965-67; field engr. IBM Corp., 1967-68; pres., gen. mgr. V.G. Systems Inc., Chgo., 1968-72; employment cons. Computer Centre, Chgo., 1973-74; asso. partner, gen. mgr. TEC Inc., Chgo., 1974-77; founder, pres. J. Thomas & Assos., Inc., Chgo., 1977—. Coordinator activities Original New Breed Com., 1968-72. Mem. Nat. Employment Assn. Office: J Thomas & Assos Inc 2315 E 103d St Chicago IL 60617

THOMAS, JIMMY LYNN, fin. exec.; b. Mayfield, Ky., Aug. 3, 1941; s. Alben Stanley and Emma Laura (Alexander) T.; B.S. (Ashland Oil Co. scholar), U. Ky., 1963; M.B.A. (Samuel Bronfman fellow, McKinsey scholar), Columbia U., 1964; m. Nancy Nelson Danforth, June 5, 1964; children—James Nelson, Carter Danforth. Fin. analyst Ford Motor Co., Detroit, 1964-66; asst. treas. Joel Dean Assos., N.Y.C., 1966-67; asst. controller TWA, N.Y.C., 1967-73; v.p. fin. services, treas. Gannett Co., Inc., Rochester, N.Y., 1973—; dir. Gannett Supply Corp., Gannett Fla., Gannett Pacific, Guam Publs., Newspaper Printing Corp., Nashville, Pacific Media, Inc., Marine Midland Bank, Charlevoix Paper Co.; treas. Frank E. Gannett Found. Bd. overseers Strong Meml. Hosp.; trustee Harley Sch.; co chmn. United Negro Coll. Fund of Rochester. Served with AUS, 1967-68. Mem. Fin. Execs. Inst., Inst. Newspaper Controllers and Fin. Officers, Rochester C. of C., Alumni Assn. U. Ky., Alumni Assn. Columbia U., Beta Gamma Sigma, Omicron Delta Kappa, Sigma Alpha Epsilon. Democrat. Mem. Chirstian Ch. Clubs: Genesee Valley, Country of Rochester. Home: 13 New England Dr Rochester NY 14618 Office: Lincoln Tower Rochester NY 14604

THOMAS, JON CAYSON, fin. advisor; b. St. Louis, June 22, 1947; s. Jefferson C. and Edna W. Thomas; B.S., U. Mo., 1971; M.B.A., So. Ill. U., 1978; m. Alma DeBasio, Aug. 31, 1968; children—Jennifer Anne, Jon Cayson, II. Div. mgr. pensions and mut. funds Safeco Securities Co./Safeco Life Ins. Co., St. Louis, 1970-74; v.p. fin. planning dept. A.G. Edwards & Sons, Inc., St. Louis, 1974-77; pres. Intermark Fin. Services, Inc., St. Louis, 1978—; founder, 1980, thereafter prin. Monetary Mgmt. Group, St. Louis. Cert. fin. planner. Mem. Nat. Assn. Securities Dealers (registered investment adv.), Internat. Assn. Fin. Planners, Inst. Cert. Fin. Planners, Beta Theta Pi. Office: 232 S Meramac Clayton MO 63105

THOMAS, LEE BALDWIN, mfg. co. exec.; b. Alma, Nebr., Sept. 17, 1900; s. Rees and Fannie (Baldwin) T.; B.B.A., U. Wash., 1923; m. Margaret T. Thomas, 1924 (dec. 1976); children—Lee Baldwin, Margaret Ellen Thomas Dunbar, Susan Jane Thomas Hamilton; m. 2d, Elizabeth C. Bromley, 1977. Advt. mgr. Ernst Hardware Co., Seattle, 1923-24; buyer R. H. Macy Co., N.Y.C., 1924-25; sales mgr. Ernst Hardware Co., Seattle, 1926-29; dir. home goods merchandising Butler Bros., Chgo., 1929-41; pres. Ekco Products Co., mfrs. kitchen goods, Chgo., 1941-47; chmn. Am. Elevator & Machine Co., Louisville, Vt. Am. Corp.; chmn. bd. Thomas Industries Inc., Louisville, Henry G. Thompson Co., New Haven; dir. Marshall Steel Co., LaGrange, Ill. Bd. dirs. Honey Locust Found. Episcopalian. Clubs: Owl Creek Country (Anchorage, Ky.); Pendennis, Jefferson (Louisville); Union League, Mid-Day (Chgo.); Mountain Lake (Lake Wales, Fla.); Harmony Landing Country (Prospect, Ky.); Lake Region Yacht and Country (Winter Haven, Fla.); Del Ray (Fla.) Dunes

Country. Home: Evergreen Rd Anchorage KY 40223 Office: Vermont American Bldg 100 E Liberty St Louisville KY 40202

THOMAS, LEWIS EDWARD, mktg. engr.; b. Lima, Ohio, May 18, 1913; s. Lewis Edward and Ilma Kathryn (Siebert) T.; B.S., Ohio No. U., 1935; M.S., Purdue U., 1937; m. Elinda Patricia Grafton, Dec. 21, 1939; children—Linda Thomas Collins, Stephanie Thomas Pawuk, Kathryn Thomas Ramsey, Deborah Thomas Masker. Asst. prof. chemistry Va. Mil. Inst., 1940-45; devel. engr. Sun Oil Co., Toledo, 1945-49, lab. supr., 1950-69, div. supr., 1969-73, lab. mgr., 1973-78, ret., 1978; mng. dir. Toledo Symphony Orch., 1978-80; mktg. engr. Jones & Henry Labs., 1980—; dir. First Fed. Savs. & Loan Assn.; vis. scientist to area high schs. Ohio Acad. Sci., 1960-67. Lay reader Episcopal Ch., 1962; pres., treas. Harvard Elementary Sch. PTA, 1953-54; mem. Mayor's Indsl. Devel. Com., Toledo, 1963-66; mem. Gov.'s Com. Statewide Health Planning Council, 1976—; mem. Lucas County Central Com., precinct committeeman Republican Party, 1958—; trustee Toledo Pub. Library, 1966-70, pres., 1969-70; trustee Toledo Lucas County Pub. Library, 1970—, v.p., 1971-72, pres., 1972-75; trustee U. Toledo, 1967—, vice chmn. bd., 1971-75; mem. adv. bd. St. Charles Hosp.; mem. Assn. Governing Bds. of Univs. and Colls., 1969—. Named Chem. Engr. of Year, Toledo Area, 1961, 63, 76; registered profl. engr., Ohio. Mem. Nat., Ohio (chmn. state conv. 1975), Toledo (trustee 1974—) socs. profl. engrs., Am. Inst. Chem. Engrs., Am. Chem. Soc. (pres. Toledo sect. 1960), Nat. Mgmt. Assn. (trustee Toledo chpt. 1962-70, nat. dir. 1968-70), Tech. Soc. Toledo (pres. 1968-69), Explorers Club, Sigma Xi, Pi Kappa Alpha, Tau Beta Pi, Nu Theta Kappa. Clubs: Toastmasters; Toledo; Press. Home: 4148 Deepwood Ln Toledo OH 43614 Office: 2000 W Central Toledo OH 43606

THOMAS, O. PENDLETON, ret. rubber co. exec.; b. Forney, Tex., June 14, 1914; s. William Pendleton and Lottye (Trail) T.; B.S., E. Tex. State U., 1935, LL.D., 1972; M.B.A., U. Tex., 1941; grad. Advanced Mgmt. Program, Harvard U.; m. Anne Swindell; children—William Pendleton II, Alexander Cole, James Trail. With Sinclair Oil Corp., N.Y.C., 1945-69, pres., 1964-69, chief exec. officer, 1968-69; chmn. exec. com., dir. Atlantic Richfield Co., N.Y.C., 1969-71; chmn. bd. B.F. Goodrich Co., Akron, Ohio, 1971-79; trustee Mut. Life Ins. Co., N.Y.; dir. Armco Inc., Westinghouse Corp., Superior Oil Co. Bd. govs. ARC. Served as lt. USNR, 1942-45. Named Distinguished Grad., U. Tex. Coll. Bus. Adminstrn., 1964, Distinguished Alumnus, U. Tex., 1969. Mem. Alliance to Save Energy (dir., exec. com.), Am. Petroleum Inst. (hon. dir.), UN Assn. U.S. (bd. govs.). Clubs: River, Links (N.Y.C.); Blind Brook (Portchester, N.Y.); Round Hill (Greenwich, Conn.); Augusta (Ga.) Nat.; Bohemian (San Francisco); Portage Country (Akron); Pepper Pike (Ohio). Office: 500 S Main St Akron OH 44318

THOMAS, OGDEN UNDERWOOD, JR., marine industry exec.; b. Lake Charles, La., May 8, 1945; s. Ogden Underwood and Dorothy Thomas; B.S. in Mgmt., Nicholls State U., 1967; m. Linda Morella, June 17, 1967; children—Michele, Scott. With Seahorse, Inc. and predecessor firm, Morgan City, La., 1969—, beginning as controller, successively adminstrv. coordinator, gen. mgr. Brazilian subs., v.p., 1969-76, pres., 1976—; dir. St. Mary Indsl. Group. Mem. Am. Petroleum Inst., Offshore Marine Service Assn. (dir.), Morgan City C. of C. (dir.), Nat. Ocean Industries Assn. Club: Nomads. Office: PO Drawer 968 Morgan City LA 70380

THOMAS, PHILIP ROBINSON, operational mgmt. cons. co. exec.; b. Torquay, Devon, Eng., Dec. 9, 1934; s. Leslie Robinson and Margaret (Burridge) T.; came to U.S., 1963, naturalized, 1969; B.Sc., U. London, 1959, M.Sc., 1961, postgrad., 1961-64; m. Wayne Laverne Heirtzler, Apr. 6, 1973; children by previous marriage—Martin N. R., Stephen D. R. With Tex. Instruments Corp., 1961-72, ops. mgr., Dallas, 1963-72, Bedford, Eng., 1961-63; v.p., gen. mgr. MOS/LSI div. Gen. Instruments Co., N.Y.C., 1972-73; gen. mgr. MOS Products div. Fairchild Camera and Instrument Corp., Mountainview, Calif., 1973-75; v.p. Integrated Circuits div. RCA, Somerville, N.J., 1975-78; pres., chief exec. officer Thomas Group Inc., Ethel, La., 1978—. Mem. IEEE, Brit. Inst. Radio and Electronics Engrs. Contbr. articles to profl. jours.; patentee semicondrs. Home: Hwy 956 Ethel LA 70730 Office: Thomas Group Inc Route 1 Box 181-D Ethel LA 70730

THOMAS, RICHARD L., banker; b. Marion, Ohio, Jan. 11, 1931; s. Marvin C. and Irene (Harruff) T.; B.A., Kenyon Coll., 1953; postgrad. U. Copenhagen (Denmark), 1954; M.B.A., Harvard, 1958; m. Helen Moore, June 17, 1953; children—Richard Lee, David Paul, Laura Sue. Pres., dir. First Nat. Bank of Chgo., First Chgo. Corp.; dir. CNA Fin. Corp., Chgo. Bd. Options Exchange, Consol. Foods Corp. Trustee Rush-Presbyn. St. Luke's Med. Center, Northwestern U.; trustee, vice chmn. Kenyon Coll., Chgo. Council Fgn. Relations, Orchestral Assn.; trustee Glenwood Sch. for Boys. Served with AUS, 1954-56. Named 1 of 10 Outstanding Young Men, Chgo. Jr. C. of C., 1966. Mem. Harvard Bus. Sch. Assn., Phi Beta Kappa, Beta Theta Pi. Clubs: Casino, Mid-Am., Econ., Comml., Chicago (Chgo.); Indian Hill Country (Winnetka, Ill.); Old Elm (Ft. Sheridan, Ill.); Sunningdale Golf (Berkshire, Eng.). Home: 219 Leicester Rd Kenilworth IL 60043 Office: 1 First Nat Plaza Chicago IL 60670

THOMAS, ROBERT CAPRON, fin./mgmt. cons.; b. Toronto, Ont., Can., Aug. 16, 1935 (parents Am. citizens); s. Robert Mathias and Ruth Bidwell (Capron) T.; B.S. in Hotel Adminstrn., Cornell U., 1958; m. Patricia Robins Morrow, Sept. 1, 1962; children—Robert Morrow, William Russel, Lucinda Capron. With market div. Jewel Tea Co., Chgo., 1961; with Canteen Corp., Chgo., 1962, Fred Harvey Restaurants, Chgo., 1963, Pick Hotels Corp., Chgo., founder, pres., chief exec. officer Thomas Distbg. Co., Inc., instnl. food distbrs., Los Angeles, 1964-74; cons. Thomas Fin. Services, Costa Mesa, Calif., 1974—. Mem. pack com. Boy Scouts Am., 1970-73, mem. troop com., 1973—, commr. Del Mar dist. Orange County council, 1975, sustaining membership chmn., 1975-76, dist. vice chmn., 1978, dist. chmn., 1979—, award of merit, 1979, mem. Orange County council exec. bd., 1979—, nat. council mem. at large, 1980; trustee Thomas Family Trusts, Chgo., 1973—. Served to lt. U.S. Army, 1959-61. Mem. Am. Mgmt. Assn., Nat. Instnl. Food Distbrs. Assn., Cornell Soc. Hotelmen, Theta Delta Chi. Republican. Episcopalian. Clubs: Newport Harbor Yacht, Balboa Bay (Newport Beach, Calif.); Mesa Verde Country (Costa Mesa). Home: 3063 Capri Ln Costa Mesa CA 92626 Office: 500 C Newport Center Dr Newport Beach CA 92660

THOMAS, ROBERT EGGLESTON, corp. exec.; b. Cuyahoga Falls, Ohio, July 28, 1914; s. Talbott E. and Jane S. (Eggleston) T.; B.S. in Econs., Wharton Sch. Finance, U. Pa., 1936; m. Kathryn L. Thomas; children—Robert Eggleston, Barbara A. Asst. to gen. mgr., sec., mgr. R.R. investments Keystone Custodian Funds, Boston, 1936-53; v.p. The Pennroad Corp., N.Y.C., 1953-56; chmn. exec. com., dir. M.-K.-T. R.R., 1956-65; chief exec. officer MAPCO Inc., 1960-79, pres., 1960-76, chmn., 1973—, also dir., mem. exec. com.; mem. exec. com., dir. Perkin-Elmer Corp.; dir. Bank of Okla., Darnell Corp., Ltd., Willard Co. Trustee U. Tulsa. Mem. Midwest Research Inst., Transp. Assn. Am. (dir.), Am. Petroleum Inst. (dir.), Nat. Coal Assn. (dir.), NAM (dir.), Nat. Petroleum Council, Newcomen Soc., Tulsa Met. C. of C. (dir.). Episcopalian. Clubs: N.Y. Yacht, Metropolitan, The Links, (N.Y.C.); Chicago; Tulsa, Summit, So. Hills Country (Tulsa); Kansas City (Mo.); Ocean Reef (Key Largo, Fla.); Cat Cay (Bahamas). Home: Liberty Towers 1502 S Boulder Ave Tulsa OK 74119 Office: 1800 S Baltimore Ave Tulsa OK 74119

THOMAS, ROBERT RAY, JR., mgmt. cons.; b. Columbus, Ohio, Dec. 14, 1926; s. Robert Ray and Esther Susan (Wolfe) T.; B.S. in TV Engring., Am. Inst. of Tech., 1950; m. Ann Lee Estes, Nov. 24, 1973; 1 dau., Sandra Ann; 1 dau. by previous marriage, Margo Lynne. Electronic engr. Oakton Engring. Co., Evanston, Ill., 1949-50, Stewart Warner Corp., Chgo., 1950-51, Gen. Transformer Co., Homewood, Ill., 1951-53; electronic sales engr. Electronic Components Inc., Chgo., 1953-54; gen. mgr. West Coast, Miller Calson Services, Los Angeles, 1954-55; sales engr. R. Edward Steem Co., Chgo., 1955-59; dist. sales mgr. Motorola Semiconductor div. Motorola, Inc., Chgo. and Dallas, 1959-61; pres., chmn. bd. Enterprises Ltd. Co., Inc., Dallas, 1961—, pres. subs. Robert R. Thomas Co., 1961—, Rep. Mgmt. & Mktg. Counselors, 1969—; pres. Press Insulator Co., 1978—. Served with USAAF, 1945-46. Named Boss of Year, Big D chpt. Am. Bus. Womens Assn., 1965, Super Salesman by Purchasing Mag., Oct. 1975. Mem. Mfrs. Electronic Reps. Assn. (dir. S.W. chpt. 1964-69, pres. S.W. chpt. 1968-69), Sales and Mktg. Execs. of Dallas (pres. 1977-78), S.W. Found. for Free Enterprise in Dallas (pres. 1976-77). Baptist. Club: Masons (Shriner). Office: 15800 Addison Rd Addison TX 75001

THOMAS, S. PENN, investment banker; b. N.Y.C., May 2, 1940; s. Francis and Teresa (Hanley) T.; student Stanford U., 1958-61; B.S. in Bus. Adminstrn., Georgetown U., 1969; m. Mary Ann MacDonald, May 31, 1975; 1 son, Penn Clarke. Asst. to mng. partner, mgr. syndicate dept. Ferris & Co., Washington, 1969-71; asst. sec. First Washington Securities Corp., Washington, 1971; pres. Rykie Corp., Washington, 1971-77; exec. v.p. Fahnestock Co., N.Y.C., 1977—. Served with USMC, 1961-67. Decorated D.F.C., Air medal with 6 stars. Clubs: Met., Broadstreet (N.Y.C.); Manasquan River Yacht. Office: 110 Wall St New York NY 10005

THOMAS, WALTER J., business exec.; b. Atlanta, 1919; married. Regional service mgr. Dun & Bradstreet Inc., 1938-52; in charge ops. J.M. Tull Industries, Norcross, Ga., 1952-58, controller, 1958-62, v.p., sec., 1962-69, v.p., sec. metals distbn. div., from 1969, now pres., dir.; chmn. Gwinnett Bank & Trust Co.; dir. Bankhead Enterprises, Inc. Office: 4405 Old Peachtree Rd Norcross GA 30071*

THOMAS, WILLARD YOUNG, cons. co. exec.; b. Ft. Worth, Dec. 25, 1935; s. Raymond Earl and Madge Belle (Rasmussen) T.; B.A. in Journalism, U. Okla., 1958; M.S., U. Tulsa, 1971; postgrad. U. Ill., 1975-77; m. Sonja K. Russell, Apr. 4, 1958; children—Willard Ray, Keith Laurence. Student intern Halliburton Co., Duncan, Okla., 1954-58; commd. 2d lt. U.S. Marine Corps, 1958, advanced through grades to maj., 1970; served in Hawaii, Ft. Sill, Okinawa, Vietnam; tech. tng. dir. Amoco Petroleum Corp., Tulsa, 1968-71; mgr. AV Comm. Standard Oil Co. Ind., Chgo., 1971-75; pres. Organizational Media Systems, Ft. Worth, 1975—. Recipient ASTD Media Communicator Year award, 1978; Outstanding Service award Indsl. TV Assn., 1972, Internat. Tape Assn. Recognition award, 1977-78. Mem. Am. Soc. Tng. and Devel. (past chmn. media div., editor div. newsletter), Internat. Tape Assn. (video com.), Internat. Indsl. TV Assn., Internat. Soc. for Gen. Semantics, USMCR Officers Assn., Fed. Media Communicators, Assn. Ednl. Communication and Tech. Contbr. Video System mag., tng. mag., ASTD Jour., others. Home: 8700 Davis Blvd Fort Worth TX 76180

THOMASSEN, HENRY, state govt. ofcl.; b. Calgary, Alta., Can., May 6, 1929; came to U.S., 1956; s. Thomas Ankar and Jessy (Andersen) T.; B.Ed., U. Alta., 1951, B.Sc., 1953; student Boston U., 1952; M.A., Stetson U., 1954; Ph.D., U. Nebr., 1956; m. Helen Lee Cochran, Sept. 3, 1960; children—Lee, Les, Lisa, Leni, Lori. Economist, Prudential Ins. Co., Newark, 1957-58; prof. econs. Ga. State U., 1958-64, U. B.C., 1965-66, Emory U., 1967-68, U. Nebr., 1968-73; econ. adv. to Gov., State of Ga., Atlanta, 1973—; cons. So. Bell Telephone Co., Elliot & Black Cons. Engrs. Omaha. Bd. dirs. Callanwolde Found., Callanwolde Arts Center, Atlanta, 1977—; pres. DeKalb County Band Boosters Assn., Atlanta, 1978-80. Served to 1st lt., Royal Can. Provost Corps, 1952. Mem. Am. Econ. Assn., Can. Econ. Assn., Nat. Tax Assn., So. Econ. Assn., Math. Assn. Am. Methodist. Home: 2709 E Sudbury Ct Atlanta GA 30360 Office: 610 Trinity Washington Bldg Atlanta GA 30334

THOMASSON, RICHARD SAMUEL, banker; b. Wheeling, W.Va., Oct. 19, 1930; s. Samuel J. and Gladys (Stinard) T.; B.S., Ohio State U., 1953; m. Sarah Jane Arnold, June 1, 1957; children—Kathryn Ilene, Thomas Richard. Asst. cashier First Nat. Bank, Newark, Ohio, 1958-63; pres., treas. Ohio Rapid Transit, Inc., Columbus, 1963-76; pres., treas. Lake Shore System, Inc., Columbus, 1963-76; asst. v.p. BancOhio Nat. Bank, Columbus. Mem. exec. bd. Central Ohio council Boy Scouts Am.; bd. dirs. Columbus Safety Council. Presbyterian. Clubs: Masons (33 deg.), Jesters, Athletic of Columbus. Home: 4225 Camborne Rd Columbus OH 43220 Office: 1733 Westbelt Dr Columbus OH 43228

THOMETZ, MARY CHRISTINA, investment banker; b. Norfolk, Va., Aug. 21, 1947; d. Alan F. and Mary McCormick (Montanus) T.; B.A., Marymount Coll., 1969; m. John Bentley Webber, Feb. 25, 1978; 1 son, John Bentley II. Asst. v.p. First Boston Corp., N.Y.C., 1969-75; sr. corp. fin. officer Girard Bank, Phila., 1975-80; v.p. Phila. Capital Advisors, 1980—. Mem. adv. council Villanova U. Mem. Fin. Women's Assn. N.Y., Forum Exec. Women, N.Y. Soc. Security Analysts. Club: Cosmopolitan (Phila.) (treas. 1980—). Office: PNB Bldg Broad and Chestnut Sts Philadelphia PA 19101

THOMPKINS, RONALD, accountant; b. Lakeland, Fla., Jan. 31, 1949; s. James Willie and Emma Lee T.; B.A. in Acctg., Howard U., 1971; m. Charlayne Rhalette Williams, Aug. 27, 1977; children—Ronald Rashad, James Salathiel. Audit mgr. Deloitte Haskins & Sells, Miami, Fla., 1972-80; partner Koon, Thompkins & Co., C.P.A.'s, North Miami Beach, 1980—. Recipient Achiever of Yr. award Harlem br. YMCA, 1974; Profl. Achievement award Greater Miami chpt. Nat. Assn. Black Accts., 1980. Mem. Am. Inst. C.P.A.'s, Fla. Inst. C.P.A.'s (com. mem. Dade County chpt.), Nat. Assn. Accts., Miami-Dade C. of C. (sec. bd. dirs. 1980—). Democrat. Mem. Ch. of Christ. Office: 520 NW 165th St Rd Suite 204 North Miami Beach FL 33169

THOMPSON, ARNOLD WILBUR, airport cons.; b. Chgo., Oct. 26, 1926; s. Oscar and Emma S. (Terkelsen) T.; student U. Wis., 1944, U. Ky., 1945; B.S. in Architecture, U. Ill., 1950; m. Marian Harding, Dec. 30, 1950; children—Keith Arnold, Bruce Windsor, Douglas Scott. Project planner U.S. Public Housing Adminstrn., Chgo., 1950-52; cons. Bldg. and Furnishings Service YMCA, Chgo., 1952-55; regional architect Am. Airlines, Chgo., 1955-60, chief architect, 1960-64; pres. Arnold Thompson Assos., Inc., N.Y.C., 1964-72; v.p. Lester B. Knight & Assos., Inc., Riverside, Conn., 1972-77; pres. Arnold W. Thompson, P.C., Airport Facilities Cons., Hawthorne, N.Y., 1978—; chmn. bd. Omnia Corp., Paoli, Ind. Mem. New Castle Bd. Zoning Appeals, 1977-79; mem. Chappaqua (N.Y.) Bd. Continuing Edn., 1980—; bd. dirs. Bethel Nursing Home Corp., 1974-78. Served with U.S. Army, 1944-46. Registered profl. architect, N.Y., Conn., Ill., N.C., Fla. Mem. AIA, ASCE, Am. Inst. Planners, Airport Cons. Council, Scarab. Congregationalist. Clubs: Wings (N.Y.C.); Whippoorwill (Armonk, N.Y.); Birchwood (Chappaqua). Office: Arnold W Thompson P C 316 Elwood Ave Hawthorne NY 10532

THOMPSON, CAROL GILBERT, bank examiner; b. Chgo., June 27, 1945; d. Jesse Douglas and Dorothy Mae (Daccardo) Gilbert; B.S., Ohio State U., 1969. Supr., New Orleans Credit Bur. Services, 1970; welfare visitor Arabi (La.) Dept. Pub. Welfare, 1970-71; asst. office mgr. Electric Vehicles Inc., Orlando, Fla., 1971-73; bank examiner FDIC, Orlando, 1973—. Mem. Am. Inst. Banking. Home: 1402 Carlson Dr Orlando FL 32804 Office: Suite 198 Tedder Bldg 988 Woodcock Rd Orlando FL 32803

THOMPSON, CHARLES FREDERICK (RICK), II, real estate devel., financial co. exec.; b. Tampa, Fla., Mar. 12, 1942; s. Robert Shaw and Peggy (McMichael) T.; B.A., Emory U., 1964; J.D., U. Fla., 1968; postgrad. Tech. Inst. Monterrey, Mex., 1960, Coll. William and Mary/Exeter U., Eng., 1967; m. Aase Bay Duelund, Dec. 29, 1968; children—Scott Christian, Grant McMichael. Asst. to chief exec. officer RIC Internat. Industries, 1968-69; securities atty. William J. Schifino, Tampa, 1969-71; owner, developer real estate projects, Central Fla. and Ala., 1971-74, Key West, Fla., 1975-77; exec. officer Thompson Group of Cos., Gainesville, Fla., 1977—. Mem. Fla. Bar Assn., Dade County Bar Assn., Hillsborough County Bar Assn., Fla. Real Estate Brokers, Alpha Tau Omega, Phi Delta Phi, Alpha Psi Omega. Democrat. Methodist. Clubs: Ye Mystic Krewe Gasparilla-Courtier, Merrymakers, Gainesville Golf and Country. Home: 610 NW 89th St Gainesville FL 32601 Office: 5200 Newberry Rd Suite D-7 Gainsville FL 32600

THOMPSON, CRAIG SNOVER, pub. relations exec.; b. Bklyn., May 24, 1932; s. Craig F. and Edith (Williams) T.; grad. Valley Forge Mil. Acad., 1951; B.A., Johns Hopkins, 1954; m. Masae Sugizaki, Feb. 21, 1957; children—Lee Anne, Jane Laura. Newspaper and radio reporter Easton (Pa.) Express, 1954-55, 57-59, Wall St. Jour., 1959-60; account exec. Moore, Meldrum & Assos., 1960; mgr. pub. relations Central Nat. Bank of Cleve., 1961-62; account exec. Edward Howard & Co., 1962-67, v.p., 1967-69, sr. v.p., 1969-71; dir. pub. relations White Motor Corp., Cleve., 1971-76; v.p. pub. relations No. Telecom, Inc., Nashville, 1976-77; v.p. pub. relations White Motor Corp., Farmington Hills, Mich., 1977-80, v.p. corp. communications, 1980—. Bd. dirs. Shaker Lakes Regional Nature Center, 1970-73. Served from 2d lt., inf., AUS, 1955-57. Mem. Pub. Relations Soc. Am. (accredited). Home: 42367 Westmeath Northville MI 48167 Office: 34500 Grand River Ave Farmington Hills MI 48024

THOMPSON, DALE MOORE, banker; b. Kansas City, Kans., Nov. 19, 1897; s. George Curl and Ruth Anna (Moore) T.; A.B. cum laude, U. Mich., 1920; m. Dorothy Allen Brown, July 2, 1921; 1 son, William Brown (dec.). Trainee, City Bank of Kansas City (Mo.) (now United Mo. Bank Kansas City, N.A.), 1920-22, asst. cashier, 1922-27, asst. v.p., 1927-30, v.p., 1930-34; v.p., dir. City Bond & Mortgage Co. (now United Mo. Mortgage Co.), Kansas City, 1934-43, exec. v.p., 1943-48, pres., 1948-68, chmn. bd., 1968-74, hon. chmn., 1974—; chmn., mng. trustee Central Mortgage & Realty Trust, 1972-76, chmn. emeritus, 1976—; lectr. Northwestern U. Sch. Mortgage Banking, also Stanford, 1954-62. Mem. Mo. Bd. Edn., 1966—, pres., 1968; trustee Mercy Hosp.; v.p., treas. Kansas City Gen. Hosp. and Med. Center, 1962-77; chmn. Kansas City campaign United Negro Coll. Fund, 1958-59; pres. Kansas City Philharmonic Assn., 1944-54; trustee U. Kansas City, Kansas City Philharmonic Assn., Conservatory Music Kansas City, Kansas City Art Inst. Served with USN, World War I. Recipient citation Kansas City C. of C., 1954, Archbishop's Community Service citation, 1954, Mayor's citation, 1955, citation NCCJ, 1965. Mem. Mortgage Bankers Assn. Am. (past 1st v.p., pres. 1962-63, gov. 1956—, mem. exec. com. 1960-67), U. Mich. Alumni Assn. (past dir.), Trigon, Phi Beta Kappa (pres. Kansas City 1946-49), Phi Kappa Psi. Mem. Christian Ch. Clubs: River, University, Indian Hills Country (Kansas City); Monterey Peninsula Country (Pebble Beach, Calif.). Home: 221 W 48th St Kansas City MO 64112 Office: United Mo Bank Bldg Kansas City MO 64106

THOMPSON, DAVID MAXWELL, mgmt. cons.; b. Lansing, Mich., Apr. 27, 1931; s. Maxwell H. and Mary Ialeem (Prochnow) T.; B.A., U. Windsor (Ont., Can.), 1954; m. Mary Helene Pendel, May 22, 1975; children—Kelly Ann, Christopher David, Peter Maxwell, Kevin Rourke. Dir. devel. U. Windsor, 1955-58; asst. dir. Am. Alumni Council, Washington, 1958-60; asst. to pres. The Brakeley Cos., Washington, 1960-61; v.p. Duquesne U., Pitts., 1961-63, Loyola U., Los Angeles, 1963-65; asst. to pres. Calif. State U., Los Angeles, 1965-66; v.p. Robert Johnson Co., Los Angeles, 1966-68; v.p., sec.-treas. Nat. Urban Coalition, Washington, 1968-71; partner Frantreb, Pray, Ferner and Thompson, Arlington, Va., 1971-76, Thompson and Pendel Assos., cons. to non-profit orgns., Arlington, 1976—. Served with U.S. Army, 1953-55. Mem. Council for Advancement and Support of Edn., Jesuit Program in Living and Learning (vice chmn.). Democrat. Roman Catholic. Address: 911 S 26th Pl Arlington VA 22202

THOMPSON, GORDON ELLEF, mgmt. cons.; b. Wautoma, Wis., May 15, 1933; s. Ellef N. and Florence A. (Gutreuter) T.; B.S., Marquette U., 1954; M.B.A., Harvard, 1961. Instr. fin., asst. dean Sch. Bus. Adminstrn., Georgetown U., Washington, 1961-63, Found. for Econ. Edn. fellow, 1963; cons. Checchi and Co., Washington, 1963-65; investment officer Internat. Fin. Corp., Washington, 1965-69; investment officer 1st Nat. City Overseas Investment Corp., N.Y.C., 1969-70; dir. ambulatory detoxification program N.Y.C. Dept. Health, 1971-73; pres. Lindland Assos., N.Y.C., 1974—. Served from ensign to lt. USN, 1955-59. Mem. Soc. Internat. Devel., Asia Soc., Arts and Bus. Council. Club: Harvard (N.Y.C.). Home: 127 E 69th St New York NY 10021 Office: 127 E 69th St New York NY 10021

THOMPSON, GROVE GEORGE, ret. real estate exec.; b. Lynbrook, N.Y., Jan. 18, 1915; s. Grove Gruen and Phebe Albertson (Merritt) T.; M. Engring., Stevens Inst. Tech., 1935; m. Grace Cecille Fitzgerald, July 25, 1942; children—Grove George, Sherwood Arthur, Curtis Richard. Asst. mgr. area devel. Pub. Service E & G Co., Newark, 1935-59; real estate mgr. Mack Trucks, Inc., Plainfield, N.J., 1959-62; exec. dir. Area Devel. City of Plainfield, 1962; mgr. real estate services Am. Standard Inc., N.Y.C., 1962-79. Served to capt. USNR, 1941-75. Recipient cert. Appreciation, USNR, 1973. Mem. Indsl. Devel. Research Council (pres. 1970-71, dir. 1961—), Northeastern Indsl. Developers Assn., Am. Econ. Devel. Council, Indsl. Real Estate Brokers of Met. N.Y., Internat. Oceanographic Found, U.S. Naval Inst., Ret. Officers Assn., Theta Xi, Pi Delta Epsilon. Quaker. Clubs: Racquets of Short Hills (N.J.), Country Club Assn. (v.p. 1973). Home: 704 Bay Cliffs Rd Gulf Breeze FL 32561

THOMPSON, HAROLD JOSEPH, mcht., real estate exec.; b. Lander, Wyo., Sept. 1, 1945; s. Kenneth Edward and Mildred Mary (Gray) T.; student Lander public schs.; m. Jolene Kolarich, Apr. 12, 1969; children—Andre Jason, Kenneth Russell. With Western Nuclear, Inc., 1969-72; owner, operator K-Bar, Inc., Jeffrey City, Wyo., 1972—, also pres. Red Desert Devel., 1978—. Mem. Jeffrey City Sch. Bd., 1975-78, chmn., 1978; mem. City Recreation Bd.; mem. Fremont County Sch. Reorgn. Bd., 1976-78. Served with U.S. Navy,

1965-67. Mem. Wyo. Liquor Dealers Assn., Hot Springs Rural Electric Assn. (dir.). Democrat. Roman Catholic. Home: Box 9 Jeffrey City WY 82310 Office: K Bar Inc 1st and D Sts Jeffrey City WY 82310

THOMPSON, HERBERT EARL, mech. engr.; b. Twin Falls, Idaho, July 23, 1926; s. Herbert Earl and Emma Amelia (Bruveleit) T.; B.S. in Mech. Engring., U. Colo., 1957; m. Jean Grace McCully, June 11, 1954; children—William Earl, Beverly Jean, Edward James. Project engr. IBM Corp., San Jose, Calif., 1957-69; dir. engring. Memorex Corp., Santa Clara, Calif., 1969-73, Shugart Assos., Inc., Sunnyvale, Calif., 1973-78; pres., engring. cons. H.E. Thompson, Inc., Los Gatos, Calif., 1978—; co-founder Shugart Assos., Inc. Troop com. Santa Clara council Boy Scouts Am., 1970-77. Served with USAC, 1945, USAF, 1947-54. Scholar U. Colo., 1946; recipient master design award Product Engring. Mag., 1965. Republican. Patentee in field. Home and Office: 17148 Mill Rise Way Los Gatos CA 95030

THOMPSON, HERBERT ERNEST, tool and die co. exec.; b. Jamaica, N.Y., Sept. 8, 1923; s. Walter and Louise (Joly) T.; student Stevens Inst. Tech., 1949-51; m. Patricia Elaine Osborn, Aug. 2, 1968; children—Robert Steven, Debra Lynn. Foreman, Conner Tool Co., 1961-62, Eason & Waller Grinding Corp., 1962-63; owner Endco Machined Products, 1966-67, Thompson Enterprises, 1974—; pres. Method Machined Products, Phoenix, 1967—; pres., owner Quality Tool, Inc., 1967—. Served to capt. USAAF, 1942-46. Decorated D.F.C., Air medal with cluster. Home: 14009 N 42d Ave Phoenix AZ 85023 Office: 4223 W Clarendon Ave Phoenix AZ 85019

THOMPSON, JAMES HOMER, ins. exec.; b. Henrietta, Tex., Sept. 11, 1926; s. James Hite and Virginia (Marberry) T.; student U. Okla., 1944-45; Ph.B., U. Chgo., 1947, M.B.A. in Fin., 1950; m. Ilene Kriss, Mar. 15, 1979; 1957; children by previous marriage—Julie A., Laurie J. Dist. sales mgr. Studebaker Corp., South Bend, Ind., 1951-55; asso. gen. agt. State Mut. Life Assurance Co. Am., Denver, 1955—; instr. U. Colo. 1964—. Mem. nat. cabinet U. Chgo., 1969—; bd. dirs. Denver Adult Edn. Council, 1976—. C.L.U., C.P.C.U., registered health underwriter. Mem. C.L.U. (v.p. Rocky Mountain 1967, pres. 1968-69, mem. nat. inst. bd. 1969-72, nat. dir. 1972—), Denver Assn. Life Underwriters (dir. 1963-66). Home: 180 Ivanhoe Denver CO 80220 Office: 252 Clayton Denver CO 80206

THOMPSON, JAMES MILTON, mfg. cons. co. exec.; b. Cambridge, Mass., Dec. 19, 1944; s. Milton Alvin and Elizabeth Jane (Alleyne) T.; B.A., Lawrence U., Appleton, Wis., 1966; M.B.A. (univ. fellow), Washington U., St. Louis, 1969; div. Accountant, Shell Oil Co., Chgo., 1966-67; mktg. rep. IBM Corp., St. Louis, 1969-74; exec. v.p. William Savage & Assos., Inc., St. Louis, 1974—; guest lectr. Washington U. Grad. Sch. Bus.; seminar speaker. Fellow Am. Prodn. and Inventory Control Soc. (pres. St. Louis chpt. 1978-80), Delta Sigma Pi, Beta Theta Pi. Republican. Congregationalist. Author articles in field. Home: 326 N Euclid Saint Louis MO 63108 Office: 1865 Mason Rd Saint Louis MO 63131

THOMPSON, JERE WILLIAM, retail food and dairy co. exec.; b. Dallas, Jan. 18, 1932; s. Joe C. and Margaret (Philp) T.; grad. high sch., 1950; B.B.A., U. Tex., 1954; m. Peggy Dunlap, June 5, 1954; children—Michael, Jere W., Patrick, Deborah, Kimberly, Christopher, David. With Southland Corp., Dallas, 1954—, v.p. stores, 1962-73, exec. v.p., 1973-74, pres., 1974—, dir., 1962—; dir. Merc. Nat. Bank at Dallas, Jack Eckerd Corp., United Fidelity Life Ins. Co. Bd. dirs. St. Paul Hosp. Endowment Fund. Served to lt (j.g.) USNR, 1954-56. Home: 4217 Armstrong Pkwy Dallas TX 75205 Office: 2828 N Haskell Ave Dallas TX 75204

THOMPSON, JOHN CLIFFORD, accountant; b. Pitts., Oct. 6, 1949; s. Kenneth Eugene and Dorothy Mae (Hamilton) T.; student U. Ariz., 1967-69; B.A., Westminster Coll., 1976; postgrad. U. Detroit, 1977—; m. Barbara Louise Goettle, Nov. 18, 1972; children—Julie, Joel. Accountant, Arthur Andersen & Co., Detroit, 1976; cost analyst Rockwell Internat., Troy, Mich., 1976-77, sr. analyst, 1977, pricing supr., 1978-79, staff mfg. engr. truck axle div., 1979, gen. mfg. supr., 1979—. Advisor, Jr. Achievement; mem. Indsl. Commn., Rockwood, Mich. Mem. Soc. Automotive Engrs., Nat. Assn. Accountants, Omicron Delta Epsilon. Republican. Presbyterian. Club: Masons. Home: 444 La Salle Dr Winchester KY 40391 Office: 708 Rockwell Rd Winchester KY 40391

THOMPSON, JOHN P., retail food co. exec.; b. Dallas, Nov. 2, 1925; s. Joe E. and Margaret (Philp) T.; B.B.A., U. Tex., 1948; m. Mary Carol Thomson, June 5, 1948; children—Mary Margaret, Henry Douglas, John P. With Southland Corp., 1948—, pres., 1961-69, chmn. bd., chief exec. officer, 1969—. Office: 2828 N Haskell Ave Dallas TX 75221*

THOMPSON, JOHN ROBERT, bank exec.; b. Denver, Mar. 24, 1936; s. Samual Henry and Corrinne Iris (Stearns) T.; B.S. in Fin. and Mktg., U. Colo., 1958; postgrad. Ind. U., 1958-59, N.Y. Inst. Fin., 1961, U. Calif. at Berkeley, 1963; m. Joan Marion Hutton, Oct. 10, 1957; children—Steven H., Tracy L. Asst. investment officer, security analyst Bank of Calif., San Francisco, 1963-67; v.p., dir. research Julian D. Weiss and Assos., Los Angeles, 1967-69, exec. v.p., 1969-71; v.p. trust investment officer, mgr. trust investment and investment mgmt. services dept. Lloyds Bank Calif., Los Angeles, 1972—. Bd. dirs. Marin County br. Am. Cancer Soc., 1963, 64. Served with U.S. Army, 1959-61. Chartered fin. analyst. Mem. Calif. Bankers Assn. (com. trust investments 1975—, chmn. 1980—), Los Angeles Soc. Fin. Analysts, Inst. Chartered Fin. Analysts, Fin. Analysts Fedn. Republican. Congregationalist. Club: Los Angeles Athletic. Editorial adv. panel Pensions and Investments Jour., 1975—. Home: 11745 Woodley Ave Granada Hills CA 91344 Office: 612 S Flower Los Angeles CA 90017

THOMPSON, JOHN SILVEY, JR., banker, bus. exec.; b. Upland, Pa., Feb. 20, 1935; s. John Silvey and Ruth Anna (Dutton) T.; B.S.E., Princeton, 1957; postgrad. Claremont U., 1961-62, Aspen Inst., 1976; children—John Silvey III, Robin John Christopher, Michael John Stuart. Mgmt. trainee Union Carbide Corp., 1957-59; Western region mgr. Avisun Corp., Phila. and Los Angeles, 1959-63; asso. McKinsey & Co., N.Y.C., Los Angeles, London and Amsterdam, 1963-67; v.p., gen. mgr. Sealed Air Corp., N.Y.C. and Los Angeles, 1968-69; asst. to chmn., dir. adminstrn. Transamerica Corp., San Francisco, 1969-74, also pres. Transamerica Research Corp., Pyramid Investment Corp.; sr. v.p., planning officer Crocker Nat. Bank, San Francisco, 1974—. Former bd. assos. Golden Gate U.; trustee West Coast Cancer Found., San Francisco; chmn. basic engring. council Princeton U. Served with U.S. Army, 1957-58. Republican. Episcopalian. Clubs: Princeton, Union League (Phila.); First Phila City Troop Cavalry; Ivy (Princeton). Office: Crocker Nat Bank One Montgomery St San Francisco CA 94104

THOMPSON, LAWRENCE, promotion exec.; b. Boston, Dec. 29, 1946; s. Earl F. and G. Eleanor (Lawrence) T.; student in bus. adminstrn. and electronics engring. N.Y.C. Community Coll., 1975-77. Disc jockey New Faces, J. Murray Yonkers Roller Disco, La Higuana, El Lobo, N.Y.C., 1972-76; co-founder, treas. Bklyn. Mobile Jocks Assn., 1976-79, v.p. record co. communications, 1977-79; adminstrv. asst. to pres. After Hours Promotions, N.Y.C., 1978-80; nat. dir. promotion Versatile Records Ltd., N.Y.C., 1980—; pres. The Funky Mind, N.Y.C., 1973—; promotion cons. clubs and discos. Home: 343 Ashford St Brooklyn NY 11207 Office: 517 W 151st St New York NY 10036

THOMPSON, LEE BENNETT, lawyer, bus. exec.; b. Miami, Indian Ter., Mar. 2, 1902; s. P.C. and Margerie Constance (Jackson) T.; B.A., U. Okla., 1925, LL.B., 1927; m. Elaine Bizzell, Nov. 27, 1928; children—Lee Bennett, Ralph Gordon, Carolyn Elaine. Admitted to Okla. bar, 1927, since practiced in Oklahoma City; sec., gen. counsel, dir. Mustang Fuel Corp.; spl. justice Okla. Supreme Ct., 1967-68. Former mem. bd. dirs. Oklahoma County Tb Assn., Inc.; former sec. Masonic Charity Found. Okla.; chmn. Okla. Co. chpt. ARC, 2 terms, chmn. resolutions com., nat. conv., 1953; past dir. Community Fund, Symphony Orch., Oklahoma City. Served from capt. to col. AUS, 1940-46. Decorated 5 campaign stars, Legion of Merit; recipient Distinguished Service citation U. Okla., 1971. Fellow Am. Bar Found. (past state chmn.), Am. Coll. Trial Lawyers (former state chmn.); mem. Oklahoma City (past dir.), Oklahoma City Jr. (past pres.), U.S., Jr. (past dir., v.p.) chambers commerce, Am. (ho. of dels. 1971-72, spl. com. fed. rules procedure, standing com. on law and nat. security), Okla. (past mem. ho. dels., pres. 1972), Oklahoma County (past pres.) bar assns., Okla. Bar Found. (trustee 1973-79), U. Okla. Alumni Assn. (past exec. com.), U. Okla. Meml. Student Union (pres.), Am. Legion, Beta Theta Pi (past v.p., trustee), Phi Beta Kappa. Democrat. Mem. Christian Ch. (past deacon and elder). Clubs: Masons (33 deg.), Shriners, Jesters, Seventy Five, Rotary (past pres.), Men's Dinner (past exec. com.), Beacon, Oklahoma City Golf and Country; Univ. (Norman, Okla.). Home: 539 NW 38th St Oklahoma City OK 73118 Office: 2120 First Nat Bldg Oklahoma City OK 73102

THOMPSON, LOHREN MATTHEW, oil co. exec.; b. Sutherland, Nebr., Jan. 21, 1926; s. John M. and Anna (Ecklund) T.; student U. Denver; m. Ruth A. Stammer, Jan. 2, 1959; children—Terrence M., Sheila M., Clark M. Spl. rep. Standard Oil Co., Omaha, 1948-56; gen. sales mgr. Frontier Refining Co., Denver, 1956-68, v.p. mktg., 1967-68 mgr. mktg. U.S. region Husky Oil Co., Denver, 1968-72; pres. Colo. Petroleum Products Co., Denver, 1972—. Vice pres. Westar Stas., Inc., Denver, 1967-71. Served with USAAF, 1944-46. Mem. Denver Petroleum Club, Colo. Petroleum Council, Denver Oilman's Club, Am. Legion. Democrat. Lutheran. Lion. Home: 10161 Melody Dr North Glenn CO 80221 Office: 4080 Globeville Rd Denver CO 80216

THOMPSON, RALPH NEWELL, chem. co. exec.; b. Boston, Mar. 4, 1918; s. Ralph and Lillian (Davenport) T.; B.S., Mass. Inst. Tech., 1940; m. Virginia Kenniston, Jan. 31, 1942; children—Pamela, Nicholas, Diana. Research engr. Middlesex Products Corp., Cambridge, Mass., 1940-42; tech. dir. Falulah Paper Co., Fitchburg, Mass., 1945-48; staff engr. Calgon div. Hagan Corp., Pitts., 1948-54, research mgr. Calgon div., 1954-58; mgr. chem. research and devel. Hagan Chems. & Controls, Inc., Pitts., 1958-63; dir. research and engring. Calgon Corp. (successor co.), 1963-67, v.p., 1967-70; mgr. corporate devel. Pa. Indsl. Chem. Corp., Clairton, 1970-71, v.p. corporate devel., 1971-74; gen. mgr. chem. div. Thiokol Corp., Trenton, N.J., 1974-76, group v.p., Newtown, Pa., 1976—; dir. Mulford Co., Inc. (Boston), Thiokol (Can.) Ltd., Thiokol Chems. Ltd. (Eng.), Toray-Thiokol Ltd. (Japan), Nisso-Ventron K.K. (Japan), S.W. Chem. Services Inc. (Tex.), S.W. Plastics Europe, S.A. (Belgium), Dynachem Corp. (Calif.), Dynachem Deutschland GmbH (W. Ger.), Thiokol Photochems., N.V. (Belgium), Carstab Corp. (Ohio). Mem. Mt. Lebanon Civic League, 1950-73. Served from ensign to lt., USNR, 1942-45; now lt. comdr. Res. (ret.). Recipient medal in chemistry Goodreau Meml. Fund, 1936. Fellow Am. Inst. Chemists; mem. TAPPI, N.Y. Acad. Scis., Soc. Chem. Industry, Soc. Rheology, AIM, Mil. Order World Wars, Pa. Soc. Presbyterian. Home: 1006 Lehigh Dr Yardley PA 19067 Office: Yardley-Newtown Rd PO Box 1000 Newtown PA 18940

THOMPSON, ROBERT HICKMAN, food co. exec.; b. Dyer County, Tenn., Nov. 11, 1920; s. Lemuel Herbert and Mary Elizabeth T.; student U. Pa., Northwestern U.; m. Miriam Ebling, May 2, 1942; children—Estella, Robert Hickman. With Campbell Soup Co., 1942—, dir. corporate planning, 1970-76; v.p., controller, asst. sec. subs. Pepperidge Farms, Inc., Norwalk, Conn., 1976-79; controller div. ops. Campbell Soup Co., Camden, N.J., 1979—. Mem. Planning Execs. Inst., Nat. Accountants Assn. Home: 201 Hickory Ln Moorestown NJ 08057 Office: Campbell Soup Co Camden NJ 08101

THOMPSON, ROY STEELE, JR., ins. co. exec.; b. Bluefield, W.Va., Dec. 19, 1917; s. Roy Steele and Trula Belle (Kiser) T.; B.S. in Commerce, Washington & Lee U., 1939; m. Virginia Marshall Lewis, Apr. 11, 1942; children—Scott G., Gregory S., Mark W., Philip M. Pres., Am. So. Ins. Co., Atlanta, 1952-78, chmn., 1978—; pres., owner Rate-o-Gram, Inc., Francesca, Inc., Thompson Ins. Enterprises, Inc.; dir. Flat Top Ins. Agy., W.Va., Ky., Va., Tenn., Ohio; mem. Lloyd's of London. Trustee Pace Acad.; bd. dirs. So. Council Internat. and Pub. Affairs. Served to lt. comdr. USNR, 1941-46. Mem. Commerce Club. Republican. Methodist. Club: Capital City. Home: 3438 Rilman Rd NW Atlanta GA 30327 Office: 2045 Peachtree Rd NE Atlanta GA 30309

THOMPSON, SIDNEY ORVILLE, ins. co. exec.; b. Leonard, N.D., Mar. 20, 1920; s. Sabien Oliver and Anna (Benson) T.; jr. coll. degree State Sch. Sci., Wahpeton, N.D., 1939; B.C.S., Benjamin Franklin U., Washington, 1949; m. Mercedes Huppeler, Apr. 14, 1941; children—Pamela Gene, Gretchen Marie, Craig Sidney. With Internal Revenue Service, 1940-42, 45-50; mgr. pension dept. New Eng. Life Ins. Co., N.Y.C., 1950-61, treas. Leaders Assn., Boston, 1959; v.p., treas. Langson Corp., N.Y.C., 1960—; pres. Thompson Pension Employee Plans, N.Y.C., 1964—; asso. gen. agt. New Eng. Life Ins. Co.; organizer, chmn. bd. Hudson Valley Nat. Bank, Yonkers, N.Y.; lectr. pension and profit sharing systems Purdue U., 1953, 54, U. Conn., 1961, U. P.R., 1961, U. N.H., 1962. Active local Community Chest, ARC; trustee Dominican Sisters of Sick Poor, Ossining, N.Y., St. Joseph Hosp., Yonkers, N.Y. Served to chief petty officer USNR, 1941-45; PTO. Mem. Leaders Assn. Boston (pres. 1963). Clubs: Union League (N.Y.C.); Winged Foot Country (Mamaroneck, N.Y.); Goodyear Golf and Country (Litchfield, Ariz.); Wigwam Country (Litchfield Park, Ariz.); Adirondack League (Old Forge, N.Y.); Camp Fire of Am. Contbr. to ins. publs. Home: Route 1 Box 54 S Bedford Rd Pound Ridge NY 10576

THOMPSON, STEVE D., broadcasting exec.; b. Cin., Nov. 1, 1949; s. Max B. and Lenore E. (Whitehead) T.; student Pierce Jr. Coll., Woodland Hills, Calif., 1969; diploma Don Martin Sch. Radio and TV, Hollywood, Calif., 1970; m. Colleen H. McClure, Nov. 21, 1971; children—Kelly S., Alexa L. Sales rep. sta. KIAK, Fairbanks, Alaska, 1972-78; TV engr. staf. KTVF, Fairbanks, 1972-73; gen. mgr. sta. KBRW, Barrow, Alaska, 1979—; bd. dirs. Alaska Public Radio Network, 1979. Served with U.S. Army, 1971-73. Mem. Alaska Broadcasters Assn. (dir.), Alaska Public Broadcasting Commn. Home: Box 33 Barrow AK 99723 Office: Box 109 Barrow AK 99723

THOMPSON, VICTOR MONTGOMERY, JR., banker; b. Thomas, Okla., Nov. 12, 1924; s. Victor Montgomery and Helen S. (Sanders) T.; B.S., U. Okla., 1948; m. Betty J. McNeill, July 3, 1946; children—Victor Bruce, Robert, J., Jean Ann. Vice pres. Am. State Bank, Thomas, 1948-57; pres., chief exec. officer First Nat. Bank & Trust Co., Stillwater, Okla., 1957-72, vice-chmn., 1972-77; chmn., chief exec. officer Utica Nat. Bank & Trust Co., Tulsa, 1970—, also dir.; dir. Sooner Life Ins. Co., Oklahoma City br. Fed. Res. Bank. Pres., Stillwater Indsl. Found., 1964-65, Payne County Indsl. Found., 1967-70, YMCA, Stillwater, 1967-70; vice chmn. Okla. State U. Edn. and Research Found., 1971—; bd. govs. Okla. State U. Devel. Found.; bd. dirs. Higher Edn. Alumni Council Okla., Met. Tulsa YMCA, Tulsa Psychiat. Center, St. John's Hosp., Gilcrease Inst. Am. History, Hillcrest Hosp., Tulsa, Philbrook Art Center, Tulsa Bi-centennial Commn., Tulsa Airport Authority 1978—, Salvation Army, 1979—; trustee Children's Med. Center. Served with USMCR, 1942-46. Mem. Okla. Bankers Assn. (exec. council 1954-55, 61-62, dir. 1978—), Met. Tulsa (dir. 1971—, v.p. 1976—), Stillwater (pres. 1961-62) chambers commerce, Sigma Delta Pi, Am. Legion. Baptist (deacon 1972—). Clubs: Southern Hills Country, Tulsa, Summit (Tulsa), Masons. Home: 2736 E 69th Pl Tulsa OK 74136 Office: PO Box 1559 Tulsa OK 74101

THOMPSON, WALTER WILLIAM, bond salesman; b. S.I., N.Y., June 29, 1927; s. Walter Harold and Rose Veronica (Dugan) T.; B.S. magna cum laude, Wagner Coll., 1950; m. Margaret Ellen Coulson, Mar. 5, 1956; 1 dau., Kathleen. Commd. officer USAF, 1951, advanced through grades to lt. col., 1967, ret., 1970; govt. bond salesman Merrill Lynch Pierce Fenner & Smith, Salt Lake City, 1970-73; staff Blythe, Eastman & Dillon, Salt Lake City, 1973-74, v.p., office mgr., 1974; v.p., mgr. Dean Witter & Co., Spokane, Wash., 1974; sr. govt. bond specialist Merrill Lynch Pierce Fenner & Smith, Seattle, 1975-76; v.p. sales Bache & Co., Seattle, 1976, sr. govt. bond specialist Loeb Rhodes Hornblower, Phoenix, 1976—; treas. Creative Realty, Salt Lake City, 1974—; sec.-treas. M & W Indsl. Enterprises, Salt Lake City, 1974—; pres., chmn. Thompson Fin. Cons., 1978—; apptd. to Com. to Amend the Investment Laws, Utah, 1973, Airz., 1979. Republican. Roman Catholic. Home: 8667 Via del Palacio Scottsdale AZ 85258 Office: 8667 Via del Palacio Scottsdale AZ 85258

THOMPSON, WAYNE DOUGLAS, real estate broker; b. Roanoke, Va., July 8, 1944; s. Curtis and Ellen (Fogle) T.; student public schs., Roanoke; m. Marzetta Hunt, Sept. 23, 1963; 1 son, Wayne Douglas. Police officer, Salem, Va., 1963-64; asst. supt. Walker Machine & Foundry, Roanoke, 1964-68; agt. Perry Realty Co., Roanoke, 1968-70; v.p. Hite-Thompson Realtors, Roanoke, 1970-72; sales mgr., sec., treas. Davis, Cox & Thompson, Vinton, Va., 1972-74; pres., real estate broker W.D. Thompson Realty Co., Inc., Roanoke, 1974—. Mem. Nat., Va. home builders assns., Roanoke Valley Bd. Realtors, Nat., Va. realtors assns. Republican. Morman. Home: 5048 Cherokee Hills Dr Salem VA 24153 Office: 4137 Brandon Ave SW Roanoke VA 24018

THOMPSON, WILLIAM ALBERT, JR., cons. co. exec.; b. Bluefield, W.Va., June 9, 1930; s. William Albert and Mary (Draper) T.; B.S. in Civil Engring., Va. Mil. Inst., 1952; m. Betty Presley Atkins, Aug. 1, 1952; children—William Albert, James Carroll, Robert Ryland. Founder, prin. Thompson & Litton, Inc., Wise, Va., 1956—, pres., 1956—; dir. First Nat. Exchange Bank, St. Paul, Va. Chmn. adv. bd. Sch. of Mine Mgmt. Clinch Valley Coll., Wise; chmn. bd. trustees Eads Pension Trust, St. Louis. Served to 1st lt. USAF, 1952-55. Registered profl. engr., Md., D.C., Va., N.C., W.Va., Ky., N.J., Tenn., Fla.; registered land surveyor, Ky. Fellow ASCE. Engrs.; mem. Nat. Soc. Profl. Engrs. Presbyterian. Home: 128 Orchard Ln Wise VA 24293 Office: PO Box 1307 Wise VA 24293

THOMPSON, WILLIAM MITCHELL, JR., banker; b. Bridgeton, N.J., July 21, 1940; s. William Mitchell and Ethel Jean (Smith) T.; B.A., Stetson U., 1963; m. Shirley Jane Pomeroy, Jan. 20, 1968; children—Huntleigh Carol. Mem. personnel staff Boeing Co., Cocoa Beach, Fla., 1966-68, Schlumberger Co., Sarasota, Fla. and Houston, 1968-72; dir. personnel Palmer Bank Corp., Sarasota, 1972-76; sr. v.p. personnel Flagship Banks Inc., Tampa, 1976—; tchr. U. South Fla., Fla. Bankers Assn. Supervision Acad. Campaign mgr., county commr., 1970; asst. campaign mgr. Pres. Ford, Sarasota County. Served to 1st. lt. U.S. Army, 1964-65. Mem. Stetson U. Alumni Assn. (dir. 1976), Sarasota Personnel Assn. (pres.), Am. Soc. Personnel Adminstrn., Fla. Bankers Assn., Delta Sigma Phi. Republican. Presbyterian. Clubs: St. Petersburg Racquet, Commerce Tampa. Author: Supervision, 1977. Home: 3330 Maple St NE St Petersburg FL 33704 Office: Box 3303 Madison and Franklin Sts Tampa FL 33601

THOMPSON, WILLIS HERBERT, JR., oil co. exec.; b. Mpls., Apr. 19, 1934; s. Willis Herbert and Wilma (Brookshire) T.; B.A. in Geology, U. Minn., 1956, M.S., 1959; m. Byrdie A. Herring, Feb. 23, 1968; children—Barbara, Nancy, Kim, Roger, Michael. Exploration geologist, geophysicist Standard Oil Co. Tex., Midland, Houston, 1959-64; with Signal Oil and Gas Co., 1964-73, mgr. internat. exploration, 1970-71, sr. v.p., 1970-71, exec. v.p., chief operating officer, 1971-72, pres., 1972-74, chief exec. officer, 1973-74, dir., 1970-74, dir. subs., 1972-74, pres., chief exec. officer Burmah Oil and Gas Co., 1974-76; v.p., dir. Burmah Oil, Inc., N.Y.C., 1974-76; pres., chief exec. officer Aminoil U.S.A., Inc., 1976; pres., chief operating officer MAPCO, Inc., Tulsa, 1976—, chief exec. officer, dir., 1980—; dir. 1st Nat. Bank of Tulsa, 1st Nat. Bancorp. Bd. dirs. Tulsa YMCA, Tulsa Philharmonic, Salvation Army, St. John's Med. Center. Served with C.E., U.S. Army, 1956-57. Mem. Am. Petroleum Inst. (dir.), Ind. Petroleum Assn. Am. (dir.), Okla. Petroleum Council (dir.), Am. Assn. Petroleum Geologists, Tex. Mid-Continent Oil and Gas Assn. (dir.), Tulsa Geol. Soc., Young Pres.'s Orgn. Republican. Presbyterian. Clubs: Tulsa, So. Hills Country (Tulsa). Office: Mapco Inc 1800 S Baltimore Ave Tulsa OK 74119*

THOMPSON, WINSTON PAGE, accountant; b. Jamaica, W.I., Sept. 19, 1949; s. Reuben and Adina T.; B.Sc., St. Francis Coll., 1976; M.B.A., Pace U., 1979; m. Clare Pinnock, June 12, 1976; 1 son, Mark. Sr. acct. Arthur Andersen & Co., N.Y.C., 1976—. C.P.A., N.Y. Mem. Nat. Assn. Black Accts., Am. Inst. C.P.A.'s. Home: 5413 Kingshwy Apt C-5 Brooklyn NY 11203 Office: 1345 Ave of Americas New York NY 10019

THOMSON, ARTHUR CHASE, livestock sales exec.; b. Girard, Kans., Oct. 11, 1908; s. Charles James and Nell Elizabeth (Gemmel) T.; B.S., Kans. State U., 1933; m. Emma Anna Hatesohl, June 18, 1935; children—Marita Thomson Knief, Gordon. Mem. editorial staff Hoards Dairyman, 1938-41; pres. Thomson-Knief Sales Service, Burlington, Ill., 1956—; export coordinator U.S. Holstein Services. Recipient Presdl. E for export service, 1974. Mem. Holstein Friesian Assn. Am. (past pres.), Ill. Holstein Assn. (past pres.), Chicagoland Angus Assn. (past v.p.). Club: Burlington Lions. Home: Box 306 Burlington IL 60109

THOMSON, DOUGLAS, trade assn. exec.; b. N.Y.C., Sept. 24, 1924; s. Alexander Gordon and Katherine (Constintine) T.; A.B., Dartmouth Coll., 1949, M.C.S., Amos Tuck Sch. Bus. Adminstrn., 1950; P.M.D., Harvard U. Sch. Bus. Adminstrn., 1966; m. Betty Culver, Dec. 29, 1951; children—Brooke Culver, Alexander Gordon. With U.S. Rubber/UniRoyal, 1950-78, v.p. mfg., Naugatuck, Conn.,

1972-75, divisional pres., Middlebury, Conn., 1975-78, corp. v.p., Middlebury, 1975-78; pres. Toy Mfrs. Am., N.Y.C., 1978—. Exec.-on-Loan to Pres. Carter's Reorgn. Project, 1978—; pres. ARC, Naugatuck, 1954-55, United Way, Thomson, Ga., 1963-65; mem. Woodbury (Conn.) Hist. Commn., 1967-70. Served with USMC, 1943-46; PTO. Republican. Congregationalist. Clubs: Dartmouth (N.Y.C.); Dartmouth (Conn.) (pres. 1955-59), Country of Waterbury; Univ. (Washington); Belle Meade Country (Thomson, Ga.). Office: 200 Fifth Ave New York NY 10010

THOMSON, RICHARD M., banker; b. Winnipeg, Can., Aug. 14, 1933; s. H.W. and Mary T.; B.A.Sc. in Engring., U. Toronto, 1955; M.B.A., Harvard, 1957; fellow course banking, Queen's U., 1958; m. Heather Lorimer; children—Robin, Elizabeth, Mary Dawn, Richard. With Toronto Dominion Bank, 1957—, sr. asst. mgr., St. James and McGill, Montreal, 1961, asst. to pres., head office, 1963, chief gen. mgr., 1968, v.p., chief gen. mgr. and dir., 1971, pres., 1972, pres., chief exec. officer, 1977, chmn. bd., chief exec. officer, 1978; dir. Can. Gypsum Co. Ltd., Toronto-Dominion Bank, Eaton's of Can., S.C. Johnson & Son, Ltd., Texasgulf, Inc., Union Carbide Can., Cadillac Fairview Corp. Ltd., Prudential Ins. Co. Am., Midland & Internat. Banks Ltd. Trustee Hosp. for Sick Children. Office: Toronto Dominion Bank PO Box 1 Toronto Dominion Center Toronto ON M5K 1A2 Canada

THOMSON, WILLIAM HENRY, ins. co. exec.; b. Toronto, Ont., Can., Mar. 27, 1933; s. William Murray and Helen Margaret (Davis) T.; B.B.A., U. Western Ont., 1957; m. Helen P. Morrison, Dec. 19, 1959; children—William D., Susan J., M. Peter. Br. mgr. data processing IBM Can., Ltd., London, Ont., 1957-68; info. systems exec. London Life Ins. Co., 1969-78; sr. v.p. Am. Bankers Ins. Group, Miami, Fla., 1978—; dir. MCM Computers Ltd., SDF Assos. Pres., United Way of Greater London, 1976-77. Mem. Canadian Assn. Data Processing Service Assn., Life Office Mgmt. Assn. (systems and ops. council). Episcopalian. Clubs: London, Doral Country. Home: 7731 SW 131 St Miami FL 33156 Office: 600 Brickell Ave Miami FL 33131

THORNDIKE, WILLIAM NICHOLAS, investment mgmt. co. exec.; b. Boston, Mar. 28, 1933; s. Augustus and Olivia L.; grad. Phillips Acad., 1951; A.B., Harvard U., 1955; m. Joan Ingram, July 29, 1961; children—William Nicholas, Alexander Lowell. With Seattle Trust and Savs. Bank, 1956-57; with Fidelity Mgmt. and Research, Boston, 1957-60; with Wellington Mgmt. Co./Thorndike, Doran, Paine & Lewis, Boston, 1960—, chmn. bd. dirs., 1960—; trustee Provident Instn. for Savs. Trustee, Mass. Gen. Hosp., 1969—; Jackson Lab., 1975—; Marine Biol. Lab., 1977—; asso. trustee New Eng. Conservatory of Music, 1970—. Mem. Boston Security Analysts Soc. Office: 28 State St Boston MA 02109

THORNE, FRANCIS XAVIER, real estate broker, builder; b. Hays, Kans., Dec. 20, 1925; s. Francis Xavier and Blanche M. (Gabriel) T.; B.S. in Bus. Adminstrn., Rockhurst Coll., 1949; student U. Minn., 1944-46; m. Kathleen Marie Keller, Feb. 11, 1950; children—Mary, Beverly, Christine, Frank Xavier III, Mark, Joseph, Teresa, Anne, Rosemary, Catherine. Real estate broker, Leavenworth County, Kans., 1973—; owner, operator Francis X. Thorne Realty, Lansing, Kans. and Leavenworth, Kans., 1974-75; founder Del. Land Devel., Inc., 1977—, Xavier Custom Homes, Inc., 1979—. Served to lt. (j.g.) USNR, 1946-50. Cert. residential broker Nat. Assn. Realtors; mem. Inst. Residential Mktg.; named Boss of Year Am. Bus. Women's Assn., 1977. Mem. Nat. Assn. Realtors, Nat. Assn. Real Estate Appraisers, Kans. Assn. Realtors, Levenworth County Bd. Realtors, Kansas City Home Builders Assn., Sales and Mktg. Council, Inst. Residential Mktg., Home Builders Assn. Am., Leavenworth C. of C. (dir. 1980), Lansing Planning Commn. Democrat. Roman Catholic. Clubs: K.C., Eagles, Kiwanis. Home: Box 117H Rural Route 2 Leavenworth KS 66048 Office: 100 Highland Rd Lansing KS 66043

THORNHILL, WILLIAM THOMAS, acctg. co. exec.; b. Washington, Oct. 14, 1926; s. William Joseph and Gartha Fay (Duncan) T.; student Md. U., 1947; B.C.S., Strayer Coll., 1949, M.C.S., 1950; student Am. U., 1950-51, Richmond U., 1961; m. Janet Marie Eustace, Nov. 23, 1957 (div.); children—Thomas, William, Karen Marie; m. 2d, Barbara Jean Allen, Dec. 20, 1969 (div.); m. 3d, Rosemary T. Di Costanzo, Mar. 6, 1976. Sr. auditor Ernst & Ernst, Balt. and Washington, 1950-53; fgn. supervisory auditor Standard-Vacuum Oil Co., White Plains, N.Y., 1953-60; mgmt. trainee Bank Va., Richmond, Va., 1960-61; audit supr. C.I.T. Financial Corp., N.Y.C., 1961-62; v.p. U.S. Indsl. Corp. and U.S. Indsl. Leasing Corp. subsidiaries U.S. Industries, Inc., N.Y.C., 1962-63, asst. controller U.S. Industries, Inc., 1963-65, gen. mgr. 6 Continents Travel Service subsidiary, 1964-65; exec. controller Central Charge Service, Inc., Washington, 1965-67, treas., asst. sec., 1966-67; asst. v.p. First Nat. Bank, Chgo., 1967-70, v.p., 1970-79; mgr. profl. edn. div. Arthur Andersen & Co., St. Charles, Ill., 1980—. Served with AUS, 1944-46. Mem. Fin. Mgrs. Soc. Savs. Instns., Am. Accounting Assn., Am. Mgmt. Assn. (past mem. finance planning council), Nat. Assn. Accountants, Inst. Internal Auditors, Assn. Systems Mgmt., Am. Legion, Phi Theta Pi. Frequent speaker and writer on bus. mgmt. Home: 220 Pine Crest Circle Barrington IL 60010 Office: Saint Charles IL

THORNTON, CHARLES BATES, diversified mfg. exec.; b. Knox County, Tex., July 22, 1913; s. W.A. and Alice (Bates) T.; B.C.S. Columbus U., 1937; LL.D., Tex. Tech. Coll., 1957, U. So. Calif. Pepperdine U., 1971; D.C.S. (hon.), George Washington U., 1964; m. Flora Laney, Apr. 10, 1937; children—Charles Bates, William Laney. Dir. planning Ford Motor Co., 1946-48; v.p., asst. gen. mgr. Hughes Aircraft Co., Culver City, Calif., 1948-53; v.p. Hughes Tool Co., 1948-53; pres. Litton Industries, Inc., 1953-61, chmn. bd., chief exec. officer, 1953—; dir., mem. fin. com. Trans World Airlines, Inc.; dir. Western Bancorp., MCA, Inc., United Calif. Bank; cons. in field. Mem. Bus. Council, Emergency Com. for Am. Trade, Internat. Bus. Adv. Com. to Sec. Commerce, nat. execs. com. Nat. Council on Crime and Delinquency; co-vice chmn. U.S. Internat. Transp. Expn. Com.; vice chmn. United Crusade Campaign. Nat. bd. dirs. Jr. Achievement; bd. dirs. So. Calif. Visitors Council; pres. Los Angeles World Affairs Council; nat. adv. council Religious Heritage Am.; life trustee U. So. Calif.; mem. Headmaster's Council Harvard Sch.; mem. U. Calif. Assos. Served as col. USAAF, World War II; cons. to comdg. gen. AAF, 1946, to undersec. Dept. State, 1947. Decorated D.S.M., Legion of Merit, Commendation ribbon with two oak-leaf clusters; recipient Merit award Albert Einstein Coll. Medicine, 1963; Nat. Bus. Industry Leader award B'nai Brith, 1967, Outstanding Achievement award in bus. U. So. Calif., 1967, Bus. Leadership award U. Mich., 1968, Big Bro. Community Service award Jewish Big Bros. Assn. Los Angeles County, 1975, Community Leadership award United Way, 1976, named Salesman of Year, Los Angeles Sales Execs. Club, 1959, Texan of Year, Tex. Press Assn., 1964, Man of Year, Beverly Hills C. of C., Bus. Statesman of Year, Harvard Bus. Sch. Alumni Assn. So. Calif., 1964; Horatio Alger award Am. Assn. Schs. and Colls., 1964; Man of Hope award City of Hope, 1965; medal of achievement Western Electronic Mfrs. Assn., 1965; Golden Plate award Am. Acad. Achievement, 1966; Industrialist of Year, Soc. Indsl. Realtors, 1966, numerous others. Mem. Tex. Technol. Coll. Century Club, Sigma Alpha Epsilon (life), Beta Gamma Sigma (hon.). Clubs: Hollywood (Calif.) Turf (dir.) Army-Navy (Washington); Beach (Santa Monica); Calif., Los Angeles Country, One Hundred (Los Angeles); Army-Navy. Office: 360 N Crescent Dr Beverly Hills CA 90213

THORNTON, EDMUND B., mining co. exec.; b. Chgo., Mar. 9, 1930; s. George A. and Suzanne W. Thornton; B.A., Yale U., 1954; div.; children—Thomas and Jonathan (twins), Susan and Amanda (twins). With No. Trust Co., Chgo., 1957-59; asst. sec., asst. treas. Ottawa Silica Co. (Ill.), 1959-61, v.p. corporate devel., 1961-62, pres., chief exec. officer, 1962-75, chmn. bd., chief exec. officer, 1975—; dir., v.p. Ottawa Nat. Bank. Del., Republican Nat. Conv., 1968, precinct committeeman, 1978—; chmn. LaSalle County Rep. Central Com. Served to lt. USMCR, 1954-56. Recipient Conservation Service award U.S. Dept. Interior, 1973. Mem. Ill. Mfrs.' Assn. (dir. 1969-75, chmn. 1975), NAM, Ill. State C. of C. (dir. 1972-78), U.S. C. of C., Nat. Indsl. Sand Assn. (dir. 1968-73). Republican. Congregationalist. Clubs: Capitol Hill (Washington); Chgo., Yale of Chgo., U. Chgo., Elks. Author various articles on historic preservation, history and mil. subjects. Home: PO Box 1 Ottawa IL 61350 Office: PO Box 577 Ottawa IL 61350

THORNTON, RICHARD ELMER, mfg. co. exec.; b. Cin., Dec. 12, 1935; s. John Ransom McGarry and Alice Mae (Naylor) T.; B.S., U. Cin., 1974; m. Margaret June Blackman, Dec. 12, 1959; children—Richard Matthew, John David Charles. Research asst., then sr. research asst. Marley Co., Kansas City, Mo., 1962-67; tech. rep., then systems specialist Honeywell, Inc., Cin., 1967-76, field service supr., 1976—; cons. energy mgmt. Asst. troop scoutmaster Dan Beard council Boy Scouts Am., 1973—, adult tng. adv., 1978, 80, Philmon crew adv., 1976, 78, 80; 1st asst. troop scoutmaster Nat. Boy Scout Jamboree, 1977. Served with USNR, 1955-57, USAF, 1957-61. Recipient various awards Boy Scouts Am. Mem. Heart of Am. Geneal. Soc. Methodist. Club: Masons. Home: 3354 Felicity Dr Cincinnati OH 45211 Office: 4350 Malsbary Rd Cincinnati OH 45242

THORPE, JAMES ALFRED, utilities exec.; b. Fall River, Mass., Apr. 19, 1929; s. James and Charlotte Ann (Brearley) T.; B.S., Northeastern U., 1951; m. Maxine Elva Thompson, Mar. 4, 1950; children—James Alfred, Peter R., David T., Carol L., Mark W. Asst. supt. prodn. Fall River Gas Co., 1951-55; chief engr. Lake Shore Gas Co., Ashtabula, Ohio, 1955-57; cons. Stone & Webster Mgmt. Corp., 1958-67; dir. spl. services Wash. Natural Gas Co., Seattle, from 1967, mgr. and v.p. So. div., to 1971, sr. v.p., 1971-72, pres., 1972—, chief exec. officer, 1974—, chmn. bd., chief exec. officer Washington Energy Co. and subs.'s; dir. Puget Sound Mut. Savs. Bank, Sea First Corp., Unigard Ins. Group, Seattle 1st Nat. Bank. Bd. dirs. Salvation Army; pres. United Way King County, 1980; bd. dirs. Downtown Devel. Assn., Corp. Council for Arts, Western region NCCJ, Found. for Pvt. Enterprise Edn. Mem. Am. (dir. 1977-78), Pacific Coast (dir., chmn. 1977-78) gas assns., Inst. Gas Tech. (dir.). Methodist. Clubs: Rainier, Wash. Athletic, Masons, Rotary (Seattle). Home: 11160 SE 59th St Bellevue WA 98006 Office: 815 Mercer St Seattle WA 98111

THORSEN, RICHARD PIERCE, banker, lawyer; b. Winnetka, Ill., May 12, 1945; s. Robert and Frances (Pierce) T.; B.S. in Bus. Adminstrn., Northwestern U., 1967, J.D., 1971. Admitted to Ill. bar, 1971; credit analyst Continental Bank, Chgo., 1972-73; asst. v.p. Hyde Park Bank, Chgo., 1973-75; v.p. Water Tower Bank, Chgo., 1975-76; asst. v.p. Bank of Ravenswood, Chgo., 1976—; dir. McCormick Commodities Co.; partner N.W. Profl. Leasing Co., Chgo., 1974—; instr. fin. Am. Inst. Banking, 1974—; instr. bus. law Northwestern U., 1975—; columnist Chgo. Daily Law Bull., 1975—. Served with U.S. Army, 1969. Mem. Am. Bar Assn., Ill. Bar Assn., Chgo. Bar Assn., Am. Inst. Banking. Episcopalian. Club: Univ. (Chgo.). Office: 1825 W Lawrence St Chicago IL 60640

THORSEN, ROBERT, lawyer; b. Winnetka, Ill., July 8, 1912; s. Henry T. and Catherine (Henrich) T.; B.S.L., Northwestern, 1932; LL.D., U. Chgo., 1934; m. Frances Adele Pierce, Apr. 28, 1935; children—Frances Adele, Robert Lloyd, Richard Pierce. Admitted to Ill., Mo. bars, 1935; br. atty. Nat. Bond Investment Co., St. Louis, 1935-37; asso. with Edward P. Madigan, 1937-40; partner Madigan & Thorsen, Chgo., 1941—; asst. sec., dir. Tee-2-Green Corp.; v.p., asst. sec., dir. McCormick Commodities Inc.; sec. Kerr Wireryte Co., Kerr Wire Products Co.; sec., dir. Tingstol Co.; mem. Chgo. Bd. Trade. Mem. Am. Judicature Soc., Am., Ill., Chgo. bar assns., Chgo. Real Estate Bd., Chgo. Assn. Commerce and Industry. Clubs: University, Executives, Westmoreland Country (past pres.), John Henry Wigmore (past pres.). Home: 145 Bertling Ln Winnetka IL 60093 Office: 1 First Nat Plaza Chicago IL 60603

THRASH, JESSE NEWTON, JR., banker; b. Charlotte, N.C., Nov. 22, 1940; s. Jesse Newton and Annie Laura (Goodale) T.; B.B.A., U. Ga., 1963; grad. Sch. Banking of South, La. State U., 1970; m. Judith Gail Wooten, Aug. 31, 1963; 1 son, Christopher Sean. With Fed. Res. Bank, Charlotte, 1957-58, Citizens & So. Nat. Bank, Atlanta, 1963-67, Nat. Bank Ga., Atlanta, 1967-70, Peoples Bank of S.C., Florence, 1970-74; pres. Peoples Nat. Bank, Smithfield, N.C., 1974-80; v.p., loan adminstr. Citizens Nat. Bank, Concord, N.C., 1980—; instr. Am. Inst. Banking. Chmn. fin. com., trustee Cabarrus Acad. Mem. Bank Adminstrn. Inst., N.C. Bankers Assn. (mgmt. com., chmn. Group III), Robert Morris Assos. Presbyterian. Club: Cabarrus Country. Home: 565 Windsor Pl NE Concord NC 28025 Office: 26 Union St S Concord NC 28025

THRASHER, JAMES PARKER, leasing co. exec.; b. Waltham, Mass., Jan. 15, 1932; s. Linus James and Doris Melissa (Parker) T.; B.S. in Indsl. Adminstrn., Yale, 1953; m. Mary Patricia Mayer, Dec. 31, 1965; children—Deborah Anne, Linda Carol, Anne Elizabeth. With U.S. Steel Corp., Cleve., 1953-60; cons. Booz, Allen & Hamilton Internat., London, 1960-65; mgmt. cons. McKinsey & Co., Inc., London, 1965-67; v.p. for Europe, Integrated Container Service, Inc., London, 1967-69, pres., chief exec. officer, N.Y.C., 1970-75; v.p., dir. Interway Corp., N.Y.C., 1969-75, pres., chief exec. officer, dir., 1975-79, Transam. Interway, Inc. subs. Transam. Corp., San Francisco, 1979—. Clubs: Yale, Am. of London. Home: 2 Topsail Ln Rye NY 10580

THULEEN, ROLAND HOWARD, banker; b. Mpls., July 21, 1917; s. Albert Axel and Ruth Blanche (Hanson) T.; ed. Stonier Grad. Sch. Banking of Rutgers U., U. Minn. Extension; cert. Am. Inst. Banking; m. Eileen Lora Walvatne, Sept., 1942; children—Pamela (Mrs. G. Scott Giebink), Randall Howard, Scott Allan. With 1st Nat. Bank of Mpls., 1936—, beginning as bellhop, successively asst. cashier, asst. v.p., v.p., v.p. and sr. comml. banking officer, sr. v.p., 1936-75, vice chmn. bd., 1975—. Pres., United Cerebral Palsy Greater Mpls., 1963-72, bd. dirs., 1955—, mem. fin. com., 1973; bd. dirs. YMCA, chmn. 1974; bd. dirs., former pres. Met. Y's Men; former trustee Gethsemane Luth. Ch. Served to 1st lt., USAF, 1942-54. Recipient Sta. WCCO Radio Good Neighbor award. Mem. Robert Morris Assos., Assn. Res. City Bankers, Am. Inst. Banking, Citizens League. Clubs: Mpls., Minikahda. Office: First National Bank of Minneapolis First Bank Pl Minneapolis MN 55480

THULSIRAJ, RAJ, mfg. co. exec.; b. India, Sept. 6, 1949; s. P. and V. (Vijayalakshmi) Venugopal; B.S. in M.E., Indian Inst. Tech., Madras, 1970; M.S. in Indsl. and Systems Engring., U. So. Calif., 1972; M.S. in Fin., West Coast U., 1974, M.S. in Mktg., 1975, M.B.A. in Multinat. Corp., 1978; m. Ana Maria Valencia, Dec. 17, 1978. Asso. indsl. engr. Xerox Corp., Pasadena, 1972-73; indsl. engr. Xerox Corp., El Segundo, 1973-74, sr. indsl. engr., 1974-76; chief indsl. engr. Intercraft Industries, Carson, Calif., 1977—. Nat. Sci. Talent Search scholar; Archimedes Circle fellow, 1971-72. Mem. Am. Inst. Indsl. Engrs., Ops. Research Soc. Am., Am. Mgmt. Assn. Home: 6272 Heil Ave Huntington Beach CA 92647 Office: 771 E Watsoncenter Rd Carson CA 90745

THUMM, FRED WILLIAM, lighting fixture co. exec.; b. Teaneck, N.J., Nov. 20, 1937; s. Fred Albert John and Dorothea (Niehaus) T.; student Fairleigh Dickinson U., 1956-64; m. Margaret Ann Dievler, July 15, 1961; children—Fred William, Donna Lynn. Chief draftsman Indsl. Gauges, West Englewood, N.J., 1956-59; project engr. Fed. Design & Service Co., Riveredge, N.J., 1959-64; chief engr. N.Y. Pressing Machine Co., Paterson, N.J., 1965-69; plant mgr. Kurt Versen Co., Westwood, N.J., 1969-80; v.p. mfg. Moldcast Lighting, Pine Brook, N.J., 1980—; partner, cons. engr. Prend, Inc.; cons. Enair, Inc. Past pres. N. Jersey Ref. Ch. Young Adults. Mem. Soc. Advancement Mgmt. Patentee in field. Home: 407 Ridgewood Ave Wyckoff NJ 07481 Office: Maple Ave at Route 80 Pine Brook NJ 07058

THURMOND, GERALD PITTMAN, lawyer; b. Madison, Ga., Aug. 20, 1936; s. Gilbert Duard and Viola Elnora (Pittman) T.; B.B.A., U. Ga., 1958, J.D. cum laude, 1964; m. Ann Sexton, May 21, 1960; children—Gerald Pittman, William R., Susan A. Admitted to Ga. bar, 1963, Pa. bar, 1970, D.C. bar, 1976, to practice before Ga. and Pa. Supreme Cts., D.C. Ct. Appeals, U.S. Dist. Ct. No. Dist. Ga., U.S. Ct. Appeals 5th Dist., U.S. Dist. Ct. Western Dist. Pa.; atty. Troutman, Sams, Schroder & Lockerman, Atlanta, 1964-68; staff atty. gen. counsel Gulf Oil Corp., Pitts., 1963-73, asst. to exec. (chmn. bd., pres. and exec. v.p.'s), 1973, adminstrv. v.p., 1974-75, Washington counsel, 1975—. Gulf Oil Co. employee chmn. United Fund of Houston, 1975. Served to 1st lt. AUS, 1958-60. Mem. Am., D.C., Ga., Allegheny County bar assns., Ga. State Soc. (dir.), Houston C. of C., C. of C. of U.S. (council on antitrust policy), NAM (com. on corp. governance and competition, com. on regulatory reform), Phi Kappa Phi. Presbyterian. Clubs: Kenwood Golf and Country, Nat. Lawyers, Internat., Capitol Hill. Home: 5207 Falmouth Rd Washington DC 20016 Office: 1025 Connecticut Ave NW Washington DC 20036

THURSTON, FRED STONE, printing co. exec.; b. Oak Park, Ill., Apr. 1, 1931; s. Fred Stone and Marie (Stemen) T.; student Eastern Ill. State Coll., 1948-50; B.A., N.Mex. Highlands U., 1954; postgrad. exec. program U. Chgo., 1975-76; m. Barbara Coy Carnes, Nov. 6, 1954; children—Fredric Kent, Bruce Edward, Janice Marie. Asst. plant mgr. UARCO, Inc., Watseka, Ill., 1955-63; asst. to pres. Joe Daley & Sons, Inc., Los Angeles, 1963-64; div. mgr. manifold forms Diamond Internat. W.G.A.D., San Francisco, 1964-65, gen. mgr. Uniform Printing & Supply div. Courier Corp., Chgo., 1965-69; dir. mfg. Bus. Forms div. Control Data Corp., Phila., 1969-70; pres., gen. mgr. Printing Services Inc. div. Am. Standard Co., Detroit, 1970-71; exec. v.p., gen. mgr. Workman Bus. Forms div. John Blair & Co., Chgo., 1971-72; exec. v.p., mktg. mgr. Forms Corp. Am., Spring Grove, Ill., 1972—. Vice pres. Iroquois County (Ill.) Young Republicans, 1960-61. Served to capt. AUS, 1951-53, USAR, 1953-64. Certified forms cons. Mem. Mensa, Sigma Tau Gamma. Republican. Home: 1238 Wildwood Ct Libertyville IL 60048 Office: PO Box 278 Rt 12 Spring Grove IL 60081

THWAITS, JAMES ARTHUR, mfg. co. exec.; b. London, Apr. 3, 1923; s. Arthur Roper and Iris Maud (Mason) T.; grad. East-Ham Coll. Tech., London, 1939, Thames Poly., London, 1942; came to U.S., 1958, naturalized, 1973; grad. East-Ham Coll. Tech., London, 1939, Thames Poly., London, 1942; Higher Nat. Cert. in Elec. Engring., Cert. Higher Math., Poly. of South Bank, London, 1944; m. Joyce Holmes, July 26, 1947; children—Joanna, Philip, David, Steven. Project engr. Standard Telephones and Cables Ltd., Eng., 1945-46; plant engr. Kelvinator Ltd., Eng., 1946-49; with 3M, St. Paul, 1949—, v.p. Afro-Asian and Can. areas, 1968-71, v.p. Tape and Allied Products Group, 1972-74, v.p. Internat. Group, 1974-75, pres. Internat. Ops., 1975—, also dir. 3M; dir. First Trust Co., St. Paul. Mem. Inst. Elec. Engrs. (London). Clubs: St. Paul Athletic; White Bear (Minn.) Yacht; North Oak; (Minn.) Golf; King Solomon's Lodge (London, Ont., Can.). Office: 3M Co PO Box 3388 Saint Paul MN 55101*

THYSEN, JANICE DARROW, import co. exec.; b. Hammond, Ind., Mar. 24, 1941; d. Jack M. and Ruth Thelma (Bush) Darrow; B.J., U. Mo., 1963; m. Benjamin Thysen, Aug. 12, 1962 (div. Feb. 1970); 1 son, Gregory Eden Darrow. Asst. editor Bus. Week Mag., 1963-66; creative dir. Frank Block Assos., 1966-69; account exec. Wright & Manning, Inc., St. Louis, 1970-75; founder, dir. U.S. Metric Plans Bd., 1974-75; pres. Thysen Communications Cons., 1970—, Thysen Imports, 1971—, J.D. Thysen & Assos., 1972-74; lectr. New Bus. for Women Seminars, St. Louis Community Coll., Meramec. Mem. CLASP sect. St. Louis White House Conf. on Edn., 1973-76. Recipient award of commendation U. Mo. Sch. Journalism, 1963, Hon. Scholarship, U. Mo. Curators, 1960; William Randolph Hearst fellow, 1963. Mem. Nat. Sch. Pub. Relations Assn., St. Louis Women's Advt. Club, Women in Communications, Sigma Delta Tau. Republican. Book reviewer Kansas City Star, 1963-64, St. Louis Globe Democrat, 1974-77. Home: 5 W Walling Dr St Louis MO 63141 Office: 7405 Manchester Ave St Louis MO 63143

TICHENOR, CHARLES BECKHAM, beverage co. exec.; b. Indpls.; s. Norman Beckham and Esther (Bremer) T.; B.S., Duke, 1948; postgrad. Harvard, 1949; m. Suzanne Nelson Stevens; children—Charles Beckham III, Peter S., Suzanne P., Melissa N. Vice pres. Sealtest Inc., Phila.; sr. corp. v.p., chief ops. officer Iroquois Brands Ltd., Greenwich, Conn.; pres. Champale Inc.; dir. Angostura Doughty Foods Inc., Motor Coils Co., Inc.; Pres., Phila. Little League; vice chmn. N.Y.C. Heart Fund; trustee Rider Coll., Lawrenceville, N.J., Trinity Coll., Washington. Served to lt. (j.g.) USNR, 1945-46; PTO, CBI. Mem. Duke Alumni Assn. (past pres.), U.S. Brewers Assn. (dir.), Am. Mgmt. Assn. Clubs: Biltmore Country (Chgo.); Union League, Merion Cricket (Phila.). Mem. U.S. Davis Cup Tennis Team, 1941-42. Home: 201 Country Gate Rd Wayne PA 19087

TICHENOR, WILLIAM GEILEY, savs. and loan exec.; b. Terre Haute, Ind., Aug. 28, 1917; s. William Taylor and Ause (Geiley) T.; B.S., Ind. State U., Terre Haute, 1939; m. Margaret Brown, May 4, 1941; 1 son, William Taylor II. With Internat. Harvester Co., 1939-41; pres. Ind. Savs. & Loan Assn., Terre Haute, 1941—. Sec.-treas., bd. dirs. Spirit of Terre Haute. Mem. Nat. Assn. Realtors, Pi Omega Pi. Methodist. Clubs: Masons, Shriners, Kiwanis, Elks. Home: Terre Haute IN 47803 Office: 100 S 7th St Terre Haute IN 47808

TIDWELL, THOMAS TATE, lumber co. exec.; b. Memphis, Jan. 5, 1923; s. Hearn Williford and Allie Lee (Tate) T.; B.A., Southwestern at Memphis, 1947; m. Valerie Lynch, Mar. 30, 1967; children—Clyde Tidwell Austin, Thomas Tate, Christopher, Daniel, Catherine Tidwell Frye. Dist. mgr. Procter & Gamble, Richmond, Va., 1951-62; pres. Triple T Co., Atlanta, 1962-68; ops. mgr. Chiclecraft, Knoxville, Tenn., 1968-71; pres., chmn. bd. City Lumber Co., Knoxville, 1971—. Bd. dirs. Met. YMCA, Gt. Smoky Mountain council Boy Scouts Am.

Served to lt. (j.g.) USNR, 1943-46; PTO. Mem. Archtl. Woodwork Inst. (dir. 1974—, chpt. pres. 1973; chmn. nat. hdqrs. bldg. com., mem. exec. com., chmn. nat. conv. planning com. 1977). So. Woodwork Assn. (pres.), Kappa Alpha Order, Sigma Phi Omega. Roman Catholic. Clubs: City, Le Conte, Concord Yacht, Rotary (pres. 1967, dist. gov., rep. to Australia 1974, pres. elect Knoxville 1980—, Paul Harris fellow). Home: 9505 Mobile Dr Knoxville TN 37919 Office: 214 W Morelia Ave Knoxville TN 37917

TIEDEMANN, CARL HANS, securities co. exec.; b. Cleve., June 3, 1926; s. Carl Hans and Mary Owen (Glenn) T.; B.A., Trinity Coll., Hartford, Conn., 1950; M.S., Columbia; m. Mary B. Cumming, Oct. 24, 1959; children—Carl H., Mark B., Leigh C., Michael G. Salesman, Am. Cyanamid Co., 1950-57; with Stone & Webster Securities Co., 1957-62; with Donaldson, Lufkin & Jenrette, Inc., N.Y.C., 1962—, chmn. bd., until 1974, vice chmn. bd., 1974—; dir. Curtice-Burns, Inc., Rochester, N.Y. Bd. govs. Am. Stock Exchange. Served with USNR, 1944-46. Mem. Nat. Assn. Security Dealers. Clubs: Univ. (N.Y.C.); Maidstone (Easthampton, N.Y.). Office: 140 Broadway New York NY 10005*

TIEDGE, LOUIS ALFRED, labor relations cons.; b. South Bend, Ind., June 9, 1913; s. Fred Louis and Anna Maude (Hazen) T.; student Acme Inst. Tech., 1940-42, Notre Dame U., 1943-44, Ind. U.-South Bend, 1954-56; m. Agnes Anna Vogel, Aug. 15, 1930; children—Delores Francis Cleghorn, Geneva Mae Barnes, Sharon Louise Grall, Deborah Ann Peters. Gen. foreman mfg. Bendix Corp., South Bend, 1939-51, staff asst. indsl. relations, 1952-58, mgr. labor relations, 1959-61, dir. indsl. relations, 1962-78; freelance arbitrator, cons. employee and labor relations South Bend, 1978—; mgmt. cons. City of South Bend, St. Joseph County, Michiana Area CETA Consortium. Mem. South Bend-Mishawaka Labor Mgmt. Commn., 1963—; gen. chmn. United Fund St. Joseph County Campaign, 1966-67; chmn. Ind. Gov.'s Task Force for Employment of Handicapped, 1970-75; mem. Ind. Blue Cross Hosp. Rate Rev. Com., 1978—; trustee St. Joseph Hosp., South Bend, 1977—. Mem. Inst. Cert. Profl. Mgrs. (accredited), Am. Soc. Personnel Adminstrn. (accredited exec. personnel), Ind. C. of C. (chmn. labor relations and personnel com. 1975-77), U.S. C. of C. (mem. labor relations com. 1964-69), South Bend-Mishawaka Area C. of C., Ind. Mfrs. Assn. Republican. Roman Catholic. Club: Rotary (pres. South Bend South 1976-77). Home: 19400 Sundale Dr South Bend IN 46614 Office: 712 County City Bldg South Bend IN 46601

TIEMANN, K. GABRIELLE, title ins. co. exec.; b. Brunn, Bohemia/Ger., July 19, 1941; d. Heinrich Otto Wilhelm and Adelheid Clara (Kirchhoff) T.; came to U.S., 1959, naturalized, 1965; A.A. in Bus., Foothill Coll., 1966, A.A. in Real Estate, 1968; LL.B., Lincoln Law U., 1972. Flexo typist Carson, Pirie Scott & Co., Chgo., 1960-61; sec. Pitney-Bowes, San Francisco, 1961-62; with Transam. Title Ins. Co., 1962-79, escrow officer, Palo Alto, Calif., 1964-67, sr. escrow officer, 1967-78, chief title officer for San Diego County, 1978-79, regional chief title officer for So. Calif., Los Angeles, 1979, mgr. Palo Alto and Los Altos (Calif.) brs., 1973-79; No. Calif. counsel, asst. v.p. USLife Title Ins. Co., Dallas, 1979—; faculty San Jose City Coll., 1973—, San Diego City Coll., 1978—. Mem. Assn. Profl. Mortgage Women (pres. 1975), Escrow Assn. Santa Clara Valley, Am. Bar Assn., Nat. Ass. Realtors. Home: 1524 Arbor Ave Los Altos CA 94022 Office: 1301 Main St Dallas TX

TIEN, JAMES M., educator, policy analyst; b. N.Y.C., Mar. 27, 1945; s. Yu Shih and Tien Lun (Li) T.; B.E.E., Rensselaer Poly. Inst., 1966; Ph.D., Mass. Inst. Tech., 1972. Mem. tech. staff Bell Telephone Labs., Holmdel, N.J., 1966-69; project dir. Rand Corp., N.Y.C., 1970-73; sr. scientist Urban Systems Research & Engring. Inc., Cambridge, Mass., 1973-75; exec. v.p. Pub. Systems Evaluation Inc., Cambridge, 1975—; vis. lectr. Mass. Inst. Tech., Cambridge, 1973-77; asso. prof. computer and systems engring. Rensselaer Poly. Inst., 1977—; cons. to local, state, fed. agencies. Recipient Excellence in Teaching award Mass. Inst. Tech., 1972; Bell Telephone Labs. fellow, 1966-77. Mem. IEEE, AAAS, Ops. Research Soc. Am., Evaluation Research Soc., Eta Kappa Nu, Tau Beta Pi. Contbr. articles to profl. jours. Home: 69 Meadowlark Dr Cohoes NY 12047 Office: Rensselaer Poly Inst Troy NY 12181 also Pub Systems Evaluation 929 Massachusetts Ave Cambridge MA 02139

TIERNEY, CECILIA VERONICA, accountant; b. Newark, Del., July 13, 1922; d. William Aloysius and Helen Irene (O'Rourke) T.; B.A., U. Del., 1943; M.B.A., U. Pa., 1952; Ph.D., U. Tex., Austin, 1970. Mem. audit staff Price Waterhouse & Co., Phila., 1944-47; mem. faculty U. Del., 1947-50, Syracuse U., 1950-51, Bridgeport U., 1953-55, U. Tex., 1955-60, U. Wash., 1966-68, U. Calif., Berkeley, 1974-75, Wash. State U., 1968-77: mem. internal audit staff RCA Service Co., Gloucester City, N.J., 1952-53; with acctg. research div. Am. Inst. C.P.A.'s, 1960-66; with tech. activities div. Financial Accounting Standards Bd., Stamford, Conn., 1975-76; research acct., comptroller Phillips Petroleum Co., Bartlesville, Okla., 1977—. Vice-chmn. research adv. council Office of Bus. Research, U. Tulsa. C.P.A., N.Y. Mem. Am. Inst. C.P.A.'s, Am. Accounting Assn., Okla. Soc. C.P.A.'s, Desk and Derrick Club, Beta Alpha Psi. Democrat. Roman Catholic. Home: 2074 SE Osage St Bartlesville OK 74003 Office: 330 PBA Bartlesville OK 74004

TIERNEY, JOHN PATRICK, wholesale co. exec.; b. Bloomington, Ind., July 12, 1926; s. John Leo and Mae Christene (Stark) T.; B.S. in B.A., U. Notre Dame, 1949; m. Joyce Romayne Oesch, Dec. 26, 1948; children—Mike, Pat, Tom, Tim, Jim. Br. mgr. Great Lakes Distbg., South Bend, Ind., 1950, br. mgr., 1951-59; v.p. Wabash Wholesale, Inc., Logansport, Ind., 1959-62, pres., 1963—, also dir.; sec., treas., dir. Asphalt Supplies, Inc., Logansport. Del. Ind. Democratic State Conv., 1974; bd. dirs. Cass County United Fund, 1965-67. Mem. Nat. Bldg. Materials Distbrs. Assn., Air Force Assn. Clubs: Rotary (dir. 1957), Kiwanis (dir. 1961), Elks, K.C., Logansport Country, Moose. Home: 117 Orchard Hill St Logansport IN 46947 Office: PO Box 508 Logansport IN 46947

TIERRA, MANUEL MARK, fin./investment cons.; b. N.Y.C., Mar. 9, 1932; s. Casimir R. and Sarah (Carlucci) T.; B.S., CCNY, 1951, M.S., 1952; M.B.A., N.Y. U., 1956, LL.D., 1966; J.D., N.Y. Law Sch., 1962; m. Rosemary C. McClutchy, July 8, 1978; children—Lisa Marie, Gary Cass. In various staff and mgmt. positions Gen. Motors Corp., 1954-68, dir. state, local and fgn. taxes, 1965-68, dir. tax dept., N.Y.C., 1968; pres. Garlis Mgmt. Services, Woodbridge, N.J., 1968-78; prin. partner Kimro Assos., Ocean, N.J., 1978-79; prin. partner Selective Venture Assos., Ocean, 1979—; admitted to N.Y. State bar, 1962; instr. econs. CCNY, 1955-56; instr. acctg. N.Y. U., 1957-58; instr. law Fordham U., 1965-67. Chmn. fin. United Fund of Central Jersey, 1970-72; fin. cons. Boys Club Am., Trenton, N.J., 1978-80; fin. mgr. Vis. Nurse Assn., Middlesex County, N.J., 1974-76. Served with U.S. Army, 1952-54. Decorated Silver Star, Purple Heart. Author books in field, including: History and Development of Sales Finance and Morris Plan Companies, 1956; Computation of Effective Yields on Financial Transactions, 1968; contbr. articles to profl. publs. Office: Plaza East Bldg Suite 103 Franklin Ave at Hwy 35 Ocean NJ 07712

TIETYEN, DAVID EARL, advt. exec.; b. Milw., May 3, 1940; s. Elben Edward and Viola T.; B.S. in Journalism, U. Wis., 1965; m. Mary Hoban, Nov. 15, 1975. Account exec. Klau Van Pietersom-Dunlap, Milw., 1966-69; account supr. Ketchum, MacLoed & Grove, Pitts. and Los Angeles, 1969-71; sr. account exec. Burson-Marstellar, Los Angeles, 1971; pres. PR Mix, Los Angeles, 1972-75; dir. advt. Hal Leonard Pub. Co., Milw., 1975-77; freelance author, Los Angeles, 1977-78; v.p., creative dir. Darryl Lloyd, Inc., North Hollywood, Calif., 1978—. Served with USCGR, 1960. Mem. Public Relations Soc. Am., Los Angeles Ad Club. Author: The Illustrated Disney Songbook, 1979. Office: 5118 Vineland Ave North Hollywood CA 91601

TIETZ, WILLIAM ALBERT, advt./public relations firm exec.; b. Detroit, Aug. 31, 1938; s. Alfred Albert and Doris Charlotte (Henke) T.; B.B.A., U. Tex., 1961, M.B.A., 1962. Supervising auditor Texaco, Inc., Western Hemisphere, 1962-68; mgr. internal audit Anderson Clayton Co., Houston, 1968-70; controller Bekins Co., Los Angeles, 1970-74; v.p. fin. Regis McKenna, Inc., Palo Alto, Calif., 1977—; tax and fin. cons. Served with USAR, 1962. Republican. Methodist. Home: 999-87 Evelyn Terr W Sunnyvale CA 94086 Office: 1800 Embarcadero St Palo Alto CA 94301

TIGER, HYMAN SIDNEY, microwave co. exec.; b. Bklyn., Aug. 17, 1918; s. Samuel and Mary (Banis) T.; student RCA Inst., 1950; B.E.E., Bklyn. Poly. Inst., 1957; m. Shirley Bezoza, Jan. 11, 1957; children—Neil, Abbe. Engr., Narda Microwave Corp., L.I., N.Y., 1955-57, Airborne Instruments Lab., L.I., 1957-60, Loral Electronics Corp., 1960-63, Blass Antenna Corp., N.Y.C., 1963-65, Honeywell Radiation Center, Boston, 1965-66, RCA Aerospace Div., Burlington, Mass., 1966-68; chief engr. Diamond Antenna & Microwave Corp., Winchester, Mass., 1968-77; with Weinschel Engring. Co., Inc., Gaithersburg, Md., 1977-78, Maury Microwave Corp., Cucamonga, Calif., 1978-79, Microwave Assos., Burlington, Mass., 1979—. Served with Signal Corps, AUS, 1941-45; ETO. Decorated Bronze Star with 3 oak leaf clusters; lic. profl. engr., Mass. Mem. N.Y. Acad. Scis., IEEE, AAAS, Profl. Group Microwave Theory and Techniques. Office: South St Burlington MA 01803

TIGRAK, MEHMET FUAT, structural engr.; b. Istanbul, Turkey, Aug. 26, 1911; s. M. Suleyman and Hediye (Harputlu) T.; Diploma, Mil. Coll., Habiye, Istanbul, 1932, Diploma Mil. Engring., 1934; Certificate, U. Berlin (Germany), 1938; student Technische Hochschule, Berlin, 1938-39; B.S., U. Ill., 1942, M.S., 1943, Ph.D., 1945; m. Mary Louise Evans; children—William M.U., James A.F., Hediye Louise. Came to U.S., 1958, now naturalized. With Turkish Army Corps Engrs., 1934-51; resigned as sr. maj.; tech. dir. Turk Yapi Ltd. Co., Ankara, Turkey, 1951; dept. head Metcalf, Hamilton, Grove, Kansas City, Mo., 1951-53; prin. engr., project co-ordinator Hamilton Co., Kansas City, Mo., 1953-54; owner, mgr. Tigrak Cons. Engr. Co., Tigrak Constrn. Co., Ankara, 1954-58; prin. partner, mgr. Tigrak & Kolbasi, engrs.-contractors, Ankara, 1956-58; asso. Clark, Daily & Dietz, 1958-62; prin. v.p. charge structures and hwys. div. Clark, Dietz & Assos., Engrs., Inc., Urbana, Ill., 1962-66, v.p. in charge fed. and r.r. projects, 1966—. Recipient hon. mention for Findlay Bridge, U.S. Army Corps. Engrs., Shelbyville Lake, Ill., 1969. Registered profl. engr., Ill., Wis., Mo., Tenn., Ind., Ky., Turkey; registered structural engr., Ill., Ky., Turkey. Mem. ASCE (life), Nat., Ill. socs. profl. engrs., Am. Concrete Inst., Am. Ry. Engring. Assn., Soc. Am. Mil. Engrs., A.A.A.S., Ill. Assn. Professions, Chamber Architects and Engrs. Turkey, Sigma Xi, Chi Epsilon, Phi Kappa Epsilon. Mason (32 deg., Shriner). Home: 23 Briarcliff Rural Route 1 Mahomet IL 61853 Office: 211 N Race St Urbana IL 61801

TILDEN, GEORGE WILLIAM, JR., banker; b. Clayton, Mo., Aug. 1, 1926; s. George William and Dolores Gretrude (Needham) T.; B.S., Central Meth. Coll., 1950; m. Mary Ann Ellis, Apr. 28, 1951; children—Lynda Sue Tilden Higgins, David Ellis, Martha Ann. Asst. to controller Terminal RR Assn. St. Louis, 1950-65; with St. Louis Union Trust Co., 1965—, pension trust adminstr., 1969, asst. sec., 1970, asst. v.p., 1971-74, v.p., 1974—. Active Boy Scouts Am., 1970—; treas., dir. United Methodist Children and Family Services of Mo., 1971—. Served with USN, 1944-46, 50-54. Mem. Nat. Assn. State Retirement Adminstrs. Republican. Methodist. Clubs: Mo. Athletic, Sunset Country, Masons. Home: 303 Oakley Ln Kirkwood MO 63122 Office: 510 Locust St Saint Louis MO 63101

TILLE, CHARLES HERMAN, accountant; b. Decatur, Ill., Aug. 3, 1926; s. Herman Carl and Grace Alice (Cummings) T.; B.S. in Engring. Adminstrn., Millikin U., 1950; m. 2d, Betsy Lou Rucker, May 26, 1973; children—Alice Jean, James E. Accountant, Marvel-Schebler Products div. Borg-Warner Corp., Decatur, 1952-54, supr. inventory control, 1954-60, purchasing buyer, 1960-66; sr. accountant Richardson, Karloski, Pinkley & Kuppler, C.P.A.'s, Decatur, 1966-76; controller Fleetwood Oil Co. Inc., Moweaqua, Ill., 1976; prin. Charles Tille Accounting & Tax Service, Decatur, 1976-78; sr. accountant Graves, Moody & Co., C.P.A.'s, Decatur, 1978-79, Nalefski & Catlin, C.P.A.'s, Decatur, 1979—. Coach Little League, Decatur, 1960, mgr., 1961, commr., 1962, sec., 1963; mental health vol., Decatur, 1973. Served with USN, 1944-46. Recipient Accounting award Murphy, Jenne & Jones, 1950. Mem. Am. Legion, 40 and 8 Soc. Republican. Clubs: Elks, Masons (local treas. 1968-78), Shriners. Home: 1735 Country Club Rd Apt 103 Decatur IL 62521 Office: 600 Citizens Bldg Decatur IL 62523

TILLEY, JON, mortgage banker; b. Kenosha, Wis., Aug. 13, 1945; s. Lawrence E. and Myra B. (Johnson) T.; B.S., U. Wis., 1967, J.D., 1970; postgrad. Sch. Mortgage Banking, Stanford U., 1972; m. Lorna Moseley, June 8, 1968; 1 son, Jeffrey. Admitted to Wis. bar, 1970, D.C. bar, 1976; asso. firm DeWitt, McAndrews & Porter, Madison, Wis., 1970-72; v.p., gen. counsel Kensington Mortgage & Fin. Corp., Milw., 1972-74; sr. v.p., gen. counsel Evans Fin. Corp., Washington, 1974-75, pres., 1975—. Mem. Am., D.C. bar assns., Mortgage Bankers Assn., Assn. Manufactured Housing Mortgage Bankers (pres. 1973-74), Phi Gamma Delta, Phi Alpha Delta. Articles editor Wis. Student Bar Jour., 1969-70. Home: 700 New Hampshire Ave Washington DC 20037 Office: 1101 30th St Georgetown DC 20007

TILLINGHAST, CHARLES CARPENTER, III, publishing co. exec.; b. N.Y.C., Nov. 16, 1936; s. Charles Carpenter, Jr. and Lisette (Micoleau) T.; B.S. in Mech. Engring., Lehigh U., 1958; M.B.A., Harvard, 1963; m. Cynthia Branch, Sept. 28, 1974; children by previous marriage—Avery D., Charles W., David C. Asst. to dir. devel. Lehigh U., Bethlehem, Pa., 1958-61; adminstrv. asst. Boise Cascade Corp., Portland, Oreg., 1961-63, asst. to v.p., Boise, Idaho, 1964-65, gen. mgr. office supply div., 1965-67, gen. mgr. paper distbn. div., 1966, v.p., 1967-68, v.p. bus. services and products, 1967-69, sr. v.p. housing group, 1969-71, sr. v.p., 1971-73; pres. CRM div. Ziff-Davis Pub. Co., Inc., Del Mar, Calif., 1971-75; pres., treas. Value Communications, Inc., La Jolla, Calif., 1975-76; pres. Oak Tree Publs., Inc., San Diego, 1976—, A.S. Barnes & Co., 1980—; dir. Leisure Dynamics Corp. Served to 2d lt. AUS, 1959. Home: 1762 Nautilus St LaJolla CA 92037 Office: 11175 Flintkote Ave San Diego CA

TILSON, JORJ LIENERT, econ. devel. assn. exec.; b. Buffalo, Apr. 28, 1938; d. George Day and June Rhoda (Magwood) Lienert; B.A., San Jose (Calif.) State U., 1966, M.A., 1969; postgrad. SUNY, Stony Brook, 1970-74; 1 son, Stephen. Instr., Sonoma (Calif.) State Coll., 1969-70; cons. Tri-U. group, Clark U., Yale, SUNY, Stony Brook, 1974-76; dep. dir. San Jose Mexican-Am. C. of C., 1976-79; mktg. analyst Nat. Econ. Devel. Assn., San Jose, 1979—. Mem. airport planning adv. com., San Jose, 1977-80; mem. Mex./Calif. Trade Conf. Task Force. Mem. Fed. Govt./Industry SBA No. Calif., Peninsula Mktg. Assn., San Jose SBA. Democrat. Co-author: America Through the Looking Glass, 2 vols., 1974; editor: Quien es Quien: Hispanic-Americans of Santa Clara County, 1980. Office: 510 N First St Suite 210 San Jose CA 95112

TILSON, ROBERT RAY, mfg. co. exec.; b. Asheville, N.C., Apr. 4, 1932; s. Robert Yates and Lena Catherine (Ray) T.; B.S., N.C. State U., 1959; M.B.A., Case Western Res. U., 1971; m. Joan Arlene Murphy, July 18, 1964; children—Robert Burton, John Ray, David Neill. Methods engr. Gen. Electric Co., Cin., 1952-56; devel. engr. TRW, Inc., Cleve., 1959-64; mgr. product planning Reliance Electric Co., Cleve., 1964-71; mgr. corporate projects A. O. Smith, Inc., Milw., 1971-72; dir. mergers and acquisitions and internat. affairs Sundstrand Corp., Rockford, Ill., 1972—; instr. indsl. engring. N.C. State U., 1957-59; guest lectr. internat. bus. No. Ill. U., DeKalb, 1974-75. Bd. dirs. Community Ednl. Council, Rockford, Ill., 1975-76. Mem. Assn. for Corp. Growth (pres. 1977-78), Aerospace Industries Assn., Internat. Trade Club Chgo., Machinery and Allied Products Inst., ASME, World Trade Club No. Ill., U.S.-U.S.S.R. Trade and Econ. Council. Patentee in field. Home: 6743 Squire Ln Rockford IL 61111 Office: 4751 Harrison Ave Rockford IL 61101

TILTON, CLYDE DUANE, savs. and loan exec.; b. Holland, Mich., Feb. 7, 1942; s. Morley L. and Edith Vivian T.; B.A. in Bus. Adminstrn., Hope Coll., 1965; m. Esther Meyering, Aug. 20, 1965; children—Tracy Lynn, Thomas Brian. Mgmt. trainee Ottawa Savs. and Loan Assn., Holland, Mich., 1965-70, asst. v.p., 1970-79, v.p., 1980—. Vice-chmn. bd. Central Wesleyan Ch., 1976, 77, 78; active Legion Band, 1958-76. Served with U.S. Army Band, 1967. Recipient Exec. Devel. award Mich. Savs. and Loan League, 1974; named Layman of Year, Noon Kiwanis Club, 1977. Mem. Mich./Ind. chpt. Fin. Officers, Holland/Zeeland Personnel Club, Inst. Fin. Edn. (dir. Western Mich. chpt.), C. of C. Republican. Home: A-4679 Cherry St Holland MI 49423 Office: 245 Central Ave Holland MI 49423

TILTON, WEBSTER, JR., gen. contractor; b. St. Louis, Sept. 11, 1922; s. Webster and Eleanor (Dozier) T.; student St. Marks Prep. Sch., 1936-40, Pawling Prep. Sch., 1940-42; master brewers degree, U.S. Brewers Acad., 1949; m. Grace Drew Wilson, Feb. 14, 1948 (div. Oct. 1959); 1 son, Webster III; m. 2d, Nancy McBlair Payne, Jan. 5, 1963. Asst. brewing technologist F&M Schaffer Brewing Co., Bklyn., 1948-52; factory sales rep. Cole Steel Equipment Co., N.Y.C., 1957-68; dist. sales mgr. Scantlin Electronics, Inc., Washington, 1968-70; sales rep. Comml. Washer & Dryer Sales Co., Washington, 1970-72; propr. Webster Tilton, Jr., contractor, Washington, 1972—. Served from cadet to chief mate Mcht. Marine Res.-USNR, 1942-45. Episcopalian. Home: 3719 Fulton St NW Washington DC 20007 Office: 940 Bender Bldg 1120 Connecticut Ave NW Washington DC 20036

TILY, STEPHEN BROMLEY, III, banking exec.; b. Phila., July 7, 1937; s. Stephen Bromley and Edith Helen (Straub) T.; B.A., Washington & Jefferson Coll., 1960; postgrad. Temple Sch. of Law, 1962-63; m. Janet Anita Walz, July 10, 1965; children—Deborah Powell, Stephen Bromley, James Charles. Trust officer Indsl. Valley Bank & Trust Co., Phila., 1968-71; v.p. Farmers Bank of the State of Delaware, Wilmington, 1971-77; exec. v.p., chief operating officer Del. Charter Guarantee & Trust Co., 1977-80, pres., chief operating officer, dir., 1980—; chief exec. officer, dir. G.&T. Incorporators, Ltd.; tchr. Am. Inst. of Banking, Valley Forge chpt. Served in USAR, QMC, 1960-61. Mem. Fin. Analysts of Wilmington, Inc., Internat. Found. of Employee Benefit Plans. Home: 410 Churchill Dr Berwyn PA 19312 Office: PO Box 8963 Wilmington DE 19899

TIMKEN, WILLIAM ROBERT, JR., mfg. co. exec.; b. 1938; B.A., Stanford U., 1960; M.B.A., Harvard U., 1962; married. With Timken Co. (formerly Timken Roller Bearing Co.), 1962—, asst. to v.p. sales, 1964-65, dir. corp. devel., 1965-68, v.p., 1968-73, vice chmn. bd., chmn. fin. com., 1973-75, chmn. bd., chmn. fin. com., 1975—, also dir.; dir. La. Land & Exploration Co., Libbey-Owens-Ford Glass Co. Vice pres. Timken Found. Office: Timken Co 1835 Dueber Ave SW Canton OH 44706*

TIMMERMAN, JAMES MCKISSIC, JR., ins. co. exec.; b. Montgomery, Ala., Nov. 13, 1946; s. James McKissic and Nalda (Williams) T.; B.S. in Bus. Adminstrn., U. Ala., 1969; m. Margaret Lynn Addison, July 18, 1970; 1 dau., Melinda Lea. Registered rep. Waddell & Reed, Sacramento, 1973; brokerage mgr. Mfrs. Life Ins. Co., Sacramento, 1973-76, mktg. mgr., 1976—. Served with USAF, 1969-73. Mem. Gen. Agents and Mgrs. Assn., Nat., Sacramento (dir. 1975—) assns. life underwriters. Home: 9005 Caldera Way Sacramento CA 95825 Office: 2233 Watt Ave Suite 360 Sacramento CA 95825

TIMONER, ELI, airline exec.; b. N.Y.C., Dec. 12, 1928; s. Bertram and Rae (Edelman) T.; student U. Ill.; grad. in Bus. Adminstrn., U. Miami, 1950; m. Elissa Doane, Dec. 4, 1966; children—Pamela, Rachel, Andrea, David. Co-founder, Laura Lee Candy Co., 1950-63; pres., chmn. bd. Giffen Industries, 1963-70; pres., chief operating officer Air Florida, Miami, 1971—; dir., exec. com. Sunset Comml. Bank. Bd. dirs. Greater Miami Jewish Fedn., Met. Dade County Inst. of Art at Miami, Palm Beach Festival; mem. citizens bd. U. Miami. Office: 3900 NW 79th Ave Miami FL 33166

TIMOTHY, ROBERT KELLER, telephone co. exec.; b. Gilcrest, Colo., June 27, 1918; s. Virge and Alice (Patterson) T.; A.B., U. No. Colo., 1941; m. Elaine Hurd, Oct. 23, 1941; children—Kristen, Robert Alan. High Sch. sci. tchr., Ft. Lupton, Colo., 1941-42; with Mountain State Telephone Co., 1946—, dist. mgr., Colorado Springs, Colo., 1956-59, Wyo. traffic mgr., Cheyenne, 1959-60, Colo. comml. mgr., Denver, 1960-62, v.p., gen. mgr. Idaho, Boise, 1962-65, v.p. pub. relations, Denver, 1965-68, v.p. operations, 1968-70, pres., 1970—, also dir.; dir. United Bank of Denver, United Banks of Colo. Pres., campaign chmn. United Fund, Boise, 1962-64. Bd. dirs. Air Force Acad. Found., Bus.-Industry Polit. Action Com., Lutheran Med. Center; v.p. bd. dirs. Nat. Safety Council, 1971-80; trustee Colo. Women's Coll.; mem. founding bd. Civilian/Mil. Inst. Served to capt. Signal Corps, AUS, 1943-46. Mem. Telephone Pioneers Am. (pres. 1978), Denver C. of C., Alliance Businessmen (regional chmn. 1974), Newcomen Soc. in U.S. (Colo. chmn.). Republican. Clubs: Univ. Denver, Denver Country, Rotary (Denver). Home: 2155 E Alameda Denver CO 80209 Office: 931 14th St Denver CO 80202 Office: 931 14th St Denver CO 80202

TIMPANY, ROBERT DANIEL, business exec.; b. Panama, Ill., Feb. 24, 1919; s. Robert Gibson and Mary (Daily) T.; B.S.C.E., U. Ill., 1940; m. Margaret Jane Robey, 1960; children—Mary Suzanne, Robert Gibson. Mining engr. Peabody Coal Co., Marion, Ill., 1940-41;

asst. engr. N.Y. Central R.R., Indpls., 1941-42, successively asst. engr., trainmaster, asst. supt., asst. master mechanic, supt., gen. mgr., asst. v.p., Indpls., Springfield, Ohio, Albany, N.Y., Watertown, N.Y., Boston, Syracuse, N.Y., Cleve. and N.Y.C., 1946-68; asst. v.p. Penn Central R.R., Phila., 1968-71; trustee Central R.R. of N.J., Newark, 1971-79; pres., chief exec. officer, dir. Central Jersey Industries, Inc., 1979—; pres., dir. N.Y. and Long Branch R.R. Co., 1976—. Registered profl. engr., Ill. Mem. Am. Ry. Engrs. Assn., Am. Soc. Traffic and Transp., Nat. Def. Transp. Assn. Presbyterian. Clubs: Masons; Aronimink (Newtown Square, Pa.); Innisbrook (Tarpon Springs, Fla.). Home: 737 Camp Woods Rd Villanova PA 19085 Office: Suite 501 Gateway 1 Newark NJ 07102

TINCHER, WILLIAM R., corp. exec.; b. Wichita, Kans., 1926; B.S., Wichita U., 1950; J.D., Washburn U., 1953. Admitted to Kans. bar, individual practice law, Topeka; with FTC, Washington; with Purex Corp., Lakewood, Calif., 1961—, corporate v.p., 1963, chmn. corporate study group, 1962, sr. v.p., 1963-65, chmn. corporate devel. com., 1965, pres. chief exec. officer, 1965—, chmn. bd., chmn. exec. com., 1968—. Dir. First Western Bank and Trust Co., C.H.B. Foods, Inc. Bd. dirs. Martin Luther Hosp.; bd. councilors U. So. Calif. Sch. Bus. Adminstrn. Mem. N.A.M. (dir., mem. exec. com.), Soap and Detergent Assn. (dir.). Office: Purex Industries Inc 5101 Clark Ave Lakewood CA 90712*

TINDALL, ROBERT EMMETT, lawyer, educator; b. N.Y.C., Jan. 2, 1934; s. Robert E. and Alice (McGonigle) T.; B.S. in Marine Engring., SUNY, 1955; postgrad. Georgetown U. Law Sch., 1960-61; LL.B., U. Ariz., 1963; LL.M., N.Y. U., 1967; Ph.D., City U., London, 1975; children—Robert Emmett IV, Elizabeth Mary. Mgmt. trainee Gen. Electric Co., Schenectady, N.Y., Lynn, Mass., Glen Falls, N.Y., 1955-56, 58-60; law clk. firm Haight, Gardner, Poor and Havens, N.Y.C., 1961; admitted to Ariz. bar, 1963; prin., mem. firm Robert Emmett Tindall & Assos., Tucson, 1963—; asso. prof. mgmt. U. Ariz., Tucson, 1969—; vis. prof. Grad. Sch. of Law, Soochow U., Republic of China, 1972, Nat. Chengchi U., Republic of China, 1972, Schiller Coll., London, 1973, Grad. Bus. Centre, London, 1974; dir. grad. profl. programs Coll. Bus. and Public Adminstrn., U. Ariz., Tucson, 1980—; lectr. USIA in Eng., India, Middle East, 1974; lectr. bus. orgn. and regulatory laws Southwestern Legal Found., Acad. Am. and Internat. Law, 1976-80. Actor community theatres of Schenectady, 1955-56, Harrisburgh, Pa., 1957-58, Tucson, 1961-71; appeared in films Rage, 1971, Showdown at OK Corral, 1971, Lost Horizon, 1972; appeared in TV programs Gunsmoke, 1972, Petrocelli, 1974. Served to lt. USN, 1956-58. Ford Found. fellow, 1965-67; Asia Found. grantee, 1972-73. Mem. Am. Bar Assn., State Bar of Ariz., Internat. Bar Assn., Am. Bus. Law Assn., Acad. Internat. Bus., Honourable Soc. of Middle Temple (London), Phi Delta Phi, Beta Gamma Sigma (pres. Alpha chpt. Ariz. 1979-80). Club: Racquet (Tucson). Author: Multinational Enterprises, 1975; contbr. articles on legal aspects of domestic and internat. bus. to profl. jours. Home: 2020 Elm St Tucson AZ 85719 Office: Coll Business and Public Adminstrn U Ariz Tucson AZ 85721

TINDELL, BARRY ROSS, automobile cooling accessory mfg. co. exec.; b. Glendale, Calif., Dec. 22, 1948; s. Otto James and Beverly Jean (Archibault) T.; A.A., Los Angeles Pierce Coll., 1969; B.S., U. So. Calif., 1971; LL.B., LaSalle U., 1974. With mktg. dept. Mobil Oil Corp., Los Angeles, 1969-70; gen. mgr. Weland Automotive Industries, Los Angeles, 1970-72; pres. T.P.P. Cooling Industries, Burbank, Calif., 1972—; cons. to small bus. Mem. Am. Mktg. Assn., Commerce Assos., Am. Mgmt. Assn. Office: 830 N Lake St Burbank CA 91502

TINEN, JOHN VICTOR, concrete additives sales co. exec.; b. Berwyn, Ill., Jan. 24, 1922; s. John Victor and Jane (Mills) T.; B.B.A., Northwestern U., 1946; m. Lois Jean Heicher, Jan. 23, 1943; children—Susan J., Diane E., Mary E., Brian R. Controller, Howard Foundry Co., 1954-58; regional acctg. dir. U.S. Post Office, 1958-60; exec. v.p., treas. Walter N. Handy Co., Inc., Springfield, Mo., 1960-63, pres., 1963—, also dir.; chmn. bd. Fly Ash Sales Co., 1969—, Ozark Concrete Co., 1969—, Handy Trucking Co., 1973—. Served with USAAF, 1942-46. C.P.A., Ill. Mem. Am. Inst. C.P.A.'s, Mo. Soc. C.P.A.'s, Beta Alpha Psi, Sigma Nu. Methodist. Club: Hickory Hills. Home: 2721 Glendale St Springfield MO 65804 Office: Walter N Handy Co Inc 1948 (C) Glenstoen St Springfield MO 65804

TINGLEY, KENNETH ELLIOTT, telecommunications co. exec.; b. Wolfville, N.S., Can., Oct. 12, 1932; s. Llewellyn Elliott and Greta Laura (Wilson) T.; came to U.S., 1958; diploma in applied sci., Acadia U., 1955; B.E.E., N.S. Tech. Coll., 1957; M.B.A., Harvard U., 1962; m. Donna Jean Shaw, May 17, 1957; children—Scott, Heather, Megan. With Canadian Gen. Elec., 1957-58, Linde div. Union Carbide, 1958-60; successively gen. mgr. Asia-Africa-Australasia sales region, mktg. mgr. Microwave div. Hewlett-Packard, Palo Alto, Calif., 1962-70; gen. mgr. European mktg. div., dir. bus. planning Schlumberger Instruments et Systemes S.A., Montrouge, France, 1970-73; v.p. mktg. N.E. Electronics div. No. Telecom, Inc., Concord, N.H., 1974-77, pres., 1977—. Home: Gage Hill Rd Hopkinton NH 03301 Office: Airport Rd Concord NH 03301

TINKER, ROBERT DALE, trade assn. exec.; b. Durango, Colo., Nov. 1, 1948; s. George Henry and Ruby Lavina (Whitley) T.; B.A. in Architecture, U. N.Mex., 1976; m. Elizabeth Ann Poplawski, Aug. 19, 1972; 1 son, Erek Matthew. Mechanic, Hwy Materials Trucking Co., South Lansing, N.Y., 1972; apprenticeship dir. Bldg. Contractors Assn. N.Mex., Albuquerque, 1976; exec. v.p. Albuquerque Home Builders Assn., 1976—; adv. constrn. trades programs local high sch., 1977—; pub. Sphere mags., Albuquerque, 1976—. Served with U.S. Army, 1968-71. Mem. Assn. Execs. N.Mex., Am. Soc. Assn. Execs., Albuquerque C. of C. Office: 4807 Menaul St NE Albuquerque NM 87110

TINSLEY, C. RICHARD, banker; b. Dublin, Ireland, Oct. 10, 1947; s. Charles Henry and Evelyn Maud (Boucher) T.; came to U.S., 1969; diploma with honors, Haileybury Sch. of Mines, Can., 1968; B.S. with high honors, Mich. Tech. U., 1971; M.S. (Henry Krumb fellow), Columbia U., 1972; m. Dana Patricia Hiken, Oct. 27, 1973. Asso. editor Metals Week, McGraw-Hill Corp., N.Y.C., 1972-74, mng. editor Metals Sourcebook, 1973-74; specialist non-ferrous commodities Chrysler Corp., Detroit, 1974-76; v.p. mining div. Continental Bank of Chgo., 1976—; advisor NOAA, 1977, Congl. Budget Office, 1977-78; tech. cons. UN Law of the Sea Conf., 1973. Recipient grad. citation Columbia U., 1972, spl. award Inst. Quantity Surveyors, 1966. Mem. Am. Inst. Mining, Metall. and Petroleum Engrs. (chmn. mineral resource mgmt. com. 1979—, mem. council of econs. 1980—), Nat. Assn. Bus. Economists, Inst. Mgmt. Sci. Author and editor articles in profl. jours. Home: 601 E Lake Shore Dr Barrington IL 60010 Office: Continental Bank 231 S LaSalle St Chicago IL 60693

TINSLEY, THOMAS VINCENT, JR., accounting co. exec.; b. Wilkes-Barre, Pa., Oct. 16, 1940; s. Thomas Vincent and Mary Clare (Green) T.; B.S. in Accounting, U. Scranton, 1963; grad. in programming Electronic Computer Programming Inst., 1966; m. Katherine Alice Swan, Oct. 15, 1966; children—Sara Elisabeth, Tracy Swan. Jr., accountant Peat, Marwick, Mitchell & Co., Balt., 1963-64; accounts receivable mgrr., import accounting mgr. Aimcee Wholesale Corp., N.Y.C., 1964-65; sr. accountant Richards, Ganly, Fries & Preusch, N.Y.C., 1965-66, Morris J. Weinstein, Groothius & Co., N.Y.C., 1966-69; supr. Brach Lane Hariton & Hirshberg, N.Y.C., 1969-70; owner mgr. Thomas V. Tinsley, Jr., C.P.A., Wilkes Barre, Pa. and N.Y.C., 1970—; notary pub., Luzerne County, Pa.; mem. faculty bank Found. for Acctg. Edn. Div. chmn. United Way Campaign of Wyoming Valley, 1975. Served with USMCR, 1960-66. C.P.A., N.Y., Pa., N.J. Mem. Am. Arbitration Assn., Am. Accounting Assn., Am., Pa. insts. C.P.A.'s, Accounting Research Assn., Nat. Assn. Accountants, N.J., N.Y. State socs. C.P.A.'s, Am. Numis. Assn., Nat. Rifle Assn., U. Scranton Nat. Alumni Soc. (bd. govs. 1979-81). Democrat. Roman Catholic. Clubs: N.Y. Athletic, World Trade Center, Union League (N.Y.C.); K.C. Home: Box 366 White Birch Ln Glen Summit Mountaintop PA 18707 Office: Suite 500 10 W Northampton St Wilkes Barre PA 18701

TIPPETT, W(ILLIS) PAUL, JR., mktg. exec.; b. Cin., Dec. 27, 1932; s. Willis Paul and Edna Marie (Conn) T.; A.B., Wabash Coll., Crawfordsville, Ind., 1953; m. Carlotta Prichard, Jan. 24, 1959; children—Willis Paul III, Holly. Brand mgr. Procter & Gamble, Cin., 1958-64; dir. sales and mktg. Ford Motor Co., Dearborn, Mich., Phila. and Essex, Eng., 1964-75; pres. STP Corp., Ft. Lauderdale, Fla., 1975-76; exec. v.p., dir. Singer Co., N.Y.C., 1976-78; pres., chief operating officer, dir. Am. Motors Corp., 1978—. Trustee Wabash Coll. Served to lt. USNR, 1953-58. Mem. Am. Mgmt. Assn. (dir.), Nat. Minority Purchasing Council (dir.), Fgn. Policy Assn., Motor Vehicle Mfrs. Assn. (dir.), Econ. Club Detroit (dir.). Methodist. Clubs: Princeton, Univ. Office: Am Motors Corp 27777 Franklin Rd Southfield MI 48034

TIPTON, BILLY GENE, mfg. co. exec.; b. Paris, Mo., June 27, 1926; s. Stribling Burl and Lucille Elizabeth (Murphy) T.; student Rutgers U., 1962-63, Newark Coll. Engring., 1964; m. Madeline Lucille Cairns, Feb. 21, 1952; children—Elizabeth, William, Michele, Pamela, Melissa, Stephanie. Utilities engr. Ford Motor Co., Metuchen, N.J., 1960-63, mgr. plant engring., 1963-69, mgr. plant engring. and maintenance, 1969-75, mgr. facilities, 1975-78, mgr. prodn. and facilities, 1978-80, mgr. strategic planning for energy and environ., 1980—; cons. in field. Chmn. indsl. devel. com. City of Middletown (N.J.), 1971-74; chmn. Monmouth County transp. bus. com., 1975—; bd. dirs. Bayshore Community Hosp., 1972-75, United Way, Monmouth, 1979—. Mem. Middletown C. of C. (pres. 1972), Am. Inst. Plant Engrs. (Civic Betterment award, spl. achievement award, Cert. of Plant Engrs.), Nat. Soc. Profl. Engrs., Nat. Assn. Energy Engrs. Contbr. articles in field to profl. jours. Office: Hwy 35 Holmdel NJ 07733

TIPTON, JAMES MCCALL, educator; b. Knoxville, Tenn., July 20, 1948; s. James Reed and Lois (McCall) T.; B.S. in Econs., U. Tenn., Knoxville, 1971; M.B.A. in Fin. (Public Utility Research Center fellow 1976), U. Fla., 1976, M.A. in Econs., 1978; Ph.D. in Econs., 1980; m. Barbara Ann, June 11, 1976. Treasury analyst Chgo. Northwestern R.R., Chgo., 1974; research analyst Public Utility Research Center, U. Fla., Gainesville, 1976, instr. dept. econs., 1977-79; asst. prof. fin. and econs. Baylor U., Waco, Tex., 1980—; cons. in field. Served with U.S. Army, 1971-74. Recipient Fla. Public Utility Research award, 1978. Mem. Am. Fin. Assn., Am. Econ. Assn., Omicron Delta Kappa, Omicron Delta Epsilon, Sigma Chi. Baptist. Co-author articles in field. Home: 312 Guittard Waco TX 76703 Office: Dept Econs Hankamer School of Business Baylor U Waco TX 76703

TIPTON, JERE TAYLOR, lawyer; b. Covington, Tenn., Oct. 10, 1904; s. John Applewhite and Kate (Coward) T.; A.B., U. Tenn., 1926; m. Jean Blackburn, Apr. 1, 1972. Admitted to Tenn. bar, 1934, U.S. Supreme Ct. bar, 1947; practiced in Chattanooga, 1934—; asso. firm Shepherd, Garden, Curry & Levine, 1937-42; partner firm Shepherd & Tipton, 1945-47, Miller, Martin, Hitching & Tipton, 1947-49; sr. partner Miller, Martin, Hitching, Tipton, Lenihan & Waterhouse, 1949-79, Miller & Martin, 1979—; dir. Vol. State Life Ins. Co., Porter Warner Industries, Inc. Charter mem. Tenn. Law Revision Commn., 1965-68. Served to maj. USMC, 1942-45. Decorated Bronze Star. Mem. Am. Bar Assn., Tenn. Bar Assn., Chattanooga Bar Assn., Assn. Life Ins. Counsel (pres. 1968-69), Kappa Sigma. Presbyterian. Clubs: Lookout Mountain (Tenn.)-Fairyland, Lookout Mountain Golf, Chattanooga Golf and Country, Mountain City (pres. 1966-68). Contbr. articles to legal jours. Home: 100 Scenic Hwy Lookout Mountain TN 37350 Office: 10th Floor Volunteer Bldg Chattanooga TN 37402

TIPTON, JOHN HOWARD, JR., ins. co. exec.; b. Chattanooga, Nov. 9, 1926; s. John Howard and Blanche Gertrude (Viall) T.; B.S. in Engring., Vanderbilt U., 1950. With Nat. Life & Accident Ins. Co., Nashville, 1950—, v.p., mgr. investments, 1967-74, dir., 1970—, exec. v.p. fin., 1974-77, pres., 1977-80, also dir.; vice chmn., chief fin. officer NLT Corp., 1980—, also dir.; dir. Guardsman Life Ins. Co., Intereal Co., WSM, Inc. Served with USN, 1944-46. Mem. Am. Inst. Real Estate Appraisers, Omicron Delta Kappa, Tau Beta Pi. Presbyterian. Club: Belle Meade Country. Office: Nat Life Center Nashville TN 37250

TIRET, HORACE MEDLIN, accountant; b. Pacific Grove, Calif., Oct. 23, 1915; s. Auguste Hubert and Annie Blaine (Eliot) T.; student Am. Inst. Banking, 1933-35; B.A., San Francisco Inst. Accountancy, 1941; postgrad. Golden Gate U., 1948-49; m. Elsie Christine Bleuss, Nov. 5, 1938; children—Sharon Lee, Jeffrey, Steven, Daniel, Michael. Bond cashier, Investment dept., Wells Fargo Bank, San Francisco, 1933-41; owner Horace M. Tiret & Assos., San Francisco, 1946—, pres., 1976-77, partner, 1977—; pres. Concise Contact Lens Co., San Leandro, Calif., 1949-78, v.p., sec., 1978—, also dir. Chmn. troop com. Boy Scouts Am., San Francisco, 1955-60. Served with AUS, 1945-46. C.P.A., Calif. Mem. Calif. C.P.A. Soc., Am. Inst. C.P.A.'s, Am. Fuchsia Soc., Nat. Fuchsia Soc. Presbyn. Patentee in fuchsia field. Home: 168 Lunado Ct San Francisco CA 94127 Office: 2225 Taraval St San Francisco CA 94116

TISCH, LAURENCE ALAN, business exec.; b. N.Y., Mar. 5, 1923; s. Al and Sadye (Brenner) T.; B.Sc. cum laude, N.Y.U., 1942; M.A. in Indsl. Engring., U. Pa., 1943; student Harvard Law Sch., 1946; m. Wilma Stein, Oct. 31, 1948; children—Andrew, Daniel, James, Thomas. Chmn. exec. com. Loews Corp., N.Y.C., 1959-65, chmn. bd., 1960, pres., 1965-69, chief exec. officer, chmn. bd., 1969—; chmn. CNA Fin. Corp.; Automatic Data Processing, Inexco Corp., CNA. Chmn. bd. trustees N.Y. U., Whitney Mus. Am. Art; trustee-at-large Fedn. Jewish Philanthropies N.Y.; trustee Legal Aid Soc. Home: Manursing Island Rye NY 10580 Office: Loews Corp 666 Fifth Ave New York NY 10020

TISCH, PRESTON ROBERT, bus. exec.; b. Bklyn., Apr. 29, 1926; s. Abraham Solomon and Sayde (Brenner) T.; student Bucknell U., 1943-44; B.A., U. Mich., 1948; m. Joan Hyman, Mar. 14, 1948; children—Steven E., Laurie M., Jonathan M. Pres., chmn. exec. com., dir. Loew's Corp., N.Y.C.; chmn. Lorillard Corp.; chmn., dir., Loew's Hotels, Inc.; chmn. exec. com., dir. CNA Fin., Bulova Watch Co. Chmn. N.Y. Conv. Bur.; vice chmn. Assn. for a Better N.Y. Served with AUS, 1943-44. Mem. Am. Hotel Assn., Theatre Owners Am., Young Pres.'s Orgn., Sigma Alpha Mu. Clubs: Harrison (N.Y.); Rye Racquet; Century Country. Home: 5 Timber Trail Harrison NY 10580 Office: 666 Fifth Ave New York NY 10019

TISCHLER, MORRIS, bioengr., bus. exec.; b. Newark, Mar. 28, 1922; s. David and Sarah (Bach) T.; student Johns Hopkins U., 1946-50, Morgan State U., 1954; B.S., U. Md., 1950, M.A., 1952, postgrad., 1956-58; m. Maureen Hayman Siegel, Sept. 25, 1977; children by previous marriage—Joel, Alan, Bruce, Mark, Joanne. Electronics instr. Forest Park High Sch., Balt., 1948-57, Balt. Poly. Inst., 1958-59; cons. to Westinghouse Electric Co., 1960; instr. electronics Community Coll. Balt., 1960-62, head dept. electronics, 1962-64; cons. on pacemakers to personal physician of Pres. Dwight D. Eisenhower, 1958-60; dir. med. electronics dept. exptl. surgery U. Md. Sch. Medicine, 1956-63; founder Training Aids Co., Balt., 1958, pres., 1958-72, dir. tng. courses, 1964-71; founder Career Edn. Assos., Inc., Balt., 1972, pres., 1972—; vis. lectr. in over 400 univs. in U.S., Can., and Europe, 1962—; cons. in med. electronics, 1958—, communication systems, 1950—, tng. aids devel. and mfg., 1957—, tchr. tng., 1953—; internat. ednl. cons., 1962—. Served with U.S. Army, 1943-46. Decorated Bronze Star with oak leaf cluster. Mem. IEEE, NEA, Am. Vocat. Assn. Author 3 books on linear integrated circuits, also tech. tng. manuals on electronics, communications, circuit design and motor control; contbr. numerous articles on bioengring. to med. and tech. jours.; producer ednl. films and videotapes on use of electronic instruments; patentee in field; inventor solid-state cardiac pacemaker (exhibited Smithsonian Instn.), cardiomatic monitor; developed biometer, physiol. monitor with biofeedback. Home: 7704 Eden Roc Way Baltimore MD 21208 Office: CEA Inc 6122 Reisterstown Rd Baltimore MD 21215

TISHLER, JAMES HOWARD, mgmt. cons.; b. Detroit, Sept. 5, 1946; s. Earl James and Gladys Marie (Groh) T.; B.S. in Indsl. Engring., U. Mich., 1968, M.B.A. in Fin., 1970. Indsl. engr. Am. Can Co., San Francisco, 1970-71; with Kaiser Steel Co., 1971-78, plant engr. Fontana Steel Mill (Calif.), 1974-75, fin. planner, Oakland, Calif., 1975-76, prodn. mgr. Myers Drum Co. subs., Los Angeles, 1976-78; mgmt. cons. Oatman Assos., 1978—. Mem. Inst. Mgmt. Cons.'s, Assn. Iron and Steel Engrs. Clubs: Olympic of San Francisco, Bachelors (San Francisco). Office: Oatman Assos 311 California St Suite 800 San Francisco CA 94104

TITTEL, FRIEDRICH WILHELM, mgmt. cons.; b. Germany, June 11, 1918; came to U.S., 1956, naturalized, 1962; s. Friedrich Wilhelm and Maria Notburga (Waha) T.; M.S., West Coast U., 1976, M.B.A. summa cum laude, 1978; m. Ilse Abel, Sept. 19, 1943; children—Regina, Susanne. Foreman, Sherman Industries, Flushing, N.Y., 1957-61; asst. plant mgr. J. Stern & Co., Mt. Vernon, N.Y., 1961-71; plant mgr. Tre Metal Processing Co., Santa Ana, Calif., 1971-76; gen. mgr., v.p. C.S. Industries, Long Beach, Calif., 1977; mgmt. cons., Tustin, Calif., 1978—; sr. lectr. West Coast U., 1976—. Mem. Republican Nat. Com., 1978. Cert. engring. technician; pvt. pilot. Mem. Am. Soc. Metals, U. Calif. Irvine Exec. Assn. Home: 13771 Browning Ave Tustin CA 92680

TIVY, ROBERT CLIFFORD, mfg. co. exec.; b. Fenelon Falls, Ont., Can., Oct. 16, 1923; s. Clifford and Meta (Moffat) T.; B.S. (Royal Can. Engrs. Meml. scholar), Queen's U., 1951; m. Ethel Vivian Wilson, June 2, 1945; children—Jane W. Johnston, Mary E. Tradesman, Can. Gen. Electric Co., Peterborough, Ont., 1939-42; various staff and line positions in engring. and mfg. Automatic Electric div. GTE, Brockville, Ont., 1951-70; v.p. mfg. Black & Decker Mfg. Co. Ltd., Brockville, 1970-72, v.p., gen. mgr., 1972-74, pres., 1974—, chief exec. officer, 1978—, chmn., 1979—, v.p. Can. Pacific ops., 1979—. Mem. Brockville Dist. High Sch. Bd., 1960-64. Served with Royal Can. Inf. Corps, 1942-46. Decorated Can. Forces Decoration, Centennial medal. Mem. Nat. Council on Bus. Issues, Assn. Profl. Engrs. Ont., Royal Can. Mil. Inst. Clubs: Brockville Country, Bel Aire. Home: 12377 Ridge Circle Brentwood Los Angeles CA 90049 Office: 5400 Alla Rd Los Angeles CA 90066

TOAL, DESMOND J., business exec. Vice pres., gen. mgr. Metals div. ITT Thompson Industries, Inc., Valdosta, Ga. Office: PO Box 928 Valdosta GA 31601*

TOBEY, CARL WADSWORTH, publisher; b. Meriden, Conn., Nov. 18, 1923; s. Carl W. and Prudence (Wadsworth) T.; ed. U.S. Mcht. Marine Acad.; m. Charlotte Butterworth, Aug. 19, 1944; children—Peter Wadsworth, Carl Eric, Cheryl L. Regional sales mgr. Northeastern div. Dell Pub. Co., Inc., 1953-58, sales mgr. Dell Books, 1958-64, v.p. co., 1964-68, sr. v.p., 1968, exec. v.p., dir., 1968-76, pres., 1976—. Served with U.S. Mcht. Marine, 1943-46. Republican. Congregationalist. Club: Woodway Country. Home: Deacons Way New Canaan CT 06840 Office: 1 Dag Hammarskjold New York NY 10017

TOBIA, ERNESTO ALESSANDRO, constrn. co. exec.; b. Arsita-Teramo, Italy, July 11, 1932; came to Can., 1958, naturalized, 1966; s. Ermenegildo and Immacolata Margherita (Giannantonio) T.; diploma geometra, Mario Pagano Sch., Italy, 1952; m. Lucia Sebastiano, July 11, 1959; children—Piero, Tania, Lisa. Archtl. designer, Italy, 1953-56; rds. designer and constrn. mgr., Italy, 1956-58; with Faludi Cons., Toronto, Ont., 1958-62, Scarborough Twp. Engring. Dept., 1962-66; Can. tech. advisor and constrn. mgr. Maccaferri Gabions, Toronto, 1966-68; co-founder, pres. Key Masonry Ltd., Weston, Ont., 1968—; founder, pres. Tobern Constrn. Ltd., Downsview, Ont., 1977—; co-founder, sec. CO.S.T.I., Can. Center of Edn. for Emigrants, Toronto, 1961—; dir. Can. Masonry Constrn. Assns., 1975—, 2d v.p., 1979-80, pres., 1981—; tchr. math., drafting, blueprint reading Central Tech. Inst. Toronto, 1960-64. Served with Italian Arty., 1955-56. Recipient Ont. award of Excellence for Masonry Workmanship, 1972. Mem. Met. Masonry Constrn. Assn. (pres. 1979-80), Ont. Masonry Constrn. Assn. (dir. 1979-80), Can. Standards Assn., Italian C. of C. (dir. 1979-80), Can. Masonry Constrn. Assn., Ont. Assn. Cert. Engring. Technicians and Technologists, Can. Italian Bus. and Profl. Assn. Toronto, Toronto Constrn. Assn., Masonry Contractors Assn. Am., Can. Constrn. Assn. Liberal. Roman Catholic. Clubs: The Skyline, Mayfair Racquet, Abrusz. Home: 69 Golfwood Heights Weston ON M9P 3L8 Canada Office: 78 Martin Ross Ave Downsview ON M3J 2L4 Canada

TOBIN, MICHAEL E., banker; b. Newtown Square, Pa., Jan. 17, 1926; s. Michael Joseph and Emma (Roberts) B.; B.S. in Econs., U. Pa., 1948; m. Judith Anne Brown; children—Michael E., Allegra, Corey. Cons. Philco, RCA, Ebasco Service, Inc., 1950-56; sr. cons. Arthur Young & Co., N.Y.C., 1956-59, Midwest dir. cons. services, Chgo., 1959-68; pres. Midwest Stock Exchange, Chgo., 1968-78; pres. Am. Nat. Bank & Trust, Chgo., 1978, chmn. bd., chief exec. officer, 1979—. Mem. exec. bd. Chgo. Theatre Group, Inc.; mem. governing bd. Orchestral Assn. of Chgo. Symphony Orch., Lyric Opera Chgo. Served with U.S. Army, World War II; ETO. Mem. Chgo. Assn. Commerce and Industry (dir.), Bus. Adv. Council, Chgo. Urban League. Office: Am Nat Bank & Trust 33 N LaSalle St Chicago IL 60690

TOBOLOWSKY, JACK LEHMAN, textile co. exec.; b. Dallas, Jan. 16, 1917; s. Reuben and Etta Gertrude (Tobolowsky) T.; B.B.A., U. Tex., 1937; m. Josephine Pergament, Feb. 7, 1943; children—Dona (Mrs. Robert Stiffel), Ira, George, Myra (Mrs. Stuart Prescott). Sr. engr. Western Electric Co., N.Y., 1944-49; gen. mgr. Tex Style Mfg. Co., Midlothian, 1949-59; pres. Midlo Textile Co., Midlothian and Dallas, 1959-63; pres. Wolf Textile Co., Dallas, 1963—; also engaged in ranching. Served with AUS, 1942-44. Mem. Phi Sigma Delta. Home: 5909 Waggoner Dr Dallas TX 75230 Office: 2214 Pacific Ave Dallas TX 75201

TODA, AUGUST ALBERT, computer co. exec.; b. Farrell, Pa., Dec. 11, 1934; s. August B. and Minnie (Teice) T.; B.S., Ohio State U., 1962; postgrad. Harvard Bus. Sch., 1973; m. Marilyn Jean Sandstrom, Nov. 24, 1965 (div. Oct. 1980); 1 dau., Ann Marie. Dept. mgr. Federated Dept. Stores, Columbus, Ohio, 1961-65; program mgr. Gen. Electric Co., Phoenix, 1965-69; founder, dir. Citicorp Systems, Inc., Cambridge, Mass., 1969-70; pres. Toda Data Systems, Manchester, Mass., 1970-71; pres. Vertel, Inc., Clifton, N.J., 1976-79, now dir.; pres. Datassure, Inc., North Andover, Mass., 1979—; session mgr. IEEE conf. on computer terminals, 1969. Served with U.S. Army, 1957-59. Mem. IEEE, Assn. Computer Machinery, Am. Soc. for Indsl. Security, Solar Energy Industries Assn., Am. Wind Energy Assn., Aircraft Owners and Pilots Assn. Clubs: Harvard (N.Y.C.) (Boston), Harvard Bus. Sch., Boston Lit. Hour (Boston). Home: 23 Mill St Manchester MA 01944 Office: 451 Andover St North Andover MA 01845

TODD, CURTIS LINN, meat processing co. exec.; b. Ft. Madison, Iowa, June 15, 1948; s. Homer Lee and Iva Parleigh (Faw) T.; B.B.A. in Acctg., U. Iowa, 1970; m. Judith Mae Boltz, June 24, 1972; 1 son, Kieran. Sr. asst. accountant Haskins & Sells, C.P.A.'s, N.Y.C., 1970, Omaha, 1972-74; asst. controller Am. Beef Packers, Inc., Omaha, 1974-77; staff accountant Buesing & Schleisman, C.P.A.'s, Omaha, 1977; with Omaha Steaks Internat., Omaha, 1977—, v.p., controller, 1978—. Served with U.S. Army, 1970-72. C.P.A., Nebr., Iowa. Mem. Am. Inst. C.P.A.'s, Nebr. Soc. C.P.A.'s, Iowa Soc. C.P.A.'s, Nat. Assn. Accountants (chpt. pres. 1981-82). Home: 14019 Madison Circle Omaha NE 68137 Office: 4400 S 96th St Omaha NE 68127

TODD, LLOYD ALLEN, systems analyst; b. Omaha, Mar. 13, 1942; s. Billy Eugene and Dorothy Lucille (Kinsley) T.; student U. Nebr. at Omaha, 1959-61, Electronic Computer Programming Inst., 1966-67; m. Barbara Elaine Hall, May 16, 1970; 1 dau., Jennifer. Ops. staff Central Nat. Life Ins. Co., Omaha, 1967-68; mgr. Output Computer Services, Omaha, 1968-70; systems analyst NW Bell Telephone Co., Omaha, 1970—. Active mem. Omaha Jaycees, 1968-69, Millard (Nebr.) Jaycees, 1973-75. Served with U.S. Army, 1964-66. Mem. Systems and Procedures Assn., Am. Legion. Baptist. Clubs: Eagles, Toastmasters. Home: PO Box 59 Kennard NE 68034

TODD, STANTON WESLEY, III, life ins. exec.; b. Grand Rapids, Mich., Feb. 23, 1941; s. Stanton Wesley, Jr., and Rosemary T.; B.A., Lake Forest (Ill.) Coll., 1963; m. Gail Walker, Mar. 1, 1969; children—Cortney Walker, Stanton Wesley IV, Kaley Clark, Kathryn Gayl. Sales rep. Northwestern Mut. Life Ins. Co., 1963-74; chief exec. officer, dir. Early Am. Life Ins. Co., 1974-78; sr. v.p., sr. mktg. officer Globe Life Ins. Co., Chgo., 1978—. Mem. Avoka Cocus, New Trier (Ill.) Twp.; bd. dirs. Nat. Child Labor Com. (N.Y.C.); bd. govs. Lake Forest Coll.; chmn. leadership council Ravenswood Hosp. (Chgo.). Life mem. Million Dollar Round Table. Home: 52 Woodley Rd Winnetka IL 60093 Office: 222 N Dearborn St Chicago IL 60601

TODD, ZANE GREY, utility exec.; b. Hanson, Ky., Feb. 3, 1924; s. Marshall Elvin and Kate (McCormick) T.; student Evansville Coll., 1947-49; B.S. summa cum laude, Purdue U., 1951, D.Eng. (hon.), 1979; m. Marysnow Stone, Feb. 8, 1950. Fingerprint classifier FBI, 1942-43; electric system planning engr. Indpls. Power & Light Co., 1951-56, spl. assignments supr., 1956-60, head elec. system planning, 1960-65, head substa. design div., 1965-68, head distbn. engring. dept., 1968-70, asst. to v.p., 1970-72, v.p., 1972-74, exec. v.p., 1974-75, pres., 1975—, chmn. bd., 1976—; gen. mgr. Mooresville Pub. Service Co., Inc. (Ind.), 1956-60; dir. Indpls. Power & Light Co., Am. States Ins. Cos., Mchts. Nat. Bank. Mem. adv. bd. St. Vincent Hosp.; bd. dirs. Greater Indpls. Progress Com., Commn. for Downtown, 500 Festival Assos., Corporate Community Council; bd. dirs. United Way Greater Indpls., chmn. gen. fund drive, 1978; trustee Ind. Central U.; trustee, mem. adv. council Christian Theol. Sem. Served as sgt. AUS, 1943-47. Named Distinguished Engring. Alumnus, Purdue U., 1976. Fellow IEEE (past chmn. application of probability methods com., past chmn. power system engring. com.); mem. Ind. (dir.), Indpls. (dir.), Mooresville (past pres.) chambers commerce, Ind. Soc. Profl. Engrs., Nat. Assn. Mfrs. (dir.), Am. Mgmt. Assn. (gen. mgmt. council), Ind. Electric Assn. (chmn. 1976, dir.), Eta Kappa Nu, Tau Beta Pi. Clubs: Rotary, Lions (past pres.), Columbia, Indianapolis Athletic, Meridian Hills Country; La Coquille (Palm Beach, Fla.). Contbr. to tech. jours. and mags. Originator probability analysis of power system reliability. Home: 7645 Randue Ct Indianapolis IN 46278 Office: 25 Monument Circle Indianapolis IN 46206

TOELLE, ROBERT MAYNARD, risk mgmt. cons.; b. Waukegan, Ill., June 29, 1912; s. Hugh Christopher and Belle (Fulton) T.; student Northwestern U., 1931-33; m. Gladys Chocol, May 7, 1937. Asst. mgr. ins. agy., 1929-43; bond mgr. Fireman's Fund, 1946-48; Chgo. mgr. Am. Fgn. Ins. Assn., 1948-51, sec., 1951-61; nat. risk exec. Kemper Group, Chgo., 1961-63, v.p. Corp. Policyholders Counsel, 1963-76; risk mgmt. cons., Sun City Center, Fla., 1976—. Served with AUS, 1943-46. Mem. Inst. Risk Mgmt. Cons. (exec. sec.), Chartered Property and Casualty Underwriters (treas.), Soc. Chartered Property and Liability Underwriters. Home: 703 Thunderbird Ave Sun City Center FL 33570

TOEWS, ALVAN WARREN, mfg. co. exec.; b. Giroux, Man., Can., Apr. 7, 1928; came to U.S., 1953, naturalized, 1965; m. Peter R. and Katharine (Reimer) T.; diploma Success Bus. Coll., Winnipeg, Man., 1948; m. Katherine L. Penner, Apr. 30, 1949; children—Terri M. Toews Hansen, Sheri Ann Toews Baltzer, Glenn Alvan. With Can. Pacific Steamships Ltd., Winnipeg, 1948-53; office mgr. Heimann Co., Mpls., 1954-58; with Indsl. Spray Painting Co., Mpls., 1958—, pres., owner, 1961—. Mem. Chem. Coaters Assn., Minn. Assn. Commerce and Industry, Fridley C. of C. Evangelical. Club: Karpe's Court (Anoka, Minn.). Office: 8251 Ashton Ave NE Fridley MN 55432

TOFFEY, H. JAMES, investment banker; b. Summit, N.J., Nov. 8, 1930; s. Harold James and Madeleine Constance (Weston) T.; A.B., Dartmouth Coll., 1952; m. Salley Jane Needles, Apr. 9, 1955; children—James W., Debora Lynn. In govt. bond sales and trading First Boston Corp., N.Y.C., 1957-66, govt. bond. sales mgr., 1966-68; partner-in-charge govt. bond dept. dePont, Glore, Forgan, N.Y.C., 1969-70; v.p. govt. securities Merrill Lycnh, Pierce, Fenner & Smith, N.Y.C., 1971-73, sr. v.p., dir. in charge govt. securities, 1973-78, exec. v.p., 1978—; dir. Taxable Fixed Income Securities Groups, 1978—. Served to lt. (j.g.) USN, 1952-55. Mem. Assn. Primary Dealers in Govt. Securities (pres.), Pub. Securities Assn. (dir.). Republican. Episcopalian. Home: Featherbed Ln Green Village NJ 07935 Office: First Boston Corp 20 Exchange Pl New York NY 10005

TOFTNER, RICHARD ORVILLE, environ. mgmt. cons.; b. Warren, Minn., Mar. 5, 1935; s. Orville Gayhart and Cora Evelyn (Anderson) T.; B.A., U. Minn., 1966; M.B.A., Xavier U., 1970; m. Jeanne Bredine, June 26, 1960; children—Douglas, Scott, Kristine, Kimberly, Brian. Sr. economist Federated Dept. Stores, Inc., Cin., 1967-68; dep. dir. EPA, Washington and Cin., 1968-73; mgmt. cons. environ. affairs, products and mktg., 1973-74; prin. PEDCo Environ., Cin., 1974-80; trustee PEDCo trusts, 1974-80; pres. ROTA Mgmt., Inc., Cin., 1980—; adj. prof. U. Cin.; lectr. Grad. fellowship rev. panel Office of Edn., 1978—; advisor, cabinet-level task force Office of Gov. of P.R., 1973; subcom. Nat. Safety Council, 1972. Served with AUS, 1954-57. Mem. Am. Inst. Cert. Planners, Soc. Advancement Mgmt., Water Pollution Control Fedn., Water Resources Council of Ohio. Contbr. articles to mgmt. planning and environ. to periodicals, chpts. in books. Home: 9175 Yellowwood Dr Cincinnati OH 45239 Office: 4700 Lakeview Tower Cincinnati OH 45241

TOGNONI, HALE CHRISTOPHER, lawyer, mineral devel. cons., engr.; b. Preston, Nev., Apr. 16, 1921; s. Joseph Russell and Ina B. (Cates) T.; student Va. Mil. Inst., 1943-44, Colo. Sch. Mines, summer 1947; B.S. in Geol. Engring., U. Nev., 1948; law student Am. U., 1950-52; J.D., U. Ida., 1953; m. George-Ann Neudeck, Mar. 13, 1947; children—Becky Lou, Brian Hale, David Quentin, Sandra-Ann, Jeffrey R. Foreman, Molina sect. New Idria Quicksilver Mining Co. (Calif.), 1940-41; geol. asst. U.S. Geol. Survey, Steamboat Springs, Nev., 1946-48; geol. engr. Anaconda Copper Mining Co., Butte, Mont., also Darwin, Calif., 1948-50; staff asst. Carnegie Inst. Tech., Dept. Terrestrial Magnetism, Washington, 1950; hwy. testing engr., C.E., Ft. Belvoir, 1951; geologist Magna Mine, Superior, Ariz., 1953; asst. dir. research Ariz. Legis. Council, 1953-54; state mineral examiner Ariz. Land Dept., 1954-55; in pvt. practice as lawyer, also cons. engr., Phoenix, 1954—, partner law firm Tognoni, Parsons and Gooding (later Tognoni, Parsons, Birchett & Gooding, then Tognoni and Pugh), 1956-71; pres. Mineral Econs. Corp., Multiple Use, Inc., Minerals Trust Corp.; v.p., dir. Gunsight Mining Co., Mineral Services Corp., Wollastonite Copper Corp., Tonto Basin Uranium Corp., Tognoni Fine Arts Inc. Faculty asso. engring. Ariz. State U., 1962-74. Formerly active Boy Scouts Am.; chmn. Ariz. State Land Law Study Com., 1954-56; mem. Flood Protection Improvement Com. representing Maricopa County, 1957-59; chmn. Gov.'s Com. on Arid Lands, 1959-60. Served from pvt. to 1st lt. C.E., AUS, 1942-46; res. officer, 1946-53. Mem. Ariz. Soc. Profl. Engrs. (sec. Central chpt. 1958-60, pres. 1961; chmn. state legis. com. 1959-68, state pres. 1968-69, nat. dir. 1970-73), Ariz. Council for Edn. (sec. 1957-58), Am., Ariz., Maricopa County bar assns., Petroleum Devel. Assn. (pres. 1969), Am. Inst. Mining and Metall. Engrs. (chmn. Maricopa subsect. 1974-75, program chmn. S.W. mineral industry conf. 1973). Kiwanian (pres. N.W. Valley 1961, chmn. vocat. guidance com., chmn. S.W. dist. agr. and conservation com. 1968). Club: Kiva. Author articles in field. Home: 1525 W Northern Ave Phoenix AZ 85021 Office: Suite 1260 Del Webbs Town House Phoenix AZ 85013

TOKAR, LOUIS JOHN, constrn. co. exec.; b. Sioux City, Iowa, July 21, 1923; s. John S. and Mary T. (Homa) T.; B.S., Morningside Coll., 1952; m. Mary J. Trafton, Aug. 30, 1947; children—Mary L., Robert L. Asst. to pres. Tower Communications, 1950-60; pres. Advance Industries, Inc., Sioux City, 1961—. Served with USNR, 1942-46. Mem. Electronic Industries Assn., Petroleum Assn., R.R. Assn. Elk, Rotarian. Club: Sioux City Country. Home: 3817 Country Club St Sioux City IA 51104 Office: 2301 Bridgeport Dr Sioux City IA 51102

TOLL, DANIEL ROGER, fin. services co. exec.; b. Denver, Dec. 3, 1927; s. Oliver W. and Merle D'Aubigne (Sampson) T.; A.B. magna cum laude, Princeton U., 1949; M.B.A. with distinction (Baker scholar), Harvard U., 1955; m. Sue Andersen, June 15, 1963; children—Daniel Andersen, Matthew Mitchell. Asst. mgr. product supply and distbn. Deep Rock Oil Corp., 1949-51; with Helmerich & Payne, Tulsa, 1955-64, fin. v.p., 1961-64; treas., dir. corp. planning Sunray DX Oil Co., Tulsa, 1964-66, v.p. corp. planning and devel., 1966-68; v.p. Sun Oil Co., 1969; sr. v.p. fin., dir., mem. exec. com. Walter E. Heller Internat. Corp., Chgo., 1970-79, exec. v.p., 1979-80, pres., 1980—; exec. v.p. Walter E. Heller & Co., Chgo., 1976—; dir. Lincoln Nat. Direct Placement Fund, Inc. Vice chmn., mem. budget com. Tulsa Community Chest, 1964-66; v.p., dir. Tulsa Opera, 1960-69; dir., chmn. play choosing and casting coms. Tulsa Little Theatre, 1963-69; chief crusader Chgo. Crusade Mercy, 1972—; bd. dirs. Inroads, Inc., 1973—; chmn. fin. and profl. fund raising Chgo. area council Boy Scouts Am., 1974-76, bd. dirs., 1976—, exec. v.p., 1980—, pack master Kenilworth Cub Scouts, 1972-75; mem. Sch. Bd. Dist. 38, Kenilworth, Ill., 1975—, pres., 1978—, also chmn. fin. com. Served to lt. (j.g.) USNR, 1951-52. Mem. Chgo. Assn. Commerce and Industry (dir.), Phi Beta Kappa. Clubs: Union League, Economic, Harvard Bus. Sch. (past pres. local chpt., dir. 1971—) (Chgo.); Indian Hill (Winnetka). Home: 125 Abingdon Ave Kenilworth IL 60043 Office: 105 W Adams St Chicago IL 60690

TOLLE, WAYNE FRANCIS, apparel co. exec.; b. Mansville, Ky., Aug. 3, 1941; s. James Wayne and Mary Edna (Bussell) T.; B.S. in Commerce, U. Ky., 1964; M.B.A., U. Ga., 1969; m. Mary Judith Porter, Dec. 17, 1966; children—Jeffrey Wayne, Mary Elizabeth, Julie Lynne. With Blue Bell Inc., 1969—, asst. div. mgr., Greensboro, N.C., 1971-74, mfg. mgr. Wrangler South Africa, 1974-75; gen. mgr. Blue Bell Scotland, Falkirk, 1975-78; chief exec., mfg. dir. Wrangler Australia, Chatswood, 1978—; dir. Blue Bell Apparel Scotland. Served with USAF, 1964-68. Decorated Air Force Commendation medal. Mem. Am. Apparel Mfg. Assn., Am. Inst. Indsl. Engrs. Republican. Methodist. Office: Wranger Australia 21A Smith St Chatswood 2067 Australia*

TOLLEMACHE, CEDRIC REGINALD, auto parts distbn. co. exec.; b. Johannesburg, South Africa, Dec. 16, 1944; came to U.S., 1979; s. Laurence Alfred Reginald and Evelyn Alice (Paddock) T.; grad. U. Witwatersrand, 1963-68; m. Catrina Valerie Gourlay, Jan. 16, 1970; children—Andrew, Sarah, Victoria. Articled clk. to sr. audit clk George Mackenzie & Co., also P.A. Becker & Co., 1963-69; successively group acct., dir., group mktg. dir., Diesel-Elec. Orgn. South Africa, 1969-76, group chief exec. officer, 1976-79; pres., chief exec. officer Am. Oanag Orgn., Houston, 1979—; pres., chief exec. officer Oanag U.S.A. Corp.; exec. chmn. Oanag Can. Corp. Chartered acct., South Africa. Fellow Inst. Cost and Mgmt. Accts. (London); mem. Transvaal Soc. Chartered Accts. Office: 15534 W Hardy Rd Houston TX 77660

TOLLENAERE, LAWRENCE ROBERT, indsl. products co. exec.; b. Berwyn, Ill., Nov. 19, 1922; s. Cyrille and Modesta (Van Damme) T.; B.S. in Engring., Iowa State U., 1944, M.S. in Engring., 1949; M.B.A., U. So. Calif., 1969; LL.D. (hon.), Claremont Grad. Sch., 1978; m. Mary Hansen, Aug. 14, 1948; children—Elizabeth, Homer, Stephanie, Caswell Ann, Jennifer Mary. Asst. prof. engring. Iowa State U., 1947-50; sales rep. Ameron (formerly Am. Pipe & Constrn. Co.), South Gate, Calif., 1950-53, spl. rep., Santiago, Chile, 1953-54, 2d v.p., div. mgr., Bogota, Colombia, 1955-57, v.p., mgr., South Gate, Calif., 1958-63, v.p. corporate offices, Monterey Park, Calif., 1963-64, pres., 1965—, chief exec. officer, 1967—, dir., 1966—; dir. Gifford-Hill-Am., Inc., Dallas, chmn., 1966-76; dir. Avery Internat., Norris Industries, Newhall Land & Farming Co., Valencia, Calif., Pacific Mut. Life Ins. Co., Parsons Corp. Bd. fellows Claremont U. Center; bd. govs. Iowa State U. Found.; bd. dirs. Beavers; trustee Henry A. Huntington Library Art Gallery and Bot. Gardens, 1973-78, life mem. Soc. Fellows. Served from ensign to lt. (j.g.), USNR, 1944-46. Mem. Soc. Advancement Mgmt., Mchts. and Mfrs. Assn. (exec. com.), NAM, Calif. C. of C., Newcomen Soc., Alpha Tau Omega. Clubs: California; San Gabriel (Calif.) Country; Jonathan (Los Angeles); Lincoln; Pauma Valley Country. Home: 1400 Milan Ave South Pasadena CA 91030 also Kaanapali Plantation Lahaina Maui HI 96761 Office: 4700 Ramona Blvd PO Box 3000 Monterey Park CA 91754

TOLLESON, JOHN CARTER, bank exec.; b. Ennis, Tex., Aug. 16, 1948; s. Cecil H. and Frances Louise (Carter) T.; m. Debra June Stewart, Jan. 8, 1977; 1 son, John Carter. Sr. v.p. Nat. Bank of Commerce, Dallas, 1969-75, Mercantile Nat. Bank, Dallas, 1975-77; pres. Am. Nat. Bank, Austin, Tex., 1977—; dir. Am. Bank, Affiliated Computer Services, Citizens Bank of Austin, 1978— sr. v.p. Mercantile Tex. Corp., 1978—. Bd. dirs. Austin C. of C., 178-79, treas., 1978, chmn. budget & fin. com., 1978-79; mem. adv. bd. Knights of Symphony, Brackenridge Hosp., 1978—; trustee Capital Area United Way, 1978-81. Mem. Tex. Bankers Assn. (chmn. edn. com.), Am. Inst. Bankers, Am. Bankers Assn. Methodist. Clubs: Admirals, Headliners (mem. exec. bd.). Office: PO Box 2266 Austin TX 78780

TOLLIVER, JONATHAN COOPER, mktg. research exec.; b. Flemingsburg, Ky., Oct. 21, 1925; s. John Cooper and Bessilene (Hysong) T.; grad. high sch. Producer, Children's Fine Arts Guild, N.Y.C., 1959-63; treas. region 14, Children's Theatre Conf., N.Y.C., 1963-66, regional gov., 1966-68; comptroller, mem. exec. com. nat. governing bd. Children's Theatre Assn., Washington, 1968-74; exec. v.p., sec. Miller & Taliaferro Inc., N.Y.C., 1973—. Bd. dirs. Children's Performing Arts Center, N.Y.C. Mem. Am. Mktg. Assn., Geneal. Soc. of Original Wilkes County, Episcopal Actors Guild, English-Speaking Union. Translator: (pseudonym John D. Cooper) Ruy Blas (Victor Hugo), 1956. Home and office: 1270 Fifth Ave New York NY 10029

TOLMIE, JOHN STRATTON, JR., real estate investor and developer; b. Rockland, Mass., Apr. 18, 1946; s. John Stratton and Mary Agnes (O'Connell) T.; B.S., U.S. Naval Acad., 1969; M.B.A., Pepperdine U., 1974; m. Linda Ann Bailey, June 7, 1969; children—John Stratton, Erin Marie. Sales rep. Xerox Corp., Honolulu and Hilo, Hawaii, 1974-76, Hawaii Land Realty, 1976-77, Hirota-Griffin & Assos., 1977-79; pres. J.T. Trading Co., Ltd., Hilo, 1976—. Served to capt. USMC, 1969-74. Named Salesman of Year, Honolulu br. Xerox Corp., 1975. Mem. Nat. Assn. Realtors, Farms and Land Inst. Democrat. Roman Catholic. Club: Exchange. Home: 1069 Laulima Pl Hilo HI 96720 Office: 175 Banyan Dr Hilo HI 96720

TOLSON, DARRELL GRAY, travel agt.; b. Elizabeth City, N.C., Apr. 25, 1947; s. Arnold G. and Inez G. Tolson; student public schs.; m. Evelyn R. Hodgin, Apr. 20, 1969; children—Laura, Gray. Vice pres. mktg. Am. Travel Corp., 1969-73, Travel Cons., 1973-74; pres. So. Internat. Travel Corp., Raleigh, N.C., 1974—. Served with USCGR, 1966-68. Mem. Am. Soc. Assn. Execs., Internat. Assn. Travel Agts., Internat. Trade Assn. Office: 4300 Six Forks Rd Raleigh NC 27609

TOMBROS, JAMES RUSSELL, pharm. co. exec.; b. Vineland, N.J., Aug. 13, 1946; s. Nicholas Russell and Eleanor Emma (Brown) T.; B.S. in Mktg. Mgmt., Syracuse U., 1969; M.B.A., Pace U., 1973; cert. pharm. seminar Dartmouth Coll., 1974; m. Barbara Lehmann, June 28, 1970; children—Meredith, Allison. Mgr. hosp. products Winthrop Labs., N.Y.C., 1972-75; mktg. mgr. Hermal Labs., Elmsford, N.Y., 1976-77, dir. mktg., 1978-79, v.p., gen. mgr., Oak Hill, N.Y., 1979—, also dir. Mem. alumni career devel. com. Pace U., 1975—. Mem. Am. Mktg. Assn., Am. Mgmt. Assn., Assn. M.B.A. Execs., Pharm. Advt. Council, Tau Kappa Epsilon. Office: Hermal Labs Route 145 Oak Hill NY 12460

TOMES, JAMES STEEL, mfg. co. exec., lawyer; b. Milw., Apr. 30, 1927; s. William Austin and Elizabeth (Steel) T.; B.S., Northwestern U., 1951; LL.B., Chgo. Kent Coll. Law, 1957; m. Joann Witmeyer Raymaley, June 26, 1954; children—Robert Steel, Elizabeth Austin, John Wilson, Julia Hall. Admitted to Ill. bar, 1957; asso. law firm Petit, Olin, Overmyer & Fazio, Chgo., 1957-60; asst. counsel Bell & Howell Co., Chgo., 1960-61, counsel, 1961-65, v.p. product mgmt., 1965-67; v.p., gen. mgr. audio visual products div., 1967-69; pres. Ventron Instruments Corp. subs. Ventron Corp., 1969-70; corporate v.p., pres. Internat. group Bell & Howell Co., 1970-72, corporate v.p., pres. consumer products group, 1972-73, sr. corp. v.p., pres. consumer and audiovisual products group, 1973-74; sr. corp. v.p., chief exec. consumer group U.S. Industries, 1975-76; pres., chief exec. officer Filtertek, Inc., Hebron, Ill., 1977-79, dir., 1972-80; pres., chief exec. officer, dir., Bijur Lubricating Corp., Oakland, N.J., 1980—. Bd. dirs. Ill. div. ACLU, 1965-72. Served with AUS, 1945-47, USAF, 1950-53. Mem. Am., Ill., Chgo. bar assns., Phi Delta Phi. Home: 714 Washington St Wilmette IL 60091 Office: 112 Bauer Dr Oakland NJ 07436

TOMISEK, THOMAS NEAL, automobile parts store exec.; b. Chgo., July 22, 1948; s. James Joseph and Bessie Georgiana (Severa) T.; B.S., U. Tenn., 1970; children—Thomas Neal, Timothy Alan. Supr., Atlas Paper Box Co., Chattanooga, 1972-73; prodn. planner Combustion Engring. Co., Chattanooga, 1973-77; salesman Mass. Mut. Life Ins. Agy., Chattanooga, 1977-78; owner, operator TNT Auto Parts, Inc., Chattanooga, 1978—. Scoutmaster troop 90 Boy Scouts Am. Served with U.S. Army, 1970-72. Mem. Am. Service Assn., Ind. Garage Assn., Chattanooga Jaycees (v.p.). Home: 1006 Teeside Rd Chattanooga TN 37421 Office: TNT Auto Parts Inc 2103 E 23d St Chattanooga TN 37404

TOMKINSON, ORION HARRY EDWARD, ret. govt. exec.; b. Phila., Aug. 19, 1918; s. Henry T. and Emilie Louise (Knoedler) T.; student Am. U., 1958-59; m. Dorris Grey Chrisman, June 21, 1941; children—Richard Lee, Harry Allan, Sue Ellen Tomkinson, Kenneth Chrisman. With U.S. Treasury Dept., Washington, 1962—, mgmt. analysis officer, 1962-72, asst. to dep. treas. of U.S., 1972-74, asst. to commr. Bur. Govt. Fin. Ops., 1974-75, dep. asst. commr. banking and cash mgmt., 1975-80. Democrat. Mem. Ch. of Christ (Bible class tchr., elder, lay preacher). Office: US Treasury Dept Bur Govt Financial Operations Room 206 Annex 1 Washington DC 20226

TOMKO, ANDREW DAVID, aerospace co. exec.; b. Roznava, Czechoslovakia, Feb. 3, 1919; s. Andrew and Maria (Davidova) T.; B.S. (Ohio Bd. Realtors scholar), Ohio State U., 1949; M.A. (Air Force Advance Programs grantee), U. Okla., 1970; m. Mary Louise McAdams, Sept. 2, 1943; children—Lawrence Andrew, Margaret Ann, Mary Jean, Tamara Sue. Civil servant U.S. Air Force, 1950-76, fgn. mil. sales program br. chief, Oklahoma City, 1959-65, program mgr. for procurement methods, 1965-76; pres. Govt. Contractors Co., Oklahoma City, 1976—; dir. Astro Mktg. Co. and Internat. Mil. Sales Corp. (both Oklahoma City). Sustaining mem. Republican Nat. Com., 1978—, asst. party dist. chmn., 1978-80. Served with USAAF, 1940-45. Decorated D.F.C., Air medal with 4 oak leaf clusters. Mem. Air Force Assn. (chmn. indsl. com. Oklahoma City chpt. 1978—), Mfrs. and Agts. Nat. Assn., Nat. Contract Mgmt. Assn., 8th Air Force

Hist. Soc., Czechoslovak Nat. Council Am., Ohio State U. Alumni Assn., U. Okla. Alumni Assn., Am. Legion. Lutheran. Clubs: Edmond (Okla.) Tennis; Tinker Air Force Base Officers, Moose. Home: 201 Country Club Terr Midwest City OK 73110 Office: Govt Contractors Co PO Box 10794 Oklahoma City OK 73140

TOMLINSON, ALLAN JOHN, JR., chem. co. exec.; b. Houston, Aug. 30, 1932; s. Allan John and Edyna Mae (Kuehn) T.; B.S.Chem.E., Tex. Tech. U., 1954; M.B.A., Harvard U., 1960; m. Helen E. Nebeker, July 7, 1960; children—Allan John, III, Laura Ellen, William Marc. Engr., Shell Oil Co., 1954-58; mktg. mgr. Dow Chem. Co., Midland, Mich., 1960-66; cons. McKinsey & Co., Cleve., 1966-68; exec. v.p. Diamond Shamrock Corp., Cleve., 1968-80, pres., chief operating officer, 1980—. Vice pres. Shaker Heights (Ohio) Bd. Edn.; trustee Cleve. Ballet, St. Lukes Hosp., Cleve. Served with USAF, 1955-58. Office: Diamond Shamrock Corp 1100 Superior Ave Cleveland OH 44114*

TOMLINSON, J. RICHARD, railroad exec.; b. Newton, Pa., Mar. 26, 1930; s. Robert K. and Margaret (Wright) T.; B.A., Swarthmore, 1952; postgrad. George Washington U., 1952-53, U. Mich., 1955-57, Drexel Inst. Tech., 1954-57, Am. U., 1965; m. Barbara Elizabeth Brazill, Apr. 30, 1955; children—Karin Kathleen, Kimberly Ann. Mgmt. analyst Dept. State, Washington, 1952-53; with Old Republic Life Ins. Co., Washington, 1953-54; supr. fin. analysis Ford Motor Co., Detroit, 1954-61; cons. McKinsey & Co., Washington, 1961-65; v.p. finance, dir. passenger services, Reading Co., Phila., 1965-69, v.p. finance Rollins Internat., Inc., 1969-71; exec. v.p. Amtrak, Washington, 1972-74; partner Louis T. Klander & Assos., Phila., 1974-75; exec. v.p. Penn Central Transp. Co., 1975-79; partner L.T. Klamber & Assos., 1979—. Named Man of Month, Phila. C. of C., 1967. Clubs: Union League (Phila.); Stone Harbor (N.J.) Yacht. Home: 1656 Susquehanna Rd Rydal PA 19046 Office: PNB Bldg Broad and Chestnut St Philadelphia PA 19107

TOMMASSELLO, ROBERT, ins. cons.; b. Hazleton, Pa., Sept. 20, 1939; s. Salvatore Adam and Carmella Irene (Basile) T.; A., St. Joseph's Coll., 1960; Asso. degree U. Pa., 1963, B.S., 1965; m. Jean Marie Bednarchik, May 16, 1971; children—Robert Adam, Nicole Marie. Regional dir. Pa. Dept. Public Welfare, 1960-69; v.p. Phila. Wood Carving Co., Inc., 1969-73; ins. cons. Mut. of N.Y., Hazelton, 1973—, mem. agy. adv. bd., field cons., 1974—. Charter mem., founder Hazleton Diabetic Assn., 1974, former pres., chmn. bd.; pres., bd. dirs. Lower Luzerne County Drug and Alcohol Abuse Program, 1975; bd. dirs. Anthracite council Boy Scouts Am. Mem. Mut. of N.Y. Hall of Fame, Million Dollar Round Table, Pa. Leaders Round Table; recipient Nat. Sales Achievement award, other ins. awards. Mem. Nat. Assn. Life Underwriters. Roman Catholic. Club: Rotary. Home: Saint Johns PA 18247 Office: Mutual of New York 29th and N Church Sts Hazleton PA 18201

TOMPKINS, DONALD FREDERICK, motor transp. co. exec.; b. Paterson, N.J., Sept. 15, 1930; s. Daniel and Mary Ester (Sindle) T.; B.S., Fairleigh Dickenson U., Teaneck, N.J., 1959; J.D., St. Johns U., Bklyn., 1969; m. Sadako Umetsu, Oct. 2, 1956; children—Edward, Nancy, Judith. Credit mgr. Comml. Credit Corp., Paterson, 1956-61, Appliance Buyers Credit Corp., East Orange, N.J., 1962-64, Arrow Group Industries, Inc., Haskell, N.J., 1965-68; claims and credit mgr. Gilbert Flexi-Van Corp., N.Y.C., 1968-70; admitted to N.J. bar, 1969; atty., v.p. finance, dir. Nelson Resource Corp., Secaucus, N.J., 1970—; dir. A & B Garment Delivery, Inc., Tri-State Transp. Co., Inc., Linco Leasing Corp., Vineland, N.J. and Phila., Bradleys Express Co., Inc., Berlin, Conn., Nelson Air Internat., Inc., Nelson Distbn. Corp., Marking Services Corp., Secaucus. Served with AUS, 1955-56. Mem. Am., N.J. bar assns. Home: 2 Lenox Rd Wayne NJ 07470 Office: 20 Enterprise Ave Secaucus NJ 07094

TOMPKINS, DONALD ROBERT, telephone co. exec.; b. Portchester, N.Y., June 9, 1941; s. Reed Pershing and Lucille Marion (Radcliffe) T.; A.A.S., Western Conn. State Coll., 1974; postgrad. Fairleigh Dickinson U., 1977-79; children—Brian Dale, Kathleen Kim, Colleen Joy. Engring. supr. AT & T Long Lines, White Plains, N.Y., 1968, ops. supr., 1968-71, ops. cutover chmn., 1971-73, ops. cutover chmn., Bridgeport, Conn., 1973-75, ops. mgr., White Plains, 1975-77, industry mgr. sales, Newark, 1977-78, nat. account mgr. sales, White Plains, 1978-80, dist. mktg. mgr. sales, 1980—. Com. chmn. Fairfield County council Boy Scouts Am., 1965-70, scoutmaster, 1970-78; sch. supt. Meth. Ch., Danbury, Conn., 1965-72. Served with U.S. Navy, 1960-64. Mem. Am. Mgmt. Assn., Am. Mktg. Assn. Republican. Methodist. Club: Green Mountain Hiking. Home: 42 Outlook Ave Hawthorne NJ 07506 Office: 445 Hamilton Ave White Plains NY 10601

TOMPKINS, JAMES GLOVER, III, steamship co. exec.; b. Washington, Sept. 26, 1926; s. James Glover and Ruth Lee (Kunkel) T.; B.S.M.T., U.S. Mcht. Marine Acad., 1947; B.S.F.S., Georgetown U., 1950; m. Margaret Susan Bader, Mar. 12, 1954; children—Fredrica Clare, James Glover, Lucy Elizabeth. With Lykes Bros S.S. Co., Inc., 1945-48, 51—, dir. U.K., Lykes Lines Agy., Inc., London, 1961-64, dir. Continental-U.K., Antwerp, Belgium, 1965-73, v.p. Continental-U.K., Antwerp, 1974-75, v.p., W. Gulf div., Houston, 1975, sr. v.p., Houston, 1976—; mem. Nat. Def. Exec. Res.; v.p. Nat. Def. Transp. Assn. Benelux; adv. com. Tex. A&M U.-Tex. Transp. Inst. Named adm. Tex. Navy. Mem. Am. C. of C. Belgium (dir.), German-Am. C. of C. (adv. bd.), Am. Belgium Assn., West Gulf Maritime Assn. (dir., chmn.), Houston World Trade Assn. (dir.). Episcopalian. Office: Lykes Bros Steamship Co PO Box 1339 Houston TX 77001

TOMPKINS, STEPHAN, film co. exec.; b. St. Louis, Jan. 15, 1937; s. Tom Louis and Ella Mae T.; A.A., Sacramento City Coll.; student Sacramento State Coll., 1963; B.A., U. Calif. at Berkeley, 1960; postgrad. U. Calif. at Los Angeles, 1965; children—David, Pam. Film dir. MGM Studios, 1973, Acad. Films, 1974; pres. Stephans Tompkins Prodns., Hollywood, Calif., 1969—; producer, dir. Teamed for Laughter, Warner Bros. Studios, 1975, The Children of Sisyphus, 1978. Served with AUS, 1959. Mem. Dirs. Guild, Writers Guild, Ind. Producers Assn., Smithsonian Instn. Office: PO Box 69425 Hollywood CA 90069

TOMS, CLINTON LEE, mgmt. cons.; b. Albany, N.Y., May 1, 1928; s. Adrian G. and Ruby (Rymer) T.; student Sampson Coll., 1946-48; B.S. Indsl. Engring., Rutgers U., 1952; m. Clara L. Metcalf, June 26, 1949 (div. Oct. 1980); children—Donna, Scott, Kevin, Laura, Tracey. Plant supt. Owens Illinois Co., Columbus, Ohio, 1952-55; dir. inventory control and market research James Lees & Sons, Norristown, Pa., 1955-60; pres. Perkup Co., Pottstown, Pa., 1960-63; co-founder, sr. v.p. K. W. Tunnell Co., Inc., King of Prussia, Pa., 1963-69; pres. Exec. Forums, Inc., Norristown, 1969-74, Center for Applied Mgmt., Inc., Greenfield, Wis., 1974—, Micro Mgmt. Systems, Inc., Milw., 1977—; lectr. numerous univs., colls. Chmn. bd. suprs. Lower Providence Twp., Montgomery County, Pa., 1960-66. Mem. Am. Mgmt. Assn., Am. Prodn., Inventory Control Soc. (founder), Inst. Mgmt. Cons. (founding), Am. Inst. Indsl. Engring., Am. Soc. Tng. Dirs., Am. Arbitration Assn. Republican. Contbr. numerous articles to profl. jours.; author textbook set 1960-78; patentee in field.

TONER, JOHN FRANCIS, mfg. co. exec.; b. Providence, Sept. 25, 1926; s. Edward J. and Florence J. (Smith) T.; B.S., Mt. St. Mary's Coll., 1950; m. Tommye Comer, Sept. 25, 1964; 1 dau., Ann Kathryn. Sales rep. Avondale Mills, N.Y.C., 1955-76, v.p. merchandising, 1976-78, sr. v.p. mktg., 1978—. Trustee, Pound Ridge (N.Y.) Library. Served with USN, 1944-46. Mem. Am. Arbitration Assn., Am. Textile Mfrs. Inst. Clubs: Waccabuc Country, Princeton. Home: Bender Way Pound Ridge NY 10576 Office: 1430 Broadway New York NY 10018

TONEY, ILA VERNE, realtor; b. McNeil, Ark., Apr. 2, 1934; d. William Edwin and Bertha Oleta (Jameson) Brasher; B.A., U. Houston, 1968; A.A., Alvin Jr. Coll., 1965; m. Rayford B. Toney, Apr. 28, 1953; children—Tina Rey Thorson, Ivy Lynn Lambert. Sales agt. Houstonian Realty, Houston, 1973-74, Jim Tucker Realty, Houston, 1974-77, office mgr., dir. tng., 1976-77; sales agt. ERA First Realty of Houston, 1977—, broker asso., 1975-80. Precinct exec. committeeman Republican Party, Harris County, Tex., 1975-80; reader in taping for the blind, Library of Congress, 1976-80. Cert. real estate specialist. Mem. Nat. Assn. Realtors, Tex. Assn. Realtors, Nat. Assn. for Hist. Preservation. Republican. Mormon. Clubs: Meadowbrook Civic, Order Eastern Star. Home: 8354 Bonner St Houston TX 77017 Office: 8035 Gulf Freeway Houston TX 77017

TONEY, ROBERT LELAND, air force officer; b. Chelsea, Mich., Mar. 27, 1932; s. Clarence Rueben and Mary Almeda (Bradbury) T.; B.B.A., Mich. State U., 1954; M.S., George Washington U., 1966; m. Carolynn Ann Bates, May 8, 1954; children—Steven Robert, Lori Ann, Marianne, Christopher Leland. Jr. underwriter Boston and Old Colony Ins. Co., Lansing, Mich., 1952-55; payroll auditor Oldsmobile div. Fischer Body Corp., Lansing, 1955; commd. 2d lt. USAF, 1955, advanced through grades to col., 1976; comptroller 26th Tactical Reconnaisance Wing, Zweibrucken (W. Ger.) AFB, 1971-73, 86th Tactical Fighter Wing, Ramstein (W. Ger.) AFB, 1973-75, systems accountant Plans and Programs div. Hdqrs. Air Force Accounting and Fin. Center, Lowry AFB, Colo., 1976-77, chief pay and travel systems div., 1977, dir. mil. pay ops., 1977-79; dep. controller Air Tng. Command, Randolph AFB, Tex., 1979—; mgmt. instr. So. Colo. State Coll., 1965-66. Decorated Bronze Star, Legion of Merit. Mem. Am. Soc. Mil. Comptrollers, Air Force Assn., Theta Xi. Lutheran. Home: 2 S Park Randolph AFB TX 78148

TONGUE, PAUL GRAHAM, banker; b. Phila., Dec. 30, 1932; s. George Paul and Florence (Kogel) T.; B.S., Drexel Inst. Tech., 1957; M.B.A., N.Y. U., 1966; m. Marjorie Joan Meyers, May 26, 1954; children—Suzanne Marjorie, Douglas Paul. With Burroughs Corp., Paoli, Pa., 1956-57; with Chase Manhattan Bank, N.Y.C., 1957—, asst. v.p., 1963-68, v.p., 1968—, div. exec. Bankamericard div., 1969-72; group exec. Issuer Securities Services, 1972, sr. v.p., 1972—, area exec. data processing, 1974-77, group exec. retail banking prodn., 1977—. Faculty, N.Y. chpt. Am. Inst. Banking, 1966—. Mem. Republican County Com., Richmond County, N.Y., 1961-63. Served with AUS, 1954-55. Mem. N.Y. State Bankers Assn. (chmn. open end consumer credit com. 1971-72), Am. Bankers Assn. (exec. com. bank card div. 1970-72), Am. Mgmt. Assn. (mgmt. scis. and systems council 1975-80, exec. com. installment lending div. 1980—). Home: 792 Park Ave Manhasset NY 11030 Office: 1211 Ave of Americas New York NY 10018

TOOKEY, ROBERT CLARENCE, cons. actuary; b. Santa Monica, Calif., Mar. 21, 1925; s. Clarence Hall and Minerva (Anderson) T.; B.S., Calif. Inst. Tech., 1945; M.S., U. Mich., 1947; m. Marcia Louise Hickman, Sept. 15, 1956; children—John Hall, Jennifer Louise, Thomas Anderson. Jr. actuarial asst. Prudential Ins. Co., Newark, 1947-49; asso. actuary Pacific Mut. Life Ins. Co., Los Angeles, 1949-55; asst. v.p. Lincoln Nat. Life, Ft. Wayne, Ind., 1955-61; dir. actuarial services Peat, Marwick, Mitchell, Chgo., 1961-63; mng. prin. M&R Inc., Pasadena, Calif., 1963-76; pres. Robert Tookey Assos., Inc., Pasadena, 1977—. Mem. Re-elect the Pres. Com., 1972. Served to lt. (j.g.), USN, 1943-45, 51-52. Fellow Soc. Actuaries, Conf. of Actuaries in Public Practice; mem. Am. Acad. Actuaries. Republican. Clubs: Union League (Chgo.); San Gabriel Country, Rotary, Pasadena, Los Angeles Actuarial (pres. 1966-67). Contbr. articles to profl. jours. Home: 1249 Descanso Dr LaCanada CA 91011 Office: 251 S Lake Ave Suite 107 Pasadena CA 91101

TOOLE, ROBERTA LDUISE GLENNON, fin. exec.; b. Miller, S.D., Jan. 1, 1937; d. Robert Pearsall and Irene Elizabeth (Hatch) Glennon; B.S., St. Louis U., 1959, Ed.M., 1962; postgrad. Washington U., 1962-64, M.B.A., 1977; m. William J. Toole, Aug. 2, 1961 (div. Jan. 1976); children—Mary, Douglas, William Timothy. Tchr. biology and chemistry St. Louis Bd. Edn., 1959-62; office mgr. Wm. J. Toole Co., Clayton, Mo., 1963-75; adminstrv. asst. to dean Washington U. Sch. Bus., St. Louis, 1976-77; mgmt. trainee Profl. Econ. Services, Clayton, 1977-78; v.p., controller Multiphasic Health Services, Clayton, 1978; supr. acctg. Charter Nat. Life Ins. Co., Clayton, 1978-79; mgr. fin. and adminstrn. Stolz Advt. Co., Clayton, 1979-80, v.p. fin. and adminstrn., 1980—. Chmn., Keep Informed on Dist. Schs., 1974-75; mem. Parks and Recreation Commn., Des Peres, Mo., 1976-78; mem. hon. degree com. Washington U., 1976-77; exec. bd. Jr. Great Books Found. Greater St. Louis. NSF grantee, 1962-64. Mem. Assn. M.B.A. Execs., Advt. Fedn. St. Louis, D.A.R., Mensa. Contbr. articles to profl. jours. and mags. Home: # 3 Briarbrook Trail Des Peres MO 63131 Office: 7701 Forsyth Ave Clayton MO 63105

TOOTHMAN, EDWIN HUGH, acoustical engr.; b. Mannington, W.Va., Oct. 1, 1932; s. Charles Adam and Syvilla May (Fluharty) T.; B.S., Fairmont State Coll., 1960; postgrad. U. Pitts., 1960-62; m. Anita Louise Antel, June 16, 1955; children—Connie Louise, Eric Edwin, Kim Lynette, Wendy Lynae. Proposal engr. Pa. Transformer Co., Canonsburg, 1957-58; research asst. U. Pitts., 1958-62; dir. noise and radiation control Bethlehem Steel Corp. (Pa.), 1962—; chmn. tech. task group Fastener Industry Noise Control Research Program, 1975—. Pres. East Hills Civic Assn., 1971-72; pres. Gov. Wolf Sch. PTA, 1968-69. Served with USAF, 1950-53. Mem. Am. Indsl. Hygiene Assn., Acoustical Soc. Am. (pres. Delaware Valley chpt. 1971-72), Engrs. Club Lehigh Valley, Am. Iron and Steel Inst. (chmn. subcom. on noise 1974—). Home: 2932 Avon Rd Bethlehem PA 18017 Office: Bethlehem Steel Corp Room B-238 Martin Tower Bethlehem PA 18016

TOOTHMAN, FRED REES, r.r. ofcl.; b. Hepzibah, W.Va., Oct. 26, 1918; s. Glenn J. R. and Elsie H. (Rees) T.; B.S. in Mining Engring., W.Va. U., 1941, M.S. in Mining Engring., 1946; postgrad. aerology U.S. Naval Acad., 1945; m. Velma S. Neale, Nov. 16, 1973; children—Brent H., Stephen B. Mining engr. C. & O. Ry. Co., Huntington, W.Va., 1946-50, adminstrv. asst. engr., 1957-58, engr. coal properties, 1959-65, dir. coal devel. C. & O. Ry.-B. & O. R.R., Huntington, 1966-72, asst. v.p. Chessie System, Huntington, 1973—; first chmn. Huntington Model R.R. Show, 1956. Mem. advisory bd. W.Va. U.; elder Enslow Park Presbyterian Ch., Huntington. Served to lt. comdr. USNR, 1941-46. Registered profl. engr., W.Va., Ky. Mem. Nat. W.Va. (pres. 1966, Engr. of Yr. award 1977) socs. profl. engrs., Am. Inst. Mining and Metall. Engrs. (chmn. coal div. 1966), W.Va. C. of C., Huntington C. of C., Sigma Gamma Epsilon, Tau Beta Pi. Home: 44 Fairfax Dr Huntington WV 25705 Office: 801 Madison Ave Huntington WV 25704

TOPPER, J. RAY, glass corp. exec.; b. Waynesboro, Pa., May 8, 1928; s. Clarence E. and Sarah Frances (Stahley) T.; B.S. in Elec. Engring., Brown U., 1952; m. Mary Helen Bromage, July 25, 1953; children—Mary Kathleen, Sarah Helen, Joseph Ray, James Michael. With Gen. Electric Co., Fairfield, Conn., 1952-71, gen. mgr. personal appliances dept., 1968-71; with Anchor Hocking Corp., Lancaster, Ohio, 1972—, exec. v.p., 1977-78, pres., chief operating officer, 1978—, also dir. Chmn. bd. trustees Lancaster-Fairfield County Hosp. Served with USN, 1946-48. Mem. IEEE, Nat. C. of C., Am. Mgmt. Assn., Glass Packaging Inst., Am. Glassware Assn. (chmn. 1977-78). Republican. Roman Catholic. Club: Lancaster Country. Office: 109 N Broad St Lancaster OH 43130

TOREM, CHARLES, lawyer; b. Newark, Sept. 30, 1914; s. Jacob and Hannah (Koslow) T.; A.B., Amherst Coll., 1935; LL.B., Harvard, 1938; m. Susannah Wilshire, July 1969; 1 son (by previous marriage), Christopher. Admitted to N.Y. bar, 1939, Fla. bar, 1941; practiced law, N.Y.C., 1938-41, Miami, Fla., 1941-42; joined Coudert Freres, internat. lawyers, Paris, 1946, partner, 1949—, now sr. partner; dir. Procter & Gamble France, Ashland Chem. (France) S.A. Vice chmn. arbitration ct. ICC; chmn. council Am. Chambers Commerce in Europe, 1967-68; panelist Practising Law Inst. N.Y. Pres., Am. C. of C. in France, 1966-69; gov. Am. Hosp. in Paris. Served from ensign to lt. comdr., USNR, 1942-46. Decorated chevalier Legion of Honor (France); spl. commendation U.S. Navy (Oran), 1945. Mem. Am., N.Y.C., Fed. bar assns., Am. Fgn. Law Assn., Am. Soc. Internat. Law, Harvard Law Sch. Assn. (mem. council), Phi Beta Kappa, Delta Sigma Rho. Clubs: American (London); Amherst; University (France); Harvard (N.Y.); Travellers, Automobile, Polo, Cercle Interallie (Paris). Contbr. articles to profl. jours. Home: 4 Rue Marbeuf Paris 8 France Office: 52 Ave des Champs Elysees Paris France

TORNEDEN, ROGER L(EE), retail chain exec.; b. Lawrence, Kans., Feb. 2, 1944; s. William E. and Lelia M. (Kindred) T.; B.S. in Indsl. Mgmt., U. Kans., 1966, M.S. in Ops. Research, 1967; Ph.D. in Internat. Bus., N.Y. U. 1974; m. Karan L. Rodgers, July 1, 1967; children—Jennifer, Stephanie. Corp. planning analyst ARCO, N.Y.C., 1967-69; sr. fin. analyst J.C. Penney, N.Y.C., 1969-72, dir. ops. analysis Sarma-Penney, Brussels, 1972-74, Japan project dir., Kobe, 1974-77, dir. internat. devel., N.Y.C., 1977—; asst. prof. mktg. Baruch Coll., 1978—; internat. cons. disposal fgn. ops. Bd. dirs. Am. C. of C. in Japan, 1976-77. Served with USNR, 1961-65. Recipient Outstanding Performance award Bd. Govs. Am. C. of C. in Japan, 1977. Mem. Nat. Retail Mgmt. Assn. (internat. com.), Soc. Applied Econs., Japan Soc. Republican. Lutheran. Author: Foreign Disinvestments by U.S. Multinational Corporations, 1975; contbr. articles to profl. jours. Office: 1301 Ave Americas New York NY 10019

TOROK, TIBOR, mfg. co. exec.; b. Budapest, Hungary, May 27, 1935; s. Joseph and Piroska (Szegedi) T.; came to U.S., 1957, naturalized, 1962; B.S. in M.E., Poly. Inst. (Budapest), 1954; M.S. in Indsl. Engring., Tech. U. Budapest, 1956; m. Helen Odum, July 4, 1967; children—Derek, Marika. Mgr. mfg. and engring. Greenwald Industries, Bklyn., 1967-72; v.p. mfg. Wing Industries, Inc., Linden, N.J., 1972-77; v.p. ops. The Valtronic Corp., Bronx, 1977—. Pres., Workers Revolutionary Council, Budapest, 1956. Mem. Am. Def. Preparedness Assn., Am. Security Council, Am. Mgmt. Assn. Home: 102 Cresci Blvd Hazlet NJ 07730

TORONTO, JOHN JOSEPH, bus. equipment co. exec.; b. Columbus, Ohio, Feb. 2, 1930; s. Larry and Maude (Hoover) T.; student Remington Word Processing Sch., 1976; m. Patricia Shoemaker, Dec. 8, 1978; children—Carol S., James E. City salesman Borden Co., Columbus, 1950-61; dist. mgr. Sperry-Remington, Columbus, 1961-73; founder, pres. Toronto Bus. Equipment, Inc., Columbus, 1973—; cons. Casio, Inc., Remington Bus. Systems, Inc.; mem. dealer adv. council Sperry Remington, 1964, 69, 71, 73, 77, 79, Casio, Inc., 1978, 79. Named Nat. Dealer Sales Leader, Sperry-Remington, 1973, 74, 75, 76, 77, 78. Mem. Nat. Office Machines Dealers Assn. Republican. Clubs: Columbus Maennerchor, Masons, Shriners. Home: 1273 Ducrest Dr S Columbus OH 43220 Office: 1159 W Broad St Columbus OH 43222

TORRENCE, (JOHN) RICHARD, mktg. exec.; b. Ottumwa, Iowa, Oct. 12, 1936; s. John W. and Louise Lucy (Willey) T.; B.S., U. Wis., 1958. Pres., Richard Torrence Mgmt., N.Y.C., 1962-72, WTM Inc., Englewood, N.J., 1966-71; dir. pub. relations Rodgers Organ Co., Hillsboro, Oreg., 1971-75, v.p. mktg., 1975; pres. Torrence-Perrotta Mgmt. Inc., N.Y.C., 1972-76, Torrence Assos., N.Y.C., 1976-78; chmn. Performance Mktg. Corp., N.Y.C., 1978—; pres. Centerline Prodns., Inc., 1980—; cons. Pantheon Audience Network, Nat. Endowment for the Arts; mktg. cons. Fratelli Ruffatti, Padua, Italy; exec. chmn. Albert Schweitzer Centenary Concert, 1975; exec. sec. Albert Schweitzer Music Award Com., 1975—; project coordinator Carnegie Hall, Internat. organ series, 1972-75; founding mem. Carnegie Hall Nat. Endowment Fund; mem. adv. bd. Van Cliburn Internat. Piano Competition; N.Y. producer Fanfare for Organ, Lincoln Center, 1969-70, Heavy Organ, 1970, Mind Over Matter, 1976, Umabatha, 1979, A Katherine Dunham Gala, 1979. Mem. Assn. Coll. and Community Arts Adminstrs. (liaison com. Am. Symphony Orch. League). Democrat. Office: One Harkness Plaza New York NY 10023

TORRES, EUGENIO, controls engr.; b. San Juan, P.R., May 14, 1950; s. Eugenio and Pura (Agosto) T.; A.E.E., U. P.R., 1971; E.E.T., Wentworth Inst. Tech., Boston, 1973; children—Eugenio F., Herbert. Prodn. supr. Union Carbide, Inc., P.R.; automation specialist Honeywell, Inc., Rio Piedras, P.R.; account mgr. Mal del Caribe, Santurce, P.R.; applications engr. comml. mktg. Carrier Corp., Syracuse, N.Y.; now controls engr. internat. group Rapistan div. Lear Seigler, Grand Rapids, Mich. Served with P.R. Air N.G., 1975-78, USNG, 1978—. Cert. engring. technician. Mem. IEEE, ASHRAE, SIEPR, Delta Phi Theta, Alpha Phi Omega. Roman Catholic. Clubs: Exchange, Nyang NCO, Prang NCO. Home: 2501 Longmeadow NW Grand Rapids MI 49504

TORRES, JOSE EDUARDO, banker; b. Cayey, P.R., Dec. 16, 1939; s. Eduardo and Rosalina (Ortiz) Torres-Besosa; B.B.A., U. P.R., 1962; postgrad. Stonier Grad. Sch. Banking, Rutgers U. Indsl. rep. P.R. Econ. Devel. Adminstrn., San Juan, 1963-71; asst. v.p. bus. devel. Banco de Ponce, N.Y.C., 1971—. Bd. dirs. Inst. Comptmporary Hispanic Arts, N.Y.C., 1976—. Mem. P.R. C. of C. in U.S. (dir. 1976—, sec. 1980-81), Friends of P.R. (dir.), Internat. Assn. Bus. and Econ. Students, AIESEC, U. P.R. Alumni Assn., Phi Eta Mu. Roman Catholic. Clubs: N.Y. Athletic, Masons. Home: 185 West End Ave New York NY 10023 Office: 10 Rockefeller Plaza New York NY 10020

TORRES, RENE, services conglomerate exec.; b. N.Y.C., June 17, 1943; s. Herminio and Mercedes (Gonzalez) T.; A.B. in Physics, U. P.R., 1962; M.B.A., Harvard U., 1974; m. Cheryl Schwichtenberg, Oct. 25, 1965; children—Cheryl Amanda, Michael Rene. Resident metrologist Calverton Standards Lab., Grumman Aerospace Corp., Bethpage, N.Y., 1967-68; adminstrv. mgr. Sir Vess, Inc., Saddle Brook, N.J., 1968-69; sr. mgmt. cons. Touche Ross & Co., San Juan, P.R., 1969-70; pres. Rene Torres Assos., San Juan and Boston,

1970-76; pres., chief exec. officer Intrex Corp., Hato Rey, P.R., 1976—; lectr. bus. adminstrn. Northeastern U., Boston, 1976-77; dir. various corps. Served to capt. USAF, 1962-67. Recipient Journalism award Air Force Times, 1962; Best Young TV Actor of Yr. awards, P.R., 1956, 57; Lever Bros. fellow, 1972-74. Mem. Am. Assn. for Contamination Control (sr. mem., mem. nat. bio-sci. com. 1967-69), P.R. Inst. Appraisers, Soc. Real Estate Appraisers (asso.), Phi Sigma Alpha. Roman Catholic. Clubs: Harvard (Boston) (N.Y.C.); Century (San Juan). Editor Contrails mag., 1960-62. Home: 212 Diez de Andino Apt 1003 Santurce PR 00912 Office: Pan Am Bldg Suite 203 Hato Rey PR 00917

TOSTENRUD, DONALD BOYD, banker; b. Estherville, Iowa, Mar. 24, 1925; s. Oswald Morris and Irene Cecilia (Connell) T.; B.B.A., U. Minn., 1948; diploma Rutgers U. Grad. Sch. Banking, 1957; m. Arlene Girg, Jan. 12, 1950; children—Eric, Amy. Nat. bank examiner, Mpls., 1948-58; v.p. First Nat. Bank Black Hills, Rapid City, S.D., 1958-59; with Ariz. Bank, Phoenix, 1959—, sr. exec. v.p., then pres., 1969-78, chmn. bd., chief exec. officer, 1978—, dir., 1967—; dir. VISA, U.S.A., Southwest Gas Corp. Trustee Am. Grad. Sch. Internat. Mgmt., Heard Mus., Mus. No. Ariz., Grand Central Art Galleries N.Y., Ariz. Heart Inst.; pres. Compas 6, 1978; adv. bd. Compas 7, 1980; pres. Phoenix Art Mus., 1980—; bd. govs. Western Art Assos.; bd. dirs. Samaritan Health Service; mem. Ariz. Commn. on the Arts. Served with U.S. Army, 1943-45. Mem. Am. Bankers Assn. (gov. 1974-75), Robert Morris Assos. (past chpt. pres., past nat. dir.), Ariz. Bankers Assn. (past pres.), Tucson C. of C. (past pres.). Office: 101 N 1st Ave Phoenix AZ 85003

TOTARO, RICHARD, fin. services exec.; b. Buffalo, Feb. 20, 1939; s. Vincent and Marguerite (Phillips) T.; B.S. (Alcoa Found. scholar), Canisius Coll., 1963; student Grad. Sch. Consumer Banking, U. Va., 1968; m. Elizabeth A. Best, June 14, 1970; children—Doreen, Donald, Douglas, James, Richard, Steven. Asst. v.p., mgr. Marine Midland Banks, Buffalo, 1959-70; fin. factors v.p. Foremost Ins. Co., Harrisburg, Pa., and Walnut Creek, Calif., 1970-75; sr. v.p., dir. Sebrite Corp., Boise, Idaho, and Pitts., 1975—; instr. Am. Inst. Banking. Chmn. West Seneca United Fund, 1967; chmn. Res. Hose Fund Raising, 1968. Mem. Am. Bankers Assn. Home: 4143 Timberlane Dr Allison Park PA 15101 Office: 4084 Mount Royal Blvd Allison Park PA 15101

TOTH, ALEX STEPHEN, trade co. exec.; b. Bradenton, Fla. Apr. 6, 1944; s. Alex and Dorothy T.; B.A., Johns Hopkins U., 1966; M.B.A., Case Western Res. U., 1974; m. Kathryn Jones, Oct. 23, 1976; children—Piper, Amanda. Pres., PBM Office Products Co., Independence, Ohio, 1974—. Served to capt., USAF, 1967-71. Mem. Nat. Office Products Assn., Beta Gamma Sigma, Alpha Epsilon Delta. Home: 377 Miles Rd Chagrin Falls OH 44022 Office: PBM Office Products Co 7820 E Pleasant Valley Independence OH 44131

TOTH, STEPHEN JOSEPH, indsl. mfg. co. exec.; b. N.Y.C., June 2, 1925; s. Stephen Joseph and Viola Caroline (Schaefer) T.; B.S., M.I.T., 1950; m. Kathryn N. Toth. Div. gen. mgr. Hughes Aircraft Co., Culver City, Calif., 1967-70; group v.p. Wyle Labs., El Segundo, Calif., 1970-72; pvt. cons., Sherman Oaks, Calif., 1972-74; pres. Crydom div. Internat. Rectifier Co., Los Angeles, 1974-76; pres., chief exec. officer Pacific Scientific Co., Anaheim, Calif., 1976—, also dir. Served with USAAF, 1944-45. Mem. Am. Mgmt. Assn., C. of C. Clubs: Balboa Bay; Calif. Home: 25 Lochmoor Ln Newport Beach CA 92660 Office: 1350 S State College Blvd Anaheim CA 92803

TOTIN, MARY ANN, banker; b. Fairbank, Pa., Apr. 7, 1930; d. Charles and Anna Romanchak; student Mercer County Community Coll., 1977; m. Peter George Totin, Jr., Aug. 7, 1948; children—Marlene, Leonard G., Mary Margaret, Gail Ann. Bookkeeper, Fayette Nat. Bank, Uniontown, Pa., 1950-53; teller William Penn Savs. & Loan, Levittown, Pa., 1970; clk., sec., asst. sec., dept. mgr., sr. loan officer Morrisville Bank (Pa.), 1970-80, sr. installment loan officer, dept. mgr., 1980—. Leader, Girl Scouts U.S.A., 1952-73; treas. St. Ignatius Sodality, 1976-80. Cert. consumer credit exec. Mem. Nat. Assn. Banking Women, Am. Inst. Banking, Bucks County Bankers Assn., N.J. Installment Lenders Assn., Nat. Fedn. Bus. and Profl. Women's Club (treas., 2d v.p., 1st v.p., fin. chmn. 1974-80), African Violet Soc. Home: 11 Richie Ln Yardley PA 19067 Office: 2 E Bridge St Morrisville PA 19067

TOUPS, JOHN MELBURN, civil engr.; b. Wichita Falls, Tex., Jan. 10, 1926; s. Sidney and Alice (Bryant) T.; B.S.C.E., U. Calif., Berkeley, 1949; m. Mary Pat Powers, Jan. 30, 1950; children—Paul, Charles, Dana, Ellen. Engr., Calif. Div. Hwys., Los Angeles, 1949, Asso. Oil Co., Ventura, Calif., 1949-52, United Water Conservation Dist., Santa Paula, Calif., 1952-53; city engr. City of Seal Beach (Calif.), 1953-55, City of Fullerton (Calif.), 1955-56; dist. engr. Orange County Water Dist., Orange, Calif., 1956-58; founder, pres. Toups Corp., Santa Ana, Calif., 1958-74; sr. v.p. Planning Research Corp., Los Angles, 1974-77, pres., chief exec. officer, Washington, 1977—. Served with U.S. Army, 1944-45. Decorated Silver Star, Purple Heart. Registered profl. engr. Mem. Nat. Soc. Profl. Engrs., Cons. Engrs. Assn. Calif., Am. Cons. Engrs. Council, Am. Water Works Assn. Clubs: Internat., Washington Golf and Country (Washington). Office: 1850 K St NW Suite 1100 Washington DC 20006

TOURNILLON, NICHOLAS BRADY, diversified co. exec.; b. New Orleans, Sept. 1, 1933; s. Samuel C. and Anna Mae (Brady) T.; B.A., Southeastern La. U., 1958; M.B.A., La. State U., 1960; m. Audrey Nicosia, Dec. 15, 1956; children—Brady, Linda, Tracy, Jeffrey, Gregory, Lori. Loan officer Export Import Bank of U.S., Washington, 1960-66; adminstrv. asst. to exec. officers Atlantic Gulf & Pacific Co. of Manila, Philippines, 1966-68; asst. treas. GTE Internat., Stamford, Conn., 1968-76, treas., 1976—; internat. adv. bd. Union Trust Co.; bd. govs. War Risk Reciprocal. Chmn., Conn. Dist. Export Council of U.S. Dept. Commerce; mem. monetary com. U.S. council Internat. C. of C. Served with USN Air Reserves, 1953-54; Korea. Named Outstanding Alumnus of Yr., Southeastern La. U., 1976. Mem. Fin. Execs. Inst., Soc. Internat. Treasurers, Acad. Internat. Bus., Phi Kappa Phi. Home: Midwood Dr Greenwich CT 06830 Office: 1 Stamford Forum Stamford CT 06904

TOUSSIE, MICHAEL ISAAC, accountant; b. Bklyn., Dec. 10, 1949; s. Isaac Samuel and Marie (Sasson) T.; B.B.A. cum laude (Bernard Baruch scholar), Coll. City, N.Y., 1970. Staff accountant J.K. Lasser & Co. (C.P.A.'s), N.Y.C., 1970-71; sr. accountant Arthur Andersen & Co., N.Y.C., 1971-73, v.p. finance Toussie World Enterprises, Inc., N.Y.C., 1971—, v.p. accounting, dir. Toussie Enterprises, Inc., Medford, N.Y., 1975—; v.p. finance and accounting, dir. Levitt House, Inc., Medford, 1976-77; dir. Environ. Solutions, Inc.; adj. lectr. acctg. Queens Coll., 1979-80. Mem. Council Concerned Youth, Bklyn., 1976—. Bernard M. Baruch scholar, 1976; C.P.A. Mem. Am. Inst. C.P.A.'s, N.Y. Soc. C.P.A.'s, Mensa. Democrat. Jewish. Home: 2014 E 5th St Brooklyn NY 11223 Office: 2014 E 5th St Brooklyn NY 11223

TOUSSIE, SAMUEL ROOSEVELT, investment banker; b. Bklyn., May 9, 1934; s. Isaac Samuel and Marie (Sasson) T.; grad. high sch.; m. Nancy Hanan, Dec. 26, 1966; children—Marie, Victoria, Isaac, Ralph, David. Sec., dir. Merry Mites, Hiline, Small Talk, N.Y.C., to 1966; pres. Toussie Devel. Co., Toussie Land Co., Toussie Enterprises, Inc., Toussie World Enterprises, Inc., Toussie Oil & Gas Co., Medford, N.Y., 1966—. Editor, Community Jour., 1950-60; chief exec., chmn. bd., pres. Levitt House, Inc., Environ. Solutions, Inc., Nat. Housing Corp. Bd. dirs. NAACP; chmn. Heart Fund. Mem. Nat. Assn. Securities Dealers. Jewish. Clubs: Masons; Bklyn. Yacht Sports; Jogging. Home: 2014 E 5th St Brooklyn NY 11223 Office: PO Box 80 500 Expressway Dr S Medford NY 11763

TOVEY, JOSEPH, investment banker; b. Tel Aviv, Israel, Nov. 5, 1938; s. Samuel and Rachel (Weiman) T.; came to U.S., 1940, naturalized, 1947; B.S. summa cum laude, Bklyn. Coll., 1959; M.B.A., N.Y.U., 1961, Ph.D., 1969; m. Anita Beverly Losice, Feb. 20, 1961; children—David, Debra, Nissan Chaim, Seth Reuven, Shayna Nava. Staff accountant Machtiger, Green & Co., N.Y.C., 1959-60, Loeb & Troper, N.Y.C., 1960-61; tax researcher Lybrand, Ross Bros. & Montgomery, 1961-63; planning asso. Mobil Oil Corp., N.Y.C., 1963-67; asst. v.p. A.G. Becker & Co., N.Y.C., 1967-70; asso. Roth, Gerard & Co., N.Y.C., 1970-73; v.p. Faulkner, Dawkins & Sullivan Inc., 1973-76; v.p. Shields Model Roland, Inc., N.Y.C., 1976-77; partner Tovey & Co., N.Y.C., 1977—; pres. Joint Trading Inc., 1977—, Tovey & Co., Inc., 1978—, Lee-Tovey Oil Co., 1980—. Mem. exec. bd. Agudath Israel Am., 1963-67. C.P.A., N.Y. Mem. Newcomen Soc. N.Am., Am. Fin. Assn., Am. Inst. C.P.A.'s, Fgn. Policy Assn., N.Y.U. Alumni Assn., Bklyn. Coll. Alumni in Fin. Jewish religion. Club: N.Y. Univ. (N.Y.C.). Author: (with H.C. Smith) Federal Tax Treatment of Bad Debts and Worthless Securities, 1964. Asso. editor Tax Letter, 1961-66. Contbr. articles to profl. jours. Home: 1170 E 19th St Brooklyn NY 11230 Office: 20 Exchange Pl New York NY 10005

TOW, LEONARD, cable TV exec.; b. N.Y.C., May 30, 1928; s. Louis and Estelle Tow; B.A., Bklyn. Coll., 1950; M.A., Columbia U., 1952, Ph.D. (Nat. Acad. Sci.-NRC fellow), 1960; m. Claire Schneider, Aug. 10, 1952; children—Frank, Andrew, Emily. Vice pres. Intervest, Inc., N.Y.C., 1961-64; mgmt. cons. Touche Ross & Co., 1964-65; sr. v.p. Teleprompter Corp., 1965-73; pres. Century Communications Corp., New Canaan, Conn., 1973—. Mem. Nat. Cable TV Assn., Calif. Cable TV Assn., Conn. Cable TV Assn., Va. Cable TV Assn., W.Va. Cable TV Assn., N.Y. Cable TV Assn. Author: The Manufacturing Economy of Southern Rhodesia, Problems and Prospects, 1960. Home: West Ln Pound Ridge NY 10576 Office: 51 Locust Ave New Canaan CT 06840

TOWER, RAYMOND CAMILLE, mfg. co. exec.; b. N.Y.C., Feb. 20, 1925; s. Raymond C. and Elinor (Donovan) T.; B.S., Yale U., 1945; grad. Advanced Mgmt. Program, Harvard U., 1964; m. Jaclyn Bauerline, Feb. 7, 1948; children—Raymond, Patricia, Christopher, Robert, Mary, Michael, Victoria. Research chemist Westvaco Chem. Co., 1946-48; mktg. positions Chem. div. FMC Corp., N.Y.C., 1948-65, v.p., gen. mgr. organic chem. div., 1965-67, exec. v.p., mgr. chem. group, 1967-77, pres., 1977—, dir. corp.; dir. Marathon Oil Co., Phila. Nat. Bank. Served to lt. USNR, 1944-46, 51-53. Mem. Harvard Advanced Mgmt. Assn., A.T.M.I., Greater Phila. C. of C. (dir.). Clubs: Sky (N.Y.C.); Phila. Country, Urban, Union League (Phila.); Country of N.C. Office: 200 E Randolph St Chicago IL 60601*

TOWERMAN, STANFORD BERNARD, life ins. underwriter; b. St. Louis, Mar. 16, 1930; s. Louis and Ida T.; B.S. in Commerce magna cum laude, St. Louis U., 1952; M.S. in Fin. Services, Am. Coll., 1979; m. Elaine Richman, Dec. 23, 1951; children—Craig, Michael, Robyn. Exec. trainee Weil-Kalter Mfg. Co., St. Louis, 1954-55; agt. Phoenix Mut. Life Ins. Co., St. Louis, 1955—. Served as lt. USAF, 1952-54. C.L.U.; life mem. Million Dollar Round Table; named to Portrait Hall of Fame, Phoenix Mut. Life Ins. Co., 1973. Mem. Soc. C.L.U.'s (past pres. St. Louis chpt.), Nat. Assn. Life Underwriters. Jewish. Home: 11592 New London St Creve Coeur MO 63141 Office: 7777 Bonhomme Ave Clayton MO 63105

TOWERS, JOHN, business exec.; b. Scotland, 1921; B.S. in Metall. Engring., Mich. Coll. Mining and Tech., 1943; M.S. in Metallurgy, U. Notre Dame, 1949; D.Engring., Mich. Technol. U., 1978; married. With AMAX Inc. (formerly Am. Metal Climax, Inc.), Greenwich, Conn., 1946—, pres., dir. subs. U.S. Metals Refining Co., 1963-74, dir. parent co., 1969—, group v.p. base metals div., 1967-75, exec. v.p. parent co., 1975-77, pres. parent co., 1977—; dir. Amax Found. Inc., Amax Mich., Inc., Makgadikgadi Soda Ltd., O'okiep Copper Co. Ltd., Tsumeb Corp., Ltd. Trustee, Mich. Tech. Fund, Minerals Industry Ednl. Found. Served to capt. AUS, 1943-46. Clubs: Belle Haven (Greenwich); Mining (past gov.) (N.Y.C.); Saugatuck Harbor Yacht (Westport, Conn.); Ocean Reef (Fla.). Office: AMAX Center Greenwich CT 06830

TOWEY, JAMES FISCHER, chem. co. exec.; b. Wood River, Ill., Mar. 1, 1916; s. James Keener and Anna (Fischer) T.; B.S. in Gen. Bus., U. Ill., 1939; LL.D. (hon.), Morehouse Coll., 1973; m. Virginia Elnor Anderson, Mar. 30, 1940; children—James Mayo, Susan Kay. With Western Cartridge Co., East Alton, Ill., 1939-47; chief accountant Olin Industries, Inc., East Alton, 1947-51, plant controller, 1951-55; asst. controller Olin Mathieson Chem. Co., N.Y.C., 1955-58, fin. officer aluminum div., 1958-64, v.p. brass operation, 1964-70; v.p., chief fin. officer Olin Corp., Stamford, Conn., 1970-71, sr. v.p., 1971-72, pres., 1972-73, chmn. bd., 1972—, chief exec. officer, 1972-78; dir. Olin-Am., Inc. Trustee Atlanta U. Served with Signal Corps, AUS, 1945-46. Mem. Financial Execs. Inst., Conf. Bd., Bus. Roundtable. Clubs: Darien (Conn.) Country; Lockhaven Country (Alton, Ill.). Home: 40 Charter Oak Ln New Canaan CT 06840 Office: 120 Long Ridge Rd Stamford CT 06904

TOWLER, WILLIAM ALBERT, III, mgmt. cons. co. exec.; b. Charlottesville, Va., Nov. 19, 1935; s. William Albert, Jr. and Jane Nolan (Cotten) T.; B.A. cum laude in Econs., Washington and Lee U., Lexington, Va., 1958; M.A. in Bus. Adminstrn., U. N.C., Charlotte, 1970; m. Martha Lois Jackson, Dec. 19, 1971; children—Bill, Mark. Fin. trainee internat. div. Gen. Electric Co., N.Y.C., 1960-61; v.p. Wachovia Bank & Trust Co., Charlotte, N.C., 1961-69, Communications Inst. Am., Inc., Dallas, 1970-71; v.p., gen. mgr., then exec. v.p. Rattikin Title Co., Ft. Worth, 1971-77; pres. Am. First Title & Trust Co., Oklahoma City, 1977—, also dir.; pres. Am. First Corp., Oklahoma City, 1979-80, Towler & Assos. Inc., 1980—; dir. First Life Assurance Co. Served as officer U.S. Army, 1958-60. Named Tex. Land Titleman of Yr., Tex. Land Title Assn., 1977. Mem. Am. Land Title Assn. (vice chmn. abstractors/agts. sect. 1980), Okla. Land Title Assn. (dir.), Oklahoma City Bd. Realtors. Episcopalian. Club: Beacon (Oklahoma City). Office: Towler and Assos Am First Corp PO 6325 N Villa St Suite 127 Oklahoma City OK 73112

TOWNES, JAMES ARMISTEAD, JR., plantation mgr.; b. Greenwood, Miss., Dec. 7, 1934; s. James Armistead and Ruth Dent (Alexander) T.; B.A. in Polit. Sci., Delta State U., 1960; m. Mary Anne Fedric, Dec. 27, 1977; 1 dau., Caroline Cooke. With Evans Townes Plantation, Minter City, Miss., 1960—, gen. mgr., 1974—; sec.-treas. Palo Alto Plantation, Inc., Minter City, 1974—; v.p. Deermound Gin Co., Minter City, 1974—. Commr., Tallahatchie County Vol. Fire Dept., 1974—; mem. Tallahatchie County Sch. Bd., 1977-81; bd. dirs. Greenwood Little Theater, 1978-81, Cottonlandia Mus., Greenwood. Mem. Internat. Fire Chiefs Assn. (state v.p.), Miss. Fire Chiefs Assn. (sec.-treas. 1977—), Internat. Fire Brigade Soc., Miss. Numismatic Assn. (life), Delta Council. Democrat. Episcopalian. Home: Palo Alto Plantation Minter City MS 38944 Office: Evans Townes Plantation Minter City MS 38944

TOWNSEND, EDWARD ALLEN, bank exec.; b. Brazil, Mar. 9, 1942; s. Charles H. T. and Elsa (Seiffert) T.; B.A. in Econs., U. Tex., 1964, B.B.A. in Fin., 1965, M.B.A. in Fin., 1967; m. Patricia Nulty, June 26, 1965; children—Jennifer, Leslie, Lara. With First Nat. Bank, Dallas, 1967-79, sr. v.p., 1973-79, exec. v.p., chief fin. officer, head fin. div., 1979; vice chmn. bd., chief adminstrv. officer First Internat. Bank, Houston, 1979—. Mem. asso. bd. dirs. So. Methodist U. Grad. Sch. Bus. Mem. Robert Morris Assos. Republican. Episcopalian. Clubs: Dallas Petroleum, Meml. Country.

TOWNSEND, J. RUSSELL, JR., employee benefit plans co. exec.; b. Cedar Rapids, Iowa, Nov. 21, 1910; s. Jay Russell and Mabel Helen (Ferguson) T.; B.S. in Natural Sci., Butler U., 1931; M.B.A., Wharton Sch., U. Pa., 1933; m. Virginia Kathryn Holt, Aug. 1, 1938; 1 son, John Holt. Gen. agt. Equitable Life Ins. Co. Iowa, 1950—; owner, mng. asso. J. Russell Townsend & Assos., Indpls., 1969—; asso. prof. ins. Butler U., Indpls., 1933—; mem. Ind. Ho. of Reps., 1946-48; mem. Ind. Senate, 1956-64; cons. Ind. State Ins. Dept., 1946-64. Former pres. Childrens Bur. Indpls., Indpls. Lit. Club. Served to lt. comdr. USNR, 1942-70. Recipient Distinguished Service award Internat. Assn. Accident Health Underwriters, 1960; C.L.U.; registered health underwriter. Mem. Chartered Life Underwriters Assn. (past pres. Indpls. chpt.), Ind. (past dir.), Indpls. (past dir.) life underwriters assns. Republican. Club: Kiwanis (past pres.). Contbr. articles to ins. publs. Home: 8244 N Pennsylvania St Indianapolis IN 42640 Office: 715 Board Trade Bldg Indianapolis IN 46204

TOWNSEND, M. WILBUR, mfg. co. exec.; b. Oyster Bay, N.Y., Jan. 17, 1912; s. M.W. and Alberta (Say) T.; A.B., Wesleyan U., 1934; m. Barbara White Hayden, Oct. 1, 1938; children—Barrett Say, Philip Hayden. With sales dept. Handy & Harman, N.Y.C., 1946—, pres., 1964, chmn. bd., 1967—, chief exec. officer, 1979—; dir. Lazare Kaplan & Sons, N.Y.C. Mem. Jewelry Indsl. Council. Clubs: Union League, 24 Karat (pres.). Office: 850 3d Ave New York NY 10022

TOWNSEND, THOMAS P., JR., constrn. co. exec.; b. Laurens, S.C., Sept. 28, 1937; s. Thomas P. and Virginia (Taylor) T.; B.S., Clemson U., 1959; B.A., Emory U., 1969; grad. Advanced Mgmt. Program, Harvard U., 1980; m. Lucie Sparkman, July 14, 1962; children—Thomas P. III, William Bacot, Julia Randolph. Mech. engr. Daniel Internat. Corp., Greenville, S.C., 1959-63, asst. mgr. mech. div., 1963-65, asst. gen. mgr. Caribbean, 1965-69, v.p. internat., 1969-73, group v.p., 1973—. Served with USMC, 1961-62. Episcopalian. Club: Greenville Country. Home: 10 Rock Creek Ct Greenville SC 29605 Office: Dainiel Internat Corp Daniel Bldg Greenville SC 29602

TOWNSON, WILLIAM DAVID, JR., lumber co. exec.; b. Murphy, N.C., Sept. 30, 1922; s. William David and Winnie (Sneed) T.; student Young Harris Coll., 1940-42, Ga. Inst. Tech.; children—William David, Grace Winifred Townson Grasty, Barbara Whichard Townson Keeter, Jerry Morgan. Pres., Townson Lumber Co., Inc., Edenton, N.C., 1957—, Townson Pallets, Inc., Edenton, 1963-75, Townson Homes, Inc., 1975—, Carrson Products, Inc., Edenton, 1965—, Carson Products, Inc., Atlanta, Townson Funeral Homes, Inc., Murphy, Robbinsville, Andrews and Haysville, N.C., Northside Properties, Edenton, Townson Lumber Co., Inc. P.R., Mayaguez. Patentee in field. Home: PO Box H Edenton NC 27932 Office: Industrial Park Edenton NC 27932 also 11 Cypress St Mayaguez PR 00708

TOYOMURA, DENNIS TAKESHI, architect; b. Honolulu, July 6, 1926; s. Sansuke and Take (Sata) T.; B.S., Chgo. Tech. Coll., 1949; postgrad. U. Ill. Extension, 1950, 53, 54, Ill. Inst. Tech., 1954-55, U. Hawaii, 1966-67, 73; m. Charlotte Akiko Nakamura, May 27, 1949; children—Wayne J., Gerald F., Amy J., Lyle D. Designer draftsman James M. Turner, Hammond, Ind., 1950-51, Wimberly & Cook, Honolulu, 1952, Gregg & Briggs, Chgo., 1952-54; architect Holabird, Root and Burgee, 1954-55; prin. Dennis T. Toyomura, AIA, 1954—; with Loebl, Schlossman and Bennett, 1955-62; sec., dir. Maiko of Hawaii, Inc., 1972; dir. Pacific Canal Hawaii, Inc., 1972—; archtl. cons. Honolulu Redevel. Agy., Kapahulu dist. City and County of Honolulu, 1967-71; fallout shelter analyst Dept. Def.; mem. Hawaii Bd. Registration Profl. Engrs., Architects, Surveyors and Landscape Architects, 1974—, Nat. Council Archtl. Registration Bds., 1974—, Nat. Council Engring. Examiners, 1974—; mem. adv. com. drafting tech. Leeward Community Coll., U. Hawaii, 1968-81; western region del. Nat. Council Archl. Registration Bds., 1975-80, nat. del., 1976, 78, 79, 80. Del. commr. State Assembly, Synod of Ill. Presbyn. Ch., 1958, Los Angeles Presbytery, 1965. Registered profl. architect, Ill., Hawaii; real estate broker, Ill. Served with AUS, 1945-46. Recipient Outstanding Citizen Recognition award Cons. Engrs. Council Hawaii, 1975. Mem. AIA (office mgmt. com. 1977, practice mgmt. com. 1978; dir. Hawaii soc. 1973-74, treas. 1975), Am. Concrete Inst., Acad. Polit. Sci., Chgo. Nat. History Mus., Chgo. Art Inst., Am. Acad. Polit. and Social Scis., Ill. Assn. Professions, Honolulu C. of C., Constrn. Specifications Inst., Brab Bldg. Research Inst. of Nat. Acad. Scis., AAAS, ASTM, Council Ednl. Facility Planners Internat. (regional bd. govs. 1980-81), Lyon Arboretum Assn. (dir. 1975, treas. 1976), Constrn. Industry Legis. Orgn. (dir. 1973—, treas. 1976-77), Kappa Sigma Kappa. Presbyterian (elder, trustee 1964-66, 69-72, sec. 1965). Clubs: Malolo Mariners; Purser (treas. 1964); Skipper (pres. 1965). Home: 2602 Manoa Rd Honolulu HI 96822 Office: 1370 Kapiolani Blvd Honolulu HI 96814

TOZER, W. JAMES, JR., banker; b. Salt Lake City, Feb. 9, 1941; s. W. James and Virginia (Somerville) T.; B.A. cum laude, Trinity Coll., 1963; M.B.A., Harvard, 1965; m. Elizabeth Farran, July 30, 1965; children—Farran Virginia, Katharine Coppins. With Citibank, N.A., 1964-77, v.p. corporate devel., N.Y.C., 1970-71, sr. v.p. and head Citicorp subs. group, 1971-74, sr. v.p./gen. mgr., head mcht. banking group, 1974-75, head N.Y. banking div., consumer services group, 1975-77; sr. exec. v.p., dir. Shearson Hayden Stone Inc., N.Y.C., 1978-79; exec. v.p. Marine Midland Bank, also Marine Midland Banks, Inc., N.Y.C., 1979—; asso. mem. N.Y. Stock Exchange. Trustee, chmn. fin. com. Community Service Soc. N.Y., 1974—; chmn. bd. fellows Trinity Coll., 1972-78. Mem. Mktg. Sci. Inst. (trustee 1975-77), Pi Gamma Mu, Theta Xi. Clubs: University, Bond (N.Y.C.); Lawrence Beach (Atlantic Beach, N.Y.); Marhomack Fish and Game Preserve (Shelter Island, N.Y.). Home: 1112 Park Ave New York NY 10028 Office: 767 Fifth Ave New York NY 10022

TOZER, WILLIAM THOMAS, ins. co. exec.; b. Petersburg, Ill., Jan. 19, 1934; s. Clarence W. and Winona (Armstrong) T.; B.S., U. Ill., 1956; m. Joan Marie Heberlein, July 31, 1955; children—Barbara, Theodore, Marilyn. Acturial asst. State Farm Life Ins. Co., Bloomington, Ill., 1956-60; actuary, sr. v.p. Am. Republic Ins. Co., Des Moines, 1960-70; v.p., actuary Am. Republic Assurance Co., Des Moines, 1967-70, dir., 1967-70; v.p., actuary United Ins. Co. of Am. Chgo., 1970-72; v.p., chief actuary Ky. Central Life Ins. Co., 1972—; v.p. Ky. Central Ins. Cos., 1975—. Frequent speaker on computers at profl. meetings, seminars. Mem. actuarial adv. bd. Drake U., 1967-70; chmn. computer adv. com. Iowa Ins. Dept., 1967-68. Mem. Polk County Tax Payers Computer Com., 1965; mem. budget com. United Way of Bluegrass, 1973—. Named Ky. col. C.L.U. Fellow Soc. Actuaries, Life Office Mgmt. Inst.; mem. Southeastern Actuaries Club, Am. Acad. Actuaries, Internat. Actuarial Assn., Am. Council Life Ins. (com. mem. 1974-79), Lexington C. of C., Phi Kappa Phi, Phi Eta Sigma, Beta Gamma Sigma. Presbyterian (elder, deacon, trustee). Club: Actuarial (pres. 1965) (Des Moines). Contbr. articles to profl. jours. Home: 647 Tateswood Dr Lexington KY 40502 Office: Kincaid Towers Lexington KY 40508

TRAA, RICHARD LOUIS, restaurant co. exec.; b. Pitts., June 8, 1942; d. Louis Arthur and Ruth Christine (Kirschner) T.; B.A., Wilmington Coll., 1965; M.B.A., Miami U. (Ohio), 1966; m. Ruth Melinna Dildilian, Aug. 27, 1966; children—Andrew Richard, Matthew Ara. Instr. econ. and bus. Wilmington (Ohio) Coll., 1966-68; pres. Traa Corp., Pleasantville, N.J., 1976—; dir. Fiber Glass Industries, Inc., Amsterdam, N.Y., 1976—. Mgmt. adv. council Wilmington Coll., 1978—; bd. govs. Shore Meml. Hosp., Somers Point, N.J., 1975—, v.p., 1978-81; councilman City of Linwood (N.J.), 1976; mem. Linwood Planning Bd., 1977—, pres., 1977, 80; bd. dirs. Linwood Nursery Sch., 1973—, pres., 1978—; bd. dirs. Children's Oncology Services, Inc. of Phila., 1975—, pres., 1977-81, mem. nat. adv. bd., 1977—. Recipient Nat. Found. March of Dimes Service award, 1970; Phila. Eagles Touchdown award against Leukemia, 1976; Am. Cancer Soc. Service award, 1977; Wond Sports award, 1977; Wall St. Jour. Student Achievement award, 1965. Mem. Am. Mgmt. Assn., Restaurant Bus. Adv. Panel. Club: Atlantic City Country. Home: 214 Morris Ave Linwood NJ 08221 Office: 776 Black Horse Pike Suite 3 Pleasantville NJ 08232

TRACE, WILLIAM FREDERICK, credit co. exec.; b. Meadville, Pa., June 30, 1928; s. James Bennett and Marion Rebecca (Ewing) T.; B.A., Allegheny Coll., 1953; m. Helen Irene Britton, Sept. 25, 1946; children—Karen Rylander, Kim Larr, Gary B. Treasury rep. Westinghouse Electric Corp., Pitts. and Chgo., 1953-61; regional mgr. Westinghouse Credit Corp., Chgo., 1961-69; regional v.p. 1st Mortgage Adv. Corp., South Bend, Ind., 1969-71, sr. v.p., Miami Beach, Fla., 1971-73; chmn. bd., pres. USI Credit Corp., Los Angeles and N.Y.C., 1973—. Served with U.S. Army, 1946-48, 50-51. Mem. Nat. Consumer Fin. Assn. Clubs: Union League (N.Y.C.); Shore Haven Golf (Norwalk). Home: 12 Prospect Ave Darien CT 06820 Office: 733 Third Ave New York NY 10017

TRACY, EUGENE ARTHUR, utility exec.; b. Oak Park, Ill., Dec. 14, 1927; s. Arthur Huntington and Emily Margaret (Groff) T.; B.S. in Bus. Adminstrn., Northwestern U., 1951; M.B.A., DePaul U., Chgo., 1958; m. Irene Walburga Kacin, June 30, 1951; children—Glen Eugene, Diane Emily, Janet Freda. With Peoples Gas Light & Coke Co., Chgo., 1951-69, 77—, pres., 1977—, also dir.; with Peoples Gas Co., Chgo., 1969-77, v.p., 1973-77, controller, 1974-77, also dir.; pres., dir. N. Shore Gas Co., Waukegan, Ill., 1977—; dir. First Fed. Savs. & Loan Assn. Chgo., Natural Gas Pipeline Co. Am. Trustee Taxpayers Fedn. Ill., 1973-77; bd. dirs. Civic Fedn. Chgo., 1976-77; bd. dirs. Central YMCA Community Coll., Chgo., 1971—, treas., 1972-77, chmn. bd., 1977-79; treas. St. David's Episcopal Ch., Glenview, Ill., 1970-79; bd. dirs. Jr. Achievement, Chgo., 1978—; trustee Inst. Gas Tech., Chgo., 1978—. Served with U.S. Army, 1946-47. Mem. Am. Midwest (dir.) gas assns., Chgo. Assn. Commerce and Industry (dir. 1979—). Clubs: Sunset Ridge Country (Northbrook, Ill.); Econ., Univ., Chicago (Chgo.). Home: 1424 Sequoia Trail Glenview IL 60025 Office: 122 S Michigan Ave Chicago IL 60603

TRAEGER, ROBERT HOIT, elec. mfg. co. exec.; b. Auburn, Wash., July 11, 1926; s. Henry G. and Margaret P. (Hoit) T.; B.S. in Mech. Engring., U. Wash., 1950, B.S. in Indsl. Engring., 1951; m. Betty Rae Peirce, Sept. 7, 1949; children—Lisa, Paul, John. With Gen. Electric Co., 1951-74, pres., mng. dir. Gen. Electric Consumer Electronics Pvt., Ltd., Singapore, 1971-74; v.p. tech. ops. Sony Corp. Am., N.Y.C., 1974-77; v.p., gen. mgr. mfg. div. Toshiba Am., Inc., Lebanon, Tenn., 1977—. Trustee Cumberland Coll., Lebanon, 1979—; mem. Gov. Tenn. adv. bd. to S.E., U.S.-Japan Assn. Served with USNR, 1944-46. Mem. Lebanon C. of C. Club: Lebanon Rotary. Home: 3635 Knollwood Rd Nashville TN 37215 Office: 1420 Toshiba Dr Lebanon TN 37087

TRAGER, BERNARD HAROLD, lawyer; b. New Haven, July 18, 1906; s. Harry and Ida (Ruttenberg) T.; LL.B., N.Y. U., 1928; m. Mina Rubenstein, Aug. 25, 1929; children—Roberta E. (Mrs. Ralph L. Cohen), Philip S. Admitted to Conn. bar, 1929; sr. partner firm Trager & Trager, 1965—; trustee People's Savs. Bank. Chmn. Bridgeport Mayor's Commn. on Human Rights, 1958-62, Nat. Community Relations Adv. Council, 1953-57; pres. Conn. Conf. Social Work, 1948-49; v.p. Am. Jewish Congress, 1958-60; mem. Nat. Exec. Council United Synagogue Am., 1957-59; mem. Bridgeport Fin. Adv. Commn. 1966-76; chmn. Conn. Bd. Pardons, 1959-73. Life trustee U. Bridgeport; bd. dirs. Council Jewish Fdns. and Welfare Funds, 1954-61, United Hias Service, 1956-58; trustee Nat. Health & Welfare Retirement Assn., 1955-68, Bridgeport Area Found., Inc.; bd. dirs. Bridgeport Hosp. Mem. Am. (ho. of dels. 1964-66), Conn. (pres. 1964-65), Bridgeport (pres. 1959-61) bar assns., N.Y. U. Law Alumni Assn. (dir. 1958-62). Clubs: Algonquin (pres. 1978-79), Birchwood Country, N.Y. U., Nat. Lawyers. Home: 25 Cartright St Bridgeport CT 06604 Office: 1305 Post Rd Fairfield CT 06430

TRAINA, MICHAEL JAMES, camera co. exec.; b. N.Y.C., July 9, 1949; s. Edward and Lillian (Francis) T.; B.B.A., CCNY, 1972; m. Randie Parker, May 2, 1976; 1 dau., Michele Nicole. Order processing mgr. Berkey Mktg. Co., Woodside, N.Y., 1971-77; dir. order service Olympus Camera Corp., Woodbury, N.Y., 1977—. Mem. Am. Mgmt. Assn., Photo Mktg. Assn. Roman Catholic. Home: 9 Conifer Ct Northport NY 11768 Office: Olympus Camera Corp 145 Crossway Park W Woodbury NY 11797

TRAINOR, CHARLES JOSEPH, concrete forming equipment co.; b. New Brunswick, N.J., Dec. 13, 1937; s. John J. and Elizabeth H. (deRussy) T.; B.S. in Econs., St. Peter's Coll., 1961; m. Karen Ann Hughes, Dec. 27, 1961; children—Charles, John, Patrick, Ann; m. 2d, Kay Logan Russell, May 5, 1979. Salesman, Symons Mfg. Co., Des Plaines, Ill., 1963-68; dist. mgr. Simplex Form Co., Chgo., 1968-69; founder, pres. Conesco Industries, Ltd., Little Ferry, N.J., 1969—. Served to 1st lt. C.E., U.S. Army, 1961-63. Mem. Little Ferry C. of C. (pres.), Asso. Constrn. Distbrs. Internat., Sales Exec. Club. Club: The Moles. Home: 160 Park St Montclair NJ 07042 Office: 214 Gates Rd Little Ferry NJ 07643

TRAINOR, DAVID BRUCE, oil co. exec.; b. Phila., Feb. 28, 1942; s. John F. and Gertrude (Rhoads) T.; B.A., LaSalle Coll., 1964; postgrad. Temple U. and U. Pa., 1964-65; m. Kathleen McNichol, June 11, 1976; children—David B., Daniel H., Elizabeth K. Account exec. Butcher & Sherrerd, Phila., 1965-69; pres. Tax Shelter Advisory Service Inc., Narberth, Pa., 1970-73; pres., chmn. World Resources Corp., Radnor, Pa., 1973—; pres., chmn. Omni-Exploration, Inc., Radnor, 1974—; dir. VicJet Corp., Narberth, Pa. Mem. Ind. Petroleum Assn. Am. Republican. Roman Catholic. Clubs: Union League, Overbrook Golf, Houston Petroleum. Office: 3 Radnor Corporate Center 100 Matson Ford Rd Radnor PA 19087

TRAMAGLINI, SALVATORE LAWRENCE, JR., cable and wire mfg. co. ofcl.; b. Ossining, N.Y., Dec. 4, 1941; s. Salvatore Lawrence and Barbara Ann (Pekic) T.; B.B.A., Pace U., 1972, M.B.A., 1979; 1 dau., Kimberly Ann. Lead operator IBM Corp., Yorktown, N.Y., 1965-69; ops. mgr., programmer Technicon Corp., Tarrytown, N.Y., 1969-72; mgr. data processing ops. Empire Nat. Bank, Newburgh, N.Y., 1972-74; mgr. info. systems dept. Phelps Dodge Cable & Wire Co., Yonkers, N.Y., 1974-80, dir. mgmt. info. services, 1980—. Served with USNR, 1962-64. Mem. Data Processing Mgmt. Assn., Am. Prodn. and Inventory Control Soc. (chpt. pres.). Home: 3004 Ferncrest Dr Yorktown NY 10598 Office: PO Box 391 Yonkers NY 10702

TRAN, CUNG DO, food retailer; b. Vietnam, Mar. 28, 1922; s. Luong Huu and Nguyet Thi (Do) T.; came to U.S., 1975, naturalized, 1978; B.Engring., Salon-de-Provence, France, 1953; B.A., French U. Hanoi, 1945; m. Bao Nguyen, Apr. 19, 1949; children—Thanhhuong, Bich Thuy, Tuananh, Minh Chau, Tuan Tai. Dep. minister economy Republic of Vietnam, 1966-67, dep. dir. rehab. handicapped, 1967-69; expert adviser Asian Parliamentarians Union, 1970-72; expert cons. Ministry Planning, 1972-74; sales clk. J.C. Penney Co., 1975; owner 7-Eleven Market, Seaside, Calif., 1976—, also Salinas, Calif., 1978—. Served to lt. col. Vietnamese Air Force, 1953-74. Mem. Small Bus. Assn. Republican. Buddhist. Home: 9735 Maul Oak Pl Oakhills Salinas CA 93907 Office: 1391 Fremont Blvd Seaside CA 93955 also 1305 N Main St Salinas CA 93901

TRANTER, GEORGE THOMAS, JR., non-profit orgn. exec.; b. Chgo., July 30, 1954; s. G. Thomas and Mary Ellen (Sanders) T.; B.S. in Econs. (Merit scholar 1974, 75), Elmira Coll., 1976; grad. Health Exec. Devel. program Cornell U., 1979; M.P.S. in Community Service Adminstrn., Alfred U., 1980; m. Elizabeth Blake, Oct. 11, 1975; 1 son, Michael David. Planner, Chemung County, Elmira, N.Y., 1973-74; CETA dir. Chemung County, 1974-76; exec. dir. Chemung County chpt. ARC, Elmira, 1976—. Bd. dirs. Econ. Opportunity Program, 1974-76, Planned Parenthood of So. Tier, 1977-80; chmn. adv. council CETA, Chemung County, 1978-80; chmn. med. com. N.Y. State Spl. Olympics, 1979-80; sec. Multiple Sclerosis Soc., 1979-80. Recipient Disting. Community Service award Chemung County, 1976. Mem. Chemung County C. of C., Elmira Rotary. Republican. Club: Downtown Health. Home: 329 Glen Ave Elmira NY 14905 Office: 462 W Church St Elmira NY 14901

TRANTHAM, WALTER EARL, JR., transp., mfg. exec.; b. Cuero, Tex., July 4 1920: s. Walter Earl and Mabel (Duffey) T.; student Rice Inst., 1937-39; B.A.E., Tex. A. and M. U., 1942; student Am. U., 1943-44; Sc.D., Hamilton U., 1974; m. Eleanor MacDougall, Oct. 30, 1943. Dir. ops. Microwave Tube div. Hughes Aircraft Co., Los Angeles, 1959-61; v.p., dir. mktg. Radcom group Litton Industries, Silver Spring, Md., 1961-63; dir. southeast ops. U.S. Def. group ITT, Washington, 1963-66; pres., chief exec. officer Tasker Industries, Van Nuys, Calif., 1966-68; v.p., dir. advanced programs Canoga Electronics Corp., 1968-70; mgr. transp. control systems Transp. and Indsl. div. GTE Info. Systems, Inc., subs. Gen. Telephone & Electronics, Inc., Bedford, Mass., 1970-72; dir. govt. ops. Servo Corp. Am., Hicksville, N.Y., 1972-75; v.p. Marine Electric Ry. Products div. Marine Electric Corp., 1975-80; pres., chief exec. officer Trac Products Inc., Falls Church, Va., 1980—; dir. MicroCom Inc. Bd. regents Casa Loma Coll., 1966-71. Served to col. USMC, 1942-55; with USMCR, 1955-75. Fellow AIM, mem. IEEE, Am. Inst. Aeros. and Astronautics, Am. Mgmt. Assn., Electronic Industries Assn. (dir. 1966-70, chmn. Mass. transp. bd. 1968-72), Armed Forces Communications Electronics Assn. (v.p., nat. treas. 1959-62, v.p. 1967-70), Nat. Security Indsl. Assn. (mgmt. adv. bd. 1966-68), Marine Corps Res. Officers Assn. (v.p. 1971—), Assn. Am. Railroads, Am. Ry. Engring. Assn., Transp. Research Bd., R.R. Info. Services, Locomotive Maintenance Officers Assn. Home: 2605 Faber Ct Falls Church VA 22046

TRAPP, DONALD WILLIAM, mfg. co. exec.; b. Hampton, Va., Sept. 28, 1946; s. Chester A. and Ida L.; B.A., Va. State Coll., 1968; M.B.A., Ind. U., 1973; m. Shirley A. Stokes, May 29, 1971; children—Rashaad, Brandon. Mgr. treasury Irwin Mgmt. Co., Columbus, Ind., 1973-75; fin. specialist Cummins Engine Co., Columbus, 1976-77, asst. treas., 1977-78, dir. pricing, 1978—. Bd. dirs., audit com. Columbus United Way Am., 1976—; v.p. William R. Laws Found., 1975—. Served with U.S. Army, 1968-70. Recipient Achievement award Wall St. Jour., 1968, Disting. Service citation United Negro Coll. Fund, 1977. Mem. Ind. U. Sch. Bus. Alumni Assn., Kappa Alpha Psi. Office: Cummins Engine Co 1000 5th St Columbus IN 47201

TRAPP, ROBERT FRANK, electronics co. exec.; b. Taylorville, Ill., Nov. 4, 1932; s. Frank Henry and Alice (Rountree) T.; B.S. in Engring. Physics, U. Ill., 1954, postgrad., 1954; postgrad. Ohio State U., 1955-56, UCLA, 1957-60; children—Robert Frank, Stephen M., David J. Chief nuclear project engr. Douglas Missile and Space Systems, Santa Monica, Calif., 1956-62; chief advance concepts NASA Hdqrs., Washington, 1962-68; dir. research div. Arms Control and Disarmament Agy., Washington, 1968-70; mfrs. rep., Fairfax, Va., 1971-76; dir. tech. research Panasonic Co., Secaucus, N.J., 1976-77; pres. Microelectronics Tech. Corp., Palo Alto, Calif., 1977—. Served with USAF, 1954-56. Mem. IEEE, Soc. Automotive Engrs., ASME, Am. Mgmt. Assn., Internat. Soc. for Hybrid Microelectronics, Soc. for Info. Display, Soc. Photo-optical Instrumentation Engrs. Republican. Contbr. tech. papers to publs. Home: San Jose CA Office: 2446 Watson Ct Palo Alto CA 94303

TRAPPENBURG, HERBERT, import co. exec.; b. Gorinchem, Netherlands, July 19, 1919; came to U.S., 1951; s. Cornelis and Pietje (Ouderdorp) T.; student Christelyk Lyceum, Hilversum, Vereniging van Accountants; m. Flora Thieme, Jan. 8, 1947; children—Cornelis Willem, Johanna Margot, Pieter Frans, Liesbeth. Engaged in acctg., Netherlands, 1939-44; adminstr. Hosp. Naarden, 1944-46; with N.V. Amsta, export-import, 1946-49, N.V. P. de Jong Wormerveer, export, 1950, Europe Am. Trading Co. Inc., Hilversum, Netherlands, 1965; pres. Del. Mercantile Co. Inc., Stamford, N.Y., 1965—. Served with Dutch Army, 1939-40. Mem. Am. Importers Assn., Bicycle Wholesalers and Distbrs. Assn. Club: Stamford Rotary. Home: 1 Park Ave Stamford NY 12167 Office: Del Merchantile Co Inc Railroad Ave Stamford NY 12167

TRAUTLEIN, DONALD HENRY, steel co. exec.; b. Sandusky, Ohio, Aug. 19, 1926; s. Henry Francis and Lillian Amelia (Russell) T.; student Bowling Green State U., 1946-47; B.S. in Bus. Adminstrn., Miami U., Oxford, Ohio, 1950; m. Mary Rankin, Apr. 28, 1956; children—John Russell, James Rankin, Katherine. Bus. trainee Gen. Electric Corp., Bridgeport, Conn., 1950-51; partner Price Waterhouse & Co., N.Y.C., 1951-76; comptroller Bethlehem Steel Corp. (Pa.), 1977-80, sr. v.p. acctg., 1977-80, exec. v.p., 1979-80, chmn., chief exec. officer, 1980—, also dir. Served with USNR, 1945-46. C.P.A., N.Y., Pa., others. Mem. Am. Inst. C.P.A.'s, N.Y. State Soc. C.P.A.'s. Episcopalian. Clubs: Univ. (N.Y.C.); Tokeneke (Darien, Conn.); Saucon Valley Country; Bethlehem. Home: RD 1 Coopersburg PA 18036 Office: Bethlehem Steel Corp 8th and Eaton Aves Bethlehem PA 18016

TRAUTMAN, GERALD HOUGH, transp. exec., lawyer; b. Petoskey, Mich., Aug. 27, 1912; s. Newton Ellsworth and Madeline (Hough) T.; B.A., Stanford, 1934; LL.B., Harvard, 1937. Admitted to Calif. bar, 1937, since practiced in San Francisco; partner firm McCutchen, Doyle, Brown, Trautman & Enersen, San Francisco, 1937-65; pres., chief exec. officer, dir. Greyhound Corp., 1966-70, chmn. exec. com., 1968, chmn. bd., chief exec. officer, 1970, pres., 1977-79, chief exec. officer, 1970-80; pres., dir. Greyhound de Mexico, S.A. de C.V.; dir. Greyhound Computer Corp., Armour & Co., Greyhound Fin. & Leasing Corp. A.G., Greyhound Leasing & Financial Corp., Aircraft Service Internat., Inc., Brewster Transport Co. Ltd., Greyhound Food Mgmt., Inc., Greyhound World Tours, Inc., Greyhound Lines, Inc., Greyhound Lines of Can. Ltd., Greyhound Rent-A-Car, Inc., Air Service Internat. Inc., Motor Coach Industries, Inc., Motor Coach Industries Ltd., Post Houses, Inc., Prophet Foods Co., Red Top Sedan Service, Inc., Travelers Express Co., Inc., Armour-Dial Inc., Am. Sightseeing Tours, Inc., Calif. Parlor Car Tours Co., Eastern Can. Greyhound Lines, Ltd., Ry. Equipment Leasing Co., Verex Corp., Restaura, S.A., Lehman Corp., N.Y.C., 20th Century Fox. Served to lt. USNR, 1944-46. Mem. Am. Bar Assn., U.S. C. of C., Nat. Council of Salk Inst., Delta Kappa Epsilon. Clubs: Links (N.Y.C.); Arizona, Camelback Country, Phoenix Country, Plaza (Phoenix). Office: Greyhound Tower Phoenix AZ 85077

TRAVAGLINI, BARBARA CARLSON (MRS. ALFONSO FREDERICK TRAVAGLINI), steel co. exec.; b. Easton, Pa., Nov. 4, 1925; d. Gunard Oscar and Margaret Bailey (Berry) Carlson; Bryn Mawr Coll., 1943-44, Moore Coll. Art, 1944-48; m. Alfonso Frederick Travaglini, June 15, 1946; children—Gunard Carlson, Frederick Carlson, Mark Carlson. Dir., vice-chmn., sec. G.O. Carlson, Inc., Thorndale, Pa., 1956—. Pres. Coatesville Hosp. Aux., 1967-72, 1st v.p., 1972—; sec. Chester County Airport Authority. Exec. dir., sec., treas. Gunard Berry Carlson Meml. Found.; trustee Saint Francis Coll., Lafayette Coll. Republican. Roman Catholic. Author: The Kelly Green Cow, 1949; Henry Hippo, 1972; columnist A Woman's Pen and As I See It. Home: 4000 Hazelwood Ave Thorndale PA 19372 Office: G O Carlson Inc Thorndale PA 19372

TRAVELL, CLARK, corp. exec.; b. N.Y.C., Aug. 29, 1923; s. J. Willard (M.D.) and Edith (Talcott) T.; A.B., cum laude, Princeton, 1945; m. Joan Agnes Balch, Oct. 9, 1945 (div. June 1966); children—Susan Talcott (Mrs. Haynes Johnson), Blair Bates (Mrs. Thomas McMorrow), Jill Gordon (Mrs. Richard Benner), Phyllis Balch; m. 2d, Philippa Walter Breckenfeld, July 19, 1980. Export dept. Phelps Dodge Cooper Products Corp., N.Y.C., 1948-50; asso. William A.M. Burden & Co., N.Y.C., 1951-62; exec. v.p., sec. Austral Oil Co., Inc., 1951-67; cons. oil, gas and mineral investments, 1967—. Asst. treas. United Republican. Finance Com. for N.Y. State, 1955-59. Trustee Solebury Sch., New Hope, Pa., 1950-56, 61-65; trustee, treas. The Browning Sch., N.Y.C., 1953-74, trustee, v.p., 1974-75, pres., 1975—. Served as capt., pilot USAAF, 1942-45. ETO. Decorated Air Medal with 5 clusters (U.S.); Croix de Guerre avec palme (France). Clubs: University (N.Y.C.); Quandrangle (Princeton). Office: Watrous Point Old Saybrook CT 06475

TRAVELSTEAD, COLEMAN, internat. banker; b. Lexington, Ky., May 21, 1942; s. Chester Coleman and Marita (Hawley) T.; B.A., U. N.Mex., 1969. Area adminstr. for Japan, Bank of Am., San Francisco, 1969-71, asst. mgr. loans Osaka (Japan) br., 1971-73, asst. mgr. bus. devel. Tokyo br., 1974-75, v.p., sect. head, internat. banking office, N.Y.C., 1976-79; v.p., group head for fgn. and personal banking groups Bank of Am. Internat. of Fla., Miami, 1979—. Served with U.S. Army, 1961-64. Mem. U. N.Mex. Alumni Assn. (bd. dirs. 1980—). Home: 11155 SW 135th Ct Miami FL 33186 Office: 1000 Brickell Ave Miami FL 33131

TRAVER, SPENCER J., rubber co. exec.; b. New Brighton, Pa., July 13, 1929; s. Harry G. and Ruth J. (Gowell) T.; student Ohio State U., 1948-52; B.B.A. in Fin., Northwestern U., 1971; postgrad. U. Chgo., Kent State U.; m. Kathleen M. Gaines, Nov. 3, 1973; children—Jeanette, Jeffrey, John. Casualty underwriting mgr. Nationwide Mut. Ins. Co., Columbus, Ohio, 1952; spl. agt. Prudential Ins. Co., Columbus, 1953-55, Hartford Ins. Group, Columbus, 1955-57; account exec. Weisenberger Ins. Agy., Chillicothe, Ohio, 1957-67; corp. ins. mgr. Brunswick Corp., Skokie, Ill., 1967-70; corp. ins. mgr. Baxter Labs., Morton Grove, Ill., 1970-73, dir. risk mgmt., Deerfield, Ill., 1973-74; dir. risk mgmt. B.F. Goodrich, Akron, Ohio, 1974-78, asst. treas., 1978—; lectr. Akron U., N.Y. U., U. Dallas, Am. Grad. Sch. Internat. Mgmt.; cons. ins., risk mgmt., appraisal, large losses. Served with USNR, 1947-51. Asso. in Risk Mgmt., Ins. Inst. Am.; C.P.C.U., Am. Inst. Property Liability Underwriters. Mem. Soc. C.P.C.U.'s, Risk and Ins. Mgmt. Soc., Lake Cable Recreation Assn. Republican. Presbyterian. Club: Shady Hollow Country (Massillon, Ohio). Home: 5309 Island Dr Canton OH 44718 Office: 500 S Main St Akron OH 44318

TRAVERS, THOMAS JOSEPH, mfg. co. exec.; b. Boston, Jan. 13, 1918; s. Daniel A. and Mary H. (McGarry) T.; A.B. cum laude, Boston Coll., 1939, M.S. in Labor Relations, 1941; m. Katherine O'Leary, June 29, 1946; children—Thomas Joseph, Stephen, Maureen, Damiel, Richard, Robert. Mgmt. service rep. Ernst & Ernst, C.P.A.'s, Boston, 1946-49; with Comml. Shearing, Inc., Youngstown, Ohio, 1949—, v.p., sec., 1971-75, chmn. bd., 1975—, also dir.; dir. Am. Welding & Mfg. Co., Dollar Savs. & Trust Co., Youngstown; trustee Youngstown Community Corp.; pres., trustee Indsl. Info. Inst. Trustee Youngstown Hosp. Assn., Youngstown Ednl. Found. Mem. Nat. Fluid Power Assn. (dir.). Clubs: Youngstown, Youngstown Country. Home: 230 N Cadillac Dr Youngstown OH 44512 Office: PO Box 239 Youngstown OH 44501

TRAVIS, DEMPSEY JEROME, mortgage banker; b. Chgo., Feb. 25, 1920; s. Louis and Mittie (Strickland) T.; B.A., Roosevelt U., 1949; grad. Sch. Mortgage Banking, Northwestern U., 1969; Ph.D. in Econs. (hon.), Olive Harvey Coll.; Ph.D. (hon.), Daniel Hale Williams U.; m. Moselynne Hardwick, Sept. 17, 1949. Pres., Travis Realty Co., 1949—, Travis Ins. Agy., 1951—; pres., owner Sivart Bldg.; pres. Urban Research Inst., Inc.; dir. Sears Bank & Trust Co., Chgo. Pres., Dearborn Real Estate Bd., 1957-59, 70-72; mem. adv. bd. Non-Profit Housing Partnership, Washington; chmn. HUD/PUSH Nat. Housing Task Force, 1975; past mem. adv. bd. Fed. Nat. Mortgage Assn., Washington. Mem. Presdl. Task Force Urban Renewal, 1970—, Mayor's adv. com. Bldg. Code Amendments, 1970—; mem. Mayor's Com. on Rent Control, Ill. Ins. Consumers Adv. Panel, 1970; mem. Presdl. Task Force Inflation, 1974; mem. Fed. Energy Adminstrn.'s Constructive Adv., 1974-75. Life mem. Field Mus. Natural History, Chgo. Art Inst.; mem. adv. com. Urban Am. Bd. dirs. Nat. Housing Conf., Washington, Chgo. Econ. Devel. Corp.; trustee Northwestern Meml. Hosp., Central YMCA Community Coll., 1969—; mem. Mayor's Commn. for Preservation Chgo.'s Hist. Bldgs.; voting mem. Met. Chgo. YMCA. Served with Ordance Corps, AUS, 1942-46. Mem. Mortgage Bankers Assn. Am. (pres.), United Mortgage Bankers Am. (founder 1961, pres. 1961-74), NAACP (pres. Chgo. 1959-60), Nat. Assn. Real Estate Brokers (1st v.p. 1959-60), Am. Soc. Real

Estate Counselors, Cosmopolitan C. of C. (dir., vice chmn. ins. com.), Beta Gamma Sigma, Lambda Alpha Internat. Clubs: Executives, Economics, Forty (Chgo.), Cliff Dwellers, Met. Author: Don't Stop Me Now; A 100-Year Odyssey on Black Housing, Chicago, 1900-2000, 1977. Fin. editor Dollars and Sense. Contbr. articles to profl. jours., popular mags. Home: 8001 S Champlain Ave Chicago IL 60619 Office: 840 E 87th St Chicago IL 60619

TRAVIS, WHITNEY, pvt. club mgr.; b. Peekskill, N.Y., Jan. 18, 1920; s. Elias Whitney and Helen (McCutchen) T.; B.S., Cornell U., 1942; m. Marjorie Doreen Tudor, Feb. 1, 1947; children—John Whitney, Brion Derek, Elizabeth Tudor. Field auditor Horwath & Horwath, N.Y.C., 1947-49; controller Bear Mountain Inn, N.Y., 1949-60; gen. mgr. The Yale Club of N.Y.C., 1960-74; gen. mgr. The Stock Exchange Luncheon Club, N.Y.C., 1974—. Employer trustee local 6 Club Employees Pension & Ins. Funds, 1964-75, chmn. bd., 1973-75. Served with Med. Adminstrn. Corps, U.S. Army, 1942-46; ETO. Named Club Mgr. of the Yr., Yale Club of N.Y.C., 1971. Mem. Club Mgrs. Assn. Am. (nat. pres. 1979). Republican. Episcopalian. Club: Masons (32 deg.). Home: Cloudbank Garrison NY 10524 Office: 11 Wall St New York NY 10005

TREEGER, THOMAS CARL, mfg. co. exec.; b. N.Y.C., Feb. 26, 1932; s. Clarence R. and Helen Elizabeth (Felstiner) T.; A.B. in Econs., Mich. U., 1954; M.B.A., Harvard U., 1958; m. Marjorie Ann Lawrence, Oct. 15, 1962; children—Jennifer Grant, Anne Elizabeth. Project mgr. product devel. St. Regis Paper Co., N.Y.C., 1958-62, mgr. new product planning, 1962-67, mgr. corporate new ventures dept., 1967-68, gen. mgr. environ. systems div., 1968-72; div. mgr. Angelica Corp., St. Louis, 1972-75, group v.p., 1975—. Co-chmn. Environment Com., Scarsdale, N.Y., 1970-71. Served to lt. U.S. Army, 1954-56. Mem. Am. Mktg. Assn., (v.p. 1970-72), Nat. Assn. Corporate Planning. Republican. Jewish. Clubs: Harvard, Harvard Bus. Sch. Home: 44 Broadview Dr Clayton MO 63105 Office: Corporate Sq Saint Louis MO 63132

TREES, JAMES FREDERICK, investment co. exec.; b. Glencoe, Ill., Feb. 15, 1939; s. Harry A. and Eleanor (Smith) T.; B.A., DePauw U., 1961; M.B.A., Harvard U., 1963, D.B.A., 1971. Mem. faculty Harvard Bus. Sch., 1963-65; asst. mgr. Brown Bros. Harriman & Co., N.Y.C., 1965-69; asso. New Court Securities Corp., N.Y.C., 1969-70; cons. J. Henry Schroder Banking Corp., N.Y.C., 1969-71; founder, chmn. bd., chief exec. officer Charter Atlantic Corp. and subsidiaries, Fischer, Francis, Trees & Watts, Inc., and Charter Atlantic Securities Co., Inc., N.Y.C., 1972—; dir. Lombard Odier Internat. Portfolio Mgmt., Ltd. (London). Bd. dirs., mem. fin. com. City at 42d St., Inc., 1979—; bd. dirs. Group for the South Fork, 1980—; trustee C.G. Jung Found. for Analytical Psychology, 1980—. Mem. Council Fgn. Relations, Center Inter-Am. Relations. Office: 717 Fifth Ave New York NY 10022

TREGENZA, NORMAN HUGHSON, investment banker; b. Morristown, N.J., Feb. 1, 1937; s. Norman J. and Marion Esther (Hughson) T.; B.A., St. Lawrence U., 1959; M.B.A., N.Y. U., 1963; m. Alyce Virginia Bruene, Aug. 27, 1966; children—Norman Arthur, Suzanne Carol. Sr. investment officer Tchrs. Ins. & Annuity Assn., N.Y.C., 1960-71; sr. v.p. Republic Funding Corp., N.Y.C., 1971—; co-founder, dir. Satellite Syndicated Systems, Inc., So. Satellite Systems, Inc., Tulsa. Chmn. stewardship com. Presbyn. Ch., Morristown, N.J., 1978, ruling elder, 1979, pres. bd. trustees, 1981. Mem. St. Lawrence U. Alumni Assn. N.J. (pres. 1970-72). Club: Baltusrol Golf. Home: 9 Beechwood Dr Convent Station NJ 07961 Office: 645 Madison Ave New York NY 10022

TREIMAN, EDWARD F., elec. engr.; b. Toledo, Iowa, July 29, 1910; s. Samuel E. and Dorothy (Walker) T.; B.S. in E.E., Iowa State Coll., 1933, E.E., 1943; m. Selma White, June 24, 1942; children—Paul, Rosalind, Ann. With Western Electric Co., Chgo. and N.Y., engring., research and transcontinental line experimentations, 1933-37; asst. pruchasing agt. Allied Machinery Corp., Feb.-Sept. 1937; with Internat. Western Electric Co., 1938-39; mng. dir. Nat. Electric Light Assn., 1946-52; cons. engr., Chgo., 1952—. Sec., St. Lawrence Commn. U.S., 1944-46, 2d Nat. Radio Conf., 1945. Commd. 1st lt., Signal Corps, U.S. Army, 1937, later capt.; served in U.S. and France. Mem. Am. Inst. Elec. Engrs., Edison Electric Inst., NAM, Tau Beta Pi, Delta Upsilon. Clubs: Union League, Univ., Recess (N.Y.C.); Univ. (Chgo.). Address: 2918 W Fargo St Chicago IL 60645

TREMBLAY, CLAUDE, business exec.; b. Montreal, Que., Can., July 17, 1941; s. Alphonse and Albina (Drolet) T.; student public schs., Montreal. Sr. cons. SGI Ltee, Montreal, 1969-73; officer in charge of Dept. Edn. budget Quebec Treasury Bd., 1973-75; treas. Olympic Installation Bd., Montreal, 1976-77; v.p. fin. and planning Que.'s Nat. Asbestos Corp., 1978—; pres. Lupel-SNA Inc., Cap-De-La-Madeleinc, Que. Served with M.C. Canadian Army, 1959-62. Mem. Que. Chartered Accts. Inst. (Silver medal 1966), Data Processing Mgmt. Assn., World Future Soc., Canadian Public Adminstrn. Inst., Canadian Tax Found. Home: 1 Jardins de Merici 404 Quebec PQ G1S 4M4 Canada Office: 845 Boul St-Cyrille ouest Quebec PQ G1S 1T5 Canada

TREMBLAY, PETER V., razor co. exec.; b. Oldbury, Eng., Jan. 22, 1918; s. Albert Vilmont and Gladys Evelyn (Durrant) T.; grad. high sch.; m. Dorothy Cicely Cartwright, Jan. 16, 1943; children—Joan Dorothy, Gillian Cicely. Asst. purchasing agt. Can. Broadcasting Corp., Montreal, Que., 1946-51; gen. purchasing agt. Dominion Dairies, Ltd., Montreal, 1952-54; mgr. purchasing Gillette of Can., Montreal, 1954-59; exec. asst. Gillette Safety Razor Co., Boston, 1960-65, v.p.-purchasing, 1968—; mgr. purchasing Gillette Industries, Ltd., London, 1966-67. Served as flight lt. RCAF, 1940-45; ETO. Mem. Nat. Assn. Purchasing Mgmt., Purchasing Mgmt. Assn. Boston (dir.). Episcopalian. Contbg. author: Purchasing Handbook, 3d edit., 1973. Home: 8 Eastgate Ln Hingham MA 02043 Office: Gillette Park Boston MA 02106

TRENCHER, MARK L., ins. co. ofcl.; b. Bad Nauheim, Germany, July 12, 1948; s. Naftali and Toni (Landau) T.; came to U.S., 1951; naturalized, 1956; B.A. cum laude, Bklyn. Coll., 1969; M.S., N.Y. U., 1971; m. Sandra Kaminetsky, Sept. 15, 1970; children—Steven, Elana. Ordained rabbi, 1971; mgr. research and long range planning Prudential Property and Casualty Ins. Co., Woodbridge, N.J., 1972-76; mgr. corp. planning Aetna Life & Casualty Co., Hartford, Conn., 1976-80, dir. market research and devel., 1980—; adj. prof. Kean Coll., N.J., 1974-75, Rutgers U., 1975-76, U. Hartford, 1977—; cons. in operations research and mgmt. sci. Treas. Young Israel of West Hartford, 1977-78, v.p., 1978-80, chmn. rabbinical bd., 1980—; dir., mem. religious and secular bds. edn. Hebrew Acad. of Greater Hartford, 1977—, chmn. religious bd. edn., 1980—. Mem. Am. Statis. Assn., Soc. Ins. Research, N. Am. Soc. for Corp. Planning Nat. Assn. Bus. Economists. Developer computer statistical and econ. analysis systems. Home: 50 Miamis Rd West Hartford CT 06117 Office: Aetna Life & Casualty Co 151 Farmington Ave Hartford CT 06156

TREND, KENNETH NOLAN, computer co. exec.; b. Shaker Heights, Ohio, July 24, 1942; s. Raymond W. and Marilyn J. (Brouker) T.; B.A. cum laude, Muskingum Coll., 1964; postgrad. U. Tex., 1964-66. Asso. prof. Monmouth Coll., Long Branch, N.J., 1966-68; asst. to pres. Bookshelf of Am., N.Y.C., 1968-69; field engr. Acoustic Research, Inc., Cambridge, Mass., 1969-72; sr. orgn. devel. specialist Digital Equipment Corp., Maynard, Mass., 1972-79, Prime Computer, Inc., Framingham, Mass., 1979—; civic and indsl. cons.; adj. prof. orgn. behavior Boston U. Mem. Am. Soc. Tng. and Devel., Organization Devel. Network. Home: PO Box 44 Concord MA 01742 Office: 145 Pennsylvania Ave Framingham MA 01701

TRESSLER, DAVID L., banker; b. South Connellsville, Pa., Apr. 30, 1936; s. Albert and Anna Mary (Fallon) T.; B.S., Pa. State U., 1958; M.S., U. Pitts., 1965; postgrad. Stonier Grad. Sch. Banking, Rutgers U., 1967-69; m. Joyce Mack, Aug. 9, 1958; children—David L., James M. Vice-pres., regional mgr. Pitts. Nat. Bank, 1963-74; sales rep. REA Express, Pitts., 1962-63; with Northeastern Bank, Scranton, Pa., 1975—, exec. v.p., 1978, chief exec. officer, 1978—, pres., dir., 1978—. Bd. dirs. Lackawanna County United Way, Catholic Social Services, Economic Devel. Council N.E. Pa., Johnson Sch. Tech., Mercy Hosp. Mem. Eastern States Bankcard Assn. (dir.), Scranton C. of C. (dir., treas., mem. exec. com.), Scranton Lackawanna Indsl. Bldg. Co. (mem. exec. com., dir. v.p.), Pa. Bankers Assn. (2d vice-chmn.), Lackawanna Indsl. Fund Enterprises (trustee, mem. exec. com.), Am. Inst. Banking. Clubs: Lions, Scranton Country, Elks. Office: Penn Ave and Spruce St Scranton PA 18503

TRETLER, RICHARD STERLING, toy co. exec.; b. Bklyn, Aug. 13, 1944; s. Nathan Burton and Virginia L. (Saper) T.; B.S. in Econs., U. Pa., 1966; M.B.A., Syracuse U., 1968; m. Marcia J. Stein, Aug. 19, 1967; children—Jonathan David, Elizabeth Dana. Asst. to v.p. corp. control Revlon, Inc., N.Y.C., 1968-70, asst. controller profl. products div., 1970-71, controller profl. products div., 1971-79; v.p. fin. Knickerbocker Toy Co. Inc., Middlesex, N.J., 1979—. N.Y.C. fund raising chmn. Syracuse U. Grad Sch. Bus., 1976. Mem. Beta Gamma Sigma. Home: 3 Coachman Dr Roslyn NY 11576 Office: 207 Pond Ave Middlesex NJ 08846

TREVITHICK, RONALD JAMES, fin. exec.; b. Portland, Oreg., Sept. 13, 1944; s. Clifford Vincent and Amy Lois (Turner) T.; B.B.A., U. Wash., 1966; m. Delberta Russell, Sept. 11, 1965; children—Pamela, Carmen, Marla, Sheryl. Mem. audit staff Ernst & Ernst, Anchorage, 1966, 68-70; pvt. practice accounting, Fairbanks, Alaska, 1970-73; with Touche Ross & Co., Anchorage, 1973-78, audit partner, 1976-78; treas., dir. VECO, Inc., 1978—; exec. v.p. fin., dir. VECO Internat., Inc., 1979—; chmn. bd. P.S. Contractors A/S, 1978—; sec.-treas., dir. Norcon, Inc., 1978—, VECO Drilling, Inc., 1978—, VEMAR, Inc., 1979—; instr. accounting U. Alaska; lectr. accounting and taxation Am. Coll. Life Underwriters. Bd. dirs., fin. chmn. Anchorage Arts Council, 1975-78; campaign div. chmn. United Way, 1976-77. Served with U.S. Army, 1967-68. C.P.A., Alaska, La., N.C., Va. Mem. Alaska Soc. C.P.A.'s, Am. Inst. C.P.A.'s, Petroleum Accountants Soc., Fin. Execs. Inst., Beta Alpha Psi. Clubs: Rotary, Petroleum, Tower Commonwealth North. Home: SRA Box 372W Anchorage AK 99507 Office: 5151 Fairbanks St Anchorage AK 99503

TREVOR, BRONSON, economist, corp. exec.; b. N.Y.C., Nov. 12, 1910; s. John Bond and Caroline Murray (Wilmerding) T.; A.B., Columbia Coll., 1931; m. Eleanor Darlington Fisher, Nov. 8, 1946; children—Eleanor, Bronson, Caroline. Own bus., 1931—; dir., asst. sec. Northwestern Terminal R.R., 1952-58; chmn. bd. Texinia Corp., Advanced Drilling Systems, Inc. Former dir. chmn. fin. com. Gen. Hosp. of Saranac Lake; mem. Council for Agrl. and Chemurgic Research, Am. Forestry Assn. Mem. Republican County Com. of N.Y. County, 1937-39; leader in primary election campaigns N.Y. County, 1937, 38, 39 to free local Rep. party orgn. from leftwing affiliations; mem. Nat. Rep. Club. Served with U.S. Army, 1942, World War II. Mem. N.Y. State C. of C., S.A.R., Soc. Colonial Wars. Clubs: Union, Knickerbocker, Racquet and Tennis, Piping Rock. Author: (pamphlet) The United States Gold Purchase Program, 1941; also numerous articles on econ. subjects. Home: Paul Smith's NY 12970 Office: POB 182 Oyster Bay NY 11771

TRIBULL, CHRISTOPH, bus. exec.; b. W. Ger., Feb. 25, 1941; student in econs. U. Cologne (W. Ger.); M.B.A., INSEAD, Fontaine-bleu, France, 1969. Mgr., Commerzbank A.G., Cologne, 1965-68; fin. dir. Dow Chem., Sao Paulo, Brazil, 1969-74; chmn. bd., chief exec. officer Sierracin Corp., Sylmar, Calif., 1976—; dir. various Brazilian ranching, chem. and steelmill cos. Served with W. German Navy, 1959-60. Office: 12780 San Fernando Rd Sylmar CA 91342

TRICE, EZRA B., business exec.; b. 1921; married. Gen. mgr. Radcliff Gravel Co., 1947, 54-56; with Bay Towing & Dredging Co., 1952-54; pres. Radcliff Materials Inc., 1956-64, 68-74; v.p. So. Industries Corp., Mobile, Ala., 1964-68, exec. v.p., 1976-79, pres., 1979—, also dir. Served with U.S. Army. Office: PO Box 1685 Mobile AL 36601*

TRIGAUX, GEORGE ARILLE, flavor and fragrance industry mgmt. cons.; b. Charleston, W.Va., Mar. 1, 1925; s. George Sylvan and Mary Elizabeth (Holmes) T.; B.Chem.Engring., Ga. Inst. Tech., 1945; m. June Moree, Sept. 1, 1946; children—David, Susan, Robert. Engr., Union Carbide Corp., N.Y.C., 1946-70; various corporate mgmt. positions, 1955-70, mgr. corporate devel., 1970; founder, pres. Norfield Corp., Danbury, Conn., 1970-72; pres. Firmenich Inc., Princeton, N.J., 1972-77; pres. PFW Inc., Middletown, N.Y., 1977-80; prin. George A. Trigaux Assos., Inc., 1980—; dir. PFW Inc. Bd. dirs. Research Inst. for Fragrance Materials; trustee Nutrition Found.; mem. U.S. Senatorial Bus. Adv. Bd., 1980—. Served with USN, 1943-45. Mem. Essential Oil Assn. (dir.), Am. Inst. Chem. Engrs., Am. Chem. Soc., Am. Mgmt. Assn., Alpha Chi Sigma, Beta Theta Pi. Clubs: Weston (Conn.) Field; Board Room, Met., Marco Polo (N.Y.C.). Home: RD 2 Clove Rd Lagrangeville NY 12540

TRIMBLE, HAROLD GUYON, JR., Realtor; b. Oakland, Calif., June 16, 1926; s. Harold Guyon and Esther Evelyn (Kushins) T.; student Menlo Coll., 1949, U. Calif., Berkeley, 1951; m. Ann Malloy, Mar. 15, 1968; children—Harold, Sandra, Scott, Jay, Randolph. Vice-pres. C.J. Duncan Co., Oakland, 1955-58; v.p. Duncan Korb and Trimble Realtors, Oakland, 1958-65; pres. Toddy Investment Co., San Francisco, 1960-78; owner Harold G. Trimble and Assos., San Francisco, 1978—; trustee 1st Western Income Realty Trust. Pres., East Bay Diabetic Youth Found., 1978; chmn. Community Relations Council, Alameda and Contra Costa counties, 1968. Served with USNR, 1944-47. Mem. Realtors Nat. Mktg. Inst. (v.p. 1980, chmn. comml. investment div.), Nat. Assn. Realtors, Internat. Real Estate Fedn., Internat. Council Shopping Centers, San Francisco Bd. Realtors, Oakland Bd. Realtors. Republican. Jewish. Club: B'nai B'rith. Office: 115 Sansome St Suite 1200 San Francisco CA 94104

TRIMBLE, LINDA FRANCES, devel. co. exec.; b. Dallas, Feb. 11, 1948; d. Joseph Leon and Frances Elise (Manship) T.; student Stephen F. Austin U., 1966-67; B.B.A., N. Tex. State U., 1970; M.B.A., U. South Fla., 1980. Sr. control analyst Southwestern States Bankcard Assos., Dallas, 1970-72; mgmt. acct. Redman Devel. Corp., Dallas, 1972-74; exec. officer, asst. mgr. accounts payable Lincoln Property Co., Dallas, 1974-75; mgr. acctg. and internal auditor, Tampa, Fla., 1975-76; mgr., acctg. and data services S.E. div. Duo Fast Corp., Tampa, 1976-80; acctg. mgr. W & G Devel. Corp., Sun City Center, Fla., 1981—. Mem. Am. Mktg. Assn., Nat. Assn. Accts., LWV, Phi Chi Theta (nat. officer 1973-78). Democrat. Methodist. Club: Pilot. Home: 2812 Ebony Pl Seffner FL 33584 Office: PO Box 5698 Sun City Center FL 33570

TRINGALE, ANTHONY ROSARIO, life ins. co. exec.; b. Syracuse, N.Y., Apr. 20, 1942; s. Anthony and Susan Marie (Cerio) T.; B.S.F.S., Georgetown U., 1967; CLU, Am. Coll. Life Underwriters, 1973; m. Myranda Lou Atwell, Aug. 1, 1964; children—Anthony William, Michael Paul, Mark David, Amber Marie. Office mgr. trainee N.Y. Life Ins. Co. No. Va., 1965-66, office mgr., Fairfax office, 1966, field underwriter, 1966-68, asst. mgr., 1968-73, mgmt. asst., home office, N.Y.C., 1973, gen. mgr. Pitts. gen. office, 1973-76; gen. mgr. Acacia Mut. Life Ins. Co., Annandale, Va., 1976—; lectr. in field. Founding vice chmn. Fairfax Orgn. Christians/Jews United in Service (FOCUS); lector Nat. Shrine of Immaculate Conception, St. Leo's Ch.; vol. ARC; bd. dirs. Jeane Dixon's Children to Children Found.; mem. VIP panel United Cerebral Palsy campaign; panelist Washington Multiple Sclerosis Soc. C.L.U. Mem. No. Va. Assn. Life Underwriters (treas. 1972), Sales Marketing Execs. Met. Washington (pres. 1979-80), Nat. Assn. Life Underwriters (nat. mgmt. award Gen. Agts. and Mgrs. Conf., 1976-79; life), No. Va. Estate Planning Council, No. Va. Gen. Agts. and Mgrs. Assn. (pres. 1980-81), Fairfax County C. of C. (legis. com.). Roman Catholic (lector, instr.). Home: 8805 Sandy Ridge Ct Fairfax VA 22031 Office: 7700 Little River Turnpike Suite 600 Annandale VA 22003

TRINKLE, JAMES LEWIS, real estate broker; b. Roanoke, Va., Apr. 2, 1929; s. Elbert Lee and Helen (Sexton) T.; B.A., Hampden-Sydney Coll., 1950; LL.B., U. Va., 1953; m. Betty Francis, Dec. 27, 1950; children—James Lewis, William Francis, David Ball. Admitted to Va. bar, 1952; asso. firm Woodrum, Staples & Gregory, Roanoke, 1953-56; sales rep. C.W. Francis & Son, Inc., Roanoke, 1956-61, v.p., 1961-66, pres., 1966—; dir. The Colonial-Am. Nat. Bank of Roanoke; chmn. bd., dir. Peoples Fed. Savs. & Loan Assn. of Roanoke. Pres. Central YMCA, Roanoke, 1971-73, Roanoke Fine Arts Center, 1968-70, United Fund of Roanoke Valley, 1963, Downtown Roanoke, Inc., 1962; mem. project com. Roanoke Civic Center, 1964-71; mem. Roanoke City Charter Study Commn., 1961; pres. Young Democratic Clubs of Va., 1959; chmn. Roanoke City Democratic Com., 1962; bd. dirs. Roanoke Symphony Soc., Roanoke chpt. Am. Cancer Soc., Roanoke Hist. Soc.; trustee Hampden-Sydney Coll. Recipient Distinguished Service award Roanoke Jr. C. of C., 1961. Mem. Roanoke Valley, Va., Nat. real estate bds., Am. Va., Roanoke bar assns., Gen. Alumni Assn. U. Va. (pres.), Gen. Alumni Assn. Hampden-Sydney Coll. (pres.), Omicron Delta Kappa, Pi Kappa Alpha, Phi Alpha Delta. Presbyterian. Clubs: Roanoke Country, Shenandoah, Hunting Hills Country, Farmington Country. Home: 5270 Flintlock Rd SW Hunting Hills Roanoke VA 24014 Office: 120 W Kirk Ave Roanoke VA 24011

TRIPLETT, GARY J., lawyer, chem. co. exec.; b. Van, W. Va., May 17, 1926, s. General Francis and Vivian Ethel (Eastep) T.; student Ala. Poly. Inst., 1944-45; A.B., W.Va. U., 1949, LL.B., 1951; m. Loretta James Findley, Apr. 18, 1953; children—Martha Sloan, Grace Stout. Admitted to W.Va. bar, 1951; law clk. U.S. Dist. Ct., Charleston, W.Va., 1951-52; mem. firm Jackson, Kelly, Holt & O'Farrell, Charleston, 1952-58; atty. Union Carbide Corp., South Charleston, 1958-69, atty. in charge South Charleston regional office law dept., 1969-72, energy, environ. affairs counsel, N.Y.C., 1972-75, counsel chems. and plastics group, 1975-76, sr. group counsel, 1976-78, sr. regional counsel W.Va. and Gulf Coast, 1978—; instr. comml. law Am. Inst. Banking, 1956-57; pres. W.Va. State Bar, 1970-71, chmn. bd., 1971-72; mem. Jud. Conf. 4th Circuit. Bd. dirs. Kanawha-Clay chpt. ARC, vice chmn., 1971-72. Served with USNR, 1945-46. Mem. Am. Bar Assn. (mem. standing com. assn. communications 1972-75), Phi Delta Phi, Psi Chi, Delta Nu Tau, Beta Theta Pi. Presbyterian. Mem. editorial bd. W.Va. Law Rev., 1949-51. Home: 909 Chestnut Rd Charleston WV 25314 Office: Union Carbide Corp Law Dept 437 MacCorkle Ave South Charleston WV 25303

TRIPLETT, RAYMOND FRANCIS, underwriter; b. Detroit Lakes, Minn., Oct. 14, 1921; s. Raymond LeRoy and Barbara A. (Wambach) T.; grad. U.S. Maritime Acad., 1943; Am. Coll. Life Underwriters, 1957; m. Shirley J. Koenig, Feb. 14, 1942; children—Kathleen Triplett Hayes, Barbara K. Triplett Sullivan, Joan D. Triplett Noyes, Therese M. Triplett Corman, Raymond J. Western sales mgr. Minn. and Ont. Paper Co., 1950-53; pres. Triplett Planning and Service Corp., San Jose, Calif., 1953—. Mem. Santa Clara Personnel Bd., 1965-66, Jud. Adv. Selection Bd., 1967-74; bd. fellows U. Santa Clara; bd. dirs. O'Connor Hosp. Found., San Jose. C.L.U. Mem. Am. Soc. C.L.U.'s (nat. pres. 1972-73), Nat. Assn. Life Underwriters, San Jose Life Underwriters Assn. (pres. 1962), Santa Clara County Estate Planning Council (pres. 1958), Cath. Layman's Retreat Assn. (past pres.). Republican. Roman Catholic. Contbr. articles to jours. Office: 777 N 1st St Suite 520 San Jose CA 95112

TRIPP, MARCIA BIXBY, greeting card publishing co. exec.; b. Peterborough, N.H.; d. Thomas Edward and Joan (Avery) Bixby; student U. N.H., 1963-66, 67-68; m. Wallace W. Tripp, Sept. 18, 1965; children—Banjamin, Loren, Samuel. Artist's agt., 1972-78; pres. Pawprints, Inc., Jaffrey, N.H., 1978—, also dir., developer Top Drawer Designs subs., 1979-80. Office: Pawprints Inc Pierce Crossing Rd Jaffrey NH 03452

TRIPP, MARIAN BARLOW LOOFE, pub. relations co. exec.; b. Lodge Pole, Nebr., July 26, 1921; d. Lewis Rockwell and Cora Dee (Davis) Barlow; B.S., Iowa State U., 1944; m. James Edward Tripp, Feb. 9, 1957; children—Brendan Michael, Kevin Mark. Writer, Dairy Record, St. Paul, 1944-45; head, product promotion div., pub. relations dept. Swift & Co., Chgo., 1945-55; mgmt. supr., v.p. pub. relations J. Walter Thompson Co., N.Y.C. and Chgo., 1956-74; v.p. consumer affairs, Chgo., 1974-75; pres. Marian Tripp Communications Inc., Chgo., 1976—. Mem. Pub. Relations Soc. Am., Soc. Consumer Affairs Profls., Am., Ill. home econs. assns., Chgo. Home Economists in Bus. (consumer affairs com.), U.S. C. of C. Episcopalian. Club: Fortnightly. Office: 70 E Walton Pl Chicago IL 60611

TRIPP, MICHAEL EDWARD, fin. exec.; b. Ann Arbor, Mich., Oct. 10, 1946; s. Edward Sequist and Mary (Hanchy) T.; B.S. in Edn., Central Mich. U., 1968; children—Joseph Edward, Stacy Lyn. Gen. mgr. Sun Valley Devel. Corp., Tarpon Springs, Fla., 1971-73; ops. mgr. U.S. Home Mobilife Corp., Dunedin, Fla., 1974; owner Moisture Balancing Inc., Dunedin, 1975-76; exec. v.p. Briar Creek Devel. Corp., Clearwater, Fla., 1977-80; v.p. Dynamic Investments, Inc., Clearwater, 1980—. Bd. dirs. Briar Creek Mobile Home Community I, Clearwater, 1979-80. Recipient award of merit Sertoma Internat., 1974; Outstanding Service award Dunedin Breakfast Sertoma 1974; cert. of appreciation Tarpon Springs C. of C., 1974, Future Bus. Leaders of Am., 1979. Mem. C. of C., Clearwater Largo Dunedin Bd. Realtors, Fla. Assn. Realtors, Sigma Tau Gamma. Republican. Episcopalian. Clubs: Ed Dart Sertoma, Masons. Office: 3175 McMullen Booth Rd Clearwater FL 33519

TRIPP, ROGER MICHAEL, electronic engr.; b. Derby, Conn., May 5, 1943; s. Roger Edwin and Tessie (Wasilkowich) T.; B.S. in Elec. Engring., Northeastern U., 1966; m. Carole Jeane Roberts, Mar. 31, 1973; children—Jon Christopher, Kimberly Lauren. Electronic devel. engr. ordnance systems Gen. Electric Co., Pittsfield, Mass., 1966-69; circuit devel. engr. nuclear instruments Consol. Controls Co., Bethel, Conn., 1969—, sr. project engr. in electromech. design mfg. pressure/temperature transducers, 1972—; cons. electronic engr., 1973—. Sec. bd. trustees 1st Congl. Ch., Waterbury, Conn., 1980—, leader Pilgrim Fellowship, 1979—. Registered profl. engr., Conn. Mem. Instrument Soc. Am., Eta Kappa Nu. Republican. Co-author: Standard Amplifier Assembly, 1966. Home: 213 Oronoke Rd Waterbury CT 06708 Office: 15 Durant Ave Bethel CT 06801

TRIPP, RUSSELL MAURICE, medical instruments co. exec.; b. Holten, Kans., July 12, 1916; s. Maurice Hall and Alma Belle (Cottrelle) T.; Geol. Engr., Colo. Sch. Mines, 1939, M. Geophys. Engring. (pres.'s fellow), 1942; 1Sc.D., Mass. Inst. Tech., 1949; m. Catherine Graham Burr, Aug. 12, 1937; children—Catherine Ann, Peggy Marie, Elizabeth Belle, R. Maurice II, David Graham, Timothy Lane, Mary Alice. Asst. to pres., dir. research Geotechnical Corp., Cambridge, Mass., 1944-46; dir. Geochem. Research Lab., Boston U., 1947-49; v.p. Research, Inc., Dallas, 1949-54; pres. Tripp Research Corp., Saratoga, Calif., 1955—. SKIA Corp., San Jose, Calif., 1972—; dir. Cimota Exploration, Torginol of Am., Exploration, Inc., Sonic Research Corp.; pres. El Camino Trust. Bd. dirs. Boy Scouts Am.; chmn. Calif. State Park Citizens Adv. Com.; Tex. Gov.'s appointee to Atomic Energy Com.; pres. Saratog High Sch. PTA; v.p. Girl Scout Council. Recipient Carbett Award, Sight Conservation Found. Mem. AAAS, Am. Inst. Mining Engrs., Am. Assn. Petroleum Geologists, Geol. Soc. Am., Soc. Exploration Geophysicists, Soc. Info. Display, Soc. for Crystal Growing, Assn. Advancement Med. Instrs., Soc. Photog. Scientists and Engrs., Soc. Econ. Paleontologists and Mineralogists, Calif. Acad. Science, Sigma Xi, Tau Beta Pi. Republican. Patentee mineral dressing, radiography, bldg. materials, microscopy, 3 dimensional photography. Contbr. articles to profl. jours. Home: 15231 Quito Rd Saratoga CA 95070 Office: 960 Remillard Ct San Jose CA 95122

TRITTEN, RAY ALBERT, mfg. co. exec.; b. Utica, N.Y., Feb. 21, 1919; s. Charles Albert and Hazel (Chapman) T.; B.S.Chem. Engring., U. Mich., 1942; m. Shirley Elaine Johnson, Sept. 19, 1942; children—Craig A., Stephen E. With Day & Night Mfg. Co. div. Carrier Corp., La Puente, Calif., 1955-70, pres., 1965-70, pres. Payne Co. div., 1965-70; with AMF Inc., White Plains, N.Y., 1970—, pres. Ben Hogan Co. div., 1970, pres. Cuno div., 1971-72, group exec. liquid conditioning group, 1972-73, corp. v.p., 1973-78, group exec. motorcycle products group, 1974-78, exec. v.p.-ops./leisure products, 1978-79, pres., chief operating officer, dir., 1979—. Served in USNR, 1942-45. Mem. Sigma Xi, Tau Beta Pi. Club: Country of Darien (Conn.). Office: 777 Westchester Ave White Plains NY 10604

TRIVELPIECE, ALVIN WILLIAM, research co. exec.; b. Stockton, Calif., Mar. 15, 1931; s. Alvin Stevens and Mae (Hughes) T.; B.S., Calif. Poly. Coll., San Luis Obispo, 1953; M.S., Calif. Inst. Tech., 1955, Ph.D., 1958; m. Shirley Ann Ross, Mar. 23, 1953; children—Craig Evan, Steve Edward, Keith Eric. Asst. prof., then asso. prof. U. Calif. at Berkeley, 1959-66; prof. physics U. Md., College Park, 1966-76; on leave as asst. dir. research div. controlled thermonuclear research AEC, Washington, 1973-75; v.p. Maxwell Labs., Inc., San Diego, 1976-78; corp. v.p. Sci. Applications Inc., LaJolla, Calif., 1978—; dir. Fusion Power Assos.; mem. fusion adv. panel to energy research and prodn. subcom. U.S. Ho. of Reps. Com. Sci. and Tech., 1979—. Fulbright scholar Delft (Netherlands) U., 1958-59; Guggenheim fellow, 1966; recipient Distinguished Alumnus award Calif. Poly. State U., San Luis Obispo, 1978. Fellow Am. Phys. Soc., AAAS, IEEE; mem. Washington Philos. Soc., Am. Nuclear Soc., Ams. for Energy Independence, AAUP, Sigma Xi. Author: Slow Wave Propagation in Plasma Wave Guides, 1966; (with N.A. Krall) Principles of Plasma Physics, 1973; also articles. Patentee in field. Home: 7080 Caminito Estrada LaJolla CA 92037 Office: 1200 Prospect St LaJolla CA 92038

TROCKE, JOHN KENDALL, educator, cons.; b. Detroit, Oct. 3, 1924; s. Theodore G. and Letha E. (O'Harrow) T.; B.S., Albion Coll., 1949; M.S., Mich. State U., 1957; LL.B., Blackstone Coll. Law, 1960, J.D., 1963; m. Carol B. Albertson, June 18, 1977; children—Linda, Stephen, Tom, Sue, Theodore, James, Chris, Matthew, Kirk, Amy. Vice pres. mktg. Thompson's Inc.; div. gen. mgr. Frito-Lay Co.; mktg.-mgmt. specialist, coop. extension service Mich. State U., Ann Arbor, Washtenaw County Service Center, from 1976; speaker, writer, lectr., cons. agr., horticulture, resource devel.; bd. dirs. twelve orgns. Mem. local sch. bd., 1968-72, city planning comm., 1972-74, zoning bd., 1974.; chmn. bd. trustees, lay leader Meth. Ch. Served with U.S. Army, 1942-43. Named Mich. Minute Man. Fellow Am. Found. Econ. Edn., Assn. Social Psychology; mem. Am. Soc. Tng. and Devel., Am. Mgmt. Assn., Nat. Assn. County Agrl. Agts., Phi Kappa Phi, Sigma Chi. Author: Managing for Profit, 1968; Motivation for Modern Man, 1970; Financial Management and Planning, 1972; contbr. research reports and articles to publs. Home: 1191 Stamford St Ypsilanti MI 48197 Died Sept. 2, 1978.

TROGDON, DEWEY LEONARD, textile co. exec.; b. Summerfield, N.C., Feb. 17, 1932; s. Dewey Leonard and Ethel (Miller) T.; A.B. in Econs., Guilford (N.C.) Coll., 1958; postgrad. U. N.C., Greensboro, 1967-68, U. Va., 1970, Harvard U., 1978; m. Barbara Jean Ayers, Sept. 10, 1955; children—Mark, Leonard. With Cone Mills Corp., 1958—, v.p., then exec. v.p., 1977-79, pres., Greensboro, 1979—, now chmn., chief exec. officer, also dir.; dir. Textile Hall Corp. Served with USNR, 1949-53. Mem. Am. Textile Mfrs. Inst. (dir.), N.C. Textile Mfrs. Assn. (dir.). Methodist. Office: 1201 Maple St Greensboro NC 27405

TROIANI, JOSEPH EDWARD, psychologist; b. Chgo., Sept. 21, 1949; s. Edward H. and Josephine (Gall) T.; B.A., Northeastern Ill. U., 1967-71, postgrad., 1971; M.A. in Health Sci. Adminstrn., Govs. State U., 1974; postgrad. in indsl. psychology, Ill. Inst. Tech., 1975-78, Fielding Inst., Calif., 1978—. Psychiat. aide dept. psychiatry Grant Hosp., Chgo., 1969-78; alcoholism counselor and group therapist Chgo. Alcoholism Treatment Program, Grant Hosp., 1971; group co-therapist Austin Counseling Center, 1970; rehab. counselor drug cure program West Side VA Hosp., Chgo., 1971-72; staff psychologist Outpatient Mental Health Clinic, Loretto Hosp., Chgo., 1972-73; program coordinator alcoholism and drug treatment Forest Hosp., Des Plaines, Ill., 1973-74; dir., supervisory psychologist Alcohol Program and Edn. Center, Loretto Hosp., Chgo., 1974—; cons. on alcoholism Ingalls Meml. Hosp., Harvey, Ill., Norridge (Ill.) Nursing Center, also indsl. firms; pres., dir. Way Back Inn, Maywood, Ill; adv. bd. alcoholism sci. curriculum council Govs. State U. Served with USNR; mem. Res. Mem. Am. Soc. Advancement Tension Control, Biofeedback Soc. Am., Biofeedback Soc. Ill. (bd. dirs.), Assn. Labor Mgmt. Adminstrs. on Consultants on Alcoholism, Ill. Assn. Alcoholism and Drug Dependency, Alcohol and Drug Problems Assn. N. Am., Ill. Alcoholism Counselors Alliance, Ill. Group Psychotherapy Soc., Am. Soc. Psychical Research, Inc., Mensa. Office: Loretto Hospital 645 S Central Ave Chicago IL 60644

TRONE, CURVIN J., JR., financial cons.; b. York, Pa., May 15, 1921; s. Curvin J. and Velma (Geltz) T.; A.B., Brown U., 1948; M.A., Harvard, 1949; postgrad. U. Mich. Law Sch., 1949-50; m. Alice Louise Young, Sept. 9, 1950. Asst. to pres., ops. controller Whirlpool Corp., Benton Harbor, Mich., 1953-63, pres. S.A. Royal Corp. subs., Paris, 1961-62; dir. planning consumers group Westinghouse Electric Corp., Pitts., 1963; dir. corporate, fin. planning and control Hunt Foods & Industries, Fullerton, Calif., 1963-67; v.p. Allis-Chalmers Corp., Milw., 1967-71, v.p. finance, 1967-71, also group exec., v.p. Consumer Products Group, 1969-71; exec. v.p. Penn-Pacific Corp., Phoenix, 1971-74; pres. Trone & Co., Allis-Chalmers Credit Corp., Allis-Chalmers Internat. Credit Corp., Allis-Chalmers Leasing Corp.; dir. Brastemp, S.A., Sao Paulo, Brazil, S.A. Royal Corp., Paris, Allis-Chalmers U.K., Allis-Chalmers France, Allis-Chalmers Australia, Air Calif., Dyna-Shield, Inc., Milw. County Bank, Allis-Chalmers-Siemens Electric Products Corp.; trustee in reorgn. Westgate-Calif. Corp. Mem. pres.'s select com. Brown U., bd. dirs. 3d Century Fund; trustee Allis-Chalmers Found. Fellow Fin. Analysts Fedn.; mem. Phoenix Soc. Fin. Analysts, Nat. Assn. Accountants, Am. Inst. Indsl. Engrs. (sr.), Fin. Execs. Inst. Clubs: Arizona, Cuyamaca, Brown U. Home: 7343 E Marlette Ave Scottsdale AZ 85253 Office: 1010 2d Ave San Diego CA 92101

TRONE, ROBERT WILLIAM, investment banker; b. N.Y.C., Apr. 9, 1930; s. William Andrew and Oneta Ione (Norcross) T.; B.A., Williams Coll., 1952; m. Nancy Ann Dale, Sept. 8, 1951; children—Linda Susan, Leslie Ann, Cynthia Dale. With Merrill Lynch, 1954—, investment banker, 1956-70, dir. research, 1970-75, dir. investment banking, 1975-78, mng. dir. Merrill Lynch White Weld Capital Markets Group, N.Y.C., 1977—; dir. Merrill Lynch Pierce Fenner & Smith, 1970-79, Merrill Lynch Leasing, 1976—. Served with AUS, 1952-54. Clubs: Baltusrol Golf, City Midday. Office: 165 Broadway New York NY 10080

TROSSMAN, DON C., mortgage banker; b. Chgo., Sept. 14, 1946; s. Harold and Doris (Cole) T.; B.S. in Psychology, Tulane U., 1968; M.B.A., Loyola U., Chgo., 1971; m. Janis Norman, June 14, 1969; 1 dau., Jill Elisabeth. Asst. v.p. Heitman Mortgage Co., Chgo., 1972-74; loan officer B.B. Cohen & Co., Chgo., 1974-75; v.p., regional mgr. Banco Mortgage Co., Chgo., 1975—. Served with USAF, 1968-73. Mem. Mortgage Bankers Assn. Am., Assn. Indsl. Real Estate Brokers, Nat. Assn. Office and Indsl. Parks, Internat. Council Shopping Centers, Ill. Mortgage Bankers Assn. Clubs: Standard (Chgo.); Lake Shore Country (Glencoe, Ill.). Office: 55 W Monroe St Chicago IL 60603

TROTTER, ARTHUR CLARENCE, corrugated containers mfg. co. ofcl.; b. Newburg, Mo., Aug. 9, 1933; s. Arthur Clarence and Velma Mae (Knapp) T.; B.S. in Commerce, St. Louis U., 1955; m. Carol Dianne Bunfill, Apr. 2, 1960; children—Steven Douglas, Philip Jeffrey. Auditor, P.B. Radloff, C.P.A., St. Louis, 1954-57; internal auditor Crown Zellerbach, St. Louis, 1957-61, sr. acct., Los Angeles, 1961-64, office mgr., 1964-67, adminstrv. asst. to regional mgr., Orinda, Calif., 1968-70, adminstrv. asst. to regional mgr., Fullerton, Calif., 1970-74, asst. to regional mgr., 1974-77, regional controller, Los Angeles, 1977-79, plant controller, City of Industry, Calif., 1979—. Baptist. Home: 740 W Country Hills Dr LaHabra CA 90631 Office: 440 N Baldwin Park Blvd Industry CA 91749

TROTTER, JOHN FRANCIS, geology and oil co. exec.; b. Minatare, Nebr., Sept. 2, 1926; s. Burton Ellsworth and Notie Louise (Cope) T.; B.S. with honors, U. Wyo., 1952; M.A., 1954; m. Leona Caroline Batcher, May 3, 1947. Exploration geologist Rocky Mountain div. Mobil Oil Co., Casper, Wyo., 1954-61; ind. geologist, Casper, 1961-70; v.p. Power Resources Corp., Casper, 1972-73, dir., 1972-76; v.p., sec. Aquarius Resources Corp., Casper, 1970-73, pres., 1973—, dir., 1970—; dir. Consolidated Royalty Bldg., Inc., Casper, 1967—. City councilman, Sundance, Wyo., 1950. Served with USAAF, 1945. Registered profl. geologists. Mem. Am. Assn. Petroleum Geologists, Am. Inst. Profl. Geologists, Wyo. Geol. Assn. Methodist. Asso. editor Wyo. Geol. Assn. Guidebook 1968. Home: 3781 Carmel Dr Casper WY 82601 Office: Suite 307 Conroy Bldg Casper WY 82601

TROUP, FRANK FLEISHER, lawyer; b. Pitts., Sept. 20, 1905; s. Charles Baldwin and Myrtle May (Fleisher) T.; A.B., U. Pitts., 1926, LL.B., 1929, J.D., 1968; m. Margaret Gertrude Pickering, Dec. 25, 1939. Admitted to Pa. bar, 1929, also U.S. Supreme Ct., 1965; pres., dir. Homewood Masonic Hall Assn., 1954-67; Allegheny County agt. Berks Title Ins. Co., 1949-75. Past bd. dirs. Allegheny Acad. Mem. Am., Pa., Allegheny County bar assns., Internat. Acad. Law and Sci., Pi Kappa Alpha. Republican. Lutheran. Club: Pitts. Athletic Assn. Home: 1014 Blackridge Rd Pittsburgh PA 15235 also Newton Lake Carbondale PA 18407 Office: 732 Frick Bldg Pittsburgh PA 15219

TROUP, THOMAS JAMES, chem. co. exec.; b. Council Bluffs, Iowa, Sept. 4, 1923; s. Ralph Leslie and Ruth (Beaumont) T.; B.S. in Chem. Engring., U. Wis., 1945; M.B.A. with high distinction, Harvard, 1952; m. Marjory Alice Suelflow, Feb. 2, 1946; children—Robert, Patricia, James. Asst. to gen. mgr. Internat. Mineral & Chem. Corp., San Jose, Calif., 1945-49, Chgo., 1952-53; sales rep. Foxboro Co., Los Angeles, 1949-50; with W.R. Grace Co., 1954-68, controller Cryovac div., Cedar Rapids, Iowa, 1954-56, v.p., treas., Cambridge, Mass., 1956-60, Duncan, S.C., 1961-64, v.p. chem. group, N.Y.C., 1965-68; treas. Burr-Brown Research Corp., Tucson, 1968-71, now dir.; v.p., treas. Akzona, Inc., Asheville, N.C., 1971—, also dir.; dir. Microelectrics Center of N.C., 1980—. Trustee Warren Wilson Coll., Swananoa, N.C. Mem. Psi Upsilon. Clubs: University (N.Y.C.); Biltmore Forrest Country (Biltmore, N.C.); Red Fox Country (Tryon, N.C.); Asheville Downtown City; Farmer's (London). Home: Route #1 Red Ridge Farm Landrum SC 29356 Office: PO Box 2930 Asheville NC 28802

TROUT, ROBERT RAYLE, economist; b. Kansas City, Mo., Feb. 21, 1942; s. John Truman and Marie Louise (Busch) T.; B.S., U. Oreg., 1964; M.B.A., UCLA, 1971, Ph.D. (Hellman doctoral fellow), 1978; m. Rebecca Sue Frederick, Nov. 26, 1978. Treasury supr. Pacific Telephone Co., Los Angeles, 1967-71; sr. economist Nat. Econ. Research Assos., Inc., N.Y.C., 1974-76; lectr. U. Calif., Irvine, 1977-78; sr. asso. Resource Planning Assos., Inc., San Francisco, 1978—. Served with USAR, 1964-70. Recipient 1st prize Iowa State U. Regulatory Conf., 1974. Mem. Am. Fin. Assn., Nat. Assn. Bus. Economists. Mem. Marin Covenant Ch. (dir.). Co-author: Modern Practices in Retail Rate Design, 1980; contbr. articles to profl. jours. Home: 1325 Mar West St Tiburon CA 94920 Office: Suite 2080 Three Embarcadero Center San Francisco CA 94111

TROUTMAN, H. LELAND, devel. corp. exec.; b. Seattle, Oct. 24, 1918; s. Harry White and Dora (Leland) T.; student U. Wash., 1938-40; m. Doris Helen Brown, May 28, 1945; children—David L., Stephen B. Asst. to the v.p. Columbia Valley Lumber Co., Bellingham, Wash., 1948-50, 54-57; sales mgr. Bellingham (Wash.) Builders Supply Co., 1950-53; account exec. Pacific Northwest Co., Seattle, 1953-54; regional mgr. Utah Internat., San Francisco, 1957-65; v.p. Foster Calif., Foster City, Calif., 1965-69; v.p. Avco Community Developers, Inc., San Diego, Calif., 1969—; exec. com., dir. Mission Park Corp., San Diego, Econ. Devel. Corp.; adv. com. Calif. Office Econ. Devel., 1978—. Served to lt. col. U.S. Army, 1941-47. Recipient Nesh Memorial award, 1975. Mem. Nat. Assn. Indsl. Parks, Am. Indsl. Devel. Council, Indsl. Devel. Execs. Assn., Calif. C. of C. (chmn. econ. developers com. 1976—), San Diego C. of C. (dir., 1976-78), So. Calif. Econ. and Job Devel. Council (exec. com.). Republican. Home: 7590 Caminito Avola S La Jolla CA 92037 Office: Security Pacific Plaza Suite 424 San Diego CA 92101

TROWBRIDGE, EDWARD KENNETH, ins. co. exec.; b. Phila., Nov. 17, 1928; s. Cecil Roman and Lillian Rose (Biester) T.; B.S. in Bus. Adminstrn., U. Pa., 1956; grad. Advanced Mgmt. Program, Harvard Bus. Sch., 1977; m. Marie Cassidy, Nov. 4, 1950; children—Lynn Marie, Edward Kenneth, Glenn Thomas. Fire ins. trainee, then underwriter Fire Assn. Phila., 1945-48; marine ins. underwriter William H. McGee & Co., Phila., 1951-52; with The Atlantic Cos., N.Y.C., 1952—, sr. exec. v.p., 1977—; trustee Atlantic Mut. Ins. Co.; dir. Centennial Ins. Co., J.A. Blondeu, Ltd. Trustee N.Y. councils Boy Scouts Am. Served with U.S. Army, 1948-51. Mem. Am. Inst. Marine Underwriters (dir.), Am. Hull Ins. Syndicate (bd. mgrs.), Bd. Underwriters N.Y. (dir.), Security Bur. (dir.), U.S. Salvage Assn. (bd. mgrs.), Nat. Cargo Bur. (dir.), Maritime Law Assn. U.S., India House (gov.). Clubs: Met. (N.Y.C.); Springbrook Country (Morristown, N.J.). Home: 7 Springbrook Rd Morris Twp NJ 07960 Office: 45 Wall St New York NY 10005

TROXELL, JAMES DANE, lawyer, petroleum co. exec.; b. Akron, Ohio, Mar. 5, 1946; s. Delmont and Katherine T.; B.A., U. Akron, 1968, J.D., 1975; m. Sandra L. Coey, June 14, 1969. Trainee, Goodyear Aerospace Co., Akron, Ohio, 1969-70; legal counsel Babcock & Wilcox Co., Barberton, Ohio, 1970-76; admitted to Ohio bar, 1976, U.S. Supreme Ct. bar, 1979; asso. firm Hershey & Browne, Akron, 1976-78; corp. counsel Gen. Tire & Rubber Co., Akron, 1979-80; pres. Ohio Petroleum Energy Co., Cuyahoga Falls, Ohio, 1978—. Past bd. dirs. United Cerebral Palsy of Summit County and Akron. Mem. Am. Bar Assn., Ohio State Bar Assn., Akron Bar Assn., Ohio Oil and Gas Assn., Psi chi. Republican. Club: Cascade (Akron). Office: PO Box 266 Cuyahoga Falls OH 44222

TROXELL, WILLIAM HARLAND, retail photo and sound electronics co. exec.; b. Jo Davies County, Ill., Jan. 1, 1916; s. Edward Copeland and Odessa May (Flickinger) T.; B.A., U. Dubuque, 1938; m. Margaret Jean Maxwell, Nov. 5, 1939; children—Suzanne, James, April. Mgr. still dept. Harfilms Motion Pictures, New Orleans, 1938; sales mgr. Interstate Power Co., Dubuque, Iowa, 1939-40; budget mgr. Firestone Tire and Rubber Co., Dubuque, 1941; dist. mgr. World Book, Des Moines, 1942; auditor, acct. U.S. Army, 1942-44, civilian head fiscal dept. Navajo Ordnance, Ariz., 1946; founder, owner, chmn. bd., mgr. Jean and Trox Supply Co. Inc., Flagstaff, Ariz., 1946—; daily news analyst Sta. KCLS, 1949—; tchr. photography, 1950—. Sponsor, Happy Farm Orphanage; scoutmaster Boy Scouts Am.; mem. Ariz.-Mex. Commn., 1974—. Served to lt. (j.g.) USNR, 1944-45. Recipient nat. awards Brand Names Found., 1964-68; named to Flagstaff Hall of Fame, 1968; named Brand Name Retailer of Yr., 1969, 1972; Alumnus of Distinction, U. Dubuque, 1969; One of 60 Leading Arizonans of 1960's, Ariz. Mag., 1979; recipient Nat. medal of honor DAR, 1979. Mem. Nat. Small Bus. Assn. (dir.), Nat. Fedn. Ind. Businesses, Am. Soc. Mag. Photographers, Flagstaff C. of C. (dir.), Downtown Flagstaff Bus. Assn. (past pres.), Ariz. Retailers Assn., Bipac, Am. Legion, VFW. Clubs: Elks, Masons, Shriners. Contbr. articles to nat. boating and travel mags. Home: 3601 N Paradise Rd Flagstaff AZ 86002 Office: 8 and 17 N Leroux St Flagstaff AZ 86002

TROY, B(ERNARD) THEODORE, apparel co. exec.; b. Huntington Park, Calif., Jan. 16, 1932; s. Bernard and Florence Ruth (Stillman) T.; B.A. in Econs., U. Calif., Santa Barbara, 1953; B.Fgn. Trade, Am. Grad. Sch. Internat. Mgmt., 1957; m. Pauline Pearson, Feb. 25, 1960; 1 son, Kevin Bernard. With Procter & Gamble Brand Mgmt., overseas, 1957-61; account exec. McCann Erickson, Los Angeles, 1961-62; with R.J. Reynolds, 1962-77, pres. Mexican subs., 1968-75, Brazil subs., 1976-77; pres. Export div. Burlington Industries, N.Y.C., 1977-78; pres. Kayser-Roth Internat., N.Y.C., 1978—. Trustee U. Calif. Santa Barbara Found. Served to 1st lt. U.S. Army, 1953-55. Office: 1221 Ave of the Americas New York NY 10020

TROYER, BRYCE DUANE, corp. exec.; b. Arnold, Nebr., Apr. 11, 1936; s. William Ivan and Elsie Ethyl (Coen) T.; B.S. in Chem. Engring. (J.V.N. Dorr scholar, 1957), S.D. Sch. Mines and Tech., 1958; M.S. in Chem. Engring. (fellow, 1959), U. Colo., 1960; M.B.A., U. Chgo., 1977; m. Lois Jean Newman, Feb. 6, 1965; 1 son, Michael. Devel. engr. Union Carbide Corp., Institute, W.Va., 1959-60; chem. engr., group leader Dow Chem. Co., Golden, Colo., 1961-66, group leader, asst. supt., Midland, Mich., 1966-69; prodn. supt., engring. mgr. No. Petrochem. Co., Morris, Ill., 1969-79; pres. Dunhill of Joliet (Ill.), Inc., 1979—. Mem. Am. Inst. Chem. Engrs. (treas. Joliet sect., 1970-71), Plastics Soc. Am., Am. Mgmt. Assn., Exec. Program Club, Sigma Xi, Sigma Tau, Beta Gamma Sigma, Tau Beta Pi. Republican. Clubs: Am. Contract Bridge League (life master), Mensa, Elks, Masons. Patentee in field. Home: 516 Tana Ln Joliet IL 60435 Office: 288 Barney Dr Joliet IL 60435

TRUBY, JOHN LOUIS, business exec.; b. New Kensington, Pa., Nov. 28, 1933; s. George Neal and Bertha Louise (Deyber) T.; B.B.A. cum laude, U. Pitts., 1959; m. Mary Ann Holmes, Dec. 10, 1952; children—Leslie Ann, Jacque Lee, Barbara Holmes. Mgr. adminstrn. Westvaco Co., Luke, Md., 1964-70; controller Lehigh Portland Cement Co., Allentown, Pa., 1970-72, v.p. finance, 1972-74; pres. J. Truby Co., 1974—, Irish Ridge Coal Co., 1977—. Class agt. U. Pitts. Class of 1959; bd. dirs. Willow Lake Assn. Served as 1st lt. AUS, 1953-56. Mem. Fin. Execs. Inst., Nat. Assn. Accountants, Ohio Coal and Energy Assn. (dir.). Address: 225 W Willow Dr Zanesville OH 43701 Office: PO Box 2519 Zanesville OH 43701

TRUDEL, JOHN DAVIS, electronics co. exec.; b. Trenton, N.J., Aug. 1, 1942; s. LeRoy Renee and Elizabeth Etta (Reading) T.; B.E.E. cum laude (Western Electric scholar, State of N.J. scholar, McLendon scholar), Ga. Inst. Tech., 1964; M.S.E.E. (NDEA grad. fellow), Kans. State U., 1966; m. Barbara Banks Beaty, Sept. 1, 1973; 1 stepson—Michael Gene Beaty. Research and devel. project engr. Collins Radio Co., Richardson, Tex., 1966-67; sr. engr. Sanders Assos., Inc., Nashua, N.H., 1967-68; sr. electronic system engr. LTV Electrosystems, Inc., Greenville, Tex., 1968-69; sr. engr. Collins Radio Co., Richardson, 1969-70; project engr. F & M Systems, Co., Dallas, 1970-71; pres. Sci. System Tech., Inc., Richardson, 1971-74; product mgr. Tektronix, Beaverton, Oreg., 1974—; cons. computer aided design. Mem. nat. adv. bd. Am. Security Council, 1974—. Recipient Scholastic award Lambda Chi Alpha, 1963, 64. Mem. IEEE, Automatic R.F. Techniques Group, Am. Electronics Assn., Am. Mktg. Assn., Assn. Old Crows, Nat. Avionics Soc., Aircraft Owners and Pilots Assn., Tau Beta Pi, Eta Kappa Nu. Roman Catholic. Clubs: Private Pilot, Ski. Primary author of MAGIC, gen. purpose microwave computer aided design package; contbr. articles to profl. jours. Home: 14755 S W 144th St Tigard OR 97223 Office: PO Box 500 Beaverton OR 97077

TRUEBENBACH, MARVIN ERWIN, compressor mfg. co. exec.; b. Milw., Dec. 11, 1933; s. Erwin Louis and Emily Wilhelmina (Lof) T.; B.S., U. Wis., 1956; postgrad. U. Pa., 1978—; m. Ellowene Pipkorn, July 21, 1956; children—Tracey, Eric, Kristy. Methods engr., mgmt. trainee Joy Mfg. Co., Pitts., 1956-60; various positions Cooper Bessemer, Mt. Vernon, Ohio, 1960-67, dir. mfg. Europe, Hengelo, Netherlands, 1968-76; gen. mgr. pump plant Cooper Energy Services div. Cooper Industries, Easton, Pa., 1976—. Republican. Lutheran. Home: Rural Delivery 7 Quarter Mile Rd Bethlehem PA 18015 Office: Northwood Ave Easton PA 18042

TRUESCHLER, BERNARD CHARLES, utility exec.; b. Balt., Jan. 3, 1943; s. Philip Joseph and Gertrude Cecilia (Carey) T.; B.A., Johns Hopkins U., 1947; LL.B., U. Md., 1952; m. Helen Rita Golley, Nov. 19, 1956; children—John Gregory, Jeanne Carey, Paul Conrad, Mary Kathryn. Admitted to Md. bar; with Balt. Gas & Electric Co., 1948—, v.p. gas ops., 1971-72, v.p. distbn., 1972-74, pres., 1974—, chmn., chief exec. officer, 1980—, also dir.; dir. Monumental Corp., Monumental Life Ins. Co., Union Trust Co. Md., Union Trust Bancorp; mem. adv. bd. Nat. Alliance Businessmen. Trustee, Balt. Opera Co., Coll. Notre Dame of Md.; bd. dirs. Bus. Industry Polit. Action Com., Greater Balt. Com., United Way Central Md.; mem. Vol. Council on Equal Opportunity. Served with U.S. Army, 1942-44. Mem. Md. C. of C. (dir.), Am. Gas Assn., Internat. Dist. Heating Assn., Southeastern Electric Exchange (dir.), Engring. Soc. Balt., Tau Beta Pi, Kappa Alpha. Republican. Roman Catholic. Clubs: Balt. Country, The Center. Office: PO Box 1475 Baltimore MD 21203

TRUEX, GEORGE ROBERT, JR., banker; b. Red Bank, N.J., May 29, 1924; s. George Robert and Elsie D. (White) T.; A.B. in Econs., Rutgers U., 1949; m. Nancy Carroll Burt, May 10, 1947; children—Peter Barclay, Amy Dinsmore. Sr. v.p. Irving Trust Co., N.Y.C., 1949-66; exec. v.p. Bank of Am., San Francisco, 1966-73, vice chmn. subs. Small Bus. Enterprises Co., 1968-72; chmn. bd., chief exec. officer Rainier Bancorp., Seattle, 1973—, Rainier Nat. Bank, 1973—; dir., mem. exec. com. Nat. Airlines, Miami, Fla., 1962-80, INA Life Ins. Co., N.Y.C., 1965-68; dir. Pvt. Export Funding Corp., N.Y.C., 1978-80, Pan Am. World Airways, N.Y.C., 1980—; regional adv. com. 13th Nat. Bank Region, 1975-77. Fin. chmn. Calif. Gov.'s Task Force on Flood Relief, 1969-73; mem. orthopedic council Orthopedic Hosp., Los Angeles, 1969-72; trustee Calif. Inst. Arts, Los Angeles, 1968-72, Bank of Am. Found., 1973; mem. fin. adv. com. CAB, 1970-71; bd. dirs. Jr. Achievement So. Calif., 1967-72, pres., 1968-70, Western regional bd. dirs., 1968-72; nat. bd. dirs. Jr. Achievement, Inc., 1968-75; bd. dirs. Jr. Achievement Greater Seattle, 1976-77; div. chmn. United Way, Inc., Los Angeles, 1970, 71; asso. gen. campaign chmn. United Way of King County, 1976-78, gen. chmn., 1979; mem. adv. bd. Grad. Sch. Bus. Adminstrn., U. Wash., 1975—; bd. dirs. Walt Disney Assos. of Calif. Inst. Arts, 1972—, Virginia Mason Hosp., 1976—, bd. regents Seattle U., 1976—. Served to capt. U.S. Army, World War II; ETO. Mem. Assn. Res. City Bankers, Seattle C. of C. (trustee 1975-78); San Francisco Planning and Urban Renewal Assn. (dir. 1973). Clubs: Calif. (Los Angeles); Bankers, Bohemian (San Francisco); Seattle Golf, Wash. Athletic, Rainier, Broadmoor Golf (Seattle); Bellevue (Wash.) Athletic. Office: Rainier Nat Bank PO Box 3966 Seattle WA 98124

TRUITT, WILLIAM JAMES, economist; b. Dallas, Mar. 4, 1940; s. William Alton and Nova Merle (Hamilton) T.; B.A., So. Methodist U., 1960; M.S. (Ford Found. fellow 1960-62), Purdue U., 1962; Ph.D., U. Ill., 1968; m. Catherine Cecile Butts, Aug. 25, 1962; children—Susan Narceille, Catherine Nova. Asst. prof. econs. La. State U., 1965-68; mem. faculty Baylor U., 1968—, prof. econs. and fin., chmn. dept. Hankamer Sch. Bus., 1971—; dir. Onmark Builders Supply, Inc., Red River Timberline, Inc., Trumas, Inc. Chmn. Common Edn., 1971—; pres. Men for Missions, 1979—; mem. adminstrv. bd., personnel com., council ministries First United Meth. Ch., Waco; mem. dist. council ministries, ann. conf. Council Ministries, United Meth. Ch. Mem. Am. Econs. Assn., So. Econs. Assn. Club: Fish Pond Country. Home: 701 Forest Oaks Waco TX 76710 Office: Hankamer Sch Bus Baylor Univ Waco TX 76706

TRULUCK, JEFFERSON RAY, ins. exec.; b. Blackville, S.C., Jan. 9, 1922; s. Claude Isadore and Ruby Beryl (Ray) T.; B.S., Newberry Coll., 1947; m. Mary Lucile Willis, Nov. 26, 1949; children—Jefferson Ray, Lynda, Lea, Paul. With Motors Ins. Corp., 1949, Nationwide Ins. Co., 1949-59, dist. service office mgr., 1952-59; admitted to S.C. bar, 1958; asst. claims mgr. Canal Ins. Co., Greenville, S.C., 1959-66, asst. v.p., 1966-69, v.p., 1969—; v.p. Canal Indemnity Co. Treas. Greenville County ARC, 1968-69, Botany Woods Homes Assn., 1966-71, Wade Hampton PTA, 1968-69; active Greenville Travelers Aid, Greenville County Democratic Party. Served with USNR, 1943. Recipient humanities award ARC, 1970. Mem. Truck and Heavy Equipment Claims Council (past pres.), Piedmont Claims Assn. (pres. 1956), S.C. Assn. Property and Casualty Ins. Cos. (pres. 1977-78), Fedn. Ins. Counsel, S.C. Council Safety Suprs., Greater Greenville C. of C., Exec. Sales Club (chmn. 1971), S.C., Greenville County bar assns. Democrat. Methodist. Clubs: Elks, Rotary. Home: 303 Bridgewater Dr Greenville SC 29615 Office: PO Box 7 Greenville SC 29602

TRUMBO, PHILIP WALTER, motel mgr.; b. Ouray, Colo., June 9, 1933; s. Walter Ray and Marjorie Ruth (Morgan) T.; B.S., Iowa State U., 1954; m. Reda May Ellis, Oct. 19, 1962; children—Susan Elizabeth, Walter Ray, Rebecca Ruth. Petroleum reservoir engr. Shell Oil Co., Denver, 1954-61; chem. engr. Cameron Engrs., Denver, 1961-64; owner, mgr. Best Western Red Arrow Motel, Montrose, Colo., 1965—, bd. govs. Best Western, 1978—; dir. United Bank of Montrose. Ind. cons. engr., Montrose, 1965—. Formerly active Nat. Ski Patrol; mem. bus. adv. council Colo. State U.; mem. Colo. Tourism Adv. Council. Served with USNR, 1955-57. Registered profl. engr., Colo. Mem. Innkeepers Assn. (dir. 1968-76), Montrose Motel Assn. (pres. 1966-67, 68-70), Am. Hotel and Motel Assn. Colo.-Wyo. Hotel and Motel Assn. (dir. 1978—), Aircraft Owners and Pilots Assn., C. of C. (dir. 1969-72), Tau Beta Pi, Pi Mu Epsilon. Elk, Rotarian. Club: Colo. Mountain (dir. 1962-64). Patentee in field. Home: PO Box 236 Montrose CO 81401

TRUMP, ALLAN E., pension cons.; b. Somerville, Mass., Apr. 24, 1930; s. George A. and Doris D. (Robinson) T.; B.B.A., Northeastern U., 1961; m. Elaine J. Croy, Apr. 25, 1953; children—Debbra L. Trump Hurd, Gary A., Marsha A. Benefit clk. benefit cons. div. F.B. Hall & Co., Inc., Boston, 1954-56, benefit admnstr., 1956-58, account exec., 1958-63, asst. mgr., 1963-66, sec. 1966-77, v.p., 1977—; founding dir. N.E. Pension Forum, Boston, 1963—. Trustee First Congregational Ch., Rockland, Mass., 1960-72; treas. Rockland Republican Com., 1961-69; mem. parents conf. Clark Sch. for Deaf, Northampton, Mass., 1966—. Served with USN, 1946-48, with USCG, 1948-54. Recipient advance pension planning certificate Am. Coll., 1977. Mem. Am. Pension Conference, Mass. Assn. for Deaf and Hard of Hearing; asso. mem. Am. Soc. Pension Actuaries. Republican. Congregationalist. Clubs: Abington Ferternal (treas. 1966-70), Mason. Home: Maritime Dr Wareham MA 02571 Office: 89 Broad St Boston MA 02110

TRUNCELLITO, JOSEPH J., lumber and millwork corp. exec.; b. Union City, N.J., Nov. 14, 1908; s. John and Maria (Mainieri) T.; certificate Mech. Inst., N.Y.C., 1928; cert. indsl. arts Rutgers U., 1929; m. Yolanda Viola Leo, Sept. 22, 1935; children—Joan (Mrs. Joseph Oliva), Elena (Mrs. John Santoro), Maria (Mrs. Lawrence Pfaadt II). Salesman Mastro Lumber/Millwork Co., Union City, 1930—, mgr., 1948-55, exec. officer, 1955—, now pres.; mem. staff extension div. Coll. City N.Y., 1955-70, Rutgers U., 1954-59. Adv. com. to mayor Ft. Lee (N.J.), 1955-70; adv. com. Ft. Lee Bd. Edn., 1955-70. Mem. N.J. Lumber and Bldg. Materials Assn. (trustee), Hudson County Lumbermen's Assn. (trustee), Bldg. Supply Dealers Assn. (pres. 1970), Archtl. Woodwork Inst. (pres. 1963). Club: Lions (pres. 1970). Home: 275 McElroy Ave Fort Lee NJ 07024 Office: 124 43d St Union City NJ 07087

TRUSTMAN, ALAN ROBERT, pvt. investor, screenwriter, lawyer; b. Boston, Dec. 16, 1930; s. Benjamin Arthur and Julia Bertha (Myerson) T.; A.B. magna cum laude, Harvard, 1952, LL.B. magna cum laude, 1955; m. Deborah Weisgall, June 15, 1969; children—John W., Laurie Sue, Steven W. Admitted to Mass. bar, 1955; asso. firm Nutter, McClennen & Fish, Boston, 1955-59, jr. partner, 1959-60, sr. partner, 1960-69, ret., 1977—; gen. counsel, dir. Damon Corp., Needham, Mass., 1961-69; acquisition counsel King's Dept. Stores, Inc., Newton, Mass., 1964-69; screenwriter motion pictures The Thomas Crown Affair, 1968; Bullitt, 1969; They Call Me Mr. Tibbs, 1970; Lady Ice, 1972; Hit!, 1973; Crime and Passion, 1975; The Next Man, 1976; dir. exec. com. World Jai-Alai, Inc., Miami, Fla., 1972-77. Former trustee Combined Jewish Philanthropies, Boston, Temple Ohabei Shalom, Brookline, Mass.; former chmn. Brookline drive Am. Cancer Soc.; former mem. bd. dirs. Jewish Vocat. Service, Boston; residential chmn. Brookline United Fund; former sec., bd. dirs. United Cerebral Palsy Assn. Greater Boston; vice chmn., treas. Brookline Redevel. Authority; former mem. Brookline Town Meeting; founding mem. Mass. Draft Goldwater Com. Recipient Edgar Allen Poe award Mystery Writers Am., 1969. Mem. Writers Guild Am., Acad. Motion Picture Arts and Scis. Home and Office: Berry Hill Farm Lincolnville ME 04849 also Parkman Tavern Concord MA 01742

TRUTTER, JOHN THOMAS, telephone co. exec.; b. Springfield, Ill., Apr. 18, 1920; s. Frank L. and Frances (Mischler) T.; A.B., U. Ill., 1942; postgrad. Northwestern U., U. Chgo.; m. Edith English Woods, June 17, 1950; children—Edith English II, Jonathan Woods. With Ill. Bell Telephone Co., Chgo., 1946-55, 58—, gen. traffic mgr. 1959-62, asst. v.p. pub. relations, 1962-65, asst. v.p. suburban ops., 1965-67, gen. mgr. north suburban ops., 1967-69, v.p. pub. relations, 1969-71, v.p. operator services, 1971-80, v.p. community affairs, 1980—; mem. personnel relations staff Am. Tel. & Tel. Co., N.Y.C., 1955-58; dir. State Nat. Bank Evanston (Ill.). Mem. City of Evanston Zoning Amendment Bd., 1968-70; pres. 1st Ward Non-Partisan Civic Assn., 1970-71; mem. adv. bd. Internat. Visitors Center, Chgo. 1963—; mem. regional bd. NCCJ, Chgo., 1963-72, v.p., chmn. exec. com., 1969-72, pres. co-chmn., 1973—, nat. trustee, 1967—; various leadership assignments Met. Crusade Mercy, 1968-72; mem. adv. bd. Citizenship Council Met. Chgo., 1969—; mem. exec. bd. Chgo. Area council Boy Scouts Am., 1969-75; chmn. justice task force Chgo. United Inc.; bd. dirs. Chgo. Crime Commn., 1976—, chmn. membership com., 1978—, sec., 1980, v.p., 1981—; trustee Children's Home and Aid Soc. Ill., v.p., 1976-79, pres., 1979—; trustee, mem. exec. com. Hull House Assn., 1970, pres., 1972-74, hon. chmn. 90-yr. campaign fund, hon. trustee, 1978—; trustee U. Ill. YMCA, 1975—; treas., mem. exec. com. Nat. Minority Purchasing Council, 1976-77; bd. govs. Chgo. Heart Assn., 1967-71; bd. dirs., mem. exec. com. United Cerebral Palsy, 1974—, pres., 1975-77, chmn. bd., 1977—, nat. bd. dirs., 1975—, nat. campaign chmn., nat. v.p., 1977—; bd. dirs. Lyric Opera, Vol. Interagency Assn., Chgo. Conv. and Tourism Bur., 1979—, mem. exec. com., 1980—; bd. dirs., chmn. fin. com. Chgo. City Ballet Co., 1980—; exec. bd. Northwestern U. Library; chmn. subcom., com. on case flow Cook County Circuit Ct., 1980—; chmn. Com. on Chgo. Sch. Truancy, 1980—. Served to lt. col. AUS, 1942-46; CBI. Decorated Legion of Merit. Mem. Ill. Hist. Soc. (v.p. 1978-79), Sangamon County Hist. Soc. (1st pres. 1961-62), Chgo. Com., Pub. Relations Soc. Am., Alpha Sigma Phi (Nat. Award Delta Beta Xi). Clubs: Mid-America, Tavern (gov.), Economic (Chgo.). Author: (with others) Handling Barriers in Communications, 1957; The Governor Takes a Bride, 1977. Contbr. articles to profl. jours.; mem. adv. council Weekly Rev. newspaper. Home: 630 Clinton Pl Evanston IL 60201 Office: 225 W Randolph St Chicago IL 60606

TSAO, JAMES TSENG-HU, economist; b. Nanking, China, Nov. 6, 1936; s. Yi Shan and Si (Wen) T.; M.A., Centro Escolar U., 1968; A.M., U. Pa., 1972, Ph.D., Wharton Sch., 1976; came to U.S., 1969, naturalized, 1976; m. Elly Hsiao-Min Yin, Apr. 30, 1961; children—Henry, Hensin. Chief cons. Yi-Shan Entertainment Enterprise, Taipei, 1960-62; dir. Translation and Interpretation Service, Taipei, 1963-65; chief tech. asst. sect. Pa. Div. Health Planning, Harrisburg, 1974-77; statis. staff supr. long lines AT & T, Bedminster, N.J., 1977-78; economist U.S. Internat. Trade Commn., Washington, 1979—; lectr. Trenton State Coll., parttime, 1978. Pres., Central South Pa. Chinese Assn., 1976. Mem. Am. Econ. Assn., Eastern Econ. Assn. (D.C. rep.), Am. Statis. Assn., Am. Translators Assn., Mark IV Users Club. Episcopalian. Home: 11416 Georgetowne Dr Potomac MD 20854 Office: US Internat Trade Commn Washington DC 20436

TSCHAPPAT, DOUGLAS WILSON, electric utility co. exec.; b. Martins Ferry, Ohio, Dec. 30, 1927; s. Charles Wesley and Bertha Mae (Anshutz) T.; B.S. in Mech. Engring., Chgo. Tech. Coll., 1951; m. Ellen L. Phillips, Feb. 6, 1949; children—Kay Tschappat Chamberlain, Karen Tschappat Gerber. With Balt. & Ohio R.R., Lorain, Ohio, 1948-51; with Ohio Edison Co., 1951—, prodn. maintenance, tech. engr., Akron, 1964-69, chief mech. engr., 1969-71, chief elec. and mech. engr., 1971-75, mgr. constrn. budgeting, 1975-76, v.p., 1976-78, sr. v.p., 1978-80, exec. v.p., chief operating officer, 1980—, dir., 1980—; dir. Pa. Power Co. Served with USN, 1946-48. Mem. ASME, IEEE, Am. Nuclear Soc., Atomic Indsl. Forum. Club: Cascade. Home: 1248 Ridgewood Rd Wadsworth OH 44281 Office: Ohio Edison Co 76 S Main St Akron OH 44308

TSCHUDIN, HUGO, mktg. cons.; b. Lausen, Switzerland, May 16, 1929; s. Wilhelm and Elisa (Fink) T.; came to U.S., 1958, naturalized, 1964; LL.D. magna cum laude, U. Basel (Switzerland), 1954; postgrad. in social psychology and philosophy Sorbonne U. Paris, 1958; m. Ruth Anne Olnowich, Nov. 10, 1967; 1 dau., Elisa Grace. Atty. and civil ct. substitute, Basel, 1954-56; lit. agt. Tschudin Press, Basel, 1957-58; asst. new projects dir. Vick Internat. div. Richardson-Merrell, N.Y.C., 1958-59; asst. to pres. Brown Boveri Corp., N.Y.C., 1960-64; owner, mgr. Key Tng. Service, Jersey City, 1965-66; pres., cons. Watchmakers of Switzerland Info. Center/Mktg. Inst., N.Y.C., 1966-69; pres. Dr. H. Tschudin Assos., River Vale, N.J., 1970—; condr. numerous mktg. seminars, N. Am., Europe. Mem. Am. Mgmt. Assn., Am. Mktg. Assn., Sales Execs. Club, Conf. Bd., Swiss-Am. C. of C., German-Am. C. of C., Am. C. of C. in Germany. Clubs: Rotary, Swiss Soc. (past pres.) (N.Y.C.); Efficiency of Basel (past pres.). Author: Handbuch fuer den Geschaeftsverkehr mit den USA, 1971. Office: 215 River Vale Rd River Vale NJ 07675

TSUAYAMA, MASAO, bank exec.; b. Manchuria, China, Mar. 19, 1918; s. Eikichi and Masako (Egi) T.; M.A. in Econs., Keio U.; m. Eiko Chigira; children—Maki, Kay. With Yokohama Specie Bank (now Bank of Tokyo, Ltd.), Tokyo, Bank of Tokyo of Calif., San Francisco; with Calif. First Bank (merger Bank of Tokyo of Calif. with So. First Nat. Bank), San Francisco, chmn. bd., 1978—. Bd. dirs. World Affairs Council No. Calif., Japan Soc. San Francisco. Mem. Overseas Bankers Assn. No. Calif. (chmn.). Office: 350 California St San Francisco CA 94104

TSUKIJI, RICHARD TAKEO, fin. services cons.; b. Salt Lake City, Jan. 31, 1946; s. Isamu and Mitsuie (Hayashi) T.; grad. Sacramento City Coll., 1966; A.A., U. Pacific, McGeorge Sch. Law, 1970-72; m. Laura Elaine Gomes, Aug. 1976; children—Angela Jo, Richard Michael. Grocery mgr. Food Mart, Inc., Sacramento, 1963-65; agy. supr. Takehara Ins. Agy., Sacramento, 1965-68; sales rep. Kraft Foods Co., Sacramento, 1969-71; sales mgr. Olivetti Corp., Sacramento, 1972-73; co-founder Mktg. Devel. and Mgmt. Coll., Sacramento, 1973, pres., 1973-74; pres. Richard Tsukiji Corp., Sacramento, 1974-77; chief exec. officer, chmn. bd. Assos. Investment Group, Sacramento, 1978—; chmn. bd. RichColor Corp. Sacramento, 1978—, E.J. Sub Factories, Inc., Elk Grove, Calif., 1978—; dir. Hunt & Johnson, Inc., LeRich Enterprises; gen. agt. Comml. Bankers Life Ins. Co., 1974—. Mem. Yolo County Oral Rev. Bd., 1975-76; bd. dirs. Valley Area Constrn. Opportunity Program, 1972-76, chmn., 1976-77; active ARC, Sane and Orderly Devel., Inc. Served with U.S. Army, 1962-63. Recipient Commendation, Calif. Senate, 1978. Mem. Internat. Assn. Fin. Planners, Associated Gen. Contractors, Sacramento Jaycees (dir. 1977-78), Asian Alliance, Japanese Am. Citizens League, Sacramento Urban League. Democrat. Roman Catholic. Office: 2522 Claremont Dr #303 San Diego CA 92117

TSUN, STEPHEN BING-KEUNG, mfg. co. exec.; b. Hong Kong, Jan. 19, 1942; came to U.S., 1966; B.S. in Elec. Engring., U. Mich., 1970; M.B.A., U. Dayton (Ohio), 1974; m. Nena S.Y. Lee, July 26, 1973; children—Angela W.Y., Ryan W.K. With Gen. Electric Co., 1970-80, product planner semicondr. products dept., Syracuse, N.Y., 1976-78, mgr. signal product sales semicondr. products dept., Auburn, N.Y., 1978-80; product mktg. mgr. Unitrode Corp., Lexington, Mass., 1980—. Home: 15 Pierce Ave Westford MA 01886 Office: 5 Forbes Rd Lexington MA 02173

TUBBS, EDWARD LANE, banker; b. Delmar, Iowa, Apr. 17, 1920; s. Clifton Marvin and Mary Ellen (Lane) T.; B.S., Iowa State U., 1941; m. Grace Barbara Dyer, Nov. 27, 1941; children—Steven, Alan, William. With Iowa State U. Agrl. Extension Service, Newton, 1942; farm owner and mgr., 1944—; instr. Vets. On-Farm, DeWitt (Iowa) schs., 1957-58; v.p., dir. Jackson State Bank, Maquoketa, Iowa, 1959-66; chmn., pres., dir., trust officer Maquoketa State Bank, 1966—; pres., dir. Ohnward Bancshares, Inc.; chmn., dir. First Central State Bank, DeWitt; lectr. banking schs.; Exchange del. USSR, 1959. Pres. Elwood (Iowa) Sch. Bd., 1956-62; treas. City of Maquoketa, 1975—; mem. Maquoketa Indsl. Devel. Bd., 1970-77; treas. Maquoketa Community Services, 1967—. Served with AUS, 1942-43. Recipient 4H Club Alumni award, 1962, Century Farm award Iowa Dept. Agr., 1976; named Jaycee Boss of Year, 1970. Mem. Bank Adminstrn. Inst., Iowa Bankers Assn. (treas. 1978-79, pres. 1980-81), Iowa Transfer System (dir. 1978—), Iowa Ind. Bankers, Am. Legion, Isaac Walton League, Farm Bur., Iowa State U. Alumni Assn., Maquoketa C. of C. (dir. 1966-69), Order of Knoll (Iowa State U.), Internat. Platform Assn., Gamma Sigma Delta. Republican. Mem. United Ch. Christ. Author articles in field. Home: 820 Niles St Maquoketa IA 52060 Office: 203 N Main St Maquoketa IA 52060

TUBBS, JOHN TOWNSEND, lumber contracting co. exec.; b. Selbyville, Del., Feb. 2, 1918; s. John Asbury and Edith Mae (Townsend) T.; B.A., Yale U., 1940; m. Jean Wire, Nov. 25, 1967; 1 son, John Townsend. With Selbyville Mfg. Co., Rehoboth, Del., 1945—, pres., 1972—; pres. Seaside Villages, Bethany Beach, Del., 1964—; v.p. Balt. Trust Co., 1968—, also dir.; sales asso. Lingo Real Estate, 1978—. Bd. dirs. Delmarva Rehab. Center, 1955—, Rehoboth Art League, 1978—. Served with USNR, 1940-45; ETO, PTO. Republican. Methodist. Home: 78 Oak Ave Rehoboth DE 19971 Office: Selbyville Mfg Co Box 199 Rehoboth DE 19971

TUCCI, GERALD FRANK, mfg. co. exec.; b. N.Y.C., Sept. 9, 1926; s. Frank and Mary (Fattizzi) T.; student Dartmouth Coll., 1944; Sc.B. in Naval Sci., Brown U., 1946; Sc.B. In Mech. Engring., 1948; M.B.A. with distinction, Harvard U., 1950; m. Eva G. Gyllander, May 14, 1968; children—Francis Henrik, Michael Fredrik, Amy Christina. Mfg. trainee Am. Can Co., Jersey City, 1950-51; asst. v.p., plant mgr. Artcraft Hosiery Mills, Inc., Darby, Pa., 1951-53; v.p. Leach & Garner Co., Attleboro, Mass., 1953-63, Gen. Findings, Inc., Attleboro, 1953-63; pres. Micro Contacts Inc., Hicksville, N.Y., 1963—; v.p. Mold-A-Matic Corp., Oneota, N.Y., 1965—; chmn. bd., chief exec. officer Hallmark Findings, Inc., Warwick, R.I., 1965—; pres. Micro Pneumatic Logics, Inc., Ft. Lauderdale, Fla., 1975—. Served to lt. (s.g.) USNR, 1944-47. Mem. ASME, Am. Soc. Mfrs., Beta Theta Pi. Republican. Roman Catholic. Clubs: North Hempstead Country, Harvard Bus. Sch. N.Y. Office: 62 Alpha Plaza Hicksville NY 11801

TUCH, EUGENE, mfg. co. exec.; b. Jersey City, June 3, 1940; s. Samuel and Belle Geraldine (Feldman) T.; B.S., Rutgers U., 1961; m. Lorraine T. Winkler, May 31, 1964; children—Sherry, Debra, David. Accountant, J.K. Lasser & Co., N.Y.C., 1961-68; controller Am. Metal Market, N.Y.C., 1968-72; v.p. fin. Childcraft Edn. Corp., Edison, N.J., 1972—; pres. Rylco Rubber Products, Trenton, N.J., 1980—. Served with U.S. Army, 1961. Mem. Rutgers U. Alumni Fedn. (pres. 1977-79, Am. Inst. C.P.A.'s (exec. com. continuous profl. edn., industry and govt. com.), N.J. Soc. C.P.A.'s (sec. 1978-79, trustee 1976-78), Rutgers Sch. Bus. Alumni Assn. (pres. 1976-77), Am. Inst. C.P.A.'s. Editorial bd. C.P.A. Jour., 1971-75. Home: 20 Johnson Rd Somerset NJ 08873 Office: 1218 Walnut Ave Trenton NJ 08629

TUCK, NOEL BARTON, JR., ins., real estate and investment co. exec.; b. Henderson, N.C., Jan. 3, 1938; s. Noel Barton and Emily (Barnette) T.; student Campbell Jr. Coll., 1956-58; B.S., U. N.C., 1960; m. Linda Anthony, Sept. 20, 1975; children by previous marriage—Kathy, Emily, Linda, Noel. Accountant, S.D. Leidesdorf, Greenville, S.C., 1960-66; account exec. Harris, Upham, Greenville, 1966-70; founder Fin. Planning Assos., Greenville, 1970-72; founder, pres. U.S. Shelter Corp., Greenville, 1972—; dir. H.G. Smithy Co., Washington, S.C. Nat. Bank, Greenville. Bd. dirs. St. Francis Hosp., Greenville. active United Fund. C.P.A., S.C., N.C. Mem. Am. Inst. C.P.A.'s, N.C., S.C. assns. C.P.A.'s, Greater Greenville C. of C. (exec. com., chmn. fin. com.). Clubs: Greenville Country, Poinsett. Home: 4 Brookside Way Greenville SC 29605 Office: 1000 Executive Center Dr Greenville SC 29615 also PO Box 6725 Greenville SC 29606

TUCKER, ALLEN BROWN, JR., computer scientist; b. Worcester, Mass., Feb. 19, 1942; s. Allen Brown and Louise (Woodberry) T.; B.A., Wesleyan U., 1963; M.S., Northwestern U., 1968, Ph.D., 1970; m. Maida Somerville, Dec. 19, 1965; children—Jennifer, Brian. Programmer, Norton Co., Worcester, 1963-67; asst. prof. computer sci. U. Mo., Rolla, 1970-71; asst. prof. computer sci. Georgetown U., Washington, 1971-76, asso. prof., dir. Computer Sci. Program,

1976—, dir. Acad. Computation Center, 1976—; cons. Pan Am. Health Orgn., 1973—. Mem. Assn. for Computing Machinery, Sigma Xi. Author: Programming Languages, 1977; Text Processing, 1979. Home: 6520 Dryden Dr McLean VA 22101 Office: Computer Sci Program Georgetown U Washington DC 20057

TUCKER, CARL ALFRED, office supplies mfg. co. exec.; b. Charlotte, N.C., Oct. 30, 1932; s. Carl A. and Radie Naomi (Mullis) T.; Asso. in Sci., U. Md., 1953, B.S.B.A., 1979; student U. Syracuse, 1971-72; m. Harriett Yvonne Jordon, Feb. 18, 1956; children—Devin Scott, Harriett Paige. Ter. mgr. Gen. Electric Supply Corp., Norfolk, Va., 1953-56; sales tng. mgr. Revlon, Norfolk, 1956-59; dist. mgr. U.S. Rubber Co., Balt., 1959-61; area sales mgr. Sheaffer Pen Co., Detroit, 1961-69; gen. sales mgr. McDonald Products Corp., Buffalo, 1969-78; v.p. mktg. Wite-Out Office Products, Inc., Beltsville, Md., 1979—. Served with USAF, 1949-53. Named Mr. Revlon, 1958, Area Mgr. for Year Sheaffer Pen Co., 1968. Mem. Sales and Mktg. Execs. Internat. (trustee), Am. Mgmt. Assn., U. Syracuse Alumni Assn. (pres. 1978). Republican. Presbyterian. Clubs: Masons (32 deg.), Shriners. Home: 624 Shore Acres Rd Arnold MD 21012 Office: 10114 Bacon Dr Beltsville MD 20705

TUCKER, DONALD MICHAEL, med. group adminstr.; b. Muncie, Ind., Feb. 22, 1947; s. Kenneth V. and Helen C. T.; student U. Ill., 1965, U. Md., 1966, U. Tokyo, 1967, U. Okla., 1968, Ohio U., 1973, Ill. Central Coll., 1973-74; m. Nelly Tucker, May 19, 1978; children—Michael Allen, Bradley Michael. Buyer, expediter Berekley Davis Co., 1965; program analyst Caterpiller Tractor Co., 1969-73; dist. sales mgr. Litton Industries, Peoria, Ill., Orlando and Tampa, Fla., 1973-76; bus. adminstr. Tampa Bay Radiology, Tampa, 1976—; cons. med. computer billing. Served with U.S. Army, 1966-69; Vietnam. Mem. Med. Group Mgmt. Assn., Radiology Bus. Mgrs. Assn. Republican. Club: Sertoma. Home: 2486 Indian Trail Palm Harbor FL 33563 Office: Tampa Bay Radiology 4530 Armenia St Tampa FL 33603

TUCKER, EVERETT, JR., indsl. devel. co. exec.; b. Tucker, Ark., July 7, 1912; s. Dewitt Everett and Will Lynn (Alexander) T.; B.S., Washington and Lee U., 1934; postgrad. Harvard Bus. Sch., 1942-43, U. N.Mex., 1947-48; m. Francis Marion Williams, Oct. 9, 1943; children—Robert W., Everett III, Marion C. Mgmt. trainee Standard Oil Co., Little Rock, 1934-36; cotton farmer, 1936-41; indsl. mgr. Little Rock (Ark) C. of C., 1949-59; pres., dir. Indsl. Devel. Co. of Little Rock, 1960—; mng. partner S.E. Tucker Cotton Plantation, Tucker, Ark. dir. Ark. Nat. Stockyards, Capital Cable Co., Austin, Tex., Comml. Nat. Bank, Commonwealth Fed. Savs. & Loan Assn. Mem. Little Rock Sch. Bd., 1958-65, pres., 1959-63. Served to maj. USAAF, 1942-46. Mem. Am. (pres. 1967-68), So. (pres. 1957-58) Indsl. Devel. Council. Episcopalian. Clubs: Little Rock Country, Little Rock, XV. Home: 4601 Kavanaugh Blvd Little Rock AR 72207 Office: 1780 Tower Bldg Little Rock AR 72201

TUCKER, GEORGE MAXWELL, bldg. maintenance co. exec.; b. Bainbridge, Ga., Jan. 17, 1950; s. John Pierce, Sr., and Isabel (Slade) T.; A.B. in Polit. Sci. and Christianity, Mercer U., 1972, postgrad. Sch. Theology, 1972-74. Mem. exec. staff Internat. Devel. Campaign and spl. field rep. for pres. Campus Crusade for Christ Internat., San Bernardino, Calif., 1972-77; dir. pub. relations, acting adminstr., Shepherd Prodns., Inc., Denver, 1977-78; personnel mgr. Riverside Mfg. Co., Moultrie, Ga., 1978; sales mgr. Western U.S., Plains Mfg. Co., Sidney, Nebr., 1978-79; asst. to pres. for spl. projects Campus Crusade for Christ, Internat., San Bernardino, Calif., 1979-80, asso. staff exec. ministries, 1980—; owner, mgr. Environ. Control Bldg. Maintenance Co., Decatur, Ga., 1980—; speaker civic clubs, ch. confs., retreats; Bibl./family counseling; fund raising cons. small Christian orgns. Recipient Youth Leadership award, Elks Club, 1968. Mem. Christian Business Men's Com., Alpha Tau Omega. Baptist. Author: A Resource Manual for Church Youth Workers, 1976. Home: Atlanta GA Office: 1924 Clairmont Rd Decatur GA 30033

TUCKER, GEORGE MCKINLEY, JR., constrn. co. exec.; b. Balt., Apr. 7, 1934; s. George McKinley and Carolyn Elizabeth (Simmons) T.; B.E., Johns Hopkins U., 1954; m. Patricia Jane Smith, Aug. 6, 1955; children—Michael Spencer, Barrett Lee. With Whiting-Turner Contracting Co., Towson, Md., 1957—, div. mgr., 1969-73, v.p., 1973—. Mem. ch. vestry Trinity Episcopal Ch., Long Green, Md., 1971-76, coordinator youth confirmation program, 1972—, sr. warden, 1973-76, head usher, 1978—; coach, mgr. Community Little League Baseball, Optimist Basketball and Football, Jacksonville, Md., 1968-75; active Balt. area council Boy Scouts Am., 1971-74. Served to 1st lt. C.E., U.S. Army, 1955-57. Mem. ASCE, Republican. Episcopalian. Home: 4207 Ravenhurst Cr Glen Arm MD 21057 Office: 300 E Joppa Rd Towson MD 21204

TUCKER, GORDON LOCKE, meteorologist; b. Peeksill, N.Y., Dec. 19, 1932; s. Edwin Locke and Eleanor Wardwell (Ramsdell) T.; B.S. in Elec. Engring., U. Mass., 1955; B.S. in Meteorology, St. Louis U., 1956; M.S. in Meteorology, U. Wis., 1962; M.S. in Systems Mgmt., U. So. Calif., 1976; m. Marlene Rae Culli, Nov. 22, 1959; children—Lisa Marie, Glenn Locke, Lori Sue. Commd. lt. USAF, 1955, advanced through grades to maj., 1975; staff meteorologist USAF Space and Missile Test Center, Vandenberg AFB, Calif., 1971-75, ret., 1975; mgr. phys. scis. sect., air quality specialist, sr. meteorologist HDR Scis. div. Henningson, Durham & Richardson, Santa Barbara, Calif., 1975—. Decorated Air Force Commendation medal with oak leaf cluster, Air Force Meritorious Service medal. Mem. Am. Meteorol. Soc., Air Force Assn., Air Pollution Control Assn., Ret. Officers Assn. Club: Kiwanis. Contbr. profl. publs. Home: 458 Merida Dr Santa Barbara CA 93111

TUCKER, HARRELL FRANKLIN, credit union exec.; b. Malvern, Ark., June 22, 1917; s. Isac Franklin and Maybell (Moye) T.; student U. Ill., 1936-40; Fin. and Adminstrn. degree, U. Chgo., 1949; m. Nina Katherine Lambert, Dec. 19, 1937; children—Harrell G., Tommy L., Sandra K., Angela G. Asst. mgr. Met. Life Ins. Co., Little Rock, 1940-46; gen. mgr. Sterling Drug Co., N.Y.C., 1949-55; Little Rock regional dir. Allstate Ins. Co., Ft. Smith, Ark., 1955-59; owner, operator Tucker Pharm. Co., Little Rock, 1959-69; pres. Ark. Sch. Nursing, Little Rock, 1970-73; treas. Wesemp Fed. Credit Union, Little Rock, 1973—, mgr., 1975—, trust officer, 1977—, loan officer, 1978—. C.P.A., Calif., Ark., N.Y., Wash. Mem. Ch. of Christ. Club: Mason (32 deg., Shriner). Home: 3209 Katherine St Little Rock AR 72204 Office: 6227 Asher Ave Little Rock AR 72204

TUCKER, HUBERT E., paper co. exec.; b. Bridgeport, Ohio, July 6, 1931; s. Hubert E. and Leona A. (Nightengale) T.; B.S. cum laude, Marion Coll.-Ind. No. U., 1967, M.B.A., 1969; asso. with distinction, Nat. Inst. Credit, 1975; m. Imogene L. Sontchi, July 22, 1956; children—Michael, Robert. With Bricker Co., Marion, Ind., 1956-59; internal auditor, asst. controller Bell Fibre Products Corp., Marion, 1959-71, dir. corp. credit, 1971, asst. treas., 1975, treas., 1978—. Mem. adv. council on vocat. edn. C.O.E. Programs, 1977—. Served with U.S. Army, 1951-53. Mem. Assn. M.B.A. Execs., Nat. Paper Package Group, Nat. Assn. Accts., Nat. Assn. Credit Mgmt., Am. Legion. Presbyterian. Clubs: Elks, Masons. Home: 4041 Creston Dr Marion IN 46952 Office: Bell Fibre Products Corp PO Box 3333 3102 S Boots St Marion IN 46952

TUCKER, JAMES DAVID, bus. mgr., mfg. co. exec.; b. Mpls., Jan. 24, 1937; s. Gordon and Margaret Ann (Pilney) T.; B.A. cum laude in Econs., U. Minn., 1960; M.B.A. in Fin., U. Pa., 1961; m. Katherine Ann Hart, Nov. 28, 1964; children—Molly, Scott, Kevin. Mgmt. cons. A.T. Kearney, Inc., 1965-70; pres., chief exec. officer Nimrod Inc., 1970-74; mgmt. cons., 1975-76; gen. partner Cadre Partners, Newport Beach, Calif., 1977—; interim exec. spl. projects HammerBlow Corp., Wausau, Wis., 1977-80; chief exec. officer Dakota Bake N Serv, Jamestown, N.D., 1978-79; chmn. bd., chief exec. officer Laguna Mfg. Co., Irvine, Calif. 1980—; v.p., dir. Taylor Chain Co., Hammond, Ind., 1980—. Recipient Design citation Am. Iron and Steel Inst., 1973. Mem. Assn. Corp. Growth. Roman Catholic. Club: Balboa Yacht. Home 1824 Port Sheffield Pl Newport Beach CA 92660

TUCKER, MARSHALL DANIEL, wholesale indsl. pipes, valves and fittings supply co. exec.; b. Dresden, Tenn., Mar. 30, 1932; s. Marshall J. and Julia I. (Travis) T.; B.B.A., U. Tenn., 1954; m. Gloria Shelwitt, Aug. 30, 1959; children—Susan, Karen, Mark. Asst. plant acct. Paperboard div. Mead Corp., Knoxville, Tenn., 1955-58, corp. staff acct., Dayton, Ohio, 1966-68, corp. fin. planning anlayst, 1969-70, asst. to group pres. Mead Interiors Group, Stanleytown, Va., 1971-74, controller Stanley Furniture div., 1975-76, asst. treas. parent co., Dayton, 1977-79; chief fin. officer Devel. and Resources Corp., N.Y.C., 1959-64, Ahwaz, Iran, 1959-64; internal auditor Burlington Industries, Greensboro, N.C., 1965; v.p. fin. McJunkin Corp., Charleston, W.Va., 1979—; dir. Mfrs. Equipment Co., Middletown, Ohio. Bd. dirs. Bronco Junction, Charleston. Served with U.S. Army, 1956-57. Home: 5313 Stoneybrook Rd Charleston WV 25313 Office: 1400 Hansford St Charleston WV 25301

TUCKER, NICHOLAS JOEL, abrasives mfg. co. exec.; b. Evanston, Ill., Feb. 27, 1951; s. William Ruggles, Jr. and Janet (Boogher) T.; B.A., Monmouth (Ill.) Coll., 1973. Inside domestic sales and service rep. Buehler, Ltd., Evanston, Ill., 1974-77, sales engr., microstructural analyst, Milw., 1977-80; tech. sales rep. CBN products Diamond Abrasives div. Carborundum Co., Niagara Falls, N.Y., 1980—. Asst. scout master Evanston chpt. Boy Scouts Am., 1967-68. Recipient Eagle Scout award Boy Scouts Am., 1967. Mem. Am. Soc. Metals, Soc. Mfg. Engrs., Abrasive Engring. Soc., Zeta Beta Tau (chpt. treas., chmn. fin. com. 1972-73), Zeta Beta Tau Alumni Assn. (founding mem. Chgo. chpt.). Republican. Congregationalist. Home: 317 Nora Ave Glenview IL 60025 Office: PO Box 403 Bldg 5-1 Bonded Abrasives Div Niagara Falls NY 14302

TUCKER, PAUL WILLIAM, petroleum co. exec.; b. Liberty, Mo., Dec. 21, 1921; s. Nova William and Georgia May (Cuthbertson) T.; A.B., William Jewell Coll., 1942, LL.D., 1968; M.S., La. State U., 1944; postgrad. U. Ill., 1945-46; Ph.D. (George Breon fellow), U. Mo., 1948; m. Beverly Caryl Livingston, June 2, 1943; children—Ann Caryl (Mrs. John T. Worland), Linda Louise (Mrs. J. Hale Smith). Chemist, spectroscopist Tenn. Eastman Corp., Oak Ridge, 1944-46; chemist Phillips Petroleum Co., Bartlesville, Okla., 1948-49, tech. rep., 1949-60, asst. dir. pub. affairs, 1960-62, mng. dir. Phillips Petroleum Co. U.K. Ltd., London, 1962-68, v.p. gas and gas liquids Phillips Petroleum Co. Europe-Africa, London, 1969-73, v.p. gas and gas liquids pub. affairs and govt. relations Phillip Petroleum Co. Europe-Africa, London, 1973-74, mgr. internat. gas and gas liquids Phillips Petroleum Co., Bartlesville, 1974-78, v.p. gas and gas liquids div. Natural Resources Group, 1978-80, v.p. gas and gas liquids group, 1980—. Registered profl. engr., Okla. Fellow Inst. Petroleum (U.K.), Inst. Gas Engrs. (U.K.); mem. Am. Chem. Soc., Nat., Okla. socs. profl. engrs., N.Y. Acad. Sci., Sigma Xi, Phi Lambda Upsilon, Kappa Alpha, Alpha Chi Sigma. Clubs: American (London); Hillcrest Country (Bartlesville). Author numerous articles on safety, storage, transp. and handling of liquefied petroleum gas, anhydrous ammonia, natural gas in Europe. Home: 1533 Pecan Pl Bartlesville OK 74003 Office: 17 Phillips Bldg Bartlesville OK 74004

TUCKER, RICHARD LYON, steel co. exec.; b. Greensboro, N.C., Mar. 22, 1939; s. Lewis Lyon and Mary Lea (Jones) T.; B.S., N.C. State U., 1962; Prodn. coordinator Carolina Steel Corp. Greensboro, 1963-70, indsl. engr., 1970- 73, structural mgr. Greenville (S.C.) Steel Co. div., 1973-75, asst. gen. mgr., 1975-76, gen. mgr., 1976-77, v.p., gen. mgr., 1978—. Mem. Am. Inst. Indsl. Engrs., Va./Carolinas Structural Steel Fabricators Assn., Am. Inst. Steel Constrn. Methodist. Club: Rotary. Home: 10 Applejack Ln Taylors SC 29687 Office: Greenville Steel Co PO Box 128 Greenville SC 29602

TUCKER, THOMAS JAMES, finance and leasing co. exec.; b. Atlanta, Sept. 5, 1929; s. Thomas Tudor and Carol (Govan) T.; B.A., Univ. of the South, 1952; student Ga. State U., 1957-59; m. Mary Ann Garland, Nov. 24, 1953. Credit analyst CIT Corp., Atlanta, 1957-59; dist. credit mgr., Jacksonville, Fla., 1959-62, asst. sec., San Francisco, 1962-71, Atlanta, 1971-72; pres., chief exec. officer Alabanc Fin. Corp., Birmingham, Ala., 1972—, also dir. Served with USAF, 1952-56. Mem. Assn. Bank Holding Cos., Am. Assn. Equipment Lessors. Episcopalian. Clubs: The Club, The Relay House, Birmingham Canoe (pres. 1979). Contbr. articles to fin. jours. Home: Route 1 Box 57 B Maylene AL 35114 Office: PO Box 2545 Birmingham AL 35202

TUDOR, BARRY REUBEN, computing services exec.; b. Somerville, N.J., Feb. 9, 1952; s. Sidney and Ida (Axelrod) T.; B.S. cum laude in Econs., U. Pa., 1974; m. Wanda M. Dudley, Apr. 11, 1976. Cost acct. Burroughs Corp., Paoli, Pa., 1974-75; mktg. rep. STSC, Inc., N.Y.C., 1975-78, br. mgr., Phila., 1978—; instr. APL computer lang. Active, Woodmere Park Civic Assn., 1979—. Recipient STSC Pres.'s award for outstanding corp. contbns., 1977. Mem. Assn. Computing Machinery, Am. Mgmt. Assn. Office: Bourse Bldg Suite 530 Independence Mall East Philadelphia PA 19106

TUDOR, WILLIAM PAUL, computer software co. exec.; b. Detroit, June 12, 1945; s. Paul M. and Margaret I. (David) T.; B.B.A., U. Detroit, 1974; m. Mary Lou Coons, Aug. 25, 1967; children—Lori Marie, Robert William. Systems analyst Hygrade Food Products, Detroit, 1968-70; data processing mgr. Hungerford, Cooper, Luxon & Co., C.P.A.'s, Taylor, Mich., 1970-73; pres. Metro Beverage Distbrs., Inc., Ann Arbor, Mich., 1973-75, Tudor Systems, Inc., Charlotte, N.C., 1975—. County committeeman Tega Cay Republican Party, 1980. Served with U.S. Army, 1965-67. Mem. Jaycees (pres. Chelsea 1976-77), Delta Sigma Pi. Roman Catholic. Home: 8010 Windjammer Fort Mill SC 29715 Office: One Woodlawn Green Charlotte NC 28210

TUFTS, JOHN MITCHELL, corrugated fibreboard co. exec.; b. Atlanta, May 16, 1949; s. Rutledge and Mimi Mitchell T.; B.A., Vanderbilt U., 1971; M.B.A., So. Methodist U., 1974; m. Kathryn Hutchison, Nov. 26, 1971; children—Joseph Rutledge, Kathryn Cole. Nat. sales mgr. John E. Mitchell Mfg., Dallas, 1976-77; pres. Francis Tufts Investments, Dallas, 1978-79; asst. fin. chmn. Gov. Bill Clements of Tex., 1979; pres., chief exec. officer Voidco Mfg. Co., Dallas, 1979—. Mem. fin. com. Young Life, 1976—; mem. fin. com. Grady Spruce YMCA Camp. Mem. Dallas C. of C., Associated Gen. Contractors. Episcopalian. Club: So. Methodist Univ Mustang. Office: Voidco Inc Box 29407 11282 Leo Ln Dallas TX 75229

TUGANDER, DENNIS, broadcasting exec.; b. Bronx, N.Y., July 12, 1949; s. Morris P. and Frances E. Tugander; student Ohio State U., 1966-68; A.A., Lehman Coll., 1970; m. Diane F. Rinaldi, Sept. 13, 1970; children—Elisa Christine, Andrea Dawn, Laura Beth. Mut. funds adminstr. Bank of N.Y., 1968-70; accountant, gen. ledger supr. CBS, Inc., N.Y.C., 1970-72, adminstr. accounting, 1972-74; fin. analyst WBBM-TV, Chgo., 1974-76, mgr. bus. affairs, 1976-78, mgr. budgets/forecasts, 1978-79, dir. bus. affairs, 1979—. Mem. fin. adv. com. Sch. Dist. 63, 1977-78. Mem. Broadcast Fin. Mgmt. Assn., Broadcast Credit Assn., Am. Mgmt. Assn. Jewish. Clubs: Moose; Our Lady of Ransom Varsity Booster. Home: 8899 Grand St Niles IL 60648 Office: CBS Inc 630 N McClurg Ct Chicago IL 60611

TULIPANO, EMILIO JOHN, businessman; b. Rome, Italy, June 20, 1946; s. Saverio and Lucy Tulipano; came to U.S., 1953, naturalized, 1961; 1 dau., Lisa C. Treas., owner The Needham Clipper Inc. (Mass.), hairstyling, 1975—. Served with USMC, 1963-67. Mem. Nat. Small Bus. Assn., Needham Bus. Assn. Roman Catholic. Office: 1095 Great Plain Ave Needham MA 12192

TULLER, WENDY JUDGE, cons.; b. Cranston, R.I., Dec. 17, 1943; d. Alfred Carman and Anna Louise (Waterman) Judge; A.B., Brown U., 1965; M.L.S., U. R.I., 1969. Elementary sch. librarian Providence Pub. Sch. System, 1965-69; mgr. Xerox Corp., various locations, 1969-75, Carter Hawley Hale Stores, Inc., Los Angeles, 1975; cons. Sibson & Co., Inc., Princeton, N.J., 1975-78; cons. equal opportunity affairs Atlantic Richfield Co., Los Angeles, 1978—. Mem. Am. Soc. Personnel Adminstrn., Am. Soc. Tng. and Devel., Internat. Assn. Personnel Women. Home: 222 S Figueroa St Los Angeles CA 90012 Office: 515 S Flower St Los Angeles CA 90071

TULLIS, JOHN LEDBETTER, wholesale distbn. co. exec.; b. Quanah, Tex., May 9, 1911; s. John Ledbetter and Coral (Horton) T.; B.S. in Elec. Engring., U. Tex., 1933; m. Bettye Bishop, Mar. 22, 1980. Sales engr. AMF Beaird, Inc., 1947, sales mgr., 1948-54, v.p. sales, 1954-57, exec. v.p., 1957-58, pres., gen. mgr., 1959-62, pres., chmn., 1962-68; v.p. AMF, Inc., 1963, group exec., products group, 1963-68, exec. v.p., 1968, pres., 1970—; pres., chief operating officer, dir. AMF Inc., 1970-73; sr. officer, gen. mgr. Interstate Electric Co., Inc., Shreveport, La., 1974—. Chmn. devel. council Schumpert Meml. Center. Recipient Disting. Engring. Grad. award U. Tex., 1963. Mem. Tex. Hist. Assn. Presbyterian. Clubs: Shreveport Country, Shreveport, Univ. Home: 1806 Hunter Circle Shreveport LA 71119 Office: PO Box 31094 Shreveport LA 71130

TULLIS, RICHARD BARCLAY, communications and info. handling equipment co. exec.; b. Western Springs, Ill., July 12, 1913; s. Lauren Barclay and Izelah (Gilmore) T.; A.B., Principia Coll., Elsah, Ill., 1934; m. Chaille Handy, Aug. 17, 1935; children—Sarah (Mrs. Charles deBarcza), Barclay J., Garner H. With Miller Printing Machinery Co., Pitts., 1936-56, pres., 1952-56; with Harris Corp., Melbourne, Fla., 1956—, exec. v.p., 1957-61, pres., 1961-72, chief exec. officer 1968-78, chmn., 1972-78, chmn. exec. com., 1978—; also dir.; dir. Cleve. Electric Illuminating Co., Gen. Tire and Rubber Co. trustee First Union Real Estate Investment Trust. Chmn., Univ. Circle Inc., Cleve.; trustee Principia Coll., Mus. Arts Assn., Cleve. Home: 221 Indian Harbor Rd Vero Beach FL 32960 Office: Melbourne FL 32919

TULLOCH, JAMES MACDONALD, ins. co. exec.; b. Racine, Wis., Mar. 5, 1924; s. Thomas MacDonald and Mabel (Peterson) T.; B.A., Carleton Coll., Minn., 1949; m. Shirley Jordan, May 19, 1943; children—Tara Nancy, Thomas Scott, Gail Jean. Underwriter, Federated Mut. Ins. Cos., Owatonna, Minn., 1949-53; casualty underwriting mgr. Integrity Mut. Casualty Ins. Co., Appleton, Wis., 1953-57; actuarial and underwriting mgr. Nat. Farmers Union Ins. Cos., Denver, 1957-67, dir. research and planning, 1967-68; actuary Dairyland Ins. Co., Madison, Wis., 1968-69, v.p. and actuary, 1969-71, pres., Scottsdale, Ariz., 1971—, also dir.; chmn. and dir. Dairyland County Mut. Ins. Co.; dir. Sentry Life Ins. Co., Sentry Indemnity, United Bank. Bd. dirs. Scottsdale YMCA, Dairyland Found., Scottsdale Baptist Ch. Served with USAF, 1942-46; PTO. Mem. Phoenix Met. C. of C. (dir.), Nat. Assn. Ind. Insurers (dir.), Am. Mgmt. Assn. Clubs: Rotary, Ariz. Country, Camelback Golf, Mesa Country. Office: 9501 E Shea Blvd Scottsdale AZ 85258

TUNC, DEGER CETIN, research scientist; b. Izmir, Turkey, Apr. 2, 1936; came to U.S., 1957, naturalized, 1966; s. Hulusi and Saadet (Gokce) T.; B.S., Columbia U., 1963; M.A., Fairleigh Dickinson U., 1966; Ph.D., Rutgers U., 1972; m. Gunay Gokmen, Nov. 4, 1963; children—Feza, Aysan. Research chemist ITT-Rayonier Research, Whippany, N.J., 1963-66; with Johnson & Johnson, New Brunswick, N.J., 1966—, research surg. dressings, 1966-72, sr. research scientist biopolymers in medicine and surgery, 1972—; UN lectr. Ege U., Izmir, summer 1979. Mem. Am. Chem. Soc., Soc. for Biomaterials, Turkish Architects, Engrs. and Scientists Am. (bd. dirs. 1970-72, pres. 1972-74). Moslem. Patentee in U.S., U.K., Can. Office: 501 George St New Brunswick NJ 08903

TUNNICLIFFE, WILLIAM WARREN, graphics co. exec.; b. Washington, Apr. 22, 1922; s. Homer Warren and Christine (Hobbs) T.; B.E.E., Worcester Poly. Inst., 1943; A.M. in Engring. Scis. and Applied Physics, Harvard, 1951; m. Ruth Loretto Loftus, June 23, 1951; children—Peter Warren, Virginia Warren, Elizabeth Loftus, William Loftus. Staff mem. Mass. Inst. Tech. Radiation Lab., 1943-44; head electronics sect. Boston U. Optical Research Lab., 1946-51; electronics engr. Barkley & Dexter Labs., Inc., Fitchburg, Mass., 1953-55; mgr. Eastern engring. office Offner Electronics, Inc., Somerville, Mass., 1955-56; systems engr., project mgr., program mgr. Raytheon Co., Wayland, Mass., 1956-63; v.p. Info. Dynamics Corp., Reading, Mass., 1963-65; program mgr. Courier-Citizen Co., Lowell, Mass., 1965-68, v.p., 1969-72; nat. sales mgr. Graphic Services subs. Am. Standard, 1972, Warren, Mich., pres., 1973-74; pres. Tunnicliffe Assos., Inc., Winchester, Mass., 1974—; gen. mgr. Woodland Communications Co. subs. W.E. Andrews Co., Bedford, Mass., 1975; program dir. pre-press systems Graphic Communications Computer Assn., Arlington, Va., 1976-77; v.p. research and devel. Walter T. Armstrong, Inc., Phila., 1977-78; program mgr. Bobst Graphic Inc., Bohemia, N.Y., 1979, dir. market research, 1979-80, mktg. mgr., 1980-81; mktg. mgr. graphic arts div. Imlac Corp. subs. Hazeltine, Needham, Mass., 1981—; cons. Raytheon Co., 1964-66, Courier-Citizen Co., 1972, Chrysler Corp., 1974; organizing chmn., dir. Printing Research Inst. for New Tech., Inc., Washington, 1968-69, chmn., dir., pres., 1970-74; instr. grad. physics dept. Boston U., 1949-51. Vice pres., bd. dirs. Horace L. and Florence E. Mayer Found., Balt. Served as lt. (j.g.) USNR, 1944-46, lt., 1951-53, capt. Res., 1967. Mem. Am. Soc. Info. Scis., Armed Forces Communications and Electronics Assn., Internat. Word Processing Assn., Assn. Computing Machinery, IEEE, Nat. Micrographics Assn., Soc. Info. Display, Soc. Motion Picture and TV Engrs., Inst. Printing (London), Printing Industries Am., Graphic Communications Computer Assn. (chmn. character generation com. 1967-74, dir. 1970-74, v.p. 1973-74), Research and Engring. Council Graphic Arts Industry, Nat. Composition Assn., Naval Res. Assn., Res. Officers Assn., U.S. Naval Inst., Sci. Research Soc. Am., Sigma Xi, Sigma Alpha Epsilon. Club: Harvard of Boston. Home: 39 Central St Winchester MA 01890 Office: 150 A St Needham MA 02194

TUOHEY, CONRAD GRAVIER, lawyer; b. N.Y.C., Dec. 27, 1933; s. James J. and Rose (Gravier) T.; B.A., George Washington U., 1957; J.D., U. Mich., 1960; m. Judith Octavia Jeeves, July 7, 1956; children—Octavia Jeeves, Heather Gravier, Meighan Judith, Caragh Rose. Admitted to Calif. bar, 1962, N.Y. bar, 1980, D.C. bar, 1980; sr. mem. firm Tuohey & Barton; dir. Walker & Lee, Inc., Fed. Home Loan Bank, San Francisco. Mem. citizens adv. bd. Orange County Transit Com., 1966-68; pres. Calif. Alliance Partners for Progress, 1969-72, Friends of Calif. State U. at Fullerton, 1969-71; mem. InterAm. bd. Partners Alliance for Progress, 1969-72, nat. bd. dirs., 1970-72. Served with AUS, 1951-54. Decorated Combat Infantryman's Badge, Korean Service medal with 3 battle stars; named Outstanding Young Man of Year, Fullerton Jr. C. of C., 1967. Mem. State Bar Calif., Am. (antitrust, internat., corp., banking and bus. law sects.), Los Angeles, Orange County bar assns., Calif. Trial Lawyers Assn., Kent Inn of Phi Delta Phi, Phi Sigma Kappa. Home: 24762 Red Lodge Pl Laguna Hills CA 92653 Office: Suite 800 1200 N Main St Santa Ana CA 92701

TUPPER, ALLISON DOUGLAS, cons. forensic engr.; b. Truro, N.S., Can., Jan. 15, 1942; s. Douglas B. and Janet Pierce (Vincent) T.; engring. cert. Mt. Allison U., 1962; B.Eng. in Chem. Engring., N.S. Tech. Coll., 1964; m. Helen Jean Vincent, May 28, 1966; children—Ted Vincent, Kristin Margaret. Engr., Gulf Oil Can. Ltd., Ont. and N.S., 1967-73; asso. cons. Provincial Indsl. Services Ltd., Halifax, N.S., 1973-75; pres. A.D. Tupper & Assos., Ltd., Cons. Forensic Engrs., Halifax, 1975—, Applied Tech. (Can.) Ltd., Mgmt. and Planning Cons., Halifax, 1978—; dir. Eastcan Fin. Services Ltd., Halifax. Served as officer Corps of Elec. and Mech. Engrs., Royal Canadian Army, 1959-67. Registered profl. engr., N.S., N.B., P.E.I., Nfld. Mem. Arbitrators Inst. Can. (dir. Atlantic br. 1979—), ASHRAE, Canadian Soc. Chem. Engrs. (sec. conf. 1978), Chem. Inst. Can., Engring. Inst. Can., Ins. Inst. Can., Internat. Assn. Arson Investigators, N.B. Assn. Profl. Engrs., Nfld. Assn. Profl. Engrs., N.S. Assn. Profl. Engrs., P.E.I. Assn. Profl. Engrs., Photog. Soc. Am. (dist. rep. 1980—). Mem. United Ch. of Can. Club: Rotary (sec., dir. Port Hawkesbury chpt. 1969-71). Home: 60 Lorne Ave Dartmouth NS B2Y 3E7 Canada Office: PO Box 71 Halifax NS B3J 2L4 Canada

TURBIDY, JOHN BERRY, mfg. co. exec.; b. Rome, Ga., Oct. 18, 1928; s. Joseph Leo and Louyse (Berry) T.; grad. Darlington Sch., 1945; B.A., Duke, 1950; postgrad. N.Y.U., 1952, Emory U., 1954-56; m. Joan Marsales, Dec. 19, 1958; children—John Berry, Trevor Martin. Various indsl. relations positions Lockheed Aircraft Ga. Co., Marietta, 1951-56; gen. mgmt. cons. McKinsey & Co., N.Y.C. and London, 1956-63; v.p. adminstrn. ITT Europe, Inc., Brussels, Belgium, 1963-64, v.p., group exec. European consumer products, 1964-65, v.p., group exec. for No. Europe, 1965-67; corporate v.p. adminstrn. Celanese Corp., N.Y.C., 1967-68, pres. SIACE, S.P.A., subs., Milan, Italy, 1968-69; chmn. bd. The Vecta Group, Dallas, 1970-74; v.p. corp. devel. IU Internat. Corp., Phila., 1974-76, sr. v.p., 1976-78, exec. v.p., 1978—. Served with USNR, 1952. Clubs: Racquet (Phila.); Atrium (N.Y.C.); Windham (N.Y.) Mountain; Merion Golf, Merion Cricket (Ardmore, Pa.). Home: 909 Morris Ave Bryn Mawr PA 19010 Office: 1500 Walnut St Philadelphia PA

TURBYFILL, JOHN RAY, ry. exec.; b. Newland, N.C., Sept. 28, 1931; s. Thomas Manuel and Della Isabell (Braswell) T.; B.A., Roanoke Coll., 1953; LL.B., U. Va., 1956; m. Joyce Lorraine Wainwright Bolton, Aug. 14, 1954; children—Karen Denise, John Ray. Admitted to Va., N.Y. bars, 1956; asso. mem. firm Cravath, Swaine & Moore, N.Y.C., 1956-60; mem. law dept. Norfolk & Western Ry. Co., Roanoke, Va., 1960-70; sr. v.p. Erie Lackawanna Ry. Co. and Delaware & Hudson Ry. Co., Cleve., 1970-72; v.p. Dereco, Inc., Cleve., 1970-72, 73—; v.p. adminstrn. Norfolk & Western Ry. Co., Roanoke, 1972-74, v.p. finance, 1974-80, exec. v.p., 1980—; v.p. Va. Holding Corp., Roanoke, 1973—; dir. Ill. Terminal R.R. Co., St. Louis, Fairport, Painesville & Eastern Ry. Co., Fairport Harbor, Norfolk, Franklin & Danville Ry. Co., Suffolk, Pocahontas Land Corp., Roanoke. Mem. Am. Bar Assn., Roanoke Valley C. of C. (v.p. 1974-76, pres. 1976), Phi Delta Phi. Democrat. Home: 2860 S Jefferson St Roanoke VA 24014 Office: 8 N Jefferson St Roanoke VA 24042

TURELL, ROBERT LAWRENCE, ins. agy. exec.; b. Far Rockaway, N.Y., May 12, 1938; s. Norman I. and Annette (Lichter) T.; B.S., Am. U., 1960; m. Marjorie Steisel, June 7, 1961; children—Laurence B., Jeffrey L., Laura B. Agt., N.Y. Life Ins. Co., 1961—, charter mem. of chmn.'s council; pres. Ins. Design Assos., N.Y.C., 1974—. Served with U.S. Army, 1960-61. C.L.U. Mem. Life Underwriters Assn. N.Y.C. (dir.), Million Dollar Round Table. Home: Stratford Rd Harrison NY 10528 Office: 2 Penn Plaza New York NY 10001

TURI, LEONARD FRANK, data processing cons. and mktg. co. exec.; b. Camden, N.J., Jan. 16, 1939; s. Frank Joseph and Rose Ann (Altimore) T.; A. Arch., Temple U., 1959; B.S. in Bus. Adminstrn., Rutgers U., 1970; LL.B., LaSalle Extension U., 1977; certificate in data processing Inst. for Certification Computer Profls., 1977; m. Irene Turi; children—Lorraine, Leonard. Mgr. programming Gen. Electric Co., Phila., 1962-67; mgr. N.Y.C. office Keystone Computer Assos., 1967-72; mgr. dept. computer applications CACI, Inc., N.Y.C., 1972-77; founder, pres. TMS Tech. Mktg. Services, Inc., N.Y.C., 1977—; pres. Profit Mgmt. Systems, Inc., 1978—; tchr. in field. Chmn. Ocean United Soccer Assn., 1978—. Author: A Quick Look at Database Technology, 1977; (with M. Daniels) Privacy Legislation—Trends and Impact on Computerized Information, 1977; Can a Small Business Computer System Improve Your Profits?, 1978. Office: 122 E 42d St New York NY 10017

TURIACE, FRANK ANTHONY, JR., appliance distbr., mfg. exec.; b. Los Angeles, Sept. 13, 1931; s. Frank Anthony and Josephine (Smaldino) T.; A.A., Glendale Coll., 1957; m. Eleanor Hlipala, July 14, 1973; children—Donella Angela, Joni Ann, Kenneth Anthony. Mem. Los Angeles Police Dept., 1954-64; pres., chmn. bd. Tap-King Corp., Los Angeles, 1964—; mem. distbrs. council Fedders Corp., Edison, N.J.; mem. pres.'s club Gibson Appliance Corp., Greenville, Mich. Served to staff sgt. USMC, 1950-54; Korea. Decorated Purple Heart. Life mem. 1st Marine Div. Assn. Republican. Roman Catholic. Patentee combined portable bar and soda fountain, portable soda fountain, fishing rod-holding sand spike.

TURNER, ARTHUR PAUL, savs. and loan exec.; b. Steele, Ala., June 13, 1914; s. Norman John and Eleanor Lou (Bryant) T.; student Jacksonville State Coll., 1931-32; A.B., U. Ala., 1936, M.A., 1952; postgrad. Howard Coll., Birmingham, Ala., 1939; m. Nancy Lee Holladay, Oct. 1, 1938; 1 son, Robert Paul. Tchr., prin. St. Clair County (Ala.) Schs., 1936-42, asst. supt., 1946-58; pres., mng. officer St. Clair Fed. Savs. & Loan Assn., Pell City, Ala., 1959—. Mem. St. Clair County Democratic Exec. Com., 1960-72; mem. City Council, Pell City, 1971—; chmn. bd. St. Clair County Library, Coosa Valley Regional Library; mem. exec. com. Choccolocco council Boy Scouts Am. Served to capt. AUS, 1942-46; PTO. Mem. U.S. (dir. 1971-73), Ala. (exec. com. 1968-69, pres. 1969-70) savs. and loan leagues, Ala. Sch. Transp. Assn. (pres. 1955), U. Ala. Alumni Assn. (pres. St. Clair County chpt., past dist. v.p.), Am. Legion, VFW, Kappa Phi Kappa, Phi Delta Kappa. Baptist (deacon). Mason, Rotarian. Home: 927 25th St N Pell City AL 35125 Office: 1920 First Ave N Pell City AL 35125

TURNER, CARL JEANE, electronics engr.; b. Sevierville, Tenn., July 27, 1933; s. Kenneth Albert and Lenna Faye (Christopher) T.; B.S.Ed., B.S.E.E., Columbia Pacific U.; m. Flossie Pearl Ingram, Dec. 11, 1954; children—Marcia, Kenneth, Theresa, Christopher. Enlisted in Fla. Air N.G., 1948, active duty in USAF, 1950, advanced through ranks with service in Korea and Vietnam; ret., 1972; with Itek Corp., 1972-77, 78—, program devel. mgr. Optical Systems div., Athens, Greece, 1978-79, resident program mgr. Applied Tech. div., Ulm, W. Ger., 1979—; sr. engr. analyst, chief instr. E-Systems, Inc., Greenville, Tex., 1977-78. Recipient George Washington Honor medal Freedoms Found., 1965. Mem. IEEE, Assn. Old Crows, Air Force Assn., Armed Forces Communications and Electronics Assn., Order Seasoned Weasels. Republican. Baptist. Author, editor electronic warfare mgmt. courses. Office: 645 Almanor Ave Sunnyvale CA 94086

TURNER, CHARLES LAWRENCE, coll. dean; b. St. Louis, Feb. 27, 1936; s. Seneca B. and Lester (McRae) T.; B.A., So. Ill. U., Carbondale, 1962; M.S., So. Ill. U., Edwardsville, 1976; Cert. of completion Bus. Mgmt. Inst., Stanford U., 1980; m. Karen Kaegel, Sept. 4, 1971. Mktg. rep. Shell Oil Co., St. Louis, 1966-70; dir. planning Human Devel. Corp., St. Louis, 1970-73; asst. to pres. State Community Coll., East St. Louis, Ill., 1973-77, dean adminstrv. services, 1977—; cons. community relations and communications. Bd. dirs. Alliance for Regional Community Health, 1974-75, Ill. Coll. Relations Council, 1975-77. Served with USMC, 1954-57. Mem. Nat. Assn. Coll. and Univ. Bus. Officers (editorial bd.), Assn. Sch. Bus. Ofcls., Ill. Community Coll. Bus. Adminstrs. Democrat. Episcopalian. Club: Kappa Alpha Psi. Office: 417 Missouri Ave East Saint Louis IL 62201

TURNER, EUGENE ANDREW, glass container co. exec.; b. Bridgeton, N.J., Aug. 7, 1928; s. Benjamin and Pearl (Wolbert) T.; ed. Mich. State U., 1968, Columbia U. Bus. Sch., 1980; m. June McHenry, Dec. 3, 1950; 1 dau., Mary Ann. With Owens Ill. Corp., Toledo, Ohio, 1951-73; v.p., gen. mgr. Anchor Hocking Corp., v.p. adminstrn. Midland Glass Co., Cliffwood, N.J., 1973-76, pres., 1981—, also dir. Lancaster, Ohio, 1976-81. Club: Seaview Country (Absecon, N.J.). Office: PO Box 557 Cliffwood NJ 07721

TURNER, GERALD ALLEN, engring. co. exec.; b. Cleve., Feb. 11, 1948; s. Rudolph Allen and Betty Jean Turner; A.S. in Elec.-Electronic Tech. (scholar), Cuyahoga Community Coll., 1968; B.S. in Elec.-Mech. Engring. (Cleve. Electric Illuminating Co. scholar), Cleve. State U., 1975; M.B.A., Baldwin-Wallace Coll., 1981. Elec. engr. Cleve. Electric Illuminating Co., 1968-78; research cons., instr. biomed. sci. and parapsychology New Age Centre Hdqrs., Toronto, Ont., Can., 1978-79; cons. indsl. br. Ont. Ministry Industry and Tourism, 1978-79; pres. Turner & Knight, Inc., engrs., Cleve., 1979—; instr. electronic tech. Cuyahoga Community Coll., Cleve., 1976—; instr. elec.-electronic tech., elec. power systems design Cleve. State U., 1980—. Served with USN, 1970-71. Mem. Nat. Soc. Profl. Engrs., IEEE, Cleve. Engring. Soc., Assn. Energy Engrs., Greater Cleve. Growth Assn., Council Smaller Enterprises (Cleve. and state legis. coms. 1980—). Inventor biofeedback brainwave monitor. Home and Office: 17722 Tarkington Ave Cleveland OH 44128

TURNER, GUYON WOLF, broadcast co. exec.; b. N.Y.C., Feb. 20, 1942; s. Frank and Barbara Kemp (Buehler) T.; student Carnegie Mellon U., 1960-62; B.A. in Econs., Washington and Jefferson Coll., 1964; M.B.A., Rutgers U., 1971; m. Judith Ann Wible, June 29, 1968; children—Elizabeth Wynne, Katherine Barbara. Sr. investment analyst Prudential Ins. Co. Am., Newark, 1967-71; gen. mgr. Greater Phila. Venture Capital Corp., Inc., 1971-75; v.p., treas. Broadcast Enterprises Nat., Inc., Phila., 1975—; dir. Capital Corp. Am. Chmn. acad. com.-ABC in Lower Merion, Inc., Ardmore, Pa., 1973-77, fin. com., 1977—. Served with U.S. Army, 1964-66. Mem. Broadcast Fin. Mgmt. Assn., TV and Radio Advt. Club, Am. Judicature Soc., Beta Gamma Sigma, Omicron Delta Epsilon. Club: Raquet (Phila.). Home: 400 N Ithan Ave Rosemont PA 19010 Office: 1211 Chestnut St Suite 202 Philadelphia PA 19107

TURNER, HENRY BROWN, govt. ofcl.; b. N.Y.C., Sept. 3, 1936; s. Henry Brown and Gertrude (Adams) T.; A.B., Duke U., 1958; M.B.A., Harvard U., 1962; m. Sarah Jean Thomas, June 7, 1958; children—Larua Eleanor, Steven Bristow, Nancy Carolyn. Controller, Fin. Corp. Ariz., Phoenix, 1962-64; treas., dir. corp. planning Star-Kist Foods, Terminal Island, Calif., 1964-67; 1st v.p., dir. Mitchun, Jones & Templeton, Los Angeles, 1967-73; asst. sec. Dept. Commerce, Washington, 1973-74; v.p. fin. N-Ren Corp., Cin., 1975-76; v.p. Oppenheimer & Co., N.Y.C., 1976-78; exec. v.p., mng. dir. corp. fin. Shearson Hayden Stone Inc., N.Y.C., 1978-79; sr. mng. dir. Ardshiel Assos. Inc., N.Y.C., 1980—; dir. Mobex, Cousteau Group, Korn/Ferry Internat., Redken Labs., Exec. Confs., Ltd., Swift-Ships Inc., Shirley of Atlanta, Inc., Monroc, Inc., MacDonald & Co., Daltmans Internat. Sponsor, Jr. Achievement, 1964-67. Served to lt. USNR, 1958-60. Mem. Fed. Govt. Accts. Assn. (hon.), Omicron Delta Kappa. Club: Harvard Bus. Sch. of So. Calif. (dir.). Office: 200 Park Ave New York NY 10017

TURNER, JAMES THOMAS, paper mfg. co. exec.; b. Hendersonville, N.C., Aug. 17, 1944; s. Robert W. and Billie T.; B.S., Va. Poly. Inst. and State U., 1967, M.S., 1971; m. Judith Luxton, Dec. 30, 1967; children—Hilary E., Scott C., Sarah R., Martha C. Tchr. Radford (Va.) pub. schs., 1968; instr. Va. Inst. Tech., 1969-70, grad. teaching asst., 1971; mem. faculty, asst. to head economics dept. U. Akron, 1972-73; indsl. relations Packaging Corp. Am., Rittman, Ohio, 1973-74, corp. dir. manpower, 1975-76; mgr. manpower and orgn. devel. Mead Corp., Dayton, Ohio, 1976-77, mgr. corp. staff personnel, 1977—; labor cons. Ohio State Labor Edn. Program, 1972. Chmn., Chippawa Dist. council Boy Scouts Am., 1976; v.p. Rittman United Way, 1974, campaign chmn., 1975. Chmn. bd. dirs. Multiple Sclerosis Soc. Dayton. Mem. Internat. Register Orgn. and Devel. Profls., Am. Soc. Tng. and Devel., Am. Soc. Personnel Adminstrn. Republican. Lutheran. Author: Introduction to Labor, 1975. Contbr. articles to profl. jours. Home: 629 Johnson Rd Chillicothe OH 45601 Office: No 12 Paper Machine Chillicothe OH 45601

TURNER, JOHN ALFRED, JR., lawyer; b. Washington, Sept. 10, 1948; s. John Alfred and Lois (Pair) T.; B.A., Howard U., 1970; J.D., Georgetown U., 1973, LL.M., 1977; m. Cecelia Wirtz, Aug. 31, 1974; 1 son, John Alfred III. Admitted to Pa. bar, 1973, D.C. bar, 1974, U.S. Supreme Ct. bar, 1977; law clk. to assoc. judge D.C. Ct. Appeals, 1974-75; asso. counsel Fed. Privacy Protection Commn., Washington, 1975-77; partner firm Dixon and Turner, Washington, 1978—. Mem. exec. bd. Washington Urban League. Named Man of Yr., Alpha chpt. Omega Psi Phi, 1969. Mem. Washington Bar Assn. (v.p.). Office: 1420 N St NW Washington DC 20005

TURNER, LEON L., JR., transp. exec.; b. Columbus, Ohio, Feb. 21, 1948; s. Leon L. and Mildred C. Turner; B.S. cum laude, Lowell Tech. Inst., 1970; M.B.A., Stanford U., 1973. Fin. analyst Standard Oil Co. of Calif., San Francisco, 1972-76; venture capitalist Hurt, Hurt & Turner, Cambridge, Mass., 1976-77; planning mgr. Sperry and Hutchinson Co., N.Y.C., 1977-78; joint ventures mgr. Sea-Land Industries, Inc., Menlo Park, N.J., 1978—. Mem. Am. Mgmt. Assn., Stanford Bus. Alumni, Omega Psi Phi. Home: 307 Prospect Ave Apt 3H Hackensack NJ 07601 Office: PO Box 900 Edison NJ 08817

TURNER, LINDA VILLEGAS, data processor; b. McAllen, Tex., Feb. 26, 1949; d. Macario Bernardo and María DeJesús (Palacios) Villegas; B.A. in Chemistry (Univ. scholar 1966-69), Our Lady of Lake Coll., San Antonio, 1969. Programmer/analyst Spiegel Inc., Chgo., 1969-72; programming cons. Programming Methods, Inc., Chgo., 1972-73; sr. programmer/analyst Conti Commodities Services, Chgo., 1973-74; sr. systems analyst Combined Ins. Co. Am., Chgo., 1974-76; tech. specialist Applied Info. Devel. Co., Oakbrook, Ill., 1976-77; data processing generalist Berger, Vernay & Co., Houston, 1977-79; mgr. bus. systems and programming Rohr Industries, Chula Vista, Calif., 1979—; cons. in field. Chmn. service com. exploring div. South Bay Area council Boy Scouts Am., 1980. Mem. Am. Prodn. and Inventory Control Soc., Nat. Mgmt. Assn. Roman Catholic. Home: 6304 Friars Rd Apt 343 San Diego CA 92108 Office: Rohr Industries Foot of H St Chula Vista CA 92010

TURNER, LOYD LEONARD, corp. exec.; b. Claude, Tex., Nov. 5, 1917; s. James Richard and Maude (Brown) T.; B.A., Baylor U., 1939, M.A., 1940; postgrad. U. Pa., 1940-42; m. Lee Madeleine Barr, Apr. 13, 1944; children—Terry Lee, Loyd Lee. Instr., U. Pa., 1940-42; pub. relations coordinator Consol. Vultee Aircraft Corp., San Diego, 1946-48, dir. pub. relations, Ft. Worth, 1948-53; asst. to pres. Ft. Worth div. Gen. Dynamics Corp., 1953-72; exec. asst. to chmn. bd. and pres. Tandy Corp., Ft. Worth, 1972-76; v.p. Tandy Corp., 1976—. Pres., Ft. Worth Pub. Library Bd., 1958-63; v.p. Ft. Worth Bd. Edn., 1962-65, pres., 1965-71; mem. exec. com. Tex. Assn. Sch. Bds., 1966-71, v.p., 1970-71; mem. steering com., council big city bds. Nat. Sch. Bds. Assn., 1967-69, mem. Gov's Com. on Pub. Sch. Edn., 1966-69; pres. Tex. Council Maj. Sch. Dists., 1968-69, Baylor U. Devel. Council, 1975-77, Casa Mañana Musicals, 1978-80; bd. dirs. Tarrant County chpt. A.R.C., 1956-59, Tex. Com. Pub. Edn., 1961-69, bd. dirs. Ft. Worth Parenting Guidance Center, 1975-78, Ft. Worth Child Study Center, 1975—, Longhorn council Boy Scouts Am., 1977—, Assn. Grad. Edn. and Research, 1978-80, One Broadway Plaza, 1978—, Tex. Research League, 1979—, Ft. Worth Safety Council, 1980—, Arts Council Ft. Worth and Tarrant County, 1980—; trustee Pub. Communication Found. N. Tex., 1970-76; mem. planning and research council United Way, 1977—; mem. Christian Edn. Coordinating Bd., 1977-80; v.p. Ft. Worth Crime Resistance Task Force, 1977—. Served with USAAF, 1942-46. Named Library Trustee of Year, Tex. Library Assn., 1961, Pres. of Best Bd. of Large Sch. Systems in U.S., NEA, 1968; recipient citation Air Force Assn., 1962; Leadership awards W. Tex. C. of C., 1966, 69, Distinguished Service award Tex. Assn. Sch. Bds., 1971. Mem. Pub. Relations Soc. Am. (pres. N. Tex. chpt. 1977, recipient Paul M. Lund public service award 1980), Tex. Assn. Bus. (dir. 1977—), Air Force Assn., Nat. Mgmt. Assn., Friends of Fort Worth Library (v.p. 1971), Advt. Club Ft. Worth (dir. 1975-79, pres. 1977-78), Ft. Worth C. of C. (dir. 1974-76, 78—, chmn. edn. com. 1976), Baylor U. Alumni Assn. (dir. 1958-61), Assn. Higher Edn. (v.p. 1980—), Sigma Delta Chi (pres. Ft. Worth 1961-62). Baptist. Rotarian (dir. Ft. Worth 1972-76, pres. 1974-75). Clubs: Ft. Worth Press, Knife and Fork (dir. 1963-66, pres. 1965-66), Colonial Country, Century II. Author: The ABC of Clear Writing, 1954. Home: 3717 Echo Trail Fort Worth TX 76109 Office: 1800 One Tandy Center Fort Worth TX 76102

TURNER, LYLE WILLIS, JR., brokerage firm account exec.; b. Buffalo, Dec. 11, 1933; s. Lyle Willis and Minnie Mae Turner; B.S. in Bus. Adminstrn., U. Tulsa, 1956; m. Kay Lenore Burleson, Nov. 20, 1959; children—Lyle Willis III, Lisa Kay. With Merrill Lynch, Pierce, Fenner & Smith, Tulsa, 1960—, sr. account exec., 1968-73, asst. v.p., 1973-77, v.p., 1977—; adv. dir. Western Nat. Bank, Bigheart Drilling Co.; stock market and econ. talk show host Sta. KXXO. Program chmn. Indian Nations council Boy Scouts Am., 1975—, bd. dirs., 1980—, chmn. Scout-o-rama, 1976-78. Served to lt. USN, 1956-60. Paul Harris fellow, 1972; Tulsa Community fellow, 1975. Methodist. Clubs: Cedar Ridge Country, Petroleum, Rotary, Merrill Lynch Chmn.'s (charter), Charles E. Merrill Circle. Office: Suite 3960 One Williams Center Tulsa OK 74172

TURNER, MARSHALL CHITTENDEN, JR., med. products co. exec.; b. Santa Monica, Calif., Oct. 10, 1941; s. Marshall Chittenden and Winifred Keating (Hudson) T.; B.S.M.E., Stanford U., 1963, M.S. in Product Design, 1965; M.B.A. with distinction, Harvard U., 1970; m. Jane Ann Curran, Feb. 6, 1965; children—Erin Ross, Benjamin Curran, Brian Marshall. Summer asso. McKinsey & Co., N.Y.C. and Los Angeles, 1969-70; White House fellow, Washington, 1970-71; asst. to adminstr. EPA, Washington, 1971-73; venture capital asso. Crocker Assos., also fin. Sierra R.R. Co., San Francisco, 1973-75; pres., chmn. bd., chief exec. officer Liquid Crystal Tech., Inc., San Leandro, Calif., 1975—; dir. Robert Parker, S.A., Geneva, Hallcrest Products, Inc., Chgo., Bethesda Research Labs. (Md.). Trustee, Reed Union Sch. Dist., Tiburon, Calif., 1977—, chmn., 1978-79; bd. dirs. KQED, Inc., San Francisco. Served to lt. USPHS, 1966-68. Recipient Creative Design award Machinery Inst., 1963. Republican. Contbr. articles on heart assistance to profl. jours.; designer left ventricular bypass pump. Office: 14692 Wicks Blvd San Leandro CA 94577

TURNER, RICHARD LAZEAR, bus. exec.; b. Huntington, W.Va., Feb. 22, 1925; s. Clyde Baker and Jess L. (Lazear) T.; B.A., Yale U., 1948, LL.B., 1951; m. Nancy Elena Riford, June 9, 1951; children—Richard R., Sarah L., James R., Molly L. Admitted to N.Y. bar, 1952; asso. firm Nixon, Hargrave Devans & Dey, from 1951, partner, to 1962; chmn. bd. Schlegel Mfg. Co. (name changed to Schlegel Corp. 1974), Rochester, N.Y., 1962—, chief exec. officer, 1964—, pres., 1972—; dir. Forbes Products Corp., Genesee Brewing Co., Rochester Telephone Corp. (all Rochester); regional bd. dirs. Marine Midland Bank. Trustee, Genesee Country Museum, Mumford, N.Y., Preservation League N.Y. State, Albany, U. Rochester; bd. dirs., past chmn. Hochstein Sch. Music; bd. dirs. Vis. Nurse Service Rochester and Monroe County. Served with USMCR, 1943-46. Mem. Indsl. Mgmt. Council (dir., chmn.), Rochester Area C. of C. (trustee). Office: 400 East Ave PO Box 23113 Rochester NY 14692

TURNER, RODERICK L., consumer packaged products mfg. co. exec.; b. Mineola, N.Y., June 1, 1931; s. Claude E. and Eulalia (Rodriguez) T.; B.A., Cornell U., 1952; m. Teresa C. Vadetaire, May, 1957; children—R. Bradford, Melissa A. Vice pres. Benton & Bowles, Inc., N.Y.C., 1958-63; group product mgr. personal products div. Colgate-Palmolive Co., N.Y.C., 1963-67, group product mgr. h.p. div., 1967-68, pres., gen. mgr. Colgate Canadian Co., 1969-72, v.p. mktg. services div., 1973, corp. v.p., gen. mgr. Western hemisphere div. Colgate-Palmolive Co., 1974-76, gen. mgr. European div., 1976-78, group v.p. internat., 1979—. Served to 1st lt. AUS, 1952-54; Korea. Clubs: Vertical, Cornell (N.Y.C.). Home: 36 Cornwell Beach Rd Sands Point NY 11050 Office: Colgate Palmolive Co 300 Park Ave New York NY 10020

TURNER, VANGIE LUELLA, elec. wholesale and lighting co. exec.; b. Lawndale, N.C., June 26, 1920; d. Lawrence Thomas and Lillie Mae (Norman) T.; student Blantons Bus. Coll., Asheville, N.C., 1940-41, U. S.C., 1960, LaSalle U., 1967-70, S.C. Sch. Real Estate, 1977. Supr. proof dept. Citizen & So. Nat. Bank, Spartanburg, S.C., 1941-43; supr. bookkeeping dept., cashier First Nat. Bank, Morganton, N.C., 1943-47; asst. to clerical supr., jr. accountant Durham (N.C.) City and County Health Dept., 1950-52; sr. accountant Greensboro (N.C.)

County Welfare dept., 1952-53; office mgr., accountant Dodge-Plymouth Dealer, Shelby, N.C., 1953-58; corporate accountant Capital Electric Supply Co., Columbia, S.C., 1959—, exec. sec.-treas., 1965—, also dir., trustee retirement plans. Trustee Coll. Place United Methodist Ch., Columbia, 1976-78. Mem. Nat., Eau Claire (treas. 1978-79) bus. and profl. women's clubs. Democrat. Club: Off-Beat Organ, Bridge. Home: 600 Glenthorne Rd Columbia SC 29203 Office: 2015 Marion St Columbia SC 29201

TURNER, WILLIAM COCHRANE, cons. economist; b. Red Oak, Iowa, May 27, 1929; s. James Lyman and Josephine (Cochrane) T.; B.S., Northwestern U., 1952; m. Cynthia Dunbar, July 16, 1955; children—Scott Christopher, Craig Dunbar, Douglas Gordon. Pres., dir. Western Mgmt. Cons., Inc., Phoenix, 1960-74, Western Mgmt. Cons. Europe, S.A., Brussels, 1968-74; U.S. ambassador, permanent rep. OECD, Paris, 1974-77, vice chmn. exec. com., 1976-77, U.S. rep. Energy Policy Commn., 1976-77; mem. U.S. dels. internat. meetings, 1974-77; chmn. Argyle Atlantic Corp., Phoenix, 1977—; dir. Pullman, Inc., 1977—, Nabisco, Inc., 1978—, Energy Transition Corp., 1978—, Goodyear Tire & Rubber Co., 1978—; mem. European adv. com. IBM World Trade Europe, Africa, Middle East Corp., 1977—; mem. Gen. Electric of Brazil adv. council Gen. Electric Co., Coral Gables, Fla., 1979—; mem. Caterpillar of Brazil adv. council Caterpillar Tractor Co., Peoria, Ill., 1979—. Bd. dirs. Atlantic Council U.S., 1977—, Am. Grad. Sch. Internat. Mgmt., 1970—; bd. govs. Atlantic Inst. Internat. Studies, Paris, 1977—; adv. bd. Center Strategic and Internat. Studies, Georgetown U., 1977—; bd. govs. Am. Hosp. of Paris, 1974-77; trustee Nat. Symphony Orch. Assn., Washington, 1973—, Am. Sch., Paris, 1974-77, Orme Sch., Mayer, Ariz., 1970-74, Phoenix Country Day Sch., 1971-74; mem. nat. councils Salk Inst., 1978—; mem. U.S. Adv. Com. Internat. Edn. and Cultural Affairs, 1969-74; nat. rev. bd. Center Cultural and Tech. Interchange between East and West, 1970-74; mem. vestry Am. Cathedral, Paris, 1976-77; pres., bd. dirs. Phoenix Symphony Assn., 1969-70; chmn. Ariz. Joint Econ. Devel. Com., 1967-68; exec. com., bd. dirs. Ariz. Dept. Econ. Planning and Devel., 1968-70; chmn. bd. Ariz. Crippled Children's Services, 1964-65; treas. Ariz. Republican Com., 1956-57. Recipient East-West Center Distinguished Service award, 1977. Mem. Internat. C. of C. (trustee, exec. com. U.S. council 1977—), Council Fgn. Relations, Phoenix 40. Episcopalian. Clubs: Travellers (Paris); Metropolitan (N.Y.C.); Paradise Valley (Ariz.) Country. Home: Paradise Valley AZ Office: 4350 E Camelback Rd Suite 240-B Phoenix AZ 85018

TURNEY, WILLIAM OTTIS, JR., co. exec.; b. Decatur, Ala., Oct. 3, 1945; s. William O. and Libbie (Legg) T.; B.S., Austin Peay State U., 1966; M.B.A., Memphis State U., 1968; m. Patricia Maroney, Feb. 28, 1970; children—Robert Travis, Karen Marie. Asst. to v.p. fin. LTV Aerospace Corp., Dallas, 1968-71; dir. planning and bus devel. Addressograph Multigraph Corp., Cleve., 1971-73; dir. fin. services Internat. Systems and Controls Corp., Houston, 1973-74; exec. v.p., sec., chief fin. officer Stratford of Tex., Inc., Houston, 1974-79; sr. v.p. fin. and adminstrn. Ridgway's Inc., Houston, 1979—; dir. Glazier Foods Co., Houston, Independence Isle Corp., New Orleans, Brazos Capital Corp., Houston, Uddo Co., New Orleans. Served to 2d lt. USAR, 1967. Republican. Episcopalian. Clubs: Westside Tennis, Met. Tennis, Met. Racquet, Houston City. Home: 11623 Highgrove Dr Houston TX 77077 Office: 5711 Hillcroft Houston TX 77036

TUROV, DANIEL, fin. writer, investment exec.; b. Bklyn., Jan. 15, 1947; s. Bernard and Mildred (Stevelman) T.; B.A. in Econs., CCNY, 1969; m. Rosalyn B. Kalishock, Aug. 25, 1968; 1 son, Joshua Nathaniel. Account exec. Walston & Co., 1969-72, Thomson McKinnon Securities, 1972-75; sr. v.p. Faulkner Dawkins & Sullivan, 1975-77, Cowen & Co., N.Y.C., 1977-80; dir. Turov Investment Group div. Moore & Schley, Cameron & Co., N.Y.C., 1980—; chmn. Philtrum Advt. Corp., 1980—; editor New Innovations Pub. Corp., 1979—. faculty N.Y. Inst. Fin., New Sch. Social Research. Mem. N.Y. Instl. Options Soc. Author: Investment Hedging: The Conservative Approach to Aggressive Investing, 1980; author Turov on Investments and Hedging, monthly, 1972-80. Contbr. articles to Fin. Analysts Jour., N.Y. Times, Barrons, chpt. in book. Home: Box 58 Ramsey NJ 07446 Office: Turov Investment Group 26 Broadway New York NY 10004

TURPIN, THOMAS EMBURY, bank data processing exec.; b. Columbus, Ind., Aug. 18, 1942; s. Harold Willard and Louella Jeanette (Empey) T.; B.S., Ind. U., 1965, M.A.T., 1966; m. Karon Sue Squier, June 9, 1966; children—Tanya Anne, Christine Jo. Programmer, account sales mgr. NCR Corp., Muncie, Ind., 1967-72, sr. instr. fin. sales edn., mem. fin. systems mktg. staff, 1972-76, fin. dist. mgr., 1977-78; regional v.p. Banking div. Computer Services, Inc., Paducah, Ky., 1978—; secondary tchr. YMCA fund chmn., 1976. Served to sgt., ROTC, 1962-63. Mem. Nat. Automated Bank Servicers, Am. Mgmt. Assn., Paducah C. of C., Theta Chi. Methodist. Clubs: Lions, Rolling Hill Country, Masons. Developed fin. devel. course for fin. edn., 1973-74. Home: PO Box 1602 Audubon Dr Paducah KY 42001 Office: PO Box 60 13th and Broadway Paducah KY 42001

TURRELL, RICHARD HORTON, banker; b. Kingston, Pa., Apr. 9, 1925; s. George Henry and Sarah Margaret (Clark) T.; student Cornell U., Ithaca, N.Y., 1943; B.S. in Commerce with honors, Washington and Lee U., 1949; m. Sally Ann Wolfe, May 28, 1955; children—Richard Horton, David Clark, Douglas Wolfe. Asst. to pres. Delaware Lackawanna & Western Coal Co., N.Y.C., 1949-58; registered rep. Auchincloss, Parker & Redpath, N.Y.C., 1958-61; with Fiduciary Trust Co. of N.Y., N.Y.C., 1961—, v.p., 1965-68, sr. v.p., 1968-71, sr. v.p., sec., 1971—; adv. council Lehigh Portland Cement Co.; dir. Wittemann Co., Duchamp Corp., Pine-Raleigh Corp. Treas., trustee Simon's Rock Coll., 1968-79, Monmouth Coll., 1980—; pres. Millburn-Short Hills (N.J.) Republican Club, 1969-71, chmn., 1971-73, 74—. Served with Signal Corps U.S. Army, 1943-46. Mem. Newcomen Soc., Pa. Soc., Chatham Fish and Game Protective Assn., Washington and Lee Alumni (pres. 1971-72), Phi Beta Kappa, Omicron Delta Kappa, Beta Gamma Sigma, Phi Eta Sigma, Alpha Kappa Psi. Episcopalian. Clubs: Baltusrol Golf, Capitol Hill, Masons, Shriners. Home: 26 Hobart Gap Rd Short Hills NJ Short Hills NJ 07078 Office: Two World Trade Center Suite 9400 New York NY 10048

TURRENTINE, ROBERT CLEVELAND, boot mfg. co. exec.; b. Steubenville, Ohio, 1925; s. Chesley Dean and Grace Lillian (Evans) T.; student Austin Peay State U., 1946-47; m. Imogene Morgan, May 31, 1951; children—Carol, Richard, Ross Grace. With Acme Boot Co., Clarksville, Tenn., 1947—, v.p. ops., 1950-62, pres., 1962—, chief exec. officer, 1970—. Served with USAAF, 1943-46. Mem. Am. Footwear Industries Assn., Tenn. Mfrs. Assn., Taxpayers Assn. Methodist. Office: PO Box 749 Clarksville TN 37040

TUSCHMAN, JAMES MARSHALL, steel co. exec.; lawyer; b. Toledo, Nov. 28, 1941; s. Chester and Harriet (Harris) T.; B.S. in Bus., Miami U., Oxford, Ohio, 1963; J.D., Ohio State U., 1966; m. Ina S. Cheloff, Sept. 2, 1967; children—Chad Michael, Jon Stephen, Sari Anne. Admitted to Ohio bar, 1966; since practiced in Toledo, partner firm Shumaker, Loop & Kendrick, 1966—; chmn. bd., sec. Tuschman Steel Co., Toledo, 1969-76; vice chmn. bd. Kripke Tuschman Industries, Inc., Toledo, 1976—; chmn. bd., sec. Toledo Steel Supply Co., 1969—; pres. Tuschman Realty and Investment Co., 1977—; partner Starr Ave. Co., Toledo; dir. Superior Cos., Inc., Ft. Wayne, Ind., Physicians Insuring Exchange, Toledo. Mem. Am. (com. on law and medicine), Ohio, Toledo bar assns., Def. Research Inst., Soc. Hosp. Attys., Zeta Beta Tau, Phi Delta Phi. Jewish. Clubs: Glengary Country, Toledo. Home: 5240 Coldstream Rd Toledo OH 43623 Office: 500 Libbey-Owens-Ford Bldg Toledo OH 43624

TUSH, MASON LEE, distilling and importing co. exec.; b. Louisville, Dec. 26, 1918; s. John Otha and Elsa Louise (Stein) T.; A.B., U. Louisville, 1941; M.B.A. (scholar), Northwestern U.; m. Anna Lucille Coldiron, June 24, 1946; children—Lesleigh Ann, Mason Lee, John William, Patti Lynn. Dir. mktg. research Reynolds Metals, Louisville, 1946-48; asst. prof. econs. U. Louisville, 1948-50; dir. promotion Ky. C. of C., Louisville, 1950; with Brown-Forman Distillers Corp., Louisville, 1951—, v.p., area dir., 1966-69, v.p., 1966—; with Joseph Garneau Co., Louisville, 1951—, exec. v.p., 1969-71, dir. mktg., 1971—, pres., 1971—, also dir.; dir. Jaggers Equipment Co., Inc. Mem. psychiat. council Norton Meml. Infirmary Psychiat. Clinic. Served to maj. AUS, 1941-46. Decorated Bronze Star. Mem. Confrerie de la Chaine des Rotisseurs, Confrerie des Chevaliers du Tastevin, Sovereign and Noble Order of Ancient Recioto, Mensa. Club: Masons. Home: 6358 Limewood Circle Louisville KY 40222 Office: PO Box 1080 Louisville KY 40201

TUTHILL, SAMUEL JAMES, utility exec.; b. San Diego, Sept. 6, 1925; s. Marvin James and Nancy Irene (Morgan) T.; A.B., Drew U., Madison, N.J., 1951; M.S. (NSF fellow), Syracuse (N.Y.) U., 1960; M.A. (NDEA fellow, Rodger Dennison 1st prize for research), U. N.D., 1963, Ph.D. (NSF sci. faculty fellow), 1969; m. Constance Huntington Howell, Sept. 7, 1952; children—Susan, James, John. Geologist, N.D. Geol. Survey, 1963-64; asst. prof. geology Muskingum Coll., New Concord, Ohio, 1964-68; leader expdns. to Central Alaska, 1965, 67, 68; state geologist, dir. Iowa Geol. Survey, 1969-75; sci. adv. to sec. interior, 1975; asst. adminstr. Fed. Energy Adminstrn., 1976; sr. v.p. Iowa Electric Light and Power Co., Cedar Rapids, 1977—; pres. Tuthill, Inc., geol. cons., 1979—; adj. prof. geology U. Iowa, 1970-75; collaborating prof. geology Iowa State U., 1971-75. Mem. nat. council Boy Scouts Am., 1976—; public mem. Iowa Energy Policy Council, 1978-79; bd. dirs. Iowa Natural Heritage Found., 1979; Iowa commr. Upper Miss. River Basin Commn., 1980—. Served with USAAF, 1943-45; ETO. Decorated Air medal (3). Fellow Geol. Soc. Am., Explorers Club; mem. Am. Assn. Policy Advisers (dir.), Midwest Gas Assn. (dir.), Sigma Xi. Republican. Episcopalian. Club: Cedar Rapids Country. Contbr. articles to profl. jours. Office: PO Box 351 Cedar Rapids IA 52406

TUTINS, ANTONS, electronics/audio engr.; b. Ludza, Latvia, May 2, 1933; s. Francis and Veronika (Seipulniks) Tutins; came to U.S., 1950, naturalized, 1963; student U. Minn., 1951-55; B.S. in Elec. Engring., Ill. Inst. Tech., 1970; M.B.A., U. Chgo., 1974; m. Raita Snebergs, July 8, 1961; 1 son, Robert. With Motorola Communications div., Chgo., 1964-73; applications engring. supr. Knowles Electronics, Inc., Franklin Park, Ill., 1973-77, product engring. mgr., 1977—. Served with USN, 1955-57. Mem. IEEE, Acoustical Soc. Am., Chgo. Acoustical and Audio Group (pres. 1977-78), Audio Engring. Soc., Midwest Acoustics Soc. (exec. com., pres. 1980), Latvian Cath. Student Assn. Dzintars (pres. 1979—), Am. Latvian Cath. Assn. (sec. 1975-77), Motorola Engring. Club (pres. 1970-71). Roman Catholic. Home: 1338 Briar Ct Des Plaines IL 60018 Office: 3100 N Mannheim St Franklin Park IL 60131

TUTTLE, GORDON MUIR, diversified co. exec.; b. Orange, N.J., Oct. 31, 1922; s. Pierson Muir and Anna Lucille (Libby) T.; A.B., Yale U., 1943; LL.B., Harvard U., 1948; m. Alice Wyker, Jan. 26, 1957; children—Garrett, David, Ann. Admitted to N.Y. bar, 1948; asso. firm Gould & Wilkie, 1948-50, Pruitt, Coursen, Cechler & McLaughlin, 1950-55; with Avco Corp., Greenwich, Conn., 1955—, sec., 1964-68, sr. v.p., 1975—, gen. counsel, 1968—. Served with AUS, 1943-45. Mem. N.Y. State Bar Assn., Assn. Bar City N.Y. Home: 366 Hollow Tree Ridge Rd Darien CT 06820 Office: 1275 King St Greenwich CT 06830

TUTTLE, ROBERT R., chem. co. exec.; b. Prairie Home, Mo., Apr. 10, 1929; s. Joseph Morton and Rylie (Ellis) T.; B.S., U. Mo., 1951; m. Mary A. Mathews, July 15, 1951; children—Barbara J., Mary J., Susan L. Partner, Woodland Farms, 1953-55; sales rep. Am. Agrl. Chem. Co., Higginsville, Mo., 1955-61; sales rep. Calif. Chem. Co., Kansas City, Mo., 1961-66; regional sales asst. Chevron Chem. Co., Ft. Madison, 1966-69, br. mgr., Toledo, 1969-70, dist. mgr., 1970-79, regional mgr., Richland, Wash., 1979—; past pres. Mo. Agrl. Industries Council; dir., pres. Woodland Farms Inc. Served as arty. officer U.S. Army, 1951-53. Mem. Nat. Agrl. Mktg. Assn. Clubs: Brandywine, Maumee Valley Thunderbird. Office: 6148 Kennewick WA 99336

TWEEDIE, LEONARD CHRISTIE, container co. exec.; b. Chgo., May 4, 1932; s. David and Isabel (Heddle) T.; B.A., Coe Coll., 1953; m. Eathel Darnell, Feb. 19, 1954; children—Sherry Lynn, Jack, Douglas. Mgmt. trainee Am. Boxboard Co., Chgo., 1955-58; regional sales mgr. packaging div. Olin Corp., Joliet, Ill., 1958-68; regional mgr. Time Container, Chgo., 1968-69; gen. mgr. Menasha Corp., Chgo., 1969-70, Neenah, Wis., 1970-74, pres. Hartford Container subsidiary, 1972—, also v.p. and gen. mgr. container div., 1976—. Cubmaster, 1955-59, 74—, scoutmaster, 1959-60; pres. PTA, 1974-75. Served with USAF, 1953-55. Mem. T.A.P.P.I., Soc. Packaging and Handling Engrs., Rotary Internat., Tau Kappa Epsilon. Presbyn. Mason, Elk; mem. Order Eastern Star (asso. patron). Home: 1226 Lynrose Ln Neenah WI 54956 Office: PO Box 367 Neenah WI 54956

TWEEDLE, CHARLES E., cons.; b. Pitts., July 3, 1905; s. Charles Ralph and Lillie (Gillen) T.; E.E., Armour Inst. Tech., 1925; postgrad. bus. Northwestern U., U. Chgo., 1925-27; pvt. studies electronics; m. Barbara Bryant, Dec. 31, 1946; 1 dau., Barbara Anne. Asso. tech. sales, 1925-35; pres. Air Devices Corp., Tex., 1935-37; v.p., gen. mgr. Polar Air, Inc., 1937-39; pres. Coastal Engrs., 1939-42; exec. v.p. Askania Regulator Co., 1946-50; gen. mgr. Ga. Kaolin Co., 1950-55; exec. v.p. Birdsey Flour & Feed Mill, Macon, Ga., 1955-65; former chmn. bd. E.A. Issa & Bros. Ltd., Kingston; now cons. First Cayman Bank Ltd., Grand Cayman, B.W.I.; dir. Jacques Scott & Co. Ltd., Terminal Services Ltd., Cayman Tours & Travel Ltd., Security & Alarms Ltd. (all Grand Cayman). Served as lt. comdr. USN, 1942-46; comdr. USNR. Rotarian. Home and office: PO Box 1418 Grand Cayman BWI

TWELLS, JOHN LAWRENCE, mktg. and distbg. co. exec.; b. Flint, Mich., Feb., 1934; s. Robert and Margaret Shaw (MacKillop) T.; B.B.A., U. Toledo, 1957; postgrad. Marquette U., 1975; m. Mary Jane Jentzen, Nov., 1961; children—Linda, John Lawrence, Robert William. Ter. mgr., nat. accounts rep. Motorcraft/Autolite div. Ford Motor Co., Dearborn, Mich., 1950-63; regional sales mgr. MOPAR div. Chrysler Corp., Detroit, 1963-67; asst. gen. mgr. NAPA Genuine Parts Co., Atlanta, 1967-68; gen. mgr. John MacKillop & Co., Inc., Milw., 1968—; mgr. replacement parts Baker Material Handling Corp., a joint venture of Linde AG (W. Ger.) and United Technologies Corp., Cleve., 1976-78, gen. sales mgr. Amweld Bldg. Products div. Am. Welding & Mfg. Co., Niles, Ohio, 1978—; lectr. in field. Deacon, Immanuel Presbyterian Ch., Milw., 1974-76. Served with U.S. Army, 1957-59. Recipient Disting. Mktg. award Sales & Mktg. Mgmt., 1980. Mem. Am. Def. Preparedness Assn., Am. Inst. Indsl. Engrs., Am. Legion, VFW. Republican. Club: Rotary. Contbr. articles on microfiche, inventory control, personnel selection, motivation and evaluation to profl. jours. Home: 8996 Sherwood Dr NE Warren OH 44484 Office: 100 Plant St Niles OH 44446

TWIGG-SMITH, THURSTON, newspaper pub. co. exec.; b. Honolulu, Aug. 17, 1921; s. William and Margaret Carter (Thurston) T.-S.; B.E., Yale U., 1942; m. Bessie Bell, June 9, 1942; children—Elizabeth Twigg-Smith Jenkins, Thurston, William, Margaret Twigg-Smith Fivash, Evelyn Twigg-Smith Fried. With Honolulu Advertiser, 1946—, managing editor, 1954-60, asst. bus. mgr., 1960-61, pub., pres., dir., 1961—; pres., dir. Persis Corp., Honolulu, 1961—; chmn., dir. Asa Properties, 1970—, Shiny Rock Mining Corp., 1974—, Pacific Comml. Inc., 1977—; dir. Hawaiian Electric Co., Am. Trust Co., Kamehameha Investment Co., First Fed. Savs. & Loan of Honolulu, Tongg Pub. Co. Trustee, Punahou Sch., 1955—, Honolulu Acad. Arts, 1969—; chmn. Honolulu Symphony, 1979—. Served with U.S. Army, 1942-46. Decorated Bronze Star. Congregationalist. Clubs: Oahu Country, Waialae Country, Pacific. Office: Box 3110 Honolulu HI 96802

TWITCHELL, ERVIN EUGENE, constrn. co. exec.; b. Salt Lake City, Mar. 4, 1932; s. Irvin A. and E. Alberta (Davis) T.; student Brigham Young U., 1954, 55; B.A., Calif. State U., Long Beach, 1959; J.D., UCLA, 1966; m. Joyce Newey, Aug. 9, 1957; children—Laurie, Robert, David, Michael. Contracts adminstr. Rockwell-N. Am. Aviation, Seal Beach, Calif., 1966-68; sr. contracts adminstr. McDonnell Douglas Corp., Long Beach, 1968-73; in-house counsel Albert C. Martin & Assos., Los Angeles, 1973-77; admitted to Mich. bar, 1977; corp. counsel, asst. sec. Barton-Malow Co., Detroit, 1977—; instr. bus. law Golden West Coll., Huntington Beach, Calif., 1973-74. Pres., Corona Musical Theatre Assn., 1976; dist. chmn. North Trails dist. Boy Scouts Am., 1978—; various lay leadership positions Mormon Ch. Served with USAF, 1950-52; Korea. Mem. Am. Bar Assn., Am. Trial Lawyers Assn., Mich. Bar Assn., Oakland County Bar Assn., Detroit Bar Assn., Detroit EEO Forum. Republican. Home: 4069 Middlebury Dr Troy MI 48098 Office: Barton-Malow Co 13155 Cloverdale St Oak Park MI 48237

TWOMEY, STEPHEN PAUL, telephone co. ofcl.; b. Newburyport, Mass., Mar. 4, 1948; s. George Edmund and Doris Marie (Creeden) T.; B.S., Ricker Coll., 1972; M.P.A., Suffolk U., 1979; m. Stella Marie Gincauskis, May 1, 1977; children—Danielle Lise, Stephen Paul, Jason Matthew. Communications cons. New Eng. Telephone Co., Boston, 1972-74, account rep., 1974-75, 75-79, service cons., 1975, mgr. mktg. staff, 1979—; instr. mktg. Newbury Jr. Coll., 1974-76. Pres., Turning Point, Inc., Newburyport, 1978—, public speaker, 1979. Recipient Bell Profl. award, 1977, 78. Home: 86 Bignell Rd Billerica MA 01821 Office: 185 Franklin St Room 1408 Boston MA 02110

TYLEN, DONALD JAMES, tax and pension cons.; b. Muskegon, Mich., June 15, 1932; s. Theodore Lewis and Florence Marie (Tardy) T.; B.B.A., Detroit Inst. Tech., 1959. Agt., IRS, Detroit, 1959-68; agt. Penn Mut. Life Ins. Co., 1968-74; pension cons., 1974—; tax and pension cons. Arrowhead Packaging Co., Detroit, 1979—; dir. Adair St. Warehouse, Adair Land Co., Thunderbird Mfg. Co., Ralph Vigliotti Realty Inc. Served with AUS, 1949-52. Office: Arrowhead Packaging Co 210 Adair St Detroit MI 48207

TYLER, CHAPLIN, mgmt. cons.; b. Washington, Mar. 28, 1898; B.Chem. Engring., Northeastern U., 1920, Sc.D. (hon.), 1961; B.B.A., Boston U., 1922; S.M., M.I.T., 1923; m. Harriet Adelia Scott, June 12, 1925; children—Joan, Richard, Jack. Research asst., research asso. M.I.T., 1920-24; asst. editor McGraw-Hill Pub. Co., 1924-27; research supr., research mgr., sales devel. mgr., asst. dir. public relations, dir. public relations Remington Arms Co. subs. E.I. du Pont de Nemours & Co., 1927-41, sr. mem. devel. dept., 1942-62; mgmt. cons., Wilmington, Del., 1963—; asso. in journalism Columbia U., 1926-27; lectr. U. Del., 1946-49; cons. President's Materials Policy Commn., 1950-51; mem. bd. Compressed Gas Assn., 1946-53; dir. Sterling Inst., 1970-75, Roger Williams Tech. & Econ. Services, 1963-79. Bd. dirs. Boys' Club Wilmington, 1938—, past pres.; mem. Del. Higher Ednl. Aid Adv. Commn., 1970-74; mem. corp., trustee Northeastern U., 1967—. Served with U.S. Army, 1917-19; AEF in France. Recipient Modern Pioneer award NAM, 1939, award of merit Am. Assn. Cost Engrs., 1960. Mem. Am. Chem. Soc. (50 yr. emeritus), Am. Inst. Chem. Engrs. (50 yr. emeritus), Tau Beta Pi, Phi Kappa Phi. Republican. Episcopalian. Clubs: Greenville Country, Wilmington (Wilmington); M.I.T. Faculty (Cambridge). Author: Chemical Engineering Economics, 1926, 38, 46, 59; (with Edwin A. Gee) Managing Innovation, 1976; patentee fertilizer manufacture field. Home: Box 8 Cokesbury Village Hockessin DE 19707

TYLER, RICHARD DALE, JR., bearing mfg. co. exec.; b. Binghamton, N.Y., Aug. 21, 1944; s. Richard Dale and Irene Elizabeth (Brown) T.; B.A., Amherst Coll., 1967; M.B.A., Harvard U., 1971; m. Mary Jane Salamone, Apr. 12, 1969; children—Richard Dale III, Matthew James, Christopher Frank, Luke Michael. With Fin. Mgmt. Program, Gen. Electric Co., Schenectady, 1967-69; pres. Fin. Mgmt. Program Assn., 1968-69; owner, pres. Tyler Mgmt. Co., Boston, 1970-76; pres., co-owner KuBar Bearings, Inc., Cambridge, Mass., 1976—. Mem. Anti-Friction Bearing Mgmt. Assn., Am. Assn. Indsl. Mgmt., Assn. M.B.A. Execs. Club: Harvard of Boston. Office: 21 Erie St Cambridge MA 02139

TYLER, ROBERT DIXON, JR., foods co. exec.; b. Greenwich, Conn., July 1, 1940; s. Robert Dixon and Helen Elizabeth (Fagan) T.; B.A., Cornell U., 1962; J.D., Northwestern U., 1965. Admitted to Ill. bar, 1965; asso. firm Winston & Strawn, Chgo., 1968-74; atty. Beatrice Foods Co., Chgo., 1975—. Bd. govs. Orchestral Assn. Chgo., 1978—; mem. adv. bd., jr. governing bd. Chgo. Symphony Orch., 1971—; mem. Cornell Adv. Com. on Performing Arts, 1980—. Served to capt. AUS, 1966-68. Mem. Am. Bar Assn., Ill. Bar Assn., Chgo. Bar Assn. Republican. Roman Catholic. Clubs: University, Cornell (pres. 1973-74) (Chgo.). Home: 1448 Lake Shore Dr Chicago IL 60610 Office: Beatrice Foods Co 2 N LaSalle St Chicago IL 60602

TYLER, ROBERT RALPH, retail jewelry co. exec.; b. Cleve., Sept. 18, 1939; s. Ralph Weston and Marion Anna (Kostir) T.; B.S. in Bus. Adminstrn., Ohio State U., 1962; m. Alice Ann Weed, Mar. 17, 1962; children—Robert Glenn, Kimberly Marie. Staff acct. Arthur Andersen & Co., Cleve., 1962-68; controller Great Scot Supermarkets, Findlay, Ohio, 1968-72; v.p., chief fin. officer J.B. Robinson Jewelers, Cleve., 1972—. C.P.A., Ohio. Mem. Am. Inst. C.P.A.'s, Ohio Soc. C.P.A.'s, Nat. Acctg. Assn. Club: Civitan (treas. 1971) (Findlay). Office: 811 Citizens Federal Tower Cleveland OH 44115

TYMINSKI, FRANK STEPHEN, cosmetic chemist; b. Balt., Nov. 4, 1946; s. Frank Stephen and Dorothy I. (Coulter) T.; A.A. in Chemistry, Johns Hopkins U., 1973, B.S. in Life Scis., 1976; m. Carroll Rountree, Oct. 21, 1972. Research lab. technician FMC Corp., Balt., 1967-72; process devel. chemist Noxell Corp., Balt., 1972—.

Mem. Soc. Cosmetic Chemists (chmn. Middle Atlantic chpt.). Club: Lions. Office: 11050 York Rd Baltimore MD 21030

TYNER, NEAL EDWARD, ins. co. exec.; b. Grand Island, Nebr., Jan. 30, 1930; s. Edward Raymond and Lydia Dorothy (Kruse) T.; B.S. in Bus. Adminstrn., U. Nebr., 1956; m. Leota Faye Butler, May 6, 1953; children—Karen, Morgan. Loan counselor Federated Fin. Co., Lincoln, Nebr., 1955-56; jr. securities analyst Bankers Life Ins. Co. Nebr., Lincoln, 1956-62, asst. v.p. securities, 1962-67, v.p. securities, treas., 1967-69, fin. v.p., treas., 1969-72, sr. v.p. fin., treas., 1972—; pres., dir. Lincoln Gateway Shopping Center, Inc., 1971—; dir., chmn. audit com., mem. exec. com. Spencer Foods, Inc. (Iowa), 1973-78. Trustee Lincoln Found., U. Nebr. Found.; advisor City of Lincoln Investment Com.; envoy Nebr. Diplomats. Served to capt. USMC, 1950-54. Mem. Chartered Fin. Analysts Soc., Omaha-Lincoln Soc. Fin. Analysts, Lincoln C. of C. (mem. public utilities study com.), Am. Council Life Ins. (mem. subcom. on fiscal and monetary policy). Republican. Lutheran. Clubs: Lincoln Country (bd. dirs.), Nebraska, Wall Street. Home: 2734 O'Reilly Dr Lincoln NE 68502 Office: Cotner & O Sts Lincoln NE 68501

TYREE, JAMES EDWARD, gas co. exec.; b. Sperry, Okla., 1922; B.S., U. Okla., 1948; m. Bonnie Tyree; children—Terry, Lana; stepchildren—Steve Cook, Russell Kroll. With Okla. Natural Gas Co. (name changed to ONEOK Inc. 1980), 1949—, asst. dist. operating supr., 1954-55, dist. operating mgr., 1955-64, dist. v.p., Shawnee, Okla., 1964-68, Oklahoma City, 1968-72, exec. v.p., Tulsa, 1972-76, pres., 1976—, also dir.; dir. Bank of Okla., Tulsa. Bd. dirs. Industries for Tulsa, Inc., Inst. Gas Tech. Mem. So. Gas Assn. (dir.), Tulsa C. of C. (dir.). Office: ONEOK Inc 624 S Boston Ave Box 871 Tulsa OK 74102

TYREE, TOM REX, ins. co. exec.; b. Chgo., Sept. 6, 1942; student Joliet (Ill.) Jr. Coll., 1963-65, Ill. Wesleyan U., 1965-67; 1 dau., Tamara Marie. With Conn. Gen. Life Ins. Co., Davenport, Iowa, 1967—, now estate and bus. planning cons.; prof. ins. and estate planning St. Ambrose Coll., 1967-73. Bd. dirs. Humane Soc. Scott County (Iowa), 1972—, pres., 1974-76. Served with USN, 1960-63. Named Man of Yr., Conn. Gen. Life Ins. Co., 1970-75; C.L.U. Mem. Chartered Life Underwriting Assn., Nat. Life Underwriters Assn., Million Dollar Round Table Assn. Club: Rotary. Home: 4150 E 60th St Davenport IA 52807 Office: Suite 800 Kahl Bldg Davenport IA 52801

TYRRELL, BRENNISS G., mfg. co. exec.; b. Windsor, Conn., May 21, 1910; s. Brenniss H. and Lena (Sampson) T.; m. Clara M. Jacobsen, June 21, 1932; 1 son, Donald J. Acct., Colts Patent Fire Arms Mfg. Co., Inc., 1930-42, chief acct., 1942-44; controller Whitney Chain Co., 1944-52, treas., 1952-56, exec. v.p., treas., 1956-59, dir., 1953-59; exec. v.p. The Hanson-Whitney Co., Hartford, Conn., 1959-64, pres., 1964—, dir., 1959—; dir. J.C. Glenzer Co., W.M. Ziegler Tool Co. Mem. Fin. Execs. Inst., Nat. Assn. Accts. Home: 26 Cold Spring Dr Bloomfield CT 06002 Office: 169 Bartholomew Ave Hartford CT 06101

TYRRELL, JAMES ANTHONY, rec. co. exec.; b. N.Y.C., Dec. 15, 1931; m. Ruby Belk; children—Milton, Cheryl, Joi Nandra. Profl. musician, record producer, 1954-69; v.p. Internat. Tape Cartridge Corp., 1965-70; v.p. mktg. and sales CBS, N.Y.C., 1973-74, v.p. mktg., 1974-79; pres., chmn. bd. T-Electric Records Co., Inc., N.Y.C., 1979—. Mem. Black Music Assn. (dir., mem. exec. com., treas. 1980—), Fraternity Rec. Execs. (founder and pres. N.Y. chpt. 1970), Nat. Acad. Rec. Arts and Scis. (2d v.p., gov. N.Y. chpt. 1979—, nat. trustee 1980—). Established scholarship and PACE career guidance awards for N.Y.C. high sch. students. Office: T-Electric Records Co Inc 450 W 54th St New York NY 10019

TYSON, JOHN CAIUS, III, judge; b. Montgomery, Ala., Oct. 7, 1926; s. John Caius and Virginia Bragg (Smith) T.; student Gulf Coast Mil. Acad., Gulfport, Miss., 1942-43, Baylor Sch., Chattanooga, 1943-44; student U. Ala., 1944, 46-51, B.S. and LL.B.; m. Mae Martin Bryant; children—Mary Harmon, Marc John. Admitted to Ala. bar, 1951, since practiced in Montgomery; asso. Jones, Murray & Stewart, 1951; individual practice, 1952-56; asso. C. H. Wampold, Jr. in gen. practice law, 1956-60; asst. atty. gen. State of Ala., 1959-71; judge Ct. Criminal Appeals, 1972—, presiding judge, 1976-77; developer Beaumont Estates. Served with USCG, 1944-46, mem. Res., 1947-52. Mem. Ala. State Bar (lectr. continuing legal edn. program), Am., Montgomery County (exec. com. 1963) bar assns., Am. Judicature Soc., SAR (past pres. Montgomery County chpt., 1st v.p. Ala.), Soc. Pioneers Montgomery (past pres., dir.), Am. Legion, Montgomery C. of C. Democrat. Episcopalian (vestryman 1957-60, 70-73). Clubs: Masons, Shriners, Kiwanis, Montgomery Country, Beauvoir. Home: 3114 Jasmine Rd Montgomery AL 36111 Office: Judicial Bldg Rm 306 Montgomery AL 36101

TYSON, LYNN CARLTON, ins. co. exec.; b. Charlotte, Mich., Jan. 31, 1943; s. George Carlton and Wilma (Barnes) T.; B.A., Western Mich. U., 1965; m. Nan Betty Cochran, Aug. 27, 1966; children—Melanie, Jamie. Tchr., coach Mendon (Mich.) Community Schs., 1965-69; ins. salesman Coll. Life Ins. Co., Kalamazoo, 1969-71; agency mgr. Nat. Life and Accident Ins. Co., Lansing, Mich., 1971-73; regional sales dir. Aetna Life & Casualty, San Diego, 1973-75; dist. mgr. Calif. Casualty, 1975-76; regional mktg. mgr. Security First Group, Valencia, Calif., 1976-79, div. v.p., 1979—, also scholarship coordinator; instr. life underwriter tng. council classes. Sec., Valencia Racquet Club Homeowners Assn., 1976-77, pres., 1977-78. Recipient Okemos Athletic Club award, 1972, 73; recipient various ins. sales awards. Mem. Nat., Calif., Los Angeles assns. life underwriters, Gen. Agents Mgmt. Assn., United State Golf Assn. Methodist. Club: Optimists (bd. dirs. 1974, pres. 1975). Home: 15838 Falconrim Canyon Country CA 91351 Office: 4640 Admiralty Way Suite 219 Marina Del Ray CA 90291

TYSON, THEODORE ROBERT, mktg. mgmt. cons.; b. N.Y.C., Sept. 10, 1926; s. Charles Randolph and Irene M. (Jansen) T.; student U. Calif. at Los Angeles, 1946-49; m. Marilyn Joan Macdonald, June 8, 1968; children—Lawrence, Christopher, Pamela, Randall. Regional sales mgr. Am. Hosp. Supply Corp., N.Y.C., 1959-65; v.p. mktg. Standard Sci., N.J., 1965-69; corp. v.p. mktg. Telco Mktg. Services Inc., Chgo., 1969-75; mktg. cons. T.R. Tyson, Buffalo Grove, Ill., 1978—; cons. health care, bus. orgns., 1975—. Served with USNR, 1944-46. Republican. Presbyterian. Contbr. articles to profl. jours. Home: 612 White Pine Rd Buffalo Grove IL 60090

TZELIOS, CHRISTOS GEORGE, accountant; b. Politsani, No. Epirus, Oct. 12, 1934; s. George Demetrios and Sevasti (Papachronis) T.; came to U.S., 1956, naturalized, 1962; student Athens U. Law Sch., 1954-56; B.B.A. in Pub. Accountancy, City Coll. N.Y., 1963; m. Vivi Rigas, Jan. 16, 1972; children—Aristotle, Alexander. Accountant, AMF Pinspotters, N.Y.C., 1958-60; tax accountant Royal McBee Corp. subs. Litton Industries, N.Y.C., 1961-65, Agrico Chem. subs. Continental Oil Co., N.Y.C., 1965, Colt Industries, N.Y.C., 1966-68; owner, operator Tzelios Bus. Service, bus. cons. and planning, Astoria, N.Y., 1968—; owner, pres. Hellenic Book Club, 1973—. A founder, mem. bd. dirs. Astoria Restoration Assn., 1977—; treas. Greek-Am. Democratic Com., 1976—. Mem. City Coll., Baruch Coll. alumni assns. Greek Orthodox. Club: Hellenic Univ. Office: 22-55 31st St Astoria NY 11105

UDA, JOAN A., lawyer; b. Dubuque, Iowa, July 21, 1939; d. Warren William and Alice B. (Carlton) McAllister; student Cornell Coll., 1956-58; B.A., North Central Coll., 1959; postgrad. U. Chgo., 1960; M.F.A. (Univ. fellow), U. Iowa, 1967; J.D. (Univ. fellow), U. Mont., 1975; m. Lowell Masato Uda, Feb. 2, 1963; children—Carolyn Sue, Michael John, Elizabeth Teruko, Lowell Takeo. Admitted to Mont. bar, 1975; atty./adviser HEW, Balt., 1975-76; staff atty. Gov.'s Office of Budget and Program Planning, State of Mont., Helena, 1976-77, chief legal counsel Dept. Social and Rehab. Services, 1977-78, chief legal counsel, spl. asst. for human services to Gov., 1978; with firm Zion, Zion, Uda, Reynolds & Perlmutter, Helena, 1979—; lectr. in field; counsel Mont. House Majority Leader, 1979. Bd. dirs. Helena Film Soc., 1979—, Helena Learners Exchange, 1979—; pres. Women's Law Caucus, U. Mont., 1973-75. Recipient Outstanding Service award Student Bar Assn., 1975. Mem. State Bar of Mont., Mont. Trial Lawyers Assn. Club: Zonta. Author: Montana Working Woman: Your Job Rights, 1980; comments editor Mont. Law Rev., 1974-75; contbr. articles to profl. jours. Office: Suite 201 Power Block PO Box 1255 Helena MT 59601

UDELL, MICHAEL BENNETT, lawyer; b. N.Y.C., Apr. 6, 1951; s. Jack Alex and Janet (Abrams) U.; A.A., Miami Dade Jr. Coll., 1971; B.A., U. Fla., 1973; postgrad. Fla. Internat. U., 1974; J.D., S. Tex. Coll. Law, 1978; m. Helene Joyce Bookman, Mar. 28, 1980. Admitted to Tex. bar, 1978, Fla. bar, 1979; Congl. student intern, Washington, 1973; asst. to pres. J.A.S.P. Nursing Home Group, Miami, Fla., 1974; chief operating officer Truco Med. Supplies, Inc., Miami, 1975; tchr. Houston Ind. Sch. Dist., 1976-77; law clk. firm Stolbun & Shaw, Bellaire, Tex., 1978, Franklin, Ullman, Entin & Kimler, N. Miami Beach, Fla., 1978; pvt. practice law, N. Miami, Fla., 1979—; mem. Gov.'s Com. on Juvenile Justice, Fla., 1978; mem. staff mayor, Gainesville, Fla., 1973. Mem. Environ. Action Group, Gainesville, 1973; registered lobbyist Young Democrats, Fla. Senate and Ho. Reps., 1971. Recipient Student Bar Assn. Merit award, 1977; Am. Jurisprudence Book awards, 1977. Mem. Am. Bar Assn., Tex. Bar Assn., Fla. Bar Assn., Assn. Trial Lawyers Am., Am. Judicature Soc., Nat. Assn. Criminal Def. Attys., Dade County Fla. Bar Assn., Dade County Trial Lawyers Assn., N. Dade Bar Assn., Acad. Fla. Trial Lawyers, N. Miami Beach C. of C., Sigma Lambda Phi, Pi Sigma Alpha. Clubs: Kiwanis, B'nai B'rith, K.P. Home: 3905 Parkside Ln Hollywood FL 33021 Office: 2020 NE 163rd St Suite 204 North Miami Beach FL 33162

UEBELHOER, GARY PHILLIP, environ. services corp. ofcl.; b. Ft. Wayne, Ind., Nov. 3, 1953; s. U.L. and Irma C. U.; B.S. in Interdisciplinary Engring., Purdue U., 1975, M.S. in Indsl. Adminstrn., 1976. With solid waste collection project Office of Mayor Indpls., 1975; intern, asst. environ. mgr. Minnamax project in Minn., Environ. Services Group, AMAX Inc., 1976-77; project environ. mgr., Central Fla. phosphate project, AMAX Environ. Services, Inc., Lakeland, 1977-80; dir. environ. and community affairs AMAX Phosphate, Inc., Lakeland, 1980—. Active, Environ. Awareness Center-Fla.; founder club Fla. Audubon Soc. Mem. Am. Mgmt. Assn., Omicron Delta Kappa. Clubs: Purdue Alumni Assn., Sigma Chi. Home: 210 Hollingsworth Dr #1702 Lakeland FL 33803

UHL, EDWARD GEORGE, mfg. exec.; b. Elizabeth, N.J., Mar. 24, 1918; s. Henry and Mary (Schiller) U.; B.S., Lehigh U., 1940, D.Sc. (hon.), 1975; m. Maurine B. Keleher, July 19, 1942; children—Carol, Kim, Scott, Cynthia; m. 2d, Mary Stuart Brugh, Sept. 17, 1966. With Martin Co., 1946-59, successively engr. guided missile sect., chief project engr., v.p. engring., 1953-55, v.p. operations, 1955-56, v.p., gen. mgr. Orlando div. (Fla.), 1957-59; v.p. tech. adminstrn. Ryan Aero. Co., 1959-61; chmn., chief exec. officer Fairchild Industries, 1961—, also dir.; dir. Am. Satellite Corp., Bunker Ramo Corp., Md. Nat. Corp., Md. Nat. Bank. Trustee, mem. vis. coms. Lehigh U.; trustee Johns Hopkins U. Served from 2d lt. to lt. col. Ordnance Corps, AUS, 1941-46. Recipient Hamilton Holt award Rollins Coll., 1959. Fellow Am. Inst. Aeros. and Astronautics; mem. Am. Def. Preparedness Assn. (dir., John C. Jones award 1975), Air Force Assn., Soc. Automotive Engrs., Phi Beta Kappa Assos., Phi Beta Kappa, Tau Beta Pi. Clubs: Fountain Head Country, Assembly (Hagerstown); Wings, Sky, Union League (N.Y.C.); Burning Tree, Safari (Washington); Nat. Space (bd. govs.). Co-inventor bazooka. Home: PO Box 2161 Hagerstown MD 21740 Office: Sherman Fairchild Technology Center Germantown MD 20767

UHLIR, NORMAN CLARENCE, aerospace and indsl. products co. exec.; b. Cleve., Mar. 23, 1937; s. Clarence Stephen and Gladys Katherine (Vanek) U.; B.B.A., Western Res. U., 1960; m. Frances Joan Braun, June 20, 1959; children—Shelly Marie, Dennis John, Scott Michael. Cost, fin. analyst Ford Motor Co., Cleve., 1960-63; asst. div. controller Hupp Corp., Cleve., 1963-65; mgr. fin. analysis TRW, Inc., Cleve., 1965-69; sr. cons. Peat, Marwick, Mitchell & Co., Cleve., 1969-71; corporate controller Huffman Mfg. Co., Dayton, Ohio, 1971-75; controller advanced tech. group Sundstrand Corp., Rockford, Ill., 1975—. Mem. Fin. Execs. Inst., Planning Execs. Inst., Am. Mgmt. Assn. Clubs: Masons, Shriners. Home: 1810 Jonquil Circle Rockford IL 61107 Office: 4747 Harrison Ave Rockford IL 61101

UHRBROCK, F. BECTON, retail exec.; b. N.Y.C., Sept. 19, 1930; s. E. Frederick Jr. and Edith Davis (Becton) U.; B.A., Columbia U., 1952; m. Jenny Hinkelthein, Apr. 28, 1966; 1 dau., Christiana Becton. Asst. dir. research C.&N.W. Ry., also New Haven R.R., 1958-65; transp. analyst Am. Cynamid Co., Wayne, N.J., 1968-70; documentation mgr. Seatrain Lines, Wehawkan, N.J., 1970-73; transp. mgr., analysis and internat. div. K-Mart Apparel Corp., North Bergen, N.J., 1973—. Dir. pub. relations Jr. C. of C., Guilford, Conn., 1961-63. Served with CIC, U.S. Army, 1952-55; Korea; with USAR, 1966-67; Vietnam. Mem. Am. Importers Assn. (chmn. transp. com. 1977—), Internat. Apparel Importers Assn. (chmn. internat. transp. com. 1975—). Republican. Presbyterian. Club: N.Y. Athletic. Home: 36 Wendt Ln Wayne NJ 07470 Office: K-Mart Apparel Corp 7373 Westside Ave North Bergen NJ 07470

UIHLEIN, HENRY HOLT, elec. co. exec.; b. Milw., Aug. 17, 1921; s. Herman Alfred and Claudia (Holt) U.; student U. Va., 1941-43; B.A., Babson Sch. Bus. Adminstrn., 1946; m. Marion Strauss, June 13, 1942; children—Henry Holt, James Christopher, Philip, Richard. Pres., gen. mgr. Ben Hur Mfg. Co., Milw., 1947-62, Quic Frez, Inc., Fond du Lac, Wis., 1955-60; with U-Line Corp., Milw., 1962—, pres., gen. mgr., 1962—, chmn. bd., treas., 1977—; pres. Jensen Service Corp., 1962—; bus. cons., 1962-75. Pres. Herman A. Uihlein Sr. Found., Inc., Milw., 1955—. Served with USMCR, 1944-46. Named to the Wis. Hockey Hall of Fame, 1978. Republican. Christian Scientist. Clubs: Milw. Country, Milw. Athletic. Home: 8500 N Green Bay Ct Milwaukee WI 53209 Office: 8900 N 55th St Milwaukee WI 53223

UKAOGO, AGU AGU, accountant; b. Aba, Nigeria, July 20, 1951; came to U.S., 1974; s. Lazarus Ukaogo Agu and Christiana Enyinne Nwosu; student Ala A&M U., 1975-76; B.S. in Bus. Adminstrn., U. Nebr., Omaha, 1977. Account supr. City of Council Bluffs (Iowa), 1977-79; asst. to dir. Nebr. Gov.'s Spl. Grants Office, Lincoln, 1979-80; sr. acct. Nelson, Peters & Assos., Inc., Omaha, 1980—; dir., partner ACA, Inc.; dir. L.U. Agu & Sons Ltd., AMNI, Inc., Energy Resources Inc. Mem. Assn. Minority and Women in Bus. Nebr., Nat. Assn. Accts., Minority Accts. Nebr., Douglas County Young Republicans, NAACP, Internat. Students Orgn. (v.p. memberships). Presbyterian. Home: 2909 S 93d Plaza #4 Omaha NE 68124 Office: Keeline Bldg Suite 500 319 S 17th St Omaha NE 68102

ULLMARK, WILLIAM ARVID, brokerage firm exec.; b. East Chicago, Ind., Nov. 30, 1928; s. William Arvid and Margaret Holly U.; student UCLA, 1953-56; m. Leana Esposito, Mar. 25, 1959; 1 son, William. Investment exec. Hornblower, Weeks, Hemphill-Noyes, Inc. (name changed to Shearson Loeb Rhoades Inc.), Los Angeles, 1961-65, resident mgr., Glendale, Calif., 1965-74, corp. v.p., N.Y.C., 1974-75, corp. v.p., resident mgr., Buffalo & Williamsville, N.Y., 1975—; instr. Hornblower selling skills program, 1974-79. Bd. dirs., sec. Glendale (Calif.) C. of C., 1970-73; bd. govs. Glendale (Calif.) Symphony Orch., 1971-74; trustee Buffalo Neighborhood Reinvestment Program, 1979—; bd. dirs. Buffalo Philharm. Orch.; mem. budget and mgmt. adv. bd. Erie County (N.Y.). Served with USCG, 1947-51. Clubs: Bond of Buffalo, Buffalo. Home: 255 Nottingham Terr Buffalo NY 14216 Office: Statler Bldg Suite 1730 Buffalo NY 14202

ULM, RONALD JOSEPH, personnel exec.; b. Evanston, Ill., Aug. 3, 1935; s. William J. and Geraldine E. (Reich) U.; B.A. in Psychology, U. Ill., 1959; M.S., Loyola U., Chgo., 1963; m. Rosemary A. Walsh, July 3, 1965; children—Stacey, Lisa. Mgr. labor relations Spiegel, Inc., Chgo., 1960-68; dir. personnel Ben Franklin div. City Products Corp., Des Plaines, Ill., 1968-71, v.p. personnel, 1971-73; asst. dir. personnel City Products Corp., Des Plaines, 1973-79, dir. personnel, 1979—. Mem. bus. adv. bd. Oakton Community Coll.; mem. adv. bd. Newman Found., U. Ill. Mem. Am. Mgmt. Assn., Des Plaines C. of C. (dir.). Republican. Roman Catholic. Clubs: Valley Lo Country, Ill. Athletic. Home: 1500 Sequoia Trail Glenview IL 60025 Office: City Products Corp 1700 S Wolf Rd Des Plaines IL 60018

ULMER, DANIEL C., JR., banker; b. Louisville, Dec. 15, 1932; s. Daniel C. and Marie Ulmer; B.S., U. Louisville; postgrad. Stonier Grad. Sch. Banking, Stanford Exec. Program; children—Gary C., Elizabeth Asman, Mary Kathleen. With Citizens Fidelity Bank, Louisville, v.p., 1965-70, sr. v.p., 1970, now pres. Bd. overseers U. Louisville; mem. adv. council U. Louisville Sch. Bus.; bd. dirs. Metro Park and Recreation Bd., Louisville Orch. Mem. Assn. Res. City Bankers. Office: 5th and Jefferson Sts Louisville KY 40202*

ULUSAN, AYDIN, banker; b. Ankara, Turkey, Jan. 13, 1941; came to U.S., 1977; s. Aziz and Nilufer (Dincay) U.; B.A., Istanbul Turkey, 1967; M.A., Mich. State U., 1971, Ph.D., 1973; m. Enise Atesdagli, July 13, 1967; 1 dau., Cigdem. Chmn. dept. econs. Bosphorus U., Istanbul, Turkey, 1973-75, dean Sch. Adminstrv. Scis., 1975-76; vis. research economist Princeton (N.J.) U., 1977; N.Y. rep. Yapi ve Kredi Bank of Turkey, N.Y.C., 1977—. Bd. dirs. N.Y. U. Grad. Sch. Bus. Mgmt. Game, 1978-79. Served with Turkish Army, 1961-63. Recipient Duncan S. Bllantine award, Robert Coll., 1967; Chrysler Corp. Internat. fellow, 1967. Mem. Turkish Mgmt. Assn., Edn. Found. Editor: The Political Economy of Income Distribution in Turkey, 1980; contbr. articles to profl. jours. Home: 1680 York Ave Apt 5E New York NY 10028 Office: 645 Fifth Ave Suite 902 New York NY 10022

UMANS, ALVIN ROBERT, mfg. co. exec.; b. N.Y.C., Mar. 11, 1927; s. Louis and Ethel (Banner) U.; student U. Rochester, 1944-45; m. Nancy Jo Zadek, June 28, 1953 (div.); children—Kathi Lee Umans Lind, Craig Joseph. Sales mgr. Textile Mills Co., Chgo., 1954-56; regional sales mgr. Reflector Hardware Corp., Melrose Park, Ill., 1957-59, nat. sales mgr., 1959-61, v.p., 1961-66, pres., treas., 1966—, also dir.; dir. Concepts, Inc., Mpls., Fine Arts Broadcasting, Inc., Miami, Fla.; chmn. bd., pres. Garcy Corp., Chgo.; v.p., dir. Midland Industries, Wichita, Kans., Goer Mfg. Co., Inc., Charleston, S.C., Servicomex (Mexico); pres., treas., dir. Spacemaster Corp., Chgo.; pres., treas Spacemaster-Garcy Corp., Chgo.; pres. Ringo Corp., Chgo.; dir. Banner Press, N.Y.C. Trustee Mt. Sinai Hosp. Med. Center, 1972—; bd. dirs. Milton and Rose Zadek Fund, 1965-79. Served with U.S. Army, 1945-46. Mem. Nat. Assn. Store Fixture Mfrs. (dir. 1969-70), Chgo. Pres.'s Orgn., Young Pres.'s Orgn. Jewish. Club: Standard (Chgo.). Home: 260 E Chestnut Chicago IL 60611 Office: 1400 N 25th Ave Melrose Park IL 60160

UMBERHAUER, MAURICE EDWIN, outerwear mfg. co. exec.; b. Schuylkill Haven, Pa., May 21, 1938; s. George Edwin and Eleanor Ann (Schaeffer) U.; student Ford Sch. Bus., 1965, Am. Mgmt. Assn., 1966; grad. Dale Carnegie Course, 1972; m. Shirley Ann Roeder, June 1, 1957; children—Denise, George, Melissa. With Am. Argo Corp., Schuylkill Haven, 1956—, dir. systems, 1975-76, v.p. distbn./customer service, 1976—. Mem. Vol. Fire Dept., Schuylkill Haven; pres. Grace Evang. Congregational Ch., Schuylkill Haven. Recipient Christian Growth and Achievement award Grace Evang. Ch. Mem. Schuylkill Haven Fish and Game Assn. Clubs: East End Gun, Buck Horn Hunting Lodge. Home: PO Box 472 RD 3 Schuylkill Haven PA 17972 Office: Am Argo Corp Market and Margaretta Sts Schuylkill Haven PA 17972

UMLAUF, JAMES LEWIS, investment banker; b. Key West, Fla., Jan. 8, 1945; s. Otto Dezso and Joyce Evelyn (Taylor) U.; B.A. (scholar), U. Wis., 1968; M.B.A. (scholar), Columbia U., 1969; m. Frances Stuart, June 11, 1976. Asst. to pres. Spencer Foods, Inc. (Iowa), 1970-72; asst. v.p. duPont Glore Forgan, N.Y.C., 1972-73; v.p. W.P. Carey & Co., Inc., N.Y.C., 1973-76, sr. v.p., San Francisco, 1976-80, exec. v.p., 1980—, also mng. dir. Office: Transamerica Pyramid 600 Montgomery St San Francisco CA 94111

UNDERHILL, JACOB BERRY, III, ins. co. exec.; b. N.Y.C., Oct. 25, 1926; s. Jacob Berry, Jr., and Dorothy Louise (Quinn) U.; A.B., Princeton U., 1950; m. Cynthia Jane Lovejoy, Sept. 9, 1950 (div.); children—David Lovejoy, Kate Howell Underhill Kerwin, Benedict Quinn; m. 2d, Lois Beachy, Nov. 2, 1963. Editor, Potsdam (N.Y.) Courier & Freeman, 1950-53; reporter Rochester (N.Y.) Democrat & Chronicle, 1953-56; chief editorial writer St. Petersburg (Fla.) Times, 1956-59; asso. editor McGraw Hill Pub. Co., N.Y.C., 1959-61; asso. editor Newsweek, N.Y.C., 1961-63; asst. press sec. to Gov. of N.Y., 1963-67; dep. supt. to 1st dep. supt. N.Y. Ins. Dept., 1967-72; successively v.p., sr. v.p., exec. v.p., dir., vice chmn. bd. N.Y. Life Ins. Co., N.Y.C., 1972—. Bd. dirs. Manhattan Eye, Ear and Throat Hosp., Better Bus. Bur. Met. N.Y.; trustee retirement system ARC, Nat. Trust Hist. Preservation. Served with USNR, 1944-46. Clubs: Links, Players (N.Y.C.); Noyac Golf and Country (Sag Harbor, N.Y.). Office: 51 Madison Ave New York NY 10010

UNDERKOFLER, JAMES RUSSELL, utilities co. exec.; b. Baraboo, Wis., Oct. 25, 1923; s. Ray S. and Margaret (Thompson) U.; LL.B., U. Wis., 1950; m. Dorothy A. Paske, Nov. 16, 1946; children—James H., Thomas R., R. Craig, Kevin S., Cynthia M. With Wis. Power and Light Co., Madison, 1941—, exec. v.p., 1967-68, pres., chief exec. officer, 1968—; dir. S. Beloit Water, Gas and Electric Co., 1st Wis. Nat. Bank of Madison, 1st Wis. Corp., Milw., H.C.

Prange Co., Sheboygan, Wis., Am. Family Ins. Group, Madison. Bd. dirs. Meth. Hosp., Madison, 1967-75; pres. Wis. Utilities Assn. Research Found., 1970-73; pres. United Way, Madison, 1971; trustee Milton (Wis.) Coll., 1971-75. Served with U.S. Army, 1943-45. Decorated Purple Heart. Mem. Edison Elec. Inst. (past chmn. environ. and energy div.), Wis. Utilities Assn. (past chmn.), Wis. Mfrs. and Commerce, Wis. Bar Assn., Dane County Bar Assn. Lutheran. Clubs: Madison, Maple Bluff Country, Rotary. Office: 222 W Washington Ave Madison WI 53703

UNDERWEISER, IRWIN PHILIP, lawyer, mining co. exec.; b. N.Y.C., Jan. 3, 1929; s. Harry and Edith (Gladstein) U.; B.A., Coll. City N.Y., 1950; LL.D., Fordham U., 1954; LL.M., N.Y. U., 1961; m. Beatrice J Kortchmar, Aug. 17, 1959; children—Rosanne, Marian, Jeffrey. Admitted to N.Y. bar, 1954; asso. Scribner & Miller, N.Y.C., 1951-54, 56-62; practice law, N.Y.C., 1962—; partner Feuerstein & Underweiser, 1962-73, Underweiser & Fuchs, 1973-77, Underweiser & Underweiser, 1977—; v.p., sec., dir. Sunshine Mining Co., Kellogg, Idaho, 1965-70, chmn. bd., 1970-78, pres., 1971-74, v.p., 1978—; sec., dir. Berel Industries, Inc., N.Y.C., 1964—; vice chmn. Underwriters Bank and Trust Co., N.Y.C., 1969-73; dir. Anchor Post Products, Inc., chmn. bd., 1976-77. Gen. counsel, mem. bus. council Friends City Center Music and Drama, N.Y.C., 1966-67; pres. West Quaker Ridge Assn., Scarsdale, N.Y., 1969-70; treas. Scarsdale Neighborhood Assn. of Pres.'s, 1970-71; bd. dirs. Silver Inst., also mem. exec. com. Served with AUS, 1954-56. Mem. Am., N.Y. State bar assns., Assn. Bar City N.Y., Phi Beta Kappa, Phi Alpha Theta. Home: 7 Rural Dr Scarsdale NY 10583 Office: 250 Park Ave New York NY 10017 also 405 Park Ave New York NY 10022

UNDERWOOD, DAVID MILTON, security co. exec.; b. Houston, Mar. 5, 1937; s. Milton Ramon and Catherine (Fondren) U.; B.A., Yale, 1958; postgrad. Inst. Investment Banking, Wharton Sch. Finance, U. Pa., 1969; m. Lynda Knapp, Nov. 21, 1964; children—David Milton, Catherine F., Duncan Knapp. With Morgan Stanley & Co., N.Y.C., 1962; with Underwood, Neuhaus & Co., investment bankers, Houston, 1962—, v.p., 1966-74, sr. v.p., 1974—, dir., 1968—; pres. Feliciana Corp., Houston, 1966—, Pano Tech Exploration Co., Houston, 1972—; dir. Fannin Bank. Trustee, Fondren Found., Meth. Hosp., Kinkaid Sch.; bd. dirs. Tex. Med. Center, Inc. Served to capt. AUS, 1958-60, 61-62. Decorated Army Commendation medal. Mem. Zeta Psi. Republican. Episcopalian. Clubs: Houston Country, River Oaks Country, Bayou, Ramada, Houston, Allegro, Sarabande (Houston); Yale (N.Y.C.). Home: 3645 Willowick Rd Houston TX 77019 Office: 724 Travis St Houston TX 77002

UNRUH, JAMES ARLEN, financial exec.; b. Goodrich, N.D., Mar. 22, 1941; B.S., Jamestown Coll., 1963; M.B.A., U. Denver, 1964; m. Virginia Taylor; children—Jeffrey A., Julie A. Vice pres. treasury and corp. devel. Fairchild Camera & Instrument Co., 1975-79, v.p. fin., 1979-80; v.p. fin. Memorex Corp., Santa Clara, Calif., 1980—; dir. Magnuson Computer Systems, Santa Clara. Mem. Fin. Execs. Inst., Internat. Assn. Treas.'s. Office: Memorex Corp San Tomas at Central Expressway Santa Clara CA 95051

UNWIN, RICHMOND WOLCOTT, JR., mfg. co. exec.; b. Chgo., May 2, 1924; s. Richmond Wolcott and Marguerite (Ludeman) U.; B.S., U. Wis., 1949; m. Muriel F. Dixon, May 27, 1950; children—William R., Nancy. Sales mgr. Am. Tire Machinery Co., Muncie, Ind., 1953-54; advt. supr. E.I. DuPont Co., Wilmington, Del., 1955-64; advt. mgr. NL Industries, Inc., N.Y.C., 1964-66, dir. public affairs and corp. communications, 1966—; v.p., mgr. NL Industries Found. Bd. dirs. N.Y. Bd. of Trade. Served with USAAF, 1943-45. Mem. U.S. Power Squadron (comdr. 1961-62), Nat. Investor Relations Inst., Pub. Relations Soc. Am., Pub. Relations & Soc. N.Y. (pres. 1976), Internat. Pub. Relations Assn., Kappa Sigma. Club: N.Y. Yacht. Home: 76 Beekman Rd Summit NJ 07901 Office: 1230 Ave of Americas New York NY 10020

UPBIN, HAL J., real estate exec.; b. Bronx, N.Y., Jan. 15, 1939; s. David and Evelyn (Sloan) U.; B.B.A., Pace U., 1961; s. Shari Kiesler, May 29, 1960; children—Edward, Elyse, Danielle. Tax mgr. Price Waterhouse, N.Y.C., 1965-71; treas. Wheelabrator-Frey Inc., N.Y.C., 1971-74; pres. Wheelabrator Fin. Corp., N.Y.C., 1974-75; with Triton Group Ltd. (formerly Chase Manhattan Mortgage & Realty Trust), N.Y.C., 1975—, chmn., 1978—, trustee, 1980—; dir. Isomedics, Inc.; trustee Realty Growth Investors. Mem. N.Y. State Soc. C.P.A.'s, Am. Inst. C.P.A.'s. Jewish (pres. temple). Home: 45 E 89th St New York NY 10028 Office: One Pennsylvania Plaza New York NY 10001

UPDEGRAFF, DAVID EDWIN, marine transp. co. exec.; b. Detroit, Dec. 14, 1941; s. Frank Murray and Kathryn Florence (Abel) U.; student Principia Coll., 1959-61; B.A. Wayne State U., 1963, M.A., 1968; M.M., Northwestern U., 1975; m. Nancy Ida Durie, June 15, 1968; children—Elizabeth Suzanne, David Prescott. Credit mgr. Crandall Wholesale Co., Detroit, 1964-65; teaching and research asst. Wayne State U., 1965-68; lectr. econs. Eastern Mich. U., 1968-70; economist Fed. Res. Bank of Chgo., 1970-73, mgr., 1973-77; mgr. resource planning Hannah Marine Corp., Lemont, Ill., 1977-79, v.p. ops., 1979—. Mem. Am. Econ. Assn. Club: Propeller (Chgo.). Home: 1124 W 187th Homewood IL 60430 Office: Kingery Rd at Archer Ave Lemont IL 60439

UPSON, STUART BARNARD, advt. agy. exec.; b. Cin., Apr. 14, 1925; s. Mark and Alice (Barnard) U.; B.S., Yale, 1945; m. Marguerite Barbara Jussen, Nov. 2, 1946; children—Marguerite, Anne, Stuart. With Dancer-Fitzgerald-Sample, Inc., N.Y.C., 1946—, exec. v.p., 1966-67, pres., chief exec. officer, 1967-74, chmn. bd., 1974—; dir. Manhattan Life Ins. Co. Served with USNR, 1943-46. Mem. St. Elmo Soc. Presbyterian. Clubs: Sky; Yale; Blind Brook Country; Weeburn. Home: 68 Stephen Mather Rd Darien CT 06820 Office: 405 Lexington Ave New York NY 10017

UPTON, EUGENE HARRY, real estate exec.; b. Dayton, Minn., Oct. 21, 1930; s. Russell Arnold and Anna Rose (Lehn) U.; B.A. in Acctg., U. Minn., 1956; children—Michael, Betsy. Acct., Century 21 Upton Assos. Realtors, Inc., Sunnyvale and Saratoga, Calif.; engaged in real estate, 1962—; owner, operator Century 21 Upton, Sunnyvale and Saratoga. Served with USN, 1948-52. Mem. Nat. Assn. Realtors, Calif. Assn. Realtors (regional v.p. 1974), Calif. Real Estate Assn. (dir. 1964-74), Sunnyvale Real Estate Bd. (pres. 1971; Realtor of Year 1979). Republican. Roman Catholic. Office: Century 21 Upton Assos 156 W El Camino Sunnyvale CA 94087

UPTON, HOWARD BLAIR, JR., assn. exec.; b. Tahlequah, Okla., May 17, 1922; s. Howard Blair and Marjorie (Ross) U.; B.A., U. Okla., 1943, LL.B., 1948; m. Jean Devereaux, July 14, 1945; children—Pamela, Barbara, Martha, Brian. Admitted to Okla. bar, 1948; indsl. relations dir. Western Petroleum Refiners Assn., Tulsa, 1948-51; exec. v.p., gen. counsel Petroleum Equipment Inst., Tulsa, 1951—; dir. Telex Corp., 1974—. Served with USNR, 1943-48. Mem. Am. Bar Assn., Am. Soc. Assn. Execs. (past dir.), Am. Petroleum Inst., Okla. Bar Assn., Tulsa Soc. Assn. Execs. (past pres.), Soc. Scribes, Order of Coif. Clubs: Tulsa, Cedar Crest Country. Address: 5133 E 25th Ct Tulsa OK 74114

URBINE, ROBERT WILLIAM, ins. sales co. exec.; b. Ft. Wayne, Ind., Aug. 18, 1935; s. Herman Joseph and Violet Elaine Urbine; student U. Cin. Sowell Sch. Aviation, 1978; m. Kay F. Archibald, Sept. 3, 1953; children—Kevin, Kent, Kerry. Pres., Urbine/Beard Ins., Ft. Wayne, 1955-69; v.p. Nat. Aviation Underwriters, St. Louis, 1969-74; pres. Aviation Ins. Unltd. Inc., Greensboro, N.C., 1975—, Aviation Ins. Underwriters Inc., Aviation Claims Center Inc.; pres. Ft. Wayne Ins. Bd., 1969—. Mem. Warbird Am., Quiet Birdman, Valient Air Command, Exptl. Aircraft Assn., Aircraft Owners and Pilots Assn. Democrat. Roman Catholic. Home: 4101 Ponce de Leon High Point NC 27260 Office: PO Box 19022 Greensboro Regional Airport Greensboro NC 27410

URCIUOLI, J. ARTHUR, investment banker; b. Syracuse, N.Y., Nov. 13, 1937; s. Joseph R. and Nicoletta Anne (Phillips) U.; B.S., St. Lawrence U., 1959; J.D., Georgetown U., 1966; m. Margaret Jane Forelli, Aug. 13, 1966; children—Karen Sloan, Christian Arthur. Admitted to N.Y. bar, 1966; atty. firm Brown, Wood, Fuller, Caldwell & Ivey, N.Y.C., 1966-69; asso., investment banking div. Merrill Lynch, Pierce, Fenner & Smith, N.Y.C., 1969-70, v.p., mgr. internat. fin. dept., 1970-72; pres. Merrill Lynch, Pierce, Fenner & Smith Securities Underwriter Ltd., Paris, 1972-74; v.p., dir. internat. fin. Merrill Lynch, Pierce, Fenner & Smith Inc., N.Y.C., 1974-76, mng. dir. Merrill Lynch Capital Markets Group, 1977-78, pres. Merrill Lynch Internat., Inc., 1978—; dir. Trident Internat. Fin. Ltd., Hong Kong, 1975-77, Merrill Lynch Internat. Bank, London, 1976—. Trustee St. Lawrence U., 1976—; bd. dirs. United Way, Greenwich, Conn., 1978—. Served to capt. USMC, 1959-63. Republican. Congregationalist. Clubs: City Midday (N.Y.C.); Riverside (Conn.) Yacht; Rocky Point (Old Greenwich, Conn.). Contbr. articles to profl. jours. Home: 14 Fairgreen Ln Old Greenwich CT 06870 Office: 1 Liberty Plaza 165 Broadway New York City NY 10006

URFER, RICHARD PETERSON, investment banker, cattle breeder; b. Spring Green, Wis., June 28, 1936; s. Walter Chester and Alice Mae (Peterson) U.; B.S., U. Wis., 1958; M.B.A., Harvard U., 1964; m. Cynthia Leigh Vaughan, June 22, 1968; children—Jocelyn Leigh, Gilbert Fielding, Courtney Vaughan. Asst. to treas. Allis-Chalmers Mfg. Co., Milw., 1960-62; asso. Morgan Stanley & Co., N.Y.C., 1964-67; pres., chief exec. officer, dir. DCL, Inc., Jersey City, 1967-69; dir. office fgn. direct investments Dept. Commerce, Washington, 1969-70; spl. cons. to Sec. Commerce for Internat. Fin. Affairs, Washington, 1971; sr. v.p., dir. Blyth Eastman Dillon & Co., N.Y.C., 1971-73; sr. v.p., dir. Atlantic Capital Corp., N.Y.C., 1973—; owner, operator, Urfer Farms, 1973—; dir. United Silk Mills, Ltd., WJS Inc. Mem. nat. council Salk Inst. Served to 2d lt. U.S. Army, 1959. Mem. N.Y. Soc. Security Analysts, Council Fgn. Relations. Republican. Clubs: Union (N.Y.C.); India House, Harbor, Morris County Golf, Seal Harbor Yacht. Contbr. articles to profl. jours. Home: Willow Brook Farm Blue Mill Rd Morristown NJ 07960 Office: 40 Wall St New York NY 10005

UROSHEVICH, MIROSLAV, solar energy co. exec.; b. Belgrade, Yugoslavia, Aug. 29, 1933; s. Spasoje and Nevenka (Pretic) Urosevic; B.S. equivalent, U. Belgrade, 1956; postgrad. Beaux Arts and Ecole Polytechnique, Paris, 1957-58; m. Ingrid Schwarzpaul, Dec. 31, 1963; children—Marko, Steven, Yvette, Nicole. Chief designer Panhard et Levassor SA, Paris, 1956-58; chief devel. engr. Keco Industries, Cin., 1958-60; pres. Alpha Designs Inc., cons., Cin., 1960-77; pres. Alpha Solarco Inc., Cin., 1977—; speaker and lectr. on solar energy and related subjects. Mem. Internat. solar Energy Soc., Solar Energy Industries Assn. Serbian Orthodox. Patentee. Home: 2505 Fleetwood Ave Cincinnati OH 45211 Office: 1014 Vine St Suite 2530 Cincinnati OH 45202

URQUHART-FISHER, CAROL LOANNE, banker; b. Tex., Dec. 15, 1949; d. John Earl and Marguerite Loanne (Urquhart) Fisher; B.A., Rice U., 1970; M.A., U. Pa., 1973, M.B.A., Wharton Sch., 1975. Mgmt. Trainee Young & Rubicam, Australia, 1973; with Am. Express Internat. Banking Corp., 1974—, dep. dir. Am. Express Bank A/S, Copenhagen, Denmark, 1975-77; asst. v.p., chief staff global treasury, N.Y.C., 1977—. Mem. Republican Nat. Com., 1977—; founder Center for Internat. Security Studies of Am. Security Council Ednl. Found., 1977. Mem. Am. Mktg. Assn., Fin. Women of N.Y., Assn. M.B.A. Execs. Episcopalian. Club: Jr. League. Home: 200 E 24th St New York NY 10010 Office: 125 Broad St New York NY

URREA, PETRONIO DAVID, JR., soft contact lens co. exec.; b. San Francisco, Nov. 8, 1939; s. Petronio David and Martha Herren (Clark) U.; student San Francisco City Coll., 1957-60; student U. Calif. at Berkeley, 1960-62; Pharm.D. with honors, U. Calif. Med. Center, San Francisco, 1966; m. Eileen Patricia Morley, Apr. 12, 1979; children—Cheryl Lynn, Kimberly Lnn, Deborah Lynn, Wayne Maurice, Karen Lynn, Tina Marie. Clin. liaison Barnes-Hind Pharms., Sunnyvale, Calif., 1967-68, mgr. clin. liaison, 1968-69; dir. med. affairs Barnes-Hind Pharms., 1970-72, dir. med. and tech. affairs, 1972-73, v.p. med. and tech. affairs, 1972-73, v.p. research and product devel., 1973-76; v.p. ops. Continuous Curve Contact Lenses, Ind., San Diego, 1976-79; pres. Hydron Australia Pty. Ltd., Sydney, Australia, 1979—. Served with USCGR, 1958-66. Recipient highest Coast Guard award for athletic excellence, 1958, named to All-Am. coll. swimming team, 1959; licensed pvt. single/multiengine pilot. Mem. Acad. Pharm. Scis., Am. Nat. Standards Inst., Am., Calif., Contra Costa pharm. assns., Nat. Assn. Retail Druggist, U. Calif. Sch. Pharmacy Alumni Assn., Kappa Psi. Roman Catholic. Research, inventions and publs. regarding contact lenses. Home: 27 Buena Vista Terr San Francisco CA 94117 Office: Hydron Australia Pty Ltd Capital Centre Bldg 255 Pitt St Sydney Australia 2000

URSIN, BJARNE ELLING, mfg. co. exec.; b. Bridgeport, Conn., Aug. 8, 1930; s. Bjarne and Esther (Schiott) U.; B.S. in Physics, Mass. Inst. Tech., 1957; m. Mary Elizabeth Locke, July 26, 1969; children—Stephanie, Lara, Matthew. Project engr. Raytheon, Andover, Mass., 1957-60; prin. investigator Gen. Dynamics, San Diego, 1960-62; sr. scientist Philco-Ford, Newport Beach, Calif., 1962-67; with McDonnell Douglas Corp., Huntington Beach, Calif., 1967-76, sr. ops. project mgr., mgr. mfg., 1967-76; prodn. mgr. Eldec Corp., Lynnwood, Wash., 1976-78; v.p. mfg. TCS Inc., 1978-80; chief exec. officer Westechnology, Bellevue, Wash., 1980—; v.p. Nor'west Reps, Bellevue, 1980—; pres. BJI, Mercer Island, Wash., 1968—. Commn. chmn. City of Huntington Beach, 1975-76. Served with AUS, 1951-53. Mem. Am. Inst. Physics, IEEE, Am. Assn. Physics Tchrs., Am. Inst. Aeros. and Astronautics, AAAS, U.S. Internat. Sailing Assn., Am. Mgmt. Assn. Republican. Roman Catholic. Clubs: M.I.T. of Wash. (dir. 1979—); Mercer Island Yacht (commodore 1977-80, dir. 1977-80); Mercer Island Jogging and Sculling Assn. (adm. 1978-80); Bahia Corinthian Yacht (bd. dirs. 1972-76, rear commodore 1974, vice commodore 1975, commodore 1976) (Corona Del Mar); Royal Norwegian Yacht (Oslo). Home: 9520 SE 61st Pl Mercer Island WA 98040 Office: PO Box 596 Mercer Island WA 98040 also 4320 150th Ave NE Redmond WA 98052

USELDINGER, RONALD EUGENE, health orgn. exec.; b. Warren, Minn., Dec. 16, 1932; s. John Jack and Ellen Josephine (Wickum) U.; B.A., Lewis and Clark Coll., 1954; M.A. in Phys. Edn., San Jose State Coll., 1965; children—Krista, Kevin, Kurt, Karole. Tchr., athletic coach Milwaukie High Sch., Portland, Oreg., 1955-59, Cupertino (Calif.) High Sch., 1959-62, Homestead High Sch., Sunnyvale, Calif., 1962-68; dist. dir. Am. Phys. Fitness, San Jose, Calif., 1968-71; regional dir. Phys. Fitness Inst. Am., San Jose, 1976-77; exec. dir. Fitness Motivation Inst. Am., San Jose, 1976-78, nat. dir., 1977-78; internat. dir. Fitness Motivation Inst., Inc., San Jose, 1978—; pres. FMI, Inc., 1978—; lectr. Mem. AAHPER, Calif. Coaches Assn., Nat. Small Bus. Men's Assn., Nat. Speakers Assn. (CSP award), Lewis and Clark Alumni Assn., Am., No. Calif. socs. of assn. execs., Amateur Athletic Union (mem. nat. council phys. fitness). Republican. Contbr. articles in field to various publs. Patentee exercise equipment. Home: 9331 Hwy 17 Santa Cruz CA 95060 Office: 36 Harold Ave San Jose CA 95117

USSERY, ALBERT TRAVIS, lawyer, banker; b. Gulfport, Miss., Mar. 12, 1928; s. Walter Travis and Rosamond (Sears) U.; A.B., Washington U., St. Louis, 1950; LL.B., U. N.Mex., 1951, J.D., 1968; LL.M., Georgetown U., 1955; m. Margaret Grosvenor Paine, Nov. 22, 1950; children—Margaret Rosamond, John Travis, Marilyn Ann, Meredith Lee. Admitted to N.Mex. bar, 1951; since practiced in Albuquerque; mem. firm Gallagher and Ussery, 1951-53, Threet, Ussery & Threet, 1957-60; asso. with Alfred H. McRae, 1961-63; partner McRae, Ussery, Mims, Ortega & Kitts, 1964-65; chmn. Am. Bank Commerce, 1966-70, pres., 1967-70; chmn. Rio Grande Valley Bank, Albuquerque, 1972—; partner Ussery, Burciaga & Parrish, 1969-79; pres. Ussery & Parrish, P.A., 1980—, Albuquerque Small Bus. Investment Co., 1977—; spl. counsel on water law City of Albuquerque, 1956-66. Lectr. mil. law U. N.Mex., 1956, instr. corp. finance, 1956-57, lectr. bus. law, 1960-61. Chmn. water adv. com. Albuquerque Indsl. Devel. Service, 1960-66; vice chmn. N.Mex. Council on Econ. Edn., 1969-74; chmn. bd. advisors Lovelace Med. Found., 1976-78, trustee, 1978—; mem. N.Mex. Regional Export Expansion Council, 1969-74. Bd. dirs. Goodwill Industries N.Mex., 1957-65, Albuquerque Travelers Assistance, 1956-66, Family Consultation Service, 1961-64, Albuquerque Symphony Assn., 1964-68, N.Mex. Arthritis Found., 1969—. Served as 1st lt. Judge Advocate Gen. Corps. AUS, 1953-55. Mem. Am., Fed., Albuquerque (treas. 1957-60) bar assns., State Bar of N.Mex., Estate Planning Council Albuquerque (pres. 1962), N.Mex. Bankers Assn., N.Mex. Zool. Soc. (pres. 1977-78), Am. Legion (comdr. 1962-63), Lawyers Club, Delta Sigma Pi. Club: Kiwanis (dir. 1957-60). Home: PO Box 487 Albuquerque NM 87103 Office: 200 Rio Grande Valley Bank Bldg 501 Tijeras Ave NW PO Box 487 Albuquerque NM 87103

USSERY, HARRY MACRAE, engring. and construction co. exec.; b. Rockingham, N.C., Jan. 27, 1920; s. Robert Roy and Maggie Estelle (MacRae) U.; A.A., Wake Forest U., 1947; J.D., George Washington U., 1950; m. Olive Dual Simmons, Mar. 19, 1949. Admitted to D.C. bar, 1950; asso. firm Geiger & Harmel, Washington, 1950-52; partner firm McNeill & Ussery, Washington, 1952-53; gen. counsel, dir. Harry R. Byers, Inc., Washington and Denver, 1953-59; procurement counsel Martin Marietta Corp., Denver, 1959-62; authorized agent RCA, Camden, N.J., 1962-69; staff counsel, mgr. internat. subcontract operations Burns and Roe Construction Corp., Paramus, N.J., 1969-74; legal counsel, mgr. internat. subcontract operations Burns and Roe Indsl. Services Corp., Paramus, 1975—; cons. in field. Served with USAF, 1941-45. Recipient Community Chest Campaign awards, 1951, 52; named to Aviation Hall of Fame. Mem. Am. Bar Assn., Am. Judicature Soc., Nat. Contract Mgmt. Assn., George Washington Law Assn., Wake Forest Alumni Assn., Delta Theta Phi. Republican. Presbyterian. Clubs: St. Andrew's Soc., Clan MacRae Soc., Delaware Valley Jaguar, Colony (Medford Lakes, N.J.). Chief moderator and dir. District Roundtable, WWDC Radio Station, Washington, 1950-53. Home: 306 Village Pl Wyckoff NJ 07481 Office: PO Box 663 Paramus NJ 07652

UTZ, JOHN EDWARD, mktg. cons.; b. Dayton, Ohio, Mar. 13, 1945; s. David William and Ailene Abbie (Meyers) U.; B.A. and B.S. in History and Econs., U. Ill., 1967; M.B.A., U. N.H., 1973; m. Christina L. Imsick, Sept. 11, 1971. Product specialist, computer products div. Nashua Corp. (N.H.), 1971-73, distbr., sales mgr., 1973-74, worldwide mktg. mgr., 1974-77; pres. Mktg. Decisions, Inc., 1977—; guest lectr. bank direct mktg., office output and productivity. Served as lt. USNR, 1968-71. Mem. Internat. Word Processing Assn., Sigma Chi (Kappa Kappa chpt.). Republican. Contbr. articles to profl. publs. Home: 69 Haines Terr Merrimack NH 03054

UZELAC, GEORGE, JR., steel co. exec.; b. Gary, Ind., Sept. 26, 1942; s. George and Ann Marie (Stofega) U.; student Ind. U., 1961-70; children—Stacey Lynn, Todd Allen. Research asst. Sch. Bus., Ind. U. N.W., Gary, 1968-70; dir. govt. tax research Gary C. of C., 1969-72; pres. Info. Research Assos., Inc., Merrillville, Ind., 1972-76; tax rep. U.S. Steel Corp., Gary, 1976—; cons. Ind. Commn. on Tax and Fin. Policy, Town of Schererville (Ind.), Town of Dyer (Ind.), Town of St. John (Ind.), Govt. of Lake County (Ind.). Served with USAF, 1963-67; Vietnam. Mem. Am. Mgmt. Assn., Greater Gary C. of C., Lake County Community Devel. Com., Lake County Research Bur. Mem. Serbian Orthodox Ch. Author: Crime Within Our Society, 1971; A Comparative Review of Seven Indiana Public School Systems, 1971. Office: 1 N Broadway Gary IN 46402

VACCA, JOHN JOSEPH, broadcasting exec.; b. Chgo., Apr. 7, 1922; s. John Joseph and Caroline (Bain) V.; student Northwestern U., 1940-42, Internat. Corr. Schs., 1950-54; m. Alice Isabel Ure, May 2, 1944; children—John Joseph, Dawn Susan, Kim Frances. Editor, Midwest Times, Chgo., 1940-41; with prodn. dept. NBC Radio, 1946-47; news dir. Sta. KECK, Odessa, Tex., 1947-49, chief announcer, 1948-49; program mgr. KOSA-Radio, Odessa, 1949-55, sta. mgr. KOSA-TV, 1955-61, gen. mgr., 1962-72; sec. Odessa Broadcasting Co., 1950-72; v.p., dir. Trigg-Vaughn Stas., Inc., Odessa, 1962-67; asst. sec. Doubleday Broadcasting Co., Inc., Odessa, 1967-78, v.p., 1967-75, sr. v.p., 1975-78; gen. mgr. KDTV, Dallas, 1972-73; v.p., gen. mgr. MCI Prodns., Dallas, 1978-79; TV cons., 1979—. Bd. dirs. Better Bus. Bur., Odessa, 1956-72, Odessa Community Chest, 1965-72; campaign maj. ARC, 1951-72; publicity adviser Ector County chpt. Nat. Found. for Infantile Paralysis, 1949—; campaign coordinator Civic Music Assn., 1950-72; sponsor, adviser Permian Playhouse, 1959-72, v.p., 1971-72; city councilman, Odessa, 1962-64; bd. dirs. Am. Cancer Soc. Served with USAAF, 1942-46. Recipient Zeus award Epsilon Sigma Alpha, 1971. Mem. Nat., Tex. assns. broadcasters, Tex. AP Broadcasters Assns., Advt. Club Odessa (pres. 1960-61, dir. 1960-63), C. of C. (publicity adviser 1950-72), Holy Name Soc. Roman Catholic. Club: K.C. (sec. Odessa 1950-51). Home: 9872 Dale Crest Dallas TX 75220

VAGELL, CRAIG WILLIAM, real estate appraiser; b. Passaic, N.J., Mar. 1, 1949; s. William Michael and Rose Marie V.; student U. Dayton (Ohio), 1967-68; B.A., Rutgers U., 1971, M.B.A., 1973; m. Marilyn C. Ippolito, July 16, 1972; 1 dau., Kristy Lynn. Sr. real estate credit analyst 1st Nat. State Bank of N.J., 1972-74; dir. residential appraising pvt. real estate appraisal firm, Morristown, N.J., 1974-78; pvt. practice as real estate appraiser, 1978—; adj. faculty mem. Somerset Community Coll., 1978—; cons. bd. dirs. Greater Morristown Area Jaycees, 1977, v.p., 1978, counsel to bd., 1979; radio officer charge emergency communications Garfield Civil Def., 1967-74; communications officer Hanover Twp., 1980—. Licensed real estate salesman, N.J. Mem. Soc. Real Estate Appraisers (sr. residential appraiser), Wireless Inst. Northeast, Am. Radio Relay

League, Morris County Bd. Realtors. Roman Catholic. Club: Split Rock Amateur Radio. Home: 6 Crest Rd Cedar Knolls NJ 07927 Office: PO Box 1032R Morristown NJ 07960

VAIANA, PAUL FRANKLIN, farm equipment mfg. co. exec.; b. Moline, Ill., Oct. 24, 1940; s. Joseph and Crystal K. Vaiana; student Blackhawk Jr. Coll., Moline, Ill., 1958; m. Sally E. Ronk, Dec. 26, 1960; children—Lisa, Thomas, Shawn, Jon, Jennifer. IBM trainee Deere & Co., Moline, 1959-60; IBM operator Internat. Harvester Co., Rock Island, Ill., 1960-61, Eagle Food Center, Milan, Ill., 1961-62; IBM operator, then specifications clk. John Deere Harvester Works, East Moline, Ill., 1963-67; microfilm analyst Deere & Co., Moline, 1967-76, mgr. microfilm systems div., 1976—. Mem. Nat. Micrographics Assn. (past chpt. pres., standards bd. 1979-80), Internat. Micrographics Assn., Comtec Assn. Address: 2919 28th Ave A Moline IL 61265

VAIKUTIS, JOHN PAUL, lead smelting and refining co. exec.; b. Chgo., Jan. 1, 1918; s. Peter P. and Frances M. (Poska) V.; B.S., Ill. Inst. Tech., 1944; m. Denise Alkim, Nov. 3, 1956; children—Jeanne, Judith, John, Joseph, Joyce. Founder, partner Continental Smelting & Refining Co., McCook, Ill., 1946-65; corp. project engr. DeSoto, Inc., DesPlaines, Ill., 1965-70; phys. plant dir. ARA Services, St. Charles, Ill., 1970-76; v.p., founder, partner Mincon, Muncie, Ind., 1976—. Water commr. Village of Indian Head Park, Ill., 1966—. Registered profl. engr., Ill., Ind. Mem. Am. Inst. Mech. Engrs., ASME, Chgo. C. of C. Republican. Roman Catholic. Clubs: K.C., Legion of the Moose; Edgewood Valley Country. Home: 6544 Pontiac Dr Indian Head Park IL 60525 Office: Mincon Corp 2601 W Mount Pleasant Blvd Muncie IN 47302

VAIL, JOE FRANKLIN, mktg. co. exec.; b. Indpls., Mar. 24, 1928; s. Frank Albert and Trixie May (Hawley) V.; B.S., Purdue U., 1951; 1 son, Kevin Joe. Treas., Apex Corp., Indpls., 1953-60; owner, operator Bus. Service Co., Indpls., 1961-63; partner Pulse Publs., Indpls., 1963-64; pres. Unique, Inc., Indpls., 1965-70; owner, operator Mid-Am. Advt. Co., Indpls., 1970-73; pres. Mid-Am. Mktg., Inc., Indpls., 1973—. Mem. Chgo. Assn. Direct Mktg.; Nat. Fedn. Ind. Bus., Am. Bus. Club. Clubs: John Purdue, Masons. Editor, pub.: Land Opportunity Review, 1970—. Author: Keys to Wealth, 1971; Your Fortune in Mail Order, 1972; How to Get Out of Debt and Live Like a Millionaire, 1977; Money-Where It is and How to Get It, 1981. Home: 1720 Wellington Ave Indianapolis IN 46219 Office: 1150 N Shadeland Ave Indianapolis IN 46219

VAIL, RICHARD CARTER, instrument co. exec.; b. Sterling, Ill., Dec. 14, 1930; s. Cecil Sterling and Ida Simpson Panther; B.S. in Indsl. Econs., Iowa State U., 1952; m. Janet S. Sullivan, Mar. 4, 1967; children—Rebecca, Robert, David. Mgr. spacecraft communications mfg. dept. Collins Radio Co., Cedar Rapids, Iowa, 1961-67; dir. prodn. ops., systems div. Harris Corp., Melbourne, Fla., 1967-73; dir. mfg., computer div. Harris Corp., Ft. Lauderdale, Fla., 1973-75; v.p. mfg., instrument group Sybron Corp., Rochester, N.Y., 1975—. Served with USAF, 1954-56. Republican. Presbyterian. Club: Rotary (dir.) (Rochester). Office: Sybron Corp 95 Ames St Rochester NY 14601

VAIL, ROBERT WILLIAM, cons. co. exec.; b. Columbus, Ohio, Oct. 29, 1921; s. Robert David and Dorothy (Mosier) V.; student Ohio State U., 1938-39; m. Martha Henderson, Apr. 7, 1939; children—William N., Veronica Vail Fish, David A., Ashley M., Victor H., Lorelei Meade, Hilary W. Chemist, Barnebey-Cheney Engring. Co., 1941-44; sr. chemist Pa. Coal Products Co., Petrolia, 1944-51; abrasive engr. Carborundum Co., Niagara Falls, N.Y., 1951-54; tech. sales Allied Chem. Corp., Cleve., 1954-59; head research lab. U.S. Ceramic Tile Co., Canton, Ohio, 1960-62; sales mgr. Ferro Chem. div. Ferro Corp., Walton Hills, Ohio, 1962-70; pres. R. William Vail Inc., Cleve., 1971-72; mgr. tech. services Manpower Inc., Cleve., 1972-74; owner, mgr. Vail, Shaker Heights, Ohio, 1974-78; sr. cons. Hayden, Heman, Smith & Assos., Cleve., 1978—. Recipient Am. Security Council Bus. Citizenship Competition Excellence award, 1967. Mem. Amateur Radio Relay League. Republican. Presbyterian. Clubs: Shriners, Masons. Author: Teardrops Falling, 1963; contbg. author: Ency. of Basic Materials for Plastics, 1967. Home: 1701 E 12th St #20T West Cleveland OH 44114 Office: 3260-100 Erieview Plaza Cleveland OH 44114

VALCHAR, JERRY EDWARD, ins. co. exec.; b. Oakland, Tex., Dec. 13, 1917; s. Jerry Joe and Annie (Malinovsky) V.; student Blinn Jr. Coll., 1953, Temple (Tex.) Jr. Coll., 1954; student in farm mut. prins. U. Tex., 1966-67; m. Vlasta Ermis, Jan. 21, 1946; children—Gladys Ann, Bernice Jane (Mrs. Nicolas K. Henry). Sec.-adjuster lodge Farmers Mut. Protective Assn., Weimar, Tex., 1947-52, treas., Temple, 1953-58, pres., 1959—, also dir.; pres. Tex. R.V.O.S. Ins. Co., 1978—. Notary pub., Bell County (Tex.), 1953—; translator birth certificates from Czech lang. Dist. Social Security Office, Temple, 1966—. Mem. Temple Citizens Adv. Com., 1962-67; mem. housing study group, Temple, 1966-67; mem. nat. council U.S.O., 1971—, v.p. Temple council, 1971-72, pres., 1973. Sec., Planning Commn., Temple, 1968-71, mem. City Zoning Bd., 1970-71. Bd. dirs. Temple United Fund. Served with AUS, 1941-45; PTO. Decorated Bronze Star. Adm., Tex. Navy, 1969—. Mem. Tex. Assn. Mut. Fire and Storm Ins. Cos. (pres. 1965-67), Western Fraternal Life Assn., Slavonic Benevolent Order Tex., V.F.W. Mem. Ch. of Brethren (ch. bd. 1954-55, pres. Men's Brotherhood 1965-66). Modern Woodman. Club: Farm and Ranch. Contbr. articles to co. publs. Home: 12 E Young St Temple TX 76501 Office: PO Box 426 Temple TX 76501

VALENTA, JOSEF, investment casting mfg. co. exec.; b. Bruck, Austria, Dec. 15, 1925; s. Franz and Cecilia (Krassnitzer) V.; came to Can., 1957; Chemotechniker, Corr. Sch. Berlin, 1943; m. Elfriede Sorger, Nov. 7, 1952; children—Jose Kurt Fernando, Enrique, Frank. Lab. technician Geb. Boehler & Co. AG, Bohler, Austria, 1947-51; Clip S.A., Buenos Aires, Argentina, 1951-52; partner, tech. dir. Durometal Societad Responsibilitad, Ltd., Buenos Aires, 1952-56; co-founder Cercast Inc., Montreal, Que., Can., 1958, sec.-treas., 1958-69; co-founder Vestshell Inc., Montreal, 1964, sec. treas., 1964-69, pres., owner, 1969—; pres. Canus Tool & Machine Inc., Montreal, Vestshell Vermont Inc., St. Albans, Vt. Served with German Army, 1943-45. Home: 2255 Dudemaine St Montreal PQ H3M 1R4 Canada Office: 10351 Pelletier St Montreal North PQ H1H 3R2 Canada

VALENTINE, ROGER LEE, electronics co. exec.; b. Akron, Ohio, Nov. 20, 1941; s. Leland Leolan and Anna Mae Thelma Blanche (Snook) V.; B.S. in Mech. Engring., Brigham Young U., 1973; m. Joanne Probst, Sept. 10, 1964; children—Deborah, Carey, Ryan, Anne. Prodn. coordinator Alpha Corp., Salt Lake City, 1971; mgr. Sanford Heilner Inc., Provo, Utah, 1971-72; mgr. Valentine Engring. Inc., Oren, Utah, 1972-78; mech. engr., research and devel. dept. Ivie Electronics Inc., Orem, 1978-79, mgr. Fabrication div., 1979—. Chmn. Planning Commn., Highland City, Utah, 1980—. Mem. Soc. Mfg. Engrs. (sr. mem.). Republican. Mormon. Home: 11161 N 5730 W Highland UT 84003 Office: 500 W 1200 S Orem UT 84057

VALENTINO, FLAVIO, chem. co. exec.; b. Albona, Italy, Sept. 11, 1924; s. Cesare and Gemma (Brun) V.; came to U.S., 1973; student U. Milan, 1944-48. Lab. tech. Madeco, Santiago, Chile, 1950-56; tech. sales coordinator internat. div. Montecatini, Milan, 1957-61; mng. dir. Montedison U.K., London, 1961-73; exec. v.p. Montedison U.S.A., N.Y.C., 1973—; chmn. Galileo Corp. Am., Fiorucci Inc.; v.p. Datamount USA, 1976—; cons. in field. Mem. Inst. Dirs. Roman Catholic. Office: 1114 Ave of Americas New York NY 10036

VALENTINO, HARRY NICHOLAS, meat packing co. exec.; b. New Castle, Pa., June 9, 1944; s. Harry Edward and Louise Philomena (Toscano) V.; B.A., Allegheny Coll., 1966; M.B.A., U. Chgo., 1968; m. Michele Mae Malley, Dec. 26, 1970; children—Roslyn, Roxanne, Nicholas. Asst. exec. dir. Deaconess Hosp. Inc., Evansville, Ind., 1971-76; adminstr. Massillon (Ohio) Community Hosp., 1976-79; adminstrv. v.p. Superior's Brand Meats, Inc., Massillon, 1979—. Bd. dirs. Mental Health Assn., Massillon; mem. exec. com. U. Chgo. Grad. Program In Hosp. Adminstrn. Served with Med. Service Corps, USN, 1968-71. Fellow Am. Coll. Hosp. Adminstrs.; mem. Am. Hosp. Assn. Office: PO Box 571 Massillon OH 44646

VALENZUELA, THOMAS, JR., mortgage banking exec.; b. Pasadena, Calif., Sept. 9, 1940; s. Thomas and Juanita Anita (Ruiz) V.; B.S. in E.E., Calif. State U., Long Beach, 1963; M.B.A., Woodbury U., Los Angeles, 1974. Pres., Advanced Recovery Systems, Los Angeles, 1969—; pres., chmn. Accrutek Engring. Co., Los Angeles, 1970—; exec. v.p. Beverly Hills (Calif.) Finding, Inc., 1977—; exec. v.p., chief. fin. officer Chelsea Pictures Internat., Beverly Hills, 1979—. Served with USAF, 1963-67. Decorated D.S.M., Legion of Merit with 1 oak leaf cluster, D.F.C., Air medal with 4 oak leaf clusters, Silver Star, Bronze Star. Registered profl. safety engr., profl. electronic engr. Office: 9440 Santa Monica Blvd Beverly Hills CA 90210

VALICENTI, SHIRLEY MARGUERITE, alloy co. exec.; b. Brookline, Mass.; d. Henry Joseph and Marguerite Leontine (Marshall) Halpin. Gen. mgr. Friedman Metal Co. (name changed to Freecast Alloys Inc.), Bklyn., 1965-74, v.p., 1974—. Mem. children's com. against mental illness Bklyn. Assn. Mental Health, 1968-70; pres. Bklyn. chpt. Am. Soc. Mentally Ill Children, 1966-69; mem. Mayors Com. on Mental Health, N.Y.C., 1970-72; pres. PTA Summit Sch. for Spl. Children, Queens, N.Y., 1965-68. Mem. Zinc Alloyers Assn. (pres. 1978), Soc. Die Casting Engrs. Office: 310 McGuinness Blvd Brooklyn NY 11222

VALINET, STANLEY S., diversified co. exec.; b. Indpls., Nov. 13, 1916; s. Arthur and Mary (Bernstein) V.; student Ind. U., 1933-40; div.; children—Stephen, Pamela, Greg. Founder, chmn. bd. Tru-Lite Research Labs., Indpls., 1937-75; chmn. bd. Stanley Realty and Devel. Co., Indpls., 1939-76; chmn. bd., pres. NRC Corp., Indpls., 1940—, Valley Devel. Co., Indpls., 1939—. Mem. Profl. Farmers Am., Future Farmers Am., Am. Soybean Assn. Republican. Club: Columbia (Indpls.). Office: PO Box 40789 Indianapolis IN 46240

VALK, ROBERT JAMES, ins. co. exec.; b. Middletown, Conn., Jan. 13, 1948; s. Henry James and Catherine (Dougherty) V.; B.A. in Math., St. Michael's Coll., 1970; M.S. in Math, Central Conn. State Coll., 1974; m. Denise Ann Battis, Nov. 4, 1978. Tchr., Windsor (Conn.) Bd. Edn., 1970-73; programmer, analyst Aetna Life & Casualty, Hartford, Conn., 1974-76, sr. analyst, 1976-78, devel. supt., 1978—. Democrat. Home: 70 Steep Rd South Windsor CT 06074 Office: 151 Farmington Ave Hartford CT 06115

VALLE, ANTHONY JOSEPH, govt. mgmt. ofcl.; b. Newark, Mar. 24, 1944; s. Anthony Thomas and Marie Cathrine (Peltz) V.; B.A., Seton Hall U., 1965; m. Claire Ellen Picknally, Dec. 30, 1967; children—Anthony J. Jr., Mary Elizabeth, Michael T., Barbara Ann, Daniel S. Supply systems analyst U.S. Navy Internat. Logistics Control Office, Bayonne, N.J., 1967-71, head of evaluation div., 1971-75, dir. performance evaluation div., 1975-77, dir. mgmt. engring. div., Phila., 1977—. Served with arty. U.S. Army, 1965-67; Viet Nam. Decorated Army Commendation medal. Mem. Am. Mgmt. Assn., Methods Time Measurement Assn. for Standards and Research (Certificate of Recognition 1968). Roman Catholic. Home: 1523 Longfellow Dr Cherry Hill NJ 08003 Office: 700 Robbins Ave Philadelphia PA 19111

VALLELY, BARBARA ANN, banker; b. N.Y.C., Nov. 13, 1946; d. Joseph Leon and Mary Josefa (Jablonski) Breton; B.A., St. John's U., 1968; M.B.A. with distinction, Pace U., 1974; m. Thomas J. Vallely III, Oct. 3, 1970; 1 dau., Christine Michelle. Caseworker Dept. Scoial Services, Bklyn., 1968-69; adminstrv. asst. Internat. div. Irving Trust Co., N.Y.C., 1970-73, credit analyst, Asia dist. mgr., 1973-74, corp. lending trainee, asst. sec., 1974-76, asst. v.p. Comml. Banking div., 1978—. Mem. Delta Mu Delta. Club: Welcome Wagon.

VALLERIO, SAMUEL ROBERT, financial corp. exec.; b. Phila., Apr. 9, 1931; s. Samuel and Virginia (Cipparone) V.; B.A., U. Pa., 1953; m. Bernardine Rosemary Poplaski, May 7, 1966; children—Robert William, Keith Stephen. Underwriter trainee Pa. Fire Ins. Co., Phila., 1956; div. ops. mgr. CIT Corp., Phila., 1956—. Served with U.S. Army, 1953-55. Mem. World Affairs Council Phila., U. Pa. Alumni Assn. Republican. Roman Catholic. Home: 60 Kingsclere Rd Southampton PA 18966 Office: 2 Penn Center Plaza Philadelphia PA 19102

VALLERY, JERRY LOUIS, computer services co. exec.; b. Phila., Jan. 29, 1945; s. Jerry and Mary Etta (Pope) V.; B.S., Fisk U., 1966; postgrad. in physics (fellow) Howard U., 1967-68; J.D., Cath. U. Am., 1977; m. Madelyn Louise Hicks, Apr. 16, 1965; children—Jerry Louis Jr., Kia Kilolo. Aerospace engr. Dept Navy, Washington, 1966-68; mktg. rep., systems engr. IBM Corp., Arlington, Va., 1968-72; data processing cons. Internat. Bus. Services, Washington, 1972-73; mktg. mgr. Grumman Data Systems Corp., Washington, 1973-75; dir. mktg. Informatics Inc., McLean, Va., 1975—; admitted to D.C. bar, 1977, U.S. Dist. and Appeals Cts. bars, 1977; dir. Career Systems Inc., Synergy Data Systems Inc. Mem. exec. com. Ward 4 Democrats, 1978-79; chmn. fund raising Fisk Alumni, Washington; bd. dirs. HOPE Inc.; del. 10th anniversary ceremony Republic Tanzania, 1971; chmn. Commn. on Christian Social Relations. Mem. D.C., Am., Washington, Fed. bar assns., Washington C. of C., Internat. Traders, Computer Law Assn., Nat. Assn. Housing and Redevel. Ofcls., Phi Alpha Delta, Kappa Alpha Psi. Baptist. Contbr. articles to profl. jours. Home: 1773 Verbena St NW Washington DC 20012 Office: 7926 Jones Branch Dr Suite 272 McLean VA 22101

VALLONE, EDWARD BARCALO, II, investment banker; b. Harrisburg, Pa., Nov. 23, 1939; s. Edward Barcalo and Helen Ethel (Congrove) V.; student Trinity Coll., Hartford, Conn., 1957-59, U. Ariz., 1961-64; m. Donna Joan Smith, Aug. 2, 1968; children—Edward Barcalo, Berkley. Dir. sales Camelback Inn, Scottsdale, Ariz., 1964, resident mgr., 1965; trainee, rep. E.F. Hutton & Co., Phoenix, 1966-67; rep., asst. mgr. Bache & Co., Phoenix, 1967-69; with Young, Smith & Peacock, Inc., Phoenix, 1969—, sr. v.p., mgr. retail div., 1974-78, pres., chief exec. officer, 1978—; pres. Phoenix Giants, 1980—; dir. MNORX, Inc., Hartford. Founder, Project 35, YMCA, bd. dirs., 1968-70. Mem. Nat. Security Traders Assn., Phoenix Stock and Bond Club, Ariz. Security Traders, Young Pres.'s Orgn., Beta Theta Pi. Republican. Episcopalian. Clubs: Paradise Valley Country, Plaza (founding gov.), Kiva, Ariz., Execs. (Phoenix); Head Honchos Parada Del Sol (Scottsdale); Pine Valley Golf (N.J.). Home: 6613 E Exeter Blvd Scottsdale AZ 85251 Office: 3443 N Central St Suite 100 Phoenix AZ 85012

VALTOS, WILLIAM, advt. agy. exec.; b. Scranton, Pa., Aug. 18, 1937; s. James Anthony and Mary (Rukat) V.; student U. Scranton; m. Maria Rosario Cecilia Tolentino Vallarta, Sept. 2, 1959; children—William, Catherine, Anthony, Michael. Copy chief R.H. Macy & Co., N.Y.C., 1959-61; copy chief, v.p., prin. Rockmore, Garfield & Shaub, Inc., 1961-65; creative dir., v.p. Clinton E. Frank, Inc., N.Y.C. and Chgo., 1965-75; creative dir., sr. v.p. D'Arcy, McManus & Masius, Chgo., 1975—. Served with USAF, 1955-59. Home: 420 High Ridge Rd Barrington IL 60010 Office: 200 E Randolph St Chicago IL 60601

VAN, GEORGE PAUL, diversified co. exec.; b. Isle Maligne, Que., Canada, Feb. 12, 1940; s. Raymond Murdoch and Germaine Marie (Brassard) V.; B.A. in Psychology, McGill U., 1961; D.H.A., U. Toronto, 1963; m. Janine Marie Irene Therese Yvette Boily, Sept. 15, 1962; children—John, Robert, Caroline. Sr. cons. Agnew, Peckham & Assos., Toronto, Ont., Can., 1963-65; chief exec. officer, exec. dir. Misericordia Corp., Edmonton, Alta., Can., 1965-68; chief exec. officer, exec. v.p., dir. Texpack, Ltd. subs. Am. Hosp. Supply Corp., Brantford, Ont., 1968-70; group v.p., Will Ross, Inc. (now subs. G.D. Searle), Milw., 1970-73; exec. v.p., chief operating officer, dir. Nortek, Inc., Cranston, R.I., 1973-77; pres., chief operating officer, mem. exec. com., dir. Bd. Hosp. Affilates Internat., Inc. (now subs. INA Corp.), Nashville, 1977—; lectr. in field; cons., participant numerous profl. coms., advisory councils, workshops, coms. involving collective bargaining. Bd. dirs. Tulane U. Med. Center; asso. trustee U. Pa., also bd. overseers Sch. Nursing. Mem. Am. Mgmt. Assn. (pres.'s assn.), Internat., Am. hosp. assns., Am. Coll. Hosp. Adminstrs., Am. Pub. Health Assn. Fedn. Am. Hosps. Clubs: Hillwood Country, Seven Hills Swim, Nashville Racquet. Contbr. numerous articles to profl. jours. Home: 4509 Shys Hill Rd Nashville TN 37215 Office: 4525 Harding Rd Nashville TN 37205

VAN ABRAHAMS, RON, electronics co. exec.; b. Chgo., Oct. 18, 1935; s. Charles and Myrtle (Van Flymen) Abrahams; student Lake Forest Coll., 1953-55; B.A., U. Chgo., 1959; m. Nancy Elaine Adam, Oct. 3, 1973; children—Justin Trent, Meagan Royce. Asst. export mgr. Apeco Corp., Evanston, Ill., 1960-62; staff asst. Westinghouse Electric Corp., Pitts., 1962-66; mgr. adminstrn. Republic Corp., Beverly Hills, Calif., 1966-70; br. mgr. Fundamental Investment Corp., Lafayette, Calif., 1970-72; v.p. adminstrn. Pioneer Electronics Am., Long Beach, Calif., 1972—. Served with USAF, 1955-59. Mem. Am. Mgmt. Assn., Am. Soc. Personnel Adminstrn., Assn. Electronic Importers. Christian Scientist. Office: 1925 E Dominguez St Long Beach CA 90810

VANAGS, INTIS, benefits cons.; b. Jaunrauna, Latvia, July 24, 1939; s. Janis and Dzidra Laima (Sauleskalns) V.; came to U.S., 1950, naturalized, 1958; A.B., Amherst Coll., 1962; m. Mara Ozolins, June 8, 1968; children—Liza Laima, Eriks Intis. Reporter, photographer Memphis Press-Scimitar, summers 1961, 62; tchr. Fla. Air Acad., Melbourne, 1962-63; with Conn. Gen. Life Ins. Co., various locations, 1965-76, dist. mgr., group pension, San Francisco, 1972-76; field rep., retirement and ins. Air Line Pilots Assn., Washington, 1976-79; v.p., mgr. employee benefit plan cons. Cin. Office, Johnson & Higgins, 1979—. Served with U.S. Army, 1963-65. Republican. Lutheran. Home: 6265 Hollow Wood Circle Loveland OH 45140

VAN ALSTYNE, VANCE BROWNELL, arbitration mgmt. cons.; b. Rochester, N.Y., Feb. 3, 1924; s. Guy Brownell and Jessie Cary Van A.; B.A., U. Rochester, 1948; LL.B., Blackstone Coll. Law, 1964; m. Jane Kotary, Aug. 12, 1950; children—Cary B., Stacey E. Research asst. Gilbert Assos., Inc., N.Y.C., 1950-56; corp. sec., v.p., dir. R.C. Simpson & Staff, Inc., Newark and Ridgewood, N.J., 1956-74, chmn., pres., dir. R.C. Simpson, Inc., Ridgewood, 1975—. Served to 2d lt. USAF, 1943-45. Decorated Air medals. Mem. Am. Mgmt. Assn., Indsl. Relations Research Assn., Am. Arbitration Assn., Atlantic, Swiss-Icelandic salmon assns. Home: 175 Brush Hill Rd Kinnelon NJ 07405 Office: United Jersey Bank Bldg PO Box 567 Ridgewood NJ 07451

VAN ANDEL, BETTY JEAN, household products co. exec.; b. Mich., Dec. 14, 1921; d. Anthony and Daisy (Van Dyk) Hoekstra; A.B., Calvin Coll., 1943; m. Jay Van Andel, Aug. 16, 1952; children—Nan Elizabeth, Stephen Alan, David Lee, Barbara Ann. Elementary sch. tchr., Grand Rapids, Mich., 1943-45; service rep. and supr. Mich. Bell Telephone Co., Grand Rapids, 1945-52; dir.-stockholder Amway Corp., Grand Rapids, 1972—. Treas., LWV, 1957-60; chmn. Eagle Forum, Mich., 1975—. Mem. Nat. Trust Hist. Preservation, St. Cecelia Music Soc., Smithsonian Assos. Republican. Club: Women's City of Grand Rapids. Home: 7186 Windy Hill Rd SE Grand Rapids MI 49506 Office: PO Box 172 Ada MI 49301

VANCE, HERBERT A., publishing exec.; b. Bklyn., Aug. 29, 1901; s. William and Jane (Brown) V.; B.S., St. Lawrence U., 1924, L.H.D., 1978; m. Dorothy J. Jones, Dec. 18, 1942; children—Herbert A., William Colekin. Statistician, Bankers Trust Co., N.Y.C.; sec., treas. Ault & Wiborg Co., Cin.; gen. mgr. R. H. Donnelley Corp., N.Y.C.; chmn. Vance Pub. Co.; dir. Hartford Plaza Bank, Chgo. Past mem. bd. dirs. Asso. Bus. Publs., N.Y.; trustee Lincoln Coll. Served as comdr. USN, 1943-46. Recipient Navy Citation Commendation with ribbon; U.S. Treasury award War Fin., 1945. Clubs: Chgo., Union League, Racquet (Chgo.); St. Lawrence U.; Farmington Country (Charlottesville, Va.); Onwentsia (Lake Forest, Ill.). Home: 791 N Hawthorne Ln Lake Forest IL 60045 Office: 300 W Adams St Chicago IL 60606

VANCE, JAMES, mfg. co. exec.; b. Cleve., May 20, 1930; B.A. cum laude, Baldwin Wallace Coll., 1955; J.D. magna cum laude, Cleve. Marshall Law Sch., 1960; m. Dolores Bernadette Doyle, July 6, 1957; 1 son, James J. Asst. treas., asst. to v.p. fin. and adminstrn., fin. analyst Republic Steel Corp., 1956-58; treas. Addressograph and Multigraph Corp., Cleve., 1968-72; v.p. fin. Cin. Milacron Inc., 1972-76; exec. v.p. fin., treas., dir. Dayton-Walther Corp., Dayton, Ohio, 1977—; dir. Amertool Corp., Gen. Automation Corp., Citation Cos., DWISA Internat.-France, Fiday-France, Dayton-Est-France, Mincer-Mex.; lectr. bus. law Baldwin Wallace Coll., 1961-63. Vice chmn. United Appeal, 1959; mem. Citizens League Cleve., 1960; fin. com. YMCA, 1961; mem. Greater Cleve. Growth Center, 1963; vice chmn. fin. com. Cuyahoga Republican Party, 1968-69. Served with inf. AUS, 1951-52. Decorated Bronze Star. Mem. Cleve. Soc. Security Analysts, Am. Bar Assn., Ohio Bar Assn., Fin. Execs. Inst., Am. Ordnance Assn., Nat. Machine Tool Builders Assn., Machinery and Allied Products Inst., Am. Mgmt. Assn., Cin. Indsl. Inst., Ohio C. of C., Cleve. Treasurers Club (dir.), Alpha Tau Omega, Delta Theta Phi. Home: 6600 Wyman Ln Cincinnati OH 45243 Office: PO Box 1022 Dayton OH 45401

VANCE, ROBERT MERCER, banker, textile mfr.; b. Clinton, S.C., July 9, 1916; s. Robert Berly and Mary Ellen (Bailey) V.; B.S. in Bus. Adminstrn., Davidson Coll., 1937; H.H.D., Presbyn. Coll., Clinton, 1968; m. Virginia Sexton Gray, Dec. 27, 1949; children—Mary Bailey

Vance Patterson, Robert Mercer, Russell Gray. Paymaster, Lydia Cotton Mills, Clinton, 1937-41, v.p., 1953-58, pres., treas., 1958-64; with M.S. Bailey & Sons, bankers, Clinton, 1946—, pres., 1948-75, chmn. bd., 1975—; asst. treas. Clinton Cotton Mills (S.C.), 1948-53, v.p., 1953-58, pres., treas., 1958-64; v.p., asst. treas. Clinton Cottons, Inc., N.Y.C., 1953-58, treas., 1958-64; pres., treas. Clinton Mills, Inc. (merger Lydia Cotton Mills and Clinton Cotton Mills 1964), 1964-79, chmn. bd., 1979—; dir. Textile Hall Corp., Greenville, S.C. Pres. Community Chest Greater Clinton, 1958; trustee Inst. Textile Tech., Charlottesville, Va., 1959—; trustee Presbyn. Coll., Clinton, 1953-76, chmn., 1956-67, 78—; bd. visotors Davidson (N.C.) Coll., 1959-62, 77—; mem. State Commn. on Higher Edn., 1967—, chmn., 1968-71; elder-deacon First Presbyterian Ch., Clinton, 1950—, deacon, treas., 1950-58. Served with U.S. Army, 1941; served to lt. comdr. USNR, 1941-46. Named Man of Yr., Lions Club Clinton, 1955; Textile Man of Yr., N.Y. Bd. Trade, 1978. Mem. Am. Bankers Assn. (v.p. S.C. 1953-55), Am. Textile Mfrs. Inst. (dir. 1965-68, 70—), S.C. Textile Mfrs. Assn. (dir.), S.C. Bankers Assn. (pres. 1963-64), S.C. Textile Mfrs. Assn. (pres. 1967-68), Am. Legion, Kappa Alpha. Clubs: Piedmont (Spartanburg, S.C.); Poinsett (Greenville, S.C.); Lakeside Country, Kiwanis (pres. 1955) (Clinton). Home: 311 S Broad St Clinton SC 29325 Office: M S Bailey & Son Clinton SC 29325 also Clinton Mills Inc Clinton SC 29325

VAN CLEAVE, NOLL ALLEN, timber co. exec.; b. Mobile, Ala., Sept. 8, 1925; s. Noll Allen and Georgia Theresa (Ernest) V.; B.S. in Forestry, Auburn U., 1950; m. Elizabeth Jane Steber, Apr. 26, 1952; children—Jane, Devery, Noll Allen. Forester, Union Camp Paper Co., Savannah, Ga., 1945-51; procurement supr. St. Regis Paper Co., Pensacola, Fla., 1951-58; pres. Valley Wood, Inc., Richland, Ga., 1959—, Navco Timberlands, Inc., Columbus, Ga., 1962—, Callaway Old Cadillac, Inc., 1976—; sec.-treas. Maddox Chevrolet Co., Lumpkin, Ga., 1969—; chmn. bd. Colonial Nursing Home, Columbus, 1970—; pres. Valley Land, Inc., Richland, 1960—; dir. Fourth Nat. Bank, Columbus. Mem. Muscogee County Bd. Foresters, 1970—; mem. Gov.'s Adv. Bd. State and Local Govt., 1973; chmn. bd. Westville Handy Craft and Art, Inc., Lumpkin, 1973; mem. Muscogee County Sch. Bd., 1976—. Served with USAAF, 1944-45. Mem. Ga. Forestry Assn. (pres. 1971-73, chmn. bd. 1973-74), Soc. Am. Foresters, Am. Pulpwood Assn., Ga., Fla. (dir. 1952) forestry assns. Clubs: Moose, Lions (pres. 1954-55), Rotary, Big Eddy, Columbus Country. Home: 2406 Downing Dr Columbus GA 31906 Office: Box 127 Richland GA 31825

VAN CURLER, DONALD EDWARD, architect; b. Pontiac, Mich., Apr. 13, 1931; s. Raymond and Cornelia (Vanderzyl) Van C.; B.Arch., U. Mich., 1960. Mem. tool design dept. P.R. Mallory & Co., Indpls., 1951-52; draftsman, designer Charles M. Valentine Architect, Marysville, Mich., 1954-55; draftsman Wyeth & Harmon, Inc., Port Huron, Mich., 1955-56; designer James H. Livingston Architect, Ann Arbor, Mich., 1956-59; partner Hammett Assos. in Architecture, 1959-61; practice as Donald E. Van Curler, Architect, 1961—; pres. Flying Dutchman Mgmt. Inc., Amsterdam, Inc., Flying Dutchman Motor Inn Inc.; v.p., dir. Hwy. Club Systems, Inc. Exec. dir. Ann Arbor Research Inst., Modular Bldg. Research Found. Served with AUS, 1952-54. Recipient Best Home for Money award Am. Home mag., 1962, 63; Award of Excellence, Am. Inst. Steel Constrn., 1969; registered architect, Mich., Ind., Ohio, Pa., Ill., Ga., Ky., Miss., Wis., Tenn., Ala., Tex., S.C., Ark., Iowa. Mem. Soc. Am. Registered Architects, AIA, Nat. Rifle Assn., Soc. Archtl. Historians, Mich. Soc. Architects, Nat. Council Archtl. Registration Bds., Urban Land Inst., Nat. Hist. Soc., Engring. Soc. Detroit, Am. Def. Preparedness Assn., Korean Tae Kwon Do Assn., Phi Kappa Phi, Tau Sigma Delta. Republican. Baptist. Important works include restaurants, apt. bldgs., shopping centers. Office: 2004 Hogback Rd Ann Arbor MI 48104

VANDAGRIFF, DAVID PETER, electronic and elec. products mfg. co. exec., lawyer; b. Ames, Iowa, Oct. 25, 1947; s. Warren Williams and Marguerite Lucille (Morgan) V.; B.S., Northwestern U., 1969; J.D. cum laude, Pepperdine U., 1976; m. Gail Valerie Gibson, Oct. 21, 1972; 1 son, Morgan McGill. Research project dir. dept. econs. and mktg. research CNA Fin. Corp., Chgo., 1969-72; account exec. J. Walter Thompson Co., Chgo., 1972-73; pres. Corp. Info. Assos., Los Angeles, 1973-74; admitted to Calif. bar, 1976; asso. firm Robert V. Gibson, Los Angeles, 1974-76; v.p., gen. counsel Wanlass Techs. Inc., Tustin, Calif., 1976-79; pvt. practice, 1979—; dir. Valentine Orgn., Inc., Los Angeles, Wanlass Service Corp., Santa Ana, Calif., United Mo. Industries, Pierce City; bus. counsel Radiographic Devel. Corp., Santa Ana. Recipient Am. Jurisprudence award for corp. law Pepperdine U., 1976. Mem. Calif. Bar Assn., Orange County C. of C. Mormon. Office: 200 W Broadway Monett MO 65708

VANDENBERG, JAMES DAVID, publisher; b. Cleve., Jan. 8, 1949; s. W. James and Thais E. Vandenberg; B.S. in Journalism, Bowling Green State U., 1975. Founder, Flatlands Trader Newspaper, Bowling Green, Ohio, 1976, expanded edits., Findlay, Fostoria, Fremont, Tiffin, Ohio, 1977-79; pres. Flatlands Newspapers, Inc., Bowling Green, 1979—, also engaged in photo-typesetting, data processing, book pub., resume services; pres. Student Post Direct Distbn. System, 1980. Mem. Nat. Assn. Advt. Pubs., Community Papers Ohio and W.Va. Office: PO Box 647 Bowling Green OH 43402

VAN DEN HOUTEN, HANS, investment ser. exec.; b. The Hague, Netherlands, Aug. 6, 1940; s. Johannes Nicolaas and Magdalena (Schuil) van den H.; came to U.S., 1967, naturalized, 1973; License es Scis. Economiques et Sociales, U. Lausanne, Switzerland, 1964; m. Carola Lydia Cutler, Sept. 4, 1965; children—Tania Carola, Andrew Nicolas Rembert. With Royal Shell Dutch/Netherlands, Congo, South Africa, 1964-67; asst. treas. Chase Manhattan Bank, N.Y.C., 1970, v.p. corp. devel. group, 1973-75; dir. fin. Mus. Modern Art, N.Y.C., 1970-73; div. exec. instl. and corp. div. Africa Banking Group, 1975-76; dir. Nigeria Indsl. Devel. Bank, 1975-76; v.p., internat. dir., chmn. internat. rating com., Moody's Investors Services Inc., N.Y.C., 1976-79; v.p., regional mgr. Latin-Am. Dun & Bradstreet Internat., N.Y.C., 1979—. Dir. Netherlands-Am. Community Assn., N.Y.C. Served to 1st lt., Royal Dutch Army, 1958-60. Home: 390 West End Ave New York NY 10024

VAN DERBUR, FRANCIS STACY, ins. co. exec.; b. Victor, Colo., Sept. 30, 1907; s. Francis Carl and Pearl Fredericks (McDaniel) Van D.; B.A., U. Denver, 1929; m. Gwendolyn Olinger, June 13, 1930; children—Gwendolyn (Mrs. Ernest Mitchell), Valerie (Mrs. John Horan), Nancy (Mrs. Richard Knowlton), Marilyn (Mrs. Lawrence Atler). Vice-pres. Old Homestead Bread Co., Denver, 1929-36; exec. Olinger Mortuaries, Denver, 1929-44, pres., 1940—; chmn. bd. Olinger Life Ins. Co., 1949—; pres. Eastlawn Cemetery, Evergreen Cemetery, Mount Lindo Cemetery, Tower of Memories Mausoleum, Niagara Corp., Cherry Creek Corp., Purple Shield Corp.; dir. Central Bank of Denver. Bd. dirs., pres. Denver Center for Performing Arts, 1972—; chmn. bd. Nat. Internat. Found., 1962—; pres. Denver Area council Boy Scouts Am., 1971-73, pres. Old West Trails area, 1978-80; chmn. bd. Kappa Sigma Endowment Fund; trustee Frederick G. Bonfils Found., U. Denver, Wallace Village for Children, Denver; chmn. bd. Denver Better Bus. Bur., 1961-63; bd. dirs. Nat. Fund for Med. Edn., 1977—; pres. Bonfils Theatre, 1960— Mem. Roundup Riders of the Rockies, Kappa Sigma (internat. pres. 1949-51), Nat. Interfrat. Conf. (chmn. 1957-58), Interfrat. Research and Adv. Council (chmn. 1960-66). Mason (33 deg.), Rotarian. Clubs: Denver Athletic, Press, Mount Vernon Country, Gyro. Denver, Cherry Hills Country, Garden of the Gods. Home: 2100 E 8th Ave Denver CO 80206 Office: Box 11128 Highlands Station Denver CO 80211

VANDER KNYFF, JACOBUS JOHANNES MARIUS, engring. co. exec.; b. Arnhem, Holland, Oct. 18, 1943; s. Jacobus Johannes Marius and Johanna (Limburg) Vander K.; came to U.S., 1956, naturalized, 1967; B.S. in Engring. Sci., U. Redlands, 1965; M.B.A., Calif. State U. at Fullerton, 1971; m. Janice Merle Taylor, June 6, 1964; children—Lauri A., Bradley J. Sr. engr. Gulton Industries, Rochester, N.Y., 1967-69, Pulse Engring. subs. Varian Assos., San Diego, 1969-71; plant mgr. Pemcor, Tijuana, Mex., 1971-73; mgr. internat. ops. Pulse Engring., San Diego, 1973-75, gen. mgr., 1975-79, pres., 1979—. Mem. Am. Electronics Assn. (dir.), Beta Gamma Sigma. Home: 1815 Bailey Dr Oceanside CA 92054 Office: PO Box 12235 San Diego CA 92112

VAN DER MEULEN, BARRY EDWIN, energy and securities co. exec., cons.; b. Waukegan, Ill., Jan. 4, 1937; s. George Y. and Adelle (Cary) Van Der M.; B.S., M.S. in Psychology, Coll. Universal Truth, Chgo. and Los Angeles, 1956, D.D., 1957, Ph.D., 1958; m. Ellen C. Smith, Apr. 1, 1978; children by previous marriage—Cary K., John E., Colette Y. From dist. agt. to dist. mgr. Prudential Ins. Co. Am., 1959-67; v.p. Equity Funding Corp. Am., Los Angeles, 1967-68; cons. in securities and ins. mgmt., Indpls., Atlanta, Los Angeles, Detroit, 1968-72; cons., zone v.p. Hamilton Internat. Corp., 1970-71; chmn. bd. Havoco of Am. Ltd., Chgo., 1972—. Mem. Internat. Assn. Fin. Planners (adv. bd.), Chgo. Assn. Commerce and Industry, Smithsonian Assos., Am. Mgmt. Assn. (pres.'s club), Life Underwriters Assn. Mgmt. Orgn. (v.p., organizer Indpls.), C.L.U.'s Tng. and Life Underwriters Tng. Council. Home: 155 Harbor Dr Unit 813 Chicago IL 60601 Office: 155 Harbor Dr Chicago IL 60601

VANDERPOOL, WARD MELVIN, mgmt., marketing cons.; b. Oakland, Mo., Jan 20, 1915; s. Oscar B. and Clara (McGuire) V.; M.E.E., Tulane U.; m. Lee Kendall, July 7, 1935; v.p. charge sales Van Lang Brokerage, Los Angeles, 1934-38; mgr. agrl. div. Dayton Rubber Co., Chgo., 1939-48; pres., gen. mgr. Vee Mac Co., Rockford, Ill., 1948—; pres., dir. Zipout, Inc., Rockford, 1951—, Wife Saver Products, Inc., 1959—; chmn. bd. Zipout, Internat., Kenuan, Inc., 1952—, Shevan Corp., 1951—, Atlas Internat. Corp.; pres. Global Enterprises Ltd., Global Assos. Ltd.; chmn. bd. Atlas Chem. Corp.; chmn. bd. Merzat Industries Ltd.; trustee Ice Crafter Trust, 1949—; dir. Atlas Chem. Internat., Ltd., Shrimp Tool Internat. Ltd. Cons., Am. Heart Assn. Mem. swim com. Central Amateur Athletic Union; dir. Central and Midwestern Amateur Athletic Union Open. Adv. bd. Nat. Security Council. Honored by Internat. Swimming Hall of Fame. Mem. Nat. (dir. at large), Rock River (past pres.) sales execs., Sales and Marketing Execs. Internat. (dir.), Am. Mgmt. Assn., Rockford Engring. Soc., Am. Tool Engrs., Internat. Acad. Aquatic Art (dir.), A.I.M. (president's council), Am. Ordnance Assn., Internat. Platform Assn., Ill. C. of C. Mason (Shriner), Elk. Clubs: Rockford Swim, Forest Hills Country, Executive, Elmcrest Country, Pyramid, Jester, Dolphin, Marlin. Home: 374 Parkland Dr SE Cedar Rapids IA 52403 Office: Panorama Ct Toronto ON Canada also 120 Adelaide St W Toronto ON Canada

VANDERSLICE, THOMAS AQUINAS, elec. mfg. co. exec.; b. Phila., Jan. 8, 1932; s. Joseph R. and Mae (Daly) V.; B.S. in Chemistry and Philosophy, Boston Coll., 1953; Ph.D. in Chemistry and Physics, Catholic U. Am., 1956; m. Margaret Hurley, June 9, 1956; children—Thomas Aquinas, Paul Thomas Aquinas, John Thomas Aquinas, Peter Thomas Aquinas. With Gen. Electric Co., 1956—, gen. mgr. electronic components bus. div., 1970-72, v.p., 1970—, group exec. spl. systems and products group, Fairfield, Conn., 1972-77, sr. v.p., sector exec. Power Systems Sector, 1977-79, exec. v.p., sector exec., 1979; pres., chief operating officer, dir. Gen. Telephone & Electronics Corp., Stamford, Conn., 1979—; mem. com. on energy Aspen Inst. Humanistic Studies; mem. Oxford Energy Policy Club, Oxford U. Trustee, Boston Coll., Fairfield U., Com. Econ. Devel.; chmn. Design Com. on Tech. Policy; bd. dirs. Jr. Achievement Onondaga and Madison counties, N.Y., 1971-72, Phoenix, 1968-70. Fulbright scholar, 1953-56; recipient Golden Plate award Acad. Achievement, 1963; Bicentennial medallion Boston Coll., 1976. Mem. Nat. Acad. Engring., Conn. Acad. Sci. and Engring., Am. Vacuum Soc., ASTM, Am. Chem. Soc., Am. Inst. Physics, Sigma Xi, Tau Beta Pi, Alpha Sigma Nu, Sigma Pi Sigma. Clubs: Conn. Golf (Easton); Patterson (Fairfield); Oxford U. Energy Policy. Co-author: Ultra High Vacuum and Its Applications, 1963; reviser: Scientific Foundations of Vacuum Technique, 1960. Contbr. to profl. jours. Patentee low pressure gas measurements and analysis, gas surface interactions and elec. discharge. Office: Gen Telephone & Electronics Corp 1 Stamford Forum Stamford CT 06904

VANDER VEEN, ARVIN LAURENCE, real estate exec.; b. Sioux Falls, S.D., Nov. 8, 1945; s. Arthur and Laura (Wehling) Vander Veen; student in real estate Highline Jr. Coll., Kent, Wash., 1973, 79, 80; m. Karen Marie Kennon, Oct. 3, 1978. Pres., Northwest Central Corp., Federal Way, Wash., 1972-73; Midwest regional sales mgr. KSM div. Omark Industries, 1973-77; dist. dir. World Wide Products Co., 1977-78; sales mgr. Competion Specialities Co., 1978-79; pres., prin. Frankenfield & Co., comml. real estate, Seattle, 1979—; v.p. engring., prin. Slam-Dunk Inc., mfrs. basketball rims, 1980—. Served with USAR, 1966-68. Mem. Seattle Seafair Commodores, Nat. Hot Rod Assn. Republican. Home: 915 SW Dash Point Rd Federal Way WA 98003 Office: 6000 Southcenter Blvd Suite 225 Seattle WA 98188

VANDER VELDEN, EDWARD LEENDERT, machine tool and environ. equipment mfg. co. exec.; b. Flint, Mich., June 7, 1934; s. Neil Paul and Aileen Jeanette (Cunningham) Vander V.; B.S. in Indsl. Engring., U. Mich., 1957; m. Diane M. Oldenburg, Aug. 30, 1968; children—Anne, Cynthia, Michael, Amy. Sales, engr., office mgr. Allen Bradley Co., Detroit, 1960-65; estimator, project engr. Detroit Broach & Machine Co., 1965, Valley Tools Sales Inc., Flint, Mich., 1966-74; pres., chmn. bd. Vander Velden, Inc., Grand Blanc, Mich., 1974—, Venturmation, Inc., 1978—. Past mem. Regional Planning Commn., Grand Blanc, Twp. Planning Commn. Served to lt. (j.g.) USN, 1957-60. Mem. Soc. Mfrs. Reps. Club: Warwick Hills Golf and Country. Home: 8498 Bush Hill Ct Grand Blanc MI 48439 Office: G-3465 Pollock Rd Grand Blanc MI 48439

VAN DERVORT, JUDSON BENTON, computer supply co. exec.; b. San Francisco, Feb. 15, 1940; s. Edmund Harold and Mary Elizabeth (Lennon) Van D.; B.A., Rutgers U., 1963; M.S.E., U. Pa., 1973; postgrad. Temple U., 1974-76; m. Mary A. Ciavarelli, Dec. 28, 1963; children—Judson Benton, Anthony Edmund, Mary Michelle, Kristin. Programmer RCA Corp., 1963; sr. systems design specialist Philco Ford, 1963-69; cons., computer devel. specialist Keystone Computer Assos., Fort Washington, Pa., 1969-75; pres. Keystone Data Systems, Maple Shade, N.J., 1975-80, Nat. Info. Systems, 1979—, Keystone Info., 1980—; chmn. bd. Keytime, Inc., 1980—, Computer Works, 1980—. Served with USAF, 1959-61. Mem. IEEE, Am. Mgmt. Assn. Home: 116 W Walnut Ave Moorestown NJ 08057 Office: Park Ave Maple Shade NJ 08052

VAN DOOIJEWEERT, WILLY NICO, retail luggage co. exec.; b. Tricht, Netherlands, Apr. 17, 1952; came to U.S., 1971; s. Arie and Margaretha (Voet) van D.; A.A. with honors, Netherlands Sch. Bus., 1971; B.A., Mich. State U., 1972, M.B.A. with honors, 1974; m. Linda Joyce Hashimoto, May 27, 1977. Asso. buyer women's moderate sportswear Dayton's Dept. Stores, Mpls., 1974-76, buyer luggage and leather goods, 1976-78; founder, pres. Great Luggage! Inc., St. Paul, 1978—; mem. Nat. Retail Adv. Bd., 1978—, cons. various luggage cos. Mem. U.S. Soccer Assn. (cert. nat. referee), N. Am. Soccer League (profl. referee), Minn. Soccer Referee Assn. (pres. 1979—, soccer referee instr. 1979—), Japan Am. Soc., Friends of St. Paul Chamber Orch., Beta Gamma Sigma. Home: 1112 Benton Way Arden Hills MN 55112 Office: 1120 Maplewood Mall Saint Paul MN 55109

VAN DYCK, KENNETH ARTHUR, indsl. designer, lectr.; b. Pitts., June 18, 1916; s. Arthur F. and Edith A. (Soderston) Van D.; B.S., Carnegie Inst. Tech., 1939; postgrad. Harvard U., 1941, M.I.T., 1942; m. Phyliss T. Norten, June 18, 1978; children—Wayne, Stephen, Bruce, Peter, Marcia, Lisa. Asst. dir. design Eastman Kodak Co., 1945-55; pres. Van Dyck Assos. div. Enrichment Found., Woodbury, Conn., 1955—; dir. Gen. Security Systems, Auberge Inc.; lectr. in field, 1970—. Served with USAAF, 1942-45. Recipient Small Businessman of Yr. award SBA, 1968; gold design awards Design mag., 1962, 64, 70. Mem. Internat. Oceanographic Found., Am. Def. Preparedness Assn. Club: N.Y. Yacht. Contbr. articles to tech. publs.; patentee in field; pioneer programmed invention. Home: 154 Bueford Ct Goshen CT 06756 Office: 717 Main St Woodbury CT 06798

VAN DYKE, STEVE, computer co. exec.; b. Oklahoma City, Mar. 29, 1947; s. Denver M. and Evelyn B. (Young) Broam; B.S. in Math., Okla. State U., 1969; m. Anne C. Dunlap, July 10, 1975. Systems programmer Tex. Instruments, Dallas, 1969-72; systems programmer Teleswitcher Corp., Dallas, 1972-73; sr. systems programmer Action Communications, Dallas, 1973-75; dir. programming systems Datapoint Corp., Dallas, 1975—. Republican. Methodist. Home: 9731 Burleson Dr Dallas TX 75243 Office: 4300 Alpha Suite 200 Dallas TX 75234

VAN EECKHOUT, GERALD DUANE, heart pacemaker co. exec.; b. Fargo, N.D., Sept. 29, 1940; s. Edward Cornelius and Rose Ella (Tuchscherer) Van E.; B.A., U. N.D., 1962; postgrad. exec. program Stanford U., 1976; m. Carolyn Rush, Aug. 22, 1964; children—Jill, Pam, Kim. Audit mgr. Touche Ross & Co., Mpls., 1962-70; dir. corp. audit Pillsbury Co., Mpls., 1970-71, chief fin. officer internat., 1971-74; v.p. fin. and adminstrn. Medtronic, Inc., Mpls., 1975—. Mem. econ. community adv. com. Mpls. Public Schs., C.P.A., Minn. Mem. Fin. Execs. Inst. (dir. Twin Cities chpt. 1978—), Am. Inst. C.P.A.'s, Minn. Soc. C.P.A.'s (dir.). Roman Catholic. Clubs: Mpls. Rotary, Minneapolis; North Oaks (Minn.) Country. Home: 9 Ironwood Ln North Oaks MN 55110 Office: 3055 Old Hwy 8 PO Box 1453 Minneapolis MN 55440

VAN EERDEN, NEIL, cosmetics co. exec.; b. Ogden, Utah, June 22, 1932; s. Peter C. and Louise (Chase) Van E.; Asso. Sci., Weber State Coll., 1958; student Boston U., 1958-60; m. Eleanor O'Shea, Aug. 21, 1954; children—Kristin, Heidi, Peter. Mgr., Zareh, Inc., Boston, 1959-64; dir. sales dept. Store div. Faberge, N.Y.C., 1964-77; v.p. sales Coparel, Inc., N.Y.C., 1978—. Served with USAF, 1952-56. Mem. N.Y. Cosmetic Assn., New Eng. Cosmetic Assn., Cleve. Cosmetic Assn., Phila. Cosmetic Assn., Nat. Assn. Cosmetic Drug Stores. Democrat. Home: 370 Indian Rd Wayne NJ 07470 Office: 437 Madison Ave New York NY 10022

VANERSTROM, CARL LEVIN, indsl. engr.; b. Kane, Pa., Aug. 28, 1919; s. Oscar Conrad and Alma Edith (Johanson) V.; student Pa. State U., Franklin and Marshall Coll., Corning (N.Y.) Community Coll., LaSalle Extension U.; m. Donna M. Painter, Mar. 25, 1939; children—Donna E., Judith, Larry L. Indsl. engr., then mem. mgmt. staff Dresser Industries, 1960; supr. mfg. engring. Ingersoll-Rand Corp., Painted Post, N.Y., 1965; with York (Pa.) div. Borg Warner Corp., 1967—, sr. indsl. engr. charge all service replacement parts, also mfg. engr. cost improvement, 1977—. Mem. exec. council local Boy Scouts Am., 1960-62; cons. Sheltered Workshop, 1976-78. Served with AUS, 1944-46. Mem. Am. Inst. Indsl. Engrs. (sec.-treas. 1975), Soc. Carbide and Tool Engrs. (treas. 1979-80). Republican. Presbyterian. Club: Masons. Home: 2156 Yale Ave Camp Hill PA 17011 Office: PO Box 1592 York PA 17405

VAN ETTEN, JOSEPH ELMER, contrn. co. exec.; b. Bronx, N.Y., Mar. 5, 1933; s. Elmer E. and Margaret A. (Fiesel) Van E.; B.C.E., Manhattan Coll., 1957; m. Jeanne I. Brown, Feb. 21, 1959; children—Craig H., Patricia Jeanne. Supt., George F. Driscoll Co., N.Y.C., 1957-68; gen. supt. LeFrak Orgn., Forest Hills, N.Y., 1968-75; project mgr. NICO, N.Y.C., 1975-78, gen. supt., 1979—; v.p. RAMCO, N.Y.C., 1978-79. Commr. and chmn. city planning commn. City of Mt. Vernon (N.Y.), 1968-69, commr. and chmn. housing and bldg. code appeal bd., 1969—; past gen. chmn. United Fund; past pres. Young Men's Republican Club; active Boy Scouts Am. Recipient Service to Youth award B'nai B'rith, 1964, Outstanding Citizenship award United Fund, 1966, Wood badge Boy Scouts Am., 1965. Mem. ASCE, Nat. Soc. Profl. Engrs. Republican. Roman Catholic. Clubs: Rock Glen Golf, Elks (past exalted ruler). Home: PO Box 147 Fleetwood NY 10552 Office: 750 3d Ave New York NY 10017

VAN FLEET, G. NELSON, mortgage banker; b. Scranton, Pa., May 10, 1936; s. George N. and Loretta R. (Bachman) Van F.; B.S., Pa. State U., 1958; J.D., Georgetown U., 1966; m. Patricia Ann Thomas, June 15, 1958; children—Margaret Meredith, Thomas Allen, Elizabeth Allison. Admitted to D.C. bar, 1966, Pa. bar, 1968, Kans. bar, 1971; with U.S. Securities and Exchange Commn., Washington, 1961-68; atty. firm Ringe, Peet & Mason, Phila., 1968-70; v.p., gen. counsel Beacon Resources Corp., Wichita, Kans., 1970-72; pres. Amortibanc Investment Co., Inc., Wichita, 1972—; dir. Garvey Industries, Inc. Bd. dirs. Medicalodges Inc. Served to lt. U.S. Navy, 1958-61. Mem. Am. Bar Assn., Mortgage Bankers Assn., Nat. Assn. Home Builders, Chgo. Bd. Trade. Club: Rotary. Home: 7014 Timberon Ln Wichita KS 67206 Office: 300 W Douglas St Wichita KS 67202

VAN FOSSAN, ROBERT V., ins. co. exec.; b. Breckenridge, Minn., Sept. 24, 1926. Agy. cashier Northwestern Nat. Life Ins. Co., Mpls., 1947-49, agt., 1949-51, supr. central div., Chgo., 1951, supt. agys., Spokane, Wash., Mpls., v.p., agy. dir., 1966-69, sr. v.p., agy. dir., 1969-72; pres. Mut. Benefit Life Ins. Co., Newark, 1972-78, chmn. bd., chief exec. officer, 1978—; dir. Pub. Service Electric & Gas, Amerada Hess Corp. Commr., Port Authority N.Y. and N.J.; chmn. Renaissance Newark Inc., Com. on Efficiency in Operation Cts.; bd. dirs. Regional Plan Assn.; trustee Newark Mus.; exec. com. Coalition N.E. Gov.'s, NCCJ. Mem. N.J. C. of C. (dir.), Greater Newark C. of C. Office: 520 Broad St Newark NJ 07101

VAN FRANK, ROGER MERRILL, architect; b. Newburgh, N.Y., Oct. 13, 1924; s. Leslie Keats and Edna Ensign (Merrill) van F.; student U. Cin., 1946-49; B.Arch. with distinction, U. Okla., 1949-52; m. Sheila Margaret Alison Watkins, June 28, 1947; children—Mereth, Kevin, Gweneth, Leslie, Alison, Megan. Draftsman, Sidney

Schleman, Middletown, N.Y., 1936, Gordon Marvel, Newburgh, 1937-42, Ed Beiting, Ky., 1947, Wilkens-Schrand Wilkens, Ohio, 1948-49, Hixson-Tartar, Ohio, 1949, Mendel Gluckman, Okla., 1950-52, George Cannon Young, Utah, 1950, Noftsger & Lawrence, Okla., 1952-54; architect Reynolds & Morrison, Okla., 1955, Young & Hansen, Utah, 1956, Roger Merrill van Frank, Salt Lake City, 1957-58, 61-66; partner Moyes & van Frank, Salt Lake City, 1959-60, van Frank & Giusti, Salt Lake City, 1967-68; v.p., dir. Bernson, van Frank & Giusti, Salt Lake City, 1969-72; pres., chmn. bd. van Frank & Assos., architects, engr., Salt Lake City, 1973—. Served with USN, 1942-45; PTO. Recipient various design awards; registered architect, Utah, Wyo.; cert. Nat. Council Archtl. Registration Bd. Club: Rotary (chmn. youth exchange com.). Pioneer in energy conservation, constrn. techniques, processes and methods. Home: 1445 Michigan Ave Salt Lake City UT 84105 Office: 1549 South 1100 East Salt Lake City UT 84105

VANGI, JOSEPH MICHAEL, electronic security systems co. exec.; b. San Paolo, Brazil, Feb. 23, 1954; came to U.S., 1959, naturalized, 1965; s. Michael and Anna V.; student Teterboro Sch. Aeros., Bergen, N.J., 1972-74; m. Catherine DiGeloromo, Sept. 3, 1977; 1 son, Michael. Mgr., Radio Shack, various locations, N.Y., 1974-78; v.p. ABI Security, Little Neck, N.Y., 1978—; cons. in field. Mem. Met. Burglar Alarm Assn., Nat. Bus. Assn. Democrat. Roman Catholic. Home: 17-16 149th St Whitestone NY 11357

VAN GILDER, BARBARA JANE DIXON, interior designer, cons.; b. South Bend, Ind., Dec. 6, 1933; d. Vincent Alan and Wanda Anita (Rapell) Dixon; student Mich. State U., 1951-55; postgrad. St. Mary's Coll., 1956-57, N.Y. Sch. Design, 1956-58; m. Erwin Delton VanGilder, May 25, 1959; children—Eric Dalton, Marc David. Factory color cons. Smith-Alsop Paint Co., Terre Haute, Ind., 1955-56; archtl. design cons., Mishawaka, Ind., 1956-58; residential-comml. designer, South Bend, Chgo., 1958-63; designer industrialized housing industry, Ga., Fla., Ind., Mich., 1962—; v.p. design Treasure Chest Corp., Sturgis, Mich., 1969, also dir.; pres., dir. Sandpiper Art, Inc.; v.p. T.C.I. Ltd.; design cons. C.O. Smith Ind. Peachtree Housing, Moultrie, Ga., Nobility Homes, Ocala, Fla.; head merchandising and design Sandpiper Originals, clothing boutique, 1978—; public relations dir., v.p. Lake Aire Vending Service, Vangi Assos.; also coordinator trade show displays; writer series on decorating for 2 Mich. newspapers, 1961-63. Officer, Shoreham Village (Mich.) Bd. Zoning, 1960-63. Named Woman of Year, Profl. Model's Club, 1952; recipient 1st pl. furniture design hardwoods Nat. Hardwoods Assn., 1956; 1st pl. Best in Show award, Louisville, Atlanta, 1964-65, 66, 69, 70-74, 76; others. Mem. Design Council Industrialized Housing (award 1974), Nat. Soc. Interior Designers, Mich. State U. Alumni Assn., Internat. Platform Assn., Internat. Biog. Assn. Permanent guest editor, contbr. Today's Home mag., 1974—. Home: 3630 S Lakeshore Dr Saint Joseph MI 49085

VAN GORDER, JOHN FREDERIC, found. exec.; b. Jacksonville, Fla., Mar. 22, 1943; s. Harold Burton and Charlotte Louise (Anderson) Van G.; grad. Dover (Eng.) Coll., 1961; A.B., Dartmouth Coll., 1965; postgrad. Air Force Inst. Tech., 1967-68; M.S. in Adminstrn., George Washington U., 1973; postgrad. U. Va., Coll. William and Mary, Cath. U. Am., Northeastern U., Babson Coll., Fordham U. Sch. Law, 1977—; m. Sandra Joan Hagen, June 4, 1977; children—Alyssa Jane. Weapons controller Aerospace Def. Command, Ft. Lee, Va., 1965-67; buyer electronics systems div. Air Force Systems Command, Bedford, Mass., 1968-69; project mgr. research and devel. Hdqrs. U.S. Air Force, Washington, 1969-73, br. chief personnel, 1973-74; Presdl. social aide The White House, Washington, 1970-73; asso. Louis C. Kramp & Assos., Washington, 1975; program officer J.M. Found., N.Y.C., 1975—; chmn. N.Y.C. steering com. Nat. Congress on Volunteerism and Citizenship, 1976; mem. exec. com. Mayor's Vol. Action Council, 1977-78; bd. govs., 4th v.p. First Assembly Dist. Republican Club, 1977—. Served to capt. USAF; maj. Res. Named Outstanding Young Man of Va., 1974. Mem. Internat. (senator; v.p. 1975; rep. to UN 1976), U.S. (nat. v.p. 1973-74), D.C. (pres. 1972-73) N.Y.C. (bd. govs. 1978-79) Jaycees (bd. govs. found. 1978-79), S.A.R., Soc. Mayflower Descs., Student Bar Assn. (class pres. 1978-81), Alpha Delta Phi. Republican. Episcopalian. Clubs: Young Republican (N.Y.C.); Toastmasters (local pres. 1969-70, area gov. 1970-71) (Bedford, Mass.); Masons; Bergenfield Swim. Home: 30 Woods Ave Bergenfield NJ 07621 Office: JM Foundation 60 E 42d St New York NY 10165

VAN GORDER, SANDRA HAGEN, banker, investment analyst; b. N.Y.C., Apr. 19, 1947; d. George G. and Mildred (Albert) Hagen; B.S., St. John's U., 1969, M.B.A., 1976; m. John Frederic Van Gorder, June 4, 1977; 1 dau., Alyssa Jane. Investment analyst Chase Manhattan Bank, N.Y.C., 1969-75, asst. treas., 1975-77, 2d v.p., 1977-79. Recipient Outstanding Jaycees award, 1976. Mem. N.Y.C. (dir. 1976-77), Manhattan (treas. 1977-78) Jaycees. Club: Bergenfield Jr. Women's (social services chmn. 1980-81). Roman Catholic. Home: 30 Woods Ave Bergenfield NJ 07621

VAN GORKOM, JEROME WILLIAM, corp. exec.; b. Denver, Aug. 6, 1917; s. A.G. and Elizabeth (Laux) Van G.; B.S., U. Ill., 1939, J.D., 1941; m. Betty Jean Alexander, June 27, 1942; children—Gayle, Lynne. Law asso. KixMiller, Baar & Morris, Chgo., 1945-47; accountant Arthur Andersen & Co., 1947-54, partner, 1954-56; treas., controller Trans Union Corp., Chgo., 1956-58, v.p., treas., 1958-60, exec. v.p., 1960-63, pres., 1963-78, dir., 1957—, chmn. bd., 1978—, also chmn exec. com.; dir. I.C. Industries, Ill. Central Gulf R.R. Co., Schering-Plough, Champion Internat. Trustee Tax Found.; bd. dirs. Lyric Opera of Chgo. Served with USNR, 1941-45. C.P.A., Ill. Mem. Am. Bar Assn., Am. Inst. C.P.A.'s. Clubs: Chicago, Mid-Am., Comml. (Chgo.); Old Elm; Onwentsia; Pauma Valley Country. Home: 908 Ringwood Rd Lake Forest IL 60045 Office: 90 Half Day Rd Lincolnshire IL 60015

VAN KAMPEN, ROBERT CORNELIUS, publisher; b. Chgo., July 5, 1910; s. John Dow and Angelena (Hoving) Van K.; grad. Chgo. Christian High Sch., La Grange Jr. Coll., Northwestern U., La Salle Extension Inst., Chgo.; m. Darthe Payne Ruisch, Sept. 15, 1933; children—Warren L., Evelyn B., Robert D. With Hitchcock Pub. Co., Chgo., 1927-66, pres. and gen. mgr., 1940-60, chmn. bd. 1960-66; pres. Morton Printing Co., Pontiac, Ill., 1946-62; chmn. bd. Mdse. Service Co., 1962-78; v.p. Evergreen Dept. Store, Evergreen Park, Ill., 1939-72; v.p., dir. Gary Wheaton Bank, 1950-64; dir. Club Aluminum Products Co., 1942-60, Hawthorn Bank of Wheaton, 1965-72; partner Stream Assos.; v.p., treas. Developers Finance Corp., 1971-74; dir. Radio Sta. KAIM, Honolulu, 1951—, Bell Savs. & Loan Assn., 1961—. Mem. U.S. Exec. Res., 1958—. Pres. bd. Aedus Community Center, Chgo., 1945-46; chmn. bd. Wheaton (Ill.) Acad., 1945-60; trustee Wheaton Coll., 1948, Northwestern Schs., Mpls., 1948-53, Westmont Coll., 1962—; bd. dirs. Billy Graham Evangelistic Assn., 1957—, Direct Relief Found. Internat., Billy Graham Found., 1970—; bd. dirs. Sansum Research Found., 1974—, v.p., 1977—; sec. Samarkand Found. Mem. Gideons (pres. Chgo. chpt. 1940-42, internat. treas. 1947-52, exec. com. 1942-45), Nat. Indsl. Advt. Assn., Chgo. Bus. Pub. Assn., World Wide Prayer and Missionary Union (dir.), Young Life Campaign (mem. bd. 1943-47), Christian Service Brigade (v.p. bd. 1944-46; pres. 1947-52), Nat. Assn. Evangelicals (treas. 1948-58, 63-66), Evang. Alliance Mission (dir.). Mem. Evang. Free Ch. (chmn. bd. 1954-60). Clubs: Union League (Chgo.); Valley. Home: 171 Coronada Circle Santa Barbara CA 93108

VAN KERSEN, PHILIP LIONEL, thermometer mfg. co. exec.; b. South Haven, Mich., Nov. 13, 1926; s. Edward Philip and Mildred Irene (Whitney) Van K.; B.A., Western Mich. U., 1949; postgrad. U. Mich., 1949-50; children—Philip William, Christopher Ashley, Melissa Dee, Eric Philip, Matthew Christopher. Field sales rep. Pitman-Moore Co., 1950-62; product promotion mgr. Dow Pharms., 1962-64, product mgr., sr. product mgr., 1964-69; founder, mgr., owner Robert J. Scott Assos., sales promotion agy., Indpls., 1969-73, Temperature Dynamics, mfrs. liquid temperature devices, Indpls., 1973-79; with Clinitemp, Inc., Indpls., 1975—, chmn., 1979—; cons. on sr. citizen needs Indpls. C. of C., 1970-77. Served with Hosp. Corps, USN, 1945-46. Mem. Health Industries Mfrs. Assn., Pharm. Advt. Club N.Y., Midwest Pharm. Advt. Club. Republican. Episcopalian. Author: Aunt Belle's Famous Bread Cookbook, 1980; patentee thermochromic liquid crystal devices; inventor forehead fever detector, bath, wine, yeast thermometers, fever detector for dogs. Home: PO Box 40273 Indianapolis IN 46240 Office: 8549 Zionsville Rd Indianapolis IN 46268

VAN LANDINGHAM, LEANDER SHELTON, JR., patent lawyer; b. Memphis, July 15, 1925; s. Leander Shelton Van L.; B.S. in Chemistry, U. N.C., 1948, M.A. in Organic Chemistry, 1949; J.D., Georgetown U., 1955; m. Henrietta Adena Stapf, July 5, 1959; children—Ann Henrietta, Leander Shelton III. Patent adviser Dept. Navy, Washington, 1953-55; admitted to D.C. bar, 1955, since practiced in Washington. Cons. patent, trademark and copyright law, chem. patent matters, 1955—. Served to lt. USNR, 1943-46, 1951-53. Mem. Am. Chem. Soc., Sci. Assn., Fed., Am., D.C. bar assns., Am. Patent Law Assn., Am. Judicature Soc., Sigma Xi, Phi Alpha Delta. Methodist. Home: 10726 Stanmore Dr Potomac Falls Potomac MD 20854 Office: 2001 Jefferson Davis Hwy Arlington VA 22202

VAN LEEUWEN, WILLIAM HAROLD, ins. co. exec.; b. Paducah, Ky., July 4, 1923; s. William Harold and Virginia Marie (Charles) Van L.; B.A., U. Ill., 1947, LL.B., 1948; m. Lois Bolle, Aug. 18, 1948; children—Barbara, Thomas Melton. Admitted to Ill. bar, 1948; with Sentry Ins. Co., 1948-65, resident v.p., Grand Rapids, Mich., 1955-59, Mpls., 1959-65; successively asst. v.p., 2d v.p., v.p. Kemper Ins. Group, Long Grove, Ill., 1965-73; chmn. bd., chief exec. officer, exec. com. Kemper Investors Life Ins. Co., Los Angeles, 1972-76, dir., 1972-78; pres., chief exec. officer, exec. com., dir. Nat. Automobile and Casualty Ins. Co., Pasadena, Calif., 1972—; adv. bd. U. San Diego Sch. Bus. Adminstrn.; bd. dirs. Assn. Calif. Ins. Cos. Served to 1st lt., inf., U.S. Army, 1943-46. C.P.C.U.; C.L.U. Mem. Soc. C.P.C.U.'s, Am. Soc. C.L.U.'s, Pasadena C. of C., Sigma Alpha Epsilon, Phi Delta Phi. Republican. Episcopalian. Clubs: Rotary, Jonathan (Los Angeles); Annandale Golf (Pasadena). Office: 150 S Los Robles Ave Pasadena CA 91101

VANMETER, ABRAM DEBOIS, JR., banker; b. Springfield, Ill., May 16, 1922; s. Abram DeBois and Edith (Graham) VanM.; B.S., Kings Point Coll., Great Neck, N.Y., 1946; J.D., Northwestern U., 1948; m. Margaret Schlipf, Dec. 1, 1956; children—Abram DeBois IV, Alice, Ann. Admitted to Ill. bar, 1949; partner firm VanMeter, Oxtoby & Funk, Springfield, 1949—; dir. Ill. Nat. Bank of Springfield, 1960—, v.p., 1964-65, pres., 1965—; dir. Toledo, Peoria & Western R.R. Co. Chmn. bd. dirs. Ill. Housing Devel. Authority; bd. dirs., exec. com. Meml. Med. Center; trustee So. Ill. U.; vice chmn. Ill. State Bd. Investment. Served with USNR, 1944-59. Mem. Am. Bar Assn., Am. Bankers Assn., Ill. Bar Assn., Assn. Modern Banking in Ill. Methodist. Clubs: Illini Country, Sangamo, Masons. Office: 1 Old Capitol Plaza N Springfield IL 62701

VAN METER, ROBERT ALLEN, nuclear engr.; b. Grant Town, W.Va., Dec. 2, 1949; s. Beatrice Virginia Van Meter; B.S. in Aerospace Engring., W.Va. U., 1971; m. Christine Mary Babcock, Mar. 16, 1974. Systems design engr. Knolls Atomic Power Lab., Schenectady, 1975-80; sr. engr. Rockwell Hanford Operation, Richland, Wash., 1980—. Served with USAF, 1971-74. Mem. Am. Nuclear Soc., Tau Beta Pi, Sigma Gamma Tau. Home: 5123 Chukar Dr West Richland WA 99352 Office: Rockwell Hanford Operation PO Box 800 Area 200E Bldg 2750E Room 0254 Richland WA 99352

VANNAN, HARLEY BENSON, ins. co. exec.; b. Schreiber, Ont., Can., Oct. 1, 1920; s. Harley George and Katheryn Ethel (Benson) V.; diploma Daniel McIntyre Collegiate Inst.; m. Audrey Isabella Wright, June 21, 1947; children—Harley Wright, Jeffrey Robert, Lisa Katheryn, Mark Allan, Gillian leah. With 20th Century Fox Film Co., Winnipeg, Man., Can.; with Canadian Indemnity Co., 1947—, v.p. underwriting, Toronto, 1963-70, pres., 1970—, dir., 1966—; dir. United Canadian Shares Ltd., 1966—. Bd. dirs. Ont. Found Diseases of Liver. Served to sub-lt. Canadian Navy, World War II. Mem. Panam. Surety Assn. (pres.), Ins. Bur. Can. (dir.), Ind. Insurers Assn. (dir.), Underwriters Adjustment Bur. (dir.), Centre for Study Ins. Ops. (dir.). Clubs: Manitoba, Ontario, Donalda. Office: Suite 3130 South Tower Royal Bank Plaza Toronto ON M5J 2J1 Canada

VAN NESS, MARVIN LEONARD, pump mfg. exec.; b. Welsh, La., Dec. 1, 1903; s. Marvin Brown and Alice Elizabeth (Archer) van N.; student Asbury Coll., 1922-24, McKendree Coll., 1925-26, Rice Inst. Tech., 1926-27; m. Mabel Guzman, Apr. 26, 1929; 1 son, Joseph Leonard. Machinist Tex. Co., Port Arthur, 1929-30, Welsh Machine Shops, 1930-50; owner Lo-Lift Pump Co., Inc., Welsh, 1951—, pres., mgr., 1976—; owner, operator van Ness Bldgs., Welsh, 1950—; owner, mgr. Lady Fair, Welsh. Alderman, Welsh, 1959-62; bd. dirs. La. Intracoastal Seaway Assn., 1967, Welsh Gen. Hosp., 1957-60 Lion (pres. 1950, dep. dist. gov. 1953). Home: 602 E South St Welsh LA 70591 Office: PO Box 745 Welsh LA 70591

VAN NESS, RICHARD JAMES, mgmt. cons.; b. Troy, N.Y., Nov. 16, 1943; s. Raymond Kenneth and Lillian B. Van Ness; B.A., Russell Sage Coll., 1969; M.A., Coll. St. Rose, 1972, M.S., 1981; m. Mary H. Sawicki, June 15, 1967; children—Richard James, Michael P., Robert K. Adminstr., controller Sofarelli Assos., Inc., Albany, N.Y., 1967-80; pres., chief exec. officer Execuguide Bus. Services, Inc., Albany, 1980—. Mem. citizens adv. com. Capital Dist. Regional Planning Commn., 1975-79; mem. citizens adv. com. Albany County Planning Bd., 1977. Served with USMC, 1965-67. Mem. Am. Mgmt. Assn., Inst. Mgmt. Acctg., Metroland Execs. Roman Catholic. Office: Exec Park E PO Box 5121 Albany NY 12205

VANNIER, ARLENE LINN, investment banker, wholesale tea dealer; b. N.Y.C., Apr. 22, 1933; d. Milton M. and Frances (Stern) Linn; A.B., U. Miami, 1952; postgrad. U. Pa., 1952-53, N.Y. Inst. Fin., 1964; m. Joseph Dale Vannier, Dec. 21, 1969; 1 son by previous marriage, Bruce Mason Malamut. Mannequin, Coronet Agy., Fla., Dior Collections, Cuba, France, 1956-58; owner cattle bus., Colombia, S.Am., 1959-60; account exec. Ted Worner Assos., N.Y.C., 1960-61; v.p. investments Internat. Devel. Corp., N.Y.C., 1962-63; portfolio mgr., registered rep. Oppenheimer & Co., N.Y.C., 1964-71; owner, operator Vannier Ranch, Cool, Calif., 1968—; founder, pres., dir. Vannier Group, Inc., N.Y.C., 1969, Folks Mgmt. Inc., N.Y.C., 1971—; founder, sec., treas., dir. Vannier Tea Inc., N.Y.C., 1970—. Mem. Women's Econ. Roundtable, N.Y. Acad. Scis. Republican. Clubs: Westchester Country (Rye, N.Y.); Atrium (N.Y.C.). Home: 25 E 83d St New York NY 10028 Office: 445 Park Ave New York NY 10022

VAN NOSTRAND, MORRIS ABBOTT, JR., publishing co. exec.; b. N.Y.C., Nov. 24, 1911; s. Morris Abbott and Margaret Adrianna (Edwards) Van N.; B.A., Amherst Coll., 1934; m. Jane Alexander, Dec. 28, 1934 (dec. 1944); children—Pamela George, Patricia Abbott; m. 2d, Julia de la Roche Eaton, July 3, 1953; children—Abbie Eaton, Deborah Randall. With Samuel French, Inc., N.Y.C., 1934—, sec., 1948-52, pres., 1952—; pres. Samuel French (Can.) Ltd., Toronto, Ont., since 1952—, Walter H. Baker Co., Boston, 1952—, Hugo and Luigi-Samuel French Music Pubs., N.Y.C., 1970—; chmn. bd. Samuel French Ltd., London, 1975—; trustee Lincoln Savs. Bank, Bklyn. Bd. dirs. Travelers Aid Soc.; trustee Kew Forest Sch.; mem. council Friends of Amherst (Mass.) Library. Mem. ANTA (dir.), New Dramatists Com. (dir.). Clubs: Lambs, Amherst, El Morocco, Doubles (N.Y.C.); Nassau Country (gov.) (Glen Cove, N.Y.); Les Ambassadeurs, Clermont (London). Home: 131 E 66th St New York NY 10021 Office: Samuel French Inc 25 W 45th St New York NY 10036

VANNUCCI, JOSEPH WILLIAM, food service co. exec.; b. Williamsport, Pa., Nov. 18, 1933; s. Joseph William and Kathleen Jane (McGee) V.; B.S., Pa. State U., 1955; grad. Advanced Mgmt. Program, Harvard U., 1979; m. Marilynn Raymond, Aug. 1, 1978; children—Joseph W., Todd Christopher. With ARA Services, Inc., 1958—, v.p. sales and mktg., v.p. Mid-Atlantic area, now pres. N.E. area, White Plains, N.Y.; adj. asso. prof. Pa. State U. Served with U.S. Army, 1956-58. Mem. Pa. State Alumni Assn., Soc. Food Service Mgmt. Roman Catholic. Clubs: Ridgewood Country, Harvard (Boston, N.Y.C.), Mont Tremblant Lodge. Office: ARA Service Co 6 Corporate Dr White Plains NY 10604

VAN NUIS, EDGAR LYLE, career and retirement planning cons.; b. New Brunswick, N.J., Jan. 30, 1923; s. Percy Lyle and Clara Margaret (Weigel) Van N.; B.S. in Indsl. Engring., Va. Poly. Inst., 1947, B.S. in Metall. Engring., 1949; m. Jane Le Cato, June 18, 1949; children—Martha Paterson, Peter Lyle, Cary Weigel. Engr., Am. Smelting & Refining Co., 1949-51; mgr. bldg. products div. Cronk Mfg. Co., 1951-55; asso. Drake, Startzman, Sheahan & Barclay, 1955-57; mgr. packaging dept. Products div. Bristol Myers, 1957-60; br. office mgr. Bernard Haldane Assos., 1960-69; v.p. THinc. Career Planning Corp., 1969-76; pres. The Van Nuis Co., Inc., South Dennis, N.J., 1976—; speaker. Pres. United Neighbors Assn., 1961-63. Served with AUS, 1943-45. Decorated Purple Heart. Mem. Mgmt. Devel. Forum, Soc. Advancement Mgmt., Holland Soc. N.Y., SAR. Republican. Dutch Reformed. Author: Your Job Finding Manual, 1977. Home and office: 922 Delsea Dr South Dennis NJ 08245

VAN RODEN, DONALD, business exec.; b. 1924; B.S. in Bus. Adminstrn., Lehigh U., 1948; married. With Smith Kline Corp., 1948—, v.p. adminstrn. and fin., 1967-69, group v.p. pharm., 1969-71, pres. Smith Kline & French Labs. div., 1971-74, corp. exec. v.p., 1974—, vice chmn. bd., 1980—, also dir. Served with U.S. Army, World War II. Office: 1500 Spring Garden St Philadelphia PA 19101*

VANROSSEM, ARNOLD, mfg. co. exec.; b. Delft, Netherlands, Dec. 11, 1925; came to U.S., 1954, naturalized, 1958; s. Arnold and Beatrix Isabel (Lusted) vanR.; M.Sc., State Agrl. U., Wageningen, Netherlands, 1953; postgrad. U. Minn., 1953-54; m. Joan E. Harris, Aug. 10, 1954; children—Christopher, Mark, James, Elizabeth. Feed salesman Gen. Mills Inc., 1955-58, dir. internat. ops. feed div., Mpls., 1958-62; mgr. feed div. Midland Coop., Mpls., 1962-65; v.p., gen. mgr. Pillsbury-Venezuela, 1965-71; exec. v.p. Big Dutchman Co., Zeeland, Mich., 1971-75; pres. Chickmaster Incubator Co., Medina, Okla., 1975—. Served with Dutch Air Force, 1947-50. Grantee Van Leer Inst., 1953. Club: Chippewa Yacht. Home: 7512 Standing Oak St Medina OH 44256 Office: 945 LaFayette Rd Medina OH 44256

VAN SANT, ARTHUR DALE, energy resources co. exec.; b. Tomah, Wis., Feb. 24, 1928; s. Arthur Dale and Elizabeth (Hoppe) Van S.; B.S.M.E., Ill. Inst. Tech., 1963; m. Anne H. Miller, Oct. 7, 1978; children by previous marriage—David, Torrence, Daniel, Ann. Chief engr. Portec, Inc., Oak Brook, Ill., 1963-70; cons. Dept. Transp., Washington, 1970-72; asst. mgr. railway sales CF&I 1972-74, asst. supt. steel ops., 1974-77, gen. mgr. CF&I Energy Resources, Pueblo, Colo., 1977—. Mem. Am. Ry. Engring. Assn., Triangle Fraternity. Home: 302 Elm Circle Colorado Springs CO 80906 Office: PO Box 316 Pueblo CO 81002

VAN TETERING, JACOBUS JOHANNES, pump co. exec.; b. Bussum, the Netherlands, Sept. 3, 1932; came to Can., 1967, naturalized, 1978; s. Adriaan and Johanna Christina (Hagendoorn) van T.; student Middelbare Technische Sch., 1958; Ing., Hogere Technische Sch., 1961; m. Mina Hendrika Scherphof, June 22, 1956; children—Monique, Saskia, Caroline. Mech. engr. Philips, Huizen, Holland, 1952-55; application engr. Stork Pompen, Hengelo, Holland, 1955-67; engring. supr. Worthington Can., Ltd., Brantford, Ont., 1967-69; v.p. Stork Pumps Div., Mississauga, Ont., 1969—; dir. Stork Werkspoor Can. Ltd., 1975—. Home: 1789 Sherwood Forrest Circle Mississauga ON L5N 2H7 Canada Office: 5122 Timberlea Blvd Mississauga ON L4W 2S5 Canada

VAN TETS, RIJNHARD WILLEM FERDINAND, investment banker; b. The Hague, Holland, Apr. 7, 1947; s. Dirk Arnold W. and Nancy M. van T.; came to U.S., 1975; LL.B., U. Leiden (Holland), 1967, M.B.A., 1970; m. Elsbeth van Tienhoven, July 5, 1975. Asst. syndicate mgr. Amsterdam-Rotterdam Bank N.V., Amsterdam, 1972-74; spl. asst. to gen. mgr. BEC, Brussels, 1974-75; sr. v.p. corp. fin. SoGen-Swiss Internat. Corp., N.Y.C., 1975-79; v.p. First Boston, Inc., N.Y.C., 1979—; dir. 21 E. 90th St. Apt. Corp. Accredited statis. analyst; banker's diploma Dutch Bankers Assn. Club: Meadowbrook. Home: 21 E 90th St New York NY 10028 Office: 20 Exchange Pl New York NY 10005

VAN TIEM, FLORENTINE URBAN STEWART (MRS. RICHARD L. VAN TIEM), bus. exec.; b. Detroit, Sept. 15, 1928; d. Joseph Stephen and Helen (Reinowski) Urban; A.B., Wayne U., 1948; m. John Slagle, June 15, 1950 (dec.); 1 son, John Gerard (dec.); m. 2d, Dr. Maitland Newman Stewart, May 4, 1957 (div. 1965); children—Joseph Gerald, Victoria Helen; m. 3d, Richard L. Van Tiem, Apr. 22, 1972. Copywriter and publicity dir. of the W. B. Doner Co., 1946-48; account exec. Wolfe, Jickling, Dow & Conkey, 1948-51; exec. v.p. Ruse & Urban, Inc., 1951-55; pres. Splty. Bakers Services, Inc., 1954—; owner Scope Advt. Agy., 1955—, Christopher Gerard & Asso., 1963—, Hilltop Farm Products Inc., 1968—, Specialized Investment Co., 1968—, Victoria Farms, Inc., 1968—. Dir. Ednl. Found., trustee Louis K. Buell Scholarship and Award Found. Recipient numerous awards including Crusade for Freedom, Capital V Viscountess. Mem. Catholic Theatre Detroit, Navy League, Am. Inst. Mgmt., Am. Bakers Assn., Am. Women Radio and TV, Women's Advt. Club, Fashion Group, Detroit Symphony Orch. Women's Assn., Theta Sigma Phi. Republican. Roman Catholic. Clubs: Pilot, Western Golf and Country, Women's City, Young Republicans, Bakers of Chicago, Edgewood Country; Lapeer Golf and Country. Home: Hilltop Farms 1779 E Brocker Rd Metamora MI 48455 also

Troumassee Estate St Lucia WI Office: 280 N Washington St Oxford MI 48051

VAN TIEM, PHILLIP MICHAEL, hosp. ofcl.; b. Grosse Pointe, Mich., Oct. 4, 1935; s. August Gerard and Margaret Mary (Power) Van T.; B.A., Mich. State U., 1963; M.P.A., Central Mich. U., 1978; m. Darlene Miriam Roff, Apr. 4, 1964; children—Bradford, Adrienne. With Gen. Motors Acceptance Corp., 1963-68, credit and collections mgmt., 1965-68; comml. sales rep. Goodyear Tire & Rubber Co., 1968-69; mgr. accounts receivable Lansing (Mich.) Gen. Hosp., 1969-70; mgr. patient accounting Sinai Hosp., Detroit, 1971-72, St. John Hosp., Detroit, 1972-80, asst. controller, 1980—. Bd. dirs. Lansing Gen. Hosp. Credit Union, 1969-70, treas., 1970; chmn. supr. com. Sinai Hosp. Credit Union, 1971-72; vol. social worker Family to Family Movement, 1965-71; mem. vol. program Mich. Dept. Social Services, 1965-71; publicity chmn. Grosse Pointe Park Civic Assn., 1976-78, area del., 1978—. Served with AUS, 1958-60. Recipient hon. mention for suggestion Mich. Hosp. Assn., 1972. Mem. Patient Accounting Mgmt. Assn., Hosp. Fin. Mgmt. Assn. (advanced mem.; chairperson social com. 1975-77, mem. membership com. 1975-77, G.L.D. awards chmn. 1977-78, publicity chmn. 1978-80, dir. 1979-81, del. to Mich. Coordinating Council for Eastern Mich. chpt., Graham L. Davis award 1978, award Eastern Mich. chpt. 1978). Roman Catholic. Home: 1310 Kensington Rd Grosse Pointe MI 48230 Office: 22101 Moross Rd Detroit MI 48236

VAN VELKINBURGH, CLARENCE JOSEPH, ins. co. exec.; b. Decatur, Ill., Oct. 21, 1919; s. Clarence and Linda (Butler) Van V.; B.A., U. Calif., Berkeley, 1951; m. Lula B. Martin, May 31, 1958; children—Danny Joe, Michael Joe. Office mgr. Hildreth Mining Co., Cross Roads, Calif., 1939-41; credit mgr. Mecco and Ceazan Tire Co., Los Angeles, 1945-49; owner, mgr. Carisade Co., boarding house, Berkeley, 1949-54; staff accountant, field auditor C.P.A. firms, 1954-58; nat. and internat. news editor Evansville (Ind.) Courier, 1958-63; field auditor Employer Liability Ins. Cos., New Orleans and Jackson, Miss., 1963-75; sec.-treas., mgr. Miss-Lou Ins. Services, Inc., Jackson, 1975—. Active local Episcopalian Ch., PTA, Babe Ruth League. Served with AUS, 1941-45. Decorated Bronze Star. Mem. Nat. Ins. Auditors Assn. (a founder), Southwest Ins. Auditors Assn. (a founder), Southeastern Ins. Auditors Assn., Miss. Ins. Auditors Assn., New Orleans Ins. Auditors Assn. (a founder), New Orleans Accountants Assn., VFW (life), DAV (life). Clubs: Kiwanis, Lions, Rotary. Home: 160 Beechrest Dr Jackson MS 39211 Office: PO Box 16198 Jackson MS 39206

VAN VLECK, JAMES, paper, furniture and indsl. forest products co. exec.; b. Oklahoma City, May 10, 1930; s. Charles L. and Lula Grace (Mahanke) Van V.; B.A., Principia Coll., 1952; M.B.A., Harvard U., 1956; m. Joan Amery, July 19, 1952; children—Susan, Betsy. Mem. mktg. staff Mead Papers, Dayton, 1957-62; asst. to dir. Mead SA, Zug, Switzerland, 1962-63, dir., 1963-65; dir. Mead European Paper Ops., Belgium, 1965-66, mng. dir. Mide Europe, S.A., Belgium, 1966-68; exec. asst. corp. strategy Mead Corp., Dayton, 1968-69, exec. v.p. Mead Interior Furnishings, Stanleytown, Va., 1969-71; pres. Stanley Furniture Co., Stanleytown, 1971-76; pres. Mead Interior Furnishings, 1976, group v.p. corp. staff, 1976-80, group v.p. indsl. products, 1980—. Bd. dirs. United Way Martinsville-Henry County, 1974-75, City-Wide Devel. Corp., 1977—, Dayton Performing Arts Fund, 1979; mem. Pvt. Industry Council, 1980. Served with U.S. Army, 1952-54. Mem. Martinsville-Henry County C. of C. (past pres.). Office: Courthouse Plaza NE Dayton OH 45463

VAN VLEET, WILLIAM BENJAMIN, JR., lawyer, ins. co. exec.; b. Milw., Dec. 4, 1924; s. William Benjamin and Irene (Peppey) Van V.; student Lawrence Coll., 1943-44; J.D., Marquette U., 1948; m. Marilyn Nilles Dec. 26, 1946; children—Terese (Mrs. Edward Svetich), Susan (Mrs. Paul Waldo), William Benjamin III, Monica, Mark. Admitted to Wis. bar, 1948, Ill. bar, 1950; gen. counsel George Rogers Clark Mut. Casualty Co., Rockford, Ill., 1948-59; gen. counsel Pioneer Life Ins. Co., Rockford, 1950-59, v.p., gen. counsel, 1959-68; dir. exec. v.p., gen. counsel Pioneer Life Ins. Co. of Ill., Rockford, 1968—. Mem. Boylan Central Cath. High Sch. Council of Adminstrn., 1965-72; mem. Diocesan Bd. Edn., Rockford, 1970-78; v.p. Nat. Assn. Bds. Edn., 1972-74, pres., 1974-76; dir. Nat. Catholic Edn. Assn., 1975-78; bd. adv. Marion Coll., 1976-79, St. Anthony's Hosp., 1978—. Served to lt. (j.g.) USNR, 1944-46. Mem. Am., Ill., Wis. bar assns. Roman Catholic. Home: 811 Coolidge Pl Rockford IL 61107 Office: 127 N Wyman St Rockford IL 61101

VAN WART, DONALD TURNER, banker; b. Wis., Mar. 1, 1943; s. Donald Reitler and Louise (Turner) Van W.; B.A., Beloit Coll., 1965; M.B.A., U. Pa., 1967; m. Linda Williams, Dec. 28, 1964; children—Donald, Tara, Justin. Asst. mgr. Citibank N.A., Asuncion, Paraguay, 1968-70, mgr., Buenos Aires, Argentina, 1970-74, gen. mgr., Rio de Janeiro, Brazil, 1974-77, unit head-v.p., N.Y.C., 1977—. Home: 52 Oakhill Rd Chappaqua NY 10514 Office: 399 Park Ave New York NY 10043

VAN WINKLE, ARTHUR D., real estate and ins. exec.; b. Rutherford, N.J., Mar. 11, 1911; s. Charles A. and Helen (Decker) Van W.; grad. Babson Inst., 1932; m. Gretchen Horn, Feb. 23, 1934 (div. Oct. 1973); children—Joan (Mrs. David F. Cunningham), Daniel Horn, Linda (Mrs. Thomas W. Watkins III); m. 2d, Adelaide Shaffer Campbell, Nov. 1, 1973. Past pres. A.W. Van Winkle & Co., 1932-49; chmn. bd. Van Winkle & Liggett, gen. real estate, ins. brokers, 1949-76, chmn. bd., 1976—; pres. Central Guaranty Mortgage & Title Co., 1958-68, Rutherford Equities, 1972—; pres., treas. Rutherford Investment Co., 1972—, Mystic Island Co., 1960—; v.p., dir. Chelsea Title & Guaranty Co., Atlantic City, 1968—; dir. United Jersey Bank, United Jersey Banks Holding Co. Past pres., mem. N.J. Assn. Real Estate Bds., N.J. chpt. Am. Inst. Real Estate Appraisers, South Bergen County Bd. Realtors. Past pres. Rutherford YMCA. Trustee Centenary Coll. for Women, Hackettstown, N.J.; gov. Hackensack (N.J.) Hosp.; mem. adv. bd. Ladies Residence, Hackensack, N.J. Mem. Holland Soc. N.Y., Inst. Real Estate Mgmt., Nat. Assn. Real Estate Brokers, Rutherford C. of C. (dir. 1943). Republican. Presbyn. (past trustee). Mason, Elk Rotarian (past. pres.). Clubs: Masons Island Yacht (past commodore) (Mystic, Conn.); Hackensack Golf; Boca Raton Hotel. Home: 125 Prospect Ave Hackensack NJ 07601 also Masons's Island Mystic CT 06355 also 600 S Ocean Blvd Boca Raton FL 33432 Office: 85 Orient Way Rutherford NJ 07070

VAN WINKLE, PETER KEMBLE, bank exec., portfolio mgr.; b. Providence, Dec. 30, 1941; s. Kingsland and Kate Louise (Vondermuhll) Van W.; B.A. in History, Denison U., 1964; M.B.A. in Fin., Columbia U., 1968; C.F.A., U. Va., 1979; m. Prudence Anderson Bridges, Aug. 16, 1969; children—Trintje Anderson, Prudence Elizabeth. Trust officer U.S. Trust Co., N.Y.C., 1969-70, Boston State St. Bank & Trust, 1970-72; v.p., dir. Lemire Van Winkle & Co., investment counselors, Boston, 1972-73; chief investment officer Choate Hall & Stewart, Boston, 1973-75, v.p. trust investments, portfolio mgr., security analyst First Nat. Bank, Palm Beach, Fla., 1975-80, sr. v.p. Sun Banks, 1980—; instr. bus. Palm Beach Atlantic Coll., 1976-78; cons. Vt. Anesthesia Assos. Inc. Bd. dirs. March of Dimes, Palm Beach, 1977—; treas. Parents and Tchrs. Montessori Children, Palm Beach, 1977—; asst. treas., mem. vestry Bethesda by-the-Sea Episcopal Ch., Palm Beach, 1980—; pres. Palm Beach Water Sports, Inc. Served to 1st lt. U.S. Army, 1964-70. Mem. Fin. Analysts Fedn., Inst. Chartered Fin. Analysts, Boston Soc. Security Analysts, So. Fla. Security Analysts Soc., Bond Club Miami, Fla. Bankers Assn. Republican. Episcopalian. Pub. books of rules and instrns. on water hockey; patentee curved water hockey stick. Home: 110 Seaspray Ave Palm Beach FL 33480 Office: 302 East Atlantic Ave Delray Beach FL 33444

VAN ZON, JACK, conveyor mfg. co. exec.; b. Haarlem, Holland, Nov. 18, 1924; grad. Tech. Sch. Haarlem, 1941; m. Jacoba Allegonda Spiekerman, Feb. 22, 1951; children—Yvonne, Pauline, Carol, Rick. Engring. apprentice Conrad Stork, Haarlem, 1941-47; design-draftsman N.V. Vuilafvoermaatschappy, Amsterdam, Holland, 1947-51; project engr. Dominion Steel & Coal Co., Sydney, N.S., Can., 1951-53; squad leader, chief draftsman, asst. mgr. engring., mgr. engring. Mathews Conveyor Co., Port Hope, Ont., Can., 1953-75; dir. engring., v.p. engring. MidWest Conveyor Co., Kansas City, Kans., 1975—. Vice pres. Children's Aid Soc., Port Hope, 1972-74. Patentee in field. Office: Midwest Conveyor Co 450 E Donovan Rd Kansas City KS 66115

VARLEY, ARTHUR JOSEPH, JR., condominium conversion co. exec.; b. Jacksonville, Fla., June 21, 1949; s. Arthur Joseph and Ula Mary (Maville) V.; B.S. with honors, San Diego State U., 1971; M.D., U. Fla., 1975. Intern, U. Calif., San Diego, 1975-76; resident in orthopedic surgery U. So. Calif., Orthopedic Hosp., 1976-80; founder, pres. Varley Enterprises, San Diego, 1977—; prin. Kopple-Varley Properties, Los Angeles, 1979—, also dir.; pres. Grass Mountain Ski Parks of Am., Inc., Los Angeles, 1980—; v.p. Alutro Enterprises, Inc., San Diego, 1975—; med. adv. Nat. Ski Patrol, Far West Region, 1980. Mem. AMA, San Diego County Med. Assn. Roman Catholic. Office: 7314 Summertime Ln Culver City CA 90230

VARNDELL, CHARLES ROBERT, cons. engring. exec.; b. Uniontown, Pa., July 5, 1924; s. Jacob Richard and Ruth O. (Brown) V.; B.S., U. Md., 1946; m. Elinor Power, July 10, 1954; children—Carolyn R., John P. Asst. bridge engr. Md. State Rds. Commn., Balt., 1946-50; civil engr. CAA, Anchorage, 1950-51; structural engr. Alaska R.R., Anchorage, 1951-52; structural engr. Rummel, Klepper & Kahl, Balt., 1952-55, head bridge dept., 1955-64, asso., 1964-68, partner, 1968—. Fellow ASCE; mem. Soc. Am. Mil. Engrs., Engring. Soc. Balt., Inst. Rapid Transit (asso.), Md. Acad. Scis. (asso.), Am. Railway Engring. Assn., Am. Rd. Builders Assn., Prestressed Concrete Inst., Am. Concrete Inst., Tau Beta Pi. Methodist. Club: Monument River Sportsmen's Association (Houlton, Me.). Home: 2117 Fernglen Way Baltimore MD 21228 Office: 1035 N Calvert St Baltimore MD 21202

VARNER, DAVID EUGENE, lawyer, bus. exec.; b. Dallas, Oct. 9, 1937; s. E.C. and D. Evelyn V.; B.A., So. Meth. U., 1958, J.D., 1961; m. Joan Paula Oransky, Aug. 13, 1962; children—Michael A., Kevin E., Cheryl L. Admitted to Tex. bar, 1961, Fla. bar, 1974, Okla. bar, 1977, U.S. Supreme Ct. bar, 1978; mem. firm Eldridge, Goggans, Davidson & Silverberg, Dallas, 1962-65; atty., asst. sec. Redman Industries, Inc., Dallas, 1965-66; asso. gen. atty. Tex. Instruments Inc., Dallas, 1966-73; sr. atty., asst. sec. Fla. Gas Co., Winter Park, 1973-76; sec., gen. counsel Facet Enterprises, Inc., Tulsa, 1976—, v.p., 1977—; v.p.-legal, sec. Summa Corp., Las Vegas. Served with U.S. Army, 1961-62. Mem. Am. Bar Assn., Am. Soc. Corporate Secs. Mng. editor Southwestern Law Jour., 1960-61. Office: 4045 S Spencer St Las Vegas NV 89109

VARNER, STERLING VERL, oil co. exec.; b. Ranger, Tex., Dec. 20, 1919; s. George Virgle and Christina Ellen (Shafer) V.; student Murray State Sch. Agr., Tishomingo, Okla., 1949, Wichita (Kans.) State U., 1949; m. Paula Jean Kennedy, Nov. 17, 1945; children—Jane Ann, Richard Alan. With Kerr-McGee, Inc., 1941-45; with Koch Industries, Inc., 1945—, pres., chief operating officer, Wichita, 1945—, also dir. mem. exec. com.; dir. 4th Nat. Bank, Wichita, Bd. dirs. NCCJ, Wesley Med. Center, Wichita. Mem. Assn. Oil Pipelines, Nat. Petroleum Refiners Assn., Petroleum Industry Twenty-Five Yr. Club. Mem. Ch. of Christ. Clubs: Wichita, Crestview Country. Office: 4111 E 37th St North Wichita KS 67220

VARNEY, CHARLES WESLEY, JR., ins. exec.; b. Rochester, N.H., Nov. 17, 1912; s. Charles Wesley and Matilda (Shepherd) V.; student New Hampton Sch., 1931; A.B., Dartmouth Coll., 1935; m. Marjorie Wainwright, Mar. 4, 1938; children—Cynthia Bisbee, Susan Helfenstein. Partner, Charles W. Varney & Co., Rochester, 1935, sr. partner, 1948-63, sole owner, 1963-66, pres., treas., 1966-78, chmn. bd., 1978—; asst. treas. Grange Mut. Ins. Co., 1941, treas., 1942, pres., dir., 1948—; pres. Rockingham Farmers Mut. Fire Ins. Co., Grange Ins. Bldg., Inc.; pres., treas. Varney Realty, Inc.; dir. Rochester Savs. Bank & Trust Co., Heritage Banks Inc.; adv. bd. Peerless Ins. Co. Bd. overseers Old Sturbridge Village; trustee Nute High Sch. and Library, Frisbee Meml. Hosp., Eastern States Expn., Gafney Home for Aged. Mem. N.H. Lesislature, 1937-38, N.H., Rochester hist. socs. Republican. Methodist. Clubs: Masons, Shriners, Elks, Odd Fellows, Rotary. Home: 2 Dartmouth Ln Rochester NH 03867 Office: 17 Wakefield St Rochester NH 03867

VARZALY, LAIRD ALAN, trade co. exec.; b. Pitts., Jan. 31, 1947; s. George and Mildred (Tishko) V.; B.S. in Elec. Engring., U. Pitts., 1968; M.S. in Nuclear Engring., Purdue U., 1970; M.B.A., U. Santa Clara, 1975; m. Afsaneh Mavaddat, July 5, 1974. Project engr. Gen. Electric Nuclear Div., San Jose, 1972-76; pres. Ataollah Mavaddat Co., 1976—. Served to lt. USAF, 1970-72. Mem. San Jose C. of C. Club: Santa Clara Valley World Trade Assn. Home: 706 Albanese Circle San Jose CA 95111 Office: 111 W Saint John St #724 San Jose CA 95113

VASA, HARK MANILAL, mgmt. cons. co. exec.; b. Bombay, India, Feb. 8, 1944; s. Manilal Panachand and Prabha M. (Dholakia) V.; came to U.S., 1967, naturalized 1976; B.S., Victoria Jubilee Tech. Inst., Bombay, 1966; M.S., W. Va. U., 1968; m. Kusum B. Doshi, Nov. 8, 1970; children—Anita, Sarita. Indsl. engr. Union Carbide Co., Charleston, W.Va., 1968-69; mgr. sales and systems Dialog Computing Co., Phila., 1969-70; cons. Decision Scis. Corp., Jenkintown, Pa., 1970-74, dir. mgmt. scis. div., 1974-78, v.p. mgmt. scis. and info. systems div., 1978—. Mem. Ops. Research Soc. Am., Assn. Field Service Mgrs., Alpha Pi Mu. Contbr. articles to profl. jours. Home: 48 Twin Brooks Dr Willow Grove PA 19090 Office: Box 1010 Benjamin Fox Pavilion Jenkintown PA 19046

VASCHE, JON DAVID, economist; b. Auburn, Calif., Oct. 11, 1945; s. Joseph Burton and Gertrude A. (Hoekenga) V.; A.B., U. Calif., Riverside, 1967; M.A. in Econs., U. Calif., Berkeley, 1968, Ph.D., 1975; m. Janet DeValois, June 14, 1975; 1 dau., Jennifer Ann. Instr., Calif. State U., San Francisco, 1970-73, acting instr. U. Calif., Berkeley, 1973; lectr. U. Calif., Santa Barbara, 1974-75; instr. Calif. State U., Sacramento, 1978-79; program budget analyst Joint Legis. Budget Com., State of Calif., 1975-77; sr. economist Office of Legis. Analyst, State of Calif., 1977—. Woodrow Wilson fellow, 1968-71; Ford Found. grantee, 1968-69; NSF fellow, 1970-71. Mem. Soc. Govt. Economists, Western Tax Assn., Nat. Tax Assn., Nat. Assn. Bus. Economists, Phi Beta Kappa. Presbyterian. Contbr. articles to profl. jours. Home: 5212 Shelato Way Carmichael CA 95608 Office: 925 L St 805 Sacramento CA 95814

VASCONI, VINCENT PETER, fin. exec.; b. San Francisco, July 1, 1933; s. Theodore and Georgette (Tuerlay) V.; B.S., U. Santa Clara, 1955, M.B.A., 1969; m. Rosemarie Sitra, Feb. 20, 1955; children—Theresa Marie, Anthony Vincent, Vicky Rose, Tina Ann, Andrew Joseph. Dept. mgr. J.C. Penney, Santa Clara, Calif., 1957-59; fin. analyst Westinghouse Corp., Sunnyvale, Calif., 1959-64; mgr. cost analysis Philco Ford, Santa Clara, 1964-68; cost acctg. mgr. Nat. Semiconductor Corp., Santa Clara, 1968-70, dir. acctg., 1974-78, dir. fin. Dyna-Craft, Inc. subs., 1978—; group controller Fairchild Camera and Instrument Corp., Santa Clara, 1970-74; dir. SAMP, Inc. Chmn. sch. bd. Queen of Apostle Elem. Sch., 1976-77. Served to 1st lt. U.S. Army, 1955-57. Mem. Fin. Exec. Inst., Nat. Assn. Accts., Am. Mgmt. Assn. Democrat. Roman Catholic. Home: 521 Park Meadow Ct San Jose CA 95129 Office: 2900 Semiconductor Dr Santa Clara CA 95051

VASQUEZ, CORRADO, fin. exec.; b. Ragusa, Italy, Nov. 20, 1933; came to U.S., 1949; s. Giuseppe and Francesca (Parisi) V.; B.B.A., City Coll. N.Y., 1959; M.B.A., City U. N.Y., 1962; postgrad. N.Y. U., 1963-65, Coll. of Ins., 1978-79, Pace U., 1974-80; m. Edith Santana, Dec. 26, 1954; children—Dianne, Carol, Joseph. Exec. trainee Port Authority of N.Y. and N.J., Jersey City, 1959-60, cost acct., 1960-61, mgmt. analyst, 1961-63, property acctg. supr., 1963-64, asst. to dir. world trade, 1964-66, constrn. mgmt. specialist, 1966-68; mgmt. cons., med. adminstr., 1970-78, mgr. risk mgmt. div., 1978—; internat. controller, v.p., gen. mgr. Europe Marriott Corp., 1968-70; lectr. C.W. Post Coll., Wagner Coll., Am. Mgmt. Assn. Bd. dirs. Prospect Hosp. Med. Found., 1975-78. Served with USN, 1951-55. Named Med. Adminstr. of Yr., Am. Acad. Med. Adminstrs., 1976. Fellow Am. Acad. Med. Adminstrns.; mem. Risk and Ins. Mgmt. Soc., Nat. Assn. Accts., Am. Pub. Health Assn., Internat. Assn. Bridges, Tunnels and Turnpikes. Roman Catholic. Contbr. articles to profl. jours. Home: 45 Yacht Club Cove Staten Island NY 10308 Office: 1 Path Plaza Jersey City NJ 07306

VASSELL, GREGORY S., utility exec.; b. Moscow, Russia, Dec. 24, 1921; came to U.S., 1951, naturalized, 1957; s. Gregory M. and Eugenia M. Wasiljeff; Dipl.Ing., Tech. U. Berlin, 1951; M.B.A., N.Y. U., 1954; m. Martha E. Williams, Apr. 26, 1957; children—Laura Kay, Thomas Gregory. Asst. engr. Am. Electric Power Service Corp., N.Y.C., 1951, head high voltage planning, 1962, chief planning engr., 1967, asst. v.p. bulk power supply planning, 1968, v.p. system planning, 1973, sr. v.p. system planning, 1976—, also dir. Fellow IEEE; mem. Nat. Acad. Engring., Internat. Conf. on Large High Voltage Electric Systems, U.S. Nat. Com. of World Energy Conf. Contbr. articles to profl. jours. Office: 180 E Broad St Columbus OH 43215

VASSILIOU, EUSTATHIOS, chemist, chem. mfg. co. exec.; b. Athens, Greece, Aug. 22, 1934; s. Theodore and Evlalia (Porfiriou) V.; came to U.S., 1966, naturalized, 1972; B.S. in Chem. Engring., Nat. Tech. U. Athens, 1958; Ph.D. in Chemistry, Victoria U., Manchester, Eng., 1964; m. Kleoniki I. Parri, Dec. 22, 1960; children—Theodore, Helen, Evelyn. Research scientist Nuclear Research Center, Athens, 1964-66, Research Lab. D.S. Bersis, Athens, 1964-66; research fellow in chemistry Harvard U., Cambridge, Mass., 1966-67; research chemist E.I. Du Pont de Nemours & Co., Inc., Wilmington, Del., 1967-73, staff chemist Marshall Research and Devel. Lab., Phila., 1973-78, research asso., 1978-79, research supr. Exptl. Sta. Lab., Wilmington, 1979-80, research asso., 1980—; cons. internal on fluropolymers, 1973-79. Served with Greek Army, 1959-60. NATO grantee, 1963-64. Mem. Am. Chem. Soc., Assn. Harvard Chemists. Greek Orthodox. Contbr. articles to profl. jours.; research in properties on indsl. products, product devel.; patentee in field. Home: 12 S Townview Ln Newark DE 19711 Office: E I DuPont de Nemours Exptl Sta Wilmington DE 19898

VAUGHAN, DAVID JOHN, distbn. co. exec.; b. Detroit, July 17, 1924; s. David Evans and Erma Mildred V.; A.B., U. Ill., 1950; m. Anne McKeown Miles, Aug. 21, 1975; children by previous marriage—David John, Melissa Ann, Julia Crawford McLaughlin. Chemist, Midland Electric Colleries, 1950-52; pres. Varrco Distbg. Co., Peoria, Ill., 1953—; prin. David J. Vaughan, investment adv., Peoria, 1970—; instr. Carl Sandburg Coll., Peoria, 1968—. Served to lt. USAAF, 1942-46, USAF, 1951-52; Korea. Registered investment adv. Republican. Presbyterian. Clubs: Peoria Country, Northport Point (Mich.); Peoria Skeet, Masons, Shriners, Jesters. Home: 4510 N Miller Ave Peoria IL 61614

VAUGHAN, HERBERT WILEY, lawyer; b. Brookline, Mass., June 1, 1920; s. David D. and Elzie (Wiley) V.; student U. Chgo., 1937-38; A.B. cum laude, Harvard, 1941, LL.B. 1948; m. Ann Graustein, June 28, 1941. Admitted to Mass. bar, 1948; asso. firm Hale and Dorr, Boston, 1948-54, jr. partner 1954-56, sr. partner, 1956—, co-mng. partner, 1976-80; corporator Boston Five Cents Savs. Bank. Fellow Am. Bar Found.; mem. Am., Boston, Mass. bar assns., Am. Coll. Real Estate Attys. Clubs: Union (Boston), Badminton and Tennis, Longwood Cricket; Bay; Coral Beach and Tennis. Home: 119 Jericho Rd Weston MA 02193 Office: Hale & Dorr 60 State St Boston MA 02109

VAUGHAN, OLIVER WILBERN, pharm. co. exec.; b. Leland, Mass., Aug. 25, 1928; s. Jasper Wilbern and Mattie Lou V.; B.S., Miss. State U., 1953, M.S. in Nutrition, 1954; Ph.D. in Biochemistry, U. Calif., Berkeley, 1959; m. Mary C. Mills, June 3, 1950; children—Oliver, Richard, Cynthia. Research scientist, dir. biochem. lab. Ross Labs., Columbus, Ohio, 1959-64; dir. quality control, dir. internat. mfg. Miles Labs., Elkhart, Ind., 1965-70, v.p. mfg. Ames div., 1970—. Served with U.S. Army, 1951-52. Mem. Am. Chem. Soc., Am. Inst. Nutrition, Phi Kappa Phi. Club: Elkhart Racquet. Office: Miles Labs Elkhart IN 46515

VAUGHAN, RICHARD ALLEN, life ins. underwriter; b. Sherman, Tex., July 18, 1946; s. John W. and Margaret Ann (Fires) V.; student U. Tex., Austin, 1964-68; B.B.A., N. Tex. State U., 1969; m. Terence Hall Thompson, Jan. 12, 1968; children—Shannon, Elizabeth, Todd. Mgr., Vaughan Dept. Stores, Sherman, 1968-73; asso. Fallon Co., Sherman, 1973-76; partner Fallon & Vaughan, C.L.U.'s, Sherman, 1976—; founder, dir. Consol. Printing, Inc.; v.p. Fiserco Inc.; instr. Life Underwriter Tng. Council, Washington. Bd. dirs. Grayson County (Tex.) chpt. Am. Cancer Soc., 1973-77, pres., 1976-77; bd. dirs. Salvation Army, 1975-77; mem. Sherman City Council, 1977-79. Qualifying and life mem. Million Dollar Round Table; named Agt. of Yr., Indpls. Life Ins. Co., 1975; C.L.U. Mem. Am. Soc. C.L.U.'s, Nat. Assn. Life Underwriters, Life Underwriters Assn. (dir.), Tex. Assn. Life Underwriters, Sigma Alpha Epsilon. Baptist. Office: 111A N Travis Sherman TX 75090

VAUGHAN, RICHARD HAMILTON, distbn. co. exec.; b. Pottstown, Pa., Jan. 8, 1928; s. Jacob Oldfield and Ruth Lewis (Winter) V.; B.S., Coll. of William and Mary, 1949; m. Florence Elizabeth Carty, Nov. 25, 1950; children—Douglas Carty, Elizabeth Hamilton. Operating supt. Sears Roebuck & Co., Phila., 1947-60; v.p. ops. Consol. Sun Ray Drug Co. Inc., Phila., 1960-62; v.p. mktg. Vendo Co., Kansas City, Mo., 1962-71; v.p. sales and mktg. Litton

Microwave Cooking Products, Mpls., 1971-76; pres. Sefco Distbg. Co. Inc., Hanover, Md., 1976—. Served with U.S. Army, 1950-52. Mem. Internat. Foodservice Mfrs. Assn., Nat. Automatic Merchandising Assn., Amusement and Music Operators Am. Republican. Roman Catholic. Clubs: Elks, Civitan. Home: 10 Theo Ln Towson MD 21204 Office: 7255 Standard Dr Hanover MD 21076

VAUGHN, CHARLES LECLAIRE, psychologist, mgmt. cons.; b. Emporia, Kans., Oct. 5, 1911; s. Charles and Anna (Jones) V.; B.S., Kans. State Tchrs. Coll., 1931; Ph.D., U. Chgo., 1936; m. Kathleen Inez Thayer, Nov. 5, 1935; children—Michael Thayer, Charles Robert, Kathleen Virginia Vaughn Wright, Richard James. Asst. dir. market research Psychol. Corp., N.Y.C., 1946-60; sr. research asso. Dunlap & Assos., Stamford, Conn., 1960-61; dir. bus. research to dir. Office of Spl. Programs, Boston Coll., 1961-77; pres. Vaughn Co., Needham, Mass., 1977—; bd. dirs. Communicare, Inc., Lacy Sales Inst. Served to lt. USNR, 1943-46. Recipient spl. awards Internat. Franchise Assn., Boston chpt. Am. Mktg. Assn.; lic. psychologist, Mass., Conn., N.Y. Fellow Am. Psychol. Assn.; mem. N.Y. Psychol. Assn. (dir.). Republican. Methodist. Author: Franchising: Its Nature, Scope, Advantages and Development, 2d edit., 1979; also several vols. of Franchising Today, Marketing in the Defense Industries. Address: 41 Stratford Rd Needham MA 02192

VAUGHN, FRED J., limousine service exec.; b. South Bend, Ind., May 1, 1948; s. Fred W. and Mary Ellen (Steele) V.; student Ind. U., 1966-67, Cleary Coll., 1967-69; m. Sharon Sue Nusbaum, Dec. 12, 1970; children—Dawn Elain, Amy Marie, Daniel Russell. Clk.-typist Comml. Motor Freight, South Bend, 1966-67; sales rep., Elkhart Brass Mfg. Co. (Ind.), 1969-71, Nat. China & Equipment, Marion, Ind., 1971-72, Indpls., 1972-73; buyer Continental Byman, Calumet City, Ill., 1973-74; pres., gen. mgr. Metro. Rental Service, Inc., South Bend, 1974—. Pres., Town Bd. of Roseland, 1980—. Club: Masons (master 1979). Address: 120 W Cripe St South Bend IN 46637

VAUGHN, LEWIS CANDLER, automotive equipment exec.; b. Conyers, Ga., Mar. 10, 1900; s. Roland Bennett and Lucy (Anderson) V.; B.S. in Elec. Engring. with honors, Auburn U., 1919; m. Varina Goynes Webb, Aug. 26, 1930. Elec. engr. Westinghouse Electric Co., East Pittsburg, Pa., 1919-22; pres. Vaughn & Wright, Inc., West Palm Beach, Fla., 1922—, chmn. bd., 1922—. Chmn. bd. dirs. Am. Orchid Soc.'s Fund for Edn. and Research, Cambridge, Mass., 1967—. Served with A.C., AUS, 1918. Recipient Gold medal of Achievement Am. Orchid Soc., 1967; award of Distinction South Fla. Orchid Soc., 1963. Mem. Am. Orchid Soc. (pres. soc. 1964-66, chmn. Fifth World Orchid Conf. 1966). Contbr. articles to various publs. Patentee in field. Home: 6001 S Flagler Dr PO Box 3091 West Palm Beach FL 33402 Office: 100 Palmetto St W Palm Beach FL 33405

VAUGHN, MICHAEL JEFFERY, banker, educator, lawyer; b. Palestine, Tex., May 26, 1943; s. J.E. and Catherine W. (Wright) V.; B.A., Baylor U., 1964, J.D., 1966; LL.M., Yale, 1967; m. Martha Ballenger, July 5, 1967; children—Russ Wright, Mary Elizabeth, Sarah Eleanor, Clay Ballenger. Admitted to Tex. bar, 1966, since practiced in Waco; mem. firm Vaughn and Sullivan, 1971-74; asso. prof. law Baylor U., Waco, 1967-71; vis. prof. law South Tex. Coll. Law, Houston, 1971, prof. law, 1979—; chmn. bd. Lott (Tex.) State Bank, 1974-77, First State Bank, Chilton, Tex., 1974-77; chmn. bd. Consol. Bankers Life Ins. Co., Waco, pres., 1972-74; pres., chief exec. officer First Security State Bank of Cranfills Gap (Tex.), 1973-75, chmn. bd., 1976-77; chmn. exec. com., chief exec. officer Am. Bank of Waco, 1974-76; v.p. Coracorp Mortgage Services, Inc., 1978. Justice of peace Anderson County (Tex.), 1964-67; mem. Henderson County Hist. Survey Com., 1968-71. Mem. Internat. Acad. Forensic Psychology (bd. govs. 1968-71), Assn. Am. Law Schs., State Bar Tex., SCV. Club: Masons. Author: History of Cayuga and Crossroads, Texas, 1967; (with William Q. de Funiak) Principles of Community Property, 2d rev. edit., 1971; contbr. articles to profl. jours. Home: 3501 Austin Ave Waco TX 76710 Office: South Tex Coll Law 1303 San Jacinto Houston TX 77002

VAUTHEROT, RICHARD, apparel retail exec.; b. Colmar, France, Oct. 1, 1951; s. Robert and Marie Therese (Moulieras) V.; came to U.S., 1978; B.S., U. So. Calif., 1974; M.B.A., 1975. Tech. cons. Metra Proudfoot Inc., Brussels, Belgium, 1976; internat. sales mgr. HL Chapuis Co., Cannes, France, 1977-78; mktg. mgr. Mediterranean Fashions, Inc., Beverly Hills, Calif., 1977-78; v.p. mktg., 1979—. Mem. U. So. Calif. Entrepreneur and Venture Mgmt. Alumnus Assn. Home: 2111 N Beverly Glen Los Angeles CA 90024 Office: 9511 Brighton Way Beverly Hills CA 90210

VAWTER, WALLACE READ, JR., overseas banking adminstr.; b. Indpls., Feb. 8, 1928; s. Wallace Read and Helen (Cripe) V.; B.S. in Bus. Adminstrn., U. Colo., 1951; M.B.A., Fordham U., 1974. With Am. Express Co., 1956—, dist. mgr., Am. Express Internat. Banking Corp., Taiwan, Philippines, Vietnam, 1964-70, mgr. ops., mil. banking div., 1970-72, asst. treas., mil. banking div., 1972-75, asst. treas. dist. mgr., mil. banking offices, Japan, 1976-79; asst. v.p., dep. regional mgr. Mil. Banking Facilities-Pacific, 1979—. Served as lt. (j.g.) USNR, 1951-55; capt. Res. Mem. Navy Supply Corps Assn. (past nat. dir.), Am. C. of C. in Saigon, Am. C. of C. in Taipei. Baptist. Office: American Express International Banking Corp Military Banking Facilities APO San Francisco CA 96301

VEALE, JOHN EDMOND (JACK), business exec.; b. Winchester, Mass., July 12, 1954; s. Edmond John and Margaret Louise V.; B.S. in Bus. Adminstrn., Norwich U., 1976; m. Laurie Jean Howard, Apr. 29, 1978. With Southwest Hide Co., Boise, Idaho, 1976—, acct., 1977-78, office mgr., corp. office, 1978-79, corp. controller, 1979-81, chief fin. officer, 1981—. Mem. Idaho Assn. Commerce and Industry, Alpha Kappa Psi. Republican. Clubs: Full Gospel Businessmen's Internat., Nat. Ski Patrol Home: 4062 Patton St Boise ID 83704 Office: Box 7946 Boise ID 83707

VEASY, EUGENE BRIAN, food co. exec.; b. Phila., Oct. 23, 1939; s. John P. and Nora T. (Moran) V.; B.S., Drexel U., 1963; M.B.A., Harvard U., 1965; 1 son, Sean Richard. With Honeywell, Inc., Ft. Washington, Pa., 1965-67; cons. A.T. Kearney & Co., N.Y.C., 1967-69; mgr. new ventures and ops. research Purolator, Inc., Rahway, N.J., 1969-70; asst. to pres. Gen. Cinema Corp., Boston, 1970-74; asst. v.p. Folger & Co., Boston, 1974-75; v.p., chief fin. officer Golden Eye Seafoods, Inc., Fairhaven, Mass., 1975-80; exec. v.p., chief operating officer New Bedford Seafood Coop. Assn., Inc., 1980—; lectr. in field; notary pub., Mass., 1977—. Licensed real estate broker, Mass. Mem. Am. Inst. Indsl. Engrs. (v.p. 1967-69), Harvard Bus. Sch. Assn. Boston (pres. 1978-79), New Bedford C. of C. (dir. 1981—), Sigma Pi. Club: Harvard. Author: (with others) Computer Time Sharing: Dynamic Information Handling for Business, 1966. Home: 10 Dexter Rd Marion MA 02738 Office: PO Box J4028 New Bedford MA 02741

VEBELIUNAS, VYTAUTAS, tax counselor, bus. exec.; b. Lithuania, July 26, 1930; s. Kazys and Juze (Kalvaitis) V.; came to U.S., 1950, naturalized, 1953; B.S., Pace Coll., 1956; m. Vanda Tamsevicius, Dec. 30, 1967; children—Daiva, Gina, Rima, Aras, Tauras, Rytas. Accountant Am. Chickle Co., N.Y.C., 1956-61; asst. to treas. and tax mgr. Panagra-Braniff Airways, N.Y.C. and Dallas, 1961-69; pres. Litas Group, N.Y.C., 1969—; chmn. bd. Litas Investing Co., Inc. lectr. in field. Served with USMC, 1951-53. Enrolled pub. accountant N.Y. State; admitted to practice as agt. before IRS. Republican. Roman Catholic. Home: 304 Bayville Rd Lattington NY 11560 Office: 120 Wall St New York NY 10005

VECCHIO, DONALD ANTHONY, pharmacy exec.; b. Denver, Apr. 29, 1932; s. Dominic Marion and Mary Asunta (Perry) V.; B.S. in Pharmacy, Colo. U., 1954; m. Nellie Louise Lines, Jan. 11, 1959; children—Mary Louise, Nellie Ann, Donna Marie. Pharmacist, mgr. Owl Drug, Denver, 1957-61; owner, mgr. Dons Prescription Shop, Inc., Wheatridge, Colo., 1961—; partner, founder Allied Surg. Supply, 1971—; pres. Don Lin Pharmacy, Wheatridge, 1974—; instr. clin. pharmacy practice U. Colo. Coll. Pharmacy, 1979—; dir. Allied Surg. Supply; mem. Colo. Rx Com. Dept. Social Services Drug Review Bd.; advisor to Jefferson County Schs. on drug edn.; teaching staff drug abuse seminars; chmn. Operation Drug Alert. Served with M.C., U.S. Army, 1955-57. Named Pharmacist of the Yr., 1971, Denver Area Pharm. Assn.; recipient Kiwanis Appreciation award, 1974; City of Arvada Image award, 1976; A.H. Robbins Bowl of Hygea award, 1977; named Man of Year, Arvada, 1978. Mem. Am., Denver area pharm. assns., Nat. Assn. Retail Druggists, Am. Coll. Apothecaries, Allied Retail Druggist Assn. Republican. Methodist. Club: Kiwanis. Home: 7068 Parfet Ct Arvada CO 80004 Office: 4485 Wadsworth St Wheatridge CO 80033

VEDDER, BLAIR, advt. exec.; b. Chgo., Dec. 4, 1924; s. Beverly B. and Helen (Morse) V.; B.A., Colgate U., 1946; m. Geraldine Bovbjerg, Feb. 1, 1947; children—Nicholas B., Nancy N., Richard D. Salesman, Radio Sta. WOSH, Oshkosh, Wis., 1947-48; asso. media dir. Needham, Louis & Brorby, Chgo., 1948-55; v.p., media dir. Needham, Harper & Steers Advt., Inc., Chgo., 1955-64, sr. v.p. adminstrn., corporate media, 1964-66, sr. v.p. internat., London, 1966-67, exec. v.p., Chgo., 1967-74, chmn. bd., 1974-76, pres., 1976-80, chmn. exec. com., chief operating officer, 1980—; pres. Pioneer Farm Corp., 1978—. Dir. Nat. Outdoor Advt. Bur., N.Y.C., 1955-60. Served to lt. USNR, 1942-46; PTO. Clubs: N.Y. Yacht, Chicago Yacht, Tavern. Home: 2714 Lincoln St Evanston IL 60201 Office: 401 N Michigan Ave Chicago IL 60611

VEGA, ALBERTO LEON, mfg. co. exec.; b. Havana, Cuba, Apr. 11, 1947; s. Alberto and Ofelia Gregoria (Perez) V.; came to U.S., 1961, naturalized, 1971; B.B.A. cum laude, U. Miami, 1969; m. Rosa Maria Alvarez, June 26, 1971. Sr. accountant Ernst & Ernst, Miami, Fla., 1969-73; asst. treas. Amcourt Systems, Inc., Coral Gables, Fla., 1973-74; v.p.-fin. Heinicke Instruments Co., Hollywood, Fla., 1974—, dir., 1975—. C.P.A., Fla. Mem. Am., Fla. insts. C.P.A.'s, Fin. Execs. Inst., Beta Alpha Psi. Club: Exchange of S.W. Miami. Office: 3000 Taft St Hollywood FL 33021

VEIL, G. SHELDON, chem. co. exec.; b. Cleve., June 24, 1927; s. George W. and Emma K. Veil; B.S. in Bus. Adminstrn., Miami U., Oxford, Ohio, 1950; postgrad. Cleve.-Marshall Law Sch., 1950, 51; m. Alice Anne Veil, Aug. 28, 1974; children by previous marriage-Mark W., Scott, Michael, Mark B., Brent. Auto sales mgr. Glidden Co., Detroit, 1950-68; pres. Grow Chem. Co., Troy, Mich., 1972—; exec. v.p. Grow Group, Inc., Troy, 1972—, dir., 1976—. Served with USN, 1945-46. Mem. Soc. Automotive Engrs., Engring. Soc. Detroit, Nat. Paint and Coatings Assn., Chem. Coatings Assn. Clubs: Detroit Athletic, Recess, Grosse Pointe Hunt. Home: 1390 Willow Ln Birmingham MI 48009 Office: Grow Group Inc 3155 W Big Beaver Rd Troy MI 48084

VEITH, RICHARD LEE, oil co. exec.; b. Harrisburg, Pa., May 9, 1940; s. Leroy Oscar and Hester Dowler (Meek) V.; B.A., Cornell U., 1963; M.B.A. (First Pa. Ednl. Fund fellow), U. Pa., 1965; m. Carolyn Rickards, June 27, 1964; children—Barbara Wainwright, Charles Douglas. With Sun Oil Co., Phila., auditor, 1965-70, mgr. cash adminstrn., 1970-72, fin. adminstr., P.R., 1972-75, project mgr., 1975-76, treas. Sun Ventures, Inc., 1976-78, fin. coordinator enterprises group, 1977-79; v.p. fin., dir. Sun Carriers, Inc., 1978—. Bd. mgrs. Boys' Club Met. Phila. Mem. Fin. Execs. Inst., Phi Delta Theta. Republican. Presbyterian. Clubs: Phila. Skating, Martin's Dam. Home: 436 Timber Ln Devon PA 19333 Office: 2000 Market St Philadelphia PA 19103

VELIOTIS, PANAGIOTIS TAKIS, shipbldg. co. exec.; b. Kranidion, Greece, Aug. 11, 1926; s. Eleutherios George and Joanna (Zarifis) V.; B.A., St. Paul Coll., Greece; postgrad. Nat. U., Athens, Greece; degree in Engring., Royal Naval Acad. Greece; D.Sci. (hon.), Nat. U., San Diego; m. Paulette Dupuis, children—Eleutherios George, Joanna. Engr., E.G. Veliotis Shipowners, 1948-53; engr., draftsman Davie Shipbldg. Ltd., Que., Can., 1953, supt. gen. engring. div., 1954, mgr. gen. engring. div., 1955-59, asst. gen. mgr., 1959-62, dir., gen. mgr., 1962-72, pres., gen. mgr., dir., 1972; v.p. Gen. Dynamics Corp., pres., gen. mgr. Quincy Shipbldg. div. (Mass.), 1973-77, gen. mgr. Electric Boat div., 1977-80, exec. v.p.-marine, 1980—. Served as officer Royal Hellenic Navy, World War II. Mem. Soc. Naval Architects and Marine Engrs., Shipbuilders Council Am., Am. Bur. Shipping, Lloyd's Register of Shipping. Greek Orthodox. Clubs: Quebec Garrison, Quebec Yacht. Home: 1431 Brush Hill Rd Milton MA 02186 Office: Eastern Point Rd Groton CT 06340

VELLA, RUTH ANN, Realtor; b. Chester, Pa., Aug. 18, 1942; d. Eric and Carmella Tanberg; children—Michele Francette Vella, Nicole Renae Vella. Real estate sales asso. Reeve Realty, Wilmington, Del., 1966-72; owner, Realtor, Heritage Realty, Wilmington, 1972—; instr. sales Wilmington Coll., 1978—; mem. faculty Del. State Coll., 1979—. Mem. New Castle County Bd. Realtors (ednl. chmn.), Womens Council Realtors (past state pres., gov.), Nat. Assn. Realtors (nat. speaker, energy conservation instr.), Ind. Fee Appraisers Assn., Newark Profl. Womens Assn., Zonta. Roman Catholic. Office: 3619-B Kirkwood Hwy Wilmington DE 19808

VELMANS, LOET ABRAHAM, pub. relations exec.; b. Amsterdam, Netherlands, Mar. 18, 1923; s. Joseph and Anna (Cohen) V.; grad. U. Amsterdam, 1947. Info. officer Dutch Govt. in Singapore, 1945-47; with Hill & Knowlton, Inc., 1953—, v.p. Hill Knowlton Internat., Geneva, 1959-60, pres., 1960-74, vice chmn., London, 1969-76, pres., N.Y.C., 1976—, chief exec. officer, 1979—, chmn., 1980—. Recipient Commendatore dell'Ordine Merito della Repubblica Italiana, 1976. Mem. Legal Aid Soc. N.Y. (dir.). Office: Hill and Knowlton 633 3d Ave New York NY 10017

VELZY, DAVID WALTER, indsl. engr.; b. Columbus, Ohio, Apr. 30, 1951; s. Walter Earl and Jane Allison (Stewart) V.; B.S. in Indsl. Systems Engring., Ohio State U., 1975, postgrad., 1975-77. Mgr. biomechanics lab., engring. mechanics dept. Ohio State U., Columbus, 1974-77; indsl. engr. Bowen Assos., Newark, Ohio, 1975-77; sr. mfg. engr./systems Diebold Inc., Newark, 1977-78, product change engr., 1978-80, plant project coordinator, 1980—; mem. Modern Plastics Adv. Council, 1979-80. Mem. Instrument Soc. Am., Am. Soc. Nondestructive Testing, Am. Mgmt. Assn. Home: 162 W Weber Rd Columbus OH 43202 Office: PO Box 2328 Newark OH 43055

VENABLE, CHARLES RICHARD, III, agrl. co. exec.; b. Kingsport, Tenn., May 24, 1948; s. Charles Richard and Jean Elizabeth (Herndon) V.; B.A. summa cum laude, Harding Coll., 1970; M.B.A. with honors (fellow), So. Meth. U., 1972; m. Katherine Fay Julian, Nov. 26, 1970; children—Mark Tyler, Jeffrey Austin. Accountant, Arthur Andersen & Co., Dallas, 1970-71; asst. controller Cambridge Cos., Inc., Dallas, 1972-74; v.p. fin. Robert B. Watson & Assos., Jackson, Miss., 1974; corp. controller McCarty-State Pride Farms, Inc., Magee, Miss., 1975—. Mem. pres.'s devel. council Harding Coll., 1970—. Recipient award Wall Street Jour., 1970; C.P.A., Miss., Tex. Mem. Am. Inst. C.P.A.'s, Tex. Soc. C.P.A.'s, Southeastern Poultry and Egg Assn., Beta Gamma Sigma. Republican. Mem. Ch. of Christ. Club: Simpson County Country. Home: Route 1 Box 77A Magee MS 39111 Office: PO Box 366 Magee MS 39111

VENABLE, W(ILLIAM) HENRY, lawyer; b. Cin.; s. William Mayo and Jessie (Tuckerman) V.; B.S., Carnegie Inst. Tech., 1928. C.E., 1937; LL.B., Duquesne U., 1945; m. Eva Edna Nicholson, Oct. 1931; children—William Henry, Beatrice. Design engr. Blaw-Knox Co., Pitts., 1928-37, asst. to mgr. devel. dept., 1937-46, patent counsel, 1946-68; admitted to Pa. bar, 1946; pvt. practice law, Pitts., 1968—. Mem. com. on internat. protection indsl. property U.S. council Internat. C. of C., del. to XIX-XXII congresses, 1963, 65, 67, 69, 75. Registered profl. engr., Pa. Mem. Am., Pa. bar assns., Am. Patent Law Assn., Patent Law Assn. Pitts. (bd. mgrs. 1972), A.A.A.S., History Sci. Soc. (del. VIII-XII congresses). Soc. for History Tech., Am. Arbitration Assn. (nat. panel arbitrators), Am. Soc. Internat. Law, Engrs. Soc. Western Pa., Pa. Soc., N.Y. Acad. Scis. Republican. Presbyn. Clubs: University, Field, Duquesne (Pitts.). Home: 610 Park Pl Pittsburgh PA 15237 Office: Union Trust Bldg Pittsburgh PA 15219

VENDETTE, VINCENT JOSEPH, securities co. exec.; b. Phila., Jan. 14, 1953; s. Vincent Victor and Louise Ann (Napoli) V.; A.B., U. Pa., 1976, B.B.A., 1980; m. Diane Cona, May 26, 1977. Option specialist Dean Witter Reynolds Co., Phila., 1975—; mem. Phila. Stock and Option Exchange, 1975—. Home: 67 Hillside Rd Turnersville NJ 08012 Office: Dean Witter Reynolds Co Philadelphia Stock Exchange Philadelphia PA 19103

VENIT, WILLIAM BENNETT, lighting cons.; b. Chgo., May 28, 1931; s. George B. and Ida (Shaffell) V.; student U. Ill., 1949; m. Nancy Jean Carlson, Jan. 28, 1956; children—Steven Louis, April Ann. Sales mgr. Coronet Inc., 1952-55, pres., 1955-74, chmn. bd., 1960-74; pres. Roma Wire Co., Inc., Chgo., 1963-74, chmn. bd., 1973-74; pres. William Wire Co., Inc., Chgo., 1974—; chmn. bd., pres. William B. Venit, Sales and Consulting, Chgo., 1977—. Bd. dirs. Horner Park and River Park Athletic Assn., Luther High Sch. Booster Club, Henry Hart Jewish Community Center. Served with Q.M.C., U.S. Army, 1949-52. Mem. Lamp and Shade Inst. (dir.). Jewish. Patentee in lighting industry. Home: 4850 N Monticello Ave Chicago IL 60625

VENT, RICHARD HENRY, hotel and airline catering co. exec.; b. Kittanning, Pa., Jan. 8, 1941; s. Henry J. and Alice Vent; B.S., Duquesne U., 1966; M.B.A., Ind. U., 1970; m. Sonja M. Roncher, Apr. 1, 1967. Investment researcher Mellon Nat. Bank, Pitts., 1966-67; v.p. ARA Services Co., Phila., 1967-77; v.p. food service mgmt. Marriott Corp., Washington, 1977-79, v.p. internat., 1979—; dir. Servair, Paris; mem. adv. bd. Western Carolina U. Bd. dirs. Kensington Hosp., Phila., 1971-73. Served with USN, 1958-62. Mem. Am. Mgmt. Assn. Republican. Roman Catholic. Home: 1666 Chimney House Rd Reston VA 22090

VENTRESCA, BENJAMIN JOSEPH, JR., mgmt. cons.; b. Phila., Apr. 2, 1948; s. Benjamin Joseph and Mary Angela Ventresca; B.Civil Engring., Villanova (Pa.) U., 1970, M.Structural Engring., 1974; m. Elinor Marie DeLany, June 1, 1974; children—Benjamin Ryan, Gregory Joseph. Instr., Villanova U., 1971-74; mgr. data processing services STV, Inc., Pottstown, Pa., 1974-76; mgr. mgmt. systems and ops. Altemose Enterprises, Centre Square, Pa., 1976-77; prin. Krall Mgmt., Inc., Radnor, Pa., 1977—. Mem. counseling and recruiting program Villanova U., Republican Com. of Chester County; active Charter Chase Community Assn., East Mt. Airy Neighbors Assn. Registered profl. engr., Pa. Mem. ASCE (past chpt. pres.), Nat. Soc. Profl. Engrs., Am. Soc. Info. Scis., Am. Mgmt. Assn., Am. Inst. Steel Constrn., Data Processing Mgrs. Assn., Engring. Joint Council (chpt. chmn. 1972-74), Nat. Geog. Soc., LaSalle Alumni Assn. Roman Catholic. Clubs: Pa. Athletic Rowing, Villanova U. Rowing. Home: 1398 Morstein Rd West Chester PA 19380 Office: 2 Radnor Corp Center Suite 310 Radnor PA 19087

VERANO, ANTHONY F., banker; b. West Harrison, N.Y., Jan. 4, 1931; s. Frank and Rose (Viscome) V.; student Am. Inst. Banking, 1956-60, Bank Adminstrn. Inst., U. Wis., 1962-64, N.J. Bankers Data Processing Sch., 1966-68; m. Clara Cosentino, July 8, 1951; children—Rosemarie, Diana Lynn. Clk., The County Trust Co., White Plains, N.Y., 1949, teller, 1949-52, jr. teller, 1952-53, sr. teller, 1953-57, asso. auditor, 1957-60, sr. auditor, 1960-61; asst. auditor State Nat. Bank Conn., Bridgeport, 1961, auditor, 1962-79, exec. auditor, 1979—; instr. Am. Inst. Banking. Served with USN, 1951-52. Chartered bank auditor. Mem. Bank Adminstrn. Inst., Inst. Internal Auditors, Am. Accounting Assn. Home: PO Box 1205 SM Sta Fairfield CT 06430 Office: 2834 Fairfield Ave Bridgeport CT 06605

VERBLAAUW, RODNEY T., bank exec.; b. Hawthorne, N.J., Mar. 1, 1938; s. Tunis and Wilma V.; A.A., Fairleigh Dickinson U., 1960; grad. Nat. Trust Sch., Northwestern U., 1968; m. Geraldine J. Prol, June 3, 1959; children—Kathleen, Janice, Richard, Robert. With Citizens First Nat. Bank, Ridgewood, N.J., 1955—, v.p., 1966-76, sr. v.p., 1976-79, exec. v.p., 1979-80, pres., 1980—. Mem. N.E. Jersey Bankers Assn. (pres.), N.J. Bankers Assn. (past chmn. trust legis. com.; exec. com.), No. N.J. Fiduciary Assn. (past pres.). Club: Ridgewood Lions (past pres.). Office: 208 Harristown Rd Glen Rock NJ 07452

VERDERBER, JOSEPH ANTHONY, business machines mfg. co. exec.; b. Cleve., Nov. 30, 1938; s. Joseph Arthur and Dorothy Louise (Buchta) V.; B.S. (Nat. Merit scholar), M.S. in Mech. Engring. (NSF fellow), M.I.T., 1961; m. Anita Barto, Sept. 10, 1960; children—Joseph Anthony, Lisa, Paul. With Product Research Lab., Addressograph-Multigraph Corp., Cleve., 1961-70, mgr. labs., 1966-70; dir. engring. Varityper Corp., East Hanover, N.J., 1970-72, product mgr., 1972-77; dir. advanced devel. AM Internat., Mt. Prospect, Ill., 1977—; lectr. mech. engring. Cleve. State U., 1962-67. Registered profl. engr., Ohio. Mem. ASME, Fox Point Homeowners Assn. (tennis com. 1979-80). Patentee in field. Home: 315 S Valley Rd Barrington IL 60010 Office: 1800 W Central Rd Mount Prospect IL 60056

VEREEN, WILLIAM JEROME, clothing co. exec.; b. Moultrie, Ga., Sept. 7, 1940; s. William Coachman and Mary Elizabeth (Bunn) V.; B.S. in Indsl. Mgmt., Ga. Inst. Tech., 1963; m. Lula Evelyn King, June 9, 1963; children—Elizabeth King, William Coachman. With Riverside Mfg. Co., Moultrie, 1967—, plant mgr., 1970, v.p., 1970-73, exec. v.p., 1973-77, pres., 1977—, also dir.; v.p. dir. Moultrie Cotton Mills, Inc., 1967—; v.p. dir. Riverside Industries, Inc., 1967-79, pres., 1979—; v.p. dir. Riverside Uniform Rentals, Inc., 1967-79, pres.,

1979—; pres., dir. Riverside Mfg. Co. (Ireland) Ltd., 1977—, Riverside Mfg. Co. GmbH (W. Ger.). Bd. dirs. Moultrie-Colquitt County United Givers, 1967-74, Colquitt County Cancer Soc., 1967-70, Moultrie YMCA, 1969—, Moultrie Colquitt County Devel. Authority, 1972-74; trustee Community Welfare Assn., 1968—, Pineland Sch., 1970—. Mem. Moultrie-Colquitt County C. of C. (dir. 1969-72), Young Pres.'s Orgn., Am. Apparel Mfgrs. Assn., Nat. Assn. Uniform Mfgrs., Sigma Alpha Epsilon. Presbyterian (chmn. bd. deacons). Club: Elks, Kiwanis. Home: 21 Dogwood Circle Moultrie GA 31768 Office: PO Box 460 Moultrie GA 31768

VERGNE, LUÍS JESUS, internat. cons.; b. Orocovis, P.R., Dec. 18, 1929; s. Jesús José and Josephine (Latorre) V.; B.A., Tulane U., 1956; postgrad. exec. program Stanford U., 1979; m. Frances Mayo Goss, Dec. 19, 1953; children—Stewart, Cecilia, Valerie. Asst. to pres. Transcontinental Import-Export Corp., New Orleans, 1952-54; mgr. Transoceanic Shipping Co., New Orleans, 1954-56; sales rep. Phosphate div. Internat. Minerals & Chem. Corp., Chgo., 1957-59, sales mgr. for Latin Am., Chgo., 1963-75, v.p. overseas sales Fertilizer Group, Northfield, Ill., 1976—; mng. dir. IMC S.A., San Juan, P.R., 1959-63; cons. on internat. ops., 1980—. Mem. Chgo. Council Fgn. Relations, Chgo. Assn. Commerce and Industry, Internat. Trade Club Chgo., Japan-Am. Soc., U.S.-Mex. C. of C. Roman Catholic. Club: Exmoor Country (Highland Park, Ill.).

VERITY, CALVIN WILLIAM, JR., steel co. exec.; b. Middletown, Ohio, Jan. 26, 1917; s. Calvin William and Elizabeth (O'Brien) V.; B.A., Yale U., 1939; m. Margaret Burnley Wymond, Apr. 19, 1941; children—Jonathan George, Peggy Wymond (Mrs. John Power), William Wymond. With Armco Steel Corp. (now Armco Inc.), Middletown, 1940—, dir. public relations, 1961-62, asst. to pres., 1962-63, v.p., gen. mgr., 1963-65, exec. v.p., dir., 1965, pres., chief exec. officer, 1965-71, chmn. bd., 1971—, also dir.; dir. Chase Manhattan Bank, Mead Corp., Dayton, Ohio, Bus. Internat., N.Y.C., First Nat. Bank, Middletown, Boston Co., Taft Broadcasting Co., Cin. Chmn. bd. govs. Ford's Theater; chmn. U.S.-USSR Trade and Econ. Council; mem. Pres.'s Export Council; bd. dirs. Nat. Council for U.S.-China Trade, Internat. Iron and Steel Inst.; trustee Colgate Darden Grad. Sch. Bus. at U. Va.; hon. trustee U. Dayton; chmn. bd. trustees Ford's Theatre, Washington. Mem. Middletown C. of C. (past pres.), U.S. C. of C. (chmn. 1980—), Cin. Council World Affairs, SAR. Clubs: Brown's Run Country (Middletown); Moraine (Dayton); Laurel Valley (Ligonier, Pa.); Queen City, Camargo (Cin.). Office: Armco Inc 703 Curtis St Middletown OH 45042

VERMEER, RICHARD DOUGLAS, oil drilling contractor; b. Bronxville, N.Y., July 2, 1938; s. Albert Casey and Helen Valentine (Casey) V.; B.S., Fairleigh Dickinson U., 1960; M.B.A., LeHigh U., 1967; m. Grace Dorothy Ferguson, May 22, 1960; children—Carin Dawn, Catherine Jeanne, Robert Brooke. Mgmt. trainee Gen. Electric Co., Phila., 1961-63; auditor Campbell Soup Co., Camden, N.J., 1963-64; sr. systems analyst Air Products & Chems. Inc., Allentown, Pa., 1964-67; mgr. fin. systems Trans World Airlines, N.Y.C., 1967-71; dir. mgmt. services Kaufman & Broad Inc., Los Angeles, 1971-73, group controller, 1974-76; asst. to pres. Global Marine, Inc., Los Angeles, 1976-77, v.p., mgr. corp. planning, controller, 1977—. Adviser, Jr. Achievement Phila., 1962-63. Served with AUS, 1960. Recipient awards Am. Legion, 1956, Am. Mktg. Assn., 1960. Mem. Allentown Jr. C. of C. (dir. 1966), Nat. Assn. Accountants, Fin. Execs. Inst., Assn. Systems Mgmt., Am. Mgmt. Assn., Mensa. Republican. Home: 32009 Foxmoor Ct Westlake Village CA 91361 Office: 811 W 74th St Los Angeles CA 90017

VERNON, DUANE RICHARD, credit bur. exec.; b. Ithaca, Mich., Sept. 3, 1931; s. Wesley Robert and Leah Amelia (Smith) V.; B.A. in Personnel Adminstrn., Mich. State U., 1953; m. Virginia Louise Graff, Apr. 4, 1954 (dec. 1975); children—Rick, Nancy, Mary Jo. Asst. mgr. affiliated divs. Mich. Retailers Assn., Lansing, 1956-59; dir. sales and pub. relations Credit Bur. Greater Lansing, 1959-74, pres., gen. mgr., 1974—; active in enactment Mich. Equal Credit Opportunity Act, 1977; lectr. Mich. State U., Lansing Community Coll., Cooley Law Sch. Pres., Lansing Jaycees, 1961-62; bd. dirs., capital area div. campaign chmn. United Way, Lansing, 1962-68; pres. Lansing Vol. Bur., 1967-68; bd. dirs. Easter Seal Soc. Mid-Mich., 1975—, Mich. State U. Devel. Council, 1977—, Camp Highfields; exec. bd. Chief Okemos council Boy Scouts Am.; charter bd. dirs. Mid-Mich. chpt. Nat. Football Found. and Hall of Fame; Mid-Mich. chmn. Olympathon '79. Served with U.S. Army, 1954-56. Recipient Lansing Jaycees Key Man award, 1960, Lansing Outstanding Young Man of Year award, 1963, Jaycee Internat. Senator award, 1978; Outstanding Club Pres.'s award Mich. State U. Alumni Assn., 1969; Disting. Alumni award Delta Tau Delta, 1978, Vandervoort Meml. award Downtown Coaches Club of Lansing, 1978, others. Mem. Asso. Credit Burs. Mich. (pres. 1979-80, Gold Key Leadership award 1978, Exec. Achievement award 1979), Pub. Relations Assn. Mich., Retail Credit Grantors Assn. Lansing (pres. 1961-62), Mid-Mich. Personnel Assn., Lansing Assn. Credit Mgmt. (dir. 1977—), Lansing Regional C. of C., Mich. State U. Alumni Club (pres. 1969). Methodist. Clubs: Rotary (pres. 1980-81), Downtown Coaches, Greater Lansing Bull-Pen (pres. 1972), Waverly High Sch. Sideliners Athletic Boosters (pres. 1977-78), Waverly Swim (dir. 1977—), Box 23 of Lansing (vice chief). Home: 4315 Wagon Wheel St Lansing MI 48917 Office: 520 S Washington St Lansing MI 48901

VERNON, LACY S., granite quarry and fabricating co. exec.; b. Fries, Va., Aug. 17, 1931; s. Troy J. and Minnie E. (Bond) V.; student U. Md., 1954-56; grad. Draughon's Bus. Coll., 1957, Internat. Acctg. Assn., 1959; m. Annie Lee Collins, Dec. 22, 1951; children—Terry Ellen Vernon Hooker, David Lee, Penny Elizabeth. Sect. chief U.S. Army Security Agy., Arlington Hall, Va., 1952-56; with N.C. Granite Corp., Mount Airy, N.C., 1957—, estimator, 1960-61, dept. mgr., 1961-69, exec. officer, 1969-72, exec. v.p., 1972-75, pres., chief exec. officer, 1975—. Vice-chmn. elders Grace Moravian Ch.; bd. dirs., fin. chmn. Salvation Army; bd. dirs., treas. United Fund; bd. dirs., sec. YMCA. Mem. Building Stone Inst. (dir.), Nat. Bldg. Granite Quarriers (pres.). Democrat. Moravian. Club: Ruritan (sec.). Home: 114 Laila Ln Route 9 Stonehenge Mount Airy NC 27030 Office: Box 151 Mount Airy NC 27030

VEROST, PATRICIA MARIE, broadcasting exec.; b. Bklyn., Nov. 28, 1941; d. Alan Vincent and Marjorie Marie (Colclough) Hinton; B.A. in English, St. John's U., Bklyn., 1963; M.B.A. in Fin., Fairleigh Dickinson U., Rutherford, N.J., 1976; m. Robert Verost, Apr. 17, 1971; 1 son, Robert. Asst. to dir. advt. Hilton Reservation Service, N.Y.C., 1961-65; from sec. to fin. adminstr. Ford Found., N.Y.C., 1965-76; sr. fin. analyst Sta. WNET, Ednl. Broadcasting Corp., N.Y.C., 1976-79, mgr. fin. reporting and control, 1979—; cons. in field. Mem. Am. Mgmt. Assn., M.B.A. Assn. Roman Catholic. Author manual. Home: 532 Passaic Ave Nutley NJ 07110 Office: 358 W 58th St New York NY 10019

VERROCHI, WILLIAM ANTHONY, utilities co. exec.; b. Boston, Nov. 14, 1921; s. Antonio and Mary Rose (Di San Bernardo) V.; B.S., M.I.T., 1947; m. Gloria Maria Todino, Oct. 3, 1953; children—Elizabeth A., Suzanne J., Kathryn J., Barbara M. Project engr., project mgr. Jackson & Moreland, Boston, 1947-61; supt. prodn. Pa. Electric Co., Johnstown, 1961-69, asst. v.p. tech., Parsippany, N.J., 1969-71, pres., Johnstown, 1977—, dir.; v.p. design and constrn. GPU Service Corp., Parsippany, 1971-74, v.p. generation, 1974-77; dir. GPU Service Corp., Utilities Mut. Ins. Co., U.S. Nat. Bank, Johnstown. Bd. dirs. Greater Johnstown YMCA, Johnstown Symphony Orch., Mercy Hosp. Johnstown, Johnstown Area Econ. Devel. Corp.; mem. adv. bd. Johnstown Flood Mus.; mem. adv. com. Pa. State Inst. for Research on Land and Water Resources; past chmn. Greater Johnstown Com.; hon. mem. Penns Woods council Boy Scouts Am. Served to 1st. lt. C.E., U.S. Army, 1943-46. Lic. profl. engr., Mass., N.J., Pa. Mem. Air Pollution Control Assn., ASME (recipient outstanding leadership award for energy resources devel. 1975), Pa. Soc. Profl. Engrs., Pa. Electric Assn. (exec. com.), Pa. Council Econ. Edn. Roman Catholic. Club: Sunnehanna Country. Office: 1001 Broad St Johnstown PA 15907

VERSER, DAN WALTER, electronics/metals mfg. co. exec.; b. Winona, Minn., Apr. 3, 1943; s. Walter Frank and Lydia Emma (Hilke) V.; B.Ch.E. (Nat. Merit Scholar), U. Louisville, 1966; Ph.D. (Univ. fellow), Princeton U., 1970; M.B.A. (Baker Scholar), Harvard U., 1975; m. Gertrude Grace Casselman, Mar. 18, 1973; 1 son, MacAndrew Dan. Asso. devel. scientist B.F. Goodrich Chem. Co., Avon Lake, Ohio, 1970-73; asst. to chmn. bd. Gould, Inc., Rolling Meadows, Ill., 1975-76, dir. ops., metals div. Mendota Heights, Minn., 1976-78, pres., gen. mgr., metals div., 1979—. Mem. allocations com., mem. panel United Way, St. Paul. Mem. Am. Inst. Chem. Engrs., Am. Phys. Soc., AAAS, Lead Industries Assn. (dir.). Home: 13809 High Dr Burnsville MN 55337 Office: Metals Div Gould Inc 1110 Hwy 110 Mendota Heights MN 55118

VERSIC, RONALD JAMES, indsl. scientist; b. Dayton, Ohio, Oct. 19, 1942; s. Charles and Volunta Henrietta (Sherman) V.; B.S., U. Dayton, 1964; M.A., Johns Hopkins U., 1968; Ph.D., Ohio State U., 1969; m. Linda Joan Davies, June 11, 1966; children—Kathryn Clara, Paul Joseph. Sr. physicist GAF Corp., Binghamton, N.Y., 1969-70; program mgr. Systems Research Labs., Dayton, 1970-71; sr. scientist The Standard Register Co., Dayton, 1971-76; dir. chem. research and devel. Monarch Marking Systems, Inc., Dayton, 1976-79; materials sci. mgr. Mead Corp., Dayton, 1979—. Mem. Citizens' Housing Com., Oakwood, Ohio, 1978—, Precinct 1 Republican committeeman, Oakwood Ward, 1973—. Named distinguished outstanding lt. gov. Ohio Dist. Optimist Internat., 1975-76. Mem. Kettering-Moraine Mus. and Hist. Soc., Am. Chem. Soc., Soc. Photographic Scientists and Engrs., Am. Def. Preparedness Assn., Am. Inst. Physics, Am. Assn. Physics Tchrs., Am. Crystallographic Assn., AAAS, Soc. Photo-Optical Instrumentation Engrs., Dayton Art Inst., Nat. Rifle Assn., Sigma Xi. Roman Catholic. Clubs: Johns Hopkins, Washington Square Optimist, Engrs. of Dayton, Yugoslav of Greater Dayton, Walter P. Chrysler, Inc. Contbr. articles to profl. jours. Home: 1601 Shafor Blvd Dayton OH 45419 Office: 1368 Research Park Dr Dayton OH 45432

VER STANDIG, JOHN DAVID, lawyer, broadcasting exec.; b. Washington, Feb. 1, 1947; s. Maurice Belmont and Helen (Van Stondeg) V.; B.S., U. Pa., 1970, J.D., 1974. Admitted to Pa. bar, 1974, D.C. bar, 1975; v.p. VerStandig, Inc., Washington, 1969-74; 76-78; individual practice law, Washington, 1975-78; pres. VerStandig Broadcasting Inc., Washington, 1977—, also dir.; dir. M.B. VerStandig Inc., 1970—, Equity Fin. Corp. Inc., 1975—, Family Jewels of Westview Inc., 1975—. Active vol. with area youth programs in soccer. Mem. D.C., Am., Pa. bar assns., Tau Epsilon Phi. Jewish. Clubs: Bala Country Of Phila.; Washington Golf and Country. Home: 7362 Montcalm Dr McLean VA 22101 Office: 4850 Connecticut Ave Washington DC 20008

VERVILLE, NORBERT JOSEPH, excavator mfg. co. exec.; b. Hancock, Mich., June 16, 1936; B.Sc. in Bus. Adminstrn., Mich. Technol. U., 1960; married; children—Stephen, Catherine, Joseph, Patrick. With Bucyrus-Erie Co., South Milwaukee, Wis., 1960-71; dir. Ruston-Bucyrus Ltd. Excavator Works, Lincoln, Eng., 1972—; mng. dir. Ruston-Bucyrus Ltd., 1978—. Home: 1 Lee Rd Lincoln LN2 4BJ England Office: Excavator Works Lincoln LN6 7DJ England

VESCI, JOSEPH VINCENT, accountant; b. Phila., Dec. 26, 1940; s. Joseph Francis and Susie Ann (Visco) V.; B.S., LaSalle Coll., 1965, M.B.A., 1981; m. Lorraine D'onofrio, Nov. 21, 1970; children—Susan C., Joseph C., Rosemarie, Christopher M. Supr. trainee I-T-E Imperial Corp. (subs. Gould, Inc. 1976), Phila., 1967-68, financial analyst, 1968-71, supr. budgets and reporting, 1971-74, mgr. gen. accounting, 1974-77; dir. corp. budget and accounting systems Extra Corporeal Med. Specialities, Inc. subs. Johnson & Johnson, 1978—. Republican. com. rep., Phila., 1967-71, 60-64. Served with USN, 1964-67. Mem. Pa. Assn. Notaries. Roman Catholic. Club: The Drexelbrook. Home: 2517 Marshall Rd Drexel Hill PA 19026 Office: Royal and Ross Rds King of Prussia PA 19406

VESECKY, JACK J., retailer; b. Chgo., May 14, 1946; s. Herbert J. and Ruth Vesecky; B.B.A., So. Ill. U., 1967; B.A. cum laude, Drake Coll. of Fla., 1969; m. Laura Maze, Aug. 20, 1967; children—Marc, Robyn. Buyer, Troy Dept. Stores, Elmwood Park, Ill., 1969-72, v.p., 1972-75, exec. v.p., 1975—. Bd. dirs. Berwyn (Ill.) United Way. Mem. Cermak Rd. Bus. Assn. (dir.), North Riverside Park Mchts. Assn. (dir.), Spl. Agts. Assn., Ill. Retail Mchts. Assn., Am. Fedn. Police. Clubs: West Suburban Exec. Breakfast, Berwyn Kiwanis. Office: Troy Dept Stores 7216 W Grand Ave Elmwood Park IL 60635

VEST, CAROL ANN, retail franchise exec.; b. Jackson, Miss., Mar. 21, 1940; d. John William and Dorothy (Crowe) V.; B.A. cum laude, Belhaven Coll., 1962; postgrad. U. N.Mex., 1963-64, U. Espirito Santo, Brazil, 1965-66. With ARC, Fort Jackson, S.C., 1963; Peace Corps vol., Espirito Santo, Brazil, 1964-65; with Office Econ. Opportunity, Jackson, Miss., 1966-67; tennis profl., 1967-79; owner Vest Racquet Shop, Jackson, 1974—, owner Sportique, Inc., Jackson, 1975—. Named Miss Tennis Profl. of Yr., 1977, 79. Mem. U.S. Profl. Tennis Assn. Club: First Ladies Civitan. Home: 5125 Old Canton Jackson MS 39211 Office: Maywood Mart Jackson MS 39211

VESTAL, ADDISON ALEXANDER, estate mgr.; b. Whitewright, Tex., May 30, 1905; s. Rolla C. and Lora A. (Robinson) V.; B.A., Baylor U., 1927; M.S., Columbia, 1928; m. Lillian Cooper, July 3, 1937; children—William A., Gwen Vestal Davis, Richard C. Estate mgr. R.K. Mellon & Sons, Pitts., 1938—; chmn. bd. Blue Danube, Inc., Oil City, Pa. Pres., Ingomar (Pa.) Little League Baseball, 1945-60. Bd. dirs. Albert Schweitzer Hosp., Deschapelles, Haiti, Grant Found., Pitts.; trustee Laughlin Children's Center, Sewickley, Pa. Home: Box 1138 Pittsburgh PA 15230 Office: 525 William Penn Pl Pittsburgh PA 15219

VETTER, ERIC WILLIAM, elec. products co. exec.; b. Detroit, Aug. 14, 1932; s. Ruth A. Vetter; A.B. in Econs., M.B.A. in Indsl. Relations, Ph.D., all U. Mich.; m. Virginia Vetter, Jan. 18, 1957; children—Karen, Eric William. Asso. dean, prof. mgmt. Tulane U. Grad. Sch. Bus. Adminstrn., New Orleans, 1962-75; sr. v.p. human resources Gould Inc., Rolling Meadows, Ill., 1976—. Bd. dirs. Met. Chgo. Crusade of Mercy; bd. dirs., 1st v.p. United Way/Crusade of Mercy. Served with U.S. Army, 1954-56. Mem. Acad. of Mgmt., Conf. Bd., Phi Gamma Delta. Author: Manpower Planning for High Talent Personnel, 1967. Home: 630 Elm Rd Barrington IL 60010 Office: Gould Inc 10 Gould Center Rolling Meadows IL 60008

VETTER, MARY MARGARET (PEGGY), bank exec., mgmt. cons.; b. Richmond, Va., June 7, 1945; d. Robert Joseph and Miriam Thomas V.; B.A., Catholic U. Am., 1967; M.B.A. with distinction, N.Y. U., 1978; m. Dimitri Yannacopoulos, May 24, 1980. Asst. to controller N.C. Trading Co., N.Y.C., 1972-74; asst. controller Shaheen Natural Resources Inc., N.Y.C., 1974-76; fin. coordinator mining div. Nat. Bulk Carriers, Inc., N.Y.C., 1976-77; corporate cons. mktg. and strategic planning Gen. Electric Co., Bridgeport, Conn., 1978-80; v.p., internat. mktg. strategy Bankers Trust Co., N.Y.C., 1980—; mgmt. cons. Urban Bus. Assistance Corp., N.Y.C. Named Woman of Yr., N.Y. U. Alumnae Assn., 1978. Mem. Women in Mgmt., Beta Gamma Sigma. Republican. Roman Catholic. Home: 330 Merwin Ave #G2 Milford CT 06460 Office: 280 Park Ave 14W New York NY 10017

VIANA, FERNANDO, ins. broker; b. La Paz, Bolivia, Feb. 13, 1928; s. Carlos Viana and Lily Estenssoro de Viana; came to U.S., 1961, naturalized, 1971; B.C.E., Rensselaer Poly. Inst., 1951; certificate as ins. broker Siena Coll., 1964; m. Jacquelyn MacNulty, Aug. 11, 1951; children—M. Fernanda, J. Carlos, Kevin A. Vice pres. Banco Popular Colombo-Boliviano, La Paz, 1954-60; chmn. bd. Andes Ins. Co., La Paz, 1958-59; mgr. Mfrs. Reps. Co., Ltda., La Paz, 1961; N.Y. state regional mgr. Am. Progressive Ins. Co. N.Y., Albany, 1961-68; gen. agt. Am. Progressive Health Ins. Co. N.Y., Albany, 1968-79, Gerber Life Ins. Co., Albany, 1977-79; mgr. Albany office Am. Life Ins. Co., 1979—; hon. chancellor Bolivian Consulate, N.Y.C., 1952. Served to lt. Engrng. Corps, Bolivian Army, 1951. Recipient ins. awards, including as Top Producer, Am. Progressive Health Ins. Co., 1961-68, Loyal Representation award Am. Progressive Ins. Co. N.Y., 1977, Service award K.C. Ins., 1976; Very Important Performance award Mut. of N.Y., 1968. Mem. Fgn. Money Collectors Assn. Roman Catholic. Clubs: Univ., K.C. (Albany). Home and Office: 41 Patroon Pl Loudonville Albany NY 12211

VIANI, ALAN ROCCO, labor union ofcl.; b. N.Y.C., Jan. 13, 1936; s. Paul Anthony and Elizabeth Rose (Coccaro) V.; B.S., Kans. State U., 1958. Pres., Social Services Local Union 371, Am. Fedn. State, County and Municipal Employees, AFL-CIO, N.Y.C., 1964-67, asst. dir. research and negotiations Dist. Council 37, 1967-69, asso. dir. research and negotiations, 1969-73, dir. research and negotiations, 1973—, adj. faculty Coll. New Rochelle (N.Y.), 1976. Mem. exec. com. Mayor's Voluntary Action Council, N.Y.C., 1978—, mem. labor task force, 1973; mem. N.Y. State Gov.'s Human Services Task Force, 1975. Served with USAR, 1954-62. Nat. Endowment for Humanities fellow, 1978. Mem. Am. Soc. Pub. Adminstrn., Indsl. Relations Research Assn., Nat. Civil Service League, Nat. Municipal League. Democrat. Home: 102 Buena Vista Dr Dobbs Ferry NY 10522 Office: 140 Park Pl New York NY 10007

VIAR, JOSEPH FRANKLIN, JR., computer cons. co. exec.; b. Phila., June 15, 1941; s. Joseph Franklin and Alice Lee (Williams) V.; B.S., Hampden-Sydney (Va.) Coll., 1963; m. Penelope Lusby; children—Elizabeth Anne, Amy Laura. Mgr., IBM Corp., Research Triangle Park, N.C., 1967-69; v.p. Systems Engrng. Corp., Richmond, Va., 1969-71; dir. environ. programs Chase, Rosen & Wallace, Inc., Alexandria, Va., 1971-76; pres. Viar and Co., Inc., Alexandria, 1976—. Episcopalian. 8710 Highgate Rd Alexandria VA 22308 Office: 114 N Columbus St Alexandria VA 22314

VICK, JONATHAN CHAPIN, hosp. supply co. exec.; b. Rochester, N.Y., Jan. 9, 1943; s. William and Louise (Stockard) V.; B.A., Hamilton Coll., 1964; LL.B., La Salle U., 1969; M.A.E., U. Okla., 1970; m. June 12, 1965; children—Cecilia Lyon, Nathaniel Sawyer. Mktg. mgr. Soflens div. Bausch & Lomb, Rochester, N.Y., 1970-77; v.p., dir. mktg. Sauflon Internat., Los Angeles, 1977-78; mktg. sales mgr. Med. Optics Center, Am. Hosp. Supply Corp., Irvine, Calif., 1978—. Served with USAF, 1965-70. Mem. Airplane Owners and Pilots Assn. Republican. Episcopalian. Author: Life at High Altitudes, 1964; Use and Re-use of Land and Land Resources, 1970. Home: 20532 Sycamore Gulch Trabuco Canyon CA 92678 Office: 1402 E Alton Ave Irvine CA 92714

VIDALIS, ORESTIS EFTHIMIOS, fiberglass co. exec.; b. Argos, Greece, Sept. 24, 1917; s. Efthimios John and Anthi Aristotelis (Kastritis) V.; came to U.S., 1968; B.S., Greek Mil. Acad., 1937; postgrad. U.S. Army Command Gen. Staff Coll., 1952-53; M.A. in Polit. Sci., Georgetown U., 1957; m. Matina Vamvakaris, Jan. 15, 1950; 1 son, Efthimios O. Served to lt. gen. Greek Army, 1937-67, mem. staff standing group NATO, Washington, 1954-57; sr. planner, corporate planning Owens-Corning Fiberglas Corp., Toledo, 1968-69, dir. orgn. procedures, 1969-73, dir. new bus. devel. internat, 1973-75, mng. dir. Middle E. Regional Hdqrs., Athens, Greece, 1975-78, v.p. Middle East ops., Athens, 1978—. Decorated Hellenic medal of Valor (Greece), Order British Empire. Greek Orthodox. Office: Owens Corning Fiberglas Middle East Operations Athens Tower Athens Greece 610

VIEHE, KARL WILLIAM, educator, cons. firm exec.; b. Allentown, Pa., Aug. 12, 1943; s. John Sage and Margaret (Higgs) V.; M.A., Am. U., 1968, postgrad., 1968-72; J.D., Howard U., 1980. Instr. math. and Russian St. Alban's Sch., Washington, 1967-68; exec. dir. Investment-Futures Group, Washington, 1968—; asst. prof. math. and statistics U. D.C., Washington, 1970—; chmn. bd. dirs. Nat. Ednl. Trust, Washington, 1971—; internat. advt. dir. Washingtonian Mag., 1972-75; professorial lectr. math., statistics Am. U., Washington, 1972—. Office: Investment Futures Group 3520 Van Ness St NW Washington DC 20008

VIEIRA, SHARON ANN, mfg. co. exec.; b. New Bedford, Mass., Aug 23, 1954; s. Daniel Thomas and Norma Dorothy (McCabe) V.; B.S. in Acctg. cum laude, Providence Coll., 1976; M.B.A., Northeastern U., 1977. Staff acct., M.B.A. intern Laventhol & Norwath, C.P.A., Providence, 1977; jr. fin. analyst Polaroid Corp., Waltham, Mass., 1977-78, fin. analyst, Freetown, Mass., 1978-79, fin. analyst, Cambridge, 1979—; lectr. in fin. acctg. Southeastern Mass. U., 1979—; adj. prof. acctg. Northeastern U., 1980—; cons. in field. Chairperson public support and fund raising ARC, New Bedford, Mass. Mem. Nat. Assn. Female Execs. (dir. 1978—), Univ. Coll. Faculty Soc., Phi Sigma Tau. Roman Catholic. Home: 226 Rockland St South Dartmouth MA 02748 Office: 565 Technology Square Cambridge MA 02139

VIEMEISTER, PETER EMMONS, business exec.; b. Mineola, N.Y., Feb. 15, 1929; s. August Louis and Janet (Emmons) V.; B.M.E. (Grumman scholar), Rensselaer Poly. Inst., 1950; S.M. (Sloan Fellow), Mass. Inst. Tech., 1969; m. Suzanne Neelands, 1951 (div. 1965); children—Clay N., Read L., Susan B., Katherine A.; m. 2d, Revelle Hamilton, 1975. With Lippincott & Margulies, N.Y.C., 1945; with Grumman Aircraft, Bethpage, N.Y., 1946-57, mgr. bus. planning, 1960-65, asst. to pres. and chmn. bd., 1965-69; pres. Grumman Data Systems Corp., Bethpage, 1969-73; chmn. bd. Computility, Inc., Boston, 1971-73; v.p. Grumman Corp., 1973-79; dir. Grumman Allied Industries, 1975-79, Paumonack Leasing Corp., 1976-79; adj. asso. prof. Dowling Coll., 1972-73. Chmn. Empire State Coll. Found., 1975—; trustee Huntington (Dist. 3) Pub. Schs., 1964-66; bd. dirs.

Energy Research Inst. S.C., 1977—; overseer Lynchburg Coll., 1979—; adv. com. Inst. Energy Analysis, Oak Ridge, 1980—. Mem. Sigma Xi, Tau Beta Pi. Author: The Lightning Book, 1961; Psychosystems, 1973. Contbr. articles to profl. jours. Inventor behavior simulator. Office: Solaridge Bedford VA 24523

VIENER, MAURICE A., metals co. exec.; b. Charles Town, W.Va., Nov. 29, 1916; s. Hyman and Rebecca G. (Mozenter) V.; B.S. in Econs., U. Pa., 1938; m. Evelyne B. Gittleman, Nov. 12, 1939; children—Cynthia D. (Mrs. H.J. Hoff), Pamela D. (Mrs. R.B. Hariton). With Hyman Viener & Sons, Charles Town, 1938—, partner, 1939—; chmn. bd., dir. Blakeley Bank & Trust Co. W.Va., 1961—. Chmn. W.Va. Athletic Commn., 1966-69. Mem. Iron and Steel Inst., World Boxing Assn., Nat. Assn. Recycling Industries, U. Pa. Alumni Washington Area (pres., Key Alumnus, 1963). Democrat. Club: Winchester Country. Home: 2906 Ellicott St NW Washington DC 20008 also Briar Patch Farm Route 1 Charles Town WV Office: Box 55 Charles Town WV 25414

VIERA, JOSEPH, ins. co. exec.; b. New Bedford, Mass., Oct. 11, 1923; s. Michael and Theresa (Moreira) V.; student Columbia U., 1947-49, Coll. of Ins., 1949-51; m. Theresa Mary Orlando, Oct. 16, 1949; children—Michael Joseph, Susan Marie. Partner, Lakeville Assos. & Kolvie Realty, Inc., New Hyde Park, N.Y., 1951-53; sales rep. Singer Co., Plainview, N.Y., 1953-55; sales mgr. Sentry Ins., Morris Plains, N.J., 1955—. Pres., Brooklawn Civic Assn., Morris Plains, N.J., 1973-75. Served with Signal Corps, U.S. Army, 1943-46. C.L.U., C.P.C.U., N.J. Mem. Soc. C.L.U.'s, Soc. Chartered Property and Liability Underwriters. Club: Toastmasters. Home: 71 Brooklawn Dr Morris Plains NJ 07950 Office: 202 Johnson Rd Morris Plains NJ 07950

VIEWEG, ROBERT ARTHUR, lawyer; b. New Brunswick, N.J., Aug. 8, 1940; s. Hermann Frederick and Alice (McNulty) V.; B.A., Earlham Coll., 1963; J.D., U. Mich., 1966; m. Jane Edith Johnson, Feb. 24, 1973. Admitted to Mich. bar, 1967; asso. firm Levin, Levin, Garvett & Dill, 1968-72; adminstrv. v.p., gen. counsel Avis Enterprises, 1972-73; atty. firm Helm, Schumann & Miller, 1973-79; partner firm Hoops & Hudson, 1979-80; Heywell & Rosenfeld, Troy, Mich., 1980—; instr. law Macomb County Community Coll. Active Detroit Com. Fgn. Relations. Mem. Am. Bar Assn., Mich. Bar Assn., Fed. Bar Assn., Detroit Bar Assn. Republican. Episcopalian. Clubs: Detroit Athletic, Univ., Detroit Boat, Detroit Torch. Office: 3221 W Big Beaver Suite 309 Troy MI 48084

VIGNIERI, CHARLES JOSEPH, meat packing co. exec.; b. Chgo., Oct. 7, 1924; s. Frank and Rosario (Saporito) V.; student pub. schs., Kenosha, Wis.; m. Lorraine Vander Warn, June 29, 1946; children—Allan, Susan, Dennis, Richard, Patricia, Joseph, Thomas, Daniel, Mark. With Frank Vignieri & Sons, Kenosha, 1936-54; with Kenosha Packing Co., 1954—, pres., 1960—; pres. Birchwood Meat & Provision, Inc., Kenosha, 1960—; dir. Kenosha Savs. & Loan Assn.; sec. Milw. Meat Council, 1965-67; guest lectr. Carthage Coll., Kenosha, 1970-75, bd. assos., 1970—. Co-chmn. March of Dimes Campaign, Kenosha, 1964; chmn. Paris-Kenosha County Plan Commn., 1965; co-founder, chmn. Kenosha Youth, Inc., 1968-70; bd. dirs. United Way, Kenosha, 1966-68, 72-75, campaign gen. chmn., 1972, pres., 1973-74; mem. adv. bd. Dominican Sisters of Bethany, Kenosha, 1963-71. Served with AUS, 1943-46; PTO. Mem. Kenosha C. of C. (dir. 1965-68), Nat. Meat Assn. (dir. 1965-77, v.p. central div. 1974-77, 1st v.p. 1978, chmn. 1980-82). Roman Catholic (trustee, treas. 1952-66, parish chmn. archibishops fund appeal 1952-66). Clubs: Elks, Rotary (dir. 1965-70, pres. 1967-68). Contbr. articles to profl. jours. Home: 4001 5th Pl Kenosha WI 53142 Office: PO Box 639 Kenosha WI 53141

VIGNOLA, ANDREW MICHAEL, banker; b. N.Y.C., Sept. 6, 1938; s. Michael John and Mary Elizabeth (Romano) V.; student in Bus. Adminstrn., Coll. City N.Y., 1956-59; m. Barbara Francis Hummel, Aug. 22, 1959; children—Ellen Ann, Andrew Michael, Robert Eugene. Programmer trainee Citibank, N.Y.C., 1959-60; programmer analyst Soc. for Savs., Hartford, Conn., 1960-63; mgr. on-line data center NCR Corp., Boston, 1963-67; cons., sr. partner Computer Assistance, Inc., Hartford, 1967-72; v.p., info. systems service div. Soc. for Savs., Hartford, 1972-80, pres. subs. Solar Services, Inc., 1977-80; info. sers. dir. Dime Savs. Bank N.Y., 1980—; lectr. in field. Mem. Data Processing Mgmt. Assn. (pres., chmn. bd. Hartford chpt. 1976-77), Assn. System Mgmt. (profl.), Contbr. articles to profl. jours. Home: 161 N Timber Ln Cheshire CT 06410 Office: Green Acres Shopping Center Valley Stream NY

VILARDI, VIVIENNE E., communications co. exec.; b. N.Y.C.; d. Gabriel and Iolanda (Signore) V.; B.A. in English, Marymount Coll., 1965; M.A., Fordham U., 1972; M.B.A., Adelphi U., 1977. Tchr. secondary schs., 1965-70; mktg. cons. Prentice Hall Media Group, Inc., White Plains, N.Y., 1971-73; asst. to v.p. mktg., mktg. analyst SCM Corp., New Canaan, Conn., 1976-79; account exec. AT&T Long Lines, White Plains, 1979-80; dir. corp. planning Eastern States Bankcard Assn., Lake Success, N.Y., 1980—; cons. Kimun Lee Assos. Mem. Planning Execs. Inst. (v.p. programs), Am. Mktg. Assn., Am. Mgmt. Assn. Home: 51 Whittlesey Dr Bethel CT 06801 Office: Eastern States Bankcard Assn Inc 4 Ohio Dr Lake Success NY 11042

VILLERE, ROGER FRANCIS, JR., florist; b. New Orleans, Aug. 16, 1949; s. Roger Francis and Ursula (Wattigny) V.; student U. New Orleans, 1968, Delgado Coll., New Orleans, 1968; m. Donna Gunckel, Apr. 12, 1969; children—Roger Francis III, Mark Charles, Jacques Philip. With Scheinuck the Florist, New Orleans, 1966-68; chief clk. I.C. R.R., 1968-70; owner Villere Florist, Metairie, La., 1969-78; pres. Villere Corp., Metairie, 1978—; bd. dirs. New Orleans Floral Trail, 1978—. Mem. Acad. Am. Florists, Profl. Floral Designers Assn. (past pres.), Soc. Am. Florists, La. Florists Assn. (past pres.), New Orleans Orchid Soc., New Orleans Retail Florists Assn., Young Mens Bus. Club Greater New Orleans, Jaycees Internat., U.S. Jaycees, La. Jaycees (past v.p. individual devel., Metairie Jaycees (past pres.; Outstanding New Jaycee award 1975, Outstanding Pres. award 1977). Roman Catholic. Office: 928 Homestead Ave Metairie LA 70005

VILLI, PHILIP VINCENT, ins. co. exec.; b. Bklyn., Jan. 2, 1930; s. Anthony George and Pearl (Goldner) V.; B.A., N.Y. U., 1953; m. Lois Manson, May 6, 1951; children—Robert, Roger, Russ, Lori. With Aetna Life Ins. Co., N.Y.C., 1957-63; brokerage supr. Berkshire Life, N.Y.C., 1963-68; v.p. Windsor Life, N.Y.C., 1968-71; mng. dir. Bankers Life, N.Y.C., 1971—; pres. Park Ave. Brokerage, Inc., N.Y.C. Served with U.S. Army, 1951-53. C.L.U. Mem. Life Underwriters Assn., Life Suprs. Assn. Home: 67 15 102d St Forest Hills NY 11375 Office: 230 Park Ave New York NY 10169

VIÑAS, RICARDO HÉCTOR, naval architect; b. Mendoza, Argentina, Jan. 5, 1933; came to U.S., 1962, naturalized, 1967; s. Fernando Agustín Viñas Diaz and Úrsula Clelia Monsch Rusca; student (scholar) Argentina Naval Acad., 1949-53; M.Mech. Engring. and Naval Architecture, U. Buenos Aires, 1955-60; postgrad. in data processing Tulane U., 1967-68; m. Noemí T. Schiaffino Caimi, Sept. 10, 1958; 1 dau., María Noemí. Served as naval architect, mech. engr. Argentine Navy, 1949-61; mech. engr. Chrysler Corp., Argentina, 1962; naval architect Avondale Shipyards, New Orleans, 1964-66, Breit Engring. Co., New Orleans, 1966-68, Friede & Goldman, New Orleans, 1968-71; v.p., owner Gulf Marine Design, Inc., Metairie, La., 1971—. Mem. Soc. Naval Architects and Mech. Engrs. (Elmer A. Sperry award 1975), Soc. Profl. Engrs. (Argentina). Club: Metairie Country. Designer Lash vessel. Home: 3708 Tolmas Dr Metairie LA 70002 Office: 3100 Ridgelake Dr Metairie LA 70002

VINCENT, ALBERT VERNON, real estate exec.; b. Rector, Ark., Sept. 4, 1921; s. Albert Wesley and Helen (Wilcher) V.; student pub. schs.; m. Kay Tokie Nagata, Sept. 4, 1960; children—Armond Vernon, Linda Carol, Sharon Lynn, Albert Vernon, Wendi Vernelle. Supr., Naval Supply Center, Pearl Harbor, 1942-48; div. mgr. Century Metalcraft Corp., 1948-54; gen. mgr. Saladmaster of Hawaii, 1954-56; realtor, 1957-60; pres. Tropic Shores Realty, Ltd., Honolulu, 1960—. Bd. dirs. Real Estate Securities and Syndication Inst., 1973—. Mem. Nat. Assn. Realtors (dir., regional v.p. 1970), Hawaii Assn. Real Estate Bds. (hon. pres.), Nat. Inst. Real Estate Brokers (gov.), Honolulu Bd. Realtors (pres.), Inst. Real Estate Mgmt., Nat. Inst. Farm and Land Brokers (gov. 1970, gov. comml. and investment div. 1967—), Am. Soc. Real Estate Counselors (gov. 1978—), Realtors Nat. Mktg. Inst. (gov. 1978—), Hawaii Assn. Realtors (pres. 1978), Internat. Real Estate Fedn., Calif. Real Estate Assn., Internat. Platform Assn. Clubs: Honolulu, Plaza, Honolulu Press, Pacific, Internat. Traders Club (gov.). Home: 1920 Laukahi St Honolulu HI 96821 Office: 33 S King St Honolulu HI 96813

VINCENT, DONALD GEORGE, oil service co. exec.; b. Somerville, Mass., May 12, 1929; s. George Daniel and Margreta Janet (Johnston) V.; A.B., Harvard U., 1951, M.B.A., 1953; m. Jennie McKeage Patchin, May 3, 1976; children—Donald George, Deborah Ann, Clifford Joseph, Christine Elaine. Pres. W.R. Ames Co., subsidiary Rucker Co., San Franscso, 1969-70, Kobe, Inc., subs. Baker Internat. Corp., Los Angeles, 1970-73; v.p. ops. Newpark Resources, New Orleans, 1974-75; prin. Vincent Assos., Inc., Houston, 1974—; chmn. bd., chief exec. officer Baker Gas Lift, Inc., Houston, 1980—, Aegean Internat., Inc., Houston, 1980—; cons. in field. Trustee Republican Assos. Calif., 1972-74. Recipient Cordiner award Gen. Electric Co., 1965. Presbyterian. Clubs: Los Angeles Yacht, Houston Yacht, Masons. Home: 14 Carolane Trail Houston TX 77024 Office: 4512 Pinemont St Houston TX 77018

VINCENT, EDNA F., retail co. exec.; b. Boston, Apr. 8, 1941; d. Robert Louis and Marietta (Wallace) Craig; A.A., Fisher Jr. Coll., 1950; B.A., Boston U., 1952; m. James W. Vincent, May 7, 1955. Trainee, Jordan Marsh Co., Boston, 1952-54, asst. buyer, 1954-56, buyer cosmetics, 1956-62; buyer cosmetics Wm. Filene and Sons, Boston, 1962-66; buyer cosmetics Marshall Field & Co., Chgo., 1966-72, asst. v.p., 1972—. Active United Fund, Boston; bd. dirs. Fontbonne Acad., Braintree, Mass., 1964-66. Republican. Roman Catholic. Home: 16488 Brockton Oak Forest IL 60452

VINCENT, EDWARD PORTER, sales and service co. exec.; b. Franklin, Pa., Dec. 31, 1928; s. Arthur Porter and Leila F. (Watson) V.; B.S. in Chemistry, Grove City Coll., 1952; P.M.D., Harvard U., 1966; m. Sophie Harwood, Oct. 16, 1954; children—Mark P., Gregory S., Shawn E. Asst. supt. furnace dept. PPG Industries, Creighton, Pa., 1952-57; mgr. tech. sales Refractory div. Kaiser Aluminum and Chem. Corp., Oakland, Calif., 1957-66; exec. v.p. E.S.M., Inc., Valencia, Pa., 1966-69; v.p. mktg. Zedmark, Inc., Valencia, 1969-75, now dir.; pres. E.P. Vincent, Inc., Gibsonia, Pa., 1975—; engring. cons. to industry, 1975—; incorporator Vincent Assos., retail sales microcomputers, 1980. Bd. dirs., pres. Butler County Mental Health Assn., 1977-79. Mem. Am. Ceramic Soc. Republican. Clubs: Butler Country, Masons, Shriners. Home: 1221 North Dr Butler PA 16001 Office: 5499 William Flynn Hwy Gibsonia PA 15044

VINCENT, HARRY L., JR., business exec.; b. Chaumont, N.Y., 1919; grad. U.S. Naval Acad., 1941, Calif. Inst. Tech., 1946. Vice chmn. Booz, Allen & Hamilton, Inc., N.Y.C.; mem. policyholders adv. com. New Eng. Mut. Life Ins. Co.; mem. exec. com., dir. Marriott Corp.; mem. compensation com., dir. Bank of Va. Co. Office: 245 Park Ave New York NY 10017*

VINCENT, JAMES LOUIS, health care co. exec.; b. Johnstown, Pa., Dec. 15, 1939; s. Robert Clyde and Marietta Lucille (Kennedy) V.; B.S.M.E., Duke U., 1961; M.B.A. in Indsl. Mgmt., U. Pa., 1963; m. Elizabeth M. Matthews, Aug. 19, 1961; children—Aimee Archelle, Christopher James. Far East div. mgr. Tex. Instruments, Inc., also pres. Tex. Instruments Asia, Ltd., Tokyo, 1970-72; v.p. diagnostic ops., pres. diagnostics div. Abbott Labs., North Chicago, Ill., 1972-74, group v.p., from 1974, now exec. v.p., chief operating officer, dir. Bd. dirs. Chgo. Hort. Soc. Recipient Young Exec. Achievement award Young Execs. Club Chgo., 1976; named Ky. col. Mem. Econ. Club Chgo., Am. Mgmt. Assn. Republican. Presbyterian. Clubs: Shoreacres Country, Forge. Office: Abbott Labs Abbott Park North Chicago IL 60064

VINCENT, THOMAS SCOTT, fin. exec.; b. Dallas, Feb. 6, 1941; s. Thomas Henry and Martha (Bolton) V.; B.B.A., N. Tex. State U., 1964; m. Pamela Louise Frandsen, Aug. 31, 1968; 1 son, Brenton Warren. Real estate appraiser N.Y. Life Ins. Co., Mpls., Chgo., 1966-68; v.p. Larwin Reit Mgmt. Corp., Dallas and Beverly Hills, Calif., 1970-76; sr. v.p. HIC of Fla., Miami, 1976-78; pres., chief exec. officer Union Realty Mortgage Co., Inc., subs. Central Nat. Chgo. Corp., Chgo., 1978—, also dir.; cons. in field. Served with USNR, 1964. Mem. Mortgage Bankers Assn. Republican. Lutheran. Address: 100 W Monroe St Chicago IL 60603

VINCENT, WILLIAM SELBY, acct.; b. St. George's, Nfld., Can., Oct. 8, 1948; s. Alice Mary Young; m. Ann Theresa McNeil, Jan. 7, 1978. Audit supr. David Curtis & Co., Corner Brook, Nfld., 1973-76; audit supr. Thorne, Riddell & Co., Corner Brook, 1975-77; asst. mgr. Steers Ltd., Corner Brook, 1977-79; pvt. practice acctg., Labrador City, Nfld., 1979—. Chartered acct. Mem. Inst. Chartered Accts. Nfld., Canadian Inst. Chartered Accts., Am. Mgmt. Assn. Address: PO Box 216 Labrador City NF A2V 2K5

VINCENZO, JAMES JOSEPH, consumer products mfg. co. exec.; b. Chester, Pa., May 25, 1946; s. John Joseph and Agnes Lydia Vincenzo; B.S. in Math., Villanova (Pa.) U., 1968; M.B.A. in Fin. (Catherine Sharpe fellow 1973, Wharton Pub. Policy fellow 1972), Wharton Sch., U. Pa., 1973; m. Denise Susan Racz, Oct. 5, 1975. Ops. analyst Travelers Ins. Co., Hartford, Conn., 1968-71; internat. analyst, then mgr. internat. fin. analysis Johnson & Johnson, New Brunswick, N.J., 1973-76, mgr. corp. fin. analysis, 1976-78, controller Devro div., 1978—. Mem. Nat. Assn. Accountants (pres. Raritan chpt.), Am. Fin. Assn., Math. Assn. Am., Beta Gamma Sigma. Democrat. Roman Catholic. Address: 51 Wood Lake Dr Piscataway NJ 08854

VINES, CHARLES CARSON, oil co. exec.; b. Rocky Mount, N.C., Aug. 7, 1944; s. Charles Carson and Gladys Maude (Verney) V.; B.A. in Econs., Harvard Coll., 1966; M.B.A. in Fin., U. Pa., 1968. Asst. v.p., sr. cons. Citibank, N.Y.C., 1968, 1970-73; v.p. New Court Securities Corp., N.Y.C., 1973-79; v.p. fin., sec. Wainoco Oil Corp., Houston, 1979—; dir. Murray Hill Oil & Gas, N.Y.C., Wainoco Internat., Inc., Houston. Served with U.S. Navy, 1968-70. Clubs: Houstonian and Plaza (Houston); Harvard, Roadrunners (N.Y.C.). Office: 1200 Smith St Suite 1500 Houston TX 77002

VINH, JOHN NGUYEN DINH, food mfg. co. exec.; b. Ha Nam, Vietnam, Mar. 12, 1949; s. Nghi Dinh and Thuoc Thi (Dinh) Nguyen; B.S., St. John's U., 1972; M.S. in Chemistry, U. Wis., 1975; m. Janie Dzung, Nov. 25, 1977; 1 son, John Nguyen Dinh. Sanitarian, ITT Continental Baking Co., St. Paul, 1975-77, quality mgr., Natick, Mass., 1977-78; dir. sanitation and product safety Rohtstein Corp., Woburn, Mass., 1978, v.p., gen. mgr., 1978—. Mem. Inst. Food Technologist, Am. Chem. Soc. Home: 55 Polaris Ln Tewksbury MA 01876 Office: 70 Olympia Ave Woburn MA 01888

VINK, PIETER CAREL, mfg. co. exec.; b. E'ndhoven, Holland, Sept. 18, 1919; s. Hermanus and Catherina (Pellekaan) V.; grad. Lorenz Lyceum, Eindhoven, 1937; m. Thea Fluijt, June 7, 1945. With N.Am. Philips Corp., or subsidiary cos., 1939—, mng. mgr. Phillips South Africa, chmn., mng. dir. ops. Iran, India, Australia, 1948-65, pres. N.Am. Philips Co., 1965-69, N.Am. Philips Corp., N.Y.C., 1969—, chmn., chief exec. officer, 1976—, also dir.; dir. PEPI, Inc., Borden Inc. Served with Brit. Army, 1944-45. Decorated Order Brit. Empire. Mem. Newcomen Soc. N.Am. Clubs: Stanwich (Greenwich, Conn.); Indian Harbor Yacht (Greenwich, Conn.); Economic, Sky (N.Y.C.); Blind Brook (Port Chester, N.Y.). Office: 100 E 42d St New York NY 10017*

VINSON, JOHN CHARLES, real estate broker; b. Phoenix, Mar. 5, 1946; s. Julian T. and Doris Vinson; student Sacramento City Coll., 1966-67, Sacramento State U., 1968; m. Taeko Kanno, Mar. 5, 1972; children—Jarica, Christopher J. Sales mgr. Heinemann Realty Co., Tempe, Ariz., 1972-73; pres./broker Century 21, John Vinson Realty, Inc., Tempe, 1974—; partner Vinson Mgmt. Co., Vinson Devel. Co. Mem. Century 21 Broker's Council Maricopa County (dir., past pres.), Young Realtors Assn. (past v.p.), Nat. Assn. Realtors, Ariz. Assn. Realtors, Century 21 Investment Soc. Clubs: Mesa Country, Tempe Rotary, Tempe Toastmasters (officer). Home: 438 E Carson St Tempe AZ 85282 Office: 949 E Guadalupe Rd Tempe AZ 85283

VINT, ROBERT JAMES, constrn. co. exec.; b. Washington, Jan. 30, 1934; s. Thomas Chalmers and Mary Alice (Waring) V.; A.B., Colgate U., 1956; postgrad. U. Ariz., 1961-65; m. Katherine Lois Brown, Aug. 18, 1956; children—Thomas Arthur, Robert Walter, Mary Katherine, James Michael, William Waring. Computer programmer Hughes Aircraft Co., Tucson, 1959-61; sr. computer programmer Pan Am. World Airways, Tucson, 1961-62; programmer-analyst Bunker-Ramo Corp., Ft. Huachuca, Ariz., 1962-65; mgr. computer services Bell Aerospace Co., Tucson, 1965-76; v.p. data processing M.M. Sandt Constrn. Co., Tucson, 1976—, also dir. Vestryman, St. Michaels Episc. Ch., 1965-76. Served with U.S. Army, 1957-59. Republican. Home: 7409 Calle Antigua Tucson AZ 85710 Office: 4101 E Irvington Rd Tucson AZ 85726

VIRUS, JOHN ROBERT, perfume co. exec.: b. Johnstown, Pa., July 1; s. John and Christina (Urias) V. Founder, Brandy Harvest Colognes of N.Y.C., 1962; appearing as singer The Broadway Troubadour, N.Y.C. Office: 53-06 39th Ave Woodside New York NY 11377

VISCEGLIA, FRANK DIEGO, real estate exec.; b. Jersey City, Mar. 22, 1942; s. Frank and Rosalie V.; B.A. in Fin., U. Notre Dame, 1964; postgrad. N.Y. U.; m. Linda Lee Jerzykowski, July 23, 1966; children—Frank Diego, Nicole Christine. Exec. v.p. Fed. Storage Warehouse, Edison, N.J., 1964—; dir. Raritan Center, Inc., 1976—; gen. partner Center Realty, Edison, 1975—. Trustee Endowment Fund for Delbarton Sch., 1977—. Mem. Nat. Assn. Indsl. and Office Parks (past regional v.p., past pres. N. Jersey chpt.), Delbarton Alumni Assn. (pres., dir. 1975-76), Jaycees, U.S., N.J., Raritan Valley, Edison (treas., dir.) chambers commerce, Notre Dame Alumni Assn. N.J., Small Bus. Assn. Alliance for Action, Blue Badge Assn., Nat. Assn. Bus. and Ednl. Radio. Club: K.C. Office: Federal Business Centers 300 Raritan Center Pkwy Edison NJ 08817

VISHNEY, RENE, computer co. exec.; b. Paris, Jan. 2, 1936; s. Jules Alan and Anna Rose (Lazarus) V.; A.A.S., N.Y. U., 1955; student Hofstra U., 1958; B.S., Ohio State U., 1961; postgrad. Northwestern U., 1963; m. Lois Helene Preis, Jan. 25, 1963; children—Jared, Shawn, Debra. Sr. data processing analyst Fairchild Semiconductor, Mountain View, Calif., 1966-68; mgr. info. systems Caelus Memories, San Jose, Calif., 1968-70; owner, operator RLD Assos., Los Gatos, Calif., 1970-79; pres. Continental Computer Systems, San Jose, 1980; dir. Compunetics Computer Corp., N. Am. Computer Systems. Pack leader Boy Scouts Am., Los Gatos, 1980—; officer Belwood Home Owners Assn., 1976-77; cons. on consumer protection, County of Santa Clara, 1975; pres. Computer Literacy Studies, 1978. Mem. Data Processing Mgmt. Assn., Assn. of Computing Machinery, Forth User Group. Home: 181 Belwood Gateway Los Gatos CA 95030 Office: 97 Boston Ave San Jose CA 95128

VITA, FRANCIS KEANE, internat. banker; b. Union City, N.J., May 16, 1939; s. Frank Joseph and Helen Galvin (Keane) V.; grad. Am. Community Sch., Paris, 1955; student Georgetown U., 1955-58; B.A., U. Pitts., 1962; B.S., Fairleigh Dickenson U., 1961; M. Pub. and Internat. Affairs, U. Pitts., 1963; A.M., Harvard, 1965, M. Pub. Adminstrn., 1974, doctoral cand. Grad. Sch. Bus., 1974-76; m. Lise K. Christensen, May 31, 1968; children—Lisa Helen, Christina Keane, Nicholas Keane. Project officer, UN Devel. Program, N.Y.C., 1966-68, dep. resident rep., Caracas, Venezuela, 1968-70; loan officer World Bank, Washington, for Eastern Africa, 1970-71, for Uruguay and Chile, 1971-73, ops. adviser financial devel. unit, 1975-77, economist and sr. ops. officer devel. finance companies, indsl. and finance dept., 1977-80, sr. economist capital markets, 1980—. Served with U.S. Army, 1959-61. Ford Found. fellow, 1962-64. Mem. Soc. Internat. Devel., Assn. MBA Execs., Harvard Club Local Citizens Assn. (exec. council), Pi Delta Phi, Gamma Rho Sigma. Roman Catholic. Home: 6314 Kenhowe Dr Bethesda MD 20034 Office: 1818 H St NW Washington DC 20433

VITALE, ALPHONSE JOHN, electronics co. exec.; b. Waltham, Mass., June 7, 1937; s. Angelo Guy and Angelina Josephine (Giuliano) V.; B.S., Boston Coll., 1960, M.B.A., 1963; m. Marilyn Viera, Aug. 26, 1979; children—John Lawrence, Daniel Joseph, Edward Geary, Ellen Theresa. Analyst, Raytheon Corp., Waltham, Mass., 1957-61; asst. controller, mgr. info. systems Baird Atomic, Inc., Cambridge, Mass., 1961-65; gen. mgr. Atomic Accessories, Inc., Valley Stream, N.Y., 1965-66; controller Bush Transformer Corp., Westwood, Mass., 1966-67; gen. mgr., dir. Wall Industries, Cambridge, 1967-68; v.p., treas., cir. Control Logic, Inc., Natick, Mass., 1968-71, pres., 1971—; lectr. Boston Coll. Grad. Sch. Bus., 1963-64; instr. Northeastern U., 1965-68. Chmn. fin. adv. com. to Sch. Com., Town of Stow, Mass., 1975. Roman Catholic. Office: 9 Tech Circle Natick MA 01760

VITALIS, WILLIAM NELSON, fin. exec.; b. Greenfield, Mass., Sept. 11, 1929; s. Joseph S. and Genevieve Salome (Feyrer) V.; B.A., Dartmouth Coll., 1953; cert. of completion Harvard Bus. Sch. Advanced Mgmt. Program, 1972; m. Jean Buchanan, Dec. 28, 1957; children—William N., Rita G. Tchr., Deerfield (Mass.) Acad.,

1956-57; fin. assignments W.R. Grace & Co., N.Y.C., 1955-56; asso. Morgan Stanley Co., Inc, N.Y.C., 1957-61; co-founder, dir., officer Lombard, Vitalis, Paganucci & Nelson, Inc., N.Y.C., 1961-72; v.p. Smith Barney, Harris Upham & Co., Inc., N.Y.C., 1972-75; pres., dir. Activest Capital Corp. and Activest Resources Corp., Cornwall Bridge, Conn., 1975—; mng. partner Ellsworth Hill Farm, Sharon, Conn., 1974—; trustee Midland Mortgage Investment Trust, Oklahoma City, 1969—; dir. Albany (N.Y.) Internat. Corp., 1974—, Outagamie Corp., 1975—. Served with USMC, 1953-55. Home: Dibble Hill Rd West Cornwall CT 06796 Office: PO Box 76 Cornwall Bridge CT 06754

VITE, FRANK ANTHONY, realtor; b. Aurora, Ill, Feb. 9, 1930; s. Frank A. and Rose (Cosentino) V.; grad. Marmion Mil. Acad., 1948; student U. Notre Dame Sch. Mgmt., 1958; hon. dr. Hillsdale Coll., 1972; m. Barbara Ann Decio, Oct. 23, 1954; children—Bradley Scott, Mark Steven, Michael Lee, Leslie Ann, Lisa Ann. Plant engr. Lyon Metal Products, Aurora, 1951-52, purchasing agt., 1953-54; became sales mgr., exec. v.p., owner, dir. Skyline Homes, Inc., Elkhart, Ind., 1954; pres., owner B & F Realty, Inc., No. Ind. Appraisal Co., Golden Falcon Homes, Inc.; real estate broker; dir. 1st Nat. Bank, Elkhart, Ind. Mem. Ind. Commn. for Higher Edn.; trustee Hillsdale, Mich. Served with AUS, 1952-53, Korea. Mem. Elkhart Bd. Realtors, Nat. Sales Execs. Assn., Ind. Real Estate Assn., Nat. Inst. Real Estate Brokers, Holy Name Soc. Republican. Clubs: K.C. (4 deg.), Knights Malta, Elks. Home: 23236 Shorelane Elkhart IN 46514 Office: 1300 Cassopolis St Elkhart IN 46514

VITELLO, JOHN PETER, med. supply co. exec.; b. Buffalo, Oct. 31, 1935; s. John and Rose Marie (Caretti) V.; B.S., U. Buffalo, 1960; postgrad. State U. Coll. N.Y. at Buffalo, 1966, Harvard, 1969, 70; m. Shirley Ann Mogavero, Nov. 13, 1954; children—Jonathan, Mark, Melissa, Christopher. Chemist, Union Carbide Corp., Tonawanda, N.Y., 1960-61, Harris Research Labs., Washington, 1961-64; dir. planning and devel. Sterilon div. Gillette Co., Braintree, Mass., 1964-70; pres., chmn. bd. Paramed. Disposables, Inc., Needham, Mass., 1970—. Co-commr. Newton Centennial, 1973-74; mem. Library Civic Com., 1973-74. Mem. Am. Chem. Soc., Soc. Plastics Engrs., Am. Soc. Testing Materials, State U. N.Y. at Buffalo Alumni Assn. (Boston chmn., 1972—), Am. Assn. Med. Instrumentation, Nat. Assn. Intravenous Therapy. Patentee in field med. products and consumer products. Home: 22 Church St Weston MA 02193 Office: 570 Pleasant St Watertown MA 02172

VITOR, KENNETH MARIAN, oil industry exec.; b. Chgo., May 30, 1942; s. Mariano A. and Susan V. Vitor; B.S.C., DePaul U., 1964; m. Mary L. Blasberg, Feb. 17, 1979; children—Lisa, Bruce. Mfg. and planning mgr. Johnson & Johnson, Chgo., 1965-72, sales and distbn. mgr., Tex., 1972-75; v.p. ops. Texstar Automotive Distbn. Group, St. Louis, 1975-79, pres., chief exec. officer, 1979—; pres., chief exec. officer Freedom Freightways Inc., 1979—. Served with U.S. Army, 1964-65. Home: 66 Crestwood St Clayton MO 63105 Office: 9060 Latty St Saint Louis MO 63134

VITT, SAM B., advt. co. exec.; b. Greensboro, N.C., Oct. 23, 1926; s. Bruno Caesar and Gray (Bradshaw) V.; A.B., Dartmouth, 1950; m. Marie Foster, Oct. 30, 1955; children—Joanne Louise, Michael Bradshaw, Mark Thomas. Exec. asst. TV film CBS, N.Y.C., 1950-52; broadcast media buyer Benton & Bowles, Inc., N.Y.C., 1952-54; broadcast media buyer Biow Co., N.Y.C., 1954-55, asso. account exec., 1955-56; broadcast media buyer Doherty, Clifford, Steers & Shenfield, Inc., N.Y.C., 1956-57, media supr., 1958-59, v.p., media supr., 1960, v.p., asso. media dir., 1960, v.p., media dir., 1960-63, v.p. in charge media and broadcast programming, 1963-64; v.p., exec. dir. media-program dept. Ted Bates & Co., Inc., N.Y.C., 1964-66, sr. v.p., exec. dir. mediaprogram dept., 1966-69; founder, pres. Vitt Media Internat., Inc., N.Y.C., 1969—; advt. dir. Banking Law Jour., 1955-69; dir. Advt. Info. Services, Inc., 1964-65; mktg. and media workshop panel Ind. Buying Service, 1979; mem. Media Dirs. Council, 1964-65; lectr. advt. N.Y. U., 1973, 74, Am. Mgmt. Assn., 1974, 75, Assn. Nat. Advertisers, 1967, 69, 70, Advt. Age Media Workshop, 1975, 77. Chmn. radio-TV reps. div. Greater N.Y. Fund, 1962, chmn. pub. div., 1963; mem. com. Nat. UN Day, 1973, vice chmn., 1974, asso. chmn., 1975, co-chmn., 1976; bd. govs. N.Y. Young Republican Club, 1957-58, editor Directory, 1956-57; bd. dirs. N.Y.C. Comml. Devel. Corp., 1968-70. Recipient Media award Sta. WRAP, Norfolk, Va., 1962; award of Merit, Greater N.Y. Fund, 1963; Gold Key Advt. Leadership award Sta. Reps. Assn., 1967; certificate of merit Media/Scope, 1967, 69, ann. honors Ad Daily, 1967. Mem. Am. Assn. Advt. Agys. (broadcast media com. corr. 1958-63, media operating com. on consumer mags. 1964-65), Internat. Radio and TV Soc. (time buying and selling seminar com. 1961-62), UN Assn. U.S. (dir. 1977—), Nat. Acad. TV Arts and Scis., Sigma Alpha Epsilon. Clubs: N.Y. Athletic (N.Y.C.); Roxbury Run Country (Denver, N.Y.); Larchmont Manor Beach. Presbyterian. Contbr. chpts. to books; contbg. editor, columnist Madison Ave., 1963-68; editorial cons. Media/scope, 1968-69; producer record album The Body in the Seine. Home: 3 Roosevelt Ave Larchmont NY 10538 Office: 1114 Ave of Americas New York NY 10036

VITTY, RODERIC BEMIS, ins. co. exec.; b. St. Johnsbury, Vt., July 28, 1933; s. Clarence Lucian and Leota (Cobleigh) V.; B.S., U.S. Mil. Acad., 1955; M.S. in Fin. Services, Am. Coll., Bryn Mawr, Pa., 1977; m. Virginia Gable, Mar. 5, 1960; children—Roderic G., Virginia A., David P., Suzanne L. With Conn. Gen. Life Ins. Co., 1960—, mgr. br. office, Cherry Hill, N.J., 1968—, Greater Phila. office, 1981—. Served with inf. U.S. Army, 1955-59, Pa. N.G., 1961-68. C.L.U. Mem. West Point Soc. Phila. (bd. govs., pres. 1969-71), Nat. Assn. Life Underwriters, Estate Planning Council, Am. Soc. C.L.U. (South Jersey chpt.), So. N.J. Gen. Agts. and Mgrs. Assn. (pres. 1979-80), Assn. Grads. U.S. Mil. Acad., Army Athletic Assn. Lutheran. Clubs: Sunnybrook Swim, Cherry Hill Tennis, Riverton Country, Millside Racquet, Masons (32 deg.), Shriners. Home: New Albany Rd Moorestown NJ 08057 Office: Conn Gen Life Ins Co Suite 800 One Cherry Hill Office Bldg Cherry Hill NJ 08002

VLACHOS, ESTELLA MARIA, constrn. co. exec.; b. Santa Monica, Calif., Oct. 24, 1939; d. Rudolph John and Estelle Smith (Scott) Carlson; A.A., Long Beach City Coll., 1959; student Long Beach State Coll., 1959-60; m. Emanuel James Vlachos, Feb. 19, 1966. Accountant, Smith & Smith, pub. accountants, Long Beach, 1959-65; auditor, tax accountant Lyons, Bandell & Bryant C.P.A.'s, Santa Ana, Calif., 1965-67, Diehl, Evans & Co., Santa Ana, 1967-69; controller, C.R.S. Inc., Mikkelson Enterprises Inc., and San Bernardino Bus. Men's Assn., computerized credit reporting and collection, 1969-73; controller Griffith Bros., constrn., farming and fruit packing houses, Placentia, Calif., 1973—. Mem. parish council Greek Orthodox Ch., also ch. treas. Mary E. Baker Meml. scholar, 1957; Am. Soc. Women Accountants scholar, 1959. Licensed collector, tax preparer. Mem. Am. Soc. Women Accountants (pres. chpt.), Nat. Notary Assn., Taxpreparers Assn. Calif. (charter), Soc. Calif. Accountants, Nat. Soc. Pub. Accountants, Smithsonian Assos. Designer computerized accounting program for collection agencies. Home: PO Box 6094 Anaheim CA 92807 Office: 181 W Orangethorpe Ave B Placentia CA 92660

VODIAN, RONALD HUGH, banker; b. Pueblo, Colo., Jan. 5, 1942; s. George and Evelyn B. (Gorshow) V.; B.A., U. Colo., 1964; M.B.A., U. N.Mex., 1967; postgrad. U. Calif., 1967-68, Yale U., 1968-69, Pacific Coast Banking Sch., 1980; m. Jacqueline J. Shipman, June 24, 1968; 1 dau., Nicole Lynn. Adminstrv. dir. Gen. Dynamics Corp., San Diego, also Groton, Conn., 1967-69; dir. market pricing and adminstrn. Samsonite Corp., Denver, 1969-72; investment banker Merrill Lynch, Pierce, Fenner & Smith, N.Y.C. and Denver, 1972-75; corp. v.p. Western Bancorp., Albuquerque, 1975-81; sr. v.p. N.Mex. Banquest Corp. (N.Mex. Bancorp.), 1981—. Mem. exec. com., state bd. dirs. Am. Cancer Soc., United Way. Mem. Am. Bankers Assn., Bank Mktg. Assn., Am. Mgmt. Assn., Am. Mktg. Assn., Planning Execs. Inst. Contbr. numerous articles to profl. jours. Home: 2201 Dietz Pl NW Albuquerque NM 87107 Office: PO Box 6107 Santa Fe NM 87502

VOESTE, NEALY CORNELIUS, food service equipment cons.; b. Corpus Christi, Tex., Feb. 24, 1925; s. Frank W. and Annie (Buckley) V.; student Del Mar Coll.; m. Valerie W. Voeste, July 7, 1950; 1 dau., Julie A. Mem. sales staff Gardner Hotel Supply Co., Houston, 1948-50, Southwestern Hotel Supply Co., Corpus Christi, 1950-59; pres. Central Kitchen Equipment Co., Corpus Christi, 1959-75; distbr. Scotsman Ice Machine, 1964-75; owner, pres. So. Food Equipment, Inc., Corpus Christi, 1978—. Served with USAF, 1941-45; CBI. Recipient awards from various civic groups. Mem. Tex. Restaurant Assn., Corpus Christi Restaurant Assn. Roman Catholic. Home: 3228 Crestwater St Corpus Christi TX 78415 Office: 5829 Ayers St Corpus Christi TX 78415

VOGEL, ALLEN HAROLD, accountant; b. Kingston, N.Y., July 30, 1949; s. Jack and Claire (Salutsky) V.; B.S., N.Y. Inst. Tech., 1972; M.S., L.I. U., 1974. Auditor, A.J. Armstrong Co., Inc., N.Y.C., 1972-73; staff accountant Unishop's, Inc., Jersey City, 1973-76; controller, asst. sec. Askin Service Corp., N.Y.C., 1976—; pvt. practice accounting, tax adviser. Office: 459 W 15th St New York NY 10011*

VOGEL, CARL EDWARD, property adminstrn. exec.; b. Chgo., Oct. 21, 1919; s. Eugene E. and Madeline (Keim) V.; student Wilson Jr. Coll., Chgo., 1937-39, Northwestern U., 1940-41; m. Frances Stevens Terrell, Mar. 17, 1945; children—Cynthia, Susan, Meredith, Kirkland. With Nat. Bur. Property Adminstrn., Inc., Chgo., 1939—, chmn. bd., exec. v.p., 1958-63, chmn. bd., pres., 1963—; chmn., bd., pres. Kirkland Corp., Chgo., 1969—. Active in local fund-raising drives. Served to 1st lt. USAAF, 1942-46. Mem. Chgo. Assn. Commerce and Industry, Internat. Assn. Assessing Officers, Nat. Tax Assn. Clubs: Executives, Mid-America (Chgo.); North Shore Country (Glenview). Home: 720 Glenayre Dr Glenview IL 60025 Office: Prudential Plaza Chicago IL 60601

VOGEL, DAVID AGNEW, patent lawyer; b. New Castle, Ind., Dec. 27, 1925; s. Karl Conrad and Josephine (Agnew) V.; B.S. in Chem. Engring., Purdue U., 1945, M.S., 1948; LL.B., Chgo. Kent Coll. Law, 1951; postgrad. John Marshall Law Sch., 1953-54; M.B.A., Ill. Inst. Tech., 1977; m. Josephine Farrell, May 29, 1952; children—David Agnew, Walter C. Farrell, Sarah J., Ellan A. Instr. chemistry Purdue U., 1947-48; admitted to Ill. bar, 1951, U.S. Supreme Ct., 1957; patent lawyer, Chgo., 1951—; partner firm Prangley, Clayton & Vogel, 1954-57, firm Smith, Prangley, Baird & Clayton, 1957-58, Prangley, Baird, Clayton, Miller, & Vogel, 1958-69, Prangley, Clayton, Mullin, Dithmar & Vogel, 1969-72, Prangley, Dithmar, Vogel, Sandler & Stotland, 1972-77, Vogel Dithmar, Stotland, Stratman & Levy, 1977—; partner Gurnee Apts. (Ill.), 1969—, Big Oak Assos., Gurnee, 1970—; dir., sec. Gravi-Mechanics Co., High Hopes Stables, Inc.; treas., dir. HSV Corp., 1970-73; dir. Acoustic Fiber Sound Systems. Vice pres. Young Republican Orgn. Ill., 1953-55; trustee Chgo.-Kent Coll. Law, 1967-69, sec., 1968-69; trustee Kendall Coll., vice chmn., 1970—; chmn. adv. bd. Chgo.-Kent Coll. Law, Ill. Inst. Tech., 1971—. Fellow AAAS; mem. Am. Chem. Soc., Am., Ill., Chgo. bar assns., Chgo.-Kent Alumni Assn. (pres. 1963-64), Am., Chgo. patent law assns., Assn. Trial Lawyers Am., Ill. Trial Lawyers Assn., Sigma Xi, Sigma Iota Epsilon, Tau Beta Pi, Omega Chi Epsilon, Phi Lambda Upsilon, Tau Kappa Epsilon, Phi Alpha Delta. Methodist (chmn. ofcl. bd. 1958-60, pres. bd. trustees 1960-61). Club: Masons. Home: 1136 Long Valley Rd Glenview IL 60025 Office: 189 W Madison St Chicago IL 60602

VOGEL, JOHN HOLLISTER, banker; b. N.Y.C., May 24, 1917; s. Howard H. and Edith V. (Eiseman) V.; B.S., N.Y. U., 1939, M.B.A., 1941; grad. advanced mgmt. program Harvard U., 1964; m. Helen W. Wolff, Dec. 20, 1947; children—Virginia Vogel Zanger, John Hollister, Thomas H. With C.I.T. Fin. Corp. and subs., N.Y.C., 1934-65; with Nat. Bank N.Am., N.Y.C., 1965—, pres., chief exec. officer, 1971-77, chmn., 1977—; dir. Nat. Westminster Bank Ltd.; mem. N.Y. Clearing House Com. Bd. dirs. N.Y.C. Landmarks Conservancy, Futura House, White Plains, N.Y., N.Y.C. Community Preservation Com., Pan Pacific Community Assn., Washington; mem. Westchester County (N.Y.) Exec. Blue Ribbon Transp. Commn. Served with USAAF, 1942-46.

VOGEL, LAURENCE, lawyer; b. N.Y.C., Dec. 17, 1936; s. Moe and Sylvia (Miller) V.; A.B. cum laude, U. City N.Y., 1957; J.D., U. Va., 1960; LL.M., N.Y. U., 1964; m. Anna Lise Andreasen, May 24, 1973; children—Peter Andrew, Carsten Dyhr. Admitted to N.Y. State bar, 1961; asso. firm Cadwalader, Wickersham & Taft, N.Y.C., 1960-64; asst. U.S. atty., chief civil div. So. Dist. of N.Y., N.Y.C., 1964-69; mem. firm Schaeffer, Dale & Vogel, N.Y.C., 1970-76, Greenbaum, Wolff & Ernst, N.Y.C., 1976—; v.p., gen. counsel Duty Free Shoppers Group Ltd., 1979—. Served with AUS, 1960-61. Mem. Am. Bar Assn., Fed. Bar Council (pres. 1968-70), Order of the Coif. Jewish. Home: Beaverkill NY 12758 also 430 E 86th St New York NY 10028 also 3056 La Pietra Circle Honolulu HI 96815 Office: Greenbaum Wolff Ernst 437 Madison Ave New York NY 10022 also 841 Bishop St Honolulu HI 96813

VOGEL, PHILLIP THOMAS, pharm. co. exec.; b. Henderson, Ky., Dec. 16, 1939; s. Fred George and Eileen (Beal) V.; B.S. in Elec. Engring., Ga. Inst. Tech., 1963; M.B.A., Wharton Sch., U. Pa., 1964; m. Neil Lowery, July 29, 1972; children—George Thomas, David Park, Deion Lowery. Plant and ops. mgr. Tex. Instruments Co., Dallas, also W. Ger., Italy and Singapore, 1964-73; v.p. bus. Lowery Bros. Constrn. Co., Daytona, Fla., 1973-74; div. v.p., gen. mgr. diagnostic products Abbott Labs., North Chicago, Ill., 1974—. Republican. Home: 220 Homewood St Libertyville IL 60048 Office: Abbott Park AP6C North Chicago IL 60064

VOGEL, SHELDON L., recording co. exec.; b. Long Branch, N.J., Feb. 8, 1932; s. Harry and Nettie (Gottlieb) V.; B.S. in Econs., Wharton Sch. Fin., U. Pa., 1953; m. Anne Monica Purcell, June 17, 1962. Controller, Vogel's Dept. Store, Long Branch, 1955-60, Barney's Clothes, N.Y.C., 1960-62; with Atlantic Rec. Corp., N.Y.C., 1962—, sr. v.p. fin., 1971-74, exec. v.p., 1974-80, vice chmn. bd., 1980—; cons. Cosmos Soccer Club. Served with U.S. Army, 1953-55. Office: 75 Rockefeller Plaza New York NY 10019

VOGEL, WERNER PAUL, machine co. exec.; b. Louisville, June 15, 1923; s. Werner George and Emma (Bartman) V.; B. Mech. Engring., U. Louisville, 1950; m. Helen Louise Knapp, Oct. 2, 1954. With Henry Vogt Machine Co., Louisville, 1942—, asst. plant supt., 1957-60, plant supt., 1961-73, v.p., 1974—. Trustee, City of Strathmoor Village, Ky., 1959-61; clk. City of Glenview Manor, Ky., 1967-73, trustee, 1974-75; bd. dirs. Louisville Protestant Altenheim, 1979—. Served with USAAF, 1944-46. Mem. ASME, Am. Welding Soc., Am. Def. Preparedness Assn., Tau Beta Pi, Sigma Tau. Republican. Methodist. Home: 29 Glenwood Rd Louisville KY 40222 Office: 1000 W Ormsby St Louisville KY 40210

VOGELPOEL, ANTHONY PETER, mfg. co. exec.; b. Amsterdam, Netherlands, Apr. 7; s. Johannes Anthonius and Anna Catharina (Van D.) V.; came to U.S., 1960, naturalized, 1966; certificate, Ryerson Inst. Tech. (Can.), 1956; certificate, U. Toronto (Can.), 1959; B.S. cum laude, Boston U., 1964; postgrad. Northeastern U., 1964-65; m. Ilse Lina Kuhn, Jan. 7, 1969; children—Amelie, Louise. Quality control technician Raytheon Can., Kitchener, Ont., 1959-60; sr. quality control engr. Raytheon Co., Newton, Mass., 1960-66; corporate quality cons. The Singer Co., Elizabeth, N.J., 1966-69; corporate mgr. quality assurance and reliability N. Am. Philips Corp., N.Y.C., 1969-80, dir. product assurance, 1980—. Sec., Meadow Ridge Civic Assn. Registered profl. engr., Calif. Mem. Nederlandse Genealogische Vereniging (co-founder, 1st pres. 1946), Arbeitskreis Siegen (W. Germany), Deutsche Gesellschaft Fuer Qualitaet, Am. Soc. for Quality Control, Boston U. Alumni Assn. Republican. Lutheran. Contbr. articles to profl. jours. Home: 7896 Red Fox Dr Manlius NY 13104 Office: 100 Fairgrounds Dr Manlius NY 13104

VOGT, BRUCE THEODORE, pharm. co. exec.; b. Ashford, Conn., Sept. 19, 1948; s. William Harold and Elizabeth V.; B.A. in Theology, Berkshire Christian Coll., Lenox, Mass., 1969; postgrad. SUNY, Albany, 1969-70; m. Catherine Ann Karker, Feb. 3, 1973; children—Bruce William, Nathan Michael. Sales rep. Searle Labs., 1970-78, dist. sales mgr., Catharpin, Va., 1978—. Recipient various sales awards. Mem. Am. Pharm. Assn. Republican. Baptist. Address: 3607 Sanders Ln Catharpin VA 22018

VOGTLE, ALVIN WARD, JR., electric utility exec.; b. Birmingham, Ala., Oct. 21, 1918; s. Alvin Ward and Ollie (Stringer) V.; B.S., Auburn U. 1939; LL.B., U. Ala. 1941; m. Kathryn Drennen, Apr. 20, 1945 (dec.); children—Kathryn D., Anne Moore (Mrs. Baldwin), Alvin Ward, III; m. 2d, Rachael Giles, 1966; children—Bryant Wade, William Patrick, Rachael Giles, Robert Jackson. Admitted to Ala. bar, 1941; asso. Martin, Vogtle, Balch & Bingham and predecessor firms, Birmingham, 1945-50, mem. firm, 1950-62; exec. v.p., dir. Ala. Power Co., 1962-65; pres. So. Electric Generating Co., 1960-62, dir., 1962—; exec. v.p. So. Co., 1966-69, pres., dir., 1962—, now also chief exec. officer; chmn. bd., dir. So. Co. Services, Inc.; dir. CSX Corp., Protective Life Ins. Co., Union Camp Corp.; v.p., dir. Ala., Ga., Gulf, Miss. power cos. Advisory bd. visitors Mary Baldwin Coll., trustee Tax Found., Com. Econ. Devel; YMCA Met. Atlanta. Served from 2d lt. to capt. USAAF, 1941-45. Mem. Newcomen Soc. Eng., Newcomen Soc. N.Am., Soc. of Colonial Wars, The Conf. Bd., SAR, Ala. Hist. Assn., Am. Legion, Sigma Nu. Episcopalian. Home: King's Lea Farms 3189 Batesville Rd Woodstock GA 30188 Office: 64 Perimeter Center E Atlanta GA 30346

VOIGT, JOHN JACOB, trading co. exec.; b. Atlantic City, Apr. 2, 1942; s. Jacob Joseph and Mary Margret (Camp) V.; grad. Lawrenceville Sch., 1960; student U. Pitts., 1960-61; B.S. in Economics, Wharton Sch. Fin. and Commerce U. Pa., 1963, postgrad., 1964; m. Glenna Fitzsimons, Sept. 22, 1962; children—Bridget Glenna, John Jacob. Pres., Nat. Accessories Co., Phila., 1970—; pres. Howard Butcher Trading Corp., Phila., 1976—; dir. Atlantic Metal Finishing Co., Butcher Foods Inc., Cont. Quality Industries; cons. Compagnie Generale d'Electricite, Paris, Matra Group, Paris. Bd. govs. Betty Bacharach Hosp., 1976—; mem. vestry, sr. warden Ch. of Epiphany, Ventnor, N.J., 1975—. Republican. Clubs: Union League Phila., Princeton N.Y.C.; Atlantic City Country. Home: 8705 Ventnor Ave Margate City NJ 08402 Office: Suite 400 1516 Atlantic Ave Atlantic City NJ

VOLCKER, PAUL A., banker, govt. ofcl.; b. Cape May, N.J., Sept. 5, 1927; s. Paul A. and Alma Louise (Klippel) V.; A.B. summa cum laude, Princeton U., 1949; M.A., Harvard U., 1951; postgrad. London (Eng.) Sch. Econs., 1951-52; m. Barbara Marie Bahnson, Sept. 11, 1954; children—Janice, James. Economist, Fed. Res. Bank N.Y., 1952-57, pres., 1975-79; economist Chase Manhattan Bank, 1957-61, v.p., dir. planning, 1965-68; with Dept. Treasury, 1961-65, 69-74, dep. under sec. monetary affairs, 1963-65, under sec., 1969-74; chmn. bd. govs. Fed. Res. Bd., Washington, 1979—; mem. Fed. Open Market Com., 1975—, chmn., 1979—. Sr. fellow Woodrow Wilson Sch. Pub. and Internat. Affairs, 1974-75. Office: Office Chmn Fed Res Bd 20th and Constitution Ave NW Washington DC 20551

VOLCKHAUSEN, WILLIAM ALEXANDER, lawyer; b. N.Y.C., Mar. 13, 1937; s. William Louis and Jessie Anderson (Rankin) V.; A.B., Princeton U., 1959; A.M., U. Calif., Berkeley, 1963; J.D., Harvard U., 1966; m. Grace E. Lyu, Aug. 2, 1968; children—Sharon Lyu, Alexander Louis. Instr., Tunghai U., Taichung, Taiwan, 1959-61; program officer Asia Found., N.Y.C., San Francisco, 1966-69; admitted to N.Y. bar, 1967; atty., mng. atty. MFY Legal Services, N.Y.C., 1969-73; atty., spl. counsel, gen. counsel N.Y. State Banking Dept., N.Y.C., 1973-79; spl. counsel Hughes Hubbard & Reed, N.Y.C., 1979-80; exec. v.p., gen. counsel Dime Savs. Bank of N.Y., N.Y.C., 1980—; adj. prof. law Cardozo Sch. Law, N.Y.C., 1980—. Bd. dirs. Asian-Am. Legal Def. Fund, 1978—; trustee Carroll Street Sch., 1974—, pres., 1975-76. Mem. N.Y. County Lawyers Assn., Bar Assn. City N.Y. Home: 262 President St Brooklyn NY 11231 Office: 589 Fifth Ave New York NY 10017

VOLDNESS, ARLEN RALPH, home for aging adminstr.; b. Chgo., Sept. 1, 1932; s. Albin Olie and Edna L. (Olsen) V.; student No. Ill. U., 1955-56; m. Helen Ferguson, Oct. 27, 1956; children—James R., Barbara A., Paul E., H. Katrina, Mark A., Francis D. Research engr. HRB-Singer, State College, Pa., 1961-65, tng. dir., 1965-66; sr. research engr. Technology, Inc., Dayton, Ohio, 1967; owner, mgr. Arby's Franchise, Winter Park, Fla., 1968-69; nat. electronic adminstr. Bell & Howell, Chgo., 1970-71, prin. Elec. Engr. Magnacraft div., Chgo., 1972-76; owner, mgr. Hopkins Electric & Maintenance Co., Cin., 1977-78; adminstr. St. Francis Village, Crowley, Tex., 1978—; cons. electronic controls. Regional minister 3d Order of St. Francis; founder, St. Francis Hospice, 1979. Served with USAF, 1951-55. Mem. Associated Builders and Contractors, Internat. Assn. Elec. Inspectors, Tex. Assn. Homes for Aging. Democrat. Roman Catholic. Club: K.C. Co-inventor unicolor photo process. Home: 6316 Whitman St Fort Worth TX 76133 Office: 1 Chapel Plaza Crowley TX 76036

VOLK, HARRY J., banker; b. Trenton, N.J., July 20, 1905; s. Michael T. and Susan (Harkins) V.; A.B., Rutgers U., 1927, LL.B., 1930, L.H.D., 1958; m. Marion E. Waters, Oct. 12, 1931 (dec. 1972); children—Robert H., Richard R., Carolyn E. (Mrs. Jacques); m. 2d, Marjorie L. Hale, Aug. 14, 1976. With Prudential Ins. Co., 1927-57, v.p. in charge western operations, 1947-57; pres., dir. Union Bank, Los

Angeles, 1957-69, chmn. bd., dir., 1969—; chmn., dir. Union Bancorp, Inc., 1969-79; dir. Standard Chartered Bancorp. Served as div. chief U.S. Strategic Bombing Survey, World War II. Trustee Calif. Inst. Tech., Hosp. of Good Samaritan; alumni trustee Rutgers U., 1942-47. Mem. Nat. Alumni Assn. Rutgers U. (pres. 1940-45), Calif. Clearing House Assn., Music Center (founder). Clubs: California, Bohemian, Los Angeles Country; Los Angeles, Los Angeles County Mus. Art, U. So. Calif. Assos. Club: Calif., Bohemian, Los Angeles, Los Angeles Country. Home: 1110 Maytor Pl Beverly Hills CA 90210 Office: 445 S Figueroa St Los Angeles CA 90017

VOLK, ROBERT HARKINS, lawyer; b. E. Orange, N.J., Nov. 27, 1932; s. Harry j. and Marion (Waters) V.; B.A., Stanford U., 1954, LL.B., 1958; m. Barbara June Klint, Sept. 10, 1954. Admitted to Calif. bar, 1959; asso., then partner firm Adams, Duque & Hazeltine, Los Angeles, 1958-67; commr. corps., State of Calif., 1967-69; chmn. bd. Unionamerica, Inc., Los Angeles, 1969-79; of counsel firm Nossaman, Krueger & Marsh, Los Angeles, 1980—; owner, pres. Martin Aviation, Inc., Orange County, Calif., 1980—; dir. Host Internat., Western Airlines. Chmn., Calif. Bd. Investment, 1967; mem. Calif. World Trade Authority, 1969; bd. overseers Hoover Inst. on War, Revolution and Peace. Served with USAF, 1955-57. Mem. Am. Bar Assn., Calif. Bar Assn., Los Angeles Bar Assn., Calif. C. of C. (dir. 1972—). Clubs: Los Angeles, Los Angeles Country, Calif., Beach, Los Angeles Yacht. Author: (with Harold Marsh, Jr.) Practice Under the Corporate Securities Law of 1968, 1969. Address: 445 S Figueroa St Los Angeles CA 90071

VOLLBEER, FRED H., fin. exec.; b. Davenport, Iowa, Jan. 3, 1944; s. Walter H. and Fern J. (Holst) V.; B.B.A., U. Iowa, 1966; m. Bonnie J. Deur, Dec. 28, 1968; 1 son, Robert Scott. With Berlage Bernstein Builders, Alexandria, Va., 1971-72; v.p. finance L.A. Clarke & Son, Inc., Washington, 1972-76, also dir.; controller Micro Systems, Inc., Vienna, Va., 1976-77; chief fin. officer Williams Lumber Co. Inc., Rocky Mount, N.C., 1977-78; personal bus. mgr. to Roy J. Carver, founder, chmn. bd. Bandag, 1978—; gen. mgr. Carver Enterprises, Miami, Fla., 1978—; owner Fred H. Vollbeer Financial Services; dir. Lancaster Masonry, Inc. (Fairfax, Va.), Carver Pump Co., Muscatine, Iowa, Carver Foundry, Muscatine, Carver Med. Research Found., Iowa City. Served with USAF, 1968-71. Mem. Alpha Kappa Psi. Club: Benvenue Country (Rocky Mount). Home: 6885 Cassia Pl Miami Lakes FL 33014 Office: 880 NE 69th St Suite 1E Miami FL 33138

VOLLMER, DONALD WALTER, fin. cons. co. exec.; b. New Rochelle, N.Y., July 12, 1934; s. Walter E.B. and Olive (Griffin) V.; B.A., Colby Coll., 1956; M.B.A., N.Y. U., 1963; A.M.P., Harvard U., 1973; m. Judith Ann Dunnington, Aug. 25, 1962; children—Victoria Ann, Ian Douglas. Comml. loan analyst Chase Manhattan Bank, N.Y.C. and Frankfurt, 1960-64; credit officer Wells Fargo Bank, San Francisco, 1964-65; fin. analyst World Bank, Washington, 1965-68; v.p. nat. div. Bank of Am., San Francisco, 1968-70, multinat. div., London, Eng., 1970-73; pres. Banque Ameribas, Paris, France, 1973-74; sr. v.p., internat. head Rainier Nat. Bank, Seattle, 1974-77; sr. v.p., mgr. internat. Seattle First Nat. Bank, 1977-79; pres. Banc Research, Inc., Seattle, 1979—; dir. Bankers Assn. for Fgn. Trade, Wash. (State) Council on Internat. Trade. Served to lt. USNR, 1956-59. Mem. Nat. Assn. Accts. Speaker profl. groups Europe; contbr. articles to publs. Office: 2737 77th St Mercer Island WA 98040

VOLPE, ROBERT WOODARD, elec. engr.; b. Chgo., Dec. 3, 1923; s. Lewis Philip and Inez (McGinity) V.; student Knox Coll., 1941-43, N.Y. U., 1944; B.S. in Elec. Engring., Northwestern U., 1947; m. Kathleen Sue Voslow, children—Catherine, Barbara, Robert David, Patricia. Control systems engr. Gen. Electric Co., Erie, Pa., 1947-48, supr. engring. adminstrn. 1950-51, research application engr., 1951-66; mgr. product planning Unit Rig & Equipment Co., Tulsa, 1966-69, asst. to pres., 1969—. Served with AUS, 1943-46. Registered profl. engr., Pa., Okla. Mem. Soc. Automotive Engrs., IEEE, Am. Inst. Mining and Metall. Engrs. Republican. Baptist. Contbr. articles to profl. jours. Clubs: Oaks Country, Petroleum (Tulsa). Home: 842 Lynwood Ln Broken Arrow OK 74012 Office: 5400 S 49 W Ave Tulsa OK 74101

VOLPERT, HOWARD ALAN, dept. store exec.; b. Syracuse, N.Y., May 7, 1934; s. Myron and Marian G. (Berman) V.; grad. Syracuse U., 1959; m. Judith Ann Schmidt, July 27, 1969; children—Molly Anne, Adam Raphael. Exec. trainee, asst. buyer, buyer Open Dey Bros. Home Store, 1961-65; buyer, store mgr. Burdines Federated Dept. Store, Hollywood, Fla., 1970-76, mdse. mgr. Dadeland div., 1965-67, gen. mgr., 1967-69, now v.p., regional mgr. Burdines Central Fla., Orlando, also dir.; dir. Sun Bank. Bd. dirs., head mchts. div. Combined Jewish Appeal; bd. dirs. Loch Haven Art Center, also chmn. fin. com.; vice chmn. United Fund. Served as capt. AUS, 1959-61. Mem. Hollywood Fashion Center Mchts. Assn. (pres.), Hollywood C. of C. (past pres.), Greater Orlando C. of C. (dir.), Res. Officers Assn., Zeta Beta Tau (trustee). Clubs: Masons, Rotary. Home: 203 River View Dr Sweetwater Club Longwood FL 32750 Office: 1 Orlando Fashion Sq Orlando FL 32814

VON AMMON, CARL, exec. search cons.; b. Winnetka, Ill., Nov. 30, 1911; s. Ernst Carl and Ida (Kroeschell) von A.; student Williams Coll., Mass., 1929-32; B.A. in Econs., North-western U., 1933; m. Mary Ellen Herron, Oct. 1, 1938; children—Stephanie, Victoria, Eric. Buyer, Sears Roebuck & Co., Chgo., 1933-42; asst. chief consumer durables goods br. War Prodn. Bd., 1942-43; asst. dir. advt. Ekco Products Co., Chgo., 1946-48; v.p. and asst. to pres. Grant Advt., Inc., Chgo., 1948-51; v.p. and mgmt. supr. J. Walter Thompson Co., Chgo., 1951-66; v.p. mktg. Internat. Minerals & Chems. Corp., Chgo., 1966-68; asso. Boyden Assos., Inc., Chgo., 1968-71; v.p. Eastman & Beaudine, Inc., Chgo., 1971—. Vice-pres., bd. dirs. Northwestern Univ. Settlement; active Boy Scouts Am., United Way Chgo., ARC, Cancer Soc., Winnetka Caucus. Served to lt. USN, 1943-46. Republican. Mem. Christian Ch. Clubs: Indian Hill (Winnetka); Univ. (Chgo.). Office: 111 W Monroe St Chicago IL 60603

VON BERG, WILLIAM GEORGE, mfg. co. exec.; b. N.Y.C., May 8, 1919; s. William and Margaretha (Kreidler) von B.; B.S. in Accounting cum laude, Syracuse U., 1940; m. Barbara J. Fleckenstein, May 3, 1947; children—William George, Susan C., Carol A., Barbara C., Steven E. Sr. accountant, audit staff Ernst & Ernst, 1939-42, 45-48; controller W.B. Coon Co., 1948-52; with Sybron Corp., Rochester, N.Y., 1952—, exec. v.p., 1970-71, pres., 1971-75, pres., chief exec. officer, 1975-78, chmn. bd., chief exec. officer, 1978—; dir. Rochester Gas & Electric Corp., Lincoln First Bank, Inc. Bd. dirs. United Way of Greater Rochester, chmn. bd., chief exec. officer, 1978-80; bd. dirs. Rochester Hosp. Service Corp., Genesee Valley Group Health Assn., Indsl. Mgmt. Council, Rochester Conv. and Publicity Bur.; trustee Center for Govtl. Research, Inc., U. Rochester, Syracuse U. Served to capt., inf., AUS, 1942-45; ETO. C.P.A., N.Y. Mem. Conf. Bd., Rochester Area C. of C. (trustee, pres. 1977), Beta Gamma Sigma, Alpha Kappa Psi. Clubs: Rochester Country, Univ.; Genesee Valley. Home: 8 Old Landmark Dr Rochester NY 14618 Office: Sybron Corp 1100 Midtown Tower Rochester NY 14604

VON BOECKLIN, RICHARD AUGUST, banker; b. Tacoma, June 3, 1942; s. August R. and Helen (Fochtman) von B.; License en Sciences Economiques Appliques, U. Louvain (Belgium), 1968; A.B. cum laude, U. Notre Dame, 1964; M.B.A., U. Chgo., 1967; Asst. v.p. Wells Fargo Bank, London, 1968-73; with Seattle 1st Nat. Bank, 1973—, v.p., mgr. multinational dept., 1976-78, sr. v.p., mgr. internat. dept., 1979—. Mem. vis. com. Sch. Internat. Studies, U. Wash., 1979—. Mem. Bankers Assn. Fgn. Trade, Nat. Com. Internat. Trade Documentation, Robert Morris Assn., Wash. Council Internat. Trade, Seattle Com. Fgn. Relations, Wash, Internat. Trade Fair. Clubs: Rainier, Wash. Athletic, Harbor. Office: 1001 4th Ave Seattle WA 98154

VON DER LINDEN, ARTHUR FELIX, JR., fin. planner; b. Orange, N.J., Jan. 9, 1942; s. Arthur F. and Frances E. (Mathey) von der L.; B.S. in Mech. Engring., Rensselaer Poly. Inst., Troy, N.Y., 1963; M.B.A., Wharton Sch., U. Pa., 1972; M.S. in Taxation, Bentley Coll., Waltham, Mass., 1976; m. Nancy Clarke, Oct. 31, 1964; children—James, Gregory, Eric. Self-employed fin. planner, Boston area, 1972-77; sr. couselor Personal Capital Planning Group Inc., Boston, 1977—. Properties chmn. S. Acton Congl. Ch., Acton, Mass., 1977—. Served as officer USN, 1963-70; mem. Res. Clubs: Bentley Tax Luncheon, Action Lions (dir.). Office: 1 Beacon St Boston MA 02108

VON DER WENSE, BODO, mfg. co. exec.; b. Berlin, W. Ger., Dec. 6, 1940; came to U.S., 1962; s. Horst Georg and Ursula Olga (Wodtke) von der W.; M.B.A., U. Hamburg (W. Ger.), 1962; grad. cum laude Sch. for Export Trade in Hamburg, 1962; married; children—Gero, Nicholas. Salesman, Scriptomatic, Inc., various locations, 1963-64, salessupr., 1965-66, br. mgr., 1967-68, dist. mgr., 1969-70, regional sales mgr., 1971-73; gen. mgr. Scriptomatic Can. Ltd., Toronto, Ont., 1974-78; v.p. mktg. Scriptomatic Inc., Phila., 1979—. Mem. Direct Mail Mktg. Assn., Nat. Office Machine Dealers Assn., Rocky Mt. Ski Instrs. Assn., N.Am. Yacht Racing Union, U.S. Squash Assn. Clubs: Berwyn Squash, Internat. Laser Class Assn. Contbr. articles to profl. jours. Home: 465 Garrison Way Gulph Mills PA 19428 Office: 1 Scriptomatic Plaza Philadelphia PA 19131

VON GEHR, GEORGE HENRY, JR., corp. exec.; b. Evanston, Ill., June 5, 1941; s. George Henry and Lois Agnes (Barnes) VonG.; B.S.E., Princeton, 1963; J.D., Stanford, 1966, M.B.A., 1968; m. Joan C. Comroe, Dec. 20, 1965; children—Karla, David. Cons., McKinsey & Co., Inc., 1968-69; asst. to pres., v.p. mktg. U.S. Natural Resources, Inc., 1969-73; v.p. fin. Dynapol, Palo Alto, Calif., 1974-78; sr. v.p. fin. and adminstrn. Spectra-Physics, Inc., Mountain View, Calif., 1978—. Mem. Am., Calif. bar assns. Home: 301 Stockbridge Ave Atherton CA 94025 Office: Spectra-Physics Inc 1250 W Middlefield Rd Mountain View CA 94042

VON HARZ, JAMES LYONS, elec. mfg. co. exec.; b. Palatine, Ill., Feb. 9, 1915; s. Ben C. and Honore Regina (Lyons) von H.; B.S. in Mech. Engring., Purdue U., 1938; m. Mary Jane Patterson, Oct. 31, 1938; children—John, Patricia, Rosanne, Jane, Kathleen, Sheila. Gen. mgr. Gen. Engring. & Mfg. Co., Des Plaines, Ill., 1938-41; exec. v.p., Oak Mfg. Co., Crystal Lake, Ill., 1941-62; v.p. Waller Corp., Crystal Lake, 1962-63; gen. mgr. Internat. Resistor Corp.-TRW, Burlington, Iowa, 1963-68; group exec. v.p. Transitron Electronic Corp., Wakefield, Mass., 1968-71; pres. ITT Cannon Electric, Santa Ana, Calif., 1971-75, gen. mgr. ITT Components Group, 1974—, dir. ITT Cannon, France, Germany, Italy, 1971—, corp. v.p. ITT. Mem. Western Electric Mfg. Assn. (dir. Orange, Calif.), Nat. Alliance Businessmen (regional chmn.). Home: 70 Monarch Bay S Laguna CA 92677 Office: ITT Cannon Electric 666 E Dyer Rd Santa Ana CA 92702

VON HOLZHAUSEN, FRANK JOHN, indsl. designer; b. Tarrytown, N.Y., Aug. 10, 1944; s. Marie (Eberhardt) Von H.; B.Indsl. Design, Syracuse U., 1967; m. Jane Fryatt, Aug. 20, 1966; children—Franz, Kurt, Ingrid. Staff designer Indsl. Design Cons., Farmington, Conn., 1967-69, staff supr., 1969-72, asso. partner, 1970-72; owner, officer Group Four, Inc., Avon, Conn., 1972—. Mem. Indsl. Designers Soc. Am., Am. Inst. Graphic Arts. Republican. Christian Scientist. Home: 29 Canton Rd W Simsbury CT 06092 Office: 147 Simsbury Rd Avon CT 06001

VON HORN, KNUT RAOUL LEOPOLD ROBERT, govt. ofcl., farmer; b. Stockholm, Nov. 28, 1907; s. Robert and Elizabeth (Bohnstedt) von H.: student U. Cambridge, 1927; B.A., U. Stockholm, 1930, LL.B., 1934; m. Birgitta von Horn, June 1, 1940; children—Johan, Edward, Michaela. Sec., Swedish State Commn. of Trade, 1939-41; chief sec. Ministry Supply, 1942-46, Ministry Commerce, 1946-48; mem. State-Commn. Agr., 1950-56; chmn. Swedish State Seed Testing Sta., 1959-74, Gullspang Power AB, 1973—; chamberlain at Royal Ct., 1946; dep.-marshall Diplomatic Corp., 1950-59; first surveyor at Royal Ct., 1956; Swedish del. internat. econ. confs. GATT, ECE, 1946-55; mem. bd. Korsnas AB, Investment AB Kinnevik, AB Swedish Lithographic Industries. Mem. Royal Swedish Acad. Agr. and Forestry (chmn. 1972-75), Swedish Milling Assn. (chmn. 1973-80). Office: Hjelmarsnas Stora Melloesa Sweden

VON JACOBI, VICTOR THEODOR, pharm. mfg. co. exec.; b. Gomel, Russia, Nov. 17, 1918; s. Theodor Woldemar and Catharina (Froloff) von J.; came to U.S., 1953, naturalized, 1962; B.S. in Pharmacy, St. Batory U., Wilno, Poland, 1939; Ph.D., Friedrich Schiller U., Jena, Germany, 1945; m. Ursula Huebert, Apr. 7, 1945; children—Victoria-Irina, Christian. Supr. lab. Wyeth Labs. Inc., Evanston, Ill., 1954-58, chief chemist, 1958-62, mgr. lab., 1962-72, mng. dir., 1972—. Mem. Am. Chem. Soc., Tech. Assn. Chgo. Home: 760 Greenbay Rd Highland Park IL 60035 Office: 8100 McCormick Blvd Evanston IL 60202

VON MAKNASSY, HARRO BRENNER, advt. and public relations firm exec.; b. Berlin, Germany, Feb. 27, 1939; B.A., Johannesburg, LL.B., 1962; M.B.A., U. Wuerzburg, 1967. With Deutsche Bank AG, Frankfurt Main, W. Ger., 1967-75, lending officer, v.p., 1970-75; sr. lending officer, v.p. Barclays Bank Internat. Ltd., N.Y.C., 1976-77; sr. v.p. fin. and corp. affairs Garth Assos., Inc., N.Y.C., 1978-80; exec. v.p., treas. The Garth Group, Inc., N.Y.C. Office: The Garth Group Inc 745 Fifth Ave New York NY 10151

VON PETERFFY, GEORGE ALBERT, communications products co. exec.; b. N.Y.C., Dec. 17, 1929; s. Ernst Zoltan and Louise Caroline (Schober) von P.; B.A., Dartmouth Coll., 1952; M.B.A., Harvard U., 1957; m. Ulrike Marianne Angelika Risch, Nov. 27, 1976; children—George F. W., Alexandra H., Walter O., Ferdinand, Anouschka. Partner, Hillyer Assos., Milan, Italy, 1960-61; staff cons. Arthur D. Little, Cambridge, Mass., 1961-63; asso. prof. Harvard U. Bus. Sch., Boston, 1963-71; dep. asst. sec. Dept. State, Washington, 1971-73; v.p. Kidder Peabody, N.Y.C., 1974; chmn. bd. Hubertus GmbH, Cologne, W. Ger., 1975-77; v.p. Gen. Telephone and Electronics Co., Stamford, Conn., 1977—; cons. Dept. State. Served to 1st lt. U.S. Army, 1952-55. Mem. Internat. Inst. Strategic Studies (London). Republican. Clubs: Knickerbocker (N.Y.C.); Brooks (London). Author: Engineering Manpower: How To Improve Its Productivity, 1952; (with others) Power and The Business Environment, 1968. Office: 1 Stamford Forum Stamford CT 06904

VON SCHLEGELL, VICTOR, III, insulation mfg. co. exec.; b. Aurora, Ill., June 17, 1947; s. Victor and Rosemary von Schlegell; B.A., Stanford U., 1969, M.B.A., 1971; m. Abbie J. Hicks, Sept. 24, 1968; 1 dau., Gretchen. Prin., Cresap, McCormick & Paget, Inc., San Francisco, 1973-79; chmn., pres. Forty-Eight Insulations, Aurora, 1979—. Office: Forty-Eight Insulations PO Box 1148 Aurora IL 60507

VON SEE, ROBERT-JOHN, pollution control co. exec.; b. New Brunswick, N.J., June 7, 1940; s. John J. and Hildegarde (Kappauf) von S.; A.A., Keystone Coll. Engring., 1960; B.S. in Mktg. and Econs., Lehigh U., 1963. Cost accountant, Western Electric, Allentown, Pa., 1963; asst. to pres. U.S. Foundry Corp., Reading, Pa., 1964-66; indsl. salesman, Glidden Paint Co., Reading, 1966-68; partner Cast Marble Products, Reading, 1968-69; asst. to pres. Mid-City Steel Corp. and Gitlin Industries, Westport, Mass., 1969—, dir. Petro-Trap div. Gitlin Industries, 1973—; owner Pollution Tech Service, Westport, 1974—; owner, dir. Petro-Trap Service, Westport, 1976—; pollution cons. to City of Providence; designer lobster and fish traps; vol. instr. fish trap building clinics for profls. Pres. Internat. Mgmt. Council Fall River, Mass., 1973; bd. dirs. Fall River YMCA, 1974—; asst. scoutmaster Watchung Council Boy Scouts Am. Served with N.G., 1963-69. Recipient citizenship award, Lions Club, Middlesex, N.J., 1954, silver award in exploring, Eagle Scouts, 1954. Mem. Inst. Scrap Iron and Steel (sec. No. N.Eng. Chpt., 1969-76, pub. relations com., Washington, 1969—), Mass. Lobstermens Assn., ASTM (pollution control com.). Lutheran. Lodge: Masons (jr. warden Blue Lodge), Scottish Rite. Co-inventor Petro-Trap; condr. research pollution control materials and techniques, aquaculture methods and equipment design, recycling methods. Home: Box 91 Westport MA 02790 Office: Petro-Trap Westport MA 02790

VON SELDENECK, JUDITH METCALFE, employment co. exec.; b. High Point, N.C., June 6, 1940; d. Frederick Maurice and Harriet (Curtis) Metcalfe; B.A., U. N.C., 1962; postgrad. Am. U. Coll. Law, 1963-64; m. George Clay von Seldeneck, Apr. 8, 1980; children—Rodman Clay, Kevin Clay. Senatorial asst., 1963-72; pres. Distaffers, Inc., Phila., 1973—; dir. Central Penn Nat. Bank, Greater Phila. Partnership; mem. Mayor Phila. Small Bus. Adv. Council. Mem. Phila. Tourism Commn., Phila. Tricentennial Com.; trustee St. Mary's Coll., Raleigh, N.C. Mem. Forum Exec. Women (founder, dir.). Democrat. Episcopalian. Clubs: Phila. Cricket, Sunneybrook Golf. Address: 2 Girard Plaza Suite 1804 Philadelphia PA 19102

VON SUMMER, ALEXANDER CARL, JR., real estate exec.; b. Teaneck, N.J., Nov. 2, 1938; s. Alexander Carl and Edith Marion (Spencer) von S.; B.A., Dartmouth, 1960; m. Sally Louise Pierce, Sept. 21, 1963; children—Kristen Pierce, Alexander Carl 3d, Hollis Marion Dene. Propr., Alexander Summer Co., Realtors and property devel., Teaneck and West Orange, 1962—; v.p. Alexander Summer Mortgage Co., Teaneck, 1963-73, chmn. bd., v.p. property mgmt. Alexander Summer, Inc., Teaneck, 1962-74, exec. v.p., 1974—; dir. United Jersey Mortgage Co., United Jersey Bank. Mem. legislative com. Bd. Realtors Eastern Bergen County, 1964-72, chmn., 1965-72, bd. dirs., 1970-75, pres., 1973. Mem. Conservation Commn., Saddle River, N.J., 1970-71; jury commr. Bergen County, 1971-75; mem. real estate adv. com. Bergen Community Coll.; trustee Teterboro Aviation Hall of Fame. Served with N.J. N.G., 1960-64. Mem. N.J. Builders, Owners and Mgrs. Assn. (pres. 1971—, dir. 1966—), N.J. Builders Assn. (dir. 1971—, mem. legislative com. 1971—), N.J. Assn. Realtors (mem. legislative com. 1969-75, dir. 1973-75), Am. Arbitration Assn., Chamber Commerce and Industry of No. N.J. (dir., vice-chmn. 1980), Alpha Delta Phi (v.p. 1959-60). Clubs: Arcola Country (Paramus, N.J.); Dartmouth of Greenwich (Conn.); Campfire Am. (Chappaqua, N.Y.). Home: 19 Pilot Rock Ln Riverside CT 06878 Office: 222 Cedar Ln Teaneck NJ 07666

VOORHES, WILLIAM GORDON, machinery co. exec.; b. Brownsville, Tex., Aug. 6, 1929; s. Marion Irwin and Mary (Conrard) V.; B.S., U. Ky., 1949, M.S., 1950; M.A. in Econs., Trinity Coll., 1963; m. Avis M. Bercin, Aug. 21, 1954; children—Mary Margaret, David William, Amy Jennifer, John William. Shift supr. E.I. duPont de Nemours & Co., Inc., Aiken, S.C., 1951-55; shop supt. Combustion Engring., Windsor, Conn., 1955-60; mgr. advanced engring. Pratt & Whitney Machine Tool Co., W. Hartford, Conn., 1960-65; chief engr. Elox Corp., Troy, Mich., 1965-70; pres. Wanskuck Co., Providence, 1970—, also dir.; dir. Plasar Industries, Inc. Mem. E. Greenwich (R.I.) Devel. Commn., 1973-76, E. Greenwich Planning Bd., 1976-77, E. Greenwich Democratic Town Com., 1976—. Registered profl. engr., Conn., R.I. Mem. Am. Soc. Metals, Soc. Mfg. Engrs., Wire Assn., Metal Powder Industries Fedn., Aluminum Extruders Council. Democrat. Unitarian. Club: Turk's Head. Patentee in field; contbr. articles to profl. jours. Home: 98 Cindyann Dr East Greenwich RI 02818 Office: 304 Pearl St Providence RI 02907

VORA, SHANTILAL AMRITLAL, cons. actuary; b. Bombay, India, July 21, 1928; s. Amritlal Keshavji and Triveni Hargovind (Doshi) V.; arrived U.S., 1966; B.S. with honors, Ramnarain Ruia Coll. of Bombay, 1949; m. Shanta Goculdas Mehta, Mar. 17, 1952; children—Pragna, Swati, Rita. Sr. officer Life Ins. Corp. of India, Bombay and Nairobi, 1965; actuary, mgr. Jubilee Ins. Co., Mombasa, Kenya, Africa, 1965-66; cons. actuary Bruce & Assos., Inc., Lake Bluff, Ill., 1966—; cons. all aspects ins.; exec. v.p. Kenya Ins. Inst., Mombasa, 1966, bd. dirs., 1963-64. Enrolled actuary Joint Bd. Enrollment of Actuaries, U.S. Depts. Treasury and Labor. Fellow Inst. Actuaries of London, Can. Inst. Actuaries, Conf. Actuaries in Public Practice (Chgo.), Fraternal Actuarial Assn.; mem. Am. Acad. Actuaries, Chgo. Actuarial Club. Mem. Internat. Soc. Krisna Consciousness. Contbr. articles on African life ins. to E. African publs.; contbr. research paper to profl. conf. Home: 218 Greentree Pkwy Libertyville IL 60048 Office: 916 Sherwood Dr Lake Bluff IL 60044

VORHAUER, BRUCE WARD, research co. exec.; b. Johnstown, Pa., Nov. 22, 1941; s. Raymond W. and Dorothy C. (Westover) V.; B.S., Va. Poly. Inst. and State U., 1964; M.S., W.Va. U., 1966, Ph.D., 1968; M.B.A., Northeastern U., 1973; 1 son, Scott Douglas. Engr., Esso Research & Engring. Co. and Esso Internat., Florham Park, N.J., 1968-70; program mgr. research div. USM Corp., Beverly, Mass., 1970-72; founder Medapex Corp., Boston, 1972-73; v.p. research and devel. Edwards Labs., Am. Hosp. Supply Corp., Santa Ana, Calif., 1973-75, group v.p., 1975-76; founder, pres. Vorhauer Labs., Inc., Newport Beach, Calif., 1976—; founder, prin. INVENTA, Internat. Ventures Assos., Costa Mesa, Calif., 1978—; mem. State Dept. Investment Missions to Southeast Asia, 1978, So. Europe, 1979; industry rep. FDA cardiovascular devices panel, 1974-76, obstetrics/gynecology devices panel, 1976-77. NSF fellow, 1964-68; registered profl. engr., Va. Mem. Sigma Xi, Tau Beta Pi, Beta Gamma Sigma. Contbr. articles in field to profl. jours. Home: 17902 Butler Irvine CA 92715 Office: 130 McCormick Bldg 104 Costa Mesa CA 92626

VORIS, WILLIAM, ednl. adminstr.; b. Neoga, Ill., Mar. 20, 1924; s. Louis K. and Faye H. (Hancock) V.; student U. N.C., 1943-45; B.S., U. So. Calif., 1947, M.B.A., 1948; Ph.D., Ohio State U., 1951; LL.D. (hon.), Sung Kyun Kwan U., Seoul, Korea, 1972, Eastern Ill. U., 1976; m. Mavis Myre, Mar. 20, 1949; children—Charles William, Michael K. Asst. prof. mgmt. Calif. State U., Los Angeles, 1952-56, asso. prof., 1956-59, prof., 1959-63, head dept. mgmt., 1956-63; dean Coll. Bus. and Public Adminstrn., U. Ariz., 1963-71; pres. Am. Grad. Sch. Internat. Mgmt., 1971—; mem. task force Joint Am. Assembly Collegiate Schs. Bus.-European Found. Mgmt. Devel., 1976—. Treas., Palo Verde Mental Found., Tucson, 1964-68; chmn. Tucson Community Goals Com., 1965-66; founding commn. mem. King Abdul Aziz U., Jeddah, Saudi Arabia, 1966; chmn. Phoenix Com. Fgn. Relations, 1976-78. Served with USN, 1942-45. Fellow Acad. Mgmt. (chmn. div. internat. mgmt., 1976-77); mem. Am. Assembly Collegiate Schs. Bus. (chmn. com. internat. affairs 1975-77), Western Acad. Mgmt., Nat. Acad. Mgmt., Western Assn. Collegiate Schs. Bus., Alpha Kappa Psi, Beta Gamma Sigma. Club: Circumnavigators. Author: Management of Production, 1960; Production Control, 1966. Office: Pres's Office Am Grad Sch Internat Mgmt Thunderbird Campus Glendale AZ 85306

VORNLE, PAUL, fin. services co. exec.; b. Vienna, Austria, Oct. 1, 1929; came to U.S., 1949, naturalized, 1954; s. R. and Elisabeth Haas (Iben-Haagenfels) V.; B.S. in Bus. Adminstrn., U. Ill., 1951; M.S., Columbia U., 1954; m. Rita Szigetter, Sept. 13, 1954; children—Steven, John. Exec. positions with Gen. Electric Co., 1954-61, ITT, 1961-66; exec. dir. European distbg. cos. ITT, Brussels, 1971-76; mng. dir. European aluminum ops. Hunter-Douglas Corp., Rotterdam, Netherlands, 1966-71; sr. v.p. internat. Am. Express Co., N.Y.C., 1976—; dir. Alliance Corp. Served with U.S. Army, 1951-53. Republican. Office: Amex Plaza New York NY 10004

VOS, HUBERT DANIEL, health care co. exec.; b. Paris, Aug. 2, 1933 (parents U.S. citizens), s. Marius and Aline (Porge) V.; B.A., Inst. d'Etudes Politiques, U. Paris, 1954; M.Public Affairs, Princeton U., 1956; m. Susan Hill, Apr. 18, 1958; children—Wendy, James. Internal auditor, dir. fin. Internat. Packers, Ltd., 1957-64; asst. to controller, then controller internat. div. Monsanto Corp., 1964-69; v.p. planning and fin. Smith Kline & French, 1969-72; sr. v.p. fin. and adminstrn., dir. Norton Simon Inc., 1974-79; sr. v.p. fin., dir. Becton Dickinson Co., Paramus, N.J., 1979—; dir. Rowe Price New Era Fund, Inc., Roe Price Prime Res. Fund. Mem. Am. Mgmt. Assn., Fin. Execs. Inst. Office: Mack Centre Dr Paramus NJ 07652

VOSBURGH, KENNETH VERNON, food brokerage co. exec.; b. Auburn, N.Y., Aug. 20, 1933; s. Stanley Alvin and Anne (Moravec) V.; B.A. in Bus. Adminstrn., St. Lawrence U., 1956; m. Betty Mueller, May 4, 1957; children—Kenneth E. (dec.), Karen, Kay. Telephone directory rep. L.M. Barry Co., Rochester, N.Y., 1956-57; wholesale foods rep. Brewster-Crittenden & Co., Rochester, 1957-59; food service rep. Carnation Co., Syracuse, N.Y., 1959-64; terr. candy rep. E.J. Brach & Sons, Buffalo, 1964-74; owner, mgr. K-Vee Sales Co., Buffalo, 1974—. Mem. Assn. for Research of Childhood Cancer (pres. 1972-78, 79-80, treas. 1974-75, public relations dir. 1976-77), Empire State Candy Club. Republican. Lutheran. Club: Masons. Home and Office: 206 Temple Dr Cheektowaga NY 14225

VOSMEIER, LEONARD FRANCIS, printing co. exec.; b. Richmond, Ind., Nov. 29, 1925; s. Leonard Henry and Ruth M. (Miller) V.; A.B., Ind. U., 1950; m. Monabelle Romaine Brockmyer, Aug. 26, 1950; children—Valerie, Mark, Mary (dec.), Ned, Matthew. Vice-pres. Mulhaupt Printing Co., Inc., Ft. Wayne, Ind., 1951-55; pres. Ft. Wayne (Ind.) Printing Co., Inc., 1955—; dir., treas. Mulhaupt Printing Co., Inc. Div. chmn. United Way, 1974; co-chmn. patriotism com. Bicentennial Com., 1974-76; admissions rep. U.S. Mil. Acad. Served to col. AUS, 1943-46. Recipient Ind. Commendation medal Mil. Dept. Ind., 1969. Mem. Res. Officers Assn. (pres. 1967, 76), Mil. Order World Wars (Fort Wayne Cadre Comdr. 1978), VFW, DAV, SAR, Sons and Daus. of Pilgrims, Am. Legion, Fort Wayne Printing House Craftsman, Allen County-Fort Wayne Hist. Soc., C. of C., Phi Kappa Theta. Republican. Roman Catholic. Clubs: Masons, Shriners, Olympia Country (pres. 1973-76), Serra (pres. 1976) (Ft. Wayne). Home: 2705 Whitegate Dr Fort Wayne IN 46805 Office: 340 E Berry St Fort Wayne IN 46802

VOSS, WENDELL GRANT, ceramic engr.; b. Omaha, Sept. 16, 1927; s. Walter Andrew and Carroll Alcestis (Schell) V.; B.S., Iowa State U., 1950; M.B.A., Case Western Res. U., 1957; m. Ann Terry Miller, May 6, 1951; children—Katherine Evelyn, William Wendell. Ceramic engr. Spinks Clay Co., Paris, Tenn., 1950-53; supr. research and devel. Ferro Corp., Cleve., 1953-61; project engr. Aeronca Mfg., Middletown, Ohio, 1961-65; mgr. ceramic sales Leco Corp., St. Joseph, Mich., 1965-71; plant mgr. Flo-Con Systems, Champaign, Ill., 1971-72; mgr. process control Gen. Refractories, Warren, Ohio, 1972-74; asst. to gen. mgr. Ferro Engrng. div. Oglebay Norton Co., Cleve., 1974-80; owner, sec.-treas. Portsmouth (Ohio) Casting, Inc., 1980—. Pres. adv. council St. Joseph (Mich.) Public Schs., 1967, mem. bd. edn., 1968-71. Served with U.S. Army, 1945-47. Mem. Am. Ceramic Soc., Nat. Inst. Ceramic Engrs., Iron and Steel Soc., Am. Inst. Mech. Engrs. Republican. Lutheran (pres. 1978-80). Patentee in field. Home: 2429 Grandview Ave Portsmouth OH 45662 Office: Portsmouth Casting Inc 618 11th St Portsmouth OH 45662

VOURNAS, CHRIS NICHOLAS, marine shipping co. exec.; b. Athens, Greece, May 8, 1938; came to U.S., 1967, naturalized, 1980; s. Nicholas D. and Constantina C. V.; B.B.A. in Econs. and Acctg., Athens U., 1963, postgrad. in law, 1966-67; M.B.A. in Acctg. and Mgmt., George Washington U., 1973. Mgr. acctg. dept. Athenian Distillery, Inc., Athens, 1966-67; acct. Geico Ins. Co., Washington, 1974; chief acct. Winco Tankers, Inc., N.Y.C., 1974-77; controller Lexington Transport (N.Y.), Inc., N.Y.C., 1977—. Served with Greek Army, 1964-65. Mem. Am. Mgmt Assn., Am. Hellenic Ednl. Progressive Assn. Club: Hellenic Univ. Grads. Office: Lexington Transport 551 Fifth Ave Suite 910 New York NY 10017

VRABLIK, EDWARD ALLEN, computer services co. exec.; b. Chgo., May 20, 1937; s. Edward Matthew and Helen Bertha (Felzan) V.; B.S. in Physics, M.I.T., 1959; M.S., Northeastern U., 1963; m. Carol Ann Kinzie, Apr. 29, 1961; children—Kevin Allen, Scott Edward. Research staff mem. Arthur D. Little, Inc., Cambridge, Mass., 1959-64; staff mem. M.I.T. Lincoln Lab., Lexington, Mass., 1964-67; asst. chief engr. Datatech, Watertown, Mass., 1967-69; pres. Dimensional Systems, Watertown, 1969-73; mgr. CAD, Digital Equip. Corp., Maynard, Mass., 1973-78; v.p. software engrng. Autotrol Tech. Co., Denver, 1978-79; v.p. research and devel. Computer Graphics Co., Denver, 1979—. Gen. Motors scholar, 1955-59. Mem. IEEE (design automation tech. com.), Am. Mgmt. Assn., IEEE Computer Soc., Kappa Sigma. Patentee in field. Office: 5200 E Evans St Denver CO 80222

VREELAND, JAMES ALBERT, financial exec.; b. East Orange, N.J., June 23, 1927; s. Albert L. and Helen (Aeschbach) V.; student Stevens Inst. Tech., 1947-50; B.B.A., Upsala Coll., 1952; grad. Exec. Mgmt. Program N.Y. U., 1964; M.B.A. magna cum laude, Fairleigh Dickinson U., 1972; m. Laura Price, June 10, 1949 (div. Nov. 1971); children—Elizabeth Ann, Stephen, Keith; m. 2d, Joyce Kessel, Dec. 10, 1977. Supr. chem. div. Celanese Corp., Newark, 1952-55; div. controller Kelsey-Hayes Co., Clark, 1955-59; asst. corp. comptroller Ametek, Inc., Newark, 1959-61; controller Graver Water Conditioning Co. div. Ecodyne Corp., N.J., 1961-70, v.p., 1970-72, v.p., controller Unitech Co. div., 1968-72; v.p., treas. Cascade Industries, Inc., Edison, N.J., 1972-75; v.p. fin. Belco Pollution Control Corp., Parsippany, N.J., 1975—. Mem. Short Hills-Millburn Republican Club, 1953-62. Fund drive dir. finance com. Rahway YMCA, 1954-56, Overlook Hosp., 1959-60, Knollwood Assn., 1959-61; mem. adv. com. Somerset Coll., 1969-75; mem. steering com. Human Resources Inst., U. Mich., 1972-77. Served with USNR, 1945-47; officer mil. intelligence CIC, 1955-61. Public acct., N.J. Mem. Nat. CIC Assn., Nat. Rifle Assn. (life), Mil. Order World Wars (past state comdr., life), Union C. of C. (industry com. 1968-72), Am. Mgmt. Assn. (chmn., speaker seminars), Fin. Execs. Inst. (past pres. N.J. chpt., vice chmn. conf. 1977), Holland Soc. N.Y., U.S. Power Squadron, Silver Beach Assn. Mason (K.T.). Club: Garden Bay Country. Home: 181 Long Hill Rd Little Falls NJ 07424 Office: 119 Littleton Rd Parsippany NJ 07054

VUSI, TSIAMBU IBRAHIM-SIXTUS, devel. banker; b. Big Babanki, Cameroon, May 30, 1947; s. Gabriel and Anastasia (Maki) V.; B.A. in Physics, Amherst Coll., 1972; M.S. in Math., Rensselaer Poly. Inst., 1973; Ph.D., U. Pitts., 1978. Asst. prof. bus. adminstrn. U. Pitts., 1978-79; fin. analyst African Devel. Bank, Abidjan, Ivory Coast, 1979—. Amherst Meml. fellow, 1972-73. Mem. Am. Inst. Decision Scis., Inst. Mgmt. Scis. Office: ADB 01 BP 1387 Abidjan 01 Ivory Coast West Africa

WAAK, RICHARD WALTER, mfg. and distbn. co. exec.; b. Wisconsin Rapids, Wis., Dec. 21, 1946; s. Heimo Walter and Marceline Sylvia (Barney) W.; B.S., Mich. State U., 1972; J.D., U. Detroit, 1975; m. Barbara Lynn Henderson, Dec. 26, 1969; children—Brian David, Heather Kristin. Legal research clk. Mich. State Appellate Defender Office, Detroit, 1974-75; staff editor West Pub. Co., St. Paul, 1975-78; admitted to Mich. bar, 1976; staff atty. corp. services Amway Corp., Ada, Mich., 1979—. Served with U.S. Army, 1969-71; Vietnam. Decorated Army Commendation medal. Mem. Am. Bar Assn., Mich. Bar Assn., Grand Rapids Bar Assn. Home: 1741 Edgewood St SE Grand Rapids MI 49506 Office: Amway Corp 7575 E Fulton Rd Ada MI 49355

WABER, HARRY EDWARD, ins. agy. exec.; b. Phila., May 2, 1911; s. Max and Hattie (Sonnenfeld) W.; B.S. in Econs., U. Pa., 1933; m. Raechal Krantz, Oct. 8, 1935 (dec.); children—Beth Rebecca Waber VanHollander, Michael David. With Montgomery Scott & Co., Phila., 1933-35, Waber & Co., 1935-56, Waber-Odell, 1956-75, Trio Mgmt., 1963-75; founder, chmn. Main Line Agy., Inc., Wynnewood, Pa., 1960—; founder Montgomery Gen. Agy., Inc., Wynnewood, 1962. Trustee Fedn. Jewish Agys.; vice chmn. Allied Jewish Appeal; bd. dirs. Akiba Acad., Torah Acad., Beth Jacob Schs. Served with U.S. Army, 1943-46. Decorated Army Commendation medal; recipient cert. of merit Big Bros., 1961; C.P.C.U. Mem. Soc. Chartered Property and Casualty Underwriters (life). Jewish. Clubs: Locust; White Manor Country (past pres.), Bryn Mawr Kennel (past gov.), B'nai Brith. Home: 1001 City Line Ave Apt WA-704 Lower Merion PA 19151 Office: Main Line Agy Inc 300 E Lancaster Ave Wynnewood PA 19096

WACHNER, LINDA JOY, cosmetics co. exec.; b. N.Y.C., Feb. 3, 1946; d. Herman and Shirley W.; B.S. in Econs. and Bus., U. Buffalo, 1966; m. Seymour Appelbaum, Dec. 21, 1973. Buyer, Foley's Federated Dept. Store, Houston, 1968-69; sr. buyer R.H. Macy's, N.Y.C., 1969-74; v.p. Warner div. Warnaco, Bridgeport, Conn., 1974-77; corp. mktg. v.p. Caron Internat., N.Y.C., 1977-79; pres. U.S. div. Max Factor & Co., Hollywood, Calif., 1979—. Named Women's Equity Action League Outstanding Woman in Bus., 1980. Office: 1655 N McCadden Pl Hollywood CA 90028

WACHTELL, THOMAS, oil co. exec.; b. Crestwood, N.Y., Mar. 27, 1928; s. Theodore and Caroline (Satz) W.; B.S., Syracuse U., 1950; LL.B., J.D., Cornell U., 1958; m. Esther Carole Pickard, Jan. 27, 1957; children—Roger Bruce, Wendy Ann, Peter James. Admitted to N.Y. bar, 1958; asso. Livingston, Wachtell & Co. C.P.A.'s, N.Y.C., 1958-60; pres. Allied Homeowners Assn., Inc., White Plains, N.Y., 1960-63, Gen. Factoring Co., White Plains, 1960-63; exec. asst. to pres. Occidental Petroleum Corp., Los Angeles, 1963-65, v.p., exec. asst. to chmn. bd., 1965-72, exec. v.p., 1972-73, officer, dir. numerous subs.'s; pres. Hydrocarbon Resources Corp., Los Angeles, 1973—; pres., dir. Cayman Petroleum Corp., 1974-75; dir. IBEX Films, 1975-79, IMEG (U.K.) Ltd., 1975-79; panelist, lectr. Nat. Indsl. Conf. Bd., 1969. Bd. dirs. Los Angeles Music Center Opera Assn.; bd. govs. Performing Arts Council, Los Angeles Music Center; trustee Good Hope Med. Found., Los Angeles, 1974—. Served to lt. USNR, 1952-56. Mem. Am. Mgmt. Assn., Los Angeles World Affairs Council, Choate Alumni Assn. So. Calif. (chmn. 1969—), Confrérie des Chevaliers du Tastevin, Beta Theta Pi, Phi Delta Phi. Home: 35 Crest Rd E Rolling Hills CA 90274 Office: 609 Deep Valley Dr Rolling Hills Estates CA 90274

WACHTER, JAMES JOSEPH, fin. exec.; b. N.Y.C., Apr. 1, 1939; s. Ferdinand and Edna (Connelly) W.; B.B.A. cum laude, St. Francis Coll., 1960; m. Elizabeth Ann Collison, June 15, 1963; children—John, Carol Ann, Joseph. Sr. acct. Price Waterhouse & Co., N.Y.C., 1960-64; with SCM Corp., N.Y.C., 1964-65; with Cities Service Co. and subs., 1965-74, mgr. fin. Columbian Carbon Co., 1965-69, chief fin. officer Copebras, Brazil, 1969-73, asst. to corp. controller, 1973-74; with Internat. Platex, N.Y.C., 1974-76; chief fin. officer Central Resources Corp., N.Y.C., 1976-80; sr. v.p., chief fin. officer, dir. Food Fair, Inc. Ft. Lauderdale, Fla., 1980—. Address: 2118 NW 19th Way Boca Raton FL 33431

WACHUKU, CHUKU ANABA N., business cons.; b. Nbawsi, Nigeria, Aug. 13, 1947; s. Benjamin Anaba and Lily (Towanidiary) W.; came to U.S., 1971; naturalized, 1973; B.S. in Econs., Eastern Mich. U., 1975; m. Gayle McMillian, Sept. 1, 1972; children—Chuku, Tuowoanidiari. Salesman, J. Lewis Cooper, Detroit, 1973; ter. sales mgr. Milan Wineries, Detroit, 1974-76; pres., operator United Bros. Internat., bus. cons. co., Ypsilanti, Mich., 1976—; dir. Anwa & Sons, Ltd., Nigeria, 1975—, mng. dir., 1979—; dir. Sorrento Hotels, Ltd., 1975—. Mem. Am. Mgmt. Assn. Club: Aba Country. Address: 1354 Elmwood Dr Ypsilanti MI 48197

WACKER, FREDERICK GLADE, JR., tool mfg. co. exec.; b. Chgo., July 10, 1918; s. Frederick Glade and Grace Cook (Jennings) W.; grad. Hotchkiss Sch., 1936; B.A., Yale, 1940; student Gen. Motors Inst. Tech., 1940-42; m. Ursula Comandatore, Apr. 26, 1958; children—Frederick Glade III, Wendy, Joseph Comandatore. With AC Spark Plug div. Gen. Motors Corp. 1940-43, efficiency engr., 1941-43; with Ammco Tools, Inc., North Chicago, Ill., 1947—, pres., 1948—, chmn. bd., 1948-68, 78—; founder, pres., chmn. bd. Liquid Controls Corp., N. Chgo., 1954—; ltd. partner Francis I. duPont & Co., N.Y.C., 1954-70; dir. Liquid Controls Europe, Zurich, Switzerland, Moehlenpah Industries, Inc., St. Louis. Condr., Freddie Wacker and His Orch., 1955-70, which appeared on TV and radio, now rec. with Cadet Records. Trustee, Warren Wilson Coll., Chgo. chpt. Multiple Sclerosis Soc.; mem. Eastern exec. council Conf. Bd., 1974; bd. dirs. Ch. League Am., Rockford Inst. Served to lt. (j.g.) USNR, 1943-45. Mem. NAM, Sports Car Club Am. (pres. 1952-53), Ill. Mfrs. Assn. (chmn. 1975, mem. bd.), Chief Execs. Forum, Chgo. Presidents Orgn. (dir., pres. 1972-73). Presbyterian. Clubs: Racquet (pres. 1960-61), Casino, Chicago, Mid-Am. (Chgo.); N.Y. Yacht; Shore-acres, Onwentsia (Lake Forest). Home: 1600 Green Bay Rd Lake Bluff IL 60044 Office: 2100 Commonwealth Ave North Chicago IL 60064

WACKERLE, FRED WILLIAM, mgmt. cons.; b. Chgo., June 25, 1939; s. Fred and Babette (Buck) W.; B.A., Monmouth (Ill.) Coll., 1961; m. Elaine Gately, Apr. 28, 1962; children—Jennifer, Ruth. Prin., A.T. Kearney & Co., Chgo., 1964-66; v.p. Berry Henderson & Aberlin, Chgo., 1966-68, also dir.; v.p. R.M. Schmitz & Co., Chgo., 1968-70; partner McFeely, Wackerle Assos., Chgo., 1970—. Bd. dirs. Wilmette United Fund; pres. alumni bd., senate dir. Monmouth Coll. Served with USAF, 1957-62. Mem. Tau Kappa Epsilon. Office: 20 N Wacker Dr Chicago IL 60606

WADDELL, GUILFORD THOMAS, III, ins. broker; b. Charlotte, N.C., Sept. 10, 1949; s. Guilford Thomas and Ella Frances (Cochrane) W.; B.A., U. N.C., 1971, M.B.A., 1974; m. Mary Gwendolyn Hightower, Aug. 20, 1972. Asso., Chris C. Crenshaw & Assos., ins. brokers, Durham, N.C., 1974-75; mng. partner Easton & Waddell, Chapel Hill, N.C., 1975-79; pres. Waddell Benefit Plans, Inc., Chapel Hill, 1979—; vis. lectr. U. N.C., Chapel Hill, 1978—. Ruling elder Univ. Presbyn. Ch., 1980—, co-chmn. bldg. fund campaign, 1979; dist. chmn. Carolina Ann. Giving, 1979, United Way, 1978; mem. U. N.C. Ednl. Found., 1976—. Recipient Disting. Service award Nat. Assn. Life Underwriters, 1979; C.L.U. Mem. N.C. Assn. Life Underwriters (ethics com. 1979), Durham Assn. Life Underwriters (pres.-elect), Am. Soc. C.L.U.'s, Assn. M.B.A. Execs., Chapel Hill-Carrboro C. of C., Durham C. of C., Million Dollar Round Table, Order Golden Fleece. Democrat. Club: Chapel Hill Country (golf com. 1978, tennis com. 1979). Contbr. articles to profl. pubis. Home: 109 Longwood Dr Chapel Hill NC 27514 Office: 500 Eastowne Dr Suite 80 Chapel Hill NC 27514

WADDELL, MARTHA J., stockbroker, fin. planner; b. Birmingham, Ala., Apr. 25, 1944; d. Aubrey Vincent and Ruth (Dyer) Hoover; A.B., U. N.C., 1964; diploma with honors, Goethe Inst., Germany, 1965; grad. N.Y. Inst. Fin., 1975; m. Joseph Martin Waddell, Nov. 11, 1966 (dec. Aug. 1978). Asst. news dir. Sta. WDNG, Anniston, Ala., 1967-68; ops. dir. Adventure Vacations, Boston, 1969-70; asst. mgr. Colpitts Travel Center, Eatontown, N.J., 1971-72; regional dir. sales Travel Mktg. Systems, San Francisco, 1972-75; account exec. E.F. Hutton, San Francisco, 1975—; instr. fin. planning U. Calif., Berkeley, San Francisco Community Coll.; leader fin. planning seminars; past pres. Friends of Commn. on Status Women. Cert. fin. planner. Mem. San Francisco Fin. Women's Club (pres.), Embarcadero Women's Forum, Bay Area Exec. Women's Forum, San Francisco C. of C. (women's council), Stockbroker Soc. Home: 1250 Vallejo Apt 2 San Francisco CA 94109 Office: 400 California 15th Floor San Francisco CA 94104

WADDICK, DANIEL MICHAEL, advt. exec.; b. Indpls., June 14, 1946; s. William Anthony and Mary Elizabeth (Dolan) W.; B.S., U. Dayton, 1968; M.B.A., Ind. U., 1970. Auditor, Peat Marwick & Mitchell, Chgo., 1970-71; mem. fin. staff Quaker Oats Co., Chgo., 1972-74, product mgr., 1974-76; product mgr. Alberto Culver Co., Chgo., 1976-77; product mgr. new products Swift & Co., Chgo., 1977-78, dir. planning, 1979; account mgr. Don Costello & Co. Advt., Chgo., 1979-80; pres. Waddick & Assos., mgmt. and advt. cons., Chgo., 1980—. Served to capt. USAR, 1968-76. Chaffee W. Shirk fellow, 1970. Mem. Am. Mgmt. Assn., Soc. Advancement Mgmt., Alpha Kappa Psi. Home: 2850 N Sheridan Rd Chicago IL 60657 Office: 620 N Michigan Ave Chicago IL 60611

WADE, DUDLEY FREEMAN, investment mgmt. co. exec.; b. Boothbay Harbor, Maine, Aug. 8, 1918; s. William Merrill and Caroline (Dudley) W.; B.S. in Commerce, U. Va., 1942; M.B.A., U. Pa., 1943; M.S., Grad. Sch. Bus., Columbia U., 1949; m. Marie A. Obernesser, Apr. 15, 1960; 1 son, Nicholas D. Asst. mgr. investment research Old Colony Trust Co., Boston, 1949-51; investment analyst State Street Research & Mgmt. Co., Boston, 1951-58, partner, 1958—; v.p. Federal Street Fund, Inc., Boston, 1968—, State Street Investment Corp., Boston, 1972—. Chartered fin. analyst. Mem. Boston Security Analysts Soc. Unitarian. Club: Down Town (Boston). Home: 66 Williamsburg Ln Scituate MA 02066 Office: 225 Franklin St Boston MA 02110

WADE, JOHN KENNETH, telephone co. exec.; b. Los Angeles, Apr. 15, 1933; s. Jay Kenneth and Estella Lucile (Hanson) W.; B.S. in Engring., U. Calif., Los Angeles, 1960, M.S. in Engring., 1964; postgrad. Exec. Program, U. Va., 1975; m. Nancy Ann Gordon, Feb. 9, 1962; children—Timothy Gordon, Christopher Brent. Sr. engr., supr. div. traffic Pacific Telephone Co., Los Angeles, 1961-65, 68-69, staff mgr., San Francisco, 1965-68, 69-76; dist. mgr., Bell of Nev., Reno, 1976—; pres., mng. partner Wade Assos., 1973—. Registered profl. engr., Calif. Republican. Home: 881 Donna Dr Incline NV 89450 Office: 1005 Terminal Way Reno NV 89520

WADE, MICHAEL ROBERT ALEXANDER, economist; b. N.Y.C., June 29, 1945; s. Burton Jean and Celia (Handleman) W.; student U. Rennes, France, 1964; A.B., U. Chgo., 1967; postgrad. in pub. adminstrn., Am. U., 1967-71; M.B.A. in Fin., N.Y. U., 1975; m. Carole Kay West, Aug. 25, 1974. Program analyst, mgmt. intern HUD, 1967-71; dep. dir. Mgmt. Communications and Briefing Center, U.S. Price Commn., 1972; asst. exec. sec. policy coordination U.S. Cost of Living Council, 1973-74; asso. dir. U.S. Indochina Refugee Program, 1975-76; pres. China Trade Devel. Corp. of Chgo., 1977—; participant with W.R. Grace & Co. in Okla. oil and gas prodn. Recipient Meritorious Service award Exec. Office of the Pres., 1972, Distinguished Service award U.S. Cost of Living Council, 1974. Mem. Soc. Contemporary Art, Internat. Trade Club of Chgo. (policy and legis. action com.), Chgo. Council Fgn. Relations. Club: U. Chgo. (sec. bd. dirs. Washington 1970-73). Home: 900 Lake Shore Dr Chicago IL 60611 Office: 25 E Washington St Chicago IL 60602

WADHAMS, CHARLES HASTINGS, JR., ins. co. exec.; b. Brockport, N.Y., Aug. 31, 1926; s. Charles Hastings and Marian Dorothy (Shafer) W.; student U.S. Navy Postgrad. Sch., 1950; B.S., Rochester U., 1950; m. Anne Taylor Schaaff, Sept. 6, 1950; children—Jean Wadhams Warren, Charles Hastings, Peter S., Andrew W., William G. Enlisted USNR, 1944-46, commd. ensign, 1950, advanced through grades to comdr., 1965; staff comdr. in chief Pacific Fleet, 1950-52; res. adviser to comdr. Naval Security Group, 1971-73; agt. Mass Mut. Life Ins. Co., Rochester, N.Y. and Washington, 1952-69, gen. agt., Bethesda, Md., 1970-73, Fresno, Calif., 1973-76; gen. agt. C.H. Wadhams & Asso., Bethesda and Fresno, 1971-76; sales exec. N.Y. Life Ins. Co., 1976—; lectr. in field. Bd. dirs. Nat. Found., 1956-67, Nat. Council Crime and Delinquency; del. Episcopal Diocese Washington, 1970-73, Episcopal Diocese San Joaquin, 1974. Recipient John Dublin award Pub. Service, Nat. Assn. Life Underwriters, 1965; C.L.U., 1959. Mem. Am. Soc. C.L.U.'s (pres. Rochester chpt. 1966), Nat. Assn. Life Underwriters (v.p. N.Y. 1967), Gen. Agts. and Mgrs. Assn., Psi Upsilon. Clubs: Genesee Valley

(Rochester); Sierra Racquet (Fresno); Soc. Descs. Mayflower. Home: 5365 Thorne Ave Fresno CA 93711 Office: 1300 W Shaw St Suite 1 Fresno CA 93711

WADMAN, LORAN WOOD, mfg. co. exec.; b. Peekskill, N.Y., July 8, 1929; s. Loran Wood and Viola May (Bacon) W.; student Taft Coll., 1949-51; children—Roxanne, Loran Wood III, Randall. Gen. sales mgr. Brunton Corp., Gardena, Calif., 1966-70; partner W&W Co., San Jose, Calif., 1970-71; gen. sales mgr. nationwide Kynell Industries, Inc., San Jose, 1971—, also mfrs. rep. Lic. gen. engring. contractor, Calif. Home: PO Box 53107 San Jose CA 95153 Office: 1817 Stone San Jose CA 95125

WADSWORTH, CHARLES NOEL, textile mfr.; b. Prattville, Ala., Dec. 13, 1935; s. Charles D. and Margaret (McCrary) W.; B.S., Auburn U., 1960; m. Kathryn Dickinson, Dec. 31, 1958; children—Margaret Dana, Jennifer Kathryn. Asst. design chief Cabin Crafts, West Point Pepperell, Dalton, Ga., 1960-63; dir. products Coronet Industries, Dalton, 1963-67; chmn. Wadsworth-Greenwood Corp., Dalton, 1968-79, chmn. emeritus, 1979—; pres. N. Wadsworth Co., Atlanta, 1979—; mem. govtl. affairs com. Gulf Oil Corp. Bd. dirs. Ga. Mus. Art; mem. nat. campaign com. Generations Fund, Auburn U. Served with U.S. Army, 1955-57. Episcopalian. Home: 725 Riverknoll Dr Atlanta Country Club Marietta GA 30067

WAGAR, JAMES LEE, pharm. and consumer products mfg. co. exec.; b. Port Chester, N.Y., Oct. 10, 1934; s. Legrand and Anna W.; B.S., Fordham U., 1956; M.B.A., N.Y. U., 1966; m. Rita Cosenza, May 30, 1961; children—Peter, Alba, Paul, Anthony. With Sealtest Foods, 1959-72; v.p., treas. Carter Wallace, Inc., N.Y.C., 1973—. Served with U.S. Army, 1957-59. Mem. Nat. Assn. Accts., Treas.'s Group, Short Term Investment Group, Risk Ins. Mgmt. Soc. Office: 767 Fifth Ave New York NY 10022

WAGER, EARL RUPERT, JR., planning and devel. co. exec.; b. Watertown, N.Y., Aug. 3, 1935; s. Earl R. and Marion (Greene) W.; B.S. in Bus. Adminstrn., U. Vt., 1958; M.A. in Organizational Devel., W.Ga. Coll., 1979; m. Rose Anne Ryan, July 15, 1970; children—Della Dewitt, Barbara Brink, Carrie Greene. Project mgr. Wager Constrn. Co., Watertown, 1958-63, v.p., 1963-67, pres., 1967-75; pres. M/R of Atlanta Center Inc., 1976-78; constrn. mgr. Gilbanie Bldg. Co., Providence, 1978-79; exec. McBro Planning and Devel. Corp., St. Louis, 1979—. Mem. St. Lawrence Eastern Ont. Commn., 1969—. Clubs: Masons, Elks; Black River Valley (Watertown); Lake Placid (N.Y.); Crescent Yacht (Chaumont, N.Y.). Home: 11240 Tureen Dr Saint Louis MO 63141

WAGMAN, FRED LYLE, cable TV exec.; b. Regina, Sask., Can., Feb. 6, 1937; s. Alex and Belle (Junker) W.; ed. Campion Coll., Regina, 1954, U. Alta., 1956, U. Sask., 1973; m. Anita J. Polasek, June 8, 1959; children—Lisa, Troy. With Sta. CKCK-TV, Regina, 1957-66; coordinator radio and TV Regina Separate Sch. System, 1966-76; gen. mgr., sec. bd. Cable Regina, Sask., 1976—. Active United Appeal, Regina, Regina Hist. Soc. Mem. Canadian Cable TV Assn., Sask. Cable TV Assn., Adminstrv. Mgmt. Soc., Regina C. of C. Roman Catholic. Clubs: Regina Rotary, Regina Curling, Regina Press. Contbr. in field. Office: 102-1911 Park St Regina SK S4N 5Y4 Canada

WAGNER, ALAN BURTON, mfg. exec.; b. Balt., June 8, 1938; s. Robert Ellsworth and Anna Margaret (Schnitzlein) W.; B.Engring. Sci. (scholastic leadership award) John Hopkins, 1960; M.M.E., Case-Western Res. U., 1962, Ph.D. in Bus. Mgmt., 1965; m. Lynn Felton Wynant, June 26, 1964; children—Brian Alan, David Scott, Elizabeth Lynn. Mgr. orgn. planning and devel. Internat. Minerals & Chem. Corp., Libertyville, Ill., 1964-67, dir. indsl. relations, 1967-70, v.p. div. orgn. and indsl. relations, 1970-73, corp. v.p. adminstrn., 1973—; v.p. IMC Coal Corp., Lexington, Ky., 1977-79; pres. Taylor Tot Products, Inc., Frankfort, Ky., 1979—, also dir.; dir. Crescent Industries Inc., So. Elkhorn Coal Corp.; lectr. in field. Fellow Alfred P. Sloan Nat. Found.; mem. Chgo. Assn. Commerce and Industry, Chem. Industries Council of Midwest, ASME, Am. Mgmt. Assn., ASHRAE, (Homer Addams award), AAAS, Ky. Coal Assn. (dir.), Sigma Xi, Omicron Delta Kappa. Clubs: Knollwood (Lake Forest, Ill); Greenbrier, Lafayette (Lexington). Home: 1523 Lakewood Ct Lexington KY 40502 Office: Box 636 Taylor Tot Rd Frankfort KY 40602

WAGNER, GORDON CARL, banker; b. Plymouth, Wis., May 20, 1933; s. Elray Walter and Mayme A. (Luth) W.; B.S. in Dramatics and English, Lawrence U., 1956; grad. Central States Grad. Sch. Banking, U. Wis., Madison, 1968; m. Peggy Arlene Rankin, Feb. 16, 1980; children—Amy Lynn, Betsy Lynn, Kurt Gordon, Melissa Rae, Brandon Scott. Asst. cashier First Nat. Bank Elkhorn (Wis.), 1959-65; v.p., sec. to bd. Bank Watertown (Wis.), 1965-68; v.p. First Nat. Bank Janesville (Wis.), 1968-71; exec. v.p. Heritage Bank Whitefish Bay, Milw., 1971-74, also dir.; pres., chief exec. officer Hillcrest Bank and Trust, Lyndhurst, Ohio, 1974-75; chmn. bd., pres., chief exec. officer Community Nat. Bank, Warrensville, Ohio, 1975-77; chmn. bd., pres., chief exec. officer Comml. Nat. Bank, Tiffin, Ohio, 1977—. Bd. dirs. Tiffin C. of C. Mayor's Com. on Revitalization of Downtown Tiffin; treas., bd. dirs. Betty Jane Rehab. Center, Tiffin, 1978—; trustee Tiffin Hist. Trust, 1978-79; mem. long range planning com. Trinity United Ch. of Christ, Tiffin. Recipient Spl. commendation Nat. Trust Hist. Preservation, Chgo., 1978; named Boss of Yr., Tri-County chpt. Nat. Secs. Assn., 1979. Mem. Am. Bankers Assn. (cert. comml. lender; community bankers adv. bd. 1978-80), Ohio Bankers Assn. (econ. devel. com. 1978-79, dir. BankPac 1978-80), Seneca County Bankers Assn. (sec.-treas. 1978-79, v.p. 1979-80, pres. 1980-81), Am. Inst. Banking, Bank Adminstrn. Inst. Clubs: Mohawk Golf, Elks. Office: 79 S Washington St Tiffin OH 44883

WAGNER, HARRY JOHN, mfg. co. exec.; b. Bklyn., Aug. 15, 1945; s. Harry Fred and Frieda (Friebolin) W.; B.B.A. cum laude, Pace U., 1974; m. Carol Ann Handy, Aug. 19, 1967; children—Laura, Maryann. Asst. market mgr. Acme Air Appliance Co. div. Ideal Corp., Bklyn., 1969-73; sales mgr. Maxwell I. Rothbell Co., Inc., Massapequa, N.Y., 1975-76; sales mgr. N.E. region Clayton Mfg. Co., Ridgefield, N.J., 1976—. Active Am. Tng. Corps, Inc., 1966-72. Served with U.S. Army, 1965-68. Mem. Nat. Model R.R. Assn. (pres. 1960—), Am. Mensa (pres. 1978—). Republican. Lutheran. Home: 51 Ringwood Ave Pompton Lakes NJ 07442 Office: 663 Grand Ave Ridgefield NJ 07657

WAGNER, JERALD FORD, music rec. co. exec.; b. Balt., May 9, 1944; s. Ford Morrison and Miriam (Stimson) W.; A.B. in History and Econs., U. N.C., Chapel Hill, 1965; postgrad. in Law Harvard U., 1965-66; m. Mary Clare Egidi Galvin, July 23, 1977. Dist. sales mgr. RCA, Atlanta, 1967-69; nat. promotion dir. Ampex, N.Y.C., 1969-71; v.p. sales Jubilee Records Co., N.Y.C., 1971-73; v.p., gen. mgr. Babylon Records Co., N.Y.C., 1973-76; pres., chief exec. officer CTI Records, N.Y.C., 1976—. Mem. Phi Beta Kappa, Delta Upsilon. Republican. Episcopalian. Clubs: Baileys Beach (Newport, R.I.); Bath and Tennis (Palm Beach, Fla.); N.Y. Athletic (N.Y.C.); Friars. Home: 56 W 71st St New York NY 10023 Office: 1 Rockefeller Plaza New York NY 10020

WAGNER, LOUIS EDWARD, chem. systems corp. exec.; b. Buffalo, Mar. 12, 1937; s. Louis F. and Lucille S. (Olson) W.; A.A.S. in Chemistry, U. Buffalo, 1961, B.S. in Mgmt., 1963, M.B.A., 1964; m. Mary M. Fitzgerald, Sept. 13, 1958; children—Meribeth, Thomas F. Research chemist, asst. lab mgr. Amercoat Corp. (now Ameron Corrosion Control div.), Buffalo, 1954-63, plant supt., Buffalo and Ont., Can., 1963-65, plant mgr., Buffalo, 1965-69; founder, pres. Chem-Trol Pollution Services, Inc., Blasdell, N.Y., 1969-76; founder, pres. NEWCO Chem. Waste Systems, Inc., Niagara Falls, N.Y. and Cin., 1976-79; founder, pres. LEW, Inc., 1979—; designer secure landfills facility, Model City, N.Y., 1971; condr. research polymer chemistry, plastics, hazardous waste disposal; cons. in fields. Mem. Spl. Corp. Environ. Tasks, Buffalo. C. of C. Mem. Am. Chem. Soc., N.Y. State Conservation Assn., Western N.Y. Air and Water Pollution Control Socs., Nat. Solid Waste Mgmt. Assn. (hazardous waste com.), Fed. Water Pollution Assn., Jacques Cousteau Soc., Young Presidents' Assn., Am. Forestry Assn., Com. 107 for Proper Handling of Materials Containing Polychlorinated Biphenyls, Asso. Industries N.Y. State, Am. Nat. Standards Inst. Club: Park Country (Buffalo). Lectr. in fields, confs.; contbr. articles to profl. publs.; patentee processes in waste treatment. Home: 8 Eltham Dr Eggertsville NY 14226 Office: 4242 Ridge Lea Rd Amherst NY 14226

WAGNER, MICHAEL GRAFTON, investor, corp. exec.; b. Greenville, Ohio, May 31, 1935; s. Chester and Mary Elizabeth (Palmer) W.; B.A., Vanderbilt U., 1957, asso. (hon.) Grad. Sch. Bus., 1969; m. Aubrey Chastain Wagner, Aug. 5, 1980; children by previous marriage—Kurt McIlwain, Charles Hammock, Krista Kathleen, Kerstin Kayne, Mary Gretchen, Michael Grafton. With Henny Penny Corp., Eaton, Ohio, 1957-76, sales, 1957-60, dir. advt., 1960-63, dir. mktg., 1963-68, pres., chief exec. officer, 1968-76, also of Henny Penny, Ltd., Toronto, Ont., Can.; pvt. investor, 1976—; pres. Schaefer Corp., Madison, Ala., 1979—. Area chmn. Vanderbilt U. Endowment Fund, Nashville, 1961-66, 70-74; chmn. Tobacco Bowl, Hartsville, Tenn., 1969; fin. chmn. Tenn. Republican Party, 1977-78. Mem. Am. Rifle Assn., Am. Ordnance Assn., Am. Forestry Assn., Am. Mgmt. Assn. (Pres.'s Assn.), Nat. Restaurant Assn., Nat. Assn. Food Equipment Mfgrs., Internat. Food Service Mfgrs. Assn., Nat. Commadore Club, Alpha Tau Omega. Episcopalian (sec., treas., warden 1969-71). Clubs: Ill. Athletic, Monte Sano, Green Hills Golf and Country (dir.). Home: PO Box 2124 Huntsville AL 35804 Office: Schaefer Corp 1200 Wall Triana Rd Madison AL 35758

WAGNER, MICHAEL JAMES, pipeline industry exec.; b. Omaha, Oct. 29, 1946; s. James Edward and Laura Caroline (Leubbert) W.; B.S. in Civil Engring., U. Nebr., 1968, M.B.A., 1973; postgrad. U. Alta.; m. Jacqueline Maxine Schlecht, Aug. 31, 1968; children—Matthew James, Tracey Maureen. Engr., No. Natural Gas Co., Omaha, 1968-70, project engr., 1970-71, sr. project engr., 1971-73; project mgr. Banister Pipelines, Edmonton, Alta., Can., 1973-74, mng. engr., 1974-75; v.p. N.Am. Pipeline div. Banister Continental Ltd., Edmonton, 1975-77; v.p. O.J. Pipelines Ltd., Edmonton, 1977—; pres., chmn. Mustang Mgmt. Ltd., Edmonton, 1977—. Served with USAFR, 1969-73. Lic. comml. pilot; cert. flight instr.; registered profl. engr., Alaska, Nebr., Tex., Alta. Mem. Am. Gas Assn., ASCE, Can. Constrn. Assn., Can. Gas Assn. (chmn. pipeline contractors div.), Can. Pipeline Contractors Assn. (labor negotiations com.), United Assn. Nat. Pipeline Industry (legis com., trustee, sec. bd.), Can. Soc. Terrain Vehicle Systems, Engring. Inst. Can., Air Civil Engrs., Slurry Transport Assn., Edmonton C. of C. (natural resources com.). Roman Catholic. Clubs: Royal Glenora, Edmonton Petroleum. Author numerous research papers. Home: 27 Greenwich Crescent Edmonton AB T8N 0Z5 Canada Office: 130 6325 103d St Edmonton AB T6H 5H6 Canada

WAGNER, ROMAN FRANK, ins. agy. exec.; b. Sheboygan, Wis., Mar. 16, 1927; s. Roman N. and Clara C. (Ott) W.; B.S. in Bus. Adminstrn., Marquette U., 1950; m. Jacqueline Anne Randall, Aug. 13, 1949; children—Kenneth, Katherine, Julie, Lisa, Janine, Jodi, Randall. With Bankers Life Co., Sheboygan, 1950—; spl. agt. Sheboygan Falls (Wis.) Mut. Ins. Co., 1953-54; treas. Sheboygan Town & Country, Inc., 1963—; pres. Roman Wagner Agy., Inc., Sheboygan, 1964—, Scorpio, Inc., Sheboygan, 1979—; dir. Wis. Cycle Supply Co., Sheboygan, 1979—; instr. Ins. Inst. Am., Lakeshore Tech. Inst., 1966—; condr. workshops in field; mem. Wis. Ins. Agts. Adv. Council, 1974-80. Active, United Fund drs., Sheboygan, 1963-68; mem. City of Sheboygan Police and Fire Commn., 1968-75, sec., 1970-75. Served with USN, 1945-47. Named Wis. Mr. Mut. Agt., 1966; Jaycees Key Man, 1960. Mem. Sheboygan County Ind. Ins. Agts., Chartered Life Underwriters Soc., Soc. Chartered property and Casualty Underwriters, Ind. Ins. Agts. of Wis-(Agt. of Yr.-award 1978), Wis. Assn. Life Underwriters, Profl. Ins. Agts. of Wis., Wis. Found. for Ins. Edn. (Disting. Service award 1975), Sheboygan C. of C., Alpha Kappa Psi, Beta Gamma Sigma, Alpha Phi Omega. Republican. Roman Catholic. Clubs: Econ. (pres. 1980), K.C. (4th degree), Rotary. Home: 2730 N 28th St Sheboygan WI 53081 Office: 611 New York Ave Sheboygan WI 53081

WAGNER, RUSSELL LEE, ins. co. exec.; b. Marengo, Iowa, June 17, 1916; s. Charles and Katherine (Schweitzer) W.; B.S., State U. Iowa, 1938, M.S., 1940. With Nat. Life and Accident Ins. Co., 1940—, mathematician, 1944-47, asst. actuary, 1947-54, actuary, 1954-58, v.p., 1958-65, sr. v.p., chief actuary, 1965-69, exec. v.p., 1969-72, pres., 1972-77, chmn. bd., chief exec. officer, 1977—, also dir.; pres., dir. NLT Corp., Nashville, after 1972, now chmn., chief exec. officer; chmn. Nat. Property Owners Ins. Co., Great So. Life Ins. Co.; chmn., dir. WSM, Inc., Nashville; chmn. Guardsman Life Ins. Co.; dir. NLT Computer Services, Beatrice Foods, J. Ray McDermott & Co., Kroger Foods. Mem. Met. bd. Nashville YMCA, 1972—; nat. bd. Jr. Achievement, Inc., 1973—. Fellow Soc. Actuaries; mem. Southeastern Actuaries Club (pres. 1953-54), Home Office Life Underwriters Assn. (pres. 1963-64), Acad. Actuaries, Nashville C. of C. (bd. govs. 1971). Presbyn. Clubs: Cumberland, Belle Meade Country (Nashville); International (Chgo.); New York Athletic. Office: Nat Life Center Nashville TN 37250

WAGONER, EDDIE JACK, acct.; b. Bogata, Tex., May 31, 1943; s. Jack Clifton and Ora (Waldean) W.; B.B.A. in Acctg., So. Meth. U., 1969; m. Sharron Lee Nunn, May 22, 1964; 1 dau., Stefani Lee. Mgmt. trainee, acct. J.C. Penney Co., Dallas, 1961-65; mgr. acctg. dept. Braniff Airways, Inc., Dallas, 1965-69; sr. acct. Alford, Meroney & Co., C.P.A.'s, Dallas, 1969-76; owner, mgr. E.J. Wagoner, C.P.A., Mesquite, Tex., 1976—. C.P.A., Tex. Mem. Am. Inst. C.P.A.'s, Tex. Soc. C.P.A.'s. Baptist. Club: Mesquite Host Lions. Home: 10222 Kilkenny Pl Dallas TX 75228 Office: 3230 Hwy 67E Suite 105 Mesquite TX 75150

WAIDELICH, CHARLES J., oil co. exec.; b. Columbus, Ohio, May 2, 1929; s. Bernard Howard and Alberta (Poth) W.; B.S., Purdue U., 1951, D.Eng. (hon.), 1978; m. Margaret Ellen Finley, Jan. 26, 1952; children—Michael Brian, Sharon Ann. Engr., Cities Service Oil Co., Bartlesville, Okla., 1951-54; asst. to pres. Cities Service Pipeline Co., Bartlesville, Okla., 1956-59; pipeline coordinator Cities Service Co., N.Y.C., 1959-65, transp. coordinator, 1965-66, staff v.p. ops. coordination, 1966-68, exec. v.p. ops., dir., 1970-71, pres., 1971—; v.p. ops. Tenn. Corp., N.Y.C., 1968-70; chmn. bd. Colonial Pipeline Co., Atlanta, 1967-70; dir. Bank of Okla. Bd. dirs. Transp. Assn. Am., Tulsa Area United Way; mem. pres.'s council Purdue U.; bd. govs. Purdue Found. Served with C.E., AUS, 1954-56. Mem. Am. Petroleum Inst., Am. Inst. Mining Engrs., Econ. Club N.Y., Theta Xi. Clubs: Sky (N.Y.C.); Internat. (Washington); So. Hills Country, Tulsa, Summit, Utica 21 (Tulsa). Home: 2161 Forest Blvd Tulsa OK 74114 Office: Cities Service Bldg Tulsa OK 74102

WAINWRIGHT, RICHARD ADOLPH, elec. engr.; b. Creston, Ia., Apr. 15, 1931; s. Theodore Lee and Annetta (Schlepp) W.; Engr.dipl., Capitol Inst. Tech., 1954, D.Sc., 1976; law cert. George Washington U., 1968; m. June 18, 1976; children by previous marriage—Richard, Deborah, Jonathan, Stephen, David; stepchildren—Ronald Alexander, Douglas Alexander. Lectr., Capitol Inst. Tech., Kensington, Md., 1954-59; sr. engr. Page Engring. Co., Washington, 1956-57; staff cons. Rixon Electronics, Laguna Beach, Calif., 1957-60; chief research Telonic Engring. Co., Laguna Beach, 1960-62; founder, pres. I-Tel Inc., Kensington, Md., 1962-71; founder, owner Cirqtel, Inc., Kensington, 1962-71, chmn. bd., pres., 1971—. Trustee, Capitol Inst. Tech., 68—, vice-chmn. bd., 1975-76, chmn., 1976-80. Served with USN, 1948-52. Recipient cert. of meritorious service Capitol Inst. Tech., 1979. Mem. IEEE, ASME, AAAS, Numerical Control Soc., N.Y. Acad. Sci. Club: Columbia Country. Contbr. articles to profl. jours.; patentee in field. Home: 3333 University Blvd W Kensington MD 20795 Office: 10504 Wheatley St Kensington MD 20795

WAITE, LOUIS EDWARD, driver leasing co. exec.; b. Roaring Springs, Pa., Feb. 11, 1926; s. Clarence Earl and Bessie Ruth (Hoover) W.; student Oberlin (Ohio) Coll.; m. Frances Clara Jackson, Dec. 26, 1950; children—Yvonne Bessie, Louis Edward, Duane Douglas, John Thomas. Diesel engr. City of Oberlin, 1948-50; from driver to regional mgr. REA Express, 1950-70; truck transp. mgr. Inland Container Corp., Indpls., 1970-76; v.p. T.L.I. Inc., St. Louis, 1976—, also dir.; dir. I.T.I. Drayage Co., Transco Logistics Co. Served with inf. AUS, 1944-45; ETO. Decorated Combat Inf. badge; named Ky. col., 1972. Mem. Am. Trucking Assn. (dir. pvt. carrier conf.), Driver Leasing Council Am., Mo. Truck and Bus Assn., S.P.E.B.S.Q.A. Republican. Baptist. Clubs: High Hat (life) (Indpls.); Shriners. Home: 2265 Brook Dr Florissant MO 63033 Office: 8 Progress Pkwy Saint Louis MO 63043

WAITE, RICHARD CRAIG, cons. co. exec.; b. Tulsa, Okla., July 15, 1949; s. Robert G. and Katherine E. (Cavanaugh) W.; M.A. in Bus. Adminstrn., U. Mass., 1975. Prodn. supr. Carapace, Inc., Tulsa, 1975-76; pres. RCW, Hinsdale, N.H., 1977—; lectr. U. Mass. Served with U.S. Army, 1967-69. Decorated Bronze Star, Purple Heart. Mem. Nat. Pilots Assn., VFW. Author: Into the Darkness, 1974; Black Virgin Mountain, 1976. Office: 14 Dale Dr Hinsdale NH 03451

WAKEFIELD, CORNELIUS WILLIAM, ins. broker; b. Union City, Tenn., Aug. 16, 1920; s. Cornelius William and Mary (Mayo) W.; B.A. in Econs., Vanderbilt U., 1942; B.S., U.S. Mil. Acad., 1945; m. Betty Ruth Williams, Mar. 2, 1950; children—Cornelius William, Mary Adair, Sallie Staten. Ins. broker, El Paso, Tex. and McLean, Va., 1955—; pres. John D. Williams Co., El Paso, 1965—. Commr., El Paso Housing Authority, 1974-76; mem. nat. fin. com. Democratic Party, 1979—. Served to lt. col. U.S. Army, 1945-55. Mem. Soc. C.L.U.'s, El Paso Assn. Ins. Agts. (past pres.), Million Dollar Roundtable. Democrat. Baptist. Club: Kiwanis (dir. El Paso). Office: J D Williams Co 1330 E Yandell St El Paso TX 79902

WAKENIGG, RICHARD PAGE, elec. appliance mfg. exec.; b. Bridgeport, Conn., Aug. 3, 1940; s. John H. and Marion (Burbank) W.; B.S., U. Ariz., 1963; m. Jo B. Keegan; children—Michael, Richard, Stephen. Trainee, Colgate Palmolive Co., Dallas, 1963, salesman, Austin, Tex., 1964-65, Fort Worth, 1966-67, spl. rep., Fla., 1968, key account mgr., Washington, 1969-70; dist. sales mgr. Yardley Cosmetics Co., Atlanta, 1971-73; regional mgr. GiftAmerica (Western Union), Atlanta, 1973-74; regional sales mgr. Clairol Co., Atlanta, 1974-76; regional sales mgr. Norelco Inc., Decatur, Ga., 1977—. Chmn. com. Cub Scouts, 1975-76; mem. Republican Campaign Com. Md. Home: 4362 Mink Livsey Rd Lithonia GA 30058 Office: 4151 Memorial Dr Suite B119 Decatur GA 30032

WALBERT, RICHARD B., stock exchange exec.; b. Milford, Ill., 1916; ed. Northwestern U. Chmn., chief exec. officer Midwest Stock Exchange, Chgo.; dir. Northwestern Steel & Wire Co. Office: 120 S LaSalle St Chicago IL 60603*

WALBY, MICHAEL DAVID, social welfare agy. adminstr.; b. Bklyn., Nov. 25, 1947; s. Benjamin and Anna Walby; B.S. in Edn., U. Kans., 1971; M.S.W., Hunter Coll., 1978; m. Nancy McCully, Aug. 15, 1970; children—Matthew David, Jacqueline Louise. Dir. day hosp. service S. Beach Psychiatric Center, Bensonhurst, S.I., N.Y., 1972-78; exec. dir. Seaside Industries, Inc., S.I., 1978—; treas. N.Y. State Industries for Handicapped. Cert. social worker, N.Y. Mem. Nat. Alliance Social Workers. Home: 1902 E 51st St Brooklyn NY 11234 Office: 28 Bay St Staten Island NY 10305

WALD, BERNARD JOSEPH, lawyer; b. Bklyn., Sept. 14, 1932; s. Max and Ruth (Mencher) W.; B.B.A. magna cum laude, Coll. City N.Y., 1953; J.D. cum laude, N.Y. U., 1955; m. Francine Joy Weintraub, Feb. 2, 1964; children—David Evan, Kevin Mitchell. Admitted to N.Y. bar, 1955, since practiced law in N.Y.C.; mem. firm Herzfeld & Rubin, 1964—. Mem. Am., N.Y. State bar assns., N.Y. County Lawyers Assn., Assn. Bar City N.Y., Beta Gamma Sigma, Beta Alpha Psi. Home: 520 La Guardia Pl New York NY 10012 Office: 40 Wall St New York NY 10005

WALD, MICHAEL H., lawyer; b. Oceanside, N.Y., Feb. 11, 1952; s. Morton Lee and Janice W.; B.S. magna cum laude, Wharton Sch. Finance, U. Pa., B.A. magna cum laude; postgrad. London Sch. Econs., 1974; J.D., Duke U., 1977. Admitted to N.Y. bar, 1978, Va. bar, 1978, D.C. bar, 1978, Fla. bar, 1979, Tex. bar, 1980; asso. firm Ballard, Spahr, Andrews & Ingersoll, Phila., 1976; atty. FTC, Washington, 1977-78; asso. firm Dunaway, McCarthy & Dye, Washington, 1979; corp. counsel Datapoint Corp., San Antonio, 1980—. Eli Lilly Found. grantee, 1974. Mem. Am. Bar Assn., Va. State Bar, Fla. State Bar, Tex. State Bar, Phi Beta Kappa, Beta Gamma Sigma. Home: 15718 Blue Creek San Antonio TX 78232 Office: 7900 Callaghan San Antonio TX 78229

WALDENBERG, TOBY, assn. exec.; b. N.Y.C.; d. Nathan and Mamie (Nettler) Waldenberg; B.B.A., Coll. City N.Y., 1948; M.B.A., N.Y. U., 1957, systems certificate, 1960. Adminstr., indsl. engr. Western Union Telegraph Co., 1948-60; mgmt. cons., 1960-62; personnel adminstr. Kinney Assos., 1962-64; systems analyst Girl Scouts U.S.A., N.Y.C., 1964-68, bus. mgr., 1968-74, field adminstr., 1976-77, dir. methods and procedures, 1974-76, bus. ops. dir., 1977—. Mem. deans day and fund raising coms. N.Y. U. Grad. Sch., 1957-70. Mem. Word Processing Assn., Am. Inst. Indsl. Engrs. Club: N.Y. U. Alumnae (past dir., v.p.). Author: Business Management in Girl Scouting; contbr. articles to personnel jours. Home: 251 E 51st St New York NY 10022 Office: 830 3d Ave New York NY 10022

WALDFOGEL, RUTH, retail co. exec.; b. Munich, Germany, Dec. 27, 1948; came to U.S., 1951, naturalized, 1955; d. Abram and Golda (Geld) W.; student Mich. State U., 1966-67; B.A., Northwestern U., 1970; m. Fred Fahrbach, June 20, 1975. With Bloomingdale's, N.Y.C., 1970-74, buyer, until 1974; buyer Workbench, N.Y.C., 1975-77; adminstr. Macy's N.Y.C., 1977-79, v.p. home furnishings, 1979—. Mem. Nat. Retail Mchts. Assn. (dir.), Mensa. Democrat. Jewish. Office: 151 W 34th St New York NY 10001

WALDMAN, BARBARA LEE, packaging co. exec.; b. Akron, Ohio, Sept. 15, 1947; d. Jack L. and Betty C. (Klusner) W.; B.A., U. Mich., 1969; postgrad. Sloan Sch., M.I.T., summers 1975, 76; P.M.D., Harvard U., 1978. Systems and procedures asst. Loomis Sayles & Co., Boston, 1969-71; procedures analyst, applications specialist Continental Can Co., Chgo., 1972-74, systems analyst, planning analyst, 1974-76, mgr. adminstrn., asst. to pres., Stamford, Conn., 1976-78, mgr. planning analysis, 1978-79, mgr. mktg. services and licensing, 1979—. Mem. Women in Mgmt. (founding mem.). Club: Harvard Bus. Sch. of N.Y. Home: 237-15 Strawberry Hill Ave Stamford CT 06902 Office: 72 Cummings Point Rd Stamford CT 06904

WALDMAN, GILBERT DONALD, indsl. supply co. exec.; b. Hillside, N.J., Sept. 7, 1931; s. Irving and Elsie (Brooks) W.; A.B., SUNY, Albany, 1953, M.A., 1954; student Albany Law Sch., 1955-56; LL.B., U. Tulsa, 1960; m. Nancy Bellin, June 16, 1957; children—Vincent, Douglas. Admitted to Okla. bar, 1960; public adminstrn. intern N.Y. State Dept. Commerce, 1955, Bur. Planning, 1956-57; with Indsl. Uniform and Towel Supply, Tulsa, 1957—, pres., 1970—; pres. Dusttex Internat. Assn., 1977-79. Mem. Gov.'s Com. Employment of Handicapped, Okla., 1972—. Served with USNR, 1949-60. Mem. Inst. Indsl. Launderers (dir. 1965-67), Southwestern Linen and Indsl. Supply Assn. (dir.), Okla. Assn. Textile Services (v.p.), Am. Bar Assn., Okla. Bar Assn., Tulsa County Bar Assn. Home: PO Box HH Tulsa OK 74112 Office: PO Box 15798 Tulsa OK 74112

WALDMAN, SAMUEL, indsl. gas co. exec.; b. N.Y.C., Dec. 9, 1934; s. David and Bella (Harbatkin) W.; B.S., N.Y. U., 1956; m. Lorraine E. Sklarin, Mar. 1, 1959; children—David, Mindy. Sr. accountant S.F. Bauer & Co., C.P.A.'s, 1956-60; controller Arrow Welding Supply Co., Farmingdale, N.Y., 1960-64; mgr. budget and evaluations Airco Indls. Gases, San Francisco, 1964-69; v.p. finance Airco Cryogenics, Irvine, Calif., 1969-74; v.p. finance and adminstrn. Airco Indsl. Gases, Murray Hill, N.J., 1974-79, sr. v.p. staff, 1980—. Mem. Bd. Edn., Hayward, Calif., 1968-69; chmn. com. Watchung council Boy Scouts Am., 1975. Mem. Nat. Assn. Accountants, Am. Mgmt. Assn. Republican. Home: 113 Crest Dr Summit NJ 07901 Office: 575 Mountain Ave Murray Hill NJ 07974

WALDMANN, EDWARD BERNARD, physician; b. Council Bluffs, Iowa, Feb. 6, 1926; s. Edward Bernard and Carolyn Gertrude (Spitznagle) W.; B.S., Creighton U., 1946, M.D., 1948, M.S., 1950; m. Ethel Mackey, Sept. 2, 1971; children by previous marriage—Mary Kathleen, Mary Patricia, Stephen, Margaret Ellen, Christine. Extern, Jennie Edmundson Meml. Hosp., Council Bluffs, 1946-47, St. Josephs Meml. Hosp., Omaha, 1948; intern Hosp. of Good Samaritan, Los Angeles, 1948-49; research fellow physiology Creighton U. Grad. Sch., 1949-50; resident psychiatry St. Bernards Hosp., Council Bluffs, 1950; fellow in medicine Mayo Found., 1953-55; staff Mayo Clinic, 1956, cons. in medicine, 1956-59; mem. staff Rochester Methodist Hosp., 1956-59; practice medicine, specializing in internal medicine, Phoenix, 1959-68, cons. practice in internal medicine and nephrology, 1968—; mem. active staff St. Joseph Hosp. and Med. Center, 1963, chmn. Outpatient Clinic, 1962-65, med. dir. Mercy Clinic, 1968—, chmn. pharmacy and therapeutics com., 1962-68, chief adult sect. nephrology, dept. medicine, 1969-76, sec. med. com., 1971-72, also dir. employee health services; mem. vis. staff Good Samaritan Hosp., John C. Lincoln Hosp., St. Lukes Hosp. Med. Center; asst. in chemistry Creighton U., 1944, lectr. physiology Sch. Nursing, 1948, asst. in medicine Sch. Medicine, 1950-56; instr. medicine Grad. Sch., U. Minn., 1957-59; asso. in medicine U. Ariz. Sch. Medicine, Tucson, 1973—; instr. Grad. Sch. Nursing, Ariz. State U., Tempe; pres., dir. Osborn Med. Bldg., 1964-67; cons. Ariz. Poison Control Centers, 1968—, Med. Emergency Communication Assistance, 1970-74, Asso. Ambulance, Phoenix, 1969-74; chief examiner Minn. Mut. Life Ins. Co., Gt. So. Life Ins. Co.; co-chief examiner N.Y. Life Ins. Co. Dir. med. edn. Aero. Med. Emergency Services Project, 1969; chmn. emergency med. services, transp com. Health Services Area I, 1976—. Served to capt. USNR, 1945—. Diplomate Nat. Bd. Med. Examiners, Am. Bd. Internal Medicine, Pan Am. Med. Assn. Fellow A.C.P., Am. Coll. Chest Physicians, Am. Coll. Clin. Pharmacology; mem. Internat., Am., Ariz. (sec.-treas. 1975-76) socs. internal medicine, Internat., Am. socs. nephrology, Am. Soc. Enologists, Am. (pres. Maricopa div. 1975-76), Ariz. (chmn. physicians edn. com. 1972-73), Maricopa (dir. 1962-64) heart assns., Nat., Ariz. (mem. med. adv. com. 1964-72) kidney founds., Renal Physicians Assn., U.S. and Mexico Med. Soc., Central Ariz. Arthritis Found., Maricopa Found. for Med. Care, Phoenix Chpt. Hemophilia Found. (mem. med. adv. com. 1969-72), AMA, Ariz. Med. Assn., Maricopa County Med. Soc., Aerospace Med. Assn., Naval Res. Assn., Naval Order U.S. Roman Catholic. Clubs: Elks. Contbr. articles to med. jours. Home: 7033 N 10th Ave Phoenix AZ 85021 Office: 350 W Thomas Rd Phoenix AZ 85013

WALDO, RALPH EMERSON, ins. co. exec.; b. Portsmouth, Ohio, Jan. 16, 1918; s. Ralph Emerson and Margaret Ruth (Van Meter) W.; B.S., Ohio State U., 1940, C.L.U., 1955; m. Lorna Broome, Feb. 14, 1941; children—Ralph III, Douglas, Kim. Agt., Equitable of Iowa, Columbus, Ohio, 1940-49; mktg. dept. Columbus (Ohio) Mut. Life Ins. Co., 1949-63, v.p., dir. agys., 1963-68, pres., 1968—; dir. Columbia Electric Co., So. Ohio Electric Co., SCOA Industries, Inc., BancOhio, State Auto Ins. Co. Bd. dirs. Columbus Boys Club; trustee Franklin U. Served to maj. U.S. Army, 1941-46. Decorated Bronze Star. Mem. Nat. Assn. Life Underwriters, Am. Council Life Ins. (dir. 1979). Republican. Baptist. Clubs: Scioto Country, Columbus Athletic, Masons. Office: 303 E Broad St Columbus OH 43215

WALDO, ROBERT LELAND, mortgage guaranty ins. co. exec.; b. Pittsville, Wis., Sept. 1, 1923; s. Elmer Harley and Edith (Senter) W.; B.S., U. Wis., 1949, J.D., 1951; m. Elaine Anne Jossie, June 4, 1947; children—Daniel Robert, Thomas Parker, Susan Jeanne. Admitted to Wis. bar, 1951; asso. firm Miller, Mark & Fairchild, Milw., 1951-59; asst. sec., asst. gen. counsel Wis. Gas Co., Milw., 1959-69; v.p., gen. counsel Continental Mortgage Ins. Inc., Madison, Wis. (predecessor of Verex Corp.), 1969-72; exec. v.p., sec. Verex Corp. and subs., 1972-78, pres., 1978—; pres., mem. exec. com. Mortgage Ins. Cos. Am.; dir. Marine Trust Co. N.A., Milw. Chmn. Dane County (Wis.), chpt. ARC, 1977-78; bd. dirs., mem. exec. com. Dane County chpt. United Way, 1980—. Served with U.S. Army, 1943-46. Mem. Wis. Bar Assn., Am. Bar Assn. Methodist. Clubs: Madison, Maple Bluff Country. Office: PO Box 7066 Madison WI 53707

WALDO, SALLY (MRS. CLAUDE A. WALDO), real estate, ins. broker; b. Seattle, Jan. 8, 1903; d. Hyman and Lena (Kaplan) Rosenstein; student Modesto Jr. Coll., 1930; m. Claude A. Waldo, Nov. 6, 1925 (dec. June 1969). Exec. sec., co-owner, exec. sec. firm Claude A. Waldo, land surveyor, Martinez, Calif., 1945-69; bus. opportunity broker, real estate broker, 1949—, ins. broker, 1950—. Mem. Calif. 50-50 Bill Com., 1937; mem. committeewoman, 1937-39, 1st v.p., 1936-37, chmn. woman's activities, 1936; Calif. chmn. circulation Nat. Young Dem. Paper, 1937; adv. bd. women's div. Calif. Dem. Central Com., 1936-38; organizer three young Dem. clubs in Stanislaus County, 1935; mem. Calif. Dem. Campaign Com., 1936; v.p. San Joaquin dist. Fed. Dem. Women's Study Clubs, 1940. Mem. San Joaquin Dist. Conv. Fedn. Women's Clubs (pub. chmn. 1935, legis. chmn. Stanislaus County 1934), Women's Improvement Club Modesto (Calif.; sec. 1933), Women's Progressive Club (charter Modesto, sec. 1933), Tres Artes (organizer 1935), Modesto Art League (charter), Martinez Grange, San Francisco Press Club (hon.), Patrons Art and Music San Francisco, DeYoung Mus. Art, U. Calif. Hosp. Aux., Mt. Zion Hosp. Aux., Nat. League Women's Service Calif., Women's City Club San Francisco, Berkeley Polit. Sci. Club, Irish-Israeli-Italian Soc., Toastmistress Club (charter Modesto), Walnut Creek Civic Arts League, Internat. Platform Assn., AIM (asso.), Town Hall Forum Los Angeles. Mem. Order Eastern Star. Club: City Commons (Berkeley). Office: PO Box 1023 Lafayette CA 94549

WALDRON, HICKS BENJAMIN, food and beverage co. exec.; b. Amsterdam, N.Y., Oct. 31, 1923; s. Hicks Benjamin and Dorothy S. (Clearwater) W.; B.S. in Mech. Engring., U. Minn., 1944; m. Evelyn L. Rumstay, May 8, 1976; children—Janet Waldron Ambrose, Hicks Benjamin, III (dec.). With Gen. Electric Co., 1946-73, v.p., 1970-71, group exec., 1971-73; pres., chief operating officer Heublein, Inc., Farmington, Conn., 1973—, also dir.; dir. Conn. Gen. Ins. Co., Conn. Bank & Trust Co. Bd. dirs. United Way, Hartford Hosp., Hartford Easter Seal Rehab. Center; pres. Jr. Achievement of N. Central Conn.; pres. Greater Hartford Arts Council; trustee Green Mountain Coll., Poultney, Vt., Hartford Grad. Center, Western New Eng. Coll. Served to ensign USNR, 1944-46. Mem. Greater Hartford C. of C. (dir.), Phi Gamma Delta. Episcopalian. Clubs: Hartford Golf; Farmington Country. Home: 88 Prattling Pond Rd Farmington CT 06032 Office: Heublein Inc. Munson Rd Farmington CT 06032

WALIA, BALBIR SINGH, ins. co. exec.; b. Lyallpur, India, July 1, 1945; came to U.S., 1969; s. Piara Singh and Gurcharan (Kaur) W.; B.S. with honors in Chem. Engring., India Inst. Tech., Kharagpur, 1968. Sales rep. Equitable Life Assurance Soc. U.S., N.Y.C., 1970-74, dist. mgr., 1974—. Recipient Disting. Performance Citation award in sales Equitable Life Assurance Soc. U.S., 1972, Nat. Citation award for mgmt., 1976. Mem. Sikh Cultural Soc. N.Y. Club: Matterhorn Sports (N.Y.C.). Office: 1633 Broadway 15th Floor New York NY 10019

WALINSKY, ADAM, lawyer; b. N.Y.C., Jan. 10, 1937; s. Louis J. and Michele (Benson) W.; A.B., Cornell U., 1957; LL.B., Yale U., 1961; m. Jane Rosenhirsch, Aug. 25, 1961; children—Peter Lee, Cara Anne. Admitted to N.Y. bar, 1962; law clk. U.S. Ct. Appeals, 2nd Circuit, New Haven, 1961-62; asso. firm Winthrop, Stimson, Putnam & Roberts, N.Y.C., 1962-63; with U.S. Dept. Justice, Washington, 1963-64; legis. asst. Robert F. Kennedy, 1964-68; partner Kronish, Lieb, Shainswit, Weiner & Hellman, N.Y.C., 1971—; chmn. N.Y. State Commn. of Investigation, 1979—; vis. lectr. SUNY, Stony Brook, 1971. Served with USMCR, 1958. Mem. Assn. Bar of City of N.Y., Lehrman Inst., Council on Fgn. Relations. Democrat. Jewish. Office: 1345 Ave of Americas New York NY 10019

WALKER, AUBREY MAX, telephone co. exec.; b. Hinton, W.Va., Apr. 25, 1922; s. Audrey Oakley and Nannie E. (Dobbins) W.; student U. Richmond, 1940-42; B.S. in Bus. Adminstrn., U. S.C., 1948; m. Patricia Koger, Sept. 2, 1954; children—Mark Koger, Susan Lynn, Terri Anne. Accountant, So. Bell Tel. & Tel. Co., Nashville, 1948-58, 63-65; with comptroller's dept. Am. Tel. & Tel. Co., N.Y.C., 1959-62, with regulatory dept., 1966-67; v.p., treas. So. Bell Tel. & Tel. Co., Atlanta, 1968—; chmn. bd. Hatteras Income Securities, Inc., Charlotte, N.C., 1973—; dir. Liquid Capital Income, Inc., Cleve., Blue Cross and Blue Shield Ga., Atlanta, Ga. Telco Credit Union, Atlanta; mem. nat. employee benefits and compensation com. Blue Cross/Blue Shield, Chgo. Active, United Way campaigns, Atlanta, 1977-79; trustee Atlanta Acad. and Inst. Reading; mem. pres.'s nat. adv. council U. S.C. Served to lt. USN, 1943-46. Mem. Fin. Execs. Inst., So. Pension Conf., Theta Chi. Baptist. Clubs: Capital City, Commerce, Stadium (all Atlanta). Home: 6215 Riverwood Dr N W Atlanta GA 30328 Office: PO Box 2211 Atlanta GA 30301

WALKER, BERNARD MELVIN, broadcasting co. exec.; b. Houston, Aug. 17, 1928; s. Julius Lloyd and Bernice Mary W.; B.S. in Tech. and Indsl. Edn., So. U., 1949; postgrad. in graphic arts Tex. So. U., 1951; postgrad. U. Md., Overseas, 1951-52; m. Sept. 15, 1956; children—Cindi Marie, Kelly Bernard, Fern Cecelia, David Bernard. Territorial rep. Carnation Co., Houston, 1953-60, sales promotion mgr., 1961-64, dir. personnel and indsl. relations, 1965-69; asst. gen. mgr. Sta. KYOK-AM, Houston, 1970-72, pres., gen. mgr., 1975-77, dir. mktg./mgmt. Starr Broadcasting Group Inc., parent co., New Orleans, 1973-74, v.p., 1975-77; v.p. broadcasting Shamrock Broadcasting Co., Hollywood, Calif., 1978—; cons. mktg. mgmt.; dir. Standard Savs. Assn., Houston. Bd. dirs. Manpower Adv. Planning Council, City of Houston, 1977—; trustee Tex. So. U. Found., 1977—; chmn. media com. Mayor's Full Count Com.-Census '80, 1979—. Served with U.S. Army, 1951-53; ETO. Mem. Houston Retail Grocers Assn., Houston C. of C., Houston Vis.'s and Conv. Bur., Savs. and Loan League, Am. Mgmt. Assn., Nat. Assn. Broadcasters (asso. chmn. census com. 1980), Nat. Radio Broadcasters Assn., Nat. Assn. Market Developers, Omega Psi Phi. Roman Catholic. Office: 3001 LaBranch St Houston TX 77004

WALKER, CHARLES HERBERT, JR., telephone co. exec.; b. Newark, Nov. 11, 1922; s. Charles Herbert and Helen (Rothacker) W.; student Rutgers U., 1974-75; m. Berenice Estelle Snellen, Dec. 11, 1952; children—Patricia Lee, W. Virginia. Apprentice painter, 1946-47; salesman Supreme Fuel Co. & Heating Equipment, Newark, 1948-49, Smith-Corona Typewriters, Newark, 1949-50; sales mgr. Scott & Fetzer, Orange, N.J., 1951-52; with N.J. Bell Telephone, Maplewood, N.J., 1953—, sales mgr., 1957-72, dist. mgr. local sales, 1972-77, dist. mgr. nat. sales, 1977—. Vice pres. Bus. and Residential Orgn. of Middletown (N.J.), 1971-72; co-chmn. Middletown Bicentennial Commn., 1975-76; mem. Bicentennial Park Commn., 1976-80; mem. Homeowners and Taxpayers Assn. of Middletown, 1975-76; mem. Democratic Com. Middletown, 1979-80. Served with USMC, 1943-46; PTO. Recipient Middletown VFW award, 1971; Bicentennial Commn. award Middletown Twp., 1976; Good Citizenship award Middletown Police Dept., 1977; Yellow Pages Sales Leadership award, 1977. Mem. VFW (public relations chmn. 1975, sr. vice comdr. of post 1976), Newark C. of C., Nat. Yellow Pages Service Assn., Mktg. Communications Execs. Internat., Futurist Soc., Nat. Geog. Soc. Democrat. Presbyterian. Clubs: N.J. Bell Pioneers, Sales Execs. of Newark, Advt. of No. N.J., Masons (past master, 32d degree), K.T. Home: 36 Harvey Ave Lincroft NJ 07738 Office: 50 Burnett Ave Maplewood NJ 07040

WALKER, CHARLES STEWART, fin. exec.; b. Calgary, Alta., May 16, 1936; s. Stewart and Rita (Ranger) W.; student U. Man., 1956; m. Beverley Hunter, Feb. 2, 1963; children—Shannon Michele, Scott Stewart. With Edmonton (Alta.) Jour., 1956-59; field rep. GMAC, Edmonton, 1959-63; sales mgr. FMCC, Edmonton and Vancouver, 1963-66; v.p. Seaboard Life Ins., Vancouver, 1966—; pres. Chuck Walker & Assos., Ltd., Vancouver, 1966—. Liberal Party. Roman Catholic. Clubs: Capilano Golf and Country, Terminal City, N. Shore Winter. Office: 1900 W Broadway Vancouver BC V6J 1Z2 Canada

WALKER, DALE RUSH, banker; b. High Point, N.C.; s. Raymon Lowe and Virginia (Rush) W.; B.S. in Math. cum laude, Wake Forest U., 1965; M.B.A., U. N.C., 1967; m. Maedell Goodson, Aug. 13, 1966; children—Ashley, Whitney. Asst. cashier Citibank, N.Y.C., 1967-70; with Union Bank, 1970—, asst. v.p., San Francisco, 1970-71, v.p., sr. loan officer, 1971-74, sr. v.p., 1974-75, regional v.p., No. Calif. Hdqrs. Banking Office, San Francisco, 1975-78, regional v.p. East Bay Regional Head Office, Oakland, Calif., 1978-80; sr. v.p. Wells Fargo Leasing Corp., San Francisco, 1980—. Bd. dirs. Pacific Vision Found., 1977-80. Mem. Robert Morris Assos. Democrat. Methodist. Club: University (v.p. 1979-80, dir. 1977-80). Home: 195 Vagabond Way Danville CA 94526 Office: 460 Hegenberger Rd Oakland CA 94621

WALKER, DANIEL CRAIG, motel exec.; b. N.Y.C., May 10, 1935; s. James G. and Anne L. (Craig) W.; B.S. in Hotel Adminstrn., Cornell U., 1957; m. Joan E. Comer, Nov. 19, 1960; children—Ellen, James, Daniel, Nancy, Anne. Asst. to pres. Food & Lodging Div., Holiday Inns, Inc., Memphis, 1971-74; gen. mgr. Hilton Inn, Logan Airport, Boston, 1974-75; pres. Inn Control Mgmt. Co., Greenwich, Conn., 1975-76; exec. v.p. Continental Corp. of Mich., Kalamazoo, 1976-78; gen. mgr. Helmsely-Spear, Inc., Newark, 1978—. Adv. bd. Taylor Bus. Inst., 1980-81. Served with USAF, 1957-63. Mem. Cornell Soc. Hotelmen, Iron-Bound Mfrs. Assn., Newark C. of C. N.J. Hotel-Motel State Assn. Republican. Roman Catholic. Clubs: Cornell of Central N.J., Rotary. Address: 600 Route 1 Newark NJ 07114

WALKER, DANIEL JOSHUA, JR., lawyer; b. Gibson, N.C., Nov. 27, 1915; s. Daniel Joshua and Annie (Hurdle) W.; A.B., U. N.C., 1936, J.D., 1948; m. Sarah Elizabeth Nicholson, June 14, 1941. Claim dept. Barnwell Bros. Trucking Co., Burlington, N.C., 1936-42; admitted to N.C. bar, 1948; clk. Superior Ct. Alamance County, Graham, N.C., 1948-53; partner Long, Ridge, Harris & Walker, Graham, 1953-67; sr. mem. firm Walker Harris, Graham, 1967-71; partner Allen, Allen, Walker & Washburn, Burlington, 1977—; county atty. Alamance County, Graham, 1964-77, county mgr., 1971-76; Mem. Human Relations Council, Alamance County, 1963-71, chmn., 1970. Pres., Alamance County Young Democratic Club, 1950; chmn. Alamance County Dem. Exec. Com., 1956-58; mem. N.C. Dem. Exec. Com., 1958-66. Trustee Tech. Inst. of Alamance, 1964-71; mem. N.C. Environ. Mgmt. Commn., 1972-77; bd. dirs. Alamance County United Fund, Cherokee council Boy Scouts Am., Community YMCA, Burlington; trustee Presbyn. Found., Presbyn. Ch. U.S., 1969-73, mem. exec. com. 1971-73; mem. council Orange Presbytery, 1972-74, moderator, 1980. Served with AUS, 1942-46. Decorated Bronze Star. Mem. Am. Judicature Soc., Alamance C. of C. (v.p. 1979, pres.-elect 1980), Am., N.C., Alamance County (pres. 1977-78) bar assns., N.C. Assn. County Attys. (v.p. 1971, pres. 1972 named county atty. of yr. 1971), Phi Alpha Delta. Democrat. Presbyn. (elder; trustee ch.). Kiwanian. Home: 215 Long Ave Graham NC 27253 Office: PO Box 29 Burlington NC 27215

WALKER, DOUGLAS MCDONALD, agrl. engr.; b. Edinburgh, Scotland, Feb. 4, 1928; s. James and Mary (Barton) W.; nat. diploma agr. Edinburgh Sch. Agr., 1947; m. Helen Grant Bell, Aug. 18, 1951; children—Morag McDonald, Ian Grant, Duncan Andrew. Lectr. farm machinery Lancashire Inst. Agr., 1949-51; lectr. agrl. engring. Shuttleworth Coll., Bedford, Eng., 1951-54; asst. export sales mgr. David Brown Tractors Ltd., Huddersfield, Eng., 1954-65; sales mgr. John Deere Ltd., Nottingham, 1965-68, mng. dir., Eng., 1968—. Mem. mktg. adv. com. Nat. Coll. Agrl. Engring., Eng., 1969—; mem. engring. advisory com. Nat. Inst. Agrl. Engring. Dep. pres. Motor and Cycle Trades Benevolent Fund. Freeman, City of London; liveryman Worshipful Co. Farmers. Mem. Instn. Agrl. Engrs., Nottingham C. of C. (council), Agrl. Engrs. Assn. (council mem. 1970—), Brit. Inst. Mgmt. Club: Farmers (London). Contbr. articles to profl. jours. Home: 17 Dovedale Rd West Bridgford Nottingham NG2 6JB England Office: Langar Nottingham NG 13 9HT England

WALKER, EVELYN, ret. ednl. TV exec.; b. Birmingham, Ala.; d. Preston Lucas and Mattie (Williams) W.; A.B., Huntingdon Coll., 1927, L.H.D., 1974; postgrad. Cornell U., 1927-29; spl. courses U. Ill., 1955; M.A., U. Ala., 1963. Speech instr. Phillips High Sch., Birmingham, 1930-34; head speech dept. Ramsay High Sch., Birmingham, 1934-52; chmn. radio and TV, Birmingham Pub. Schs., 1944-75, head instructional TV programming services, 1969-75; Miss Ann, broadcaster daily children's program WSGN Birmingham, 1946-57; producer Our Am. Heritage radio series, 1944-54; TV staff producer programs shown daily Ala. Pub. TV Network, 1954-76; cons. Gov.'s Ednl. TV Legislative Study Com., 1953; nat. del. Asian-Am. Women Broadcasters Conf., 1966; chmn. Creative TV-Radio Writing Competition. Mem. Nat. Def. Adv. Com. on Women in Services; TV-radio co-chmn. Gov.'s Adv. Bd. Safety Com.; TV chmn. Festival of Arts; audio-visual chmn. Ala. Congress, also Birmingham council P.T.A.; mem. Obelisk Awards Acad. of Jurors; media chmn. Gov.'s Commn. on Yr. of the Child; bd. dirs. Freedom Ednl. Found., Women's Army Corps Found. Recipient Alumnae Achievement award Huntingdon Coll., 1958; Tops in Our Town award Birmingham News, 1957; Air Force Recruiting plaque, 1961; Spl. Bowl award for promoting arts through Ednl. TV., 1962; citation 4th Army Corps., 1962; certificate appreciation Ala. Multiple Sclerosis Soc., 1962; Freedoms Found. Educator's medal award, 1963; Top TV award A.R.C., 1964; Ala. Women of Achievement award, 1964; Bronze plaque Ala. Dist. Exchange Clubs, 1969; certificate of appreciation Birmingham Bd. Edn., 1975; Obelisk award Children's Theatre, 1976; 20-Yr. Service award Ala. Ednl. TV Commn.; named Woman of Year, Birmingham, 1965; named Ala. Woman of Year, Progressive Farmer mag., 1966; Hon. col. Ala. Mem. Nat. Assn. Ret. Persons, Am. Women in Radio and TV (area trustee Ednl. Found. Bd., chpt. pres. 1959-60), Huntingdon Coll. Alumnae Assn. (former internat. pres.), Ala., Arlington (dir., pres. 1981—) hist. assns., Nat. Trust Hist. Preservation, Magna Charta Dames (past state sec.-treas.), D.A.R. (former pub. relations com. Ala., TV chmn., state program chmn. 1979—), Colonial Dames 17th Century, U.S. Daus. 1812 (past state TV chmn.), Daus. Am. Colonists (former 2d v.p. local chpt., state chmn. TV and radio), Arms. Royal Descent, Royal Order Garter, Plantagenets Soc. Am., Salvation Army Women's Aux., Symphony Aux., Humane Soc. Aux., Greater Birmingham Arts Alliance, Eagle Forum, Nat. League Am. Pen Women, Com. of 100 Women (dir.), Royal Order Crown, Women in Communications (past local pres., nat. headliner 1965), English Speaking Union, Birmingham-Jefferson Hist. Soc. (trustee), Internat. Platform Assn., Delta Delta Delta. Methodist. Clubs: Downtown, Birmingham Country, Press, The Club. Home: 744 Euclid Ave Mountain Brook Birmingham AL 35213

WALKER, FRED WILLIAM, mortgage banker; b. Detroit, Nov. 29, 1929; s. Russell W. and Elsie May (Handy) W.; student pub. schs., Detroit; m. Erma C. Bell, Jan. 29, 1969; children by previous marriage—Dona Sue, Barry Lee. Gen. mgr. M-M Driveway Service, 1950-54; owner Walker Driveway, 1954-55; real estate broker, Colorado Springs, Colo., 1958—; real estate appraiser condemnation, 1957—; gen. mgr. Central Mortgage & Investment Co., 1958-61, sec.

treas., 1961-64, exec. v.p., 1964-67, pres., 1967—; dir., 1958—; pres. Prairie Corp., 1976—, The Mortgage Center, Inc., 1980—. Instr. extension div. U. Colo., 1964-73. Rotarian. Home: 1425 E Hwy 105 Monument CO 80132 Office: 1569 Briargate Blvd Colorado Springs CO 80908

WALKER, HERBERT JOHN, data systems exec.; b. Winnipeg, Man., Can., Sept. 5, 1934; s. George Harry and Hilda (Denman) W.; came to U.S., 1967; student U. Man., 1952-53; m. Patricia Tustin, Sept. 10, 1955; children—Linda, Mark. Western regional systems mgr. Recognition Equipment Inc., San Francisco, 1969-71; project dir. Crocker Nat. Bank, San Francisco, 1971-73; dir. internat. mktg. Microform Data Systems, Mountain View, Calif., 1973-80; v.p. mktg. Boles & Co., Foster City, Calif., 1980—. Mem. Am. Soc. Machinery, Internat. Micrographic Congress, Mechanics Inst., Assn. Systems Mgmt. Club: Masons (asst. chmn. youth activities 1978, chmn. 1979). Home: 211 Colibri Ct San Jose CA 95119

WALKER, JAE LEROY, banker; b. St. George, Utah, Nov. 30, 1942; s. J. LeRoy and Aileen (Worthen) W.; student Utah State U., 1960-62; B.A. in Bus. Adminstrn., U. Utah, 1969; m. Kathleen Ann Pettit, July 9, 1965; children—Brent, Jason, Amy, John, Aaron. Br. mgmt. trainee Wells Fargo Bank, San Jose, Calif., 1969-70, credit officer, San Jose, 1970-72, loan officer, Oakland, Calif., 1972-74, asst. v.p., Los Angeles, 1974-77, v.p., 1977—, mgr. So. Calif. loan adjustment dept., El Monte, 1976—. Missionary, Ch. of Jesus Christ of Latter-day Saints, So. Germany, 1962-65. Mem. Am. Mgmt. Assn. Democrat. Office: 9000 E Flair Dr El Monte CA 91735

WALKER, JAMES LESTER, ins. and health services co. exec.; b. Pitts., June 28, 1935; s. John M. and Marie Irene (Gordon) W.; A.B., Princeton U., 1957; M.B.A., Harvard U., 1961; m. Nancy Belle Vincent, Aug. 6, 1960; children—James Lester, William Frederick. Investment analyst Mellon Bank, Pitts., 1957-59, 61-62; investment analyst White Weld & Co., Phila., 1962-64; comml. asst. First Pa. Bank, Phila., 1964-66; investment research mgr. Ins. Co. N. Am., Phila., 1966-69; mgr. Ins. Portfolios Group, I.N.A., Phila., 1969-72; asst. treas. corp. fin. INA Corp., Phila., 1972-75, v.p., treas., 1975-80, sr. v.p., chief fin. officer, 1980—, also chmn. fin. affairs and reserves coms.; dir. Phila. Investment Corp. Trustee, chmn. fin. com. Carmel Presbyterian Ch., Glenside, Pa. Mem. Fin. Analysts Phila., Phila. Treas. Club. Club: Union League Phila. Office: 1600 Arch St Philadelphia PA 19101

WALKER, JOHN BRYAN, investment analyst; b. Lubbock, Tex., Feb. 1, 1946; s. Daniel Bryan and Nora Lena (O'Connell) W.; B.B.A., Tex. Tech. U., Lubbock, 1968; M.B.A., N.Y. U., 1972; m. Nancy Elizabeth Hicks, Aug. 1, 1970; 1 son, Judson Bryan. Fin. analyst oil service industry Smith Barney Co., N.Y.C., 1972-75, Paine Webber Micthell Hutchins, N.Y.C., 1975—; pres. Walker Energy Co., 1979—. Served to lt. USNR, 1968-70; Vietnam. Decorated Letter of Commendation. Mem. Ind. Petroleum Assn. Am., Nat. Assn. Petroleum Investment Analysts, Oil Analysts Group N.Y., N.Y. Soc. Security Analysts, Fin. Analysts Fedn. Author energy industry reports. Office: 140 Broadway New York NY 10005

WALKER, JOHN BUCHANAN, corp. exec.; b. Balt., Apr. 10, 1938; s. John Frederick and Louise Snowdon (Buchanan) W.; B.A., Trinity Coll., Hartford, Conn., 1960; m. Anita MacMillen, Sept. 14, 1963 (div.); children—Wendy Snowdon, John Buchanan; m. 2d, Virginia Wendell, Nov. 26, 1977; stepchildren—Hilary Ellis Kline, Jenilee Kline. Trust adminstr. Bank of N.Y., N.Y.C., 1962-64; account mgr. Am. Bank Note Co., N.Y.C., 1964-67, 77—; account exec. Herold Kastor & Gerald, Inc., N.Y.C., 1967-69; mgr. investment counsel div. Value Line, N.Y.C., 1969-73; dir. pension fund investments Carrier Corp., Syracuse, N.Y., 1973-75; v.p. Nielson Instl. Services, Inc., N.Y.C., 1975-76; v.p. Brougham Cons., Ltd., N.Y.C., 1976. Served with USNG, 1961. Mem. Am. Mgmt. Assn., Psi Upsilon. Episcopalian. Club: Coral Beach and Tennis (Bermuda). Home: 16 Sycamore Hill Rd Bernardsville NJ 07924 Office: 70 Broad St New York City NY 10004

WALKER, LYNN, oil co. exec.; b. Port Arthur, Tex., Jan. 26, 1925; s. GroverC. and Lavanna M. (Lynn) W.; B.S., Baylor U., 1949; postgrad. U. Tex., 1949-50; m. Bettye Ruth Broussard, Aug. 27, 1948; children—Randal, Damon, Kevin. Engring. coordinator joint interest operations Creole Petroleum Corp., Caracas, Venezuela, 1950-56; with Felmont Oil Corp., N.Y.C., 1956—, pres., dir., 1972—; dir. Case, Pomeroy & Co., Inc., Case-Pomeroy Oil Corp., Essex Offshore, Inc., Monagas Oil Corp. Served with AUS, 1943-46; ETO. Decorated Purple Heart. Mem. Soc. Petroleum Engrs., AIME, Am. Assn. Petroleum Geologists, Am. Petroleum Inst., Ind. Petroleum Assn. Am., Assn. Ex-Mems. Squadron A, Inc. Republican. Office: 6 E 43d St New York NY 10017

WALKER, MAXINE CANFIELD (MRS. JORDAN C. WALKER), real estate developer; b. Boise, Idaho, June 29, 1933; d. Max M. and Alice Irene (Chamberlin) Armstrong; student Williamette U., 1950-51, Sacramento Jr. Coll., 1951-52; m. Jordan C. Walker, Aug. 4, 1967; children—Karen Joanne Walker Brown, Mark A. Canfield, Leslie Canfield. Real estate salesman MacBride Realty, Sacramento, 1961-63; propr., broker Canfield and Assos. Realtors, Sacramento, 1963-66; partner Canfield Hurst & Walker Realtors, Sacramento, 1966-67; propr., broker Canfield & Assos. Realtors, Sacramento, 1968—; pres. Jordan Devel. Co., 1976—. Mem. Calif. Real Estate Assn., Nat. Assn. Real Estate Bds., Sacramento Bd. Realtors. Home: 4330 Sierra Madre Dr Sacramento CA 95825 Office: Jordan Devel Co Inc 1721 Eastern Ave Suite 8 Sacramento CA 95825

WALKER, MAYNARD BARTRAM, dock co. exec.; b. Ashtabula, Ohio, Aug. 22, 1930; s. Wade Osborne and Beryl Louise (Bartram) W.; B.C.E., Ohio State U., 1954; m. Emily May Hartley, July 1, 1951; children—Rebecca Lee, Diana Lou, Valerie Lynn, Lisa Celeste. Laborer, Pinney Constrn. Co., Ashtabula, 1948-49; surveyor N.Y.C. R.R., Erie, Pa., 1950-51; successively foreman, supt., exec. v.p., dir., pres. Pinney Dock & Transport Co., Ashtabula, 1954; pres., dir. Ashtabula Stevedore Co., Tajon Transport Co.; dir. Farmers Nat. Bank. Mem. Great Lakes Terminal Operators Assn. (dir., past pres.), Nat., Ohio socs. profl. engrs. Republican. Methodist. Clubs: Ashtabula Country (past trustee); Sharon (Pa.) Golf; Cleve. Athletic, Elks. Home: 6426 Jefferson Rd Ashtabula OH 44004 Office: 1149 E 5th St Ashtabula OH 44004

WALKER, P(ERCIVAL) DUANE, hosp. mgmt. co. exec.; b. McKeesport, Pa., June 5, 1931; s. Percy Theodore and Bertha I. (Westerberg) W.; B.S., Pa. State U., 1953; M.B.A., N.Y. U., 1969; m. Doris Jane McClymont, Dec. 12, 1959; children—Jeannine Cherie, Andrea Lee, Edward Duane. Systems engr. IBM Corp., Pitts., 1955-58; cons. corporate controller's staff Westinghouse Elec. Co., Pitts., 1958-59; mgr. mgmt. adv. services Price Waterhouse & Co., Pitts., 1959-62; successively mgr. market analysis-programming systems, mgr. info. systems planning and arch., mgr. bus. systems planning IBM Corp., Poughkeepsie and White Plains, N.Y., 1962-74; sr. v.p. mgmt. systems Humana, Inc., Louisville, 1974—, also mem. mgmt. and compensation coms.; dir., chmn. compensation com. Kurfees Coatings, Inc., Louisville; lectr., speaker univs., nat. profl. soc. meetings. Pa. state v.p. Jaycees, 1957; chmn. Hire the Physically Handicapped, 1957, Fund for the Arts, Louisville, 1976; dir. Jr. Achievement; mem. athletic com. Ky. Country Day Sch.; mem. Louisville Schs. and Bus. Coordinating Council, 1979-80; mem. Leadership Louisville, 1979-80; com. vice chmn. Boy Scouts Am., 1981. Mem. Soc. Mgmt. Info. Systems, Am. Inst. Indsl. Engrs., Kappa Delta Rho. Presbyterian. Clubs: Penn State Alumni, Penn State of Ky., Nitanny Lions, Pitts. Playhouse, N.Y. U., Harmony Landing Country, Jefferson (Louisville). Home: 1309 N Buckeye Ln Goshen KY 40026 Office: PO Box 1438 Louisville KY 40201

WALKER, ROBERT CHARLES, arts mgmt. exec.; b. Alameda, Calif., Oct. 29, 1944; s. Robert and Charlotte (McKinster) W.; B.A., U. Calif., Berkeley, 1966; M.B.A., UCLA, 1973; M.A., San Francisco State U., 1967; m. Diana Kehrig, Oct. 26, 1974; 1 dau., Kira Rose. Fin. adminstr. N.Y.C. Opera, Lincoln Center, 1973-77; mgr. San Francisco Opera Assn., 1977—. Trustee Am. Guild Mus. Artists Pension and Welfare Fund, 1975-77, Internat. Alliance Theatrical Stage Employees Pension and Welfare Fund; bd. dirs. Opera America, 1975-77. Served with USN, 1967-71. Nat. Opera Inst. fellow, 1973. Mem. Am. Mgmt. Assn., Opera America. Christian Scientist. Office: War Memorial Opera House San Francisco CA 94102

WALKER, ROBERT EDWARD, audio visual co. exec.; b. Waxahachie, Tex., Apr. 17, 1951; s. William Campbell and Frances Utley W.; B.B.A., Tex. Christian U., 1973; m. Caryn Jane Henderson, Apr. 10, 1976; 1 son, Christopher Robert. Sales exec. Sta. KXOL, 1973-74; account exec. Sta. WFAA, Dallas, 1974-76; nat. sales mgr. AVW Audio Visual, Dallas, 1976-80, v.p. prodn. services, 1980—. Mem. Dallas Advt. League, Lambda Chi Alpha. Republican. Office: 2241 Irving Dallas TX 75207

WALKER, ROBERT GERALD, diversified corp. exec.; b. Austin, Tex., Feb. 25, 1925; s. Robert Gerald and Bess Woodrin (Patterson) W.; B.B.A., U. Tex., 1950; m. Pauline Burleson, Feb. 11, 1949; children—Keith, Mark, Susan, Wayne, Sally. Mfg. mgr. R.H. Folmar Bldg. Products Co., Austin, 1950-55; prodn. control mgr. Waste King Corp., Los Angeles, 1955-56, 56-59, mfg. services mgr., 1956-59, mgr. mfg., Chgo., 1959-60; mgr. mfg. Digital Computer div. Litton Industries Inc., Los Angeles, 1960-63, gen. mgr., Lubbock, Tex., 1963-64, mgr. Econ. Devel. Corp. div., Beverly Hills, Calif., 1964-65, gen. mgr. Atherton div., Mpls., 1965-67; v.p. Allis-Chalmers Mfg. Co., Milw., 1967-72; pres., chmn. bd. Kin-Ark Corp., Tulsa, 1972—, also dir.; dir. Boyles Galvanizing Corp., Ft. Worth, Camelot Inns of Am. Mayor, city councilman, LaMirada, Calif., 1959-60. Served with USAAF, 1943-46, 50-51. Home: 3855 S Birmingham Pl Tulsa OK 74105 Office: 7060 S Yale Ave Tulsa OK 74177

WALKER, RONALD FREDERICK, ins. co. exec.; b. Cin., Apr. 9, 1938; B.B.A., U. Cin., 1961; married. Trainee in fin. Hobart Mfg. Co., 1961-62; v.p. fin. Kroger Co., 1962-72; v.p., dir. Am. Fin. Corp., 1973—; from exec. v.p. to pres. Gt. Am. Ins. Co., 1973—, also dir.; pres., dir. Am. Nat. Fire Ins.; exec. v.p. Gt. Am. Life Ins. Co.; exec. v.p., dir. Republic Indemnity Co.; dir. Stone Wall Ins. Co. Office: 580 Walnut St Cincinnati OH 45202*

WALKER, THOMAS CHARLES, business exec.; b. Trenton, N.J., Jan. 19, 1933; s. Thomas Charles and Anne Marie (Reagan) W.; B.S. in Indsl. Engring., Lafayette Coll., 1954; m. Carolyn Francis Wolff, Apr. 13, 1957; children—Thomas Charles, Joseph Fredrick. With Gen. Electric Co., 1954, 59, Tex. Instruments Inc., 1959-66; pres. Superior Curciuits, Inc., Dallas, 1966-68; chmn. bd. dirs., chief exec. officer Intermed Corp., Dallas, 1968-71; pres. Waste Resources Inc., Phila., 1971-72; v.p. Browning Ferris Industries, Inc., Houston, 1972-76, Criterion Capital Corp., Houston, 1976-77; dir. new ventures Rockwell Internat., Dallas, 1977-79; pres. Thomas C. Walker Assos., Dallas, 1979—. Served to lt. USNR, 1955-59. Mem. NAM. Republican. Roman Catholic. Clubs: Dallas Country, Dallas City, T Bar M Tennis. Home: 4353 Edmondson Ave Dallas TX 75205 Office: 3626 N Hall St Dallas TX 75219

WALKER, THOMAS DAVID, bus. services co. exec.; b. Memphis, Apr. 25, 1942; s. Joseph H. and Ruth (Cooprider) W.; B.A., Tex. Christian U., 1965, M.A., 1967; postgrad. U. London, 1971; m. Danielle Medina Rome; 2 children. Surety assurance account exec. Traveller's Ins. Co., 1969-70; asst. dean Schiller Coll., Paris, 1970-72; edn. dir. Alliance for Franco-Am. Grad. Studies, N.Y.C., 1972-73; tng. coordinator Chase Manhattan Bank, Paris, 1973-77; dir. program adminstrn. Systran Corp., Chgo., 1977-79, dir. proposals, 1979-80, dir. internat. projects, 1980—; prof. English, U. Paris, 1968-69, Coll. des Sciences Sociales et Economiques, Paris, 1974-75, L'Ecole Superieure d'Electricite, Gif-sur-Yvette, France, 1974-76. Institut Francais du Petrole, 1975-76, L'Institut National des Sciences Politiques, Paris, 1976-77. Mem. Nat. Assn. Fgn. Student Affairs, Am. Soc. Tng. and Devel., Phi Alpha Theta. Home: 719 Washington St Wilmette IL 60091 Office: 70 W Hubbard St Chicago IL 60610

WALKER, WELMON (RUSTY), JR., publisher; b. Chgo., Dec. 28, 1947; s. Welmon and Mary Ann (Brefford) W.; student U. Alaska, 1970-74, Tanana Valley Community Coll., 1975; m. Nedra K. Carlson, Dec. 30, 1972; 1 son, Welmon III. Coordinator, Future Classics Program Sta. KUAC-FM, U. Alaska, Fairbanks, 1971, founding gen. mgr. Sta. KMPS, 1971-74, duty dir. Sta. KUAC-TV, 1973-74; chmn., pres., dir. NW Horizons, Inc., Fairbanks, 1973-78; head, photo dept., Sta. KFAR-TV, Fairbanks, 1974-75; instr. TV prodn., Fairbanks Native Assn., 1975-76; treas., bus. mgr. Nat. Painting Corp., Fairbanks, 1976; founder, owner, W. Walker Enterprises, Fairbanks, 1975-79; chmn. pres. That New Publishing Co., 1978—; instr. Tanana Valley Community Coll., 1978, 79, 80; dir. Alaska Coll. Students, 1973—, Minds Eye Inc., 1976-78; nat. sales mgr. Intercollegiate Broadcasting System, 1975. Bd. dirs. Fairbanks Crisis Clinic Found., 1975-77; v.p. Midnight Sun council Boy Scouts Am., 1977-80; statewide rep., Univ. Assembly, Alaska, 1972, 73, 74. Mem. Inst. Certified Photographers. Baptist. Author: Alaska Corporation Manual, 1977, 2d edit., 1979. Office: 1525 Eielson St Fairbanks AK 99701

WALKER, WILLIAM HARWOOD, II, instrumentation service co. exec.; b. Montreal, Que., Can., July 19, 1944; s. William Hawrood and Violet Muriel (Feeney) W.; Chartered Acct., McGill U., 1967; m. Anita Mae Frenca, Dec. 30, 1968; children—William Hamilton Harwood, Richard Lloyd. Prof. acctg. McGill U., 1970-78; partner Thorne Riddell & Co., Montreal, 1975-77; v.p. fin., treas. Walsh Process Control Ltd., Montreal, 1977-79, exec. v.p., 1980—, also dir.; dir. Walsh Instrumentation, Ross A Graham Co. Ltd.; Mem. Inst. Chartered Accts. Que. Club: Beaconsfield Golf. Home: 44 Waverley Rd Pointe Claire PQ H9S 4W5 Canada Office: 4999 Saint Catherine St W Suite 305 Montreal PQ H3Z 1T3 Canada

WALKUP, WILLIAM EDMONDSON, business exec.; b. Nashville, May 31, 1918; s. John Pegram and Marion (Edmondson) W.; student U. Calif. at Los Angeles, 1936-38; m. Dorothy Elizabeth Sanborn, Sept. 2, 1939; children—William Sanborn, Marion Elena, Frank Sanborn. With Signal Oil & Gas Co., Los Angeles, 1939—, dir. finance dept., 1955—, group v.p. staff, 1962-64, sr. exec. v.p., 1964-68; vice chmn. bd., exec. v.p. Signal Cos., Inc., 1968-69, chmn. bd., exec. v.p., 1969-80 chmn. exec. com., 1980—. Clubs: Los Angeles Country; California. Office: 9665 Wilshire Blvd Beverly Hills CA 90212

WALL, JAMES CURTIS, bank exec.; b. Los Angeles, Mar. 31, 1945; s. Charles J. and Myrtle (Lynch) W.; B.A. in English, Stanford U., 1967; M.A. in English, Calif. State U., San Diego, 1969; m. Anne Fuller, July 8, 1967; children—Christopher, Matthew. Vice pres. Wells Fargo Bank, N.A., 1969-80; pres. Univ. Nat. Bank & Trust Co., Palo Alto, Calif., 1980—. Club: Los Altos Golf and Country. Office: 361 Lytton Ave Palo Alto CA 94301

WALL, NORBERT FRANK, real estate cons. co. exec.; b. Chgo., Sept. 29, 1934; s. Frank M. and Rose (Cepa) Wolsztyniak; A.A., Chgo. City Coll., 1958; B.S., Roosevelt U., 1963; m. Rita Blaze, June 16, 1956; children—James, Amanda. Sr. v.p. Real Estate Research Corp., Washington, 1969-74; pres. Am. Realty Consultants, Chgo., 1974-75, Larry Smith and Co., Chgo., 1975-78, Am. Realty Consultants Ltd., Chgo., 1978—, EVP Clayton Towers Devel. Co.; dir. Unico, Cairo, Namesa, Paris, Glasser/Am. Co., Larry Smith & Co. Ltd., others; host syndicated radio show Norb Wall's Real Estate Corner. Served with USNR, 1952-54. Mem. Internat. Soc. Real Estate Appraisers (sr. real estate appraiser), Am. Inst. Real Estate Appraisers (v.p.), Nat. Assn. Corporate Real Estate Execs. (founding), Urban Land Inst. (sustaining). Roman Catholic. Author: Real Estate Investment by Objective, 1979. Contbr. articles to profl. publs. real estate. Home: 261 Steeplechase Rd Barrington Hill IL 60010 Office: 120 Lageshulte St Barrington IL 60010

WALL, STEPHEN JAMES, organizational psychologist; b. Wallasy, Gt. Brit., Aug. 25, 1947; came to U.S., 1955, naturalized, 1966; s. John and Margaret M. (Dixon) W.; B.A., SUNY, 1969; M.A. in Psychology, U. Akron, 1971; M.A. in Indsl./Organizational Psychology, N.Y. U., 1980; m. Margaret Mary King, Aug. 26, 1978; 1 dau., Alissa Gabrielle. Cons., Human Resources Lab., Am. Tel. & Tel., N.Y.C., 1972-73, personnel supr., mgmt. selection and devel. research, 1973-75; profl. devel. asso. Union Carbide Corp., N.Y.C., 1975-76, mgr. profl. devel., 1976-77, dir. corp. mgmt. devel., 1977—. Contbr. articles to profl. jours. Home: 100 Hope St Unit 48 Stamford CT 06906 Office: 270 Park Ave New York NY 10017

WALLACE, ANDREW CHARLES, mktg. and distbn. co. exec.; b. Lexington, Ky., Apr. 30, 1934; s. Andrew Conroy and Bertha Elisabeth (Peoples) W.; B.S., U. Ky., 1966, M.A., 1967; postgrad. U. Iowa, 1967-69; m. Anita Louise Wylds, July 29, 1960; children—Diane, Andrea. Nat. sales mgr. Lite Vent Industries, Oak Park, Mich., 1960-64; v.p. sales Banner Metal Products Co., Taylor, Mich., 1964-65; instr. mktg. U. Iowa, Iowa City, 1967-69; asst. prof. mktg. U. S. Fla., Tampa, 1969-75; pres. Mktg. Systems & Distbn., Inc., Tampa, 1975—; cons. and speaker, various nat. trade assns. Served with USAF, 1953-57. Recipient nat. editorial award Am. Soc. Personnel Adminstrs., 1971; named 1 of top 10 tchrs. U. S.Fla., 1975. Mem. Sales and Mktg. Execs. Internat. (dir. Tampa 1973). Home: Route 1 Box 42A Tampa FL 33618 Office: Mktg Systems & Distbn Inc 16310 Shagbark Pl Tampa FL 33618

WALLACE, ARNOLD DELANEY, univ. adminstr.; b. Salisbury, Md., Feb. 1, 1932; s. George Linwood and Margaret Elizabeth (Townsend) W.; B.A., Howard U., 1952; B.S. magna cum laude, Rutgers U., 1977, postgrad., 1977—; m. Theresa Fredericks Brooks, Sept. 27, 1950; children—Deborah, Terry, Arnold, Michael, Stephen, Stephanie. Communications engr. WCAU-TV, Phila., 1963-72, dir. pub. affairs, 1972-79; dir. univ. relations Howard U., Washington, 1979-80, gen. mgr. Sta. WHMM-TV, Howard U., 1980—; adj. prof. adminstrv. studies Rutgers U., 1978-79. Mem. Pennsauken (N.J.) Bd. Edn., 1971—, v.p., 1973-75, pres., 1975-76; bd. dirs. N.J. Com. for the Humanities, Phila. Mayor's Drug and Alcohol Commn., Phila. Urban League; Coadj. mktg. and pub. relations Rutgers U. trustee Merabash Mus. Black History, New Egypt, N.J., also bd. dirs. Recipient award Phila. Human Relations Commn., 1976, Negro Trade Union Leadership Council, 1976, nat. award Juvenile Diabetes Found., 1978. Mem. N.J. Sch. Bds. Assn. (ednl. fin. com.), Negro Airmen Internat. (internat. publicity chmn. 1969—), Aircraft Owners and Pilots Assn., World Affairs Council, TV and Radio Advt. Club, Corp. Social Responsibility Assn. Delaware Valley. Mem. A.M.E. Ch. (vice chmn. bd. trustees). Clubs: Masons, Shriners, Kiwanis, Willingboro Country. Producer, dir. documentary film Journey to Paradise-Barbados; exec. producer documentary film 2000 and Beyond; contbr. to Rutgers U. Lit. Mag. Home: 802 DeVere Dr Silver Spring MD 20903 Office: Howard U 2400 6th St NW Washington DC 20001

WALLACE, DAVID OLIVER, grocery distbn. co. exec.; b. Portland, Oreg., Mar. 19, 1938; s. Dean Leslie and Adelaide Ellen (Oliver) W.; B.A. in Econs., Western Wash. U., 1966; grad. Northwestern U. Transp. Center, 1967; m. Donna Rae Brunett, Sept. 3, 1961; children—Jeffrey John, Julie Suzanne. Market research analyst mktg. dept. Gt. No. Ry., St. Paul, 1966-70; dir. personnel Western Farmers Co., Seattle, 1970; income tax cons., G. J. Isaccson, Lynnwood, Wash., 1970-73; wholesale and retail salesman dairy div. Foremost-McKesson Co., Seattle, 1971-73; key account area salesman Purex Corp., Spokane, 1973-75; dir. advt. U.R.M. Stores, Inc., Spokane, 1975-78, cons. store devel. dept., 1978—; owner, operator Sign Design, advt. co. Bd. dirs. Nat. Jr. Ski-Nordic, St. Paul, 1969; vice chmn. Spokane Sch. Dist. 81 Citizen Adv. Council, 1976-78, chmn., 1978-80; mem. exec. com. Western Art Show, Museum Native Am. Cultures, Spokane, 1978-79. Served with U.S. Army, 1959-61. Clubs: The Spokane, Eagles (Spokane); Toastmasters (exec. v.p. club); Elks (Bellevue, Wash.). Home: W 448 25th St Spokane WA 99203 Office: 7511 N Freya St Spokane WA 99220

WALLACE, JAMES ALFONSO, educator; b. Clearwater, Fla., Oct. 11, 1948; s. Willie James and Ernestine Marion (Hamm) W.; B.A. in Bus. Adminstrn., Bethune-Cookman Coll., 1970; M.B.A. in Acctg. and Fin. (Gen. Foods fellow), So. Meth. U., 1971; m. Joyce Ann Battles, Apr. 13, 1979; children—Dwanetta, Kenneth. Field specialist Opportunities Industrialization Centers Am., Dallas, 1971-74, sr. field specialist, 1974-75, project officer, 1975-76; exec. dir. Oklahoma County Opportunities Industrialization Center, Inc., Oklahoma City, 1976—. Bd. dirs. Oklahoma City N.E., Inc., 1978—, 1st vice chmn., 1979—; bd. dirs. NAACP, Urban League Oklahoma City; mem. Last Frontier council Boy Scouts Am. Mem. Assn. M.B.A. Execs. (charter), Exec. Dirs. Assn. Opportunities Industrazlization Centers Am. (treas. 1979—), Oklahoma City C. of C., Alpha Phi Omega, Alpha Phi Alpha. Club: Rotary. Office: 400 N Walnut St Oklahoma City OK 73104

WALLACE, JAMES EDWARD, paint mfg. co. exec.; b. Cleve., Apr. 18, 1933; s. Joseph P. and Margaret C. (Black) W.; A.B., Kenyon Coll., 1955; student advanced mgmt. program Case Western Grad. Sch. Mgmt., 1973; m. June C. Kysela, Feb. 5, 1955; children—Thomas E., John P., Catherine M., Carolyn A., James J., William C. Mgr., gen. cost dept. Sherwin-Williams Co., Cleve., 1969-70, group controller chems., 1970-73, group controller coatings, 1973-75, asst. to sr. v.p., 1975, v.p. adminstrn., 1975-79, v.p., corp. controller, 1979—. Served with USN, 1955-58. Mem. Fin. Execs. Inst., Case Western Reserve U. Sch. Mgmt. Alumni (dir.). Republican. Roman Catholic. Club: Cleve. Athletic. Office: 101 Prospect Ave NW Cleveland OH 44115

WALLACE, JAMES THOMAS, automobile mfg. co. exec.; b. Astoria, Oreg., Oct. 30, 1939; s. James Clinton and Martha Sylvia (Sarpola) W.; A.B., Whitman Coll., 1960; M.B.A., U. Calif., Berkeley,

1962; m. Sonja May Ronn-Johannessen, Aug. 13, 1977; children—Clinton, Scott, Aniki, Chelsia. With Ford div. Ford Motor Co., 1962-74, zone mgr., distbn. mgr., car merchandising mgr., bus. mgmt. mgr., San Jose, Calif., 1963-71, met. market mgr. Los Angeles Dist. Sales Office, 1971-74; gen. sales mgr. Vista Ford, Woodland Hills, Calif., 1974-76; v.p., gen. mgr. Cortese Ford, Richmond, Calif., 1976-77, also dir.; v.p. ops. Irontree Mgmt. Co., Palm Desert, Calif., 1977-80, also dir.; v.p. sales and mktg. Clenet Coachworks, Inc., Santa Barbara, Calif., 1980—. Pres., bd. dirs. Ironwood Owners Assn., 1974-78; bd. overseers Whitman Coll., Walla Walla, Wash., 1972-75. Mem. Community Assn. Inst., Whitman Coll. Alumni Assn. (pres., dir. 1968-75). Club: Ironwood Country. Home: 72-749 Haystack Rd Palm Desert CA 92260

WALLACE, JOHN FREDERICK, III, bond broker; b. Bklyn., Jan. 20, 1954; s. John Frederick and Loretto Therese W.; A.B. in Polit. Sci., Fordham U., 1976; m. Brenda Donelan Wallace, Dec. 30, 1978. Congressional asst. U.S. Ho. of Reps., 1972-77; prin. S.B. Cantor Co., Inc., N.Y.C., 1977-78; mcpl. bond broker Brean Murray, Foster Securities, Inc., N.Y.C., 1978—; founder, chmn. bd. Wall St. Workshops Found., Inc., N.Y.C., 1979—. Bd. dirs. Washington Workshops Congressional Found., Inc.; mem. legis. adv. com. N.Y. State Assembly; mem. Nassau County (N.Y.) Republican Com. Recipient Congressional Medal of Merit, 1972; named to Outstanding Young Men Am., U.S. Jaycees, 1977. Mem. N.Y. Mcpl. Bond Assn., Eagle Scout Assn. Clubs: N.Y. Athletic, Westchester Country. Office: 90 Broad St New York NY 10004

WALLACE, JOSEPH E., travellers checks co. exec.; b. Chgo., Sept. 14, 1932; s. Edward M. and Zeta M. (O'Donnell) W.; B.S.C., Loyola U., Chgo., 1955; student U. Chgo., 1961-65. Dist. mgr. Bell & Howell Co., Lincolnwood, Ill., 1959-61; partner Drexel Harriman Ripley Inc., Chgo., 1964-70; pres. Original Devel. Corp., Chgo., 1970-75, Internat. Travelers Cheque Co., Chgo., 1974—; v.p. W.T. Grimm & Co., Chgo., 1975-78. Served to 2d lt. U.S. Army, 1955-57. Mem. Assn. for Corp. Growth, Bond Club Chgo. Republican. Roman Catholic. Clubs: Metropolitan, Snowchase.

WALLACE, KENNETH ALAN, real estate devel. exec., rancher; b. Gallup, N.Mex., Feb. 23, 1938; s. Charles Garrett and Elizabeth Eleanor (Jones) W.; A.B. in Philosophy, Cornell U., 1960; postgrad. U. N.Mex., 1960-61; m. Rebecca Marie Odell; children—Andrew McMillan, Aaron Blue, Susanna Garrett. Comml. loan officer Bank of N.Mex., Albuquerque, 1961-64; asst. cashier Ariz. Bank, Phoenix, 1964-67; comml. loan officer Valley Nat. Bank, Phoenix, 1967-70; pres. WWW, Inc., Houston, 1970-72; v.p. fin. Hometels of Am., Phoenix, 1972-77, Precision Mech. Co., Inc., 1972-77; partner Schroeder-Wallace Co., Phoenix, 1977—, Pala Partners, San Diego, Wallace Enterprises, Mobile, Ala., Sommer-Wallace, Johannesburg, S. Africa; v.p., dir. Roosevelt Royale, Inc., Cedar Rapids; dir. Schroeder Constrn. Co., Inc., Phoenix; v.p., dir. C.G. Wallace Co., Albuquerque, Diamond W Ranch, Sanders, Ariz. Loaned exec. Phoenix United Way, 1966, Tucson United Way, 1967; big brother Valley Big Brothers, 1970—; fin. dir. Ret. Sr. Vol. Program, 1973—; mem. Phoenix Men's Arts Council, 1974—. Campaign committeeman Republican Gubernatorial Race, N.Mex., 1964; treas. Phoenix Young Republicans, 1966. Bd. dirs. Devel. Authority for Tucson, 1967. Mem. Soaring Soc. Am. (Silver badge), Am. Rifle Assn. (life), Nat. Mktg. Assn. (Mktg. Performance of Year award 1966), Nat. Assn. Skin Diving Schs., Pima County Jr. C. of C., (dir. 1967), Phoenix Little Theatre, Phoenix Musical Theatre, S.W. Ensemble Theatre (dir.), Men's Symphony Council, Alpha Tau Omega. Clubs: Univ., Plaza (Phoenix), Masons, Shriners. Home: 409 E Keim Dr Phoenix AZ 85012 Office: 3606 N 24th St Phoenix AZ 85016

WALLACE, LARRY WILLARD, lumber co. exec.; b. Reston, Man., Can., Mar. 29, 1943; s. Lloyd Oliver and Dorothy May (Henden) W.; m. Olive Ann Elliott, June 1, 1963; children—Michele Arlene, Sean Gordon, Colleen Nicole, Kent Elliott. Mgmt. trainee Monarch Lumber Co. Ltd., Elrose, Sask., Can., 1963-64; asst. mgr. Revelstoke Bldg. Materials Ltd., Rosetown, Sask., 1964-65, mgr., Watrous, Sask., 1965-67, Portage Laprairie, Man., 1967-72; mgr. Revelstoke Cos. Ltd., The Pas, Man., 1973-75, Brandon, Man., 1975-76; pres. Yellowhead Bldg Supplies Ltd., Langenburg, Sask., 1976—. Mem. Langenburg C. of C., Western Retail Lumbermen's Assn., Mchts. Consol. Ltd. Home: 304 March Ave Langenburg SK S0A 2A0 Canada Office: 335 Kaiser William Ave Langenburg SK S0A 2A0 Canada

WALLACE, ROBERT GLENN, petroleum co. exec.; b. Webb City, Okla., Oct. 8, 1926; s. Glenn McKinsey and Sarah Elizabeth W.; B.S. Ch.E., Tex. A&M U., 1950; A.M.P., Harvard U./U. Hawaii, 1972; m. Kelmor Teichman, Oct. 9, 1954; 1 son, John. Mgr. internat. sales and devel. Phillips Petroleum Co., Bartlesville, Okla., 1970-71, v.p. plastics, 1974-78, sr. v.p., 1978-80, exec. v.p., 1980—; pres. Sealright Co., Inc., Kansas City, Mo., 1972-73; dir. Applied Automation Inc., Pier 66 Corp., Acurex Corp., Phillips P.R. Core, Inc., Phillips-Imperial Petroleum Ltd., Petrochim, Papago Chems., Am. Fertilizer & Chem. Co., Phillips Pacific Chem. Co. Mem. council Tex. A&M U. Coll. Bus. Adminstrn. Served with USN, 1944-46. Registered profl. engr., Okla. Republican. Office: Phillips Bldg 18th Floor Bartlesville OK 74004

WALLACE, THOMAS EDGAR, JR., elec. utility mgr.; b. Latrobe, Pa., Sept. 20, 1942; s. Thomas Edgar and Lucille Elva (Sweitzer) W.; B.S.E.E., U. Pitts., 1967, M.S. in Indsl. Engring., 1980; m. Jennifer Elaine Nichols, Oct. 15, 1966; 1 son, Timothy William. Successively cadet engr., constrn. engr., plant engr. West Penn Power Co., Greensburg, Pa., 1966-70; power engr. Allegheny Power Service Corp., Greensburg, 1970-73, sr. power engr., 1973-78, mgr. start up and quality assurance, 1978—. Registered profl. engr., Pa., W.Va., Md. Republican. Methodist. Office: 800 Cabin Hill Dr Greensburg PA 15601

WALLACE, THOMAS PECKHAM, banker; b. Cranston, R.I., Apr. 8, 1926; s. Andrew and Margaret Marian (Peckham) W.; B.S. in Bus. Adminstrn., Bryant Coll., 1949; Grad. Certificate in Comml. Banking, Am. Inst. Banking, 1960. With Citizens Trust Co./Citizens Savs. Bank, 1949—, mgr., 1958-65, asst. treas., 1965-70, asst. v.p., 1970—. Asst. dist. commr. Narragansett council Boy Scouts Am., 1950-55, mem. air scout squadron com., 1948-58, scoutmaster, 1952-58, mem. dist. com., 1950-62. Served with USAAF, 1944-46, 50. Mem. Am. Inst. Banking (pres. Providence chpt. 1972-73), R.I. Hist. Soc., Soc. Mayflower Descs., Air Force Assn. Republican. Congregationalist. Club: Lions. Home: 226 Beckwith St Cranston RI 02910 Office: 1086 Willett Ave Riverside RI 02915

WALLACE, WILLIAM FARRIER, JR., lawyer, banker; b. Dallas, Apr. 2, 1918; s. William Farrier and Mary Ethel (Pope) W.; student U. Tex., 1935-41; m. Ruth Saunders, Aug. 2, 1956. Admitted to Tex. bar, 1941; practiced in Corpus Christi, 1941, 44—; chmn. bd. Hondo (Tex.) Nat. Bank, 1964—, 1st State Bank, Bishop, Tex., 1964—; pres. Wondob Corp., Corpus Christi, 1965—. Founder, chmn. Exec. Audial Rehab. Soc., 1966—. Served to 2d lt. AUS, 1942-44. Named Handicapped Texan of Yr., 1961; recipient Pres.'s citation for aid to handicapped, 1961. Mem. Tex. Bar Assn., Tex. Bankers Assn., Ind. Bankers Assn. Tex., Tex. Assn. Bank Counsel (charter), S.W. Legal Found. (founding mem.), Oil and Gas Inst. (founding mem.), Corpus Christi C. of C. Episcopalian. Clubs: Corpus Christi Town, Corpus Christi Country, Rotary (Corpus Christi); Nueces; Dallas Petroleum. Office: 500 Guaranty Bank Plaza Corpus Christi TX 78403

WALLACE, WILLIAM HENRY, bus. systems co. exec.; b. Washington, N.C., Oct. 4, 1942; s. William Henry and Hilda Mae (Braddy) W.; B.A. in Bus., E. Carolina U., 1965; m. Roberta Ann Eason, July 4, 1965. Mgr. zone sales Burroughs Corp., Chgo., 1965-72; sales mgr. Philips Bus. Systems, Inc., Chgo., 1972-73; gen. mgr. Safeguard Bus. Systems, Dallas, 1973-80; dir. franchising MicroAge Computer Stores, Tempe, Ariz., 1980—. Mem. EDP Mgrs. Assn. Episcopalian. Home: Route 2 Box 301A McKinney TX 75069

WALLACE, WILLIAM KEITH, restauranteur; b. Montreal, Que., Can., Feb. 11, 1932; s. W.H. and Elcy (Harrison) W.; B.A., St. Lawrence U., Canton, N.Y., 1955; advanced mgt. course Exec. Devel. Inst., Montreal; 1959; m. Marjorie Conkling, Apr. 7, 1956; children—William, Kimberly, Kathleen. Vending machine salesman Seven-Up Montreal Ltd., 1955-59, mgr. vendor dept., 1959-61, asst. gen. mgr., 1961-64, pres., 1964-80; owner; pres. Golden Griddle Pancake House; Mississauga; Ont., Can., 1980—. Bd. dirs. Zeller Osteo. Clinic, Canadian Osteo. Assn., Council for Canadian Unity Mem. Young Pres.'s Orgn., Mem. United Church Can. (past pres. men's club, past dir. Dorval United Ch., Mount Royal United Ch.). Clubs: Kiwanis of Toronto (past pres. Montreal Club), Mississauga Golf and Country. Home: 2375 Mississauga Rd N Mississauga ON L5H 2L3 Canada Office: Golden Griddle Pancake House 2155 Leanne Blvd Mississauga ON L5K 2K8 Canada

WALLACH, NEAL LLOYD, retail co. mgr., acct.; b. Bronx, N.Y., Nov. 1, 1947; s. Lawrence and Lena W.; student Harvard U., summers 1965-68; B.A. cum laude, Boston U., 1969; M.B.A. in Fin. and Acctg., U. Houston, 1977; student S. Tex. Coll. Law; 1 dau. by previous marriage, Jacqueline Beth. With Foley's div. Federated Dept. Stores, Houston, 1970—, corp. expense cons., 1974, selling supt. Downtown Store, 1975, dir. corp. compensation, 1975-76, mgr. human resources info., 1976-78, mgr. internal audit, 1979—; acctg. instr. Houston Community Coll., U. Houston; chmn. bd. Foley's Asso. Credit Union. Mem. budget allocation com. United Way, employee chmn. Foley's, 1976-78. Served with USAR, 1969-75. C.P.A., Tex.; cert. mgmt. acct. Mem. Nat. Assn. Accts., Am. Inst. C.P.A.'s, Tex. Soc. C.P.A.'s, Inst. Mgmt. Acctg., Inst. Internal Auditors, Data Processing Mgmt. Assn., EDP Auditors Assn., Am. Compensation Assn. (cert. compensation profl.), Am. Soc. Personnel Adminstrn., Analyzer Internat. Users Group (sec.), Houston C. of C. Home: 2021 Spenwick Dr #215 Houston TX 77055 Office: 1110 Main St Houston TX 77002

WALLACH, PHILIP, mfg. co. exec.; b. N.Y.C., May 29, 1928; s. Morris and Lillian (Levy) W.; B.S., U.S. Mcht. Marine Acad., 1950; postgrad. N.C. State Grad. Sch. Engring., N.Y. U. Grad. Sch. Bus.; m. Florence O'Neil, Apr. 8, 1951; children—Ruth, Sandra, Louis, David. Sales engr., regional mgr. Nordberg Mfg. Co., 1955-67; v.p. mktg., pres. Engine div. Fairbanks Morse subs. Colt Industries, Inc., Beloit, Wis., 1967-71, corporate v.p., group exec., 1971, group v.p., 1972—; pres. Colt Industries Internat., Inc. Served to lt. USNR, 1953-55. Recipient Outstanding Profl. Achievement award U.S. Mcht. Marine Acad., Marine Man of Yr. award. Mem. Am. Soc. Naval Engrs., Soc. Naval Architects and Marine Engrs. Club: Economic (N.Y.C.). Home: 3211 Montlake Dr Rockford IL 61111 Office: 701 Lawton Ave Beloit WI 53511

WALLER, BILL EDWARD, JR., talent agy. exec.; b. Cin., Aug. 8, 1950; s. Bill E. and Frances Hope W.; B.S., Xavier U., 1969, M.B.A., 1972. Profl. football player New Orleans Saints, 1969-71; with Procter & Gamble, 1969-70, Avco Broadcasting Co., 1970-72; probation officer, Cin., 1973-75; pres. Pro-Talents Inc., Cin., 1975—; tchr. U. Cin., 1977-78. Mem. Nat. Film Inst., Nat. Sports Reps. Assn. Republican. Roman Catholic. Office: Pro-Talents Inc 414 Walnut St Suite 920 Cincinnati OH 45202

WALLER, CHARLES PAYTON, oil and gas exploration co. exec.; b. Dallas, Mar. 5, 1939; s. Lorenzo Payton and Pearl Cleo W.; B.S., North Tex. State U., 1970, postgrad. in clin. psychology, 1971-72; m. Linda Kay Scott, Nov. 22, 1968; children—Michael Payton, Kristin Elizabeth. Cost accounting specialist Fleming & Sons, Dallas, 1962-66; exec. asst. to pres. Fabricators, Dallas, 1964-68; mgmt. cons. FMB Assos., Dallas, 1972; cons. mgmt., Arlington, Tex., 1972-76; corp. tng. dir. Atlantic Pacific Marine Corp., Houston, 1977-80, Dixilyn-Field Drilling Co., Houston, 1980—; cons to industry on mfg. systems, human resource devel. Recipient Spoke award Nat. Jr. C. of C., 1961. Mem. Internat. Assn. Drilling Contractors, Am. Soc. Tng. and Devel., Am. Soc. Personnel Adminstrn. Republican. Baptist. Subject of industry mag. interviews; developer 1st skills tng. center, 1st video tng. tapes, 1st comprehensive entry-level skills-tng. program in drilling industry in U.S. Home: 1003 Apache Falls Dr Katy TX 77450 Office: 2425 Fountainview Suite 300 Houston TX 77057

WALLER, HENRY BUFORD, telephone co. exec.; b. Los Angeles, Sept. 18, 1944; s. Henry Buford and Virginia Lockhart (Watson) W.; B.S., U. So. Calif., 1966, M.B.A., 1976; m. Frances Elizabeth Stoufer, Apr. 6, 1966; children—Henry Buford, Amanda Ruth. Mgmt. trainee Gen. Telephone Co. Calif., Santa Monica, 1969, unit supr., 1970, accounting supr., 1970-71, staff accountant, 1972, spl. accountant, 1973-75, accounting adminstr., 1975-77, accounting mgr., 1977—. Served with U.S. Army, 1966-69. Decorated Army Commendation medal. Mem. Nat. Assn. Accountants, Commerce Assos., GTC Mgmt. Assn., Theta Chi. Democrat. Congregationalist. Club: Sunset Hills Country. Home: 2325 E Otono Circle Thousand Oaks CA 91360 Office: 12211 Washington Blvd Los Angeles CA 90066

WALLERICH, PETER KENNETH, banker; b. Tacoma, Mar. 4, 1931; s. Clarence W. and Ellen (Hansen) W.; B.A.A., U. Wash., 1953; m. Marylu Ann Oakland, July 9, 1954; children—Karen, Kristen, Karla, Kaari. Investment officer N. Pacific Bank, Tacoma, 1956-59, exec. v.p., 1959-71, chmn. bd., 1971-73; pres., chief exec. officer, 1973—; dir. N. Pacific Bank, Western Finance Co., Mountain View Devel. Co. Pres., Design for Progress, 1970-71. Bd. dirs., pres. Mary Bridge Children's Hosp., trustee, treas. U. Puget Sound; bd. visitors Sch. Law U. Puget Sound; gen. chmn. Tacoma-Pierce County United Way, 1981. Mem. Am. Bankers Assn. (nat. exec. planning com., dir. Community bankers div.), Washington Bankers Assn. (treas., dir.), C. of C. (dir.), Mensa, Beta Gamma Sigma (chpt. award 1980). Home: 12111 Gravelly Lake Dr SW Tacoma WA 98499 Office: 5448 S Tacoma Way Tacoma WA 98409

WALLFESH, HENRY MAURICE, editor, publisher, retirement counselor; b. The Bronx, N.Y., June 15, 1937; s. David Shibe and Rose (Silk) W.; student Rutgers U., 1954-55; B.S., Cornell U., 1958; m. Suzanne Krakowitch, Dec. 26, 1960; children—Saundra Kay, Gerald Bruce. Editor, co-pub. Indsl. Relations News, N.Y.C., Stamford, Conn., 1960-67; with Retirement Advisors, N.Y.C., 1968—, exec. v.p., dir., 1974-80, pres., 1981—; dir. V.S.O.P. Mktg. and Sales, Boston; lectr. Columbia, Princeton, Duke univs., others, also profl. groups; mem. steering com. on pre-retirement edn. N.Y. State Office on Aging. Served with USAR, 1958-67. Mem. Indsl. Relations Inst. (past pres.), Soc. Pre-Retirement Program Planners (sec., dir.). Club: Roxbury Swim (dir.) (Stamford, Conn.). Contbr. studies in human resources. Home: 1616 Long Ridge Rd Stamford CT 06903 Office: 720 Fifth Ave New York NY 10019

WALLIN, GARY PHILLIP, communications equipment co. exec.; b. Newark, Nov. 8, 1940; s. Irving and Rose (Greenberg) W.; B.S., Upsala Coll., 1958-62; children—Ian Robert, Amy Gwen, Michael Adam. Engr., Welch Communications Corp., Dover, N.J., 1962-64; asst. to v.p. Edison Electronics, Boonton, N.J., 1965; service mgr. Motorola, Inc., Franklin Park, Ill., 1965-69; owner, pres. Comex Systems, Inc., Comex, Inc., Manchester, N.H., 1969—; dir. Exec. Exchange, Inc., Communications Engrs. Co., Inc., Mchts. Savs. Bank, Telecator Network Am.; cons. in field. Justice of the peace, Manchester, 1971—; bd. dirs. Jewish Community Center, Jewish Community Council, N.H. Performing Arts Center; treas. Federated Arts Manchester; asso. chmn. nat. young leadership cabinet United Jewish Appeal; dir. local temple. Mem. IEEE, Radio Club Am., Electronic Industries Assn., AAAS, Soc. Am. Magicians, Internat. Brotherhood Magicians (sec. 1964), Hundred Club N.H. Clubs: Manchester Country, Exchange. Patentee in field. Office: Comex Inc 720 Union St Manchester NH 03104

WALLIN, WINSTON ROGER, mfg. co. exec.; b. Mpls., Mar. 6, 1926; s. Carl A. and Theresa (Hegge) W.; B.B.A., U. Minn., 1948; m. Maxine Houghton, Sept. 10, 1949; children—Rebecca, Brooks, Lance, Bradford. With Pillsbury Co., Mpls., 1948—, v.p. commodity ops., 1971-76, exec. v.p., 1976, pres., chief ops. officer, 1977—; dir. Medtronic, Inc., Soo Line R.R., 1st Mpls. Bank. Bd. dirs. United Way, Mpls., 1977, Downtown Council Mpls., 1977. Served with USN, 1944-46. Mem. Chgo. Bd. Trade, Mpls. Grain Exchange (bd. dirs. 1977—), Kansas City Bd. trade. Clubs: Mpls., Interlachen, Minikahda. Office: Pillsbury Co 608 2d Ave S Minneapolis MN 55435*

WALLIS, GORDON TODD, banker; b. Salt Lake City, Aug. 15, 1919; s. James Benjamin and Jessie (McAlister) W.; B.A., Columbia, 1940; LL.B., N.Y. U., 1948; m. Dorothy Jean Merrill, June 15, 1946. With Irving Trust Co., N.Y.C., 1940—, asst. sec., 1948-53, asst. v.p., 1953-55, v.p., 1955-64, sr. v.p., 1964-65, exec. v.p., 1965-69, vice-chmn., 1969-70, chmn., chief exec. officer, 1970—, dir., 1969—; pres., chief exec. officer Irving Bank Corp., 1970, chmn., chief exec. officer, 1972—, also dir.; dir. Wing Hang Bank Ltd., Internat. Comml. Bank, JWT Group, Inc., Sterling Drug Inc., F.W. Woolworth Co., Gen. Telephone & Electronics Corp., Fed. Res. Bank of N.Y. Bd. dirs. United Way of N.Y.C., United Way of Tri-State; chmn., bd. dirs. Downtown-Lower Manhattan Assn.; chmn. Econ. Devel. Council N.Y.C. Served to capt. USAAF, 1942-46. Mem. N.Y. Clearing House Assn. (pres.), Council on Fgn. Relations, Conf. Bd., Internat. C. of C. (trustee U.S. council), N.Y. C. of C. Club: Links (N.Y.C.). Office: 1 Wall St New York NY 10015

WALLIS, WILLIAM TURNER, III, bank exec.; b. Jacksonville, Fla., Jan. 23, 1929; s. William Turner and Margaret (Phillips) W.; student Washington and Lee U., 1946-50; B.S., Fla. State U., 1951; postgrad. U. Ind., 1960; m. Jean M. Wallis (dec.); children—William Turner, Laura Day, Michael Munro, Marshall Bennett; m. 2d, Joanne Cook; stepchildren—Robin, Patricia, Christine, John. Trainee, First Fed. Savs. and Loan Assn. of the Palm Beaches, West Palm Beach, Fla., 1955, loan service officer, to 1958; with First Fed. Savs. and Loan Assn. Osceola County, Kissimmee, Fla., 1958-76, exec. sec., 1958-59, exec. v.p., 1959-68, pres., 1968-76, also dir.; pres. First Fed. Savs. and Loan Assn. Martin County, Stuart, Fla., 1977—, also dir.; dir. Fed. Home Loan Bank of Atlanta, 1975-78. Chmn., E. Central Fla. Planning Commn., 1961-69; mem. City of Kissimmee Planning Commn.; bd. suprs. Reedy Creek Improvement Dist., 1974-75; v.p., bd. dirs. Fla. Tech. U. Found., 1974-76; bd. dirs. Osceola (Fla.) Art and Culture Center, Kissimmee; sr. warden St. John's Episcopal Ch. Served with USNR, 1951-55. Mem. Fla. Savs. and Loan League (pres. 1967), U.S. League Savs. Assns. (dir. 1968-69, exec. com. 1980—), Fla. C. of C., Greater Kissimmee C. of C. Democrat. Home: 19 W Highpoint Rd Sewalls Point Jensen Beach FL 33457 Office: 989 S Federal Hwy Stuart FL 33494

WALLMAN, CHARLES JAMES, money handling products co. exec.; b. Kiel, Wis., Feb. 19, 1924; s. Charles A. and Mary Ann (Loftus) W.; student Marquette U., 1942-43, Tex. Coll. Mines, 1943-44; B.B.A., U. Wis., 1949; m. Charline Marie Moore, June 14, 1952; children—Stephen, Jeffrey, Susan, Patricia, Andrew. Sales promotion mgr. Brandt, Inc., Watertown, Wis., 1949-65, v.p., 1960-70, exec. v.p., 1970-80, v.p. corp. devel., 1980—, also dir.; v.p. corp. devel., dir. Brandt Mfg. Co., Inc., Pell City, Ala., 1973—, Brandt-PRA, Inc., Bensalem, Pa., 1976, Brandt Systems, Inc., Watertown, 1976. Exec. bd. Potawatomi council Boy Scouts Am., also former v.p. council. Trustee, Joe Davies Scholarship Found. Served with armored inf. AUS, 1943-45; ETO. Decorated Bronze Star. Mem. Am. Legion, East Central Golf Assn. (past pres.), Wis. Alumni Assn. (local past pres.), Phi Delta Theta. Republican. Roman Catholic. Elk (past officer). Club: Watertown Country (past dir.). Home: 700 Clyman St Watertown WI 53094 Office: 705 12th St Watertown WI 53094

WALLNER, NICHOLAS, investor; b. Chgo., Aug. 30, 1929; s. Nickolaus and Mary (Miller) W.; B.S., U.S. Naval Acad., 1953; M.B.A., U. So. Calif., 1959; Ph.D., Calif. Pacific U., 1979; m. Sally Elizabeth Sullivan, Jan. 23, 1955; children—Scott Sullivan, Bruce Garrett, Kimberly Nicolette. Chmn., The Wallner Co., 1967—, Epcom, Inc., 1975—, LaSalle-Deitch Co., Inc., 1980—; vice chmn. Digital Sci. Corp., 1980—, Sparta Instrument Corp., 1980—. Faculty, U. So. Calif., Los Angeles, 1963-67, Calif. Tech. Inst., Pasadena, 1965-66, U. Calif. at San Diego, La Jolla, 1967—, Nat. U., San Diego, 1976—. Served with USAF, 1953-58. Mem. Young Presidents Orgn., U. So. Calif. Commerce Assos., World Bus. Council, U.S. Naval Acad. Alumni Assn., Beta Gamma Sigma. Home: 100 Coast Blvd LaJolla CA 92037 Office: 1205 Prospect St Suite 542 La Jolla CA 92037

WALLS, JOHN WILLIAM, assn. exec.; b. Knightstown, Ind., Mar. 25, 1927; s. Otto F. and Ruth M. W.; A.B., Ind. U.; M.P.A., Wayne State U.; m. Phyllis Hardin, June 20, 1948; children—Ann, Kathryn, Elizabeth, Timothy. Exec. dir. Greater Indpls. Progress Com., 1965-68; sr. dep. mayor City of Indpls., 1968-73; v.p. Mchts. Nat. Bank, 1973-78; pres. Ind. State C. of C., 1978—; chmn. Indpls. Public Transp. Corp., 1973-76, Met. Devel. Commn., 1976-80, Ind. Public Transp. Adv. Com., 1979-80. Served with USAAF, 1945-46. Mem. Council State C. of C. (treas.), Am. Inst. Cert. Planners. Republican. Quaker. Office: 143 N Meridian Indianapolis IN 46204

WALLSTROM, WESLEY DONALD, bank exec.; b. Turlock, Calif., Oct. 4, 1929; s. Emil Reinhold and Edith Katherine (Lindberg) W.; student Modesto Jr. Coll., 1955-64; cert. Pacific Coast Banking Sch., U. Wash., 1974; m. Marilyn Irene Hallmark, May 12, 1951; children—Marc Gordon, Wendy Diane. Bookkeeper, teller First Nat. Bank, Turlock, 1947-50; v.p. Gordon Hallmark, Inc., Turlock, 1950-53; asst. cashier United Calif. Bank, Turlock, 1953-68, regional v.p., Fresno, 1968-72, v.p., mgr., Turlock, 1972-76; founding pres., dir. Golden Valley Bank, Turlock, 1976—. Campaign chmn. United Crusade, Turlock, 1971; founding dir. Covenant Vill., retirement home, Turlock, 1973—; founding pres. Turlock Regional Arts Council, 1974, dir., 1975-76. Served with U.S. N.G., 1948-56. Mem.

Nat. Soc. Accts. for Coops., Ind. Bankers No. Calif., Am. Bankers Assn., U.S. Yacht Racing Union, No. Calif. Golf Assn., Turlock C. of C. (dir. 1973-75), Stanislaus Sailing Soc. (commodore). Republican. Mem. Covenant Ch. Clubs: Turlock Golf and Country (pres. 1975-76, v.p., dir. 1977), Rotary. Home: 1720 Hammond Dr Turlock CA 95380 Office: 301 E Main St Turlock CA 95380

WALRATH, JOHN FREDERICK, diversified mfg. exec.; b. Evans Mills, N.Y., May 18, 1916; s. Edson J. and Emma (Hoffer) W.; B.S. in Accounting cum laude, Syracuse (N.Y.) U., 1937. With Gen. Electric Co., 1937-63; v.p., controller Univac div. Sperry Rand Corp., N.Y.C., 1963-66; v.p. finance, sec., treas. Escambia Chem. Corp., N.Y.C., 1966-68; v.p. finance, treas., dir. Andrew Jergens Co., Cin., 1968-71; with Am. Brands, Inc., N.Y.C., 1971—, pres., 1977-80, chief operating officer, 1974-80, vice chmn., 1981—, also dir.; dir. Acme Visible Records, Inc., Am. Tobacco Internat. Corp., Sunshine Biscuits Inc., Andrew Jergens Co., James B. Beam Distilling Co., Daffy-Mott Co., Inc., Gallaher Ltd., Master Lock Co., Swingline Inc., Wilson Jones Co., Acushnet Co. Mem. Beta Gamma Sigma (dirs. table), Alpha Kappa Psi, Phi Kappa Phi. Methodist. Clubs: Burning Tree Country (Greenwich); Queen City (Cin.); Shriners. Office: 245 Park Ave New York NY 10167

WALSH, CHARLES RICHARD, bank exec.; b. Bklyn., Jan. 30, 1939; s. Charles John and Anna Ellen W.; B.S., Fordham U., 1960; M.B.A., St. John's U., 1966; m. Marie Anne Goulden, June 21, 1961; children—Kevin C., Brian R., Gregory M. Credit and collection mgr. Texaco Inc., N.Y.C., 1961-67; mgr. credit research Trans World Airlines, N.Y.C., 1967-71; dir. br. ops. Avon Products Inc., N.Y.C., 1971-74; sr. v.p., officer-in-charge of retail card services dept. Mfrs. Hanover Trust Co., Hicksville, N.Y., 1974—; chmn. bd. dirs. Eastern States Monetary Services, Lake Success, N.Y., 1978—. Sustaining mem. Republican Nat. Com., 1978—. Served with USAR, 1960, 61-62. Cert. Soc. Cert. Consumer Credit Execs. Mem. N.Y. State Bankers Assn. (dir., mem. gov. council), Am. Bankers Assn. (mem. exec. com., chmn. edn. com.), Am. Mgmt. Assn., N.Y. Credit & Fin. Mgmt. Assn. Republican. Clubs: Forest Estates (Oyster Bay, N.Y.). Office: 100 Duffy Ave Hicksville NY 11801

WALSH, DANIEL JOHN, III, ins. agy. exec.; b. Phila., Nov. 11, 1939; s. Daniel J. and Rosemary (Gallagher) W.; B.S., Villanova U., 1961; m. Cynthia Connell, Feb. 3, 1968; children—Michelle, R. Bruce, Marni, Allison. With Daniel J. Walshs Sons, Inc., Phila., 1961—, exec. v.p., 1977—; v.p., dir. Howe Life Ins. Co. of Am., Phila., 1964-76; dir. Howe Protective Co., Phila., 1974-76; dir. Home Protective Co., Phila., 1974-76. Active Cath. Charities, Phila., 1967-76; bd. dirs. Agape Camp Fire Girls, 1976-78; mem. com. for deferred giving Archdiocese of Phila., 1976-78; mem. Lower Merion-Narberth Republican Fin. Com. Mem. Phila., Nat. assns. life underwriters, Am. Soc. C.L.U.'s. Republican. Roman Catholic. Clubs: Phila. Country, Union League, Peale, Atlantic City Country. Home: 1610 Mount Vernon Circle Gladwyne PA 19035 Office: 1700 Race St Philadelphia PA 19103

WALSH, EDMUND CARROLL, III, mfg. co. exec.; b. Clinton, Iowa, Mar. 25, 1913; s. Edmund Carroll and Hazel Marie (Hill) W.; A.B., Harvard U., 1935, postgrad. law, 1935-36; m. Miriam M. Holleran, Sept. 1, 1937; children—Judith Walsh Houley, David E. With Johns-Manville Corp., Chgo., 1937-52; with Steel Parts Corp., Tipton, Ind., 1952—, pres., 1965-79, chmn. bd., chief exec. officer, 1979—; dir. City Machine Tool & Die. Trustee Little Sisters of the Poor; bd. dirs., trustee St. Vincent Hosp. Found., Indpls. Served with USNR, 1943-45. Clubs: Woodstock (dir., pres.), University, Indpls. Athletic, Harvard (Indpls.); Recess (Detroit). Home: 7475 Holliday Dr E Indianapolis IN 46260 Office: 9000 Keystone Crossing Suite 945 Indianapolis IN 46240

WALSH, EDWARD, JR., life ins. exec.; b. Bronx, May 28, 1941; s. Edward Arthur and Marion (Bundock) W.; student U.S. Naval Acad., 1962-63; m. Marna Putt, Mar. 21, 1975; children from previous marriage—Katherine, Edward, Maureen, Eileen. Agy., Fidelity Mut. Life Ins. Co., Wilmington, Del., 1967-70, agy. mgr., 1970-72; dir. advanced underwriting Continental Am. Life Ins. Co., Wilmington, 1972-76; gen. agt., owner S&W Assos., Quakertown, Pa., 1976—. Vice chmn. Perkasie Planning Commn., 1978-79. Served with USMC, 1960-63. Mem. Lehigh Valley Assn. Life Underwriters, Lehigh Valley Estate Planning Council, Am. Soc. C.L.U.'s. Home: 129 Ridge Ave Perkasie PA 18944 Office: PO Box 458 Quakertown PA 18951

WALSH, EDWARD JOSEPH, food co. exec.; b. Mt. Vernon, N.Y., Mar. 18, 1932; s. Edward Aloysius and Charlotte Cecilia (Borup) W.; B.B.A., Iona Coll., 1953; M.B.A., N.Y. U., 1958; m. Patricia Ann Farrell, Sept. 16, 1961; children—Edward, Megan, John, Robert. With Armour & Co., 1961—, v.p. toiletries div. Armour Dial Co., 1973-76, exec. v.p., 1976-78, pres. Armour Internat. Co., Phoenix, 1978—. Served with U.S. Army, 1953-55. Mem. Am. Mgmt. Assn., Nat. Meat Canners Assn. (past pres.). Republican. Roman Catholic. Office: 111 W Clarendon Phoenix AZ 85077

WALSH, F. HOWARD, oil producer, rancher; b. Waco, Tex., Feb. 7, 1913; s. P. Frank and Maude (Gage) W.; B.B.A., Tex. Christian U., 1933, LL.D. (hon.), 1979; m. Mary D. Fleming, Mar. 13, 1937; children—Richard F., F. Howard, D'Ann E. (Mrs. William F. Bonnell), Maudi Walsh Willson, William Lloyd. Self employed in oil prodn., ranching, 1942—; pres. Walsh & Watts, Inc.; past dir. 1st Nat. Bank of Ft. Worth. Past mem. Jud. Qualifications Commn. State of Tex.; pres. Walsh Found.; v.p. Fleming Found.; trustee Tex. Christian U.; past trustee Southwestern Bapt. Theol. Sem.; bd. dirs. Southwestern Expn. and Fat Stock Show; past bd. dirs. So. Bapt. Found.; guarantor Ft. Worth Ballet, Ft. Worth Arts Council, Ft. Worth Opera, Ft. Worth Symphony Orch., Tex. Boys Choir, Community Theatre. Recipient Valuable Alumnus award Tex. Christian U., 1967, spl. recognition for support U. Ranch Tng. Program, Royal Purple award, 1979; (with wife) Distinguished Service award So. Bapt. Radio and TV Commn., 1972; named (with wife) Edna Gladney Internat. Grandparents, 1972; co-recipient Brotherhood citation NCCJ, 1978; named (with wife) Patron of Arts in Ft. Worth, 1970; donor (with wife) Walsh Med. Bldg., Southwestern Bapt. Theol. Sem., (with wife) Wurlitzer Organ to Casa Manaña, 1972, (with wife) bldgs. and land to Tex. Boys Choir, 1971; library bldg. Tarrant County Jr. Coll., NW campus, named in his and wife's honor, 1978; 1978-79 season of Ft. Worth Ballet dedicated in his and wife's honor. Mem. Tex.-Mid-Continent, West Central Tex., North Tex. oil and gas assns., Ind. Petroleum Assn. Am., Tex. Ind. Producers and Royalty Owners, Am-Internat. Charolais Assn., Tex. Christian U. Ex-Lettermen's Assn. Baptist (bd. sr. deacons). Clubs: Garden of the Gods (Colorado Springs); Colorado Springs Country; Steeplechase, Fort Worth, Ridglea, Rivercrest Country, Breakfast, Frog, Colonial Country, Shady Oaks Country, Century II. Tng. center at So. Bapt. Radio and TV Commn. named for biographee and his wife, 1976. Home: 2425 Stadium Dr Fort Worth TX 76109 also 1801 Culebra Colorado Springs CO 80907 Office: First Nat Bank Bldg Fort Worth TX 76102

WALSH, FRANCIS HERBERT, III, mgmt. cons.; b. Bethlehem, Pa., Apr. 17, 1945; s. Francis Herbert, Jr., and Marie Geraldine (Girouard) W.; S.B. in Aero. and Astronautical Engring., M.I.T., 1967; M.S.M.E., U. Calif., Berkeley, 1969; M.B.A., Harvard U., 1973; m. Linda Anne Lawn, Nov. 30, 1974. Research engr. guidance and navigation systems C.S. Draper Lab., M.I.T., Cambridge, 1968-73; mgmt. cons. Temple, Barker & Sloane, Inc., Lexington, Mass., 1973—. Mem. Harvard Bus. Sch. Assn. Boston, Tau Beta Pi, Sigma Gamma Tau. Home: 23 Fletcher Rd Lynnfield MA 01940 Office: 33 Hayden Ave Lexington MA 02173

WALSH, FRANCIS JOSEPH, JR., transp. and leasing co. exec.; b. Weehawken, N.J., Jan. 26, 1947; s. Francis Joseph and Frances Valerie (Rieman) W.; student public schs., Jersey City; m. Donna Kolpin, Feb. 13, 1965; children—Jacqueline, Suzanne, Francis Joseph. With Walsh Trucking Co., Inc., Jersey City, 1965-79, North Bergen, 1980—, exec. v.p., 1968-78, pres., 1978—. Republican. Roman Catholic. Club: Lions (pres. club 1977). Home: 24 Jean Dr Englewood Cliffs NJ 07632 Office: 2820-16th St North Bergen NJ 07302

WALSH, GEOFFREY THOMAS, petroleum engr.; b. London, Dec. 20, 1931; s. Arthur Aloysius and Elizabeth Louise (Sewel) W.; B.Sc., U. Alta., 1971; m. Patricia Colleen Keddie, June 3, 1978; children by previous marriage—Deborah, Sandra. Plant supr. Egerton Tool & Instrument Co., London, 1952-57; plant foreman Flame-Master Furnace Co., Edmonton, Alta., 1957-59; plant supr. McCready Products, Edmonton, 1959-64; sr. engring. technologist (petroleum) U. Alta., Edmonton, 1964—; pres. GMW Mfg. & Design Ltd., Edmonton, 1970—. Served with Brit. Army, 1950-52. Mem. Alta. Soc. Engring. Technologists. Conservative. Anglican. Author publs., patentee devices for use in chem. and petroleum engring. Home: 3240 105th St Edmonton AB T6J 3A2 Canada Office: U Alta Mineral Engring Edmonton AB T6G 2G6 Canada

WALSH, JAMES EDWARD, constrn. co. exec.; b. Sioux City, Iowa, July 3, 1927; s. Daniel L. and Dorothy M. (Thill) W.; student Loyola U., Los Angeles, 1950-51; m. Frances D. Dorsett, Feb. 17, 1952; children—John A., Helen M. Supr. N. Am. Aviation, Inc., Los Angeles, 1947-52; v.p., owner Columbia Export Packers, Inc. div. MPS, Inc., Los Angeles, 1952-62; owner, sec.-treas. ABCO Constrn. Co., Torrance, Calif., 1962—; gen. partner Vi-Roi Oil and Drilling Co., Duncan, Okla.; dir. Torrance Nat. Bank. Chmn. com. South Bay council Boy Scouts Am., 1969-73. Bd. dirs. Palos Verdes (Calif.) Little League, 1967-68; trustee Chadwick Sch., Palos Verdes, 1973-77. Served with USMC, 1944-47. Roman Catholic. Clubs: Palos Verdes Country (dir. 1968-70); Pauma Valley (Calif.) Country. Home: 12 Rawhide Ln Rolling Hills CA 90274 Office: 2535 Maricopa St Torrance CA 90503

WALSH, JAMES JOSEPH, ins. co. exec.; b. Sharon, Pa., Aug. 23, 1921; s. James Joseph and Margaret Mary (Kelch) W.; student St. Vincent Coll., 1939-41, Okla. Bapt. U., 1943; A.B., Youngstown (Ohio) State U., 1948; m. Jean Herald, Oct. 23, 1948; children—Maurya Walsh Johnson, James J., Kevin H., Megan M. With labor gang U.S. Steel, 1940; fireman Mercer Valley R.R., 1941-42; student/employee, transp. dept. Sharon (Pa.) Steel, 1949; ins. agt., agy. tng. supr., brokerage mgr., gen. agt., pvt. practice cons., advanced underwriting specialist, Columbus, Ohio, 1949-62; v.p. Columbus Mut. Life Ins. Co., 1970—; cons. in field 1972—; faculty Am. Coll. Life Underwriters, 1964-76. Served to 1st lt. USAAF, 1943-45. Decorated Air medal with three oak leaf clusters, Presdl. citation with two clusters. C.L.U. Mem. Am. Soc. C.L.U.'s, Internat. Assn. Health Underwriters, Disability Ins. Council (trustee), Nat. Assn. Life Underwriters, Estate Planning Council. Republican. Author 13 books in field, including: What You Should Know About Split Dollar Life Insurance, 1972; Applications of Life and Health Insurance to Business Needs, 1975; contbr. articles to fin. mags.; speaker, condr. seminars in field. Office: 303 E Broad St Columbus OH 43216

WALSH, JAMES PATRICK, ins. cons., actuary; b. Ft. Thomas, Ky., Mar. 7, 1910; s. James Patrick and Minnie Louise (Cooper) W.; comml. engring. degree U. Cin., 1933; m. Evelyn Mary Sullivan, May 20, 1939. Accountant, Firestone Tire & Rubber Co., Gen. Motors Corp., 1933-36; rep. ARC, 1937, A.F. of L., 1938-39; dir. Ohio div. minimum wages, Columbus, 1939-42; asst. sec.-treas. union label trades dept. AFL, Washington, 1946-53; v.p. sales and adminstrn. Pension and Group Cons., Inc., Cin., 1953—. Mem. Pres.'s Commn. on Jud. and Congressional Salaries, 1953, Gov. Ohio Commn. on Employment of Negro, 1940, Hamilton (Ohio) County Welfare Bd., 1954—, council long term illness and rehab. Cin. Pub. Health Fedn., 1957-62; bd. dirs. U. Cin., 1959-67; bd. govs. St. Xavier High Sch., Cin., 1958-68; trustee Brown Fund, Newman Found.; mem. Green Twp. Republican Club, Rep. Club Hamilton County (life), War Vets. Rep. Club. Served to lt. col. AUS, 1942-46; col. Res. Decorated Legion of Merit; named Ky. Col., 1958; Ky. Adm., 1966; recipient U. Cin. Coll. Engring. Distinguished Alumni award, 1969; St. Xavier High Sch. Insignis award, 1974. Fellow Am. Soc. Pension Actuaries; mem. Am. Acad. Actuaries, Res. Officers Assn. (life), Am. Legion (life), Assn. U.S. Army (trustee), Am. Fedn. State, County and Employees Union, Nat. Assn. Uniformed Services (life), Internat. Alliance Theatrical Stage Employees (sgt. at arms), Internat. Hodcarriers, Bldg. and Common Laborers Union, Ins. Workers Internat. Union, Office Workers Internat. Union, Friendly Sons St. Patrick (past pres.), Am. Pub. Welfare Assn., VFW, Covington Latin Sch. (past pres.), U. Cin. (life) alumni assns., Soc. for Advancement Mgmt., Health Ins. Council S.W. Ohio, Am. Soc. Mil. Engrs., Ancient Order Hibernians (past pres.), Order Alhambra, Allied Constrn. Industries, Internat. Assn. Health Underwriters, Alumni Assn. St. Xavier High Sch., Am. Arbitration Assn. (nat. community dispute settlement panel), Alpha Kappa Psi. Roman Catholic. Clubs: K.C. (4 deg.), Elks, Cuvier Press, St. Antoninus Athletic, Global Sportsmen's, Scuttlebutts, Travelers, U CATS, Cincinnatian Table, U. Cin. Boosters, U. Cin. Pres.'s, Newman (Cin.), Cin. (life, past pres.), pres.), Queen City, Nat. Travel, Am.-Irish, Insiders, Bengal Boosters, Bankers (life), Engrs., Roundtable, Scuttlebutts, Mil. (life), Carriage Makers of Ohio. Home: 5563 Julmar Dr Cincinnati OH 45238 Office: 6 E 4th St Cincinnati OH 45202

WALSH, JOHN ROBERT, mfg. co. exec.; b. Boston, Apr. 17, 1930; s. Edward Robert and Alice Imelda (McMahon) W.; B.S. in Engring., M.I.T., 1953, postgrad. process metallurgy, 1953; m. Christiane Bernadette Septier, Feb. 25, 1955; children—Mary Anne, John Robert, Marie-Noelle, Thomas M. Sr. partner Stephenson, Walsh & Assos., Cons. Engrs., Paris, 1958-61; mgr. licensing, acquisitions Borg-Warner Internat. Corp., N.Y.C., Chgo., 1961-64, asst. to pres. Borg-Warner Corp., 1964-65, gen. mgr. York Shipley, Ltd. subs., London, 1965-67, v.p. internat. ops. York (Pa.) div., 1967-68, pres. York Europe div., Geneva-Brussels, 1969-77, pres. York Internat. (pa.), 1978—; dir. Le Froid Industriel York, S.A., France, 1967—, Brown Boveri-York Kalte-Und Klimatechnik GmbH, Germany, 1970—, chmn. mgmt. com., 1974—; dir. Borg-Warner A.G., Zug, Switzerland, 1971—, chmn. bd., 1975—; joint mng. dir., dir. Borg-Warner Ltd., U.K., 1976—; dir. York Internat. Corp., York Aire, S.A., Mex., Recold S.A. de C.V., Mex., Refrigeracion York, S.A., Venezuela, McFarland Co., Harrisburg, Pa., OYL Condair Industries Sdn. Bhd., Malaysia, Marco Ltd., Saudi Arabia. Mem. ednl. council M.I.T., 1968—. Served to 1st lt., C.E., AUS, 1954-58. Registered profl. engr., Mass. Mem. Am. Mgmt. Assn. (pres.'s council 1975—), Machinery and Allied Products Inst. (internat. ops. council 1978—). Roman Catholic. Clubs: Beaufort Hunt, Country of York, Lafayette, Rose Tree Fox Hunting. Office: York Internat Borg-Warner Corp PO Box 1592 York PA 17405

WALSH, JULIA MARGARET CURRY (MRS. THOMAS M. WALSH), investment co. exec.; b. Akron, Ohio, Mar. 29, 1923; d. Edward A. and Catherine U. (Skurkay) Curry; B.B.A. magna cum laude, Kent State U., 1945; postgrad. N.Y. Inst. Finance, 1956; grad. Advanced Mgmt. Program, Harvard, 1962; LL.D., Hood Coll., 1969; Regis Coll., 1973; m. John G. Montgomery, Apr. 7, 1948 (dec. Dec. 1957); children—John, Stephen, Michael, Mark; m. 2d, Thomas M. Walsh, May 18, 1963; 1 dau., Margaret; stepchildren—Mary Francis (Mrs. Steven Ferencie), Patrick Joseph, Kathleen, Thomas D., Joan, Daniel, Ann. Personnel officer Am. counsulate gen., Munich, Germany, 1945-48; probation officer Wash. State Sch. Girls, Centralia, 1948-50; exec. officer U.S. Ednl. Commn., Ankara, Turkey, 1952-54; registered rep. Ferris & Co., Inc., Washington, 1955-59, gen. partner, 1959-70, sr. v.p., 1971-73, vice chmn. bd., 1973-77; dir. Pitney Bowes; chmn. Julia M. Walsh & Sons, Inc., Washington, 1977—; mem. Am. Stock Exchange, 1965—, bd. govs., 1972-74; adv. bd. 1st Am. Washington; mem. Sec. State's Spl. Adv. Com. on Public Opinion; mem. Tax Revision Commn. D.C. Bd. dirs. Kent State U. Found., Nat. Shrine Immaculate Conception, St. Mary of the Woods Coll., Georgetown U., Greater Washington Bus. Center; dir.-at-large Met. Washington Bd. Trade; bd. govs. East-West Center, Honolulu; adv. com. Grad. Program Women in Mgmt., Simmons Coll.; mem. Pres.'s Exec. Exchange Commn. Recipient Disting. Alumna award Kent State U., 1967. Mem. Bus. and Profl. Women's Club Potomac, U.S. C. of C. (dir.), AAUW (trustee Ednl. Found.), Harvard Bus. Sch. Assn. (exec. council). Democrat. Clubs: Women's Nat., Am. Newspaper Women's, Harvard Bus. Sch. (past pres.), Zonta, Internat. (Washington). Home: 5001 Millwood Ln NW Washington DC 20016 Office: Julia M Walsh & Sons Inc 910 17th St NW Washington DC 20006

WALSH, LINDA ELIZABETH, banker; b. Shelbyville, Ill., Jan. 22, 1947; d. Bernard Robert Schaefer and Elizabeth McKinsey; student Gulf Park Coll., 1965-66, U. Madrid, summer 1966; B.S., U. Ariz., 1969; M.B.A., Keller Grad. Sch. Mgmt., 1980. Asst. buyer mgr. Bullocks Dept. Store, Santa Ana, Calif., 1969-70; asst. to dir. Japan Nat. Tourist Orgn., Chgo., 1970-72; asst. mktg. dir. Nat. Security Bank, Chgo., 1972-74; personal banking officer, banking dept. No. Trust Co., Chgo., 1974-80; asst. v.p. Heritage County Bank & Trust, Blue Island, Ill., 1980—. Pres. bd. Martha Washington Home for Dependent Crippled Children, 1978—; mem. asso. bd. Chgo. Lung Assn., 1980—; bd. dirs. Children's Meml. Hosp.; bd. dirs., treas. Friends of the Handicapped Riders, 1979-80; bd. dirs., chmn. fin. com. Americana Towers Condominium Assn. Lic. real estate broker, Ill. Mem. Chgo. Fin. Advertisers, Nat. Assn. Bank Women, Am. Soc. Tng. and Devel., Ill. Hunters and Jumpers Assn., English Speaking Union, Alpha Chi Omega. Episcopalian. Club: Lake Shore Center. Home: 1636 N Wells St Chicago IL 60614 Office: 12015 S Western Ave Blue Island IL 60406

WALSH, PETER JOHN, ins. co. exec.; b. Darby, Pa., Jan. 28, 1939; s. Peter Joseph and Nora Ann (Hallinan) W.; B.S., Villanova U., 1962; M.B.A., Seton Hall U., 1971; m. Eileen Elizabeth Whelan, Apr. 25, 1964; children—Ellen Marie, Suzanne, Juliann, Sean Peter. Staff accountant Ernst & Ernst, N.Y.C., 1962-63, George E. Marucci & Co., Upper Darby, Pa., 1963-65; sr. auditor Univac div. Sperry Rand, Blue Bell, Pa., 1966; sr. auditor Merck & Co., Inc., Rahway, N.J., 1967, analyst, 1967-68, sr. consolidation accountant, 1969-70; dir. internal audit Western Union Corp., Upper Saddle River, N.J., 1970-77; controller Fgn. Credit Ins. Assn., N.Y.C., 1977—. Served with U.S. Army, 1963. Mem. Am., Pa. insts. C.P.A.'s, Fin. Execs. Inst. Republican. Roman Catholic. Club: K.C. Home: 780 Albemarle St Wyckoff NJ 07481 Office: One World Trade Center 9th Floor New York City NY 10048

WALSH, VINCENT JAMES, SR., corp. exec.; b. Teaneck, N.J., Jan. 2, 1943; s. Michael J. and Jane G. W.; B.A. in Mktg., Fairleigh Dickinson U., 1966; student law Felician Coll., Lodi, N.J., 1978; m. Dorothy Jane Campman, Aug. 10, 1962; children—Vincent J., Charles M., Alyson Lee, Jennifer Jill, Courtney Jill. Pres., chief operating officer Hackensack News Co., Carlstad, N.J., 1966—; chief exec. officer Queen Anne Services and Big Apple Delivery Systems, 6 other corps., Teaneck, 1962—. Pres., Valley Cottage Engine Co. 1, 1968-69. Mem. Suburban Wholesalers Assn. (1st v.p.), Met. Rt. Dealers Assn. (pres. 1978-80). Democrat. Roman Catholic. Home: 605 Standish Rd Teaneck NJ 07666 Office: 230 US Rt 46 Little Ferry NJ 07643

WALSH, WALTER JOSEPH, ins. co. exec.; b. N.Y.C., Jan. 5, 1929; s. Walter Gordon and Anna (Mullins) W.; A.B., Allegheny Coll., 1955; M.B.A., U. Pitts., 1960; m. Sally Kloppman, June 9, 1956; children—Terence Allen, Brian Patrick, Laurie Ann. Reporter, Meadville (Pa.) Tribune, 1953-55; asst. to public relations dir. Welch Grape Juice Co., Westfield, N.Y., 1955-57; supr. editorial services Dravo Corp., Pitts., 1957-60; asst. to public relations dir. Oscar Mayer & Co., Madison, Wis., 1960-67; dir. public relations Bankers Life, Des Moines, 1967-80, v.p. public relations, 1980—. Pres., Des Moines Symphony Assn., 1974-76; bd. dirs. Community Blood Bank of Iowa, 1968—, pres., 1977—; bd. dirs. Des Moines YMCA. Served with U.S. Navy, 1948-52. Mem. Public Relations Soc. Am. (chmn. Midwest 1972-73, pres. Iowa chpt. 1977-79, dir. 1979—), Des Moines C. of C., Am. Council Life Ins., Life Ins. Advertisers Assn. Roman Catholic. Club: Des Moines Golf and Country (dir.). Office: 711 High St Des Moines IA 50307

WALSTAD, PAUL JAMES, lawyer; b. Great Falls, Mont., Aug. 27, 1944; s. Berner M. and Elsie Bernadine (Vancil) W.; B.A., Am. U., 1966; J.D., Am. U., 1969; m. Nancy J. Walstad, Mar. 9, 1963; children—Kimberly, Paul James, Peter, Phillip, Michael, Susan, Karen, Catherine, Kirsten. Asst. to Congressman Charles E. Bennett, Washington, 1963-69; legis. asst. Bldg. and Constrn. Trades Dept., AFL-CIO, Washington, 1969-70; admitted to Va. bar, 1969; asso. firm Lewis, Mitchell & Moore, Vienna, Va., 1970-73, partner, 1974; partner, Walstad, Wickwire, Peterson, Gavin & Asselin, Washington and Vienna, Va., 1974-78, Walstad, Kasimer, Tansey & Ittig, Vienna and Washington, 1979—; chmn. 4th circuit contrn. com. Am. Bar Assn. litigation sect., 1976—. Mem. Loudoun County Bd. suprs., 1971-74; commr. No. Va. Planning Dist. Commn., 1971-74, vice chmn. 1973-74; chmn. legis. com., 1972-73, chmn. pub. safety com. Metro D.C. Council Govts., 1973-74. Named Outstanding Young Man, Sterling Park Jr. C. of C., 1974. Mem. Am. (chmn. 4th circuit constrn. com. litigation sect. 1976—), Va. bar assns., Bar Assn. D.C., Assn. Trial Lawyers Am., No. Va. Trial Lawyers Assn., Am. Judicature Soc., U.S. Jaycees. Republican. Mormon. Contbr. articles to profl. jours. Home: 2237 Hunter Mill Rd Vienna VA 22180 Office: 1607 New Hampshire Ave NW Washington DC 20009

WALSTEN, MICHAEL COLE, agrl. editor; b. Galesburg, Ill., Feb. 18, 1947; s. Curtis Howard and Mildred Gertrude (Cole) W.; B.S., U. Ill., 1970, M.B.A., 1972; m. Judith Kay Sims, Feb. 21, 1970; children—Sarah Elizabeth, Timothy Michael. Asso. editor Farm Jour., Phila., 1972-74; mng. editor Livestock Publs., Farm Jour.,

Phila., 1974-75; asso. editor Profl. Farmers of Am., Cedar Falls, Iowa, 1975-78, mng. editor, 1978-79, exec. editor, 1979—. Mem. Soc. Profl. Journalists, Am. Agrl. Editors Assn., Am. Soc. Farm Mgrs. and Rural Appraisers, Sigma Delta Chi. Presbyterian. Club: Lions. Home: 4024 Horseshoe Dr Cedar Falls IA 50613 Office: 219 Parkade St Cedar Falls IA 50613

WALTER, JAMES MICHAEL, engr.; b. Neenah, Wis., Nov. 11, 1946; s. Milton Michael and Marie Helen (Dryer) W.; B.S. in Engring., Purdue U., 1968, M.S. in Indsl. Engring., 1969; m. Susan Marguerite Albrecht, June 15, 1968; children—Tara Sue, Michael John. Indsl. engr. Kimberly Clark Corp., Neenah, 1968-71, project mgr., 1971-73, mill engr., Beech Island, S.C., 1973-74, ops. supt., Memphis, 1974-77, mill planner, Neenah, 1977-79, project engr., 1979—; instr. U. Wis., 1969-70. Bd. dirs. St. John Parochial Sch., Menasha, Wis., 1972, pres., 1973. Mem. Theta Tau, Tau Beta Pi, Sigma Phi Alpha, Phi Eta Sigma. Club: K.C. Contbr. articles to profl. jours. Home: 2219 Gmeiner Rd Appleton WI 54911 Office: PO Box 999 Neenah WI 54952

WALTER, JAMES W., mfg. co. exec.; b. Lewes, Del., 1922; m. Monica Saraw, 1946; children—James W., Robert. Chmn. bd., chief exec. officer, dir. Jim Walter Corp., 1955—; dir. Walter E. Heller Internat. Corp., Gen. Telephone & Electronics Co., Biejerinvest, Sweden. Office: 1500 N Dale Mabry St Tampa FL 33607

WALTER, JOSEPH C., JR., oil co. exec. Chmn., Houston Oil & Minerals Corp. Office: 1212 Main St Houston TX 77001*

WALTER, NOLA JANICE, rental co. exec.; b. Eau Claire, Wis., Mar. 29, 1934; d. Robert Emmet and Adeline Victoria (Johnson) Rossman; student Dist. 1 Tech. Inst., Eau Claire, 1977-78; 1 dau., Rhea Carol. Exec. sec. W.H. Hobbs Supply Co., Eau Claire, 1952-54; jr. accountant C.A. Irwin Co., Eau Claire, 1954-61; legal sec. various attys. in Eau Claire, Mpls., 1963-73; office mgr. Bearson-Steinmetz Rentals, Eau Claire, 1974—. Recipient Gregg Shorthand certificate of merit, 1952; certificates of award in oil painting, 1977, 78; Silver and Bronze awards in competitive dancing, 1979. Mem. Smithsonian Assos., Nat. Wildlife Fedn., Nat. Trust for Hist. Preservation, Mpls. Soc. Fine Arts, Am. Film Inst. Democrat. Congregationalist. Home: 825 Barland St Eau Claire WI 54701 Office: 315 E Madison St Eau Claire WI 54701

WALTER, TERRY LYNN, psychologist; b. Gt. Bend, Kans., Dec. 23, 1928; s. Clifton William and Helen Naudia (Rusco) W.; B.S., Kans. State U., 1952; M.Ed., U. Mo., 1969, Ph.D., 1979; m. Evelyn Margaret Evans, July 3, 1949; children—Marcia Jeanne, Sandra Alice, Michael Kent, Steven Craig. Chemist, Halliburton Oil Well Cement Co., Gt. Bend, 1945-47; research asst. Dept. Agr., Manhattan, Kans., 1948-52; extension tchr. math. and sci. U. Md., 1953-54; elem. sch. tchr. Fairview Sch., Norton, Kans., 1955-56; cons. engr. Walter Cons. Engring. Services, Tribune, Kans., 1954—; exec. v.p. Asso. Personnel Technicians, Inc., Wichita, Kans., 1975-79, pres., 1979—; owner, operator Mineral Exploration & Devel. Unlimited, Wichita, 1975—; pres. Walter Exploration & Devel. Unltd., Inc., 1976—; chmn. bd. PAT, N.V., W.E.D.U., Inc.; dir. KAW Cons., Pool Petroleum Co., Inc. Chmn. bd. Wichita Child Guidance Center, 1979-80, Christian Community Services, Inc., 1975-77; bd. dirs. Am. Baptist Chs. U.S.A., 1976-79. Served with USAF, 1952-54. Registered profl. engr., Kans. Mem. Am. Personnel and Guidance Assn., Am. Coll. Personnel Assn., Am. Psychol. Assn., Am. Soc. Personnel Adminstrs., Adminstrv. Mgmt. Soc., Kans. Ind. Oil and Gas Assn., Kans. Profl. Engrs. Assn. Clubs: Petroleum, Crestview Country. Home: 6700 Abbotsford Pl Wichita KS 67206 Office: 1650 E Central St Wichita KS 67214

WALTERS, GEORGE WILLIAM, JR., ins. agt.; b. Bridgeport, Conn., Sept. 3, 1950; s. George William and Marjorie Ellen (Lopes) W.; student South Central Community Coll. Conn., 1969-70; grad. various ins. insts.; student Huebner Sch. C.L.U. Studies, Am. U., 1977—. Agt., dist. rep., asst. br. mgr., field tng. supr. Certified Life Ins. Co. Calif., Oakland, 1973-75; dist. rep., San Francisco, 1975-77, agt., Marin County, Calif., 1977; agt. Bankers Life & Casualty Co., North Haven, Conn., 1977—; asso. MacArthur Ins. Group, Calif. and Conn., 1973-81, Prudential Ins. Am., New Haven, 1981—. Hon. mem. New Haven County Dep. Sherriffs Assn. Recipient Grand award Certified Life Ins. Co. Calif., 1974, 75, 76, Wall of Fame award, 1976, named to Pres.'s Club, 1974—. Mem. Nat. Assn. Life Underwriters, Nat. Notaries Soc. Democrat. Episcopalian. Home: 70 Fountain Terr New Haven CT 06515 Office: 47 College St Suite 202 New Haven CT 06510

WALTERS, HAROLD WALLACE, assn. exec.; b. Amarillo, Tex., Apr. 17, 1929; s. Leslie Alva and Nellie (Jackson) W.; B.S., Purdue U., 1955; grad. Inst. Assn. Mgmt., Mich. State U.; m. Donna, Aug. 25, 1979; children—Michael, David, Cynthia, Nancy, Diane. With Nat. Assn. Mut. Ins. Cos., Indpls., 1955—, exec. sec.-mgr., then exec. v.p.-gen. mgr., 1963-72, pres., gen. mgr., 1972—; mem. bd. electors Ins. Hall of Fame; dir. Hoosier Travel Service. Chartered assn. exec. Mem. Am. Soc. Assn. Execs., Conf. Casualty Ins. Cos. (exec. v.p.), Ind. Soc. Assn. Execs. (past pres.). Republican. Club: Downtown Indspls, Kiwanis. Office: 7931 Castleway Dr Indianapolis IN 46250

WALTERS, HOYLE SAGER, wholesale co. exec., developer; b. Danville, Va., May 9, 1924; s. Archie Hoyle and Mabel Cathryn (Lindsay) W.; B.S., Va. Commonwealth U., 1950; m. Ruby G. Merriman, Nov. 20, 1948; children—Wendra Leigh, Joanne. Salesman, Welmont Electric Corp., 1949-52; advt. mgr. Goldberg Co., Inc., Richmond, Va., 1952-54, territory mgr., 1952-63, sales mgr., 1963-64, v.p. sales, from 1964; v.p. 7200 Corp., from 1963; partner DDW Assos., Land and Devel., Richmond, 1979—, hh Assos., Apt. Aquisition, Richmond, 1979—. Served with AUS, 1943-46; ETO. Lutheran (v.p. council 1964-65). Home: 4301 Shirley Rd Richmond VA 23225 Office: 4377 Carolina Ave Richmond VA 23222

WALTERS, JEFFERSON BROOKS, musician, real estate broker; b. Dayton, Ohio, Jan. 22, 1922; s. Jefferson Brooks and Mildred Frances (Smith) W.; student U. Dayton, 1947; m. Mary Elizabeth Espey, Apr. 6, 1963; children—Dinah Christine Basson, Jefferson Brooks. Composer, cornetist, Dayton, 1934—; real estate broker, Dayton, 1948—; founder Am. Psalm Choir, 1965; music counselor BHA, Inc., Dayton, 1979. Vice-chmn. bd. dirs. Friends of the Library, Wright State U. Served with USCGR, 1942-45; PTO, ETO. Mem. S.A.R., Greater Dayton Antique Study Club (past pres.), Dayton Art Inst., Montgomery County Hist. Presbyn. Mason (32 deg.). Condr., composer choral, solo voice settings of psalms and poetry Alfred Lord Tennyson; composer Crossing the Bar (meml. performances U.S. Navy band), 1961. Home: 400 Ridgewood Ave Dayton OH 45409 Office: 53 Park Ave Dayton OH 45409

WALTERS, RONALD OGDEN, consumer fin. corp. exec.; b. Holcombe, Wis., July 13, 1939; s. Ogden Eugene and Anna Josephine (Hennekens) W.; student U. Wis., Madison, 1957-59; grad. Nat. Installment Bankers Sch., Boulder, Colo., 1974; m. Margaret Ellen Weisheipl, July 14, 1962; children—Laurie Ann, Cheryl Leigh, Michael Ogden, Patrick Ronald. Trainee, Thorp Fin. Corp., Chippewa Falls, Wis., 1959-63, mgr., La Crosse, Wis., 1963-65, regional mgr., Milw., 1965-69; regional mgr. ITT Consumer Fin. Corp. (purchased Thorp Fin. Corp.), Milw., 1969-74, div. dir., Milw., 1974-76, v.p., area gen. mgr., Milw., 1976—; pres. Aetna Indsl. Bank, Denver, 1980—. Pres. Wis. Consumer Fin. Assn., 1980. Roman Catholic. Office: 150 N Sunnyslope Rd Brookfield WI 53005

WALTERS, ROY WASHINGTON, JR., mgmt. cons.; b. Chattanooga, Oct. 22, 1918; s. Roy Washington and Ruth (Gokey) W.; B.S. in Engring., U. Pitts., 1941; m. Mary Annette Campbell, Aug. 23, 1941; children—Roy Washington III, Christine, Carolyn, Ruth. With Bell Telephone Co. of Pa., 1941-60; dir. employment and devel. A.T. & T., N.Y.C., 1960-68; pres. Roy W. Walters & Assos., Inc., Mahwah, N.J., 1968—. Served with USAAF, 1942-46; CBI. Cert. mgmt. cons.; accredited personnel diplomat. Mem. Inst. Mgmt. Consultants, Am. Soc. Tng. and Devel., Am. Soc. Personnel Adminstrn., Sales Execs. Club. Club: Masons. Author: Job Enrichment for Results, 1975. Home: 344 Grandview Circle Ridgewood NJ 07450 Office: Whitney Industrial Park Mahwah NJ 07430

WALTERSDORF, JOHN MAURICE, elec. supply co. exec.; b. Washington, Pa., Mar. 1, 1926; s. Maurice and Elizabeth (Crapster) W.; B.A., Yale U., 1948; M.B.A., U. Chgo., 1949; m. Margaret Canby Stott, Sept. 15, 1951; children—John Galt, Elizabeth Grayson, Margaret O'Neal, Roberta Annan. Sales and advt. Waltersdorf Furniture Co., Hanover, Pa., 1949-52; sales promotion mgr. Tristate Elec. Supply Co., Balt., 1952-54, exec. v.p., Hagerstown, Md., 1956-58, pres., 1958—; pres. Graybills, Inc., Hagerstown, 1954-56; chmn. bd. Antietam Bank Co., Hagerstown, 1975—. Chmn. bd. Hagerstown Regional Airport, 1977—; trustee Washington County Mus. Fine Arts, Hood Coll., 1978—. Served with Signal Corps, U.S. Army, 1946-47; ofcl. photographer Admiral Byrd Naval Antarctic Expdn. Mem. Council on Capital Formation (dir.), Nat. Assn. Wholesaler-Distbrs. (pres. 1974, 75, chmn. bd. trustees 1975-76), Nat. Assn. Elec. Distbrs. (pres. 1970, 71), Small Bus. Adv. Council, Phi Gamma Delta. Episcopalian. Clubs: Assembly, Fountain Head Country, Center. Home: 947 The Terrace Hagerstown MD 21740 Office: PO Box 469 Hagerstown MD 21740

WALTHALL, JOHN H. T., savs. and loan exec.; b. Roanoke, Va., Nov. 27, 1923; s. John Henry and Annabel Lee (Jordan) W.; B.S. in Commerce, U. Ky., 1949; m. Elizabeth Ann Callihan, May 6, 1954; 1 dau., Ann Mitchell. Salesman, Gevedon Realty Co., 1949-58; sec.-treas. Ashland Fed. Savs. and Loan Assn. (Ky.), 1958-66, v.p., 1966-71, pres., mng. officer, 1971—; dir. Savs. and Loan Data Corp., Ky. Ohio Gas Co. Bd. dirs. Ashland Urban Renewal and Community Devel. Agy., Ashland Rehab. and Conservation of Housing Bd. Served with C.E., U.S. Army, 1943-46. Mem. Ashland Area C. of C. (past dir.), Home Builders Assn., Ashland Area Bd. Realtors. Presbyterian. Office: 344 17th St Ashland KY 41101

WALTON, ROBERT WHEELER, trade assn. exec.; b. Melfort, Sask., Can., Sept. 6, 1919; came to U.S., 1925; s. James Nathaniel and Blanche Stella (Wheeler) W.; B.S., Ind. U., 1948; postgrad. Nat. Inst. Comml. and Trade Orgn. Execs., Northwestern U., 1949-52; m. Janet Ewing Langam, Oct. 2, 1948; children—William Lanham, Lucinda. Pres. Walton & Assos., Inc., Indpls., 1948—; exec. v.p. Nat. Precast Concrete Assn.; exec. dir. Archtl. Precast Assn.; exec. sec. Great Lakes Ice Assn., Mid-west Ready Mixed Concrete Assn.; exec. dir. Ind. Concrete Masonry Assn.; exec. v.p. Ind. Soc. Public Accts. Elder Presbyterian Ch. Served to capt. USAF, 1941-47; PTO. Recipient Robert E. Yoakum award Nat. Precast Concrete Assn., 1978; named to Great Lakes Ice Assn. Hall of Fame, 1979. Mem. Am. Concrete Inst., ASTM, U.S. C. of C., Can. C. of C., Nat. Fedn. Ind. Bus., Internat. Concrete Assn. Execs. (dir.), Am. Soc. Assn. Execs., Inst. Assn. Mgmt. Cos. Republican. Clubs: Elks, Indpls. Athletic. Contbr. to Modern Concrete Mag., Concrete Products Mag. Office: 825 E 64th St Indianapolis IN 46220

WALTUCH, NORTON DONALD, brokerage exec.; b. N.Y.C., Apr. 25, 1932; s. Joseph and Ruth (Haber) W.; B.S., FairleighDickinson U., 1953; m. Anita RuthZuckerman, June 24, 1956; children—Randall Eric, Denise Jill. With Bache & Co., N.Y.C., 1958-63; commodity futures specialist Hayden Stone Inc., N.Y.C., 1963-70; commodity futures specialist, v.p. Conti Commodity Services Inc., N.Y.C., 1970—; dir. Conti Capital Mgmt.; bd. govs. Citrus Assos. and Petroleum Assos. of N.Y. Cotton Exchange; mem. arbitration and bus. conduct cons. N.Y. Merc. Exchange. Served with U.S. Army, 1954-56. Mem. Chgo. Bd. Trade, Interat. Monetary Market Chgo. Merc. Exchange, N.Y. Merc. Exchange, N.Y. Cotton Exchange, Commody Exchange, Inc., N.Y. Coffee, Sugar and Cocoa Exchange, London Cocoa Terminal Market. Jewish. Clubs: Commodity N.Y., Mason. Home: 180 S Woodland St Englewood NJ 07631 Office: 4 World Trade Center New York NY 10048

WALUKONIS, EDWARD MATTHEW, data processing exec.; b. Shenandoah, Pa., Sept. 30, 1951; s. Albert Edward and Elizabeth Claire (Lutz) W.; student Intext Computer Inst., Allentown, Pa., 1969-70, Northampton County Community Coll., 1972; m. Maria S. Alfieri, Oct. 7, 1972. Systems engr. Computer Action, Inc., Souderton, Pa., 1972-73; programmer-analyst Lehi Dairy, Allentown, Pa., 1973-74; dir. info. systems Reading (Pa.) Hosp. and Med. Center, 1974—. Bd. dirs. Reading Hosp. and Med. Center Fed. Credit Union, 1977—, pres., 1977-79. Mem. Smithsonian Inst. Assos., Data Processing Mgmt. Assn. Republican. Roman Catholic. Home: 815 Rainbow Ave Fox Chase Reading PA 19605 Office: 6th and Spruce St Reading PA 19603

WALVOORD, R. WAYNE, mgmt. cons.; b. Beaver, Utah, Mar. 4, 1944; s. Oliver Wendall and Evelyn Elizabeth (Greenway) W.; B.A. in Internat. Affairs cum laude, U. Colo., 1970; M. Internat. Mgmt., Am. Grad. Sch. Internat. Mgmt., 1971; diploma Am. Bankers Assn., 1974; m. Lady DiIenno, Oct. 6, 1973; children—Laura Grace, Damon Oliver, Adrianne Elizabeth. With Peace Corps, Turkey and Afghanistan, 1965-66; export bus. devel. officer Provident Nat. Bank, Phila., 1971-74; resident banker Export Import Bank U.S., 1973; asst. v.p., mgr. internat. dept. Security Trust Co., Rochester, N.Y., 1974-77; pres., founder Internat. Trade Mgmt. Co., Inc., Rochester, also mng. dir., founder Trade Mgmt. Co. N.V. (Netherland Antilles), 1979—; chmn., lectr., writer Am. Mgmt. Assn. Bd. dirs. Rochester Assn. UN, Rochester Confedn. Internat. Orgns.; former pres. and chmn. Rochester World Trade Council; past mem. Rochester com. Council Fgn. Relations. Mem. Rochester C. of C., Am. Mgmt. Assn., Nat. Assn. Fgn. Trade Zones, Nat. Com. Internat. Trade Documentation, Am. Wine Soc. Republican. Contbg. editor Am. Import Export Bull., 1979—. Home: 62 Waterford Way Fairport NY 14450 Office: 2550 Baird Rd Penfield NY 14526

WAMBOLDT, DONALD GEORGE, fin. exec.; b. Sterling, Colo., Oct. 23, 1932; s. J. George and Marie K. (Schneider) W.; B.A., U. Calif., Berkeley, 1953; m. Helen L. Moore, June 26, 1954; children—Alan Dale, Carol Anne. With State Farm Fire & Casualty Co., 1955—, underwriter, Berkeley, Calif., 1955-58, underwriting supt., Santa Ana, Calif., 1958-63, regional fire mgr., Greeley, Colo., 1963-68, v.p. underwriting, Bloomington, Ill., 1968—. Served with U.S. Army, 1953-55. Cert. property and casualty underwriter; C.L.U. Mem. Soc. Cert. Property and Casualty Underwriters, Soc. C.L.U.'s, McLain County C. of C. Republican. Lutheran. Home: Rural Route 4 Bloomington IL 61701 Office: 112 E Washington St Bloomington IL 61701

WAMBOLT, THOMAS EUGENE, fin. cons.; b. Scottsbluff, Nebr., Aug. 9, 1938; s. Andrew, Jr. and Anne (Altergott) W.; B.S., Met. State Coll., Denver, 1976; m. Linda E. Shifflett, Oct. 31, 1967; 1 son, Richard Duane King. Pres. Universal Imports Co., Westminster, Colo., 1967-71; printer Rocky Mountain News, Denver, 1967-78; propr., accountant Thomas E. Wambolt Co., Arvada, Colo., 1974-77, fin. adviser, 1977—. Baptist. Address: 6035 Garrison St Arvada CO 80004

WAND, RICHARD WALTON, paper co. exec.; b. Shelbyville, Ind., Sept. 20, 1939; s. J. Harold and Josephine Katharine (Harvey) W.; B.S. in Mech. Engring., Purdue U., 1961; M.B.A., Ind. U., 1964; m. Sharon Brierly, June 21, 1964; children—Brian James, Katharine. Project engr. Combustion Engring., Inc., 1961-63; mgr. tech. ops. Aerospace Research Applications Center, Ind. U., 1963-65; with Bergstrom Paper Co., Neenah, Wis., 1965—, adminstrv. v.p., 1972-79, exec. v.p.-ops., 1979-80; v.p. adminstrn. P.H. Glatfelter Co., Spring Grove, Pa., 1980—. Bd. dirs. Jr. Achievement of York County (Pa.). Mem. Nat. Assn. Recycling Industries (dir., exec. com.), Am. Paper Inst. (chmn. deinking mills sect., dir. pulp consumers div.), Solid Waste Council, Beta Theta Pi. Republican. Presbyterian. Clubs: University (Chgo.); Wynfield (York, Pa.). Contbg. editor Infosystems mag., 1972-73. Home: 45 E Springettsbury Ave York PA 17403 Office: PH Glatfelter Co 228 S Main St Spring Grove PA 17362

WANDERS, HANS WALTER, banker; b. Aachen, Germany, Apr. 3, 1925; came to U.S., 1929, naturalized, 1943; s. Herbert and Anna Maria (Kusters) W.; B.S., Yale U., 1947; grad. cert. Rutgers U. Grad. Sch. Banking, 1964; m. Elizabeth Knox Kimball, Apr. 2, 1949; children—Crayton Kimball, David Gillette. Trainee, Gen. Electric Co., 1947-48; mgmt. trainee to Chgo. dist. sales mgr. plastic products Plaskon div. Libbey-Owens-Ford Glass Co., 1948-53, Plaskon div. (acquired by Allied Chem. Co. 1953) Allied Chem. Co., 1953-55; asso. McKinsey & Co., Inc., 1955-57; asst. cashier No. Trust Co., Chgo., 1957-59, 2d v.p., 1959-62, v.p., 1962-65; v.p. Nat. Blvd. Bank, Chgo., 1965-66, pres., 1966-70; exec. v.p. Wachovia Bank and Trust Co., N.A., Winston-Salem, N.C., 1970-74, chmn. bd., 1977—; pres. Wachovia Corp., Winston-Salem, 1974-76, chmn. bd., 1977—, also dir.; trustee Wachovia Realty Investments; v.p., dir. Winton Mineral Co.; dir. Hanes Dye & Finishing Co., N.C. Textile Found., Inc., N.C. Engring. Found., Inc. Pres., N.C. Sch. Arts Found., Inc., 1972-73; chmn. Winston-Salem Found. Com., 1981—; N.C. area chmn. Campaign for Yale, 1976-78; chmn. Salem Acad. and Coll. Challenge Campaign, 1979—. Served to lt. USNR, 1943-46, 51-53. Mem. Am. Bankers Assn. (chmn., dir. Communications Council 1971-73, chmn. mktg. div. 1979-80), Assn. Res. City Bankers, Assn. Bank Holding Cos. (dir. 1980—), Conf. Bd. (mem. So. regional adv. council 1974—), Internat. C. of C. (trustee U.S. Council 1974-80), Newcomen Soc. N.Am. Episcopalian. Clubs: Yale (N.Y.C.); Chgo. Commonwealth; Old Town (Winston-Salem); Roaring Gap (Roaring Gap, N.C.). Office: 301 N Main St Winston-Salem NC 27101

WANG, CHARLES JOSEPH, business exec.; b. Fushan, China, Nov. 3, 1943; s. Joseph C. and Mary (Chao) W.; student Manhattan Coll., 1962; B.A., U. Wash., 1969; postgrad. Seattle U., 1971; m. Patricia C. Hedrick, June 20, 1970; children—Stephen, Kristin, Jeffrey, Michael. Mktg. rep. Info. Services Bus. div. Gen. Electric Co., Seattle, 1969-71, tech. cons., Bethesda, Md., 1971-72; dir. systems and programming Robert Hall Co., N.Y.C., 1972-75; pres. Wang Assos., Amityville, N.Y., 1973-76, Wang Systems Inc., N.Y.C., 1976—, Tekkon Computer Services Corp., 1980—. Roman Catholic. Home: 6 Willa Way Massapequa NY 11758 Office: 380 N Broadway Jericho NY 11753

WANG, CHEN CHI, electronics co. exec., real estate exec.; b. Taipei, Taiwan, China, Aug. 10, 1932; s. Chin-Ting and Chen-Kim (Chen) W.; came to U.S., 1959, naturalized, 1970; B.A., Nat. Taiwan U., 1955; B.S.E.E., San Jose State U., 1965; M.B.A., U. Calif. at Berkeley, 1961; m. Victoria Rebisoff, Mar. 5, 1965; children—Katherine Kim, Gregory Chen, John Christopher. With IBM Corp., San Jose, Calif., 1965-72; founder, mgr. Electronics Internat. Co., Santa Clara, Calif., 1968-72, owner, gen. mgr., 1972—; dir. Systek Electronics Corp., Santa Clara, 1970-73; founder, sr. partner Wang Enterprises, Santa Clara, 1974—; founder, sr. partner Hanson & Wang Devel. Co., Woodside, Calif., 1977—; founder, sr. partner Alpha Enterprises, Hillsborough, Calif., 1979—; mng. partner Woodside Acres-Las Pulgas Estate, Woodside, 1980—. Served to 2d lt., Nationalist Chinese Army, 1955-56. Mem. Internat. Platform Assn., Tau Beta Pi. Mem. Christian Ch. Author: Monetary and Banking System of Taiwan, 1955; The Small Car Market in the U.S., 1961. Home: 195 Brookwood Rd Woodside CA 94062 Office: PO Box 4082 Woodside CA 94062

WANG, DONALD TED, computer systems co. exec.; b. Chgo., May 7, 1942; s. Harold Sigurd and Eleanor Marie (Andresen) W.; B.A., So. Ill. U., 1966. Systems analyst Mid-Am. Computer Corp., 1971-73, sr. mfg. systems con., 1974-75, mgr. data base adminstrn., Bensenville, Ill., 1976—. Served with USAF, 1967-71. Mem. IEEE, Assn. Computing Machinery. Office: Mid America Dr Bensenville IL 60106

WANG, LU-WEI (ROBERT), hobby and handicraft import co. exec.; b. China, Dec. 12, 1948; s. D.C. and Wen (Huang) W.; M.A., Memphis State U., 1975; m. Susie Lee Wang, Apr. 10, 1975; children—Eugene Lee, Robert Lee. Pres., Wang's Internat., Inc., Memphis, World of Handicraft, Inc., Memphis. Mem. Hobby Industry Assn. Am. Address: 1437 Eastridge Dr Memphis TN 38138

WANG, SAMSON, bank exec.; b. Chungking, China, Aug. 10, 1944; s. Edward Fang and Grace (Chang-Ling) W.; B.A., Yale U., 1967; M.B.A., Columbia U., 1969; m. Pauline Fung; children—Andrew, Christopher. Security analyst Kidder Peabody & Co., N.Y.C., 1969-71; sr. security analyst Coll. Retirement Equities Fund, N.Y.C., 1973; v.p. Bank of N.Y., N.Y.C., 1974-77, sr. v.p., 1977—; guest lectr. New Sch., N.Y.C. Mem. N.Y. Soc. Security Analysts, Fin. Analysts Fedn., Inst. Quantitative Research, Yale Alumni Assn. Mem. Christian Ch. Office: 48 Wall St New York NY 10005

WANG, THOMAS KELIANG, city ofcl., community service adminstr.; b. Yin-chun, Hu-Hsien, Shensi, China, June 26, 1920; s. Chin Hsun and Yinn C. (Wang) W.; came to U.S., 1947, naturalized, 1956; B.A., Nat. Northwestern U., China, 1944; M.A., N.Y. U., 1951; m. En-Ming Chen, Apr. 27, 1951; children—George Hansen, John Linson, Aveline Enming. Pvt. sec. to pres. of Control Yuan, Chinese Nat. Govt., 1944-47; gen. mgr. Peking and Canton restaurant, Bklyn., 1951-55; office mgr. Trade Union Courier Pub. Corp., N.Y.C., 1955-56, comptroller, 1956-61, chief exec. officer, 1962-64, dir., sec. treas., 1959-63; comptroller World Wide Press Syndicate, 1955-62; housing adviser Dept. Social Services, City of N.Y., 1966-69, spl. asst. to dep. commr. for adminstrn., 1969-75; chmn. bd. Chinatown Service Center, Inc., N.Y.C., 1971—; chmn. bd. N.Y. Chinatown Sr. Citizen Coalition Center, Inc., 1976—; founder of Chinatown Daycare Center, Inc., N.Y.C., 1970, chmn., 1970—. Mem. Com. for Formation of Siking Coll., N.Y.C., 1972—; pres. of Chinese-Am. Republican

Club of N.Y. State, 1975—. Mem. Am. Soc. Pub. Adminstrn., Asian Am. Assembly for Policy Research, Harry S. Truman Library Inst., Smithsonian Assos. Home: 34 Crooke Ave Brooklyn NY 11226 Office: 35-37 37 1/2 Division St New York NY 10002

WANSING, WILLIAM JOSEPH, automobile co. exec.; b. St. Louis, Feb. 2, 1950; s. Joseph and Grace (Klenke) W.; B.A., St. Louis U., 1978. With Chrysler Corp., Fenton, Mo., 1968—, sr. adv. mgmt. programs, 1980—. Served with U.S. Army, 1969-71. Mem. Mo. Real Estate Assn., Personnel Adminstrn. St. Louis. Home: 80 Jefflyn Dr Valley Park MO 63088 Office: 931 St Louis Ave East Saint Louis IL 62201

WANTA, LEO EMIL, mgmt. cons.; b. Stevens Point, Wis., June 11, 1940; s. Emil William and Ethel Mary (Aanonsen) W.; Indsl. Engr., Milw. Inst. Tech.; grad. Metals Engring. Inst., Am. Soc. Metals; grad. network methods program U. Wis., Oshkosh; grad. Lincoln Inst., Cleve.; m. Joanne Elizabeth Ramstack, Aug. 5, 1961; children—Brian Michael, Christine Elizabeth, Michael Lee. Supr. mfg. engring. Wis. Centrifugal Foundry and Machining, Inc., 1970-72; plant mgr. S.C. Johnson EEE Corp., Racine, Wis., 1972-74; gen. mgr., chief exec. officer Freeman div. Allied Products, Peru, Ind., 1974-76; mgr. ops. Kimberly Clark Corp., Neenah, Wis., 1976-78; pres. Leo E. Wanta Assos., Appleton and Menomonee Falls, Wis., 1970—. Bd. dirs. YMCA. Mem. ASME (vice chmn. 1971), Soc. Mfg. Engrs., Am. Metal Stamping Assn., Farm Equipment Mfrs. Assn., Soc. Packaging and Handling Engrs., Ind. C. of C. Republican. Roman Catholic. Club: K.C. Address: 2101 N Edgewood Ave Appleton WI 54911

WARD, GARY BRABANDER, mfg. co. exec.; b. Chgo., Nov. 22, 1939; s. William George and Lorraine (Dittus) W.; B.A., Colgate U., 1961; M.B.A., U. Pa., 1970; m. Mary Anne Doherty, Sept. 14, 1968; children—Amanda, Sarah, Elizabeth. Asst. dir. corp. devel. ITT Corp., 1971-78; v.p. AMF, Inc., White Plains, N.Y., 1978—. Asso. vestryman Christ's Ch., Rye, N.Y. Served with USNR, 1962-65. Mem. Fin. Execs. Inst. Club: Apawamis (Rye). Home: 100 Mendota Ave Rye NY 10580 Office: 777 Westchester Ave White Plains NY 10604

WARD, GEORGE DOUGLAS, financial co. exec.; b. Rochester, N.Y., Dec. 30, 1922; s. George Merritt and Ruth (Everest) W.; B.Chem. Engring., Cornell U., 1947; m. Carol Van Dorn Mygatt, Sept. 19, 1946; children—Charles Everest, Helen Terry, George Douglas. Engr., Esso Research & Engring. Co., Linden, N.J., 1947-59, mgr. European engring. office, The Hague, Netherlands, 1959-62, asst. gen. mgr. engring., Florham Park, N.J., 1962-64, dep. v.p. research, 1964-66; v.p. Esso Chem. Co., N.Y.C., 1967-71; pres. Ward Douglas & Co., Inc., Marbledale, Conn., 1971—, Westkey Petroleum Corp., Bowling Green, Ky., 1980—; dir. Linden Chems. & Plastics Corp. Served to 1st lt. AUS, 1943-46. Mem. Am. Inst. Chem. Engrs., Cornell Soc. Engrs., Tau Beta Pi, Delta Upsilon. Episcopalian. Clubs: Union League (N.Y.C.); Washington (Conn.). Home: Route 202 Box 276 Marbledale CT 06777

WARD, JOHN EDWARD, chem. co. exec.; b. Chgo., Feb. 7, 19—; s. Maxwell Andrew and Loretta (Watt) W.; A.B., Wabash Coll., 1943; M.S. (scholar), Inst. of Paper Chemistry, Appleton, Wis., 1948, Ph.D., 1951; m. Ada Lovinger, Nov. 2, 1946; children—Marianne Irene, Elizabeth Laura, Kitty, Johanna, Andrew John, Thomas Raoul. Research chemist P.H. Glatfelter Co., Spring Grove, Pa., 1950-51; research chemist Nopco Chem. Co., Harrison, N.J., 1951-55, tech. mgr. fgn. dept., 1955-59; mgr. Nopco Chimie S.A., Fribourg, Switzerland, 1959-76; mng. dir. Diamond Shamrock Chimie S.A., Fribourg, Switzerland, 1976—, also dir.; dir. Diamond Shamrock Electrosearch, Diamond Shamrock Chem. Products, Switzerland, Diamond Shamrock Process Chems. Ltd., Eng., Diamond Shamrock Eytesa S.A., Spain, Diamond Shamrock France S.A., Diamond Shamrock Italia S.p.A., Diamond Shamrock Schandinavia A/S, Norway, Munzing Chemie G.m.b.H., Germany. Served with AUS, 1943-46. Mem. Am. Chem. Soc., TAPPI, Phi Beta Kappa. Contbr. articles on paper making and paper coating to profl. jours; patentee indsl. chem. specialties. Home: 24 route de la Veveyse CH-1700 Fribourg Switzerland Office: Diamond Shamrock Chimie SA Case Postale 643 CH-1701 Fribourg Switzerland

WARD, JOHN VINES, assn. exec.; b. Indpls., Feb. 26, 1932; s. John W. and Eva (Vines) W.; B.S. in C.E., Purdue U., 1954; M.B.A., U. Wis., 1962; m. Virginia Costigan, Feb. 13, 1971; children—John P., Mark D., Scott S., Alexandra L. Sales engr., market analyst Aluminum Co. Am., Milw. and Pitts., 1956-62; mgmt. cons. McKinsey & Co., Chgo., 1963-66; dir. bus. devel. Boise Cascade, Portland, Oreg., 1965-69; v.p., exec. v.p. S.W. Forest Industries, Phoenix, 1969-73; pres. Tellus Corp., Coral Gables, Fla., 1973-74; sr. v.p. Ryland Group, Columbia, Md., 1974-78; v.p. internat. trade Nat. Forest Products Assn., Washington, 1978—. Bd. dirs. Family Life Center, Columbia, Md., 1977-80, Phoenix Housing Commn., 1972-74. Served to 1st lt. C.E., U.S. Army, 1954-56. Republican. Roman Catholic. Home: 9213 May Day Ct Columbia MD 10045 Office: 1619 Massachusetts Ave NW Washington DC 20036

WARD, LEW O., oil producer; b. Oklahoma City, July 24, 1930; s. Llewellyn Orcutt and Addie (Reisdorph) W. II; student Okla. Mil. Acad. Jr. Coll., 1948-50; B.S., Okla. U., 1953; m. Myra Beth Gungoll, Oct. 29, 1955; children—Casidy Ann, William Carlton. Dist. engr. Delhi-Taylor Oil Corp., Tulsa, 1955-56; partner Ward-Gungoll Oil Investments, Enid, Okla., 1956—; owner L.O. Ward Oil Ops., Enid, 1963—; v.p. 1420 Lahoma Rd. Inc., Enid, 1967—, also dir.; dir. Pulse Mag., Community Bank & Trust Co. Enid; mem. Okla. Gov.'s Adv. Council on Energy. Chmn. Indsl. Devel. Commn., Enid, 1968—; dir. Enid Indsl. Devel. Found.; chmn. bd. dirs. Okla. Polit. Action Com., 1974—, Bass Hosp.; active YMCA; chmn. Garfield County Republican party, 1967-69 adv. council Sch. Bus. Phillips U. Served as 1st lt. C.E., AUS, 1953-55. Registered profl. engr., Okla. Mem. Am. Inst. Mining and Metall. Engrs., Ind. Petroleum Assn. Am. (dir., area v.p.), Okla. Ind. Petroleum Assn. (dir., pres.), Am. Bus. Club (pres. 1964), Enid C. of C. (v.p., pres.-elect), Order Ky. Cols., Alpha Tau Omega. Methodist. Clubs: Masons, Shriners, Rotary, Toastmasters (pres. Enid 1966). Home: 900 Brookside Dr Enid OK 73701 Office: 502 S Fillmore Enid OK 73701

WARD, RALPH E., JR., corp. exec.; b. Scotch Plains, N.J., 1921; m. Eugenia Elizabeth McManigal, Sept. 28, 1944; children—Sarah Elizabeth, Richard Reynolds, Thomas Dudley, John Bessom, James Ralph. Chmn., pres., chief exec. officer, dir. Chesebrough-Pond's, Inc.; dir. Stauffer Chem. Co. Trustee Lafayette Coll. Office: 33 Benedict Pl Greenwich CT 06830*

WARD, SAMUEL JOSEPH, JR., banker; b. Savannah, Ga., Jan. 7, 1928; s. Samuel Joseph and Frankie Inez (Ward) W.; Asso. Sci., Armstrong Coll., 1949; B.S. in Indsl. Mgmt., Ga. Inst. Tech., 1951; postgrad. Indsl. Coll. Armed Forces, 1974-75; m. Barbara Sue McDuffee, June 27, 1951; children—Samuel Joseph III, Raymond Curtis, Dana Reginald, James Grady, Robert Edwin, Glenn William. Asst. mgr. Savannah Area C. of C., 1954-59; asst. to pres. Savannah Gas Co., 1959-66; v.p. sales promotion First Nat. Bank of Atlanta, 1966-70; v.p. mktg. First Ga. Bank, Atlanta, 1970-72; v.p. mktg., dir. pub. relations Bank of Va. Co., Richmond, 1972—. Mem. So. Indsl. Devel. Council, 1972—. Mem. Ga. Tech. Athletic Recruitment, 1966—; v.p., treas. Va. Boy Scouts Am., 1973—. Mem. Chatham County (Ga.) Bd. Edn., 1959-60. Trustee Ga. Found. Ind. Colls., 1962-72. Served with AUS, 1946-47, USAF, 1951-53 (col. Res.). Recipient Outstanding Man of Year award Savannah and Ga. State Jr. C. of C., 1960; Savannah Hist. Found., 1962; Community Relations award Am. Gas Assn., N.Y.C., 1962, 63. Mem. Bank Mktg. Assn. (chmn. public relations council), Ga. Inst. Tech. Alumni Assn. (past pres.), Richmond Pub. Relations Soc., Pub. Relations Soc. Am., Am. Soc. Tng. and Devel. (pres. Ga. chpt. 1970-71). Presbyn. (chmn.). Home: 2635 Radstock Rd Midlothian VA 23113 Office: Bank of Va Co 7 N 8th St Richmond VA 23260

WARD, WILLIAM HERBERT, mfg. co. exec.; b. Bodines, Pa., Jan. 18, 1931; s. William H. and Mary D. (West) W.; B.A., Upsala Coll., 1963; M.B.A., Fairleigh Dickinson U., 1978; m. Nancy Anne Taylor, Jan. 24, 1958; children—Kurt, Karen, Jennifer, Scott. Planning engr., test set designer Western Electric Co., 1956-62; sales engr., sales mgr. Agastat div. Amerace Corp.; pres. Amerace Ltd., Toronto, Buchanan Elec. Products Corp., Control Products div. Amerace Corp., Elastimold div. Amerace Corp., 1962—. Football coach Upsala Coll., 1956-57. Served with USMC, 1947-50. Mem. Am. Mgmt. Assn., Pres.'s. Assn., Am. Mktg. Assn. Republican. Bretheren. Clubs: Spring Brook County; Seaview Country; Suburban Country. Author electronic Tng. manual. Home: 21 Runnymede Rd Chatham NJ 07928 Office: Newburgh Rd Hackettstown NJ 07840

WARD, WILLIAM JOSEPH, banker; b. N.Y.C., Oct. 25, 1946; s. William J. and Marjorie (Mellick) W.; B.S., St. John's U., 1968, M.B.A., 1971; m. Claire M. Vahey, Aug. 7, 1971; 1 son, William J. With Esso Chem. Co., N.Y.C., 1969; trainee Citibank, N.Y.C., 1971, systems officer ops., 1972, asst. v.p., 1973, personnel policy devel. officer, 1974-76, v.p., chief of staff corp. personnel relations, dir. personnel services, 1977-79; v.p., Western regional services mgr. Citicorp U.S.A., San Francisco, 1979—, dir., treas. Citicorp Mgmt. Services div. Mem. Beta Gamma Sigma. Home: 72 Surfwood Circle San Rafael CA 94901 Office: Citicorp 44 Montgomery St San Francisco CA 94104

WARDELL, CHARLES WILLARD BENNETT, JR., petroleum corp. exec.; b. Bklyn., June 2, 1913; s. Charles Willard Bennett and Emma Chambers (Lakeland) W.; A.B., Princeton U., 1935; postgrad. N.Y. U., 1944-45; m. Elsa Talbot Adam, Jan. 16, 1937; children—Wendy T., Charles W.B., Christopher C., David A. Sales rep. Tidewater Oil Co., N.Y.C., 1936-42; pres. Deltec Corp., N.Y.C., 1946-60; pres. Willard Internat. Fin. Corp., N.Y.C., 1960-65; dep. to chmn. Republic Nat. Bank, N.Y.C., 1966-71; chmn., pres. Barrons Resources, Inc., N.Y.C., 1971—; dir. Abstracta Systems, Inc., Geneco Petroleum Corp. Bd. dirs. Multiple Sclerosis Soc. for Suffolk County, 1973-78, Com. for Responsible Health Care, Washington, 1978—. Served to lt. USNR, 1942-45. Mem. Tex. Ind. Producers Assn. Episcopalian. Clubs: Cold Spring Harbor Beach; Princeton, University (N.Y.C.); Huntington Country. Home: 26 Spring Hill Rd Cold Spring Harbor NY 11724 Office: 919 3d Ave New York NY 10022

WARDEN, KENT DALE, ins. co. exec.; b. Grantsburg, Wis., Nov. 26, 1942; s. Harry Eugene and Helen Elizabeth (Anderson) W.; student Minn. Sch. Bus., 1961-62, U. Minn., 1967-68; m. Ruth Ann Siegel, Apr. 5, 1969; children—Kelly Andrea, Adam Judson. Purchasing asst. N.W. Nat. Life Ins. Co., Mpls., 1962-65, job analyst, 1965-71, property mgr., 1971—. Mem. Mpls. Citizens Com. Pub. Edn., 1970-76, Mpls. del. Minn. Assn. Vo-Tech Schs., 1970-76; dist. dir. Mpls. Area United Fund, 1971; precinct vice chmn. Excelsior Republican Com., 1976—; bd. dirs. Eden Rehab. and Treatment Facility, Inc., Mpls., Mpls. Jaycees Housing, Inc., Mpls. Suburban Community Services, 1979—; mem. adv. com. Mpls. Tech. Inst., 1979—. Served with USNR, 1965-67. Certified real property adminstr. Bldg. Owners and Mgrs. Inst. Mem. Bldg. Owners and Mgrs. Assn. (officer, dir. 1978—), Bd. Bldg. Owners, Mpls. Jaycees (dir. 1971-73), Minn. Jaycees (v.p. 1973-74), Mortgage Bankers Assn. (treas. Minn. chpt. 1976-77), Inst. Real Estate Mgmt. (certified property mgr.), Minn. Assn. Realtors (asso.). Club: Minn. Toastmasters. Home: 4395 N Shore Dr Mound MN 55364 Office: NW Nat Life Ins Co 20 Washington Ave S Minneapolis MN 55440

WARDLOW, ERVIN E., retail co. exec.; b. 1921. With K Mart Corp. (name formerly S.S. Kresge Co.), Detroit, 1939—, store mgr., 1951-55, supt. stores, 1955-58, asst. sales dir., 1958-61, sales dir., gen. merchandise mgr., 1961-68, v.p. sales, 1968-70, exec. v.p. mdse., 1970-72, pres., chief operating officer, 1972—, also dir. Office: 3100 W Big Beaver Rd Troy MI 48084*

WAREHAM, HAROLD CHARLES, ins. co. exec.; b. Wellsburg, W.Va., Dec. 31, 1926; s. Elmer and Margaret Emily (Swank) W.; student W. Liberty State Coll., 1944, Mich. State Coll., 1947; B.B.A., Westminster Coll., 1950; postgrad. in Bus. Adminstrn., U. Conn., 1974; m. Dec. 24, 1950; children—Miles, John, Elizabeth Ann. Casualty adjuster, reg. supr., field auditor, claim mgr. Aetna Casualty & Surety (Aetna Life & Casualty), Hartford, Conn., 1950-67, v.p. Aetna Tech. Services, dir. claims Aetna Casualty Co., 1970-75; sr. v.p. Security Ins. Group, Hartford, 1968-70; sr. v.p. Equitable Gen. Ins. Co., Ft. Worth, 1975—. Bd. dirs. Ft. Worth Assn. Retarded Citizens, Tarrant County Mental Health Mental Retardation Services, Tarrant Council Alcoholism and Drug Abuse; mem. subcom. on allocations to mem. agys. United Way. Served with USNR, 1944-46. Home: 4029 Clayton Rd E Fort Worth TX 76116 Office: 1 Equitable General Pl Fort Worth TX 76151

WARGIN, JOHN EMERSON, petroleum co. exec.; b. Williston Park, N.Y., July 29, 1938; s. Emerson John and Dolores Mary (Hughes) W.; student Hofstra U., 1957-59, George Washington U., 1959-62, Boston Coll., 1971-74; m. Jo Ann Sergi, Sept. 7, 1962; children—Gregory J., Michael E., David N., Kathy M., Dennis G. With Texaco, Inc., 1962-75; pres. Cray Energy, Inc., Bellows Falls, Vt., 1976—, Energy Mind Systems, Inc., Hanover, N.H., 1980—; v.p. C & O Oil Co., Inc.; treas. Green Mountain Mini-Markets, Inc. Served with U.S. Army, 1959-62. Mem. Ind. Oil Men's Assn. (dir. 1976—), Am. Petroleum Inst. (N.H. exec. bd. 1975-77), Nat. Assn. Texaco Wholesalers (treas. 1976—), Small Businessmen's Assn., Nat. Oil Jobbers Council, Republican Congressional Leadership Council, Am. Polled Hereford Assn. Republican. Roman Catholic. Clubs: Lions, K.C. Home: Juniper Hill Farm Walpole NH 03608 Office: 173 Main St NW Bellows Falls VT 05101 also 37 S Main St Hanover NH 03755

WARGO, JAMES LOUIS, mgmt. cons.; b. Warren, Ohio, Aug. 24, 1930; s. William D. and Julia (Shaley) W.; student St. Vincent Coll., 1950; B.S.B.A., Geneva Coll., 1952; m. Ellen N. Stubble, Sept. 11, 1951; children—Kathleen, LuAnn, Colette, Jeffrey, Kerry, Robyn. Mgmt. trainee U.S. Steel, Elwood City, Pa., 1952-54, div. analyst, maintenance of standards supr. Homestead Works, 1954-62, sr. analyst corp. hdqrs., 1962-65; sr. mgmt. cons. Ernst & Ernst, 1965-67, supr. mgmt. cons. service, 1967-69, mgr., 1969-75; partner Ernst & Whitney, Cleve., 1975—; gen. chmn. Cleve. Bus. Show. Mem. Greater Cleve. Growth Assn., Pleasant Hills (Pa.) CSC, Pleasant Hills Republican Club. C.P.A., Ohio. Mem. Ohio Soc. C.P.A.'s, Am. Inst. C.P.A.'s, Nat. Assn. Accts. (nat. dir., pres. Cleve. chpt., chmn. Ohio council), Am. Foundrymen's Soc., Council Smaller Enterprises, Am. Prodn. and Inventory Control Soc. Republican. Roman Catholic. Clubs: Cleve. Athletic, Lakewood Country, Mid Day, Playhouse, Downtown Toastmasters (pres.), Rotary. Office: 1300 Union Commerce Bldg Cleveland OH 44115

WARGO, PETER, mgmt. cons.; b. Linden, N.J., May 14, 1922; s. John and Anna (Simchak) W.; B.S. in Engring. Physics, U. Ill., 1950; Ph.D., U. Minn., 1955; m. Ramona Arlene Nelson, Dec. 22, 1950; children—Rebecca, John, Elena, Gail, Thomas. Research asso. Gen. Elec. Co., Schenectady, 1955, mgr. engring., cathode ray tube dept., Syracuse, N.Y., 1960, mgr. engring. X-ray dept., Milw., 1964-68, gen. mgr. biomed. equipment bus., Milw., 1968-69; gen. mgr. Ferrite div. Allen-Bradley Co., Milw., 1969-70; v.p., group exec. Allis-Chalmers Corp., Milw., 1970-74; pres. Wargo & Co., Milw., 1974—. Mem. exec. engring. extension adv. bd. U. Wis. (Milw.); mem. Milw. Mayor's Sci. and Tech. Advt. Council, 1974—. Served to 1st lt. USAAF, 1943-46. Recipient Emmy award for outstanding tech. achievement Acad. TV Arts and Scis., 1960. Mem. IEEE, AAAS. Home: N65W30745 Beaver Lake Rd Hartland WI 53029 Office: 2300 N Mayfair Rd Milwaukee WI 53226

WARKENTIN, ERVIN JOHN, union ofcl.; b. Corn, Okla., Dec. 14, 1919; s. Detrict M. and Anna Esther (Gunther) W.; student Reedley Jr. Coll., 1941; m. June Esther Heinze, Dec. 29, 1946; children—Donald Ray, John Ervin, Timothy Wayne. Contractor, E.J. Constrn. Co., Reedley, Calif., 1950-58; carpenter, supr., foreman Rutledge Constrn. Co., 1958-76; fin. sec., dispatcher Carpenters Local 1109, Visalia, Calif., 1976—; tchr. adult edn. Cloves Unified Sch. System, 1972-77. Active Cub Scouts, Little League, Boys Brigade, Reedley Swim Team. Mem. Calif. Lic. Contractors Assn., United Brotherhood Carpenters Am. Democrat. Mennonite. Clubs: Men's Fellowship (v.p. 1977-79), Fresno Madeia Kings and Tulare Bldg. and Trades Council, Squoia Dist. Council Carpenters. Address: 319 N Church St Visalia CA 93217

WARMBOLD, HERMAN PETER, exec. recruiting cons.; b. Berlin, Germany, Apr. 21, 1927; came to U.S., 1956, naturalized, 1961; m. Hermann and Leonor Margarita (Wagemann) W.; B.S., N.Y. U., 1959, M.B.A., 1960; m. Grace Marion Staub, Oct. 26, 1963; 1 dau., Kimberly Nicole. With Pacific Steel Mills, 1950-60, dir. materiel, 1960; partner Robert Manley & Assos., Inc., N.Y.C., Mexico City, 1960-62; exec., v.p., dir. Staub, Warmbold & Assos., Inc., N.Y.C., 1962—. Mem. Assn. Exec. Recruiting Cons., IEEE, N.Y. U. Alumni Assn. Republican. Presbyterian. Home: 20 Sutton Pl S New York NY 10022 Office: 655 3d Ave New York NY 10017

WARNE, ALLAN HENDERSON, JR., sales and finance cons.; b. Indpls., June 6, 1929; s. Allan Henderson and Esther (Forkner) W.; student Ind. U., 1947-48, Purdue U., 1948-49; m. Jacqueline Joyce Bauer, Sept. 7, 1949; children—Karen Yvonne Warne Pfeiffer, James Brian, John Allan. Vice pres. ABC Constrn. Corp., Indpls., 1949-58; pres. ABC Mortgage & Investment Corp., Indpls., 1958-59; v.p. Marsh Homes, Inc., Indpls., 1960-61; with Acme Bldg. Materials, Inc., Indpls., 1962-70, chmn. bd., 1967-70; pres. Precision Built Homes, Inc., 1970—; sales and fin. cons., Indpls., 1966—; dir. ABC Constrn. Corp., Acme Bldg. Materials, Inc. Served with CIC, AUS, 1952-54. Mem. Builders Assn. Greater Indpls. (dir. 1965-68), Home Builders Assn. Ind. (dir. 1966-72), Indpls. Home Builders Assn. (pres. 1965-66, sec. 1973-74). Clubs: Masons, Grotto, Shriners; Columbia (Indpls.). Home: 8843 Walma Dr Indianapolis IN 46219 Office: 910 N Shadeland Indianapolis IN 46219

WARNECKE, JOHN CARL, architect; b. Oakland, Calif., Feb. 24, 1919; s. Carl I. and Margaret (Esterling) W.; B.A. cum laude, Stanford U., 1941; M.A., Harvard U., 1942; children—John Carl, Rodger C., Margaret E., Frederick P. Architect, Miller & Warnecke, Oakland, 1945; prin. John Carl Warnecke & Assos., San Francisco, 1946-58, chmn. bd., chief exec. officer, San Francisco, N.Y.C., Boston, Washington and Los Angeles, 1958—; partner Warnecke & Warnecke, San Francisco, 1951-58. Mem. Fine Arts Commn., Washington, 1963-67. Recipient Arnold Brunner prize Nat. Inst. Arts and Letters, 1957; numerous awards won by firm. Fellow AIA; mem. NAD (asso.). Democrat. Clubs: Olympic, Pacific Union (San Francisco); Doubles, N.Y. Athletic (N.Y.C.); Fed. City (Washington); Hawaii Canoe. Major projects include: John F. Kennedy Grave, Arlington (Va.) Nat. Cemetery, Hawaii State Capitol, Honolulu, Lafayette Sq., Washington, master plan Michelson and Chauvenet Halls, U.S. Naval Acad., Annapolis, Md., Philip A. Hart Senate Office Bldg., Washington, AT&T Long Lines, Hdqrs., Bedminster, N.J., USSR Embassy Complex, Washington, Neiman-Marcus, Washington, South Terminal, Logan Airport, Boston, Am. Hosp., Paris, Royal Saudi Naval Acad., Jubail, Saudi Arabia. Office: 417 Montgomery St San Francisco CA 94104 also 745 Fifth Ave New York NY 10051 also 2029 Century Park E Los Angeles CA 90067 also One Farragut Sq S NW Washington DC 20006 also 148 State St Boston MA 02109

WARNER, ADDISON WHEELOCK, corp. exec.; b. Geneva, Ill., June 5, 1899; s. Henry Dimock and Harriette King (Young) W.; student Dartmouth, 1917; B.S., Stanford, 1922; m. Helen Christopher, Dec. 25, 1924; children—Ann Wheelock (Mrs. Kimball), Addison Wheelock. Mgr. investor's aid dept. Chgo. Jour. Commerce, 1922-26; mgr. statis. dept. Stevenson, Perry & Stacy, 1926-27; sales mgr. Robert Stevenson & Co., 1927-28; gen. mgr. Kissell, Kinnicutt & Co., Chgo., 1929-30; sr. partner Addison Warner & Co., 1930-38, pres., 1938-43; now oil producer; pres., chmn. bd. Imco Inc.; treas., dir. Aviation Industries. Trustee Union League Boys' Club, 1933-53, pres. 1938-40; chmn. fin. com., trustee South Side Boys' Club, 1938-53. Served as flying cadet U.S. Army, 1918-19; apptd. 2d lt., A.S.S. Res. Corps, 1919. Mem Order of Founders and Patriots Am., Chgo. Stanford Alumni Assn. (pres. 1938-47), S.A.R., Mayflower Soc., Chi Psi. Clubs: Adventurers, Union League, Econ. (life mem.) (Chgo.); Petroleum (Ft. Worth). Office: 6119 Thorp Spring Rd Weatherford TX 76086

WARNER, CHARLES ANDERSON, mfg. and distbg. co. exec.; b. Balt., Oct. 29, 1941; s. Charles Raymond and Ruth (Anderson) W.; student public schs., Altoona, Pa.; m. Gloria Jean Shoenfelt, July 1, 1961; children—Douglas Charles, Rebbecca Mae. Sales clk. Claster Lumber Co., Bellfonte, Pa., 1964-65, outside sales mgr., 1965-66, prodn. mgr., 1966, asst. store mgr., 1966-67; sales rep. Busy Beaver Remodelers, Inc., Pitts., 1967-68, prodn. mgr., 1968, asst. sales mgr., 1968-69, sales mgr., 1969-70; sales rep. Curtis Industries, Inc., Eastlake, Ohio, 1971-72, cert. trainer, 1972-75, dist. mktg. mgr., 1975-78, regional mktg. mgr., 1978—. Home: 208 Coleridge Ave Altoona PA 16602 Office: 34999 Curtis Blvd Eastlake OH 44094

WARNER, CHARLES ARTHUR, mfg. co. exec.; b. Waynesboro, Pa., Apr. 22, 1928; s. Charles Anderson and Helen (DeLawter) W.; B.S., Maryville Coll., 1950; P.M.D., Harvard U., 1961; m. Undine Bridgers, Jan. 23, 1954; children—Melissa Beth, Rebecca Jane, Charles Anderson. Controller, Landis Tool Co., Waynesboro, 1950-64; exec. v.p. Grove Mfg. Co., Shady Grove, Pa., 1964—; dir. CircleSteel Corp., Taylorville, Ill., Grove Internat. Corp., Shady Grove. Bd. mgrs. Waynesboro Hosp., 1978—; bd. dirs. Easter Seal Soc. of Franklin County, Pa., 1975—. Mem. Am. Mgmt. Assn., Waynesboro C. of C. Republican. Presbyterian. Clubs: Elks,

Waynesboro Country (pres. 1980—, dir. 1975—). Home: 10204 Amsterdam Rd Waynesboro PA 17268 Office: PO Box 21 Shady Grove PA 17256

WARNER, FRANK CHARLES, market and distbn. analyst; b. Washington, July 14, 1939; s. Francis Reybold and Ruth S. (Steiger) W.; B.S. in Bus. Adminstrn., U. Del., 1971; M.S. in Mgmt., Memphis State U., 1975; m. Marian Jean Anderson, Dec. 23, 1962; 1 son, Michael Allen. Sr. instr. Naval Mgmt. Schs., Millington Naval Air Sta., Tenn., 1972-74; leader seminars in supervision and mgmt. theories and principles U. Tenn. Center for Govt. Tng., Memphis and Nashville, 1974-77; owner, pres. Balmoral Cinema, Inc., Memphis, 1975—; cons. in motion picture antitrust litigation. Active Boy Scouts Am. Served with USAF, 1959-63, USN, 1971-74. Mem. Beta Gamma Sigma. Republican. Club: Masons. Home: 3898 Pippin St Memphis TN 38128 Office: 3606 Austin Peay Suite 311 Memphis TN 38128

WARNER, HAROLD CLAY, JR., banker; b. Knoxville, Tenn., Feb. 24, 1939; s. Harold Clay and Mary Frances (Waters) W.; B.S. in Econs., U. Tenn., 1961, Ph.D., 1965; m. Patricia Alice Rethorst, Sept. 1, 1961; children—Martha Lee, Carol Frances. Asst. to pres. First Fed. Savs., Savannah, Ga., 1965-67; v.p. and economist No. Trust Co., Chgo., 1967-73; sr. v.p. and chief economist Crocker Nat. Bank, San Francisco, 1974-79, sr. v.p., mgr. liability mgmt. dept., 1979—; lectr. dept. econs. U. Tenn., 1962-63, Grad. Sch. Bus., Loyola U., Chgo., 1969-73, Pacific Coast Banking Sch., U. Wash., 1978-79. Bd. dirs. Chgo. Commons Assn., 1973-74. NDEA fellow, 1961-64. Mem. Nat. Assn. Bus. Economists (past pres. Chgo. chpt. 1971-72, San Francisco chpt. 1976-77), Phi Gamma Delta, Phi Eta Sigma, Omicron Delta Kappa, Phi Kappa Phi. Clubs: Peninsula Golf and Country (San Mateo, Calif.). Home: 350 Georgetown Ave San Mateo CA 94402 Office: 1 Montgomery St San Francisco CA 94104

WARNER, RAWLEIGH, JR., oil co. exec.; b. Chgo., Feb. 13, 1921; s. Rawleigh and Dorothy (Haskins) W.; student Lawrenceville Sch., 1937-40; A.B. cum laude, Princeton, 1944; m. Mary Ann deClairmont, Nov. 2, 1946; children—Alison H. Pyne, Suzanne de C. Parsons. Sec.-treas., Warner Bard Co., Chgo., 1946-48; asst. to treas. Continental Oil Co., Ponca City, Okla., 1948-49, sec., N.Y.C., 1949-51, asst. to pres., Houston, 1951-52, asst. treas., 1952-53; treas. Socony-Vacuum Overseas Supply Co., Ft. Lee, N.J., 1953-55; asst. treas. Mobil Overseas Oil Co., Ft. Lee, 1955-56; mgr. econs. Socony Mobil Oil Co., Inc., N.Y.C., 1956-57, mgr. Middle East, 1958-59; regional v.p. Mobil Internat. Oil Co., N.Y.C., 1959-60, exec. v.p., 1960-63, pres., 1963-64; exec. v.p., dir Mobil Oil Corp., 1964-65, pres., 1965-69, chmn., chief exec. officer, 1969—; chmn., chief exec. officer Mobil Corp., 1976—; dir. Wheelabrator Frye Co., Caterpillar Tractor Co., Am. Express Co., AT & T, Chem. N.Y. Corp. Mem. Bus. Council; bd. dirs. Am. Petroleum Inst. Served to capt. F.A., AUS, 1943-46. Decorated Silver Star, Bronze Star, Purple Heart. Republican. Presbyterian. Clubs: Country of New Canaan (Conn.); Augusta Nat. Golf; Seminole; Pinnacle, The Links (N.Y.C.); Blind Brook (Port Chester, N.Y.); Chicago; The Island (Hobe Sound, Fla.) Office: 150 E 42d St New York NY 10017

WARNER, THOMAS PAYTON, heating, cooling, ventilating equipment mfg. co. exec.; b. Pitts., May 9, 1932; s. John C. and Louise (Hamer) W.; B.S., Carnegie Mellon U., 1954; m. Gloria Guynes, 1977; children—Ann E., William S. Project engr., Union Carbide, Charleston, W.Va., 1954-55; gen. mill foreman U.S. Steel, Homestead, Pa., 1957-65; plant supt. Screw & Bolt Corp., Mt. Pleasant, Pa., 1965-68; plant mgr. Teledyne Linair Engring. Co., Dania, Fla., 1968-70; ops. mgr. Climate Master Products, Fort Lauderdale, Fla., 1970-75; plant mgr. Mammoth div. LSI, Holland, Mich., 1975—. Served to 1st lt. U.S. Army, 1955-57. Mem. Am. Soc. Tool and Mfg. Engrs. (sr.). Republican. Home: 73 Country Club Rd Holland MI 49423 Office: 341 E 7th St Holland MI 48423

WARNOCK, FREDERICK WILLIAM, electronic distbn. co. exec.; b. Pendleton, Oreg., Oct. 8, 1940; s. Chester L. and Seville M. (Sloan) W.; B.S., U. Oreg., 1962; student Oreg. State U., 1959; m. Cheryl A. Becker, June 15, 1968; 1 son, Brian. With Almac/Stroum Electronics, Seattle, 1966—, pres., 1975—. Served with USAF, 1962-66. Mem. Nat. Electronics Distbr. Assn., Electronics Distbr.'s Research Inst. Home: 14044 SE 44th Pl Bellevue WA 97006 Office: 5811 6th Ave S Seattle WA 98108

WARNSBY, JACQUELYN ELAINE, govt. ofcl.; b. Memphis, July 20, 1948; d. Lee and Laura Jeannette (Young) Anderson; student LeMoyne-Owen Coll., Memphis, 1966, So. Ill. U., Carbondale, 1967-68. Supervisory bookkeeper Union Planters Bank, Memphis, 1968-72; taxpayer service rep. IRS, Ottawa, Ont., Can. and Memphis, 1972-74, intern, Washington, 1974-75, program analyst Western region, San Francisco, 1975-78, Southwest region, Dallas, 1978-79, br. chief taxpayer service div., 1979—, also EEO investigator; lectr. in field. Vice-chmn., Western Regional Commrs. Com. Affirmative Action, 1976-77. Recipient Spl. Achievement award IRS, 1973, 75. Mem. Children's Writers Guild (asso.), Am. Mgmt. Assn., Am. Astrol. Soc., Nat. Writers Assn. (asso.). Home: 14833 Spring Creek Rd Dallas TX 75248 Office: 7839 Churchill Way LB-70 Dallas TX 75251

WARREN, C(HAMP) DEE, JR., architect, planner; b. Lubbock, Tex., Feb. 14, 1930; s. Champ Dee and Maggie (Palmer) W.; student Centenary Coll., 1946-47; B.Arch., U. Tex., 1955; m. Cathy L. Eastham, 1975; children by previous marriage—Champ Dee III, Christopher Darrell, Marshall K., Brett Bivin; 1 stepdau., Camille Darcy. Designer, planner Victor Gruen & Assos., Beverly Hills, Calif., 1959-62, Daniel Mann Johnson & Mendenhall, Los Angeles, 1962; v.p., dir. planning Glenn Abbogast & Assos., 1963-65; designer Irving R. Klein & Assos., Houston, 1965-67; prin. C. Dee Warren, AIA, Architect and Planner, Houston, 1967—; asso., dir. planning and design The Klein Partnership Inc., Houston. Bd. dirs. Harris County Com. on Aging. Served with AUS, 1953-54. Mem. AIA (urban design com. Los Angeles chpt. 1962-64), Tex. Soc. Architects, Am. Inst. Fine Arts Los Angeles, Nat. Council Archtl. Registration Bds. Home: 9404 Stonehouse Ln Houston TX 77025

WARREN, CARTEN AUTHORLON, diversified co. exec.; b. Franklinton, La., Feb. 9, 1948; s. Angus M. and Angie (Bell) W.; B.S., So. U., 1966, M.A. in Math., 1967; Ph.D. in Math., Brown U., Providence, 1970. Tchr., Montgomery, Ala., 1971, Ill. Inst. Tech., Chgo., 1971-72, Montgomery County Schs., Rockville, Md., 1972-74; chief exec. Warren Corp., Washington, 1974—. La. Legislature grantee, 1963; Named Ebony's Most Eligible Bachelor, 1969. Mem. NEA, Entrepreneurs Assn. Am., Nat. Small Bus. Assn. Author: The Clouds of Joy, 1969; Become Slim and Stay Slim, 1980; composer: I'll Always Love You, 1971; Baby It's You, 1972; Don't Lose Your Good Thing, 1973; Hot Pants Break Down, 1974; Big Legged Women, 1975; writer producer musical comedy Don't Bite the Hand That Feeds You, 1976.

WARREN, CHARLES DEWEY, mgmt. cons.; b. Gill, Colo., Oct. 2, 1938; s. Charles Laybourn and Edna M. (Dewey) W.; B.A. in Economics, U. Denver, 1968; m. Judith Bryant, June 22, 1963. Tng. systems analyst LTV Aerospace Corp., Dallas, 1968-70; curriculum design mgr. Philco-Ford Corp., Pasadena, Calif., 1971-72; dir. mgmt. and organizational devel., internal cons. Host Internat., Santa Monica, Calif., 1972—; cons. in field to businesses and non-profit orgns.; lectr. on free-enterprise economics. Chpt. leader W. Los Angeles chpt. Com. for Freedom of Choice in Cancer Therapy, 1975-76. Served with USAF, 1956-60. Mem. Am. Soc. Tng. and Devel., Am. Mgmt. Assn. Participant, Valdez Glacier Expdn., 1980. Author various mgmt. models, including: The Essence of Leadership, 1975; Planning and Evaluating Performance, 1980. Home: 11206 Woolford St Culver City CA 90230 Office: 3402 Pico Blvd Santa Monica CA 90406

WARREN, DOUGLAS KENT, real estate co. exec.; b. Newberg, Oreg., July 16, 1948; s. Vernon James and Margaret Louise (Holzmeyer) W.; B.S., in Civil Engring. with honors, Oreg. State U., 1971. Supt. CPM Constrn. Co., Newport, Oreg., 1971-72; partner Warren Realty Group, Inc., Newport, 1972—; instr. Instr. real estate Linn-Benton Community Coll., 1974—. Sec./treas. Lincoln County (Oreg.) Multifamily Housing Council, 1980-81. Mem. Nat., Oreg. (chmn. real estate div. liason com. 1975, dir. 1976) assns. Realtors, Lincoln County Bd. Realtors (pres. 1976, Realtor of Yr. award 1976), Oreg. Coast Exchangors, Nat., Oreg. State (dir. 1973-74), County (pres. 1973-74, dir. 1975) home builders assns., Scabbard and Blade, Sigma Tau, Tau Beta Pi, Phi Eta Sigma. Clubs: Kiwanis, Optimists (lt. gov. Pacific NW dist. 1980-81). Co-author: The Real Estate Exchange Market and How it Operates. Home and office: PO Box 179 Newport OR 97365

WARREN, FOREST GLEN, agrl. consultant, economist; b. Kouts, Ind., Dec. 15, 1913; s. Joseph Allen and Mary Imogene (Philpott) W.; B.S., Purdue U., 1937; Ph.D., U. Ill., 1945; m. Olive Louise Lauterbach, Nov. 21, 1942; children—Mary Anne, Richard Henry. Economist, U.S. Dept. Agr. Chgo., 1941-42; Lend Lease Adminstrn., Washington, 1942-45; U.S. Dept. Commerce, Washington, 1945-59; Export-Import Bank U.S., Washington, 1959-66; U.S. Dept. Agr., Washington, 1966-73; cons. agr., Itasca, Ill. and Valparaiso, Ind., 1973—; pres. Warren Lands, Inc., 1949—. Mem. Am. Econ. Assn., Am. Farm Econs. Assn., Internat. Assn. Agrl. Economists, Sigma Xi. Methodist. Club: Blue Ridge Mountain Country. Contbr. articles to profl. jours. Home and Office: 603 N 50 W Valparaiso IN 46383

WARREN, GEORGE HENRY, outdoor advt. co. exec.; b. Walker County, Ala., Nov. 16, 1941; s. Daniel W. and O. Marie (Savage) W.; A.A., Freed-Hardeman Coll., 1962; m. Reba Palmer, July 21, 1961; children—Wayne, Kimberly. Ordained to ministry Ch. of Christ, 1962; minister various churches, 1962-69; with Creative Displays, Inc., Tuscaloosa, Ala., 1965—, plant supr., 1972-80, v.p., 1972-75, exec. v.p., 1975-77, pres., 1977—. Mem. adv. bd. Freed-Hardeman Coll., Henderson, Tenn. Mem. Outdoor Advt. Assn. Am. (nat. dir., chmn. Southeastern region bd. dirs., chmn. mems. action com., mem. legis. com.), Inst. Outdoor Advt. (Southeastern regional coordinator plans bd.), C. of C. Clubs: Toastmasters, Northport Athletic Boosters. Home: 1604 Briarcliff Northport AL 35476 Office: PO Box 2389 Tuscaloosa AL 35403

WARREN, LAWRENCE DALE, ins. and trade cos. exec.; b. Scottsburg, Ind., Jan. 4, 1944; s. Lionel G. and Edna Marie (Hollin) W.; student Purdue U., 1961-65; m. Esther Sibal, Aug. 7, 1976; children—Alana Kay, Douglas Dale, Kirsten. Owner, pres. Products Unltd., Inc., Houston, 1967-69; territory mgr. W. R. Grace & Co., Houston, 1970-76; owner Larry Warren & Co., Houston, 1965—; owner, pres. Warren Internat., Inc., 1976—; dir. Delta Gulf Industries, Houston, Continental Casing Inc. Mem. Producers Council, Inc. (pres. 1975-76), Constrn. Specifications Inst. (membership chmn. 1973-74), Million Dollar Round Table. Republican. Methodist. Home: 506 Magic Oaks Dr Spring TX 77373 Office: 3400 Montrose St Suite 718 Houston TX 77006

WARREN, LILLIE BELLE WATSON, real estate exec.; b. Ico, Ark., Feb. 24, 1909; d. Finis Bascum and Maude Eleanor (Ashe) Watson; B.S., Ark. State Tchrs. Coll., 1933; m. Truman John Warren, Sept. 9, 1939 (dec. 1964); children—Mary Louise, Truman John, Eleanor Ruth. Tchr. home econs. Mabelvale (Ark.) High Sch., 1929-33; asst. buyer, mgr. ready-to-wear dept. Gus Blass Stores, Little Rock, 1933-39; pres. Warren Enterprises, Inc., Morrilton, Ark., 1964—. Cub Scout leader, 1952-60; Girl Scout leader, 1951-62; chmn. com. preservation nat. hist. places in Conway County, Ark. Arts Center, 1973—. Mem. Nat. Retail Mchts. Assn., Ark. Retail Mchts. Assn., Morrilton Retail Mchts. Assn., U.S. C. of C., Morrilton C. of C., Nat. Small Bus. Assn., Ark. Small Bus. Assn., Democrat. Presbyterian. Clubs: Morrilton Garden (pres. 1940-42); Pathfinder (pres. 1939-43). Home: 201 W Church St Morrilton AR 72110 Office: PO Box 517 Morrilton AR 72110

WARREN, PATRICIA ARMSTRONG, fin. cons.; b. Los Angeles, Jan. 29, 1932; d. Paul Lincoln and Marie (Collison) Armstrong; student Mills Coll., 1949-51, U. Calif. at Berkeley, 1951-52; B.A., Calif. State U. at Los Angeles, 1965, M.A., 1967; M.B.A., Pepperdine U., 1978; postgrad. UCLA, 1979—; children—William, Tiffany, John, Wendy Warren Mullender. Hist. curator County Los Angeles Dept. Arboreta and Bot. Gardens, Arcadia, Calif., 1967-75; account exec. Merrill Lynch, Pierce, Fenner and Smith, Sherman Oaks, Calif., 1975-77; v.p. Armstrong Investments Co., Marina del Rey, Calif., 1977—; pres. Armstrong Warren Assos., 1977—; instr. Pasadena City Coll., 1968-75, UCLA, 1969—. Mem. adv. com. Los Angeles City Hist. and Cultural Resources Survey, 1978—. Recipient Grant, Nat. Mus. Act, 1973. Mem. Internat. Assn. Fin. Planners, Inst. Cert. Fin. Planners, Am. Soc. Women Accts., Nat. Assn. Women Bus. Owners, Am. Mgmt. Assn., Am. Assn. Museum, Soc. Archtl. Historians (treas. So. Calif. chpt. 1978-80), Calif. Hist. Soc. (merit award 1974, Associated Hist. Socs. Los Angeles County (pres. 1971-73), Hist. Soc. So. Calif. (v.p. 1971), Conf. Calif. Hist. Socs. (awards chmn./museums chmn. 1971-73), Women of Wall St. West (dir. 1978-81), Phi Alpha Theta. Author: California Architecture, 1971; Santa Anita Depot, 1970; Elias Jackson Baldwin, 1973; A Time of Change; Hugo Reid, 1973; Motivation and the Museum Volunteer, 1978; Financial Planning Through Time Management, 1980. Office: 2601 Ocean Park Blvd Suite 204 Santa Monica CA 90405

WARREN, RENNY DEBEVOISE, mfg. co. exec.; b. Flushing, N.Y., Aug. 4, 1942; s. Edward L. and Helen Q. Warren; B.S., U. Conn., 1964; grad. Advanced Mgmt. Program, Harvard U., 1979; m. Susan J. Ferguson; children—Timothy Scott, Christopher Edward. With Citibank, N.A., N.Y.C., 1966-72, asst. v.p., 1972; mgr. banking, then asst. treas. Phelps Dodge Corp., N.Y.C., 1972-79, treas., 1979—. Served to capt. USAR, 1964-66. Mem. AIME, Sigma Alpha Epsilon. Clubs: Wee Burn Country (Darien, Conn.); Mining, Treasurer's Group, Harvard Bus. Sch. (N.Y.C.). Office: 300 Park Ave New York NY 10022

WARREN, THOMAS JEFFERSON, JR., real estate investments, oil and gas exploration exec.; b. Dallas, Dec. 31, 1949; s. Thomas J. and Rita Elizabeth (Powell) W.; B.B.A., U. Tex., Austin, 1974; postgrad. Tex. A&M U., 1976-78; m. Julie Surrey; children—Kelli, Clent. Real estate broker, 1974-76; founder, pres., chmn. Warren Investments, Dallas, 1976—; owner Petroleum Resources Recovery, 1978—; charter organizer S.W. Nat. Bank, 1979. Mem. Soc. Real Estate Developer-Counselors, Nat. Assn. Realtors, Tex. Assn. Realtors, Dallas Assn. Realtors. Club: North Park Exchange. Contbr. articles to profl. publs.; contbg. author: Tax Aspects of Real Estate Investments, 1978. Office: 5954 Sherry Ln Dallas TX 75225

WARREN, TIMOTHY MATLACK, publishing co. exec.; b. Stamford, Conn., Dec. 9, 1923; s. Keith Faulkner and Barbara (Matlack) W.; student Harvard U., 1942; A.B. cum laude, Bowdoin Coll., 1945; m. Phyllis Faber, Aug. 14, 1946; children—Timothy Matlack, Elizabeth Faulkner, Peter Grenelle. Pres., Warren Pub. Corp., Boston, 1970—, also dir.; editor Bankers Publ. Co., Boston, 1955, v.p., 1956-70, pres., 1970—, also dir.; dir. Concept Devel. Inc. Trustee, Concord Free Pub. Library. Served to 1st lt. U.S. Army, 1942-46. Democrat. Unitarian. Clubs: Concord Country, Harvard, Hubbard St. Athletic (dir. 1959). Home: 53 Hubbard St Concord MA 01742 Office: 210 South St Boston MA 02111

WARRINER, ROBERT STANLEY, farmer, constrn. co. exec., real estate agt.; b. Morristown, N.J., June 21, 1944; s. Reuel Edward and Susanne Doris (Stanley) W.; student Rutgers U., 1962-64; m. Katherine Ellen Baker, Oct. 15, 1966; children—Edgar T., Doris S., Rachel A., Raymond C. Owner, gen. mgr. Agawam Assos., dairy farming and constrn., Montrose, Pa., 1964—; sales agt. Arndmont Realty, Montrose. Mem. Profl. Farmers Am., Am. Guernsey Cattle Club, Holstein Friesian Assn. Am. Episcopalian. Club: Shriners. Address: Agawam RD4 Montrose PA 18801

WARRINGTON, FRANCIS CARLTON, steel co. exec.; b. Garden Grove, Iowa, Mar. 27, 1913; s. Frank E. and Nannie P. W.; B.S. in Civil Engring., Iowa State U., 1937; m. Lois Jane Jones, Aug. 24, 1940; children—Frank, Nancy, Linda, Terri. Trainee in constrn., engring. shop and sales, 1937-42; with Cleve. lab. NASA, 1942-45; mem. staff, sales office Pitts.-Des Moines Steel Co., Dallas, 1945-53, sales mgr. plate div., dist. sales office, Des Moines, 1953-60, sales mgr., central div., Des Moines, 1960-63, v.p., gen. mgr. So. div., Birmingham, Ala., 1963-78, v.p. staff work with subsidiaries, Birmingham, 1978—, dir., 1972—; dir. PDM Hydrostorage. Mem. bd. Vestavia Hills United Methodist Ch., 1968-76, trustee, 1980. Mem. ASCE, Am. Water Works Assn., Steel Plate Fabricators Assn., Mfrs. Assn. of Am. Waters Works Assn., Iowa State U. Alumni Soc. (pres. Pitts. 1938-39), Tau Beta Pi Alumni (pres. Birmingham 1977-78). Republican. Methodist. Clubs: Vestavia Country, The Club, Downtown (Birmingham). Home: 1348 Turnham Ln Birmingham AL 35216 Office: Pitts-Des Moines Steel Co 401 Ave W Birmingham AL 35218

WARRINGTON, HOWARD MOODY, pub. co. exec.; b. Pocahontas, Iowa, Nov. 6, 1912; s. Winfield W. and Nell (Robinson) W.; B.A., Grinnell Coll., 1934. With Prentice-Hall, Inc., Englewood Cliffs, N.J., 1935—, editor, 1939-45, editor in chief, 1945-65, pres. coll. div., 1965-71, exec. v.p., 1971-74, chmn. bd., 1974—, also dir.; chmn. bd. Prentice-Hall of Can., Robert J. Brady Co., Deltak, Inc., Goodyear Pub. Co., Reston Pub. Co. Mem. Assn. Am. Pubs. (dir.), Am. Ednl. Pubs. Inst. Clubs: Bronxville Field; Princeton (N.Y.C.). Office: Prentice-Hall Inc Englewood Cliffs NJ 07632

WARSHAWSKY, ALBERT, accountant; b. Asbury Park, N.J., Oct. 2, 1935; s. Harry and Eva (Holland) W.; B.B.A., U. Mich., 1957, M.B.A., 1958; m. Felicia Dawn Jacob, Aug. 14, 1966; children—David Sereno, Leah Vanessa. Sr. accountant Apfel & Englander, C.P.A.'s, N.Y.C., 1959-65; mgr. Price Waterhouse & Co., N.Y.C., 1965-79; controller Marymount Manhattan Coll., N.Y.C., 1979—. Served with USMCR, 1958. Mem. Am. Inst. C.P.A.'s, N.Y. State Soc. C.P.A.'s, Nat. Assn. Accountants, Beta Alpha Psi, Alpha Epsilon Pi. Home: 200 E 78th St New York NY 10021 Office: 221 E 71st St New York NY 10022

WARTHEN, JOHN EDWARD, leasing and finance co. exec.; b. Cedar City, Utah, May 8, 1922; s. Mark Tew and Emma (Simkins) W.; student Branch Agrl. Coll. So. Utah, Cedar City, 1940-41; m. Norma Jane Hansen, June 22, 1943; children—Russel Edward, John Merrill, Judith Damus, Linda Fahringer, Carla Jean, Lauri Janette. Pres., mgr. St. George Service, Inc. (Utah), 1945-61, Warthen Constrn. Co., Las Vegas, 1961—, Warthen Buick, 1961—; pres., gen. mgr. Diversified Investment & Leasing Corp., Las Vegas. Councilman, City of St. George, 1950-54. Trustee, treas. Latter Day Saint Br. Geneal. Library, Las Vegas, 1964—; co-founder Center for Internat. Security Studies; dist. dir. Freeman Inst.; nat. dir. Liberty Amendment Com.; dist. chmn. Citizens for Pvt. Enterprise, Las Vegas; mem. Council Inter-Am. Security, Americanism Ednl. League; dist. fin. chmn. Boy Scouts Am.; state chmn. Nev. Dealer Election Action Com.; mem. Nev. Devel. Authority. Mem. S.A.R. Mem. Ch. of Jesus Christ of Latter-day Saints (bishop 1957-61). Rotarian, Kiwanian. Home: 2475 Viking St Las Vegas NV 89121 Office: 3025 E Sahara Ave Las Vegas NV 89104

WASCHKA, RONALD WILLIAM, ind. oil and gas producer; b. Memphis, Sept. 2, 1932; s. Frederick William and Hazel Celeste (Guidroz) W.; B.A., U. Miss., 1960; M.A., Memphis State U., 1970, Ph.D., 1977; m. Patricia Janet Sinclair Hanney, July 27, 1963; children—Michael, John, Anne Marie, Helen Marissa. Service asst. Memphis State U., 1970, teaching asst., 1972-75; with Legis. Reference Service, Library of Congress, Washington, 1955; founder, owner Ronald Co., Inc., Memphis, 1963—; ind. oil and gas producer, Germantown, Tenn., 1972—; cons. in field. Com. mem. Boy Scouts Am., Germantown, 1975—. Served with USAF, 1955-59, Tenn. Air N.G., 1963-69. Mem. Res. Officers Assn., Am. Petroleum Inst., Am. Econ. History Assn., Am. Hist. Assn., Orgn. Am. Historians, So. Hist. Assn. Republican. Roman Catholic. Clubs: Farmington Country, Summit, Rotary. Home: 7750 Dogwood Rd Germantown TN 38138 Office: 5050 Poplar Ave Suite 816 Memphis TN 38157

WASHA, ARTHUR JOHN, bus. exec.; b. Milw., Sept. 23, 1943; s. Arthur Antone and Elizabeth (Harrison) W.; B.S., U. Wis., 1969, M.S., 1971; m. Cheryl Ann Schuepferling, Sept. 2, 1969 (dec.); children—Andrew John, Wendy Ann, Kristen Ann. Instr., U. Wis. Center System, 1970-71; instr. U. Wis., Milw., 1969-71; investigator Wis. Dept. Justice, 1971; instr. Kei,n C 1971-72; dir. edn., publs. and edn. div. Am. Appraisal Co., Milw., 1972-74; owner, operator Appraisal Assos., West Bend, Wis., 1973-74; exec. dir. edn. Nat. Assn. Ind. Fee Appraisers, St. Louis, 1975-79, Service awards, 1973, 74; pres., dir. Inst. Real Estate Tech., St. Louis, 1979-80; pres., owner Am. Valuation Services Co., Milw., 1980—; exec. producer, host, television series How To Buy A Home, 1975. Served with USMC, 1962-65. Recipient Hatcher award U. Wis., 1970. Mem. Am. Soc. Appraisers, Am. Soc. for Tng. and Devel., Adult Edn. Council of St. Louis, Inst. Real Estate Tech. Club: Rotary Internat. Author: Residential Real Estate Appraisal: Techniques of Capitalization, 1974; Residential, Commercial and Industrial Building Cost Estimating, 1972. Office: 4030 N 93d St Milwaukee WI 53222

WASHBURN, DONALD ARTHUR, hotel exec., lawyer; b. Mankato, Minn., Sept. 24, 1944; s. Donald and Geraldine Helen (Pint) W.; B.B.A. with high honors, Loyola U., Chgo., 1971; M.B.A., Northwestern U., 1973, J.D. cum laude, 1978; m. Christine Carvell, Aug. 24, 1968; children—Timothy, Abigail. Prodn./contract adminstr. J.T. Ryerson & Sons, Chgo., 1963-68; group project mgr. Intec, Inc., Chgo., 1969-72; product mgr. The Quaker Oats Co., Chgo., 1972-74, asst. to v.p. and gen. mgr. corn products and mixes div., 1974-75, adviser to sr. v.p. law and corp. sec., 1975-78, atty., 1978-79; sr. cons. Booz, Allen & Hamilton, Inc., Chgo., 1979-80; v.p. hotel planning Marriott Corp., 1980—; spl. lectr. mktg. and antitrust Northwestern U., 1973—; lectr. mgmt. and mktg. Loyola U., Chgo., 1978—. Mem. urban action commn. Met. YMCA, Chgo., 1968-69. Mem. Am. Bar Assn., Ill. State Bar Assn., Chgo. Bar Assn., Beta Gamma Sigma, Alpha Sigma Nu, Blue Key. Contbr. articles to profl. jours. Office: One Marriott Dr Washington DC 20058

WASHBURN, GREGORY GEORGE, printing co. exec.; b. LaGrange, Ill., Jan. 7, 1947; s. George Burton and Doris W.; student U. Notre Dame, 1965-66; B.A. in Bus. Adminstrn., Coe Coll., 1968; m. June 21, 1969; children—Brian Gregory, Kristin Belle, Clayton Gerard. With mktg. div. Midwest regional office IBM, Chgo., 1969-70; co-owner, v.p. Washburn Graficolor, Inc., Lisle, Ill., 1970—; instr. adult coll. graphic arts program Ill. Benedictine Coll.; co-instr. undergrad. mktg. studies George Williams Coll. Mem. pres.'s adv. council Ill. Benedictine Coll. Recipient award Printing Industry Am., 1972, 76; Outstanding Service award Ill. Benedictine Coll., 1978. Mem. Bus./Profl. Advt. Assn., Phi Kappa Tau. Roman Catholic. Club: Rotary. Office: Washburn Graficolor Inc 1975 University Ln Lisle IL 60532

WASHBURN, JERRY MARTIN, bus. exec.; b. Powell, Wyo., Dec. 31, 1943; s. Roland and Lavon (Martin) W.; B.S., Brigham Young U., 1969; m. Pamela Ruth Palmer, June 11, 1965; children—Garth, Gavin, Tina. Staff accountant Arthur Andersen & Co., Seattle, 1969-71, sr. auditor, Boise, Idaho., 1971-73, audit mgr., Boise and Portland, Oreg., 1973-79; prin. Washburn Enterprises, Phoenix, 1979—. C.P.A., Wash., Idaho, Oreg., Ariz. Mem. Inst. Internal Auditors (past pres. Boise, dir. Boise, Portland), Am. Mgmt. Assn., Am. Inst. C.P.A.'s, Wash. Soc. C.P.A.'s. Mormon. Home: 4830 E Altadena St Scottsdale AZ 85254 Office: 4510 N 16th St Phoenix AZ 85016

WASHBURN, SETH HARWOOD, utility research exec.; b. Kansas City, Mo., Oct. 24, 1921; s. Benjamin Martin and Henrietta Tracy (de Selding) W.; student Dartmouth Coll., 1939-42; B.S. in Elec. Engring., M.I.T., 1944, M.S. in Elec. Engring., 1947; m. Janet Higginbotham, June 24, 1944; children—John B., Rebecca, Kate B., Stephen T., Peter C. With Bell Telephone Labs., 1947—, exec. dir. div. switching, Columbus, Ohio, 1966-73, exec. dir. tech. employment, edn. and salary adminstrn., Murray Hill, N.J., 1973-79, v.p. personnel and public relations, Murray Hill, 1979—. Mem. Columbus Community Relations Commn., 1968-73; jr. warden St. Stephen's Protestant Episcopal Ch., Columbus, 1968-71, sr. warden, 1971-73. Served with USN, 1942-46. Mem. Am. Mgmt. Assn., Sigma Xi, Tau Beta Pi. Author: (with Keister and Ritchie) The Design of Switching Circuits, 1951; contbr. articles to profl. jours. Office: 600 Mountain Ave Murray Hill NJ 07974

WASHINGTON, CHARLES EDWARD, educator; b. Little Rock, Nov. 27, 1933; s. David D. and Hzel M. Washington; B.A., Philander Smith Coll., Little Rock, 1958; M.Ed., U. Okla., 1962; postgrad. U. So. Calif.; m. Ruby N. Jones, Sept. 4, 1956 (div. 1965); 1 dau., Toni Regail. Tchr. public schs., Ft. Smith, Ark., 1958-60, Oklahoma City, 1960-69, Los Angeles, 1979—; registered rep. ITT Hamilton Mgmt. Corp., 1963-70; fin. counselor Fin. Congeneric Corp., 1971-74, Am. Inst. Property and Liability Underwriters; spl. agt. Welsh & Assos., Ins. Services, Walnut, Calif., 1979—. Mem. Crenshaw Christian Center. Served with USMC, 1951-54; Korea. Mem. NEA, Calif. Tchrs. Assn., United Tchrs. Los Angeles, Ind. Ins. Assn. Calif., U. Okla. Alumni Assn. (class rep. 1964-67), Nat. Dunbar Alumni Assn., Philander Smith Coll. Alumni Assn., Nat. Notary Assn. Omega Psi Phi. Democrat. Home: 20023 Alvo Ave Carson CA 90745 Office: 959 Fairway Dr Walnut CA 91789

WASHINGTON, EARL WARNER, ins. co. exec.; b. Long Beach, Miss., Dec. 22, 1918; s. Earl Warner and Edith (Gates) W.; grad. U. N.C.; postgrad. in Bus. Adminstrn., Harvard U., 1957; m. Minnie Olen Day, Feb. 16, 1943; children—Virginia, Martha. Gen. agt. Franklin Life Ins. Co., 1945-47; v.p., agy. dir. Nat. Equity Life Ins. Co., 1947-53; v.p., gen. mgr. Jackson Life Ins. Co., 1953-55; pres. Continental Life Ins. Co., 1955-59; pres., chief exec. officer, dir. State Res. Life Ins. Co., Ft. Worth, 1959—; dir. Western Savs. & Loan Assn. Pres., Jr. Achievement Tarrant County (Tex.), 1965-66, also bd. dirs. Served with USAAF. Republican. Episcopalian. Clubs: Ft. Worth, Petroleum, Shady Oaks Country, Masons, Shriners. Office: 115 W Seventh St Fort Worth TX 76102

WASHINGTON, GENE EDWARD, fin. exec.; b. Birmingham, Ala., Aug. 12, 1931; s. Horace Webster and Dorothy Grace (Henderson) W.; B.S., Okla. State U., 1952; M.B.A., U. Chgo., 1970; m. Jacqualin Ann Kaiser, Jan. 26, 1952; children—Robert Todd, James Allen, Steven Lee, Darren Scott. Sr. mktg. rep. IBM, Dallas, 1956-63, mktg. mgr., Detroit, 1963-67; v.p. Greyhound Computer Corp., Chgo., 1967-68, exec. v.p., 1969-70; v.p. Boothe Computer Corp., San Francisco, 1971-72, sr. v.p., group exec., 1972-73; chmn., pres. and chief exec. officer Environ. Chemic Systems, Inc., Novato, Calif., 1974-78; chmn., pres. Systems Assurance & Fin. Corp., Novato, 1978—; dir. Systems Assurance & Fin. Corp., Environ. Chemic Systems, Inc., Greyhound Computer Corp., Greyhound Time-Sharing Corp., Greyhound Computer of Can., Ltd., Computer Personnel Cons., Inc., Boothe Computer of Can., Ltd., Boothe Mgmt. Systems, Inc., Boothe Computer Mktg., Inc., Boothe, A.G. (Zurich), Computer Leasing Services, Ltd. of S. Africa. Dir., Jr. Achievement, Dallas, 1958; precinct treas. Republican Party, 1965-66; mem. Pop Warner Com., 1976-80. Served to capt. USAF, 1952-56. Named Mgr. of Yr., IBM Dist., 1964, Industry Leader, 1962, Regional Mgrs. award, 1963. Mem. Arnold Air Soc. (treas. 1951-52), Data Processing Mgmt. Assn., Computer Lessors Assn., Blue Key, Mu Kappa Tau, Gamma Theta Psi, Alpha Kappa Psi, Sigma Chi (treas. 1951-52), Scabbard and Blade. Republican. Presbyterian. Clubs: Marin Country, Commonwealth. Home: 1427 Buchanan St Novato CA 94947 Office: 46A Hamilton Dr Novato CA 94947

WASILEWSKI, ROBERT JOSEPH, chem. mfg. co. exec.; b. Kenosha, Wis., Aug. 5, 1939; s. Joseph Henry and Ann (Helinski) W.; B.S., Gannon Coll., 1970, M.B.A., 1972. Sales corr. Lord Kinematics Co., Erie, Pa., 1965; computer systems specialist Lord Corp., Erie, 1967-70, fin. analyst, 1970-72; gen. mgr. Lord Indsl. Ltd. and Kinematics Indsl. Ltd., Jundiai and São Paulo, Brazil, 1972—. Served with U.S. Army, 1963-65. Mem. Brazilian Tech. Rubber Assn. (sec. 1975—), Am. C. of C. for Brazil, Jundiai (Brazil) Mfrs. Assn., São Paulo Mfrs. Assn. Republican. Roman Catholic. Club: Mannechor (Erie); Pineiras do Morumby (São Paulo). Home: Rua Senador Padua Sales 56 Andar São Paulo SP Brazil 01233 Office: Rua Major Sertorio 422-6 Andar São Paulo SP Brazil

WASSÉN, KURT OLOF, lumber and real estate co. exec.; b. Kingston, N.Y., Oct. 15, 1929; s. Kurt and Gertrude (Middewer) W.; B.S., Lafayette Coll., 1951; M.B.A., Harvard U., 1955; m. Joan Wappler, Feb. 14, 1952; children—Judy Ann, Carolyn, Jane, Kurt O. With Westvaco Corp., various locations, 1955—, gen. mgr. mill carton div., Richmond, Va., 1970-74, pres. Westvaco Devel. Corp., Summerville, S.C., 1974—. Pres., Summerville YMCA, 1976-78, v.p., 1979-80. Served with AUS, 1951-53. Mem. So. Forest Products Assn., Am. Land Devel. Assn. Republican. Presbyterian. Clubs: Summerville Tennis, Summerville Tennis Assn., U.S. Tennis Assn. Home: 111 Willow Oaks Ln Summerville SC 29483 Office: PO Box 2078 Summerville SC 29483

WASSER, SIDNEY, acct., corp. exec.; b. N.Y.C., Aug. 18, 1929; s. Benjamin and Rose (Klein) W.; B.S., Syracuse U., 1950; m. Florence Samler, Apr. 15, 1950; children—Leslie Gale, Andrew Scott, David Bennet. Dir. fin. and adminstrn. Lehigh Valley Industries, Inc., N.Y.C., 1966-71; v.p. fin. Scottex Corp., N.Y.C., 1971-73; treas., dir. Decorator Industries, Inc., Pitts., 1973-76; v.p., corp. controller Ampco-Pitts. Corp., 1976—. Mem. Am. Mgmt. Assn., Am. Inst. C.P.A.'s, N.Y. State Soc. C.P.A.'s, Pa. Inst. C.P.A.'s, Fin. Execs. Inst. Office: 700 Porter Bldg Pittsburgh PA 15219

WASSERMAN, HERBERT, hotel, real estate exec.; b. N.Y.C., July 30, 1931; s. William and Clara (Cobrinik) W.; A.B., Harvard U., 1952, LL.B., 1955; m. Cecille Goldberg, May 20, 1956; children—Emily, Stefanie, Wendy. Admitted to N.Y. bar, 1956; pvt. practice law, N.Y.C., 1957; v.p. Schnine Enterprises, N.Y.C., N.Y., 1958-60, Transcontinental Investing Corp., N.Y.C., 1961-66; bus. cons., investor, N.Y.C., 1967-69; exec. v.p. Hurok Concerts, N.Y.C., 1969-74; theatrical producer Pirandello's Henry IV, Broadway and maj. cities, 1973, Los Muchachos Internat. Circus, 1974, Jerusalem Symphony Orch., 1975, Arthur Miller's The American Clock, N.Y.C., 1980; investor hotel and real estate, 1974—; owner, mgr., dir. hotels, real estate throughout U.S., 1966—. Served with U.S. Army, 1955-57. Democrat. Jewish. Home: 60 Beach Ave Larchmont NY 10538 Office: 211 E 51st St New York NY 10022

WASSERMAN, JACK, lawyer; b. N.Y.C., Feb. 20, 1913; s. Samuel and Sabina (Hoffman) W.; A.B., Coll. City N.Y. 1932; J.D. cum laude, Harvard, 1935; m. Marie Krempa, June 7, 1941; children—Lorraine DeVera, Michael Owen. With Harvard Legal Aid Soc., 1934-35; admitted to N.Y. bar, 1936, D.C. bar, Pa. bar, U.S. Supreme Ct. bar, Bd. Immigration Appeals, ICC, FCC; practiced in N.Y., 1936-41; atty. Bd. Immigration Appeals, 1941-42; sr. atty. Alien Enemy Control Unit, 1942-43; mem. Bd. Immigration Appeals, 1943-46; atty. Alien Enemy Litigation Sect., 1946-47; asst. gen. counsel Citizens Com. on Displaced Persons, 1947-48; partner firm Wasserman, Orlow, Ginsberg & Rubin, Washington. Mem. Assn. Immigration and Nationality Lawyers (nat. pres., legis. rep.), N.Y. State, D.C., Pa., Fed., Am. bar assns., Nat. Lawyers Club, Phi Beta Kappa. Author: Immigration Law and Practice. Contbr. articles on immigration to mags. Home: 4405 Sedgwick St Washington DC 20016 Office: 1707 H St NW Washington DC 20006

WASSERMAN, JERRY, mgmt. cons.; b. Bklyn., Sept. 22, 1931; B.S. cum laude, CCNY, 1951, M.A., 1953; M.S. in Elec. Engring., Newark Coll. Engring., 1957; m. Maxine E. Kaplan, June 14, 1952; children—Allen, David, Terri. Sales engr. S-J Sales Assos., N.Y.C., 1958-61; mktg. mgr. Lambda Electronics Corp., Melville, N.Y., 1961-67; gen. mgr. electronics dept. Amerex Trading Corp., N.Y.C., 1967-70; pres. Intertrade Tech. Inc., Lexington, Mass., 1970; dir. electronics mgmt. activities Arthur D. Little, Inc., Cambridge, Mass., 1971—. Served with Signal Corps, U.S. Army, 1953-55. Mem. Electronic Industries Assn. (chmn. export assistance com.). Home: 11 Winthrop Rd Lexington MA 02173 Office: Arthur D Little Inc Acorn Park Cambridge MA 02140

WASSERMAN, LEW R., business exec.; b. Cleve., Mar. 15, 1913; m. Edith Beckerman, July 5, 1936; 1 dau., Lynne Kay (Mrs. Myers). Nat. dir. advt. and publicity Music Corp. Am., Chgo., 1936-38, v.p., 1938-39, became v.p. charge motion picture div., 1940; now chmn. bd. chief exec. officer, MCA, Inc., also chmn. bd., chief exec. officer, dir. subs. corps.; dir. Am. Airlines. Mem. adv. council Presdl. Election Campaign Fund; mem. nat. com. Lyndon Baines Johnson Meml. Grove of Potomac; trustee John F. Kennedy Library, John F. Kennedy Center Performing Arts, Calif. Inst. Tech.; hon. chmn. bd. Center Theatre Group Los Angeles Music Center; bd. dirs. Lyndon Baine Johnson Found., Research to Prevent Blindness. Democrat. Home: Beverly Hills CA Office: MCA Inc Universal City Studios Universal City CA 91608

WASSON, WILLIAM GEORGE, oil co. exec.; b. Bradford, Pa., Sept. 10, 1918; s. Albert Dorr and Fleury Clara (Morris) W.; student pub. schs., Bradford; m. Betty Jean Irons, July 10, 1940; children—William Barry, Thomas Lee. With Felmont Oil Corp., Olean, N.Y., 1968—, v.p., 1978—; automobile dealer, 1937-68; air taxi operator, 1964-70; pres. Wasson Motors Inc., Olean, 1967—, Jadeland Devel. Inc., Olean, 1967—; v.p. Chrysler Dealer Advt. Assn., 1960-68. Pres. Olean United Fund, 1958-72, Seneca council Boy Scouts Am., 1960-61; mem. Olean Bd. Edn., 1955-60, Olean Planning Commn., 1968. Served with USAAF, 1942-45. Recipient Silver Beaver award Boy Scouts Am., 1960. Mem. Am. Petroleum Inst., Pa. Oil and Gas Assn., N.Y. State Oil Producers Assn., Olean C. of C. (v.p., dir. 1952—; Community Service award 1972), N.Y. State Auto Dealers Assn. (v.p. 1952-68). Republican. Methodist. Clubs: Bartlett, Rotary (past pres. Olean), Shriners. Home: 1605 Stardust Ln Olean NY 14760 Office: 1446 Buffalo St Olean NY 14760

WASTAL, PATRICK HENRY, business co. exec.; b. Los Angeles, Mar. 8, 1932; s. Zigmond Henry and Goldie (Wastal) W.; grad. parochial schs.; grad. various packaging courses; Ph.D. (hon.), Hamilton State U., 1974. Vice pres. Continental Packaging, Los Angeles, 1955-64; pres. Sands Supply Corp., Glendale, Calif., 1965-66; pres. P. H. Wastal & Assos., Glendale, 1966—, LAD Sales & Service, Los Alamitos, 1968—, Opti-Man Products, Los Alamitos, 1970—, The Professionals, Anaheim, Calif., 1970—; owner, breeder thoroughbred race horses. Sustaining patron Huntington Hartford Theatre Assn.; founder Orange County Cultural Center. Recipient U.S. Inventors and Scientists Achievement award. Mem. Mfrs. Agts. Nat. Assn., Soc. Indsl. Packaging and Handling Engrs., Instrument Soc. Am., Am. Yachting Assn., Am. Power Boat Assn., U.S. Coast Guard Aux., Internat. Platform Assn., Am. Ordnance Assn. (life), Acad. Magical Arts, Calif. Thoroughbred Assn., German Wine Soc., Soc. Wine Educators (instr.). Roman Catholic. Clubs: Old Ranch Tennis, Hollywood Turf, Santa Anita Turf, Del Mar Turf. Patentee in field plastics products. Office: PO Box 5219 Buena Park CA 90622

WASYLOWSKY, WALTER PHILIP, farming equipment mfg. co. exec.; b. Chgo., Aug. 27, 1937; s. Philip Theodore and Anna Rose (Woloszyn) W.; B.S.B.A., Roosevelt U., 1960; M.B.A., U. Chgo., 1980; m. Elaine Alice Trisilla, Aug. 8, 1959; children—Jeffrey Dean, Laura Jean. With Internat. Harvester, 1964—, asst. dir. fin. Internat. Harvester Germany, Neuss, 1971-74, dir. fin., 1974-77, v.p. fin. components group, Chgo., 1977—; dir. Internat. Harvester Singapore, Iowa Indsl. Hydraulics Co. Office: 401 N Michigan Ave Chicago IL 60611

WAT, JAMES KAM-CHOI, mfg. co. exec.; b. Hong Kong, Sept. 9, 1949; came to U.S., 1977; s. Biu and Yuk-ping (Tang) W.; gen. cert. of edn. U. London, 1969; m. Miranda Kwai-fong Leong, Oct. 6, 1974; children—Bryan Kar-yan, Vincent Kar-shun. Sales exec. Tonan Mdse., Ltd., Hong Kong, 1969-70; asst. bus. exec. Texwood Ltd., Hong Kong, 1970-72, asst. mgr., 1972-74, sales mgr., 1974-77; gen. mgr. Texwood, Inc., N.Y.C., 1977-79, exec. v.p., dir., 1980—; v.p. Jive Sportswear, Inc., N.Y.C., 1978—; exec. v.p. Drager Industries, N.Y.C., 1980—; exec. v.p., dir. Amtex Sportswear Inc., N.Y.C., 1981—. Home: 17 Capi Ln Port Washington NY 11050 Office: 1441 Broadway Suite 1440 New York NY 10018

WATERBURY, JACKSON DEWITT, advt. agy. exec.; b. Evanston, Ill., Feb. 4, 1937; s. Jackson D. and Eleanor (Barrows) W.; A.B., Brown U., 1959; m. Suzanne Butler, Aug. 27, 1958 (div. Jan. 1970); children—Jackson D. III, Arthur Barrows; m. 2d, Lynn Hardin, Mar. 17, 1971; 1 son, Timothy Bradford. Account exec. D'Arcy Advt. Co., St. Louis, 1958-63, Batz-Hodgson-Neuwoehner, Inc., St. Louis, 1963-66; exec. v.p., sec., dir. Lynch, Phillips & Waterbury, Inc., St. Louis, 1966-68; pres. Jackson Waterbury & Co., St. Louis, 1968-73; v.p., partner Vinyard & Lee & Partners, 1973-74; pres. Waterbury Inc., 1975—, Bright Ideas, Inc., 1977—. Football coach Mo. High Sch. All-Stars, 1966-67, St. Louis U., 1968-70. Mem. Ducks Unltd., Am. Motorcycle Assn., St. Louis Advt. Producers Assn. (steering com., negotiating com. 1977—), Nat. Rifle Assn. Beta Theta Pi. Episcopalian. Clubs: Racquet, Strathalbyn Farms (dir.). Home: 2 Colonial Hills Dr Saint Louis MO 63141 Office: 149 N Meramec Saint Louis MO 63105

WATERHOUSE, GARY GEORGE, retail food chain exec.; b. McKeesport, Pa., Jan. 23, 1942; s. George Henry and Hazel Rhoda (Stevens) W.; B.A., Grove City Coll., 1963; m. Alice Adele Wilcox, Oct. 15, 1966; children—Camille Alice, Chrstie Adele. Mgmt. trainee Three Rivers Bank & Trust Co., 1965-66; with Great A & P Tea Co., Inc., various locations, 1966—, internal auditor, 1970-72, asst. treas. Altoona div., 1972-73, treas. Pitts. div., 1974-75, controller, 1976-78, mgr. fin. reporting and analysis Keystone Regional Adminstrv. Center, Valley Forge, Pa., 1978, dir. acctg. ops., 1978-79, asst. controller Plus Discount Foods, Inc., subs. Great A & P Tea Co., Inc., Florence, N.J., 1979—, also sec. exec. bd. Chmn. finance and stewardship com. Wilson United Presbyn. Ch., 1972, elder, 1972—. Served with USN, 1963-65. Home: 1280 Bluestone Dr Yardley PA 19067 Office: 707 Railroad Ave Florence NJ 08518

WATERS, EDNA F., advt. agy. exec.; b. Downers Grove, Ill., May 17, 1946; d. Walter G. and Helene (Banks) Wilson; B.A., Northwestern U., 1967, M.A., 1968; m. George L. Waters, Aug. 15, 1971; 1 dau., Margaret Anne. Asst. copywriter Clinton E. Frank Advt., Chgo., 1968-72; copywriter Foot, Cone & Belding, Chgo., 1974-78, copy supr., 1978-80, creative dir., 1980—. Active United Way, Girl Scouts U.S. Recipient various advt. awards. Mem. Chgo. Women in Advt. Democrat. Presbyterian. Home: 8215 S Bishop Chicago IL 60620

WATERS, FRANCIS P., investment adviser; b. N.Y.C., Apr. 21, 1931; s. Francis J. and Nora (Hegarty) W.; B.A. cum laude, St. John's Coll., 1953; LL.B., St. John's U., 1955; LL.M., Columbia, 1956; m. Nuala M. Kilbride. Admitted to N.Y. bar, 1956, U.S. Supreme Ct. bar, 1960; asso. firm Barr, Robbins & Palmer, N.Y.C., 1960-61, Hawkins, Delafield & Wood, N.Y.C., 1961-64; individual law practice, N.Y.C., 1964-67; chmn. bd. Internat. Investment Counsellors. Served as 1st lt. Judge Advocate Gen.'s Corp., AUS, 1957-60. Mem. Am., N.Y. State bar assns. Home: 45-55 41st St Long Island City NY 11104 Office: 1 Hainault Park Foxrock Dublin 18 Ireland

WATERS, GEORGE FRANKLIN, mfg. co. exec.; b. Mpls., Dec. 17, 1920; s. Glen Myers and Carolyn (Waite) W.; B.S., Harvard, 1943, vet.'s certificate Bus. Sch., 1947; m. Jean Frances Dain, May 18, 1946; children—Dain Katherine, Brenda Lorraine, Anne Welles. Sales mgr. Waters-Conley Co., Rochester, Minn., 1947-54; with Waters Co., Rochester, 1954-61, pres., 1958-61; with Waters Instruments Inc. (formerly Flo-Tronics, Inc.), Mpls., 1961—, pres., 1963-69, chmn. bd., chief exec. officer, 1969-71, pres., 1971-74, chmn. bd., 1974—; dir. First Nat. Bank Rochester. Bd. dirs. Indsl. Opportunities, Inc., Rochester, 1958. Served to 1st lt. AC, AUS, 1943-46. Mem. Rochester C. of C. Clubs: Rotary, Minneapolis. Home: 825 3d St SW Rochester MN 55901 Office: PO Box 6117 Rochester MN 55901

WATERS, WILLIAM ERNEST, microelectronics exec.; b. Toronto, Ont., Can., Aug. 18, 1928; s. Charles Lacy and Margaret (Boulden) W.; B.A.Sc., U. Toronto, 1950; m. Evelyn Elizabeth Phillips, Jan. 18, 1952; children—Kenneth Geoffrey, Brian Gregory, Kimberly William. Gen. mgr. Hoskins Alloys of Can. Ltd., Toronto, 1953-59; pres. Waters Metal Products Ltd., Toronto, 1960—, Waters Metal Products, Inc., Buffalo, 1960-69, Watmet Inc., Niagara Falls, N.Y., 1968—, Microtectonics, Inc., Buffalo, 1968-71. Served with RCAF, 1946-52. Mem. Engring. Inst. Can., Ont. Assn. Profl. Engrs., Canadian Soc. for Elec. Engring., Internat. Soc. Hybrid Microelectronics, Mfrs. and Agts. Nat. Assn., Beta Theta Pi (dir. 1973-77). Rotarian. Club: Niagara Falls Golf and Country. Home: 5060 Woodland Dr Lewiston NY 14092

WATFORD, JOHN HARDIN, banker; b. Hagerman, N.Mex., Oct. 8, 1931; s. Angus Elwood and Emma Joyce (West) W.; B.S. in Bus., U. Colo., 1954; m. June Joan Onarati, Aug. 31, 1952; children—Bill C., Lois A., Bob E., Jim A., Linda K. Asst. dir. data processing United Calif. Bank, Los Angeles, 1960-67; sr. v.p., dir. data processing div. Seattle 1st Nat. Bank, 1967-75; pres., chmn. bd. Atlantic Ops. Inc. subs. Atlantic Bancorp., Jacksonville, Fla., 1976—; dir. Computer Systems Inc., Seattle. Mem. Wash. Data Processing Authority, 1974-75. Served with AUS, 1955-57, 58-60. Mem. Data Processing Mgmt. Assn., Bank Adminstrn. Inst. Am. Banking Assn. (mem. nat. automation com. 1970-73), Beta Alpha Psi. Clubs: Wash. Athletic, Sawgrass Country Home: 3607 Ocean Dr South Jacksonville Beach FL 32250 Office: Atlantic Bank Bldg Jacksonville FL 32231

WATKINS, DEEMS CHRISTOPHER, oil co. exec.; b. Oakland, Calif., Oct. 18, 1946; s. George Edward and Marie Elizabeth W.; B.S. in Indsl. Mgmt. (ROTC scholar), U. Nev., 1968; M.B.A. in Mgmt. (Consortium fellow), U. So. Calif., 1973. Mem. staff M.B.A. exec. devel. program Hughes Aircraft Co., Los Angeles, 1973-75, project control adminstrn., El Segundo, Calif., 1975-76; mgmt. control analyst Atlantic Richfield Co., Pasadena, Calif. 1976, sr. services coordinator, Prudhoe Bay, Alaska, 1976-78, material control supr., 1978-79, sr. materials mgmt. supr., 1979—; cons. in mgmt. and mktg. to small bus. Loaned exec. Los Angeles United Crusade, 1973. Served to capt. U.S. Army, 1968-72. Decorated Bronze Star with 2 oak leaf clusters, Air medal with 2 oak leaf clusters, Purple Heart, Army Commendation medal. Mem. Am. Mgmt. Assn., Delta Sigma Pi. Home: PO Box 922 Anchorage AK 99510 Office: 3201 C St Suite 560 Anchorage AK 99503

WATKINS, EDWIN HERREN, financial exec.; b. Evanston, Ill., Mar. 12, 1924; s. Frank Alonzo and Julia (Herren) W.; B.A., Amherst Coll., 1947; m. Carol Frances Burtis, Nov. 3, 1951; children—Frank, Cynthia, Nancy, Ann, David. With U.S. Gypsum Co., Chgo., 1947-50; time study engr., chief indsl. engr. Mather Stock Car Co., Chgo., 1950-55; steel buyer, div. buyer U.S. Gypsum, Chgo., 1955-59; investment analyst Duff, Anderson & Clark, Chgo., 1959-65; investment mgr. Field Enterprises, Inc., Chgo., 1965-71, v.p., 1971—; dir. Mathers Fund, Inc., Chgo., 1971—; v.p. Amfund, Inc., Chgo., 1972-76, pres., 1976—. Served to ensign USNR, 1945-46. Chartered fin. analyst. Mem. Inst. Chartered Fin. Analysts, Investment Analysts Soc. Chgo., Chgo. Sci. Analysts. Congregationalist. Clubs: East Bank (charter), Univ. (Chgo.); Skokie Country (Glencoe, Ill.). Home: 576 Ash St Winnetka IL 60093 Office: Room 700 401 N Wabash Ave Chicago IL 60611

WATKINS, HAYS THOMAS, r.r. exec.; b. Fern Creek, Ky., Jan. 26, 1926; s. Hays Thomas and Minnie Catherine (Whiteley) W.; B.S. in Accounting, Western Ky. U., 1947; M.B.A., Northwestern U., 1948; m. Betty Jean Wright, 1950; 1 son, Hays Thomas III. With C.&O. Ry., Cleve., 1949—, v.p. finance, 1964-67, v.p. adminstrv. group, 1967-71, pres., chief exec. officer, 1971-73, chmn., chief exec. officer, 1973-80, chmn., pres., 1975-80; chmn. Chessie System, Inc., 1973-75; pres. CSX Corp., 1980—; pres. B.&O. R.R., 1971-73, vice chmn. bd., 1973-75, pres., chief exec. officer, 1975-80; dir. Black & Decker Mfg. Co., Westinghouse Electric Corp. Sponsor, William and Mary Coll. Sch. Bus. Adminstrn., 1971—. Trustee St. Luke's Hosp., Mus. Arts Assn. (Cleve. Orch.), Johns Hopkins U., Baldwin-Wallace Coll. Served with AUS, 1945-47. C.P.A., Ill. Mem. Nat. Assn. Accountants, Am. Inst. C.P.A.'s, Ohio Soc. C.P.A.'s. Clubs: Center (Balt.); Commonwealth (Richmond, Va.); Sky (N.Y.C.); Union (Cleve.). Home: 70 Quail Hollow Dr Moreland Hills OH 44022 Office: Fed Res Bank Bldg 15th Floor Richmond VA

WATKINS, MARIE CARMELLA, materials co. ofcl.; b. New Rochelle, N.Y., July 22, 1937; d. Nicholas and Theresa (Martinetti) Chimento; student Iona Coll., 1974—; children—Edward, Diane, Robert. Exec. sec., 1965-69; mem. acctg. staff J.F. Jelenko Co. div. Penwalt Corp., 1969-76; adminstrv. mgr. Cora Materials Corp., New Rochelle, 1976—. Adminstrv. dir. Brewster Camp Assn., 1967-69. Mem. Am. Mgmt. Assn., Bus. and Profl. Women's Club. Office: 2525 Palmer Ave New Rochelle NY 10801

WATKINS, OLIVER TIMBERLAKE, newspaper advt. sales exec.; b. Wilmington, N.C., Aug. 30, 1928; s. Edison Lee and Maysie Carlton (Crunter) W.; B.S., U. N.C., 1952; Advt. promotion mgr. Hawaii Newspaper Agy. Inc., Honolulu, 1960-65, Detroit Free Press, 1965-68; v.p. research and sales promotion Story & Kelly-Smith, Inc., N.Y.C., 1968-76; v.p. sales Gannett Newspaper Advt. Sales, N.Y.C., 1976—. Served with AUS, 1946-48. Mem. Newspaper Advt. Sales Assn. (past pres. N.Y. chpt.). Republican. Presbyterian. Office: 200 Park Ave New York NY 10017

WATKINS, RICHARD ALLEN, soft drink co. exec.; b. Balt., Oct. 11, 1930; s. Fielding Lucas and Emma Blanche (Hayes) W.; student Balt. City Coll., 1945-48; A.A., Eastern Coll., 1951; m. Mary Ellen Kirkpatrick, Apr. 22, 1949; children—Richard Allen, Deborah Lea (Mrs. Charles Allen Kennedy), Marsha (Mrs. William Roberts), Glenn, David. Asst. to pres. Albert F. Goetze, Inc. meat packer, Balt., 1949-67; div. mgr. Allegheny Pepsi Cola Bottling Co., Balt., 1967-74, v.p., gen. mgr., 1975-81, pres., 1981—. Mem. Md. C. of C., Restaurant Assn. Md., Va., Md. soft drink assns., Advt. Club Balt., Md. Automatic Merchandising Council, Coin-Op Laundry Assn. Md., Retail Grocers and Food Dealers Assn. Home: The Summit Cross Junction VA 22625 Office: 2216 N Charles St Baltimore MD 21218

WATKINS, RICHARD VENABLE, govt. ofcl., civil engr.; b. Richmond, Va., Feb. 7, 1940; s. Charles Baskerville and Rebekah (Stephenson) W.; B.S. in Civil Engring., Va. Poly. Inst. and State U., 1964; M.S. in Environ. Engring., U. Mo., 1966; postgrad. Va. Poly. Inst. and State U., 1976—; m. Nana Sue Via, Nov. 29, 1969; children—Gregory Joseph, Jeffrey Lee, Kristin Venable, Jonathan Venable. Sanitary engr. Black & Veatch Cons. Engrs., Kansas City, Mo., 1966; prof. Finlay Engring. Coll., Kansas City, Mo., 1966-68; phys. sci. adminstr. EPA, Kansas City, Mo., 1966-68, Charlottesville, Va., 1968-71, Washington, 1971-75; sr. environ. project mgr. U.S. Nuclear Regulatory Commn., Washington, 1975-79; dep. dir. office environ. affairs U.S. Geol. Survey, Reston, Va., 1979—. Dist. commr. Stonewall Jackson council Boy Scouts Am., 1969-70; ordained deacon Presbyterian Ch., 1975, elder, 1978. Recipient Silver Medal award U.S. EPA, 1975, Bronze Medal award, 1974; diplomate Am. Acad. Environ. Engrs.; registered profl. engr., Va., D.C. Mem. ASCE, Water Pollution Control Fedn., Nat., Va. socs. profl. engrs. Club: Toastmasters. Contbr. articles on environ. engring. to profl. jours. Home: 933 Jaysmith St Great Falls VA 22066 Office: US Geol Survey Reston VA

WATKINS, WAYNE BENJAMIN, chem. co. exec.; b. El Dorado, Ark., June 15, 1932; s. William Benjamin and Carlee Inez (Pearson) W.; B.S. in Chem. Engring., U. Ark., 1955; m. Zada Lucille Trull, Aug. 29, 1954; children—Michael, Elizabeth, Janet, Benjamin. Production engr. Union Carbide Co., Port Lavaca, Tex., 1955-60, dept. head, 1960-68, asst. plant mgr., 1968-70, plant mgr., 1970-72, v.p. Union Carbide Caribe, Ponce, P.R., 1972-73, pres., 1973-75, nat. sales mgr. Union Carbide Chems. & Plastics, N.Y.C., 1975-79; v.p. ops. and tech. coating materials div., 1980—; dir. 1st State Bank, Port Lavaca, 1970-72; dir. Union Carbide Caribe, 1972-75. Active, Boys Club Am. Recipient Gov.'s Award for Safety, P.R., 1974; Indsl. Devel. award Assn. Mktg. Execs. P.R., 1975; registered profl. engr., Tex. Mem. Am. Inst. Chem. Engrs. Methodist. Club: Rotary. Home: 84 Remington Rd Ridgefield CT 06877 Office: 270 Park Ave New York NY 10017

WATKINS, WAYNE COURTNEY, mgmt. cons.; b. Derry, Pa., Aug. 1, 1937; s. Charles James and Viola Mae (Stauffer) W.; B.S., U. N.D., 1959; M.A., U. Pa., 1971, M.B.A., 1973. Commd. 2d. lt., inf. U.S. Army, 1959, advanced through grades to capt., 1967, resigned, 1969; dir. ops. div. various cons. cos., 1974-78; founder, pres., chmn. bd. Wayne C. Watkins Concepts Co., mgmt. cons., Sicklerville, N.J., 1978—. Decorated Bronze Star. Mem. Am. Prodn. and Inventory Control Soc., Am. Inst. Indsl. Engrs., Nat. Assn. Accts. Club: Masons. Office: 36 Peoria Ln Sicklerville NJ 08081

WATLINGTON, JOSEPH, JR., ins. broker; b. Phila., Aug. 22, 1924; s. Joseph and Susie (Banks) W.; B.A., Temple U., 1947; m. Marion Spencer, July 9, 1949; children—Joseph Richard, Leigh Ellen. Visitor, Pa. Dept. Pub. Assistance, Phila., 1947-48; sales agt. N.C. Mut. Life Ins. Co., Phila., 1948; with Watlington & Cooper, Inc., Phila., 1948—, pres., 1967—; pres. Personnel Resources, Inc., 1974-80; chmn. Nat. Urban Ins. Co., 1971-74; broker 1st Pa. Bank Ins. cons. Sch. Dist. Phila., others; instr. Community Coll. Phila., 1972; mem. ins. adv. council City of Phila., 1980—; chmn. adv. com. Office of Employment and Tng., City of Phila. Vice pres. Afro-Am. Hist. and Cultural '76 Bicentennial Corp. Phila., 1975-77. Bd. dirs., pres. Lighthouse, 1971-72; bd. dirs. Urban Studies Center, LaSalle Coll., 1969-72, Nat. Bonding Service Found., 1969-75, Upward Exec. Tng. Inst., 1969; trustee W. Kuhn Day Camp, Coll. Settlement Phila.; pres. Black Unitarian-Universalist Caucus Delaware Valley, 1970-71; chmn. the Citizens, 1972-80; chmn. Phila. Allied Action Commn., 1976-79; bd. dirs., treas. Edn. to Work Council, 1979—. Served with AUS, 1943-45. Recipient Disting. Sales award Sales Mktg. Execs. of Phila., 1980; non-resident ins. broker, N.J., Md., Va., D.C. Mem. Nat. Assn. Ins. Agts., Pa. Assn. Ins. Agts., Profl. Ins. Agts. Assn., Greater Phila. C. of C. (dir.), Ins. Soc. Phila. (dir.), Alpha Phi Alpha. Unitarian (past trustee, ann. fund chmn.). Clubs: Downtown, Urban. Home: 6447 Magnolia St Philadelphia PA 19119 Office: 100 S Broad St Philadelphia PA 19110

WATREL, WARREN GEORGE, pharm. co. exec.; b. N.Y.C., Jan. 5, 1935; s. John and Julia (Rock) W.; B.S. in Zoology and Microbiology, Syracuse U., 1957, M.S. in Microbiology and Biochemistry, 1958, postgrad., 1958; m. Louisa Vetri; children—Marc, Justin, Stephen. Gen. sales mgr. PharmaciaAB, Sweden, 1964-65, dir. mktg. and sales, gen. mgr., 1965-72; v.p., gen. mgr. Damon Corp., Vineland, N.J., 1972-74; ops. and mktg. exec. Pharmachem Corp., Bethlehem, Pa., 1974-75; exec. v.p., chief operating officer, dir. Newton Industries, Inc. (N.J.), 1976—; instr. bacteriology Syracuse U.; cons. to industry. Served to capt. AUS, 1959-60. Recipient award for sci. advertisement Litton-Reihold Pub. Co., 1968, 69. Mem. Am. Mgmt. Assn., Sales and Mktg. Execs. Internat., Am. Chem. Soc., AAAS, Am. Soc. Microbiology, Animal Health Inst., N.Y. Acad. Scis., Am. Inst. Chemists. Contbr. to Ency. of Chemistry, 3d edit., 1971. Patentee in field. Home: 1174 Sherlin Dr Bridgewater NJ 08807

WATSON, DOROTHY MAAHS, restaurant exec.; b. Dayton, Ohio, July 21, 1934; d. Henry H. and Velma J. (Bower) Maahs; student public schs., Dayton, Ohio; m. Harry B. Watson, Sept. 10, 1952; children—Christine Marie, Harry B. Clk., bookkeeper Keowee Sweet Shoppe, Dayton, 1945-54; with Burger Chef of Ohio, Dayton, 1965-68, Rax Roast Beef, Dayton, 1965-68; with Ponderosa System, Inc., Dayton, 1965—, asst. controller, 1970, asst. sec., dir. risk mgmt., 1977—. Mem. Nat. Assn. Accts. (pres. chpt.), Am. Soc. Women Accts. (past pres. chpt., past nat. sec.), Risk and Ins. Mgmt. Soc. (pres. chpt.), Nat. Restaurant Assn., Eintracht Singing Soc. (fin. sec.). Home: 6351 Shull Rd Dayton OH 45424 Office: PO Box 578 Dayton OH 45401

WATSON, ELBERT, pipe line co. exec.; b. Little Rock, Feb. 23, 1926; s. Elbert Lycurgus and Irma (Hooker) W.; student U. South, 1943-44, 46-47, U. Ark., 1947-49; m. Adeline Elliott, Jan. 1, 1953; children—Elbert Elliott, Laura Adeline. Sr. v.p. Houston Natural Gas Corp., 1974—; pres. Oasis Pipe Line Co., Houston, 1975—, H-T Gathering Co., Houston, 1975—; exec. v.p. HNG Fossil Fuels, Houston, 1976—; dir. HNG and subs., 1968—, Pargas, Inc., 1977—. Served with USN, World War II. Republican. Episcopalian. Home: 6138 Cedar Creek Houston TX 77057 Office: 1200 Travis St Houston TX 77002

WATSON, ESTELL MILFORD, elec., indsl. and photog. engr.; b. Otterville, Ill., June 23, 1903; s. Dr. James Edwin and Rose (Milford) W.; B.S., Purdue U., 1925, E.E., 1929; M.S., Case Inst. Tech., 1932, M.S. in Indsl. Engring., 1951; m. Harriet Brink, Aug. 6, 1925; children—John Estell, Marilyn Rose (Mrs. Wilford H. Cheetham), Richard Milford, Margery Edith. Engr. research lab. Gen. Electric Co., Nela Park, Cleve. 1925-28, lamp developing lab., 1928-41, Cleve. Equipment Works, 1944-58; cons. engr. Warner & Swasey Co., 1959-60, E.M. Watson, High Speed Photography, 1961—, NASA Lewis Research Center, 1962—. Mem. Cleve. council Boy Scouts Am. Served as capt. ordnance AUS, 1941-42, AC, 1942-44. Mem. Soc. Motion Picture and Television Engrs., Cleve. Physics Soc., Cleve. Engring. Soc., Am. Legion. Republican. Presbyterian. Clubs: Masons, Rotary. Address: 874 Medford Dr Cleveland Heights OH 44121

WATSON, HOWARD LEE, chem. co. exec.; b. Louisville, July 16, 1927; s. Clarence James and Annie (Lynch) W.; B.S., U. Louisville, 1949; m. Lorraine Virginia Wagner, Dec. 31, 1948; children—Connie Ann, Sandra Lee, Marc Alan, Gregory Thomas, Barbara Lynn. Plant engr. Nat. Carbide, Louisville and Calvert City, Ky., 1949-56; utilities project engr. Gen. Electric Co., Evendale, Ohio, 1956-57; operations Mgr. Air Products & Chems., Inc., Calvert City, Ky., 1957-71, plant mgr., 1971-73, group prodn. mgr., Allentown, Pa., 1973-77, technology mgr.-emulsions, 1978—. Served with USNR, 1945-46. Registered profl. engr., Ky., N.J., Ohio. Mem. Am. Inst. Chem. Engrs. (chpt. pres. 1963). Republican. Presbyterian. Club: Rotary (pres. 1973). Home: PO Box 282A RD 2 River Bend Rd Allentown PA 18103 Office: PO Box 538 Allentown PA 18105

WATSON, JAMES A., food chain exec.; b. Mpls., 1919; B.A., U. Minn., 1942. Chmn. bd. Red Owl Stores, 1946-72; pres. Gamble Skogmo, Inc., 1960-72; v.p.-retail and wholesale ops. George Weston Ltd., 1972-73; pres., chief exec. officer Nat. Tea Co., Rosemont, Ill., 1973, now chmn. bd.; dir. Northwestern Nat. Bank, K-Tel Internat. Inc., George Weston Ltd. Office: 9701 W Higgins Rd Rosemont IL 60018*

WATSON, K. BERT, gas co. exec.; b. Ranger, Tex., June 22, 1925; s. Max K. and Elizabeth (Slaughter) W.; B.Ch.E., U. Colo., LL.B., 1948; postgrad. Grad. Sch. Bus. Columbia U.; m. Joy Willhoite, Dec. 29, 1947; children—Sandra (Mrs. M. Lewis Browder), Randall, Kenneth, Delk, David. Admitted to Tex. bar, 1948; asst. atty. gen. State of Tex., 1949-52; atty. Amarillo (Tex.) Oil Co., 1952-53; corp. sec., atty. Pioneer Natural Gas Co., Amarillo, 1955-65, dir., 1965—, v.p., gen. counsel, 1965-71, exec. v.p., 1971-73, pres., 1973—, also chmn. bd., chief exec. officer; chmn. bd. Pioneer Gas Products Co.; chmn. bd., chief exec. officer Pioneer Corp.; dir. Amarillo Oil Co., Pioneer Nuclear Inc., Pinaga, Pioneer Transmission Corp., Pioneer Prodn. Corp.; mem. exec. com. Water, Inc. Active Boy Scouts Am. Served with USNR, 1942-45. Mem. West Tex., Amarillo chambers commerce, So., Am. (dir.) gas assns., Tex. Tech. Law Sch. Found., Phi Delta Phi, Pi Kappa Alpha. Office: PO Box 511 Amarillo TX 79163*

WATSON, KENNETH WILLIAM, fin. co. exec.; b. White Plains, N.Y., Nov. 18, 1942; s. Lionel William and Loretta Ann (Hagele) W.; B.S. in Econs., Villanova U., 1964; M.B.A., Pace U., 1967; m. Margaret, May 28, 1966; children—Michelle, Nicole. Product mgr. CPC Internat., Englewood Cliffs, N.J., 1966-69; mktg. mgr. Hunt Wesson Foods, Fullerton, Calif., 1968-72; v.p. United Beverages, Pepsico, Purchase, N.Y., 1972-76; pres., chief exec. officer Internat. Gold Corp., N.Y.C., 1976—. Club: Winged Foot. Home: 64 Hanson Rd Darien CT 06820 Office: 645 Fifth Ave New York NY 10022

WATSON, R. WARD, business exec. Chmn., dir. MBPLX Corp., Wichita. Office: PO Box 2519 Wichita KS 67201*

WATSON, ROLAND HENRY, minerals and chem. co. exec.; b. Ferndale, Mich., Dec. 13, 1928; s. Henry Ralph and Golda Ellen (Sisson) W.; B.S. in M.E., Purdue U., 1952, M.S. in Indsl. Engring., 1952; m. Carolyn Sue Marshall, Nov. 1, 1954; children—David Bradford, Bruce Robert. With Aluminum Co. Am., Pitts., 1955-77; corporate mgr. safety, health and loss prevention SCM Corp., N.Y.C., 1977-80; corp. dir. safety and loss prevention Engelhard Minerals & Chems. Corp., N.Y.C., 1980—. Active Boy Scouts Am., various locations. Served to lt. (j.g.) U.S. Navy, 1948-55. Registered profl. engr.; cert. safety profl. Mem. Am. Soc. Safety Engrs., Am. Soc. Metals, Am. Mgmt. Assn., Purdue Alumni Assn., Delta Upsilon. Republican. Presbyterian. Home: 17 Middlesex Rd Darien CT 06820 Office: 1221 Ave of Americas New York NY 10020

WATSON, STEWART CHARLES, constrn. co. exec.; b. Brock, Sask., Can., Sept. 17, 1922; s. Samuel Henry and Elva Jane (St. John) W.; student U. Buffalo; m. Irene Lillian Ahrens, Aug. 4, 1943; children—Judith Gail (Mrs. David Stafford), Wendy Carolyn (Mrs. Rocco Amuso), Ronald James. With Acme Steel & Malleable Iron Works, Buffalo, 1940-42; with Acme Hwy. Products, Buffalo, 1946-69, internat. marketing mgr., 1955-69; pres. Watson-Bowman Assos., Inc., Buffalo, 1970—. Internat. lectr. on kinetics of civil engring. structures; mem. U.S. Transp. Research Bd. Served with AUS, 1943-45; ETO. Fellow Am. Concrete Inst.; mem. ASTM, Nat. Acad. Sci. Mason (32 deg., Shriner). Home: 178 Sherbrooke Ave Williamsville NY 14221 Office: 95 Pineview Dr Amherst NY 14120

WATTENGEL, HARVEY JAMES, health care products co. exec.; b. Glendale, Calif., Aug. 22, 1942; s. Charles James and Mildred (Pollard) W.; B.S. in Aero. Engring., Calif. State Poly. Coll., 1964; M.B.A. in Fin., U. So. Calif., 1972; m. Maria Estela Zertuche-Segrove, July 29, 1967; children—Adriane Michelle, Christopher James. Engr./scientist McDonnell-Douglas Astronautics, Santa Monica, Calif., 1964-71; cons. Mgmt. Services Co., Sacramento, 1972-74; with Abbott Labs., North Chicago, Ill., 1974-78, sr. fin. analyst, 1976-78; mgr. spl. fin. studies, consumer products unit Johnson & Johnson do Brazil, Sao Paulo, 1978—. Democrat. Home: Rua Albuquerque Lins 100 Ed Ouro Preto 34 05663 Sao Paulo SP Brazil Office: Rua Gerivativa 55 Butanta 05501 Sao Paulo SP Brazil

WATTLES, JOHN CHARLES, banker; b. South Bend, Ind., Jan. 6, 1931; s. Charles P. and Carmen (Irvin) W.; B.B.A., Western Mich., U. 1955; m. Helen Statler Fischer, Feb. 26, 1955; children—Charles, Sara, Katie. Trust officer, v.p. First Nat. Bank & Trust Co. of Mich., Kalamazoo, 1957-69; pres. W.J. Upjohn Mgmt. Co., Kalamazoo, 1969-75; sr. v.p., trust officer Indsl. State Bank & Trust Co., Kalamazoo, 1975—; vice chmn., dir. Wells Mfg. Corp.; dir. APM, Inc., FCF, Inc., Wells-Index Corp. Bd. dirs. Lakeside Children's Home, Inc., Western Mich. U. Found. trustee YMCA, Howe Mil. Sch.; pres. Civic Auditorium Trustee Corp. Served as 1st lt., Q.M.C., U.S. Army, 1955-57. Mem. Investments Analyst Soc. Chgo. Presbyterian. Club: Park. Office: 151 S Rose St Kalamazoo MI 49007

WATTS, JOHN DANIEL (J. DAN), map co. exec.; b. Knoxville, Tenn., Sept. 29, 1942; s. Daniel Monroe and Bernice C. (Creel) W.; student U. Alaska, 1962-63. Supr., J & R Map Co., Van Buren, Ark., 1967-70; exec. Security Fin. Co., Spartanburg, S.C., 1971-73, BP Industries, Midland, Tex., 1974-75; pres., chief exec. officer Impact Map Co., Lubbock, Tex., 1975-80; gen. mgr. Mosher-Adams Inc., Oklahoma City, 1980—. Served with USAF, 1960-64; Vietnam. Recipient ednl. achievement award USAF, 1963, presdl. unit citation, 1963, award of merit, 1964; photog. excellence award (6), Photo Five Photog. Soc., 1968-74; named Mgr. of Yr., Security Fin. Co., 1973; cert. fin. analyst. Mem. Profl. Photographers Tex., Nat. Free Lance Photographers Assn., Associated Photographers Internat., Printing Industries Am., U.S. C. of C. Republican. Methodist. Home: 648 W Beam Ave Yukon OK 73099 Office: 400 W Commerce St Oklahoma City OK 73109

WATTS, JOHN MCCLEAVE, ins. and investment co. exec.; b. Salt Lake City, July 20, 1933; s. Newell Edward and Mildred (McCleave) W.; B.S., Mass. Inst. Tech., 1956; m. Janis Marie Duncan, July 4, 1971; children—John McCleave, Christopher A., Kelly Lee; 1 stepson, Kenneth D. McCoy. Engaged in ins. bus., 1957—; dir. life ins. mktg. Channing Cos., Inc., Houston, 1968-71; dir. mktg. Waddell & Reed, Inc., Kansas City, Mo., 1971-74, exec. v.p., dir., 1974-79; exec. v.p., dir. subs. Research Mgmt. Assos., Inc., Kansas City, 1974-79; v.p. nat. ins. dept. E. F. Hutton & Co., N.Y.C., 1979—, pres. 17 mktg. subs., 1979—. Councilman, City of Leawood, Kans., 1973-78, pub. safety commr., 1973—; chmn. Nueces County (Tex.) Republican Party, 1962-65. Served to capt. AUS, 1957. Recipient Life Ins. Mktg. Inst. Achievement award Purdue U., 1970; C.L.U. Mem. Am. Soc. Pension Actuaries, Internat. Assn. Fin. Planners, Nat. Assn. Life Underwriters, Internat. Found. Employee Benefit Plans. Republican. Club: Torrey (LaJolla, Calif.). Contbr. articles to profl. jours. Home: 16307 Woodson View Rd Poway CA 92064 Office: 11011 N Torrey Pines Rd Box 2700 LaJolla CA 92038

WATTS, ROSS LESLIE, educator, acctg. cons.; b. Hamilton, Australia, Nov. 10, 1942; came to U.S., 1966; s. Leslie R. and Elsie B. (Horadam) W.; B. Commerce with honors (Commonwealth Govt. scholar 1960-65), U. Newcastle (Australia), 1966; M.B.A. (Ford Found. fellow 1967-68), U. Chgo., 1968, Ph.D., 1971; m. Helen Clare Firkin, Jan. 15, 1966; children—Andrew David, James Michael. Audit clk. Forsythe & Co., Newcastle, Australia, 1960-64, acct., 1964-66; instr. Grad. Sch. Bus., U. Chgo., 1969-70; asst. prof. Grad. Sch. Mgmt., U. Rochester (N.Y.), 1971-78, asso. prof., 1978—; prof. commerce U. Newcastle, 1974-75; cons. to bus. firms, 1972—. Recipient Notable Contbn. award Am. Inst. C.P.A.'s, 1979, 80. Mem. Am. Acctg. Assn., Am. Fin. Assn., Am. Econs. Assn., Inst. Chartered Accts. in Australia. Contbr. articles on acctg. research to profl. jours.; asso. editor Jour. Acctg. Research, 1972-78, Jour. Fin. Econs., 1974—, Australian Jour. Mgmt., 1976—; co-editor Jour. Acctg. and Econs., 1979—. Home: 17 Burncoat Way Pittsford NY 14534 Office: GSM Wilson Blvd Rochester NY 14627

WAUGH, CAROL ANN, pub. co. exec.; b. Rockville Center, N.Y., Oct. 29, 1948; s. Donald Randolph and Maida Sizer W.; B.A., N.Y. U., 1971; M.B.A., Pace U., 1980. Adminstrv. asst. Interbank Card Assn., 1972; account exec. Action Letter, N.Y.C., 1972-73; dist. sales mgr. U.S. Fleet Leasing, N.Y.C., 1974-75; dir. ednl. products Butterick Pub., N.Y.C., 1975-80; v.p., dir. ednl. products Maclean Hunter Learning Resources, N.Y.C., 1980—. Bd. dirs. Environ. Action Coalition, 1977. Mem. Assn. Media Producers, Women in Communications, Advt. Women N.Y., Womens Direct Response Group. Co-author: The Patchwork Quilt Coloring and Design Book, 1977; Rollerskating: A Sport of a Lifetime, 1979. Home: 165 W 20th St New York NY 10011 Office: 708 3d Ave New York NY 10017

WAX, GEORGE LOUIS, lawyer; b. New Orleans, Dec. 6, 1928; s. John Edward and Theresa (Schaff) W.; LL.B., Loyola U. of South, 1952, B.C.S., 1960; m. Patricia Ann Delaney, Feb. 20, 1965; children—Louis Jude, Joann Olga, Therese Marie. Admitted to La. bar, 1952, practiced in New Orleans, 1954—. Served with USNR, 1952-54. Mem. Am., La., New Orleans bar assns., Am. Legion. Roman Catholic. Kiwanian. Clubs: New Orleans Athletic, Suburban Gun and Rod, Pendennis. Home: 5635 Pratt Dr New Orleans LA 70122 Office: Nat Bank Commerce New Orleans LA 70112

WAXMONSKY, RONALD JOHN, bus. planner; b. Pittston, Pa., Apr. 12, 1949; s. Jacob Joseph and Catherine Rose W.; B.I.E., Gen. Motors Inst., 1972; M.C.E., Pa. State U., 1973; M.B.A., Wayne State U., 1976; m. Delia Accettola, Apr. 22, 1978. Supr. material dept. assembly div. Gen. Motors Corp., Wilmington, Del., 1973-74, sr. mktg. engr. transp. systems div., Gen Motors Tech. Center, Mich., 1974-76, sr. engr. auto assembly, product planning and tooling, 1977-79, coordinator bus. planning Gen. Motors de Mexico, Mexico City, 1980—; traffic and transp. cons. Pa. State U./Fed. Hwy. Adminstrn. fellow, 1972; Wayne State U. fellow, 1976; registered profl. engr., Mich. Mem. Inst. Transp. Engrs., Soc. Automotive Engrs., Mich. Soc. Profl. Engrs., Internat. Entrepreneurs Assn., Tau Beta Pi. Clubs: Gen Motors Ski, Tech Center Ski. Address: Gen Motors de Mexico Apartado 107-BIS Mexico 1 DF Mexico

WAY, ALVA OTIS, III, credit card co. exec.; b. Schenectady, Apr. 27, 1929; s. Alva Otis and Margaret (Sigsbee) W.; A.B., Brown U., 1951; m. Eleonore Maurer; children—Peter, Karin Andrea, Cynthia Helena. With Gen. Electric Co., various locations, 1951-70, 73-79, v.p., 1973-77, sr. v.p. fin., 1977-79; v.p. Honeywell Info. Systems, Inc., 1973-77; vice chmn. Am. Express Co., N.Y.C., 1979—; dir. Am. Express Internat. Banking Corp., Fireman's Fund Life Ins. Co., Amex Credit Corp., Warner Amex Cable Corp. Served with U.S. Army, 1952-54. Trustee, Brown U.; bd. dirs. Columbia Presbyn. Hosp., N.Y.C., Lower Manhattan Downtown Assn. Mem. Sigma Chi. Club: Union League. Office: 125 Broad St New York NY 10004

WAYNE, GAIL MOVENE, motion picture producer, real estate investment co. exec.; b. Calgary, Alta., Can., Oct. 11, 1922; d. Earl Ransom and Ida Movene (Helgeson) Tamblin; student Los Angeles City Coll., 1939, Lumbleau Real Estate Sch., 1956; m. Steve Wayne, May 28, 1948 (div. Nov. 1952); 1 son, Christopher Stephen. Motion picture actress, Hollywood, Calif., 1938-46; owner Gail Wayne Splty. Shop, Farmers Market, Los Angeles, 1946-54; real estate broker, Los Angeles, 1958—; pres. Sun State Lands, Inc., Los Angeles, 1958—; pres. Asia-Am. Land Investments, Ltd., Hong Kong, 1965—, chmn. bd., 1966—; exec. producer, v.p. Hagen-Wayne Prodns., Inc., Hollywood, 1973—; pres. Hagen-Wayne Film Orgn., Inc., Hollywood, 1974—. Del. Hawaii State Republican Conv., 1970. Bd. dirs. Hawaii chpt. WAIF div. Internat. Social Service. Mem. Honolulu Bd. Realtors, Nat. Assn. Realtors. Clubs: Hawaii Polo (social chmn. 1973-74) (Honolulu); Diamond Head Tennis, Outrigger Canoe (Waikiki, Hawaii). Home: 2957 Kalakaua Ave Honolulu HI 96815 Office: 1040 N Las Palmas Ave Hollywood CA 90038 also Room 77 New Henry House Hong Kong China

WEAKLEY, GEORGE DAVID, equipment co. exec.; b. Battle Creek, Mich., May 8, 1930; s. Harry M. and Hazel May W.; student Mich. State U., 1949-50; m. Patricia Anne McAllister, Dec. 27, 1952; children—Beverly, Deborah, David, Elizabeth. With Clark Equipment Co., 1956—, adminstrv. mgr., Chgo., 1969-72, parts sales mgr., 1973-76, gen. mgr. depots, Atlanta, 1977—. Mem. Oak Forest (Ill.) Sch. Bd., 1970-73. Served with USAF, 1951-55. Life mem. Delta Tau Delta. Club: K.C. Home: 2372 Oxbow Circle Stone Mountain GA 30083 Office: Clark Equipment Co 1155 Southern Rd Morrow GA 30260

WEARLY, W(ILLIAM) L(EVI), bus. exec.; b. Warren, Ind., Dec. 5, 1915; s. Purvis Gardner and Ethel Ada (Jones) W.; B.S., Purdue U., 1937; m. Mary Jane Riddle, Mar. 8, 1941; children—Patricia Ann, Susan Riddle, Beth Ann, William L. Student engr. C.A. Dunham Co., Michigan City, Ind., 1936; mem. elec. design staff Joy Mfg. Co., Franklin, Pa., 1937-57, v.p. in charge coal machinery sales, 1947, exec. v.p., 1956-57, pres., dir. 1957-62; cons. engr., 1962-64; v.p., dir. Ingersoll-Rand Co., N.Y.C., 1964-66, exec. v.p., 1966-67, chmn. bd., chief exec. officer, 1967—; dir. Sperry Corp., Bank N.Y., Am. Smelting & Refining, Am. Cyanamid. Mem. AIEE, Am. Inst. Mining Engrs., NAM (dir.), Eta Kappa Nu, Tau Beta Pi, Beta Theta Pi. Republican. Methodist. Clubs: Duquesne (Pitts.); Sky (N.Y.C.); Indian Harbor Yacht (Greenwich, Conn.); Blind Brook Golf; Masons, Shriners. Author tech. publs. relating to mining; speaker before engring. groups; inventor. Home: 170 Round Hill Rd Greenwich CT 06830 Office: Woodcliff Lake NJ 07675

WEARN, JAMES POWELL, elec. mfg. co. exec.; b. Wayne, Pa., Apr. 19, 1927; s. George E. and Mabel A. (McCabe) W.; B.S. in Adminstrv. Engring., Lafayette Coll., 1950; cert. in bus. adminstrn. U. Va., 1972; m. Virginia C. Freeman, Sept. 15, 1951; children—James Powell, Joanne A. Mfg. engr. power generation divs. Westinghouse Elec. Corp., Phila., 1950-56, supervisory mfg. engr., 1956-66, mgr. plant planning, 1966-68, mgr. ops., 1968-70, mgr. multi-plant ops., 1970-74, corp. dir. mfg. services, 1974-77, dir. capital appropriations, 1977-79, dir. mfg. industry equipment group, Pitts., 1979—. Served with USN, 1944-46. Mem. ASME, Soc. Mfg. Engrs., Am. Inst. Indsl. Engrs. Republican. Club: Wildwood Golf. Home: 3242 Maine Dr Allison Park PA 15101 Office: Industry Equipment Group Westinghouse Electric Corp Pittsburgh PA 15222

WEARSTLER, EARL FORD, bank equipment/systems mfg. co. exec.; b. North Canton, Ohio, Mar. 1, 1924; s. Russell John and Goldie Marie (Young) W.; student Northwestern U., 1942, Kent State U., 1946; m. Catherine Nora Duren, Apr. 19, 1974; 1 dau., Joyce Ann. With Diebold, Inc., 1947—, regional mgr., Atlanta, 1955-56, southeast area mgr., 1957-64, v.p., gen. mgr., Canton, Ohio, 1965-76, exec. v.p., North Canton, Ohio, 1977—, dir., 1976—; dir. Diebold of Can., Ltd. Served with AC, USNR, 1942-46. Republican. Clubs: Brookside Country (Canton); Congress Lake Country (Hartville, Ohio); Union (Cleve.); Prestwick Country (Uniontown, Ohio); Masons. Contbr. articles to fin. and trade related jours. Home: 3124 Sussex St NW Canton OH 44718 Office: Diebold Inc 5995 Mayfair Rd North Canton OH 44720

WEATHERHEAD, ALBERT JOHN, III, bus. exec.; b. Cleve., Feb. 17, 1925; s. Albert J. and Dorothy (Jones) W.; A.B., Harvard, 1950, postgrad., 1951; m. Celia Scott, Jan. 1, 1975; children—Dwight S., Michael H., Mary H. Prodn. mgr. Yale & Towne, Stamford, Conn., 1951-54, Blaw-Knox, Pitts., 1954-56; plant mgr. Weatherhead Co., Cleve., 1957-59, gen. mgr., 1959-61, v.p., gen. mgr., 1962-66, gen. sales mgr., 1962-63, v.p. mfg., 1964-66; v.p., dir. Weatherhead Co. of Can., Ltd. 1960-63, pres., chief exec. officer, dir., 1964-66; pres., dir. Weatherchem Corp., 1971—; dir. Weatherhead Co., Protane Corp., L.P.G. Leasing Corp., Leasepac Corp., Leasepac Can., Ltd., Creative Resources, Inc. Mem. Univ. Sch. Alumni Council, trustee Univ. Sch.; trustee, mem. resources com. Case Western Res. U.; mem. vis. com. Ohio U., Athens; v.p. nat. adv. com. Rollins Coll., Winter Park, Fla.; mem. com. univ. resources Harvard U.; adv. trustee Pinecrest Sch., Ft. Lauderdale, Fla.; mem. capital campaign steering com. Laurel Sch.; trustee Vocat. Guidance and Rehab. Services, Hwy. Safety Found.; v.p. Weatherhead Found. Served with USAAF, 1943-46. Mem. Am. Newcomen Soc., Beta Gamma Sigma. Clubs: Union (Cleve.); Country (Shaker Heights, Ohio); Ottawa Shooting (Freemont, Ohio); Ocean (Delray, Fla.); Everglades (Palm Beach, Fla.); Codrington (Oxford, Eng.). Author: The New Age of Business, 1965. Home: 19601 Shelburne Rd Shaker Heights OH 44118 Office: 2222 Highland Rd Twinsburg OH 44087

WEATHERLY, MONNY LESTER, JR., lawyer, acct.; b. Buttahatchee, Ala., Nov. 2, 1926; s. Monny Lester and Eugie Mitt (Gregg) W.; B.S. in Acctg., Ariz. State U., 1961, M.S., 1962, postgrad. 1965-66, J.D., 1970; postgrad. U. Ariz., 1962-64; m. Nancy Rae Gales, Mar. 8, 1969; 1 son, Gregory Wray. Cotton gin mgr. S. Mt. Gin Co., Laveen, Ariz., 1952-58; acct. Dennis Schmich & Co., Phoenix, 1964-69; dep. county atty. Maricopy County, Phoenix, 1969-70; admitted to Ariz. bar, 1970; controller, house counsel Ray Industries, Inc., Phoenix, 1970-72; partner Nelson, Weatherly, Lambson & Olvis, C.P.A.'s, Mesa, 1972—. Camping dir. Boy Scouts Am., Phoenix, 1956; bd. dirs. Mesa Area Retarded Citizens, 1978-80. Served with USAF, 1944-48, U.S. Army, 1949-52. C.P.A., Ariz. Mem. Ariz. Soc. C.P.A.'s, Am. Inst. C.P.A.'s, Phi Kappa Phi, Phi Eta Sigma, Delta Sigma Pi. Democrat. Baptist. Clubs: Masons (Shriner). Home: 2016 E Gary Circle Mesa AZ 85203 Office: 77 W University Dr Mesa AZ 85201

WEATHERS, K. RUSSELL, agrl. exec.; b. Harrison County, Mo., June 21, 1942; s. W. Kenneth and Mildred G. (Fitzpatrick) W.; B.S. in Agrl. Edn., U. Mo., Columbia, 1964; m. Judith C. Cain, Aug. 12, 1961; children—Vince S., Kent A., Joy L. Vocat.-agrl. tchr. North Platte Schs., Dearborn, Mo., 1964-66, Centralia (Mo.) Public Schs., 1966-67; with Farmland Industries, Inc., Kansas City, Mo., 1967—, public relations exec., 1980—. Mem. Liberty (Mo.) City Council, 1977—; bd. dirs. Mo. 4-H Found., Agrl. Hall of Fame; pres. bd. dirs. Shepherd Youth Center, Liberty. Recipient Service award Nat. Future Farmers Am., 1978. Mem. Internat. Agribus. Club (chmn. bd. dirs. Kansas City chpt.), Northland (Mo.) C. of C., Guest Relations Assn., U. Mo. Alumni Assn. Mem. Christian Ch. (Disciples of Christ). Home: 1907 Clay St Liberty MO 64068 Office: PO Box 7305 Kansas City MO 64116

WEAVER, A. VERNON, govt. ofcl.; b. Miami, Fla.; B.E.E., U.S. Naval Acad. Vice-pres., So. Venetian Blind Co., 1949-60; pres. Lanotan, 1960-61; registered rep. Stephens, Inc., investment banking, 1960-63; with Hollis Co.; pres. Union Mgmt. Corp., mut. funds mgmt., 1964-69; v.p. sec. Intersci. Capital Mgmt. Corp., 1969-71; v.p. Union Life Ins. Co., 1971-72, pres., 1972-77; adminstr. SBA, Washington, 1977—; Served to lt. j.g. USN, 1946-49, 51-53. Office: SBA 1441 L St NW Washington DC 20416

WEAVER, ARTHUR J., banker; b. Falls City, Nebr., Nov. 19, 1912; s. Arthur J. and Maude E. (Hart) W.; m. Harriet Elizabeth Walt; children—Walt F., Arthur, John H., James T. Chmn. bd. Nishna Valley State Bank, Riverton, Iowa; ret. v.p. Alexander & Alexander Inc., N.Y.C.; dir. Comml. Fed. Savs. & Loan Assn., HOC Internat. Ltd., Denver, Kimberly Pines Inc., Davenport, Iowa, N.W. Investors, Inc., Nebrado Ltd., Nassau, Bahamas. Spl. U.S. ambassador independence of Republic of Togo, Africa, 1960. Mem. exec. com., v.p. Lancaster chpt. A.R.C.; active YMCA. Trustee U. Nebr. Found; Bd. dirs. Lincoln Found., Lincoln Center Devel. Assn. Mem. City Council of Lincoln, 1939-51, v.p.; chmn. Bd. of Equalization, Utility Tax Com., Post-War Aviation Planning Com.; mem. jud. nominating commn. Supreme Ct. Nebr.; mem. Nebr. State Forestry Adv. Commn. Del.-at-Large Rep. Nat. Conv., 1944, 56, 60. Rep. candidate for Gov. Nebr., 1946; del. at-large, chmn. Nebr. Del. to Rep. Nat. Conv., 1948, 1952. Bd. dirs. Lincoln Found., St. Elizabeth Hosp. Recipient Masters Certificate of Honor and Merit, U. Neb., 1965, Nebr. Builder award, 1971. Mem. Nat. Assn. Ins. Agts., Nebr. Alumni Assn., C. of C., Newcomen Soc. N. Am. Presbyn. Clubs: Lincoln Country, University, Nebraska. Home: 3519 Allendale Dr Lincoln NE 68516 Office: Nishna Valley State Bank Riverton IA 51650

WEAVER, BILL THOMAS, furniture co. exec.; b. Nashville, Dec. 6, 1925; s. Frank L. and Mamie Sue (Black) W.; B.S., Manchester Coll., 1952; M.A., Ball State U., 1964; LL.B., Blackstone Sch. Law, 1971, J.D., 1975; m. Kathryn Eloise Smith, Dec. 7, 1946; children—Kim William, Kevin Todd (dec.), Jan Kathryn, Noel Thomas, Valerie Jill. With Gen. Tire & Rubber Co., Wabash, Ind. and Akron, Ohio, 1944-60, govt. sales-tech. rep., 1959-60; with Firestone Indsl. Products Co., various locations, 1960-67, West coast sales mgr., San Leandro, Calif., 1966-67; with Graham Mfg. Inc., Auburn, Ky., 1967-78, pres., 1977-78, agt., 1967—; owner, mgr. Weaver Enterprises, Bowling Green, Ky., 1952—; asst. prof., head dept. furniture prodn. mgmt. Vincennes U., 1978-80; v.p. Tri-State Bedding Co., Inc., Bowling Green, 1979-80; agt. G/L Industries, 1978—. Mem. Warren County (Ky.) Election Commn., 1972-76; scoutmaster, explorer adv. Boy Scouts Am.; chmn. Republican City Com. Wabash (Ind.), 1958-59; mem. exec. com., Warren County Rep. Com., 1977—; bd. dirs. S. Union Shaker Assn., Inc. (Ky.), v.p., 1975; bd. dirs. Shakertown Revisited, Inc. Japanese Soc. N.Y. fellow, 1959. Mem. Soc. Auto Engrs., Nat. Assn. Furniture Mfrs., Travelers Protective Assn., Kappa Delta Rho. Episcopalian (warden, vestryman). Clubs: Kiwanis, Auburn Rotary (pres. 1973-74). Home: 619 Ironwood Dr Bowling Green KY 42101

WEAVER, GEORGE SPERRY, JR., securities dealer; b. Wheeling, W.Va., May 29, 1934; s. George Sperry and Eleanor DuBois (Holloway) W.; student Yale U., 1952-53; diploma Stockbridge Sch., U. Mass., 1953-55; m. Shirley Ann McElhinney, Sept. 10, 1955; children—George III, John, David, Mary. Mgr., Virginia Hurst Farm, Triadelphia, W.Va., 1955-64; registered rep., 2d v.p. Bache Halsey-Stuart Co., Wheeling, 1964- 73; pres. Hazlett, Burt & Watson, Inc., Wheeling, 1973—. Pres., Oglebay Inst., 1975-78, Wheeling Soc. for Crippled Children, 1979-80; v.p. Ohio Valley Med. Center, Inc., 1980; chmn. Ohio County Republican Exec. Com., 1970-76; alt. del. Rep. Nat. Conv., 1968, 1976. Mem. Nat. Assn. Security Dealers. Episcopalian. Club: Ft. Henry. Home: RD 1 Virginia Hurst Wheeling WV 26003 Office: 1 Central Union Bldg Wheeling WV 26003

WEAVER, JOHN RANDALL, mfg. co. exec.; b. Glendale, Calif., Aug. 16, 1945; s. John Hibbard and Lois Gimmel (Reed) W.; student Los Angeles Valley Coll., 1970; B.S., U. So. Calif., 1972; m. Linda Louise Shirley, June 17, 1972. Staff acct. Arthur Young & Co., Los Angeles, 1972-1974; sr. v.p. fin. Anadex, Inc., Chatsworth, Calif., 1974—, also dir. Served with USN, 1967-68. C.P.A., Calif. Mem. Am. Inst. C.P.A.'s, Calif. Soc. C.P.A.'s. Office: 9825 DeSoto Ave Chatsworth CA 91311

WEAVER, JOHN WILLIAM HAPPEL, telephone co. ofcl.; b. Harrisburg, Pa., Aug. 14, 1931; s. Edwin F. and Christine G. (Happel) W.; B.A., Ursinus Coll., 1953; postgrad. Pa. State U., 1957-58, U. Mich., 1964, U. Kans., 1971-72; M.B.A., U. Mo., 1975; m. Alma M. Swartz, May 11, 1971; children—David, John. Traffic engr. United Telephone Co. Pa., Carlisle, 1957-68, traffic engring. mgr., 1968-72; staff dir. equipment engring. United Telecommunications, Kansas City, Mo., 1972-78, staff dir. traffic ops., 1978-79; comml./traffic staff dir. United Telephone Co., Overland Park, Kans., 1979—. Active fund drives YMCA, United Fund, savs. bonds. Served with U.S. Army, 1953-56. Mem. U.S. Ind. Telephone Assn. (chmn. operator services com.), Internat. Mgmt. Club (pres. 1970-71), Nat. Assn. Computer Users, Telephone Pioneers (pres. Heart of Am.). Mem. United Ch. of Christ. Contbr. articles to Telephony mag. Home: 12706 Pembroke Ln Leawood KS 66209 Office: 6666 W 110th St Overland Park KS 66211

WEAVER, KEVIN CARL, auditor; b. Bronx, N.Y., July 2, 1954; s. Wilbur H. and Mildred Weaver; B.S. in Acctg., William Paterson Coll., Wayne, N.J., 1976. With MetPath Inc., Teterboro, N.J., 1976—, staff internal auditor, 1977, sr. internal auditor, 1978—. Mem. Inst. Internal Auditors. Club: Adventure. Home: 748 Maywood Ave Maywood NJ 07607 Office: 1 Malcolm Ave Teterboro NJ 07608

WEAVER, WILLIAM CLAIR, JR. (MIKE), mgmt. cons. firm exec.; b. Indiana, Pa., Apr. 11, 1936; s. William Clair and Zaida (Bley) W.; B.S. in Aero. Engring., Rensselaer Poly. Inst., 1958; M.B.A., Washington U., St. Louis, 1971; postgrad. Rutgers U., Pa. State U.; m. Janet Marcelle Boyd, Sept. 18, 1963; 1 son, William Michael. Aerodynamics engr. N.Am. Aviation, Los Angeles, 1958-60; lead flight test ops. engr. Vertol div. Boeing Co., Phila., 1963-66; flight test project engr. Lockheed Electronics Co., Plainfield, N.J., 1966-69; advanced systems project engr. and sr. staff engr. Electronics and Space div. Emerson Electric Co., St. Louis, 1969-72; pres. Achievement Assos. Inc., St. Louis, 1972—. Mem. adv. com. Boy Scouts Am., Bridgeton, Mo., 1974—. Served with USAF, 1960-63. Registered profl. engr., Pa. Mem. Nat. Soc. Profl. Engrs., Am. Ordnance Assn., Am. Inst. Aeros. and Astronautics, Am. Helicopter Soc., Am. Soc. Bus. and Mgmt. Cons.'s, Assn. M.B.A. Execs., Air Force Assn., Assn. U.S. Army, St. Louis C. of C., Mensa, Acacia, Beta Gamma Sigma. Lutheran. Office: Suite M-3 The Montmartre 8600 Delmar St Louis MO 63124

WEBB, ARTHUR CLAYTON, ins. co. exec.; b. Madison, Ill., Mar. 14, 1922; s. William B. and Elsie (Fine) W.; student U. Wis., 1955-56, U. Chgo., 1968-69; m. Sarah E. Walton, Jan. 2, 1946; children—William Bruce, Ruth Ellen, Linda J., Emily Sue, Arthur C. Clk., Nickel Palte R.R., Madison, Ill., 1941-57; with Cuna Mut. Ins. Soc., Madison, Wis., 1957—, v.p., 1971—. Served with C.E., U.S. Army, 1943-45. Mem. Sales and Mktg. Execs. Madison. Club: Mason. Home: 2310 Tawhee Dr Madison WI 53711 Office: 5910 Mineral Point Rd Madison WI 53701

WEBB, ERNEST PACKARD, publisher; b. Junta, W.Va., Aug. 30, 1907; s. Robert Moses and Josephine (Harvey) W.; student advt. Internat. Corr. Schs., 1946-48, Alexander Hamilton Bus. Sch., 1948-52. Artist, Mountain State Engraving Co., 1929, Huntington Engraving Co. (W.Va.), 1930, Charleston Engraving Co. (W.Va.), 1931; owner, mgr. Profl. Art Studio, Roanoke, Va., 1931-40; v.p., treas. Roanoke Engraving Co., 1940-48; pres. Va. Engraving Co., Richmond, 1947—, W & H Corp., 1968—; v.p. Dixie Engraving Co., Roanoke, 1961—. Served with USAAF, 1942-45. Mem. Va., Richmond chambers commerce, Am. Photoplatemakers Assn., Master Printers Am., Printing Industries Virginias, Internat. Craftsman's Club. Republican. Baptist. Clubs: Willow Oaks Country, Westwood Tennis (Richmond). Home: 2000 Riverside Dr Richmond VA 23225 Office: 2003 Roane St Richmond VA 23222

WEBB, J. RICHARD, appliance co. exec.; b. Orlando, Fla., Feb. 28, 1940; s. L.C. and C.M. (Campbell) W.; B.S. in Indsl. Mgmt., Fla. State U., 1962; postgrad. in Mgmt. Devel., Harvard, 1971; m. Judith A. Paulsen, Dec. 21, 1963; children—Scott R., Craig A. With corporate purchasing program Westinghouse Electric Corp., Pitts., 1963-71, mgr. purchasing home comfort div., Edison, N.J., 1971-73, exec. asst., v.p. mktg. maj. appliance group, 1973-75; mgr. nat. distbn. White-Westinghouse Appliance Co., Pitts., 1975-76, mgr. bus. planning, 1976-77; pres. Luxaire, Inc. subs. Westinghouse, Elyria, Ohio, 1978-80; gen. mgr. Westinghouse Air Conditioning, Staunton, Va., 1980—; pvt. cons. distbn. and purchasing. Mem. Harvard PMD Assn., Nat. Assn. Purchasing Mgmt., Nat. Council Phys. Distbn. Mgmt. Office: PO Box 2510 Staunton VA 24401

WEBB, JAMES SIDNEY, JR., mfg. co. exec.; b. Salt Lake City, Oct. 14, 1919; s. James Sidney and Josephine Isabel (Hornung) W.; B.S. in Bus. Adminstrn., San Jose (Calif.) State U., 1941; m. Lucille Marian Gardner, June 28, 1941; children—Janet Webb Sippi, James Sidney. With Shell Chem. Co., 1945-48, U.S. Steel Corp., 1948-52, Varian Assos., 1952-54; with TRW Inc., 1954—, gen. mgr. electronics group, corp. v.p., 1963-66, exec. v.p., 1966-78, vice chmn. bd., 1978—, also dir.; dir. DeSoto, Inc., May Dept. Stores Co. Bd. dirs. Los Angeles Philharmonic Assn., TRW Found., Ind. Colls. of So. Calif., Estelle Doheny Eye Found.; trustee City of Hope; bd. govs. Hugh O'Brian Youth Found. Served to lt. USNR, 1942-45. Office: TRW Inc 23555 Euclid Ave Cleveland OH 44117*

WEBB, JOHN HOWARD, mfg. co. exec.; b. Belfast, Me., Oct. 1, 1926; s. John Howard and Myra Berenice (Harriman) W.; student Dartmouth Coll., 1944-46; B.S. in M.E., U. Maine, 1953; M.S., Northeastern U., 1964; m. Constance Dawn Frazier, June 20, 1953; children—Gary, Dawn, Jill, Lynn. Engr., Eastman Kodak Co., Rochester, N.Y., 1953-69; mgr. Polaroid Corp., Cambridge, Mass., 1969-73; v.p., treas. Indico, Inc., Needham, Mass., 1973-76; pres. Jodice Controls Corp., Waltham, Mass., 1976-78; asst. to pres. W.H. Nichols Co., Waltham, 1978-79; gen. mgr. Nichols/De Hoff, Cranston, R.I., 1979—. Served with USN, 1944-46. Registered profl. engr., Mass. Club: Masons. Contbr. articles to profl. jours. Office: 15 Worthington Rd Cranston RI 02920

WEBB, JOHN PALMER, music store exec.; b. Hopkinsville, Ky., May 24, 1944; s. Richard Parker and Iyone Delphine (Leas) W.; student U. Minn., 1965; m. Randi Pamela Royce, Apr. 2, 1970; children—Melissa, Amy, Jonathan. Mdse. mgr. Wickes Corp., Fridley, Minn., 1971-77; v.p. TSM Corp., Minnetonka, Minn., 1977-79; pres. Mr. Bojangles Music Sta., Columbia Heights, Minn., 1979—. Served with USN, 1964. Mem. Nat. Fedn. Ind. Businessmen, Minn. Progressive Trade Assn., U.S. C. of C. Office: 2303 37th Pl NE Columbia Heights MN 55421

WEBB, JOSEPH HERBERT, electronics co. exec.; b. Mt. Holly, N.J., Nov. 22, 1938; s. Ira Prickett and Anna Elizabeth (Worrell) W.; student Rider Coll., 1958-59; m. Betty Jo Enck, July 13, 1957; 1 dau., Linda Kelsey. Sales rep. Liberty Mutual Ins. Co., 1962-70; sales mgr. Town Hall Stationers, Mt. Holly, N.J., 1970-72; dist. sales mgr. Internat. Election Systems, Burlington, N.J., 1972-74, nat. sales mgr., 1974-75, v.p., gen. mgr., 1975-77; mfr.'s rep., 1977; fleet mgr. Garden State Motors, 1977-79; pres. Electronic Elections, Inc., Willingboro, N.J., 1979—. Mem. Mcpl. Planning Bd., Eastampton Twp., N.J., 1967-73, mcpl. treas., 1961-64. Served with USAF, 1961-63. Mem. Am. Mgmt. Assn. Clubs: Elks, Kiwanis. Home: 2 S Ave W Mt Holly NJ 08060 Office: PO Box 484 Willingboro NJ 08046

WEBB, RICHARD CLARK, investment banking exec.; b. New Gulf, Tex., June 12, 1933; s. Harry Charles and Ruth (Brown) W.; B.B.A., U. Tex., 1955; postgrad. Inst. Investment Banking, 1966-68; m. Sara Slaton, Oct. 29, 1955; children—Karen Elaine, Janice Ann, R. Clark. With trust investment dept. Republic Nat. Bank, Dallas, 1955-56; registered rep. Underwood Neuhaus & Co., 1959-60; mgr. Houston office Goodbody & Co., 1960-71; sr. registered option prin. Rotan Mosle Co., Houston, 1971—. Pres., Chinquapin Sch., St. James House of Baytown; trustee St. Lukes Hosp. Served to lt. (j.g.) USN, 1956-59. Mem. Houston Option Soc. (charter, dir., pres.), Nat. Option Soc. (dir.), Houston Stock and Bond Club, Phi Delta Theta. Republican. Episcopalian. Home: 10615 Twelve Oaks Houston TX 77024 Office: 1500 South Tower Pennzoil Pl Houston TX 77002

WEBB, ROBERT S., constrn. co. exec.; b. Murray, Utah, Oct. 26, 1930; s. Robert Traylen and Mildred Elizabeth (Simpson) W.; B.S. in Civil Engring., U. Utah, 1955; m. Colleen Foy, June 10, 1955; children—Cindy, Gordon Robert. Office mgr. Chgo. Bridge & Iron Co., Salt Lake City, 1956-58, contracting sales engr., San Francisco, 1958-67, nuclear product mgr., Oak Brook, Ill., 1967-72, dist. sales mgr., Phila., 1972-74, exec. v.p., Tokyo, 1974-78, area sales v.p., San Francisco, 1978—. Mem. planning commn. City of Belmont, Calif., 1966-68. Served with U.S. Army, 1951-53. Mem. ASCE (chmn. constrn. com. on nuclear constrn. 1971-72), Am. Petroleum Inst., Pacific Coast Gas Assn., Pacific Coast Elec. Assn. Mormon. Clubs: World Trade, Moraga Country. Home: 187 Cypress Point Way Moraga CA 94556 Office: 160 Sansome St San Francisco CA 94104

WEBB, TED WARNER, welding co. exec.; b. Richmond, Va., June 2, 1935; s. Frank N. and Stella T. Webb; student Bryant Trade Sch., Catonsville Community Coll.; m. Margaret E. Rupert, Jan. 9, 1959; children—Jann Marie, Kim Ann. Successively gen. mgr. Sheet Metal Constrn. Co., Inc., Balt., Anti-Air Pollution Systems, Inc., Balt., mgr. engring. dept. Kelco Corp., Balt., owner, pres. Arc Welding Service

Co., Balt., Fabricators & Welding Specialists, Inc., Balt., 1978—; tchr. drafting, sheet metal layout and shop. Served with C.E., U.S. Army, 1957-59. Mem. Air Pollution Control Assn., Sue Island Power Squadron (asst. sec. 1969-70, lt. comdr. 1970-73, comdr. 1973-74). Democrat. Methodist. Clubs: Balt. Yacht, Boumi Temple Yacht, Masons, Boumi Temple, York Rite, Towson Shrine, Steel of Balt., Chesapeake Cruiser Assn., Green Spring Inn. Home: 12501 Sagamore Forest Ln Reisterstown MD 21136 Office: 2713 North Point Blvd Baltimore MD 21222

WEBBER, MICHAEL DAVID, mgmt. cons.; b. Enid, Okla., May 27, 1940; s. Mike E. and Lorine L. (Loomis) W.; B.B.A., U. Okla., 1962; M.B.A. (fellow), U. Pa., 1964; m. Janet Dodson, June 30, 1962; children—Michael David, Meredith. Vice pres. A.T. Kearney, Inc., Chgo., 1967-77; pres., dir. Kearney: Mgmt. Cons.'s, Ltd., Toronto, Ont., Can., 1975-77; v.p. Booz-Allen & Hamilton, Inc., N.Y.C., 1977—. Served to 1st lt., USAF, 1964-67. Cert. mgmt. cons. Inst. Mgmt. Consultants U.S. and Ont. Mem. Inst. Mgmt. Scis., Ops. Research Soc. Am., Am. Mktg. Assn., Am. Prodn. and Inventory Control Soc., Nat. Council Phys. Distbn. Mgmt. Clubs: Greenwich Country; Milbrook Country; Internat. (Chgo.); Union League (N.Y.C.). Contbr. articles to profl. jours. Home: 18 Woodside Dr Greenwich CT 06830 Office: 245 Park Ave New York NY 10017

WEBER, DAVID MILLER, wholesale grocery exec.; b. Marshfield, Wis., July 27, 1948; s. Donald Valentine and Bette Ruth W.; student U. Wis., Madison, 1966-67, Highlands U., 1968, U. N.Mex., 1972-74; m. Wendy Jane Jorgenson, Nov. 12, 1977; children—Rachel Maria, Jesse Julian. Retail supr. Hub City Foods, Inc., Marshfield, 1974-75, buyer, 1975-76, gen. mgr., 1976-78, pres., 1979—, also dir.; dir. Freedom Foods, Marshfield R & W. Mem. Nat.-Am. Wholesale Grocers Assn., Wis. Assn. Food Dealers, Food Mktg. Inst., Greater Marshfield, Inc. Office: Hub City Foods Inc 1700 Laemle Ave Marshfield WI 54449

WEBER, DONALD BELDEN, advt. exec.; b. Jersey City, Nov. 6, 1932; s. John W. and Rose Ann (Sarosi) W.; B.A., Rollins Coll., 1954; M.B.A., Northwestern U., 1959; m. Ann Elizabeth McDermaid, Nov. 26, 1955; children—Martha Elizabeth, Margaret Ann. With Leo Burnett Co., Inc., Chgo., 1958-63, account exec., 1961-63; with Foote, Cone & Belding Inc., Chgo., 1963-75, account supr., 1965-69, v.p., 1969-75, mgmt. supr., 1969, sr. v.p., dir., 1972-75; pres., dir. Blau/Bishop & Assos., Chgo., 1975-79; v.p. Russel Reynolds Assos., Chgo., 1979—; lectr. mktg. Northwestern U., Evanston, 1959—. Served to lt. USNR, 1954-57. Mem. Am. Mktg. Assn., Sigma Nu. Republican. Episcopalian. Clubs: Econ., Plaza, Execs., Northwestern, Rollins Alumni (v.p. 1959—) (Chgo.); Exmoor Country, Plaza. Home: 2540 Riverwoods Rd Lincolnshire IL 60015 Office: 230 W Monroe St Chicago IL 60606

WEBER, GEORGE RICHARD, accountant; b. The Dalles, Oreg., Feb. 7, 1929; s. Richard Merle and Maud (Winchell) W.; B.S., Oreg. State U., 1950; M.B.A., U. Oreg., 1962; m. Nadine Hanson, Oct. 12, 1957; children—Elizabeth Ann, Karen Louise, Linda Marie. Sr. trainee U.S. Nat. Bank of Portland (Oreg.), 1950-51; jr. accountant Ben Musa, C.P.A., The Dalles, 1954; tax and audit asst. Price Waterhouse, Portland, 1955-59; sr. accountant Burton M. Smith, C.P.A., Portland, 1959-62; pvt. C.P.A. practice, Portland, 1962—; lectr. accounting Portland State Coll. Sec.-treas. Mt. Hood Kiwanis Camp, Inc., 1965. Served with AUS, 1951-53. Decorated Bronze Star; C.P.A., Oreg. Mem. Am. Inst. C.P.A.'s, Beta Alpha Psi, Pi Kappa Alpha. Republican. Episcopalian. Clubs: Kiwanis, Portland Track, City (Portland); Multnomah Athletic. Contbr. to profl. publs. and poetry jours. Home: 2603 NE 32d Ave Portland OR 97212 Office: 5520 SW Macadam Portland OR 97201

WEBER, JOHN BENEDICT, banker; b. Buffalo, Apr. 11, 1926; s. John August and Loretta (Kolkmeyer) W.; B.B.A., Canisius Coll., 1952, M.B.A. in Accounting, 1976; m. Frances J. Steck, June 4, 1949; children—John Benedict, William T., Paul J., Christopher R., Richard A., Mary Frances, Edward C. Asst. title officer Abstract & Title Ins. Corp., 1946-56; asst. sec., asst. controller Transcontinent Television Corp., 1956-65; treas., controller, asst. sec. Crescent Niagara Corp., 1960-68; treas., asst. sec. Northeastern Pa. Broadcasting, Inc., 1958-68; treas., asst. sec., dir. Bridgeport Hardware Mfg. Corp., 1964-68; exec. v.p., treas., dir. Frontier Savs. & Loan Assn., 1969-73, pres., 1973-74; chmn. adv. bd. Erie Savs. Bank, 1974—; sec., dir. Taylor Travel Service Inc., 1969—; dir. McCoy Med. Enterprises Inc., 1971—; bus. cons., 1968—; mem. faculty Canisius Coll., 1970—, SUNY, Fredonia, 1971—; mem. N.Y. State Bd. Public Accountancy, 1974—. Treas., Citizens Com. for Observance of Lord's Day, 1961—. Served with USAAF, 1944-45. Mem. Christian Family Movement (nat. treas. 1961-68), Financial Mgmt. Assn., Financial Exec. Inst. (nat. dir. 1969-70, nat. adv. council 1970-73), Nat. Assn. Accountants, Am. Accounting Assn., Nat. Assn. State Bds. Accountancy, Air Force Assn. Roman Catholic. Club: Lancaster Country (treas. 1973-78). Home: 149 Wickham Dr Williamsville NY 14221 Office: 30 S Cayuga Rd Williamsville NY 14221

WEBER, LAWRENCE KIRKWOOD, JR., real estate broker; b. San Francisco, May 20, 1930; s. Lawrence Kirkwood and Grace (Laile) W.; B.A., U. Calif., Berkeley, 1951; m. Owene Phillips Hall, Nov. 26, 1954; children—Owene, Lawrence Kirkwood III, Cathleen, Nicholas, Louise. Investment exec. Wells Fargo Bank, 1951; commd. ensign U.S. Navy, 1953, advanced through grades to comdr., 1967, ret., 1972; real estate broker, property mgr., Orange Park, Fla., 1973-76; v.p. Walter Dickinson, Inc., Jacksonville, Fla., 1976-78; pres., dir. United Property Investors, Inc., Jacksonville, 1978—; dir., pres. Security Research Cons., Inc., Jacksonville. Mem. Nat. Assn. Corporate Real Estate Execs. Episcopalian. Office: United Property Investors Suite 932 200 W Forsyth St Jacksonville FL 32202

WEBER, MATTHEW, food processing corp. exec.; b. N.Y.C., Mar. 11, 1940; s. Benjamin and Victoria (Bobroff) W.; B.B.A., U. City N.Y., 1961; Staff acct. Eisner & Lubin C.P.A.'s, N.Y.C., 1961-65; v.p. Continental Seafoods, Inc. div. Ward Foods, Inc., N.Y.C., 1965-71; v.p. Marine Internat. Inc., Newark, 1971-73; v.p. internat. dept. Gortons div. Gen. Mills Corp., v.p., gen. mgr. Trans World Seafood Inc. subs., N.Y.C., 1973—. Mem. N.Y. State Soc. C.P.A.'s, Inst. Dirs. London. Jewish. Home: 1 Gracie Terr New York NY 10028 Office: Trans World Seafood Inc 600 3d Ave New York NY 10016

WEBER, MILAN GEORGE, mgmt. cons., business broker; b. Milw., Oct. 15, 1908; s. Adam George and Frances (Lehrbaumer) W.; B.S., U.S. Mil. Acad., 1931; grad. various mil. schs.; grad. Nat. War Coll., 1952; m. Mary Agness Keller, Sept. 2, 1931; 1 son, Milan George. Commd. 2d lt. U.S. Army, 1931, advanced through grades to col., 1944; service in Philippines, ETO, Argentina and Japan; global strategic planner J.C.S., 1952-54; dep. comdr. 2d region U.S. Air Def. Command, Ft. Meade, Md., 1958-60, ret., 1960; mgr. electronic countermeasures Loral Electronics Corp., N.Y.C., 1960-62; product mgr. electronic countermeasures Hallicrafters Corp. (now Northrop Corp.), Chgo., 1962-64; partner Weber Assos., acquisitions and mergers, Deerfield, Ill., 1964-69; pres., dir. Milan G. Weber Assos., Inc., advisors to large corps. on acquisitions, bus. brokers and mgmt. cons., Deerfield, 1969—. Chmn., Citizens Com. Honesty in Govt., 1969—, Gt. Lakes Ecology Assn., 1974—; mem. Ill. Drivers Safety Adv. Com., 1975—; bd. dirs. Deerfield Library, 1976-78; mem. Deerfield Caucus, 1978—, vice-chmn., 1979—. Decorated Bronze Star, Legion of Merit, Army Commendation medal with oak leaf cluster. Mem. Assn. Old Crows, Assn. Grads. U.S. Mil. Acad. Clubs: Army Navy (Washington); Army-Navy Country (Arlington, Va.); West Point Soc. (Chgo.). Author articles on mgmt. and nat. strategy; weekly column Gleanings. Home: 611 Colwyn Terr Deerfield IL 60015 Office: Box 81 Deerfield IL 60015

WEBER, ROBIN MICHAEL, bus. equipment mfg. co. exec.; b. Pitts., Mar. 3, 1947; s. Henry Paul and Rosine Marie (Carney) W.; B.S., Ithaca Col., 1969; M.B.A., U. Conn., 1972; m. Mary-Evan Keenan, June 6, 1970; children—Mark Christopher, Carrie Gwynn. Sales rep. Xerox Corp., N.Y.C., 1972-73, facsimile products specialist, 1974, sales tng. specialist, Leesburg, Va., 1975-76, sr. sales tng. specialist, 1976-77, office systems sales mgr., 1977-79, forward products sales tng. mgr., Dallas, 1980—. Served with USAR, 1969-76. Home: 6911 Windy Ridge Dallas TX 75247 Office: Xerox Corp 1341 W Mockingbird Ln Dallas TX 75248

WEBER, RONALD RICHARD, mgmt. cons.; b. N.Y.C., May 4, 1937; s. Richard Dillon and Gertrude W.; B.A., Queens Coll., 1960; postgrad. N.Y. U., 1962; m. Patricia Devlin, Dec. 3, 1977; children—Dawn, Glenn, Allison, Richard. Asst. v.p. Crum & Forster, 1960-71; v.p. adminstrn. Frank B. Hall & Co., N.Y.C., 1971-74; v.p. Parallel Planning Corp., N.Y.C., 1974-77; pres. Weber Mgmt. Cons., Inc., Great Neck, N.Y., 1977—. Home: 8 Radcliff Dr Huntington NY 11743 Office: 287 Northern Blvd Rm 204 Great Neck NY 11021

WEBER, VALENTINE ANDREW, lawyer; b. Madison, Wis., Feb. 16, 1933; s. Valentine Andrew and Margaret Ellen (Murphy) W.; B.S., Yale, 1955; LL.B., Harvard, 1958; m. Deonne Wilson Koch, Sept. 27, 1958; children—Charles, Scott, Christopher. Admitted to Ill. bar, 1958, practiced in Chgo., 1958-68; asso. firm Keck, Mahin & Cate, Chgo., 1958-65, partner, 1965-68; pres. James Capel (U.S.), Chgo., 1969-74; partner firm Reuben & Proctor, Chgo., 1978—. Pres. Kenilworth (Ill.) Bd. Edn., 1970-76. Mem. Sigma Xi, Phi Gamma Delta, Tau Beta Pi. Republican. Roman Catholic. Club: Mid-Day (Chgo.). Home: 221 Warwick Rd Kenilworth IL 60043 Office: 19 S LaSalle St Chicago IL 60603

WEBSTER, BRUCE JAMES, aviation safety cons.; b. Indpls., Sept. 16, 1950; s. James R. and Patricia (Morrison) W.; student U. Southwestern La., 1974-76, U. So. Calif., 1976. Pilot, spl. asst. Petroleum Helicopters, Inc., Lafayette La., 1971-76; safety mgr. Helicopter Assn. Am., Washington, 1976-80; v.p., partner Internat. Air Safety Ltd., Alexandria, Va., 1980—; aircraft accident investigation and prevention cons.; lectr. in field. Mem. Pres.'s Com. for 75th Anniversary of Powered Flight, 1977-78; mem. aviation sub com. Nat. Safety Council, 1979. Served with U.S. Army, 1968-71. Decorated D.F.C., Air Medal. Named U.S. Jaycees Outstanding Young Man, 1980. Mem. Internat. Soc. Air Safety Investigators, Profl. Aviation Maint. Assn., Exptl. Aircraft Assn., Fedn. Aeronautique Internat., Nat. Assn. for Search and Rescue, Hon. Order Ky. Cols. Republican. Episcopalian. Club: Helicopter. Columnist: Rotor and Wing mag., 1980—; contbr. articles to profl. jours. Home: 9132 Santayana Dr Fairfax VA 22030 Office: 4660 Kenmore Ave Alexandria VA 22304

WEBSTER, CHARLES LINSLEY, oil co. exec.; b. Cleve., Mar. 12, 1930; s. Paul Towslee and Mary (Carran) W.; B.A., Babson Coll., Boston, 1953; m. Mary Joyce Dant, Sept. 15, 1956; children—Mary Virginia, Charles Linsley, Edwin Dant. Asst. to dir. bd. research Babson Inst., 1953-54; v.p., gen. mgr. Central Petroleum Co., Cleve., 1956—. Served with AUS, 1954-56. Mem. Am. Soc. Lubrication Engrs., Cleve. Engring. Soc., Ind. Oil Compounders. Republican. Presbyterian. Clubs: Shriners, Cleve. Petroleum (dir.), Towslee Hill Hunt. Home: 1022 S Belvoir St South Euclid OH 44121 Office: 548 Standard Bldg Cleveland OH 44113

WEBSTER, DAVID ARTHUR, life ins. co. exec.; b. Downs, Ill., July 20, 1937; s. Harold Sanford and Carmen Mildred (Moore) W.; B.S., U. Ill., 1960; m. Anna Elizabeth Prosch, June 10, 1956; children—Theodore David, Elizabeth Anna, Arthur Lee, William Harold. Actuarial asst. Mass. Mut. Life Ins. Co., Springfield, 1960-64; cons. actuary George Stennes & Assos., Mpls., 1964-68; v.p., actuary Piedmont Life Ins. Co., Atlanta, 1968-72, Pacific Fidelity Life Ins. Co., Los Angeles, 1972-74; v.p., chief actuary U.S. Life Corp., N.Y.C., 1974-76, exec. v.p., 1976-78; dir., 1976-78; exec. v.p., dir. Beneficial Standard Life, Los Angeles, 1978—; v.p., treas., dir. Beneficial Assurance Co.; pres., dir. Am. Exec. Life, BPS Agy., Inc., Beneficial Pension Services; asst. sec., dir. Beneficial Computer Services; treas. Tel-Assurance. Mem. ins. council City of Hope. Fellow Soc. Actuaries; mem. Am. Acad. Actuaries, Los Angeles Actuaries Club, Actuarial Club Pacific States. Club: Woodland Hills Country. Home: 5131 Encino Ave Encino CA 91316 Office: 3700 Wilshire Blvd Los Angeles CA 90010

WEBSTER, DONALD ALBERT, mfg. exec.; b. Rochester, N.Y., Dec. 9, 1930; s. Albert C. and Madeline M. (Vanden Bush) W.; B.A., Hamilton Coll., 1953; M.A., Johns Hopkins U., 1955; m. Helen Long, Mar. 29, 1959. Minority staff dir. Joint Econ. Com., U.S. Congress, 1962-68; asst. to sec. U.S. Treasury, 1969-70, dep. asst. sec., 1970-71; pvt. practice cons., Washington, 1972-74; mem. staff White House, 1974-75; v.p. govt. relations AMF, Inc., Washington, 1975—. Served with USN, 1956-60. Mem. Nat. Economists Club, Bus.-Govt. Relations Council, Phi Beta Kappa. Republican. Clubs: Internat., Capitol Hill (Washington). Home: 2810 29th St NW Washington DC 20008 Office: 1701 K St NW Washington DC 20006

WEBSTER, GEORGE C., mgmt. cons.; b. Washington, Mar. 21, 1921; s. John Garnett and Jessie Mary (Conner) W.; B.S.M.E., Md. U., 1943; J.D., Georgetown U., 1948, LL.M., 1955; M.B.A., Harvard U., 1951; 1 dau., Letitia. Pres., J.G. Webster & Sons, Inc., Washington, 1945-55, Wilson Supply Co., Inc., Washington, 1952-60, George C. Webster and Assos., Washington, 1955—, Evelyn Wood Reading Dynamics, 1962-68; dir. Credit Card Service Bur. Am., Inc., 1970-78; lectr. in field. Served with USN, 1943-45. Mem. Am. Bar Assn. Episcopalian. Clubs: Harvard U., Univ., Columbia Country. Author: The Strategy of Bus. Perpetuation, 1974; ESOP'S, 1975; High Performance Wholesaling, 1976; Controlling Payroll Costs in Distribution, 1976; Sales Productivity: Crisis in Distribution, 1977; Organizing People for Profit, 1978; Telephone Selling, 1979. Home: PO Box 1048 Riverview House Beaufort SC 29902 Office: 207 Hancock St Beaufort SC 29902

WEBSTER, GEORGE DRURY, lawyer; b. Jacksonville, Fla., Feb. 8, 1921; s. George D. and Mary Gaines (Walker) W.; B.A., Maryville Coll., 1941; LL.B., Harvard, 1948; children—Aen Walker, George Drury III, Hugh Kilpatrick. Admitted to Ga. bar, 1950, D.C. bar, 1952; atty. tax div. Dept. Justice, Washington, 1949-51; partner firm Webster & Chamberlain; vice chmn. bd. First Western Financial Corp., Las Vegas. Lectr. numerous tax insts. Spl. ambassador to Liberia, 1972. Trustee U.S. Naval Acad. Found., Maryville Coll. Served from ensign to lt., USNR, 1942-46. Mem. Am. Law Inst., Am. Bar Assn. Presbyn. Clubs: Chevy Chase (Md.); Harvard (N.Y.C., Washington); Metropolitan (Washington); Racquet and Tennis (N.Y.C.). Author: Law of Associations, 1981. Author articles on fed. taxation. Home: 5305 Cardinal Ct Washington DC 20016 also Webster Angus Farms Rogersville TN 37857 Office: 1747 Pennsylvania Ave NW Washington DC 20006

WEBSTER, JOHN KIMBALL, investment exec.; b. N.Y.C., June 7, 1934; s. Reginald Nathaniel and Lillian (McDonald) W.; B.A., Yale U., 1956; postgrad. Wharton Sch. Finance and Commerce, 1957-58; m. Katherine Taylor Mulligan, Jan. 28, 1967; children—John McDonald, Katherine Kimball. With Dominick & Dominick, N.Y.C., 1961-73, v.p., 1968-73; v.p., sec. Dominick Fund, Inc., Barclay Growth Fund, N.Y.C., 1971-73; v.p. Dominick Mgmt. Corp., N.Y.C., 1971-73, Monumental Capital Mgmt., Inc., Balt., 1974-75, Bernstein-Macaulay, Inc., N.Y.C., 1975-78; v.p., dir. Penmark Investments, Inc., Chgo., 1978-79, sr. v.p., 1979-80, exec. v.p., 1980—; mem. no-load com. Investment Co. Inst., Washington, 1971-73; mem. exec. com. No Load Mut. Fund Assn., N.Y.C., 1971-73, treas., 1972-73. Served to capt. USAF, 1958-61. Episcopalian. Clubs: Mid-Day (Chgo.); Church, Yale (N.Y.C.); Rumson (N.J.) Country; Seabright (N.J.) Lawn Tennis. Office: Penmark Investments Inc 222 N Dearborn St Chicago IL 60601

WEBSTER, WALTER C., JR., graphic arts cons. co. exec.; b. Phila., Mar. 6, 1919; s. Walter C. and Louise Florence Webster; student U. Pa., 1939-40, Mulvey Inst. Advt., 1939; spl. edn. M.I.T., 1958, Dartnell Inst., Chgo., 1962; m. Virginia W. Wagnor, May 12, 1945; 1 son, Walter C. III. Asst. advt. mgr. Supplee-Biddle, Phila., 1939-40; advt. copywriter Philco Corp., Phila., 1940-41; salesman Dennison Mfg. Co., Phila., 1946-49, Richmond, Va., 1949-56, merchandising mgr. Ind. div., 1956-62, dist. sales mgr., Chgo., 1962-69, product mgr. consumer div., 1969-71; regional sales mgr. Flexcon Co., Inc., 1971—; pres. Walter C. Webster Assos., Inc., Chadds Ford, Pa., 1977—. Active, Benjamin Franklin council Boy Scouts Am., Phila., 1947-48, asst. scoutmaster, Sudbury, Mass., 1957; mgr. Sudbury Little League, 1958-61; fire commr. City of North Barrington (Ill.), 1965-66. Served with USAAF, 1941-46; PTO. Methodist. Patentee self-locking device blister packages. Home: RD 1 Hillendale Rd Chadds Ford PA 19317 Office: PO Box 156 Chadds Ford PA 19317

WEBSTER, WILLIAM OGRAM, JR., stockbroker; b. Columbus, Ohio, July 5, 1943; s. William Ogram and Elizabeth (Dorman) W.; B.A., Dartmouth Coll., 1965; M.B.A., N.Y. U., 1971; m. Victoria Drewes, Oct. 8, 1967; children—William O., Scott Tyler. Sales trainee, salesman Riegel Paper, 1967-72; with Blyth Eastman Dillon, Wilton, Conn., 1972-79, asst. v.p., 1976-79; v.p., asst. mgr. Paine Webber, Bridgeport, Conn., 1979—. Mem. Internat. Assn. Fin. Planners, Fairfield County Stockbrokers Assn., Inst. Cert. Fin. Planners. Republican. Club: Dartmouth (pres.) (New Canaan-Wilton, Conn.). Home: 28 Juniper Pl Wilton CT 06897 Office: 1261 Post Rd Fairfield CT 06430

WECHSLER, HARRY C., chem. co. exec.; b. Jassy, Roumania, Dec. 24, 1919; came to U.S., 1946, naturalized, 1950; s. Carol and Betty Wechsler; B.S., Victoria U. (Eng.), 1939; M.Sc., Hebrew U., Jerusalem, 1945; Ph.D., Bklyn. Poly. Inst., 1948; m. Ruth Reiser, Oct. 29, 1949; children—Mia, Dana, Sharon. Project leader DeBell & Richardson, Hazardville, Conn., 1951-53; research dir. Am. Monomer Co., Leominster, Mass., 1953-55; gen. mgr. polyvinyl chloride dept. Borden Chem. Co., Leominster, 1956-59, v.p., N.Y.C., 1959-64, group v.p., 1964-66, exec. v.p., 1966-68, pres., 1968-71; exec. v.p., chief operating officer Beatrice Chem. div. Beatrice Foods, Wilmington, Mass., 1972-77, pres. div., 1977—. Trustee Poly. Inst. N.Y., named Disting. Alumnus, 1969. Mem. Am. Mgmt. Assn., (internat. council), Am. Chem. Soc., Soc. Plastics Engrs. Club: Univ. Contbr. articles to profl. publs.; patentee in field. Office: 730 Main St Wilmington MA 01887

WECKERLE, JOSEPH FREDERICK, IV, ins. co. exec.; b. Hempstead, N.Y., Mar. 29, 1936; s. Joseph Frederick and Catherine Erna (Anderson) W.; student U. Oreg., 1958, Coll. of Idaho, 1958-59; m. Barbara Joyce Kalemba, Apr. 28, 1962; children—Laura Ann, Joseph Frederick V. From trainee to asst. v.p. Continental Casualty Co., Chgo., 1960-74; exec. v.p. Loveless and Co., Atlanta, 1974-75; chmn. pres. H & W Ins. Services, mem. The Continental Group, Los Angeles, 1975—. Served with USN, 1954-58. Mem. Nat. Assn. Profl. Surplus Lines Offices, Calif. Surplus Lines Assn. (exec. com.). Republican. Office: 16255 Ventura Blvd Suite 406 Encino CA 91436

WECKESSER, PAUL MAURICE, civil and traffic engr.; b. Rochester, N.Y., June 20, 1933; s. Joseph Louis and Marie Margaret W.; B.S.C.E., U. Detroit, 1956; M.S.C.E., Purdue U., 1958; m. Mildred Jacqueline Schreiber, Sept. 13, 1958; children—Gerard, Wendy M., Melissa A., Paul M. Sr. traffic engr. City of Rochester, N.J., 1958-59; traffic engr. N.J. Turnpike Authority, New Brunswick, 1959—, dir. ops., 1976—; prin. Paul M. Weckesser, P.E., Traffic Engring. Cons., 1978—. Registered profl. engr., N.J., Calif. Fellow Inst. Transp. Engrs.; mem. ASCE, Nat. Soc. Profl. Engrs., Am. Assn. Hwy. and Transp. Ofcls., Internat. Bridge Tunnel and Turnpike Assn. Roman Catholic. Home: 3 Hillwood Rd East Brunswick NJ 08816 Office: PO Box 1121 New Brunswick NJ 08903

WEDDLE, L. STEVE, banker; b. Jasper, Ala., July 12, 1948; s. I. Hershel and Margaret D. (Daniel) W.; B.A., U. Ala., 1970; diploma Vanderbilt U. Banking Sch., 1972; J.D., Nashville Law Sch., 1978; m. Patricia Rich, Aug. 18, 1979. Mgmt. trainee Am. Nat. Bank, Chattanooga, 1970, banking officer, 1971-73; asst. v.p. Commerce Union Bank, Chattanooga, 1974, v.p., 1975, sr. v.p., 1976, exec. v.p., dir., 1977-81, pres., chief operating officer, dir., 1981—, also mem. exec. and trust coms.; dir. Chattanooga World Trade Council, Chattanooga Speech and Hearing Center, C. U. Leasing Corp. Treas. Cherokee Regional chpt. Tenn. Easter Seal Soc.; bd. dirs. Chattanooga Jr. Achievement; co. chmn., mem. allocations com. United Fund Chattanooga; chmn. banking div. Heart Fund of Chattanooga; mem. Chattanooga Youth Commn. Mem. U. Ala. Alumni Assn., Phi Sigma Kappa Alumni Assn., Mcpl. Treas.'s Assn. U.S. and Can., Am. Inst. Banking, Nashville Law Sch. Alumni Assn. Methodist. Clubs: Chattanooga Golf and Country, Jaycees, Chattanooga Rotary, Walden (dir.). Author articles in field (2d pl. award Robert Morris Assos. Fin. Inst. 1972). Home: 720 Bacon Trail Estate 30 Chattanooga TN 37412 Office: Commerce Union Tower 633 Chestnut St Chattanooga TN 37450

WEDER, ERWIN HENRY, corp. exec.; b. Highland, Ill., Dec. 13, 1904; s. August and Julia (Brunner) W.; student pub. schs.; m. Florence Louise (Graham), July 19, 1938; children—Mary Kay, Dona Lee, Donald Erwin, Wanda May, Janet Marie. Office work Highland Dairy Farms, 1923-25; detective Fla. East Coast Hotel Co., 1927-29; auto salesman, broker L.E. Anderson Co., 1930-32; salesman Metal Goods Corp., 1933-41; product devel., sales mgr., pres., Highland Supply Corp., 1941—; pres., sales and products mgr. Highland Products, Inc., 1948—; pres., sales and products mgr. Highland Mfg. Co., 1944—; mng. partner, sales and products mgr. Highland Mfg. & Sales Co., 1952—; pres. Weder Farms, Inc., 1950—, Quality Motors, Inc., 1946—; sr. partner Seven W. Enterprises, 1958—; owner, operator Six Bar X ranch, Jordan, Mont. Mem. St. Louis Media Club. Republican. Clubs: DX-5, Mo. Athletic; Capitol Hill; Masons. Home:

1304 Washington St Highland IL 62249 Office: 6th and Zschokke Sts Highland IL 62249

WEED, BYRON ELLSWORTH, II, real estate broker, builder; b. Ann Arbor, Mich., June 18, 1938; s. Cecil Max and Hannah (Chappell) W.; B.S., Eastern Mich. U., 1961, M.A., 1963; children—Dalana S., Anissa E. Tchr. high sch. Dearborn Heights, Mich., 1961-63; partner Paige-Weed Realty, Ann Arbor, 1964-69; owner Weed Realty, Ann Arbor, 1969—; sales mgr. new home constrn. Guenther Bldg. Co., 1977-79, 80—; dir. sales Candid Realty, Inc., 1979—. Lectr., instr. U. Mich., Ann Arbor, 1968—. Served with USNR, 1954-63. Mem. C. of C., Ann Arbor Bd. Realtors (dir., sec. 1973-74), Real Estate Securities and Syndication (dir. 1973), Real Estate Alumni Mich., Phi Sigma Epsilon. Author: Papermaking: A New Process, 1963. Home: 2817 Laurel Hill Ann Arbor MI 48103 Office: 1300 S Main St Ann Arbor MI 48103

WEED, EDWARD REILLY, mfg. co. exec.; b. Chgo., Jan. 25, 1940; s. Cornelius Cahill and Adelaide E. (Reilly) W.; student Fordham U., 1959-61, Loyola U., 1961-62; m. Lawrie Irving Bowes, Feb. 2, 1969. Account exec. Leo Burnett Co., Chgo., 1961-71; pres. GDC Ad Inc., Gen. Devel. Corp., Miami, Fla., 1971-74, corp. asst. v.p., 1971-74; v.p., account supr. D'Arcy Mac Manus & Masius, Chgo., 1975; group v.p. mktg. Hart Schaffner & Marx, Chgo., 1975—; dir. First Nat. Bank So. Miami. Trustee, Latin Sch. Found., 1976—; bd. dirs. North Ave. Day Nursery, 1969-73; pres. Northwestern Mil. and Naval Acad., 1972-74. Served with Ill. N.G. Republican. Roman Catholic. Club: Cliff Dwellers. Office: 101 N Wacker Dr Chicago IL 60606

WEEDEN, ALAN NORMAN, former investment banker; b. Oakland, Calif., May 16, 1924; s. Frank and Mabel (Henrickson) W.; B.A., Stanford U., 1947; m. Barbara Elliott, Mar. 19, 1950; children—Donald Alan, Robert Elliott, Helen Leslie. With Weeden & Co. Inc., N.Y.C., 1949-79, v.p., 1958-66, pres., chief exec. officer, 1967-76, chmn. bd., 1978-79; v.p., dir. Moseley Hallgarten Estabrook & Weeden Holding Corp., N.Y.C., 1979-80; mem. Mcpl. Securities Rulemaking Bd. Trustee Stanford U., 1970-80, Edward John Noble Found., Served to lt. (j.g.) USNR, 1943-46. Mem. Explorers Club, Phi Beta Kappa. Clubs: Am. Yacht, Apawamis. Home: Upper Dogwood Ln Rye NY 10580

WEENIG, FRED (CHRISTIAN FREDERICK MORONI), civic worker; b. Salt Lake City, July 19, 1906; s. Christian Frederick Everdinas, Jr. and Elizabeth (Goudriaan) W.; student U. Utah, 1934; m. Raola Fern Seely, Apr. 3, 1935; children—Eileen, Ruth. Missionary, Church Jesus Christ of Latter Day Saints, Netherlands, 1929-32; with Ford Motor Co., Salt Lake City, 1935-42, Electrolux Vacuum Cleaners, 1945-53; rep. Curtis Circulation Co., 1953-71; ordnance worker Mormon Latter Day Saints Temple, Salt Lake City, 1971—. Fund raiser various schs., Utah, Nev., Ariz., Colo., Calif., 1953-71; usher Salt Lake Tabernacle, 1948—, host Tabernacle Square visitors center, 1978—; active Boy Scouts Am., Salt Lake City, 1919-60. Served with USAAF, 1942-45. Recipient Paul Harris award, 1978. Republican. Club: Rotary (sec. 1967-68, v.p. 1968-69, pres. 1969-70, now exec. sec.). Address: 1324 Logan Ave Salt Lake City UT 84105

WEEREN, MILO PERSHING, savs. and loan assn. exec.; b. Burton, Tex., Sept. 16, 1918; s. William Henry and Jennie Ellis (Laas) W.; student Blinn Coll., Brenham, Tex., 1936-37; m. Agnes Winifred Beaumier, Apr. 19, 1952; children—Gayle Nichols, Lana Kendall Weeren Plunkett. Material coordinator Brown Shipbuilding Co., Greens Bayou, Tex., 1941-44; work schedule coordinator Hughes Tool Co., Houston, 1944-47; mgr.-coordinator sales and pub. relations, materials insp. So. Inspection Service, Houston, 1947-56, 57-59; multi-state expediter, coordinator Austin Co., Houston, 1956-57; account exec. Top Value Enterprises, Houston, 1959-64; exec. v.p. Heights Savs. Assn., Houston, 1964—, also dir., officer; dir., officer Heights Developers, Inc., 1971—, Old Bridge Lake Community Service Corp., 1972—. Mem. speaker's adv. com. Tex. Ho. of Reps., 1970, Champions Community Improvement Action, 1968-76. Mem. Tex. Savs. and Loan League, Inst. Fin. Edn., Greater Houston Home Builders Assn. Democrat. Baptist. Clubs: 100 Club of Houston, Champions Golf, Masons. Home: 13802 Jupiter Hills Dr Houston TX 77069 Office: 204 W 19th St Houston TX 77008

WEGGELAND, ROBERT LAYNE, china co. exec.; b. Washington, June 20, 1936; s. Dan W. and Marjorie A. W.; B.A., Drew U., 1961; postgrad. N.Y. U., 1963-65; m. Grace K. Onderdonk, June 6, 1959; 1 dau., Monique A. Gen. mgr. G.A. Nelson, Inc., 1961-65; fin. cons. Louis Berger, Inc., East Orange, N.J., 1965-69; v.p. fin. and adminstrn. Paillard, Inc., Linden, N.J., 1969-73; gen. mgr. Paul B. Williams, Inc., Millburn, N.J., 1973-75; v.p. corp. devel. Estee Lauder, Inc., N.Y.C., 1975-81; pres. Royal Worcester Spode, Inc., N.Y.C., 1981—. Trustee, treas. Knox Sch., St. James, N.Y. Served with U.S. Army, 1953-55. Mem. Fin. Execs. Inst., Planning Execs. Inst., N.Am. Soc. Corp. Planning. Contbg. editor: Dow/Jones Irving Handbook Budgeting, 1980. Office: New York NY

WEGNER, ARTHUR EDUARD, aircraft engine mfg. co. exec.; b. Madison, Wis., June 23, 1937; s. Arthur Eduard and Elynore (Bell) W.; B.S., U.S. Naval Acad., 1960; M.B.A., Harvard U., 1969; m. Patricia J. Vining, Oct. 20, 1960; children—Meleda Ann, Elisabeth Kirsten. Sr. asso. mgmt. cons. Cresap, McCormack & Paget, 1967-70; mktg. mgr. Hewitt-Robbins, 1970-72; v.p. adminstrn. and planning Rust Engring. Co., 1972-73; dir. ops. analysis United Techs. Corp., 1973-76, dir. fin. planning, 1976; exec. v.p. mfg. div. Pratt & Whitney Aircraft Group, East Hartford, Conn., 1976—; dir. Hartford Savs. & Loan Assn., 1978—. Corporator, St. Francis Hosp., 1977—. Served with USN, 1960-67. Republican. Episcopalian. Office: 400 Main St East Hartford CT 06108

WEGNER, HERBERT GAIRD, assn. exec.; b. San Francisco, Sept. 20, 1929; s. Armin and Ethel (Slater) W.; B.A. in Polit. Sci., San Francisco State U., 1951; postgrad. U. Calif., 1953, Am. Inst. Fgn. Trade, 1952, m. Susan Aitken, Dec. 28, 1957; children—Steven, Susan, David. Statewide budget officer U. Cal. at Berkeley, 1957-59; internat. relations officer AID, Quito, Ecuador, 1959-61, Washington, 1961-62; spl. projects officer Peace Corps, Washington, 1962-64; Latin Am. dir. Credit Union Nat. Assn., Panama, 1964-71, mng. dir., 1971-79; pres. CUNADATA Corp., Madison, Wis., 1973-79; pres. CUNA Service Group, Inc., Madison, 1973-79; exec. vice chmn. ICU Services Corp., Madison, 1971-79; mng. dir. CUNA Supply Coop., Madison, 1971-79; pres. Wegner Ryan Group Inc., Washington, 1979-81; pres., dir. Network EFT Inc., Elk Grove, Ill., 1981—; v.p. Concord Computing Corp., 1981—; vice chmn. Nat. Commn. Electronic Funds Transfer, 1975-77. Mng. dir. World Council Credit Unions, 1971-75; ex-officio mem. Congress Central Credit Union, 1973—; dir. U.S. Central Credit Union. Bd. dirs. CUNA Internat. Found., Inc.; trustee Internat. Devel. Conf., CARE, Vol. Devel. Corps. Served to lt. USNR, 1953-57. Recipient Key Man award Jr. C. of C., Berkeley, 1951. Home: 7902 Lawndale Dr Silver Spring MD 20901 Office: Network EFT Inc 1715 Carmen Dr Elk Grove IL 60007

WEHLER, WALTER OLIVER, check verification co. exec.; b. Aurora, Ill., Jan. 15, 1934; s. Oliver Wendel and Elizabeth (Overberger) W.; B.B.A., U. Portland, 1962; m. Doris Ann Rukke, Mar. 1, 1963; children—Kristin Elizabeth, Garrick Eugene. Auditor, Safeco Ins. Co., Portland, Oreg., 1965-73, Oreg. Auto Ins. Co., Portland, 1973-78; pres. Telecheck Oreg., Inc., Portland, 1978—. Mem. Wilsonville (Oreg.) City Council, 1968-75; mem. West Linn Sch. Dist. Sch. Bd., 1976—, chmn. 1978-80. Served with USAF, 1952-56. Mem. Wilsonville Jr. C. of C. (life, Disting. Service award 1968, Walter E. Holman award 1969). Club: Rotary. Home: 6855 S W Boeckman Rd Wilsonville OR 97070 Office: Telecheck Oreg Inc Suite 222 Cascade Plaza 2828 S W Corbett St Portland OR 97201

WEHRLY, JACK RUSSELL, mfg. co. exec.; b. Ft. Wayne, Ind., Aug. 28, 1928; s. Wilfred R. and Lillian R. (Schmidt) W.; B.S., Purdue U., 1952; M.B.A., Rutgers U., 1958; A.M.P., Harvard U., 1968; m. Geraldine A. Fitzgerald, Dec. 28, 1948; children—Donna, Diana, Dennis. Research engr. Dow Corning Corp., 1952-55, regional sales/mktg. mgr., 1960-62, product mktg. mgr., 1962-67, dir. planning, 1967-71, bus. mgr., 1971-72, dir. tech. service and devel., 1972-77, new ventures bus. gen. mgr., 1977-80, v.p. govt. relations and public affairs, 1980—. Councilman-at-large, West Lafayette, Ind., 1950-52; pres. United Community Fund, 1970-72; others. Served with U.S. Army, 1946-48. Mem. Am. Chem. Soc., Am. Mgmt. Assn., Am. Inst. Chem. Engrs. Clubs: Midland Country (sec. 1973-78), Internat., Univ., Capitol Hill. Patentee in Silicone field. Home: 3301 39th St NW Washington DC 20036 Office: 1800 M St NW Suite 710 S Washington DC 20036

WEIANT, WILLIAM MORROW, investment banker; b. Perth Amboy, N.J., Nov. 30, 1938; s. Monroe Alden and Lois May (Dayer) W.; B.A. with honors, Amherst Coll., 1960; M.B.A., N.Y. U., 1963; m. Joan Claire Eberstadt, June 10, 1967; children—Clarissa Leigh, Pamela Anne. Salesman, T.L. Watson & Co., Perth Amboy, 1961-62; 1st v.p. investment research Blyth Eastman Dillon & Co., Inc., N.Y.C., 1963-75; mng. dir. First Boston Corp, N.Y.C., 1975—. Mem. Chartered Fin. Analysts, Fin. Analysts Fedn., N.Y. Soc. Sec. Analysts, Bank and Fin. Analysts Assn (pres. 1975-76). Clubs: City Midday, Seabright Lawn Tennis and Cricket, Seabright Beach, Mantaloking Yacht. Home: 524 Little Silver Point Rd Little Silver NJ 07739 Office: 20 Exchange Pl New York NY 10005

WEIDA, LEWIS DIXON, mktg. analyst; b. Moran, Ind., Apr. 23, 1924; s. Charles Ray and Luella Mildred (Dixon) W.; student Kenyon Coll., 1943, Purdue U., 1946; B.S., Ind. U., 1948; M.S., Columbia U., 1950. Mgr. statis. analysis unit Gen. Motors Acceptance Corp., N.Y.C., 1949-55; asst. to exec. v.p. Am. Express Co., 1955—. Served with USAAF, 1943-46; PTO. Mem. Am. Mktg. Assn., Travel Research Assn., Internat. Platform Assn. Democrat. Club: Masons. Office: Am Express Co 1350 Ave of Americas New York NY 10019

WEIDEN, PAUL LUDWIG, lawyer; b. Frankfurt am Main, Germany, Jan. 28, 1908; s. Joseph and Selma (Mayer) Welden-Baum; LL.D., U. Frankfurt, 1931; M.L., U. England, 1936; m. Gerda Kaufmann, July 12, 1937; 1 son, Paul Lincoln; m. 2d, Helga Zindel, Feb. 28, 1953 (div.); children—Peter Joseph, Michael David; came to U.S., 1936, naturalized, 1942. Chief legal sect. Liberated Areas Br., Bd. Econ. Warfare, 1943-44; admitted to bar Eng., 1936, Oreg. bar, 1938, D.C. bar, 1943, N.Y. bar, 1947; in law practice, Portland, Oreg., 1938-42; with Weiden, Grosswell & Gunnigle (name changed to Weiden & Gunnigle, 1960), N.Y.C., 1947—; atty. SEC, 1944-45; chmn. bd. various European and Am. corps.; chmn. Steinberg & Vorsaenger Corp., Wilag Corp. (Wiesbaden) Ltd. Contbr. European, Am. legal publs. Home: 920 Park Ave New York NY 10021 Office: 200 Park Ave New York NY 10017 also Bockenheimer Anlage 38 Frankfort Federal Republic of Germany

WEIDT, GEORGE WILLIAM, sales rep.; b. Paterson, N.J., Mar. 17, 1917; s. George Albert and Nellie Ellen (Miller) W.; student Drake's Bus. Coll., Paterson, N.J., 1936-38, U. Louisville, 1952, 55, U. Md., 1959; m. Gisela Sauter, Oct. 16, 1948; children—Debra E., Nancy E. Inducted into U.S. Army with N.G., 1941; commd. 2d lt., 1943, advanced through grades to lt. col., 1961, ret., 1964; with Army and Air Force Exchange Service, 1964-79, successively mgr., store supr., retail ops. mgr., gen. mgr., exchange mgr.; Tex. rep. Bastian Bros. Mem. Defense Supply Assn. (pres. Paris chpt. 1962-63). Republican. Roman Catholic. Home: 9107 Balcones Club Dr Austin TX 78750

WEIERSTALL, GUNTHER JOHN, cons.; b. Elberfeld, Germany, May 27, 1925; s. William Frederick and Selma Anna (Erlenbruch) W.; came to U.S., 1927, naturalized, 1947; student Upsala Coll., 1946-47; B.S., N.Y. U., 1949; m. Lillian Eleanor Weixler, Mar. 17, 1946; children—John Gunther, Carol Jeanne. Asst. purchasing agt. Leewal Co., Bergenfield, N.J., 1949-50; buyer GAF Corp., N.Y.C., 1950-52, sr. buyer, 1952-62, asst. purchasing agt., 1962-67, mgr. purchasing, 1967-72, corp. dir. purchasing, 1972-79; cons., 1979—; pres. Weierstall Assos., Inc., 1980—. Served with U.S. Army, 1943-46; ETO. Decorated Bronze Star, Purple Heart. Lutheran. Mem. Sigma Gamma Phi, Nat. Assn. Purchasing Mgmt. (cert.). Home and Office: 621 Mazur Ave Paramus NJ 07652

WEIGEL, ROBERT LEWIS, JR., printing co. exec.; b. St. Louis, Sgpt. 7, 1944; s. Robert Lewis and Georgene Nancy (Walbancke) W.; student St. Petersburg Jr. Coll., 1963-64; m. Mary Ann Davis, Nov. 4, 1967; children—John Christopher, Debra Lynn. Sec.-treas. Creative Interiors, Clearwater, Fla., 1967-69; office mgr. Consol. Hotel Equipment, Clearwater, 1969; store mgr. Am. Nat. Stores, St. Louis, 1970-72; sec.-treas. Weigel Screen Process, Eureka, Mo., 1972-76, pres., 1976—. Served with U.S. Army, 1964-66. Mem. Nat. Space Inst., Screen Printing Assn., Eureka C. of C. (dir.). Episcopalian. Home: PO Box 307 Marthasville MO 63357 Office: 141 S Central Eureka MO 63025

WEIGELE, GEORGE CHARLES, mfg. co. exec.; b. Bklyn., Apr. 23, 1920; s. William Joseph and Elsie Lucille (Kramer) W.; student U. Evansville, 1947-49; m. Dorothy Elizabeth Millay, Jan. 10, 1946; children—Karen Ann, Andrea Jo, Barbara Jean, Brian Joseph. Purchasing agt. VA, 1946-48; cost estimator Internat. Havester Co., 1948-56; div. controller Whirlpool Corp., Evansville, Ind., 1956—. Chmn. small bus. div. United Fund Drive, 1971. Served with U.S. Army, 1942-45. Decorated Bronze Star. Mem. Nat. Assn. Accts. (past nat. dir., past chpt. pres.), Evansville C. of C. Roman Catholic. Clubs: Turners, Eagles. Home: 7900 Ridgemont Dr Newburgh IN 47630 Office: Whirlpool Corp Evansville IN 47727

WEIGHT, MELVIN E., book binding co. exec.; b. Salt Lake City, Jan. 14, 1942; s. Sheldon James and Florence Beatrice (Brailsford) W.; student Latter Day Saints Bus. Coll., 1964-65; m. Diane K. Ellis, Mar. 19, 1962; children—Cheri Suzanne, Jeffrey Paul, Melissa Danielle. With Mountain States Bindery, Salt Lake City, 1958-64, Nat. Sales Inc., div. Mountain States Bindery, Salt Lake City, 1964-68; with Coast Book Cover Co., Los Angeles, 1968-78; Western regional sales mgr. nat. cover div. Ga.-Pacific Corp., St. Louis, Los Angeles office, 1978—. Active Jr. C. of C., Salt Lake City, 1964-68, chmn. 24th of July Breakfast, 1966. Mem. Bank Stationers Assn., Binding Industries Am. (dir. 1973-78, Outstanding Service award 1975, 76, 77), Sales and Mktg. Execs. Assn. of Los Angeles. Republican. Mormon. Keynote speaker nat. seminars in field; contbr. articles to profl. publ. Office: 9760 El Greco Circle Fountain Valley CA 92708

WEIL, DAVID MAXWELL, packaging co. exec.; b. Chgo., Apr. 23, 1912; s. Joseph and Blanch (Falter) W.; B.A. magna cum laude, Harvard, 1933; m. Aase Pedersen, Feb. 28, 1950; children—Lise Weil, Greta Weil, Kari. Chmn. bd., treas. Cromwell Paper Co.; chmn. bd. Thomas Tape Co., 1968—; fgn. editor Chgo. Jour. Commerce, 1939-42; book reviewer Chgo. Sun, 1946-48; consul ad honorem El Salvador, 1940-42, 46—; financial adviser Royal Embassy of Yugoslavia. Gov. mem. Library Internat. Relations; sponsor Chgo. Council Fgn. Relations. Served with AUS, 1942-45. Decorated comdr. Order St. Sava (Yugoslavia); officer Order Homayoun (Iran); Order Merit 1st class (Iran). Mem. Alliance Franciase, Pan Am. Soc., Phi Beta Kappa. Clubs: Adventurers, Arts, Lake Shore Country, Standard (Chgo.); Harvard (Chgo. and N.Y.C.). Home: 1540 N Lake Shore Dr Chicago IL 60610 Office: 35 E Wacker Dr Chicago IL 60601

WEIL, ROBERT LEONARD, food service distbn. co. exec.; b. Denver, Oct. 13, 1922; s. Felix Leon and Frances Bernice (Levy) W.; B.Sci. Bus., U. Colo., 1947; m. Debra Sue New, Dec. 6, 1952; children—Ronald Leon, Richard Floyd, Linda Marie. Ind. ins. agt., Denver, 1947-52; Pres. Westman Commn. Co., Denver, 1952—, also dir.; pres., dir. Continental Orgn. Distbr. Enterprises, Inc., Pitts., 1979—; dir., mem. exec. com. Nat. Cooking Inst., 1976—. Bd. dirs. Denver and Colo. Conv. and Visitors Bur., 1979-80, Children's Asthma Research Inst. and Hosp., Denver, 1965-74. Served with USNR, 1943-46. Mem. Foodservice Orgn. Distbrs. (treas., dir. 1979-80), Nat. Restaurant Assn., Colo.-Wyo. Restaurant Assn. (dir., treas., Disting. Service award 1972), Denver C. of C., Colo. Chefs de Cuisine Assn., Colo.-Wyo. Hotel and Motel Assn., Foodservice Industry Gourmet Soc., Zeta Beta Tau (trustee Beta Alpha chpt. 1947-54, citation of merit 1960). Jewish. Clubs: Town (dir., v.p., pres. 1969-75), Mile-Hi Stadium (dir. 1979), Optimist, Lowry Field Commd. Officers (Denver). Mem. editorial adv. bd. Instnl. Distbn. mag., 1975—. Office: 4450 Lipan St Denver CO 80211

WEIL, S. DOUGLAS, real estate investments exec.; b. Cleve., Apr. 21, 1936; s. Robert Nathaniel and Jean (Schaffner) W.; B.A., Princeton, 1958; M.B.A., Harvard, 1960; m. Judith R. Schimmel, Dec. 23, 1963; children—Deborah Lynne, David Louis, Elizabeth Ann. Econ. analyst Larry Smith & Co., Washington, 1960-61; asst. v.p. Webb & Knapp, N.Y.C., 1962-64, Kirkey-Natus Corp., N.Y.C., 1964-66; mgr. real estate investments Irwin Mgmt. Co., Columbus, Ind., 1966-70; sr. v.p. Property Capital Trust, also sr. v.p., dir. Property Capital Advisors, Boston, 1970-78; sr. v.p., dir. Capital for Real Estate, Boston, 1975-78; pres., dir. Paine Webber Properties Inc., Boston, 1978—; lectr. Harvard Bus. Sch., Mass. Inst. Tech., N.Y. U., Babson Inst.; cons. Pres. Johnson's Com. on Urban Housing Mem. town meeting City of Wellesley (Mass.), 1973-77, mem. by-laws com., 1975-78; mem. nat. exec. council Am. Jewish Com., vice chmn. Boston chpt.; trustee synagogue; trustee Jewish Community Council of Greater Boston; bd. dirs. United Fund. Mem. Nat. Realty Com. (v.p.), Internat. Council Shopping Centers. Club: Hazel H. Wightman Tennis Center (Weston, Mass.). Home: 22 Cartwright Rd Wellesley MA 02181 Office: 100 Federal St Boston MA 02101

WEILAND, CARL WALTER, mech. engr.; b. Zurich, Switzerland, Aug. 13, 1909; s. Josef and Maria (Wiederkehr) W.; M.E., Inst. Tech., Barcelona, 1933; D.Sc.; m. Irene Meta Moesch, Mar. 8, 1944; children—Herbert, Philipp. Mech. engr. designing spl. machines for Swiss, German, Am., Spanish industries, 1933—; work on ground effect machines, 1956—; cons. Reynolds Metals Co., Zurich, 1960, later with product devel. div., Richmond, Va., then aircraft div. Douglas Aircraft Co., Inc., Long Beach, Calif.; now pres. Weiland Machine Co., Detroit. Office: 1769 Golfridge Dr Bloomfield Hills MI 48013

WEILAND, FRANK A., mfg. co. exec.; b. Bergen County, N.J., July 4, 1945; s. Donald L. and Eleonor M. Weiland; B.B.A., Central Conn. State Coll., 1970; M.B.A., Wescon State Coll., 1979; m. Joanne M. Weiland, June 26, 1963; children—Colleen A., Michael D. With Union Carbide Corp., 1966—, plant acct., Linden, N.J., 1969-72, mgr. cost acctg., fin. analyst-systems, 1972-74, controller, 1974-77, asst. group controller, 1977-79, group controller subsidiaries, N.Y.C., 1979—, dir. 25 Union Carbide subs. corps. Bd. dirs. Barkwood Falls Assn.; commr. Brookfield Youth Soccer Club. Served with USN, 1962-65. Mem. Smithsonian Instn. (asso.). Democrat. Roman Catholic.

WEILL, SANFORD I., banker; b. N.Y.C., Mar. 16, 1933; s. Max and Etta (Kalika) W.; B.A., Cornell U., 1955, student Grad. Sch. Bus. and Public Adminstrn., 1954-55; m. Joan Mosher, June 20, 1955; children—Marc P., Jessica M. Chmn. bd., chief exec. officer Carter, Berlind & Weill (name changed to CBWL-Hayden, Stone, Inc. 1970, to Hayden Stone, Inc. 1972, to Shearson Hayden Stone 1974, to Shearson Loeb Rhoades Inc. 1979), N.Y.C.; mem. Midwest Stock Exchange, Chgo. Bd. Trade; asso. mem. N.Y. Stock Exchange. Bd. dirs. Nat. Energy Found.; rep. of N.Y. State comptroller to bd. dirs. Mcpl. Assistance Corp. City N.Y.; trustee Brandeis U. Mem. N.Y. Soc. Security Analysts, Securities Industry Assn. (dir.), Young Presidents Orgn. Clubs: Bond (bd. govs.), Cornell, Harmonie (N.Y.C.); Sunningdale Country (Scarsdale, N.Y.); Lucullus Circle. Home: 50 E 79th St New York NY 10021 Office: Shearson Loeb Rhoades Inc 14 Wall St New York NY 10005

WEINBERG, ALEXANDER, civil engr.; b. Warsaw, Poland, Sept. 5, 1921; s. Hanan and Natalia (Friedman) W.; came to U.S., 1964, naturalized, 1971; B.S., Politechnic of Silesia, 1948; m. Anita Bergerman, June 11, 1957; children—Annette, Ohr, Shirley. Resident engr., project mgr. J. Lustig Constrn. Co., Tel Aviv, Israel, 1948-54; dist. engr. Israeli Ministry Def. Constrn. Dept., 1954-59; chief engr. Nigersol Constrn. Co., Ibandan, Nigeria, 1959-63; chief engr. Nat. Constrn. Co., Kathmandu, Nepal, 1963-64; project mgr. R. Chuckrow Constrn. Co., N.Y.C., 1964-65; chief engr. Diesel Constrn. Co., N.Y.C., 1965-68; pres. Amis Constrn. and Cons. Services, Inc., N.Y.C., 1968—. Mem. Am. Mil. Engrs. Assn., Am. Value Engrs. Club: Capitol Hill. Home: 482 E Royal Flamingo Dr Sarasota FL 33577 Office: 21 W 38th St New York NY 10018

WEINBERG, HERSCHEL MAYER, lawyer; b. Bklyn., Oct. 13, 1927; s. Jacob and Gertrude (Wernick) W.; B.A., Bklyn. Coll., 1948; LL.B., Harvard, 1952. Admitted to N.Y. bar, 1952; atty. Payne & Steingarten, N.Y.C., 1952-57, Jacobs, Persinger & Parker, N.Y.C., 1957-61; partner firm Rubin, Rubin, Weinberg & Di Paola, N.Y.C., 1961-78, Pearlman Weinberg Tauber & Bernstein, N.Y.C., 1979—; dir. Milgray Electronics, Inc. Served with AUS, 1946-47. Mem. Assn. Bar City N.Y. Club: Harvard (N.Y.C.). Home: 50 Sutton Pl S New York NY 10022 Office: 575 Madison Ave New York NY 10022

WEINBERG, JOHN LIVINGSTON, investment banker; b. N.Y.C., Jan. 5, 1925; s. Sidney James and Helen (Livingston) W.; A.B. cum laude, Princeton U., 1948; M.B.A., Harvard U., 1950; m. Sue Ann Gotshal, Dec. 6, 1952; children—Ann K. (dec.), John, Jean. With Goldman, Sachs & Co., N.Y.C., 1950—, partner, 1956-76, sr. partner, co-chmn. mgmt. com., 1976, now chmn. bd.; mem. Chgo. Bd. Trade; mem. industries adv. com. Advt. Council Inc.; dir. Capital Holding Corp., Witco Chem. Corp., B.F. Goodrich Co., Dart & Kraft, Inc., Knight-Ridder Newspapers, Inc., Cluett, Peabody & Co., Inc., Seagram Co. Ltd. Bd. govs., mem. exec. com. N.Y. Hosp.; trustee

Deerfield Acad.; bd. dirs. Josiah Macy, Jr. Found. Served to 2d lt. USMCR, 1942-46, capt., 1951-52. Fellow Inst. Jud. Adminstrn. (treas., chmn. fin. com.). Clubs: Econ., Princeton, Harvard Bus. Sch. (N.Y.C.); Blind Brook; Century Country; Lyford Cay. Office: Goldman Sachs & Co 55 Broad St New York NY 10004

WEINBERG, LORETTA LEONE, govt. ofcl.; b. N.Y.C., Feb. 6, 1935; d. Murray M. and Raya (Hamilton) Isaacs; B.A., U. Calif., Los Angeles, 1956; M.P.A., Fairleigh Dickinson, 1977; m. Irwin Weinberg, July 25, 1961; children—Daniel, Francine. Congressional aide U.S. Congressman Henry Helstoski, Washington, 1968-72; legis. asst. N.J. State Assemblyman Byron Baer, Trenton, N.J., 1972-73; asst. county adminstr. Bergen County, Hackensack, N.J., 1975—. Bergen County, 1970-72; Mem. twp. adv. bd. on bus. and industry, Bergen County, 1970-72; mem. employment tng. adv. council, Bergen County, 1979-80, adv. bd. on handicapped, Bergen County, 1979-80. Mem. Am. Soc. Public Adminstrs., Am. Mgmt. Assn., Internat. Inst. Mcpl. Clks., Nat. Council Jewish Women. Home: 866 Queen Anne Rd Teaneck NJ 07666 Office: Adminstrv Bldg Hackensack NJ 07601

WEINBERG, SIDNEY JAMES, JR., investment banker; b. N.Y.C., Mar. 27, 1923; s. Sidney James and Helen (Livingston) W.; B.A. in Pub. and Internat. Affairs, Princeton U., 1945; M.B.A., Harvard U., 1949; m. Elizabeth Houghton, June 30, 1951; children—Elizabeth Livingston, Sydney Houghton, Peter Amory. Vice pres. textile div. Owens-Corning Fiberglas Corp., N.Y.C., 1949-65, Goldman, Sachs & Co., N.Y.C., 1965—, partner, 1967—; dir. Corning Internat. Corp., J.P. Stevens & Co., Inc., Tejon Ranch Co., Norris Industries, Inc., Tecumseh Products Co., Sigma-Aldrich Corp., Eagle-Picher Industries, Inc. Trustee, Found. Center, 1968-74, Com. Econ. Devel., WNET-13 Ednl. Broadcasting Corp., 1965-79, Carnegie Found. Advancement of Teaching, 1965-78, Presbyn. Hosp. of City N.Y., Scripps Coll., Claremont, Calif.; cons. panel Comptroller Gen. of U.S. Served to 1st lt. F.A., U.S. Army, 1943-46. Clubs: River, Recess (N.Y.C); Century Country (Purchase, N.Y.); Eldorado Country (Indian Wells, Calif.); Calif. (Los Angeles). Home: Greenwich CT 06830 Office: 55 Broad St New York NY 10004

WEINBERGER, DONALD CHARLES, fin. public relations co. exec.; b. Jersey City, N.J., Oct. 27, 1942; s. Bernard and Rae (Glanzer) W.; B.S., Fairleigh Dickinson U., 1965, M.B.A., 1969; m. Sue Linda Schultz, June 23, 1974; children—Marc Bennett, Jay Steven. Purchasing asso. Foster Wheeler Corp., Livingston, N.J., 1966-69; fin. div. asso. Harshe Rotman & Druck, N.Y.C., 1969-72; exec. v.p., Howard Bronson & Co., N.Y.C., 1972—. Office: 708 Third Ave New York NY 10017

WEINBLATT, MYRON BENJAMIN, broadcasting co. exec.; b. Perth Amboy, N.J., June 10, 1929; s. Barney and Renee (Kempner) W.; B.S., Syracuse U., 1951; m. Annie Weitz, Sept. 25, 1956; children—Marc, Richard. Purchasing agt. Kramer-Trenton Co., Trenton, N.J., 1953-56; with NBC, 1957—, dir. participating program sales, N.Y.C., 1964-68, v.p., Eastern sales mgr., 1968-69, v.p. talent and program adminstrn., 1969-73, v.p. sales, 1973-75, sr. v.p. sales, 1975, exec. v.p., 1975—, exec. v.p., gen. mgr., 1977—, pres. Entertainment div., 1978-80, pres. NBC Enterprises, 1980—. Served with CIC, AUS, 1951-53; Japan. Mem. Internat. Radio and TV Soc., Nat. Acad. TV Arts and Scis., Internat. Acad. TV Arts and Scis. (bd. govs.), Syracuse Alumni Assn. Office: NBC 30 Rockefeller Plaza New York NY 10020*

WEINEL, JOAN MARY, engring. co. exec.; b. East St. Louis, Ill., Jan. 30, 1934; d. Charles Everett and Josephine Theresa (Wessell) Threlkeld; ed. high sch.; m. Robert Phillip Weinel, Feb. 5, 1954; 1 dau., Julia Weinel Wood. Partner, Weinel Co., O'Fallon, Ill., 1954—; sec.-treas. Metro Land Developers Inc., O'Fallon, 1962—, Bob Weinel Builder Inc., O'Fallon, 1966—. Pres. O'Fallon Econ. Devel. Commn., 1974-76, chmn., 1976-77; mem. environ. task force East-West Gateway Coordinating Council, 1978—; bd. dirs. St. Louis Bi-State chpt. St. Clair County region ARC, 1977—. Mem. O'Fallon C. of C. (pres. 1974-76). Home: 204 Wesley Dr E O'Fallon IL 62269 Office: 103 N Oak St O'Fallon IL 62269

WEINER, GARY ALAN, service industry exec.; b. Miami Beach, Fla., Oct. 6, 1953; s. Al and Sally Weiner; B.A. in Mgmt., Duke U., 1974; M.B.A., U. Pa., 1976; m. Susan R. Baker, Dec. 24, 1976. Regional mktg. mgr., sr. corp. planner Food Fair, Inc., Phila., 1976-79; v.p. fin. and corp. planning Renard Mfg. Co., Inc., Miami, Fla., 1979-80; v.p. fin. Aero. Enterprises div. ARA Services Inc., Miami, 1980—. Mem. Am. Mktg. Assn., Fla. Solar Energy Coalition. Club: Kiwanis. Office: 1596 NW 159th St Miami FL 33169

WEINER, JOSEPH JACOB, mortgage banker; b. Phila., Apr. 24, 1937; s. Abraham and Bertha (Cohen) W.; B.A., U. Pa., 1958; m. Sharon Cooper, July 5, 1970; children—Andrew, Scott. Engaged in comml. fin. industry, 1958-66; v.p. Friedman-Drew Corp., N.Y.C., 1966-71; exec. v.p., dir. Horowitz Fin. Corp., Irvington, N.J., 1971—; partner S.C. Realty Investment Co., Hamilton Center Assos., 1977—; dir. Horowitz-Weiner Investment Co., Horowitz Funding Corp., Horowitz & Weiner Fin. Services, Inc. Trustee Temple B'nai Abraham, Livingston, N.J., treas., 1981—. Mem. Mortgage Bankers Assn. N.Y., Young Mortgage Bankers Assn. N.Y. Republican. Jewish. Home: 18 Goodhart Dr Livingston NJ 07039 Office: 50 Union Ave Irvington NJ 07111

WEINER, PETER RICHARD, financial analyst; b. Danbury, Conn., May 23, 1950; s. William and Marcia (Smith) W.; B.S. magna cum laude, Boston U., 1972; M.B.A., Cornell U., 1974. Ops. officer 1st Nat. City Bank, N.Y.C., 1974-75; account exec. Merrill Lynch, N.Y.C., 1975-76; fin. analyst F. & M. Schaefer, N.Y.C., 1976-77; mng. dir. Ashmont Arms Realty Trust, Milton, Mass., 1977—. Mem. Am. Mgmt. Assn., Assn. M.B.A. Execs., Beta Gamma Sigma. Home: 800 W Roxbury Pkwy Chestnut Hill MA 02167

WEINERT, FRED JOSEPH, business exec.; b. Dayton, Ohio, Apr. 20, 1947; s. Fred Joseph and Eileen A. Weinert.; B.S. in Acctg., U. Dayton, 1969; married, children—Stephanie, Thomas. Staff auditor Arthur Andersen & Co., Chgo., 1969-71; controller Lease-A-Plane Internat., Chgo., 1971-73; v.p. Waste Mgmt. Internat., London, 1973-79, dir. constrn., Saudi Arabia, 1977-78; regional controller Waste Mgmt., Inc., 1973-75, asst. to pres., 1976-77; pres. Waste Mgmt. Argentina S.A., Buenos Aires, 1980—. Roman Catholic. Office: Leandro N Alem 1110 Piso 11 1001 Buenos Aires Argentina

WEINGARTEN, SAUL MYER, lawyer; b. Los Angeles, Dec. 19, 1921; s. Louis and Lillian Dorothy (Alter) W.; A.B., U. Calif. at Los Angeles, 1942; certificate diesel engring. Cornell U., 1944; J.D., U. So. Calif., 1949; m. Miriam Ellen Moore, Jan. 21, 1949; children—David, Steven, Lawrence, Bruce. Admitted to Calif. bar, 1950, also U.S. Supreme Ct. bar; instr. law Naval Postgrad. Sch., Monterey, Calif., also Naval Sch. Justice, Newport, R.I., 1950-54, Monterey Peninsula Coll.; counsel Mountain Plains Ednl. and Econ. Devel. Program Inc., 1971-77; pres. Saul M. Weingarten Inc.; gen. counsel Redevel. Agy. of Seaside, 1963-77; spl. counsel Monterey County Bd. Edn.; faculty Monterey Peninsula Coll. U.S. del. Internat. Union Local Authorities, 1963-64, 73; past pres. Family Service Agy.; bd. dirs. Lyceum of Monterey Peninsula (Calif.), Monterey County Symphony Assn., Monterey Peninsula Inst. of Fgn. Studies; instr. law Naval Res. Officers Sch.; past pres. Monterey County Citizens Planning Assn., Vets. Coordinating Council, 1954; past dir. Monterey County Tb and Health Assn.; mem. Monterey County Council; Bd. dirs. ARC, Seaside Civic League; bd. dirs., pres. Alliance on Aging. Served as lt. USNR, 1942-46, 50-54, comdr. Res. (ret.). Coro Found. fellow, 1949-50. Mem. Calif., Monterey County bar assns., Am., Calif. trial lawyers assns., Amvets (post comdr. 1953-54), Comml. Law League Am. (world trade and commerce com.). Clubs: Rotary (pres. Seaside club 1972), Commonwealth, Meadowbrook. Author five motion pictures on law. Home: 4135 Crest Rd Pebble Beach CA 93953 Office: Fremont Profl Center Seaside CA 93955 also El Rancho Bldg Box 22855 Carmel CA 93922

WEININGER, HARRY DOV, real estate holding co. exec.; b. Czernovitz, Russia, Sept. 28, 1933; s. Shicku and Regina (Klinger) W.; B.A., U. Chgo., 1962; m. Suzanne Talmy, Aug. 29, 1957 (div. 1966); children—Carmi Jan, Nehama Ellen. Prin., NTJC Sch., Skokie, Ill., 1961-63; gen. mgr. Kaufman's Stores, Berkeley, Calif., 1963-65; owner/mgr. Carpet Center, Berkeley, 1965—; gen. partner Trust Security Mgmt. Co., Berkeley, 1976—. Treas. Better Berkeley Campaign Com.; mem. Berkeley Civic Arts Commn., 1975-78; pres. Civic Arts Found. Berkeley, 1976—; v.p. Berkeley Dem. Club, 1977—; mem. Commn. Employment and Tng. Berkeley, 1977-78. Served to 1st. lt., inf., U.S. Army. Mem. Am. Mgmt. Assn. Democrat. Jewish. Office: 921 Parker St Berkeley CA 94710

WEINROTH, DONALD MELVIN, engring. and fin. cons., investment co. exec.; b. Phila., Feb. 25, 1931; s. Max and Frances (Schwartzman) W.; student (Univ. scholar), U. Pa., 1947-51; B.S.C.E., U. Md., 1958, postgrad., 1959-61; M.C.E., Catholic U. Am., 1964, postgrad. in engring. (NSF fellow, Washington Consortium Univs. fellow) 1960-77; m. Marcia B. Hankin, Aug. 26, 1962; children—Susan Charlotte, Nan Linda. With Groll-Beach Assos., architects, engrs., 1956-62, chief engr., Washington, 1960-62; v.p., gen. mgr. Weinroth Assos., Inc., engring. cons., Washington, 1962-75; sr. staff officer Bldg. Research Adv. Bd., also program mgr. program on U.S./USSR cooperation in field of housing and other constrn. Nat. Acad. Scis., Washington, 1976-79; exec. sec. U.S. Nat. Com. on Bldg. Research Studies and Documentation, 1977-78; pres., treas. Weinroth Assos., Inc., real estate, fin. instns. and bldg. products investments, Washington, 1975—; prin. Donald M. Weinroth, P.E., engring. fin. counsel, Washington, 1976—; cons.; co-chmn. U.S./USSR Seminar on Industrialized Bldgs., Moscow, 1978, U.S./USSR Seminar on Bldg. Utility Systems, Washington, 1979; mem. Greater Washington Bd. Trade. Pres., Chinese-Am. Lions Club, Washington, 1970-71. Served with U.S. Army, 1951-54; Korea. Registered profl. engr., Md., D.C., Va., Mass.; real estate cert., Md., D.C., Va. Mem. Nat. Soc. Profl. Engrs., D.C. Soc. Profl. Engrs. (pres. 1978-79), D.C. Profl. Council (pres. 1979), ASCE, Am. Ry. Engrs. Assn., Marine Tech. Soc., Am. Planning Assn., Am. Oceanic Assn., Alpha Epsilon Pi (pres. chpt. 1954-55), Chi Epsilon. Club: George Washington U. Home: 5009 Battery Ln Bethesda MD 20014 Office: Weinroth Assos Inc PO Box 30183 Washington DC 20014

WEINSTEIN, HOWARD JAY, constrn. and real estate co. exec.; b. Bklyn., Dec. 18, 1941; s. Maurice and Yetta W.; A.A.S. in Acctg., Bronx Community Coll., 1964; B.B.A., CUNY, 1968; m. Bernice B. Zaslow, Aug. 25, 1963; children—Jennifer Robin, Daniel Lawrence. Asst. controller Conforti & Eisele, Inc., N.Y.C., 1969-72; sr. staff mem. J.K. Lasser & Co., Lake Success, N.Y., 1972-73; controller Conforti & Eisele, Inc., N.Y.C., 1973-77, Kerschner Cos., Norwalk, Conn., 1977-80, Klein & Eversoll, Inc., Happauge, N.Y., 1980—. Adv., Reach Out for Youth with Inflammatory Bowel Disease, Jericho, N.Y.; treas. East Meadow (N.Y.) Towne House Condominium Assn. C.P.A., N.Y. Mem. N.Y. State Soc. C.P.A.'s. Club: East Meadow Soccer. Home: 1810-48 Front St East Meadow NY 11554 Office: 350 Vanderbilt Motor Pkwy Hauppauge NY 11787

WEINSTEIN, MORTON ELLIOTT, retail co. exec.; b. N.Y.C., Aug. 19, 1931; s. Harry and Betty (Tellis) W.; B.B.A., CCNY, 1953; M.S., N.Y. U., 1960; m. Serafina Corsello, June 23, 1974; children—Frederick, Kenneth, Paola. Asst. to v.p. Allied Stores Corp., N.Y.C., 1954-68; v.p. Diana Stores Corp., North Bergen, N.J., 1968-78; pres., chief exec. officer W&L Apparel Corp., N.Y.C., 1978—; tchr. Lab. Inst. of Merchandising, 1959-61, Fashion Inst. Tech., 1961-62. Mem. Nat. Retail Mchts. Assn. Clubs: N.Y. U., Masons. Home: 234 Beverly Rd Huntington NY 11746 Office: 275 7th Ave New York NY 10001

WEINSTEIN, STANLEY HOWARD, real estate exec.; b. N.Y.C., Oct. 27, 1948; s. George and Shirley Beatrice (Greenberg) W.; B.S., U. Ill., 1970; J.D., St. John's Sch. Law, 1973; m. Lenore Marsha Bienenfeld, May 25, 1975; children—Moshe, Ronni Leah. Staff acct. M.J. Weinstein Groothuis & Co., N.Y.C., 1969-70; asst. treas. Nat. Diversified Industries Inc., Great Neck, N.Y., 1970-73; partner Weinstein Assos., N.Y.C. and Milw., 1973—; admitted to N.Y. bar, 1975, D.C. bar, 1979; exec. v.p., sec., owner REIT Property Mgrs., Ltd., Milw., 1975—, also dir.; chmn. bd. RPM/Preiss Real Estate Inc., Milw., 1979—, also dir.; pres. 925 E. Wells Corp., Milw., 1976—, also dir.; pres. Weinstein Assos. Ltd., Milw.; sec. Hudson Valley Corp. Treas., bd. dirs. Hillel Acad., 1978—; bd. dirs. Anshe Sfard Synagogue, Beth Judah Synagogue, Milw. Jewish Community Center; asso. chmn. Acharai II-Fedn. Young Leadership Mission to Israel; mem. budget and planning com. Milw. Jewish Fedn.; mem. Milw. Kosher Restaurant Com. C.P.A., Ill. Mem. Assn. for Torah Advancement (sec., dir.), Am. Inst. C.P.A.'s, N.Y. State Soc. C.P.A.'s, N.Y. State Bar Assn., Assn. Bar City N.Y., Nat. Assn. Rev. Appraisers, Am. Bar Assn., Delta Sigma Pi, Jewish. Office: Weinstein Assos Ltd 925 E Wells St PO Box 92219 Milwaukee WI 53202 also Israel

WEINSTOCK, GERARD, baking ingredients and equipment mfg. exec.; b. Bklyn., Mar. 18, 1919; s. Louis and Celia (Dubowy) W.; A.B., Harvard, 1939, LL.B., 1942; m. Margaret M. Epstein, Dec. 15, 1945; children—Douglas, William S., Katherine L. Admitted to N.Y. bar, 1942; practiced in N.Y.C., 1946-51; pres. Basic Foods div. Mallinckrodt, Inc., Englewood, N.J., 1951—; v.p., dir. Grossman Publishers, Inc., N.Y.C., 1964-68; dir., exec. com. Mchts. Bank of N.Y.C., 1949—; lectr. on mergers and acquisitions N.Y. U. Sch. Continuing Edn. Mem. Human Rights Commn., New Rochelle, N.Y., 1963-65; chmn. Am. Field Service, New Rochelle, 1961-63; pres. Guidance Center, New Rochelle, 1972-75. Trustee, treas. Windward Sch., White Plains, N.Y., 1956-59; mem. Radio Free Europe del., Portugal, Germany, 1960; mem. armed forces and vets. service com. Nat. Jewish Welfare Bd.; bd. dirs. Wildcliffe Children's Mus., New Rochelle, 1963-65, Citizens for Pub. Edn., New Rochelle, 1961-65; trustee Westchester Jewish Community Services, Larchmont-Mamaroneck Center Continuing Edn.; chmn. bd. trustees, bd. govs., chmn. retirement com. Am. Jewish Com.; mem. adminstrv. council Jacob Blaustein Inst. for Advancement Human Rights; adv. bd. Fedn. Employment and Guidance Service, N.Y.C.; nat. major gifts com., N.Y. area co-chmn. The Harvard Campaign; nat. chmn. Harvard Center for Jewish Studies; mem. com. to nominate overseers Harvard U.; mem. Harvard overseers vis. com. on univ. resources; mem. com. to visit Center for Middle Eastern Studies and Near Eastern Langs. and Civilizations; mem. steering com. Friends of Harvard Judaica Collection, Widener Library; trustee Am. Schs. Oriental Research; bd. dirs. Children's Village, Dobbs Ferry, N.Y. Served with CIC, AUS, 1942-46. Mem. Nat. Bakery Suppliers Assn. (dir. 1970—), Am. Soc. Bakery Engrs., Asso. Harvard Alumni (dir.). Jewish. Clubs: Harvard (bd. mgrs.), Bakers (N.Y.C.); Beach Point (Mamaroneck N.Y.); Rotary (Englewood, N.J.). Mem. publ. com. Commentary mag. Home: 1 Knollwood Dr Larchmont NY 10538 Office: 53 Bancker St Englewood NJ 07631

WEINTRAUB, LOUIS, pub. relations exec.; b. Montreal, Que., Can., June 4, 1922; s. Samuel and Bella (Silverman) W.; student pub. schs., N.Y.C.; m. Renee Arum, Nov. 4, 1951; children—Toby, Joel, Judy. Came to U.S., 1923, naturalized, 1946. Washington bur. mgr. Pix, Inc., 1940-41; asst. to picture editor Washington Post, 1940-41; news photographer Office War Information, 1941-42; picture editor Keystone Pictures, Inc., N.Y.C., 1947-49; asst. to pub. N.Y. Age, 1949-50; dir. News Press Service, 1950-54; dir. pub. relations Pavelle Color and Pavelle Labs., Inc., 1951-57; pres. Weintraub & Fitz-Simons, Inc., pub. relations counsel, N.Y.C., 1958—; pres. Photo Communications Co., Inc., visual cons., N.Y.C., 1958—. Pub. relations adviser Hon. W. Averell Harriman, 1954-60. N.Y. State Goodwill Ambassador, Brussels World's Fair, 1958; mem. Pres. Com. on Employment of Handicapped, 1958—; vice chmn., mem. bd. Citizen's Budget Commn., 1967—; v.p., mem. bd. Greater N.Y. Safety Council, 1969—. Served to cpl., Signal Corps, AUS, 1942-45. Decorated Croix de Guerre with Palms (France). Recipient Medal, City of Orleans, France, 1948, Pub. Service award Philippines Lions Internat., 1959. Mem. Pub. Relations Soc. Am., Silurians, Fgn. Press Assn., Am. Legion, V.F.W., Nat. Press Photographers Assn. Mem. B'nai B'rith. Clubs: Nat. Press, Overseas Press, K.P. Home: 11 Maytime Dr Jericho NY 11753 Office: 488 Madison Ave New York City NY 10022

WEINTRAUB, RONALD HARVEY, pub. co. exec.; b. Cleve., Mar. 29, 1934; s. Sam A. and Beatrice (Sindell) W.; B.S. in Econs., U. Pa., 1955; m. Diane Rosenblatt, Nov. 22, 1958; children—Steven, Beth, Arlene. Acct. exec. E.F. Hutton & Co., Beverly Hills, Calif., 1959-65; pres. Communication Skill Builders, Inc., Tucson, 1966—. Vice pres. Jewish Community Center, Tucson, 1969-70; pres. Temple Emanu-el, Tucson, 1977-78; trustee Palo Verde Found. for Mental Health, 1976—. Served with USAR, 1957. Mem. Direct Mail Mktg. Assn., Tucson C. of C., Nat. Sch. Supply and Equipment Assn. Office: PO Box 42050 Tucson AZ 85733

WEIR, ALEXANDER, JR., engr.; b. Crossett, Ark., Dec. 19, 1922; s. Alexander and Mary Eloise (Feild) W.; B.S. in Chem. Engring., U. Ark., 1943; M.Ch.E., Poly. Inst. Bklyn., 1946; Ph.D., U. Mich., 1954; certificate U. So. Calif. Grad. Sch. Bus. Adminstrn., 1968; m. Florence Forschner, Dec. 28, 1946; children—Alexander III, Carol Jean, Bruce Richard. Analyst, chemist Am. Cyanamid and Chem. Corp., summers 1941, 42, chem. engr. Am. Cyanamid Co., Stanford Research Labs., 1943-47; with U. Mich., 1948-58, as research asst., research asso., asso. research engr., project supr. Aircraft Propulsion Lab., Engring. Research Inst., 1948-57, lectr. chem. and metall. engring. dept., 1954-56, asst. prof., 1956-58; cons. Ramo-Wooldridge Corp., Los Angeles, 1956-57, mem. tech. staff, 1957-58, with Space Technology Labs., as sect. head, asst. mgr., 1958-60, in charge Atlas Missile Captive test program, 1957-60; asst. to sr. v.p., tech. Northrop Corp. Corporate Office, Beverly Hills, Calif., 1960-62, corporate devel. planning, 1962-64, tech. adviser to pres., 1964-65, corporate sr. sci. and tech. adviser, 1965-67, asst. dir. tech. applications, 1969-70; dir. plans and programs Northrop Corporate Labs., Hawthorne, Calif., 1967-69; prin. scientist for air quality So. Calif. Edison Co., Los Angeles, 76, mgr. chem. systems research and devel., 1976—; rep. Am. Rocket Soc. to Detroit Nuclear Council, 1954-57; chmn. session on chem. reactions Nuclear Sci. and Engring. Congress, Cleve., 1955; U.S. del. AGARD (NATO) Combustion Colloquium, Liege, Belgium, 1955; Western U.S. rep. task force on environmental research and devel. goals Electric Research Council, 1971. Bd. govs., past pres. Civic Union Playa del Rey, chmn. sch., police and fire, nominating, civil def., army liaison coms.; mem. Senate, Westchester YMCA, chmn. Dads sponsoring com., active fund raising; chmn. nominating com. Paseco del Rey Sch. P.T.A., 1961; mem. Los Angeles Mayors Community Adv. Com.; asst. chmn. advancement com., merit badge dean Centinella dist. Los Angeles Area council Boy Scouts Am. Mem. Am. Geophys. Union, Navy League U.S. (v.p. Palos Verdes Peninsula council 1961-62), N.Y. Acad. Scis., Sci. Research Soc. Am., Am. Chem. Soc., Am. Inst. Chem. Engrs., A.A.A.S., Combustion Inst., Air Pollution Control Assn., Assn. U.S. Army, U.S. Power Squadron, Sigma Xi, Phi Kappa Phi, Phi Lambda Upsilon, Alpha Chi Sigma, Lambda Chi Alpha. Club: Santa Monica Yacht. Author: Two and Three Dimensional Flow of Air through Square-Edged Sonic Orifices, 1954; (with R. B. Morrison and T. C. Anderson) Notes on Combustion 1955; also tech. papers. Inventor Weir power plant stack scrubber. Office: So Calif Edison Co PO Box 800 Rosemead CA 91770

WEIR, BETTY JO, real estate/mobile home co. exec.; b. McAlester, Okla., Dec. 12, 1929; d. James Franklin and Alice (Clifton) Woodley; B.A. in Edn., E. Central State Coll., Ada, Okla., 1952; postgrad. Calif. State Coll., Fullerton, San Fernando State Coll., Reseda, Calif., 1968, Wis. State U., Eau Claire, 1969; m. Robert Knowlton Weir, Jan. 9, 1970; children—Robin Ray Carney, James Kevin Carney. Asst. editor Latimer County News Tribune, W. Burton, Okla., 1952-53; high sch. tchr., Okla., 1953-57; owner, operator Youth Shop, Roswell, N.Mex., 1957-63; corp. sec. Antah Aboha Developers, Roswell, 1963-64; account exec. Sta. KGFL, Roswell, 1964-65; tchr. high schs. in Calif. and Minn., 1966-71; Southeastern sales mgr. Mobile Home Communities Denver, 1972-73; mgr. Tavares Cove Mobile Home Sales, W. Palm Beach, Fla., 1972-75, Lord & Lord, Inc., mobile homes and real estate, Stuart, Fla., 1975-76; property mgr. Aristek Corp., also mgr. Aristek Homes, Denver, 1976-78; pres. Housing Profls. Inc., real estate, Denver, 1978—; founder, 1978, since v.p. Shelter Maintenance Corp., Denver. Pres. Little League Aux., Roswell, 1962. Named Forensic Coach of Yr., Mar Monte (Calif.) Speech League, 1970. Mem. Women Owners Bus. Denver (organizer 1980), Nat. Assn. Realtors, Colo. Assn. Realtors. Republican. Baptist. Address: 500 E 84th St Thornton CO 80229

WEIR, JOHN HOWARD, real estate and banking exec.; b. Binghamton, N.Y., Jan. 18, 1925; s. Milton N. and Mildred L. (Young) W.; student pub., pvt. schs.; m. Jamesena G. Hardee, Aug. 31, 1950; children—Deborah Suzanne, John Howard. Gen. mgr. Weir & Sons of Fla., Inc., Boca Raton, 1952-58, 61—; v.p., gen. mgr. Arvida Corp., 1958-61; exec. v.p., dir. Boca Raton Nat. Bank, 1961—; v.p., dir. Castleton Industries, Inc., 1967-70; pres., dir. Citizens Nat. Bank, Boca Raton, 1969—. Trustee, vice chmn. Boca Raton Community Hosp. Served with USNR, 1943-46. Mem. Am. Legion. Republican. Presbyterian. Clubs: Masons; Wings (N.Y.C.); Boca Raton Bath and Tennis, Royal Palm Yacht and Country (Boca Raton). Home: 2840 Banyan Blvd Circle NW Boca Raton FL 33431 Office: 77 E Camino Real Boca Raton FL 33432

WEIR, ROBERT H., lawyer; b. Boston Dec. 7, 1922; s. Abraham and Beatrice (Stern) W.; A.B., Harvard, 1944, LL.B., 1948; m. Ruth Hirsch, July 2, 1954 (dec. Nov. 1965); children—Anthony, David, Michael H.; m. 2d, Sylvia T. Frias, Mar. 29, 1969; children—Nicole F., Daniella F. Admitted to Mass. bar, 1948, Wash. bar, 1952, Calif.

bar, 1957; spl. asst. to atty. gen. U.S. Dept. Justice, Seattle, 1948-53, Washington, 1953-56; practiced in San Jose, also Palo Alto, Calif., 1957—. Instr. taxation of real estate U. Calif. at San Jose and Palo Alto, 1957—; lectr. U. So. Calif. Tax Inst.; instr. taxation, life ins. Chartered Life Underwriters Assn., San Jose, 1960—; Speaker taxation annual meetings Nat. Assn. Real Estate Bds., 1958-60. Mem. prison com. Am. Friends Service Com. Served with AUS, 1942-45. Mem. Am., Santa Clara County bar assns., State Bar Calif., Am. Judicature Soc. Author: Advantages in Taxes, 1960; Taxes Working for You, 1966; How to Make the Most of Depreciation Write Off. Tax columnist Rural Realtor, Chgo., 1959—. Contbr. articles to profl. jours. Office: 93 W Julian St San Jose CA 95150

WEIS, ARTHUR MARTIN, lawyer, aero. engr., mfg. co. exec.; b. Passaic, N.J., Apr. 3, 1925; s. Jerome and Lillie (Feier) W.; B.Aero. Engring., Rensselaer Poly. Inst., 1949; student U.S. Naval Acad.; J.D., Rutgers U., 1968; postgrad. N.Y. U. Sch. Law; m. Bernice Miriam Shapiro, July 29, 1947; 1 son, Eric Matthew. Research engr., project engr., mktg. mgr. Curtiss-Wright Corp., Woodridge, N.J., Quehanna, Pa., 1947-59; mgr. mktg. and sales Nuclear Materials & Equipment Corp., Apollo, Pa., 1959-64; pres. Brevatome-U.S.A., N.Y.C., 1964-67, now dir.; founder, pres. Capintec Inc., Montvale, N.J., 1967—, also dir.; admitted to N.J. bar, 1952; cons. French AEC, Mitsubishi, Italian AEC. Served with USN, 1943-46. Mem. Soc. Nuclear Medicine, Am. Mgmt. Assn., N.J. Bar Assn. Patentee nuclear thermionic generator. Research on analysis of radioisotope calibrators in nuclear medicine. Office: 136 Summit Ave Montvale NJ 07645

WEISBACH, JERRY ARNOLD, pharm. exec.; b. N.Y.C., Dec. 23, 1933; s. Louis and Nettie W.; B.S., Bklyn. Coll., 1955; M.A. (NSF fellow), Harvard U., 1956, Ph.D. (Eastman Kodak Co. fellow), 1959; m. Elise Jane Isaacs, June 15, 1958; children—Michael, David, Deborah. Research chemist Sun Oil, 1959-60, sr. med. chemist, 1960-65, group leader, 1965-67, asso. dir. chemistry, 1967-71; dep. dir. research U.S. Pharm. Products, 1971-77; v.p. research for U.S., Smith, Kline & French Labs., 1977-79; pres. pharm. research div. Warner-Lambert/Parke-Davis, Ann Arbor, Mich., 1979—. Mem. Am. Chem. Soc., Brit. Chem. Soc., N.Y. Acad. Sci., AAAS, Am. Soc. Microbiology, Indsl. Research Inst., Pharm. Mfrs. Assn., Phi Beta Kappa, Sigma Xi. Mem. editorial bd. Japanese Jour. Antibiotics, 1975, Antimicrobiol. Agts. and Chemotherapy, 1976—: contbr. articles to profl. jours. Patentee in field. Office: 2800 Plymouth Rd Ann Arbor MI 48105

WEISBERG, HARRY MICHAEL, leasing co. exec.; b. N.Y.C., Jan. 12, 1932; s. Abe and Helen W.; A.B. in Econs., Marietta Coll., 1954; J.D., Cornell U., 1957; m. Elinor V. Purinton, Feb. 15, 1959; children—Karen, Steven. Admitted to N.Y. bar, 1957; asso. firm Paul V. Rudden, Mineola, N.Y., 1957-65; gen. counsel Nat. Equipment Rental Ltd., Lake Success, N.Y., 1965-67, v.p., gen. counsel, 1967-72, exec. v.p., 1972-73, pres., 1973—; v.p. Tiger Leasing Group Inc., 1974—. Mem. Computer Lessors Assn., Am. Assn. Equipment Lessors. Home: 31 Fairbanks Blvd Woodbury NY 11797 Office: Nat Equipment Rental Ltd 410 Lakeville Rd Lake Success NY 11042

WEISBERG, LEONARD R., physicist, govt. ofcl.; b. N.Y.C., Oct. 17, 1929; s. Emanuel E. and Esther (Raynes) W.; B.A. magna cum laude, Clark U., 1950; M.A., Columbia, 1952; m. Francis Simon, Mar. 23, 1980; children—Glenna Raynes, Orren Beth, Frances Barnett. Research asst. Watson labs. IBM, N.Y.C., 1953-55; with RCA Labs., Princeton, N.J., 1955-71, mem. tech. staff, 1955-66, head research group, 1966-69, dir. semicondr. device research lab., 1969-71; dir. materials research lab. Itek Corp., Lexington, Mass., 1972-74, v.p., dir. central research lab., 1974-75; dir. electronics tech. Dept. Def., Washington, 1975-79; v.p. sci. and tech. Honeywell Inc., Mpls., 1980—. Fellow IEEE; mem. Am. Phys. Soc., Materials Research Soc., Sigma Xi. Contbr. articles to profl. jours. Home: 1225 LaSalle Ave No 1407 Minneapolis MN 55403 Office: Honeywell Plaza Minneapolis MN 55408

WEISENBERGER, JOAN DENISE, investment adviser; b. Indpls., June 30, 1924; d. Francis Grove and Vera (Merz) W.; Ph.B., Barry Coll., Miami, Fla., 1947. Spl. events coordinator L.S. Ayres & Co., dept. store, Indpls., 1950-56; staff writer Indpls. Times, 1956-57; trainee, stockbroker Paine, Webber, Jackson & Curtis, Indpls., 1957-58, registered rep., 1958-65; registered rep. Walston & Co., Indpls., 1965-67; registered rep., mgr. 1st women's investment dept. in Ind., Hornblower & Weeks, 1967-72; organizer, dir. br. Rowland & Co., stockbrokers, Indpls., 1972-73; prin. J.D. Weisenberger & Co., Inc., Indpls., 1973—; pres. J.D. Bishop Assos., Inc., constrn., 1979—. Mem. council Immaculate Heart Mary Ch. Registered investment adviser SEC. Mem. Indpls. Soc. Fin. Analysts, Indpls. Art Mus., Econ. Club Indpls. Roman Catholic. Republican. Clubs: St. Mary's Alumnae; Manor House; Immaculate Heart Mary Women's. Home: 5630 Washington Blvd Indianapolis IN 46220 Office: 6100 N Keystone St Suite 230 Indianapolis IN 46220

WEISER, NORMAN SIDNEY, music pub. co. exec.; b. Mpls., Oct. 1, 1919; s. Simon and Rosa (Davidson) W.; B.A., Northwestern U., 1939; m. Ruth Miller, Mar. 23, 1943; children—Judith Ann, Richard Alan. Reporter, Radio Daily, N.Y.C., 1938-42; reporter, editor Billboard Mag., N.Y.C. and Chgo., 1947-52; pub. Down Beat Mag., Chgo., 1952-59; v.p. United Artists, N.Y.C., 1959-62, 64-68, Twentieth Century Fox, N.Y.C., 1962-64; v.p., dir. European ops., Music div. Paramount, London, 1968-69; v.p., gen. mgr. Chappell Music Co., 1969-73, pres., 1973-77; sr. v.p. Polygram Corp., 1974-77; pres. Sesac, Inc., N.Y.C., 1978—. Bd. dirs. UNICEF. Served to capt. USAAF, 1942-47. Decorated Purple Heart, Commendation medal; recipient Ben Gurion award Bonds for Israel, 1975. Mem. ASCAP (dir. 1974-78), Nat. Music Pubs. Assn. (v.p., dir. 1974-78), Country Music Assn. (chmn. bd. 1976-77). Club: B'nai B'rith. Author: Writers' Radio Theater, 1940; Writers' Radio-TV Theater, 1942; Under the Big Top, 1947; History AAF, World War II, 1947. Home: 58 W 58th St New York NY 10019 Office: 10 Columbus Circle New York NY 10019

WEISNER, MORRIS CLINTON, bus. exec.; b. Durham, N.C., Nov. 21, 1938; s. Thomas Clinton and Eleanor (Morris) W.; B.S.M.E., Duke U., 1960; M.S., Case-Western Res. U., 1964; m. J. Paulette Peters, Jan. 30, 1960; children—Carl, Anne. Mktg. research analyst Babcock & Wilcox Co., Barberton, Ohio, 1960-65; mgr. corp. devel. R.J. Reynolds Industries, Inc., Winston-Salem, N.C., 1965-72; v.p. Brenner Industries, Inc., Winston-Salem, 1972-77; exec. v.p. fin. and adminstrn. Hampshire Designers, Inc., Manchester, N.H., 1977-78; pres., chief operating officer Cormier Hosiery Mills, Inc., Laconia, N.H., 1978-80; sr. v.p. Mgmt. Improvement Corp. Am., Durham, 1980—; chmn. bd. Winston Industries, 1968-69. Former bd. dirs. Forsyth County Hosp. Authority, Forsyth County Health Planning Council, Piedmont Triad Health Planning Council, Winston-Salem Citizens Coalition, Forsyth County Econ. Devel. Corp., Forsyth County Investment Corp. Mem. Fin. Execs. Inst., Nat. Assn. Accts., Fin. Mgmt. Assn. Republican. Episcopalian. Office: 617 Morehead Ave Durham NC 27707

WEISS, FLORENCE, research co. exec.; b. N.Y.C., Nov. 8, 1938; d. Jules J. and Pearl (Finklestein) W.; student (Woodrow Wilson fellow) Columbia, 1959-60; B.A. magna cum laude, Syracuse U., 1959. Econ. research asst. Nat. Econ. Research Assos., N.Y.C., 1960-63, econ. analyst, 1964-68, supr. research, 1968-71, asst. v.p., 1971-73, v.p., 1973-77; mgr. antitrust studies AT&T, N.Y.C., 1977—. Mem. Am. Econ. Assn. (com. on status of women in econs. profession), Nat. Assn. Bus. Economists, Phi Beta Kappa, Phi Kappa Phi. Home: 101 W 12th St New York NY 10011 Office: AT&T 195 Broadway New York NY 10007

WEISS, MAX TIBOR, aerospace co. exec.; b. Hajdunanas, Hungary, Dec. 29, 1922; s. Samuel and Anna (Hornstein) W.; came to U.S., 1929, naturalized, 1936; B.E.E., CCNY, 1943; M.S., M.I.T., 1947; Ph.D., 1950; m. Melitta Newman, June 28, 1953; children—Samuel Harvey, Herschel William, David Nathaniel, Deborah Beth. Research asso. M.I.T., 1946-50; mem. tech. staff Bell Telephone Labs., Holmdel, N.J., 1950-59; asso. head applied physics lab. Hughes Aircraft Co., Culver City, Calif., 1959-60; dir. electronics research lab. The Aerospace Corp., Los Angeles, 1961-63, gen. mgr. labs. div., 1963-67, gen. mgr. electronics and optics div., 1968-78, v.p., gen. mgr. lab. ops., 1978—; asst. mgr. engring. ops. TRW Systems, Redondo Beach, Calif., 1967-68. Served with USNR, 1944-45. Fellow Am. Phys. Soc., IEEE; mem. Sigma Xi. Contbr. articles to physics and electronics jours. Patentee electronics and communications. Home: 2185 Guthrie Dr Los Angeles CA 90034 Office: PO Box 92957 Los Angeles CA 90009

WEISS, PAUL WILLIAM, mfg. co. exec.; b. Elmhurst, Ill., Feb. 22, 1939; s. Arthur John and Clara W.P. (Beckman) W.; m. Norma Jean Weiss, Sept. 3, 1960; children—Sarah, Paul, Faith. With Wyco Tool Co., Chgo., 1960—, East Coast regional sales mgr., 1964—; pres., owner Weiss Enterprises, Emmaus, Pa., 1964—. Served with U.S. Army, 1958-60. Republican. Home: Rt 1 Box 185 Augusta WV 26704 Office: Box 205 229 Adrain St Emmaus PA 18049

WEISS, PETER, business exec. Chmn., chief exec. officer, dir. Compo Industries, Inc., Waltham, Mass. Office: 125 Roberts Rd Waltham MA 02254

WEISSE, FLOYD EARL, elec. engr.; b. Victoria, Tex., July 6, 1947; s. Frank Walter Edward, Jr. and Opal Leona (Caraway) W.; B.S. in Elec. Engring., Tex. A&M U., 1970. With Central Power & Light Co., Corpus Christi, Tex., 1970-75, Brown & Root Inc., 1976-80; transmission/substa. constrn. supr. J.A. Jones Co., Anderson, Tex., 1980—. Registered profl. engr., Tex.; lic. elec. contractor, Fla. Mem. IEEE. Democrat. Baptist. Home: 1400 Plantation Oaks St Apt 853 College Station TX 77840 Office: PO Box 229 Anderson TX 77830

WEISSER, HERMAN MARTIN, investment banker, mortgage broker, hotel corp. exec.; b. N.Y.C., Apr. 26, 1926; s. Israel and Rose (Adler) W.; student City U. N.Y.; B.S. in Aero. Engring, U. Md. Vice pres. Powers Enterprises, Inc., N.Y.C., 1946-55; real estate builder and investor Rose Realty Co. and Daytona Motel Corp., N.Y.C. and Daytona Beach, Fla., 1952-70; pvt. practice fin. cons., motel, investment real estate, motels, 1954—; co-owner, co-operator Desert Inn, Daytona Beach, 1957-67; pres., chmn. bd. Daytona Motel Corp., 1960—; dir. Day Realty Corp., Fla. Security Service, Inc., 800 Orange, Inc., Gwaltney Motels, Inc.; lectr. on accommodations, real estate, financing. Mem. Motel Industry Fla., 1965, bd. dirs., 1966, 67; v.p. Halifax Area Council Assns., 1962, pres., 1963, 64, bd. dirs., 1962-65, chmn. coms., 1963-64; mem. Daytona Beach Mayor's Study Com., 1963, City Mgr.'s Adv. Com., 1965; mem. Daytona Beach Com. of 100. Named to Motel Hall of Fame, Hospitality mag., 1967; recipient Key to City of Daytona Beach, 1966. Mem. A-1-A Motel Assn. (v.p. 1962, pres. 1963-65, dir. 1964-65, Daytona Man of Year 1963), Motel Assn. Am. (dir. 1967-69), Nat. Assn. Rev. Appraisers (sr.), Fla. Assn. Mortgage Brokers (dist. v.p. 1980), Nat. Assn. Mortgage Brokers, Fla. Real Estate Exchangors, Ormond Beach C. of C., Am. Mgmt. Assn., UN Assn. (com. mem. 1976, 77), Nat. Realty Club. Clubs: Kiwanis, Halifax. Author: Manual for Operations and Control of the Complete Resort, 1968; Hotel Sales Promotion, 1969. Home: 1108 Waverly Dr Daytona Beach FL 32018 Office: Box 5631 Daytona Beach FL 32018

WEISSLER, EDWIN MAURICE, electronics co. ofcl.; b. Chgo., Feb. 3, 1932; s. Mark and Rose W.; student U. Ill., 1950-51, B.S. in Elec. Engring., 1961, M.S. in Elec. Engring., 1971; m. Carol Ruth Klein, July 5, 1953; children—Mark, Lisa, Paul, Lynn. Enlisted U.S. Air Force, 1952, commd. lt., 1953, advanced through grades to col., 1973, served as navigator, command pilot, sr. project engr., Europe, Far East, U.S., Arctic, Central and S. Am., ret. 1976; program mgr. TRW Colo. Electronics, Colorado Springs, 1977—. Decorated Legion of Merit, Bronze Star. Mem. IEEE, Armed Forces Communications-Electronics Assn., Am. Mgmt. Assn., Air Force Assn. Republican. Jewish. Home: 6457 Mesedge Ln Colorado Springs CO 80919 Office: 3450 N Nevada Ave Colorado Springs CO 80907

WEISSMAN, CLARK, computer co. exec.; b. Bklyn., June 12, 1934; s. Max and Ella Dorothy (Vogel) W.; B.S. in Aero. Engring., Mass. Inst. Tech., 1956; postgrad U. So. Calif., 1956-57, U. Calif. at Los Angeles, 1957-58, 61-63; m. Elaine; children—Ellin, Hillary, Wendy, Philip, Suzanne, Eric. Systems analyst N.Am. Aviation, Los Angeles, 1956-58; project leader System Devel. Corp., Paramus, N.J., 1958-60, mem. computer research staff, Santa Monica Calif., 1960-69, mgr. research and devel. dept., 1969-71, chief technologist, 1971-73, 76—, mgr. computer security dept., 1973-76, dep. mgr. research and devel. div., 1976—, mgr. ind. research and devel. program, 1976—. Instr., U. Calif. at Los Angeles, 1966-71. Cons., U.S. Govt., 1971-72, 80; mem. adv. com. to Sec. Commerce on Computer Security, 1974-77; mem. computer security panel Adv. Research Project Agy., Dept. Def., 1975—; bd. dirs. Los Angeles Songmakers, Inc., 1978-80, pres., 1979-80. Mem. Assn. Computing Machinery (editor operating systems dept. of commn. 1973-75), Fedn. Am. Scientist, AAAS, IEEE, Research Soc. Am. Author: Lisp 1.5 Primer, 1967, Japanese edit., 1971. Home: 4401 Trancas Pl Tarzana CA 91356 Office: 2500 Colorado Ave Santa Monica CA 90406

WEISSMAN, GEORGE, tobacco co. exec.; b. N.Y.C., July 12, 1919; s. Samuel and Rose (Goldberg) W.; student Townsend Harris Prep. Sch., 1933-35; B.B.A., City Coll. N.Y., 1939; postgrad. N.Y. U., U. Ill., 1942; m. Mildred Stregack, June 4, 1944; children—Paul Jonathan, Ellen Victoria, Daniel Mark. Editor, Raritan Valley News, also reporter Newark Star Ledger, Newark Sunday Call, 1939-41; publicist Brit. Am. Ambulance Corps, 1941-42; publicity and advt. Samuel Goldwyn Prodns., N.Y.C., 1946-48; public relations account exec. Benjamin Sonnenberg, N.Y.C., 1948-52; asst. to pres. Philip Morris, Inc., N.Y.C., 1952, v.p. 1953-59, dir. mktg., 1957-60, exec. v.p., 1959-66, pres., chief operating officer, 1967-73, vice chmn., 1973-78, chmn., chief exec. officer, 1978—, dir., 1958—, mem. exec. com., 1964—; chmn. bd., chief exec. officer Philip Morris Internat., 1960-66; dir. Miller Brewing Co., Chem. N.Y. Corp., Chem. Bank, Avnet Inc. Mem. Bus. Com. for Arts, Conf. Bd.; bd. visitors CCNY; chancellor's adv. com. City U. N.Y.; bd. dirs. Lincoln Center, Lincoln Center Film Soc., Econ. Devel. Council; trustee Lincoln Center Fund, Whitney Mus. Am. Art, Com. Econ. Devel., Baruch Coll. Fund; mem. Swarthmore Coll. Council. Served with U.S.S. Horace A. Bass, APD 124. Decorated comdr. Order of Merit (Italy); recipient Exec. of Yr. award Nat. Assn. Tobacco Distbrs., 1954; award Fedn. Jewish Philanthropies, 1963. Mem. N.Y. C. of C. and Industry (dir.), CCNY Alumni Assn. (recipient Townsend Harris medal 1968, medallion 1973), Beta Gamma Sigma. Office: Philip Morris Inc 100 Park Ave New York NY 10017

WEISSMAN, MORTON ARTHUR, real estate broker; b. Pitts., July 19, 1918; s. Felix A. and Radie W.; B.S., U. Pitts., 1940; m. Elaine R. Weissman, Oct. 12, 1968. Mgr. luggage dept. Rosenbaum Co., Pitts., 1952-59; real estate broker, v.p. indsl. dept. Arnheim & Neely, Inc., Pitts., 1960—; instr. real estate Allegheny Community Coll., Weaver Sch. Real Estate, U. Pitts. Bd. dirs. United Cerebral Palsy, Pitts. Served with Med. Service Corps, AUS, 1941-46, also Korean War. Mem. Nat. Assn. Realtors, Greater Pitts. Bd. Realtors, Soc. Indsl. Realtors (nat. dir., pres. Western Pa. chpt. 1974, 81), Omicron Delta Kappa, Pi Lambda Phi. Home: 128 N Craig St Apt 605 Pittsburgh PA 15213 Office: Arnheim & Neely Inc 820 Grant Bldg Pittsburgh PA 15219

WEISZ, WILLIAM JULIUS, electronics co. exec.; b. Chgo., Jan. 8, 1927; s. George R. and Minnie (Riff) W.; B.S. in Elec. Engring., Mass. Inst. Tech., 1948. With Motorola, Inc., Chgo., then Schaumburg, Ill., 1948—, exec. v.p., 1969-70, pres., 1970—, chief operating officer, 1972—, vice chmn. bd., 1980—, also dir.; pres. Motorola Communications Internat., 1966-69, Motorola Communications and Electronics, Inc., 1966-69. Mem. exec. com. land mobile adv. com. to FCC. Com. chmn. Cub Scout pack Evanston council Boy Scouts Am., 1960-62. Trustee Mass. Inst. Tech., also chmn. elec. engring. and computer scis. vis. com., mem. Sloan Sch. vis. com.; mem. devel. com. MIT Corp., 1970—. Served with USNR, 1945-46. Recipient award of merit Nat. Electronics Conf. Fellow IEEE (past nat. chmn. vehicular communications group); mem. Electronic Industries Assn. (past chmn. bd. govs.), Econ. Club Chgo., Sigma Xi, Tau Beta Pi, Eta Kappa Nu, Pi Lambda Phi. Club: M.I.T. (dir.) (Chgo.). Office: 1303 E Algonguin Rd Schaumburg IL 60196

WEITHAS, WILLIAM V., JR., advt. agy. exec. Pres., chief operating officer SSC&B Advt., Inc., N.Y.C. Office: One Dag Hammarskjold Plaza New York NY 10017*

WEITHERS, JOHN GREGORY, business exec.; b. Chgo., 1933; ed. U. Notre Dame, DePaul U. With Midwest Stock Exchange, 1958—, sec., 1962, v.p., 1963, sr. v.p., sec., 1967, exec. v.p., 1972, pres., 1980—. Office: Midwest Stock Exchange Inc 120 S La Salle St Chicago IL 60603*

WEIZER, EDWARD CARL, stockbroker; b. Trenton, N.J., May 10, 1919; s. Otto Ernst and Veronica (Mandl) W.; certificate Wharton Sch. U. Pa., 1940; mgmt. student George Washington U., 1951; grad. Inst. Investment Banking, U. Pa., 1955; m. Diana Fraser Dilatush, Jan. 14, 1954; children—Barbara Lynn, Diana Darryl, Leslie Ann, Edward Carl. With Merrill Lynch, Pierce, Fenner & Smith, 1940—, br. office mgr., Trenton, 1952-56, resident mgr., v.p., Newark, 1957—, also dir. Vice pres. Jr. Achievement, Trenton, 1956-57; vice chmn. Union County Coordinating Agy. for Higher Edn., 1968-71; gen. campaign chmn. Robert Treat council Boy Scouts Am., 1972-73; mem. N.J. Securities Adv. Commn., 1970—; mem. N.J. Republican State Fin. Com., 1968-73; trustee United Community Fund of Essex and West Hudson, Boys' Clubs, Newark, N.J. Hist. Soc., United Hosps. Newark, 1973-76; mem. pres.'s council Monmouth Coll. Served to maj. USAAF, 1941-45; ETO; with Air Staff, Washington, 1951-52. Mem. Greater Newark C. of C. (dir.), Sales Execs. Club of No. N.J., N.J. Bond Club. Clubs: Essex, Downtown (Newark); Baltusrol Golf (Springfield, N.J.); Rock Spring (West Orange, N.J.); Beacon Hill (Summit, N.J.); 200 (Essex County), Rotary. Home: 100 Whittredge Rd Summit NJ 07901 Office: Gateway 1 Newark NJ

WEKESSER, ROBERT ALEXANDER, banker; b. Lincoln, Nebr., Jan. 2, 1919; s. Alexander and Minnie Mae (Kleinschmidt) W.; B.S., U. Nebr., 1941; M.S. in Banking, Columbia U., 1942; m. Edith Elaine Knight, Dec. 12, 1943; children—Ann, Robert Alexander, Edward, Thomas. Various positions to sr. v.p. Nat. Bank of Commerce, Lincoln, 1946-67; pres. Evergreen Corp., 2d Evergreen Corp., Prairie Home, Inc., and Farmers Ins. Agy., Inc., Lincoln, 1959—; pres. Farmers State Bank, Sargent, Nebr., Farmers & Mchts. Bank, Comstock, Nebr.; chmn. bd. dirs. Bank of Panama, Farmers Bank, Prairie Home, Nebr. Chmn. S.E. Community Coll.; former pres. Lincoln Sch. Bd. Served to lt. USNR, 1943-46. Mem. Nebr. Ind. Bankers Assn., Ind. Bankers Assn., Bank Mktg. Assn., Beta Gamma Sigma. Republican. Presbyterian. Clubs: Masons (trustee Grand Lodge State of Nebr.), Shriners. Home and Office: 5301 A St Lincoln NE 68510

WELCH, HERBERT EUGENE, physicist, educator; b. Gainesville, Tex., Aug. 22, 1933; s. John Arthur and Virginia Pearl (White) W.; B.S., Tex. Tech. U., 1965, M.S., 1968, Ph.D., 1969; m. Nedra Jo Thorn, Sept. 15, 1951; children—Randy Eugene, Pamela Denise. Electronics technician KCBD-TV, Lubbock, Tex., Nunn Electric Supply Corp., Lubbock, 1948-63; research asst. Tex. Tech. U., 1963-64, 65-68; sr. physicist, dir., product devel. Collins Radio Group, Rockwell Internat., Richardson, Tex., 1969—; adj. prof. U. Tex. at Arlington, 1973—. Chmn. programs Richardson Orchestra Club, 1971, v.p., 1972, pres., 1973; coach Little League Baseball-Football, 1960-71. Served with USNR, 1951-58. NDEA fellow, 1966-68. Mem. IEEE (program com., session chmn. 1974, program chmn. 1975, edn. chmn. 1976), Am. Phys. Soc., AAUP, AAAS. Democrat. Baptist. Patentee color TV, tape systems. Home: 412 Fairview Richardson TX 75081 Office: 1200 N Alma Rd Richardson TX 75080

WELCH, JOHN FRANCIS, JR., elec. mfg. co. exec.; b. Peabody, Mass., Nov, 19, 1935; s. John Francis and Grace (Andrews) W.; B.S. in Chem. Engring., U. Mass., 1957; M.S., U. Ill., 1958, Ph.D., 1960; m. Carolyn B. Osburn, Nov. 21, 1959; children—Katherine, John, Anne, Mark. With Gen. Electric Co., Fairfield, Conn., 1960—, v.p., 1972, v.p., group exec. components and materials group, 1973-77, sr. v.p., sector exec., consumer products and services sector, 1977-79, vice chmn., exec. officer, 1979-81, chmn. bd., 1981—, also dir.; dir. Gen. Electric Credit Corp. Recipient award U. Mass. Engring. Alumni Assn., 1974. Patentee in field. Office: 3135 Easton Turnpike Fairfield CT 06431

WELCH, LOUIE, assn. exec.; b. Lockney, Tex., Dec. 9, 1918; s. Gilford E. and Nora (Shackelford) W.; B.A. magna cum laude, Abilene Christian Coll., 1940; m. Iola Faye Cure, Dec. 17, 1940; children—Guy Lynn, Gary Dale, Louie Gilford, Shannon Austin, Tina Joy. Pres. Louie Welch & Co., Inc., real estate and investment brokers; pres. Houston C. of C., 1974—; dir. Gibraltar Savs., Imperial Corp.; trustee Kanaly Trust Co. Pres., Tex. Mcpl. League, 1959-60, U.S. Conf. Mayors, 1972-73; councilman-at-large City of Houston, 1950-52, 56-62, mayor, 1963-73. Trustee, Abilene Christian U.; bd. dirs. Goodwill Industries, Houston Symphony, Houston Grand Opera, Energy Research and Edn. Found., Named Key Houstonian, 1973, Distinguished Eagle Scout, 1974; recipient Kennedy Peace medal, 1971, Internat. B'nai B'rith Humanitarian award, 1973, Am. Med. Center Humanitarian award, 1975. Home: The Briar Pl 803 21 Briar Hollow Houston TX 77027 Office: Houston C of C Houston TX 77001

WELCH, NATHANIEL, trade assn. exec.; b. Selma, Ala., Mar. 23, 1920; s. William Pressley and Lucille (Burt) W.; A.B. cum laude, Furman U., 1942; postgrad. U. N.C., 1942, U. Ala., 1946; m. Gloria Constance Ljunglof, Sept. 11, 1948; children—Gustaf Lindstrom, Shannon Constance, Melanie Rebecca. Advt. rep. So. Farm & Home Mag., Montgomery, Ala., 1947-52; account exec. WABT, Birmingham, Ala., 1952-53; v.p. sales Orradio Industries, Opelika, Ala., 1953-58; mgr. mktg. Orr div. Ampex Corp., Opelika, 1958-60; exec. v.p. Electronics for Edn., Kensington, Md., 1961-63; fed. rep. So. Interstate Nuclear Bd., Atlanta, 1963-68; exec. dir. Community Relations Commn., Atlanta, 1968-74; exec. v.p. Ga. Freight Bur., 1974—. Mem. gov. com. Investigation Voter Registration of Vets, State of Ala., 1950; mem. Nat. Citizens Com. for Community Relations, 1964-68; bd. dirs. Ala. Council Human Relations, 1959-66, pres., 1965-66; bd. dirs. So. Region Council, 1962-70; mem. Charter Commn. Democratic Party Ga., 1974-75; alt. del. Dem. Nat. Conv., 1956; chmn. Urban Action Inc., North Ga. Conf. United Methodist Ch., 1975-78; mem. alumni bd. dirs. Furman U., 1967-72; exec. com. Nat. Small Shipments Traffic Conf., 1976-78. ICC practitioner, Mem. U.S. Ry. Assn. (dir. 1978—), So. Traffic League (bd. govs. 1980—), Nat. Indsl. Traffic League, Ga. Am. Humanics Bd. Clubs: Rotary, Commerce (Atlanta). Home: 2112 Castleway Dr Atlanta GA 30345 Office: 1622 Healey Bldg Atlanta GA 30303

WELKER, CAROL EVALEE, banker; b. Cambridge, Ohio, Sept. 11, 1940; d. Carl Everett and Elsie (Hahn) W.; B.S. in Landscape Architecture, Ohio State U., 1963, M.S., 1970; M.B.A., Claremont Coll., 1977. Program cons. Calif. Gov.'s Office, Sacramento, 1970-73; v.p. engring. Lampman & Assos., Pomona, Calif., 1973-75; mgmt. cons. Inst. Advanced Systems, Pomona, 1976; account officer Bank of Am., Los Angeles, 1976-78, v.p., planning officer, 1978-80, v.p., San Francisco, 1980—; cons. in field. HUD fellow, 1966. Unitarian. Home: 1825 Scott St San Francisco CA 94115 Office: 555 California St San Francisco CA 94137

WELLBROCK, WILLIAM D., paint, coatings and wallcovering distbg. co. exec.; b. Bklyn., Feb. 18, 1939; s. Richard and Helen W.; B.S. in Bus. Adminstrn., Norwich U., 1962; m. Samantha Barbara Hart, Sept. 3, 1960; children—Samantha Lee, Deborah Ann, Amy Lynn. Mgr. pigments group Celanese Coating Co. div. Celanese Corp., Louisville, 1975-77; corp. v.p. mktg. Grow Group, Inc., N.Y.C., 1977-78, exec. v.p. U.S. Paint div., St. Louis, 1978-79; pres., chief exec. officer The Gilman Co., Inc., Chattanooga, 1979—. Mem. allocations com. United Fund, Chattanooga. Mem. Nat. Paint Conf. (trade sales steering com.), NAM, Tenn. Mfrs. Assn., So. Paint Soc. Republican. Episcopalian. Clubs: Chattanooga Golf and Country, Walden (Chattanooga); Media (St. Louis). Office: 540 McCallie Ave Suite 300 Chattanooga TN 37401

WELLER, HARRY DEETS, JR., indsl. mfg. co. exec.; b. Lancaster, Pa., Feb. 26, 1913; s. Harry Deets and Sara Ada (Stively) W.; B.S., Franklin-Marshall Coll., 1934; m. Betty Jane Allenbaugh, Apr. 6, 1940; children—Harry Deets III, Charles D., Judith Lynne. With Firestone Tire & Rubber Co., Akron, Ohio, 1935-48, 49-52; pres. Gengras Motors, Hartford, 1948-49; with White Motor Co., Cleve., 1952—, lease sales div., asst. regional mgr., asst. to v.p. sales, regional mgr., N.Y.C., regional v.p., v.p. sales, v.p. marketing, exec. v.p. sales and product planning; now pres. truck group White Consol. Industries, Inc., Cleve., also pres. Hupp, Inc. div.; dir. Great Lakes Diesel Corp. Trustee, Cleve. Health Mus. Mem. Pvt. Truck Council Am. (dir.), Am. Ordnance Assn., Soc. Automotive Engrs., Cleve. C. of C., Transp. Assn. Am. (dir.), Phi Kappa Psi. Presbyn. Mason. Clubs: Mayfield Country (past pres.), Union, Pepper Pike Golf, Cleveland Athletic (Cleve.); Pine Lake Trout Farm (Chagrin Falls, Ohio); Sea Pines Plantation (Hilton Head, S.C.). Home: 2728 Claythorne Rd Shaker Heights OH 44120 also 344 Greenwood Dr Hilton Head Island SC 29928 Office: White Consol Industries 11770 Berea Rd Cleveland OH 44111

WELLIN, KEITH SEARS, investment banker; b. Grand Rapids, Mich., Aug. 13, 1926; s. Elmer G. and Ruth (Chamberlin) W.; B.A., Hamilton Coll., 1950; M.B.A., Harvard U., 1952; m. Carol D. Woodhouse, Sept. 5, 1951 (dec. 1970); children—Cynthia, Peter, Marjorie; m. 2d, Ariane Y. Reed, July 6, 1974. With E.F. Hutton & Co., Inc., Chgo., 1952-71, regional v.p., dir., 1962-66, pres., N.Y.C., 1967-71, vice chmn., 1970-71; sr. v.p., treas., dir. Reynolds Securities, Inc., 1971-74, pres., dir., 1974-77; exec. v.p., dir. Dean Witter Reynolds Orgn. Inc., N.Y.C., 1978—; chmn., chief exec. officer Dean Witter Reynolds InterCapital Inc.; former gov., mem. exec. com. Assn. Stock Exchange Firms; former gov. Securities Industry Assn. Vice chmn. Christian Herald and its affiliated charities; former trustee Hamilton Coll., chmn. investment com.; former trustee N.Y.C. Police Found. Served to 2d lt., inf. AUS, 1945-47. Clubs: Chgo.; Racquet and Tennis, Recess, Blind Brook, Knickerbocker (N.Y.C.); Clove Valley Rod and Gun (N.Y.). Home: 22 Round Hill Club Rd Greenwich CT 06830 Office: 130 Liberty St New York NY 10006

WELLINGTON, ROBERT HALL, mfg. co. exec.; b. Atlanta, July 4, 1922; s. Robert H. and Ernestine V. (Vossbrinck) W.; B.S. in Mech. Engring., Northwestern Tech. Inst., 1943; M.S. in Bus. Adminstrn., U. Chgo., 1958; m. Marjorie Jarchow, Nov. 15, 1947; children—Charles R., Robert H., Christian J., Jeanne L. With Griffin Wheel Co. subs. Amsted Industries, Inc., Chgo., 1946-61, asst. to pres., 1958-60, v.p., 1960-61; v.p. Amsted Industries, Inc., Chgo., 1961-74, exec. v.p., 1974-80, pres., 1980—, chief exec. officer, 1981—; dir. L.E. Myers Co., Chgo., Signode Corp., Chgo. Served to lt. USN, 1943-46. Clubs: Chgo., Chgo. Athletic Assn., Econ., Mid-Am. Office: 3700 Prudential Plaza Chicago IL 60601

WELLS, ALAN KELLER, fin. cons. co. exec.; b. Decatur, Ill., June 14, 1945; s. Arthur M. and Louise K. Wells; B.A. in Econs., DePauw U., 1967; M.B.A., Dartmouth Coll., 1973; m. Josephine A. Muzzy, June 3, 1973; children—Erin, Blair Arthur, Grandel Robert. Vice pres., corp. sec. Niederhoffer, Cross & Zeckhauser, Inc., N.Y.C., 1973-77, also dir.; pres., treas. Select A Spring Corp., Jersey City, 1975-77, also dir., pres., treas. Multi-Parts Inc., Hamilton, Ill., 1975-77, also dir.; pres. Bollinger, Wells, Lett & Co., Inc., N.Y.C., 1977—. Mem. exec. com. Muscular Dystrophy Assn. N.Y.C. Served to lt. U.S. Navy, 1967-71. Club: Dartmouth of N.Y. Home: 61 Glenwood Rd Upper Montclair NJ 07043 Office: Suite 303E 200 Park Ave New York NY 10017

WELLS, CHARLES W(ESLEY), real estate exec.; b. Petersburg, Va., Oct. 6, 1893; s. Beauregard Lee and Bessie (Adams) W.; student pub. and pvt. schs.; m. Laura Booth Tucker, Oct. 7, 1924. Owner, Wells Realty; pres. Petersburg Holding Corp., 1942—, Mt. Erin Corp., 1948—; pres. Sycamore Shopping Center, Inc., 1956. Served in World War I. Mem. Am. Legion. Mason (Shriner), Kiwanian. Home: 1622 Westover Ave Walnut Hill Petersburg VA 23803 Office: 36-40 S Union St PO Box 790 Petersburg VA 23803

WELLS, DAMON, JR., investment co. exec.; b. Houston, May 20, 1937; s. Damon and Margaret Corinne (Howze) W.; B.A. magna cum laude, Yale, 1958; B.A., Oxford U., 1964, M.A., 1968; Ph.D., Rice U., 1968. Owner, chief exec. officer Damon Wells Interests, Houston, 1958—. Bd. dirs. Child Guidance Center of Houston, 1970-73, Jefferson Davis Assn., 1973—; trustee Christ Ch. Cathedral Endowment Fund, 1970-73, Kinkaid Sch., 1972—. Mem. Sr. Common Room, Pembroke Coll., Oxford U., 1972—; trustee Camp Allen retreat of Episc. Diocese of Tex., 1976-78; founding bd. dirs. Brit. Inst. U.S., 1979—. Mem. English-Speaking Union (nat. dir. 1970-72, v.p. Houston br. 1966-73), Phi Beta Kappa, Pi Sigma Alpha. Episcopalian. Clubs: Coronado, Houston Country, Houston; Yale (N.Y.C.). Author: Stephen Douglas: The Last Years, 1857-1861, 1971. Home: 1861 Post Oak Park Dr Houston TX 77027 Office: River Oaks Bank Bldg Suite 806 2001 Kirby Dr Houston TX 77019

WELLS, DONALD THOMAS, electronics mfg. co. exec.; b. Henderson, Ky., Dec. 26, 1931; s. Melvin Jackson and Laura Bell Wells; B.S. in Fin. and Mktg., U. Ky., 1957; postgrad. Ind. U., 1957-59; m. Josephine Gibbs, June 12, 1954; children—Renetta G., Kathy L. Asst. sec. treas. Von Hoffmann Press, Inc., St. Louis, 1963-68; gen. mgr., treas. Amelco Leasing Corp., St. Louis, 1968-71; group controller Interlake Steel Co., Dallas, 1971-73; corp. controller, asst. sec. treas. Multi-Amp Corp., Dallas, 1973—; chmn. bd., treas. Prairie Creek Bottery Inc.; dir. Wells, Inc.; lectr., fin. cons. Deacon, office of adv. council, chmn. budget com., chmn. fin. com. Baptist Ch. Served with U.S. Army, 1951-53. Mem. Nat. Assn. Accountants, Am. Mgmt. Assn., C. of C. Clubs: Kiwanis, Masons. Office: Multi-Amp Corp 4271 Bronze Way Dallas TX 75237

WELLS, HARRY KENNADY, food processing co. exec.; b. Balt., Sept. 4, 1922; s. Clifton Kennady and Ruth Jones (Coale) W.; B.S. in Mech. Engring., U. Md., 1943; m. Lois Luttrell, Sept. 8, 1946; children—Katherine Wells Witbeck, Robert Grayson, David Kennady. Asst. plant supr. McCormick & Co., Balt., 1946-50, plant supr., 1950-56; plant mgr. Schilling div., San Francisco, 1956-64, asst. gen. mgr. div., 1964-66, v.p., gen. mgr. div., 1966-68, v.p. corp., 1968-69, pres., 1969-79, chief exec. officer, 1970—, chmn., 1977—, also dir.; chmn. McCormick de Mexico S.A., Mexico City, McCormick/Lion, Ltd., Tokyo; dir. Gilroy Foods, Inc., Calif., McCormick Properties, Inc., Hunt Valley, Balt. Gas & Electric Co., Inc., PHH Group, Inc., Hunt Valley, Md. Nat. Bank, Balt., Loyola Fed. Savs. & Loan Assn., Balt., Armstrong World Industries, Inc., Lancaster, Pa., McCormick Foods (U.K.) Ltd., London, McCormick Foods Australia. Chmn., Md. State Bd. for Higher Edn., Annapolis; bd. dirs. Nat. Assn. for Sport and Phys. Edn., Washington; mem. nat. adv. council Salvation Army; trustee St. Joseph Hosp., Towson, Md. Served to lt. USN, 1943-46. Recipient Disting. Engring. Alumnus award U. Md., 1976. Mem. Food and Drug Law Inst. (chmn. 1980-81, trustee), Grocery Mfrs. Am. (dir.), NAM (past chmn., dir.), Am. Soc. Plant Engrs., Alpha Tau Omega. Methodist. Clubs: Balt. Country, Center, Maryland, Hunt Valley Golf, Towson, Seaview Country, Stone Harbor Yacht, San Francisco World Trade, San Francisco Commercial, Masons (32 deg.), K.T., Shriners. Home: 1311 Gateshead Rd Towson MD 21204 Office: 11350 McCormick Rd Hunt Valley MD 21031

WELLS, JAMES DORING, food co. exec.; b. Quincy, Mass., July 9, 1920; s. Harry Clement and Mabel Eleanor (Doring) W.; A.B., Dartmouth Coll., 1943, M.B.A., 1947; m. Jane Augusta Page, Jan. 30, 1944; children—Susan Jane Wells Ferrante, Nancy Jane Wells Silvester. With Procter & Gamble Distbg. Co., 1947-53; with Wm. Underwood Co., Westwood, Mass., 1953-73, 78—, exec. v.p., 1965-73, pres., 1978—, chief exec. officer, 1980—; pres. Colombo Inc., Metheun, Mass., 1973-78; dir. Superior Pet Foods Inc., Baybank Norfolk County Trust Co. Served to lt. USNR, 1943-46. Republican. Clubs: Weston Golf, Bald Peak Colony, Union, Cumberland. Home: 110 Oxbow Rd Weston MA 02193

WELLS, JAMES THOMAS, real estate mgmt. and cons. co. exec.; b. Salt Lake City, Mar. 24, 1939; s. Calvin Y. and Arvilla (Thomas) W.; B.A. in Econs., U. Utah, 1964, M.B.A. in Finance and Accounting, 1966; grad. Calif. Assn. Realtors Inst., 1976; m. Luana Pearl Sharp, July 7, 1967; children—Rebecca, Elizabeth, Rachel, Jamie, Eden, Don Carlos. Financial analyst corp. staff, budget adminstr. RCA, N.Y.C., 1966-67, Los Angeles, 1967-68; mgr. third-party leasing and finance Xerox Data Systems, Inc., El Segundo, Calif., 1968-70; v.p. finance and adminstrn. Holstein Industries, Inc., Costa Mesa, Calif., 1971-72; pres. J.T. Wells & Assos., real estate cons., Costa Mesa, 1973—; dir. Investors Realty, Inc., Salt Lake City; cons. Boise Cascade Bldg. Co., Los Angeles, 1970, Am. Mobilehome Co., Los Angeles, 1970-71. Mem. Financial Execs. Inst., Nat., Calif. realtors assns., Assn. M.B.A. Execs., Interstake Bus. and Profl. Assn., Lambda Delta Sigma, Alpha Kappa Psi. Mem. Ch. of Jesus Christ of Latter-day Saints. Author: Recent Real Estate Activity. Address: 1797 Oriole Dr Costa Mesa CA 92626

WELLS, MICHAEL TREVOR, communications co. exec.; b. London, Apr. 6, 1928; came to U.S., 1959; s. George and Lilian Grace (Williams) W.; ed. Eng.; m. Mary Farkass, July 16, 1960; children—Lilian Grace, Michael Anthony. Sr. auditor Haskins & Sells, Paris, France, 1952-55; audit mgr. Price Waterhouse, Sao Paulo, Brazil, 1956-59; with ITT, 1959—, area gen. mgr., S.Am., Buenos Aires, 1967-75, exec. dir. external relations ITT World Communications Inc., N.Y.C., 1976—. Served with Royal Arty., 1946-48. Fellow Inst. Chartered Accts. Eng.; mem. Canadian Inst. Chartered Accts. (Ont.), Assn. Cert. Accts. (U.K.). Episcopalian. Clubs: Royal Auto (London); Met. (N.Y.C.); Jockey Argentino (Buenos Aires); Jockey Brasileiro (Rio de Janeiro). Contbr. articles and papers to profl. lit. Office: 67 Broad St New York NY 10004

WELLS, PETER GERALD, mfg. co. exec.; b. Clacton-on-Sea, Eng., Mar. 29, 1929; came to Can., 1966, naturalized, 1972; s. Bert Lawrence and Doris Winifred (Keen) W.; M.S., Enfield Tech. Coll., London, 1954; postgrad. Cranfield Aero. Coll., 1956; m. Barbara Wells, Dec. 20, 1952; children—Christopher, Alison, Helen, Robyn. Indsl. engr. G.W.G. Co., Edmonton, Alta., Can., 1966-70; plant mgr. Formfit Internat., Toronto, Ont., 1970-73; v.p. Imperial Leather Co., Winnipeg, Man., 1973-77; prodn. dir. Monarch Wear Ltd., Montreal, Que., Can., 1977—. Served with RAF, 1947-49. Mem. Am. Mgmt. Assn., Am. Inst. Indsl. Engrs. Baptist. Home: 428 Darwin Crescent Thunder Bay ON P7B 5S2 Canada Office: 1202 5800 Rue St Denis Montreal PQ Canada

WELLS, PETER SCOVILLE, stock exchange ofcl.; b. N.Y.C., Apr. 25, 1938; s. Jonathan Godfrey and Eleanore Shannon (Scoville) W.; student U. Va., 1956-58, Columbia U., 1959-61; m. Patricia Ann Trent, Dec. 8, 1973; 1 son by previous marriage, Peter Scoville. Asst. to controller Laird & Co., N.Y.C., 1961-63; asst. to partner charge ops. Goldman Sachs, N.Y.C., 1963-64; mgr. new bus. dept. B.J. Herkimer Co., N.Y.C., 1964-67; divisional policy and procedures adminstr. Paine, Webber, Jackson & Curtis, Inc., N.Y.C., 1967-70, asst. to exec. cashier, 1970-73, asst. v.p., mgr. employment services, adminstr. equal employment opportunity, 1973-80; personnel officer, exec. recruiter N.Y. Stock Exchange, 1980—. Bd. dirs. Harlem Interfaith Counseling Service. Cons. human affairs Gracie Sq. Hosp.; adv. bd. Mayor's Office for Handicapped. Served with AUS, 1958. Mem. Employment Mgmt. Assn., Securities Industries Assn., Wall St. Employment Mgrs., Uptown C. of C., N.Y.C. C. of C., SAR, Phi Kappa Psi. Home: 449 E 78th St New York NY 10021 Office: 11 Wall St New York NY 10021

WELLS, WILLIAM HENDERSON, pollution engring. co. exec.; b. Larbert, Scotland, Oct. 30, 1922; s. William Henderson and Agnes (MacAulay) W.; came to U.S., 1973, naturalized, 1977; engring. certificate Stirlingshire Edn. Authority, 1939; m. Dorothy Irene Keeble, May 6, 1943; children—Kenneth William, Carol-Anne. Tech. mgr. Reunert & Lenz Ltd., Johannesburg, South Africa, 1952-57; works-sales mgr. J. Brockhouse S.A. Ltd., Johannesburg, 1957-66; mgr., dir. Engelhard Industries, Johannesburg, 1966-73; gen. mgr. Engelhard Exhaust Controls Inc., Union, N.J., 1973—. Served with RAF, 1940-46. Mem. Soc. Aircraft Engrs., Instrument and Control Soc. South Africa, Air Pollution Control Assn., Denver Mining Club, Material Handling Inst., Union C. of C., Am. Mining Congress, Soc. Mining Engrs. Home: 35 Lenape Trail Chatham NJ 07928 Office: 2655 Route 22 W Union NJ 07083

WELPTON, SHERMAN SEYMOUR, III, investment banker; b. Omaha, June 6, 1934; s. Sherman Seymour and Dorothy Virginia (Felber) W.; B.A., Stanford U., 1956, M.A., 1957; children—Marie Elizabeth, Sherman Blakemore. With Sutro & Co., San Francisco, 1961-71, Drexel Firestone, San Francisco, 1971-73; with Kidder, Peabody, San Francisco, 1973-77; v.p. R.L. Crary, San Francisco, 1977-78, Paine Webber, 1978—. Active Easter Seal Found., Lincoln Child Center Found. Served with U.S. Army, 1958-60. Mem. Guardsmen of San Francisco, Phi Gamma Delta. Episcopalian. Club: Bohemian. Home: 222 Sunnyside Ave Piedmont CA 94611 Office: 555 California St San Francisco CA 94104

WELS, RICHARD HOFFMAN, lawyer; b. N.Y.C., May 3, 1913; s. Isidor and Belle (Hoffman) W.; A.B., Cornell, 1933; J.D., Harvard, 1936; naval student U. Ariz., 1944; m. Marguerite Samet, Dec. 12, 1954; children—Susan, Amy Elizabeth. Admitted to N.Y. bar, 1936; spl. asst. dist. atty. N.Y. County, 1936-37; asso. Handel & Panuch, N.Y.C., 1937-38; mem. legal staff, asst. to chmn. SEC, Washington, 1938-42; spl. asst. to atty. gen. U.S. and spl. asst. U.S. atty., 1941-42; spl. counsel Com. Naval Affairs, U.S. Ho. of Reps., 1943, Sea-Air Commn., Nat. Fedn. Am. Shipping, 1946; partner firm Moss, Wels & Marcus, 1946-63, Sulzberger, Wels & Marcus, N.Y.C., 1968-72, Moss, Wels & Marcus, 1972-79, Sperry, Weinberg, Wels, Waldman & Rubenstein, 1979—; gen. counsel Bowling Proprs. Assn. Am., Acad. Psychoanalysis, N.Y. State Bowling Proprs. Assn.; v.p., dir. Petronav, Inc.; dir. Broadcast Data Base, Inc., H-R TV Inc. Commr. Interprofl. Commn. on Marriage and Divorce. Chmn. bd. trustees Bleuler Psychotherapy Center; chmn. bd. govs. Islands Research Found.; trustee, sec. William Alanson White Inst. Psychiatry, N.Y.C., 1946—; vice chmn. Am. Parents Com., Am. Jewish Com. Trustee, chmn. bd. Daytop Village, Inc.; bd. dirs. Nine Eleven Park, Inc. Served as ensign to lt. USNR, 1942-46; mem. staff Under Sec. Forrestal, 1943-44; PTO, 1944-46. Mem. Am. (chmn. ann. meeting planning com. family law sect.), Fed., N.Y. State (chmn. family law sect.) bar assns., Bar Assn. City N.Y. (chmn. spl. com. on improvement family law), N.Y. County Lawyers Assn. (vice chmn. com. on pub. relations), Am. Legion, Naval Order U.S., Mil. Order World Wars, Res. Officers Assn., Assn. ICC Practitioners, Pi Lambda Phi, Sphinx Head. Clubs: Harmonie (bd. govs.), Harvard, Cornell (N.Y.C); Nat. Lawyers (Washington); Sunningdale Country, Statler (Ithaca, N.Y.). Co-author: Neurotic Interaction in Marriage; Sexual Behavior and the Law. Author articles to profl. jours. Home: 911 Park Ave New York NY 10021 Office: 6 E 43d St New York NY 10017

WELSFORD, WALTER DUTHIE, lumber wholesale co. exec.; b. Vancouver, B.C., Can., Nov. 26, 1934; s. Walter Giles and Ellen Philip (Duthie) W.; B.Sc. in Forestry, U. B.C., 1958; m. Lorraine Claire Mulvihill, Sept. 5, 1959; children—Michael Duthie, David William. N.Y. br. mgr. Cooper-Widman Ltd., 1962-66, U.S. sales mgr., 1967-69; v.p. Can. Am. Industries Ltd., Vancouver, 1969-73, pres., 1973—, also dir. Mem. B.C. Wholesale Lumber Assn. (pres. 1980-81), Western Lumber and Mktg. Assn., N.Am. Wholesale Lumber Assn. Conservative. Clubs: Vancouver, Vancouver Lawn Tennis. Home: 6836 East Blvd Vancouver BC V6P 5R3 Canada Office: 1670 W 8th Ave Vancouver BC V6J 4N9 Canada

WELSH, JOHN RICHARD, bank exec.; b. Neillsville, Wis., May 27, 1938; s. Francis Richard and Bernice Margaret (Schneider) W.; B.B.A., Loyola U., 1977; m. Carol Kay Ableidinger, Sept. 30, 1961; children—Tony, Becky, Cathy, Mike, Shelley. Mgr. dept. accident and health George F. Brown & Sons, Inc., Chgo., 1968-69; benefits adminstr. Marsh & McLennan Inc., Chgo., 1969-71; mgr. adminstrv. services Kemper Ins. Co., Long Grove, Ill., 1972-73; benefits adminstr. First Nat. Bank of Chgo., 1973-79, Ariz. Bank, Phoenix, 1979—. Mgr., coach Portage Park Baseball Program, Chgo., 1971-79, coach football program, 1972-79; leader Chgo. Area council Boy Scouts Am., 1973-75; high sch. football ofcl., 1980—. Served with U.S. Navy, 1956-59. Mem. Am. Mgmt. Assn., Am. Soc. Personnel Adminstrn., Phoenix Personnel Mgmt. Assn., Western Pension Conf., Phoenix Life, Health Claims Assn., Ariz. Interscholastic Assn. Club: K.C. Home: 4141 W Hayward Ave Phoenix AZ 85021 Office: 101 N 1st Ave Phoenix AZ 85003

WELSH, JUDSON BOOTH, bank exec.; b. Rochester, N.Y., Oct. 22, 1945; s. Frederic Sager and Helen (Groves) W.; B.A. in Econs., St. Lawrence U., 1964-67; M.Internat. Mgmt., Thunderbird Grad. Sch. Internat. Mgmt., 1972-73. Statistician, Eastman Kodak, Ltd., London, 1966; ter. rep. Eastman Kodak Co., Rochester, 1970-73; asst. v.p. Chem. Bank Internat., 1973-77, regional rep. W. Africa, Abidjan, Ivory Coast, 1977-79, internat. officer, 1979-80; asst. v.p. 1st Nat. Bank of Boston, 1980—, founder, dir. Boston Bank Cameroon, 1980, dir. credit of mktg., 1981—; leader seminars for W. African nations. Served to lt. USN, 1967-70; Vietnam. Decorated D.S.M. (Vietnam). Mem. Am. Mgmt. Assn., Airplane Owners and Pilots Assn. Acad. Polit. Sci., Table Round Abidjan (charter). Author internat. credit seminar. Home: 38 Valley Beach Ave Hull MA 02045 Office: PO Box 1939 Boston MA 02105

WELSH, LESLIE THOMAS, mfr., accountant; b. Bradford, Ill., Nov. 29, 1922; s. Leslie Edward and Anna (Holden) W.; B.S. in Accountancy, U. Ill., 1944; m. Mary Lee Weaver, Aug. 12, 1950; children—Leslie Thomas, Robert Weaver, Barbara Jo Ann, Cynthia Lee. Partner, Arthur Andersen & Co., Chgo., 1944-63; pres. Welsh Sporting Goods Corp., Iowa Falls, Iowa, 1964-72; v.p. finance, chief financial officer Studebaker-Worthington, Inc., 1967-69, sr. v.p., 1969-71, pres., 1971—. Trustee, Village of Barrington Hills, Ill., 1963-67. C.P.A. Clubs: Chicago; Barrington Hills Country (dir., pres.). Author film and articles in profl. jours. Home: 33 Lake View Ln Barrington IL 60010 Office: 1300 Grove Ave Barrington IL 60010

WELTMAN, SOL RUBIN, computer services cons.; b. Bklyn., July 19, 1932; s. Meyer and Dora W.; student Queens Coll., 1950-51; m. Marilyn Vivian Schneider, Sept. 1, 1951; children—Aster Deborah, Michael. Elec. engr. ASEA Electric, Inc., Armonk, N.Y., 1964-66, Parsons-Jurden Corp., N.Y.C., 1967; interactive computer systems software specialist Davis Computer Systems Co., N.Y.C., 1968-69, On-Line Systems, Inc., Pitts., 1970-74, Time Sharing Resources Co., Gt. Neck, N.Y., 1974-75, First Data Corp., Waltham, Mass., 1975; on-line minicomputer specialist Monchik-Weber Assos., N.Y.C., 1975-77, Datronics, Inc., N.Y.C., 1977-78; ind. on-line minicomputer software cons. to industry, Bklyn., 1978-79; pres. Modern Solutions, Inc., N.Y.C., 1980—. Address: 382 E 2d St Brooklyn NY 11218

WELTON, THEODORE M., mfg. co. exec.; b. 1918; A.B., U. Nebr., 1940; M.B.A., Harvard Bus. Sch., 1942. With Chevron Chem. Co. (subs. Standard Oil Calif.), 1947-67, v.p., 1963-67; exec. v.p. Calgon Corp. (subs. Merck & Co., Inc.), 1967-69, pres., 1969-72, also dir.; v.p. Water Mgmt. Carborundum Co., Niagara Falls, N.Y., 1972-73, group v.p. research, devel. and Water Mgmt., 1973; v.p. non-mineral new bus. devel. Kennecott Copper Corp., 1973-78, pres. Kennecott Devel. Co. div., Stamford, Conn., 1978—. Served with AUS, 1942-46. Office: 3 High Ridge Park Stamford CT 06905

WEMPLE, WILLIAM BARENT, mgmt. cons.; b. Washington, June 22, 1946; s. William and Dorothea (Dutcher) W.; B.S. Yale U., 1968; M.B.A., Harvard U., 1973; m. Sylvia A. Eriksen, Aug. 30, 1973. Asso., Reynolds Securities, N.Y.C., 1973-74; officers asst. Morgan Guaranty Trust Co., N.Y.C., 1974-78; sr. asso. Case & Co., Stamford, Conn., 1978—. Served with USMC, 1968-71. Mem. Inst. Mgmt. Cons. Republican. United Ch. of Christ. Club: Harvard Bus. Sch. Home: 6 Hood Ct Hartsdale NY 10530 Office: 1111 Summer St Stamford CT 06905

WENDELL, DAVID TAYLOR, investment counselor; b. Hackensack, N.J., Dec. 8, 1931; s. Edward Nelson and Eunice (Taylor) W.; A.B. cum laude, Harvard U., 1955, M.B.A., 1958; children—Karen, Erica. With Nat. Shawmut Bank of Boston, 1958-59; with David L. Babson & Co. Inc., Boston, 1959-79, sr. v.p., 1977-79, editor weekly staff letter, 1967-79; individual practice investment counseling, 1979—. Mem. corp. Northeastern U. Served with U.S. Army, 1951-54. Recipient award Valley Forge Freedom Found., 1974. Mem. Inst. Chartered Fin. Analysts, Boston Security Analysts Soc., Boston Econ. Club. Home: Quarry Farm North Edgecomb ME 04556 Office: 304 Cross Point Rd North Edgecomb ME 04556

WENDER, IRA TENSARD, lawyer, banker; b. Pitts., Jan. 5, 1927; s. Louis and Luba (Kibrick) W.; student Swarthmore Coll., 1942-45; J.D., U. Chgo., 1948; LL.M., N.Y. U., 1951; m. Phyllis Bellows, June 24, 1966; children—Justin, Sarah; children (by previous marriage)-Theodore, Mathew, Abigail, John. Asso. Lord, Day & Lord, N.Y.C., 1950-52, 54-59; asst. dir. internat. program in taxation Harvard Law Sch., 1952-54; lectr. N.Y. U. Sch. Law, 1954-59; partner Baker & McKenzie, Chgo., 1959-61, sr. partner, N.Y.C., 1961-71; partner firm Wender, Murase & White, N.Y.C., 1971—; chmn. C. Brewer & Co., Ltd., Honolulu, 1969-75; pres., chief exec. officer Warburg Paribas Becker, Inc. and A.G. Becker, Inc., 1978—; dir. IU Internat., Paribas Internat. S.A., Mercury Securities, Ltd., London; lectr. numerous law insts. Vis. com. U. Chgo. Law Sch.; bd. mgrs. Swarthmore Coll. Mem. Am., N.Y. State bar assns., Assn. Bar City N.Y. Clubs: Board Room (N.Y.C.); Pacific (Honolulu). Author: (with E.R. Barlow) Foreign Investment and Taxation, 1955. Home: 555 Park Ave New York NY 10021 Office: 55 Water St New York NY

WENDLINGER, ROBERT MATTHEW, communications cons.; b. N.Y.C., July 20, 1922; s. Harry and Rose (Pollock) W.; B.S., Columbia U., 1952; children—David, Marcella, Marta. Script editor Radio Free Europe, N.Y.C., 1950-52; asso. editor Ind. Film Jour., N.Y.C., 1953-57; gen. mgr. Kermit Rolland and Assos., Princeton, N.J., 1957-59; exec. asst. in charge editorial services United Hosp. Fund of N.Y., N.Y.C., 1959-60; mgr. info. sect. Com. for Air and Water Conservation Am. Petroleum Inst., N.Y.C., 1966-67; with Bank of America NT & SA, San Francisco, 1967-78, asst. v.p. communications, 1972-78; pres. The Wendlinger Group, San Francisco, 1978—; mem. faculty St. Mary's Coll., Moraga, Calif., 1975-78; mem. Astron Corp. Served with AUS, 1943-46. Fellow Am. Bus. Communication Assn.; mem. Indsl. Communication Council (past pres.). Author: (with James M. Reid, Jr.) Effective Letters: A Program in Self-Instruction, 1964, 3d edit., 1978. Contbr. to Everbody Wins; TA Applied to Organizations, 1973; Affirmative Action for Women, 1973; McGraw-Hill Ency. Professional Management, 1978. Office: 44 Montgomery St San Francisco CA 94104

WENDT, CHARLES MARCUS, mfg. co. exec.; b. Sterling, Colo., Nov. 22, 1942; s. Marcus F. and Donna Beth (Bell) W.; B.S. in Bus. Adminstrn., U. Denver, 1965, M.B.A., 1968; m. Dorothy M. Whitaker; children—Eric Marcus, Ellen Marie. Materials coordinator Samsonite Corp., Denver, 1964-65; regional production planner Owens-Ill. Inc., Chgo., 1965-67, salesman glass container div., 1968-70; Eastern area liquor mgr. Anchor-Hocking Corp., Louisville, 1970-75, dist. sales mgr., 1975-80; product mgr. Liquor & Wine Industries, Lancaster, Ohio, 1980—. Home: 7680 Heatherwood Dr Canal Winchester OH 43110 Office: 1749 W Fair Ave Lancaster OH 43130

WENGER, JEROME MAXWELL, publisher; b. Phila., Oct. 19, 1945; s. Harry and Mona (Albert) W.; B.S., U. Ala., 1969; postgrad. Johns Hopkins U., 1975; m. Susan Tarken, Nov. 23, 1969; 1 dau., Beth Ann. Asst. controller Container Corp. Am., Phila., 1970-71; with Polaroid Corp., Cambridge, Mass., 1975—, sr. tech. mktg. rep., 1977—; pub. Penny Markets Rev., Penny Stock Newsletter, Columbia, Md., 1980—. Club: Masons. Office: Oakland Mills Village Center Columbia MD 21045

WENGLER, ROBERT EUGENE, research and devel. co. exec.; b. Hollywood, Calif., Mar. 5, 1933; s. George Aloys and Evelyn Margaret (Stump) W.; B.S. (Bd. Regents scholar), UCLA, 1961, M.S., 1964. Research scientist Atomics Internat., Canoga Park, Calif., 1961-62; group leader Garrett Corp., Los Angeles, 1964-65; dir. Northrop Corp. Labs., Hawthorne, Calif., 1965-67; staff mem. Gen. Research Corp., Santa Barbara, Calif., 1967-69; v.p. Effects Tech., Inc., Santa Barbara, 1969-71, pres., 1971—, chmn. bd., 1973—, also dir.; dir. tech. applications group Flow Gen., Inc., 1979—; cons. in field; dir. Moseley Assos., Inc. Served with USN, 1952-56. Mem. Sigma Pi Sigma, Pi Mu Epsilon. Contbr. articles to profl. jours.; inventor in field. Home: 1018 Belmonte Dr Santa Barbara CA 93101 Office: 5383 Hollister Ave Santa Barbara CA 93111

WENIGER, SIDNEY N., real estate investor and developer; b. Bklyn., Apr. 20, 1920; s. Morris and Rose (Swerling) W.; B.C.E., Cooper Union Inst. Tech., 1941; M.M.E., Poly. Inst. Bklyn., 1949; L.H.D. (hon.), Graceland Coll., 1978; m. Lenore E. Sternick, Dec. 28, 1941; children—Earl Douglas, Bruce Gilbert, Cynthia Sue. Pres. various home bldg. corps. and pvt. utility cos., L.I., Fla., 1949-61; v.p. Kirkeby-Natus Corp., N.Y.C., 1962-65; v.p. Standard Financial Corp., N.Y.C., 1965-67; owner, pres. Sidney N. Weniger Orgns., 1967—; pres. Gen. Resources Assos. Inc., 1967—, The Wengroup Cos., 1979—; nat. comml. panel Am. Arbitration Assn., 1958—; mem. Nat. Assn. Real Estate Investment Funds; mem. adv. bd. Apt. Builder/Developer Conf.; dir. Pulaski Bank & Trust Co., Little Rock. Trustee, Optometric Center N.Y., Drs. Hosp., Little Rock. Served to lt. USNR, 1944-46. Registered profl. engr., N.Y., N.J. Mem. Nat. Soc. Profl. Engrs., Am. Water Works Assn., Mortgage Bankers Assn. N.Y., Assn. Navy Civil Engr. Corps Officers. Clubs: Marco Polo (N.Y.C.); Little Rock; Capital City, Montgomery. Home: 40 E 80th St New York NY 10021 Office: 745 Fifth Ave New York NY 10151 also 500 S University Little Rock AR 72205

WENTLING, JAMES WESTFALL, banker; b. Ashtabula, Ohio, Jan. 10, 1924; s. Orva Olean and Vera Helene (Westfall) W.; B.A., U. Ala., 1949, M.A., 1950; grad. Sch. Bank Mktg., Northwestern U., Chgo., 1964, Stonier Grad. Sch. Banking, Rutgers U., 1969; m. Ann Houston, Nov. 27, 1947; children—Carol Beth, David James. Mgr., Painesville studio Sta. WICA, Ashtabula, 1941-42; pres., treas. Wentling's Pharmacy, Inc., Astabula, 1950-61; v.p. Northeastern Ohio Nat. Bank, Ashtabula, 1962-70; v.p., economist, dir. mktg. Bank Ohio Corp., Columbus, 1970-76; corp. v.p. mktg. Flagship Bansk, Inc., Miami, Fla., 1977—; instr. econs. and mktg. Kent State U., Ashtabula, 1959-68; instr. Ohio Sch. Banking, 1967-69; v.p. Printcraft, Inc., Conneaut, Ohio; past v.p., dir. Midwest Econometrics, Inc., Columbus; dir. Flagship Services Corp., Tampa, Fla., Seaforth, Inc., Tampa. Past pres. Ashtabula Area C. of C.; past treas. Ashtabula Indsl. Corp., Ashtabula County chpt. Nat. Found.; past sec.-treas. Ashtabula Area Coll. Com. Served with AUS, 1943-46; PTO. Recipient Disting. Service award Kent State U., 1970, Ashtabula Area C. of C., 1970. Mem. Bank Mktg. Assn. (treas.), Am. Mktg. Assn., Am. Bankers Assn., Fla. Bankers Assn., Alpha Kappa Psi, Beta Gamma Sigma, Omicron Delta Kappa. Republican. Mem. Disciples of Christ. Office: 777 Brickell Ave Miami FL 33131

WENTWORTH, CLARE G., mfg. co. exec.; b. Dryden, Mich., July 29, 1939; s. Gail C. and Pauline M. (Lyons) W.; B.S. in Engring. Sci., Oakland U., 1964; m. Shirley G. Grondin, July 23, 1960; children—Christopher, Pamela, Nathan. Project engr. Vickers, Inc., Troy, Mich., 1964-65; systems engr. IBM, Flint, Mich., 1965-68; pres. R&R Smith Co., Mayville, Mich., 1968-70; dir. purchasing, v.p. Champion Home Builders, Dryden, 1970—. Active in community activities. Served with USMC, 1958-61. Registered profl. bus. programmer. Mem. Manufactured Housing Industries. Republican. Roman Catholic. Clubs: Dryden Vets., Dryden Boosters.

WENTWORTH, DAVID FRANK, accountant; b. Fairfield, Iowa, Aug. 7, 1924; s. Harry David and Eva May (Anderson) W.; B.S.C., U. Iowa, 1948; m. Lillian Estelle Kraemer, June 10, 1944; children—Ellen, Ann, Jill, Karen, Nancy. With McGladrey, Hendrickson & Co., and predecessor, C.P.A.'s, 1948—, resident partner, Davenport, Iowa, 1951-66, adminstrv. partner, 1966—; dir. Hon Industries, Inc. Served with U.S. Army, 1943-46. C.P.A., Iowa (Sells Silver medal 1950). Mem. Am. Inst. C.P.A.'s, Iowa Soc. C.P.A.'s (past pres.), Davenport C. of C. Republican. Methodist. Clubs: Davenport (past pres.), Davenport Optimist (past pres.), Davenport Country (past dir.). Office: Davenport Bank Bldg Davenport IA 52803

WENTWORTH, TIMOTHY FAIR, publisher; b. Rochester, N.Y., Dec. 31, 1943; s. Paul Roberts and Margaret (Fair) W.; B.A., Lehigh U., 1965; m. Margaret Louise French, Apr. 29, 1967; children—Katherine Jane, Jessica Fair. Asst. advt. mgr. Hamilton Watch Co., Lancaster, Pa., 1965-70; asst. advt. mgr. Pennwalt Corp., Phila., 1970-71; v.p. Fondren Advt., Lancaster, 1971-74; pres. Range Industries, Inc., Lancaster, 1974-76; owner Wentworth Publ. Co., Lancaster, 1976—. Mem. Lancaster Advt. Club (past pres.), Bank Mktg. Assn. Elder, 1st Presbyterian Ch. Club: Lancaster Aero (past pres.). Home: 1746 Longview Dr Lancaster PA 17601 Office: 24 W King St Lancaster PA 17603

WENTZ, SIDNEY FREDERICK, ins. co. exec.; b. Dallas, Mar. 27, 1932; s. Howard Beck and Emmy Lou (Cawthon) W.; A.B., Princeton, 1954; LL.B., Harvard, 1960; m. Barbara Strait, Sept. 9, 1961; children—Eric, Jennifer, Robin. Admitted to N.Y. State bar, 1961; atty. firm White & Case, N.Y.C., 1960-65, Western Electric Co., 1965-66, Am. Tel. & Tel. Co., 1966-67; with Crum & Forster Ins. Cos., Morristown, N.J., 1967—, dir., 1968—, sr. v.p., gen. counsel, 1971-73, vice chmn. bd., 1973—; with Crum & Forster, N.Y.C., 1967—, dir., 1969—, exec. v.p., 1972-73, pres., 1973—; pres., dir. Crum & Forster Corp., Morris Twp., N.J., 1978—; chmn., vice chmn., pres. or dir. numerous affiliated cos. Trustee Morristown Meml. Hosp., 1974—. Served to lt. (j.g.) USNR, 1954-57. Clubs: Morris County Golf; Morristown Field; Sakonnet (R.I.) Golf; Baltusrol Golf. Office: PO Box 2387 305 Madison Ave Morristown NJ 07960

WENTZ, THEODORE EMORY, heavy equipment mfg. co. exec.; b. Pitts., Aug. 10, 1931; s. Welker Wallace and Kathryn Ebberts) W.; B.A. cum laude, Amhest Coll., 1953; B.S. magna cum laude, U. Buffalo, 1958, M.B.A., 1960; m. Eleanor Frances Donald, July 23, 1955; 1 son, Donald Richard. Asso. cons. Touche Ross & Co., San Francisco, 1960-65; div. controller Varian Assos., Palo Alto, Calif., 1965-69; dir. fin. Symbolic Control, Inc., San Mateo, Calif., 1969-70; controller Clementina Ltd., San Francisco, 1971-73; dir. fin. Probe Systems, Inc., Sunnyvale, Calif., 1973-76; v.p. fin. Viking Industries, Inc., Chatsworth, Calif., 1976-78; chief fin. officer Calovar Corp., Santa Fe Springs, Calif., 1979-80. Served with USNR, 1953-55. C.P.A., Calif. Mem. Calif. Soc. C.P.A.'s, Calif. C.P.A. Found. Edn. and Research. Home and Office: 20850 NE 26th Pl Redmond WA 98052

WENZLAU, JOHN NORBERT HANS, real estate exec.; b. Meissen, W. Ger., Aug. 20, 1946; came to U.S., 1965; s. Otto Olgerd and Ursula Jutta (Schumann) W.; B.A., U. Oreg., 1968, M.A., 1970; M.Div., Southwestern Baptist Sem., Ft. Worth, 1981; m. Katherine Kickliter, Dec. 28, 1968; 1 son, Matthew Brian. Salesman, mem. mktg. staff Xerox Corp., Calgary, Alta., Can., 1971-74; br. mgr., then regional sales mgr. Rentway Can., Calgary, 1974-76; v.p., gen. mgr. Maple Leaf Enterprises, Inc., Phoenix, 1977—, also dir.; pres., dir. MLE, Inc., Arlington, Tex., 1978—. Republican. Baptist. Club: Woodhaven Country (Ft. Worth). Address: 4409 Woodland Park Blvd Arlington TX 76013

WERD, GREGORY FRANCIS, steel co. exec.; b. Chgo., Aug. 17, 1938; s. Frank and Jean J. (Weinert) W.; B.A., Vanderbilt U., 1960; m. Margaret Rose Paulsel, July 16, 1960; children—Daphne Frances, Gregory Francis, Matthew Brooks. With U.S. Steel Corp., various locations, 1960—, sr. sales rep., Birmingham, Ala., 1968-73, product sales rep., Pitts., 1973-74, market planning rep., 1974-75, asst. mktg. mgr., Chgo., 1975-76, asst. mgr. sales, 1976—; mem. Ill. adv. com. Employees Good Govt. Fund. Am. Iron and Steel Inst. teaching fellow, 1974. Mem. Am. Iron and Steel Inst. Assn. Iron and Steel Engrs., Chgo. Assn. Commerce and Industry. Republican. Club: Exchange. Home: 1348 Crestwood Dr Northbrook IL 60062 Office: 208 LaSalle St S Suite 1300 Chicago IL 60604

WERDEN, JAMES EDWARD, health care adminstr.; b. Detroit, Nov. 15, 1941; s. Irvin Ira and Lottie Marie (Brodie) W.; B.A. in Bus., U. Md., 1972; M.B.A., Calif. Western U., 1979; m. Diane Kay Dalman, June 25, 1960; children—Carmen, James Edward II, Karen, Michael. Joined Med. Service Corps, U.S. Army, 1959, ret., 1972; head dept. cardiology Providence Hosp., Waco, Tex., 1972-75; dir. cardiology Meml. Med. Center, Corpus Christi, Tex., 1975—; partner Profl. Services Assos.; cons. health care mgmt.; project coordinator Am. Coll. Cardiology, 1976. Bd. dirs. Coastal Bend chpt. Am. Heart Assn., 1976; com. mem. Boy Scouts Am. Mem. Am. Mgmt. Assn., Am. Coll. Hosp. Adminstrs., Am. Cardiology Technologists Assn., Am. Soc. Cardiopulmonary Technologists, Corpus Christi C. of C. Republican. Baptist. Club: Lions. Home: 1021 S Bay Dr Corpus Christi TX 78412 Office: 2606 Hospital Blvd PO Box 5280 Corpus Christi TX 78405

WERMERT, JAMES FRANCIS, mgmt. cons.; b. Worcester, Mass., Nov. 12, 1949; s. Francis Henry and Eleanor June (Flading) W.; B.A. in Polit. Sci., Cornell U., 1971; M.B.A., Harvard U., 1978; postgrad. Johns Hopkins U., 1972-74; m. Diana Gayle Goldberg, July 12, 1975; 1 dau., Anastasia Marie (Stacey). Systems analyst Nat. Med. Care, Boston, 1976-77; mgmt. cons. Kurt Salmon Assos., Atlanta, 1978—; guest lectr. Hillsborough County Community Coll., Tampa, Fla. Co-founder, Serendipity, Balt. Area Social Service Orgn., Foster Parents Plan; instr. ARC. Served to capt. U.S. Army, 1971-75. Roman Catholic. Clubs: N.Y. Road Runners; Balt. Free Rugby. Office: 400 Colony Sq Atlanta GA 30361

WERNER, BURTON KREADY, ins. co. exec.; b. St. Louis, Apr. 24, 1933; s. Elmer L. and Helen (Kready) W.; A.B. cum laude, Amherst Coll., 1954; M.B.A., Wharton Grad. Sch., U. Pa., 1958; m. Joanna Catherine Hill, Oct. 17, 1959; children—Lisa Anne, Cynthia Catherine, Bradford Kready. Sec., Insurers Service Corp., St. Louis, 1958-65, exec. v.p., 1965-75, pres., 1975—, also dir.; v.p. Safety Mut. Casualty Corp., 1958-75, exec. v.p., 1975—, pres., 1976—, also dir.; underwriting mem. Lloyd's of London. Guarantor, St. Louis Mcpl. Opera; active YMCA. Served to capt. USAF, 1954-56. Named Ky. col.; C.P.C.U. Fellow Truman Library; mem. Nat. Assn. Safety and Claims Orgns. (sec. 1966, 67, pres. 1968-71, dir. 1967—), Arts and Edn. Council St. Louis, Asso. Industries Mo., Better Bus. Bur. St. Louis, Humane Soc. Mo., Mo. Bot. Garden, St. Louis Zoo Assn., St. Louis Symphony Soc., City Art Mus. St. Louis, Landmarks Assn. St. Louis, McDonnell Planetarium, Delta Kappa Epsilon. Episcopalian. Clubs: Casa Y Pesca Las Cruces (Mex.); Napili Kai Beach; Indian Lake (Fla.); Racquet (St. Louis); University, Sugar Tree. Home: 14 Clermont Ln Saint Louis MO 63124 Office: University Club Tower 1034 S Brentwood Blvd Saint Louis MO 63117

WERNER, ELMER LOUIS, JR., ins. co. exec.; b. St. Louis, Nov. 21, 1927; s. Elmer Louis and Helen M. (Kready) W.; A.B., Princeton U., 1948; B.S., Washington U., St. Louis, 1950, LL.B./J.D., 1952; m. Sandra M. Johnston, Dec. 3, 1966; children—Louis, Eric, Matthew. Admitted to Mo. bar, 1952, U.S. Mil. Ct. Appeals bar, 1963, U.S. Supreme Ct. bar, 1963. served to col. JAGC, U.S. Army, 1952-55; asst. v.p. Insurers Service Corp., St. Louis, 1955-59, v.p., gen. counsel, 1959-76, chmn., 1976—; asst. sec. Safety Mut. Casualty Corp., St. Louis, 1955-59, sec./treas., gen. counsel, 1959-76, exec. v.p., gen. counsel, 1976—; v.p., dir. Butch Baird Enterprises, Inc., 1979. Bd. dirs. Playgoers of St. Louis, Inc.; mem. Better Bus. Bur. St. Louis, Associated Industries Mo.; ruling elder Ladue Chapel, 1980—. Mem. Am. Soc. C.P.C.U.'s, Nat. Assn. Safety and Claims Orgns., Fed., Mo., St. Louis bar assns. Presbyterian. Clubs: Mo. Athletic, St. Louis Indoor Soccer (dir. 1981), Forest Hills Golf and Country (sec., dir. 1980), Ambassadors, St. Louis, Lawyers, Dome. Home: 7 Barclay Woods Dr Saint Louis MO 63124 Office: 1034 S Brentwood Blvd Saint Louis MO 63117

WERNER, JESSE, chem. co. exec.; b. N.Y.C., Dec. 5, 1916; s. Louis and Clara (Karan) W.; B.S. cum laude, Bklyn. Coll., 1935; M.A., Columbia, 1936, Ph.D., 1938; m. Edna Lesser, Aug. 16, 1943; children—Kenneth M., Nancy E. Asst. chemistry Columbia, 1936-38; with GAF Corp. (formerly Gen. Aniline & Film Corp.), N.Y.C., 1938—, research chemist, group and sect. leader, asst. mgr. process devel., asst. to v.p. operations, 1938-52, dir. comml. devel., 1952-59, v.p., 1959-62, pres., 1962-77, chmn., 1964—, also chief exec. officer, dir.; dir. Curtis-Wright Corp., Kennecott Corp. Trustee, Sackler Sch. Medicine; bd. dirs. Chamber Mus. Soc. Lincoln Center, Young Concert Artists. Fellow Am. Inst. Chemists, AAAS; mem. Am. Chem. Soc., Am. Inst. Chem. Engrs., Chem. Market Research Assn., Comml. Devel. Assn., Soc. Chem. Industry (chmn. Am. sect. 1968-69), Film Soc. Lincoln Center (dir.), Bus. Com. for Arts, Sigma Xi, Pi Mu Epsilon, Phi Lambda Upsilon. Clubs: Econ. of N.Y. (pres. 1968-69), Hemisphere. Office: 140 W 51st St New York NY 10020

WERNER, JOHN C., corp. staff cons.; b. Jamestown, N.D., July 9, 1920; s. Fern Clifford and Bessie Christine (Nord) W.; A.A., Santa Monica City Coll., 1941; m. Persis V. Hite, Oct. 18, 1947 (dec. 1977); children—William J., Wendy P. Production control mgr. Cherry Rivet Co., Los Angeles, 1947-51; tool and prodn. control supr. Bendix Aviation Corp., N. Hollywood, Calif., 1951-58; tooling mgr. Cannon Electric Co., Los Angeles, 1959-61; facilities mgr. Martin Marietta Corp., Vandenberg AFB, Calif., 1961-65; production control mgr. Jostens, Inc., Attleboro, Mass., 1965-67; dir. indsl. ops. Performance Tech. Corp., Los Angeles, 1967-70; corp. staff cons. Sundstrand Corp., Rockford, Ill., 1970—; cons. mktg. and ops. mgmt., U.S. and Europe; cons. program mgmt. USAF. Cons. Gov's. Commn. on Sch., Ill., 1972. Served with USAF, 1942-45, to maj. with USAFR, 1945-70, ret. 1970. Decorated Air Medal. Certified nat. security mgr., Indsl. Coll. Armed Forces; certified multi-engine comml. pilot, USAF and Dept. Transp. Mem. Am. Inst. Indsl. Engrs. (certified sr. indsl. engr.), Experimental Aircraft Assn. Club: Am. Ex-Prisoners of War. Contbr. program mgmt. criteria U.S. Dept. Defense, 1967; developer, author Adminstrv. Value Analysis Implementation Guide, 1973; Adminstrv. Planning and Tng. (APT), Zero Base Budgeting for Production Oriented Industry, Operations Control for Productivity Improvement. Home: 215 Shore Ln Rockton IL 61072 Office: 4751 Harrison Ave Rockford IL 61101

WERRELL, TERRY SHERMAN, auto and appliance supply co. exec.; b. Janesville, Wis., Mar. 5, 1936; s. Daniel and Vivian Virginia (Sherman) W.; B.I.E., Gen. Motors Inst., 1960; m. Sandra E. Samuelson, July 6, 1957; children—Daniel D., Diana D., Linda L., Pamela L. Engr., Fisher Body div. Gen. Motors Corp., Janesville, 1959-66, prodn. engring. supt., Lordstown, Ohio, 1968-70, maintenance shift supt., 1970-72; maintenance supt. assembly div., Lordstown, 1972-75, maintenance supt. Vega and van plant, 1975-76: dir. facilities and process Delorean Motor Co., Bloomfield Hills, Mich., 1976-78; mfg. mgr. Delorean Motors Cars Ltd., Belfast, No. Ireland, 1978—; gen. mgr. Hardy div. Sheller Globe Corp., Union City, Ind., 1980—, chmn. decorative zinc and plastics subcom. of product planning com. Mem. budget com., chmn. audit com. Trinity Lutheran Ch., Union City. Recipient Grad. Key award Gen. Motors Inst., 1960. Mem. Union City C. of C., Am. Soc. Electroplated Plastics (dir.), Soc. Mfg. Engrs. (cert.). Clubs: Elks, Masons (officer). Home: 812 N Columbia Union City IN 47390 Office: 1225 W Pearl Union City IN 47390

WERT, JAMES W., banker; b. Chgo., Sept. 22, 1946; s. Andrew J. and Clair C. Wert; B.A. in Fin., Mich. State U., 1971; postgrad. Grad. Sch. Mgmt., Northwestern U., 1971-75, Stonier Grad. Sch. Banking, Rutgers U., 1977—; m. Candace M. Cronwall, Apr. 2, 1976. Second v.p. Continental Ill. Nat. Bank of Chgo., 1971-75; v.p. Society Nat. Bank/Society Corp., Cleve., 1976-77; sr. v.p., sr. investment officer, economist Society Nat. Bank of Cleve., 1977—; sr. v.p. Society Corp., 1980—; guest lectr. Grad. Sch. Mgmt., Northwestern U., 1974-75; mem. faculty Grad. Sch. Banking, U. Wis., 1978—; guest speaker at nat. confs., 1975—. Served with U.S. Army, 1965-68. Mem. Greater Cleve. Growth Assn., Am. Bankers Assn., Cleve. Bus. Economists Club, Cleve. Bond Club, Leadership Cleve. Republican. Clubs: Union (Cleve.); Canterbury Golf. Contbr. articles on bank asset and liability mgmt. to profl. jours. Home: One Bratenahl Pl Bratenahl OH 44108 Office: 127 Public Sq Cleveland OH 44114

WERT, JOHN HOWARD, investment co. exec.; b. Mt. Holly, N.J., July 3, 1936; s. Howard Milton and Sarah Wood (Brecht) W.; B.A. in History, Princeton U., 1957; m. Martha Ellen Stevenson, Sept. 10, 1959; children—John Howard, Robert, Stephen, Elizabeth. With First Nat. City Bank, N.Y.C., 1957-58, Nat. Bank of Detroit, 1958-69; with Bache Halsey Stuart, and predecessors, 1969—, v.p., mgr. Grand Rapids (Mich.) office, 1975—. Bd. dirs. Grand Rapids Symphony, 1976—, Kendall Sch. of Design, 1978—. Served with USAF, 1959. Mem. Mich. Assn. Fin. Analysts, Bond Club Mich. Republican. Episcopalian. Clubs: Merion Golf (Ardmore, Pa.); Kent Country; Peninsular (Grand Rapids); Detroit; Orchard Lake (Mich.) Country. Office: 511-M Water Bldg Grand Rapids MI 49502

WERTHEIM, JOHN TAYLOR, bank exec.; B.B.A., Kent State U., 1965; M.B.A., Ohio State U., 1966; student Grad. Sch. Banking, U. Wis., 1977-79. Mgmt. cons. Arthur Andersen & Co., N.Y.C., 1969-73; v.p., sec.-treas. Peoples Bancshares, Inc., Canton, Ohio, 1973-76; sr. v.p. Peoples Merchants Trust Co., Canton, Ohio, 1976-78; pres., chief exec. officer Ameritrust of Portage County, Kent, Ohio, 1978—, also dir. President-elect United Way of Portage County, 1980. Served with U.S. Army, 1967-69, C.P.A., Ohio, N.Y. Mem. Bank Adminstrn. Inst., Am. Bankers Assn. Office: 115 S Water St Kent OH 44240

WERTZ, MARCUS EMMONS, JR., mfg. co. exec.; b. Belleville, N.J., Dec. 29, 1917; s. Marcus Emmons and Roberta Chapman (Struble) W.; B.S., Lehigh U., 1939; m. Georgieanna Cecile Campbell, Apr. 24, 1943 (dec. Nov. 1972); children—Nancy Jeanne (Mrs. James G. Kerridge), Roberta Carol (Mrs. C.M. Sutter), Marcus Emmons III; m. 2d, Constance Josephine Weil, June 23, 1973. With Lehigh Structural Steel Co., Allentown, Pa., 1949-54, 57-60, asst. supt., 1953-54, dir. indsl. relations, 1958-59, asst. to exec. v.p., 1959-60; v.p., dir. Crandall Corp., Warren, N.H., 1954-57; prodn. mgr. Gulf States Tube Co., Rosenberg, Tex., 1961-66, gen. mgr., 1966-67; cons., Houston, 1967-69; plant mgr. Rheem Superior div. Rheem Mfg. Co., Pearland, Tex., 1969-70; contract mgr. Bethelehem Fabricators Inc. (Pa.), 1970, adminstrv. v.p., 1970-72, sr. v.p., 1972-74, exec. v.p., 1974-76, chief operating officer, 1974-76, also dir.; v.p. Whitehead & Kales Co., Detroit, 1975-76; pres., dir. Gulfport Steel Co. (Miss.), 1976—. Bd. dirs. Lehigh Valley chpt. Nat. Safety Council, Bethlehem, 1971. Served to lt. comdr. USNR, 1941-45. Me. Assn. Iron and Steel Engrs., Am. Welding Soc., Newcomen Soc., Pa. Soc., Gulfport Area C. of C., Navy League, Beta Theta Pi. Republican. Clubs: Gulfport Rotary, Mason (32 deg.). Home: 113 Lakeview Dr Biloxi MS 39531 Office: Lorraine Rd PO Box 2097 Gulfport MS 39503

WERWAISS, JOHN ANDREW, real estate exec.; b. N.Y.C., May 10, 1942; s. Frederick W. and Julia L. Werwaiss; A.B., Georgetown U., 1964; m. Beth A. Nielsen, Jan. 25, 1966; children—Gretchen N., John A., Christian W. Vice pres. W. A. White & Sons, N.Y.C., 1964-74; pres. Werwaiss & Co., Inc., N.Y.C., 1975—; chmn. bd. Realty Growth Investors, Towson, Md., 1979—; guest lectr. real estate N.Y. U. Trustee, treas. James Weldon Johnson Community Centers, Inc., N.Y.C.; trustee Pine Island Park Assn., Bayville, N.Y. Mem. Real Estate Bd. N.Y., Young Men's Real Estate Assn. N.Y., Nat. Realty Club. Roman Catholic. Clubs: Union (N.Y.C.); Piping Rock. Home: 1107 Fifth Ave New York NY 10028 Office: 509 Madison Ave New York NY 10022

WESCOE, W(ILLIAM) CLARKE, physician, drug co. exec.; b. Allentown, Pa., May 3, 1920; s. Charles H. and Hattie G. (Gilham) W.; B.S., Muhlenberg Coll., 1941, Sc.D., 1957; M.D., Cornell U., 1944; m. Barbara Benton, Apr. 29, 1944; children—Barbara, William, David. Intern, N.Y. Hosp., 1944-45, resident, 1945-46; asst. prof. pharmacology Cornell U. Med. Coll., 1949-51; prof. pharmacology and exptl. medicine U. Kans. Med. Center, 1951—, dir., 1953-60, dean sch. medicine, 1952-60; chancellor U. Kans., 1960-69; vice chmn. bd. Sterling Drug Inc., N.Y.C., 1970-74, chmn. bd., 1974—, also dir.; dir. Phillips Petroleum Co., Hallmark Cards, Inc., Irving Trust Co., Irving Bank Corp. Chmn. China Med. Bd. of N.Y., N.Y.C., 1972—. Trustee, Samuel Kress Found., Columbia U., John Simon Guggenheim Meml. Found.; bd. dirs. Tinker Found. Served as capt., pharmacol. sect., med. div. Army Chem. Center, M.C., AUS, 1946-48. Markle scholar med. scis., 1949-54. Fellow A.C.P.; mem. Am. Soc. Pharmacology and Exptl. Therapeutics, Phi Beta Kappa, Sigma Xi, Alpha Omega Alpha, Alpha Tau Omega, Nu Sigma Nu. Editor: Jour. Pharmacol. and Exptl. Therapeutics, 1952-57. Home: 828 Traylor Dr Allentown PA 18103 Office: 90 Park Ave New York NY 10016

WESOLOWSKI, ADOLPH JOHN, elec. engr.; b. Chelsea, Mass., June 4, 1916; s. Joseph A. and Adamina (Ploharska) W.; B.S., Harvard, 1938; postgrad. Pa. State U., 1958-59; M.S. in Engring., Ariz. State U., 1964; m. Eleanor Louise Currier, June 3, 1939 (div. 1967); children—Mary Eleanor (Mrs. Harold A. Downing), Eleanor Louise (Mrs. John Tennyson), Joseph Walter, Allen Joseph, Frank James, Steven Michael; m. 2d, Gabrielle Bourgon, 1968. Turbine engr. Gen. Electric Co., Lynn, Mass., 1938-41; field engr., Boston, 1941-45, motor design engr., Lynn, 1945-50, chief aircraft generator engr., Lynn, also Erie, Pa., 1950-59; sr. design engr. AiResearch Mfg. Co., Phoenix, 1959-66; project engr. Garrett Mfg. Ltd., Rexdale, Ont., Can., 1966-68, Leland Airborne Products, Vandalia, Ohio, 1968-70; chief engr. Dyna Corp., Dayton, Ohio, 1970-75; pres. World Wide Artifacts Inc., 1975—; cons. engr. electro-mech. design. Registered profl. engr., Mass. Mem. I.E.E.E. (chmn. aerospace energy conversion com. 1962-64), Internat. Aerospace Elec. Conf. (chmn. 1964), Phoenix, Greater Erie chambers commerce, Ohio Archaeol. Soc., Central States Archaeol. Soc., Artifact Soc. (founder). Club: Point of Pines Yacht (past financial sec.) (Revere, Mass.). Patentee in field. Home: 7125 E Fanfol Rd Paradise Valley AZ 85253

WESP, ARTHUR PHILIP, mfg. co. exec.; b. Bklyn., Jan. 30, 1947; s. Arthur Philip and Virginia Helen (Marshall) W.; B.S. in Chemistry, Ohio U., 1969; m. Karen Sue Werner, Aug. 23, 1969; children—Scott, Laurie, Carrie. Sales rep. Shell Chem., Cin., 1971-73, Cleve., 1973-76, product sales mgr. oxo alcohols, Houston, 1976-78, product sales mgr. IPA/OMK-MEK, Houston, 1978-79, sales mgr. Central region, 1979—. Vice pres. Louetta Rd. Mun. Utility Dist., 1978-80; pres. Bd. Equalizations, 1979; chmn. maintenance com. Terra Nova, 1978-79; program dir. Rd. Runners, 1980—. Served with U.S. Army, 1969-71. Mem. Am. Mgmt. Assn., Assn. Water Bd. Dirs. Presbyterian. Home: 885 Deepwood Dr Medina OH 44256 Office: 7123 Pearl Rd Cleveland OH 44130

WESSEL, MILTON RALPH, lawyer, educator; b. N.Y.C., Aug. 19, 1923; s. Harry N. and Elsie (Stettiner) W.; A.B., Yale, 1944; J.D., Harvard, 1948; m. Joan Strauss, Jan. 29, 1953; children—Douglas C., Kenneth L., Michael R. Admitted to N.Y. bar, 1949, U.S. Supreme Ct. bar, 1956; partner firm Kaye, Scholer, Fierman, Hays and Handler, 1960-73; gen. counsel Assn. Data Processing Service Orgn., Montvale, N.J., 1966—, Am. Fedn. Info. Processing Socs., Montvale, N.J., 1968-75, gen. counsel Chem. Industry Inst. of Toxicology, Research Triangle, N.C., 1975—; counsel Parker Chapin Flattau & Klimpl, 1980—; vis. prof. law N.Y. U., 1975-78, Columbia U., 1972—, Stanford U., 1978; spl. litigation counsel The Dow Chem. Co., 1974-78. Dir., pres. Henry Kaufmann Campgrounds, Inc., Pearl River, N.Y., 1956-73; v.p., trustee Westchester Reform Temple, Scarsdale, N.Y., 1965-72. Served with U.S. Army, 1942-45. Mem. Am., N.Y. State bar assns., Assn. Bar City N.Y. Author: Federal Pretrial and Jury Trial Procedure, 1955; (with Dr. Bruce Gilchrist) Government Regulation of the Computer Industry, 1972; Freedom's Edge: The Computer Threat to Society, 1974; The Rule of Reason; A New Approach to Corporate Litigation, 1976; Science and Conscience, 1980; contbr. articles in field to profl. jours. Home: One Tall Tree Ln Pleasantville NY 10570 Office: 530 Fifth Ave New York NY 10036

WESSEL, PAUL CHARLES, pub. co. exec.; b. Pitts., Feb. 24, 1948; s. Paul Charles and Rosemary W. (Rebel) W.; B.A., Dickinson Coll., 1970; M.B.A., Rutgers U., 1971; m. Judith Kern Seifert, July 31, 1970; children—Geoffrey David, James Conover. With Price Waterhouse & Co., N.Y.C., 1971-77, audit mgr., 1975-77; dir. internal auditing Harcourt Brace Jovanovich, Inc., N.Y.C., 1977-80, controller, 1980—. C.P.A., N.Y. Mem. Am. Inst. C.P.A.'s, N.Y. State Soc. C.P.A.'s, Inst. Internal Auditors. Club: Jaycees. Office: 757 3d Ave New York NY 10017

WESSELS, ROBERT ROGERS, cons. engr.; b. Atlanta, Oct. 27, 1922; s. Theodore Francis and Mildred Mayrant (Thatcher) W.; B.S., U.S. Mil. Acad., 1944; postgrad. Cornell U., 1948-49; m. Mary Jane Luethke, Aug. 21, 1946; children—William Robert, Kirtley. Commd. 1st lt. C.E., U.S. Army, 1946, advanced through grades to col., 1965; ret., 1973; dir. shuttle constrn. office, dir. facilities NASA Marshall Space Flight Center, Huntsville, Ala., 1972-76; cons. engr. in pvt. practice, Huntsville, 1976—; pres. Wescope Corp., 1977—. Active Boy Scouts Am.; bd. dirs. Aid to Retarded Citizens Assn., 1975—. Registered profl. engr., Ala., Pa. Mem. Soc. Am. Mil. Engrs., Nat. Soc. Profl. Engrs., Assn. U.S. Army, SAR. Republican. Episcopalian. Home: 2005 Shadecrest Rd Huntsville AL 35801 Office: PO Box 204 Huntsville AL 35804

WEST, BILL GRAYUM, mgmt. and tng. cons.; b. Paducah, Tex., May 24, 1930; s. Kade and Ruth (Grayum) W.; B.A., Baylor U., 1951; Th.D., Southwestern Sem., 1957; postgrad. U. Houston, 1970; m. Ann Radnor, June 12, 1976; 1 son, Jason. Ordained to ministry Baptist Ch., 1951; minister First Bapt. Ch., Okmulgee, Okla., 1957-65, River Oaks Bapt. Ch., Houston, 1965-72; asso. prof. Houston Bapt. U., 1972-75; profl. speaker and mgmt. cons., 1975—; pres. West and Assos., Houston, 1975—. Bd. dirs. Baptist Conv. Okla., 1958-65; trustee Houston Bapt. U., 1966-72, mem. exec. com., 1970-71. Mem. Am. Soc. Tng. and Devel., Nat. Speakers Assn., Tex. Soc. Assn. Execs., Houston Speakers Assn. (dir.). Republican. Author: Free To Be Me, 1971; How To Survive Stress, 1980; contbg. editor Indsl. Distbn. mag., 1979—; contbr. articles to various publs. Office: PO Box 218551 Houston TX 77218

WEST, DANIEL JONES, JR., hosp. ofcl.; b. Coaldale, Pa., Sept. 19, 1949; s. Daniel Jones and Mildred Elizabeth Wilkinson (Kreiger) W.; B.S. cum laude, Pa. State U., 1971, Ed.M. summa cum laude, 1972, postgrad., 1974—; m. Linda Jean Werdt, Sept. 18, 1971; children—Jeffrey Bryan, Christopher Jones. Psychol. services asso. Harrisburg (Pa.) State Hosp., 1972; adminstrv. dir./counselor Good Samaritan Hosp., Pottsville, Pa., 1972-74, adminstrv. dir. Alcoholism and Drug Counseling Center, 1975-79, dir. ambulatory and outreach services, 1979—; instr. continuing edn. Pa. State U., Schuylkill campus, 1973—; instr. edn. Pa. State U., University Park campus, 1974-75; cons. drug abuse and alcoholism programming, 1974—; mem. Schuylkill County (Pa.) Drug and Alcohol Exec. Commn., 1977—. Chmn., drug advisory task force Gov.'s Council on Drug and Alcohol Abuse in Pa., 1975-78, mem. treatment com., 1975—; mem. Schuylkill County Criminal Justice System Task Force, 1975—; mem. Pa. Statewide Coordinating Council; mem. local advisory bd. Holy Family Home Health Care Agy. of Schuylkill County, 1977—; mem. Task Force of Child and Family Resource Devel. Program of Schuylkill County, 1973—; bd. dirs. Catherine Caron House, Pottsville, Pa., v.p., 1976—; bd. dirs. Health Systems Agy. N.E. Pa., Inc., 1977—. Cert. rehab. counselor, addictions counselor. Mem. Nat., Pa. rehab. assns., Am. Hosp. Assn. (asso.), Hosp. Assn. Pa., Nat. Rehab. Adminstrn. Assn. (chmn. subcom. on ethics), Am., Pa. personnel and guidance assns., Nat., Pa. vocat. guidance assns., Am., Pa. psychol. assns., Assn. for Advancement Behavior Therapy, Council Rehab. Counselor Educators, Assn. Advancement of Psychology, Alcohol and Drug Problems Assn. N.Am., Am. Pub. Health Assn., Am. Ednl. Research Assn., Assn. Mental Health Adminstrs., Alcoholism Assn. Pa., Nat. Assn. Alcoholism Counselors, Pa. Assn. Tchr. Educators, N. Atlantic Regional Assn. for Counselor Edn. and Supervision, Schuylkill County Mental Health Assn., St. David's Soc. of Schuylkill and Carbon Counties (dir. 1976—), Pa. State, Eastern Pa. Inst. of Alcohol Studies alumni assns., Iota Alpha Delta, Phi Kappa Phi. Clubs: Elks, Masons. Contbr. articles to jours. Home: PO Box 4425 Elmer St RD 4 Pottsville PA 17901 Office: 727 E Norwegian St Pottsville PA 17901

WEST, ERIC, banker; b. Keyser, W.Va., Dec. 26, 1943; s. Frederick and Harriet Miller (Fisher) Sheetz; B.S., Rensselaer Poly. Inst., 1966; M.B.A., Dartmouth, 1968. With Citibank, N.Y.C., 1967—, asst. v.p., 1971-73, v.p., 1973—. Served with AUS, 1968-69. Club: Univ. (N.Y.C.). Home: 160 E 65th St New York NY 10021 Office: 55 Water St New York NY 10043

WEST, FREDERIC W., JR., steel co. exec.; b. Phila.; B.S., Cornell U. With Bethlehem Steel Corp. (Pa.) 1941—, asst. gen. mgr. sales, Bethlehem, 1969-70, v.p. manufactured products, sales, 1970-73, exec. v.p., 1973-74, pres., 1974-77, dir., 1973—, vice chmn., 1977—; dir. Iron Ore Co. Can. Mem. adv. council Grad. Sch. Bus. and Pub. Adminstrn., Cornell U.; trustee St. Luke's Hosp. Served with ordnance AUS, World War II, 1942-46, procurement officer, 1950-52. Mem. Am. Iron and Steel Inst., Conf. Bd., Advt. Council (industries adv. com.). Clubs: Econ. of N.Y., Sky, Chicago, Bethlehem, Saucon Valley Country, Links, Laurel Valley Golf, Blooming Grove Hunting and Fishing. Office: Bethlehem Steel Corp Bethlehem PA 18016

WEST, HAROLD TRUMAN, Realtor; b. Clarksville, Ark., Oct. 26, 1922; s. Dave and Mary Dell (Tucker) W.; grad. Realtors Inst.; m. Ellen Jane Baldwin, Oct. 18, 1968; children (by previous marriage)—Patricia, Martha (Mrs. Mike Lemon), Susanna (Mrs. Richard Roberts), Rebecca. Real estate broker-developer, Redding, Calif., 1952-60; broker, Marin County, Calif., 1960—; pres., Baldwin West & Assos., San Rafael, Calif., 1971—; sec. Ramac Co., Inc., San Rafael, 1974-75; pres. Rancho Parks, Inc., Redding, 1958-61. Served with USMC, 1942-45, 51. Decorated Bronze Star; cert. residential specialist. Mem. Nat. Assn. Real Estate Bds., Marin County Bd. Realtors. Club: Rotary. Home: 16 Galleon Way San Rafael CA 94903 Office: 200 Northgate Shopping Center San Rafael CA 94903

WEST, JOHN ANTHONY, bldg. materials co. exec.; b. Saulte Sainte Marie, Ont., Can., Jan. 2, 1928; s. John Alexander and Adela Catharine (Lewis) W.; B.S., U. Toronto, Ont., 1953; m. Anne Evelyn Forster, Nov. 26, 1954; children—Carol Patricia, David John, Sandra Allison. Constrn. supt. W.A. Mackey Co., Toronto, Ont., 1954-56, King Paving Co. Ltd., Oakville, Ont., 1956-72, various positions to v.p. constrn. King Paving & Materials Ltd., 1972; corporate constrn. mgr. Flintkote Co., Stamford, Conn., 1972-75, pres. subs. Campanella Corp., 1973-75, exec. v.p. H.T. Campbell Sons Co. div., 1975-76, div. pres., 1976-79, pres. Flintkote Stone Products Co. div., 1979—; dir. Balt. Life Ins. Co. Mem. Greater Balt. Com. Inc., 1975—; active United Fund; bd. dirs. Assn. Independent Colls. in Md., 1978—, Commerce and Industry Combined Health Appeal, 1978—, Towson State U. Found., 1978—; bd. govs. Balt. Goodwill Industries. Registered profl. engr., Ont. Mem. Nat. Sand and Gravel Assn. (dir.). Anglican. Clubs: Baltimore Country, Greenspring Inn, Towson. Home: 12 Bafford Ct Glen Arm MD 21057 Office: Flintkote Stone Products Co Executive Plaza IV Hunt Valley MD 21031

WEST, KENNETH ALLEN, accountant; b. Tulsa, Oct. 31, 1946; s. Donald A. and Wanda W.; student U. Tulsa, 1964-66, Met. State Coll., Denver, 1972-74; m. Judith A. Long, Jan. 16, 1971; children—Jennifer, Julie. Acct., Claude Holland, P.A., Denver, 1971-74; audit staff Fox & Co., Denver, 1974-75; fin. reporting mgr. Blue Cross Blue Shield, Denver, 1975-76; mgr. small bus. dept. Combellick, O'Connor & Reynolds, Englewood, Colo., 1976-79; mgr. Zaveral, Boosalis & Raisch, Denver, 1979—. Referee, Little League Soccer; treas. Faith Community Center, 1978-80. Served with USAF, 1967-71. Colo. scholar, 1973. Mem. Colo. Soc. C.P.A.'s, Am. Inst. C.P.A.'s. Club: Optimist (treas.). Home: 7604 S Lamar Ct Littleton CO 80123 Office: 360 S Monroe St Suite 500 Denver CO 80209

WEST, PEARL LEONARD, retail music co. exec.; b. Dean, Iowa, Sept. 18, 1914; s. Clarence Aubry and Lydia Ocle (Rachford) W.; student Centerville Jr. Coll., 1935; B.A. in Music, U. Iowa, 1940; m. Eleanor Louise Bosworth, Mar. 15, 1940; children—Shari Ann, Stephen Leonard. With Paul Wendel Music Co., Des Moines, 1939-41; organized West Music Co., Iowa City, 1941; woodwind instr. Iowa City Public Schs., 1942-44; founder, pres. West Music Co., Inc., Coralville, Iowa, 1945-79, chmn. bd., 1980—; v.p. Everett's Music Co., Washington, Iowa, 1977—; dir. Hawkeye State Bank, Iowa City. Mem. Nat. Assn. Music Mchts. (dir.), Nat. Assn. Sch. Music Dealers, U.S. C. of C., Iowa City C. of C., SCORE (Service Corps Ret. Execs.). Democrat. Methodist. Clubs: Rotary, Elks. Home: 1655 Ridge Rd Iowa City IA 52240 Office: West Music Co Inc 1212 5th St Coralville IA 52241

WEST, PERRY DOUGLAS, lawyer; b. Meadville, Pa., May 16, 1947; s. William Merrill and Rose Marie (Tate) W.; B.A. in Govt. and Econs., Fla. State U., 1968, J.D., 1974; m. Barbara Janet Luecking, June 8, 1974; 1 son, Taylor Benton. Investment counselor Investors Fin. Services, Washington, 1972; admitted to Fla. bar, 1974; practice in Cocoa, 1974-78, Merritt Island, 1978—; partner firm Perry Douglas West, P.A., 1978—, Daly, Ballew, Gaich & West, developers, 1978—; devel. cons., corp. officer Seville, Inc., Beach Club Investments, Inc.; corp. officer Phila. Land Trust, First Combat Corp., Marine Habors, Inc., Port Royal Marine Co. Bd. dirs., counsel Fla. 4-H Found.; bd. dirs. Brevard ALPHA. Served as officer USAR, 1969-72. Mem. Am. Bar Assn., Acad. Trial Lawyers Am., Fla. Public Defenders Assn., Fla. State Bar, Acad. Fla. Trial Lawyers, Brevard County Bar Assn., Porsche Club Am., Phi Delta Phi. Democrat. Clubs: Suntree Country, Indian River Yacht. Contbr. articles to legal publns. Office: 10 N Sykes Creek Pkwy Suite 200 Merritt Island FL 32952

WEST, ROBERT VAN OSDELL, JR., petroleum co. exec.; b. Kansas City, Mo., Apr. 29, 1921; s. Robert Van Osdell and Alma Josephine (Quistgard) W.; B.S., U. Tex., 1942, M.S., 1943, Ph.D., 1949; children—Robert Van Osdell, III, Kathryn Anne, Suzanne Small, Patricia Lynn. Pres., Slick Secondary Recovery Corp., San Antonio, 1956-59, Texstar Petroleum Co., San Antonio, 1959-64; pres. Tesoro Petroleum Corp., San Antonio, 1964-71, chmn. bd., 1971—; dir. Frost Nat. Bank of San Antonio, Commonwealth Oil Refining Co., San Antonio, Continental Telephone Corp., Atlanta, Trinidad-Tesoro Petroleum Co. Ltd., Port-of-Spain, Trinidad, High Stoy Technol. Corp., Gladstone, N.J. Pres., chmn. exec. com. Caribbean/Central Am. Action, Washington; past sr. warden St. Lukes Episcopal Ch., San Antonio; chmn. bd. Tiwanaku Archeol. Found., La Paz, Bolivia; past trustee City Pub. Service Bd., San Antonio; mem. Engring. Found. Adv. Council, U. Tex., Austin; mem. adv. council Sch. Bus. Adminstrn., St. Mary's U., San Antonio; trustee SW Research Inst., San Antonio; chmn. San Antonio Econ. Devel. Found.; bd. dirs. Cascia Hall Prep. Sch., Tulsa. Mem. Am. Petroleum Inst. (nat. dir.), Ind. Petroleum Assn. Am. (dir.), Tex. Mid-Continent Oil and Gas Assn. (dir.), All-Am. Wildcatters, 25 Year Club of Petroleum Industry. Home: 2602 Country Hollow San Antonio TX 78209 Office: 8700 Tesoro Dr San Antonio TX 78286

WEST, SAM, refrigeration co. exec.; b. Glen Ullen, N.D., Jan. 6, 1916; s. Avedis M. and Jessie (Harris) W.; A.B., State Tchrs. Coll., Mayville, N.D., 1938; M.C.S., Amos Tuck Sch., Dartmouth, 1947; grad. econ. mblzn. course Indsl. Coll. Armed Forces, 1953; m. Ruth Driskill, Aug. 27, 1948; children—Gay Anne (Mrs. Ralph Trottier), Sara Elizabeth (Mrs. Roobik Azarnia), Linda Lee. Instr. comml. subjects schs. in McIntosh, Minn., 1938-40, Wadena, Minn., 1941; with Tyler Refrigeration Corp., Niles, Mich., 1947-55, pres. Tyler Refrigeration Internat. subs. Tyler Refrigeration Corp., 1976—. Active local United Fund. Served with USAAF, 1941-45; CBI. Mem. Am. Ordnance Assn., Mich. World Trade Club (sec., past treas.), Kappa Sigma. Republican. Presbyterian. Club: Lions. Home: 532 Cedar St Niles MI 49120 Office: 1329 Lake St Niles MI 49120

WEST, THOMAS LEE, bus. brokerage exec.; b. Chgo., June 17, 1936; s. Raymond Russell and Mary Elizabeth (Thomas) W.; student Pa. State U., 1955-57, Temple U., 1957-59; m. Barbara Ann Wright, Apr. 1, 1972; children—Patricia, Jennifer, Susan, James, Ronald. Founder, pres. United Bus. Investments, Inc., subs. Triple Check, Inc., Paramount, Calif., 1964-79; founder, pres. VR Bus. Brokers, Inc., Needham Heights, Mass., 1979—. Served with U.S. Army, 1959-61. Mem. Internat. Franchise Assn., Am. Mgmt. Assn. (pres.'s club), Smaller Bus. Assn. N.Eng., Phi Gamma Delta. Speaker in field. Home: 118 Silver Hill Rd Concord MA 01742 Office: 197 1st Ave Needham Heights MA 02194

WEST, WILLIAM JOSEPH, JR., indsl. reprographics co. exec.; b. Dayton, Ohio, Oct. 2, 1945; s. William Joseph and Helen Jeanette (Hetzel) W.; student U. Cin., 1968-69, also Bowling Green State U. Pres., Saxon's Sandwich Shops, Columbus, Ohio, 1969-70, Craft Showcase, Dayton, 1970-71, Shirt Gallery, Dayton, 1971—, Engraf Co., Cin.; reprographic cons. to architects, engrs. Mem. Mini Max Internat., Internat. Reprographic Assn. Office: 850 E Ross Ave Cincinnati OH 45217

WESTBROOK, ALBERT G., banker; b. Demopolis, Ala., Nov. 21, 1929; s. Albert G. and Lessie G. (Crockett) W.; B.S. in Bus. Adminstrn., Auburn U., 1951; m. Hazel Solomon, June 3, 1951; children—Rebecca Lynn, Albert Gary. Partner, Emaculate Cleaners, 1956-60; personnel mgr. Marengo Mills div. Vanity Fair, Inc., 1960-68; exec. v.p. Comml. Nat. Bank, Demopolis, 1968-69, pres., 1969—, chmn. bd., 1975—. Mem. Demopolis City Council, 1968-76; former pres. Demopolis Jaycees. Served with USAF, 1951-56. Mem. Demopolis Area C. of C. (pres. 1966). Baptist. Club: Kiwanis. Office: 201 N Main Ave Demopolis AL 36732

WESTBROOK, WILLIAM GALE, mfg. co. exec.; b. Columbus, Ohio, Jan. 7, 1927; s. William Gale and Elizabeth Lucille (Loren) W.; student Ohio State U., 1947-48. With Battelle Meml. Inst., 1950-74, project leader, Bangkok, Thailand, 1967-70, group leader, researcher, Columbus, 1970-74; prodn. mgr. Aerospace Materials Inc., Columbus, 1974-76; v.p., gen. mgr. Clydesbale Aircraft, Inc., aircraft engine remfg., Columbus, 1976—. Mem. Columbus Public TV Task Force, 1974; pres. bd. public affairs City of Hilliard (Ohio), 1954-60, dir. public service, 1960-62. Served with USAAF, 1945-47. Recipient Outstanding Young Man of Yr. award U.S. Jr. C. of C., 1957. Home: 500 Liberty Ln Westerville OH 43081 Office: 3850 E 5th Ave Columbus OH 43219

WESTCOTT, ROBERT FREDERICK, mgmt. cons.; b. Detroit, Sept. 22, 1922; s. Edgar Cecil and Lois (Strongman) W.; B.S. in Agr., Mich. State U., 1948; M.B.A., U. Detroit, 1953; m. Peggy A. Cooper, Sept. 1977; children—Mark A., Robert F., Douglas K., Craig M., Evan D. Cons., Booz Allen and Hamilton, Chgo., 1955-59; v.p. Spencer Stuart and Assos., Chgo., 1959-66, also dir.; pres., treas. Westcott Assos. Inc., Chgo., 1966—; lectr. on interviewing, mgmt. selection. Served with U.S. Army, 1943-45. Clubs: Union League, Monroe. Office: 135 S LaSalle St Chicago IL 60603

WESTENDORF, DAVID RICHARD, produce shipping co. exec.; b. Twin Falls, Idaho, May 6, 1945; s. Richard Henry and Berniece (Brandon) W.; B.Agr., U. Idaho, 1967; M.Agr., U. Calif., Davis, 1968; m. Carolyn D. Casebolt, Sept. 3, 1965; children—David, Eric, Ryan. Salesman, Albers Milling Co., Stockton, Calif., 1968-69, Boise Cascade Co., Sunnyvale, Calif., 1969-72; account exec. corrugated div. Continental Can Co., Los Angeles, 1972-76; sales mgr. produce packaging Continental Forest Industries (formerly Continental Can Co.), Los Angeles, 1976-78; mng. partner G & W Produce Sales Co., Santa Ana, Calif., 1978-79; pres. Dave Westendorf Produce Sales, Inc., Oceanside, Calif., 1979—. Vice pres. Westlake Hills Sch. PTA, Westlake Village, Calif., 1973; bd. dirs. Westlake Hills Property Owners Assn., v.p., 1976; trustee Conejo Future Found., Thousand Oaks, Calif., 1977-78. Club: Rotary. Home: 105 Via Zapata San Clemente CA 92672 Office: PO Box 2297 2521 Oceanside Blvd Oceanside CA 92054

WESTERHOLM, JOHN RUDOLPH, mgmt. cons.; b. N.Y.C., Nov. 28, 1936; s. John W. and Helen A. (Henkel) W.; B.S. in Chem. Engring., U. Detroit, 1965; M.B.A., Pepperdine U., 1975; m. Lois Drake, July 14, 1972. Materials mgr. The Traub Co., Detroit, 1966-69; mgr. ops., chief fin. officer Chemelex, Inc., Redwood City, Calif., 1969-75; pres. Viking Bus. Services, Inc., Los Gatos, Calif., 1975—; chmn. bd. Enviropol Corp., Sunnyvale, Calif., 1975-78; dir. Elint Semicondr. Inc., Santa Clara, Calif.; adj. prof. acctg. and fin. Pepperdine U. Sch. Bus. and Mgmt., 1979—. Bd. dirs. Calif. Acad. Drafting, 1977—, Eshmun Found., San Jose, Calif., 1978—; v.p. Santa Clara Assn. Pvt. Schs. Served with USNR, 1958-60. Certified community coll. instr. in accounting and bus./indsl. mgmt., Calif. Mem. Profl. and Tech. Cons. Assn. Club: Elks. Office: 120 Montclair Rd Los Gatos CA 95030

WESTERMANN, DAVID, lawyer, electronic industry exec. and cons.; b. N.Y.C., Mar. 2, 1920; s. John Jacob and Margaret (Maher) W.; A.B., Columbia, 1941, LL.B., 1943; LL.D. (hon.), Adelphi U., 1979; m. Edith E. West, Mar. 11, 1972; children by previous marriage—Nancy, John Jacob, David. Admitted to N.Y. bar, 1943; asso. firm Donald A. Gray, N.Y.C., 1947-48, William P. McCool, N.Y.C., 1948-50; lawyer Hazeltine Corp., Green Lawn, N.Y., 1950—, v.p., gen. counsel, 1961-66, pres., chief exec. officer, 1966-80, chmn. also dir.; pres. Hazeltine Research, Inc., Chgo., 1963-66, dir., 1963-78; prof. James Forrestal Chair, Def. Systems Mgmt. Coll., Ft. Belvoir, Va., 1981—; dir. Nat. Bank N. Am., Mem. bd. edn. S. Huntington Schs., Union Free Sch. Dist. 13, 1956-59, pres., 1959-60; bd. dirs., 1st v.p. Urban League L.I.; bd. dirs. Action Com. L.I.; chmn. bd. dirs. Performing Arts Found. L.I.; trustee Poly. Inst. N.Y. Served to 1st lt. AUS, 1942-46. Mem. Columbia Coll. and Columbia Law Sch. alumni assns., Nat. Security Indsl. Assn. (trustee 1969—, chmn. 1975-76), Nat. Contract Mgmt. Assn. (bd. advs.), L.I. Forum Tech. (founding chmn. 1977—), Am. Bar Assn., Urban League L.I., Am. Legion, Air Force Assn., Delta Psi, Phi Delta Phi. Clubs: Mariner Sands Country, Wings, Westhampton Country. Home: 3050 Palm Aire Dr N Pompano Beach FL 33060 also 15 Meadow Ln Westhampton Beach NY 11978

WESTFALL, DEAN PAUL, internat. trade cons.; b. Akron, Ohio, May 18, 1920; s. Donald Edmond and Rissa May (Black) W.; student Hammel Bus. Coll., 1938-39, Actual Bus. Coll., 1946-47, Internat. Corr. Schs., 1949-51; m. Pauline Kornas, Aug. 22, 1941; children—Richard Dean, John Thomas, Shirley Anne. Dept. mgr. waste control and methods investigation Goodyear Aircraft Corp., Akron, 1941-42, 45-46; warehouse contractor War Surplus Adminstrn., Dallas, 1946; asst. indsl. engr. Luscombe Aircraft Co., Garland, Tex., 1946-47; traffic mgr., purchasing agt. Moncreif-Lenoir, Houston, 1947-52; owner Mgmt. & Cons. Services, Houston, 1952-60; port dir., mgr. indsl. park Warren County Port Commn., Vicksburg, Miss., 1960-66; cons. on water traffic, 1949-66; regional mgr. Nissho-Iwai Am. Corp., 1966-71; owner D.P. Westfall, Memphis, 1971—, Cambridge, Ohio, 1980—. Mem. Warren County Indsl. Com., 1964-66; mem. Nat. Def. Exec. Res. Mem. Warren County Republican Exec. Com., 1964—. Served with AUS, 1942-45. Decorated Bronze Star. Mem. Vicksburg C. of C., Miss. Rivers and Harbors Assn., Nat. Def. Transp. Assn., Am. Assn. Port Authorities, Central Miss. Traffic Club, Delta Nu Alpha. Presbyterian. Kiwanian. Home: 1123 Stewart St Cambridge OH 43725 Office: PO Box 248 Cambridge OH 43725

WESTGAARD, ODIN EVERETT, instructional design co. exec.; b. Cody, Wyo., Dec. 9, 1936; s. Olaf and Willie Ruth (Brim) W.; B.A., Western State of Colo., 1962; M.A., U. No. Colo., 1968, Ed.D., 1970; m. Goldie Jane Schmid, Aug. 17, 1958; children—Olaf, Orville, Oscar. Tchr. public schs., Craig, Colo., 1962-66, elem. sch. tchr., 1966-67; instr. U. No. Colo., Greeley, 1968-70; asst. prof. Central Wash. State U., Ellensburg, 1970-75; asst. prof. U. Victoria (B.C., Can.), 1975-76; instructional designer Advanced Systems, Inc., Elk Grove, Ill., 1976—; cons. to mgmt. Precinct committeeman Republican Party, 1969-70; cons. East Wenatchee (Wash.) Bd. Edn., 1972-75; chief negotiator, chmn. chpt. welfare com. NEA, 1965-67. Served with U.S. Army, 1958-62. Recipient Bausch & Lombe Sci. award, 1955; Continental Oil scholar, 1955-60. Mem. Am. Chem. Soc., Nat. Soc. Performance and Instruction, Am. Soc. Tng. and Devel., Phi Delta Kappa. Republican. Mem. United Ch. of Christ. Contbr. articles to profl. jours. Home: 316A Easton Ave Prairie View IL 60069 Office: 1601 Tonne St Elk Grove Village IL 60007

WESTON, STANLEY ROBERT, JR., real estate appraisal co. exec.; b. Cedarhurst, N.Y., Sept. 23, 1919; s. Stanley Robert and Hulda (Jackson) W.; B.S. in Fin., N.Y. U., 1949; postgrad. Rutgers U., 1956, Dartmouth Coll., 1957; m. Verna A. Brush, July 9, 1942; children—Nancy A., Robert F., Lauren A. With Rockaway Savs. Bank (merged with Jamaica Savs. Bank), Far Rockaway, N.Y., 1937-62, comptroller, 1948-57, trustee, 1951-57, v.p., 1956-57, asst. sec., 1957-62; treas. Joseph J. Blake & Assos., Inc., Woodbury, N.Y., 1962—, v.p., 1966-70, sr. v.p., 1970—, also dir. Trustee Grace United Methodist Ch., Valley Stream, N.Y. Served to capt. U.S. Army, 1941-46. Decorated Bronze Star. Mem. Am. Inst. Real Estate Appraisers, L.I. Bd. Realtors, Internat. Right of Way Assn. (pres. N.Y. state chpt. 1975), Nat. Assn. Accts. Clubs: Exchange (pres. 1959), Sky Island. Home: 63 E Fenimore St Valley Stream NY 11580 Office: 100 Crossways Park W Woodbury NY 11797

WESTON, WILLARD GALEN, bus. exec.; b. Eng., Oct. 29, 1940; s. W. Garfield and Reta L. W.; student U. Western Ont. (Can.); m. Hilary M. Frayne, 1965; 2 children. Founder, owner, operator food co. and dept. store, Ireland, 1960-73; chief exec. officer Loblau Ltd., 1973-74; pres., chief exec. officer Loblau Cos. Ltd., 1974; chmn., mng. dir. George Weston Ltd., Toronto, Ont., 1974-78, chmn. bd., pres., 1978—. Office: 22 Saint Clair Ave E Toronto ON M4T 2S7 Canada

WESTPHAL, RAINER JOHN, data processing co. exec.; b. Huntington Station, N.Y., July 7, 1935; s. Frank and Gertrude W.; B.S. in Bus. Adminstrn., Drexel U., 1959; m. Antoinette Westphal, May 7, 1960; children—Jeffrey, Stefanie, Amanda. Programmer/analyst RCA, Camden, N.J., 1960-61; systems mgr. Ednl. Testing Service, Princeton, N.J., 1961-68; sr. mgmt. cons. Peat, Marwick, Mitchell & Co., Phila., 1968-72; v.p. Vertex Systems Inc., King of Prussia, Pa., 1972-78, pres., 1978—. Mem. Jaycees (sec. 1967). Roman Catholic. Clubs: Martin's Dam Swim and Tennis (Wayne, Pa.); Chester Valley Golf (Frazer, Pa.). Home: 460 Woodcrest Rd Wayne PA 19087 Office: 222 Lancaster Ave Devon PA 19333

WESTPHAL, ROGER ALLEN, grain merchandising exec.; b. Hillsboro, Ill., Aug. 5, 1942; s. Clarence Charles and Marguerite Lucille (Brakenhoff) W.; B.S. in Fin., U. Ill., 1971, M.B.A., 1973. Gen. office employee Rieke Elevator & Supply, Nokomis, Ill., 1961-64, asst. mgr., 1973-77, gen. mgr., chief adminstrv. officer, 1977—. Mem. adv. com. Krannert Center for Performing Arts, 1971-73. Served with USAF, 1964-68. Decorated AF Commendation medal. Mem. Grain Elevator and Processing Soc., Am. Mgmt. Assn., Assn. M.B.A. Execs., U. Ill. Alumni Assn., Sigma Iota Epsilon. Republican. Lutheran. Home: Route 1 Box 36 Harvel IL 62538 Office: Route 1 Box 108 Nokomis IL 62075

WESTRAN, ROY ALVIN, ins. co. exec.; b. Taft, Oreg., Apr. 30, 1925; s. Carl A. and Mae E. (Barnhardt) W.; B.B.A., Golden Gate Coll., 1955, M.B.A., 1957; m. Dawn M. Oeschger, Oct. 18, 1952; children—Denise, Thomas, Michael, Dawna. Mem. sales staff C.A. Westran Agy., Taft, 1946-49; underwriter Fireman's Fund Group, San Francisco, ins. mgr. Kaiser Aluminum Chem., Oakland, 1952-65; pres., dir. Citizens Ins. Co. Am., Howell, Mich., 1967—; pres., dir. Am. Select Risk Ins. Co. and Beacon Mut. Indemnity Co., Columbus, Ohio, 1969—; v.p. Hanover Ins. Co.; dir. Worcester Mut. Ins. Co. (Mass.), 1st Nat. Bank, Howell. Mem. ins. adv. council Salvation Army, San Francisco, 1957-60; chmn. drive United Fund, 1970. Bd. dirs., exec. com. Portage Trails council Boy Scouts Am., 1970-72; trustee Traffic Safety Assn. Detroit, 1967, Traffic Safety for Mich., 1967, McPherson Health Center, Howell; mem. bus. adv. council Central Mich. U. Served with AUS, 1943-46. C.P.C.U. Mem. Ins. Inst. Am., Mich. C. of C. (dir. 1968-71), Am. Soc. Ins. Mgmt. (pres. 1960-62), Soc. C.P.C.U. (nat. pres. 1968-69), Mich. Catastrophic Claims Assn. (vice chmn.). Home: 5835 Griffith Dr Brighton MI 48116 Office: 645 W Grand River Howell MI 48843

WESTROM, ROBERT GEORGE, microfilm and mosquito control co. exec.; b. Des Moines, Feb. 4, 1925; s. Fred William and Grace Marie (Canady) W.; B.A. in Bus. Adminstrn., N. Central Coll., Naperville, Ill., 1951; m. Thelma Jean Robertson, July 1948; children—Dean Robert, Brad Canady, Lee Francis, Jan Lisa. Supt. personnel dept. Studebaker Corp., Chgo., 1951-55; owner, operator Shoe Tree, West Chicago, Ill., 1955-65, Tifa Sales Corp., West Chicago, 1965-79; owner, pres., dir. Microchem, Inc., West Chicago, 1979—. Mem. Bd. Edn. Dist. 94, West Chicago, 1969—, pres., 1974-78; dep. chief West Chicago Fire Protection Dist., 1971-74. Served with USN, 1942-45. Named Citizen of Yr., West Chicago C. of C., 1957. Mem. Am. Mosquito Control Assn., Ill. Pest Control Assn., Ill. Mosquito Control Assn., Nat. Micrographics Assn., Ind. Sanitarians, Ind. Vector Control Assn., Ill. Sch. Bds. Assn. Republican. Methodist. Club: Rotary (past pres.). Home: 426 E Washington St West Chicago IL 60185 Office: Microchem Inc 185 W Washington St West Chicago IL 60185

WESTWOOD, ALBERT RONALD CLIFTON, research adminstr.; b. Birmingham, U.K., June 9, 1932; came to U.S., 1958, naturalized, 1974; s. Albert Sydney and Ena Emily (Clifton) W.; B.Sc. with honors, U. Birmingham, 1953, Ph.D., 1956, D.Sc., 1968; m. Jean Mavis Bullock, Dec. 8, 1956; children—Abigail, Andrea. Tech. officer I.C.I. Metals div., U.K., 1956-58; with Martin Marietta Labs., Balt., 1958—, head materials sci. dept., 1964-69, dep. dir., 1969-74, dir., 1974—; mem. rev. com. Nat. Bur. Standards, 1972-75, Argonne Nat. Labs., 1976—; mem. nat. materials adv. bd. Nat. Acad. Scis., 1979—; vis. lectr. Acad. Scis., USSR, 1969, 76, 78. Johns Hopkins U. fellow, 1965—; recipient Beilby Gold medal Royal Inst. Chemistry, Soc. Chem. Industry and Inst. Metals, U.K., 1970; Tewksbury lectr. Melbourne U., Australia, 1974. Fellow Inst. Metallurgists (U.K.), Inst. Physics (U.K.), Am. Soc. Metals; mem. Nat. Acad. Engring., AIME (dir. Metall. Soc. 1980—), AAAS. Author numerous publs. on environ.-sensitive mech. behavior. Home: 908 E Joppa Rd Towson MD 21204 Office: 1450 S Rolling Rd Baltimore MD 21227

WETHERILL, EIKINS, lawyer; b. Phila., Oct. 3, 1919; s. A. Hecksher and Edwina (Brunner) W.; LL.B., U. Pa., 1948. Practiced in Phila., 1948-55, Norristown, 1955—; asso. firm Evans, Bayard & Frick, 1948-50; partner firm Reilly, Hepburn, Earle & Wetherill, 1950-55, firm Henderson, Wetherill, O'Hey & Horsey, 1955—; pres. Phila. Stock Exchange, Inc., 1965-81; dir. Norfolk So. Ry. Co., Germantown Savs. Bank; fin. commentator CBS-TV News, 1966-68; chmn. bd. Sta. WHYY-TV, 1970-76, dir., 1976—; dir. 1st Pa. Corp., 1st Pa. Bank; solicitor to lt. gov. Pa., 1951-55; asst. U.S. atty. gen., 1953-55; treas. Montgomery County, 1956-59; pres. Montgomery County Bd. Commrs., 1960-63; chmn. Pa. Securities Commn., 1963-65; commr. Delaware Valley Regional Planning Commn., 1965—, chmn., 1968-69, 70-71, 78-79. Bd. dirs. Greater Phila. Partnership Pa. Economy League; chmn. Phila. Drama Guild, 1975-79. Served to capt., cav., Signal Corps, OSS, AUS, 1941-45. Mem. Am., Phila. bar assns., Phila. Greater C. of C. (dir.), Delta Psi. Episcopalian. Clubs: Phila., Racquet (Phila.). Office: 17th St and Stock Exchange Pl Philadelphia PA 19103

WETHERN, JAMES DOUGLAS, pulp and paper co. exec.; b. Mpls., July 12, 1926; s. Rudolph Jesse and Ida Oliva (Nelson) W.; B.S.Ch.E., U. Wis., 1947; M.S., Inst. Paper Chemistry, 1949, Ph.D., 1952; m. Yvonne Marie Zuelko, Sept. 11, 1948; children—Mary, Michael, Jeffrey, Thomas. Chief pulp sect., chief paper sect., coordinator applied research Crown Zellerbach, Camas, Wash., 1951-58; tech. dir., mgr. mfg. service Riegel Paper, Acme, N.C., 1959-65, v.p. La. ops., Port Hudson, 1965-68, v.p. mfg., pulp and paper div., N.Y.C., 1968-72; v.p. mfg. Brunswick Pulp & Paper (Ga.), 1972-80, pres., 1980—. Active United Fund; bd. dirs. Hunterdon Med. Center, 1970-72; chmn. Cape Fear Tech. Inst., 1962-65. Served with USN, 1944-46. Mem. TAPPI, Am. Mgmt. Assn., Can. Pulp and Paper Assn. Episcopalian. Clubs: Rotary, Kiwanis. Contbr. articles to profl. jours.; patentee in field. Home: 218 Devonwood St Saint Simons Island GA 31522 Office: PO Box 1438 Brunswick GA 31520

WETHINGTON, CHARLES MICHAEL, security products co. exec.; b. Lebanon, Ind., June 26, 1949; s. Charles Thomas and Betty Louise (Bowman) W.; student Purdue U., 1968-69, Midwestern State U., Wichita Falls, Tex., 1973, Ind. U./Purdue U., Indpls., 1977—; m. Barbara Ann Austin, Mar. 11, 1972; children—Michelle Jennifer, Heather Nicole. Installer, Mosler Safe Co., Indpls., 1973-77, project installation mgr., 1978-80, br. installation/service mgr., 1980—; service customer ops. rep. Honeywell, Inc., Indpls., 1977-78. Served with USAF, 1969-73. Mem. N.G. Assn. U.S. Baptist. Office: Mosler Safe Co 2231 Distributors Dr Indianapolis IN 46241

WETMORE, JAMES RUSSELL, cutting tools mfg. co. exec.; b. Roxbury, Conn., Feb. 24, 1910; s. Frank Edward and Martha Elizabeth (Holden) W.; student public schs.; m. Frances Walker, May 30, 1949; children—James Edward, Ralph Fredrick, Richard Lawrence. Various positions State of Conn., 1924-42; with Wetmore Cutting Tools, Pico Rivera, Calif., 1950—, pres., chmn. bd., 1978—. Served with N.G., 1930-35. Mem. Cutting Tool Mfrs. Assn. (dir. 1975—), Pico Rivera C. of C. (dir. 1974—), Nat. Tool and Die Assn., NAM. Republican. Clubs: Masons, Shriners, K.T. Office: Wetmore Cutting Tools PO Box 68 9129 Perkins St Pico Rivera CA 90660

WETSEL, BILLY DWAIN, accountant; b. Mangum, Okla., Feb. 9, 1953; s. Robert Carroll and Melvena (Riddle) W.; B.S., Southwestern Okla. State U., 1975; m. Monica Pauline Todd, Apr. 22, 1978; 1 son, Todd Dwain. Internal auditor Phillips Petroleum Co., Bartlesville, Okla., 1975-77; mgr. accounting unit Southwestern Bell Telephone Co., Oklahoma City, 1977-78; staff acct. Luton & Co., Inc., Oklahoma City, 1977-78; property acct., tax mgr. TRG Drilling Corp., Oklahoma City, 1978; acct. Phillips Petroleum Co., Bartlesville, 1978—. Mem. Jr. C. of C. Democrat. Lutheran. Home: 1711 Orchard Ln Bartlesville OK 74003 Office: 9B-2 Adams Bldg Bartlesville OK 74004

WETZEL, ALBERT JOHN, univ. adminstr., systems analyst, cons.; b. New Orleans, Dec. 29, 1917; s. Albert John and Emelie (Willoz) W.; B.Engring., Tulane U., 1939; M.S., Johns Hopkins U., 1950; postgrad. UCLA, George Washington U., 1952, 1956; m. Helen Elizabeth Zurad, Sept. 7, 1946; children—Albert John, Elizabeth Ann, Joan Clark, Edward Russel. Commd. 2d lt. C.E., U.S. Army, 1941, advanced through grades to col. USAF, 1956; service in Europe, Asia, Middle East; wing comdr. SAC, 1955-57; dir. Titan ICBM and Gemini Space Program, 1957-62; exec. dir. USAF Council, 1962-63; dir. strategic programs, def., research and engring. Office Sec. of Def., 1963-65; ret., 1965; dir. research and sponsored programs, then dir. univ. devel. Tulane U., 1965-76, v.p. alumni and univ. affairs, 1976-80, sr. adv. to pres., 1980—, adj. prof. mgmt. and engring. mgmt., 1965—; mem. rocket and space panel Pres.'s Sci. Adv. Com., 1965—; bd. dirs. Gulf South Research Inst., Inst. Def. Analysis, Washington; del. Nat. Conf. Advancement Research. Bd. dirs. Walter Clark Teagle Found. (N.Y.C.), Oak Ridge Asso. Univs., Navy League U.S., Crippled Children's Hosp., New Orleans, La. Council Music and Performing Arts, Council. Devel. French in La.; trustee Delgado Jr. Coll.; v.p., bd. dirs. New Orleans Catholic Found.; bd. dirs. Girl Scouts U.S.A.; exec. com. local Boy Scouts Am.; commr. La. Ednl. Authority. Decorated Legion of Merit, Armed Forces and AF Commendation Medal. Registered profl. engr., Ohio. Mem. Greater New Orleans Area C. of C. (v.p.), Sigma Xi, Kappa Sigma, Tau Beta Pi, Omicron Delta Kappa. Clubs: Internat. House, Bienville, Plimsoll (New Orleans); Univ. (N.Y.C.); Army-Navy (Washington); Rotary. Contbr. articles on aeros., strategic mil. weapons and strategy to profl. jours. Home: 7 Richmond Pl New Orleans LA 70115 Office: Tulane University University Station New Orleans LA 70118

WETZEL, EDWARD THOMAS, pub. co. exec.; b. Indpls., Apr. 16, 1937; s. Edward George and Sarah Catherine W.; B.A., Bethany (W.Va.) Coll., 1959; M.B.A., U. Mass., Amherst, 1962; m. Stanlee Lucille Nott, June 26, 1965; children—Raymond, Cynthia. Market research analyst Gen. Electric Co., Pittsfield, Mass., 1960-63; editor, spl. projects dir., asst. v.p. DMS, Inc., Greenwich, Conn., 1964-70; pres. Industry News Service, Inc., Wilton, Conn., 1970—; pres. Emergency Care Info. Center div. Industry News Service, Inc. Pres. Wilton Vol. Ambulance Corps, 1976—; bd. dirs. Norwalk-Wilton chpt. ARC. Served to 2d lt. USAFR, 1959-65. Mem. Tech. Mktg. Soc. Am., Am. Assn. Automotive Medicine. Club: Kiwanis (v.p., dir. chpt.). Editor various def. industry publs. Home: 701 Ridgefield Rd Wilton CT 06897 Office: Industry News Service Inc PO Box 457 Wilton CT 06897

WETZEL, ELLEN LIVELY, bus. devel. co. exec., pub. exec.; b. Fayette County, W.Va., Jan. 22, 1936; d. Alfred French and Sarah Ellen (Pritchard) L.; student N.Mex. State U., 1962-74; m. Harold Bernard Wetzel, Aug. 10, 1968; children—Gregory Benjamin Pake, Seana Ellen Pake. Civilian adminstrv. officer Dept. Army, White Sands Missile Range, N.Mex., 1962-67; mgr. Kelly Services Inc., Las Cruces, N.Mex., 1967—; pres. Lively Enterprises, Inc., Las Cruces, 1967-76; sec., treas. Adam II, Ltd., Las Cruces, 1973-77; pres. Dr. Romero's Symposium Internat. Inc., Las Cruces, 1977-78, Asset & Resource Mgmt. Corp., Organ, N.Mex., 1978—; lit. agt., prin. Ellen Lively Wetzel & Assos., 1979—; advt. dir. for South and Southwest, Conservative Digest, 1980—. Served with USAF, 1954-57. Mem. Internat. Assn. Fin. Planners, Sales & Mktg. Execs. Internat., Am. Mgmt. Assn., D.A.R. Republican. Episcopalian. Club: Order Eastern Star; Assn. (Las Cruces). Home and Office: San Augustine Pass Organ NM 88052

WETZEL, HARRY HERMAN, JR., mfg. co. exec.; b. Howard, Pa., Jan. 27, 1920; s. Harry Herman and Maude Caroline (Thomas) W.; B.S., Cornell U., 1941; m. Margaret Kirkpatrick, July 23, 1945; children—Sally, Harry Herman III, Katherine, John. With Garrett Corp., Los Angeles, 1946—, mgr. airesearch div., 1958-62, exec. v.p., 1962-63, pres., 1962-67, pres., 1967-79, chmn., 1967—, chief exec. officer, 1979—, also dir., mem. exec. com.; dir., mem. exec. com. Signal Cos.; dir. Thiokol Corp., UOP Inc., Nat. Semicondr. Corp. Vice chmn. bd. govs. Performing Arts Council of Music Center, Los Angeles; trustee Donald Douglas Mus. and Library, Calif. Inst. Tech. Served to capt. pilot USAAF, 1941-45. Mem. Aerospace Industries Assn. (gov.), Am. Inst. Aeros. and Astronautics, Conquistadores del Cielo, Confrerie des Chevaliers du Tastevin, U. So. Calif. Assos., Beta Theta Pi. Episcopalian (vestry). Home: 401 Via Media Palos Verdes Estates CA 90274 Office: 9851 Sepulveda Blvd Los Angeles CA 90009

WETZEL, JAMES LEWIS, chem. co. exec.; b. Greenfield, Mo., Sept. 23, 1916; s. Lewis A. and Lillian (Lyngar) W.; student U.S. Naval Acad., 1934-36; m. Mary Louise Hill, Dec. 31, 1938; children—James Lewis, John H. With Atlas Powder Co., Wilmington, Del., 1937-43, 46-59, dist. sales mgr., 1951-55, regional sales mgr., 1956-59; v.p., gen. mgr. explosives ops., Olin Mathieson Chem. Corp., N.Y.C., 1959-63; pres. A. M. Byers Co., Pitts., 1963-73, also dir.; group v.p. chems. Gen. Tire & Rubber Co., Akron, Ohio, 1973-77, pres. GTR Chem. Co., Chem./Plastics div. Gen. Tire & Rubber Co., 1977—; dir. Fenix & Scisson, Tulsa; bd. dirs. Internat. Inst. Synthetic Rubber Producers, Houston. Served to lt. (s.g.) USNR, 1943-46. Clubs: Duquesne (Pitts.); Allegheny Country (Sewickley, Pa.); Sharon Golf (Sharon Center, Ohio). Office: PO Box 1829 Akron OH 44329

WETZEL, JOHN KEITH, banking exec.; b. White Plains, N.Y., Feb. 1, 1933; s. William McKinley and Zella Gertrude (Mason) W.; B.A., Dartmouth Coll., 1955, M.B.A., 1956; m. Elizabeth Louise Griffin, Dec. 26, 1954; children—Daniel M., James M., Susan L., Deborah L., Thomas K. Sec., Fyr-Fyter Co., N.Y.C., 1959-64; v.p. Irving Trust Co., N.Y.C., 1964-71; pres. Goldsmith Bros., N.Y.C., 1971-73; v.p., head met. banking Morgan Guaranty Trust Co., N.Y.C., 1973—. Served with USAF, 1956-58. Home: 633 Valley Rd Watchung NJ 07060 Office: Morgan Guaranty Trust Co 40 Rockefeller Plaza New York NY 10020

WEXLER, MELVIN JAY, mfg. co. exec.; b. Los Angeles, Dec. 1, 1940; s. Arnold H. and Marilyn (Lazarof) W.; B.A. (Stanley Morse scholar 1962), San Francisco State U., 1963; M.B.A., Stanford U., 1970; m. Betty Jean Keller, Dec. 21, 1969; children—Jennifer Lynn, David Elliott. Systems asso. So. Pacific R.R., 1963-67; sr. systems analyst Stanford U., 1967-68; instr. data processing DeAnza Coll., Cupertino, Calif., 1968-70; product planner Ford Motor Co., Dearborn, Mich., 1970-75; sr. mgr. market analysis Nissan Motor Corp., Carson, Calif., 1975—; tchr. bus. Orange Coast Coll., Costa Mesa, Calif., 1978—. Pres. Sunridge Community Assn., 1978-80, Turtlerock Village Assn., 1980—. Mem. Am. Mktg. Assn., Automotive Mktg. Research Council. Home: 7 Rimrock Irvine CA 92715 Office: PO Box 191 Gardena CA 90247

WEXNER, LESLIE HERBERT, retail co. exec.; b. Dayton, Ohio, Sept. 8, 1937; s. Harry Louis and Bella (Cabakoff) W.; B.S., Ohio State U., 1959, postgrad. Law Sch., 1959-61. Founder, pres., chmn. bd. Ltd. Stores, Inc., fashion chain, Columbus, Ohio, 1963—. Founder Orphan's Day at Ohio State Fair; bd. dirs. Hillel Found.; trustee Columbus Jewish Fedn., 1972—, Heritage House-Columbus Jewish Home for Aged, 1972-76; bd. dirs. St. Anthony's Hosp., Agudas Achim Synagogue; mem. bus. adminstrn. adv. council Ohio State U. Named One of 10 Outstanding Young Men, Columbus Jaycees, 1971; Man of Yr., Am. Mktg. Assn., 1974. Mem. Young Pres. Orgn., Columbus Area C. of C. (dir. 1979-80), Sigma Alpha Mu. Jewish. Club: B'nai B'rith (dir. 1972; dir. Project Hope/Men's Div.). Office: One Limited Pkwy Columbus OH 43230

WEYERHAEUSER, GEORGE HUNT, forest products co. exec.; b. Seattle, July 8, 1926; s. John Philip and Helen (Walker) W.; B.S. with honors in Indsl. Engring., Yale, 1948; m. Wendy Wagner, July 10, 1948; children—Virginia Lee, George Hunt, Susan W., Phyllis A., David M., Merrill W. With Weyerhaeuser Co., Tacoma, 1949—, successively mill foreman, br. mgr., 1949-56, v.p., 1957-62, exec. v.p., 1962-66, pres., 1966—, also chief exec. officer, dir.; dir. Boeing Co., SAFECO Corp., Standard Oil Co. Calif., Weyerhaeuser Can., Ltd. Office: Weyerhaeuser Co Tacoma WA 98477

WEYGAND, LAWRENCE RAY, ins. broker; b. South Haven, Mich., Jan. 5, 1940; s. Ray and Lorraine (Berkins) W.; B.A., Drake U., 1962, postgrad., 1962-63; m. Lois Henderson, Dec. 22, 1962; 1 son, Chad C. Comml. multi-peril ins. underwriter Aetna Casualty & Surety Co., Mpls., also Indpls., 1964-66, Safeco Ins. Co., Denver, 1966-69; pres., chmn. bd. Weygand & Co., ins. agts., brokers and consultants, Denver, 1969—; pres. Transatlantic Underwriters, Inc., Homeowners Ins., Inc., Scottsdale, Ariz. and Denver, Weygand & Co. of Ariz., Inc., Scottsdale; owner U.S. Insurors, Inc., Ariz. Dealers Ins. Services, Inc., Colo. Dealers Ins. Services, Inc., Denver, Storage Pak Ins., Inc.; asst. to Gov. State of Iowa, 1961-62. Mem. bus. community adv. council Regis Coll., 1976-77. Mem. Ind. Ins. Agts. Colo. (chmn. fair and ethical practice com.), Ind. Ins. Agts. Am., Profl. Ins. Agts. Colo., Profl. Ins. Agts. Ariz., Profl. Ins. Agts. Am., Alpha Tau Omega. Republican. Congregationalist. Clubs: Denver Athletic. Home: 10703 E Crestline Ave Englewood CO 80110 also 8415 E San Candido Dr Scottsdale AZ Office: 1582 S Parker Rd Denver CO 80231 also 6991 E Camelback Ave Suite B-301 Scottsdale AZ 85251

WEYGAND, LEROY CHARLES, security exec.; b. Webster Park, Ill., May 17, 1926; s. Xaver William and Marie Caroline (Hoffert) W.; B.A. cum laude, U. Md., 1964; grad. Command and Gen. Staff Coll., 1965, Indsl. Def. Sch., 1965; m. Helen Bishop Bangs, Aug. 28, 1977; children by previous marriage—Linda M. Weygand Vance (dec.), Leroy C., Cynthia R., Janine P. Commd. 2d lt. U.S. Army, 1949, advanced through grades to lt. col., 1969, ret., 1969; chief phys. security U.S. Army, Washington, 1965-69; exec. v.p. Taurus Assos., Alexandria, Va., 1970-71; pres. Weygand Security Cons., Washington, also Anaheim, Calif., 1971—; security dir. Jeffries Banknote Co., Los Angeles, 1972-78; exec. v.p., dir. Mind PSI Biotics Inc., Anaheim, 1977—; pres. W & W Devel. Corp., Anaheim, 1979—. Decorated Legion of Merit. Mem. Am. Soc. Indsl. Security (cert. protection profl. award 1977). Inventor office equipment locking device and automatic radio volume control; contbr. articles to Nat. Locksmith Mag.; editor Insights Mag., 1976—. Home: Star Route 1 Box 800-89 Tehachapi CA 93561 Office: 125 E Ball Rd Anaheim CA 92805

WHALEN, DONALD ROBERT, electronics and communications co. exec.; b. Bklyn., June 4, 1936; s. Henry C. and Ethel (Jenkins) W.; B.S., N.Y. U., 1962; m. Arlene Campbell, Sept. 27, 1957; children—Christopher, Paul, Timothy. Audit mgr. Deloitte Haskins & Sells, N.Y.C., 1962-72; corp. comptroller ABC, Inc., N.Y.C., 1972-76; staff v.p. ops. analysis RCA Corp., N.Y.C., 1976—. Served with USNR, 1976-79. C.P.A., N.Y. Mem. N.Y. State Soc. C.P.A.'s (chmn. non-profit orgns. com. 1971-72), Fin. Execs. Inst., Am. Inst. C.P.A.'s. Methodist (chmn. adminstrv. bd. 1975-77). Club: Rockefeller Center Luncheon. Office: 30 Rockefeller Plaza New York NY 10020

WHALEN, JOHN SYDNEY, financial exec.; b. Moncton, N.B., Can., Sept. 26, 1934; s. Harry Edward and Sarah Maude (Bourgeois) W.; grad. Canadian Inst. Chartered Accountants, 1959; m. Margaret Joan Carruthers, May 3, 1958; children—Bradley Graham, Elizabeth Ann. Chartered accountant McDonald, Currie & Co., St. John, N.B., 1954-63; with Kaiser Services, Oakland, Calif., 1963-75, telecommunications mgr., 1966, asst. controller, 1969, controller, 1970-74; mgr. corporate accounting Kaiser Industries Corp., Oakland, 1975, controller Kaiser Engrs. div., 1975-76, v.p., controller Kaiser Engrs. div., 1976-77, v.p. finance and adminstrn., 1977—. Bd. dirs. Mt. Diablo council Boy Scouts Am., 1974-75. Mem. Fin. Execs. Inst. Club: Round Hill Country. Home: 2216 Nelda Way Alamo CA 94507 Office: 300 Lakeside Dr Oakland CA 94623

WHATLEY, LISA GOULART, business exec.; b. Rio de Janeiro, Brazil, Nov. 4, 1940; d. Adhemar Vieira and Elzira V. Ramos Goulart; came to U.S., 1964, naturalized, 1970; B.A., U. Rio de Janeiro, B.S., 1962; postgrad. Conservatorio Giusepi Verdi, Milan, Italy, 1958-60, Columbia U., 1964-66; m. William J. Whatley, Apr. 5, 1976; children—Lee Adhemar G. Feldshon. Vice pres. fin., dir. internat. div. W. J. Whatley, Inc., Commerce City, Colo., 1975-80, pres., chief exec. officer, 1980—. Tutor, Adams County High Sch. Recipient award Family Orphanage Brazil, 1960. Home: 1300 Green Meadow Ln Littleton CO 80121 Office: 6980 E 54th Pl Commerce City CO 80022

WHATMOUGH, J. JEREMY T., r.r. co. exec.; b. Boston, Sept. 24, 1934; s. Joshua and Cerona (Taylor) W.; A.B., Harvard U., 1956; m. Myrna Ferrell, Nov. 5, 1960; children—Jeremy, Jocelyn. With Ford Motor Co., Dearborn, Mich., 1956-70; with Am. Motors Corp., Detroit, 1970-79, exec. dir. quality and reliability, 1976-79, dir. mfg., 1979; v.p. materials and purchasing Conrail, Phila., 1979—. Served with U.S. Army, 1957. Mem. Soc. Automotive Engrs., Am. Soc. for Quality Control, Nat. Assn. Purchasing Mgmt., Purchasing Mgmt. Assn. Phila. Clubs: Phila. Country, Union League (Phila.); N.Y. Traffic. Home: 641 Morris Ave Bryn Mawr PA 19010 Office: 1528 Walnut St Philadelphia PA 19102

WHEAT, HARRY LEWIS, natural gas liquids co. exec.; b. Bath, S.C., July 19, 1933; s. Harry Dell and Mary Louise (Jones) W.; grad. Palmer Bus. Coll., Charleston, S.C., 1959; m. Audrey Eleanor Gordon, June 13, 1951; children—Harry Leonard, Hiram Anthony, Christopher Dell, Richard Alan. Owner, Valley Fuel Co. and Val-E-Lane, Inc., 1954-65; dist. mgr. Suburban Propane Gas Corp., 1965-67; v.p., gen. mgr. Texgas Corp., 1967-76; gen. mgr. hydrocarbon supply and distbn. Union Tex. Petroleum div. Allied Chem. Corp., Houston, 1976—; tchr. industry mgmt. seminars. Served with USN, 1950-54. Mem. Nat., S.C. (past pres.), Fla. (past pres.) LP gas assns. Republican. Baptist. Clubs: Masons (32d deg.), Elks. Home: 3007 Triway Ln Houston TX 77043 Office: PO Box 2120 Houston TX 77001

WHEATON, JOHN RODGERS, energy co. exec.; b. San Francisco, Mar. 12, 1938; s. George and Virginia (Murphy) W.; B.A., Dartmouth Coll., 1960, M.S., 1961; M.B.A., Stanford U., 1969; m. Jane Railton, Feb. 4, 1967; children—Calbraith Rodgers, Mele Elizabeth. Engr., Nat. Engring. Sci. Co., Pasadena, 1964; project mgr. Oceanographic Inst., Waimanaco, Hawaii, 1965-67; dir. corporate devel. Dillingham Corp., Honolulu, 1969-74; v.p. devel. Calif. Liquid Gas Corp., Sacramento, 1974-79; pres. Dillingham Energy Services, Sacramento, 1979—. Pres. bd. trustees Sacramento Country Day Sch., 1976-78; adv. bd. Nat. Alliance Bus., Sacramento, 1979—. Served to 1st lt. Ordnance Corps, U.S. Army, 1961-64. Mem. Nat. LPG Assn. Republican. Clubs: Outrigger Canoe, Waialae Country, Rotary. Office: PO Box 28397 Sacramento CA 95828

WHEELER, CALVIN WELLINGTON, ins. co. exec.; b. Des Moines, Dec. 26, 1920; s. Walter Arthur and Esther Lydia (Antrim) W.; student Centenary Coll., 1938; J.D., Creighton U., 1947; m. Virginia Grace Brown, Oct. 18, 1942; children—Candace Lynn Wheeler Kommers, Judith Lane Wheeler Collester, Thomas Clinton. Admitted to Nebr. bar, 1948; with Mut. of Omaha Ins. Co., 1947—, asst. v.p., policy counsel, 1959-67, 2d v.p., policy counsel, 1967-68, v.p., policy counsel, 1968-72, v.p. regulatory affairs, 1972—; chmn., dir. N.Mex. Life Ins. Guaranty Assn.; vice chmn. dir. Nebr. Life and Health Ins. Guaranty Assn.; dir. Kans. Life and Health Ins. Guaranty Assn.; pres. Insurers Action Council, Inc. Co-founder Omaha Zool. Soc., 1951, pres., 1955-57; bd. dirs. Omaha Civic Music Assn., 1960-62; elder Presbyterian Ch. Served to capt. U.S. Army, 1943-46. Decorated Purple Heart; recipient awards Omaha Jr. C. of C.; certs. of appreciation from various agys., civic groups, assns. Mem. Nebr. Bar Assn., Omaha Bar Assn., Health Ins. Assn. Am., Nebr. Assn. Commerce and Industry, Ins. Fedn. Nebr., Omaha C. of C., Am. Legion, Alpha Sigma Nu. Republican. Clubs: Nebr.; Offutt AFB Officers. Home: 3107 S 104th Ave Omaha NE 68124 Office: Mut of Omaha Ins Co Mutual of Omaha Plaza Omaha NE 68175

WHEELER, CHRISTOPHER, stockbroker; b. N.Y.C., Feb. 19, 1928; s. Frank Walker and Winifred (Lenihan) W.; A.B., Harvard U., 1951; m. Rosemarie Piombino, July 17, 1954; children—David, Kenneth, Christopher, Brian. Commd. 2d lt. U.S. Army, 1951, advanced through grades to lt. col., 1966; service in Korea, Panama and Vietnam; ret., 1969; account exec. Reynolds Securities, Inc., Sarasota, Fla., 1969-78; v.p. Smith Barney Harris Upham, Inc., Sarasota, 1978—; chmn. bd. Siesta Key Utilities Authority, Inc., 1976—. Pres. Siesta Key Assn., 1970-75; treas. Asolo Theatre Festival Assn., 1973-80, Key Gate Library Assn., 1978. Decorated Legion of Merit, Bronze Star, Army Commendation medal with oak leaf cluster. Mem. Ret. Officers Assn. Republican. Clubs: University, Ivy League (Sarasota). Home: 4925 Primrose Path Sarasota FL 33581 Office: Sarasota Bank Bldg 1605 Main St Sarasota FL 33577

WHEELER, RICHARD SPICE, lawyer; b. Utica, N.Y., June 22, 1946; s. Everett Jesse and Marjorie Elizabeth (Spice) W.; B.A., Colgate U., 1968; J.D., Union U., 1971; m. Barbara June Curtis, Oct. 12, 1968; children—Andrew Colin, Daniel Ethan. Admitted to N.Y. bar, 1972; confidential law asst. Appellate Div. N.Y. Supreme Ct., Rochester, N.Y., 1971-73; asso. firm Harter, Secrest & Emery, Rochester, 1973-76; asso. counsel Dairylea Coop., Inc., Pearl River, N.Y., 1976-79, gen. counsel, 1979-80, v.p., gen. counsel, 1980—. Bd. trustees Packanack Community Ch., Wayne, N.J., 1979—. Mem. Am. Bar Assn., N.Y. Bar Assn. Club: Packanack Lake Country and Community Assn. Contbr. articles to profl. jours. Office: 1 Blue Hill Plaza Pearl River NY 10965

WHEELER, ROBERT NASH, banker; b. New London, N.H., July 14, 1942; s. Wayne Keith and Alice Margaret (Nash) W.; B.A., U. N.H., 1963, M.B.A., 1968; m. Linda Peltola, June 15, 1963; children—Karen, R. David, Margaret. Chemist, Gen. Electric Co., Waterford, N.Y., 1963-64; loan officer, Worcester County Nat. Bank (Mass.), 1968-71; gen. mgr. Manchester Mgmt. Corp., 1971-76; exec. v.p. Sundeen Lumber Co., Manchester, N.H., 1976-78; pres., dir. Bedford Bank (N.H.), 1978—. Chmn. budget com. Town of Bedford (N.H.), 1972—, auditor, 1976—; trustee, treas. Bethany Covenant Ch., Bedford, 1975-78; bd. dirs. Eastman Community Assn., Grantham, N.H., 1973-76, Easter Seals of N.H., 1979—, N.H. Higher Edn. Found., 1981—, Better Bus. Bur., 1979—. Served to lt. AUS, 1964-66. U. N.H. fellow, 1966-68. Mem. Phi Kappa Phi, Tau Kappa Epsilon (nat. Teke of year 1963). Republican. Home: RFD 2 Perry Rd Bedford NH 03102 Office: 106 S River Rd Bedford NH 03102

WHEELER, WARREN G(AGE), JR., pub. co. exec.; b. Boston, Dec. 6, 1921; s. Warren Gage and Helen (Hoagland) W.; B.S., Bowdoin Coll., 1943; B.J., U. Mo., 1947, M.A., 1948; m. Jean Frances Moseley, Feb. 22, 1945; children—Richard, Michael, Ann, Duncan. With South Bend (Ind.) Tribuen (name changed to Schurz Communications, Inc. 1976), 1948—, gen. mgr., 1964-71, exec. v.p., 1971-75, pres., 1975—; dir. Evergreen Communications, Inc., Bloomington, Ill. Campaign chmn. United Community Services, South Bend, 1960, pres., 1964; treas. South Bend Urban League, 1962-63; trustee St. Joseph's Hosp., South Bend, 1969-77; gen. chmn. St. Joseph County (Ind.) Hosp. Devel., 1969-71; deacon, elder, pres. session 1st Presbyn. Ch., South Bend. Served with USN, 1943-46. Protestant recipient Brotherhood award South Bend-Mishawaka chpt. NCCJ, 1970. Mem. Am. Newspaper Pubs. Assn., Am. Mgmt. Assn., Newspaper Personnel Relations Assn. (pres. 1955-56), Hoosier State Press Assn. (dir. 1967-70), Inland Daily Press Assn. (pres. 1972, pres. found. 1974-78), Sigma Delta Chi, Kappa Tau Alpha, Kappa Mu. Clubs: South Bend Press, Goose and Duck, Chikaming Country, Summit. Editor: Newspaper Personnel Relations Assn. News, 1953-54. Home: 1311 E Woodside St South Bend IN 46614 Office: 225 W Colfax Ave South Bend IN 46626

WHEELER, WILMOT FITCH, JR., diversified mfg. co. exec.; b. Southport, Conn., June 5, 1923; s. Wilmot Fitch and Hulda Day (Chapman) W.; grad. St. Paul's Sch., 1941; B.A., Yale U., 1945; student N.Y. U., 1947-48; m. Barbara Rutherfurd, Sept. 30, 1944 (dec. Sept. 1971); children—Wilmot Fitch III, James Alexander, John R., Susan; m. 2d, Nonnye Landers, Dec. 20, 1973; children—Tracy Lynne, Alexa Margaret. Staff engr. Stevenson, Jordan & Harrison, Inc., mgmt. cons., 1946-51; with Am. Chain & Cable Co., Inc., N.Y.C., 1951—, asst. to pres., 1953-55, v.p., 1955-59, dir., 1958—, exec. v.p., 1959-65, pres., 1965-67, chief exec. officer, chmn., 1967-76, also dir.; chmn. Jelliff Corp., 1976; mgmt. cons. Case & Co. Inc.; dir. Am. Mut. Liability Ins. Co., Am. Dist. Telegraph Co., Manhattan Life Corp., Hersey Products Inc., Pratt-Read Corp., Am. Policyholders Ins. Co.; trustee Dollar Savs. Bank, People's Savs. Bank. Trustee U. Bridgeport, Bridgeport Hosp.; bd. dirs. William T. Morris Found., Wilmot Wheeler Found.; adv. trustee Outward Bound. Served with AUS, 1943-46. Decorated Bronze Star. Mem. Machinery and Allied Products Inst. (exec. com. 1971-76). Episcopalian. Clubs: Yale, Links, Sky (N.Y.C.); Country of Fairfield. Home: 328 Sasco Hill Rd Southport CT 06490 Office: Jelliff Corp 354 Pequot Rd Southport CT

WHEELER-JENKINS, DONNA IRENE, govt. ofcl.; b. Washington, June 7, 1947; d. Howard Anthony and Virginia Pauline (Wilson) Maxwell; A.A., Fed. City Coll., 1975, B.A. in Psychology, 1975; postgrad. Ga. State Coll., 1977-78; m. Jack Hutchinson Jenkins, Oct. 20, 1979; children—Denita Wheeler, James A. Wheeler, Troy M. Wheeler. Various secretarial positions HUD, Washington, 1965-72, housing intern, 1973-74, housing mgmt. asst., 1974-75, employee devel. specialist Atlanta regional office, 1975-77, spl. asst. to area mgr., 1978-79, govt. liaison to state, city, county on community planning and devel. block grant program and related programs, 1979—; pres. Correspondence and Assistance, Atlanta, 1978—; asso. prof. Philander Smith Coll., Little Rock, 1978. Sec., Parent's Adv. Council to Fulton County Bd. Edn.; den mother Boy Scouts Am. Mem. Southeastern Assn. Black Fed. Employees (public relations chmn.), Federally Employed Women, Am. Fedn. Govt. Employees (v.p. local 1568), NAACP, SCLC. Home: 120 Traverse Ct College Park GA 30349

WHELAN, WILLIAM ANTHONY, forest products co. exec.; b. Bklyn., Aug. 18, 1921; s. Daniel and Catherine (Pugh) W.; B.S.M.E., U. Calif., Berkeley; m. Marcia M. McCorkle, Nov. 14, 1948; children—Michael, Greer, Daniel, Ann. Vice pres. Klamath Machine & Locomotive Works, 1948-58; plant and dist. mgr. U.S. Plywood, 1959-68; v.p. West Coast ops. Champion Internat., 1968-74; v.p. exec. Roseburg Lumber Co., 1975-77; exec. v.p. Pope & Talbot, Inc., Portland, Oreg., 1978, pres., 1979—, also dir. Mem. Western Wood Products Assn. (1st v.p., mem. operating com., exec. com., dir.), Nat. Forest Products Assn. (dir., exec. com.). Served in U.S. Army, 3 years; Okinawa. Republican. Episcopalian. Club: Arlington. Office: 1700 SW Fourth Ave Portland OR 97201*

WHELIHAN, ALAN STUART, govt. ofcl.; b. Phila., Sept. 17, 1932; s. John Franklin and Dorothy (Dodge) W.; B.S.E., Princeton, 1954; M.B.A., U. Pa., 1960; m. Joan Carol Murrell, June 20, 1959; children—Pamela, Deborah Linda, Jacqueline. Engr., Philco Corp., Phila., 1954-55; product line mgr. RCA Corp., Camden, N.J., 1959-65; gen. mgr. Chem. Micro Milling Co., Phila., 1965-66; mgr. mgmt. cons. Peat Marwick Mitchell & Co., Washington, 1966-72; asst. commr. fed. supply service GSA, Washington, 1973-75, engring. policy adviser, 1975-80; dir. planning and coordination U.S. Metric Bd., Arlington, Va., 1980—; dir. Am. Nat. Standards Inst.; cons. Can. Dept. Nat. Def., U.S. Navy Labs. Trustee, McAuley Park Citizens Assn. Served with USN, 1955-58. Recipient Phila. Sci. Council award, 1950. Fellow Washington Acad. Scis.; mem. IEEE (sr.), Nat. Contract Mgmt. Assn., Am. Soc. Pub. Adminstrn. Republican. Episcopalian. Club: Congressional Country. Home: 9417 Kentsdale Dr Potomac MD 20854 Office: US Metric Bd 1600 Wilson Blvd Arlington VA 22209

WHELPLEY, JAMES DIX, investment mgr.; b. Cin., Mar. 16, 1936; s. James Albert and Ruth Francis (Dix) W.; B.A., Yale, 1958; postgrad. N.Y. Grad. Sch. Bus. Adminstrn., 1958-59, Am. U. Beirut, 1961-62; m. Sandra Jo Young, Jan. 17, 1959; children—James Linvill, Tarik Thomas, Tamara Jo. Ofcl. asst. First Nat. City Bank N.Y., head office overseas div., N.Y.C., 1958-61, Beirut br. office, 1961-62; salesman Laird, Inc., N.Y.C., 1962-64, mgr. spl. research, 1964-68, v.p., dir. research, 1968-70; exec. v.p. Bay Securities Corp., San Francisco, 1970; sr. v.p., mgr. investments ISI Corp., San Francisco, 1970-74, pres., investment mgr., dir., 1974—; pres., dir. Whelpley Assos., Inc., ISI Corp., 1975—. Mem. N.Y. Soc. Security Analysts, Delta Kappa Epsilon. Republican. Clubs: Yale (N.Y.C.); World Trade, Olympic (San Francisco); Oakland Athletic. Home: 321 Hillside Ave Piedmont CA 94611 Office: 1608 Webster St Oakland CA 94612

WHIPPLE, KENNETH, automobile co. exec.; b. Detroit, Sept. 28, 1934; s. Kenneth and Margaret Ames (Bearse) W.; B.S., M.I.T., 1958; m. Denise L. Fuller, Aug. 29, 1973; children—Kay, Lynn, David, Michael, Deborah, Matthew, Martha. With Ford Motor Co., Dearborn, Mich., 1958—, v.p. fin., then exec. v.p. diversified fin. Ford Motor Credit Co., 1973-80, pres., 1980—; pres., dir. Ford Credit Co. U.S., Ford Credit Co. Can., Am. Rd. Ins. Co., Ford Life Ins. Co., Vista Ins. Co. Vol. leader Detroit United Fund, 1979-80. Office: Ford Motor Credit Co American Rd Dearborn MI 48121

WHIPPS, EDWARD FRANKLIN, lawyer; b. Columbus, Ohio, Dec. 17, 1936; s. Rusk Henry and Agnes Lucille (Green) W.; B.A., Ohio Wesleyan U., 1958; LL.B., Ohio State U., 1961, J.D., 1968; children—Edward Scott, Rusk Huot, Sylvia Louise, Rudyard Christian. Admitted to Ohio bar, 1961; partner George, Greek, King, McMahon & McConnaughey, Columbus, Ohio, 1961-79, McConnaughey, Stradley, Mone & Moul, Columbus, 1979-81, Thompson, Hine & Flory, Columbus, 1981—. Pres., Upper Arlington Bd. Edn., 1972-81; trustee Upper Arlington Swimming Pool, 1972—, Upper Arlington C. of C., 1979-81; bd. alumni dirs. Ohio Wesleyan U., 1975-78; moderator TV program Upper Arlington Plain Talk, 1979—. Mem. Am. Bar Assn., Ohio Bar Assn., Columbus Bar Assn., Assn. Trial Lawyers Am., Ohio Acad. Trial Lawyers, Franklin County Trial Lawyers Assn., Am. Judicature Soc. Republican. Clubs: Lawyers of Columbus, Barristers, Columbus Athletic, Ohio State U. Faculty. Home: 3771 Lyon Dr Columbus OH 43220 Office: 100 E Broad St Columbus OH 43215

WHISTLER, JAMES EDWIN, life ins. exec.; b. Independence, Kans., Apr. 20, 1948; s. Olen J. and Donna Lucille (Lightner) W.; B.B.A., U. Idaho, 1970, J.D., 1973; M.Fin., Am. Coll., 1979; m. Kathryn Anne Skok, July 4, 1969; 1 son, James Michael. Spl. agt. Northwestern Mut. Life Ins. Co., Moscow, Idaho, 1969-73, agy. supr., San Francisco, 1973-75, asst./regional dir., Milw., 1975-80, gen. agt., San Diego, 1980—; admitted to Idaho bar, 1973, Calif. bar, 1974; instr. Milw. Stratton Bus. Coll., 1975-78. C.L.U. Mem. Nat. Assn. Life Underwriters, Am. Soc. C.L.U.'s, Calif. Bar Assn., Idaho Bar Assn., Am. Bar Assn., Gen. Agts. and Mgrs. Assn., Phi Alpha Delta, Phi Gamma Delta. Republican. Club: Univ. of San Diego. Contbr. to legal and ins. publs. Home: 11435 Fuerte Farms Rd El Cajon CA 92020 Office: 233 A St Suite 800 San Diego CA 92101

WHITAKER, GILBERT RILEY, JR., bus. economist, univ. adminstr.; b. Oklahoma City, Oct. 8, 1931; s. Gilbert Riley and Melodese (Kilpatrick) W.; B.A., Rice U., 1953; postgrad. So. Meth. U., 1956-57; M.S. in Econs., U. Wis., Madison, 1958, Ph.D. in Econs.

(Ford Found. dissertation fellow), 1961; m. Ruth Pauline Tonn, Dec. 18, 1953; children—Kathleen, David Edward, Thomas Gilbert. Instr., Northwestern U. Sch. Bus., Evanston, Ill., 1960-61, asst. prof. bus. econs., 1961-64, asso. prof., 1964-66, research asso. Transp. Center, 1962-66; asso. prof. Washington U., St. Louis, 1967-68, prof., 1968-76, adj. prof. econs., 1967-76, asso. dean Grad. Sch. Bus. Adminstrn., 1969-76; dean, prof. bus. econs. M.J. Neeley Sch. Bus., Tex. Christian U., Ft. Worth, 1976-79; dean, prof. Grad. Sch. Bus. Adminstrn., U. Mich., Ann Arbor, 1979—; dir. La Barge Inc., 1972—, Nat. Bank and Trust Ann Arbor (Mich.), 1979—, Detroit Bank Corp., 1979—, Hoover Universal, 1980—; sr. economist banking and currency com. U.S. Ho. of Reps., 1964; trustee Grad. Mgmt. Admissions Council, 1972-75, chmn., 1974-75. Served with USN, 1953-56. Mem. Am. Econ. Assn., Am. Fin. Assn., Nat. Assn. Bus Economists. Club: Ft. Worth Boat. Author books, including: (with Marshall Colberg and Dascomb Forbush) Business Economics, 5th edit., 1975, 6th edit., 1981; (with Roger Chisholm) Forecasting Methodist, 1971. Office: U Mich Grad Sch Bus Adminstrn Ann Arbor MI 48109

WHITCHURCH, CHARLES RANDALL, engring. co. exec.; b. Evanston, Ill., Aug. 29, 1946; s. Charles Goldwin and Jane Dorothy (Christensen) W.; B.A. cum laude in Econs., Beloit Coll., 1968; M.B.A., Stanford, 1973; m. Jane Ann Neutzling, Feb. 21, 1976. Corporate fin. cons. Harris Trust & Savs. Bank, Chgo., 1973-76; chief fin. officer Resinoid Engring. Co., Skokie, Ill., 1976—. Served to 1st lt. U.S. Army, 1969-71. Mem. Phi Beta Kappa. Home: 3536 Hillside Rd Evanston IL 60201 Office: 3445 Howard St Skokie IL 60076

WHITCOMB, JOHN MERVIN, mfg. co. exec.; b. Danbury, Conn., Aug. 25, 1949; s. Mervin Wesley and Ella Elisabeth (Hallington) W.; B.S. in Mgmt. Sci., Rensselaer Poly. Inst., 1972; M.B.A., U. Wis., 1975; m. Barbara Ann Liyana, June 20, 1970; 1 dau., Joy Ellen. Counselor, T. E. Bell Employment Agy., Latham, N.Y., 1972; mgmt. trainee Albany Internat. Corp., (N.Y.), 1972, personnel asst., personnel mgr., Appleton, Wis., 1973-74, mgr. personnel and purchasing, 1975; labor relations rep. Plough, Inc., Memphis, 1975-77, asst. dir. indsl. relations, 1977-78, dir. labor relations, 1979-81, dir. labor relations worldwide, 1981—. Mem. City of Germantown (Tenn.) Personnel Adv. Com., 1978, 79. Mem. Am. Soc. Personnel Adminstrn. (v.p. Memphis chpt. 1978, pres. 1979; charter mem. internat. chpt., nat. public affairs com. 1978—), Memphis C. of C. (govtl. affairs com.). Home: 1530 Stonegate Pass Germantown TN 38138 Office: PO Box 377 Memphis TN 38151

WHITE, ALEXANDER PATRICK, lawyer, labor contracting exec.; b. Chgo., Mar. 30, 1932; s. Alexander Patrick and Eleanor Marion W.; B.S. in Fin., No. Ill. U., 1959; J.D. cum laude, Ill. Inst. Tech. Chgo.-Kent Coll. Law, 1964; LL.M., John Marshall Sch. Law, 1976; M.S., DePaul U., 1977; m. Marilyn Karen Samuelsen, Aug. 23, 1958; children—Bradley Jonathan, Christy Lynn, Laura Susan, Julie Kathleen. Admitted to Ill. bar, 1964, U.S. Supreme Ct. bar, 1968; law clk. Appellate Ct. Ill., 1st Dist., 1964-67; with firm McKay, Moses, McGarr, Gibbons and Fox, Chgo., 1962-67; legal asst. Cook County Bd. Commrs., 1966-69; exec. asst. to gov. State of Ill., 1969-70; chmn. Ill. Indsl. Commn., 1970-73; individual practice law, Chgo., 1973, 77—; regional dir. Dept. Labor, 1973-77; pres. Atlantic Plant Maintenance, Inc., Chgo., 1977—; fed. defender U.S. Dist. Ct., No. Dist. Ill., 1966—; counsel Ill. Dept. Labor, 1973; spl. asst. atty. gen., counsel Ill. Bd. Investment, 1977—; adj. prof. Ill. Inst. Tech. Chgo.-Kent Coll. Law, 1977—. Treas., Cook County Young Republicans, 1966, chmn., 1967; precinct capt., mem. exec. bd. 37th Ward Regular Rep. Orgn., 1966-70; precinct capt. Maine Twp. Regular Rep. Orgn., 1970-73, bd. dirs., 1970-71; del. Ill. Rep. Conv., 1968, 72; exec. dir. Citizens Com. for Improvement of Cook County Jail, 1968; exec. dir. Ill. Sesquicentennial. Served with USMCR, 1954-58. Recipient cert. of appreciation Dept. Labor, 1973. Mem. Am. Soc. Pub. Adminstrn., Am. Bar Assn., Fed. Bar Assn. (pres. Chgo. chpt. 1980), Ill. Bar Assn., Chgo. Council Lawyers, Chgo. Bar Assn., Am. Trial Lawyers Assn., Ill. Trial Lawyers Assn., Nat. Legal Aid and Defender Assn., Am. Judicature Soc., Nat. Lawyers Club, Judge Advocates Assn. (sec. 1977), Naval Res. Lawyers Assn., N.W. Suburban Bar Assn., Ill. Chamber of Commerce, Chgo. Assn. Commerce and Industry, Res. Officer Assn., Marine Corps League, Marine Corps Res. Officer Assn. (1st v.p. Glenview chpt. 1968-71), Am. Legion, Chgo.-Kent Coll. Alumni Assn. (v.p. 1977-79). Home: 1300 River Dr Des Plaines IL 60018 Office: Atlantic Plant Maintenance Inc 10 S LaSalle St Chicago IL 60602

WHITE, BRANDON CLARK, JR., banker; b. Detroit, Mar. 15, 1933; s. Brandon Clark and Mabel Helman (Wilkins) W.; ed. U. Mich.; grad. Grad. Sch. Banking, U. Wis., 1967, Stonier Grad. Sch. Banking, Rutgers U., 1974; m. Mary Annette Turner, Nov. 17, 1956; children—Brandon Clark III, Mark Norman, Michelle Abby. Cashier, dir. Dexter Savs. Bank (Mich.), 1956-63; asst. cashier, comml. loan Ann Arbor Bank (Mich.), 1963-66; exec. v.p., dir. Central Nat. Bank, St. Johns, Mich., 1966-69; adminstrv. v.p., dir. Clinton Bank and Trust Co., St. Johns, 1969-74, pres., chief exec. officer, dir., 1974—; dir. Saylor Beall Mfg. Co., Koebco Foods, Inc., AVISO, Inc. Served with U.S. Army, 1953-55. Mem. Mich. Bankers Assn., St. Johns Area C. of C. (pres. 1969-70). Republican. Congregationalist. Clubs: Walnut Hills Country (Lansing, Mich.); Rotary (pres. 1973-74) (St. Johns); Renaissance (Detroit); Masons. Office: Clinton Bank and Trust Co 200 N Clinton Ave Saint Johns MI 48879

WHITE, DENZIL WILMOT, petroleum equipment co. exec.; b. East Palestine, Ohio, June 10, 1916; s. Frank and Ethel (Akenhead) W.; B.S. in Edn., Kent State U., 1939; diploma, Case Sch. Applied Sci., 1942; m. Louise E. Stump, Aug. 18, 1940; children—Robert D., Richard K. Instr., East Palestine (Ohio) public schs., 1939-41; field engr. Shell Oil Co., Cleve., 1941-46; div. engr. Amco Corp., Cleve., 1946-50; mgr. pump and filter div. Telco, Inc., 1950-61; mfg. agt. Denny White & Co., Cleve., 1961-65; pres. Denny White, Inc., Cleve., 1965—. Mem. Am. Soc. Petroleum Ops. Engrs., Cleve. Engring. Soc., Am. Mgmt. Assn., Am. Petroleum Inst., Petroleum Equipment Inst., Mfg. Agts. Nat. Assn. Republican. Lutheran.

WHITE, DONALD ALLEN, mfg. co. exec.; b. Toronto, Ont., Can., June 7, 1913; s. Frederick Charles and Mabel Clair (Griswold) W.; student Stratford (Ont.) Coll. Inst., 1926-28, Shaw Bus. Sch., Toronto, 1928; m. Xeita Alberta Mason, Aug. 6, 1938; children—Donald Richard, Dennis James. Clk., C.N. Railways, 1929-33; mgr. Standard Tube Co. Ltd., 1933-38; gen. mgr. Metal Fabricators Ltd., Woodstock and Tillsonburg, Ont., 1939-49; with Huntington Labs. of Can. Ltd., Bramalea, Ont., 1949—, pres., 1956—. Bd. govs. Humber Coll. of A.A. & T., Toronto, 1967-75, chmn. bd. govs., 1976-77. Served with Canadian Army, 1942-45. Mem. Can. Sanitation Standards Assn. Conservative. Mem. United Ch. Can. Clubs: Kiwanis (pres. Music Festival Assn. of Toronto 1962-63). Home: 58 Riverwood Pkwy Toronto ON M8Y 4E3 Canada Office: 15 Victoria Crescent Bramalea ON L6T 1E3 Canada

WHITE, DONALD GRAHAM, pub. co. exec.; b. Polson, Mont., Dec. 10, 1936; s. James P. and Mabel Helen (Douglas) W.; B.S., U. Mont., 1961, M.S. in Teaching (NSF grantee), 1965; M.B.A., U. Chgo., 1981; children—Thomas James, Daniel Richard. Tchr., Central Valley Sch. Dist., Spokane, Wash., 1961-65; coll. salesperson Harcourt Brace Jovanovich, Inc., Denver, 1965-71, Midwestern mgr. coll. dept., Chgo., 1971-77; gen. mgr. coll. dept. Rand McNally & Co., Skokie, Ill., 1977—. Served with U.S. Army, 1954-56. Mem. Am. Mgmt. Assn., Assn. Am. Publishers. Presbyterian. Club: U. Chgo. Exec. Office: Rand McNally & Co 8255 Central Park Skokie IL 60076

WHITE, EDWARD GEORGE, mgmt. cons.; b. Flushing, N.Y., July 13, 1943; s. Edward P. and Agnes (Timlin) W.; B.S., Loyola U., Chgo., 1965; M.A., Manhattan Coll., 1972; cert. fin. mgmt. N.Y. U., 1977; m. Frances X. Maraventano, Sept. 26, 1970; children—Kristen Elizabeth, Justin. Auditor, Dow Jones Inc., N.Y.C., 1971-73; budget analyst Consol. Edison N.Y., N.Y.C., 1973-78; owner, mgr. Gen. Bus. Services Nutley (N.J.), 1977—; instr. small bus. mgmt. Nutley Adult Sch., 1978—. Bd. dirs. Nutley Family Service Bur., chmn. long range planning com., 1979—; treas. Nutley Democratic County Com., 1979—, Nutley Dem. Club, 1978—. Served with USMC, 1967-71; Vietnam. Mem. VFW, Nat. Small Bus. Assn., Inst. Bus. Appraisers, Am. Mgmt. Assn., Active Core Execs. SBA. Roman Catholic. Clubs: K.C., Lions. Office: 310 Washington Ave Nutley NJ 07110

WHITE, EDWARD W., JR., oil producer; b. West Palm Beach, Fla., Feb. 21, 1933; s. Edward W. and Jeanne Mary (Kraft) W.; student Loyola U., Chgo., 1951-54; m. M. Carol Anderson, Sept. 8, 1956 (div. May 1972); 1 son, Michael Dennis; m. 2d, Margaret Patricia Rush, Mar. 31, 1973; 1 son, William Fletcher. Owner, E. W. White & Assos., Chgo., 1956-65; founder, pres. Pointer Oil Co., Chgo., 1965—, Pointer Oil Co. Fla., 1971—, Mineral Leasing, Inc., 1970—, K-B Oil Co., 1973—, Trishco Oil Co., 1977—. Home: 550 Ocean Dr Key Biscayne FL 33149 Office: 104 Crandon Blvd Key Biscayne FL 33149

WHITE, ELIZABETH DERRICK, direct mktg. cons.; b. Atlanta, Dec. 11, 1940; d. Andrew O. and J. Elizabeth (Rawlins) Derrick; LL.B., U. New South Wales (Australia), 1974; m. Oct. 1958 (dec.); children—Deborah Helene, Terry Ingram. Pres., Edmund Strange Assos. Ltd., Atlanta, 1958-62; gen. mgr. Associated Brokerage Corp., Atlanta, 1962-66; trust officer Stewart Title Co. Ga., Atlanta, 1964-66; advt. mgr. Barkers Inc., N.Y.C., 1967-68; pres. White, Hamilton & Young Ltd., Atlanta, 1978—. Mem. Direct Mktg. Assn. Australia (dir. mktg. group 1974-76), Consultants Assn. (founder, pres.), Direct Mktg. Assn. S.E. (organizer). Republican. Episcopalian. Author trade and tech. articles. Office: 2971 Flowers Rd S #100 Atlanta GA 30341

WHITE, FRANK JOSEPH, JR., constrn. industry assn. exec.; b. Worcester, Mass., Jan. 23, 1939; s. Frank Joseph and Celia (Carrigan) W.; B.S. with honors, Columbia, 1964; M.A. in Econs., Trinity Coll., 1976; m. Flora V. Conte, June 17, 1962; children—Kristin Lynn, Alison Jennifer, Hilary Ellen. Asst. exec. dir. Gen. Bldg. Contractors N.Y. State, Inc., Albany, 1964-65; legislative dir., asst. dir. safety and tng. Asso. Gen. Contractors Am., Washington, 1965-66; exec. v.p. Asso. Gen. Contractors Conn., Inc., Woodbridge, 1966-77, pres., 1977—; dir. Conn. Bldg. Congress, 1969-72; vis. lectr. Sch. Orgn. and Mgmt., Yale U., New Haven, 1981; mem. Gov.'s Constrn. Adv. Council; mem. steering com. tech. and prequalification div. Nat. Inst. Bldg. Scis. Vice chmn. New Haven Equal Employment Opportunity Plan, 1971-75; pres., dir. Conn. Bldg. Congress Scholarship Fund, 1974—; mem. citizens adv. com. vocational edn. Eli-Whitney Regional Vocational and Tech. Sch., New Haven, 1969—; mem. Woodbridge Bd. Edn., 1975-79, vice-chmn.; mem. Conn. Assn. Bds. Edn., 1975-79; mem. state commn. higher edn. evaluation team archtl. tech. program Hartford State Tech. Coll., 1976; bd. govs. Constrn. Inst., U. Hartford, 1976—. Trustee, Iron Workers locals 15 and 424 Pension Fund, Extended Benefit Fund, Vacation Fund, Annuity Fund, Apprenticeship and Tng. Fund, Meriden, Conn., Conn. State Bldg. Trades Hospitalization and Ins. Fund, West Haven, Conn., Conn. Laborers Legal Services Fund, Carpenters Local 43 Supplemental Pension Benefit Fund. Mem. Nat. Inst. Bldg. Scis., Am. Soc. Assn. Execs., New Eng. Soc. Assn. Execs. Club: Quinnipiack (New Haven). Home: 7 Evergreen Dr Woodbridge CT 06525 Office: 6 Lunar Dr Woodbridge CT 06525

WHITE, FRANKLIN MORSE, elec. co. exec.; b. Fairbury, Nebr., Dec. 6, 1920; s. Chesley Franklin and Nellie Blanch (Smith) W.; B.S.E.E., U. Nebr., 1943; m. Lydia Worster, Oct. 8, 1948; 1 dau., Janet Louise. Partner, gen. mgr. White Electric Supply Co., Lincoln, Nebr., 1946-65, pres., gen. mgr., 1965—. Pres., Lincoln Family Service Assn., 1962-65; mem. Lincoln Lancaster County Planning Commn., 1962-68. Served with Signal Corps, U.S. Army, 1943-46. Mem. Nat. Assn. Elec. Distributors (bd. govs. 1966-71), Nebr.-Iowa Elec. Council (pres. 1980-81), Res. Officers Assn., U. Nebr. Alumni Assn. Republican. Mem. Christian Ch. Clubs: Sertoma, Elks, Univ., Nebr., Mo. River (pres. 1969-70). Home: 2701 Bonacum Dr Lincoln NE 68502 Office: 427 S 10th St Lincoln NE 68501

WHITE, GEORGIA JOANNE JABER, banker; b. Springfield, Mass., Nov. 13, 1941; d. George Samuel and Margaret (Arnold) Jaber; student U. Fla., 1973, Jacksonville U., 1977; m. Bevis Valine White, Aug. 14, 1959; children—Daniel Edward, Stephen Samuel, Debra Anne. Clk., Atlantic Nat. Bank, Jacksonville, 1959-65; adminstrv. asst. Fairfield County Trust Co., Danbury, Conn., 1965-69; asst. tax officer Atlantic Nat. Bank, Jacksonville, 1969-76, asst. ops. officer, 1976; asst. tax officer Barnett Banks Trust Co., Jacksonville, 1977, tax officer, estate tax specialist, 1978—; lectr. in field; class dir. Fla. Bankers Assn. Trust Sch. Bd. fin. Gateway council Girl Scouts U.S., 1974—; bd. fin. St. Paul United Meth. Ch., Jacksonville, 1977—, trustee found., 1978—. Mem. Fla. Bankers Assn. Democrat. Clubs: Captains, Jacksonville Offshore Sport Fishing. Home: 2310 Shipwreck Circle W Jacksonville FL 32224 Office: Barnett Banks Trust Co PO Box 40200 Jacksonville FL 32231

WHITE, GERALD RAE, mgmt. cons.; b. Lewiston, Idaho, Aug. 28, 1930; s. Everett Miller and Ruth Alberta (Huff) W.; B.S.E.D., U. Idaho, 1956, M.Ed., 1960; m. Constance L. Freeman, Aug. 5, 1952; children—Allen R., Jerry L., Charles V., Karen A. White Snyder. Tchr., Idaho, Nev., Calif., 1956-62; tchr./adminstr., Idaho, 1958-60; tng. specialist N. Am., Rockwell, Downey, Calif., 1960-66; mgr. manpower devel. ITT Cannon Electric, Los Angeles, 1966-69; regional mgr./adminstr. Madison Convalescent Center, Spokane, Wash., 1969-70; owner, mgr. M.D.A. Co., Spokane, 1970—, Mgmt. Tng. Center, Spokane, 1978—, M.D.A. Fin. Planning Brokerage, Spokane, 1975—. Vice pres., treas. Comprehensive Health Planning Council, Spokane, 1970-74; chmn. bd. Family Counseling of Spokane, 1977—; mem. Spokane CETA Bd., 1971-79; overall chmn. Spokane County Overall Econ. Devel. Planning Commn., 1972-80. Served with USAF, 1948-52. Mem. Internat. Assn. Fin. Planners, Internat. Platform Assn., DAV, Phi Delta Kappa. Home: W 810 Teal Ave Spokane WA 99218 Office: Bldg 7 Spokane Indsl Park Spokane WA 99216

WHITE, GLENN EDWARD, automobile co. exec.; b. Grand Rapids, Mich., Aug. 21, 1926; s. Hugh A. and Edna (Close) W.; A.B. and M.B.A., U. Mich., 1947; m. Ruth Evelyn Snyder, June 27, 1947; children—Charles E., David B., Nancy E. White Bergsma. Credit analyst Nat. Bank Detroit, 1947-53; with Chrysler Corp., 1953—, v.p. Chrysler-Plymouth div., 1968-71, v.p. Latin Am., 1971-73, v.p. mgmt. services, 1973-76, v.p. personnel and adminstrn., 1976—. Past pres. Detroit Area council Boy Scouts Am; trustee Spring Arbor Coll., Children's Hosp. Served to lt. USNR, 1944-45, 52-53. Mem. Am. Inst. C.P.A.'s, Mich. Assn. C.P.A.'s, Nat. Alliance Bus. (chmn. Detroit area). Free Methodist. Clubs: Detroit Golf, Detroit Athletic. Office: PO Box 1919 Detroit MI 48288

WHITE, HARVEY, investment banker; b. Boston, July 31, 1925; s. Murray and Rose (Polakowich) W.; B.A., Dartmouth Coll., 1946; m. Dorothy Berkowitz, Apr. 20, 1947; children—Marian Louise, Stanley Martin, Edward Robert. Pres., treas., chmn. bd. Puritan Aerosol Corp., Berkley, R.I., 1959-69; v.p. corp. fin. Clark, Dodge & Co., Boston, 1969-71; pres. Harvey White and Assos., Inc., Boston, 1980—; cons. Investment Banking div. H.C. Wainwright & Co., Boston, 1977—; dir. Packaging Systems Corp., Butler Automatic Inc., Outlet Co. Served with USNR, 1943-46. Mem. Chief Execs. Forum. Republican. Clubs: N.Y. Yacht, Beverly Yacht, Cruising of Am., Harvard of Boston, Sippican Tennis. Office: One Boston Pl Boston MA 02108

WHITE, HENRY WALTER, plant engr.; b. Waterville, Maine, Feb. 11, 1949; s. Paul Merwood and Alberta Frances (Wright) Rollins; student in marine engring. Maine Maritime Acad., 1967-68; m. Mary Theresa Williams, Dec. 27, 1971; children—Theresa Marie, Jason Anthony, Michelle Frances. Third engr. maritime service Sun Oil Co., Marcus Hook, Pa., 1968-70; supr. in charge plant automation Wilmington (Del.) Med. Center, 1970; chief engr. Maine Med. Center, Portland, 1970-75; dir. phys. plant Columbus Services Inc., Allentown, Pa., 1975-79; dir. mfg. and facilities Stonhard Inc., Maple Shade, N.J., 1979—; instr. candidates for engring. licensing. Cert. indsl. accident prevention, Maine. Mem. Nat. Assn. Power Engrs. (pres. Maine chpt. I), Am. Inst. Plant Engrs. Roman Catholic. Home: 104-G Bennett Ct Newport DE 19804 Office: Route 73 and Park Ave Maple Shade NJ 08052

WHITE, JACK DUANE, elec. co. exec.; b. Surprise, Nebr., June 25, 1924; s. George Dempsey and Mildred Evaline (Brown) W.; B.Sc., U. Nebr., 1949, M.Sc., 1951; m. Harriet Elma Williams, Aug. 31, 1947; children—Scott Duane, Brett Donald, Kent Dempsey. Instr., U. Nebr., 1948-51; quality control coordinator Ford Motor Co., Chgo., 1951; dir. quality control Birtman Elec. Co., Chgo., 1952-57; chief indsl. engr. Electra Mfg. Co., Independence, Kans., 1957-63, dir. mfg., Mineral Wells, Tex., 1963-68; v.p. passive ops. Sprague Elec. Co., North Adams, Mass., 1968-77, Clinton, Tenn., 1977—. Served with USAAF, 1943-45. Decorated D.F.C., Purple Heart, Air Medal with 12 oak leaf clusters. Mem. U.S. C. of C., Nat. Rifle Assn., Sigma Xi, Pi Tau Sigma, Sigma Tau. Republican. Office: Eagle Bend Industrial Park Clinton TN 37716

WHITE, JAMES FRANCIS, county ofcl.; b. Niagara Falls, N.Y., Apr. 13, 1948; s. Daniel John and Helen Margaret (Collins) W.; B.A., Niagara U., 1970; fellow in urban planning U. Buffalo, 1978. Research asst. to minority leader N.Y. State Assembly, 1973; sr. planner Niagara County (N.Y.) Govt., 1974, dep. dir. manpower program, 1975, 1st dep. county exec., 1976-77, chmn. econ. devel. com., 1976-77; with Donald Dillon Agy., securities and ins., Buffalo, 1979—. Democratic county committeeman Niagara County, 1970—, dir. County Democratic Exec. Bd., 1970—. Served to 2d lt. C.E., U.S. Army, 1976-78. Mem. Nat. Assn. Securities Dealers, Nat. Assn. Life Underwriters, Alumni Assn. Niagara U., Jr. C. of C., Ancient Order Hibernians. Roman Catholic. Clubs: Moose, LaSalle Sportsman, Premier of Bankers Life Ins. Co., Sertoma Internat. Home: 2201 Ontario Ave Niagara Falls NY 14305 Office: 661 Delaware Ave Buffalo NY 14202

WHITE, JAMES FRANCIS, Realtor, realty and bus. appraiser; b. Bayonne, N.J., Sept. 6, 1917; s. Michael and Mary (Duffy) W.; student Columbia U., 1940-42, N.Y. U., 1941-42, New Sch. for Social Research, 1945; m. Ermalinda Russo, July 19, 1947; children—Janet Lynn, Judith Ann, Joan Ellen. Real estate appraiser Byrne, Bowman & Forshay, N.Y.C., 1941-42; officer in charge VA, Jersey City and New Brunswick, N.J., 1944-49; chief contact services VA Hosp., Lyons, N.J., 1949-52; owner, Realtor, appraiser James F. White Realty Co., Union, N.J., 1950—. Bd. dirs. Boys Club of Union, 1969-76; mem. N.J. Developmental Disabilities Council, 1971-78; pres. Epilepsy Found. N.J., 1971-73, chmn. bd. dirs., 1973-74; mem. adv. bd. Child Study Inst., Kean Coll. of N.J., 1973-76. Served with Mil. Police, AUS, 1942-44. Recipient Nat. Citation plaque DAV, 1952; Realtor of Year award Eastern Union County Bd. Realtors, 1970, 72; Resolutions of commendation Twp. Union, 1970, 72, N.J. Legislature, 1972; Nat. Service award Epilepsy Found. Am., 1972, Leadership award, 1974. Mem. Columbia Soc. Real Estate Appraisers, Nat., N.J. assns. Realtors, Profl. Ins. Agts. Assn. C. of C., DAV of N.J. (chmn. rehab. 1952), DAV of Jersey City (past comdr.), Vets. Alliance (past comdr.), Am. Legion (service officer 1967—). Episcopalian. Author fed., state programs aiding handicapped. Home: 9 Hayes Rd Union NJ 07083 Office: 1423 Stuyvesant Ave Union NJ 07083

WHITE, JOHN BARTLETT, glass co. exec.; b. Toledo, Feb. 26, 1924; s. Wilbur McKee and Helen Ruth (Bartlett) W.; B.S.M.E., Ohio State U., 1952; m. Helen Florence Collins, Mar. 22, 1952; children—Kenneth M., Ann C., Susan J., David J. With PPG Industries, Inc., 1952—, v.p. mfg., Pitts., 1967-73, v.p. Flat Glass Group, 1973-77, v.p. primary glass products flat glass div., 1977—; adv. bd. New Kensington campus Pa. State U., 1970-73; adv. bd. mech. engring. dept. Ohio State U., 1970—, chmn. steering com. Com. for Tomorrow, 1978—. Bd. dirs. Allegheny Valley Library, Tarentum, Pa., 1965-73, Pa. State U., New Kensington, 1970-73. Recipient Benjamin G. Lamme award Ohio State U., 1974, Meritorious Service citation, 1980; registered profl. engr., Ohio, Pa. Mem. ASME (Pitts. sect. Outstanding Engr. 1979), Soc. Automotive Engrs., Nat. Soc. Profl. Engrs. Clubs: Rotary (v.p. club 1960), Masons, Elks. Home: 127 Oak Manor Dr Natrona Heights PA 15065 Office: One Gateway Center Pittsburgh PA 15222

WHITE, JOHN MCLEAN, electronics co. exec.; b. N.Y.C., Nov. 18, 1927; s. John McLean and Frances (Gibson) W.; B.S. in Chemistry, Queens Coll., 1950; postgrad. U. Fla., 1955-58; m. Marie Grande, May 30, 1952; children—Laurie Ann, John McLean. Materials engr. Sperry Rand, Gainesville, Fla., 1952-56, materials mgr., 1956, spl. products mgr., 1958, dir. engring., 1964-75; v.p., dir. ops. ITT Electro-Optical Products Div., Roanoke, Va., 1975—; cons. waste/water treatment, Fla. Fallout shelter chmn., Gainesville, 1965-70. Served with U.S. Army, 1946-47, 50-52. Mem. Am. Mgmt. Assn., Am. Ceramic Soc., IEEE. Republican. Club: Masons. Patentee ceramic metal seals. Home: 3726 Tomley Dr Roanoke VA 24018 Office: 7635 Plantation Rd Roanoke VA 24019

WHITE, JOHN ROBERT, elec. mfg. co. exec.; b. Phoenix, Aug. 27, 1942; s. Howard and Alma Hazel (Railey) W.; B.A. in Liberal Arts, Brigham Young U., 1968, M.B.A., 1970; postgrad. Miami U., Oxford, Ohio, 1970, N.Y. U., 1971; m. Dorothy Jeanne Cozzens, Aug. 25, 1965; children—Christen, Tamra Lee, Nathan Howard, Bryan Robert. Auditor, Ernst & Ernst, N.Y.C., 1970-73; auditor Westinghouse Corp., Union, N.J., 1973-74, mgr. Latin Am. audit zone, San Juan, P.R., 1974—; sec.-treas. Westinghouse Electric Corp. S.Am., 1975-77, also dir.; corporate audit mgr. internat. Westinghouse Electric Corp., Pitts., 1977-79, controller, 1979—; instr. accounting Upsala Coll., 1973-74; cons. in field. C.P.A., N.Y. Mem. Am. Inst.

C.P.A.'s, N.Y. State Soc. C.P.A.'s, Nat. Accountants Assn. (asst. dir. N.Y. chpt. 1972), Assn. M.B.A.'s. Republican. Mormon. Home: 3331 Benden Dr Murrysville PA 15668 Office: 2040 Ardmore Blvd Pittsburgh PA

WHITE, JOSEPH ALLEN, JR., chem. co. exec.; b. Essex Fells, N.J., Feb. 26, 1920; s. Joseph Allen and Elizabeth (Skidmore) W.; Ph.B., U. Vt., 1942; postgrad. U. Pitts., 1950; m. Charlene Elgin, Nov. 29, 1952; children—Joseph Allen III, Andrew Clayton, Charles Edward. With Stanvac, 1947-62, ty. mgr. North China, 1947-49, sales mgr. Hong Kong, 1950-51, Malaya/Thailand, 1952-58, employee relations adviser Mobil Internat. Oil Co., N.Y.C., 1959-62; mng. dir. Mobil Oil Malaya Ltd., subsidiary Mobil Oil Co., N.Y.C., 1962-63; dir. internat. sales Hooker Chem. Corp. subsidiary Occidental Petroleum Corp., N.Y.C., 1963-73, dir. internat. marketing, 1967-73; v.p. internat. Oxy Metal Industries (INTRA), Inc., 1973-75; pres. Chemwood Internat., Inc., Stamford, Conn., 1975-79, Conn. Bulk Carriers, Inc., Stamford, 1979—. Served to maj., USMCR, 1942-46. Episcopalian (vestryman, lay reader). Mason, Rotarian. Home: Saddle Hill Rd Stamford CT 06903 Office: 460 Summer St Stamford CT 06901

WHITE, KENNETH ROGER, sales exec.; b. Richey, Mont., Jan. 1, 1929; s. Edward Brown and Emma Amanda W.; student Portland State Coll., 1954-56; B.S.E.E., Oreg. State U., 1956-58; m. Elsie Ann Sobolewski, Aug. 27, 1955; children—Ski Patrick, Julie Marie, Jill Ann, Scott Joseph. Asso. design engr. substas. Portland Gen. Electric Co. (Oreg.), 1958-61, mktg. specialist heating and air conditioning, 1961-67; sales engr. McGraw Edison Power System, Portland, 1967-71; sales engr. RTE Corp., Portland, 1971-72, sales mgr. Western region, 1972-79, sales mgr. Western area, 1980—. Served with USN, 1950-54. Mem. IEEE, N.W. Electric Light and Power Assn., N.W. Public Power Assn., Pacific Coast Elec. Assn., Elec. Club Oreg. Office: 12600 SW Hall Blvd Portland OR 97223

WHITE, KIRK, mfg. co. exec.; b. Pasadena, Calif., Apr. 2, 1926; s. Wells Newkirk and Genevieve Margaret (Moore) W.; student U. Calif., Berkeley, 1943-47, Ecole des Beaux Arts, Fontainebleau, France, 1948; m. Barbara Carolyn D'Arcy, Apr. 30, 1966. Head interior design studio W. & J. Sloane, N.Y.C., 1960-66; dir. design Medallion Ltd., N.Y.C., 1966-72, Directional Industries, N.Y.C., 1972-77; dir. design, furnishings div. Sperry and Hutchinson Co., N.Y.C., 1977—; v.p. funding Nat. Home Fashion League Ednl. Found. Served with USAAF, 1943-45, USAF, 1948-50. Mem. Am. Soc. Interior Designers (profl.), So. Furniture Club. Republican. Episcopalian. Club: U. Calif. Alumni. Home: 400 E 56th St New York NY 10022 Office: Sperry and Hutchinson Co 330 Madison Ave New York NY 10017

WHITE, LEWIS JAMES, bank exec.; b. Mayville, Mich., Mar. 20, 1938; s. Maurice and Dorothy Marie (Thompson) W.; student public schs., Mich.; m. Evelyn Lucile Hanes, Nov. 9, 1957; children—Jill Marie, Melanie Sue. Cashier, The Peoples State Bank of Caro (Mich.), 1969-72, v.p., 1972-78, pres., 1978—. Treas., Rotary Club, 1974—, Tuscola County Republican Commn., 1965-79. Office: 171 N State St Caro MI 48723

WHITE, MAX STEWART, banker; b. Lewisport, Ky., June 13, 1939; s. Jesse Moore and Martha Elizabeth (Stewart) W.; B.S. in Agr., U. Ky., 1961, postgrad. 1961-63; m. Carolyn Brauns, May 19, 1963; children—Stephen, Susan, Jennifer. Sr. appraiser real estate investment dept. Prudential Ins. Co., Louisville and Lexington, Ky., 1964-70; asst. v.p. Louisville Mortgage Service Co., 1970-73; v.p. T.F.A.C., Inc., Indpls., 1973-76; v.p. First Nat. Bank of Louisville, 1976—. Served with U.S. Army, 1963. Democrat. Club: Hunting Creek Country. Home: 6919 Wythe Hill Circle Prospect KY 40059 Office: PO Box 36000 Louisville KY 40232

WHITE, PETER COOPER, railroad exec.; b. Seattle, Nov. 30, 1929; s. Frank E. and Ruth F. White, B.C.E., U. Wash., Seattle, 1953; M.B.A., Northwestern U., 1972; m. Gwen Goodwin, Dec. 26, 1952; children—Katherine R., Peter C., Edward G. With Milw. R.R., 1953—, v.p. corp. services, Chgo., 1976-78, v.p. planning, 1979-80, v.p. mktg., 1980—; dir. Wash., Idaho & Mont. Ry. Co., Chgo., Terre Haute & Southeastern Ry. Co., Bedford Belt Ry. Co., Am. Rail Box Co., Trailer Train Co., So. Ind. Ry. Co., Milw. Motor Transp. Co. Vestryman, Redeemer Episcopal Ch., Elgin, Ill., 1979, treas., 1980—. Served with USAF, 1954-56. Registered profl. engr., Washington. Mem. Am. Ry. Engring. Assn., Nat. Freight Transp. Assn., Am. Ry. Devel. Assn., Transp. Research Forum, Milw. Rd. Polit. Action Com., Chgo. Traffic Club. Clubs: Union League (Chgo.); Met., Old Wayne Golf, Elks. Office: 516 W Jackson Blvd Chicago IL 60606

WHITE, RALPH DALLAS, health ins. exec.; b. Oklahoma City, Feb. 11, 1919; s. Ralph Allen and Ora Della (Lamberson) W.; grad. Okla. Sch. Bus., 1938; B.Comml.Sci., Okla. Sch. Accountancy, Law and Finance, 1941; postgrad. U. Tulsa, 1947-48, U. Mich., 1965-66; m. Ramona Corrine Caffee, Aug. 29, 1943; children—Richard Dallas, Linda Diane. With Gen. Motors Acceptance Corp., Tulsa, 1939-42, Douglas Aircraft Corp., Tulsa, 1942-45; accounting supr. Blue Cross & Blue Shield of Okla., Tulsa, 1945-50, mgr. personnel and systems, 1950-51, office mgr., 1951-57, dir. adminstrn., 1957-62, sec.-treas., 1962-67, v.p., sec.-treas., 1967-70, v.p., treas., 1970-74, exec. v.p., treas., 1974-79, sr. v.p., spl. cons. to pres., 1980—; v.p., treas. Mems. Service Life Ins. Co., 1977-79. Mem. Internat. Com. of Tulsa, 1967-68, Ark. Basin Devel. Assn., 1968—. Recipient Merit award key Nat. Office Mgrs. Assn./Adminstrv. Mgmt. Soc., 1958, Diamond Merit Award key, 1968; Boss of Year award Am. Bus. Women's Assn., 1961. Mem. Nat. Office Mgmt. Assn./Adminstrv. Mgmt. Soc. (pres. 1957-58), C. of C. Methodist. Clubs: Tulsa Farm, Kiwanis. Contbr. articles to profl. jours. Home: 4709 E 22 Pl Tulsa OK 74114 Office: 1215 S Boulder St Tulsa OK 74119

WHITE, RALPH DUDLEY, music co. exec.; b. Buffalo, Aug. 25, 1934; s. Menno Delbert and Hilda W.; student SUNY, Buffalo, 1952-58, U. Rochester (N.Y.), 1977, U. Colo., 1978, Harvard U., 1979; m. Margaret Jean Chapman, Aug. 18, 1956; 1 son, David Daniel. Missile test tech. Bello Aero., Buffalo, 1954-58; engring. tech. Sylvania Electric Engring. Research Lab., Buffalo, 1958-69, cons. engr. to purchasing dept., 1964-69, field sales engr., 1969-70; field sales engr. J. D. Ryerson, Rochester, 1969-70; owner, mgr. April Instruments, Batavia, N.Y., 1970-72; field sales mgr. Nycom, Syracuse, N.Y., 1973-76; dir. material mgmt. Moog Music, Inc., Cheektowaga, N.Y., 1976—. Served with U.S. Army, 1952-54. Mem. Am. Mgmt. Assn., Nat. Assn. Purchasing Mgrs., Purchasing Mgmt. Assn. Buffalo. Home: 860 N Forrest Rd Williamsville NY 14221 Office: 2500 Walden Ave Buffalo NY 14225

WHITE, ROBERT FREEMAN, mfr.'s agt.; b. Atlanta, Dec. 5, 1945; s. William Emmett and Elizabeth (Freeman) W., Jr.; student U. Houston, 1963-64, 72; m. Betty Ruth Horton, June 11, 1971; children—Shannon, Dara, Tracy, Trudi, Kendra. Pres., A-1 Coffee Break, Inc., Houston, 1972-76; partner Kershaw-White Co., Houston, 1976-77, MWB Assos., Houston, 1977—. Served with USN, 1964-72. Mem. Mktg. Agts. for Foodservice Industry, Tex. Restaurant Assn. Republican. Presbyterian. Club: N.W. Houston Kiwanis. Home and Office: 3823 Pineleaf St Houston TX 77068

WHITE, ROBERT MILES FORD, life ins. co. exec.; b. Lufkin, Tex., June 9, 1928; s. Sullivan Miles and Faye Clark (Scurlock) F.; B.A., Stephen F. Austin State U., 1948; B.B.A., St. Mary's U., San Antonio, 1955; postgrad. Am. Coll. Fin. Services, 1981; m. Mary Ruth Wathen, Nov. 10, 1946; children—Martha, Robert, Benedict, Mary, Jesse, Margaret, Maureen, Thomas. Tchr., Douglas (Tex.) Pub. Schs., 1946-47, Houston Pub. Schs., 1948-51; office mgr. Heat Control Insulation Co., San Antonio, 1951-53; accountant S.W. Acceptance Co., San Antonio, 1953-55; sec.-treas. Howell Corp., San Antonio, 1955-64; agent New Eng. Mutual Life Ins. Co., San Antonio, 1964-71; br. mgr. Occidental Life Ins. Co. of Calif., San Antonio, 1971—. Mem. citizens liaison com. San Antonio Ind. Sch. Dist., 1972-78, Equal Employment Opportunity Council, 1974—; active Wolverine Boys Council, 1969—. Mem. San Antonio Estate Planners Council, S.W. Pension Conf., Nat., Tex., San Antonio assns. life underwriters, Am. Soc. Chartered Life Underwriters, Gen. Agts. and Mgrs. Assn., Am. Risk and Ins. Assn., Tex. Hist. Soc., East Tex. Hist. Soc., San Antonio, S.E. Tex. geneal. and hist. socs., Sons of Republic of Tex., SAR, Kappa Pi Sigma. Republican. Roman Catholic. Home: 701 Sunshine Dr E San Antonio TX 78228 Office: 6243 IH 10 North Suite 330 San Antonio TX 78201

WHITE, ROBERT ROY, chem. engr., cons., educator; b. Bklyn., Mar. 1, 1916; s. Laurance Samuel and Grace Alma (Diffin) W.; B.S. in Chem. Engring., Cooper Union Inst., 1936; M.S. in Chem. Engring., U. Mich., 1938, Ph.D., 1940; postgrad. Law Sch., DePaul U., 1941-42; postgrad. Sr. Exec. Program., M.I.T., 1960; m. Elizabeth Rachel Clark, July 2, 1940; children—Robert Roy, William Wesley, Elizabeth Anne, Margaret. Chem. engr. legal dept. Universal Oil Products Co., Chgo., 1940-42; prof. dept. chem. engring., asso. dean Sch. Grad. Studies, dir. Inst. Sci. and Tech. and Gt. Lakes Research Inst., U. Mich., Ann Arbor, 1942-59; v.p., dir., gen. mgmt. Research and Devel., Atlantic Refining Co., Phila., 1959-62; v.p. corp. devel. Champion Papers, Inc., Hamilton, Ohio, 1962-66; pres. research div. W.R. Grace and Co., Clarksville, Md., 1966-67; dean Sch. Mgmt., Case Western Res. U., Cleve., 1967-73; dir. Academy Forum, spl. asst. to pres. Nat. Acad. Scis., Washington, 1971—; chem. engring. cons., 1942-59; mgmt. and tech. cons., 1967—; adj. prof. Am. U., Cath. U. Am.; dir. Ferro Corp., Cleve., ASC Inc., Lake Bluff, Ill. Served with sci. adv. commn. U.S. Army. Recipient Russell award U. Mich., 1945; George Westinghouse award Am. Soc. Engring. Edn., 1955; Sesquicentennial award U. Mich., 1967; Alumni award for Disting. Profl. Achievement, Cooper Union, 1974. Fellow Am. Inst. Chem. Engrs. (Profl. Progress award 1956); mem. Am. Chem. Soc., Ops. Research Soc. Am., Société Chimie Industrielle, AAAS, Am. Mgmt. Assn., Sigma Xi, Tau Beta Pi. Club: Cosmos. Contbr. articles to tech. and sci. publs. Home: 2440 Virginia Ave NW Suite D-1106 Washington DC 20037 Office: National Academy Sciences 2101 Constitution Ave Washington DC 20418

WHITE, RUTH MIRIAM WEIHS (MRS. PAUL WHITE), trade and fin. co. exec.; b. Vienna, Austria; d. Hugo and Ilka (Herzog) Weihs; came to U.S., 1947, naturalized, 1952; B.A. in Bus. Adminstrn., St. John's U., Shanghai, China, 1947; postgrad. N.Y.U., Coll. City N.Y.; m. Paul White, Sept. 18, 1949. Exec. sec. to chmn. bd. Pan Am. Trade Devel. Corp., N.Y.C., 1947-49, mgr., 1949-53, asst. v.p., 1953-58, v.p., 1958-75, sr. v.p., 1975—; also pres. Indsl. Crystal Corp. Office: 2 Park Ave New York NY 10016

WHITE, TERRANCE LEE, mfg. co. exec.; b. Akron, Ohio, June 12, 1947; s. Donald Allan and Audrey May (Bryan) W.; B.A., Ohio State U., 1970; m. Toni Suzanne Bell, Nov. 24, 1971. Vice pres. Long Beach Surplus Sales, Westminster, Calif., 1972—; pres. TP Mfg., T & T Cycle, B & T Auto Body, Westminster, 1976—. Life mem. Republican Nat. Com. Served with U.S. Army, 1966-68. Mem. Associated Surplus Dealers, Associated Mdse. Dealers, Sierra Club, Nat. Audubon Soc., Friends of Met. Opera Soc. Roman Catholic. Clubs: South Coast Racquet, John Wayne Tennis. Shark Island Yacht. Home: 9571 Orient St Huntington Beach CA 92646 Office: 7550 Garden Grove Westminster CA 92683

WHITE, TIMOTHY LEE, constrn. co. exec.; b. Brush, Colo., Sept. 6, 1949; s. George Robert and Corrine Ellen (Gray) W.; B.S., Colo. State U., 1972; postgrad. Denver U., Colo. State U.; m. Angelika Hansch, Sept. 14, 1969; 1 dau., Courtney. Estimator, project mgr. Lembke Constrn. Co., Denver, 1972-73; br. ops. mgr. B.B. Andersen Constrn. Co., Inc., Topeka, 1973-75; project mgr. Pinkard Constrn. Co., Denver, 1975-77; pres., owner Fischer-White Contractors, Inc., Castle Rock, Colo., 1977—. Trustee Castle Rock City Council, 1978-80; mem. Douglas County Variance Com., 1979—; mem. Castle Rock Planning Commn., 1978-80; mayor Town of Castle Rock, 1980—. Mem. Asso. Builders and Contractors. Republican. Lutheran. Club: Castle Rock Optimist (pres. 1978-79). Home: 82 Moore Dr Castle Rock CO 80104 Office: 312 Wilcox St Castle Rock CO 80104

WHITE, WILLIAM GREGG, ret. transp. exec.; b. San Francisco, Apr. 7, 1913; s. William Lee and Elsie (Gallagher) W.; student U. Calif., 1931-33; B.S., George Washington U., 1936; advanced mgmt. program Harvard, 1952; m. Mary Widdowfield, Oct. 28, 1939; children—William Lee, Ralph Gregg (dec.). With D.L. & W.R.R. Co., 1935-60, successively yard clk., supr. freight claim prevention, operating insp., trainmaster, div. supt., gen. supt., gen. mgr., 1935-54, v.p. operation, 1954-60; pres., dir. Consol. Freightways, Inc., San Francisco, 1960-75, chmn. bd., 1966-78; dir. Santa Fe Internat. Corp.; Howard lectr. George Washington U. Sch. Engring., 1959; guest lectr. Stanford U., U. Calif., Berkeley, George Washington U., 1979. Mem. adv. panel U.S. Army Transp. Corps, 1954-58. Bd. dirs. Guide Dogs for the Blind, San Rafael, Calif.; trustee George Washington U. Served from maj. to lt. col. Transp. Corps, World War II. Recipient outstanding alumnus award George Washington, U., 1959, alumni achievement award, 1965; Salzburg Meml. medal for distinguished service to transp. Syracuse U., 1973. Mem. Nat. Def. Transp. Assn., Western Hwy. Inst. (exec. com.), Alpha Kappa Lambda. Presbyterian. Clubs: Menlo Country (Calif.); Palo Alto (Calif.); Masons, Shriners. Office: Box 1708 Palo Alto CA 94302

WHITE, WILLIS SHERIDAN, JR., utilities exec.; b. nr. Portsmouth, Va., Dec. 17, 1926; s. Willis Sheridan and Carrie (Culpepper) W.; B.S., Va. Poly. Inst., 1948; M.S., M.I.T., 1958; m. LaVerne Behrends, Oct. 8, 1949; children—Willis Sheridan III, Marguerite Louise White Spangler, Cynthia Diane. With Am. Electric Power Co. System, 1948—; asst. egr. Am. Electric Power Service Corp., N.Y.C., 1948-52, asst. to pres., 1952-54, office mgr., 1954-57, adminstrv. asst. to operating v.p., 1958-61; div. mgr. Appalachian Power Co., Lynchburg, Va., 1962-66, asst. gen. mgr., Roanoke, Va., 1966-67, asst. v.p., 1967-69, v.p., 1969, exec. v.p., dir., 1969-73; sr. exec. v.p. ops., dir. Am. Electric Power Service Corp., N.Y.C., 1973-75, vice chmn. ops., also dir.; chmn. bd., chief exec. officer, Am. Electric Power Co., 1976—, Am. Electric Power Service Corp., 1976—; chmn., dir. Appalachian Power Co., Columbus & So. Ohio Electric Co., Ind. & Mich. Electric Co., Mich. Power Co., Ohio Power Co., Ky. Power Co., Kingsport Power Co., Wheeling Electric Co.; pres., dir. Beech Bottom Power Co., Blackhawk Coal Co., Cardinal Operating Co., Cedar Coal Co., Central Appalachian Coal Co., Central Coal Co., Central Ohio Coal Co., Central Operating Co., Franklin Real Estate Co., Ind. Franklin Realty Co., Mich. Gas Exploration Co., Price River Coal Co., Kanawha Valley Power Co., So. Appalachian Coal Co., So. Ohio Coal Co., Twin Br. R.R. Co., W.Va. Power Co., Windsor Power House Coal Co., Ohio Valley Electric Corp., Ind.-Ky. Electric Corp. Trustee, Randolph-Macon Woman's Coll.; asso. trustee Battelle Meml. Inst. Served with USNR, 1945-46. Sloan fellow, 1957-58. Mem. Edison Electric Inst. (adv. com.), Assn. Edison Illuminating Cos. (exec. com.), Nat. Coal Assn. (dir.), NAM (dir.), Downtown-Lower Manhattan Assn. (dir.), IEEE, Eta Kappa Nu. Methodist. Office: 180 E Broad St Columbus OH 43215

WHITEAKER, STANLEY CYRIL, accountant; b. Hurdland, Mo., Nov. 24, 1918; s. Roscoe E. and Marie (Surry) W.; evening student Rockhurst U., 1955-58; m. Justine M. Warford, Dec. 25, 1938; 1 dau., Linda J. Accountant, Mo. Pub. Service Commn., 1942-51; utility cons., 1951-58; partner Troupe, Kehoe, Whiteaker & Kent, C.P.A.'s, Kansas City, Kans. and Kansas City, Mo., 1958—; cons. Kans. Corp. Commn., Mo. Pub. Service Commn. and maj. industries in midwest on natural gas usage; cons. to Sec. Air Force; dir. T.K.W. Supply Co., Inc., Westboro Builders, Inc., Bichelmeyer Meat Co., Interstate Investments, Inc. Bd. mem., exec. council Greater Kansas City Council on Alcoholism. Served as sgt. USNR, 1943-45. Mem. Kansas City C. of C., Am. Inst. C.P.A.'s (chmn. regulated industries com.), Kans. Soc. C.P.A.'s, Nat. Assn. Pub. Accountants, Internat. Platform Assn. Clubs: Odd Fellows, Kansas City, Country of Mo., Milburn. Contbr. articles to profl. jours. Home: 6008 W 86th Terr Overland Park KS 66204 Office: Power & Light Bldg Kansas City MO 64105

WHITED, JOHN WALLACE, III, real estate broker; b. Beckley, W.Va. Mar. 18, 1941; s. John Wallace and Jessie A. (Wauhop) W.; student Gulf Coast Community Coll., Panama City, Fla., 1959-60, Tenn. Tech. U., 1960-63; m. Dorothy Anne Pringle, June 22, 1961; children—John Wallace, James Robert, Elizabeth Victoria, Kristi Marie. Div. mgr. Sears Roebuck & Co., 1960-70; v.p. Belle Isle Corp., Inc., Panama City, 1970—; pres. Whited Wilhite & Assos., Inc. and Four Star Investment Corp., Panama City, 1974—, First Fla. Comml. Realty, Inc., 1980—. Bd. dirs. Salvation Army, Panama City, 1977-78. Mem. Nat. Bd. Realtors, Associated Photographers Internat., Panama City Bd. Realtors. Republican. Methodist. Clubs: Masons, Shriners. Office: 1815 W 15th St Panama City FL 32401

WHITEHAIR, GARY M., steel co. exec.; b. Clarksburg, W.Va., Jan. 31, 1945; s. Garland M. and Mary E. (Ball) W.; B.S. in Acctg., U. Balt., 1963-67; M.B.A., U. Pa., 1970; m. I. Lorraine Whitehair, Apr. 22, 1961; children—Dawn, Michael, Christopher. Pres., Alarm Data Corp., Balt., 1970-73; regional controller truck div. The Hertz Corp., Balt., 1973-74; asso. Booz, Allen & Hamilton, N.Y.C., 1974-79; chmn. bd., chief exec. officer Steelworkers, Inc., Balt., 1979—; dir. Minn. Tax Exempt Bond Fund. Mem. Nat. Assn. Accts. Republican. Club: Univ. Home: 4614 Roundhill Rd Ellicott City MD 21043 Office: 1334 Sulphur Spring Rd Baltimore MD 21227

WHITEHEAD, FREDERICK BURNETT, consumer cons.; b. Newark, Sept. 23, 1915; s. Gustav Burnett and Mary Louise (Kuhn) W.; B.B.A., Rutgers U., 1940; m. Rita Dunlap, Apr. 19, 1942; children—Frederick Burnett, Janis Lanne Wallace. With Prudential Ins. Co., 1934-46; traffic mgr. Fuller, Smith & Ross Advt. Agy., N.Y.C., 1945; advt. editor Good Housekeeping mag., N.Y.C., 1947-80, dir. consumer affairs, 1970-80; pres. Cause for Consumer Concern, Florham Park, N.J., 1980—. Mem. council Borough of Florham Park 1963-72, pres. council, 1968-72; mem. Hanover Park Regional High Sch. Bd. Edn. Served to maj. Q.M.C., U.S. Army, 1941-45. Recipient Citizen of Yr. award Jaycees, 1970. Mem. Soc. Consumer Affairs Profls. in Bus. (nat. dir. 1975-77, pres. N.Y. chpt. 1977-78, spl. achievement award 1980), Am. Legion. Republican. Presbyterian. Clubs: Kiwanis (pres.), Florham Park Country, West Essex Camera, Masons. Office: Cause for Consumer Concern Inc PO Box 248 Florham Park NJ 07932

WHITEHEAD, MARGARET HAROLD, publishing co. exec.; b. Chattanooga, Aug. 18, 1928; M.A., U. Chattanooga, 1950. Editor/pub. New Woman mag. Episcopalian. Compiler: Best of Show in Flower Arrangements series; Prize-Winning Painting series; Prize-Winning Graphics series; Prize-Winning Water Colors series; Prize-Winning Sculpture series. Author: Daddy is a Doctor. Office: 214 Royal Poinciana Plaza Palm Beach FL 33480

WHITEHEAD, STEPHEN ROBERT, publishing co. exec.; b. Des Moines, Mar. 7, 1940; s. Glenn Edwin and Shirley Adelle (Hildahl) W.; student S.D. State U., 1962-64; m. Myrna Gene Owen, Aug. 18, 1962; children—Lori Lynn, Julie Ann, Marcie Kay, Stacie Elizebeth. With composing dept., Perry (Iowa) Daily Chief, 1954-58, mem. advt. dept., 1961-64, gen. mgr., co-publisher, 1964—. Served with USNR, 1959-61. Mem. Iowa Daily Press (dir. 1968-71, news com. 1972-74), Printing Industry Iowa (dir. 1974-75). Mem. Perry C. of C. (dir. 1977—, pres. 1979). Presbyterian. Elk, Rotarian. Home: 2321 Iowa St Perry IA 50220 Office: 1323 2d St Perry IA 50220

WHITEHILL, HENRY DAVID, diversified co. exec.; b. Vienna, Austria, Mar. 29, 1923; came to U.S., 1938, naturalized, 1943; s. Charles and Katherine W.; student CCNY, 1940-41, Columbia U., 1941, Rutgers U., 1949-50; m. Margery Werner, May 23, 1943; 1 son, Thomas. With Gen. Cigar Co. Inc. (co. name changed to Culbro Corp. 1975), N.Y.C., 1947—, dist. mgr., 1961-64, asst. v.p. prodn., 1965-68, v.p. purchasing, 1969-74, sec., 1975—, sr. v.p., 1979—; dir. Am. Mayflower Life Ins. Co. Served with AUS, 1943-46. Mem. Soc. Corp. Secs. Home: 300 E 57th St New York NY 10022 Office: Culbro Corp 605 3d Ave New York NY 10016

WHITEHORNE, ROBERT ALVIN, bus. educator; b. Portsmouth, Va., June 20, 1925; s. Stanford Laferty and Ruth (Speight) W.; B.E.E., Va. Poly. Inst., 1948, M.E.E., 1951; m. Margaret Kirby, Sept. 6, 1946; children—Lynn Whitehorne Sacco, Robert Alvin, Cynthia Leigh. Engr., IBM Corp., Poughkeepsie, N.Y., 1950-54, lab. adminstr., Kingston, N.Y., 1954-56, dir. employee relations, Armonk, N.Y., 1956-72, resident mgr. Mid-Hudson Valley, Poughkeepsie, 1972-74; v.p.-personnel and orgn. planning Sperry & Hutchinson Co., N.Y.C., 1976-79; exec. v.p. Michelin Tire Corp., Grenville, S.C., 1974-76; dir. CODESCO, Inc., SPAN-America, Inc.; mem. faculty Coll. Bus. Adminstrn., U. S.C., Columbia, 1980—. Former trustee U. S.C. Bus. Partnership Found.; mem. plans for progress com. Pres.'s Commn. on Equal Employment Activity, 1963-68. Served with USMCR, 1944-46. Methodist. Clubs: Quail Hollow, Princeton. Home: 2400 Owl Circle West Columbia SC 29169 Office: U SC Coll Bus Columbia SC 29208

WHITEHOUSE, ALTON WINSLOW, JR., oil co. exec.; b. Albany, N.Y., Aug. 1, 1927; s. Alton Winslow and Catherine (Lyda) W.; B.S., U. Va., 1949, LL.B., 1952; m. Helen MacDonald, Nov. 28, 1953; children—Alton, Sarah, Peter. Admitted to Ohio bar, 1953; asso. partner firm McAfee, Hanning, Newcomer, Hazlett & Wheeler, Cleve., 1952-68; v.p., gen. counsel Standard Oil Co. (Ohio), Cleve., 1968-69, sr. v.p., gen. counsel, 1969-70, pres., chief operating officer, 1970-77, vice chmn., 1977-78, chmn. bd., chief exec. officer, 1978—, also dir., mem. exec. com.; dir. Cleve. Trust Co., Midland-Ross Corp., Cleve.-Cliffs Iron Co. Trustee Cleve. Clinic Found., Case Western Res. U., Cleve. Mus. Art; bd. dirs. Hwy. Users Fedn. Mem. Cleve.,

Ohio, Am. bar assns., Am. Petroleum Inst. (dir.). Episcopalian. Office: Standard Oil Co (Ohio) 1750 Midland Bldg Cleveland OH 44115

WHITEHOUSE, HENRY REMSEN, II, s.s. co. exec.; b. N.Y.C., Aug. 5, 1931; s. Guill Schenck and Frances Josephine (Burke) W.; B.A., Princeton U., 1954; m. Rosalia M. Ferrer, Apr. 7, 1962; children—Joan Marie, Christina. Mgmt. trainee Grace Line, 1957-62; traffic mgr., mgr., ops. mgr. Grace y Cia (Colombia) S.A., Cali, Buenaventura, Barranquilla, 1962-67; mgr. South Atlantic & Caribbean Lines, San Juan, P.R., 1968-73; gen. mgr. Motorships of P.R. Inc., San Juan, 1974-75; pres. Motorships Inc., Englewood, Colo., 1975-76; dir. sales for Latin Am., Prudential Lines Inc., N.Y.C., 1976-77; exec. v.p. Grancolombiana (N.Y.) Inc., N.Y.C., 1977—, also dir.; dir. JSP Agy. Inc., N.Y.C. Served to lt. comdr. USNR, 1954-57. Mem. N.Y. Shipping Assn. (dir.), U.S. Naval Inst., Nat. Def. Transp. Assn., Am. Mgmt. Assn., N.Y. C. of C. and Industry. Republican. Episcopalian. Clubs: Princeton (N.Y.C.); Cap and Gown (Princeton, N.J.). Office: One World Trade Center Suite 1667 New York NY 10048

WHITEHOUSE, HUGH LORD, air tools mfg. co. exec.; b. Erie, Pa., Dec. 10, 1924; s. Irving Percival and Helen (Lord) W.; A.B., Harvard U., 1946, A.M., Grad. Sch. Arts and Scis., 1949; m. Martha Linton, June 29, 1946; children—Katherine, Daniel, Stephen, David. With Rotor Tool Co. (now div. Cooper Industries), Cleve., 1951-63, sec., 1956-60, v.p. sales and engring., 1960-63; founder, gen. mgr. Stanley Air Tools div. The Stanley Works, Cleve., 1963—, pres., 1976—. Mem. Compressed Air and Gas Inst. (dir., 2d v.p.). Patentee air tool field. Office: 700 Beta Dr Cleveland OH 44143

WHITEHOUSE, JACK PENDLETON, pub. relations cons.; b. Los Angeles, Aug. 18, 1924; s. Marvin and Lola Katherine (Gerber) W.; student The Principia Coll., 1942-43, UCLA, 1945-49; m. Phyllis Jeanne Stockhausen, Mar. 6, 1964; 1 son, Mark Philip. Editor, Los Angeles Ind. Pub. Co., 1946-48; writer UCLA Office Pub. Info., 1948-51; mng. editor Yuma (Ariz.) Daily Sun, 1951-53; asso. editor Desert Mag., 1953-54; owner Whitehouse & Assos., Los Angeles, 1954-55; dir. West Coast press relations Shell Oil Co., Los Angeles, 1955-56; pub. relations dir. Welton Becket & Assos., Los Angeles, 1956-58; owner, pres. Whitehouse Assos., Inc., Encino, Calif., 1958—; owner, pres. Internat. Pub. Relations Co. Ltd. (Calif.), Los Angeles, 1959—; dir. Japan Steel Info. Center, Los Angeles, 1966—; univ. guest lectr. pub. relations, internat. bus. Advisor, Japanese Philharmonic Soc., 1975—. Served with USAAC, 1943-45. Mem. Pub. Relations Soc. Am., Japan Am. Soc. (mem. exec. council 1968—), Fgn. Trade Assn. (dir. 1978—), World Affairs Council, Calif. Council Internat. Trade, Japan-Calif. Assn. Republican. Clubs: Internat. Los Angeles, Greater Los Angeles Press. Author: International Public Relations, 1978; contbr. article to profl. jour. Office: 15720 Ventura Blvd Encino CA 91436

WHITEHURST, WILLIAM WILFRED, JR., mgmt. cons.; b. Balt., Mar. 4, 1937; s. William Wilfred and Elizabeth (Hogg) W.; B.A., Princeton, 1958; M.S., Carnegie Inst. Tech., 1963; m. Linda Joan Potter, July 1, 1961; children—Catherine Elizabeth, William Wilfred, III. Mathematician Nat. Security Agy., Fort George G. Meade, Md., 1961-63; mgmt. cons. McKinsey & Co., Inc., Washington, 1963-66; partner L.E. Peabody & Assos., Washington, 1966-69, exec. v.p., dir. L.E. Peabody & Assos., Inc., Lanham, Md., 1969—. Served to lt. USNR, 1958-61. Mem. Operations Research Soc. Am., Inst. Mgmt. Scis., Washington Soc. Investment Analysts. Episcopalian. Clubs: University, Princeton (Washington); Princeton (N.J.) Quadrangle. Home: 12421 Happy Hollow Rd Cockeysville MD 21030 Office: 8200 Professional Pl Landover MD 20785

WHITESEL, JAMES WARREN, lawyer; b. Crosskeys, Va., Dec. 4, 1921; s. James Brown and Lillian Mae (Shaver) W.; B.S. cum laude, Wake Forest U., 1943; J.D. with distinction, George Washington U., 1948, LL.M., 1950; M.B.A., U. Chgo., 1964; m. Patricia Aylward, Dec. 27, 1948; children—James Eric, Cheryl Eileen, Mary Jennifer. Admitted to D.C. bar, 1948, N.Y. State bar, 1951, Ill. bar, 1959, U.S. Supreme Ct. bar, 1955, U.S. Ct. Customs and Patent Appeals bar, 1950; examiner U.S. Patent Office, 1948-50; trademark counsel Stromberg-Carlson, Rochester, N.Y., 1950-58; Midwest area patent counsel ITT, Chgo., 1959-70; sr. partner firm Laff, Whitesel & Rockman, patent attys., Chgo., 1970—. Served with U.S. Army, 1943-46. Mem. Am. Bar Assn., Ill. Bar Assn., Chgo. Bar Assn., Am. Patent Law Assn. Home: 5313 Grand Ave Western Springs IL 60558 Office: Laff Whitesel & Rockman 875 N Michigan Ave Chicago IL 60611

WHITESELL, JAMES CLARENCE, food broker; b. St. Joseph, Mo., Apr. 13, 1931; s. David Earl and Emma Gertrude (Derks) W.; student St. Joseph Jr. Coll., 1949-50, U. Mass., 1956-57, Alexander Hamilton Inst., 1960-62; m. Melita Ann Hogan, Sept. 14, 1955; children—Bart, Beth Ann, Susan, Patricia. Salesman, Procter & Gamble, 1950-54, Rath Packing Co., 1954-62, Food Merchandisers, 1962-64; pres., gen. mgr. Splty. Food Sales Co., Inc., Atlanta, 1964—; dir. Belcraft Constrn. Co., Hadacol Corp. Served with USMCR, 1951-53. Mem. Frozen Food Council Ga. (v.p. 1972-73, pres. 1974-75). Clubs: Elks, K.C. Home: 155 Old College Way Atlanta GA 30328 Office: 57 14th St NE Atlanta GA 30309

WHITING, CARSON ROSS, mfg. co. exec.; b. Cin., Nov. 15, 1910; s. William Alexander and Stella Jane (Hitz) W.; comml. engring. degree U. Cin., 1933; m. Kathryn May Townsley, Apr. 23, 1937; children—Clair Ann Whiting Sharpless, Richard Townsley, David Ross (dec.). With Cin. & Suburban Bell Telephone Co., 1933-34; with Gano & Cherrington, C.P.A.'s, Cin., 1934-35; home furnishings buyer McAlpin Dept. Stores, Cin., 1935-41; nat. home furnishings buyer Montgomery Ward & Co., N.Y.C., 1941-49; founder, pres. Whiting Mfg. Co., Inc., Cin., 1949-80; dir. Madison Bldg. Assn., Citizens State Bank, Ohmart Corp. Mem. Ohio Bedding Adv. Bd., 1961-68; mem. endowment com., chmn. bd. trustees Knox Presbyterian Ch.; chmn. U. Cin. Corp. Fund Drive, 1973; trustee Gen. Protestant Orphan Home, 1956-77, pres., 1966-74, reception chmn. Ann. Orphan Feast, 1977, officer of the day Orphan Feast, 1978, mem. orphan home adv. com., 1977-80; Bd. dirs. Cin. Zool. Soc., 1956-80, pres., 1959-65, chmn. long-range planning com. Cin. Zoo, 1972-80. Recipient Wildlife and Conservation award Green Valley of Cin., 1979; Disting. Alumni award U. Cin., 1969. Mem. Cin. Hist. Soc. Clubs: Masons, Jesters. Office: Whiting Mfg Co Inc 9999 Carver Rd Cincinnati OH 45242

WHITING, CLAUDETTE JULIA, chem. co. exec.; b. Phila., Mar. 3, 1943; d. Olive Jennings Mitchell; B.S. in Chemistry, Morgan State U., Balt., 1965; m. Reginald Whiting, July 16, 1966; children—Valeria, Kristina. Gen. mgr. Princeton Info. Tech. (N.J.), 1969-72; mgr. tech. info. J.D. Williams Co., N.Y.C., 1972-74; dir. communications Apollo Technologies, Inc., Whippany, N.J., 1975-79, asst. v.p., 1979—. Mem. Am. Chem. Soc., Chem. Communicators Assn., Spl. Library Assn., Bus. and Profl. Communicators Assn., Publicity Club N.Y., Gamma Sigma Sigma. Democrat. Baptist. Author: Dyeing Synthetic Textiles, 1975. Home: 139 S Munn Ave East Orange NJ 07018 Office: 1 Apollo Dr Whippany NJ 07981

WHITMAN, GUY ED, JR., box and pallet mfg. co. exec.; b. Sidney, Ohio, Apr. 25, 1921; s. Guy Ed and Lucille (Simmons) W.; student Ind. Bus. Coll., 1946; m. Marilynn Eileen Andress, Oct. 18, 1941; children—Don Edward, Mark Eliot. With various tool and die design shops, Dayton, Ohio, 1954; salesman The State Stationers, Inc., Indpls., 1954-79; outside salesman Area Box & Pallet Mfg. Co., Indpls., 1978—; owner, operator Odon Box & Pallet, Inc. (Ind.), 1979—. Served with U.S. Army, 1943-44; with USAAF, 1944-45; PTO. Decorated Air medal with 7 oak leaf clusters. Mem. Odon Bus. and Profl. Assn., Odon C. of C. Republican. Methodist. Club: Masons. Home: 310 S Spring St Odon IN 47562 Office: 313 S Spring St Odon IN 47562

WHITMAN, JEANNETTE CECILIA, transp. exec.; b. Aiken, S.C., Dec. 22, 1947; d. Harlan George and Ruth Hilda (Andrews) Zweep; grad. high sch.; m. Charles A. Whitman, Oct. 22, 1966; children—Charles F., Susan D. With Whitman Aviation, Waukesha, Wis., 1973—, v.p., 1974—. Mem. Nat. Air Transp. Assn., Exptl. Aircraft Assn., Waukesha Aviation Club (dir.), Aircraft Owners and Pilots Assn. Home: 2918 West View Ct Waukesha WI 53186 Office: 24151 W Bluemound Rd Waukesha WI 53186

WHITMAN, MARTIN J., investment banker; b. N.Y.C., Sept. 30, 1924; s. Irving and Dora (Cukier) W.; B.S. magna cum laude, Syracuse U., 1949; M.A., New Sch. for Social Research, 1956; postgrad. Princeton U., 1949-50; m. Lois M. Quick, Mar. 10, 1956; children—James Q., Barbara E., Thomas I. Research analyst, buyer Shearson Hammill & Co., N.Y.C., 1950-56; analyst William Rosenwald Co., N.Y.C., 1956-58; head research Ladenburg, Thalmann & Co., N.Y.C., 1958-60; gen. partner Gerstley Sunstein & Co., Phila., 1960-67; v.p., dir. Blair & Co., Inc., N.Y.C., 1967-68; pres. M.J. Whitman & Co. (now Inc.), N.Y.C., 1969—; dir. Mathematica Inc., Princeton, N.J.; vice-chmn. GNMR, Inc., N.Y.C.; adj. prof. fin. Yale U., New Haven, 1972—; cons. disclosure study SEC, 1968; cons. Pres.'s Commn. on Accident at Three Mile Island, 1979. Served with USNR, 1942-46. Chartered fin. analyst. Mem. N.Y. Soc. Security Analysts, Phila. Econ. Soc. Jewish. Author: (with M. Shubik) The Aggressive Conservative Investor, 1979; contbr. numerous articles to profl. publs., also booklets. Home: 285 Central Park W New York NY 10024

WHITMARSH, THEODORE FRANCIS, lawyer, investor; b. Englewood, N.J., Sept. 25, 1918; s. Karl Russell and Catherine (Clarke) W.; A.B., Harvard, 1942; LL.B., Fordham U., 1950; m. Mary Louise Ward, Feb. 19, 1944; children—Linda L., Carol P., Dorothy S. Admitted to N.Y. bar, 1950; asst. sec., dir. Frances H. Leggett & Co., 1950-52, v.p., sec., dir., 1955-59; sec., dir. Thames & Hudson Pub. Co., N.Y.C., 1952-53; v.p., gen. mgr., asst. sec., dir. Hogan-Faximile Corp., 1959-64, pres., dir. Hogan Faximile Corp. of Can. Ltd., 1962-64, 103 E. 75th St. Apts., Inc., 1957-70, Audley Clarke Co., 1968—. Served with AUS, 1942-46. Mem. Am., N.Y. State bar assns., Assn. Bar City N.Y., Huguenot Soc. Am. (pres., dir. 1975-78). Clubs: River, Union, Church (N.Y.C.); Piping Rock. Home: 183 Linden Ln Glen Head NY 11545 Office: 99 Madison Ave New York NY 10016

WHITMORE, GEORGE MERLE, JR., mgmt. cons. co. exec.; b. Tarrytown, N.Y., Jan. 1, 1928; s. George Merle and Elizabeth Helen (Knodel) W.; B.E., Yale, 1949; M.B.A., Harvard, 1951; m. Priscilla Elizabeth Norman, Mar. 30, 1963; children—Elizabeth Lawrence, George Norman, Stephen Bradford. Test engr. Gen. Electric Co., Bridgeport, Conn., Erie, Pa., 1949; research asso. Harvard Bus. Sch., Boston, 1951-52; asso. Cresap, McCormick Paget Inc., N.Y.C., 1954-59, prin., 1959-61, partner, 1961-69, v.p., dir., 1969-79, mng. dir., chief exec. officer, 1979—; dir. Philo Smith & Co., Inc., Stamford, Conn. Trustee Hackley Sch., Tarrytown, N.Y.; chmn. bd. trustees Greenwich (Conn.) Acad.; dir. Yale Alumni Fund. Served with USAF, 1952-53. Mem. Inst. Mgmt. Cons. Inc. (founding mem., dir.), Assn. Cons. Mgmt. Engrs. (dir.), Newcomen Soc., Tau Beta Pi. Presbyterian. Clubs: Stanwich (Greenwich); Yale (N.Y.C.). Home: 4 Cedarwood Dr Greenwich CT 06830 Office: Cresap McCormick Paget 245 Park Ave New York NY 10017

WHITMORE, JOHN EDWIN, III, public relations cons.; b. Alburquerque, Sept. 2, 1930; s. John Edwin and Gwen Lee (Wilson) W.; B.A. in Journalism, Tex. A&M U., 1952; m. Brenda Morris, Aug. 16, 1975; children by previous marriage—James Timothy, Erik D. Gustafson, John Alexander. Bur. chief Bus. Week Mag., 1957-67; asst. dir. Inst. Texan Cultures, San Antonio, 1967-69; v.p. 1st Mktg. Group, Inc., of Houston, 1972-75; owner, operator Whitmore Co. Public Relations, Houston, 1969-72, 75—; dir. Sugar Creek Nat. Bank; lectr. U. Houston. Pres., Learning Devel. Center, 1978—. Served to 1st lt. AUS, 1952-54. Recipient 1st place award for newswriting AP Mng. Editors, 1955. Mem. Public Relations Soc. Am. (accredited), Press Club Houston. Republican. Episcopalian. Clubs: Sugar Creek Country, Warwick, Rotary (Houston). Home: 631 Montclair Blvd Sugar Land TX 77478 Office: 11700 Southwest Freeway Suite 200 Houston TX 77031

WHITNEY, ADELBERT GRANT, merc., ins. co. exec.; b. Lowell, Mass., July 25, 1917; s. Adelbert Howard and Julia (Sheehan) W.; B.S. in Bus. Adminstrn., Boston U., 1940; m. Lillian Ritch DeArmon, Nov. 17, 1950; children—Julia Woodley, A. Grant, Frank DeArmon. Asst. to v.p. Belk Stores, Charlotte, N.C., 1946-52, asst. to pres., 1952-55; v.p., sec.-treas. Belk Stores Ins. Reciprocal, Belk Underwriters, Inc., Charlotte, 1950-58, exec. v.p., sec.-treas., 1958—; gen. mgr. ins. dept. Belk Stores, 1951—; sec., mem. exec. com. Belk Stores Services, 1959-68, v.p., 1964-68, employee ins. operating com., 1971-72; v.p., sec.-treas. Providence Realty Corp., Charlotte, 1950-63, pres., 1959-60, pres., sec.-treas., 1964-75; v.p. Queen City Investors, Inc., Charlotte, 1959-62; sec. Thrifty Investors, Inc., Charlotte, 1961-62, investment chmn., 1964-65, v.p., 1967-68; sec.-treas. Archdale Mut. Ins. Co., 1962-65, exec. v.p., sec.-treas., 1965; speaker Internat. Ins. Seminars, Inc., 1972—; mem. advisory com. on state workmen's compensation laws to Council State Govts. Mem. exec. com., dir. Arthritis and Rheumatism Found., Charlotte, 1959-60; mem. exec. bd. Mecklenburg council Boy Scouts Am., 1949—, v.p., 1962-66, chmn. exploring, 1970-72, mem. exec. bd. S.E. region, 1973—, mem.-at-large nat. council, 1974—; chmn. N.C. U.S.O., 1959-73; chmn. Charlotte Third U.S. Army Advisory Com., 1953-68, civilian adviser, 1968—; vice chmn. Shrine Bowl of Carolinas, 1963-66, gen. chmn., 1967-69; creator, dir. Charlotte's Festival in the Park, 1964—; industry chmn. laymen's nat. com. Nat. Bible Week, 1967-70, asso. chmn., 1971—; chmn. adv. com. Charlotte Youth for Christ; crusade chmn. N.C. div. Am. Cancer Soc., 1969-70, chmn. spl. gifts com., 1967, mem. exec. com., bd. dirs., 1968—, 3d v.p., 1970, pres., 1972-73; mem. ins. advisory council U. Tex., 1968-69; internat. bd. electors Ins. Hall of Fame, 1968-70, mem. chamber of electors, 1972—; mem. Mayor's Com. Better Charlotte, 1974—; gen. chmn. Billy Graham Appreciation Day, 1968, Pres. Eisenhower's Visit to Charlotte; program chmn. Charlotte/Mecklenburg Bicentennial Celebration Com., 1968, chmn. com., 1974—; gen. chmn. Mecklenburg Declaration of Independence-Freedom Celebration, 1975, 76; chmn. host com. Billy Graham 60th Birthday Party, Nov. 4, 1978; bd. dirs. Jr. Achievement, Inc., Charlotte Council on Alcoholism, Mecklenburg Citizens Better Libraries, 1967-71, Contact of Charlotte, Goodwill Industries Charlotte, Inc., Govern, Union, N.C. Multiple Sclerosis Soc., Rescue Mission, United Arts Council, Charlotte Symphony Soc., 1949-55; v.p. bd. dirs. Christian Rehab. Center, 1979—; chmn. Sun Belt Conf. Festival Worship Service, 1978; trustee United Community Services, Elmira (N.Y.) Coll., 1978; bd. visitors Brevard Music Center; bd. govs. Am. Found. Religion and Psychiatry, 1959-72, Insts. Religion and Health, 1972—; trustee United Community Services; mem. parents council Davidson Coll., 1972-73. Served as officer U.S. Army, 1940-45; col. Res. ret., 1945-70; NATOUSA. Decorated Soldiers medal for heroism U.S. Army; recipient Disting. Service award Jaycees, 1952; Freedoms Found. Bronze medal, 1954; Silver Beaver Award Boy Scouts Am., 1956; Disting. Service award Charlotte Rotary, 1966, Disting. Service award Charlotte Exchange Club, 1967; Disting. Service award Jungle Aviation and Radio Service, Inc., 1971; named to Exec. and Profl. Hall of Fame, 1966 (mem. selection com. 1967—); named Charlotte Young Man of Year, 1952; Exemplary Service award N.C. Soc. Prevention of Blindness, 1972; Franklin Medallion award Printing Industry Carolinas, Inc., 1973; Certificate of appreciation Bd. Govs. U.S.O., 1973; Disting. Service award Hornet's Nest council Girl Scouts Am., 1976, 77; Service to Mankind award Sertoma Clubs, Charlotte, 1977. others; named Man of Yr., Charlotte News, 1975; cert. of commendation U.S. Conf. Mayors, 1976; A. Grant Whitney Day named for him, City of Charlotte, 1977. Mem. Risk and Ins. Mgmt. Soc. (pres. Va.-Carolinas chpt. 1957-58, pres. Carolinas chpt. 1963-64, mem. nat. nominating com. for officers 1964-65, nat. v.p., conf. activities 1965-66, 1st v.p. 1966-67, pres. 1967-68, nat. dir. 1968-70, nat. legis. com., joint industry/risk mgr. com., named man of year 1971, Pres.'s award 1971), Am. Mgmt. Assn., Nat. Assn. Ind. Insurers (v.p. 1953-67, dir. 1968—, vice chmn. 1977-78, chmn. 1978-79, chmn. fin. com. 1980), Property Casualty Ins. Council, Captive Ins. Cos. Assn. (v.p. 1973-74, sec. 1974), U.S. (ins. com. 1967-69), Charlotte chambers commerce, Am. Legion, Carolinas Carrousel (dir. 1952-57, 70-71), Mil. Order World Wars, Carolina Clowns (hon.), Royal Soc. Knights of Carrousel, Inc., (pres. 1954-64, chmn. governing council 1964-68, chmn. exec. com. 1968-69), Downtown Charlotte Assn. (chmn. promotional activities planning com. 1965-68), Ky. Cols., Newcomen Soc. N.Am. (N.C. com.), Soc. 1st Div. Infantry, Assn. U.S. Army, Res. Officers Assn., French Fgn. Legion (hon.). Presbyterian (elder). Mason (Shriner, 33 deg.). Clubs: Boston Univ. Alumni of the Carolinas (pres. 1949-51, nat. alumni council 1962—), Execs. (pres. 1963-64), Charlotte City Club, Myers Park Country, Lions, Goodfellows (Charlotte). Home: 684 Colville Rd Charlotte NC 28207 Office: 308 E 5th St Charlotte NC 28202

WHITNEY, RALPH ROYAL, JR., financial exec.; b. Phila., Dec. 10, 1934; s. Ralph Royal and Florence Elizabeth (Whitney) W.; B.A., U. Rochester, 1957, M.B.A., 1972; m. Fay Wadsworth, Apr. 4, 1959; children—Lynne Marie, Paula Sue, Brian Ralph. Spl. agt. Prudential Ins. Co., Rochester, N.Y., 1958-59, div. mgr., 1959-63; gen. agt. Nat. Life of Vt., Syracuse, N.Y., 1963-64; controller Wadsworth Mfg. Assos. Inc., Syracuse, 1964-65, v.p., 1965-68, pres., 1968-71; pres. Warren Components Corp., Warren, Pa., 1968—; partner Hammond Kennedy & Co., N.Y.C., 1972—; dir. Regency Electronics Inc. Mfg. Co., Displays, Inc., Diemolding, Inc., Securities Industries, Inc. Trustee Onondaga Community Coll. Served with AUS, 1958. Episcopalian. Clubs: N.Y. Yacht, Lotos (N.Y.C.); Century (Syracuse). Home: 7099 Frank Long Rd RD 2 Jamesville NY 13078 Office: 230 Park Ave New York NY 10017

WHITSELL, MARGARET MAUDE, lumber co. exec.; b. Charleston, N.Y., Apr. 24, 1930; d. Edward Carl and Mabel (Clarke) Bruce; student pub. schs., Jericho and Winooski, Vt.; m. Darrell Michael Whitsell, Sept. 22, 1947; children—Darrell, Cheryel, Bruce, Bonnie, Thomas, Melody, Fred, Don. Co-owner, bookkeeper Whitsell Co., Springfield, Oreg. Mem. Nat. Fedn. Ind. Bus., Nat. Wildlife Fedn., Ams. Against Union Control of Govt., Western Forestry Center, Springfield C. of C. Republican. Seventh-Day Adventist. Home: 36663 Camp Creek Rd Springfield OR 97477 Office: Whitsell Co 3411 Marcola Rd Springfield OR 97477

WHITT, PAUL J. C., textile co. ofcl.; b. High Point, N.C., Mar. 10, 1919; s. Fred O'Cas and Mary Lena (Jones) W.; B.A., Guilford Bus. Coll., 1938; m. Virginia Jean Pugh, Oct. 4, 1940; children—Robert Carleton, Frederick Keith, Parker Brian. Asst. supt. dyeing Cloverdale Dye Works, High Point, N.C., 1938-40; supt. dyeing Morgan Mills, Inc., Lauringburg, N.C., 1940-43, Chester H. Roth, Burlington, N.C., 1946-52; asst. supt. Standard-Coosa-Thatcher Co., Chattanooga, 1952-58; tech. sales rep. Ciba Co., Inc., 1958-72; dir. dyeing Am. and Efird Mills, Inc., Mt. Holly, N.C., 1972—. Mayor, City of Mt. Holly, 1973-75, 75-77, mem. city council, 1969-73; elder Presbyn. Ch. Served with AC, U.S. Army, 1943-46. Mem. Am. Assn. Textile Colorists and Chemists (vice chmn. Piedmont sect.). Democrat. Clubs: Masons, Shriners. Home: 225 Dogwood Dr Mount Holly NC 28120 Office: PO Box 926 Mount Holly NC 28120

WHITTAKER, ALFRED EVERTON WINSTON, ins. agt.; b. Kingston, Jamaica, Nov. 7, 1951; came to U.S., 1970; s. Ira and Maisie (Powell) W.; B.A. in Polit. Sci., Allegheny Coll., 1976. Underwriter, Am. Internat. Group, N.Y.C., 1977-78; regional casualty underwriter Wausau Ins. Cos., N.Y.C., 1978—. Mem. Soc. C.P.C.U.'s (charter mem.). Office: Wausau Ins Cos 1633 Broadway New York NY 10019

WHITTEMORE, LAURENCE FREDERICK, banker; b. Bangor, Maine, Mar. 7, 1929; s. John Cambridge and Elizabeth Payson (Prentiss) W.; student Balliol Coll., Oxford U., 1950; B.A., Yale U., 1951; M.B.A., Harvard U., 1953; m. Sarah Lee Arnold, Aug. 9, 1958; children—Arianna, Gioia, Lia, Nike. Account mgr. Brown Bros. Harriman & Co., N.Y.C., 1956-72, gen. mgr., 1972-73, partner, 1974—; dir. Manhattan Life Ins. Co., Otto Wolff U.S. Holding Co., Hurricane Industries, Inc.; mem. fin. com. Uniglobal, Frankfurt, Germany, Guardian Royal Exchange Assurance; mem. Midwest Stock Exchange. Mem. Yale Alumni Fund, 1957—, Am. Trauma Soc., 1976—, Art Inst. Chgo., 1977—, Harvard Bus. Sch. Fund, 1979—. Served to comdr. USNR, 1953-56. Mem. Fin. Analysts Fedn., Investment Analysts Soc. Chgo., N.Y. Soc. Security Analysts. Republican. Episcopalian. Clubs: Econ., Chgo., Attic (Chgo.); Links, 29, Yale (N.Y.C.). Office: Brown Bros Harriman & Co 135 S LaSalle St Chicago IL 60603

WHITTEN, DONALD GILBERT, oil co. exec.; b. Munday, Tex., June 11, 1929; s. Gilbert L. and B. Louise (Yarborough) W.; B.S., U. Okla., 1956; m. Marye Louise LaGarde, Apr. 26, 1947; children—Donna Lou, Susan Beth, Donald Gilbert. With Brit. Am. Oil Producing Co., Tulsa and Oklahoma City, 1947-58; regional petroleum engr. Am. Petrofina of Tex., Dallas, 1958-62, div. mgr. exploration and prodn., Big Spring, 1963-72, mgr. exploration and prodn. for U.S., 1972-74; sr. v.p. oil and gas ops. Mitchell Energy Corp., Houston, 1974-77; chmn. bd., owner W. J. Oil Co., Inc., Houston, 1977—. Recipient Spl. Service award Oil Info. Commn., Tex. Mid-Continent Oil and Gas Assn., 1968. Mem. Am. Petroleum Inst., Soc. Petroleum Engrs., Tex. Ind. Producers and Royalty Assn., Tex. Mid-Continent Oil and Gas Assn., W. Central Tex. Oil and Gas Assn., Permian Basin Petroleum Assn. (dir. 1964-72), Ind. Assn. Oil Drilling Contractors, Kans. Ind. Oil and Gas Assn., Pi Epsilon Tau, Petroleum Engrs. Club (pres. 1956). Office: 3 Northpoint Dr Suite 102 Houston TX 77090

WHITTIER, EDWARD JAMES, ins. co. exec.; b. Superior, Wis., Aug. 12, 1928; s. Edward Joseph and Anna Marie (Haglund) W.; B.S., U. Wis., 1952; m. Marilyn Diane Growell, June 27, 1959; children—Michael James, Mary Diane. With Pacific Mut. and subs., 1954—, pres. PM Mgmt. Services Co., Santa Ana, Calif., 1980—. C.L.U. Fellow Life Office Mgmt. Assn. Republican. Home: 1301 Sea Crest Dr Corona Del Mar CA 92625 Office: 400 N Tustin Ave PO Box 11873 Santa Ana CA 92711

WHITTINGHAM, CHARLES ARTHUR, publisher; b. Chgo., Feb. 11, 1930; s. Charles Arthur and Virginia (Hartke) W.; B.S. in English Lit. cum laude, Loyola U., Chgo., 1951; m. Jean Bragger Whittingham, June 4, 1955; children—Mary Elizabeth, Charles Arthur III, Philip Alexander, Leigh Ann. With McCall Corp., Chgo., 1956-59, Time, Inc., Chgo., 1959-62; pub.'s rep. Fortune mag., Time, Inc., N.Y.C., 1962-65, mgr. San Francisco Office, 1965-69; asst. to pub. Fortune, N.Y.C., 1969-70, asst. pub., 1970-78, pub. Life mag., 1978—. Served to lt. (j.g.) USNR, 1951-55. Named to Athletic Hall of Fame, Loyola U., 1960. Clubs: Univ. (N.Y.C. and San Francisco); Mt. Kisco (N.Y.) Country. Home: 11 Woodmill Rd Chappaqua NY 10514 Office: Fortune Mag Time and Life Bldg Rockefeller Center New York City NY 10020

WHITTINGTON, FLOYD LEON, ret. oil co. exec., ret. fgn. service officer, economist, bus. cons.; b. Fairfield, Iowa, May 27, 1909; s. Thomas Clyde and Ora E. (Trail) W.; A.B., Parsons Coll., 1931; M.A., U. Iowa, 1936; student U. Minn., 1940, Northwestern U., 1941-42; m. Winifred Carol McDonald, July 31, 1933; children—Susan Carol (Mrs. West), Thomas Lee. Econs., speech instr. Fairfield High Sch., 1931-36, Superior (Wis.) High Sch., 1936-40; supr. tchr. tng. Superior State Tchrs. Coll., 1936-40; econs., fin. instr. Carroll Coll., Waukesha, Wis., 1940-42; price exec. OPA, Wis. and Iowa, 1942-46; indsl. relations mgr. Armstrong Tire & Rubber Co., Des Moines, 1946-48; dir. price and distbn. div. SCAP, Tokyo, Japan, 1948-51; Far East economist ODM, Washington. 1951-52; asst. adviser to sec. on Japanese fin. and econ. problems Dept. State, Washington, 1952-53; chief Far Eastern sect. Internat. Finance div., bd. govs. Fed. Res. System, Washington, 1953-56; officer charge econ. affairs Office Southeast Asian Affairs, Dept. State, 1956-57, dep. dir. Office Southeast Asian Affairs, 1957-58; became counselor of embassy, Am. embassy, Bangkok, Thailand, 1958; counselor, polit. officer Am. embassy, Djakarta, Indonesia, 1962-65; counselor of embassy for econ. affairs, Seoul, Korea, 1965-66; v.p. Pacific Gulf Oil, Ltd., Seoul, from 1966; exec. v.p. Southeast Asia Gulf Co., Bangkok, Thailand, Gulf Oil Co. Siam, Ltd., Bangkok, 1967-72; v.p. Gulf Oil Co.-South Asia, Singapore, 1970-72; now Asian bus. cons.; pres. Olympus Internat., Inc., Olympus U.S., Inc. Trustee, World Affairs Council, Seattle. Recipient meritorious civilian service citation Dept. Army, 1950. Mem. Am. Econ. Assn., Am. Acad. Polit. Sci., Pi Kappa Delta, Theta Alpha Phi, Presbyterian. Clubs: Royal Bangkok (Thailand) Sports; Rainier (Seattle); Everett Yacht; Masons, Shriners. Address: 900 W Rocky Point Dr Camano Island WA 98292

WHITTLE, MELVIN IRVIN, exec. recruiter; b. N.Y.C., Jan. 16, 1936; s. Melvin Joseph and Mildred Alice (Raines) W.; B.S.E.E., Sussex Coll., Eng., 1968; m. Betty Lou Caison, Jan. 27, 1956; children—Deborah, Richard, Linda. Gen. mgr., v.p. Tower Fin. Co., 1964-68; sales exec. Pitney Bowes, Inc., Columbia, S.C., 1965-75; exec. v.p., dir. Mgmt. Recruiters of Columbia, Inc., 1975-77; pres., chmn. bd. Mgmt. Dirs., Inc., Charleston, S.C., 1977—. Chmn. St. Andrews Baptist Sch. Bd.; former chmn. bd. deacons St. Andrews 1st Bapt. Ch. Served with U.S. Army, 1955-57. Mem. Jay Strack Assn. (vice chmn. bd.). Home: 28 Shadowmoss Pkwy Charleston SC 29407 Office: Fairfield Office Park Suite 21 Charleston SC 29407

WHITWORTH, W. ROYCE, chem. co. exec.; b. Delta County, Colo., Jan. 28, 1920; s. Winston Lafayette and Ethel Irene (Watts) W.; A.B., U. Denver, 1948; student Va. Poly. Inst., 1943; m. Eileen Patience Christian, July 19, 1944; children—Sandra, Linnea. Operations supr. Union Carbide Corp., Oak Ridge, 1946-47, cost estimator, supr. estimating, Paducah, Ky., 1951-62; cost estimator Rocky Flats plant AEC, Golden, Colo., 1962—, mgr. estimating, 1970-78; sand chemist Am. Brake Shoe Co., Denver, 1948-51. Bd. dirs. Westdale Townhomes Assn., Arvada, Colo., 1976—, v.p., 1976—. Served with AUS, 1942-45. Certified cost engr.; certified profl. estimator. Mem. Am. Assn. Cost Engrs., Am. Soc. Profl. Estimators, Nat. Estimating Soc., Nat. Mgmt. Assn., Order Engrs. Democrat. Methodist. Clubs: Aviation, Mason (Shriner), Order Eastern Star. Home: 7957 Chase Circle 189 Arvada CO 80003 Office: PO Box 464 Golden CO 80401

WHOLEBEN, BRENT EDWARD, educator; b. Olean, N.Y., July 7, 1946; s. Bernard Edward and Mildred Florence (Camp) W.; B.S. in Mathematics, St. Bonaventure U., 1968; M.Ed. in Psychology, U. Hawaii, 1972, M.Ed. in Adminstrn., 1974; Ph.D. in Ednl. Adminstrn. U. Wis., 1979; m. Judith Ann Braun, June 22, 1968; 1 dau., Melissa Anne. Tchr. mathematics, coordinator student activities, dir. guidance services Hawaii Dept. Edn., 1970-75; family psychotherapist, vocat. guidance specialist interim dept. supr. Family Tng. Center, Glasgow, Mont., 1975-77; project asst., research cons. U. Wis., Madison, 1977-79, teaching asst. computer applications in edn., 1978-79; systems evaluation cons. to sch. dists., 1978-79; asst. prof. ednl. adminstrn., asso. dir. Research Bur., U. Wash., 1979—. Served with arty. U.S. Army, 1968-70; Vietnam. Mem. Am. Ednl. Research Assn., Wash. Ednl. Research Assn., Wash. Assn. Supervision and Curriculum Devel., Phi Delta Kappa. Democrat. Roman Catholic. Club: K.C. Author articles in field; manuscript and publs. reviewer N.W. Regional Ednl. Labs., Assn. Ednl. Data Systems. Home: 14110 81st Pl NE Bothell WA 98011 Office: U Wash 144A Lewis Annex DV-10 Seattle WA 98195

WHYTE, THOMAS JOSEPH, lawyer; b. Wheeling, W.Va., Dec. 31, 1932; s. Frank James and Katherine (Hack) W.; B.A., Ohio State U., 1954; LL.B., W.Va. U., 1960; m. Margaret Ann Brown, Aug. 31, 1954; children—Christopher, Lynn Ann, Kevin, Kathleen, Elizabeth. Admitted to W.Va. bar, 1960; law clk. U.S. Dist. Ct., Fairmont, W.Va., 1960; partner firm Furbee, Hardesty, Critchfield & Whyte, Fairmont, 1960-67; of counsel Furbee, Amos, Webb & Critchfield, 1967-77; exec. v.p. Consol. Coal Co., Pitts., 1967-77; partner firm Rose, Schmidt, Dixon, Hasley, Whyte & Hardesty, Pitts., 1977—. Chmn. bd. dirs. Wheeling Coll., 1974-79; chmn. vis. com. W.Va. U. Law Sch. Served to lt. comdr. USNR, 1954-57. Mem. W.Va. Coal Assn. (past dir., past chmn. bd.), Soc. Mining Engrs., Am., Pa., W.Va., D.C., Allegheny County bar assns., Am. Judicature Soc., W.Va. U. Coll. Law Alumni Assn. (pres.), Order of Coif, Phi Delta Phi. Editor-in-chief W.Va. Law Rev., 1960. Clubs: Duquesne, St. Clair Country (Pitts.); Williams Country (Weirton, W.Va). Home: 136 Warwick Dr Pittsburgh PA 15241 Office: 9th Floor Oliver Bldg Pittsburgh PA 15222

WICHERSKI, JOSEPH LOUIS, sales, mktg. and corporate communications exec.; b. New Bedford, Mass., Aug. 7, 1936; s. Stanley Matthew and Helen Catherine (Turbak) W.; B.S. summa cum laude, Boston U., 1963; M.S. with honors, Columbia, 1964; M.B.A. with highest honors, N.Y. U., 1969. Pub. relations officer, asst. dir. advt. and promotion Chase Manhattan Bank, N.Y.C., 1964-70; mgr. corporate communications Northrop Corp., Century City, Calif., 1971; mgr. corporate info. Litton Industries, Beverly Hills, Calif., 1972-80; co-founder, v.p. Himolene Sales Corp., 1980—. Recipient Clapp and Poliak Bus. Writing award Columbia, 1964. Home: 13900 Tahita Way Marina Del Rey CA 90291

WICK, KEITH RAY, fin. and estate planning cons.; b. Darke County, Ohio, Apr. 19, 1939; s. George Lester and Glenna (Miller) W.; student pub. schs., Pitsburg, Ohio; m. Joyce Irene Hulett, July 18, 1959; children—Lynda, Douglass, Brent Alan. Sanitary insp., Montgomery County (Ohio) Health Dept., 1966-67; environmentalist Springfield (Ohio) Health Dept., 1967-71; ter. mgr. Ralston Purina Co., Darke and Miami Counties, Ohio, 1971-73, dist. mgr., W.Va., 1973-75, western Pa., Mercer, 1975-78, mem. Chow div. gen. sales adv. bd., 1975-76; with Ohio Nat. Life Ins. Co., Dayton, 1978—; gen. agt. Bob Vann and Assos., Dayton, 1978—; resource person at agr. and vocat. tech. schs. Recipient profl. awards. Mem. Nat., Ohio, Dayton assns. life underwriters. Republican. Baptist. Home: 3959 Shields Rd Arcanum OH 45304 Office: 3131 S Dixie Dayton OH 45439

WICKS, LORNE FREDERICK, coll. adminstr.; b. Wolsey, Sask., Can., Dec. 5, 1918; s. Frederick and Martha (Suggitt) W.; diploma indsl. mgmt. LaSalle Extension U., 1955; m. Ella Margaret Urbach, Mar. 16, 1940; children—Donna Margaret, Wayne Frederick Donald Albert. Turret lathe operator Can. Gen. Electric Co., 1942-45; with Union Carbide Can. Ltd., 1953-55, plant mgr., 1955-79; v.p. bus. affairs Winnipeg Bible Coll. (now Ont. Bible Coll.), Otterburne, Man., 1979-80, asst. to pres. for adminstrn., 1980—. Mem. Conservative Party. Home: 12 Alanadale Ave Markham ON L3P 1S3 Canada Office: 201 Steeles Ave Willowdale ON M2M 4B3 Canada

WIEDEMANN, GLADYS H. GARDNER, investment co. exec.; b. Mpls.; d. Charles Henry and Delia Margaret (Blair) Gardner; student Minn. U., 1945-47, Wichita U., 1958-59; H.H.D. (hon.), Friends U., 1980; m. Karl T. Wiedemann, July 22, 1950 (dec. Jan. 1961). Sec., Pioneer Rim & Wheel Co., Mpls., 1925-35, Socony-Vacuum Oil Co., St. Paul, 1935-42, Rosemount War Plant, Minn., 1942-44, Tankar Gas, Inc., Mpls., 1944-50; v.p. Beaumont Petroleum Co., El Dorado, Kans., 1950-61, pres., 1961—; pres. K.T. Wiedemann Trust Co., El Dorado, 1961—, trustee, 1962—. Mem. research bd. Wesley Med. Center, Wichita, Kans., 1966—; mem. research bd., student nurse com. Wesley Hosp.; adv. bd. Wichita YWCA, 1968—; v.p. Wichita Symphony Inc., Music Theatre Wichita; pres. K.T. Wiedemann Found., Wichita; bd. dirs. Wichita area Girl Scouts U.S.A., Wichita State U. Endowment Assn., Crime Commn., Salvation Army, Booth Meml. Hosp.; trustee emeritus Friends U.; Mem. Wichita Art Assn. (chmn. bd.), Women's Aux. Wichita Logopedics (dir.), Wichita Petroleum Club, Wichita Hist. Mus. Assn., P.E.O., Mu Phi Epsilon. Presbyn. Clubs: Soroptimist, 20th Century, Saturday Music, Organ Aires, Wichita, Petroleum, Wichita Country (Wichita); Mpls. Athletic. Home: 8615 Shannon Way Wichita KS 67206 also 4200 Estero Blvd Fort Myers Beach FL 33931 Office: PO Box 1296 El Dorado KS 67042

WIEGAND, KENNETH ALLAN, bus. systems cons.; b. Sheboygan, Wis., Aug. 24, 1947; s. Arno A. and Marion D. (Janisse) W.; B.S. in E.E., U. Wis., 1970; M.B.A., Xavier U., 1975; m. Sandra, Nov. 7, 1970. Devel. engr. Western Electric Co., Columbus, Ohio, 1970-73; tech. analyst N. Electric, Galion, Ohio, 1973-75; project leader N.Am. Van Lines, Ft. Wayne, Ind., 1975-76, mgr. fin. systems, 1976-80; bus. systems cons. Hammermill Paper Co., Erie, Pa., 1980—. Mem. Assn. for Systems Mgmt., IEEE. Home: 5606 Swanville Rd Erie PA 16506 Office: PO Box 1440 Erie PA 16533

WIEGNER, EDWARD ALEX, utility exec.; b. Waukesha, Wis., Dec. 13, 1939; s. Roy Edward and Margaret Mary (Kuehnlein) W.; B.B.A., U. Wis., 1961, M.S., 1965, Ph.D., 1968; m. Cathryn Mullens, Oct. 16, 1970; children—Carlin Edward, Ryan Mathew. Pres.'s staff U. Wis., Madison, 1963-64, vis. asso. prof. Grad. Sch. Bus., 1971-73; adminstrv. and faculty Marquette U., Milw., 1964-71; sec. Wis. Dept. Revenue, Madison, 1971-73; sr. v.p. consumer, pub. and fin. affairs Wis. Power & Light, Madison, 1974—. Mem. Edison Electric Inst., Electric Power Research Inst., Am. Gas Assn., Utility Modeling Forum. Home: 1415 W Skyline Dr Madison WI 53705 Office: 222 W Washington Ave PO Box 192 Madison WI 53701

WIESE, NORMAN EUGENE, controller; b. Council Bluffs, Iowa, July 25, 1930; s. Clarence T. and Frances C. (Bachman) W.; student Los Angeles Harbor Coll., 1960-63; m. Phyllis A. Whitbeck, June 5, 1955; children—David, Karen, Larry. Asst. controller Lion Clothing Co., San Diego, 1969-75; controller Southland Envelope Co., El Cajon, Calif., 1975-77; v.p., controller, dir. Heliotrope Gen., Inc., Spring Valley, Calif., 1977—. Served with AUS, 1951-53; Korea. Home: 728 Safford Ave Spring Valley CA 92077 Office: 3733 Kenora Dr Spring Valley CA 92077

WIESE, WALTER RODNEY, retail co. exec.; b. Glendale, Calif., Feb. 28, 1937; s. Walter H. and Dorothy Jean W.; B.S. in Fin., Calif. State U., 1969; m. Margaret Ann Munford, June 23, 1962; children—Clark M., Brett N. With Bon Marche Co., Seattle, 1969—, dir. loss prevention, 1975—. Organizer, pres. Consumer Awareness Council, Seattle, 1970, chairperson, 1970-78; advisor Wash. Crime Watch Anti-Shoplifting Program, 1977-78. Recipient Seattle Downtown Devel. Assn. New Look award, 1973. Mem. Inst. Internal Auditors. Club: Sno-King Hockey Assn. (treas. 1977-78, pres. 1978-79). Office: Bon Marche 3d and Pine Sts Seattle WA 98111

WIESNER, ARTHUR RICHARD, retail distbg. exec.; b. Teaneck, N.J., Apr. 18, 1932; s. Adolph Julius and Margaret Florence (Hoffman) W.; grad. high sch., Park Ridge, N.J.; m. Mary Lou Etcheberry, Sept. 12, 1953; children—Michele Ann, Craig Andrew. Vice pres. Fenwick Machinery, Wharton, N.J., 1960-73; mgr. Western region Liebherr Am., Newport News, Va., 1973-75; ter. mgr. Interstate Tractor, Portland, Oreg., 1975-77; gen. mgr. Case Power & Equipment, Sacramento, also J.I. Case, Racine, Wis., 1977—. Mem. Nat. Utility Contractors Assn., Underground Contractors Assn. Republican. Roman Catholic. Home: 5098 Keane Dr Carmichael CA 95608 Office: 7849 Stockton Blvd Sacramento CA 95823

WIESNER, ERHARD, mgmt. cons.; b. Giersdorf, Ger., Sept. 22, 1943; came to U.S., 1969; s. Herbert A. and Margarete C. (Hartelt) W.; B.S., Tech. U. Hannover (W. Ger.), 1964; Diplom Kaufmann, Georgia Augusta U., Goettingen, W. Ger., 1969; M.B.A., Columbia U., 1970; m. Marian Jean Koopman, May 6, 1978. Asst. prof. mktg. Georgia Augusta U., 1969; sr. cons. Quickborner Team, internat. mgmt. and planning cons., Hamburg, 1970-72, v.p., Millburn, N.J., 1972-78, partner, Hamburg, 1972—; pres., treas. Plan-Consult, Inc., Evergreen, Colo., 1978—; leader seminars, lectr. in field. German Acad. Exchange Program fellow, 1969, 70. Mem. Am. Mgmt. Assn., Adminstrv. Mgmt. Soc. Contbr. articles to profl. jours., chpt. to textbook. Address: 2641 Pinehurst Dr Evergreen-Hiwan CO 80439

WIGGINS, BENJAMIN STINSON, Realtor; b. Columbia, S.C., May 20, 1932; s. Stinson Oliver and Sophia Harriett (Alford) W.; B.S., Clemson U., 1956; m. Barbara Jean Conder, Mar. 17, 1956; children—Michael Benjamin, Lauri Denise. Owner, operator Wiggins Equipment Co., Columbia, 1959-62; owner, pres. Imperial Realty Co., Inc., Columbia, 1962—; dir. Townhouse Constrn., Inc.; lectr. in field; pres. Columbia Bd. Realtors, 1980. Bd. dirs. Cancer Soc., 1970-71, S.C. Edn. Found.; mem. adv. com. real estate Midlands Tech. Coll. pres. Columbia Multiple Listing Service, 1974. Served with USAF, 1956-59. Named Realtor of Year, Columbia, 1977. Mem. S.C. Assn. Realtors (dir. 1976—), Nat. Assn. Realtors, Columbia Homebuilders Assn., Nat. Assn. Homebuilders, Realtors Nat. Mktg. Inst. Methodist. Clubs: Sertoma (pres.; award of merit 1970; (life), S.C. Master. Author: Real Estate Training Manual, 1979. Developer comprehensive tng. program in real estate. Home: 2046 Shady Ln Columbia SC 29206 Office: Imperial Realty Co Inc 3508 Devine St Columbia SC 29205

WIGGINS, GWENDOLYN ANN, accountant; b. Bklyn., May 25, 1950; d. Francis and Ann Lee (Jackson) W.; B.A., City U. N.Y., 1972; M.B.A., L.I. U., 1976. Analyst, Equitable Life Assurance Soc., N.Y.C., 1973-76; auditor Mitchell & Titus, N.Y.C., 1976-77; chief accountant Nat. Commn. on Observance of Internat. Women's Year, N.Y. State Meeting, 1977-78; controller Port Royal Communications Network, Inc., N.Y.C., 1978-79; internal auditor Port Authority N.Y. and N.J., 1979—; resident lectr. Malcolm King Coll., 1976-77; lectr. Medgar Evers Coll., 1978—. Chmn. bd. dirs. young peoples dept. Ch. Ushers Assn. N.Y. State, Inc., 1968-76; v.p. Nat. United Ch. Ushers Assn. Am., Inc., 1970-72; pres. young peoples dept. Ch. Ushers Assn. of Bklyn. and L.I., 1970-75, supr., 1977—, co-chmn. bd. dirs. assn.; mem. Coalition of 100 Black Women, Inc.; adv. bd. acctg. dept. Borough of Manhattan Community Coll. Thomas A. Ellis Oratorial scholar, 1968, PTA scholar, 1968. Mem. Nat. Assn. Accountants, Nat. Assn. Black Accountants, Inc. (nat. dir., pres. N.Y. chpt. 1978—), Nat. Black M.B.A.'s Assn., Council of Concerned Black Execs., Inc. (treas. 1978—), N.Y. Assn. C.P.A. Candidates. Democrat. Baptist. Home: 325 Clinton Ave Brooklyn NY 11205

WIGGINS, WALTON WRAY, publisher; b. Roswell, N.Mex., May 13, 1924; s. Miles Burgess and Mona Cecil (Brown) W.; grad. Motion Picture Cameraman Sch., Astoria, N.Y., 1945; m. Roynel Fitzgerald, Apr. 30, 1963; children—Walton Wray, Kimberly Douglas, Lisa Renée. Free-lance photo-journalist for nat. mags., 1948-60; dir. public relations Ruidoso Racing Assn., Ruidoso Downs, N.Mex., 1960-69, v.p., 1967-68; founder, pub. Speedhorse Publs., Roswell, N.Mex. and Norman, Okla., 1969-78; owner/operator Wiggins Galleries Fine Art, 1978—; pres. Quarter Racing World, 1970-78, Am. Horse Publs., Washington, 1978; del. leader People to People, Internat. Served with U.S. Army, 1943-46. Recipient Detroit Art Dirs. award, 1955, Greatest Contbr. award Quarter Racing Owners Am., 1974. Mem. Overseas Press Club, Am. Soc. Mag. Photographers, Am. Horse Publs. Republican. Author: The Great American Speedhorse, 1978; Cockleburs and Cowchips, 1975; Alfred Morang-A Neglected Master, 1979; Ernest Berke - Paintings and Sculptures of Old West, 1980. Home: PO Box 1597 Roswell NM 88201 Office: 209 W First St Roswell NM 88201

WIGGLESWORTH, DAVID CUNNINGHAM, bus. and mgmt. cons.; b. Passaic, N.J., Sept. 23, 1927; s. Walter Frederick and Janet (Cunningham) W.; B.A., Occidental Coll., 1950, M.A., 1953; postgrad. U. de las Ams., 1954-56; Ph.D., U. East Fla., 1957; L.H.D. (hon.), Arubaanse Handels Academie, 1969; m. Rita Dominguez, Mar. 15, 1956 (dec.); children—Mitchell Murray, Marc David, Miles Frederick, Janet Rose. Dir., Spoken English Inst., Mexico City, also lectr. Mexico City Coll., 1954-56; headmaster Harding Acad., Glendale, Calif., also lectr. Citrus Jr. Coll., 1956-58; dir. Burma-Am. Inst., Rangoon, 1958-60; project dir. Washington Ednl. Research Assos., Washington, Conakry, Guinea, Benghazi, Libya, Carbondale, Ill., 1960-64; mng. editor linguistics div. T. Y. Crowell Pub. Co., N.Y.C., 1964-66; dir. linguistic studies Behavioral Research Labs., Palo Alto, Calif., 1966-67; pres. D.C.W. Research Assos., Los Altos, Calif., 1967—; mem. faculty external degree program St. Mary's Coll., Moraga, Calif., 1979—. Trustee, City U. Los Angeles; mem. adv. bd. Martin Luther King Reading Acad., Los Angeles; ordained minister Universal Life Ch., 1969. Served with U.S. Army, 1945-46, 52-54. Mem. Am. Mgmt. Assn., Orgn. Devel. Network, Am. Soc. Tng. and Devel., Soc. Internat. Edn. Tng. and Research, 1st World Congress Internat. Orgn. Devel., Orgn. Devel. Forum, Peninsula Orgn. Devel. Support, Mideast Am. Bus. Conf., World Future Soc. Clubs: Peninsula Exec. (Los Altos); SEDUMEX (Mexico City); Benghazi Sailing; Orient (Rangoon). Author: PI/LT-Programmed Instruction/Language Teaching, 1967; Career Education, 1976; contbr. articles to profl. publs. Home: 1438 Firebird Way Sunnyvale CA 94087 Office: PO Box 1062 Los Altos CA 94022

WIGMORE, DAVID, JR., pharm. co. exec.; b. Rotterdam, Netherlands, Mar. 18, 1937; s. David and Lena Cornelia (Van Den Bosch) W.; came to U.S., 1946, naturalized, 1949; B.S. (Gold scholarship medal), Seton Hall U., 1965; m. Marie E. Ippolito, Dec. 3, 1967; 1 son, David. Accountant, Gen. Foods Corp., Hoboken, N.J., 1956-62, auditor, 1962-69; cost engring. mgr. E.R. Squibb & Sons, Inc., New Brunswick, N.J., 1969-77, dir. cost ops. worldwide engring. and constrn., Princeton, N.J., 1978—, dir. and v.p. Mfg. Enterprises div. E.R. Squibb & Sons, Inc., 1978—. Mem. rent leveling bd. Twp. Highland Pk. (N.J.), 1977—. Certified cost engr. Mem. N.J. Soc. Profl. Engrs., Am. Assn. Cost Engrs., Nat. Assn. Accountants, Am. Mgmt. Assn., Am. Arbitration Assn., Jr. C. of C., Order of DeMolay. Republican. Club: Masons. Home: 18 Johnson St Highland Park NJ 08904

WIGNALL, ERNEST CARL, banker; b. Norwich, Conn., Jan. 22, 1927; s. Thomas John and Anna Margaret (Meyer) W.; grad. Wentworth Inst., Boston, 1950; postgrad. Grad. Sch. Savs. Banking, Brown U., 1960-62, Dartmouth and Amherst colls., 1966-67; m. Laura B. Saeger, June 24, 1959. Asst. sec. Norwich Savs. Soc., 1952-63; asst. v.p. Binghamton (N.Y.) Savs. Bank, 1963-71; v.p. Mechanics Savs. Bank, Hartford, Conn., 71-75, sr. v.p., 1975—; dir. Capitol Towers, Inc. Chmn., Binghamton City Planning Commn., 1966-71; dir., chmn. budget and fin. N.Y. Penn Health Planning Council, Inc., 1969-70; housing cons. Broome County Community Resources Found., Inc., 1970-71; adviser Broome County Housing Devel. Corp., 1970-71; housing adviser Found. of State U. N.Y. at Binghamton, 1970. Corporator, Inst. of Living, Hartford, 1972—, Hartford Hosp., 1972—; active United Way Greater Hartford, YMCA of Met. Hartford; trustee, mem. exec. com. Boys' Clubs of Hartford, 1973—; mem. adv. bd. and exec. com. Salvation Army, Hartford, 1973—. Served with USNR, 1945-46. Mem. Greater Hartford, Manchester bds. realtors, Nat. Assn. Mut. Savs. Banks, Savs. Banks Assn. Conn., Mortgage Bankers Assn. Am., Savs. Bank Housing Corp. Conn. (dir.), Hartford County Home Builders Assn. (dir.), Greater Hartford C. of C. Republican. Lutheran. Clubs: Masons; Univ. (Hartford). Home: 1 Gold St Hartford CT 06103 Office: 80 Pearl St Hartford CT 06103

WIJESINHA, SHIRLEY PATRICK, assn. exec.; b. Mt. Lavinia, Sri Lanka, June 18, 1940; s. Srikantha and Pearl Beatrice (Jayawardana) W.; came to U.S., 1975; ed. St. Thomas' Coll., Mt. Lavinia, 1960; m. Naomi Therese Marina Delilkhan, Feb. 1, 1969; children—Dinusha, Shyanika, Eshanthika. Chief accountant Ceylon Nutritional Foods, Ltd., Colombo, Sri Lanka, 1962-75; exec. dir. fin. and adminstrn. Jaycees Internat., Inc., Coral Gables, Fla., 1975—. Nat. pres. Sri Lanka Jaycees, 1973; v.p. Jaycees Internat., 1975. Fellow Brit. Inst. Mgmt.; mem. Inst. Cost and Mgmt. Accountants of London (affiliate),

Am. Mgmt. Assn., Sri Lanka Astron. Assn. Home: 6301 SW 39th St Miami FL 33155 Office: 400 University Dr Coral Gables FL 33134

WILAND, HARRY ALAN, film producer, dir.; b. N.Y.C., July 30, 1944; s. Nathan E. and Lillian (Packer) W.; B.A. in Chemistry, Bklyn. Coll., 1964; postgrad. in biology U. Mass., 1965; M.F.A. in Film, Columbia U., 1968; m. Ellen Starr, Apr. 10, 1970 (separated 1979); 1 dau., Julia Rebeeca. Film producer, dir. Amram Nowak Assos., N.Y.C., 1970-74; film producer, dir., sec./treas. Varied Directions, Rockport, Maine, 1974-78; pres. Amesbury Hill Prodns., Rockport, 1978—; instr. film Hofstra U., 1974-75; Served with USAR, 1966-71. Mem. TV Acad. Producer films: Johnny Cash, 1971, Nashville Sound, 1971; producer TV spl. Earl Scruggs, 1972, Sing Sing Thanksgiving, 1976, Couples, 1980. Home: Camden ME 04856 also New York NY

WILAYTO, HENRY JOHN, mfg. co. transp. exec.; b. Nashua, N.H., Jan. 4, 1917; s. Alexander Matheuw and Genevieve (Michnevitch) W.; B.A. magna cum laude, Boston U., 1952; postgrad. Babson Coll., 1978—; m. Helen Mary Butchard, June 17, 1946; children—Anne-Marie Christine Wilayto Bishop, Philip Henry, Allan John, Kathryn Helen Wilayto MacDonald, Margaret Elizabeth. Field rep., asst. disaster dir. ARC, Boston, 1952; flight test facility bus. mgr. Mass. Inst. Tech., Concord, 1952-55; asst. to controller, purchasing agt. Allied Research Assos., Boston, 1955-57; purchasing agt. Lab. for Electronics, Boston, 1957-63; mgr. freight consolidation and analysis Honeywell Info. Systems, Billerica, Mass., 1963—; conducted purchasing, transp. and packaging panels and seminars. Served with U.S. Army, 1940-48. Mem. New Eng. Purchasing Agts. Assn. (dir. 1960-65), Am. Defenders of Bataan and Corregidor (life; vice nat. comdr. 1964-67), Soc. Packaging and Handling Engrs. (Merit and Service awards for conducting seminars 1972—), Nat. Com. for Internat. Documentation, VFW, DAV (life), Delta Nu Alpha (regional v.p. 1979—). Democrat. Roman Catholic. Contbr. articles to profl. jours. Office: Honeywell 250 Merrimack St (MS-461) Lawrence MA 01843

WILBANKS, RICHARD PAUL, real estate appraiser; b. Coalinga, Calif., Feb. 19, 1921; s. Joseph Olney and Marie Antionette (Flynn) W.; student pub. schs., Placerville, Calif.; m. Leta Marjorie Ross, Feb. 20, 1942; 1 dau., Pamela Jeanne. Appraiser, dep. assessor El Dorado County (Calif.), 1953-61; appraiser, loan officer, corp. officer, trust officer Financial Fedn., Inc., Marysville, Calif., 1962-76; pvt. practice as real estate appraiser and cons., Marysville, 1976—. Pres., Cathedral Oaks Mut. Water Co., 1974-75; chmn. Cathedral Oaks Subdiv. Archtl. Control Com., 1974—. Served with AC, U.S. Army, 1940-45, USAF, 1950-51. Mem. Nat. Assn. Rev. Appraisers, Am. Assn. Cert. Appraisers. Republican. Episcopalian. Editor, El Dorado County Sportsmans paper, 1955-56; outdoor sports editor Placerville Times, 1955-56, columnist, 1955-56. Home and Office: 4626 Pat Ln Marysville CA 95901

WILBER, ROBERT EDWIN, oil and gas co. exec.; b. Boston, Dec. 15, 1932; s. Charles Edwin and Mary Charles (Gay) W.; B.S. in Bus. Adminstrn., Bowling Green State U., 1954; m. Bonnie Marilyn Jones, Aug. 5, 1954; children—Debra, Kathleen, Robert Edwin, Thomas, Jeffrey, Mark, Matthew. Asst. treas. Glens Falls Ins. Co. (N.Y.), 1963-66; controller Penobscot Co., Boston, 1966-67; v.p. fin. and adminstrn. S.S. Pierce Co., Boston, 1967-73, Samson Ocean Systems, Inc., Boston, 1973-79; v.p., chief acctg. and controls officer ENSERCH Corp., Dallas, 1979—; dir. Greater Boston Credit Bur., 1967-70. Bd. dirs. Washingtonian Center for Addictions, 1969-79. C.P.A., Mass. Mem. Am. Inst. C.P.A.'s, Mass. Assn. C.P.A.'s, Fin. Execs. Inst., Am. Petroleum Inst. Republican. Club: Chaparral. Office: 301 S Harwood St Dallas TX 75201

WILBURN, VICTOR HUGO, architect, developer; b. Omaha, Jan. 23, 1931; student U. Chgo., 1950; M. Arch., Harvard, 1959; postgrad. U. Pa., 1960. Owner, architect, developer Victor H. Wilburn & Asso., Washington and Phila., 1962—; pres. Urban Devel. Group, Inc., 1962—; asst. prof. architecture Howard U., Washington, 1973-74, U. Va., 1972-73, Drexel Inst., 1971-72. Mem. Am. Inst. Planners, AIA. Home: PO Box 4379 Washington DC 20012 Office: 4301 Connecticut Ave NW Washington DC 20008 also 1920 Chestnut St Philadelphia PA 19103

WILCOX, CONNY ALBURTA, accountant; b. Toronto, Ont., Can., July 24, 1944; d. Arthur and Alice Alberta (Trumbull) Boxall; student pub. schs., Haliburton, Ont.; m. Benjamin Albert Wilcox, Aug. 18, 1973; 1 dau., Laura Ann. Asst. to trustee Dunwoodco Ltd., Toronto, 1969-72; officer, dir. Hammond Organ Studios & OSSCO Ltd., Toronto, 1972-75; regional controller Atlantic region Thorne Riddell, Halifax, N.S., 1975-77, regional dir. fin. and adminstrn., 1977—. Founder, pres. New Horizons for Children, 1979-80; mem. job expln. for students program com. Halifax Bd. Trade, 1979, mem. civic affairs com., 1979-80. Mem. Am. Mgmt. Assn. Home: 36 Raymoor Dr Dartmouth NS B2X 1G7 Canada Office: Thorne Riddell 1690 Hollis St Halifax NS B3J 3J9 Canada

WILCOX, EDWARD DONALD, JR., packaging machinery mfr.; b. Mpls., July 5, 1926; s. Edward Donald and Elsa (Hultgren) W.; B.M.E., Worcester Poly. Inst., 1949; student Northeastern U., 1950-51; m. Arlene Silva, May 26, 1956; 1 dau., Allison Hadley. Mgr. mech. engring. Lever Bros. Co., 1952-56; mgr. corp. packaging engring. Union Camp Corp., Wayne, N.J., 1965-69, div. gen. mgr., 1969-80; v.p., dir. Inglett & Co., Augusta, Ga., 1970-80; v.p., gen. mgr. packaging div. Howe Richardson Scale Co., Clifton, N.J., 1980—. Served with USNR, 1944-46. Mem. ASME, Packaging Inst., Packaging Machinery Mfrs. Inst. (pres., dir.). Club: Univ. (N.Y.C.). Home: 35 Sutton Pl New York NY 10022 Office: Clifton NJ

WILCOX, GEORGE LATIMER, elec. mfg. exec.; b. N.Y.C., Jan. 20, 1915; s. Thomas and Louise (Latimer) W.; B.E.E., Poly. Inst. Bklyn., 1939; m. Edith Leah Smallshaw, Sept. 2, 1939; children—Leslie, Holly, George. Elec. engr. Consol. Edison Co., 1930-42; design engr. Westinghouse Electric & Mfg. Co., 1942-43; gen. mgr. Windsor Mfg. & Repair Cor., 1946-50, Westinghouse Internat. Devel. Co., 1950-51; asst. mgr. central sta. dept. Westinghouse Elec. Internat. Co., 1943-46, successively mgr. projects div., gen. sales mgr., v.p. sales, 1951-53, v.p. ops., dir., 1953-56; pres. Westinghouse Can. Ltd., 1956-61; v.p., asst. to pres. Westinghouse Electric Corp., 1961, v.p., dep. exec. v.p., 1962, exec. v.p., 1963-69, vice chmn. corp. affairs, 1969-75, dir.-officer, 1975-80; dir. Kaiser Steel Corp., Pitts. Nat. Corp., Pitts. Nat. Bank, Kaiser Resources, Ltd. Chmn., pres. Pa. Economy League. Trustee Com. for Econ. Devel. Clubs: Duquesne (Pitts.); Univ. (N.Y.C.); Rolling Rock, Laurel Valley (Ligonier, Pa.). Home: Weavers Mill Rd Rector PA 15677 Office: Westinghouse Bldg Gateway Center Pittsburgh PA 15222

WILCOX, KENNETH ROBERT, advt. agy. exec.; b. Hartford, Conn., Feb. 24, 1951; s. Whiting Jerome and Rosanne (Dufresne) W.; student Central Conn. State Coll., 1973. Lithographer, Heminway Printing Co., Waterbury, Conn., 1970-72; salesman Allied Printing Services, Inc., Manchester, Conn., 1972-74; account exec., advt. designer Concepts, Inc., Hartford, 1974-76; pres. Wilcox Group, Ltd., Wethersfield, Conn., 1976—; cons. in field. Advt. judge Distributive Edn. Club Am. Mem. Am. Mgmt. Assn., Am. Inst. Graphic Art, Conn. Art Dirs. Club, Advt. Club Greater Hartford. Office: Wilcox Group Ltd 915 Silas Deane Hwy Wethersfield CT 06109

WILCOX, THOMAS ROBERT, comml. banker; b. N.Y.C., Aug. 23, 1916; s. Thomas and Louise (Latimer) W.; student N.Y. U., 1934-38; B.A., Princeton U., 1940; m. Jane Collette, Mar. 28, 1943; children—Thomas R., Kirby C., Andrew McK. With First Nat. City Bank, 1934-71, beginning as page, successively asst. cashier, asst. v.p., v.p. charge domestic branches, 1954-57, exec. v.p., 1957-67, vice chmn., 1967-71; vice chmn., dir. Blyth Eastman Dillon & Co., Inc., 1971-73; pres. Crocker Nat. Bank, San Francisco, 1974, chmn., pres., chief exec. officer, 1974—; dir. Colgate-Palmolive Co., Hilton Hotels Corp.; trustee Mut. Life Ins. Co. N.Y. Trustee Marine Hist. Assn., Mystic, Conn. Mem. Conf. Bd. (sr.). Clubs: University, Links (N.Y.C.); Bohemian, Pacific Union, San Francisco Golf (San Francisco); Los Angeles Country, Calif. (Los Angeles). Office: One Montgomery St San Francisco CA 94104 also 611 W 6th St Los Angeles CA 90017

WILDE, CHARLES BROADWATER, investment banker; b. Oakland, Calif., July 22, 1940; s. Willard Henry and Elizabeth M. (Broadwater) W.; A.B., U. Calif. at Berkeley, 1962; m. Molly Burnett, June 23, 1962; children—Charles Broadwater, Stephen Burnett. Salesman Procter & Gamble, San Francisco, 1963-64, dist. head salesman, 1964-65, unit mgr., 1965-67; account exec. Dean Witter, Reynolds, Inc., Hayward, Calif., 1967-70, asst. v.p., divisional syndicate mgr., 1972-74, v.p., nat. dir. tax advantaged investments, 1974-79; v.p. Winthrop Fin. Co. Inc., San Francisco, 1979—; sr. v.p. Winthrop Securities Co. Inc., 1979—; dir. Allen & Dorward Advt.; cons. indsl. solar energy conversions Dept. Energy; co-founder, dir., exec. v.p. Interflight Corp., Long Beach, Calif., 1970-72. Vice pres. Tahoe Pines Assn., 1968-71. Finance chmn. No. Calif. com. for Brian Van Camp, candidate Calif. sec. state, 1974. Bd. dirs. Golden Bear Athletic Found., pres., 1980—; bd. dirs. No. Calif. chpt. Nat. Multiple Sclerosis Soc. Mem. Big C Soc. (dir. 1972-77, finance chmn. 1973-77), U. Calif. Young Alumni Assn. (dir. 1968-70). Clubs: Bohemian (San Francisco); Claremont Country (Oakland). Home: 67 Lynwood Pl Moraga CA 94556 Office: 595 Market St Suite 2950 San Francisco CA 94105

WILDE, WILLIAM JAMES, printing and engraving co. exec.; b. Milw., Sept. 13, 1927; s. Henry Herman and Anna Margaret (Lamp) W.; Ph.B., Marquette U., 1951; m. Jeanne G. Gearhard, June 14, 1952 (dec.); children—James, Anne, Joan, Charles, Denise, Daniel, Mary, Mark. Sales and prodn. Gillfoy Printing Co., Inc., Milw., 1951-64, pres., 1972—; v.p. Advertisers Litho Co., 1964-66; pres. Williston Wilde Graphics Inc., Milw., 1979—. Served with U.S. Army, 1945-46. Mem. Printing Industry Am. Home: 202 Division St Thiensville WI 53092 Office: 407 E Michigan St Milwaukee WI 53202

WILDEBUSH, JOSEPH FREDERICK, economist, former trade assn. exec.; b. Bklyn., July 18, 1910; s. Harry Frederick and Elizabeth (Stolzenberg) W.; A.B., Columbia, 1931, postgrad Law Sch., 1932; LL.B., Bklyn. Law Sch., 1934, J.D., 1967; m. Martha Janssens, July 18, 1935; children—Diane Elaine (Mrs. Solon Finkelstein), Joan Marilyn (Mrs. Bobby Sanford Berry); m. Edith Sorensen, May 30, 1964. Admitted to N.Y. State bar, 1934, Fed. bar, 1935; practice law, N.Y.C., 1934-41; labor relations dir. Botany Mills, Passaic, N.J., 1945-48; exec. v.p. Silk and Rayon Printers and Dyers Assn. Am., Inc., Paterson, N.J., 1948-70; exec. v.p. Textile Printers and Dyers Labor Relations Inst., Paterson, 1954-70; mem. panel labor arbitrators Fed. Mediation and Conciliation Service, N.Y. State Mediation Bd., N.J. State Mediation Bd., N.J. Pub. Employment Relations Commn., Am. Arbitration Assn.; co-adj. faculty Rutgers U., 1948—; lectr. Pres. Pascack Valley Hosp., Westwood, N.J., 1950-64, chmn. bd., 1964-67, chmn. emeritus, 1967—; pres. Group Health Ins. N.J., 1962-65, chmn. bd., 1965-80; dir. Group Health Ins. N.Y., 1950—. Served as maj. Engrs. Corps, AUS, 1941-43. Mem. N.Y. County Lawyers Assn., Am. Acad. Polit. and Social Sci., Indsl. Relations Research Assn., Ret. Officers Assn., Nat. Geog. Soc. Lutheran. Contbr. articles profl. jours. Home and office: 37 James Terr Pompton Lakes NJ 07442

WILDER, ALTUS E., III, bank holding co. exec.; b. Austin, Tex., Oct. 14, 1944; s. Altus E. and Lillian A. Wilder; B.B.A. in Acctg., N. Tex. State U.; m. Linda Dawn Fry, Dec. 11, 1970. Acctg. mgr., First Internat. Bankshares, Dallas, 1971-74; asst. controller Merc. Bancorp. Inc., St. Louis, 1974-77; pres. Republic Bancorp. Inc., Tulsa, 1977—; dir. corps. C.P.A., Tex., Okla. Mem. Okla. Soc. C.P.A.'s, Tex. Soc. C.P.A.'s, Am. Inst. C.P.A.'s. Methodist. Office: PO Box 1656 Tulsa OK 74101

WILDER, CHARLES MOULTON, door mfg. co. exec.; b. Stamford, Conn., Apr. 9, 1928; s. Frank Edwin and Julia (Gould) W.; B.Mech.Engring., Cornell U., 1951; m. Christine Clark, Mar. 24, 1951 (div.); children—David, Anne, John. Sr. exptl. engr. Gen. Motors Corp., Detroit, 1953-58; v.p. Clark Door Co., Cranford, N.J., 1958-62, pres., 1962—, dir., 1959—, v.p., dir. Mesker-Clark Inc., St. Louis, 1971—; pres. Clark Door of Can., Markham, Ont., 1974—; chmn. bd. Clark Door Ltd., Carlisle, Eng., 1974—; dir. Nippon-Clark Ltd., Japan. Bd. dirs. United Fund of Cranford, 1965-71. Served with arty. AUS, 1951-53. Decorated Bronze Star; registered profl. engr., N.J. Mem. Soc. Automotive Engrs., Internat. Inst. Refrigeration, ASHRAE, World Trade Assn. N.J. (dir. 1974-79), Cranford C. of C. (dir. 1970-71). Clubs: Rotary, Bay Head Yacht, Echo Lake Country. Patentee in field. Home: PO Box 733 Cranford NJ 07016 Office: Clark Door Co 69 Myrtle St Cranford NJ 07016

WILDER, DUANE EDWARD, cons., co. exec.; b. Warren, Pa., Feb. 5, 1929; s. Clinton Eugene and Fannie (Kornreich) W.; A.B., Princeton U., 1951; M.B.A., N.Y. U., 1954. Exec. v.p., dir. Nat. Forge Co., Irvine, Pa., 1957-61; chmn. fin. com. Nat. Forge Co., Irvine, 1961-64; partner Wilder Deem Assos., consultants, N.Y.C., 1969—; chmn., treas. WDP Inc., Wilmington, Del., 1973—, Swank Refractories Co., Pitts., 1973—, Hyde Park Foundry & Machinery Co. (Pa.), 1974—; chmn. Am. Tar Co., Seattle, 1976—. Bd. dirs., treas. Circle Repertory Co., Nat. Scholarship Service and Fund for Negro Students; bd. dirs. Waverly Consort, Ednl. Products and Info. Exchange, 1969-75; mem. Pa. Bd. Edn., 1962-68, Pa. Gov.'s Library Commn., 1960-62. Served with U.S. Army, 1954-56. Democrat. Presbyterian. Club: Rainier (Seattle). Home and office: 121 Washington Pl New York NY 10014

WILDER, MICHAEL STEPHEN, lawyer; b. New Haven, Sept. 8, 1941; s. Harry and Ann (Castroll) W.; B.A., Yale U., 1963; J.D., Harvard U., 1966; m. Marjorie Levitin, June 13, 1965; children—Kathryn, Amanda. Admitted to Conn. bar, 1966; atty. Hartford Fire Ins. Co. (Conn.), 1967-69, asst. gen. counsel, 1969-71, asso. gen. counsel, 1971-75, gen. counsel, sec., 1975—; gen. counsel mem. cos. Hartford Ins. Group. Steering com. Vol. Action Center Capitol Region, 1978-80; sec. Citizens' Com. Effective Govt., Inc., 1978—; vice chmn. Greater Hartford Arts Council Fund Drive, 1977—; com. reps. New Eng. Whalers Hockey Club, 1975-80; corporator Mt. Sinai Hosp., 1979—. Mem. Conn. Bar Assn. Club: Yale of Hartford (v.p.). Home: 11 Fernwood Rd West Hartford CT 06119 Office: Hartford Plaza Hartford CT 06115

WILDERMUTH, ROGER GREGORY, printing and pub. co. exec.; b. Sandwich, Ill., July 15, 1944; s. Richard Eli and Ruth Viola (Gregory) W.; B.S. in Accountancy, U. Ill., 1966; m. Anna S. Chin, May 12, 1974; 1 son, Eric. From staff acct. to audit mgr. Arthur Andersen & Co., Chgo., 1966-76; v.p. adminstrn., sec.-treas. Dreis & Krump Mfg. Co., Chgo., 1976-78; corp. controller Rand McNally & Co., Skokie, Ill., 1978-80, group v.p.-systems, 1980—. Served with USN, 1966-67. C.P.A., Ill. Mem. Am. Inst. C.P.A.'s, Ill. Soc. C.P.A.'s, Fin. Execs. Inst. Republican. Mormon. Clubs: Cedardell Golf; Oak Brook Bath and Tennis. Home: 498 Hampshire St Elmhurst IL 60126 Office: 8255 N Central Park Skokie IL 60076

WILDEY, JAMES ALLEN, mfg. co. exec.; b. Binghamton, N.Y., Feb. 13, 1943; s. Leon Earl Wildey and Constance Evelyn (Springer) Nelson; A.A.S., Rochester Inst. Tech., 1964, B.S., 1965; M.S. (fellow), Pa. State U., 1967; grad. IBM Systems Sci. Inst., 1979; m. Barbara Ann Marold, Sept. 10, 1966; children—J. Dane, Eric E. Buyer, systems rep. IBM, Boca Raton, Fla., 1967-69, corp. staff mem. systems planning group, Portchester, N.Y., 1969-72; owner, mgr. GUIDE Farms, Inc., Myerstown, Pa., 1972-77; sr. staff mem. EDP quality assurance GPU Service Corp., Reading, Pa., 1977-80; mgr. info. systems and cost acctg. Quaker Alloy Casting Co., Myerstown, 1980—; cons. on small systems applications-mfg., 1967—. Chmn. stewardship com. Myerstown Grace Brethren Ch., 1976—; bd. dirs. Youth for Christ Internat., 1977-79; sec. sch. bd., chmn. public relations com. Grace Christian Sch., 1978—. Recipient On the Move award Rochester Inst. Tech. Alumni Assn., 1979. Mem. Data Processing Mgmt. Assn. (asso.), Assn. Systems Mgmt. Home: 101 S College Ave Myerstown PA 17067 Office: Quaker Alloy Casting Co 720 S Cherry St Myerstown PA 17067

WILDHACK, WILLIAM AUGUST, JR., lawyer; b. Takoma Park, Md., Nov. 28, 1935; s. William August and Martha Elizabeth (Parks) W.; B.S., Miami U., Oxford, Ohio, 1957; J.D., George Washington U., 1963; m. Martha Moore Allston, Aug. 1, 1959; children—William III, Elizabeth. Agt., IRS, No. Va., 1957-65; admitted to bar; mem. firm Morris, Pearce, Gardner & Beitel, Washington, 1965-69; individual practice law, Washington, 1969; corp. counsel, v.p. B.F. Saul Co. and affiliates, Chevy Chase, Md., 1969—; sec. B.F. Saul Real Estate Investment Trust, Chevy Chase; pres. MHC Corp., Chevy Chase. Chmn. mediation com., vice chmn. Arlington Tenant Landlord Commn., 1976—; pres. Arlington unit Am. Cancer Soc., 1970-71. Mem. Am. Soc. Corp. Secs., Am., D.C., Va., Arlington County bar assns., Phi Alpha Delta. Presbyterian. Office: 8401 Connecticut Ave Chevy Chase MD 20015

WILEY, RAY NELSON, ins. agy. exec.; b. Airville, Pa., Apr. 1, 1923; s. J. Ross and Grace E. (Kilgore) W.; grad. high sch.; m. 2d, Jean Seifred, Feb. 13, 1971; children by previous marriage—Ray Nelson Jr., Barbara L. Wiley Martenson. Various factory jobs, until 1945; bakery delivery route, 1945-50; ins. agt. Hardware Mutuals, Landisville, Pa., 1950-55; local ind. agt., 1955-65; owner Ray N. Wiley Agency Inc., Mount Joy, Pa., 1965—, also pres.; v.p. Old Guard Mut. Ins. Co.; pres. Sigma Electronics Inc., East Petersburg, Pa.; dir. Red Rose Mut. Co., others. Vice pres. Mut. Ins. Edn. Found., 1978—. Mem. Profl. Ins. Agts. Assn., Profl. Ins. Agts. of Pa., Md. and Del. (pres. 1969-70, named outstanding agt. of yr. 1977-78), Lancaster County Agts. Assn. (pres. 1968-69), Ins. Fire Mark Soc. (v.p. 1976-78, pres. 1978-79), Soc. Cert. Ins. Counselors. Republican. Methodist. Club: Rotary (pres. 1957-58). Home: RD 1 Box 40 Mount Joy PA 17552 Office: RN Wiley Agency Inc 323 W Main St Mount Joy PA 17552

WILEY, RONALD, mfg. co. exec.; b. Lexington, Ky., Nov. 30, 1942; s. Earl Smith and Edith Mae(Robinson) W.; m. Bernice Kay Vancil, Dec. 16, 1963; children—Janene, Jolene, Ronald Alan. Charter comml. pilot, Frankfort, Ky., 1964-66; sales rep. Gillette Safety Razor Co., Boston, 1966-69; sales mgr., dir. tng. Carter-Wallace, Inc., Cranbury, N.J., 1969-78; corp. dir. devel. Hartz Mountain Corp., Harrison, N.J., 1978-80; dir. sales and market devel. Akwell Industries, Tinton Falls, N.J., 1980—. Active local Boy Scouts Am. Served with USAF, 1960-64. Mem. Am. Mgmt. Assn., Nat. Soc. Sales Tng. Execs., Nat. Assn. Flight Instrs. Baptist. Home: 52 Bar Harbor Rd Freehold NJ 07728 Office: 78 Apple St Tinton Falls NJ 07724

WILEY, WILLIAM BRADFORD, publisher; b. Orange, N.J., Nov. 17, 1910; s. William Carroll and Isabel (LeCato) W.; A.B., Colgate U., 1932, LL.D. (hon.), 1966; m. Esther T. Booth, Jan. 4, 1936; children—William Bradford II, Peter Booth, Deborah Elizabeth. With John Wiley & Sons, Inc., N.Y.C., 1932—, sec., v.p. and sec., exec. v.p., treas., 1938-56, pres., 1956-71, chmn., 1971—, dir., 1942—; chmn., dir. John Wiley & Sons, Can., Wiley Pubs. Can., John Wiley & Sons Ltd., London, Jacaranda-Wiley, Ltd., Brisbane; dir. Limusa, S.A., Mexico. Trustee Drew U., Colgate U. Episcopalian. Clubs: Players, University (N.Y.C.); Sakonnet Golf, Sakonnet Yacht (R.I.); Baltusrol (N.J.) Golf. Home: 57 Prospect Hill Ave Summit NJ 07901 also Bailey's Ledge Little Compton RI 02837 Office: 605 3d Ave New York NY 10016

WILEY, WILLIAM CHARLES, instrument mfg. co. exec.; b. Monmouth, Ill., Aug. 7, 1924; s. Samuel E. and Vashti (Sorenson) W.; B.S., U. Ill., 1949; m. Margaret Kurtz, Mar. 15, 1944; children—Kurt M., Mark S. Supervisory physicist Bendix Corp., Southfield, Mich., 1949-65, dir. applied sci. lab., 1965-67, asso. dir. planning, research labs., 1968-69, asst. gen. mgr. sci. instruments and equipment div., Rochester, N.Y., 1969-71; v.p., chief tech. officer Leeds & Northrup Co., North Wales, Pa., 1971—. Bd. dirs. Univ. City Sci. Center, Phila. Served with USAAF, 1943-45. Recipient Mich. Outstanding Living Inventors award Mich. Patent Law Assn., 1963, Outstanding Alumni award U. Ill., 1975. Mem. AAAS, Am. Phys. Soc., IEEE, Instrument Soc. Am. Contbr. articles to profl. jours.; patentee in field. Home: 2 Kinder Rd Conshohocken PA 19428 Office: Dickerson Rd North Wales PA 19454

WILFLEY, GEORGE MERRITT, mfg. co. exec.; b. Denver, May 23, 1924; s. Elmer R. and Margaret W.; B.A., U. Colo., 1950, postgrad., 1977; m. Eleanore Breitenstein; children—George Michael, John Frederick. With A.R. Wilfley & Sons, Inc., Denver, 1950—, pres., 1958—, also dir.; pres., dir. Western Foundries, Inc.; chmn. bd., dir. Conveying Industries, Inc.; dir. First Nat. Bank of Denver. Vice pres. bd. trustees U. Denver; chmn. bd. Boys Club of Denver, Inc. Served with F.A., AUS, 1943-46. Mem. AIME, Nat. Assn. Corrosion Engrs., Colo. Mining Assn. Home: 34 Polo Club Circle Denver CO 80209 Office: PO Box 2330 Denver CO 80201

WILFORD, WALTON TERRY, economist, educator; b. Murray, Ky., Sept. 27, 1937; s. Jasper Dekalb and Rebecca (Sykes) W.; B.B.A., So. Meth. U., 1958, Ph.D., 1964; Asst. prof. econs. U. Ga., Athens, 1962-63, U. Idaho, Moscow, 1963-65; econ. adviser AID, Bolivia and Guatemala, 1965-68; prof. econs. and fin. U. New Orleans, 1968—, chmn. dept., 1972—. Vis. prof. Calif. State U., San Jose, 1972. Ford Found. fellow, 1964. Mem. Am., So., Western econ. assns., Southeastern Conf. Latin Am. Assn., Fin. Mgmt. Assn., Omicron Delta Epsilon. Author: (with Raul Moncarz) Essays in Latin American Economic Issues, 1970. Editorial bd. Miss. Valley Jour. Bus., 1970—. Contbr. numerous articles to profl. jours. Home: 404

Eden Isles Dr Slidell LA 70458 Office: Dept Economics and Finance University of New Orleans New Orleans LA 70122

WILKENFELD, JEROME, oil co. exec.; b. Bklyn., Oct. 25, 1920; s. Elias and Pauline (Nadel) W.; B. in Chem. Engring., Coll. City N.Y., 1943; m. Rhoda B. Barandes, Dec. 21, 1969; children—Richard S., Robert M. With Hooker Chems. & Plastics Corp., 1943-78, operating and tech. assignments, dir. process engring. group, quality control and product specification, also mgr. research and control, 1943-65, dir. corp. program in environ. health, 1966-78, dir. environ. health, 1970-78; dir. health and environ. Occidental Petroleum Corp., Los Angeles, 1978—; mem. N.Y. State Air Pollution Control Bd., 1958-70, N.Y. State Environ. Bd., 1970-80; N.Y. State Health Planning Adv. Council, 1972-76; mem. EPA Solvents Adv. Com., 1970-72. Bd. dirs. Am. Lung Assn., 1971-78. Mem. Mfg. Chemists Assn. (chmn. air quality com., water resources com.), Chlorine Inst. (chmn. environ. mgmt. com.), Niagara Frontier Sect. Air Pollution Control Assn. (chmn., Outstanding Contbn. award for Air Pollution Control 1964), Environ. Health Commn. (chmn.), N.Y. State Chem. Industries Council, Am. Inst. Chem. Engrs., Am. Chem. Soc., Air Pollution Control Assn., Water Pollution Control Fedn. Clubs: Younstown Yacht, Niagara. Contbg. author Waste Management and Control, 1966; Industrial Pollution Control Handbook, 1971; Occupational Safety & Health Handbook. Home: 5757 Owensmouth Ave Woodland Hills CA 91367 Office: 10889 Wilshire Blvd Los Angeles CA 90024

WILKERSON, CLAUDE DAN, cons. engring. co. exec.; b. Alexandria, La., July 18, 1928; s. Claude DeVille and Hazel Margret (Dunn) W.; B.S. in Mech. Engring., La. State U., 1950; m. Julie Ensue Jung, May 24, 1961; children—Daniel, Claudia Carol. Chief mech. engr. Japan Central Exchange, Japan, Korea, 1953-55, Adrian Wilson & Assos., Japan, Korea, 1955-56, Daniel, Mann Johnson & Mendenhall, Japan, Korea, 1956-57; pres. Trans-Asia Engring. Assos. Inc., Japan, Korea, 1957-62, sr. v.p., Japan, Korea, Philippines, 1962-70, dir., 1970—; chmn. bd. dirs. Trans-Asia Singapore Pvt. Ltd., Singapore, Indonesia, 1970—; dir. Resco Corp., Trasen Assos. Inc.; dir., v.p. Hood Internat. Inc. Served with U.S. Army, 1950-52; Korea, Japan. Recipient Achievement Outstanding Service certificate Japan Central Exchange, 1952; Letter of Appreciation Ministry Constrn., S. Korea, 1970; registered profl. engr., La., Tex., Republic Singapore. Mem. ASME, La. Engring. Soc., Profl. Soc. Tex. Engrs., Seoul (Korea) Foreigners Club (pres. 1968-69), Petroleum Club Singapore. Home: 746 Jacaranda Circle Hillsborough CA 94010

WILKERSON, OWEN THOMAS, public relations counsel; b. Halifax County, Va., Mar. 22, 1943; s. Ernest Baxter and Lucille Francis (Owens) W.; B.S. in Edn., W.Va. State Coll., 1965; m. Cheryl F. Tynes Pelzer, Nov. 1969. News reporter N.J. Afro-Am., 1966-68; reporter Newark Evening News, 1968-71; exec. editor Encore Am. and Worldwide mag., N.Y.C., 1972-73; nat. news exec. Boy Scouts Am., 1973-77; mgr. media relations Sperry & Hutchinson Co., N.Y.C., 1977-80; public relations counsel, N.Y.C., 1980—; asso. adj. prof. journalism Rutgers U., 1970-72; lectr. Dillard U., New Orleans, 1975; guest prof. U. Kans., 1976. Bd. dirs. James Varick Community Center, N.Y.C., Essex County (N.J.) OICs of Am.; mem. Essex (N.J.) council Boy Scouts Am. Ford Found. fellow Columbia U. Grad Sch. Journalism, 1969, Harvard U. Alumni Coll., 1976; Nat. Endowment Humanities fellow Tufts U. Fletcher Sch. Law and Diplomacy, 1978. Mem. Public Relations Soc. Am. (co-chmn. minorities com. N.Y. chpt., dir. chpt.), Am. Acad. Social and Polit. Sci., UN Assn., Fgn. Policy Assn., Nat. Conf. Social Welfare, Publicity Club N.Y.C., Alpha Phi Omega. Club: Overseas Press (N.Y.C.). Home: 351 Broad St Apt B1810 Newark NJ 07104 Office: 507 Fifth Ave Suite 903 New York NY 10017

WILKES, FRANKLIN JOHN, ins. co. exec.; b. N.Y.C., June 15, 1909; s. Nathaniel R. and Anna M. W.; student Princeton U., 1932; m. Floreine J. Nelson, Oct. 31, 1979; children—Franklin John, Lawrence Bruce. With Mfrs. Hanover Trust Co., 1932-50, adminstrv. officer, 1950; founder, chmn., chief exec. officer F.J. Wilkes & Co., Inc., N.Y.C., 1950—; mem. Lloyd's of London, 1977—; thoroughbred horse owner. Mem. Sherriff's Jury First Panel. Served to maj. USAF, 1942-46. Mem. Ins. Fedn. N.Y. (past pres.). Clubs: Downtown Assn., Brook, Union, River, Piping Rock. Office: 1 World Trade Center Suite 10217 New York NY 10048

WILKES, HAROLD ARTHUR, grocery chain exec.; b. Cambridge, Ohio, May 16, 1936; s. James and Hester May (Wharton) W.; student Ohio State U., 1963-64, Marietta Coll., 1966; m. Carol J. Denny, Sept. 17, 1958; children—Curtis H., Mark A. With Big Bear Stores Co., 1960-67; pres. Vienna Food Giant Inc., 1967—; Mini-Giants Inc., Vienna, W.Va., 1970—. Served with USN, 1956-60. Mem. Nat. Assn. Convenience Stores, Nat. Assn. Retailers, Human Resources Devel. Assn., W.V. Assn. Retail Grocers, Am. Motorcycle Assn. Clubs: Ohio Valley Ski (pres. 1978, dir. 1979), Elks. Home: 3800 Grand Central Vienna WV 26105 Office: 3005 Grand Central Vienna WV 26105

WILKES, ROBERT BURTON, bus. appraisals corp. exec.; b. Tex., July 13, 1920; s. Jeff Key and Stella Florence (Thomas) W.; student George Washington U., 1938-41, UCLA, 1958-60; B.A., U. Tex., 1943; m. Montjoy Elizabeth Lodge, Aug. 17, 1952; children—Robert Lodge, Gary Edwin. With Convair div. Gen. Dynamics Corp., San Diego, 1951-57; gen. auditor Hughes Aircraft Co., Culver City, Calif., 1957-60; sec.-treas., controller Los Angeles Soap Co., treas., controller, dir. White King, Inc., exec. v.p., dir. Calif. Rendering Co., Ltd. (all Los Angeles), 1960-62; with Am. Electronics, Inc., Fullerton, Calif., 1962-63; partner, exec. v.p. Taylor & Wilkes, Inc., Anaheim, Calif., 1964-73; pres., owner, founder United Motor Inn, Inc., Dallas, 1973-75; pres., founder Corp. Devel., Inc., Sacramento, 1977—; exec. v.p. United Motor Inss, Inc., Dallas and Ind. Appraisal, Inc., Corp. Devel., Inc., Sacramento, 1964-73, sec.-treas., 1960-62, controller, 1962-63, pres., 1973—, dir., 1964—; lectr., panel mem. for continuing edn., 1966—. Served to capt. USAAF, 1942-46. Mem. Fin. Execs. Inst. (employee benefits nat. com. 1977-80), Am. Soc. Appraisers, Employee Stock Ownership Plan Assn. Am. (valuation com. 1978-80), Sacramento C. of C., Nat. Fedn. Ind. Bus. (action com. 1976-80, White House Conf. on Small Bus. 1979-80). Republican. Presbyterian. Home: 6745 Bertran Ct Citrus Heights CA 95610 Office: Ind Appraisal Inc Corp Devel Inc Suite 390 2255 Watt Ave Sacramento CA 95825

WILKESHESKI, GERALD MICHAEL, fin. exec.; b. Humboldt, Sask., Can., May 30, 1944; s. Michael and Victoria Catharine (Samoleski) W.; B.A., U. Sask., 1965, M.A., 1966; m. Sharon Anne Lund, Oct. 5, 1968. Importer-exporter, Saskatoon, Sask., 1965-66; pvt. practice tax preparation and acctg. services, Saskatoon, 1970-76; pvt. investment specialist/investor/counsellor, Regina, Sask., 1976—; fin. cons. Exec. asst. to provincial opposition leader Sask. Legis. Assembly, 1978-79. Recipient cert. for service to jailed inmates Hoffman Howard Soc., 1977. Liberal Party. Roman Catholic. Club: K.C. Contbr. articles to profl. jours. Address: 22-26 Shaw St Regina SK S4R 3M4 Canada

WILKINSON, DONALD ELLSWORTH, govt. agrl. adminstr.; b. Benton, Wis., May 4, 1922; s. Fred William and Edna (Turnbull) W.; student U. Dubuque, 1940-42; B.S., U. Wis.-Madison, 1947; m. Elizabeth Koehler, June 14, 1947; children—David T., Nancy E., Karen E. Tchr. vocat. agr. Waukesha (Wis.) High Sch., 1947-48; info. officer Wis. Dept. Agr., Madison, 1948-51, dir. commodity promotion, 1951-54, chief div. mktg., 1955-64, asst. sec. dept., 1965-69, sec., 1969-75; adminstr. Agrl. Mktg. Service, U.S. Dept. Agr., Washington, 1975-77; gov. Farm Credit Adminstrn., Washington, 1977—. Mem. mktg. advisory com. to U.S. sec. agr., 1964-68; pres. Mid-Am. Internat. Agr. Trade Council, Chgo., 1969-71. Asso. campaign chmn. Madison United Givers, 1968. Pres. bd. dirs. Meth. Hosp., Madison, 1972-75. Served to 1st lt. USAAF, 1942-46. Decorated D.F.C. Mem. Nat. Assn. Mktg. Ofcls. (pres. 1964), Nat. Assn. State Depts. Agr. (pres. 1974). Methodist (del. gen. conf. 1972). Kiwanian. Office: Farm Credit Adminstrn 490 L'Enfant Plaza SW Washington DC 20578

WILKINSON, MICHAEL CHARLES, engring. cons.; b. Milw., Dec. 14, 1935; s. Joseph Henry and Lauretta (Larson) W.; B.S. in Civil Engring., U. Minn., 1958; m. Barbara Jean Jones, July 16, 1960 (div. Oct. 1977); children—Lisa, Katy, Megan; m. 2d, Mary E. Moras, Dec. 6, 1979. Structural test engr. Boeing Airplane Co., Seattle, 1958-60; project engr. Morrison-Knudsen, Honolulu, 1960-64; estimator, project engr. and tunnel supt. Al Johnson Constrn. Co., Mpls., 1964-70; project mgr. Mich. Sewer Constrn. Co., Detroit, 1970; div. mgr. Kellogg Corp., Denver, 1970—. Mem. Nat. Ski Patrol, 1965—. Recipient Bausch & Lomb Sci. award, 1953. Registered profl. engr., Colo. Mem. Nat. Soc. of Profl. Engrs. (chmn. com. on Denver rapid transit 1975), ASCE (chmn. com. on inspection), Brit. Tunnelling Soc., Am. Inst. Constructors, Am. Underground Assn., Am. Arbitration Assn., Beta Theta Pi. Republican. Lutheran. Home: 481 W Prentice Littleton CO 80120 Office: 5601 S Broadway Littleton CO 80121

WILL, CHARLES AUGUSTUS, ins. co. exec.; b. N.Y.C., Apr. 10, 1917; s. Charles and Gertrude (Zauner) W.; B.S., N.Y. U., 1951; m. Kathleen O'Donnell, Aug. 7, 1943; children—John Barry, Mary Kathleen, Peter Joseph. Chief underwriter Guardian Life Ins. Co. Am., 1948-50, asst. underwriting sec., 1950-60, underwriting sec., 1960-67; v.p. underwriting Cologne Life Reins. Co., Stamford, Conn., 1967-71, sr. v.p., 1971—. Served with USNR, 1944-46. Mem. Home Office Life Underwriters Assn., Inst. Home Office Underwriters (pres. 1957-58), Assurance Med. Soc. Gt. Britain, S. African Assn. Med. Underwriters. Club: Nyack Field. Home: 81 River Rd Grandview-on-Hudson NY 10960 Office: 1200 Bedford St Stamford CT 06905

WILLARD, JOHN GERARD, multi-nat. co. adminstr., lectr.; b. Pitts., Nov. 20, 1952; s. Cornelius Merle and May E. (Hinds) W.; B.A. in Journalism, Duquesne U., Pitts., 1974; m. Lorraine L. Franze, Sept. 2, 1978. Producer, dir. art talent Sta. WDUQ-FM, Pitts., 1971-73; master control tech. dir. Sta. KDKA-TV, Pitts., 1973; cons. communications Better Bus. Bur., Pitts., 1974; asst. account exec. Marc & Co., Advt., Pitts., 1975; adminstr. employee benefit adminstrn. Rockwell Internat. Corp., Pitts., 1975-80, adminstr. relocation and corp. personnel procedures, 1980—. Mem. Am. Mensa Ltd., Internat. Platform Assn., Smithsonian Nat. Instn., Nat. Rifle Assn. (markmanship instr.), Stage 62, Kappa Tau Alpha, Alpha Tau Omega. Office: 600 Grant St Suite 5083A Pittsburgh PA 15219

WILLARD, RICHARD WESLEY, motel exec.; b. Pittsburg, Kans., Nov. 4, 1929; s. Russell Orville and Vada (Robertson) W.; B.Gen. Studies, U. Nebr., Omaha, 1970. Pres. Willard & Baughman Inc., Omaha, 1966-73, Starlite and Mansard Motels Inc., Council Bluffs, Iowa, 1973—; regional coordinator Friendship Inns Internat., 1973—. Served with AUS, 1951-54. Named Man of Year, Friendship Inns Internat., 1976. Mem. Iowa Hotel, Motel and Motor Inn Assn. (dir. 1974-78, 3d v.p. 1976-77, 2d v.p. 1977, 1st v.p. 1978), U. Nebr. Alumni Assn., Iowa Civil Liberties Union, Newberry Library (Chgo.), Am. Hotel and Motel Assn., Omaha Lodging Assn., Council Bluffs C. of C. (chmn. conv. com.). Address: 10 Plaza Sq Saint Louis MO 63103

WILLARD, ROBERT WAID, pub. co. exec.; b. Denver, June 18, 1938; s. Oscar Waid and Evelynne Leslie (Kirk) W.; B.S. in Bus. Adminstrn., U. Denver, 1961, M.B.A., 1962; m. Margie A. Adams, Jan. 29, 1962; children—Kirk, Christian, Sean, Brooke. Advt. rep. Dow Jones & Co., San Francisco, 1965-69, advt. mgr., Houston, 1969-71, advt. mgr., Cleve., 1971-74; mgr. Rocky Mountain region PENTON/IPC, Cleve., Englewood, Colo., 1974-76; pub. cons. Titsch Pub., Denver, also FRS Publs., San Jose, Calif., 1977-78; regional mgr. Tech. Pub. Co. div. Dun & Bradstreet Co., 1979—. Chmn., Cleve. Tomorrow Com., 1972-73. Recipient 1st pl. Creative award Am. Advt. Fedn., 1965, Maggie award Western Pubs. Assn. Mem. Denver Advt. Fedn. (dir.), Bus. Profl. Advt. Assn., Chgo. Athletic Assn. Episcopalian. Address: 7272 E Davies Pl Englewood CO 80112

WILLCOX, NORTON C., aerospace co. exec.; b. Buffalo, 1920; ed. U. Buffalo. Formerly v.p. fin., controller Bell Aerosystems Co.; now pres. Bell Aerospace Textron. Office: PO Box 1 Buffalo NY 14240*

WILLES, MARK HINCKLEY, food co. exec.; b. Salt Lake City, July 16, 1941; s. Joseph Simmons and Ruth (Hinckley) W.; A.B., Columbia U., 1963; Ph.D., 1967; m. Laura Fayone, June 7, 1961; children—Wendy Anne, Susan Kay, Keith Mark, Stephen Joseph, Matthew Bryant. Mem. com. staff banking and currency com. Ho. of Reps., Washington, 1966-67; asst. prof. fin. U. Pa., 1967-69; economist Fed. Res. Bank, Phila., 1967, sr. economist, 1969-70, dir. research, 1970-71, v.p., dir. research, 1971, 1st v.p., 1971-77; pres. Fed. Res. Bank of Mpls., 1977-80; exec. v.p., chief fin. officer Gen. Mills Inc., Mpls., 1980—. Office: 9200 Wayzata Blvd Minneapolis MN 55426

WILLETT, THOMPSON A.L., distillery exec.; b. Bardstown, Ky., Jan. 27, 1909; s. Aloysius Lambert and Mary Catherine (Thompson) W.; B.A., Xavier U., Cin., 1931; m. Mary Virginia Sheehan, Jan. 14, 1942; children—Mary Tabitha (Mrs. Frank J. Fisher, Jr.), James (dec.), Martha Harriet (Mrs. Even Kulsveen), John David, Susan Virginia (Mrs. Thomas C. Dawson), Richard Francis, Alice Jane. Editor Loveland (Ohio) Herald, 1931-32; comptroller Ky. Hwy. Dept., 1932-33; asst. supt. Bernheim Distilling Co., Louisville, 1933-36; pres. Willett Distilling Co., Bardstown, Ky., 1936—, also dir. Chmn. Bardstown-Nelson County Hist. Commn., 1938; Ky. advisor Nat. Trust for Historic Preservation, Washington, 1940. Bd. dirs. Xavier U., 1960-63; bd. dirs. Bellarmine Coll., 1964—. Mem. Ky. Distillers Assn. (pres. 1960), Newcomen Soc. N.Am., Distilled Spirits Council U.S. (dir. 1940—). K.C. Club: Old Kentucky Home Country (Bardstown). Contbr. articles to various publs. Home: Beechwold E Stephen Foster Bardstown KY 40004 Office: Box 10 Bardstown KY 40004

WILLEY, DOUGLAS JEROME, automobile co. exec.; b. Arlington, Va., Feb. 17, 1924; s. Addison Henry and Lena (Warner) W.; student U. Md., 1941-43, Amherst Coll., 1943-44; A.A. in Fgn. Affairs, George Washington U., 1949; m. June Elizabeth Butscher, Nov. 4, 1944; children—Allen, Ronald, Linda (Mrs. John B. Lowe). With Buick Motor div. Gen. Motors Corp., 1949-57, asst. mgr., Detroit, 1957, cons., 1957-58; pres. Doug Willey Pontiac, Inc., Birmingham, Ala., 1958—; chmn. bd. Crown Pontiac, St. Petersburg, Fla., 1968—; chmn. bd., pres. Crown Automobile, Birmingham, 1971—; sec. Action Toyota, Atlanta, 1978—; chmn. Action Toyota, Birmingham, 1976—; pres. SE Bankers Life Ins. Co., 1977—; founder Dealer Mgmt. Analysis Corp., Birmingham, 1967, pres., until 1971; vis. instr. Gen. Motors Inst., 1961-63; cons. in field. Mem. Gen. Motors President's Dealer Adv. Council, 1972-73; mem. retail adv. com. Brand Names Found., 1959—. Served to 1st lt. AUS, World War II. Decorated Bronze Star; Medalha de Companha, Medal of Peacemaker (Brazil); knighted by Pope Paul VI, 1969, named knight of St. Gregory. Hon. mem. Soc. 1st Div. Clubs: The Club, Inverness, Downtown, Relay House, Shoal Creek; Tennis Ranch (Scottsdale, Ariz.). Home: 1002 Carnoustic Shoal Creek AL 35223 Office: 1640 Hwy 31 S Birmingham AL 35216

WILLIAMS, AUDREY ARTHUR, JR., architect; b. Dallas, Mar. 25, 1925; s. Audrey Arthur and Helen Myrtle (Stark) W.; B.S. in Archtl. Constrn., Tex. Agrl. and Mech. U., 1951; m. Martha Louise Thomas, July 2, 1943; 1 dau., Sally Ann (Mrs. James Richard Hewell, Jr.). Architect, Art Williams Jr. & Assos., Architects, Dallas, 1954—; owner Art Williams Jr. Interiors; owner Motor Hotel Consultants; pres., dir. Standard Constrn. Co. Waco (Tex.), Am. Motor Inns, Inc., Americana Mortgage & Leasing Corp.; designer numerous bldgs. including motor hotels, restaurants. Served with USAF, 1942-45; ETO. Mem. Nat., Am. insts. architects, Constrn. Specifications Inst., Tex. Soc. Architects. Republican. Home: 14140 Rawhide Parkway Dallas TX 75234 Office: 2880 LBJ Freeway Dallas TX 75234

WILLIAMS, BARBARA LYNN, Realtor; b. Montrose, Colo., Nov. 25, 1944; d. Joe H. and Elsie Arlene Baldwin; grad. Am. Acad. Real Estate, 1973, Wyo. Real Estate Inst., 1977, Realtor Inst., 1979; m. Joe A. Williams, Oct. 3, 1965; children—Christine, Anisa Jo. Saleswoman, Western Realty Co., Durango, Colo., 1970-72; mng. broker Wedgwood Ltd., Realtors, Durango, 1973-74, pres., 1974-75; sales mgr. Coulter Agency, Gillette, Wyo., 1976-77, gen. mgr., 1977-78; owner/operator Barbara Williams Brokerage with the Real Estate Exchange, 1978—. Vice chmn. LaPlata County Republican Central Com., 1973-75; mem. Region 9 Housing Com., 1974-75; mem. steering com. Sch. Dist. 9R, 1973-74. Licensed real estate broker, Colo., Wyo. Mem. Campbell County Bd. Realtors (profl. standards com. 1979), Wyo. Assn. Realtors (pres.-elect 1981), Nat. Assn. Realtors (equal opportunity com. 1980—), Realtors Nat. Mktg. Inst., Farm and Land Inst., Durango, Gillette (housing com. 1977-78) chambers commerce. Clubs: Rep. Women's; Emblem (past sec., trustee); Newcomers (past dir.); Empire Investment (pres. 1977). Home: 3 Grandview Circle Gillette WY 82716 Office: 802 E 3d St Suite A Gillette WY 82716

WILLIAMS, CHARLES D., farm products co. exec. Chmn., dir. Gold Kist, Inc., Atlanta. Office: 244 Perimeter Center Pkwy NE Atlanta GA 30346*

WILLIAMS, CHARLES LOUIS (RUSTY), bank exec.; b. San Angelo, Tex., June 13, 1944; s. Albert B. and Betty G. (Dozier) W.; B.B.A. in Fin., U. Tex., 1966; student Stonier Grad. Sch. Banking, 1971-73; m. Sandra Pace, Feb. 24, 1967; children—Ashley, Brooke. Vice pres. comml. loans Tex. Commerce Bank, Houston, 1966-73; treas. Walter W. Scarborough, Inc., Houston, 1973-74; sr. v.p., sr. loan officer Southwestern Savings Assn., Houston, 1974-75; sr. v.p. mktg. bus. devel., corr. banking So. Nat. Bank, Houston, 1975-78; exec. v.p., sr. credit officer N. Side Bank, Houston, 1978-79; pres. Nat. Bank of Commerce of Houston, 1979—. Mem. Robert Morris Assn. (com. chmn.), Fin. Execs. Inst. (sec.), Pin Oak Charity Horse Show Assn. (pres.). Office: PO Box 36190 Houston TX 77036

WILLIAMS, CHARLES MOLTON, mortgage banking exec.; b. Birmingham, Ala., June 21, 1930; s. Elliott Tuttle and Gertrude (Molton) W.; B.S., Washington and Lee U., 1952; postgrad. U. Ala., 1954; m. Pauline Hope White, Oct. 19, 1954; children—Charles Molton, John Thomas Hunter, John White, Kate Hope. With Molton, Allen and Williams, Inc., Birmingham, Ala., 1954—, pres., chief exec. officer, 1968-78, chmn. bd., 1978—; dir. Nat. Bank Commerce. Mem. exec. bd. Birmingham Area council Boy Scouts Am.; mem. adv. council Salvation Army Home and Hosp.; past pres. Birmingham Festival of Arts Assn. Served with U.S. Army, 1952-54. Mem. Am., Ala. mortgage bankers assns., Nat. Assn. Home Builders, Birmingham Bd. Realtors, Young Presidents' Orgn. Presbyterian. Clubs: Shoal Creek Country, Country of Birmingham, Quarterback, Relay House, The Club, Kiwanis, Redstone. Home: 3924 Royal Oak Dr Birmingham AL 35243 Office: 2008 3d Ave N Birmingham AL 35203

WILLIAMS, CHARLES RALPH, III, fin. and mktg. cons.; b. Pitts., Oct. 26, 1946; s. Ralph G. and LaVaughn M. (Hurd) W.; A.B. (Harvard Club scholar, 1964-68), Harvard U., 1968, M.B.A., 1972; postgrad. Law Sch., Columbia U., 1971; m. Lisette de Knocke van der Meulen, Sept. 14, 1973; 1 son, Jason Charles. Sr. cons. Arthur D. Little, Inc., Cambridge, Mass., 1972-77; dir. fin. instn. mgmt. services Touche Ross & Co., Boston, 1977-78; pres., chief exec. officer Charles Williams & Co., Cambridge, from 1978—; exec. v.p., chief fin. officer Fed. Home Loan Mortgage Corp., 1979—; dir. Travel Design Corp., Cambridge. Touche Ross & Co. fellow, 1970-72. Mem. Harvard Bus. Sch. Assn. Boston, Nat. Urban League, Internat. Relations Council, Phi Alpha Phi. Club: Harvard. Author: Market Research in Banking, 1973; Managing Working Capital in an Inflationary Environment, 1975; co-author: Bankers Handbook on EFT, 1976; Marketing Effectiveness in the Banking Environment, 1978. Office: 1776 G St NW Washington DC 20013

WILLIAMS, CLYDE EZRA, real estate appraiser; b. Farnum, Idaho, Jan. 22, 1920; s. John Ezra and Harriet Rhoda (Miller) W.; student Weber Coll., 1938-41, U. Utah, Eastern Wash. State Coll., U. San Francisco, Purdue U.; m. Geraldine (Jeri) Hadley, June 2, 1950; children—Deborah Lynn (Mrs. Arbon Nordgran), Jon Timothy. Partner, Williams Sewing Machine Co., Salt Lake City, 1947-49; contractor, Bountiful, Utah, 1949-54; pres. Clyde E. Williams Co., Bountiful, 1954-70; pres. Willindco Co., Bountiful, 1971—; owner, mgr. Williams Appraisal Co., Bountiful, 1975—. Mem. Bountiful City Planning Commn., 1957-65, chmn., 1959-65; mem. Bountiful Capital Improvements Com., 1958-61. Served with USAAF, 1942-47. Decorated Air medal, DFC. Mem. Soc. Real Estate Appraisers (past pres.), S. Davis Home Builders Assn. (past pres.). Mormon. Club: Sertoma Internat. Home and Office: 868 East 1050 North Bountiful UT 84010

WILLIAMS, DAVID PERRY, automotive co. exec.; b. Detroit, Nov. 16, 1934; s. Marshall Sears Perry and Virginia Ballard (Hayes) W.; B.A., Mich. State U., 1956; M.B.A., Mich. State U., 1964; LL.B., LaSalle U., 1978; m. Eleanor Schneider, Aug. 7, 1972; children—Tracy, Perry, David. Vice pres. sales Kelsey Hayes Co., Romulus, Mich., 1958-71; v.p. ITT, N.Y.C.; product line mgr. Worldwide Automotive, N.Y.C., 1971-76; sr. v.p. ops. Budd Co., Troy, Mich., 1976—, also dir. Served with USAF, 1956-58. Mem. Soc. Automotive Engrs., Engrs. Soc. Detroit, Advanced Mgmt. Club of Mich. State U. Beta Gamma Sigma. Republican. Episcopalian. Clubs: Bloomfield Hills Country, Detroit Athletic, Country of Detroit, Yondotega. Home: 333 Lincoln St Grosse Pointe MI 48230 Office: Budd Co Troy MI 48084

WILLIAMS, DAVID ROGERSON, JR., civil engr.; b. Tulsa, Oct. 20, 1921; s. David Rogerson and Martha Reynolds (Hill) W.; B.S. in Civil Engring., Yale U., 1943; m. Pauline Bolton, May 28, 1944; children—Pauline Bolton Williams d'Aquin, David Rogerson III, Rachel Katharine. Constrn. engr., foreman, supt. Williams Bros. Corp., Tulsa, 1939-49; co-founder Williams Companies, 1949, v.p., 1949-56, exec. v.p., 1956-66, chmn. exec. com., 1966-70; chmn. Williams Bros. Engring. Co., Tulsa, 1957—, Williams Bros. Can. Ltd., Calgary, Alta., 1957—, The Resource Scis. Corp., Tulsa, 1970—, Holmes & Narver, Inc., Orange, Calif.; dir. Pima Savs. & Loan Assn., Tucson, Ariz., Patagonia Corp., Tucson, Great Western Bank & Trust Co., Tucson, Alaskan Resource Scis. Corp., Anchorage, Filtrol Corp., Los Angeles, No. Resources Inc., Billings, Mont., Burlington No. Inc., St. Paul, U.S. Filter Corp., N.Y.C., Western Am. Mortgage Co., Phoenix, Williams Bros. Engring. Ltd., London. Trustee, Nat. Symphony Orch., Washington, Desert Research Inst., Reno, Hudson Inst., Croton-on-Hudson, N.Y. Served to capt. USAF, World War II. Fellow ASCE; mem. Am. Petroleum Inst., Am. Gas Assn., Ind. Natural Gas Assn., Royal Arts Soc. (London), Yale Engring. Assn., Alta. Assn. Profl. Engrs. Episcopalian. Clubs: Ranchmen's (Calgary); Toronto; Chagrin Valley Hunt (Gates Mill, Ohio); Petroleum, Southern Hills Country, Summit (Tulsa); Racquet and Tennis, Sky, Yale (N.Y.C.); Rolling Rock (Ligonier, Pa.); Springdale Hall (Camden, S.C.); Union (Cleve.). Office: 6600 S Yale Tulsa OK 74177

WILLIAMS, DAVID SAMUEL, ins. co. exec.; b. Purcell, Okla., Oct. 16, 1926; s. David Skelton and Mattie Carolyn (Kimberlin) W.; B.A., U. Okla., 1950; LL.B., LaSalle Extension U., 1968; m. Gloria Jean Trudgeon, Jan. 14, 1951; children—Mellanie K., David R., Gary B., Kimberly R. With U.S. Fidelity & Guaranty Cos., various locations, 1952-73, asst. mgr., Albuquerque, 1963-66, mgr., San Jose, Calif., 1966-73; v.p. Eldorado Ins. Co., Palo Alto, Calif., 1973-77, exec. v.p., chief operating officer, 1977—; v.p. Eldorado Mgmt. Co., 1973-77, chief operating officer, exec. v.p., 1978; mng. dir. Eldorado Service Corp., 1973-76, exec. v.p., 1976-78; partner Williams Ranch Co., 1977—, Williams Pecan Co., 1977—; chmn. bd., pres. Homeland Gen. Corp., Homeland Ins. Co. and Homeland Indsl. Corp., San Jose, Calif., 1978—; pres. Homeland Mgmt. Corp. (Cayman) Ltd., 1980; past dir. Westlands Bank, San Jose; adv. bd. Pacific Valley Bank, 1975—; tchr. Albuquerque U., 1957-58, N.Mex. U., 1958-59; mem. indsl. panel Stanford Research Inst., 1968; mgmt. cons. County Santa Clara Edn. Dept., 1968-73; mem. Calif. Adv. com. Ins. Services Office. Committeeman Pioneer council Boy Scouts Am., 1968. Served to maj. A.C. AUS, 1944-46, 50-52. Recipient Outstanding Fieldman's award for N.Mex., N.Mex. Insurors Assn., 1959. Mem. Central Coast Fieldmen's Assn., Ins. Mgrs. Assn. No. Calif. (pres. 1974), Assn. Calif. Ins. Cos. (dir.), Sigma Alpha Epsilon. Lutheran. Clubs: Rotary (pres. 1974); Univ. San Jose, British-Am., Center, San Francisco Comml. Home: 14198 Juniper Ln Saratoga CA 95070 Office: Homeland Insurance Co San Jose CA

WILLIAMS, DOLORES (DOLLY) LORELEI LYNN, cons.; b. Valley City, N.D., June 7, 1932; d. Edgar Sidney and Evelyn Bonita (Taylor) Freborg; Banking Degree, U. Wis., 1978; m. Billy Joe Williams, Jan. 15, 1977; children—Stephen, Cheryl, Daniel, Shawn. With First Nat. Bank, Portland, Oreg., 1950-55, First Nat. Bank, Denver, 1955-61, Central Bank, Denver, 1961-68, Jefferson Bank & Trust Co., Lakewood, Colo., 1971-72; with South Denver Nat. Bank, 1972-74, asst. v.p., personnel adminstr., asst. to pres., 1972-74; v.p., cashier Comml. Nat. Bank, Longview, Tex., 1974-80; ind. tng. cons., Longview, 1980—. Treas., March of Dimes; bd. dirs. YMCA. Mem. Am. Inst. Banking (dir. 1975-80), Nat. Assn. Bank Women, Am. Mgmt. Assn., NOW. Democrat. Christian Ch. Clubs: Civitan, Toastmasters. Home: 1205 Columbia Dr Longview TX 75601 Office: 420 FN Bank Bldg Longview TX 75601

WILLIAMS, DONALD CLINTON, mgmt. cons.; b. St. Louis, Feb. 27, 1929; s. R. Arthur and Deborah (Catlin) W.; B.A., Hamilton Coll., 1951; M.B.A., Harvard U., 1953; m. Suzanne Talbot, Aug. 10, 1957; children—Donald Clinton, Bradford H., Bruce T. Sales rep. U.S. Steel Corp., Detroit, 1957-62; gen. mgr. Mich. div. Interstate United Corp., Detroit, 1962-65; with Heidrick & Struggles, Inc., 1965-78, sr. v.p., mgr. Midwest, dir., Chgo., 1973-78; pres. Donald Williams Assos. Inc., Chgo., 1978—; dir. Cavendish Investing Ltd. Served with USNR, 1953-56. Mem. Alpha Delta Phi. Clubs: Glen View; Chicago, Economic, Harvard Bus. Sch. (Chgo.). Home: 222 Leicester St Kenilworth IL 60043 Office: 233 S Wacker Dr Chicago IL 60606

WILLIAMS, DWIGHT BRADLEY, lawyer; b. Salt Lake City, Oct. 27, 1943; s. Dwight James and Janet (Jardine) W.; student Stanford U., 1961-62; B.A., U. Utah, 1967; J.D., Columbia U., 1970; m. Nan Romney, Sept. 1, 1967; children—Dwight Bradley, W. Romney, Ann Marie, Elisabeth. Admitted to N.Y. bar, Utah bar; asso. atty. Chadbourne, Parke, Whiteside & Wolff, N.Y.C., 1970-71, VanCott, Bagley, Cornwall & McCarthy, Salt Lake City, 1971-74; individual practice law, 1974-76; mem. firm Williams, Hansen & Luster, Salt Lake City, 1977-79; pres. Dwight B. Williams, P.C., Salt Lake City, 1979—; adj. prof. bus. law U. Utah; dir. various corps. Mem. Dist. Export Council, 1976—; pres. Utah World Trade Assn., 1979-80, Utah Council for Internat. Visitors, 1980—. Served to capt. U.S. Army, 1971. Mem. Internat. Bar Assn., Am. Bar Assn., Utah Bar Assn. Mormon. Office: 225 N State St Salt Lake City UT 84103

WILLIAMS, EDWARD ARTHUR, mgmt. cons.; b. New Britain, Conn., Nov. 9, 1919; s. Arthur Merwin and Lorraine (Frost) W.; B.S., U. Conn., 1941; M.B.A., Stanford U., 1947; m. Florence Belle Jayne, Aug. 19, 1948 (dec. Dec. 1979); 1 son, David Edward; m. 2d, Charlotte Lee Bell, Oct. 24, 1980. With firm Webster, Blanchard & Willard, Hartford, Conn., 1946; with firm Haskins & Sells, San Francisco, 1947-48, L. H. Penny & Co., San Francisco, 1948; with Collins Radio Co., Dallas, 1949-71, v.p., controller, 1961-64, v.p. control and finance, dir., 1964-71; v.p. finance, dir. Tucker Electronics Co., Garland, Tex., 1971-73; v.p. adminstrn. U. Dallas, 1974-75; v.p. Corporate Bus. Systems, Dallas, 1976-78; v.p., sec.-treas. Elevations Design, Inc., Dallas, 1980—. Served to capt. AUS, 1941-46. C.P.A., Calif., Iowa, Tex. Mem. Fin. Execs. Inst., Am. Inst. C.P.A.'s, Nat. Assn. Accountants. Home: 3616 Wellington Pl Plano TX 75075 Office: Elevations Design Inc 4384 Sunbelt Dr Dallas TX 75248

WILLIAMS, EDWARD EARL, JR., educator, financial exec.; b. Houston, Aug. 21, 1945; s. Edward Earl and Doris Jewel (Jones) W.; B.S. (Benjamin Franklin scholar, Jesse Jones scholar), U. Pa., 1966; Ph.D. (Tex. Savs. and Loan League fellow, NDEA fellow), U. Tex., 1968. Asst. prof. econs. Rutgers U., New Brunswick, N.J., 1968-70; asso. prof. fin. McGill U., Montreal, Que., Can., 1970-73; v.p., economist Service Corp. Internat., Houston, 1973-77; prof. adminstrv. sci. Rice U., Houston, 1978—; chmn. bd. Service Tech. Internat., Inc., Houston, 1976—; chmn. bd., pres. Trust Corp. Internat.; dir. Willwhite Industries, Inc., Equus Internat. Inc. Chmn. 15th Senatorial dist. Republican Party Tex. Mem. Fin. Mgmt. Assn., So. Fin. Assn., Southwestern Fin. Assn., Beta Gamma Sigma, Alpha Kappa Psi. Republican. Presbyterian. Club: Tex. Nat. Country. Author: An Integrated Analysis for Managerial Finance, 1970; Investment Analysis, 1974; contbr. articles to profl. jours. Home: 1400 Hermann Dr 8C Houston TX 77004 Office: Jesse H Jones Grad Sch Adminstrn Rice U Houston TX 77001

WILLIAMS, EDWARD JOSEPH, mfg. co. exec.; b. St. Louis, Aug. 3, 1922; s. Edward J. and Bertha Louise (Gerberding) W.; cert. accountancy, Washington U., St. Louis, 1952; m. Mary Ellen Justice, June 7, 1952; children—Linda Kay, Karen Ann, Mark Edward, David Justice. With Price Waterhouse & Co., C.P.A.'s, St. Louis, 1947-50; controller, sec., treas. Laclede Christy Co., St. Louis, 1951-54; controller, asst. sec. Magic Chef, Inc., St. Louis, 1955-56; with Gen. Aniline & Film Corp., N.Y.C., 1957-61, v.p. financial planning and control, 1960-61; v.p. finance, treas. Interlake, Inc., Chgo., 1962-63, exec. v.p., chief operating officer, 1963-64, also dir.; exec. v.p., chief operating officer Jos. Schlitz Brewing Co., Milw., 1964-69; exec. v.p., mem. mgmt. com. dir. GAF Corp., N.Y.C., 1969-72; pres., dir. McGraw-Edison Co., Elgin, Ill., 1972-73, chmn. bd., pres., chief exec. officer, dir., 1973—; dir., chmn. audit com. Interlake Steel Corp., Chgo.; dir. L.E. Myers Co., L.E. Myers Co. Internat. Ltd., Dukane Corp. Chmn., Jr. Achievement Chgo.; trustee Thomas Alva Edison Found. Served with U.S. Army, 1942-46. C.P.A., Mo. Mem. Am. Inst. C.P.A.'s, NAM (dir.), Ill. Mfrs. Assn. (dir.). Clubs: Mid-America, Economic, Chicago, Executives (Chgo.); Barrington Hills Country (Barrington); Butler Nat. Golf. Office: McGraw-Edison Co 333 W River Rd Elgin IL 60120*

WILLIAMS, EDWARD KENNETH, mfg. co. exec.; b. Schenectady, Aug. 19, 1941; s. Richard Raymond and Ruth Anna (Yarter) W.; grad. Gen. Electric Tech. Mfg. Apprentice Program, 1963, other mfg. tech. courses; m. Frances Z. Stevens, June 15, 1978; children—Karen, Judith, Phillip, Eric, Wendy. With Gen. Electric Co., Schenectady, 1959—, specialist in machine tool and process equipment, 1969—. Recipient Merit award Gen. Electric Co., 1973, 74. Mem. Christian Ch. Home: RD 1 Box 482 Schoharie Turnpike Delanson NY 12053 Office: Bldg 273 Room 2140 N Ave Schenectady NY 12345

WILLIAMS, FREDRIC DENNIS, communications and fin. cons. co. exec.; b. Madison, Wis., Dec. 27, 1943; s. Harry Albert and Jacquelyn Adoree (Phillips) W.; B.A., U. Wis., Madison, 1965; M.A., U. Iowa, 1972. Instr. English, Carnegie-Mellon U., 1968-71; public affairs officer NASA, 1972-77; dir. communications Sperry div. Sperry Corp., 1977-79; pres. Sunlight Corp., Washington, 1979—. Recipient Exceptional Service medal NASA, 1975. Mem. Mensa. Libertarian. Author poetry, newspaper and mag. articles. Home: 1748 Q St NW Washington DC 20009 Office: 1611 Connecticut Ave Washington DC 20009

WILLIAMS, GORDON BRETNELL, constrn. co. exec.; b. Phila., Apr. 3, 1929; s. Thomas W. and Helen (Berryman) W.; B.S., Yale, 1951; m. Susan M. Cunningham, June 20, 1953; children—Lucy Chase, Marcus Bretnell. Chief indsl. engr. Chrysler div. Chrysler Corp., Detroit, 1954-57; pres., dir. Cunningham-Limp Co., Birmingham, Mich., 1957-76; v.p. mktg. H.K. Ferguson Co., Cleve., 1976-78; pres. H.K. Ferguson Co., 1979—; dir. Arco Industries. Trustee Cranbrook Ednl. Community Retirement Plan, 1969; chmn. adv. bd. St. Joseph Mercy Hosp., 1970-74. Served as ensign USNR, 1951-54. Registered profl. engr., Calif., Mich., Ohio, Tex. Mem. Phi Gamma Delta. Clubs: Yale of Ohio, Union of Cleve. Home: 2761 Sherbrooke Shaker Heights OH 44122 OFfice: HK Ferguson Co One Erieview Plaza Cleveland OH 44114

WILLIAMS, HAROLD MARVIN, govt. ofcl., former univ. dean; b. Phila., Jan. 5, 1928; s. Louis W. and Sophie (Fox) W.; A.B., U. Calif. at Los Angeles, 1946; J.D., Harvard, 1949; postgrad. U. So. Calif. Grad. Sch. Law, 1955-56. Admitted to Calif. bar, 1950; practiced in Los Angeles, 1950, 53-55; with Hunt Foods and Industries, Inc., Los Angeles, 1955-68, v.p. 1958-60, exec. v.p., 1960-68, pres., 1968; gen., mgr. Hunt-Wesson Foods, 1964-66, pres., 1966-68; chmn. finance com. Norton Simon, Inc., 1968-70, chmn. bd., 1969-70, dir., 1959-77; prof. mgmt., dean Grad. Sch. Mgmt., U. Calif. at Los Angeles, 1970-77; pres., dir. Special Investments & Securities Inc., 1961-66; chmn. SEC, Washington, 1977—. Mem. Commn. for Econ. Devel. State of Calif., 1973-77; energy coordinator City of Los Angeles, 1973-74; pub. mem. Nat. Advt. Review Bd., 1971-75; co-chmn. Pub. Commn. on Los Angeles County Govt. Served as 1st lt. AUS, 1950-53. Mem. State Bar Calif. Office: SEC Washington DC 20549

WILLIAMS, HAROLD MILTON, trade assn. exec.; b. Lemmon, S.D., Oct. 10, 1907; s. William Daniel and Lillian (Jackson) W.; B.A., U. Wis., 1929; M.B.A., U. Chgo., 1947; m. Alice Rosamond Fox, Jan. 20, 1931; children—Rosemary Williams DeMore, Martha E., Maudie G. Williams Bremer, David H., Daniel J. With Swift & Co., Chgo., 1929-31, Williams Packing Co., Chgo., 1931-43; plant mgr. Hofhers Meat Co., Chgo., 1943-44; v.p. Fox De Luxe Foods, Inc., Chgo., 1944-57; pres., dir. Inst. Am. Poultry Industries, Chgo., 1958-71, Inst. Am. Poultry Industries Internat., 1968—; pres. Poultry and Egg Inst. Am., Chgo., 1971—; dir. Poultry and Egg Nat. Bd., 1959—; treas. Asso. Poultry and Egg Industries, 1967-69. Mem. U.S. Pres.'s Food for Peace Com., 1962—; adminstr. coop. program between Fgn. Agr. Service of U.S. Dept. Agr. and Inst. Am. Poultry Industries, 1958; del. European Am. Symposium on Agr. Trade, Amsterdam, Holland, 1963; del. White House Conf. on Food and Nutrition, 1969; del., speaker Nat. Symposium on Salmonella, 1964. Named hon. citizen Kansas City, Mo., 1963, New Orleans, 1968. Mem. U.S. Livestock San. Assn., Inst. Food Technologists, Assn. Food and Drug Ofcls. U.S., Def. Supply Assn. Inst. Sanitation Mgmt., Food Packaging Council (gov.), Chgo. Assn. Commerce and Industry, Am. Freedom from Hunger Found., Phi Kappa Phi. Clubs: Serra of North Shore, Executive, Lake Shore (Chgo.); University (Washington); Executive Program (U. Chgo.). Home: 2842 W Chase Ave Chicago IL 60645 Office: 135 S LaSalle St Chicago IL 60603

WILLIAMS, HAROLD MURDOCH, adhesive mfg. co. exec.; b. Oswego, N.Y., July 13, 1922; s. George Walter and Verna Ida (Murdoch) W.; B.M.E., Cleve. State U., 1955; m. Gladys Bell, Mar. 15, 1947. Project engr. Bailey Meter Co., Wickliffe, Ohio, 1959-61, mgr. spl. design dept., 1961-65, contract adminstr., 1965-70; mgr. process devel. Fasson Co. div. Avery Internat., Painesville, Ohio, 1970-74, mgr. indsl. systems, 1974—. Served with USAF, 1942-45. Mem. Cleve. Engring. Soc., U.S. Yacht Racing Union, Highlander Nat. Assn., Order of Engr. Clubs: Mentor Harbor Yacht, Cedarwood Beach (past pres.). Home: 6142 Cedarwood Rd Mentor OH 44060 Office: 205 Chester St Painesville OH 44077

WILLIAMS, HARRY JOHN, JR., accountant; b. Marion, Ill., Mar. 10, 1924; s. Harry John and Helita (Durham) W.; B.B.A., Tulane U., 1948; m. Joanne Elizabeth Schwartz, Nov. 1, 1947; children—Kathleen W. Trenchard, Marianne W. Antoine, Barbara W. Moose, Harry John III. With Peat, Marwick, Mitchell and Co., St. Louis, 1948-53; pvt. practice acctg., New Orleans, 1953-76; mng. partner Harry Williams and Co., New Orleans, 1976—; lectr. Tulane U., 1953-56; co-founder Asso. Regional Accounting Firms, chmn., 1969-71. Served with USNR, 1943-46. Mem. Am. Inst. C.P.A.'s, Soc. La. C.P.A.'s (pres. New Orleans chpt. 1964-65, parliamentarian 1971-72, dir. 1964-65, 71-72, mem. trial bd. 1972-76, chmn. 1972-73, chmn. numerous coms.), Acctg. Research Assn., New Orleans Estate Planning Council (treas. 1970-71), New Orleans Bd. Trade, Chamber New Orleans and River Region, Econ. Devel. Council, Com. of 50, Pi Kappa Alpha. Clubs: Pickwick, So. Yacht, Internat. House-World Trade Center (dir. 1975—, v.p. 1979—), Rotary (New Orleans). Methodist. Democrat. Editor La. C.P.A., 1961-62. Contbr. articles to profl. jours. Home: 6824 Vicksburg St New Orleans LA 70124 Office: 5110 One Shell Sq New Orleans LA 70139

WILLIAMS, JAMES BRYAN, banker; b. Sewannee, Tenn., Mar. 21, 1933; s. Eugene G. and Ellen B. Williams; A.B., Emory U., 1955; m. Betty G. Adams, July 11, 1980; children—Ellen, Beth, Bryan. Pres., Peachtree Bank & Trust Co., Chamblee, Ga., 1962-64; chmn. bd. 1st Nat. Bank & Trust Co., Augusta, Ga., 1971-73; pres., chmn. bd. Trust Co. of Ga. Assos., Atlanta, 1973—; vice chmn. bd. Trust Co. Ga., Atlanta, 1977—; dir. affiliated banks throughout Ga., Coca-Cola Co., Genuine Parts Co., Rollins, Inc., Ga. Internat. Life Ins. Co., Merry Cos., Inc. (Augusta). Bd. trustees Emory U., Westminster Schs., Henrietta Egleston Hosp. for Children, Woodruff Med. Center; bd. visitors Berry Coll. (Rome, Ga.). Served to lt., USAF, 1955-57. Mem. Assn. Res. City Bankers, Am. Bankers Assn., Ga. Bankers Assn. Presbyterian. Clubs: Piedmont Driving, Capital City, Oglethorpe, Augusta Country. Office: PO Box 4418 Atlanta GA 30302

WILLIAMS, JAMES PATRICK, automotive repair co. exec.; b. N.Y.C., Aug. 20, 1942; s. William Joseph and Aida (Losco) W.; A.A., Westchester Community Coll., 1968; B.S. in Bus., Pace Coll., 1970; m. Tangerine Forkas, Dec. 15, 1978; children—Randi, Tammy-Joy, Gina. Acct. exec. Howard Lawrence & Co., N.Y.C., 1972-74, mgr. Newark office, 1974-75; trainee Littman Jewelers, Menlo Park, N.J., 1975, mgr., 1975-76; mgr. Carol Jewelers, Suffolk County, N.Y., 1976-78; v.p., gen. mgr. Midas Muffler Shops of Suffolk County, 1978—. Served with U.S. Army, 1963-66. Mem. Nat. Franchise Assn. Coalalition, Nat. Midas Dealers Assn., Am. Mgmt. Assn., U.S. Coast Guard Aux. Club: Senatorial. Office: 207 E Sunrise Hwy Lindenhurst NY 11757

WILLIAMS, JAMES PAUL (JAY), JR., broadcasting co. exec.; b. Harvey, Ill., Oct. 19, 1944; s. James Paul and Lucille (Larson) W.; student Ind. U., 1966-67; A.B., Wabash Coll., 1966. Announcer, music dir. Sta. WAVI, Dayton, Ohio, 1967-68; music dir., personality Sta. WXLW, Indpls., 1968-69; account exec. Fairbanks Broadcasting, Sta. WNAP, Indpls., 1970-71; gen. sales mgr. Sta. WVBF, Boston, 1971-74, v.p., sta. mgr., 1974-75, v.p., gen. mgr., 1975—; pres. Broadcasting Unltd., cons. Mem. Nat. Radio Broadcasters Assn., New Eng. Broadcasting Assn. Republican. Methodist. Home: 16 Coltsway Wayland MA 01778 Office: 100 Mt Wayte Ave Framingham MA 01701

WILLIAMS, JOHN BRAXTON, JR., real estate devel. exec.; b. Indpls., Aug. 10, 1933; s. John Braxton and Jeanette Jane (Webb) W.; B.S. in Civil Engring., So. Meth. U., 1957; 1 son, John Kevin. Pres., co-owner Isles Constrn. Co., Dallas, 1955-58; chief civil engr. Wyatt C. Hedrick Architect/Engr., Dallas, 1958-60; asso., Don Fleming & Assos. Architects/Engrs., Dallas, 1961-62; constrn. engr., overseas projects, M.W. Kellogg Co., N.Y.C., 1963-65; constrn. mgr. J.C. Penney Co., Atlanta, 1966-79; chmn. bd. Arco Properties Inc., Atlanta, 1971—; dir. Trader Investment Co., Dallas, Creative Properties, Atlanta/Dallas. Republican. Unitarian. Contbr. articles to engring. jours. Office: Box 54032 Atlanta GA 30308

WILLIAMS, JOHN BRYANT, engr.; b. Narrows, Va., Apr. 23, 1925; s. John Bryant and Grace (Topper) W.; B.S., Mass. Inst. Tech., 1947; B.S., Stevens Inst. Tech., 1946, M.S., 1949, M.E., 1950; M.S., Rutgers U., 1970. Electronic engr. Hazeltine Electronics Corp., 1949-51; project devel. engr. atomic energy div. Am. Machine & Foundry Co., N.Y.C., 1951-65, tech. adviser gen. engring. lab., 1963, spl. assignment new product analysis and devel., 1964-65, mem. tech. staff Research Center, Ingersoll-Rand Co., Princeton, N.J., 1965—. Served as ensign USN, 1947-48. Registered profl. engr., Conn. Mem. Mensa, Ops. Research Soc. Am. Contbr. articles on gravity research to profl. jours. Patentee in field. Home: PO Box 177 Rocky Hill NJ 08553 Office: PO Box 301 Princeton NJ 08540

WILLIAMS, JOHN LEE, ins. co. exec.; b. Orange, N.J., June 26, 1921; s. Samuel Crane and Edna Newman (Fowler) W.; A.B., Dartmouth Coll., 1942, M.B.A., 1947; m. Beverly Margaret Schofield, June 30, 1945; children—John Lee, Jeffrey, Adrienne. Service rep. Dun & Bradstreet, N.Y.C., Newark, 1947-48; with Prudential Ins. Co., Newark, 1948-67, underwriting cons., 1967; mgr. group underwriting Blue Shield Calif., San Francisco, 1967-70; mgr. underwriting Calif. Physicians Ins. Corp., San Francisco, 1970—. Mem. Citizens Budget Advisory Com., South Orange, N.J., 1960-67; dist. leader Citizens Party League, South Orange, 1965-66. Served to capt. USMC. Mem. Western Home Office Underwriters Assn., Group Underwriters Assn. Ret. Officers Assn., Res. Officers Assn., Zeta Psi. Club: Commonwealth of Calif. Episcopalian. Home: 27 Millstone Terr San Rafael CA 94903 Office: 2 Northpoint San Francisco CA 94133

WILLIAMS, JOSEPH DALTON, pharm. mfg. co. exec.; b. Washington, Pa., Aug. 15, 1926; s. Joseph Dalton and Jane (Day) W.; B.Sc. in Pharmacy, U. Nebr., 1950, D.Pharmacy (hon.), 1978; m. Mildred E. Bellaire, June 28, 1973; children—Terri Williams, Daniel Williams. Pres., Parke-Davis Co., Detroit, 1973-76; pres. pharm. group Warner-Lambert Co., Morris Plains, N.J., 1976-77, pres. Internat. Group, 1977-79, pres., dir. Warner-Lambert Corp., 1979—, chief operating officer, 1980—; dir. Fidelity Union Bank. Served with USNR, 1943-46. Mem. Pharm. Mfrs. Assn., Am. Pharm. Assn., N.J. Pharm. Assn., Am. Soc. Hosp. Pharmacists Research and Edn. Found. Clubs: Met. (N.Y.C.); Baltusrol Golf (Springfield, N.J.). Office: Warner Lambert Co 201 Tabor Rd Morris Plains NJ 07950*

WILLIAMS, JOSEPH HILL, diversified industry exec.; b. Tulsa, June 2, 1933; s. David Rogerson and Martha Reynolds (Hill) W.; diploma St. Paul's Sch., 1952; B.A., Yale, 1956, M.A. (hon.), 1977; postgrad. Sch. Pipeline Tech. U. Tex. 1960; children—Joseph Hill Jr., Peter B., James C.; m. Terese T. Ross, May 7, 1977; stepchildren—Margot Ross, Jennifer Ross. Field employee domestic constrn. div. Williams Cos., Tulsa, 1958-60, project coordinator engring. div., 1960-61, project supt., Iran, 1961-62, asst. resident mgr., Iran, 1962-64, project mgr., 1964-65, resident mgr., 1965-67, exec. v.p., 1968—, pres., chief operating officer, 1971-78, chmn., chief exec. officer, 1979—; dir., chmn. Fed. Res. Bank of Kansas City; dir. Parker Drilling Co. Bd. dirs. Industries for Tulsa, Tulsa Area United Way, Okla. C. of C.; mem. adv. com. Jr. Achievement; fellow, trustee Yale Corp. Served with AUS, 1956-58. Mem. Am. Petroleum Inst. (dir.), Young President's Orgn., Council on Fgn. Relations, Nat. Petroleum Council, Conf. Met. Tulsa C. of C. (dir.). Episcopalian. Clubs: Southern Hills Country, Summit, Tulsa, Yale (sec.) (Tulsa); Springdale Hall (Camden, S.C.); Augusta (Ga.) Nat. Golf; Links (N.Y.); Grandfather Golf and Country (Linville, N.C.). Office: One Williams Center PO Box 2400 Tulsa OK 74103

WILLIAMS, JUDSON FINLON, investment banker; b. Ft. Worth, June 19, 1913; s. Samuel Jones Tilden and Emily Beaty (Clugston) W.; B.A., Hardin Simmons U., 1934; B.J., M.A., U. Mo., 1940; Ph.D., U. Tex., 1952; m. Jackie Roe, June 15, 1941; children—Judith Williams Ridley, Jeanne Williams Fowler, Jerith Williams Clarence, Judson Charles. High sch. prin. and coach, Rochester, Tex., 1935-36, Grandfalls, Tex., 1936-39; dir. pub. relations, instr. journalism Tex. Coll. Mines, 1940-52; dean students, prof., chmn. dept.

journalism-radio-TV, Tex. Western Coll., 1942-56, v.p., dir. White House Dept. Stores, El Paso, Tex., 1956—; v.p., dir. First Savs. & Loan Assn., El Paso, 1957—; mayor of El Paso, 1963-69; pres. Uptrends, Inc., investment bankers, 1969—; dir. Arkansas Western Gas Co., So. Union Prodn., Aero Systems, Inc., So. Union Gas Co., Mountain Bell, Bus. Products & Services, Inc.; cons. Hogg Found., 1946—, also U. Tex.; bd. advisers Mountain States Telephone Co., 1958-63. Vice pres., dir. S.W. Sun Country Assn., 1960-63; bd. dirs., mem. exec. com. Tex. Municipal League Cities, 1963, pres., 1967-69; exec. com. urban affairs So. Conf. Council State Govts., 1967—; pres. El Paso Jr. C. of C., 1947, El Paso C. of C., 1962, Southwestern Sun Carnival Assn., 1957, El Paso County Bd. Devel., 1960-62, El Paso Indsl. Devel. Corp., 1964, United Fund El Paso, 1961; bd. dirs. Lee Moore Children's Home, Energy Found. Tex.; bd. regents Tex. Tech. U. Named El Paso's Young Man of Year, 1946, El Paso's Outstanding Citizen, 1966; elected to El Paso Hall of Honor, 1973; recipient Medallion of Merit, U. Tex., 1967, Headliner of Year award by Press, 1967, Outstanding State of Tex. award Tex. Inst. Traffic Engrs., 1973. Mem. Acad. Polit. Sci., Nat. League Cities, El Paso Rancheros (past pres.), Sigma Delta Chi, Phi Delta Kappa, Kappa Tau Alpha, Alpha Phi Gamma, Alpha Epsilon Rho. Presbyterian (trustee). Clubs: Kiwanis (past pres.), Touchdown (past pres.), El Paso, El Paso Country, Coronado Country (El Paso). Contbr. articles to profl. jours. Home: 4200 O'Keefe Dr El Paso TX 79902 Office: 506 N Mesa El Paso TX 79902

WILLIAMS, LOUIS BOOTH, coll. pres.; b. Paris, Tex., Oct. 15, 1916; s. William Louis and Maggie Jo (Booth) W.; A.A., Paris (Tex.) Jr. Coll., 1935; B.B.A., U. Tex., 1951; M.B.A., E. Tex. State U., 1961; LL.D.(hon.), Tex. Wesleyan U., 1976; m. Mary Lou Newman, Oct. 15, 1939; children—Joanne Williams Click, Louis Booth. Profl. local C. of C. exec., Austin, Navasota and Paris, Tex., 1938-44; mgr. Bireley's Beverages, Denison, Tex., 1946-49; asst. to pres. Paris Jr. Coll., 1949-52, pres., 1967—; personnel mgr. Paris Works, Babcock & Wilcox Co., 1952-67; dir. Liberty Nat. Bank, Paris. Served with USNR, lt. comdr. ret. Recipient Silver Beaver award Boy Scouts Am., 1956; Paul Harris fellow Rotary Internat., 1974. Mem. Am. Assn. Community Jr. Colls., Tex. Assn. Colls. and Univs. (pres. elect 1980), Assn. Tex. Jr. Colls., Theta Kappa Omega, Delta Sigma Pi, Phi Theta Kappa (hon.). Democrat. Methodist. Club: Rotary. Author: The Organization, Functions, and Administration of a Local Chamber of Commerce, 1937. Home: 3170 Laurel Ln Paris TX 75460 Office: Paris Jr Coll Clarksville St Paris TX 75460

WILLIAMS, LOUIS STANTON, glass and chem. mfg. co. exec.; b. Honolulu, Oct. 7, 1919; s. Urban and Amelia (Olson) W.; A.B., Amherst Coll., 1941; M.B.A., Harvard, 1943; m. Dorothy Webster Reed, June 12, 1943; children—Eric Reed, Timothy Howell, Steven Neil, Deborah Reed Sawin. With PPG Industries (formerly Pitts. Plate Glass Co.), 1946—, chief accountant Creighton factory, 1948-50, div. accountant glass div., 1950-53, mgr. cost planning, glass accounting, 1953-56, asst. controller, 1956, became controller, 1956, v.p. finance, 1963-75, dir. 1975—, exec. v.p., 1975-76, vice chmn., 1976-78, chmn., chief exec. officer, 1979—; chmn. Fed. Home Loan Bank, Pitts., 1971-73; dir. Pitts.-Corning Corp., PPG Industries Can. Ltd., Duplate Can. Ltd., Dravo Corp., Rubbermaid Inc. Trustee Family and Children's Service, Pitts., 1955-61; treas. YMCA, Pitts., 1959-65, dir., 1959—, v.p., 1966-75, pres., 1975-77, mem. nat. council, 1967—, mem. nat. bd., 1973—; mem. exec. com. Allegheny Conf. on Community Devel., 1978—; bd. dirs. Community Chest Allegheny County, 1961-67, St. Margaret's Meml. Hosp., Pitts., 1969—, Pitts. Symphony Soc., 1978—; div. chmn. United Way Campaign of Allegheny County, 1975-77, bd. dirs., 1978—; trustee Carnegie-Mellon U., Carnegie Inst. Served to lt. USNR, 1943-46. Mem. Fin. Execs. Inst. (pres. Pitts. 1965-66, nat. dir. 1968-73, nat. v.p. 1972-73), Phi Beta Kappa. Presbyn. Clubs: Duquesne, Fox Chapel Golf, Harvard-Yale-Princeton (Pitts.); Laurel Valley Golf, Rolling Rock (Ligonier, Pa.); Iron City Fishing (Can.). Office: PPG Industries 1 Gateway Center Pittsburgh PA 15222*

WILLIAMS, LUKE GLADSTONE, sign mfg. co. exec.; b. Spokane, Wash., Oct. 4, 1923; s. Luke Campbell and Grace Colby (Murray) W.; student Eastern Wash. State Coll., 1940-41; m. Beuletta M. Nordby, Oct. 19, 1947; children—Brenda, Louise, Mark Edward. Co-founder, v.p. Am. Sign & Indicator Corp., Spokane, 1952-63, pres., 1963—, chief exec. officer, 1963—, also chief exec. officer of subsidiaries; dir. Seattle 1st Nat. Bank. Mem. Spokane City Council, 1962-66; chmn. Wash. State Commn., mem. exec. com. EXPO 1974; chmn. Spokane Sports Entertainment Arts and Conv. Advisory Bd.; founder Am. economy program Pacific Lutheran U., 1968; bd. dirs. Wash. State Council on Econ. Edn. Found.; trustee Comstock Found.; founder United for Wash., 1970. Served with USN, 1942-46. Named Industrialist of Yr., Wash. State Realtor's Assn., 1969; recipient Outstanding Service award Assn. Wash. Bus., 1970, Others award Salvation Army, 1970. Mem. Nat. Aswn. Mfrs. (exec. com.), Assn. Wash. Bus. (pres. 1967-69), Nat. Assn. Mfrs. (dir.), Bus., Industry Polit. Action Com. (state treas., dir.), Spokane C. of C. (chmn. 1979). Republican. Presbyterian. Clubs: Shriners (Shrine Merit award 1974), Masons, Jesters. Home: 931 Comstock Ct Spokane WA 99203 Office: 2310 N Fancher Way Spokane WA 99206

WILLIAMS, MARY LEE, mktg. exec.; b. Auxvasse, Mo., Nov. 19, 1942; d. James Jonathan and Martha Helen (Roberts) Gentry; B.S., Central Mich. U., 1978, postgrad., 1978—; m. Ralph Emerson Williams, Dec. 25, 1974; 1 dau., Shari Lee. Adminstrv. asst. to mgr. new bus. McDonnell Aircraft Co., St. Louis, 1960-63; adminstrv. asst. to corp. sec. and pres. Midland Management Co., Clayton, Mo., 1963-66; adminstrv. sec. to ops. mgr. Chrysler Corp., Cape Canaveral, Fla., 1966-69; mgr. mktg. services Travco Corp., Mt. Clemens, Mich., 1970—; guest lectr. various high schs., bus. and jr. colls., 1970—; sec. Apollo Contractors Info. Center, 1968-69. Mem. Nat. Assn. Female Execs., Nat. Bus. Edn. Assn., Nat. Secs. Assn. (Macomb County Sec. of Yr. 1971), Am. Bus. Women's Assn. (pres. Cranbrook chpt. 1978-79), Central Mich. U. Alumni Assn., Alpha Delta Pi. Home: 31524 Schoenherr Rd Warren MI 48093 Office: 26750 23 Mile Rd Mount Clemens MI 48045

WILLIAMS, MICHAEL DAVID, electronics co. exec.; b. Detroit, July 14, 1944; s. Raymond Otis and Virginia Anne (Hoener) W.; B.B.A., Eastern Mich. U., 1974, M.B.A., 1975; children—Sara Anne, Susannah. Program dir. Bur. of Bus. Services and Research, Eastern Mich. U., Ypsilanti, 1974-75, instr. bus., 1974-75; logistics planner support equipment Trident Missile System, Lockheed Missile & Space Co., Sunnyvale, Calif., 1975-78; program mgr. mfg. and test Digital Image Generation Systems, Singer-Link Advanced Products, Sunnyvale, 1978, dir. material control World Airways, Oakland, Calif., 1979-80; prodn. control mgr. linear div. Fairchild Corp., Mountain View, Calif., 1980—; cons. in logistics; pres. Logistics Inc., Santa Clara, Calif., 1977—. Vice chmn. Santa Clara Schs. Sch. Site Com., 1978. Served with U.S. Army, 1966-73. Decorated Bronze Star medal, Air medal, Purple Heart, Army Commendation medal. Mem. Soc. Logistics Engrs. (chmn.), Assn. U.S. Army. Contbr. articles to profl. jours. Home: 4874 Scarlett Wood Terr San Jose CA 95129 Office: 464 Ellis St Mountain View CA 94042

WILLIAMS, PHILIP BANNATYNE, accounting and fin. exec.; b. Waukegan, Ill., Aug. 22, 1925; s. Philip Bannatyne and Estelle Louise W.; B.S.B.A., Northwestern U., 1948; m. Marion Miles Mifflin, Mar. 25, 1960; children—Carol, Barbara, Deborah. Cons., supr. Mobil Oil Corp., N.Y.C., 1949-69; pres. Slater, Williams & Co., Inc., N.Y.C., 1969-74; controller, dir. data processing Protinal, C.A., Valencia, Venezuela, 1974-76; v.p., dir. Norcon Group Internat., N.Y.C., 1976—; dir. Norcon Corp., African-Am. Enterprises Ltd. Bd. dirs. YMCA, N.Y.C., 1960-65; treas., bd. dirs. Valencia Community Ch., 1974-76. Served with USN, 1943-46. Mem. Am. Mgmt. Assn., Systems and Procedures Assn. Baptist. Clubs: Oyster River, Cochecho Country, Rainbow Springs Farm. Author: Inflation Accounting Concepts, 1954; Profit Improvement Systems, 1970. Home: 10 Crestview Dr Dover NH 03820

WILLIAMS, PHILIP GARY, mfg. distbn. exec.; b. Davenport, Iowa, Nov. 29, 1939; s. William Ludman and Betty Jane (Blankenburg) W.; B.A., St. Ambrose Coll., 1966; m. Celia Anne Weaver, Sept. 1, 1961; children—Andrew, David. Mgmt. trainee Aluminum Co. Am., Davenport, 1966-68, supr. traffic office, 1968-70, traffic mgr., 1970-74; corp. traffic mgr. Valmont Industries, Inc., Valley, Nebr., 1974—; Nebr. state chmn. Nat. Transp. Week, 1977, 78. Chmn. bd. dirs. San. Improvement Dist. 6 Saunders County, 1976—; treas. Nebr. Dist. 11 Sch. Bd., 1976-79. Named Transp. Man of Yr., Omaha Transp. Club, 1977; recipient Nat. 1st Pl. award Nat. Transp. Week Competition, 1978. Mem. Omaha Transp. Club, Traffic Clubs Internat. (bd. dirs. Nebr. 1980—), Midwest Shipper Carrier Conf., Nebr. Motor Carrier Assn. (dir.), Nat. Maritime Council (nat. vice chmn. shippers adv. bd.), Indsl. Traffic Mgrs. Assn., Midwest Internat. Trade Assn., Delta Nu Alpha (dir. Omaha chpt.). Republican. Baptist. Clubs: Kiwanis, Masons. Home: Rural Route 5 Douglas Dr Fremont NE 68025 Office: Valmont Industries Inc Hwy 275 Valley NE 68064

WILLIAMS, RICHARD L., III, lawyer; b. Oct. 30, 1940; s. Richard L. and Ellen (Muster) W.; B.A. in History, Princeton U., 1962; LL.B., U. Va., 1965; m. Karen Carmody, Nov. 11, 1967. Admitted to Ill. bar; asso. Winston & Strawn, Chgo., 1968-74, partner, 1974-79; sr. v.p., gen. counsel Gould, Inc., Rolling Meadow, Ill. Vice pres., dir. Chgo. Tennis Patrons, 1969-74. Served to lt. USNR, 1965-68. Mem. Am. Bar Assn., Chgo. Bar Assn., Ill. Bar Assn. Clubs: Meadow, Saddle and Cycle; Midtown Tennis. Office: 10 Gould Center Rolling Meadows IL 60008

WILLIAMS, ROBERT BERESFORD, ins. exec.; b. San Francisco, June 23, 1921; s. Frank Beresford and Margaret Berkeley (Beatie) W.; B.S.E.E., U.S. Naval Acad., 1944; M.A., Stanford U., 1951; m. Vanessa Thornton, Sept. 19, 1978; children—Cara Taylor, Betsey Williams. Commd. ensign U.S. Navy, 1944, advanced through grades to lt. comdr., 1954; resigned, 1954; internat. life ins. sales, Menlo Park, Calif., 1955—, Beirut, 1965-75, London, 1954—; pres. Willinsure Ins. Services Co., Menlo Park and London, 1978-80, Robert Beresford Williams Ins. Agy., Inc., Menlo Park and London, 1979-80; industry speaker, U.S., Europe, Middle East; underwriting mem. Lloyd's of London; incorporator Empire Life Ins. Co. Trustee, U.S. Naval Acad. Found., 1968—, The Am. Coll., Bryn Mawr, Pa., 1977—; bd. dirs. Pan Pacific Music and Art Soc., 1978—. Mem. Am. Soc. C.L.U.'s (pres. 1978-79), Assn. Advanced Life Underwriters, Palo Alto Fin. Forum, Peninsula Estate Planning Council (pres. 1960-61), Nat. Assn. Life Underwriters, Leading Life Producers No. Calif. (pres. 1966-67), Million Dollar Round Table, Top of the Table, Seven Million Dollar Forum, U.S. Naval Acad. Class Assn. (pres. 1942—), Profits Unltd., Delta Upsilon. Republican. Clubs: Menlo Country, Menlo Town. Home: 414 Sand Hill Circle Menlo Park CA 94025 Office: 873 Santa Cruz Ave Menlo Park CA 94025

WILLIAMS, ROBERT FINE, business exec.; b. Los Angeles, Feb. 24, 1949; s. Donald Odeal and Janice Elaine (Fine) W.; B.A., U. Calif., Los Angeles, 1971; M.B.A., U. So. Calif., 1974; m. Kim Porter, May 30, 1976; 1 son, Sean Albert. Cons. in bus. devel., Los Angeles, 1971-74; exec. v.p. Ski-Pak, Inc., Marine Del Rey, Calif., 1973-75; v.p. Me-Books Publs. Co., Inc., Burbank, Calif., 1975-77; mktg. mgr. McCulloch Corp., Los Angeles, 1977-79, dir. interco. services, 1979—; instr. U. Calif., Los Angeles and other univs; univ. curriculum advisor. Mem. Commerce Assos., U. So. Calif. MBA Alumni Assn., U. Calif., Los Angeles MBA Alumni Assn., Assn. Internationale des Estudiants en Sciences Economiques et Commerciales Alumni Assn., Los Angeles C. of C., Los Angeles Jr. C. of C., Alpha Kappa Psi Alumni Assn. Club: Internat. Trade. Author publs. in field. Office: 5400 Alla Rd Los Angeles CA 90066

WILLIAMS, RONALD BOAL, JR., cons. co. exec.; b. Lake Forest, Ill., Dec. 23, 1938; s. Ronald Boal and Dorothy (Herreman) W.; B.A., U. Wis., 1961; M.B.A., Northwestern U., 1969; m. Sue Ellen White, Dec. 23, 1961; children—Elizabeth, Anna, Abigail. Fin. analyst Richardson Co., Melrose Park, Ill., 1965-68; adminstrv. asst. Beatrice Foods Co., Chgo., 1968-72, exec. coordinator, 1972-75, v.p.-mfg. divs., 1975-77, dir. corporate planning, 1977-80; exec. v.p. Systema Corp., Chgo., 1980—. Mem. Downers Grove (Ill.) Dist. Sch. Bd., 1976-79. Served with U.S. Navy, 1961-65. Mem. Planning Execs. Inst., Soc. Long Range Planning. Home: 4825 Seeley Ave Downers Grove IL 60515 Office: 150 N Wacker Dr Chicago IL 60602

WILLIAMS, RONALD DAVID, mining co. exec.; b. Marshall, Ark., Mar. 15, 1944; s. Noble Kentucky and Elizabeth (Karns) W.; B.A., Columbia U., 1966, B.S., 1967, M.B.A., 1973; m. Beth L. Williams, Nov. 1977; 1 dau., Stephanie Noble. Process engr. DuPont, Deepwater, N.J., 1966; design engr. Combustion Engring. Co., Hartford, 1971; cons. Arthur Andersen & Co., N.Y.C., 1973-76; corp. planner Amax Inc., Greenwich, Conn., 1976-77, group planning adminstr., 1978-80, mgr. corp. planning and analysis, 1980—; project mgr. Olin Corp., Stamford, Conn., 1977-78. Served with USN, 1967-70: Vietnam. NASA traineeship, 1971; S.W. Mudd scholar, 1971. Mem. AAAS, Am. Chem. Soc., Am. Mgmt. Assns. Democrat. Club: Appalachian Mountain. Home: 65 Glenbrook Rd Stamford CT 06902 Office: Amax Inc Amax Center Greenwich CT 06830

WILLIAMS, RUSSELL, mgmt. cons.; b. Muncie, Ind., Mar. 19, 1925; s. Russel Stanley and Gertrude Jane (Miedema) W.; B.S. in Bus. Adminstrn. and Mktg., Ind. U., 1948; m. Laura Elizabeth Evans, Jan. 14, 1950; children—Laura Christine, Sandra Lynn, Lee Anne. Exec. v.p. Gaseteria, Inc., Indpls., 1948-58; owner, mgr. Williams Investments, encompassing Fidelity Leasing, Appliance City, real estate holdings, Phoenix, 1958—; mgmt. cons., Phoenix, 1975—; pres. Western Techs., Inc., Phoenix, 1978—, also dir.; dir. S.W. Savs. & Loan, Engrs. Testing Labs.; trustee Samaritan Health Services; chmn. Ariz. Corp. Commn., 1970-73. Chmn. dean's adv. council Ariz. State U., 1971-73, founding dir. Productivity Inst., 1975; mem. bd. Community Orgn. for Drug Abuse Control, 1968-69; bd. dirs. San Pablo Home for Boys, 1970-76; chmn. investment com. Ariz. Compensation Fund, 1968-69; Republican candidate for gov. Ariz., 1974; sr. warden, vestryman All Saints Episcopal Ch., 1976-78. Served with USAAF, 1942-46. Mem. Nat. Petroleum Inst., Profl. Soc. Mgmt. Assn., Phoenix C. of C., Delta Sigma Pi. Clubs: Masons, Valley of Sun Kiwanis (pres. 1969).

WILLIAMS, SAM JOSEPH, retail trade co. exec.; b. Des Moines, Mar. 7, 1919; s. Isadore and Esther Leah (Aaron) W.; A.A., Long Beach Jr. Coll., 1940; B.S., UCLA, 1951; teaching credential Long Beach State Coll., 1952; m. Sharon Sherman, Jan. 16, 1955; children—Lisa R., Brian S. Photographer, Balboa, Calif., 1937-42; owner Dave's, Fun Zone, Balboa, 1940-42; owner Lewellyn's Restaurant, Anaheim, Calif., 1947-50; pres. The Williams Co., Fullerton and Anaheim, Calif., 1952—. Served with AUS, 1942-46. Mem. Anaheim C. of C. (dir. retail div. 1958), Alpha Delta Sigma. Lion. Home: 416 S Redwood Dr Anaheim CA 92806 Office: 112 E Commonwealth Ave Fullerton CA 92632

WILLIAMS, SANDRA VIRGINIA, bus. machines mfg. co. ofcl.; b. N.Y.C., May 14, 1945; d. Edward Barnwell and Miriam Virginia (Anderson) Williams; B.S. in Edn., Northwestern U., 1967. With IBM, 1967—, regional equal opportunity program mgr., N.Y.C., 1973-75, Gen. Bus. Group/Internat. personnel programs adv., White Plains, N.Y., 1975-77, Gen. Bus. Group/Internat. mgr. exec. compensation, 1977-78, adminstrv. asst. to IBM corp. dir. personnel programs, Armonk, N.Y., 1979, mgr. personnel resources Systems Product div., White Plains, 1979-80, hdqrs. personnel mgr., 1980—. Episcopalian.

WILLIAMS, THOMAS GARDNER, foods co. exec.; b. Kans. City, Mo., Dec. 16, 1939; s. Thomas Aaron and Viola Emelie (Schloeman) W.; B.S.B.A., U. Mo., 1962; m. Carol Ann Hunt, Sept. 26, 1965; children—Mark Thomas, Mary Elizabeth. Mgmt. trainee Guaranteed Foods, Inc., 1963-64, food sales mgr., 1964-66, non-foods mgr., 1966-67, exec. v.p., gen. sales mgr., 1968-71, v.p., ops. mgr., 1967-68, dir., 1970—, pres., gen. mgr., 1972, pres., chmn. bd., 1974—; dir. Oak Park Nat. Bank, Overland Park, Kans. Bd. commrs., v.p. Kans. Retail Council, 1976—; dir. v.p. Youth Services Bur., 1972-74; mem. Planning Commn., 1978-80; chmn. Heart Fund Campaign, Johnson County Commn., 1974; bd. dirs. City Union Mission, 1979—. Named Outstanding Young Man of Lenexa, 1975. Mem. Am. Assn. Meat Processors, Advt., Mktg. Club, Kans. Assn. Commerce and Industry, Kans. Retail Council, Frozen Food Council (dir.), Lenexa C. of C., Better Bus. Bur., Am. Royal Assn. (bd. govs. 1979—), Delta Tau Delta. Republican. Lutheran. Home: 12100 W 148th St Olathe KS 66061 Office: 8901 Rosehill Rd Lenexa KS 66215

WILLIAMS, THOMAS OLDHAM, JR., bldg. material mfg. co. exec.; b. Charleston, W.Va., Apr. 2, 1943; s. Thomas Oldham and Elizabeth (Reed) W.; B.S., Wake Forest Coll., 1964; M.B.A., U. Pa., 1966; m. Mary Elizabeth Fobert, May 3, 1960; children—Thomas Oldham III, Kathryn Elizabeth. Trainee to asst. personnel mgr. FMC Corp., Meadville, Pa., 1966-69, personnel mgr., Fredericksburg, Va., 1969-70, mfg. supt., 1970-74; adminstrv. asst. Gen. Products Co., Inc., Fredericksburg, 1974-79, v.p. mktg., 1979—; mem. faculty Pa. State U., 1966-70, Va. Community Coll., 1970-76. Mem. exec. com., bd. dirs. United Givers Fund, 1970-75; bd. dirs. New Sch., 1972-77, Hist. Fredericksburg Found., 1972-76, YMCA, 1973-77; bd. advisors Germanna Coll., 1970-76. Mem. Va. Coll. Placement Assn., Va. Mfrs. Assn., Va. C. of C., Nat. Mfrs. Assn., Fredericksburg Area C. of C. (dir. 1970-76), Fredericksburg Jr. C. of C. (pres. 1970-72), Va. Assn. Realtors. Republican. Presbyterian. Club: Rotary (pres. 1970). Home: 515 Harrison Rd Fredericksburg VA 22401 Office: Gen Products Co Inc PO Box 887 Fredericksburg VA 22401

WILLIAMS, THOMAS RICE, banker; b. Atlanta, Sept. 14, 1928; s. George Ketchum and Isabel (Rice) W.; B.S. in Indsl. Engring., Ga. Inst. Tech., 1950; M.S. in Indsl. Mgmt., M.I.T., 1954; m. Loraine Plant, Mar. 18, 1950; children—Janet Williams Osborne, Susan I., Thomas Rice. Indsl. engr. Dan River Mills, Danville, Va., 1950-53; dir. indsl. engring. Riegel Textile Corp., Ware Shoals, S.C., 1954-59; v.p. Bruce Payne & Assos., Inc., N.Y.C., 1959-64; asst. to pres. Patchoque-Plymouth Co., N.Y.C., 1964-65; v.p. Nat. City Bank Cleve., 1965-69, exec. v.p. 1969-72; pres. First Nat. Bank of Atlanta, 1972-76, chief exec. officer, 1976—, chmn. bd., 1977—; pres. First Nat. Holding Corp. (now First Atlanta Corp.), 1974—, chmn. bd., 1977—; dir. Nat. Service Industries, Inc., Equifax, Inc., ConAgra, Inc., VISA U.S.A. Inc., Nat. Life Vt. Trustee YMCA Met. Atlanta, Atlanta U. Center, Ga. Inst. Tech. Found., Agnes Scott Coll., Atlanta Arts Alliance, So. Center Internat. Studies; bd. dirs. Central Atlanta Progress, Fulton County unit Am. Cancer Soc.; mem. adv. bd. Christian Council Met. Atlanta; treas. Concerned Businessmen's Congressional Forum. Mem. Assn. Bank Holding Cos., The Conf. Bd., Assn. Res. City Bankers (dir. 1979—), Am. Bankers Assn. (governing council 1979—), Atlanta C. of C. (pres. 1980). Episcopalian. Clubs: Capital City (governing bd. 1977-80), Commerce (dir. 1976—), Piedmont Driving, Peachtree Golf; Farmington Country (Charlottesville, Va.); Union (Cleve.); Rotary (club dir. 1976-79). Office: 2 Peachtree St NW Atlanta GA 30303

WILLIAMS, TYLER EDWARD, JR., govt. ofcl.; b. Chgo., July 10, 1926; s. Tyler Edward and Anne (Salmon) W.; B.S., Ill. Inst. Tech., 1951, M.S., 1956; M.Ed., U. Va., 1972; postgrad. U. Iowa; m. Frances M. Reif, Aug. 27, 1949; children—Tyler Edward, Michael, Thomas, Margaret, Gerard, Joseph (dec.), John, Mary Frances. Dept. supr. Oscar Mayer and Co., Chgo., 1949-52; indsl. engr. Am. Gage and Machine Co., Chgo., 1952-54; sr. indsl. engr. Bendix Aviation Corp., Davenport, Iowa, 1954-55; engr., engring. exec. Ordnance Corps, U.S. Army, Rock Island Arsenal (Ill.), 1955-63, Office of Sec., Dept. Commerce, Washington, 1963-65, Office Comptroller of Army, Washington, 1965-70; fed. mid-career fellow U. Va., 1970-71; with Safeguard System Office, Hdqrs. Dept. Army, 1971-73; asst. dir. Office Sec. Def., 1973-75; asst. controller bd. govs. FRS, 1975-77; with Office Asst. Sec. Conservation, Dept. Energy, 1977—; professorial lectr. George Washington U., Washington. Commr., Fairfax County (Va.) Devel. Authority, 1975—. Served from seaman to capt. USNR, 1944—. Registered profl. engr., Iowa, Ind. Mem. AAAS, Soc. Gen. Systems Research, Am. Soc. Engring. Edn., Am. Soc. Mil. Comptrollers, Council Basic Edn., Am. Inst. Indsl. Engrs., Washington Ops. Research Soc. Contbr. articles to profl. and tech. jours. Home: 3312 Prince William Dr Mantua Hills Fairfax VA 22031 Office: Office Asst Sec Conservation US Dept Energy Washington DC 20585

WILLIAMS, W. R., accountant; b. Lena Station, La., Mar. 15, 1930; s. Eddie S. and Edna (Rashall) W.; B.S., U. Ark., 1956; m. Lovene Arlene Parker, June 30, 1956; children—Julie Marie, Janet Lynn. Mng. partner Peat, Marwick, Mitchell & Co., C.P.A.'s, 1959-74, sr. partner W. Ger., Frankfurt, 1974-78, vice chmn. S.W., Houston, 1978—. Bd. govs. Houston Grand Opera Assn., 1979—. Served with USAF, 1948-52. C.P.A., Okla. Mem. Am. Inst. C.P.A.'s, Nat. Assn. Accts., Am. Acctg. Assn., Okla. Soc. C.P.A.'s (past dir.), U. Ark. Alumni Assn. (life). Clubs: Houston, Houston Athletic, Houston Racquet, Houstonian, Brae Burn Country. Office: 4300 1 Shell Plaza Houston TX 77002

WILLIAMS, WALTER FRED, steel co. exec.; b. Upland, Pa., Feb. 7, 1929; s. Walter James and Florence (Stott) W.; B.Civil Engring. summa cum laude, U. Del., 1951; m. Joan Bernice Carey, Aug. 26, 1950; children—Jeffrey F., Richard C., Douglas E. With Bethlehem Steel Corp. (Pa.), 1951—, chief engr. constrn., Burns Harbor (Ind.) plant, 1966-67, mgr. engring. in charge projects, design and constrn., 1967-68, asst. to v.p. engring., 1968, asst. v.p. shipbldg., 1968-70, v.p., shipbldg., 1970-75, v.p. steel ops., 1975-77, sr. v.p. steel ops., 1978-80, pres. and chief ops. officer, 1980—, also dir. Served to 1st lt. U.S. Army, 1951-53. Mem. Am. Iron and Steel Inst. Methodist. Clubs: Saucon Valley Country (Bethlehem); Laurel Valley Country (Ligonier, Pa.). Home: Saucon Valley Rd 4 Bethlehem PA 18015 Office: Bethlehem Steel Corp Bethlehem PA 18016

WILLIAMS, WILLIAM EUGENE, business services co. exec.; b. Phila., Sept. 16, 1926; s. Nye and Ruth Francis (Beeker) W.; B.S., Temple U., 1949; m. Mary Jane White, May 12, 1951; children—William Nye, Wendy Ann. Propr., Nye & Parker Co., Camden, N.J., 1949-52; dist. mgr. Sinclair Oil Co., Pa., N.J. and Md., 1952-54; chief analyst Sindlinger Co., Swathmore, Pa., 1954-58; v.p. P.M.M. Inc., Haddonfield, N.J., 1958-63, pres., 1963—; dir. Para-Ml. Co., Collegeville, Md. Mem. N.J. Adv. Bd., 1973-75, N.J. Exec. Bd., 1976-78. Recipient various grants, commendation awards. Mem. Am. Soc. Tng. Dirs., Profl. Engring. Club Phila., Creative Behavior Inst., Indsl. Mgmt. Soc., State Dirs. Assn. Lutheran. Clubs: Square Circle Gun, Masons, Shriners. Author tng. manuals. Home: 211 Elm Ave Haddonfield NJ 08033 Office: 77 Ellis St Haddonfield NJ 08033

WILLIAMS, WILLIAM ROSS, real estate broker, investment counselor, developer; b. Grand Junction, Colo., Sept. 7, 1950; s. Wilbur Deloss and Theresa Louise (Turman) W.; student Colo. State U., 1968-69; m. Deborah Ann Plass, July 23, 1971 (div.); children—William Ryan, Amy Marie, Trevor Patrick. Machinery salesman Schloss and Shubart Co., Denver, 1970-72; land salesman The Pinery, Denver, 1972-73; real estate salesman Greater Denver Properties, 1974, Grubb and Ellis, 1975; pres. Property Resources, Inc., Denver, 1975—; v.p. Devel. Resources Inc., Denver; prin. William R. Williams Investments; cons. real estate investment, apt. mgmt. Mem. Nat. Assn. Realtors, Denver Art Mus., Denver Polic Protective Assn. Republican. Episcopalian. Club: Masons. Home: 6495 Happy Canyon Rd Denver CO 80237 Office: 50 S Steele St Denver CO 80209

WILLIAMS, WILLIAM WARNER, banker; b. Opelika, Ala., July 1, 1933; s. Richard D. and Marye (Warner) W.; B.S. in Indsl. Mgmt., Auburn U., 1955; grad. Banking Sch. of South, La. State U., 1976; postgrad. sr. bank officers seminar Harvard U. Grad. Sch. Bus. Adminstrn., 1977; m. Alice Paxson, Nov. 23, 1957; children—William Warner, Robert Clayton. Various sales promotion assignments Owens Corning Fiberglas Corp., Houston, 1955-60, Richmond, Va., 1960-62, Greenville, S.C., 1962-63, Columbia, S.C., 1963-64, Birmingham, Ala., 1964-65; sales mgr. Caststone Corp., Opelika, Ala., 1965-67; personnel dir. West Point Pepperell Inc., Opelika, 1967-70; exec. v.p., cashier Farmers Nat. Bank, Opelika, 1970—, also dir. Chmn. Opelika United Appeal Campaign, 1971-72; chmn. Opelika Community Chest, 1973-74. Bd. dirs. Ala. Soc. Crippled Children and Adults; chmn. bd. Jr. Achievement Chattahoochee-Lee, 1973-74; chmn. adv. com. Opelika Achievement Center, 1973-74; chmn. trustees Opelika Arts Assn., 1974—. Served with AUS, 1955-57. Mem. Opelika C. of C. (dir. 1976-77, pres. 1978), Opelika Downtown Bus. Assn. (dir. 1972-74), Alpha Tau Omega. Methodist. Clubs: Elks, Kiwanis (dir. 1976), Saugahatchee Country. Office: Farmers Nat Bank 707 Ave A Opelika AL 36801

WILLIAMS, WINTON HUGH, civil engr.; b. Tampa, Fla., Feb. 14, 1920; s. Herbert DeMain and Alice (Grant) W.; grad. Adj Gens. Sch., Gainesville, Fla., 1943; student U. Tampa, 1948; grad. Transp. Sch., Ft. Eustis, Va., 1949; B.C.E., U. Fla., 1959; grad. Command and Gen. Staff Coll., Ft. Levenworth, Kans., 1964, Engrs. Sch., Ft. Belvoir, 1965, Indsl. Coll. Armed Forces, Washington, 1966, Logistics Mgmt. Center, Ft. Lee, Va., 1972; m. Elizabeth Walser Seelye, Dec. 18, 1949; children—Jan, Dick, Bill, Ann. Constrn. engr. air fields C.E., U.S. Army, McCoy AFB, Fla., 1959-61, Homestead AFB, Miami, Fla., 1961-62; civil engr. C.E., Jacksonville (Fla.) Dist. Office, 1962-64, chief master planning and layout sect., mil. br., engring. div., 1964-70; chief master planning and real estate div. Hdqrs. U.S. Army So. Command, Ft. Amador, C.Z., 1970-75, spl. asst. planning and mil. constrn. programming Marine Corps Air Bases Eastern Area, Marine Corps Air Sta., Cherry Point, N.C., 1975—. Active Boy Scouts, C.Z.; mem. nat. council U. Tampa. Served with AUS, World War II, Korean War; ETO, Korea; col. Res. Decorated Breast Order of Yun Hi (Republic of China); presdl. citation, Meritorious Service medal (Republic of Korea); eagle scout with gold palm; registered profl. engr., Fla., N.C., C.Z. Fellow ASCE; mem. Res. Officers Assn. (life, v.p. C.Am. and S.Am.), Nat. Soc. Profl. Engrs., Profl. Engrs. N.C., Prestressed Concrete Inst. (profl.), Soc. Am. Mil. Engrs. (engr.), Nat. Eagle Scout Assn., Nat. Rifle Assn. Am., Am. Legion (life), Order Arrow, Theta Chi. Presbyterian. Lion. Clubs: Fort Clayton Riding (pres.), Fort Clayton Golf, Gamboa Golf and Country, Balboa Gun, Am. Bowling Congress. Home: 4408 Coral Point Dr Morehead City NC 28557 Office: Facilities Devel Dept Office of Dir Installations and Logistics Marine Corps Air Station Cherry Point NC 28533

WILLIAMSON, CALEB RICHMOND, investments and real estate devel. co. exec.; b. Danville, Va., Oct. 24, 1928; s. Thomas Spencer and Mary Dodson (Richmond) W.; A.B. in English, Washington and Lee U., 1951. Partner, Piedmont Builders Co., 1954-57; pres., owner Southeastern Services Corp., 1958-59, Asso. Services, Corp., Danville, 1959—. Served to lt. (j.g.) USCG, 1951-53. Mem. Soc. of Cincinnati, Beta Theta Phi. Presbyterian. Office: 227 Lynn St Danville VA 24541

WILLIAMSON, CLARENCE WILLIE, bank exec.; b. Ft. Benning, Ga., Oct. 15, 1949; s. Clarence and Edda Ree (Farmer) W.; B.A., Morris Brown Coll., 1971; m. Gloria Elaine Mattison, June 10, 1972; 1 dau., Tannis Jenine. With The Citizens and So. Nat. Bank, Atlanta, 1971—, v.p. community banking, 1978—. Bd. dirs. Dekalb Metro Fair Housing Assn. Mem. Morris Brown Coll. Alumni Assn., Nat. Bankers Assn., Atlanta Urban Bankers Assn., Robert Morris Assos., Alpha Phi Alpha. Methodist. Home: 115 Green Mountain Trail College Park GA 30349 Office: 603 North Ave Atlanta GA 30312

WILLIAMSON, FLETCHER PHILLIPS, real estate broker; b. Cambridge, Md., Dec. 16, 1923; s. William Fletcher and Florence M. (Phillips) W.; student U. Md., 1941, 42; m. Betty June Stoker, Apr. 1943; 1 son, Jeffrey Phillips; m. 2d, Helen B. Morris, Aug. 28, 1972. Test engr. Engring. Lab. Glen Martin Co., 1942-43; with Corkran Ice Cream Co., Cambridge, 1946-50; real estate broker, 1950—; pres. Williamson Real Estate, Dorchester Corp.; dir., v.p. Cargo Handlers, Inc., Colonial Consultants Ltd.; dir. Cam-Storage, Inc.; chmn. bd. Nat. Bank Cambridge, 1979—; co-receiver White & Nelson, Inc. Pres., Cambridge Hosp., United Fund Dorchester County. Served with Ordnance Tech. Intelligence, AUS, 1943-46; U.S., ETO. Mem. Md. Assn. Realtors (gov. 1956-60), Outdoor Writers Assn., Nat. Rifle Assn., Am. Ordnance Assn., Cambridge Dorchester C. of C. (dir. 1955—), Power Squadron (comdr. 1954-56). Methodist. Mason (Shriner). Clubs: Explorers, Shikar Safari, Camp Fire, Soc. of the South Pole, Chesapeake Bay Yacht, Md., Tred Avon Yacht; Anglers. Home: 310 Wildwood Dr E San Antonio TX 78212 Office: The Point US 50 PO Box 715 Cambridge MD 21613

WILLIAMSON, JAMES GASTON, JR., banker; b. Little Rock, Dec. 7, 1944; s. James Gaston and Wrenetta (Worthen) W.; B.A., Emory U., 1966; m. Carole Ridgely McCann, May 30, 1967; children—Edith R., Mary Wrenetta. Asst. comptroller Twin City Bank, North Little Rock, Ark., 1970-73, v.p., comptroller, 1973-76, v.p., cashier, 1976-78, sr. v.p. and chief fin. officer, 1978—; dir. Twin City Agency, Datamatic Services, Inc. Mem. budget com. Pulaski County United Way, Little Rock, 1972-78; bd. dirs. Pulaski County unit ARC, 1977—; vice chmn. bd. dirs. Pulaski County unit Am. Heart Assn., 1972-76; treas. Ark. Opera Theatre, Little Rock, 1978; bd. dirs. United Cerebral Palsy, Better Bus. Bur. Ark., 1978, Ark. Symphony Orch.; trustee Ark. Coll., 1976—. Served as 1st lt. U.S. Army, 1966-69. Decorated Army Commendation medal. Mem. Bank Adminstrn. Inst. (sec. Central Ark. chpt. 1971, v.p. 1978, pres. 1979), Ark. Soc. Fin. Mgrs. Presbyterian. Club: North Little Rock Optimist (sec.-treas. 1970-74). Home: 606 Shady Valley Dr North Little Rock AR 72116 Office: # 1 Riverfront Pl North Little Rock AR 72115

WILLIAMSON, JAMES THOMAS, JR., automobile agy. exec.; b. Mobile, Ala., Aug. 4, 1935; s. James Thomas and Sadie Louise (Yerkes) W.; student U. Ala., 1953-54, Spring Hill Coll., 1954; m. Mary Long (dec. Dec. 1979); children—Sandra, Tom III, Renee. Office mgr. Rowe Engring. Co., Mobile, 1956-58; chief estimator Folmar & Flinn Inc., Montgomery, Ala., 1958-59; v.p., gen. mgr. Jack Hamel Volkswagen, Montgomery, 1960-72; owner, pres. Roebuck Volkswagen Mazda Inc., Birmingham, Ala., 1973—. Mem. Automobile Dealers Assn., Ala. Automobile Dealers Assn., Birmingham Automobile Dealers Assn. (dir.), Mazda Motors of Am. East (chmn. nat. dealer council). Republican. Roman Catholic. Home: 3512 Kingshill Rd Mountain Brook AL 35223 Office: Roebuck Volkswagen Mazda Inc 9008 Parkway E Birmingham AL 35206

WILLIAMSON, ROBERT JOSEPH, forest products mfg. co. exec.; b. Punxsutawney, Pa., May 11, 1935; s. John Leo and Dorothy Lou (Duganier) W.; A.A. in Engring., Big Bend Community Coll., 1965; B.A. in Bus., Bellevue Coll., 1971; m. Patricia Lou Thomas, Oct. 15, 1955; children—Susan Kae, Robert J., David M., Linda D., Karen L., Gregory J., Denise M. Served as enlisted man U.S. Air Force, 1953-73; advanced through grades to chief master sgt., 1970, ret., 1973; prodn. supr. Boise Cascade Co., St. Louis, 1974, dept. mgr., 1974-75, prodn. mgr., 1975-77, plant mgr., 1977-79, plant mgr. East Greenville (Pa.) plant, 1979—. Bd. dirs. Oil City Hosp.; chmn. Tri County Vo-Tech Crafts Com. Decorated Meritorious Service award with 1 oak leaf cluster, Air Force Commendation medal with 3 oak leaf clusters, Bronze Star with 1 oak leaf cluster. Mem. Am. Mgmt. Assn., Soc. Indsl. Accts. Republican. Roman Catholic. Clubs: Wenango Country, Adelphoi Business Men's (dir.), Rotary. Home: 708 Lehigh St Quakertown PA 18951 Office: Boise Cascade State Rd East Greenville PA 18041

WILLIG, BILLY WINSTON, foundry and machine shop exec.; b. Temple, Tex., Mar. 11, 1929; s. Bruno William and Mary Sophia (Barth) W.; B.S.M.E., U. Tex., 1951; m. Lanelle Brooks, Sept. 11, 1951; children—Bruce Wayne, Jana Lynn. Mgr., owner Western Iron Works, San Angelo, Tex., 1951-71, inc., 1971, pres., mgr., 1971—. Pres., YMCA, 1980, San Angelo Industries, Inc., 1975-80; pres., dir. West Tex. Devel. Corp., 1980; council commr. Boy Scouts Am. Concho Valley Council, 1980, Silver Beaver award, 1976. Served with C.E., U.S. Army, 1952-54. Named Citizen of Year, City of San Angelo, 1979. Mem. Am. Foundrymen's Soc., Tex. Assn. Bus., San Angelo C. of C. (pres. 1978). Presbyterian. Clubs: Concho Yacht, Shriners, Masons, San Angelo Rotary (pres. 1980). Home: 1618 Shafter St San Angelo TX 76901 Office: 21 E 6th St San Angelo TX 76903

WILLING, JAMES ROBERT, investment broker; b. Boston, Mar. 6, 1936; s. James Burland and Marion Lane (Smith) W.; B.A., Dartmouth Coll., 1958; grad. N.Y. Inst. Fin., 1960; m. Sarane Wilcox Symonds, Feb. 13, 1960; children—James Bradford, Deborah Anne, Patricia Lane. With Loeb Rhoades, Hornblower & Co. and predecessors, Boston, 1960—, v.p. sales, until 1967, v.p., N.E. instl. head, 1967-79; v.p., instl. equity sales head Bache Halsey Stuart Shields, Boston, 1979—; trustee, mem. bd. investment Winchester (Mass.) Savs. Bank; dir. Clin. Chem. Labs. Inc. Trustee Children's Hosp., Boston, 1968—, Winchester Trust Funds, 1974—, Scholarship Funds Winchster, 1977—; chmn. trustees Winchester Hosp. Served with U.S. N.G., 1959-66. Mem. Bond Club Boston. Republican. Episcopalian. Club: Winchester Country. Home: 6 Clearwater Rd Winchester MA 01890 Office: 99 High St Boston MA 02110

WILLINGHAM, BEN HILL, JR., mgmt. co. exec.; b. Nashville, Aug. 6, 1937; s. Ben Hill and Dorothy (Wells) W.; B.S. in Indsl. Mgmt., Ga. Inst. Tech., 1956; m. Virginia Marie Schulte, June 27, 1960 (div. 1974); children—Ben Hill III, Kirby Shields, Katrina Marie; m. 2d, Erika Maria Wey, Mar. 15, 1979; Raw material controller Kingsboro Mills, Inc., Chattanooga, 1961-62, became adminstr., v.p., Nashville, 1963; v.p. Formfit-Rogers Co., N.Y.C. 1965-69; area dir. Europe, Genesco Inc., 1969-72; pres. Genesco Europe, AG, Zurich, Switzerland, 1969-72; pres. Robertson Assos. AG, Zurich, 1972-79, AGFIA AG, Zollikon, Switzerland, 1979—. Served as lt. USNR, 1956-61. Clubs: Union League, The Leash (N.Y.C.); Baur au Lac (Zurich). Home: Alte Landstrasse 78 8702 Zollikon Switzerland Office: Dufourstrasse 65 8702 Zollikon Switzerland

WILLIS, ARTHUR BURGESS, lawyer; b. Washington, May 22, 1914; s. Robert Chadwick and Mary Ermine (Burgess) W.; B.C.S., Benjamin Franklin U., 1933, M.C.S., 1935; postgrad. George Washington U., 1935-38, George Washington U. Sch. Law, 1938-39, Loyola U. Sch. Law, Chgo., 1939-41; J.D., Loyola U., Los Angeles, 1942; m. Evelyn Marjorie Davis, Aug. 11, 1939; children—Jean Louise, Allen Lloyd. Mgr. tax dept. Arthur Andersen & Co., C.P.A.'s, 1936-45; admitted to Calif. bar, 1943; practiced in Los Angeles, 1945—; partner firm Dempsey, Thayer, Deibert & Kumler, Attys., 1945-47, Willis, Butler, Scheifly, Leydorf & Grant, Attys. and predecessors, 1947—. Vis. lectr. U. Calif. at Berkeley, 1964—; instr. U. So. Calif. Sch. Law, Los Angeles, 1951-60, mem. planning com. Inst. Fed. Taxation, 1954-69; mem. adv. com. N.Y. U. Inst. Fed. Taxation, 1962-66; chmn. adv. group to Mills subcom. Ways and Means Com., U.S. House Reps., 1956-61; chmn. ann. tax and probate forum Title Ins. & Trust Co., Los Angeles, 1966—; chmn. Commn. to Revise Tax Structure 1969—. Trustee exec. com., investment com. U. of Redlands, 1964-76, J.W. and Ida M. Jameson Found. Recipient Distinguished Alumni award Benjamin Franklin U., Washington, 1964; Dana Latham Meml. award for contbn. to community and tax bar. Fellow Am. Bar Found., Am. Judicature Soc., Am. Law Inst. (tax adv. group estate and gift taxation); mem. Am., Calif., Los Angeles County, Orange County bar assns., Phi Alpha Delta. Republican. Presbyterian (elder). Club: California (Los Angeles). Author: Handbook of Partnership Taxation, 1957; Willis on Partnership Taxation, 1971; Partnership Taxation, 1976. Editor: Studies in Substantive Tax Reform, 1969. Contbr. numerous articles to law jours. Home: 800 W 1st St Box 158 Los Angeles CA 90012 Office: Willis Butler Scheifly Leydorf & Grant Attys 606 S Olive St Los Angeles CA 90014

WILLIS, CLIFFORD LEON, engring. co. exec.; b. Chanute, Kan., Feb. 20, 1913; s. Arthur Edward and Flossie Duckworth (Fouts) W.; B.S., U. Kans., 1939; Ph.D., U. Wash., 1950; m. Serreta Margaret Thiel, Aug. 21, 1947; 1 son, David Gerard. Asst. prof. geology U. Wash., 1950-54; chief geologist Harza Engring Co., Chgo., 1954-67, v.p., 1967—. Cons. geologist. Served to lt. USCG, 1942-46. Recipient Haworth distinguished alumnus award U. Kan., 1963. Fellow Geol. Soc. Am., Geol. Soc. London; mem. Am. Soc. Petroleum Geologist, Assn. Engring. Geologists, Am. Inst. Mining Metall. and Petroleum Engrs. Internat. Soc. Soil Mechanics and Found. Engring., Internat. Soc. Rock Mechanics, Sigma Xi, Tau Beta Pi, Sigma Tau, Theta Tau. Roman Catholic. Home: 16 Briar Rd Golf IL 60029 Office: 150 S Wacker Dr Chicago IL 60606

WILLIS, FREDERICK WYBORN, bldg. and consumer products co. exec.; b. Toledo, Apr. 5, 1928; s. Francis W. and Mildred B. (Rowland) W.; B.B.A., U. Mich., 1951; m. Ada E. Crouch, June 12, 1949; children—Frederick R., Robin Lynn, William Todd. Mgr. materials Willis-Overland, Inc., Toledo, 1951-64; v.p. Harris Intertype, Inc., Cleve., 1964-71; corporate v.p., pres. Bldg. and Consumer Products div. Leigh Products, Inc., Coopersville, Mich., 1971—. Bd. dirs. Jr. Achievement, Cleve., 1967-71, Project Youth 70; mem. bus. adv. bd. Wilberforce U., 1970-71. Mem. Coopersville C. of C., Fin. Execs. Inst., Phi Sigma Kappa. Republican. Lutheran. Clubs: Spring Lake (Mich.) Country, Masons. Home: 16230 Woodcrest St Spring Lake MI 49456 Office: Leigh Products Inc Coopersville MI 49404

WILLIS, GLENN HARRY, oil co. exec.; b. Magnolia, Ark., Apr. 18, 1922; s. Bernard B. and Irene (Thornton) W.; B.S. in Petroleum Engring., U. Okla., 1950; m. Louise McKinney, May 11, 1948; children—Stephen, Susan, Mary Lynn, Glenda. Oil buyer Standard Oil of Ind., New Orleans, 1950-55; oil buyer Clark Oil & Refining Corp., Dallas, 1955-66, v.p. crude oil supply and transp. dept., 1966-76; v.p., dir. Intercontinental Petroleum Corp. Inc., 1976-77; pres., dir. Dorchester Petroleum Co., Dallas, 1977—; v.p. Dorchester Refining Co., 1977—, Dorchester Pipeline Co., 1977—, Dorchester Gas Corp., 1977—; exec. v.p. Clark Maritime Inc.; dir. Southcap Pipe Line Co., Chgo. Pipeline Co., Clark Pipeline Co. Active precinct worker Democratic party 1959—. Served with AUS, 1940-45. Decorated Combat Infantryman's badge. Mem. Am. Inst. Mining Engrs. Clubs: Petroleum of Dallas, Dallas Athletic; Austin (Tex.). Home: 11084 Erhard Dr Dallas TX 75228 Office: 5735 Pineland Dr Dallas TX 75231

WILLIS, HAROLD WENDT, SR., dairy and gas sta. chain exec.; b. Marion, Ala., Oct. 7, 1927; s. Robert James and Della (Wendt) W.; student Loma Linda U., 1960, various courses San Bernardino Valley Coll.; m. Patsy Gay Bacon, Aug. 2, 1947 (div. Jan. 1975); children—Harold Wendt II, Timothy Gay, April Ann, Brian Tad, Suzanne Gail; m. 2d, Vernette Jacobson Osborne, Mar. 30, 1980. Partner, Victoria Guernsey, San Bernardino, Calif., 1950-63, co-pres., 1963-74, pres., 1974—; owner Quik-Save, 1966—, K-Mart Shopping Center, San Bernardino, 1969—; pres. Energy Delivery Systems, Food and Fuel, Inc. San Bernardino City water commr., 1965—. Bd. councillors Loma Linda (Calif.) U., 1968—, pres., 1971-74. Served as officer U.S. Mcht. Marine, 1945-46. Recipient Silver medal in 3000 meter steeplechase Sr. Olympics, U. So. Calif., 1979; lic. pvt. pilot. Mem. Calif. Dairy Industries Assn. (pres. 1963, 64), Liga Internat. (2d v.p. 1978). Seventh-day Adventist (deacon 1950-67). Home: 1155 E Ponderosa Dr San Bernardino CA 92404 Office: PO Box 5607 San Bernardino CA 92412

WILLIS, ROBERT ERWIN, financial exec.; b. Atlanta, Jan. 2, 1942; s. William Leslie and Margaret Louise (Nail) W.; B.S., So. Ill. U., Edwardsville, 1968; m. Sherrin Newsome, Oct. 26, 1973; children—Robert Erwin II, William Eugene, Valerie Lorene. Supr. mail service So. Ill. U., 1962-66; accountant Prince Gardner Co., St. Louis, 1966-68; controller Northwestern Constrn. Co., Chamblee, Ga., 1968-69; sr. accountant Touche Ross & Co., Charlotte, N.C., 1969-72; controller Savannah Foods & Industries (Ga.), 1972-78; corporate group controller Rollins, Inc., Atlanta, 1978—. C.P.A., Ga., N.C. Mem. Nat. Assn. Accountants (pres. chpt. 1975—), Am. Inst. C.P.A.'s, Am. Accounting Assn. Home: 2761 Breckenridge Ct Atlanta GA 30345 Office: 2170 Piedmont Rd Atlanta GA 30324

WILLIS, WILLIAM ERVIN, lawyer; b. Huntington, W.Va., Oct. 11, 1926; s. Asa Hannon and Mae (Davis) W.; student Ind. U., 1944, N.Y. U., 1945; A.B., Marshall U., 1948; J.D., Harvard, 1951; m. Joyce Litteral, Sept. 1, 1949; children—Kathryn Willis Cunningham, Anne Willis Dresser, William. Admitted to N.Y. bar, 1952; practiced in N.Y.C., 1951—; mem. firm Sullivan & Cromwell, 1951—; lectr. Practising Law Inst., 1963—; trustee Fed. Bar Council, 1968-72; mem. 2d Circuit commn. on reduction burdens and costs of civil litigation, 1977—. Served with AUS, 1944-46. Fellow Am. Coll. Trial Lawyers, Am. Bar Found.; mem. Am., N.Y. State (chmn. antitrust sect. 1976-77, exec. com. 1976—) bar assns., Assn. Bar City N.Y., Am. Judicature Soc., Am. Arbitration Assn. (arbitrator), Fed. Bar Council, N.Y. County Lawyers Assn., N.Y. Law Inst. Clubs: Broad St., Internat. (Washington). Contbg. editor N.Y. CPLR & Forms, 1963; contbr. articles to profl. jours. Home: Dogwood Ln Alpine NJ 07620 also 62 Otterhole Rd West Milford NJ 07480 Office: 125 Broad New York NY 10004

WILLIS, WILLIAM HAROLD, JR., mgmt. cons., exec. search specialist; b. Harrisburg, Pa., Dec. 19, 1927; s. William Harold and Elizabeth Tilford (Keferstein) W.; B.A., Yale U., 1949; m. Pauline Sabin Smith, Oct. 15, 1955; children—Wendell, Christopher, Gregory. Mktg. mgr. Owens-Corning Fiberglas Corp., N.Y.C., 1956-62; div. mgr. AMF, Inc., Greenwich, Conn., 1962-65; partner Devine, Baldwin & Willis, N.Y.C., 1965-70; pres. William H. Willis, Inc., N.Y.C., 1970—. Bd. dirs. Girls Clubs Am., Inc., N.Y.C., 1962-80, treas., chmn. fin. com., 1961-76, chmn. devel. com., 1976-77; vestryman St. Barnabas Episcopal Ch., Greenwich, Conn., 1978-81. Served with U.S. Army, 1950-52. Mem. Assn. Exec. Recruiting Cons. (past chmn. admissions com., dir. 1979—), Am. Mgmt. Assn. Republican. Clubs: Yale, Racquet and Tennis (N.Y.C.). Home: 275 Round Hill Rd Greenwich CT 06830 Office: 445 Park Ave New York NY 10022

WILLMAN, JOHN NORMAN, hosp., lab. and med. equipment mfg. co. exec.; b. St. Joseph, Mo., Jan. 19, 1915; s. John N. and Frances (Potter) W.; student St. Benedict's Coll., 1936; B.A., St. Louis U., 1979; m. Victoria King, May 9, 1941; 1 dau., Victoria. With Am. Hosp. Supply Co., 1940-59; v.p., 1954-59; with Brunswick Corp., St. Louis, 1959-68, v.p., 1961-68, pres. health and sci. div., 1961-68; v.p., dir. Sherwood Med. Industries, Inc., St. Louis, 1961-67, pres., dir., 1967-72, vice chmn., dir. 1972-73; pres., chief exec. officer, dir. IPCO Hosp. Supply Corp., White Plains, N.Y., 1973-78; mgmt. cons., 1978—; dir. Nat. Patent Devel. Corp., 1980—. Clubs: Nonday, St. Louis, Old Warson Country (St. Louis). Home: 530 N Spoede Rd Creve Coeur MO 63141

WILLMANN, CAMILLA CLAUDIA, tax preparation co. exec.; b. Greenville, Ill., Jan. 27, 1916; d. Charles Harrison and Dorcas Camilla (Foulon) McLean; m. Frederick E. Willmann, Jan. 27, 1945; children—Charles L., Mary S., William E., Max Louie. Owner, mgr. H & R Block, Greenville. Treas. Bond County Health Improvement; sec. Utlaut Hosp. Aux.; sponsor Illini Mid-State Tumblers; sponsor women's slowpitch softball team. Mem. Greenville C. of C., Bond County Bus. and Profl. Club (charter; treas., chmn. fin. com.),

Greenville Retailers Assn. Republican. Roman Catholic. Home: Rt 2 Pocahontas IL 62275 Office: 217 S 3d St Greenville IL 62246

WILLNER, EUGENE BURTON, beverage co. exec.; b. Chgo., July 27, 1934; s. Fred and Mae (Goodhartz) W.; B.A., Northwestern U., 1956; m. Karen Nell Kaye, Feb. 22, 1962; children—Tracy Fran, Kelly Kaye. Pres., World Wide Fisheries Inc., Chgo., 1956-60; merchandiser Edison Bros. Stores Inc., St. Louis, 1960-66; v.p. Mo. Supreme Life Ins. Co., St. Louis, 1966-67; exec. v.p. Exec. Agys., Inc., St. Louis, 1966-67; pres. Bluff Creek Industries, Inc., Ocean Springs, Miss., 1967-69, Purse String Stores, Inc., Miami, Fla., 1968-69, World Wide Fisheries, Inc., Miami, Fla., 1969-73, Universal Fisheries, Inc., Miami, 1974—; chmn. bd. Astral Liquors, Inc., Miami, 1977—; chmn. bd., pres. Renwill Corp. Am., Miami and Beverly Hills, Calif., 1976—; chmn. bd. Prime Universal Seafood Corp., Miami, also Key West, Fla., Caracas, Venezuela, San Juan del Sur, Nicaragua, Quito, Ecuador. dir. Mo. Supreme Life Ins. Co., Lite Am. Corp. Clubs: Cricket, Kingsbay Country, Jockey. Home: 8400 SW 146th St Miami FL 33158 Office: 3000 Biscayne Blvd Miami FL 33137

WILLNER, JAY R., cons. co. exec.; b. Aurora, Ill., Sept. 22, 1924; s. Charles R. and Ida (Winer) W.; student U. Calif. at Los Angeles, 1946-48; B.S., Mass. Inst. Tech., 1950; M.B.A., Rutgers U., 1959; m. Suzanne Wehmann, July 17, 1958; 1 son, Adam Wehmann. Lab. researcher Andrew Brown Co., Los Angeles, 1950-52; tech. salesman Glidden Co., Los Angeles, 1952-54; market researcher Roger Williams Inc., N.Y.C., 1954-59; sr. market analyst Calif. Chem. Co., San Francisco, 1959-63; mgr. planning Chem. Coatings div. Mobil Chem. Co., N.Y.C., 1963-68; pres. WEH Corp., San Francisco, 1968—; lectr. U. Calif. at Berkeley, 1962—; adj. faculty U. San Francisco, 1977—. Served from pvt. to 2d lt., A.C., AUS, 1943-46. Mem. Am. Chem. Soc., Chem. Market Research Assn., Golden Gate Paint and Coatings Assn., Chem. Coaters Assn. Clubs: Chemists (N.Y.C.); M.I.T. No. Calif. Home: 2011 Vallejo St San Francisco CA 94123 Office: WEH Corp PO Box 40066 San Francisco CA 94140

WILLOUGHBY, ERNEST DWIGHT, govt. ofcl.; b. Flint, Mich., Mar. 6, 1932; s. Ernest Clyde and Marion Amelia (Fletcher) W.; B.S., Wayne State U., 1955, postgrad. in Humanities, 1960-65; m. Ann Harper, June 11, 1960; 1 son, Ernest Frank. With Mich. Employment Security Commn., Detroit, 1959-72, 73—, mgr. occupational research, 1975—; tech. expert in occupational research UN, Tanzania and Ethiopia, 1972-73; lectr. occupational analysis Wayne State U., Oakland U.; mem. career-job placement service advisory bd. Detroit Pub. Schs., 1976-79; mem. Fed. Occupational Analysis Coordinating Com., 1980—, Mich. Adv. Com. on Occupational Info. for Disabled. Chmn. Mich. Combined Episcopal Services Appeal, 1972. Served with U.S. Army, 1955-57. Recognized for career edn. work Mich. Legislature, 1977. Mem. Am. Welding Soc. (nat. com. on classification welders 1974-76), Econometric Soc., Internat. Assn. Personnel in Employment Services, Mensa. Episcopalian. Author: Occupational Analysis and Classification, Tanzania, 1975; contbr. occupational definitions to Dictionary of Occupational Titles, 1965, 77. Home: 15945 Curtis St Detroit MI 48235 Office: Mich Employment Security Commn 7310 Woodward Ave Detroit MI 48202

WILLOUGHBY, KEITH GODWIN, banker; b. Milw., Feb. 5, 1927; s. Geoffrey and Marian van Arsdale (Helliwell) W.; B.A. in Econs., U. Wis., 1950, M.A., 1951; diploma Stonier Sch. Banking, 1966; m. Lieselotte Haack; children—Geoffrey, Gregory. Mcpl. credit analyst Dun & Bradstreet, Inc., 1955-59; with Govt. Bond House, N.Y.C., 1959-61; 2d v.p. Chase Manhattan Bank, N.Y.C., until 1968; with Mut. Bank for Savs., and predecessor, Newton Centre, Mass., 1968—, exec. v.p., 1971-73, pres., 1973—; mem. Gov. Mass. Capital Task Force, 1976; dir. Adams Fiduciary Bond Fund, 1977—. Trustee, Lasell Jr. Coll., Newton, Mass., 1977—; bd. dirs. YMC Union, Boston, 1976—. Mem. Nat. Assn. Mut. Savs. Banks (chmn. com. assets and liability mgmt. 1976-79), Savs. Banks Econ. Forum, Savs. Banks Assn. Mass. (chmn. securities com. 1971-75, chmn. planning com. 1979, now 2d vice chmn.). Address: 1188 Centre St Newton Centre MA 02159

WILLS, CLIFFORD ROBERT, govt. ofcl.; b. Milw., May 15, 1920; s. Elias and Grace (Simon) W.; student Layton Sch. Art, 1945, U. Wis., 1960-70; m. Alice M. Nelson, Dec. 1, 1945; children—Thomas Robert, Rodger James, Dianne Marie. Photographer, Sturgeon Bay, Wis., 1938-42, 45-48; officer Door County (Wis.) Vets. Service, 1951-55; with Dept. Vets. Affairs, 1955—, dep. sec., Madison, 1966—. Active Boy Scouts Am., 1955-65, Youth Baseball, 1955-62; mem. City of Monoma Sts. and Transp. Commn., 1962—. Served with USAAF, 1942-43. Recipient Nat. Meritorious Service awards VFW, 1975, Polish Legion Am. Vets., 1976, Nat. Assn. Concerned Vets., 1978, Am. Legion, 1979, others. Mem. DAV, Am. Legion, Amvets. Roman Catholic. Address: 77 N Dickinson St Madison WI 53702

WILLS, LARRY GENE, oil securities co. exec.; b. Cape Girardeau, Mo., Sept. 27, 1937; s. Tillman E. and Glenda (Thompson) W.; B.S., S.E. Mo. State U., 1958; J.D., U. Mo., 1961; diploma Coll. Fin. Planning; m. Sharon Van Sciver, Sept. 7, 1961; children—Heidi Jo, Rebecca Jane, Julie Katherine, Daniel Thomas, Christopher Bradley. Spl. agt. FBI, Washington, Pitts., Monterey, Calif. and Phila., 1961-67; rep. Raymond, James & Assos., Inc., St. Petersburg, Fla., 1967-68, br. office mgr., Orlando, Fla., 1968-70, v.p. Planning Corp. Am. subs., St. Petersburg, 1970-71; v.p. Petro Lewis Securities Corp., Denver, 1971—, also dir. Former regent, former chmn. bd. regents Coll. Fin. Planning. Mem. Internat. Assn. Fin. Planners (past nat. dir., mem. exec. com.), Am., Mo. bar assns., Inst. Certified Fin. Planners. Republican. Lutheran. Club: Kiwanis. Home: 6744 Alpine Dr Parker CO 80134 Office: PO Box 2250 717 17th St Denver CO 80201

WILLSON, EDWIN LLOYD, truck mfg. co. exec.; b. Pasadena, Calif., July 5, 1942; s. Edwin Lloyd and Evelyn Edine (Frye) W.; B.S., U. So. Calif., 1964; m. Janet Lee Downey, June 26, 1970; 1 son, Bradley Dean. Owner, operator restaurant/bar, Los Angeles, 1967-69; sales trainee Internat. Harvester Co., Los Angeles, 1969-70, salesman, 1970-71, asst. br. mgr., 1971-72, zone mgr., 1972-74, br. sales mgr., Anaheim, Calif., 1974-75, br. service mgr., Norwalk, Calif., 1975, bus. mgr., Oakland, Calif., 1975-77, dist. mgr., 1977-79, sales trainer, 1980—. Served as capt. USMC, 1964-67. Mem. Delta Chi. Republican. Presbyterian. Clubs: SAR, Masons, Elks, Ft. Douglas/Hidden Valley Country (Salt Lake City). Home: 3721 E Blue Jay Ln Salt Lake City UT 84121 Office: 8393 Capwell Dr Oakland CA 94621

WILLSON, FRED E., advt. exec.; b. Kansas City, Mo., Oct. 22, 1917; s. Fred E. and Hazel I. (Tarter) W.; B.S. in Bus., U. Ill., 1940; m. Pat Mary Draper, July 12, 1947; children—Michael, Haley (Mrs. Richard Lowe), Jill (Mrs. Harold Landem), Laurie, Peter, Mark. Writer, salesman radio sta. WDWS, Champaign, Ill., 1940-42; program dir. radio sta. WIND, Chgo., 1942-45; with Ivan Hill, Inc., advt., Chgo., 1945-50; with PKG/Cunningham & Walsh, advt., Chgo., 1950—, sr. v.p., gen. mgr., 1970—, also dir., mem. exec. com.; dir. Ad-Pro Computer Services, Inc., Chgo. Bd. dirs. Kidney Found. Ill.; rep. End Stage Renal Disease Network 15. Episcopalian. Office: 875 Michigan Ave Chicago IL 60611

WILLSON, JAMES KERN, air conditioner mfg. co. exec.; b. Milw., Sept. 9, 1943; s. Donald James and Virginia Kern (Toelle) W.; B.S.C.E., Purdue U., 1965; M.B.A., Northwestern U., 1967; m. Constance Lou, Oct. 14, 1967; children—Eric Donald, Victoria Lynn, Bradley James. With The Trane Co., La Crosse, Wis., 1967—, product mktg. mgr. process div., 1980—. Mem. Am. Mgmt. Assn., La Crosse Jr. C. of C. Congregationalist. Clubs: La Crosse Purdue Alumni (pres. 1976), Toastmasters (pres. La Crosse chpt. 1971, area gov. 1972), Masons. Home: 120 S 17th St La Crosse WI 54601 Office: 3600 Pammel Creek Rd La Crosse WI 54601

WILLSON, ROBERT BELLOWS, honey dealer, importer and exporter co. exec.; b. N.Y.C., June 8, 1894; s. John George and Nettie Elzada (Bellows) W.; B.S., Cornell U., 1917; m. Wilma Elizabeth Harris, Jan. 12, 1934; children—Robert C., John P., Lloyd H. Instr. biology dept. Miss. State Coll., 1919-22; instr. dept. biology Cornell U., 1922-26; founder, chmn. R. B. Willson, Inc., N.Y.C., 1946—. Chmn. bd. Am. Honey Industry Council, 1951-53. Served to 1st lt., inf., U.S. Army, 1918. Recipient City of Merida (Mexico) Gold medal, 1971. Mem. Nat. Honey Packers and Dealers Assn. (past pres.), Am. Legion (past comdr., gold medal Americanism award 1974). Clubs: Cornell (bd. govs.) (Westchester); Larchmont Shore; Cornell of N.Y. (v.p. 1972). Home: 2 Garmany Pl Yonkers NY 10710 Office: 222 Mamaroneck Ave White Plains NY 10605

WILMOUTH, ROBERT KEARNEY, commodity exec.; b. Worcester, Mass., Nov. 9, 1928; s. Alfred F. and Aileen E. (Kearney) W.; B.A., Holy Cross Coll., Worcester, 1949; M.A., U. Notre Dame, 1950; grad. Rutgers U. Stonier Grad. Sch. Banking, 1961; m. Ellen Mary Boyle, Sept. 10, 1955; children—Robert J., John J. and James P. (twins), Thomas G., Anne-Marie. With First Nat. Bank Chgo., 1950—, sr. v.p., 1966-72, exec. v.p., dir., 1972-75; pres., chief adminstrv. officer Crocker Nat. Bank, 1975-77; pres., chief exec. officer Chgo. Bd. Trade, 1977—; dir. Victoria Sta., LaSalle Bank Pvt. Export Funding Corp. Vice pres. lay adv. bd. Holy Family Hosp., Des Plains, Ill., 1964-67; trustee Mundelein Coll., Chgo., 1967-79, U. Notre Dame. Served to 1st lt. USAF, 1951-53. Recipient Distinguished Service award Chgo. Jr. Assn. Commerce and Industry, 1961; named One of Ten Outstanding Young Mem. in Chgo., U.S. Jr. C. of C. Mem. Am. Bankers Assn. (chmn. automation com. 1963-79), Chgo. Assn. Commerce and Industry (dir.). Roman Catholic. Clubs: Mid-Day (trustee), Econ., Execs. (Chgo.); Barrington Hills Country. Home: Caesar Dr Route 5 Barrington Hills IL 60010 Office: 141 W Jackson Blvd Chicago IL 60604

WILSON, ALBERT OLOF, JR., steel co. exec.; b. Watertown, Mass., Nov. 27, 1916; s. Albert Olof and Anita Karen (Bagge) W.; B.S., M.I.T., 1938; m. Carol P. Doty, May 31, 1941; children—Raymond T., Anita P. With Bethlehem Steel Co. (Pa.), 1938-39; with A.O. Wilson Structural Co., Cambridge, Mass., 1939—, pres., chmn. bd. dirs., 1955—; dir. Peter Gray Corp., Reliance Coop. Bank, trustee Wilson-Cambridge Trust (Realty), John Hancock Cash Mgmt. Trust. Chmn., Mt. Auburn Hosp., 1980—. Mem. Cambridge C. of C. (pres. 1967-68), Am. Inst. Steel Constrn. (dir. 1963-64), Asso. Industries of Mass. (dir., treas. 1969-78). Club: Rotary, (pres. 1958-59). Office: 40 Smith Pl Cambridge MA 02138

WILSON, ALEXANDER MURRAY, mining co. exec.; b. Tulare, Calif., May 17, 1922; s. Alexander Murray and Grace Ethel (Creech) W.; B.S. in Metall. Engring., U. Calif., Berkeley, 1948; m. Beverlee Elaine Forsblad, Jan. 4, 1948; children—Shelley Blaine, Kristin Holly Wilson Keyes, Alexis Elaine Wilson Kjellstrom. With Bradley Mining Co., Stibnite, Idaho, 1948-51, Molybdenum Corp. Am., Nipton, Calif., 1951-54; with Utah Internat. Inc. subs. Gen. Electric Co., San Francisco, 1954—, pres., 1971-79, chief exec. officer, 1978—, chmn., 1979—, also dir.; chmn., dir. Utah Devel. Co.; dir. First Security Corp., Fireman's Fund Ins. Co. Served with U.S. Army, 1944-46; CBI. Mem. Am. Mining Congress (dir.), Nat. Coal Assn. (dir.), Mining and Metall. Soc. Am., Soc. Mining Engrs., Pacific Basin Econ. Council (chmn. U.S. nat. com.). Office: 550 California St San Francisco CA 94104

WILSON, BRUCE PAGE, corp. exec.; b. Binghamton, N.Y., Jan. 12, 1920; s. Thomas A. and Gertrude (Page) W.; B.A., Princeton U., 1942; m. Laura Dell Meacham, June 1, 1946; children—Jay MacLean, Barbara Wilson Schweizer, Katharine Wilson Denby, Laura Campbell. Sec.-treas. Steeltin Can Corp., 1946-48; pres. Balt. and Annapolis R.R. Co., 1949-61; regional v.p., div. v.p. Carling Brewing Co., 1961-70; exec. v.p. Mercantile Bankshares Corp., Balt., 1970-76; chmn. exec. com. Mercantile Safe Deposit and Trust Co., Balt., 1970-76, pres., 1976—; dir. Balt. and Annapolis R.R., Sta. WMAR-TV, Walker-Wilson Travel, Steeltin Can Corp., Ward Machinery Co., Nat. Distbg. Properties, Bd. dirs. United Way of Central Md., Union Meml. Hosp. Served to maj., U.S. Army, World War II. Decorated Bronze star. Office: Mercantile Safe Deposit and Trust Co 2 Hopkins Plaza Baltimore MD 21201

WILSON, CARY ROBERT, computer industry co. exec.; b. Chgo., Feb. 28, 1942; s. Robert John and Lucille W.; B.A. cum laude, Ariz. State U., 1964, M.A. magna cum laude, 1969; m. Virginia Anstrand, Sept. 3, 1968; children—Amy Louise, Geoffrey Clayton. Regional sales mgr. Plenum Pub. Co., N.Y.C., 1967-68; sales rep. RCA Computer Systems Co., Seattle, 1969-71; account mgr. Burroughs Co., Los Angeles, 1971-73; br. mgr. Telex Co., Los Angeles, 1973-76; internat. mktg. mgr. Nat. Semiconductor Co., Sunnyvale, Calif., 1976-78; pres. Redwood Fin. Industries, Atherton, Calif., 1978—. Pres., Young Democrats, 1960. Served with USN, 1966. Laverne Noyes fellow U. Chgo., 1964-65. Mem. Data Processing Mgmt. Assn., Assn. Computing Machinery, Phi Delta Theta, Blue Key. Anglican. Home and Office: 178 Almendral St Atherton CA 94025

WILSON, CHARLES RAYMOND, JR., constrn. co. exec.; b. Los Angeles, June 16, 1926; s. Charles Raymond and Persis Pauline (Leamer) W.; student U. Redlands, 1944, U. So. Calif., 1946-47; m. Audrey Mae Griesinger, Jan. 10, 1953; children—Debra Kay, Nancy Lee. Estimator, C.W. Wilson & Sons, Los Angeles, 1947-50; corp. sec. Crowell-Wilson Co., Los Angeles, 1951-54, Ray Wilson Co., Los Angeles, 1955-64, pres., 1964—; exec. v.p. Balasem Coantracting Co., Kuwait, Arabia, 1978—. Bd. dirs. Hollywood Presbyn. Med. Center, 1979—; trustee Westmont Coll., 1979—. Served with USN, 1944-46. Mem. U. So. Calif. Archtl. Guild (dir. 1976-79). Republican. Presbyterian. Office: 4660 Colorado Blvd Los Angeles CA 90039

WILSON, DARYL CHARLES, fin. ofcl.; b. St. John, N.B., Can., July 27, 1949; s. Maurice Heber and Evelyn Margaret (Galbraith) W.; B.Comm., Mt. Allison U., 1971; m. Sharon Louise Thomas, Oct. 4, 1975; children—Craig, Christine. Audit mgr. Clarkson, Gordon & Co., St. John, 1973-77; dep. commr. fin. City of St. John, 1977—. Chartered acct., 1973. Mem. N.B. Inst. Chartered Accts. Mem. Ch. Brethren. Office: PO Box 1971 St John NB E2L 421 Canada

WILSON, DAVID ALEXANDER, accountant; b. Toronto, Ont., Can., June 24, 1941; s. John Robertson McKay and Lois (Girvan) W.; B. Commerce, Queen's U., 1964; M.B.A., U. Cal. at Berkeley, 1965; Ph.D., U. Ill., 1972; m. Marsha Jane Murray McCarroll, Apr. 17, 1976; children—Sean Alexander, Bennett Bolton McCarroll. Staff accountant Arthur Young/Clarkson, Gordon & Co., London, Ont., 1965-68; asst. prof. accounting and finance Queen's U., Kingston, Ont., 1968-70; teaching asst. accounting U. Ill. at Urbana, 1970-72; asst. prof. accounting U. Tex. at Austin, 1972-76, asso. prof., 1976-78; prin. Arthur Young & Co., Houston, 1978—; vis. asso. prof. bus. adminstrn. Harvard, 1976-77; cons. financial mgmt. in industry and in costing telecommunication services to govt. agys., 1969—; instr. exec. devel. programs Duke, 1973-75. Am. Acctg. Assn. Doctoral Consortium fellow, 1971, dir., 1975. Recipient Outstanding Teacher award U. Ill., 1972, Coll. Bus. Adminstrn. U. Tex., 1973. Chartered accountant, Can.; C.P.A., Tex. Mem. Am. Acctg. Assn. (research editorial bd. 1976—), Inst. Chartered Accts. Ont., Can. Inst. Chartered Accts., Tex. Soc. C.P.A.'s, Am. Inst. C.P.A.'s. Club: Houstonian. Author: (with Welsch, Zlatkovich and Zin) Intermediate Accounting, 1974, 78; (with Shank and Frolin) Contemporary Financial Reporting, 1978; (with Minard) Forbes Numbers Game, 1980; contbr. articles to profl. jours. Home: 927 Ivy Wall Dr Houston TX 77079 Office: 2500 Pennzoil Pl Houston TX 77002

WILSON, DONALD A., fin. exec.; b. Pitts., Jan. 20, 1923; s. Herbert C. and Etta P. (Ross) W.; student Robert Morris Sch. Accountancy; m. Elizabeth L. Martindale, Sept. 4, 1946; children—James E., Mary Etta. Acct., H.J. Heinz Co.; acct., material mgr. Rockwell Mfg. Co.; acct. Rockwell Internat.; controller Scott & Fetzer Co.; v.p. fin. The Kirby Co. div. Scott & Fetzer, Cleve. Served with USAF, 1942-45. Mem. Am. Legion, Nat. Assn. Accts. Republican. Presbyterian. Clubs: Sertoma, Elks. Home: 12900 Lake Ave Apt 502 Lakewood OH 44107 Office: 1920 W 114th St Cleveland OH 44102

WILSON, DONALD HURST, III, mfg. co. exec.; b. Balt., Mar. 1, 1946; s. Donald Hurst and Winifred L. Wilson, Jr.; A.B., Yale U., 1968; M.B.A., Harvard U., 1976, J.D., 1976; m. Beverly L. Wright, Oct. 3, 1975. Mgmt. cons. The Boston Cons. Group, Inc., 1976-78; dir. bus. analysis Black & Decker Mfg. Co., 1978-80, dir. mktg. planning and research indsl./constrn. div. Black & Decker (U.S.) Inc., 1980—; admitted to Mass. bar, 1976. Served to lt. Supply Corps, USNR, 1969-72. Home: 3915 Dance Mill Rd Phoenix MD 21131 Office: 626 Hanover Pike Hampstead MD 21074

WILSON, DURWARD EARL, steel co. exec.; b. Macon, Ga., Sept. 23, 1925; s. Sam and Eunice (Scoggins) W.; B.S. in Indsl. Engring., Ga. Inst. Tech., 1950; m. Sara Ann Saunders, Dec. 20, 1946; children—Beth, Jan, Mark, John. Indsl. engr. E.I. duPont Co., Chattanooga, 1950-54, div. prodn. asst., Wilmington, Del., 1954-56; sr. mgmt. cons. John M. Avent & Assn., Atlanta, 1956-58; planning mgr. Tex. Steel Co., Ft. Worth, 1958-59, asst. v.p., 1959-66, v.p., 1966-72, exec. v.p., 1972-75, pres., 1975—; pres., chmn. bd. Tex. Steel Co. Can., Ltd., St. Stephen, N.B.; pres., dir. L & M Mfg. Co., Steel Casting Machine Co., S.W. Steel Casting Co., Bus. Communications, Inc.; dir. Liberty Mfg. Co. Tex., Armstrong Oil & Land Co. Served with USAAF, 1943-46. Mem. Steel Founders' Soc. Am. (pres., dir.), Cast Metals Fedn. (bd. dirs., chmn. environ. com., Tex. chmn. governmental affairs), Nat. Foundry Assn. (dir.), Am. Foundrymen's Soc., Concrete Reinforcing Steel Inst., Steel Bar Mill Assn., Am. Iron and Steel Engrs. Republican. Episcopalian. Clubs: Shady Oaks Country, Ridglea Country, Century II, Fort Worth. Home: 1 Bounty Rd W Fort Worth TX 76132 Office: 3901 Hemphill St Fort Worth TX 76110

WILSON, E. C., JR., acct., machinery co. exec.; b. Richlands, Va., Feb. 6, 1940; s. E. C. and Buelah M. (Newberry) W.; Asso. Nat. Bus. Coll., Roanoke, Va., 1964; m. Hazel Loretta Billings, May 5, 1962; children—Michael Anthony, Matthew Scott. Owner, E.C. Wilson & Co., C.P.A.'s, Richland, 1971-73; treas. Pyott-Boone, Inc., Tazewell, Va., 1973-74; exec. v.p. Pyott-Boone Machinery Corp., Saltville, Va., 1974-75; pres. Wil-Jon Machinery Corp., Saltville, 1975—; chmn. bd. Miners & Mfrs. Ins. Co.; dir. Denson Corp. Mem. Sequoyah council Boy Scouts Am., 1976; treas. Tazewell County Republican Com., 1972; mem. Cedar Bluff (Va.) Town Council, 1970; bd. visitors Emory (Va.) and Henry Coll., 1977; mem. Smyth County Planning Commn., 1976. Served with AUS, 1957-60. C.P.A., Va. Mem. Am. Inst. C.P.A.'s, Va. Soc. C.P.A.'s. Presbyterian. Clubs: Rotary, Shriners. Address: Box 1321 Richlands VA 24641

WILSON, EARL COLEMAN, contracting co. exec.; b. Cynthiana, Ind., Dec. 22, 1925; s. Edmund Smith and Vera Cynthia (Robbins) W.; B.S., U. Evansville, 1949; M.B.A., Ind. State U., 1969; m. Jo Anne Freshley, June 14, 1953; children—Mark Shane, Shanna Lynn. Office mgr. Posey County Farm Bur., Mt. Vernon, Ind., 1949-50; asst. sec., treas. Charles E. Day Engring. Co., Evansville, Ind., 1950-53; auditor U.S. Navy, Evansville, 1953-54; budget mgr. Mead Johnson Internat. div., Evansville, 1954-69; treas., chief fin. officer Indsl. Contractors, Inc., Evansville, 1970-80, v.p. fin., 1980—. Solicitor, United Way Southwestern Ind., 1974-75, 76. Served with USAAF, 1944-46. Mem. Adminstrv. Mgmt. Soc., Nat. Assn. Accountants. Methodist. Clubs: Masons, Shriners. Home: 13250 Woodland Ln Evansville IN 47711 Office: 401 NW 1st St Evansville IN 47708

WILSON, EDWARD, bank mktg. cons.; b. Pasadena, Calif., Aug. 20, 1924; s. Elmer M. and Regina (Veale) W.; B.A., Stanford U., 1950; m. Mary Ellen Lovemark, Jan. 21, 1961; children—Scott, Robert, Jeffrey, Terry, Pamela. Vice-pres. Foote, Cone & Belding, Los Angeles, 1951-68; sr. v.p. United Calif. Bank, Los Angeles, 1968-79; v.p. Boylhart, Lovett & Dean, Los Angeles, 1980—; mem. faculty U. Colo. Sch. Bank Mktg., Boulder, 1977-79. Pres., Pasadena Tournament of Roses, 1973-74. Served with AUS, 1943-46. Mem. Bank Mktg. Assn. (dir. 1973-76), Hollywood Radio and TV Soc. (dir. 1974-77), Acad. Magical Arts. Clubs: Annandale Golf, Variety Arts. Overland. Home: 1134 Glen Oaks Blvd Pasadena CA 91105 Office: 680 Wilshire Pl Los Angeles CA 90005

WILSON, FRANCIS SERVIS, JR., securities dealer; b. Chgo., Oct. 7, 1906; s. Francis Servis and Caroline (Seigfried) W.; student Dartmouth Coll., 1925-26; Ph.B., U. Chgo., 1930; m. Kathryn A. Wilson, June 1, 1945; children—Grace E., Francis Servis III, John G., William P., Thomas S. With investment firms, 1930-40; with War Dept., Washington, 1942-43; analyst Standard & Poors Corp., Chgo., 1943-53; chief analyst Bache & Co., Chgo., 1954-63; exec. v.p. Woolard & Co., Chgo., 1963—; dir. Qualair Corp., Sacramento, Casualty Ins. Co., Chgo., Spin Plastics Co., South Bend, Ind., Stenograph Corp., Skokie, Ill., CIC Financial Corp., Chgo., Energy Absorption Systems, Chgo. Mem. Delta Kappa Epsilon. Episcopalian. Clubs: University, Tavern, Attic (Chgo.); Chikaming Country (Lakeside, Mich.); Everglades, Bath and Tennis (Palm Beach, Fla.). Home: 199 E Lake Shore Dr Chicago IL 60611 Office: 135 S La Salle St Chicago IL 60603

WILSON, FREDERICK ARNELL, JR., ins. co. ofcl.; b. Bklyn., Aug. 6, 1946; s. Frederick and Annie T. (Wood) W.; B.A. in Psychology, Johnson C. Smith U., 1969; m. Patricia Bridges, Nov. 28, 1968; children—Jacqueline Diane, Deidre Renee. Test adminstr. and evaluator N.Y. State Dept. Labor, 1970-71; sales agt. N.Y. Life Ins. Co., Bklyn., 1971-74, asst. sales mgr., 1974—; dir. Okon Internat. Import-Export Corp. Recipient Black Achievers in Industry award YMCA Greater N.Y., 1977. Mem. Nat. Life Underwriters Assn., N.Y. Life Underwriters Assn., Nat. Assn. Security Dealers, U.S. Jaycees, N.Y. Jaycees, 100 Blackmen, Over the Hill Athletic Assn.,

Omega Psi Phi. Home: 359 Skidmore Rd Deer Park NY 11729 Office: 9512 3d Ave Brooklyn NY 11209

WILSON, HAROLD KERMIT, mfg. co. exec.; b. Mpls., June 12, 1940; s. Kermit Houchins and Lavina Jesse (Blatterman) W.; student U. Minn., 1958-62; m. Maria Malaya Manalansan, Jan. 7, 1977; children—Leilani, Jocelyn, Sarah; children by previous marriage—Mary Angela, Christopher. With SICO, Inc., Mpls., 1963—, exec. v.p., 1973-77, pres., 1977—, also dir. Co-founder, Pony Colt League, St. Louis Park, 1963; bd. dirs. Edina Hockey Assn., 1975-77. Mem. Edina Hist. Soc., Young Pres.'s Orgn., AMA Pres.'s Assn., Am. Hotel Assn. Club: Rotary (dir. 1972-73, dist. internat. youth exchange com. 1972-73). Office: Box 1169 Minneapolis MN 55440

WILSON, HARVEY J., data processing co. exec.; b. Lousia, Ky., Jan. 7, 1939; s. Frederick Earl and Goldia Ellen (Workman) W.; B.S., Pa. State U., 1962; m. Marlynn A. Turki, June 9, 1962; children—Gregory Lawrence, Mitchell Grant. Civil engr. Dravo Corp., Pitts., 1955-62; mem. sales staff med. systems div. IBM, Phila., 1965-69; founder, v.p. Shared Med. Systems Corp., King of Prussia, Pa., 1969-80, pres., 1980—, also dir. Served to lt. USNR, 1963-65; PTO. Office: 650 Park Ave King of Prussia PA 19406

WILSON, HILLSMAN VAUGHAN, food co. exec.; b. Crewe, Va., Dec. 29, 1928; s. Joseph Henry and Lucy (Vaughan) W.; B.A., Coll. William and Mary, 1951; B.C.L., Marshall Wythe Law Sch., 1953; m. Anne Steuart Gantt, May 15, 1965; children—Pamela Hunt, Richard Hillsman, Daniel Vaughan, Robert Vaughan. Admitted to Va. bar, 1952, Md. bar, 1956; practiced law, Crewe, 1955; with McCormick & Co., Inc., 1955—, v.p. fin., 1973-77, exec. v.p., 1977-79, pres., chief operating officer, Hunt Valley, Md., 1979—, mem. exec. com., sec., 1969—, also dir.; chmn. bd., dir. McCormick Properties, Inc.; dir. Grocery Products div. McCormick & Co. Inc., McCormick de Mexico S.A., McCormick Foods Australia Pty., Ltd., McCormick GmbH., McCormick-Lion Ltd., Union Trust Bancorp, Balt. Life Ins. Co. Trustee, Endowment Assn., Coll. William and Mary; bd. dirs. Ind. Coll. Fund Md.; trustee McDonogh Sch. Served to 1st lt. U.S. Army, 1953-55. Mem. Am. Bar Assn. Methodist. Clubs: Balt. Country, Seaview Country, Center, Towson. Office: 11350 McCormick Rd Hunt Valley MD 21031

WILSON, J. TYLEE, tobacco co. exec.; b. Teaneck, N.J., June 18, 1931; s. Eric J. and Florence Q. Wilson; A.B. in Govt., Lafayette Coll., 1953; m. Patricia F. Harrington, July 17, 1970; children—Jeffrey J., Debra L., Christopher. Group v.p., dir. Chesebrough-Pond, Inc., Greenwich, Conn., 1960-74; pres., chief exec. officer, dir. RJR Foods, Inc., Winston-Salem, N.C., 1974-76, chmn., chief exec. officer R.J. Reynolds Tobacco Internat., Inc., 1976-78, exec. v.p., dir. R.J. Reynolds Industries, Inc., 1976-79, pres., dir., 1979—; dir. Sonoco Products Co., Firestone Tire & Rubber Co., Wachovia Corp., Wachovia Bank & Trust Co. Trustee, Lafayette Coll., U.S. Council of Internat. C. of C.; bd. dirs. Met. YMCA of Winston-Salem and Forsyth County; bd. visitors Wake Forest Coll., 1977—; mem. Gov.'s Bus. Council on Arts and Humanities, 1979—; bd. dirs. Reynolda House, 1980; trustee Lafayette Coll., Forsyth Country Day Sch. Served with U.S. Army, 1954-56. Mem. Internat. C. of C. (trustee U.S. council), U.S. C. of C. (internat. policy com.). Clubs: Old Town, Twin City (Winston-Salem); Apawanis (Rye, N.Y.); Sawgrass, Ponte Vedra (Ponte Vedra Beach, Fla.); Sky (N.Y.C.). Home: 2585 Club Park Rd Winston-Salem NC 27104 Office: World Hdqrs RJ Reynolds Industries Inc Winston-Salem NC 27102

WILSON, JAMES JOHN, constrn. and real estate exec.; b. N.Y.C., Apr. 18, 1933; s. Daniel J. and Mary (O'Donnell) W.; B.C.E., Manhattan Coll., 1955; m. Barbara A. Wilson, July 27, 1957; children—Kevin John, Elizabeth Ann, Thomas Brian, Mary Patricia, James Michael, Brian Joseph. Pres., chmn. Interstate Gen. Corp., Hato Rey, P.R., 1965—; pres., chmn. Wilson Securities Corp.; chmn. Interstate Land Devel. Corp., Inc., Interstate St. Charles, Inc.; dir. Va. Stallion Sta. Inc.; adv. council Banco Popular de P.R., 1968-70. Pres., Buck Hill Falls Community Assn. Recipient Alumni award for outstanding businessman Manhattan Coll., 1969. Mem. New Communities Council, Urban Land Inst., Am. Arbitration Assn., Va. Thoroughbred Assn., No. Va. Angus Assn., Soc. Am. Mil. Engrs. (pres. 1958), Nat. Assn. Home Builders (pres. P.R. chpt. 1963, dir. 1962-65), Young Pres. Orgn. (pres. Caribbean chpt. 1968-69), Manhattan Coll. Alumni Assn. Clubs: Caparra Country; N.Y. Athletic (N.Y.C.); University (Washington). Middleburg (Va.) Tennis; Banker's of P.R. Home: Dresden Farm Box 392 Middleburg VA 22117 also Buck Hill Falls PA Office: 336 Post Office Rd St Charles MD 20601 also Box 3908 San Juan PR 00936

WILSON, JAMES RAY, agrl. products co. exec.; b. Hamilton, Ohio, Mar. 7, 1930; s. Ray Crawford and Ruth Lee (Walthers) W.; B.A. (U.S. Navy Coll. Tng. Program scholar), Miami U., Oxford, Ohio, 1952, postgrad., 1967-68; M.A., Ohio State U., 1956; m. Carolyn Dempsey, Feb. 1, 1952; children—Robin E., Victoria, Mark, Jamie. Grad. asst. Ohio State U., 1955-56; grain mcht. Cargill Inc., Balt., 1956-58; pres. Granexport Corp., Manila, Philippines, 1959-66; mng. dir. Tradax Graanhandel B.V., Amsterdam, 1966-67; instr. in geography Miami U., 1967-68; pres. Cargill Agricola S.A., Sao Paulo, Brazil, 1968-78; dir. indsl. div. Tradax Geneve S.A., Geneva, 1978-80; corp. v.p. Cargill Inc., Mpls., 1980—. Served with USN, 1952-55. Mem. Assn. Am. Geographers, Am. Geog. Soc. Congregationalist. Home: 16224 Ice Circle Dr Wayzata MN 55391 Office: PO Box 9300 Minneapolis MN 55440

WILSON, JAMES REID, JR., publishing co. exec.; b. Phila., Aug. 5, 1934; s. James Reid and Florence S. (Dunn) W.; B.S. in Econs., U. Pa., 1956; m. Eve-Ann Jones, Apr. 4, 1970; children—Suzanne Winters, Diantha Curtis. Asso. dir. Western Hemisphere promotion N.Y. Times, 1966-69; indsl. advt. mgr., 1969-74; corp. advt. mgr. U.S. News & World Report, N.Y.C., 1974—. Pres. Pa. Assn. for Retarded Citizens, 1969-71; sr. vp. Nat. Assn. for Retarded Citizens, 1975-77, pres. 1977-79. Recipient humanitarian award Phila. Assn. for Retarded Citizens, 1973. Mem. Pub. Relations Soc. of Am. Republican. Presbyterian. Clubs: Union League of Phila., St. Nicholas Soc. of N.Y. Office: US News & World Report 45 Rockefeller Plaza New York NY 10020

WILSON, JOHN ALAN, lawyer; b. Glen Ridge, N.J., Sept. 1, 1917; s. Robert and Adelaide Anna (Streubel) W.; A.B., Princeton, 1939; LL.B., Yale, 1942; m. Dorothy Francisco, Aug. 9, 1947; children—Robert Alan, Anne Elizabeth. Admitted to Ohio bar, 1950; house counsel Dresser Industries, Inc., 1949-50; sec. Affiliated Gas Equipment, Inc., 1950-55; dir. law Diamond Shamrock Corp., Cleve., 1956-61, sec., 1961-79, gen. counsel, 1964—, v.p., 1967—; legis. asst. to Senator Taft, 1946-49. Mem. trustees devel. council St. Luke's Hosp. Assn. Served with AUS, 1942-45. Mem. Am., Fed., Cleve. bar assns., Am. Soc. Corp. Secs. Clubs: Cleve., Union, Skating, Clevelander; Princeton of N.Y.; Sea Pines (Hilton Head Island, S.C.). Home: 2684 Leighton Rd Shaker Heights OH 44120 also 14 Harleston Green Hilton Head Island SC 22928 Office: 1100 Superior Ave Cleveland OH 44114

WILSON, JOHN CORNELL, JR., lumber co. exec.; b. San Jose, Calif., June 24, 1937; s. John Cornell and Helen (Bechtel) W.; A.B., U. Calif., Berkeley, 1959, M.B.A., 1963; m. Kristin Buck, June 13, 1964; children—Mary Katherine, John III, Christian Coleman. Acct., Touche, Ross & Co., San Francisco, 1963-69; investment banker Dean Witter Co., San Francisco, 1969-77; v.p. fin. C.P. National Co., San Francisco, 1977-79; v.p. fin. Pacific Lumber Co., San Francisco, 1980—; dir. Cost Plus, Inc. Served with U.S. Army, 1960-61. C.P.A., Calif. Mem. Am. Inst. C.P.A.'s, Fin. Execs. Inst., Calif. Soc. C.P.A.'s. Republican. Episcopalian. Clubs: San Francisco Golf, Bohemian. Home: 156 Commonwealth Ave San Francisco CA 94118 Office: PO Box 7406 San Francisco CA 94118

WILSON, JOHN DONALD, banker, economist; b. McKeesport, Pa., Feb. 8, 1913; s. John Johnston and Katherine A. (Hollerman) W.; B.A. magna cum laude in Econs. and History, U. Colo., 1935; M.A. in Econs., Tufts Coll., 1937; M.A. in Econs., Harvard, 1940; m. Danesi Matthews Hilton, Nov. 3, 1951; children—Nina Marie, John Douglas, David Matthews, Mary Danesi. Instr. econs. Harvard, 1937-40; editor Survey Current Bus., Dept. Commerce, Washington, 1940-42; economist, editor, founder Am. Letter, McGraw-Hill Pub. Co., N.Y.C., 1946-50; with research and devel. staff N.Y. Life Ins. Co., 1950-51; v.p. charge ops. Inst. Internal Edn., N.Y.C., 1951-53; bus. cons., v.p. econs. research Chase Manhattan Bank, N.Y.C., 1953-55, v.p., dir. econ. research div., pub. relations div., now sr. v.p., dir. econs. group; dir. Chase Econometric Assos., Inc., chmn., 1971-75. Trustee, Inst. Internat. Edn.; bd. dirs. United Neighborhood Houses, 1955-78; trustee, treas. Found. Library Center, 1956-63. Served to lt. (j.g.) USNR, 1943-46; MTO, ETO. Mem. N.Y.C. C. of C. (monetary and fin. com.), Council Fgn. Relations, C. of C. U.S. (banking, monetary and fiscal policy com.), Am. Econ. Assn., Am. Statis. Assn., Internat. C. of C. (exec. com., trustee U.S. council), Am. Mgmt. Assn. (pres.'s council), Nat. Assn. Bus. Economists, Phi Beta Kappa, Sigma Chi. Mem. Dutch Reformed Ch. Clubs: Econ., Harvard (N.Y.C.). Contbr. articles on econs. and bus. to profl. and trade publs. Home: 6 Sunset Ave Bronxville NY 10708 Office: 1 Chase Manhattan Plaza New York NY 10015

WILSON, JOHN HART, constrn. co. exec.; b. Seattle, June 11, 1922; s. Richard Hagan and Agnes Josephine (Hart) W.; student Stanford, 1940-43; B.S. in Civil Engring., Calif. Inst. Tech., 1944; m. Barbara Elizabeth Wells, Jan. 22, 1949; 1 dau., Wendy Wilson Smull. Engr., supt. Harms Bros. Co., Sacramento, 1946-52; dist. engr. Morrison-Knudsen Co., Inc., Los Angeles, 1960-64, dist. mgr., Los Angeles, 1964-67, chief engr., 1968-69, v.p. engring., 1970-74, v.p. spl. assignment, 1975—. Served with C.E., USNR, 1943-46. Mem. ASCE, Am. Inst. Constructors, Soc. Am. Mil. Engrs., Beavers, Delta Kappa Epsilon. Republican. Club: Hillcrest Country. Home: 3904 Hillcrest Dr Boise ID 83705 Office: 1 Morrison-Knudsen Plaza Boise ID 83729

WILSON, JOHN HUMAN, geologist, geophysicist; b. Wills Point, Tex., Feb. 24, 1900; s. James Thomas and Birdie Alice (Blanks) W.; E.M., Colo. Sch. Mines, 1923; m. Harriette Fromhart, Sept. 8, 1924; children—Mary Alice, John Human. Geologist, geophysicist Midwest Mfg. Co., Denver, 1923-26, Huasteca Petroleum Corp., Tampico, Mex., 1926-28; asst. prof. geophysics Colo. Sch. Mines, 1928-29; cons. geologist, Golden, Colo., 1929-37; v.p. Ind. Exploration Co., Houston, 1937-50; pres. Piper Petroleum Co., Fort Worth, Tex., 1950—; pres., dir. Wilson Exploration Co. Mem. Am. Assn. Petroleum Geologists, Soc. Exploration Geophysicists, AIME. Clubs: Fort Worth, River Crest Country, Petroleum, Century. Home: 7921 White Settlement Rd Fort Worth TX 76108 Office: 1212 West El Paso Fort Worth TX 76102

WILSON, JOHN MURRAY, JR., instrument mfr.; b. Los Angeles, May 22, 1933; s. J. Murray and Elizabeth E. (Reese) W.; B.S.M.E., U. Calif., Berkeley, 1956; M.B.A., Harvard U., 1960; m. Marily A. Purkiss, July 14, 1955 (div.); children—John Murray, Craig A., Kimberley R., Durinda C. Prodn. engr. Hewlett-Packard, Palo Alto, Calif., 1960-61; stockbroker Shuman, Agnew & Co., San Francisco, 1961-63; fin. planning mgr. Aeronutronic div. Ford Motor Co., Newport Beach, Calif., 1963-65; gen. mgr. Disc Instruments, Inc., Newport Beach, 1965-69; pres. Telcor Instruments, Inc., Irvine, Calif., 1969—; dir. Cortron Corp.; founder Biotronik GmbH, W. Ger. Active Newport Harbor Art Mus. Served to lt. (j.g.) USNR, 1956-58. Mem. So. Calif. Marine Assn., Harvard Bus. Sch. Assn. Republican. Presbyterian. Clubs: Balboa Bay, Balboa Racquet. Office: Telcor Instruments Inc 17785 Sky Park Circle Irvine CA 92714

WILSON, JOHN ROGERS, automobile dealer; b. Fond du Lac, Wis., Jan. 8, 1931; s. John S. And Vivian M. (Luby) Wacynski; B.S. in Econs., Carroll Coll., 1955; grad. Am. Inst. Banking, Milw., 1956; m. Daine T. Bryne, May 6, 1968; children—Jacalyn, Holly, Denise, Dawn, Michael. Mgr., Bernard Chevrolet, Libertyville, Ill., 1958-61; with Libertyville Auto Sales, 1963-68; pres. Wilson V.W., Florence, S.C., 1969-76; pres. Imports of Florence, 1969-76; pres. Myrtle Beach (S.C.) Imports, 1973-76, Brit. Cars, Inc., Pensacola, Fla., 1976—; pres. Full Line Brit. Leland NW Fla., 1976—; pres. D & J Inc., 1977—. Served with USAF, 1951-52. Mem. Fraternal Order Police. Democrat. Roman Catholic. Address: 1069 Laguna Ln Gulf Breeze FL 32561

WILSON, JOHN TRUESDELL, banker; b. Faubush, Ky., July 23, 1898; s. William Floyd and Doretta (Combest) W.; student Jefferson Sch. Law, 1929-31, Stonier Grad. Sch. Banking, Rutgers U., 1956-68; m. Evangeline Cooper, Apr. 28, 1917; children—John Dave (dec.), James Truesdell (dec.), Eva Elizabeth (Mrs. Ollie Caplin, Jr.). Partner Truesdell Wilson Sales & Service, Somerset, Ky., 1945-52; farmer, Ky., 1921-49; salesman Swift & Co., Somerset, 1923-24; plant mgr., engr. Wood-Mosiac Co., Monticello, Ky. and Louisville, 1931-35; with First Farmers Nat. Bank, Somerset, 1933—, pres., 1961-73, chmn. exec. bd., 1973—, also dir.; dealer Chevrolet Co., Somerset, 1937-39, Chrysler Co., Somerset, 1945-52; owner, pres., operator Ky. Oil Co., Somerset, 1935-52; dir., pres. Farmers Tobacco Warehousing Corp., 1948—, Peoples State Bank, Monticello, Ky., 1934-35. Mgr. various Democratic campaigns, 1935-58; bd. dirs. Somerset-Pulaski County Airport, 1948—, chmn., 1952—. Mem. Am., Ky. bankers assns., Ky. (dir. 1950-69), Somerset-Pulaski County (pres. 1957) chambers of commerce. Mason, Kiwanian (pres. 1955, lt. gov. 1958). Author: History of Banking in Pulaski County, 1970. Home: Dutton Hill PO Box 103 Somerset KY 42501 Office: One Fountain Sq Somerset KY 42501

WILSON, KEITH, JR., lawyer; b. Independence, Mo., Mar. 3, 1928; s. Keith and Elizabeth (Baxter) W.; B.A., U. Kans., 1949, LL.B., 1951; m. Yvonne Camille Josserand, June 30, 1951; 1 dau., Leslie Yvonne. Admitted to Mo. bar, 1951, Kans. bar, 1951; practiced in Kansas City, Mo., 1951—, Independence, 1955—; asso. firm Stinson, Mag, Thomson, McEvers & Fizzell, Kansas City, 1951-54; partner Shaffer & Wilson and predecessor firms, Independence, 1955—; lectr. U. Kans. Sch. Law, Lawrence, 1953; pres. P.B. Wilson, Inc., Independence, 1953—; v.p. Burlington Mfg. Co., 1965-70, gen. counsel, 1965—; v.p., sec., gen. counsel Luzier Cosmetics, 1977—. Dep. election commr., Jackson County, Mo., 1954-60; asst. atty. gen. State Mo., 1961; city counselor, Kansas City, Mo., 1961-63; spl. counsel City of Independence, 1966-67, city mgr., 1967-68, 80—; mem. Jackson County Redevel. Commn., 1975—. Sec., Big Bros. Kansas City; trustee, gen. counsel Kansas City Coll. Osteo. Medicine, 1962—; hon. consul People's Republic of Benin, 1978—. Served to maj., inf. AUS, 1949-55. Mem. Am., Kansas City, Independence bar assns., Lawyers Assn. Kansas City, Internat. City Mgrs. Assn., Jackson County Hist. Soc. (dir.), Nat. Inst. Municipal Law Officers (v.p. 1962-63, chmn. com. on civil liberties), Phi Gamma Delta Alumni Assn. (pres.), Mil. Order World Wars, Phi Gamma Delta, Omicron Delta Kappa, Phi Delta Phi, Delta Sigma Rho. Democrat. Clubs: Masons, K.T., Shriners, Jesters; Kansas City, Carriage. Author: Search and Seizure, 1951; Whither Weather, 1951; The Origin of the Antitrust Cause of Action, 1953; also articles in law revs. Home: 1215 W 63d Street Terrace Kansas City MO 64113 Office: Chrisman-Sawyer Bank Bldg Independence MO 64050

WILSON, KENNETH ALLEN, pharm. co. exec.; b. Orange, N.J., Jan. 2, 1932; s. Harry and Amelia (Hartung) W.; B.S. in Bus. Adminstrn., Rutgers U., 1953; M.B.A., N.Y. U., 1972; m. Sara Blair Rosekrans, June 4, 1955; children—David, Katherine, Sara. Auditor, Price Waterhouse & Co., C.P.A.'s, Newark, 1954-55; accountant Nordson Pharm. Co., Irvington, N.J., 1957-60; chief accountant, then comptroller Purdue Frederick Co., Norwalk, Conn., 1960-76, group comptroller, 1976—. Treas. Littleton Civic Assn., 1958-62; warden St. Paul's Episcopal Ch., Montvale, N.J., 1980. Served with AUS, 1955-57. Mem. Fin. Execs. Inst. Home: PO Box 256 40 Brown Dr Pearl River NY 10965 Office: 50 Washington St Norwalk CT 06856

WILSON, KERMIT HOUCHINS, mfg. co. exec.; b. Mpls., Mar. 3, 1916; s. Arthur and Grace May (Houchins) W.; student U. Minn., 1946-47; m. LaVonne Esther Bettner, Dec. 31, 1961; children—Harold, LaVaan, Bonnita, Michael, Tereasa. With Cargill Inc., Albany, N.Y. and Mpls, 1934-45; co-founder, partner Waco Steel Scaffolding Co., Mpls., 1945-51; founder, owner SICO, Inc., Mpls., 1951—, chmn. bd., chief exec. officer, 1977—. Chmn. Hennepin County 3rd Dist. Republican Party Neighbor-to-Neighbor campaign, 1964; del. state and county Rep. Party convs., 1968; mem. first trade mission to Eastern Europe and Soviet Union, 1967; chmn. Edina Govtl. Commn., 1973-74; pres. Edina Found., 1978-79; Sunday sch. supt. Fremont Congregational Ch., 1936-38, chmn. bd. trustees, 1938, 62. Recipient Fgn. Trade cert. Dept. Commerce, 1967; Cert. of Appreciation, Govt. Yugoslavia, 1973; Edina C. of C. Bus. award, 1978. Paul Harris fellow Rotary Internat., 1973. Mem. Edina C. of C., Greater Mpls. C. of C., Upper Midwest Council, NAM, Nat. Fedn. Ind. Bus., Nat. Sch. Supply and Equipment Assn. Republican. Clubs: Edina Country, Classic Car of Am., Rotary (founding pres. Edina, 1957), Masons, K.T. Patentee in field. Office: 7525 Cahill Rd Edina MN 55435

WILSON, LARRY LESTER, community action agy. exec.; b. Norfolk, Va., Feb. 6, 1954; s. Lester and Ladye Evelyn (Jordan) W.; B.A. cum laude, Harding U., 1976; M.A., Tex. A. and M. U., 1978, postgrad., 1980—; m. Evelyn Lee Garton, May 21, 1976; 1 dau., Ladye Rachel. Stock asso. J.C. Penney Co., Searcy, Ark., 1976; grad. asst. dept. polit. sci. Tex. A. and M. U., College Station, 1976; adminstrv. asst. Brazos Valley Community Action Agy., Bryan, Tex., 1977, dep. dir., 1978—. Mem. youth sub-com. Regional Adv. Council on Employment and Tng., 1979-80; precinct del. Brazos County Democratic Conv., 1980. Mem. Brazos Valley Personnel Assn. (chmn. wage and salary survey com. 1980). Ch. of Christ. Home: 2201 Echols St Bryan TX 77801 Office: 413 Varisco Bldg Bryan TX 77801

WILSON, LEROY, corp. exec.; b. Indpls., July 15, 1928; s. Paul Allison and Lula (Berry) W.; B.S. in M.E., Purdue U., 1950; m. Claudie Leenaert, Aug. 9, 1968; children—Paul Neil, Daniel Stuart, Benjamin. With Corning Glass Works (N.Y.), 1950—, European gen. sales mgr., Zurich, Switzerland, 1965-68, dep. area mgr. for Europe, Brussels, 1968-70, v.p. Corning Internat., area mgr. Can. and Latin Am., Corning, 1970-75, corporate v.p., gen. mgr. electronic products div., Corning, 1975-80, dir. Corning France, Avon, Corning Internat. Corp., N.Y.C. and pres. Corning Europe Inc., Nevilly, France, 1980—; chmn. bd. Siecor Optical Cables, Inc., Horseheads, N.Y., 1977-80; chmn. bd., chief exec. officer Superior Cable Corp., Hickory, N.C., 1980; dir. Sovcor S.A., LeVesinet, France, Siecor GmbH, Munich, Germany. Served with Chem. Corps, AUS, 1954-56. Episcopalian. Club: Union (N.Y.C.). Home: 62 Blvd de Courcelles 75017 Paris France Office: Corning Europe Inc 185 Ave Charlesde Gaulle Neuilly France

WILSON, LLOYD LEE, housing co. exec.; b. Elkton, Md., Sept. 14, 1947; s. Clifton Laws and Betty Raye (Bare) W.; B.S., M.I.T., 1969, M.S., 1977. Bus. mgr. med. clinics Mass. Gen. Hosp., Boston, 1970-73; partner Willow Co., mgmt. cons.'s, Cambridge, Mass., 1974-77; dir. community relations Wilson Neuropsychiat. Hosp., Charlottesville, Va., 1977-78; exec. dir. Jefferson Area United Transp. Inc., Charlottesville, 1978-80, Va. Mountain Housing Inc., Blacksburg, 1980—; pres., dir. Va. Housing Coalition, Inc., 1981—. Vice-chmn., Montgomery County Community Services Commn., 1980—. Bd. dirs. Interfaith Housing Corp., 1975-77, treas., 1976-77; mem. corp. Cambridge Friends Sch., 1970-77; bd. dirs. Am. Friends Service Com., Inc., Phila., 1980—; mem. permanent bd. New Eng. Yearly Meeting of Friends, 1975-77, human resources assembly, 1978-80; regional exec. com. Am. Friends Service Com., 1975-77; ednl. council MIT, 1978—. Home: No 4 Wingo Pembroke VA 24136 Office: 400 Draper Rd Blacksburg VA 24060

WILSON, LOCKRIDGE WARD, investment counselor; b. Roswell, N.Mex., Jan. 14, 1919; s. William Lockridge and Freda (Brough) W.; M.S., U. So. Calif., 1953; m. Fern Pauline Brown, Mar. 14, 1942; children—Larry Ward, David Brown. Tchr., adminstr. Los Angeles Unified Sch. Dist., 1942-73; investment cons., pres. Am. Bus. Corp. Universal, Carlsbad, Calif., 1973—. Served to lt. USNR, 1942-46; Philippines. Cert. sch. adminstr., Calif. Mem. Delta Upsilon. Republican. Mem. Christian Ch.-Disciples of Christ. Club: Kiwanis (pres. local club 1963). Home: 4798 Hillside Dr Carlsbad CA 92008

WILSON, LOUISE LOEFFLER, metals co. exec.; b. Pitts., May 15, 1931; d. Emil F. and Hilda (Beck) Loeffler; B.A., Chatham Coll., 1952; m. Robert K. Wilson, 1952 (div.); children—Kenneth Taft, Lesley Louise. Actuary, Marsh & McLennan, Boston and Pitts., 1952-53, 57-58; freelance writer, 1953-54, 58-59; asst. dir., acting dir. pub. relations Chatham Coll., Pitts., 1955-57; budget analyst Allstate Ins., Pitts., 1960-61; dir. publs. and research asso. Found. for Study Cycles, Pitts., 1961-66; info. retrieval specialist U. Pitts., 1967; coordinator info. center Alcoa, Pitts., 1967-76, internat. forecaster, 1969-76, fin. analyst, 1969-76, asso. economist, 1976—; mem. Nat. Materials Adv. Bd., I.E.P.A.; mem. commn. on sociotech. systems NRC. Trustee Chatham Coll., 1976-78; bd. dirs. UN Assn. Pitts., 1975-78. Mem. Pitts. Econ. Club, Nat. Economists Club, Council of the Americas, Bus. Roundtable (econ. com.), Chatham Coll. Alumnae Assn. (exec. council), Nat. Assn. Bus. Economists, 4th Dist. Fed. Res. Roundtable, Am. Council for Capital Formation, Soc. Govt. Economists, Aluminum Assn. (econ. com.). Republican. Presbyterian. Author: Catalogue of Cycles: Part I-Economics, 1964; contbr. articles to profl. jours. Home: 704 S Pitt St Alexandria VA 22314 Office: 1200 Ring Bldg Washington DC 20036

715 WHO'S WHO IN FINANCE AND INDUSTRY

WILSON, PATRICIA POPLAR, elec. mfg. exec.; b. Chgo., Sept. 20, 1931; d. George and Leona (O'Brien) Poplar; B.S., U. Wash., 1966, M.A., 1967, Ph.C., 1977; m. Chester Goodwin Wilson, Jan. 30, 1960; children—Susan Spadafora, Chester Wilson. Instr., U. Wash., Seattle, 1967-74; women's editor Nor'westing Mag., Seattle, 1969—, now editor; pres. Wilson & Assos. Northwest Inc., Seattle, 1974—; v.p. Northwest Mfg. & Supply, Inc., 1977—, Northwest Mfg. & Supply Ltd., 1980—; dir. Trydor Sales Ltd.; lectr. in field. Mem. Electric League. Episcopalian. Club: Seattle Yacht. Author: Household Equipment, A Guide to Surplus Equipment. Contbr. articles to profl. jours. Home: 1612 22d E Seattle WA 98112 Office: 2400 6th Ave S Suite 254 Seattle WA 98134

WILSON, PAUL JOHN STUART, trust co. exec.; b. Surbiton, Eng., Sept. 10, 1940; came to U.S., 1977, naturalized, 1978; m. Leslie Trayton and Elizabeth Anne (Whiting) W.; student McGill U., 1960-61; B.A. in English Lit., Concordia U., Montreal, Que., Can., 1965; m. Pamela Jane Todds, June 7, 1967: children—Jane, Andrew. Mgr. advt. and public relations Allis-Chalmers Can. Ltd., Montreal, 1963-67; mgr. advt. Cominco Ltd., Vancouver, B.C., Can., 1967-73; sr. public relations adv. The Royal Bank of Can., Montreal, 1973-77; v.p. corp. communications Bankers Trust Co., N.Y.C., 1977—. Mem. Internat. Advt. Assn., Publicity Club N.Y. Clubs: N.Y. Athletic (N.Y.C.); Royal St. Lawrence Yacht (Montreal). Home: 140 E 56th St New York NY 10022 Office: 280 Park Ave New York NY 10017

WILSON, RAY CLARENCE, banking exec.; b. Houston, July 10, 1929; s. Rogers C. and Hattie (Schumacher) W.; A.A., Blinn Coll., 1947; B.B.A., U. Tex., 1949, M.B.A., 1951; m. Lucy Ann Reid, Mar. 23, 1951; children—Reid Carroll, Cynthia Ann, Lisa Ann. Asst. mgr. mortgage loan dept. Richard Gill Co., San Antonio, 1951-54; loan insp. Nat. Life Ins. Co., Montpelier, Vt., 1954-58; regional supr. Jefferson Standard Life Ins. Co., Greensboro, N.C., 1958-63; v.p. Am. Nat. Ins. Co., Galveston, Tex., 1963-69, sr. v.p., 1969-72; pres. ANREM Corp., 1969-72; chmn. bd., mng. trustee Diversified Mortgage Investors, Boston, 1972-74; pres. Diversified Advisers, Inc., Coral Gables, Fla., 1972-74; chmn., chief exec. officer Rotan Mosle Mortgage Co., Houston, 1974-77, also pres. Rotan Mosle Realty Investments, 1974-77; sr. v.p. Soc. for Savs., Hartford, Conn., 1977-78, San Antonio Savs., 1978—; pres. Mortgage Corp. Tex., 1978—; lectr. Realtors Inst., U. N.C., 1960-63, Mortgage Banking Seminar Mich. State U., 1961-68, So. Meth. U., 1969-71, Sch. Mortgage Banking, Northwestern U., 1964-66, Chmn. acquisitions and preservations com. Galveston Hist. Found., 1965-66. Bd. dirs. Galveston YMCA, 1964-68; trustee Trinity Episcopal Sch., 1965-72. Mem. Am. Inst. Real Estate Appraisers, Urban Land Inst., Tex. Mortgage Bankers Assn. (dir. 1966-72), Mortgage Bankers Assn. Am., Internat. Council Shopping Centers, Phi Sigma Kappa. Republican. Episcopalian. Clubs: Hartford; Galveston Artillery (pres. 1971); Oak Hills Country. Home: 207 Sheffield Pl San Antonio TX 78213 Office: 601 NW Loop 410 San Antonio TX 78216

WILSON, RICHARD AMOS, mgmt. cons.; b. Tacoma, July 25, 1926; s. Amos S. and Elizabeth A. (Giblett) W.; B.S. in Elec. Engring., U. Wash., 1947, M.S. in Elec. Engring., 1949; m. Frances J. Elliott, Nov. 28, 1958; children—Richard D., Susan E., Lorinne A., Erin A. Teaching fellow U. Wash., Seattle, 1947-49; project engr. Sperry Gyroscope Co., N.Y.C., 1949-50; sr. engr. Canoga Corp., Los Angeles, 1950-54; pres. Redcor Corp., Los Angeles, 1956-65; gen. mgmt. cons. March Assocs., Los Angeles, 1965—; chmn. exec. com. Britt Corp., Los Angeles, 1973—. Served to lt. USNR, 1944-45, 54-56. Mem. Sigma Xi, Tau Beta Pi. Home: 7612 March Ave Canoga Park CA 91304 Office: 11707 W Exposition Blvd Los Angeles CA 90064

WILSON, RICHARD JOSEPH, steel co. exec.; b. Chgo., Nov. 5, 1925; s. Clarence and Catherine (Curley) W.; B.S. in Metall. Engring., U. Minn., 1949; m. Mary Louise Movius, Aug. 5, 1946; children—Thomas R., Stephen J., Catherine M., Robert M., Therese M., Richard K., Mary P., James F., Kevin J. Blast furnace engr., trainee Inland Steel Co., East Chicago, Ind., 1949-55, asst. supt. blast furnaces, 1955-68, mgr. iron prodn., 1968-71, mgr. steel prodn., 1971, asst. gen. mgr. primary prodn., 1971—. Served to ensign USN, 1943-46. Mem. Am. Iron and Steel Inst. (recipient Tech. award 1957), AIME (J.E. Johnson award 1961), Western States Blast Furance and Coke Assn. Roman Catholic. Club: Woodmar Country. Home: 8311 Linden Munster IN 46321 Office: Inland Steel Co 3210 Watling East Chicago IN 46312

WILSON, ROBERT FRANCIS, lawyer; b. Fitzsimons, Colo., Nov. 16, 1943; s. Robert Wilbur and Alice J'Leane (Beasley) W.; B.S. in Bus. Adminstrn., U. Denver, 1966, M.S. in Bus. Adminstrn., 1967; J.D., U. So. Calif., 1970; m. Jane Harwell Trotter, Mar. 7, 1970; children—Graham Buchanan, Kirsten Marshall. Admitted to Calif. bar, 1972, Colo. bar, 1973; tax accountant Arthur Young & Co., San Diego, 1970-72; partner firm Gorsuch, Kirgis, Campbell, Walker & Grover, Denver, 1972-81; shareholder Pendleton, Sabian & Craft, P.C., 1981—. C.P.A. Mem. Am. (taxation, corp., banking, bus. law sects.), Colo., Denver bar assns., State Bar Calif., Beta Alpha Psi. Home: 3860 S Narcissus Way Denver CO 80237

WILSON, ROBERT JAMES, lawyer, assn. exec.; b. Grand Rapids, Mich., June 2, 1902; s. James Alexander and Annie E. (McAlpine) W.; A.B., U. Mich., 1925, J.D., 1929; m. Helen Ruth Gillespie, Aug. 22, 1959. Admitted to Mich. bar, 1929, D.C. bar, 1961; partner firm Warner, Norcross & Judd, Grand Rapids, Mich., 1931-42; v.p., gen. counsel Capital Airlines, Inc. (now United Airlines), Washington, 1947-61; dir., chmn. bd. Airlines Nat. Terminal Corp., 1961-66; pres., dir., chmn. bd. Universal Airlines, Inc., Detroit, 1966-69; exec. v.p., sec.-treas. Nat. Alliance Businessmen, 1969—; partner Patterson, Belknap & Webb, N.Y.C. and Washington; dir. Eastide Terminal Corp., W. Side Terminal Corp., Airlines Nat. Terminal Service Co.; chmn. Loudoun County (Va.) Indsl. Adv. Bd., 1971-72. Commr. City of Grand Rapids (Mich.), 1936-42; sr. warden Episcopal Ch., Oatlands, Va. Recipient U.S. Presdl. citations, 1972, 76, 78. Mem. Mich. Bar Assn., D.C. Bar, Mich. Assn. of Professions. Republican. Clubs: Internat. (Washington), Peninsular (Grand Rapids), Belle Haven Country (Alexandria, Va.). Home: Grapelands Farm Route 2 Box 394 Leesburg VA 22075

WILSON, ROBERT L., architect; b. Tampa, Fla., Oct. 17, 1934; s. Ashbert and Flossie M. (Jones) W.; B.Arch., Columbia U., 1963, M.Arch., 1969, M.Urban Design, 1971; m. Mary A. Davis, Aug. 12, 1961; children—Kevin, Brian, Bret. Draftsman, Robert J. Reilly Architect, N.Y.C., 1956-57; archtl. draftsman Voorhees, Walker, Smith, Smith & Hynes, N.Y.C., 1957-59; project architect, designer Emery Roth & Sons, N.Y.C., 1959-63; project architect Charles Luckman Assos., N.Y.C., 1963-66; pres. Robert L. Wilson Assos., Architects/Planners, Stamford (Conn.), Boston, Tampa, 1966—; lectr. Yale U., 1970—, U. Kans., 1976—, U. Tex., 1977—, Hampton Inst., 1977—; cons. Nat. Acad. Scis., Nat. Endowment for Arts, 1977—. Bd. dirs. Stamford Family and Children Services, 1971-75. Registered architect, Tex., La., Calif., Miss., Conn., N.Y., N.J., Mass., R.I., Ga., Fla. Mem. AIA (dir. 1975, nat. v.p. 1976-77), Conn. Soc. Architects (design award 1973, pres. 1975), Nat. Orgn. Minority Architects (co-founder, dir. 1971-75), N.Y. Coalition Black Architects (founder). Prin. works include office bldgs., apts., transp., New Hope Towers Apts., Stamford, 1970. Office: 733 Summer St Stamford CT 06901

WILSON, ROBERT MCALLISTER, energy co. exec.; b. Detroit, Sept. 1, 1925; s. Robert Willett and Nan (McAllister) W.; A.B., Princeton, 1947; m. Christine J. Crouse, May 26, 1951; children—Lawrence Boyd, Lindsay W. Bibler. Public relations and advt. positions Inland Steel Co., 1949-54, No. Trust Co., 1954-66, Youngstown Sheet & Tube Co., 1966-70; v.p. corp. communications Peoples Energy Corp., 1970—. Mem. Chgo. Crime Commn.; mem. citizens bd. Loyola U.; bd. dirs. DuSable Mus. African Am. History. Mem. Pub. Relations Soc. Am. (pres. Chgo. chpt. 1971), Pub. Relations Clinic Chgo. (pres. 1961). Clubs: Chicago Press, Univ., Valley-Lo Sports. Home: 1545 Winnetka Rd Glenview IL 60025 Office: 122 S Michigan Ave Chicago IL 60603

WILSON, TERRENCE RAYMOND, corporate exec.; b. St. Louis, July 1, 1943; s. Raymond Lemuel and Eula Ellen (Sutton) W.; student Drury Coll., 1961-62, St. Louis Jr. Coll., 1962-64, Mo. U., 1965-67; m. Judy Marie Coleman, May 23, 1964; children—John Scott, Dustin Martin. Program control planning adminstr. McDonnell Aircraft, St. Louis, 1962-65, 67; mgmt. control mgr. Vitro Labs., Silver Spring, Md., 1966; mgr. customer service Teledyen Wis. Motor Co., Milw., 1968-69, dir. ops., 1970-71, dir. mktg., 1972-73; gen. mgr. Teledyne Still-Man, Cookeville, Tenn., 1973-74, pres. multiplant div., 1975-78, group exec. Teledyne, Inc., 1979—. dir. Citizens Bank. Bd. dirs. Community Symphony, Tenn. Tech. U. Coll. Bus. Found. Mem. Nat. Mgmt. Assn. (Leadership award 1970), Cookeville C. of C., Am. Mgmt. Assn., Sales and Mktg. Execs., Systems and Procedures Assn., Beta Gamma Sigma. Roman Catholic. Clubs: K.C., Rotary, Cookeville Golf and Country. Home: 1430 Pilot Dr Cookeville TN 38501 Office: PO Box 789 1011 Volunteer Dr Cookeville TN 38501

WILSON, THOMAS EVANS, JR., constrn. co. exec.; b. Darlington, S.C., Oct. 27, 1909; s. Thomas Evans and Bertha Lesesne (Briggs) W.; B.S. in Civil Engring., The Citadel, 1931; m. Maudine Lamar Arnau, May 13, 1944; children—Suzanne Lamar, Thomas Evans III, Alexa Spain. Instrumentman, resident engr. S.C. Hwy. Dept., 1931-42; engr., supt. William F. Bowe Co., Augusta, Ga., 1946-52; with reorganized co. So. Roadbuilders, Inc., 1952—, pres., 1966—; owner Roadbuilders Leasing Co., Augusta, 1966—; partner Hillside Devel. Co., Augusta, 1952—; hon. dir. Ga. R.R. & Banking Co., Augusta, Ga. R.R. Bank & Trust Co. Past bd. dirs. United Way Richmond, Columbia Counties and N. Augusta; pres. Richmond County Hist. Soc.; pres., trustee Tuttle Newton Home, Augusta; mem. exec. com. Univ. Hosps. Health Care Found., Augusta. Served to maj. AUS, 1942-46. Registered profl. engr., Ga. Mem. Nat. Soc. Profl. Engrs. (life), Ga. Soc. Profl. Engrs., ASCE (life), Ga. Hwy. Contractors Assn. (pres. 1972-73), Am. Rd. Builders Assn. (past pres. contractors div.), Nat. Constrn. Industry Assn. (chmn.), Am. Concrete Paving Assn. (past pres.), Huguenot Soc. S.C. Episcopalian (past sr. warden). Rotarian (past pres. Augusta). Clubs: Augusta Country, Pinnacle, Westlake Country (Augusta). Home: 3067 Hillside Dr Augusta GA 30904 Office: 2312 Walden Dr Augusta GA 30903

WILSON, THORNTON ARNOLD, airplane co. exec.; b. Sikeston, Mo., Feb. 8, 1921; s. Thornton Arnold and Daffodil (Allen) W.; student Jefferson City (Mo.) Jr. Coll., 1938-40; B.S., Iowa State Coll. 1943; M.S. Calif. Inst. Tech., 1948; Sloan fellow Mass. Inst. Tech., 1952-53; m. Grace Miller, Aug. 5, 1944; children—Thornton Arnold III, Daniel Allen, Sarah Louise. With Boeing Co., Seattle, 1943—, asst. chief tech. staff, project engring. mgr., 1957-58, v.p., mgr. Minuteman br. aerospace div., 1962-64, v.p. ops. and planning, 1964-66, exec. v.p., then pres., dir., 1966-72, chief exec. officer, 1969—, chmn. bd., 1972—; mem. bus. council, dir. Seattle First Nat. Bank; dir. PACCAR, Inc., U.S. Steel. Bd. govs. Iowa State U. Found.; mem. corp. M.I.T. Fellow Am. Inst. Aeros. and Astronautics; mem. Beta Theta Pi. Clubs: Rainier, Seattle Golf. Office: The Boeing Co PO Box 3707 Seattle WA 98124

WILSON, WILLIAM DALE, travel mgmt. exec.; b. Los Angeles, Sept. 24, 1938; s. William Burnett and Rose Marie (Rendinell) W.; A.A., Santa Monica Coll., 1962; B.S., UCLA, 1964; M.B.A., Calif. State U., Long Beach, 1968; m. Virginia Ellen Barth, July 20, 1968; children—Travis Blythe, Ross William. Asst. mgr. bus. mgmt. Ford div. Ford Motor Co., Los Angeles, 1964-70; mgmt. cons. Peat, Marwick, Mitchell & Co., C.P.A.'s, Los Angeles, 1970; West Coast fin. mgr. Macmillan Co., Beverly Hills, Calif., 1970-71; fin. mgr. and asst. corp. sec. Benziger Bruce & Glencoe, Inc., Beverly Hills, 1970-75; treas./controller Bowne of Los Angeles, Inc., 1975-80; dir. fin. Decker Internat., Los Angeles, 1980—; instr. bus. mgmt. Santa Monica Coll., 1971—, El Camino Coll., 1975-77. Served with U.S. Army, 1958-60. Mem. Bruin Bench, UCLA Alumni Assn., Beta Theta Pi. Republican. Presbyterian. Office: 515 S Flower St Suite 325 Los Angeles CA 90071

WILSON, WILLIAM FEATHERGAIL, petroleum co. ofcl., geologist; b. San Antonio, Dec. 25, 1934; s. Glenn Caldwell and Marion (Hord) W.; B.A., U. Tex., Austin, 1957, B.S. with honors, 1960, M.A., 1962; m. Elizabeth Gail Harmison, Mar. 17, 1979; children—Douglas Hord, Clayton Hill, Wendy Elanore. With dept. geology U. Tex., 1958-61, Texaco, Inc., 1961-65, El Paso Natural Gas Co., 1965-66; ind. petroleum geologist, rancher, real estate exec., 1966-70; environ. geologist Alamo Area Council Govts., 1970; account exec. Merrill Lynch Fenner & Smith, 1970-74; sr. exploration geologist Tesoro Petroleum Corp., San Antonio, 1974, exploration mgr. Tex. dist., 1974-76, Eastern hemisphere, 1976-78; exploration mgr. Placid Oil Co., San Antonio, 1978—; adj. instr. geology U. Tex., San Antonio, 1976—. Mem. Am. Assn. Petroleum Geologists (cert.), Geol. Soc. Am., Assn. Profl. Geol. Scientists (cert.), S. Tex. Geol. Soc. (pres., editor bull. 1976—), AAAS, Sigma Gamma Epsilon. Contbr. stories to San Antonio mag., articles to profl. jours. Home: 422 Fantasia San Antonio TX 78216 Office: 1635 NE Loop 410 Suite 803 San Antonio TX 78209

WILTSE, DORR NORMAN, ins. exec.; b. Caro, Mich., Sept. 20, 1911; s. Norman Anson and Evie Markham (McCartney) W.; student Eastern Mich. U., 1931-33; teaching cert. Central Mich. U., 1933-37; m. Gladys May Garner, Nov. 11, 1932; children—Dorr Norman, Saire Christina. Tchr., Tuscola County (Mich.) Public Schs., 1931-42; br. mgr. Mich. Mut. Ins. Co., Caro, 1942-75; city assessor, Caro, 1964—, also casualty ins. cons., Caro, 1975-79. Vice pres. Caro Devel. Corp., 1975-79; adv. bd. DeMolay Found. of Mich., 1965-67; founder, pres. Watrousville-Caro Area Hist. Soc., 1972-75, 78; pres. Caro Hist. Commn., 1975-79; chmn. Caro Bicentennial Commn., 1975-76; mem. Com. to Elect Pres. Gerald R. Ford, 1975-76; mem. Indianfields-Caro-Almer Planning Commn., 1972-79. Named Citizen of Year, Caro C. of C., 1975. Mem. Mich. Assessors Assn., Caro Masonic Bldg. Assn., Inc. (pres. 1974-79), Nat. Trust Hist. Preservation, Nat. Hist. Soc., Hist. Soc. Mich., Huguenot Soc. Mich., Saginaw Geneal. Soc., Mich. Archaeol. Soc. Democrat. Presbyterian (elder). Clubs: Caro Lions (pres. 1946), Mich. Mut. Quarter Century, Masons (past master), Shriners. Author: The First Hundred Years, 1978; The Hidden Years of the Master, 1976; The Wiltse Saga, 1980. Home: 708 W Sherman St Caro MI 48723 Office: 247 S State St Caro MI 48723

WIMBERLY, WILLIAM FINCH, agrl. co. exec.; b. Brandon, Tex., Dec. 30, 1928; s. William Finch and Oral Magdalene (Gibson) W.; B.S., Tex. A. and M. U., 1959; m. Ruth Elder, Aug. 12, 1974; children by previous marriage—William Finch III, Brenda Sue. Mgr., High Plains Sesame Growers, Inc. (Tex.), 1959-62; v.p. Tex. Sesame Growers, Inc., 1962-66; exec. v.p. Tex. Sesame div. Paris Milling Co., Muleshoe, Tex., 1966-78; gen. mgr. Agrow Swine, Houston, 1979—, Bobby Free Farms, Inc., Muleshoe, 1980—; sec., dir. Tidwell's, Inc.; exec. v.p., dir. Mountain Mills, Lubbock, Tex. Served with USAF, 1952-56. Mem. Nat., Tex. feed and grain assns., Grain Sorghum Producers Assn. (past dir.), Muleshoe C. of C. (dir.), Phi Kappa Phi, Phi Eta Sigma, Alpha Zeta. Methodist. Home: PO Box 690 Muleshoe TX 79347

WINDELS, PAUL, JR., lawyer; b. Bklyn., Nov. 13, 1921; s. Paul and Louise E. (Gross) W.; A.B., Princeton, 1943; J.D., Harvard, 1948; m. Patricia Ripley, Sept. 10, 1955; children—Paul III, Mary Hyde, James H.R., Patrick Dillon. Admitted to N.Y. State bar, 1949; spl. asst. counsel N.Y. State Crime Commn., 1951; asst. U.S. atty. Eastern Dist. N.Y., 1953-56; N.Y. regional adminstr. SEC, 1956-61, also spl. asst. U.S. atty. for prosecution securities frauds, 1956-58; lectr. law Am. Inst. Banking, 1950-57; partner Windels, Marx, Davies & Ives, and predecessors, 1961—; pres. Franklin Custodian Funds, Inc., 1962-66. Trustee Fedn. French Alliances French Inst./Alliance Française; v.p. Bklyn. Law Sch.; chmn. bd. Lycée Français de N.Y. Served from pvt. to capt. F.A., AUS, 1943-46; ETO; maj. Res. Decorated officer Nat. Order Merit (France). Mem. Am., N.Y. State, N.Y. County bar assns., Fed. Bar Council, Assn. Bar City N.Y., Harvard Law Sch. Assn. (v.p.), Am. Soc. French Acad. Palms (pres.). Republican. Presbyterian. Author: Our Securities Markets—Some SEC Problems and Techniques, 1962. Home: 1220 Park Ave New York NY 10028 Office: Windels Marx Davies & Ives 51 W 51st St New York NY 10019

WINDHEIM, PAUL, coating fabrics co. exec.; b. Bklyn., Nov. 27, 1919; s. Leonard and Sara Reva (Markun) W.; B.A. with hons., U. Pa., 1941, M.A., 1942; certificate Army Specialized Tng. Program, U. Minn., 1944; m. Gertrude Marion Kramer, June 8, 1948; children—Susan Jean, Amy Debra. Plant mgr. White Mountain Mfg. Co., Plymouth, N.H., 1946-49; pres., treas. Markun Bros., Inc., Boston, 1950-66; pres. Windmill Fashions Co., Boston, 1954-66; treas. Mr. J. Sportswear, Boston, 1962-64; dir. purchasing Shutzer Industries, Lawrence, Mass., 1966-75; gen. mgr. Pyrotex Corp. Leominster, Mass., 1976-79; exec. Kaplan-Symon Co., Braintree, Mass., 1979—; cons. in field; notary pub. Commonwealth of Mass. Served with U.S. Army, 1942-46. Mem. Convas Products Assn. Internat., Am. Soc. Notaries. Republican. Jewish. Club: B'nai B'rith (charter mem., past pres.). Home: 132 Hagen Rd Newton Centre MA 02159 Office: 115 Messina Dr Braintree MA 02184

WINDHORST, DONALD EUGENE, advt. co. exec.; b. Louisville, Dec. 18, 1933; s. Andrew and Anna Pearl (Miller) W.; student public schs., Louisville, m. Bobbie Ann Scott, June 5, 1959; children—Donald Eugene, Mark A., Janet L., Sandra L. With Gen. Outdoor Advt. Co. Louisville, 1952-55; v.p. Windhorst Sign Co., Inc., Louisville. 1955-60; pres. Louisville Outdoor Advt. Co., Inc., 1960-72; sales Naegele Outdoor Advt. Co. Louisville, 1972-77, v.p., sales mgr., 1977-79, pres. and gen. mgr., 1979—; mem. exec. com. Maj. Media, Inc. Recipient 1st pl. Addy award Am. Advt. Fedn., 1974. Republican. Baptist. Clubs: Masons, Shriners, Advt. Louisville, Jefferson, Hurstbourne Country. Home: 2203 Stannye Dr Louisville KY 40222 Office: 1501 Lexington Rd Louisville KY 40206

WINDLINGER, JEROME LEO, oil co. exec.; b. San Antonio, Tex., Aug. 29, 1926; s. Herman J. and Amanda Marie (Sueltenfus) W.; B.B.A., St. Mary's U., 1948; postgrad. U. Houston, 1949-50, S. Tex. Coll. Law, 1950-51; m. Mary A. Howard, June 18, 1949; children—Susan, Jerome L., John, Joan, Jane, James, Sarah. Accountant, Humble Oil & Refining Co., Houston, 1948-49; with Exxon Co., Houston, 1966—, chief tax agent, property tax mgr., 1972-79; cons. tax policy, 1979—. Served with USN, 1944-46. Mem. Houston C. of C. (chmn. edn. com. 1974-76), Inst. Property Taxation (founder, bd. govs. 1976—), Tax Research Assn. Harris County (pres. 1979—), Tex. Mid-Continent Oil and Gas Assn., Am. Petroleum Inst., Sons of Hermann of Tex. Roman Catholic. Democrat. Clubs: Alto Lakes Golf and Country, K.C. Home: 7806 Hiawatha St Houston TX 77036 Office: PO Box 392 Houston TX 77001

WINDSOR, ROBERT WILKS, JR., beer distbg. co. exec.; b. Wilmington, Del., Oct. 8, 1918; s. Robert Wilks and Mary Bethany (Hackett) W.; student U. Va., 1937; B.S., U.S. Naval Acad., 1941; postgrad., U.S. Naval Test Pilot Sch., 1950-51, George Washington U., 1963-64; m. Elizabeth Foster, Oct. 29, 1946; 1 son, Robert Grover. Commd. ensign U.S. Navy, 1941, advanced through grades to capt., 1958; test pilot; various commands VC-68, VF-32, VF-24; comdg. officer USS Currituck, USS Independence; ret., 1967; exec. asst. to pres. Vought Corp., Dallas, 1967-76; partner Windward Co., Deer Park, Tex., 1976—, also dir. Decorated D.F.C., Bronze Star medal, Vietnamese Cross of Gallantry; recipient Thompson trophy as 1st pilot to fly over 1000 MPH in other than exptl. aircraft, 1956. Assn. fellow Soc. Exptl. Test Pilots; mem. Navy League (dir., Dallas 1967-68), Assn. Naval Aviation (trustee), Air Force Assn., Smithsonian Assos., Naval Inst. Clubs: New York Yacht, Brook Hollow Golf, American (London), Army-Navy Country, Las Colinas Country, Princess Anne Country. Home: 27 River Hollow Houston TX 77027 Office: Windward Co Box C Deer Park TX 77536

WINEGARDNER, ROY E., hotel corp. exec.; b. 1920. Contractor and developer Holiday Inn franchise, from 1959, past 1st vice chmn. bd., chief operating officer, Holiday Inns, Inc., now chmn. bd., chief exec. officer. Office: Holiday Inns Inc 3742 Lamar Ave Memphis TN 38195

WINFIELD, NIGEL JOHN, aircraft co. exec.; b. Bilaspur, India, June 23, 1937; came to U.S., 1948, naturalized, 1959; s. Malcolm Henry and Ena Mary (Burns) W.; student public schs., Boston; m. Patricia Holmberg, June 26, 1971; 1 dau., Nikki. Owner, operator Winfield Jet Center, Ft. Lauderdale, Fla., 1977—; owner Winfield Racing Stables, Ft. Lauderdale, 1975—; pres. Comml. Airtransport Sales Corp., Ft. Lauderdale, 1972—. Served with USAF, 1960-61. Republican. Roman Catholic. Home: 13920 Stirling Rd Fort Lauderdale FL 33330 Office: 701 SW 48th St Fort Lauderdale Internat Airport Fort Lauderdale FL 33315

WING, JERRY WINSTON, mfg. co. exec.; b. Tulsa, May 27, 1944; s. Jerome Sidney and Miriam Carolyn (Chapman) W.; B.A., Okla. State U., 1972, M.B.A., 1975; postgrad. U. Okla., 1976-77; m. Terttu M. Kuusela, July 16, 1977. Program mgr. Nat. Alliance of Bus., Tulsa, 1972-73; pres. Wing/Compu-Dine Corp., Norman, Okla., 1975-77; program dir. Nat. Alliance of Bus., Washington, 1977-80; dir. internat. mktg. Tracor, Inc., Alexandria, Va., 1980—; mem. adv. com. Office of Fed. Contract Compliance Programs, Washington, 1979, Council for Exceptional Children, Washington, 1978-79, Indochina Refugee program, Washington, 1980. Served with USMC, 1966-69. Recipient Presdl. Commendation, 1980. Mem. Am. Mktg. Assn., Assn. MBA Execs., Fin. Mgmt. Assn., Beta Gamma Sigma. Republican. Methodist. Contbr. articles to profl. jours. Home: 17 S Ingram St

Alexandria VA 22304 Office: Skyline East Bldg Off Route 7 Alexandria VA 22302

WINGERTER, LAURENCE ADRIAN, JR., motor freight transp. exec.; b. N.Y.C., Apr. 30, 1942; s. Laurence Adrian and Mary Margaret (Willman) W.; A.B., Stanford, 1964; m. Jeanie Pinkston, Feb. 14, 1966. Terminal supr. Red Arrow Freight Lines, Dallas, 1965-66, Corpus Christi, Tex., 1966-67, field supr., San Antonio, 1967-70, customer service mgr., 1970-73, v.p., 1973-75, v.p. adminstrn., 1975—, also dir., dir. affiliated cos.; v.p. Southwestern Claim Conf., 1973-74; bd. govs. Regular Common Carrier Conf., Am. Trucking Assn., 1979—. Unitarian. Home: Route 3 PO Box 1022 San Antonio TX 78218 Office: PO Box 1897 3901 Seguin Rd San Antonio TX 78297

WINIARZ, JEAN ELAINE, real estate broker; b. Old Town, Maine, Aug. 27, 1934; d. Orland Kent and Helen Louise Taylor; Real Estate Broker, Onondaga Community Coll., 1976; m. Joseph Winiarz, Apr. 26, 1972; children—Robert, Frank, Sue, Kimberly Ming. Beauty counselor Vanda Beauty Counselor Cosmetics Co., Orlando, Fla., 1959-62; dist. mgr. Luzier Inc., Kansas City, Mo., 1969-73; distbr. cons. Neo Life Corp., LaJolla, Calif., 1970-75; pres. Guild Fashionata, Syracuse, 1976-77; distbr. Shaklee, 1981—; cons. beauty, fashion model, coordinator. Active United Heart Assn. Mem. Greater Syracuse Bd. Realtors, Nat. Assn. Realtors.

WINKLER, JAMES HAROLD, investment adviser; b. Malersdorf, W. Ger., July 20, 1950; came to U.S., 1950, naturalized, 1956; s. Jack and Maria Winkler; A.B. magna cum laude, Brown U., 1968; J.D., Northwestern U., 1977; m. Susan R. Swire, Jan. 6, 1980. Sr. asso. ENI Corp., research and sales of tax shelters, Portland, Oreg., 1974-76; propr. Winkler Investments, venture capital and tax shelters, Portland, 1976: pres. Entax Corp., Portland, 1978—; admitted to Oreg. bar, 1978. Mem. allocations and campaign coms. Russian resettlement program Jewish Fedn. Portland. Mem. Oreg. Bar Assn. Club: Multnomah Athletic (Portland). Office: 900 SW 5th St Portland OR 97204

WINKLER, JAN JOSEF, constrn. co. exec.; b. Gottwaldov, Czechoslovakia, July 24, 1940; s. Jan and Stepanka (Obracajova) W.; grad. archtl. technologist Inst. Archtl. Engring., Gottwaldov, 1958; m. Alena Stechova, June 23, 1962; children—John, Iveta. Constrn. supt., project mgr., porject supr., Czechoslavakia, 1958-68; laborer Klymenko Masonry, Thunder Bay, Ont., Can., 1968-69; draftsman J.P. St. Jacques, architect, Thunder Bay, 1969-70; constrn. and planning asst. Confedn. Coll., Thunder Bay, 1970-74; pres. Projecta Engring. & Constrn. Inc., Thunder Bay, 1974—. Mem. adv. com. Confedn. Coll.; chmn. Thunder Bay Motocross Assn., 1971-76. Served with Czechoslovakia Army, 1958-60. Mem. Assn. Archtl. Technologists Ont., Ont. Nordic Assn. (treas. 1976-79), Can. Ski Assn. Mem. United Ch. of Can. Office: Projecta Engring & Constrn Inc Box 416 Thunder Bay ON P7C 4V2 Canada

WINN, WILLIS JAY, banker; b. Plattsburg, Mo., Apr. 26, 1917; s. Sam J. and Emma (Sell) W.; A.B., Central Coll., 1939, LL.D., 1959; M.A., U. Pa., 1940, Ph.D., 1951; m. Lois Gengelbach, Nov. 25, 1942; children—Judith Ann, Steven Jay. Research asso. Nat. Bur. Econ. Research, N.Y.C., 1942-46; with U. Pa., 1946-71, beginning as instr. finance, successively asst. prof., asso. prof., 1946-57, prof. finance, 1957-71, vice dean Wharton Sch. Finance and Commerce, 1955-57, acting dean, 1957-58, dean, 1958-71, vice provost univ., 1958-71; pres. Fed. Res. Bank, Cleve., 1971—. Chmn. Fed. Res. Bank of Phila. Dir. Nat. Bureau Econ. Research, Inc., 1959—. Mem. Am. Finance Soc., Am. Royal econ. socs. Office: Federal Reserve Bank Cleveland OH 44101

WINNINGHAM, JAMES LEWIS, bank exec.; b. Fayette, Mo., Jan. 17, 1931; s. Jesse and Helen M. W.; B.S. in Bus. Adminstrn., Central Mo. State U., Warrensburg, 1955; m. Janet L. Jurgens, Aug. 21, 1958; children—Rick E., Rhonda Lee. Engring. planner N. Am. Aviation, Los Angeles, 1955-57; indsl. relations supr. Servomechanisms, Inc., Hawthorne, Calif., 1957-60; trust officer State Bank of Arthur (Ill.), 1960, now pres., dir.; dir. Schrock Bros. Mfg. Co., Progress Industries, Inc. Served with U.S. Army, 1952-54. Mem. Ind. Community Banks of Ill. (pres.), Ill. Bankers Assn. (past pres. agri. div.), Bank Adminstrn. Inst. Methodist. Clubs: Kaskaskia Country, Decatur, Shrine-Ansar Temple, Arthur Lodge.

WINNINGSTAD, CHESTER NORMAN, computer co. exec.; b. Berkeley, Calif., Nov. 5, 1925; s. Chester Hafdan and Phyllis Ame (Whichello) W.; B.S. in Elec. Engring., U. Calif., Berkeley, 1948; M.B.A., Portland (Oreg.) State U., 1972; m. Dolores Constance Campbell, Mar. 24, 1948; children—Richard Norman, Dennis Steven, Joanne Marie. Project engr. Lawrence Berkeley Labs., 1950-58; mgr. info. display group Tektronix, Inc., Beaverton, Oreg., 1958-70; chmn., pres., chief exec. officer Floating Point Systems, Inc., Portland, 1970—. Bd. dirs. Oreg. Mus. Sci. and Industry. Served with USNR, 1942-44. Recipient Howard Vollum Sci. and Tech. award Reed Coll., 1978. Mem. IEEE, AAAS, Beaverton Area C. of C. (dir.). Club: Colombia Aviation Country. Patentee in field. Office: PO Box 23489 Portland OR 97223

WINSHIP, HENRY DILLON, trucking industry exec.; b. Macon, Ga., July 27, 1929; s. Henry Dillon and Anne (Chichester) W.; B.S. in Transp., U. Tenn.; m. Sarah Patricia Cortelyou, Sept. 28, 1951; children—Adrian C., Henry Dillon, Blanton C. With Ga. Hwy. Express, Inc., Atlanta, now chmn. bd., chief exec. officer. Served with U.S. Army, 1953-55. Mem. Transp. Assn. of Am. (dir., past chmn.), Chief Execs. Forum, Inc., World Bus. Council, Inc. Presbyterian. Clubs: Commerce, Capital, Cherokee Country. Office: 2090 Jonesboro Rd SE Atlanta GA 30315

WINSHIP, WADLEIGH CHICHESTER, express co. exec.; b. San Francisco, Oct. 3, 1940; s. Henry Dillon and Anne Eliza (Chichester) W.; student Woodberry Forest (Va.) Sch., 1954-56; grad. Darlington Sch., Rome, Ga., 1959; B.A., U. Ga., 1964; m. Lynne McPherson, Dec. 28, 1970. Exec. trainee G. Hwy. Express, Inc., Atlanta, 1964-68; exec. v.p., 1968—, also dir., mem. exec. com.; pres., chmn. SurfAir, Inc., Atlanta, 1970—; v.p., dir. Transus, Inc. Chmn. transp. com. A.R.C., Atlanta, 1968—; bd. dirs. Ga. Soc. Prevention of Blindness, Alliance Theatre Co. Mem. Am. Trucking Assn. (dir. regular common carrier conf., v.p., dir. local and short haul carriers conf.), Atlanta Air Cargo Assn. (charter), Ga. Bus. and Industry Assn. (dir.), Chi Phi. Clubs: Peachtree Golf, Capital City, The Nine O'Clocks, German. Home: 3296 Rilman Rd NW Atlanta GA 30327 Office: 2090 Jonesboro Rd SE Atlanta GA 30315

WINSLOW, ROBERT ALBERT, petroleum co. exec.; b. Carthage, Ind., Feb. 5, 1922; s. William Howard and Ione (Morris) W.; B.S. in Chem. Engring., Purdue U., 1943; m. Totsye Harper, June 14, 1944; children—A. Robert, M. Craig, Judith Winslow Huchton. Engring. and managerial positions Exxon Co. USA, 1946-66; sr. v.p. Essochem Europe, 1966-68, pres., 1968-70; pres. Exxon Chem., USA, 1970-74; exec. v.p. Exxon Chem., Inc., also v.p. Exxon Corp., 1974-79; pres. Exxon Enterprises Inc., 1979—. Served with USN, 1943-46. Mem. Mfg. Chemists Assn., Soc. Chem. Industry. Presbyterian. Clubs: Stanwich (Greenwich, Conn.); Riverhill (Kerrville, Tex.); Italian (Stamford, Conn.). Office: Exxon Enterprises Inc 1251 Ave of Americas New York NY 10020

WINSTON, ARTHUR WILLIAM, physicist, indsl. controls and microwave products co. exec.; b. Toronto, Ont., Can., Feb. 11, 1930; came to U.S., 1951, naturalized, 1959; s. Maurice and Alma (Freedman) W.; B.A.Sc., U. Toronto, 1951; Ph.D., M.I.T., 1954; m. Lily Baum, Sept. 4, 1949; children—Leslie, Pamela, David, Matthew. Physicist, NRC, Toronto, 1949-51; research asst. M.I.T., Cambridge, 1951-54; sr. engr. Schlumberger Corp., Houston, 1954-57; physicist Nat. Research Corp., Cambridge, 1957-59; chief scientist Allied Research Assos., Boston, 1959-61; pres. Space Scis., Inc., Waltham, Mass., 1961-65, Ikor Inc., Burlington, Mass., 1965-75, Wincom Corp., Lawrence, Mass., 1979—; v.p. Omni-Wave Electronics Corp., Gloucester, Mass., 1976-78; dir. Granite State Controls, Inc.; asso. prof. Northeastern U., 1978—; mem. U.S. Dept. Commerce European Pollution Control Trade Mission, 1971; chmn. Electro Conf., 1960. Judge, Mass. State Sci. Fair, 1957—; chmn. internat. intercultural programs com. Lexington chpt. Am. Field Service, 1977—. Recipient cert. of appreciation U.S. Dept. Commerce, 1971; Wallberg Meml. scholar, 1949; Assn. Profl. Engrs. scholar, 1949; others. Mem. Am. Phys. Soc., IEEE, AIAA, Am. Geophys. Union, Air Pollution Control Assn., AIME, Sigma Xi. Clubs: M.I.T., Appalachian Mountain. Contbr. numerous articles to profl. jours. Home: 18 Winchester Dr Lexington MA 02173 Office: 23 Shepard St Lawrence MA 01842

WINSTON, MORTON MANUEL, oil co. exec.; b. N.Y.C., Dec. 9, 1930; s. Myron Hugh and Minna (Schneller) W.; A.B., U. Vt., 1951; M.A., U. Conn., 1953; LL.B. magna cum laude, Harvard U., 1958; m. Katherine Tupper Winn, Feb. 3, 1979; children by previous marriages—Gregory Winston, Livia Winston; stepchildren—Wesley Hudson, Laura Hudson. Admitted to D.C. bar, 1961; law clk. to Justice Frankfurter, Supreme Ct. U.S., 1959-60; asso. firm Cleary, Gottlieb, Steen & Hamilton, N.Y.C., Washington, 1960-67; v.p. Tosco Corp., N.Y.C., 1964-67, exec. v.p., 1967-71, pres., 1971—, chief exec. officer, 1976—; dir. Baker Internat. Corp., 1976—. Chmn. bd. trustees Craft and Folk Art Mus., Los Angeles, 1976—; trustee City of Hope, Los Angeles, 1977—; bd. govs. Performing Arts Council, Los Angeles. Served to lt. (j.g.) USCGR, 1953-55. Office: 10100 Santa Monica Blvd Los Angeles CA 90067

WINTER, HENRI LEONARD-MAURICE, optical co. exec.; b. Vevey, Switzerland, Dec. 21, 1943; came to U.S., 1953, naturalized, 1959; s. Adolphe and Czypa (Kalisher) W.; B.A., N.Y. Inst. Tech., 1969; M.B.A., St. Johns U., 1973; m. Sari Spilky, May 19, 1964; 2 children. With Marshall Granger & Co., Mamaroneck, N.Y., 1968-79, partner, 1977-79; v.p. fin., chief fin. officer Carl Zeiss, Inc., N.Y.C., 1979—, asst. treas., 1979—, also mem. exec. com.; dir. Carl Zeiss of Am. Holding Corp. C.P.A., N.Y. Mem. Am. Inst. C.P.A.'s, N.Y. State Soc. C.P.A.'s. Office: 444 Fifth Ave New York NY 10018

WINTER, MARTIN, lawyer, builder; b. N.Y.C., Dec. 29, 1907; s. Louis and Rose W.; B.A., Columbia U., 1928; LL.B, Fordham U., 1930; m. Adele Godfrey, Feb. 2, 1941; children—Carolyn Anderson, Marjorie Krieger. Admitted to N.Y. State bar, 1933; trust dept. exec. Central Hanover Bank, N.Y.C., 1932-33; asso. firm Seligsberg & Lewis, N.Y.C., 1933-35; founder, partner firm Chorosh & Winter, N.Y.C., 1935-77; builder housing projects, L.I., N.Y., 1947—; mem. faculty Columbia U.; lectr. Practicing Law Inst. Ofcl. adviser Mayor Lindsay's Office of S.I. Devel., 1966-72; chmn. bldg. com. Village Russell Gardens, Nassau County, N.Y. Mem. Regional Plan Assn., Nassau County Bar Assn. Club: North Shore Country (Glen Head, N.Y.). Author: Inside Staten Island, 1964.

WINTER, RICHARD ERWIN, physician, health care co. exec.; b. N.Y.C., Jan. 10, 1923; s. Leo and Sylvia (Hirschberg) W.; A.B., Lafayette Coll., 1942; M.D., N.Y. U., 1945; m. Marlys Johnson, Sept. 12, 1960 (div. Dec. 1976); children—William, Victoria, Gregory; m. 2d, Bella B. Broneman, July 16, 1979. Intern, Bellevue Hosp., N.Y.C., 1945-46, resident in internal medicine, 1946-47; practice medicine specializing in preventive medicine, N.Y.C., 1945-53, 55-59; chmn. Exec. Health Examiners Group Inc.; chmn. Nat. Health Services, Inc., N.Y.C., 1959—; med. dir. U.S. Lines, Ford Found., Govt. Employees Ins. Co. N.Y., Batten, Barton, Durstine & Osborn. Trustee, Childrens Aid Soc. Served to capt. USAF, 1953-55. Mem. N.Y. State N.Y. County med. socs., AMA, Aerospace Med. Assn., Am. Pub. Health Assn., Pan Am. Med. Assn., Am. Occupational Med. Assn. Author: Your Body and Its Care, 1959. Office: Executive Health Examiners 777 3d Ave New York NY 10017

WINTER, RONALD EUGENE, cons. engring. co. exec.; b. Toronto, Ont., Can., Aug. 10, 1926; s. Redvers Buller and Margaret Agnes (Cronmiller) W.; B.A.Sc., U. Toronto, 1949; m. Jenny Isobel Carton, Apr. 26, 1952; children—Alan Eugene, Cheryl Lee, Lori Lynn. Partner, Browne & Cavell, Engrs. & Surveyors, Toronto, 1952-53; pres., dir. R.E. Winter & Assos. Ltd., Mississauga, Ont., 1955—; dir. S.B. McLaughlin Assos. Ltd., Mississauga, 1962—; v.p. Kingscross Estates Ltd. Mem. Borough of York (Ont.) Devel. Com., 1962-65. Bd. dirs. North York Social Planning Council, 1967-68, YMCA, 1957-62. Mem. Assn. Profl. Engrs. Ont. and B.C., Assn. Cons. Engrs. Can., Cons. Engrs. Ont. Presbyterian. Home: 96 Betty Ann Dr Willowdale ON M2N 1X2 Canada Office: 77 City Centre Dr Mississauga ON Canada

WINTERER, WILLIAM G., hotel exec.; b. St. Louis, July 7, 1934; s. Herbert O. and Dorothy (Sprengnether) W.; B.A., U. Fla., 1956; M.B.A., Harvard U., 1962; m. Victoria Thompson, Sept. 2, 1967; children—William, Andrew, Britton, Mark. Mgr. corporate fin. dept., partner Goodbody & Co., 1966-69; pres. Fla. Capital Corp., Greenwich, Conn., 1969-72; owner Griswold Inn, Essex, Conn., Town Farms Inn, Middletown, Conn., 1972—; dir. Fla. Capital Corp., Zimmer Homes Corp., Jack's Food Systems, Valley R.R. Co., Cashion Systems, Inc.; mem. adv. bd. United Bank and Trust. Trustee, founding pres. Conn. River Found. at Steamboat Dock; trustee Ivoryton Playhouse Found.; corporator Middlesex Hosp.; bd. dirs. Conn. Hist. Commn., Gov.'s Vacation Travel Council. Mem. Asso. Restaurants Conn. (dir.). Republican. Roman Catholic. Clubs: N.Y. Yacht, Seawanhaka Corinthian Yacht, Essex Yacht (gov.), Pettipaug Yacht; Harvard (N.Y.C.); Old Lyme Beach; English Speaking Union. Home: Turtle Bay Essex CT 06426 Office: Main St Essex CT 06426

WINTERS, EDWARD WILLIAM, data systems co. exec.; b. Bronxville, N.Y., May 23, 1947; s. Edward and Caroline (Hanson) W.; B.S., Richmond Coll., City U. N.Y., 1970; M.S., N.Y. U., 1973; m. Ann Marie Eller, Jan. 25, 1969; 1 dau., Elizabeth. Computer applications engr. Norden div. United Aircraft, 1970; staff asst. AT&T Long Lines, White Plains, N.Y., 1970-72, mem. programming staff, 1972-74, data systems design supr., 1974—; system mgr. PSL System, 1974-80; mgr. info. systems AT&T, Piscataway, N.J., 1980—; lectr. Assn. Computing Machinery Profl. Devel. Seminars, 1975, 76; del. USA-USSR Sci. and Tech. Exchange Program, NSF, 1979. Goodwin Watson Inst. for Research and Program Devel. fellow, 1978. Mem. Am. Mgmt. Assn., Human Factors Soc., Soc. for Mgmt. Info. Systems (jour. reviewer 1977—), Assn. Computing Machinery, IEEE. Contbr. articles to bus. and profl. jours. Home: 415 Windmill Way Somerville NJ 08876 Office: Piscataway NJ 08854

WINTERS, WAYNE, editor; b. Council Bluffs, Iowa, Oct. 16, 1915; s. James Chester and Mary (Potter) W.; student pub. schs.; m. Violet Agnew, June 7, 1937 (div. 1970); children—Frances Jeannine (Mrs. John Chapman), Carl Wayne, James Curtis; m. 2d, Mary T. Martinez, 1970 (div. 1976); m. 3d, Vijaya Swamidoss, 1980. Apprentice printer Nonpareil, Council Bluffs, 1935-41; tramp printer-reporter-photographer many newspapers, 1941-46; editor, pub. Douglas (Wyo.) Budget, 1946-49; sec. Malpais Mining & Holding Co., 1951—; pres. Piedras del Sol Mining Co., 1957—; owner Nugget Pub. Co., 1960—; pub. Western Prospector and Miner; editor Tombstone (Ariz.) Epitaph. Mem. Ariz. Newspaper Assn., Ariz. Multiple Use Assn. (sec.-treas.), Am. Inst. Mining Engrs., Ariz. Small Mine Operators Assn. (pres.). Republican. Author: Blood and Gold in the Land of Enchantment, 1952; Campfires Along the Treasure Trail, 1963; Forgotten Mines and Treasures of the Great Southwest, 1972. Contbr. articles to profl. jours. Home: Box 657 Diamond Acres Tombstone AZ 85638 Office: Box 657 Tombstone AZ 85638

WINTHROP, JOHN, brokerage and investment co. exec.; b. Boston, June 22, 1936; s. Nathaniel Thayer and Serita (Bartlett) W.; B.A., Harvard Coll., 1958; M.B.A., Columbia, 1962; children—John, Henry Grenville, Bayard. Journalist, Atlantic Council U.S., Washington, 1962-63; chmn. exec. com. Wood, Struthers & Winthrop, N.Y.C., from 1964, also mem. exec. com., dir.; past chmn. Wood Struthers & Winthrop Mgmt. Corp.; chmn. deVegh Mut. Fund; founder John Winthrop & Co., investments, 1980; dir. Nat. Utilities & Industries, Elizabeth, N.J., Ivanhoe Corp., Alliance Capital Res. Fund, firm Donaldson, Lufkin and Jenrette. Former bd. dirs. Ednl. Policy Center, N.Y.C.; past trustee Greenwich Country Day Sch., St. Marks Sch., Southborough, Mass.; mem. corp. Greenwich Hosp.; vis. com. history Harvard; bd. dirs. Fresh Air Fund, N.Y.C.; bd. govs. Investment Co. Inst., Washington. Served with USNR, 1958-60. Mem. N.Y. Soc. Security Analysts, Bond Club N.Y., Nat. Audubon Soc. (dir.). Clubs: Round Hill, Field (Greenwich, Conn.); Bond, City Midday, Knickerbocker, Harvard (N.Y.); Procellian (Cambridge, Mass.). Contbr. articles to Barrons, Wall St. Jour., Trusts and Estates, Boston Globe, others. Home: John St Greenwich CT 06830 Office: 120 Broadway New York NY 10005

WINTON, THOMAS STEPHEN, oil co. exec.; b. Duncan, Okla., May 8, 1933; s. Charlie Josiah and Ila Mae (Mangum) W.; B.B.A., U. Okla., 1956; m. Norma Lee Parkhurst, June 9, 1956; 1 son, William Scott. Mgr. adminstrv. services Continental Pipeline Co., Ponca City, Okla., 1963-67, fin. coordinator, N.Y.C., 1967-71; asst. v.p. Consolidation Coal Co., Pitts., 1971-73, v.p., 1973-74; treas. Continental Oil Co., Stamford, Conn., 1974-76; v.p., treas. Conoco, Inc., Stamford, 1976—; dir. Continental Carbon Co. Bd. dirs. Stamford United Way, 1979—, mem. campaign cabinet, 1979; dir. Pitts. C. of C., 1973-74. Served to 1st lt. Transp. Corps, AUSR, 1958-67. Mem. Fair Chester Treasurers Group, Soc. Internat. Treasurers, Fin. Execs. Inst., Am. Petroleum Inst. Office: High Ridge Park Stamford CT 06904

WINZEN, JOHN PETER, mfg. co. exec.; b. Cologne, Germany, Apr. 20, 1920; came to U.S., 1938, naturalized, 1943; s. Christian Otto and Lilly J. Winzen; Abitur, Realgymnasium, Cologne, 1938; M.E. in Aero. Engring., U. Detroit, 1942; m. Mary L. Daley, Nov. 4, 1957; children—Peter, Moira, Christopher. Exec. v.p. Permanent Filter Corp., Los Angeles, 1956-60; pres. Aerospace Components Corp., Los Angeles, 1961-63; founder, owner Wintec Corp., Los Angeles, 1964-76; dir. valves and controls group, technetics div. Brunswick Corp., Anaheim, Calif., 1976—. Served with AUS, 1944-46. Decorated Commendation medal; recipient cert. of recognition NASA, 1974, Shuttle Orbiter award, 1979. Club: Palos Verdes Breakfast. Patentee in field. Home: 2872 Via Victoria Palos Verdes Estates CA 90274 Office: 1111 N Brookhurst St Anaheim CA 92801

WINZENRIED, JESSE DAVID, oil co. exec.; b. Byron, Wyo., June 13, 1922; s. Fritz and Margaret (Smith) W.; B.S., U. Wyo., 1945; M.S. (Sloan fellow), U. Denver, 1946; Ph.D. (fellow), N.Y. U., 1955; m. Marion Jacobson, Mar. 15, 1945; children—Suzan Winzenried Carlston, Jay Albert, Keith Frederic. Research dir. Tax Found., N.Y.C., 1947-56; sr. v.p. Husky Oil Ltd., Cody, Wyo., 1956-65, Calgary, Alta., Can., 1965-67; v.p. Booz, Allen, Hamilton, Cleve., 1968-69; v.p. Coastal States Gas Corp., Houston, 1969-74; group v.p., dir. Crown Central Petroleum Corp., Balt., 1974—; lectr. N.Y. U.; cons. fin. and adminstrn. State of Wyo. Mem. Govtl. Research Assn., Am. Petroleum Inst., Nat. Petroleum Refiners Assn., Ind. Petroleum Assn. Am. Republican. Mormon. Home: 220 Charmuth Rd Timonium MD 21093 Office: One N Charles St Baltimore MD 21203

WINZER, BETTY DAVENPORT, exploration co. ofcl.; b. Houston, Mar. 2, 1935; d. Travis Lamar and Ila Grace (Odom) Davenport; student pub. schs., Houston; 1 dau., Betty Kathleen. Sec. various depts. Exxon, 1953-60; legal sec. firm Liddell, Austin, Dawson & Sapp, 1961-62; legal sec., land sec., exec. sec. TransOcean Oil Co., Inc., Houston, 1962-74; exec. sec. Michel T. Halbouty, Houston, 1974-75; office mgr., exec. sec. IMC Exploration Co., Houston, 1975—. Baptist. Home: 2102 McDuffie St Houston TX 77019 Office: PO Box 55583 Houston TX 77055

WINZER, RICHARD SELLERS, cons. co. exec.; b. Sellersville, Pa., July 18, 1927; s. Fred Arnold and Bertha Leah (Sellers) W; student U. Richmond, Duke U.; m. Mary Elizabeth Lesher, Oct. 24, 1945; children—Paula K., Karen N. Ind. ins. adjuster, Reading, Pa., 1947-48; underwriter Am. Casualty Co., Reading, 1948-51, underwriter to asst. br. mgr., Chgo., 1951-56; salesman to v.p. James S. Kemper Co., Chgo., 1956-66, pres., from 1970, also dir.; pres. Central div. James S. Kemper Agy., Inc., 1966-70. Founding pres. Lutheran Ch. of Holy Spirit, Elk Grove Village, Ill. Served with USN, 1945-46. Mem. Nat. Assn. Ins. Brokers (dir.), Research Inst. Am. (dir. sales and mktg. div., award for contbn. to effective mktg.), Ind. Ins. Agts. Am., Am. Inst. Property and Liability Underwriters, Econs. Club Chgo. Club: Medinah Country. Office: Corporate Cons Inc 999 Plaza Dr Suite 400 Schaumburg IL 60195*

WIRTH, RAYMOND LUCAS, corp. exec.; b. Milw., Oct. 1, 1918; s. Reinhardt A. and Emma (Schimelpfening) W.; Ph.B., U. Wis., 1942; M.B.A, Northwestern U., 1943; m. Delaine Thisted, Aug. 31, 1946; children—Barry, Craig, Bradley. Sales research analyst Standard Oil Co. Ind., Chgo., 1943-47; v.p., gen. mgr. Thisted Motor Co., Great Falls, Mont., 1946-61; v.p. Thisted Co., 1962—; v.p., dir. Great Falls Fed. Savs. & Loan Assn., 1953-62, pres., mng. officer, dir., 1962—; pres., dir. Service Corp. Mont., 1974—; dir. Fed. Home Loan Bank San Francisco, Fed. Home Loan Bank Seattle, U.S. Savs. and Loan League; pres. Mont. Savs. and Loan League, 1972-73, now dir.; lectr. real estate, faculty Coll. Great Falls. Chmn., City-County Flood Control Commn., Mont. Auto Dealers Ins. Trust, 1958; bd. dirs., pres. Great Falls Neighborhood Housing Service, 1980—; bd. dirs., v.p. Beautification Assn., Great Falls, 1980—; mem. devel. com. Coll. of Great Falls, 1980—; mem. Great Falls Citizens Adv. Com., 1980—; Mem. Mont. (pres. 1958), Great Falls (pres. 1952) auto dealers assns., Great Falls C. of C. (dir.), Alpha Delta Sigma. Rotarian (pres. 1952-54). Home: Park Plaza 6D 405 Park Dr Great Falls MT 59401 Office: Box 2327 Great Falls MT 59401

WIRTH, RUSSELL D.L., JR., investment banker, real estate investor; b. Milw., June 30, 1930; s. Russell and Mary (McMahon) W.; B.A. summa cum laude, Yale U., 1951; M.A. with honors, Sch. Advanced Internat. Studies, Johns Hopkins U., 1954; postgrad. N.Y. U. Grad. Sch. Bus. Adminstrn., 1957-59; grad. with honors Airborne and Spl. Forces Officers Sch., 1980; m. Alice Guion Ardrey, Jan. 4, 1958 (div. Jan. 1971); children—Mary Elizabeth, Russell III. Staff, U.S. Senate Fgn. Relations Com. and aide to Senator Alexander Wiley, Washington, 1954-55; mem. corporate underwriting dept. Blyth & Co., Inc., 1957-59; loan officer for Latin Am., U.S. Devel. Loan Fund, 1960-61; co-founder, pres. Saint-Phalle Spalding & Wirth Inc., Buenos Aires, Argentina, 1962-63; exec. v.p. Internat. Investment Co., Washington, 1963-64; investment officer Chase Internat. Investment Co., 1965-66; originator, co-founder Western Am. Bank (Europe) Ltd., London, Eng., 1967; founder, pres. Puerto Rican Fin. Group (PRFG), San Juan, 1968-79; co-founder Hemisphere Oil Co., San Juan, 1976; co-founder, partner Wirth & Co. and Wirth & Wirth, Calif. real estate investment, 1979—. Republican candidate for Congress from 5th dist. of Milw., 1956. Served to capt. USMCR, Korean War; maj. Spl. Forces, U.S. Army Res. and N.G., 1977—. Decorated Bronze Star, Silver Star, Purple Heart, U.S. Korean Presdl. Unit citations. Mem. Phi Beta Kappa. Episcopalian.

WIRTHS, WALLACE RICHARD, elec. co. exec.; b. Englewood, N.J., July 7, 1921; s. Rudolph and Dorothy (Berls) W.; B.S., Lehigh U., 1942; postgrad. Fordham U. Law Sch., 1942-43; LL.D. (hon.), Upsala Coll., 1980; Asst. indsl. relations mgr. Aluminum Co. Am., Edgewater, N.J., 1943-54; pub. relations project mgr. Sylvania Elec. Products, Inc., N.Y.C., 1954-56; mgr. pub. relations Westinghouse Electric Corp., Bloomfield, N.J., 1956—; dir. Inter-Continental Enterprises, Bloomfield; owner Twin Ponds Farm Exptl. Dairy Farm, Sussex, N.J., 1958-79; v.p. Twin Ponds Excavating & Landscaping Corp.; pres. Unique Homeowners Am., 1973-79; dir. Colonial Decorators; trustee Nat. Lighting Bur., 1976-79. Mem. Nat. Council on Crime and Delinquency, 1966—; mem. Tocks Island Regional Adv. Council, 1966-75; mem. N.J. Employers Legis. Com., 1959-79; mem. com. on subliminal projection N.J. Legislature, 1962-63; mem. pres.'s adv. council Bloomfield Coll., 1971-76; mem. publs. com. Lehigh U., 1971-74; chmn. Sussex County Heart Fund, 1979-80; mem. Sussex County Soc. for Prevention Cruelty to Animals, 1970—, Sussex County Arts Council, 1973—, Sussex County Big Bros., 1974—, Nat. Trust for Historic Preservation; del. Easter Seal Soc. N.J., 1973-76. Sussex County Republican committeeman, 1962—; mem. Sussex County Soil Conservation Dist.; co-chmn. N.W. N.J. Citizens for Pres. Ford Com., 1976; trustee Alexander Linn Hosp., Sussex; donor estate to Upsala Coll. for satellite campus in Sussex County, N.J. (now Wirths campus), 1978. Served with USNR, 1950-54. Commd. Ky. col.; recipient Westinghouse Electric Community Service award, 1976, Ortho Nat. Community Service award, 1976; Sussex County Man of Yr. award Radio Sta. WSUS, 1979. Mem. Urban League, NAACP, Jamaican-Am., N.J. chambers commerce, Trinidad and Tobago C. of C. U.S.A. (v.p., dir.), N.J. Farm Bur., Acad. Polit. Sci., Sussex County Hist. Soc. (life), N.J. Press Assn., N.J. Agrl. Soc., N.J. Hosp. Assn., Bloomfield Fedn. Music, N.J. Mfrs. Assn., Watsessing Businessmen's Assn., Illuminating Engring. Soc., Alexander Linn Hosp. Assn. (life), Old Sturbridge Village Assn., Bloomfield C. of C., Dairy Herd Improvement Assn., Land Improvement Contractors Am. (exec. sec. N.J. chpt. 1975-77). Club: Republican Congressional. Author syndicated polit. newspaper column Candidly Speaking, 1970-74. Home: Twin Ponds Farm RD 3 Sussex NJ 07461 Office: 1 Westinghouse Plaza Bloomfield NJ 07003

WIRTSCHAFTER, IRENE NEROVE, tax cons., real estate salesperson; b. Elgin, Ill., Aug. 5; d. David A. and Ethel G. Nerove; B.C.S., Columbus U., 1942; m. Burton Wirtschafter, June 2, 1945 (dec. 1966). Commd. ensign Supply Corps, U.S. Navy, 1944, advanced through grades to capt., 1975; sea duty, 1956; comdg. officer Res. Supply Unit, 1974-75; ret., 1976; agt. office internat. ops. IRS, 1967-76, internat. banking specialist, 1972-75; now pvt. practice tax cons., Washington. Past troop leader Girl Scouts U.S.A.; lt. col. and mission pilot CAP; comml. instrument pilot; chmn. College Park Airport Johnny Horizon Day, 1975; co-chmn. Internat. Women's Year Take Off Dinner, Washington, 1976; mem. Nat. Com. Internat. Forest of Friendship, Atchison, Kans. Named hon. citizen of Winnipeg (Can.), 1966, Atchison, 1978; Ky. col., La. col. Mem. Naval Res. Assn. (nat. treas. 1975-77, adv. com.), Ninety Nines (past chpt. and sect. officer; Achievement award), Naval Order U.S. First female Supply Corps officer to be assigned sea duty. Home: 1825 Minutemen Causeway Cocoa Beach FL 32931 Office: 2500 Q St NW Apt 641 Washington DC 20007

WIRTZ, ARTHUR M(ICHAEL), corp. ofcl., real estate exec.; b. Chgo., Jan. 23, 1901; s. Fredrick C. and Leona (Miller) W.; B.A., U. Mich., 1922; m. Virginia Wadsworth, Mar. 1, 1926; children—Cynthia Wirtz MacArthur, William, Arthur Michael, Elizabeth V. Founder, chmn., chief exec. officer Wirtz Corp., realtors, Chgo., 1927—; chmn. Forman Realty Corp., Chgo.; chmn. bd. Consol. Enterprises, Inc., Chgo.; chmn. bd., chief exec. officer Am. Mart Corp., Chgo.; chmn. Griggs-Cooper & Co., Inc., St. Paul, Rathjen Bros., Inc., San Francisco, 1st Nat. Bank South Miami (Fla.), Chgo. Stadium Corp., Chgo. Blackhawk Hockey Team, Inc.; dir. Met. Fair and Expn. Authority, operators McCormick Pl. Chgo. Pres., trustee Chgo. Urban Transit Dist. Mem. Hockey Hall of Fame; named Man of Year, Chgo. Boys Club, 1976. Clubs: Racquet, Chgo. Athletic, Saddle and Cycle, Tavern, Chgo. Yacht (Chgo.); Knollwood Country (Lake Forest, Ill.). Home: 1420 Lake Shore Dr Chicago IL 60610 Office: 666 Lake Shore Dr Chicago IL 60611

WISE, CHARLES WILLIAM, III, fin. exec.; b. York, Pa., Oct. 7, 1951; s. Charles William and Charlotte Louise (Mundis) W.; B.S. in B.A., Ind. U. of Pa., 1973; grad. Young Execs. Program, Coll. Bus. Adminstrn., Pa. State U., 1981; m. Holly Sue Smith, Dec. 7, 1974; 1 dau., Heather Britta. Staff, sr. acct. Miller, Miller & Co., C.P.A.'s, York, Pa., 1973-77; audit supr. Pa. Blue Shield, Camp Hill, Pa., 1977-79, mgr. internal audit, 1979—; chmn. continuing edn. and profl. devel. com. Blue Cross & Blue Shield, Region II; pvt. practice public acctg., Camp Hill; cons. in field. Corp. dir. York White Rose Jr. Drum and Bugle Corps; active Salvation Army Softball Leagues; vol. Girl Scouts U.S.A.,; active PTO. C.P.A., Pa. Mem. Am. Inst. C.P.A.'s, Pa. Inst. C.P.A.'s, Ins. Internal Audit Group, Inst. Internal Auditors, Nat. Assn. Accts. Republican. Methodist. Home: 515 Alton Ln York PA 17402 Office: Senate Ave Camp Hill PA 17011

WISINSKI, STANLEY JOSEPH, III, real estate broker; b. Grand Rapids, Mich., Sept. 10, 1940; s. Stanley Joseph, Jr. and Mary Stella (Goleniewski) W.; student Aquinas Coll., Grand Rapids, 1958-60; certificate real estate U. Mich., 1972; grad. Realtor Inst.; m. Phyllis June White, Aug. 29, 1968; step-children—Steve Glupner, Sue Glupker, Carol Gluper; 1 dau., Maryanne. With Westdale Co., Grand Rapids, 1960—, mgr. comml. dept., 1968-72, v.p., gen. mgr. comml. investment div., 1972-76; pres. Westdale Comml. Investment Co., 1976—. Mem. adv. bd. Marywood Acad., Grand Rapids, 1973—. Served with N.G., 1964-70. Certified comml. investment mem. Nat. Assn. Realtors. Recipient Distinguished Sales award Sales and Mktg. Exec. Club Grand Rapids, 1971. Mem. Soc. Indsl. Realtors, Grand Rapids C. of C. Home: 8080 Wilderness Lake Trial NE Ada (Grand Rapids) MI 49301 Office: 3435 Lake Eastbrook Blvd SE Grand Rapids MI 49506

WISLER, NORMAN ELMON, pub. co. exec.; b. Phila., Mar. 26, 1943; s. Norman and Frances Cecilia (Chase) W.; B.S., Temple U., 1964; diploma Charles Morris Price Sch. Advt. and Journalism, 1965. Copy contact Tricebock Advt., Huntington Valley, Pa., 1965; advt. asst. KSM div. Omark Industries, Moorestown, N.J., 1965-67; advt. mgr. Amchem Products, Inc., Ambler, Pa., 1967-73; regional mktg. mgr. Hitchcock Pub. Co., Wheaton, Ill., 1973—; instr. bus./profl. advt. Charles Morris Price Sch., Phila., 1971-76. Recipient Alumnus award Charles Morris Price Sch., 1965. Mem. Bus. and Profl. Advt. Assn. (dir. 1968-72, 80—, cert. bus. communicator), Poor Richard Alliance. Republican. Roman Catholic. Contbr. articles to trade publs. Home: 2139 Clay St Philadelphia PA 19130 Office: 964 3d Ave Suite 2300 New York NY 10022

WISNIEWSKI, JOSEPH BERNARD, JR., electronics service co. exec.; b. Shamokin, Pa., Nov. 3, 1928; s. Joseph Bernard and Angeline (Zaniewska) W.; m. Marianne Mitterweger, Dec. 14, 1951; children—Karen A., Nina M., Vera A., Marc J. Enlisted Signal Corps, U.S. Army, 1945, advanced through grades to chief warrant officer, 1955, ret., 1969; communications specialist Gilbo Industries, Springfield, Va., 1969-70; gen. mgr. Electronic Service Co., Springfield, 1971-79, pres., gen. mgr., 1979—; owner, operator Logistics Consultants Co.; treas., dir. 8th Dist. Service Corp. Mem., treas. No. Va. Planning Dist. Commn., 1976—; mem. Bd. of Rds., Fairfax County, Va., 1976—; vice chmn. Fairfax County Democratic Party, 1976-79; chmn. precinct ops. Annandale (Va.) Dist. Dems., 1976—; treas. Congressman Herb Harris campaign, 1979—; del. White House Conf. on Small Bus., 1980. Decorated Bronze Star, Army Commendation medal. Mem. Nat. Fedn. Ind. Bus., VFW. Roman Catholic. Home: 7311 Foxe Pl North Springfield VA 22151 Office: Electronic Service Co 6566 Backlick Rd Springfield VA 22150

WISOTSKY, JERRY JOSEPH, graphic arts co. exec.; b. N.Y.C., Oct. 22, 1928; s. Abraham I. and Anna P. (Slipoy) W.; student CCNY, 1946-48; m. Helen E. Lerner, Nov. 12, 1949; children—Pearle Eve (Mrs. Malcolm H. Marr), Ronald Ian. Apprentice, Triplex Lithographic Corp., N.Y.C., 1949-51; pres. Kwik Offset Plate Inc., N.Y.C., 1952-59; pres. Imperial Lithographers Inc., Phoenix, 1959-69, chmn. bd., 1970—. Partner M.J. Enterprises, Phoenix, 1959—. Mem. bd. appeals, Phoenix, 1974-76; pres. Ariz. Found. for Handicapped, 1976—; campaign chmn. corp. div. United Way, 1975, gen. campaign chmn., 1977, pres. Phoenix-Scottsdale, 1981; pres. trusteeship St. Luke's Hosp. Med. Center; pres. Phoenix Jewish Community Center, 1970-71; v.p. bd. dirs. United Way; trustee St. Luke's Hosp.; chmn. Ariz. bd. dirs. Anti-Defamation League, also nat. commr.; pres. Metro-Phoenix Citizens Council; bd. dirs. Boys Clubs Phoenix. Recipient Torch of Liberty award Anti-Defamation League, 1977; 12 Who Care-Hon Kachina award, 1980. Home: 7520 N 1st St Phoenix AZ 85020 Office: 210 S 4th Ave Phoenix AZ 85003

WISTER, WILLIAM DAVID, investment co. exec.; b. N.Y.C., Oct. 24, 1938; s. William Ducasse and Helen Francis (Albrecht) W.; B.A., Lafayette Coll., 1960; m. Carol Lynne Weeks, July 27, 1963; children—William David, Heather Lynne. Sr. portfolio mgr. U.S. Trust Co. of N.Y., N.Y.C., 1963-67; asst. sec./sr. portfolio mgr. Naess & Thomas, N.Y.C., 1967-69; sr. v.p., dir., mem. exec. com. Cyrus J. Lawrence, N.Y.C., 1969—. Chmn. bd. trustees 1st Congl. Ch., Old Greenwich, Conn., 1975—. Served to capt. USMCR, 1960-63. Mem. Fin. Analysts Fedn., Inst. Chartered Fin. Analysts, N.Y. Soc. Security Analysts. Clubs: Mchts. (N.Y.C.); Rocky Point Yacht (Old Greenwich, Conn.). Home: 19 Midbrook Ln Old Greenwich CT 06870 Office: 115 Broadway New York NY 10006

WIT, HAROLD MAURICE, investment banker, investor; b. Boston, Sept. 6, 1928; s. Maurice and Martha (Bassist) W.; A.B. magna cum laude, Harvard, 1949; J.D., Yale, 1954; children—David Edmund, Hannah Edna. Admitted to N.Y. bar, 1954; asso. Cravath, Swaine & Moore, N.Y.C., 1954-58; asst. sec. One William St. Fund, Inc., N.Y.C., 1958-59, v.p., sec., 1959-60; asso. Allen & Co., Inc., 1960—, v.p., 1965-71, exec. v.p., 1971—, also dir., mem. exec. com.; pres., dir. Wit Securities Corp.; mem. exec. com., dir. DPF Inc.; v.p., dir. Omni Communications Corp.; dir. Interstate Brands Corp., Allegheny & Western Energy Corp., Toys "R" Us. Bd. dirs. Group for America's South Fork, Inc., South Fork Land Fedn.; mem. Gov.'s Panel of Future of Govt. in N.Y.; bd. advisers Nat. Taxpayers Union. Served as cpl. Mass. N.G., 1948-50, lt. (j.g.) USNR, 1951-53. Mem. VFW, Phi Beta Kappa, Phi Delta Phi. Clubs: Harvard (N.Y.C. and Boston); Univ., Yale (N.Y.C.). Editor Yale Law Jour. Home: 160 E 65th St New York NY 10021 also Cross Hwy East Hampton NY 11937 Office: 711 Fifth Ave New York NY 10022

WITHERS, CHRIS, systems analyst; b. Pierre, S.D., June 8, 1938; d. Henry and Marie (Danzer) Huckfeldt; B.S.B.A., U. of S.D., 1976. Owner, operator Withers Oil Co., Pierre, 1962-72; fiscal officer State of S.D., Pierre, 1973-74; allocations officer S.D. Office Energy, Pierre, 1974; underwriter personal lines Employers Mut., Des Moines, 1976-77; acct. Iowa Dept. Environ. Quality, Des Moines, 1977-78, systems analyst-programmer, 1978-79; systems analyst Rockwell Hanford, Richland, Wash., 1979—; instr. Am. Inst. Bus. Mem. Am. Mgmt. Assn., Bus. and Profl. Women, Assn. Systems Mgrs. Address: PO Box 152 Richland WA 99352

WITHERS, W. RUSSELL, JR., broadcast exec.; b. Cape Girardeau, Mo., Dec. 10, 1936; s. W. Russell and Dorothy Ruth (Harrelson) W.; A.B., SE Mo. State U., 1958; 1 dau., Dana Ruth. With radio sta. KGMO, Cape Girardeau, 1955-59, co-owner sta. KGMO AM-FM, 1973—; with sta. WGGH, Marion, Ill., 1959-60, sta. WMAK, Nashville, 1960-62; v.p. LIN Broadcasting Corp., Nashville, N.Y.C., 1962-69; exec. v.p. Laser Link Corp., N.Y.C., 1969-71; dir. Theatre-vision, Inc., N.Y.C., 1970-71; chmn., chief exec. officer Withers Beverage Corp., Mobile, Ala., 1973-79; pres., owner Royal Hawaiian Radio Co., Inc., Honolulu, 1975-80; owner sta. WDTV, Clarksburg, W.Va., 1973—, sta. KAUS AM-FM, Austin, Minn., 1974-78, sta. WMIX AM-FM, Mt. Vernon, Ill., 1973—; pres. Productos de Atlanticos, S.A., San Jose, Costa Rica; v.p. Turneffe Island Lodge, Ltd., Belize, C. Am.; dir. Ina State Bank (Ill.), Rend Lake Bank, Union City, Tenn.; mem. affiliate adv. bd. MBS; dir. Jennings Broadcast and Creative, San Francisco. Served with U.S. Army, 1958-59. Mem. Ill. (dir.), Nat. radio broadcasters assns., Nat. Assn. Broadcasters, AMVETS, Mt. Vernon C. of C. (dir. 1974-76), Sigma Chi. Republican. Christian Scientist. Clubs: Monroe, Plaza (Chgo.); Stadium, Mo. Athletic (St. Louis); Elks. Home: 1 Sleepy Hollow Mount Vernon IL 62864 Office: PO Box 1238 Mount Vernon IL 62864

WITHERSPOON, WILLIAM, investment co. exec.; b. St. Louis, Nov. 21, 1909; s. William Conner and Mary Louise (Houston) W.; student Washington U., St. Louis, eves. 1928-47; m. Margaret Telford Johanson, June 25, 1938; children—James Tomlin, Jane Witherspoon Peltz, Elizabeth Witherspoon Vodra. With research dept. A.G. Edwards & Sons, 1928-31; pres. Witherspoon Investment Co., St. Louis, 1931-34; head research dept. Newhard Cook & Co., St. Louis, 1934-43, 45-53, limited partner, 1964-68; chief price analysis St. Louis Ordnance Dist., 1943-45; owner Witherspoon Investment Counsel, St. Louis, 1953-64; v.p. investment research Stifel Nicolaus & Co., St. Louis, 1968—; dir. Eota Realty Co., 1946—; lectr. investments Washington U., 1948-67. Mem. Clayton (Mo.) Bd. Edn., 1955-68, treas., 1956-68, pres., 1966-67; mem. Clayton Park and Recreation Commn., 1959-60. Trustee sta. KETC, ednl. TV, 1963-64; mem. investment com. Gen. Assembly Mission Bd. Presbyterian Ch. U.S., 1976-79. Mem. St. Louis Soc. Financial Analysts (pres. 1949-50), Inst. Chartered Financial Analysts. Club: Mo. Athletic (St. Louis). Home: 6401 Ellenwood St St Louis MO 63105 Office: 500 N Broadway St Louis MO 63102

WITHERUP, TERRENCE LEE, systems analyst; b. Butler, Pa., Dec. 17, 1952; s. Lewis Aubrey and Ruby Belle (Stewart) W.; B.S. in Computer Sci., Pa. State U., 1974; M.B.A., U. Pitts., 1980. Asst. systems engr., Armco Steel Corp., Ambridge, Pa., 1974-77; jr. systems analyst Blue Cross of Western Pa., Pitts., 1977-79; programmer/analyst Dollar Savs. Bank, Pitts., 1979-81; sr. programmer/analyst Copperweld Corp., Pitts., 1981—. Telephone coordinator Beaver County for Common Cause, 1977—; pres. Christian Young Adults Beaver County, 1976-77, co-pres., 1977-78. Mem. Assn. M.B.A. Execs., Am. Mgmt. Assn., Pa. State Alumni Assn., Sierra Club, Pitts. Symphony Soc. Democrat. Clubs: Gaimy Investment (treas. 1978—), Number One Investment (v.p. 1979—). Computerized credit union accounting system, Armco, 1976. Home: 1500 Gringo Rd Aliquippa PA 15001 Office: Two Allegheny Center Pittsburgh PA 15212

WITHROW, ARTHUR CHAUNCEY, oil co. exec.; b. Dubuque, Iowa, Oct. 8, 1897; s. James William and Harriet (Simpson) W.; m. Clare Margaret Miller, June 21, 1927; 1 son, Arthur Chauncey. Pres., Arthur C. Withrow Co., cons., chemists, engrs., Los Angeles, 1937—. Mem. Director's Circle, Gerontology Center, U. So. Calif. Mem. Soc. Automotive Engrs., Am. Soc. Mfg. Engrs. (life), Am. Soc. Metals, Am. Soc. Lubrication Engrs., ASTM, Am. Soc. Tool Engrs., AAAS, Four Way Test Assn. (v.p.). Methodist. Clubs: Masons, Shriners, Rotary (past dist. gov.); Valley Hunt, Annandale Golf (Pasadena, Calif.); Springs (Rancho Mirage, Calif.); Seven Lakes Country (Palm Springs, Calif.). Research on specialized forging and metal working lubricants, space-age lubricants. Office: 5511 District Blvd Los Angeles CA 90040

WITT, NEIL ORAND, educator; b. Milw., Oct. 30, 1941; s. Orand A. and Ruth E. W.; A.S., Clark County Community Coll., 1974; B.S., U. Nev., 1976; M.B.A., Golden Gate U., 1980; student Nev. So. U., 1965. Radiol. tech. So. Nev. Meml. Hosp., Las Vegas, 1965-79; instr. in mgmt. Clark County Community Coll., North Las Vegas, 1976—, instr. CETA program, 1979-80; tech. cons. Lincoln County Hosp., Caliente, Nev., 1974; mgmt. cons. MCS Assos., 1979—; coordinator bus. lab. Clark County Community Coll.; instr. bus. mgmt. Nev. State Prison, 1981—; public relations Radio Sta. KVEG, Las Vegas, 1980—. Mem. Nat. Bus. Edn. Assn., AAUP, Am. Registry Radiologic Techs., Am. Soc. Radiologic Techs. Home: 5809 Granada Ave Las Vegas NV 89107 Office: 3200 E Cheyenne Ave North Las Vegas NV 89030

WITT, ROBERT, JR., steel co. exec.; b. Irvine, Ky., June 9, 1921; s. Robert and Lula Bell (Wilcox) W.; student Eastern Ky. State U., 1938-42; B.S., U. Ky., 1951; m. Mary Louise Hillis, Apr. 10, 1948; children—Roberta Louise, Ruth Ann. Lab. instr. mineral beneficiation U. Ky., Lexington, 1945-48; chief chemist, metallurgist Fluorspar dist. U.S. Steel Co., Mexico, Ky., 1951-54, preparation engr., coal div., Corbin, Ky., 1954-66; supt. coal preparation Frick dist. U.S. Steel Corp., Uniontown, Pa., 1968-74, dist. engr. Frick dist., 1974-77, chief engr., 1978—. Mem. AIME (vice chmn. coal preparation subcom. 1970-71), Am. Mining Congress, Am. Forestry Assn., Tau Beta Pi, Sigma Gamma Epsilon. Mason. Home: 340 S Lombard St Uniontown PA 15401 Office: Fayette Bank Bldg Uniontown PA 15401

WITT, ROBERT EDWARD, oil co. exec.; b. El Dorado, Ark., June 28, 1909; s. Edward Nathan and Lula Rebecca (Rankin) W.; student Davidson Coll., 1926-27, 29-30, Washington U., 1927-28; A.B., U. Ark., 1934; M.A., 1934; m. Zoe Elizabeth O'Ferrall, Feb. 22, 1938; 1 dau., Zoe Ann. Chemist, Lion Oil Co., El Dorado, 1934-36, with asphalt sales dept., 1936-56, mgr. asphalt sales dept., 1956-58; pres. Witt Oil Prodn. Co., Shreveport, La., also El Dorado, 1957—. Pres., El Dorado Community Chest Bd., 1955; chmn. Community Chest Campaign, 1953; pres. Sr. Teen Age Club Bd., 1956, El Dorado Community Concert Assn., 1956, El Dorado Library Bd., 1946-76. Trustee Sem. of Southwest, 1965—, mem. exec. com., 1965-69; mem. corp. Warner Brown Hosp.; trustee U. South, 1952-55; vice chmn. Sewanee All Saint Campaign, 1952-54; chmn. dept. finance Exec. Council Diocese Ark., 1953-54, mem. steering com., 1958—; dep. gen. conv. Episcopal Ch., 1953, 56; bd. dirs., exec. v.p. Shreveport Symphony Soc. Mem. Am. Petroleum Inst., Ind. Petroleum Assn. Am. (Ark. v.p. 1960-63, exec. com., 1963-67, dir. 1967-69), Asphalt Inst. (mem. mgmt. com. Div. III 1950-58), Petroleum Administrn. War (mem. asphalt sub-com. 1942-44), Shreveport C. of C., Assn. Asphalt Paving Technologists, Sigma Chi, Sigma Upsilon. Democrat. Episcopalian. Clubs: Shreveport, Shreveport Petroleum. Author: Another Autumn and Other Poems, 1977; Indian Summer and More, 1980. Home: 710 N Madison Ave El Dorado AR 71730 Office: Commercial Nat Bank Bldg Shreveport LA 71101

WITT, ROBERT LOUIS, corp. exec.; b. Vallejo, Calif., Feb. 22, 1940; s. Charles L. and Encie L. (Bates) W.; A.A., Solano (Calif.) Coll., 1959; student Oreg. State U., 1959-61; J.D., San Francisco Law Sch., 1968; m. Myrna D. Harvey, Feb. 11, 1960; 1 son, Mark Louis. Buyer, Lenkurt Electric Co., San Carlos, Calif., 1961-63; contract adminstr. Litton Industries, 1963-67, Kaiser Aerospace & Electronics Co., 1967-69; admitted to Calif. bar, 1969; sec., counsel Hexcel Corp., Dublin, Calif., 1969—, v.p., 1976—, also dir. subsidiaries. Winner prize for excellence Am. Jurisprudence Soc., 1966; judge San Francisco Law Sch. Moot Ct., 1968. Mem. Am., Calif., San Francisco bar assns., Am. Soc. Corporate Secs. Home: 7858 Kentwood St Pleasanton CA 94566 Office: 650 California St Suite 1400 San Francisco CA 94108

WITT, T. FOSTER, JR., trust exec.; b. Richmond, Va., Nov. 4, 1927; s. T. Foster and Isabel (Luke) W.; grad. St. Christopher's Sch., 1946; B.A., Va. Mil. Inst., 1950; LL.B., U. Va., 1955; m. Ann Lane Crittenden, Apr. 13, 1971; children—T. Foster III, Anne Lane, Andrew Luke; step-children—Janet Kirsten Griffiths, P. David Griffiths. Registered rep. Scott & Stringfellow, 1955-61; trust planner United Va. Bank, Richmond, 1961—; dir. Commonwealth Lab., Inc. Active United Givers Fund; past pres. Children's Home Soc. Va.; former vestryman St. Stephen's Episcopal Ch. Served to 1st lt., inf. AUS, 1951-53. Chartered financial analyst. Mem. Va. Bar Assn., Richmond Soc. Financial Analysts (past pres.), Va. Mil. Inst. Alumni Assn., English Speaking Union (past treas. Richmond br.), Sons of the Revolution (past sec. Va.), Assn. Preservation of Va. Antiquities (past br. pres.), Kappa Alpha, Phi Alpha Delta. Clubs: Country of Va., Commonwealth, Downtown (past pres.); The Cohoke (past pres.); Focus (past treas.). Home: 7603 Cornwall Rd Richmond VA 23229 Office: 900 E Main St Richmond VA 23219

WITTEN, JAMES CURTIS, mining co. exec.; b. Johnson County, Ky., July 26, 1920; s. Chester and Virgie (Welch) W.; student Mayo State Vocat. Sch., 1939-40; m. Dolores Van Hoose, Apr. 4, 1942;

children—James Curtis, William D., Robert W. Pres. Witten Coal & Mining Co., Paintsville, Ky., 1948—; chmn. bd. First Nat. Bank, Paintsville, 1980—, also dir.; dir. TEMCO Mining Co., Paintsville. County judge, Johnson County, Ky., 1975-77; mem. nat. fin. council Dem. Nat. Com., 1977—; bd. dirs. Paintsville Hosp., 1977-78, Big Sandy Area Devel. Dist. Bd., 1975-77. Served with USAAF, 1942-45. Decorated 6 Bronze Star medals. Democrat. Christian Ch. Clubs: Kiwanis, Lafayette, Masons (Shriners, Jesters). Home: Paintsville and Lexington KY Office: 482 Church St Paintsville KY 41240

WITTEN, WESLEY MYRON, mfg. co. exec.; b. King City, Calif., June 20, 1928; s. Earl H. and Virginia T. (Scolari) W.; B.S., Calif. State U., 1950; m. Thelma Ruth Hamilton, July 22, 1950; children—Steven, Eric, Susan. Engr., Pacific Gas & Electric Co., San Francisco, 1950-56; with Atlantic Richfield Co., 1956-79, sr. v.p., dir. Arco Pipeline Co., Los Angeles, 1977-79; v.p., dir. Alyeska Pipeline Service Co., Anchorage, 1979-80; v.p. crude supply Arco Petroleum Products Co., Los Angeles, 1980—; pres. Arco Trading Co. Mem. ASME, Am. Petroleum Inst., Cal Poly Alumni Assn. Republican. Office: 515 S Flower St Los Angeles CA 90071

WITTENBORN, HAROLD WALTER, state ofcl.; b. Chgo., Jan. 5, 1917; s. Walter G. and Lottie (Mossler) W.; student U. Wis., 1936-37, DeForest Tng. Sch., Chgo., 1946-47, U. Chgo., 1961-62; m. Alice V. Smith, Oct. 31, 1940 (dec.); 1 dau., Linda Jean; m. 2d, Margery Ortengren Kjelstad, Aug. 14, 1970. Machine operator Kimberley-Clark Corp., 1935-36, 40-42, 45-46; accountant Faust Motor Co., Neenah, Wis., 1937-40; with Cook Electric Co., Chgo., 1947-72, asst. mgr. indsl. relations, 1953-54, dir. personnel, 1954-60, v.p. indsl. relations, 1960-72; pres. Wittenborn Electronics, Inc., Columbia, Mo., 1972-76; contract service rep. Mo. Div. Employment Security, 1977—. Past mem. adv. council on plans for progress Pres.'s Com. Equal Employment Opportunities; chmn. Plans for Progress 3d Nat. Conf., 1965, past chmn. employment and guidance com. Chgo. Urban League; exec. sec. Congo Gospel Mission; past dir. No. Ill. area Youth for Christ; past mem. adv. employment com. Chgo. Commn. Human Relations. Past bd. dirs. Family Financial Counseling Service of Chgo. Served with USAAF, 1942-45. Decorated Bronze Star medal. Fellow Am. Acad. Personnel Execs.; mem. Am. Soc. Personnel Administrn., Indsl. Relations Assn. Chgo. (past pres.), Columbia Mo. C. of C., Gideons Internat., Am. Mgmt. Assn., Broadway Shopping Center Assn. (pres.), Acad. Polit. Sci., Newcomen Soc., Field Mus. Natural History. Home: 800 Steamboat Dr Washington MO 63090 Office: Highway 47 and 100 Washington MO 63090

WITTERN, FRANCIS ARTHUR, SR., mfr.; b. Cushing, Iowa, Oct. 19, 1900; s. Frank Heinrich and Sophia Meta (Petersen) W.; student U. Minn., 1920-23; m. Viola Katherine Dutton, Oct. 13, 1934; children—Francis Arthur, Terry Richard (dec.). Founder, chmn. bd. Hawkeye Novelty, Des Moines, and successor firm Fawn Engring. Corp., 1931—. Established Flandreau Scholarship Trust Fund. Recipient E award for export excellence Office of Pres., 1975, award for employment handicapped vets. Am. Legion, 1965, Hyatt House award for community service and leadership, 1970, recognition award for excellence Gov. State of Iowa, 1973, cert. of merit Am. Cancer Soc., 1976, World Meeting award for trade lit. Affiliated Advt. Agencies Internat., 1970. Mem. Soc. Mfg. Engrs. Republican. Lutheran. Clubs: Embassy, Hyperion, Masons, Shriners. Patentee (30). Home: 1616 Casady Dr Des Moines IA 50315 Office: PO Box 1333 8040 University St Des Moines IA 50305

WITTNER, JEAN GILES, savs. and loan assn. exec.; b. Atlanta, Oct. 29, 1934; d. James H. and Lucile W. West; student public schs.; m. Ted P. Wittner, Mar. 5, 1979; 1 son, James Alan Giles. With St. Petersburg Fed. Savs. & Loan Assn. (Fla.), 1954—, pres., dir., 1975—; dir. Fla. Power Corp., 1977—. Bd. dirs. Fla. Gulf Coast Symphony, 1976—, 2d v.p., 1977-80; chmn. NCCJ Brotherhood Awards Dinner, 1980; pres. United Way Pinellas County, 1978, Vol. Activisit award, 1978; mem. Downtown Improvement Authority, 1979-80; bd. dirs. St. Petersburg Jr. Coll. Devel. Found., 1980—, Pinellas Assn. Retarded Children, 1980—. Recipient Bus. and Profl. Women and YWCA Mgmt. award, 1980. Mem. Fla. Savs. and Loan League (dir. dist. II 1978-80), St. Petersburg Area C. of C. (pres. 1979-80), U.S. League Savs. Assns., Pinellas Suncoast C. of C. (adv. bd. 1980—), St. Petersburg Sales and Mktg. Execs. (Top Mgmt. Disting. Service award 1976), Nat. Fedn. Bus. and Profl. Women, Christian Bus. and Profl. Women's Council (pres. 1973). Democrat. Club: Midday Group, Commerce, St. Petersburg Yacht, Hadassah (life mem.). Office: St Petersburg Fed Savs and Loan Assn 33 6th St S Saint Petersburg FL 33701

WITTNER, TED PHILIP, ins. exec.; b. Tampa, Fla., Sept. 17, 1928; s. Jacob and Helen (Goldman) W.; B.S. in Bus. Adminstrn., U. Fla., 1950; m. Sylvia Heller, Apr. 3, 1954 (dec. May 1975); children—Sharyn Wittner Jacobson, Pamela Anne; m. 2d, Jean Giles, Mar. 5, 1979. Mgr., Bell Luggage Co., Tampa, 1953-54; gen. agt. Crown Life Ins. Co., St. Petersburg, Fla., 1956—; pres. Ted P. Wittner & Assos., St. Petersburg, 1964-67; pres. Wittner & Co., St. Petersburg, 1968—; chmn. Profit Programs Co., St. Petersburg, 1969-76; chmn. bd., dir. Nat. Bank St. Petersburg, 1970-75; chmn. Pinellas Bank. Bd. dirs. Com. of 100, Pinellas County; mem. St. Petersburg Civic Adv. Com. Bd. dirs., Pinellas Assn. Retarded Children; bd. dirs., sec.-treas. Menorah Center, Inc. Served to 2d lt. USAF, 1950-53. Life and qualifying mem. Million Dollar Round Table. Mem. Gen. Agts. and Mgrs. Conf. (pres. St. Petersburg chpt. 1957), Nat. Assn. Life Underwriters, Crown Life Brokerage Gen. Agts. Assn. (pres. 1968—), St. Petersburg Area C. of C. (v.p. 1969-72), Fla. Blue Key, Tau Epsilon Phi. Jewish (pres. Congregation 1966-68, chmn. bd. 1964-66). Club: Commerce of Pinellas County (pres., dir.). Home: 1220 Park St N St Petersburg FL 33710 Office: 5999 Central Ave St Petersburg FL 33710

WITZKE, RICHARD ALLAN, dentist, dental and med. products exec.; b. Bklyn., Feb. 4, 1941; s. Dorward C. and Eva Clare (Kirkwood) W.; B.S., Muskingum Coll., 1963; D.M.D., U. Pitts., 1968; M.B.A., Case Western U., 1977; m. Janet Anne Williams, Aug. 17, 1963; children—Kevin, Scott, Kristi. Individual practice dentistry, New Philadelphia, Ohio, 1970-73; asst. prof. Sch. Dentistry Case Western Res. U., 1973-77; dir. advanced products Dentsply Internat., Inc., 1977—. Pres. Tuscarawas County (Ohio) Comprehensive Health Planning Council, 1971-72; cons. Group Health Plan Northeast Ohio. Bd. dirs. Seven County Health Planning Council, 1971-72, Ohio Outdoor Drama Assn., Tuscarawas County United Fund, Oldtown Colonial Estates Homeowners Com., Tuscarawas County United Fund Health Found., Boy Scouts Am. Served with AUS, 1968-70; Vietnam. Decorated Bronze Star. Mem. York County Dental Soc., Am., Pa. dental assns., Am. Assn. Dental Schs., Internat. Am. assns. dental research, Am. Mktg. Assn., New Philadelphia (pres. 1972-73), Ohio (dist. v.p. 1973-74, award of honor) Jaycees. Home: 3335 Harrowgate Rd York PA 17402 Office: 570 W College Ave York PA 17404

WITZKY, HERBERT K. V., mgmt. cons.; b. N.Y.C., May 26, 1919; s. Kurt Emil and Anna M. (Zueger) von Witzky; B.S. in Personnel Mgmt. and Indsl. Relations, N.Y. U., 1949, M.B.A. in Mgmt., 1962, postgrad.; m. Melva Annabel Good, Dec. 19, 1953; children—Annaliese Magdalena, Christopher Herbert Kurt. Clk., Dry Dock Savs. Bank, N.Y.C., 1937-42; asst. dir. Bur. Employment, N.Y. U., 1942-44; asst. personnel dir. United Parcel Service, N.Y.C., 1944-45, Vocat. Service, 1943-46; dir. Womrath's Book Shops, 1946-47; personnel dir. Plaza Hotel, Hilton Hotels Corp., 1947-50; dir. adminstrn. and planning Pan Am. World Airways, Intercontinental Hotels Corp., 1950-56; pres. Herbert K. Witzky & Assos., New Fairfield, Conn., 1950—; owner, developer Shortwoods Estates, 1953-78; head hotel and restaurant mgmt. program N.Y. U., 1960-66; vis. prof. Cornell U., 1966-72; chmn. spl. bus. programs, head hotel and restaurant mgmt. program Bucks County Community Coll., 1967-74; dir. Mgmt. Inst., 1967-74; pres. Friendly Inns of Am., New Fairfield, 1971—; prof. mgmt., dir. hotel and restaurant mgmt. program Fairleigh Dickinson U., Rutherford, N.J., 1974—; adv. bd. hotel/restaurant mgmt. Brandywine Coll. (Del.), Essex Community Coll. (N.J.). Named Educator of Year in N.J., N.J. Hotel Assn., 1978. Mem. Acad. Mgmt., Council Hotel, Restaurant and Instnl. Edn., Hotel-Motel-Restaurant Mgmt. Soc. Am. (founder, pres.), Mgmt. Inst. (founder, pres.), Indsl. Relations Research Assn., Soc. Advancement Food Service Research, Internat. Brotherhood Magicians, Order of Merlin, N.J. Restaurant Assn. (hon. life dir.), Alpha Kappa Delta, Alpha Kappa Psi, Omicron Delta Epsilon. Republican. Lutheran. Author: What Executives and Department Heads Are Paid in Hotels in United States, Canada and Puerto Rico, 9 edits., 1955—; Modern Hotel-Motel Management Methods, 5th edit., 1971; Hotel-Restaurant Management Cases, 1962; The Advertising Guide, 1955-66; Practical Hotel-Motel Cost Reduction Handbook, 1970; Your Career in Hotels and Motels, 1971; Labor-Management Relations Handbook, 1976; The Changing Role of the Manager, 1981; Developing Employees and Managers, 1981; Compensating Innkeeping Executives, 1962; The Witzky Survey, 1978—. Home and Office: Meeting House Hill Box 8888 New Fairfield CT 06810

WIXOM, THEODORE MERSHON, linen rental co. ofcl.; b. Galesburg, Ill., June 15, 1937; s. Robert Nelson and Doris (Cox) W.; B.S. in Indsl. Mgmt., Miami U., Oxford, Ohio, 1960; m. Carolyn Sue Masson, Aug. 26, 1962; children—Elizabeth Kay, Margaret Marie. Plant mgr. F.W. Means & Co., Lexington, Ky., 1964-66, South Bend, Ind., 1966-68; staff plant mgr. Assn. Linen Services, Utica, N.Y., 1968-70, gen. mgr., 1970-74; v.p. ops. Community Linen Rental Services, Los Angeles, 1974-76; v.p., dir. Spalding's Services Ltd., Louisville, 1976-78; gen. mgr. N.Y. area Morgan Services, Inc., Buffalo, 1978—. Instr. driving course Nat. Safety Council, Utica, 1972-73. Served to lt. (j.g.) USNR, 1960-62. Named engr. year Joint Engrs. Council Mohawk Valley, 1971. Certified Mfg. eng. Mem. Am. Inst. Indsl. Engrs. (v.p. region 5; sr. mem.; nat. bd. dirs.), Mohawk Valley Joint Engrs. Council (chmn. pub. relations com.), Soc. Mfg. Engrs., Linen Supply Assn. Am. (mem. nat. ops. com.), Alpha Kappa Psi, Theta Chi. Clubs: Masons, Rotary. Contbr. articles to profl. jours. Home: 91 Huntington Ct Williamsville NY 14221 Office: 325 Louisiana St Buffalo NY 14204

WNUK, WADE JOSEPH, mfg. co. exec.; b. St. Louis, Sept. 2, 1944; s. Edward Joseph and Helen Evelyn (Millick) W.; B.S. magna cum laude in Math., St. Louis U., 1966; M.S. in Engring. Sci. (NSF trainee), Calif. Inst. Tech., 1966-67; M.B.A., Harvard, 1974; m. Judith Kay Yohe, May 3, 1969; children—Russell Nicholas, Wade Gregory. Govt. research analyst, Washington, 1967-69; planner FMC Corp., Chgo., 1974-75, mgr. bus. devel. petroleum equipment div., Houston, 1975-77, group planning mgr., petroleum equipment group, 1977-78, ops. mgr. FMC Petroleum Equipment SE Asia, 1978-80, subsea mgr. FMC Wellhead Equipment div., Houston, 1980—. Served with U.S. Army, 1969-72. Mem. Internat. Bus. Club (past v.p.), Am. Mgmt. Assn., AAAS, Nat. Geog. Soc., Smithsonian Assos., St. Louis U., Calif. Inst. Tech., Harvard alumni assns. Club: Harvard (Houston). Home: 5510 Kingswick Ct Houston TX 77069 Office: FMC Wellhead Equipment Div PO Box 3091 Houston TX 77001

WOELFLE, ARTHUR WILLIAM, food co. exec.; b. Dunkirk, N.Y., Mar. 8, 1920; s. Arthur and Agnes (Johnson) W.; B.A., U. Buffalo, 1943; m. Ruth Godden, Dec. 29, 1943; children—Gretchen, Christine, Ann. Sec.-treas. Bedford Products (acquired by Kraft, Inc. 1955), Dunkirk, N.Y., 1946-55; sr. v.p. Bedford Products div. Kraft Foods, Chgo., 1955-59; chief exec. officer Kraft-Germany, 1966-69; chmn. Kraft-U.K., 1969-73; vice chmn. Kraft, Inc., Glenview, Ill., 1973, pres., 1973—, also chief operating officer; dir. Santa Fe Industries, Inc., First Chgo. Corp., 1st Nat. Bank Chgo., Atchison, Topeka & Santa Fe Ry. Co. Office: Kraft Inc Kraft Ct Glenview IL 60025

WOERNER, EDGAR WILLIAM, machine and tool co. exec.; b. Elizabeth, N.J., Jan. 5, 1935; s. William Anton and Liesel (Schwarz) W.; B. Mgmt. Engring., Rensselaer Poly. Inst., 1956; m. Diane Caird, May 18, 1957 (separated): children—Caroline Caird, Stephanie Caird. Constrn. engr. Aluminum Co. Am., Evansville, Ind., Massena, N.Y., and Pitts., 1956-58; sales devel. engr. Alcoa, New Kensington, Pa., 1958-60; with Woerner Machine & Tool Co. Inc., Dunellen, N.J., 1960—, v.p., 1966-71, pres., 1971—; pres. Block Industries Supply Co., Dunellen. Served with U.S. Army, 1957. Mem. Piscataway C. of C., Republican. Episcopalian. Home: 119 E 6th St Plainfield NJ 07060 Office: 100 S Washington Ave Dunellen NJ 08812

WOFFENDEN, DAVID LLOYD GEORGE, printing co. exec.; b. Montreal, Que., Can., Jan. 2, 1922; s. John Henry and Elsie Kathleen (Denham) W.; B.A., McGill U., 1951; m. Maria Petronella Kousbroek, Sept. 26, 1945; children—Robert Alexander, Ronald Alan, Deborah Ellen. With CN Telegraphs, 1938, No. Electric Co., 1938-41, Montreal Engring. Co. Ltd., 1951-62; pres. Wade Reprodn. Services Inc., Montreal, 1962—, Wade Repro Ltd., Calgary, Alta., 1962—. Served with Royal Can. Elec. and Mech. Engrs., 1941-46. Mem. Employing Printers Assn. Montreal (dir. 1972-75), Graphic Arts Industries Assn., Printing Industries Am. Home: 6595 Mackle Rd Apt 322 Cote Saint Luc PQ H4W 2Y1 Canada Office: 380 St Antoine St W Montreal PQ H2Y 1J9 Canada

WOGLOM, JAMES RUSSELL, environ. planner; b. Glen Ridge, N.J., May 17, 1926; s. Russell Stanley and Viola Ruth (Herslow) W.; B.S. in Adminstrv. Engring., A.B. in Econs., Lafayette U., 1950; M.A. in Polit. Sci., Lehigh U., 1960; certs. in advanced mgmt. Northeastern U., 1971-77; m. Eleanor I. Crockett, June 7, 1952; children—David L., Russell C., George N., Maryellen. Asst. dir. city planning div. Morris Knowles, Pitts., 1950-61; dir. community planning, v.p. Metcalf and Eddy, Boston, 1961-75; v.p., pres. environ. planning Camp Dresser and McKee, Boston, 1975—. Active Boy Scouts Am., Little League, Twilight Soccer League, Town Com.; asso. trustee Lafayette Coll., 1978—. Served in U.S. Army, 1944-46; ETO. Registered profl. engr., 42 states, D.C.; NCEE cert.; lic. or cert. planner, 44 states. Mem. Am. Inst. Cert. Planners, Mass. Cons. Planners (pres. 1972-75), Am. Soc. Cons. Planners (dir. 1974-75), ASCE, Soc. Am. Mil. Engrs., Nat. Soc. Profl. Engrs., Am. Planning Assn., Inst. Transp. Engrs., Pi Gamma Mu, Alpha Phi Omega. Episcopalian. Contbr. articles to profl. jours. Home: 9 Ledgetree Rd Medfield MA 02052 Office: Camp Dresser & McKee One Center Plaza Boston MA 02108 also 1945 The Exchange NW Suite 290 Atlanta GA 30339 also 710 S Broadway Walnut Creek CA 94596 also One World Trade Center Suite 2637 New York NY 10048 also Ford Bldg Suite 1300 Detroit MI 48226 also 8500 W Capitol Dr Milwaukee WI 53222 also Twin Sixties Office Bldg N Central Expy Dallas TX 75206

WOHL, LAWRENCE BRADLEY, painting co. exec.; b. N.Y.C., Jan. 10, 1931; s. Maurice and Rose Wohl; B.S. in Civil Engring., N.Y. U.; m. Millicent G. Levy, June 10, 1956; children—Jonathan, Nina, David. Project mgr., civil engr. Western Electric Co., 1957-59; v.p., chief estimator H.R. Ruback Constrn. Co., White Plains, N.Y., 1959-61; pres. Modern Protective Coatings, Inc., Port Chester, N.Y., 1961—; pres. Lawrence B. Wohl, Inc., 1961—. Chmn. Joint Apprenticeship Fund, Westchester Painters; chmn. Westchester Painters Annuity Fund. Served with U.S. Army, 1951-53. Mem. Painting and Decorating Contractors Am. (nat. v.p.), N.Y. U. Alumni Assn. Jewish. Clubs: Canyon Country (Armonk, N.Y.), Masons. Office: 325 Olivia St Port Chester NY 10573

WOHL, ROBERT ALLEN, aerospace exec., lawyer; b. Chgo., June 21, 1931; s. Max and Frieda (Friedmann) W.; student U. Wis., 1948-50; B.A., San Diego State U., 1952; postgrad. U. Calif. at Berkeley, 1954-56; J.D., U. San Diego, 1960; m. Christine Allison, 1974; children—Melissa, Suzanne. Admitted to Calif. bar, 1961; mgr. contracts Gen. Dynamics Corp., San Diego, 1956-62, mgr. program control, space programs, 1962-63, asst. to v.p., N.Y.C., 1963-68, corporate dir. contracts, 1968-70; v.p. adminstrn., sec. Canadair Ltd., Montreal, Que., Can., 1970-79, sr. v.p. adminstrn. and legal, 1979—. Served with USAF, 1952-54; 1st lt. Res. Mem. Am. Bar Assn., Am. Soc. Internat. Law, Union Internat. des Avocats, Nat. Mgmt. Assn. (chpt. 1st v.p. 1962), Blue Key, Phi Alpha Delta (chpt. pres. 1956). Club: Wings N.Y. Home: 21 Pacific Ave Senneville PQ H9X 1A2 Canada Office: 1800 Laurentian Blvd St Laurent PQ H3C 3G9 Canada

WOHLGEMUTH, EDWARD WARREN, publishing co. exec.; b. Cin., Dec. 24, 1915; s. Albert Joseph and Francis Louise (Bell) W.; A.B. in Lit., U. Mich., 1937; M.B.A., Harvard, 1939; m. Virginia Nulsen Balke, Nov. 29, 1940; children—Virginia N. (Mrs. Gary Fritts), Barbara B. (Mrs. Edward Blaine), Edward Warren. Salesman Nat. Underwriter Co., Cin., 1938; salesman The Rough Notes Co., Inc., Indpls., 1939—, mgr. circulation dept., 1940-41, mgr. pictorial div., 1945-58, dir., sec., 1950-59, pres., 1959—; dir. John C. Nulsen Investment Co., St. Louis, RN-AAA Co., Inc., Indpls., Ronaco Realty Co., Indpls. Served to capt. U.S. Army, 1941-45. Mem. Phi Delta Theta. Presbyterian. Club: Kiwanis. Home: 180 E 71st St Indianapolis IN 46220 Office: 1200 N Meridian St Indianapolis IN 46204

WOHLSTEIN, JEROME LASZLO, mgmt. cons.; b. N.Y.C., Oct. 16, 1922; s. Morr and Helen Sarah (Czerpakov) W.; B.S., U.S. Mcht. Marine Acad., 1943; M.B.A., Pace U., 1975; D.B.A., Western Colo. U., 1977; m. Florence Brier, Nov. 27, 1943; children—Michael Stuart, Karen Sue. From engr. to chmn. bd. Rogil Constrn., Uher Holding Corp., Peekskill, N.Y., 1946-51, 54-76; coordinator constrn. and facilities mgmt. programs Iona Coll., New Rochelle, N.Y., 1976—; mgmt. cons., Peekskill, 1970—; pres. U. Indsl. Mgmt., Dania, Fla., 1980—. Served with USN, 1943-46, 51-54. Mem. Am. Inst. Constructors, Am. Mgmt. Assn., Nat. Safety Council (profl. mem.), U.S. Power Squadron (chmn. coop. charting 1972-74), Peekskill Power Squadron (comdr. 1971). Club: Cortland Yacht (commodore 1967). Contbr. articles to profl. jours. Address: Box 661 Peekskill NY 10566

WOJCIK, CAROLYN, retail exec.; b. Bayonne, N.J., June 20, 1942; d. Albert and Regina (Kaczka) W.; B.A. in English, Notre Dame Coll., 1964. Children's buyer Lord & Taylor, N.Y.C., 1970-73; children's central dress buyer Frederick Atkins, N.Y.C., 1973-74, children's import coordinator/buyer, 1974-78, divisional mdse. mgr., 1978—. Roman Catholic.

WOJCIK, CASS, decorative supply co. exec., former city ofcl.; b. Rochester, N.Y., Dec. 3, 1920; s. Emil M. and Casimira C. (Krawiecz) W.; student Lawrence Inst. Tech., 1941-43, Yale, 1943-44, U.S. Sch. for European Personnel, Czechoslovakia, 1945; m. Lilliam Leocadia Lendzion, Sept. 25, 1948; 1 son, Robert Cass. Owner Nat. Florists Supply Co., Detroit, 1948—; owner Nat. Decorative, Detroit, 1950—; co-owner Creation Center, Detroit, 1955-60; cons.-contractor hort.-bot. design auto show displays, TV producers, designers and decorators. Mem. Regional Planning and Evaluation Council, 1969—; city-wide mem. Detroit Bd. Edn., 1970-75; commr. Detroit Pub. Schs. Employees Retirement Commn., until 1975; mem. Area Occupational Ednl. Commn., Ednl. Task Force; chmn., grand marshall Ann. Gen. Pulaski Day Parade, Detroit, 1970, 71; mem. Am. Polish Action Council; co-chmn. Friends of Belle Isle; co-chmn., fund raiser ann. Polish Day Parade; mem. Detroit Archdiocesan Pastoral Assembly, Polish Day Parade Com. Served with AUS, 1944-46. Decorated Bronze Star; recipient citation Polish-Am. Congress, 1971. Mem. S.E. Mich. Council Govts., Mich., Nat. sch. bd. assns., Big Cities Sch. Bd. Com., Nat. Council Great Cities Schs., Municipal Finance Officers Assn. U.S., Nat. Council Tchr. Retirement, Central Citizens Com. Detroit, Founders Soc. Detroit, Internat. Platform Assn., Nat. Heritage Groups, Nat. Geog. Soc. Roman Catholic. Club: Polish Century (Detroit). Home: 451 Lodge Dr Detroit MI 48214

WOJCIK, RICHARD THOMAS, bank exec.; b. Blue Island, Ill., Dec. 8, 1938; s. Joseph John and Jane Catherine (Falejczyk) W.; B.S. in Bus. Adminstrn., St. Mary's Coll., 1960; m. Barbara A. Elliott, June 19, 1965; children—Richard A., Erika A., Kirsten M. With Heritage County Bank & Trust Co., Blue Island, 1955—, now pres., chief exec. officer, dir. Served with U.S. Army, 1961-63. Office: 12015 S Western Ave Blue Island IL 60406

WOJEWODZKI, RICHARD STEPHEN, real estate cons.; b. Jersey City, Dec. 4, 1952; s. Richard Alexander and Irene Alfrieda (Wichowski) W.; B.S. in Bus. Adminstrn., Monmouth Coll., 1978; m. Victoria J. Czesnik, Apr. 3, 1976. Field supr. Municipal Revaluations, Avon, N.J., 1973-74; appraiser, cons., v.p. Walker Appraisal Assn., Shrewsbury, N.J., 1974-77; 2d v.p. real estate fin. dept. Chase Manhattan Bank, N.Y.C., 1977-80; asst. v.p. realty ops. Equitable Life Assurance Soc., N.Y.C., 1981—. Recipient Herbert B. Nelson award Nat. Assn. Realtors, 1976. Mem. Soc. Real Estate Appraisers (pres. Central Jersey chpt. 1979-80), Am. Inst. Real Estate Appraisers, Lambda Sigma Tau. Home: 2 Colony Ct Hazlet NJ 07730 Office: 1285 Ave of Americas 32d Floor New York NY 10019

WOJTA, GERALD CHARLES, pharm. co. exec.; b. Manitowoc, Wis., Aug. 17, 1930; s. Charles J. and Agnes (Stefl) W.; student U. Wis., 1948-51; children—Pamela, Jerold, Daniel, James, Ann, Kimberly, Melissa. Salesman, Dorsey Labs., Inc., Lincoln, Nebr., 1953-55, asst. sales mgr., 1956, sales mgr., 1957-61; dir. mktg. Philips Roxane Lab., Inc., Columbus, Ohio, 1962-64, v.p., gen. mgr., 1965, pres., 1967—; dir. Mediplex, Inc. Trustee, Coll. Osteo. Medicine and Surgery, Des Moines, Columbus Day U.S.A. Assn. Fellow Am. Coll. Osteo. Obstetricians and Gynecologists; mem. Am., Ohio pharm. assns., Drug Chem. and Allied Trades Assn., Am. Soc. Hosp. Pharmacists. Clubs: Scioto Country, Columbus Athletic, Columbus Touchdown. Office: 330 Oak St Columbus OH 43216

WOLANIN, SOPHIE MAE, civic worker; b. Alton, Ill., June 11, 1915; d. Stephen and Mary (Fijalka) W.; student Pa. State Coll., 1943-44; cert. secretarial sci. U. S.C., 1946, B.S. in Bus. Adminstrn. cum laude, 1948; Ph.D. (hon.), Colo. State Christian Coll., 1972. Clk., stenographer, sec. Mercer County (Pa.) Tax Collector's Office, Sharon, 1932-34; receptionist, social sec., nurse-technician to doctor, N.Y.C., 1934-37; coil winder, assembler Westinghouse Electric Corp., Sharon, 1937-39, duplicator operator, typist, stenographer, 1939-44, confidential sec., Pitts., 1949-54, exec. sec., charter mem. Westinghouse Credit Corp., 1954-72, sr. sec., 1972-80, reporter WCC News, 1967-68, asst. editor, 1968-71, asso. editor, 1971-75; student office sec. to dean U. S.C. Sch. Commerce, 1944-46, instr. math., bus. adminstrn. and secretarial sci., 1946-48. Publicity and pub. relations chmn., corr. sec. S. Oakland Rehab. Council, 1967-69; charter mem. pres's. council, fellow U. S.C. Ednl. Found., 1972—; mem. nat. voter adv. bd. Am. Security Council; founder Center Internat. Security Studies Am. Security Council Ednl. Found. Recipient Gold Lyre Music award Sharon High Sch., 1933; Gold plaque Westinghouse, 1968; citation in Congl. Record, 1969; Girl Friday citation TWA, 1969, numerous others. Fellow, patron Intercontinental Biographical Assn. (life); fellow Internat. Inst. Community Service (life), U. S.C. Alumni Assn. Ednl. Found. (gen. chmn. Tri-State area 1959, Pa. state fund chmn. 1967-68); mem. Allegheny County Scholarship Assn. (life), Allegheny County LWV, AAUW (life), Internat. Fedn. Univ. Women, N.E. Hist. Geneal. Soc., Hypatian Lit. Soc., Acad. Polit. Sci. (Columbia) (life), Bus. and Profl. Women's Club Pitts. (dir. 1963-77, editor Bull. 1963-65, treas. 1965-66, historian 1969-70, pub. relations chmn. 1971-76, Woman of Year award 1972), Liturgical Conf. N. Am. (life), Nat., Pa. fedns. bus. and profl. women's clubs, Westinghouse Vet. Employees Assn., Am. Acad. Polit. and Social Sci., Am. Judicature Soc., Am. Mus. Natural History (asso.), Internat. Platform Assn., Am. Bible Soc., Mercer County Hist. Soc. (life), Société Commemorative de Femmes Celebres, Nat. Trust Hist. Preservation, Polish Am. Ednl. and Cultural Soc., Anglo-Am. Hist. Soc., Nat. Hist. Soc. (founding), Am. Counselors Soc. (life), Am. Hort. Soc., Smithsonian Assos., UN Assn. U.S., St. Paul's Cathedral Altar Soc., Assos. Nat. Archives, Nat. Soc. Lit. and Arts, Early Am. Soc., Nat. Assn. Exec. Secs., Friends Churchill Meml. Library in U.S.; asso. Met. Opera Guild. Republican. Roman Catholic. Clubs: Jonathan Maxcy of U. S.C. (charter), Univ. Catholic of Pitts., College of Sharon (hon.); Key of Pa. Contbr. articles to newspapers. Home: 5223 Smith-Stewart Rd SE Girard OH 44420

WOLANSKI, THOMAS JOSEPH, constrn. co. exec.; b. Phila., Aug. 3, 1945; s. Thomas T. and Dorothy (Orzewchowski) W.; B.S.C.E., Pa. State U., 1965; m. Cirila Bernvi, Jan. 8, 1970; children—Michelle, Joseph. Pres., Bucks County Constrn. Corp., 1970-72; asst. v.p. Hylton Enterprises, Woodbridge, Va., 1972-77; gen. mgr. Bellemah Corp., Albuquerque, 1977-79; asst. v.p. Robert E. McKee, Inc., El Paso, 1980—. Served to 1st lt. USMC, 1965-70. Mem. Am. Soc. Quality Control, ASCE. Home: 734 Mesa Hills Dr El Paso TX 79912 Office: 1918 Texas Ave El Paso TX 79901

WOLAVER, CARL LEROY, bus. exec.; b. Balt., Aug. 22, 1941; s. Walter E. and Harriett (Clark) W.; B.S. in Indsl. Engring., U. Cin., 1964; M.B.A., U. Fla., 1967; m. Marna J. Terry, Apr. 26, 1969; children—Nathan Edward, Alex Walter. Indsl. engr. Delco Div. Gen. Motors, Dayton, Ohio, 1964-65; sales supr., market analyst, mil. specialist Corning Glass Works (N.Y.), 1967-70; mktg. mgr., communications mgr., product mgr., foam div. Scott Paper Co., Chester, Pa., 1970-76; dir. sales and mktg., Soundcoat, N.Y.C., 1976—; cons. GarDoc, Inc. Mem. Acoustical Soc. Am. Contbr. articles to profl. jours. Home: 35 Magnolia Ave Garden City NY 11530

WOLCOTT, EUGENE AARON, plastics co. exec.; b. Fountain City, Wis., Sept. 23, 1923; s. Clair Chester and Murriel Alice (Irmscher) W.; grad. Henderson Jr. Coll., Athens, Tex., 1960; student U. Tex. at Arlington, 1976—; m. Nannie John Knipp, June 11, 1944; 1 dau., Nancy Eileen. Supr. plant ops. analysis Ford Motor Co., Dallas, 1947-70; controller Sterling Packing & Gasket subs. Texstar Corp., 1970, controller Texstar Plastics Co. Grand Prairie, Tex., 1970—, v.p., 1976—, treas., 1978—. Mayor, Terrell, Tex., 1956-57; Democratic precinct chmn., 1965-69. Recipient Ford Citizen of Year award, 1959-60. Mem. Nat. Assn. Accountants, Terrell C. of C. (dir. 1960-65). Methodist. Clubs: Civitan (pres. Terrell 1958), Masons (33 deg.). Home: 2702 Ashbury Dr Arlington TX 76015 Office: PO Box 1530 Grand Prairie TX 75051

WOLD, JOHN SCHILLER, former Congressman, mineral exploration and prodn. exec.; b. East Orange, N.J., Aug. 31, 1916; s. Peter Irving and Mary Helen (Helff) W.; B.A., Union Coll., Schenectady, 1938; Exchange scholar St. Andrew's (Scotland) U., 1936-37; M.S., Cornell U., Ithaca, N.Y., 1939; m. Jane Adele Pearson, Sept. 28, 1946; children—Peter, Priscilla, John. Geologist, Magnolia Petroleum Co., Okla. and Tex., 1939-40; cons. physicist Bur. Ordnance USN, Washington, 1942; mgr. exploration Rocky Mountain div. Barnsdall Oil Co. and Sunray Oil Co., Casper, Wyo., 1946-50; cons. geologist, Casper, 1950-68; owner, chief exec. officer Wold Nuclear Co., 1974—, Wold Mineral Exploration Co., 1971—, J & P Corp., BTU Inc.; dir. Kans.-Nebr. Natural Gas Co., First Nat. Bank Casper, Empire State Oil Co.; founding pres. Central Wyo. Ski Corp. Mem. Wyo. Ho. of Reps., 1957-59; mem. at large 91st Congress, 1969-71; Wyo. Republican state chmn., 1960-64; mem. exec. com. Rep. Nat. Com., 1962-64; chmn. Western State Rep. State Chmn. Assn., 1962-64; Rep. candidate for U.S. Senate from Wyo., 1964, 70; trustee Casper Coll., 1977—, pres. bd., 1979—. Served to lt. USNR, 1941-46. Recipient Watchdog of Treasury award Nat. Assn. Businessmen, 1970; named AP-UPI Wyo. Man of Year, 1968; Wyo. Mineral Man of Year, 1978. Fellow AAAS; mem. Wyo. Geol. Assn. (pres. 1959), Rocky Mountain Oil and Gas Assn. (v.p. for Wyo. and S.D. 1967-68), Fedn. Rocky Mountain States (dir.), Am. Assn. Petroleum Geologists, Ind. Petroleum Assn. Am., Am. Petroleum Inst., Wyo. Mining Assn., Sigma Xi, Alpha Delta Phi. Episcopalian. Clubs: Wigwam Country (Ariz.); Casper Country, Casper Petroleum. Contbr. articles to profl. jours. Home: PO Box 114 Casper WY 82602 Office: Mineral Resource Center Casper WY 82601

WOLF, CARL THEODORE, food co. exec.; b. Newark, July 7, 1943; s. Samuel and Irma (Wiener) W.; B.A., Rutgers U., 1965; M.B.A., U. Pitts., 1966; m. Marion Frances Karp, Oct. 31, 1965; 1 dau., Karen. Sr. acquisitions analyst Sperry & Hutchinson Co., N.Y.C., 1966-69; pres. Sci. Restaurant Mgmt. Corp., Mountainside, N.J., 1969-71; v.p., gen. mgr. Brooke Bond Foods Inc., Lake Success, N.Y., 1971-77, also dir.; pres. Market Finders, Inc., South Orange, N.J., 1978—; pres., dir. Carl Wolf Sales, Inc., South Orange, 1980—; v.p., dir. East/West Mktg. Co., Inc., South Orange; dir. Cheez Co., Wisconsin Rapids, Wis.; mem. pres.'s com. Internat. Cheese and Deli Seminar; instr. econs. Newark State Coll., Union, N.J., 1967-68. Served with N.J. Army N.G., 1966-72. Food Fair scholar, 1961-65; N.J. State scholar, 1961-65; U. Pitts. Tuition fellow, 1965-66; Henry Rutgers scholar, 1964-65. Mem. Assn. Corp. Growth, Nat. Food Distbrs. Assn., L.I. Assn. World Trade Club, Cheese Importers Am., Rutgers Alumni Assn., Eastern Dairy Deli Assn., Am. Entrepreneurs Assn., Phi Beta Kappa, Beta Gamma Sigma. Club: Unity (Maplewood, N.J.). Home: 20 Collinwood Rd Maplewood NJ 07040 Office: 76 S Orange Ave South Orange NJ

WOLF, CHARLES ROBERT, educator; b. Mason City, Iowa, Oct. 9, 1933; s. Harry Ralph and Mildred W.; A.B., Harvard U., 1955, M.B.A., 1960, D.B.A., 1965. With bond dept. 1st Western Bank, San Francisco, 1956-58; economist Fed. Res. Bank N.Y., 1960-61; research asst., research asso., research fellow Harvard U. Bus. Sch., 1962-66; asst. prof. bus. Columbia U., 1966-69, asso. prof., 1969-77, prof., 1977—. Mem. Am. Econ. Assn., Am. Fin. Assn. Clubs: Harvard, Harvard Bus Sch. (N.Y.C.). Author: (with Eli Shapiro) The Role of Private Placements in Corporate Finance, 1972. Home: 560 Riverside Dr Apt 16C New York NY 10027 Office: 410 Uris Hall Columbia Univ New York NY 10027

WOLF, CLARENCE, JR., stockbroker; b. Phila., May 11, 1908; s. Clarence and Nan (Hogan) W.; student Pa. Mil. Prep. Sch., 1921; grad. Swarthmore (Pa.) Prep. Sch., 1923; m. Alma C. Backhus, Sept. 11, 1942. Founder French-Wolf Paint Products Corp., Phila., 1926, pres. until 1943; admitted to Phila.-Balt. Stock Exchange, 1937; asso. Reynolds Securities Inc. (name now Dean Witter Reynolds Inc.), 1944—, rep., Miami Beach, Fla., 1946-63, spl. rep., 1963-77, v.p. sales, 1977, v.p. investments, 1977—; dir., vice chmn. bd., mem. exec. com. Amcord, Inc.; dir. George S. MacManus Co., Rand Broadcasting Co., owners radio and TV stas., also hotels, 1946-68. Pres. Normandy Isles Improvement Assn., Miami Beach, 1952-53; mem. Presidents Council Miami Beach, 1952—. Mem. Alumnus Assn. Pa. Mil. Coll. (Fla. dir. 1961—). Clubs: Clermont (London, Eng.), Variety, Standard, Miami Shores Country, Jockey, Cricket (Miami, Fla.). Author: $even Letter$, 1980. Home: Jockey Club Apt 901-2 Biscaya Point 11111 Biscayne Blvd Miami FL 33161 Office: care Dean Witter Reynolds Inc 700 Brickell Ave 6th Floor Miami FL 33131

WOLF, CRAIG JOSEPH, systems analyst; b. Washington, Iowa, Aug. 18, 1937; s. Bernard Owen and Anna Marie Wolf; A.B. in Philosophy cum laude, Cath. U. Am., 1959; M.S. in Personnel Adminstrn., George Washington U., 1965; m. Susan Irene Hartenstine, May 24, 1969; children—Melissa Dawn, Evan Curtis Owen. Sr. systems analyst Nera Systems, Washington, 1970-78; stockbroker various firms, N.Y.C., 1971-72; v.p. retail sales Bear Stearns, N.Y.C., 1972-76; stockbroker Dean Witter & Co., Kahuluis, Maui, Hawaii, 1976-77; stockbroker L.F. Rothschild, N.Y.C., 1977-79; sr. systems analyst Andrea Raab, N.Y.C., 1979—; sci. adv. bd. cybernetics Explorers Club N.Y.; tech. com. Info. Resource Dictionary System, Am. Nat. Standards Inst. Mem. Aux. Mounted Police of N.Y.C., 1974-75; treas. St. George Civic Assn., 1974, pres., 1975; Whale Watchers coordinator, Maui, 1977. Served to lt. USNR, 1960-69; lt. comr. Res. Cert. data processor; qualitifed floor trader N.Y. Futures Exchange; br. office mgr. qualified N.Y. Stock Exchange; commodity solicitor Chgo. Bd. Trade, 1971-77. Mem. Explorers Club. Roman Catholic. Fin. columnist Maui Sun, 1977. Office: 4702 Glenwood Rd Brooklyn NY 11234

WOLF, FRANCES LORETA SMITH (MRS. MILTON HARRY WOLF), banker, civic worker; b. Cleve., Sept. 3, 1917; d. Francis William and Laura Barrett (Smitha) Smith; grad. Sch. Public Relations and Mktg., Northwestern U., 1965; m. Milton Harry Wolf, Feb. 14, 1935 (dec. Aug. 1954); children—Henry George II, Jacqueline Jeanne (Mrs. Ralph Matthew Gruenewald). Writer, visuals, asst. to producer comml. films Ray Waters Inc., 1950-55; adminstrv. asst. to Willard Johnson, NCCJ, 1955-57; craft stylist Chgo. Printed String Co., 1956-59; free lance advt., pub. relations, commls., 1959-60; dir. pub. relations Ave. State Bank (now Ave. Bank & Trust Co. Oak Park), Oak Park, Ill., 1961-68, asst. cashier, pub. realtions and advt., 1968-71, asst. v.p. pub. relations, 1971-75, dir. community services and public relations, 1975—. Co-chmn. publicity Santa Claus Event, Oak Park, 1961-69; publicity chmn. Frank Lloyd Wright Festival, Oak Park-River Forest, 1969, chmn. pub. relations com. Frank Lloyd Wright Home and Studio Found., 1974-77; chmn. pub. relations Oak Park-River Forest Antique Show and Sales, 1967-70; bd. dirs. Oak Park-River Forest Symphony, 1965-67; incorporator Cultural Arts Center, Oak Park, 1970. Bd. dirs. Sr. Citizens' Oak Park-River Forest; bd. dirs., mem. exec. bd. Thatcher Woods council Boy Scouts Am., 1977—; mem. Camp Shin-Go-Beck Fire Dept., Amundsen Park Community Council, N.W. Austin Community Council. Recipient fund raising award Thatcher Woods council Boy Scouts Am., 1976. Mem. Nat. Assn. Bank Women, Hist. Soc. Oak Park and River Forest (1st v.p., program chmn. 1973-78), Women in Communications (chmn. Jacob Scher awards 1977), Ave.-Lake Plaza Assn. (pres. 1969-70, v.p., treas. 1970-77), Woman's Advt. Club Chgo. (pub. relations com. mem. 1969—), Oak Park-River Forest C. of C. (co-chmn. ann. dinner 1963—, dir. 1980—), Art Inst. Chgo., Publicity Club Chgo. (dir. 1975-77), Zonta Internat. (dir. Oak Park chpt. 1976-77, chmn. community affairs 1976-77), 19th Century Woman's Club Assn. (spl. events com. 1969-70), D.A.R. (vice regent chpt. 1981), St. Andrew Soc. Ill., Am. Clan Gregor Soc., Meml. Soc. Germanna Colonies of Va., Ky. Hist. Soc. Clubs: Chgo. Press, Suburban Press, Chgo. Shell, Zonta, Exec. Home: 151 N Kenilworth Ave Oak Park IL 60301 Office: 104 N Oak Park Ave Oak Park IL 60303

WOLF, HERBERT LEONARD, elec. equipment mfg. co. exec.; b. Bklyn., Sept. 6, 1940; s. Arnold M. and Fanny (Lashkevitz) W.; B.S., in M.E., Bklyn. Poly. Inst., 1962; m. Maxine Wasserman, Mar. 22, 1964; children—Ellen, Barbara, Richard. Packaging engr. Western Union Tel., N.Y.C., 1962-63; ground support engr. Grumman Aircraft, Bethpage, N.Y., 1963-64; v.p. Pelham Sheet Metal Works, Inc., Bronx, 1964-68; with Electrospace Corp., North Bergen, N.J., 1968-74, v.p., 1969-74, gen. mgr. Nanasi Co. div., 1968-74, corp. dir., 1972-74; div. mgr. Elec. Fittings Corp. div. ITE Imperial Corp., East Farmingdale, N.Y., 1975-76; gen. mgr. EFCOR Products div., 1976; v.p., gen. mgr. Gould Ind. Elec. Components div., East Farmingdale, N.Y., 1976-77; gen. mgr. electronics mfg. COLECO Industries Inc., Amsterdam, N.Y., 1977-79, v.p. electronics ops., 1978-79; v.p. ops. Lesney Products Corp., Moonachie, N.J., 1979—, sr. v.p. ops., 1980—. Mem. Am. Mgmt. Assn., ASME, Am. Soc. Heating, Refrigeration and Air Conditioning Engrs. Home: 10 Woodhaven Rd Parsippany NJ 07054 Office: 141 W Commercial Ave Moonachie NJ 07074

WOLF, MAURICE, lawyer; b. London, Eng., Oct. 15, 1931; came to U.S., 1947; s. D.I. and Esther (deMiranda) W.; B.A. with honors, UCLA, 1959; LL.B. (Harlan Fiske Stone scholar 1962), Columbia U., 1962; m. Yolanda Pazmino, May 4, 1963; children—J. David, Monica M. Admitted to N.Y. bar, 1962, D.C. bar, 1964, U.S. Supreme Ct. bar, 1980; atty., advisor Office Satellite Communications, FCC, Washington, 1962-66; project atty. Interamerican Devel. Bank, Washington, 1966-72, sr. atty., 1972-74, sr. counsel, 1974-77; sr. partner firm Wolf, Arnold & Cardoso, P.C., Washington, 1977—; dir. Interam. Coffee Corp., N.Y.C., 1979—; lectr. internat. fin. Am. Mgmt. Assn., 1977-80. Pres. Riverside Civic Assn., Fairfax, Va., 1969-70, 1977-78, v.p., 1976-77; co-chmn. Mt. Vernon Council Civic Assn., 1969-70. Mem. Columbia Soc. Internat. Law (pres. 1961-62), N.Y. Bar Assn. (chmn. internat. investment and fin. subcom. nat. fin. com.), D.C. Bar Assn., Fed. Bar Assn., Inter-Am. Bar Assn., Am. Soc. Internat. Law. Club: International (Washington). Home: 8354 Wagon Wheel Rd Alexandria VA 22309 Office: Suite 1225 1850 K St NW Washington DC 20006

WOLF, ROBERT CHARLES, mktg. and sales exec.; b. Teaneck, N.J., Nov. 9, 1942; s. Robert, Jr., and Julia Mary (Reichenbach) W.; B.A., St. Francis Coll., 1965; postgrad. in mktg. Fairleigh Dickinson U.; m. Rita Ann Giretti, July 16, 1966; children—Kenneth Robert, Anthony Robert. Key account mgr. Thomas J. Lipton, Englewood Cliffs, N.J., 1965-67; sales supr., patient care div. Johnson & Johnson, New Brunswick, N.J., 1967-71; v.p. Justco Co., N.Y.C., 1971-72; v.p. mktg. and sales Chaston Med. and Surg. Products, 1972-77; pres. Sales Mktg. and Research Trends, Inc., Rockville Centre, N.Y., 1978-80; pres. Athletic Conditioning Products Inc., Rockville Centre, 1980—. Mem. Health Industry Mfrs. Assn., Am. Mgmt. Assn., Porsche Club Am., BMW Club Am. Roman Catholic. Clubs: K.C., Rockville Centre Soccer. Home: 28 Muirfield Rd Rockville Centre NY 11570 Office: PO Box 531 Rockville Centre NY 11571

WOLF, ROSE BARRY, tax cons.; b. Colchester, Ct., Apr. 27, 1921; d. Samuel David and Lena Sylvia (Hoffman) Barry; grad. in acctg. Pace Inst., 1946; m. Lester Wolf, Sept. 28, 1947 (dec.); children—Beverly Sheila, Perry Stewart. Office mgr. HY & D. Agar Realty, Inc., Bklyn., 1946-47, Joseph Love, Inc., N.Y.C., 1947-48; real estate accountant, tax accountant Benjamin Passilia, N.Y.C., 1948-67; accountant Val Stream Volkswagen, Valley Stream, N.Y., 1967-67; sr. tax accountant Columbia Pictures Industries, Inc., N.Y.C., 1968-73; comptroller Matthews, Inc., Beverly Hills, Calif., 1973-74, Alexander & Friends., Inc., El Segundo, Calif., 1974-76; tax cons., pres. Group Services Internat., Tarzana, Calif., 1976—; treas. Travel Group Inc., Anaheim, Calif.; employment sec.-treas. Midway Energy Inc., Tarzana, 1978. Accredited in accountancy; enrolled to practice before IRS. Mem. Tarzana C. of C., Nat. Soc. Pub. Accountants, Am. Soc. Women Accts. (corr. sec.), Nat. Assn. Enrolled Agts. (chmn. Yellow Pages advt. Los Angeles chpt.), Am. Bus. Women's Assn. (treas.). Democrat. Clubs: B'nai B'rith, Seaford Dramatic. Columnist, Weekend mag., San Fernando Valley. Office: 19644B Ventura Blvd Tarzana CA 91356

WOLF, SEYMOUR (SY), sales exec.; b. Chgo., May 12, 1921; s. Charles K. and May (Lando) W.; LL.B., Northwestern U., Coll. Pacific, 1943; m. Ellie Schreiber, Oct. 28, 1945; children—Susan, Stephen, Charles. Pres., Ceramic World, Northfield, Ill., 1980—; v.p. Selected Brands, Northfield, 1980—. Staff, Magistrate Ct., Justice Peace Ct.; active City of Hope. Served with U.S. Army, 1942-46; PTO. Recipient Idealism award City of Hope, 1979. Mem. Am. Assn. Ret. Persons, Profl. Golfers Assn., World Golfers Hall of Fame. Jewish. Home: 2245 Vista Ct Northbrook IL 60062 Office: 550 Frontage Rd Northfield IL 60093

WOLF, TED HOWARD, real estate exec.; b. N.Y.C., June 7, 1944; s. Lester and Bella (Gordon) W.; student Coll. City N.Y., 1962-65, Columbia U., 1967-69; m. Harriet Schilkraut, Nov. 25, 1967; 1 dau., Lauren Samantha. Asst. inward freight mgr. Black Diamond S.S. Line, Inc., N.Y.C., 1963-65; gen. mgr. Thomas F. Ryan, Inc., N.Y.C., 1969-71; pres. Corporate Staffers, Inc., N.Y.C., 1971-74; pres. N.Am. Condominium Mgmt., Inc., N.Y.C., 1975—; instr. Rockland and Nassau community colls., 1976-77; mem. N.Y. State Atty. Gen. Joint Legis. Com., 1973-74. Mem. Westchester Apt. Owners Adv. Council Co-op. and Condo Conversion Com. Served with U.S. Army, 1965-67. Mem. Westchester Builders Inst., Rockland County Builders Assn. (dir.), Nat. Assn. Home Builders. Republican. Jewish. Home: 68 Tamarack Ln Pomona NY 10970 Office: 200 E Eckerson Rd Spring Valley NY 10977

WOLF, WILLIAM MARTIN, corp. exec.; b. Watertown, N.Y., Aug. 29, 1928; s. John and Rose (Emrich) W.; B.S. in Physics, St. Lawrence U., 1950; M.S., U. N.H., 1951; postgrad. U. Pa., 1951-52, Mass. Inst. Tech., 1952-54; children—Rose Mary, Sylvia Marie, William John. Mathematician, Frankford Arsenal, Phila., 1951-52; staff mem. Mass. Inst. Tech., 1952-54; pvt. practice as math. cons., Boston; pres. William M. Wolf Co., 1956-59, Wolf Research and Devel. Corp., West Concord, Mass., 1959-69, Wolf Computer Corp., 1969—, Computer Bus. Mgmt. Corp., 1969—; dir. Design Sci. Inst.; cons. in digital computer field to FAA, USN, USAF, NASA, Mass. Inst. Tech. Named one of outstanding young men of Boston, 1962. Home: PO Box 21 Cambridge MA 02142

WOLF, WILLIAM MILTON, advt. exec.; b. N.Y.C., July 4, 1923; s. Saul and Bertha (Dryer) W.; B.A., City Coll. N.Y., 1942; postgrad. N.Y. U., 1946-48; m. Norma Miller, July 7, 1956; children—Adam Jason, Leonard Mark. Vice pres. Leonard Wolf & Assos., N.Y.C., 1950-60; advt. mgr. Barth's of L.I., Valley Stream, 1960-62; sr. copywriter Fairfax Advt., N.Y.C., 1962-63; with William Douglas McAdams Inc., N.Y.C., 1963—, exec. v.p., 1973—, also mem. exec. com. Served with USAAF, 1942-45. Mem. Pharm. Advt. Club, Jewish War Vets. Author short stories. Home: 489 Grenville Ave Teaneck NJ 07666 Office: 110 E 59th St New York City NY 10022

WOLF, ZVI, merchant; b. Panevez, Lithuania, Dec. 11, 1930; came to Can., 1963, naturalized, 1968; s. Leo and Sarah (Sklar) W.; student public schs., Lithuania, Israel; m. Sarah Ben-Israel, Dec. 27, 1950; children—Ronald, Jeffrey. Pres., Z. Wolf Inc., Montreal, Que., Can., 1963—. Served to maj. Israeli Army, 1948-59. Liberal Party. Jewish. Author: Belahan Hamered, 1952; journalist for Cheirut newspaper, Tel Aviv, 1961. Home: 2372 Frenette St Montreal PQ H4R 1M4 Canada Office: 9064 Saint Laurent Blvd Montreal PQ H2N 1M7 Canada

WOLFE, ALEXANDER MCWHORTER, JR., banker; b. Balt., May 31, 1926; s. Alexander McWhorter and Sarah (Clark) W.; B.A. in Math., Bowdoin Coll., 1950; m. Diana Alys Paterson, July 16, 1954; children—Diane Elizabeth, Robert McWhorter. With 1st Nat. Bank of Boston, 1952-76, sr. v.p., div. head internat. dept., 1972-76; chmn. bd., chief exec. officer SE 1st Nat. Bank of Miami, 1976—; pres. banking group, chief operating officer SE Banking Corp. Pres., United Way of Dade County, 1980—; bd. dirs. Council of Americas, 1977—, also vice chmn.; pres. Greater Miami Opera Assn., 1979—. Served to lt. USNR, 1946-52. Mem. Assn. Res. City Bankers, Greater Miami C. of C., Bankers Assn. Fgn. Trade (past pres.), Am. Bankers Assn. (mem. exec. com. internat. banking). Clubs: Bankers, Miami (Miami); La Gorce Country (Miami Beach; Key Biscayne Yacht; Ocean Reef (Key Largo, Fla.). Office: 100 S Biscayne Blvd Miami FL 33131

WOLFE, DANE ADAM, coll. ofcl.; b. Annville, Pa., Nov. 24, 1952; s. Paul C. and Marian L. W.; B.S. in Econs. and Bus. Adminstrn., Lebanon Valley Coll., Pa., 1974. Bookkeeper, Paul C. Wolfe Ins. Agy., Cleona, Pa., 1970-74; mgmt. trainee Farmers Bank & Trust Co., Hummelstown, Pa., 1974-75, asst. cashier, br. mgr., installment loan officer, 1975-77; asst. controller, bus. mgr. Lebanon Valley Coll., Annville, Pa., 1977—. Mem. citizens adv. council Lebanon County (Pa.) Child Welfare Dept., 1970-74; treas. Annville Free Library Assn., Inc., 1977—. Recipient Wall St. Jour. award, 1974, Outstanding Young Men Am. award U.S. Jaycees, 1977, 79. Mem. Am. Inst. Banking (certified). Republican. Home: 325 W Penn Ave Cleona PA 17042 Office: Lebanon Valley Coll Annville PA 17003

WOLFE, EDWARD CLARE, ret. investment co. account exec.; b. Horton, Kans., Feb. 16, 1922; s. Roland John and Mary Clella (Braley) W.; student pub. schs., Lincoln, Nebr.; m. Julia Teran, Apr. 12, 1965. Tool and die maker, designer Boeing Co., Wichita, Kans. and Seattle,

1947-52, Torrington Mfg. Co., Van Nuys, Calif., 1952-60; registered rep. Dempsey-Tegeler & Co., Glendale, Calif., 1960-70, Mitchum Jones & Templeton, Pasadena, Calif., 1970-71, Wagenseller & Durst, Pasadena, Calif., 1971-72; registered rep. Schumacher & Assos., Glendale, Calif., 1975—; account exec., Universal Stock Transfer, Woodland Hills, Calif., 1976-78; loan officer Sutto Mortgage, Inc., Los Angeles, 1978-79. Served with USNR, 1944-46. Republican. Home: 21315 Kingsbury St Chatsworth CA 91311

WOLFE, ESTEMORE ALVIS, ins. co. exec.; b. Crystal Springs, Miss., Dec. 29, 1919; s. Henry and Vinia (Crump) W.; B.S., Jackson State Coll., 1947; student Fla. Meml. Coll., 1948-49, N.Y.U., 1952-53; M.Ed., Wayne State U., 1951; M.A., Purdue U., 1953; D.Ed., Boston U., 1958; L.H.D., Wilberforce U., 1959; Litt.D., Creighton U., 1961; L.H.D., Syracuse U., 1963; postgrad. Purdue U., 1964; divorced. Dir. med. technicians Detroit Tb Sanitorium, 1947-48; ednl. cons., mass media specialist Detroit Bd. Edn., 1948—; v.p., sec. Wright Mut. Ins. Co., Detroit, 1955—; mem. internat. adv. Hamilton Funding Corp.; dir. Ind. Prodns. Corp., also chmn. nat. edn. com. for educators. Lectr., guest prof. Gt. Lakes Coll., Assumption Coll. (Can.), Wayne U., 1953-56, Jackson State Coll., Bethany Coll., U. Detroit, Wis. State U., Stevens Point, So. U. (La.); writer column Detroit Times; cons. to pres. P. Lenud & Co. Mem. White House Conf. of Children and Youth, 1960; mem. Council on Aging, 1965-66; campaign chmn. Jackson State Coll. Devel. Fund Drive, 1970-71. Organizer, pres. Detroit chpt. Friends of AMISTAD, 1972, nat. v.p., 1972—. Chmn. bd. trustees Detroit Met. Symphony Orch.; trustee Jackson State U. Devel. Fund, Nat. Negro Archives Mus., Washington, Mich. council Arts, Scis. and Letters, Bethany (W.Va.) Coll. Served with AUS, 1942-46. Recipient Nat. Human Relations award Clark U., 1969, citation Am. Airlines in recognition of contbns. to devel. air transp. and nat. air power, 1969, Presidential citation for performance beyond call of duty, 1945, citation and plaque outstanding service and leadership City of Detroit, 1973; Achievement award Jackson State U. Alumni Assn., also Centennial medallion; plaque Kiwanis Clubs, 1978, Am. Heritage Found. award, 1980, numerous other plaques and citations for leadership in bus., civic orgns., edn. devel.; CASE TWO award Council for Advancement and Support for Higher Edn., 1979; plaque U. Detroit, 1979; 2d Century award Jackson State U., 1979; Spirit of Detroit award, 1980; Key to City of New Orleans, 1980; Outstanding Alumnus award Boston U., 1980; numerous others; named hon. staff col. Gov. Miss., 1977. Mem. NAACP, Nat. Soc. Visual Edn., Nat. Geog. Soc., Am. Acad. Social and Polit. Sci., Nat. Ins. Assn., Detroit Fedn. Tchrs., Detroit Assn. Radio and TV, Detroit Assn. Film Tchrs., Internat. Platform Assn., Detroit Schoolmen's Club, Detroit Roundtable, Nat. Congress Parents and Tchrs., Orgn. Alumni Assn. Wayne State U. (pres.), Nat. Alumni Assn. Jackson State U. (pres. 1976—, regional dir.). Democrat. Methodist (trustee ch.). Office: 2995 E Grand Blvd Detroit MI 48202

WOLFE, GOLDIE BRANDELSTEIN, real estate co. exec.; b. Linz, Austria, Dec. 20, 1945; d. Albert and Regina (Sandman) Brandelstein; student U. Ill., 1963-64; B.S. with honors in Bus. Adminstrn., Roosevelt U., 1967; postgrad. U. Chgo. Grad. Sch. Bus., 1968-69; 1 dau., Alicia Danielle Schuyler. Account research mgr. J. Walter Thompson Advt., Chgo., 1967-71, asso. account exec., 1971-72; account exec. Needham, Harper & Steers, Advt., Chgo., 1972; real estate broker office leasing dept. Arthur Rubloff & Co., Chgo., 1972—, asst. v.p., 1975-77, v.p. office leasing, 1977-80, sr. v.p., 1980—. Bd. dirs. realty div. Jewish United Fund, 1976-77; bd. dirs. Michael Reese Hosp. Med. Research Inst. Council, 1979—; chmn. services group Chgo. Public TV, 1974-75. Mem. Chgo. Real Estate Bd., Ill. Assn. Realtors, Nat. Assn. Realtors, Am. Mktg. Assn., Young Exec. Club (program v.p. 1980-81). Home: 1332 Sutton Pl Chicago IL 60610 Office: Arthur Rubloff & Co 69 W Washington St Chicago IL 60602

WOLFE, JACK, investment banker; b. New London, Conn., Mar. 15, 1922; s. Sam and Anne (Lazaroff) W.; B.S. in Chemistry, U. Calif., Los Angeles, 1941; postgrad. Pratt Inst., 1942-43, U. Pitts., 1943-44, Med. Coll. Va., 1944-46; m. Jewel Nussbaum, Aug. 26, 1944; 1 dau., Barbara Lee. Pres., Gen. Leasing Corp., Los Angeles, 1952-54; exec. v.p., gen. mgr. Fed. Leasing, Los Angeles, 1954-60; pres. Capital Reserve Corp., Los Angeles, 1960-63, Carry-Phone Corp., Los Angeles, 1964-76; chmn. bd. ECI-Internat. Banking, Inc., Los Angeles, 1967—. Served with U.S. Army, 1942-46. Republican. Jewish religion. Home: 4856 Mahalo Dr Eugene OR 97405

WOLFE, JOHN ALLEN, cons. firm exec.; b. Riverton, Iowa, June 3, 1920; s. Asa Allen and Alice (Thomas) W.; Geol. Engr., E.M., Colo. Sch. Mines, 1947, M.S., 1954; children—James Perry, Cynthia Wolfe Burke; m. 2d, Lenora Irvin, 1969. Dir. exploration Ideal Cement Co., Denver, 1948-65; geol. cons., Philippines, Latin Am., 1965-68; pres. Mineral Resources Cons., Houston, 1968-72; partner Schoenike, Wolfe & Assos., Houston, 1970-75; pres. Taysan Copper, Inc., Manila, 1973—; lectr., cons. in field; mem. Colo. Mining Industry Devel. Bd., 1963-65. Fellow Geol. Soc. Am.; mem. Am. Mining Congress (gov. 1963-65), Colo. Mining Assn. (pres. 1963), Am. Inst. Mining Engrs., Geol. Soc. Philippines, Am. Geophys. Union, Assn. Geologists for Internat. Devel., Soc. Econ. Geologists, Am. Inst. Profl. Geologists. Republican. Contbr. articles to profl. jours. Home: care Taysan Copper Inc CCPO Box 1868 Makati Rizal Philippines Office: 5133 Richmond Ave Suite 1 Houston TX 77027

WOLFE, JOHN BINNIE, banker; b. Macomb, Ill., Feb. 25, 1907; s. Edward Clark and Eleanor (Binnie) W.; B.S., Knox Coll., 1930; postgrad. Northwestern U., 1931-32; m. Sara Kramer, Aug. 15, 1936 (dec. 1969); 1 dau., Mary Eleanor Wolfe Satter; m. 2d, Alice Findley Reno, Aug. 22, 1970. Asst. examiner FDIC, 1933-34; bookkeeper, teller Citizens Nat. Bank Macomb, 1935-36, asst. cashier, 1936-37, cashier, 1938-50, dir., 1938—, exec. v.p., 1950-51, pres., 1951-73, chmn. bd., 1966—. Bd. dirs. Western Ill. U. Found., 1944—, pres., 1973-74; treas. McDonough County March of Dimes, 1938-77. Recipient Community Service award Macomb Area C. of C. and Western Ill. U. Sch. Bus., 1975. Mem. Macomb C. of C. (past dir.). Clubs: Macomb Country, Macomb Rotary. Republican. Presbyterian. Home: 646 Lincoln St Macomb IL 61455 Office: 127 S Side Sq Macomb IL 61455

WOLFE, LOUIS, publisher; b. N.Y.C., Mar. 2, 1935; s. Nathan and Goldie (Cohen) W.; B.A., CCNY, 1956; m. Emily Gordon, Sept. 16, 1957; children—Barbara, Debra. Vice pres., gen. sales mgr. New Am. Library, N.Y.C., 1959-70; dir. Australasia, Times Mirror Co., Sydney, Australia, 1970-72; gen. mgr. Gordon & Breach, N.Y.C., 1972-75; mktg. dir. Ballantine Books, N.Y.C., 1975-77; exec. v.p., gen. mgr. Avon Books, N.Y.C., 1976-80; chmn. bd., chief exec. officer Bantam Books, N.Y.C., 1980—; dir. Bertelsmann, Inc., others; cons. Franklin Book programs, 1973. Mem. U.S. Book Assn., Assn. Am. Publishers. Jewish. Office: Bantam Books 666 Fifth Ave New York NY 10303

WOLFE, MANUEL, mgmt. cons.; b. N.Y.C., Apr. 26, 1919; s. Max and Rebecca (Weisler) W.; B.S. in Acctg., DePaul U., Chgo., 1948; m. Annette Morris, Apr. 17, 1944; children—Laurence A., Robert S. Exec. v.p. Patt Engring. and Mfg. Co., Gardena, Calif., 1948-68; cons. Metaframe Corp., Gardena, 1968-74; ind. mgmt. cons., Los Angeles, 1974—. Pres., Alhambra Synagogue Center (Calif.), 1956-58, B'nai Tikvah Congregation, Los Angeles, 1965-66. Served with USAAF, 1942-46.

WOLFE, ROBERT KENNETH, educator; b. Chattanooga, Sept. 5, 1929; s. Robert Earl and May Bell (Hicks) W.; B.Chem.Engring., Ga. Inst. Tech., 1952, Ph.D., 1955; m. Mary Chacharonis, Oct. 31, 1959; children—Robert Kenneth, Ann Marie. Project engr. Mallinckrodt Chem. Works, St. Louis, 1955-60; mgr. systems engring. IBM, Chgo., 1960-68; mgr. operations research Owens Ill., Toledo, 1968-73; prof. indsl. engring., computer sci. and engring., chmn. Ph.D. systems program U. Toledo, 1973—; cons. engr. Bd. dirs. YMCA, N. Suburban Chgo., 1965-68. Tenn. Eastman Research fellow, 1952-54; registered profl. engr., Ohio. Mem. Am. Inst. Chem. Engrs., Am. Inst. Indsl. Engring., Ops. Research Soc., Inst. Mgmt. Sci., Phi Lambda Upsilon, Sigma Xi, Phi Kappa Phi, Pi Kappa Alpha (advisor 1975—). Baptist. Club: Sylvania Country. Contbr. articles in field to profl. jours. Home: 4930 Spring Mill Ct Toledo OH 43615 Office: U Toledo 2800 W Bancroft St Toledo OH 43606

WOLFF, THOMAS CONRAD, JR., real estate developer; b. Fall River, Mass., July 28, 1924; s. Thomas Conrad and Edith Dorothy (Stewart) W.; A.B., Duke U., 1947; postgrad. Johns Hopkins U., 1948-49; m. Mary Elizabeth MacDonald, Oct. 11, 1952; children—Elizabeth Barry, Meredith Anne, Thomas Neil. Vice pres. Rouse Co., Columbia, Md., 1960-72; exec. v.p. Irvine Co., Newport Beach, Calif., 1972-77; partner Newport Devel. Co., Newport Beach, 1977—; dir. Peterson, Howell & Heather, Inc., Balt., Bata Land Co., Belcamp, Md. Trustee Newport Harbor Art Mus. Served to lt. (j.g.) USNR, 1943-46. Mem. Nat. Assn. Indsl. and Office Parks, Soc. Indsl. Realtors, Urban Land Inst. Home: 56 Royal St George Rd Newport Beach CA 92660 Office: 900 Cagney Ln Newport Beach CA 92663

WOLFLEY, ALAN, coal co. exec.; b. Rockford, Ill., Dec. 23, 1923; s. Chester E. and Lois K. (Karlson) W.; student Middlebury (Vt.) Coll., 1941-42, A.B. cum laude, 1947; M.B.A., Harvard U., 1949; m. Joanne Higgins, Jan. 6, 1945; children—C. Alan, Susan (Mrs. Peter Baumgartner), E. William. Budget supr. Merck & Co., Rahway, N.J., 1949-52; asst. to treas. Standard Vacuum Oil Co., White Plains, N.Y., Tokyo, Japan, 1952-59; asst. treas. Parke-Davis & Co., Detroit, 1959-64; v.p. finance Carborundum Co., Niagara Falls, N.Y., 1964-68; v.p. finance, dir. Scovill Mfg. Co., Waterbury, Conn., 1968-71; exec. v.p., dir., mem. exec. com. Cerro Corp., N.Y.C., 1971-76; chmn., dir. Incontrade, Inc., Stamford, Conn., 1973—; pres. Cerro Coal Trading Co., 1976-78; pres., dir. Inconcoal Corp., N.Y.C., 1976—, Inconcoal Internat. Ltd., Ghent, Belgium, 1980—, Greenley Energy Corp., 1978—; dir. Am. Coal Industries Inc., Marmon Group Inc., Chgo., Solar-En Corp., Denville, N.J. Mem. nat. adv. council Salk Inst., La Jolla, Calif., 1980—. Served to capt. USAAF, 1942-45. Decorated Silver Star medal, D.F.C., Air medal, Purple Heart. Mem. Chi Psi. Republican. Methodist. Clubs: Harvard, Racquet and Tennis (N.Y.C.); Wee Burn Country (Darien, Conn.); Pine Valley Golf (Clementon, N.J.). Home: 22 Canaan Close New Canaan CT 06840 Office: 123 Main St PO Box 218 New Canaan CT 06840

WOLFORD, WILLIAM GRANE, banker; b. Ashland, Oreg., Apr. 15, 1926; s. Benjamine Edward and Anna Dorthia (Grane) W.: A.A., So. Oreg. Coll., 1948; B.S., Oreg. State U., 1950; m. Adele J. Schmidt, Sept. 6, 1975; children by previous marriage—Douglas, Bruce, Monica. Credit reporter Dun & Bradstreet, Inc., Portland, Oreg., 1950-51; bank examiner Fed. Deposit Ins. Corp., Seattle, 1952-58; v.p. Security State Bank, Ephrata, Wash., 1958-68; pres., chmn. bd. Security Bank Wash., Ephrata, 1968—. Pres. Ephrata C. of C., 1962-63; mem. Wash. State Water Resources Bd., 1973, Wash. State Energy Council, 1974; commr. Wash. State Dept. Ecology, 1975-77. Served with USN, 1944-46; PTO. Mem. Community Banks Wash. (pres. 1976), Wash. Bankers Assn. (pres. 1977-78), Am. Bankers Assn. (governing council 1979-80), Columbia Basin Devel. League (pres. 1972-73, hon. life mem.). Republican. Lutheran. Clubs: Elks, Am. Legion. Office: PO Box 1177 Ephrata WA 98823

WOLFSON, FRANKLIN ALLEN, apparel importing co. exec.; b. Queens, N.Y., Jan. 20, 1943; s. Leon Bernard and Ruth (Levine) W.; B.B.A. (Bernard Baruch Meml. scholar 1962), CCNY, 1966; M.B.A., N.Y. U., 1969. Mktg. and fin. cons. Kayser Roth Corp., 1970-75; mktg. mgr. Roland Shirts, 1977; pres., dir. Kostar, Inc., North Hollywood, Calif., 1977-80; pres. Buckeroo Internat., Chatsworth, Calif., 1980—. Served with USAR, 1963-69. Home: 358 S Roxbury Dr Beverly Hills CA 90212 Office: 9723 Eton Ave Chatsworth CA 91311

WOLFSTON, G. WILLIAM, JR., advt. exec.; b. Phila., Aug. 16, 1922; s. George William and Margaret (Mayer) W.; B.A., Lehigh U., 1943. Dir. radio-TV, Lefton Co., N.Y.C., 1949-52, account exec., 1952-55, v.p., account supr., 1956—, v.p., partner, mem. exec. com., 1960—; v.p. N. Am. Land Co., Phila., 1959—; dir. Dillon, Agnew, Marton, Internat. Sales Promotion Agy., Amsterdam, Netherlands, 1962-76. Bd. dirs. Fedn. Jewish Philanthropies N.Y.C., 1965—; pres. Poyntelle-Ray Hill Camp, Poyntelle, Pa., 1971-74; v.p. Asso. Camps of N.Y.C., 1966—. Served with USN, 1943-46. Recipient Melvin Block award Asso. Y's of N.Y.C., 1971. Clubs: West Hampton Yacht Squadron, Lehigh of N.Y.C. Home: 360 E 55th St New York NY 10022 Office: 71 Vanderbilt Ave New York NY 10017

WOLFUS, DANIEL EDWARD, investment banker; b. Buenos Aires, Argentina, Mar. 3, 1946; s. Jack and Joanne Ida (Shapiro) W.; came to U.S., 1957, naturalized, 1962; B.A., U. Calif. at Los Angeles, 1967, M.B.A., 1969; m. Christine Mary Marshall, Aug. 27, 1967; 1 dau., Stephanie Melissa. Research analyst Econ. Research Assos., Los Angeles, 1968-69; corporate fin. asso. E.F. Hutton & Co., Inc., Los Angeles, 1969-71, asst. v.p., 1971-73, v.p., 1974-78, 1st v.p., 1979-81, sr. v.p., 1981—; dir., mem. audit com. Rossmoor Corp.; pres., dir. EFH Plaza, Los Angeles; chmn. bd. Hancock Savs. & Loan Assn.; lectr. in field. Bd. mgrs. Wilshire YMCA. Clubs: Jonathan, Bond (Los Angeles). Home: 423 S Las Palmas St Los Angeles CA 90020 Office: 888 W 6th St Los Angeles CA 90017

WOLL, ROBERT HENRY, mcht., banker; b. San Jose, Ill., Sept. 7, 1900; s. Henry and Catherine (Neikirk) W.; grad. San Jose High Sch., 1920; m. Amanda Williams, Dec. 25, 1925; 1 son, Robert Nicolas. With N. Woll & Co. (established 1867), San Jose, Ill., 1920—, mgr., 1928-38, sole owner, 1938-69, partner, 1969—; sr. v.p. San Jose Tri-County Bank, 1944-75, pres., 1975-80; mem. adv. com. Happy Hour Stores, 1947-53; treas. Green Hill Cemetery Assn., 1938-56; established Amanda's Antique Shop, 1959. School dir., 1937-40; Committeeman, Boy Scouts Am., 1920-46; mem. Community Council, Mason County Pub. Welfare Com., Mason County Planning Commn.; chmn. Mason County Housing Bd., 1959-74; auditor Allen Grove Township, Mason County, Ill., 1973-77; committeeman Salvation Army. Mem. adv. bldg. com. Sch. Dist. 122; sec., treas. Green Hill Cemetery Assn. Mem. Am. Legion, Ill. Hist. Soc., Ill. Retail Grocers Assn., Farm Bur., Nat. Assn. Housing and Redevel. Ofcls., Nat. C. of C. Republican. Methodist (trustee 1938-66, pres. bd. 1959-62, hon. trustee 1966—, trustee sustaining fund, sec. treas. Meth. Men 1973—). Office: N Woll & Co PO Box 154 San Jose IL 62682

WOLLERT, GERALD DALE, food co. exec.; b. LaPorte, Ind., Jan. 21, 1935; s. Delmar Everette and Esther Mae W.; B.S., Purdue U., 1957; m. Carol Jean Burchby, Jan. 26, 1957; children—Karen Lynn, Edwin Del. With Gen. Foods Corp., 1959—, dir. consumer affairs, White Plains, N.Y., 1973-74, mng. dir. Cottee Gen. Foods, Sydney, Australia, 1974-76, gen. mgr. Gen. Foods Mexico, Mexico City, 1978-79, pres. Asia/Pacific ops., corp. v.p., Honolulu, 1979—; dir. Gen. Food's cos., Australia, Japan, Korea, Singapore, Philippines. Webelos leader Boy Scouts Am., Mexico City, 1978-79; co. gen. chmn. United Fund Campaign, Battle Creek, Mich., 1964-65, White Plains, N.Y., 1972-73. Served with U.S. Army, 1958. Mem. Asian-U.S. Bus. Council. Office: Gen Foods Corp 615 Piikoi St Honolulu HI 96814

WOLPE, ROBERT NEIL, real estate developer; b. Washington, Oct. 22, 1946; s. Allen M. and Eleanor B. Wolpe; B.S. cum laude in Bus. Adminstrn., Am. U., 1970; m. Marcy Shear, Oct. 1, 1971. Pres., Robert N. Wolpe Enterprises, Inc., Washington, 1974—, Washington Realty Group, Inc., 1977—; guest lectr. Georgetown U. Sch. Law, Am. U. Grad. Sch. Bus. Served with U.S. Army, 1967-73. Am. U./Dow Jones scholar, 1970. Office: 1140 19th St NW Washington DC 20036

WOLPER, MARSHALL, ins. cons.; b. Chgo., Nov. 19, 1922; s. Harry B. and Bessie (Steiner) W.; B.A. in Polit. Sci. and Econs., U. Ill., 1942; m. Thelma R. Freedman, Apr. 15, 1957 (div. Oct. 1968); m. Jacqueline Miller, Sept. 19, 1969 (div. Jan. 1976). With Marshall Industries, Chgo., 1947-52; life underwriter Equitable Life Assurance Soc., Miami Beach, Fla., 1953—, nat. sales cons., 1967—; sr. partner Wolper and Katz, life ins. and employee benefit plans consultants, Miami Beach, 1958—; mem. faculty life underwriting U. Miami, 1959—; pres. Family Ins. Plans Am. 1961—, Marshall Wolper Co., 1963—, Marshall Wolper Pension Services, Inc., 1977—; chmn. bd. M.W. Computer Systems, 1972—; mng. dir. Wolper, Ross & Co. Inc., 1980—; lectr. life ins., employee benefit plans, taxes, estate planning to various univs., spl. meetings, 1957—; faculty Practising Law Inst., 1968—. Pres., Estate Planning Council Greater Miami, Greater Miami Tax Inst.; chmn. bd. C.L.U. Inst. Bd. dirs. Dade County chpt. A.R.C. Served to 1st lt. AUS, World War II; ETO. Decorated Bronze Star, Purple Heart. C.L.U. Mem. Am. Soc. C.L.U. (com. faculty and curriculum inst. bd.; pres. Miami chpt., nat. v.p.), Nat. Assn. Life Underwriters, Million Dollar Round Table (exec. com. 1974-78, pres. 1977), U.S. (dir. 1956), Miami Beach (pres. 1957) jr. chambers commerce, Assn. for Advanced Life Underwriting (pres.), Nat. Assn. Pension Consultants and Adminstrs. (treas.), Am. Soc. Pension Actuaries (dir.), Zeta Beta Tau. Author: Tax and Business Aspects of Professional Corporations and Associations, 1968. Contbr. articles to profl. publs. Home: 714 W DiLido Dr Miami Beach FL 33139 Office: 444 Brickell Ave Miami FL 33131

WOLTZEN, HUGH ANDREWS, comml. fin. co. exec.; b. Peoria, Ill., Nov. 29, 1945; s. Louis A. and Elizabeth A. Woltzen; B.A., U. Ill., 1967; postgrad. Dartmouth Coll. Grad. Sch. Credit and Fin. Mgmt., summers 1975-76, Johns Hopkins U., 1976; m. Donna, Sept. 19, 1970; children—Hugh Andrews, Elizabeth Marie. Vice pres. comml. banking div. Md. Nat. Bank, Towson, 1970-77, v.p., head credit services div., 1977-80, v.p. adminstrn. and planning Md. Nat. Corp., 1979-80, sr. v.p., Western group mgr. Md. Nat. Indsl. Fin. Corp., Oak Brook, Ill., 1979—. Served to 1st lt. U.S. Army, 1967-70. Mem. Am. Inst. C.P.A.'s, Md. Assn. C.P.A.'s. Roman Catholic. Home: 22 W 358 Glen Valley Dr Glen Ellyn IL 60137 Office: Md Nat Indsl Fin Corp 1315 W 22d St Oak Brook IL 60521

WOMBOLD, DANNY DARRELL, personnel adminstr.; b. Dayton, Ohio, June 18, 1951; s. Vernon Darrell and Dorothy Jean (Clunk) W.; B.Indsl. Adminstrn., Gen. Motors Inst., 1974; M.B.A., U. So. Calif., 1974; m. Brenda Jean McCabe, Nov. 4, 1972; 1 dau., Tara Lynn. Mfg. foreman Inland div. Gen. Motors Corp., Dayton, 1974-76, labor relations rep., 1976-78, mgr. employee relations, 1978-80, supr. health and safety, 1980—. Mem. U. So. Calif., Gen. Motors Inst. alumni assns., Foreman's Club, Theta Xi, Beta Gamma Sigma, Sigma Alpha Chi. Clubs: USC-MBA's, Masons, Alpha. Home: 6690 Roberta Dr Tipp City OH 45371 Office: PO Box 1224 Dayton OH 45401

WONDER, RICHARD JOHN, edn. services co. exec.; b. Bklyn., Dec. 1, 1951; s. John Edward and Regina (Smutek) W.; student Bklyn. Coll.; m. Pamela Wonder; children—Patricia Ann, Theresa Marie. Stock chartist Kalb, Voorhees, N.Y.C., 1967-68; computer operator IBM, N.Y.C., 1969-70; ops. mgr., dir. SARK, Univ. Applications Processing Center, Bklyn., 1970—; guest lectr. Pace U., N.Y.C. Bd. Edn. Recipient Certificate of Service, Community Hosp., Bklyn., 1967. Office: 2001 Oriental Blvd Brooklyn NY 11235

WONG, ARNO, clin. lab. scientist; b. Canton, China, Jan. 26, 1950; s. William and Helen (Lai) W.; came to U.S., 1971, naturalized, 1977; B.S., Morgan State U., 1977. Staff clin. lab. scientist VA Hosp., Balt., 1977—. Mem. Am. Soc. Clin. Pathologists, Phi Theta Kappa, Alpha Kappa Mu. Home: 5126 Tennis Court Circle Tampa FL 33617 Office: VA Hosp Lab Service Tampa FL 33612

WONG, BENJAMIN WINGNIN, fin. exec.; b. Hong Kong, June 20, 1949; came to U.S., 1970; s. Ding Lun and Ling Sik (Lui) W.; B.S. with high honors, U. Wis., Stevens Point, 1973; M.B.A. with distinction, Northwestern U., 1974; m. Cecilia Y. Wong, Mar. 22, 1974; 1 dau., Vivian. Fin. analyst Chemed Corp., Cin., 1974-76, mgr. fgn. exchange, 1976-78, asst. treas., 1978—. Recipient Disting. Scholar award Northwestern U., 1974. Mem. Assn. M.B.A. Execs., Bankers Club. Home: 1216 Bobwhite Ct Edgewood KY 41018 Office: 1200 DuBois Tower Cincinnati OH 45202

WONG, JAMES PAN, restaurant exec.; b. Canton, China, Oct. 10, 1914; s. Jaw and Toy (Shee) W.; came to U.S., 1923, naturalized, 1923; student pub. schs., Ellensburg, Wash.; m. Cynthia Chan, June 6, 1956; children—Ella, Rosalind, Lisa. Partner, Nan Yan Restaurant, Chgo., 1947-50, owner, mgr., 1950—; owner, mgr. Jimmy Wong's Restaurant, Chgo., 1959—, Jimmy Wong's N., Chgo., 1965—; dir. James A. Shanahan & Assos., Chgo., Bank of Chgo. Overseas Chinese adviser Republic China, 1973-74, 71—; Midwest chmn. Hip Sing Benevolent Assn. Served with USAAF, W.W. II; ETO. Recipient award recognition Ann. Nat. Restaurant Conv., 1962; Medal of Merit award VFW, 1971; Chgo. Press Photographers Assn. award, 1973; Ill. Man of Yr. award Combined Vets Assn., 1975; Energy award State of Israel Bonds, 1976. Mem. Wabash Ave. Assn. Club: Chinese Passenger (pres., Chgo.). Home: 9217 N Kenton St Skokie IL 60076 Office: 426 S Wabash Ave Chicago IL 60605

WONG, JEFFREY JOSEPH, lawyer; b. San Francisco, July 24, 1943; s. Joe Bing and Lili Phyllis (Jew) W.; A.B. in Politics, Princeton U., 1965; J.D., U. Calif., San Francisco, 1968; m. Julianne Bryant, Mar. 30, 1980. Admitted to Calif. bar, 1969; asso. firm Dinkelspiel & Dinkelspiel, San Francisco, 1969-75, partner, 1975—; mem. attys. com. Am. Assn. Equipment Lessors, 1978—, participant legal seminars on equipment leasing law, 1978—; participant seminar on uniform comml. code Calif. Bus. Law Inst., 1979; instr. workshop leader Coll. Advocacy, Hastings Coll. Law, U. Calif., San Francisco, 1976. Mem. housing and urban devel. com. Human Rights Commn. San Francisco, 1976-79; dir. San Francisco Lawyers Com. for Urban Affairs, 1974—; bd. dirs. Golden Gate chpt. ARC, 1972-78, Vis. Nurse Assn. San Francisco, 1975—, Charilla Found., 1977—. Mem. Am. Bar Assn., State Bar Calif., Bar Assn. San Francisco (editor In Re newsletter 1976-78, del. to state bar convs. 1976, 77). Democrat.

Clubs: Princeton U. Canon; Bohemian, 20-30 (pres. 1969) (San Francisco). Office: care Dinkelspiel & Dinkelspiel One Market Plaza San Francisco CA 94105

WONHAM, FREDERICK STAPLEY, bank exec.; b. N.Y.C., Apr. 8, 1931; s. Wilson Stapley and Mary Knight (Lincoln) W.; B.A., Princeton U., 1953; postgrad. N.Y. U., 1955-59; m. Ann Hayden Brunie, June 18, 1953; children—Stapley, Henry, Lincoln. Various positions G.H. Walker & Co., investment bankers, N.Y.C., 1955-71, pres., 1971-74; with White, Weld & Co. Inc., N.Y.C., 1974-78, pres., 1975-78; sr. v.p., mgr. personal trust and investment div. U.S. Trust Co., N.Y.C., 1979—; dir. Conrac Corp.; chmn. Provident Loan Soc., N.Y.C., 1974-77. Trustee Community Service Soc., Brunswick Sch. Served to 1st lt. AUS, 1953-55. Mem. Investment Assn. N.Y. (pres. 1961). Clubs: Bond (gov. 1974-77) (N.Y.C.); Roundhill (Greenwich, Conn.). Home: 238 June Rd Cos Cob CT 06807 Office: 45 Wall St New York NY 10005

WOO, GLENN FRANK, stockbroker; b. Honolulu, June 8, 1945; s. Francis H.T. and Mabel S. (Lee) W.; B.B.A., U. Notre Dame, 1967; M.B.A., Baruch Coll. City U. N.Y., 1968, doctoral fellow, 1969; m. Linda Lew, June 21, 1970. With Amswiss Internat. Corp., N.Y.C., securities dealers, 1968—, pres., 1974—, also dir.; pres. Met. Philatelic Supply. Mem. Security Traders Assn. N.Y., Am. Stamp Dealers Assn., U. Notre Dame Lacrosse Team Alumni. Club: L.I. Akita Kennel. Home: RD5 Box 102 Flemington NJ 08822 Office: 30 Montgomery St Room 1401 Jersey City NJ 07302

WOOD, ARLETTA RENEE, booking agy. exec.; b. Columbus, Ohio, Apr. 19, 1945; d. Clem and Sarah Jane Elizabeth Hairston; B.S. in Bus. Adminstrn., Howard U., 1967; student Montgomery County Jr. Coll., 1977-78, spl. courses; m. Larry Keith Wood, May 20, 1970 (div. 1981). Exec. sec. to dept. head Ohio Dept. Edn., 1963-64; adminstrv. sec. to head botany dept. Howard U., 1964-66; adminstrv. asst., exec. and adminstrv. sec. various locations, 1967-79; adminstrv. sec. Air Transport Assn. Am., Washington, 1979—; founder, pres. Affiliated Enterprises, Inc., artists mgmt. and fin. brokerage, Silver Spring, Md., 1967—, B.I. Prodns., 1971-79, Renee's Beauty Boutique, 1974-79. Mem. Air Transport Assn. Am. Employees Assn. (pres. 1980-81), Am. Soc. Profl. and Exec. Women, UN Assn. U.S., Pres.'s Assn., Am. Mgmt. Assn., Nat. Trust Hist. Preservation, Smithsonian Instn., Am. Film Inst., Am. Fedn. Musicians. Spiritualist. Home: 2418 Homestead Dr Silver Spring MD 20902 Office: PO Box 13037 Washington DC 20009

WOOD, BRIAN, financial corp. exec.; b. Stretford, U.K., Sept. 29, 1920; s. James William and Constance (Medcalf) W.; came to U.S., 1947, naturalized, 1957; student Manchester U., 1935-38, Royal Coll. Tech., Manchester, 1946; m. Carolyn Elizabeth Wilber, May 31, 1945; children—Christine Elizabeth, Robin Ann. Salesman export div. J.P. Stevens & Co., Inc., 1947-54; v.p. Walker Bros. (N.Y.) Inc., 1954-62; export sales mgr. Warner Bros. Inc., 1962-63; exec. v.p., dir. Fenchurch Corp. (name changed to Tozer Kemsley & Millbourn U.S.A., Inc.), N.Y.C., 1964-77; exec. v.p., dir. S.H. Lock, Inc., N.Y.C., 1964-74, pres., 1975—; exec. v.p., dir. Tozer Kemsley & Millbourn (Can.) Ltd., 1966-73, TKM Pacific Ltd., 1972-74; joint mng. dir. Fenchurch NV, Curacao, 1972-77; chmn. S.H. Lock (Can.) Ltd., 1980—; dir. James Finlay Internat. Inc. Served to lt. comdr. Air br. Royal Navy, 1940-45. Mem. Trinidad and Tobago C. of C. N.Y. (dir., 1st v.p. 1970-73, pres. 1975—). Republican. Clubs: Patterson (Fairfield, Conn.); Jamaica (Kingston, Jamaica); Union (Port of Spain, Trinidad). Home: 109 Mill River Rd Fairfield CT 06430 Office: 535 Fifth Ave New York NY 10017

WOOD, DAVID BAKER, JR., furniture store co. exec.; b. Asheville, N.C., Sept. 7, 1941; s. David Baker and Mildred C. (Riley) W.; student Cath. U. Am., 1959-62; m. Margaret Heath, Dec. 21, 1963 (div. 1977); children—David Baker, III, William Riley. Owner Adams Morgan Gallery, Washington, 1962-64; salesman, store mgr. Wood Shop, Washington, 1963-66; mgr. Shelf Shop, Cleve., 1966-69; contract mfr. Design Assos., Cleve., 1969-71; pres. Design Union, Inc., 1971—; pres. Holmes County Chair Co. Inc., 1981—; dir. Digetrends Inc., Cleve. Bd. dirs. Peoples and Cultures, Cleve., 1974-75. Mem. U.S. C. of C., Greater Cleve. Growth Assn., Council of Smaller Enterprises. Home: 3205 Rumson Rd Cleveland Heights OH 44118 Office: 1330 Old River Rd Cleveland OH 44113

WOOD, DENNIS LEROY, computer co. exec.; b. Carthage, N.Y., Aug. 24, 1932; s. LeRoy Alfred and Mary Geneva (Adner) W.; B.S. in Math., Syracuse U., 1956, postgrad., 1957; postgrad. U. Calif., 1963; m. Jeannine Helen Shaw, Jan. 28, 1962; 1 son, Bruce Sibelius. Physicist, Am. Car and Foundry, Washington, 1956-57; aero. research scientist NASA, Edwards AFB, Calif., 1958-60; sr. computer programmer System Devel. Corp., Santa Monica, Calif., 1960-63; mem. tech. staff Logicon, Inc., San Pedro, Calif., 1963-64; sr. mem. adv. staff Computer Scis. Corp., El Segundo, Calif., 1965-69; pres. Software Enterprises Corp., Westlake Village, Calif., 1970—, also chmn. bd. dirs.; lectr. George Washington U., U. Calif., Los Angeles, Royal Mil. Coll. Can., fed. govt. and industry; cons. Dept. Def. and industry for mgmt. of computer-based systems. Mem. Am. Def. Preparedness Assn. Fine arts painter; works exhibited publicly, 1962-70; contbr. papers in computer mgmt. to profl. publs. Home: 11654 Presilla Rd Camarillo CA 93010 Office: 2239 Townsgate Rd Westlake Village CA 91361

WOOD, DENNIS ROGER, banker; b. Waterloo, Iowa, Mar. 16, 1947; s. Marvin F. and Ruth K. W.; B.S. in Animal Sci., Iowa State U., 1969, M.S. in Econs., 1971; m. Deborah J. Estell, Aug. 16, 1969. Vice pres. corr. banking and credit Omaha Nat. Bank, 1971-74; pres. 2d Nat. Bank of Eldora (Iowa), 1974-77; pres. Packers Nat. Bank, Omaha, 1977—. Sec., bd. dirs. Omaha Girls Club; bd. govs. Omaha Boys Club; chmn. bd. Omaha Housing Authority Services, Inc. Served with U.S. N.G., 1968-74. Named one of 10 Outstanding Young Omahans, 1979. Mem. Nebr. Bankers Assn. (exec. council), Omaha Bankers Assn. (2d v.p.). Republican. Office: 4710 S 23d St Omaha NE 68107

WOOD, DOUGLAS RAYMOND, food products co. exec.; b. Wayzata, Minn., Nov. 7, 1944; student St. Johns U., Collegeville, Minn., 1967-69, U. Minn., Mpls., 1970-72. Accountant, Aluma Craft Corp., Mpls., 1964-67; div. asst. Supersweet div. Internat. Multifoods Inc., Mpls., 1969-71, Century Communications Corp., Mpls., 1971-74; internal auditor Pacific Gamble Robinson Inc., Seattle, 1974-76, div. accountant shipping ops. Pacific Fruit and Produce, Los Angeles, 1977-80; acct. milling div. Carnation Co., Los Angeles, 1980—. Home: 2416 Bellevue Ave Apt 204 Los Angeles CA 90026 Office: 5045 Wilshire Blvd Los Angeles CA 90046

WOOD, GEORGE MARK, JR., investment banker; b. Montgomery, Ala., Sept. 6, 1925; s. George M. and Mattie Maxwell (Pegues) W.; student Starke U., 1937-41, U. Ill., 1942-43, Auburn U., 1942; B.S., U. Tex., 1946; student U. Ala., 1946; m. Marguerite McDaniel Wood; 1 dau., Meri. Chmn., pres., sec. George M. Wood & Co., Inc., Montgomery, 1946—, also dir.; dir., vice-chmn. bd. Thermal Components, Inc., Montgomery. Chmn. Operation Drug Alert, 1969-70. Bd. dirs. Montgomery Area Mental Health, 1969-72, South Ala. State Fair, 1969-73. Served with USNR, 1942-46, 51-52. Mem. Nat., Ala. security dealers assns., Kappa Sigma. Episcopalian. Kiwanian (pres.). Clubs: Pioneers, Montgomery Country. Home: 3425 Thomas Ave Montgomery AL 36111 Office: 8 Commerce St Montgomery AL 36102

WOOD, GLENN FORD, real estate appraiser, broker; b. Oak Pk., Ill., Sept. 16, 1925; s. Charles James and Juanita Marie (Boutet) W.; educated Elmhurst Coll., 1949-51, Northwestern U., 1951-52; m. Eldonna Mary Baker, June 26, 1948; children—Glenn Geoffrey, Paul Charles, Lowell Andrew, Chelle Jean, Ronald Spencer; foster child, Gerard Lawrence Crawford. Real estate broker Wood Realty Co. Lombard, Ill., 1947-58; real estate appraiser Equitable Life Assurance Soc., Chgo., 1952-55, 1st Fed. Savs., Chgo., 1955-56; owner operator Accurate Appraisal Service, Lombard, Ill., 1954—, appraiser Fairfield Savings, Chgo., 1958—; ins. broker, 1950-77, real estate develop, 1958—; cons. in field. Pres. local chpt. and council PTA, 1961-63; precinct committeeman, 1960-66; treas. Lombard Vets. Meml. Hall, 1975-78; past pres. Methodist Men, past lay del. Ann. Conf.; candidate for Ill. Legis., 1964-66. Served with USN, 1943-46; ETO, PTO. Mem. Ill. Real Estate Brokers, Soc. Real Estate Appraisers, Am. Legion (comdr. 1963-64), VFW, Phi Alpha Delta. Republican. Clubs: Jaycees (dir. 1950), Masons. Home: 428 Eugenia St Lombard IL 60148 Office: 1601 Milwaukee Ave Chicago IL 60647

WOOD, HAROLD GRAY, marketing exec.; b. Jackson, Tenn., Aug. 6, 1926; s. Irby Gray and Lessie (Holland) W.; B.S., Union U., 1948; B.S. in Elec. Engring., U. Tenn., 1950; postgrad. Tex. Coll. Arts and Industries, 1956-59; m. Kaye Anne Lloyd, June 7, 1956; children—Lloyd Gray, Kenneth Martin. Commd. 2d lt. U.S. Army Signal Corps, 1952, advanced through grades to capt., 1960; asst. to planning engr. Western Union Telegraph Co., N.Y.C., 1960; Eastern regional mgr. Mil. Products div. Hoffman Electronics Corp., Los Angeles, 1960-64; mgr. Monmouth office Ling Temco Vought, Inc., 1964-69, mgr. area office LTV Electrosystems Inc., Long Branch, N.J., 1969-72, mgr. area office E-Systems, Inc., 1972—. Mem. Assn. U.S. Army, Armed Forces Communications and Electronics Assn., Am. Def. Preparedness Assn., Assn. Old Crows, Army Aviation Assn. Am., Nat. Contracts Mgmt. Assn., Aircraft Owners and Pilots Assn. Democrat. Baptist. Clubs: Deal Golf and Country, Masons. Home: 45 Sydney Ave Deal NJ 07723 Office: 776 Shrewsbury Ave Tinton Falls NJ 07724

WOOD, JACK WELDON, petroleum co. exec.; b. Santa Maria, Calif., June 15, 1925; s. Jack B. and Margaret (Weldon) W.; student Central Wash. Coll. Edn., 1943-44, Southwestern U., 1949-50, U. Calif. at Los Angeles, 1951-54; m. Catherine Susan Lagomarsino, June 25, 1949; children—Thomas Joseph, John Anthony. Oil and gas leaseman, oil operator, producer, 1954—; chmn. bd. Pyramid Oil Co., Santa Fe Springs, Calif., 1969—, also dir.; partner Assn. Developers, real estate, Ventura, 1959—, Arbolito Pacifico, farms, Ventura, 1959—; v.p. Malotto Dig Service, Consulcorp Inc.; sec., dir. Ventura Realty Co.; dir. Thailand-Pacific Exploration Co., Instrumatic, Inc., Gen. Petroleum & Devel. Co. Bd. dirs. 31st Agrl. Dist., State of Calif. Served with USAAF, 1943-46. Mem. Am. Assn. Petroleum Geologists, Coast Geol. Soc., Palm Soc., Internat. Oil Scouts. Clubs: Ventura Yacht (dir., past commodore), Rotary. Office: PO Box 2131 Santa Fe Springs CA 90670 also PO Box 1666 Ventura CA 93001

WOOD, JAMES, chain store exec.; b. Newcastle upon Tyne, Eng., Jan. 19, 1930; s. Edward and Catherine Wilhelmina (Parker) W.; came to U.S., 1974; student St. Joseph's Roman Cath. Ch., Newcastle upon Tyne; m. Colleen Margaret Taylor, Aug. 14, 1954; children—Julie, Sarah. Chief food chain Newport Coop. Soc., South Wales, Eng., 1959-62, Grays Food Coop. Soc. (Eng.), 1962-66; dir., joint dep. mng. dir. charge retailing Cavenham, Ltd., Hayes, Eng., 1966-80, pres. Grand Union Co., Elmwood Park, N.J., 1973-79, chief exec. officer, dir., 1973—, chmn., 1979—; chmn. bd., chief exec. officer Gt. Atlantic & Pacific Tea Co., Inc., 1980—; chmn. Allied Suppliers, Ltd.; mng. dir. retail div. Cowenham Ltd., 1979—; dir. Irma Fabrikerne A/S, Denmark. Served with Brit. Army, 1948-50. Mem. Food Mktg. Inst. Roman Catholic. Home: 394 Minoma Ln Franklin Lakes NJ 07417 Office: 2 Paragon Dr Montvale NJ 07645

WOOD, JESSE JAMES, blueprint and photography co. exec.; b. Des Moines, Apr. 29, 1935; s. Jesse James and Anna (Jones) W.; A.A., Sacramento City Coll., 1955; Engring. Tech. degree Sierra Community Coll., 1970-75; m. Barbara Tillie Sterba, Dec. 27, 1955; children—Deborah Lee, Terry Keith. Drafting supr. Spink Corp., Sacramento, 1958-69; mgr. Raymond Vail & Assos., Sacramento, 1970-76; pres., owner Atlas Blueprint & Reprographics, Inc., Sacramento, 1976—; advisor drafting bd. Sierra Coll. Served with AUS, 1955-57. Mem. Bldg. Inst. Am., Nat. Ind. Bus. Assn., Small Bus. Assn. Club: Lions. Home: 8716 Fallbrook Way Sacramento CA 95826 Office: 1323 J St Sacramento CA 95814

WOOD, JOHN HERBERT, banker; b. Worcester, Mass., Apr. 2, 1932; s. Herbert A. and Mary A. (Handfield) W.; B.S. in Econs., Holy Cross Coll., 1954; J.D., Suffolk U., 1970; postgrad. in Econs., Clark U., 1956-57; m. Mary Theresa Nee, Nov. 27, 1957; children—Michelle, Tamasine, Christopher, Anne-Mary. Admitted to Mass. bar, 1971; with State St. Bank & Trust Co., Boston, 1957-73; v.p./gen. mgr. State St. Boston Leasing Co., 1967-73; pres., chief exec. officer Melrose Savs. Bank, Boston, 1973—; instr. Holy Cross Coll., 1956-57, Am. Inst. Banking, 1958—, also Grad. Sch. Banking Brown U.; dir. Mass. Higher Edn. Assistance Corp.; pres., dir. Mass. Automated Transfer System. Former trustee, former mem. exec. com. Melrose-Wakefield (Mass.) Hosp. Assn.; alderman City of Melrose, 1972-73; chmn. Republican ward com., Melrose, 1965-73. Served with AUS, 1954-56. Mem. Nat. Assn. Mut. Savs. Banks, Arden House Credit Com., Savs. Banks Officers Assn., Mass. Savs. Bank Assn. (former chmn. consumer loan com.). Roman Catholic. Clubs: Bellevue Golf; Rotary (Melrose). Home: 40 Rivers Ln Melrose MA 02176 Office: Melrose Savs Bank 476 Main St Melrose MA 02176

WOOD, JOHN WALTER, advt. agy. exec.; b. N.Y.C., July 7, 1941; s. John Walter and Suzanne (Cort) W.; B.A. magna cum laude Trinity Coll., Ireland, 1962; M.A., U. So. Calif., 1978; postgrad. Oxford (Eng.) U., 1979—; m. Charlotte M. Cusack-Jobson; 1 son, William Duncan. Chief copy dept. C.P.V. Kenyon & Eckhardt, Ltd., London, 1965; asso. creative dir. Pritchard Wood & Partner, London, 1965-68; chmn. Wood Brigdale & Co., London, 1968—; cons. internat. relations. Recipient various advt. awards, including Cannes Film, Venice Film, Cork Film, Hollywood Broadcast, N.Y. Broadcast festivals. Fellow Inst. Dirs.; mem. Anglo-Am. C. of C., Westminster C. of C., Anglo-Dutch C. of C., Royal Inst. Internat. Affairs, Internat. Inst. Strategic Studies, Mind Assn., Aristotelian Soc. Clubs: Hurlingham, Oxford, Cambridge, Royal Automobile, American Club London, Union, Shinnecock Yacht. Author: The Instrument of Advertising, 1977; The Question of Costs, 1978; Human Needs and World Society, 1977; The Nature of International Relations, 1979. Office: Wood Brigdale & Co Ltd Kent House Market Pl London W1 England

WOOD, JOSEPH BARBER, trust and savs. and loan assn. exec.; b. Tuscaloosa, Ala., Apr. 1, 1938; s. James Garland and Charlene Elizabeth (Swanzey) W.; student U. Ala., 1955-63, Tulane U., 1957-58, U. No. Ariz., 1960-61; m. Patricia Ann Sturgis, July 15, 1967; children—Joseph Barber, Courtney Elizabeth. Owner, Asso. Consultants, Inc., Germantown, Tenn., 1972-76; treas. Germantown Trust Savs. & Loan Assn., 1974-79, pres., 1979—. Mem. Rules and Regulations com. Dept. Ins., State of Tenn., 1978; mem. City of Germantown Investment Com., 1978-79; mem. spl. planned unit developments com. Shelby County Planning Commn., 1969-70. Mem. Tenn. State Savs. and Loan League, U.S. Savs. and Loan League (dir.), Tenn. State Savs. and Loan Assn. Republican. Baptist. Clubs: Trumpt, Rotary, Farmington Country, Ducks Unlimited. Office: 7770 Poplar Ave Germantown TN 38138

WOOD, LARRY (MARYLAIRD), journalist, pub. relations exec., environ. cons., educator; b. Sandpoint, Idaho; d. Edward Hayes and Alice (McNeel) Small; B.A. magna cum laude, U. Wash., 1938, M.A., 1940; postgrad. Stanford U., 1941-42; postgrad. U. Calif. at Berkeley, 1943-44, certificate in photography, 1971; postgrad. in journalism U. Wis., 1971-72, U. Minn., 1971-72, U. Ga., 1972-73, U. Calif., Santa Cruz, 1974-76; children—Mary, Marcia, Barry. By-line columnist Oakland (Calif.) Tribune, San Francisco Chronicle, 1946—; contbg. editor Mechanixs Illus., 1946—, Popular Mechanics, 1948—; feature writer Western region Christian Sci. Monitor, CSM Radio Syndicate and Internat. News, 1973—, Des Moines Register and Tribune Syndicate, 1973—; contbg. editor Traveldays mag., 1976—; regional corr. Spokane mag.; Calif. corr. Money mag., Portland Oregonian, Seattle Times Sunday mag.; Far West contbg. editor Fashion Showcase, Dallas; byline features writer/photographer Parade, 1960—; feature writer Indsl. Progress, Calif. Today, 1977—; travel feature writer San Jose Mercury News, 1977—; work syndicated feature synopses on radio stas. in N. Am., CSM Radio News Service; freelance writer mags. including Parents, Sports Illustrated, Oceans and Sea Frontiers, Accent, People on Parade, House Beautiful, Am. Home, Off-Duty, 1946—; dir. pub. relations No. Calif. Assn. Phi Beta Kappa, 1969—; asst. prof. journalism San Diego State U., 1975—; prof. journalism San Jose State U., spring 1976; asst. prof. journalism Calif. State U., Hayward; prof. environ. journalism U. Calif., Berkeley, 1979; dir. pub. relations/cons. in field of sci., environ. affairs and recreation to firms, instns., assns. Pub. relations dir. YWCA, YM-YW USO, Seattle, 1942-46, YWCA, Oakland, 1946-56, Childrens's Home Soc. Calif., 1946-56, Children's Med. Center No. Calif., 1946-70, Eastbay Regional Park Dist., 1946-58, Calif. Spring Garden Shows, 1946-58, Girl Scouts U.S.A., Oakland, 1946-56; speaker ednl. insts., profl. groups, 1946—; sec. Oakland Jr. Arts Center, 1952—; vol. pub. relations Am. Cancer Soc., Oakland YMCA, 1946-52; pub. relations writer ARC, 1946-56; trustee Calif. State Parks Foun ., 1976—. Recipient citations U.S. Forest Service, 1975, Nat. Park Service, 1976, Oakland Mus. Assn., 1979, 80; Nat. Headliner award Mercury News, 1979, 80; Daisy citation, 1980. Mem. Pub. Relations Soc. Am., Nat. Sch. Pub. Relations Assn., Internat. Environ. Cons.'s, Environ. Cons.'s N.Am., Oceanic Soc., Internat. Oceanographic Soc., Am. Assn. Edn. in Journalism (nat. exec. bd. mag. div. 1979—, nat. chmn. travel writing contest for Am. univ. students 1978—), Advt. and Mktg. Assn., Nat. Assn. Sci. Writers, Travel Writers Am., Soc. Profl. Journalists, Women in Communications, Calif. Acad. Environ. News Writers, Nat. Press Club, Nat. Press Photographers Assn., Sigma Delta Chi. Author: English for Social Living; Tell the Town. Address: 6161 Castle Dr Oakland CA 94611

WOOD, NICHOLAS BURGWIN, warehouse developer; b. N.Y.C., July 8, 1931; s. Richardson King and Mildred Burgwin W.; B.A., Cornell U., 1952; m. Sanko Kamiyama, May 8, 1954; children—Olivia Midori, Francesca Ayame, John Kamiyama. With various firms engaged in redevel. of downtown areas, New Haven and Bridgeport, Conn., Buffalo, 1957-68; pres. Nicholas Wood & Assos., Inc., nat. warehouse and office developer, Bridgeport, 1968—; guest lectr. Harvard U., Yale U., CCNY. Del., White House Conf. on Small Bus., 1980. Served with 1st Radio Broadcast and Leaflet Group, 1953-54. Mem. Warehousing Edn. and Research Council (founding mem.), Nat. Council Phys. Distbn. Mgmt. Democrat. Author: The Family Firm, 1964. Created new form of operating lease financing using tax exempt bonds. Office: Nicholas Wood & Assos Inc 1016 Broad St Bridgeport CT 06604

WOOD, RALPH BRIGGS, constrn. exec.; b. Lane, Okla., July 15, 1940; s. Ralph Roy and Opal Eugenia (Shoemake) W.; B.S., U. Ariz., 1962; postgrad. bus. U. So. Calif., 1968-69; m. Ilka Ilona Molitor, Aug. 18, 1977; children—Jeffrey Briggs, Suzanne Jane, Tanya Natalie. Plant supr. Mountain States Telephone Co., 1962-64; maintenance engr. Signal Oil & Gas Co., Bakersfield, Calif., 1964-71; v.p., sec., dir. Timeo Co., Bakersfield, 1971—; sec., dir. Petrochem Insulation Inc., Richmond, Calif., 1975-79; pres., dir. Sierra Allied Contractors, Richmond, 1976—; v.p., dir. Indsl. Pipe & Mfg. Co., Bakersfield, 1978—; cons. mech. engr., 1969—. Served with USAR, 1963-64. Registered profl. engr., Calif. Mem. ASME, Western Oil and Gas Assn., Sigma Chi. Republican. Office: 601 8th St S Richmond CA 94803

WOOD, RICHARD DONALD, pharm. mfg. co. exec.; b. Brazil, Ind., Oct. 22, 1926; s. Howard T. and Dorothy (Norfolk) W.; B.S. in Engring., Purdue U., 1948, LL.D., 1973; M.B.A., U. Pa., 1950; LL.D., De Pauw U., 1972; D.Sc., Butler U., 1974; LL.D., Phila. Coll. Pharmacy and Scis., 1975, Ind. State U., 1978; m. Billie Lou Carpenter, Dec. 29, 1951; children—Catherine Ann, Marjorie Elizabeth. Gen. mgr. Argentina, Eli Lilly Internat. Corp., 1961-62, Mexico, 1962-64, pres., Indpls., 1970-71, now dir.; dir. market research Eli Lilly & Co., Indpls., 1964-66, exec. dir. market devel., 1966-68, exec. dir. sales Eastern regions, 1968-69, exec. dir. indsl. relations, 1969-70, exec. v.p., 1971-72, pres., 1972-73, chmn. bd., chief exec. officer, dir., 1973—; dir. IVAC Corp., Cardiac Pacemakers, Inc., Physio-Control Corp., Elanco Products Co., Elizabeth Arden, Inc., Standard Oil Co. (Ind.), Dow Jones & Co., Lilly Endowment, Inc., Chem. N.Y. Corp., Chem. Bank. Bd. dirs. Am. Enterprise Inst. for Public Policy Research, Ind. State Symphony; chmn. bd. govs. Asso. Coll. Ind.; bd. govs. Purdue Found.; trustee U.S. Council Internat. C. of C., Com. Econ. Devel., Indpls. Mus. Art, DePauw U. Mem. Pharm. Mfrs. Assn. (dir.), Bus. Roundtable, Conf. Bd., Council Fgn. Relations. Presbyn. Clubs: Links (N.Y.C.); Indpls. Athletic; Meridian Hills Country. Home: 5715 Sunset Ln Indianapolis IN 46208 Office: 307 E McCarty St Indianapolis IN 46285

WOOD, RICHARD GENE, phys. fitness chain exec.; b. Lima, Ohio, Jan. 23, 1948; s. Richard D. and Vera June (Bryant) W.; student N.Mex. Jr. Coll., 1972, Ohio State U., Lima, 1967-70; m. Cinthia Olson, Apr. 3, 1979. Jr. mfg. engr. XLO Corp., Lima, 1968-69; mgr. New Life Health Spa, Lima, 1969-71; pres. Golden Life Phys. Fitness Centers, Inc., Midland and Odessa, Tex., Hobbs and Roswell, N.Mex., 1971—; pres. Golden Life Franchise Mgmt. Inc., 1980—. Pres., Grenhill Terrace Community Assn., 1980. Mem. Assn. Phys. Fitness Centers (Disting. Service award), N.Mex. Mounted Patrol. Democrat. Lutheran. Home: 4700 Tattenham Midland TX 79703 Office: 3200 Andrews Hwy Midland TX 79701

WOOD, RICHARD ROBINSON, real estate exec.; b. Salem, Mass., Nov. 8, 1922; s. Reginald and Irene (Robinson) W.; A.B., Harvard, 1944; postgrad. Mass. Inst. Tech., 1948; m. Pamela Vander Wiele, Mar. 3, 1951; children—Christopher Robinson, Bryant Cornelius, Marcella Jeffries; m. 2d, Jane Philbin Dreyfuss, Sept. 19, 1970. Research and marketing Godfrey L. Cabot Corp., 1948-49, 61—; sales promotion asst. Wm. S. Merrell Co., Cin., 1949-55; salesman Macalaster-Bicknell Co., Cambridge, Mass., 1955-59; mgr. investment dept. Hunneman & Co., Boston, 1959-61, v.p., 1961-72, sr. v.p., 1972; chmn. bd., pres. Continental Real Estate Equities, Inc., 1972-74; exec. v.p. Itel Real Estate Corp., 1975; v.p. Baird & Warner, 1976—, Renwood of Savannah, 1979—, Renwood of Ark., 1980—; pres. Renwood of Ill., Inc., 1977—, Convest Mgmt.; trustee Suffolk Franklin Savs. Bank, 1965-76. Mem. Beacon Hill Civic Assn., 1958-74, Mayor's Adv. Com., Boston, 1965-69; dir. Boston Municipal Research Bur., 1966-74, vice chmn., 1967-70; pres. Boston Republican Com., 1968-72; mem. Mass. State Rep. Com., 1964-72, asst. treas., 1964-72; candidate Mass. Ho. of Reps., 1956. Dir. White Mountain Ski Runners, pres., 1960-62; trustee Mass. Real Estate Investment Trust. Served with U.S. Army, 1944-45. Mem. Boston (dir. 1963-67), Chgo. (pres. comml. M.L.S. 1980—) real estate bds., Rental Housing Assn. (dir. 1961-67), Brokers Inst. (v.p., dir. 1964-67), Nat. Inst. Real Estate Brokers, Mass. Assn. Real Estate Bds. (dir. 1965-70), Nat. Assn. Indsl. and Office Parks, Internat. Council Shopping Centers, Real Estate Securities Syndication Inst. (bd. govs. 1973—, pres. 1977). Clubs: Longwood Cricket, White Mountain Ski Runners, Monroe, Down Town, Harvard (N.Y.C.). Home: 60 E Scott St Chicago IL 60610 Office: 115 S LaSalle St Chicago IL 60603

WOOD, ROBERT EDWIN, ins. co. exec.; b. Seattle, Nov. 20, 1904; s. Galen and Agnes (Irvine) W.; B.B.A., U. Wash., 1928; m. Marjorie May Kuhnley, June 19, 1935 (dec. 1959); 1 dau., Barbara L. Acker; m. 2d, Esther Schelenberg, Aug. 6, 1966. Sec.-treas., buyer Gene Hatton, 1918-29; with Phoenix Mut. Life Ins. Co., 1929-36, office supr., N.Y., 1936-40, br. mgr., San Francisco, 1940-44, personal prodn., 1944—; v.p. First San Francisco Planning Corp.; Calif. chmn. anti-inflation campaign Am. Council Life Ins. Cos., 1980—. Vice pres. San Francisco Estate Planning Council, 1963-64; treas. San Francisco Easter Seal Soc.; sec. Million Dollar Round Table Found.; San Francisco finance chmn. Adventures Unlted.; mem. U.S. Olympic Games Com., 1972, 76, 80; treas. Royal Towers Apt. Corp.; asso. chmn. Laymen's Nat. Bible Com., N.Y.C. Recipient Orr award, 1948, Heron award, 1956 for outstanding service to life ins. industry; charter mem. Phoenix Mut. Hall of Fame. Mem. Nat. (past trustee, chmn. nominating com.), Calif. (past pres., hon. dir. 1979), San Francisco (past pres.) assns. life underwriters, Am. Soc. C.L.U.'s (past regional v.p.), Million Dollar Round Table (life mem., mem. organizing bd. Found.). Mason (hon. award, 32 deg., Shriner). Contbr. articles to profl. publs. Home: Royal Towers 1750 Taylor St San Francisco CA 94133

WOOD, ROBERT JAMES, public relations exec.; b. Syracuse, N.Y., Nov. 27, 1918; s. John Marshall and Anna Mae (Wood) W.; student U. Toronto, 1936-37, Syracuse U., 1937-38, Columbia U. Grad. Sch. Bus., 1953; m. Jean K. Buchanan, Feb. 22, 1945; children—Judith Ann, Robert James, Maureen Elizabeth. Reporter, Syracuse Herald Jour., also Central N.Y. corr. AP, 1939-43; with Carl Byoir & Assos., N.Y.C., 1947—, exec. v.p., 1961-65, pres., 1965—, chief exec. officer, 1976—. Trustee Ill. Coll., Jacksonville. Served with USAAF, 1943-46. Mem. Public Relations Soc. Am., Found. Public Relations Research and Edn. (v.p., treas.). Republican. Roman Catholic. Clubs: Winged Foot Golf (Mamaroneck, N.Y.); Pinnacle, Board Room (N.Y.C.). Office: 380 Madison Ave New York NY 10017

WOOD, ROBERT RAY, machine tool mfg. co. exec.; b. Coffeyville, Kans., Dec. 19, 1942; s. Robert Gould and Geraldine Rosalie (Newman) W.; B.S., U. Wyo., 1966; M.B.A., No. Ill. U., 1974; m. Nola Jean Freouf, June 7, 1964; children—Robert Dean, Todd Ray. With Ingersoll Milling Machine Co., Rockford, Ill., 1966—, controller, 1972-76, v.p. fin., 1976—. Asst. state chief Y-Indian guide program; mem. mgmt. adv. bd. Rock Valley Coll.; bd. dirs. Civic League Winnebago County, 1975, Wesley Willows Retirement and Nursing Center, 1975-78; bd. dirs. YMCA, 1976—, treas., 1979—, recipient Vol. of Yr. award, 1975; pres. NW Community Nursery Sch., 1971. Mem. Nat. Assn. Accountants, Fin. Council Machine and Allied Products Inst., Fin. Execs. Inst. (charter, 2d v.p. 1978-79, pres. 1979-80), Ill. Mfrs. Assn. (fin. council), Alpha Kappa Psi. Methodist (fin. com.). Home: 813 Prestwick Pkwy Rockford IL 61107 Office: 707 Fulton Ave Rockford IL 61101

WOOD, ROGER SAMUEL, real estate broker; b. Parsons, Kans., June 12, 1952; s. Richard Warren and Betty Marie W.; B.B.A. in Econs., Pittsburg State U., 1980; m. Terri Lynne Fearmonti, May 25, 1974; children—Tiffany Renae, Regina Marie. Asso. broker Wood, Realtors, Pittsburg, Kans., 1974—. Cert. residential salesman; Grad. Realtors Inst. Mem. Nat. Assn. Realtors, Realtors Nat. Mktg. Inst., Pittsburg Bd. Realtors, Omicron Delta Epsilon. Republican. Mem. Christian Ch. Clubs: Optimist (pres. 1977-78), Kiwanis, Lions (Pittsburg). Home: 701 Thomas Pittsburg KS 66762 Office: Wood Realtors 2422 S Broadway Pittsburg KS 66762

WOOD, THOMAS HARVEY, elec. contractor; b. Rockford, Ill., Oct. 5, 1936; s. Cecil B. and Mabel M. (Nicholson) W.; student U. Ill., 1954-55; B.E.E., Chgo. Tech. Coll., 1958; m. LaVeda B. Bowden, Mar. 8, 1973; children—Thomas, William, Todd, Vickie, Jackie. Pres., Cecil B. Wood Inc., Rockford, dir., 1958—; owner Mid-States Traffic Supply Co., Rockford, 1966—; owner Sam's Pl., Rockford; lectr. in field. Lic. elec. contractor, Ill., Wis. Mem. Rock River Valley Electric Assn. (pres. 1972-73), Nat. Elec. Contractors Assn. (pres. No. Ill. chpt.), Nat. Fire Protection Assn., Internat. Assn. Elec. Insps. Mason (Shriner). Home: 4524 Olde Lyme Dr Rockford IL 61111 Office: 1610 Kilburn Ave Rockford IL 61103

WOOD, WESLEY THOMAS, pub. and music exec.; b. Queens, N.Y., Jan. 25, 1943; s. Wesley B. and Catherine (Rudy) W.; B.S., N.Y. U., 1964; m. Mary Catherine Piliero, Nov. 7, 1964; children—Lisa, Robert, Christina. Account exec. Arthur Falconer Assos., N.Y.C., 1964-66; dir. mktg. Investors Funding Corp. N.Y., 1966-72; exec. v.p. Dowre Communications, Inc., N.Y.C., 1972-74, also dir.; pres. Candlelite Music Inc., N.Y.C., 1974—; pres., dir. Country Music mag., 1979—; dir. PSI Industries, N.Y. Realty, CMI Group Inc. Mem. Direct Mktg. and Mail Assn. Roman Catholic. Home: 24 Timber Ridge Dr Laurel Hollow Oyster Bay NY 11771 Office: CMI Group Inc Nursery Ln Rye NY 10580

WOOD, WILLIAM ANDREW, JR., printing co. exec.; b. Atlanta, Sept. 13, 1919; s. William A. and Naomi (Majors) W.; student U. Ga., 1948; m. Helen C. Kelley, Nov. 19, 1940; children—Elaine Wood Norris, Susan, Shirley Wood Lanham, Margaret Wood Duggan. With Foote & Davies, Doraville, Ga., 1938—, v.p. sales, 1955-69, exec. v.p., 1969-73, v.p. S.E. sales, 1973-74, v.p. spl. projects, 1974-78; pres. Stein Printing Co., Atlanta, 1978—; dir. Graphic Industries, Atlanta. Bd. dirs. DeKalb County chpt. Am. Cancer Soc. Served with USAAF, 1942-45. Mem. Atlanta C. of C., Atlanta Advt. Club, Commerce Club. Kiwanian. Club: Atlanta Athletic. Home: 2050 Amberwood Way NE Atlanta GA 30345 Office: 2161 Monroe Dr Atlanta GA 30324

WOODARD, EDWARD JOSEPH, JR., bank exec.; b. Portsmouth, Va., Mar. 9, 1943; s. Edward Joseph and Catherine Gay W.; student Frederick Coll., 1961-64, Old Dominion U., 1967-72, Am. Inst. Banking, 1967-72; m. Sharon Williamson, Oct. 14, 1967; 1 son, T. Brandon. Credit mgr. American Finance System, Norfolk, Va., 1964-67; asst. v.p. First Virginia Bank of Tidewater, 1967-72; pres., chief exec. officer Bank of the Commonwealth, Norfolk, 1972—, also dir., chmn. exec. com., mem. investment and salary adminstrv. coms. Mem. Fin. and Budget com. Tidewater chpt. Am. Heart Assn., also bd. dirs.; bd. dirs., mem. exec. com. Downtown Norfolk Assn., 1972—, pres., 1978—; mem. study team Norfolk City Planning Commn., 1979—; mem. Granby Mall Adv. Commn., 1976—; mem. City of Norfolk Mayor's Task Force for Econ. Devel., 1979—. Mem. Tidewater Heart Assn., Downtown Norfolk Assn., Norfolk C. of C. Baptist (mem. fin. com.). Clubs: Kiwanis, Harbor. Office: PO Box 1177 Norfolk VA 23501

WOODBRIDGE, RICHARD CARVETH, patent atty., research and devel. exec.; b. Niagara Falls, N.Y., Nov. 15, 1943; s. Richard George and Marie Josephine (Carveth) W.; B.E.E., Princeton, 1965; J.D. with honors, George Washington U., 1971; m. Karen L. Moore, Apr. 3, 1971; children—Jennifer Carveth, Richard George, Janie Fleming. Project engr. Procter & Gamble Co., Cin., 1965-67; patent examiner U.S. Patent Office, Washington, 1968-72; admitted to Va. bar, 1971, D.C. bar, 1972, N.J. bar, 1974; asso. firm Baker & McKenzie, Washington, 1972-73; partner firm Behr & Woodbridge, Princeton, N.J., 1973-77; individual practice, 1978-80; partner firm Mathews, Woodbridge, Goebel, Laughlin & Reichard, P.A., 1980—; v.p., dir. Transspace Lab., Inc., Princeton Junction, 1976—, Princeton Venture Capital Corp., 1979—. Mem. Princeton Borough Council, 1977—; v.p. Princeton Rep. Club, 1975-77; police commr. Princeton Borough, 1977—. Recipient Spl. Achievement award U.S. Patent Office, 1971, 72. Mem. IEEE, Am., N.J., Va., D.C., Mercer County, Princeton bar assns., N.J. Patent Law Assn. (chmn. pub. relations com. 1976-77, 80—), Washington Soc. Engrs., Princeton Area Alumni Assn. (treas. 1975-77, v.p. 1977-79), Explorers Club. Episcopalian. Club: Pretty Brook Tennis. Patentee in field. Home: 56 William St Princeton NJ 08540 Office: 357 Nassau St Princeton NJ 08540

WOODBURY, KENNETH DONALD, bank exec., lawyer; b. Pembroke, N.H., Aug. 9, 1918; s. Kenneth M. and Ruth C. (Johnson) W.; B.S., U. N.H., 1940; J.D., Boston U., 1947, LL.M., 1948; m. Zdeny Forst, May 28, 1946; 1 son, James Kenneth. Admitted to Mass. bar, 1948, N.H. bar, 1949; partner firm Tomassian & Woodbury, Watertown, Mass., 1947-48, Woodbury & Woodbury, Suncook, N.H., 1948—; owner Woodbury Ins. Agency, Suncook, N.H., 1958-67; pres. The Suncook Bank, 1970—, also dir.; treas., dir. Pembroke Investment Corp., Hooksett Industries, Inc.; dir., clk. Osborne Transp. Inc., F.W. Saltmarch & Sons, Inc.; dir. Huckins Oil Co., Agrafiotis Assos., Inc. Mem. N.H. Ho. of Reps., 1957-59; tax collector Town of Pembroke, 1948-54, corp. counsel, 1952-79; corp. counsel Allenstown (N.H.), 1952-72, Hooksett (N.H.), 1948-72. Served with USAAF, 1942-46. Mem. Am. Bar Assn., Bar Assn. N.H., Am. Judicature Soc., N.H. Water Works Assn., Am. Bankers Assn., N.H. Bankers Assn., Nat. Trust Hist. Preservation, Delta Theta Phi. Home: Pembroke St Suncook NH 03275 Office: 50 Glass St Suncook NH 03275

WOODCOCK, CLIFTON ELBERT, ret. accounting firm exec.; b. Albia, Iowa, Feb. 9, 1919; s. Earl E. and Edith P. (Callen) W.; B.S., U. Iowa, 1942; m. Mary A. Eastman, Dec. 31, 1941; children—Joel, Susan, Virginia. Accountant, Haskins & Sells, N.Y.C. and Denver, 1942-43; tax accountant Malco Refineries, Inc., Roswell, N.Mex., 1943-46; accountant firm Linder, Burk & Stephenson, Albuquerque, 1946-56, partner, 1949-56, Peat, Marwick, Mitchell & Co., Albuquerque, 1956—, mng. partner, 1961-68, Detroit, 1969-77; fin. v.p. Bill C. Carroll Co. Inc., Albuquerque, 1977—; dir. Bank Securities Inc. Sec., U. N.Mex. Found.; exec. com. Lovelace Med. Center; bd. dirs. N.Mex. Rehab. Center, Albuquerque; mem. budget com. Mich. United Fund, Lansing; mem. exec. com. Detroit Met. Fund; chmn. bd. dirs. Camp Fire Girls, Inc., N.Y.C., 1973; mem. N.Mex. Govs. Tax Advisory Com., 1963-69. Fellow Aspen Inst. Humanistic Studies; mem. N.Mex. Soc. C.P.A.'s (past pres.), Mich. Assn. C.P.A.'s, Am. Inst. C.P.A.'s, Mich. Assn. Professions. Clubs: Albuquerque Country (pres. 1979), Rotary (Albuquerque); Pres. of U. Mich. Home: 1815 Princeton St NE Albuquerque NM 87106

WOODFIN, GENE MACK, mfg. co. exec.; b. Paris, Tex., Feb. 7, 1919; s. John Elmer and Alma Kathryn (Smiley) W.; grad. U. Tex. Law Sch., Austin, 1940; m. Jane Gentry, 1941 (dec. 1969); children—William S., Kathryn Jane; m. 2d Judith Frankel Kaplan, July 31, 1970. Admitted to Tex. bar, 1941; asso. firm Vinson, Elkins, Weems & Searls, Houston, 1940-59, partner, 1946-59; sr. partner Loeb, Rhoades & Co., 1959-73, limited partner, 1973-75; pres., chief exec. officer Marathon Mfg. Co., Houston, 1973, chmn. bd., 1974-76, chmn. bd., chief exec. officer, 1976—, also dir.; dir. Houston br. Fed. Res. Bank of Dallas, Jim Walter Corp., Studebaker-Worthington, Inc., Penn Central Corp., Big Three Industries, Inc. Served to lt. USNR, 1942-46. Mem. Am., Tex. bar assns., U. Tex. Found. (past pres., dir.). Clubs: Houston Country; Nat. Golf Links of Am., Links (N.Y.C.); Annabelles (London); Ramada, Coronado, Petroleum (Houston); Quaker Hill; Back of Beyond (Pawling, N.Y.). Office: 600 Jefferson St Houston TX 77002*

WOODHALL, JOHN ALEXANDER, JR., constrn. co. exec.; b. Peoria, Ill., Oct. 10, 1929; s. John Alexander and Marion Ellen (Solstad) W.; B.B.A., U. Minn., 1952; m. Donna Irene Simmons, Aug. 21, 1948; children—John Alexander, Susan, Cheryl, Douglas, Robert. Project supt. Central States Constrn. Co., Willmar, Minn., 1953-57, v.p., project mgr., 1957-60; v.p., area mgr. Allied Enterprises, Willmar, 1960-69; exec. v.p. Central Allied Enterprises, Inc., Canton, Ohio, 1969-74, chmn., chief exec. officer, 1974—; chmn. bd. Clark Irrigation Co., Schory Cement Block, Inc.; dir. 1st Nat. Bank Willmar; dir. Road Info. Program. Mem. exec. com. constrn. sect. Nat. Safety Council; mem. Minn. Gov.'s Occupational Safety Health Adv. Council; bd. dirs., vice-chmn. Minn. Safety Council; pres. W. Central Safety Council, 1979; dist. commr. Viking council Boy Scouts Am., 1969-71. Mem. Am. Mgmt. Assn., Vets. of Safety, Am. Arbitration Assn., Asso. Gen. Contractors Am. (dir.), Asso. Gen. Contractors Minn. (pres. 1977), Lutheran. Clubs: Kiwanis (Willmar); Masons, Shriners, Mpls. Athletic. Home: 190 Lake Ave E Spicer MN 56288 Office: PO Box 1317 Willmar MN 56201 also PO Box 1387 Sta C Canton OH 44708

WOODHEAD, ROBERT KENNETH, constrn. and engring. co. exec.; b. Wendell, Idaho, Feb. 11, 1925; s. Albert Arthur and Clara Elizabeth W.; B.S., U. Idaho, 1948, D.A.S., 1980; m. Dolores Lucille Calvert, May 29, 1951; 1 dau., Linda D. With Morrison Knudsen Co. Inc., Boise, Idaho, 1948—, treas. NAMCO, 1968-70, v.p. corporate affairs, 1970-72, sr. v.p., 1972—, also dir.; dir. Nat. Steel & Shipbldg. Co., Broadway Ins. Co., H.K. Ferguson Co., Internat. Engring. Co. Served to 1st lt. USAAF, 1943-46. Mem. Fin. Execs. Inst. Home: 3509 Woodacres Dr Boise ID 83705 Office: 400 Broadway Boise ID 83729

WOODHULL, REMINGTON BROWN, merchant; b. North Bennington, Vt., Nov. 17, 1909; s. Joel Brown and Eliza (Remington) W.; ed. pub. schs. Vt.; m. Gladys A. Benner, Nov. 17, 1930; children—Elizabeth Jean (Mrs. Anthony Charles Maiola), Roberta Ann (Mrs. Vernon Violette). With A. & P. Tea Co., 1929-32; owner, operator Woodhull's Market, 1932-70; pres. Newport Industries, Inc., 1955-58; trustee, chmn. Newport Savs. Bank. Mem. N.H. Ho. of Reps., 1947-48; mem. Sullivan County Commn., 1963—; pres. N.H. County Assn., 1968-71. Trustee, chmn. New Eng. Kurn Hattin Homes, Westminster, Vt.; pres. S.W. Employment Tng. Program, Cheshire and Sullivan Counties, N.H.; trustee Newport (N.H.) Hosp. Mem. Asso. Grocers N.H. (dir. 1955-61), Ind. Food and Grocers Assn. N.H. (pres. 1958-58), C. of C. Republican. Congregationalist. Clubs: Masons, Moose. Address: 28 Pleasant St Newport NH 03773

WOODLAND, GORDON CARTER, yacht mfg. co. exec.; b. Aberdeen, Wash., Oct. 29, 1924; s. Earle Clement and Marian Alma (Carter) W.; student U. Oreg., 1942, Tex. A. and M. U., 1943, Princeton U., 1945, U. Willamette, 1945, U. Colo., 1946; A.B., U. Wash., 1949; Cour Pratique, U. de Grenoble (France), 1950, Centre Univ. de Mediterraneen, 1950; m. Joanne Katherine Bouse, May 7, 1955; children—Michael Sean, Leslie Denise, Kristyn Ann, Kimberly Diane. Self employed in logging, Aberdeen, 1946-50; mgr. C. of C., Anacortes, Wash., 1951-54; mgr. sales and promotion Skagit Plastics, La Conner, Wash., 1955-60; west coast mgr. Traveler Boat div. Stanray Corp., Chgo., 1961-62, field sales mgr., 1962-63, gen. sales mgr., 1963-64, v.p. sales, 1964-66; gen. sales mgr. Pearson Yachts div. Grumman Allied Industries, Inc., Portsmouth, R.I., 1966-74, asst. gen. mgr., dir. mktg., 1974-76, gen. mgr., 1976—; cons. seminars Am. Mgmt. Assn.; speaker seminars Sales Execs. Clubs N.Y., Chgo. Pres. Pheasant Hill Assn., Portsmouth, 1976; mem. local sch. bd. adv. com., 1971, Title I Reading Inst., Portsmouth Sch. Dist.; bd. dirs. Seaport '76, 1976—; campaign chmn. Wash. Gov. Arthur B. Langlie for U.S. Senate, 1956. Served with USN, 1941-45, to lt. comdr. USNR, 1948-72; comdr. R.I. Naval Militia. Recipient certificate of appreciation Am. Sail Tng. Assn., 1976, commendation Sales Execs. Club N.Y., 1965, Plankowner's certificate Seaport '76, 1978; notary pub., R.I. Mem. Nat. Assn. Engine and Boat Mfrs., Boating Industry Assn. (dir.), Boat Mfrs. Assn. (dir.), Nat. Marine Mfrs. Assn. (dir., fin. shows coms.), Am. Sail Tng. Assn. (dir.), Boat Mfrs. Assn. (chmn.), C. of C. Newport County (dir.), Naval Res. Assn., Nat. Athletic Scholastic Soc., U. Wash. Alumni Assn., Sigma Nu. Republican. Roman Catholic. Clubs: Twenty Hundred (vice commodore); Barrington (R.I.) Yacht. Home: 78 Pheasant Dr Portsmouth RI 02871 Office: West Shore Rd Portsmouth RI 02871

WOODRICH, GLENN CARL, mfg. co. exec.; b. Oak Harbor, Ohio, Sept. 4, 1926; s. Carl John and Alma Augusta (Leiske) W.; student U. Toledo, 1946-48; B.S. in B.A., Bowling Green State U., 1950; m. Karis Elaine Baker, June 12, 1948; children—Kirk, Carol. Acct., Acme Industries, Jackson, Mich., 1950-51; salesman Ditto Inc., Denver, 1951-54; br. mgr. Duplicator Supply Co., Denver, Salt Lake City, 1954-57; dist. sales mgr. Bohn Bus. Machines, Inc., 1958, br. mgr., N.Y.C., to 1964; mktg. team mgr. Xerox Corp., Stamford, Conn., 1964-68; corp. officer, v.p. mktg. Writing Products div. Joseph Dixon Crucible Co., Jersey City, 1968—. Mem. Planning and Zoning Commn. Weston (Conn.), 1974-79; sr. mktg. exec. panel mem. The Conf. Bd., 1979; mem. N.Y. Sales Execs. Ednl. Speakers Bur., 1976-79. Served with USAAF, 1945-46. Recipient commendations Xerox Corp., 1966; Radio Sta. WICC merit award, 1968; Cert. of Appreciation, Town of Weston, 1979. Mem. Writing Instrument Mfrs. Assn. (dir. 1974—), Wholesale Stationers Assn. (govt. relations com. 1973), Nat. Office Products Assn., Pencil Makers Assn., Nat. Sch. Supply Edn. Assn., Internat. Blueprint and Reprographics Assn., Research Inst. Am., Hudson County C. of C. Republican. Episcopalian. Clubs: Sales Exec., Weston Field, Masons. Contbr. articles to profl. jours. Home: 33 High Acre Rd Weston CT 06883 Office: 167 Wayne St Jersey City NJ 07303

WOODRING, COOPER COOLIDGE, indsl. designer; b. Washington, Feb. 10, 1937; s. Harry Hines and Helen (Coolidge) W.; B.F.A., U. Kans., 1960; M.F.A., Cranbrook Acad. Art, 1962; m. Sue Elmore, July 28, 1960; children—Marcus, Sarah. Designer, F. Eugene Smith Assos., Bath, Ohio, 1962-65; product designer B.F. Goodrich Co., N.Y.C., 1965-69; mgr. product design J.C. Penney Co., Inc., N.Y.C., 1969—; guest lectr. Dartmouth Coll., Pratt Inst., U. Kans., Purdue U., 1973—. Dep. mayor Village of Plandome (N.Y.), 1977—, trustee, 1977—, hwy. commr., 1977—. Recipient Disting. Service and Achievement citation U. Kans., 1979. Mem. Indsl. Designer's Soc. Am. (dir., chmn. N.Y. chpt. 1977-78, chmn. 1979 ann. conf., v.p. 1980). Democrat. Editorial adv. Indsl. Design mag.; patentee in field. Home: 12 South Dr Plandome NY 11030 Office: 1301 Ave of the Americas New York NY 10019

WOODROW, FITZ WILLIAM MCMASTER, JR., marine officer; b. Washington, Dec. 9, 1929; s. Fitz William McMaster and Cicely (Bowman) W.; B.S.E.E., U.S. Naval Acad., 1954; M.S.I.M., Ga. Inst. Tech., 1970; postgrad. George Washington U.; m. Faye Martin, Oct. 19, 1957; children—Shera, Cicely, Fitz William III. Commd. 2d lt., U.S. Marine Corps, 1954, advanced through grades to col., 1978—, dir. morale support activities, 1974—, mem. USMC Non-Appropriated Fund Bd.; mem. adj. faculty Pepperdine U.; mem. faculty No. Va. Community Coll. Bd. dirs. United Services Automobile Assn. (Group), also mem. audit com.; elder Presbyn. Ch., 1974—, supt. ch. sch., 1976—. Decorated Bronze Star, Purple Heart, Navy commendation. Mem. Am. Mgmt. Assn. Democrat. Clubs: Army Navy Country, Army and Navy Town. Home: 4201 Stanby Ct Alexandria VA 22312 Office: Hdqrs US Marine Corps Code MSMS Washington DC 20380

WOODROW, ROBERT HENRY, JR., banker, lawyer; b. Birmingham, Ala., Nov. 24, 1920; s. Robert Henry and Carrie (Shaw) W.; A.B., U. of South, 1941; LL.B., U. Va., 1947; postgrad. Rutgers U. Stonier Grad Sch. Banking, 1955; m. Martha Glaze, Mar. 31, 1944; children—Robert Henry III, John P., Catherine, Philip C. With First Nat. Bank Birmingham, 1947—, asst. trust officer, 1950-53, trust officer, 1953-57, v.p., trust officer, 1957-61, sr. v.p., trust officer, 1961-66, exec. v.p., trust officer, 1967-70, exec. v.p., 1970-71, chmn. bd., 1972-76; vice chmn. bd. Ala. Bancorp., 1976—; admitted to Ala. bar, 1948. Served with AUS, 1942-46. Home: 3308 Hermitage Rd Birmingham AL 35223 Office: Alabama Bancorp PO Box 11007 Birmingham AL 35288

WOODRUFF, DALE L., life ins. co. exec.; b. Roseburg, Oreg., July 24, 1922; s. Glen E. and Georgia Grace (Sargent) W.; B.S. in Fin. (Bronze Medallion award), U. Oreg., 1950; m. Betty L. Moore, June 21, 1947; children—Nancy Lucinda, Pamela Anne, Scott Glen. Agt., then gen. agt. Franklin Life Ins. Co.; with Am. Guaranty Life Ins. Co., 1st v.p., then pres., chief exec. officer, from 1961, now chmn. bd., also dir.; dir. Am. Guaranty Fin. Corp., Sentinel Life Ins. Co., Nickerson Fleet Mgmt. Co., Internat. King's Table Co., Dimensions Computer Corp., K/P Graphics Co., Guaranty Acceptance Corp. Past bd. dirs. Rotary Found., Boy Scouts Am., Multiple Sclerosis Soc., Linfield Coll. Served with USNR, 1942-45. Mem. Million Dollar Round Table. Mem. Nat. Assn. Life Cos. (dir.). Office: 1430 SW Broadway Portland OR 97201

WOODRUFF, EDWIN TOWNSEND, TV producer; b. N.Y.C., Aug. 6, 1915; s. Frank and Maybelle (Beadle) W.; student Newark Sch. Engring.; m. Sarah Jane Davis, Oct. 23, 1964; children—Richard S., Barbara S. Woodruff Keats. Procurement officer, TV producer Dumont Network, N.Y.C.; pres. Cinetel Ltd., London, N.Y.C., Paris; pres. Bahama Public Relations Ltd., Nassau and Miami, Fla., 1962—, El Salvador Resorts, Ltd., Nassau, 1972—; cons. Devel. Corp. Bahamas, 1972-74. Served with USN, 1938-42. Recipient Service to Youth award Kiwanis K Clubs of Bahamas, 1970. Mem. TV Producers

Assn. (founding pres.). Club: Rotary (Nassau). Home: 46 George St Nassau Bahamas Office: PO Box 523281 Miami FL 33152

WOODS, JOHN L., mgmt. cons.; b. Oxford, Ohio, Feb. 18, 1912; s. George B. and Helen (Smith) W.; student Am. U., 1929-31; B.S. in Commerce, Northwestern U., 1933; m. Mary Torkilson, Apr. 2, 1938; children—Thomas George, Judith Ann, Jean Katharine, John Franklin. Asst. Cashier Mackubin, Legg & Co., 1933-34; accountant Arthur Andersen & Co., 1934-42; office mgr. Bauer & Black, 1942-44; v.p. finance and adminstrn., dir. Amphenol Corp., until 1968, mem. exec. com., 1961-68; v.p. finance Bunker-Ramo Corp. (merged with Amphenol Corp.), 1968-71; mgmt. cons., Chgo., 1971—; dir. Tower Products, Inc.; treas., dir. Valuation Counselors, Inc. Pres., dir. Borg Investment, 1964-71; pres., dir. Northview Pub. Co., 1950-53. Mem. Glenview Sch. Bd., 1945-51; commr., v.p. Glenview Park Bd., 1953-60; pres. Northfield Twp. High Sch. Bd. Edn., 1947-51, Glen Oak Acres Community Assn., 1947-48; bd. dirs. Chgo. Dist. Golf Assn. C.P.A., Ill., Washington. Mem. Fin. Execs. Inst., Am. Inst. Accountants, Ill. Soc. C.P.A.'s, Am. Soc. Appraisers, Am. Mgmt. Assn., Newcomen Soc. N.Am. Republican. Clubs: Midday, Knollwood (pres. 1970-72), Executive, Union League, Economic (Chgo.); Wall Street (N.Y.C.). Home: 5 Ct of Bucks County Lincolnshire IL 60015 Office: Suite 556 230 W Monroe St Chicago IL 60606

WOODS, JOHN RUSSELL, minerals co. exec.; b. Ottawa, Ont., Can., May 10, 1930; s. Shirley Edwards and Catherine (Guthrie) W.; student pvt. schs.; m. Denovan Elizabeth Braden, Aug. 29, 1953; children—James, Jennifer. Vice pres. S.E. Woods Ltd., Hull, Que., Can., 1954-59; pres., gen. mgr. Holden Mfg. Co. Ltd., Hull, 1959-66; v.p. Lynx Can. Exploration Ltd., Toronto, Ont., 1970—; chmn. Columbia Lime Products, Ltd., Ottawa, 1972—, Eaglet Mines Ltd., Ottawa, 1971—; chmn., dir. Can-cast Cement Co. Ltd., pres. Scolo Pax Ltd. Texada Lime Ltd.; v.p. Cogper Ltd., Ottawa, 1971—; dir., chmn. Can. Korea Ventures Ltd., Ottawa, ETS Tool Corp., Pub. Affairs Internat. Ltd.; dir. Carinex Resources Ltd. Nat. dir. fin. Liberal Party Can., Ottawa, 1968-72; chmn. Hull Red Cross, 1963, Canadian Nat. Inst. Blind, Ottawa, 1968; chmn. bd. govs. Ashbury Coll. Served to lt., inf. Canadian Army, 1950-53; Korea. Decorated knight comdr. Order Lazarus of Jerusalem, Mil. medal Korea. Mem. Canadian Sport Fishing Inst. (pres. 1969—, now chmn.), Can. Horse Council (dir.). Clubs: Rideau, Country (pres.), Maganassippi Fish and Game, Shitepoke (pres.), Ottawa Valley Hunt (Ottawa); Cavalry and Guards (London). Home: Kildare Farm Route 1 Pakenham ON KOA 2XO Canada Office: 130 Slater St Ottawa ON K1P 5H6 Canada

WOODS, MAURICE GLENN, mfg. co. exec.; b. Oklahoma City, Oct. 31, 1926; s. Roy G. and Esther C. (Marrs) W.: B.S., U. Okla., 1950; m. Teresa Jean Wright, Feb. 20, 1968; children—Pamela, Virginia, Robert, Lance, Brooke, Maurice Glenn, Tyler. Vice pres. So. Scholastic Mfg. Co., 1950-52; asst. to pres. Hap Drilling Co., also Calvert Drilling Co., 1952-54; pres., owner Wedgewood Amusement Park, Oklahoma City, 1954-69, Waste Systems, Inc., solid waste disposal and energy recovery, Oklahoma City, 1969—; v.p. Waste & Energy Recovery, Inc., Tulsa, 1980—. Deacon, elder First Christian Ch., Oklahoma City; past pres. Greater Oklahoma City United Cerebral Palsy; charter dir. Oklahoma City Open Golf Tournament. Served with U.S. Army, 1945-47, USAF, 1950-51. Recipient various service awards. Mem. Internat. Assn. Amusement Parks Sigma Chi. Republican. Patentee in field. Home: 6420 N Hillcrest St Oklahoma City OK 73116 Office: 2601 NW Expressway Oklahoma City OK 73112

WOODS, NANCY CHEYNE, banker; b. Cambridge, Mass.: d. Hugh Innes and Martha (MacCully) Cheyne; grad. in Journalism, Westbrook Coll., 1947; m. Carlton M. Woods, Jr., June 7, 1948; 1 son, Carlton M. Mem. advt. staff Wellesley (Mass.) Townsman, 1948-51; reporter Concord (Mass.) Jour., 1951-54; bus. mgr., dir. devel., dir. pub. relations, trustee, treas. Sea Pines Sch., East Brewster, Mass., 1965-73, Friendship Sch., 1973—; dir. advt., chmn. adv. bd. 1st Nat. Bank Cape Cod, Orleans, 1976—. Mem. New Eng. Assn. Schs. and Colls. Congregationalist. Clubs: Chatham Beach and Tennis, Monomoy Yacht, Eastward Ho, Country. Home: 270 Whidah Rd North Chatham MA 02650 Office: 1st Nat Bank Cape Cod Orleans MA 02653

WOODS, ROBERT LAWRENCE, life ins. exec., mgmt. cons.; b. Los Angeles, May 17, 1911; s. Walter A. and Alice (Strang) W.; A.B., U. Calif. at Los Angeles, 1933; C.L.U., Am. Coll. Life Underwriters, 1937; m. Dorothy Welbourn, Oct. 10, 1942; children—Robert Lawrence, Susan Welbourn. With Los Angeles agy. of Mass. Mut. Life Ins. Co., 1934—, asst. gen. agt., 1938-46, asso. gen. agt., 1946-49, gen. agt. in partnership, 1949-57, sole gen. agt., 1957-73, owner Woods Agy., 1973—, gen. agt. emeritus, mgmt. cons. Fund raising chmn. Los Angeles chpt. A.R.C., 1961, dir., 1960-63. Trustee Am. Coll. Life Underwriters, 1958-61, 71-79. Served to lt. col. inf. AUS, 1941-46. Recipient John Newton Russell Meml. award Nat. Assn. Life Underwriters, 1971; Will G. Farrell award Los Angeles Life Ins. Industry Orgns., 1974; elected to Mgmt. Hall of Fame, Nat. Gen. Agts. and Mgrs. Conf., 1974. Mem. Am. Soc. C.L.U.'s (pres. Los Angeles 1953-54, nat. pres. 1959-60), Mass. Mut. Gen. Agts. Assn. (pres. 1959-60), Gen. Agts. and Mgrs. Assn. (pres. Los Angeles 1957-58, nat. pres. 1967-68), Phi Gamma Delta. Home: 720 N Oakhurst Dr Beverly Hills CA 90210 Office: 4401 Wilshire Blvd Los Angeles CA 90010

WOODS, ROBERT WILLIAM, real estate co. exec.; b. Statesville, N.C., May 12, 1912; s. Harold and Bertha Hazel Woods; student public schs., N.C. and Va.; m. Kathryn Blunt, Feb. 22, 1936; children—Robert William, Valinda Woods Ashworth, Susan Woods Jennings. With Woods Bros. Coffee Co., Roanoke, Va., 1978, pres., 1968-78, pres. Woods Devel. co. real estate subs., 1978—; mem. adv. bd. Colonial Am. Nat. Bank, 1968-78. Mem. adv. bd. Salvation Army, Roanoke; fund raiser Roanoke Community Fund, 1978; mem. bd. Greene Meml. United Meth. Ch. Mem. Grocery Mfrs. Reps. Assn. (pres. 1968-69), Nat. Coffee Assn., So. Coffee Assn. (adv. bd.), Va. Assn. Mfrs., Roanoke Area Mfrs. Assn. (dir. 1970-74), Roanoke Valley C. of C. (dir. 1972-73). Republican. Clubs: Optimists, (v.p.), Rotary, Elks (Roanoke). Home: 1122 Clearfield Rd SW Roanoke VA 24015 Office: 3404 Aerial Way Dr SW PO Box 13167 Roanoke VA 24031

WOODS, RONALD HOSEA, oil co. exec.; b. Bklyn., Sept. 24, 1933; s. Victor V. and Viola (Mischke) W.; B.A. cum laude, St. Lawrence U., 1960; M.Indsl. Labor Relations, Cornell U., 1962; m. Kathryn Coughlin, June 13, 1959; children—Jerilee S., Karen J., Kristina S., Sean B., Maureen K. Asst. prof. St. Lawrence U., Canton, N.Y., 1962-66; supr. indsl. relations Union Carbide Corp., Charleston, W.Va., 1966-72; mgr. employee relations Crown Central Petroleum Co., Houston, 1972-75; mgr. tng. and devel. Brown & Root, Inc., Houston, 1976-78; mgr. tng. and devel. Tenneco Oil Co., Houston, 1978—. Served with USCG 1952-54. Lily Found. fellow, 1965. Mem. Am. Soc. Tng. and Devel., Indsl. Relations Research Assn., Beta Beta Beta, Psi Chi. Office: PO Box 2511 Houston TX 77001

WOODS, WILLIAM J., JR., corp. exec.; b. Lewistown, Pa., Oct. 15, 1921; s. William and Myrtle (Sebrell) W.; A.B., Princeton, 1944; m. Colette Ivel, July 17, 1947 (div.); 1 dau., Colette; m. 2d, Barbara Trent, July 25, 1973. Asst. sec., asst. treas. Pa. Glass Sand Corp., Pitts., 1948, sec.-treas., 1949-50, v.p. charge of sales, 1950-62, exec. v.p., 1962-69, also dir.; chmn., pres., chief exec. officer Unimin Corp., New Canaan, Conn., 1970—, Unisil Corp., 1970—; pres. Winchester and Western R.R., 1977—. Presbyterian. Home: 317 Country Club Rd New Canaan CT 06840 Office: 50 Locust Ave New Canaan CT 06840

WOODSIDE, WILLIAM STEWART, mfg. co. exec.; b. Columbus, Ohio, Jan. 31, 1922; s. William Stewart and Frances (Moorman) W.; B.S. in Bus. Adminstrn., Lehigh U., 1947; M.A. in Econs., Harvard, 1950. With Am. Can Co., 1950—, asst. to v.p., gen. mgr. Dixie Cup div., Easton, Pa., 1962-64, adminstrv. asst. to chmn. bd., 1964-66, v.p., 1966-69, sr. v.p. packaging, 1969-74, exec. v.p. ops., 1974-75, pres., chief operating officer, 1975—, chmn. bd., 1980—. Office: American Ln Greenwich CT 06830

WOODSON, DENNIS MARSHALL, 2D, accountant, developer; b. Atlanta, Apr. 30, 1949; s. Wesley Sloan and Noel (Johnson) W.; student U. Pa., 1968-69, Orlando (Fla.) Jr. Coll., 1969-70; B.B.A., Emory U., 1972, M.B.A., 1974; M.S.A., Fla. Tech. U., 1977. Pres., Sloan Land Co., Maitland, Fla., 1975-77; auditor Coopers & Lybrand, Atlanta, 1978; v.p. Marshall & Wesley, Inc., Maitland, 1978—; propr. Dennis M. Woodson II C.P.A., Maitland, 1978—; dir. Hison, Inc., 1975—; registered real estate salesman. Mem. Am. Inst. C.P.A.'s, Fla. Inst. C.P.A.'s, Maitland-South Seminole C. of C. (chmn. legis. action com. 1980). Episcopalian. Home and Office: 2923 Cove Trail Maitland FL 32751

WOODSON, HENRY LEE, JR., electronics co. exec.; b. Roanoke, Va., Apr. 12, 1908; s. Henry L. and Estelle (Hancock) W.; B.S. in Elec. Engring., Va. Mil. Inst., 1932; m. Dicie May Cassady, July 1, 1950; children—Douglas Lee, James Neal, Patricia Lea. Asst. city mgr., Roanoke, 1937-45; chief maintenance and operations N.W. Pacific area VA, Seattle, 1945-48; engring. rep. G. F. Muth Co., Washington, 1948-52; chief, property mgmt., orgn., methods examiner Office U.S. Housing Adminstrn., Washington, 1952-55; adminstrv., field mgmt. officer USOM, Pakistan, 1955-56; exec. officer, Turkey, 1956-57; mgr. Washington office Bendix Radio div. Bendix Corp., 1957-67, regional mgr. communications div., 1967-73; mgmt. cons., 1973—; dir. ACLS Corp. Served to lt. col. AUS, 1941-46. Mem. I.E.E.E., Am. Helicopter Soc., Am. Congress on Mapping & Surveying, A.A.A.S., Soc. Am. Mil. Engrs., Nat. Assn. Housing Ofcls., Internat. City Mgrs. Assn., Am. Marketing Assn., Aero Club Washington, U.S. Naval Inst., Internat. Platform Assn., Fedn. Aeronautique Internationale, AIAA, Air Traffic Control Assn., Radio Tech. Commn. for Aeros., Smithsonian Instn., Assn. Old Crows, Nat. Space Club, Armed Forces Communications and Electronics Assn., Am. Def. Preparedness Assn., Armed Forces Mgmt. Assn., Air Force Assn., Navy League U.S., Assn. U.S. Army. Rotarian. Clubs: Nat. Aviation, Gaslight, Army and Navy. Home: 2401 N Vernon St Arlington VA 22207 Office: PO Box 7140 Arlington VA 22207

WOODSON, RICHARD PEYTON, III, ins. co. exec.; b. Albuquerque, Mar. 1, 1923; s. Richard Peyton and Katherine (McMillen) W.; B.A. cum laude, Princeton U., 1945; postgrad. in Bus., Stanford U., 1949-50; m. Martha Avison, Sept. 18, 1954; children—Sheila Prentice, Richard Peyton, Martha Winslow. Treas., Occidental Life Ins. Co. of N.C., Raleigh, 1955-59, v.p. and treas., 1959-62, chmn. bd., chief exec. officer, 1962-69, chmn. bd., pres., chief exec. officer, 1969-71, chmn. bd., 1974—; chmn. bd. McMillen Corp., Jacksonville, Fla., 1972-77, Peninsular Life Ins. Co., Jacksonville, 1977—, McM Corp., Raleigh, 1977—, Brit.-Am. Ins. Co., Ltd., Nassau, Bahamas, 1974—. Chmn., Raleigh Community Relations Com., 1965-69, dir., 1964-70; chmn. N.C. Housing Corp., 1969-73; bd. visitors Davidson Coll., 1967-71; trustee Shaw U., 1964-71, St. Mary's Coll., Raleigh, 1979—, N.C. Symphony, Raleigh, 1977—. Served to maj. USAAC and USAF, World War II. Decorated Air medal with three clusters. Mem. Inst. Life Ins. (dir. 1970-72, spl. com. concept rev. 1970-72, research com. 1970-72), Life Office Mgmt. Assn. (chmn. bd. 1968-69, vice-chmn. 1967-68, dir. 1966-70), Chief Execs. Forum, World Bus. Council, Young Pres.'s Orgn. Democrat. Presbyterian. Clubs: Rotary, Capital City, Sphinx, Carolina Country (Raleigh); Lyford Cay (Nassau); Marco Polo, Princeton, Sky (N.Y.C.). Office: PO Box 12346 Raleigh NC 27605

WOODWARD, GARY LEE, banker; b. Circleville, Ohio, Oct. 26, 1946; s. Robert Harold and Florence Elizabeth (Woodruff) W.; student Wright State U., 1965-67, U. Dayton, 1967-69; grad. Am. Inst. Banking, 1974; m. Diana Lynn Crawford, Nov. 28, 1969; children—Elizabeth Jane, Melody Rebecca. Mailing supt. George A. Pflaum, Pub., Dayton, Ohio, 1965-71; asst. v.p., mgr. First Nat. Bank, Dayton, 1971—; asst. v.p., mgr. consumer lending dept. Huntington Banks, Dayton; notary pub. State of Ohio, 1975—. Vice pres. Youth Welfare, Dayton, 1974; pres. Old North Dayton Bus. Assn., 1978-79; meto mfg. chmn. United Way campaign, 1978, div. chmn. met. comml., 1979—; mem. Dayton Comml. Revitalization Bd., 1979—; mem. Ind. Bus. Council, 1978-79; bd. dirs., treas. Dayton Area Heart Assn. Served with USAF, 1964; served to capt. Ohio Air N.G., 1964—. Recipient Outstanding Service award United Way, 1978; High Twelve Internat. Ambassador award, 1978; Number One award First Nat. Bank of Dayton, 1978. Mem. Am. Inst. Banking, N.G. Assn. U.S.A., Ohio N.G. Assn., Greater Dayton Jr. C. of C., Dayton Area C. of C. (life), Nat. Rifle Assn. Methodist. Clubs: 1000, Northmont High Twelve (pres. 1978-79), Northmont Pres., Masons, Shriners, Order Eastern Star. Contbr. articles to profl. jours. Home: 1361 Timberwyck Ct Fairborn OH 45324 Office: 1100 American Bldg 45 Main St Dayton OH 45402

WOODWARD, HARRY HASTINGS, JR., rehab. agy. exec.; b. Augusta, Ga., Apr. 14, 1933; s. Harry Hastings and Almena (Preacher) W.; A.B., U. S.C., 1955; M.A. (George A. Schulze fellow), U. Chgo., 1960; m. Violeta Pabarcius, Sept. 9, 1966; 1 child, Zigmas H. Center dir. City of Chgo. Com. on Urban Opportunity, 1945-67; program officer W. Clement & Jessie V. Stone Found., Chgo., 1967-77; supr. nat. program of end. in correctional instns. Spl. Services Center, Lewis U., Chgo., 1977; exec. dir. Goodwill Industries Chgo. and Cook County, 1978—; mem. faculty Northeastern U., Chgo. Served with USNR, 1956-57. NIMH fellow, 1958-59. Mem. Nat. Assn. Social Workers, Am. Public Health Assn., Ill. Assn. Rehab. Facilities. Baptist. Clubs: Cliff Dwellers, Chgo. Press, Carlton. Home: 5810 N Kingsdale Ave Chicago IL 60646 Office: Goodwill Industries Chgo and Cook County 120 S Ashland Blvd Chicago IL 60607

WOODWARD, JACK CARLTON, pottery co. exec.; b. Roseville, Ohio, July 26, 1923; s. Floyd Harris and Clara Marie (Ungemach) W.; B.B.A., lMeredith Coll., 1942; m. Janice Colleen Harper, Nov. 8, 1962: children—Jon, Jo Ellen, Sharon, Vickie, Jane. With Robinson Ransbottom Pottery Co., Roseville, 1937—, treas., 1970-72, exec. v.p., 1972-78, pres., gen mgr., 1978—, also dir. Mem. Republican Central Com., Zanesville, 1949-53. Served with U.S. Army, 1943-46. Mem. Pottery, China and Glass Assn., Southeastern Ohio Ceramic Assn., U.S. C. of C., Ohio C. of C., Zanesville Area C. of C. (dir. 1976). Presbyterian. Clubs: Elks, Masons (32 deg.), Eagles. Office: Roseville OH 43777

WOODWARD, M. CABELL, JR., fin. exec.; b. Pitts., Jan. 29, 1929; s. M. Cabell and Anne (Cary) W.; B.A., Princeton U., 1951; M.B.A., N.Y. U., 1962; m. Helen Marie Boushee, July 24, 1954; children—Margaret Beale, Anne Cary. Asst. v.p. Hanover Bank, N(Y.C., 1954-61; asst. treas. ITT Continental Baking Co., Rye, NY., 1961-62, treas., 1962-66, v.p. fin., 1966-69, exec. v.p., 1969, pres., 1969-79, chief exec. officer, 1971-79, exec. v.p. chief fin. officer ITT, N.Y.C., 1979—. Served to capt. USMC, 1951-53. Office: 320 Park Ave ITT New York NY 10022

WOODWARD, MADISON TRUMAN, JR., lawyer; b. New Orleans, Feb. 15, 1908; s. Madison Truman and Maude (Weill) W.; LL.B., Tulane U., 1927; postgrad. U. Mich., 1927-28; m. Elvina Bernard, June 30, 1937 (dec. 1964); children—Anne Carol (Mrs. David G. Baker), Elizabeth H. (Mrs. James Ryan III), Lucie B. (Mrs. John P. Cavaroc), Margaret E., Madison Truman III; m. 2d, Ethel Dameron, June 24, 1977. Admitted to La. bar, 1929, since practiced in New Orleans; asso. firm Milling, Benson, Woodward, Hillyer, Pierson & Miller and predecessors, 1929-36, mem. firm, 1937—; dir. Valencia, Inc., 1960-74, pres., 1963-65; dir. Petroleum Helicopters, Inc., Offshore Nav. Inc. Chmn., La. Bar Found., 1980—, Victor Bernard Found., 1965—. Fellow Am. Coll. Probate Counsel, Am. Bar Found., Am. Coll. Trial Lawyers; mem. Am. (ho. of dels.), La. (pres. 1973-74), New Orleans bar assns., Am. Law Inst., La. Law Inst. (council 1957—, pres. 1979—), Am. Judicature Soc. (dir. 1973-76), Nat. Conf. Bar Pres.'s (exec. council 1973-75), 5th Circuit Jud. Conf. (del. 1966), Jud. Council Supreme Ct. La. Clubs: Pickwick, New Orleans Country, Stratford, Petroleum, Internat. House, Plimsoll (New Orleans); City (Baton Rouge). Author: Louisiana Notarial Manual 1952, rev. edit., 1962, supplement, 1973; also articles. Home: 1234 6th St New Orleans LA 70115 Office: Whitney Bldg New Orleans LA 70130

WOODWARD, OSCAR JAMES, III, lawyer, real estate devel. co. exec.; b. Oakland, Calif., Oct. 14, 1935; s. Oscar James and Beatrice (Denke) W., II; A.B., U. Calif., Berkeley, 1958, J.D., 1964; M.B.A., Stanford U., 1961; children—Baron James, Skye Lynne. Teaching asst. U. Calif., Berkeley, 1962-64, asst. gen. counsel to regents, 1966-67; admitted to Calif. bar, 1965; partner firm Gallagher, Baker, Manock & Woodward, Fresno, Calif., 1967-72; regional mgr., counsel Kaiser Aetna Co., real estate devel., Newport Beach, Calif., 1972-77; v.p., counsel 1st Savs. and Loan Assn., Fresno, 1977—; exec. v.p. Uniservice Corp., Fresno, 1977—. Pres., Fresno Arts Center, 1968-69, Storyland of Fresno, 1970; treas., United Crusade, Fresno, 1972, Fresno Taxpayer's Assn., 1980; bd. dirs. Urban Coalition, 1969-71, Fresno Community Theatre, 1969-72, Fresno Public Radio, 1979—; mem. County Condominium Conversion Task Force, County Bd. of Rev. Served to capt. U.S. Army, 1958-66. Community coll. teaching credential, Calif. Mem. Am. Bar Assn. (mem. real estate mgmt. com.), State Bar Calif., Fresno County Bar Assn., Estate Planning Council, Fresno C. of C. (chmn. legis. action and local govt. adv. coms. 1970-79), Urban Land Inst., Phi Delta Phi, Phi Delta Theta. Republican. Baptist. Clubs: Sierra Sport and Racquet, Fig Garden Swim and Racquet, Stanford, Commonwealth; Golden Bear (U. Calif.). Home: 5044 N Wishom Ave Fresno CA 93704 Office: 1515 E Shaw St Fresno CA 93710

WOODWORTH, ALFRED SKINNER, JR., investment banker; b. Boston, Jan. 1, 1948; s. Alfred Skinner and Beatrice (Hardon) W.; A.B., Harvard Coll., 1970; M.B.A., Dartmouth Coll., 1976. Analyst, State St. Bank & Trust Co., Boston, 1973-74, v.p. corp. fin., 1976—. Served to lt. USN, 1970-73. Home: 61 Sparks St Cambridge MA 02138

WOOLDRIDGE, DABNEY ELLIS, JR., former utility exec.; b. Clifton Forge, Va., Mar. 28, 1913; s. Dabney Ellis and Lula May (McCoy) W.; student Fenn Coll., 1937-38; grad. utility exec. program U. Mich., 1963; m. Naomi Georgia Withrow, Sept. 12, 1933; children—Georgia (Mrs. H. Bruce Cobbs), Dabney Ellis III, Kenneth L. Apprentice C. & O. Ry., Clifton Forge and Cleve., 1932-38; civilian supr. Norfolk Naval Yard (Va.), 1938-46; service engr. B.F. Sturtevant div. Westinghouse Corp., Hyde Park, Mass., 1946-47; mech. engr. Ohio Edison Co., Akron, 1947-53, prodn. maintenance engr., 1953-59, plant supt. R.E. Burger Plant, 1959-63, gen. supt. power prodn., 1964-67, gen. supt. prodn. and transmission, 1967-69, v.p., 1969-78, ret., 1978. Chmn. subcom. Edison Electric Inst.; chmn. fossil fuel task force Electric Power Research Inst., 1972—; mem. U.S.A./USSR Sci. and Tech. Cooperation Com. Scoutmaster Akron council Boy Scouts Am., 1967—; trustee, sec. North Summit County (Ohio) Hosp. Assn., 1957-68. Mem. ASME, Nat. Ash Assn. (pres. 1973-75). Mem. United Ch. of Christ. Clubs: Fairlawn Country, Akron City, Cascade, Masons, Shrine, Elks, Kiwanis. Home: 2294 Criston Dr Newport News VA 23602

WOOLF, JACK JACOB, food co. exec.; b. Bklyn., Aug. 24, 1933; s. Pincus and Minnie (Epstein) W.; B.B.A., CCNY, 1954, M.B.A, 1962; m. Vera Altschuler, Dec. 25, 1957; children—Laurie, Elizabeth, Malcolm. Asst. accounting mgr. Sonotone Corp., 1958-61; budget mgr. Rayco div. B.F. Goodrich Co., 1961-63; with Gen. Foods Corp., White Plains, N.Y., 1963-79, v.p. finance and adminstrn. Kohner Brothers Inc. subs., Elmwood Park, N.J., 1971-75, controller grocery group devel., 1976-79; v.p. fin., treas. Hilti Inc., Tulsa, 1979—. Bd. dirs. Assn. for Mentally Ill Children, 1975-79. Served with U.S. Army, 1954-56. Mem. Nat. Assn. Accountants (pres. Westchester chpt. 1976-77, chmn. edn. subcom. on pricing policies 1977-78, nat. dir. 1980—; E.J. Kelly award, 1966), Fin. Execs. Inst., Am. Mgmt. Assn. Club: Masons. Home: 6949 S Delaware Pl Tulsa OK Office: PO Box 45400 Tulsa OK 74136

WOOLF, JEROME ALAN, chem. co. exec.; b. N.Y.C., May 31, 1933; s. Harry H. and Lilyan (Schutzman) W.; A.A., Los Angeles Community Coll., 1954; B.A., U. So. Calif., 1956, M.A., 1971; B.A., Calif. State U., 1965; certificate U. Calif. at Los Angeles, 1969; LL.B., Williams Coll., 1971; Ph.D., Calif. Western U., 1976; m. Waltraud E. Trampenau, Feb. 24, 1974; 1 dau., Jamie Susan. Research and devel. chemist Chem-Seal Corp., Los Angeles, 1956-58; dir. tech. devel. Mesa Plastics Co., Los Angeles, 1958-61; exec. c.p. Techform Labs., Inc., Los Angeles, 1961-67, pres., 1967—; pres., dir. Alpha Chem. Co., Los Angeles, Omnia Corp., Los Angeles; dir. Consol. Gen. Corp., Los Angeles. Vice pres. Communications Exec. Program U. Calif. at Los Angeles. Fellow Am. Inst. Mgmt.; mem. Am. Oil Chemists Assn., AAAS, Soc. Plastics Industry, Am. Inst. Aeros. and Astronautics, Soc. Coatings Tech., Polymer Group So. Calif., Am. Chem. Soc. Contbr. articles to profl. jours. Patentee in field. Home: 16363 Royal Hills Dr Encino CA 91436 Office: 215 W 131st St Los Angeles CA 90061

WOOLF, PRESTON G., lawyer; b. Indpls., Oct. 10, 1906; s. Merritt Edgar and Bertha E. (Stone) W.; B.S., U. Fla., 1928; LL.B., Ind. U., 1932; grad. in material resources Indsl. Coll. Armed Forces; m. Phoebe Ann Cummins, Nov. 9, 1937. Export mgr. Hurty-Peck & Co., Indpls., 1932-36, asst. sec., 1936-47, sec., 1947-76; asst. sec. Hurty-Peck & Co. of Calif., Orange, 1942-46, sec., 1946-76; pres. Am. Beverage and Supply Corp., Indpls., 1945-76, chmn. bd., 1976—; sec. Costa Rican Devel. Co., San Jose, Hurty-Peck Eastern, Inc., Union, N.J., Blanke-Baer Co., St. Louis, Gt. Am. Trading Corp., St. Louis, Mfrs. Fin. Corp., Indpls., Remi Foods Corp., Chgo., Universal Falvors

Ill., Chgo., 1959-77; dir. Woolf Internat., Ltd., Hong Kong, 1961—, Ambesco de Mexico, S.A. de C.V., Mexico City, Universal Flavors Corp., Universal Flavors, Calif., Inc., Universal Flavors N.J., Inc., Universal Flavors Mo., Inc., 1959-77; spl. fgn. corr. Indpls. Star, 1959—; columnist chain S. Am. newspapers, 1960—; mem. world trade adv. com. U.S. Dept. Commerce, 1958-60, mem. Midwest regional com., 1960-67. Leader, Republican polit. study mission to Arabian world, 1966; leader Ind. Bankers and Indsl. Leaders study tour around world, 1967, to Africa, 1968, to China, 1976; cons. on Oriental affairs; mem. Trade Missions subcom. Council Fgn. Relations; mem. Ind. Fgn. Lang. Adv. Com.; pres. Indpls. Council World Affairs, 1958-60; dir. Internat. Bldg., Ind. State Fair, 1958-60; dir. Internat. Sch. Bus., Ind. U., 1961-67; mem. adv. council State Ind. Fgn. Lang. Program; 1st v.p. Ind. Econ. Edn. Found., 1965-77; chmn. Ind. Peoples World Affairs Com., 1961—; dir. Citizen's Com. for Free Cuba, 1965—; mem. bd. strategy Episcopal Diocese Indpls., 1961-66. Decorated Gold Cross Merit, 1st class (Fed. Republic W.Ger.); recipient citation Indpls. C. of C., 1960; Rabbi Stephen S. Wise Meml. citation Am. Jewish Congress, 1959. Mem. English-Speaking Union, Japan Soc., Asia Soc., U.S. C. of C. (world trade com.), Pan Am. Soc., AIM, Am. Bar Assn., Am. Security Council Washington, Inter-Am. Lawyers Assn. (founder 1935, pres. 1935-38), Am. Legion, Indpls. C. of C. (leader trade missions to Orient 1963, Latin Am. 1965), Delta Chi, Sigma Delta Chi, Sigma Delta Kappa. Republican. Episcopalian. Clubs: Rotary (dir., chmn. internat. contacts com.), Athletic, Press, Literary (Indpls.); Overseas Press (N.Y.C.); Am. (Hong Kong, Singapore); Fgn. Corrs. (Tokyo); Masons. Mem. around-the-world Flight Pan Am. Airways, 1976, N. and S. Poles Expdn., 1977. Home: 14825 Allisonville Rd Noblesville IN 46060 Office: 5700 W Raymond St Indianapolis IN 46241

WOOLLEY, MERLE EDWARD, mfg. co. exec.; b. Blackwell, Okla., June 29, 1941; s. Edgar Hamilton and Ada Joy (Beck) W.; student public schs., Ponca City, Okla.; m. Patricia Lynn Nicholson, Dec. 20, 1969; children—Mark Alan, Kimberly Kae. Area sales mgr. Mid-Continent Permanent Co., Perry, Okla., 1962-66; sales and mktg. cons., 1966-72; pres., owner S.W. Safety Systems, Inc., Tulsa, 1972-75, Mapakam, Inc., Springfield, Mo., 1975—, MPI Industries Inc., Springfield, 1980—; speaker on motivation, bus. cons., 1972—. Baptist. Home: Route 2 Box 166D Nixa MO 65714 Office: 2001 E Dale St Springfield MO 65803 also 1840 E Meadowmere Springfield MO 65804

WOOTTEN, EDMUND BERNARD, mfg. co. exec.; b. Malvern, Worcester, Eng., June 12, 1929; s. Ernst Dodd and Mary Jane (Waite) W.; B.Sc., Nottingham (Eng.) U., 1954; A.M.P., Harvard Bus. Sch., 1968; m. Linda Mary Allen, Sept. 19, 1955. Sales engr. Goodyear Aviation Div., Wolverhampton, Eng., 1954-57; with Lucas Industries, 1957—, pres., Troy, Mich., 1977—; chmn. Lucas Industries Can., Aris Industries Ltd., Ill.; dir. Siliconix Inc., Calif., Joseph Lucas Ltd., U.K. Served with RAF, 1947-49. Mem. Inst. Mgmt., British Am. C. of C. (dir.), Inst. Mktg., Soc. Automotive Engrs. Clubs: Renaissance, Detroit Athletic, Econ. (Detroit); Royal Air Force, Royal Automobile; Bloomfield Hills (Mich.) Country. Home: 311 Cranbrook Ct Bloomfield Hills MI 48013 Office: 5500 New King St Troy MI 48098

WOOTTEN, JOHN ROBERT, investor; b. Chickasha, Okla., Feb. 5, 1929; s. Henry Hughes and Ella Gayle (Ditzler) W.; B.S., Colo. A. and M. U., 1953; m. Mary Lou Schmausser, Mar. 15, 1952 (div.); children—Pamela Jean, Robert Hughes. Sec., S.W. Radio & Equipment Co., Oklahoma City, 1953-55; pres. Belcaro Homes, Inc., 1955-60, Bob Wootten Ford, Yukon, Okla., 1960-68, Bus. Data Systems, 1968-72; chmn., chief exec. officer 1st Nat. Bank, Moore, Okla., 1970-72; pres. Communications Enterprises, Inc., Liberal, Kans., 1967-79, Trebor Leasing Co., 1965—, Okla. Sch. Book Depository, Inc., Oklahoma City, 1976-80, S.W. Sch. Book Depository, Inc., Dallas, 1976—; chmn., chief exec. officer Exchange Nat. Bank Del City (Okla.), 1976-78; dir. S.W. Bancshares Corp., Oklahoma City. Pres., Okla. chpt. Am. Cancer Soc., 1966-67, Okla. chpt. Arthritis Found., 1973-76, Lyric Theater Okla., 1976-77; chmn. bd. trustees Bone and Joint Hosp., 1976—; bd. dirs. Okla. Theater Center, Dallas Theater Center; trustee Oklahoma City U.; pres. Last Frontier council Boy Scouts Am., 1968-70, Silver Beaver award, 1971; Republican nominee for Lt. Gov. of Okla., 1966. Mem. Ind. Bankers Assn., Am. Bankers Assn., Tex. Bookmen's Assn., Okla. Bookmen's Assn., Tex. Assn. Sch. Adminstrs., Econ. Club Okla., Navy League. Republican. Episcopalian. Club: Oklahoma City Rotary (pres. 1963-64). Home: 6784 E Northwest Hwy Dallas TX 75231 Office: 9259 King Arthur Dr Dallas TX 75247

WORKMAN, LEWIS CHAFFEE, ins. co. exec.; b. Mt. Clemens, Mich., Apr. 12, 1929; s. Harry Chaffee and Ilah (Lewis) W.; B.S., Drake U., 1951; m. Sally Ann Spence, Feb. 7, 1960; children—Diane, Douglas, Deborah. With Central Life Assurance Co., Des Moines, 1951—, asst. actuary, 1957-62, asso. actuary, 1962-64, actuary, 1964—, actuarial v.p., 1967—; mem. actuarial sci. adv. com. Drake U. Active Boy Scouts Am., PTA Iowa. Recipient Wall St. Jour. student achievement award, 1951. Fellow Soc. Actuaries; mem. life office Mgmt. Assn. (chmn. exam. com.), Des Moines C. of C., Am. Acad. Actuaries, Am. Soc. Pension Actuaries, Iowa Home Office Life Underwriters Assn., Beta Gamma Sigma. Mem. Disciples of Christ. Clubs: Izaak Walton League, Mens Garden of Polk County, Des Moines Actuaries. Author: (with Floyd S. Harper) Fundamental Mathematics of Life Insurance, 1970; Workbook for Fundamental Mathematics of Life Insurance, 1970. Home: RTE 5 Des Moines IA 50317 Office: 611 5th Ave Des Moines IA 50309

WORMLEY, LORENTZ ENGLEHART, SR., ret. civil engr., sch. adminstr.; b. Savoy, Ill., Oct. 29, 1899; s. Edwin and Katherine (Grove) W.; B.S. in Mining Engring., U. Ill., 1921; postgrad. U. Calif., 1930-40; extension work U. Chgo., 1925-26, Purdue U., 1926-28, Stanford, 1942-43; m. Geneva A. Stillman, Mar. 9, 1921; children—Lorentz, Phyllis Jeanne Wormley Adams. Mining engr. Roane Iron Co., Rockwood, Tenn., 1922-23; resident engr. Ill. Div. Hwys., East St. Louis, 1923-24; instr., athletic coach Du Quoin (Ill.) Twp. High Sch., 1923-26; instr., dept. head Hammond (Ind.) Tech. High Sch., 1926-28; constrn. and plant engr., field engring. unit Columbia Steel Corp., Pittsburg, Calif., 1928-29; asst. bridge engr., resident engr. Calif. State Hwy. Dept., Sacramento, 1929-30; constrn. engr., asst. to mgr. Austin Co., Oakland, Calif., 1930; dir. adult edn. Monterey (Calif.) Union High Sch., 1930-40; asst. state supr. trade and indsl. edn. Bur. Trade and Indsl. Edn., Calif. State Dept. Edn., Sacramento, 1940-41; dir. trade and indsl. tng. Unified Sch. Dist., San Francisco, 1941-42; supervising engr. Def. Plant Corp., San Francisco, 1942-43; area tng. specialist civilian personnel div. office Sec. of War, San Francisco, 1943-46; tng. officer-in-charge VA, San Francisco, 1946-47; supr. edn. Calif. Dept. Corrections, Sacramento, 1947-69; sec. Calif. Interagy. Com. for Correctional Inmate Tng. and Placement, 1955-69. Mem. Calif. Gov.'s Statewide Com. for Equal Opportunity in Apprenticeship and Tng. for Minority Groups, 1960-69. Mem. Calif. Assn. Adult Edn. Adminstrs. (life), Am. Correctional Edn. Assn. (past pres.), Alumni Assn. U. Ill. (life), Ret. Pub. Employees Calif., Nat., Calif. ret. tchrs. assns., Vets. World War I, SAR, Pi Kappa Phi. Clubs: Masons, Comstock. Contbr. articles to profl. jours. Home: 2360 Purinton Dr Sacramento CA 95821

WORMSER, ERIC SIGMUND, mfg. co. exec.; b. Germany, July 31, 1926; s. Arthur and Hedie (Brettauer) W.; came to U.S., 1939, naturalized, 1944; B.S. in Chemistry, Purdue U., 1946; M.B.A., Ind. U., 1947; m. Dorothy M. Hendrickson, Oct. 19, 1952; children—David A., Randall J., Heidi M. Chemist, chief chemist Lehon Co., Chgo., 1947-50; tech. dir. waterproofing div. Battenfeld Grease & Oil Corp., Kansas City, Mo., 1950-56; dir. research Gibson-Homans Co., Cleve., 1956-61, v.p. research and prodn., 1961-76, chmn. bd., 1976—. Mem. Nat. Paint and Coatings Assn., Adhesive and Sealant Council, Am. Chem. Soc., ASTM. Home: 2951 Attleboro Rd Shaker Heights OH 44120 Office: 1755 Enterprise Pkwy Twinsburg OH 44087

WORNE, HOWARD EDWARD, chem. co. exec.; b. Phila., Mar. 1, 1914; s. Edward H. and Lillian G. (Greene) W.; B.S., U. Mex., 1938; M.D., Universidad Libre Mexicana, 1940; Ph.D. in Biochemistry, Instituto Polytechnico Nacional, 1962; m. Phyllis Dolores Garofalo, Sept. 14, 1962; 1 dau., Elinor D. Pres., Nat. Solvents Corp., Elizabeth, N.J., 1942-45; v.p. Synthetic Resins, Inc., Toms River, N.J., 1943-47; v.p. Pentavir div. A.P. DeSanno & Sons, Phoenixville, Pa., 1947-48; sci. dir. Robinson Found., N.Y.C., 1950-55; pres. Pharm. Industries, Inc., Cherry Hill, N.J., 1955-62; pres. Enzymes, Inc., Cherry Hill, 1963-72, dir. Enzymes Japan, Inc., 1969-76; pres. Worne Biochemicals Inc., Berlin, N.J., 1973—, chmn. bd., 1973—; chmn. bd. Worne Biochems. (Europe), Ltd., 1976—, Fermentation Industries, Cherry Hill, N.J., 1977—, Biotech. de P.R., San Juan, 1978; pres. Bioferm Internat., Moorestown, N.J., 1977. Nat. Grain Yeast Corp fellow, 1935-37. Mem. Am. Chem. Soc., N.J. Acad. Sci., N.Y. Acad. Sci., AAAS, Pan Am. Med. Assn., Soc. Cosmetic Chemists, Fed. Water Pollution Control Assn. Republican. Presbyterian. Author: Soil Microbiology, 1975; editor in chief Archives of Research, 1953-55; contbr. sci. papers in field to profl. jours.; patentee in field. Home: 205 Sunny Jim Dr Medford NJ 08055 Office Lyon Industrial Park RTE 73 Berlin NJ 08009

WORRAL, GORDON JAMES, publishing co. exec.; b. Toledo, Dec. 21, 1923; s. William and Ruth Irene (Tippett) W.; grad. high sch.; m. Mary Winona Winch, Oct. 16, 1948; children—Donald James, Douglas Walter, David William, Kevin Lewis, Bernard Martin. Printer apprentice William Worral Typesetting, Kenmore, N.Y., 1941-42; sec., treas. West Side Pub. Co., Inc., 1946-62, pres., 1962-73; editor, pub. Riverside Rev., Buffalo, 1967—, Ema (N.Y.) Rev., 1979—; pres. Worral Pub., Inc., Buffalo, 1973—; pres., dir. Printing Industries Assn., Buffalo, 1969-70. Pres. Riverside Businessmen's Assn., 1972-74; pres., co-founder Local Devel. Co., 1977—, city-wide dir., 1978—; mem. Urban Waterfront Adv. Com. Western N.Y., 1975-76. Named Man of Year Riverside Businessmen's Assn., 1974. Served with AUS, 1943-45. Lutheran (pres. 1959-60; elder 1961-62, treas. 1975-76, trustee 1979—, del. Mo. Synod Eastern dist. conv. 1976). Kiwanian (pres. 1969-70). Home: 1371 Bowen Rd Elma NY 14059 Office: 946 Hertel Ave Buffalo NY 14216

WORRALL, BRUCE KENNETH, printing co. exec.; b. Doylestown, Pa., July 8, 1951; s. William K. Worrall and Mary L. Scott; grad. Valley Forge Mil. Acad.; student Embry Riddle Aero. U., 1969-71; m. Betti L. Tobin, Sept. 9, 1972; 1 dau., Brienne Marie. Vice pres. mktg. Keystone Offset Printing Co., King of Prussia, Pa., 1975-77: pres. Centennial Printing Corp., King of Prussia, 1977—. Mem. Graphic Arts Assn. Delaware Valley, Greater Valley Forge C. of C., Valley Forge Mil. Acad. Alumni Assn. (dir.). Republican. Home: 162 Farmhouse Dr Audubon PA 19403 Office: 558 W De Kalb Pike King of Prussia PA 19406

WORRELL, ANNE EVERETTE ROWELL (MRS. THOMAS EUGENE WORRELL), newspaper exec.; b. Surry, Va., Mar. 7, 1920; d. Charles Gray and Ethel (Roache) Rowell; student Va. Intermont Coll., 1937-39; m. Thomas Eugene Worrell, Sept. 12, 1941; 1 son, Thomas Eugene. Instr., VIRanch Camp, Bristol, Tenn., 1938-39, dir., 1942, 47-51; sec. Gen. Motors Acceptance Corp., Richmond, Va., Washington, 1939-41; feature writer, fashion editor Bristol Herald Courier, Va. Tennessean, Bristol, after 1963; sec.-treas., fashion dir., dir. Bristol Newspapers, Inc., after 1958, now v.p. Pres., Bristol Border Guild, 1959; mem. Va. Mus., 1960—, Carroll Reece Mus., 1968—; bd. dirs., sec. Bristol chpt. ARC, 1966-70; chmn. adv. bd., trustee Va. Intermont Coll.; patron Charlottesville-Albemarle Found. for Encouragement Arts, 1978—; mem. adv. bd. Virginia Highlands Community Coll. Mem. DAR, Assn. Preservation Va. Antiquities, Nat. Trust for Hist. Preservation. Presbyterian. Home: 7 Sunset Circle Farmington Charlottesville VA 22901 Office: Pantops PO Box 5386 Charlottesville VA 22905

WORTH, JAMES GALLAGHER, engr., chemist; b. Phila., Sept. 20, 1922; s. Wilmon W. and Elsie (Gallagher) W.; Asso. Sci., Rochester Inst. Tech., 1949; B.S., U. Miami, 1949-51; postgrad. U. So. Calif., 1961—; m. Esther Alberta Cring, Sept. 11, 1943; children—Nancy Jeanne, Constance Anne, James Gallagher. Chem. technician Internat. Paper Co., 1942-43, Eastman Kodak Co., 1946-49; pres., founder, engr.-chemist Applied Research Labs. Fla., Inc., Hialeah, 1949—, chmn. bd., 1956—; pres., chmn. bd. Ra-Chem Lab., Inc., Hialeah, 1964—. Served to maj. USAAF, 1943-46. Registered profl. engr., Calif., Fla. Fellow Am. Inst. Chemists; mem. Am. Chem. Soc., Am. Soc. Testing Materials, Am. Metals Soc., Nat. Soc. Profl. Engrs., Fla. Engring. Soc., A.A.A.S. Democrat. Methodist. Mason. Home: 751 Oriole Ave Miami Springs FL 33166 Office: 650 Palm Ave Hialeah FL 33010

WORTHINGTON, WILLIAM ALBERT, JR., ins. co. exec.; b. Pitts., Aug. 10, 1927; s. William Albert and Beatrice (Potter) W.; student U. Pitts., 1954-55; m. Patricia Lou Reynolds, Jan. 31, 1948; children—William Albert, John Edward, Kimberly Jean. Spl. agt. Aetna Ins. Co., Hartford, Conn., Pitts., Balt., 1948-59; home office supr. Nat. Union Ins. Co., Pitts., Denver, 1959-61; prodn. mgr. Pacific dept. San Francisco, 1962-68; v.p. Sims & Grupe, Stockton, Calif., 1968-71; pres. IMCO Ins. Mgmt. Corp., San Francisco, Stockton, 1971—, also dir. Mem. Young Republicans, 1952-54; active Contra Costa Rep. party, 1968-70. Served with USCGR, 1945-46. Recipient Salvation Army Pub. Service award, 1964. Mem. San Francisco Comml. Club, Ind. Ins. Agts. Assn. Calif., Soc. Ins. Brokers (past pres.), Aircraft Owners and Pilots Assn., Nat. Pilots Assn. Methodist (chmn. bd. trustees 1970-71). Kiwanian. Clubs: Encinal Yacht; Commonwealth of Calif. (San Francisco). Home: 1064 Grayson Rd Pleasant Hill CA 94523 Office: 22 Battery St San Francisco CA 94111

WORTZ, CARL HAGLIN, III, business cons.; b. Ft. Smith, Ark., May 9, 1921; s. Carl H. Wortz and Ed Dell (Haglin) W.; grad. N.Mex. Mil. Inst., 1940, Sparton Sch. Aeronautics, 1943; B.S. in Bus., U. Ark., 1947; m. Charlotte Wacker, June 29, 1943; 1 dau., Carolyn Jane. Former pres. Wortz Co.; pres. Wortz Assos.; chmn. Intercontinental Corp. of Tex.; dir. Live Oak Research Corp. Served with AUS, 1943-46; CBI. Mem. Sigma Alpha Epsilon. Methodist. Office: PO Box 45565 Dallas TX 75245 also 260 Ledgerwood Rd Hot Springs AR 71901

WOZIWODZKI, HILTRUD ELIZABETH, research scientist; b. Eisleben, Ger., June 20, 1935; d. Franz Johann and Elizabeth Martha (Wrusch) W.; came to U.S., 1963, naturalized, 1968; Abitur, Gymnasium Eisleben, 1953; Vordiplom chemiker, U. Rostock, 1956; Diplom Chemiker, U. Munich, 1961. Chemist, Sloan-Kettering Inst. Cancer Research, N.Y.C., 1963-68; research scientist Lever Bros., Edgewater, N.J., 1968—. Mem. Am. Chem. Soc., Am. Oil Chemists Soc., AAAS, N.Y. Acad. Sci. Club: Ponte Verdra. Patentee; contbr. articles to profl. jours. Home: 8200-7 Boulevard E Apt 30J North Bergen NJ 07047 Office: 45 River Rd Edgewater NJ 07020

WOZNIAK, SAM, recreation and def. mfg. co. exec.; b. Timblin, Pa., Mar. 6, 1931; s. John and Fenyi (Fedasz) W.; B.S., U. Tulsa, 1971, M.B.A., 1972; m. Shirley J. Johnson, Dec. 28, 1961; children—Susan Rae, John David. Elec. engr., Douglass Aircraft Corp., 1955; supr. inertial instruments Bell Aircraft, 1955-58; supr., research scientist N. Am. Aviation, 1958-61; chief project engring. N. Am. Rockwell, Downey, Calif. 1961-64; engring. mgr. Rockwell Internat., Tulsa, 1964-74; dir. div. engring. Brunswick Corp., DeLand, Fla., 1973-76, tech. dir., Def. div., Skokie, Ill., 1976—; spl. adviser USAF Mission Analysis on Electronic Warfare, 1971-74; Sci. adviser low radar cross sect. aircraft/radar aboring materials USAF, 1978; adj. prof. U. Tulsa, 1971-73; mem. admissions council Carengie Mellon U., 1966-70. Vice chmn. YMCA, 1968-70. Served with USAF, 1951-55. Mem. AAAS, Am. Mgmt. Assn., Am. Inst. Aeros. and Astronautics, IEEE, Electronic Def. Assn., Am. Def. Preparedness Assn., Assn. MBA Execs., Assn. Old Crows, Delta Sigma Pi, Pi Sigma Epsilon, Beta Gamma Sigma, Sigma Iota Epsilon. Republican. Co-author: Guided Missiles Fundamentals, 1953, Radar Systems Manual, 1954; author: Radar Absorbing Materials and Radar Cross Section Analysis on Electronic Warfare, 1972; Radar Camouflage Benefits, 1975; Army Camouflage Net System, 1975, others. Home: 1168 Princess Ct Costa Mesa CA 92626 Office: One Brunswick Plaza Skokie IL 60077

WOZNIUK, LEONARD, mfg. co. fin. exec.; b. Niagara, Ont., Can., July 18, 1944; s. Isaac and Alexandra Wozniuk; came to U.S., 1971; B.S., Bob Jones U., 1968; m. Lee P. Graber, Apr. 25, 1970; children—Jill Marie, James William. Auditor, Price Waterhouse & Co., Toronto, Ont., 1968-70; fin. analyst Continental Western Industries, Des Moines, 1971-73, v.p., treas. subs. Am. Wood Corp., Commerce, Tex., 1973-74; div. acctg. mgr. Overhead Door Co. of Tex., Dallas, 1974-79; door div. controller Overhead Door Corp., Dallas, 1979—. Mem. Planning Execs. Inst., Nat. Assn. Accountants. Baptist. Home: 2729 Clover Valley Dr Garland TX 75043 Office: 6750 LBJ Freeway Dallas TX 75222

WRAGG, WILLIAM REID, JR., pharm. co. exec.; b. Newark, Aug. 28, 1929; s. William Reid and Enola K. (Haughwout) W.; B.S. in Commerce and Fin., Bucknell U., 1951; m. Elizabeth A. Dale, Sept. 5, 1953. Supr. billing and receivables Standard Brands, N.Y.C., 1953-58, staff asst., systems and procedures, 1958-62, regional mgr., eastern accounting ops., 1962-63, asst. to controller, 1963-64, asst. brand mgr., 1964-65; budget mgr. Schering Plough, Kenilworth, N.J., 1965-68, mgr. ops. planning and control, 1968-74, mgr. mktg. adminstrn., 1974—. Served to 1st lt. U.S. Army, 1951-53. Methodist. Home: 776 Country Club Rd Bridgewater NJ 08807

WRAITH, WILLIAM, III, mgmt. cons.; b. Anaconda, Mont., Jan. 8, 1933; s. William and Gladys (Ayers) W.; B.S., Stanford U., 1955, M.S., 1958, M.B.A., 1959; m. Leslie Wittenberg, Sept. 26, 1956; children—William IV, Stephen. With Anaconda (Mont.) Co., 1959-63; with Marcona Mining Co., Lima, Peru, 1963-70; corporate v.p. Anaconda Co., N.Y.C., 1970-75; corporate v.p. mineral ops Marcona Corp., San Francisco, 1975-77; pres. William Wraith, Inc., 1977—; v.p. David Powell, Inc., 1977—; dir. Waipipi Iron Sands Ltd. (New Zealand), Marcona Ocean Industries Ltd., Marcona Sales Inc., 1975-77. Served with USAF, 1955-57. Mem. Am. Inst. Mining and Metall. Engrs., Am. Mgmt. Assn., Am. Prodn. and Inventory Control Soc., Nat. Assn. Accountants, Stanford Grad. Sch. Bus. Alumni Assn. (dir. 1977—), Sigma Chi. Republican. Presbyterian. Clubs: Elks; Alpine Hills Tennis (Portola Valley, Calif.); Mounted Patrol of San Mateo County; Shackriders (Woodside, Calif.). Patentee in field. Home: 110 Sausal Dr Portola Valley CA 94025 Office: 3000 Sand Hill Rd Menlo Park CA 94025

WRATHER, JOHN DEVERAUX, JR., oil producer, motion picture producer, financier; b. Amarillo, Tex., May 24, 1918; s. John D. and Mazie (Cogdell) W.; A.B., U. Tex., 1939; m. Bonita Granville, Feb. 5, 1947; children—Molly, Jack, Linda, Christopher. Ind. oil producer, Tex., Ind., Ill.; pres. Evansville (Ind.) Refining Co., 1938-40, Overton Refining Co., Amarillo Producers & Refiners Corp., Dallas, 1940-49, Jack Wrather Pictures, Inc., 1947-49, Freedom Prodns., Inc., 1949—, Western States Investment Corp., Dallas, 1949—, Wrather Television Prodns., Inc., 1951—, Wrather-Alvarez Broadcasting, Inc., The Lone Ranger, Inc., Lassie, Inc., Disney-land Hotel, Anaheim, Calif., L'Horizon Hotel, Palm Springs, Calif.; owner KFMB, KERO and KEMB-TV, San Diego, KOTY-TV, Tulsa; part-owner WNEW, N.Y.C.; pres. Sgt. Preston of the Yukon, Inc.; chmn. bd. Muzak, Inc., Ind. Television Corp. and Television Programs of Am. Inc., Stephens Marine, Inc.; pres. Balboa Bay Club, Inc., Kona Kai, Inc.; pres., chmn. bd. Wrather Corp.; dir. TelePrompTer Corp., Transcontinent. Television Corp., Jerold Elec. Corp., Capitol Records, Inc. Bd. dirs. Community Television of So. Calif. Am. Found. Religion and Psychiatry, Corp. for Public Broadcasting; mem. devel. bd. U. Tex., vice chmn. chancellor's council; commr. Los Angeles County-Hollywood Mus. Served to maj. USMC Res., 1942-53. Mem. Ind. Petroleum Assn. of Am., Internat. Radio and TV Soc., Nat. Petroleum Council, Dirs. Guild Am., Motion Picture Acad. of Arts and Scis. Clubs: Dallas Athletic, Dallas Petroleum; Cat Cay Yacht (Bahamas); Players, Hemisphere (N.Y.C.); Mark's, Buck's, White Elephant (London). Motion pictures produced include: The Guilty, 1946, High Tide, Perilous Water, 1947, Strike It Rich, 1948, Guilty of Treason, 1949, The Long Ranger and The Lost City of Gold, 1958, The Magic of Lassie, 1978, The Legend of the Lone Ranger, 1981, others. Home: 172 Delfern Dr Los Angeles CA 90024 Office: 270 N Canon Dr Beverly Hills CA 90210

WRAY, JOHN LAWRENCE, cons. engring. co. exec.; b. Maryville, Mo., June 17, 1935; s. Lawrence Paul and Roberta Inez (Cook) W.; B.S., Mo. U., 1957; M.S., Stanford, 1958; M.B.A., Santa Clara U., 1966; m. Sally Blair Gerdes, Dec. 27, 1958; children—Mary, Nancy, Carolyn. With Gen. Electric Co., San Jose, Calif., 1962-78, area sales mgr., 1970-72, mgr. product planning, 1972-75, mgr. market research and planning, 1975-78; v.p. engring. Quadrex Corp., Campbell, Calif., 1978—; instr. George Mason U., Arlington, Va., 1961-62. Mem. fin. com. Elementary Sch. Dist., Saratoga, Calif., 1974-78. Served with USAF, 1958-62. AEC fellow, 1957-58. Beta Theta Pi scholar, 1956-57; registered profl. engr., Calif., Minn., Mo., Ill., N.Y., Tex. Mem. ASME, Am. Nuclear Soc., Stanford Alumni Assn., Beta Theta Pi. Mem. Federated Ch. Saratoga. Clubs: Brookside Swim and Tennis, Masons. Home: 14961 Haun Ct Saratoga CA 95070 Office: 1700 Dell Ave Campbell CA 95008

WRAY, KARL, newspaper pub.; b. Bishop, Tex., June 8, 1913; s. Ernest Paul and Gertrude (Garvin) W.; A.B., Columbia, 1935; m. Flora-Lee Koepp, Aug. 11, 1951; children—Diana, Mark, Kenneth, Norman, Thomas. Auditor, U.S. Dept. Agr., Washington and Little Rock, 1935-37; salesman O'Mara & Ormsbee, Inc., N.Y.C., 1937-42; advt. mgr. Lompoc (Calif.) Record, 1947-54; owner, pub. San Clemente (Calif.) Daily Sun-Post, 1954-67, Coastline Dispatch, San Juan Capistrano, Calif., 1956-67, Dana Point (Calif.) Lamplighter,

1966-67; cons. Lear Siegler, Inc., Washington, 1967-68; pub. Daily Star-Progress, La Habra, Calif., 1969-74; pub. Anaheim (Calif.) Bulletin, 1974—. Mem. Calif. State Park Commn., 1960-64, vice chmn., 1961-62; mem. exec. bd. Orange County Council Boy Scouts Am., 1961-64, 76-81; mem. citizens adv. com. Orange Coast Coll., 1963-66; bd. dirs. Calif. Newspaper Youth Found., 1978-80. Served to capt. USMC, 1942-46. Mem. Calif. Newspaper Advt. Exec. Assn. (pres. 1952-53), Calif. Newspaper Pubs. Assn. (dir. 1960-64), San Juan Capistrano (pres. 1966), San Clemente (pres. 1956-57), La Habra (dir. 1970-74), Anaheim (dir. 1974-81), chambers commerce, Am. Theatre Critics Assn., Football Writers Assn. Presbyterian (elder). Home: 2420 S Ola Vista San Clemente CA 92672 Office: 1771 S Lewis St PO Box 351 Anaheim CA 92805

WRAY, MARC FREDERICK, minerals co. exec.; b. Evanston, Ill., Nov. 21, 1932; s. George M. and Anabelle F. (Moriarty) W.; B.S.C., Loyola U., 1955; M.B.A., Harvard U., 1964; m. Suzanne Elliott, June 16, 1965; children—Marc Thomas, Andrew Elliott. Vice pres. Bangor Punta, N.Y.C., 1968-71; exec. v.p. Manati Industries, Inc., N.Y.C., 1971-72; dir. corp. devel. Internat. Paper Co., N.Y.C., 1972-75, v.p. and group exec. minerals and diversified bus., 1980—; v.p. diversified businesses Gen. Crude Oil Co., Houston, 1975-79; pres. GCO Minerals Co., Houston, 1979—; dir. Union Bank Houston. Served with U.S. Army, 1955-56. Mem. Am. Petroleum Inst., Houston C. of C. Roman Catholic. Clubs: Petroleum, Forest (Houston). Office: 2600 One Allen Center Houston TX 77002

WREN, PAUL INGRAHAM, JR., mfg. co. exec.; b. Cambridge, Mass., May 10, 1935; s. Paul Ingraham and Alice (Trumbull) W.; B.S. in M.E., Tufts U., 1957; M.B.A., Harvard, 1962; m. Karen Margot Westly, June 12, 1957 (div. 1978); children—Kathryn, Susan, Paul III. With Norton Co., Worcester and Wesseling, Germany, 1962—, controller Norton Internat., Worcester, 1967-70, mng. dir., Wesseling, 1970-73, dir. planning and control, diversified products, 1973-79, asst. controller, 1977—. Bd. dirs. Greater Worcester unit Am. Cancer Soc., pres., 1978-80, mem. field services com. Mass. div., bd. dirs. div., 1978—, chmn. planned giving and legacy com., 1980—. Served with USN, 1957-60. Mem. Tau Beta Pi. Clubs: Old Car Club Worcester, Model A Restorers, Model A Ford of Am., Shelby-Am. Automobile, Intermeccanica Owners. Home: 5 Hiddenwood Path Littleton MA 01460 Office: 1 New Bond St Worcester MA 01606

WRENN, GEORGE THOMAS, JR., chem. and refrigeration co. exec.; b. Norfolk, Va., July 1, 1915; s. George Thomas and Lillian Leona (Meads) W.; M.E., Va. Poly. Inst., 1937; m. Ruby L. Ackiss, Dec. 7, 1940; children—Paul Michael, Tanya Sue. Plant engr. Ford Motor Co., 1937-40; prodn. mgr. Glenn L. Martin Co., 1940-42; planning mgr. Bechtel-McCone Corp., 1943-45; with Va. Chems. Inc., Portsmouth, 1945—, plant mgr., 1963-72, v.p. engring. and refrigeration, 1972—, now v.p., gen. mgr. refrigeration; exec. v.p. Sleepy Lake Devel. Corp., Suffolk, Va., 1956—, dir., 1956—; v.p., Virchem of Japan, Tokyo. Registered profl. engr., Va. Mem. Compressed Gas Assn. (past pres.), Nat. Soc. Profl. Engrs., ASME, Am. Refrigeration Inst. Republican. Episcopalian. Clubs: Cedar Point Country, Rotary. Home: 1500 Timber Trail Box 6124 Suffolk VA 23433 Office: Virginia Chemicals Inc 3340 W Norfolk Rd Portsmouth VA 23703 also 2100 Platinum Way Dallas TX 75237

WRENN, THEODORE WOODWARD, JR., market research exec.; b. Ft. Hoyle, Md., Nov. 17, 1925; s. Theodore Woodward and Margaret (Middendorf) W.; student Colo. Sch. Mines, 1946-47; B.B.A., Denver U., 1949; m. Sara Ann Beattie, Oct. 24, 1947; children—Theodore Woodward III, Sara Virginia, Gregory Beattie. Lab. asst. Komac Paint Co., Denver, 1947-49, indsl. salesman, 1949-52; mem. sales div. Gates Rubber Co., Denver, 1952-58, sales analyst, 1958-60; media and research dir. Henderson, Buckman & Co., Denver, 1960-67; v.p. media also research dir. Dacey, Wolff & Weir Inc., Boulder, Colo., 1967-69; mng. partner Wrenn-Watson Co., Denver, 1969-72; dir. information services U. Colo. Med. Center, 1972-76; mktg. dir. Research Service, Inc., Denver, 1977—; v.p., treas. Service Office Supply Co., 1970-76. Instr. Sales Tng. Inst. Mem. East High Sch. budget adv. com., 1965-72, chmn. parent edn. com., 1967-68, chmn. East Denver Citizens for Sch. Bonds, 1968. Dist. finance chmn. Republican Party, 1964. Served with AUS, 1944-46. Mem. Am. Advt. Fedn., Advt. Club Denver (dir.), Alpha Delta Sigma, Beta Theta Pi. Episcopalian (vestryman 1963-64, jr. warden 1967-68). Home: 1601 E 3d Ave Denver CO 80218 Office: 1441 Welton St Denver CO 80220

WRIGHT, ALMA MCINTYRE, mag. editor; b. Knoxville, Tenn., July 31, 1909; d. William Mobry and Theresa (Biagiotti) McIntyre; B.S. in Edn., U. Tenn., 1932; m. Robert Oliver Wright, Feb. 17, 1931; 1 son, Robert Oliver. Writer stories, articles on African violets, house plants, 1947—; editor African Violet Mag., 1947-63; exec. dir. African Violet Soc. Am., Inc., 1960-63, also hon. life mem., rec. sec., 1946-48, nat. pres., 1948-49, membership sec., 1953-63; pres. Indoor Gardener Pub. Co., Inc., Knoxville, 1963—; editor Gesneriad-Saintpaulia News, 1963—, Am. Gesneria Soc., 1963—; editor publs., rec. sec. Saintpaulia Internat., 1963-80. Mem. Am. Horticulture Soc. (hon. v.p. 1954). Editor: The Master List of African Violets, 1962. Home: The Meadows Condominium 1075 7914 Gleason Rd Knoxville TN 37919 Office: 1800-1802 Grand Ave Knoxville TN 37901

WRIGHT, CLYDE JOE, communications cons.; b. Lockhart, Tex., May 13, 1946; s. Clyde and Celestine (Thompson) W.; B.S. in Psychology, Ariz. State U., 1968; M.A. in Internat. Relations (Sperry Rand fellow 1968-70), U. Hawaii, 1970. Vice pres. Kicks Unlimited Inc., Phoenix, 1971-72; pres. Right on Productions, Phoenix, 1972—; v.p. Valley Cable Co., Phoenix, 1977—; telecommunications cons. Telecommunications Inc., Tempe, Ariz., 1974-77; cons. Cormier & Assos., 1972—. Bd. dirs. S.W. region Black and African Cultural Festival, 1973-75, Central Ariz. Health System, Theodore Roosevelt council Boy Scouts Am.; chmn. Phoenix Black Coalition; vol. U.S. Peace Corps, Malaysia, 1969-71; Democratic precinct committeeman, Phoenix, 1971-72. Mem. Screen Actors Guild, TV and Performing Arts Guild, Nat. Black Scholar Assn. (dir.), Ariz. Minority Broadcasters Assn. (pres. 1973-75). Patentee in field. Home: 4096 W Tobira Tucson AZ 85704 Office: 2109 S 48th St Tempe AZ 85282

WRIGHT, COLIN MERVYN, resort exec.; b. Skegness, England, Sept. 8, 1945; s. Arthur Leslie and Bessie; came to U.S., 1975; grad. with honors Hendon Hotel Sch., London U., 1966; m. Nancy Elizabeth Meads, Feb. 21, 1976. Dir., Taylorplan Catering Ltd., London, 1970-74; gen. mgr. LPS, Richmond, England, 1974-75; cons. to Adda Internat. Hotels, London, 1975; exec. v.p., gen. mgr. Sapphire Valley Devel. Corp., Sapphire, N.C., 1975—; dir. Gen. Solargenic Corp., Maldenway Internat. Co. Ltd., Gt. Britain, Sweet Caroline's Inc. Trustee Highlands Hosp. Mem. Hotel and Catering Inst. of Gt. Britain. Home: Star Rte 70 Box 80 Sapphire NC 28774

WRIGHT, CURTIS LYNN, advt. agy. exec.; b. Beloit, Wis., Sept. 16, 1944; s. Kenneth Archie and Lorraine Millicent (Hanamann) W.; student Purdue U., 1963-66; m. JoAnn Margeret Korn, Apr. 16, 1966; children—Christopher Michael, Bryan Edward. Advt. prodn. mgr. L.S. Ayres & Co., Indpls., 1962-66; advt. mgr. John Bean div. FMC Corp., Tipton, Ind., 1966-67, marketing asst. Riverside (Calif.) div., 1967-68, asst. advt. mgr. ordnance div., San Jose, Calif., 1968-69; pres. Bergthold, Fillhardt & Wright, Inc., San Jose, 1969—. Bd. dirs. San Jose Symphony, 1971-72, Santa Clara (Calif.) County Performing Arts League, 1972, San Jose Community Theater, 1972, Santa Clara County Jr. Achievement, 1973—, Better Bus. Bur., 1977-78. Recipient Ad Man of Year award Am. Advt. Fedn., 1973, Andy award Advt. Club N.Y.C., 1973, 74, 75, 77, 79, 80, 1st pl. awards (12) San Francisco Soc. Communicating Arts, 1973, 75, 76, 77, 78, 79, 80, Western Art Dirs. competition award, 1973, 75, 76, 77, 78, 79, 80, Communication Arts competition award, 1974, 77, 79, others. Mem. Am. Assn. Advt. Agys. (gov. No. Calif. council 1974-75), San Jose C. of C. (chmn. communications com. 1974-76), No. Calif. Assn. Indsl. Advertisers (dir. 1973-74), San Jose Advt. Club (pres. 1974-76). Home: 15980 Jackson Oaks Dr Morgan Hill CA 95037 Office: 190 Park Center Plaza San Jose CA 95113

WRIGHT, DAVID ALLEN, stockbroker; b. Norwood, Mass., May 5, 1939; s. Laurence S. and Marry Lou (Warren) W.; B.S. in Bus., U. Colo., 1961; m. Gayla F. Monahan, June 2, 1960; children—Kim Elizabeth, William Warren, Brook, Chris. Asst. to pres. ERC Internat., 1961-62; dir. mktg. Conf. Bd., 1962-71; v.p. mktg. Investors Mgmt. Scis., Inc. subs. Standard & Poors, Englewood, Colo., 1971-73; instl. sales Boettcher & Co., 1973-76; v.p. Dain Bosworth, Denver, 1976—. Dir., v.p., sec.-treas. Castlewood Sanitation Dist. Republican. Presbyterian. Club: Union League (N.Y.C). Home: 5816 S Florence Englewood CO 80111 Office: 950 17th St Denver CO 80202

WRIGHT, FRANK LAWSON, publisher; b. Mitchell, S.D., Apr. 26, 1921; s. Gage P. and Florence Louise (Walrath) W.; m. Elizabeth Taylor, Feb., 1955; children—John, Gage, Frank, Florence, Vicky, Mary, Sally. Pioneered all-classified newspaper, 1945—; pres. Customart Press, Inc., Mamaroneck, N.Y., 1945—; pub. 12 classified newspapers. Mentioned in Simon and Schuster's book 100 Stories of Business Success, 1954, in How to Win Success Before 40 (William G. Damroth), 1956. Home: 1411 Blair Ln Tustin CA 92680 Office: Customart Press Inc 525 N Barry Mamaroneck NY 10543

WRIGHT, FRANK LESTER, ins. exec.; b. Columbia, Mo., July 9, 1920; s. Frank Lester and Pearle Eberdine (Thomas) W.; student U. Cin., 1938-41, Georgetown U., 1947-52; m. Betty Dale Rhoads, Mar. 6, 1949. Vice pres. Parker & Co., 1950-65; chmn., chief exec. officer Wright & Co., Washington, 1965—; pres. Inter-Am. Ins. Co., Ltd., Grand Cayman, B.W.I., 1969—, Wright & Co. (Ins. Brokers) Ltd., London, 1977—, TAMINCO (The Arab Middle-east Ins. Co.), Jeddah, Saudi Arabia, 1978—, Wright Internat., Grand Cayman, 1969—; underwriting name at Lloyds of London. Pres., Frank & Betty Wright Found., 1975—; elder Presbyn. Meeting House, Alexandria, Va. Served with C.I.C., USAAF, 1942-47. Mem. Internat. Wine and Food Soc. (dir., pres. emeritus; dir. N.Am. com.). Clubs: Reform (London); Internat., F St. (Washington); Washington Golf and Country (Arlington). Home: 212 S Fairfax St Alexandria VA 22314 Office: 1001 Connecticut Ave NW Washington DC 20036 also 9 Bishopsgate London EC2 England

WRIGHT, GEORGE CULLEN, electronics co. exec.; b. Anderson, S.C., June 28, 1923; s. Benjamin Norman and Essie Floride (Cole) W.; B.S., Clemson U., 1948; Elec. Engr., 1949; m. Kathleen Ashe, Oct. 19, 1947; children—Carol Ann (Mrs. John C. Marquardt), George Cullen, Florenda Jean, William Norman. Asst. supt. Duke Power Co., 1949-56; city mgr., Gaffney, S.C., 1956-60; v.p. mktg. Hubbard & Co., Chgo., 1960-65; dir. Methode Electronics, Inc., Rolling Meadows, Ill., 1965—; v.p., dir. Anchor Coupling Co., Inc., Libertyville, Ill., 1973—; pres., dir. Exec. Extension & Ventures, Inc., Barrington, Ill., 1976—; pres., dir. White Marlin Marine, Inc., Anderson, S.C., 1976—. Pres., Barrington East Assn., 1968-70. Served with AUS, 1942-45. Mem. AIEE Electron Industry Assn., Am. Mgmt. Assn. Rotarian. Club: Sertoma (pres. 1963-65) (Anderson, S.C.). Patentee in field. Home: State Rd 243 Box 87 Fair Play SC 29643

WRIGHT, GERALD WILLIAM, mfrs. rep.; b. Orange, N.J., Dec. 14, 1944; s. Wilton Frank and Mildred (Hulsart) W.; B.S., U. S.C., 1966; M.S., Rutgers U., 1969, M.B.A., 1976; m. Trudi Porter, Aug. 1, 1970; 1 son, Bradley P. Research biologist Merck & Co., Rahway, N.J., 1969-71; with W.F. Wright, Inc., Irvington, N.J., 1971—, pres., 1977—; cons. to N.J. gas utilities on energy saving indsl. equipment. Named Top Distbr., Indsl. Boiler Co., 1979; recipient sales achievement award Roberts Gordon Appliance Co., 1979. Mem. N.J. LP Gas Assn., Nat. LP Gas Assn., Nat. Rifle Assn. (life). Republican. Office: 26 Mount Vernon Ave Irvington NJ 07111

WRIGHT, GLEN LAVERE, chem. mfg. co. ofcl.; b. Walton, W.Va., May 28, 1933; s. Opie Presley and Oleta Mesa (Cottrell) W.; B.S., Morris Harvey Coll., 1963; m. Lois Jean Fisher, June 23, 1956; 1 son, Stephen Lee. Lab. technician Union Carbide Corp., S. Charleston, W.Va., 1955-58, sr. lab. technician, 1959-62, research chemist, 1963-66, tech. rep., Charlotte, N.C., 1967-69, area rep., 1970-72, account rep., 1973-74, regional mgr., Tarrytown, N.Y., 1974-77, mgr. contract formulations, Jacksonville, Fla., 1977-79, mgr. inventory planning and control, 1979—. Served in U.S. Army, 1952-55. Mem. Assn. Textile Colorists and Chemists (sr.), Am. Chem. Soc. (sr.), Alpha Chi Sigma. Republican. Baptist. Clubs: Optimists, Lions, Masons, Shriners. Home: 4440 Charter Point Blvd Jacksonville FL 32211 Office: 7825 Baymeadows Way Jacksonville FL 32216

WRIGHT, JAMES LYNN, savs. and loan co. exec.; b. Springfield, Ill., Sept. 22, 1940; s. Glenn LaRue and Freida Pearl (Bloomfield) W.; B.S., Ill. Coll., 1963; M. Accounting Sci., U. Ill., 1965, postgrad., 1969-71; m. Karen Ann Barber, Nov. 24, 1976; children—Jeffrey Michael, Timothy Lynn. Staff auditor Arthur Young & Co., Chgo., 1965-66, 68-69; teaching asst. accounting U. Ill., Urbana, 1969-70; instr. accounting Ill. State U., Normal, 1970-71; accountant Bloomington (Ill.) Fed. Savs. & Loan Assn., 1972, asst. treas., 1972-73, dir. data processing, 1974-76, v.p., 1976-78, comptroller, 1976-78, v.p., treas., 1978-81, sr. v.p., treas., 1981—. Served with U.S. Army, 1966-68. Club: Univ. (Chgo.). Home: 308 Vista Dr Bloomington IL 61701 Office: 115 E Washington St Bloomington IL 61701

WRIGHT, JEFFREY CHAPMAN, automobile mfg. co. exec.; b. Toledo, Aug. 28, 1939; s. Benjamin Strang and Ione (Chapman) W.; B.A., Yale U., 1962; m. Judith Ann Allred, June 5, 1965; Dir. sales Estern Hemisphere, Am. Motors Corp., Southfield Mich., 1976-78, gen. mgr. European-African ops., 1978-79, v.p. internat. AM Gen. Corp., Detroit, 1979—. Served with USCG, 1962-63. Office: 14250 Plymouth Rd Detroit MI 48232

WRIGHT, JOHN PEALE, banker; b. Chattanooga, Mar. 27, 1924; s. Robert Toombs and Margaret (Peale) W.; B.S., U. Chgo., 1944; M.B.A., Harvard, 1947; m. Ruth Brown Garrison, Sept. 11, 1948; children—Margaret, John, Ruth, Mary. With Am. Nat. Bank & Trust Co., Chattanooga, 1947—, pres., 1962—, also dir. Elder, Presbyterian Ch. Served to 1st lt. USAR, 1943-45. Mem. Robert Morris Assos. (past pres.), Tenn. Bankers Assn. (past pres.). Home: 1331 Scenic Hwy Lookout Mountain TN 37350 Office: Am Nat Bank Chattanooga TN 37401

WRIGHT, JOHN RICHARD, hotel co. exec.; b. Washington, Jan. 23, 1942; s. John Charles and Gladys Bell (Hartle) W.; student Old Dominion Coll., 1960-66; m. Inabelle Marlene Phillips, Apr. 17, 1965; children—Mary-Bell Lea, John Vernon. Owner, operator South Gate Motor Hotel, Inc., Arlington, Va., 1957-61; partner John C. Wright & Son, Leesburg, Va., 1964—; owner, operator Quality Motel Lake Wright, Norfolk, Va., 1964—, Lake Wright Golf Course, 1966—, Country Club Apts., Leesburg, 1970—, Quality Inn, Leesburg, Va., 1972—; sec. Tuscarora, Inc., Leesburg, 1968-79. Treas., coach Loudoun County Boy's Midget Football League, Leesburg, 1968-77; mem. Loudoun County Parks and Recreation Bd., 1972-78, Loudoun County Tourism and Econ. Devel. Com., 1973-78. Bd. dirs. John C. Wright Found. Mem. Loudoun County C. of C. (pres. 1977-78), Am., Va. (dir.) hotel and motel assns., Va. Motel Assn. (dir.), No. Va. Builders Assn., Am., Va. quarter horse assns., Va. Travel Council (dir. 1976—, vice-chmn. no. region), Presbyterian. Clubs: Optimists, Kiwanis (chpt. pres. 1973), Cosmopolitan (Norfolk). Home: Foxfield Leesburg VA 22075 Office: PO Box 1338 Leesburg VA 22075

WRIGHT, JOHN SCOTT, investment co. exec.; b. Mpls., May 21, 1951; s. Donald O. and Maria M. Wright; B.A., U. Minn., 1973; m. Joy Marie, Aug. 11, 1971; children—Jocelyn, Jonathan. Supr., Northwestern Nat. Bank, Mpls., 1973; qualified correlator fin. planning Investors Diversified Services, St. Louis Park, Minn., 1974—. Recipient Investors Diversified Services Pro awards, 1976-78. Mem. Nat. Assn. Life Underwriters. Roman Catholic. Home: 4309 Flag Ave N New Hope MN 55428 Office: Investors Diversified Services Suite 200 5353 Wayzata Blvd Saint Louis Park MN 55416

WRIGHT, JOSEPH ROBERT, JR., credit card co. exec.; b. Tulsa, Okla., Sept. 24, 1938; s. Joe Robert and Ann Helen (Cech) W.; B.S., Colo. Sch. Mines, 1961; M.I.A., Yale U., 1963. Vice pres. Booz, Allen & Hamilton, N.Y.C., 1965-71; asst. sec. Dept. Commerce, Washington, 1971-73; asst. sec. Dept. Agr., Washington, 1973-76; pres. Citicorp Retail Services, N.Y.C., 1976—, Retail Consumer Services, Inc., 1977—. Served with U.S. Army, 1963-65. Mem. Young Pres. Orgn. Republican. Office: 485 Lexington Ave New York NY 10017

WRIGHT, JOSEPH SUTHERLAND, lawyer; b. Portland, Oreg., Mar. 16, 1911; s. Joseph Alfred and Carrie (Sutherland) W.; LL.B., George Washington U., 1937; m. Ruth Lacklen, Nov. 14, 1936; children—Joseph Sutherland, Susan Jane. Sec., Senator B. K. Wheeler, 1933-36; admitted to D.C. bar, 1934; atty. FTC, 1936-42; asst. gen. counsel, chief compliance, 1947-52; asst. gen. counsel Zenith Radio Corp., Chgo., 1952-53, gen. counsel, dir., 1953-58, v.p., 1951-58, exec. v.p. 1958-59, pres., gen. mgr., 1959-68, chief exec. officer, 1965-76, 79—, chmn., 1968-76, 79—; dir. Standard Oil (Ind.), Bethlehem Steel Corp., Sunbeam Corp., Commonwealth Edison Corp. Trustee U. Chgo., George Washington U., John Crerar Library. Served to lt. comdr. USNR, 1942-45. Mem. Chgo. Bar Assn. Clubs: Comml., Tavern, Chicago, Chgo. Yacht (Chgo.); Met. (Washington); Park Ridge Country. Office: 1000 Milwaukee Ave Glenview IL 60025 also Zenith Radio Corp 1900 N Austin Blvd Chicago IL 60639*

WRIGHT, LARRIMORE, zipper co. exec.; b. Red Boiling Springs, Tenn., Sept. 26, 1933; s. Heber Theodore and Sara Mary W.; B.A. Vanderbilt U., 1954; m. Mary Manning, Jan. 20, 1960; children—Jeffrey, Theodore, Betsy, Kara. Partner in charge Carolinas practice Price Waterhouse & Co., 1956-71; exec. v.p. Texfi Industries, 1971-76; pres. Hampshire Group, 1976-79, Talon div. Textron, Meadville, Pa., 1979—; dir. Cato Corp., Spartan Foods, M-D Foods. C.P.A. Mem. Ga. Soc. C.P.A.'s, N.C. Assn. C.P.A.'s. Clubs: Roaring Gap., Charlotte City. Office: 626 Arch St Meadville PA 16335

WRIGHT, LESTER NEAL, aero. engr.; b. Joseph, Oreg., Dec. 10, 1933; s. Charles Jackson and Gladys Drucilla (Towers) W.; B.S., Northrop Inst. Tech., 1960; m. Joanne Lee Zigman, June 11, 1954; children—Lori Kathleen, Juli Suzanne. Asso. engr. Am. Missile Products Co., Lawndale, Calif., 1958-60; with N.Am. Aviation/Rockwell Internat., Anaheim, Calif., 1960—, project mgr. advanced energy mgmt. systems, 1969—. Served with USAF, 1953-57. Methodist. Contbr. articles to profl. jours.; patentee in field. Home: 829 Tula St Long Beach CA 90808 Office: 3330 Mira Loma Ave Anaheim CA 92803

WRIGHT, LINDA SHICKEL, mfg. co. exec.; b. Harrisonburg, Va., Sept. 4, 1947; d. Marcel Knicely and Helen Marie (Swestyn) Shickel; B.S. in Mathematics, Coll. William and Mary, 1969; M.S. in Computer Sci., Rutgers U., 1973; m. John William Wright III, June 22, 1968; 1 son, John William IV. Programmer, U. Va. Computer Sci. Center, Charlottesville, 1969-70; mem. info. systems staff Western Electric Co., Naperville, Ill., 1970-72; mem. tech. staff Bell Labs., Murray Hill, N.J., 1972-74; computer specialist Sun Oil Co., Phila., 1974-76, supr. computer network performance analysis, Dallas, 1976-77, projects mgr., Phila., 1977-78; mgr. systems analysis and test Digital Equipment Corp., Tewksbury, Mass., 1978-79, mgr. systems performance analysis methods and models, Maynard, Mass., 1979—; dir. Computer Measurement Group, Inc., Phoenix, 1976—. Mem. Inst. Mgmt. Scis., Assn. for Computing Machinery (spl. interest group on operating systems 1973—, spl. interest group on measurement and evaluation 1973—). Home: Still River Rd Bolton MA 01740 Office: 146 Main St Maynard MA 01754

WRIGHT, MYRON ARNOLD, oilfield equipment and forging mfg. co. exec.; b. Blair, Okla., Apr. 9, 1911; s. Charles Edgar and Hattie Susan (Dillingham) W.; student N.W. Okla. State Tchrs. Coll., 1928-30; B.S., Okla. State U., 1933; Sc.D. (hon.), U. Tulsa, 1967; LL.D. (hon.), Okla. Christian Coll., 1967; D.Eng. (hon.), Worcester Poly. Inst., 1968; m. Izetta Chattin, June 4, 1935 (dec.); 1 dau., Mary Judith Wright Reid; m. 2d, Josephine S. Primm, June 14, 1969. Petroleum engr. Carter Oil Co., Tulsa, 1933-44, chief petroleum engr., asst. mgr. prodn., 1944-46; exec. asst. producing dept. Standard Oil Co. (N.J.), N.Y.C., 1946-49, dep. coordinator, 1949-51, producing coordinator, 1954-58, dir., 1958-66, exec. v.p., 1960-66; exec. v.p. Internat. Petroleum Co., Ltd., Coral Gables, Fla., 1951-52; chmn., chief exec. Exxon Co., U.S.A., Houston, 1966-76; exec. v.p., dir. Exxon Corp., N.Y.C., 1973-76; chmn. bd., pres. Cameron Iron Works, Inc., Houston, 1977—; dir., mem. exec. com. 1st City Bancorp Tex., Houston; dir., mem. exec. and audit coms. Am. Gen. Corp., Houston. Mem. Pres.'s Nat. Water Commn., 1968-69; chmn. bd. govs. U.S. Postal Service, 1974-80, Okla. State U. Devel. Found.; bd. dirs. Houston Symphony Soc. Recipient Disting. Service award Tex. Mid-Continental Oil and Gas Assn.; named to Alumni Hall of Fame, Okla. State U., 1962, to Okla. Hall of Fame, 1980. Mem. AIME, Am. Petroleum Inst. (dir.), Nat. Wildlife Fedn. (dir.), Houston C. of C. (dir. 1978—), U.S. C. of C. (pres. 1966-67, chmn. bd. 1967-68), Fgn. Policy Assn. N.Y. (dir. 1978-80), Okla. Heritage Soc., Tau Beta Pi, Sigma Tau, Sigma Tau Gamma, Phi Kappa Phi. Clubs: Houston, Univ., River Oaks Country, Petroleum, Ramada. Office: PO Box 1212 Houston TX 77001

WRIGHT, PETER, govt. ofcl.; s. Stuyvesant Bayard and Rebecca Addison (Holland) W.; student U. of South, 1952-53, George Washington U., 1953, 57, postgrad., 1963-64, grad. intern fellow, 1965-66; M.A., Washington Labor Studies Center, Fed. City Coll.,

1977; m. Carolann Mulheron, Sept. 8, 1956; children—Peter, Andrew Sullivan, Edward Stuyvesant. Asst. exec. mgr. Truck Body Equipment Assn., Washington, 1955-57; owner, operator, chmn. Bayard's Bend Farm, Brookneal, Va., 1957-61; research analyst Naval Personnel Research, Washington, 1961-62; personnel mgmt. specialist Office Sec. Agr., Washington, 1962-66; supervisory personnel officer AID Dept. State, Washington, 1966-68; labor mgmt. advisor Am. Fedn. Govt. Employees AFC-CIO, Washington, 1968-71; personnel mgmt. specialist Dept. Commerce, Washington, 1971-73; labor relations officer Nat. Park Service, also Bur. Indian Affairs, Dept. Interior, Washington, 1973-78; dir. labor and employee relations, ACTION, Washington, 1978—; pres. Peter Wright, Inc., 1957-62; chmn. investments com. Maggies Investment Assos., 1975—; instr. labor relations to govt. execs., 1973—; condr. union tng. Washington Labor Studies Center, 1975-77; instr. labor relations and bus. adminstrn. No. Va. Community Coll., 1977—. Recipient certificate merit Dept. Agr., 1965. Mem. Soc. Labor Relations Profls., Indsl. Relations Research Assn. Episcopalian. Clubs: Old Gaffers Assn. (hon. area sec.), Rappahannock River Yacht, Windmill Point Yacht. Home: 10904 Belmont Blvd Lorton VA 22079 Office: 806 Connecticut Ave NW Washington DC 20006

WRIGHT, RICHARD DONALD, pharm. co. exec.; b. Chester, Pa., Mar. 18, 1936; s. Richard H. and Anita C. (Howery) W.; B.S. in Bus. Adminstrn., Pa. State U., 1963; m. Joan Cooke, Oct. 24, 1959; children—Richard, Paul, Susan. Trainee, corporate fin. mgmt., internal auditor, corporate staff auditor RCA, Cherry Hill, N.J., 1963-66; with Smith Kline French Labs. div. Smith Kline Corp., Phila., 1966—, mgr. budget, 1966-69, mgr. planning and control, 1969-70, mgr. fin. ops., 1970-72, controller mfg. ops., 1972-73, dir. fin. planning, 1973-74, controller pharm. ops., U.S., 1974-79; v.p. Franklin Town Corp. affiliated co., 1979—. Elder, bd. dirs. Faith Community Ch. of Christian and Missionary Alliance. Mem. Fin. Execs. Inst. (cert.), Planning Execs. Inst., Nat. Assn. Accts., Bldg. Owners and Mgrs. Assn., Sigma Tau Gamma. Lectr. and author in field. Home: 104 Shadow Lake Dr Vincentown NJ 08088

WRIGHT, ROBERT DAVID, environ. engr.; b. Bradford, Yorkshire, Eng., May 13, 1924; s. Alan and Gladys (Hudson) W.; B.Sc. in Engring., U. London, 1944; m. Carolyn Pennell Case, June 1975; children—Barbara, Jonhathan, Delia, Philippa, Carolyn. Tech. mgr. Rhodesian European Engring. & Fin. Co., Johannesburg, S. Africa, 1953-55; pres. Altacorp., Johannesburg, 1955-60; chief tech. exec. Carter Indsl. Products Ltd., Birmingham, Eng., 1960-63; exec. engr.-in-charge indsl. pollution control dept. Email Ltd., Sydney, Australia, 1963-66; mgr. air pollution control group United McGill Corp., Columbus, Ohio, 1966-71; pres. Am. Van Tongeren & Associated Cos., Clumbus, 1971-76; pres., dir. Aerex Corp., Scotstown, Que., Can., 1976—, Canadian Bioreactors Ltd., Scotstown, 1976—; sr. partner R.D. Wrights & Assos., cons., 1976—. Layreader, Episcopal Ch. Diocese S. Ohio, 1968-76; mem. diocesan order layreaders Anglican Ch. Can. Diocese Que., 1976—. Served as officer Brit. Army, 1943-47. Chartered tech. engr., Eng. Fellow Mine Ventilation Soc. South Africa, Instn. Engring. Tech. Eng.; mem. ASME, Air Pollution Control Assn.; Assn. Inst. Elec. Engrs. South Africa, Inst. Mech. Engrs. South Africa. Clubs: Eccentric (London), Masons. Author papers in field. Home: Rural Route 3 Sisyphus Farm Bury PQ J0B 1J0 Canada Office: 147 Victoria Rd Scotstown PQ J0B 3B0 Canada

WRIGHT, TENNYSON JAMES, contract mgmt. co. exec.; b. Aiken, S.C., Sept. 26, 1948; s. Leroy James and Miriam Bertha (Johnson) W.; B.S. in Math., Livingstone Coll., 1970; M.Ed. in Rehab. Counseling, U. Ga., 1972, Ph.D. in Rehab. Counseling, 1976; m. Gwendolyn Moon, Nov. 26, 1975; 1 dau., Gwendolyn Kristina. Community sch. dir. Clake County Bd. Edn., Athens, Ga., 1971-72; lectr. San Diego State U., 1973-74; asst. prof. Fla. State U., 1976-78; research and tng. mgr. Edn. div. Singer Co., Rochester, N.Y., 1978-80; pres. Pan Am, Inc., 1980—. adj. prof. Syracuse U. Delegate White House Conf. on Handicapped, 1977. HEW Rehab. Services Adminstrn. grantee, 1971-72. Mem. Am. Personnel and Guidance Assn., Am. Rehab. Counseling Assn., Nat. Rehab. Counseling Assn., Vocat. Evaluation and Work Adjustment Assn., Am. Soc. Tng. and Devel., Kappa Alpha Psi. Democrat. Baptist. Home: 330 Providence Rd Athens GA 30606 Office: 151 Nellie B Ave Athens GA 30606

WRIGHT, WILLIAM FRANKLIN, aerospace co. exec.; b. Licking County, Ohio, Aug. 22, 1924; s. Gerald Stafford and Ina Mae (Clark) W.; B. Aero. Engring., Ohio State U., 1948, M.S., 1951; m. Sharon Jane Newman, June 5, 1971; children—Craig Allen, Carol Ann. Research analyst N. Am. Aviation Co., Downey, Calif., 1954-55; program mgr. Lockheed lfissiles & Space Co., Sunnyvale, Calif., 1960-70, chief engr., 1972-76, v.p., program mgr., 1977—. Served with USN, 1942-46, USAF, 1951-55. Fellow Am. Inst. Aeros. and Astronautics (asso.). Republican. Home: 1174 Hyde Ave San Jose CA 95129 Office: Lockheed Missiles and Space Co Bldg 562 Sunnyvale CA 94088

WRIGLEY, WILLIAM, corp. exec.; b. Chgo., Jan. 21, 1933; s. Philip Knight and Helen Blanche (Atwater) W.; B.A., Yale U., 1954; m. Alison Hunter, June 1, 1957 (div. 1969); children—Alison Elizabeth, Philip Knight, William. With Wm. Wrigley Jr. Co., Chgo., 1956—, v.p., 1960-61, pres., chief exec. officer, 1961—, dir., 1960—; dir. Wrigley Espana S.A. (Spain), Wrigley Co., Ltd. (U.K.), Wrigley Co. (N.Z.), Ltd. (Auckland, New Zealand), Wrigley Co. Pty., Ltd. (Australia), Wrigley N.V. (Netherlands), Wrigley Philippines, Inc., The Wrigley Co. (H.K.) Ltd. (Hong Kong), Wrigley Co. (East Africa) Ltd. (Kenya), Wrigley & Co. Ltd., Japan; dir., mem. audit com., chmn. exec. com. Chgo. Nat. League Ball Club, Inc.; dir., mem. salary and auditing com., mem. com. non-mgmt. dirs., mem. spl. com. non-mgmt. dirs., chmn. nominating com. Texaco, Inc.; dir., mem. compensation com. Nat. Blvd. Bank Chgo.; dir., v.p., chmn. exec. com. Santa Catalina Island Co. Bd. dirs. Wrigley Meml. Garden Found.; bd. dirs., mem. personnel com. Northwestern Meml. Hosp.; benefactor mem. Santa Catalina Island Conservancy; trustee Chgo. Latin Sch. Found.; bd. dirs., exec. com. Geneva Lake Water Safety Com.; adv. bd. Center for Sports Medicine, Northwestern Med. Sch. Served from ensign to lt. (j.g.), USNR, 1954-56; Pacific; lt. comdr. Res. (ret.). Mem. Chgo. Hist. Soc., U.S.C. Oceanographic Assos., Wolf's Head Soc., Field Mus. Natural History, Art Inst. Chgo., Antiquarian Soc. Art Inst. Chgo., Navy League U.S., Catalina Island Mus. Soc., Delta Kappa Epsilon. Clubs: Saddle and Cycle, Racquet, Tavern, Chicago Yacht, Commercial (Chgo.); Lake Geneva (Wis.) Country, Lake Geneva Yacht; Catalina Island Yacht; Brook (N.Y.C.); Catalina Island (Calif.) Gun; Tuna (Catalina). Office: 410 N Michigan Ave Chicago IL 60611

WRISTON, WALTER BIGELOW, banker; b. Middletown, Conn., Aug. 3, 1919; s. Henry M. and Ruth (Bigelow) W.; B.A. with distinction, Wesleyan U., Middletown, Conn., 1941; postgrad. Ecole Francaise Middlebury, Vt., 1941, Am. Inst. Banking, 1946; M.A., Fletcher Sch. Internat. Law and Diplomacy, 1942; LL.D., Lawrence Coll., 1962, Tufts U., 1963, Brown U., 1969, Columbia U., 1972, Fordham U., 1977; D.C.S., Pace U., 1974, St. John's U., 1974, N.Y. U., 1977; D.H.L. Lafayette Coll., 1975; m. Barbara Brengle, Oct. 24, 1942 (dec.); 1 dau., Catherine B.; m. 2d, Kathryn Ann Dineen, Mar. 14, 1968. Officer spl. div. Dept. State, Washington, 1941-42; jr. insp. comptrollers div. Citibank, N.A., 1946-50, asst. cashier, 1950-52, asst. v.p., 1952-54, v.p., 1954-58; sr. v.p., 1958-60, exec. v.p., 1960-67, pres., 1967-70, chmn., 1970—, also dir.; chmn., dir. Citicorp; dir. J.C. Penney Co., Gen. Electric Co., Chubb Corp., Minerals & Resources Corp. Ltd.; trustee Rand Corp. Mem. Nat. Commn. on Productivity, 1970-74, Labor-Mgmt. Adv. Com., Nat. Commn. for Indsl. Peace, 1973-74, Adv. Com. on Reform Internat. Monetary System. Bd. govs. N.Y. Hosp.; bd. visitors Fletcher Sch. Law and Diplomacy; bd. dirs. Assos. Harvard Bus. Sch.; trustee Am. Enterprise Inst.; joint bd. N.Y. Hosp.-Cornell Med. Center. Served with AUS, 1942-46. Mem. Council Fgn. Relations Bus. Council. Clubs: Links, River, Sky, Citicorp Center (N.Y.C.); Met. (Washington). Office: 399 Park Ave New York NY 10043

WROBEL, LEONARD JOSEPH, city ofcl.; b. Erie, Pa., May 17, 1943; s. Stanley Joseph and Hedwig (Ulanowski) W.; Russian Lang. Certificate, Ind. U., 1962; B.S. in Math., Gannon Coll., 1969; M.S. in Math. (grad. teaching fellow), St. Louis U., 1971. Equipment engr. Gen. Telephone of Pa., Erie, 1969, 70, planning engr., 1971-77; city controller City of Erie, 1978—. Bd. dirs. Boys Clubs of Greater Erie, 1977—. Served with USAF, 1961-65. Mem. Pi Mu Epsilon, Alpha Sigma Nu. Democrat. Roman Catholic. Clubs: Polish Falcons Am., Polish Nat. Alliance, Maennerchorr. Home: 831 E 44th St Erie PA 16504 Office: 304 Municipal Bldg Erie PA 16501

WU, ANDREW JUNG ERH, restaurateur; b. Ping Tung, Taiwan, Nov. 18, 1940; s. Ting Tze and Chung Ing (Chiu) W.; came to U.S., 1967, naturalized, 1977; B.A., Tam Kong Coll. Arts and Scis. (Taiwan), 1964; M.A., Faith Sem., Elkins Park, Pa., 1972. Tchr. Ping Tung Girls' High Sch., 1961-64; mgr. Yeps Chinese Food, Phila., 1972-74; mgr., pres. Ho Sai Gai Chinese Food, Phila., 1975—; guest lect. Potpourri Sch. Cooking, Bryn Mawr, Pa. Served to 2d lt. Republic of China Army, 1962-64. Restaurant named Best Chinese Restaurant of Phila., Phila. mag., 1977, 78. Mem. Pa., Phila., Delaware Valley restaurant assns. Home: 1000 Race St Philadelphia PA 19107

WU, LI-PEI, banker; b. Taiwan, Sept. 9, 1934; came to U.S., 1968, naturalized, 1976; s. Yin-Su and Chiaw-Mei Wu; B.A. in Econs., Nat. Taiwain U., 1957; M.B.A., Ft. Hays (Kans.) State U., 1969; m. Jenny S. Lai, Mar. 24, 1963; children—George T., Eugene Y. Officer, Changhwa Comm. Bank, Taipei, 1960-67; mgr. fin. dept. Elite Indsl. Corp., Taiwan, 1967-68; v.p., controller, then sr. v.p. Nat. Bank Alaska, 1973-78; chmn. exec. com., chief adminstrv. officer Alaska Nat. Bank of North, Anchorage, 1978-80, pres., chief operating officer, 1980—. Mem. budgetary adv. com. City of Anchorage, 1974; bilingual adv. Anchorage Sch. Dist., 1978. Mem. Am. Bankers Assn., Am. Banking Inst., Alaska Bankers Assn., Asian Am. Assn. (adv. bd.). Home: SRA 807 Anchorage AK 99502 Office: Pouch 7-010 Anchorage AK 99510

WUERFELE, ALBERTA IRENE, banker; b. Burlington, Kans., Oct. 29, 1918; d. George and Fonda Ethel (Graham) W.; student Kans. State Tchrs. Coll., Emporia, 1937-41. With Am. Nat. Bank & Trust Co. Chgo., 1946—, asst. comptroller, 1967-68, 2d v.p., 1968-70, comptroller, 1970—, v.p., 1975—, also dir. and treas. subs.; dir. Chgo. Fin. Exchange. Bd. dirs., treas. Met. YMCA, Chgo. Served with WAC, 1943-46. Recipient Outstanding Achievement in Field of Bus. award YWCA, Chgo., 1973. Mem. Fin. Execs. Inst. (dir.), Chgo. Network, Women's Forum. Clubs: Econ., Exec. Home: 1406 Scotdale Rd LaGrange Park IL 60525 Office: 33 N LaSalle St Chicago IL 60690

WUESTHOFF, WINFRED WILLIAM, investment counselor; b. Milw., July 10, 1922; s. Oscar and Louise (Schuettler) W.; Ph.B., U. Wis., 1947; m. Louise June Wesle, Sept. 16, 1950; children—Anne Louise, Lynn Elsbeth. With Marine Nat. Exchange Bank, Milw., 1947-72, exec. v.p., 1963-72, also dir.; founder, pres. W.W. Wuesthoff, Inc., Milw., 1972—; dir. Data Retrieval Corp., Wetzel Bros., Inc. Am. Active Local Community Services, Boys Club; bd. dirs. Todd Wehr Found., Carthage Coll. Mem. Fin. Analysts Fedn., Fin. Execs. Inst., Am. Fin. Assn. Clubs: Univ., Kiwanis, Milw. Country (Milw.). Home: 940 E Wye Ln Milwaukee WI 53217 Office: 250 E Wisconsin Ave Milwaukee WI 53202

WUNDER, DAVID HART, govt. ofcl.; b. Argo, Ill., Dec. 6, 1925; s. Mylton Bowerman and Marion Antoinette (Richcreek) W.; grad. Wabash Coll., 150; J.D., Chgo. Kent Coll. Law, 1962; m. Mary Ann Koestner, May 9, 1980; children—Rebecca Anne Wunder Thomson, David Hart, Theodore Joseph. Sales rep. Edward Hines Lumber Co., Chgo., 1950-54; sec.-treas. M. Wunder Homes, Inc., Oak Lawn, Ill., 1954-63; enforcement atty., mgr. Chgo. office securities dept. Office of Sec. of State Ill., 1963-72; securities commr. State of Ill., Springfield, 1972—; lectr.; admitted to Ill. bar, 1963. Served in U.S. Army, 1944-46. Recipient various decorations. Mem. Am. Bar Assn., Ill. State Bar (corp. and securities council, chmn. 1978-79), Chgo. Bar Assn., N.Am. Securities Adminstrs. Assn. (1st v.p. 1980-81), Midwest Securities Commrs. Assn. (pres. 1977-78), Central Securities Adminstrs. Council (chmn. 1978-79), SAR, Soc. Mayflower Descs., Am. Legion (dist. comdr. 1971-72), Delta Tau Delta, Delta Theta Phi. Methodist. Office: 151 Bruns Ln Suite 102 Springfield IL 62702

WUNDER, GENE CARROLL, educator, bus. cons.; b. Waterloo, Iowa, Feb. 11, 1939; s. Lloyd Carl and Alice Marie (Reed) W.; B.B.A., U. Iowa, 1969; M.B.A., U. Mo., 1971; postgrad. U. Mo., 1972-75; grad. asso. in Econs., U. Ark., 1977-78; m. Judy Kay Stone, Dec. 16, 1966; children—Lara Anne, Sara Elizabeth. Agt., Security Mut. Life, 1964-69; mgmt. trainee State Farm Mut. Ins., 1969-71; instr. bus. adminstrn. N.E. Mo. State U., Kirksville, 1972-75, asst. prof. bus. adminstrn., 1976—; cons. in field. Chmn. supervisory com. N.E. Mo. Credit Union, 1976—. Recipient Alpha Kappa Psi Outstanding Alumni award, 1968. Mem. S.W. Fin. Assn., Midwest Fin. Assn., Am. Mktg. Assn., Am. Risk Mgmt. Assn., So. Regional Bus. Law Assn., AAUP, Alpha Kappa Psi, Phi Alpha Delta, Phi Delta Kappa. Republican. Methodist. Clubs: Masons (32 deg.), Shriners, Kiwanis. Contbr. articles to profl. jours. Home: 908 Fairview Dr Kirksville MO 63501 Office: 152 Violette Hall NE Mo State Univ Kirksville MO 63501

WURTZBURGER, JON ALAN, investment banker; b. Balt., May 5, 1934; s. Alan and Janet (Cohn) W.; B.A., U. Pa., 1957, student Wharton Sch., 1957-58; m. Reva Sara Sprafkin, Dec. 25, 1957; children—Wendy, Jan. With Merrill Lynch, Pierce, Fenner & Smith, N.Y.C. and Balt., 1958-64; with Stein Bros. & Boyce, Inc., Balt., 1964-70, exec. v.p., 1967-70; 1st v.p. Bache & Co., N.Y.C., 1970-74; mem. N.Y. Stock Exchange, 1974—; dir. Growth Properties, Inc.; pres. J.E.C.W., Inc. Mem. arbitration com. N.Y. Stock Exchange. Mem. Tax Commn. Balt., Balt. Airport Bd., Md. Airport Commn., Balt. Council Internat. Visitors. Mem. bd. Md. Children's Aid Soc., Jewish Family and Children's Service. Served with AUS, 1957. Named Outstanding Young Man of Year, Balt. Jaycees, 1968. Am. Home: 19 E 72d St New York City NY 10021 Office: care Spear Leeds & Kellogg 111 Broadway New York City NY 10006

WYATT, ROBERT BYRON, editor; b. Miami, Okla., May 19, 1940; s. Byron A. and Harriett Elizabeth (Botts) W.; B.A., U. Tulsa, 1962. Asst. editor Avon Books, N.Y.C., 1964, editor, 1965-67, sr. editor, 1967-69, exec. editor, 1971-78, v.p., editorial dir., 1978—; editor-in-chief Books for Young Readers, Delacorte Press, 1969-71. Home: Woodstock NY 12498 Office: 959 8th Ave New York NY 10019

WYATT, WILSON WATKINS, lawyer; b. Louisville, Nov. 21, 1905; s. Richard Henry and Mary (Watkins) W.; J.D., U. Louisville, 1927, LL.D. (hon.), 1948; LL.D. (hon.), Knox Coll., 1945, Centre Coll. Ky., 1979; m. Anne Kinnaird Duncan, June 14, 1930; children—Mary Anne, Nancy Wyatt Zorn, Wilson Wyatt. Admitted to Ky. bar, 1927; individual practice law, 1927—; mayor City of Louisville, 1941-45; lt. gov. State of Ky., 1959-63; sr. partner firm Wyatt, Grafton & Sloss, Louisville, 1947-80, Wyatt, Tarrant & Combs, Louisville, 1980—; dir. Louisville Courier-Jour., Louisville Times Co., Standard Gravure Corp., WHAS, Inc.; presdl. emissary from Pres. Kennedy to Pres. Sukarno of Indonesia, 1963; chmn. 6th Circuit Jud. Nominating Commn., 1977-80. Nat. campaign chmn. Adlai E. Stevenson, 1952; chmn. Regional Cancer Center Corp., 1977—, Bellarmine Coll., 1979—, U. Louisville, 1951-55; chmn. Leadership Louisville Found., 1978—; chmn. nat. council Nat. Mcpl. League, 1978—; pres. Louisville Area C. of C., 1972, Gold Cup award for community service, 1975; chmn. Ky. Econ. Devel. Commn., 1960-63, Nat. Conf. on Govt., 1975-78. Recipient Gov.'s Disting. Service Medallion, Commonwealth of Ky., 1980. Mem. Am. Bar Assn., Ky. Bar Assn., Louisville Bar Assn., Am. Law Inst. Democrat. Presbyterian. Clubs: Century (N.Y.C.); Louisville Country, Pendennis, Wynn Stay, Jefferson (Louisville). Home: 1001 Alta Vista Rd Louisville KY 40205 Office: Wyatt Tarrant & Combs 28th Floor Citizens Plaza Louisville KY 40202

WYMAN, PAUL BARTRAM, lawyer; b. Three Rivers, Mich., Oct. 8, 1913; s. Charles Bartram and Bertha (Gesaman) W.; student Kalamazoo Coll., 1932-35; LL.B., Duke, 1938; m. Louise Cabell Warren, June 10, 1940; children—Warren Bartram, Michael Louis. Admitted to Colo. bar, 1939, Mich. bar, 1943; gen. law practice in Colo., 1939-42; pros. atty. Kalkaska County, Mich., 1943-55; spl. asst. atty. gen., Mich., 1950; asst. pros. atty. Wexford County, Mich., 1955-57; friend of ct. for 28th Jud. Circuit of Mich., 1948—; spl. asst. pros. atty. Wexford County, 1962; city atty. City of Cadilac, Mich., 1959-64. Mem. exec. bd. Scenic Trails council Boy Scouts Am., asst. dist. commr. for So. Dist. Pres., Kalkaska Sch. Bd., 1943-46. Mem. Am., Mich., Wexford-Missaukee (pres. 1957) bar assns., Mich. Pros. Attys. Assn. (1st v.p. 1954), Mich. Friends Ct. Assn. (exec. bd. 1977—), Nat. Reciprocal and Family Support Enforcement Assn. Nat. Rifle Assn., Am. Judicature Soc. Presbyterian (pres. 1957, chmn. bd. trustees 1958), Mich Assn. Professions, Am. Cancer Soc. (exec. bd. Wexford Unit). Clubs: Rotary (pres. 1958-59), Cadillac, Caberfae Ski, Masons (32 deg.). Contbr. articles to profl. jours. Home: 426 Crippen St Cadillac MI 49601 Office: Court House Annex Cadillac MI 49601

WYMAN, RICHARD HODGSON, ins. mgmt.; b. Winchester, Mass., Aug. 5, 1946; s. Wayne W. and Marjorie J. (Hodgson) W.; B. in Math., U. Maine, 1969; M.B.A., Babson Coll., 1973; m. Maryellen Stanley, Aug. 2, 1970; children—Michelle Jean, Christine Ann. Computer systems analyst Prudential Ins. Co., Boston, 1969-74, methods analyst, planning, 1975, mgr. electronic data processing, 1976-77, mgr. investment property acctg., 1977-78, mgr. investment property ops., 1979—, co. rep. New Eng. Council Shopping Center Mgrs., 1980; instr. fin., 1977, ins. acctg., 1978-79. Fin. advisor Jr. Achievement, 1975-77; loaned exec. Boston C. of C., 1975-76, recipient certificate of commendation, 1975; loaned exec. Gov.'s Mgmt. Task Force, 1979; mem. Gov.'s Adv. Com., 1979-80; chmn. Channel Two Auction, 1980. Fellow Life Office Mgmt. Assn. Roman Catholic. Home: 260 Edgell Rd Framingham MA 01701 Office: 800 Boylston St Boston MA 02199

WYMAN, ROBERT JAMES, city ofcl.; b. Chester, Vt., May 5, 1938; s. Clarence David Uriah and Hazel Isabelle (Martin) W.; student public sch., Chester; m. Anita Marie Hitchings, Apr. 7, 1962; children—Debra Lee, James Uriah. Asst. mgr. Frisch's Big Boy, Athens, Ohio, 1964-65; honing machine operation MPB Corp., Keene, N.H., 1965; buyer Twin States Indsl. Dist., Keene, 1965-72; purchasing agt. City of Keene, 1972—. Mem. Vets. Council, City of Keene, 1977—. Served with USN, 1956-64. Mem. Nat. Purchasing Inst., Twin States Purchasing Mgmt. Assn., Nat. Assn. Purchasing Mgmt., Am. Legion. Clubs: Owls, Elks, Masons, Eagles, Moose. Home: 9 Sullivan St Keene NH 03431 Office: 3 Washington St Keene NH 03431

WYMAN, THOMAS HUNT, food processing co. exec.; b. St. Louis, Nov. 30, 1929; s. Edmund Allan and Nancy (Hunt) W.; grad. Phillips Acad., Andover, Mass., 1947; B.A. magna cum laude, Amherst Coll., 1951; student Mgmt. Devel. Inst., Lausanne, Switzerland, 1960-61; m. Elizabeth Minnerly, Dec. 3, 1960; children—Peter Hunt, Michael Barry, Thomas Hunt, Elizabeth Baldwin. Mgmt. trainee First Nat. City Bank N.Y., 1951-53; asst. to pres., also new products div. mgr. Nestle Co., White Plains, N.Y., 1955-60; mktg. dir. Findus Internat. S.A. (Nestle), Vevey, Switzerland, 1961-65; v.p. Polaroid Corp., Cambridge, Mass., 1965—, sr. v.p.; gen. mgr., 1972-75; pres., chief exec. officer Green Giant Co., 1975-79; dir. Toro Co., N.W. Bancorp., Scott Paper Co., Nat. Exec. Service Corps. Mem. Presdl. Commn. World Hunger, 1978—. Trustee Amherst Coll., Mpls. Soc. Fine Arts; bd. dirs. United Way Mpls. Area; nat. bd. advisers Goodwill Industries; nat. advisory council Multiple Sclerosis Soc. Served to 1st lt. C.E., AUS, 1953-55; Korea. Named one of 200 Rising World Leaders Time mag., 1974. Mem. Conf. Bd. (dir.), Assos. Grad. Sch. Bus. Adminstrn. Harvard U., Phi Beta Kappa. Home: 3610 Northome Rd Wayzata MN 55391 Office: Pillsbury Co 608 2d Ave S Minneapolis MN 55402

WYNN, GRACE ROSE, ins. agt.; b. Milw., Feb. 7, 1937; d. Joseph Frank and Evelyn Valerie Wysocki; student U. Wis., Milw., 1961-63. Office mgr. A.R. Korbel, C.L.U., Milw., 1961-65; sales asst. Korbel Corp., Milw., 1961-68; ins. agt. Central Life Assurance Co., Milw., 1968-72; agt., partner Wynn & Mottl, C.L.U.'s, Milw., 1972—. Recipient Nat. Sales Achievement awards Nat. Assn. Life Underwriters, 1972—, Nat. Quality awards, 1971—; C.L.U. Mem. Assn. Life Underwriters (dir.), Million Dollar Round Table (life), Women's Leader Round Table (life), Estate Counselors Forum, Milw. Chpt. C.L.U.'s. Republican. Roman Catholic. Home: 929 N Astor St Milwaukee WI 53202 Office: Wynn & Mottl CLU's 400 N Broadway Milwaukee WI 53202

WYNNE, WILLIAM FRANCIS, paper co. exec.; b. N.Y.C., Feb. 23, 1922; s. Patrick Edward and Mary (Cunningham) W.; B.B.A. cum laude, Miami U., Oxford, Ohio, 1949; m. Catherine Glynn, Oct. 14, 1950; children—William Francis, Thomas, Pamela, Diana, Deborah, Donald, Walter. Group ins. rep. Zurich Ins. Co., 1950-53; brokerage cons. Conn. Gen. Ins. Co., 1953-55; ins. asst., mgr. Am. Standard Corp., 1955-67; dir. risk mgmt. Champion Internat., N.Y.C., 1967—. Troop chmn. Boy Scouts Am., River Edge, N.J., 1963-65. Bd. dirs. River Edge Swim Club, 1966-68. Served with USAAF, 1942-45. Mem. Am. Soc. Ins. Mgmt. (nat. dir., past pres. N.Y.), Am. Legion. K.C. Home: 773 Summit Ave River Edge NJ 07661 Office: 1 Champion Plaza Stamford CT 06921

WYSLOTSKYI, IHOR, engring. co. exec.; b. Kralovane, Czechoslovakia, Dec. 22, 1930; s. Ivan and Nadia (Alexiew) W.; came to U.S., 1958, naturalized, 1961; M.E., Sch. Aeros., Buenos Aires, Argentina, 1955; m. Maria Czechut, Nov. 22, 1958; children—Katria, Bohdan. Design engr. Kaiser Industries, Buenos Aires, 1955-58; cons. design engr., Newark, 1959-64; chief engr. Universal Tool Co., Chgo., 1964-69; pres. CBC Devel Co., Inc., Chgo., 1969-74; pres. Thermoplastics Engring. Co., Chgo., 1972—; engring. adviser to bd. Biosystems Assos., Inc., La Jolla, Calif. Chmn., Ukrainian studies com. U. Ill. Mem. Packaging Inst. U.S., Am.-Israeli C. of C., Brit. Engring. Assn. Plate River, Soc. Mfg. Engrs. Club: Michigan City Yacht. Patentee in field. Mgmt. adv. bd. Modern Plastics Publs. Home: 18630 Golfview Dr Hazel Crest IL 60429 Office: 5328 W 123d Pl Alsip IL 60658

WYSOCKI, ROBERT ADAM, telephone co. exec.; b. Syracuse, N.Y., Apr. 29, 1945; s. Adam Joseph and June Pauline (Guenthner) W.; B.S., U.S. Mil. Acad., 1967; m. Mary D. Tapogna, Feb. 8, 1969; children—Christopher, Lauren. Commd. 2d lt. U.S. Army, 1967, advanced through grades to capt., 1969; Vietnam; resigned, 1971; with N.Y. Telephone Co., 1971—, regional treasury mgr., Albany, N.Y., 1973-76, cash mgr., N.Y.C., 1976-79, pension fund mgr., 1980—. Decorated Bronze Star, Commendation medal. Mem. West Point Soc. N.Y. (treas.). Republican. Roman Catholic. Home: 16 Cherokee Dr Brookfield Center CT 06805 Office: 1095 Ave Americas New York NY 10036

WYSOCKI, ROBERT JOSEPH, stained glass artisan; b. Alpena, Mich., Dec. 25, 1919; s. Edmund Leo and Frances Barbara (Zielinski) W.; m. Frances Overton, Apr. 6, 1946; children—Theresa, Timothy, Annette. Apprentice stained glass studio, Winston-Salem, N.C., 1951-54; prin., owner Stained Glass Assos., Raleigh, N.C., 1958—. Served to 1st lt. U.S. Army, 1941-46. Mem. Stained Glass Assn. Am., Interfaith Forum on Religion, Art and Architecture. Republican. Roman Catholic. Clubs: K.C., Moose. Home: 618 Mial St Raleigh NC 27608 Office: PO Box 1531 Raleigh NC 27602

XANDER, ALBERT FREDRICK, fluid power components distbg. exec.; b. Oil City, Pa., Oct. 4, 1921; s. Albert Fredrick and Elda (Stephens) X.; grad. high sch.; m. Iva Zimmerman, Nov. 14, 1943; children—John Albert, Thomas George, Gary Mark, Steven Scott, Albert Fredrick. Store mgr. Triangle Shoe Co., Pa., 1941-45; owner, operator City Cab & Trucking Co., Corry, Pa., 1945-53; founder, pres. Al Xander Co., Inc., Corry, 1953—; chmn. bd. Corry Rubber Corp.; dir. Airtek, Inc. Mem. Fluid Power Distbrs. Assn. Republican. Episcopalian. Clubs: Corry Country, Tarpon Woods Golf and Country, Elks, Masons, Order of Police, Order Ky. Cols. Home: 1 N Hillcrest Dr RD 4 Corry PA 16407 Office: 36 E South St Corry PA 16407

XYDES, CHRIST JOHN, computer engr.; b. Chgo., Feb. 26, 1955; s. Leonidas and Lena (Maniates) X.; B.S., U. Ill., 1975, M.S., 1977. Sr. programmer Mgmt. Info. Div. State of Ill., Springfield, 1973-74; research asst. Info. Engring. Lab., U. Ill., 1974-77; computer engr. IBM, San Jose, Calif., 1977—. Mem. IEEE, Assn. Computing Machinery, Soc. Profl. Engrs., U. Ill. Alumni Assn., Sigma Xi, Tau Beta Pi, Phi Kappa Phi, Sierra Club. Office: 5600 Cottle Rd San Jose CA 95193

YADAV, DHARAM VIR SINGH, fin. co. exec.; b. Ismailpur, India, July 10, 1936; s. Bharat Singh and Brahmo (Devi) Y.; B.Com., Agra U., 1955; M.B.A., U. Oreg., 1966; m. Aruna Yadav, May 17, 1962; children—Ruchira, Alpana. Asst. to exec. v.p. fgn. ops. Evans Products Co., Portland, Oreg., 1970-71, pres., gen. mgr. subs. Maderas Centro America, Matagalpa, Nicaragua, 1971-78, chmn. bd. dirs., 1971-77; pres. Yadav & Feuerstein P.C., Portland, 1977—. C.P.A., Oreg. Mem. Am. Inst. C.P.A.'s, Oreg. Soc. C.P.A.'s, Oreg. Accts. for Public Interest. Clubs: Lions, Optimists. Home: 7280 SW Lara St Portland OR 97223 Office: 4536 NE 42d Ave Portland OR 97218

YADDOF, ELMER, JR., apiarist; b. Jackson County, Iowa, May 10, 1931; s. Elmer Justus and Norma (Rutchozke) Y.; grad. high sch.; m. Carol Jean Meyer, Feb. 21, 1953; children—Steven, Christina (Mrs. Ray Johnson Jr.), Thomas, William. Owner, Elmer Yaddof Jr. Apiaries, Preston, Iowa, 1950—. Mem. Preston Community Fire Dept., 1953-74. Active in Boy Scouts and Little League, 1963-74. Mem. Mid-Am. Honey Producers, Am. Honey Producers Assn., Am. Beekeeping Fedn., Iowa Honey Producers. Republican. Lutheran. Home and office: Box 608 Preston IA 52069

YAFFE, GERALD JERRY, indsl. safety cons. exec.; b. Toronto, Ont., Can., July 10, 1944; s. David and Lillian Y.; M.A. in Bus. Adminstrn., U. Toronto, 1968; m. Elain Schwartz, Feb. 5, 1967; children—Jacqueline, Adrienne, Samantha Hope. Founder, pres. Safety House Can., Toronto, 1961—; pres. Safe-Tex Mfg. Co., 1971—, Safety House Internat., 1965—, Enyco Safety Co. Ltd., 1974—; dir. Canadian ORT. Bd. govs. Fedn. Cerebral Palsied, Participation House Internat.; treas. Arts Can. Mem. Can. Standards Assn. (dir.), Canadian Safety Equipment Distbrs. Assn. (chmn.). Office: 1275 Castlefield Ave Toronto ON M6B 1G4 Canada

YAFFE, JOSEPH X., lawyer; b. Phila., May 6, 1913; s. Samuel and Rose (Schaffer) Y.; A.B., U. Pa., 1929-33; J.D., Temple U., 1936; m. Silvia F. Fishbein, July 21, 1940; children—Roy, Peter M., Lisa Jo. Admitted to Pa. bar, 1937; spl. dep. atty. gen. Commonwealth of Pa., 1937-54; partner Yaffe and Gould, Phila., 1954—; pres. Commonwealth Insular Devel., Inc. Counsel, bd. dirs. Police Athletic League, 1948—; counsel, bd. dirs. Elder Craftsmen Phila., 1959—, pres., 1965-66, chmn. bd., 1966-67; mem. exec. com. Nat. Community Relations Adv. Council, 1956-64, treas., 1960-64; pres. Jewish Community Relations Council Greater Phila., 1956-59, hon. pres., 1959—; commr. Pa. Fair Employment Practices Commn., 1960-61; bd. dirs. Phila. Fellowship Commn., 1956-76, v.p., 1960-63; commr. Pa. Human Relations Commn., 1961—, vice chmn., 1967-74, chmn., 1974—; counsel, bd. dirs. Soc. Handicapped Children and Adults Phila. Area, counsel, dir., 1949—, pres., 1962-63; bd. dirs. Pa. Easter Seal Soc. Crippled Children and Adults, 1969-73; mem. nat. council Joint Distbn. Com., 1964-77; v.p. Internat. Assn. Ofcl. Human Rights Agys., 1967-68, counsel, 1973-76. Served as ensign USCGR, 1942-45. Recipient Easter Seal Pres.'s medallion, 1965, Police Athletic League Founder's award, 1966, Distinguished Service award, 1970, Humanitarian award Salem Bapt. Ch., 1968, Service award Pa. Ho. of Reps., 1971, Distinguished Merit award NCCJ, 1976, Martin Luther King, Jr. Human Rights award Salem Baptist Ch., 1980, Police Athletic League Hall of Fame award, 1980. Mem. Am., Pa., Phila. bar assns. Clubs: Masons, Shriners, Meadowlands Country (gov. 1963—, pres. 1971-73). Home: 1006 Arboretum Rd Wyncote PA 19095 Office: Two Penn Center Plaza Philadelphia PA 19102

YAFFE, MONTE EARL, mfg. co. exec.; b. Boston, July 24, 1933; s. George Hellman and Rosa Irene (Tobin) Y.; B.B.A., Clark U., 1956; m. Judith Saltman, May 5, 1959; children—Eric Lloyd, Donna Merle. Vice pres., gen. mgr. Crown Container Corp., Whitman, Mass., 1959-69; pres., chmn. bd. Golf-In Equip., Golf-In of Am. and Golf-In of Can., Canton, Mass., 1971—; pres., chmn. bd. Graphic Circuits, Inc., Woburn, Mass., 1978—. Served with U.S. Army, 1956-58. Jewish. Home: 65 Mary Ellen Rd Newton MA 02168 Office: 5-7 6th St Woburn MA 01801

YAHAGI, TSUNEO, mfg. co. exec.; b. Tokyo, Feb. 27, 1942; s. Toshio and Kimiko Y.; B.S., Keio U., Tokyo, 1965; M.B.A. with honor, Stanford U., 1974, Ph.D. in Bus. Adminstrn. (AACSB award), 1979; m. Reiko Shinjo, Apr. 7, 1967; children—Tamako, Naohisa, Tomozo. With Mitsubishi Corp., Tokyo, 1965-72; v.p. Fuji Die Co., Tokyo, 1972—, exec. rep. U.S., 1976—. Trustee AFS Internat./Intercultural, N.Y.C., 1976—, AFS Japan Assn., 1965—. Mem. Am. Mktg. Assn. Home: 700 College Ave Menlo Park CA 94025 Office: 2-17-10 Shimomaruko Ota-ku Tokyo Japan

YALE, JORDAN PRODROMOU, investment co. exec., mgmt. cons.; b. Thessaloniki, Greece, Mar. 28, 1928; s. Prodromos and Melpomeni (Inzipecoglou) Yeleyenides; came to U.S., 1947, naturalized, 1962; B.S., New Bedford Textile Inst., 1950; B.S., Lowell Textile Inst., 1952; M.B.A., Rutgers U., 1957; Ph.D., N.Y.U., 1965; m. Demetra Arapakis, Sept. 6, 1953; children—Robert Alexander, Donna Louise, Melanie Diane. Statistician, Chemstrand Corp., N.Y.C., 1957-60, economist, 1960-66; mgr. new investments, fibers Esso Chem. Co., Inc., N.Y.C., 1966-72; pres. Statistikon Corp., East Norwich, N.Y., 1972—; asso. prof. Hofstra U., 1979—; asso. prof. econs. C.W. Post Coll., Brookville, N.Y. Founder, chmn. Com. Beautification of East Norwich. Recipient Am. Heritage award J.F. Kennedy Library for Minorities. Mem. Am. Econ. Assn., A.A.A.S. Author: The Economic Structure of the Textile Industry. Home: 81 Peachtree Dr East Norwich NY 11732 Office: PO Box 246 East Norwich LI NY 11732

YAMAMOTO, SHIGERU, chem. co. exec.; b. Hawaii, Aug. 23, 1919; s. Sanzuchi and Iyo (Ichiyama) Y.; student Yamaguchi Coll. Commerce, 1937; m. Yoshie Fujii, Mar. 17, 1948; children—Masashi, Kumiko. With Nichiman Shoji Co., Ltd., Manchuria, 1941-46, Yamaguchi Liaison Office, Iwakuni, Japan, 1947-48; with Teijin Precision Machinery Co. Ltd., 1948-50; sec. dirs. Teijin Ltd., 1950-52, adminstrn. and planning chief, 1952-54, mgr. fgn. relations, 1954-60, sec. to dirs., 1960-73, dir., sec., 1973—. Served to lt. Japanese Army, 1941-46. Mem. French C. of C. (dir. 1973-76). Home: 5-8-7 Kamisoshigaya Setagaya-ku Tokyo Japan 157 Office: 2-1-1 Uchisaiwai-cho Chiyoda-ku Tokyo Japan 100

YAMASHITA, BRUCE NOBORU, utility exec.; b. Molokai, Hawaii, June 21, 1947; s. Henry Noboru and Marie (Tanemura) Y.; B.S. in Elec. Engring., Kans. State U., 1969; M.S., Calif. State U., Long Beach, 1970; M.B.A. (honors), Calif. State U., Fullerton, 1971. Nuclear/environ. engr. Bechtel Power Corp., Los Angeles, 1971-75; exec. v.p., gen. mgr., dir. Molokai Electric Co., 1975—; lectr. Maui Community Coll. Dist. chmn. Molokai Boy Scouts Am. Registered profl. engr., Calif., Hawaii. Mem. IEEE, Nat., Hawaii socs. profl. engrs., Molokai C. of C. (dir.). Club: Masons. Office: Box 378 Kaunakakai HI 96748

YAMMINE, RIAD NASSIF, oil co. exec.; b. Hammana, Lebanon, Apr. 12, 1934; s. Nassib Nassif and Emilie (Daou) Y.; came to U.S., 1952, naturalized, 1963; B.S. in Petroleum Engring., Pa. State U., 1956; grad. Advanced Mgmt. Program, Harvard U., 1977; m. Beverly Ann Hosack, Sept. 14, 1954; children—Kathleen, Yammine Griffiths, Cynthia, Michael. Engr., Trans-Arabian Pipe Line Co., Saudi Arabia, 1956-61; with Marathon Pipe Line Co., 1961-75, mgr. Western div., Casper, Wyo., 1971-74, mgr. Eastern div., Martinsville, Ill., 1974-75; mgr. div. mktg. ops. Marathon Oil Co., Findlay, Ohio, 1975—, also officer, dir. subsidiaries. Mem. council, chmn. fin. com. First Lutheran Ch., Findlay, 1976—. Registered profl. engr., Ohio. Mem. ASME, Am. Petroleum Inst. Republican. Club: Findlay Country. Patentee in field. Home: 624 Winterhaven Dr Findlay OH 45840 Office: 539 S Main St Findlay OH 45840

YANACEK, FRANK JOSEPH, diversified mfg. co. exec.; b. Lansford, Pa., May 24, 1931; s. John Joseph and Caroline (Pavlick) Y.; B.S. in Bus., Central Mich. U., 1962; M.A. in Social Sci., William Paterson Coll., 1973; m. Jacqueline Ann Sipko, Dec. 26, 1954; children—James, Richard, Kathryn, Janice Carolyn. Mgr. distbn. and traffic Eastern region Dow Chem. Co., Chgo., Midland, Mich. and Bloomfield, N.J., 1954-65; mgr. traffic ops. Westvaco Corp., N.Y.C., 1965-73; dir. transp. and distbn. SCM Corp., N.Y.C. and Cleve., 1973—; adj. prof. Passaic County Community Coll., Paterson, N.J., Cleve. State U.; guest lectr. transp. and distbn. workshops N.Y. C. of C. and Industry. Active econ. edn. seminars U.S. C. of C., 1976. Served with Security Agy., U.S. Army, 1951-53. Mem. Am. Soc. Traffic and Transp. (cert.; pres. N.Y. State chpt. 1974-75), ICC Practitioners Assn., Nat. Council Phys. Distbn. Mgmt., Cleve. Traffic Club. Republican. Roman Catholic. Home: 3660 Kings Post Pkwy Rocky River OH 44116 Office: 900 Union Commerce Bldg Cleveland OH 44115

YANCEY, BYRON TAYLOR, JR., fin. exec.; b. Austin, Tex., Feb. 19, 1947; s. Byron Taylor and Ruth (Phelps) Y.; B.S., Berry Coll., 1969; M.B.A., U. Ga., 1970; m. Rebecca Camp, Sept. 8, 1968; children—Byron Taylor, Tiffany and Heather (twins). With Citibank, N.Y.C., 1973—, fin. analyst, 1975-79; dir. relationships Southeastern region Thrift Resources, Inc., Atlanta, 1980—. Served with USAF, 1970-73. Home: 6497 Rose Common Dr Norcross GA 30092 Office: 60 Perimeter Center E Suite 6000 Atlanta GA 30346

YANCEY, ROBERT EARL, oil co. exec.; b. Cleve., Ohio, July 15, 1921; s. George W. and Mary (Gutzwiller) Y.; B.E., Marshall U., 1943; m. Mary Estelline Tackett, July 25, 1941; children—Robert Earl, Susan Carol Yancey Farmer. With Ashland Oil Inc. (Ky.), 1943—, chief operating officer, from 1969, pres., 1972—, also dir.; pres. Ashland Petroleum Co., 1969—; dir. Ashland de Venezuela, C.A., Australian Carbon Black (Pty.) Ltd., Oleofina S.A., Belgium United Carbon de Venezuela, C.A., United Carbon India Ltd., 3d Nat. Bank, Ashland. Past bd. dirs. Spindletop Research Center, Lexington, Ky.; adv. bd. Marshall U., Huntington. W.Va., 1977. Mem. Nat. Petroleum Refiners Assn. (dir. 1965—, pres. 1969-70), Nat. Petroleum Assn. (mfg. com.), Am. Petroleum Inst. (dir.), Ky. Soc. Profl. Engrs. (dir. 1970—). Office: PO Box 391 Ashland KY 41101

YANCEY, ROBERT EARL, JR., petroleum co. exec.; b. Ashland, Ky., June 16, 1945; s. Robert Earl and Estelline (Tackett) Y.; B.Ch.E., Cornell U., 1969; m. Nina Carol McGee, June 16, 1962; children—Robert Earl III, Yvonne Carol, Elizabeth Lynn. Tech. service engr. Ashland Oil Inc., Buffalo, 1969-71, tech. service engr., St. Paul Park, Minn., 1971-72, operating supt., 1972-74, asst. to v.p. in charge refineries, Ashland, Ky., 1974-75, supt. Catlettsburg Refinery, 1975-80, asst. to pres., 1980—. Mem. Am. Inst. Chem. Engrs., Am. Petroleum Inst. Home: 1033 Brentwood Dr Russell KY 41169 Office: Ashland Oil Inc 1409 Winchester Ave Ashland KY 41101

YANCY, ROBERT JAMES, paint mfg. co. exec.; b. Tifton, Ga., Mar. 10, 1944; s. Preston Martin and Margaret (Robinson) Y.; B.A., Morehouse Coll., 1964; M.B.A., Atlanta U., 1966; Ph.D. (fellow) Northwestern U., 1973; m. Dorothy Yvonne Cowser, Sept. 8, 1967; 1 dau., Yvonne Cowser. Instr. Albany State Coll. (Ga.), 1966-67, So. U., Baton Rouge, 1965-66; Hampton (Va.) Inst., 1967-69; chmn., pres. Zebra Corp., Atlanta, 1972—; asso. prof. Atlanta U., 1971—. Research asst. Nat. Adv. Council Minority Bus. Enterprise; cons. Nat. Task Force Minority Bus. Tng. and Edn.; mem. alumni bd. Leadership Atlanta, 1976—. Bd. dirs. Met., Atlanta Girls Clubs. Named Young Man of Yr. in Bus., YMCA, 1977. Ford Found. urban studies fellow, 1971-72. Mem. Sales and Marketing Execs. Atlanta, C. of C. Author: Federal Government Policy and Black Business Enterprise, 1974. Home: 3056 Pomona Way East Point GA 30344 Office: 698 Echo St NW Atlanta GA 30318

YANKOVOY, MICHAEL SAMUEL, fin. analyst; b. Phila., Sept. 23, 1953; s. Samuel Walter and Marguerite Mary (Donnelly) Y.; B.S. in Econs., U. Pa., 1975; M.B.A., Temple U., 1977. Corp. planning analyst Amax, Inc., Greenwich, Conn., 1977-78; fin. analyst, ops. analyst Air Products and Chems., Allentown, Pa., 1978-80, supr. fin. planning and analysis, 1980—. Mem. Am. Mgmt. Assn. Home: 1516 N 2d St Philadelphia PA 19122 Office: Box 538 Allentown PA 18105

YANNEY, REGINALD H(OCK), mgmt. cons.; b. Alliance, Ohio, Sept. 24, 1906; s. Benjamin F. and Carolyn (Hock) Y.; student, U. Chgo., 1922-23; B.S., Wooster Coll., 1926; m. Helen Black, July 24, 1929; 1 son, Louis Edward. Accountant, Ohio Pub. Service Co., Ohio Fuel Gas Co., Am. Tel. & Tel. Co., 1926-28; accountant Hoover Co., 1928-51, controller, 1951-55, asst. treas., 1955-61; mgmt. cons., 1961—; asso. prof., chmn. dept. econs. and bus. adminstrn. Heidelberg Coll., Tiffin, Ohio, 1963-77. C.P.A., Ohio. Mem. Am. Inst. C.P.A.'s, Ohio Soc. C.P.A.'s, Am. Accounting Assn., Nat. Assn. Accountants, Financial Execs. Inst., Republican. Presbyterian. Clubs: Masons, Elks; Rotary. Home: West Torch Lake Dr Rapid City MI 49676

YARBOROUGH, ERNEST LYNWOOD, JR., ins. broker; b. Atlantic City, Nov. 13, 1944; s. Ernest Lynwood and Dolores (Stewart) Y.; B.A. in Social Sci., Moravian Coll., 1966; C.P.C.U., Wharton Sch., U. Pa., 1974; m. Carole Ann Gilliam, Sept. 3, 1964; children—Tracey Ann, Ernest Lynwood. Claim adjuster, underwriter Employers Liability Assurance Corp., Phila., 1967-68; office mgr. John H. Gilliam Agy., Bala Cynwyd, Pa., 1968-75; account rep. Cape Ins. Center, North Wildwood, N.J., 1975-76, gen. mgr., 1976-77, v.p., gen. mgr., 1977—. Bd. dirs. Cape May County United Way, 1978—. Mem. Ind. Ins. Agts. Am., Ind. Ins. Agts. Cape May County (pres. 1978), Profl. Ins. Agrs. Am., Soc. C.P.C.U., Avalon C. of C. (dir. 1978, v.p. 1980-81), Cape May C. of C. (legis. dir. 1981). Republican. Roman Catholic. Clubs: Jersey Cape Racquet, Optimists (pres. 1969) (Bala-Cynwyd); Lions (v.p. 1977, 78) (Stone Harbor, N.J.). Contbr. articles to trade mags. Home: 867 Avalon Ave Avalon NJ 08202 Office: 303 New Jersey Ave North Wildwood NJ 08260

YASNYI, ALLAN DAVID, TV prodn. co. exec.; b. New Orleans, June 22, 1942; s. Ben Z. and Bertha R. (Michalove) Y.; B.B.A., Tulane U., 1964; m. Lesley E. Behrman, Dec. 8, 1968; children—Benjamin Charles, Evelyn Judith. Free-lance exec. producer, producer, writer, actor and designer for TV, motion picture and theatre, 1961-73; dir. fin. and adminstrn. Quinn Martin Prodns., Hollywood, Calif., 1973-76, v.p. fin., 1976-77, exec. v.p. fin. and corp. planning, 1977; vice chmn., chief exec. officer QM Prodns., Beverly Hills, Calif., 1977-78, chmn. bd., chief exec. officer, 1978—. Served with U.S. Army, 1964-66. Mem. Acad. TV Arts and Scis., Am. Advt. Fedn., Am. Mgmt. Assn., Hollywood Radio and TV Soc., Hollywood C. of C. (dir.). Home: 3343 Laurel Canyon Blvd Studio City CA 91604

YATES, BILLY SUMMERS, retail appliance and furniture co. exec.; b. Gibson County, Tenn., Dec. 7, 1925; s. Arthur P. and Nettie (Summers) Y.; student Murray State U., 1946-48; m. Mary Emmalene Eidson, July 31, 1949; children—William Mark, Laura Yates Emerson, Mary Jane, Joseph Stephen. Founder, owner, mgr. Gen. Appliance & Furniture Co., Dyersburg, Tenn., 1948—; dir. First Citizens Nat. Bank, 1973—, mem. fin. and trust com., 1977—. Pres. Dyer County Fair Assn., 1965-66; chmn. Reelfoot Regional Library Bd., 1967-68; mem. bd. mgrs. Methodist Hosp., Memphis. Served with USN, 1943-46. Named Outstanding Young Man, Jr. C. of C., 1951; Creative Salesman of Yr., Ladies Home Jour.-NARDA, 1959; Tenn. Retailer of Yr., 1974; Outstanding Business Man of Yr. for Dyer County, Dyersburg C. of C., 1979. Mem. Tenn. Retail Mchts. Assn. (pres. 1980-81), Dyersburg C. of C. (dir. 1964-68, v.p. 1968-70), Nat. Assn. Retail Dealers of Am. (exec. com. 1965—), Nat. Appliance and Radio-TV Dealers Assn. (past pres.). Methodist. Home: 2001 Okeena St Dyersburg TN 38024 Office: 213-219 W Court St Dyersburg TN 38024

YATES, HOWARD NELSON, real estate exec.; b. Wingham, Ont., Can., May 21, 1931; s. Howard H. and Lucy E. (McGregor) Y.; grad. high sch., Port Elgin, Ont.; m. Mary Joan Hemstock, Feb. 24, 1951; children—Mark Howard, Mary Maureen. Asst. mgr. S.S. Kresge Co. Ltd., Oshawa, Toronto, Ont., also Calgary, Alta., 1948-53; exec. Weber Bros. Agys. Ltd., Embassy Devels. Ltd. and Asso. Cos., Edmonton, Alta., 1954-72; pres. Yates Realty Services Ltd., Yates Hawaii, Inc., Venture Mortgage Ltd., Alta. Indsl. Rental Systems Ltd., Edmonton, 1972—. Mem. Urban Devel. Inst. Alta. (pres. 1968-69), Can. Real Estate Assn., Urban Land Inst. U.S. Progressive Conservative. Mem. United Ch. of Can. Clubs: Mayfair Golf and Country, Edmonton, Edmonton Petroleum, Shriners. Home: 13904 90A Ave Edmonton AB T5R 4X3 Canada Office: 708 10240 124 St Edmonton AB T5N 3W6 Canada

YAU, ANDREW TAK-MING, import exec.; b. Hong Kong, Aug. 4, 1950; s. Tse Wah and Kwei Chee (Liang) Y.; came to U.S., 1968; B.A., UCLA, 1972; M.B.A., U. Santa Clara (Calif.), 1974. Chief exec. officer Nat. Stake, Inc., Orinda, Calif., 1975—. Mem. Assn. M.B.A. Execs., Nat. Assn. Realtors, Calif. Assn. Realtors, U. Calif. Alumni Assn., Orinda Assn., Phi Eta Sigma. Address: Box 332 Nat Stake Inc Orinda CA 94563

YAU, GLORIA VAYL, govt. ofcl.; b. N.Y.C., Jan. 26, 1941; d. John and Carmela (Vela) Pantaleo; B.A., CCNY, 1966; postgrad. Syracuse Edn. Center for IBM Systems Design, 1972; m. Bernard Yu-Kwong Yau, Dec. 6, 1974; children—Paul, Christine. Mgmt. analyst Dept. Labor, N.Y.C., 1962-75; fin. mgmt. systems cons. Div. Housing and Community Renewal, N.Y.C., 1975-76; info. systems exec. Div. Criminal Justice Services, N.Y.C., 1976—; cons., lectr. in field. Crime Control Planning Bd. grantee, 1978-80.

YAVITZ, BORIS, educator; b. Tblisi, Russia, June 4, 1923; came to U.S., 1946, naturalized, 1950; s. Simon and Miriam Y.; M.A., Trinity Coll., Cambridge U., 1943; M.S., Columbia U., 1948, Ph.D. (Ford fellow), 1964; children—Jessica Ann, Judith, Emily; m. Irene Bernhard, July 17, 1949. Econ. con. Jewish Agy. for Palestine, 1948-49; mgmt. cons. Werner Mgmt. Consultants, N.Y.C., 1949-54; owner land devel., investment orgn., 1954-61; faculty Columbia U., N.Y.C., 1964-75, prof. mgmt., 1968-75, dean Grad. Sch. Bus., 1975—; dep. chmn., dir. Fed. Res. Bank of N.Y., 1977—; dir. J.C. Penney Co., Inc., 1978—; cons. in field. Bd. dirs. Inst. Art and Urban Resources, 1977; bd. advisers Internat. Mgmt. and Devel. Inst., Washington, 1975; ex officio trustee Am. Assembly, 1975, chmn. internat. affairs com. Collegiate Schs. Bus., 1978; mem. White Plains (N.Y.) Planning Bd., 1975-76. Served to lt. Brit. Royal Navy, 1943-46. Recipient Disting. Teaching award Columbia U., 1972. Mem. ASME, Inst. Mgmt. Sci., Beta Gamma Sigma (pres. 1962-63). Clubs: Univ.

(N.Y.C.); Sheldrake Yacht (Mamaroneck, N.Y.). Author: Automation in Commercial Banking - Its Process and Impact, 1967, Electronic Data Processing in New York City - Lessons in Metropolitan Economics, 1967, Labor Markets - An Information System, 1973; contbr. chpts. to books. Office: Grad Sch Bus Columbia U 101 Uris Hall New York NY 10027

YAWORSKI, STEPHANIE EMILY, educator; b. Rome, N.Y., Jan. 17, 1940; d. Andrew and Genevieve Y.; B.S., Keuka Coll., 1961; M.S. in Bus. Edn., Syracuse U., 1968; Ph.D., U. N.D., 1974. Chmn. dept. bus. Greece Central Sch. Dist., Rochester, N.Y., 1961-71; asst. prof. bus. edn. Coll. Bus. Adminstrn., Bowling Green (Ohio) State U., 1975—; cons. data processing and word processing. Pres. Monroe County Bus. Tchrs. Assn., Rochester, 1971; area leader N.Y. State Dept. Bus. and Vocat. Edn., 1971-72. Served to 1st lt., AGC, U.S. Army, 1971-73. Carnegie grantee, 1960; Nat. Def. grantee, 1963. Mem. Nat. Bus. Tchrs. Assn., Internat. Word Processing Assn., N.Y. State, Ohio bus. tchrs. assns., Res. Officers Assn., Bus. and Profl. Women, AAUW, Delta Pi Epsilon, Pi Omega Pi, Pi Lambda Theta. Roman Catholic. Contbr. chpt. to Nat. Bus. Edn. Yearbook, 1973, articles to publs. Home: 1726 Spruce Dr #152 Bowling Green OH 43402 Office: Coll Bus Adminstn Bowling Green State U Bowling Green OH 43402

YEAGER, DAVID LEROY, utility exec.; b. Youngstown, Ohio, Feb. 12, 1935; s. LeRoy C. and Marjorie (Ballington) Y.; B.E.M.E., Youngstown U., 1959; P.M.D., Harvard U., 1973; m. Margaret Scott, Feb. 7, 1959; children—David, Karen, Ellen. Supt. elec. and steam sales Ohio Edison Co., Youngstown, 1968-70, dir. comml.-indsl. mktg., Akron, 1971-76, mgr. project coordination, 1976-78, asst. to exec. v.p., 1978-79, asst. to pres., 1980—. Vice pres. Summit County unit Am. Cancer Soc., 1979—. Registered profl. engr., Ohio. Mem. ASME (past chmn. Youngstown sect.), Nat. Soc. Profl. Engrs. (past pres. Mahoning Valley Soc.), ASHRAE. Club: Harvard Bus. Sch. (Cleve.). Home: 2878 Lakeland Pkwy Silver Lake OH 44224 Office: 76 S Main St Akron OH 44308

YEAGER, EDWARD JAMES, pharm. co. exec.; b. Phila., Nov. 1, 1919; s. W. Fiske and Euphemia Caroline (Wood) Y.; grad. Charles Morris Price Sch. Advt., 1951; cert. in mgmt. devel. Pa. State U., 1963. With McNeil Labs., Inc., Ft. Washington, Pa., 1937-78, exec. asst. advt., 1946-51, mgr. advt. promotion, 1951-60, mgr. sample advt. div., 1960-64, mgr. sample mfg., 1964-78; mgr. rep. services McNeil Consumer Products Co., Ft. Washington, 1978—. Publicity chmn. Ambler (Pa.) Adult Sch. Staff, 1975—. Served with AUS, 1942-46; ETO. Mem. Am. Mgmt. Assn. Presbyterian. Home: 402 Welsh Rd Ambler PA 19002 Office: Camp Hill Rd Fort Washington PA 19034

YEAP, JOHNNIE CHEE BENG, paint co. exec.; b. Rangoon, Burma, Oct. 21, 1943; s. Hock Tyan and Chye Lyan (Teoh) Y.; came to U.S., 1974, naturalized, 1979; B.A., U. Rangoon, 1965; m. Donata Mya Han, Dec. 21, 1969; children—Tricia, Allan. With import-export and mfg. bus., Burma, 1962-64; accounts mgr. Burmese Govt. Trade Corp., 1964-66; with Am. embassy, Rangoon, 1967-74, Synkoloid Co., Los Angeles, 1974-76; regional purchasing mgr. Glidden Coatings and Resins div. SCM Corp., San Francisco, 1976—. C.P.A., Burma. Mem. Nat., Golden Gate (dir.) paint and coatings assns. Rosicrucian. Home: 1109 Jack London Dr Vallejo CA 94590

YEATER, LAWRENCE EDWARD, editor, publisher; b. Menoken, N.D., Oct. 9, 1909; s. Waldo Emerson and Nellie Viola (Ebeling) Y.; grad. high sch.; m. Melba Lunn, Mar. 14, 1943; children—Melba Ruth (Mrs. Virgil Bippus), Marilyn (Mrs. Robert Craven), Stephen E. With Exchange Pub. Corp., New Paris, Ind., 1928—, compositor, 1928-35, prodn. mgr., 1935-40, bus. mgr., 1945-55, asst. editor, 1956-61, pub., editor, 1962-77; dir. New Paris Telephone, Inc. (Ind.). Served with C.E., AUS, 1941-45. Mem. C. of C. (pres. 1966). Lion. Home: PO Box 45 New Paris IN 46553 Office: Industrial Dr New Paris IN 46553

YEATES, JAMES OWEN, fuel distbr., banker; b. Logan, Utah, May 25, 1928; s. Richard Owen and Evalyn (Monson) Y.; B.S., Utah State U., 1953, postgrad., 1955-57; m. Iva Loo Petersen, May 23, 1952; children—Paula, Lauralee, Cordell, Angela, Anthon, Spencer, Samuel. Sales rep. Tidewater Oil Co., Los Angeles, 1957-58, asst. sales supr., 1959-61, dist. sales supr. Calif.-Nev., 1962-63; founder, owner Yeates Oil Co., Logan, Utah, 1963—; founder, chmn. bd., dir. North Park Bank of Commerce, North Logan, Utah, 1975—; founder, pres. No. Fin. and Thrift Co., Logan, 1979—. Chmn. Cache County Young Republicans, 1949-52, voting dist. chmn., 1949-50, 63-70; mem. city council City of North Logan, 1971-77; chmn. City Planning Commn., North Logan, 1978—; commr. Cache County, 1980—. Served with U.S. Army, 1953-55. Mem. Intermountain Oil Marketers Assn. (past v.p. Utah chpt.), Sigma Nu (past alumni pres. Utah State U. chpt.). Mormon. Club: Lions (past v.p.). Home: 1497 Highland Dr 1780 N North Logan UT 84321 Office: 620 W 200 N Logan UT 84321

YEDLICKA, WILLIAM GEORGE, mfg. co. exec.; b. Apollo, Pa., Dec. 25, 1922; s. Joseph Frank and Katie (Cadina) Y.; B.S., U. Pitts., 1949, M.L., 1957; m. Theresa Unger, July 17, 1970; 1 son, Monte. Asst. sales mgr. Bowers Battery & Spark Plug Co. div. Gen. Battery, sales mgr., 1965-66, s. eastern regional sales mgr., 1966-67; spl. products mgr. F. Penn Mfg. Co., Inc., Lyon Station, Pa., 1967-74, sales mgr. indsl. r.r. and mining, 1974-79, v.p. sales, indsl. r.r. and mining, 1979—. Served with USAF, 1942-46. Decorated D.F.C., Air medal with 4 clusters. Mem. Material Handling Inst., Material Handling Equipment Dealers Assn., Nat. Elec. Mfrs. Assn. Republican. Presbyterian. Clubs: Pinehurst Country, Mason, Shriner. Home: 355 Lackawanna St Reading PA 19601 Office: Deka Rd Lyon Station PA 19536

YEH, CHIAO, biostatistician; b. Sun Yuan, China, May 26, 1941; s. Chin-wen and Shun-hua (Chung) Y.; came to U.S., 1965, naturalized, 1974; B.S., Nat. Taiwan U., 1963; Ph.D., U. Minn., 1970; m. Sheria Chao-tung Chang, Mar. 17, 1968; children—Oliver, Oscar. Biostatistician, Atlas Chem. Industries, Inc., Wilmington, Del., 1970-71, Sandoz Pharms., East Hanover, N.J., 1971-72; sr. biomathematician ICI Ams., Inc., Wilmington, 1972—; cons. in field. Cubmaster Boy Scouts Am., Wilmington, 1976-77. Mem. Orgn. Chinese Ams. (exec. bd. dirs. 1977—), Am. Statis. Assn., Biometric Soc., Sigma Xi. Club: Toastmasters (treas. 1974-76). Contbr. articles to profl. jours. Home: 120 Weldin Park Dr Wilmington DE 19803 Office: ICI Americas Wilmington DE 19897

YELOVICH, ROBERT BORIS, advt co. exec.; b. Zagreb, Yugoslavia, Apr. 3, 1942; came to Can., 1970, naturalized, 1975; s. Peter and Maria (Bilac) Y.; ed. U. Zagreb Sch. Law, Advt. Art Sch., Stockholm; m. Dorothy Yelovich, May 5, 1979; 1 dau., Audessa. Layout artist Ahlens & Akerlunds, Stockholm, 1967-70; art dir. Leo Burnett Co., Toronto, Ont., 1970-71; art dir. Vickers & Benson, Toronto, 1971-74; pres., creative dir. Publicad Inc., Toronto, 1974—. Mem. Art Dirs. Club Toronto, Art Dirs. Club N.Y. Roman Catholic. Author: (with Michael Read) How To Get A Great Ad Idea; contbr. articles to profl. jours. Home: 1986 Bough Beeches Blvd Mississauga ON L4W 2J7 Canada Office: 130 Adelaide St W Suite 1818 Toronto ON M5H 3P5 Canada

YENGLING, THEODORE FRANK, mfg. co. ofcl.; b. Salem, Ohio, Oct. 16, 1938; s. Ross Herbert and Barbara (Whidden) Y.; B.A. in Edn., U. Akron, 1963; M.A., Kent State U., 1967; m. Gudrun Zierhut, Nov. 2, 1963; children—David, Erika. Speech pathologist Akron (Ohio) Bd. Edn., 1963-67; sales engr. B. F. Goodrich Indsl. Products Co., Atlanta, 1967-69, sales rep. N.Y.C., 1969, Phila., 1973, sales account rep. B.F. Goodrich Gen. Products Co., 1971-76, spl. accounts rep. Gen. Products div. B.F. Goodrich Co., Franklin Park, Ill., to 1980, region sales mgr., 1980—; sales mgr. Opex Corp., from 1976; tchr. U. Akron, 1967, Trenton State U., 1975-77, Camden County Coll., 1976. Served with U.S. Army, 1956. Mem. Am. Summit County (pres.) speech and hearing assns. Baptist. Office: 10701 Belmont Ave Franklin Park IL 60131

YEP, WALLEN LAI, regional ofcl.; b. Stockton, Calif., July 23, 1943; s. Hong Wey and Kim Chin Gee Y.; A.A., Coll. of San Mateo, 1972; B.A., Calif. State U., 1975; certificate in contract adminstrn., U. Calif. at Berkeley, 1975; M.B.A., Golden Gate U., 1977; m. Yong Sun Hwang, June 12, 1970; 1 child, Suk Kyung. Contract price analyst U.S. Army Procurement Agy., Korea, 1969; base supply supr. AAEOI, Korea, 1969-71; staff advisor In-Chang Group, Korea, 1971; adminstrv. services supr. Far West Lab., San Francisco, 1971-74; adminstrv. officer Met. Transp. Commn., Berkeley, Calif., 1974—; instr. Asian mktg. and internat. bus. mgmt. Lincoln U., 1978—; cons. internat. field. Mem. Oakland (Calif.) Unified Sch. Dist. Affirmative Action Purchasing adv. com., 1978; co-chmn. North Beach Chinatown Youth Services Center, 1977—; hon. adv. bd. Mission Coalition, 1977—; pres. Internat. Center Tech. Assistance and Devel.; adv. East Bay Asian Local Devel. Corp., 1977—; ad hoc com. Alameda United Way, 1977—, others. Served with U.S. Army, 1967-69. Cert. profl. contracts mgr., cert. purchasing mgr. Mem. Nat. Assn. Purchasing Mgmt., No. Calif. Purchasing Mgmt. Assn., Oakland World Trade Assn., Assn. M.B.A. Execs., Calif., Golden Gate alumni assns., Nat. Contract Mgmt. Assn. Republican. Home: 601 Montclair Ave Oakland CA 94610 Office: MTC Hotel Claremont Berkeley CA 94705

YERMAN, ROBERT NEIL, accountant; b. N.Y.C., Jan. 16, 1940; s. Nat W. and Tina (Barotz) Y.; student Alfred U., 1956-58; B.A., U. City N.Y., 1960; postgrad U. City N.Y., Fairleigh Dickenson U., 1962-67; m. Judith Linn, Apr. 15, 1962 (div. Dec. 1969); children—Gregory Marc, Gary Jay; m. 2d, Anne V. DeLue, May 21, 1972; children—Brant Matthew Peace, Lesley Elizabeth Hope. Pres., Exec. Exchange Office Insp. Gen., HUD, Washington, 1975-76; partner Touche Ross & Co., Washington, 1977—, now nat. services dir., communications; partner J. Linn & Co., C.P.A.'s, N.J., 1963-69. Mem. Am. Inst. C.P.A.'s, N.Y. State Soc. C.P.A.'s (chmn. internat. ops. com.), D.C. Inst. C.P.A.'s, Exec. Interchange Alumni Assn. (Pres.). Clubs: Desiree, Mason. Contbr. to various profl. jours. Home: 5430 30th St NW Washington DC 20015 Office: 1900 M St NW Washington DC 20036

YETKA, JULES, mfg. co. exec.; b. Jersey City, Jan. 15, 1920; s. Edward and Louise A. (Brandt) Y.; B.S. in Finance, Pace Coll., 1954; m. Mary B. McCarthy, June 14, 1942; children—Barbara L., Sharon L. (Mrs. Leon Robert Discavage), Brian Christopher. Controller Permutit Co., N.Y.C., 1953-58, pres., 1958-67; group exec. Parker Hannifin Co., Des Plaines, Ill., 1967-70; pres. K-G Industries, Inc., Rosemont, Ill., 1970-73; group v.p. Berwind Corp., Phila., 1973-77, sr. v.p., 1978—; v.p., dir. Sinto Berwind Corp., Nagoya, Japan; chmn. bd. Bindicator Co., Port Huron, Mich., K-G Industries, Inc., Rosemont, Mateer-Burt Co., Devon, Pa., Rietz Mfg. Co., Santa Rosa, Calif., Strong Scott Co., Mpls., Hutt GMBH, Heilbronn, Germany. Served with AUS, World War II. Mem. Process Equipment Mfrs. Assn. (pres.), Fin. Execs. Inst. Clubs: Phila. Country, Union League (Phila.). Home: 223 Hermitage Dr Radnor PA 19087 Office: West Tower-Center Square Philadelphia PA 19102

YETTER, DONALD FRANKLIN, motorcyle parts and acessories co. exec.; b. Mifflintown, Pa., July 12, 1945; s. Mae Elizabeth Grissinger Yetter; m. Sharon M. Shimp, Mar. 13, 1966; children—Tina Marie, Donald F. II, Mark Anthony. Advt. mgr. asst. Aurand's for Sports, Inc., Lewistown, Pa., 1964-65, mgr. shipping and receiving, 1965-68; sales rep. A.F.S. Distbrs., Lewistown, Pa., 1968-70, asst. mgr. motorcyle div., 1970-71; gen. mgr. Betor Am. Corp., 1971-74; v.p., gen. mgr. Magura U.S.A. Corp., Milroy, Pa., 1975—. Served with USAF, 1963-64. Mem. Motorcycle Trades Assn., Am. Motorcyle Assn., Motorcycle Industry Council, Credit Mgrs. Assn. So. Calif., DAV. Republican. Lutheran. Clubs: Rotary (dir.), Elks. Home: RD 1 Box CH-25 Woodland Circle Reedsville PA 17084 Office: PO Box 337 Milroy PA 17063

YEUTTER, CLAYTON KEITH, merc. exchange exec.; b. Eustis, Nebr., Dec. 10, 1930; s. Reinhold F. (dec.) and Laura P. Yeutter; B.S. with high distinction, U. Nebr., 1952, J.D. cum laude, 1963, Ph.D., 1966; student U. Wis., 1960; m. Lillian Jeanne Vierk, June 13, 1953; children—Brad, Gregg, Kim, Van. Operator farm and ranch in central Nebr., 1957-75; with dept. agrl. econs. Univ. Nebr., 1960-66; exec. asst. Gov. Nebr., 1966-68; dir. Univ. Nebr. Mission in Colombia, 1968-70; adminstr. consumer and mktg. service U.S. Dept. Agr., 1970-71; regional dir. Com. for Re-election of Pres., 1972; asst. sec. for mktg. and consumer services Dept. Agr., 1973-74, asst. sec. internat. affairs and commodity programs, 1974-75; dep. spl. trade rep. Exec. Office of Pres., Washington, 1975-77; admitted to Nebr. bar, 1963; sr. partner Nelson, Harding, Yeutter & Leonard, Lincoln, Nebr., 1977-78; pres., chief exec. officer Chgo. Merc. Exchange, 1978—; dir. Conagra, Inc., Omaha. Bd. dirs. Chgo. Assn. Commerce and Industry, Chgo. Council Fgn. Relations, U.S. Meat Export Fedn., Denver, Japan Am. Soc. Chgo., Inc.; bd. visitors Sch. Bus. Adminstrn., Georgetown U., Washington; trustee Internat. Agrl. Devel. Service, N.Y.C., Farm Found., Oak Brook, Ill.; mem. adv. council Found. Am. Agr. Program, Farm Found., Washington; sr. v.p. Internat. Bus. Council, Chgo.; trustee Livestock Merchandising Inst., Kansas City, Mo. Recipient Disting. Service award Am. Soc. Agrl. Cons., 1978; U. Nebr. 4-H Club Alumni award; Farm House "Master Builder of Men" award. Mem. Nebr. Soc. Washington (v.p.), Farm House Fraternity Alumni Assn. (dir.). Methodist (chmn. ofcl. bd.). Contbr. articles to profl. jours.; editorial bd. Commodities. Office: 444 W Jackson Blvd Chicago IL 60606

YLVISAKER, WILLIAM TOWNEND, bus. exec.; b. St. Paul, Feb. 25, 1924; s. Lauritz S. and Winifred Jean (Townend) Y.; B.S., Yale, 1948; children—Laurie Ellen, Elizabeth Maren, William Wendell, Amy Townend, Jon Alastair; m. 2d, Jane Penelope Mitchell, May 11, 1972. Security analyst Bank of New York, 1948-49; gen. mgr. Lake Forest Motor Sales (Ill.), 1949-52; v.p., gen. mgr. Pheoll Mfg. Co., Chgo., 1952-58; pres. Parker-Kalon div. Gen. Am. Transp. Corp., Clifton, N.J., 1958-61, exec. asst. to pres. of corp., dir., Chgo., 1961-63, v.p., 1963-64, group v.p., 1964-68, dir., 1961-68; chmn. bd., chief exec. officer Gould-Nat. Batteries, Inc., 1968; pres., chief exec. officer, dir. Gould Inc., 1968-72, chmn., pres., chief exec. officer, dir., 1972-75, chmn., chief exec. officer, 1975—; dir. 1st Nat. Bank of St. Paul, Penske Corp., Piscataway, N.J., Accumuladores Tudor S.A., Mexico, Compagnie Francaise d'Electro-Chimie, France. Bd. dirs. Bush Found., NCCJ, Nat. Alliance Businessmen, Chgo. Assn. Commerce and Industry, Hwy. Users Fedn., Washington. Served as ensign USNR, 1943-45. Mem. U.S. Polo Assn. (bd. govs.). Clubs: Chgo.; Racquet (Chgo. and N.Y.C.); Barrington (Ill.) Hills Country; Ocean (Ocean Ridge, Fla.); Oak Brook (Ill.) Polo (gov.). Home: Ridge Rd Barrington IL 60010 Office: 10 Gould Center Rolling Meadows IL 60008

YOCAM, DELBERT WAYNE, electronic products mfg. co. exec.; b. Long Beach, Calif., Dec. 24, 1943; s. Royal Delbert and Mary Rose (Gross) Y.; B.A. in Bus. Adminstrn., Calif. State U., Fullerton, 1966; M.B.A., Calif. State U., Long Beach, 1971; m. Janet McVeigh, June 13, 1965; children—Eric Wayne, Christian Jeremy. Mktg./supply changeover coordinator Automotive Assembly div. Ford Motor Co., Dearborn, Mich., 1966-72; prodn. control mgr. Control Data Corp., Hawthorne, Calif., 1972-74; prodn. and material control mgr. Bourns Inc., Riverside, Calif., 1974-76; corp. material mgr. Computer Automation Inc., Irvine, Calif., 1976-78; prodn. planning mgr. central staff ITT Cannon Electric Div., World hdqrs., Santa Ana, Calif., 1978-79; dir. materials Apple Computer Inc., Cupertino, Calif., 1979—; mem. faculty Cypress (Calif.) Coll., 1972-79; co-founder Control Data Corp. Mgmt. Assn., 1974. Active Los Angeles County Heart Assn., 1966. Mem. Am. Prodn. and Inventory Control Soc., Purchasing Mgmt. Assn. Republican. Methodist. Office: Apple Computer Inc 10455 Bandley Dr Cupertino CA 95014

YOCUM, JOHN EMERSON, food processing co. exec.; b. Mansfield, Ohio, Apr. 17, 1938; s. Emerson Phillips and Mildred Halcyian (Gerberich) Y.; B.A., Muskingum Coll., 1962; postgrad. Ohio State U., 1966; M.B.A., U. Ariz., 1969; m. Kelleen Louise Morgan, Sept. 8, 1962; 1 dau., Amy Marie. Sales mgr. Future Products Co., Columbus, Ohio, 1967; computer sales General Electric Co., Los Angeles, 1969-71, Honeywell Info. Systems Inc., Los Angeles, 1971-72; registered rep. Kidder Peabody & Co., Los Angeles, 1972-74; budget and internal audit mgr. Diamond/Sunsweet, Inc., Stockton, Calif., 1974-76, dir. systems and planning, 1976-78, dir. internal audit, 1978—. Served as officer USAF, 1962-66. Cert. internal auditor. Mem. Am. Mgmt. Assn., Inst. Internal Auditors, Amway Distbrs. Assn. Presbyterian. Home: 7005 Yorktown Ct Stockton CA 95209 Office: 1050 S Diamond St Stockton CA 95201

YODER, DAVID, real estate devel. co. exec.; b. Meyersdale, Pa., Oct. 10, 1931; s. Ernest and Lena (Bender) Y.; B.A., Goshen (Ind.) Coll., 1957; postgrad. W.Va. U., 1957-65, U. Vienna, 1962, U. Graz (Austria), 1965; m. Ruby Jeanell Shenk, Sept. 6, 1964; children—Jon, Robert. Exec. v.p. Allegheny Devel. Corp. Inc., Morgantown, W.Va., 1966—; pres. Pineview Realty, Inc., Morgantown, 1970—; sec., treas. Allegheny Realestate Sales, Morgantown, 1975—; dir. Allegheny Devel. Corp., Inc., Pineview Realty, Inc., Allegheny Realestate Sales. Mem. Morgantown Area C. of C., N. Central W.Va. Home Builders Assn. (v.p. 1976, pres. 1977-80), W.Va. Home Builders Assn. (v.p. 1979, expert witness Ways and Means com. U.S. Congress 1979). Home: Winona Ct Morgantown WV 26505 Office: 1225 Pineview Dr Morgantown WV 26505

YODER, JAMES ROBERT, computer sci. cons.; b. Albuquerque, Apr. 19, 1942; s. Robert Bingham and Catherine Louise (Meyer) Y.; B.S., U. Albuquerque, 1965; postgrad. U. N.Mex., 1969-70, 77-80; m. Dolores Mary Pfiester, May 25, 1968; 1 son, Stephen Eric. Tech. staff asst. Sandia Labs., Albuquerque, 1966-75; v.p. Property Data Systems, Inc., Albuquerque, 1970-74; tech. staff asso. Sandia Labs., Albuquerque, 1974—; dir. Property Data Systems, Inc., Albuquerque, 1970-74. Served with U.S. Army, 1966. Republican. Club: Coronado. Home: 3505 Embudito NE Albuquerque NM 87111 Office: Sandia Labs Div 2425 PO Box 5800 Kirtland AFB NM 87185

YODER, JOHN CHRISTIAN, bus. exec.; b. Newton, Kans., Jan. 9, 1951; s. Gideon G. and Stella H. Y.; B.A., Chapman Coll., 1972; J.D., U. Kans., 1975; M.B.A., U. Chgo., 1976. Admitted to Kans. bar, 1975, Ind. bar, 1976; asst. prof. bus. Goshen Coll. (Ind.), 1975-76; pvt. practice law, Hesston, Kans., 1976-77; asso. dist. judge 9th Jud. Dist., Newton, Kans., 1977-80; chmn. bd., v.p., dir. Jay Energy Devel. Co., 1978—; chmn. bd. Stone Mill Wichita, Inc., 1977-80, Stone Mill Bakeries, Inc., 1977—; jud. fellow U.S. Supreme Ct., Washington, 1980—. Bd. dirs. Showalter Villa, Hesston, 1977-80, Substance Abuse Bd. Harvey County, 1977-80. Mem. Am., Kans., Ind., Harvey County bar assns., Nat. Council Juvenile and Family Ct. Judges, Newton C. of C., Hesston C. of C., Newton Jaycees, LWV. Republican. Mennonite. Club: Optimist. Home: 320 Third St NE Washington DC 20002 Office: Office Adminstrv Asst to Chief Justice Supreme Ct US Washington DC 20543

YODICE, FRANK ANTHONY, advt. exec.; b. Paterson, N.J., Feb. 2, 1952; s. Nunzio James and Anna Eleanor (Fiorello) Y.; A.A. in Journalism, Bergen Community Coll., 1973; m. Patricia Lorraine Hancock, Oct. 3, 1971. Sales rep. Bergen Record Corp., Hackensack, N.J., 1971-73; nat. advt. mgr. Ridgewood News, Inc. (N.J.), 1973-74; v.p. prodn. Hank Forssberg, Inc., Hackensack, 1974-79; v.p., account supr. Bozell & Jacobs Advt., Union, N.J., 1979-81; v.p., gen. mgr. Etkins & Harris Advt., N.Y.C., 1981—. Former bd. dirs. Wayne Jaycees. Served with Army N.G., 1972-78. Recipient Adweek citation Advt. Age, 1978. Mem. Ad Club N.J. (dir.), North Jersey Ad Club, N.J. Art Dirs. Club (dir.). Liberal Democrat. Roman Catholic. Clubs: Elks, Knights of Aksarben. Home: 81 Gordon Ave Totowa NJ 07512 Office: Etkins and Harris 232 E 35th St New York NY 10016

YOFFE, MORRIS, health care co. exec.; b. Mt. Carmel, Pa., Aug. 8, 1929; s. Max and Sarah (Wishkin) Y.; B.S., Drexel U., 1953; m. Chickee Esther Faith Margulis, June 25, 1955; children—Seth Michael, Eve Nicole, Josh Aron and Lori Jo (twins). Sr. accountant Adler Faunce & Leonard, C.P.A.'s, Phila., 1956-58; individual practice accounting, Phila., 1958-63; pres. dir. Corp. Planners, Inc., Laverock, Pa., 1962—; sr. partner founder Yoffe, Herman & Co., C.P.A.'s, Phila., 1963-70; founder, dir., pres., chief exec. officer Am. Med Affiliates, Inc., Jenkintown, Pa., 1968—; hearing officer, appeals, HEW and Social Security Adminstrn., 1973—; mem. nat. nursing home costs study Battelle Research, 1974-75. Mem. Cheltenham Twp. (Pa.) Citizens Adv. Bd., 1974—; mem. budget adv. com. Cheltenham Sch. Dist., 1976-78; bd. dirs. Met. Hosp., Phila., 1974—, Solomon Schechter Day Sch., Wynnewood, Pa., 1975—; bd. dirs. Nat. Tay-Sachs, 1976—, Beth Sholom Synagogue, Elkins Park, Pa., 1977—, Laverock Improvement Assn., 1977—, Citizens Crime Commn., Phila., 1978—. Recipient Alexander Van Rensselaer award Drexel U., 1952, State of Israel Health Care Services Tribute award, 1978. Licensed nursing home adminstr., Pa.; C.P.A., Pa. Fellow Am. Coll. Nursing Home Adminstrs.; mem. Am., Pa. insts. C.P.A.'s, Health Care Facilities Pa. (dir.), Am. Health Care Assn., (dir.), Nat. Council Health Care Services, Blue Key, Penna Soc., Met. Phila. Anti-Defamation League (vice chmn. 1977—), Anti-Defamation League Soc. Fellows (nat. vice chmn. 1978—), Drexel U. Astra Club. Clubs: Ashbourne Country, B'nai B'rith (lodge pres. 1960-61). Home: 7724 Morgan Ln Laverock PA 19118 Office: Highland Office Center Pinetown Rd Fort Washington PA 19034

YOKELY, RONALD EUGENE, mech. engr., research corp. exec.; b. High Point, N.C., Feb. 7, 1942; s. Clarence Eugene and Grayce (Waddy) Y.; B.S. in Mech. Engring., N.C. State U., Raleigh, 1963; m. E. Joanne Williams, July 6, 1963; children—Rhonda Lynette, Rene Michelle. Test engr. McDonnell Aircraft Corp., St. Louis, 1963-67; sect. mgr. simulation products div. Singer Co., Houston, 1967-73;

engring. mgr. Aeronutronic Ford Corp., Houston, 1973-76; sr. v.p. Onyx Corp., Bethesda, Md., 1976-78; pres., treas. Acumenics Research & Tech., Inc., Bethesda, Md., 1978—; cons. FAA, 1975-76. Registered profl. engr., Tex. Mem. AIAA, IEEE, Nat. Soc. Profl. Engrs., AAAS, Reston (Va.) Homeowners Assn. (council), Omega Psi Phi. Episcopalian. Co-author: Microcomputers—A Technology Forecast and Assessment to the Year 2000, 1980. Home: 11453 Purple Beech Dr Reston VA 22091 Office: 4340 East-West Hwy Suite 808 Bethesda MD 20014

YOMINE, DANIEL JOSEPH, operations co. exec.; b. Chgo., Sept. 22, 1921; s. Nicholas D. and Josephine (Ciancio) Y.; student Northwestern U., 1943-45, Am. U., 1951-53; m. Helen Mabel Douzanis, Jan. 30, 1943; 1 son, Daniel Frank. Tool engr. No. Tool & Die Co., 1944-50; prodn. engring. mgr. ACF Industries, Riverdale, Md., 1950-55; mfg. engring. mgr. Bell & Howell Co., Chgo., 1955-59, gen. mgr., dir., Japan, 1959-62, corporate v.p., group pres., Lincolnwood, Ill., 1977—; dir., chmn. exec. com. Tomioka Optical Co., Japan, 1959-62; asst. corporate sec., also div. operations mgr. Ampex Consumer Products div. Ampex Corp., 1962-67, dir. corporate staff mfg., Redwood City, Calif., 1967-68, v.p., 1968-71; v.p. Internat. Video Corp., Sunnyvale, Calif., 1971-72, sr. v.p., 1973; pres., chief exec. officer, dir. Consolidated Video Systems, Inc., Santa Clara, 1973-75; pres., treas. Convid Internat., Santa Clara, 1974-75; corp. v.p. mfg. Bell & Howell Co., 1977—; dir. Computer Image Corp., Fernseh Inc. Mem. Am. C. of C., Tokyo, Japan, 1959-62. Mem. Mfg. Engrs. Soc., Ill. C. of C. Am. Arbitration Assn., Am. Mgmt. Assn., Peninsula Mfrs. Assn. (dir.), Western Electronic Mfr.'s Assn. Presbyn. (usher). Clubs: Executive (Chgo.); Commonwealth of Calif. (San Francisco). Patentee in field. Home: 263 W Onwentsia Rd Lake Forest IL 60045 Office: 7100 McCormick Rd Lincolnwood IL

YONEZAWA, SHIGERU, telegraph and telephone co. cons.; b. Toyama Prefecture, Japan, Feb. 1, 1911; s. Yososhichi and Kimiko (Yamazaki) Y.; B. Engring., Tokyo U., 1933, Dr. Engring., 1942; m. Tokuko Ariyoshi, Oct. 15, 1941; children—Jun-ichi, Kenji. Engr., Ministry Communications, Nippon Telegraph & Telephone Pub. Corp., Japan, 1933-53; mng. dir., 1953-60, dir., maintenance bur., 1953-56, dir. plant engring. bur., 1956-58, dir. elec. communications lab., 1958-60, sr. mng. dir., chief engr., 1960-62, exec. v.p., 1962-65, pres., 1965-77, cons., 1977—. Mem. Japan Sci. Council, 1959-65; chmn. Inst. Elec. Communication Engrs., Japan, 1960-61; pres. Internat. Conf. on Microwaves Circuit and Information Theory, Tokyo, 1964; dir. Fedn. Econ. Orgn., 1972—, mem. council sci. and tech., 1974—; dir. Assn. 1970 Expn. Fellow IEEE; mem. Telecommunications Assn. (pres. 1980—). Rotarian. Author: Microwave Communication, 1963. Home: 37-17 2-chome Denenchofu Ota-ku Tokyo 145 Japan Office: 1-6 1-chome Uchisaiwai-cho Chiyoda-ku Tokyo 100 Japan

YORK, DOUGLAS ARTHUR, mfg., constrn. co. exec.; b. Centralia, Ill., June 5, 1940; s. Harry Bernice and Violet Alvera (Johnstone) Y.; student San Diego State Jr. Coll., 1957; m. Linda Kay McIntosh, Sept. 13, 1958; children—Deborah Ann, Darren Anthony. With Meredith & Simpson Constrn. Co./DBA Pressure Cool Co., Indio, Calif., 1958—, v.p., 1968—, sec., gen. mgr., 1976—. Commr., Riverside County Parks; mem. Bldg. and Housing Appeals Bd., City of Indio. Mem. ASHRAE, Calif. Assn. Park and Recreations Commrs. and Bd. Mems. Republican. Office: 83-801 Ave 45 Indio CA 92201

YORK, JEROME BAILEY, automotive mfg. co. exec.; b. Memphis, June 22, 1938; s. Jerome Bailey and Rae Lolette (Irving) Y.; B.S., U.S. Mil. Acad., 1960; M.S., Mass. Inst. Tech., 1961; M.B.A., U. Mich., 1966; m. June 11, 1960 (div.); m. 2d, 1977; children—Lisa, Julie, Jerome Bailey III. Sr. project engr. Pontiac Motor div. Gen. Motors Corp., 1962-67; mgr. advanced bus. planning Ford Motor Co., Dearborn, Mich., 1967-70; staff v.p. bus. planning RCA Corp., N.Y.C., 1970-72, pres. Hertz Equipment Rental Corp. subs., 1972-75; group v.p. Baker Industries, Inc., Parsippany, N.J., 1976-78; pres. Delta Truck Body Co., Inc., Montgomeryville, Pa., 1978-79; dir. engring. adminstrn. Chrysler Corp., Highland Park, Mich., 1979—. Served with U.S. Army, 1956-60. Registered profl. engr., Mich. Patentee carbureation and fuel injection. Office: PO Box 1118 Detroit MI 48288

YORK, JERRY HARDING, ins. holding co. exec.; b. Brazil, Ind., June 17, 1922; s. Noble H. and Beatrice (Clift) Y.; student Butler U., 1942-44, Ind. U., 1944-46; m. Margaret Ann Rankin, Mar. 30, 1947; children—Becky Ann, Kathy Sue, Cindy Lee, Stephen Scott. Spl. agt. Prudential Life Ins. Co., Indpls., 1947-49; dist. mgr. Midwestern Life Ins. Co., Indpls., 1949-52; agt. Indpls. Life Ins. Co., 1952-54; gen. agt. Standard Life Ins. Co., Indpls., 1954-56; gen. agt., regional mgr., dir. sales, v.p. Ind. Liberty Life Ins., Mich., 1960-67; state mgr. Ind. Liberty Life Ins. Co., Ind., 1967-68; v.p. Arlington Nat. Life Ins. Co., Columbus, Ohio, 1969-70; pres. Gt. Lake Corp., Ohio and Ind., 1970-80; pres., treas., chmn. bd. Wesley Otterbein Corp., Indpls., 1973—; dir. John Wesley Corp., First City Corp., Am. Continental Corp. Mem. Carmel/Clay Concerned Citizens Com., Carmel Plan Commn., Carmel Bd. Zoning Appeals; chmn. Carmel and Indpls. Devel. Com.; mem. fin. com. Hamilton County Republican Party. Recipient various ins. awards. Mem. Nat. Assn. Life Underwriters, Nat. Assn. Securities Dealers, others. Republican. Presbyterian. Clubs: Indpls. Athletic, Woodland Country, Rotary, Masons, Shriners. Home: 40 Maple Crest Dr Carmel IN 46032 Office: 3959 Central Ave Indianapolis IN 46205

YORK, W. THOMAS, corp. exec.; b. Archdale, N.C., Oct. 14, 1933; s. Shelley Clyde and Bertie Jane (Dunn) Y.; B.S., U. N.C., 1955, M.B.A., 1958; m. Patricia Louise Permenter, June 16, 1955; children—Tucker, Jonathan, Rheney. Mgr. accounting and fin. analysis Philco-Ford, Phila., 1958-68; asst. corp. comptroller, dir. corp. acctg. AMF Inc., 1969, corp. comptroller, 1969, corp. v.p., 1970-72, v.p. fin., 1972-74, exec. v.p., 1974, pres., chief operating officer, 1975—, chmn., chief exec. officer, 1978—, also dir.; dir. Conn. Mut. Life Ins. Co., Scovill Mfg. Co., Diamond Shamrock Corp. Trustee Manhattanville Coll. Served to lt. USNR, 1955-57. Home: Hemlock Hill Rd New Canaan CT 06340 Office: AMF Inc 777 Westchester Ave White Plains NY 10604

YORKS, LYLE, mgmt. cons. co. exec.; b. Abington, Pa., July 18, 1946; s. Lyle and Emilie (Trindle) Y.; B.A., Tusculum Coll., 1968; M.A., Vanderbilt U., 1969; m. Joanne Mary Griffin, Dec. 28, 1968; children—Lyle, Tracy, Russell. Research asso. Meharry Med. Coll., Nashville, 1969-70; analyst corp. systems and methods Travelers Ins. Cos., Hartford, Conn., 1970-72; sr. asso. Drake-Beam & Assos., N.Y.C., 1972-75, v.p., 1975-77, sr. v.p., 1977—; instr. program in manpower planning New Sch. for Social Research, N.Y.C., 1974; asso. prof. mgmt. scis. Eastern Conn. State Coll., Willimantic, 1977—; guest lectr. Air Command Staff Coll. and Base Comdrs. Sch., USAF. NSF fellow, 1969. Mem. Acad. of Mgmt., Assn. for Systems Mgmt., Pi Gamma Mu. Author: A Radical Approach to Job Enrichment, 1976; Job Enrichment Revisited, 1979; Effective Communication in Real Estate Management, 1979; contbr. articles to profl. jours. Home: 281 Hanks Hill Rd Storrs CT 06268 Office: 277 Park Ave New York City NY 10017

YOSHIKAWA, TAKATOSHI, beauty, barber and dental equipment mfg. co. exec.; b. Osaka, Japan, Apr. 23, 1930; s. Hidenobu and Shizue (Morita) Y.; B.A., Tokyo U., 1954; m. Akiko Inoue, May 29, 1957; children—Takaaki, Hirokazu. Shipbldg. engr. Osk Ltd., Osaka, 1954-55; products mgr. Takara Chukosho Co. Ltd., Osaka, 1955-56, market researcher, N.Y.C., 1956; founder Takara Co. N.Y. Inc., N.Y.C., 1956—; mng. dir. Takara Belmont Co. Ltd., Osaka, 1965—; pres. Takara Co. Can. Ltd., Mississauga, Ont., 1966—, Koken Mfg. Co. Inc., St. Louis, 1969; dir. Takara Standard Co. Ltd., Osaka, Takara Belmont London Ltd., subs.'s in France, W.Ger., Brazil. Mem. Nat. Beauty and Barber Mfrs. Assn., Japan Soc. Clubs: Fiddlers' Elbow Country, Nippon. Office: 1 Belmont Dr Somerset NJ 08873

YOUGER, ROBERT WAYNE, utility exec.; b. Covington, Ky., Mar. 24, 1946; s. Robert N. and Viola (White) Y.; B.B.A. in Accounting, U. Cin., 1969; M.B.A. in Mgmt., Xavier U., Cin., 1976; m. Rose Mary Herrmann, Sept. 7, 1968; children—Jennifer, Christopher, Scott. Fin. staff asst. accounting dept. Cin. Gas Electric Co., 1969-73, adminstrv. asst. 1973-76, coordinator customers billing and collections, 1976—. Bd. dirs. Mut. Benefit Credit Union, Inc., 1972—. Office: PO Box 960 Cincinnati OH 45201

YOUMANS, PAUL EDWIN, investment banker; b. Fort Smith, Ark., June 1, 1902; s. Frank Abijah and Delia (Enroughty) Y.; B.S. in Bus. and Pub. Adminstrn., U. Mo., 1923; m. Katherine St. John Carter, June 7, 1928 (dec. Jan. 1969); 1 dau., Anne Carter (Mrs. William R. Mason). Entered investment banking through Nat. Bank of Commerce, St. Louis, 1923; joined Internat. Trust Co., Denver, 1927; with Nat. City Co., 1928-29; joined Sullivan & Co., 1930, partner, 1941-46; chmn., chief exec. officer, dir. Bosworth, Sullivan & Co., Inc., Denver; dir. Inter-Regional Fin. Group, Inc., Mpls.; v.p. Dain Bosworth, Mpls., mem. N.Y. Stock Exchange. Trustee, Blue Shield Plan, Denver, 1962-71. Mem. Investment Bankers Assn. Am. (gov. 1952-55), Nat. Assn. Securities Dealers (gov. 1960-63), Assn. Stock Exchange Firms (gov. 1963-69), Phi Delta Theta. Episcopalian. Clubs: University, Mile High, Rotary (Denver). Home: 480 S Marion St Pkwy Denver CO 80209 Office: 950 17th St Denver CO 80202

YOUNG, ALAN RICHARD, oil and gas land leasing co. exec.; b. Chester, Pa., Dec. 10, 1935; s. Lawrence Thomas and Elsie (Livesey) Y.; B.A., Calif. State U. Los Angeles, 1966, M.S., 1972; m. Judith Ruth Gartner, Sept. 17, 1954; children—Cherie, Debra, Susan. Purchasing agt. Western Dynamics Corp., Gardena, Calif., 1959; buyer Elotec Corp., El Monte, Calif., 1960; various positions Lockheed Propulsion Co., Lockheed Calif. Co., 1960-62, 65-68; bus. mgr. standard missile engring. programs Gen. Dynamics Corp., Pomona, Calif., 1962-65, 68—; pres. Westgate Resources, Inc., 1980—. Served with USAF, 1953-59. Mem. Nat. Mgmt. Assn. Republican. Home: 1342 W Hollowell St Ontario CA 91762 Office: 1675 W Mission Blvd Pomona CA 91766

YOUNG, BILLIE, pub. co. exec., author; b. Bklyn., June 27, 1933; d. Albert and Reda (Bromberg) Y.; student Bklyn. Coll., 1949-51, New Sch. Social Research, 1953-54; m. Simeon Paget, Jan. 2, 1959; children—Bruce, Richard, Dana, Laurie, Lief, Kristie. Copywriter Camp Chem. Co., Bklyn., 1950-53; reporter Cowles Communications, Deer Park, N.Y., 1968-69; pres. Ashley Books, Inc., Port Washington, N.Y., 1970—, Peerage Books Ltd.; treas. Born Blessed Publs., Los Angeles, 1973—; lectr.; guest numerous TV talk shows; promoter books, cons. in field; free-lance writer. Dir. pub. relations Am. Repertory Theatre; active North Shore Community Arts Center, 1953-59, North Shore Hosp., 1958-63. Mem. ADA, Am. Booksellers Assn., Assn. Am. Publishers, Publishers Ad Club, Cancer Care, Com. Small Mag. Editors and Pubs. Author: The Naked Chef, 1971; Vive La Difference, 1976. Contbr. articles to newspapers, popular mags. Promoted Naked Came the Stranger as author, Penelope Ashe, 1969. Office: 30 Main St Port Washington NY 11050

YOUNG, DONALD E., business equipment co. exec.; b. Pitts., July 23, 1920; s. William P. and Helen (Bollenberg) Y.; B.A., George Washington U., 1948; M.B.A., Harvard, 1951; m. Pauline Schloesser; children—Leigh, Anna Dey, Lance. Spl. agt. FBI, 1948-49; with Office Spl. Investigations, 1951-53; asst. to pres. G.H. Packwood Co., 1953; asst. to v.p. and treas., bank sales rep. regional bank mgr. The Todd Co., 1956; asst. to v.p. marketing Burroughs Corp., Detroit, then exec. asst. to pres., 1960-61, asst. v.p.-gen., 1961-66, v.p. corporate communications, 1966-76, sr. v.p., 1976-79, exec. v.p., 1980—; dir. Mich. Nat. Bank Detroit. Bd. dirs. Detroit Conv. Bur., Boys Clubs Met. Detroit, Mich. Blue Cross and Blue Shield, Civic Searchlight; bd. govs. Nat. Invest-in-Am., Greater Mich. Found.; bd. of mems. Mich. Coll. Found.; trustee Founders Soc., Detroit Inst. Arts, William Beaumont Hosp., Detroit Renaissance, Inst. Econ. Edn.; trustee Met. Fund. Served to capt. USAF, 1941-46; ETO. Decorated D.F.C. with oak leaf cluster, Air medal with 5 oak leaf clusters. Mem. Soc. Former Spl. Agts. FBI, Newcomen Soc. N.A., Mich. (charter), Greater Detroit (chmn., dir.) chambers commerce. Clubs: Harvard Business School of Detroit (dir.), Detroit, Economic, Adcraft, Harvard of New York (N.Y.C.); Bloomfield Hills Country. Home: 376 Dunston Rd Bloomfield Hills MI 48013 Office: Burroughs Corp Detroit MI 48232

YOUNG, DONALD LOUIS, accountant; b. Cherokee, Okla., Feb. 5, 1933; s. Lewis Edward and Amy Viola (Brannon) Y.; B.B.A., Northwestern Okla. State U., 1958; postgrad. So. Meth. U., 1966; m. Dorothy Marie Strawn, May 24, 1953; children—Louis Price, Craig Evan, Stephani Jill. Accountant, Neff & Assos., Albuquerque, 1958-59; sr. accountant Cosden Oil & Chem. Co., Big Spring, Tex., 1959-64; systems mgr. Am. Petrofina, Dallas, 1964-70; asst. v.p. accounting ops. Clinton Oil, Wichita, Kans., 1970-72; mgr. parent co. accounting Jack P. DeBoer Assos., Wichita, 1972; bus. mgr. Permian dist. Atlantic Richfield Co., Midland, Tex., 1972-79; dir. investment acctg. ARCO Oil & Gas Co. div. Atlantic Richfield Co., Dallas, 1979—. Active Boy Scouts Am. Served with NG, 1950-58. Mem. Petroleum Accountants Soc. (past pres. Midland). Methodist. Home: 6315 Oakleaf Ln Dallas TX 75248 Office: PO Box 2819 Dallas TX 77221

YOUNG, DOUGLAS ALBERT, JR., Realtor; b. Oxford, Miss., Mar. 1, 1939; s. Douglas Albert and Pauline (Stafford) Y.; B.A., Delta State U., Cleve., Miss., 1967; postgrad. student U. Mo. Sch. Law, Kansas City, 1969-70; m. Susan Adams, May 31, 1969; 1 son, Douglas Albert. Dir. agy. ops. central div. St. Paul Title Ins. Corp., Kansas City, Mo., 1969-73; v.p. A.W. Zimmer & Co., Kansas City, Mo., 1973-77, L.J. Baer & Co., Kansas City, Mo., 1977-79; pres. Douglas A. Young & Co., Kansas City, Mo., 1980—; 3rd dist. rep. Jackson County Legislature, 1978-82, mem. Public Works com., 1978, Land Use com., 1978; chmn. Legis. Affairs com., 1979. Mem. exec. com. Bacchus Found., 1975; mem. Jackson County Rev. Commn., 1977, Jackson County Econ. Devel. Commn., 1978; bd. dirs. Mo. Assn. Counties, 1978, Goodwill Industries of Greater Kansas City, 1979-80; adminstrv. bd. St. John's United Methodist Ch., 1978-81; mem. exec. com. Truman Med. Center, 1980. Mem. Real Estate Bd. Kans. City (dir., chmn. polit. affairs com.), Mo. Assn. Realtors (dir. 1973—, exec. com. 1977-78, trustee), Nat. Assn. Realtors, Nat. Assn. Counties (land-use steering com. 1979-80), SAR (sec. 1974—). Methodist. Office: 106 W 14th St Kansas City MO 64105

YOUNG, FRANK NOLAN, JR., constrn. co. exec.; b. Tacoma, Feb. 26, 1941; s. Frank N. and Antoinette (Mahncke) Y.; B.A., U. Wash., 1963; m. Susan E. Bayley, Aug. 13, 1965; children—Sandra Suzanne, Frank Nolan. Vice pres., dir. Strand Inc., Seattle, 1966-73; pres., chief exec. officer, treas., dir. Gall Landau Young Constrn. Co., Bellevue, Wash., 1973—; v.p., sec., dir. Cascade Structures, Kirkland, 1972—. Active YMCA, Boys Club. Served with USCGR, 1964-70. Mem. Associated Gen. Contractors (chpt. trustee). Republican. Episcopalian. Clubs: Links, Overlake, Golf and Country, Sun Valley Ski, Alpental Ski, Elks, Shriners, Masons. Home: 5005 E Mercer Way Mercer Island WA 98040 Office: 1934 132d Ave NE Bellevue WA 98005

YOUNG, GEORGE DALE, ins. co. exec.; b. Howard County, Mo., June 16, 1930; s. Herbert Overton and Hazel (Pipes) Y.; B.S., U. Mo., Columbia, 1950, Ph.D., 1958; M.S., Cornell U., 1952; m. Willie Podesta, Nov. 6, 1976; children—Melissa Ann, Melanie Kay, Magie Podesta. Adminstrv. v.p., sec. Transit Casualty Co., St. Louis, 1959-69; sr. v.p., dir. Nat. Indemn- ity Co., Omaha, 1969—; pres., dir. Columbia Ins. Co., Omaha; dir. Redwood Fire & Casualty Co., Los Angles, So. Casualty Ins. Co., Alexandria, La., Nat. Fire & Marine Co., Omaha. Mem. Mo. Ho. of Reps., 1955-61. Served with USAF, 1952-54, 61-62. Chartered property and casualty underwriter; chartered fin. analyst. Mem. Ind. Reins. Underwriters. Democrat. Methodist. Clubs: Omaha, Omaha Country. Home: 6037 Young Plaza Omaha NE 68152 Office: 3024 Harney St Omaha NE 68131

YOUNG, GERALDINE CAMPBELL, elec. co. exec.; b. Emporium, Pa., Sept. 4, 1919; d. Walter S. and Edna (Casbeer) Campbell; grad. high sch.; m. Philip S. Young, July 25, 1955 (dec. June 1960); stepchildren—Philip L., Lillian Jean (Mrs. Benjamin E. Waller III), Mary Catherine. Bookkeeper, Western Auto Store, Wellsboro, Pa., 1937-39, mgr., 1939-49; agt. Wingate Ins. Agy., Wellsboro, 1949-56; owner Young Ins. Agy., Wellsboro, 1956-60; v.p. Wellsboro, Elec. Co., 1956-60, pres., 1960—. Bd. dirs. Grow Found. Mem. Bus. and Profl. Women's Club, Am. Inst. Mgmt., Internat. Platform Assn. Episcopalian. Home: 59 Waln St Wellsboro PA 16901 Office: 19 Waln St Wellsboro PA 16901

YOUNG, J. LOWELL, city ofcl.; b. Union Utah, July 22, 1921; s. William Penn and Berenice (Dunster) Y.; student U. Utah, 1940-42, 46-47; certificate pub. fin. adminstrn. U. Wis., 1976; m. LeOra Hess, Mar. 16, 1947; children—Candy Lee, Von Lowell, Ray Lowell, Melody. Sales mgr. Guy E. Kelly Co., Frederick, Md., 1947-50; advt. salesman Deseret News, Salt Lake City, 1950-52; bldg. splty. salesman Buehner Block Co., Salt Lake City, 1952-60; office mgr. Bestway Products Co., Salt Lake City, 1960-61; sr. gen. clk. Disbursements div. Hercules, Inc., Magna, Utah, 1961-66; city treas. Murray City (Utah) Corp., 1966—; pres. Valley Arts Co. Chmn., United Way, 1976-77; mem. citizens advisory com. Murray City Sch. Bd. Mem. book com. Murray City Bicentennial project funds solicitor Murray City Amphitheater, 1975. Stake pres. Ch. of Jesus Christ of Latter Day Saints, 1968-78, bishop of Murray 6th ward, 1960-66, high councilman, 1967-68, with missionary service, N.Y., N.J., Pa., 1942-44. Mem. Murray City C. of C. (outstanding community service award). Served with USNR, 1944-46. Mem. Mcpl. Treasurers Assn. U.S. and Can. (named outstanding treas. of yr., 1976-77; recipient awards meritorious service 1972-73), Ill. Mcpl. Treasurers Assn., Wis. Mcpl. Treasurers Assn. Mem. Utah Mcpl. Treasurers Assn. (exec. dir., compiler-editor handbook). Author publs. in field. Home: 8 W Valley Dr Murray UT 84107 Office: 5461 S State St Murray UT 84107

YOUNG, JAMES CHARLES, advt., mktg. exec.; b. Shawnee, Okla., Nov. 25, 1931; s. James Carl and Evelyn Lucille (McEwen) Y.; student Oklahoma City U., 1949-50; B.B.A., Ga. State U., 1963; m. Carol Ann Gesford, Feb. 22, 1958; children—James Charles, Jr., Jennifer Lynn. Asst. exec. dir. Kappa Alpha Order, Atlanta, 1956-63; dir. info. and edn. Okla. Restaurant Assn., Oklahoma City, 1963-64; mgr. communications Oklahoma City, Aero Comdr. div. N. Am. Rockwell, 1964-68; dir. pub. relations Star Mfg. Co., Oklahoma City, 1968-72; dir. mktg. communications C-E Natco, Combustion Engring., Inc., Tulsa, 1972—; lectr. journalism U. Okla., Norman, 1969-70. Mem. Oklahoma City Beautiful Orgn., 1970-72; div. chmn. Oklahoma City United Appeal, 1969-71; budget com. Tulsa United Way, 1977; fund raising com. Oklahoma City Jr. Achievement Assn., 1970; mem. gen. bd. Tulsa March of Dimes. Served with inf. U.S. Army, 1950-52. Decorated Japanese, Korean occupation medals, Korean campaign medal with 1 battle star, unit citation. Recipient B.L. Sempter meml. award Oklahoma City United Appeal, 1969, 1970; editor of yr. award Oklahoma City chpt. Indsl. Editors Assn., 1967; 1st place advt. awards, 1971-73, 1975-77; best indsl. publ. award of excellence, 1968. Mem. Pub. Relations Soc. of Am. (accredited), Bus./Profl. Advt. Assn. (accredited), Internat. Assn. Business Communicators (pres. Oklahoma City chpt. 1968-69), Kappa Alpha (editor jour. 1959-71, exec. council 1974-75). Republican. Presbyterian. Clubs: Lakeview Country, The Summit of Tulsa, Tulsa Press, Masons (32 deg.). Editor Midsouthwest Foodservice Mag., 1965-67. Home: 7423 E 70th St S Tulsa OK 74133 Office: PO Box 1710 Tulsa OK 74101

YOUNG, JERRALD FRANCIS, fin. analyst; b. Ogden, Utah, Sept. 25, 1921; s. Johnty Flitton and Viola Elizabeth (Johnson) Y.; student Weber State Coll., 1939-40, 46; B.B.A., Utah State U., 1951; M.B.A., Harvard, 1953; m. Genevieve Schaerrer Clayton, Aug. 6, 1943; children—Jon C., Larry C. (dec.), Frances Ann, Mark C. Accountant with various firms, Utah, Okla., Calif., 1941-50; controller, dir. econ. research Pacific Airlines, San Francisco Internat. Airport, 1955-58; subcontract mgmt. specialist, fin. analyst, adminstr. Lockheed Missiles & Space Co. Sunnyvale, Calif., 1958—; prin. J. F. Young Enterprises, Introspectrum Co., Sunnyvale, 1974—; dir. 3 cos.; instr. Foothill Community Coll Dist., 1967—; lectr., cons. in field. Served with USN, 1942-45. Decorated Bronze Star; recipient seven cost performance awards, Lockheed Missiles & Space Co., named Employee of Month, 1973. Mem. Nat. Mgmt. Assn., Faculty Assn. Continuing Edn. (pres. 1973-75), Harvard Alumni Assn. Mem. Ch. of Jesus Christ of Latter-day Saints. Author: Workbook for Success in Entrepreneurship, 1974; Decision Making for Small Business Management, 1977; Human Relations for the Individual, 1980; others. Home: 1474 Wright Ave Sunnyvale CA 94087

YOUNG, JOHN ALAN, electronics co. exec.; b. Nampa, Idaho, Apr. 24, 1932; s. Lloyd Arthur and Karen Eliza (Miller) Y.; B.S. in Elec. Engring., Oreg. State U., 1953; M.B.A., Stanford U., 1958; m. Rosemary Murray, Aug. 1, 1954; children—Gregory, Peter, Diana. With Hewlett Packard Co., 1958—, gen. mgr. microwave div., 1963-68; v.p. electronics products group, Palo Alto, Calif., 1968-74, exec. v.p., 1974-77, pres., 1977—, chief exec. officer, 1978—; dir. Dillingham Corp., Wells-Fargo Bank. Nat. chmn. corp. gifts Stanford U., 1973-77, chmn. ann. fund, 1969-73, adv. council Grad. Sch. Bus., 1968-73, 75—, trustee, 1977—; bd. govs. Stanford Assos.; co-chmn. Mid Peninsula Urban Coalition. Served with USAF, 1954-56. Mem. Am. Electronics Assn. Office: 1501 Page Mill Rd Palo Alto CA 94304

YOUNG, KENNETH MARR, Realtor; b. Honolulu, Sept. 30, 1922; s. John Alexander and Alloe Louise (Marr) Y.; B.A., Stanford, 1946; m. Mary Jennie Crudele, Nov. 13, 1976; children—David Michael, Barbara Ann Morgan, Peter Thomas, Sandra Bingham. Asst. treas., mgr. land dept. Oahu Ry. & Land Co., Honolulu, 1952-61; v.p. Dillingham Corp., Honolulu, 1961-67; pres. K.M. Young & Assos., Inc., Kailua-Kone, Hawaii, 1967—. Pres. Honolulu Bd. Realtors, 1965; mem. Kona Bd. Realtors. Named Hawaii's Realtor of Yr., 1966. Mem. Nat. Assn. Realtors, Inst. Real Estate Mgmt., Nat. Inst. Real Estate Brokers, Am. Right-of-Way Assn. Office: 75-5707 B Alii Dr Kailua-Kona HI 96740

YOUNG, LEO FRANKLIN, mail order co. exec.; b. Houston, Nov. 20, 1944; s. Mamie Smith Young; grad. Elkins Inst., 1976; 1 dau., Elizabeth. Owner, pres. Baabys L.T.D., Houston, 1972—. Chmn. Civic Club, 1977-80. Served with U.S. Army, 1966-68. Recipient citation Dept. Energy, 1979. Mem. Internat. Mail Order Assn. Democrat. Baptist. Home: 8319 S Breeze St Houston TX 77071 Office: 8322 S Breeze St Houston TX 77071

YOUNG, NORMAN, psychologist, business exec.; b. Bklyn., May 30, 1925; s. Macklyn and Estelle (Carmine) Y.; Diploma in Engring., U. Dayton, 1945; B.S., Coll. City N.Y., 1948; M.A., Columbia, 1949, Ph.D., 1957; M.Ed., U. Ill., 1950; m. Myrna Lewis, Mar. 20, 1947; children—Todd, Heidi, Gretchen. Instr. psychology U. Ill., Urbana, 1949-51; analytical statistician USPHS, 1950; research psychologist Carnegie Found. Project, Columbia, 1951-53; pvt. practice psychotherapy, 1953; sr. writer ABC-TV, N.Y.C., 1953-54; adviser, dir. Anahist div. Warner Lambert Pharm. Corp., Hastings, N.Y., 1954-59; v.p. Ted Bates Advt. Agy., N.Y.C., 1959-63; sr. v.p., dir. Levitt & Sons, Inc., Lake Success, N.Y., 1963-68; pres. ITT Levitt Devel. Corp., N.Y.C., 1968-70; pres., chmn. bd. ITT Community Devel. Corp., N.Y.C., 1970-76; exec. v.p. Gen. Devel. Corp., Miami, Fla., 1976—; chmn. Neighborhood Realty Group U.S.A., 1977—; prof. psychology, math., etymology Rutgers U., New Brunswick, N.J., 1952-53, N.Y. U., 1953-54, Coll. City N.Y., 1960-61, Bklyn. Coll., 1953-54, Pace Coll., 1959-60, Hunter Coll., 1960-63; guest lectr. Princeton, U.S. Mil. Acad., U. Notre Dame, Cornell U., 1972, U. Singapore, Chulalongkorn U., Thailand; lectr. history of urban settlements, urban devel. Yale U., Princeton U., U.S. Mil. Acad., U. Teheran, U. Singapore, Bar Ilan U., Tel Aviv, 1975-78, Chulalongkorn U., Bangkok, Thailand. Bd. dirs. Insts. Religion and Health. Served with AUS, 1943-45. Mem. AAAS, Am. Psychol. Assn., N.Y., Ill. acads. sci., Psi Chi. Contbr. articles to profl. sci. jours. Home: 21 E 81st St New York City NY 10028 also 6969 Collins Ave Miami Beach FL 33141 also East Quogue NY 11942 Office: 1111 S Bayshore Dr Miami FL 33131

YOUNG, RALPH EUGENE, ins. co. exec.; b. Terry, Mont., Sept. 5, 1923; s. Ingval Ralph and Alice Elizabeth (DeVine) Y.; A.B., Carroll Coll., Helena, Mont., 1943; M.S., State U. Iowa, 1949; m. Joan P. McCarthy, Oct. 3, 1945; children—Candace (Mrs. Robert G. Frie), Barbara (Mrs. Thomas Keegan), Stephen Ralph, Karen (Mrs. Robert Shields), Robert Eugene, Richard Donald. Hydraulic engr. U.S. Geol. Survey, Helena, Mont., 1946-47; with Western Life Ins. Co., St. Paul, 1949-78, asst. actuary, 1951-56, asso. actuary, 1956-62, actuary, 1962, actuarial v.p., 1964, exec. v.p., 1969, pres., 1970, chmn., chief exec. officer, 1976-78; also dir.; pres., dir. St. Paul Life and Casualty, 1971-73, St. Paul Life Ins. Co., 1973-78, Provident Life Ins. Co., 1979—; Instr. bus. Carroll Coll., part time 1949-56; cons. State Indsl. Accident Bd. Mont., 1955-61; past dir. St. Paul Fire and Marine Ins. Co., St. Paul Investors, Inc., St. Paul Advisers, Inc. Mem. Gov.'s Com. on Hiring Physically Handicapped, 1959-61; pres. Cherry Hill Civic Assn., 1965, Dakota County chpt. Am. Field Service, 1966-68; gen. chmn. cardiovascular research and tng. center fund raising dr. Variety Heart Hosp. U. Minn., 1973-75; nat. co-chmn. parents' council Coll. of St. Catherine, St. Paul, 1973-79. Bd. dirs., treas. Kidney Found. of Upper Midwest, 1975; bd. dirs. Nat. Kidney Found., 1976-78; bd. dirs., v.p. Bismarck Devel. Assn., 1979—. Served to lt. (j.g.) USNR, 1943-46. Mem. Ins. Fedn. Minn. (chmn. bd., mem. exec. com. 1970-79), Am. Council Life Ins. (dir. 1977-79), St. Paul Area C. of C. (dir. 1977-78), Am. Acad. Actuaries, Pacific, Twin Cities actuarial clubs, St. Paul C. of C. (dir. 1976-79). Clubs: Apple Creek Country (Bismarck); Variety Internat. (hon.); Rotary. Office: 316 N 5th St Bismarck ND 58501

YOUNG, RAYMOND THEODORE, heavy equipment mfg. co. exec.; b. Waco, Tex., Dec. 29, 1922; s. John Charles and Anna Marie (Huber) Y.; student Waco Tech. Sch., 1945-47; m. Frances Marie Markum, Apr. 29, 1948; 1 dau., Mary Catherine. Pres., Young Bros. Inc., Waco, 1948-64; pres., Slurry Seal, Inc., Waco, Tex., 1964—, also dir. Mem. Pres.'s Council Export Expansion. Bd. dirs. Providence Hosp., Waco, Tex., 1966-71. Served with USNR, 1942-45. Roman Catholic. Patentee in field. Home: 1148 Knotty Oaks Dr Waco TX 76710 Office: PO Box 7677 Waco TX 76710

YOUNG, RICHARD EDWARD, JR., mgmt. cons.; b. Balt., Dec. 30, 1941; s. Richard Edward and Maggie Bell (McQueen) Y.; B.A., U. Md., 1971; M. City and Regional Planning, Rutgers U., 1973; J.D., Seton Hall U., 1979; m. Carol Emile Gette, Nov. 27, 1969; children—Joyce Ann, Jeffrey Wendell. Housing insp. Balt. Dept. Housing and Comml. Devel., 1967-71; urban planner N.J. Dept. Community Affairs, 1971-72, HUD, 1972-73; asso. dir. community planning and devel. United Way Essex and West Hudson (N.J.), 1973-74; econ. devel. dir. City of Newark, 1974—; pres. R.E. Young Assos., export mgmt. cons., New Brunswick, N.J., 1973—; instr. N.Y. U., 1973-79, Essex County Coll., 1979—. Trustee N.J. Neuropsychiat. Inst., 1977—; trustee, v.p. Joint Connection, 1976-79. Served to maj. AUS, 1964-66. Tri-State Regional Planning Commn. fellow, 1971-73; minority scholar N.J. Dept. Higher Edn., 1974. Mem. Am. Inst. Cert. Planners, N.J. Soc. Profl. Planners. Roman Catholic. Clubs: Internat. 100 Blackmen N.Y.

YOUNG, RICHARD JAMES, bus. services co. exec.; b. Syracuse, N.Y., Nov. 21, 1934; s. Carl V. and Alice K. Young; ed. high sch.; m. Shirley Landon, Oct. 18, 1958; children—Kimberley Sue, Richard C. Accounting office and sales Arco, Syracuse, 1955-59; cash register sales NCR Corp., Syracuse, 1960-65, fin. sales, 1965-76, dist. mgr. comml., med., edn. and govt. sales, 1976—. Nat. trustee Dollars for Scholars, 1972-75, pres., Chemung County, N.Y., 1972. Club: Rotary (treas. 1971). Address: NCR Corp 742 James St Syracuse NY 13203

YOUNG, RICHARD WILLIAM, camera mfg. co. exec.; b. Ridgewood, N.Y., Oct. 17, 1926; s. Charles Michael and Louise Margaret (Baust) Y.; A.B., Dartmouth, 1946, A.M., 1947; Ph.D., Columbia U., 1950; m. Sheila deLisser, Sept. 11, 1949; children—Christine, Noreen, Brian, Eileen. Sr. research chemist Chemotherapy div. Am. Cyanamid Co., Conn., 1950-56, group leader pesticide chems. Agr. div., 1956-58, dir. chem. research Agr. div., 1958-60, dir. chem. research Central Research div., 1960-62; asst. dir. research Polaroid Corp., Cambridge, Mass., 1962-69, v.p., 1963-69, sr. v.p. research and devel., 1969-72, sr. v.p. internat. div., 1972-80, exec. v.p., 1980—, dir. numerous subsidiaries. Trustee, Regis Coll., Weston, Mass., Polaroid Found., Marine Biol. Lab., Woods Hole, Mass.; trustee, chmn. sci. adv. com. Mass. Eye and Ear Infirmary, Boston; mem. corp. Northeastern U., Boston. Mem. Am. Chem. Soc., Chem. Soc. London, A.A.A.S., Soc. Photog. Scientists and Engrs., Royal Photog. Soc., Internat. C. of C. (trustee). Patentee in field. Home: 100 Royalston Rd Wellesley Hills MA 02181 Office: 730 Main St Cambridge MA 02139

YOUNG, ROBERT BRUCE, mfg. co. exec.; b. Malden, Mass., Mr. 22, 1938; s. Russell Vincent and Lena A. Young; B.S. in Indsl. Engring., Northeastern U., 1961; m. Blanche Raab, Dec. 16, 1961; children—Paula Anne, Robert Scott. Indsl. engr. Raytheon Co., Waltham, Mass., 1963-64; sr. mfg. methods engr. RCA, Burlington, Mass., 1965-66; supr. indsl. engring. Sanders Assos., Nashua, N.H., 1966-74; dir. mfg. Applicon Inc., Burlington, Mass., 1974—. Mgr., Chelmsford Little League, 1973—. Served to 1st lt. AUS, 1961-64. Recipient Outstanding Achievement award Applicon, 1977. Mem. Am. Inst. Indsl. Engrs. (sr.). Home: 7 Coach Rd Chelmsford MA 01824 Office: 32 2d Ave Burlington MA 01803

YOUNG, ROBERT HARRIS MCCARTER, JR., utilities co. exec.; b. N.Y.C., July 22, 1947; s. Robert Harris McCarter and Gloria Ann Bond (Tenney) Y.; B.A., Beloit Coll., 1970; M.B.A., Stanford U., 1975; m. Jane Victoria Peterson, Aug. 17, 1974; 1 son, Peter Bond. With Bechtel Corp., San Francisco, 1970-73, asst. to project mgr., 1973-75; with Can. Bechtel Ltd., 1975-77, sr. field engr., 1977; with Bay State Gas Co., Canton, Mass., 1977—, dir. corp. planning, 1979—, v.p. Bay State Exploration, Inc. Mem. New Eng. Gas Assn., Planning Execs. Inst. Episcopalian. Club: Dedham Country and Polo. Home: 164 Pine St Medfield MA 02052 Office: Suite 200 120 Royall St Canton MA 02021

YOUNG, ROBERT LERTON, ins. brokerage co. exec.; b. Columbus, Ohio, Feb. 21, 1936; s. Robert Lerton and Ada Beatrice (Aderholt) Y.; student Ohio State U., 1958-60, U. Ill., 1953-55. Mgr. actuarial dept. Gates McDonald & Co., Columbus, 1959-66, dist. mgr., Oakland, Calif., 1966-70; v.p., founder Nat. Compensation Services, Inc., Pleasant Hill, Calif., 1970-71; v.p. Fred S. James & Co., Inc., Pleasant Hill and San Francisco, 1971-76, sr. v.p. self-ins. service, Chgo., 1976—; cons. Los Angeles County Self-Ins. Program; mem. adv. com. Calif. Dept. Indsl. Relations; tchr. U. Calif. Extension, 1970; lectr. Am. Mgmt. Assn. Mem. Pleasant Hill Youth Commn., 1973. Served with U.S. Army, 1955-58. Recipient Service award Chartered Property and Casualty Underwriters, 1971, 75. Mem. Assn. Lloyd's Brokers, Ins. Inst. Am. (risk mgmt. diploma), Am. Soc. Safety Engrs. (indsl. safety diploma), Nat. Council Self-Insurers, Internat. Assn. Indsl. Accident Bds. and Commns., Calif., Ariz., Wash., Pa., Mass., Ga., Fla. self-insurers assns., Newcomen Soc. Clubs: Commonwealth (San Francisco); Met. (Chgo.). Contbr. articles to profl. jours. Home: 1910 N Cleveland Chicago IL 60614 Office: Fred S James & Co 230 W Monroe St Chicago IL 60606

YOUNG, SCOTT, record retailing exec.; b. Rockville Centre, N.Y., Oct. 5, 1946; s. Herbert Scott and Selma (Schultz) Y.; B.S. in Bus. Adminstrn., U. Fla., 1969; M.B.A., U. N.C., 1971; m. Linda Sloan, 1979. Auditor, Arthur Andersen & Co., Atlanta, 1970; cons. Achievement, Inc. Chapel Hill, N.C., 1971-72; prin. Matthews, Young & Assos., Chapel Hill, 1972-74; v.p. finance The Record Bar, Durham, N.C., 1974-75, exec. v.p., 1975-76, chief operating officer, 1976—, also dir.; exec. v.p. Pickwick Internat., Inc., 1980—, also gen. mgr. retailing div.; owner, pres. Young Entertainment, Inc., 1980—; chmn. bd., dir. Sam Goody, Inc., 1976—; mem. policy adv. com. Am. Can Co., 1978—; instr. U. N.C.; dir., treas., chmn. finance com. Nat. Accrediting Agy. Clin. Lab. Scis.; dir. Sam Goody, Inc. Bd. dirs. Music Bus. Inst. Singlehanded sailing champion of Va., N.C., S.C., 1974. Mem. Life Office Mgmt. Assn., Indsl. Mgmt. Soc., Am. Mgmt. Assn., Internat. Council of Shopping Centers, Nat. Assn. Rec. Merchandisers, Data Processing Mgmt. Assn. Home: 2575 Peachtree Rd NE Atlanta GA 30305 Office: 7500 Excelsior Blvd Minneapolis MN 55426

YOUNG, SUMNER SULLIVAN, bus. exec.; b. Mpls., Sept. 17, 1932; s. Sumner Bacheler and Sidney (Washburn) Y.; A.B., Brown U., 1955; m. Eris Lundin, Nov. 10, 1962; children—Katherine Dianne, Jennifer Eris. Account exec. Pidgeon, Savage, Lewis, Inc., 1957-60; advt. and market planning mgr. boat div. Brunswick Corp., 1960-62; account exec. Batten, Barton, Durstine & Osborn, N.Y.C., 1963; v.p. Erle Savage Co., Mpls., 1963-67, pres., 1967-72; chmn. bd. Larson Industries, Inc., 1972-76; pres. Gen. Boats, Inc., Mpls., 1972—, The Advt. Agy., Inc., 1972—. Served to capt. USAF, spl. agt. Office of Spl. Investigations, 1955-57. Mem. North Central Marine Assn. (pres. 1972, dir.), Minn. Execs. Orgn., Phi Gamma Delta. Clubs: Mpls.; Wayzata Yacht, Skylight. Home: 2600 Maplewoods Circle E Wayzata MN 55391 Office: 2200 Foshay Tower Minneapolis MN 55402

YOUNG, WILLIAM EDMUND, machine mfg. co. exec., mech. engr.; b. Ridgewood, N.J., Mar. 22, 1916; s. Walter and May I. (Donahue) Junge; M.E., Stevens Inst. of Tech., Hoboken, N.J., 1937; m. Barbara Shultz Stanford, Aug. 19, 1974; children—Paula Ann, David Walter. Instr., Stevens Inst. Tech., 1937-39; chief engr. Clay-Adams Co., N.Y.C., 1940-48; engring. cons., N.Y.C., 1948-51; dir. engring. Standard Packaging Corp., N.Y.C., 1951-57; partner Mahaffy Engring. Co., Little Falls, N.J., 1957-62; pres. William E. Young & Co., Neptune, N.J., 1961—; dir. Research and Devel. Associates for Mil. and Food Packaging Inc. Trustee Freedoms Found.; mem. bd. Jersey Shore Med. Center, Shore YMCA. Recipient 100th Anniversary Citation medal Stevens Inst., 1970; registered profl. engr., N.J. Mem. ASME, Am. Chem. Soc., Newcomen Soc., Packaging Inst. (profl. award 1969), Order of Lafayette. Republican. Episcopalian. Clubs: Stanford Yacht, Channel, Deal Golf and Country, Mason. Contbr. articles on packaging processes to profl. publs.; patentee in field. Home: 60 W Concourse Neptune NJ 07753 Office: 600 Essex Rd Neptune NJ 07753

YOUNGQUIST, ALVIN MENVID, JR., publisher; b. Toledo, Oct. 9, 1925; s. Alvin Menvid and Elsie W. (Bostock) Y.; B.S., Northwestern U., 1950, postgrad. Sch. Journalism, 1951; m. Judith Jackett, June 13, 1953. Editor, Bankers Monthly, Skokie, Ill., 1953-70; editor, pres., publisher, Bankers Monthly, Inc., Northbrook, Ill., 1971—. Mem. Bank Mktg. Assn., U.S. Power Squadron. Republican. Episcopalian. Clubs: White Lake (Mich.) Yacht, Glenview (Ill.) Tennis. Home: 1343 Hollywood Ave Glenview IL 60025 Office: 601 Skokie Blvd Northbrook IL 60062

YOUNGS, JACK MARVIN, cost research engr.; b. Bklyn., May 2, 1941; s. Jack William and Virginia May (Clark) Y.; B.Engring., CCNY, 1964; M.B.A., San Diego State U., 1973; m. Alexandra Marie Robertson, Oct. 31, 1964; 1 dau., Christine Marie. Mass properties engr. Gen. Dynamics Corp., San Diego, 1964-68, research engr., 1968-69, sr. research engr., 1969-80, sr. cost devel. engr., 1980—. Dist. dir. Scripps Ranch Civic Assn., 1976-79. Mem. AIAA, Nat. Mgmt. Assn. (award of honor 1975), Assn. M.B.A. Execs., Beta Gamma Sigma, Chi Epsilon, Sigma Iota Epsilon. Club: Scripps Ranch Swim and Racquet (dir. 1977-80, treas. 1978-79, pres. 1979-80). Research in life cycle costing and econ. analysis. Home: 11461 Tribuna Ave San Diego CA 92131 Office: 5001 Kearny Villa Rd San Diego CA 92138

YOUNGSTROM, EDWIN ERIC, canvas products mfg. co. exec.; b. Nassau County, L.I., N.Y., Dec. 27, 1950; s. Edwin Harold and Bertha Cecelia (Matson) Y.; A.A., Nassau Community Coll., 1969-71; student architecture N.Y. Inst. Tech., 1971-73; B.S. in Bus. Adminstrn., No. Ariz. U., 1976. Head installations, designer Bruns Products, Inc., New Hyde Park, N.Y., 1970-77; owner, founder, operator Canvas Products Co., Mineola, N.Y., 1977—; tech. cons. to bus. Mem. Canvas Products Assn. Internat., Phi Kappa Phi, Beta Gamma Sigma. Office: 234 Herricks Rd Mineols NY 11501

YOUNT, STANLEY GEORGE, paper co. exec.; b. Ketchum, Idaho, Feb. 15, 1903; s. George and Cansada (Smith) Y.; student U. Nev., 1924; m. Agnes Pratt, Feb. 17, 1944; children—Ann E., George S. Div. sales mgr. Crown Zellerbach Corp., 1926-40; pres. Southland Paper Converting Co., 1940-56; pres. Fortifiber Corp. and affiliates, Los Angeles, 1956-77, chmn., 1977—, also dir.; dir. Stanwall Corp. Served with U.S. Army, World War I; AEF in France. Mem. Nat. Flexible Packaging Assn. (pres. Indsl. Bag and Cover div. 1954-56), Barrier Paper Mfrs. Assn. Mason (Shriner). Clubs: Jonathan (Los Angeles), Rotary. Home: 2260 Robles Ave San Marino CA 91108 Office: United Calif Bank Bldg Suite 4820 707 Wilshire Blvd Los Angeles CA 90017

YU, ALBERT YEOU CHERNG, microcomputer co. exec.; b. Shanghai, China, Feb. 10, 1941; s. I. Tao and Marina (Chen) Y.; came to U.S., 1960, naturalized, 1974; B.S., Calif. Inst. Tech., 1963; M.S., Stanford, 1964, Ph.D., 1967; m. Lucia Cha, July 9, 1966. Dir. device research Fairchild Camera & Instrument Co., Palo Alto, Calif., 1967-72; dir. technology devel. Intel Corp., Santa Clara, Calif., 1972-77; pres. Umtech Inc., Santa Clara, Calif., 1977-78, C.M. Technologies, Palo Alto, 1978—; dir. Matrix Leasing, San Francisco, 1971-74, Crespi Trading, Los Angeles, 1970—; adj. faculty U. Santa Clara, 1971-74. Mem. IEEE (sr.; chmn. electron device group 1971-74), Am. Phys. Soc., Electrochem. Soc., Sigma Xi. Club: Fremont Hills Country. Contbr. articles to profl. jours. Office: 2950 Patrick Henry Dr Santa Clara CA 95050

YU, CHYANG JOHN, ceramic engr.; b. China, June 20, 1948; s. Nelson Gienying and Fen (Tao) Y.; came to U.S., 1971; B.S. in Physics, Taiwan Cheng Kung U., 1970; M.A., Wayne State U., Detroit, 1972; Ph.D. in Ceramic Engring., U. Ill., Urbana-Champaign, 1977; m. Yu-chu Grace Chiang, Dec. 22, 1974; 1 son, Albert Benjamin. Research asst. U. Ill., 1973-77; research engr. Ohio Brass Co., Wadsworth, 1977-79; research and devel. mgr. Mepco/Electra, Inc., Canandaigua, N.Y., 1979-80; Centralab, Inc., Los Angeles, 1980—. Mem. Am. Ceramic Soc., Am. Phys. Soc., Am. Chem. Soc., Keramos. Office: 4561 Colorado Blvd Los Angeles CA 90039

YUCAS, JAMES ANTHONY, architect; b. Vandergrift, Pa., July 3, 1948; s. Anthony C. and Mary C. (Cheris) Y.; B.Arch., Pa. State U., 1973, M.S. in Architecture (AIA William H. Scheick Research fellow), 1978; m. Annagene Spekis, May 27, 1972. Apprentice architect to Bruce Goff, Architect, Tyler, Tex., 1973-75; job capt. to Rea, Hayes, Large and Suckling, architects, Altoona, Pa., 1975-76; grad. asst. dept. architecture Pa. State U., University Park, 1976-78; field rep. AIA Research Corp., Washington, 1977; vis. lectr. dept. architecture Pa. State U., 1978-79, asst. prof. architecture/tech. specialist Pa. Tech. Assistance Program/Pa. State U., 1979—; prin. J. Yucas, architect, State College, Pa., 1978—. Mem. AIA, Nat. Council Archtl. Registration Bds. (cert.). Office: Dept Architecture 206 Engring Unit C Pa State Univ University Park PA 16802

YUEN, CHARLES F., fin. exec.; b. Hankow, China, Nov. 9, 1946; came to U.S., 1970, naturalized, 1978; s. Wen-Yao and Hwa-Ching Y.; B.S. in Chemistry, Nat. Chung-Hsing U., 1969; M.S. in Ops. Research, U. So. Calif., 1973, D.B.A. in Fin., 1977; m. Angela C. Hsueh, Aug. 7, 1971; children—Anita C., Jennifer I. Cost engr. Electronic Memories, Hawthorne, Calif., 1971-72; mem. div. fin. staff Xerox Corp., El Segundo, Calif., 1972-75; dir. fin. planning Northrop Corp., Hawthorne, 1975—; pres. The Fortune Co., Palos Verdes Estates, Calif., 1973—; pub., editor Yuen's Investment Letter, lectr. Yuen's Investment Seminar; mgmt. and fin. cons. Served with China Air Forces, 1969-70. Mem. Am. Mgmt. Assn., Am. Inst. Indsl. Engrs., Chinese Profl. Soc., Chinese Chemistry Soc., Northrop Mgmt. Club. Fin. writer China Times, 1979—. Office: PO Box 2335 Palos Verdes Estates CA 90274

YUNICH, DAVID LAWRENCE, consumer co. cons.; b. Albany, N.Y., May 21, 1917; s. Max A. and Bess (Felman) Y.; A.B., Union Coll., 1939, LL.D., 1964; postgrad. Harvard Sch. Bus. Adminstrn., 1939-40; m. Beverly F. Blickman, June 11, 1941; children—Robert Hardie, Peter B. Mdse. councillor L. Bamberger & Co., Newark, 1947-48, pres., dir., 1955-62; v.p. Macy's N.Y., 1941-51, sr. v.p., 1951-62, pres., 1962-71; dir. R.H. Macy & Co., Inc., 1958-73, vice chmn. bd., 1971-73; dir. Prudential Ins. Co. Am., East River Savs. Bank, N.Y. Telephone Co., J. Walter Thompson Co., W.R. Grace & Co., U.S. Industries, Inc., Perdue Farms, Inc., Harwood Cos., Inc., Fidelity Group Mut. Funds; chmn. N.Y. Gov.'s Commn. Financing Mass Transp., 1970-72, N.Y.C. Mayor's Council Econ. and Bus. Advisors, 1973-74; chmn. Met. Transp. Authority, 1974-77; mem. N.Y. State Banking Bd., 1968-74. Pres. Greater N.Y. councils Boy Scouts Am., 1972-76; bd. dirs. Regional Plan Assn., Ednl. Broadcasting Corp., 1960-68, Nat. Jewish Hosp. Denver; trustee Union Coll., 1965-72, Albany Med. Coll., 1967-74, Skidmore Coll., 1966-73, Saratoga Performing Arts, Carnegie Hall Corp.; bd. govs., trustee Rutgers U., 1958-62. Decorated chevalier Confrerie des Chevaliers du Tastevin. Mem. Retail Dry Goods Assn. (pres. 1964-69), Am. Mgmt. Assn. (dir. 1958-68), N.Y. Chamber Commerce and Industry Assn. (chmn. bd. 1970-74), Nat. Retail Mchts. Assn. (dir.), Am. Pub. Transp. Assn. (v.p.). Clubs: Harvard Business School, Harvard, University, Recess, Economic (N.Y.C.); Blind Brook, Scarsdale (Westchester); Saratoga Golf and Polo (Saratoga Springs, N.Y.); Sandy Lane Golf (Barbados, W.I.). Home: Five Birches Cooper Rd Scarsdale NY 10583 Office: 1114 Ave of Americas New York NY 10036

YURASEK, FRANK AUGUSTINE, advt. exec.; b. Newark, Oct. 30, 1939; s. Frank Augustine and Mary Elizabeth (Branch) Y.; B.A., U. Notre Dame, 1961, M.A. (teaching fellow), 1963; student law Coll. William and Mary, 1963-65; m. Leslie Turbow, May 27, 1979; 1 dau., Lauren; children by previous marriage—Amy, Michele, Mara, Andrew, Antonia, Jason. Network sales service rep. NBC, Chgo., 1965-66; dir. sales Columbia Realty, North Manchester, Ind., 1966-67; account exec. Lamport, Fox, Prell & Polk, South Bend, 1967-69, Boger Martin & Fairchild, Elkhart, Ind., 1969-70; copy chief Vivox, St. Joseph, Mich., 1970-71; account exec. Juhl Advt., Elkhart, 1971-73; asso. pub. Sportsman Pub., Southfield, Mich., 1973-75; pres. FYI, South Bend, 1975-77; v.p. Russell T. Gray, 1977-79; v.p. Grant/Jacoby, Inc., Chgo., 1979—. Public relations com. Internat. ARC; public relations dir. Fair for Gov. Com. and Dougherty for Congress Com., 1976. Recipient award for sportswriting Pa. Press Assn., 1956, Addy awards, 1977. Mem. Bus. and Profl. Advt. Assn. Clubs: Publicity of Chgo., Chgo. Press. Office: 500 N Michigan Ave Chicago IL 60611

ZABEL, ROBERT PAUL, advt. exec.; b. Abington, Pa., July 20, 1928; s. Paul and Ethel (Neuschaefer) Z.; A.B., Princeton U., 1952; m. Joan Cohee, Apr. 16, 1955; children—Nancy, Susan, Robert Paul. With N.W. Ayer & Sons, Inc., Phila., 1952—, exec. v.p., dir., Chgo., 1969-74, pres., 1974—. Mem. bd. dirs. Midwest council Am. Assn. Advt. Agencies. Bd. dirs. N.Y. council Boy Scouts Am. Served with USMCR, 1946-48. Mem. Nat. Alliance Businessmen (dir. N.Y.). Clubs: Mid-Am., Tavern (Chgo.); Indian Hill (Winnetka); Cap and

Gown (Princeton); Greenwich Country, Pine Valley Golf. Office: 1345 Ave of Americas New York NY 10019*

ZACHARIAS, JOHN ELLING, chem. co. exec.; b. Connellsville, Pa., Sept. 8, 1915; s. Johannes M. and Louise M. (Elling) Z.; A.B., Princeton, 1936; student Grad. Sch. Bus. Adminstrn., N.Y. U., 1937-38, Law Sch., 1939-40; m. Muriel C. Eckes, Sept. 21, 1946; children—Jane E., Thomas E. Estate adminstrn., U.S. Trust Co. of N.Y., 1936-43; prodn. mgr. Whitehall Pharm. Co., 1946-48; dir. operations Jamieson Pharm. Co., 1948-51; with McKesson & Robbins, Inc. (now Foremost-McKesson, Inc.), N.Y.C., 1952-77, v.p., 1956-77; pres. Cord Assos., Ltd., Wilton, Conn., 1978—. Served with USNR, 1943-46. Clubs: Princeton (N.Y.C.); Wilton (Conn.) Riding; Woodstock (Vt.) Country; Silver Spring Country. Home: Belden Hill Rd Wilton CT 06897 Office: Box 431 Wilton CT 06897

ZACHARIAS, WILLIAM PAUL, mgmt. cons.; b. Tucson, Nov. 25, 1930; s. William Paul and Mary Lou (Boyd) Z.; student So. Ill. U., 1948-50; B.A., U. Denver, 1957; m. Beverly Smith, June 5, 1971; children by previous marriage—William D. Zacharias, Janet L. Zacharias, James M., Beverly Dianne, Charles E. Calhoun. Tchr. public schs., Denver, 1957-59; dir., therapist Easter Seal Rehab. Center, Albany, Ga., 1959-64; exec. sec. S.W. Ga. Soc. for Crippled Children and Adults, Inc., Albany, 1960-64; personnel adminstr. Lilliston Corp., Albany, 1964-71; corp. dir. employee relations Builders Homes, Inc. div. Am. Standards, Inc., Dothan, Ala., 1971-72, W.C. Bradley Co., Columbus, Ga., 1972-76; pres. Zacharias & Assos., Inc., mgmt. cons., Columbus, 1976—; pres. Preferred Placements, Inc., 1978—, Employee Relations Concepts, ednl. cons.; profl. speaker. Chmn. adv. com. for vocat.-tech. edn. Musoogee County Sch. System; past pres., chmn. bd. Jr. Achievement of Columbus, Jr. Achievement of Phenix City (Ala.); mem. personnel rev. bd. Consol. Govt. of Columbus; mem. Commn. on Status Women, Commn. on Employment Handicapped, Ga. Employer-Employee Relations Council. Served in USAF, 1950-54. Recipient Leadership award Jr. Achievement Am., 1976, 77; numerous awards from various charitable and health orgns. Mem. Am. Soc. Personnel Adminstrn. (accredited personnel diplomate), Am. Mgmt. Assn., Am. Arbitration Assn., Am. Soc. Tng. and Devel., C. of C. U.S., Ga., Columbus, Cordele, LaGrange chambers commerce, Columbus Personnel Assn. Methodist. Clubs: Sertoma (Columbus); One Hundred. Contbr. articles to profl. periodicals. Home: 4718 20th Ave Columbua GA 31904 Office: PO Drawer 4408 Columbus GA 31904 also 5825 Glenridge Dr NE Bldg 1 Suite 130 Atlanta GA 30328*

ZAGAR, LAWRENCE THOMAS, financial exec.; b. Aliquippa, Pa., Apr. 17, 1921; s. Anthony and Mary (Padavich) Z.; B.S., St. Vincent Coll., Latrobe, Pa., 1944, postgrad. Southwestern U., Los Angeles, 1953, U. Calif. at Los Angeles, 1955-60; Ph.D. (hon.), 1974; m. Sylvia Louise Puskarich, May 11, 1946; 1 son, Terence Richard. Controller, Cath. Youth Orgn., Archidocese of Los Angeles, 1947-51; cost accountant Solar Mfg. Corp., 1953; cost accountant Ducommun Metals & Supply Co., Los Angeles, 1954-56, mgr. profit improvement dept., 1957-60, project control mgr., 1958-60, corporate budget mgr., 1960-62; mgr. financial planning and controls Riverside Cement Co., Los Angeles, 1962-63; v.p. finance Medallion Printers & Lithographers, Los Angeles, 1963-64, also dir.; asst. sec.-treas., controller Pacific Western Industries, Inc., Los Angeles, 1965-66, asst. sec., 1966-67; sec.-treas. Simi Valley Rock Products, Inc., 1965-70, Glenn E. Walker Corp., Walnut, Calif., 1965-67, Mountain Rock Products, Upland, Calif., 1965-67; pres. Furnishings Complete, Los Angeles, 1967-69; chief adminstrv. officer Jules Strongbow Enterprises, Inc., Los Angeles, 1968-70; v.p. Financial Communications Clearing House, Los Angeles, 1970-71, pres., 1971—, also dir.; mem. U.S. Senatorial Bus. Adv. Bd., 1980—. Mem. Calif. Athletic Commn.; mem. So. Calif. Golden Gloves Com., 1948-68; bd. dirs. Boxers and Wrestlers Fund, Inc.; bd. govs., chmn. fin. com. Vols. of Am., Los Angeles, 1978—; mem. pres.'s council Calif. State Poly. U., 1980—. Served from pvt. to 1st lt. USMC, 1942-46, comdg. officer, 1951-53, maj., 1954. Mem. St. Vincent Alumni Assn. Republican. Roman Catholic. Author articles in field. Home: 4360 W 4th St Los Angeles CA 90020 Office: 3691 Bandini Blvd Los Angeles CA 90011

ZAGER, BERNARD SOLOMON, surgeon, business group med. dir.; b. Detroit, Nov. 3, 1926; s. Phillip P. and Lena (Wandler) Z.; B.A., Wayne U., 1947; M.D., Northwestern U., 1950; m. Denise Helen Acheson, Sept. 11, 1953; children—Robert, Gerald, Martin. Intern, Grace Hosp., Detroit, 1949-50, resident in surgery, 1952-54, chief surg. resident, 1954-56, surgeon, teaching staff, 1956-68; practice medicine specializing in surgery, Detroit, 1956-64; coordinator, surg. edn. Sinai Hosp., Detroit, 1956-57, attending surgeon, 1956-68; cons. surgeon Mich. Bell Telephone Co., Detroit, 1962-64; chief physician, automotive assembly div. Ford Motor Co., Utica, Mich., 1964-68; med. dir. nuclear energy group Gen. Electric Co., San Jose, Calif., 1968—; med. dir. Civil Def. Redford Twp. (Mich.), 1956-60; mem. program com. Western Occupational Health Conf., 1977; adv. com., occupational safety and health program Chabot Coll., Hayward, Calif., 1976—. Served to capt. M.C., AUS, 1950-52. Diplomate Am. Bd. Preventive Medicine. Fellow Am. Coll. Preventive Medicine, Am. Occupational Med. Assn., Am. Acad., Occupational Medicine. Home: 4133 Mattos Dr Fremont CA 94536

ZAGORAC, MICHAEL, JR., retail co. exec.; b. Chgo., Mar. 23, 1941; s. Michael and Helen (Rush) Z.; B.S., Purdue U., 1963; M.B.A., Am. U., 1971; m. Linda F. Grubb, Mar. 7, 1970; children—Christina Lynn, Michael Paul. Dir. govt. programs Am. Pharm. Assn., Washington, 1966-68; v.p. Nat. Assn. Chain Drug Stores, Washington, 1968-76; v.p. pub. affairs Jack Eckerd Corp., Clearwater, Fla., 1976—; chmn. Retail Public Affairs Conf., 1981; dir. Prepaid Health Care, Inc. Mem. pharm. reimbursement advisory com. Dept. HEW, 1977-78; mem. council U. Tex. Found., 1978. Served with Chem. Corps, AUS, 1964-66. Decorated Army Commendation medal. Mem. Associated Industries Fla. (dir. 1976—), Fla. Retail Fedn. (dir. 1976—, chmn. 1980), Public Affairs Council (dir. 1980—), Am. Pharm. Assn., Am. Inst. History of Pharmacy (dir. 1974-76), Nat. Press Club, Omicron Delta Kappa, Rho Chi. Democrat. Methodist. Clubs: Army-Navy Country, Capital City, Clearwater Yacht. Home: 153 Palmetto Rd Belleair FL 33516 Office: PO Box 4689 Clearwater FL 33516

ZAHORIK, DONALD JEROME, med. elec. mfg. co. exec.; b. Manitowoc, Wis., Oct. 16, 1935; s. Harry J. and Ida M. Z.; B.E.E., Marquette U., 1958; m. Katherine B. Blonski, Sept. 27, 1958; children—Pamela, Steven, Scott, Michael, Mark, Matthew. Dir. mktg., mgr. product planning Nuclear Chgo. Corp., 1957-68; pres. Intertechnique Instruments, Inc., Paris, France and N.J., 1968-71; pres. Med. Dynamics Corp., Bernardsville, N.J., 1971-72; pres. Unirad Corp., Denver, 1972-76, also dir.; exec. v.p., gen. mgr. Holosonics, Richland, Wash. and Denver, 1977-79; pres. Med. Cons. Internat. Ltd., Franktown, Colo., 1979—; cons. Gen. Electric Co. Gt. Britain, 1978, Wake Forest U., NSF. Mem. Soc. Nuclear Medicine, Am. Inst. Ultrasound in Medicine, Alliance for Engring. in Medicine and Biology, Echocardiology Council, Am. Heart Assn., Triangle Frat. Roman Catholic. Home: PO Box 217 Franktown CO 80116

ZAIS, JERROLD C., mfg. co. exec.; b. Kenosha, Wis., Sept. 26, 1945; s. Carmen E. and Valeria R. (Kelnhofer) Z.; student U. Wis., 1977, Marquette U., 1978; children—Lynn, Michael. Prodn. draftsman Marshfield Homes, Inc., Marshfield, Wis., 1963-67; prodn. foreman, asst. plant mgr. Wick Homes, Mazomanie, Wis., 1967-71, plant mgr., Moberly, Mo., 1971-73; material handling mgr. Wausau Homes, Wausau, Wis., 1973-78, service parts distbn. mgr., 1978-80; inventory control mgr. Hoffer's Inc., Wausau, 1980—. Active various charitable orgns. Mem. Am. Prodn. and Inventory Control Soc., Wis. Valley Suprs. Council. Roman Catholic. Home: 805 Flieth St Apt 28 Wausau WI 54401 Office: 310 Bellis St Wausau WI 54401

ZAISER, SALLY SOLEMMA VANN (MRS. FOSTER E. ZAISER), retail book co. exec.; b. Birmingham, Ala., Jan. 18, 1917; d. Carl Waldo and Einnan (Herndon) Vann; student Birmingham-So. Coll., 1933-36, Akron Coll. Bus., 1937; m. Foster E. Zaiser, Nov. 11, 1939. Accountant, A. Simionato, San Francisco, 1956-65; head accounting dept. Richard T. Clarke Co., San Francisco, 1966; accountant John Howell-Books, San Francisco, 1967-72, sec., treas., 1972—; sec. Great Eastern Mines, Inc., Albuquerque, 1969—. Braille transcriber for A.R.C., Kansas City, Mo. 1941-45; vol. worker ARC Hosp. Program, Sao Paulo, Brazil, 1952. Mem. Book Club Calif., Soc. Lit. and Art, Calif. Hist. Soc., Theta Upsilon. Republican. Episcopalian. Club: Capitol Hill. Home: 355 Serrano Dr San Francisco CA 94132 Office: 434 Post St San Francisco CA 94102

ZAKON, ALAN JAMES, mgmt. cons.; b. Boston, Dec. 26, 1935; s. Edward and Lillian Francis (Rubenstein) Z.; B.A., Harvard U., 1957; S.M., M.I.T., 1959; Ph.D., UCLA, 1964; m. Sandra Ohrn, Nov. 27, 1972; children—David Andrew, Shari Ellen. Asso. prof. Coll. Bus., Boston U., 1962-67; with Boston Cons. Group, 1967—, chmn. mgmt. com., chief exec. officer, 1980—. Co-editor: Elements of Investments, 1967; contbr. articles to profl. publs. Office: 1 Boston Pl Boston MA 02106

ZAKRAYSEK, SHIRLEY ANN, income tax service co. exec.; b. Pitts., Aug. 3, 1931; d. Nevin Layser and Mary Barbara (Wilson) Hartman; student public schs., Pitts.; m. Louis Zakraysek, Sept. 19, 1952; children—Mary A. Zakraysek Kenny, Nancy J., Michelle A., Edward S. Travel cons. Gulf Oil Corp., Phila., 1948-52; traffic mgr. 1st Broadcasting Corp., Syracuse, N.Y., 1971; comptroller, asst. gen. mgr. Sentry Communications Inc., Baldwinsville, N.Y., 1973-78; pres., founder A To Z Income Tax Service, Inc., Cicero, N.Y., 1978—. Hostess, Republican Party, 1965-68. Mem. Cicero C. of C. Home and Office: 8432 Brewerton Rd Cicero NY 13039

ZALAZNICK, CHARLES, lawyer; b. N.Y.C., Apr. 6, 1933; s. Herman and Priscilla (Sands) Z.; B.A., N.Y. U., 1954, J.D., 1957; postgrad. Harvard U., 1954; m. Gilda Jay Gellin, June 17, 1956; children—Dana Sari, Edward Philip, Brian Harry. Admitted to N.Y. State bar, 1958, U.S. Supreme Ct. bar, 1963; asso. mem. firm Garbarini & Kroll, N.Y.C., 1956-58, Siegel & Field, N.Y.C., 1958-60; individual practice law, N.Y.C., 1960-66; asso. firm Golenbock & Barell, N.Y.C., 1966-70, Dreyer and Traub, N.Y.C., 1971-72; partner firm Golenbock and Barell, N.Y.C., 1972—; lectr. Practicing Law Inst., 1974—. Served with U.S. Army, 1956. Mem. Am., N.Y. State bar assns., Am. Arbitration Assn., Judge Advocate Gen. Alumni Assn. Republican. Jewish. Club: Masons. Author: Construction Financing. Home: 28 Brookby Rd Scarsdale NY 10583 Office: 645 Fifth Ave New York City NY 10022

ZALE, DONALD, retail co. exec.; b. 1933; student Tex. A&M U.; B.B.A., So. Meth. U., 1953; married. With Zale Corp., Dallas, 1954—, asst. treas., 1961-63, treas., 1963-64, exec. v.p., 1964-71, pres., chief exec. officer, 1971-78, vice chmn. bd., chief exec. officer, 1978—, also dir. Office: 3000 Diamond Park Dr Dallas TX 75247*

ZALEIKO, NICHOLAS STEVENSON, mgmt. cons.; b. N.Y.C., Jan. 29, 1921; s. Steven C. and Mary (Romanoff) Z.; B.S. in Chem. Engring., Bklyn. Poly. Inst., 1941; m. Hilde Leon, Feb. 13, 1954; 1 dau., Christina. Indsl. marketing specialist Owens Corning Fiberglas, N.Y.C., 1948-50, Dorr-Oliver Corp., Stamford, Conn., 1950-59; gen. mgr. DESCO, Whippany, N.J., 1959-61; cons., acting dir. air and water div. Technicon Corp., Ardsley, N.Y., 1961-68; pres. T.A.F.I., Inc., Enercol, Inc., 1968—. Engring. instr. Marquette U., 1942. Asst. chmn. Park Ridge Zoning Bd., 1959-63. Served with C.E., AUS, 1944-45. Recipient War Dept. citation, Manhattan Project, 1945. Mem. Am. Soc. for Testing and Materials (chmn. subcoms. 1967—), TAPPI, Water Pollution Control Fedn., Am. Water Works Assn., Instrument Soc. Am., Air Pollution Control Assn. Contbr. articles to tech. jours. Inventor multipurpose air pollution analyzer, 1963, apple juice process, 1956, water pollution analyzer, 1962, pollution oxidation process, 1971. Home: 01 Vista Pl Red Bank NJ 07701 Office: 157 Broad St Red Bank NJ 07701

ZAMBETIS, CLEO NICHOLAS, indsl. painting contractor; b. Samos, Greece, Nov. 23, 1925; s. John Constantine and Katina (Nicolaou) Z.; student Youngstown State U.; m. Faye Arfaras, Nov. 7, 1948; children—Kathy, Tulla. Founder, pres. Camco Painting Service, Inc., Youngstown, Ohio, 1950—. Served with USNR, 1946-48. Mem. Painting and Decorating Contractors Am. Greek Orthodox. Clubs: Order of Ahepa, Masons (Shriner). Home: 341 Montridge Dr Canfield OH 44406 Office: Camco Painting Services Box 3065 Youngstown OH 44511

ZAMBOLDI, ROBERT JOSEPH, chem. co. exec.; b. Kittanning, Pa., Nov. 16, 1940; s. Henry Francis and Florence Elizabeth (Colligan) Z.; B.S., U.S. Air Force Acad., 1963; M.B.A., Ohio State U., 1967; m. Marilyn E. Geyer, July 6, 1963; children—Melissa, Kathryn, Robert. Sales engr. Air Products & Chemicals Inc., Pitts., 1968-69, dist. mgr., 1969-74, regional mgr. Midwest, Chgo., 1974-76, mgr. mktg. Indsl. Gas div., Allentown, Pa., 1976-77, gen. mgr. bus. devel., 1977-78; gen. mgr. Nitrogen Services, Houston, 1978—. Served with USAF, 1963-67. Home: 12114 Glenway Dr Houston TX 77070 Office: 260 N Belt E Suite 200 Houston TX 77060

ZANARDO, DARRYL DUANE, bus. forms co. mgr.; b. Chgo., Oct. 27, 1950; s. Willard and Maxine A. (Schednig) Z.; B.S. in Mktg., No. Ill. U., 1972, M.B.A., 1973; m. Barbara Kolodziej, July 29, 1978. Sales rep. Moore Bus. Forms Co., Southfield, Mich., 1974-75, sales trainer, 1975-76, sales supr., 1976—. Mem. Am. Mktg. Assn., Sales and Mktg. Execs. Internat. Office: 1650 W Big Beaver Suite 200C Troy MI 48084

ZAND, JACOBO SIMON, photog. cons., illustrator; b. Mendoza, Argentina; came to U.S., 1965, naturalized, 1977; s. Adolfo and Malka (Goldzach) Z.; M. Aero. Engring., Nat. U. Cordoba, Argentina, 1957; grad. mem. Royal Aero. Soc., London, 1960; spl. studies Southall Poly., London, 1960, Boeing Co., Renton, Wash., 1967. Prof., lectr. D.F. Sarmiento, Cuyo Nat. U., San Juan, Argentina, 1958-59; postgrad. scholarship trainee Fairey Aviation, Ltd., Hayes, Middlesex, Eng., 1959-61; chief engr. hydraulic dept. Aerolineas Argentinas, Buenos Aires, 1962-63; rep., cons. Argenorah Co., Buenos Aires, 1963-65; designer Nichols Engring. and Research Corp., N.Y.C., 1965-66; service engr. Tech. Support Group, Boeing Co., Renton, 1966-68; engring. cons. Austral Airlines, Buenos Aires, 1969; tech. cons., photographer J.S. Zand Creative Photography and Zand Tech. Services, N.Y.C., 1969—; adminstrv. lead engr. Stone & Webster Engring. Corp., N.Y.C., 1975-78; tech. and photog. cons. Served with arty. Army of Argentina, 1952-53. Mem. Aero. Engrs. Profl. Council of Buenos Aires, Confedn. Brit. Industries (life), Mensa. Jewish. Patentee U.S., U.K., Japan, Germany, France, Argentina, Italy. Office: 430 W 34th St New York NY 10001

ZANDSTRA, KENNETH RAY, bank exec.; b. Linton, N.D., Oct. 9, 1932; s. Albert and Matilda Ann (Van Beek) Z.; B.S. in Bus. Adminstrn., No. State Coll., Aberdeen, S.D., 1958; student Dakota Wesleyan U., 1950-51, Wis. Sch. Banking, 1970; m. Betty Ann Meisner, June 18, 1954; children—Allen W., Kevin K. Office mgr. State Fin. Corp., Mobridge, S.D., 1958-59; ins. and installment loan officer Citizens Bank of Mobridge, 1959-62, asst. cashier, 1962-67, cashier, sec. to bd. dirs., 1968-70, v.p., cashier, 1971-72, exec. v.p., cashier, dir., 1973, pres., dir., 1974—. Treas., v.p. Mobridge Jaycees, 1961-62; treas. March of Dimes, 1967-77. Served with U.S. Army, 1954-56. Mem. S.D. Bankers Assn. Republican. Presbyterian. Clubs: Lions (v.p., pres.), Mobridge Country (dir., treas.), Rotary (treas.), Moose. Office: 320 Main St Mobridge SD 57601

ZANGARI, FRANK JOSEPH, interior designer; b. Portsmouth, N.H., Feb. 7, 1951; s. Dominick and Theresa (Truglia) Z.; student Boston Archtl. Center, 1975, Parsons Sch. Design, 1979; B.S. in Mech. Engring., Northeastern U., 1973; M.S. in Environ./Interior Design, Pratt Inst., 1977. With M.I.T. Draper Lab., Cambridge, Stone & Webster Engring. Corp., Boston, Noel Jeffrey Inc., Interior Design, N.Y.C., L.S.K. Designs, N.Y.C., Michael de Santis, Interior Design, N.Y.C., 1976-78, Angelo Donghia of Donghia/Martin Interior Design, N.Y.C., 1978; individual practice interior design, N.Y.C., N.Y., 1979—. Mem. Am. Soc. Interior Designers (profl.), ASME (asso.).

ZANGRI, SALVATORE JOSEPH, atomic corp. exec.; b. Lawrence, Mass., Mar. 25, 1920; s. Alfred and Santa Z.; B.S. in Chemistry, Tufts U., 1942; postgrad. in engring. Ohio State U., 1957-59, Ohio U., 1968; m. Helen Berger Schowengerdt, June 24, 1944; children—Alfred George, Robert Stephen, John Richard. Shift chemist Hercules Powder Co., Lawrence, Kans., 1942-44; sr. engr. Union Carbide Corp., Oak Ridge, 1944-54; with Goodyear Atomic Corp., 1954—, supr. pross engring., Portsmouth, Ohio, 1954-69, from tech. asst. to dep. gen. mgr. and gen. mgr., 1969-78, supt. engring., operation project contractors' office, Oak Ridge, 1978—; cons. in field. Asst. foreman Ross County Grand Jury, 1977. Recipient St. George medal in scouting; registered profl. engr., Tenn. Mem. Am. Inst. Chem. Engrs. Republican. Roman Catholic. Clubs: Elks, K.C. Home: 108 Antioch Dr Oak Ridge TN 37830 Office: Y-12 Plant Bldg 9106 PO Box Y Oak Ridge TN 37830

ZAPATA, WILLIAM, retail exec.; b. N.Y.C., Oct. 5, 1940; s. Santos and Dina (Hernandez) Z.; B.B.A., CCNY, 1962; m. Amparo Rosa, Feb. 6, 1973; children—Gisselle, Michelle, Julio Rafael, Dina Mariana. Sr. acct. Ernst & Ernst, N.Y.C., 1962-65, San Juan, P.R., 1965-66; treas., sec. Bargain Town Dept. Stores, San Juan, 1966-70; partner Madison Consultants, San Juan, 1970-71; fin. v.p. N.Y. Dept. Stores, Santurce, P.R., 1971-76, exec. v.p., 1976-80; exec. v.p. Caribbean div. (Barkers and Franklins Stores) div. Cornwall Equities, Ltd., San Juan, 1980-81; v.p. Caribbean div. (Barkers & Franklin Stores) div. King's Dept. Stores, Inc., San Juan, 1981—. Bd. dirs. Jr. Achievement P.R., 1976-78. Served in U.S. Army, 1963-64, N.G., 1963-67. C.P.A., P.R. Mem. Am. Inst. C.P.A.'s, P.R. Coll. C.P.A.'s, Nat. Assn. Accts., Beta Alpha Psi, Sigma Alpha. Episcopalian. Club: Rio Mar Country (Rio Grande, P.R.). Home: Poppy St EE-8 Borinquen Gardens Rio Piedras PR 00926 Office: GPO Box 4743 San Juan PR 00936

ZAPTON, DANIEL THOMAS, banker; b. Detroit, June 23, 1943; s. Steve and Anne Marie Zapton; B.B.A. cum laude in Econs. (Evans Found. scholar), U. Mich., Ann Arbor, 1965, M.B.A. in Finance, 1967. Commercial lending officer met. div. Continental Ill. Bank & Trust Co. Chgo., 1968-73, v.p. nat. div., 1973-77, v.p., regional mgr., Phila., 1977—. Varsity hockey coach Chestnut Hill Acad., 1979-81. Served with U.S. Army, 1967-68. Mem. Small Bus. Council, Greater Phila. C. of C. Roman Catholic. Clubs: Racquet, Union League, Sunnybrook, Pennlyn (Phila.); Wissahickon Skating (hockey coach 1978-79, mem. membership com. 1980-81). Home: 22 Waterman Ave Philadelphia PA 19118 Office: 3 Girard Plaza Philadelphia PA 19102

ZARECKI, THOMAS JOHN, banker; b. Chgo.; s. John Anthony and Helen Elizabeth Z.; A.A.S. with honors, Mo. Valley Community Coll., 1973; B.A., Governors State U., 1973, M.A., 1977; m. Bernadine Bruno, Nov. 9, 1963; children—Robert, Juliann. Agy. mgr. Met. Life Ins. Co., 1963-69; store systems analysts trainee Nat. Cash Register, Chgo., 1969-70; programmer, operator Midwest Stock Exchange, Chgo., 1970-73; instr. Moraine Valley Coll., Palos Hills, Ill., 1973—; audit programmer specialist Lakeview Trust & Savs., Chgo., 1975-76; EDP auditor, officer Mid-City Bank, Chgo., 1976-78, Bank of Hickory Hills, Burbank State Bank, Lemont State Bank and Worth Bank & Trust (Ill.), 1978—; v.p. EDP Audit Assos., Inc.; instr. Am. Inst. Banking. Treas. Friends of Chicago Ridge Library, 1978, pres., chmn. pro tem, 1976-78; merit badge counselor, mem. exec. council troup 351 Boy Scouts Am., 1975—; tribe leader YMCA and Indian Guides, 1971-73; 2d lt., fin. officer CAP. Served with USAF, 1958-61. Cert. data educator, bus. educator. Mem. EDP Auditors Assn. (pres., dir. Chgo. chpt.), Am. Inst. Banking, Bank Adminstrn. Inst., Inst. Internal Auditors, Assn. Computing Machinery, Governors State U., Moraine Valley Community Coll. alumni assns, Computer Sci. Library. Roman Catholic. Office: 6825 W 111th St Worth IL 60482

ZARISH, JOSEPH FREDERICK, furniture mfr.; b. Chgo., Mar. 13, 1919; s. Michael and Ursula (Petrick) Z.; B.S. in Marketing Distbn., U. Ill., 1940; postgrad. Northwestern U., 1941, 46-47, Havana (Cuba) Bus. U., 1946; m. Jane Butler, June 21, 1952. Founder export co., Havana, 1946; salesman Salmanson & Co., N.Y.C., 1946-48, mgr. Chgo. office, 1947, asst. to pres., 1948; nat. sales and merchandising mgr. Sealy, Inc., Chgo., 1948-53; exec. dir. Spring Air Co., 1953, exec. v.p., 1953-56; v.p. merchandising Schnadig Corp. and subsidiaries, Internat., Karpen, J.L. Chase, 1956, v.p. mktg. parent co., 1958-60, also dir.; pres. Flagship Enterprises, 1950-65; v.p. marketing Storkline Corp., 1961-62, also dir.; pres. Chamberline Metal Products Co., 1962-64, also dir.; dir. Sandymac Corp., 1961-63; pres. Canterbury House, Inc., Peru, Ind., 1964—, Award Exhibits, Inc., 1956-62; cons. in field; mem. White House Conf. on Small Bus., 1979-80. Mem. savs. bonds div. U.S. Sec. Treasury Staff, 1942-43; mem. steering com. NCCJ, 1953-62; membership chmn. Mississinewa Reservoir Devel. Assn., 1968-71; chmn. indsl. gifts Miami County Heart Fund, 1971-72, 80, chmn. indsl. div., 1971-74, chmn. div., 1975; sec. Grissom AFB Community Council, 1975-76, 1st v.p., 1977, pres., 1978. Bd. dirs., sec. Chgo. chpt. Am. Diabetic Assn., also mem. exec. com., treas. Chgo. and No. affiliates, 1975-76, bd. dirs., 1975—, chmn. nat. audit com., 1976-77, nat. dir., 1977—; bd. dirs. United Fund, Peru, treas., 1974; bd. dirs. Clarence Darrow Community Center, Hull House, 1969-74, hon., 1974—; chmn. Am. Diabetes Assn. Greater Chgo. and No. Ill., 1974—. Served from pvt. to maj. Signal Corps, AUS, 1941-46. Recipient Kimberly Clark Promotional Award, 1953. Mem. U. Ill. Alumni Assn., Res. Officers Assn., Soc. Gen. Semantics, Nat. Assn. Bedding Mfrs., Am. Legion (post chaplain), Peru C. of C.,

Delta Phi (trustee 1965-75), Alpha Kappa Psi. Clubs: National Sales Executives, Furniture of America (pres. 1962), Executives. Author promotional booklets, articles in sales jours. Home: 1579 Woodvale St Deerfield IL 60015 Office: 217 E Canal St Peru IL 46970

ZARTMAN, VANCE ALLEN, accountant; b. Huntington County, Ind., Nov. 7, 1936; s. Walter Austin and Alma Kimberley (Fort) Z.; B. Mus. Edn., Ind. U., 1958; M.B.A., 1967; m. Jane Marie Benedict, Aug. 25, 1957; children—Chadd Austin, Gretchen Jayne. Tchr., N. Vernon (Ind.) City Schs., 1958-59; teaching asso. Ind. U., 1965-67; mgr. adminstrv. services div. Arthur Andersen & Co., Indpls., 1967-78; founder, pres. Zartman & Assos., Inc., C.P.A.'s, Indpls., 1978—. Served with USAF, 1959-65. C.P.A., Ind. Mem. Am. Inst. C.P.A.'s, Ind. C.P.A. Soc., Planning Execs. Inst. Methodist. Clubs: Indpls. Athletic, YMCA. Home: 7424 Wood Stream Dr Indianapolis IN 46254 Office: Suite 312 9101 Wesleyan Rd Indianapolis IN 46268

ZATZMAN, JOSEPH, Can. govt. ofcl.; b. St. John, N.B., Can. Nov. 20, 1912; s. Louis and Ida (Handler) Z.; student in commerce Dalhousie U., 1933; LL.D. (hon.), St. Mary's U., N.S., 1979; m. Leah Flam, Aug. 22, 1939; children—Karla, Michael. Owner, operator grocery, Dartmouth, N.S., Can., 1934-57; chmn. Resources Devel. Bd. Province N.S., N.S. Fisheries Loan Bd., N.S. Farmers Loan Bd.; vice chmn. Indsl. Commn.; adv. bd., dir. Royal Trust Co.; bd. dirs. Atlantic Provinces Transp. Commn. Pres., Dartmouth C. of C., Maritime Provinces C. of C.; mem. Dartmouth City Council, also mayor; chmn. United Jewish Appeal, Israeli Bond Com.; regional authority chmn. Halifax-Dartmouth & County; bd. govs. St. Mary's U. Liberal. Jewish. Clubs: Curling, Dartmouth Yacht, Dartmouth Rod and Gun, Brightwood Golf, Dartmouth. Home: 102 Newcastle St Dartmouth NS B2Y 3Y5 Canada Office: 5151 George St Halifax NS B3J 2R7 Canada

ZAVADA, MARY ROBERTA, editor, writer; b. Passaic, N.J., Jan. 11, 1936; d. John Michael and Sophie Catherine (Majowicz) Z.; A.B. magna cum laude, Coll. of St. Elizabeth, 1957; M.A. in Creative Writing, De Paul U., 1959; postgrad. Breadloaf Sch. English, 1961; postgrad. (English-Speaking Union fellow 1962), London U., 1962, 63-64. Editor, Sylvania News, asso. editor The Scanner, Sylvania Electronic Systems, Waltham, Mass., 1968-69; account exec. Anderson Assos., Boston, 1969-70; editor Publs. div. Ednl. Testing Service, Princeton, N.J., 1971-74, dir. program editorial services Coll. Bd. div., 1974—; instr. Trinity Coll., Washington, 1961-63, Northeastern U., 1967-70, Mass. Bay Community Coll., 1969-70. Recipient 1st prize Prix de Paris writing contest Vogue mag., 1957. Mem. Authors Guild, Authors League Am. Roman Catholic. Contbr. stories and articles to mags. and newspapers including Vogue, Am., N.J. Weekly of N.Y. Times, Chgo. Tribune, Washington Post. Home: 161 Franklin Corner Rd Apt D-7 Lawrenceville NJ 08648 Office: Ednl Testing Service Rosedale Rd Princeton NJ 08541

ZAYTOUN, JOSEPH ELLIS, ins. agy. exec.; b. Kinston, N.C., Sept. 14, 1920; s. Ellis and Isabelle (DaKash) Z.; A.B. in Econs., U. N.C., Chapel Hill, 1943; m. Thelma Elizabeth Knuckley, Nov. 7, 1943; children—Albert Joseph, Robert Ellis, Mary Zaytoun Benton, Stephen Knuckley. Partner, Zaytoun News Agy., New Bern, N.C., 1946-54; owner, gen. mgr. Zaytoun Gift & Toy Shop, New Bern, 1951-57; agt. John Hancock Mut. Life Ins. Co., New Bern, 1957-62; pres. Joseph E. Zaytoun & Assos., New Bern, 1958-62; v.p. Associated Insurers, Inc., Raleigh, N.C., 1962—; pres. Zaytoun & Assos. Inc., 1976—; chmn. local adv. bd. United Carolina Bank, Raleigh, N.C.; founding mem., past chmn. Capitol Nat. Bank, Raleigh. Chmn. publicity and promotion com. Tryon Palace Commn., New Bern, 1979—; mem. N.C. Bd. Elections, 1961-65; chmn. City of New Bern Civil Service Commn., 1957-61. Served to 1st lt. USMCR, 1943-47. Mem. Nat. Assn. Life Underwriters, Am. Soc. C.L.U.'s, Million Dollar Round Table (life), Raleigh Assn. Life Underwriters, Wake County Estate Planning Council (pres. and chmn. 1969-71), VFW. Democrat. Roman Catholic. Clubs: MacGregor Downs Country, Capitol City, K.C., Civitan (v.p. 1980—). Home: 205 Annandale Dr Cary NC 27511 Office: Associated Insurers Inc 1033 Wade Ave Raleigh NC 27611

ZECCA, BARRY JAY, hypnosis cons.; b. Newark, Sept. 29, 1944; s. Harry G. and Viola L. (Kohn) Z.; A.A. in Bus., Union Coll., 1968; B.S. in Mktg., Fairleigh Dickinson U., 1970; postgrad. Yeshiva U., 1975-78, New Sch. Social Research, 1978—. Mktg. exec. Xerox Corp., N.J., 1970—; pres. Dynamic Concepts, South Orange, N.J., 1974—; exec. dir. Learning Dynamics, Inc., West Orange, N.J.; faculty Ethical Hypnosis Tng. Center. Probation counselor Union County Probation Dept; mem. stop smoking com. Am. Cancer Soc. Mem. Assn. to Advance Ethical Hypnosis (certified), Internat. Soc. Profl. Hypnosis, Internat. Assn. Forensic Hypnosis. Contbr. articles to Hypnosis Quar. Home: 1529 Long Meadow Mountainside NJ 07092 Office: 19 Hutton Ave West Orange NJ 07052

ZECH, THECLA ROSEMARIE KOESTERS, printing co. exec.; b. Carthagena, Ohio, July 22, 1935; d. Leander Bernard and Barbara Rose (Hess) Koesters; B.A., U. Dayton (Ohio), 1966; m. Richard Lee Zech, May 14, 1976. With Hooven-Dayton Co., 1953—, prodn. mgr., 1965-71, v.p., gen. mgr., 1971—; trustee employee edn. program Graphic Arts Internat. Union. Mem. Am. Soc. Women Accts., Nat. Fedn. Ind. Businesses (action council), Nat. Assn. Accts., Am. Mgmt. Assn., Dayton M.B.A. Club. Club: Pilot (Kettering, Ohio). Home: 3615 Laurel Fork Rd Dayton OH 45414 Office: 430 Leo St Dayton OH 45404

ZEE, TIEN PEI, toy and plastic mfg. cos. exec.; b. Shanghai, China, Aug. 13, 1936; s. Z. Z. and W. F. (Wong) Z.; came to U.S., 1956, naturalized, 1963; student Whittier Coll., Oreg. State U.; student U. So. Calif. Grad. Sch., 1961-63; m. Kimiko Haniu, Feb. 17, 1971; children—Jin Min, Jinly, Jinsen. Research engr. Emery Industries, Inc., Santa Fe Springs, Calif., 1961-63; pres. Zee Toys, Inc., Long Beach, Calif., 1965—, Intex Plastics Sales Co., Long Beach, 1971—, Intex Plastics Inc., Gardena, Calif., 1977—, also dir.; dir. Zyll Enterprises, Ltd., Minda Indsl. Corp., Taipei, Taiwan. Mem. Am. Pres.'s Assn. Republican. Home: 4 El Concho Ln Rolling Hills CA 90274 Office: 4130 Santa Fe Ave Long Beach CA 90801

ZEGAR, EUGENE, JR., automotive co. exec.; b. Newark, Apr. 12, 1946; s. Eugene and Gladys T. (Byk) Z.; B.A., Alliance Coll., 1967; J.D., U. Toledo, 1970; m. Frances Smith, Aug. 19, 1967; children—Eugene, Tracy, Kenneth, Becky. Mgr. employee benefits Am. Motors, Jeep Corp., Toledo, Ohio, 1971-73, mgr. hourly benefits and employment, 1973-78, mgr. salaried personnel and employee services, 1978-80, dir. indsl. relations Jeep Corp., 1980—. Bd. dirs. Toledo Plan, 1975—. Mem. Am., Ohio, Toledo bar assns., Toledo Personnel Mgmt. Assn., Ohio State, NW Ohio self insured assns. Roman Catholic. Home: 5143 Bridlington St Toledo OH 43623 Office: 940 N Cove Blvd Toledo OH 43657

ZEHNDER, LAWRENCE EDWARD, financial and mgmt. cons.; b. Santa Monica, Calif., Mar. 11, 1930; s. John Edward and Alice Gertrude (Weeks) Z.; B.S. in Bus. Adminstrn., U. Calif. at Los Angeles, 1952, M.B.A., 1966; m. Delores May Loper, June 5, 1955; children—Lawrence M., Linda M., Laura M. Sr. accountant Calif. Inst. Tech., 1971-73; asst. controller J. Walter Thompson Co., Los Angeles, 1973-74; controller Ear Research Inst., Los Angeles, 1974-75; dir. KM&L Industries, Los Angeles; lectr. finance Los Angeles Harbor Coll.; adj. instr. bus. U. Redlands; now financial and mgmt. cons. Mem. Father's Action Com. Westwood Sch., Los Angeles, 1967—. Mem. Financial Mgmt. Assn., Delta Upsilon. Episcopalian. Address: 2013 Veteran Ave Los Angeles CA 90025

ZEINER, EUGENE ANDREWS, molecular physicist; b. N.Y.C., Mar. 15, 1930; s. Eugene Francis and Marie (Andrews) Z.; M.S. in Mech. Engring., Cornell U., 1952, Ph.D. in Engring. Physics (NSF scholar 1957-59), 1959; m. Gwendolyn White, June 14, 1953 (div. 1957). Research engr. Jet Propulsion Lab., Pasadena, Calif., 1959-63; mgr. engring. dept. Electro-Optical Systems Co., Pasadena, 1963-66; mgr. satellite system div. Space Gen. Corp., El Monte, Calif., 1966-71; sr. scientist Aerojet Electro-Systems Co., 1971—; partner Krajan Investment Co.; cons. computer scis. and design. Served to lt. comdr. USNR, 1952-57; Korea. Decorated Air medal. Mem. Am. Inst. Aeros. and Astronautics, Inst. Environ. Scis., ASTM (exec. v.p. com. on contamination). Contbr. articles to profl. jours.; patentee adsorption power generator, air evacuation system. Home and Office: 13909 Old Harbor Ln Marina del Rey CA 90291

ZELCER, ISAAC, neckwear mfg. co. exec.; b. Havana, Cuba, May 18, 1935; s. Kiwa and Sara (Horowitz) Z.; came to U.S., 1960; naturalized, 1966; ed. U. Havana; m. Loly Shaftal, Mar. 11, 1955; children—Alan, Elena, Robin. Asst. prodn. mgr. Spiegel Neckwear, N.Y.C., 1960-62; prodn. mgr. Fabil Mfg. Co., N.Y.C., 1962-63; prodn. mgr. Randa Neckwear Corp., Hackensack, N.J., 1963-65, asst. to pres., 1965-70, v.p., 1970-73, pres., 1973-80; pres. Isaco Internat. div. Charles Jourdan Cravats, Miami, Fla., 1980—; pres. Gino Pompeii Neckwear, Geoffrey Beene Neckwear; dir. Four Star Industries, P.R., GP Spa Formia, Italy. Mem. Neckwear Assn. Am. (dir.), N.J., Italian chambers commerce. Jewish. Clubs: Empire State (N.Y.C.); Cricket (Miami, Fla.). Home: 1215 N Biscayne Point Rd Miami Beach FL 33141 Office: 599 NW 29 St Miami FL 33127

ZELDMAN, MAURICE IRVING, engring. and mgmt. cons.; b. N.Y.C., Sept. 8, 1927; s. Harry and Rae (Seligsohn) Z.; B.M.E., CCNY, 1955; M.A.S., Adelphi U., 1963; m. Phyllis Sylvia Gross, Aug. 24, 1951; children—Lewis Jeffrey, Peter David. Sr. engr. Bulova Research and Devel. Lab., 1958-63; mgr. robotics and automation AMF, 1963-66; mgr. engr. atomic absorption Perkin-Elmer, 1966-67; dir. tech. Rockwell Internat., 1967-73; pres. Emzee Assos., Pitts., 1973—; lectr. tech. mgmt. seminars Am. Mgmt. Assn. Served with USNR, 1945-46. Lic. profl. engr., N.Y. Mem. IEEE, Assn. Iron and Steel Engrs., Engrs. Soc. Western Pa. Author: The Business Future for Industrial Robots, 1973; Keeping Technical Projects on Target, 1978; Creative Concepts, 1980; inventor Versatran Robot, inertial navigation systems, mining shovel, med. devices. Office: 1401 Pueblo Dr Pittsburgh PA 15228

ZELLER, MARK STEVEN, commodity specialist; b. San Bernadino, Calif., Apr. 2, 1945; s. Albert and Faye (Merrims) Z.; student Weber State Coll., 1960-63, Brigham Young U., 1965, 69; B.S. in Journalism and Advt., U. Utah, 1967, postgrad., 1967-69; m. Harriet Lasko, Mar. 25, 1979. Bus. adv. Bus. Advisors, Inc., Ogden, Utah, 1965-70; ins. agt. Mut. Benefit Life & Fin. Service Co., N.Y.C., 1970-72; account exec. trainee Merrill Lynch, Pierce, Fenner & Smith, N.Y.C., 1972; broker Bache & Co., N.Y.C., 1973-75; commodity specialist Dean Witter Reynolds, N.Y.C., 1975—; lectr. commodity futures; registered rep. Chgo. and Amex Options Exchanges; lectr. 1st Global Conf. on Future, Toronto, Ont., Can., 1980. Mem. citizens adv. council Nat. Republican Congressional Com., 1978—; pres. Concerned Citizens, 1978—; sponsor Rep. Senatorial Club. Mem. Am. Stock Exchange Club, N.Y. Stockbrokers Forum, N.Y. Stockbrokers Club, World Future Soc., Assn. M.B.A. Execs., Alpha Kappa Psi, Sigma Delta Phi. Home: Royal York Suite East 8C 425 E 63d St New York NY 10021 Office: 5 World Trade Center 6th Floor New York NY 10048

ZELLER, NICHOLAS, sugar co. exec.; b. Auid, Transylvania, May 9, 1914; s. Isidore K. and Gisela (Gal) Z.; B.A., Ecole Superieur de Commerce, Alba Julia, Transylvania, 1932; m. Eleanore Knauer, Dec. 6, 1944; 1 son, George. With lumber and export bus. Transylvania to 1947; pres. Ferromar, S.A., Naviera Polaris, S.A.; v.p. Aceros Unidos de Cuba, Havana, 1950-60; v.p. in charge molasses dept. Amerop Corp., N.Y.C., 1963-67; v.p., treas. Central Aguirre Sugar Co, N.Y.C., 1967-68, exec. v.p., treas., 1968-72; treas. Aguirre Co., N.Y.C., 1972-78; vice chmn. bd. Westway Trading Co., 1978—. Home: 600 W 246th St Riverdale NY 10471 Office: 464 Hudson Terr Englewood Cliffs NJ 07632 also PO Box 1607 Englewood Cliffs NJ 07632

ZELLER, ROBERT GRIFFING, investment banker; b. Los Angeles, July 25, 1918; s. John Baptiste and Shirley (Emanuel) Z.; A.B., Stanford U., 1939; LL.B., Harvard U., 1942; m. Mildred Koob, Nov. 12, 1976; children by previous marriage—Avery French, Constance Elizabeth. Admitted to N.Y. bar, 1944; law clk. Wright, Gordon, Zachary, Parlin & Cahill, N.Y.C., 1943-54; partner firm Cahill, Gordon, Reindel & Ohl, N.Y.C., 1955-63; partner F. Eberstadt & Co., Inc., N.Y.C., 1963-69, chmn. bd., 1969-78, chmn. exec. com., 1978-79; chmn. bd. Chem. Fund, Inc., 1976-79; vice chmn. Surveyor Fund, F. Eberstadt Mgrs. and Distbrs. Inc., 1969-79; dir. Cunningham Drug Stores, Inc., Engelhard Minerals & Chems. Corp., S.E. Rykoff & Co. Mem. Phi Beta Kappa, Beta Theta Pi. Episcopalian. Clubs: Downtown Assn., Downtown Athletic (N.Y.C.); Nat. Arts. Home: PO Box 949 Center Harbor NH 03226

ZELTZER, LEE BARRY, small bus. cons. co. exec.; b. Bklyn., Oct. 28, 1948; s. Fred and Shirley (Marshak) Z.; B.A., SUNY, Buffalo, 1969; postgrad. Coll. Law, U. Ariz., 1977-80; m. Jennifer Ann Stark, Dec. 31, 1977; 1 son, Nicholas. Instr. anatomy and physiology Pima Jr. Coll., Tucson, 1970-71; gen. mgr. Motorless Transit Authority, Tucson, 1971-74, Flotation Concepts, Tucson, 1974-80; v.p. Small Bus. Cons. Co., Tucson, 1980—; cons. waterbeds C. B. Vanvorst Co., Los Angeles, 1978-79. Recipient award Waterbed Mfrs. Assn., 1979. Mem. Am. Bar Assn. Patentee waterbed safety liner design (2). Home: 70 Calle Encanto Tucson AZ 85716

ZEMAITIS, ALGIRDAS JONAS ALEXIS, internat. orgn. exec., cons.; b. Salniskiai Manor, Lithuania, Mar. 9, 1933; came to U.S., 1949, naturalized, 1954; s. Vincentas Petras and Bronislava (Rusecki-Ruseckas) Z. de Druck; grad. student U. Bonn (Germany), 1954-56, B.A. (hon.), Balliol Coll., Oxford (Eng.) U., 1959, M.A., 1964; m. Vanda Jadvyga Kibort-Kybartas, Apr. 5, 1956; children—Alexis-Pius-Kestutis, Maria-Birute, Rita-Vilia, Paulus-Algirdas, Julia-Dalia. Vice pres., asst. to pres. Union-Chretienne-Democrate d'Europe Centrale S/J, Paris, France, 1955-59; sr. economist Borg-Warner Internat. Corp. Chgo., 1959-61; dir. gen. Market Facts ROC Internat., Chgo., 1962-63; internat. economist Sears, Roebuck & Co., Chgo., 1963-66; sr. internat. trade officer AID, U.S. Dept. State, Washington, 1966-68; economist FAO, UN, Rome, 1968-75, country project officer, 1975—. Chmn., Bonn Komite Litauisches Welt Gemeinschaft, Bonn, Germany, 1954-56; del. Internat. Christian Democratic Movement, Europe and Latin Am., 1955-66. Served with AUS, 1952-54. Decorated knight comdr. Equestrian Order Holy Sepulchre of Jerusalem. Fellow Royal Econ. Soc.; mem. Acad. Polit. and Social Scis., Am. Polit. Sci. Assn., Am. Econ. Assn., Am. Mgmt. Assn., Soc. for Internat. Devel. Author: The Frontiers in the Region Between the Baltic and the Black Seas, 1960. Contbr. articles to profl. jours. Home: Villa Lituania Via Casalmonferrato 33 Rome Italy 00182 Office: FAO UN Via della Terme di Caracalla Rome Italy

ZENI, BETTY WAGNER, retail co. exec.; b. Chgo., Mar. 3, 1926; d. Percy E. and Elizabeth Cecelia (McGeeney) Wagner; student U. Chgo., 1942-44, U. Zurich, 1946; B.A., Vassar Coll., 1947; postgrad. Katharine Gibbs Sch., 1947-48; m. Ferdinand J. Zeni, Jr., 1974. With Marshall Field & Co., Chgo., 1950—, mem. real estate div., 1950-72, mgr. corp. ins. and property taxes, 1972—. Pres., Women's Nat. Republican Club Chgo., 1976-78, bd. dirs., 1976—; alt. del. Rep. Nat. Conv., 1968; bd. dirs. Lake Shore Condominium Assn., 1975-80; mem. adv. bd., bd. dirs. Civic Fedn.; mem. land valuation com. State St. Council. Mem. Vassar Alumnae Assn., Vassar Club Chgo., Katharine Gibbs Alumnae Assn. (past pres.), Risk and Ins. Mgrs. Soc. (dir. Chgo. chpt. 1974-77), Pewter Collectors Club Am., Midwest Pewter Collectors Club, Lambda Alpha. Home: 1440 N Lake Shore Dr Chicago IL 60610 Office: 25 E Washington St Chicago IL 60602

ZERFOSS, JAY RICHARD, semicondr. mfg. co. exec.; b. Somerset, Pa., June 5, 1934; s. James Buchanan and Maisie Pearl (Berkey) Z.; B.S., Ind. State Tchrs. Coll., 1956; M.B.A., U. Pa., 1961; m. Kay Mills, Aug. 23, 1963; 1 dau., Karen Diane. Sr. acct. Price Waterhouse & Co., Washington, 1961-67; fin. analyst Air America Inc., Washington, 1967-69; v.p., treas. Aerial Application Corp., San Francisco, 1969-70; controller Chanslor & Lyon Co., Inc., Brisbane, Calif., 1970-74; v.p. fin. and adminstrn. Pacific Ready-Mix, Inc., San Mateo, Calif., 1974-77; dir. fin. Toshiba Semicondr. (U.S.A.), Inc., Sunnyvale, Calif., 1977—; mgmt. cons.; instr. Coll. of San Mateo. Served with AC, USN, 1956-59. C.P.A., D.C. Mem. Am. Inst. C.P.A.'s. Home: 59 Roosevelt Circle Palo Alto CA 94306 Office: 1220 Midas Way Sunnyvale CA 94086

ZERFOSS, LESTER FRANK, mgmt. cons., educator; b. Mountaintop, Pa., Nov. 2, 1903; s. Clinton and Mabel (Wilcox) Z.; B.A. cum laude, Pa. State U., 1926, M.Ed., 1934, Ed.D., 1958; m. Harriet Mildred Cary, Dec. 21, 1928 (dec. Dec. 1979); children—Patricia Ann (Mrs. Thomas Sibben), Clinton Cary, Robert Williamson; m. 2d, Irma J. Allen, July 12, 1980. Coll. tchr., pub. sch. adminstr., Pa., 1928-41; supr. design, devel. Gen. Motors Inst., 1942-46; head supervisory devel. Detroit Edison Co., 1946-52; corporate tng. dir. Am. Enka Corp. (N.C.), 1952-59, dir. indsl. relations, mgmt. services, 1959-66, mgmt. cons. tech., mgmt. devel., 1966-73; prof. psychology, dir. mgmt. devel. programs U. N.C. at Asheville, 1966-74, prof. mgmt. and developmental psychology, chmn. dept. mgmt., 1974-76; pres. L.F. Zerfoss Assos., Inc., Mgmt. Consultants, 1976—; cons. on mgmt. devel. State of N.C. Mem. N.C. Personnel Bd., 1966-72, Southeastern Regional Manpower Adv. Com., 1966-71, N.C. Community Coll. Adv. Council, 1966—. Trustee Brevard Coll., Mountain Manpower Corp. Mem. Am. Mgmt. Assn. (lectr. mgmt. devel. pres.'s assn.), Nat. Soc. Advancement Mgmt. (profl. mgr. citation 1962), Am. Soc. Tng. and Devel., Phi Delta Kappa, Kappa Phi Kappa, Kappa Delta Pi, Delta Sigma Phi. Contbg. author Training and Development Handbook, 1967, Management Handbook for Plant Engineers, 1978. Author: Developing Professional Personnel in Business, and Government, 1968. Contbr. articles to profl. jours. Home: 3911 Lovett Circle Charlotte NC 28210 Office: PO Box 386 Liberty SC 29657

ZICCARELLI, SALVATORE FRANCIS, food co. exec.; b. Chgo., May 1, 1936; s. Joseph and Josephine Nancy (Scibilia) Z.; attended U. Ill., 1954-58; m. Sheila Mae Weiss, Oct. 28, 1961; children—Mark S., Kathryn J., Matthew T., Marina M., John X. Chief chemist Schutter Candy Co., Chgo., 1960-62; quality control mgr. Kitchen Art Foods Co., Chgo., 1962-65; dir. research and devel. Good-N-Rich Food Co., Chgo., 1965-67, Newlywed Cracker Co., Chgo., 1965-68; mgr. research and devel. Beatrice Foods Co., Chgo., 1969—; cons. in field. Served with USMC, 1959. Mem. Inst. Food Technologists, Am. Assn. Cereal Chemists, Am. Assn. Dairy Technologists, Am. Assn. Candy Technologists, Catholic Order Foresters (past rec. sec., fin. sec., treas.). Patentee in field. Home: Downers Grove IL 60515 Office: 1526 S State St Chicago IL 60605

ZICK, HUGH JOSEPH, fin. co. exec.; b. Columbus, Wis., Aug. 2, 1931; B.B.A., U. Wis., 1953; M.B.A., U. Chgo., 1960. C.P.A., Price Waterhouse & Co., Chgo., 1966-68; v.p. Greyhound Leasing Corp., Chgo., 1968-72; pres. Am. Fletcher Leasing Inc., Indpls., 1972-78; pres., dir. Household Fin. Co. Leasing Inc., Prospect Heights, Ill., 1978—. Served with U.S. Army, 1953-55. Mem. Am. Inst. C.P.A.'s, Ill. Soc. C.P.A.'s, Am. Assn. Equipment Lessors, Fin. Execs. Inst., Mensa. Office: 2700 Sanders Rd Prospect Heights IL 60070

ZICK, LEONARD O., mfg. exec., financial cons.; b. St. Joseph, Mich., Jan. 16, 1905; s. Otto J. and Hannah (Heyn) Z.; student Western State U., Kalamazoo; m. Anna Essig, June 27, 1925 (dec. May 1976); children—Rowene (Mrs. A. C. Neidow), Arlene (Mrs. Thomas Anton), Constance Mae (Mrs. Hilary Snell), Shirley Ann (Mrs. John Vander Ley) (dec.); m. 2d, Genevieve E. Zick, Nov. 3, 1977. Sr. partner firm Zick, Campbell & Rose, South Bend, Ind., 1928-48; sec.-treas. C. M. Hall Lamp Co., Detroit, 1948-51, pres. 1951-54, chmn. bd., 1954-56; pres., treas., dir. Allen Electric & Equipment Co., Kalamazoo, 1954-56, The Lithibar Co., Holland, Mich., 1956-61; v.p., treas. Crampton Mfg. Co., 1961-63; mgr. corporate finance dept. Manley, Bennett, McDonald & Co., Detroit, 1963-68; mgr. Leonard O. Zick & Assos., Holland, 1968—; dir. Eberhard's Foods, Inc. (Grand Rapids), Kandu Industries, Inc. Former mem. Mich. Republican Central Com. Mem. Nat. Assn. Accountants (past nat. v.p., dir.), Financial Execs. Inst., Stuart Cameron McLeod Soc. (past pres.). Lutheran. Rotarian. Clubs: Detroit Athletic, Renaissance (Detroit); Peninsular (Grand Rapids); Holland (Mich.) Country; Union League (Chgo.); Macawtawa Yacht; East Bay Country (Largo, Fla.). Home: 849 Brook Village Holland MI 49423 also Penthouse Greens 1609F The Fairway 225 Country Club Dr Largo FL 33541 Office: 21 W 16th St Holland MI 49423

ZIDER, LEROY STUART, JR., former chem. co. exec.; b. Bklyn., Feb. 25, 1912; s. Leroy Stuart and Ethel May (Bryer) Z.; student N.Y. U., Mich., N.Y. Coll. Ins.; m. Eleanor Anne Link, Nov. 11, 1939; children—Leroy Stuart, III, Robert Bruce. Gen. agt. Mut. Benefit Life Ins. Co., N.Y.C.; asst. field v.p. Acacia Mut. Life Ins. Co., then mgr. Detroit agy.; gen. agt. Continental Am. Life Ins. Co.; mgr. life dept. Johnson & Higgins Co., N.Y.C.; v.p. sales W.B. McVicker Co., indsl. chemists, Bklyn., 1965-80; past pres. L.I. br. Life Underwriters Assn. City N.Y. Dir. local Civil Def., 1953-60; chmn. bd. govs. West Hempstead (N.Y.) Republican Club, 1948-49. Served with AUS, 1943-45. Mem. Community Ch. Mem. VFW. Clubs: Hempstead Golf and Country, Masons. Home: 299 Colony St West Hempstead NY 11552

ZIEBARTH, KARL REX, railroad exec.; b. Reading, Pa., May 25, 1938; s. Robert Kurt and Leah Evelyn (DuBor) Z.; B.A., Yale, 1959; m. Gisela Hermine Hader, Nov. 13, 1970; children—Viktoria, Alexander, Elena. Analyst, Bank of N.Y., N.Y.C., 1960-63; analyst to 2nd v.p. Hayden Stone Inc., brokers, N.Y.C., 1963-70; asst. v.p. Dominick & Dominick, N.Y.C., 1970-71; v.p., sec., treas. M.-K.-T.

R.R., 1971-78, exec. v.p., 1979—, also dir.; dir. Texas City Terminal R.R., Galveston, Houston & Henderson R.R. Clubs: Mory's (New Haven); Yale (N.Y.C.); Petroleum, Dallas Athletic (Dallas); Racquet (Chgo.); Reform (London). Contbr. articles to publs. Office: 701 Commerce St Dallas TX 75202

ZIEBARTH, ROBERT CHARLES, mgmt. cons.; b. Evanston, Ill., Sept. 12, 1936; s. Charles Alvin and Marian (Miller) Z.; A.B., Princeton, 1958; M.B.A., Harvard, 1964; m. Patience Arnold Kirkpatrick, Aug. 28, 1971; children—Dana Kirkpatrick, Scott Kirkpatrick, Christopher, Nicholas. Mgr. financial analysis Bell & Howell Co., Chgo., 1964, mgr. financial planning, 1965-68, controller photo products group, 1968-69, treas., chief fin. exec., 1969-76; mgmt. cons. Ziebarth Co., 1976—; mem. dirs. adv. bd. Arkwright Boston Ins. Co., 1969—; dir. Corp. Resources, Inc., Telemedia, Inc. Asso., Community Renewal Soc., 1969—; mem. Ill. Bd. Higher Edn., 1971—, Ill. Joint Edn. Commn., 1975; trustee Choate Sch., Wallingford, Conn., Latin Sch., Chgo.; bd. dirs. Harvard Bus. Sch. Fund, U.S.O., Inc. Served to lt. USNR, 1959-62. Mem. Naval Hist. Found., Chgo. Hist. Soc., Art Inst., Mus. Modern Art. Clubs: Mid America, Economics, Executives, Racquet, Saddle and Cycle. Office: 1500 Lake Shore Dr Chicago IL 60610

ZIEGLER, GERALD RICHARD, newspaper exec.; b. Hebron, Nebr., June 15, 1930; s. Frank John and Norine Christine (Helfrich) Z.; m. JoAnne Suzanne Thompson, Sept. 22, 1952; children—Richard, Francis, Elizabeth, Jon, Patrick, Kathryn, Kenneth. Owner, mgr. Hebron (Nebr.) Airways, 1949-53; printer Hebron Jour. Register, 1952-60; printer Scottsdale (Ariz.) Daily Progress, 1960-63, prodn. mgr., 1963—. Mem. Ariz. Newspaper Assn. Roman Catholic. Clubs: K.C., Moose. Home: 8035 E Monte Vista Rd Scottsdale AZ 85257 Office: 7302 E Earll Dr Scottsdale AZ 85252

ZIEGLER, JAMES RUSSELL, cash register sales exec.; b. Warren, Pa., Oct. 10, 1922; s. LeRoy Curtis and Daisy (Gesin) Z.; B.S. in Elec. Engring., Pa. State U., 1943, M.A. in Math., 1948; m. Maxine Evelyn Hogue, Feb. 10, 1952 (dec. Nov. 1968); children—Evalinde Aurelia, Charlotte Elaine, Curtis Wayman, Bruce Allan; m. 2d, Florence M. Bowler, 1969 (div. 1975); 1 son, Scott. UHF wave guide research Norden Corp., N.Y.C., 1943-44; instr. math. Pa. State Coll., 1946-48; instr. math. U. Calif. at Los Angeles, 1948-54, research asso., statistician tchrs. characteristics study sponsored by Am. Council on Edn., 1951-54; mgr. programming services electronic computers Nat. Cash Register Co., Hawthorne, Calif., 1954-68; pres. Turn-Key Computer Applications, 1968-75; dir. So. Fed. Savs. & Loan Assn., Los Angeles, 1968-69; adv. dir. Coast Fed. Savs. & Loan Assn., Los Angeles, 1969-74; sr. cons. analyst NCR Co., San Diego, 1975-78, San Diego Cash Register Co., 1978—. Tech. cons. Office Naval Research Study; data processing cons. psychol. research projects U. So. Calif., also U. Utah. Served with USMCR, 1944-46; PTO. Mem. Tau Beta Pi, Sigma Tau, Eta Kappa Nu. Republican. Methodist. Mason. Author: Time Sharing Data Processing Systems, 1967; also numerous articles. Home: 1050 Pinecrest Ave Escondido CA 92025 Office: 3701 Bancroft Dr Spring Valley CA

ZIELINSKI, DIANNE BEVERLY, med. technologist; b. Detroit, May 6, 1953; d. Edward Joseph and Theresa Cecilia (Borkowski) Z.; B.S. in Chemistry, B.S. in Med. Tech., Detroit Inst. Tech., 1974; Ph.D., Pacific So. U., 1977; postgrad. Wayne State U., 1975-76. Med. technologist Grace Hosp., Detroit, 1973-75; supr. Spl. Chemistry Lab., Deaconess Hosp., Detroit, 1975-77; chief technologist N.W. Med. Lab., Southfield, Mich., 1977-79; gen. mgr. Mich. Med. Lab., Farmington Hills, Mich., 1979—; cons. to pathologists and clin. labs. Mem. Am. Soc. Clin. Pathologists, Clin. Lab. Mgmt. Assn. (Certificate of Recognition 1975), Am. Chem. Soc., AAAS. Office: 23900 Orchard Lake Rd Farmington Hills MI 48024

ZIGLI, RONALD MICHAEL, educator; b. Apr. 22, 1938; B.S., Ohio State U., 1961; M.B.A., Ga. State U., 1970, Ph.D., 1976; married; 2 children. Research asso. instnl. planning Ga. State U., 1970-73; asst. prof. mgmt. Appalachian State U., Boone, N.C., 1974-77, asso. prof., 1977-81, prof., 1981—, asst. dean John A. Walker Coll. Bus., 1978—, dir. Center for Mgmt. Devel.; mgr. fin. services Hunt Mfg. Co., Phila.; programmer Apollo and Nimbus project Gen. Electric Co., Daytona Beach, Fla., 1965-69; cons. in field. Served with USAF, 1962-64. Mem. Am. Inst. Decision Scis. (v.p. acad. affairs Southeastern chpt. 1980-81, v.p. membership 1977-78), Acad. Mgmt., So. Mgmt. Assn., So. Mktg. Assn., Data Processing Mgmt. Assn., Pi Sigma Epsilon, Alpha Iota Delta, Beta Gamma Sigma, Gamma Iota Sigma. Contbr. articles to profl. jours.

ZIKE, ROBERT JOSEPH, employee benefits cons.; b. Scranton, Pa., Jan. 15, 1953; s. Joseph Julian and Nellie Madeline (Cwynar) Z.; B.S. in Acctg., U. Scranton, 1974, M.B.A., 1977; cert. U. Pa., 1980; m. Jill Louise Pitman, July 26, 1980. Successively ins. broker and cons., teller, asst. v.p., head dept. employee benefits Trust div. Northeastern Bank of Pa., Scranton, 1974—; cons. ins. programs. Active Everhart Mus. Art and Natural Sci. Cert. employee benefit specialist, 1980; lic. ins. broker, Pa. Mem. Am. Acctg. Assn., Assn. M.B.A. Execs., Am. Inst. Banking, Internat. Found. Employee Benefit Plans, Corp. Three Fiduciaries. Mem. Polish National Catholic Ch. Office: PO Box 937 Scranton PA 18501

ZILBERBERG, NAHUM NORBERT, video and film prodn. exec., publisher; b. Manheim, Germany, Feb. 13, 1925; s. Mendel Max and Pasia Paula (Morgenstern) Z.; came to U.S., 1957, naturalized, 1961; grad. Sem. for Art Tchrs., Tel Aviv, 1952; B.F.A., Yale, 1960, M.F.A. (fellow), 1961; m. Rita Orechovsky, 1946 (div.); children—Oded, Doron; m. 2d, Barbara Cahn, 1968 (div.); children—Jedediah, Noah. Lectr. in printing for Printers Union of the Histadrut, Israel, 1946-52; govt. printer, Tel Aviv, 1950-52; prof. Sem. for Art Tchrs., Tel Aviv, 1952-57, Yale, 1958-61; tchr. of arts and crafts in elementary and secondary schs., Tel Aviv, 1952-57; tchr. and jr. rabbi Congregation B'nai Jacob, New Haven, 1957-60; designer of instructional materials Montgomery County (Md.) Bd. Edn., 1962-63; asst. designer Macmillan Pub. Co., N.Y.C., 1963-64; asst. designer Harcourt Brace & World, Inc. (name changed to Harcourt Brace Jovanovich, Inc. 1970), San Francisco, 1964-65, art dir. Center for Study of Instruction div., San Francisco, 1965-68, v.p. Center, 1968-72, sr. v.p., 1972-80; pres. Harcourt Brace Jovanovich Films div., 1973—; founder, pres. N2 Videodisc Prodns., Mill Valley, Calif., 1980—; adj. prof. San Francisco State U., 1978—; lectr. on spatial edn. various schs. and parent groups in Calif. 1974—; mem. policy bd. Learning Recognition Program, Armstrong Coll., Berkeley, Calif., 1975—; adj. prof. San Francisco State U., 1978—. Served with Israel Def. Forces, 1948-50. Recipient Grand award Internat. Film and TV Festival of N.Y., 1976; Cindy award Info. Film Producers Am., 1976; Gold Camera award U.S. Indsl. Film Festival, 1977; gold awards 10th Ann. Festival of Ams., 1977, 14th Ann. Chgo. Internat. Film Festival, 1978, 21st, 22d Ann. Internat. Film and TV Festival N.Y., 1978, 79, 80, Houston Internat. Film Festival, 1979, Gold Camera award 13th Ann U.S. Indsl. Film Festival, 1980. Mem. Assn. Ednl. Communications and Tech., Am. Inst. Graphic Arts, Calif. Humanities Assn., Bookbuilders West. Author and designer: Self Expression and Conduct: The Humanities Activity Kits, 1975; inventor system for printing ednl. materials for publ.; research in technol. areas of communication for edn.; conceived and produced first self-contained interactive ednl. video disc program. Home: 833 Marin Dr Mill Valley CA 94941 Office: Harcourt Brace Jovanovich Films Polk & Geary St San Francisco CA 94109

ZILKHA, ABDULLA KHEDOURI, banker; b. Baghdad, Iraq, Jan. 7, 1913; s. Khedouri A. and Louise (Bashi) Z.; m. Zmira Many, Sept. 22, 1935; children—Elie, Daniel, Ruth. With Banque Zilkha, 1929-48; dir. UFITEC, Zurich, Switzerland, 1950—. Mem. Circle Interallie. Clubs: Polo de Paris; Golf de Saint Nom la Breteche. Home: 11 bis Ave du Maréchal Manoury 75016 Paris France

ZILKHA, DANIEL ABDULLA, publisher; b. Cairo, Oct. 1, 1942; came to U.S., 1961, naturalized, 1978; s. Abdulla K. and Zmira M. Z.; B.S.E., Princeton U., 1964; M.B.A., Harvard U., 1969; m. Frances P. Rogers, Dec. 15, 1970; children—Leonora Rebecca, Nathaniel Maurice, Rebecca Rogers. Partner, Soditic S.A., Geneva, 1971-77; pres. Auction Holdings Inc., N.Y.C., 1978; pub. Art & Auction mag., N.Y.C., 1979—. Office: Art & Auction 250 W 57th St New York NY 10019

ZILKHA, EZRA KHEDOURI, banker; b. Baghdad, Iraq, July 31, 1925; s. Khedouri A. and Louise (Bashi) Z.; came to U.S., 1941, naturalized, 1950; grad. Hill Sch., Pottstown, Pa., 1943; A.B., Wesleyan U., Middletown, Conn., 1947; m. Cecile Iny, Feb. 6, 1950; children—Elias Donald, Simha Donna, Bettina Louise. Pres., Zilkha & Sons, Inc., N.Y.C., 1956—; dir. INA Corp., Phila., INA Life Ins. Co. of N.Y., Handy & Harman, N.Y.C., Mothercare Ltd., London, Mothercare Stores, N.Y.C., Newhall Land & Farming Co. Calif. Trustee ICD Rehab. and Research Center, N.Y.C., Lycee Francais de N.Y., French Inst./Alliance Francaise, Spence Sch., N.Y.C.; trustee, chmn. investment com. Wesleyan U. Decorated chevalier de la Legion d' Honneur, officer Ordre National du Merite (France). Mem. Council Fgn. Relations, Clubs: Univ., Knickerbocker, Meadow; Polo, Travellers (Paris). Home: 927 Fifth Ave New York NY 10021 Office: 30 Rockefeller Plaza New York NY 10112

ZIMINSKI, RICHARD WILLIAM, environ. cons., system design engr.; b. Mineola, N.Y., Aug. 23, 1934; s. Peter J. and Anna (Clausen) Z.; B.Sc.E.M., Lehigh U., Bethlehem, Pa., 1956; m. Mary Ann Wechtel, Feb. 12, 1955; children—Ann Marie, Peter Karl, Richard William II, Julia Elizabeth, Matthew August. Supr., N.J. Zinc Co., 1956-60; mine/quarry supt. to plant supt. Capital Cement Co. div. Martin-Marietta, 1960-67; designer modular concept in ESP's Precipitair Pollution Control, 1967-70; organizer Precipitator Group, Chem. Constrn. Co., 1970-71; v.p., partner Cambridge Root Environ. Controls, 1971-74; pres. Ambient Engring., Inc., Somerville, N.J., 1974—. Registered profl. engr., N.J., N.Y., W.Va. Mem. AIME, Air Pollution Control Assn. Contbr. to Air Pollution Control and Design Handbook, 1977. Office: 61 Reimer St Somerville NJ 08876

ZIMMER, LINDA FENNER, writer, payment services specialist; b. Balt., Nov. 9, 1942; d. John William and Harriet (Sherbon) Fenner; B.B.A., Pa. State U., 1964; M.B.A., Boston Coll., 1967; m. Dieter Zimmer, Oct. 14, 1972; 1 dau., Heidi Anne. Sr. research asso. Bank Adminstrn. Inst., Park Ridge, Ill., 1967-72; researcher, writer on fin. payment services; bd. advs. Bank Automation Assn. Delaware Valley, 1975—; co-chmn. Nat. Confs. on Automated Teller Machines, 1978—. Leader, Troop 651 Cook County council Girl Scouts U.S.A., 1968-71. Republican. Episcopalian. Author profl. articles, reports; editorial adv. bd. Mag. of Bank Adminstrn., 1980—. Home and Office: 56 Roberts Rd Marlborough CT 06447

ZIMMERMAN, EUGENE WALTER, developer, investor, owner motor hotels; b. nr. Jenner Twp., Pa., Mar. 23, 1909; s. Robert and Amanda A. (Walter) Z.; student pub. schs.; m. Eleanor Witt, Apr. 8, 1930 (div. Oct. 1965); children—Doris Joan (Mrs. James H. Mapes), Ronald E., Rosalie Eleanor (Mrs. Ralph C. Johnson); m. 2d, Irene Fabian, May 23, 1966. Developer, owner Zimmerman Motor Co., Somerset, Pa., 1938-45, Roof Garden Motor Hotel, 1941-52, Ella-Gene Apts., Ft. Lauderdale, Fla., 1946-49, Motel Harrisburg, Pa., 1950-57 (now known as Holiday Motor Hotel-East), 1957—; developer, owner Holiday Motor Hotel, West, Harrisburg, Pa., 1952—, Holiday Inn Town, 1962—; owner Gene Zimmerman's Automobilorama and Mus., Holiday West, Ft. Lauderdale, Fla., 1965—; ofcl. staff editor Clissold Pub. Co., Chgo. Cons. to motor hotel industry. Recipient Hall of Fame award Am. Motel Mag., Chgo., 1961, Merit Resolution, Pa. Ho. of Reps., 1968. Mem. Am. Hotel Assn., Pa. Motel Assn. (pres. 1953-54, dir. master hosts 1955—, ambassador master hosts 1961, 62), Am. Motor Hotel Assn., (v.p., dir. 1956), Pa., Central Pa. restaurant assns., Nat. Assn. Travel Orgn., Hotel Sales Mgrs. Assn., Hotel Greeters Am., Inter-Am., Internat. hotel assns., Hammond Organ Soc., Tall Cedars Lebanon, Harrisburg C. of C., Am. Airlines (Admiral), Acacia, Antique Automobile Club Am. (sr. judge), Classic Car Club Am., Horseless Carriage Club, Vets. Motor Car Club, Auburn-Cord-Duesenberg Club, Pierce-Arrow Soc., Rolls Royce Owners Club, S.A.R., Am. Soc. Travel Agts., Richard Nixon Assos., Pa. Soc. Republican. Lutheran. Mason (K.T., Shriner), Rotarian. Clubs: T.W.A. Ambassador (life), American Airlines Admiral (life) (N.Y.C.); Matson Mariners' (hon. navigator) (San Francisco) Curved Dash Owners (New Hope, Pa.); Executives, Zembo Luncheon (Harrisburg); Le Club International (Fort Lauderdale); Chub Cay (The Bahamas). Internat. editor: Am. Motel mag., 1962—. Office: Automobilorama Inc 1500 SE 17th St Fort Lauderdale FL 33316

ZIMMERMAN, GEORGE HERBERT, banker, financial cons.; b. N.Y.C., Sept. 10, 1895; s. George Henry and Jessie (Browne) Z.; B.C.S., N.Y. U., 1921; D.Sc. (hon.), Assumption U., Windsor, Ont., Can., 1961; m. Mary Helen Campion, July 7, 1926; children—Doris (Mrs. Andrew G. Bato), Elaine (Mrs. Rankin P. Peck), Jessie (Mrs. J. Daniel Hitchens), Georgia (Mrs. John J. Loftus), Louis. Employee N.Y. Edison Co., 1911-16, Guaranty Securities Corp., N.Y.C. and Montreal, 1916-18, Gen. Motors Acceptance Corp., N.Y.C. and Chgo., 1919-26; v.p. Comml. Credit Co., Balt., 1926-28; exec. v.p. Universal Credit Corp., 1928-41; v.p. Universal C.I.T. Credit Corp., Detroit, 1941-50; chmn. bd., pres., dir. Mich. Bank, Detroit, 1944-50; organizer, G. H. Zimmerman Co., bus. and financial cons., 1950; surveyed econ. and financial conditions in Australia and New Zealand, 1956; dir. C.I.T. Financial Corp. (N.Y.C.); cons. Dearborn Motors Credit Corp. (Birmingham, Mich.), Ford Motor Co. Can., Ltd. (Windsor, Ont.); financial cons. Gar Wood Industries, Inc., Wayne, Mich. Dir., Met. Detroit Bdlg. Found., 1954; pres., trustee Friends Assumption Found., 1955-60. Chmn. finance com. bd. regents Assumption U., Windsor, Ont., Can., 1953. Chmn. bldg. com. St. Paul Sch. and Convent, Grosse Pointe, Mich., 1950-51. Served with 30th CAC, World War I; war chest Met. Detroit, 1942; U.S. Treasury Dept. war finance com. for Mich., 1944-45. Recipient Assumption U. Alumni award, 1959. Mem. A.I.M. (charter mem. pres.'s council 1950-51), Financial Analysts Soc. Detroit, Albert Gallatin Assos. of N.Y. U., N.Y.U. Alumni Detroit (organizer, 1st pres.), Delta Sigma Pi (life). Catholic. Clubs: Grosse Point, Detroit Athletic, Detroit Country, Grosse Pointe Yacht (Detroit); Century (Chgo.); N.Y. University; Surf (Miami Beach, Fla.). Home: 125 Kenwood Rd Grosse Pointe Farms MI 48236 Office: 220 Bagley Ave Detroit MI 48226

ZIMMERMAN, JOHN ELLIOTT, corp. exec.; b. Marshfield, Wis., Sept. 7, 1918; s. George Frederick and Blanche (Crocker) Z.; Ph.B., U. Wis., 1940; J.D., U. Chgo., 1949; m. Muriel Yvonne Ramharter, June 14, 1948; 1 son, George Elliott. Cost accountant Gen. Electric Co., Bridgeport, Conn., 1940-41; asst. sec. Bear Brand Hosiery Co., Chgo., 1946-52; admitted to Ill. bar, 1949; practiced law, Chgo., 1949-52; mfg. mgr. Ford Motor Co., Dearborn, Mich., 1952-60; corporate comptroller Massey Ferguson Ltd., Toronto, Ont., Can., 1960-64; sec.-treas. King-Seeley Thermos Co., Ann Arbor, Mich., 1964-65, v.p. finance, sec., 1966-68; v.p. finance and adminstrn., dir. Air Products and Chems., Inc., Allentown, Pa., 1968-72; exec. v.p., dir. GAF Corp., N.Y.C., 1972-74; sr. v.p. Certain-Teed Corp., Valley Forge, Pa., 1974—. Served to lt. comdr. USNR, 1941-46. C.P.A., Ill. Home: 17 Chamond-Arbordeau Devon PA 19333 Office: PO Box 860 Valley Forge PA 19482

ZIMMERMAN, JOHN WALLACE, bus. cons., exec.; b. Milw., Apr. 25, 1929; s. Wallace and Gladys (Parker) Z.; student Carroll Coll., 1947-49; B.S., U. Tenn., 1951; M.B.A., U. Wis., 1952, postgrad., 1953; postgrad. U. Minn., 1958-60; m. Charlotte McCallen, Aug. 28, 1951; children—John, Paul, Mark, James. Materials handling engr. Oscar Mayer & Co., Madison, Wis., 1952-53; prodn. supr., indsl. engr. Pillsbury Co., Springfield, Ill., 1953-55, asso. tng. mgr., Mpls., 1955-57, corp. tng. mgr., 1957-61; asso. Kepner-Tregoe Inc., Princeton, N.J., 1961-69, sr. v.p., 1969—, dir., 1973—; vis. lectr. Centre d'Etudes Industrielles, Geneva, 1974—; cons. in strategy formulation, problem solving, decision making. Mem. Am. Soc. Tng. and Devel. (dir. 1980, Torch award 1977). Republican. Author: (with Benjamin Tregoe) Top Management Strategy, 1980; contbr. articles to profl. jours. and anthologies. Home: 414 Blue Spring Rd Princeton NJ 08540 Office: PO Box 704 Princeton NJ 08540

ZIMMERMAN, LARRY WAYNE, value engr.; b. Frederick, Md., Aug. 28, 1948; s. Bernard William and Mary Louise Z.; B.S.C.E., Valparaiso U., 1970; m. Susan Carol Heitmuller, Aug. 22, 1970. Project mgr. Engring. Sci., Inc., Washington, 1970-73; v.p. value engring. coordinator Arthur Beard Engrs., Inc., Chevy Chase, Md., 1973-80; asso. Smith Hinchman & Grylls, Washington, 1980—. Mem. S.W. Howard County (Md.) Park Council, 1977-78. Mem. Water Pollution Control Fedn., Am. Water Works Assn., Soc. Am. Value Engrs. (pres. Washington chpt.), Am. Mgmt. Assn. Lutheran. Office: 1050 17th St Washington DC 20036

ZIMMERMAN, M. PAUL, assn. exec.; b. N.Y.C., Apr. 22, 1934; s. Louis and Rose Z.; B.A. cum laude, Dartmouth Coll., 1955; LL.B., Yale U., 1958; m. Margot Lurie, Aug. 18, 1957; children—Jeffrey, John, Julie. Admitted to N.Y. bar, D.C. bar; gen. atty. CAB, Washington, 1959; asso. firm Wolf & Wolf, Washington, 1960-62; gen. counsel, exec. sec. Nat. Aircraft Noise Abatement Council, Washington, 1963-66; dir. Am. Peace Corps, S. India, 1966-68, Iran, 1968-71; 1st dep. adminstr. EPA, N.Y.C., 1971-74; exec. dir. Moped Assn. Am., Washington, 1975—. Served in U.S. Army, 1958-59. Mem. Internat. City Mgmt. Assn., N.Y. State Bar Assn., D.C. Bar Assn., Phi Beta Kappa. Clubs: Nat. Lawyers; City of N.Y. Contbr. introductions to books, numerous articles to profl. jours. Office: Moped Assn Am 1001 Connecticut Ave NW Washington DC 20036

ZIMMERMAN, MORTIMER FRED, financial exec.; b. Bklyn., July 17, 1922; s. Isaac and Esther (Goodman) Z.; B.B.A, Coll. City N.Y., 1947; postgrad. N.Y.U., 1964-67; m. Annette Furman, Oct. 19, 1947; children—John Mitchell, Robert Peter. Controller, L. Grossman Sons, Inc. (Mass.), 1958—; treas. ABC Consol. corp., Long Island City, N.Y., 1963-68; treas., chief financial officer, 1968; v.p. finance Nytronics, Inc., Pelham Manor, N.Y., 1968—; now v.p., treas. Russ Togs, Inc., N.Y.C. Lectr. Am. Mgmt. Assn. Served with AUS, 1943-45. C.P.A., N.Y. Mem. Financial Execs. Inst., Am. Inst. C.P.A.'s. Jewish religion (past pres. temple). Home: 5 Vista Dr Great Neck NY 11021 Office: 27-11 49th Ave Long Island City NY 11101

ZIMMERMAN, NANCY, mgmt. cons.; b. Liberty, N.Y., Oct. 9, 1948; d. Joseph D. and Shirlie L. Sardonia; B.A., George Mason U., 1970; M.L.S., U. Md., 1975. Mgr. info. sci. dept. EG&G WASC, Inc., Rockville, Md., 1971-77; pres. Zimmerman & Assos. Inc., 1977—. Office: 7700 Leesburg Pike Suite 420 Falls Church VA 22043

ZIMMERMAN, RICHARD ANSON, chocolate mfg. co. exec.; b. Lebanon, Pa., Apr. 5, 1932; s. Richard Paul and Kathryn Clare (Wilhelm) Z.; B.A. in Commerce, Pa. State U., 1953; m. Nancy J. Cramer, Dec. 27, 1952; children—Linda Joan, Janet Lee. Asst. sec. Harrisburg Nat. Bank (Pa.), 1956-58; with Hershey Foods Corp. (Pa.), 1958—, asst. to pres., 1965-71, v.p., dir., 1971-76, pres., chief operating officer, 1976—, also chief exec. officer; pres. Cory Corp., Chgo., 1971-74. Chmn. Derry Twp. Sch. Bldg. Authority. Trustee Lebanon Valley Coll. Served to lt. USNR, 1953-56. Recipient Alumni Fellow award Pa. State U., 1978. Mem. Phi Kappa Psi. Methodist. Mason, Rotarian (pres. Hershey club 1973-74). Club: Hershey Country. Home: 220 Bahia Ave Hershey PA 17033 Office: 19 E Chocolate Ave Hershey PA 17033

ZIMMERMAN, SIDNEY JACOB, financial exec.; b. N.Y.C., Nov. 17, 1918; s. William and Anita (Rosenthal) Z.; B.B.A., CCNY, 1939; J.D., N.Y. Law Sch., 1955; m. Rosaly Haines, Mar. 17, 1950; children—Edward, Harriet. Pub. accounting, N.Y.C., 1939-42; auditor Army & Air Force Exchange Service, U.S. and Europe, 1946-50; agt. IRS, N.Y.C., 1950-52; controller, asst. treas. A. C. Israel Commodity Co., Inc., N.Y.C., 1952-64, asst. v.p., controller, 1964-70; comptroller A. C. Israel Coffee Co., Inc., 1964-70; controller A. C. Israel Cocoa, Inc., 1965-70; controller M. Golodetz & Co., Inc., N.Y.C., 1970-78, fin. v.p., 1978—; fin. v.p. Golodetz Trading Corp., N.Y.C., 1980—; treas. Bucan Packing Corp., Fla., 1973-74, Recovery Industries Corp., S.C., 1979—, Reclamation Internat., Inc., S.C., 1979—; admitted to N.Y. bar, 1955. Served to capt. AUS, 1942-46, ETO. C.P.A., N.Y. Mem. N.Y. State Soc. C.P.A.'s. K.P. Office: M Golodetz & Co Inc 666 Fifth Ave New York NY 10019

ZIMNY, ROBERT WALTER, welding co. exec.; b. Chgo., June 7, 1937; s. Walter William and Francis Clara (Greskowiak) Z.; B.S. in Edn., Chgo. State U., 1971; M.A. in Adminstrn. and Supervision, Govs. State U., 1976; m. Patricia S. Tillema, June 6, 1964; children—Brian Walter, Douglas Robert, Russell Patrick. Welding leadman Elkay Mfg. Co., Broadview, Ill., 1955-63; foreman Stembridge Mfg. Co., Addison, Ill., 1963-65; welding dir. Am. Inst. Engrs., Chgo., 1965-66; welding instr., dept. chmn. Chgo. Vocational High Sch., 1966-70; welding instr. Triton Community Coll., Melrose Park, Ill., 1968-70; welding instr., dept. chmn. Washburne Trade Sch., 1970-78; pres. Zimny Welding Service, Chgo., 1978—; cons. Weldors, Inc., 1970-78. Served with U.S. Army, 1959-61. Mem. Chgo. State U. Alumni Assn., Govs. State U. Alumni Assn., Chgo. Tchrs. Union. Republican. Roman Catholic. Clubs: Downers Grove Sportsman, Salmon Unltd., Ill. Fedn. Sportsmen, Moose. Author: Welding Instructor Handbook, 1971. Office: 3314 W 47th St Chicago IL 60632

ZINDER, NEWTON DONALD, stock market analyst; b. N.Y.C., Aug. 12, 1927; s. Paul and Jennie (Feld) Z.; B.A., N.Y. U., 1948, M.B.A., 1957; M.A., Columbia U., 1949; m. Clarice Katz, Dec. 26, 1954; children—Marla, Andrea, Pamela. Securities analyst Ira Haupt & Co., N.Y.C., 1953-60; securities analyst E. F. Hutton & Co., Inc.,

N.Y.C., 1960-63; stock market analyst, 1963—, v.p., 1969-79, 1st v.p., 1979-81, sr. v.p., 1981—. Served with USN, 1945-46. Mem. N.Y. Soc. Securities Analysts, Market Technicians Assn., N.Y. U. Fin. Club, N.Y. U. Alumni Assn. (dir.). Republican. Jewish. Office: One Battery Park Plaza New York NY 10004

ZINGRAFF, MICHAEL, JR., mag. editor; b. Phila., July 4, 1920; s. Michael and Barbara (Lux) Z.; student Ursinus Coll., 1945-48; m. Nancy C. Green, Apr. 5, 1942; 1 dau., Elizabeth Michele. Ins. agt. Mut. of N.Y., Phila., 1966-67; asst. to pres. 63d St. Motors, Inc., Phila., 1955-65, agency mgr., 1965-73; wholesaler editor Motor Age Mag., Chilton Co., Radnor, Pa., 1973—; speaker in field. Served with U.S. Army, 1940-45. Recipient Distinguished Service citation Automotive Organization Team, Inc., 1978. Mem. Am. Bus. Press, Inc., Automotive Service Industries Assn. (pres. Phila. area), Automotive Orgn. Team (sec. Phila. chpt.), Automotive Booster Clubs Internat., Automotive Warehouse Distbrs. Assn. (del.), Distbrs. Inst., Middle Atlantic Regional Assn. (dir.), Pa. Assn. Notaries Public. Republican. Presbyterian. Home: 211 Drexel Ave Lansdowne PA 19050 Office: Motor/Age Chilton Way Radnor PA 19089

ZINK, PHILIP GARY, mobile home corp. exec.; b. Balt., Aug. 27, 1932; s. Philip Frantz and Mattie (Gary) Z.; student U. Bridgeport (Conn.), 1950-53, U. Conn., 1952; m. Rose Racalbuto, Aug. 28, 1954; children—Philip G., John Scott, Barbara Marie. With Ryder Mobile Homes, Inc., Milford, Conn., 1947—, pres., 1950—; mem. Milford adv. bd. Orange Nat. Bank. Mem. New Eng. Mobile Home Assn. (pres., Conn. legal and legis. com.), Milford C. of C. Republican. Clubs: Rotary (pres.), Race Brook Country, Milford, Masons, Shriners. Home: 200 Margaret Ln Orange CT 06477 Office: Ryder Mobil Homes Inc 1377 Boston Post Rd Milford CT 06460

ZINKEL, ROBERT RUDOLPH, ins. agy. exec.; b. Chgo., Oct. 19, 1931; s. Arthur H. and Elizabeth H. (Gren) Z.; B.S. in Fire Protection Engring., Ill. Inst. Tech., 1953; m. Nellie M. Holderbaum, June 27, 1953; children—Robert C., Sandra S., Nancy M. Engr., Springfield Fire & Marine Ins. Co., Chgo., 1953-56; account exec. Wineman Bros., Inc., Chgo., 1956-69; v.p. Reed Shaw Stenhouse, Inc., Chgo., 1969-78; asst. v.p. Alexander & Alexander, Chgo., 1978—. Pres. Parents Music Assn., Homewood, Ill., 1975-78, Homewood-Flossmoor High Sch. Band Parents Assn., 1978—. Mem. Soc. C.P.C.U.'s (past pres. Chgo. chpt.), Soc. Fire Protection Engrs., Nat. Fire Protection Assn. Presbyterian. Club: Union League (Chgo.) Home: 1720 W 183d St Homewood IL 60430 Office: 130 E Randolph Dr Chicago IL 60601

ZINMAN, JACQUES, ins. agy. exec.; b. Phila., Nov. 7, 1922; B.S., U. Va., 1943; postgrad. U. Pa., 1945-46. Chmn., The Zinman Group, Ins. Agy., 1950—; Watson & Schwartz, Inc., Matawan, N.J. and other locations, 1961-62, pres., 1962—; pres. Frankford Union Ins. Co., 1968—. Mem. exec. com. Pa. state Republican fin. com.; mem. Presdl. Electoral Coll. from Pa., 1972; bd. dirs. Pop Warner Nat. Football League. Served to ensign USNR, 1943-44. Recipient Outstanding Young Man Phila. award Jewish Nat. Fund, 1961. Mem. Ins. Soc. Phila., Variety Club, Theta Delta Chi. Club: Masons. Contbr. articles to profl. jours. Office: 309 Old York Rd Jenkintown PA 19046

ZINNECKER, ROBERT WALLACE, utility co. exec.; b. Cass City, Mich., Apr. 7, 1938; s. William Wallace and Helen Berniece (Bradford) Z.; student Northeastern Sch. Commerce, 1955-57, Internat. Accts. Soc., 1957-60, U. Minn., 1966; m. Elaine I. Johns, Aug. 9, 1958; children—Timothy, Karen, Diana, Bradford. Internal auditor Gen. Telephone Co. Mich., 1958-62; treas. Continental Telephone Co. Mich., 1962-66; controller Continental Telephone Co. Mo., 1966-67; div. controller Central Western Co., Wentzville, Mo., 1967-68; v.p. Contel Data Services Corp., Wentzville, 1968-77; pres. Continental Telephone Co. Iowa and Nebraska, Knoxville, Iowa, 1977—. Bd. dirs. Iowa Wesleyan Coll., Knoxville Community Hosp. Found.; trustee Knoxville Free Meth. Ch. Mem. Am. Mgmt. Assn. Pres.'s Assn., Ind. Telephone Pioneers Assn. Republican. Office: 1214 W Jackson Knoxville IA 50138

ZIRKLE, KENNETH EUGENE, telecommunications engr.; b. Champaign, Ill., Mar. 2, 1945; s. Howard Eugene and Florence Mabel (Dickason) Z.; Asso. in Electronic Tech., So. Ill. U., 1965. Lineman, installer, maintenance Eastern Ill. Telephone Co., 1965-76; traffic engr., dial office adminstr., staff engr. long range planning Mid Continent Telephone Service Corp., Rantoul, Ill., 1976—. Exec. bd. Arrowhead council Boy Scouts Am., 1975—, Dist. Award of Merit, 1977, dist. chmn. No. Dist., 1975-77; pres. Rantoul Beautification Council, 1978. Mem. So. Ill. U. Vocat. Tech. Constituent Soc., So. Ill. U. Alumni Assn. (life). Clubs: Champaign County Sports Car, Moose. Office: 300 N Maplewood St Rantoul IL 61866

ZISKIN, FREDRIC STEVEN, uniform co. exec.; b. Bklyn., May 4, 1947; s. Abraham and Rae (Dorfman) Z.; B.S. in Mktg., Calif. State U., Northridge, 1969; m. Kim Morgan, Jan. 15, 1975; children—Jeffrey, Cameron, Andrew, Joelle. Mktg. and advt. rep. Ideal Toy Corp., Los Angeles, 1970-73; sales and mktg. mgr. Barco of Calif., Los Angeles, 1973-76; nat. sales mgr. Ottenheimer & Co. Inc., Chgo., 1976-78; pres., gen. mgr. Tiffany Uniforms Co. div. Superior Surgical, Seminole, Fla., 1978—. Speaker, sponsor local bus. programs Jr. Achievement, Nassau County, N.Y. Served with USAR, 1969-75. Mem. Research Inst. Am., Am. Mgmt. Assn. Home: 1654 Sheffield Dr Clearwater FL 33516 Office: Tiffiny Uniforms 100th Terr Seminole FL 33542

ZISSELMAN, ISAAC WILLIAM, lawyer; b. Bklyn., Dec. 12, 1941; s. Jack and Sarah (Placer) Z.; B.A., Bklyn. Coll., 1963; J.D., Bklyn. Law Sch., 1967; LL.M. in Taxation, N.Y. U., 1970; m. Marcia E. Blitz, Jan. 26, 1964; children—Jeffrey, Marc. Admitted to N.Y. State bar, 1967, U.S. Supreme Ct. bar, 1975, also various fed. ct. bars; mem. firm Young, Kaplan, Ziegler & Zisselman, N.Y.C., 1972—; lectr. N.Y. U. Sch. Continuing Edn., 1977—; vis. adj. prof. law U. Miami (Fla.), 1977—; lectr. Practising Law Inst., 1971—. Mem. Assn. Bar City N.Y., N.Y. State, Am. bar assns. Democrat. Jewish. Home: 2341 Halyard Dr Merrick NY 11566 Office: Young Kaplan Ziegler & Zisselman 277 Park Ave New York NY 10172

ZIVICA, ROBERT FRANCIS, inventor, marketer; b. N.Y.C., Feb. 5, 1933; s. Frank J. and Janet (Staniecki) Z.; B.B.A. in Mktg., Hofstra U., 1958; M.B.A., Pepperdine U., 1977; m. Barbara MacDermott, May 2, 1959; children—Stephanie, Stacey. With N.Y. World Telegraph & Sun, N.Y.C., Interiors mag., Washingtonian mag., N.Y.C., Suffolk (N.Y.) Sun, Detroit Free Press; founder, owner Select Markets, Inc., Detroit; v.p., gen. mgr., dir. Pro-Sports Mktg. Inc., Concord, Calif.; founder, owner, pres. Zico Corp., 1977—. Served with USN, 1950-53; Korea. Mem. Am. Mgmt. Assn., Inventors Workshop Internat., Gamma Rho Epsilon, Pi Sigma Epsilon. Roman Catholic. Patentee in field. Home: 1045 Springfield Dr Walnut Creek CA 94598 Office: 1910 Olympic Blvd Walnut Creek CA 94596

ZIVIN, NORMAN H., lawyer; b. Chgo., Aug. 10, 1944; s. Alfred E. and Irene (Scher) Z.; E.M., Colo. Sch. Mines, 1965; J.D. cum laude, Columbia U., 1968; m. Lynn F. Fishman, Dec. 27, 1967; children—Allison, Stephen, Michael. Admitted to N.Y. State bar, 1968, Ill. bar, 1970, U.S. Supreme Ct. bar, 1975, also various fed. cts.; asso. firm Cooper, Dunham, Clark, Griffin & Moran, N.Y.C., 1968-70, 71-76, partner, 1976—. Mem. New Castle (N.Y.) Bd. Ethics, 1974-79. Mem. Am. Bar Assn., Assn. Bar City N.Y., N.Y. Patent Law Assn., Am. Patent Law Assn., Am. Inst. Mining Engrs. Clubs: Birchwood; Town (New Castle); Netherland (N.Y.C.). Mem. bd. editors Trademark Reporter, 1971-73. Home: 3 Valley Ln Chappaqua NY 10514 Office: 30 Rockefeller Plaza New York NY 10020

ZOCCOLILLO, ROGER RALPH, chem. co. exec.; b. Haledon, N.J., July 20, 1928; s. Marco and Luigia (Mattei) Z.; B.S. in Chem. Engring., Newark Coll. Engring., 1949; m. Stephanie E., Nov. 17, 1978; children—Mark, James. With Dow Chem Co., Midland, Mich., 1953—, gen. mgr. Italian ops., 1960-64, mng. dir. Dow Lepetit S.P.A., Milan, Italy, 1964-68, asst. gen. mgr. Dow Human Health Dept., Midland, 1968-72, pres. Bentex Mills Dow Badische, East Rutherford, N.J., 1973-74, v.p. bus. mgmt. Dow Badische, Williamsburg, Va., 1974-75, group v.p. fibers and yarns Badische Corp., mem. BASF Group, Williamsburg, 1975—. Served with Chem. Corp, AUS, 1951-53. Recipient Order Merit, Italian Govt., 1968. Mem. Man-Made Fiber Producers Assn. (dir.), Carpet and Rug Inst. (dir.). Home: 8 Hampton Key Williamsburg VA 23185 Office: PO Drawer D Williamsburg VA 23185

ZOELLNER, WELDON JOSEPH, real estate broker; b. Perryville, Mo., Apr. 20, 1927; s. Louis William and Albertie Mary (Renaud) Z.; grad. high sch.; m. Virginia Lee Smith, Oct. 28, 1950; children—Beverly (Mrs. Richard R. Groneck), Cynthia Zoellner Banta, Weldon P. Journeyman, St. Louis Plasterers Union Local No. 3, 1945-49, Cement Masons Local No. 1, St. Louis, 1949-54; sales mgr. Insul-Air Aluminum Products, St. Louis, 1954; partner J & J Window Sales, St. Louis, 1955-58; pres. W. J. Window Sales, St. Louis, 1959-69, Superior Color Reception, St. Louis, 1965-78, Denner Food Products, St. Louis, 1966-67, W. J. Zoellner Realty Co., St. Louis, 1969—. Recipient Distinguished Service award Bridgeton Kiwanis Club, 1970. Lic., Mo., Ark., Okla. Mem. Nat. Farm and Land Inst. (chmn. pub. relations Mo. chpt. 1974-75; accredited; Realtor of Year award 1975, 79, Most Creative Transaction of Yr. Nat. award 1977, 78, v.p. 1977, pres. 1978-79, chmn. nat. mktg. com. 1980), Nat. Assn. Real Estate Bds., Ind. Fee Appraisers, Nat. Market Inst., Am. Investment Counselors (exec. v.p. 1974, pres. 1975—), St. Louis Real Estate Exchange (pres. 1975, dir. 1974-78, Sale of Yr. award 1976), Internat. Exchangors Assn. (pres. region 7 1978—). Democrat. Roman Catholic. Clubs: K.C., Kiwanis. Patentee in field. Home: 10955 Ridgecrest Dr St Ann MO 63074 Office: 3550 McKelvey Rd Suite 206 Bridgeton MO 63044

ZOERNIG, ELIZABETH ANN, corp. exec.; b. Oklahoma City, Feb. 21, 1919; d. Herman Joseph and Elizabeth Dorothy (Berney) Zoernig; A.B. (Trustee scholar 1936-38), Mills Coll., Oakland, Calif., 1938; B.A., life teaching certificate U. Okla., 1940; certificate Blackwood Bus. Coll., Oklahoma City, 1941. Sec., Anderson-Prichard Oil Co., 1941-43, 45-46, Douglas Aircraft Co., 1943-45; sec. to chmn. bd. and chief exec. officer Kerr-McGee Corp., Oklahoma City, 1946—, corporate sec., 1972—. Dir. Oklahoma City chpt. Exec. Women Internat., 1969-73, pres., 1973, adviser, 1974; bd. dirs. Hist. Preservation of Heritage Hills, 1971—, 1st v.p., 1974; regional gov. Mills Coll., 1964-70. Recipient Outstanding Women's award YWCA, 1979. Mem. Ind. Petroleum Assn. Am., Oklahoma City C. of C. (dir.), Anton H. Classen Awards Assn., Kappa Alpha Theta. Club: Oklahoma City Mills Coll. Alumnae. Office: Kerr-McGee Center Oklahoma City OK 73102

ZOLL, WILLIAM ALBERT, contracting cons.; b. Tiffin, Ohio, Apr. 8, 1938; s. Cletus Andrew and Mary Katrine (Allman) Z.; student U. Maine, Orono, 1967-68, McMurry Coll., 1969; B.S. in Mgmt., Wright State U., 1979; m. Muriel Jean Cooper, Feb. 7, 1959; children—Sharen Marie, Michael Gray, Teri-Jo. Enlisted U.S. Air Force, 1955; advanced through grades to master sgt., 1970; inventory mgmt. supt. Wright-Patterson AFB, Ohio, 1971-72, supr. data processing, 1972-75; ret., 1975; contracting cons. Battelle Columbus Labs./USAF, Wright-Patterson AFB, Dayton, 1975—; chmn., chief exec. officer, treas. Forbees Microsystems, Inc., Fairborn, Ohio. Trustee Greater Mad River Twp. Assn., 1976-78. Decorated Air Force Commendation medal with 2 oak leaf clusters, Air Force Meritorious Service medal. Republican. Roman Catholic. Club: Rotary (Fairborn). Home: 4980 Appleridge Ct Dayton OH 45424

ZOLTY, RICHARD CHARLES, ins. co. exec.; b. Ft. Dix, N.J., Oct. 19, 1946; s. John Salvatore and Anna (Marinkos) Z.; B.S., Rutgers U., 1969; m. Linda Ann Sunderlin, Mar. 23, 1974; children—Jason Charles, Ian Gordon. Program dir. York Rd. YMCA, Hatboro, Pa., 1969-70; fire underwriter INA, Phila., 1970-74; sr. property underwriter Nat. Grange Mutual Ins., Keene, N.H., 1974-77, property underwriter, 1977-78, property mgr., 1978-79; br. mgr. A.I.G., Manchester, N.H., 1979—. Home: 29 Woburn Abbey Dr Bedford NH 03102 Office: 1750 Elm St Manchester NH 03107

ZONDERVAN, PETER JOHN (PAT), publisher, religious orgn. exec.; b. Paterson, N.J., Apr. 2, 1909; s. Louis and Nellie Petronella (Eerdmans) Z.; student public schs., Grandville, Mich.; D.Litt. (hon.), John Brown U., 1969; Litt.D., Lee Coll., 1972; m. Mary Swier, May 21, 1934; children—Robert Lee, Patricia Lucille, William J., Mary Beth. Co-founder, Zondervan Pub. House, Grandville, Mich., 1931, Grand Rapids, Mich., 1932—; Pres., Grand Rapids Camp of Gideons, 1938-41, chaplain, 1944-46, pres., 1947-48, internat. trustee, 1950-52, v.p. Gideons Internat., 1952-55, pres., 1956-59, treas., 1972-75, chaplain, 1975-78. Bd. dirs. Christian Nationals Commn., San Jose, Calif.; bd. dirs. Winona Lake Christian Assembly, Ind., 1937—, sec., 1961—; dir. Marantha Bible and Missionary Conf., Muskegon, Mich., 1961; organizer, 1st chmn. Christian Businessmen's Com., Grand Rapids, 1942; chmn. com. for city-wide Evangelistic meeting, 1946. Honored with declaration of P.J. Zondervan Day in Grand Rapids, Dec. 1973. Mem. Internat. Platform Assn. Clubs: Lotus (pres. 1949, 65-67) (Grand Rapids); Peninsular; Blythefield Country. Office: Zondervan Corp 1415 Lake Dr SE Grand Rapids MI 49506*

ZOOK, JOSEPH DUDLEY, heavy machinery mfg. co. exec.; b. Chgo., Mar. 18, 1922; s. Joseph Dudley and Louise Davis (Keeling) Z.; B.S. in Mech. Engring., Purdue U., 1949; m. Kathryn Seese, Dec. 22, 1945; children—Catherine (Mrs. Ralph Anderson), John, Caroline (Mrs. Marc Bertrand), Margaret (Mrs. Laurent Perroud). M.E., Oliver Mining div. U.S. Steel, Hibbing, Minn., 1949-50; dist. mgr. Thew Shovel Co., Lorain, Ohio, 1954-60, product devel. mgr., 1960-63, sales mgr., 1963-65; dist. mgr. Am. Hoist & Derrick Co., St. Paul, 1950-52, mfg. project engr., 1952-54, staff asst. to v.p. mfg., 1965-67, gen. mgr. Ft. Wayne Plant, 1967-71, v.p., 1968—, gen. mgr. St. Paul Plant, 1971-74, v.p., dir. ops., constrn. machinery group, 1974-79, v.p. corp. devel., 1979—; v.p. Am. Hoist Internat. Corp., 1974—. Adv. council Ft. Wayne Vocat. Tng. Center, 1968-70. Bd. dirs. St. Paul Jr. Achievement, 1972—, Am. Communications Network. Served as pilot USMCR, 1942-46. Clubs: Athletic, Univ. (St. Paul); Mendakota Country (St. Paul). Home: 702 Fairmount St Saint Paul MN 55105 Office: 63 S Robert St Saint Paul MN 55107

ZOPF, DAVID EDWARD, business exec.; b. Lansing, Mich., July 14, 1941; s. Edward Jay and Eva Mae (Bauer) Z.; B.A., Mich. State U., 1963; m. Donna Marie Thompson, May 13, 1967; children—David Edward, Amy Marie, Mary Katherine. Purchasing agt. Hager Fox Home Center, Lansing, 1964-66; purchasing agt. Ren Plastics, Lansing, 1966-72; founder, pres. Abacus Enterprises, Lansing, 1972—; founder, pres. CBS Industries, 1974—. Initiated and taught 1st purchasing courses Lansing Community Coll., 1974. Served with AUS, 1964-70. Named Alumnus of Year, Alpha Kappa Psi, 1968. Mem. Purchasing Mgmt. Assn. Central Mich. (pres. 1971). Patentee in field. Home: 2602 Rockdale Ave Lansing MI 48917 Office: 121 W Mt Hope Lansing MI 48910

ZORN, RICHARD LAURENCE, fin. exec.; b. Mt. Vernon, N.Y., Aug. 16, 1940; s. Lewis Edward and Lillian (Rubin) Z.; B.A., Yale U., 1962, LL.B., 1965; m. Frances Heller, Aug. 19, 1969; children—Daniel M., Katherine Heller. Admitted to N.Y. bar, 1965; trial atty. N.Y. regional office SEC, 1965-67; with L.M. Rosenthal & Co., Inc., N.Y.C., 1967-69; pres. R. L. Zorn & Co., N.Y.C., 1969-72; v.p. Ultrafin Internat., N.Y.C., 1972-74, Lehman Bros. Internat., N.Y.C., 1976-78; pres. Balis & Zorn, Inc., N.Y.C., 1978—; mem. N.Y. Stock Exchange; gen. partner BZ/Sommers Asso./Pelican Assos., N.Y.C., Balis & Zorn Internat., Panama, Geneva, 1979—. Pres., The Zorn Found., 1979—; bd. dirs. Nat. Choral Council, 1980—; guest condr. N.Y. String Ensemble, 1980, Manhattan Chorale, 1968-74, N.Y. Choral Soc., 1965-67. Jewish. Club: Yale. Home: 1120 Park Ave New York NY 10028 Office: 5 Hanover Sq New York NY 10004

ZOSS, ABRAHAM OSCAR, chem. co. exec.; b. South Bend, Ind., Feb. 17, 1917; s. Harry and Fannie (Friedman) Z.; B.S. in Chem. Engring., U. Notre Dame, 1938, M.S., 1939, Ph.D., 1941; m. Betty Jane Hurwich, Dec. 24, 1939; children—Roger, Joel, Hope Zoss Schladen; m. 2d, Magda Szanto, May 1978. With Gen. Aniline & Film Corp., Easton, Pa., 1941-47, tech. mgr., Linden, N.J., 1947-55, plant mgr., 1955-57; mgr. mfg. adminstrn., chem. div. Minn. Mining & Mfg. Co., St. Paul, 1957-58, prodn. mgr. chem. div., 1958-60; v.p. Photek Inc., West Kingston, R.I., 1960-62; asst. corp. tech. dir. Celanese Corp., N.Y.C., 1962-65, corp. tech. dir., 1965-66, corp. dir. comml. devel., 1966-69; v.p. corp. devel. Tenneco Chems., Inc., N.Y.C., 1969-71, Universal Oil Products Co., Des Plaines, Ill., 1971-72; group v.p. Engelhard Industries div. Engelhard Minerals & Chem. Corp., Murray Hill, N.J., 1972-74, v.p. bus. devel., 1974-77; v.p. corp. devel. CPS Chem. Co., Inc., Old Bridge, N.J., 1977, dir., v.p., chief adminstrv. officer, 1978—; mem. field info. agency Office Tech. Service, Commerce Dept., Europe, 1946; teaching asst. U. Notre Dame, 1939-41. Mem. Met. Mus. Art, N.Y.C., Mus. Modern Art, N.Y.C. Recipient Centennial Sci. award U. Notre Dame, 1965; certified profl. chemist Am. Inst. Chemists. Fellow Am. Inst. Chemists, AAAS; mem. Am. Chem. Soc., Am. Inst. Chem. Engring., N.Y. Acad. Scis., Comml. Devel Assn., Soc. Chem. Industry, Catalysis Soc. N.Y., Assn. Corp. Growth, Nat. Planning Assn., Newcomen Soc. N.Am. Clubs: Chemists' (N.Y.C.), B'nai B'rith. Contbr. articles to profl. publs. Patentee in field. Home: Claridge House I Apt 505 Verona NJ 07044 Office: PO Box 162 Old Bridge NJ 08857

ZSCHAU, JULIUS JAMES, lawyer; b. Peoria, Ill., Apr. 1, 1940; s. Raymond Ernst and Rosamond Lillian (Malicoat) Z.; B.S. in Commerce, U. Ill., 1962, J.D., 1966; LL.M., John Marshall Law Sch., 1978; m. Leila Joan Krueger, Aug. 7, 1971; children—Kristen Elisabeth, Kimberly Erna. Admitted to Ill. bar, 1966, U.S. Supreme Ct. bar, 1973, Fla. bar, 1975; atty. Ill. Central R.R. Co., Chgo., 1966-68; asso. firm Coin & Sheerin, Chgo., 1968-70, Snyder. Clarke, Dalziel, Holmquist & Johnson, Waukegan, Ill., 1970-72; counsel Ill. Center Corp., Chgo., 1972-74; v.p., gen. counsel, sec. Am. Agronomics Corp., Tampa, Fla., 1974-75; pres. firm Sorota & Zschau, P.A., Clearwater, Fla., 1975—; dir. Holopeter & Post Inc., 1974-76, SE States Mortgage Ic., 1975-77; v.p., gen. counsel, sec. Am. Internat. Land Corp., 1974-75. Candidate Ill. Constl. Conv., 1969; bd. dirs. Fla. Gulf Coast Symphony; mem. Republican exec. com. Pinellas County. Served to comdr. USNR, 1962-64. Mem. S.A.R., Am., Ill., Chgo., Clearwater, Fla. bar assns., Clearwater C. of C. (v.p.). Lutheran. Clubs: Kiwanis, Masons, Shriners. Home: 1910 Saddlehill Rd N Dunedin FL 33528 Office: 2515 Countryside Blvd Suite A Clearwater FL 33515

ZUCKER, LEON WILLIAM, financial exec.; b. N.Y.C., May 7, 1921; s. Benjamin and Helen (Schellerman) Z.; B.B.A., Coll. City, N.Y., 1940; postgrad. Stanford, 1943-44; m. Arline Davidson, June 17, 1947; children—Harold G., Ricki Glantz. Treas., Sealand Dock and Terminal Corp., Fed. Stevedoring Co., Inc., Bklyn., 1947-59, treas., dir. Containerships, Inc., N.Y.C., 1959-61; treas. Erie & St. Lawrence Corp., 1959-61; asst. treas. Meml. Sloan-Kettering Cancer Center, Sloan-Kettering Inst. for Cancer Research, Meml. Hosp. for Cancer and Allied Diseases, 1961-66, v.p. fin., 1966-76; v.p. fin. Pub. Health Trust of Dade County (Fla.), 1976—; pvt. practice C.P.A., 1940-42, 45-47; cons. HEW, 1969—; adj. prof. U. Miami, 1978—. Bd. dirs. Nassau Center for Emotionally Disturbed Children, 1965-70, treas., 1966-69, pres., 1969-70; bd. dirs. Pride of Judea Treatment Center, 1974-76; mem. U.S. Com. for Israel Environment; trustee Arnold and Marie Schwartz Coll. Pharmacy and Health Scis., L.I. U., 1976-77; vice chmn. Fla. Medicaid Advisory Com. Mem. Am. Inst. C.P.A.'s, Financial Execs. Inst. (dir.), N.Y. State Soc. C.P.A.'s, Hosp. Fin. Mgmt. Assn., Fla. Inst. C.P.A.'s. Home: 3650 N 36th Ave Hollywood FL 33021 Office: 1611 NW 12th Ave Miami FL 33136

ZUCKER, LEONARD CHARLES, trucking co. exec.; b. Bronx, June 13, 1933; s. Ralph Gilbert and Elsie (Himmelstein) Z.; B.A., Yeshiva U., 1951; postgrad. Acad. Advanced Traffic, 1955; m. Elaine Trachtman, Dec. 25, 1955; children—Anne, Esther Lynne, Rhea Miriam, Ronald Gary. Ordained rabbi, 1957; with Charlton Bros. Transp. Co., Inc., Phila., 1953-58; sales mgr. Phila.-Pitts., Carriers, Phila., 1958-61; dist. sales rep. Preston Inc., also v.p. Drake Motor Lines Inc., Cherry Hill, N.J., 1965-76; v.p., chief operating officer Pinto Trucking Service, Inc., Phila., 1976—. Bd. dirs. Motor Transport Labor Relations, Phila., 1973-76. Served with U.S. Army, 1953-55. Mem. Assn. of ICC Practitioners, Delta Nu Alpha. Democrat. Jewish. Clubs: Air Cargo, Nat. Fedn. Men's, Fifth Wheel, Traffic and Transp. Author: Why be a Transportation Specialist, 1971; Safety Guide for the Motor Carrier, 1973. Home: 321 Brookline Ave Cherry Hill NJ 08002 Office: 1414 Calcon Hook Rd Sharon Hill PA 19079

ZUCKERMAN, GORDON NATHANIEL, ins. cons.; b. Schenectady, N.Y., Mar. 18, 1942; s. George and Gloria Z.; A.A.S., Hudson Valley Community Coll., 1962; B.S., Union Coll., 1970; m. Linda Kolker, June 7, 1964; 1 dau., Miriam Michelle. Chem. technician dept. insulating materials Gen. Electric Co., 1963-67; research chemist Albany Felt Co., Menands, N.Y., 1967-70; licensed spl. agt. N.Y. Life Ins. Co., Albany, N.Y., 1970—; tchr. estate planning, adult edn. Shenendahowa High Sch. Served with U.S. Army, 1968-69. C.L.U. Mem. Nat., N.Y. State, Schenectady, Albany (dir. 1973—, pres. 1977-78) assns. life underwriters, Am. Soc. C.L.U.'s, Estate Planning Council of Eastern N.Y., Internat. Assn. Fin. Planners. Treas., Temple Gates of Heaven, pres. Temple Brotherhood. Clubs: Gideon Lodge, B'Nai B'rith. Home: 1137 Fernwood Dr Schenectady NY 12309 Office: 277 State St Box 613 Schenectady NY 12301

ZUCKERMAN, IVAN JAY, ins. co. exec.; b. Cleve., Oct. 18, 1931; s. Lester A. and Belle R. (Berk) Z.; B.B.A., So. Meth. U., 1953; m. Marjorie Anne Barker, Nov. 1, 1953; children—Faye Eileen, Karen Marie, Susan Beth, Robin Gay. Underwriter, Southwestern Life Ins. Co., Dallas, 1956-57, sr. life underwriter, 1957-60, life and health, 1960-67, chief health underwriter, 1967-72, 2d v.p. underwriting dept., 1972-74, v.p., 1975—. Active membership drs. Downtown Dallas YMCA. Served with U.S. Army, 1954-56. Mem. Inst. Home Office Underwriters, Home Office Underwriters Assn., SW Ins. Assn., Delta Sigma Pi, Sigma Alpha Mu. Jewish. Clubs: Masons, Shriners. Home: 4847 Forest Bend Dallas TX 75234 Office: PO Box 2699 Dallas TX 75221

ZUCKERMAN, PAUL HERBERT, lawyer; b. Bklyn., Mar. 7, 1935; s. Max B. and Minnie (Mendelson) Z.; B.S. in Econs., U. Pa., 1957; M.B.A. in Corp. Fin., N.Y. U., 1964; J.D., Bklyn. Law Sch., 1967; m. Sara Shiffman, Aug. 25, 1963; children—David Isaac, Daniel Mark. Security analyst U.S. Trust Co., N.Y.C., 1962-66; sr. security analyst CNA Mgmt. & Research Corp., N.Y.C., 1966-71, mgr. research, 1971-73; admitted to N.Y. bar, 1968, U.S. Supreme Ct. bar, 1973, U.S. Ct. of Appeals bar for 2d Circuit, 1972, U.S. Dist. Ct. bars, So. Dist. N.Y., 1975, Eastern Dist. N.Y., 1975, U.S. Tax Ct. bar, 1977; individual practice law, N.Y.C., 1973—. Vice chmn. bus. div. adv. bd. Borough Manhattan Community Coll., 1976—; bd. dirs. Jewish Center of Kings Highway, Bklyn. Served with Supply Corps USN, 1957-60. Mem. Am. Bar Assn., Assn. of Bar City of N.Y., Fed. Bar. Council, N.Y. Soc. Security Analysts, Bklyn. C. of C. (vice chmn. mktg. com. 1977—). Author, pub. newsletter Tax Planning and Estate Planning Concepts; speaker Harvard Bus. Sch. Club, 1980; contbr. articles to publs. in field. Office: 28 W 44th St New York NY 10036

ZUDIKER, MICHAEL HARVEY, pharm. mfg. co. ofcl.; b. Poughkeepsie, N.Y., Apr. 6, 1944; s. Hyman and Ruth Zudiker; M.S. in Chemistry, Queens Coll., 1967; Ph.D. in Chemistry, City U. N.Y., 1975; M.B.A. in Mktg., St. John's U., 1976; m. Mona Russo, June 11, 1966; 1 son, Steven. Chemist, GTE Research Lab., Bayside, N.Y., 1970; market research asso. Schering Corp., Kenilworth, N.J., 1973-77, mgr. quality control adminstrv. services, Union, N.J., 1977, mgr. quality control systems, 1978-80, mgr. new product planning, 1980—. Mem. Am. Chem. Soc., Am. Mgmt. Assn. Home: 103 W Roselle Ave Roselle Park NJ 07204 Office: 1011 Morris Ave Union NJ 07083

ZUEHLKE, WILLIAM HENRY, fin. cons., former life ins. co. exec.; b. Appleton, Wis., Apr. 19, 1915; s. William H. and Ina (Babcock) Z.; Ph.B., Lawrence U., 1936; m. Muriel Mae Heidemann, May 2, 1953. Trading and syndicate mgr. Harris, Hall & Co., investment bankers, Chgo., N.Y., 1936-46; sr. v.p., dir. investments Aid Assn. for Lutherans, Appleton, Wis., 1946-77; dir. emeritus First Nat. Bank of Appleton, Post Corp., Appleton. Trustee Lawrence U., Valparaiso U., State of Wis. Investment Bd., 1975-77; bd. dirs. Santa Cruz County Fair and Rodeo Assn. Served to lt. comdr. USNR, 1941-46. Paul Harris fellow. Mem. Chartered Financial Analysts, Fraternal Investment Assn., Soc. Tympanuchus Cupido Pinnatus, Ariz. Nature Conservancy, Heard Mus., Tucson Mus. Art, Ariz.-Sonora Desert Mus., Sigma Phi Epsilon. Republican. Lutheran. Clubs: Rotary, Old Pueblo (Tucson). Home: Tunnel Springs Ranch Sonoita AZ 85637 Office: PO Box 326 Sonoita AZ 85637

ZUKERMAN, HERBERT JAY, acct.; b. Bklyn., Dec. 31, 1943; s. Sidney Martin and Ada (Sapir) Z.; B.C.E., Cornell U., 1964, M.B.A., 1966; m. Ann Levinson, Aug. 10, 1977; children—Amy, David, Samuel, Adam, Jeffrey, Caryn. With Dayton Constrn., N.Y.C., 1969-77; chief exec. officer Tidewater Fast Foods, Inc., Norfolk, Va., 1977-79; dir. ops. Great Atlantic Mgmt. Co., Newport News, Va., 1979-80; with Edmondson Ledbetter & Ballard, C.P.A.'s, Norfolk, 1980—. Bd. dirs. Congregation Beth El, Norfolk, 1979—, Jewish Community Center, 1979—, United Jewish Fedn., 1979—; vice chmn. Tidewater Apt. Council, 1979—. Mem. ASCE, Am. Inst. C.P.A.'s, Va. Soc. C.P.A.'s. Jewish. Club: Beth El Men's (pres. 1980—). Home: 4057 Richardson Rd Virginia Beach VA 23455

ZULICH, MICHAEL JOSEPH, cons.; b. N.Y.C., Feb. 18, 1955; s. Michael and Anna Nina (Lubicich) Z.; B.S., Poly. Inst. N.Y., 1977; student Pace U., 1980—; m. Margaret Iannuzzi, July 2, 1978. Project analyst Mfrs. Hanover Trust Co., N.Y.C., 1977-78; internal cons. Morgan Guaranty Trust Co., N.Y.C., 1979—. Mem. Am. Inst. Indsl. Engrs. Home: 3656 Johnson Ave Riverdale NY 10463 Office: 30 Broad St New York NY 10015

ZUMWALT, ROSS WAYNE, feed mfg. co. exec.; b. Nebo, Ill., Oct. 6, 1929; s. Humphrey Andrew and Mossaline Euna (Allison) Z.; B.S., U. Ill., 1956, M.S. in Edn., 1959; m. Margaret Ellen Eagleton, Apr. 5, 1953; 1 dau., Tracy Ann. Tchr. vocat. agr. Jamaica Consol. Schs., Sidell, Ill., 1956-59; with Ralston Purina Co., various locations, 1959-71; v.p. Gooch Feed Mill Corp., Lincoln, Nebr., 1971-74, pres., 1974—, also dir.; dir. English River Pellets, Asso. Industries of Lincoln. Served with AUS, 1949-52. Mem. Am. Feed Mfrs. Assn. Am. Legion. Republican. Presbyterian. Clubs: Hillcrest Country, Exec., Elks. Home: 1313 Piedmont Rd Lincoln NE 68510 Office: Box 81308 Lincoln NE 68501

ZUNICH, LINDSEY H., EDP exec.; b. Denver, Oct. 4, 1927; s. Albert Eugene and Virginia (Brown) Z.; B.A., Calif. U., Long Beach, 1952; m. Barbara Jane Best, June 15, 1952; children—LeAnn, Jana Lynn, Lark O'Lee, Jay Dravan. Tchr. gifted students El Monte (Calif.) Schs., 1956-62; systems analyst Certified Grocers, City of Commerce, Calif., 1963-66; systems programmer N. Am. Aviation, Downey, Calif., 1967-73; mgr. systems programming Rockwell Internat., Downey, 1974-76, supr. service control center, Seal Beach, Calif., 1977—. Scoutmaster Cub Scouts, 1971-73; mgr. Covina Nat. Little League, 1973; pres. Covina Boys Basketball, 1973-75; counselor Boy Scouts Am., 1974-77, Girl Scouts U.S.A., 1975; instr. water safety ARC; bd. dirs. Country Club Sch. Mem. Nat. Mgmt. Assn. Republican. Mem. Moravian Ch. Home: 110 Termino 304 Long Beach CA 90803 Office: PO Box 2837 Seal Beach CA 90740

ZUNIGA, THOMAS MARK, real estate developer; b. Balize, Brit. Honduras; May 27, 1947; came to U.S., 1962, naturalized, 1970; s. John Jacob and Stella Simeona (Majia) Z.; m. Karen Elizabeth Williamson, Dec. 1, 1974; children—Mark, Malyssa, Stephanie. Tchr. math. N.Y. Bd. Edn., N.Y.C., 1968-69; real estate appraiser, mortgage underwriter N.Y. Life Ins. Co., N.Y.C., 1969-72; asst. v.p. Investors Funding Corp., N.Y.C., 1972-74; tax supr., real estate specialist Coopers & Lybrand, P.C., N.Y.C., 1974-76; v.p. Nat. Housing Partnership, Washington, 1976-80; founder, pres. Zuniga & Assos. Inc. and Rehabitat Ltd., Washington, 1980—; dir. Altomar Group, N.Y.C.; lectr. Center for Community Preservation, Howard U., Washington; cons. HUD; instr. Community Rehab. Tng. Center. Lubin fellow, 1967. Mem. Nat. Housing Conf., Assn. Home Builders. Home: 1400 Emerson St NW Washington DC 20011 Office: Zuniga & Assos/Rehabitat Ltd 1500 Massachusetts Ave NW Washington DC 20005

ZUR LOYE, DIETER, fin. exec.; b. Berlin, Ger., Sept. 26, 1928; s. Otto and Gertrud (Laux) zur L.; came to U.S., 1975; M.B.A., U. Frankfurt, W. Ger., 1952; grad. Advanced Mgmt. Program Harvard, 1970; m. Hella Elisabeth Troeger, July 20, 1957; children—Axel Otto, Hans-Conrad, Karen Hildegard. With Hoechst Aktiengesellschaft, Frankfurt/Main, W. Ger., 1955-75, mktg. dir. plastics exports, 1967-70, dir. corp. planning and coordination, 1970-75; group v.p. fin. and accounting Am. Hoechst Corp., Somerville, N.J., 1975-78, exec. v.p., 1978-80, sr. exec. v.p., 1980—, dir., 1975—, chief fin. officer, 1975-80, chief operating officer, 1980—; pres., dir. Hoechst Capital Corp., Somerville, 1975—; dir. Hoechst-Roussel Pharms., Inc. Presbyterian. Clubs: Roxiticus Golf, Deutscher Verein, Univ. Office: American Hoechst Corp PO Box 2500 Somerville NJ 08876

ZWEIBAN, HERMAN DAVID, stock broker; b. N.Y.C., Oct. 8, 1919; s. Sol and Jennie (Zelekuvitz) Z.; B.S., U. Ill., 1940; m. Ethel Reda Dupler, Dec. 13, 1942; children—Donna (Mrs. Harry R. Price), Glenn. Press., Lee's Furs, Inc., Gary, Ind., 1945-49; v.p. Nancy Lee, Inc., Gary, 1949-58; pres. Greens Furs, Inc., Gary, 1949-63; v.p. Bloom's, Inc., Hammond, Ind., 1950-56, Yousims Furs, Inc., South Bend, Ind., 1950-56; pres. Ben-Her Oil Co., Gary, 1960-63, Norge Village, Gary, 1961-63; v.p. Walston & Co., Dallas, 1964-73, Harris, Upham & Co., Inc., 1973-74, Hornblower & Weeks-Hemphill, Noyes, Inc., Dallas, 1974-78, Paine Webber Jackson & Curtis Inc., Dallas, 1978-80, Smith Barney Harris Upham Inc., Dallas, 1980—. Chmn., Lake County (Ind.) Arthritis Fund, 1960-61. Served to capt. USAAF, 1941-45. Certified fin. planner. Mem. U.S. Power Squadron, Inst. Certified Fin. Planners, Gamma Theta Phi, Kappa Tau Alpha. Jewish. Mem. B'nai Brith. Club: City (Dallas). Home: 7924 Royal Ln Dallas TX 75230 Office: 5300 1st Internat Bldg Dallas TX 75270

ZWEIG, MARTIN EDWARD, econ. cons., educator; b. Cleve., July 2, 1942; s. Sidney J. and Katherine (Schwartz) Z.; B.S., Wharton Sch., U. Pa., 1964; M.B.A., U. Miami, 1967; Ph.D., Mich. State U., 1969; m. Mollie Dee Friedman, Aug. 26, 1965; 1 son, Zachary M. Registered rep. Bache & Co., Bal Harbour, Fla., 1965; instr. U. Miami (Fla.), 1966; instr. fin. and acctg. Mich. State U., 1966-68; asst. prof. fin. and econs. Baruch Coll., City U. N.Y., 1969-74; econ. cons. Axelrod & Co.; asso. prof. fin. Iona Coll., New Rochelle, N.Y., 1975—; econ. cons. Avatar Assos., N.Y.C., 1972—; panelist Nat. Ednl. TV, 1973—. Gen. Electric fellow, 1969; City U. N.Y. research grantee, 1973. Mem. Am. Fin. Assn., N.Y. Soc. Security Analysts, Market Technicians Assn., Beta Gamma Sigma, Beta Alpha Psi. Jewish. Author: (with Gerald Appel) New Directions in Technical Analysis, 1976; contbr. booklets on stock markets and articles on fin. to profl. publs. Office: 747 3rd Ave New York NY 10017

ZWETOW, JEFFRY LYNN, real estate broker; b. St. Louis, July 10, 1947; s. Sidney and Helen Jean (Cochran) Z.; student Onslow Tech. Inst., Jacksonville, N.C., 1970; asso. degree in real estate Meremac Community Coll., 1980; m. Kath Lynn Butler, Apr. 26, 1969; children—Douglas Lynn, Jeffry Scott. Real estate agt. G. & R. McClanahan, St. Louis, 1971-76, Century 21 Kaiser-Milligan, Inc., St. Louis, 1976-79; real estate agt. Century 21 Action Properties, St. Louis, 1979-80, real estate broker, owner, 1980—. Pres., Clifton Heights Neighborhood Assn., 1978-80; v.p. South St. Louis Community Services Corp., 1978-79; pres. Dist. 4 Community Council, 1978-79, treas., 1979—. Served with USMC, 1967-71; Vietnam. Mem. Nat. Assn. Realtors, Met. Real Estate Bd. St. Louis. Methodist. Club: Art's Boys (v.p.). Home: 6243 Magnolia Ave Saint Louis MO 63139 Office: Century 21 Action Properties 6411 Chippewa Ave Saint Louis MO 63109

ZWICK, CHARLES JOHN, banker; b. Plantsville, Conn., July 17, 1926; s. Louis Christian and Mabel (Rich) Z.; B.S. in Agrl. Econs., U. Conn., 1950, M.S., 1951; Ph.D. in Econs., Harvard U., 1954; m. Joan Wallace Cameron, June 21, 1952; children—Robert Louis, Janet Ellen. Instr., U. Conn., 1951, Harvard U., 1954-56; head logistics dept. RAND Corp. 1956-63, mem. research council, 1963-65; asst. dir., then dir. U.S. Bur. Budget, 1965-69; pres., dir. SE Banking Corp., Miami, Fla., 1969—; dir. SE First Nat. Bank, Miami, SE Mortgage Co., So. Bell Tel. & Tel. Co., Johns-Mansville Corp.; chmn. President's Commn. Mil. Compensation, 1977-78; mem. cons. panel Office Controller Gen.; panel econ. advisers Congressional Budget Office. Mem. council Internat. Exec. Service Corps.; mem. Fla. Council 100; trustee Carnegie Endowment Internat. Peace. Served with U.S. Army, 1946-47. Mem. Econ. Soc. So. Fla., Assn. Res. City Bankers, Conf. Board, Greater Miami C. of C., Am. Historic and Cultural Soc. Office: Southeast Banking Corp 100 S Biscayne Blvd Miami FL 33131

ZWIERZCHOWSKA, LUCIA, apparel products co. exec.; b. Italy; d. Giovanni and Maria Teresa (Furnari) Lombardo; came to Can., 1952, naturalized, 1957; student Leonardo Da Vinci Tech. Coll., Italy, 1943, U. Sherbrooke, Can., 1967; m. Franciszek Zwierzchowski, Sept. 24, 1944; children—Richard, Sonia, George, Miriam. Mgr. Charny Clothing Mfg. Co., Jolliette, Que., 1956-59; asst. mgr. Vancor Enterprises, Montreal, Que., 1959-60; propr. Frank Sportswear, Inc., Sherbrooke, Que., 1960—; also tchr. in field. Mem. Sherbrooke C. of C. Club: Chess. Home: 2157 Albert Lozeau St Sherbrooke PQ Canada Office: 269 Bank St Sherbrooke PQ Canada

ZWILLENBERG, MELVIN LESLIE, utilities co. exec.; b. Bklyn., Aug. 3, 1938; s. Nathan Max and Rose (Berger) Z.; B.Ch.E., Cooper Union Sch. Engring., 1960; M.A., Princeton U., 1963, Ph.D., 1975; m. Myrna Kogan, Dec. 14, 1969 (div. Dec. 1980); 1 son, Daniel Eric. Chem. engr. E.I. DuPont, Seaford, Del., 1960; sr. research engr. United Aircraft Research Labs., East Hartford, Conn., 1965-70; mktg. mgr. Theta Tech. Corp., Wethersfeld, Conn., 1970; air pollution engr. Conn. Dept. Environ. Protection, 1971-72; asst. prof. mech. engring. Drexel U., Phila., 1975-76; sr. engr. research Public Service Electric & Gas Co., Newark, N.J., 1976—. Democratic committeeman 42d Congressional Dist., N.J., 1974-75, 76-77, 78-79. NSF fellow, 1961-63. Mem. AIAA, AAAS, Combustion Inst., NE Atlantic Sect. of Internat. Air Pollution Control Assn., Tau Beta Pi. Jewish. Patentee in field. Home: 21 Tekening Way Hamilton Sq NJ 08690 Office: 80 Park Plaza Newark NJ 07101